BOOK REVIEW INDEX

ISSN 0524-0581

BOOK REVIEW INDEX

2005 Cumulation

Dana Ferguson
Editor

THOMSON

GALE

Detroit • New York • San Francisco • San Diego • New Haven, Conn. • Waterville, Maine • London • Munich

THOMSON

GALE

Book Review Index 2005 Cumulation

Project Editor
Dana Ferguson

Editorial
Kristen Dorsch, Allison Marion, Kathy Meek, Kathy Nolan, Kevin Nothnagel, Tyra Phillips

Editorial Support Services
Margit Aarons, Margot Diltz, Lawrence Gee, Adelaide Hulbert, Andrea Kudzia, Alan LaVergne, Paul Lewon, Charles Nemenzo

Data Capture
Katrina Coach, Beverly Jendrowski, Elizabeth Pilette, Beth Richardson

Composition and Electronic Capture
Carolyn A. Roney

Manufacturing
Drew Kalasky

LIBRARY OF CONGRESS CATALOG CARD NUMBER 88-658021

ISBN 0-7876-7841-4
ISSN 0524-0581

Printed in the United States of America
10 9 8 7 6 5 4 3 2 1

Contents

Introduction

Book Review Index (BRI) is a master key providing access to reviews of thousands of books, audiobooks, and e-books. Representing a wide range of popular, academic, and professional interests, *BRI* guides readers and researchers to reviews appearing in over 400 publications from the United States, Canada, Europe, and Australia. *BRI* includes citations for reviews of any type of book, audiobook, or e-book that has been or is about to be published. *BRI's* definition of "review" is broad, citing reviews that provide a critical comment, a description of the book's contents, or a recommendation regarding the type of library collection for which a book is suited.

This volume cumulates the three issues for 2005. The journals and other reviewing sources have been carefully selected to ensure a wide range of subject coverage and relevancy to those interested in reviews. Sources indexed include:

- reviewing journals such as *Choice, Booklist,* and *School Library Journal;*

- national publications of general interest like *Time* and *Newsweek;*

- scholarly and literary journals such as *American Historical Review* and *The Kenyon Review;* and

- electronic publications such as *Law* and *Politics Book Review, H-Net: Humanities and Social Science Online,* and *Reference Reviews.*

Arrangement of *BRI*

Book Review Index has two major parts. The main section of the book presents book review citations arranged by the name of the author of the reviewed book. The citations include the title, illustrators or readers, name of the reviewing source, date of publication, length of the review, and in some cases the age range for which the reviewer felt the book was appropriate.

There are three size ranges: 1 to 50 words, 51 to 500 words, and over 501 words. This scheme effectively classifies reviews as "small," "medium," and "large."

Following the main section is the Title Index, which gives the user access to the citations by way of the title. This index is useful when the name of the author is unknown. Listings in the title index refer the user to the main entry section. When a title appears without an author it is an indication that the title itself is the main entry form.

For more information on the entries and definitions of codes, please consult the Users Guide following this introduction.

Available in Electronic Formats

Online. *Book Review Index* is available online from Thomson Gale via two different subscriptions: the index-only offering and the *Book Review Index Online Plus* option. The index-only resource includes more than 5 million review citations, while *Book Review Index Plus* includes not only the 5 million review citations, but also more than 664,000 full-text reviews from InfoTrac OneFile and InfoTrac Expanded Academic. Both *Book Review Index Online* and *Book Review Index Online Plus* include citations from more than 5,800 publications with over 2.5 million titles reviewed; this represents the entire backfile of *Book Review Index* print content, dating back to 1965. For more information, call 1-800-877-GALE.

BRI is also available online on DIALOG as File 137, Book Review Index and includes reviews from 1969-2004. For more information, contact The Dialog Corporation, 11000 Regency Parkway, Ste. 10, Cary, NC 27511; phone: (919) 462-8600; toll-free: 800-3-DIALOG.

Acknowledgements

The editors of *Book Review Index* would like to thank the many other Thomson Gale staff members who helped in the compilation of this issue. We would also like to express our gratitude to the publishers of the journals indexed in *BRI*. Their assistance is invaluable to the publication of *BRI*.

Comments and Suggestions Are Welcome

The editors welcome comments or suggestions on the scope and coverage of *BRI*. Please address all correspondence to:

Editor

Book Review Index

Gale Group, Inc.

27500 Drake Road

Farmington Hills, MI 48331-3535

Phone: 248-699-GALE

Toll-Free: 800-347-GALE

Fax: 248-699-8067

Users Guide

Inclusion Criteria

BRI's broad inclusion criteria are designed to allow searchers to find practically any review that has been published within the time covered by a particular issue. Coverage includes:

- Adult fiction and nonfiction books

- Poetry and song books

- Books that are intended for children

- Audio books and electronic editions (aka books on tape) of books.

- E-books for adults, young adults and children.

Sample Entry

▮1▮ Sattler, Helen R -

▮2▮ The Book of Eagles

▮3▮ (Illus. by Dore, Gustave) or (Read by Prichard, Michael)

▮4▮ c

▮5▮ CCB-B -

▮6▮ v50 - O '96 -

▮7▮ p43+

▮8▮ [51-500]

Descriptions of Numbered Elements

▮1▮ Author or Editor of work being reviewed. When a work has multiple authors, only the first or principal author is shown.

▮2▮ Title of work being reviewed. Subtitles are usually included.

▮3▮ Illustrator (if the book is intended for children or young adults) or Reader of an audiobook

▮4▮ Age or Type code. See Explanation of Age and Type Codes below.

▮5▮ Abbreviation of reviewing periodical title. See the "Publications Indexed" section for complete list of abbreviations.

▮6▮ Volume number and date or issue number

▮7▮ Page on which review appears or NA, which indicates the review is only available online. See "Page Number Designations" below for more details.

▮8▮ Approximate number of words in the review. Ranges used are 1-50, 51-500, and 500+.

Works published in several editions over the years may have the name of the editor, translator, or publisher added in parentheses after the title to clarify which version is under review.

Explanation of Age and Type Codes—

Some entries in BRI include age and/or type codes that help define the kind of work being reviewed.

Age codes

Age designations are determined by the reviewer or publisher.

"c" denotes a book for children (up to age ten)

"y" denotes a book written for young adults (ages eleven through eighteen)

Page Number Designations

Pagination for periodical articles is expressed with a starting page followed by the total number of pages in parentheses, if the article spans more than one page. For academic journals, pagination may be expressed in the same way or by a beginning page and ending page separated by a dash.

Examples

- p10

- p70(5)

- p196-199

Some periodical content that is generated from electronic feed does not contain any pagination information. In these cases, the pagination value "pNA" is used.

Abbreviations for Months and Seasons

Names of individual months and seasons are spelled out, while dates spanning across months or seasons are sometimes abbreviated.

Examples

- Annual

- April-August

- April-Dec

- Autumn

- Autumn-Spring

- Autumn-Wntr

Arrangement of Citations

The main (or Author) section is arranged alphabetically by author names. When the authorship is attributed to a corporate entity, the name of that group is interfiled among the authors. In cases where a book has no author cited, it appears in the main section under its title interfiled among the authors. A user searching for a particular entry in the author or title indexes should note the following guidelines.

- Roman and arabic numerals file in numerical order before the letter A. For example, the title *30-Minute Meals* would file before entries beginning with A; *Thirty-Minute Meals* would file in the T's.

- Acronyms and initialisms file as single words unless periods or spaces divide the letters. Letters following a period or space file as new words. Users should note that variant forms of initialisms would file separately under this arrangement. For example, U.S.A. would

appear near the beginning of the U section, while USA would file just before the word "Use."

- Initial articles are ignored in most cases for both English and non-English language titles.

Title Index

The Title Index, which follows the main section, lists all titles for which BRI has citations to reviews. It is arranged alphabetically and follows the same sorting conventions as noted above. A listing in the title index gives the author where the citations will be found in the main section. When no author is listed, the citations are listed under the title in the main (author) section.

Publications Indexed

Preceding the main section is the list of reviewing sources indexed in *BRI*. This section is arranged by the abbreviation used with the main entries to indicate the journal. Each entry in the Publications Indexed section gives the title, subscription address, frequency of publication, ISSN, and URL (Uniform Resource Locater) if the journal's publisher maintains a site on the Internet.

Publications Indexed

The periodical abbreviations used in Book Review Index citations are arranged here alphabetically in letter-by-letter sequence. The full periodical title appears to the right of the abbreviation. The following information is also provided for each publication: frequency, ISSN, subscription address, and URL if the source is available online.

A

A Aff: *Asian Affairs*
Issues per year: 3 ISSN 0306-8374
2 Belgrave Sqaure
London SW1X 8PJ United Kingdom

A Art: *American Artist*
Issues per year: 12 ISSN 0002-7375
770 Broadway, 6th Floor
New York, NY 10003 United States
http://www.vnuemedia.com/

A Lib: *American Libraries*
Issues per year: 11 ISSN 0002-9769
50 East Huron St.
Chicago, IL 60611-2795 United States

ABR: *American Book Review*
Issues per year: 6 ISSN 0149-9408
c/o Unit for Contemporary Literature
Normal, IL 61790-4241 United States

Adoles: *Adolescence*
Issues per year: 4 ISSN 0001-8449
3089C Clairemont Drive
San Diego, CA 92117 United States

Advocate: *The Advocate (The national gay & lesbian newsmagazine)*
Issues per year: 26 ISSN 0001-8996
Box 542
Mount Morris, IL 61054-7846 United States

Afr Am R: *African American Review*
Issues per year: 4 ISSN 1062-4783
St. Louis University
St. Louis, MO 63103-2007 United States

Afterimage: *Afterimage*
Issues per year: 6 ISSN 0300-7472
31 Prince St.
Rochester, NY 14607 United States

AH: *American Heritage*
Issues per year: 8 ISSN 0002-8738
60 5th Ave.
New York, NY 10011 United States

AHR: *American Historical Review*
Issues per year: 5 ISSN 0002-8762
400 A Street SE
Washington, DC 20003-3889 United States

AHS: *Australian Historical Studies*
Issues per year: 2 ISSN 1031-461X
Dept. of History
Parkville Vic 3052 Australia

AIQ: *The American Indian Quarterly*
Issues per year: 4 ISSN 0095-182X
233 N. 8th St.
Lincoln, NE 68588-0255 United States
http://www.nebraskapress.unl.edu/

AJE: *American Journal of Education*
Issues per year: 4 ISSN 0195-6744
Journals Division
Chicago, IL 60637-2954 United States
http://www.journals.uchicago.edu

AJES: *The American Journal of Economics and Sociology*
Issues per year: 4 ISSN 0002-9246
41 E. 72nd St.
New York, NY 10021 United States

AJN: *American Journal of Nursing*
Issues per year: 12 ISSN 0002-936X
555 West 57th Street
New York, NY 10019 United States

AJP: *American Journal of Philology*
Issues per year: 4 ISSN 0002-9475
2715 N. Charles Street
Baltimore, MD 21218 United States

AJPS: *Australian Journal of Political Science*
Issues per year: 3 ISSN 1036-1146
P.O. Box 25
Abingdon, Oxon 0X14 3UE United Kingdom

AJR: *American Journalism Review*
Issues per year: 6 ISSN 1067-8654
University of Maryland
Adelphi, MD 20783-1716 United States
http://www.umd.edu/

AJS: *The American Journal of Sociology*
Issues per year: 6 ISSN 0002-9602
Journals Division
Chicago, IL 60637-2954 United States
http://www.journals.uchicago.edu

AL: *American Literature*
Issues per year: 4 ISSN 0002-9831
Box 90660
Durham, NC 27708-0660 United States

Albion: *Albion*
Issues per year: 4 ISSN 0095-1390
Applachian State University
Boone, NC 28608 United States
http://www.albion.appstate.edu/

ALJ: *The Australian Library Journal*
Issues per year: 4 ISSN 0004-9670
University College & Research
Queen Victoria Terrace, Australian Capital Territory 2600 Australia

AM: *America*
Issues per year: 26 ISSN 0002-7049
106 West 56th St.
New York, NY 10019 United States
http://www.americamagazine.org

Am Ant: *American Antiquity*
Issues per year: 4 ISSN 0002-7316
900 Second St., N.W. Suite 12
Washington, DC 20002 United States

Am Bio T: *The American Biology Teacher*
Issues per year: 8 ISSN 0002-7685
11250 Roger Bacon Drive #19
Reston, VA 22090 United States

Am Craft: *American Craft*
Issues per year: 6 ISSN 0194-8008
72 Spring Street
New York, NY 10012 United States

Am Ind CRJ: *American Indian Culture and Research Journal*
Issues per year: 4 ISSN 0161-6463
Box 951548
Los Angeles, CA 90095-1548 United States

Am M: *American Music*
Issues per year: 4 ISSN 0734-4392
Journals Division
Champaign, IL 61820 United States

Am MT: *American Music Teacher*
Issues per year: 6 ISSN 0003-0112
The Carew Tower
Cincinnati, OH 45202-2814
United States
http://www.mtna.org

Am Q: *American Quarterly*
Issues per year: 4 ISSN 0003-0678
2715 N. Charles Street
Baltimore, MD 21218 United States

Am Sci: *American Scientist*
Issues per year: 6 ISSN 0003-0996
99 Alexander Dr.
Research Triangle Park, NC 27709-3975 United States

Am Spect: *The American Spectator*
Issues per year: 10 ISSN 0148-8414
1611 N. Kent St., Suite 901
Arlington, VA 22209 United States

Am St: *American Studies*
Issues per year: 2 ISSN 0026-3079
University of Kansas at Lawrence
Lawrence, KS 66045-2117 United States

Am Theat: *American Theatre*
Issues per year: 11 ISSN 8750-3255
Dist. by Eastern News Distributors, Inc.
Sandusky, OH 44870 United States

Amerasia J: *Amerasia Journal*
Issues per year: 3 ISSN 0044-7471
3230 Campbell Hall
Los Angeles, CA 90024-1546 United States

Ams: *Americas: A Quarterly Review of Inter-American Cultural History*
Issues per year: 4 ISSN 0003-1615
1712 Euclid Ave.
Berkeley, CA 94709-1208 United States

Analog: *Analog Science Fiction & Fact*
Issues per year: 13 ISSN 1059-2113
PO Box 54027
Boulder, CO 80322-4027 United States

ANQ:QJ: *ANQ*
Issues per year: 4 ISSN 0895-769X
1319 18th St., NW
Washington, DC 20036-1802 United States

Ant R: *The Antioch Review*
Issues per year: 4 ISSN 0003-5769
Box 148
Yellow Springs, OH 45387 United States

Ant&CM: *Antiques & Collecting Magazine*
Issues per year: 12 ISSN 1084-0818
Circulation Department
Chicago, IL 60605 United States

APH: *Air Power History*
Issues per year: 4 ISSN 1044-016X
1535 Command Dr., Suite A122
Andrews Air Force Base, MD 20762-7002 United States

APJ: *Air & Space Power Journal*
Issues per year: 4
401 Chennault Circle
Maxwell AFB, AL 36112-6428 United States
http://www.airpower.maxwell.af.mil/airchronicles/apje.html

Apo: *Apollo*
Issues per year: 12 ISSN 0003-6536
20 Theobald's Road
London WC1N 2LL United Kingdom

APR: *The American Poetry Review*
Issues per year: 6 ISSN 0360-3709
117 South 17th Street, Suite 910
Philadelphia, PA 19103 United States

Arch: *Archaeology*
Issues per year: 6 ISSN 0003-8113
135 William Street
New York, NY 10038 United States

Archiv: *Archivaria*
Issues per year: 2 ISSN 0318-6954
P.O. Box 2596, Station D
Ottawa, Ontario K1P 5W6 Canada

Arena: *Arena Magazine*
Issues per year: 6 ISSN 1039-1010
PO Box 18
N. Carlton, Victoria 3054 Australia

Art Bull: *The Art Bulletin*
Issues per year: 4 ISSN 0004-3079
275 Seventh Ave.
New York, NY 10001 United States

Art N: *ARTnews*
Issues per year: 10 ISSN 0004-3273
P.O. Box 2083
Knoxville, IA 50197-2083 United States

AS: *American Scholar*
Issues per year: 4 ISSN 0003-0937
1606 New Hampshire Avenue, NW
Washington, DC 20009 United States

Astron: *Astronomy*
Issues per year: 12 ISSN 0091-6358
21027 Crossroads Circle
Waukesha, WI 53187 United States
http://corporate.kalmbach.com/

Atl: *The Atlantic Monthly*
Issues per year: 12 ISSN 1072-7825
Box 2547
Boulder, CO 80322 United States

Aud: *Audubon*
Issues per year: 6 ISSN 0097-7136
Membership Data Center
Boulder, CO 80322 United States

Aztlan: *AZTLAN - A Journal of Chicano Studies*
Issues per year: 2 ISSN 0005-2604
University of California
Los Angeles, CA 90024 United States

B

B Ent: *Black Enterprise*
Issues per year: 12 ISSN 0006-4165
130 Fifth Avenue, 10th Floor
New York, NY 10011-4399 United States

Barron's: *Barron's*
Issues per year: 52 ISSN 1077-8039
Box 300
Princeton, NJ 08543-0300 United States

BCS: *Buddhist-Christian Studies*
Issues per year: 1 ISSN 0882-0945
2840 Kolowalu St.
Honolulu, HI 96822 United States
http://www.uhpress.hawaii.edu/

Beav: *The Beaver: Exploring Canada's History*
Issues per year: 6 ISSN 0005-7517
478-167 Lombard Ave.
Winnipeg, Manitoba MB R3B OT6 Canada
http://www.historysociety.ca

BHR: *Business History Review*
Issues per year: 4 ISSN 0007-6805
Book Review Coordinator
Boston, MA 02163 United States

BIC: *Books In Canada*
Issues per year: 12 ISSN 0045-2564
427 Mount Pleasant Rd.
Toronto, Ontario M4S 2L8 Canada

Biomag: *Biography*
Issues per year: 4 ISSN 0162-4962
2840 Kolowalu St.
Honolulu, HI 96822 United States
http://www.uhpress.hawaii.edu/

Bkbird: *Bookbird*
Issues per year: 4 ISSN 0006-7377
c/o Barbara A. Lehman, Ed.,
Mansfield, OH 44906 United States

Bks & Cult: *Books & Culture*
Issues per year: 6 ISSN 1082-8931
465 Gunderson Dr.
Carol Stream, IL 60188 United States
http://www.christianitytoday.com/

BL: *Booklist*
Issues per year: 22 ISSN 0006-7385
50 East Huron St.
Chicago, IL 60611-2795 United States

Bl S: *The Black Scholar*
Issues per year: 4 ISSN 0006-4246
Subscription Services
Oakland, CA 94609 United States

Black Iss: *Black Issues Book Review*
Issues per year: 6 ISSN 1522-0524
10520 Warwick Ave., #B8
Fairfax, VA 22030 United States

BooChiTr: *Books (Chicago Tribune)*
Issues per year: 52
435 N. Michigan Ave.
Chicago, IL 60611 United States

BSA-P: *Papers of the Bibliographical Society of America*
Issues per year: 4 ISSN 0006-128X
P.O. Box 397
New York, NY 10163 United States

BTB: *Biblical Theology Bulletin*
Issues per year: 4 ISSN 0146-1079
Seton Hall University
South Orange, NJ 07079-2696
United States

Bus W: *Business Week*
Issues per year: 52 ISSN 0007-7135
1221 Avenue of the Americas
New York, NY 10020 United States

BW: *Book World*
Issues per year: 52 ISSN 0006-7639
1150 15th St., N.W.
Washington, DC 20071 United States

Bwatch: *The Bookwatch*
Issues per year: 12 ISSN 0896-4521
278 Orchard Dr.
Oregon, WI 53575 United States
http://www.midwestbookreview.com

C

Callaloo: *Callaloo*
Issues per year: 4 ISSN 0161-2492
2715 N. Charles Street
Baltimore, MD 21218 United States

Can CL: *Canadian Children's Literature*
Issues per year: 4 ISSN 0319-0080
University of Guelph
Guelph, Ontario N1G 2W1
Canada
http://www.uoguelph.ca/englit/ccl

Can Hist R: *Canadian Historical Review*
Issues per year: 4 ISSN 0008-3755
340 Nagel Drive
Cheektowaga, NY 14225 United States
http://www.utpress.utoronto.ca/journal/home.htm

Can Lit: *Canadian Literature*
Issues per year: 4 ISSN 0008-4360
#223 - 2029 West Mall
Vancouver, British Columbia V6T 1Z2 Canada

CBRA: *Canadian Book Review Annual*
Issues per year: 1 ISSN 0383-770X
44 Charles St. W., Suite 3205
Toronto, Ontario ON M4Y
Canada

CC: *The Christian Century*
Issues per year: 37 ISSN 0009-5281
407 South Dearborn Street
Chicago, IL 60605-1150 United States

CCB-B: *Center for Children's Books Bulletin*
Issues per year: 12 ISSN 0008-9036
Journals Division
Champaign, IL 61820 United States

CE: *Childhood Education*
Issues per year: 6 ISSN 0009-4056
17904 Georgia Ave., Ste 215
Olney, MD 20832 United States

CEH: *Central European History*
Issues per year: 4 ISSN 0008-9389
165 First Avenue
Atlantic Highlands, NJ 07716-1289 United States

Ceram Mo: *Ceramics Monthly*
Issues per year: 10 ISSN 0009-0328
735 Ceramic Place
Westerville, OH 43086-6102 United States

CG: *Canadian Geographic*
Issues per year: 6 ISSN 0706-2168
39 McArthur Avenue
Vanier, Ontario XIL 8L7 Canada

CH: *Church History*
Issues per year: 4 ISSN 0009-6407
Box 8517
Red Bank, NJ 07701-8517
United States

CH Bwatch: *Children's Bookwatch*
Issues per year: 12
278 Orchard Dr.
Oregon, WI 53575 United States
http://www.midwestbookreview.com

Ch Rev Int: *China Review International*
Issues per year: 2 ISSN 1069-5834
2840 Kolowalu St.
Honolulu, HI 96822 United States
http://www.uhpress.hawaii.edu/

Ch Today: *Christianity Today*
Issues per year: 14 ISSN 0009-5753
P.O. Box 11617 or 11618?
Des Moines, IA 50340 United States
http://www.christianitytoday.com/

CHE: *The Chronicle of Higher Education*
Issues per year: 49 ISSN 0009-5982
Subscriptions
Marion, OH 43305 United States

Choice: *CHOICE: Current Reviews for Academic Libraries*
Issues per year: 11 ISSN 0009-4978
50 East Huron St.
Chicago, IL 60611-2795 United States

CHR: *The Catholic Historical Review*
Issues per year: 4 ISSN 0008-8080
620 Michigan Ave., N.E.
Washington, DC 20064 United States
http://cuapress.cua.edu/journals.htm

ChrSFF&H: *Chronicle*
Issues per year: 12 ISSN 0195-5365
P.O. Box 2988
Radford, VA 24143-2988 United States

CI: *Catholic Insight*
Issues per year: 10 ISSN 1192-5671
P.O. Box 625
Toronto, Ontario M5C 2J8
Canada
http://www.catholicinsight.com

CJ: *The Classical Journal*
Issues per year: 4 ISSN 0009-8353
c/o John F. Hall
Provo, UT 84602 United States

CJR: *Columbia Journalism Review*
Issues per year: 6 ISSN 0010-194X
207 Journalism
New York, NY 10027 United States

Class R: *Classical Review*
Issues per year: 1 ISSN 0009-840X
Journals Department
Eynsham, Oxford 0X8 1JJ United Kingdom

Clio: *CLIO*
Issues per year: 4 ISSN 0884-2043
2101 E. Coliseum Blvd.
Fort Wayne, IN 46805 United States

CLR: *Columbia Law Review*
Issues per year: 8 ISSN 0010-1958
435 West 116th Street
New York, NY 10027 United States

CML: *Classical and Modern Literature: A Quarterly*
Issues per year: 4 ISSN 0197-2227
PO Box 629
Terre Haute, IN 47808-0629 United States

Col Lit: *College Literature*
Issues per year: 3 ISSN 0093-3139
554 New Main
West Chester, PA 19383 United States

Comp L: *Comparative Literature*
Issues per year: 4 ISSN 0010-4124
223 Friendly Hall
Eugene, OR 97403-1233 United States

Comw: *Commonweal*
Issues per year: 22 ISSN 0010-3330
15 Dutch Street
New York, NY 10038 United States
Commonweal@msn.com

Cons: *Conscience*
Issues per year: 4 ISSN 0740-6835
1486 U Street N.W., Suite 301
Washington, DC 20009-3997 United States
http://www.catholicsforchoice.org

Cont Pac: *The Contemporary Pacific*
Issues per year: 2 ISSN 1043-898X
2840 Kolowalu St.
Honolulu, HI 96822 United States
http://www.uhpress.hawaii.edu/

CQ: *The Carolina Quarterly*
Issues per year: 3 ISSN 0008-6797
CB# 3520, Greenlaw Hall
Chapel Hill, NC 27599-3520 United States
http://www.unc.edu/depts/cqonline

CR: *Contemporary Review*
Issues per year: 12 ISSN 0010-7565
Cheam Business Centre
Cheam, Sutton, Surrey SM2 7AZ United Kingdom

Critm: *Criticism*
Issues per year: 4 ISSN 0011-1589
4809 Woodward Ave.
Detroit, MI 48201-1309 United States
http://www.lib.wayne.edu/wsupr

Critq: *CRITIQUE: Studies in Contemporary Fiction*
Issues per year: 4 ISSN 0011-1619
1319 18th St., NW
Washington, DC 20036-1802 United States

CS: *Contemporary Sociology*
Issues per year: 6 ISSN 0094-3061
1722 N Street NW
Washington, DC 20036 United States

Cur R: *Curriculum Review*
Issues per year: 9 ISSN 0147-2453
125 Patterson Ave.
Little Falls, NJ 07424 United States

CWS: *Canadian Woman Studies*
Issues per year: 4 ISSN 0713-3235
212 Founders College
North York, Ontario M3J 1P3 Canada
http://www.yorku.ca/cwscf/

D

Dal R: *The Dalhousie Review*
Issues per year: 4 ISSN 0011-5827
Sir James Dunn Building
Halifax, Nova Scotia B3H 3J5 Canada

Dance: *Dance Magazine*
Issues per year: 12 ISSN 0011-6009
P.O. Box 50470
Cicero, IL 60650 United States
http://www.dancemagazine.com/

Dance RJ: *Dance Research Journal*
Issues per year: 2 ISSN 0149-7677
State University of New York
Brockport, NY 14420 United States

Dbt: *Down Beat*
Issues per year: 12 ISSN 0012-5768
Box 1071
Skokie, IL 60076 United States

Dialogue: *Dialogue: Canadian Philosophical Review*
Issues per year: 4 ISSN 0012-2173
75 University Ave.
W. Waterloo, Ontario N2L 3C5 Canada

Dis: *Dissent*
Issues per year: 4 ISSN 0012-3846
521 5th Avenue
New York, NY 10017 United States

DroRevMy: *Drood Review of Mystery*
Issues per year: 6 ISSN 0893-0252
484 E. Carmel Dr. 378
Carmel, IN 46032 United States

E

E Mag: *E*
Issues per year: 6 ISSN 1046-8021
Box 5098
Westport, CT 06881 United States

E-A St: *Europe-Asia Studies*
Issues per year: 8 ISSN 0966-8136
875-81 Massachusetts Avenue
Cambridge, MA 02139 United States

E-Streams: *E-Streams: Electronic Reviews of Science & Technology References*
Issues per year: 12 ISSN 1098-4399
999 Maple St,
Contoocook, NH 03229 United States

Econ: *The Economist (US)*
Issues per year: 51 ISSN 0013-0613
Subscription department
Boulder, CO 80322-8524 United States
http://www.economist.com

Econ J: *Economic Journal*
Issues per year: 6 ISSN 0013-0133
Attn: Rights Department
Oxford OX4 2DQ United Kingdom
http://www.blackwellpublishers.com/

EFHM: *Everton's Family History Magazine*
Issues per year: 6 ISSN 1539-1531
P.O. Box 368
Logan, UT 84323-0368 United States

Eight-C St: *Eighteenth-Century Studies*
Issues per year: 4 ISSN 0013-2586
c/o Jeffrey Smitten
Logan, UT 84322-3730 United States

ELT: *English Literature in Transition 1880-1920*
Issues per year: 4 ISSN 0013-8339
Department of English
Greensboro, NC 26170 United States
http://www.uncg.edu/eng/elt

En Jnl: *The Energy Journal*
Issues per year: 4 ISSN 0195-6574
28790 Chagrin Blvd., Suite 350
Cleveland, OH 44122 United States

Ent W: *Entertainment Weekly*
Issues per year: 48 ISSN 1049-0434
Box 830609
Birmingham, AL 35283-0609 United States
http://www.timeinc.com

Env: *Environment*
Issues per year: 10 ISSN 0013-9157
1319 18th St., NW
Washington, DC 20036-1802 United States

ER: *The Ecumenical Review*
Issues per year: 4 ISSN 0013-0796
Publications Office
Geneva 2 CH 1211 Switzerland

Esq: *Esquire*
Issues per year: 12 ISSN 0194-9535
C.D.S.
Des Moines, IA 50315 United States
http://www.hearst.com

Essays CW: *Essays on Canadian Writing*
Issues per year: 3 ISSN 0316-0300
2120 Queen Street East
Toronto, Ontario M4E 1E2 Canada

Ethics: *Ethics*
Issues per year: 4 ISSN 0014-1704
Journals Division
Chicago, IL 60637-2954 United States
http://www.journals.uchicago.edu

Ext: *Extrapolation*
Issues per year: 4 ISSN 0014-5483
University of Texas at Brownsville, Department of English
Brownsville, TX 78520 United States

F

Fam in Soc: *Families in Society: The Journal of Contemporary Human Services*
Issues per year: 4 ISSN 1044-3894
11700 W. Lake Park Dr.
Milwaukee, WI 53224-3099 United States
http://www.alliance1.org/

Fed Prob: *Federal Probation*
Issues per year: 4 ISSN 0014-9128
Superintendent of Documents
Pittsburgh, PA 15250-7954 United States

Film Cr: *Film Criticism*
Issues per year: 3 ISSN 0163-5069
Film Criticism Office
Meadville, PA 16335 United States

Five Owls: *The Five Owls*
Issues per year: 4 ISSN 0892-6735
2004 Sheridan Ave., S.
Minneapolis, MN 55405 United States

Folkl: *Folklore*
Issues per year: 3 ISSN 0015-587X
University College
London WC1E 6BT United Kingdom

For Aff: *Foreign Affairs*
Issues per year: 6 ISSN 0015-7120
58 East 68th St.
New York, NY 10021 United States
http://www.foreignaffairs.org

Forbes: *Forbes*
Issues per year: 27 ISSN 0015-6914
P.O. Box 10048
Des Moines, IA 50340-0048 United States
http://www.forbes.com

Fortune: *Fortune*
Issues per year: 25 ISSN 0015-8259
Box 60190
Tampa, FL 33660-0001 United States
http://www.timeinc.com

FQ: *Film Quarterly*
Issues per year: 4 ISSN 0015-1386
Journals Division
Berkeley, CA 94720 United States

FS: *French Studies*
Issues per year: 4 ISSN 0016-1128
c/o Prof. A.W. Raitt, ed., Taylor
Oxford OX1 3NA United Kingdom

Fut: *The Futurist*
Issues per year: 10 ISSN 0016-3317
7910 Woodmont Avenue
Bethesda, MD 20814 United States
http://www.wfs.org/wfs

G

G&L Rev W: *The Gay & Lesbian Review Worldwide*
Issues per year: 4 ISSN 1532-1118
Box 180300
Boston, MA 02118 United States

Ga R: *The Georgia Review*
Issues per year: 4 ISSN 0016-8386
The Georgia Review
Athens, GA 30602 United States
http://www.law.uga.edu

Ger Q: *The German Quarterly*
Issues per year: 4 ISSN 0016-8831
112 Haddontowne Court
Cherry Hill, NJ 08034-3662
United States

GJ: *The Geographical Journal*
Issues per year: 3 ISSN 0016-7398
1 Kensington Gore
London SW7 2AR United Kingdom

Globe & Mail: *Globe & Mail (Toronto, Canada)*
Issues per year: 312 ISSN 0319-0714
720 King Street West
Toronto, Ontario M5V 2T3
Canada
www.globeandmail.com

GSR: *German Studies Review*
Issues per year: 3 ISSN 0149-7952
Center for Business Research
Tempe, AZ 85287-4406 United States

H

HAHR: *Hispanic American Historical Review*
Issues per year: 4 ISSN 0018-2168
Box 90660
Durham, NC 27708-0660 United States

Har Bus R: *Harvard Business Review*
Issues per year: 6 ISSN 0017-8012
60 Harvard Way
Boston, MA 02163 United States

Hast Cen R: *The Hastings Center Report*
Issues per year: 6 ISSN 0093-0334
The Hastings Center
Garrison, NY 10524-5555 United States
http://www.yearbooknews.com/

HB: *The Horn Book Magazine*
Issues per year: 6 ISSN 0018-5078
56 Roland St., Suite 200
Boston, MA 02129 United States

HER: *Harvard Educational Review*
Issues per year: 4 ISSN 0017-8055
Graduate School of Education
Cambridge, MA 02138 United States

HER: *The English Historical Review*
Issues per year: 5 ISSN 0013-8266
Great Clarendon Street
Oxford OX2 6DP United Kingdom

Hisp R: *Hispanic Review*
Issues per year: 4 ISSN 0018-2176
Romance Languages Department
Philadelphia, PA 19104-6204
United States

Hist Geo: *Historical Geography*
Issues per year: 1 ISSN 1091-6458
43 Allen Hall
Baton Rouge, LA 70803-5005
United States

HJAS: *Harvard Journal of Asiatic Studies*
Issues per year: 2 ISSN 0073-0548
2 Divinity Avenue
Cambridge, MA 02138 United States

HLR: *Harvard Law Review*
Issues per year: 8 ISSN 0017-811X
Gannett House
Cambridge, MA 02138 United States

HM: *Harper's Magazine*
Issues per year: 12 ISSN 0017-789X
P.O. Box 7511
Red Oak, IA 51591-0511 United States

HNet: *H-Net: Humanities and Social Sciences Online*
Issues per year: 12 ISSN 1538-0661
Michigan State University, 310 Auditorium Bldg
East Lansing, MI 48824 United States

HR: *The Hudson Review*
Issues per year: 4 ISSN 0018-702X
684 Park Avenue
New York, NY 10021 United States

HR Mag: *HRMagazine*
Issues per year: 12 ISSN 1047-3149
1800 Duke Street
Alexandria, VA 22314 United States
http:www.shrm.org/

HRNB: *History: Review of New Books*
Issues per year: 4 ISSN 0361-2759
1319 18th St., NW
Washington, DC 20036-1802
United States

HT: *History Today*
Issues per year: 12 ISSN 0018-2753
20 Old Compton Street
London W1V 5PE United Kingdom

Hum: *The Humanist*
Issues per year: 6 ISSN 0018-7399
7 Harwood Dr.
Amherst, NY 14226-7188 United States
http://www.americanhumanist.org/

I

IBMR: *International Bulletin of Missionary Research*
Issues per year: 4 ISSN 0272-6122
P.O. Box 3000
Denville, NJ 07834 United States

IJAHS: *International Journal of African Historical Studies*
Issues per year: 3 ISSN 0361-7882
270 Bay State Road
Boston, MA 02215 United States

IJCM: *International Journal of Commerce and Management*
Issues per year: 4 ISSN 1056-9219
Indiana University of Pennsylvania (IUP)
Indiana, PA 15705 United States

IJMES: *International Journal of Middle East Studies*
Issues per year: 4 ISSN 0020-7438
40 West 20th Street
New York, NY 10011-4211 United States
http://www.cambridge.org

ILR: *International Labour Review*
Issues per year: 6 ISSN 0020-7780
Marketing & Licensing Section/ Publications Branch
1211 Geneva 22 Switzerland

ILS: *Irish Literary Supplement*
Issues per year: 2 ISSN 0733-3390
2592 North Wading River Road
Wading River, NY 11792-1404
United States

IndRev: *Independent Review*
Issues per year: 4 ISSN 1086-1653
100 Swan Way
Oakland, CA 94621-1428 United States

Inst: *Instructor (1990)*
Issues per year: 8 ISSN 1049-5851
1 East First Street
Duluth, MN 55802 United States
http://www.scholastic.com

Intpr: *Interpretation*
Issues per year: 4 ISSN 0020-9643
Dept. of Mgmt. Marketing & Logistics
University Heights, OH 44118
United States

Isis: *Isis*
Issues per year: 4 ISSN 0021-1753
Journals Division
Chicago, IL 60637-2954 United States
http://www.journals.uchicago.edu

J

J Am St: *Journal of American Studies*
Issues per year: 3 ISSN 0021-8758
40 West 20th Street
New York, NY 10011-4211 United States
http://www.cambridge.org

J Bl St: *Journal of Black Studies*
Issues per year: 6 ISSN 0021-9347
2455 Teller Road
Thousand Oaks, CA 91320
United States
http://www.sagepub.com

J Broadcst: *Journal of Broadcasting & Electronic Media*
Issues per year: 4 ISSN 0883-8151
1771 N Street NW
Washington, DC 20036 United States

J Ch St: *Journal of Church and State*
Issues per year: 4 ISSN 0021-969X
Baylor University
Waco, TX 76798-7308 United States

J Chem Ed: *Journal of Chemical Education*
Issues per year: 12 ISSN 0021-9584
Subscription Department
Easton, PA 18042 United States

J Film & Vid: *Journal of Film and Video*
Issues per year: 4 ISSN 0742-4671
Department of Communications
Atlanta, GA 30303-3080 United States

J Hi E: *Journal of Higher Education*
Issues per year: 6 ISSN 0022-1546
1070 Carmack Rd.
Columbus, OH 43210-1002 United States
http://www.ohiostatepress.org

J Hist G: *Journal of Historical Geography*
Issues per year: 4 ISSN 0305-7488
High Street
Sidcup, Kent DA14 5HP United Kingdom

J Mil H: *The Journal of Military History*
Issues per year: 4 ISSN 0899-3718
George C. Marshall Library
Lexington, VA 24450 United States
http://www.smh-hq.org/

J Phil: *The Journal of Philosophy*
Issues per year: 12 ISSN 0022-362X
Business Manager
New York, NY 10027 United States

J POP F&TV: *Journal of Popular Film and Television*
Issues per year: 4 ISSN 0195-6051
1319 18th St., NW
Washington, DC 20036-1802 United States

J Rehab: *The Journal of Rehabilitation*
Issues per year: 4 ISSN 0022-4154
633 South Washington Street
Alexandria, VA 22314-4109 United States

J Soc H: *Journal of Social History*
Issues per year: 4 ISSN 0022-4529
George Mason University
Fairfax, VA 22030-4444 United States
http://chnm.gmu.edu/jsh

J Urban H: *Journal of Urban History*
Issues per year: 6 ISSN 0096-1442
2455 Teller Road
Thousand Oaks, CA 91320 United States
http://www.sagepub.com

JAAC: *The Journal of Aesthetics and Art Criticism*
Issues per year: 4 ISSN 0021-8529
Journal Division
Madison, WI 53711-2059 United States

JAAL: *Journal of Adolescent & Adult Literacy*
Issues per year: 12 ISSN 1081-3004
800 Barksdale Road
Newark, DE 19714-8139 United States
http://www.reading.org

JAAR: *Journal of the American Academy of Religion*
Issues per year: 4 ISSN 0002-7189
P.O. Box 15399
Atlanta, GA 30333-0399 United States

JAH: *Journal of American History*
Issues per year: 4 ISSN 0021-8723
Executive Secretary
Bloomington, IN 47408-4199 United States

JAS: *The Journal of Asian Studies*
Issues per year: 4 ISSN 0021-9118
University of Michigan at Ann Arbor
Ann Arbor, MI 48109 United States

JC: *Journal of Communication*
Issues per year: 4 ISSN 0021-9916
Journals Department
Eynsham, Oxford 0X8 1JJ United Kingdom

JEGP: *The Journal of English and Germanic Philology*
Issues per year: 4 ISSN 0363-6941
Journals Division
Champaign, IL 61820 United States

JEH: *The Journal of Economic History*
Issues per year: 4 ISSN 0022-0507
40 West 20th Street
New York, NY 10011-4211 United States
http://www.cambridge.org

JEL: *Journal of Economic Literature*
Issues per year: 4 ISSN 0022-0515
2014 Broadway
Nashville, TN 37203 United States

JGS: *Journal of Gender Studies*
Issues per year: 3 ISSN 0958-9236
P.O. Box 25, Abingdon
Oxfordshire, England OX14 3UE United Kingdom

JIH: *The Journal of Interdisciplinary History*
Issues per year: 4 ISSN 0022-1953
Five Cambridge Center, Suite 4
Cambridge, MA 02142-1493 United States

JMH: *The Journal of Modern History*
Issues per year: 4 ISSN 0022-2801
Journals Division
Chicago, IL 60637-2954 United States
http://www.journals.uchicago.edu

JNE: *Journal of Negro Education*
Issues per year: 4 ISSN 0022-2984
1240 Randolph St., N.E.
Washington, DC 20017 United States

JNES: *Journal of Near Eastern Studies*
Issues per year: 4 ISSN 0022-2968
Journals Division
Chicago, IL 60637-2954 United States
http://www.journals.uchicago.edu

JouAmCul: *Journal of American Culture (Malden, MA)*
Issues per year: 4 ISSN 1540-1847
Attn: Rights Department
Oxford OX4 2DQ United Kingdom
http://www.blackwellpublishers.com/

JPC: *Journal of Popular Culture*
Issues per year: 4 ISSN 0022-3840
Attn: Rights Department
Oxford OX4 2DQ United Kingdom
http://www.blackwellpublishers.com/

JPR: *Journal of Peace Research*
Issues per year: 6 ISSN 0022-3433
1 Oliver's Yard, 55 City Road
London EC1Y 1SP United Kingdom
http://www.sagepub.com

JR: *The Journal of Religion*
Issues per year: 4 ISSN 0022-4189
Journals Division
Chicago, IL 60637-2954 United States
http://www.journals.uchicago.edu

JRAI: *Journal of the Royal Anthropological Institute*
Issues per year: 4 ISSN 1359-0987
Distribution Centre
Letchworth, Hertsfordshire SG6 1HN United Kingdom
http://www.therai.org.uk/

JSH: *Journal of Southern History*
Issues per year: 4 ISSN 0022-4642
Journal of Southern History MS 45
Houston, TX 77251-1892 United States
http://www.uga.edu/˜sha

JTWS: *Journal of Third World Studies*
Issues per year: 2 ISSN 8755-3449
PO Box 1232
Americus, GA 31709 United States

JWH: *Journal of Women's History*
Issues per year: 3 ISSN 1042-7961
601 N. Morton St.
Bloomington, IN 47404-3797 United States

K

Ken R: *The Kenyon Review*
Issues per year: 4 ISSN 0163-075X
Kenyon College
Gambier, OH 43022 United States
http://www.kenyonreview.org

Kliatt: *Kliatt*
Issues per year: 6 ISSN 1065-8602
33 Bay Street
Wellesley, MA 02481 United States

KR: *Kirkus Reviews*
Issues per year: 24 ISSN 0042-6598
770 Broadway, 6th Floor
New York, NY 10003 United States
http://www.vnuemedia.com/

L

Lam Bk Rpt: *Lambda Book Report*
Issues per year: 12 ISSN 1048-9487
PO Box 73910
Washington, DC 20056-3910 United States

Lang Soc: *Language in Society*
Issues per year: 4 ISSN 0047-4045
110 Midland Ave.
Port Chester, NY 10573 United States
http://www.cambridge.org

Lat Ant: *Latin American Antiquity*
Issues per year: 4 ISSN 1045-6635
900 Second St., N.W. Suite 12
Washington, DC 20002 United States

Law Q Rev: *Law Quarterly Review*
Issues per year: 4 ISSN 0023-933X
South Quay Plaza
London E14 9FT United Kingdom

Law&PolBR: *Law and Politics Book Review*
Issues per year: 12 ISSN 1062-7421
1527 New Hampshire Avenue NW
Washington, DC 20036 United States

Legacy: *Legacy: A Journal of American Women Writers*
Issues per year: 2 ISSN 0748-4321
233 N. 8th St.
Lincoln, NE 68588-0255 United States
http://www.nebraskapress.unl.edu/

LHT: *Library Hi Tech*
Issues per year: 4 ISSN 0737-8831
P.O. Box 1808
Ann Arbor, MI 48106 United States

Lib & Cul: *Libraries & Culture*
Issues per year: 4 ISSN 0894-8631
P.O. Box 7819
Austin, TX 78713-7819 United States
http://www.utexas.edu/utpress

LibMed: *Library Media Connection*
Issues per year: 5 ISSN 1542-4715
Subscription Department
Worthington, OH 43085-2372 United States

LJ: *Library Journal*
Issues per year: 21 ISSN 0363-0277
Box 59690
Boulder, CO 80322-9690 United States
http://www.cahners.com/

Lon R Bks: *London Review of Books*
Issues per year: 24 ISSN 0260-9592
28-30 Little Russell St.
London WC1A 2HN United Kingdom

LQ: *Library Quarterly*
Issues per year: 4 ISSN 0024-2519
Journals Division
Chicago, IL 60637-2954 United States
http://www.journals.uchicago.edu

LRTS: *Library Resources & Technical Services*
Issues per year: 4 ISSN 0024-2527
50 East Huron St.
Chicago, IL 60611-2795 United States

M

M Ed J: *Music Educators Journal*
Issues per year: 6 ISSN 0027-4321
1806 Robert Fulton Dr.
Reston, VA 20191 United States
www.menc.org/index2.html

M Lab R: *Monthly Labor Review*
Issues per year: 12 ISSN 0098-1818
Superintendent of Documents
Pittsburgh, PA 15250-7954 United States

MA: *Modern Age*
Issues per year: 4 ISSN 0026-7457
14 South Bryn Mawr Avenue
Bryn Mawr, PA 19010-3275 United States
http://www.isi.org

Mac: *Maclean's*
Issues per year: 52 ISSN 0024-9262
777 Bay St.
Toronto, Ontario M5W 1A7 Canada
www.cardmedia.com

Mag Antiq: *The Magazine Antiques*
Issues per year: 12 ISSN 0161-9284
Box 10547
Des Moines, IA 50340 United States

Magpies: *Magpies*
Issues per year: 5 ISSN 0817-0088
P.O. Box 98
Grange, Queensland 4051 Australia

MAQ: *Medical Anthropology Quarterly*
Issues per year: 4 ISSN 0745-5194
4350 N. Fairfax Dr., Suite 640
Arlington, VA 22203-1621 United States

Mar Crp G: *Marine Corps Gazette*
Issues per year: 12 ISSN 0025-3170
PO Box 1775
Quantico, VA 22134 United States

Math T: *Mathematics Teacher*
Issues per year: 9 ISSN 0025-5769
1906 Association Drive
Reston, VA 22091-1593 United States

Med R: *Medieval Review*
Issues per year: 12 ISSN 1096-746X
Western Michigan University,
Walwood Hall, 1903 W Michigan,
Kalamazoo, MI 49008-5432 United States

MEJ: *The Middle East Journal*
Issues per year: 4 ISSN 0026-3141
Indiana University Press
Bloomington, IN 47404 United States

MEP: *Middle East Policy*
Issues per year: 4 ISSN 1061-1924
1730 M. Street N.W., Suite 512
Washington, DC 20036-4505 United States

MEQ: *Middle East Quarterly*
Issues per year: 4 ISSN 1073-9467
1500 Walnut St., Ste 1050
Philadelphia, PA 19102-3523 United States
ww.mequarterly.org

MFSF: *Modern Fiction Studies*
Issues per year: 4 ISSN 0026-7724
Department of English
West Lafayette, IN 47907 United States

MFSF: *The Magazine of Fantasy and Science Fiction*
Issues per year: 11 ISSN 1095-8258
P.O. Box 3447
Hoboken, NY 07030 United States
www.fsfmag.com

MHR: *Medical Humanities*
Issues per year: 2 ISSN 1468-215X
BMA House
London WC1H 9JR United Kingdom

MLN: *MLN*
Issues per year: 5 ISSN 0026-7910
2715 N. Charles Street
Baltimore, MD 21218 United States

MP: *Modern Philology*
Issues per year: 4 ISSN 0026-8232
Journals Division
Chicago, IL 60637-2954 United States
http://www.journals.uchicago.edu

Ms: *Ms. Magazine*
Issues per year: 6 ISSN 0047-8318
135 W. 50th St.
New York, NY 10020 United States

MT: *Musical Times*
Issues per year: 4 ISSN 0027-4666
22 Gibson Sq
London N1 0R United Kingdom

N

NACEJou: *NACE Journal*
Issues per year: 4 ISSN 1542-2046
62 Highland Avenue
Bethlehem, PA 18017 United States

NAR: *The North American Review*
Issues per year: 6 ISSN 0029-2397
1222 West 27th Street
Cedar Falls, IA 50614-0516 United States

Nation: *The Nation*
Issues per year: 47 ISSN 0027-8378
33 Irving Place
New York, NY 10003 United States

Nature: *Nature*
Issues per year: 51 ISSN 0028-0836
Box 1733
Riverton, NJ 08077-7333 United States

NCFS: *Nineteenth-Century French Studies*
Issues per year: 2 ISSN 0146-7891
233 N. 8th St.
Lincoln, NE 68588-0255 United States
http://www.nebraskapress.unl.edu/

NEQ: *The New England Quarterly*
Issues per year: 4 ISSN 0028-4866
Northeastern University
Boston, MA 02115 United States

New ER: *New England Review*
Issues per year: 4 ISSN 1053-1297
23 South Main Street
Hanover, NH 03755-9886 United States

New Or: *New Orleans Magazine*
Issues per year: 12 ISSN 0897-8174
111 Veterans Blvd., 18th Floor
Metairie, LA 70005 United States

New R: *The New Republic*
Issues per year: 48 ISSN 0028-6583
P.O. Box 602
Mount Morris, IL 61054 United States
http://www.thenewrepublic.com/

New Sci: *New Scientist*
Issues per year: 51 ISSN 0262-4079
Quadrant House
Sutton, Surrey SM2 5AS United Kingdom

New York: *New York*
Issues per year: 50 ISSN 0028-7369
One International Blvd., Suite 444
Mahwah, NJ 07495-0017 United States

NH: *Natural History*
Issues per year: 12 ISSN 0028-0712
36 West 25th St., Fifth Floor
New York, NY 10010 United States

Nine-C Lit: *Nineteenth-Century Literature*
Issues per year: 4 ISSN 0891-9356
Journals Division
Berkeley, CA 94720 United States

NL: *The New Leader*
Issues per year: 6 ISSN 0028-6044
275 Seventh Ave.
New York, NY 10001 United States

Notes: *Notes*
Issues per year: 4 ISSN 0027-4380
8551 Research Way, Suite 180
Middletown, WI 53562 United States
http://www.musiclibraryassoc.org

NRJ: *Natural Resources Journal*
Issues per year: 4 ISSN 0028-0739
University of New Mexico
Albuquerque, NM 87131-1431 United States

NS: *New Statesman (1996)*
Issues per year: 50 ISSN 1364-7431
52 Grosvenor Gardens, 3rd Floor
London SW1W 0AU United Kingdom
http://

NW: *Newsweek*
Issues per year: 52 ISSN 0028-9604
Newsweek
Livingston, NJ 07039 United States

NWCR: *Naval War College Review*
Issues per year: 4 ISSN 0028-1484
U.S. Naval War College
Newport, RI 02841-1027 United States
http://www.nwc.navy.mil/press/

NWSA Jnl: *NWSA Journal*
Issues per year: 3 ISSN 1040-0656
601 N. Morton St.
Bloomington, IN 47404-3797 United States

NY: *The New Yorker*
Issues per year: 52 ISSN 0028-792X
750 Third Ave., 3rd Floor
New York, NY 10017 United States
http://www.condenet.com/condenast/

NYRB: *The New York Review of Books*
Issues per year: 21 ISSN 0028-7504
P.O. Box 420384
Palm Coast, FL 32142-0384 United States

NYT: *The New York Times*
Issues per year: 365 ISSN 0362-4331
1133 Sixth Avenue
New York, NY 10036 United States

NYTBR: *The New York Times Book Review*
Issues per year: 52 ISSN 0028-7806
1133 Sixth Avenue
New York, NY 10036 United States

O

ON: *Opera News*
Issues per year: 10 ISSN 0030-3607
70 Lincoln Center Plaza
New York, NY 10023 United States

OOB: *off our backs*
Issues per year: 11 ISSN 0030-0071
2337B 18th St., N.W.
Washington, DC 20009 United States

OS: *The Other Side*
Issues per year: 6 ISSN 0145-7675
300 West Apsley St.
Philadelphia, PA 19144-4285 United States

P

Pac A: *Pacific Affairs*
Issues per year: 4 ISSN 0030-851X
#223 - 2029 West Mall
Vancouver, British Columbia V6T 1Z2 Canada

PAJ: *PAJ: A Journal of Performance and Art*
Issues per year: 3 ISSN 1520-281X
Five Cambridge Center, Suite 4
Cambridge, MA 02142-1493 United States

Parabola: *Parabola*
Issues per year: 4 ISSN 0362-1596
656 Broadway
New York, NY 10012 United States

Parameters: *Parameters*
Issues per year: 4 ISSN 0031-1723
122 Forbes Ave.
Carlisle, PA 17013-5238 United States
Carlisle-www.army.mil/usawc/parameters

People: *People Weekly*
Issues per year: 51 ISSN 0093-7673
P. O. Box 30603
Tampa, FL 33630-0603 United States
http://www.timeinc.com

Per Psy: *Personnel Psychology*
Issues per year: 4 ISSN 0031-5826
Attn: Rights Department
Oxford OX4 2DQ United Kingdom
http://www.blackwellpublishers.com/

Pers PS: *Perspectives on Political Science*
Issues per year: 4 ISSN 1045-7097
110 Midland Ave.
Port Chester, NY 10573 United States
http://www.cambridge.org

PetPho: *Petersen's Photographic*
Issues per year: 12 ISSN 0199-4913
2400 E. Katella, 7th Floor
Anaheim, CA 92806 United States

PG: *Political Geography*
Issues per year: 8 ISSN 0962-6298
The Boulevard
Kidlington, Oxford 0X5 1GB United Kingdom

PhiKapP: *Phi Kappa Phi Forum*
Issues per year: 4 ISSN 1538-5914
c/o Dr. James P Kaetz, Ed.
Auburn, AL 36849-5306 United States

Phil R: *The Philosophical Review*
Issues per year: 4 ISSN 0031-8108
Sage School of Philosophy
Ithaca, NY 14853 United States

PHR: *Pacific Historical Review*
Issues per year: 4 ISSN 0030-8684
Journals Division
Berkeley, CA 94720 United States

Phys Today: *Physics Today*
Issues per year: 12 ISSN 0031-9228
One Physics Ellipse
College Park, MD 20740-3843 United States

Physics T: *The Physics Teacher*
Issues per year: 9 ISSN 0031-921X
Subscription Department
College Park, MD 20740-4100 United States

PMS: *Popular Music and Society*
Issues per year: 4 ISSN 0300-7766
11 New Fetter Lane
London EC4P 4EE United Kingdom

Poet: *Poetry*
Issues per year: 12 ISSN 0032-2032
60 West Walton Street
Chicago, IL 60610 United States

Pres St Q: *Presidential Studies Quarterly*
Issues per year: 4 ISSN 0360-4918
208 East 75th Street
New York, NY 10021 United States

Prog: *The Progressive*
Issues per year: 12 ISSN 0033-0736
409 East Main Street
Madison, WI 53703 United States

PSQ: *Political Science Quarterly*
Issues per year: 4 ISSN 0032-3195
475 Riverside Drive
New York, NY 10115-0012
United States

PSQ: *Prairie Schooner*
Issues per year: 4 ISSN 0032-6682
233 N. 8th St.
Lincoln, NE 68588-0255 United States
http://www.nebraskapress.unl.edu/

Pub Hist: *Public Historian*
Issues per year: 4 ISSN 0272-3433
Journals Division
Berkeley, CA 94720 United States

Pub Int: *Public Interest*
Issues per year: 4 ISSN 0033-3557
1112 16th St. N.W., Suite 140
Washington, DC 20036 United States

Pub Op Q: *Public Opinion Quarterly*
Issues per year: 4 ISSN 0033-362X
Journals Department
Eynsham, Oxford 0X8 1JJ United Kingdom

PW: *Publishers Weekly*
Issues per year: 55 ISSN 0000-0019
Box 6457
Torrance, CA 90504-0457 United States
http://www.cahners.com/

Q

QRB: *Quarterly Review of Biology*
Issues per year: 4 ISSN 0033-5770
Journals Division
Chicago, IL 60637-2954 United States
http://www.journals.uchicago.edu

Quad: *Quadrant*
Issues per year: 10 ISSN 0033-5002
PO Box 1495
Collingwood, Victoria 3066 Australia

Queens Q: *Queen's Quarterly*
Issues per year: 4 ISSN 0033-6041
144 Barrie Street
Ottawa, Ontario K7L 3N6 Canada
http://www.queensu.ca/quarterly/

R

R Today: *Reading Today*
Issues per year: 6 ISSN 0737-4208
800 Barksdale Road
Newark, DE 19714-8139 United States
http://www.reading.org

R&R Bk N: *Reference & Research Book News*
Issues per year: 4 ISSN 0887-3763
5739 N.E. Sumner St.
Portland, OR 97218 United States

R&USQ: *Reference & User Services Quarterly*
Issues per year: 4 ISSN 1094-9054
50 East Huron St.
Chicago, IL 60611-2795 United States

RAH: *Reviews in American History*
Issues per year: 4 ISSN 0048-7511
Journals Publishing Division
Baltimore, MD 21211-2190 United States

RCF: *The Review of Contemporary Fiction*
Issues per year: 3 ISSN 0276-0045
4241 Illinois State University
Normal, IL 61790-4241 United States

Reason: *Reason*
Issues per year: 11 ISSN 0048-6906
P.O. Box 526
Mount Morris, IL 61054 United States

Ref Rev: *Reference Reviews*
27500 Drake Road
Farmington Hills, MI 48331 United States
http://www.gale.com

Rel St: *Religious Studies*
Issues per year: 4 ISSN 0034-4125
40 West 20th Street
New York, NY 10011-4211 United States
http://www.cambridge.org

Ren Q: *Renaissance Quarterly*
Issues per year: 4 ISSN 0034-4338
The Graduate School and University Center
New York, NY 10016-4309 United States
http://www.r-s-a.org/

RES: *The Review of English Studies*
Issues per year: 5 ISSN 0034-6551
Journals Department
Eynsham, Oxford 0X8 1JJ United Kingdom

Res Links: *Resource Links*
Issues per year: 5 ISSN 1201-7647
P.O. Box 9
Pouch Cove, New Foundland A0A 3L0 Canada
http://www.atcl.ca

RM: *The Review of Metaphysics*
Issues per year: 4 ISSN 0034-6632
Catholic University of America
Washington, DC 20064 United States

RocksMiner: *Rocks & Minerals*
Issues per year: 6 ISSN 0035-7529
1319 18th St., NW
Washington, DC 20036-1802 United States

Roundup M: *Roundup Magazine*
Issues per year: 6 ISSN 1081-2229
P.O. Box 29, Star Route
Encampment, WY 82325 United States

RT: *The Reading Teacher*
Issues per year: 8 ISSN 0034-0561
800 Barksdale Road
Newark, DE 19714-8139 United States
http://www.reading.org

Russ Rev: *The Russian Review*
Issues per year: 4 ISSN 0036-0341
Attn: Rights Department
Oxford OX4 2DQ United Kingdom
http://www.blackwellpublishers.com/

S

S Liv: *Southern Living*
Issues per year: 12 ISSN 0038-4305
P.O. Box 830119
Birmingham, AL 35201 United States

S&S: *Science & Society*
Issues per year: 4 ISSN 0036-8237
72 Spring Street
New York, NY 10012 United States

S&T: *Sky & Telescope*
Issues per year: 12 ISSN 0037-6604
49 Bay State Rd.
Cambridge, MA 02138 United States
http://www.skypub.com

SB: *Science Books & Films*
Issues per year: 6 ISSN 0098-342X
P.O. Box 2033
Marion, OH 43305-2033 United States
http://www.aaas.org/

Scan St: *Scandinavian Studies*
Issues per year: 4 ISSN 0036-5637
3003 JKHB
Provo, UT 84602 United States

Sch Lib: *School Librarian*
Issues per year: 4 ISSN 0036-6595
Unite 2, Lotmead Business Village
Wanborough, Swindon SN4 0UY United Kingdom

Sci: *Science*
Issues per year: 51 ISSN 0036-8075
P.O. Box 2033
Marion, OH 43305-2033 United States
http://www.aaas.org/

Sci Teach: *The Science Teacher*
Issues per year: 9 ISSN 0036-8555
1840 Wilson Blvd.
Arlington, VA 22201-3000 United States

SciTech: *SciTech Book News*
Issues per year: 4 ISSN 0196-6006
5739 N.E. Sumner St.
Portland, OR 97218 United States

SE: *Social Education*
Issues per year: 7 ISSN 0037-7724
3501 Newark St. N.W.
Washington, DC 20016 United States

SEP: *Saturday Evening Post*
Issues per year: 6 ISSN 0048-9239
1100 Waterway Blvd.
Indianapolis, IN 46202 United States

Sew R: *The Sewanee Review*
Issues per year: 4 ISSN 0037-3052
University of the South
Sewanee, TN 37375-1000 United States

SF: *Social Forces*
Issues per year: 4 ISSN 0037-7732
P.O. Box 2288
Chapel Hill, NC 27515-2288
United States

SFS: *Science Fiction Studies*
Issues per year: 3 ISSN 0091-7729
Arthur B. Evans
Greencastle, IN 46135-0037
United States

Shakes Q: *Shakespeare Quarterly*
Issues per year: 4 ISSN 0037-3222
201 East Capitol Street S.E.
Washington, DC 20003 United States

SHQ: *Southwestern Historical Quarterly*
Issues per year: 4 ISSN 0038-478X
Richardson Hall 2-306
Austin, TX 78712 United States

Si & So: *Sight and Sound*
Issues per year: 12 ISSN 0037-4806
Sight and Sound Subscriptions
Harborough, Leicestershire LE16 9EF United Kingdom

SIAM Rev: *SIAM Review*
Issues per year: 4 ISSN 0036-1445
3600 University City Science
Philadelphia, PA 19104-2688
United States

Signs: *Signs*
Issues per year: 4 ISSN 0097-9740
Journals Division
Chicago, IL 60637-2954 United States
http://www.journals.uchicago.edu

Six Ct J: *The Sixteenth Century Journal*
Issues per year: 4 ISSN 0361-0160
MC 111L
Kirksville, MO 63501 United States

Slav R: *Slavic Review*
Issues per year: 4 ISSN 0037-6779
Jordan Quad-Acacia
Stanford, CA 94305-4130 United States
http://www.fas.harvard.edu/~aaass

SLJ: *School Library Journal*
Issues per year: 12 ISSN 0362-8930
Box 57559
Boulder, CO 80322-7559 United States
http://www.cahners.com/

Soc: *Society*
Issues per year: 6 ISSN 0147-2011
Rutgers - The State University of New Jersey
Piscataway, NJ 08854-8042 United States
http://www.transactionpub.com/cgi-bin/transactionpublishers.storefront

Soc Ser R: *Social Service Review*
Issues per year: 4 ISSN 0037-7961
Journals Division
Chicago, IL 60637-2954 United States
http://www.journals.uchicago.edu

South CR: *South Carolina Review*
Issues per year: 2 ISSN 0038-3163
Department of English
Clemson, SC 29634-1503 United States

South HR: *Southern Humanities Review*
Issues per year: 4 ISSN 0038-4186
9088 Haley Center
Auburn, AL 36849 United States

South R: *The Southern Review*
Issues per year: 4 ISSN 0038-4534
43 Allen Hall
Baton Rouge, LA 70803-5005 United States

SPA: *Bulletin of the Atomic Scientists*
Issues per year: 6 ISSN 0096-3402
6042 South Kimbark
Chicago, IL 60637 United States

Spec: *Spectator*
Issues per year: 52 ISSN 0038-6952
56 Doughty Street
London WC1N 2LL United Kingdom
http://www.spectator.co.uk

Spectr: *Spectrum: the Journal of State Government*
Issues per year: 4 ISSN 1067-8530
2760 Research Park Drive
Lexington, KY 40578-1910 United States
http://www.statesnews.org

Specu: *Speculum: A Journal of Medieval Studies*
Issues per year: 4 ISSN 0038-7134
1430 Massachusetts Avenue
Cambridge, MA 02138 United States

SS: *The Social Studies*
Issues per year: 6 ISSN 0037-7996
1319 18th St., NW
Washington, DC 20036-1802 United States

SSJ: *Sociology of Sport Journal*
Issues per year: 4 ISSN 0741-1235
Box 5076
Champaign, IL 61825-5076 United States

Storyworks: *Storyworks*
Issues per year: 6 ISSN 1068-0292
557 Broadway
New York, NY 10012-3999 United States
http://www.scholastic.com

Stud Hum: *Studies in the Humanities*
Issues per year: 2 ISSN 0039-3800
110 Leonard Hall
Indiana, PA 15705 United States

T

T&C: *Technology and Culture*
Issues per year: 4 ISSN 0040-165X
Journals Division
Chicago, IL 60637-2954 United States
http://www.journals.uchicago.edu

TC Math: *Teaching Children Mathematics*
Issues per year: 9 ISSN 1073-5836
1906 Association Drive
Reston, VA 22091-1593 United States

TCR: *Teachers College Record*
Issues per year: 9 ISSN 0161-4681
525 W. 120th St.
New York, NY 10027 United States

TDR: *TDR (Cambridge, Mass.)*
Issues per year: 4 ISSN 1054-2043
Five Cambridge Center, Suite 4
Cambridge, MA 02142-1493 United States

Teach Lib: *Teacher Librarian*
Issues per year: 5 ISSN 1481-1782
4501 Forbes Blvd., Suite 200
Lanham, MD 20706 United States

Teach Mus: *Teaching Music*
Issues per year: 6 ISSN 1069-7446
1806 Robert Fulton Dr.
Reston, VA 20191 United States
www.menc.org/index2.html

Tec Teach: *The Technology Teacher*
Issues per year: 8 ISSN 0746-3537
1914 Association Drive, Suite 201
Reston, VA 20191-1539 United States

TES: *Times Educational Supplement*
Issues per year: 52 ISSN 0040-7887
Admiral House
London E1 9XY United Kingdom

Theat J: *Theatre Journal*
Issues per year: 4 ISSN 0192-2882
2715 N. Charles Street
Baltimore, MD 21218 United States

Theol St: *Theological Studies*
Issues per year: 4 ISSN 0040-5639
P.O. Box 465
Hanover, PA 17331 United States

Tikkun: *Tikkun*
Issues per year: 6 ISSN 0887-9982
2342 Shattuck Ave., Suite 1200
Berkeley, CA 94704 United States

Time: *Time*
Issues per year: 52 ISSN 0040-781X
P O Box 60001
Tampa, FL 33660-0001 United States
http://www.timeinc.com

TimHES: *Times Higher Education Supplement*
Issues per year: 52 ISSN 0049-3929
Admiral House
London E1 9XY United Kingdom

TLS: *TLS. Times Literary Supplement*
Issues per year: 52 ISSN 0307-661X
Admiral House
London E1 9XY United Kingdom

TSWL: *Tulsa Studies in Women's Literature*
Issues per year: 2 ISSN 0732-7730
Tulsa Studies in Women's Literature
Tulsa, OK 74104-3189 United States

TT: *Theology Today*
Issues per year: 4 ISSN 0040-5736
Princeton Theological Seminary
Princeton, NJ 08542 United States

TV Q: *Television Quarterly*
Issues per year: 4 ISSN 0040-2796
111 West 57th Street
New York, NY 10019 United States

U

USNews & Wrld Rpt: *U.S. News & World Report*
Issues per year: 50 ISSN 0041-5537
P.O. Box 55929
Boulder, CO 80322-5929 United States
http://www.usnews.com

V

Veg J: *Vegetarian Journal*
Issues per year: 6 ISSN 0885-7636
P.O. Box 1463
Baltimore, MD 21203 United States
www.vrg.org

VOYA: *Voice of Youth Advocates*
Issues per year: 6 ISSN 0160-4201
4501 Forbes Blvd., Suite 200
Lanham, MD 20706 United States

VQR: *The Virginia Quarterly Review*
Issues per year: 4 ISSN 0042-675X
One West Range
Charlottesville, VA 22903 United States

VS: *Victorian Studies*
Issues per year: 4 ISSN 0042-5222
601 N. Morton St.
Bloomington, IN 47404-3797 United States

W

W&M Q: *The William and Mary Quarterly*
Issues per year: 4 ISSN 0043-5597
P.O. Box 8781
Williamsburg, VA 23187-8781 United States

WestFolk: *Western Folklore*
Issues per year: 4 ISSN 0043-373X
9420 Carrillo Avenue
Montclair, CA 91763-2412 United States

WHQ: *The Western Historical Quarterly*
Issues per year: 4 ISSN 0043-3810
Utah State University
Logan, UT 84322-0740 United States

Wil Q: *The Wilson Quarterly*
Issues per year: 4 ISSN 0363-3276
Wilson Center Membership Dept.
Palm Coast, FL 32142-9860 United States

WLT: *World Literature Today*
Issues per year: 4 ISSN 0196-3570
Center for Economic and
Norman, OK 73019 United States

Wom HR: *Women's History Review*
Issues per year: 4 ISSN 0961-2025
Attn: Roger Osborn-King
Wallingford, Oxford OX10 0YG United Kingdom

Wom R Bks: *The Women's Review of Books*
Issues per year: 11 ISSN 0738-1433
Wellesley College
Wellesley, MA 02481 United States
http://www.wellesley.edu/WomensReview/

World&I: *World and I*
Issues per year: 12 ISSN 0887-9346
3600 New York Ave NE
Washington, DC 20002 United States

WP: *World Politics*
Issues per year: 4 ISSN 0043-8871
2715 N. Charles Street
Baltimore, MD 21218 United States

Y

YR: *Yale Review*
Issues per year: 4 ISSN 0044-0124
Attn: Rights Department
Oxford OX4 2DQ United Kingdom
http://www.blackwellpublishers.com/

Z

Zygon: *Zygon*
Issues per year: 4 ISSN 0591-2385
Attn: Rights Department
Oxford OX4 2DQ United Kingdom
http://www.blackwellpublishers.com/

A

Abele, Jon R. - *Medical Errors and Litigation: Investigation and Case Preparation*
    SciTech - v28 - i3 - Sept 2004 - p11(1) [501+]

Abell, Martha L. - *Differential Equations with Mathematics, 3rd Ed.*
    TimHES - v0 - i1668 - Nov 26 2004 - pXVI(1) [501+]

Abelmann, Nancy - *The Melodrama of Mobility: Women, Talk, and Class in Contemporary South Korea*
    JAS - v63 - i3 - August 2004 - p807-808 [501+]
    R&R Bk N - v19 - i2 - May 2004 - p136 [51-500]

Abeloff, Martin D. - *Clinical Oncology, 3rd Ed.*
    SciTech - v28 - i4 - Dec 2004 - p91(1) [51-500]

Abelson, John R. - *Amorphous and Nanocrystalline Silicon-Based Films--2003*
    SciTech - v28 - i1 - March 2004 - p160(1) [51-500]

Abelson, Robert P. - *Experiments with People: Revelations from Social Psychology*
    CS - v33 - i5 - Sept 2004 - p621-621 [501+]

Abercrombie, Nicholas - *Sociology*
    Choice - v42 - i3 - Nov 2004 - p570(1) [1-50]

Aberg, Martin - *Social Capital and Democratization: Roots of Trust in Post-Communist Poland and Ukraine*
    Slav R - v63 - i3 - Fall 2004 - p626-627 [501+]

Aberjhani - *Encyclopedia of the Harlem Renaissance*
    y VOYA - v27 - i3 - August 2004 - p246(1) [1-50]

Aberle, Doug - *Earth Stories: Paleontology, Vol. 1*
    LibMed - v22 - i5 - Feb 2004 - p55(2) [501+]

Abernathy, Donzaleigh - *Partners to History: Martin Luther King Jr., Ralph David Abernathy, and the Civil Rights Movement*
    y VOYA - v27 - i4 - Oct 2004 - p321(2) [51-500]

Abernethy, David B. - *The Dynamics of Global Dominance: European Overseas Empires, 1415-1980*
    HER - v119 - i483 - Sept 2004 - p1085(3) [501+]

Abersek, B. - *How Gears Break*
    SciTech - v28 - i4 - Dec 2004 - p145(1) [501+]

Aberyratne, Ruwantissa I.R. - *Aviation in Crisis*
    R&R Bk N - v19 - i2 - May 2004 - p109(1) [51-500]

Abeysekara, Ananda - *Colors of the Robe: Religion, Identity, and Difference*
    Pac A - v77 - i2 - Summer 2004 - p364(2) [501+]

Abikoff, William - *In the Tradition of Ahlfors and Bers, III: Proceedings*
    SciTech - v28 - i3 - Sept 2004 - p39(1) [51-500]

Abildskov, Marilyn - *The Men in My Country*
    BL - v101 - i3 - Oct 1 2004 - p296(1) [51-500]
    KR - v72 - i17 - Sept 1 2004 - p843(1) [51-500]
    LJ - v129 - i19 - Nov 15 2004 - p68(1) [501+]

Abisaab, Rula Jurdi - *Converting Persia: Religion and Power in the Safavid Empire*
    Choice - v42 - i1 - Sept 2004 - p170(1) [501+]

Abish, Walter - *Double Vision*
    BW - v34 - i12 - March 21 2004 - p4(1) [501+]

Abley, Mark - *Spoken Here: Travels Among Threatened Languages*
    CBRA - Annual 2003 - p269(1) [501+]
    Globe & Mail - August 21 2004 - pD13 [1-50]
    IBMR - v29 - i1 - Jan 2005 - p46(1) [501+]
    TLS - i5265 - Feb 27 2004 - p29-29 [501+]
    World&I - v19 - i2 - Feb 2004 - p225 [501+]

Ablow, Keith - *Murder Suicide*
    Ent W - i775 - July 23 2004 - p82 [51-500]

Abnett, Dan - *Double Eagle*
    ChrSFF&H - v26 - i10 - Oct 2004 - p25(1) [51-500]
    Lone Wolves
    ChrSFF&H - v26 - i10 - Oct 2004 - p28(1) [51-500]

Abney, Lisa - *Twenty-First-Century American Novelists*
    R&R Bk N - v19 - i4 - Nov 2004 - p240(1) [501+]

Aboff, Marcie - *The Giant Jelly Bean Jar (Illus. by Billin-Frye, Paige)*
    c SLJ - v50 - i9 - Sept 2004 - p154(1) [51-500]

Abou El Fadl, Khaled - *Islam and the Challenge of Democracy: A Boston Review Book*
    Choice - v42 - i4 - Dec 2004 - p735(1) [1-50]

Abou Zahab, Mariam - *Islamist Networks: The Afghan-Pakistan Connection*
    R&R Bk N - v19 - i3 - August 2004 - p18(1) [1-50]

Abraham, Arthur - *An Introduction to the Precolonial History of the Mende of Sierra Leone*
    R&R Bk N - v19 - i1 - Feb 2004 - p51(1) [51-500]

Abraham, Carolyn - *Possessing Genius: The Bizarre Odyssey of Einstein's Brain*
    TimHES - v0 - i1660 - Oct 1 2004 - p24(1) [501+]

Abraham, Henry David - *What's a Parent To Do?: Straight Talk on Drugs and Alcohol*
    LJ - v129 - i16 - Oct 1 2004 - p106(1) [51-500]
    LJ - v129 - i17 - Oct 15 2004 - p80(2) [51-500]

Abraham, Pearl - *The Seventh Beggar*
    KR - v72 - i14 - July 15 2004 - p643(1) [51-500]
    NYTBR - March 6 2005 - p17 [501+]
    PW - v252 - i1 - Jan 3 2005 - p34(2) [501+]

Abraham, Philip - *Cars*
    y SLJ - v51 - i1 - Jan 2005 - p139(2) [51-500]
    Firefighter
    c LibMed - v22 - i6 - March 2004 - p76(1) [501+]
    Television and Movies
    y SLJ - v51 - i1 - Jan 2005 - p139(2) [51-500]

Abraham, Rebecca - *Organizational Cynicism: Definitions, Bases and Consequences*
    R&R Bk N - v19 - i3 - August 2004 - p106(1) [1-50]

Abraham, Susan Gonzales - *Cecilia's Year*
    y BL - v101 - i9-10 - Jan 1 2005 - p856(1) [1-50]
    CH Bwatch - Jan 2005 - pNA [51-500]

Abrahams, Debbie - *25 Cushions to Knit: Fantastic Cushions for Every Room in Your Home*
    LJ - v129 - i13 - August 2004 - p77(1) [51-500]

Abrahams, Marc - *IgNobel Prizes 2: Why Chickens Prefer Beautiful Humans*
    New Sci - v184 - i2477 - Dec 11 2004 - p51(1) [501+]

Abrahams, Peter - *Down the Rabbit Hole: An Echo Falls Mystery*
    y Kliatt - v39 - i2 - March 2005 - p6(1) [51-500]
    Oblivion
    KR - v72 - i24 - Dec 15 2004 - p1151(1) [501+]
    LJ - v129 - i20 - Dec 1 2004 - p86(1) [1-50]
    LJ - v130 - i3 - Feb 15 2005 - p113(1) [51-500]

Abrahamson, Eric - *Change Without Pain: How Managers Can Overcome Initiative Overload, Organizational Chaos, and Employee Burnout*
    Per Psy - v57 - i4 - Winter 2004 - p1062(3) [501+]

Abramo, J.L. - *Counting to Infinity*
    KR - v72 - i14 - July 15 2004 - p661(1) [51-500]
    PW - v251 - i29 - July 19 2004 - p148(1) [51-500]

Abrams, Anne Collins - *Clinical Drug Therapy: Rationales for Nursing Practice, 7th Ed.*
    SciTech - v28 - i4 - Dec 2004 - p116(1) [1-50]

Abrams, Brad - *.NET Framework Standard Library Annotated Reference, Vol. 1*
    SciTech - v28 - i3 - Sept 2004 - p18(1) [501+]

Abrams, Bradley F. - *The Struggle for the Soul of the Nation: Czech Culture and the Rise of Communism*
    Choice - v42 - i4 - Dec 2004 - p716(1) [1-50]
    For Aff - v83 - i5 - Sept-Oct 2004 - p164 [501+]
    R&R Bk N - v19 - i3 - August 2004 - p171(1) [501+]

Abrams, Douglas Carl - *Selling the Old-Time Religion: American Fundamentalists and Mass Culture, 1920-1940*
    HNet - Sept 2004 - pNA [501+]

Abrams, Floyd - *Speaking Freely: Trials of the First Amendment*
    KR - v73 - i3 - Feb 1 2005 - p157(1) [501+]
    LJ - v129 - i20 - Dec 1 2004 - p90(1) [1-50]
    PW - v252 - i7 - Feb 14 2005 - p65(1) [51-500]

Abrams, Fran - *Freedom's Cause: Lives of the Suffragettes*
    TimHES - v0 - i1650 - July 23 2004 - p28(2) [501+]

Abrams, Liesa - *Divorce*
    y SLJ - v50 - i10 - Oct 2004 - p182(2) [51-500]

Abrams, Michael T. - *Research Training in Psychiatry Residency: Strategies for Reform*
    SciTech - v28 - i1 - March 2004 - p98(1) [51-500]

Abrams, Pare - *Now I Eat My ABC's (Illus. by Wolf, Bruce)*
    c PW - v251 - i38 - Sept 20 2004 - p64(1) [51-500]

Abrams, Robert E. - *Landscape and Ideology in American Renaissance Literature: Topographies of Skepticism*
    Choice - v42 - i1 - Sept 2004 - p98(1) [501+]

Abrams, S.A. - *Stable Isotopes in Human Nutrition: Laboratory Methods and Research Applications*
    QRB - v79 - i3 - Sept 2004 - p345(1) [501+]

Abrams, Sabrina Fuchs - *Mary McCarthy: Gender, Politics, and the Postwar Intellectual*
    R&R Bk N - v19 - i4 - Nov 2004 - p243(1) [501+]

Abramson, Ian - *Oracle Database 10g: A Beginner's Guide*
    LJ - v129 - i16 - Oct 1 2004 - p104(1) [51-500]

Abramson, John - *Overdosed America: The Broken Promise of American Medicine*
    BW - v34 - i41 - Oct 10 2004 - p4(1) [501+]
    Bwatch - March 2005 - pNA [51-500]
    PW - v251 - i39 - Sept 27 2004 - p54(1) [51-500]
    SciTech - v28 - i4 - Dec 2004 - p76(1) [51-500]

Abramson, Paul R. - *Sexual Rights in America: The Ninth Amendment and the Pursuit of Happiness*
    Choice - v41 - i7 - March 2004 - p1371(1) [501+]

Abramson, Stephen - *Financial Professional's Guide to Qualified Retirement Plans: Planning, Implementation, Operation, and Compliance, 2004 Ed.*
    R&R Bk N - v19 - i1 - Feb 2004 - pNA [51-500]

Abt-Perkins, Dawn - *Making Race Visible: Literary Research for Cultural Understanding*
    TCR - v106 - i5 - May 2004 - p901(4) [501+]

Abu El-Haj, Nadia - *Facts on the Ground: Archaeological Practice and Territorial Self-Fashioning in Israeli Society*
    HNet - Sept 2004 - pNA [501+]
    Isis - v95 - i3 - Sept 2004 - p523(2) [501+]

Abu-Ghazaleh, Talal - *Intellectual Property Laws of the Arab Countries*
    R&R Bk N - v19 - i3 - August 2004 - p209(1) [1-50]

Abu-Jaber, Diana - *The Language of Baklava*
    Ent W - i812 - March 25 2005 - p76 [51-500]
    KR - v73 - i1 - Jan 1 2005 - p27(1) [51-500]
    LJ - v130 - i2 - Feb 1 2005 - p109(1) [51-500]
    PW - v252 - i3 - Jan 17 2005 - p43(1) [51-500]

Abu-Jamal, Mumia - *We Want Freedom: A Life in the Black Panther Party*
    Choice - v42 - i3 - Nov 2004 - p545(1) [1-50]
    R&R Bk N - v19 - i3 - August 2004 - p66(1) [51-500]

Abu-Kandil, Abu - *Matrix Riccati Equations in Control and Systems Theory*
    SIAM Rev - v46 - i4 - Dec 2004 - p753-754 [501+]

Abu-Laban, Yasmeen - *Selling Diversity: Immigration, Multiculturalism, Employment Equity, and Globalization*
    CBRA - Annual 2003 - p354(1) [501+]

Abu-Rabi, Ibrahim M. - *Contemporary Arab Thought: Studies in Post-1967 Arab Intellectual History*
    Choice - v41 - i11-12 - July-August 2004 - p2103(1) [501+]

Abu-Sahlieh, Sami A. - *Muslims in the West: Redefining the Separation of Church and State*
    IJMES - v36 - i3 - August 2004 - p508-509 [501+]

AbuKhalil, As'ad - *The Battle for Saudi Arabia: Royalty, Fundamentalism, and Global Power*
    MEJ - v59 - i1 - Wntr 2005 - p151(2) [501+]

Abulafia, David - *Italy in the Central Middle Ages: 1000-1300*
    TimHES - v0 - i1680 - Feb 25 2005 - pXI(1) [501+]
    The Mediterranean in History
    TimHES - v0 - i1669 - Dec 3 2004 - p24(1) [501+]

Aburish, Said K. - *Nasser: The Last Arab*
    Spec - v295 - i9178 - July 3 2004 - p37(1) [501+]

Aburish, Said K, - *Saddam Hussein: The Politics of Revenge*
    Globe & Mail - Feb 26 2005 - pD15 [501+]

Abusch, Tzvi - *Riches Hidden in Secret Places: Ancient Near Eastern Studies in Memory of Thorkild Jacobsen*
    JNES - v64 - i1 - Jan 2005 - p71(2) [501+]

Academic de Droit International de la Haye - *Recueil des cours, Vol. 300*
    R&R Bk N - v19 - i4 - Nov 2004 - p158(1) [501+]
    Recueil des cours, Vol. 301
    R&R Bk N - v19 - i4 - Nov 2004 - p159(1) [501+]

Acamovic, T. - *Poisonous Plants and Related Toxins: Proceedings*
    SciTech - v28 - i3 - Sept 2004 - p132(1) [51-500]

Acampora, Christa Davis - *A Nietzschean Bestiary: Becoming Animal Beyond Docile and Brutal*
    Choice - v42 - i2 - Oct 2004 - p307(1) [51-500]

Accattoli, Luigi - *John Paul II: A Pope for the People*
    CR - v285 - i1664 - Sept 2004 - p185(1) [51-500]

Acebes, Hector - *Hector Acebes: Portraits in Africa, 1948-1953*
    Choice - v42 - i7 - March 2005 - p1221(1) [51-500]
    LJ - v129 - i19 - Nov 15 2004 - p56(1) [51-500]
    R&R Bk N - v19 - i4 - Nov 2004 - p248(1) [501+]

Acello, Barbara - *Nursing Assisting: Essentials for Long-Term Care, 2nd Ed.*
    SciTech - v28 - i4 - Dec 2004 - p121 [51-500]

Acereda, Alberto - *Modernism, Ruben Dario, and the Poetics of Despair*
    Choice - v42 - i7 - March 2005 - p1233(1) [51-500]
    R&R Bk N - v19 - i4 - Nov 2004 - p232(1) [501+]

Acham, Christine - *Revolution Televised: Prime Time and the Struggle for Black Power*
 Black Iss - v7 - i2 - March-April 2005 - p57(1) [501+]
 PW - v251 - i33 - August 16 2004 - p50(2) [51-500]

Acharya, Tinku - *JPEG 2000 Standard for Image Compression: Concepts, Algorithms and VLSI Architecture*
 SciTech - v28 - i4 - Dec 2004 - p155(1) [51-500]

Achcar, Gilbert - *Eastern Cauldron: Islam, Afghanistan, Palestine and Iraq in a Marxist Mirror*
 R&R Bk N - v19 - i3 - August 2004 - p48(1) [51-500]

Achebe, Chinua - *Collected Poems*
 y BL - v100 - i22 - August 2004 - p1891(1) [51-500]

Achenbach, Joel - *The Grand Idea: George Washington's Potomac and the Race to the West*
 BW - v34 - i27 - July 4 2004 - p4(1) [501+]
 LJ - v129 - i13 - August 2004 - p92(1) [501+]

Acheson, James M. - *Capturing the Commons: Devising Institutions to Manage the Maine Lobster Industry*
 NRJ - v44 - i3 - Summer 2004 - p916-921 [501+]

Achinstein, Peter - *The Book of Evidence*
 Dialogue - v43 - i1 - Wntr 2004 - p184-186 [501+]

Achinstein, Sharon - *Literature and Dissent in Milton's England*
 Clio - v33 - i3 - Spring 2004 - p336(6) [501+]
 JR - v84 - i3 - July 2004 - p508(2) [501+]
 Ren Q - v57 - i3 - Fall 2004 - p1173(3) [501+]

Achuthan, Lakshman - *Beating the Business Cycle: How to Predict and Profit from Turning Points in the Economy*
 Choice - v42 - i3 - Nov 2004 - p531(1) [1-50]
 Har Bus R - v82 - i4 - April 2004 - p28(1) [501+]

Acidini Luchinat, Cristina - *The Medici, Michelangelo, and the Art of Late Renaissance Florence*
 JIH - v34 - i4 - Spring 2004 - p645-647 [501+]
 Six Ct J - v34 - i4 - Winter 2003 - p1266-1267 [501+]

Aciman, Andre - *The Proust Project*
 BL - v101 - i4 - Oct 15 2004 - p379(1) [51-500]
 PW - v251 - i33 - August 16 2004 - p49(2) [51-500]

Acito, Marc - *How I Paid for College: A Novel of Sex, Theft, Friendship, and Musical Theater*
 NYTBR - Oct 10 2004 - p20 [501+]
 How I Paid for College: A Novel of Sex, Theft, Friendship & Musical Theater (Read by Woodman, Jeff). Audiobook Review
 y Kliatt - v39 - i2 - March 2005 - p53(1) [51-500]
 LJ - v130 - i3 - Feb 15 2005 - p168(1) [51-500]
 How I Paid for College: A Novel of Sex, Theft, Friendship & Musical Theater
 Advocate - Nov 23 2004 - p96(1) [501+]
 y BL - v100 - i22 - August 2004 - p1895(1) [51-500]
 Ent W - Sept 10 2004 - p170 [51-500]
 LJ - v129 - i16 - Oct 1 2004 - p66(1) [51-500]
 People - v62 - i13 - Sept 27 2004 - p56 [501+]
 PW - v251 - i36 - Sept 6 2004 - p47(1) [51-500]
 y SLJ - v50 - i9 - Sept 2004 - p234(1) [51-500]

Acker, James R. - *Two Voices on the Legal Rights of America's Youth*
 Law&PolBR - August 2004 - p688(4) [501+]

Acker, Kerry - *Dorothea Lange*
 VOYA - v27 - i5 - Dec 2004 - p421(1) [51-500]

Ackerly, Brooke - *Political Theory and Feminist Social Criticism*
 Signs - v30 - i2 - Wntr 2005 - p1674(4) [501+]

Ackerman, Alan R. - *Investing under Fire: Winning Strategies from the Masters for Bulls, Bears, and the Bewildered*
 R&R Bk N - v19 - i3 - August 2004 - p137(1) [51-500]

Ackerman, Bruce - *Deliberation Day*
 NYRB - v51 - i16 - Oct 21 2004 - p51(3) [501+]
 Pub Op Q - v68 - i4 - Winter 2004 - p641(4) [501+]
 Voting with Dollars: A New Paradigm for Campaign Finance
 Law&PolBR - Sept 2004 - pNA [501+]

Ackerman, Diane - *An Alchemy of Mind: The Marvel and Mystery of the Brain*
 BL - v101 - i9-10 - Jan 1 2005 - p768(1) [51-500]
 NYTBR - August 29 2004 - p15 [501+]
 People - v62 - i12 - July 12 2004 - p46 [51-500]
 SB - v40 - i3 - May-June 2004 - p117(1) [501+]
 Wom R Bks - v22 - i3 - Dec 2004 - p11(2) [501+]

Ackerman, Forrest J. - *Worlds of Tomorrow: The Amazing Universe of Science-Fiction Art*
 BW - v34 - i46 - Nov 14 2004 - p13(1) [1-50]
 Bwatch - Jan 2005 - pNA [51-500]

Ackerman, Frank - *Priceless: On Knowing the Price of Everything and the Value of Nothing*
 R&R Bk N - v19 - i4 - Nov 2004 - p88(1) [51-500]

Ackerman, Karen - *Bean's Big Day*
 c LibMed - v23 - i3 - Nov-Dec 2004 - p65(1) [51-500]

Ackerman, Kenneth David - *Boss Tweed: The Rise and Fall of the Corrupt Pol Who Conceived the Soul of Modern New York*
 LJ - v130 - i3 - Feb 15 2005 - p138(1) [51-500]

Ackerman, Lillian A. - *A Necessary Balance: Gender and Power among the Indians of the Columbia Plateau*
 Am Ind CRJ - v28 - i1 - Winter 2004 - p103-105 [501+]

Ackermann, Denise M. - *After the Locusts: Letters from a Landscape of Faith*
 HNet - Sept 2004 - pNA [501+]
 TT - v61 - i1 - April 2004 - p87-88 [501+]

Ackermann, Karen L.T. - *African American Experience: Personal and Social Activism in the 19th and 20th Centuries*
 Bwatch - v26 - i8 - August 2004 - p9(1) [51-500]

Ackermann, Marsha E. - *Cool Comfort: America's Romance with Air-Conditioning*
 T&C - v45 - i2 - April 2004 - p452-454 [501+]

Ackers, Louise - *A Community for Children?: Children, Citizenship, and Internal Migration in the EU.*
 R&R Bk N - v19 - i3 - August 2004 - p151(1) [51-500]

Ackland, Michael - *Henry Handel Richardson: A Life*
 TLS - i5307 - Dec 17 2004 - p24(1) [501+]

Ackoff, Russell L. - *Redesigning Society*
 CS - v33 - i1 - Jan 2004 - p125-125 [501+]

Ackroyd, Peter - *The Beginning*
 c CH Bwatch - v14 - i11 - Nov 2004 - pNA [501+]
 c LibMed - v22 - i7 - April-May 2004 - p76(1) [501+]
 Chaucer
 LJ - v129 - i20 - Dec 1 2004 - p116(1) [51-500]
 BL - v101 - i9-10 - Jan 1 2005 - p802(1) [51-500]
 Ent W - Feb 4 2005 - p141 [51-500]
 Globe & Mail - July 17 2004 - pD14 [1-50]
 KR - v72 - i19 - Oct 1 2004 - p945(1) [501+]
 PW - v251 - i42 - Oct 18 2004 - p55(2) [51-500]
 TLS - i5303 - Nov 19 2004 - p4(2) [501+]
 CR - v285 - i1665 - Oct 2004 - p245(3) [501+]
 Cities of Blood
 y BL - v101 - i9-10 - Jan 1 2005 - p837(1) [501+]
 The Clerkenwell Tales
 BL - v101 - i1 - Sept 1 2004 - p54(1) [501+]
 KR - v72 - i13 - July 1 2004 - p587(1) [501+]
 NYTBR - Oct 31 2004 - p27 [501+]
 PW - v251 - i29 - July 19 2004 - p142(1) [51-500]
 Escape from Earth
 y SLJ - v50 - i7 - July 2004 - p114(1) [501+]
 The Lambs of London
 Globe & Mail - Jan 29 2005 - pD8 [501+]
 Spec - v295 - i9181 - July 24 2004 - p31(2) [501+]
 TLS - i5287 - July 30 2004 - p19(1) [501+]

Acland, Charles R. - *Screen Traffic: Movies, Multiplexes and Global Culture*
 TimHES - v0 - i1647 - July 2 2004 - p29(1) [501+]

Acorn, Annalise - *Compulsory Compassion: A Critique of Restorative Justice*
 Choice - v42 - i4 - Dec 2004 - p740(1) [1-50]
 Law&PolBR - June 2004 - p446(3) [501+]
 R&R Bk N - v19 - i3 - August 2004 - p169(1) [501+]

Acorn, John - *Bugs of Ontario*
 CBRA - Annual 2003 - p398(1) [51-500]

Acosta, Teresa Palomo - *Las Tejanas: 300 Years of History*
 JSH - v70 - i4 - Nov 2004 - p892(2) [501+]

Acs, Zoltan J. - *Handbook of Entrepreneurship Research: An Interdisciplinary Survey and Introduction*
 JEL - v41 - i4 - Dec 2003 - p1397(2) [501+]
 R&R Bk N - v19 - i1 - Feb 2004 - p79(1) [51-500]

Acton, Lesley - *Practical Ceramic Conservation*
 Ceram Mo - v52 - i2 - Feb 2004 - p28(1) [501+]
 Repairing Pottery & Porcelain: A Practical Guide
 Ceram Mo - v52 - i3 - March 2004 - p32(1) [501+]

Actus Independent Comics - *Actus Presents Dead Herring Comics*
 BL - v101 - i1 - Sept 1 2004 - p76(1) [501+]

Acuff, Jerry - *The Relationship Edge in Business*
 Bus W - i3890 - July 5 2004 - p86 [501+]
 HR Mag - v49 - i8 - August 2004 - p141(1) [501+]

Acuna, Rodolfo F. - *Occupied America: A History of Chicanos, 5th Ed.*
 R&R Bk N - v19 - i1 - Feb 2004 - p57(1) [51-500]

U.S. Latino Issues
 LibMed - v23 - i1 - August-Sept 2004 - p82(1) [51-500]
 R&R Bk N - v19 - i1 - Feb 2004 - p57(1) [51-500]

Aczel, Amir D. - *Chance: A Guide to Gambling, Love, the Stock Market, and Just about Everything Else*
 BL - v101 - i5 - Nov 1 2004 - p450(1) [51-500]
 KR - v72 - i18 - Sept 15 2004 - p897(1) [51-500]
 LJ - v129 - i17 - Oct 15 2004 - p84(1) [51-500]
 NYTBR - Nov 7 2004 - p17 [501+]
 PW - v251 - i37 - Sept 13 2004 - p66(1) [51-500]

Ad-House Books - *Project Power*
 LibMed - v22 - i4 - Jan 2004 - p89(1) [501+]

Ad-House Books - *Project: Telstar*
 c SLJ - v50 - i8 - August 2004 - p149(1) [501+]

Ada, Alma Flor - *Authors in the Classroom: A Transformative Education Process*
 SLJ - v50 - i10 - Oct 2004 - pS70(2) [51-500]
 I Love Saturdays y Domingos
 c RT - v57 - Dec 2003 - p395 [51-500]
 Mama Goose: A Latino Nursery Treasury/Un Tesoro de Rimas Infantiles (Illus. by Suarez, Maribel)
 c KR - v73 - i5 - March 1 2005 - p283(1) [51-500]

Adair, Cherry - *On Thin Ice*
 BL - v100 - i22 - August 2004 - p1908(1) [51-500]

Adair, Gilbert - *The Dreamers*
 NYRB - v51 - i17 - Nov 4 2004 - p52(1) [501+]

Adair, Vivyan Campbell - *Reclaiming Class: Women, Poverty, and the Promise of Higher Education in America*
 TCR - v106 - i2 - Feb 2004 - p274-276 [501+]

Adam, Anthony J. - *Black Populism in the United States: An Annotated Bibliography*
 Choice - v42 - i5 - Jan 2005 - p832(1) [1-50]
 R&R Bk N - v19 - i4 - Nov 2004 - p59(1) [51-500]

Adam, Barbara - *Time*
 Choice - v42 - i4 - Dec 2004 - p699(2) [1-50]

Adam, John A. - *Mathematics in Nature: Modeling Patterns in the Natural World*
 Am Sci - v92 - i5 - Sept-Oct 2004 - p479(2) [501+]
 Choice - v41 - i11-12 - July-August 2004 - p2063(2) [501+]
 SB - v40 - i3 - May-June 2004 - p113(2) [501+]

Adam, Magda - *The Versailles System and Central Europe*
 R&R Bk N - v19 - i4 - Nov 2004 - p38(1) [51-500]

Adam, Robert - *Screenprinting*
 Bwatch - Oct 2004 - pNA [51-500]

Adamec, Ludwig W. - *Historical Dictionary of Afghanistan, 3rd Ed.*
 R&R Bk N - v19 - i1 - Feb 2004 - p46(1) [51-500]

Adams, Alison - *A Bibliography of French Emblem Books*
 Six Ct J - v34 - i4 - Winter 2003 - p1181-1181 [501+]
 Webs of Allusion: French Protestant Emblem Books of the Sixteenth Century
 Ren Q - v57 - i4 - Winter 2004 - p1440(2) [501+]

Adams, Amy - *Muscular System*
 SciTech - v28 - i4 - Dec 2004 - p70(1) [51-500]

Adams, Anna - *Flying Under Water*
 y Sch Lib - v52 - i4 - Winter 2004 - p220(1) [51-500]

Adams, Byron - *Vaughan Williams Essays*
 M Ed J - v91 - i3 - Jan 2005 - p62(2) [501+]

Adams, Carol J. - *Living Among Meat Eaters: The Vegetarian's Survival Handbook*
 R&R Bk N - v19 - i1 - Feb 2004 - p253(1) [51-500]

Adams, Charles - *When in the Course of Human Events: Arguing the Case for Southern Secession*
 RAH - v32 - i2 - June 2004 - p184-12 [501+]

Adams, Colin Conrad - *Knot Book: An Elementary Introduction to the Mathematical Theory of Knots*
 SciTech - v28 - i4 - Dec 2004 - p43(1) [51-500]

Adams, Cynthia L. - *Food and Drug Book of Lists for Regulated Substances*
 SciTech - v28 - i1 - March 2004 - p179(1) [51-500]

Adams, Dave J. - *Chemistry in Alternative Reaction Media*
 SciTech - v28 - i1 - March 2004 - p57(1) [51-500]

Adams, David - *Colonial Odysseys: Empire and Epic in the Modernist Novel*
 Choice - v41 - i11-12 - July-August 2004 - p2041(1) [501+]

Adams, David J. - *Introduction to Galaxies and Cosmology*
 SciTech - v28 - i4 - Dec 2004 - p46(1) [51-500]

Adams, Denise Wiles - *Restoring American Gardens: An Encyclopedia of Heirloom Ornamental Plants, 1640-1940*
Ref Rev - May 2004 - pNA [501+]
SciTech - v28 - i3 - Sept 2004 - p129(1) [51-500]

Adams, E. Charles - *Protohistoric Pueblo World, A.D. 1275-1600*
R&R Bk N - v19 - i4 - Nov 2004 - p55(1) [51-500]

Adams, Francis D. - *Alienable Rights: The Exclusion of African Americans in a White Man's Land, 1619-2000*
R&R Bk N - v19 - i1 - Feb 2004 - p57(1) [51-500]

Adams, Gerry - *A Farther Shore: Ireland's Long Road to Peace*
Choice - v41 - i11-12 - July-August 2004 - p2113(1) [501+]

Adams, Gregg A. - *Surgery Clerkship Guide*
SciTech - v28 - i1 - March 2004 - p109(1) [51-500]

Adams, Hazard - *Critical Theory Since Plato, 3rd Ed.*
R&R Bk N - v19 - i4 - Nov 2004 - p12(1) [51-500]

Adams, Henry - *Eakins Revealed: The Secret Life of an American Artist*
PW - v252 - i9 - Feb 28 2005 - p54(1) [51-500]

Adams, J.N. - *Bilingualism and the Latin Language*
Lang Soc - v33 - i3 - June 2004 - p456-459 [501+]
Bilingualism in Ancient Society: Language Contact and the Written Word
AJP - v125 - i2 - Summer 2004 - p279-283 [501+]
Class R - v54 - i1 - May 2004 - p134(3) [501+]

Adams, Jad - *Hideous Absinthe: A History of the Devil in a Bottle*
Choice - v42 - i2 - Oct 2004 - p279(1) [501+]
ELT - v48 - i2 - Spring 2005 - p124(3) [501+]
NYTBR - August 1 2004 - p12 [51-500]

Adams, James Eli - *Encyclopedia of the Victorian Era, Vols. 1-4*
BL - v101 - i9-10 - Jan 1 2005 - p780(1) [1-50]
Choice - v42 - i1 - Sept 2004 - p78(1) [501+]
LJ - v130 - i4 - March 1 2005 - p110(1) [51-500]
R&USQ - v44 - i1 - Fall 2004 - p87(2) [501+]

Adams, Jane - *Fighting for the Farm: Rural America Transformed*
CS - v33 - i2 - March 2004 - p213-215 [501+]

Adams, Jane A. - *Heatwave*
BL - v101 - i6 - Nov 15 2004 - p563(1) [51-500]
KR - v72 - i24 - Dec 15 2004 - p1165(1) [501+]

Adams, John - *Managerial Economics for Decision Making*
JEL - v42 - i1 - March 2004 - p233(1) [501+]

Adams, John Luther - *Winter Music: Composing the North*
Choice - v42 - i7 - March 2005 - p1235(2) [51-500]

Adams, Jonathan - *Scandinavia and Europe 800-1350: Contact, Conflict, and Coexistence*
R&R Bk N - v19 - i4 - Nov 2004 - p37(1) [51-500]
Scan St - v76 - i4 - Winter 2004 - p567(5) [501+]

Adams, Julian - *Proteasome Inhibitors in Cancer Therapy*
SciTech - v28 - i3 - Sept 2004 - p92(1) [51-500]

Adams, Lorraine - *Harbor*
y BL - v100 - i21 - July 2004 - p1815(1) [51-500]
BW - v34 - i36 - Sept 5 2004 - p3(2) [501+]
Ent W - i779 - August 20 2004 - p129 [501+]
NY - v80 - i27 - Sept 20 2004 - p102(1) [51-500]
NYTBR - Sept 5 2004 - p7 [501+]
NYTBR - Sept 19 2004 - p22 [501+]
People - v62 - i9 - August 30 2004 - p50 [51-500]
USNews & Wrld Rpt - v137 - i8 - Sept 13 2004 - p56 [501+]
NYTBR - Sept 12 2004 - p26 [501+]

Adams, LuAnn - *Jaws, Paws & Claws: Animal Wisdom Tales (Read by Adams, LuAnn). Audiobook Review*
BL - v100 - i21 - July 2004 - p1857(1) [1-50]

Adams, Margaret - *The Work-Life Balance Trainer's Manual: 15 Ready-Made Development Activities for Trainers*
R&R Bk N - v19 - i1 - Feb 2004 - p112(1) [501+]

Adams, Michael - *Fire and Ice: The United States, Canada, and the Myth of Converging Values*
CBRA - Annual 2003 - p300(1) [501+]
Slayer Slang: A Buffy the Vampire Slayer Lexicon
JPC - v38 - i2 - Nov 2004 - p427(2) [501+]

Adams, Michael C.C. - *Echoes of War: A Thousand Years of Military History in Popular Culture*
Pub Hist - v26 - i2 - Spring 2004 - p100(102) [501+]

Adams, Neal - *Batman Illustrated by Neal Adams, Vol. 2 (Illus. by Adams, Neal)*
y BL - v101 - i2 - Sept 15 2004 - p216(2) [51-500]
LJ - v130 - i1 - Jan 1 2005 - p87(1) [51-500]

Adams, Noah - *The Flyers: In Search of Wilbur and Orville Wright*
Choice - v41 - i7 - March 2004 - p1 [501+]

Adams, Paul - *Frank Hardy and the Literature of Commitment*
AHS - v35 - i124 - Oct 2004 - pNA412-2 [501+]
Summer of the Heart: Saving Alexandre
CBRA - Annual 2003 - p33(1) [501+]

Adams, Rick A. - *Bats of the Rocky Mountain West: Natural History, Ecology, and Conservation*
Choice - v41 - i11-12 - July-August 2004 - p2072(1) [501+]
E-Streams - Nov 2004 - pNA [501+]
SciTech - v28 - i3 - Sept 2004 - p66(1) [51-500]

Adams, Scott Charles - *Never Dream*
LJ - v129 - i19 - Nov 15 2004 - p55(1) [501+]

Adams, Simon - *Causes and Consequences - World War One*
y Sch Lib - v52 - i3 - Autumn 2004 - p163(1) [501+]
Code Breakers
c RT - v57 - Oct 2003 - p176 [1-50]
DK Geography of the World: The Essential Family Guide to Geography and Culture
RT - v58 - i3 - Nov 2004 - p290(1) [1-50]
Winston Churchill
c LibMed - v22 - i4 - Jan 2004 - p73(1) [501+]

Adams, Tim - *On Being John McEnroe*
KR - v73 - i2 - Jan 15 2005 - p91(1) [51-500]
PW - v252 - i11 - March 14 2005 - p59(1) [51-500]

Adams, W. Royce - *Developing Reading Versatility, 9th Ed.*
R&R Bk N - v19 - i4 - Nov 2004 - p185(1) [501+]

Adams, Walter - *The Bigness Complex: Industry, Labor, and Government in the American Economy*
R&R Bk N - v19 - i3 - August 2004 - p114(1) [51-500]

Adams, William Howard - *Gouverneur Morris: An Independent Life*
JAH - v91 - i3 - Dec 2004 - p996(1) [501+]
Reason - v36 - i3 - July 2004 - p59(5) [501+]
VQR - v80 - i2 - Spring 2004 - p254-254 [501+]

Adams, William M. - *Against Extinction: The Story of Conservation*
Choice - v42 - i3 - Nov 2004 - p506(1) [1-50]
Nature - v429 - i6990 - May 27 2004 - p346(2) [501+]
SciTech - v28 - i3 - Sept 2004 - p56(1) [1-50]
TimHES - v0 - i1677 - Feb 4 2005 - p30(2) [501+]

Adamson, Bob - *China's English: A History of English in Chinese Education*
Choice - v42 - i6 - Feb 2005 - p1071(1) [51-500]

Adamson, Glenn - *Industrial Design Strength: How Brooks Stevens Shaped Your World*
TimHES - v0 - i1654 - August 20 2004 - p26(1) [501+]

Adamson, Isaac - *Kinki Lullaby*
y BL - v101 - i1 - Sept 1 2004 - p67(1) [51-500]
BW - v34 - i44 - Oct 31 2004 - p13(1) [501+]
KR - v72 - i17 - Sept 1 2004 - p819(1) [51-500]
PW - v251 - i39 - Sept 27 2004 - p41(1) [501+]
SLJ - v51 - i2 - Feb 2005 - p156(1) [51-500]

Adamson, Robert - *Inside Out: An Autobiography*
TLS - i5297 - Oct 8 2004 - p28(1) [501+]
Reading the River: Selected Poems
TLS - i5297 - Oct 8 2004 - p28(1) [501+]

Adamson, Thomas K. - *Earth*
c SB - v40 - i6 - Nov-Dec 2004 - p265(1) [51-500]
Jupiter
c SB - v40 - i6 - Nov-Dec 2004 - p265(1) [51-500]
Mars
c SB - v40 - i6 - Nov-Dec 2004 - p265(1) [51-500]
Mercury
c SB - v40 - i6 - Nov-Dec 2004 - p265(1) [51-500]
Neptune
c SB - v40 - i6 - Nov-Dec 2004 - p265(1) [51-500]
Pluto
c SB - v40 - i6 - Nov-Dec 2004 - p265(1) [51-500]
Saturn
c SB - v40 - i6 - Nov-Dec 2004 - p265(1) [51-500]
Uranus
c SB - v40 - i6 - Nov-Dec 2004 - p265(1) [51-500]
Venus
c SB - v40 - i6 - Nov-Dec 2004 - p265(1) [51-500]

Adamy, David L. - *EW 102: A Second Course in Electronic Warfare*
SciTech - v28 - i4 - Dec 2004 - p172(1) [51-500]

Aday, Lu Ann - *Evaluating the Healthcare System: Effectiveness, Efficiency, and Equity, 3rd Ed.*
SciTech - v28 - i4 - Dec 2004 - p80(1) [51-500]

Addams, Jane - *Women at the Hague: The International Congress of Women and Its Results*
HNet - Sept 2004 - pNA [501+]

Addinall, Nigel - *A Study of Major Political Thinkers in France from the Seventeenth to the Twentieth Century: From Absolutism to Socialism*
R&R Bk N - v19 - i3 - August 2004 - p173(1) [501+]

Addis, Cameron - *Jefferson's Vision for Education, 1760-1845*
AHR - v109 - i4 - Oct 2004 - p1223(2) [501+]
Choice - v41 - i7 - March 2004 - p1343(2) [501+]
JAH - v91 - i1 - June 2004 - p225-225 [501+]
JSH - v70 - i3 - August 2004 - p646(2) [501+]

Addison, Doug - *Small Websites, Great Results*
Bwatch - March 2005 - pNA [51-500]

Addison, John T. - *International Handbook of Trade Unions*
Choice - v41 - i11-12 - July-August 2004 - p2089(1) [501+]

Addison, Paul - *Churchill: The Unexpected Hero*
LJ - v130 - i3 - Feb 15 2005 - p138(1) [51-500]

Adebajo, Adekeye - *West Africa's Security Challenges: Building Peace in a Troubled Region*
Choice - v42 - i5 - Jan 2005 - p932(1) [51-500]
R&R Bk N - v19 - i3 - August 2004 - p59(1) [51-500]

Adelekan, Tokunbo - *African Wisdom: 101 Proverbs from the Motherland*
Black Iss - v6 - i5 - Sept-Oct 2004 - p38(1) [501+]

Adeleke, Tunde - *Without Regard to Race: The Other Martin Robison Delany*
Black Iss - v6 - i4 - July-August 2004 - p54(1) [51-500]
Choice - v42 - i1 - Sept 2004 - p171(1) [501+]

Adelman, Gary - *Naming Beckett's Unnamable*
Choice - v42 - i1 - Sept 2004 - p105(1) [501+]

Adelson, Leone - *The Mystery Bear: A Purim Story (Illus. by Howland, Naomi)*
c BL - v101 - i3 - Oct 1 2004 - p346(1) [51-500]
c SLJ - v50 - i12 - Dec 2004 - p96(1) [51-500]

Ader, Clement - *Military Aviation*
J Mil H - v68 - i2 - April 2004 - p658(2) [501+]

Adger, Carolyn T. - *What Teachers Need to Know about Language*
TCR - v106 - i2 - Feb 2004 - p251-254 [501+]

Adi, Hakim - *Pan-African History: Political Figures from Africa and the Diaspora since 1787*
JEL - v41 - i4 - Dec 2003 - p1443(1) [501+]

Adichie, Chimamanda Ngozi - *Purple Hibiscus*
BW - v34 - i1 - Jan 4 2004 - p8(1) [501+]
y Kliatt - v39 - i1 - Jan 2005 - p12(1) [51-500]
Lon R Bks - v26 - i20 - Oct 21 2004 - p21(4) [501+]
WLT - v79 - i1 - Jan-April 2005 - p84(1) [501+]
Wom R Bks - v21 - i10-11 - July 2004 - p9(2) [501+]

Adil, Janeen - *Great Story Teller*
c SLJ - v50 - i12 - Dec 2004 - p125(1) [51-500]

Adjarian, M.M. - *Allegories of Desire: Body, Nation, and Empire in Modern Caribbean Literature by Women*
Choice - v42 - i2 - Oct 2004 - p290(1) [501+]

Adkin, Neil - *Jerome on Virginity: A Commentary on the 'Libellus de Virginitate Servanda'*
R&R Bk N - v19 - i1 - Feb 2004 - p18(1) [51-500]

Adkins, Jan - *What If You Met a Pirate? (Illus. by Adkins, Jan)*
c BL - v101 - i4 - Oct 15 2004 - p404(1) [51-500]
c KR - v72 - i17 - Sept 1 2004 - p859(1) [51-500]
c SLJ - v50 - i12 - Dec 2004 - p125(1) [51-500]

Adkins, Lesley - *Empires of the Plain: Henry Rawlinson and the Lost Languages of Babylon*
LJ - v129 - i20 - Dec 1 2004 - p129(1) [51-500]
BL - v101 - i5 - Nov 1 2004 - p450(1) [51-500]
KR - v72 - i18 - Sept 15 2004 - p897(1) [501+]
New Sci - v184 - i2472 - Nov 6 2004 - p53(1) [51-500]
PW - v251 - i41 - Oct 11 2004 - p64(1) [51-500]
TimHES - v0 - i1654 - August 20 2004 - p30(2) [501+]

Adkins, Roy - *Trafalgar: The Biography of a Battle*
Spec - v296 - i9190 - Sept 25 2004 - p53(1) [501+]

Adl, Sina M. - *The Ecology of Soil Decomposition*
QRB - v79 - i4 - Dec 2004 - p448(2) [501+]
SciTech - v28 - i1 - March 2004 - p76(1) [51-500]

Adleman, Robert H. - *The Devil's Brigade*
R&R Bk N - v19 - i3 - August 2004 - p33(1) [51-500]

Adler, Bill - *The Eloquent Jacqueline Kennedy Onassis: A Portrait in Her Own Words*
  y   VOYA - v27 - i4 - Oct 2004 - p324(1) [51-500]
Adler, David A. - *Bones and the Big Yellow Mystery (Illus. by Newman, Barbara Johansen)*
  c   BL - v101 - i4 - Oct 15 2004 - p409(1) [51-500]
  c   CCB-B - v58 - i3 - Nov 2004 - p112(1) [501+]
  c   KR - v72 - i16 - August 15 2004 - p801(1) [51-500]
  c   SLJ - v50 - i10 - Oct 2004 - p108(1) [51-500]
  Bones and the Dog Gone Mystery (Illus. by Newman, Barbara Johansen)
  c   SLJ - v50 - i12 - Dec 2004 - p96(1) [501+]
  Enemies of Slavery (Illus. by Smith, Donald A.)
  c   BL - v101 - i3 - Oct 1 2004 - p325(1) [51-500]
  c   KR - v72 - i20 - Oct 15 2004 - p1001(1) [51-500]
  George Washington: An Illustrated Biography
  c   BL - v101 - i2 - Sept 15 2004 - p235(2) [51-500]
  y   CCB-B - v58 - i6 - Feb 2005 - p242(1) [51-500]
  y   HB - v81 - i1 - Jan-Feb 2005 - p105(2) [51-500]
  c   KR - v72 - i18 - Sept 15 2004 - p909(1) [51-500]
  y   SLJ - v50 - i12 - Dec 2004 - p155(1) [51-500]
  c   VOYA - v27 - i5 - Dec 2004 - p412(1) [51-500]
  Heroes of the Revolution
  c   CE - v80 - i5 - Mid-Summer 2004 - p275(1) [51-500]
  The Kids' Catalog of Hanukkah
  c   PW - v251 - i43 - Oct 25 2004 - p46(1) [501+]
  One Yellow Daffodil
  c   RT - v57 - Dec 2003 - p392 [51-500]
Adler, David Gray - *The Presidency and the Law: The Clinton Legacy*
  Pres St Q - v34 - i3 - Sept 2004 - p693(3) [501+]
Adler, E. - *Vergil's Empire: Political Thought in the Aeneid*
  Class R - v54 - i2 - Nov 2004 - p376(3) [501+]
Adler, Ed - *Departed Angels: Jack Kerouac: The Lost Paintings*
  PW - v251 - i45 - Nov 8 2004 - p48(1) [501+]
Adler, Elizabeth - *The Hotel Riviera (Read by MacDuffie, Carrington). Audiobook Review*
  BL - v101 - i3 - Oct 1 2004 - p351(1) [51-500]
  Kliatt - v38 - i6 - Nov 2004 - p47(1) [51-500]
  Invitation to Provence
  BL - v100 - i22 - August 2004 - p1895(1) [51-500]
  KR - v72 - i13 - July 1 2004 - p587(1) [501+]
Adler, Frederick R. - *Modeling the Dynamics of Life: Calculus and Probability for Life Scientists, 2nd Ed.*
  SciTech - v28 - i4 - Dec 2004 - p39(1) [51-500]
Adler, Jeffrey S. - *African-American Mayors: Race, Politics, and the American City*
  J Urban H - v30 - i4 - May 2004 - p616-626 [501+]
Adler, Karen - *The BBQ Queens's Big Book of Barbecue*
  PW - v252 - i9 - Feb 28 2005 - p59(1) [51-500]
Adler, Patricia A. - *Paradise Laborers: Hotel Work in the Global Economy*
  Choice - v42 - i6 - Feb 2005 - p1066(1) [51-500]
Adler, Peter H. - *The Black Flies (Simuliidae) of North America*
  Choice - v42 - i6 - Feb 2005 - p1049(1) [51-500]
Adler, Robert E. - *Medical Firsts: From Hippocrates to the Human Genome*
  Choice - v42 - i2 - Oct 2004 - p324(1) [51-500]
  y   SB - v40 - i4 - July-August 2004 - p168(1) [51-500]
Adler, Ronald B. - *Looking Out/Looking In, 11th Ed.*
  R&R Bk N - v19 - i3 - August 2004 - p9(1) [1-50]
Adler, Stephen L. - *Quantum Theory as an Emergent Phenomenon: The Statistical Mechanics of Matrix Models as the Precursor of Quantum Field Theory*
  SciTech - v28 - i4 - Dec 2004 - p49(1) [51-500]
Adler, Steven - *On Broadway: Art and Commerce on the Great White Way*
  Am Theat - v22 - i1 - Jan 2005 - p92(3) [501+]
Adler, Susan - *Critical Issues in Social Studies Teacher Education*
  R&R Bk N - v19 - i3 - August 2004 - p90(1) [51-500]
Adler, William - *The Chronicle of George Synkellos: A Byzantine Chronicle of Universal History from the Creation*
  Class R - v53 - i2 - Nov 2003 - p396-397 [501+]
Adlgasser, Franz - *Die Aehrenthals: Eine Familie in ihrer Korrespondenz 1872-1911*
  JMH - v76 - i4 - Dec 2004 - p990(3) [501+]
Adlington, Robert - *Louis Andriessen: De Staat*
  Choice - v42 - i5 - Jan 2005 - p860(2) [1-50]
  R&R Bk N - v19 - i4 - Nov 2004 - p196(1) [501+]
Adobe Creative Team - *Adobe Illustrator CS: Classroom in a Book*
  SciTech - v28 - i1 - March 2004 - p135(1) [51-500]

Adobe Premier Pro: Classroom in a Book
  SciTech - v28 - i1 - March 2004 - p176(1) [51-500]
Adobe Premiere 6.5: Classroom in a Book
  SciTech - v28 - i1 - March 2004 - p176(1) [51-500]
Adoff, Jaime - *Names Will Never Hurt Me*
  y   HB - v80 - i4 - July-August 2004 - p445(1) [51-500]
  The Song Shoots Out of My Mouth: A Celebration of Music (Illus. by French, Martin)
  c   SLJ - v50 - i12 - Dec 2004 - p60(1) [501+]
Adonis, Andrew - *Roy Jenkins: A Retrospective*
  Spec - v296 - i9189 - Sept 18 2004 - p52(1) [501+]
  TLS - i5299 - Oct 22 2004 - p36(1) [501+]
Adorno, Rolena - *The Narrative of Cabeza de Vaca*
  JSH - v70 - i3 - August 2004 - p637(3) [501+]
  SHQ - v107 - i4 - April 2004 - p615(3) [501+]
Adorno, Theodor W. - *Beethoven: The Philosophy of Music*
  JAAC - v61 - Winter 2003 - p90 [501+]
Adrian, Bonnie - *Framing the Bride: Globalizing Beauty and Romance in Taiwan's Bridal Industry*
  Choice - v42 - i1 - Sept 2004 - p144(1) [501+]
Adshead, S.A.M. - *T'ang China: The Rise of the East in World History*
  Choice - v42 - i6 - Feb 2005 - p1076(1) [51-500]
Adunis - *Identite Inachevee*
  Nation - v280 - i1 - Jan 3 2005 - p23 [501+]
  If Only the Sea Could Sleep: Love Poems
  Nation - v280 - i1 - Jan 3 2005 - p23 [501+]
  Toucher La Lumiere
  Nation - v280 - i1 - Jan 3 2005 - p23 [501+]
Advincula, Rigoberto C. - *Polymer Brushes: Synthesis, Characterization, Applications*
  SciTech - v28 - i4 - Dec 2004 - p55(1) [51-500]
Aebischer, Pascale - *Shakespeare's Violated Bodies*
  TLS - i5301 - Nov 5 2004 - p35(1) [51-500]
Aers, David - *Sanctifying Signs: Making Christian Tradition in Late Medieval England*
  Choice - v42 - i2 - Oct 2004 - p278(1) [501+]
Aeschylus - *Aeschylus: Oresteia*
  Class R - v54 - i1 - May 2004 - p27(2) [501+]
Afey, Philip - *The Professional Development of Teachers: Practice and Theory*
  TES - v0 - i4576 - March 26 2004 - psss17(1) [501+]
Afolayan, Funso S. - *Culture and Customs of South Africa*
  R&R Bk N - v19 - i3 - August 2004 - p84(1) [51-500]
African-American Leaders
  LibMed - v22 - i7 - April-May 2004 - p65(1) [501+]
African Development Bank - *African Development Report 2003: Africa in the World Economy, Globalization and Africa's Development, Economic and Social Statistics on Africa*
  JEL - v42 - i1 - March 2004 - p320(1) [501+]
Afshar, Rod - *Advergaming Developer's Guide: Using Macromedia Flash MX 2004 and Director MX*
  SciTech - v28 - i3 - Sept 2004 - p24(1) [51-500]
Afuah, Allan - *Innovation Management: Strategies, Implementation, and Profits*
  TimHES - v0 - i1666 - Nov 12 2004 - p29(1) [501+]
Agamben, Giorgio - *State of Exception*
  Lon R Bks - v26 - i24 - Dec 16 2004 - p3(3) [501+]
Agar, Jon - *The Government Machine: A Revolutionary History of the Computer*
  PSQ - v119 - i3 - Fall 2004 - p558(2) [501+]
  TimHES - v0 - i1661 - Oct 8 2004 - p30(1) [501+]
Agard, John - *From Mouth to Mouth (Illus. by Wright, Annabel)*
  c   Sch Lib - v52 - i4 - Winter 2004 - p210(1) [51-500]
Agarwal, Ravi P. - *Nonoscillation and Oscillation: Theory for Functional Differential Equations*
  SciTech - v28 - i4 - Dec 2004 - p40(1) [51-500]
  Oscillation Theory for Second Order Dynamic Equations
  SIAM Rev - v46 - i4 - Dec 2004 - p748-751 [501+]
Agassiz, Jean Louis Rodolphe - *Essay on Classification*
  SciTech - v28 - i4 - Dec 2004 - p66(1) [51-500]
Agatston, Arthur - *The South Beach Diet: The Delicious, Doctor-Designed Plan for Fast and Healthy Weight Loss*
  Lon R Bks - v26 - i15 - August 5 2004 - p16(3) [501+]

Agawu, Kofi - *Representing African Music: Postcolonial Notes, Queries, Positions*
  IJAHS - v37 - i1 - Wntr 2004 - p145-147 [501+]
  Notes - v61 - i1 - Sept 2004 - p106(3) [501+]
Agee, Joel - *In the House of My Fear: An Adventure*
  PW - v251 - i40 - Oct 4 2004 - p82(2) [51-500]
Agee, Jon - *Palindromania! (Illus. by Agee, Jon)*
  c   RT - v57 - Oct 2003 - p174 [1-50]
Agenbroad, Larry D. - *Mammoths: Ice-Age Giants*
  c   RT - v57 - Oct 2003 - p177 [1-50]
Aggarwal, Vinod K. - *The Strategic Dynamics of Latin American Trade*
  R&R Bk N - v19 - i3 - August 2004 - p125(1) [51-500]
  Winning in Asia, U.S. Style: Market and Nonmarket Strategies for Success
  R&R Bk N - v19 - i2 - May 2004 - p111(1) [51-500]
Aggelis, Steven L. - *Conversations with Ray Bradbury*
  MFSF - v108 - i3 - March 2005 - p30(5) [501+]
Agger, Ben - *Speeding Up Fast Capitalism: Cultures, Jobs, Families, Schools, Bodies*
  R&R Bk N - v19 - i4 - Nov 2004 - p122(1) [51-500]
  The Virtual Self: A Contemporary Sociology
  Choice - v41 - i11-12 - July-August 2004 - p2128(1) [501+]
Aggs, Patrice - *Strawberry Squirt*
  c   Sch Lib - v52 - i3 - Autumn 2004 - p129(1) [501+]
Agha, Hussein - *Track-II Diplomacy: Lessons from the Middle East*
  MEQ - v11 - i4 - Fall 2004 - p86(1) [501+]
Agha, Irfan A. - *The Washington Manual Nephrology Subspecialty Consult*
  SciTech - v28 - i3 - Sept 2004 - p108(1) [51-500]
Agha-Jaffar, Tamara - *Women and Goddesses in Myth and Sacred Text: An Anthology*
  R&R Bk N - v20 - i1 - Feb 2005 - p12(1) [51-500]
Agha, Salih Said - *The Revolution Which Toppled the Umayyads: Neither Arab nor 'Abbasid*
  R&R Bk N - v19 - i1 - Feb 2004 - p41(1) [51-500]
Aghaie, Kamran Scot - *The Martyrs of Karbala: Shi'i Symbols and Rituals in Modern Iran*
  PW - v251 - i46 - Nov 15 2004 - pS17(1) [51-500]
Agigian, Amy - *Baby Steps: How Lesbian Alternative Insemination Is Changing the World*
  LJ - v129 - i13 - August 2004 - p103(1) [51-500]
Agile Development Conference - *Agile Development: Proceedings*
  SciTech - v28 - i4 - Dec 2004 - p23(1) [51-500]
Agius, Dionisius A. - *In the Wake of the Dhow: The Arabian Gulf and Oman*
  IJMES - v36 - i3 - August 2004 - p469-470 [501+]
Agliati, Carlo - *Il Ritratto Carpito Di Carlo Cattaneo*
  TLS - i5291 - August 27 2004 - p4-6 [501+]
Agnew, Eleanor - *Back from the Land: How Young Americans Went to Nature in the 1970s, and Why They Came Back*
  BL - v100 - i22 - August 2004 - p1878(1) [51-500]
  NYTBR - Dec 19 2004 - p10 [501+]
Agnew, Elizabeth N. - *From Charity to Social Work: Mary E. Richmond and the Creation of an American Profession*
  Choice - v42 - i1 - Sept 2004 - p144(1) [501+]
  Soc Ser R - v78 - i4 - Dec 2004 - p675(3) [501+]
Agnew, John A. - *Geopolitics: Revisioning World Politics*
  PG - v23 - i6 - August 2004 - p797-798 [501+]
  Place and Politics in Modern Italy
  JIH - v35 - i2 - Autumn 2004 - p303(4) [501+]
Agnew, Vijay - *Where I Come From*
  HNet - Sept 2004 - pNA [501+]
Agnon, S.Y. - *A Guest for the Night*
  LJ - v129 - i19 - Nov 15 2004 - p103(1) [51-500]
  In the Heart of the Seas
  LJ - v129 - i19 - Nov 15 2004 - p103(1) [51-500]
Agnon, Shmuel Yosef - *Two Tales: Betrothed & Edo and Enam*
  LJ - v130 - i2 - Feb 1 2005 - p126(1) [1-50]
Agosin, Marjorie - *Cartographies: Meditations on Travel*
  R&R Bk N - v20 - i1 - Feb 2005 - p81(1) [51-500]
Agostoni, Claudia - *Monuments of Progress: Modernization and Public Health in Mexico City, 1876-1910*
  CBRA - Annual 2003 - p280(2) [501+]
Agou, Christophe - *Life Below: The New York City Subway*
  PW - v251 - i41 - Oct 11 2004 - p74(1) [51-500]
Agrawal, Govind P. - *Lightwave Technology: Components and Devices*
  SciTech - v28 - i3 - Sept 2004 - p143(1) [51-500]
Agricola, Rudolph - *Letters*
  Isis - v95 - i2 - June 2004 - p287(2) [501+]

Agronin, Marc E. - *Dementia: A Pracitcal Guide*
SciTech - v28 - i1 - March 2004 - p100(1) [51-500]

Aguilar, Ana Paulina Malavassi - *Entre la marginalidad social y los origenes de la salud publica: Leprosos, curanderos y facultativos en el valle central de costa rica*
AHR - v109 - i4 - Oct 2004 - p1283-1284 [501+]

Aguilar, Marie-Isabel - *HPLC of Peptides and Proteins: Methods and Protocols*
SciTech - v28 - i1 - March 2004 - p75(1) [51-500]

Aguilar, Paloma - *Memory and Amnesia: The Rule of the Spanish Civil War in the Transition to Democracy*
HER - v119 - i483 - Sept 2004 - p1096(2) [501+]

Aguilo, Isabel - *Artificial Intelligence Research and Development: Proceedings*
SciTech - v28 - i4 - Dec 2004 - p14(1) [1-50]

Aguinis, Herman - *Regression Analysis for Categorical Moderators*
Choice - v42 - i5 - Jan 2005 - p888(1) [1-50]
SciTech - v28 - i4 - Dec 2004 - p38(1) [51-500]
Test Score Banding in Human Resource Selection: Technical, Legal, and Societal
R&R Bk N - v19 - i2 - May 2004 - p118 [51-500]

Aguirre, Adalberto, Jr. - *Racial and Ethnic Diversity in America: A Reference Handbook*
R&R Bk N - v19 - i1 - Feb 2004 - p57(1) [51-500]

Aguirre, Forrest - *Leviathan 4: Cities*
BL - v101 - i4 - Oct 15 2004 - p395(1) [51-500]
PW - v251 - i42 - Oct 18 2004 - p52(1) [51-500]

Aguirre-Molina, Marilyn - *Latina Health in the United States: A Public Health Reader*
E-Streams - June 2004 - pNA [501+]

Aguirre, V.H. Mendez - *El modo de Vida Idoneo en la Republica de Platon*
Class R - v54 - i2 - Nov 2004 p566-567 [501+]
Filantropia Divina en la Etica de Aristoteles? Lectura desde la Hermeneutica Analogica
Class R - v54 - i2 - Nov 2004 - p566-567 [501+]

Agyeman, Opoku - *The Failure of Grassroots Pan-Africanism: The Case of the All-African Trade Union Federation*
HNet - Sept 2004 - pNA [501+]
R&R Bk N - v19 - i1 - Feb 2004 - p100(1) [1-50]

Ahad, Zalmai - *Return, Afghanistan*
PW - v251 - i31 - August 2 2004 - p66(1) [51-500]

Aharoni, Yisrael - *Sandwich*
Globe & Mail - Oct 16 2004 - pL13 [51-500]

Aharonian, F.A. - *Very High Energy Cosmic Gamma Radiation: A Crucial Window on the Extreme Universe*
SciTech - v28 - i4 - Dec 2004 - p46(1) [51-500]

Aharonian, Gregory - *Patenting Art and Entertainment: New Strategies for Protecting Creative Ideas*
R&R Bk N - v19 - i4 - Nov 2004 - p169(1) [501+]

Ahem, Cecelia - *Rosie Dunne*
BL - v101 - i9-10 - Jan 1 2005 - p811(1) [1-50]

Ahern, Cecelia - *Irish Girls Are Back in Town*
PW - v252 - i9 - Feb 28 2005 - p43(1) [51-500]
PS, I Love You (Read by Dunne, Bernadette). Audiobook Review
c Kliatt - v38 - i4 - July 2004 - p55(1) [51-500]
Rosie Dunne
LJ - v130 - i1 - Jan 1 2005 - p93(1) [51-500]
PW - v252 - i1 - Jan 3 2005 - p34(1) [51-500]

Ahl, Diane Cole - *The Cambridge Companion to Masaccio*
Med R - July 2004 - pNA [501+]

Ahlberg, Allan - *Half a Pig (Illus. by Ahlberg, Jessica)*
c BL - v100 - i22 - August 2004 - p1932(1) [51-500]
c BooChiTr - May 9 2004 - p2(1) [501+]
c CCB-B - v58 - i1 - Sept 2004 - p4(1) [51-500]
c CH Bwatch - v14 - i8 - August 2004 - p6(1) [51-500]
c HB - v80 - i4 - July-August 2004 - p433(2) [51-500]
c NYTBR - Sept 19 2004 - p16 [51-500]
c Sch Lib - v52 - i3 - Autumn 2004 - p129(1) [501+]
c SLJ - v50 - i8 - August 2004 - p82(1) [51-500]
The Improbable Cat (Illus. by Bailey, Peter)
c CCB-B - v58 - i2 - Oct 2004 - p58(2) [51-500]
c KR - v72 - i13 - July 1 2004 - p625(1) [51-500]
c PW - v251 - i32 - August 9 2004 - p251(1) [51-500]
c SLJ - v50 - i8 - August 2004 - p115(1) [51-500]
The Little Cat Baby (Illus. by Wegner, Fritz)
c BooChiTr - May 23 2004 - p5(1) [501+]
c CCB-B - v58 - i2 - Oct 2004 - p59(1) [51-500]
c SLJ - v50 - i10 - Oct 2004 - p108(1) [51-500]
The Woman Who Won Things (Illus. by McEwen, Katharine)
c RT - v57 - Oct 2003 - p175 [1-50]

Ahlborn, Boye K. - *Zoological Physics: Quantitative Models of Body Design, Actions, and Physical Limitations of Animals*
Choice - v42 - i3 - Nov 2004 - p510(1) [1-50]

Ahlers, Rolf - *System and Context: Early Romantic and Early Idealistic Constellations = System und Kontext, Fruhromantische und Fruhidealistische Konstellationen*
R&R Bk N - v19 - i4 - Nov 2004 - p6(1) [51-500]

Ahles, Scott R. - *Our Inner World: A Guide to Psychodynamics and Psychotherapy*
SciTech - v28 - i4 - Dec 2004 - p98(1) [51-500]

Ahlrichs, Nancy S. - *Competing for Talent: Key Recruitment and Retention Strategies for Becoming an Employer of Choice*
HR Mag - v50 - i2 - Feb 2005 - pS10(1) [501+]
Manager of Choice: 5 Competencies for Cultivating Top Talent
HR Mag - v49 - i7 - July 2004 - pS20(1) [501+]
HR Mag - v50 - i2 - Feb 2005 - pS9(1) [501+]

Ahlstrand, Amanda L. - *Workplace Education for Low-Wage Workers*
JEL - v41 - i4 - Dec 2003 - p1400(2) [501+]

Ahmad, Eqbal - *Terrorism: Theirs and Ours*
IJMES - v36 - i3 - August 2004 - p530-533 [501+]

Ahmad, Feroz - *Turkey: The Quest for Identity*
Choice - v41 - i11-12 - July-August 2004 - p2103(2) [501+]
TLS - i5267 - March 12 2004 - p22-22 [501+]

Ahmad, Irfan - *Digital and Conventional Dental Photography: A Practical Clinical Manual*
SciTech - v28 - i3 - Sept 2004 - p169(1) [51-500]

Ahmed, Akbar S. - *Islam under Siege: Living Dangerously in a Post-Honor World*
MEQ - v12 - i1 - Wntr 2005 - p71(8) [501+]
Mr. Jinnah: The Making of Pakistan
LJ - v129 - i14 - Sept 1 2004 - p199(1) [501+]

Ahmed, Anne - *Iron Town Boy*
c Sch Lib - v52 - i4 - Winter 2004 - p191(1) [51-500]

Ahmed, Farid E. - *Testing of Genetically Modified Organisms in Foods*
SciTech - v28 - i3 - Sept 2004 - p74(1) [51-500]

Ahmed, Hafiz - *Principles and Reactions of Protein Extracting, Purification, and Characterization*
SciTech - v28 - i4 - Dec 2004 - p72(1) [51-500]

Ahmed, Iqbal - *Sorrows of the Moon: A Journey through London*
TLS - i5304 - Nov 26 2004 - p33(1) [51-500]

Ahner, Joachim W. - *Advanced Data Storage Materials and Characterization Techniques: Proceedings*
SciTech - v28 - i3 - Sept 2004 - p163(1) [51-500]

Ahonen, Pertti - *After the Expulsion: West Germany and Eastern Europe, 1945-1990*
Choice - v42 - i2 - Oct 2004 - p364(1) [51-500]
HNet - Oct 2004 - pNA [501+]

Ahonen, Tiina - *Transformation through Compassionate Mission: David J. Bosch's Theology of Contextualization*
IBMR - v28 - i4 - Oct 2004 - p184(1) [501+]

Ahrens, C. Donald - *Essentials of Meteorology: An Invitation to the Atmosphere, 4th Ed.*
SciTech - v28 - i4 - Dec 2004 - p53(1) [51-500]

Ahsanullah, Mohammad - *Record Values: Theory and Applications*
SciTech - v28 - i3 - Sept 2004 - p37(1) [51-500]

Ahvenainen, Jorma - *The European Cable Companies in South America before the First World War*
BHR - v78 - i3 - Autumn 2004 - p569(3) [501+]

Aichele, K. Porter - *Paul Klee's Pictorial Writing*
GSR - v27 - i3 - Oct 2004 - p635(2) [501+]

Aidarous, Salah - *Managing IP Networks: Challenges and Opportunities*
E-Streams - June 2004 - pNA [501+]

Aide, William - *Sea Voyage with Pigs*
CBRA - Annual 2003 - p207(2) [51-500]

Aidells, Bruce - *Bruce Aidells's Complete Book of Pork: A Guide to Buying, Storing, and Cooking the World's Favorite Meat*
BL - v101 - i1 - Sept 1 2004 - p35(1) [51-500]
LJ - v129 - i15 - Sept 15 2004 - p78(1) [51-500]
NW - Dec 6 2004 - p88 [501+]
PW - v251 - i31 - August 2 2004 - p67(1) [51-500]

Aidinoff, Elsie V. - *The Garden*
c BL - v101 - i3 - Oct 1 2004 - p345(1) [51-500]
y HB - v80 - i4 - July-August 2004 - p445(2) [51-500]
c SLJ - v50 - i8 - August 2004 - p115(1) [51-500]

Aigner, T. - *Laufen: Texte, Ubersetzungen, Kommentar*
Class R - v53 - i2 - Nov 2003 - p464-465 [501+]

Aik Yew-gob - *The Hugo Masters: An Anthology of Chinese Classical Music*
Teach Mus - v12 - i1 - August 2004 - p61(2) [501+]

Aiken, Clay - *Learning to Sing: Hearing the Music in Your Life*
Ent W - i793 - Nov 19 2004 - p87 [501+]
NW - Nov 22 2004 - p72 [501+]

Aiken, Don - *It Happened in Manitoba: Stories of the Red River Province*
Beav - v84 - i5 - Oct-Nov 2004 - p46(1) [501+]

Aiken, Joan - *Ghostly Beasts*
c Sch Lib - v52 - i4 - Winter 2004 - p192(1) [51-500]
Midwinter Nightingale
c CH Bwatch - v14 - i7 - July 2004 - p7(2) [501+]
y PW - v252 - i4 - Jan 24 2005 - p246(1) [51-500]
c Sch Lib - v52 - i3 - Autumn 2004 - p135(1) [501+]
c TES - v0 - i4577 - April 2 2004 - p35(1) [501+]
The Witch of Clatteringshaws
c BL - v101 - i8 - Dec 15 2004 - p742(1) [51-500]
c KR - v73 - i1 - Jan 1 2005 - p47(1) [51-500]
y PW - v252 - i4 - Jan 24 2005 - p244(1) [51-500]
y SLJ - v51 - i1 - Jan 2005 - p122(1) [51-500]
The Wooden Dragon
c KR - v73 - i1 - Jan 1 2005 - p47(1) [51-500]
c Sch Lib - v52 - i3 - Autumn 2004 - p134(2) [501+]

Aiken, Tonia Dandry - *Legal, Ethical, and Political Issues in Nursing, 2nd Ed.*
SciTech - v28 - i1 - March 2004 - p126(1) [1-50]

Aikman, David - *Jesus in Beijing: How Christianity Is Transforming China and Changing the Global Balance of Power*
IBMR - v29 - i1 - Jan 2005 - p47(2) [501+]
A Man of Faith: The Spiritual Journey of George W. Bush. Audiobook Review
LJ - v129 - i17 - Oct 15 2004 - p96(1) [51-500]

Aimi, Antonio - *La "vera" visione dei vinti e la conquista del Messico nelle fonti azteche*
Lat Ant - v15 - i4 - Dec 2004 - p469(2) [501+]

Ainger, Michael - *Gilbert and Sullivan: A Dual Biography*
Albion - v36 - i2 - Summer 2004 - p347(3) [501+]

Ainsworth, Peter - *Regions and Landscapes: Reality and Imagination in Late Medieval and Early Modern Europe*
HER - v119 - i483 - Sept 2004 - p1047(2) [501+]
HER - v119 - i483 - Sept 2004 - p1047(2) [501+]

Airth, Rennie - *The Blood-Dimmed Tide*
Globe & Mail - Nov 27 2004 - pD16 [51-500]
Spec - v296 - i9197 - Nov 13 2004 - p46(2) [501+]
TLS - i5299 - Oct 22 2004 - p23(1) [501+]

Aisbitt, Sally - *Developments in Country Studies in International Accounting - Europe, 2nd Ed.*
R&R Bk N - v19 - i3 - August 2004 - p131(1) [51-500]

Aitchison, Catherine J. - *The Birder's Guide to Vancouver and the Lower Mainland*
BIC - v33 - i5 - August 2004 - p28(3) [501+]

Aitken, A.J. - *Leading for Change: A Renewed Focus on Teaching and Learning*
CBRA - Annual 2003 - p392(1) [51-500]

Aitken, Jonathan - *Psalms for People under Pressure*
NS - v133 - i4716 - Nov 29 2004 - p48(1) [51-500]

Aitken, Judie - *Secret Shadows*
BL - v101 - i7 - Dec 1 2004 - p640(1) [51-500]

Aitken, Peter G. - *Camera Phone Obsession*
SciTech - v28 - i4 - Dec 2004 - p167(1) [51-500]

Aitken, R. - *Defect and Fault Tolerance in VLSI Systems: Proceedings*
SciTech - v28 - i4 - Dec 2004 - p158(1) [51-500]

Aitken, Rosemary - *Against the Tide*
BL - v101 - i5 - Nov 1 2004 - p462(1) [51-500]

Aizenberg, Edna - *Books and Bombs in Buenos Aires: Bergers, Gerchunoff, and Argentine-Jewish Writing*
MFSF - v50 - i2 - Summer 2004 - p498-500 [501+]

Aizenberg, Joanna - *Biological and Bioinspired Materials and Devices: Proceedings*
SciTech - v28 - i4 - Dec 2004 - p72(1) [51-500]

Ajayan, Pulickel M. - *Nanocomposite Science and Technology*
SciTech - v28 - i1 - March 2004 - p141(1) [51-500]

Ajayi, James Olaitan - *The HIV/AIDS Epidemic in Nigeria: Some Ethical Considerations*
Theol St - v65 - i3 - Sept 2004 - p684(1) [501+]

Ajhar, Brian - *Home on the Range (Illus. by Ajhar, Brian)*
c BL - v101 - i2 - Sept 15 2004 - p247(1) [51-500]
c KR - v72 - i16 - August 15 2004 - p801(1) [51-500]
c SLJ - v50 - i12 - Dec 2004 - p125(2) [51-500]

Ajmera, Maya - *Back to School*
c SLJ - v50 - i7 - July 2004 - p45(1) [51-500]
Be My Neighbor
c BL - v101 - i9-10 - Jan 1 2005 - p865(1) [51-500]
c HB - v81 - i1 - Jan-Feb 2005 - p106(1) [51-500]
c KR - v72 - i19 - Oct 1 2004 - p955(1) [501+]
c PW - v252 - i1 - Jan 3 2005 - p57(1) [51-500]
c SLJ - v51 - i1 - Jan 2005 - p100(1) [51-500]
To Be an Artist
c LibMed - v23 - i3 - Nov-Dec 2004 - p77(1) [51-500]
c SLJ - v50 - i10 - Oct 2004 - pS22(1) [1-50]

Akahira, Masafumi - *Joint Statistical Papers of Akahira and Takeuchi*
SciTech - v28 - i4 - Dec 2004 - p37(1) [51-500]

Akamatsu, Ken - *A.I. Love You*
Kliatt - v38 - i6 - Nov 2004 - p26(1) [501+]
Love Hina
y LibMed - v22 - i5 - Feb 2004 - p73(2) [501+]
Negima! Vol. 2
ChrSFF&H - v26 - i10 - Oct 2004 - p30(1) [51-500]

Akbar, Yusaf H. - *The Multinational Enterprise, EU Enlargement and Central Europe: The Effects of Regulatory Convergence*
JEL - v41 - i4 - Dec 2003 - p1355(1) [501+]

Akbari, Suzanne Conklin - *Seeing through the Veil: Optical Theory and Medieval Allegory*
R&R Bk N - v19 - i3 - August 2004 - p259(1) [51-500]

Akcam, Taner - *From Empire to Republic: Turkish Nationalism and the Armenian Genocide*
Choice - v42 - i4 - Dec 2004 - p718(2) [1-50]

Ake, David - *Jazz Cultures*
Callaloo - v27 - i2 - Spring 2004 - p570(572) [501+]
Can Lit - i181 - Summer 2004 - p96-97 [501+]

Ake, Kevin - *Information Technology for Manufacturing: Reducing Costs and Expanding Capabilities*
SciTech - v28 - i3 - Sept 2004 - p170(1) [51-500]

Akenson, Donald Harman - *An Irish History of Civilization*
Globe & Mail - March 19 2005 - pD4 [501+]
Small Differences: Irish Catholics and Irish Protestants, 1815-1922: An International Perspective
JMH - v76 - i3 - Sept 2004 - p721(2) [501+]

Aker, Don - *The First Stone*
y BIC - v33 - i2 - March 2004 - p43(2) [501+]
y CBRA - Annual 2003 - p472(1) [51-500]

Akers, Donna L. - *Living in the Land of Death: The Choctaw Nation, 1830-1860*
R&R Bk N - v19 - i4 - Nov 2004 - p55(1) [51-500]

Akers, Ronald L. - *Criminological Theories: Introduction, Evaluation, and Application, 4th Ed.*
R&R Bk N - v19 - i3 - August 2004 - p163(1) [501+]
Social Learning Theory and the Explanation of Crime: A Guide for the New Century
CS - v33 - i6 - Nov 2004 - p716(2) [501+]

Akhavan, Jacqueline - *The Chemistry of Explosives, 2nd Ed.*
Choice - v42 - i5 - Jan 2005 - p882(1) [1-50]

Akhmatova, Anna Andreevna - *The Word That Causes Death's Defeat: Poems of Memory*
Choice - v42 - i6 - Feb 2005 - p1027(1) [51-500]
NL - v87 - i6 - Nov-Dec 2004 - p40(3) [501+]

Akhtar, Shamshad - *Demutualization of Stock Exchanges: Problems, Solutions and Case Studies*
JEL - v42 - i1 - March 2004 - p267(1) [501+]

Akib, Jamel - *Monsoon*
LibMed - v22 - i6 - March 2004 - p57(1) [501+]

Akino, Matsuri - *Pet Shop of Horrors, Vol. 1*
y Kliatt - v39 - i1 - Jan 2005 - p24(1) [51-500]
Pet Shop of Horrors, Vol. 8
y Kliatt - v39 - i1 - Jan 2005 - p24(1) [501+]

Akins, Chana K. - *Laboratory Animals in Research and Teaching: Ethics, Care, and Methods*
SciTech - v28 - i3 - Sept 2004 - p132(1) [51-500]

Akiyama, Takamasa - *Rural Development and Agricultural Growth in Indonesia, the Philippines and Thailand*
R&R Bk N - v19 - i4 - Nov 2004 - p127(1) [51-500]

Akler, Howard - *Toronto: The Unknown City*
CBRA - Annual 2003 - p20(1) [51-500]

Akpunonu, Peter Damian - *The Vine, Israel, and the Church*
R&R Bk N - v19 - i1 - Feb 2004 - p19(1) [51-500]

Akroyd, H. David - *Agriculture and Rural Development Planning: A Process in Transition*
R&R Bk N - v19 - i2 - May 2004 - p132 [51-500]

Aks, Judith - *Women's Rights in Native North America: Legal Mobilization in the US and Canada*
Law&PolBR - August 2004 - p627(4) [501+]
R&R Bk N - v19 - i3 - August 2004 - p195(1) [51-500]

Aksu, Esref - *The United Nations, Intra-State Peacekeeping and Normative Change*
Choice - v42 - i3 - Nov 2004 - p559(2) [1-50]

Aktar, Ayhan - *Varlik Vergisi: Ve Turklestirme Politikarlari*
IJMES - v36 - i3 - August 2004 - p483-485 [501+]

Akunin, Boris - *The Turkish Gambit*
Globe & Mail - March 19 2005 - pD15 [51-500]

Al-Azzawi, Fadhil - *Miracle Maker: The Selected Poems of Fadhil Al-Azzawi*
Comw - v131 - i21 - Dec 3 2004 - p30(2) [501+]

Al-Duaij, Nada - *Environmental Law of Armed Conflict*
R&R Bk N - v19 - i4 - Nov 2004 - p163(1) [501+]

Al-Gailani, Noorah - *The Islamic Year: Surahs, Stories and Celebrations (Illus. by Williams, Helen)*
c SLJ - v51 - i1 - Jan 2005 - p56(1) [51-500]

Al-Haj, Majid - *Immigration and Ethnic Formation in a Deeply Divided Society: The Case of the 1990's Immigrants from the Former Soviet Union in Israel*
R&R Bk N - v19 - i1 - Feb 2004 - p43 [51-500]

Al-Hijji, Yaqub Yusuf - *The Art of Dhow-Building in Kuwait*
IJMES - v36 - i4 - Nov 2004 - p678(2) [501+]

Al-Qirim, Nabeel A.Y. - *Electronic Commerce in Small to Medium-Sized Enterprises: Frameworks, Issues and Implications*
R&R Bk N - v19 - i1 - Feb 2004 - p109(1) [51-500]

Al Tamimi, Essam - *Practical Guide to Litigation and Arbitration in the United Arab Emirates*
R&R Bk N - v19 - i1 - Feb 2004 - pNA [51-500]

Al-Windawi, Thura - *Thura's Diary: My Life in Wartime Iraq*
y HB - v80 - i4 - July-August 2004 - p464(2) [51-500]
y SLJ - v50 - i7 - July 2004 - p114(1) [51-500]
y VOYA - v27 - i3 - August 2004 - p236(1) [1-50]

Al-Zayyat, Montasser - *The Road to Al-Qaeda: The Story of Bin Laden's Right-Hand Man*
Bwatch - v26 - i7 - July 2004 - p9(1) [51-500]

Alaca, Saban - *Introductory Algebraic Number Theory*
Choice - v42 - i4 - Dec 2004 - p696(2) [501+]

Alagappa, Muthiah - *Asian Security Order: Instrumental and Normative Features*
Pac A - v77 - i3 - Fall 2004 - p547(3) [501+]

Alagna, Magdalena - *The Great Fire of London of 1666*
y SLJ - v51 - i1 - Jan 2005 - p140(1) [51-500]
Lawman of the American West
c SLJ - v50 - i12 - Dec 2004 - p126(1) [51-500]
The Louisiana Purchase: Expanding America's Boundaries
c SLJ - v50 - i8 - August 2004 - p132(1) [501+]
Mac Jemison: The First African American Woman in Space
c SLJ - v50 - i7 - July 2004 - p114(1) [1-50]
The Monroe Doctrine: An End to European Colonies in America
c SLJ - v50 - i8 - August 2004 - p132(1) [501+]

Alam Eldin, Mohie Eldin - *Arbitral Awards of the Cairo Regional Centre for International Commercial Arbitration*
R&R Bk N - v19 - i3 - August 2004 - p191(1) [501+]

Alaolmolki, Nozar - *Life after the Soviet Union: The Newly Independent Republics of the Transcaucasus and Central Asia*
IJMES - v36 - i3 - August 2004 - p521-522 [501+]

Alarcon, Daniel - *War by Candlelight: Stories*
LJ - v129 - i20 - Dec 1 2004 - p86(1) [51-500]
LJ - v130 - i2 - Feb 1 2005 - p72(2) [51-500]
PW - v252 - i8 - Feb 21 2005 - p155(1) [51-500]
War by Candlelight: Stories
KR - v73 - i1 - Jan 1 2005 - p3(1) [501+]

Alazard, Florence - *Art vocal, Art de gouverner: La musique, le prince et la cite en Italie a la fin du XVIe siecle*
Ren Q - v57 - i3 - Fall 2004 - p1093(2) [501+]

Alba, Richard - *Germans or Foreigners? Attitudes Toward Ethnic Minorities in Post-Reunification Germany*
Choice - v42 - i1 - Sept 2004 - p146(1) [501+]
Remaking the American Mainstream: Assimilation and Contemporary Immigration
AJS - v110 - i3 - Nov 2004 - p835(2) [501+]
CS - v33 - i4 - July 2004 - p404(4) [501+]
CS - v33 - i4 - July 2004 - p404(4) [501+]
CS - v33 - i4 - July 2004 - p408(3) [501+]

Albahari, David - *Drugi jezik*
WLT - v79 - i1 - Jan-April 2005 - p105(1) [501+]

Gotz and Meyer
Globe & Mail - Feb 26 2005 - pD13 [1-50]
Snow Man
Globe & Mail - March 19 2005 - pD7 [501+]

Albala, Ken - *Eating Right in the Renaissance*
JIH - v34 - i3 - Wntr 2004 - p465(2) [501+]
Food in Early Modern Europe
Six Ct J - v35 - i3 - Fall 2004 - p884-886 [501+]

Albanese, Jay S. - *Organized Crime in Our Times, 4th Ed.*
R&R Bk N - v19 - i3 - August 2004 - p165(1) [501+]

Albaret, Celeste - *Monsieur Proust*
TLS - i5283 - July 2 2004 - p29(1) [501+]

Albarran, Alan Brett - *Media Economics: Understanding Markets, Industries and Concepts*
JEL - v42 - i1 - March 2004 - p233(1) [501+]

Albee, Edward - *The Collected Plays of Edward Albee, Vol. 1*
NYRB - v51 - i14 - Sept 23 2004 - p44(3) [501+]
The Collected Plays of Edward Albee, Volume 1: 1958-65
Am Theat - v21 - i8 - Oct 2004 - p139(4) [51-500]
The Collected Plays of Edward Albee, Volume 2: 1966-77
Am Theat - v21 - i8 - Oct 2004 - p139(4) [51-500]
The Goat, or Who is Sylvia?
TLS - i5263 - Feb 13 2004 - p20-20 [501+]

Alberigo, Giuseppe - *History of Vatican II, Vol. IV*
Comw - v132 - i4 - Feb 25 2005 - p26(3) [501+]
Theol St - v66 - i1 - March 2005 - p201(2) [501+]

Alberro, Alexander - *Conceptual Art and the Politics of Publicity*
Afterimage - v32 - i4 - Jan-Feb 2005 - p15(1) [51-500]

Albers, Anni - *On Weaving*
R&R Bk N - v19 - i1 - Feb 2004 - p252(1) [51-500]

Albers, Jan - *Hands on the Land: A History of the Vermont Landscape*
Hist Geo - v32 - Annual 2004 - p219(2) [501+]

Albert, Daniel M. - *Clinical Atlas of Procedures in Ophthalmic Surgery*
SciTech - v28 - i1 - March 2004 - p113(1) [51-500]

Albert, G. Peter - *Intellectual Property Law in Cyberspace, 2003 Cumulative Supplement*
SciTech - v28 - i3 - Sept 2004 - p11(1) [501+]

Albert, Jim - *Teaching Statistics Using Baseball*
Math T - v97 - i4 - April 2004 - p302-302 [501+]

Albert, Peter J. - *Post Office Jobs: How to Get a Job with the U.S. Postal Service*
JEL - v41 - i4 - Dec 2003 - p1386(1) [501+]

Albert, Richard K. - *Clinical Respiratory Medicine, 2nd Ed.*
SciTech - v28 - i4 - Dec 2004 - p104(1) [51-500]

Albert, Steven M. - *Public Health and Aging: An Introduction to Maximizing Function and Well-Being*
SciTech - v28 - i1 - March 2004 - p83(1) [51-500]

Albert, Susan Wittig - *Dead Man's Bones*
KR - v73 - i5 - March 1 2005 - p259(1) [51-500]
The Tale of Hill Top Farm: The Cottage Tales of Beatrix Potter
BL - v101 - i5 - Nov 1 2004 - p466(1) [51-500]
LJ - v129 - i16 - Oct 1 2004 - p62(1) [51-500]
SLJ - v50 - i12 - Dec 2004 - p174(1) [51-500]

Albert, Toni - *Saving the Rain Forest with Cammie and Cooper*
CH Bwatch - v14 - i11 - Nov 2004 - pNA [51-500]

Alberti, Leon Battista - *Momus*
Six Ct J - v35 - i3 - Fall 2004 - p889-890 [501+]
Renaissance Fables
R&R Bk N - v19 - i4 - Nov 2004 - p215(1) [501+]
Renissance Fables
Choice - v42 - i3 - Nov 2004 - p479(2) [1-50]

Alberti, Theresa Jarosz - *Out and About at the Planetarium (Illus. by Shipe, Becky)*
c SB - v40 - i4 - July-August 2004 - p172(1) [51-500]

Alberto, Daisy - *Pete for President! (Illus. by Sims, Blanche)*
c SLJ - v50 - i12 - Dec 2004 - p96(1) [501+]

Alberts, Bruce - *Essential Cell Biology, 2nd ed.*
E-Streams - Oct 2004 - pNA [501+]
QRB - v79 - i4 - Dec 2004 - p417(2) [501+]

Albertson, Chris - *Bessie*
Notes - v61 - i2 - Dec 2004 - p458(3) [501+]

Albinati, Edoardo - *Coming Back: Diary of a Mission to Afghanistan*
KR - v72 - i13 - July 1 2004 - p609(1) [501+]

Albo, Mike - *The Underminer, or the Best Friend Who Casually Destroys Your Life*
    Ent W - Feb 4 2005 - p140 [51-500]
    KR - v72 - i23 - Dec 1 2004 - p1099(1) [501+]
    NYTBR - Feb 27 2005 - p26 [501+]

Albom, Mitch - *Tuesdays with Morrie: An Old Man, a Young Man, and Life's Greatest Lesson (Read by Albom, Mitch). Audiobook Review*
    LJ - v130 - i3 - Feb 15 2005 - p169(1) [51-500]

Alborough, Jez - *Duck's Key, Where Can It Be?*
    c KR - v73 - i2 - Jan 15 2005 - p115(1) [51-500]
Some Dogs Do
    c BooChiTr - Feb 1 2004 - p5(1) [501+]
    c Sch Lib - v52 - i4 - Winter 2004 - p186(1) [51-500]

Albrecht, Donald - *Glass and Glamour: Steuben's Modern Moment 1930-1960*
    Am Craft - v64 - i1 - Feb-March 2004 - p49(1) [501+]

Albrecht, Gloria - *Hitting Home: Feminist Ethics, Women's Work, and the Betrayal of "Family Values"*
    TT - v61 - i2 - July 2004 - p226(3) [501+]

Albrecht, Karl - *The Power of Minds at Work: Organizational Intelligence in Action*
    Per Psy - v57 - i4 - Winter 2004 - p1071(3) [501+]

Albrecht, M. von - *Jamblich: Itepi Toy Ityoatopeioy Bioy. Pythagoras: Legende-Lehre-Lebensgestaltung*
    Class R - v54 - i1 - May 2004 - p84(3) [501+]

Albrecht, Stephan - *Die Inszenierung der Vergangenheit im Mittelalter: Die Kloster Glastonbury und Saint-Denis*
    HNet - August 2004 - pNA [501+]

Albrecht, W. Steve - *Accounting Concepts and Applications, 9th Ed.*
    R&R Bk N - v19 - i2 - May 2004 - p119 [51-500]
Financial Accounting, 9th Ed.
    R&R Bk N - v19 - i2 - May 2004 - p119 [51-500]

Albright, Carol Bonomo - *Republican Ideals in the Selected Literary Works of Italian-American Joseph Rocchietti, 1835-1845*
    R&R Bk N - v19 - i4 - Nov 2004 - p242(1) [501+]

Albright, Harry - *Pearl Harbor: Japan's Fatal Blunder, the True Story Behind Japan's Attack on December 7, 1941, Illustrated Edition*
    R&R Bk N - v19 - i4 - Nov 2004 - p33(1) [51-500]

Albright, S. Christian - *Spreadsheet Modeling and Applications: Essentials of Practical Management Science*
    R&R Bk N - v19 - i3 - August 2004 - p102(1) [501+]

Albright, Thomas L. - *Accounting: Managing Business Information, Preliminary Ed., Vol. 1*
    R&R Bk N - v19 - i4 - Nov 2004 - p114(1) [51-500]
Accounting: Managing Business Information, Preliminary Ed., Vol. 2
    R&R Bk N - v19 - i4 - Nov 2004 - p114(1) [51-500]

Albritton, Robert - *Phases of Capitalist Development*
    S&S - v68 - i1 - Spring 2004 - p102-105 [501+]

Albuquerque, Severino J. - *Tentative Transgressions: Homosexuality, AIDS, and the Theater in Brazil*
    Choice - v42 - i4 - Dec 2004 - p665(2) [1-50]

Alcaly, Roger - *The New Economy: What it Is, How It Happened, and Why It Is Likely to Last*
    VQR - v80 - i1 - Wntr 2004 - p267-267 [501+]

Alcamo, Joseph - *Ecosystems and Human Well-being: A Framework for Assessment*
    R&R Bk N - v19 - i1 - Feb 2004 - p71(1) [1-50]

Alchon, Suzanne Austin - *A Pest in the Land: New World Epidemics in a Global Perspective*
    Ams - v61 - i2 - Oct 2004 - p274(2) [501+]
    HAHR - v84 - i4 - Nov 2004 - p717(3) [501+]
    JIH - v35 - i1 - Summer 2004 - p140-141 [501+]

Alciatore, David G. - *The Illustrated Principles of Pool and Billiards*
    BL - v101 - i1 - Sept 1 2004 - p45(1) [501+]

Alcock, John - *The Triumph of Sociobiology*
    Am Bio T - v66 - i3 - March 2004 - p227(1) [501+]

Alcock, Pete - *Work to Welfare: How Men Become Detached from the Labour Market*
    AJS - v110 - i2 - Sept 2004 - p501(2) [501+]

Alcock, Susan E. - *Side-by-Side Survey: Comparative Regional Studies in the Mediterranean World*
    R&R Bk N - v19 - i4 - Nov 2004 - p39(1) [51-500]

Alcorn, Randy - *Heaven*
    Ch Today - v49 - i2 - Feb 2005 - p89(1) [51-500]
    y LJ - v129 - i18 - Nov 1 2004 - p89(1) [51-500]
    PW - v251 - i35 - August 30 2004 - p50(1) [51-500]

Alcott, Louisa May - *Little Women (Read by Radio Theatre Performers). Audiobook Review*
    c SLJ - v50 - i11 - Nov 2004 - p82(1) [51-500]
Little Women; Little Men; Jo's Boys
    LJ - v130 - i1 - Jan 1 2005 - p172(1) [1-50]
Little Women
    c RT - v57 - Sept 2003 - p97 [51-500]

Alcover, Joan - *Elegies (Illus. by Arranz-Bravo, Eduardo)*
    WLT - v78 - i3-4 - Sept-Dec 2004 - p149(1) [501+]

Alda, Arlene - *The Book of ZZZs (Illus. by Alda, Arlene)*
    c PW - v252 - i8 - Feb 21 2005 - p173(1) [51-500]
Morning Glory Monday (Illus. by Kovalski, Maryann)
    c CBRA - Annual 2003 - p445(1) [51-500]

Aldag, Ramon J. - *Mastering Management Skills: A Manager's Toolkit*
    R&R Bk N - v19 - i3 - August 2004 - p108(1) [51-500]

Aldama, Arturo J. - *Disrupting Savagism: Intersecting Chicana Mexican Immigrant, and Native American Struggles for Self-representation*
    Am St - v45 - i1 - Spring 2004 - p164-165 [501+]
Violence and the Body: Race, Gender, and the State
    HNet - Nov 2004 - pNA [501+]

Aldama, Fredrick Luis - *Postethnic American Criticism: Magicorealism in Oscar "Zeta" Acosta, Ana Castillo, Julie Dash, Hanif Kureishi, and Salman Rushdie*
    Aztlan - v29 - i2 - Fall 2004 - p227-231 [501+]

Aldamer, Shafi - *Saudi Arabia and Britain: Changing Relations, 1939-1953*
    R&R Bk N - v19 - i1 - Feb 2004 - p33(1) [1-50]

Aldana, Patricia - *Under the Spell of the Moon: Art for Children from the World's Great Illustrators*
    y BL - v101 - i8 - Dec 15 2004 - p733(1) [51-500]
    c Globe & Mail - Dec 11 2004 - pD28 [51-500]
    c HB - v81 - i1 - Jan-Feb 2005 - p117(2) [51-500]
    c PW - v251 - i51 - Dec 20 2004 - p58(2) [51-500]
    c Res Links - v10 - i3 - Feb 2005 - p1(2) [51-500]
    c SLJ - v51 - i1 - Jan 2005 - p100(3) [51-500]

Alder, Elizabeth - *Crossing the Panther's Path*
    c RT - v57 - Nov 2003 - p276 [51-500]

Alderman, John - *Sonic Boom: Napster, MP3, and the New Pioneers of Music*
    T&C - v45 - i4 - Oct 2004 - p890(2) [501+]

Alderman, M. Kay - *Motivation for Achievement: Possibilities for Teaching and Learning, 2nd Ed.*
    R&R Bk N - v19 - i1 - Feb 2004 - p182(1) [51-500]

Alderman, Sharon - *Mastering Weave Structures: Transforming Ideas into Great Cloth*
    LJ - v129 - i13 - August 2004 - p77(1) [51-500]

Alderson, Brian - *Edward Ardizzone: A Bibliographic Commentary*
    R&R Bk N - v19 - i1 - Feb 2004 - p205(1) [51-500]

Alderson, Kevin - *Grade Power: The Complete Guide to Improving Your Grades through Self-Hypnosis*
    Globe & Mail - Oct 9 2004 - pF6 [501+]

Alderton, David - *Encyclopedia of Aquarium and Pond Fish*
    LJ - v130 - i3 - Feb 15 2005 - p156(1) [51-500]

Aldis, Anne C. - *Russian Military Reform, 1992-2002*
    R&R Bk N - v19 - i1 - Feb 2004 - p256(1) [51-500]

Aldrich, Mark - *A Catalog of Folk Song Settings for Wind Band*
    Teach Mus - v12 - i1 - August 2004 - p60(1) [501+]

Aldrich, Richard J. - *Witness to War*
    Spec - v296 - i9193 - Oct 16 2004 - p63(1) [501+]

Aldrich, Robert - *Colonialism and Homosexuality*
    AHR - v109 - i3 - June 2004 - p866(2) [501+]

Aleas, Richard - *Little Girl Lost*
    PW - v251 - i43 - Oct 25 2004 - p33(1) [51-500]

Aleinikoff, T. Alexander - *From Migrants to Citizens: Membership in a Changing World*
    PG - v23 - i2 - Feb 2004 - p213-219 [501+]

Alemany-Fernandez, Manuel - *Heterogender Homosexuality in Honduras*
    CS - v33 - i2 - March 2004 - p178-179 [501+]

Alers, Rochelle - *Let's Get It On*
    BL - v101 - i5 - Nov 1 2004 - p462(1) [51-500]
    PW - v251 - i45 - Nov 8 2004 - p36(1) [501+]

Alesina, Alberto - *Fighting Poverty in the US and Europe: World of Difference*
    Choice - v42 - i4 - Dec 2004 - p706(1) [1-50]
The Size of Nations
    JEL - v42 - i1 - March 2004 - p270(2) [501+]
    JPR - v41 - i5 - Sept 2004 - p637-637 [501+]

Alexander, Alison - *Media Economics: Theory and Practice, 3rd Ed.*
    R&R Bk N - v19 - i1 - Feb 2004 - p211 [51-500]

Alexander, Amir R. - *Geometrical Landscapes: The Voyages of Discovery and the Transformation of Mathematical Practice*
    Six Ct J - v34 - i4 - Winter 2003 - p1231-1232 [501+]

Alexander, Ann Field - *Race Man: The Rise and Fall of the 'Fighting Editor' John Mitchell Jr.*
    NYRB - v51 - i12 - July 15 2004 - p50(2) [501+]

Alexander, Arthur J. - *In the Shadow of the Miracle: The Japanese Economy Since the End of High-Speed Growth*
    JEL - v41 - i4 - Dec 2003 - p1422(1) [501+]

Alexander, Bevin - *Korea: The First War We Lost*
    R&R Bk N - v19 - i4 - Nov 2004 - p50(1) [51-500]
Lost Victories: The Military Genius of Stonewall Jackson
    R&R Bk N - v19 - i3 - August 2004 - p68(1) [51-500]

Alexander, Brian - *Rapture: How Biotech Became the New Religion*
    TimHES - v0 - i1668 - Nov 26 2004 - p24(2) [501+]

Alexander, Bruce - *Rules of Engagement*
    KR - v73 - i2 - Jan 15 2005 - p83(1) [51-500]
    LJ - v129 - i16 - Oct 1 2004 - p64(1) [51-500]
    LJ - v130 - i2 - Feb 1 2005 - p56(1) [501+]
    NYTBR - March 13 2005 - p28 [501+]
    PW - v252 - i2 - Jan 10 2005 - p41(1) [51-500]

Alexander, Bruce E. - *802.11 Wireless Network Site Surveying And Installation*
    Bwatch - Feb 2005 - pNA [501+]

Alexander, Carly - *The Eggnog Chronicles*
    LJ - v129 - i19 - Nov 15 2004 - p47(1) [501+]

Alexander, Caroline - *The Bounty: True Story of the Mutiny on the Bounty (Read by Prebble, Simon). Audiobook Review*
    Kliatt - v38 - i6 - Nov 2004 - p54(2) [501+]
The Bounty: True Story of the Mutiny on the Bounty
    BIC - v33 - i2 - March 2004 - p18(4) [501+]

Alexander, Catherine M.S. - *Shakespeare and Race*
    MP - v102 - i1 - August 2004 - p110(5) [501+]

Alexander, Cecil Frances - *All Things Bright and Beautiful (Illus. by Vojtech, Anna)*
    c CH Bwatch - v14 - i8 - August 2004 - p4(1) [51-500]
    c SLJ - v50 - i11 - Nov 2004 - p121(1) [51-500]

Alexander, Charles C. - *Breaking the Slump: Baseball in the Depression Era*
    Am St - v45 - i1 - Spring 2004 - p160-162 [501+]

Alexander, Charles N. - *Transcendental Meditation in Criminal Rehabilitation and Crime Prevention*
    R&R Bk N - v19 - i1 - Feb 2004 - p145(1) [51-500]

Alexander, Christine - *The Oxford Companion to the Brontes*
    Choice - v42 - i2 - Oct 2004 - p264(1) [51-500]
    BL - v101 - i2 - Sept 15 2004 - p276(1) [501+]

Alexander, David - *Miller European Accounting Guide, 5th Ed.*
    R&R Bk N - v19 - i1 - Feb 2004 - p112(1) [51-500]
Miller International Accounting / Financial Reporting Standards Guide: 2004
    R&R Bk N - v19 - i1 - Feb 2004 - p113(1) [51-500]

Alexander, Dean C. - *Business Confronts Terrorism: Risks and Responses*
    Bwatch - Nov 2004 - pNA [501+]
    Choice - v42 - i7 - March 2005 - p1272(2) [51-500]

Alexander, Hanan A. - *Spirituality and Ethics in Education: Philosophical, Theological and Radical Perspectives*
    R&R Bk N - v19 - i3 - August 2004 - p14(1) [1-50]

Alexander, J. - *Going Up! The No-Worries Guide to Secondary School*
    y Sch Lib - v52 - i3 - Autumn 2004 - p166(1) [501+]

Alexander, Jonathan - *Bisexuality and Transgenderism: InterSEXions of the Others*
    R&R Bk N - v19 - i3 - August 2004 - p148(1) [51-500]

Alexander, Kern - *The Law of Schools, Students, and Teachers in a Nutshell, 3rd Ed.*
    R&R Bk N - v19 - i3 - August 2004 - p201(1) [1-50]

Alexander, Lloyd - *The Black Cauldron (Read by Langton, James). Audiobook Review*
    c SLJ - v50 - i10 - Oct 2004 - p85(1) [51-500]
Castle of Llyr (Read by Langton, James). Audiobook Review
    c SLJ - v51 - i2 - Feb 2005 - p74(1) [501+]
The Chronicles of Prydain
    y Sch Lib - v52 - i4 - Winter 2004 - p212(1) [51-500]

The Remarkable Journey of Prince Jen
    PW - v251 - i51 - Dec 20 2004 - p62(1) [501+]
Time Cat
  c CH Bwatch - v14 - i8 - August 2004 - p3(1) [51-500]
The Xanadu Adventure
  c CCB-B - v58 - i5 - Jan 2005 - p196(1) [51-500]
  y HB - v81 - i2 - March-April 2005 - p196(1) [51-500]
  y KR - v73 - i4 - Feb 15 2005 - p225(1) [51-500]
  y SLJ - v51 - i2 - Feb 2005 - p132(1) [51-500]
Alexander, Lynn M. - *Women, Work, and Representation: Needlewomen in Victorian Art and Literature*
    TSWL - v23 - i1 - Spring 2004 - p138-139 [501+]
    VS - v46 - i3 - Spring 2004 - p514(2) [501+]
Alexander, M.C. - *The Case for the Prosecution in the Ciceronian*
    Class R - v54 - i1 - May 2004 - p91(3) [501+]
Alexander, Marc - *A Companion Guide to the Folklore, Myths & Customs of Britain*
    Folkl - v115 - i3 - Dec 2004 - p366(2) [501+]
Alexander, Max - *Man Bites Log: The Unlikely Adventures of a City Guy in the Woods.*
    KR - v72 - i17 - Sept 1 2004 - p843(1) [501+]
    LJ - v129 - i17 - Oct 15 2004 - p69(1) [51-500]
    PW - v251 - i41 - Oct 11 2004 - p66(1) [51-500]
Alexander, Meena - *Raw Silk*
    LJ - v129 - i13 - August 2004 - p84(2) [501+]
Alexander, Michael - *Knocking on Heaven's Door: American Religion in the Age of Counterculture*
    JIH - v35 - i2 - Autumn 2004 - p324(2) [501+]
Alexander, Neville - *An Ordinary Country: Issues in the Transition from Apartheid to Democracy in South Africa*
    HNet - July 2004 - pNA [501+]
Alexander, Paul - *The Candidate*
    NYTBR - August 15 2004 - p11 [501+]
Alexander, R. McNeill - *Human Bones: A Scientific and Pictorial Investigation (Illus. by Diskin, Aaron)*
    LJ - v129 - i16 - Oct 1 2004 - p106(2) [51-500]
    New Sci - v185 - i2486 - Feb 12 2005 - p48(2) [501+]
Alexander, Robert - *Re-Writing the French Revolutionary Tradition*
    Choice - v42 - i2 - Oct 2004 - p360(1) [51-500]
Alexander, Robert J. - *A History of Organized Labor in Brazil*
    Choice - v41 - i7 - March 2004 - p1352(1) [501+]
Alexander, Rosemary - *The Essential Garden Design Workbook*
    Bwatch - March 2005 - pNA [51-500]
Alexander, S.L. - *Media and American Courts: A Reference Handbook*
  y Ref Rev - Oct 2004 - pNA [501+]
Alexander, Sally Hobart - *On My Own (Read by Toren, Suzanne). Audiobook Review*
    Kliatt - v38 - i4 - July 2004 - p61(1) [51-500]
Alexander, Victoria - *The One That Got Away*
    PW - v251 - i43 - Oct 25 2004 - p33(1) [51-500]
A Visit from Sir Nicholas
    PW - v251 - i47 - Nov 22 2004 - p44(1) [51-500]
Alexander, Victoria D. - *Sociology of the Arts: Exploring Fine and Popular Forms*
    CS - v33 - i4 - July 2004 - p454(2) [501+]
Alexander, William - *Erectile Dysfunction and Related Disorders*
    SciTech - v28 - i1 - March 2004 - p106(1) [51-500]
Alexanderson, B. - *Le texte des Confessions de saint Augustin Manuscrits et stemma*
    Class R - v54 - i2 - Nov 2004 - p414(2) [501+]
Alexandra, Lou - *Teaching TV Soaps*
    Sch Lib - v52 - i4 - Winter 2004 - p220(1) [51-500]
Alexandrou, Aris - *Mission Box*
    TLS - i5302 - Nov 12 2004 - p31(1) [51-500]
Alexi, Robert Arthur - *The Pale Indian*
    Globe & Mail - Feb 19 2005 - pD7 [501+]
Alexievich, Svetlana - *Voices from Chernobyl*
    PW - v252 - i9 - Feb 28 2005 - p50(1) [51-500]
Alexiou, M. - *The Ritual Lament in Greek Tradition*
    Class R - v54 - i1 - May 2004 - p61(2) [501+]
Alexis, Jacques Stephen - *In the Flicker of an Eyelid*
    Callaloo - v27 - i2 - Spring 2004 - p563(564) [501+]
Alexopoulos, Golfo - *Stalin's Outcasts: Aliens, Citizens, and the Soviet State, 1926-1936*
    AHR - v109 - i3 - June 2004 - p1008(2) [501+]
    Russ Rev - v63 - i2 - April 2004 - pNA [501+]
    Slav R - v63 - i2 - Summer 2004 - p412(2) [501+]
Alfeld, Beverly Ellen Schoonmaker - *The Jamlady Cookbook*
    PW - v251 - i27 - July 5 2004 - p52(1) [51-500]

Alfonso, Isabel - *Building Legitimacy: Political Discourses and Forms of Legitimation in Medieval Societies*
    R&R Bk N - v19 - i1 - Feb 2004 - pNA [51-500]
Alfred, Agnes - *Paddling to Where I Stand: Agnes Alfred, Qwiqwasutinuxw Noblewoman*
    R&R Bk N - v19 - i3 - August 2004 - p62(1) [51-500]
Algar, Hamid - *Wahhabism: A Critical Essay*
    J Ch St - v46 - i4 - Autumn 2004 - p890(2) [501+]
Ali, Daniel - *Inside Islam: A Guide for Catholics*
    CI - v12 - i11 - Dec 2004 - p48(2) [501+]
Ali, Maryum - *I Shook Up the World: The Incredible Life of Muhammad Ali (Illus. by Johnson, Patrick)*
  c Black Iss - v6 - i4 - July-August 2004 - p60(1) [51-500]
Ali, Monica - *Brick Lane (Read by Sastre, Elizabeth). Audiobook Review*
    Kliatt - v38 - i4 - July 2004 - p48(2) [51-500]
Brick Lane
    HR - v57 - i2 - Summer 2004 - p311-316 [501+]
    WLT - v78 - i3-4 - Sept-Dec 2004 - p91(1) [501+]
Ali, Muhammad - *The Soul of a Butterfly: Reflections on Life's Journey*
    LJ - v129 - i20 - Dec 1 2004 - p129(1) [51-500]
    BL - v101 - i4 - Oct 15 2004 - p362(1) [51-500]
    PW - v251 - i43 - Oct 25 2004 - p36(1) [51-500]
Ali, Saleem H. - *Mining, the Environment, and Indigenous Development Conflicts*
    R&R Bk N - v19 - i1 - Feb 2004 - p53(1) [51-500]
Ali, Samina - *Madras on Rainy Days*
    Wom R Bks - v22 - i3 - Dec 2004 - p18(1) [51-500]
Ali, Shaheen Sardar - *Gender and Human Rights in Islam and International Law: Equal Before Allah, Unequal Before Man?*
    R&R Bk N - v19 - i4 - Nov 2004 - p175(1) [501+]
Ali, Taisier M. - *Durable Peace: Challenges for Peacebuilding in Africa*
    Choice - v42 - i6 - Feb 2005 - p1091(1) [51-500]
    R&R Bk N - v19 - i4 - Nov 2004 - p50(1) [51-500]
Ali, Tariq - *Bush in Babylon: The Recolonisation of Iraq*
    BW - v34 - i1 - Jan 4 2004 - p4(1) [501+]
    BW - v34 - i42 - Oct 17 2004 - p12(1) [501+]
    MEQ - v11 - i3 - Summer 2004 - p82(1) [501+]
Ali, Thalassa - *A Beggar at the Gate*
    PW - v251 - i40 - Oct 4 2004 - p69(1) [51-500]
Alien, Brooke - *Capote Reconsidered*
    Wil Q - v29 - i1 - Wntr 2005 - p103(2) [501+]
Alighieri, Pietro - *Pietro Alighieri, 'Comentum Super Poema 'Comedie Dantis'': A Critical Edition of the Third and Final Draft of Pietro Alighieri's 'Commentary on Dante's 'The Divine Comedy''*
    R&R Bk N - v19 - i1 - Feb 2004 - p232(1) [51-500]
Alikhan, Shahid - *Intellectual Property and Competitive Strategies in the 21st Century*
    R&R Bk N - v19 - i3 - August 2004 - p190(1) [501+]
Aliki - *Ah, Music! (Illus. by Aliki)*
    SLJ - v50 - i12 - Dec 2004 - p59(1) [501+]
Marianthe's Story
  c RT - v57 - Dec 2003 - p395 [51-500]
William Shakespeare and the Globe
  c Teach Lib - v32 - i3 - Feb 2005 - p21(1) [51-500]
Alin, Lou - *Bush Poodles are Murder*
    CBRA - Annual 2003 - p149(1) [51-500]
Aliprantis, Charalambos D. - *Assets, Beliefs, and Equilibria in Economic Dynamics*
    JEL - v42 - i1 - March 2004 - p238(1) [501+]
Alisen, Paige - *Finding Courage to Speak: Women's Survival of Child Abuse*
    SciTech - v28 - i1 - March 2004 - p102(1) [51-500]
Alison, James - *On Being Liked*
    TLS - i5299 - Oct 22 2004 - p32(1) [501+]
Aliteri, Charles - *The Particulars of Rapture: An Aesthetics of the Affects*
    VQR - v80 - i3 - Summer 2004 - p260(2) [501+]
Alkhafaji, Abbass F. - *Strategic Management: Formulation, Implementation, and Control in a Dynamic Environment*
    JEL - v41 - i4 - Dec 2003 - p1333(2) [501+]
All Night, All Day: A Child's First Book of African-American Spirituals.
  c SLJ - v50 - i12 - Dec 2004 - p59(1) [501+]
Allaby, Ailsa - *Oxford Dictionary of Earth Sciences, 2nd Ed.*
    SciTech - v28 - i1 - March 2004 - p58(1) [51-500]
Allaby, Michael - *Fog, Smog and Poisoned Rain (Illus. by Garratt, Richard)*
    LibMed - v22 - i5 - Feb 2004 - p55(1) [51-500]

Allahar, Anton - *Carribean Charisma: Reflections on Leadership, Legitimacy and Populist Politics*
    JTWS - v21 - i1 - Spring 2004 - p316(3) [501+]
Allan, Barbara - *Developing Library Staff through Work-Based Learning*
    ALJ - v53 - i4 - Nov 2004 - p409(1) [501+]
Project Management: Tools and Techniques for Today's ILS Professional
    R&USQ - v44 - i2 - Winter 2004 - p179(1) [51-500]
Allan, Edward L. - *Civil Gang Abatement: The Effectiveness and Implications of Policing by Injunction*
    R&R Bk N - v19 - i4 - Nov 2004 - p173(1) [501+]
Allan, Graham - *Social Relations and the Life Course*
    CS - v33 - i4 - July 2004 - p436(2) [501+]
Allan, J.A. - *The Middle East Water Question: Hydropolitics and the Global Economy*
    GJ - v170 - i3 - Sept 2004 - p282(1) [501+]
Allan, Nicholas - *Where Willy Went*
  c Globe & Mail - Feb 12 2005 - pD11 [51-500]
  c KR - v72 - i24 - Dec 15 2004 - p1197(1) [501+]
  c PW - v252 - i4 - Jan 24 2005 - p243(1) [51-500]
Allan, T.R.S. - *Constitutional Justice: A Liberal Theory of the Rule of Law*
    Law&PolBR - June 2004 - p449(4) [501+]
Allan, Tony - *Rain Forests*
  y SB - v40 - i3 - May-June 2004 - p122(2) [501+]
The Troubles in Northern Ireland
  y SLJ - v50 - i12 - Dec 2004 - p155(2) [501+]
Allan, W. - *Euripides: Medea*
    Class R - v54 - i1 - May 2004 - p36(2) [501+]
Allard-Nelson, Susan K. - *An Aristotelian Approach to Ethical Theory: The Norms of Virtue*
    R&R Bk N - v19 - i4 - Nov 2004 - p3(1) [51-500]
Alldritt, Keith - *David Jones: A Life*
    TLS - i5265 - Feb 27 2004 - p25-25 [501+]
Alleman, Richard - *Hollywood: The Movie Lover's Guide*
    Globe & Mail - Feb 26 2005 - pD13 [51-500]
    LJ - v130 - i1 - Jan 1 2005 - p172(1) [1-50]
New York: The Movie Lover's Guide
    LJ - v130 - i1 - Jan 1 2005 - p172(1) [1-50]
Allen, Angela C. - *Dark Thirst*
    BL - v101 - i2 - Sept 15 2004 - p214(2) [501+]
    LJ - v129 - i15 - Sept 15 2004 - p53(1) [51-500]
    PW - v251 - i37 - Sept 13 2004 - p63(1) [51-500]
Allen, Barbara L. - *Uneasy Alchemy: Citizens and Experts in Louisiana's Chemical Corridor Disputes*
    CS - v33 - i5 - Sept 2004 - p621-621 [501+]
    Law&PolBR - June 2004 - p402(4) [501+]
Allen, Barry - *Knowledge and Civilization*
    R&R Bk N - v19 - i1 - Feb 2004 - p6(1) [51-500]
Allen, Brooke - *Artistic License: Three Centuries of Good Writing and Bad Behavior*
    BL - v101 - i2 - Sept 15 2004 - p193(1) [501+]
    KR - v72 - i13 - July 1 2004 - p609(1) [501+]
    LJ - v129 - i13 - August 2004 - p75(1) [51-500]
    R&R Bk N - v19 - i4 - Nov 2004 - p233(1) [501+]
    Sew R - v112 - i3 - Summer 2004 - pXC-XCIII [501+]
Twentieth-Century Attitudes: Literary Powers in Uncertain Times
    Sew R - v112 - i3 - Summer 2004 - pXC-XCIII [501+]
Allen, Chadwick - *Blood Narrative: Indigenous Identity in American Indian and Maori Literary and Activist Texts*
    AL - v76 - i2 - June 2004 - p405(3) [501+]
    Comp L - v56 - i3 - Summer 2004 - p279-3 [501+]
Allen, Charles - *Duel in the Snows: The True Story of the Younghusband Mission to Lhasa*
    A Aff - v35 - i2 - July 2004 - p229-230 [501+]
Allen, Christopher - *French Painting in the Golden Age*
    Apo - v161 - i516 - Feb 2005 - p76(2) [501+]
Allen, Conrad - *Murder on the Salsette*
    BL - v101 - i9-10 - Jan 1 2005 - p824(1) [1-50]
Allen, D.E. - *Assessing Exchange Rate Hypothesis within Southern Africa*
    R&R Bk N - v19 - i3 - August 2004 - p136(1) [51-500]
Allen, Dana G. - *Handbook of Veterinary Drugs, 3rd Ed.*
    SciTech - v28 - i4 - Dec 2004 - p127 [51-500]
Allen, David - *Windows Linux Migration Toolkit*
    Bwatch - Jan 2005 - pNA [51-500]
    Bwatch - Feb 2005 - pNA [51-500]
Allen, David (b. 1961 -) - *The Facilitator's Book of Questions: Tools for Looking Together at Student and Teacher Work*
    TCR - v107 - i2 - Feb 2005 - p333(3) [501+]
Allen, David E. - *Medicinal Plants in Folk Tradition: An Ethnobotany of Britain and Ireland*
    E-Streams - Dec 2004 - pNA [501+]
    SciTech - v28 - i3 - Sept 2004 - p6(1) [501+]

Allen, Debra J. - *The Oder-Neisse Line: The United States, Poland, and Germany in the Cold War*
Choice - v41 - i7 - March 2004 - p1346(1) [501+]

Allen, Derek R. - *Customer Satisfaction Research Management: A Comprehensive Guide to Integrating Customer Loyalty and Satisfaction Metrics in the Management of Complex Organizations*
R&R Bk N - v19 - i3 - August 2004 - p126(1) [51-500]
Linking Customer and Employee Satisfaction to the Bottom Line: A Comprehensive Guide to Establishing the Impact of Customer and Employee Satisfaction on Critical Business Outcomes
Bwatch - Oct 2004 - pNA [51-500]

Allen, Dick - *The Day Before*
HR - v57 - i2 - Summer 2004 - p325-334 [501+]

Allen, Douglas W. - *The Nature of the Farm: Contracts, Risk, and Organization in Agriculture*
JEL - v41 - i4 - Dec 2003 - p1432(1) [501+]
JEL - v42 - i4 - Dec 2004 - p1164(2) [501+]

Allen, Eddie B. - *Low Road: The Life and Legacy of Donald Goines*
BL - v101 - i1 - Sept 1 2004 - p38(1) [51-500]
Black Iss - v6 - i5 - Sept-Oct 2004 - p47(1) [501+]
KR - v72 - i13 - July 1 2004 - p609(2) [501+]
PW - v251 - i32 - August 9 2004 - p241(1) [51-500]

Allen, Edward - *Fundamentals of Building Construction: Materials and Methods, 4th Ed.*
E-Streams - Sept 2004 - pNA [501+]

Allen, Emily - *Theater Figures: The Production of the Nineteenth-Century British Novel*
VS - v46 - i3 - Spring 2004 - p542(3) [501+]

Allen, Frederick - *A Decent, Orderly Lynching: The Montan Vigilantes and Their Troublesome Legacy*
LJ - v129 - i17 - Oct 15 2004 - p71(2) [51-500]

Allen, Gerald - *Reef Fish Identification: Tropical Pacific*
Choice - v41 - i7 - March 2004 - p1322(1) [501+]

Allen, Horace E. - *Thinking with the Heart: Principle, Practice and Purpose for Spiritual Wellness*
Black Iss - v7 - i2 - March-April 2005 - p61(1) [501+]

Allen, James - *Without Sanctuary: Lynching Photography in America*
J Bl St - v34 - i5 - May 2004 - p719-733 [501+]

Allen, James E. - *Assisted Living Administration: The Knowledge Base, 2nd Ed.*
SciTech - v28 - i4 - Dec 2004 - p7(1) [1-50]

Allen, Jean - *Airplanes*
c LibMed - v22 - i5 - Feb 2004 - p86(1) [501+]

Allen, John - *Lost Geographies of Power*
AJS - v110 - i3 - Nov 2004 - p794(2) [501+]
CS - v33 - i1 - Jan 2004 - p125-125 [501+]

Allen, John D. - *Gay, Lesbian, Bisexual, and Transgender People with Developmental Disabilities and Mental Retardation: Stories of the Rainbow Support Group*
R&R Bk N - v19 - i1 - Feb 2004 - p128(1) [51-500]

Allen, John L., Jr. - *All the Pope's Men: The Inside Story of How the Vatican Really Thinks*
AM - v191 - i10 - Oct 11 2004 - p37 [501+]
Econ - v373 - i8405 - Dec 11 2004 - p83US [501+]
All the Pope's Men: The Inside Story of How the Vatican Really Works
Comw - v131 - i21 - Dec 3 2004 - p33(3) [501+]

Allen, Joseph R. - *Metamorphosis of the Private Sphere: Gardens and Objects in Tang-Song Poetry*
. HJAS - v64 - i2 - Dec 2004 - p441-448 [501+]

Allen, Kathryn Madeline - *This Little Piggy's Book of Manners (Illus. by Wolff, Nancy)*
c LibMed - v22 - i6 - March 2004 - p56(1) [501+]

Allen, L. Dean - *Rise Up, O Men of God: The "Men and Religion Forward Movement" and the "Promise Keepers"*
CH - v73 - i4 - Dec 2004 - p893(3) [501+]

Allen, L.J.S. - *An Introduction to Stochastic Processes with Applications to Biology*
SIAM Rev - v46 - i3 - Sept 2004 - p583(2) [501+]

Allen, Leslie C. - *Psalms 101-150, revised*
Intpr - v59 - i1 - Jan 2005 - p86(2) [501+]

Allen, Linda - *Understanding Market, Credit, and Operational Risk: The Value at Risk Approach*
R&R Bk N - v19 - i2 - May 2004 - p124 [51-500]

Allen, Loyd V. - *Ansel's Pharmaceutical Dosage Forms and Drug Delivery Systems, 8th Ed*
SciTech - v28 - i4 - Dec 2004 - p119(1) [1-50]

Allen, M.E. - *Gotta Get Some Bish Bash Bosh*
y BL - v101 - i9-10 - Jan 1 2005 - p842(1) [51-500]
y CCB-B - v58 - i5 - Jan 2005 - p197(1) [51-500]
y Kliatt - v39 - i1 - Jan 2005 - p16(1) [51-500]
y KR - v72 - i24 - Dec 15 2004 - p1197(1) [501+]
y PW - v252 - i5 - Jan 31 2005 - p69(1) [51-500]

Allen, Mariette Pathy - *The Gender Frontier*
Lam Bk Rpt - v13 - i1-2 - August-Sept 2004 - p36(1) [501+]

Allen, Michael J.B. - *Marsilio Ficino: Platonic Theology*
VQR - v80 - i1 - Wntr 2004 - p278-278 [501+]

Allen, Michael Thad - *The Business of Genocide: The SS, Slave Labor, and the Concentration Camps*
BHR - v78 - i1 - Spring 2004 - p163(6) [501+]
GSR - v27 - i1 - Feb 2004 - p187-188 [501+]
JMH - v76 - i3 - Sept 2004 - p728(2) [501+]
T&C - v45 - i1 - Jan 2004 - p199(3) [501+]

Allen, Mitchell - *German Parliamentary Debates, 1848-1933*
HNet - Oct 2004 - pNA [501+]

Allen, Nancy Kelly - *Whose Food Is This? A Look at What Animals Eat--Seeds, Bugs, and Nuts (Illus. by Alderman, Derrick)*
c BL - v101 - i5 - Nov 1 2004 - p486(1) [51-500]

Allen, Pam - *Scarf Style: Innovative to Traditional, 31 Inspirational Styles To Knit and Crochet*
LJ - v129 - i20 - Dec 1 2004 - p108(1) [51-500]

Allen, Pamela - *Mr McGee and the Big Bag of Bread*
c Magpies - v19 - i5 - Nov 2004 - p26(2) [501+]

Allen, Patricia - *Together at the Table: Sustainability and Sustenance in the American Agrifood System*
Fut - v39 - i2 - March-April 2005 - p61(1) [51-500]

Allen, Paula Gunn - *Pocahontas: Medicine Woman, Spy, Enterpreneur, Diplomat*
Choice - v41 - i7 - March 2004 - p1357(2) [501+]

Allen, Pauline - *Maximus the Confessor and His Companions: Documents from Exile*
CHR - v90 - i4 - Oct 2004 - p746(2) [501+]

Allen, Peter - *A Geological Survey in Transition*
Isis - v95 - i2 - June 2004 - p301(2) [501+]

Allen, Prudence - *The Concept of Woman*
Specu - v79 - i3 - July 2004 - p729-731 [501+]

Allen, Richard C. - *David Hartley on Human Nature*
Isis - v95 - i2 - June 2004 - p290(1) [501+]

Allen, Robbie - *Active Directory Cookbook*
SciTech - v28 - i1 - March 2004 - p155(1) [51-500]

Allen, Robert C. - *Farm to Factory: A Reinterpretation of the Soviet Industrial Revolution*
Slav R - v63 - i4 - Winter 2004 - p841(9) [501+]

Allen, Robert E. - *First Battalion of the 28th Marines on Iwo Jima: A Day-by-Day History From Personal Accounts and Official Reports, with Complete Muster Rolls*
R&R Bk N - v20 - i1 - Feb 2005 - p33(1) [51-500]

Allen, Robert G. - *Multiple Streams of Income, 2nd Ed.*
R&R Bk N - v19 - i3 - August 2004 - p134(1) [1-50]

Allen, Robert W. - *Churchill's Guests: Britain and the Belgian Exiles During World War II*
PSQ - v119 - i3 - Fall 2004 - p550(2) [501+]

Allen, Ronald J. - *Preaching and Practical Ministry*
Intpr - v58 - i4 - Oct 2004 - p438(1) [501+]
Preaching the Gospels without Blaming the Jews: A Lectionary Commentary
Intpr - v59 - i1 - Jan 2005 - p109(1) [51-500]

Allen, Ronald Jay - *Comprehensive Criminal Procedure: 2004 Supplement*
R&R Bk N - v19 - i4 - Nov 2004 - p173(1) [501+]

Allen, Ronald L. - *Signal Analysis: Time, Frequency, Scale, and Structure*
SciTech - v28 - i1 - March 2004 - p153(1) [51-500]

Allen, Rosamund - *Lazamon: Contexts, Language, and Interpretation*
Specu - v79 - i4 - Oct 2004 - p1018(3) [501+]

Allen, Sheila - *Making Connections: Reading and Understanding College Textbooks, 2nd Ed.*
R&R Bk N - v19 - i4 - Nov 2004 - p185(1) [501+]

Allen, Ted - *Queer Eye for the Straight Guy: The Fab 5's Guide to Looking Better, Cooking Better, Dressing Better, Behaving Better and Living Better*
y SLJ - v50 - i8 - August 2004 - p146(2) [501+]

Allen, Thomas - *A Traveler's Guide to Mars*
Mac - Jan 26 2004 - p46(1) [51-500]

Allen, Thomas B. - *George Washington, Spymaster: How the Americans Out-Spied the British and Won the Revolutionary War (Illus. by Harness, Cheryl)*
SLJ - v50 - i10 - Oct 2004 - pS31(1) [51-500]

Allen, Tony - *A Summer in the Park: A Journal of Speakers' Corner*
NS - v133 - i4700 - August 9 2004 - p39(2) [501+]
TLS - i5301 - Nov 5 2004 - p35(1) [51-500]

Allen, Valerie - *The Age of Chaucer*
y Sch Lib - v52 - i3 - Autumn 2004 - p166(1) [501+]

Allen, William Barclay - *Habits of Mind: Fostering Access and Excellence in Higher Education*
Choice - v41 - i7 - March 2004 - p1344(1) [501+]

Allende, Isabel - *Kingdom of the Golden Dragon (Read by Brown, Blair). Audiobook Review*
y Kliatt - v39 - i1 - Jan 2005 - p46(1) [51-500]
Kingdom of the Golden Dragon
y VOYA - v27 - i3 - August 2004 - p226(1) [1-50]
My Invented Country
Globe & Mail - July 3 2004 - pD13 [1-50]
Zorro (Read by Brown, Blair). Audiobook Review
KR - v73 - i4 - Feb 15 2005 - p187(1) [501+]
Zorro
LJ - v130 - i4 - March 1 2005 - p74(1) [51-500]
PW - v252 - i9 - Feb 28 2005 - p39(1) [51-500]

Allender, Dan B. - *To Be Told: Know Your Story, Shape Your Future*
PW - v252 - i4 - Jan 24 2005 - p239(2) [501+]

Allendorf, Mark Donald - *Chemical Vapor Deposition XVI and EUROCVD 14, Vols. 1-2*
SciTech - v28 - i1 - March 2004 - p178(1) [51-500]

Aller, Susan Bivin - *Beyond Little Women: A Story about Louisa May Alcott (Illus. by Wang, Qi Z.)*
c SLJ - v50 - i8 - August 2004 - p104(2) [501+]
George Eastman
c CH Bwatch - v14 - i7 - July 2004 - p2(2) [51-500]

Allerfeldt, Kristofer - *Race, Radicalism, Religion, and Restriction: Immigration in the Pacific Northwest, 1890-1924*
JAH - v91 - i3 - Dec 2004 - p1062(2) [501+]

Alley, Alvin - *Alley Spirit: The Journey of an American Dance Company*
Black Iss - v7 - i1 - Jan-Feb 2005 - p66(1) [501+]

Alley, Michael - *The Craft of Scientific Presentations: Critical Steps to Succeed and Critical Errors to Avoid*
Phys Today - v57 - i7 - July 2004 - p59-60 [501+]

Alley, Roderic - *Internal Conflict and the International Community: Wars without End?*
R&R Bk N - v19 - i3 - August 2004 - p212(1) [1-50]

Allgower, Eugene L. - *Numerical Analysis: A Mathematical Introduction*
SIAM Rev - v46 - i1 - March 2004 - p149-150 [501+]

Allie, Scott - *B.P.R.D.: The Soul of Venice & Other Stories*
PW - v251 - i37 - Sept 13 2004 - p60(1) [501+]
The Dark Horse Book of Witchcraft
BL - v101 - i5 - Nov 1 2004 - p473(1) [501+]
PW - v251 - i30 - July 26 2004 - p41(1) [501+]
Weird Tales, Vol. 2
y BL - v101 - i6 - Nov 15 2004 - p572(1) [51-500]

Allieres, Nathalie Des - *Saint Exupery: Art, Writings and Musings*
Choice - v41 - i11-12 - July-August 2004 - p2031(1) [501+]

Allin, Lou - *A Little Learning Is a Murderous Thing*
KR - v73 - i4 - Feb 15 2005 - p198(1) [501+]

Allin, Shawn B. - *Polymer Science and Technology, 2nd Ed.*
J Chem Ed - v81 - i6 - June 2004 - p809-810 [501+]

Alling, Annika Morte - *Le Desir Selon l'Autre: Etude du 'Rouge et le Noir' et de la ' Chartreuse de Parma' A la Lumiere du desir triangulaire' de Rene Girard*
FS - v58 - i2 - April 2004 - p271(2) [501+]

Allison, Catherine - *Brown Paper Teddy Bear (Illus. by Reed, Neil)*
c BL - v100 - i22 - August 2004 - p1940(1) [51-500]
c KR - v72 - i19 - Oct 1 2004 - p955(1) [501+]
c PW - v251 - i51 - Dec 20 2004 - p58(1) [51-500]
c SLJ - v51 - i1 - Jan 2005 - p85(1) [51-500]

Allison, Glen C. - *Netblue: An Al Forte Mystery*
LJ - v129 - i12 - July 2004 - p64(1) [51-500]

Allison, Graham - *Nuclear Terrorism: The Ultimate Preventable Catastrophe*
BL - v100 - i22 - August 2004 - p1878(1) [51-500]
BW - v34 - i35 - August 2004 - p5(1) [501+]
For Aff - v84 - i1 - Jan-Feb 2005 - p156 [501+]
NYTBR - Sept 5 2004 - p8 [501+]
NYTBR - Sept 12 2004 - p26 [501+]
NYTBR - Sept 19 2004 - p22 [501+]
PW - v251 - i27 - July 5 2004 - p48(1) [501+]
SPA - v61 - i2 - March-April 2005 - p67(2) [501+]

Allison, Lon - *Going Public with the Gospel: Reviving Evangelistic Proclamation*
IBMR - v28 - i3 - July 2004 - p144(1) [501+]

Allison, Simon P. - *Metabolic Issues of Clinical Nutrition*
SciTech - v28 - i4 - Dec 2004 - p115(1) [1-50]

Allister, Mark - *Eco-Man: New Perspectives on Masculinity and Nature*
R&R Bk N - v19 - i4 - Nov 2004 - p132(1) [1-50]

Allitt, Patrick - *I'm the Teacher, You're the Student: A Semester in the University Classroom*
AM - v192 - i5 - Feb 14 2005 - p25 [501+]
LJ - v129 - i17 - Oct 15 2004 - p71(1) [51-500]
Religion in America Since 1945: A History
J Ch St - v46 - i4 - Autumn 2004 - p900(2) [501+]
JR - v84 - i4 - Oct 2004 - p613(2) [501+]
TLS - i5303 - Nov 19 2004 - p12-13 [501+]
CHR - v90 - i3 - July 2004 - p583(2) [501+]

Allman, Barbara - *Musical Genius: A Story about Wolfgang Amadeus Mozart (Illus. by Hamlin, Janet)*
c SLJ - v50 - i8 - August 2004 - p104(2) [501+]

Allman, Jean - *"I Will Not Eat Stone": A Women's History of Colonial Asante*
JWH - v16 - i3 - Autumn 2004 - p213(8) [501+]

Allman, Toney - *Tapeworms*
c SB - v40 - i5 - Sept-Oct 2004 - p224(1) [501+]

Allmers, Nancy M. - *Appleton and Lange's Review for the Surgical Technology Examination, 5th Ed.*
SciTech - v28 - i1 - March 2004 - p109(1) [51-500]

Allnutt, Gillian - *Sojourner*
TLS - i5301 - Nov 5 2004 - p34(1) [51-500]

Allon, Hagit - *The Mystery of the Dead Sea Scrolls (Illus. by Abolafia, Yossi)*
c SLJ - v50 - i7 - July 2004 - p90(1) [51-500]

Allport, Alan - *Freedom of Speech*
LibMed - v22 - i4 - Jan 2004 - p82(1) [501+]

Allwood, Mel - *Mountain Bike Maintenance: The Illustrated Manual*
R&R Bk N - v19 - i4 - Nov 2004 - p247(1) [501+]

Allwood, Melanie - *Mountain Bike Maintenance: The Illustrated Manual (Illus. by Allwood, Mel)*
LJ - v129 - i20 - Dec 1 2004 - p156(1) [51-500]

Allyn, David - *I Can't Believe I Just Did That: How Embarrassment Can Wreak Havoc in Your Life and What You Can Do to Conquer It*
Globe & Mail - Nov 6 2004 - pF8 [51-500]

Allyn, Doug - *The Burning of Rachel Hayes*
BL - v101 - i4 - Oct 15 2004 - p391(2) [51-500]
KR - v72 - i19 - Oct 1 2004 - p940(1) [501+]
PW - v251 - i43 - Oct 25 2004 - p31(2) [51-500]

Almasi, Zsolt - *The Problematics of Custom as Exemplified in Key Texts of the Late English Renaissance*
R&R Bk N - v19 - i4 - Nov 2004 - p233(1) [501+]

Almeida, Guilherme de - *Navigating the Night Sky: How to Identify the Stars and Constellations*
Choice - v42 - i1 - Sept 2004 - p126(1) [501+]

Almeida, Miguel Vale de - *Earth-Colored Sea: "Race", Culture, and the Politics of Identity in the Postcolonial Portuguese-Speaking World*
R&R Bk N - v19 - i4 - Nov 2004 - p42(1) [51-500]

Almeria, Sally - *RCRA Regulations and Keyword Index, 2004 Ed.*
R&R Bk N - v19 - i3 - August 2004 - p201(1) [1-50]

Almodovor, Pedro - *Boys 2 Men*
New York - v37 - i41 - Nov 22 2004 - p82(2) [501+]

Almond, David - *The Fire-Eaters (Read by Gerroll, Daniel). Audiobook Review*
c BL - v101 - i2 - Sept 15 2004 - p261(1) [51-500]
The Fire-Eaters
CC - v121 - i25 - Dec 14 2004 - p24(1) [51-500]
HB - v81 - i1 - Jan-Feb 2005 - p15(1) [51-500]
y SLJ - v50 - i10 - Oct 2004 - pS68(1) [51-500]
y VOYA - v27 - i4 - Oct 2004 - p312(2) [51-500]
Kate, the Cat and the Moon (Illus. by Lambert, Stephen)
c Magpies - v19 - i5 - Nov 2004 - p28(1) [501+]
Skellig
c WLT - v79 - i1 - Jan-April 2005 - p69(4) [501+]

Almond, Gabriel A. - *Strong Religion: The Rise of Fundamentalisms around the World*
Theol St - v65 - i4 - Dec 2004 - p905(1) [501+]

Almond, Steve - *Candyfreak: A Journey through the Chocolate Underbelly of America*
BL - v101 - i9-10 - Jan 1 2005 - p771(1) [501+]
R&R Bk N - v19 - i3 - August 2004 - p118(1) [51-500]
The Evil B.B. Chow and Other Stories
KR - v73 - i2 - Jan 15 2005 - p63(1) [51-500]
LJ - v130 - i4 - March 1 2005 - p81(1) [51-500]
PW - v252 - i7 - Feb 14 2005 - p167(1) [51-500]

Alnasrawi, Abbas - *Iraq's Burdens: Oil, Sanctions, and Underdevelopment*
MEQ - v11 - i3 - Summer 2004 - p86(2) [51-500]

Aloff, Brenda - *Aggression in Dogs: Practical Management, Prevention and Behaviour Modification*
Bwatch - Oct 2004 - pNA [51-500]

Aloian, Molly - *The Life and Cycle of a Flower*
y SB - v40 - i5 - Sept-Oct 2004 - p213(1) [51-500]

Alonso, Harriet Hyman - *Growing Up Abolitionist: The Story of the Garrison Children*
HNet - June 2004 - pNA [501+]

Alonso, Irma T. - *Caribbean Economies in the Twenty-First Century*
JEL - v41 - i4 - Dec 2003 - p1321(2) [501+]

Alper, Debi - *Nirvana Bites*
KR - v72 - i16 - August 15 2004 - p755(1) [501+]

Alper, Gerald - *Self Defense in a Narcissistic World: The New Everyday Addiction to Power Trips*
R&R Bk N - v19 - i3 - August 2004 - p9(1) [1-50]

Alperovitz, Gar - *America beyond Capitalism: Reclaiming Our Wealth, Our Liberty, and Our Democracy*
BL - v101 - i2 - Sept 15 2004 - p185(1) [51-500]

Alpers, Benjamin L. - *Dictators, Democracy, and American Public Culture: Envisioning the Totalitarian Enemy, 1920s-1950s*
AHR - v109 - i2 - April 2004 - p553(1) [501+]

Alpha, Delta - *The Shorter Encyclopedia of Real Estate Terms*
Choice - v42 - i2 - Oct 2004 - p277(1) [501+]

Alphabet Flash Cards (Illus. by Nelson, Beth)
c PW - v251 - i31 - August 2 2004 - p72(2) [501+]

Alphin, Elaine Marie - *Dwight D. Eisenhower*
c SLJ - v51 - i1 - Jan 2005 - p101(1) [51-500]

Alrich, Corinna Brown - *Echoes from a Distant Frontier: The Brown Sister's Correspondence from Antebellum Florida*
Choice - v42 - i6 - Feb 2005 - p1079(1) [51-500]

Alsop, Rachel - *Theorizing Gender*
JGS - v13 - i1 - March 2004 - p87-88 [501+]

Alsop, Ronald J. - *The 18 Immutable Laws of Corporate Reputation: Creating, Protecting and Repairing Your Most Valuable Asset*
R&R Bk N - v19 - i3 - August 2004 - p107(1) [1-50]

Alspach, Jennifer - *Adobe Acrobat for Windows and Macintosh*
Bwatch - March 2005 - pNA [501+]

Alston, R. - *The City in Roman Byzantine Egypt*
Class R - v54 - i2 - Nov 2004 - p514-516 [501+]

Alstott, Anne L. - *No Exit: What Parents Owe Their Children and What Society Owes Parents*
Choice - v42 - i4 - Dec 2004 - p740(2) [1-50]

Altbach, Philip G. - *The Decline of the Guru: The Academic Profession in Developing and Middle-Income Countries*
TCR - v106 - i2 - Feb 2004 - p287-290 [501+]

Alter, Cathy - *Virgin Territory: Stories from the Road to Womanhood*
y VOYA - v27 - i4 - Oct 2004 - p322(1) [51-500]

Alter, Judy - *Discovering Australia's Land, People, and Wildlife*
y SLJ - v50 - i11 - Nov 2004 - p158(1) [51-500]
Discovering North America's Land, People, and Wildlife
y SLJ - v50 - i11 - Nov 2004 - p158(1) [51-500]

Alter, Michael J. - *Science of Flexibility, 3rd Ed.*
SciTech - v28 - i3 - Sept 2004 - p70(1) [51-500]

Alter, Robert - *The Five Books of Moses: A Translation with Commentary*
BW - v34 - i43 - Oct 24 2004 - p15(1) [501+]
LJ - v129 - i18 - Nov 1 2004 - p89(2) [51-500]
NYTBR - Oct 17 2004 - p8 [501+]
Spec - v296 - Dec 18 2004 - p86(1) [501+]

Alter, Stephen - *Elephas Maximas: A Celebration of the Indian Elephant*
SciTech - v28 - i3 - Sept 2004 - p66(1) [501+]

Alterman, Eric - *The Book on Bush: How George W. (Mis)Leads America*
ABR - v25 - i6 - Sept-Oct 2004 - p1(4) [501+]
BW - v34 - i5 - Feb 1 2004 - p8(2) [501+]
When Presidents Lie: A History of Official Deception and Its Consequences
BL - v101 - i2 - Sept 15 2004 - p181(1) [51-500]
KR - v72 - i16 - August 15 2004 - p783(1) [501+]
NYTBR - Oct 10 2004 - p25 [501+]
PW - v251 - i34 - August 23 2004 - p48(1) [501+]
When Presidents Lie: A History of Official Deceptoin and Its Consequences
NY - v80 - i31 - Oct 18 2004 - p203(1) [501+]

Alterman, Glenn - *The Perfect Audition Monologue*
Choice - v42 - i1 - Sept 2004 - p107(1) [501+]

Alterman, Jon B. - *Egypt and American Foreign Assistance, 1952-1956*
IJMES - v36 - i1 - Feb 2004 - p145-146 [501+]

Alterman, Richard - *Cognitive Science Society: Proceedings, Vols. 1-2*
SciTech - v28 - i3 - Sept 2004 - p15(1) [51-500]

Alterowitz, Ralph - *Intimacy with Impotence: The Couple's Guide to Better Sex After Prostate Disease*
LJ - v129 - i12 - July 2004 - p105(1) [51-500]

Althaus, Scott L. - *Collective Preferences in Democratic Politics: Opinion Surveys and the Will of the People*
Choice - v42 - i2 - Oct 2004 - p371(1) [51-500]
JEL - v42 - i1 - March 2004 - p249(1) [501+]

Althoff, Gerd - *Medieval Concepts of the Past: Ritual, Memory, Historiography*
GSR - v27 - i2 - May 2004 - p364-365 [501+]

Althoff, Gred - *Family, Friends and Followers: Political and Social Bonds in Medieval Europe*
Choice - v42 - i6 - Feb 2005 - p1088(1) [51-500]

Althoff, William F. - *USS Los Angeles: The Navy's Venerable Airship and Aviation Technology*
SciTech - v28 - i1 - March 2004 - p179(1) [51-500]

Altieri, Miguel Angel - *Biodiversity and Pest Management in Agroecosystems*
E-Streams - August 2004 - pNA [501+]

Altig, David E. - *Evolution and Procedures in Central Banking*
JEL - v42 - i1 - March 2004 - p256(1) [501+]

Altman, Ann M. - *Early Visitors to Easter Island 1864-1877*
New Sci - v184 - i2468 - Oct 9 2004 - p49(1) [501+]

Altman, Arnold J. - *Supportive Care of Children with Cancer: Current Therapy and Guidelines from the Children's Oncology Group, 3rd Ed.*
E-Streams - Nov 2004 - pNA [501+]

Altman, Daniel - *Neoconomy: George Bush's Revolutionary Gamble with America's Future*
BW - v34 - i35 - August 2004 - p4(1) [501+]
Har Bus R - v82 - i10 - Oct 2004 - p32(1) [501+]
NS - v133 - i4711 - Oct 25 2004 - p53(2) [501+]
R&R Bk N - v19 - i4 - Nov 2004 - p89(1) [51-500]
TimHES - v0 - i1675 - Jan 21 2005 - p24(2) [501+]

Altman, John - *The Watchmen*
PW - v251 - i30 - July 26 2004 - p39(1) [501+]

Altman, Linda J. - *African Mythology*
LibMed - v22 - i5 - Feb 2004 - p81(2) [501+]

Altman, Linda Jacobs - *The American Civil Rights Movement: The African-American Struggle for Equality*
c SLJ - v50 - i8 - August 2004 - p132(2) [51-500]
The Politics of Slavery: Fiery National Debates Fueled by the Slave Economy
y SLJ - v50 - i12 - Dec 2004 - p156(1) [51-500]

Altman, Rick - *Silent Film Sound*
Bwatch - Feb 2005 - pNA [51-500]
LJ - v129 - i17 - Oct 15 2004 - p64(1) [51-500]

Altman, Rochelle - *Absent Voices: The Story of Writing Systems in the West*
R&R Bk N - v19 - i4 - Nov 2004 - p213(1) [501+]

Altman, Steven-Elliot - *Deprivers (Read by Lane, Christopher). Audiobook Review*
Kliatt - v38 - i5 - Sept 2004 - p56(2) [51-500]

Altmann, Barbara K. - *Christine de Pizan: A Casebook*
Specu - v79 - i4 - Oct 2004 - p1020(5) [501+]

Altmeyer, M. - *Unzeigemasses Denken bei Sophokles*
Class R - v54 - i1 - May 2004 - p30(3) [501+]

Altom, Laura Marie - *Sleep Tight*
y BL - v101 - i1 - Sept 1 2004 - p71(1) [51-500]

Altschul, Jeffery H. - *Islanders and Mainlanders: Prehistoric Context for the Southern California Bight*
Am Ant - v70 - i1 - Jan 2005 - p195(2) [501+]

Altschuler, Glenn C. - *All Shook Up: How Rock 'n' Roll Changed America*
RAH - v32 - i1 - March 2004 - p105(9) [501+]

Altshuler, Mordechai - *Soviet Jewry on the Eve of the Holocaust: A Social and Demographic Profile*
Russ Rev - v63 - i2 - April 2004 - pNA [501+]

Alunik, Ishmael - *Across Time and Tundra: The Inuvialuit of the Western Arctic*
Choice - v41 - i11-12 - July-August 2004 - p2104(1) [501+]
PHR - v73 - i3 - August 2004 - p505(506) [501+]
R&R Bk N - v19 - i1 - Feb 2004 - p53(1) [51-500]

Alvarez, A. - *The Writer's Life*
Globe & Mail - Feb 5 2005 - pD10 [501+]
The Writer's Voice
BL - v101 - i6 - Nov 15 2004 - p545(2) [51-500]
LJ - v129 - i16 - Oct 1 2004 - p79(1) [51-500]
PW - v251 - i37 - Sept 13 2004 - p65(1) [51-500]
Spec - v297 - i9210 - Feb 12 2005 - p39(1) [501+]

Alvarez, Julia - *Before We Were Free (Read by Alvarez, Julia). Audiobook Review*
  c BL - v101 - i6 - Nov 15 2004 - p607(1) [501+]
  y Kliatt - v39 - i2 - March 2005 - p46(2) [51-500]
  y SLJ - v50 - i11 - Nov 2004 - p80(2) [51-500]
  Before We Were Free
  c RT - v57 - Nov 2003 - p276 [51-500]
  Finding Miracles (Read by Rubin-Vega, Daphne). Audiobook Review
  y Kliatt - v39 - i2 - March 2005 - p52(1) [51-500]
  Finding Miracles
  y BL - v101 - i4 - Oct 15 2004 - p397(1) [51-500]
  y CCB-B - v58 - i4 - Dec 2004 - p158(1) [51-500]
  c CH Bwatch - Feb 2005 - pNA [51-500]
  y Kliatt - v38 - i5 - Sept 2004 - p4(2) [501+]
  y KR - v72 - i19 - Oct 1 2004 - p955(1) [501+]
  c PW - v251 - i48 - Nov 29 2004 - p41(1) [51-500]
  y SLJ - v50 - i10 - Oct 2004 - p154(1) [51-500]
  y VOYA - v27 - i5 - Dec 2004 - p378(1) [501+]
  The Woman I Kept to Myself
  y SLJ - v50 - i7 - July 2004 - p132(1) [51-500]

Alvarez-Junco, Jose - *Emergence of Mass Politics in Spain: Populist Demagoguery and Republican Culture, 1890-1910*
  AHR - v109 - i2 - April 2004 - p621(2) [501+]

Alvear, Michael - *Alexander the Fabulous: The Man Who Brought the World to Its Knees*
  G&L Rev W - v12 - i1 - Jan-Feb 2005 - p46(1) [501+]
  Men Are Pigs but We Love Bacon
  Lam Bk Rpt - v13 - i1-2 - August-Sept 2004 - p44(2) [501+]

Alvermann, Donna E. - *Adolescents and Literature in a Digital World*
  TCR - v106 - i? - Feb 2004 - p409-411 [501+]

Alvesson, Mats - *Studying Management Critically*
  R&R Bk N - v19 - i1 - Feb 2004 - p88(1) [51-500]

Alvey, James E. - *Adam Smith, Optimist or Pessimist?: A New Problem Concerning the Teleological Basis of Commercial Society*
  JEL - v42 - i1 - March 2004 - p240(1) [501+]

Alvi, Suroosh - *Vice Guide to Sex and Drugs and Rock and Roll*
  CBRA - Annual 2003 - p372(1) [501+]

Alvic, Philis - *Weavers of the Southern Highlands*
  JSH - v70 - i3 - August 2004 - p709(2) [501+]

Alweiss, Lilian - *The World Unclaimed: A Challenge to Heidegger's Critique of Husserl*
  Choice - v41 - i7 - March 2004 - p1308(1) [501+]

Alzofon, Frederick E. - *Two Methods for the Exact Solution of Diffraction Problems*
  SciTech - v28 - i1 - March 2004 - p50(1) [51-500]

Amabile, George - *Ideas of Shelter*
  Globe & Mail - July 17 2004 - pD15 [501+]

Amable, Bruno - *Diversity of Modern Capitalism*
  R&R Bk N - v19 - i4 - Nov 2004 - p85(1) [51-500]

Amacher, Ryan C. - *Faulty Towers: Tenure and the Structure of Higher Education*
  R&R Bk N - v19 - i4 - Nov 2004 - p184(1) [501+]

Amadae, S.M. - *Rationalizing Capitalist Democracy: The Cold War Origins of Rational Choice Liberalism*
  BHR - v78 - i1 - Spring 2004 - p139(4) [501+]
  Isis - v95 - i3 - Sept 2004 - p524(2) [501+]
  JEH - v64 - i1 - March 2004 - p281(2) [501+]
  JEL - v41 - i4 - Dec 2003 - p1341(2) [501+]

Amado, Elisa - *Cousins*
  c Res Links - v10 - i1 - Oct 2004 - p1(2) [501+]

Amaki, Amalia K. - *A Century of African American Art: The Paul R. Jones Collection*
  LJ - v130 - i4 - March 1 2005 - p82(1) [51-500]

Amano, Kozue - *Aria, Vol. 1.*
  LJ - v129 - i18 - Nov 1 2004 - p64(1) [501+]

Amano, Masanao - *Manga*
  Globe & Mail - Dec 18 2004 - pD14 [1-50]

Amarillo Slim - *Amarillo Slim in a World of Fat People*
  TLS - i5262 - Feb 6 2004 - p8(1) [501+]

Amaro, A. - *Modelling Forest Systems*
  QRB - v79 - i3 - Sept 2004 - p326(1) [501+]
  SciTech - v28 - i1 - March 2004 - p131(1) [51-500]

Amat, Nuria - *Queen Cocaine*
  KR - v72 - i24 - Dec 15 2004 - p1151(2) [501+]
  LJ - v130 - i4 - March 1 2005 - p74(1) [501+]
  PW - v252 - i7 - Feb 14 2005 - p53(2) [51-500]

Amato, Ivan - *Super Vision: A New View of Nature*
  Sci - v305 - i5688 - August 27 2004 - p1241(1) [51-500]
  Sci Teach - v71 - i3 - March 2004 - p86-86 [501+]

Amato, Joseph - *Mounier and Maritain: A French Catholic Understanding of the Modern World*
  Theol St - v65 - i3 - Sept 2004 - p676(2) [501+]

Amato, Mary - *Snarf Attack, Underfoodle, and the Secret of Life: The Riot Brothers Tell All (Illus. by Long, Ethan)*
  c BL - v100 - i21 - July 2004 - p1841(1) [1-50]
  c SLJ - v50 - i7 - July 2004 - p66(1) [51-500]

Amatuzio, Janis - *Forever Ours: A Forensic Pathologist's Perspective on Immortality and Living*
  BL - v101 - i2 - Sept 15 2004 - p181(1) [51-500]

Amazing Science
  LibMed - v23 - i3 - Nov-Dec 2004 - p62(1) [51-500]

Amazing Science: Weather
  LibMed - v22 - i7 - April-May 2004 - p76(1) [501+]

Amberson, M. Margaret McAllen - *I Would Rather Sleep in Texas: A History of the Lower Rio Grande Valley and the People of the Santa Anita Land Grant*
  SHQ - v107 - i3 - Jan 2004 - p474(1) [501+]
  WHQ - v35 - i2 - Summer 2004 - p235-236 [501+]

Ambrose, Ann - *SBI: Small Business Institute: Advanced Word Processing Simulation, 2nd Ed.*
  R&R Bk N - v19 - i4 - Nov 2004 - p254(1) [501+]

Ambrose, Kevin - *Washington Weather: The Weather Sourcebook for the D.C. Area*
  HNet - June 2004 - pNA [501+]

Ambrose, Stephen - *This Vast Land*
  LibMed - v22 - i7 - April-May 2004 - p62(1) [501+]

Ambrosio, Luigi - *Tropics on Analysis in Metric Spaces*
  SciTech - v28 - i4 - Dec 2004 - p43(1) [51-500]

Ambrosius, Lloyd E. - *Writing Biography: Historians and Their Craft*
  Biomag - v27 - i3 - Summer 2004 - p599(4) [501+]

Ameling, W. - *Martyrer und Martyrerakten*
  Class R - v54 - i1 - May 2004 - p207(2) [501+]

Amendola, Dana - *A Day at the New Amsterdam Theatre (Illus. by Domenico, Gino)*
  c SLJ - v51 - i1 - Jan 2005 - p101(1) [51-500]

Ament, Deloris Tarzan - *600 Moons: Fifty Years of Philip McCracken's Art*
  Choice - v42 - i6 - Feb 2005 - p1012(1) [51-500]
  LJ - v130 - i1 - Jan 1 2005 - p105(1) [51-500]

America in Words and Song
  LibMed - v22 - i7 - April-May 2004 - p80(1) [501+]

American Academy of Orthopaedic Surgeons - *Airway Management: Paramedic*
  SciTech - v28 - i1 - March 2004 - p89(1) [51-500]

The American Adventure
  LibMed - v23 - i1 - August-Sept 2004 - p74(1) [51-500]

American Animal Hospital Association - *Financial and Productivity Pulsepoints: Vital Statistics for Your Veterinary Practice, 3rd ed.*
  SciTech - v28 - i4 - Dec 2004 - p126 [51-500]

American Association of Cardiovascular and Pulmonary Rehabilitation - *Guidelines for Cardiac Rehabilitation and Secondary Prevention Programs, 4th Ed.*
  E-Streams - June 2004 - pNA [501+]
  SciTech - v28 - i1 - March 2004 - p104(1) [51-500]

The American Catholic Philosophical Association - *Philosophy and Intercultural Understanding: Proceedings*
  R&R Bk N - v19 - i4 - Nov 2004 - p27(1) [501+]

American Diabetes Association - *A Field Guide to Type 2 Diabetes: The Essential Resource from the Diabetes Experts*
  Bwatch - v26 - i7 - July 2004 - p3(1) [51-500]

American Geriatrics Society - *Doorway Thoughts: Cross-Cultural Health Care for Older Adults*
  SciTech - v28 - i4 - Dec 2004 - p83(1) [51-500]

American Girl - *Sticker Art*
  c PW - v251 - i37 - Sept 13 2004 - p81(1) [51-500]

American Grasslands
  LibMed - v22 - i6 - March 2004 - p92(1) [501+]

The American Heritage College Dictionary, 4th Ed.
  R&R Bk N - v19 - i4 - Nov 2004 - p217(1) [501+]

The American Heritage College Thesaurus
  R&R Bk N - v19 - i4 - Nov 2004 - p217(1) [501+]

American History by Decade
  LibMed - v23 - i1 - August-Sept 2004 - p74(1) [51-500]

American Indian Biographies
  c LibMed - v23 - i3 - Nov-Dec 2004 - p78(1) [51-500]

American Institute of Aeronautics and Astronautics - *Recommended Practice: Calibration of Subsonic and Transonic Wind Tunnels*
  SciTech - v28 - i3 - Sept 2004 - p163(1) [51-500]
  Recommended Practice: Wind Tunnel Testing, Pt. 1, Management Volume
  SciTech - v28 - i3 - Sept 2004 - p164(1) [51-500]

American Library Association - *ALA Annual Meeting: Abstracts, Vol. 27: Proceedings*
  R&R Bk N - v19 - i3 - August 2004 - p85(1) [51-500]

American Lives, Set 2
  LibMed - v22 - i6 - March 2004 - p74(1) [501+]

American Medical Association - *American Medical Association Family Medical Guide, 4th Ed.*
  LJ - v129 - i16 - Oct 1 2004 - p109(1) [51-500]
  PW - v251 - i39 - Sept 27 2004 - p52(1) [51-500]
  Code of Medical Ethics: Current Opinions with Annotations, 2004-2005 Ed.
  SciTech - v28 - i4 - Dec 2004 - p77(1) [51-500]
  GMED Companion: An Insider's Guide to Selecting a Residency Program 2004-2005
  SciTech - v28 - i3 - Sept 2004 - p87(1) [51-500]
  Graduate Medical Education Directory: 2004-2005
  SciTech - v28 - i3 - Sept 2004 - p78(1) [51-500]
  State Medical Licensure Requirements and Statistics, 2005
  SciTech - v28 - i4 - Dec 2004 - p80(1) [51-500]

American Pharmacists Association - *Diabetes Management Services: A Pharmacist's Resource Guide*
  E-Streams - Sept 2004 - pNA [501+]

American Psychiatric Association - *American Psychiatric Association Practice Guidelines for the Treatment of Psychiatric Disorders, Compendium 2004*
  SciTech - v28 - i3 - Sept 2004 - p97(1) [51-500]
  Quick Reference to the American Psychiatric Association Practice Guidelines for the Treatment of Psychiatric Disorders, Compendium 2004
  SciTech - v28 - i3 - Sept 2004 - p98(1) [1-50]

American Psychological Association - *Graduate Study in Psychology, 2005 25th Ed.*
  Choice - v42 - i4 - Dec 2004 - p638(1) [1-50]

American Society for Testing and Materials - *Annual Book of ASTM Standards 2004: Section 3: Metals Test Metals Mechanical Testing, Elevated and Low-Temperature Tests, Metallography*
  SciTech - v28 - i4 - Dec 2004 - p133 [51-500]
  Annual Book of ASTM Standards 2004: Section 3, Metals Test Methods and Analytical Procedures: Vol. 03.03
  SciTech - v28 - i4 - Dec 2004 - p133 [51-500]

American Society of Mechanical Engineers - *Advances in Electronic Packaging 2003: Proceedings, Vols. 1-2*
  SciTech - v28 - i1 - March 2004 - p160(1) [51-500]
  Proceedings of 2004 ASME Power
  SciTech - v28 - i4 - Dec 2004 - p151(1) [51-500]
  Proceedings of the ASME Dynamic Systems and Control Division-2003
  SciTech - v28 - i1 - March 2004 - p150(1) [51-500]
  Recent Advances in Nondestructive Evaluation Techniques for Material Science and Industries: Proceedings
  SciTech - v28 - i4 - Dec 2004 - p134 [51-500]

American Water Works Association - *2004 Water Utility Compensation Survey, 9th Annual Ed.*
  SciTech - v28 - i4 - Dec 2004 - p7(1) [1-50]
  Problem Organisms in Water: Identification and Treatment, 3rd ed.
  SciTech - v28 - i3 - Sept 2004 - p146(1) [51-500]
  Recommended Practice for Backflow Prevention and Cross-Connection Control, 3rd Ed.
  SciTech - v28 - i3 - Sept 2004 - p147(1) [51-500]
  Sizing Water Service Lines and Meters, 2nd Ed.
  SciTech - v28 - i1 - March 2004 - p148(1) [51-500]
  Water Fluoridation Principles and Practices, 5th Ed.
  SciTech - v28 - i3 - Sept 2004 - p145(1) [51-500]

Ames, Brian - *Eighty-Sixed*
  y BL - v101 - i3 - Oct 1 2004 - p307(1) [51-500]
  PW - v251 - i37 - Sept 13 2004 - p57(1) [501+]

Ames, Jonathan - *Wake Up, Sir! A Novel*
  BW - v34 - i28 - July 11 2004 - p4(1) [501+]
  LJ - v129 - i12 - July 2004 - p66(1) [51-500]
  NYTBR - August 1 2004 - p10 [501+]
  NYTBR - August 8 2004 - p18 [501+]

Ames, Kevin - *Adobe Photoshop CS: The Art of Photographing Women*
  SciTech - v28 - i4 - Dec 2004 - p166(1) [51-500]

Ames-Lewis, Francis - *Reactions to the Master: Michelangelo's Effect on Art and Artists in the Sixteenth Century*
  Ren Q - v57 - i3 - Fall 2004 - p993(3) [501+]

Amherdt, D. - *Sidoine Apollinaire: Le quatrieme livre de la correspondance*
  Class R - v53 - i2 - Nov 2003 - p388-389 [501+]

Amherst, David Dadge - *Casualty of War: The Bush Administration's Assault on a Free Press*
  IndRev - v9 - i3 - Wntr 2005 - p451(3) [501+]

Amick, Steve - *The Lake, the River, and the Other Lake*
KR - v73 - i4 - Feb 15 2005 - p187(1) [501+]
PW - v252 - i11 - March 14 2005 - p43(1) [51-500]

Amico, Tom - *The Day the Dog Dressed Like Dad (Illus. by Proimos, James)*
c KR - v72 - i16 - August 15 2004 - p801(1) [51-500]
c PW - v251 - i41 - Oct 11 2004 - p79(1) [51-500]
c SLJ - v50 - i10 - Oct 2004 - p108(1) [51-500]

Amidon, Stephen - *Human Capital*
BL - v101 - i1 - Sept 1 2004 - p54(1) [51-500]
BL - v101 - i9-10 - Jan 1 2005 - p768(1) [51-500]
Globe & Mail - Nov 6 2004 - pD20 [501+]
KR - v72 - i14 - July 15 2004 - p643(1) [501+]
LJ - v129 - i15 - Sept 15 2004 - p47(1) [51-500]
NYTBR - Oct 3 2004 - p10 [501+]
PW - v251 - i30 - July 26 2004 - p35(1) [51-500]
Spec - v297 - i9209 - Feb 5 2005 - p43(1) [501+]

Amiel, Yoram - *Inequality, Welfare and Poverty: Theory and Measurement*
JEL - v41 - i4 - Dec 2003 - p1341(1) [501+]

Amin, Ash - *The Blackwell Cultural Economy Reader*
R&R Bk N - v19 - i1 - Feb 2004 - p122(1) [51-500]
Placing the Social Economy
JEL - v41 - i4 - Dec 2003 - p1391(2) [501+]

Amin, Kamal - *Reflections from the Shining Brow: My Years with Frank Lloyd Wright and Olgivanna Lazovich*
R&R Bk N - v19 - i4 - Nov 2004 - p202(1) [501+]

Amin, Mahul B. - *Gleason Grading of Prostate Cancer: A Contemporary Approach*
SciTech - v28 - i1 - March 2004 - p91(1) [51-500]

Amin, Samir - *The Liberal Virus: Permanent War and the Americanization of the World*
Bwatch - Oct 2004 - pNA [51-500]
R&R Bk N - v19 - i4 - Nov 2004 - p152(1) [501+]

Amineh, Mehdi Parvizi - *Central Eurasia in Global Politics: Conflict, Security, and Development*
R&R Bk N - v19 - i3 - August 2004 - p182(1) [501+]

Aminzade, Ronald R. - *Silence and Voice in the Study of Contentious Politics*
JIH - v34 - i4 - Spring 2004 - p617-619 [501+]

Amirav, Hagit - *Rhetoric and Tradition: John Chrysostom on Noah and the Flood*
R&R Bk N - v19 - i3 - August 2004 - p22(1) [1-50]

Amiry, Suad - *Sharon and My Mother-in-Law: Ramallah Diaries*
NS - v134 - i4725 - Jan 31 2005 - p52(2) [501+]

Amis, Martin - *Money: A Suicide Note*
Critq - v44 - Winter 2003 - p136 [501+]
Yellow Dog
Globe & Mail - Feb 26 2005 - pD13 [1-50]
World&I - v19 - i4 - April 2004 - p230 [501+]

Amit, Vered - *Biographical Dictionary of Social and Cultural Anthropology*
Choice - v42 - i1 - Sept 2004 - p76(2) [501+]
R&R Bk N - v19 - i3 - August 2004 - p82(1) [51-500]

Ammaniti, Niccolo - *I'm Not Scared*
y Kliatt - v38 - i5 - Sept 2004 - p18(2) [501+]

Ammer, Christine - *The Facts on File Dictionary of Music*
BL - v101 - i1 - Sept 1 2004 - p170(2) [1-50]
Choice - v42 - i2 - Oct 2004 - p264(1) [51-500]
y SLJ - v50 - i10 - Oct 2004 - p91(1) [501+]

Ammon, Richard - *Valley Forge (Illus. by Farnsworth, Bill)*
c BL - v101 - i2 - Sept 15 2004 - p236(1) [51-500]
c KR - v72 - i15 - August 1 2004 - p737(1) [51-500]
c SLJ - v50 - i10 - Oct 2004 - p184(1) [51-500]

Ammons, A.R. - *Bosh and Flapdoodle*
LJ - v130 - i1 - Jan 1 2005 - p116(1) [51-500]
PW - v252 - i4 - Jan 24 2005 - p236(1) [501+]

Amodio, Mark C. - *Unlocking the Wordhord: Anglo-Saxon Studies in Memory of Edward B. Irving, Jr.*
Med R - Sept 2004 - pNA [501+]
RES - v55 - i220 - June 2004 - p448-450 [501+]

Amoia, Alba - *Multicultural Writers Since 1945: An A-to-Z Guide*
BL - v101 - i1 - Sept 1 2004 - p174(1) [501+]
LJ - v129 - i15 - Sept 15 2004 - p81(2) [501+]
Women Travel Writers from 1750 to the Present
LJ - v130 - i4 - March 1 2005 - p86(1) [51-500]

Amoretti, Ugo M. - *Federalism and Territorial Cleavages*
Choice - v42 - i4 - Dec 2004 - p730(1) [1-50]
R&R Bk N - v19 - i3 - August 2004 - p174(1) [501+]

Amos, Tori - *Tori Amos, Piece by Piece*
LJ - v130 - i4 - March 1 2005 - p86(1) [51-500]
PW - v252 - i5 - Jan 31 2005 - p62(1) [501+]

Amponsah, Peter Nkrumah - *Libel Law, Political Criticism, and Defamation of Public Figures: The United States, Europe, and Australia*
R&R Bk N - v19 - i3 - August 2004 - p190(1) [501+]

Amsden, Alice H. - *Beyond Late Development: Taiwan's Upgrading Policies*
JEL - v41 - i4 - Dec 2003 - p1416(1) [501+]

Amselle, Jean-Loup - *Affirmative Exclusion: Cultural Pluralism and the Rule of Custom in France*
JRAI - v10 - i3 - Sept 2004 - p738(2) [501+]

Amsterdam, Ezra A. - *Contemporary Diagnosis and Management of the Post-MI Patient*
SciTech - v28 - i4 - Dec 2004 - p103(1) [51-500]

Amyot, Chantal - *Country Post: Rural Postal Service in Canada, 1880 to 1945*
CBRA - Annual 2003 - p272(1) [51-500]

Amyx, Jennifer - *Japanese Governance: Beyond Japan Inc.*
JAS - v63 - i2 - May 2004 - p506(3) [501+]

An, Shuhua - *Middle Path in Math Instruction: Solutions for Improving Math Education*
SciTech - v28 - i3 - Sept 2004 - p17(1) [501+]

An, Zhiqiang - *Handbook of Industrial Mycology*
SciTech - v28 - i4 - Dec 2004 - p164(1) [51-500]

Ana, Otto Santa - *Tongue-Tied: The Lives of Multilingual Children in Public Education*
Choice - v42 - i3 - Nov 2004 - p537(1) [1-50]
JAAL - v48 - i1 - Sept 2004 - p87(1) [501+]

Anacker, John - *The Raven's Ring Pin*
c SLJ - v50 - i8 - August 2004 - p115(1) [51-500]

Anand, R.P. - *Studies in International Law and History: An Asian Perspective*
R&R Bk N - v19 - i3 - August 2004 - p210(1) [1-50]

Anand, Vijay - *Cisco IP Routing Protocols: Troubleshooting Techniques*
SciTech - v28 - i3 - Sept 2004 - p155(1) [51-500]

Anandarajan, Murugan - *Personal Web Usage in the Workplace: A Guide to Effective Human Resources Management.*
R&R Bk N - v19 - i1 - Feb 2004 - p111(1) [51-500]

Ananta, Aris - *The Indonesian Crisis: A Human Development Perspective*
Pac A - v77 - i2 - Summer 2004 - p375(2) [501+]

Ananthasuresh, G.K. - *Optimal Synthesis Methods for MEMS*
SciTech - v28 - i1 - March 2004 - p163(1) [51-500]

Anastaplo, George - *On Trial: From Adam and Eve to O.J. Simpson.*
R&R Bk N - v19 - i4 - Nov 2004 - p161(1) [501+]

Anastasios, Archbishop of Tirana and All Albania - *Facing the World: Orthodox Christian Essays on Global Concerns*
IBMR - v28 - i4 - Oct 2004 - p182(1) [501+]

Anatol, Giselle Liza - *Reading Harry Potter: Critical Essays*
LibMed - v22 - i4 - Jan 2004 - p86(1) [501+]

Anaya, Rudolfo - *Jemez Spring*
LJ - v129 - i20 - Dec 1 2004 - p96(1) [51-500]
The Santero's Miracle
CH Bwatch - Feb 2005 - pNA [51-500]
Serafina's Stories
LJ - v129 - i17 - Oct 15 2004 - p56(2) [51-500]
Roundup M - v12 - i3 - Feb 2005 - p24(1) [51-500]

Anaya Valencia, Reynaldo - *Mexican Americans and the Law: El Pueblo Unido Jamas Sera Vencido!*
Choice - v42 - i5 - Jan 2005 - p935(1) [51-500]
Law&PolBR - August 2004 - p676(7) [501+]

Ancess, Jacqueline - *Beating the Odds: High Schools as Communities of Commitment*
TCR - v106 - i2 - Feb 2004 - p362-365 [501+]

Ancient Leaders: Leaders of Ancient Greece
c LibMed - v23 - i3 - Nov-Dec 2004 - p78(1) [51-500]

The Ancient Olympics: A History
Globe & Mail - August 7 2004 - pD4 [501+]
NYRB - v51 - i16 - Oct 21 2004 - p19(3) [501+]

Ancient West and East, Vol. 2, No. 1
R&R Bk N - v19 - i1 - Feb 2004 - p12(1) [51-500]

Ancient West and East, Vol. 2, No. 2
R&R Bk N - v19 - i3 - August 2004 - p14(1) [1-50]

Ancona, Deborah - *Managing for the Future: Organizational Behavior and Processes*
R&R Bk N - v19 - i3 - August 2004 - p130(1) [51-500]

Ancona, Eligio - *The Martyrs of Anahuac*
R&R Bk N - v19 - i1 - Feb 2004 - p233(1) [501+]

Anda, Natsumi - *Zodiac P.I.*
y Teach Lib - v32 - i1 - Oct 2004 - p17(2) [501+]

Andall, Jacqueline - *Gender and Ethnicity in Contemporary Europe*
CS - v33 - i6 - Nov 2004 - p660(3) [501+]

Andel, Tjeerd H. van - *Neanderthals and Modern Humans in the European Landscape During the Last Glaciation: Archaeological Results of the Stage 3 Project*
R&R Bk N - v19 - i4 - Nov 2004 - p76(1) [501+]

Anderegg, Michael - *Cinematic Shakespeare*
Choice - v41 - i11-12 - July-August 2004 - p2029(1) [501+]
R&R Bk N - v19 - i1 - Feb 2004 - p237(1) [51-500]

Anderlini-D'Onofrio, Serena - *Women and Bisexuality: A Global Perspective*
R&R Bk N - v19 - i1 - Feb 2004 - p128(1) [51-500]

Anders, Freia - *Bialystok in Bielefeld: Nationalsozialistische Verbrechen vor dem Landgericht Bielefeld 1958 bis 1967*
HNet - June 2004 - pNA [501+]

Andersen, Bjorn - *Bringing Business Ethics to Life: Achieving Corporate Social Responsibility*
R&R Bk N - v19 - i3 - August 2004 - p107(1) [1-50]

Andersen, Christopher - *American Evita: Hillary Clinton's Path To Power*
NS - v133 - i4716 - Nov 29 2004 - p43(1) [51-500]

Andersen, Francis I. - *Micah: A New Translation with Introduction and Commentary*
Intpr - v59 - i1 - Jan 2005 - p88(2) [501+]

Andersen, H. Hellmuth - *Barbar Temples, Vols. 1-2*
R&R Bk N - v19 - i4 - Nov 2004 - p46(1) [501+]

Andersen, Hans Christian - *The Emperor's New Clothes (Illus. by Rowe, John Alfred)*
c PW - v251 - i44 - Nov 1 2004 - p64(1) [501+]
c SLJ - v51 - i1 - Jan 2005 - p85(1) [51-500]
Fairy Tales
NS - v133 - i4718 - Dec 13 2004 - p70(2) [501+]
For Sure! For Sure! (Illus. by Czernecki, Stefan)
c CCB-B - v58 - i2 - Oct 2004 - p59(1) [51-500]
c KR - v72 - i14 - July 15 2004 - p681(1) [51-500]
c Res Links - v10 - i1 - Oct 2004 - p2(1) [501+]
c SLJ - v50 - i11 - Nov 2004 - p90(1) [51-500]
The Little Mermaid (Illus. by Zwerger, Lisbeth)
c BL - v101 - i3 - Oct 1 2004 - p328(1) [51-500]
c BW - v34 - i39 - Sept 26 2004 - p11(1) [501+]
c PW - v251 - i36 - Sept 6 2004 - p62(1) [51-500]
c SLJ - v50 - i12 - Dec 2004 - p96(1) [501+]
Tales of Hans Christian Andersen (Illus. by Stewart, Joel)
y BL - v101 - i9-10 - Jan 1 2005 - p848(1) [1-50]
c CCB-B - v58 - i4 - Dec 2004 - p159(1) [51-500]
y HB - v81 - i1 - Jan-Feb 2005 - p88(2) [51-500]
KR - v72 - i19 - Oct 1 2004 - p956(1) [501+]
y Magpies - v19 - i5 - Nov 2004 - p20(4) [501+]
c PW - v251 - i50 - Dec 13 2004 - p69(2) [501+]
Thumbelina (Illus. by Sneed, Brad)
c BW - v34 - i39 - Sept 26 2004 - p11(1) [501+]
c PW - v251 - i44 - Nov 1 2004 - p64(1) [501+]
c SLJ - v50 - i10 - Oct 2004 - p108(1) [51-500]
The Ugly Duckling (Illus. by Ingpen, Robert)
c BL - v101 - i7 - Dec 1 2004 - p657(2) [501+]
c CCB-B - v58 - i5 - Jan 2005 - p197(1) [51-500]
c PW - v252 - i6 - Feb 7 2005 - p61(2) [501+]

Andersen, Jens - *Andersen: en biografi*
c Bkbird - v42 - i3 - July 2004 - p46(1) [501+]
y Scan St - v76 - i4 - Winter 2004 - p535(14) [501+]

Andersen, Linda - *The Too-Busy Book: Slowing Down to Catch Up with Life*
PW - v251 - i35 - August 30 2004 - p52(1) [51-500]

Andersen, M. J. - *Portable Prairie: Confessions of an Unsettled Midwesterner*
BL - v101 - i9-10 - Jan 1 2005 - p801(2) [51-500]

Andersen, M.J. - *Portable Prairie: Confessions of an Unsettled Midwesterner*
KR - v72 - i22 - Nov 15 2004 - p1073(1) [501+]
People - v63 - i3 - Jan 24 2005 - p52 [51-500]
PW - v251 - i47 - Nov 22 2004 - p49(1) [51-500]

Andersen, Margaret L. - *Sociology: The Essentials, 3rd Ed.*
R&R Bk N - v19 - i3 - August 2004 - p142(1) [51-500]

Anderson, L.W. - *Classroom Assessment: Enhancing the Quality of Teacher Decision Making*
  CE - v80 - i5 - Mid-Summer 2004 - p277(1) [51-500]

Anderson, Lars - *The All Americans*
  BL - v101 - i3 - Oct 1 2004 - p296(1) [51-500]
  KR - v72 - i17 - Sept 1 2004 - p843(2) [501+]

Anderson, Laurie Halse - *Prom*
  y BL - v101 - i9-10 - Jan 1 2005 - p852(1) [1-50]
  y CCB-B - v58 - i6 - Feb 2005 - p242(2) [51-500]
  y HB - v81 - i2 - March-April 2005 - p196(2) [51-500]
  y Kliatt - v39 - i2 - March 2005 - p6(1) [51-500]
  y KR - v73 - i2 - Jan 15 2005 - p115(1) [51-500]
  y PW - v252 - i4 - Jan 24 2005 - p245(1) [51-500]
  y SLJ - v51 - i2 - Feb 2005 - p132(1) [51-500]
  Thank You, Sarah (Illus. by Faulkner, Matt)
  c RT - v57 - Nov 2003 - p275 [51-500]

Anderson, Leona M. - *Women and Religious Traditions*
  Choice - v42 - i3 - Nov 2004 - p503(1) [1-50]

Anderson-Levitt, Kathryn - *Local Meanings, Global Schooling: Anthropology and World Culture Theory*
  JRAI - v10 - i3 - Sept 2004 - p716(2) [501+]

Anderson, Liam - *The Future of Iraq: Dictatorship, Democracy, or Division?*
  MEQ - v11 - i3 - Summer 2004 - p84(2) [501+]

Anderson, Lindsay - *The Diaries*
  Spec - v296 - i9201 - Dec 11 2004 - p39(3) [501+]
  TimHES - v0 - i1675 - Jan 21 2005 - p22(2) [501+]
  Never Apologise: The Collected Writings
  TimHES - v0 - i1675 - Jan 21 2005 - p22(2) [501+]

Anderson, Lisa - *Pursuing Truth, Exercising Power: Social Science and Public Policy in the Twenty-First Century*
  Soc Ser R - v79 - i1 - March 2005 - p189(2) [501+]

Anderson, M.T. - *Feed*
  c CH Bwatch - v14 - i9 - Sept 2004 - p3(1) [51-500]
  The Game of Sunken Places
  y CCB-B - v58 - i1 - Sept 2004 - p5(1) [51-500]
  c NYTBR - July 11 2004 - p19 [51-500]
  c PW - v251 - i28 - July 12 2004 - p64(1) [51-500]
  y SLJ - v50 - i9 - Sept 2004 - p198(1) [51-500]
  Strange Mr. Satie (Illus. by Mathers, Petra)
  BooChiTr - Jan 18 2004 - p5(1) [501+]
  c SLJ - v50 - i12 - Dec 2004 - p59(1) [501+]
  Whales on Stilts (Illus. by Cyrus, Kurt)
  y HB - v81 - i2 - March-April 2005 - p197(1) [51-500]

Anderson, Marcella Fisher - *Young Patriots: Inspiring Stories of the American Revolution*
  c CE - v80 - i5 - Mid-Summer 2004 - p273(1) [51-500]
  c CH Bwatch - v14 - i7 - July 2004 - p6(1) [51-500]
  c CH Bwatch - v14 - i12 - Dec 2004 - pNA [51-500]

Anderson, Marcia K. - *Foundations of Athletic Training: Prevention, Assessment, and Management, 3rd Ed.*
  SciTech - v28 - i3 - Sept 2004 - p111(1) [51-500]

Anderson, Margaret J. - *Aristotle: Philosopher and Scientist*
  c SLJ - v50 - i7 - July 2004 - p115(1) [51-500]

Anderson, Marlow - *Sherlock Holmes in Babylon and Other Tales of Mathematical History*
  Choice - v41 - i11-12 - July-August 2004 - p2081(1) [501+]
  Isis - v95 - i3 - Sept 2004 - p465(2) [501+]
  SB - v40 - i4 - July-August 2004 - p157(1) [51-500]
  SB - v40 - i6 - Nov-Dec 2004 - p240(2) [51-500]

Anderson, Mary J. - *The Life Writings of Mary Baker McQuesten: Victorian Matriarch*
  Bwatch - v26 - i9 - Sept 2004 - p5(1) [51-50]
  Globe & Mail - August 14 2004 - pD12 [1-50]
  R&R Bk N - v19 - i3 - August 2004 - p78(1) [51-500]

Anderson, Marynita - *Physician Heal Thyself: Medical Practitioners of Eighteenth-Century New York*
  SciTech - v28 - i4 - Dec 2004 - p76(1) [51-500]

Anderson, Max - *Digger*
  TLS - i5291 - August 27 2004 - p26(1) [501+]

Anderson, Max Elliot - *Mountain Cabin Mystery*
  c CH Bwatch - v14 - i12 - Dec 2004 - pNA [51-500]
  North Wood Poachers
  c Teach Lib - v32 - i3 - Feb 2005 - p54(1) [1-50]
  Secret of Abbot's Cave
  c CH Bwatch - March 2005 - pNA [51-500]

Anderson, Michael - *Monkey See, Monkey Do*
  SLJ - v50 - i10 - Oct 2004 - p88(1) [51-500]

Anderson, Misty G. - *Female Playwrights and Eighteenth-Century Comedy: Negotiating Marriage on the London Stage*
  Theat J - v56 - i1 - March 2004 - p141(3) [501+]

Anderson, Neil D. - *A Definitive Study of Evidence Concerning John Wesley's Appropriation of the Thought of Clement of Alexandria*
  R&R Bk N - v19 - i4 - Nov 2004 - p28(1) [501+]

Anderson, Norman B. - *Encyclopedia of Health & Behavior*
  BL - v101 - i1 - Sept 1 2004 - p168(2) [501+]
  Choice - v41 - i11-12 - July-August 2004 - p2022(1) [501+]
  E-Streams - August 2004 - pNA [501+]
  LJ - v129 - i12 - July 2004 - p116(1) [51-500]
  R&USQ - v44 - i2 - Winter 2004 - p169(1) [501+]

Anderson, P.F. - *Diseases and Disorders: Mental Health and Mental Disorders, Vol. 2*
  Choice - v42 - i2 - Oct 2004 - p271(2) [501+]
  Health and Wellness: Life Stages and Reproduction
  Choice - v42 - i2 - Oct 2004 - p271(2) [501+]
  The Medical Library Association Encyclopedic Guide to Searching and Finding Health Information on the Web, Vols. 1-3
  BL - v100 - i22 - August 2004 - p1980(2) [501+]
  Choice - v42 - i2 - Oct 2004 - p271(2) [501+]
  LJ - v129 - i12 - July 2004 - p119(1) [501+]
  SciTech - v28 - i3 - Sept 2004 - p80(1) [51-500]

Anderson, Pamela - *Star*
  Ent W - i778 - August 13 2004 - p93 [501+]
  PW - v251 - i34 - August 23 2004 - p39(1) [51-500]

Anderson, Patrick L. - *Business Economics and Finance with MATLAB, GIS and Simulation Models*
  R&R Bk N - v19 - i4 - Nov 2004 - p92(1) [501+]

Anderson, Paul Allen - *Deep River: Music and Memory in Harlem Renaissance Thought*
  Black Iss - v6 - i6 - Nov-Dec 2004 - p20(4) [501+]

Anderson, Paul Christopher - *George Armstrong Custer: The Indian Wars and the Battle of the Little Big Horn*
  c SLJ - v50 - i7 - July 2004 - p115(1) [1-50]

Anderson, Paul Irving - *Ehrgeiz und Trauer: Fontanes Offiziose Agitation 1859 und ihre Wiederkehr in Unwiederbringlich*
  Ger Q - v77 - i1 - Wntr 2004 - p102(2) [501+]
  GSR - v27 - i1 - Feb 2004 - p153-154 [501+]

Anderson, Paul Thomas - *Hunger's Brides: A Novel of the Baroque*
  Globe & Mail - Oct 2 2004 - pD14 [501+]

Anderson, Peggy Perry - *We Go in a Circle (Illus. by Anderson, Peggy Perry)*
  c SLJ - v50 - i10 - Oct 2004 - p108(1) [51-500]

Anderson, R.G.W. - *Enlightening the British: Knowledge, Discovery and the Museum in the Eighteenth Century: Proceedings*
  R&R Bk N - v19 - i2 - May 2004 - p194(1) [51-500]

Anderson, Richard E. - *Medical Malpractice: A Physician's Sourcebook*
  SciTech - v28 - i4 - Dec 2004 - p10(1) [1-50]

Anderson, Rick - *Buying and Contracting for Resources and Services: A How-to-Do-It Manual for Librarians*
  BL - v100 - i21 - July 2004 - p1859(1) [1-50]

Anderson, Rob - *Dialogue: Theorizing Difference in Communication Studies*
  Choice - v41 - i11-12 - July-August 2004 - p2037(1) [501+]
  R&R Bk N - v19 - i1 - Feb 2004 - p211 [51-500]

Anderson, Robert - *Little Fugue*
  BL - v101 - i6 - Nov 15 2004 - p551(1) [51-500]
  KR - v72 - i22 - Nov 15 2004 - p1059(1) [501+]
  People - v63 - i5 - Feb 7 2005 - p53 [501+]
  PW - v251 - i42 - Oct 18 2004 - p47(1) [51-500]

Anderson, Robert E. - *Just Get Out of the Way: How Government Can Help Business in Poor Countries*
  Bwatch - Dec 2004 - pNA [51-500]
  IndRev - v9 - i3 - Wntr 2005 - p454(3) [501+]

Anderson, Robert T. - *The Keepers: An Introduction to the History and Culture of the Samaritans*
  Theol St - v65 - i3 - Sept 2004 - p671(1) [501+]

Anderson, Romola - *Short History of the Sailing Ship*
  R&R Bk N - v19 - i1 - Feb 2004 - p257(1) [51-500]

Anderson, Ross - *The Forgotten Front: The East African Campaign, 1914-1918*
  Choice - v42 - i6 - Feb 2005 - p1075(2) [51-500]
  HRNB - v33 - i1 - Fall 2004 - p32(1) [501+]

Anderson, S. Catherine - *Southern Fried*
  BooChiTr - April 18 2004 - p6(1) [501+]

Anderson, Sarah - *Sarah Anderson's Travel Companion: Africa and the Middle East*
  LJ - v130 - i4 - March 1 2005 - p101(2) [501+]

Anderson, Scoular - *Space Pirates: A Map-Reading Adventure (Illus. by Anderson, Scoular)*
  c Res Links - v10 - i3 - Feb 2005 - p11(1) [51-500]
  c SLJ - v51 - i1 - Jan 2005 - p101(1) [51-500]

Anderson, Sheila B. - *Serving Older Teens*
  SLJ - v50 - i8 - August 2004 - p150(1) [501+]
  Teach Lib - v32 - i2 - Dec 2004 - p39(1) [1-50]
  VOYA - v27 - i4 - Oct 2004 - p267(1) [51-500]

Anderson, Stephen E. - *Improving Schools through Teacher Development: Case Studies of the Aga Khan Foundation Projects in East Asia*
  TCR - v106 - i2 - Feb 2004 - p293-298 [501+]

Anderson, Stephen R. - *Doctor Dolittle's Delusion: Animals and the Uniqueness of Human Language*
  Choice - v42 - i7 - March 2005 - p1253(1) [51-500]
  LJ - v130 - i1 - Jan 1 2005 - p142(1) [51-500]

Anderson, T.J. - *Notes to Make the Sound Come Right: Four Innovators of Jazz Poetry*
  R&R Bk N - v19 - i4 - Nov 2004 - p240(1) [501+]

Anderson, Teoti - *The Super Simple Guide To Housetraining*
  Bwatch - Jan 2005 - pNA [51-500]

Anderson, Terry H. - *The Pursuit of Fairness: A History of Affirmative Action*
  BW - v34 - i29 - July 18 2004 - p3(1) [1-50]
  Choice - v42 - i6 - Feb 2005 - p1079(1) [51-500]
  The Sixties, 2nd Ed.
  R&R Bk N - v19 - i1 - Feb 2004 - p62(1) [501+]

Anderson, Terry L. - *The Not So Wild, Wild West: Property Rights on the Frontier*
  Choice - v42 - i3 - Nov 2004 - p531(1) [1-50]
  HRNB - v33 - i1 - Fall 2004 - p14(1) [501+]
  Law&PolBR - August 2004 - p643(2) [501+]
  Property Rights: Cooperation, Conflict, and Law
  JEL - v42 - i4 - Dec 2004 - p1161(2) [501+]
  You Have to Admit It's Getting Better: From Economic Prosperity to Environmental Quality
  Choice - v42 - i4 - Dec 2004 - p709(1) [1-50]

Anderson, Troy - *The Way of Go: 8 Ancient Strategy Secrets for Success in Business and Life*
  BL - v100 - i22 - August 2004 - p1883(1) [51-500]

Anderson, Virginia DeJohn - *Creatures of Empire: How Domestic Animals Transformed Early America*
  BL - v101 - i3 - Oct 1 2004 - p290(1) [51-500]
  CHE - v51 - i13 - Nov 19 2004 - pA18 [501+]
  LJ - v129 - i15 - Sept 15 2004 - p67(1) [51-500]

Anderson, Warwick - *The Cultivation of Whiteness: Science, Health, and Racial Destiny in Australia*
  Isis - v95 - i3 - Sept 2004 - p497(2) [501+]

Anderson, Wayne - *The Dragon Machine*
  LibMed - v22 - i4 - Jan 2004 - p62(1) [501+]

Anderson, William - *River Boy: The Story of Mark Twain (Illus. by Anderson, William)*
  RT - v58 - i3 - Nov 2004 - p289(1) [1-50]

Andersson, Kjell - *Emigrantforska! Steg for Steg*
  EFHM - v58 - i2 - March-April 2004 - p88(1) [1-50]

Andjelic, Neven - *Bosnia-Herzegovina: The End of a Legacy*
  Choice - v41 - i7 - March 2004 - p1350(1) [501+]

Andler, Edward C. - *The Complete Reference Checking Handbook: The Proven (and Legal) Way to Prevent Hiring Mistakes*
  Per Psy - v57 - i3 - Autumn 2004 - p823(4) [501+]

Ando, Nisuke - *Towards Implementing Universal Human Rights: Festschrift for the Twenty-Fifth Anniversary of the Human Rights Committee*
  R&R Bk N - v19 - i4 - Nov 2004 - p151(1) [501+]

Andra-Warner, Elle - *Hudson's Bay Company Adventures: The Rollicking Saga of Canada's Fur Traders*
  y Res Links - v10 - i1 - Oct 2004 - p36(2) [501+]

Andrade, Jackie - *Instant Notes: Cognitive Psychology*
  SciTech - v28 - i3 - Sept 2004 - p2(1) [501+]

Andre, Rae - *Take Back the Sky: Protecting Communities in the Path of Aviation Expansion*
  LJ - v129 - i17 - Oct 15 2004 - p84(1) [51-500]

Andrea, Alfred J. - *Encyclopedia of the Crusades*
  Choice - v41 - i11-12 - July-August 2004 - p2024(1) [501+]

Andreae, Giles - *Dinosaurs Galore! (Illus. by Wojtowycz, David)*
  c KR - v73 - i5 - March 1 2005 - p283(1) [51-500]

Andreas-Salome, Lou - *You Alone Are Real to Me: Remembering Rainer Maria Rilke*
  Sew R - v111 - i3 - Summer 2003 - p455-462 [501+]

Andreasen, Dan - *A Special Day for Mommy (Illus. by Andreasen, Dan)*
  c SLJ - v50 - i7 - July 2004 - p66(1) [51-500]

Andreescu, Titu - *Mathematical Olympiads 2000-2001: Problems and Solutions from around the World*
Math T - v97 - i3 - March 2004 - p222-222 [501+]
USA and International Mathematical Olympaids 2003
Choice - v42 - i5 - Jan 2005 - p890(1) [1-50]
USA and International Mathematical Olympiads 2003
SciTech - v28 - i4 - Dec 2004 - p16(1) [1-50]

Andrejevic, Mark - *Reality TV: The Work of Being Watched*
R&R Bk N - v19 - i1 - Feb 2004 - p224(1) [51-500]

Andreoli, Richard - *Mondo Homo: Your Essential Guide to Queer Pop Culture*
Advocate - Nov 23 2004 - p96(1) [51-500]

Andreoli, Thomas E. - *Cecil Essentials of Medicine, 6th Ed.*
SciTech - v28 - i1 - March 2004 - p88(1) [51-500]

Andres, Steven - *Security Sage's Guide to Hardening the Network Infrastructure*
SciTech - v28 - i3 - Sept 2004 - p33(1) [51-500]

Andress, David - *The French Revolution and the People*
HRNB - v33 - i1 - Fall 2004 - p29(1) [501+]

Andrew, Anita M. - *Autocracy and China's Rebel Founding Emperors: Comparing Chairman Mao and Ming Taizu*
Ch Rev Int - v11 - i1 - Spring 2004 - p1(8) [501+]

Andrew, Elizabeth J. - *On the Threshold: Home, Hardwood, and Holiness*
PW - v252 - i7 - Feb 14 2005 - p70(1) [51-500]

Andrew, Joe - *Two Hundred Years of Pushkin, Vol. 1*
Russ Rev - v63 - i3 - July 2004 - pNA [501+]
Two Hundred Years of Pushkin, Vol. 2
Russ Rev - v63 - i3 - July 2004 - pNA [501+]

Andrew, Meredith - *Fresh and Tired Metaphors*
Can Lit - i182 - Autumn 2004 - p89(2) [501+]

Andrew, Paige G. - *Cataloging Sheet Maps: The Basics*
LRTS - v48 - i3 - July 2004 - p229(3) [501+]

Andrews, Beth - *Why Are You So Sad? (Illus. by Wong, Nicole)*
c CH Bwatch - v14 - i11 - Nov 2004 - pNA [51-500]

Andrews, Corey - *Literary Nationalism in Eighteenth-Century Scottish Club Poetry*
R&R Bk N - v19 - i4 - Nov 2004 - p238(1) [501+]

Andrews, David M. - *Governing the World's Money*
JEL - v42 - i3 - Sept 2004 - p850(3) [501+]

Andrews, Donna - *Access Denied*
BL - v101 - i8 - Dec 15 2004 - p710(1) [51-500]
KR - v72 - i20 - Oct 15 2004 - p985(1) [51-500]
PW - v251 - i48 - Nov 29 2004 - p26(2) [51-500]
Owl's Well That Ends Well
KR - v73 - i4 - Feb 15 2005 - p198(1) [51-500]
We'll Always Have Parrots (Read by Dunne, Bernadette). Audiobook Review
y Kliatt - v38 - i5 - Sept 2004 - p66(2) [51-500]

Andrews-Goebel, Nancy - *The Pot That Juan Built (Illus. by Diaz, David)*
c SLJ - v50 - i11 - Nov 2004 - p65(1) [51-500]

Andrews, J.E. - *An Indroduction to Enviromental Chemistry*
Choice - v41 - i11-12 - July-August 2004 - p2074(1) [501+]

Andrews, James T. - *Science for the Masses: The Bolshevik State, Public Science, and the Popular Imagination in Soviet Russia, 1917-1934*
AHR - v109 - i3 - June 2004 - p872(1) [501+]
Isis - v95 - i3 - Sept 2004 - p498(2) [501+]
Russ Rev - v63 - i3 - July 2004 - pNA [501+]
Slav R - v63 - i3 - Fall 2004 - p661-662 [501+]
T&C - v45 - i1 - Jan 2004 - p206(2) [501+]

Andrews, Jane - *Zoe and the Magic Harp*
c Sch Lib - v52 - i3 - Autumn 2004 - p129(1) [501+]

Andrews, Jonathan - *Customers and Patrons of the Mad-Trade: The Management of Lunacy in Eighteenth-Century London*
Albion - v36 - i1 - Spring 2004 - p143(2) [501+]

Andrews, Josephine T. - *When Majorities Fail: The Russian Parliament, 1990-1993*
Russ Rev - v63 - i3 - July 2004 - pNA [501+]

Andrews, Judith - *Digital Libraries: Policy, Planning, and Practice*
R&R Bk N - v19 - i4 - Nov 2004 - p260(1) [501+]

Andrews, Linda Boerger - *Core Competencies for Psychiatric Education: Defining, Teaching, and Assessing Resident Competence*
SciTech - v28 - i3 - Sept 2004 - p97(1) [51-500]

Andrews, Linda Wasmer - *Emotional Intelligence*
y SLJ - v51 - i2 - Feb 2005 - p144(1) [51-500]
Meditation
c SLJ - v50 - i7 - July 2004 - p116(1) [51-500]

Andrews, Mary Kay - *Hissy Fit*
BL - v100 - i22 - August 2004 - p1895(1) [51-500]
Ent W - i781 - Sept 3 2004 - p79 [501+]
KR - v72 - i16 - August 15 2004 - p755(1) [51-500]
LJ - v129 - i12 - July 2004 - p66(1) [51-500]
PW - v251 - i27 - July 5 2004 - p36(1) [51-500]

Andrews, Midas - *Midas*
PW - v252 - i6 - Feb 7 2005 - p42(1) [501+]

Andrews, P. Gayle - *Leaders for a Movement: Professional Preparation and Development of Middle Level Teachers and Administrators*
R&R Bk N - v19 - i3 - August 2004 - p220(1) [1-50]

Andrews, Robert - *The New Penguin Dictionary of Modern Quotations*
Choice - v42 - i2 - Oct 2004 - p261(1) [51-500]

Andrews, Robert (b. 1937 -) - *A Murder of Justice*
KR - v72 - i16 - August 15 2004 - p778(1) [51-500]
PW - v251 - i32 - August 9 2004 - p231(1) [51-500]

Andrews, Russell - *Aphrodite (Read by Schirner, Buck). Audiobook Review*
y Kliatt - v38 - i5 - Sept 2004 - p52(2) [51-500]
LJ - v129 - i14 - Sept 1 2004 - p200(1) [51-500]
Aphrodite
BooChiTr - Jan 11 2004 - p3(1) [501+]
Midas (Read by Lawlor, Patrick G.). Audiobook Review
KR - v73 - i4 - Feb 15 2005 - p188(1) [501+]

Andrews-Speed, Phillip - *Energy Policy and Regulation in the People's Republic of China*
R&R Bk N - v19 - i3 - August 2004 - p118(1) [51-500]

Andrews, Stuart - *Unitarian Radicalism: Political Rhetoric, 1770-1814*
AHR - v109 - i2 - April 2004 - p609(2) [501+]

Andrews, Tamra - *Wonders of the Sky*
y SB - v40 - i6 - Nov-Dec 2004 - p256(1) [51-500]
y Sch Lib - v52 - i4 - Winter 2004 - p217(1) [51-500]

Andrews, William L. - *North Carolina Slave Narratives: The Lives of Moses Roper, Lunsford Lane, Moses Grandy, and Thomas H. Jones*
JSH - v71 - i1 - Feb 2005 - p153(2) [501+]

Andreyev, Alexandre - *Soviet Russia and Tibet: The Debacle of Secret Diplomacy, 1918-1930s*
Choice - v41 - i7 - March 2004 - p1350(1) [501+]

Andreyev, Catherine - *Russia Abroad: Prague and the Russian Diaspora, 1918-1938*
Choice - v42 - i5 - Jan 2005 - p910(2) [1-50]
TLS - i5284 - July 9 2004 - p28-29 [501+]

Andrianov, I.V. - *Asymptotical Mechanics of Thin-Walled Structures*
SIAM Rev - v46 - i3 - Sept 2004 - p586(2) [501+]

Andricacos, P.C. - *Electrochemical Processing in ULSI Fabrication III: Proceedings*
SciTech - v28 - i1 - March 2004 - p162(1) [51-500]

Andriessen, Jerry - *Arguing to Learn: Confronting Cognitions in Computer-Supported Collaborative Learning Environments*
R&R Bk N - v19 - i1 - Feb 2004 - pNA [51-500]

Andronik, Catherine - *School Library Management, 5th Ed.*
R&R Bk N - v19 - i1 - Feb 2004 - p259(1) [51-500]

Andronikof, Anne - *Rorschachiana 26: Yearbook of the International Rorschach Society*
SciTech - v28 - i4 - Dec 2004 - p96(1) [51-500]

Andy Warhol Museum - *Andy Warhol, 365 Takes: The Andy Warhol Museum Collection*
BL - v100 - i22 - August 2004 - p1888(1) [51-500]
Choice - v42 - i3 - Nov 2004 - p473(1) [1-50]
LJ - v129 - i16 - Oct 1 2004 - p76(1) [51-500]

Anfinson, John O. - *The River We Have Wrought: A History of the Upper Mississippi*
JIH - v35 - i1 - Summer 2004 - p152-153 [501+]
Pub Hist - v26 - i1 - Wntr 2004 - p161(3) [501+]
T&C - v45 - i2 - April 2004 - p432-433 [501+]

Ang, Tom - *Digital Photography: An Introduction*
y Kliatt - v38 - i5 - Sept 2004 - p51(2) [501+]
KISS Guide to Digital Photography
y Kliatt - v38 - i5 - Sept 2004 - p51(2) [501+]

Angel, Michael - *Preserving the Sacred: Historical Perspectives on the Ojibwa Midewiwin*
Can Hist R - v85 - i3 - Sept 2004 - p576(3) [501+]

Angel, Sara - *The Museum Called Canada*
Globe & Mail - Oct 12 2004 - pR1 [501+]

Angel, Solly - *The Tale of the Scale: An Odyssey of Invention*
Choice - v41 - i11-12 - July-August 2004 - p2076(1) [501+]
SB - v40 - i5 - Sept-Oct 2004 - p206(1) [51-500]
SB - v40 - i6 - Nov-Dec 2004 - p244(1) [51-500]

Angel Stations
New Sci - v184 - i2477 - Dec 11 2004 - p50(1) [501+]

Angeletti, Norberto - *Magazines That Make History: Their Origins, Development, and Influence*
LJ - v129 - i14 - Sept 1 2004 - p163(1) [51-500]
PW - v251 - i39 - Sept 27 2004 - p53(1) [51-500]

Angelika Kauffman: "Mir Traumte vor ein Paar Nachten, ich Hatte Briefe von Ihnen Empfagen" Gesammelte Briefe in den Originalsprachen
Eight-C St - v37 - i3 - Spring 2004 - p478-482 [501+]

Angelike, Karin - *Louis-Francois Mettra: Ein Franzosischer Zeitungsverleger in Koln, 1770-1800*
Eight-C St - v37 - i3 - Spring 2004 - p483-486 [501+]

Angelis, Milo De - *Between the Blast Furnaces and the Dizziness: A Selection of Poems, 1970-1999*
Ant R - v62 - i4 - Fall 2004 - p777(2) [501+]

Angell, Jeannette L. - *Callgirl*
PW - v251 - i31 - August 2 2004 - p63(2) [51-500]
Madam
KR - v73 - i3 - Feb 1 2005 - p131(1) [501+]

Angell, Marcia - *The Truth about the Drug Companies: How they Deceive Us and What to Do about It (Read by Reading, Kate). Audiobook Review*
y Kliatt - v39 - i1 - Jan 2005 - p54(1) [51-500]
The Truth about the Drug Companies: How they Deceive Us and What to Do about It
Am Sci - v93 - i1 - Jan-Feb 2005 - p68(3) [501+]
BL - v100 - i22 - August 2004 - p1883(1) [51-500]
BW - v34 - i41 - Oct 10 2004 - p4(1) [501+]
Globe & Mail - Sept 11 2004 - pD4 [501+]
Hast Cen R - v34 - i5 - Sept-Oct 2004 - p44(2) [501+]
LJ - v129 - i12 - July 2004 - p110(1) [501+]
New R - Sept 27 2004 - p33 [501+]
NYTBR - Nov 14 2004 - p8 [501+]
PW - v251 - i31 - August 2 2004 - p63(1) [51-500]
Sci - v306 - i5705 - Dec 24 2004 - p2192(2) [501+]

Angelo, Joseph A. - *Facts on File Dictionary of Space Technology, Rev. Ed.*
E-Streams - Dec 2004 - pNA [501+]
SciTech - v28 - i1 - March 2004 - p170(1) [51-500]

Angelo, Rocco M. - *Hospitality Today: An Introduction, 5th Ed.*
R&R Bk N - v19 - i4 - Nov 2004 - p251(1) [501+]

Angelou, Maya - *Angelina of Italy (Illus. by Rockwell, Lizzy)*
c BL - v101 - i6 - Nov 15 2004 - p589(1) [51-500]
c PW - v251 - i36 - Sept 6 2004 - p62(1) [51-500]
Hallelujah! The Welcome Table: A Lifetime of Memories with Recipes
BL - v101 - i1 - Sept 1 2004 - p35(1) [51-500]
LJ - v129 - i14 - Sept 1 2004 - p181(1) [51-500]
PW - v251 - i35 - August 30 2004 - p49(1) [501+]
Hallelujah! The Welcome Table (Read by Angelou, Maya). Audiobook Review
PW - v251 - i40 - Oct 4 2004 - p29(1) [501+]

Anger
Globe & Mail - Jan 1 2005 - pD13 [501+]
HM - v310 - i1856 - Jan 2005 - p96(6) [501+]

Angevine, Robert G. - *The Railroad and the State: War, Politics, and Technology in Nineteenth-Century America*
Choice - v42 - i6 - Feb 2005 - p1068(1) [51-500]
SciTech - v28 - i4 - Dec 2004 - p8(1) [1-50]

Anggabrata, Ian - *I Wish I Had a Dinosaur (Illus. by Sheehan, Peter)*
c Magpies - v19 - i5 - Nov 2004 - p27(1) [501+]

Anghelaki-Rooke, Katerina - *Translating into Love Life's End*
TLS - i5287 - July 30 2004 - p25(1) [501+]

Anghinolfi, M. - *GDH 2002 ... Gerasimov-Dreil-Hearn Sum Rule and the Spin Structure of the Nucleon: Proceedings*
SciTech - v28 - i4 - Dec 2004 - p52(1) [501+]

Angioli, Roberto - *Chemotherapy for Gynecological Neoplasms: Current Therapy and Novel Approaches*
SciTech - v28 - i3 - Sept 2004 - p92(1) [51-500]
SciTech - v28 - i3 - Sept 2004 - p92(1) [51-500]

Angold, Michael - *The Fourth Crusade: Event and Context*
Choice - v42 - i1 - Sept 2004 - p161(1) [501+]

Argenti-Pillen, Alex - *Masking Terror: How Women Contain Violence in Southern Sri Lanka*
MAQ - v18 - i1 - March 2004 - p104(4) [501+]

Argod-Dutard, Francoise - *Des signes au sens: Lectures du livre III des Essais*
Ren Q - v57 - i3 - Fall 2004 - p1020(2) [501+]

Argueta, Jorge - *Xochitl and the Flowers/Xochitl, La Nina De Las Flores (Illus. by Angel, Carl)*
c CE - v81 - i2 - Winter 2004 - p107(1) [51-500]

Argula, Anne - *Homicide My Own*
KR - v73 - i2 - Jan 15 2005 - p83(1) [51-500]
LJ - v130 - i2 - Feb 1 2005 - p56(1) [51-500]

Argur, Anne M.R. - *Grant's Atlas of Anatomy, 11th Ed.*
SciTech - v28 - i3 - Sept 2004 - p67(1) [51-500]

Argveta, Jorge - *Trees are Hanging from the Sky (Illus. by Yockteng, Rafel)*
c LibMed - v22 - i4 - Jan 2004 - p56(1) [501+]

Argy, Fred - *Where to from Here? Australian Egalitarianism under Threat*
JEL - v41 - i4 - Dec 2003 - p1426(1) [501+]

Argyle, Bob - *Observing and Measuring Visual Double Stars*
Choice - v41 - i11-12 - July-August 2004 - p2068(1) [501+]
S&T - v109 - i1 - Jan 2005 - p119(2) [501+]

Argyrous, George - *Growth, Distribution, and Effective Demand: Alternatives to Economic Orthodoxy: Essays in Honor of Edward J. Nell*
JEL - v42 - i1 - March 2004 - p243(1) [501+]

Arianoutsou, Margarita - *Ecology, Conservation and Management of Mediterranean Climate Ecosystems: Proceedings*
SciTech - v28 - i3 - Sept 2004 - p50(1) [1-50]

Arianrhod, Robyn - *Einstein's Heroes*
New Sci - v184 - i2477 - Dec 11 2004 - p51(1) [501+]

Arieti, James A. - *The Scientific and the Divine: Conflict and Reconciliation from Ancient Greece to the Present*
Rel St - v40 - i3 - Sept 2004 - p374(4) [501+]

Ariew, Roger - *Historical Dictionary of Descartes and Cartesian Philosophy*
R&R Bk N - v19 - i1 - Feb 2004 - p3(1) [51-500]

Aris, Stephen - *Close to the Sun: How Airbus Challenged America's Domination of the Skies*
R&R Bk N - v19 - i3 - August 2004 - p120(1) [51-500]

Arise, John C. - *The Hope, Hype and Reality of Genetic Engineering: Remarkable Stories from Agriculture, Industry, Medicine, and the Environment*
QRB - v79 - i3 - Sept 2004 - p306(2) [501+]

Aristophanes - *Aristophanes, Vol. 4*
VQR - v79 - i1 - Winter 2003 - p13 [51-500]

Aristotle - *Aristotle: Nicomachean Ethics*
Phil R - v112 - i4 - Oct 2003 - p567(4) [501+]
Aristotle on Poetics
Class R - v53 - i2 - Nov 2003 - p304-305 [501+]

Ariyur, Kartik B. - *Real Time Optimization by Extremum Seeking Control*
Choice - v41 - i7 - March 2004 - p1325(1) [501+]

Arjouni, Jakob - *Idiots: Five Fairy Tales and Other Stories*
KR - v73 - i5 - March 1 2005 - p241(1) [501+]

Arkadie, Bryan Van - *Viet Nam: A Transition Tiger?*
JEL - v42 - i4 - Dec 2004 - p1160(2) [501+]

Arkes, Hadley - *Natural Rights and the Right to Choose*
Ethics - v115 - i2 - Jan 2005 - p435(2) [501+]

Arkin, Frieda - *Hedwig and Berti*
BL - v101 - i7 - Dec 1 2004 - p634(1) [51-500]
KR - v72 - i22 - Nov 15 2004 - p1059(2) [501+]
NYTBR - March 13 2005 - p31 [501+]
PW - v251 - i47 - Nov 22 2004 - p38(1) [51-500]

Arkins, Diane C. - *Halloween: Romantic Art & Customs of Yesteryear*
Ant&CM - v108 - i8 - Oct 2003 - p16(1) [51-500]

Arledge, Garnette - *On Angel's Eve: Making the Most of Your Final Time Together*
LJ - v129 - i13 - August 2004 - p102(1) [51-500]

Arledge, Roone - *Roone: A Memoir*
TV Q - v34 - i2 - Wntr 2004 - p67-69 [501+]

Arlene, Davila - *Barrio Dreams: Puerto Ricans, Latinos, and the Neoliberal City*
Choice - v42 - i6 - Feb 2005 - p1103(2) [51-500]

Arlon, Penelope - *DK First Animal Encyclopedia*
c SB - v40 - i5 - Sept-Oct 2004 - p222(1) [51-500]
c SLJ - v51 - i2 - Feb 2005 - p81(1) [51-500]
How People Live
c LibMed - v22 - i7 - April-May 2004 - p82(1) [501+]

Armani, Giuseppe - *Gli Scritti Su Carlo Cattaneo*
TLS - i5291 - August 27 2004 - p4-6 [501+]

Armantrout, Rae - *Up to Speed*
Poet - v185 - i2 - Nov 2004 - p135(2) [501+]
Wom R Bks - v21 - i10-11 - July 2004 - p6(2) [501+]

Armatage, Kay - *Girl from God's Country: Nell Shipman and the Silent Cinema*
CBRA - Annual 2003 - p102(2) [501+]

Armentrout, David - *China*
c Teach Lib - v32 - i3 - Feb 2005 - p42(1) [51-500]
The Emancipation Proclamation
c BL - v101 - i4 - Oct 15 2004 - p412(1) [51-500]
The Mayflower Compact
c BL - v101 - i4 - Oct 15 2004 - p412(1) [51-500]
Timelines of Ancient Civilizations
LibMed - v22 - i7 - April-May 2004 - p72(1) [501+]

Armerding, Paul L. - *Doctors for the Kingdom: The Work of the American Mission Hospitals in the Kingdom of Saudi Arabia--1913-1955*
CH - v73 - i3 - Sept 2004 - p704(2) [501+]

Armingeon, Klaus - *The OECD and European Welfare States*
R&R Bk N - v19 - i3 - August 2004 - p175(1) [501+]

Armintor, Marshall Needleman - *Lacan and the Ghosts of Modernity: Masculinity, Tradition, and the Anxiety of Influence*
R&R Bk N - v19 - i4 - Nov 2004 - p221(1) [501+]

Armistead, John - *The Return of Gabriel*
y SLJ - v50 - i10 - Oct 2004 - p66(1) [1-50]

Armitage, Allan M. - *Armitage's Garden Annuals: A Color Encyclopedia*
SciTech - v28 - i3 - Sept 2004 - p129(1) [51-500]

Armitage, Chistopher J. - *Planned Behavior: The Relationship between Human Thought and Action*
Choice - v42 - i6 - Feb 2005 - p1102(1) [51-500]

Armitage, David - *The British Atlantic World 1500-1800*
Albion - v36 - i1 - Spring 2004 - p193(3) [501+]
Greater Britain, 1516-1776: Essays in Atlantic History
R&R Bk N - v19 - i4 - Nov 2004 - p35(1) [51-500]

Armitage, Doreen - *From the Wheelhouse: Tugboats Tell Their Own Stories*
CBRA - Annual 2003 - p437(1) [51-500]

Armor, David J. - *Maximizing Intelligence*
Choice - v41 - i7 - March 2004 - p1374(1) [501+]

Arms, Myron - *Servants of the Fish: A Portrait of Newfoundland after the Great Cod Collapse*
Globe & Mail - Dec 24 2004 - pD13 [1-50]

Armstead, Myra B. Young - *"Lord, Please Don't Take Me in August": African Americans in Newport and Saratoga Springs, 1870-1930*
J Urban H - v31 - i1 - Nov 2004 - p106-114 [501+]

Armstead, Robert - *Black Days, Black Dust: The Memories of an African American Coal Miner*
Black Iss - v6 - i5 - Sept-Oct 2004 - p42(2) [501+]

Armstrong, Anne-Marie - *Instructional Design in the Real World: A View from the Trenches*
R&R Bk N - v19 - i1 - Feb 2004 - p181(1) [51-500]

Armstrong, C. Michael - *A Handbook of Human Resource Management in Practice, 9th Ed.*
R&R Bk N - v19 - i1 - Feb 2004 - p111(1) [51-500]
TimHES - v0 - i1666 - Nov 12 2004 - p29(1) [501+]

Armstrong, Carol - *Ocean Flowers: Impressions from Nature*
Am Sci - v92 - i6 - Nov-Dec 2004 - p573(3) [501+]
Apo - v161 - i516 - Feb 2005 - p78(2) [501+]
Bwatch - Oct 2004 - pNA [51-500]
New Sci - v183 - i2460 - August 14 2004 - p46(1) [51-500]

Armstrong, Carol M. - *Odd Man Out: Readings of the Work and Reputation of Edgar Degas*
R&R Bk N - v19 - i4 - Nov 2004 - p200(1) [501+]

Armstrong, Charles K. - *The North Korean Revolution, 1945-1950*
AHR - v109 - i2 - April 2004 - p497(3) [501+]

Armstrong, Douglas V. - *Creole Transformation from Slavery to Freedom: Historical Archaelogy of the East End Community, St. John, Virgin Islands*
Choice - v41 - i11-12 - July-August 2004 - p2085(2) [501+]

Armstrong, Eileen - *Fooly Booked! Reader Development and the Secondary School LRC*
Sch Lib - v52 - i4 - Winter 2004 - p221(1) [51-500]

Armstrong, Elisabeth - *The Retreat from Organization: U.S. Feminism Reconceptualized*
NWSA Jnl - v16 - i3 - Fall 2004 - p226(4) [501+]

Armstrong, Elizabeth A. - *Forging Gay Identities: Organizing Sexuality in San Francisco*
CS - v33 - i1 - Jan 2004 - p84-85 [501+]

Armstrong, Elizabeth M. - *Conceiving Risk, Bearing Responsibility: Fetal Alcohol Syndrome and the Diagnosis of Moral Disorder*
MAQ - v18 - i3 - Sept 2004 - p397-399 [501+]
SciTech - v28 - i3 - Sept 2004 - p116(1) [51-500]

Armstrong, Gary - *Football in Africa*
TLS - i5262 - Feb 6 2004 - p10(1) [501+]

Armstrong, Jeannette - *Whispering in Shadows*
Can Lit - i181 - Summer 2004 - p99-100 [501+]

Armstrong, Jennifer - *Magnus at the Fire (Illus. by Smith, Owen)*
c Globe & Mail - Feb 26 2005 - pD11 [501+]
Photo By Brady: A Picture of the Civil War
KR - v73 - i2 - Jan 15 2005 - p115(1) [51-500]
What a Song Can Do: 12 Riffs on the Power of Music
y BL - v100 - i22 - August 2004 - p1921(1) [51-500]
y CCB-B - v58 - i1 - Sept 2004 - p5(2) [51-500]
c LibMed - v23 - i3 - Nov-Dec 2004 - p74(1) [51-500]
c SLJ - v50 - i7 - July 2004 - p98(1) [51-500]
y SLJ - v50 - i12 - Dec 2004 - p60(1) [501+]
y VOYA - v27 - i3 - August 2004 - p226(1) [1-50]

Armstrong, John - *Jim*
BIC - v33 - i2 - March 2004 - p25(2) [501+]
The Secret Power of Beauty: Why Happiness is in the Eye of the Beholder
TimHES - v0 - i1663 - Oct 22 2004 - p26(1) [501+]

Armstrong, Karen - *A History of God; The 4,000-Year Quest of Judaism, Christianity and Islam (Read by Armstrong, Karen). Audiobook Review*
LJ - v129 - i18 - Nov 1 2004 - p130(1) [51-500]
The Spiral Staircase: My Climb Out of Darkness (Read by Armstrong, Karen). Audiobook Review
LJ - v129 - i15 - Sept 15 2004 - p89(1) [51-500]
The Spiral Staircase: My Climb Out of Darkness
Globe & Mail - March 12 2005 - pD17 [1-50]
y SLJ - v50 - i7 - July 2004 - p132(1) [51-500]
Theol St - v66 - i1 - March 2005 - p239(1) [501+]
TimHES - v0 - i1670 - Dec 10 2004 - p27(1) [501+]
TLS - i5295 - Sept 24 2004 - p25(1) [501+]
Wom R Bks - v22 - i1 - Oct 2004 - p17(2) [501+]

Armstrong, Kelley - *Industrial Magic*
PW - v251 - i44 - Nov 1 2004 - p49(1) [501+]

Armstrong, Lance - *Lance Armstrong: Images of a Champion*
R&R Bk N - v19 - i4 - Nov 2004 - p81(1) [51-500]

Armstrong, Luanne - *The Bone House*
Can Lit - i181 - Summer 2004 - p100-102 [501+]

Armstrong, Marian - *Peoples of Eastern Asia, Vols. 1-11*
c SLJ - v51 - i2 - Feb 2005 - p81(1) [51-500]

Armstrong, Mary - *Seven Eggs Today: The Diaries of Mary Armstrong, 1859 and 1869*
Globe & Mail - August 14 2004 - pD12 [1-50]
R&R Bk N - v19 - i3 - August 2004 - p78(1) [51-500]

Armstrong, Nancy - *Fans in Spain*
Choice - v42 - i3 - Nov 2004 - p470(1) [1-50]

Armstrong, Sally - *Veiled Threat: The Hidden Power of the Women of Afghanistan*
Globe & Mail - Oct 16 2004 - pD31 [501+]

Armstrong, Sara - *Information Literacy*
LibMed - v23 - i3 - Nov-Dec 2004 - p62(1) [51-500]

Armstrong, Tammy - *Translations: Aistreann*
CBRA - Annual 2003 - p150(2) [51-500]

Armstrong, Vivien - *Murder between Friends*
BL - v101 - i2 - Sept 15 2004 - p211(1) [501+]

Armus, Diego - *Entre medicos y Curanderos: Cultura, Historia y Enfermedad en la America Latina*
HAHR - v84 - i3 - August 2004 - p511(3) [501+]

Arn, Mary-Jo - *Charles D'Orleans in England*
JEGP - v103 - i3 - July 2004 - p395-398 [501+]

Arnaldez, Jean-Jacques - *Collection of ICC Arbitral Awards, 1996-2000*
R&R Bk N - v19 - i1 - Feb 2004 - pNA [51-500]

Arnall, William - *The Case of Opposition Stated, Between the Craftsman and the People*
R&R Bk N - v19 - i1 - Feb 2004 - p32(1) [1-50]

Arnason, David - *Demon Lover*
CBRA - Annual 2003 - p193(2) [51-500]

Arnason, Johann P. - *Civilization in Dispute: Historical Questions and Theoretical Traditions*
R&R Bk N - v19 - i1 - Feb 2004 - p26(1) [51-500]

Arnds, Peter O. - *Representation, Subversion, and Eugenics in Gunter Grass's The Tin Drum*
Choice - v42 - i5 - Jan 2005 - p856(1) [1-50]

Arnesen, Eric - *The Human Tradition in American Labor History*
R&R Bk N - v19 - i2 - May 2004 - p106(1) [51-500]

Arnesen, Liv - *No Horizon Is So Far: Two Women and Their Historic Journey Across Antarctica*
y Kliatt - v39 - i2 - March 2005 - p40(2) [51-500]

Arnheim, Michael - *The Handbook of Human Rights Law: An Accessible Approach to the Issues and Principles*
CR - v285 - i1666 - Nov 2004 - p315(2) [501+]
R&R Bk N - v19 - i3 - August 2004 - p194(1) [501+]

Arnold, Bruce - *The Spire and Other Essays in Modern Irish Culture*
ILS - v24 - i1 - Fall 2004 - p29(2) [501+]

Arnold, Caroline - *Birds: Nature's Magnificent Flying Machines (Illus. by Wynne, Patricia)*
c SLJ - v50 - i10 - Oct 2004 - pS37(2) [51-500]
Pterosaurs: Ruler of the Skies in the Dinosaur Age (Illus. by Caple, Laurie)
c KR - v72 - i22 - Nov 15 2004 - p1087(1) [51-500]
Pterosaurs: Rulers of the Skies in the Dinosaur Age (Illus. by Caple, Laurie)
c BL - v101 - i7 - Dec 1 2004 - p665(1) [51-500]
The Skeletal System
c SLJ - v51 - i2 - Feb 2005 - p114(1) [51-500]
Uluru, Australia's Aboriginal Heart (Illus. by Arnold, Arthur)
c LibMed - v22 - i7 - April-May 2004 - p68(1) [501+]
c Sci Teach - v71 - i4 - April 2004 - p72-72 [501+]
c SLJ - v50 - i10 - Oct 2004 - pS32(1) [51-500]
Who Has More? Who Has Fewer?
c PW - v251 - i31 - August 2 2004 - p72(2) [501+]
Who Is Bigger? Who Is Smaller?
c PW - v251 - i31 - August 2 2004 - p72(2) [501+]

Arnold, Dana - *Architecture as Experience: Radical Changes in Spatial Practice*
R&R Bk N - v19 - i4 - Nov 2004 - p203(1) [501+]

Arnold, David - *Gandhi*
HER - v119 - i482 - June 2004 - p828(2) [501+]
SOAS since the Sixties
TimHES - v0 - i1670 - Dec 10 2004 - p31(1) [501+]

Arnold, Ed - *Hockey Town: Life Before the Pros*
Globe & Mail - Oct 30 2004 - pD18 [501+]

Arnold, Edwin L. - *Gullivar of Mars: Commemorative Edition*
SFS - v31 - i2 - July 2004 - p301-302 [501+]

Arnold, Frances H. - *Directed Enzyme Evolution: Screening and Selection*
SciTech - v28 - i3 - Sept 2004 - p72(1) [51-500]

Arnold, J.R. Tony - *Introduction to Materials Management, 5th Ed.*
SciTech - v28 - i4 - Dec 2004 - p168(1) [51-500]

Arnold, James R. - *Chickamauga 1863: The River of Death*
R&R Bk N - v19 - i4 - Nov 2004 - p62(1) [51-500]
Shiloh, 1862: The Death of Innocence
R&R Bk N - v19 - i4 - Nov 2004 - p61(1) [51-500]
Tet Offensive 1968: Turning Point in Vietnam
R&R Bk N - v19 - i4 - Nov 2004 - p48(1) [1-50]

Arnold, Jeffrey - *Field-Programmable Custom Computing Machines*
SciTech - v28 - i4 - Dec 2004 - p19(1) [1-50]

Arnold, K. - *Medicine Man: The Forgotten Museum of Henry Wellcome*
J Hist G - v30 - i3 - July 2004 - p580(3) [501+]

Arnold, R. Douglas - *Congress, the Press, and Political Accountability*
Choice - v42 - i5 - Jan 2005 - p933(1) [51-500]

Arnold, Richard - *English Hymns of the Nineteenth Century: An Anthology*
R&R Bk N - v19 - i3 - August 2004 - p26(1) [1-50]

Arnold, Tedd - *Catalina Magdalena Hoopensteiner Wallendiner Hogan Logan Bogan Was Her Name (Illus. by Arnold, Tedd)*
y CCB-B - v58 - i1 - Sept 2004 - p6(1) [51-500]
c LibMed - v23 - i3 - Nov-Dec 2004 - p65(1) [51-500]
c PW - v251 - i31 - August 2 2004 - p72(2) [501+]
c SLJ - v50 - i8 - August 2004 - p105(1) [51-500]
Even More Parts: Idioms from Head to Toe (Illus. by Arnold, Tedd)
c BW - v34 - i41 - Oct 10 2004 - p12(1) [501+]
c KR - v72 - i15 - August 1 2004 - p737(1) [51-500]
c SLJ - v51 - i1 - Jan 2005 - p85(1) [51-500]
No Jumping on the Bed!
c PW - v251 - i38 - Sept 20 2004 - p64(1) [51-500]

Arnold, Vladimir I. - *Lectures on Partial Differential Equations*
Choice - v42 - i5 - Jan 2005 - p888(1) [501+]

Arnosky, Jim - *All About Sharks*
c LibMed - v22 - i6 - March 2004 - p71(1) [501+]
Beachcombing: Exploring the Seashore (Illus. by Arnosky, Jim)
c BL - v100 - i21 - July 2004 - p1848(1) [1-50]
c SLJ - v50 - i7 - July 2004 - p90(1) [51-500]
Coyote Raid in Cactus Canyon
KR - v73 - i1 - Jan 1 2005 - p47(1) [51-500]

Arnot, Bob - *Seven Steps to a Healthy Heart*
PW - v251 - i47 - Nov 22 2004 - p56(1) [51-500]
Seven Steps to Stop a Heart Attack
LJ - v129 - i20 - Dec 1 2004 - p148(1) [51-500]

Arnott, Jake - *Truecrime*
BL - v101 - i1 - Sept 1 2004 - p67(1) [51-500]
Globe & Mail - Sept 25 2004 - pD30 [1-50]
KR - v72 - i15 - August 1 2004 - p699(1) [51-500]
PW - v251 - i40 - Oct 4 2004 - p71(1) [51-500]

Arnott, Robert - *Oil Company Crisis: Managing Structure, Profitability, and Growth*
En Jnl - v25 - i1 - Jan 2004 - p109(3) [501+]

Arnould, Jean-Claude - *Premiere poesie francaise de la Renaissance: Autour des Puys poetiques normands*
Ren Q - v57 - i3 - Fall 2004 - p1013(3) [501+]

Arnould, M. - *Nuclear Physics V: Proceedings*
SciTech - v28 - i3 - Sept 2004 - p49(1) [1-50]

Arnove, Robert F. - *Comparative Education: The Dialectic of the Global and the Local, 2nd Ed.*
R&R Bk N - v19 - i1 - Feb 2004 - pNA [51-500]

Aron, Melanie - *Les Memoires de Madame de Motteville: du devouement a la devotion*
FS - v58 - i3 - July 2004 - p409-409 [501+]

Aron, Paul - *Verite et Litterature au XVIIIe Siecle: Melanges Rassembles en l'Honneur de Raymond Trousson*
Eight-C St - v37 - i3 - Spring 2004 - p500-504 [501+]

Aron, Paul (b. 1956-) - *More Unsolved Mysteries of American History*
R&R Bk N - v19 - i4 - Nov 2004 - p57(1) [1-50]

Aron, Paul (b. 1956) - *Did Babe Ruth Call His Shot? and Other Unsolved Baseball Mysteries*
PW - v252 - i3 - Jan 17 2005 - p43(1) [51-500]

Aron, Raymond - *The Dawn of Universal History: Selected Essays from a Witness to the Twentieth Century*
Soc - v41 - i3 - March-April 2004 - p94(3) [501+]
Peace and War: A Theory of International Relations
JEL - v41 - i4 - Dec 2003 - p1443(2) [501+]

Aronowitz, Stanley - *How Class Works: Power and Social Movement*
AJS - v110 - i1 - July 2004 - p236(3) [501+]
Implicating Empire: Globalization and Resistance in the 21st Century World Order
R&R Bk N - v19 - i3 - August 2004 - p187(1) [501+]

Aronson, Harvey B. - *Buddhist Practice on Western Ground: Reconciling Eastern Ideals and Western Psychology*
LJ - v129 - i15 - Sept 15 2004 - p62(1) [51-500]

Aronson, Marc - *Beyond the Pale: New Essays for a New Era*
y VOYA - v27 - i3 - August 2004 - p248(1) [1-50]
y VOYA - v27 - i4 - Oct 2004 - p266(2) [51-500]
John Winthrop, Oliver Cromwell, and the Land of Promise
y CCB-B - v58 - i1 - Sept 2004 - p6(2) [51-500]
y HB - v80 - i4 - July-August 2004 - p465(1) [51-500]
y LibMed - v23 - i3 - Nov-Dec 2004 - p80(1) [51-500]
c SLJ - v50 - i9 - Sept 2004 - p221(1) [51-500]
y VOYA - v27 - i4 - Oct 2004 - p322(1) [51-500]

Aronson, Ronald - *Camus and Sartre: The Story of a Friendship and the Quarrel that Ended It*
Lon R Bks - v27 - i2 - Jan 20 2005 - p20(3) [501+]
TLS - i5290 - August 20 2004 - p28(1) [51-500]

Aronsson, Lars - *The Development of Sustainable Tourism*
GJ - v170 - i3 - Sept 2004 - p282(1) [501+]

Arora, Dilip K. - *Fungal Biotechnology in Agricultural, Food, and Environmental Applications*
E-Streams - June 2004 - pNA [501+]
SciTech - v28 - i1 - March 2004 - p172(1) [51-500]
Handbook of Fungal Biotechnology, 2nd Ed., Rev. and Expanded
E-Streams - June 2004 - pNA [501+]
SciTech - v28 - i1 - March 2004 - p173(1) [51-500]

Arora, Rajeev - *Adaptations and Responses of Woody Plants to Environmental Stresses*
SciTech - v28 - i4 - Dec 2004 - p126 [51-500]

Arp, David - *No Time for Sex: Finding the Time You Need for Getting the Love You Want*
LJ - v129 - i15 - Sept 15 2004 - p72(1) [51-500]

Arp, Thomas R. - *Perrine's Sound and Sense: An Introduction to Poetry, 11th Ed.*
R&R Bk N - v19 - i3 - August 2004 - p259(1) [51-500]

Arratia, Gloria - *Catfishes, Vols. 1-2*
SciTech - v28 - i4 - Dec 2004 - p66(1) [51-500]

Arredondo, Gabriela F. - *Chicana Feminisms: A Critical Reader*
Choice - v41 - i7 - March 2004 - p1334(1) [501+]
SHQ - v107 - i4 - April 2004 - p633(2) [501+]

Arrow, Kenneth J. - *Handbook of Social Choice and Welfare, Vol. 1*
JEL - v42 - i1 - March 2004 - p175(2) [501+]

Arroyo, Madeline - *Calie's Gift (Illus. by Vavak, S. Dean)*
c CH Bwatch - v14 - i7 - July 2004 - p2(1) [51-500]

Arruda, Suzanne Middendorf - *The Girl He Left Behind: The Life and Times of Libbie Custer*
c SLJ - v50 - i10 - Oct 2004 - p184(1) [51-500]

Arscott, David - *East Sussex Events: Death, Disaster, War and Weather*
R&R Bk N - v19 - i1 - Feb 2004 - p31(1) [1-50]

Arsenault, Elaine - *Doggie in the Window (Illus. by Fanny)*
c PW - v252 - i2 - Jan 10 2005 - p55(2) [51-500]
c SLJ - v51 - i1 - Jan 2005 - p85(1) [51-500]

Arsenault, Mark - *Speak Ill of the Living*
BL - v101 - i9-10 - Jan 1 2005 - p824(2) [1-50]
KR - v72 - i23 - Dec 1 2004 - p1118(1) [51-500]
PW - v252 - i3 - Jan 17 2005 - p37(2) [51-500]

Arseneau, Mary - *Recovering Christina Rossetti: Female Community and Incarnational Poetics*
Choice - v42 - i4 - Dec 2004 - p658(1) [1-50]

Arshamm, Gary - *Diabetes: A Guide To Living Well*
Bwatch - Jan 2005 - pNA [51-500]

Arsuaga, Juan Luis - *The Neanderthal's Necklace: In Search of the First Thinkers*
JRAI - v10 - i3 - Sept 2004 - p710(2) [501+]

Art and Artifice: Japanese Photographs of the Meiji Era: Selections from the Jean S. and Frederic A. Sharf Collection at the Museum of Fine Arts, Boston
R&R Bk N - v19 - i4 - Nov 2004 - p248(1) [501+]

Art, Henry Warren - *Woodswalk: Peepers, Porcupines and Exploding Puff Balls!: What You'll See, Hear and Smell When Exploring the Woods*
c LibMed - v22 - i5 - Feb 2004 - p54(1) [501+]

Art, Robert J. - *A Grand Strategy for America*
Choice - v41 - i7 - March 2004 - p1367(1) [501+]
VQR - v80 - i1 - Wntr 2004 - p267-267 [501+]
International Politics: Enduring Concepts and Contemporary Issues, 7th Ed.
R&R Bk N - v19 - i3 - August 2004 - p159(1) [501+]
The United States and Coercive Diplomacy
PSQ - v119 - i3 - Fall 2004 - p536(2) [501+]

Artemiadis, Nikolaos K. - *History of Mathematics: From a Mathematician's vantage point*
SciTech - v28 - i4 - Dec 2004 - p16(1) [1-50]

Arter, David - *The Scottish Parliament: A Scandinavian-Style Assembly?*
CR - v285 - i1666 - Nov 2004 - p307(2) [501+]
The Scottish Parliment: A Scandinavian-Style Assembly?
Choice - v42 - i5 - Jan 2005 - p926(1) [1-50]

Arterburn, Stephen - *Josiah*
c BL - v101 - i3 - Oct 1 2004 - p341(1) [51-500]

Arthorne, John - *Official Eclipse 3.0 FAQs*
SciTech - v28 - i4 - Dec 2004 - p27(1) [51-500]

Arthur, C.J. - *The New Dialectic and Marx's Capital*
S&S - v68 - i4 - Winter 2004 - p513-3 [501+]
R&R Bk N - v19 - i3 - August 2004 - p94(1) [51-500]

Arthur, Catherine Rogers - *Homewood House*
Choice - v42 - i7 - March 2005 - p1219(1) [51-500]

Arthur, Liz - *Robert Stewart: Design, 1946-95*
TLS - i5266 - March 5 2004 - p26-26 [501+]

Arthur, Wallace - *Biased Embryos and Evolution*
Nature - v430 - i6997 - July 15 2004 - p294(1) [501+]

Arthurson, Wayne - *Final Season*
CBRA - Annual 2003 - p151(1) [51-500]

Arthus-Bertrand, Yann - *Yann Arthus-Bertrand: Being a Photographer*
PW - v251 - i50 - Dec 13 2004 - p61(1) [51-500]
LJ - v129 - i20 - Dec 1 2004 - p113(1) [51-500]

Ashworth, Sue - *Desserts and Sweets from around the World*
     Sch Lib - v52 - i3 - Autumn 2004 - p149(1) [501+]

Ashworth, William J. - *Customs and Excise: Trade, Production, and Consumption in England*
     BHR - v78 - i3 - Autumn 2004 - p571(3) [501+]

Asian, Reza - *No God but God: The Origins, Evolution, and Future of Islam*
     KR - v73 - i1 - Jan 1 2005 - p27(2) [501+]

Asimov, Isaac - *I, Robot (Read by Brick, Scott). Audiobook Review*
     BL - v101 - i7 - Dec 1 2004 - p677(1) [1-50]
I, Robot
     SEP - v276 - i6 - Nov-Dec 2004 - p38(1) [501+]
Isaac Asimov's 21st Century Library of the Universe: The Solar System
  c LibMed - v22 - i5 - Feb 2004 - p57(1) [501+]
Robot Dreams
     Bwatch - v26 - i7 - July 2004 - p5(2) [51-500]

Asimov, Janet Jeppson - *Isaac Asimov: It's Been a Good Life*
     Physics T - v42 - i8 - Nov 2004 - p511(1) [501+]
     SEP - v276 - i6 - Nov-Dec 2004 - p38(1) [501+]

Asimow, Michael - *Law and Popular Culture: A Course Book*
     R&R Bk N - v19 - i4 - Nov 2004 - p161(1) [501+]

Askadskii, Andrey A. - *Lectures on the Physico-Chemistry of Polymers*
     SciTech - v28 - i1 - March 2004 - p55(1) [51-500]

Askari, Hossein G. - *Case Studies of U.S. Economic Sanctions: The Chinese, Cuban, and Iranian Experience*
     R&R Bk N - v19 - i1 - Feb 2004 - p106(1) [51-500]

Askari, Jafar - *A Soldier's Story: From Ottoman Rule to Independent Iraq: The Memoirs of Jafar Pasha Al-Askari*
     R&R Bk N - v19 - i3 - August 2004 - p50(1) [51-500]

Askegren, Pierce - *Human Resource*
     LJ - v130 - i3 - Feb 15 2005 - p122(1) [51-500]

Askew, Thomas A. - *The American Church Experience: A Concise History*
     Choice - v42 - i4 - Dec 2004 - p676(1) [1-50]

Askwith, Richard - *Feet in the Clouds: A Tale of Fell-Running and Obsession*
     NS - v133 - i4695 - July 5 2004 - p51(2) [501+]
     Spec - v295 - i9181 - July 24 2004 - p35(2) [501+]

Aslam, Nadeem - *Maps for Lost Lovers*
     Econ - v372 - i8382 - July 3 2004 - p70US [501+]
     KR - v73 - i5 - March 1 2005 - p241(1) [501+]
     PW - v252 - i10 - March 7 2005 - p47(1) [51-500]
     TLS - i5285 - July 16 2004 - p22(1) [501+]

Aslan, Reza - *No God but God: The Origins, Evolution, and Future of Islam*
     LJ - v130 - i4 - March 1 2005 - p90(1) [51-500]
     PW - v252 - i7 - Feb 14 2005 - p73(1) [51-500]

Asleson, Robyn - *Notorious Muse: The Actress in British Art and Culture 1776-1812*
     Albion - v36 - i2 - Summer 2004 - p318(2) [501+]

ASME/IEEE Joint Rail Conference: Proceedings
     SciTech - v28 - i3 - Sept 2004 - p148(1) [51-500]

Asmus, A. Nunnerich - *Heiligtumer und Romanisierung auf der iberischen Halbinsel. Uberlegungen zu Religion und kultureller Identitat*
     Class R - v53 - i2 - Nov 2003 - p436-437 [501+]

Asmus, Ronald D. - *Progressive Internationalism: A Democratic National Security Strategy*
     Nation - v279 - i13 - Oct 25 2004 - p29 [501+]

Aspden, Philip - *Patient Safety: Achieving a New Standard for Care*
     SciTech - v28 - i3 - Sept 2004 - p80(1) [51-500]

Aspen-Baxter, Linda - *Plants*
  c SB - v40 - i3 - May-June 2004 - p131(2) [501+]

Aspen Publishers Directory of Corporate Counsel, 2004-2005, Vols. 1-2
     R&R Bk N - v19 - i4 - Nov 2004 - p168(1) [501+]

Aspen Publisher's Inc. - *The Lawyer's Almanac 2004: The Leading Reference to Vital Facts and Figures About the Legal Profession*
     R&R Bk N - v19 - i3 - August 2004 - p195(1) [501+]

Aspin, Diana - *Ordinary Miracles*
  y CBRA - Annual 2003 - p472(2) [51-500]

Aspiz, Harold - *So Long! Walt Whitman's Poetry of Death*
     Choice - v41 - i11-12 - July-August 2004 - p2042(1) [501+]

Asprin, Robert - *Wartorn Resurrection*
  y BL - v101 - i8 - Dec 15 2004 - p714(1) [51-500]

ASQ Statistics Division - *Glossary and Tables for Statistical Quality Control, 4th ed.*
     SciTech - v28 - i4 - Dec 2004 - p168(1) [51-500]

Assaf, David - *The Regal Way: The Life and Times of Rabbi Israel of Ruzhin*
     Slav R - v63 - i2 - Summer 2004 - p391(2) [501+]

Assani, Idris - *Chapel Hill Ergodic Theory Workshops: Proceedings*
     SciTech - v28 - i4 - Dec 2004 - p39(1) [51-500]

Asselin, Pierre - *A Bitter Peace: Washington, Hanoi, and the Making of the Paris Agreement*
     J Mil H - v68 - i2 - April 2004 - p654(2) [501+]

Assembly of States Parties to the Rome Statute of the International Criminal Court, 2d Session, New York, September 8-12, 2003: Official Records
     R&R Bk N - v19 - i1 - Feb 2004 - pNA [1-50]

Assenova, Margarita - *Debate on NATO's Evolution: A Guide.*
     R&R Bk N - v19 - i1 - Feb 2004 - p255(1) [51-500]

Assie-Lumumba, N'Dri - *Cyberspace, Distance Learning, and Higher Education in Developing Countries: Old and Emergent Issues of Access, Pedagogy, and Knowledge Production*
     R&R Bk N - v19 - i4 - Nov 2004 - p185(1) [501+]

Assiniwi, Bernard - *The Beothuk Saga*
     Can Lit - i181 - Summer 2004 - p181-182 [501+]

Assiter, Alison - *Revisiting Universalism*
     Choice - v42 - i2 - Oct 2004 - p305(1) [51-500]

Assmann, Jan - *Jenseits und Identitat*
     HNet - June 2004 - pNA [501+]

Association for Computing Machinery - *Proceedings, 26th International Conference on Software Engineering: ICSE 2004: May 23-28, 2004, Edinburgh International Conference Centre, Edinburgh, Scotland*
     SciTech - v28 - i3 - Sept 2004 - p19(1) [501+]

Association for Library Service to Children - *The Newbery and Caldecott Awards: A Guide to the Medal and Honor Books*
     Adoles - v39 - i156 - Winter 2004 - p827(2) [51-500]

Association of African Universities - *Guide to Higher Education in Africa, 3rd Ed.*
     Choice - v42 - i4 - Dec 2004 - p640(1) [1-50]

Associations USA: A Directory of Contact Information for National Associations, Foundations, and Other Nonprofit Organizations in the United States and Canada
     Choice - v42 - i4 - Dec 2004 - p625(1) [51-500]
     R&R Bk N - v19 - i3 - August 2004 - p159(1) [51-500]

Astell, Ann W. - *Joan of Arc and Spirituality*
     Choice - v41 - i11-12 - July-August 2004 - p2114(1) [501+]

Aster, Rick - *Professional SAS Programmer's Pocket Reference, 5th Ed.*
     SciTech - v28 - i4 - Dec 2004 - p37(1) [1-50]

Astier, Martin - *Lartigue: Album of a Century*
     TLS - i5290 - August 20 2004 - p18(1) [501+]

Astin, Sean - *There and Back Again*
     Ent W - i786 - Oct 1 2004 - p77 [51-500]
     LJ - v129 - i14 - Sept 1 2004 - p151(2) [51-500]
     PW - v251 - i39 - Sept 27 2004 - p48(1) [51-500]

Astle, Dave - *Beginning OpenGL Game Programming*
     SciTech - v28 - i3 - Sept 2004 - p136(1) [51-500]

Astley, Jeff - *Creation: A Reader*
     R&R Bk N - v19 - i3 - August 2004 - p13(1) [1-50]
Evil: A Reader
     R&R Bk N - v19 - i3 - August 2004 - p13(1) [1-50]
War and Peace: A Reader
     R&R Bk N - v19 - i3 - August 2004 - p13(1) [1-50]

Astley, Neil - *Being Alive*
  y Sch Lib - v52 - i4 - Winter 2004 - p220(1) [51-500]
Staying Alive: Real Poems for Unreal Times
     Poet - v184 - i5 - Sept 2004 - p392(2) [51-500]

ASTM Committee E-34 on Occupational Health and Safety - *ASTM International Metalworking Industry Standards: Environmental Quality and Safety, Fluid Performance and Condition Monitoring Tests*
     SciTech - v28 - i1 - March 2004 - p152(1) [51-500]

ASTM Committee E12 on Color and Appearance - *ASTM Standards on Color and Appearance, 7th Ed.*
     SciTech - v28 - i4 - Dec 2004 - p134 [51-500]

ASTM Committee F-16 on Fasteners - *ASTM International Standards for Mechanical Fasteners and Related Standards for Fastener Materials, Coatings, Test Methods, and Quality*
     SciTech - v28 - i4 - Dec 2004 - p147(1) [501+]

ASTM International - *ASTM Standards on Medical Transcription, 2004*
     SciTech - v28 - i4 - Dec 2004 - p78(1) [51-500]

Aston, Diana Hutts - *When You Were Born (Illus. by Lewis, E.B.)*
  c PW - v251 - i34 - August 23 2004 - p53(1) [501+]

Aston, Dianna Hutts - *When You Were Born (Illus. by Lewis, E.B.)*
  c BL - v101 - i7 - Dec 1 2004 - p658(1) [51-500]
  c Black Iss - v7 - i1 - Jan-Feb 2005 - p70(2) [501+]
  c KR - v72 - i16 - August 15 2004 - p802(1) [51-500]

Aston, Elaine - *Feminist Views on the English Stage: Women Playwrights, 1900-2000*
     Theat - v56 - i4 - Dec 2004 - p708-2 [501+]
Feminist Views on the English Stage: Women Playwrights, 1990-2000
     TLS - i5292 - Sept 3 2004 - p30(1) [501+]

Aston, Elizabeth - *The Exploits and Adventures of Miss Alethea Darcy*
     LJ - v130 - i3 - Feb 15 2005 - p113(1) [51-500]

Aston, Nigel - *Religion and Revolution in France, 1780-1804*
     HER - v119 - i483 - Sept 2004 - p1070(1) [501+]
     HER - v119 - i483 - Sept 2004 - p1070(2) [501+]

Astren, Fred - *Karaite Judaism and Historical Understanding*
     R&R Bk N - v19 - i4 - Nov 2004 - p16(1) [51-500]

Astroth, Sue - *Fast, Fun and Easy Scrapbook Quilts: Create a Keepsake for Every Memory*
     LJ - v129 - i13 - August 2004 - p77(1) [501+]

At the Global Crossroads: The Sylvia Ostry Foundation Lectures
     R&R Bk N - v19 - i4 - Nov 2004 - p107(1) [51-500]

Atala, Anthony - *Bladder Disease: Research Concepts and Clinical Applications, Vols. 1-2*
     SciTech - v28 - i1 - March 2004 - p107(1) [51-500]

Atalay, Bulent - *Math and the Mona Lisa: The Art and Science of Leonardo da Vinci*
     A Art - v68 - i744 - July 2004 - p75(2) [501+]
     Choice - v42 - i1 - Sept 2004 - p85(1) [501+]

Atals, Nava - *The Vegetarian Family Cookbook*
     Veg J - v23 - i4 - July-August 2004 - p32(1) [501+]

Atangan, Patrick - *The Silk Tapestry and Other Chinese Folktales*
  y BL - v101 - i6 - Nov 15 2004 - p572(1) [51-500]
     LJ - v130 - i1 - Jan 1 2005 - p87(1) [51-500]
     PW - v251 - i47 - Nov 22 2004 - p40(1) [51-500]
The Silk Trapestry and Other Chinese Folktales: Songs of Our Ancestors
     Bwatch - Feb 2005 - pNA [51-500]

Atarodi, Habibollah - *Great Powers, Oil and the Kurds in Mosul (Southern Kurdistan/Northern Iraq), 1910-1925*
     R&R Bk N - v19 - i1 - Feb 2004 - p41(1) [51-500]

Athens, Lonnie - *Sociology of Crime Law, and Deviance, Vol. 4*
     CS - v33 - i6 - Nov 2004 - p720(2) [501+]

Atherton, Mark - *Celts and christians: New Approaches to the Religious approaches to the Traditions of Britain and Ireland*
     HER - v119 - i483 - Sept 2004 - p1024(2) [501+]
Celts and Christians: New Approaches to the Religious Traditions of Britain and Ireland
     HER - v119 - i483 - Sept 2004 - p1024(2) [501+]

Atherton, Nancy - *Aunt Dimity and the Next of Kin*
     BL - v101 - i9-10 - Jan 1 2005 - p825(1) [1-50]

Athreya, K.B. - *Branching Process*
     SciTech - v28 - i3 - Sept 2004 - p36(1) [51-500]

Atkin, Denny - *Sony CLIE for Dummies*
     LJ - v129 - i14 - Sept 1 2004 - p182(1) [501+]

Atkin, Douglas - *The Culting of Brands: When Customers Become True Believers*
     LJ - v129 - i12 - July 2004 - p94(2) [51-500]

Atkin, Jonathan - *A War of Individuals: Bloomsbury Attitudes to the Great War*
     RES - v55 - i220 - June 2004 - p478-480 [501+]

Atkin, Nicholas - *Priests, Prelates and People: A History of European Catholicism since 1750*
     JR - v85 - i1 - Jan 2005 - p117(2) [501+]

Atkins, Caroline - *Country Living Shortcuts to Decorating Country Style*
     LJ - v129 - i15 - Sept 15 2004 - p56(1) [51-500]

Atkins, Catherine - *Alt Ed*
  c PW - v251 - i37 - Sept 13 2004 - p81(1) [51-500]

Atkins, E. Taylor - *Jazz Planet*
     Am St - v45 - i1 - Spring 2004 - p158-159 [501+]

Atkins, Gary - *Gay Seattle: Stories of Exile and Belonging*
JAH - v91 - i1 - June 2004 - p331-332 [501+]
WHQ - v35 - i2 - Summer 2004 - p229-230 [501+]
Atkins, Peter - *Galileo's Finger: The Ten Great Ideas of Science*
J Chem Ed - v81 - i10 - Oct 2004 - p1423(1) [501+]
Atkins, Robert - *Atkins Diabetes Revolution: The Groundbreaking Approach to Preventing and Controlling Type 2 Diabetes*
PW - v251 - i29 - July 19 2004 - p158(1) [51-500]
Atkins, Robert (American physician) - *Atkins for Life: The Next Level, Permanent Weight Loss and Good Health*
Lon R Bks - v26 - i15 - August 5 2004 - p16(3) [501+]
Atkins, Stephen E. - *Encyclopedia of Modern Worldwide Extremists and Extremist Groups*
BL - v101 - i4 - Oct 15 2004 - p437(2) [51-500]
Choice - v42 - i3 - Nov 2004 - p459(2) [1-50]
R&R Bk N - v19 - i3 - August 2004 - p145(1) [51-500]
y SLJ - v51 - i2 - Feb 2005 - p81(1) [51-500]
Atkins, Veronica - *Atkins for Life Low-Carb Cookbook*
LJ - v129 - i18 - Nov 1 2004 - p112(1) [51-500]
PW - v251 - i45 - Nov 8 2004 - p46(1) [501+]
Atkinson, Barbara F. - *Atlas of Diagnostic Cytopathology, 2nd Ed.*
SciTech - v28 - i1 - March 2004 - p86(1) [51-500]
Atkinson, Bill - *Within the Stone*
R&R Bk N - v19 - i4 - Nov 2004 - p249(1) [501+]
Atkinson, Brian - *Fantastic New Brunswick*
CBRA - Annual 2003 - p335(1) [51-500]
Atkinson, Gordon - *Reallivepreacher.com*
Ch Today - v48 - i10 - Oct 2004 - p113(1) [51-500]
Atkinson, James R. - *Splendid Land, Splendid People: The Chickasaw Indians to Removal*
Choice - v42 - i3 - Nov 2004 - p545(1) [1-50]
Atkinson, Jay - *Legends of Winter Hill: Cops, Con Men, and Joe McCain, the Last Real Detective*
KR - v73 - i2 - Jan 15 2005 - p91(1) [501+]
PW - v252 - i3 - Jan 17 2005 - p44(1) [51-500]
Atkinson, Kate - *Case Histories*
BL - v100 - i22 - August 2004 - p1870(1) [51-500]
BL - v101 - i9-10 - Jan 1 2005 - p768(1) [51-500]
BW - v34 - i51 - Dec 19 2004 - p3(1) [501+]
Globe & Mail - Dec 18 2004 - pD23 [51-500]
KR - v72 - i16 - August 15 2004 - p755(2) [501+]
LJ - v129 - i15 - Sept 15 2004 - p47(1) [51-500]
Lon R Bks - v26 - i18 - Sept 23 2004 - p27(1) [501+]
NYTBR - Dec 5 2004 - p65 [501+]
People - v62 - i24 - Dec 13 2004 - p56 [51-500]
PW - v251 - i43 - Oct 25 2004 - p27(2) [51-500]
Spec - v296 - i9187 - Sept 4 2004 - p35(1) [501+]
TLS - i5293 - Sept 10 2004 - p20(1) [501+]
Ent W - i792 - Nov 12 2004 - p128 [501+]
Atkinson, Kenneth - *Judaism*
y SLJ - v50 - i12 - Dec 2004 - p157(1) [51-500]
Atkinson, Leslie - *Attachment Issues in Psychopathology and Intervention*
SciTech - v28 - i1 - March 2004 - p96(1) [51-500]
Atkinson, Michael - *Tattooed: The Sociogenesis of a Body Art*
CBRA - Annual 2003 - p373(1) [51-500]
Choice - v41 - i7 - March 2004 - p1336(1) [501+]
Atkinson, Neill - *Adventures in Democracy: A History of the Vote in New Zealand*
R&R Bk N - v19 - i1 - Feb 2004 - pNA [501+]
Atkinson, Paul - *Key Themes in Qualitative Research: Continuities and Change*
JRAI - v10 - i4 - Dec 2004 - p915(2) [501+]
Atkinson, Phillip S. - *Medical Office Practice, 7th Ed.*
SciTech - v28 - i1 - March 2004 - p79(1) [51-500]
Atkinson, Rick - *By Their Deeds Alone: America's Combat Commanders on the Art of War*
Parameters - v34 - i4 - Winter 2004 - p142(2) [501+]
In the Company of Soldiers: A Chronicle of Combat
APH - v51 - i4 - Winter 2004 - p55(2) [501+]
BooChiTr - April 11 2004 - p5(1) [501+]
Parameters - v34 - i3 - Autumn 2004 - p143(2) [501+]
Atkinson, William Illsey - *Nanocosm: The Big Change That's Coming from the Very Small*
CBRA - Annual 2003 - p444(1) [51-500]
Atlas, James - *My Life in the Middle Ages: A Survivor's Tale*
BL - v101 - i9-10 - Jan 1 2005 - p789(1) [1-50]
KR - v72 - i24 - Dec 15 2004 - p1173(1) [501+]
PW - v252 - i2 - Jan 10 2005 - p45(1) [51-500]

Atlas, Ronald M. - *Handbook of Microbiological Media, 3rd Ed.*
SciTech - v28 - i3 - Sept 2004 - p73(1) [51-500]
Atleo, E. Richard - *Tsawalk: A Nuu-Chah-Nulth Worldview*
Choice - v42 - i5 - Jan 2005 - p864(1) [1-50]
R&R Bk N - v19 - i3 - August 2004 - p62(1) [51-500]
Atran, Scott - *In Gods We Trust: The Evolutionary Landscape of Religion*
Lon R Bks - v26 - i20 - Oct 21 2004 - p15(2) [501+]
Atria, Fernando - *Law and Legal Interpretation*
R&R Bk N - v19 - i1 - Feb 2004 - pNA [51-500]
ATS 2003: 12th Asian Test Symposium: Proceedings
SciTech - v28 - i1 - March 2004 - p160(1) [51-500]
Attaway, William - *Blood on the Forge*
LJ - v130 - i4 - March 1 2005 - p126(1) [1-50]
Attebery, Brian - *Decoding Gender in Science Fiction*
SFS - v31 - i2 - July 2004 - p291-294 [501+]
Attema, Martha - *Hero*
c CBRA - Annual 2003 - p473(1) [51-500]
When the War Is Over
y Can CL - i111-112 - Fall-Winter 2003 - p128(7) [501+]
Atterton, Peter - *Levinas and Buber: Dialogue and Difference*
R&R Bk N - v20 - i1 - Feb 2005 - p4(1) [51-500]
Attia, John Okyere - *Electronics and Circuit Analysis Using MATLAB, 2nd Ed.*
SciTech - v28 - i4 - Dec 2004 - p155(1) [51-500]
Attias, Jean-Christophe - *Israel, the Impossible Land (Illus. by Emanual, Susan)*
AHR - v109 - i2 - April 2004 - p655(2) [501+]
Attridge, Derek - *James Joyce's 'Ulysses': A Casebook*
ELT - v47 - i3 - Summer 2004 - p366(2) [51-500]
A Writer's Life: J.M. Coetzee's Elizabeth Costello
VQR - v80 - i4 - Fall 2004 - p254-265 [501+]
Attridge, Harold W. - *Psalms in Community; Jewish and Christian Textual, Liturgical, and Artistic Traditions*
R&R Bk N - v19 - i3 - August 2004 - p23(1) [1-50]
Psalms in Community: Jewish and Christian Textual, Liturgical, and Artistic Traditions
R&R Bk N - v19 - i4 - Nov 2004 - p22(1) [51-500]
Attridge, Steve - *Nationalism, Imperialism, and Identity in Late Victorian Culture: Civil and Military Worlds*
Albion - v36 - i2 - Summer 2004 - p339(2) [501+]
HNet - Sept 2004 - pNA [501+]
Attwood, Bain - *Rights for Aborigines*
AHS - v35 - i124 - Oct 2004 - p401(2) [501+]
Thinking Black: William Cooper and the Australian Aborigines' League
R&R Bk N - v19 - i4 - Nov 2004 - p77(1) [51-500]
Attwood, Philip - *Italian Medals c. 1530-1600 in British Public Collections*
Ren Q - v57 - i3 - Fall 2004 - p1004(4) [501+]
Six Ct J - v35 - i3 - Fall 2004 - p853-854 [501+]
Atwater, Harry A. - *Integration of Heterogeneous Thin-Film Materials and Devices: Proceedings*
SciTech - v28 - i1 - March 2004 - p140(1) [51-500]
Atwater-Rhodes, Amelia - *Snakecharm*
y KR - v72 - i17 - Sept 1 2004 - p859(1) [51-500]
y SLJ - v50 - i10 - Oct 2004 - p154(1) [51-500]
y VOYA - v27 - i5 - Dec 2004 - p398(1) [51-500]
Atwell, Mary Welek - *Evolving Standards of Decency: Popular Culture and Capital Punishment*
R&R Bk N - v19 - i4 - Nov 2004 - p148(1) [51-500]
Atwood, Christopher P. - *Encyclopedia of Mongolia and the Mongol Empire*
Choice - v42 - i3 - Nov 2004 - p460(1) [1-50]
LJ - v129 - i14 - Sept 1 2004 - p188(1) [51-500]
R&R Bk N - v19 - i4 - Nov 2004 - p49(1) [51-500]
BL - v101 - i8 - Dec 15 2004 - p757(1) [501+]
Atwood, Craig D. - *Community of the Cross: Moravian Piety in Colonial Bethlehem*
Choice - v42 - i3 - Nov 2004 - p498(1) [1-50]
W&M Q - v61 - i4 - Oct 2004 - p762-765 [501+]
The Distinctiveness of Moravian Culture: Essays and Documents in Moravian History in Honor of Vernon H. Nelson on His Seventieth Birthday
Six Ct J - v35 - i3 - Fall 2004 - p904(1) [501+]
Atwood, J.L. - *Encyclopedia of Supramolecular Chemistry, Vols. 1-2*
Choice - v42 - i3 - Nov 2004 - p458(1) [1-50]

Atwood, Jerry L. - *Encyclopedia of Supramolecular Chemistry, Vols. 1-2*
Choice - v42 - i3 - Nov 2004 - p458(1) [1-50]
E-Streams - Sept 2004 - pNA [501+]
LJ - v129 - i18 - Nov 1 2004 - p120(2) [51-500]
SB - v40 - i6 - Nov-Dec 2004 - p250(1) [501+]
SciTech - v28 - i3 - Sept 2004 - p54(1) [1-50]
Atwood, Margaret - *Bashful Bob and Doleful Dorinda (Illus. by Petricic, Dusan)*
c Globe & Mail - Dec 11 2004 - pD18 [501+]
Cat's Eye
JPC - v36 - Winter 2003 - p636 [501+]
The Handmaid's Tale
Globe & Mail - August 28 2004 - pD13 [501+]
Globe & Mail - Nov 13 2004 - pD23 [501+]
Moving Targets: Writing with Intent 1982-2004
Globe & Mail - Oct 2 2004 - pD8 [501+]
Negotiating with the Dead: A Writer on Writing
CBRA - Annual 2003 - p252(1) [51-500]
Oryx and Crake (Read by Scott, Campbell). Audiobook Review
Globe & Mail - Jan 8 2005 - pD13 [1-50]
Oryx and Crake
CBRA - Annual 2003 - p151(1) [51-500]
HR - v57 - i1 - Spring 2004 - p133-140 [501+]
Rude Ramsay and the Roaring Radishes (Illus. by Petricic, Dusan)
c BW - v34 - i45 - Nov 7 2004 - p12(1) [501+]
c CBRA - Annual 2003 - p445(2) [501+]
c KR - v72 - i16 - August 15 2004 - p802(1) [51-500]
c PW - v251 - i34 - August 23 2004 - p54(1) [501+]
c SLJ - v50 - i11 - Nov 2004 - p90(1) [51-500]
Writing with Intent: Essays, Reviews, Personal Prose: 1983-2005
KR - v73 - i2 - Jan 15 2005 - p91(2) [501+]
PW - v252 - i9 - Feb 28 2005 - p56(1) [51-500]
Atwood, Rhea Hollis - *Boston's French Secrets: Guided Walks That Reveal Boston's French Heritage*
Bwatch - Jan 2005 - pNA [51-500]
Bwatch - Feb 2005 - pNA [51-500]
LJ - v129 - i19 - Nov 15 2004 - p78(1) [501+]
Atwood, Roger - *Stealing History: Tomb Raiders, Smugglers, and the Looting of the Ancient World*
Arch - v57 - i6 - Nov-Dec 2004 - p56-56 [501+]
Art N - v104 - i1 - Jan 2005 - p94(1) [501+]
BL - v101 - i6 - Nov 15 2004 - p534(1) [51-500]
KR - v72 - i19 - Oct 1 2004 - p945(2) [501+]
LJ - v129 - i20 - Dec 1 2004 - p140(1) [51-500]
PW - v251 - i46 - Nov 15 2004 - p53(1) [51-500]
Atzeni, Stefano - *Physics of Inertial Fusion: Beam Plasma Interaction, Hydrodynamics, Hot Dense Matter*
SciTech - v28 - i4 - Dec 2004 - p65(1) [51-500]
Aubert, J.-J. - *Speculum Iuris: Roman Law as a Reflection of Social and Economic Life in Antiquity*
Class R - v54 - i1 - May 2004 - p200(3) [501+]
Aubin, Henry T. - *Rescue of Jerusalem: The Alliance Between Hebrews and Africans in 701 BC*
CBRA - Annual 2003 - p281(1) [501+]
Aubrey, John - *Brief Lives*
TLS - i5303 - Nov 19 2004 - p35(1) [51-500]
Aubrey, Merrily K. - *Naming Edmonton: From Ada to Zoie*
R&R Bk N - v19 - i4 - Nov 2004 - p71(1) [51-500]
Auch, Alison - *Welcome to Kenya*
c HNet - Sept 2004 - pNA [501+]
Auch, Mary Jane - *The Princess and the Pizza (Illus. by Auch, Herm)*
c RT - v57 - Oct 2003 - p170 [1-50]
Auchincloss, Louis - *East Side Story*
BL - v101 - i5 - Nov 1 2004 - p462(1) [51-500]
Ent W - i794 - Nov 26 2004 - p128 [51-500]
KR - v72 - i18 - Sept 15 2004 - p879(1) [501+]
LJ - v129 - i16 - Oct 1 2004 - p66(1) [51-500]
NYTBR - Dec 19 2004 - p13 [501+]
PW - v251 - i40 - Oct 4 2004 - p66(1) [51-500]
Auden, W.H. - *W.H. Auden's Book of Light Verse*
Globe & Mail - Sept 4 2004 - pD18 [1-50]
Audet, Michel - *Sante mentale et travail: L'urgence de penser autrement l'organisation*
ILR - v143 - i3 - Autumn 2004 - p284(2) [51-500]
Audi, Robert - *The Architecture of Reason: The Structure and Substance of Rationality*
Phil R - v112 - i3 - July 2003 - p432(3) [501+]
The Good in the Right: A Theory of Intuition and Instrinsic Value
Choice - v42 - i4 - Dec 2004 - p673(1) [1-50]
Choice - v42 - i4 - Dec 2004 - p673(1) [1-50]
Audoin-Rouzeau, Stephane - *14-18: Understanding the Great War*
HNet - August 2004 - pNA [501+]

Audouard, Antoine - *Farewell, My Only One*
KR - v72 - i13 - July 1 2004 - p587(2) [501+]
NYTBR - Feb 13 2005 - p8 [501+]

Audretsch, David B. - *SMEs in the Age of Globalization*
R&R Bk N - v19 - i1 - Feb 2004 - p97(1) [1-50]

Audubon, John James - *Audubon's Birds of America: The Audubon Society Baby Elephant Portfolio*
BL - v100 - i22 - August 2004 - p1886(1) [51-500]
Writings and Drawings
BL - v100 - i22 - August 2004 - p1886(1) [51-500]

Auer, Peter - *Employment Stability in an Age of Flexibility: Evidence from Industrialized Countries*
JEL - v41 - i4 - Dec 2003 - p1388(1) [501+]

Auerbach, Alan - *Handbook of Public Economics, Vol. 3*
JEL - v41 - i4 - Dec 2003 - p1301(3) [501+]
Handbook of Public Economics, Vol 4
JEL - v42 - i3 - Sept 2004 - p856(2) [501+]

Auerbach, Carl F. - *Qualitative Data: An Introduction to Coding and Analysis*
Choice - v41 - i7 - March 2004 - p1374(1) [501+]

Auerbach, Emily - *Searching for Jane Austen*
BL - v101 - i6 - Nov 15 2004 - p546(1) [51-500]
PW - v251 - i44 - Nov 1 2004 - p55(1) [501+]

Auerbach, Erich - *Mimesis: The Representation of Reality in Western Literature*
Class R - v54 - i2 - Nov 2004 - p450(4) [501+]

Auerbach, Red - *Let Me Tell You a Story: A Lifetime in the Game*
BL - v101 - i2 - Sept 15 2004 - p178(1) [51-500]
BW - v34 - i43 - Oct 24 2004 - p6(1) [501+]
LJ - v129 - i18 - Nov 1 2004 - p94(1) [51-500]

Auerbach, Scott M. - *Electron Capture Detector and the Study of Reactions with Thermal Electrons*
E-Streams - Oct 2004 - pNA [501+]

Auernheimer, Leonardo - *International Financial Markets: The Challenge of Globalization*
JEL - v41 - i4 - Dec 2003 - p1358(1) [501+]

Augar, Philip - *Player Manager: The Rise of Professionals Who Manage While They Work*
R&R Bk N - v19 - i1 - Feb 2004 - p102(1) [51-500]

Augarde, Steve - *Big Nose, Small Nose*
c PW - v251 - i41 - Oct 11 2004 - p82(1) [501+]
Hello, Moon
c PW - v251 - i41 - Oct 11 2004 - p82(1) [501+]
One Paper Hat
c PW - v251 - i41 - Oct 11 2004 - p82(1) [501+]
Purple Eyes
c PW - v251 - i41 - Oct 11 2004 - p82(1) [501+]
The Various
c LibMed - v22 - i7 - April-May 2004 - p63(1) [501+]
c NYTBR - July 11 2004 - p19 [501+]
y Sch Lib - v52 - i4 - Winter 2004 - p212(1) [51-500]
y VOYA - v27 - i4 - Oct 2004 - p312(1) [51-500]

Augen, Jeff - *Bioinformatics in the Post-Genomic Era: Genome, Transcriptome, Proteome, and Information-Based Medicine*
SciTech - v28 - i4 - Dec 2004 - p60(1) [51-500]

Auger, Catherine Volpilhac - *Montesquieu*
FS - v58 - i3 - July 2004 - p412-413 [501+]

Auger, Emily E. - *Tarot and Other Meditation Decks*
Bwatch - v26 - i7 - July 2004 - p12(1) [51-500]

Auger, Jeanette - *Passing Through: The End-of-Life Decisions of Lesbians and Gay Men*
CBRA - Annual 2003 - p373(1) [501+]

Aughton, Peter - *The Transit of Venus: The Brief, Brilliant Life of Jeremiah Horrocks, Father of British Astronomy*
Choice - v42 - i7 - March 2005 - p1246(1) [51-500]

Augspurger, Eric K. - *3Ds Max and its Applications, Release 5.x*
R&R Bk N - v19 - i1 - Feb 2004 - p252(1) [51-500]

Augspurger, Michael - *An Economy of Abundant Beauty: Fortune Magazine and Depression America*
Choice - v42 - i6 - Feb 2005 - p1016(1) [51-500]

Augst, Thomas - *The Clerk's Tale: Young Men and Moral Life in Nineteenth-Century America*
Ethics - v115 - i2 - Jan 2005 - p386(4) [501+]
NEQ - v77 - i3 - Sept 2004 - p520-522 [501+]
RAH - v32 - i4 - Dec 2004 - p518-525 [501+]

Augustin, Brian - *Go Boy 7: The Human Factor!*
PW - v251 - i2 - Jan 10 2005 - p41(1) [51-500]

Augustine, Saint, Bishop of Hippo - *De bono coniugali, De sancta uirginitate*
Specu - v79 - i3 - July 2004 - p735-736 [501+]
Saint Augustine's Conversion
BL - v101 - i3 - Oct 1 2004 - p299(1) [51-500]
KR - v72 - i18 - Sept 15 2004 - p908(1) [501+]

Augustyn, Brian - *Batman: The Mad Hatter (Illus. by Burchett, Rick)*
c SLJ - v50 - i8 - August 2004 - p82(1) [51-500]

Augustyn, Frederick J. - *Dictionary of Toys and Games in American Popular Culture*
Choice - v42 - i4 - Dec 2004 - p625(1) [1-50]
R&R Bk N - v19 - i4 - Nov 2004 - p210(1) [501+]

Aulbach, Bernd - *New Progress in Difference Equations: Proceedings*
SciTech - v28 - i4 - Dec 2004 - p42(1) [51-500]

Auld, Graeme - *Samuel at the Threshold: Selected Works of Graeme Auld*
R&R Bk N - v19 - i4 - Nov 2004 - p22(1) [51-500]

Auletta, Ken - *Media Man: Ted Turner's Improbable Empire*
Bus W - i3902 - Oct 4 2004 - p25 [501+]
BW - v34 - i41 - Oct 10 2004 - p13(1) [501+]
Fortune - v150 - i8 - Oct 18 2004 - p59 [51-500]
NYTBR - Dec 5 2004 - p67 [501+]
PW - v251 - i32 - August 9 2004 - p243(1) [51-500]

Ault, Hugh J. - *Comparative Income Taxation: A Structural Analysis, 2nd Ed.*
R&R Bk N - v19 - i4 - Nov 2004 - p164(1) [501+]

Ault, James M. - *Spirit and Flesh: Life in a Fundamentalist Baptist Church*
Bks & Cult - v10 - i6 - Nov-Dec 2004 - p9(1) [501+]
BL - v101 - i1 - Sept 1 2004 - p24(2) [51-500]
BW - v34 - i36 - Sept 5 2004 - p5(1) [501+]
Ch Today - v48 - i10 - Oct 2004 - p112(1) [51-500]
KR - v72 - i13 - July 1 2004 - p610(1) [501+]
LJ - v129 - i15 - Sept 15 2004 - p62(1) [51-500]
NYTBR - Dec 5 2004 - p69 [501+]
PW - v251 - i30 - July 26 2004 - p51(1) [501+]

Aumann, Jane - *The Christmas Tractor*
c CH Bwatch - v14 - i12 - Dec 2004 - pNA [51-500]

Aumann, Robert J. - *Handbook of Game Theory with Economic Applications, Vol. 3*
JEL - v41 - i4 - Dec 2003 - p1276(2) [501+]

Aune, David E. - *The Westminster Dictionary of New Testament and Early Christian Literature and Rhetoric*
TT - v61 - i3 - Oct 2004 - p422(1) [501+]

Auner, Joseph - *A Schoenberg Reader: Documents of a Life*
Choice - v41 - i7 - March 2004 - p1305(1) [501+]
MT - v145 - i1889 - Winter 2004 - p105-108 [501+]
Notes - v61 - i1 - Sept 2004 - p130(2) [501+]

Aurell, Martin - *L'Empire des Plantagenet, 1154-1224*
Med R - June 2004 - pNA [501+]

Aurum, Stephen Moss - *A Bird in the Bush*
Spec - v296 - i9192 - Oct 9 2004 - p55(1) [501+]

Auryle, Vincas - *Lietuviuegzodo vaiku ir jaunimo literatura 1945-1990*
c Bkbird - v42 - i3 - July 2004 - p48(1) [501+]

Aushcer, Pascal - *Heat Kernels and Analysis on Manifolds, Graphs, and Metric Spaces: Lecture Notes*
SciTech - v28 - i1 - March 2004 - p39(1) [51-500]

Auslander, Shalom - *Beware of God: Stories*
KR - v73 - i2 - Jan 15 2005 - p63(1) [501+]
PW - v252 - i9 - Feb 28 2005 - p42(1) [51-500]

Austen, Jane - *The Annotated 'Pride and Prejudice'*
R&R Bk N - v19 - i1 - Feb 2004 - p238(1) [51-500]

Austen, Siobhan - *Culture and the Labour Market*
JEL - v41 - i4 - Dec 2003 - p1385(1) [501+]

Auster, Paul - *Auggie Wren's Christmas Story*
BL - v101 - i2 - Sept 15 2004 - p205(1) [501+]
City of Glass
BW - v34 - i41 - Oct 10 2004 - p9(2) [501+]
y SLJ - v50 - i8 - August 2004 - p148(1) [501+]
Spec - v296 - Dec 18 2004 - p90(2) [501+]
Collected Novels, Vol. I
Spec - v296 - Dec 18 2004 - p90(2) [501+]
Oracle Night
ABR - v25 - i6 - Sept-Oct 2004 - p24(2) [501+]
Lon R Bks - v26 - i6 - March 18 2004 - pNA [501+]
NYTBR - Jan 30 2005 - p24 [501+]

Austin, Ann E. - *Paths to the Professoriate: Strategies for Enriching the Preparation of Future Faculty*
R&R Bk N - v19 - i3 - August 2004 - p221(1) [1-50]
TCR - v106 - i12 - Dec 2004 - p2367(5) [501+]

Austin, Barbara - *Capitalizing Knowledge: Essays on the History of Business Education in Canada*
Can Hist R - v85 - i3 - Sept 2004 - p639(3) [501+]

Austin, Dave - *Man on the Border*
Roundup M - v12 - i1 - Oct 2004 - p27(2) [51-500]

Austin, J. Luke - *General John Bratton: Sumter to Appomattox, in Letters to His Wife*
JSH - v70 - i3 - August 2004 - p693(3) [501+]

Austin, J. William, II - *Related Families of Botetourt County, Virginia, Rev. Ed.*
EFHM - v58 - i2 - March-April 2004 - p91(1) [51-500]

Austin, Lynn N. - *Candle in the Darkness (Read by Moore, Christina). Audiobook Review*
LJ - v129 - i18 - Nov 1 2004 - p129(1) [51-500]
Gods and Kings
LJ - v130 - i2 - Feb 1 2005 - p64(1) [51-500]
A Light to My Path
LJ - v129 - i18 - Nov 1 2004 - p68(1) [501+]

Austin, Mary Hunter - *The Land of Journey's Ending*
VQR - v80 - i3 - Summer 2004 - p267(2) [501+]

Austin, Mary Leman - *From the Cover: 15 Memorable Projects for Quilt Lovers*
LJ - v129 - i20 - Dec 1 2004 - p108(1) [51-500]

Austin, Robert Michael - *Artists of the Litchfield Hills*
Choice - v42 - i1 - Sept 2004 - p87(1) [501+]

Austin, Thomas - *Contemporary Hollywood Stardom*
Choice - v42 - i3 - Nov 2004 - p490(1) [51-500]

Ausubel, Ken - *Nature's Operating Instructions: The True Biotechnologies*
PW - v251 - i32 - August 9 2004 - p238(1) [51-500]

Autin-Grenier, Pierre - *Je Ne Suis Pas Un Heros*
TLS - i5263 - Feb 13 2004 - p27-27 [501+]
L' Eternite Est Inutile
TLS - i5263 - Feb 13 2004 - p27-27 [501+]
Toute Une Vie Bien Ratee
TLS - i5263 - Feb 13 2004 - p27-27 [501+]

Automated Software Engineering: Proceedings
SciTech - v28 - i4 - Dec 2004 - p150(1) [51-500]

Automatic Face and Gesture Recognition: Proceedings
SciTech - v28 - i3 - Sept 2004 - p143(1) [51-500]

Auwers, J.-M. - *The Biblical Canons: Bibliotheca Ephemeridum Theologicarum Lovaniensium*
Theol St - v65 - i4 - Dec 2004 - p909(9) [501+]

Auyang, Sunny Y. - *Engineering: An Endless Frontier*
Bwatch - Nov 2004 - pNA [51-500]
Choice - v42 - i2 - Oct 2004 - p322(1) [51-500]

Auyero, Javier - *Contentious Lives: Two Argentine Women, Two Protests, and the Quest for Recognition*
Ams - v61 - i2 - Oct 2004 - p281(3) [501+]
Biomag - v27 - i4 - Fall 2004 - p862(4) [501+]

Ava - *Ava's New Testament Narratives: When the Old Law Passed Away*
R&R Bk N - v19 - i1 - Feb 2004 - p247(1) [51-500]

Avadikyan, Arman - *The Economic Dynamics of Fuel Cell Technologies*
JEL - v41 - i4 - Dec 2003 - p1417(1) [501+]

Avalos, Hector - *Introduction to the U.S. Latina and Latino Religious Experience*
Choice - v42 - i6 - Feb 2005 - p1038(1) [51-500]
R&R Bk N - v19 - i4 - Nov 2004 - p20(1) [51-500]

Avasthi, Smita - *Day by Day: The Nineties, Vols. 1-2*
Choice - v42 - i2 - Oct 2004 - p261(1) [501+]
LJ - v129 - i13 - August 2004 - p116(1) [501+]
R&R Bk N - v19 - i3 - August 2004 - p36(1) [51-500]
BL - v101 - i2 - Sept 15 2004 - p275(1) [501+]

Avella, Adolfo - *Highlights in Condensed Matter Physics*
SciTech - v28 - i1 - March 2004 - p47(1) [51-500]
Lectures on the Physics of Highly Correlated Electron Systems VIII
SciTech - v28 - i4 - Dec 2004 - p49(1) [51-500]

Avella, Steven M. - *In the Richness of the Earth: A History of the Archdiocese of Milwaukee 1843-1958*
CHR - v90 - i3 - July 2004 - p574(3) [501+]

Aveni, Anthony - *Behind the Crystal Ball: Magic, Science, and the Occult from Antiquity through the New Age*
Isis - v95 - i3 - Sept 2004 - p466(2) [501+]

Averill, Esther - *Jenny and the Cat Club*
c Sch Lib - v52 - i4 - Winter 2004 - p201(1) [51-500]

Averill, Thomas Fox - *Ordinary Genius*
KR - v73 - i4 - Feb 15 2005 - p188(1) [501+]
PW - v252 - i9 - Feb 28 2005 - p40(1) [51-500]

Averitt, Jack N. - *Families of Southeastern Georgia Excerpted from Georgia's Coastal Plain: Family and Personal History*
EFHM - v58 - i3 - May-June 2004 - p58(1) [51-500]

Averting AIDS Crises in Eastern Europe and Central Asia: A Regional Support Strategy
JEL - v42 - i1 - March 2004 - p275(1) [501+]

Avery, Christopher - *The Early Admissions Game: Joining the Elite*
y Kliatt - v39 - i2 - March 2005 - p36(1) [51-500]
TCR - v106 - i2 - Feb 2004 - p280-283 [501+]

Avery, Derek - *Modern Architecture*
LJ - v129 - i19 - Nov 15 2004 - p56(1) [501+]

Avery, Evelyn - *The Magic Worlds of Bernard Malamud*
J Am St - v38 - i1 - April 2004 - p134-135 [501+]

Avery, Gayle C. - *Understanding Leadership: Paradigms and Cases*
R&R Bk N - v19 - i3 - August 2004 - p105(1) [1-50]

Avery, Kevin J. - *Hudson River School Visions: The Landscapes of Sanford R. Gifford*
R&R Bk N - v19 - i1 - Feb 2004 - p206(1) [51-500]

Avery-Peck, Alan J. - *When Judaism and Christianity Began: Essays in Memory of Anthony J. Saldarini, Vols. 1-2*
R&R Bk N - v19 - i3 - August 2004 - p20(1) [1-50]

Avery, Simon - *Elizabeth Barrett Browning*
CR - v285 - i1663 - August 2004 - p128(1) [501+]

Avi - *Crispin: The Cross of Lead*
y Kliatt - v38 - i4 - July 2004 - p14(1) [51-500]
y Kliatt - v38 - i5 - Sept 2004 - p18(2) [51-500]
c RT - v57 - Oct 2003 - p176 [1-50]
The End of the Beginning: Being the Adventures of a Small Snail (Illus. by Tusa, Tricia)
c BL - v101 - i2 - Sept 15 2004 - p242(1) [51-500]
c CCB-B - v58 - i3 - Nov 2004 - p113(1) [501+]
c KR - v72 - i19 - Oct 1 2004 - p956(1) [501+]
c SLJ - v50 - i10 - Oct 2004 - p154(1) [51-500]
The Good Dog (Read by Ramirez, Robert). Audiobook Review
c Kliatt - v38 - i5 - Sept 2004 - p60(2) [51-500]
c SLJ - v50 - i7 - July 2004 - p58(1) [51-500]
Never Mind! A Twin Novel
c BW - v34 - i29 - July 18 2004 - p11(1) [1-50]
y VOYA - v27 - i3 - August 2004 - p207(1) [1-50]
The True Confessions of Charlotte Doyle
y BL - v101 - i1 - Sept 1 2004 - p121(1) [501+]

Avi-Yonah, Michael - *A History of Israel and the Holy Land*
J Ch St - v46 - i4 - Autumn 2004 - p889(2) [501+]

Aviles, Ronnier J. - *Introductory Guide to Cardiac Catheterization*
SciTech - v28 - i3 - Sept 2004 - p106(1) [51-500]

Avise, John C. - *The Hope, Hype, and Reality of Genetic Engineering: Remarkable Stories from Agriculture, Industry, Medicine, and the Environment*
Choice - v42 - i1 - Sept 2004 - p128(1) [501+]
Molecular Markers, Natural History, and Evolution, 2nd Ed.
QRB - v79 - i4 - Dec 2004 - p414(2) [501+]
SciTech - v28 - i3 - Sept 2004 - p59(1) [1-50]

Avison, Charles - *Charles Avison's Essay on Musical Expression: With Related Writings by William Hayes and Charles Avison*
R&R Bk N - v19 - i4 - Nov 2004 - p198(1) [501+]

Avison, Margaret - *Always Now: The Collected Poems, Vol. 1*
CBRA - Annual 2003 - p208(1) [51-500]
Always Now: The Collected Poems, Vol. 2
Globe & Mail - Feb 19 2005 - pD5 [501+]
Concrete and Wild Carrot
CBRA - Annual 2003 - p208(1) [501+]

Avorgbedor, Daniel K. - *The Interrelatedness of Music, Religion, and Ritual in African Performance Practice*
Choice - v42 - i3 - Nov 2004 - p492(1) [51-500]
R&R Bk N - v19 - i2 - May 2004 - p193(1) [51-500]

Avorn, Jerry - *Powerful Medicines: The Benefits, Risks, and Costs of Prescription Drugs*
Am Sci - v93 - i1 - Jan-Feb 2005 - p68(3) [501+]
BL - v100 - i22 - August 2004 - p1879(1) [51-500]
BW - v34 - i45 - Nov 7 2004 - p4(1) [501+]
LJ - v129 - i12 - July 2004 - p110(1) [501+]
NYTBR - Nov 14 2004 - p8 [501+]
Sci - v306 - i5705 - Dec 24 2004 - p2192(2) [501+]

Avraham, Eli - *Behind Media Marginality: Coverage of Social Groups and Places in the Israeli Press*
R&R Bk N - v19 - i1 - Feb 2004 - p230(1) [51-500]

Avram, Wes - *Where the Light Shines Through: Discerning God in Everyday Life*
PW - v252 - i7 - Feb 14 2005 - p72(1) [51-500]

Avrech, Robert J. - *The Hebrew Kid and the Apache Maiden*
Roundup M - v12 - i3 - Feb 2005 - p25(1) [51-500]

Avriel, Mordecai - *Nonlinear Programming: Analysis and Methods*
SciTech - v28 - i1 - March 2004 - p134(1) [51-500]

Aw, Tash - *The Harmony Silk Factory*
KR - v73 - i1 - Jan 1 2005 - p3(1) [501+]
LJ - v130 - i3 - Feb 15 2005 - p113(1) [51-500]
PW - v252 - i7 - Feb 14 2005 - p52(1) [51-500]

Awde, Nicholas - *Arabic Practical Dictionary*
R&R Bk N - v19 - i3 - August 2004 - p255(1) [1-50]

Awoodey, Steve - *Catnap Brought Home: The View from Jena*
R&R Bk N - v19 - i3 - August 2004 - p5(1) [1-50]

Awsome Forces of Nature
LibMed - v22 - i7 - April-May 2004 - p76(1) [501+]

Axell, Albert - *Marshal Zhukov: The Man Who Beat Hitler*
Choice - v41 - i7 - March 2004 - p1350(2) [501+]
HNet - June 2004 - pNA [501+]

Axelrod, Alan - *Office Superman: Make Yourself Indispensable in the Workplace*
LJ - v129 - i18 - Nov 1 2004 - p98(2) [51-500]
PW - v251 - i45 - Nov 8 2004 - p46(1) [501+]

Axelrod, C. Warren - *Outsourcing Information Security*
SciTech - v28 - i4 - Dec 2004 - p32(1) [51-500]

Axelrod, Mark - *Borges' Travel, Hemingway's Garage: Secret Histories*
ABR - v26 - i2 - Jan-Feb 2005 - p31(1) [501+]
Ga R - v58 - i3 - Fall 2004 - p708-710 [501+]
NYTBR - August 15 2004 - p13 [501+]

Axelson, Eric - *The Soldier at the Crossroad: The 726th MP Battalion in World War II*
J Mil H - v68 - i3 - July 2004 - p1004-1005 [501+]

Axelsson, Per - *Preventive Materials, Methods, and Programs*
SciTech - v28 - i4 - Dec 2004 - p114(1) [1-50]

Axford, Elizabeth C. - *Song Sheets to Software: A Guide to Print Music, Software, and Web Sites for Musicians, 2nd Ed.*
Choice - v42 - i6 - Feb 2005 - p992(1) [51-500]
R&R Bk N - v19 - i4 - Nov 2004 - p194(1) [501+]

Axford, John S. - *Medicine, 2nd Ed.*
SciTech - v28 - i3 - Sept 2004 - p89(1) [51-500]

Axinn, June - *Social Welfare: A History of the American Response to Need, 6th Ed.*
R&R Bk N - v19 - i3 - August 2004 - p159(1) [51-500]

Axisa, Francois - *Discrete Systems*
SciTech - v28 - i3 - Sept 2004 - p137(1) [51-500]

Axonowitz, Stanley - *How Class Works: Power and Social Movement*
Soc Ser R - v78 - i3 - Sept 2004 - p514(3) [501+]

Axtell, Roger E. - *Gestures: The Do's and Taboos of Body Language Around the World*
HR Mag - v49 - i7 - July 2004 - pS11(1) [51-500]

Axtmann, Ronald - *Understanding Democratic Politics: An Introduction*
AJPS - v39 - i3 - Nov 2004 - p675(3) [501+]

Axworthy, Lloyd - *Navigating a New World: Canada's Global Future*
CBRA - Annual 2003 - p301(1) [501+]
Globe & Mail - Sept 4 2004 - pD18 [1-50]
HNet - July 2004 - pNA [501+]

Ayala, Cesar J. - *American Sugar Kingdom: The Plantation Economy of the Spanish Carribbean, 1898-1934*
HAHR - v84 - i3 - August 2004 - p542(2) [501+]

Ayanoglu, Byron - *Crete on the Half Shell*
CBRA - Annual 2003 - p34(1) [51-500]

Ayers, Brenda - *The Emperor's Old Groove: Decolonizing Disney's Magic Kingdom*
JPC - v38 - i1 - August 2004 - p227(3) [501+]

Ayers, David J. - *Investigating Social Problems: Using MicroCase ExplorIt*
R&R Bk N - v19 - i4 - Nov 2004 - p121(1) [51-500]

Ayers, Edward L. - *American Passages: A History of the United States, compact 2nd Ed.*
R&R Bk N - v19 - i3 - August 2004 - p64(1) [51-500]
In the Presence of Mine Enemies: War in the Heart of America, 1859-1863
J Mil H - v68 - i3 - April 2004 - p603-604 [501+]
JAH - v91 - i2 - Sept 2004 - p600(3) [501+]
JSH - v70 - i4 - Nov 2004 - p925(3) [501+]
y Kliatt - v39 - i2 - March 2005 - p38(1) [51-500]
RAH - v32 - i3 - Sept 2004 - p388-391 [501+]
Sew R - v112 - i1 - Wntr 2004 - p138-147 [501+]

Ayers, James B. - *Supply Chain Project Management: A Structured Collaborative and Measurable Approach*
R&R Bk N - v19 - i1 - Feb 2004 - p89(1) [1-50]

Ayers, John E. - *Digital Integrated Circuits: Analysis and Design*
Choice - v42 - i1 - Sept 2004 - p135(1) [501+]

Ayers, Rick - *Great Books for High School Kids: A Teacher's Guide to Books That Can Change Teens' Lives*
Kliatt - v38 - i4 - July 2004 - p35(1) [51-500]
y VOYA - v27 - i3 - August 2004 - p248(1) [1-50]

Ayers, Robert Curtis - *Baroness of the Ripetta: Letters of Augusta von Eichthal to Franz Xaver Kraus*
Theol St - v66 - i1 - March 2005 - p226(1) [501+]

Ayers, Wiliam - *Teaching the Personal and the Political: Essays and Hope and Justice*
TCR - v106 - i12 - Dec 2004 - p2349(2) [501+]

Ayers, William - *Teaching toward Freedom: Moral Commitment and Ethical Action in the Classroom*
BL - v101 - i1 - Sept 1 2004 - p25(1) [51-500]
LJ - v129 - i13 - August 2004 - p92(1) [501+]

Ayes, Linda - *Read It Again! Standards-Based Literature Lessons for Young Children*
LibMed - v22 - i5 - Feb 2004 - p82(1) [501+]

Ayittey, George - *Africa Unchained: The Blueprint for Africa's Future*
LJ - v130 - i3 - Feb 15 2005 - p146(2) [51-500]

Aykin, Nuray - *Usability and Internationalization of Information Technology*
SciTech - v28 - i3 - Sept 2004 - p33(1) [51-500]

Aykroyd, Clarissa - *Egypt*
y LibMed - v22 - i4 - Jan 2004 - p74(1) [501+]
Refugees
y SLJ - v50 - i11 - Nov 2004 - p158(1) [51-500]

Aylos, Angela - *Trust and Western-Russian Business Relationships*
R&R Bk N - v19 - i3 - August 2004 - p126(1) [51-500]

Aylward, Bruce - *Nature Tourism, Conservation, and Development in KwaZulu-Natal, South Africa*
JEL - v41 - i4 - Dec 2003 - p1393(1) [501+]

Aylward, Glen P. - *Practitioners' Guide to Behavioral Problems in Children*
R&R Bk N - v19 - i1 - Feb 2004 - p129(1) [51-500]

Ayres, Ian - *Pervasive Prejudice? Unconventional Evidence of Race and Gender Discrimination*
JEL - v41 - i4 - March 2004 - p278(1) [501+]

Ayres, Philip - *Owen Dixon*
Law Q Rev - v121 - Jan 2005 - p154-158 [501+]

Ayres, Robert U. - *Life Cycle of Copper, Its Co-Products and Byproducts*
SciTech - v28 - i1 - March 2004 - p143(1) [51-500]

Ayto, John - *Oxford Dictionary of Slang*
R&R Bk N - v19 - i1 - Feb 2004 - p217(1) [51-500]

Azeiteiro, Ulisses - *World Trends in Environmental Education*
SciTech - v28 - i3 - Sept 2004 - p5(1) [501+]

Azevedo, Mario - *Historical Dictionary of Mozambique, 2nd Ed.*
R&R Bk N - v19 - i1 - Feb 2004 - p51(1) [501+]

Azfar, Omar - *Market-Augmenting Government: The Institutional Foundations for Prosperity*
JEL - v42 - i4 - Dec 2004 - p1138(2) [501+]

Azicri, Max - *Cuba Today and Tomorrow: Reinventing Socialism*
S&S - v68 - i2 - Summer 2004 - p246-249 [501+]

Azimi, Ali - *Afghanistan's Environment in Transition*
R&R Bk N - v19 - i1 - Feb 2004 - p46(1) [1-50]

Azizollahoff, J.R. - *Oriental Rugs from A to Z*
R&R Bk N - v19 - i4 - Nov 2004 - p209(1) [501+]

Aznar, Jose Maria - *Ocho Anos de Gobierno: Una vision personal de Espana*
TLS - i5289 - August 13 2004 - p7(1) [501+]

Azra, Azyumardi - *The Origins of Islamic Reformism in Southeast Asia: Networks of Malay-Indonesian and Middle Eastern 'Ulama' in the Seventeenth and Eighteenth Centuries*
R&R Bk N - v19 - i3 - August 2004 - p17(1) [1-50]

Azuma, Kiyohiko - *Azumanga Daioh, Vol. 4.*
LJ - v129 - i14 - Sept 1 2004 - p128(1) [51-500]
y VOYA - v27 - i4 - Oct 2004 - p289(1) [51-500]

Azzarello, Brian - *100 Bullets: Samurai (Illus. by Risso, Eduardo)*
BL - v101 - i3 - Oct 1 2004 - p319(1) [51-500]
BW - v34 - i37 - Sept 12 2004 - p13(1) [501+]
Broken City (Illus. by Risso, Eduardo)
BL - v101 - i1 - Sept 1 2004 - p76(1) [501+]
Highwater
BL - v101 - i3 - Oct 1 2004 - p319(1) [501+]

Azzopardi, Trezza - *Remember Me (Read by James, Corrie). Audiobook Review*
y Kliatt - v38 - i4 - July 2004 - p55(1) [51-500]
Remember Me
TLS - i5265 - Feb 27 2004 - p23-23 [501+]
WLT - v78 - i3-4 - Sept-Dec 2004 - p91(1) [501+]
Wom R Bks - v22 - i1 - Oct 2004 - p16(1) [501+]

B

Bailey, Jonathan B.A. - *Field Artillery and Firepower*
J Mil H - v68 - i3 - July 2004 - p1017-1018 [501+]

Bailey, Kim - *The North Beach Diet*
c PW - v252 - i1 - Jan 3 2005 - p52(1) [51-500]

Bailey, Larry P. - *Miller GAAP Guide 2004: A Comprehensive Restatement Standards for Auditing, Attestation, Compilation, and Review*
R&R Bk N - v19 - i1 - Feb 2004 - p112(1) [51-500]
Miller Governmental GAAP Guide for State and Local Governments 2004
R&R Bk N - v19 - i2 - May 2004 - p124 [51-500]
Miller Governmental GAAP Practice Manual 2004: A Guide to GASB 34
R&R Bk N - v19 - i2 - May 2004 - p118 [51-500]

Bailey, Len - *Clabbernappers*
c BL - v101 - i9-10 - Jan 1 2005 - p856(1) [1-50]
c PW - v252 - i10 - March 7 2005 - p68(1) [51-500]

Bailey, Linda - *Adventures in Ancient China (Illus. by Slavin, Bill)*
c CBRA - Annual 2003 - p531(1) [51-500]
Adventures in the Ice Age (Illus. by Slavin, Bill)
c BL - v101 - i5 - Nov 1 2004 - p477(1) [51-500]
Best Figure Skater in the Whole Wide World (Illus. by Daniel, Alan)
c CBRA - Annual 2003 - p446(2) [51-500]
Stanley's Party (Illus. by Slavin, Bill)
c CBRA - Annual 2003 - p447(1) [51-500]

Bailey, Mark (b. 1960 -) - *The English Manor c. 1200-1500*
Med R - June 2004 - pNA [501+]

Bailey, Mark Warren - *Guardians of the Moral Order: The Legal Philosophy of the Supreme Court, 1860-1910*
Choice - v41 - i11-12 - July-August 2004 - p2104(1) [501+]
HNet - August 2004 - pNA [501+]
Law&PolBR - August 2004 - p634(5) [501+]

Bailey, Martin Neil - *Transforming the European Economy*
Choice - v42 - i6 - Feb 2005 - p1068(1) [51-500]

Bailey, Mary Bryant - *Jeoffry's Halloween*
c LibMed - v22 - i6 - March 2004 - p59(1) [501+]

Bailey, Michael (b. 1943 -) - *Oriental Glazes*
Ceram Mo - v53 - i2 - Feb 2005 - p66(1) [501+]

Bailey, Michael D. - *Battling Demons: Witchcraft, Heresy, and Reform in the Late Middle Ages*
CH - v73 - i3 - Sept 2004 - p691(2) [501+]
JR - v84 - i3 - July 2004 - p503(3) [501+]
Six Ct J - v35 - i1 - Spring 2004 - p274(2) [501+]
Specu - v79 - i3 - July 2004 - p736-738 [501+]
Historical Dictionary of Witchcraft
Choice - v41 - i11-12 - July-August 2004 - p2014(1) [501+]

Bailey, Michael R. - *Robert Stephenson--The Eminent Engineer*
Choice - v41 - i11-12 - July-August 2004 - p2066(1) [501+]
SciTech - v28 - i1 - March 2004 - p136(1) [51-500]
T&C - v45 - i3 - July 2004 - p650-652 [501+]

Bailey, R.A. - *Association Schemes: Designed Experiments, Algebra and Combinations*
Choice - v42 - i5 - Jan 2005 - p888(1) [501+]

Bailey, Randall C. - *Yet With a Steady Beat: Contemporary U.S. Afrocentric Biblical Interpretation*
R&R Bk N - v19 - i1 - Feb 2004 - p18(1) [51-500]

Bailey, Richard A. - *The Salvation of Souls: Nine Previously Unpublished Sermons on the Call of Ministry and the Gospel by Jonathan Edwards*
Intpr - v59 - i1 - Jan 2005 - p97(2) [501+]

Bailey, Robert C. - *Bioassessment of Freshwater Ecosystems: Using the Reference Condition Approach*
SciTech - v28 - i1 - March 2004 - p64(1) [51-500]

Bailey, Robin Wayne - *Dragonkin*
y VOYA - v27 - i3 - August 2004 - p227(1) [1-50]

Bailey, Roz - *Retail Therapy*
BL - v101 - i2 - Sept 15 2004 - p218(1) [51-500]

Bailey, Suzanne - *A Brush with Grandeur: Philip Alexius de Laszlo*
Choice - v42 - i5 - Jan 2005 - p843(1) [1-50]

Bailey, Thomas R. - *Working Knowledge: Work-Based Learning and Education Reform*
TCR - v106 - i5 - May 2004 - p979(4) [501+]

Bailin, David - *Cosmology in Gauge Field Theory and String Theory*
SciTech - v28 - i4 - Dec 2004 - p45(1) [51-500]

Bailin, Jordanna - *The Culture of Property: The Crisis of Liberalism in Modern Britian*
Choice - v42 - i6 - Feb 2005 - p1085(1) [51-500]

Baillie-de Byl, Penny - *Programming Believable Characters For Computer Games*
Bwatch - March 2005 - pNA [501+]
SciTech - v28 - i3 - Sept 2004 - p27(1) [51-500]

Baillie, Marilyn - *Amazing Things Animals Do (Illus. by Caron, Romi)*
c CBRA - Annual 2003 - p562(2) [51-500]

Baillie, Robert - *Boulevard Raspail*
Can Lit - i182 - Autumn 2004 - p144(2) [501+]

Bailo, Ben M. - *Fools in the Field*
Storyworks - v12 - i4 - Jan 2005 - p7(1) [51-500]

Baily, Jean - *Hymn for Brass: pour quintette de cuivres*
Notes - v61 - i3 - March 2005 - p870(5) [501+]

Bailyn, Bernard - *To Begin the World Anew: The Genius and Ambiguities of the American Founders*
NEQ - v77 - i2 - June 2004 - p325-327 [501+]
Sew R - v112 - i1 - Wntr 2004 - pXXVII-XXXI [501+]
W&M Q - v61 - i3 - July 2004 - p573-577 [501+]

Baiman, Ron - *Political Economy and Contemporary Capitalism: Radical Perspectives on Economic Theory and Policy*
S&S - v68 - i4 - Winter 2004 - p499-3 [501+]

Baimbridge, Mark - *Economic and Monetary Union in Europe: Theory, Evidence, and Practice*
JEL - v42 - i1 - March 2004 - p264(1) [501+]
R&R Bk N - v19 - i1 - Feb 2004 - p115(1) [1-50]

Bain, Barbara J. - *A Beginner's Guide to Blood Cells, 2nd Ed.*
SciTech - v28 - i4 - Dec 2004 - p87(1) [51-500]

Bain, David Haward - *The Old Iron Road: An Epic of Rails, Roads, and the Urge to Go West*
NYTBR - July 4 2004 - p6 [501+]

Bain, Donald - *Murder, She Wrote: A Vote for Murder*
PW - v251 - i39 - Sept 27 2004 - p41(1) [501+]

Bain, Ken - *Rethinking Childhood*
TCR - v107 - i2 - Feb 2005 - p281(4) [501+]
What the Best College Teachers Do
Am Bio T - v66 - i8 - Oct 2004 - p578(2) [501+]
CC - v122 - i4 - Feb 22 2005 - p51(2) [501+]
Wil Q - v29 - i1 - Wntr 2005 - p118(2) [501+]

Bain, Terry - *You Are a Dog*
y SLJ - v51 - i1 - Jan 2005 - p158(1) [51-500]

Bainbridge, Beryl - *The Birthday Boys (Read by Griffin, Gordon). Audiobook Review*
y Kliatt - v39 - i1 - Jan 2005 - p38(1) [51-500]

Bainbridge, Simon - *British Poetry and the Revolutionary and Napoleonic Wars*
TLS - i5265 - Feb 27 2004 - p31-31 [501+]

Bainbridge, William Sims - *Berkshire Encyclopedia of Human-Computer Interaction, Vols. 1-2*
BL - v101 - i9-10 - Jan 1 2005 - p888(2) [501+]
Choice - v42 - i6 - Feb 2005 - p996(1) [51-500]
LJ - v130 - i1 - Jan 1 2005 - p150(1) [51-500]
SciTech - v28 - i4 - Dec 2004 - p29(1) [51-500]
The Endtime Family: Children of God
CS - v33 - i1 - Jan 2004 - p54-55 [501+]

Baines, Lyndsay S. - *Struggle for Life: A Psychological Perspective of Kidney Disease and Transplantation*
SciTech - v28 - i1 - March 2004 - p107(1) [51-500]

Bainey, Kenneth R. - *Integrated IT Project Management: A Model-Centric Approach*
SciTech - v28 - i3 - Sept 2004 - p135(1) [51-500]

Bainham, Andrew - *Children and Their Families: Contact, Rights, and Welfare*
R&R Bk N - v19 - i1 - Feb 2004 - p130(1) [51-500]

Bains, William - *Biotechnology from A to Z*
Choice - v42 - i1 - Sept 2004 - p68(1) [501+]
QRB - v79 - i3 - Sept 2004 - p307(2) [501+]

Bainum, Peter M. - *Space Activities and Cooperation Contributing to all Pacific Basin Countries: Proceedings*
SciTech - v28 - i4 - Dec 2004 - p161(1) [51-500]

Bair, Deirdre - *Jung: A Biography*
NYTBR - Jan 23 2005 - p28 [501+]
CR - v285 - i1662 - July 2004 - p61(1) [51-500]

Baird, Alison - *The Empire of the Stars: The Dragon Throne, Book II*
PW - v251 - i42 - Oct 18 2004 - p52(1) [501+]

Baird, Brian J. - *Library Collection Assessment through Statistical Sampling*
LJ - v130 - i1 - Jan 1 2005 - p160(1) [51-500]

Baird, David M. - *Lighthouses of Atlantic Canada: A Pictorial Travel Guide*
CBRA - Annual 2003 - p111(1) [51-500]

Baird, Davis - *Thing Knowledge: A Philosophy of Scientific Instruments*
Choice - v42 - i1 - Sept 2004 - p123(1) [501+]

Baird, Donal M. - *Under Tow: A History of Tugs and Towing*
Can Hist R - v85 - i4 - Dec 2004 - p881(2) [501+]
CBRA - Annual 2003 - p437(2) [51-500]

Baird, Elizabeth - *Complete "Canadian Living" Cookbook: 350 Inspired Recipes from Elizabeth Baird and the Kitchen Canadians Trust Most*
CBRA - Annual 2003 - p125(2) [501+]

Baird, Rosemary - *Mistress Of the House*
HT - v54 - i11 - Nov 2004 - p86(4) [501+]

Baird, William - *History of New Testament Research, Vol. 2*
TT - v61 - i2 - July 2004 - p228(2) [501+]

Bajalinov, Erik B. - *Linear-Fractional Programming: Theory, Methods, Applications, and Software*
SciTech - v28 - i1 - March 2004 - p134(1) [51-500]

Bajorath, Jurgen - *Chemoinformatics: Concepts, Methods, and Tools for Drug Discovery*
SciTech - v28 - i3 - Sept 2004 - p125(1) [51-500]

Bak, Richard - *Henry and Edsel: The Creation of the Ford Empire*
Choice - v41 - i7 - March 2004 - p1337(2) [501+]

Bakalar, Nicholas - *Where the Germs Are: A Scientific Safari*
SciTech - v28 - i1 - March 2004 - p75(1) [51-500]

Bakan, Joel - *The Corporation: The Pathological Pursuit of Profit and Power*
Har Bus R - v82 - i3 - March 2004 - pNA [501+]
R&R Bk N - v19 - i3 - August 2004 - p113(1) [51-500]

Baken, Robert-Jan - *Plotting, Squatting, Public Purpose, and Politics: Land Market Development, Low Income Housing, and Public Intervention in India*
R&R Bk N - v19 - i1 - Feb 2004 - p102(1) [51-500]

Baker, Alan R.H. - *Geography and History: Bridging the Divide*
Choice - v41 - i11-12 - July-August 2004 - p2097(1) [501+]
JouAmCul - v27 - i3 - Sept 2004 - p340(1) [501+]

Baker, Alisa J. - *The Stock Options Book. 6th Ed.*
HR Mag - v49 - i7 - July 2004 - pS8(1) [51-500]

Baker, Andrew R. - *Snort 2.1: Intrusion Detection, 2nd Ed.*
SciTech - v28 - i3 - Sept 2004 - p33(1) [51-500]

Baker, Barbara - *Digby and Kate 1, 2, 3 (Illus. by Winborn, Marsha)*
c BL - v101 - i1 - Sept 1 2004 - p128(1) [1-50]
c SLJ - v50 - i8 - August 2004 - p82(1) [51-500]

Baker, Brenda - *The Maleness of God*
Can Lit - i182 - Autumn 2004 - p92(2) [501+]

Baker, Catherine - *Behavioral Genetics: An Introduction to How Genes and Environments Interact through Development to Shape Differences in Mood, Personality, and Intelligence*
y SB - v40 - i6 - Nov-Dec 2004 - p260(1) [51-500]

Baker, Christopher - *Absolutism and the Scientific Revolution, 1600-1720: A Biographical Dictionary*
Six Ct J - v34 - i4 - Winter 2003 - p1187-1188 [501+]

Baker, Christopher P. - *Cuba Classics: A Celebration of Vintage American Automobiles*
BL - v101 - i7 - Dec 1 2004 - p629(1) [51-500]

Baker, Christopher W. - *Robots among Us*
c RT - v57 - Oct 2003 - p177 [1-50]

Baker, David B. - *Thick Description and the Fine Texture: Studies in the History of Psychology*
Choice - v41 - i11-12 - July-August 2004 - p2128(1) [501+]

Baker, David J. - *British Identities and English Renaissance Literature*
Six Ct J - v34 - i4 - Winter 2003 - p1157-1158 [501+]

Baker, Deirdre - *A Guide to Canadian Children's Books in English (Illus. by Denton, Kady MacDonald)*
Can CL - i113/114 - Spring-Summer 2004 - p121(9) [501+]
CBRA - Annual 2003 - p9(2) [51-500]

Baker, Donna L. - *How to Use Adobe After Effects 5.0 and 5.5*
SciTech - v28 - i1 - March 2004 - p175(1) [51-500]

Baker, Dorothy - *Cassandra at the Wedding*
Globe & Mail - Nov 13 2004 - pD21 [51-500]

Baker, E.D. - *The Frog Princess*
c PW - v251 - i45 - Nov 8 2004 - p58(1) [51-500]
Once upon a Curse
c CCB-B - v58 - i5 - Jan 2005 - p198(1) [51-500]
c SLJ - v51 - i1 - Jan 2005 - p122(1) [51-500]

Baker, Frank B. - *Item Response Theory: Parameter Estimation Techniques, 2nd Ed.*
R&R Bk N - v19 - i4 - Nov 2004 - p9(1) [51-500]

Baker, Ian - *The Heart of the World: A Journey to the Last Secret Place*
Globe & Mail - Dec 18 2004 - pT8 [501+]
PW - v251 - i42 - Oct 18 2004 - p57(2) [51-500]
Wil Q - v29 - i1 - Wntr 2005 - p121(1) [501+]

Baker, James C. - *Financing International Trade*
R&R Bk N - v19 - i1 - Feb 2004 - p116(1) [51-500]

Baker, Jean H. - *James Buchanan*
For Aff - v83 - i5 - Sept-Oct 2004 - p164 [501+]

Baker, Jeannie - *Belonging*
c   Sch Lib - v52 - i4 - Winter 2004 - p192(1) [51-500]
Home
c   HB - v81 - i1 - Jan-Feb 2005 - p12(1) [51-500]

Baker, John - *The Oxford History of the Laws of England, Vol. 6*
Law Q Rev - v120 - July 2004 - p519-522 [501+]

Baker, Kage - *The Life of the World to Come*
BL - v101 - i7 - Dec 1 2004 - p642(1) [51-500]
KR - v72 - i20 - Oct 15 2004 - p988(2) [51-500]
PW - v251 - i47 - Nov 22 2004 - p42(1) [51-500]
LJ - v129 - i19 - Nov 15 2004 - p55(1) [501+]
Mother Aegypt and Other Stories
BL - v100 - i21 - July 2004 - p1827(2) [51-500]
BW - v34 - i46 - Nov 14 2004 - p13(1) [1-50]
LJ - v129 - i12 - July 2004 - p76(1) [51-500]

Baker, Keith - *Lucky Days with Mr. and Mrs. Green*
c   KR - v73 - i3 - Feb 1 2005 - p173(1) [51-500]
c   PW - v252 - i6 - Feb 7 2005 - p61(2) [501+]

Baker, Kyle - *Plastic Man: On the Lam*
y   BL - v101 - i2 - Sept 15 2004 - p217(1) [51-500]
PW - v251 - i33 - August 16 2004 - p45(1) [51-500]

Baker, Lawrence W. - *U.S. Immigration and Migration Reference Library Cumulative Index*
y   Ref Rev - Oct 2004 - pNA [501+]
R&R Bk N - v19 - i3 - August 2004 - p185(1) [501+]

Baker, Lillian - *Plastic Jewelry of the 20th Century*
Ant&CM - v108 - i6 - August 2003 - p16(1) [501+]

Baker, Linda J. - *Asperger's Syndrome: Intervening in Schools, Clinics, and Communities*
SciTech - v28 - i4 - Dec 2004 - p113(1) [1-50]

Baker, Murray - *The Debt-Free Graduate: How to Survive College or University Without Going Broke*
Globe & Mail - Sept 4 2004 - pF6 [1-50]

Baker, Nicholson - *Checkpoint*
BL - v101 - i1 - Sept 1 2004 - p3(2) [51-500]
BW - v34 - i32 - August 8 2004 - p13(1) [501+]
Ent W - i778 - August 13 2004 - p91 [51-500]
Globe & Mail - July 3 2004 - pR12 [51-500]
Globe & Mail - August 7 2004 - pD9 [501+]
KR - v72 - i16 - August 15 2004 - p756(1) [501+]
NYRB - v51 - i17 - Nov 4 2004 - p30(1) [501+]
NYTBR - August 8 2004 - p12 [501+]
TLS - i5297 - Oct 8 2004 - p22(1) [501+]

Baker, Nigel - *Urban Growth and the Medieval Church: Gloucester and Worcester*
Choice - v42 - i4 - Dec 2004 - p725(2) [1-50]
R&R Bk N - v19 - i3 - August 2004 - p21(1) [1-50]

Baker, Patricia L. - *Islam and the Religious Art*
Choice - v42 - i3 - Nov 2004 - p470(1) [1-50]

Baker, Peter S. - *The Anglo-Saxon Chronicle, A Collaborative Edition, Vol. 8*
JEGP - v103 - i3 - July 2004 - p369-380 [501+]

Baker, Raymond William - *Islam Without Fear: Egypt and the New Islamists*
JPR - v41 - i6 - Nov 2004 - p756-757 [501+]
PSQ - v119 - i4 - Winter 2004 - p689(2) [501+]
TimHES - v0 - i1652 - August 6 2004 - p26(2) [501+]

Baker, Roberta - *Lizard Walinsky*
c   CH Bwatch - v14 - i7 - July 2004 - p4(1) [51-500]

Baker, Roger C. - *Introductory Guide to Flow Measurement*
SciTech - v28 - i1 - March 2004 - p138(1) [1-50]

Baker, Ronald J. - *Professional's Guide to Value Pricing, 4th Ed.*
R&R Bk N - v19 - i1 - Feb 2004 - p109(1) [51-500]
Professional's Guide to Value Pricing, 5th Ed.
R&R Bk N - v19 - i2 - May 2004 - p115(1) [51-500]

Baker, Sarah H. - *The Long Way Home*
LJ - v130 - i1 - Jan 1 2005 - p92(1) [51-500]

Baker, Susan P. - *Death of a Prince*
KR - v73 - i4 - Feb 15 2005 - p198(1) [51-500]

Baker, T. Lindsay - *More Ghost Towns of Texas*
WHQ - v35 - i3 - Autumn 2004 - p397(2) [501+]

Baker, Thomas Woodward - *Doubts About Darwin: A History of Intelligent Design*
Ch Today - v48 - i9 - Sept 2004 - p89(3) [501+]

Baker, Wendy - *Healing Power of Horses: Lessons from the Lakota Indians (Illus. by Vinitsky, Hope)*
Roundup M - v12 - i1 - Oct 2004 - p20(1) [51-500]

Baker, William - *Nineteenth-Century Travels, Explorations and Empires: Writings from the Era of Imperial Consolidation 1835-1910, Vols. 5-8*
R&R Bk N - v19 - i4 - Nov 2004 - p73(1) [51-500]
Redefining the Modern: Essays on Literature and Society in Honor of Joseph Wiesenfarth
Choice - v41 - i11-12 - July-August 2004 - p2046(2) [501+]

Baker's Biographical Dictionary of Popular Musicians since 1990, vols. 1-2
R&R Bk N - v19 - i1 - Feb 2004 - p194(1) [51-500]

Bakewell, Geoffrey W. - *Gestures: Essays in Ancient History, Literature, and Philosophy Presented to Alan L. Boegehold on the Occasion of His Retirement and His Seventy-Fifth Birthday*
R&R Bk N - v19 - i1 - Feb 2004 - p214 [501+]

Bakich, Michael E. - *The Cambridge Encyclopedia of Amateur Astronomy*
LibMed - v22 - i6 - March 2004 - p84(1) [501+]

Bakis, Charles E. - *Composite Materials: Testing and Design, Vol. 14*
SciTech - v28 - i1 - March 2004 - p140(1) [51-500]

Bakke, Dennis W. - *Joy at Work: A Revolutionary Approach to Fun on the Job*
PW - v252 - i10 - March 7 2005 - p64(1) [51-500]

Bakker, Age F.P. - *Capital Liberalization in Transition Countries: Lessons from the Past and for the Future*
JEL - v42 - i1 - March 2004 - p325(1) [501+]

Bakker, R. Scott - *The Darkness That Comes Before*
PW - v251 - i49 - Dec 6 2004 - p32(2) [51-500]
The Warrior-Prophet
PW - v251 - i49 - Dec 6 2004 - p48(1) [501+]

Bakopoulos, Dean - *Please Don't Come Back from the Moon*
BL - v101 - i6 - Nov 15 2004 - p551(1) [51-500]
CH Bwatch - Feb 2005 - pNA [51-500]
KR - v72 - i21 - Nov 1 2004 - p1019(1) [501+]
LJ - v129 - i19 - Nov 15 2004 - p49(1) [51-500]
NYTBR - Feb 13 2005 - p11 [501+]
People - v63 - i8 - Feb 28 2005 - p60 [501+]
PW - v251 - i46 - Nov 15 2004 - p37(1) [51-500]
Econ - v374 - i8413 - Feb 12 2005 - p83US [501+]
Ent W - i806 - Feb 11 2005 - p69 [51-500]

Bakore, Amit - *Professional Apache Tomcat*
SciTech - v28 - i3 - Sept 2004 - p158(1) [51-500]

Baktes, Ivan - *Grandma Elephant's in Charge*
LibMed - v22 - i5 - Feb 2004 - p75(1) [501+]

Balachandran, U. - *Advances in Cryogenic Engineering. Proceedings, Vol. 50*
SciTech - v28 - i3 - Sept 2004 - p168(1) [51-500]

Balajthy, Ernest - *Struggling Readers: Assessment and Instruction in Grades K-6*
CE - v81 - i1 - Fall 2004 - p49(2) [501+]
SLJ - v50 - i10 - Oct 2004 - pS71(1) [51-500]
TCR - v106 - i8 - August 2004 - p1535(3) [501+]

Balakian, Peter - *The Burning Tigris: A History of the Armenian Genocide*
TimHES - v0 - i1652 - August 6 2004 - p24(2) [501+]
The Burning Tigris: The Armenian Genocide and America's Response
CR - v285 - i1666 - Nov 2004 - p314(1) [501+]
MEJ - v59 - i1 - Wntr 2005 - p132(9) [501+]
Nation - v279 - i8 - Sept 20 2004 - p39 [501+]
R&R Bk N - v19 - i1 - Feb 2004 - p45(1) [51-500]
TLS - i5294 - Sept 17 2004 - p13(1) [501+]

Balakrishnan, Gopal - *Debating Empire*
R&R Bk N - v19 - i3 - August 2004 - p171(1) [501+]

Balance, Alison - *South Sea Islands: A Natural History*
Am Sci - v92 - i4 - July-August 2004 - p375(1) [501+]
E-Streams - August 2004 - pNA [501+]

Balbas, Paulina - *Recombinant Gene Expression: Reviews and Protocols, 2nd Ed.*
SciTech - v28 - i4 - Dec 2004 - p62(1) [51-500]

Balcells, Jose Maria - *Ilimitada voz: Antologia de Poetas Espanolas, 1940-2002*
WLT - v78 - i3-4 - Sept-Dec 2004 - p142(1) [501+]

Balch, James F. - *Prescription for Natural Cures: A Self-Care Guide for Treating Health Problems with Natural Remedies, Including Diet and Nutrition, Nutritional Supplements, Bodywork, and More*
PW - v251 - i33 - August 16 2004 - p58(1) [51-500]

Baldacci, David - *Hour Game (Read by Brick, Scott). Audiobook Review*
BL - v101 - i9-10 - Jan 1 2005 - p884(1) [51-500]
PW - v251 - i49 - Dec 6 2004 - p19(1) [51-500]
Hour Game
BL - v101 - i1 - Sept 1 2004 - p4(1) [51-500]
Globe & Mail - Nov 13 2004 - pD18 [51-500]
KR - v72 - i16 - August 15 2004 - p756(1) [501+]
LJ - v129 - i17 - Oct 15 2004 - p52(1) [51-500]
PW - v251 - i38 - Sept 20 2004 - p46(1) [51-500]

Baldacci, Leslie - *Inside Mrs. B's Classroom: Courage, Hope and Learning on Chicago's South Side*
BooChiTr - Jan 25 2004 - p5(1) [501+]

Baldacci, Sharon - *A Sundog Moment*
BL - v101 - i1 - Sept 1 2004 - p55(1) [501+]

Balderston, Theo - *Economics and Politics in the Weimar Republic*
GSR - v27 - i2 - May 2004 - p399-400 [501+]
JEH - v64 - i1 - March 2004 - p251(2) [501+]
The World Economy and National Economies in the Interwar Slump
JEH - v64 - i1 - March 2004 - p285(3) [501+]
JEL - v41 - i4 - Dec 2003 - p1402(1) [501+]

Baldez, Lisa - *Why Women Protest: Women's Movements in Chile*
CS - v33 - i2 - March 2004 - p231-232 [501+]

Baldick, Chris - *The Modern Movement, 1910-1940*
LJ - v129 - i20 - Dec 1 2004 - p116(1) [501+]

Balding, Ian - *Making the Running: A Racing Memoir*
Spec - v295 - i9180 - July 17 2004 - p32(2) [501+]

Baldoli, Claudia - *Exporting Fascism: Italian Facists and Britain's Italians in the 1930's*
AHR - v109 - i2 - April 2004 - p604(1) [501+]

Baldoquin, Hilda Gutierrez - *Dharma, Color, and Culture: New Voices in Western Buddhism*
PW - v251 - i39 - Sept 27 2004 - p58(1) [51-500]

Baldridge, W. Scott - *Geology of the American Southwest: A Journey through Two Billion Years of Plate-Tectonic History*
Choice - v42 - i5 - Jan 2005 - p882(1) [1-50]
TimHES - v0 - i1682 - March 11 2005 - p29(1) [501+]

Baldriga, Irene - *L'occhio Della Lince: I Primi lincei tra arte, Scienza e Collezionismo*
Ren Q - v57 - i3 - Fall 2004 - p1104(4) [501+]

Baldry, Cherith - *The Abbey Mysteries: The Buried Cross*
c   Sch Lib - v52 - i3 - Autumn 2004 - p135(1) [501+]
The Lake of Darkness (Illus. by Wyatt, David)
c   SLJ - v50 - i7 - July 2004 - p66(1) [51-500]

Balducchi, David E. - *Labor Exchange Policy in the United States*
R&R Bk N - v19 - i4 - Nov 2004 - p103(1) [51-500]

Baldwin, Bruce A. - *The Financial Reporting Project and Readings, 4th Ed.*
R&R Bk N - v19 - i4 - Nov 2004 - p115(1) [51-500]

Baldwin, Carol - *Acids and Bases*
y   SLJ - v50 - i10 - Oct 2004 - p184(1) [51-500]
Chemical Reactions
y   SLJ - v50 - i10 - Oct 2004 - p184(1) [51-500]
Mixtures, Compounds and Solutions
y   SLJ - v50 - i10 - Oct 2004 - p184(1) [51-500]

Baldwin, Claire - *The Emergence of the Modern German Novel: Christoph Martin Wieland, Sophie von La Roche, and Maria Anna Sagar*
Ger Q - v77 - i1 - Wntr 2004 - p94(2) [501+]

Baldwin, Douglas (b. 1944 -) - *Confederation and the West*
c   CBRA - Annual 2003 - p532(2) [51-500]
Dawn of Canada
c   CBRA - Annual 2003 - p531(2) [51-500]
A Nation's First Steps
c   CBRA - Annual 2003 - p531(2) [51-500]
New France and the Fur Trade
c   CBRA - Annual 2003 - p531(2) [51-500]
Rebellion and Union in the Canada
c   CBRA - Annual 2003 - p531(2) [51-500]
Revolution, War, and the Loyalists
c   CBRA - Annual 2003 - p531(2) [51-500]

Baldwin, Douglas (b. 1958 -) - *Algorithms and Data Structures: The Science of Computing*
Choice - v42 - i4 - Dec 2004 - p696(1) [1-50]

Baldwin, Douglas (b. 1958-) - *Algorithms and Data Structures: The Science of Computing*
SciTech - v28 - i3 - Sept 2004 - p29(1) [51-500]

Baldwin, Evelyn Briggs - *The Franz Josef Land Archipelago: E.B. Baldwin's Journal of the Wellman Polar Expedition, 1898-1899*
R&R Bk N - v19 - i3 - August 2004 - p79(1) [51-500]

Baldwin, James - *Native Sons: A Friendship That Created One of the Greatest Works of the 20th Century: Notes of a Native Son*
BL - v100 - i21 - July 2004 - p1810(1) [1-50]
BW - v34 - i36 - Sept 5 2004 - p6(1) [501+]
Globe & Mail - August 14 2004 - pD12 [1-50]
TLS - i5298 - Oct 15 2004 - p25(1) [501+]

Baldwin, Jane - *Michel Saint-Denis and the Shaping of the Modern Actor*
R&R Bk N - v19 - i1 - Feb 2004 - p227(1) [51-500]

Baldwin, John R. - *Communication Theories for Everyday Life*
R&R Bk N - v19 - i1 - Feb 2004 - p210(1) [51-500]
Innovation and Knowledge Creation in an Open Economy: Canadian Industry and International Implications
JEL - v42 - i1 - March 2004 - p317(1) [501+]

Baldwin, Kate A. - *Beyond the Color Line and the Iron Curtain: Reading Encounters between Black and Red, 1922-1963*
MFSF - v50 - i2 - Summer 2004 - p479-481 [501+]

Baldwin, Peter - *Contagion and the State in Europe, 1830-1930*
JMH - v76 - i4 - Dec 2004 - p940(4) [501+]

Baldwin, Richard - *The Economics of European Integration*
TimHES - v0 - i1675 - Jan 21 2005 - p25(1) [501+]

Baldwin, Robert E. - *The Decline of US Labor Unions and the Role of Trade*
JEL - v41 - i4 - Dec 2003 - p1386(1) [501+]

Baldwin, Scott - *Product Liability Case Digest, 2004-2005 Ed.*
R&R Bk N - v19 - i3 - August 2004 - pNA [1-50]

Baldwin, Shauna Singh - *The Tiger Claw*
BIC - v33 - i9 - Dec 2004 - p10(1) [501+]
Globe & Mail - Oct 2 2004 - pD16 [501+]

Baldwin, Stanley - *Baldwin Papers*
Spec - v296 - i9189 - Sept 18 2004 - p46(2) [501+]

Baldwin, Thomas - *The Cambridge History of Philosophy, 1870-1945*
Choice - v42 - i1 - Sept 2004 - p114(1) [501+]

Baldwin, Virginia A. - *Online Ecological and Environmental Data*
SciTech - v28 - i4 - Dec 2004 - p6(1) [1-50]
Patent and Trademark Information: Uses and Perspectives
SciTech - v28 - i3 - Sept 2004 - p135(1) [51-500]

Bale, John - *Sport and Postcolonialism*
SSJ - v21 - i2 - June 2004 - p223-226 [501+]
Sports Geography
SSJ - v21 - i2 - June 2004 - p240-242 [501+]
Writing Lives in Sport: Biographies, Life-Histories and Methods
R&R Bk N - v19 - i4 - Nov 2004 - p81(1) [51-500]

Balen, Malcolm - *The Secret History of the South Sea Bubble: The World's First Great Financial Scandal*
R&R Bk N - v19 - i1 - Feb 2004 - p119(1) [51-500]

Balentine, Samuel E. - *Leviticus*
Intpr - v59 - i1 - Jan 2005 - p67(3) [501+]

Bales, Connie Watkins - *Handbook of Clinical Nutrition and Aging*
E-Streams - July 2004 - pNA [501+]

Balfour, Bruce - *Prometheus Road*
y   BL - v101 - i5 - Nov 1 2004 - p471(1) [501+]
ChrSFF&H - v26 - i10 - Oct 2004 - p27(2) [51-500]

Balfour, Michael - *Theatre in Prison: Theory and Practice*
R&R Bk N - v19 - i4 - Nov 2004 - p148(1) [501+]

Balfour, Sandy - *Nursing America: One Year Behind the Nursing Stations of an Inner-City Hospital*
KR - v72 - i23 - Dec 1 2004 - p1127(1) [501+]
LJ - v130 - i2 - Feb 1 2005 - p108(1) [51-500]
PW - v251 - i51 - Dec 20 2004 - p44(1) [51-500]

Balfour, Sebastian - *Deadly Embrace: Morocco and the Road to the Spanish Civil War*
JMH - v77 - i1 - March 2005 - p210(3) [501+]

Bali, Philip - *Critical Mass: How One Thing Leads to Another*
New Sci - v185 - i2486 - Feb 12 2005 - p49(1) [501+]

Balibar, Etienne - *We, the People of Europe? Reflections on Transnational Citizenship*
Choice - v42 - i1 - Sept 2004 - p184(1) [501+]

Baliga, Ragavendra R. - *Self-Assessment in Clinical Medicine, 3rd Ed.*
SciTech - v28 - i1 - March 2004 - p88(1) [51-500]

Balint, Anna - *Horse Thief*
LJ - v129 - i16 - Oct 1 2004 - p75(1) [51-500]

Balint, Christine - *Ophelia's Fan*
BL - v100 - i21 - July 2004 - p1815(1) [51-500]
PW - v251 - i31 - August 2 2004 - p53(1) [501+]

Balis, Christina V. - *Visions of America and Europe: September 11, Iraq, and Transatlantic Relations*
Choice - v42 - i1 - Sept 2004 - p186(1) [501+]
For Aff - v83 - i5 - Sept-Oct 2004 - p164 [501+]

Balistreri, Maggie - *The Evasion-English Dictionary*
SLJ - v50 - i10 - Oct 2004 - pS67(1) [501+]

Balius, Andreu - *Type at Work: The Use of Type in Editorial Design*
Choice - v41 - i11-12 - July-August 2004 - p2031(1) [501+]

Balkin, Karen - *Reality TV*
y   Choice - v50 - i7 - July 2004 - p116(1) [51-500]

Balkwill, Frances R. - *Amazing Schemes Within Your Genes (Illus. by Rolph, Mic)*
c   Am Bio T - v66 - i2 - Feb 2004 - p152(152) [501+]
Cell and Things Series
c   Am Bio T - v66 - i2 - Feb 2004 - p152(152) [501+]
Cells Are Us
Am Bio T - v66 - i2 - Feb 2004 - p152(152) [501+]
DNA Is Here to Stay (Illus. by Rolph, Mic)
c   Am Bio T - v66 - i2 - Feb 2004 - p152(152) [501+]

Ball, Alan M. - *Imagining America: Influence and Images in Twentieth-Century Russia*
Choice - v41 - i7 - March 2004 - p1351(1) [501+]
R&R Bk N - v19 - i1 - Feb 2004 - p38(1) [1-50]
Slav R - v63 - i4 - Winter 2004 - p893(2) [501+]

Ball, Billy - *Red Hat Linux Fedora 3 Unleashed*
Bwatch - March 2005 - pNA [51-500]

Ball, David - *Ironfire (Read by Guidall, George). Audiobook Review*
LJ - v130 - i3 - Feb 15 2005 - p168(1) [51-500]

Ball, Edward - *Peninsula of Lies: A True Story of Mysterious Birth and Taboo Love*
Spec - v296 - i9188 - Sept 11 2004 - p39(2) [501+]

Ball, Howard - *Murder in Mississippi: United States v. Price and the Struggle for Civil Rights*
Choice - v42 - i3 - Nov 2004 - p563(1) [1-50]
The U.S.A. Patriot Act of 2001: Balancing Civil Liberties and National Security: A Reference Handbook
y   Choice - v42 - i6 - Feb 2005 - p1096(1) [51-500]
c   SLJ - v51 - i2 - Feb 2005 - p82(1) [51-500]

Ball, Jacqueline - *Volcanoes*
c   SB - v40 - i4 - July-August 2004 - p174(1) [51-500]

Ball, John Clement - *Imagining London: Postcolonial Fiction and the Transnational Metropolis*
Choice - v42 - i5 - Jan 2005 - p849(2) [1-50]

Ball, Karen - *A Test of Faith*
PW - v251 - i33 - August 16 2004 - p43(1) [51-500]

Ball, Keith - *Strange Curves, Counting Rabbits, and Other Mathematical Explorations*
Math T - v98 - i2 - Sept 2004 - p144-144 [501+]
TimHES - v0 - i1682 - March 11 2005 - p26(1) [501+]

Ball, Margaret - *Disappearing Act*
Bwatch - Dec 2004 - pNA [51-500]

Ball, Philip - *Bright Earth: Art and the Invention of Color*
Isis - v95 - i3 - Sept 2004 - p468(2) [501+]
Critical Mass: How One Thing Leads to Another
JouAmCul - v27 - i4 - Dec 2004 - p438(2) [501+]
TimHES - v0 - i1652 - August 6 2004 - p23(1) [501+]
TLS - i5289 - August 13 2004 - p25(1) [501+]
The Ingredients: A Guided Tour of the Elements
Isis - v95 - i3 - Sept 2004 - p467(2) [501+]

Ball, Simon - *The Guardsmen: Harold Macmillan, Three Friends and the World They Made*
Lon R Bks - v26 - i19 - Oct 7 2004 - p13(2) [501+]
The Guardsmen: Harold Macmillan Three Friends and the World They Made
NS - v133 - i4716 - Nov 29 2004 - p49(1) [51-500]
The Guardsmen: Harold Macmillan, Three Friends and the World They Made
TimHES - v0 - i1657 - Sept 10 2004 - p32(1) [501+]
TLS - i5286 - July 23 2004 - p36(1) [501+]

Ball, Stuart - *Mass Conservatism: The Conservatives and the Public since the 1880s*
Albion - v36 - i2 - Summer 2004 - p342(2) [501+]
Winston Churchill
J Mil H - v68 - i3 - July 2004 - p993-994 [501+]

Ball, Terence - *Ideals and Ideologies: A Reader, 5th Ed.*
R&R Bk N - v19 - i1 - Feb 2004 - p147(1) [51-500]
Political Ideologies and the Democratic Ideal, 5th Ed.
R&R Bk N - v19 - i1 - Feb 2004 - p147(1) [51-500]

Ballaigue, Christopher De - *In the Rose Garden of the Martyrs: A Memoir of Iran*
PW - v252 - i1 - Jan 3 2005 - p50(1) [51-500]

Ballanger, Francoise - *Enquete sur le roman policier pour la jeunesse*
c   Bkbird - v42 - i3 - July 2004 - p47(1) [501+]

Ballantyne, Iain - *Assessment and Development Centres*
R&R Bk N - v19 - i3 - August 2004 - p129(1) [51-500]

Ballantyne, Tony - *Orientalism and Race: Aryanism in the British Empire*
JIH - v34 - i4 - Spring 2004 - p638-639 [501+]

Ballarati, Michele - *Italian Bed and Breakfasts: A Caffelletto Guide*
LJ - v130 - i1 - Jan 1 2005 - p136(2) [51-500]

Ballard, Carol - *The Digestive System: Injury, Illness and Health*
c   LibMed - v22 - i5 - Feb 2004 - p54(1) [501+]
Heart and Blood
c   LibMed - v22 - i5 - Feb 2004 - p54(1) [501+]

Ballard, Carole - *Exercise*
c   Sch Lib - v52 - i3 - Autumn 2004 - p149(1) [501+]

Ballard, Louis W. - *Native American Indian Songs*
Teach Mus - v12 - i4 - Feb 2005 - p81(1) [51-500]
Teach Mus - v12 - i4 - Feb 2005 - p81(1) [51-500]
Teach Mus - v12 - i4 - Feb 2005 - p81(1) [51-500]
Teach Mus - v12 - i4 - Feb 2005 - p81(1) [51-500]

Ballard, Michael B. - *Autumn of Glory: The Army of Tennessee: 1862-1865*
HNet - Sept 2004 - pNA [501+]
Vicksburg: The Campaign That Opened the Mississippi
LJ - v129 - i16 - Oct 1 2004 - p93(1) [51-500]

Ballard, Mignon F. - *Too Late for Angels: An Augusta Goodnight Mystery*
PW - v252 - i8 - Feb 21 2005 - p161(2) [501+]

Ballard, Robert D. - *Return to Titanic: A New Look at the World's Most Famous Lost Ship*
BL - v101 - i6 - Nov 15 2004 - p547(1) [51-500]
Globe & Mail - Dec 18 2004 - pD14 [1-50]
PW - v251 - i44 - Nov 1 2004 - p57(1) [501+]

Ballard, Sandra L. - *Listen Here: Women Writing in Appalachia*
Choice - v41 - i7 - March 2004 - p1297(1) [501+]

Ballenberghe, Victor Van - *In The Company Of Moose*
Bwatch - Jan 2005 - pNA [51-500]

Ballenger, Cynthia - *Regarding Children's Words: Teacher Research on Language and Literacy*
TCR - v106 - i8 - August 2004 - p1529(3) [501+]

Ballenger, James C. - *Anxiety, Anxiety*
SciTech - v28 - i1 - March 2004 - p101(1) [51-500]

Ballentine, Karen - *The Political Economy of Armed Conflict: Beyond Greed and Grievance*
PSQ - v119 - i3 - Fall 2004 - p545(3) [501+]

Ballentine, Mitsy - *Machine Transcription and Dictation, 5th Ed.*
R&R Bk N - v19 - i4 - Nov 2004 - p112(1) [1-50]

Ballew, Christopher Brent - *The Impact of African-American Antecedents on the Baptist Foreign Missionary Movement, 1782-1825*
R&R Bk N - v19 - i3 - August 2004 - p27(1) [1-50]

Ballew, Joli - *Degunking Windows*
LJ - v130 - i4 - March 1 2005 - p106(1) [501+]
Degunking Your Mac
Bwatch - v26 - i9 - Sept 2004 - p5(1) [501+]
LJ - v130 - i4 - March 1 2005 - p106(1) [501+]

Balliet, Gay L. - *Lions and Tigers and Mares...Oh My!*
y   BL - v101 - i2 - Sept 15 2004 - p187(1) [51-500]
Balliett, Blue - *Chasing Vermeer (Illus. by Helquist, Brett)*
y   BL - v101 - i5 - Nov 1 2004 - p496(1) [51-500]
c   BL - v101 - i6 - Nov 15 2004 - p599(1) [501+]
c   BL - v101 - i9-10 - Jan 1 2005 - p773(1) [51-500]
c   CCB-B - v57 - i11 - July-August 2004 - p453(2) [501+]
c   HB - v80 - i4 - July-August 2004 - p446(1) [51-500]
c   SLJ - v50 - i7 - July 2004 - p98(1) [51-500]
Chasing Vermeer
y   VOYA - v27 - i5 - Dec 2004 - p398(1) [51-500]
Balliett, Whitney - *Collected Works: A Journal of Jazz, 1954-2000*
Globe & Mail - July 3 2004 - pD15 [501+]
Balling, Jakob - *Story of Christianity: From Birth to Global Presence*
R&R Bk N - v19 - i1 - Feb 2004 - p16(1) [1-50]
Ballinger, Pamela - *History in Exile: Memory and Identity at the Borders of the Balkans*
JRAI - v10 - i3 - Sept 2004 - p705(2) [501+]
Ballof, Rolf - *Geschichte des Mittelalters für unsere Zeit*
GSR - v27 - i2 - May 2004 - p368-370 [501+]
Balmaceda, Margarita M. - *Independent Belarus: Domestic Determinants, Regional Dynamics, Implications for the West*
Russ Rev - v63 - i2 - April 2004 - pNA [501+]
Balmer, Josephine - *Chasing Catullus*
Quad - v49 - i1-2 - Jan-Feb 2005 - p122(3) [501+]
Balmond, Cecil - *Informal*
TLS - i5300 - Oct 29 2004 - p10-11 [501+]
Balog, James - *Tree: A New Vision of the American Forest*
LJ - v130 - i2 - Feb 1 2005 - p112(1) [51-500]
Balogh, Mary - *Simply Unforgettable*
LJ - v129 - i20 - Dec 1 2004 - p86(1) [51-500]
LJ - v130 - i1 - Jan 1 2005 - p90(1) [51-500]
PW - v252 - i8 - Feb 21 2005 - p156(2) [51-500]
Balona, Luis - *Magnetic Fields in O, B and A Stars: Origin and Connection to Pulsation, Rotation and Mass Loss*
SciTech - v28 - i1 - March 2004 - p45(1) [51-500]
Balot, R.K. - *Greed and Injustice in Classical Athens*
Class R - v54 - i2 - Nov 2004 - p461(5) [501+]
Balsam, Kimberly - *Trauma, Stress, and Resilience among Sexual Minority Women: Rising Like the Phoenix*
SciTech - v28 - i3 - Sept 2004 - p9(1) [501+]
Balsamo, Gian - *Rituals of Literature: Joyce, Dante, Aquins,and the Tradition of Christians Epics*
Choice - v42 - i4 - Dec 2004 - p658(1) [1-50]
Balter, Alison - *Sams Teach Yourself Microsoft Office Access 2003 in 24 Hours*
SciTech - v28 - i3 - Sept 2004 - p33(1) [51-500]
Balter, Michael - *The Goddess and the Bull*
KR - v72 - i21 - Nov 1 2004 - p1033(1) [501+]
New Sci - v185 - i2482 - Jan 15 2005 - p50(1) [501+]
Baltes, H. - *Enabling Technology for MEMS and Nanodevices*
SciTech - v28 - i4 - Dec 2004 - p49(1) [51-500]
Baltes, Sabine - *The Pamphlet Controversy About Wood's Halfpence, 1722-25 and the Tradition of Irish Constitutional Nationalism*
R&R Bk N - v19 - i1 - Feb 2004 - p115(1) [51-500]
Baltimore, Elizabeth Heger Boyle - *Female Genital Cutting: Cultural Conflict in the Global Community*
AJS - v110 - i3 - Nov 2004 - p816(3) [501+]
Balwin, Elizabeth - *Paying the Piper: Music in Pre-1642 Cheshire*
Six Ct J - v35 - i1 - Spring 2004 - p255(2) [501+]
Balz, Nina - *Zwischen Schock und Spiel: Narrative Moglichkeiten in der Kuzprosa Ljudmila Petrusevskajas*
Slav R - v63 - i3 - Fall 2004 - p686-687 [501+]
Balzer-Riley, Julia - *Communication in Nursing. 5th Ed.*
SciTech - v28 - i1 - March 2004 - p126(1) [1-50]
Balzo, Sandra - *Uncommon Grounds*
KR - v72 - i18 - Sept 15 2004 - p891(2) [51-500]
LJ - v129 - i18 - Nov 1 2004 - p58(1) [51-500]
PW - v251 - i42 - Oct 18 2004 - p51(1) [51-500]
Bambach, Charles - *Heidegger's Roots: Nietzsche, National Socialism, and the Greeks*
HNet - Nov 2004 - pNA [501+]
Bamber, Greg J. - *Globalisation, Company Strategies and the Quality of Working Life in Europe*
R&R Bk N - v19 - i3 - August 2004 - p117(1) [51-500]
International and Comparative Employment Relations: Globalisation and the Developed Market Economies
Choice - v42 - i2 - Oct 2004 - p336(1) [51-500]

Bamberger, Michael - *Wonderland: A Year in the Life of an American High School*
Atl - v294 - i1 - July-August 2004 - p147(4) [501+]
Bamfield, Peter - *Research and Development Management in the Chemical and Pharmaceutical Industry. 2nd Ed.*
SciTech - v28 - i1 - March 2004 - p121(1) [51-500]
Bamford, Christopher - *An Endless Trace: The Passionate Pursuit of Wisdom in the West*
Parabola - v29 - i3 - Fall 2004 - p112(3) [501+]
Bamford, James - *A Pretext for War: 9/11, Iraq, and the Abuse of America's Intelligence Agencies*
Choice - v42 - i4 - Dec 2004 - p731(1) [1-50]
NYRB - v51 - i14 - Sept 23 2004 - p40(4) [501+]
NYTBR - July 25 2004 - p22 [501+]
Bamforth, Iain - *The Body in the Library: A Literary Anthology of Modern Medicine*
R&R Bk N - v19 - i4 - Nov 2004 - p229(1) [501+]
The Body in the Library: A Literary History of Modern Medicine
Nature - v429 - i6992 - June 10 2004 - p607(1) [501+]
Banaji, Jairus - *Agrarian Change in Late Antiquity: Gold, Labor, and Aristocratic Dominance*
Class R - v53 - i2 - Nov 2003 - p442-444 [501+]
Banaszak, Lee Ann - *Women's Movements Facing the Reconfigured State*
CS - v33 - i5 - Sept 2004 - p580-582 [501+]
Bance, Peter - *The Duleep Singhs: The Photograph Album of Queen Victoria's Maharajah*
TLS - i5300 - Oct 29 2004 - p36(1) [501+]
Bancroft, John - *Sexual Development in Childhood*
Choice - v41 - i11-12 - July-August 2004 - p2128(1) [501+]
Soc Ser R - v78 - i4 - Dec 2004 - p693(4) [501+]
Bancroft, Randy - *Microstrip and Printed Antenna Design*
SciTech - v28 - i3 - Sept 2004 - p160(1) [51-500]
Bancroft, Tony - *Growing Your Musician: A Practical Guide for Band and Orchestra Parents*
M Ed J - v91 - i1 - Sept 2004 - p13(1) [51-500]
Bandeira, Luiz Alberto Moniz - *Brazil, Argentina e Estados Unidos: Da Triplice Alianca ao Mercosul, 1870-2003*
HAHR - v84 - i4 - Nov 2004 - p775(2) [501+]
Bandele, Asha - *Daughter (Read by Taylor, Myra Lucretia). Audiobook Review*
y   BL - v101 - i1 - Sept 1 2004 - p146(1) [1-50]
BW - v34 - i1 - Jan 4 2004 - p8(1) [501+]
The Prisoner's Wife (Read by Taylor, Myra Lucretia). Audiobook Review
BL - v101 - i5 - Nov 1 2004 - p505(1) [51-500]
Bandelow, Borwin - *Social Anxiety Disorder*
E-Streams - Nov 2004 - pNA [501+]
R&R Bk N - v19 - i3 - August 2004 - p9(1) [1-50]
Bando, Mark - *Vanguard of the Crusade: The 101st Airborne Division in World War II*
J Mil H - v68 - i2 - April 2004 - p638(2) [501+]
Bandow, Doug - *Wealth, Poverty, and Human Destiny*
R&R Bk N - v19 - i3 - August 2004 - p94(1) [51-500]
Bandrauk, Andre D. - *Quantum Control: Mathematical and Numerical Challenges*
SciTech - v28 - i1 - March 2004 - p50(1) [51-500]
Bandy, Joe - *Coalitions Across Borders:Transnational Protest and the Neoliberal Order*
R&R Bk N - v19 - i4 - Nov 2004 - p122(1) [51-500]
Bandy, Mary Lea - *The Hidden God: Film and Faith*
Choice - v42 - i1 - Sept 2004 - p108(1) [51-500]
Bandy, Wayne M. - *Innovation, Creativity, and Discovery in Modern Organizations*
Per Psy - v57 - i3 - Autumn 2004 - p832(4) [501+]
Bane, Mary Jo - *Taking Faith Seriously*
LJ - v130 - i4 - March 1 2005 - p93(2) [51-500]
Banerjee, Anjali - *Maya Running*
c   BL - v101 - i6 - Nov 15 2004 - p601(1) [51-500]
y   Kliatt - v39 - i1 - Jan 2005 - p6(1) [51-500]
y   KR - v73 - i2 - Jan 15 2005 - p116(1) [51-500]
y   SLJ - v51 - i1 - Jan 2005 - p122(1) [51-500]
Banerjee, Himadri - *The Other Sikhs: A View from Eastern India*
JAS - v63 - i2 - May 2004 - p526(2) [501+]
Banerjee, Indrajit - *Rhetoric and Reality: The Internet Challenge for Democracy in Asia*
Choice - v42 - i2 - Oct 2004 - p288(1) [501+]
Banerjee, Partha P. - *Nonlinear Optics: Theory, Numerical Modeling, and Applications*
SciTech - v28 - i1 - March 2004 - p49(1) [51-500]
Banes, Sally - *Reinventing Dance in the 1960s: Everything Was Possible*
Choice - v41 - i7 - March 2004 - p1308(1) [501+]

Bang, Mary Jo - *The Downstream Extremity of the Isle of Swans*
Sew R - v111 - i3 - Summer 2003 - p470-479 [501+]
The Eye Like a Strange Balloon
BL - v101 - i6 - Nov 15 2004 - p547(1) [51-500]
LJ - v130 - i1 - Jan 1 2005 - p116(2) [51-500]
PW - v251 - i42 - Oct 18 2004 - p61(1) [51-500]
Bang, Molly - *My Light*
y   LibMed - v23 - i1 - August-Sept 2004 - p79(1) [51-500]
Bangerth, Wolfgang - *Adaptive Finite Element Methods for Differential Equations*
SIAM Rev - v46 - i2 - June 2004 - p354-356 [501+]
Bango Torviso, Isidro Gonzalo - *Remembering Sepharad: Jewish Culture in Medieval Spain*
Choice - v42 - i3 - Nov 2004 - p554(1) [1-50]
Med R - Sept 2004 - pNA [501+]
R&R Bk N - v19 - i1 - Feb 2004 - p44(1) [51-500]
Bangs, Jeremy Dupertuis - *The Seventeenth-Century Town Records of Scituate, Massachusetts, Vols. 1-3*
NEQ - v77 - i2 - June 2004 - p327-330 [501+]
Bangs, Richard - *Mystery of the Nile: The Epic Story of the First Descent of the World's Deadliest River*
PW - v252 - i4 - Jan 24 2005 - p235(1) [501+]
Bangura, Abdul Karim - *Sweden vs. Apartheid: Putting Morality Ahead of Profit*
R&R Bk N - v19 - i4 - Nov 2004 - p90(1) [51-500]
Banham, Dale - *Germany 1918-1945: A Study in Depth*
y   TES - v0 - i4586 - June 4 2004 - psss14(2) [501+]
Banham, Debby - *Food and Drink in Anglo-Saxon England*
Choice - v42 - i3 - Nov 2004 - p504(1) [1-50]
Banham, Martin - *A History of Theatre in Africa*
Choice - v42 - i4 - Dec 2004 - p673(1) [1-50]
TimHES - v0 - i1655 - August 27 2004 - p28(1) [501+]
Banham, Tony - *Not the Slightest Chance: The Defence of Hong Kong, 1941*
J Mil H - v68 - i4 - Oct 2004 - p1285-1286 [501+]
Bania, Michael - *Kumak's Fish: A Tall Tale from the Far North (Illus. by Bania, Michael)*
c   BL - v100 - i22 - August 2004 - p1940(1) [51-500]
c   HB - v80 - i5 - Sept-Oct 2004 - p563(2) [51-500]
c   SLJ - v50 - i9 - Sept 2004 - p154(1) [51-500]
Banissi, E. - *Information Visualization IV 2004*
SciTech - v28 - i3 - Sept 2004 - p162(1) [51-500]
Banissi, Ebad - *Computer Graphics, Imaging and Visualization: Proceedings*
SciTech - v28 - i3 - Sept 2004 - p143(1) [51-500]
Information Visualization IV 2004
SciTech - v28 - i3 - Sept 2004 - p162(1) [51-500]
Banister, Jim - *Word of Mouse: The New Age of Networked Media*
BL - v101 - i1 - Sept 1 2004 - p25(1) [51-500]
KR - v72 - i14 - July 15 2004 - p667(1) [501+]
PW - v251 - i27 - July 5 2004 - p50(1) [51-500]
R&R Bk N - v19 - i3 - August 2004 - p144(1) [51-500]
Bank, Barbara J. - *Contradictions in Women's Education: Traditionalism, Careerism, and Community at a Single Sex College*
TCR - v106 - i2 - Feb 2004 - p271-274 [501+]
Bank, Melissa - *The Wonder Spot*
PW - v252 - i11 - March 14 2005 - p42(1) [51-500]
Bank, Zsuzsa - *The Swimmer*
BL - v101 - i7 - Dec 1 2004 - p634(1) [51-500]
KR - v72 - i24 - Dec 15 2004 - p1152(1) [501+]
LJ - v129 - i17 - Oct 15 2004 - p52(1) [51-500]
PW - v251 - i42 - Oct 18 2004 - p45(1) [51-500]
Banker, Ashok - *Prince of Ayodhya*
WLT - v78 - i3-4 - Sept-Dec 2004 - p87(1) [501+]
Banks, Cyndi - *Criminal Justice Ethics: Theory and Practice*
R&R Bk N - v19 - i3 - August 2004 - p167(1) [501+]
Banks, Dennis - *Ojibwa Warrior: Dennis Banks and the Rise of the American Indian Movement*
Choice - v42 - i6 - Feb 2005 - p1080(1) [51-500]
Roundup M - v12 - i1 - Oct 2004 - p20(1) [51-500]
Banks, Elizabeth L. - *Campaigns of curiosity: Journalistic Adventures of an American Girl in Late Victorian London*
R&R Bk N - v19 - i1 - Feb 2004 - p33(1) [1-50]
Banks, Erik - *Alternative Risk Transfer: Integrated Risk Management through Insurance, Reinsurance, and the Capital Markets*
R&R Bk N - v19 - i3 - August 2004 - p133(1) [51-500]

The Failure of Wall Street: How and Why Wall Street Fails--and What Can Be Done about It
　　BL - v101 - i1 - Sept 1 2004 - p31(1) [51-500]
Working the Street: What You Need to Know about Life on Wall Street
　　R&R Bk N - v19 - i3 - August 2004 - p138(1) [51-500]

Banks, H. Thomas - *Bioterrorism: Mathematical Modeling Applications to Homeland Security*
　　SciTech - v28 - i1 - March 2004 - p179(1) [51-500]

Banks, Iain - *The Algebraist*
　　Globe & Mail - Nov 27 2004 - pD33 [501+]
　　New Sci - v184 - i2477 - Dec 11 2004 - p50(1) [501+]
The State of the Art
　　PW - v251 - i44 - Nov 1 2004 - p48(1) [501+]

Banks, James A. - *Diversity and Citizenship Education: Global Prespectives*
　　TCR - v106 - i8 - August 2004 - p1570(6) [501+]
Handbook of Research and Multicultural Education
　　TCR - v106 - i8 - August 2004 - p1550(18) [501+]
Handbook of Research on Multicultural Education
　　Choice - v41 - i11-12 - July-August 2004 - p2096(1) [501+]

Banks, James G. - *The Unintended Consequences: Family and Community, the Victims of Isolated Poverty*
　　R&R Bk N - v19 - i3 - August 2004 - p117(1) [51-500]

Banks, Kate - *Walk Softly, Rachel (Read by Bresnahan, Alyssa). Audiobook Review*
　　y Kliatt - v38 - i5 - Sept 2004 - p65(3) [51-500]
Walk Softly Rachel (Read by Bresnahan, Alyssa). Audiobook Review
　　y SLJ - v50 - i7 - July 2004 - p60(2) [501+]
Walk Softly, Rachel (Read by Bresnahan, Alyssa). Audiobook Review
　　y SLJ - v50 - i10 - Oct 2004 - pS68(1) [501+]
Walk Softly, Rachel (Read by Bresnahan, Alyssa)
　　y LibMed - v22 - i6 - March 2004 - p66(1) [51-500]

Banks, Kathryn - *Exposure: Revealing Bodies, Unveiling Representations*
　　R&R Bk N - v19 - i4 - Nov 2004 - p230(1) [501+]

Banks, Kenneth J. - *Chasing Empire Across the Sea: Communications and the State in the French Atlantic, 1713-1763*
　　CBRA - Annual 2003 - p281(2) [501+]
　　HNet - August 2004 - pNA [501+]
　　JMH - v76 - i4 - Dec 2004 - p962(3) [501+]

Banks, L.A. - *The Bitten: A Vampire Huntress Legend*
　　KR - v72 - i22 - Nov 15 2004 - p1069(1) [51-500]
　　PW - v251 - i50 - Dec 13 2004 - p49(2) [51-500]
The Hunted: A Vampire Huntress Legend
　　LJ - v129 - i12 - July 2004 - p76(1) [51-500]

Banks, Leslie Esdaile - *Betrayal of the Trust*
　　Black Iss - v7 - i2 - March-April 2005 - p51(1) [51-500]

Banks, Lynne Reid - *Angela and Diabola*
　　c Sch Lib - v52 - i4 - Winter 2004 - p192(1) [51-500]
Stealing Stacey
　　y Sch Lib - v52 - i3 - Autumn 2004 - p155(1) [501+]
Tiger, Tiger
　　c Sch Lib - v52 - i4 - Winter 2004 - p191(2) [51-500]

Banks, Martha E. - *Women with Visible and Invisible Disabilities: Multiple Intersections, Multiple Issues, and Multiple Therapies*
　　R&R Bk N - v19 - i1 - Feb 2004 - p139(1) [51-500]

Banks, Paul - *It's a Dog's Life (Illus. by Kirchmayr, Jakob)*
　　c KR - v73 - i5 - March 1 2005 - p283(1) [51-500]

Banks, Ray - *The Big Blind*
　　PW - v251 - i51 - Dec 20 2004 - p41(1) [51-500]

Banks, Russell - *The Darling (Read by Hurt, Mary Beth). Audiobook Review*
　　BL - v101 - i9-10 - Jan 1 2005 - p882(1) [51-500]
The Darling
　　BL - v100 - i22 - August 2004 - p1870(1) [51-500]
　　BL - v101 - i9-10 - Jan 1 2005 - p769(1) [51-500]
　　BW - v34 - i43 - Oct 24 2004 - p3(2) [501+]
　　Econ - v373 - i8406 - Dec 18 2004 - p134US [501+]
　　Ent W - i788 - Oct 15 2004 - p80 [51-500]
　　Globe & Mail - Oct 16 2004 - pD24 [501+]
　　Globe & Mail - Nov 27 2004 - pD3 [51-500]
　　KR - v72 - i14 - July 15 2004 - p643(2) [501+]
　　LJ - v129 - i14 - Sept 1 2004 - p136(1) [51-500]
　　Nation - v279 - i20 - Dec 13 2004 - p38 [501+]
　　NW - Oct 11 2004 - p56 [50+]
　　NYTBR - Oct 24 2004 - p21 [501+]
　　PW - v251 - i31 - August 2 2004 - p49(1) [501+]
　　People - v62 - i16 - Oct 18 2004 - p49 [51-500]

Banks, Steven R. - *Classroom Assessment: Issues and Practices*
　　R&R Bk N - v19 - i4 - Nov 2004 - p188(1) [51-500]

Bankston, John - *F. Scott Fitzgerald*
　　y SLJ - v51 - i1 - Jan 2005 - p140(1) [51-500]
Gregor Mendel and the Discovery of the Gene
　　y SLJ - v50 - i12 - Dec 2004 - p157(2) [51-500]
Joseph Lister and the Story of Antiseptics
　　c BL - v101 - i4 - Oct 15 2004 - p415(1) [51-500]
Karl Benz and the Single Cylinder Engine
　　y SLJ - v50 - i12 - Dec 2004 - p157(2) [51-500]
The Life and Times of Alexander the Great
　　c BL - v101 - i4 - Oct 15 2004 - p415(1) [51-500]
The Life and Times of Scott Joplin
　　y SLJ - v51 - i2 - Feb 2005 - p144(1) [51-500]
Lise Meitner and the Atomic Age
　　y SB - v40 - i3 - May-June 2004 - p121(1) [501+]
Shirley Temple
　　c CH Bwatch - Jan 2005 - pNA [51-500]
Willem Einthoven and the Story of Electrocardiography
　　y SB - v40 - i6 - Nov-Dec 2004 - p262(1) [51-500]

Bann, Stephen - *Jannis Kounellis*
　　LJ - v129 - i14 - Sept 1 2004 - p146(1) [51-500]

Bannatyne-Cugnet, Jo - *Heartland: A Prairie Sampler (Illus. by Moore, Yvette)*
　　Can Lit - i181 - Summer 2004 - p104-106 [501+]

Banner, Keith - *The Smallest People Alive*
　　Lam Bk Rpt - v13 - i1-2 - August-Sept 2004 - p25(2) [501+]
　　NYTBR - July 4 2004 - p16 [51-500]

Banner, Lois W. - *Intertwined Lives: Margaret Mead, Ruth Benedict, and Their Circle*
　　Choice - v42 - i2 - Oct 2004 - p334(1) [51-500]
　　JAH - v91 - i3 - Dec 2004 - p1068(2) [501+]
Women in Modern America: A Brief History, 4th Ed.
　　R&R Bk N - v19 - i4 - Nov 2004 - p134(1) [1-50]

Banner, Stuart - *The Death Penalty: An American History*
　　J Am St - v38 - i2 - August 2004 - p350(2) [501+]
　　J Am St - v38 - i2 - August 2004 - p350-351 [501+]
Persons of Color and Religious at the Same Time: The Oblate Sisters of Providence, 1828-1860
　　J Am St - v38 - i2 - August 2004 - p351-352 [501+]

Banning, Lance - *Liberty and Order: The First American Party Struggle*
　　Choice - v42 - i3 - Nov 2004 - p548(2) [1-50]

Bannister, Jerry - *The Rule of the Admirals: Law, Custom, and Naval Government in Newfoundland, 1699-1832*
　　CBRA - Annual 2003 - p335(2) [51-500]
　　Choice - v41 - i11-12 - July-August 2004 - p2104(2) [501+]
　　R&R Bk N - v19 - i1 - Feb 2004 - pNA [51-500]

Bannister, Jo - *Depths of Solitude: A Brodie Farrell Mystery*
　　KR - v72 - i18 - Sept 15 2004 - p892(1) [51-500]
The Depths of Solitude: A Brodie Farrell Mystery
　　LJ - v129 - i20 - Dec 1 2004 - p95(1) [51-500]
Depths of Solitude: A Brodie Farrell Mystery
　　PW - v251 - i45 - Nov 8 2004 - p39(1) [501+]

Bannon, Ian - *Natural Resources and Violent Conflict: Options and Actions*
　　JEL - v41 - i4 - Dec 2003 - p1406(1) [501+]

Bannon, Mark E. - *A Quick Reference Guide to Contemporary Criminal Procedure for Law Enforcement Officers: One Hundred Notable United States Supreme Court Decisions and Their Effect on Modern Policing in America*
　　R&R Bk N - v19 - i1 - Feb 2004 - pNA [501+]

Bansavage, Lisa - *111 Shakespeare Monologues for Teens: The Ultimate Audition Book for Teens, Vol. 5*
　　c SLJ - v50 - i7 - July 2004 - p116(1) [51-500]

Banta, Martha - *Barbaric Intercourse: Caricature and the Culture of Conduct, 1841-1936*
　　AL - v76 - i2 - June 2004 - p396(2) [501+]

Bantekas, Ilias - *Oil and Gas Law in Kazakhstan: National and International Perspectives*
　　R&R Bk N - v19 - i3 - August 2004 - p208(1) [1-50]

Banti, Alberto Mario - *Il Risorgimento Italiano*
　　TLS - i5290 - August 20 2004 - p25(1) [501+]

Banting, Erinn - *Afghanistan, the Culture*
　　c CBRA - Annual 2003 - p545(2) [51-500]
Afghanistan, the Land
　　c CBRA - Annual 2003 - p545(2) [51-500]
Afghanistan, the People
　　c CBRA - Annual 2003 - p545(2) [51-500]
Australia, the Culture
　　c CBRA - Annual 2003 - p546(1) [51-500]
Australia, the Land
　　c CBRA - Annual 2003 - p546(1) [51-500]
Australia, the People
　　c CBRA - Annual 2003 - p546(1) [51-500]
England, the Culture
　　c Res Links - v10 - i1 - Oct 2004 - p22(1) [51-500]
England, the Land
　　c Res Links - v10 - i1 - Oct 2004 - p22(1) [51-500]
England, the People
　　c Res Links - v10 - i1 - Oct 2004 - p22(1) [51-500]
Puerto Rico, the Land
　　c CBRA - Annual 2003 - p547(1) [51-500]
Puerto Rico, the People
　　c CBRA - Annual 2003 - p547(1) [51-500]

Bantock, Nick - *Griffin and Sabine: An Extraordinary Correspondence*
　　BL - v101 - i2 - Sept 15 2004 - p225(1) [501+]
Griffin & Sabine: An Extraordinary Correspondence
　　LJ - v130 - i1 - Jan 1 2005 - p174(1) [501+]
Morning Star: In Which the Extraordinary Correspondence of Griffin and Sabine Is Illuminated
　　CBRA - Annual 2003 - p194(2) [501+]
Urgent 2nd Class: Creating Curious Collage, Dubious Documents, and Other Art from Ephemera
　　LJ - v101 - i17 - Oct 15 2004 - p62(1) [51-500]
　　PW - v251 - i27 - July 5 2004 - p51(2) [51-500]

Banton, Michael - *The International Politics of Race*
　　CS - v33 - i2 - March 2004 - p161-162 [501+]

Banville, John - *Shroud*
　　NYTBR - July 18 2004 - p20 [501+]
　　Sew R - v112 - i2 - Spring 2004 - pXXXVIII(3) [501+]

Bao, Xiaolan - *Holding Up More than Half the Sky: Chinese Women Garment Workers in New York City, 1948-92*
　　Wom HR - v13 - i1 - Spring 2004 - p139(4) [501+]

Bao, Yuheng - *Ancient and Classic Art of China*
　　R&R Bk N - v19 - i2 - May 2004 - p196(1) [51-500]

Baofu, Peter - *The Future of Post-Human Consciousness*
　　R&R Bk N - v19 - i3 - August 2004 - p4(1) [1-50]

Baptiste, Baron - *My Daddy Is a Pretzel: Yoga for Parents and Kids (Illus. by Fatus, Sophie)*
　　c BL - v101 - i4 - Oct 15 2004 - p409(1) [51-500]
　　c SLJ - v51 - i1 - Jan 2005 - p85(1) [51-500]

Baptiste, Tracey - *Angel's Grace*
　　y Kliatt - v39 - i1 - Jan 2005 - p6(1) [51-500]
　　KR - v73 - i1 - Jan 1 2005 - p48(1) [51-500]
　　y PW - v252 - i2 - Jan 10 2005 - p57(1) [51-500]

Bar-el, Dan - *Things Are Looking Up, Jack (Illus. by Boake, Kathy)*
　　c CBRA - Annual 2003 - p473(2) [51-500]

Bar-Gal, Yoram - *Propoganda and Zionist Education: The Jewish National Fund, 1924-1947*
　　AHR - v109 - i4 - Oct 2004 - p1347-1348 [501+]

Bar-Simon-Tov, Yaacov - *From Conflict Resolution to Reconciliation*
　　Choice - v41 - i11-12 - July-August 2004 - p2120(1) [501+]

The Bar U: Canadian Ranching History
　　Bwatch - Feb 2005 - pNA [501+]

Bar-Yam, Yaneer - *Dynamics of Complex Systems*
　　SciTech - v28 - i1 - March 2004 - p61(1) [51-500]

Barabba, Vincent P. - *Surviving Transformation: Lessons from GM's Surprising Turnaround*
　　R&R Bk N - v19 - i4 - Nov 2004 - p105(1) [1-50]

Barahona, Renato - *Sex Crimes, Honour, and the Law in Early Modern Spain: Vizcaya, 1528-1735*
　　Ren Q - v57 - i4 - Winter 2004 - p1410(2) [501+]

Barakso, Maryann - *Governing NOW: Grassroots Activism in the National Organization for Women*
　　LJ - v130 - i2 - Feb 1 2005 - p101(1) [51-500]

Baram, Daphna - *Disenchantment: The Guardian and Israel*
　　Econ - v372 - i8386 - July 31 2004 - p72US [501+]
　　NS - v133 - i4703 - August 30 2004 - p38(2) [501+]

Baran, Khenryk - *O Khlebnikove: Konteksty, istochniki, mify*
　　Slav R - v63 - i2 - Summer 2004 - p439(2) [501+]

Baranek, Patricia M. - *Almost Home: Reforming Home and Community Care in Ontario*
  SciTech - v28 - i4 - Dec 2004 - p83(1) [51-500]
Baranko, Igor - *The Horde*
  BL - v101 - i3 - Oct 1 2004 - p320(1) [51-500]
Baranowski, Shelley - *Strength through Joy: Consumerism and Mass Tourism in the Third Reich*
  Choice - v42 - i4 - Dec 2004 - p727(1) [1-50]
  HNet - July 2004 - pNA [501+]
Barany, Zoltan - *The Future of NATO Expansion: Four Case Studies*
  Choice - v41 - i7 - March 2004 - p1367(1) [501+]
  PSQ - v119 - i4 - Winter 2004 - p704(3) [501+]
  Slav R - v63 - i3 - Fall 2004 - p625-626 [501+]
Baranzini, Andrea - *Voluntary Approaches in Climate Policy*
  SciTech - v28 - i3 - Sept 2004 - p7(1) [501+]
Barasch, Lynne - *A Country Schoolhouse (Illus. by Barasch, Lynne)*
  c BL - v101 - i1 - Sept 1 2004 - p129(1) [1-50]
  c KR - v72 - i14 - July 15 2004 - p681(1) [51-500]
  c SLJ - v50 - i8 - August 2004 - p82(1) [51-500]
  Knockin' on Wood: Starring Peg Leg Bates (Illus. by Barasch, Lynne)
  c CCB-B - v57 - i11 - July-August 2004 - p454(1) [501+]
Barasch, Marc - *Field Notes on the Compassionate Life: A Search for the Soul of Kindness*
  KR - v73 - i2 - Jan 15 2005 - p92(1) [501+]
  PW - v252 - i7 - Feb 14 2005 - p67(1) [51-500]
Baratta, Joseph Preston - *The Politics of World Federation, Vols. 1-2*
  R&R Bk N - v19 - i3 - August 2004 - p160(1) [501+]
Baratz-Logsted, Lauren - *Crossing the Line*
  BL - v100 - i21 - July 2004 - p1826(1) [1-50]
Baraz, Daniel - *Medieval Cruelty: Changing Perceptions Antiquity to the Early Modern Period*
  AHR - v109 - i2 - April 2004 - p586(2) [501+]
Barbagallo, Ralph - *Wireless Game Development in Java with MIDP 2.0*
  SciTech - v28 - i4 - Dec 2004 - p29(1) [51-500]
Barbas-Rhoden, Laura - *Writing Women in Central America: Gender and the Fictionalization of History*
  Choice - v42 - i1 - Sept 2004 - p105(1) [501+]
Barbato, Joseph - *How to Write Knockout Proposals: What You Must Know (and Say) to Win Funding Every Time*
  PW - v251 - i27 - July 5 2004 - p50(2) [51-500]
Barbazette, Jean - *Instant Case Studies: How to Design, Adapt, and Use Case Studies in Training*
  R&R Bk N - v19 - i1 - Feb 2004 - p181(1) [51-500]
Barber, Alex - *Epistemology of Language*
  Choice - v42 - i1 - Sept 2004 - p94(2) [501+]
Barber, Benjamin R. - *Fear's Empire: War, Terrorism, and Democracy*
  R&R Bk N - v19 - i1 - Feb 2004 - p63(1) [501+]
Barber, Charles - *The Alexander Siloti Collection: Editions, Transcriptions, and Arrangements for Piano Sol*
  Notes - v61 - i2 - Dec 2004 - p561(5) [501+]
  Songs from the Black Chair: A Memoir of Mental Interiors
  KR - v73 - i3 - Feb 1 2005 - p157(1) [501+]
  PW - v252 - i5 - Jan 31 2005 - p58(1) [51-500]
Barber, David W. - *Music Lover's Quotation Book*
  CBRA - Annual 2003 - p15(1) [51-500]
Barber, James G. - *Children in Foster Care*
  Soc Ser R - v79 - i1 - March 2005 - p210(1) [51-500]
Barber, James P. - *Mandela's World: The International Dimension of South Africa's Political Revolution 1990-99*
  R&R Bk N - v19 - i3 - August 2004 - p60(1) [51-500]
Barber, John - *The Soviet Defence-Industry Complex from Stalin to Khrushchev*
  JEL - v42 - i1 - March 2004 - p210(2) [501+]
Barber, Katherine - *Canadian Oxford Dictionary*
  BL - v101 - i6 - Nov 15 2004 - p613(1) [501+]
Barber, Michael - *Anthony Powell: A Life*
  Atl - v294 - i3 - Oct 2004 - p163(1) [501+]
  BL - v101 - i4 - Oct 15 2004 - p376(1) [51-500]
  KR - v72 - i14 - July 15 2004 - p667(2) [501+]
  Lon R Bks - v26 - i20 - Oct 21 2004 - p10(2) [501+]
  NYTBR - Oct 31 2004 - p28 [501+]
  PW - v251 - i29 - July 19 2004 - p153(1) [51-500]
  Spec - v295 - i9178 - July 3 2004 - p39(2) [501+]
  TLS - i5284 - July 9 2004 - p9(1) [501+]
Barber, Nicola - *Tokyo*
  c SLJ - v50 - i7 - July 2004 - p116(1) [1-50]

Barber, Nigel - *Kindness in a Cruel World: The Evolution of Altruism*
  BL - v101 - i3 - Oct 1 2004 - p284(1) [51-500]
  PW - v251 - i33 - August 16 2004 - p53(1) [51-500]
  R&R Bk N - v20 - i1 - Feb 2005 - p8(1) [51-500]
Barber, Richard - *The Holy Grail: Imagination and Belief*
  AM - v191 - i19 - Dec 13 2004 - p17 [501+]
  Choice - v42 - i2 - Oct 2004 - p278(1) [51-500]
  New R - Oct 4 2004 - p31 [501+]
  TLS - i5265 - Feb 27 2004 - p25-25 [501+]
Barber, Sotirios A. - *Welfare and the Constitution*
  Law&PolBR - July 2004 - p583(15) [501+]
  PSQ - v119 - i2 - Summer 2004 - p344(3) [501+]
Barber, Stephen M. - *Regarding Sedgwick: Essays on Queer Culture and Critical Theory*
  JGS - v13 - i3 - Nov 2004 - p282-285 [501+]
Barber, Tiki - *By My Brother's Side (Illus. by Root, Barry)*
  c BL - v101 - i1 - Sept 1 2004 - p114(1) [501+]
  c KR - v72 - i18 - Sept 15 2004 - p909(1) [51-500]
  c PW - v251 - i35 - August 30 2004 - p55(1) [51-500]
  c SLJ - v50 - i11 - Nov 2004 - p122(1) [51-500]
Barbero, Alessandro - *Charlemagne: Father of a Continent*
  Econ - v372 - i8393 - Sept 18 2004 - p88US [501+]
  Spec - v296 - i9192 - Oct 9 2004 - p49(2) [501+]
Barbetta, Marfa Cecilia - *Poetik des Neo-Phantastischen*
  GSR - v27 - i2 - May 2004 - p443-445 [501+]
Barbier, Jean Paul - *Ma Bibliotheque Poetique: Quatrieme Partie, Vol. 1*
  Six Ct J - v35 - i3 - Fall 2004 - p878-880 [501+]
Barbier, Patrick - *Vivaldi's Venice*
  R&R Bk N - v19 - i1 - Feb 2004 - p195(1) [51-500]
Barbieri, Heather - *Snow in July*
  BL - v72 - i18 - Sept 15 2004 - p205(1) [501+]
  KR - v72 - i18 - Sept 15 2004 - p880(1) [51-500]
  LJ - v129 - i18 - Nov 1 2004 - p72(1) [501+]
Barbosa, Mario A. - *Bioceramics, Vol. 16*
  SciTech - v28 - i1 - March 2004 - p80(1) [51-500]
Barbour, John D. - *The Value of Solitudes: The Ethics and Spirituality of Aloneness in Autobiography*
  R&R Bk N - v20 - i1 - Feb 2005 - p10(1) [1-50]
Barbour, Reid - *Literature and Religious Culture in Seventeenth-Century England*
  TLS - i5291 - August 27 2004 - p25(1) [501+]
  Measures of the Holy Commonwealth in Seventeenth-Century England
  Ren Q - v57 - i3 - Fall 2004 - p1122(3) [501+]
Barbour, Richmond - *Before Orientalism: London's Theatre of the East, 1576-1626*
  Ren Q - v57 - i4 - Winter 2004 - p1540(2) [501+]
  Six Ct J - v35 - i3 - Fall 2004 - p866-867 [501+]
Barca, Mehmet - *Economic Foundations of Strategic Management*
  JEL - v42 - i1 - March 2004 - p294(2) [501+]
Barcan, Ruth - *Nudity: A Cultural Anatomy*
  Globe & Mail - Jan 22 2005 - pD8 [501+]
  LJ - v129 - i14 - Sept 1 2004 - p173(1) [501+]
Barcelo, Francois - *Le Nul Et La Chipie*
  Res Links - v10 - i1 - Oct 2004 - p50(1) [51-500]
Barchas, Janine - *Graphic Design, Print Culture, and the Eighteenth-Century Novel*
  Lib & Cul - v39 - i4 - Fall 2004 - p475(3) [501+]
Barcia, Roland - *IBM WebSphere: Deployment and Advanced Configuration*
  SciTech - v28 - i4 - Dec 2004 - p151(1) [51-500]
Barclay, Byrna - *Girl at the Window*
  Globe & Mail - Feb 5 2005 - pD16 [501+]
Barclay, Donald A. - *Teaching and Marketing Electronic Information Literacy Programs: A How-to-Do-It Manual for Librarians*
  LibMed - v22 - i7 - April-May 2004 - p85(1) [501+]
  R&R Bk N - v19 - i1 - Feb 2004 - p262(1) [51-500]
Barclay, Tessa - *A Handful of Dust*
  KR - v72 - i14 - July 15 2004 - p661(1) [51-500]
Barczewski, Stephanie - *Titanic: A Night Remembered*
  Choice - v42 - i4 - Dec 2004 - p726(1) [1-50]
Bard, Allen J. - *Electroanalytical Chemistry: A Series of Advances, Vol. 22*
  SciTech - v28 - i1 - March 2004 - p54(1) [51-500]
  Electrogenerated Chemiluminescence
  SciTech - v28 - i4 - Dec 2004 - p55(1) [51-500]
  Encyclopedia of Electrochemistry, Vol. 8
  Choice - v42 - i7 - March 2005 - p1254(1) [51-500]
Bardach, Janusz - *Surviving Freedom: After the Gulag*
  Russ Rev - v63 - i2 - April 2004 - pNA [501+]

Bardell, Matthew - *La Cort d'Amor: A Critical Edition*
  Specu - v79 - i4 - Oct 2004 - p1028(3) [501+]
Bardhan-Quallen, Sudipta - *Chemotherapy*
  c CH Bwatch - Feb 2005 - pNA [51-500]
  c SLJ - v50 - i8 - August 2004 - p133(1) [51-500]
Bardwell, Leland - *Mother to a Stranger*
  WLT - v78 - i3-4 - Sept-Dec 2004 - p92(1) [501+]
Bardzell, Jeffrey - *Using Macromedia FireWorks MX, Special Ed.*
  SciTech - v28 - i1 - March 2004 - p135(1) [51-500]
Barefield, Laura D. - *Gender and History in Medieval English Romance and Chronicle*
  R&R Bk N - v19 - i1 - Feb 2004 - p234(1) [51-500]
Barell, John - *Developing More Curious Minds*
  Choice - v41 - i11-12 - July-August 2004 - p2095(1) [501+]
Barenblatt, Daniel - *A Plague upon Humanity: The Secret Genocide of Axis Japan's Germ Warfare Operation*
  CR - v285 - i1664 - Sept 2004 - p182(2) [51-500]
Barendse, R.J. - *The Arabian Seas: The Indian Ocean World of the Seventeenth Century*
  IJMES - v36 - i3 - August 2004 - p470-471 [501+]
Barfe, Louis - *Where Have All the Good Times Gone? The Rise and Fall of the Record Industry*
  TimHES - v0 - i1667 - Nov 19 2004 - p22(2) [501+]
Barfield, Claude E. - *Internet, Economic Growth and Globalization: Perspectives on the New Economy in Europe, Japan and the USA*
  JEL - v41 - i4 - Dec 2003 - p1396(1) [501+]
Barfoot, C.C. - *"A Natural Delineation of Human Passions": The Historic Moment of the "Lyrical Ballads"*
  TLS - i5299 - Oct 22 2004 - p31(1) [51-500]
Bargach, Jamila - *Orphans of Islam: Family, Abandonment and Secret Adoption in Morocco*
  IJMES - v36 - i1 - Feb 2004 - p134-135 [501+]
Barger, Jan - *Bedtime, Nelly*
  c SLJ - v50 - i8 - August 2004 - p82(1) [51-500]
Barghusen, Joan D. - *Daily Life in Ancient and Modern Cairo*
  c SLJ - v51 - i1 - Jan 2005 - p57(1) [51-500]
Barham, Nick - *Dis/connected*
  NS - v134 - i4721 - Jan 10 2005 - p52(2) [501+]
Barham, Peter - *Forgotten Lunatics of the Great War*
  CR - v286 - i1669 - Feb 2005 - p123(1) [51-500]
  LJ - v129 - i17 - Oct 15 2004 - p72(1) [51-500]
  Lon R Bks - v26 - i21 - Nov 4 2004 - p12(1) [1-50]
Baricco, Alessandro - *City*
  HR - v55 - i4 - Winter 2003 - p685 [501+]
  Without Blood
  Globe & Mail - Sept 4 2004 - pD12 [501+]
Barilleaux, Ryan J. - *Power and Prudence: The Presidency of George H.W. Bush*
  Choice - v42 - i2 - Oct 2004 - p371(1) [51-500]
Bariller, Marie - *Houses of Saint-Tropez (Illus. by Dhellemmes, Thomas)*
  LJ - v130 - i1 - Jan 1 2005 - p106(1) [51-500]
Barkai, Avraham - *"Wehr Dich!" der Centralverein deutscher Staatsbyrger judischen Glaubens (C.V.) 1893-1938*
  CEH - v37 - i2 - Spring 2004 - p300(3) [501+]
Barkdull, Larry - *Cold Train Coming*
  PW - v251 - i29 - July 19 2004 - p142(2) [51-500]
Barken, Lee - *Wireless Hacking Projects For Wi-Fi Enthusiasts*
  Bwatch - Feb 2005 - pNA [51-500]
Barker, Clive - *Abarat (Read by Ferrone, Richard). Audiobook Review*
  y Kliatt - v39 - i2 - March 2005 - p46(1) [51-500]
  Abarat
  Advocate - Dec 7 2004 - p70(1) [501+]
  Abarat: Days of Magic, Nights of War
  c BW - v34 - i50 - Dec 12 2004 - p13(1) [501+]
  Days of Magic, Nights of War
  y BL - v101 - i1 - Sept 1 2004 - p79(1) [501+]
  y Kliatt - v38 - i5 - Sept 2004 - p4(2) [51-500]
  y Kliatt - v38 - i6 - Nov 2004 - p21(1) [51-500]
  y KR - v72 - i20 - Oct 15 2004 - p1001(1) [51-500]
  y PW - v251 - i40 - Oct 4 2004 - p90(1) [1-50]
  y SLJ - v50 - i11 - Nov 2004 - p134(1) [51-500]
  y VOYA - v27 - i4 - Oct 2004 - p312(1) [51-500]
  Rare Flesh
  Lam Bk Rpt - v13 - i4-5 - Nov-Dec 2004 - p51(1) [501+]
Barker, David - *Archaeology of Industrialization*
  SciTech - v28 - i3 - Sept 2004 - p7(1) [501+]
Barker, David C. - *Rushed to Judgment: Talk Radio, Persuasion, and American Political Behavior*
  Pub Op Q - v68 - i3 - Fall 2004 - p424(3) [501+]

Barker, Derek - *Isis: A Bob Dylan Anthology*
    LJ - v129 - i16 - Oct 1 2004 - p82(1) [51-500]
Barker, Drucilla K. - *Toward a Feminist Philosophy of Economics*
    Choice - v41 - i7 - March 2004 - p1343(1) [501+]
    JEL - v41 - i4 - Dec 2003 - p1337(2) [501+]
Barker, Heidi Bulmahn - *Teachers and the Reform of Elementary Science: Stories of Conversation and Personal Process*
    R&R Bk N - v19 - i4 - Nov 2004 - p182(1) [501+]
Barker, Holly M. - *Bravo for the Marshallese: Regaining Control in a Post-Nuclear, Post-Colonial World*
    Cont Pac - v16 - i2 - Fall 2004 - p445(5) [501+]
Barker, John - *At Home with the Bella Coola Indians: T.F. McIlwraith's Field Letters, 1922-4*
    Can Hist R - v85 - i3 - Sept 2004 - p579(3) [501+]
Barker, Jonathan - *No-Nonsense Guide in Terrorism*
    CBRA - Annual 2003 - p301(2) [501+]
Barker, Margaret J. - *Guide to the Collections, Harry Ransom Humanities Research Center*
    Lib & Cul - v39 - i3 - Summer 2004 - p344(3) [501+]
Barker, Nicola - *Clear*
    Spec - v296 - i9189 - Sept 18 2004 - p48(2) [501+]
    TLS - i5294 - Sept 17 2004 - p21(1) [501+]
Barker, Nicolas - *Form and Meaning in the History of the Book: Selected Essays*
    R&R Bk N - v19 - i1 - Feb 2004 - p257(1) [51-500]
Barker, Pat - *Double Vision*
    HR - v57 - i2 - Summer 2004 - p311-316 [501+]
    Wom R Bks - v21 - i10-11 - July 2004 - p14(2) [501+]
Barker, Raffaella - *Phosphorescence*
    y Sch Lib - v52 - i4 - Winter 2004 - p211(1) [51-500]
Barkin, Roger M. - *Emergency Pediatrics: A Guide to Ambulatory Care, 6th Ed.*
    E-Streams - Dec 2004 - pNA [501+]
Barkley, Charles - *Who's Afraid of a Large Black Man?*
    LJ - v129 - i20 - Dec 1 2004 - p90(1) [51-500]
    PW - v252 - i11 - March 14 2005 - p59(2) [51-500]
Barkley, Roy R. - *The Handbook of Texas Music*
    SHQ - v108 - i1 - July 2004 - p129-129 [501+]
Barkow, Henriette - *If Elephants Wore Pants... (Illus. by Johnson, Richard)*
    c SLJ - v51 - i2 - Feb 2005 - p94(1) [51-500]
Barkun, Michael - *A Culture of Conspiracy: Apocalyptic Visions in Contemporary America*
    Choice - v41 - i11-12 - July-August 2004 - p2083(1) [501+]
    TimHES - v0 - i1659 - Sept 24 2004 - p28(2) [501+]
Barlett, Donald L. - *Critical Condition: How Health Care in America Became Big Business--and Bad Medicine*
    BL - v101 - i3 - Oct 1 2004 - p284(2) [51-500]
    BW - v34 - i45 - Nov 7 2004 - p4(1) [501+]
    PW - v251 - i39 - Sept 27 2004 - p54(1) [51-500]
Barletta, John R. - *Riding with Reagan: From the White House to the Ranch*
    PW - v252 - i5 - Jan 31 2005 - p61(1) [501+]
Barletta, Laura - *Fra Regola e Licenza: Chiesa e Vita Religiosa, Feste e Beneficenza a Napoli e in Campania*
    AHR - v109 - i4 - Oct 2004 - p1334-1335 [501+]
Barling, Julian - *Psychology of Workplace Safety*
    SciTech - v28 - i1 - March 2004 - p13(1) [51-500]
Barlough, Jeffrey E. - *Strange Cargo*
    BL - v100 - i22 - August 2004 - p1912(1) [51-500]
    ChrSFF&H - v26 - i9 - Sept 2004 - p33(1) [51-500]
    LJ - v129 - i12 - July 2004 - p75(1) [51-500]
    PW - v251 - i28 - July 12 2004 - p48(1) [51-500]
Barlow, Aaron - *The DVD Revolution: Movies, Culture and Technology*
    LJ - v129 - i20 - Dec 1 2004 - p166(1) [501+]
Barlow, Andrew L. - *Between Fear and Hope: Globalization and Race in the United States*
    Choice - v41 - i7 - March 2004 - p1376(1) [501+]
    CS - v33 - i4 - July 2004 - p451(3) [501+]
Barlow, Colin - *Modern Malaysia in the Global Economy: Political and Social Change into the 21st Century*
    AJPS - v39 - i2 - July 2004 - p446(447) [501+]
Barlow, David H. - *Abnormal Psychology: An Integrative Approach, 4th Ed.*
    SciTech - v28 - i4 - Dec 2004 - p95(1) [51-500]
Barlow, Jane A. - *Big Moose Lake in the Adirondacks: The Story of the Lake, the Land, and the People*
    Bwatch - v26 - i8 - August 2004 - p10(1) [51-500]

Barlow, Janelle - *Branded Customer Service: The New Competitive Edge*
    LJ - v129 - i19 - Nov 15 2004 - p68(2) [501+]
Barlow, John - *Eating Mammals: Three Novellas*
    BL - v100 - i22 - August 2004 - p1895(2) [51-500]
    KR - v72 - i13 - July 1 2004 - p588(1) [501+]
    y NYTBR - Sept 26 2004 - p24 [501+]
    PW - v251 - i28 - July 12 2004 - p41(2) [51-500]
    y SLJ - v51 - i1 - Jan 2005 - p158(1) [51-500]
    TLS - i5267 - March 12 2004 - p20-20 [501+]
Barlow, Maude - *Profit Is Not the Cure: A Citizen's Guide to Saving Medicare*
    CBRA - Annual 2003 - p427(2) [51-500]
Barlow, Max - *New Challenges in Local and Regional Administration*
    R&R Bk N - v19 - i3 - August 2004 - p183(1) [501+]
Barlow, Tani E. - *The Question of Women in Chinese Feminism*
    Choice - v42 - i5 - Jan 2005 - p939(1) [51-500]
Barmack, Erik - *The Virgin*
    BL - v101 - i8 - Dec 15 2004 - p707(1) [51-500]
    KR - v72 - i21 - Nov 1 2004 - p1019(1) [501+]
    PW - v252 - i1 - Jan 3 2005 - p35(1) [51-500]
Barmash, Isadore - *For the Good of the Company: The History of the McCrory Corporation*
    R&R Bk N - v19 - i1 - Feb 2004 - p109(1) [51-500]
Barme, Geremie R. - *Morning Sun*
    AHR - v109 - i3 - June 2004 - p886(2) [501+]
Barme, Scot - *Woman, Man, Bangkok: Love, Sex, and Popular Culture in Thailand*
    JAS - v63 - i2 - May 2004 - p543(2) [501+]
Barna, George - *High Impact African-American Churches: Leadership Concepts from Some of Today's Most Effective Churches*
    Black Iss - v7 - i1 - Jan-Feb 2005 - p53(1) [501+]
Barnaby, Karen - *The Low-Carb Gourmet*
    Globe & Mail - Oct 23 2004 - pL12 [501+]
Barnard, Bryn - *Dangerous Planet: Natural Disasters That Changed History*
    LibMed - v22 - i6 - March 2004 - p78(1) [501+]
Barnard, Ian - *Queer Race: Cultural Interventions in the Racial Politics of Queer Theory*
    R&R Bk N - v19 - i4 - Nov 2004 - p128(1) [1-50]
Barnard, John - *American Vanguard: The United Auto Workers During the Reuther Years, 1935-1970*
    Dis - v51 - i4 - Fall 2004 - p97(5) [501+]
    The Cambridge History of the Book in Britain, Vol. 4
    Albion - v36 - i2 - Summer 2004 - p307(2) [501+]
    HNet - June 2004 - pNA [501+]
    Six Ct J - v35 - i3 - Fall 2004 - p860-863 [501+]
Barnard, Robert - *A Cry from the Dark*
    TLS - i5264 - Feb 20 2004 - p23-23 [501+]
Barnard, Roger - *Bilingual Children's Language and Literacy Development*
    R&R Bk N - v19 - i1 - Feb 2004 - p212 [51-500]
Barnard, Toby - *The Kingdom of Ireland, 1641-1760*
    CR - v286 - i1668 - Jan 2005 - p63(1) [51-500]
    Making the Grand Figure: Lives and Possessions in Ireland, 1641-1770
    TLS - i5299 - Oct 22 2004 - p3-4 [501+]
    A New Anatomy of Ireland: The Irish Protestants, 1649-1770
    JR - v85 - i1 - Jan 2005 - p130(2) [501+]
    VQR - v80 - i1 - Wntr 2004 - p277-278 [501+]
Barner, Kenneth E. - *Nonlinear Signal and Image Processing; Theory, Methods, and Applications*
    SciTech - v28 - i3 - Sept 2004 - p153(1) [51-500]
Barner, Michael D. - *The Participating Citizen: A Biography of Alfred Schutz*
    Choice - v42 - i7 - March 2005 - p1239(1) [51-500]
Barnes, Alan - *Sherlock Holmes on Screen: The Complete Film and TV History*
    LJ - v129 - i18 - Nov 1 2004 - p86(1) [51-500]
Barnes, Burton V. - *Michigan Trees: A Guide to the Trees of the Great Lakes Region, Rev. and Updated Ed.*
    E-Streams - Nov 2004 - pNA [501+]
Barnes, Celia - *Native American Power in the United States, 1783-1795*
    AHR - v109 - i4 - Oct 2004 - p1224(2) [501+]
    Am Ind CRJ - v28 - i2 - Spring 2004 - p163(2) [501+]
Barnes, Dana R. - *Notable Sports Figures*
    LibMed - v22 - i7 - April-May 2004 - p67(1) [501+]
    LibMed - v22 - i7 - April-May 2004 - p67(1) [501+]
Barnes, Darryl E. - *Action Plan for Diabetes*
    SciTech - v28 - i4 - Dec 2004 - p102(2) [51-500]

Barnes, Dawn - *Seven Wheels of Power*
    KR - v73 - i2 - Jan 15 2005 - p116(1) [51-500]
Barnes, Derrick D. - *The Low-Down, Bad-Day Blues (Illus. by Boyd, Aaron)*
    c SLJ - v51 - i1 - Jan 2005 - p85(1) [51-500]
Barnes, Gill Gorell - *Family Therapy in Changing Times. 2nd Ed.*
    SciTech - v28 - i3 - Sept 2004 - p98(1) [51-500]
Barnes, Gordon - *Is Dualism Religiously and Morally Pernicious?*
    RM - v58 - i1 - Sept 2004 - p209(3) [501+]
Barnes, James J. - *The American Civil War through British Eyes: Dispatches from British Diplomats*
    JSH - v71 - i1 - Feb 2005 - p161(2) [501+]
Barnes, Jeb - *Overruled? Legislative Overrides, Pluralism, and Contemporary Court-Congress Relations*
    Choice - v42 - i6 - Feb 2005 - p1096(1) [51-500]
    Law&PolBR - June 2004 - p498(3) [501+]
    Pers PS - v34 - i1 - Wntr 2005 - p52(1) [501+]
    R&R Bk N - v19 - i3 - August 2004 - p197(1) [1-50]
Barnes, Jessica - *Girl Source: A Book by and for Young Women about Relationships, Rights, Futures, Bodies, Minds, and Souls*
    y SLJ - v50 - i10 - Oct 2004 - pS64(1) [501+]
Barnes, Jim - *On a Wing of the Sun*
    Sew R - v112 - i3 - Summer 2004 - p467-475 [501+]
Barnes, John - *Gaudeamus*
    BL - v101 - i5 - Nov 1 2004 - p471(2) [51-500]
    ChrSFF&H - v26 - i10 - Oct 2004 - p24(1) [51-500]
    KR - v72 - i18 - Sept 15 2004 - p896(1) [51-500]
    LJ - v129 - i17 - Oct 15 2004 - p57(1) [51-500]
    PW - v251 - i39 - Sept 27 2004 - p41(2) [51-500]
Barnes, Julia - *101 Facts About Predators*
    c LibMed - v23 - i3 - Nov-Dec 2004 - p76(1) [51-500]
Barnes, Julian - *The Lemon Table: Stories*
    Ent W - i773 - July 9 2004 - p95 [51-500]
    Globe & Mail - July 17 2004 - pD7 [501+]
    New R - Sept 13 2004 - p39 [501+]
    NYRB - v51 - i16 - Oct 21 2004 - p26(1) [501+]
    NYTBR - July 4 2004 - p18 [501+]
    NYTBR - July 11 2004 - p22 [501+]
    People - v62 - i6 - August 9 2004 - p47 [51-500]
    TLS - i5267 - March 12 2004 - p19-20 [501+]
    Metroland
    BL - v101 - i2 - Sept 15 2004 - p224(1) [501+]
Barnes, Katie - *Paediatrics: A Clinical Guide for Nurse Practitioners*
    E-Streams - Nov 2004 - pNA [501+]
Barnes-McLain, Noreen - *Theater Symposium: Representations of Gender on the Nineteenth-Century American Stage*
    Theat J - v56 - i4 - Dec 2004 - p718-719 [501+]
Barnes, Mike E. - *Contrary Angel*
    Globe & Mail - August 7 2004 - pD10 [501+]
    Syllabus
    CBRA - Annual 2003 - p152(1) [51-500]
Barnes, Robert W. - *Baltimore County Families, 1659-1759*
    EFHM - v58 - i3 - May-June 2004 - p58(2) [1-50]
Barnes, Simon - *How to Be a Bad Birdwatcher*
    Spec - v296 - i9192 - Oct 9 2004 - p55(1) [501+]
Barnes, Stephen Emory - *The Cestus Deception*
    ChrSFF&H - v26 - i9 - Sept 2004 - p33(1) [51-500]
Barnes, Susan J. - *Becoming a Digital Library*
    SciTech - v28 - i1 - March 2004 - p180(1) [51-500]
    Van Dyck: A Complete Catalogue of the Paintings
    Apo - v160 - i511 - Sept 2004 - p100(2) [501+]
    Choice - v42 - i3 - Nov 2004 - p474(2) [1-50]
    LJ - v129 - i15 - Sept 15 2004 - p55(1) [51-500]
Barnes-Svarney, Patricia - *The Handy Geology Answer Book*
    Bwatch - Nov 2004 - pNA [51-500]
    Ref Rev - Nov 2004 - pNA [501+]
Barnes, Thomas G. - *Wildflowers and Ferns of Kentucky*
    Choice - v42 - i4 - Dec 2004 - p689(1) [1-50]
Barnes, Trevor - *Archaeology*
    c BL - v101 - i1 - Sept 1 2004 - p116(1) [501+]
    y SLJ - v50 - i11 - Nov 2004 - p158(1) [51-500]
Barnes, Trevor J. - *Reading Economic Geography*
    R&R Bk N - v19 - i1 - Feb 2004 - p105(1) [501+]

Barnet, Andrea - *All-Night Party: The Women of Bohemian Greenwich Village and Harlem, 1913-1930*
    Advocate - Oct 26 2004 - p56(1) [51-500]
    Choice - v42 - i4 - Dec 2004 - p719(1) [1-50]
    R&R Bk N - v19 - i3 - August 2004 - p72(1) [51-500]

Barnet, Anne Alison - *Extravaganza King: Robert Barnet and Boston Musical Theatre*
    Bwatch - v26 - i9 - Sept 2004 - p4(1) [51-500]
    Extravanganza King: Robert Barnet and Boston Musical Theatre
    Choice - v42 - i5 - Jan 2005 - p861(1) [1-50]

Barnet, Richard D. - *The Story behind the Song: 150 Songs That Chronicle the 20th Century*
    Choice - v42 - i1 - Sept 2004 - p110(1) [501+]
    R&R Bk N - v19 - i2 - May 2004 - p192(1) [51-500]
    y   SLJ - v50 - i8 - August 2004 - p55(1) [51-500]

Barnet, Sylvan - *An Introduction to Literature: Fiction, Poetry, and Drama*
    CR - v285 - i1664 - Sept 2004 - p190(2) [51-500]

Barnett, Michael N. - *Eyewitness to a Genocide: The United Nations and Rwanda*
    CS - v33 - i1 - Jan 2004 - p87-88 [501+]

Barnett, Ola W. - *Family Violence Across the Lifespan: An Introduction, 2nd Ed.*
    R&R Bk N - v19 - i3 - August 2004 - p166(1) [501+]

Barnett, Randy E. - *Restoring the Lost Constitution: The Presumption of Liberty*
    Choice - v42 - i1 - Sept 2004 - p188(1) [501+]
    Law&PolBR - Nov 2004 - p900(12) [501+]

Barnett, Raymond - *Relax, You're Already Home: Everyday Taoist Habits for a Richer Life*
    PW - v251 - i48 - Nov 29 2004 - p38(1) [51-500]

Barnett, Ronald - *Beyond All Reason: Living with Ideology in the University*
    J Hi E - v75 - i6 - Nov-Dec 2004 - p709(4) [501+]

Barnett, Rosalind - *Same Difference: How Gender Myths Are Hurting Our Relationships, Our Children, and Our Jobs*
    Bwatch - v26 - i9 - Sept 2004 - p12(1) [51-500]
    NYTBR - Oct 24 2004 - p26 [501+]

Barnett, S.J. - *The Enlightenment and Religion: The Myths of Modernity*
    Choice - v42 - i1 - Sept 2004 - p117(1) [501+]
    CR - v285 - i1666 - Nov 2004 - p313(1) [501+]

Barnett, Thomas P.M. - *The Pentagon's New Map: War and Peace in the Twenty-First Century*
    APJ - v18 - i3 - Fall 2004 - p110(1) [501+]
    Fut - v38 - i5 - Sept-Oct 2004 - p63(1) [51-500]

Barnett, Tony - *AIDS in the Twenty-First Century: Disease and Globalization*
    CS - v33 - i5 - Sept 2004 - p621-621 [501+]

Barnett, Vic - *Environmental Statistics*
    Choice - v41 - i11-12 - July-August 2004 - p2080(1) [501+]

Barney, Betty G. - *The World According to Humphery*
    c   LibMed - v23 - i3 - Nov-Dec 2004 - p68(1) [51-500]

Barnhart, Duane - *Cartooning Basics*
    c   BL - v101 - i5 - Nov 1 2004 - p495(1) [51-500]

Barnhill, Carla - *The Myth of the Perfect Mother: Rethinking the Spirituality of Women*
    PW - v251 - i33 - August 16 2004 - p60(1) [51-500]

Barnhill, Julie Ann - *Radical Forgiveness: It's Time to Wipe Your Slate Clean!*
    PW - v251 - i43 - Oct 25 2004 - p44(1) [51-500]

Barnhill, Raymond L. - *Textbook of Dermatopathology, 2nd Ed.*
    SciTech - v28 - i3 - Sept 2004 - p120(1) [51-500]

Barnhouse, Rebecca - *Middle Ages in Literature for Youth: A Guide and Resource Book*
    y   CCB-B - v58 - i3 - Nov 2004 - p155(1) [501+]
    Middle and Junior High School Library Catalog, 8th Ed.
    c   SLJ - v50 - i8 - August 2004 - p62(1) [501+]

Barnosky, Anthony D. - *Biodiversity Response to Climate in the Middle Pleistocene: The Porcupine Cave Fauna from Colorado*
    Choice - v42 - i5 - Jan 2005 - p877(1) [1-50]

Barnouw, Jeffrey - *Odysseus, Hero of Practical Intelligence: Deliberation and Signs in Homer's Odyssey*
    Choice - v42 - i7 - March 2005 - p1225(1) [51-500]

Barnstone, Tony - *The Anchor Book of Chinese Poetry*
    LJ - v130 - i2 - Feb 1 2005 - p82(1) [51-500]

Barnstone, Willis - *The Gnostic Bible*
    Choice - v42 - i2 - Oct 2004 - p310(1) [51-500]

Barntingham, P. Jeffery - *The Early Upper Paleolithic Beyond Western Europe*
    Choice - v42 - i7 - March 2005 - p1269(1) [51-500]

Baroff, Michael - *Being Your Best*
    HR Mag - v49 - i7 - July 2004 - pS5(1) [51-500]
    Contributing to Your Company's Success
    HR Mag - v49 - i7 - July 2004 - pS5(1) [51-500]
    Getting Along with Others
    HR Mag - v49 - i7 - July 2004 - pS5(1) [51-500]

Barolsky, Paul - *Michelangelo and the Finger of God*
    Ren Q - v57 - i4 - Winter 2004 - p1387(3) [501+]

Baron, Anne-Marie - *Balzac, ou les hieroglyphes de l'imaginaire*
    NCFS - v32 - i3-4 - Spring-Summer 2004 - p392(3) [501+]

Baron, David - *The Beast in the Garden: A Modern Parable of Man and Nature*
    HM - v310 - i1858 - March 2005 - p95(7) [501+]
    New Sci - v185 - i2481 - Jan 8 2005 - p51(1) [51-500]
    Sci Teach - v71 - i7 - Sept 2004 - p97-97 [501+]
    VQR - v80 - i2 - Spring 2004 - p262-262 [501+]

Baron, Helen - *D.H. Lawrence: Paul Morel*
    ELT - v48 - i1 - Wntr 2005 - p239(6) [501+]

Baron, Jill S. - *Rocky Mountain Futures: An Ecological Perspective*
    WHQ - v35 - i3 - Autumn 2004 - p375(1) [501+]

Baron, Michael - *The Mourning Sexton*
    KR - v73 - i2 - Jan 15 2005 - p63(2) [501+]
    LJ - v129 - i20 - Dec 1 2004 - p86(1) [51-500]
    LJ - v130 - i3 - Feb 15 2005 - p113(1) [51-500]

Baron, Robert C. - *Pioneers and Plodders: The American Entrepreneurial Spirit*
    R&R Bk N - v19 - i4 - Nov 2004 - p86(1) [51-500]

Baron, Samuel H. - *Adventures in Russian Historical Research: Reminiscences of American Scholars from the Cold War to the Present*
    Lon R Bks - v26 - i16 - August 19 2004 - p7(4) [501+]

Barone, Diane M. - *Literacy and Young Children: Research-Based Practices*
    CE - v81 - i2 - Winter 2004 - p112(1) [501+]

Barone, Michael - *The Almanac of American Politics 2004: The Senators, the Representatives, and the Governors: Their Records and Election Results, Their States and Districts*
    BL - v101 - i3 - Oct 1 2004 - p358(1) [501+]

Baroody, Arthur J. - *The Development of Arithmetic Concepts and Skills: Constructing Adaptive Expertise*
    CE - v81 - i1 - Fall 2004 - p51(1) [51-500]

Barr, Catherine - *Best Books for Middle School and Junior High Readers: Grades 6-9.*
    Teach Lib - v32 - i2 - Dec 2004 - p38(1) [501+]

Barr, Colin - *Paul Cullen, John Henry Newman, and the Catholic University of Ireland, 1845-1865*
    VS - v46 - i3 - Spring 2004 - p526(4) [501+]

Barr, David L. - *Reading the Book of Revelation: A Resource for Students*
    Intpr - v58 - i3 - July 2004 - p334(1) [51-500]

Barr, Emily - *Solo*
    KR - v73 - i5 - March 1 2005 - p242(1) [501+]

Barr, Gary E. - *Pearl Harbor*
    c   SLJ - v50 - i10 - Oct 2004 - p184(2) [51-500]
    World War II Home Front
    c   SLJ - v50 - i10 - Oct 2004 - p184(2) [51-500]

Barr, Helen - *Socioliterary Practice in Late Medieval England*
    RES - v55 - i218 - Feb 2004 - p119-121 [501+]
    Six Ct J - v34 - i4 - Winter 2003 - p1214-1215 [501+]

Barr, Jeff - *1001 Golf Holes You Must Play Before You Die*
    Bwatch - March 2005 - pNA [51-500]

Barr, Marleen S. - *Oy Pioneer! A Novel*
    Ext - v45 - i2 - Summer 2004 - p204(2) [501+]

Barr, Nevada - *Hard Truth*
    BL - v101 - i9-10 - Jan 1 2005 - p782(1) [1-50]
    KR - v73 - i5 - March 1 2005 - p260(1) [51-500]
    LJ - v129 - i20 - Dec 1 2004 - p96(1) [51-500]
    LJ - v130 - i2 - Feb 1 2005 - p57(2) [51-500]
    PW - v252 - i7 - Feb 14 2005 - p57(1) [51-500]

Barr, Niall - *Pendulum of War: The Three Battles of El Alamein*
    KR - v73 - i3 - Feb 1 2005 - p157(2) [501+]

Barr, Stephen M. - *Modern Physics and Ancient Faith*
    Theol St - v66 - i1 - March 2005 - p207(3) [501+]
    TT - v61 - i2 - July 2004 - p229(4) [501+]

Barr, William - *From Barrow to Boothia: The Arctic Journal of Chief Factor Peter Warren Dease, 1836-1839*
    Can Hist R - v85 - i3 - Sept 2004 - p546(4) [501+]

Barra, Allen - *Big Play: Barra n Football*
    Nation - v280 - i8 - Feb 28 2005 - p30 [501+]
    Brushbacks and Knockout: The Greatest Baseball Debates of Two Centuries
    BooChiTr - May 9 2004 - p4(1) [501+]

Barrabes, Claude - *Singular Null Hypersurfaces in General Relativity: Light-Like Signals from Violent Astrophysical Events*
    SciTech - v28 - i3 - Sept 2004 - p46(1) [1-50]

Barranger, Milly S. - *Margaret Webster: A Life in the Theater*
    AM - v191 - i19 - Dec 13 2004 - p15 [501+]
    Am Theat - v21 - i8 - Oct 2004 - p139(4) [51-500]
    Choice - v42 - i3 - Nov 2004 - p495(1) [51-500]
    Lam Bk Rpt - v13 - i3 - Oct 2004 - p22(2) [501+]

Barrass, Robert - *Writing at Work: A Guide to Better Writing in Administration, Business and Management*
    JEL - v41 - i4 - Dec 2003 - p1444(1) [501+]

Barratt, Carrie Rebora - *Gilbert Stuart*
    LJ - v129 - i20 - Dec 1 2004 - p112(1) [51-500]

Barre, Richard - *Echo Bay*
    BooChiTr - May 2 2004 - p3(1) [501+]
    DroRevMy - v24 - i3 - May-June 2004 - p11(1) [1-50]

Barreca, Gina - *Babes in Boyland: A Personal History of Co-Education in the Ivy League*
    KR - v73 - i2 - Jan 15 2005 - p92(1) [501+]
    PW - v252 - i9 - Feb 28 2005 - p53(1) [51-500]

Barrell, Barrie R.C. - *Teaching as a Form of Artistic Expression*
    CBRA - Annual 2003 - p392(1) [51-500]
    Teaching English Today: Advocating Change in the Secondary Curriculum
    Choice - v42 - i3 - Nov 2004 - p537(1) [1-50]

Barreneche, Osvaldo - *Dentro de la Ley, Todo: La Justicia Criminal de Buenos Aires en la Etapa Formation del Sistema Penal Moderno de la Argentina*
    HAHR - v84 - i2 - May 2004 - p377(3) [501+]

Barrera, Rick - *Overpromise and Overdeliver: The Secrets of Unshakable Customer Loyalty*
    BL - v101 - i7 - Dec 1 2004 - p623(1) [51-500]

Barres, Rachilde-Maurice - *Correspondance inedite: 1885-1914*
    FS - v58 - i2 - April 2004 - p275(3) [501+]

Barrett, Amy R. - *35 Ways to Help a Grieving Child*
    CE - v81 - i2 - Winter 2004 - p116(1) [51-500]

Barrett, Angela - *The Wild Swans*
    c   PW - v252 - i8 - Feb 21 2005 - p177(1) [51-500]

Barrett, Anthony - *Livia: First Lady of Imperial Rome*
    CJ - v99 - i4 - April-May 2004 - p458-462 [501+]
    Class R - v54 - i1 - May 2004 - p177(2) [501+]

Barrett, Bill, Jr. - *Price of Christler-Coke*
    PW - v251 - i32 - August 9 2004 - p235(2) [51-500]

Barrett, Catherine - *Gastrostomy Care: A Guide to Practice*
    SciTech - v28 - i4 - Dec 2004 - p108(1) [51-500]

Barrett, Daniel J. - *Linux Pocket Guide*
    LJ - v130 - i1 - Jan 1 2005 - p148(1) [501+]

Barrett, Diane M. - *Processing Fruits: Science and Technology, 2nd Ed.*
    SciTech - v28 - i4 - Dec 2004 - p165(1) [51-500]

Barrett, Grant - *Hatchet Jobs and Hardball: The Oxford Dictionary of American Political Slang*
    CJR - v43 - i5 - Jan-Feb 2005 - p62(1) [51-500]
    Hatchet Jobs and Hardball: The Oxford Dictionary of American Political Slang
    LJ - v129 - i15 - Sept 15 2004 - p81(1) [51-500]

Barrett, James - *Staged Narrative: Poetics and the Messenger in Greek Tragedy*
    Class R - v54 - i1 - May 2004 - p39(2) [501+]

Barrett, Jerry - *Big Bush Lies: 20 Essays and a List of the 50 Most Telling Lies of George W. Bush*
    R&R Bk N - v19 - i3 - August 2004 - p71(1) [51-500]

Barrett, John G. - *Yankee Rebel: The Civil War Jounral of Edmund DeWitt Patterson*
    R&R Bk N - v19 - i4 - Nov 2004 - p62(1) [51-500]

Barrett, Judith - *Fagioli: The Bean Cuisine of Italy*
    LJ - v129 - i17 - Oct 15 2004 - p83(1) [51-500]

Barrett, Justin L. - *Why Would Anyone Believe in God?*
    Choice - v42 - i6 - Feb 2005 - p1041(1) [51-500]
    R&R Bk N - v19 - i3 - August 2004 - p12(1) [1-50]

Barrett, Margaret Dwight - *The Diaspora: Introduction to Africana Studies*
    R&R Bk N - v19 - i3 - August 2004 - p57(1) [51-500]

Barrett, Marilyn - *The Handbook of Clinically Tested Herbal Remedies, Vols. 1-2*
Choice - v42 - i7 - March 2005 - p1200(2) [51-500]
SciTech - v28 - i4 - Dec 2004 - p117(1) [1-50]

Barrett, Paula M. - *Handbook of Interventions that Work with Children and Adolescents: Prevention and Treatment*
E-Streams - Sept 2004 - pNA [501+]

Barrett, Rosemary - *Hostas*
E-Streams - July 2004 - pNA [501+]
Maples
E-Streams - August 2004 - pNA [501+]

Barrett, Scott - *Environment and Statecraft: The Strategy of Environmental Treaty-Making*
JEL - v42 - i1 - March 2004 - p335(2) [501+]

Barrick, Murray R. - *Personality and Work: Reconsidering the Role of Personality in Organizations*
Per Psy - v57 - i3 - Autumn 2004 - p804(4) [501+]

Barrie, J.M. - *Peter Pan and Wendy (Illus. by Ingpen, Robert)*
c CH Bwatch - Feb 2005 - pNA [1-50]
y Magpies - v19 - i5 - Nov 2004 - p20(4) [501+]

Barrie, J. M. - *Peter Pan (Read by Peters, Donada). Audiobook Review*
BL - v101 - i2 - Sept 15 2004 - p261(1) [501+]

Barrie, J.M. - *Peter Pan*
NS - v133 - i4716 - Nov 29 2004 - p42(1) [51-500]

Barringer, Judith M. - *The Hunt in Ancient Greece*
Class R - v54 - i1 - May 2004 - p164(3) [501+]

Barringer, William - *Gregory and Alexander (Illus. by LaFave, Kim)*
c CBRA - Annual 2003 - p447(1) [51-500]

Barrios, Angel - *Obra completa para guitarra*
Notes - v61 - i3 - March 2005 - p866(4) [501+]

Barris, Jeremy - *Paradox and the Possibility of Knowledge: The Example of Psychoanalysis*
R&R Bk N - v19 - i1 - Feb 2004 - p7(1) [1-50]

Barris, Ted - *Juno: Canadians at D-Day, June 6, 1944*
BIC - v33 - i5 - August 2004 - p26(2) [501+]
BIC - v33 - i5 - August 2004 - p41(1) [501+]

Barroll, Leeds - *Shakespeare Studies, Vol. 31*
R&R Bk N - v19 - i1 - Feb 2004 - p237(1) [51-500]

Barron, Caroline M. - *The Church and Learning in Later Medieval Society: Essays in Honour of R.B. Dobson*
Albion - v36 - i2 - Summer 2004 - p290(3) [501+]
London in the Later Middle Ages: Government and People, 1200-1500
HRNB - v33 - i1 - Fall 2004 - p23(1) [501+]

Barron-Hauwaert, Suzanne - *Language Strategies for Bilingual Families: The One-Parent-One-Language Approach*
R&R Bk N - v19 - i4 - Nov 2004 - p213(1) [501+]

Barron, Patrick - *Italian Environmental Literature: An Anthology*
HNet - Nov 2004 - pNA [501+]

Barron, Rex - *Showdown at the Food Pyramid (Illus. by Barron, Rex)*
c SLJ - v50 - i7 - July 2004 - p66(1) [51-500]

Barron, Stephanie - *Jane and His Lordship's Legacy: Being a Jane Austen Mystery*
PW - v252 - i7 - Feb 14 2005 - p57(1) [51-500]
Jane and His Lordship's Legacy
KR - v73 - i2 - Jan 15 2005 - p83(2) [51-500]
LJ - v130 - i2 - Feb 1 2005 - p57(1) [51-500]

Barron, T.A. - *Child of the Dark Prophecy*
y BL - v101 - i1 - Sept 1 2004 - p122(1) [1-50]
y CCB-B - v58 - i5 - Jan 2005 - p198(2) [51-500]
y Kliatt - v38 - i5 - Sept 2004 - p4(3) [51-500]
y KR - v72 - i18 - Sept 15 2004 - p910(1) [51-500]
c PW - v251 - i43 - Oct 25 2004 - p48(1) [51-500]
y SLJ - v50 - i10 - Oct 2004 - p154(1) [51-500]
c VOYA - v27 - i5 - Dec 2004 - p399(1) [51-500]
The Great Tree of Avalon (Read by Easton, Richard). Audiobook Review
c SLJ - v51 - i2 - Feb 2005 - p74(1) [501+]

Barron, W.R.J. - *Layamon's Arthur: The Arthurian Section of Layamon's Brut*
JEGP - v103 - i2 - April 2004 - p261-263 [501+]
The Voyage of Saint Brendan: Representative Versions of the Legend in English Translation
Specu - v79 - i4 - Oct 2004 - p1030(2) [501+]

Barros, Carlos - *History under Debate: International Reflection on the Discipline*
R&R Bk N - v20 - i1 - Feb 2005 - p31(1) [51-500]

Barros, Carlos P. - *Transatlantic Sport: The Comparitive Economics of North American and European Sports*
JEL - v42 - i3 - Sept 2004 - p864(2) [501+]

Barroux, Stephane - *Mr. Katapat's Incredible Adventure (Illus. by Barroux, Stephane)*
c SLJ - v51 - i1 - Jan 2005 - p85(2) [51-500]
Mr. Katapat's Incredible Adventures (Illus. by Barroux, Stephane)
c KR - v72 - i16 - August 15 2004 - p802(1) [51-500]
c PW - v251 - i40 - Oct 4 2004 - p87(1) [51-500]
Where's Mary's Hat? (Illus. by Barroux Stephane)
c LibMed - v22 - i4 - Jan 2004 - p56(1) [501+]

Barrow, Blanche Caldwell - *My Life with Bonnie and Clyde*
c LJ - v129 - i18 - Nov 1 2004 - p108(1) [51-500]

Barrow, C.J. - *Environmental Change and Human Development: Controlling Nature?*
TimHES - v0 - i1677 - Feb 4 2005 - p32(1) [501+]

Barrow, Ian J. - *Making History, Drawing Territory: British Mapping in India, c. 1756-1905*
AHR - v109 - i4 - Oct 2004 - p1212-1213 [501+]
Choice - v42 - i2 - Oct 2004 - p345(1) [51-500]
TimHES - v0 - i1653 - August 13 2004 - p24(1) [501+]

Barrow, John D. - *Science and Ultimate Reality: Quantum Theory, Cosmology, and Complexity*
QRB - v79 - i4 - Dec 2004 - p405(1) [501+]
TimHES - v0 - i1682 - March 11 2005 - p28(1) [501+]

Barrow, Lloyd H. - *Adventures with Rocks and Minerals: Geology Experiments for Young People, Bk. 2*
y SB - v40 - i5 - Sept-Oct 2004 - p192(1) [51-500]

Barrow, Paul - *Raising Finance: A Practical Guide to Starting, Expanding and Selling Your Business*
Bwatch - March 2005 - pNA [51-500]
R&R Bk N - v19 - i4 - Nov 2004 - p118(1) [51-500]

Barrow, Steve - *Reggae: The Rough Guide*
LJ - v130 - i2 - Feb 1 2005 - p113(1) [51-500]

Barrus, Roger M. - *The Deconstitutionalization of America: The Forgotten Frailties of Democratic Rule*
Choice - v42 - i6 - Feb 2005 - p1097(1) [51-500]

Barry, Angela - *Endangered Species and Other Stories*
WLT - v78 - i3-4 - Sept-Dec 2004 - p92(1) [501+]

Barry, Dana M. - *Science Fair Projects: Helping Your Child Create a Super Science Fair Project*
SB - v40 - i5 - Sept-Oct 2004 - p192(1) [51-500]

Barry, Dave - *Peter and the Starcatchers (Read by Dale, Jim). Audiobook Review*
y BL - v101 - i8 - Dec 15 2004 - p754(1) [1-50]
y Kliatt - v39 - i2 - March 2005 - p55(1) [51-500]
c PW - v251 - i37 - Sept 13 2004 - p36(1) [51-500]
y VOYA - v27 - i5 - Dec 2004 - p372(1) [501+]
Peter and the Starcatchers (Illus. by Call, Greg)
c BL - v101 - i1 - Sept 1 2004 - p121(1) [1-50]
c CCB-B - v58 - i3 - Nov 2004 - p113(2) [501+]
y HB - v80 - i5 - Sept-Oct 2004 - p578(1) [51-500]
y KR - v72 - i15 - August 1 2004 - p737(1) [51-500]
c PW - v251 - i34 - August 23 2004 - p55(1) [51-500]
y SLJ - v50 - i10 - Oct 2004 - p154(1) [51-500]
Peter and the Starcatchers
y VOYA - v27 - i5 - Dec 2004 - p399(1) [51-500]

Barry, Frances - *Duckie's Ducklings: A One-to-Ten Counting Book*
c KR - v73 - i1 - Jan 1 2005 - p48(1) [51-500]
c PW - v252 - i7 - Feb 14 2005 - p80(2) [501+]
Duckie's Rainbow (Illus. by Barry, Frances)
c BooChiTr - April 11 2004 - p2(1) [501+]
c SLJ - v50 - i7 - July 2004 - p66(1) [51-500]

Barry, Jim - *Gender and the Public Sector: Professionals and Managerial Change*
JGS - v13 - i2 - July 2004 - p186-187 [501+]

Barry, John M. - *The Great Influenza: The Epic Story of the Deadliest Plague in History*
Nature - v429 - i6990 - May 27 2004 - p345(2) [501+]
The Great Influenza: The Epic Story of the Deadliest Plague in History
BL - v101 - i9-10 - Jan 1 2005 - p767(1) [51-500]
Choice - v42 - i2 - Oct 2004 - p324(1) [51-500]

Barry, Quan - *Controvertibles*
LJ - v129 - i16 - Oct 1 2004 - p84(1) [51-500]

Barry, Roger - *Atmosphere, Weather, and Climate, 8th Ed.*
SciTech - v28 - i3 - Sept 2004 - p49(1) [1-50]

Barry, Sebastian - *A Long Long Way*
BL - v101 - i9-10 - Jan 1 2005 - p811(1) [1-50]
KR - v72 - i24 - Dec 15 2004 - p1152(1) [501+]
PW - v252 - i5 - Jan 31 2005 - p50(1) [51-500]

Barsam, Richard - *Looking at Movies: An Introduction to Film*
R&R Bk N - v19 - i1 - Feb 2004 - p224(1) [51-500]

Barsamian, David - *The Checkbook and the Cruise Missile: Conversations with Arundhati Roy*
R&R Bk N - v19 - i3 - August 2004 - p187(1) [501+]
Louder than Bombs: Interviews from The Progressive Magazine
Bwatch - Oct 2004 - pNA [51-500]

Barshay, Andrew E. - *The Social Sciences in Modern Japan: The Marxian and Modernist Traditions*
Choice - v42 - i3 - Nov 2004 - p541(1) [1-50]

Bart, Kathleen - *Town Teddy and Country Bear: Classic Aesop's Fable Retold*
KR - v72 - i18 - Sept 15 2004 - p910(1) [501+]

Barta, Melinda A. - *Hip to Stitch: 20 Contemporary Projects Embellished with Thread*
PW - v252 - i11 - March 14 2005 - p63(1) [51-500]

Barta, Miroslav - *Sinuhe, the Bible, and the Patriarchs*
R&R Bk N - v19 - i4 - Nov 2004 - p51(1) [51-500]

Bartee, Wayne C. - *Time to Speak Out: The Leipzig Citizen Protests and the Fall of East Germany*
JR - v84 - i3 - July 2004 - p488(2) [501+]

Bartek, Mary - *Funerals and Fly Fishing*
c CCB-B - v58 - i2 - Oct 2004 - p59(2) [51-500]
c KR - v72 - i14 - July 15 2004 - p681(1) [51-500]
c SLJ - v50 - i8 - August 2004 - p115(1) [51-500]

Bartel, Julie - *From A to Zine: Building a Winning Zine Collection in Your Library*
LJ - v129 - i19 - Nov 15 2004 - p92(1) [51-500]
MFSF - v108 - i3 - March 2005 - p28(2) [501+]
R&R Bk N - v19 - i4 - Nov 2004 - p256(1) [501+]
SLJ - v51 - i2 - Feb 2005 - p160(1) [51-500]

Bartel, T.W. - *Comparative Theology: Essays for Keith Ward*
Rel St - v40 - i4 - Dec 2004 - p511(5) [501+]

Bartelmus, Peter - *Green Accounting*
R&R Bk N - v19 - i1 - Feb 2004 - p113(1) [51-500]

Barth, J. Robert - *Romanticism and Trancendence: Wordsworth, Coleridge, and the Religious Imagination*
Theol St - v65 - i3 - Sept 2004 - p675(1) [501+]

Barth, John - *The Book of Ten Nights and a Night*
Spec - v297 - i9212 - Feb 26 2005 - p36(1) [501+]

Barth, Roland S. - *Learning by Heart*
R&R Bk N - v19 - i3 - August 2004 - p214(1) [1-50]

Barthelmas, Della Gray - *The Signers of the Declaration of Independence: A Biographical and Genealogical Reference*
R&R Bk N - v19 - i1 - Feb 2004 - p58(1) [51-500]

Barthelme, Donald - *The Dead Father*
LJ - v130 - i1 - Jan 1 2005 - p172(1) [1-50]

Bartholomew, James - *The Welfare State We're In*
NS - v133 - i4717 - Dec 6 2004 - p52(1) [501+]

Bartholomew, Lee - *Picture Framing for the First Time*
LJ - v129 - i20 - Dec 1 2004 - p156(1) [51-500]

Bartholomew, Michael - *In Search of H.V. Morton*
CR - v285 - i1666 - Nov 2004 - p314(1) [501+]
TLS - i5285 - July 16 2004 - p32(1) [501+]

Bartik, Timothy J. - *Jobs for the Poor: Can Labor Demand Policies Help?*
JEL - v41 - i4 - Dec 2003 - p1308(2) [501+]

Bartkowski, John P. - *Charitable Choices: Religion, Race, and Poverty in the Post Welfare Era*
CS - v33 - i4 - July 2004 - p459(2) [501+]
J Ch St - v46 - i4 - Autumn 2004 - p907(3) [501+]
The Promise Keepers: Servants, Solders, and Godly Men
Choice - v42 - i2 - Oct 2004 - p308(1) [51-500]

Bartle, John R. - *Evolving Theories of Public Budgeting*
JEL - v42 - i1 - March 2004 - p273(1) [501+]

Bartleman, James - *Rollercoaster: My Hectic Years as Jean Chretien's Diplomatic Advisor 1994-1998*
Globe & Mail - March 12 2005 - pD4 [501+]

Bartlett, Allison - *Honey Biscuits*
c Sch Lib - v52 - i4 - Winter 2004 - p191(1) [51-500]

Bartlett, Anne - *Knitting*
KR - v73 - i2 - Jan 15 2005 - p65(1) [501+]
LJ - v130 - i4 - March 1 2005 - p74(1) [51-500]

Bartlett, Brian - *Afterlife of Trees*
CBRA - Annual 2003 - p208(2) [51-500]
Wanting the Day: Selected Poems
BIC - v33 - i6 - Sept 2004 - p32(2) [501+]

Bartlett, David L. - *What's Good About This News? Preaching from the Gospels and Galatins*
TT - v61 - i3 - Oct 2004 - p364(2) [501+]

Bartlett, Elizabeth Ann - *Rebellious Feminism: Camus's Ethic of Rebellion and Feminist Thought*
Choice - v42 - i1 - Sept 2004 - p114(1) [501+]

Bartlett, J.R. - *Jews in the Hellenistic and Roman Cities*
Class R - v54 - i2 - Nov 2004 - p511-512 [501+]

Bass, Rick - *Caribou Rising: Defending the Porcupine Herd, Gwich-'in Culture, and the Arctic National Wildlife Refuge*
  y BL - v100 - i22 - August 2004 - p1890(1) [51-500]
     LJ - v129 - i16 - Oct 1 2004 - p108(1) [51-500]
     PW - v251 - i28 - July 12 2004 - p55(1) [51-500]
The Diezmo
     KR - v73 - i5 - March 1 2005 - p242(1) [501+]
Falling from Grace in Texas: A Literary Response to the Demise of Paradise
     PW - v252 - i3 - Jan 17 2005 - p48(1) [51-500]
Bass, Scott - *Girl vs. Wave (Illus. by Collins, Julie)*
  c PW - v252 - i11 - March 14 2005 - p70(1) [501+]
Bass, Serena - *Serena, Food and Stories: Feeding Friends Every Hour of the Day*
     Time - Sept 14 2004 - p16 [51-500]
Bass, Warren - *Support Any Friend: Kennedy's Middle East and the Making of the U.S.-Israel Alliance*
     AHR - v109 - i4 - Oct 2004 - p1258(2) [501+]
     HER - v119 - i483 - Sept 2004 - p1104(3) [501+]
     HNet - July 2004 - pNA [501+]
     JAH - v91 - i2 - Sept 2004 - p695(2) [501+]
     Parameters - v34 - i4 - Winter 2004 - p146(2) [501+]
Bass, William - *Death's Acre: Inside the Legendary Forensic Lab the Body Farm Where the Dead Do Tell Tales*
     BW - v34 - i3 - Jan 18 2004 - p9(1) [501+]
Bassan, Amy - *Mekhti*
     PW - v252 - i4 - Jan 24 2005 - p220(1) [501+]
Basset, Elizabeth - *Moments of Vision: A Memoir*
     Spec - v297 - i9205 - Jan 8 2005 - p31(1) [501+]
Bassett, Carol Ann - *Organ Pipe: Life on the Edge*
     SciTech - v28 - i4 - Dec 2004 - p59(1) [51-500]
Bassett, Nicole - *Chef in Your Backpack*
     CBRA - Annual 2003 - p126(1) [51-500]
Bassett, Ross Knox - *To the Digital Age: Research Labs, Start-Up Companies, and the Rise of MOS Technology*
     T&C - v45 - i4 - Oct 2004 - p892(2) [501+]
Bassetti, Piero - *Italic Identity in Pluralistic Contexts: Toward the Development of Intercultural Competencies*
     R&R Bk N - v19 - i3 - August 2004 - p44(1) [51-500]
Bassiouni, M. Cherif - *Introduction to International Criminal Law*
     R&R Bk N - v19 - i1 - Feb 2004 - pNA [51-500]
Bastable, Marshall J. - *Arms and the State: Sir William Armstrong and the Remaking of the British Naval Power, 1854-1914*
     R&R Bk N - v19 - i3 - August 2004 - p120(1) [51-500]
Bastedo, Jamie - *Falling for Snow: A Naturalist's Journey into the World of Winter*
     CBRA - Annual 2003 - p398(2) [51-500]
Basten, Twan - *Ambient Intelligence: Impact on Embedded System Design*
     SciTech - v28 - i1 - March 2004 - p165(1) [51-500]
Bastian, Jeannette Allis - *Owning Memory: How a Caribbean Community Lost Its Archives and Found Its History*
     LQ - v74 - i3 - July 2004 - p379(4) [501+]
Bastian, Sunil - *Can Democracy Be Designed? The Politics of Institutional Choice in Conflict-Torn Societies*
     R&R Bk N - v19 - i1 - Feb 2004 - p148(1) [51-500]
Bastianich, Lidia Matticchio - *Lidia's Family Table (Illus. by Hirsheimer, Christopher)*
     LJ - v129 - i19 - Nov 15 2004 - p82(1) [51-500]
     PW - v251 - i47 - Nov 22 2004 - p55(1) [51-500]
Bastien, Betty - *Blackfoot Ways of Knowing: The Worldview of the Siksikaitsitapi*
     R&R Bk N - v19 - i4 - Nov 2004 - p54(1) [51-500]
Bastien, Greg - *CCSP Cisco Secure PIX Firewall Advanced Exam Certification Guide*
     SciTech - v28 - i3 - Sept 2004 - p155(1) [51-500]
Baston, Lewis - *Reggie: The Life of Reginald Maudling*
     Spec - v296 - Dec 18 2004 - p97(2) [501+]
Baston, Robert - *Metrum De Praelio Apud Bannockburn*
     TLS - i5290 - August 20 2004 - p6(1) [501+]
Bastress-Dukehart, Erica - *The Zimmern Chronicle: Nobility, Memory, and Self-Representation in Sixteenth-Century Germany*
     HNet - Oct 2004 - pNA [501+]
Basu, Kaushik - *International Labor Standards: History, Theory, and Policy Options*
     JEL - v41 - i4 - Dec 2003 - p1388(2) [501+]
Prelude to Political Economy: A Study of the Social and Political Foundations of Economics
     JPR - v41 - i6 - Nov 2004 - p751-751 [501+]

Readings in Political Economy
     AJPS - v39 - i2 - July 2004 - p462(463) [501+]
Batabyal, Amitrajeet A. - *The Economics of International Trade and the Environment*
     JEL - v42 - i3 - Sept 2004 - p852(2) [501+]
Batalha, Luis - *Cape Verdean Diaspora in Portugal: Colonial Subjects in a Postcolonial World*
     R&R Bk N - v19 - i4 - Nov 2004 - p42(1) [51-500]
Batali, Mario - *Molto Italiano: Simple Italian Recipes for Cooking at Home*
     LJ - v130 - i3 - Feb 15 2005 - p151(1) [51-500]
     PW - v252 - i11 - March 14 2005 - p61(1) [51-500]
Batchelor, David - *Chromophobia*
     Globe & Mail - Oct 9 2004 - pD31 [501+]
Batchelor, Martine - *The Path of Compassion: The Bodhisattva Precepts, the Chinese Brahma's Net Sutra*
     R&R Bk N - v19 - i4 - Nov 2004 - p28(1) [501+]
Batchelor, Ronald Ernest - *Using Spanish Vocabulary*
     TimHES - v0 - i1668 - Nov 26 2004 - pX(2) [501+]
Batchelor, Tracy - *Lymphoma of the Nervous System*
     SciTech - v28 - i1 - March 2004 - p92(1) [51-500]
Batchen, Geoffrey - *Forget Me Not: Photography and Remembrance*
     R&R Bk N - v19 - i4 - Nov 2004 - p248(1) [501+]
Bate, Jonathan - *"I Am": The Selected Poetry of John Clare*
     NYRB - v51 - i14 - Sept 23 2004 - p82(4) [501+]
     NYRB - v51 - i15 - Oct 7 2004 - p42(2) [501+]
     VQR - v80 - i3 - Summer 2004 - p264(2) [1-50]
John Clare: A Biography
     Bks & Cult - v11 - i1 - Jan-Feb 2005 - p23(1) [501+]
     NYRB - v51 - i14 - Sept 23 2004 - p82(4) [501+]
     NYRB - v51 - i15 - Oct 7 2004 - p42(2) [501+]
The Oxford English Literary History
     CR - v285 - i1663 - August 2004 - p124(1) [501+]
Bateman, Colin - *Bring Me the Head of Oliver Plunkett*
  c Sch Lib - v52 - i3 - Autumn 2004 - p135(1) [501+]
Running with the Reservoir Pups
  y CCB-B - v58 - i5 - Jan 2005 - p199(2) [51-500]
  y KR - v72 - i24 - Dec 15 2004 - p1198(1) [501+]
  y PW - v252 - i2 - Jan 10 2005 - p56(2) [51-500]
  y SLJ - v51 - i1 - Jan 2005 - p122(1) [51-500]
Bateman, Ian J. - *Applied Environmental Economics: A GIS Approach to Cost-Benefit Analysis*
     JEL - v42 - i1 - March 2004 - p320(1) [51-500]
Bateman, Teresa - *April Foolishness (Illus. by Westcott, Nadine Bernard)*
  c BL - v101 - i6 - Nov 15 2004 - p584(1) [51-500]
  c BL - v101 - i9-10 - Jan 1 2005 - p774(1) [1-50]
  c KR - v72 - i19 - Oct 1 2004 - p956(1) [501+]
  c PW - v251 - i51 - Dec 20 2004 - p59(1) [51-500]
  c SLJ - v50 - i11 - Nov 2004 - p90(1) [51-500]
The Bully Blockers Club (Illus. by Urbanovic, Jackie)
  c SLJ - v50 - i11 - Nov 2004 - p90(1) [51-500]
Fluffy: The Scourge of the Sea (Illus. by Chesworth, Michael)
  c BL - v101 - i9-10 - Jan 1 2005 - p867(1) [51-500]
The Princesses Have a Ball (Illus. by Cravath, Lynne)
  c RT - v57 - Oct 2003 - p170 [1-50]
Bates, A.W. - *Effective Teaching with Technology in Higher Education*
     TCR - v106 - i5 - May 2004 - p938(3) [501+]
Bates, Brian - *The Real Middle-Earth: Exploring the Magic and Mystery of the Middle Ages, J.R.R. Tolkien and The Lord of the Rings*
     Med R - Dec 2004 - pNA [501+]
The Real Middle-Earth: Exploring the Magic and Mystery of the Middle Ages, J.R.R. Tolkien and The Lord of the Rings
     R&R Bk N - v19 - i1 - Feb 2004 - p26(1) [1-50]
Bates, Daniel G. - *Human Adaptive Strategies: Ecology, Culture, and Politics, 3rd Ed.*
     R&R Bk N - v19 - i4 - Nov 2004 - p75(1) [51-500]
Bates, David - *William the Conqueror*
     HER - v119 - i483 - Sept 2004 - p1028(2) [501+]
     HER - v119 - i483 - Sept 2004 - p1028(2) [501+]
Bates, Judy Fong - *Midnight at the Dragon Cafe*
     KR - v73 - i1 - Jan 1 2005 - p3(2) [501+]
     PW - v252 - i6 - Feb 7 2005 - p39(1) [51-500]
Bates, Katharine Lee - *America, the Beautiful (Illus. by Minor, Wendell)*
  c LibMed - v22 - i4 - Jan 2004 - p70(1) [501+]
America the Beautiful (Illus. by Gall, Chris)
  c NYTBR - Nov 14 2004 - p40 [501+]

Bates, Stephen - *A Church at War: Anglicans and Homosexuality*
     BL - v101 - i3 - Oct 1 2004 - p299(1) [51-500]
     Choice - v42 - i5 - Jan 2005 - p868(2) [1-50]
     PW - v251 - i37 - Sept 13 2004 - p76(1) [501+]
     TLS - i5292 - Sept 3 2004 - p26(1) [501+]
Bateson, Mary Catherine - *Willing to Learn: Passages of Personal Discovery*
     PW - v251 - i35 - August 30 2004 - p44(1) [51-500]
Bath, K.P. - *The Secret of Castle Cant: Being an Account of the Remarkable Adventures of Lucy Wickwrght, Maidservant and Spy*
  y VOYA - v27 - i5 - Dec 2004 - p399(1) [51-500]
The Secret of Castle Cant: Being an Account of the Remarkable Adventures of Lucy Wickwright, Maidservant and Spy (Illus. by Christiana, David)
  c BL - v101 - i6 - Nov 15 2004 - p595(1) [51-500]
  y CCB-B - v58 - i1 - Sept 2004 - p7(1) [51-500]
  y KR - v72 - i17 - Sept 1 2004 - p860(1) [51-500]
  y SLJ - v50 - i9 - Sept 2004 - p198(1) [51-500]
Bath, Kevin P. - *The Secret of Castle Cant: Being an Account of the Remarkable Adventures of Lucy Wickwright, Maidservant and Spy (Illus. by Christiana, David)*
  c PW - v251 - i42 - Oct 18 2004 - p65(1) [51-500]
Batho, Gordon R. - *The Wizard Earl's Advices to His Son*
     TLS - i5297 - Oct 8 2004 - p27(1) [501+]
Batra, Geeta - *Investment Climate around the World: Voices of the Firms from the World Business Environment Survey*
     JEL - v41 - i4 - Dec 2003 - p1367(2) [501+]
Batt, Catherine - *Malory's 'Morte Darthur': Remaking Arthurian Tradition*
     RES - v55 - i221 - Sept 2004 - p613(3) [501+]
Batt, Tanya Robyn - *The Princess and the White Bear King (Illus. by Ceccoli, Nicoletta)*
  c BL - v101 - i5 - Nov 1 2004 - p486(1) [51-500]
  c PW - v251 - i45 - Nov 8 2004 - p54(1) [51-500]
  c SLJ - v51 - i1 - Jan 2005 - p86(1) [51-500]
Battelle, John - *The Search*
     Har Bus R - v83 - i2 - Feb 2005 - p57(1) [1-50]
Batten, Jack - *The Annex: The Story of a Toronto Neighbourhood*
     BIC - v33 - i6 - Sept 2004 - p38(2) [501+]
Batten, Jonathan A. - *Social Responsibility: Corporate Governance Issues*
     JEL - v41 - i4 - Dec 2003 - p1398(1) [501+]
Battersby, Gregory J. - *2004 Licensing Update*
     R&R Bk N - v19 - i4 - Nov 2004 - p169(1) [501+]
Licensing Royalty Rates, 2004 Ed.
     R&R Bk N - v19 - i3 - August 2004 - p209(1) [1-50]
Battistini, Pierluigi - *Seventh Centenary of the Teaching of Astronomy in Bologna, 1297-1997*
     Isis - v95 - i3 - Sept 2004 - p469(2) [501+]
Battle, Conchita Y. - *Building Bridges for Women of Color in Higher Education: A Practical Guide for Success*
     R&R Bk N - v19 - i4 - Nov 2004 - p190(1) [501+]
Battle-Lavert, Gwendolyn - *Papa's Mark (Illus. by Bootman, Colin)*
  c SLJ - v50 - i10 - Oct 2004 - p65(1) [51-500]
Battle-Walters, Kimberly - *Sheila's Shop: Working-Class African American Women Talk About Life, Love, Race, and Hair*
     R&R Bk N - v19 - i4 - Nov 2004 - p60(1) [51-500]
Battle Zones
     LibMed - v22 - i7 - April-May 2004 - p70(1) [501+]
Battles, Matthew - *Library: An Unquiet History (Read by Gardner, Grover). Audiobook Review*
     Kliatt - v38 - i4 - July 2004 - p60(1) [51-500]
     LJ - v129 - i15 - Sept 15 2004 - p89(2) [51-500]
Library: An Unquiet History
     Ga R - v58 - i1 - Spring 2004 - p196-197 [501+]
Baty, Chris - *No Plot? No Problem!: A High-Velocity, Low-Stress Way to Write a Novel in 30 Days*
     LJ - v129 - i14 - Sept 1 2004 - p164(2) [501+]
Baucham, Voddie Jr. - *The Ever-Loving Truth: Can Faith Thrive in a Post-Christian Culture?*
     Ch Today - v48 - i9 - Sept 2004 - p90(1) [51-500]
Bauckham, Richard - *Bible and Mission: Christian Witness in a Postmodern World*
     IBMR - v28 - i3 - July 2004 - p144(1) [501+]
God and the Crisis of Freedom: Biblical and Contemporary Perspectives
     Intpr - v58 - i3 - July 2004 - p327(2) [501+]
Gospel Women: Studies of the Named Women in the Gospels
     TT - v61 - i1 - April 2004 - p88-89 [501+]

Bauer, Carl J. - *Siren Song: Chilean Water Law As a Model for International Reform*
R&R Bk N - v19 - i3 - August 2004 - p207(1) [1-50]

Bauer, Christian - *Hibernate in Action*
Bwatch - Oct 2004 - pNA [501-500]
SciTech - v28 - i4 - Dec 2004 - p20(1) [1-50]

Bauer, David - *Adding Arctic Animals*
c SLJ - v51 - i2 - Feb 2005 - p114(1) [51-500]
Count Your Chickens
c SLJ - v51 - i2 - Feb 2005 - p114(1) [51-500]
Let's Graph
c SLJ - v51 - i2 - Feb 2005 - p114(1) [51-500]

Bauer, Dieter R. - *Mirakel im Mittelalter: Konzeptionen, Erscheinungsformen, Deutungen*
Specu - v79 - i4 - Oct 2004 - p1088(3) [501+]

Bauer, Douglas - *Prime Times: Writers on Their Favorite TV Shows*
BL - v100 - i22 - August 2004 - p1888(2) [51-500]
Ent W - i777 - August 6 2004 - p87 [51-500]
Globe & Mail - August 21 2004 - pD13 [501+]
LJ - v129 - i13 - August 2004 - p84(1) [501+]

Bauer, Kenneth M. - *High Frontiers: Dolpo and the Changing World of Himalayan Pastoralists*
Choice - v42 - i5 - Jan 2005 - p894(1) [1-50]
R&R Bk N - v19 - i3 - August 2004 - p54(1) [51-500]

Bauer, Marion Dane - *A Recipe for Valentine's Day: A Rebus Lift-the-Flap Story (Illus. by Herbert, Jennifer)*
c PW - v251 - i49 - Dec 6 2004 - p61(2) [501+]
Wind (Illus. by Wallace, John)
c SLJ - v50 - i10 - Oct 2004 - pS23(1) [51-500]

Bauer, Michael Gerard - *Running Man*
y Magpies - v19 - i5 - Nov 2004 - p39(1) [501+]

Bauer, Ralph - *The Cultural Geography of Colonial American Literatures: Empire, Travel, Modernity*
Choice - v41 - i11-12 - July-August 2004 - p2042(1) [501+]
Ren Q - v57 - i4 - Winter 2004 - p1468(2) [501+]

Bauer, Raymond T. - *Zoological Physics: Quantitative Models of Body Design, Actions, and Physical Limitations of Animals*
Choice - v42 - i3 - Nov 2004 - p510(1) [1-50]

Bauer, Susan Wise - *The Well-Educated Mind: A Guide to the Classical Education You Never Had*
R&R Bk N - v19 - i1 - Feb 2004 - p261(1) [51-500]
The Well-Trained Mind: A Guide to Classical Education at Home, Rev. and Updated Ed.
R&R Bk N - v19 - i3 - August 2004 - p226(1) [1-50]

Bauer, Theresia - *Blockpartie und Agrarrevolution von oben: Die Demokratische Bauernpartie Deutschlands 1948-1963*
AHR - v109 - i4 - Oct 2004 - p1331(2) [501+]

Bauerle, Phenocia - *The Way of the Warrior: Stories of the Crow People*
Am Ind CRJ - v27 - i4 - Fall 2003 - p186-188 [501+]

Bauerlein, Mark - *Civil Rights Chronicle: The American Struggle for Freedom*
Choice - v41 - i11-12 - July-August 2004 - p2024(1) [501+]

Baugartner, Wilhelm - *Carl Stumpf*
Ger Q - v77 - i2 - Spring 2004 - p246-248 [501+]

Baugh, Bruce - *French Hegel: From Surrealism to Postmodernism*
MLN - v118 - i5 - Dec 2003 - p1332-1336 [501+]

Bauhn, Per - *Value of Courage*
R&R Bk N - v19 - i1 - Feb 2004 - p8(1) [51-500]

Baukal, Charles E., Jr. - *Industrial Burners Handbook*
SciTech - v28 - i1 - March 2004 - p151(1) [51-500]
Industrial Combustion Pollution and Control
SciTech - v28 - i1 - March 2004 - p148(1) [51-500]

Baulieu, Laurent - *Progress in String, Field, and Particle Theory*
SciTech - v28 - i1 - March 2004 - p52(1) [51-500]
SciTech - v28 - i1 - March 2004 - p53(1) [51-500]

Baum, Eric B. - *What Is Thought?*
Nature - v429 - i6993 - June 17 2004 - p701(2) [501+]
TimHES - v0 - i1663 - Oct 22 2004 - p26(2) [501+]

Baum, Howell S. - *Community Social Action for School Reform*
TCR - v106 - i8 - August 2004 - p1637(9) [501+]

Baum, Joel A.C. - *Geography and Strategy*
JEL - v42 - i1 - March 2004 - p341(1) [501+]

Baum, L. Frank - *The Wizard of Oz (Illus. by Denslow, W.W.)*
c RT - v57 - Sept 2003 - p98 [51-500]

Baum, Lawrence - *The Supreme Court, 8th Ed.*
R&R Bk N - v19 - i1 - Feb 2004 - pNA [51-500]

Baum, Matthew A. - *Soft News Goes to War: Public Opinion and American Foreign Policy in the New Media Age*
Pub Op Q - v68 - i4 - Winter 2004 - p644(5) [501+]

Baum, Michael - *Kontingenz und Gewalt. Semiotische Strukturen und erzahlte welt in Alfred Doblins Roman*
Ger Q - v77 - i4 - Fall 2004 - p501-502 [501+]

Baum, Neil - *Marketing Your Clinical Practice: Ethically, Effectively, Economically. 3rd Ed.*
SciTech - v28 - i3 - Sept 2004 - p78(1) [51-500]

Baum, Roger S. - *Toto in Candy Land of Oz*
c CH Bwatch - v14 - i8 - August 2004 - p8(1) [51-500]
The Wizard of Oz and the Magic Merry-Go-Round
c CH Bwatch - v14 - i12 - Dec 2004 - pNA [51-500]

Bauman, Bruce - *And the Word Was*
KR - v73 - i1 - Jan 1 2005 - p4(1) [51-500]
LJ - v129 - i20 - Dec 1 2004 - p97(1) [51-500]
PW - v252 - i9 - Feb 28 2005 - p44(1) [51-500]

Bauman, Jon R. - *Santa Fe Passage*
PW - v251 - i41 - Oct 11 2004 - p54(1) [51-500]

Bauman, Zygmunt - *Liquid Love: On the Frailty of Human Bonds*
CS - v33 - i4 - July 2004 - p494(2) [501+]
Society under Siege
CS - v33 - i2 - March 2004 - p222-223 [501+]
Wasted Lives: Modernity and Its Outcasts
Tikkun - v19 - i4 - July-August 2004 - p72(3) [501+]

Baumann, James F. - *Vocabulary Instruction: Research to Practice*
R&R Bk N - v19 - i3 - August 2004 - p218(1) [1-50]
SLJ - v50 - i10 - Oct 2004 - pS71(1) [51-500]

Baumann, Linda A. - *Health Care Fraud and Abuse: Practical Perspectives, 2003 Supplement*
SciTech - v28 - i3 - Sept 2004 - p11(1) [501+]

Baumann, Ursula - *Vom Recht auf den eigenen Tod: Die Geschichte des Suizids vom 18. bis zum 20. Jahrhundert*
JMH - v76 - i4 - Dec 2004 - p982(3) [501+]

Baumbach, Jonathan - *On the Way to My Father's Funeral: New and Selected Stories*
KR - v72 - i23 - Dec 1 2004 - p1099(2) [501+]

Baumbgert, Klaus - *Laura's Secret*
c Sch Lib - v52 - i4 - Winter 2004 - p186(1) [51-500]

Baumbich, Charlene - *Elder Wisdom*
PW - v251 - i34 - August 23 2004 - pS17(3) [501+]

Baumbich, Charlene Ann - *Dearest Dorothy, Help! I've Lost Myself!*
PW - v251 - i34 - August 23 2004 - pS16(1) [51-500]

Baumeister, Philip W. - *Optical Coating Technology*
SciTech - v28 - i3 - Sept 2004 - p171(1) [51-500]

Baumeister, Roy F. - *Handbook of Self-Regulation: Research, Theory, and Applications*
Choice - v42 - i6 - Feb 2005 - p1102(1) [51-500]
R&R Bk N - v19 - i4 - Nov 2004 - p10(1) [51-500]

Baumel, Judith Tydor - *Gender, Place and Memory in the Modern Jewish Experience: Re-Placing Ourselves*
R&R Bk N - v19 - i1 - Feb 2004 - p44(1) [51-500]

Baumer, Robert W. - *American Iliad: The 18th Infantry Regiment in World War II*
J Mil H - v68 - i4 - Oct 2004 - p1293-1294 [501+]

Baumgardner, Jennifer - *Grassroots: A Field Guide for Feminist Activism*
KR - v72 - i19 - Oct 1 2004 - p946(1) [501+]
LJ - v129 - i18 - Nov 1 2004 - p108(1) [51-500]
PW - v251 - i44 - Nov 1 2004 - p51(1) [501+]

Baumgarten, Albert I. - *Sacrifice in Religious Experience*
JRAI - v10 - i4 - Dec 2004 - p936(1) [501+]

Baumgartner, Emmanuele - *Thomas: Le Roman de Tristan Suivi de La Folie Tristan de Berne et La Folie Tristan d'Oxford*
FS - v58 - i2 - April 2004 - p237(2) [501+]

Baumgartner, Frederic J. - *Behind Locked Doors: A History of the Papal Elections*
Comw - v132 - i1 - Jan 14 2005 - p26(4) [501+]
R&R Bk N - v19 - i1 - Feb 2004 - p24(1) [1-50]

Baumgartner, Jody C. - *Checking Executive Power: Presidential Impeachment in Comparative Perspective*
Choice - v41 - i11-12 - July-August 2004 - p2116(1) [501+]
PSQ - v119 - i2 - Summer 2004 - p355(3) [501+]
R&R Bk N - v19 - i1 - Feb 2004 - p150(1) [51-500]

Baumler, Alan - *Modern China and Opium: A Reader*
Ch Rev Int - v10 - i2 - Fall 2003 - p307(20) [501+]

Baumohl, Bernard - *The Secrets of Economic Indicators: Hidden Clues to Future Economic Trends and Investment Opportunities*
LJ - v129 - i18 - Nov 1 2004 - p120(1) [51-500]

Baumol, William J. - *Downsizing in America: Reality, Causes, and Consequences*
Choice - v41 - i7 - March 2004 - p1340(1) [501+]
Har Bus R - v82 - i2 - Feb 2004 - p39(1) [501+]
JEL - v42 - i1 - March 2004 - p287(1) [501+]
SF - v83 - i2 - Dec 2004 - p878(2) [501+]
Growth, Industrial Organization and Economic Generalities
JEL - v42 - i1 - March 2004 - p237(2) [501+]
Macroeconomics: Principles and Policy, 9th ed., 2004 Update
R&R Bk N - v19 - i4 - Nov 2004 - p85(1) [51-500]

Bausch, Richard - *The Stories of Richard Bausch*
NYTBR - Jan 23 2005 - p28 [501+]
VQR - v80 - i1 - Wntr 2004 - p270-270 [501+]
VQR - v80 - i1 - Wntr 2004 - p270-271 [501+]
Wives and Lovers: Three Short Novels
BW - v34 - i31 - August 1 2004 - p13(1) [501+]
Ent W - i774 - July 16 2004 - p83 [501+]
People - v62 - i7 - August 16 2004 - p52 [51-500]

Bausum, Ann - *With Courage and Cloth: Winning the Fight for a Woman's Right to Vote*
c BL - v101 - i4 - Oct 15 2004 - p397(1) [51-500]
c CCB-B - v58 - i5 - Jan 2005 - p200(1) [51-500]
c KR - v72 - i17 - Sept 1 2004 - p860(1) [51-500]
c SLJ - v50 - i8 - August 2004 - p48(1) [51-500]
c SLJ - v50 - i9 - Sept 2004 - p221(1) [51-500]

Bautch, Kelley Coblentz - *Study of the Geography of 1 Enoch 17-19: "No one has seen what I have seen"*
R&R Bk N - v19 - i1 - Feb 2004 - p20(1) [51-500]

Bautch, Richard J. - *Developments in Genre Between Post-Exilic Penitential Prayers and the Psalms of Communal Lament*
R&R Bk N - v19 - i1 - Feb 2004 - p14(1) [51-500]

Bautze-Picron, Claudine - *The Buddhist Murals of Pagan: Timeless Vistas of the Cosmos*
TimHES - v0 - i1679 - Feb 18 2005 - p22(1) [501+]

Bauwens, Luc - *Econometric Modelling of Stock Market Intraday Activity*
JEL - v41 - i4 - Dec 2003 - p1294(3) [501+]

Bawlf, R. Samuel - *The Secret Voyage of Sir Francis Drake, 1577-1580*
BIC - v33 - i2 - March 2004 - p18(4) [501+]

Bawlf, Samuel - *The Secret Voyage of Sir Francis Drake, 1577-1580*
CBRA - Annual 2003 - p282(1) [501+]

Bawtree, Michael - *Joe Howe to the Rescue*
Res Links - v10 - i2 - Dec 2004 - p13(1) [51-500]

Baxevanis, Andreas D. - *Bioinformatics: A Practical Guide to the Analysis of Genes and Proteins, 3rd Ed.*
SciTech - v28 - i4 - Dec 2004 - p60(1) [51-500]

Baxter, Charles - *A William Maxwell Portrait: Memories and Appreciations*
LJ - v129 - i18 - Nov 1 2004 - p86(1) [51-500]

Baxter, Craig - *Historical Dictionary of Bangladesh, 3rd Ed.*
R&R Bk N - v19 - i1 - Feb 2004 - p46(1) [51-500]
Pakistan on the Brink: Politics, Economics, and Society
Choice - v42 - i3 - Nov 2004 - p561(1) [1-50]
R&R Bk N - v19 - i3 - August 2004 - p53(1) [51-500]

Baxter, Cynthia - *Putting on the Dog: A Reigning Cats and Dogs Mystery*
PW - v251 - i33 - August 16 2004 - p48(1) [51-500]

Baxter Magolda, Marcia B. - *Learning Partnerships: Theory and Models of Practice to Educate for Self-Authorship*
R&R Bk N - v19 - i3 - August 2004 - p220(1) [1-50]

Beardshaw, Rosalind - *Grandma's Beach*
c BL - v100 - i22 - August 2004 - p1940(1) [51-500]
c SLJ - v50 - i8 - August 2004 - p83(1) [51-500]
Grandpa's Surprise
c BL - v100 - i22 - August 2004 - p1940(1) [51-500]
c SLJ - v50 - i8 - August 2004 - p83(1) [51-500]

Beardslee, Karen E. - *Literary Legacies, Folklore Foundations: Selfhood and Cultural Tradition in Nineteenth- and Twentieth-Century American Literature*
Col Lit - v31 - i4 - Fall 2004 - p203(7) [501+]

Beardslee, Lois - *Rachel's Children: Stories from a Contemporary Native American Woman*
R&R Bk N - v19 - i4 - Nov 2004 - p244(1) [501+]

Beare, Geoffery - *The Art of William Heath Robinson*
Choice - v42 - i5 - Jan 2005 - p842(1) [1-50]

Bearman, P.J. - *The Encyclopaedia of Islam, New Edition: Supplement, Fascicules 7-8, Iran-Maktubat*
R&R Bk N - v19 - i3 - August 2004 - p48(1) [51-500]

Beasley, Vanessa B. - *You, the People: American National Identity in Presidential Rhetoric*
Choice - v42 - i1 - Sept 2004 - p188(1) [501+]

Beason, Dick - *The Japan That Never Was: Explaining the Rise and Decline of a Misunderstood Country*
Choice - v42 - i4 - Dec 2004 - p706(1) [1-50]
For Aff - v83 - i5 - Sept-Oct 2004 - p164 [501+]

Beastieville
c LibMed - v22 - i7 - April-May 2004 - p80(1) [501+]

Beatie, Russel H. - *Army of the Potomac, Vol. 2*
LJ - v129 - i17 - Oct 15 2004 - p72(1) [51-500]

Beato, Paulina - *Competition Policy in Regulated Industries: Approaches for Emerging Economies*
JEL - v42 - i4 - Dec 2004 - p1151(2) [501+]
R&R Bk N - v19 - i1 - Feb 2004 - p97(1) [1-50]

Beaton, Cecil - *Beaton in the Sixties: The Cecil Beaton Diaries as He Wrote Them, 1965-1969*
BL - v101 - i1 - Sept 1 2004 - p36(2) [51-500]
KR - v72 - i17 - Sept 1 2004 - p844(1) [501+]
TLS - i5262 - Feb 6 2004 - p25(1) [501+]

Beaton, Claire - *Hay una vaca entre las coies*
Inst - v114 - i3 - Oct 2004 - p74(2) [501+]

Beaton, Clare - *Make Your Own Castle*
c TES - v0 - i4587 - June 11 2004 - pssss29(1) [501+]

Beaton, M.C. - *Agatha Raisin and the Haunted House (Read by Peters, Donada). Audiobook Review*
LJ - v129 - i14 - Sept 1 2004 - p200(1) [51-500]
The Deadly Dance
Globe & Mail - Nov 27 2004 - pD16 [51-500]
KR - v72 - i19 - Oct 1 2004 - p940(1) [501+]
LJ - v129 - i18 - Nov 1 2004 - p60(1) [51-500]
Death of a Bore: A Hamish Macbeth Mystery
BL - v101 - i6 - Nov 15 2004 - p563(2) [51-500]
Globe & Mail - Feb 19 2005 - pD15 [501+]
KR - v72 - i22 - Nov 15 2004 - p1070(1) [51-500]
LJ - v130 - i1 - Jan 1 2005 - p84(1) [51-500]
Death of a Poison Pen (Read by Malcolm, Graeme). Audiobook Review
y Kliatt - v39 - i2 - March 2005 - p51(1) [51-500]
Globe & Mail - Jan 15 2005 - pD13 [1-50]
Death of a Poison Pen
y SLJ - v50 - i7 - July 2004 - p131(1) [51-500]
Hasty Death
Globe & Mail - August 7 2004 - pD12 [51-500]
LJ - v129 - i12 - July 2004 - p64(1) [51-500]
Snobbery with Violence
y VOYA - v27 - i4 - Oct 2004 - p292(2) [51-500]

Beaton, Richard - *Isaiah's Christ in Matthew's Gospel*
JR - v84 - i3 - July 2004 - p454(2) [501+]

Beaton, Roderick - *George Seferis: Waiting for the Angel*
HR - v57 - i1 - Spring 2004 - p150-158 [501+]

Beattie, Andrew - *Cairo: A Cultural History*
y BL - v101 - i6 - Nov 15 2004 - p548(1) [51-500]
LJ - v129 - i18 - Nov 1 2004 - p100(1) [51-500]
Wild Solutions: How Biodiversity Is Money in the Bank
Globe & Mail - Sept 11 2004 - pD21 [1-50]

Beattie, Ann - *Follies and New Stories*
Atl - v295 - i3 - April 2005 - p104(1) [501+]
KR - v73 - i4 - Feb 15 2005 - p188(1) [501+]
PW - v252 - i11 - March 14 2005 - p43(2) [51-500]

Beattie, Cordelia - *The Medieval Household in Christian Europe c.850-c.1550: Managing Power, Wealth, and the Body*
Med R - July 2004 - pNA [501+]
R&R Bk N - v19 - i3 - August 2004 - p149(1)

Beattie, Geoffrey - *Visible Thought: The New Psychology of Body Language. 1st Ed.*
TimHES - v0 - i1668 - Nov 26 2004 - pXVII(1) [501+]

Beattie, Owen - *Frozen in Time: The Fate of the Franklin Expedition, Rev. Ed.*
R&R Bk N - v20 - i1 - Feb 2005 - p81(1) [51-500]

Beattie, Peter M. - *The Human Tradition in Modern Brazil*
Choice - v41 - i11-12 - July-August 2004 - p2103(1) [501+]
The Tribute of Blood: Army, Honor, Race and Nation in Brazil, 1864-1945
J Soc H - v38 - i1 - Fall 2004 - p271(3) [501+]

Beattie, Tina - *Woman*
TLS - i5296 - Oct 1 2004 - p30(1) [51-500]

Beatty, Carol - *Employee Ownership: The New Source of Competitive Advantage*
CBRA - Annual 2003 - p321(2) [51-500]

Beatty, Edward - *Institutions and Investments: The Political Basis of Industrialization in Mexico before 1911*
HAHR - v84 - i2 - May 2004 - p353(2) [501+]

Beatty, Jack - *Pols: Great Writers on American Politicians from Bryan to Reagan*
CJR - v43 - i3 - Sept-Oct 2004 - p60(2) [501+]
R&R Bk N - v19 - i4 - Nov 2004 - p63(1) [51-500]

Beatty, Jeffrey F. - *Essentials of Business Law, 2nd Ed.*
R&R Bk N - v19 - i3 - August 2004 - p198(1) [1-50]

Beatty, Scott - *Catwoman: The Visual Guide to the Feline Fatale*
c SLJ - v50 - i9 - Sept 2004 - p237(1) [51-500]

Beaty, Jonathan - *The Outlaw Bank: A Wild Ride into the Secret Heart of BCCI*
R&R Bk N - v19 - i3 - August 2004 - p135(1) [51-500]

Beau, Bryan F. Le - *The Atheist: Madalyn Murray O'Hair*
JAH - v91 - i1 - June 2004 - p312-313 [501+]

Beauchamp, Monte - *Blab! Vol. 15*
BL - v101 - i9-10 - Jan 1 2005 - p835(1) [501+]

Beauchemin, Bob - *First Look at SQL Server 2005 for Developers*
SciTech - v28 - i4 - Dec 2004 - p31(1) [51-500]

Beauchemin, Raymond - *Salut! The Quebec Microbrewery Beer*
BIC - v33 - i8 - Nov 2004 - p26(2) [501+]

Beaudoin, Marie-Nathalie - *Breaking the Culture of Bullying and Disrespect, Grades K-8: Best Practices and Successful Strategies*
Choice - v42 - i2 - Oct 2004 - p342(2) [51-500]

Beaudoin, Tom - *Consuming Faith: The Phenomenon of Corporate Product "Branding"*
CC - v121 - i19 - Sept 21 2004 - p40(2) [51-500]

Beaudry, Jean-Luc - *Economic Indicators*
Choice - v42 - i4 - Dec 2004 - p636(1) [1-50]

Beaufort, Simon - *The Coiners' Quarrel*
LJ - v129 - i20 - Dec 1 2004 - p94(1) [51-500]

Beaujeu, Renaut de - *Le Bel Inconnu*
FS - v58 - i3 - July 2004 - p394-395 [501+]

Beaujolin-Bellet, Rachel - *Flexibilite et performances. Strategies d'entreprises, regulations, transformations du travail*
ILR - v143 - i3 - Autumn 2004 - p283(2) [1-50]

Beaulac, Stephane - *The Power of Language in the Making of International Law: The Word Sovereignty in Bodin and Vatel and the Myth of Westphalia*
R&R Bk N - v19 - i3 - August 2004 - p210(1iBea) [1-50]

Beaulieu, Danie - *Eye Movement Integration Therapy: The Comprehensive Clinical Guide*
SciTech - v28 - i1 - March 2004 - p73(1) [51-500]

Beaulieu, Jean-Philippe - *Le Simple, Le Multiple: La Disposition du Recueil a la Renaissance*
Six Ct J - v35 - i3 - Fall 2004 - p936-937 [501+]

Beaumont, Berry - *Care of Drug Users in General Practice: A Harm Reduction Approach. 2nd. Ed.*
SciTech - v28 - i3 - Sept 2004 - p103(1) [51-500]

Beaumont, John P. - *Runner and Gating Design Handbook: Tools for Successful Injection Molding*
SciTech - v28 - i4 - Dec 2004 - p166(1) [51-500]

Beaumont, Karen - *I Like Myself! (Illus. by Catrow, David)*
c CCB-B - v57 - i11 - July-August 2004 - p454(2) [501+]
c CE - v81 - i1 - Fall 2004 - p46(1) [51-500]
c SLJ - v50 - i7 - July 2004 - p68(1) [51-500]

Beauvoir, Simone de - *Correspondance Croisee, 1937-1940*
TLS - i5302 - Nov 12 2004 - p26(1) [501+]

Beaver, Kevin - *Practical Guide to HIPAA Privacy and Security Compliance*
SciTech - v28 - i3 - Sept 2004 - p12(1) [501+]

Beaver, Wanda - *Wanda's Pie in the Sky: Pies, Cakes, Cookies, Squares, and More*
CBRA - Annual 2003 - p126(2) [51-500]

Beazley, Hamilton - *No Regrets: A Ten-Step Program for Living in the Present and Leaving the Past Behind*
CC - v121 - i17 - August 24 2004 - p39(1) [501+]

Bebbington, D.W. - *The Mind of Gladstone: Religion, Homer, and Politics*
Bks & Cult - v11 - i1 - Jan-Feb 2005 - p32(2) [501+]
Choice - v42 - i6 - Feb 2005 - p1085(1) [51-500]
Lon R Bks - v27 - i4 - Feb 17 2005 - p27(2) [501+]
TLS - i5301 - Nov 5 2004 - p11(1) [501+]

Bebchuk, Lucian A. - *Pay Without Performance: The Unfulfilled Promise of Executive Compensation*
CHE - v51 - i15 - Dec 3 2004 - pA20-A20 [501+]
Har Bus R - v83 - i3 - March 2005 - p28(1) [51-500]
HLR - v118 - i3 - Jan 2005 - p1095(1) [1-50]

Bebczuk, Richardo N. - *Asymmetric Information in Financial Markets: Introduction and Applications*
JEL - v42 - i1 - March 2004 - p267(1) [501+]

Bebris, Carrie - *Pride and Prescience, or, a Truth Universally Acknowledged: A Mr. & Mrs. Darcy Mystery*
y VOYA - v27 - i4 - Oct 2004 - p291(2) [51-500]
Suspense and Sensibility or, First Impressions Revisited: A Mr. & Mrs. Darcy Mystery
LJ - v130 - i2 - Feb 1 2005 - p57(1) [51-500]
Suspense and Sensibility, or, First Impressions Revisited: A Mr. & Mrs. Darcy Mystery
PW - v252 - i4 - Jan 24 2005 - p224(1) [501+]

Becher, Bernd - *Typologies*
Am Sci - v92 - i6 - Nov-Dec 2004 - p572(2) [501+]

Bechstedt, F. - *Principles of Surface Physics*
Phys Today - v57 - i12 - Dec 2004 - p70-71 [501+]

Becht, Charles - *Process Piping; The Complete Guide to ASME B31.3. 2nd Ed.*
SciTech - v28 - i3 - Sept 2004 - p150(1) [51-500]

Bechtold, Richard L. - *Alternative Fuels: Transportation Fuels for Today and Tomorrow*
SciTech - v28 - i1 - March 2004 - p173(1) [51-500]

Beck, Aaron T. - *Cognitive Therapy of Personality Disorders. 2nd Ed.*
SciTech - v28 - i1 - March 2004 - p101(1) [51-500]

Beck, Alison - *Gardening Month by Month*
CBRA - Annual 2003 - p416(1) [51-500]
Gardening Month by Month in Ontario
CBRA - Annual 2003 - p416(1) [51-500]

Beck, Andrea - *Elliot's Christmas Surprise*
c CBRA - Annual 2003 - p447(2) [51-500]
Elliot's Great Big Lift-the-Flap Book
c CBRA - Annual 2003 - p448(1) [51-500]
Elliot's Noisy Night
c CBRA - Annual 2003 - p447(2) [51-500]

Beck, Barry - *Outdoor Photographer's Handbook*
Bwatch - March 2005 - pNA [51-500]

Beck, Bill - *Pride of the Inland Seas: An Illustrated History of the Port of Duluth/Superior*
R&R Bk N - v19 - i4 - Nov 2004 - p106(1) [51-500]

Beck, Carolyn - *Waiting Dog (Illus. by Beck, Andrea)*
c CBRA - Annual 2003 - p448(1) [51-500]

Beck, David E. - *Handbook of Colorectal Surgery, 2nd Rev. Ed.*
E-Streams - Dec 2004 - pNA [501+]

Beck, Hanne Richardt - *Understromme*
WLT - v78 - i3-4 - Sept-Dec 2004 - p129(1) [501+]

Beck, Ian - *Kitten Cat, a Rainy Day Book*
c Sch Lib - v52 - i3 - Autumn 2004 - p129(1) [501+]

Beck, Lois - *Women in Iran: From 1800 to the Islamic Republic*
MEJ - v59 - i1 - Wntr 2005 - p167(1) [51-500]

Beck, Martha - *Leaving the Saints: How I Lost the Mormons and Found My Faith.*
KR - v72 - i24 - Dec 15 2004 - p1174(1) [501+]
PW - v252 - i3 - Jan 17 2005 - p51(1) [51-500]

Beck, Randy - *Teen Quest*
Bwatch - March 2005 - pNA [51-500]

Beck, Scott - *Little House, Little Town*
c KR - v72 - i18 - Sept 15 2004 - p910(1) [501+]
c PW - v251 - i50 - Dec 13 2004 - p66(1) [501+]
c SLJ - v50 - i12 - Dec 2004 - p98(1) [501+]

Beck, Ulrich - *Global America?: The Cultural Consequences of Globalization*
R&R Bk N - v19 - i2 - May 2004 - p125 [51-500]

Becker, Adam H. - *The Ways That Never Parted: Jews and Christians in Late Antiquity and the Early Middle Ages*
Theol St - v65 - i3 - Sept 2004 - p641(2) [501+]

Becker, Adib A. - *An Introductory Guide to Finite Elemental Analysis*
SciTech - v28 - i1 - March 2004 - p138(1) [51-500]

Becker, Carl - *Time for Healing: Integrating Traditional Therapies with Scientific Medical Practice*
SciTech - v28 - i1 - March 2004 - p79(1) [51-500]

Becker, Carl C. - *The Heavenly City of the Eighteenth-Century Philosophers*
Sew R - v111 - i4 - Fall 2003 - pcxix-cxxi [501+]

Becker, Franklin - *Offices at Work: Uncommon Workspace Strategies That Add Value and Improve Performance*
Fut - v39 - i1 - Jan-Feb 2005 - p49(1) [51-500]

Becker, Helaine - *Boredom Blasters: Brain Bogglers, Awesome Activities, Cool Comics, Tasty Treats, and More... (Illus. by Davila, Claudia)*
c CCB-B - v58 - i4 - Dec 2004 - p159(2) [51-500]
c Res Links - v10 - i2 - Dec 2004 - p25(1) [51-500]
y SLJ - v51 - i1 - Jan 2005 - p141(1) [51-500]

Becker, Henk A. - *The International Handbook of Social Impact Assessment: Conceptual and Methodological Advances*
R&R Bk N - v19 - i1 - Feb 2004 - p126(1) [51-500]

Becker, Jasper - *Rogue Regime: Kim Jong Il and the Looming Threat of North Korea*
KR - v73 - i3 - Feb 1 2005 - p158(1) [501+]
PW - v252 - i8 - Feb 21 2005 - p163(1) [51-500]

Becker, John E. - *Gray Wolves*
c SB - v40 - i4 - July-August 2004 - p177(1) [51-500]
Green Sea Turtles
y SB - v40 - i4 - July-August 2004 - p167(2) [51-500]
Mugambi's Journey (Illus. by Clapsadle, Mark)
c KR - v72 - i14 - July 15 2004 - p682(1) [51-500]
c SLJ - v50 - i11 - Nov 2004 - p90(1) [51-500]

Becker, Kenneth Michael - *From the Treasure-House of Scripture: An Analysis of Scriptural Sources in " De imitatione Christi"*
Specu - v79 - i4 - Oct 2004 - p1031(2) [501+]

Becker, Lucinda M. - *Death and the Early Modern Englishwoman*
Ren Q - v57 - i4 - Winter 2004 - p1504(2) [501+]
R&R Bk N - v19 - i1 - Feb 2004 - p130(1) [51-500]

Becker, Nancy J. - *Challenges in Librarianship: A Casebook for Educators and Professionals*
ALJ - v53 - i4 - Nov 2004 - p410(1) [501+]

Becker, Norbert - *Mosquitoes and Their Control*
Choice - v42 - i1 - Sept 2004 - p132(1) [501+]
SciTech - v28 - i1 - March 2004 - p69(1) [51-500]

Becker, Patricia C. - *Social Change in America: The Historical Handbook, 2004*
R&R Bk N - v19 - i1 - Feb 2004 - p121(1) [51-500]

Beckerdite, Luke - *American Furniture 2002*
Ant&CM - v108 - i7 - Sept 2003 - p16(1) [501+]
Ant&CM - v109 - i3 - May 2004 - p16(1) [501+]
American Furniture 2004
Mag Antiq - v167 - i1 - Jan 2005 - p128(1) [51-500]
Mag Antiq - v167 - i2 - Feb 2005 - p54(1) [51-500]

Beckerman, Howard - *Animation: The Whole Story*
LJ - v129 - i12 - July 2004 - p80(1) [51-500]

Beckerman, Ilene - *Makeovers at the Beauty Counter of Happiness*
PW - v252 - i10 - March 7 2005 - p60(1) [51-500]

Beckett, Chris - *The Holy Machine*
Analog - v124 - i11 - Nov 2004 - p134(6) [501+]

Beckett, Francis - *The Blairs and Their Court*
KR - v73 - i1 - Jan 1 2005 - p28(1) [501+]
Enemy Within
NS - v133 - i4701 - August 16 2004 - p16(3) [501+]
Stalin's British Victims
TLS - i5296 - Oct 1 2004 - p27(1) [501+]

Beckett, I.F.W. - *The First World War: The Essential Guide to Sources in the UK National Archives*
J Mil H - v68 - i3 - April 2004 - p623-624 [501+]
The Great War, 1914- 1918
HER - v119 - i483 - Sept 2004 - p1087(1) [501+]
The Victorians at War
Choice - v41 - i11-12 - July-August 2004 - p2111(1) [501+]
TLS - i5263 - Feb 13 2004 - p25-25 [501+]

Beckett, Katharine Scarfe - *Anglo-Saxon Perceptions of the Islamic World*
Med R - June 2004 - pNA [501+]

Beckett, Katherine - *The Politics of Injustice: Crime and Punishment in America, 2nd Ed.*
R&R Bk N - v19 - i1 - Feb 2004 - p143(1) [51-500]

Beckey, Fred - *Range of Glaciers: The Exploration and Survey of the Northern Cascade Range*
E-Streams - July 2004 - pNA [501+]
PHR - v73 - i4 - Nov 2004 - p664(3) [501+]
WHQ - v35 - i3 - Autumn 2004 - p376(1) [501+]

Beckford, James A. - *Social Theory and Religion*
CS - v33 - i6 - Nov 2004 - p735(2) [501+]

Beckham, Stephen Dow - *The Literature of the Lewis and Clark Expedition: A Bibliography and Essays*
Isis - v95 - i3 - Sept 2004 - p499(2) [501+]
Pub Hist - v26 - i2 - Spring 2004 - p108(109) [501+]

Beckles, Hilary - *Chattel House Blues: Making of a Democractic Society in Barbados*
TLS - i5297 - Oct 8 2004 - p24(1) [501+]
Great House Rules: Landless Emancipation and Workers' Protest in Barbados, 1838-1938
TLS - i5297 - Oct 8 2004 - p24(1) [501+]

Beckman, James A. - *Affirmative Action: An Encyclopedia, Vols. 1-2*
BL - v101 - i4 - Oct 15 2004 - p436(1) [501+]
Choice - v42 - i5 - Jan 2005 - p832(1) [1-50]
LJ - v129 - i17 - Oct 15 2004 - p86(1) [51-500]
Ref Rev - Sept 2004 - pNA [501+]
R&R Bk N - v19 - i4 - Nov 2004 - p113(1) [51-500]

Beckman, Karen - *Vanishing Women: Magic, Film, and Feminism*
TDR - v48 - i2 - Summer 2004 - p172(3) [501+]

Beckman, Wendy Hart - *National Parks in Crisis: Debating the Issues*
y SLJ - v50 - i7 - July 2004 - p116(1) [51-500]
y VOYA - v27 - i4 - Oct 2004 - p333(1) [51-500]

Beckwith, Carol - *Faces of Africa: Thirty Years of Photography*
y BL - v101 - i1 - Sept 1 2004 - p25(2) [51-500]
Black Iss - v6 - i6 - Nov-Dec 2004 - p43(1) [51-500]

Beckwith, Christopher I. - *Koguryo, the Language of Japan's Continental Relatives: An Introduction to the Historical-Comparative Study of the Japanese Koguryoic Languages with a Preliminary Description of Archaic Northeastern Middle Chinese.*
R&R Bk N - v19 - i3 - August 2004 - p256(1) [51-500]

Beckwith, Francis J. - *The New Mormon Challenge: Responding to the Latest Defenses of a Fast-Growing Movement*
Bks & Cult - v10 - i6 - Nov-Dec 2004 - p38(3) [501+]

Beckwith, Sarah - *Signifying God: Social Relation and Symbolic Act in the York Corpus Christi Plays*
MP - v102 - i1 - August 2004 - p97(5) [501+]

Beckwith, Stacy N. - *Charting Memory: Recalling Medieval Spain*
Specu - v79 - i4 - Oct 2004 - p1032(3) [501+]

Becoming Joe DiMaggio (Illus. by Hunt, Scott)
y PW - v252 - i4 - Jan 24 2005 - p246(1) [51-500]

Bedard, Michael - *Painted Wall and Other Strange Tales*
y CBRA - Annual 2003 - p474(1) [51-500]

Bedard, Tony - *Route 666: Highway to Horror*
LibMed - v22 - i4 - June 2004 - p69(1) [501+]

Bedau, Hugo Adam - *Debating the Death Penalty: Should America Have Capital Punishment? The Experts on Both Sides Make Their Best Case*
Choice - v42 - i1 - Sept 2004 - p189(1) [501+]
Killing as Punishment: Reflections on the Death Penalty in America
R&R Bk N - v19 - i3 - August 2004 - p169(1) [501+]

Beddoes, Dick - *Pal Hal*
Globe & Mail - July 31 2004 - pD15 [51-500]

Beddoes, Thomas Lovell - *Death's Jest-Book*
TLS - i5267 - March 12 2004 - p6-6 [501+]

Bedeaux, Dick - *Optical Properties of Surfaces, 2nd Ed.*
SciTech - v28 - i4 - Dec 2004 - p48(1) [51-500]

Bedell, J.M. - *Finding Courage*
c CH Bwatch - March 2005 - pNA [51-500]

Bedford, Anthony - *Engineering Mechanics: Statics and Dynamics, 4th Ed.*
SciTech - v28 - i4 - Dec 2004 - p132 [51-500]

Bedford, David - *The Copy Crocs*
c LibMed - v23 - i1 - August-Sept 2004 - p64(1) [51-500]

Mo's Stinky Sweater (Illus. by Eaves, Edward)
c PW - v251 - i30 - July 26 2004 - p53(1) [51-500]
c SLJ - v50 - i10 - Oct 2004 - p109(1) [51-500]
The Way I Love You (Illus. by James, Ann)
c BL - v101 - i8 - Dec 15 2004 - p746(1) [51-500]
c PW - v251 - i49 - Dec 6 2004 - p59(1) [51-500]

Bedford, Deborah. - *Just between Us*
LJ - v129 - i18 - Nov 1 2004 - p68(1) [501+]

Bedford, Sybille - *Quicksands*
KR - v73 - i2 - Jan 15 2005 - p93(1) [501+]

Bedgood, Douglas - *Nalu*
Bwatch - Dec 2004 - pNA [51-500]

Bediako, Kwame - *Jesus and the Gospel in Africa: History and Experience*
IBMR - v29 - i1 - Jan 2005 - p48(2) [501+]

Bedingfield, M. Bradford - *The Dramatic Liturgy of Anglo-Saxon England*
Albion - v36 - i1 - Spring 2004 - p83(2) [501+]

Bedini, Silvio A. - *Jefferson and Science*
Isis - v95 - i2 - June 2004 - p300(2) [501+]

Bednarek, Janet Rose - *Dreams of Flight: General Aviation in the United States*
JAH - v91 - i2 - Sept 2004 - p699(2) [501+]
T&C - v45 - i3 - July 2004 - p629-630 [501+]

Bedoire, Fredric - *The Jewish Contribution to Modern Architecture, 1830-1930*
Choice - v42 - i4 - Dec 2004 - p651(1) [1-50]
R&R Bk N - v19 - i3 - August 2004 - p241(1) [51-500]

Bedorf, Thomas - *Dimensionen des Dritten. Sozialphilosophische Modelle Zwischen Ethischem und Politischem*
MLN - v119 - i3 - April 2004 - p620-627 [501+]

Bedouelle, Guy - *The History of the Church*
R&R Bk N - v19 - i3 - August 2004 - p19(1) [1-50]

Beeby, Alan - *First Ecology: Ecological Principles and Environmental Issues, 2nd Ed.*
TimHES - v0 - i1680 - Feb 25 2005 - pIII(1) [501+]

Beeby, Stephen - *MEMS Mechanical Sensors*
SciTech - v28 - i3 - Sept 2004 - p162(1) [51-500]

Beechen, Adam - *Hench*
PW - v251 - i28 - July 12 2004 - p46(1) [51-500]

Beecher, Donald - *Ariosto Today: Contemporary Perspectives*
R&R Bk N - v19 - i1 - Feb 2004 - p232(1) [51-500]

Beecroft, Simon - *The Release of Nelson Mandela*
c SLJ - v50 - i7 - July 2004 - p116(1) [51-500]

Beeman, Richard R. - *The Varieties of Political Experience in Eighteenth-Century America*
Choice - v42 - i6 - Feb 2005 - p1080(1) [51-500]
HRNB - v33 - i1 - Fall 2004 - p15(1) [501+]
RAH - v32 - i4 - Dec 2004 - p478-485 [501+]

Beer, Alexander - *The Impact of Electronic Mail on Business Processes and the Relevance of Proper English in This Context*
R&R Bk N - v19 - i4 - Nov 2004 - p106(1) [51-500]

Beer, Anna - *Bess*
TLS - i5262 - Feb 6 2004 - p23(1) [501+]

Beer, Caroline C. - *Electoral Competition and Institutional Change in Mexico*
Ams - v61 - i2 - Oct 2004 - p3392 [501+]

Beer, Dan - *Michel Foucault: Form and Power*
TLS - i5289 - August 13 2004 - p27(1) [501+]

Beer, Jeanette - *Beasts of Love: Richard de Fournival's Bestiaire d'Amour and A Woman's Response*
R&R Bk N - v19 - i1 - Feb 2004 - p231(1) [51-500]

Beer, Jeremy - *Choosing the Right College 2005: The Whole Truth about America's Top Schools*
R&R Bk N - v19 - i4 - Nov 2004 - p176(1) [501+]

Beer, Josh - *Sophocles and the Tragedy of Athenian Democracy*
Choice - v42 - i2 - Oct 2004 - p289(2) [501+]

Beer, Ralph - *In These Hills*
PSQ - v78 - i2 - Summer 2004 - p192(2) [501+]

Beer, Robert - *The Handbook of Tibetan Buddhist Symbols*
R&R Bk N - v19 - i1 - Feb 2004 - p200(1) [51-500]

Beerends, R.J. - *Fourier and Laplace Transforms. 1st Ed.*
TimHES - v0 - i1668 - Nov 26 2004 - pXVI(1) [501+]

Beermann, Jack M. - *Administrative Law*
R&R Bk N - v19 - i1 - Feb 2004 - pNA [51-500]

Beers, David - *Blue Sky Dream: A Memoir of America's Fall from Grace*
BL - v101 - i7 - Dec 1 2004 - p633(1) [51-500]

Beers, Mark H. - *The Merck Manual of Health & Aging*
  LJ - v129 - i12 - July 2004 - p118(1) [51-500]
  SEP - v277 - i2 - March-April 2005 - p45(1)
    [501+]
  BL - v101 - i2 - Sept 15 2004 - p276(1) [501+]
Beery, Barbara - *Batter Up Kids: Delicious Desserts*
  c SLJ - v51 - i2 - Feb 2005 - p114(1) [51-500]
Beevers, Sue - *Off-the-Shelf Fabric Painting: 30 Simple*
  Recipes for Gourmet Results
  LJ - v129 - i13 - August 2004 - p77(1) [501+]
Beevor, Antony - *The Mystery of Olga Chekhova*
  BL - v101 - i1 - Sept 1 2004 - p37(1) [51-500]
  Globe & Mail - Oct 9 2004 - pD18 [501+]
  Globe & Mail - Nov 27 2004 - pD3 [51-500]
  KR - v72 - i14 - July 15 2004 - p668(1) [501+]
  Lon R Bks - v27 - i4 - Feb 17 2005 - p16(1)
    [501+]
  NY - v80 - i27 - Sept 20 2004 - p102(1) [51-500]
  Paris After the Liberation, 1944-1949, Rev. Ed.
  LJ - v130 - i1 - Jan 1 2005 - p172(1) [1-50]
  R&R Bk N - v19 - i4 - Nov 2004 - p38(1) [51-
    500]
Beez, Jigal - *Geschosse zu Wassertropfen Sozio-religiose*
  Aspekte des maji-Maji-Krieges in Deutsch-Ostafika
  IJAHS - v37 - i1 - Wntr 2004 - p141-143 [501+]
Before Life
  y VOYA - v27 - i4 - Oct 2004 - p334(1) [51-500]
Befu, Harumi - *Globalizing Japan: Ethnography of the*
  Japanese Presence in Asia, Europe, and America
  JAS - v63 - i2 - May 2004 - p469(2) [501+]
Begehr, Heinrich - *Progress in Analysis: Proceedings, Vols.*
  1-2
  SciTech - v28 - i4 - Dec 2004 - p39(1) [51-500]
Begg, Roddy - *The Dialogue between Higher Education*
  Research and Practice: 25 Years of EAIR
  R&R Bk N - v19 - i1 - Feb 2004 - p185(1) [51-
    500]
Beginner's Guide to Gardening: Creating a Beautiful
  Yard from the Ground Up
  BL - v101 - i7 - Dec 1 2004 - p625(1) [51-500]
Begley, Louis - *Shipwreck*
  NYTBR - Oct 17 2004 - p26 [501+]
Behn, Aphra - *The Lover's Watch*
  TLS - i5299 - Oct 22 2004 - p31(1) [51-500]
Behn, Wolfgang - *Concise Biographical Companion to*
  'Index Islamicus': An International Who's Who in
  Islamic Studies, Vol. 1
  R&R Bk N - v19 - i4 - Nov 2004 - p17(1) [51-
    500]
Behr, Joshua G. - *Race, Ethnicity, and the Politics of City*
  Redistricting: Minority-Opportunity Districts and the
  Election of Hispanics and Blacks to City Councils
  Choice - v42 - i5 - Jan 2005 - p933(1) [51-500]
Behrbohm, Hans - *Essentials of Septorhinoplasty:*
  Philosophy-Approaches-Techniques
  SciTech - v28 - i1 - March 2004 - p110(1) [51-
    500]
Behrendt, Greg - *He's Just Not That into You: The*
  No-Excuses Truth to Understanding Guys
  Globe & Mail - Oct 9 2004 - pL3 [501+]
Behrman, Greg - *The Invisible People: How the U.S. Has*
  Slept through the Global AIDS Pandemic, the Greatest
  Humanitarian Catastrophe of Our Time
  Advocate - August 31 2004 - p64(2) [501+]
  BW - v34 - i30 - July 25 2004 - p4(2) [501+]
  G&L Rev W - v11 - i4 - July-August 2004 -
    p43(2) [501+]
  LJ - v129 - i12 - July 2004 - p102(1) [501+]
  Nation - v279 - i7 - Sept 13 2004 - p56 [501+]
  NYT - July 13 2004 - pE6 [501+]
Behrman, Jere R. - *Who's In and Who's Out: Social*
  Exclusion in Latin America
  R&R Bk N - v19 - i1 - Feb 2004 - p127(1) [51-
    500]
Behrooz, Maziar - *Rebels with a Cause: The Failure of the*
  Left in Iran
  IJMES - v36 - i3 - August 2004 - p485-486 [501+]
Beichman, Janine - *Embracing the Firebird: Yosano Akino*
  and the Birth of the Female Voice in Modern Japanese
  Poetry
  HJAS - v64 - i1 - June 2004 - p205-210 [501+]
Beidler, Philip D. - *Late Thoughts on an Old War: The*
  Legacy of Vietnam
  Choice - v42 - i3 - Nov 2004 - p468(1) [1-50]
Beier, Anne - *Crispus Attucks: Hero of the Boston*
  Massacre/Heroe de la Masacre de Boston
  c SLJ - v50 - i9 - Sept 2004 - p195(1) [51-500]
Beier, Ross C. - *Preharvest and Post-Harvest Food Safety:*
  Contemporary Issues and Future Directions
  SciTech - v28 - i3 - Sept 2004 - p74(1) [51-500]
Beig, Maria - *Hermine: An Animal Life*
  PW - v251 - i51 - Dec 20 2004 - p36(1) [51-500]

Beigbeder, Frederic - *Windows on the World*
  KR - v72 - i24 - Dec 15 2004 - p1152(2) [501+]
  LJ - v130 - i1 - Jan 1 2005 - p93(1) [501+]
  PW - v252 - i4 - Jan 24 2005 - p219(1) [501+]
  Spec - v296 - i9192 - Oct 9 2004 - p46(2) [501+]
  TLS - i5299 - Oct 22 2004 - p21(1) [501+]
  WLT - v78 - i3-4 - Sept-Dec 2004 - p116(1)
    [501+]
  Ent W - i812 - March 25 2005 - p76 [501+]
Beigbeder, Yves - *Judging Criminal Leaders: The Slow*
  Erosion of Impunity
  R&R Bk N - v19 - i3 - August 2004 - p212(1)
    [1-50]
Beike, Denise R. - *The Self and Memory*
  SciTech - v28 - i4 - Dec 2004 - p3(1) [1-50]
Beil, Karen Magnuson - *Mooove Over!: A Book about*
  Counting by Twos (Illus. by Meisel, Paul)
  c KR - v72 - i18 - Sept 15 2004 - p910(1) [501+]
  c SLJ - v50 - i10 - Oct 2004 - p109(2) [51-500]
Beilin, Yossi - *The Path to Geneva: The Quest for a*
  Permanent Agreement, 1996-2004
  Choice - v42 - i5 - Jan 2005 - p929(1) [51-500]
  Nation - v279 - i6 - August 30 2004 - p31 [501+]
Beilinson, Alexander - *Chiral Algebras*
  SciTech - v28 - i3 - Sept 2004 - p45(1) [1-50]
Bein, Thomas - *Walther von der Vogelweide*
  GSR - v27 - i1 - Feb 2004 - p135-136 [501+]
Beinart, William - *The Rise of Conservation in South*
  Africa: Settlers, Livestock, and the Environment,
  1770-1950
  Choice - v42 - i3 - Nov 2004 - p539(1) [1-50]
  Social History & African Environments
  Choice - v41 - i11-12 - July-August 2004 -
    p2100(1) [501+]
Beiner, Ronald - *Liberalism, Nationalism, Citizenship:*
  Essays on the Problem of Political Community
  CBRA - Annual 2003 - p302(1) [51-500]
Being Human: Core Readings in the Humanities:
  Readings from the President's Council on Bioethics
  SciTech - v28 - i4 - Dec 2004 - p60(1) [51-500]
Beinhart, Larry - *The Librarian*
  BL - v101 - i2 - Sept 15 2004 - p211(1) [501+]
  BW - v34 - i44 - Oct 31 2004 - p13(1) [501+]
  KR - v72 - i16 - August 15 2004 - p756(2) [501+]
  LJ - v129 - i17 - Oct 15 2004 - p52(1) [51-500]
  NYTBR - Oct 17 2004 - p12 [501+]
  PW - v251 - i36 - Sept 6 2004 - p45(1) [51-500]
  PW - v251 - i38 - Sept 20 2004 - p47(1) [51-500]
Beins, Bernard C. - *Research Methods: A Tool for Life*
  R&R Bk N - v19 - i1 - Feb 2004 - p7(1) [1-50]
Beirlein, James G. - *Principles of Agribusiness*
  Management, 3rd Ed.
  SciTech - v28 - i4 - Dec 2004 - p7(1) [1-50]
Beirman, David - *Restoring Tourism Destinations in*
  Crisis: A Strategic Marketing Approach
  R&R Bk N - v19 - i1 - Feb 2004 - p69(1) [501+]
Beiser, Frederick C. - *The Romantic Imperative: The*
  Concept of Early German Romanticism
  Choice - v41 - i11-12 - July-August 2004 -
    p2048(1) [501+]
Beisner, Robert L. - *American Foreign Relations Since*
  1600: A Guide to the Literature, 2nd Ed., Vols. 1-2
  R&R Bk N - v19 - i1 - Feb 2004 - p262(1) [51-
    500]
Beisswanger, Gabriele - *Frauen in der Pharmazie: Die*
  Geschiehte eines Frauenberufs
  Isis - v95 - i2 - June 2004 - p283(1) [501+]
Beitler, Ruth Margolies - *The Path to Mass Rebellion: An*
  Analysis of Two Intifadas
  R&R Bk N - v19 - i3 - August 2004 - p51(1) [51-
    500]
Beitman, Bernard D. - *Learning Psychotherapy: A*
  Time-Efficient, Research-Based, and Outcome-Measured
  Training Program, 2nd Ed.
  SciTech - v28 - i3 - Sept 2004 - p97(1) [51-500]
Beito, David T. - *The Voluntary City: Choice, Community,*
  and Civil Society
  JEL - v41 - i4 - Dec 2003 - p1329(3) [501+]
Beitter, Ursula E. - *Critical Essays on Contemporary*
  European Culture and Society
  R&R Bk N - v19 - i1 - Feb 2004 - p31(1) [1-50]
Bejoria, Paul - *The Printer's Devil*
  c Sch Lib - v52 - i4 - Winter 2004 - p192(1) [51-
    500]
Bek, Lise - *Reality in the Mirror of Art*
  R&R Bk N - v19 - i2 - May 2004 - p194(1) [51-
    500]
Bekaert, Geert - *Emerging Markets*
  R&R Bk N - v19 - i3 - August 2004 - p139(1)
    [51-500]

Beke, D.L. - *Nanodiffusion: Diffusion in Nanostructured*
  Materials
  SciTech - v28 - i3 - Sept 2004 - p140(1) [51-500]
Bekelman, Karl - *A Personal History of CESR and CLEO*
  Am Sci - v93 - i2 - March-April 2005 - p172(1)
    [51-500]
Beker, Jeanne - *The Big Night Out (Illus. by Dion, Natalie)*
  c PW - v252 - i11 - March 14 2005 - p70(1) [501+]
Bekman, Stas - *Practical Mod_Perl*
  SciTech - v28 - i4 - Dec 2004 - p152(1) [51-500]
Belanger, Jeff - *The Worlds Most Haunted Places: From*
  the Secret Files of Ghostvillage.com
  Bwatch - Feb 2005 - pNA [501+]
Belanger, Pamela J. - *Envisioning New England: Treasures*
  from Community Art Museums
  A Art - v69 - i750 - Jan 2005 - p77(1) [501+]
Belanger, Terry - *Lunacy and the Arrangement of Books*
  LRTS - v48 - i3 - July 2004 - p231(2) [501+]
Belasco, Kent S. - *Managing Bank Conversions: The*
  Guide to Organizing, Controlling, and Implementing
  Systems Conversions
  R&R Bk N - v19 - i2 - May 2004 - p122 [501+]
Belasco, Warren - *Food Nations: Selling Taste in*
  Consumer Societies
  JWH - v16 - i3 - Autumn 2004 - p197(9) [501+]
Belbruno, Edward - *Astrodynamics, Space Missions, and*
  Chaos
  SciTech - v28 - i4 - Dec 2004 - p162(1) [51-500]
  Capture Dynamics and Chaotic Motion in Celestial
  Mechanics: With Applications to the Construction of Low
  Energy Transfers
  SIAM Rev - v46 - i4 - Dec 2004 - p754-755
    [501+]
Belchansky, Gennady I. - *Arctic Ecology Research from*
  Microwave Satellite Observations
  SciTech - v28 - i3 - Sept 2004 - p57(1) [1-50]
Belenkiy, Vladimir - *An International Encyclopedia of*
  Land Tenure Relations for the Nations of the World, Vol.
  3
  R&R Bk N - v19 - i4 - Nov 2004 - p164(1) [501+]
  An International Encyclopedia of Land Tenure Relations
  for the Nations of the World, Vol. 4
  R&R Bk N - v19 - i4 - Nov 2004 - p164(1) [501+]
Belfiore, Francesco - *The Structure of the Mind: Outlines*
  of Philosophical System
  R&R Bk N - v19 - i3 - August 2004 - p7(1) [1-50]
Belgard, William - *Shaping the Future: The Dynamic*
  Process for Creating and Achieving Your Company's
  Strategic Vision
  R&R Bk N - v19 - i3 - August 2004 - p106(1)
    [1-50]
Belgard, William P. - *Shaping the Future*
  HR Mag - v49 - i10 - Oct 2004 - p143(2) [501+]
Belgrave, Bridget - *Zak*
  c Sch Lib - v52 - i3 - Autumn 2004 - p135(1) [501+]
Belitto, Christopher M. - *Renewing Christianity: A History*
  of Church Reform from Day One to Vatican II
  JR - v84 - i4 - Oct 2004 - p621(2) [501+]
Beljanski, Mirko - *Regulation of DNA Replication and*
  Transcription
  SciTech - v28 - i1 - March 2004 - p75(1) [51-500]
Belkin, Aaron - *Don't Ask, Don't Tell: Debating the Gay*
  Ban in the Military
  CS - v33 - i4 - July 2004 - p429(2) [501+]
Belkin, Lisa - *Tales from the Times: Real-Life Stories to*
  Make You Think, Wonder, and Smile, from the Pages of
  The New York Times
  y Kliatt - v38 - i5 - Sept 2004 - p38(3) [501+]
Belknap, Michal R. - *The Vinson Court: Justices, Rulings*
  and Legacy
  Law&PolBR - Nov 2004 - p833(4) [501+]
Bell, Adrienne Baxter - *George Inness and the Visionary*
  Landscape
  Choice - v42 - i1 - Sept 2004 - p87(2) [501+]
Bell, Alison - *Fashion 101 (Illus. by Mireault, Jerome)*
  c PW - v251 - i51 - Dec 20 2004 - p62(1) [51-500]
  Fearless Fashion
  c Res Links - v10 - i3 - Feb 2005 - p44(1) [501+]
Bell, Anthea - *The Little Mermaid (Illus. by Zwerger,*
  Lisbeth)
  c CCB-B - v58 - i4 - Dec 2004 - p159(1) [51-500]
Bell, Barry - *Bangkok u Angelic Allusions*
  A Aff - v35 - i2 - July 2004 - p247-248 [501+]
Bell, Brad - *The Social Psychology of Fundraising, 4th Ed.*
  R&R Bk N - v19 - i2 - May 2004 - p121 [51-500]
Bell, Brian - *Mediterranean Cruises*
  R&R Bk N - v19 - i4 - Nov 2004 - p35(1) [51-
    500]
  USA: The New South
  R&R Bk N - v19 - i4 - Nov 2004 - p62(1) [51-
    500]

Bell, C. Jeanenne - *Pendant and Pocket Watches*
   Bwatch - v26 - i9 - Sept 2004 - p9(1) [51-500]
Bell, Catherine - *Intercultural Dispute Resolution in Aboriginal Contexts*
   R&R Bk N - v19 - i3 - August 2004 - p191(1/2) [501+]
   Intercultural Dispute Resolution in Aboriginal Contexts
   Law&PolBR - August 2004 - p598(4) [501+]
Bell, Cece - *Sock Monkey Boogie-Woogie: A Friend Is Made (Illus. by Bell, Cece)*
   c   BL - v101 - i9-10 - Jan 1 2005 - p867(2) [51-500]
   c   SLJ - v51 - i1 - Jan 2005 - p86(1) [51-500]
Bell, Daniel A. - *The Politics of Affective Relations: East Asia and Beyond*
   R&R Bk N - v19 - i4 - Nov 2004 - p156(1) [501+]
Bell, Darrin - *Peace, Love and Latties*
   Bwatch - Feb 2005 - pNA [51-500]
Bell, David - *City of Quarters: Urban Villages in the Contemporary City*
   R&R Bk N - v19 - i3 - August 2004 - p155(1) [51-500]
Bell, David F. - *Real Time: Accelerating Narrative from Alzac to Zola*
   Choice - v41 - i11-12 - July-August 2004 - p2049(1) [501+]
Bell, Derrick A. - *Race, Racism, and American Law, 5th Ed.*
   R&R Bk N - v19 - i3 - August 2004 - p203(1) [1-50]
   Silent Covenants: Brown v. Board of Education and the Unfulfilled Hopes for Racial Reform
   BooChiTr - May 2 2004 - p1(4) [501+]
   Choice - v42 - i4 - Dec 2004 - p700(1) [1-50]
   NYRB - v51 - i14 - Sept 23 2004 - p47(4) [501+]
Bell, Ellen E. - *Understanding Early Classic Copan*
   Choice - v41 - i11-12 - July-August 2004 - p2087(1) [501+]
Bell, F.G. - *Engineering Geology and Construction*
   SciTech - v28 - i3 - Sept 2004 - p142(1) [51-500]
Bell, Hilari - *Fall of a Kingdom*
   y   Kliatt - v39 - i2 - March 2005 - p24(1) [51-500]
   The Goblin Wood
   y   Kliatt - v38 - i5 - Sept 2004 - p27(2) [51-500]
   c   LibMed - v22 - i4 - Jan 2004 - p64(1) [501+]
   The Wizard Test
   c   CCB-B - v58 - i6 - Feb 2005 - p243(1) [51-500]
   y   Kliatt - v39 - i2 - March 2005 - p6(1) [51-500]
   c   KR - v73 - i2 - Jan 15 2005 - p116(1) [51-500]
   c   PW - v252 - i10 - March 7 2005 - p68(1) [51-500]
Bell, J.S. - *Speakable and Unspeakable in Quantum Mechanics*
   TimHES - v0 - i1658 - Sept 17 2004 - p27(1) [501+]
Bell, Jack - *Civil War Heavy Explosive Ordnance: A Guide to Large Artillery Projectiles, Torpedoes, and Mines.*
   JSH - v70 - i4 - Nov 2004 - p989(1) [501+]
Bell, James Scott - *Write Great Fiction: Plot & Structure; Techniques and Exercises for Crafting a Plot That Grips Readers from Start to Finish*
   LJ - v129 - i14 - Sept 1 2004 - p164(2) [501+]
Bell, Janet Cheatham - *Stretch Your Wings: Famous Black Quotations for Teens*
   y   B Ent - v34 - i12 - July 2004 - p140(1) [501+]
Bell, Janis - *Art History in the Age of Bellori: Scholarship and Cultural Politics in Seventeenth Century Rome*
   Six Ct J - v35 - i1 - Spring 2004 - p212(3) [501+]
Bell, Jerry A. - *Chemistry: A Project of the American Chemical Society*
   J Chem Ed - v81 - i11 - Nov 2004 - p1572-1572 [501+]
Bell, Madison Smartt - *The Stone That the Builder Refused*
   BL - v101 - i2 - Sept 15 2004 - p179(1) [51-500]
   BL - v101 - i9-10 - Jan 1 2005 - p769(1) [51-500]
   BW - v34 - i51 - Dec 19 2004 - p4(2) [501+]
   KR - v72 - i19 - Oct 1 2004 - p927(2) [501+]
   LJ - v129 - i17 - Oct 15 2004 - p52(1) [51-500]
   NYTBR - Nov 14 2004 - p49 [501+]
   PW - v251 - i38 - Sept 20 2004 - p43(1) [51-500]
Bell, Martin - *Through Gates of Fire: A Journey into World Disorder*
   CR - v285 - i1665 - Oct 2004 - p244(2) [501+]
Bell, Marvin - *Rampant*
   Ga R - v58 - i2 - Summer 2004 - p484-501 [501+]
   LJ - v129 - i12 - July 2004 - p87(1) [51-500]
Bell, Mary Ann - *Internet and Personal Computing Fads*
   A Lib - v35 - i8 - Sept 2004 - p79(1) [51-500]
   Choice - v42 - i4 - Dec 2004 - p630(2) [1-50]
   E-Streams - Nov 2004 - pNA [501+]
   JouAmCul - v27 - i4 - Dec 2004 - p448(2) [501+]
   R&R Bk N - v19 - i3 - August 2004 - p143(1) [51-500]

Bell, Masha - *Understanding English Spelling*
   TimHES - v0 - i1678 - Feb 11 2005 - p25(1) [501+]
Bell, Michael Mayerfeld - *Farming for Us All: Practical Agriculture and the Cultivation of Sustainability*
   Choice - v42 - i6 - Feb 2005 - p1045(1) [51-500]
Bell, Millicent - *Shakespeare's Tragic Skepticism*
   Shakes Q - v55 - i1 - Spring 2004 - p91-93 [501+]
   Six Ct J - v35 - i1 - Spring 2004 - p319(2) [501+]
Bell, Roger - *Larger than Life*
   CBRA - Annual 2003 - p247(1) [51-500]
Bell, Roger V. - *Sounding the Abyss: Readings between Cavell and Derrida*
   R&R Bk N - v19 - i3 - August 2004 - p5(1) [1-50]
Bell, Rudolph - *The Voices of Gemma Galgani: The Life and Afterlife of a Modern Saint*
   Lon R Bks - v26 - i5 - March 4 2004 - p14(5) [501+]
Bell, Stephanie A. - *The State, the Market and the Euro: Chartalism versus Metallism in the Theory of Money*
   JEL - v41 - i4 - Dec 2003 - p1346(1) [501+]
Bell, Stewart - *Cold Terror: How Canada Nurtures and Exports Terrorism around the World*
   BIC - v33 - i6 - Sept 2004 - p17(2) [501+]
   BIC - v33 - i7 - Oct 2004 - p25(1) [501+]
   TimHES - v0 - i1655 - August 27 2004 - p24(1) [501+]
Bell, Suzanne - *Encyclopedia of Forensic Science*
   J Chem Ed - v81 - i8 - August 2004 - p1122-1122 [501+]
   LibMed - v22 - i7 - April-May 2004 - p76(1) [501+]
   R&R Bk N - v19 - i1 - Feb 2004 - p144(1) [51-500]
   The Facts on File Dictionary of Forensic Science
   Choice - v42 - i3 - Nov 2004 - p454(2) [1-50]
   R&R Bk N - v19 - i3 - August 2004 - p168(1) [501+]
   y   SB - v40 - i6 - Nov-Dec 2004 - p254(1) [51-500]
Bell, Ted - *Assassin: A Novel*
   BL - v100 - i21 - July 2004 - p1823(1) [1-50]
Bell, Trudy E. - *Sun: Our Nearest Star*
   y   SB - v40 - i4 - July-August 2004 - p163(1) [51-500]
Bell, Wade - *Destroyer of Compasses*
   CBRA - Annual 2003 - p195(1) [51-500]
Bellack, Alan S. - *Social Skills Training for Schizophrenia: A Step-by-Step Guide, 2nd Ed.*
   SciTech - v28 - i4 - Dec 2004 - p99(1) [51-500]
Bellaigue, Eric de - *British Book Publishing as a Business Since the 1960s*
   TLS - i5304 - Nov 26 2004 - p30(1) [501+]
Bellamy, Adrienne - *Departures*
   Black Iss - v6 - i6 - Nov-Dec 2004 - p74(1) [51-500]
Bellamy, Alex J. - *The Formation of Croatian National Identity: A Centuries-Old Dream?*
   Choice - v42 - i1 - Sept 2004 - p168(1) [501+]
   Understanding Peacekeeping
   Choice - v42 - i3 - Nov 2004 - p561(1) [1-50]
Bellamy, David - *David Bellamy's Developing Your Watercolours*
   LJ - v129 - i12 - July 2004 - p80(1) [51-500]
Bellamy, Dodie - *Pink Steam*
   PW - v251 - i27 - July 5 2004 - p39(2) [501+]
Bellamy, Richard - *Political Concepts*
   AJPS - v39 - i3 - Nov 2004 - p675(3) [501+]
   R&R Bk N - v19 - i1 - Feb 2004 - p147(1) [51-500]
Bellamy, Rufus - *Inside the Brain*
   c   CH Bwatch - Feb 2005 - pNA [501+]
Bellany, Alastair - *The Politics of Scandal in Early Modern England: News Culture and the Overbury Affair, 1603-1660*
   JIH - v34 - i3 - Wntr 2004 - p449-2 [501+]
Bellay, Joachim Du - *La Deffence, et illustration de la langue francoyse*
   Ren Q - v57 - i3 - Fall 2004 - p1018(2) [501+]
Bellefontaine, Kim - *ABC of America (Illus. by Gurth, Per-Henrik)*
   c   LibMed - v23 - i3 - Nov-Dec 2004 - p66(1) [51-500]
   c   SLJ - v50 - i7 - July 2004 - p90(1) [51-500]
Bellegarde-Smith, Patrick - *Haiti: The Breached Citadel*
   Globe & Mail - August 21 2004 - pD13 [1-50]
Bellen, Alfredo - *Numerical Methods for Delay Differential Equations*
   SIAM Rev - v46 - i3 - Sept 2004 - p574(2) [501+]
Bellenger, Dominic Aidan - *Princes of the Church: A History of the English Cardinals*
   Six Ct J - v34 - i4 - Winter 2003 - p1233-1234 [501+]

Bellenir, Karen - *Alzheimer's Disease Sourcebook: Basic Consumer Health Information about Alzheimer's Disease, Other Dementias, and Related Disorders..., 3rd Ed.*
   SciTech - v28 - i1 - March 2004 - p101(1) [51-500]
   Back And Neck Sourcebook
   Bwatch - March 2005 - pNA [51-500]
   Cancer Sourcebook. 4th ed.
   E-Streams - July 2004 - pNA [501+]
   Fitness Information for Teens: Health Tips about Exercise, Physical Well-Being, and Health Maintenance, Including Facts about Aerobic and Anaerobic Conditioning, Stretching, Body Shape and Body Image...
   SciTech - v28 - i4 - Dec 2004 - p85(1) [51-500]
   Fitness Information for Teens: Health Tips about Exercise, Physical Well-Being, and Health Maintenance Including Facts about Aerobic and Anaerobic Conditioning, Stretching, Body Shape and Body Image...
   y   SLJ - v51 - i1 - Jan 2005 - p141(2) [51-500]
   Infectious Diseases Sourcebook: Basic Consumer Health Information about Non-Contagious Bacterial, Viral, Prion, Fungal, and Parasitic Diseases Spread ...
   SciTech - v28 - i3 - Sept 2004 - p84(1) [51-500]
   Infectious Diseases Sourcebook
   Bwatch - Nov 2004 - pNA [51-500]
   Religious Holidays and Calendars: An Encyclopedia Handbook, 3rd Ed.
   Choice - v42 - i1 - Sept 2004 - p66(1) [501+]
   c   LibMed - v23 - i3 - Nov-Dec 2004 - p86(1) [51-500]
   Religious Holidays and Calendars: An Encyclopedic Handbook, 3rd Ed.
   BL - v100 - i22 - August 2004 - p1982(1) [51-500]
   Smoking Concerns
   Bwatch - March 2005 - pNA [51-500]
Beller-McKenna, Daniel - *Brahms and the German Spirit*
   Choice - v42 - i4 - Dec 2004 - p670(1) [1-50]
Beller, Susan Provost - *Yankee Doodle and the Redcoats: Soldiering in the Revolutionary War (Illus. by Day, Larry)*
   SLJ - v50 - i10 - Oct 2004 - pS31(1) [51-500]
Belleville, Bill - *Sunken Cities, Sacred Cenotes, and Golden Sharks: Travels of a Water-Bound Adventurer*
   NH - v113 - i7 - Sept 2004 - p67(2) [501+]
   R&R Bk N - v20 - i1 - Feb 2005 - p81(1) [51-500]
Belli, Mary Lou - *The Sitcom Career Book: A Guide to the Louder Faster Funnier World of TV Comedy*
   R&R Bk N - v19 - i4 - Nov 2004 - p222(1) [501+]
Bellinger, Charles K. - *The Genealogy of Violence: Reflections on Creation, Freedom and Evil*
   JAAR - v72 - i3 - Sept 2004 - p759-762 [501+]
Bellingeri, Marco - *Dinamicas de Antiguo Regimen y Orden Constitucional: Representacion, Justicia y Administracion en Iberoamerica. Siglos XVIII y XIX*
   HAHR - v84 - i2 - May 2004 - p330(2) [501+]
Bellingham, Brenda - *Lilly Makes a Friend (Illus. by Macdonald, Clarke)*
   c   Res Links - v10 - i2 - Dec 2004 - p14(1) [501+]
Belliotti, Raymond Angelo - *Happiness Is Overrated*
   RM - v58 - i2 - Dec 2004 - p423(3) [501+]
Bellis, Peter J. - *Writing Revolution: Aesthetics and Politics in Hawthorne, Whitman and Thoreau*
   NEQ - v77 - i4 - Dec 2004 - p665-666 [501+]
Bello, Walden - *Deglobalization: Ideas for a New World Economy*
   JEL - v41 - i4 - Dec 2003 - p1348(1) [501+]
   Dilemmas of Domination: The Unmaking of the American Empire.
   KR - v72 - i24 - Dec 15 2004 - p1174(1) [501+]
   PW - v252 - i5 - Jan 31 2005 - p56(2) [51-500]
Belloc, Hilaire - *Cautionary Verses (Illus. by B.T.B.)*
   c   Sch Lib - v52 - i3 - Autumn 2004 - p154(1) [501+]
Bellow, Adam - *In Praise of Nepotism: A History of Family Enterprise From King David to George W. Bush*
   NYTBR - July 18 2004 - p20 [501+]
   In Praise of Nepotism: A Natural History
   Choice - v41 - i11-12 - July-August 2004 - p2083(2) [501+]
   Esq - v140 - i2 - August 2003 - p24 [51-500]
   Soc - v41 - i6 - Sept-Oct 2004 - p74(6) [501+]
Bellow, Saul - *Seize the Day*
   BL - v101 - i9-10 - Jan 1 2005 - p816(1) [501+]
Bellwood, Peter - *Examining the Farming/Language Dispersal Hypothesis*
   R&R Bk N - v19 - i1 - Feb 2004 - p209(1) [51-500]
Belot, Adolphe - *Mademoiselle Giraud, Ma femme*
   NCFS - v32 - i3-4 - Spring-Summer 2004 - p404(2) [501+]
Belozerskaya, Marina - *Rethinking the Renaissance: Burgundian Arts across Europe*
   Art Bull - v86 - i3 - Sept 2004 - p599(5) [501+]

Belshaw, John Douglas - *Colonization and Community: The Vancouver Island Coalfield and the Making of the British Columbia Working Class*
WHQ - v35 - i3 - Autumn 2004 - p380(2) [501+]

Belt, Marjan Van Den - *Mediated Modeling: System Dynamics Approach to Environmental Consensus Building*
Env - v47 - i1 - Jan-Feb 2005 - p43(1) [501+]

Belting, Hans - *Art History After Modernism*
VQR - v80 - i3 - Summer 2004 - p270(1) [501+]

Belton, Benjamin Keith - *Orinoco Flow: Culture, Narrative, and the Political Economy of Information*
R&R Bk N - v19 - i1 - Feb 2004 - p67(1) [501+]

Beluge, Nancy - *Scream of the Hawk*
c   CBRA - Annual 2003 - p474(1) [51-500]

Belussi, Fiorenza - *The Technological Evolution of Industrial Districts*
R&R Bk N - v19 - i1 - Feb 2004 - p96(1) [1-50]

Belvel, Patricia Sequiera - *Rethinking Classroom Management: Strategies for Prevention, Intervention, and Problem Solving*
SLJ - v50 - i10 - Oct 2004 - pS71(1) [51-500]

Belville, J. Kevin - *LASIK Techniques: Pearls and Pitfalls*
E-Streams - Sept 2004 - pNA [501+]
SciTech - v28 - i1 - March 2004 - p113(1) [51-500]

Belyea, Barbara - *A Year Inland: The Journal of a Hudson's Bay Company Winterer*
Can Hist R - v85 - i3 - Sept 2004 - p593(2) [501+]

Belz, Corinna - *Other American Voices*
HNet - June 2004 - pNA [501+]

Belzen, Jacob A. - *Archiv fur Religionspsychologie: Archive for the Psychology of Religion, Vol. 26*
R&R Bk N - v20 - i1 - Feb 2005 - p6(1) [51-500]

Bemelmans, Ludwig - *Hotel Bemelmans*
LJ - v130 - i2 - Feb 1 2005 - p126(1) [1-50]
Madeline (Illus. by Bemelmans, Ludwig)
c   RT - v57 - Sept 2003 - p99 [51-500]

Bemrose, John - *The Island Walkers*
CBRA - Annual 2003 - p153(1) [51-500]
The Island Walkers. Audiobook Review
Globe & Mail - August 14 2004 - pD13 [1-50]
The Island Walkers
TLS - i5302 - Nov 12 2004 - p23(1) [501+]

Ben-Atar, Doron S. - *Trade Secrets: Intellectual Piracy and the Origins of American Industrial Power*
CHE - v50 - i45 - July 16 2004 - pA17(1) [501+]
Choice - v42 - i2 - Oct 2004 - p338(1) [51-500]

Ben-Chaim, Michael - *Experimental Philosophy and the Birth of Empirical Science: Boyle, Locke, and Newton*
SciTech - v28 - i4 - Dec 2004 - p13(1) [1-50]

Ben, Hammouda Hakim - *The Political Economy of Post-Adjustment: Towards New Theories and Strategies of Development*
JEL - v42 - i1 - March 2004 - p305(1) [501+]

Ben-Rafael, Eliezer - *Sociology and Ideology*
R&R Bk N - v19 - i1 - Feb 2004 - p122(1) [51-500]

Benabou, Marcel - *To Write on Tamara?*
RCF - v24 - i3 - Fall 2004 - p133(1) [501+]

Benaissa, Slimane - *The Last Night of a Damned Soul: A Novel*
BL - v101 - i2 - Sept 15 2004   p205(1) [501+]
Globe & Mail - Nov 27 2004 - pD40 [501+]
KR - v72 - i15 - August 1 2004 - p699(2) [501+]
LJ - v129 - i14 - Sept 1 2004 - p136(1) [51-500]
PW - v251 - i35 - August 30 2004 - p32(1) [501+]

Benard, Bonnie - *Resiliency: What We Have Learned*
TCR - v107 - i2 - Feb 2005 - p295(5) [501+]

Benardete, Seth - *Encounters & Reflections: Conversations with Seth Benardete: With Robert Berman, Ronna Burger, and Michael Davis*
Class R - v54 - i1 - May 2004 - p253(1) [501+]

Benatallah, Boualem - *Electronic Contracting (WEC 2004): Proceedings*
SciTech - v28 - i3 - Sept 2004 - p156(1) [51-500]

Benatar, David - *Life, Death, and Meaning: Key Philosophical Readings on the Big Questions*
R&R Bk N - v19 - i4 - Nov 2004 - p8(1) [51-500]

Benatar, Raquel - *Isabel Allende: Recuerdos para un cento/Memories for a Story (Illus. by Molinari, Fernando)*
c   SLJ - v50 - i9 - Sept 2004 - p195(1) [51-500]

Benbassa, Esther - *The Jews and Their Future: A Conversation on Judaism and Jewish Identities*
TLS - i5290 - August 20 2004 - p30(1) [501+]

Benbi, Dinesh K. - *Handbook of Processes and Modeling in the Soil-Plant System*
E-Streams - August 2004 - pNA [501+]
SciTech - v28 - i1 - March 2004 - p128(1) [51-500]

Bencastro, Mario - *Viaje a la Tierra del Abuelo*
Cur R - v44 - i5 - Jan 2005 - p12(1) [501+]

Bendaly, Leslie - *Leadership on the Run: How to Get Better Results Faster*
CBRA - Annual 2003 - p322(1) [51-500]

Bende-Nabende, Anthony - *International Trade, Capital Flows and Economic Development in East Asia: The Challenge in the Twenty-First Century*
JEL - v42 - i1 - March 2004 - p305(2) [501+]

Bender, Courtney - *Heaven's Kitchen: Living Religion at God's Love We Deliver*
CS - v33 - i4 - July 2004 - p460(2) [501+]

Bender, Daniel E. - *Sweatshop USA: The American Sweatshop in Historical and Global Perspective*
AHR - v109 - i4 - Oct 2004 - p1207-1207 [501+]
BHR - v78 - i2 - Summer 2004 - p326(3) [501+]

Bender, Frederic L. - *The Culture of Extinction: Toward a Philosophy of Deep Ecology*
QRB - v79 - i3 - Sept 2004 - p329(2) [501+]

Bender, K.A. - *Centralised Pay Setting: A Study of the Outcomes of Collective Bargaining Reform in the Civil Service in Australia, Sweden, and the UK*
R&R Bk N - v19 - i1 - Feb 2004 - pNA [501+]

Bender, Margaret - *Signs of Cherokee Culture: Sequoyah's Syllabary in Eastern Cherokee Life.*
Am Ind CRJ - v27 - i2 - Spring 2003 - p144-147 [501+]

Bender, Steven W. - *Modern Real Estate Finance and Land Transfer: A Transactional Approach, 3rd Ed.*
R&R Bk N - v19 - i3 - August 2004 - p204(1) [1-50]

Bender, Thomas - *The Education of Historians for the Twenty-First Century*
Lib & Cul - v39 - i4 - Fall 2004 - p429(17) [501+]
Rethinking American History in a Global Age
VQR - v79 - i1 - Winter 2003 - p7 [51-500]

Bender, Tisha - *Discussion-Based Online Teaching to Enhance Student Learning: Theory, Practice, and Assessment*
R&R Bk N - v19 - i1 - Feb 2004 - p182(1) [51-500]

Bender, William N. - *Learning Disabilities: Characteristics, Identification, and Teaching Strategies, 5th Ed.*
R&R Bk N - v19 - i1 - Feb 2004 - p193(1) [51-500]

Bendikowski, Tillmann - *Die Macht der Toene: Musik als Mittel politischer Identikaetsstiftung im 20 Jahrhundert*
HNet - Nov 2004 - pNA [501+]

Bending, Stephen - *The Writing of Rural England, 1500-1800*
Choice - v42 - i1 - Sept 2004 - p104(2) [501+]

Bendis, Brian Michael - *Daredevil: King of Hell's Kitchen*
PW - v251 - i40 - Oct 4 2004 - p72(1) [51-500]
Powers, Who Killed Retro Girl?
y   Teach Lib - v32 - i1 - Oct 2004 - p17(2) [501+]
The Ultimate Spider-Man. Vol. 1: Power and Responsibility
y   SLJ - v50 - i7 - July 2004 - p21(1) [501+]
Ultimate X-Men Blockbuster. Vol. 7 (Illus. by Finch, David)
y   LJ - v129 - i12 - July 2004 - p60(1) [51-500]

Bendis, Richard A. - *Overcoming Barriers to Technology Transfer and Business Commercialisation in Central and Eastern Europe: Solutions and Opportunities*
SciTech - v28 - i3 - Sept 2004 - p7(1) [501+]

Bendry, Christa - *Fish*
c   SB - v40 - i3 - May-June 2004 - p131(2) [501+]
Insects
c   SB - v40 - i3 - May-June 2004 - p131(2) [501+]

Benedek, Wolfgang - *Anti-Terrorist Measures and Human Rights*
R&R Bk N - v19 - i4 - Nov 2004 - p163(1) [501+]

Benedetti, Alessandro - *Historia corporis humani sive Anatomice*
Isis - v95 - i3 - Sept 2004 - p485(2) [501+]

Benedetti, Robert L. - *The Actor at Work, 9th Ed.*
R&R Bk N - v19 - i3 - August 2004 - p264(1) [1-50]

Benedetto, William R. - *Sailing into the Abyss: A True Story of Extreme Heroism on the High Seas*
PW - v251 - i51 - Dec 20 2004 - p43(1) [51-500]

Benedict, Barbara M. - *Curiosity: A Cultural History of Early Modern Inquiry*
MP - v102 - i1 - August 2004 - p116(5) [501+]
Six Ct J - v35 - i1 - Spring 2004 - p299(2) [501+]

Benedict, Jeff - *Out of Bounds: Inside the NBA's Culture of Rape, Violence, and Crime*
y   BW - v34 - i34 - August 22 2004 - p8(2) [501+]

Benedict, Michael - *Thrill of Victory: Best Sports Stories from the Pages of "Maclean's"*
CBRA - Annual 2003 - p147(1) [51-500]

Benedict, Philip - *Christ's Churches Purely Reformed: A Social History of Calvinism*
JMH - v77 - i1 - March 2005 - p164(3) [501+]
Six Ct J - v34 - i4 - Winter 2003 - p1268-1269 [501+]

Beneduce, Ann Keay - *Moses: The Long Road to Freedom*
LibMed - v23 - i1 - August-Sept 2004 - p78(2) [51-500]

Beneke, Jeff - *The Fence Bible*
LJ - v130 - i4 - March 1 2005 - p108(1) [51-500]

Benekos, Peter J. - *Controversies in Juvenile Justice and Delinquency*
R&R Bk N - v19 - i3 - August 2004 - p206(1) [501+]

Benenson, Etzhak - *Geosimulation: Automata-Based Modelling of Urban Phenomena*
SciTech - v28 - i4 - Dec 2004 - p7(1) [1-50]

Benenti, Giuliano - *Principles of Quantum Computation and Information: Basic Concepts. Vol. 1*
SciTech - v28 - i3 - Sept 2004 - p29(1) [51-500]

Benes, Rebecca C. - *Native American Picture Books of Change: The Art of Historic Children's Editions*
Choice - v42 - i6 - Feb 2005 - p1009(1) [51-500]
HB - v80 - i5 - Sept-Oct 2004 - p609(1) [51-500]
LJ - v129 - i12 - July 2004 - p77(1) [51-500]

Benett, Cherie - *Life in the Fat Lane*
y   Kliatt - v39 - i2 - March 2005 - p17(1) [51-500]

Benett, D. Scott - *The Behavioral Origins of War*
Choice - v42 - i2 - Oct 2004 - p367(1) [51-500]

Benfey, Christopher - *The Great Wave: Gilded Age Misfits, Japanese Eccentrics, and the Opening of Old Japan*
HR - v57 - i1 - Spring 2004 - p166-172 [501+]
NYTBR - August 15 2004 - p16 [501+]

Benford, Gregory - *The Sunborn*
KR - v73 - i2 - Jan 15 2005 - p89(1) [51-500]
LJ - v129 - i19 - Nov 15 2004 - p42(2) [501+]
PW - v252 - i7 - Feb 14 2005 - p58(1) [51-500]

Benford, Tom - *Corvette Illustrated Encyclopedia*
SciTech - v28 - i4 - Dec 2004 - p160(1) [51-500]

Bengio, Ofra - *The Turkish-Israeli Relationship: Changing Ties of Middle Eastern Outsiders*
Choice - v42 - i4 - Dec 2004 - p731(2) [1-50]

Bengtsson, Tommy - *Life under Pressure: Mortality and Living Standards in Europe and Asia, 1700-1900*
Choice - v42 - i3 - Nov 2004 - p538(1) [1-50]

Benhabib, Seyla - *The Reluctant Modernism of Hannah Arendt*
R&R Bk N - v19 - i1 - Feb 2004 - p148(1) [51-500]

Benham, Hugh - *John Taverner: His Life and Music*
MT - v145 - i1889 - Winter 2004 - p89-91 [501+]

Benigni, Helen - *Myth of the Year: Returning to the Origin of the Druid Calendar*
R&R Bk N - v19 - i1 - Feb 2004 - p12(1) [1-50]

Benioff, David - *When the Nines Roll Over and Other Stories*
BL - v100 - i22 - August 2004 - p1896(1) [51-500]
BW - v34 - i40 - Oct 3 2004 - p6(1) [51-500]
Ent W - i779 - August 20 2004 - p130 [51-500]
KR - v72 - i15 - August 1 2004 - p700(1) [501+]
People - v62 - i11 - Sept 13 2004 - p58 [51-500]
PW - v251 - i27 - July 5 2004 - p35(1) [51-500]

Benjamin, Arthur T. - *Proofs That Really Count: The Art of Combinatorial Proof*
Choice - v41 - i7 - March 2004 - p1329(1) [501+]
Math T - v97 - i5 - May 2004 - p382-382 [501+]
SIAM Rev - v46 - i3 - Sept 2004 - p562(2) [501+]

Benjamin, Carol Lea - *Fall Guy: A Rachel Alexander and Dash Mystery*
BL - v101 - i1 - Sept 1 2004 - p67(2) [51-500]
KR - v72 - i16 - August 15 2004 - p778(2) [51-500]
PW - v251 - i31 - August 2 2004 - p55(2) [501+]

Benjamin, Curt - *Lords of Grass and Thunder*
PW - v252 - i10 - March 7 2005 - p54(1) [51-500]

Benjamin, Don C. - *The Old Testament Story*
Choice - v41 - i11-12 - July-August 2004 - p2060(1) [501+]

Benjamin, Feinberg - *The Devil's Book of Culture: History, Mushrooms, and Caves in Southern Mexico*
JRAI - v10 - i4 - Dec 2004 - p909(2) [501+]

Benjamin, Geoffrey - *Tribal Communities in the Malay World: Historical, Cultural, and Social Perspectives*
JAS - v63 - i2 - May 2004 - p544(5) [501+]

Benjamin, Marina - *Rocket Dreams: How the Space Age Shaped Our Vision of a World Beyond*
SB - v40 - i4 - July-August 2004 - p155(1) [51-500]
SB - v40 - i6 - Nov-Dec 2004 - p239(1) [51-500]

Beolens, Bo - *Whose Bird?: Common Bird Names and the People They Commemorate*
Choice - v41 - i11-12 - July-August 2004 - p2020(1) [501+]
E-Streams - Nov 2004 - pNA [501+]

Beracs, Jozsef - *Marketing Theory and Practice: A Hungarian Perspective*
R&R Bk N - v19 - i3 - August 2004 - p127(1) [51-500]

Berakdar, Jamal - *Correlations Spectroscopy of Surfaces, Thin Films, and Nanostructures*
SciTech - v28 - i4 - Dec 2004 - p50(1) [51-500]

Beran, Michael Knox - *Jefferson's Demons: Portrait of a Restless Mind*
JAH - v91 - i2 - Sept 2004 - p611(2) [501+]

Berardi, Rosemary R. - *Handbook of Non-Prescription Drugs: An Interactive Approach to Self-Care, 14th Ed.*
E-Streams - Oct 2004 - pNA [501+]

Berberoglu, Berch - *Globalization of Capital and the Nation-State: Imperialism, Class Struggle, and the State in the Age of Global Capitalism*
CS - v33 - i4 - July 2004 - p471(3) [501+]
Turmoil in the Middle East: Imperialism, War and Political Instability
JTWS - v21 - i1 - Spring 2004 - p324(2) [501+]

Bercaw, Nancy - *Gendered Freedoms: Race, Rights, and the Politics of Household in the Delta, 1861-1875*
AHR - v109 - i3 - June 2004 - p919(2) [501+]
JAH - v91 - i2 - Sept 2004 - p640(2) [501+]

Berchtold, Jacques - *L'Amour dans 'La Nouvelle Heloise: texte et intertexte-Actes du colloque de Geneve*
FS - v58 - i3 - July 2004 - p415-416 [501+]

Bercovici, Ellen - *Collectibles for the Kitchen, Bath & Beyond, 2nd Ed.*
Ant&CM - v109 - i1 - March 2004 - p16(1) [501+]

Berdan, Francis F. - *The Aztecs of Central Mexico: An Imperial Society, 2nd Ed.*
R&R Bk N - v19 - i3 - August 2004 - p76(1) [51-500]

Berdanier, Carolyn D. - *Genomics and Proteomics in Nutrition*
SciTech - v28 - i4 - Dec 2004 - p62(2) [51-500]

Berdayes, Vicente - *Body in Human Inquiry: Interdisciplinary Explorations of Embodiment*
R&R Bk N - v19 - i4 - Nov 2004 - p76(1) [51-500]

Beredjiklian, Pedro K. - *Review of Hand Surgery*
SciTech - v28 - i4 - Dec 2004 - p108(1) [51-500]

Beren, Peter - *Vintage San Francisco*
Bwatch - v26 - i7 - July 2004 - p2(1) [51-500]

Berend, Ivan T. - *History Derailed: Central and Eastern Europe in the Long Nineteenth Century*
AHR - v109 - i3 - June 2004 - p996(2) [501+]
CEH - v37 - i3 - Summer 2004 - p449(3) [501+]
Choice - v41 - i7 - March 2004 - p1351(1) [501+]
HER - v119 - i483 - Sept 2004 - p1003(2) [501+]
HER - v119 - i483 - Sept 2004 - p1003(2) [501+]

Berend, Nora - *At the Gate of Christendom: Jews, Muslims, and "Pagans" in Medieval Hungary, c.1000-c. 1300*
JIH - v34 - i3 - Wntr 2004 - p444-3 [501+]

Berenger, Ralph D. - *Global Media Go to War: Role of News and Entertainment Media During the 2003 Iraq War*
R&R Bk N - v19 - i3 - August 2004 - p49(1) [51-500]

Berens, Charlyne - *Power to the People: Social Choice and the Populist/Progressive Ideal*
R&R Bk N - v19 - i3 - August 2004 - p206(1) [501+]

Berenson, James R. - *Biology and Management of Multiple Myeloma*
SciTech - v28 - i3 - Sept 2004 - p92(1) [51-500]

Berenson, Laurien - *Jingle Bell Bark: A Melanie Travis Mystery*
PW - v251 - i32 - August 9 2004 - p235(1) [51-500]

Berenstain, Jan - *Bear Essentials: Everything Today's Hard-Pressed Parent Needs to Know About Bringing Up Happy, Healthy Kids*
y PW - v252 - i4 - Jan 24 2005 - p246(1) [51-500]

Berenyi, Zsolt Endre - *Risk and Performance Evaluation with Skewness and Kurtosis for Conventional and Alternative Investments*
R&R Bk N - v19 - i1 - Feb 2004 - p118(1) [51-500]

Beresford-Kroeger, Diana - *Arboretum America: A Philosophy of the Forest*
CG - v124 - i2 - March-April 2004 - p93(1) [501+]
A Garden for Life: The Natural Approach to Deigning, Planting, and Maintaining a Noah Temperate Garden.
LJ - v129 - i13 - August 2004 - p107(1) [501+]

Berezin, Mabel - *Europe Without Borders: Remapping Territory, Citizenship, and Identity in a Transnational Age*
SF - v83 - i2 - Dec 2004 - p869(3) [501+]

Berg, Carol - *Guardians to the Keep*
y BL - v101 - i1 - Sept 1 2004 - p74(1) [51-500]

Berg, Charles Ramirez - *Latino Images in Film: Sterotypes. Subversion, and Resistance*
FQ - v57 - i2 - Winter 2003 - p57(2) [501+]

Berg, Dale - *Advanced Clinical Skills and Physical Diagnosis, 2nd Ed.*
SciTech - v28 - i3 - Sept 2004 - p90(1) [51-500]

Berg, Elizabeth - *The Art of Mending: A Novel (Read by Bean, Joyce). Audiobook Review*
BL - v101 - i1 - Sept 1 2004 - p142(1) [51-500]
Kliatt - v38 - i5 - Sept 2004 - p54(2) [51-500]
The Art of Mending: A Novel
BooChiTr - April 11 2004 - p1(2) [501+]
The Year of Pleasures
LJ - v129 - i20 - Dec 1 2004 - p86(1) [1-50]
LJ - v130 - i4 - March 1 2005 - p74(2) [51-500]
PW - v252 - i8 - Feb 21 2005 - p154(2) [51-500]

Berg, Henk de - *Freud's Theory and Its Use in Literary and Cultural Studies: An Introduction*
GSR - v27 - i2 - May 2004 - p406-407 [501+]

Berg, Herbert - *The Development of Exegesis in Early Islam: The Authenticity of Muslim Literature from the Formative Period*
IJMES - v36 - i4 - Nov 2004 - p681(2) [501+]

Berg, J.H. van den - *Two Principal Laws of Thermodynamics: A Cultural and Historical Exploration*
SciTech - v28 - i4 - Dec 2004 - p49(1) [51-500]

Berg, Jill Harrison - *Improving the Quality of Teaching through National Board Certification Theory and Practice*
TCR - v106 - i5 - May 2004 - p1029(3) [501+]

Berg, Leo van den - *City and Enterprise: Corporate Community Involvement in European and US Cities*
R&R Bk N - v19 - i1 - Feb 2004 - p127(1) [51-500]
Social Challenges and Organising Capacity in Cities: Experiences in Eight European Cities
R&R Bk N - v19 - i1 - Feb 2004 - p134(1) [51-500]

Berg, Manfred - *The Ticket to Freedom: Die NAACP und das Wahlrecht der Afro-Amerikaner*
JAH - v91 - i2 - Sept 2004 - p709(1) [501+]
Two Cultures of Rights: The Quest for Inclusion and Participation in Modern America and Germany
GSR - v27 - i3 - Oct 2004 - p662(2) [501+]

Berg, Michelle - *This Little Piggy and Old MacDonald*
c PW - v252 - i7 - Feb 14 2005 - p80(2) [501+]

Berg, Paul - *George Beadle, an Uncommon Farmer: The Emergence of Genetics in the 20th Century*
Choice - v41 - i7 - March 2004 - p1315(1) [501+]

Berg-Sobre, Judith - *San Antonio on Parade: Six Historic Festivals*
SHQ - v107 - i3 - Jan 2004 - p478(2) [501+]
WHQ - v35 - i1 - Spring 2004 - p96-97 [501+]

Berga, L. - *Roller Compacted Concrete Dams: Proceedings*
SciTech - v28 - i1 - March 2004 - p146(1) [51-500]

Bergamini, M. - *La Collezione numismatica di Emilio Bonci Casuccini. Con testi di M. Bergamini, P. Bittarelli, S.della Giovampaola*
Class R - v54 - i2 - Nov 2004 - p573(2) [501+]

Bergant, Dianne - *Lamentations*
Intpr - v58 - i4 - Oct 2004 - p422(2) [501+]

Bergemann, Kurt D. - *Brackett's Battalion: Minnesota Cavalry in the Civil War and Dakota War*
HNet - Sept 2004 - pNA [501+]
J Mil H - v68 - i4 - Oct 2004 - p1267-1268 [501+]

Bergen, Doris L. - *The Sword of the Lord: Military Chaplains from the First to the Twenty-First Century*
Choice - v42 - i5 - Jan 2005 - p907(2) [1-50]
HRNB - v33 - i1 - Fall 2004 - p37(1) [501+]
J Mil H - v68 - i4 - Oct 2004 - p1243-1244 [501+]

Bergenholtz, Gunnar - *Textbook of Endodontology*
SciTech - v28 - i1 - March 2004 - p120(1) [51-500]

Berger, Alan - *Terms and Truth: Reference Direct and Anaphoric*
Dialogue - v43 - i3 - Summer 2004 - p617-619 [501+]

Berger, Alan L. - *The continuing agony; from the Carmelite convent to the crosses at Auschwitz*
R&R Bk N - v19 - i3 - August 2004 - p16(1) [1-50]
Jewish American and Holocaust Literature: Representation in the Post Modern World
Choice - v42 - i7 - March 2005 - p1228(1) [51-500]

Berger, Ales - *The Key Witnesses: The Younger Slovene Prose at the Turn of the Millennia*
WLT - v78 - i3-4 - Sept-Dec 2004 - p140(2) [501+]

Berger, Arthur Asa - *Ads, Fads, and Consumer Culture: Advertising's Impact on American Character and Society, 2nd Ed.*
Choice - v41 - i7 - March 2004 - p1338(1) [501+]
R&R Bk N - v19 - i1 - Feb 2004 - p113(1) [51-500]
Deconstructing Travel: Cultural Perspectives on Tourism
R&R Bk N - v19 - i4 - Nov 2004 - p72(1) [51-500]
Media Analysis Techniques, 3rd Ed.
R&R Bk N - v19 - i4 - Nov 2004 - p212(1) [501+]
Media and Society: A Critical Perspective
R&R Bk N - v19 - i1 - Feb 2004 - p124(1) [51-500]
Ocean Travel and Cruising: A Cultural Analysis
R&R Bk N - v19 - i3 - August 2004 - p79(1) [51-500]

Berger, Brigitte - *The Family in the Modern Age: More than a Lifestyle Choice*
CS - v33 - i1 - Jan 2004 - p33-34 [501+]

Berger, Daniel - *In the Land of Magic Soldiers: A Story of White and Black in West Africa*
VQR - v80 - i2 - Spring 2004 - p263-263 [501+]

Berger, Helge - *Managing European Union Enlargement*
Pers PS - v34 - i1 - Wntr 2005 - p55(1) [501+]

Berger, Klaus - *Identity and Experience in the New Testament*
Theol St - v66 - i1 - March 2005 - p182(3) [501+]

Berger, Lance A. - *The Compensation Handbook: A State-of-the-Art Guide to Compensation Strategy and Design. 4th Ed.*
HR Mag - v49 - i7 - July 2004 - pS6(1) [51-500]
Talent Management Handbook: Creating Organizational Excellence by Identifying, Developing & Promoting Your Best People
HR Mag - v50 - i2 - Feb 2005 - pS17(1) [501+]

Berger, Maurice - *Masterworks of the Jewish Museum*
LJ - v129 - i20 - Dec 1 2004 - p107(1) [51-500]

Berger, Maxianne - *Sun through the Blinds: Montreal Haiku Today*
BIC - v33 - i6 - Sept 2004 - p33(1) [501+]

Berger, Melvin - *Penguins Swim but Don't Get Wet and Other Amazing Facts about Polar Animals*
c BL - v101 - i4 - Oct 15 2004 - p415(1) [51-500]
The Real Vikings: Craftsmen, Traders, and Fearsome Raiders
c LibMed - v22 - i6 - March 2004 - p78(1) [501+]
c SLJ - v50 - i10 - Oct 2004 - pS32(1) [51-500]

Berger, Patricia - *Empire of Emptiness: Buddhist Art and Political Authority in Qing China*
Ch Rev Int - v10 - i2 - Fall 2003 - p369(4) [501+]

Berger, Ron - *An Ethic of Excellence: Building a Culture of Craftsmanship with Students*
R&R Bk N - v19 - i1 - Feb 2004 - pNA [51-500]
TCR - v106 - i5 - May 2004 - p1023(4) [501+]

Berger, Roni - *Immigrant Women Tell Their Stories*
Bwatch - v26 - i9 - Sept 2004 - p10(1) [51-500]
R&R Bk N - v19 - i4 - Nov 2004 - p133(1) [51-500]

Berger, Stefan - *200 and More NMR Experiments, a Practical Course*
SciTech - v28 - i4 - Dec 2004 - p55(1) [51-500]

Berger, Tamara Faith - *The Way of the Whore*
Globe & Mail - Oct 16 2004 - pD23 [501+]

Bergeron, Alain - *Les Tempetes*
Res Links - v10 - i2 - Dec 2004 - p54(1) [51-500]

Bergeron, Bryan P. - *Case Studies in Genes and Disease: A Primer for Clinicians*
SciTech - v28 - i4 - Dec 2004 - p88(1) [1-50]
Essentials of XBRL: Financial Reporting in the 21st Century
R&R Bk N - v19 - i1 - Feb 2004 - p110(1) [51-500]

Bergeron, David Moore - *English Civic Pageantry, 1558-1642, Rev. Ed.*
R&R Bk N - v19 - i3 - August 2004 - p86(1) [51-500]
Practicing Renaissance Scholarship: Plays and Pageants, Patrons and Politics
Shakes Q - v55 - i1 - Spring 2004 - p94-98 [501+]

Bergeron, Diane - *L'atlas Mysterieux*
Res Links - v10 - i1 - Oct 2004 - p50(1) [51-500]
L'Atlas Perdu
y Res Links - v10 - i3 - Feb 2005 - p58(1) [51-500]

Bergeron, Jean-Francois - *Canada's Wild Lands*
CG - v124 - i5 - Sept-Oct 2004 - p114(1) [501+]

Bernard, Janine M. - *Fundamentals of Clinical Supervision. 3rd Ed.*
SciTech - v28 - i1 - March 2004 - p98(1) [51-500]

Bernard-Maugiron, Nathalie - *Egypt and Its Laws*
R&R Bk N - v19 - i4 - Nov 2004 - p176(1) [501+]

Bernard, Shane K. - *The Cajuns: Americanization of a People*
JAH - v91 - i1 - June 2004 - p305-306 [501+]
JSH - v70 - i3 - August 2004 - p718(2) [501+]

Bernardin, Susan - *Trading Gazes: Euro-American Women Photographers and Native North Americans, 1880-1940*
WHQ - v35 - i2 - Summer 2004 - p246-247 [501+]
Trading Gazes: Euro-American Women Photographers and Native North Americans, 1880-1940
JAH - v91 - i2 - Sept 2004 - p653(2) [501+]

Bernardini, Carlo - *Enrico Fermi: His Work and Legacy*
Choice - v42 - i6 - Feb 2005 - p1043(1) [51-500]
TimHES - v0 - i1682 - March 11 2005 - p27(1) [501+]

Bernardino, Jorge - *International Database Engineering and Applications Symposium (IDEAS 04): Proceedings*
SciTech - v28 - i3 - Sept 2004 - p30(1) [51-500]

Bernasconi, Pablo - *Wizard, the Ugly and the Book of Shame*
y Magpies - v19 - i5 - Nov 2004 - p31(1) [501+]

Bernau, Anke - *Medieval Virginities*
JGS - v13 - i3 - Nov 2004 - p285-286 [501+]

Bernauer, Thomas - *Genes, Trade, and Regulation: The Seeds of Conflict in Food Biotechnology*
Pers PS - v33 - i4 - Fall 2004 - p245(1) [501+]
PSQ - v119 - i4 - Winter 2004 - p724(3) [501+]
QRB - v79 - i4 - Dec 2004 - p450(2) [501+]

Bernault, Florence - *A History of Prison and Confinement in Africa*
IJAHS - v37 - i2 - Spring 2004 - p354-356 [501+]

Bernays, Edward - *Propaganda*
LJ - v129 - i18 - Nov 1 2004 - p134(1) [1-50]

Berner, Robert A. - *Phanerozoic Carbon Cycle: CO2 and O2*
SciTech - v28 - i4 - Dec 2004 - p53(1) [51-500]

Berneville, Guillaume de - *La Vie de Saint Gilles*
FS - v58 - i2 - April 2004 - p239(2) [501+]

Bernhard, William - *The Political Economy of Monetary Institutions*
JEL - v42 - i1 - March 2004 - p256(1) [501+]

Bernhardt, Christoph - *The Modern Demon: Pollution in Urban and Industrial European Societies*
J Urban H - v31 - i1 - Nov 2004 - p101-105 [501+]

Bernhardt, William - *Dark Eye*
KR - v72 - i22 - Nov 15 2004 - p1070(2) [51-500]
LJ - v129 - i19 - Nov 15 2004 - p49(1) [51-500]
PW - v251 - i48 - Nov 29 2004 - p22(1) [51-500]

Bernheimer, Charles - *Decadent Subjects: The Idea of Decadence in Art, Literature, Philosophy, and the Culture of the Fin De Siecle in Europe*
Comp L - v56 - i4 - Fall 2004 - p365-3 [501+]

Bernholz, Charles D. - *Kappler Revisited: An Index and Bibliographic Guide to American Indian Treaties*
R&R Bk N - v19 - i1 - Feb 2004 - pNA [51-500]

Bernier-Grand, Carmen T. - *Cesar: Si, Se Puede!=Yes, We Can! (Illus. by Diaz, David)*
c BL - v101 - i4 - Oct 15 2004 - p400(1) [51-500]
c CCB-B - v58 - i2 - Oct 2004 - p60(2) [51-500]
c KR - v72 - i17 - Sept 1 2004 - p860(1) [51-500]
c SLJ - v50 - i10 - Oct 2004 - p138(1) [51-500]

Bernier, Patrick - *Nanotube-Based Devices. Proceedings*
SciTech - v28 - i1 - March 2004 - p142(1) [51-500]

Bernier, Serge - *Canada, 1900-1950: Un pays prend sa place*
Can Hist R - v85 - i4 - Dec 2004 - p834(2) [501+]

Bernieres, Louis De - *Birds Without Wings*
Globe & Mail - July 24 2004 - pD3 [501+]
Lon R Bks - v26 - i17 - Sept 2 2004 - p16(1) [501+]
NYTBR - Oct 31 2004 - p22 [501+]
PW - v251 - i35 - August 30 2004 - p34(1) [501+]

Bernoulli, Daniel - *Die Werke von Daniel Bernoulli. Volume 5: Hydrodynamik II*
Isis - v95 - i2 - June 2004 - p293(2) [501+]

Bernstein, Art - *Oregon Byways: 75 Scenic Drives in the Cascades and Siskiyous, Canyons and Coast*
R&R Bk N - v19 - i1 - Feb 2004 - p65(1) [501+]

Bernstein, Bruce - *First American Art: The Charles and Valerie Diker Collection of American Indian Art*
BL - v101 - i3 - Oct 1 2004 - p293(1) [51-500]
LJ - v129 - i19 - Nov 15 2004 - p57(1) [51-500]
R&R Bk N - v19 - i3 - August 2004 - p61(1) [51-500]

Bernstein, David E. - *You Can't Say That! The Growing Threat to Civil Liberties from Antidiscrimination Laws*
Law&PolBR - June 2004 - p472(5) [501+]

Bernstein, George L. - *The Myth of Decline: The Rise of Britain Since 1945*
TimHES - v0 - i1675 - Jan 21 2005 - p25(1) [501+]
TLS - i5286 - July 23 2004 - p13(1) [501+]

Bernstein, Hilda - *The World That Was Ours*
Spec - v295 - i9181 - July 24 2004 - p33(2) [501+]

Bernstein, Jane A. - *Women's Voice Across Musical Worlds*
R&R Bk N - v19 - i1 - Feb 2004 - p194(1) [51-500]
Women's Voices Across Musical Worlds
Choice - v42 - i1 - Sept 2004 - p113(1) [501+]
Wom R Bks - v22 - i1 - Oct 2004 - p19(1) [501+]

Bernstein, Jeremy - *Oppenheimer: Portrait of an Enigma*
Am Sci - v92 - i5 - Sept-Oct 2004 - p473(3) [501+]
Choice - v42 - i1 - Sept 2004 - p124(1) [501+]
CR - v286 - i1669 - Feb 2005 - p121(1) [51-500]
Spec - v296 - i9200 - Dec 4 2004 - p47(1) [501+]
VQR - v80 - i3 - Summer 2004 - p253(2) [501+]

Bernstein, Jonathan Sackner - *Before It Happens to You: A Breakthrough Program for Reversing or Preventing Heart Disease*
SciTech - v28 - i1 - March 2004 - p104(1) [1-50]

Bernstein, Lee - *The Greatest Menace: Organized Crime in Cold War America*
AHR - v109 - i2 - April 2004 - p558(2) [501+]

Bernstein, Mark H. - *Without a Tear: Our Tragic Relationship with Animals*
Choice - v42 - i5 - Jan 2005 - p864(2) [1-50]

Bernstein, Mark W. - *How to Survive Your Freshman Year*
y SLJ - v50 - i10 - Oct 2004 - p186(1) [51-500]

Bernstein, Michael A. - *A Perilous Progress: Economists and the Public Purpose in Twentieth-Century America*
JEL - v42 - i4 - Dec 2004 - p1116(3) [501+]

Bernstein, Michael Andre - *Conspirators*
Comw - v131 - i22 - Dec 17 2004 - p23(2) [501+]
NYTBR - July 4 2004 - p13 [501+]
NYTBR - July 11 2004 - p22 [501+]
NYTBR - July 18 2004 - p18 [501+]

Bernstein, Nina - *Magic by the Book (Illus. by Kulikov, Boris)*
c CCB-B - v58 - i6 - Feb 2005 - p244(1) [51-500]
c KR - v73 - i4 - Feb 15 2005 - p225(1) [51-500]

Bernstein, Peter L. - *Wedding of the Waters: The Erie Canal and the Making of a Great Nation*
BL - v101 - i6 - Nov 15 2004 - p536(1) [51-500]
Bus W - i3919 - Feb 7 2005 - p20 [501+]
Econ - v374 - i8413 - Feb 12 2005 - p82US [501+]
KR - v72 - i20 - Oct 15 2004 - p991(1) [501+]
LJ - v129 - i20 - Dec 1 2004 - p134(1) [501+]
PW - v251 - i46 - Nov 15 2004 - p47(1) [51-500]

Bernstein, R.B. - *Thomas Jefferson*
HNet - Sept 2004 - pNA [501+]
PSQ - v119 - i4 - Winter 2004 - p722(2) [501+]

Bernstein, Richard B. - *Thomas Jefferson: The Revolution of Ideas*
y Ref Rev - August 2004 - pNA [501+]
c SLJ - v50 - i9 - Sept 2004 - p221(2) [51-500]

Bernstein, Seymour - *Monsters and Angels: Surviving a Career in Music*
Am MT - v54 - i3 - Dec 2004 - p72(3) [501+]

Bernstein, William J. - *The Birth of Plenty: How the Prosperity of the Modern World Was Created*
Choice - v42 - i1 - Sept 2004 - p152(1) [501+]
Globe & Mail - July 24 2004 - pD5 [501+]

Bernthal, John E. - *Articulation and Phonological Disorders. 5th Ed.*
SciTech - v28 - i3 - Sept 2004 - p95(1) [51-500]

Berold, Robert - *South African Poets on Poetry: Interviews from New Coin 1992-2001*
R&R Bk N - v19 - i1 - Feb 2004 - p220(1) [1-50]
WLT - v79 - i1 - Jan-April 2005 - p85(1) [501+]

Berrero, Mauricio - *Russia: A Reference Guide from the Renaissance to the Present*
Choice - v42 - i3 - Nov 2004 - p460(1) [1-50]

Berres, Janet - *Tarot Kit for Beginners*
Bwatch - March 2005 - pNA [51-500]

Berresford, Sandra - *Italian Memorial Sculpture, 1820-1940: A Legacy of Love*
Choice - v42 - i7 - March 2005 - p1217(1) [51-500]
TLS - i5304 - Nov 26 2004 - p33(1) [51-500]

Berrett, Joshua - *Louis Armstrong and Paul Whiteman: Two Kings of Jazz*
BL - v101 - i5 - Nov 1 2004 - p457(1) [51-500]
LJ - v129 - i17 - Oct 15 2004 - p64(1) [51-500]
PW - v251 - i42 - Oct 18 2004 - p58(1) [51-500]

Berrin, Shani L. - *The Pesher Nahum Scroll from Qumran: An Exegetical Study of 4Q169*
R&R Bk N - v19 - i4 - Nov 2004 - p23(1) [51-500]

Berry, David Carson - *A Topical Guide to Schenkerian Literature: An Annotated Bibliography with Indices*
Choice - v42 - i7 - March 2005 - p1191(1) [51-500]

Berry, F. Clifton - *United States Army at War: 9/11 through Iraq*
R&R Bk N - v19 - i1 - Feb 2004 - p42(1) [51-500]

Berry, Helen - *Creating and Consuming Culture in North-East England, 1660-1830*
R&R Bk N - v19 - i4 - Nov 2004 - p90(1) [51-500]

Berry, James - *Only One of Me*
c Sch Lib - v52 - i3 - Autumn 2004 - p154(1) [501+]

Berry, Jason - *Vows of Silence: The Abuse of Power in the Papacy of John Paul II*
Choice - v42 - i4 - Dec 2004 - p676(1) [1-50]

Berry, Jeffrey M. - *A Voice for Nonprofits*
PSQ - v119 - i2 - Summer 2004 - p380(2) [501+]
R&R Bk N - v19 - i1 - Feb 2004 - p98(1) [1-50]

Berry, John W. - *Psychology in Human and Social Development: Lessons from Diverse Cultures, a Festschrift for Durganand Sinha*
R&R Bk N - v19 - i1 - Feb 2004 - p7(1) [51-500]

Berry, Linda - *Death and the Walking Stick: A Trudy Roundtree Mystery*
BL - v101 - i8 - Dec 15 2004 - p710(1) [51-500]
LJ - v130 - i1 - Jan 1 2005 - p83(1) [51-500]

Berry, Michele - *Journey Prize Stories: From the Best of Canada's New Writers*
CBRA - Annual 2003 - p246(1) [51-500]

Berry, Paul - *The Latin Language and Christianity*
R&R Bk N - v19 - i3 - August 2004 - p19(1) [1-50]

Berry, Stephen William - *All That Makes a Man: Love and Ambition in the Civil War South*
AHR - v109 - i4 - Oct 2004 - p1233(1) [501+]
JSH - v70 - i4 - Nov 2004 - p932(2) [501+]

Berry, Steve - *The Romanov Prophecy (Read by Michael, Paul). Audiobook Review*
y Kliatt - v39 - i1 - Jan 2005 - p49(1) [51-500]
The Romanov Prophecy
KR - v72 - i14 - July 15 2004 - p644(1) [501+]
LJ - v129 - i12 - July 2004 - p66(1) [51-500]
PW - v251 - i32 - August 9 2004 - p230(1) [51-500]

Berry, Wendell - *Citizenship Papers*
WLT - v78 - i3-4 - Sept-Dec 2004 - p102(2) [501+]
Hannah Coulter
BL - v101 - i6 - Nov 15 2004 - p560(1) [51-500]
KR - v72 - i18 - Sept 15 2004 - p880(1) [51-500]
PW - v251 - i40 - Oct 4 2004 - p66(1) [51-500]
S Liv - v40 - i2 - Feb 2005 - p151(1) [51-500]

Berstein, Serge - *Les Annees Giscard: Institutions et Pratiques Politiques*
HER - v19 - i483 - Sept 2004 - p1107(2) [501+]

Bertagna, Julie - *The Ice-Cream Machine (Read by Aldrea, Sophie). Audiobook Review*
c SLJ - v51 - i1 - Jan 2005 - p76(1) [51-500]
Opposite of Chocolate
y Magpies - v19 - i5 - Nov 2004 - p39(1) [501+]
Soundtrack
y Magpies - v19 - i5 - Nov 2004 - p39(1) [501+]

Bertauski, Tony - *Designing the Landscape: An Introductory Guide for the Landscape Designer*
SciTech - v28 - i3 - Sept 2004 - p130(1) [51-500]

Bertelli, Sergio - *The King's Body: Sacred Rituals of Power in Medieval and Early Modern Europe*
JRAI - v10 - i3 - Sept 2004 - p706(2) [501+]

Bertensson, Sergei - *In Hollywood with Nemirovich-Danchenko, 1926-1927: The Memoirs of Sergei Bertensson*
R&R Bk N - v19 - i4 - Nov 2004 - p226(1) [501+]

Berth-Jones, John - *Eczema and Contact Dermatitis*
SciTech - v28 - i3 - Sept 2004 - p120(1) [51-500]

Berthier, Denis - *Urban Astronomy*
Astron - v32 - i11 - Nov 2004 - p98 [501+]

Berthier, P. - *L'Annee stendhalienne, I*
FS - v58 - i1 - Jan 2004 - p119(2) [501+]

Berthoud, Ricard - *Social Europe: Living Standards and Welfare States*
R&R Bk N - v19 - i4 - Nov 2004 - p126(1) [51-500]

Berthoud, Roger - *The Life of Henry Moore*
Choice - v42 - i1 - Sept 2004 - p88(1) [501+]

Berti, E. - *M. Annaei Lucani Bellum civile Liber X*
Class R - v54 - i2 - Nov 2004 - p400(3) [501+]

Bertine, Kathryn - *All the Sundays Yet to Come: A Skater's Journey*
    BooChiTr - Feb 1 2004 - p3(1) [501+]
Bertjan, Verbeek - *Decision-Making in Great Britain During the Suez Crisis: Small Groups and a Persistent Leader*
    R&R Bk N - v19 - i1 - Feb 2004 - p50(1) [51-500]
Bertola, Francesco - *Via Lactea: Milky Way in the History and in the Heavens*
    S&T - v109 - i1 - Jan 2005 - p118(2) [501+]
Bertolino, Bob - *Change-Oriented Therapy with Adolescents and Young Adults: The Next Generation of Respectful and Effective Processes and Practices*
    Adoles - v39 - i156 - Winter 2004 - p828(1) [51-500]
    Change-Oriented Therapy with Adolescents and Young Adults: The Next Generation of Respectful Processes and Practices
    SciTech - v28 - i1 - March 2004 - p119(1) [51-500]
Bertolotti, Mario - *The History of the Laser*
    New Sci - v185 - i2488 - Feb 26 2005 - p55(1) [51-500]
Bertolucci, Cristiano - *Animals Above and Below the Water (Illus. by Bartolozzi, Alessandro)*
    c LibMed - v22 - i5 - Feb 2004 - p54(1) [501+]
    Animals by Day and by Night (Illus. by Cucchiarini, Ferruccio)
    c LibMed - v22 - i5 - Feb 2004 - p54(1) [501+]
Berton, Albert - *Political Extremism and Rationality*
    JEL - v42 - i4 - Dec 2004 - p1119(2) [501+]
Berton, Pierre - *Joy of Writing: A Guide for Writers, Disguised as a Literary Memoir*
    CBRA - Annual 2003 - p13(1) [51-500]
    The Last Spike
    Globe & Mail - March 12 2005 - pD19 [51-500]
    Prisoners of the North
    BL - v101 - i7 - Dec 1 2004 - p627(1) [51-500]
    Globe & Mail - Oct 9 2004 - pD17 [501+]
    Globe & Mail - Nov 27 2004 - pD3 [51-500]
    KR - v72 - i23 - Dec 1 2004 - p1127(2) [501+]
Bertoni, Franco - *Minimalist Design*
    Choice - v42 - i3 - Nov 2004 - p470(1) [1-50]
Bertoti, Dolores B. - *Functional Neurorehabilitation through the Life Span*
    SciTech - v28 - i1 - March 2004 - p93(1) [51-500]
Bertotti, Bruno - *Physics of the Solar System: Dynamics and Evolution, Space Physics, and Spacetime Structure*
    SciTech - v28 - i1 - March 2004 - p44(1) [51-500]
Bertram, Christopher - *Routledge Philosophy Guidebook to Rousseau and the Social Contract*
    AJPS - v39 - i2 - July 2004 - p463(464) [501+]
Bertrand, Diane Gonzales - *My Pal, Victor/Mi amigo, Victor (Illus. by Sweetland, Robert L.)*
    c SLJ - v50 - i9 - Sept 2004 - p195(1) [51-500]
Bertrand, Dominique - *Penser la nuit*
    Ren Q - v57 - i3 - Fall 2004 - p1072(2) [501+]
Bertrand, Frederic - *L'Anthropologie Sovietique des Annees 20-30: Configuration d'une Rupture*
    Russ Rev - v63 - i2 - April 2004 - pNA [501+]
Bertrand, Michael T. - *Race, Rock, and Elvis*
    PMS - v27 - i4 - Dec 2004 - p541(2) [501+]
Berube, Michael - *The Aesthetics of Cultural Studies*
    R&R Bk N - v20 - i1 - Feb 2005 - p9(1) [501+]
Bervin, Jen - *Nets*
    ABR - v26 - i2 - Jan-Feb 2005 - p22(2) [501+]
Berwick, Donald M. - *Escape Fire: Designs for the Future of Health Care*
    E-Streams - June 2004 - pNA [501+]
    SciTech - v28 - i1 - March 2004 - p81(1) [51-500]
Berzoff, Joan - *Living with Dying: A Handbook for End-of-Life Healthcare Practitioners*
    Choice - v42 - i7 - March 2005 - p1260(1) [51-500]
Bes, Daniel R. - *Quantum Mechanics: A Modern and Concise Introductory Course*
    Choice - v42 - i6 - Feb 2005 - p1059(1) [51-500]
Besamusca, Bart - *The Book of Lancelot: The Middle Dutch "Lancelot" Compilation and the Medieval Tradition of Narrative Cycles*
    Specu - v79 - i4 - Oct 2004 - p1035(3) [501+]
Besen, Wayne R. - *Anything but Straight: Unmasking the Scandals and Lies Behind the Ex-Gay Myth*
    R&R Bk N - v19 - i1 - Feb 2004 - p23(1) [1-50]
Besier, Gerhard - *Repression und Selbstbehauptung: Die Zeugen Jehovas unter der NS- und der SED-Diktatur*
    J Ch St - v46 - i4 - Autumn 2004 - p894(3) [501+]
Bess, Michael - *The Light-Green Society: Ecology and Technological Modernity in France, 1960-2000*
    Choice - v41 - i11-12 - July-August 2004 - p2113(1) [501+]

Besse, Jean-Marc - *Les grandeurs de la Terre: Aspects du savoir geographique a la Renaissance*
    Ren Q - v57 - i4 - Winter 2004 - p1471(2) [501+]
Bessel, Richard - *Life After Death: Approaches to a Cultural and Social History of Europe During the 1940s and 1950s*
    HNet - Oct 2004 - pNA [501+]
    Nazism and War
    BL - v101 - i4 - Oct 15 2004 - p365(1) [51-500]
    KR - v72 - i17 - Sept 1 2004 - p844(2) [501+]
    LJ - v129 - i19 - Nov 15 2004 - p69(1) [501+]
    TLS - i5305 - Dec 3 2004 - p6(1) [501+]
Besser, Les - *Practical RF Circuit Design for Modern Wireless Systems, Vol. 1*
    SciTech - v28 - i1 - March 2004 - p159(1) [51-500]
Besserman, Perle - *A New Kabbalah for Women*
    LJ - v130 - i1 - Jan 1 2005 - p120(1) [51-500]
    PW - v251 - i51 - Dec 20 2004 - p56(1) [51-500]
Bessesen, Brooke - *Look Who Lives in the Desert!: Bouncing and Pouncing, Hiding and Gliding, Sleeping and Creeping*
    c SLJ - v50 - i8 - August 2004 - p105(1) [51-500]
Bessette, Richard P. - *Rods Down and Dropped Fires: Illinois Central and the Steam Age in Perspective*
    R&R Bk N - v19 - i4 - Nov 2004 - p106(1) [51-500]
Best, Antony - *British Intelligence and the Japanese Challenge in Asia, 1914-1941.*
    Albion - v36 - i1 - Spring 2004 - p183(2) [501+]
    International History of the Twentieth Century, 1st Ed.
    TimHES - v0 - i1680 - Feb 25 2005 - pX(1) [501+]
Best Book, Inc. - *The Best Books for Academic Libraries*
    Choice - v42 - i1 - Sept 2004 - p59(1) [501+]
Best, Cari - *Shrinking Violet*
    LibMed - v22 - i4 - Jan 2004 - p93(1) [501+]
Best, Constance - *America's Private Forests: Status and Stewardship*
    NRJ - v44 - i2 - Spring 2004 - p621-651 [501+]
Best, Gary Dean - *Harold Laski and American Liberalism*
    Wil Q - v29 - i1 - Wntr 2005 - p122(1) [501+]
Best, Henry - *Margaret and Charley: The Personal Story of Dr. Charles Best, the Co-Discoverer of Insulin*
    CBRA - Annual 2003 - p34(2) [51-500]
Best, Joel - *More Damned Lies and Statistics: How Numbers Confuse Public Issues*
    BL - v101 - i1 - Sept 1 2004 - p26(1) [51-500]
    New Sci - v184 - i2473 - Nov 13 2004 - p57(1) [51-500]
Best, Michael H. - *The New Competitive Advantage: The Renewal of American Industry*
    JEL - v42 - i3 - Sept 2004 - p889(2) [501+]
Best, Samuel J. - *Internet Data Collection*
    R&R Bk N - v19 - i4 - Nov 2004 - p260(1) [501+]
Best, Shaun - *A Beginner's Guide to Social Theory*
    R&R Bk N - v19 - i2 - May 2004 - p126 [51-500]
    Introduction to Politics and Society
    AJPS - v39 - i2 - July 2004 - p675(3) [501+]
Best, Stephen M. - *The Fugitive's Properties: Law and the Poetics of Possession*
    Choice - v42 - i3 - Nov 2004 - p480(1) [1-50]
Best, Steven - *Terrorists or Freedom Fighters?: Reflections on the Liberation of Animals*
    Choice - v42 - i5 - Jan 2005 - p894(1) [1-50]
Best, Victoria - *An Introduction to Twentieth-Century French Literature*
    FS - v58 - i1 - Jan 2004 - p131(1) [501+]
Besterfield, Dale H. - *Quality Control. 7th Ed.*
    SciTech - v28 - i3 - Sept 2004 - p170(1) [51-500]
Bestor, Theodore C. - *Doing Fieldwork in Japan*
    Choice - v41 - i7 - March 2004 - p1336(1) [501+]
    HNet - Sept 2004 - pNA [501+]
    Tsukiji: The Fish Market at the Center of the World
    CHE - v51 - i7 - Oct 8 2004 - pA27(1) [501+]
    Sci - v305 - i5691 - Sept 17 2004 - p1716(2) [501+]
Beswick, Stephanie - *Sudan's Blood Memory: The Legacy of War, Ethnicity, and Slavery in Early South Sudan*
    Choice - v42 - i2 - Oct 2004 - p347(2) [501+]
    IJAHS - v37 - i2 - Spring 2004 - p359-361 [501+]
Betegh, Gabor - *The Derveni Papyrus: Cosmology, Theology and Interpretation*
    Choice - v42 - i7 - March 2005 - p1239(1) [51-500]
    TLS - i5307 - Dec 17 2004 - p8-9 [501+]
Bethany, Barry - *Bead Crochet*
    BL - v101 - i8 - Dec 15 2004 - p706(1) [501+]
Bethell, John T. - *Harvard A to Z*
    Choice - v42 - i3 - Nov 2004 - p445(1) [1-50]

Bethune, James D. - *Engineering Graphics with AutoCAD, 2004*
    SciTech - v28 - i3 - Sept 2004 - p135(1) [51-500]
Betsky, Aaron - *False Flat: Why Dutch Design Is So Good*
    LJ - v130 - i1 - Jan 1 2005 - p105(1) [51-500]
Betteridge, Tom - *Sodomy in Early Modern Europe*
    AHR - v109 - i2 - April 2004 - p595(2) [501+]
Betti, Julie - *Women Without Class: Girls, Race, and Identity*
    CS - v33 - i2 - March 2004 - p170-171 [501+]
Bettig, Ronald V. - *Big Media, Big Money: Cultural Texts and Political Economics*
    JPC - v38 - i1 - August 2004 - p211(2) [501+]
Bettman, Gil - *First Time Director: How to Make Your Breakthrough Movie*
    R&R Bk N - v19 - i3 - August 2004 - p262(1) [501+]
Betts, Richard K. - *Paradoxes of Strategic Intelligence: Essays in Honor of Michael I. Handel*
    J Mil H - v68 - i3 - July 2004 - p983-985 [501+]
    R&R Bk N - v19 - i1 - Feb 2004 - p256(1) [51-500]
Betz, Cecily Lynn - *Mosby's Pediatric Nursing Reference. 5th Ed.*
    SciTech - v28 - i1 - March 2004 - p117(1) [51-500]
Betz, Frederick - *Exclusionary Violence: Antisemitic Riots in Modern German History*
    GSR - v27 - i1 - Feb 2004 - p167-169 [501+]
Beuchat, Cecilia - *Tales about the Origin of Man and the World*
    y VOYA - v27 - i3 - August 2004 - p181(1) [1-50]
Beugnet, Martine - *Claire Denis*
    TLS - i5292 - Sept 3 2004 - p31(1) [501+]
Beuka, Robert - *SuburbiaNation: Reading Suburban Landscape in Twentieth-Century American Fiction and Film*
    Choice - v42 - i1 - Sept 2004 - p83(1) [501+]
Beuter, Anne - *Nonlinear Dynamics in Physiology and Medicine*
    QRB - v79 - i3 - Sept 2004 - p346(1) [501+]
Beutler, G. - *Earth Gravity Field from Space: From Sensors to Earth Sciences: Proceedings*
    SciTech - v28 - i1 - March 2004 - p43(1) [51-500]
Beutler, Linda - *Gardening with Clematis: Design and Cultivation*
    SciTech - v28 - i4 - Dec 2004 - p125 [51-500]
Bevans, Neal R. - *Tort Law for Paralegals*
    R&R Bk N - v19 - i1 - Feb 2004 - pNA [51-500]
Beverage, Dave - *Breath Sounds Made Incredibly Easy!*
    SciTech - v28 - i4 - Dec 2004 - p104(1) [51-500]
Beveridge, Cathy - *Shadows of Disaster*
    c CBRA - Annual 2003 - p474(2) [51-500]
Beverley, Jo - *A Most Unsuitable Man*
    LJ - v130 - i1 - Jan 1 2005 - p90(2) [51-500]
Beverley, John - *Testimonio: On the Politics of Truth*
    R&R Bk N - v19 - i4 - Nov 2004 - p232(1) [501+]
Beverly-Whittemore, Miranda - *The Effects of Light*
    BL - v101 - i6 - Nov 15 2004 - p551(1) [51-500]
    KR - v72 - i24 - Dec 15 2004 - p1153(1) [501+]
    LJ - v129 - i20 - Dec 1 2004 - p97(1) [51-500]
    PW - v251 - i47 - Nov 22 2004 - p36(1) [51-500]
Bevington, David - *Shakespeare*
    Shakes Q - v55 - i1 - Spring 2004 - p71-72 [501+]
Bevir, Mark - *Critiques of Capital in Modern Britain and America: Transatlantic Exchanges 1800 to the Present Day*
    Albion - v36 - i1 - Spring 2004 - p163(4) [501+]
Bevis, William - *Ten Tough Trips: Montana Writers and the West*
    Roundup M - v12 - i1 - Oct 2004 - p20(2) [51-500]
Beyaert, Rudi - *Nuclear Factor kB: Regulation and Role in Disease*
    SciTech - v28 - i1 - March 2004 - p75(1) [51-500]
Beye, Charles Rowan - *Odysseus: A Life (Read by Bramhall, Mark). Audiobook Review*
    LJ - v130 - i1 - Jan 1 2005 - p168(2) [51-500]
Beyer, Dominique - *Emar IV: Les sceaux: Mission archeologique de Meskene-Emar, recherches au pays d'Astata*
    JNES - v64 - i1 - Jan 2005 - p68(3) [501+]
Beyer, Mark - *Amy and Jordan*
    BW - v34 - i29 - July 18 2004 - p8(1) [1-50]
    The War of 1812: The New American Nation Goes to War with England
    c SLJ - v50 - i8 - August 2004 - p132(1) [501+]
Beynon-Davies, Paul - *E-Business, 1st Ed.*
    TimHES - v0 - i1680 - Feb 25 2005 - pVII(1) [501+]

Bezchlibnyk-Butler, Kalyna Z. - *Clinical Handbook of Psychotropic Drugs. 14th Ed.*
    SciTech - v28 - i3 - Sept 2004 - p122(1) [51-500]
    Clinical Handbook of Psychotropic Drugs for Children and Adolescents
    SciTech - v28 - i3 - Sept 2004 - p118(1) [51-500]
Bezdrob, Anne Marie du Preez - *Winnie Mandela: A Life*
    HNet - August 2004 - pNA [501+]
Bezek, Lyn - *Daisy, the Cripple Creek Donkey*
    c CH Bwatch - Oct 2004 - pNA [51-500]
Bezis-Selfa, John - *Forging America: Ironworkers, Adventurers, and the Industrious Revolution*
    JAH - v91 - i3 - Dec 2004 - p1014(1) [501+]
Bezmozgis, David - *Natasha and Other Stories*
    BIC - v33 - i7 - Oct 2004 - p7(2) [501+]
    BooChiTr - May 30 2004 - p1(2) [501+]
    Globe & Mail - Nov 27 2004 - pD3 [51-500]
    Lon R Bks - v26 - i24 - Dec 16 2004 - p26(2) [501+]
    Nation - v279 - i12 - Oct 18 2004 - p38 [501+]
    NYRB - v51 - i14 - Sept 23 2004 - p75(2) [501+]
    NYTBR - July 4 2004 - p18 [501+]
    NYTBR - July 11 2004 - p22 [501+]
    People - v62 - i2 - July 12 2004 - p46 [51-500]
    y SLJ - v50 - i9 - Sept 2004 - p234(1) [51-500]
    TLS - i5291 - August 27 2004 - p20(1) [501+]
Bezner, Heinrich - *Dictionary of Electrical Engineering, Power Engineering, and Automation*
    SciTech - v28 - i3 - Sept 2004 - p151(1) [51-500]
Bhagwati, Jagdish - *Going Alone: The Case for Relaxed Reciprocity in Freeing Trade*
    JEL - v41 - i4 - Dec 2003 - p1286(3) [501+]
    In Defense of Globalization
    Choice - v41 - i11-12 - July-August 2004 - p2091(1) [501+]
    NS - v133 - i4696 - July 12 2004 - p50(2) [501+]
    Reason - v36 - i4 - August-Sept 2004 - p68(4) [501+]
Bhalla, Surjit S. - *Imagine There's No Country: Poverty, Inequality, and Growth in the Era of Globalization*
    JEL - v41 - i4 - Dec 2003 - p1288(2) [501+]
Bhamra, Tracy - *Design and Manufacturing for Sustainable Development 2004: Proceedings*
    SciTech - v28 - i4 - Dec 2004 - p168(1) [51-500]
Bhangal, Sham - *Flash Hacks*
    Bwatch - Oct 2004 - pNA [51-500]
    LJ - v129 - i20 - Dec 1 2004 - p152(1) [51-500]
    SciTech - v28 - i3 - Sept 2004 - p169(1) [1-50]
Bhanu, Bir - *Computational Algorithms for Fingerprint Recognition*
    SciTech - v28 - i1 - March 2004 - p164(1) [51-500]
Bharat, Meenakshi - *Desert in Bloom: Contemporary Indian Women's Fiction in English*
    WLT - v79 - i1 - Jan-April 2005 - p87(1) [501+]
Bhardwaj, Anish - *Handbook of Neurocritical Care*
    SciTech - v28 - i3 - Sept 2004 - p93(1) [51-500]
Bhargava, Vinay - *Challenging Corruption in Asia: Case Studies and a Framework for Action*
    JEL - v42 - i1 - March 2004 - p306(1) [501+]
Bharucha, Rustom - *Rajasthan, an Oral History: Conversations with Komal Kothari*
    JAS - v63 - i3 - August 2004 - p819-820 [501+]
Bhaskar, V. - *Root Hairs: The 'Gills' of Roots, Development, Structure and Functions*
    Choice - v41 - i7 - March 2004 - p1321(1) [501+]
Bhaskaran, Manu - *Re-Inventing the Asian Model: The Case of Singapore*
    R&R Bk N - v19 - i3 - August 2004 - p100(1) [51-500]
Bhatia, Tej K. - *The Handbook of Bilingualism*
    Choice - v41 - i11-12 - July-August 2004 - p2038(2) [501+]
Bhattacharya, Kaushik - *Microstructure of Martensite: Why It Forms and How It Gives Rise to the Shape-Memory Effect*
    Choice - v41 - i11-12 - July-August 2004 - p2076(1) [501+]
    SciTech - v28 - i1 - March 2004 - p139(1) [51-500]
Bhattacharyya, Shuvra S. - *Domain-Specific Processors: Systems, Architectures, Modeling, and Simulation*
    SciTech - v28 - i1 - March 2004 - p154(1) [51-500]
Bhattasali, Deepak - *China and the WTO: Accession, Policy Reform, and Poverty Reduction Strategies*
    Choice - v42 - i5 - Jan 2005 - p900(2) [1-50]
    R&R Bk N - v19 - i4 - Nov 2004 - p108(1) [1-50]

Bhavnani, Kum-Kum - *Feminist Futures: Re-Imagining Women, Culture and Development*
    AJS - v110 - i3 - Nov 2004 - p850(2) [501+]
    R&R Bk N - v19 - i1 - Feb 2004 - p131(1) [51-500]
Bhimani, Alnoor - *Management Accounting in the Digital Economy*
    R&R Bk N - v19 - i4 - Nov 2004 - p114(1) [51-500]
Bhushan, Bharat - *Springer Handbook of Nanotechnology*
    Choice - v42 - i2 - Oct 2004 - p324(1) [51-500]
Bhushan, Vikas - *First Aid for the USMLE Step 1, 2004: A Student to Student Guide*
    SciTech - v28 - i1 - March 2004 - p74(1) [51-500]
Biafore, Bonnie - *Online Investing Hacks*
    R&R Bk N - v19 - i4 - Nov 2004 - p117(1) [51-500]
Biagi, Shirley - *Media/Impact: An Introduction to Mass Media, 7th Ed.*
    R&R Bk N - v19 - i4 - Nov 2004 - p212(1) [501+]
Bial, Raymond - *Cow Towns*
    c SLJ - v51 - i1 - Jan 2005 - p107(1) [51-500]
    Frontier Settlements
    c SLJ - v51 - i1 - Jan 2005 - p107(1) [51-500]
    Longhouses
    c SLJ - v51 - i1 - Jan 2005 - p107(1) [51-500]
    Missions and Presidios
    c SLJ - v51 - i1 - Jan 2005 - p107(1) [51-500]
    Where Washington Walked
    c BL - v101 - i8 - Dec 15 2004 - p739(1) [51-500]
    c CCB-B - v58 - i6 - Feb 2005 - p244(2) [51-500]
    c KR - v72 - i24 - Dec 15 2004 - p1198(1) [501+]
    c SLJ - v51 - i2 - Feb 2005 - p114(1) [51-500]
Bialas, Zbigniew - *Alchemization of the Mind: Literature and Dissociation*
    R&R Bk N - v19 - i1 - Feb 2004 - p221(1) [51-500]
Biale, David - *Cultures of the Jews: A New History*
    Tikkun - v19 - i4 - July-August 2004 - p77(3) [501+]
Bianchi, Luca - *Studi sull'Aristotelismo del Rinascimento*
    Ren Q - v57 - i4 - Winter 2004 - p1368(2) [501+]
Bianchi, Roland R. - *Delivery Boy*
    Bwatch - v26 - i9 - Sept 2004 - p7(1) [51-500]
Bianconi, Lorenzo - *Opera in Theory and Practice, Image and Myth*
    Notes - v61 - i3 - March 2005 - p782(4) [501+]
Biasca, Cynthia - *Supplement to the Descendents of Albert and Arent Andriessen Bradt*
    EFHM - v58 - i2 - March-April 2004 - p88(1) [1-50]
Bibby, Reginald W. - *Restless Gods: The Renaissance of Religion in Canada*
    CS - v33 - i1 - Jan 2004 - p55-56 [501+]
Bichlbaum, Andy - *The Yes Men: The True Story of the End of the World Trade Organization*
    BL - v101 - i6 - Nov 15 2004 - p544(1) [51-500]
Bichler, Martin - *E-Commerce Technology (CEC 2004). Proceedings*
    SciTech - v28 - i3 - Sept 2004 - p31(1) [51-500]
Bick, Ilsa J. - *Well of Souls*
    y Kliatt - v38 - i4 - July 2004 - p26(1) [51-500]
Bickers, Robert - *Empire Made Me: An Englishman Adrift in Shanghai*
    Ch Rev Int - v11 - i1 - Spring 2004 - p25(3) [501+]
    TLS - i5266 - March 5 2004 - p8-9 [501+]
Bickerstaff, Linda - *Cool Careers Without College for People Who Love to Fix Things*
    y SLJ - v51 - i10 - Oct 2004 - p186(1) [51-500]
    The Red Badge of Courage and the Civil War
    y SLJ - v50 - i11 - Nov 2004 - p158(2) [51-500]
Bickman, Martin - *Minding American Education: Reclaiming the Tradition of Active Learning*
    TCR - v106 - i5 - May 2004 - p1005(3) [501+]
Bicks, Caroline - *Midwiving Subjects in Shakespeare's England*
    Albion - v36 - i2 - Summer 2004 - p297(3) [501+]
Biddle, Bruce J. - *The Untested Accusations: Principals, Research Knowledge, and Policy Making in Schools*
    CS - v33 - i1 - Jan 2004 - p103-105 [501+]
Bidermann, Gottlob Herbert - *In Deadly Combat: A German Soldier's Memoir of the Eastern Front*
    HNet - August 2004 - pNA [501+]
Bidini, Dave - *For Those about to Rock: A Road Map to Being in a Band*
    Globe & Mail - Dec 11 2004 - pD24 [501+]
    Res Links - v10 - i2 - Dec 2004 - p43(1) [51-500]
    y SLJ - v50 - i12 - Dec 2004 - p158(1) [51-500]

Bidner, Jenni - *Amphoto's Complete Book of Photography: How to Improve Your Pictures with a Film or Digital Camera*
    y Kliatt - v39 - i1 - Jan 2005 - p36(1) [51-500]
    The Kids' Guide to Digital Photography: How to Shoot, Save, Play with and Print Your Digital Photos
    y BL - v101 - i9-10 - Jan 1 2005 - p837(1) [51-500]
Bidulka, Anthony - *Amuse Bouche: A Russell Quant Mystery*
    CBRA - Annual 2003 - p153(1) [51-500]
    A Flight of Aquavit
    Globe & Mail - Jan 8 2005 - pD11 [51-500]
Bieber, Eric J. - *Hysteroscopy, Resectoscopy, and Endometrial Ablation*
    SciTech - v28 - i1 - March 2004 - p116(1) [51-500]
Bieg, Bernard J. - *South-Western's Payroll Accounting, 2004 Ed.*
    R&R Bk N - v19 - i2 - May 2004 - p120 [51-500]
Biegelbauer, Peter S. - *Innovation Policies in Europe and the US: The New Agenda*
    JEL - v42 - i1 - March 2004 - p317(1) [501+]
Bielawski, Ellen - *Rogue Diamonds: The Rush for Northern Riches on Dene Land*
    CG - v124 - i3 - May-June 2004 - p127(1) [501+]
Bielecki, Janusz - *Electricity Trade in Europe: Review of Economic and Regulatory Challenges*
    SciTech - v28 - i4 - Dec 2004 - p8(1) [1-50]
Bielefeldt, Heiner - *Symbolic Representation in Kant's Practical Philosophy*
    Ethics - v114 - i4 - July 2004 - p859(2) [501+]
Bieler, Stacey - *"Patriots" or "Traitors"?: A History of American-Educated Chinese Students*
    R&R Bk N - v19 - i1 - Feb 2004 - p192(1) [51-500]
Bieler, Stacy - *"Patriots" or "Traitors"? A History of American-Educated Chinese Students*
    IBMR - v28 - i4 - Oct 2004 - p187(2) [501+]
Bieling, Peter J. - *Ending the Depression Cycle: A Step-by-Step Guide for Preventing Relapse*
    Adoles - v39 - i154 - Summer 2004 - p397(2) [51-500]
Bielski, Nella - *The Year Is '42*
    BL - v101 - i4 - Oct 15 2004 - p388(1) [51-500]
    KR - v72 - i18 - Sept 15 2004 - p880(2) [501+]
    LJ - v129 - i20 - Dec 1 2004 - p97(1) [51-500]
    PW - v251 - i40 - Oct 4 2004 - p66(1) [51-500]
    Spec - v296 - i9197 - Nov 13 2004 - p58(1) [501+]
    TLS - i5305 - Dec 3 2004 - p23(1) [501+]
Bien, Peter - *A Century of Greek Poetry 1900-2000*
    TLS - i5284 - July 9 2004 - p5(1) [501+]
Bienenstock, John - *Allergy Frontiers and Futures: Proceedings*
    SciTech - v28 - i3 - Sept 2004 - p103(1) [51-500]
Biennial Conference on Baroque Music - *Bach Studies from Dublin: Selected Papers*
    R&R Bk N - v19 - i4 - Nov 2004 - p194(1) [501+]
Bienvenue, Louise - *Quand la jeunesse entre en scene: l'Action catholique avant la Revolution tranquile*
    Can Hist R - v85 - i4 - Dec 2004 - p852(3) [501+]
Bier, Lisa - *American Indians and African American People, Communities, and Interactions: An Annotated Bibliography*
    R&R Bk N - v19 - i4 - Nov 2004 - p54(1) [51-500]
Bierce, Ambrose - *Phantoms of a Blood-Stained Period: The Complete Civil War Writings of Ambrose Bierce*
    J Am St - v38 - i1 - April 2004 - p136-137 [501+]
Bierds, Linda - *First Hand*
    PW - v252 - i10 - March 7 2005 - p64(2) [51-500]
Bierende, Edgar - *Lucas Cranach d. A. und der deutsche Humanismus: Tafelmalerei im Kontext von Rhetorik, Chroniken und Furstenspiegeln*
    Ren Q - v57 - i3 - Fall 2004 - p1035(2) [501+]
Bierman, Harold - *Financial Management for Decision Making*
    R&R Bk N - v19 - i2 - May 2004 - p123 [51-500]
Bierman, Irene A. - *Napoleon in Egypt*
    IJAHS - v37 - i2 - Spring 2004 - p351-353 [501+]
    R&R Bk N - v19 - i1 - Feb 2004 - p36(1) [1-50]
    Text and Context in Islamic Societies
    R&R Bk N - v19 - i4 - Nov 2004 - p43(1) [51-500]
Bierman, John - *The Secret Life of Laszlo Almasy: The Real English Patient*
    BIC - v33 - i5 - August 2004 - p25(2) [501+]
    Globe & Mail - August 14 2004 - pD12 [1-50]
    TLS - i5283 - July 2 2004 - p29(1) [501+]

Bierman, Karen L. - *Peer Rejection: Developmental Processes and Intervention Strategies*
Choice - v42 - i2 - Oct 2004 - p374(1) [51-500]
R&R Bk N - v19 - i3 - August 2004 - p10(1) [1-50]
Biers, Jane - *Testament of Time: Selected Objects from the Collections of Palestinian Antiquities of the Museum of Art and Archaeology, University of Missouri -- Columbia*
R&R Bk N - v19 - i3 - August 2004 - p51(1) [51-500]
Biersdorfer, J.D. - *iPod & iTunes: The Missing Manual. 2nd Ed.*
LJ - v129 - i13 - August 2004 - p114(1) [501+]
Biesemeier, Christina K. - *Achieving Excellence: Clinical Staffing for Today and Tomorrow*
SciTech - v28 - i4 - Dec 2004 - p86(1) [51-500]
Biesta, Gert J.J. - *Pragmatism and Educational Research*
TCR - v106 - i8 - August 2004 - p1628(3) [501+]
Bigart, Robert - *Letters from the Rocky Mountain Indian Missions: Father Philip Rappagliosi*
CHR - v90 - i4 - Oct 2004 - p826(2) [501+]
Bigelow, Bill - *Rethinking Globalization: Teaching for Justice in an Unjust World*
HER - v74 - i3 - Fall 2004 - p347(3) [501+]
Bigelow, Fran - *Pure Chocolate: Divine Desserts and Sweets from the Creator of Fran's Chocolates*
LJ - v129 - i13 - August 2004 - p112(1) [51-500]
People - v62 - i21 - Nov 22 2004 - p56 [51-500]
PW - v251 - i29 - July 19 2004 - p157(2) [51-500]
Bigg, Grant R. - *The Oceans and Climate*
Choice - v42 - i1 - Sept 2004 - p142(1) [501+]
Bigg, Patricia Nina - *Understanding Mental Retardation*
LJ - v129 - i12 - July 2004 - p105(1) [51-500]
Bigg, Tom - *Survival for a Small Planet: The Sustainable Development Agenda*
Choice - v42 - i3 - Nov 2004 - p534(1) [1-50]
Biggins, Michael - *Publishing in Yugoslavia's Successor States*
Lib & Cul - v39 - i4 - Fall 2004 - p477(3) [501+]
Biggs, Chester M., Jr. - *The United States Marines in North China, 1894-1942*
Choice - v41 - i7 - March 2004 - p1349(1) [501+]
Biggs, Douglas L. - *Reputation and Representation in Fifteenth-century Europe*
R&R Bk N - v19 - i3 - August 2004 - p37(1) [51-500]
Biggs, John - *Black Hat: Misfits, Criminals, and Scammers in the Internet Age*
SciTech - v28 - i3 - Sept 2004 - p30(1) [51-500]
Biggs, Matthew - *BBC's Gardener's Question Time Plant Chooser*
Bwatch - v26 - i7 - July 2004 - p4(2) [51-500]
Bigio, Anthony G. - *Urban Environment and Infrastructure: Toward Livable Cities*
R&R Bk N - v19 - i3 - August 2004 - p148(1) [51-500]
Biglan, Anthony - *Helping Adolescents at Risk: Prevention of Multiple Problem Behaviors*
SciTech - v28 - i3 - Sept 2004 - p119(1) [51-500]
Bigler, David L. - *Fort Limhi: The Mormon Adventure in Oregon Territory, 1855-1858*
R&R Bk N - v19 - i3 - August 2004 - p75(1) [51-500]
WHQ - v35 - i4 - Winter 2004 - p520-521 [501+]
Bigolina, Giulia - *Urania*
MLN - v119 - i1 - Jan 2004 - p193-197 [501+]
Bigott, Joseph C. - *From Cottage to Bungalow: Houses and the Working Classes in Metropolitan Chicago, 1869-1929*
J Urban H - v31 - i1 - Nov 2004 - p133-144 [501+]
Bigsby, Christopher - *The Cambridge Companion to David Mamet*
Choice - v42 - i5 - Jan 2005 - p863(1) [1-50]
Biguenet, John - *The Torturer's Apprentice*
Globe & Mail - Dec 24 2004 - pD3 [1-50]
Bijlefeld, Marjolijn - *It Came from Outer Space: Everyday Products and Ideas from the Space Program*
LibMed - v22 - i6 - March 2004 - p84(1) [501+]
Bik, Aart Johames Casmir - *The Software Vectorization Handbook: Applying Multimedia Extensions for Maximum Performance*
SciTech - v28 - i3 - Sept 2004 - p28(1) [51-500]
Bikandi-Mejias, Aitor - *El carnaval de Luis Bunuel: Estudios sobre una tradicion cultural*
FQ - v57 - i2 - Winter 2003 - p62(2) [501+]
Bikker, Jacob A. - *Competition and Efficiency in a Unified European Banking Market*
R&R Bk N - v19 - i3 - August 2004 - p135(1) [51-500]
Bilal, Christian - *Townscapes*
Kliatt - v38 - i6 - Nov 2004 - p26(2) [501+]
Bilal, Enki - *The Beast Trilogy: Chapters 1 & 2:*
BL - v101 - i7 - Dec 1 2004 - p643(1) [51-500]
Bildner, Phil - *The Shot Heard 'Round the World (Illus. by Payne, C.F.)*
c KR - v73 - i4 - Feb 15 2005 - p226(1) [51-500]
c PW - v252 - i6 - Feb 7 2005 - p59(1) [51-500]
Twenty-One Elephants (Illus. by Pham, Lellyen)
c BL - v101 - i3 - Oct 1 2004 - p332(1) [51-500]
c PW - v251 - i50 - Dec 13 2004 - p67(1) [51-500]
c SLJ - v50 - i11 - Nov 2004 - p90(2) [51-500]
Bilek, Tony - *No Uncle Sam: The Forgotten of Bataan*
J Mil H - v68 - i4 - Oct 2004 - p1287-1288 [501+]
Biletzki, Anat - *(Over)interpreting Wittgenstein*
Choice - v42 - i1 - Sept 2004 - p114(1) [501+]
Bill, James A. - *Roman Catholics and Shi'i Muslims: Prayer, Passion, & Politics*
CHR - v90 - i3 - July 2004 - p521(2) [501+]
Billen, Andrew - *Samuel Johnson: The Wonderful Word Doctor*
Sch Lib - v52 - i3 - Autumn 2004 - p149(1) [501+]
Biller, Peter - *The Measure of Multitude: Population in Medieval Thought*
TimHES - v0 - i1669 - Dec 3 2004 - p26(1) [501+]
Billig, Shelley H. - *Deconstructing Service-Learning: Research Exploring Context, Participation and Impacts*
R&R Bk N - v19 - i3 - August 2004 - p227(1) [1-50]
Billinger, Robert D., Jr. - *Hitler's Soldiers in the Sunshine State: German POWs in Florida*
HNet - Sept 2004 - pNA [501+]
Billingham, Clive - *Throwing Stones*
y TES - v0 - i4586 - June 4 2004 - pssss19(1) [501+]
Billingham, Mark - *The Burning Girl*
Globe & Mail - Oct 2 2004 - pD18 [51-500]
Billinghurst, Jane - *Temptress: From the Original Bad Girls to Women on Top*
CBRA - Annual 2003 - p379(1) [51-500]
R&R Bk N - v19 - i4 - Nov 2004 - p132(1) [1-50]
Billings, Henry - *History of Our World: People, Places, and Ideas*
c CH Bwatch - v14 - i11 - Nov 2004 - pNA [51-500]
Billings, Warren M. - *A Little Parliament: The Virginia General Assembly in the Seventeenth Century*
W&M Q - v62 - i1 - Jan 2005 - p136-3 [501+]
Billingsley, Bonnie S. - *Cultivating and Keeping Special Education Teachers: What Principals and District Leaders Can Do*
Cur R - v44 - i7 - March 2005 - p13(1) [51-500]
Billingsley, ReShonda Tate - *Let the Church Say Amen*
BL - v101 - i1 - Sept 1 2004 - p55(1) [501+]
LJ - v129 - i14 - Sept 1 2004 - p130(1) [51-500]
Billington, David P. - *The Art of Structural Design: A Swiss Legacy*
T&C - v45 - i4 - Oct 2004 - p851(2) [501+]
Billington, James H. - *Russia in Search of Itself*
Choice - v42 - i4 - Dec 2004 - p716(2) [1-50]
For Aff - v83 - i5 - Sept-Oct 2004 - p164 [501+]
R&R Bk N - v19 - i3 - August 2004 - p46(1) [51-500]
Bills, David B. - *Research in the Sociology of Work, Vol. 12*
CS - v33 - i6 - Nov 2004 - p672(3) [501+]
Billups, Norman F. - *American Drug Index 2004. 48th Ed.*
SciTech - v28 - i1 - March 2004 - p123(1) [51-500]
Bilski, Emily D. - *Objects of the Spirit: Ritual and the Art of Tobi Kahn*
Choice - v42 - i3 - Nov 2004 - p470(2) [1-50]
R&R Bk N - v19 - i3 - August 2004 - p244(1) [51-500]
Bilstein, Roger E. - *Stages to Saturn: A Technological History of the Apollo/Saturn Launch Vehicles*
BL - v101 - i7 - Dec 1 2004 - p633(1) [51-500]
Choice - v41 - i7 - March 2004 - p1315(1) [501+]
Testing Aircraft, Exploring Space: An Illustrated History of NACA and NASA
Isis - v95 - i3 - Sept 2004 - p525(2) [501+]
T&C - v45 - i3 - July 2004 - p632-633 [501+]
Bilz, Rachelle Lasky - *Life Is Tough: Guys, Growing Up, and Young Adult Literature*
R&R Bk N - v19 - i4 - Nov 2004 - p258(1) [501+]
SLJ - v51 - i1 - Jan 2005 - p162(1) [51-500]
Bin Ladin, Carmen - *Inside the Kingdom: My Life in Saudi Arabia (Read by Aghdashaloo, Shohreh). Audiobook Review*
BL - v101 - i5 - Nov 1 2004 - p504(1) [51-500]
Inside the Kingdom: My Life in Saudi Arabia
BL - v100 - i21 - July 2004 - p1795(1) [51-500]
Globe & Mail - July 24 2004 - pD13 [501+]
MEJ - v58 - i4 - Autumn 2004 - p706(1) [501+]
NYT - July 1 2004 - pE10 [501+]
People - v62 - i4 - July 26 2004 - p49 [51-500]
R&R Bk N - v19 - i4 - Nov 2004 - p135(1) [51-500]
The Veiled Kingdom
Quad - v48 - i11 - Nov 2004 - p91(2) [501+]
Binchy, Dan - *Loopy: A Novel of Golf and Ireland*
KR - v73 - i5 - March 1 2005 - p242(2) [51-500]
Binchy, Maeve - *Nights of Rain and Stars (Read by Donnelly, Terry). Audiobook Review*
BL - v101 - i7 - Dec 1 2004 - p677(1) [51-500]
BL - v101 - i9-10 - Jan 1 2005 - p778(1) [1-50]
PW - v251 - i44 - Nov 1 2004 - p27(2) [501+]
Nights of Rain and Stars
BL - v100 - i21 - July 2004 - p1796(1) [51-500]
Globe & Mail - August 28 2004 - pD5 [501+]
LJ - v129 - i13 - August 2004 - p63(1) [501+]
PW - v251 - i29 - July 19 2004 - p142(1) [51-500]
Binde, Jerome - *The Future of Values: 21st Century Talks*
R&R Bk N - v20 - i1 - Feb 2005 - p9(1) [51-500]
Binde, Per - *Bodies of Vital Matter: Notions of Life Force and Transcendence in Traditional Southern Italy*
Folkl - v115 - i2 - August 2004 - p233(2) [501+]
Binder, Devin K. - *Recent Advances in Epilepsy Research*
SciTech - v28 - i3 - Sept 2004 - p94(1) [51-500]
SciTech - v28 - i3 - Sept 2004 - p94(1) [51-500]
Binder-Iijima, Edda - *Die Institutionalisierung der Rumanischen Monarchie Unter Carol I: 1866-1881*
AHR - v109 - i4 - Oct 2004 - p1337(2) [501+]
Binder, Mark - *Classic Stories for Boys and Girls*
c SLJ - v50 - i8 - August 2004 - p74(2) [51-500]
Binding, Paul - *Imagined Corners: Exploring the World's First Atlas*
TLS - i5265 - Feb 27 2004 - p9-9 [501+]
Binebine, Mahi - *Welcome to Paradise*
KR - v72 - i18 - Sept 15 2004 - p881(1) [501+]
Bines, Harvey E. - *Investment Management: Law and Regulation, 2nd Ed.*
R&R Bk N - v19 - i3 - August 2004 - p198(1) [1-50]
Binfield, Kevin - *Writings of the Luddites*
R&R Bk N - v19 - i4 - Nov 2004 - p36(1) [51-500]
Bingham, Ann - *South and Meso-American Mythology A to Z*
c SLJ - v51 - i2 - Feb 2005 - p82(1) [51-500]
c BL - v101 - i3 - Oct 1 2004 - p354(1) [51-500]
Bingham, Caroline - *Pyramid*
c BL - v101 - i2 - Sept 15 2004 - p236(2) [51-500]
Bingham, Charlotte - *The Wind Off the Sea*
BL - v100 - i21 - July 2004 - p1815(1) [51-500]
Bingham, Emily - *Mordecai: An Early American Family*
JAH - v91 - i1 - June 2004 - p229-230 [501+]
JSH - v70 - i4 - Nov 2004 - p896(3) [501+]
R&R Bk N - v19 - i4 - Nov 2004 - p30(1) [501+]
Bingham, Howard L. - *Goat: A Tribute to Muhammad Ali (Illus. by Bingham, Howard L.)*
Black Iss - v6 - i4 - July-August 2004 - p33(1) [51-500]
Bingham, Jane - *Why Do Families Break Up?*
y Sch Lib - v52 - i3 - Autumn 2004 - p163(2) [501+]
c SLJ - v51 - i2 - Feb 2005 - p145(1) [51-500]
Bingham, Sallie - *Transgressions*
South HR - v38 - i1 - Wntr 2004 - p100-102 [501+]
Binney, Marcus - *Women Who Lived for Danger: The Agents of the Special Operations Executive*
R&R Bk N - v19 - i1 - Feb 2004 - p30(1) [51-500]
Binni, Walther - *Cristologia Primitiva: Dalla Teofania del Sinai all'Io Sono Giovanneo*
Theol St - v65 - i4 - Dec 2004 - p909(9) [501+]
Binnie, Jon - *The Globalization of Sexuality*
R&R Bk N - v19 - i3 - August 2004 - p149(1) [51-500]
Binning, Alexander - *Devil's Chair*
CBRA - Annual 2003 - p153(1) [51-500]
Binns, John - *An Introduction to the Christian Orthodox Churches*
JR - v84 - i3 - July 2004 - p468(2) [501+]
Binns, Tristan Boyer - *Alfred Nobel: Inventive Thinker*
y SLJ - v50 - i12 - Dec 2004 - p158(1) [51-500]
Hermit Crabs
c SLJ - v50 - i12 - Dec 2004 - p126(1) [51-500]
Potbellied Pigs
c SLJ - v50 - i12 - Dec 2004 - p126(1) [51-500]
Binsbergen, Wim M.J. van - *Situating Globality: African Agency in the Appropriation of Global Culture*
Choice - v42 - i1 - Sept 2004 - p164(1) [501+]

Bishop, Russell - *Culture Counts: Changing Power Relations in Education*
R&R Bk N - v19 - i1 - Feb 2004 - p192(1) [51-500]

Bishop, Ryan - *Postcolonial Urbanism: Southeast Asian Cities and Global Processes*
JEL - v41 - i4 - Dec 2003 - p1406(2) [501+]

Bishop, Virginia E. - *Teaching Visually Impaired Children, 3rd Ed.*
R&R Bk N - v19 - i3 - August 2004 - p162(1) [501+]

Bisk, Tsvi - *Futurizing the Jews: Alternative Futures for Meaningful Jewish Existence in the 21st Century*
Fut - v38 - i5 - Sept-Oct 2004 - p62(1) [51-500]
Fut - v39 - i1 - Jan-Feb 2005 - p12(1) [501+]

Biskind, Peter - *Down and Dirty Pictures: Miramax, Sundance, and the Rise of Independent Film*
ABR - v26 - i1 - Nov-Dec 2004 - p27(1) [501+]
NYTBR - Feb 27 2005 - p24 [1-50]
Si & So - v14 - i8 - August 2004 - p36(2) [501+]
Spec - v296 - i9189 - Sept 18 2004 - p49(1) [501+]

Gods and Monsters: Thirty Years of Writing on Film and Culture from One of America's Most Incisive Writers
BL - v101 - i9-10 - Jan 1 2005 - p798(1) [51-500]
Ent W - i797 - Dec 17 2004 - p89 [501+]
KR - v72 - i21 - Nov 1 2004 - p1033(2) [501+]

Bissegger, Arthur - *Une paroisse raconte ses mortes: L'obituaire de l'eglise Saint-Paul a Villeneuve, XIVe-XVe siecles*
Med R - Oct 2004 - pNA [501+]

Bisseling, Rob H. - *Parallel Scientific Computation: A Structured Approach Using BSP and MPI*
Choice - v42 - i3 - Nov 2004 - p518(2) [1-50]
SciTech - v28 - i3 - Sept 2004 - p20(1) [501+]

Bissell, Sallie - *Legacy of Masks*
KR - v73 - i3 - Feb 1 2005 - p131(2) [501+]
LJ - v129 - i20 - Dec 1 2004 - p96(1) [1-50]
PW - v252 - i9 - Feb 28 2005 - p43(1) [51-500]

Bissell, Tom - *Chasing the Sea: Being a Narrative of a Journey through Uzbekistan...the Aral Sea, the World's Worst Man-Made Ecological Catastrophe*
y   Kliatt - v39 - i2 - March 2005 - p41(1) [51-500]
R&R Bk N - v19 - i1 - Feb 2004 - p39(1) [1-50]

God Lives in St. Petersburg and Other Stories
KR - v72 - i23 - Dec 1 2004 - p1100(1) [501+]
BL - v101 - i9-10 - Jan 1 2005 - p811(1) [1-50]
Ent W - i803 - Jan 28 2005 - p86 [501+]
LJ - v130 - i1 - Jan 1 2005 - p102(2) [51-500]
NW - Feb 14 2005 - p59 [501+]
NYTBR - Feb 27 2005 - p10 [501+]
PW - v251 - i49 - Dec 6 2004 - p42(1) [51-500]

Bissinger, H.G. - *Three Nights in August: Strategy, Heartbreak, and Joy, Inside the Mind of a Manager*
KR - v73 - i3 - Feb 1 2005 - p158(1) [501+]
LJ - v129 - i20 - Dec 1 2004 - p90(1) [51-500]
PW - v252 - i7 - Feb 14 2005 - p62(1) [51-500]

Bisson, Robert A. - *Modern Groundwater Exploration: Discovering New Water Resources in Consolidated Rocks Using Innovative Hydrogeologic Concepts, Exploration, Drilling, Aquifer Testing, and Management Methods*
Choice - v42 - i6 - Feb 2005 - p1052(1) [51-500]
SciTech - v28 - i3 - Sept 2004 - p5(1) [501+]

Bitel, Lisa M. - *Women in Early Medieval Europe, 400-1100*
GSR - v27 - i2 - May 2004 - p365-367 [501+]
Med R - Dec 2004 - pNA [501+]
Specu - v79 - i4 - Oct 2004 - p1037(3) [501+]

Bitterli, Urs - *Golo Mann, Instanz und Aussenseiter*
TLS - i5291 - August 27 2004 - p7(1) [501+]
WLT - v79 - i1 - Jan-April 2005 - p100(1) [501+]

Bitterman, Pamela Sisman - *Sailing to the Far Horizon: The Restless Journey and Tragic Sinking of a Tall Ship*
BL - v101 - i3 - Oct 1 2004 - p295(1) [51-500]

Bittinger, Marvin L. - *Intermediate Algebra: Graphs and Models. 2nd Ed.*
SciTech - v28 - i3 - Sept 2004 - p34(1) [51-500]

Bittman, Mark - *How to Cook Everything: Bittman Takes on America's Chefs*
LJ - v130 - i3 - Feb 15 2005 - p152(1) [51-500]
PW - v252 - i11 - March 14 2005 - p61(1) [51-500]

Bittner, Mark - *The Wild Parrots of Telegraph Hill*
New Sci - v183 - i2458 - July 31 2004 - p53(1) [51-500]

Bittner, Rosanne - *Into the Prairie: The Pioneers*
y   BL - v100 - i21 - July 2004 - p1815(1) [51-500]
Walk by Faith
LJ - v130 - i2 - Feb 1 2005 - p62(1) [51-500]

Bittner, Terrie Lynn - *Homeschooling: Take a Deep Breath-- You Can Do This!*
BL - v101 - i6 - Nov 15 2004 - p536(1) [51-500]
LJ - v129 - i20 - Dec 1 2004 - p153(1) [51-500]
PW - v251 - i47 - Nov 22 2004 - p53(1) [51-500]

Bitton-Ashkelony, Brouria - *Christian Gaza in Late Antiquity*
R&R Bk N - v19 - i4 - Nov 2004 - p21(1) [51-500]

Bitzer, Frank J. - *Benefits Facts.*
HR Mag - v49 - i7 - July 2004 - pS6(1) [51-500]
ERISA Facts 2004.
HR Mag - v49 - i7 - July 2004 - pS7(1) [51-500]

Bivar, A.D.H. - *Excavations at Ghubayra, Iran*
JNES - v63 - i4 - Oct 2004 - p313(2) [501+]

Biven, W. Carl - *Jimmy Carter's Economy: Policy in an Age of Limits*
JSH - v70 - i4 - Nov 2004 - p974(2) [501+]
Pres St Q - v34 - i4 - Dec 2004 - p905(3) [501+]

Bivins, Jason C. - *The Fracture of Good Order: Christian Antiliberalism and the Challenge to American Politics*
AHR - v109 - i2 - April 2004 - p564(2) [501+]
AJS - v110 - i3 - Nov 2004 - p827(3) [501+]
CC - v121 - i19 - Sept 21 2004 - p47(3) [501+]
JAH - v91 - i3 - Dec 2004 - p1103(2) [501+]
JSH - v70 - i4 - Nov 2004 - p973(2) [501+]

Bixler, Mark - *The Lost Boys of Sudan: An American Story of the Refugee Experience*
PW - v252 - i5 - Jan 31 2005 - p56(1) [51-500]

Bizer, Marc - *Les Lettres Romaines de Du Bellay: Les Regrets et la Tradition Epistolaire*
Six Ct J - v34 - i4 - Winter 2003 - p1239-1240 [501+]

Bizzarini, Marco - *Luca Marenzio: The Career of a Musician between the Renaissance and the Counter-Reformation*
Notes - v61 - i1 - Sept 2004 - p121(2) [501+]
Ren Q - v57 - i4 - Winter 2004 - p1402(2) [501+]

Bizzaro, Patrick - *More Lights than One: On the Fiction of Fred Chappell*
Choice - v42 - i2 - Oct 2004 - p295(1) [501+]

Bjelic, Dusan I. - *Balkan as Metaphor: Between Globalization and Fragmentation*
CS - v33 - i5 - Sept 2004 - p560-562 [501+]

Bjerga, Alan - *The Almanac of the Unelected: Staff of the U.S. Congress, 2004, 17th Ed.*
R&R Bk N - v19 - i3 - August 2004 - p179(1) [501+]

Bjerregaard, Lena - *Pre-Columbian Woven Treasures in The National Museum of Denmark*
R&R Bk N - v19 - i4 - Nov 2004 - p70(1) [51-500]

Bjorge, Gary J. - *Moving the Enemy: Operational Art in the Chinese PLA's Huai Hai Campaign*
J Mil H - v68 - i4 - Oct 2004 - p1305-1306 [501+]

Bjork, Staffan - *Patterns in Game Design*
Bwatch - March 2005 - pNA [501+]

Bjorken, James D. - *In Conclusion: A Collection of Summary Talks in High Energy Physics*
SciTech - v28 - i1 - March 2004 - p52(1) [51-500]

Bjorkman, Steve - *Supersnouts!*
c   CH Bwatch - v14 - i8 - August 2004 - p6(1) [51-500]

Bjorkman, Tom - *Russia's Road to Deeper Democracy*
Choice - v41 - i7 - March 2004 - p1363(2) [501+]
E-A St - v56 - i4 - June 2004 - p625(627) [501+]

Bjornerud, Marcia - *Reading the Rocks: The Autobiography of the Earth*
KR - v73 - i5 - March 1 2005 - p269(2) [501+]
PW - v252 - i9 - Feb 28 2005 - p50(1) [501+]

Blach, David L. - *Early Christian Families in Context: An Interdisciplinary Dialogue*
R&R Bk N - v19 - i1 - Feb 2004 - p16(1) [1-50]

Black, Amy E. - *Of Little Faith: The Politics of George W. Bush's Faith-Based Initiatives*
Bks & Cult - v10 - i5 - Sept-Oct 2004 - p32(1) [501+]
CC - v121 - i17 - August 24 2004 - p27(7) [501+]
Choice - v42 - i3 - Nov 2004 - p563(2) [1-50]
Pers PS - v33 - i4 - Fall 2004 - p230(1) [501+]

Black, Antony - *Church, State and Community: Historical and Comparative Perspectives*
HER - v119 - i483 - Sept 2004 - p1040(2) [501+]

Black, Artemis - *Explicit Content*
BL - v101 - i1 - Sept 1 2004 - p54(1) [501+]

Black, Cara - *Murder in Clichy*
KR - v72 - i21 - Nov 1 2004 - p1029(1) [501+]
PW - v251 - i51 - Dec 20 2004 - p39(1) [501+]

Black, Carolyn - *Pakistan: The Culture*
y   Can CL - i111-112 - Fall-Winter 2003 - p152(1) [501+]
c   CBRA - Annual 2003 - p545(2) [51-500]
Pakistan: The Land
y   Can CL - i111-112 - Fall-Winter 2003 - p152(1) [501+]
c   CBRA - Annual 2003 - p545(2) [51-500]
Pakistan: The People
y   Can CL - i111-112 - Fall-Winter 2003 - p152(1) [501+]
c   CBRA - Annual 2003 - p545(2) [51-500]

Black, Cheryl - *The Women of Provincetown, 1915-1922*
TDR - v48 - i2 - Summer 2004 - p178(2) [501+]
Theat J - v56 - i4 - Dec 2004 - p719-720 [501+]

Black, Conrad - *Franklin Delano Roosevelt: Champion of Freedom*
Globe & Mail - Dec 24 2004 - pD3 [1-50]
JAH - v91 - i3 - Dec 2004 - p1073(2) [501+]
R&R Bk N - v19 - i1 - Feb 2004 - p61(1) [501+]
TLS - i5267 - March 12 2004 - p7-7 [501+]

Black, Earl - *Realignment: The Theory That Changed the Way We Think about American Politics*
JAH - v91 - i3 - Dec 2004 - p1093(2) [501+]

Black, Edwin - *Banking on Baghdad: Inside Iraq's 7,000-Year-History of War, Profit and Conflict*
BW - v34 - i47 - Nov 21 2004 - p3(2) [501+]
Banking on Baghdad: Inside Iraq's 7,000-Year History of War, Profit and Conflict
LJ - v129 - i18 - Nov 1 2004 - p100(2) [51-500]
PW - v251 - i40 - Oct 4 2004 - p84(1) [501+]
War Against the Weak: Eugenics and America's Campaign to Create a Master Race
CC - v121 - i22 - Nov 2 2004 - p24(5) [501+]
VQR - v80 - i2 - Spring 2004 - p266-267 [501+]
JAH - v91 - i2 - Sept 2004 - p671(1) [501+]

Black, Ethan - *At Hell's Gate*
KR - v72 - i13 - July 1 2004 - p588(1) [51-500]
PW - v251 - i31 - August 2 2004 - p52(2) [501+]

Black, Georgina Dopico - *Perfect Wives, Other Women: Adultery and Inquisition in Early Modern Spain*
MP - v102 - i1 - August 2004 - p114(3) [501+]

Black, Holly - *Tithe: A Modern Faerie Tale*
c   BIC - v33 - i5 - August 2004 - p43(1) [501+]
y   Kliatt - v38 - i4 - July 2004 - p26(1) [51-500]

Black, J.L. - *Vladimir Putin and the New World Order: Looking East, Looking West?*
Choice - v42 - i3 - Nov 2004 - p560(1) [1-50]
R&R Bk N - v19 - i3 - August 2004 - p46(1) [51-500]

Black, Jeremy - *Britain Since the Seventies: Politics and Society in the Consumer Age*
TimHES - v0 - i1657 - Sept 10 2004 - p28(1) [501+]
Britian Since the Seventies: Politics and Society in the Consumer Age
Choice - v42 - i6 - Feb 2005 - p1085(1) [51-500]
The British Seaborne Empire
Lon R Bks - v26 - i21 - Nov 4 2004 - p12(1) [1-50]
Europe and the World: 1650-1830
Eight-C St - v37 - i4 - Summer 2004 - p689-692 [501+]
France and the Grand Tour
HNet - Oct 2004 - pNA [501+]
The Hanoverians The History of a Dynasty
HT - v54 - i12 - Dec 2004 - p56(1) [501+]
Italy and the Grand Tour
HNet - Oct 2004 - pNA [501+]
HT - v54 - i9 - Sept 2004 - p59(1) [501+]
Kings, Nobles and Commoners: States and Societies in Early Modern Europe, a Revisionist History
Choice - v42 - i4 - Dec 2004 - p727(1) [1-50]
Nineteenth-Century Britain
Albion - v36 - i2 - Summer 2004 - p322(3) [501+]
Parliament and Foreign Policy in the Eighteenth Century
CR - v285 - i1663 - August 2004 - p124(1) [501+]
HRNB - v33 - i1 - Fall 2004 - p21(2) [501+]
Visions of the World: A History of Maps
TLS - i5265 - Feb 27 2004 - p9-9 [501+]
War and the New Disorder in the 21st Century
Parameters - v34 - i4 - Winter 2004 - p129(2) [501+]

Black, Jim - *River Season*
BL - v101 - i6 - Nov 15 2004 - p556(1) [501+]
BooChiTr - Jan 4 2004 - p3(1) [501+]
y   Kliatt - v39 - i2 - March 2005 - p17(1) [51-500]

Black, Johnny - *Rock and Pop Timeline: How Music Changed the World through Five Decades*
M Ed J - v91 - i3 - Jan 2005 - p64(2) [501+]

Black, Kenneth D. - *Biogeochemistry of Marine Systems*
QRB - v79 - i3 - Sept 2004 - p321(3) [501+]

Black, Lawrence - *Affluent Society?: Britain's Post-War 'Golden Age' Revisited*
    R&R Bk N - v19 - i4 - Nov 2004 - p90(1) [51-500]
Black, Lewis - *Nothing's Sacred*
    PW - v252 - i10 - March 7 2005 - p61(2) [51-500]
Black, Lydia T. - *Russians in Alaska, 1732-1867*
    Choice - v42 - i4 - Dec 2004 - p719(2) [1-50]
    R&R Bk N - v19 - i3 - August 2004 - p76(1) [51-500]
Black, Merle - *The Rise of Southern Republicans*
    JAH - v91 - i3 - Dec 2004 - p1093(1) [501+]
Black, Naomi - *Two Sides to Every Coin*
    Bwatch - v26 - i7 - July 2004 - p4(1) [51-500]
    Virginia Woolf as Feminist
    Choice - v41 - i11-12 - July-August 2004 - p2042(1) [501+]
Black, Shirley J. - *Louis Napoleon and Strasbourg*
    HRNB - v33 - i1 - Fall 2004 - p29(1) [501+]
    R&R Bk N - v19 - i3 - August 2004 - p42(1) [51-500]
Black, Sonia W. - *Jumping the Broom (Illus. by Van Wright, Cornelius)*
    c BL - v101 - i4 - Oct 15 2004 - p409(2) [51-500]
Black, Timuel D. - *Bridges of Memory: Chicago's First Wave of Black Migration*
    Black Iss - v7 - i2 - March-April 2005 - p40(2) [501+]
    BooChiTr - March 7 2004 - p1(2) [501+]
    Choice - v41 - i11-12 - July-August 2004 - p2105(1) [501+]
Black, William R. - *Transportation: A Geographical Analysis*
    R&R Bk N - v19 - i2 - May 2004 - p108(1) [1-50]
Blackadder, Neil - *Performing Opposition: Modern Theater and the Scandalized Audience*
    Choice - v41 - i11-12 - July-August 2004 - p2055(1) [501+]
    R&R Bk N - v19 - i1 - Feb 2004 - p223(1) [51-500]
Blackburn, Carole - *Harvest of Souls: The Jesuit Missions and Colonialism in North America, 1632-1650*
    R&R Bk N - v19 - i4 - Nov 2004 - p68(1) [51-500]
Blackburn, Julia - *With Billie*
    KR - v73 - i5 - March 1 2005 - p270(1) [501+]
Blackburn, Peter - *Hitchhiker's Guide to SQL Server 2000 Reporting Services*
    SciTech - v28 - i4 - Dec 2004 - p31(1) [51-500]
Blackburn, Robin - *In Green*
    CBRA - Annual 2003 - p209(1) [501+]
Blackburn, Simon - *Lust*
    HM - v310 - i1856 - Jan 2005 - p96(6) [501+]
    JouAmCul - v27 - i3 - Sept 2004 - p344(2) [501+]
Blackburn, Thomas R. - *Getting Science Grants: Effective Strategies for Funding Success*
    J Chem Ed - v81 - i9 - Sept 2004 - p1268-1269 [501+]
Blackburne-Maze, Peter - *Fruit: An Illustrated History*
    E-Streams - July 2004 - pNA [501+]
    SciTech - v28 - i1 - March 2004 - p67(1) [51-500]
Blacker, Terence - *The Angel Factory*
    c RT - v57 - Oct 2003 - p176 [1-50]
    Boy2girl
    y Kliatt - v39 - i2 - March 2005 - p6(1) [51-500]
    c KR - v73 - i3 - Feb 1 2005 - p174(1) [51-500]
    y PW - v252 - i3 - Jan 17 2005 - p56(1) [51-500]
    y Sch Lib - v52 - i3 - Autumn 2004 - p155(1) [501+]
    c TES - v0 - i4576 - March 26 2004 - pssss19(1) [501+]
Blackhawk, Terry - *Escape Artist*
    ABR - v25 - i5 - July-August 2004 - p26(2) [501+]
Blackledge, Catherine - *The Story of V: A Natural History of Female Sexuality*
    Choice - v42 - i6 - Feb 2005 - p1054(1) [51-500]
    The Story of V: Opening Pandora's Box
    TLS - i5294 - Sept 17 2004 - p4-6 [501+]
Blacklock, Dyan - *The Roman Army: The Legendary Soldiers Who Created an Empire (Illus. by Kennett, David)*
    c LibMed - v23 - i1 - August-Sept 2004 - p74(2) [501+]
    SLJ - v50 - i10 - Oct 2004 - pS32(1) [51-500]
Blackman, Margaret B. - *Upside Down: Seasons among the Nunamiut*
    Choice - v42 - i3 - Nov 2004 - p526(1) [1-50]
Blackmarr, Amy - *Above the Fall Lines: The Trail from White Pine Cabin*
    R&R Bk N - v19 - i1 - Feb 2004 - p64(1) [501+]
    Going to Ground: Simple Life on a Georgia Pond
    R&R Bk N - v19 - i1 - Feb 2004 - p64(1) [501+]

Blackmore, Josiah - *Manifest Perdition: Shipwreck Narrative and the Disruption of Empire*
    Can Lit - i182 - Autumn 2004 - p94(2) [501+]
Blackmore, Susan - *Consciousness: An Introduction*
    Am Sci - v92 - i5 - Sept-Oct 2004 - p468(1) [501+]
Blackstock, Terri - *River's Edge*
    LJ - v129 - i14 - Sept 1 2004 - p132(1) [51-500]
    PW - v251 - i34 - August 23 2004 - pS16(1) [51-500]
Blackston, Ray - *A Delirious Summer*
    BL - v101 - i3 - Oct 1 2004 - p303(1) [51-500]
Blackstone-Ford, Jann - *Ex-Etiquette for Parents: Good Behavior after a Divorce or Separation*
    LJ - v129 - i15 - Sept 15 2004 - p71(1) [51-500]
Blackstone, Stella - *Jump into January (Illus. by Carluccio, Maria)*
    c BL - v101 - i6 - Nov 15 2004 - p589(1) [51-500]
    c KR - v72 - i19 - Oct 1 2004 - p956(1) [51-500]
    c SLJ - v50 - i12 - Dec 2004 - p98(1) [501+]
    Secret Seahorse (Illus. by Beaton, Clare)
    c SLJ - v51 - i1 - Jan 2005 - p86(1) [51-500]
    Who Are You, Baby Kangaroo? (Illus. by Beaton, Clare)
    c SLJ - v50 - i11 - Nov 2004 - p91(1) [51-500]
Blackwelder, Julia Kirk - *Styling Jim Crow: African American Beauty Training During Segregation*
    Choice - v41 - i7 - March 2004 - p1354(1) [501+]
    JAH - v91 - i2 - Sept 2004 - p673(1) [501+]
Blackwell, Carole - *Tradition and Society in Turkmenistan: Gender, Oral Culture and Song*
    A Aff - v35 - i2 - July 2004 - p234-235 [501+]
Blackwell, Edward - *How to Prepare a Business Plan*
    Bwatch - March 2005 - pNA [51-500]
Blackwell, Elise - *Hunger*
    Kliatt - v38 - i6 - Nov 2004 - p13(1) [51-500]
Blackwell, Fritz - *India: A Global Studies Handbook*
    Choice - v42 - i6 - Feb 2005 - p1000(1) [51-500]
Blackwell, Joyce - *No Peace Without Freedom: Race and the Women's International League for Peace and Freedom, 1915-1975*
    Choice - v42 - i6 - Feb 2005 - p1061(2) [501+]
Blackwell, Judith C. - *Culture of Prejudice: Arguments in Critical Social Science*
    CBRA - Annual 2003 - p374(1) [51-500]
Blackwell, Lewis - *20th-Century Type*
    Choice - v42 - i4 - Dec 2004 - p645(1) [1-50]
    LJ - v129 - i12 - July 2004 - p77(1) [51-500]
Blackwood, Alan - *Playing the Piano and Keyboards*
    CH Bwatch - Feb 2005 - pNA [51-500]
Blackwood, Algernon - *Incredible Adventures*
    PW - v251 - i34 - August 23 2004 - p42(1) [51-500]
Blackwood, Gary - *The Shakespeare Stealer Series*
    y NYTBR - Sept 19 2004 - p16 [501+]
    Shakespeare's Spy
    BooChiTr - Jan 11 2004 - p5(1) [501+]
Blackwood, Jane - *A Hard Man Is Good to Find*
    BL - v101 - i6 - Nov 15 2004 - p567(1) [51-500]
Blades-Zeller, Elizabeth - *A Spectrum of Voices: Prominent American Voice Teachers Discuss the Teaching of Singing*
    R&R Bk N - v19 - i1 - Feb 2004 - p198(1) [51-500]
Blaeser, Kimberly - *Absentee Indians and Other Poems*
    Am Ind CRJ - v27 - i2 - Spring 2003 - p103-105 [501+]
Blain, Christopher - *Isaac the Pirate, Vol. 2*
    PW - v252 - i7 - Feb 14 2005 - p55(1) [51-500]
Blain, Jenny - *Researching Paganisms*
    R&R Bk N - v19 - i4 - Nov 2004 - p14(1) [51-500]
Blaine, Michael - *The Midnight Band of Mercy*
    BL - v101 - i1 - Sept 1 2004 - p54(1) [51-500]
    DroRevMy - v24 - i4 - July-August 2004 - p4(1) [501+]
    KR - v72 - i15 - August 1 2004 - p701(1) [501+]
    LJ - v129 - i14 - Sept 1 2004 - p136(1) [51-500]
    y NYTBR - Sept 26 2004 - p16 [501+]
    PW - v251 - i31 - August 2 2004 - p51(1) [501+]
Blainey, Geoffrey - *The Fuss That Never Ended*
    Quad - v48 - i7-8 - July-August 2004 - p46(4) [501+]
Blair, Annette - *The Kitchen Witch*
    BL - v101 - i3 - Oct 1 2004 - p315(1) [51-500]
Blair, Jayson - *Burning Down My Master's House (Read by Blair, Jayson). Audiobook Review*
    LJ - v129 - i14 - Sept 1 2004 - p203(1) [51-500]
    Burning Down My Master's House
    BooChiTr - April 11 2004 - p3(1) [501+]
Blair-Loy, Mary - *Competing Devotions: Career and Family among Women Executives*
    CS - v33 - i4 - July 2004 - p437(2) [501+]
    Wom R Bks - v22 - i3 - Dec 2004 - p7(2) [501+]

Blair, Mary - *The Up and Down Book*
    c PW - v251 - i38 - Sept 20 2004 - p64(1) [51-500]
Blair, Michael - *A Hard Winter Rain*
    Globe & Mail - Dec 4 2004 - pD35 [51-500]
Blair, Sandy - *The Man in a Kilt*
    BL - v101 - i1 - Sept 1 2004 - p71(1) [51-500]
    A Rogue in a Kilt
    BL - v101 - i6 - Nov 15 2004 - p566(1) [51-500]
Blaise, Clark - *Montreal Stories*
    CBRA - Annual 2003 - p196(1) [501+]
    Pittsburgh Stories--Selected Stories 2
    Can Lit - i181 - Summer 2004 - p106-108 [501+]
Blake, Brett Elizabeth - *A Culture of Refusal: The Lives and Literacies of Out-of-School Adolescents*
    R&R Bk N - v19 - i3 - August 2004 - p230(1) [1-50]
Blake, Bronwyn - *Carrie's Song*
    y Magpies - v19 - i5 - Nov 2004 - p39(2) [501+]
Blake, John - *Children of the Movement*
    Black Iss - v6 - i5 - Sept-Oct 2004 - p45(1) [501+]
    S Liv - v39 - i8 - August 2004 - p205(1) [501+]
    The Sea Chart
    HT - v54 - i12 - Dec 2004 - p57(2) [501+]
Blake, Jon - *The Deadly Secret of Dorothy W. (Read by Sachs, Kate). Audiobook Review*
    c SLJ - v51 - i2 - Feb 2005 - p74(1) [501+]
Blake, Michelle - *The Book of Light*
    CC - v121 - i21 - Oct 19 2004 - p24(5) [501+]
Blake, N.F. - *Shakespeare's Non-Standard English: A Dictionary of His Informal Language*
    Choice - v42 - i7 - March 2005 - p1191(4) [51-500]
    R&R Bk N - v19 - i4 - Nov 2004 - p235(1) [501+]
Blake, Quentin - *Angel Pavement*
    c Sch Lib - v52 - i4 - Winter 2004 - p185(1) [51-500]
    Magic Pencil: Children's Book Illustration Today
    R&R Bk N - v19 - i1 - Feb 2004 - p205(1) [51-500]
Blake, Robert J. - *Akiak: A Tale from the Iditarod*
    c PW - v251 - i45 - Nov 8 2004 - p58(1) [51-500]
    Togo (Illus. by Blake, Robert J.)
    c RT - v57 - Nov 2003 - p274 [51-500]
Blake, Robert W., Jr. - *An Enactment of Science: A Dynamic Balance among Curriculum, Context, and Teacher Beliefs*
    TCR - v106 - i5 - May 2004 - p888(4) [501+]
Blake, Toni - *The Red Diary*
    PW - v251 - i30 - July 26 2004 - p43(1) [51-500]
Blake, Yashin - *Nowhere Fast*
    Globe & Mail - July 31 2004 - pD7 [501+]
Blakemore, Michael - *Arguments with England*
    Spec - v296 - i9188 - Sept 11 2004 - p42(2) [501+]
Blaker, Kimberly - *The Fundamentals of Extremism: The Christian Right in America*
    ABR - v25 - i5 - July-August 2004 - p12(1) [501+]
    J Ch St - v46 - i4 - Autumn 2004 - p901(2) [501+]
Blaker, Michael - *Case Studies in Japanese Negotiating Behavior*
    HNet - Sept 2004 - pNA [501+]
Blalock, Travis N. - *Microelectronic Circuit Design. 2nd Ed.*
    TimHES - v0 - i1668 - Nov 26 2004 - pXIV(1) [501+]
Blamires, Alcuin - *The Romance of the Rose Illuminated: Manuscripts at the National Library of Wales, Aberystwyth*
    FS - v58 - i1 - Jan 2004 - p77(2) [501+]
Blamires, David - *Theologia Deutsch-Theologia Germanica: The Book of the Perfect Life*
    R&R Bk N - v19 - i1 - Feb 2004 - p24(1) [51-500]
Blamires, Harry - *Compose Yourself and Write Good English*
    TimHES - v0 - i1668 - Nov 26 2004 - pIX(1) [501+]
Blanc, Nero - *Anatomy of a Crossword*
    BL - v100 - i21 - July 2004 - p1823(1) [1-50]
    Wrapped Up in Crosswords
    PW - v251 - i43 - Oct 25 2004 - p32(1) [51-500]
Blanc, Pierre - *Dynamique d'une xpansion culturelle: Petrarque en Europe, XIV-XX siecle-Actes du XXVI congres international du CEFI, Turin et Chambery, 11-15 decembre 1995*
    FS - v58 - i1 - Jan 2004 - p147(2) [501+]
Blanchard, Duncan - *Fire from Raindrops to Volcanoes*
    Bwatch - v26 - i9 - Sept 2004 - p2(1) [51-500]
Blanchard, Edward B. - *After the Crash: Psychological Assessment and Treatment of Survivors of Motor Vehicle Accidents. 2nd Ed.*
    SciTech - v28 - i1 - March 2004 - p108(1) [51-500]

Blanche-Beneveniste, Claire - *Choix de Textes de Francais Parle: Trente-six Extraits*
 FS - v58 - i1 - Jan 2004 - p151(2) [501+]

Blanchette, Peg - *Make Your Own Cool Cards: 25 Awesome Notes & Invitations! (Illus. by Hershey, Rebecca)*
 c SLJ - v50 - i9 - Sept 2004 - p222(1) [51-500]

Blanchfield, Brian - *Not Even Then: Poems*
 NYTBR - Nov 21 2004 - p26 [501+]

Blanchot, Maurice - *Faux Pas*
 Can Lit - i181 - Summer 2004 - p108-109 [501+]

Blanco, Jodee - *The Complete Guide to Book Publicity, 2nd Ed.*
 Bwatch - Oct 2004 - pNA [51-500]
Complete Guide to Book Publicity, 2nd Ed.
 Bwatch - Feb 2005 - pNA [51-500]
The Complete Guide to Book Publicity, 2nd Ed.
 R&R Bk N - v19 - i4 - Nov 2004 - p255(1) [501+]

Blancoviso, Anthony N. - *Planned Group Counseling: An Alternative Group Method for Reluctant Chemically Dependent and Psychiatric Patients*
 SciTech - v28 - i3 - Sept 2004 - p97(1) [51-500]

Blanculli, Anthony J. - *Trains and Technology: The American Railroad in the Nineteenth Century, Vol. 4*
 SciTech - v28 - i1 - March 2004 - p148(1) [51-500]

Bland, Douglas L. - *New Missions, Old Problems*
 R&R Bk N - v19 - i4 - Nov 2004 - p251(1) [501+]

Bland, Eleanor Taylor - *A Cold and Silent Dying: A Marti MacAlister Mystery*
 LJ - v129 - i20 - Dec 1 2004 - p94(1) [51-500]

Bland, Kirby I. - *Breast: Comprehensive Management of Benign and Malignant Disorders. 3rd Ed.*
 SciTech - v28 - i1 - March 2004 - p91(1) [51-500]

Bland, Matthew - *They Melted His Brain!*
 c SLJ - v50 - i8 - August 2004 - p76(1) [51-500]

Bland, Roger G. - *The Orthoptera of Michigan: Biology, Keys, and Descriptions of Grasshoppers, Katydids, Crickets*
 Choice - v41 - i11-12 - July-August 2004 - p2072(2) [501+]

Bland, Taylor - *A Cold and Silent Dying*
 PW - v251 - i45 - Nov 8 2004 - p38(2) [501+]

Blandino, Betty - *The Figure in Fired Clay*
 Ceram Mo - v52 - i2 - Feb 2004 - p30(1) [501+]

Blank, Adam - *Field Guide to the North American Bird*
 NYTBR - Jan 2 2005 - p19 [501+]

Blank, Jessica - *Living Justice: Love, Justice, and the Making of The Exonerated*
 KR - v73 - i2 - Jan 15 2005 - p93(2) [501+]
 PW - v252 - i7 - Feb 14 2005 - p67(1) [501+]

Blank, Rebecca M. - *Is the Market Moral?: A Dialogue on Religion, Economics, and Justice*
 Comw - v131 - i17 - Oct 8 2004 - p23(5) [501+]
 R&R Bk N - v19 - i3 - August 2004 - p19(1) [1-50]
The New World of Welfare
 JEL - v41 - i4 - Dec 2003 - p1303(2) [501+]

Blank, Robert H. - *Comparative Health Policy*
 Choice - v42 - i2 - Oct 2004 - p324(2) [51-500]
 SciTech - v28 - i3 - Sept 2004 - p80(1) [51-500]

Blankenhorn, David - *Does Christianity Teach Male Headship? The Equal-Regard Marriage and Its Critics*
 Intpr - v59 - i1 - Jan 2005 - p110(1) [51-500]

Blankstein, Alan M. - *Failure Is Not an Option: Six Principles That Guide Student Achievement In High-Performing Schools*
 Bwatch - Oct 2004 - pNA [51-500]

Blannbekin, Agnes - *Agnes Blannbekin, Viennese Beguine: "Life and Revelations"*
 Specu - v79 - i4 - Oct 2004 - p1039(3) [501+]

Blanpain, R. - *Comparative Labour Law and Industrial Relations in Industrialized Market Economies, 8th Ed.*
 R&R Bk N - v19 - i4 - Nov 2004 - p162(1) [501+]
Temporary Agency Work and the Information Society
 R&R Bk N - v19 - i3 - August 2004 - p115(1) [51-500]

Blanton, Carlos Kevin - *The Strange Career of Bilingual Education in Texas, 1836-1981*
 Choice - v42 - i2 - Oct 2004 - p343(1) [51-500]

Blanton, DeAnne - *They Fought Like Demons: Women Soldiers in the American Civil War*
 J Mil H - v68 - i3 - April 2004 - p611-612 [501+]

Blanton, Richard E. - *Monte Alban: Settlement Patterns at the Ancient Zapotec Capital*
 R&R Bk N - v19 - i3 - August 2004 - p76(1) [51-500]

Blasco, Andreu Lopez - *Young People and Contradictions of Inclusion: Towards Intergrated Transition Policies in Europe*
 R&R Bk N - v19 - i3 - August 2004 - p152(1) [51-500]

Blashford-Snell, John - *East to the Amazon: In Search of Great Paititi and the Trade Routes of the Ancients*
 KR - v72 - i13 - July 1 2004 - p610(2) [501+]
 LJ - v129 - i14 - Sept 1 2004 - p174(1) [51-500]

Blasi, Anthony J. - *Handbook of Early Christianity: Social Science Approaches*
 Theol St - v65 - i4 - Dec 2004 - p855(2) [501+]
Transition from Vowed to Lay Ministry in American Catholicism
 R&R Bk N - v19 - i4 - Nov 2004 - p27(1) [501+]

Blasingame, James - *How Angel Peterson Got His Name: And Other Outrageous Tales about Extreme Sports*
 JAAL - v48 - i3 - Nov 2004 - p267(2) [501+]

Blass, Thomas - *The Man Who Shocked the World: The Life and Legacy of Stanley Milgram*
 Am Sci - v92 - i4 - July-August 2004 - p368(3) [501+]
 BW - v34 - i30 - July 25 2004 - p8(1) [501+]
 Choice - v42 - i3 - Nov 2004 - p567(1) [1-50]
 Lon R Bks - v26 - i22 - Nov 18 2004 - p7(2) [501+]
 Per Psy - v57 - i4 - Winter 2004 - p1081(4) [501+]
 TimHES - v0 - i1660 - Oct 1 2004 - p26(1) [501+]
 TLS - i5306 - Dec 10 2004 - p11(1) [501+]

Blathwayt, Ben - *The Great Big Little Red Train*
 c Sch Lib - v52 - i4 - Winter 2004 - p186(1) [51-500]

Blatner, David - *Flying Book: Everything You've Ever Wondered about Flying on Airplanes*
 CBRA - Annual 2003 - p438(1) [51-500]

Blatt, Harvey - *America's Environmental Report Card: Are We Making the Grade?*
 BL - v101 - i5 - Nov 1 2004 - p447(1) [51-500]
 PW - v251 - i44 - Nov 1 2004 - p52(1) [501+]

Blatt, Sidney J. - *Experiences of Depression: Theoretical Clinical, and Research Perspectives*
 Choice - v42 - i1 - Sept 2004 - p191(1) [51-500]

Blattberg, Charles - *Shall We Dance?: A Patriotic Politics for Canada*
 CBRA - Annual 2003 - p302(1) [501+]

Blau, David - *The Child Care Problem: An Economic Analysis*
 CS - v33 - i5 - Sept 2004 - p548-550 [501+]

Blau, Francine D. - *At Home and Abroad: U.S. Labor Market Performance in International Perspective*
 CS - v33 - i1 - Jan 2004 - p37-39 [501+]

Blau, Judith R. - *Race in the Schools: Perpetuating White Dominance?*
 SF - v83 - i1 - Sept 2004 - p442(3) [501+]
 TCR - v107 - i2 - Feb 2005 - p265(2) [501+]

Blau, Peter M. - *Formal Organizations: A Comparative Approach*
 R&R Bk N - v19 - i1 - Feb 2004 - p88(1) [1-50]

Blaufarb, Rafe - *The French Army, 1750-1820: Careers, Talent, Merit*
 J Mil H - v68 - i3 - July 2004 - p953-954 [501+]
 JIH - v35 - i2 - Autumn 2004 - p298(3) [501+]

Blaufuss, Mary Schaller - *Changing Goals of the American Madura Mission in India, 1830-1916*
 IBMR - v28 - i4 - Oct 2004 - p180(1) [501+]
 R&R Bk N - v19 - i1 - Feb 2004 - p23(1) [51-500]

Blaug, Mark - *Who's Who in Economics, 4th Ed.*
 JEL - v42 - i1 - March 2004 - p232(1) [501+]
 R&R Bk N - v19 - i1 - Feb 2004 - p77(1) [501+]

Blaustein, Mordecai P. - *Cellular Physiology*
 SciTech - v28 - i3 - Sept 2004 - p61(1) [501+]

Blay-Fornarino, Mireille - *Cooperative Systems Design: A Challenge of the Mobility Age*
 SciTech - v28 - i3 - Sept 2004 - p30(1) [501+]

Blayne, Sara - *Marrying the Marquis*
 BL - v101 - i2 - Sept 15 2004 - p218(1) [51-500]

Blayney, Mary - *The Captain's Mermaid*
 y BL - v101 - i1 - Sept 1 2004 - p71(1) [51-500]

Blayney, Peter W.M. - *The Stationers' Company Before the Chapter, 1403-1557*
 BSA-P - v98 - i1 - March 2004 - p127-127 [501+]

Blayzca, George - *Restructuring Regional and Local Economies: Towards a Comparative Study of Scotland and Upper Silesia*
 JEL - v42 - i1 - March 2004 - p342(1) [51-500]

Bleaney, C.H. - *Iraq: A Bibliographical Guide*
 Choice - v42 - i3 - Nov 2004 - p460(1) [1-50]
 R&R Bk N - v19 - i4 - Nov 2004 - p44(1) [51-500]

Blease, Kathleen - *I Can't Wait to Meet My Daddy (Illus. by Fackenthal, Bruce)*
 c CH Bwatch - v14 - i12 - Dec 2004 - pNA [51-500]

Blechman, Hardy - *Disruptive Pattern Material: An Encyclopedia of Camouflage*
 Globe & Mail - Dec 18 2004 - pL5 [1-50]

Blechman, Harvey - *Disruptive Pattern Material: An Encyclopedia of Camouflage*
 New Sci - v184 - i2473 - Nov 13 2004 - p56(1) [501+]

Bleckmann, B. - *Die romische Niobilitat in Ersten Punischen Krieg. Untersuchungen zur aristokratischen Konkurrenz in der Republik*
 Class R - v54 - i2 - Nov 2004 - p487(2) [501+]

Blecourt, Willem de - *Cultural Approaches to the History of Medicine: Mediating Medicine in Early Modern and Modern Europe*
 SciTech - v28 - i3 - Sept 2004 - p82(1) [501+]

Bledsoe, Bryan E. - *Intermediate Emergency Care: Principles and Practice*
 SciTech - v28 - i3 - Sept 2004 - p90(1) [51-500]

Bledsoe, Caroline H. - *Contingent Lives: Fertility, Time, and Aging in West Africa*
 JRAI - v10 - i3 - Sept 2004 - p739(1) [501+]
 MAQ - v18 - i1 - March 2004 - p113(3) [501+]

Bleeker, Johan A.M. - *The Century of Space Science*
 S&T - v107 - i1 - Jan 2004 - p76(1) [501+]

Bleier, Inge Joseph - *Inge: A Girl's Journey through Nazi Europe*
 y VOYA - v27 - i4 - Oct 2004 - p322(1) [51-500]

Bleischwitz, Raimund - *Eco-Efficiency, Regulation, and Sustainable Business: Towards a Governance Structure for Sustainable Development*
 R&R Bk N - v19 - i4 - Nov 2004 - p87(1) [51-500]

Blenkinsopp, Joseph - *Isaiah 56-66: A New Translation with Introduction and Commentary*
 JR - v84 - i4 - Oct 2004 - p605(2) [501+]
Treasures Old and New: Essays in the Theology of the Pentateuch
 Theol St - v65 - i4 - Dec 2004 - p909(9) [501+]

Blevin, Meredith - *The Hummingbird*
 LJ - v129 - i20 - Dec 1 2004 - p186(1) [51-500]

Blevins, Brooks - *Lyon College, 1872-2002: The Perseverance and Promise of an Arkansas College*
 JSH - v70 - i3 - August 2004 - p699(2) [501+]

Blevins, Dave - *UFO Directory International: 1,000+ Organizations and Publications in 40+ Countries*
 E-Streams - Dec 2004 - pNA [501+]

Blevins, Meredith - *The Vanished Priestess: An Annie Szabo Mystery*
 LJ - v129 - i16 - Oct 1 2004 - p62(1) [51-500]
 PW - v251 - i37 - Sept 13 2004 - p62(1) [501+]

Blevins, Wiley - *Where Does Your Food Go?*
 c SB - v40 - i3 - May-June 2004 - p134(1) [501+]
You Can Use a Magnifying Glass
 c SB - v40 - i3 - May-June 2004 - p130(1) [501+]

Blevins, Winfred - *Beauty for Ashes*
 KR - v72 - i16 - August 15 2004 - p757(2) [51-500]
 PW - v251 - i42 - Oct 18 2004 - p49(1) [51-500]

Blewitt, John - *Sustainability Curriculum: The Challenge for Higher Education*
 R&R Bk N - v19 - i4 - Nov 2004 - p74(1) [51-500]

Blick, Andrew - *People Who Live in the Dark*
 R&R Bk N - v19 - i3 - August 2004 - p38(1) [51-500]
 TimHES - v0 - i1661 - Oct 8 2004 - p24(1) [501+]

Blier, Suzanne Preston - *Art of the Senses: African Masterpieces from the Teel Collection*
 Choice - v42 - i3 - Nov 2004 - p470(1) [1-50]
 LJ - v129 - i18 - Nov 1 2004 - p80(1) [501+]

Bligh, Philip - *CRM Unplugged: Releasing CRM's Strategic Value*
 R&R Bk N - v19 - i3 - August 2004 - p126(1) [51-500]

Blight, David W. - *Passages to Freedom: The Underground Railroad in History and Memory*
 y BL - v100 - i21 - July 2004 - p1814(1) [51-500]
 BL - v101 - i9-10 - Jan 1 2005 - p767(1) [51-500]
 y PW - v251 - i27 - July 5 2004 - p52(1) [51-500]

Blincoe, Nicholas - *Burning Paris*
 TLS - i5283 - July 2 2004 - p20(1) [501+]

Blinder, Alan S. - *The Quiet Revolution: Central Banking Goes Modern*
 For Aff - v83 - i5 - Sept-Oct 2004 - p164 [501+]

Bliss, Wendy - *Legal, Effective References: How to Give and Get Them*
 HR Mag - v50 - i2 - Feb 2005 - pS10(1) [501+]

Blitz, Michael - *Why Arnold Matters: The Rise of a Cultural Icon*
 R&R Bk N - v19 - i4 - Nov 2004 - p68(1) [51-500]

Blix, Hans - *Disarming Iraq*
 For Aff - v83 - i5 - Sept-Oct 2004 - p164 [501+]
 TimHES - v0 - i1658 - Sept 17 2004 - p26(1) [501+]

Blizzard, Allison - *Portraits of the 20th Century Self: An Interartistic Study of Gertrude Stein's Literary Portraits and Early Modernist Portraits by Paul Cezanne, Henri Matisse, and Pablo Picasso*
 R&R Bk N - v19 - i4 - Nov 2004 - p243(1) [501+]

Bloch, Alexia - *Red Ties and Residential School: Indigenous Siberians in a Post-Soviet State*
 Choice - v41 - i11-12 - July-August 2004 - p2086(1) [501+]

Bloch, Georges - *Picasso: The Printed Graphic Work 1966-1969*
 LJ - v130 - i2 - Feb 1 2005 - p74(1) [51-500]
 Picasso: The Printed Graphic Work 1970-1972
 LJ - v130 - i2 - Feb 1 2005 - p74(1) [51-500]

Bloch, Heinz P. - *Pump User's Handbook; Life Extension*
 SciTech - v28 - i4 - Dec 2004 - p146(1) [501+]

Bloch, Marc - *Correspondance, 2: De Strasbourg a Paris, 1934-1937*
 TLS - i5287 - July 30 2004 - p10-11 [501+]
 Correspondance, 3: Les "Annales" en crises, 1938-1943
 TLS - i5287 - July 30 2004 - p10-11 [501+]

Bloch, Michael - *F.M.: The Life of Frederick Matthias Alexander, the Founder of the Alexander Technique*
 TLS - i5293 - Sept 10 2004 - p26(1) [501+]

Bloch, R. Howard - *The Anonymous Marie de France*
 Biomag - v27 - i3 - Summer 2004 - p605(5) [501+]
 FS - v58 - i2 - April 2004 - p236(2) [501+]
 Specu - v79 - i3 - July 2004 - p738-740 [501+]

Bloch, Rene S. - *Antike Vorstellungen vom Judentum. Der Judenexkurs des Tacitus im Rahmen der Griechisch-romischen Ethnographie*
 Class R - v54 - i1 - May 2004 - p113(3) [501+]

Bloch, Robert - *The Fear Planet and Other Unusual Destinations: The Reader's Bloch. Vol. 1.*
 BL - v101 - i5 - Nov 1 2004 - p472(1) [51-500]
 PW - v251 - i43 - Oct 25 2004 - p32(1) [51-500]

Bloch, Ruth H. - *Gender and Morality in Anglo-American Culture, 1650-1800*
 AHR - v109 - i2 - April 2004 - p479(2) [501+]

Block, Alan A. - *All Is Clouded by Desire: Global Banking, Money Laundering, and International Organized Crime*
 Choice - v42 - i6 - Feb 2005 - p1068(1) [51-500]
 R&R Bk N - v19 - i4 - Nov 2004 - p146(1) [501+]
 Talmud, Curriculum, and the Practical: Joseph Schwab and the Rabbis
 R&R Bk N - v19 - i3 - August 2004 - p215(1) [1-50]

Block, Berthold - *Color Atlas of Ultrasound Anatomy*
 SciTech - v28 - i3 - Sept 2004 - p67(1) [51-500]
 Endoscopy of the Upper GI Tract: A Training Manual
 SciTech - v28 - i4 - Dec 2004 - p104(1) [51-500]

Block, Cathy Collins - *Improving Comprehension Instruction: Rethinking Research, Theory, and Classroom Practice*
 CE - v80 - i5 - Mid-Summer 2004 - p276(2) [51-500]
 Teaching Comprehension: The Comprehension Process Approach
 R&R Bk N - v19 - i1 - Feb 2004 - p182(1) [51-500]

Block, Francesca Lia - *Wasteland*
 Kliatt - v38 - i6 - Nov 2004 - p13(1) [51-500]
 y PW - v251 - i42 - Oct 18 2004 - p66(1) [51-500]

Block, Gay - *Bertha Alyce: Mother Exposed*
 Art N - v103 - i5 - May 2004 - p110(1) [501+]

Block, Geoffrey - *Richard Rodgers*
 JouAmCul - v27 - i3 - Sept 2004 - p354(3) [501+]
 Notes - v61 - i1 - Sept 2004 - p119(2) [501+]

Block, James E. - *A Nation of Agents: The American Path to a Modern Self and Society*
 AHR - v109 - i4 - Oct 2004 - p1220(2) [501+]

Block, John H. - *Wilson and Gisvold's Textbook of Organic Medicinal and Pharmaceutical Chemistry. 11th Ed.*
 SciTech - v28 - i1 - March 2004 - p125(1) [51-500]

Block, Lawrence - *All the Flowers Are Dying*
 Ent W - i808 - Feb 25 2005 - p106 [51-500]
 Globe & Mail - March 19 2005 - pD15 [51-500]
 KR - v73 - i2 - Jan 15 2005 - p84(1) [51-500]
 LJ - v129 - i19 - Nov 15 2004 - p42(2) [51-500]
 NYTBR - March 13 2005 - p28 [501+]
 PW - v252 - i7 - Feb 14 2005 - p56(2) [51-500]
 The Burglar on the Prowl (Read by Sullivan, Nick). Audiobook Review
 BL - v101 - i2 - Sept 15 2004 - p258(1) [51-500]
 The Burglar on the Prowl (Read by Block, Lawrence). Audiobook Review
 LJ - v129 - i13 - August 2004 - p128(1) [51-500]

Grifter's Game
 DroRevMy - v24 - i4 - July-August 2004 - p1(2) [501+]
 Tanner's Tiger (Read by Sullivan, Nick). Audiobook Review
 LJ - v129 - i18 - Nov 1 2004 - p129(1) [51-500]
 Tanner's Virgin
 PW - v252 - i11 - March 14 2005 - p49(1) [51-500]

Block, Richard N. - *Bargaining for Competitiveness: Law, Research, and Case Studies*
 JEL - v41 - i4 - Dec 2003 - p1386(2) [501+]
 Labor Standards in the United States and Canada
 JEL - v41 - i4 - Dec 2003 - p1389(2) [501+]

Block, Stephen R. - *Why Nonprofits Fail: Overcoming the Founder's Syndrome, Fundphobia and Other Obstacles to Success*
 R&R Bk N - v19 - i3 - August 2004 - p108(1) [501+]

Blocker, Jack S., Jr. - *Alcohol and Temperance in Modern History: An International Encyclopedia, Vols. 1-2*
 Choice - v42 - i1 - Sept 2004 - p59(1) [501+]
 Ref Rev - Sept 2004 - pNA [501+]

Blocker, Jane - *What the Body Cost: Desire, History, and Performance*
 R&R Bk N - v19 - i4 - Nov 2004 - p200(1) [501+]

Blodgett, E.D. - *Ark of Koans*
 CBRA - Annual 2003 - p209(1) [51-500]

Bloemers, Wolf - *Ethics and Social Justice*
 R&R Bk N - v19 - i1 - Feb 2004 - p127(1) [51-500]

Bloisi, Wendy - *Management and Organisational Behaviour, 1st Ed.*
 TimHES - v0 - i1680 - Feb 25 2005 - pVIII(1) [501+]

Blok, M.C. - *Nutrition and Health of the Gastrointestinal Tract*
 SciTech - v28 - i1 - March 2004 - p131(1) [51-500]

Blokhin, Alexander - *Stabililty of Strong Discontinuities in Magnetohydrodynamics and Electrohydrodynamics*
 SciTech - v28 - i1 - March 2004 - p42(1) [51-500]

Bloland, Sue Erikson - *In the Shadow of Fame: A Memoir by the Daughter of Erik H. Erikson*
 y BL - v101 - i7 - Dec 1 2004 - p620(1) [51-500]
 KR - v72 - i22 - Nov 15 2004 - p1073(2) [501+]
 PW - v252 - i5 - Jan 31 2005 - p61(1) [501+]

Blom, Ida - *Gendered Nations: Nationalisms and Gender Order in the Long Nineteenth Century*
 Signs - v30 - i2 - Wntr 2005 - p1683(6) [501+]

Blom, Philipp - *Encyclopedie: The Triumph of Reason in an Unreasonable Age*
 TimHES - v0 - i1674 - Jan 14 2005 - p25(1) [501+]
 TLS - i5302 - Nov 12 2004 - p25(1) [501+]

Blomley, Nicholas - *The Legal Geographies Reader*
 PG - v23 - i2 - Feb 2004 - p229 [501+]

Blomquist, Christopher - *Box Turtles*
 c SLJ - v50 - i9 - Sept 2004 - p184(1) [1-50]
 Gopher Tortoises
 c SLJ - v50 - i9 - Sept 2004 - p184(1) [1-50]
 Green Sea Turtles
 c SLJ - v50 - i9 - Sept 2004 - p184(1) [1-50]
 The Library of Turtles and Tortoises
 c LibMed - v23 - i3 - Nov-Dec 2004 - p76(2) [51-500]
 Spiny Softshell Turtles
 c SLJ - v50 - i9 - Sept 2004 - p184(1) [1-50]

Blomquist, William A. - *Common Waters, Diverging Streams: Linking Institutions to Water Management in Arizona, California, and Colorado*
 SciTech - v28 - i3 - Sept 2004 - p145(1) [51-500]

Blomster, Jeffrey P. - *Etlatongo: Social Complexitiy, Interaction, and Village Life in the Mixteca Alta of Oaxaca, Mexico*
 R&R Bk N - v19 - i1 - Feb 2004 - p66(1) [501+]

Blomstermo, Anders - *Learning in the Internationalisation Process of Firms*
 JEL - v41 - i4 - Dec 2003 - p1355(2) [501+]

Blomstrom, Magnus - *Structural Impediments to Growth in Japan*
 JEL - v42 - i1 - March 2004 - p320(2) [501+]

Blondel, Alain - *Tamara de Lempicka: Art Deco Icon*
 BL - v101 - i5 - Nov 1 2004 - p457(1) [51-500]
 TLS - i5288 - August 6 2004 - p16-17 [501+]

Blondel, Vincent D. - *Unsolved Problems in Mathmatical Systems and Control Theory*
 Choice - v42 - i5 - Jan 2005 - p890(1) [1-50]

Blonna, Richard - *Healthy Sexuality*
 R&R Bk N - v19 - i4 - Nov 2004 - p127(1) [51-500]

Blood-Horse Publications - *The Blood-Horse Authoritative Guide to Auctions*
 Bwatch - Oct 2004 - pNA [51-500]

Bloodlines:
 Globe & Mail - Jan 22 2005 - pD12 [51-500]

Bloodworth-Thomason, Linda - *Liberating Paris*
 BL - v100 - i22 - August 2004 - p1874(1) [51-500]
 KR - v72 - i15 - August 1 2004 - p701(1) [501+]
 LJ - v129 - i15 - Sept 15 2004 - p51(1) [51-500]
 PW - v251 - i32 - August 9 2004 - p230(1) [51-500]
 S Liv - v39 - i12 - Dec 2004 - p54(1) [501+]

Bloom, Barbara E. - *Gendered Justice: Addressing Female Offenders*
 R&R Bk N - v19 - i1 - Feb 2004 - p140(1) [51-500]

Bloom, Elizabeth - *See Isabelle Run*
 BL - v101 - i9-10 - Jan 1 2005 - p825(1) [1-50]
 KR - v73 - i1 - Jan 1 2005 - p22(1) [51-500]
 LJ - v130 - i1 - Jan 1 2005 - p85(1) [51-500]
 PW - v252 - i6 - Feb 7 2005 - p46(1) [51-500]

Bloom, Harold - *The Best Poems of the English Language*
 Poet - v184 - i5 - Sept 2004 - p392(1) [51-500]
 y SLJ - v50 - i8 - August 2004 - p147(1) [501+]
 Elizabeth Bennet
 y SLJ - v50 - i9 - Sept 2004 - p222(1) [51-500]
 The Harold Bloom Shakespeare Series
 Am Theat - v21 - i8 - Oct 2004 - p139(4) [51-500]
 Jay Gatsby
 LibMed - v22 - i7 - April-May 2004 - p73(1) [501+]
 SLJ - v50 - i10 - Oct 2004 - pS67(1) [501+]
 Peripheral Light: Selected and New Poems
 WLT - v79 - i1 - Jan-April 2005 - p86(1) [501+]
 The Rubaiyat of Omar Khayyam
 y SLJ - v50 - i10 - Oct 2004 - pS67(1) [501+]
 Truman Capote
 SLJ - v50 - i10 - Oct 2004 - pS67(1) [501+]
 The Victorian Novel
 y SLJ - v50 - i10 - Oct 2004 - pS67(1) [501+]
 Where Shall Wisdom Be Found?
 BL - v101 - i3 - Oct 1 2004 - p294(1) [51-500]
 BW - v34 - i49 - Dec 5 2004 - p14(1) [501+]
 Globe & Mail - Feb 5 2005 - pD11 [501+]
 KR - v72 - i17 - Sept 1 2004 - p845(1) [501+]
 LJ - v129 - i16 - Oct 1 2004 - p80(1) [501+]
 NYTBR - Oct 10 2004 - p16 [501+]
 PW - v251 - i35 - August 30 2004 - p40(1) [501+]

Bloom, John - *Sports Matters: Race, Recreation, and Culture*
 CS - v33 - i6 - Nov 2004 - p742(1) [1-50]
 JAH - v91 - i1 - June 2004 - p311-312 [501+]

Bloom, Ken - *Broadway: Its History, People, and Places: An Encyclopedia, 2nd Ed.*
 Am Theat - v22 - i1 - Jan 2005 - p89(2) [501+]
 Ref Rev - Dec 2004 - pNA [501+]
 Broadway Musicals: The 101 Greatest Shows of All Time
 Am Theat - v22 - i1 - Jan 2005 - p89(2) [501+]

Bloom, Marc - *God on the Starting Line: The Triumph of a Catholic School Running Team and Its Jewish Coach*
 PW - v251 - i43 - Oct 25 2004 - p45(1) [51-500]

Bloom, Nicholas Dagen - *Merchant of Illusion: James Rouse, American Salesman of the Businessman's Utopia*
 Choice - v41 - i11-12 - July-August 2004 - p2084(1) [501+]

Bloom, Paul - *Descartes' Baby: How the Science of Child Development Explains What Makes Us Human*
 Am Sci - v92 - i5 - Sept-Oct 2004 - p476(3) [501+]
 Choice - v42 - i3 - Nov 2004 - p567(1) [1-50]

Bloom, Robert M. - *Criminal Procedure: Examples and Explanations, 4th Ed.*
 R&R Bk N - v19 - i4 - Nov 2004 - p174(1) [501+]
 Searches, Seizures, and Warrants: A Reference Guide to the United States Constitution
 R&R Bk N - v19 - i1 - Feb 2004 - pNA [51-500]

Bloom, Steve - *Untamed (Illus. by Bloom, Steve)*
 PW - v251 - i45 - Nov 8 2004 - p49(1) [501+]

Bloom, Suzanne - *A Splendid Friend, Indeed (Illus. by Bloom, Suzanne)*
 c KR - v73 - i4 - Feb 15 2005 - p226(1) [51-500]

Bloomberg, Jon - *The Jewish World in the Modern Age*
 BL - v101 - i2 - Sept 15 2004 - p196(1) [501+]
 R&R Bk N - v19 - i4 - Nov 2004 - p46(1) [51-500]

Bloome, David - *Discourse Analysis & the Study of Classroom Language & Literacy Events: A Microethnic Perspective*
 R&R Bk N - v19 - i4 - Nov 2004 - p182(1) [501+]

Bochinski, Julianne Blair - *More Award-Winning Science Fair Projects*
    SB - v40 - i5 - Sept-Oct 2004 - p191(2) [51-500]

Bocij, Paul - *Cyberstalking: Harassment in the Internet Age and How to Protect Your Family*
    Bwatch - Nov 2004 - pNA [51-500]
    R&R Bk N - v19 - i4 - Nov 2004 - p146(1) [501+]
    y VOYA - v27 - i3 - August 2004 - p236(1) [1-50]

Bock, Darrell L. - *Breaking the Da Vinci Code (Read by Fabry, Chris). Audiobook Review*
    BL - v100 - i22 - August 2004 - p1952(1) [51-500]

Bock, Gisela - *Women in European History*
    Wom HR - v13 - i2 - Summer 2004 - p315-317 [501+]

Bock, Gregory - *Autism: Neural Basis and Treatment Possibilities: Proceedings*
    SciTech - v28 - i1 - March 2004 - p119(1) [51-500]
    Generation and Effector Functions of Regulatory Lymphocytes: Proceedings
    SciTech - v28 - i1 - March 2004 - p76(1) [51-500]
    Reversible Protein Acetylation: Proceedings
    SciTech - v28 - i3 - Sept 2004 - p71(1) [51-500]

Bocken, Inigo - *Conflict and Reconciliation: Perspectives on Nicholas of Cusa*
    R&R Bk N - v19 - i4 - Nov 2004 - p27(1) [501+]

Bockenhauer, Mark H. - *Our Fifty States*
    y PW - v251 - i44 - Nov 1 2004 - p64(2) [501+]
    y SLJ - v51 - i1 - Jan 2005 - p142(1) [51-500]

Bocknek, Jonathan - *Stars*
    c SLJ - v50 - i8 - August 2004 - p105(1) [51-500]

Bockstoce, John R. - *High Latitude, North Atlantic: 30,000 Miles through Cold Seas and History*
    R&R Bk N - v19 - i4 - Nov 2004 - p73(1) [51-500]

Boczkowski, Pablo J. - *Digitizing the News: Innovation in Online Newspapers.*
    BHR - v78 - i3 - Autumn 2004 - p564(3) [501+]
    Choice - v42 - i1 - Sept 2004 - p93(2) [501+]

Bodanis, David - *Electric Universe: The Shocking True Story of Electricity*
    Globe & Mail - Jan 29 2005 - pD13 [1-50]
    Econ - v374 - i8413 - Feb 12 2005 - p83US [501+]
    Ent W - i808 - Feb 25 2005 - p105 [51-500]
    KR - v73 - i2 - Jan 15 2005 - p94(1) [501+]
    LJ - v129 - i20 - Dec 1 2004 - p154(1) [51-500]
    PW - v251 - i49 - Dec 6 2004 - p50(2) [51-500]

Bodansky, David - *Nuclear Energy: Principles, Practices, and Prospects, 2nd Ed.*
    Choice - v42 - i6 - Feb 2005 - p1052(1) [51-500]

Bodansky, Yossef - *The Secret History of the Iraq War*
    NYTBR - Nov 14 2004 - p60 [501+]
    Quad - v49 - i1-2 - Jan-Feb 2005 - p125(2) [501+]

Bodce, N.E. - *The Anybodies (Illus. by Ferguson, Peter)*
    y SLJ - v50 - i7 - July 2004 - p98(1) [51-500]

Bodde, David L. - *The Intentional Entrepreneur: Bringing Technology and Engineering to the Real New Economy*
    R&R Bk N - v19 - i3 - August 2004 - p104(1) [1-50]

Boddy, Martin - *City Matters: Competitiveness, Cohesion and Urban Governance*
    R&R Bk N - v19 - i4 - Nov 2004 - p157(1) [501+]

Bode, N.E. - *The Anybodies (Illus. by Ferguson, Peter)*
    c BL - v100 - i21 - July 2004 - p1841(1) [501+]
    c CCB-B - v58 - i1 - Sept 2004 - p7(2) [51-500]
    c VOYA - v27 - i5 - Dec 2004 - p399(1) [51-500]

Bodemann, Michal Y. - *A Jewish Family in Germany Today: An Intimate Portrait*
    PW - v251 - i51 - Dec 20 2004 - p49(1) [501+]

Boden, Rebecca - *Scrutinising Science: The Changing UK Government of Science*
    Nature - v432 - i7019 - Dec 16 2004 - p806(2) [501+]
    SciTech - v28 - i3 - Sept 2004 - p13(1) [501+]

Boden, Sharon - *Consumerism, Romance, and the Wedding Experience*
    CS - v33 - i6 - Nov 2004 - p690(3) [501+]

Bodenhausen, Galen V. - *Foundations of Social Cognition: A Festschrift in Honor of Robert S. Wyer, Jr.*
    R&R Bk N - v19 - i1 - Feb 2004 - p8(1) [1-50]

Bodenhorn, Terry - *Defining Modernity: Guomindang Rhetorics of a New China, 1920-1970*
    Ch Rev Int - v10 - i2 - Fall 2003 - p372(4) [501+]

Boderhorn, Howard - *State Banking in Early America: A New Economic History*
    JIH - v34 - i4 - Spring 2004 - p650-651 [501+]

Bodett, Tom - *Norman Tuttle on the Last Frontier: A Novel in Stories*
    y BL - v101 - i7 - Dec 1 2004 - p646(1) [51-500]
    c CCB-B - v58 - i4 - Dec 2004 - p160(1) [51-500]
    c Kliatt - v38 - i6 - Nov 2004 - p6(1) [51-500]
    y KR - v72 - i21 - Nov 1 2004 - p1043(1) [51-500]
    y PW - v252 - i1 - Jan 3 2005 - p56(1) [51-500]
    c SLJ - v50 - i12 - Dec 2004 - p140(1) [501+]
    c VOYA - v27 - i5 - Dec 2004 - p378(1) [501+]

Bodger, Joan - *Tales of Court and Castle (Illus. by Lang, Mark)*
    c CBRA - Annual 2003 - p475(1) [51-500]

Bodi, Leslie - *Literatur, Politik, Identitat*
    HNet - Oct 2004 - pNA [501+]

Bodine, Echo L. - *Hands That Heal*
    Bwatch - Feb 2005 - pNA [501+]

Bodio, Stephen J. - *Eagle Dreams: Searching for Legends in Wild Mongolia*
    SciTech - v28 - i3 - Sept 2004 - p133(1) [51-500]

Bodkin, Odds - *The Harper and the King: The Story of Young David (Read by Bodkin, Odds). Audiobook Review*
    c SLJ - v50 - i9 - Sept 2004 - p82(1) [51-500]

Bodle, Wayne - *The Valley Forge Winter: Civilians and Soldiers in War*
    JAH - v91 - i1 - June 2004 - p219-220 [501+]

Bodmer, Karl - *Karl Bodmer's North American Prints*
    Choice - v42 - i4 - Dec 2004 - p648(1) [1-50]

Bodnar, Istvan - *Eudemus of Rhodes*
    Isis - v95 - i2 - June 2004 - p283(3) [501+]

Bodnar, John - *Blue-Collar Hollywood: Liberalism, Democracy, and Working People in American Film*
    JAH - v91 - i2 - Sept 2004 - p677(2) [501+]
    RAH - v32 - i1 - March 2004 - p97(8) [501+]

Bodoff, Stephanie - *J2EE Tutorial, 2nd Ed.*
    CBRA - Annual 2003 - p21(1) [51-500]
    SciTech - v28 - i4 - Dec 2004 - p21(1) [51-500]

Bodwell, Teresa - *Loving Mercy*
    y BL - v101 - i7 - Dec 1 2004 - p640(1) [51-500]

Body Matters
    LibMed - v22 - i7 - April-May 2004 - p69(1) [501+]

Boeck, Tammy Montgomery - *Connections: Writing, Reading, and Critical Thinking, 2nd Ed.*
    R&R Bk N - v19 - i4 - Nov 2004 - p216(1) [501+]

Boedoe, Geefwee - *Arrowville (Illus. by Boedoe, Geefwee)*
    c BL - v101 - i8 - Dec 15 2004 - p746(1) [51-500]
    c NYTBR - Oct 17 2004 - p21 [501+]
    c PW - v251 - i49 - Dec 6 2004 - p58(1) [51-500]
    c SLJ - v50 - i11 - Nov 2004 - p91(1) [51-500]

Boehmer-Christiansen, Sonja - *International Environmental Policy: Interests and the Failure of the Kyoto Process*
    AJPS - v39 - i3 - Nov 2004 - p669(1) [501+]

Boehrer, Bruce Thomas - *Parrot Culture: Our 2500-Year Long Fascination with the World's Most Talkative Bird*
    Choice - v42 - i5 - Jan 2005 - p880(1) [1-50]

Boekhoff, P.M. - *The Navajo*
    c SLJ - v50 - i7 - July 2004 - p117(1) [51-500]

Boelts, Maribeth - *The Firefighters' Thanksgiving (Illus. by Widener, Terry)*
    c BL - v100 - i22 - August 2004 - p1940(1) [51-500]
    c KR - v72 - i13 - July 1 2004 - p625(1) [51-500]
    c PW - v251 - i39 - Sept 27 2004 - p59(1) [51-500]
    c SLJ - v51 - i1 - Jan 2005 - p86(1) [51-500]

Boenig, Robert - *Manuscript, Narrative, Lexicon: Essays on Literary and Cultural Transmission in Honor of Whitney F. Bolton*
    JEGP - v103 - i1 - Jan 2004 - p125-127 [501+]

Boer, Jelle de - *Earthquakes in Human History: The Far-Reaching Effects of Seismic Disruptions*
    TimHES - v0 - i1682 - March 11 2005 - p29(1) [501+]

Boer, Karl W. - *Survey of Semiconductor Physics. 3rd Ed.*
    SciTech - v28 - i1 - March 2004 - p50(1) [51-500]

Boer, Roland - *Marxist Criticism of the Bible*
    R&R Bk N - v19 - i3 - August 2004 - p22(1) [1-50]

Boersma, Hans - *Violence, Hospitality, and the Cross: Reappropriating the Atonement Tradition*
    Comw - v132 - i2 - Jan 28 2005 - p38(3) [501+]
    LJ - v129 - i17 - Oct 15 2004 - p67(1) [51-500]

Boettcher, Jennifer C. - *Industry Research Using the Economic Census: How to Find It, How to Use It*
    Choice - v42 - i7 - March 2005 - p1203(1) [51-500]

Boettger, Suzaan - *Earthworks: Art and the Landscape of the Sixties*
    JAAC - v62 - i3 - Summer 2004 - p309-311 [501+]

Boeve, Lieven - *Divinising Experience: Essays in the History of Religious Experience from Origen to Ricoeur*
    R&R Bk N - v19 - i4 - Nov 2004 - p19(1) [51-500]

Boeyens, J.C.A. - *The Theories of Chemistry*
    E-Streams - Oct 2004 - pNA [501+]

Boeyens, Jan C.A. - *The Theories of Chemistry*
    Choice - v42 - i1 - Sept 2004 - p133(1) [501+]

Bogaart, W.A. - *Consequences: The Impact of Law and Its Complexity*
    CBRA - Annual 2003 - p314(1) [51-500]

Bogan, Paulette - *Momma's Magical Purse (Illus. by Bogan, Paulette)*
    c SLJ - v50 - i9 - Sept 2004 - p154(1) [51-500]
    Mummy's Magical Handbag
    c Sch Lib - v52 - i4 - Winter 2004 - p185(1) [51-500]

Bogart, Daneil B. - *Estates in Land and Future Interests: Problems and Answers, 4th Ed.*
    R&R Bk N - v19 - i3 - August 2004 - p197(1) [1-50]

Bogart, Jo Ellen - *Emily Carr: At the Edge of the World (Illus. by Newhouse, Maxwell)*
    c CBRA - Annual 2003 - p532(2) [501+]

Bogart, Leo - *Finding Out: Personal Adventures in Social Research: Discovering What People Think, Say, and Do*
    Pub Op Q - v68 - i4 - Winter 2004 - p648(3) [501+]
    How I Earned the Ruptured Duck: From Brooklyn to Berchtesgaden in World War II
    J Mil H - v68 - i2 - April 2004 - p644(3) [501+]
    Over the Edge: How the Pursuit of Youth by Marketer, and the Media Has Changed American Culture
    KR - v73 - i2 - Jan 15 2005 - p94(1) [501+]

Bogdandy, Armin von - *Max Planck Yearbook of United Nations Law, Vol. 7*
    R&R Bk N - v19 - i3 - August 2004 - p186(1) [501+]

Bogdanor, Vernon - *The British Constitution in the Twentieth Century*
    Choice - v42 - i1 - Sept 2004 - p178(1) [501+]
    HER - v119 - i483 - Sept 2004 - p1021(3) [501+]
    Law Q Rev - v121 - Jan 2005 - p168-171 [501+]
    TimHES - v0 - i1651 - July 30 2004 - p24(1) [501+]

Bogdanov, Michael - *Shakespeare: The Director's Cut*
    TimHES - v0 - i1655 - August 27 2004 - p29(1) [501+]

Bogdanov, Vladimir - *All Music Guide to Country Music: The Definitive Guide to Country Music*
    Choice - v41 - i11-12 - July-August 2004 - p2013(1) [501+]

Bogdanovich, Peter - *Who the Hell's in It: Portraits and Conversations*
    Atl - v294 - i2 - Sept 2004 - p122(2) [501+]
    BL - v100 - i22 - August 2004 - p1887(1) [51-500]
    Ent W - i787 - Oct 8 2004 - p119 [501+]
    KR - v72 - i13 - July 1 2004 - p611(1) [51-500]
    LJ - v129 - i12 - July 2004 - p84(1) [51-500]
    PW - v251 - i29 - July 19 2004 - p154(1) [51-500]

Bogel, Fredric V. - *The Difference Satire Makes: Rhetoric and Reading from Jonson to Byron*
    MP - v102 - i1 - August 2004 - p122(5) [501+]

Bogener, Steve - *Ditches Across the Desert: Irrigation in the Lower Pecos Valley*
    Choice - v42 - i1 - Sept 2004 - p171(2) [501+]

Bogeyaktuk, Anatole - *Taprarmiuni Kassiyulriit: Stebbins Dance Festival*
    R&R Bk N - v19 - i3 - August 2004 - p62(1) [51-500]

Boggs, Carl - *A World in Chaos: Social Crisis and the Rise of Postmodern Cinema*
    Choice - v42 - i1 - Sept 2004 - p108(1) [501+]
    R&R Bk N - v19 - i1 - Feb 2004 - p226(1) [51-500]

Boggs, Carol L. - *Butterflies: Ecology and Evalution Taking Flight*
    QRB - v79 - i4 - Dec 2004 - p435(2) [501+]

Boggs, Johnny D. - *Dark Voyage of the Mittie Stephens*
    Roundup M - v11 - i6 - August 2004 - p26(1) [501+]
    East of the Border
    Roundup M - v12 - i3 - Feb 2005 - p25(1) [51-500]

Bogira, Steve - *Courtroom 302: A Year Behind the Scenes in an American Criminal Courthouse*
    Econ - v374 - i8418 - March 19 2005 - p86US [501+]
    KR - v73 - i3 - Feb 1 2005 - p158(2) [501+]
    PW - v252 - i7 - Feb 14 2005 - p67(2) [51-500]

Bollinger, Martin J. - *Stalin's Slave Ships: Kolyma, the Gulag Fleet, and the Role of the West*
R&R Bk N - v19 - i1 - Feb 2004 - p145(1) [51-500]

Bollobas, Bela - *External Graph Theory*
SciTech - v28 - i4 - Dec 2004 - p35(1) [51-500]

Bollow, Ludmilla - *Dr. Zastro's Sanitarium for the Ailments of Women*
PW - v251 - i43 - Oct 25 2004 - p28(1) [51-500]

Bolognini, Stefano - *Psychoanalytic Empathy*
SciTech - v28 - i3 - Sept 2004 - p100(1) [1-50]

Bolongaro, Eugenio - *Italo Calvino and the Compass of Literature*
R&R Bk N - v19 - i1 - Feb 2004 - p232(1) [51-500]

Bolotin, Norman - *Civil War A to Z*
c RT - v57 - Nov 2003 - p276 [51-500]

Bolsover, Steven R. - *Cell Biology: A Short Course. 2nd Ed.*
SciTech - v28 - i1 - March 2004 - p65(1) [51-500]

Bolstad, Richard - *Resolve: A New Model of Therapy*
SciTech - v28 - i4 - Dec 2004 - p98(1) [51-500]

Bolstad, William M. - *Introduction to Bayesian Statistics*
Choice - v42 - i4 - Dec 2004 - p697(1) [1-50]

Bolt, Rodney - *History Play: The Lies and Afterlife of Christopher Marlowe*
Spec - v295 - i9185 - August 21 2004 - p34(1) [501+]
History Play: The Lives and Afterlife of Christopher Marlowe
CR - v286 - i1668 - Jan 2005 - p61(2) [51-500]
Lon R Bks - v26 - i16 - August 19 2004 - p11(4) [501+]
TLS - i5307 - Dec 17 2004 - p22(1) [501+]

Bolton, Andrew - *Wild: Fashion Untamed*
Globe & Mail - Dec 18 2004 - pD14 [1-50]

Bolton, Betsy - *Women, Nationalism and the Romantic Stage: Theatre and Politics in Britian, 1780-1800*
RES - v55 - i221 - Sept 2004 - p626(3) [501+]

Bolton, Charles F. - *Neurology of Breathing*
SciTech - v28 - i1 - March 2004 - p105(1) [51-500]

Bolton, John - *Clive Barker's Hellraiser: Collected Best III*
PW - v251 - i29 - July 19 2004 - p146(1) [51-500]
The Sandman Presents: The Furies
LibMed - v22 - i7 - April-May 2004 - p64(1) [501+]

Bolton, Kingsley - *Chinese Englishes: A Sociolinguistic History*
Choice - v42 - i1 - Sept 2004 - p94(1) [501+]

Bolton, Martha - *Cooking with Hot Flashes*
LJ - v129 - i15 - Sept 2004 - p72(2) [51-500]

Bolzano, Bernard - *On the Mathematical Method and Correspondence with Exner*
SciTech - v28 - i3 - Sept 2004 - p17(1) [501+]

Bomar, Perri J. - *Promoting Health in Families: Applying Family Research and Theory to Nursing Practice. 3rd Ed.*
SciTech - v28 - i1 - March 2004 - p127(1) [51-500]

Bombassaro, Luiz Carlos - *Im Schatten der Diana: Die Jagdmetapher im Werk von Giordano Bruno*
Ren Q - v57 - i3 - Fall 2004 - p1098(4) [501+]

Bombaugh, Ruth - *Science Fair Success*
SB - v40 - i5 - Sept-Oct 2004 - p192(1) [51-500]

Bomford, David - *Underdrawings in Renaissance Paintings*
Six Ct J - v35 - i3 - Fall 2004 - p906-908 [501+]

Bommel, Patrick van - *Transformation of Knowledge, Information and Data: Theory and Applications*
Choice - v42 - i7 - March 2005 - p1262(2) [51-500]
SciTech - v28 - i4 - Dec 2004 - p33(1) [51-500]

Bon, Francois - *Daewoo*
TLS - i5301 - Nov 5 2004 - p34(1) [51-500]

Bona, Constantin - *Neonatal Immunity*
SciTech - v28 - i4 - Dec 2004 - p75(1) [51-500]

Bona, Miklos - *Combinatorics of Permutations*
Choice - v42 - i7 - March 2005 - p1263(1) [51-500]
SciTech - v28 - i4 - Dec 2004 - p35(1) [51-500]

Bonaccorso, Alessandro - *Mt. Etna: Volcano Laboratory*
SciTech - v28 - i4 - Dec 2004 - p57(1) [51-500]

Bonaddio, Federico - *Crossing Fields in Modern Spanish Culture*
R&R Bk N - v19 - i4 - Nov 2004 - p231(1) [501+]

Bonanno, Bill - *The Good Guys*
KR - v72 - i21 - Nov 1 2004 - p1020(1) [51-500]
People - v63 - i3 - Jan 24 2005 - p50 [51-500]
PW - v251 - i49 - Dec 6 2004 - p44(1) [51-500]
Ent W - i798 - Dec 24 2004 - p73 [501+]

Bonans, J. Frederic - *Numerical Optimization*
SIAM Rev - v46 - i3 - Sept 2004 - p568(4) [501+]

Bonansinga, Jay - *The Sinking of the Eastland; America's Forgotten Tragedy*
LJ - v129 - i20 - Dec 1 2004 - p134(1) [51-500]
PW - v251 - i36 - Sept 6 2004 - p57(1) [51-500]

Bonavoglia, Angela - *Good Catholic Girls: How Women are Leading the Fight to Change the Church*
PW - v252 - i9 - Feb 28 2005 - p64(1) [51-500]

Bond, Alison - *How to Be Famous*
KR - v73 - i1 - Jan 1 2005 - p4(1) [501+]

Bond, Bradley G. - *Mississippi: A Documentary History*
JSH - v70 - i4 - Nov 2004 - p979(1) [501+]

Bond, Brian - *The Unquiet Western Front: Britain's Role in Literature and History*
J Mil H - v68 - i3 - April 2004 - p625-626 [501+]

Bond, David - *Future Perfect: Retirement Strategies for Productive People*
CBRA - Annual 2003 - p28(1) [51-500]

Bond, Edward L. - *Spreading the Gospel in Colonial Virginia: Sermons and Devotional Writings*
R&R Bk N - v19 - i3 - August 2004 - p20(1) [1-50]

Bond, George D. - *Buddhism at Work: Community Development, Social Empowerment and the Sarvodaya Movement*
R&R Bk N - v19 - i2 - May 2004 - p130 [51-500]

Bond, Larry - *Larry Bond's First Team (Read by Brick, Scott). Audiobook Review*
y Kliatt - v39 - i2 - March 2005 - p54(1) [51-500]

Bond, Marybeth - *A Woman's Europe*
Globe & Mail - Nov 6 2004 - pT10 [501+]

Bond, Patrick - *Against Global Apartheid: South Africa Meets the World Bank, IMF and International Finance*
HNet - Oct 2004 - pNA [501+]
South Africa and Global Apartheid: Continental and International Policies and Politics
HNet - Oct 2004 - pNA [501+]

Bond, Rebecca - *This Place in the Snow (Illus. by Bond, Rebecca)*
c BL - v101 - i7 - Dec 1 2004 - p652(1) [51-500]
c CCB-B - v58 - i4 - Dec 2004 - p160(2) [51-500]
c KR - v72 - i22 - Nov 15 2004 - p1087(1) [51-500]
c PW - v251 - i51 - Dec 20 2004 - p59(1) [51-500]
c SLJ - v50 - i11 - Nov 2004 - p91(1) [51-500]

Bond, Stephanie - *Kill the Competition (Read by McCulloh, Barbara). Audiobook Review*
LJ - v129 - i17 - Oct 15 2004 - p95(1) [51-500]
Whole Lotta Trouble
PW - v251 - i36 - Sept 6 2004 - p51(1) [51-500]

Bondanella, Peter E. - *Hollywood Italians: Dagos, Palookas, Romeos, Wise Guys, and Sopranos*
Choice - v42 - i4 - Dec 2004 - p668(1) [1-50]

Bonde, Sheila - *Saint-Jean-des-Vignes in Soissons: Approaches to Its Architecture, Archaeology and History*
CHR - v90 - i4 - Oct 2004 - p754(2) [501+]

Bondeson, Jan - *The Pig-Faced Lady of Manchester Square and Other Medical Marvels*
TimHES - v0 - i1652 - August 6 2004 - p26(1) [501+]

Bondi, Roberta C. - *Night on the Flint River: An Accidental Journey in Knowing God*
TT - v60 - i4 - Jan 2004 - p560-562 [501+]

Bonds, John Bledsoe - *Bipartisan Strategy: Selling the Marshall Plan*
JAH - v91 - i3 - Dec 2004 - p1077(2) [501+]

Bonds, Michael - *Race, Politics and Community Development Funding: The Discolor of Money*
R&R Bk N - v19 - i3 - August 2004 - p146(1) [51-500]

Bondurant, Matt - *The Third Translation*
PW - v252 - i4 - Jan 24 2005 - p218(1) [501+]
PW - v252 - i4 - Jan 24 2005 - p26(1) [501+]

Bone, Ian - *A Dangerous Secret (Illus. by Murphy, Jobi)*
c CCB-B - v58 - i4 - Dec 2004 - p161(1) [51-500]
y KR - v72 - i21 - Nov 1 2004 - p1043(1) [51-500]
y PW - v252 - i2 - Jan 10 2005 - p56(1) [51-500]
y SLJ - v51 - i1 - Jan 2005 - p122(1) [51-500]
The Song of an Innocent Bystander
c BW - v34 - i35 - August 2004 - p12(1) [51-500]
y SLJ - v50 - i9 - Sept 2004 - p198(1) [51-500]
Time Trap (Illus. by Murphy, Jobi)
c KR - v72 - i24 - Dec 15 2004 - p1198(1) [501+]
y SLJ - v51 - i2 - Feb 2005 - p132(1) [51-500]

Bonekemper, Edward H. - *A Victor, Not a Butcher: Ulysses S. Grant's Overlooked Military Genius*
LJ - v129 - i12 - July 2004 - p96(1) [51-500]

Bonfiglioli, Kyril - *Don't Point That Thing at Me*
LJ - v129 - i13 - August 2004 - p131(1) [51-500]
NY - v80 - i27 - Sept 20 2004 - p104 [501+]

Bongenaar, A.C.V.M. - *The Neo-Babylonian Ebabbar Temple at Sippar: Its Administration and Its Prosopography*
JNES - v63 - i3 - July 2004 - p214(3) [501+]

Bonger, Henk - *Life and Work of Dirck Volkertszoon Coornhert*
R&R Bk N - v19 - i4 - Nov 2004 - p41(1) [51-500]

Bonhoeffer, Dietrich - *Reflections on the Bible: Human Word and the Word of God*
PW - v251 - i33 - August 16 2004 - p61(1) [501+]

Boniface, Jacqueline - *Les Constructions des nombres reels dans le mouvement d'arithmetisation de l'analyse*
Dialogue - v43 - i1 - Wntr 2004 - p190-192 [501+]

Boniface, Priscilla - *Tasting Tourism: Travelling for Food and Drink*
R&R Bk N - v19 - i1 - Feb 2004 - p252(1) [51-500]

Bonilla-Silva, Eduardo - *Urban America and Its Police: From the Postcolonial Era through the Turbulent 1960s*
CS - v33 - i5 - Sept 2004 - p594-596 [501+]

Bonin, Hubert - *La banque nationale de credit:Histoire de la quatrieme banque de depots francaise en 1913-1932*
BHR - v78 - i2 - Summer 2004 - p352(3) [501+]

Boning, Duane S. - *Advances in Chemical-Mechanical Polishing: Proceedings*
SciTech - v28 - i4 - Dec 2004 - p169(1) [51-500]

Bonisch-Brednich, Brigitte - *Keeping a Low Profile: An Oral History of German Immigration to New Zealand*
JEL - v42 - i1 - March 2004 - p278(1) [501+]

Bonk, Thomas - *Language, Truth, and Knowledge: Contributions to the Philosophy of Rudolf Carnap*
R&R Bk N - v19 - i1 - Feb 2004 - p3(1) [51-500]

Bonner, Hannah - *When Bugs Were Big, Plants Were Strange, and Terrapods Stalked the Earth: A Cartoon Prehistory of Life before Dinosaurs (Illus. by Bonner, Hannah)*
c BL - v101 - i7 - Dec 1 2004 - p670(1) [51-500]
When Bugs Were Big, Plants Were Strange, and Tetrapods Stalked The Earth: A Cartoon Prehistory of Life before Dinosaurs (Illus. by Bonner, Hannah)
LibMed - v22 - i7 - April-May 2004 - p77(1) [501+]
SLJ - v50 - i10 - Oct 2004 - pS40(1) [51-500]

Bonner, Lori - *Putting on a Party: Adventure Parties for Kids (Illus. by Lee, Fran)*
Bwatch - Nov 2004 - pNA [51-500]
c SLJ - v50 - i7 - July 2004 - p117(2) [51-500]

Bonnet, Gilles - *L'Ecriture comique de J.-K. Huysmans*
NCFS - v33 - i1-2 - Fall-Winter 2004 - p207(3) [501+]

Bonney, Rachel A. - *Anthropologists and Indians in the New South*
Am Ind CRJ - v28 - i2 - Spring 2004 - p139(4) [501+]

Bonnie, Richard J. - *Reducing Underage Drinking: A Collective Responsibility*
Choice - v42 - i3 - Nov 2004 - p518(1) [1-50]

Bonning, Tony - *Snog the Frog*
c KR - v73 - i1 - Jan 1 2005 - p48(1) [51-500]

Bonoli, Fabrizio - *Daniela Piliarvu. I lettori di astronomia: Presso lo Studio di Bologna dal XII al XX secolo*
Isis - v95 - i3 - Sept 2004 - p469(2) [501+]

Bonsall, Thomas E. - *Cadillac Story: The Postwar Years*
SciTech - v28 - i1 - March 2004 - p166(1) [51-500]
The Lincoln Story: The Postwar Years
Choice - v42 - i1 - Sept 2004 - p124(1) [501+]
SciTech - v28 - i1 - March 2004 - p167(1) [51-500]

Bonsor, Sacha - *Dipped into Oblivion*
CR - v285 - i1662 - July 2004 - p61(2) [51-500]

Bonta, Mark - *Deleuze and Geophilosophy: A Guide and Glossary*
Choice - v42 - i7 - March 2005 - p1239(1) [51-500]

Bonta, Stephen - *Studies in Italian Sacred and Instrumental Music in the 17th Century*
R&R Bk N - v19 - i1 - Feb 2004 - p196(1) [51-500]

Bony, Anne - *Furniture and Interiors of the 1940s*
Ant&CM - v108 - i7 - Sept 2003 - p16(1) [501+]
Furniture and Interiors of the 1960s
Ant&CM - v109 - i3 - May 2004 - p16(1) [501+]
LJ - v129 - i12 - July 2004 - p77(1) [51-500]

Boogaart, Thomas A. - *An Ethnography of Late Medieval Bruges: Evolution of the Corporate Milieu 1280-1349*
R&R Bk N - v19 - i4 - Nov 2004 - p136(1) [51-500]

Booher, Dianna - *From Contract to Contract*
R&R Bk N - v19 - i1 - Feb 2004 - p109(1) [1-50]

The Book of Letters. Audiobook Review
Globe & Mail - Dec 4 2004 - pD38 [1-50]

The Book of Rule: How the World Is Governed
Choice - v42 - i3 - Nov 2004 - p460(1) [1-50]

Borjesson, Kristina - *Into the Buzzsaw: Leading Journalists Expose the Myth of a Free Press. Rev. and Expanded Ed.*
LJ - v129 - i17 - Oct 15 2004 - p69(2) [51-500]
PW - v251 - i44 - Nov 1 2004 - p53(1) [501+]
y   SLJ - v51 - i1 - Jan 2005 - p159(2) [51-500]

Bork, Robert H. - *Coercing Virtue: The Worldwide Rule of Judges*
Choice - v41 - i7 - March 2004 - p1364(1) [501+]

Borley, Lester - *Celebrating the Life and Times of Hugh Miller: Scotland in the Early Nineteenth Century*
Folkl - v115 - i2 - August 2004 - p246(1) [501+]

Borman, Anders - *Protective Gloves for Occupational Use, 2nd Ed.*
SciTech - v28 - i4 - Dec 2004 - p115(1) [1-50]

Bormans, Paul - *Ceramics Are More than Clay Alone*
Ceram Mo - v53 - i1 - Jan 2005 - p76(1) [501+]

Born, Daniel - *The Common Review*
LJ - v129 - i12 - July 2004 - p120(1) [501+]

The Born-Einstein Letters, 1916-1955: Friendship, Politics and Physics in Uncertain Times
BW - v35 - i4 - Jan 30 2005 - p8(2) [501+]

Born, Georgina - *Uncertain Vision: Birt, Dyke and the Reinvention of the BBC*
NS - v133 - i4717 - Dec 6 2004 - p50(2) [501+]
TimHES - v0 - i1666 - Nov 12 2004 - p24(2) [501+]
TLS - i5307 - Dec 17 2004 - p27(1) [501+]

Born, Hans - *The 'Double Democratic Deficit': Parliamentary Accountability and the Use of Force under International Auspices*
R&R Bk N - v19 - i3 - August 2004 - p176(1) [501+]

Born, James O. - *Shock Wave*
KR - v73 - i5 - March 1 2005 - p243(1) [51-500]
Walking Money
LJ - v129 - i12 - July 2004 - p66(1) [51-500]

Bornais, Gilles - *The Devil Lives in Glasgow*
KR - v72 - i13 - July 1 2004 - p605(1) [51-500]
PW - v251 - i27 - July 5 2004 - p41(1) [51-500]

Borneman, Walter R. - *1812: The War That Forged a Nation*
y   BL - v101 - i1 - Sept 1 2004 - p41(1) [51-500]
KR - v72 - i15 - August 1 2004 - p719(1) [501+]

Bornemann, Folkmar - *The SIAM 100-Digit Challenge: A Study in High-Accuracy Numerical Computing*
Sci - v307 - i5709 - Jan 28 2005 - p521(2) [501+]

Bornstein, David - *How to Change the World: Social Entrepreneurs and the Power of New Ideas*
AM - v191 - i6 - Sept 13 2004 - p25 [501+]
Har Bus R - v82 - i2 - Feb 2004 - p39(1) [501+]
R&R Bk N - v19 - i2 - May 2004 - p130 [51-500]

Bornstein, George - *Material Modernism: The Politics of the Page*
AL - v76 - i2 - June 2004 - p400(3) [501+]

Bornstein, Yvonne - *Eleven Days of Hell: My True Story of Kidnapping, Terror, Torture and Historic FBI & KGB Rescue*
PW - v252 - i1 - Jan 3 2005 - p50(2) [51-500]

Boros, George - *Irresistible Integrals; Symbolics, Analysis and Experiments in the Evaluation of Integrals*
Choice - v42 - i7 - March 2005 - p1623(1) [51-500]

Borovik, Alexandre V. - *Computational and Experimental Group Theory: Proceedings*
SciTech - v28 - i3 - Sept 2004 - p35(1) [51-500]
Coxeter Matroids
SIAM Rev - v46 - i3 - Sept 2004 - p577(3) [501+]

Borovitz, Mark - *The Holy Thief: A Con Man's Journey from Darkness to Light*
BL - v100 - i22 - August 2004 - p1878(1) [51-500]
LJ - v129 - i14 - Sept 1 2004 - p156(1) [51-500]
PW - v251 - i30 - July 26 2004 - p50(2) [501+]

Borowitz, Andy - *The Borowitz Report: The Big Book of Shockers*
PW - v251 - i32 - August 9 2004 - p238(1) [51-500]

Borowski, Oded - *Daily Life in Biblical Times*
R&R Bk N - v19 - i1 - Feb 2004 - p43(1) [51-500]

Borradori, Giovanna - *Philosophy in a Time of Terror: Dialogues with Jurgen Habermas and Jacques Derrida*
Dal R - v83 - i3 - Autumn 2003 - p455-457 [501+]
Globe & Mail - Oct 30 2004 - pD29 [51-500]

Borras-Almenar, Juan J. - *Polyoxometalate Molecular Science: Proceedings*
SciTech - v28 - i1 - March 2004 - p56(1) [51-500]

Borras, Susana - *The Innovation Policy of the European Union: From Government to Governance*
JEL - v42 - i1 - March 2004 - p317(1) [501+]
R&R Bk N - v19 - i1 - Feb 2004 - pNA [51-500]

Borrero, Mauricio - *Hungry Moscow: Scarcity and Uban Society in the Russian Civil War, 1917-1921*
Slav R - v63 - i3 - Fall 2004 - p656-657 [501+]
Russia: A Reference Guide from the Renaissance to the Present
y   BL - v101 - i4 - Oct 15 2004 - p439(1) [51-500]
R&R Bk N - v19 - i3 - August 2004 - p45(1) [51-500]

Borrowman, Mary - *The Rescue of Nanoose (Illus. by Wang, Jacqueline)*
c   Globe & Mail - Jan 29 2005 - pD10 [51-500]
c   Res Links - v10 - i3 - Feb 2005 - p24(1) [501+]

Borrus, Kathy - *One Thousand Buildings of Paris*
R&R Bk N - v19 - i3 - August 2004 - p42(1) [51-500]

Borsay, Peter - *Provisional Towns in Early Modern England and Ireland: Change, Convergence and Divergence*
JIH - v34 - i4 - Spring 2004 - p631-632 [501+]

Borski, Robert - *Solar Labyrinth*
ChrSFF&H - v26 - i9 - Sept 2004 - p37(1) [51-500]

Borson, Roo - *Short Journey Upriver Toward Oishida*
BIC - v33 - i8 - Nov 2004 - p26(3) [501+]
Globe & Mail - July 3 2004 - p6 [501+]

Bortolin, Matthew - *The Dharma of Star Wars*
PW - v252 - i7 - Feb 14 2005 - p70(1) [51-500]

Bortolotti, Bernado - *The Challenges of Privatization: An International Analysis*
Choice - v42 - i3 - Nov 2004 - p531(2) [1-50]

Bortolotti, Dan - *Exploring Saturn*
c   CBRA - Annual 2003 - p570(1) [51-500]
c   SLJ - v50 - i10 - Oct 2004 - pS40(1) [51-500]
c   S&T - v107 - i1 - Jan 2004 - p76(1) [501+]
Hope in Hell: Inside the World of Doctors without Borders
BL - v101 - i2 - Sept 15 2004 - p188(1) [51-500]
Globe & Mail - Oct 30 2004 - pD19 [51-500]
LJ - v129 - i16 - Oct 1 2004 - p103(1) [51-500]
PW - v251 - i32 - August 9 2004 - p237(1) [51-500]
Panda Rescue: Changing the Future for Endangered Wildlife
c   CBRA - Annual 2003 - p563(1) [51-500]
c   SLJ - v50 - i10 - Oct 2004 - pS40(1) [51-500]
Tiger Rescue: Changing the Future for Endangered Wildlife
c   CBRA - Annual 2003 - p563(1) [51-500]
c   SLJ - v50 - i10 - Oct 2004 - pS40(1) [51-500]

Bortz, Fred - *The Electron*
c   SLJ - v50 - i10 - Oct 2004 - p186(1) [51-500]
The Photon
c   SLJ - v50 - i10 - Oct 2004 - p186(1) [51-500]
The Proton
c   SLJ - v50 - i10 - Oct 2004 - p186(1) [51-500]
The Quark
c   SLJ - v50 - i10 - Oct 2004 - p186(1) [51-500]

Bortz, Jeffrey L. - *The Mexican Economy, 1870-1930: Essays on the Economic History of Institutions, Revolution, and Growth*
Ams - v61 - i2 - Oct 2004 - p292(2) [501+]
BHR - v78 - i1 - Spring 2004 - p178(3) [501+]
HAHR - v84 - i2 - May 2004 - p355(2) [501+]
JEL - v41 - i4 - Dec 2003 - p1315(2) [501+]

Boruchoff, David A. - *Isabel la Catolica, Queen of Castile: Critical Essays*
CR - v285 - i1662 - July 2004 - p59(1) [51-500]
Ren Q - v57 - i4 - Winter 2004 - p1407(2) [501+]

Borwein, Jonathan M. - *Experimentation in Mathematics: Computational Paths to Discovery*
Am Sci - v93 - i2 - March-April 2005 - p182(2) [501+]
Choice - v42 - i2 - Oct 2004 - p328(2) [51-500]
SciTech - v28 - i3 - Sept 2004 - p17(1) [501+]
Mathematics by Experiment: Plausible Reasoning in the 21st Century
Am Sci - v93 - i2 - March-April 2005 - p182(2) [501+]
Choice - v42 - i5 - Jan 2005 - p887(1) [1-50]

Borzutzky, Silvia - *Vital Connections: Politics, Social Security, and Inequality in Chile*
HAHR - v84 - i3 - August 2004 - p559(3) [501+]

Bos, E.P. - *Logica Modernorum in Prague about 1400: The Sophistria Disputation 'Quoniam Quatuor' (MS Cracow, Jagiellonian Library 686, ff. 1ra-79rb), with a Partial Reconstruction of Thomas of Cleve's 'Logica'*
R&R Bk N - v19 - i1 - Feb 2005 - p3(1) [51-500]

Bos, Frits - *The National Accounts as a Tool for Analysis and Policy: Past, Present and Future*
JEL - v42 - i1 - March 2004 - p253(2) [501+]

Bos, Timothy J. - *USMLE Road Map: Microbiology and Infectious Diseases*
SciTech - v28 - i4 - Dec 2004 - p91(1) [51-500]

Bosak, Susan V. - *Dream: A Tale of Wonder, Wisdom & Wishes*
y   BL - v101 - i9-10 - Jan 1 2005 - p842(1) [501+]
c   CH Bwatch - v14 - i12 - Dec 2004 - pNA [51-500]
c   KR - v72 - i22 - Nov 15 2004 - p1088(1) [51-500]
c   PW - v251 - i46 - Nov 15 2004 - p60(1) [51-500]
c   SLJ - v50 - i12 - Dec 2004 - p140(1) [501+]

Bosch, Lynette - *Art, Liturgy and Legend in Renaissance Toledo: The Mendoza and the Iglesia Primada*
Specu - v79 - i3 - July 2004 - p740-742 [501+]

Boschetto-Sandoval, Sandra M. - *The Imaginary in the Writing of Latin American Author Amanda Labarca Hubertson (1886-1975): Supplements to a Feminist Critique*
Choice - v42 - i5 - Jan 2005 - p857(2) [1-50]
R&R Bk N - v19 - i4 - Nov 2004 - p232(1) [501+]

Boschken, Herman L. - *Social Class, Politics and Urban Markets: The Making of Bias in Policy Outcomes*
J Am St - v38 - i1 - April 2004 - p139-140 [501+]

Bose, A.B. - *The State of Children in India: Promises to Keep*
R&R Bk N - v19 - i4 - Nov 2004 - p131(1) [1-50]

Bose, N.K. - *Multidimensional Systems Theory and Applications*
SciTech - v28 - i1 - March 2004 - p40(1) [51-500]

Bosher, William C. - *The School Law Handbook: What Every Leader Needs to Know*
R&R Bk N - v19 - i4 - Nov 2004 - p171(1) [501+]
TCR - v106 - i12 - Dec 2004 - p2253(7) [501+]

Bosk, Charles L. - *Forgive and Remember: Managing Medical Failure. 2nd Ed.*
SF - v83 - i1 - Sept 2004 - p424(3) [501+]
SF - v83 - i1 - Sept 2004 - p426(3) [501+]
SF - v83 - i1 - Sept 2004 - p428(5) [501+]

Bosko, Mark Steven - *The Complete Independent Movie Marketing Handbook: Promote, Distribute and Sell Your Film and Video*
R&R Bk N - v19 - i3 - August 2004 - p261(1) [51-500]

Boskovits, Miklos - *Italian Paintings of the Fifteenth Century*
Choice - v42 - i1 - Sept 2004 - p89(1) [501+]

Boss, Martha J. - *Biological Risk Engineering Handbook: Infection Control and Decontamination*
E-Streams - Sept 2004 - pNA [501+]

Boss, Michael - *Engaging Modernity: Readings in Irish Politics, Culture and Literature at the Turn of the Century*
ILS - v24 - i1 - Fall 2004 - p20(1) [501+]

Boss, Sarah Jane - *Empress and Handmaid: On Nature and Gender in the Cult of the Virgin Mary*
CH - v73 - i4 - Dec 2004 - p876(2) [501+]

Bosse, Malcolm - *Tusk and Stone*
c   PW - v251 - i31 - August 2 2004 - p73(1) [51-500]

Bosser, Jacques - *Most Beautiful Libraries in the World (Illus. by Laubier, Guillaume de)*
R&R Bk N - v19 - i1 - Feb 2004 - p260(1) [51-500]

Bossert, James L. - *The Supplier Management Handbook*
R&R Bk N - v19 - i3 - August 2004 - p103(1) [1-50]

Bossidy, Larry - *Confronting Reality: Doing What Matters to Get Things Right*
HR Mag - v50 - i2 - Feb 2005 - pS2(1) [501+]
BL - v101 - i4 - Oct 15 2004 - p385(1) [51-500]
Bus W - i3904 - Oct 18 2004 - p24 [501+]
PW - v251 - i38 - Sept 20 2004 - p55(2) [501+]

Bost, Brent W. - *The Hurried Woman Syndrome: A Seven-Step Program to Conquer Fatigue, Control Weight, and Restore Passion to Your Relationship*
LJ - v130 - i1 - Jan 1 2005 - p134(1) [51-500]

Boston, Carole - *Weatherford Freedom on the Menu: The Greensboro Sit-ins (Illus. by Lagarrigue, Jerome)*
c   HB - v81 - i1 - Jan-Feb 2005 - p79(1) [501+]
c   HB - v81 - i1 - Jan-Feb 2005 - p87(2) [51-500]

Boston, Robert - *Why the Religious Right Is Wrong about Separation of Church and State, 2nd Ed.*
R&R Bk N - v19 - i1 - Feb 2004 - p17(1) [51-500]

Bostridge, Mark - *Lives for Sale: Biographers' Tales*
LJ - v130 - i1 - Jan 1 2005 - p112(1) [51-500]
Spec - v296 - i9190 - Sept 25 2004 - p58(1) [501+]

Bostrom, Antonia - *The Encyclopedia of Sculpture, Vols. 1-3*
Ref Rev - Nov 2004 - pNA [501+]
R&R Bk N - v19 - i1 - Feb 2004 - p204(1) [51-500]

Bowman, William D. - *Priest and Parish in Vienna, 1780-1880*
AHR - v109 - i4 - Oct 2004 - p1333-1334 [501+]

Bown, Stephen R. - *Scurvy: How a Surgeon, a Mariner, and a Gentleman Solved the Greatest Medical Mystery of the Age of Sail*
Beav - v84 - i4 - August-Sept 2004 - p48(1) [51-500]
BIC - v33 - i2 - March 2004 - p18(4) [501+]
CG - v124 - i2 - March-April 2004 - p101(1) [501+]
E-Streams - Nov 2004 - pNA [501+]
New Sci - v185 - i2482 - Jan 15 2005 - p51(1) [501+]

Bowser, Benjamin P. - *Against the Odds: Scholars Who Challenged Racism in the Twentieth Century*
CS - v33 - i1 - Jan 2004 - p53-54 [501+]

Bowtell, David - *DNA Microarrays: A Molecular Cloning Manual*
QRB - v79 - i4 - Dec 2004 - p416(1) [501+]

Box, C.J. - *Trophy Hunt*
People - v62 - i3 - July 19 2004 - p46 [51-500]

Box, Richard C. - *Public Administration and Society: Critical Issues in American Governance*
R&R Bk N - v19 - i1 - Feb 2004 - pNA [51-500]

Boxcar, Ruby Ann - *Move Over Santa, Ruby's Doin' Christmas!*
PW - v251 - i37 - Sept 13 2004 - p72(1) [1-50]

Boxer, Andrew - *Germany 1918-1945*
y TES - v0 - i4586 - June 4 2004 - psssss14(2) [501+]

Boyarin, Daniel - *Border Lines: The Partition of Judaeo-Christianity*
Choice - v42 - i5 - Jan 2005 - p869(1) [1-50]
Queer Theory and the Jewish Question
Choice - v41 - i11-12 - July-August 2004 - p2085(1) [501+]
R&R Bk N - v19 - i2 - May 2004 - p132 [51-500]
Sparks of the Logos: Essays in Rabbinic Hermeneutics
R&R Bk N - v19 - i1 - Feb 2004 - p19(1) [51-500]

Boyce, Fredric - *SOE: The Scientific Secrets*
J Mil H - v68 - i4 - Oct 2004 - p1289-1290 [501+]

Boyce, James K. - *Natural Assets: Democratizing Environmental Ownership*
JEL - v41 - i4 - Dec 2003 - p1435(1) [501+]

Boyce, Jim - *Absolute Beginner's Guide to Microsoft Office 2003*
R&R Bk N - v19 - i4 - Nov 2004 - p112(1) [1-50]
Microsoft Office Outlook 2003 Inside Out
R&R Bk N - v19 - i1 - Feb 2004 - p110(1) [51-500]

Boyce, Robert - *Origins of World War Two: The Debate Continues*
R&R Bk N - v19 - i1 - Feb 2004 - p29(1) [51-500]

Boyd, B.W. - *Brill's Companion to Ovid*
Class R - v53 - i2 - Nov 2003 - p365-367 [501+]

Boyd, Bill - *All Roads Lead to Hockey: Reports from Northern Canada to the Mexican Border*
Globe & Mail - Oct 30 2004 - pD25 [51-500]
Res Links - v10 - i3 - Feb 2005 - p44(1) [501+]

Boyd, David R. - *Unnatural Law: Rethinking Canadian Environmental Law and Policy*
BIC - v33 - i6 - Sept 2004 - p27(2) [501+]
CG - v124 - i3 - May-June 2004 - p127(1) [501+]
Law&PolBR - June 2004 - p384(5) [501+]

Boyd, Douglas - *Eleanor: April Queen of Aquitaine*
CR - v285 - i1665 - Oct 2004 - p255(1) [501+]

Boyd, Fenice B. - *Multicultural and Multilingual Literacy and Language: Contexts and Practices*
R&R Bk N - v19 - i4 - Nov 2004 - p189(1) [501+]
SLJ - v50 - i10 - Oct 2004 - pS71(1) [51-500]

Boyd-Franklin, Nancy - *Black Families in Therapy: Understanding the African American Experience. 2nd Ed.*
SciTech - v28 - i1 - March 2004 - p95(1) [51-500]

Boyd, George - *Gideon's Blues*
BIC - v33 - i9 - Dec 2004 - p24(3) [501+]

Boyd, Gregory A. - *Repenting of Religion:Turning from Judgment to the Love of God*
Ch Today - v49 - i2 - Feb 2005 - p87(2) [501+]

Boyd, Heidi - *Simply Beautiful Beading: 40 Quick and Easy Projects*
BL - v100 - i22 - August 2004 - p1889(1) [51-500]
BL - v101 - i8 - Dec 15 2004 - p706(1) [501+]
Simply Beautiful Greeting Cards: 50 Quick and Easy Projects
BL - v101 - i8 - Dec 15 2004 - p704(1) [501+]

Boyd, Helen R. - *The Future of Tibet: The Government-in-Exile Meets the Challenge of Democratization*
R&R Bk N - v19 - i3 - August 2004 - p56(1) [51-500]

Boyd, Herb - *Pound for Pound: A Biography of Sugar Ray Robinson*
BL - v101 - i6 - Nov 15 2004 - p544(1) [51-500]
KR - v72 - i22 - Nov 15 2004 - p1074(1) [501+]
LJ - v129 - i19 - Nov 15 2004 - p66(1) [501+]
PW - v251 - i49 - Dec 6 2004 - p50(1) [51-500]
We Shall Overcome: A Living History of the Civil Rights Struggle Told in Words, Pictures and the Voices of the Participants
y BL - v101 - i5 - Nov 1 2004 - p447(1) [51-500]
Black Iss - v7 - i1 - Jan-Feb 2005 - p68(1) [501+]
PW - v251 - i44 - Nov 1 2004 - p58(2) [501+]
y SLJ - v50 - i12 - Dec 2004 - p158(1) [501+]

Boyd, Jean A. - *"We're the Light Crust Doughboys from Burrus Mill": An Oral History*
JSH - v71 - i1 - Feb 2005 - p197(2) [501+]
PMS - v28 - i1 - Feb 2005 - p125(2) [501+]

Boyd, Jeffrey H. - *Being Sick Well: Joyful Living Despite Chronic Illness*
PW - v252 - i11 - March 14 2005 - p63(2) [51-500]

Boyd, John P. - *High-Order Methods for Incomplete Fluid Flow*
SIAM Rev - v46 - i1 - March 2004 - p151-152 [501+]

Boyd, Kelly - *Manliness and the Boys' Story Paper in Britain: A Cultural History, 1855-1940*
AHR - v109 - i2 - April 2004 - p614(2) [501+]
Albion - v36 - i2 - Summer 2004 - p337(2) [501+]
JPC - v38 - i2 - Nov 2004 - p443(2) [501+]
Wom HR - v13 - i2 - Summer 2004 - p330-332 [501+]

Boyd, Martin - *The Cardboard Crown*
TLS - i5300 - Oct 29 2004 - p25(1) [501+]

Boyd, Melba Joyce - *Wrestling with the Muse: Dudley Randall and the Broadside Press*
Black Iss - v7 - i2 - March-April 2005 - p31(1) [501+]
Choice - v42 - i1 - Sept 2004 - p98(2) [501+]

Boyd, Nan Alamilla - *Wide Open Town: A History of Queer San Francisco to 1965*
WHQ - v35 - i4 - Winter 2004 - p506-507 [501+]
CS - v33 - i6 - Nov 2004 - pNA [501+]
Wide-Sex Affairs: Constructing and Controlling Homosexuality in the Pacific Northwest
JAH - v91 - i1 - June 2004 - p264-266 [501+]

Boyd, Neil - *Big Sister: How Extreme Feminism Has Betrayed the Fight for Sexual Equality*
R&R Bk N - v19 - i4 - Nov 2004 - p133(1) [51-500]

Boyd, Richard - *Uncivil Society: The Perils of Pluralism and the Making of Modern Liberalism*
R&R Bk N - v19 - i4 - Nov 2004 - p152(1) [501+]

Boyd, Susan C. - *From Witches to Crack Moms: Women, Drug Law, and Policy*
Choice - v42 - i5 - Jan 2005 - p892(2) [1-50]

Boyd, William - *Fascination*
Spec - v296 - i9195 - Oct 30 2004 - p54(1) [501+]
TLS - i5300 - Oct 29 2004 - p21(1) [501+]
Fascination: Stories
BL - v101 - i7 - Dec 1 2004 - p634(1) [501+]
KR - v72 - i21 - Nov 1 2004 - p1020(1) [501+]
LJ - v130 - i1 - Jan 1 2005 - p103(1) [501+]
NYTBR - Jan 16 2005 - p21 [501+]
PW - v251 - i46 - Nov 15 2004 - p38(1) [501+]

Boyden, Joseph - *Three Day Road*
KR - v73 - i4 - Feb 15 2005 - p189(1) [501+]

Boyer, Alain - *Hors du temps: Un essai sur Kant*
Ethics - v114 - i4 - July 2004 - p806(5) [501+]

Boyer, Allen D. - *Law, liberty and parliament; selected essays on the writings of Sir Edward Coke*
R&R Bk N - v19 - i3 - August 2004 - p194(1) [501+]
Sir Edward Coke and the Elizabethan Age
JIH - v35 - i2 - Autumn 2004 - p296(2) [501+]

Boyer, Anne - *Remy de Gourmont: L'ecriture et ses masques*
NCFS - v33 - i1-2 - Fall-Winter 2004 - p204(2) [501+]

Boyer, Christopher R. - *Becoming Campesinos: Politics, Identity, and Agrarian Struggle in Postrevolutionary Michoacan, 1920-1935*
AHR - v109 - i2 - April 2004 - p574(2) [501+]
JIH - v35 - i2 - Autumn 2004 - p330(2) [501+]

Boyer, David - *Kings and Queens: Queers at the Prom*
LJ - v129 - i16 - Oct 1 2004 - p101(2) [51-500]

Boyer, J. Patrick - *"Just Trust Us": The Erosion of Accountability in Canada*
CBRA - Annual 2003 - p303(1) [501+]

Boyer, Kenneth Karel - *Extending the Supply Chain: How Cutting-Edge Companies Bridge the Critical Last Mile into Customers' Homes*
Choice - v42 - i5 - Jan 2005 - p898(1) [1-50]

Boyer, Marie-France - *Matisse at Villa le Reve (Illus. by Adant, Helene)*
Apo - v161 - i516 - Feb 2005 - p79(1) [501+]

Boyer, Paul - *College Rankings Exposed: The Art of Getting a Quality Education in the 21st Century*
R&R Bk N - v19 - i2 - May 2004 - p180(1) [51-500]

Boyer, Rick - *Mzungu Mjinga: A Memoir of a Hunter's First Safari to Tanzania's Masai-Mara*
LJ - v129 - i19 - Nov 15 2004 - p78(1) [501+]

Boyer, Robert - *The Future of Economic Growth: As New Becomes Old*
R&R Bk N - v19 - i3 - August 2004 - p110(1) [51-500]

Boyer, Stuart A. - *Scada: Supervisory Control and Data Acquisition. 3rd Ed.*
SciTech - v28 - i3 - Sept 2004 - p135(1) [51-500]

Boyers, Sara Jane - *Teen Power Politics: Make Yourself Heard*
y SLJ - v50 - i8 - August 2004 - p48(1) [51-500]

Boyett, Joseph H. - *The Guru Guide to Marketing: A Concise Guide to the Best Ideas from Today's Top Marketers*
R&R Bk N - v19 - i2 - May 2004 - p114(1) [51-500]

Boykin, Keith - *Beyond the Down Low: Sex, Lies, and Denial in Black America*
LJ - v130 - i2 - Feb 1 2005 - p104(2) [51-500]
PW - v252 - i4 - Jan 24 2005 - p235(1) [501+]

Boylan, Anne M. - *The Origins of Women's Activism: New York and Boston, 1797-1840*
JIH - v35 - i2 - Autumn 2004 - p310(2) [501+]

Boylan, Clare - *Emma Brown*
Wom R Bks - v21 - i10-11 - July 2004 - p15(2) [501+]

Boylan, James - *Pulitzer's School: Columbia University's School of Journalism, 1903-2003*
HNet - June 2004 - pNA [501+]
JAH - v91 - i3 - Dec 2004 - p1072(1) [501+]
R&R Bk N - v19 - i1 - Feb 2004 - p229(1) [51-500]

Boylan, Jennifer Finney - *She's Not There: A Life in Two Genders*
Advocate - Nov 23 2004 - p97(1) [501+]
NYTBR - August 22 2004 - p20 [501+]

Boylan, Michael - *A Just Society*
Choice - v42 - i6 - Feb 2005 - p1034(1) [51-500]
R&R Bk N - v19 - i4 - Nov 2004 - p8(1) [51-500]

Boyle, Alistair - *They Fall Hard*
BL - v100 - i22 - August 2004 - p1904(1) [501+]
KR - v72 - i13 - July 1 2004 - p605(1) [51-500]

Boyle, David - *African Americans*
LibMed - v22 - i4 - Jan 2004 - p81(1) [501+]
The Sum of Our Discontent: 1 2 3 4 5 How Numbers Make Us Irrational
R&R Bk N - v19 - i3 - August 2004 - p77(1) [51-500]

Boyle, Elizabeth Heger - *Female Genital Cutting: Cultural Conflict in the Global Community*
HNet - Nov 2004 - pNA [501+]

Boyle, Fionna - *A Muggle's Guide to the Wizarding World: Exploring the Harry Potter Universe*
c CH Bwatch - Feb 2005 - pNA [51-500]
c Res Links - v10 - i2 - Dec 2004 - p34(2) [51-500]

Boyle, Francis A. - *Destroying World Order: U.S. Imperialism in the Middle East Before and After September 11*
R&R Bk N - v19 - i3 - August 2004 - p48(1) [51-500]

Boyle, Godfrey - *Energy Systems and Sustainability: Power for a Sustainable Future*
TimHES - v0 - i1677 - Feb 4 2005 - p32(1) [501+]

Boyle, Grant - *War with Troy: The Story of Achilles*
Sch Lib - v52 - i3 - Autumn 2004 - p167(1) [501+]

Boyle, John F. - *Free State or Republic*
ILS - v24 - i1 - Fall 2004 - p4(1) [501+]

Boyle, Kevin - *Arc of Justice: A Saga of Race, Civil Rights, and Murder in the Jazz Age*
BL - v101 - i1 - Sept 1 2004 - p26(1) [51-500]
Ent W - Sept 10 2004 - p168 [51-500]
KR - v72 - i14 - July 15 2004 - p668(1) [501+]
LJ - v129 - i16 - Oct 1 2004 - p93(1) [501+]
NYTBR - Sept 12 2004 - p30 [501+]
NYTBR - Sept 19 2004 - p22 [501+]
PW - v251 - i31 - August 2 2004 - p60(1) [501+]
Time - v164 - i22 - Nov 29 2004 - p146 [51-500]

Braving the Waves
  ILS - v24 - i1 - Fall 2004 - p32(1) [51-500]
Boyle, Richard - *Knox's Words*
  TimHES - v0 - i1666 - Nov 12 2004 - p31(1)
  [501+]
Boyle, T.C. - *The Inner Circle (Read by Kramer, Michael).*
Audiobook Review
  BL - v101 - i9-10 - Jan 1 2005 - p884(1) [51-500]
The Inner Circle
  BW - v34 - i38 - Sept 19 2004 - p15(1) [501+]
  Econ - v373 - i8400 - Nov 6 2004 - p88US [501+]
  Globe & Mail - Sept 25 2004 - pD22 [501+]
  LJ - v129 - i12 - July 2004 - p66(2) [51-500]
  NYTBR - Sept 19 2004 - p8 [501+]
  People - Sept 20 2004 - p62 [501+]
  PW - v251 - i27 - July 5 2004 - p34(1) [501+]
Nookie Monster
  Ent W - Sept 10 2004 - p166 [501+]
Boyles, Nancy N. - *Constructing Meaning through Kid-Friendly Comprehension Strategy Instruction*
  Bwatch - Oct 2004 - pNA [51-500]
Boyne, Walter J. - *The Influence of Air Power upon History*
  APJ - v18 - i3 - Fall 2004 - p118(2) [501+]
  Parameters - v34 - i3 - Autumn 2004 - p154(3)
  [501+]
Today's Best Military Writing: The Finest Articles on the Past, Present, and Future of the U.S. Military
  LJ - v129 - i14 - Sept 1 2004 - p166(1) [51-500]
The Two O'clock War: The 1973 Yom Kippur Conflict and the Airlift That Saved Israel
  APH - v51 - i4 - Winter 2004 - p54(2) [501+]
Boynton, Alice Benjamin - *Teaching Students to Read Nonfiction*
  RT - v57 - Nov 2003 - p296 [501+]
  SLJ - v50 - i10 - Oct 2004 - pS71(1) [51-500]
Boynton, Robert S. - *The New New Journalism: Conversations with America's Best Nonfiction Writers on Their Craft*
  CJR - v43 - i6 - March-April 2005 - p59(3) [501+]
  LJ - v130 - i4 - March 1 2005 - p96(1) [51-500]
  PW - v252 - i6 - Feb 7 2005 - p78(1) [501+]
Boynton, Sandra - *Consider Love: Its Moods and Many Ways*
  y PW - v252 - i2 - Jan 10 2005 - p57(1) [51-500]
Philadelphia Chickens (Read by LuPone, Patti).
Audiobook Review
  c BL - v101 - i9-10 - Jan 1 2005 - p778(1) [1-50]
Boys-Stones, G.R. - *Metaphor, Allegory, and the Classical Tradition: Ancient Thought and Modern Revisions*
  Class R - v54 - i2 - Nov 2004 - p427(4) [501+]
Post-Hellenistic Philosophy: A Study of Its Development from the Stoics to Origen
  CJ - v99 - i3 - Feb-March 2004 - p362-365 [501+]
  Class R - v54 - i1 - May 2004 - p76(2) [501+]
Boys-Stones, George - *Phaedo of Elis and Plato on the Soul*
  RM - v58 - i1 - Sept 2004 - p238(2) [501+]
Boyt, Susie - *Only Human*
  TLS - i5289 - August 13 2004 - p21(1) [501+]
Bozai, Agota - *To Err Is Divine*
  BW - v34 - i31 - August 1 2004 - p7(1) [501+]
Bozarslan, Hamit - *Violence in the Middle East: From Political Struggle to Self-Sacrifice*
  R&R Bk N - v19 - i4 - Nov 2004 - p151(1) [501+]
Bozdogan, Sibel - *Modernism and Nation Building: Turkish Architectural Culture in the Early Republic, Studies in Modernity and National Identity*
  HNet - July 2004 - pNA [501+]
  IJMES - v36 - i1 - Feb 2004 - p139-140 [501+]
Bozell, L. Brent - *Weapons of Mass Distortion: The Coming Meltdown of the Liberal Media*
  BL - v100 - i21 - July 2004 - p1804(1) [51-500]
  LJ - v129 - i12 - July 2004 - p94(1) [51-500]
Bozeman, Theodore Dwight - *The Precisianist Strain: Disciplinary Religion & Antinomian Backlash in Puritanism to 1638*
  AHR - v109 - i4 - Oct 2004 - p1196-1196 [501+]
  Choice - v41 - i11-12 - July-August 2004 -
  p2060(1) [501+]
Bozorgnia, Yousef - *Earthquake Engineering: From Engineering Seismology to Performance-Based Engineering*
  SciTech - v28 - i3 - Sept 2004 - p141(1) [51-500]
Braak, Andre - *Enlightenment Blues: My Years with an American Guru*
  Parabola - v29 - i1 - Spring 2004 - p108(2) [501+]
Braaten, Carl E. - *Jews and Christians: People of God*
  Intpr - v58 - i4 - Oct 2004 - p440(1) [501+]
Braaten, Ellen - *Straight Talk about Psychological Testing for Kids*
  SciTech - v28 - i3 - Sept 2004 - p118(1) [51-500]

Braatz, Timothy - *Surviving Conquest: A History of the Yavapai Peoples*
  Am Ind CRJ - v27 - i4 - Fall 2003 - p176-178
  [501+]
  SHQ - v107 - i3 - Jan 2004 - p479(2) [501+]
  WHQ - v35 - i1 - Spring 2004 - p84-85 [501+]
Brabec, Barbara - *Bringing in the Bucks!*
  Bwatch - v26 - i8 - August 2004 - p9(1) [51-500]
Starting Smart!
  Bwatch - v26 - i8 - August 2004 - p9(1) [51-500]
Braben, Donald W. - *Pioneering Research: A Risk Worth Taking*
  New Sci - v185 - i2486 - Feb 12 2005 - p49(1)
  [501+]
  SciTech - v28 - i3 - Sept 2004 - p14(1) [501+]
Brabenec, Robert L. - *Resources for the Study of Real Analysis*
  Choice - v42 - i7 - March 2005 - p1263(1) [51-
  500]
  SciTech - v28 - i4 - Dec 2004 - p39(1) [51-500]
Brace, Ian - *Questionnaire Design: How to Plan, Structure and Write Survey Material for Effective Market Research*
  Choice - v42 - i6 - Feb 2005 - p1066(1) [51-500]
  R&R Bk N - v19 - i4 - Nov 2004 - pNA [51-500]
Bracey, Gerald W. - *On the Death of Childhood and the Destruction of Public Schools: The Folly of Today's Education Policies and Practices*
  R&R Bk N - v19 - i1 - Feb 2004 - pNA [51-500]
  TCR - v106 - i5 - May 2004 - p958(4) [501+]
Bracher, Nathan - *Through the Past Darkly: History and Memory in Francois Mauriac's Bloc-Notes*
  Choice - v42 - i7 - March 2005 - p1233(1) [51-
  500]
Bracke, Peter M. - *Ultimate DVD: The Essential Guide to Building Your DVD Collection*
  LJ - v129 - i14 - Sept 1 2004 - p152(1) [51-500]
Bracken, Bruce A. - *The Psychoeducational Assessment of Preschool Children, 3rd Ed.*
  R&R Bk N - v19 - i4 - Nov 2004 - p181(1) [501+]
Brackett, Virginia - *A Home in the Heart: The Story of Sandra Cisneros (Illus. by Reynolds, Morgan)*
  y BL - v101 - i7 - Dec 1 2004 - p645(1) [51-500]
Restless Genius: The Story of Virginia Woolf
  y BL - v101 - i2 - Sept 15 2004 - p229(1) [51-500]
  y CCB-B - v58 - i3 - Nov 2004 - p115(1) [501+]
  y CH Bwatch - v14 - i11 - Nov 2004 - pNA [51-500]
  y SLJ - v50 - i11 - Nov 2004 - p159(1) [51-500]
Bradberry, Sarah - *Kids Knit!: Simple Steps to Nifty Projects*
  BL - v101 - i8 - Dec 15 2004 - p748(1) [501+]
  SLJ - v51 - i2 - Feb 2005 - p145(1) [51-500]
Bradburn, Norman M. - *Asking Questions: The Definitive Guide to Questionaire Design: For Market Research, Political Polls, And Social and Health Questionnaires, Rev. ed.*
  R&R Bk N - v19 - i3 - August 2004 - p90(1) [51-
  500]
Bradbury, Bruce - *The Dynamics of Child Poverty in Industrialized Countries*
  JEL - v42 - i3 - Sept 2004 - p860(2) [501+]
Bradbury, David - *Armstrong*
  TLS - i5286 - July 23 2004 - p33(1) [501+]
Bradbury, Judy - *Children's Book Corner: A Read Aloud Resource with Tips, Techniques, and Plans for Teachers, Librarians and Parents*
  LibMed - v22 - i7 - April-May 2004 - p85(1)
  [501+]
Children's Book Corner
  Cur R - v44 - i5 - Jan 2005 - p12(1) [51-500]
Bradbury, Ray - *The April Witch and Other Stories*
  y VOYA - v27 - i3 - August 2004 - p182(1) [1-50]
The Cat's Pajamas: Stories
  y BL - v100 - i21 - July 2004 - p1796(1) [51-500]
  BW - v34 - i28 - July 11 2004 - p3(1) [501+]
  SLJ - v50 - i12 - Dec 2004 - p174(1) [51-500]
Braddick, C.W. - *Japan and the Sino-Soviet Alliance, 1950-1964: In the Shadow of the Monolith*
  Choice - v42 - i3 - Nov 2004 - p537(1) [1-50]
Braddick, Michael J. - *State Formation in Early Modern England, c. 1550-1700*
  JMH - v76 - i3 - Sept 2004 - p676(3) [501+]
Braden, Susan R. - *The Architecture of Leisure: The Florida Resort Hotels of Henry Flagler and Henry Plant*
  HNet - Sept 2004 - pNA [501+]
Bradfield, Scott - *Good Girl Wants It Bad*
  BL - v100 - i22 - August 2004 - p1896(1) [51-500]
  MFSF - v108 - i2 - Feb 2005 - p39(2) [501+]
  NYTBR - August 22 2004 - p23 [501+]
Bradford, Barbara Taylor - *Unexpected Blessings*
  BL - v101 - i5 - Nov 1 2004 - p444(1) [51-500]
  KR - v73 - i1 - Jan 1 2005 - p5(1) [501+]
  PW - v251 - i49 - Dec 6 2004 - p43(1) [501+]

Bradford, Ernie - *Sword and the Scimitar: The Saga of the Crusades*
  R&R Bk N - v19 - i4 - Nov 2004 - p31(1) [51-
  500]
Bradford, Ernle - *The Great Siege: Malta 1565*
  Globe & Mail - Nov 6 2004 - pD27 [501+]
Bradford, James C. - *Oxford Atlas of American Military History*
  J Mil H - v68 - i4 - Oct 2004 - p1317-1319 [501+]
Bradford, Karleen - *Angeline*
  y BIC - v33 - i9 - Dec 2004 - p39(1) [51-500]
You Can't Rush a Cat (Illus. by Watts, Leslie Elizabeth)
  c CBRA - Annual 2003 - p449(1) [51-500]
Bradford, Nikki - *Your Premature Baby: The First Five Years*
  E-Streams - July 2004 - pNA [501+]
Bradford, Sarah - *Lucrezia Borgia: Life, Love and Death in Renaissance Italy*
  BL - v101 - i4 - Oct 15 2004 - p383(1) [51-500]
  BW - v34 - i46 - Nov 14 2004 - p8(2) [501+]
  Ent W - i790 - Oct 29 2004 - p72 [51-500]
  HT - v54 - i11 - Nov 2004 - p67(2) [501+]
  KR - v72 - i18 - Sept 15 2004 - p898(1) [501+]
  New R - Feb 21 2005 - p28 [501+]
  PW - v251 - i35 - August 30 2004 - p40(1) [501+]
  Spec - v296 - i9192 - Oct 9 2004 - p42(1) [501+]
  TLS - i5303 - Nov 19 2004 - p26(1) [501+]
Bradford, Scott - *Has Globalization Gone Far Enough?: The Costs of Fragmented Markets*
  R&R Bk N - v19 - i3 - August 2004 - p124(1)
  [51-500]
Brading, Katherine - *Symmetries in Physics: Philosophical Reflections*
  TimHES - v0 - i1673 - Jan 7 2005 - p22(2) [501+]
Bradley, Alex - *24 Girls in 7 Days*
  y BL - v101 - i9-10 - Jan 1 2005 - p842(2) [1-50]
  y CCB-B - v58 - i6 - Feb 2005 - p241(2) [51-500]
  y HB - v81 - i2 - March-April 2005 - p197(2) [51-
  500]
  y Kliatt - v39 - i1 - Jan 2005 - p6(1) [51-500]
  y KR - v73 - i2 - Jan 15 2005 - p117(1) [51-500]
  y PW - v252 - i7 - Feb 14 2005 - p78(1) [51-500]
Bradley, Celeste - *The Charmer*
  BL - v101 - i3 - Oct 1 2004 - p315(1) [51-500]
Bradley, D. Edward - *Harry's War*
  y BIC - v33 - i6 - Sept 2004 - p39(1) [501+]
Bradley, Ernestine - *The Way Home: A German Childhood, an American Life*
  KR - v73 - i2 - Jan 15 2005 - p95(1) [51-500]
  PW - v252 - i6 - Feb 7 2005 - p56(1) [51-500]
Bradley, Guy Jolyon - *Ancient Umbria, State, Culture, and Identity in Central Italy from the Iron Age to the Augustan Era*
  Class R - v53 - i2 - Nov 2003 - p411-412 [501+]
Bradley-Hole, Kathryn - *Lost Gardens of England: From the Archives of Country Life*
  BL - v101 - i5 - Nov 1 2004 - p452(1) [51-500]
  Choice - v42 - i6 - Feb 2005 - p1048(1) [51-500]
Bradley, James - *Flyboys: A True Story of Courage*
  y Kliatt - v39 - i1 - Jan 2005 - p32(2) [501+]
  Mar Crp G - v88 - i5 - May 2004 - p85(2) [501+]
Bradley, K. Sue - *Teaching Reading and Writing through Children's Literature*
  R&R Bk N - v19 - i1 - Feb 2004 - p183(1) [51-
  500]
Teaching Reading and Writing through Childsen's Literature
  TCR - v106 - i8 - August 2004 - p1532(3) [501+]
Bradley, Kimberly Brubaker - *For Freedom: The Story of a French Spy*
  y LibMed - v22 - i5 - Feb 2004 - p68(1) [51-500]
  RT - v58 - i3 - Nov 2004 - p290(1) [501+]
The President's Daughter
  y SLJ - v50 - i11 - Nov 2004 - p134(1) [51-500]
  c CCB-B - v58 - i6 - Feb 2005 - p245(1) [51-500]
  c CH Bwatch - Feb 2005 - pNA [51-500]
  y KR - v72 - i21 - Nov 1 2004 - p1043(1) [501+]
Bradley, Laura - *The Brush-Off*
  DroRevMy - v24 - i3 - May-June 2004 - p11(1)
  [1-50]
Bradley, Leo H. - *Curriculum Leadership: Beyond Boilerplate Standards*
  R&R Bk N - v19 - i1 - Feb 2004 - p183(1) [51-
  500]
Bradley, Marion Zimmer - *A Flame in Hali*
  LJ - v129 - i13 - August 2004 - p73(1) [51-500]
  PW - v251 - i28 - July 12 2004 - p49(1) [501+]
Witchlight
  Kliatt - v38 - i4 - July 2004 - p26(1) [51-500]
Bradley, Mark L. - *This Astounding Close: The Road to Bennett Place*
  Sew R - v112 - i1 - Wntr 2004 - p138-147 [501+]

Bradley, Michael - *The Female Athlete: Train for Success*
  LJ - v129 - i13 - August 2004 - p89(1) [501+]
  y VOYA - v27 - i5 - Dec 2004 - p413(1) [51-500]
Bradley, Michael J. - *Yes, Your Parents Are Crazy!: A Teen Survival Guide (Illus. by Glasbergen, Randy)*
  y SLJ - v50 - i12 - Dec 2004 - p158(1) [51-500]
Bradley, Patricia - *Mass Media and the Shaping of American Feminism, 1963-1975*
  JouAmCul - v27 - i3 - Sept 2004 - p345(2) [501+]
  Wom R Bks - v22 - i3 - Dec 2004 - p30(1) [501+]
Bradley, Patricia L. - *Robert Penn Warren's Circus Aesthetic and the Southern Renaissance*
  Choice - v42 - i6 - Feb 2005 - p1020(1) [51-500]
Bradley, Phil - *The Advanced Internet Searcher's Handbook, 3rd Ed.*
  SciTech - v28 - i4 - Dec 2004 - p172(1) [51-500]
Bradley, Richard - *Harvard Rules: The Struggle for the Soul of the World's Most Powerful University*
  Atl - v295 - i2 - March 2005 - p103(1) [51-500]
  Fortune - v151 - i5 - March 7 2005 - p40 [501+]
  KR - v73 - i2 - Jan 15 2005 - p95(1) [501+]
Bradley, Robert C. - *Science, Technology, and Criminal Justice*
  SciTech - v28 - i4 - Dec 2004 - p10(1) [1-50]
Bradley, Walter G. - *Neurology in Clinical Practice. 4th Ed.*
  SciTech - v28 - i1 - March 2004 - p93(1) [51-500]
  Pocket Companion to Neurology in Clinical Practice, 4th Ed.
  SciTech - v28 - i4 - Dec 2004 - p93(1) [51-500]
Bradman, Tony - *Final Cut*
  y Sch Lib - v52 - i3 - Autumn 2004 - p155(1) [501+]
Bradsah, Ralph A. - *Handbook of Cell Signaling*
  E-Streams - June 2004 - pNA [501+]
Bradshaw, David - *A Concise Companion to Modernism*
  RES - v55 - i219 - April 2004 - p294-296 [501+]
Bradshaw, Gillian - *Alchemy of Fire*
  BL - v100 - i22 - August 2004 - p1896(1) [51-500]
  LJ - v129 - i13 - August 2004 - p64(1) [501+]
Bradshaw, Jonathan - *Children and Social Security*
  Soc Ser R - v78 - i3 - Sept 2004 - p525(1) [51-500]
Bradshaw, Mel - *Death in the Age of Steam*
  BIC - v33 - i5 - August 2004 - p42(1) [501+]
  DroRevMy - v24 - i3 - May-June 2004 - p11(1) [1-50]
Bradshaw, Paul - *The New SCM Dictionary of Liturgy and Worship*
  ER - v56 - i3 - July 2004 - p377(2) [501+]
Bradshaw, Timothy - *The Way Forward? Christian Voices on Homosexuality and the Church*
  Intpr - v58 - i4 - Oct 2004 - p440(1) [501+]
Bradsher, Keith - *High and Mighty: SUVs--the World's Most Dangerous Vehicles and How They Got That Way*
  Lon R Bks - v26 - i19 - Oct 7 2004 - p27(1) [501+]
  High and Mighty: The Dangerous Rise of the SUV
  SciTech - v28 - i1 - March 2004 - p167(1) [51-500]
Bradt, Hale - *Astronomy Methods: A Physical Approach to Astronomical Observations*
  Choice - v41 - i11-12 - July-August 2004 - p2067(1) [501+]
Bradway, Becky - *In the Middle of the Middle West: Literary Nonfiction from the Heartland*
  ABR - v25 - i6 - Sept-Oct 2004 - p10(2) [501+]
Brady, Anne-Marie - *Making the Foreign Serve China: Managing Foreigners in the People's Republic*
  Ch Rev Int - v11 - i1 - Spring 2004 - p27(3) [501+]
  IBMR - v29 - i1 - Jan 2005 - p49(2) [501+]
  R&R Bk N - v19 - i1 - Feb 2004 - p48(1) [51-500]
Brady, Catherine - *Curled in the Bed of Love.*
  VQR - v80 - i1 - Wntr 2004 - p270-271 [501+]
  VQR - v80 - i1 - Wntr 2004 - p270-271 [501+]
Brady, David W. - *Party, Process and Political Change in Congress: New Perspectives on the History of Congress*
  J Am St - v38 - i2 - August 2004 - p353(2) [501+]
  J Am St - v38 - i2 - August 2004 - p353-354 [501+]
  Party, Process, and Political Change in Congress: New Perspectives on the History of Congress
  JIH - v34 - i3 - Wntr 2004 - p472(3) [501+]
Brady, Hugh J.M. - *Apoptosis Methods and Protocols*
  SciTech - v28 - i3 - Sept 2004 - p61(1) [51-500]
Brady, Irene. - *Illustrating Nature: Right-Brain Art in a Left-Brain World*
  LJ - v129 - i19 - Nov 15 2004 - p58(1) [51-500]
Brady, James - *The Scariest Place in the World*
  KR - v73 - i5 - March 1 2005 - p270(1) [501+]
  LJ - v129 - i20 - Dec 1 2004 - p90(1) [501+]

Brady, Joan - *Bleedout*
  KR - v72 - i23 - Dec 1 2004 - p1100(2) [501+]
  PW - v252 - i10 - March 7 2005 - p50(1) [51-500]
Brady, John Joseph - *The Interviewer's Handbook: A Guerrilla Guide; Techniques & Tactics for Reporters & Writers*
  R&R Bk N - v19 - i4 - Nov 2004 - p228(1) [501+]
Brady, Liz - *See Jane Run*
  Globe & Mail - Jan 22 2005 - pD12 [51-500]
Brady, Mary Pat - *Extinct Lands, Temporal Geographies: Chicana Literature and the Urgency of Space*
  MFSF - v50 - i2 - Summer 2004 - p469-476 [501+]
Brady, Robert F., Jr. - *Comprehensive Desk Reference of Polymer Characterization and Analysis*
  J Chem Ed - v81 - i10 - Oct 2004 - p1425(2) [501+]
Brady, Thomas A. - *The Work of Heiko A. Oberman: Papers from the Symposium on His Seventieth Birthday*
  Ren Q - v57 - i3 - Fall 2004 - p1066(3) [501+]
Braester, Yomi - *Witness Against History: Literature, Film, and Public Discourse in Twentieth-Century China*
  AHR - v109 - i2 - April 2004 - p494(1) [501+]
Braet, Herman - *Risus Mediaevalis: Laughter in Medieval Literature and Art*
  FS - v58 - i3 - July 2004 - p395-396 [501+]
Braff, Joshua - *The Unthinkable Thoughts of Jacob Green*
  y BL - v100 - i21 - July 2004 - p1815(1) [51-500]
  BL - v101 - i6 - Nov 15 2004 - p558(1) [51-500]
  Ent W - Sept 10 2004 - p171 [51-500]
  LJ - v129 - i13 - August 2004 - p64(1) [51-500]
  PW - v251 - i31 - August 2 2004 - p51(1) [501+]
  SLJ - v50 - i12 - Dec 2004 - p174(1) [51-500]
Braffet, Kelly - *Josie and Jack*
  BL - v101 - i6 - Nov 15 2004 - p551(2) [51-500]
  KR - v72 - i24 - Dec 15 2004 - p1153(1) [51-500]
  LJ - v130 - i1 - Jan 1 2005 - p93(2) [51-500]
  NYTBR - Feb 27 2005 - p17(L) [501+]
  PW - v251 - i51 - Dec 20 2004 - p36(1) [51-500]
  Ent W - Feb 4 2005 - p139 [51-500]
Brager, Bruce L. - *The Iron Curtain: The Cold War in Europe*
  c SLJ - v50 - i7 - July 2004 - p118(1) [51-500]
Bragg, Lois - *Oedipus Borealis: The Aberrant Body in Old Icelandic Myth and Saga*
  R&R Bk N - v19 - i4 - Nov 2004 - p245(1) [501+]
Bragg, Rick - *I Am a Soldier, Too: The Jessica Lynch Story*
  ABR - v25 - i5 - July-August 2004 - p9(2) [501+]
  y Kliatt - v39 - i2 - March 2005 - p33(1) [501+]
  S Liv - v39 - i3 - March 2004 - p121(1) [501+]
Bragg, Roberta - *Hardening Windows Systems*
  SciTech - v28 - i3 - Sept 2004 - p31(1) [51-500]
  MCSE Self-Paced Training Kit (Exam 70-298): Designing Security for a Microsoft Windows Server 2003 Network
  SciTech - v28 - i1 - March 2004 - p157(1) [51-500]
Bragg, Steven M. - *The New CFO Financial Leadership Manual*
  R&R Bk N - v19 - i2 - May 2004 - p123 [51-500]
  Run the Rockies: Classic Trail Runs in Colorado's Front Range
  R&R Bk N - v19 - i4 - Nov 2004 - p81(1) [51-500]
Brague, Remi - *The Wisdom of the World: The Human Experience of the Universe in Western Thought*
  Clio - v33 - i2 - Wntr 2004 - p211(5) [501+]
Brahier, Daniel J. - *Teaching Secondary and Middle School Mathematics, 2nd Ed.*
  SciTech - v28 - i4 - Dec 2004 - p15(1) [1-50]
Braibanti, Ralph - *Chief Justice Cornelius of Pakistan: An Analysis with Letters and Speeches*
  JTWS - v21 - i1 - Spring 2004 - p280(2) [501+]
Braider, Christopher - *Indiscernible Counterparts: The Invention of the Text in French Classical Drama*
  Comp L - v56 - i4 - Fall 2004 - p362-3 [501+]
  FS - v58 - i3 - July 2004 - p406-406 [501+]
  Ren Q - v57 - i4 - Winter 2004 - p1438(3) [501+]
Braidotti, Rosi - *Metamorphoses: Towards a Material Theory of Becoming*
  CS - v33 - i1 - Jan 2004 - p113-115 [501+]
Brainard, Lael - *The Other War: Global Poverty and the Millennium Challenge Account*
  JEL - v41 - i4 - Dec 2003 - p1359(1) [501+]
Brainard, Lori A. - *Television: The Limits of Deregulation*
  R&R Bk N - v19 - i1 - Feb 2004 - p105(1) [51-500]
Brainpop - *Popular Science Almanac for Kids*
  c SLJ - v50 - i12 - Feb 2005 - p51(1) [51-500]
Brainpop.com - *Brain Pop Almanac for Kids*
  y SB - v41 - i1 - Jan-Feb 2005 - p23(2) [501+]
Brainy Baby: Laugh & Learn
  SLJ - v50 - i12 - Dec 2004 - p65(1) [501+]

Brainy Baby: Peek-A-Boo
  SLJ - v50 - i12 - Dec 2004 - p65(1) [501+]
Brainy Baby: Spanish
  SLJ - v50 - i12 - Dec 2004 - p65(1) [501+]
Braithwaite, Al - *Off Screen: Four Young Artists in the Middle East*
  MEJ - v58 - i4 - Autumn 2004 - p709(1) [501+]
Braithwaite, Jill - *The Statue of Liberty*
  c LibMed - v22 - i4 - Jan 2004 - p82(1) [501+]
Braithwaite, Valerie - *Taxing Democracy: Understanding Tax Avoidance and Evasion*
  R&R Bk N - v19 - i1 - Feb 2004 - p120(1) [51-500]
Brakmann, Susanne - *Evolutionary Methods in Biotechnology: Clever Tricks for Directed Evolution*
  SciTech - v28 - i4 - Dec 2004 - p164(1) [51-500]
Brallier, Kate - *Sea Island*
  PW - v252 - i4 - Jan 24 2005 - p227(1) [501+]
Braman, Arlette - *Secrets of Ancient Cultures: The Maya: Activities and Crafts from a Mysterious Land*
  LibMed - v22 - i4 - Jan 2004 - p75(1) [501+]
Braman, Sandra - *Biotechnology and Communication: The Meta-Technologies of Information*
  SciTech - v28 - i3 - Sept 2004 - p167(1) [51-500]
Brambilla, Nora - *Quark Confinement and the Hadron Spectrum V: Proceedings*
  SciTech - v28 - i4 - Dec 2004 - p52(1) [51-500]
Bramble, Linda - *Touring Niagara Wine Country, 2nd Ed. (Illus. by Coon, Dwayne)*
  CBRA - Annual 2003 - p20(1) [51-500]
Bramble, Tom - *Rethinking the Labour Movement in the 'New South Africa'*
  R&R Bk N - v19 - i1 - Feb 2004 - p102(1) [51-500]
Bramhall, William - *Hepcat*
  c CCB-B - v57 - i11 - July-August 2004 - p455(2) [501+]
  c PW - v251 - i28 - July 12 2004 - p62(1) [51-500]
  c SLJ - v50 - i8 - August 2004 - p83(1) [51-500]
Brammer, Ethriam Cash - *The Rowdy, Rowdy Ranch*
  c CH Bwatch - v14 - i8 - August 2004 - p5(1) [51-500]
Brams, Steven J. - *Biblical Games: Game Theory and the Hebrew Bible*
  CS - v33 - i5 - Sept 2004 - p623-623 [501+]
Bramwell, Neil D. - *Ancient China*
  c SLJ - v50 - i12 - Dec 2004 - p158(1) [51-500]
  Ancient Egypt
  c SLJ - v50 - i12 - Dec 2004 - p158(1) [51-500]
  Ancient Persia
  c SLJ - v50 - i12 - Dec 2004 - p158(1) [51-500]
Bramwell, Tony - *Magical Mystery Tours: My Life with the Beatles*
  KR - v73 - i2 - Jan 15 2005 - p95(2) [51-500]
  LJ - v129 - i20 - Dec 1 2004 - p90(1) [51-500]
  LJ - v130 - i3 - Feb 15 2005 - p131(1) [51-500]
  PW - v252 - i7 - Feb 14 2005 - p62(1) [51-500]
Branca, Vittore - *Il Capolavoro Del Boccaccio e Due Diverse Redazioni, 2: Variazioni Narrative e Stilistiche*
  Specu - v79 - i4 - Oct 2004 - p1171(3) [501+]
Branch, Michael P. - *The ISLE Reader: Ecocriticsm, 1993-2003*
  R&R Bk N - v19 - i1 - Feb 2004 - p220(1) [51-500]
  Reading the Roots: American Nature Writing Before Walden
  ANQ:QJ - v17 - i4 - Fall 2004 - p49(4) [501+]
Branch, Susan - *Autumn from the Heart of the Home (Illus. by Branch, Susan)*
  PW - v251 - i29 - July 19 2004 - p157(1) [51-500]
Brand, Christianna - *Nurse Matilda: The Collected Tales*
  c PW - v252 - i8 - Feb 21 2005 - p177(1) [51-500]
Brand, Dionne - *Thirsty*
  Can Lit - i182 - Autumn 2004 - p97(2) [501+]
  What We All Long For
  Globe & Mail - Jan 22 2005 - pD6 [501+]
Brand-Miller, Jennie - *The Low GI Smart Curb Diet: The Definitive Science-Based Weight-Loss Plan*
  LJ - v130 - i1 - Jan 1 2005 - p144(3) [501+]
Brand, Paul - *Kings, Barons and Justices: The Making and Enforcement of Legislation in Thirteenth-Century England*
  AHR - v109 - i3 - June 2004 - p963(1) [501+]
Brandao, Ignacio de Loyola - *Zero*
  LJ - v129 - i13 - August 2004 - p131(1) [501+]
Brandell, Jerrold R. - *Celluloid Couches, Cinematic Client: Psychoanalysis and Psychotherapy in the Movies*
  Choice - v42 - i4 - Dec 2004 - p668(1) [1-50]

Brandenberger, David - *National Bolshevism: Stalinist Mass Culture and the Formation of Modern Russian National Identity, 1931-1956*
J Soc H - v38 - i2 - Winter 2004 - p555(3) [501+]
JMH - v76 - i3 - Sept 2004 - p740(2) [501+]
Russ Rev - v63 - i2 - April 2004 - pNA [501+]

Brandenburg, Christel Weiss - *Ruined by the Reich: Memoir of an East Prussian Family, 1916-1945*
HNet - Dec 2004 - pNA [501+]
R&R Bk N - v19 - i1 - Feb 2004 - p36(1) [1-50]

Brandenburg, Jim - *Chased by the Light*
Comw - v131 - i21 - Dec 3 2004 - p32(1) [501+]

Brander, Bruce - *Love That Works: The Art and Science of Giving*
Ch Today - v48 - i11 - Nov 2004 - p87(1) [501+]

Brandis, Marianne - *Tinderbox*
c CBRA - Annual 2003 - p475(2) [51-500]

Brandist, Craig - *The Bakhtin Circle: Philosophy, Culture and Politics*
Russ Rev - v63 - i2 - April 2004 - pNA [501+]

Brandl, Johannes L. - *Grazer philosophische studien; internationale Zeitschrift fur analytische philosophie;Vol. 67*
R&R Bk N - v19 - i3 - August 2004 - p7(1) [1-50]

Brandl, Steven G. - *Criminal Investigation: An Analytical Perpsective*
R&R Bk N - v19 - i1 - Feb 2004 - p144(1) [51-500]

Brandle, Bine - *Flusi, the Sock Monster (Illus. by Brandle, Bine)*
c CH Bwatch - v14 - i12 - Dec 2004 - pNA [51-500]
c SLJ - v50 - i11 - Nov 2004 - p91(1) [51-500]

Brandolini, Anita - *Fizz, Bubble and Flash! Element Explorations and Atom Adventures for Hands-On Science Fun!*
y SB - v40 - i3 - May-June 2004 - p121(2) [501+]

Brandon, James R. - *Kabuki Plays on Stage, Vol. 3*
Pac A - v77 - i2 - Summer 2004 - p348(2) [501+]
Kabuki Plays on Stage, Vol. 4
Pac A - v77 - i2 - Summer 2004 - p348(2) [501+]
Masterpieces of Kabuki: Eighteen Plays on Stage
Choice - v42 - i5 - Jan 2005 - p849(1) [1-50]
R&R Bk N - v19 - i3 - August 2004 - p256(1) [51-500]

Brandon, Karen - *Arnold Schwarzenegger*
c BL - v101 - i5 - Nov 1 2004 - p477(1) [51-500]
y SLJ - v50 - i11 - Nov 2004 - p160(1) [51-500]

Brandon, Paul - *The Wild Reel*
BW - v34 - i28 - July 11 2004 - p10(1) [501+]

Brandon, Rick - *High-Integrity Political Tactics for Career and Company Success*
Har Bus R - v82 - i12 - Dec 2004 - p28(1) [501+]
Survival of the Savvy: High-Integrity Political Tactics for Career and Company Success
LJ - v129 - i19 - Nov 15 2004 - p69(1) [501+]

Brandon, Ruth - *The People's Chef: Alexis Soyer: A Life in Seven Courses*
HT - v54 - i8 - August 2004 - p56(1) [501+]
Spec - v296 - i9187 - Sept 4 2004 - p41(1) [501+]
TLS - i5295 - Sept 24 2004 - p27(1) [501+]
The People's Chef: The Culinary Revolutions of Alexis Soyer
KR - v73 - i4 - Feb 15 2005 - p205(2) [501+]
PW - v252 - i10 - March 7 2005 - p60(2) [51-500]

Brandreth, Gyles - *Philip and Elizabeth: Portrait of a Marriage*
Spec - v296 - i9190 - Sept 25 2004 - p50(2) [501+]

Brands, H.W. - *Lone Star Nation: How a Ragged Army of Volunteers Won the Battle for Texas Independence--and Changed America. Audiobook Review*
BL - v100 - i21 - July 2004 - p1856(1) [1-50]
Lone Star Nation: How a Ragged Army of Volunteers Won the Battle for Texas Independence--and Changed America (Read by Montgomery, Chuck). Audiobook Review
Kliatt - v38 - i4 - July 2004 - p60(1) [51-500]
LJ - v129 - i16 - Oct 1 2004 - p119(1) [51-500]
Lone Star Nation: How a Ragged Army of Volunteers Won the Battle for Texas Independence--and Changed America
Choice - v42 - i2 - Oct 2004 - p353(1) [501+]
SHQ - v108 - i1 - July 2004 - p102-105 [501+]

Brandt, Bruce - *Where to Look for Hard-to-Find German-Speaking Ancestors in Eastern Europe: Index to 19,720 Surnames in 13 Books, with Historical Background on Each Settlement. 2nd Ed.*
EFHM - v58 - i2 - March-April 2004 - p89(1) [51-500]

Brandt, Edward R. - *Genealogical Guide to East and West Prussia*
EFHM - v58 - i2 - March-April 2004 - p89(1) [51-500]

Brandt, Jesper - *Multifunctional Landscapes*
SciTech - v28 - i3 - Sept 2004 - p6(1) [501+]

Brandt, John C. - *Introduction to Comets. 2nd Ed.*
Astron - v32 - i9 - Sept 2004 - p92 [501+]
Introduction to Comets. 2nd Ed.
Choice - v42 - i4 - Dec 2004 - p684(1) [1-50]

Brandt, Lisa - *Celebrity Tantrums!: The Official Dirt*
CBRA - Annual 2003 - p82(1) [501+]

Brandt, Patricia - *Adapting in Eden: Oregon's Catholic Minority, 1838-1986*
WHQ - v35 - i1 - Spring 2004 - p90-91 [501+]

Brandt, Steven A. - *Introduction to Aeronautics: A Design Perspective. 2nd Ed.*
SciTech - v28 - i3 - Sept 2004 - p164(1) [501+]

Brandt, William - *The Book of the Film of the Story of My Life*
Ent W - i808 - Feb 25 2005 - p107 [51-500]
KR - v72 - i21 - Nov 1 2004 - p1020(2) [501+]
LJ - v130 - i2 - Feb 1 2005 - p66(1) [51-500]
PW - v252 - i4 - Jan 24 2005 - p221(1) [501+]

Brandvold, Peter - *The Devil Gets His Due*
Roundup M - v11 - i6 - August 2004 - p26(1) [501+]

Branford, Henrietta - *Six Chicks*
c Sch Lib - v52 - i4 - Winter 2004 - p185(2) [51-500]

Branham, R. Bracht - *Bakhtin and the Classics*
Russ Rev - v63 - i3 - July 2004 - pNA [501+]

Branham, Robert J. - *Sweet Freedom's Song: "My Country 'Tis of Thee" and Democracy in America*
JAH - v91 - i1 - June 2004 - p251-252 [501+]

Branigan, Steven - *High-Tech Crimes Revealed: Cyberwar Stories from the Digital Front*
Bwatch - Feb 2005 - pNA [51-500]
SciTech - v28 - i4 - Dec 2004 - p31(1) [51-500]

Brann, Eva - *The Music of the Republic: Essays on Socrates' Conversations and Plato's Writings*
Choice - v42 - i7 - March 2005 - p1239(2) [51-500]

Brannigan, Michael C. - *Cross-Cultural Biotechnology*
SciTech - v28 - i4 - Dec 2004 - p164(1) [51-500]

Brannon, Linda - *Gender: Psychological Perspectives. 4th Ed.*
SciTech - v28 - i3 - Sept 2004 - p3(1) [501+]

Bransilver, Connie - *Wild Love Affair: Essence of Florida's Native Orchids*
SciTech - v28 - i3 - Sept 2004 - p62(1) [501+]

Branson, Gary - *Solving Home Plumbing Problems*
Bwatch - v26 - i9 - Sept 2004 - p1(1) [51-500]
E-Streams - Oct 2004 - pNA [501+]
LJ - v129 - i14 - Sept 2004 - p178(1) [51-500]

Branson, Jan - *Damned for Their Difference: The Cultural Construction of Deaf People as Disabled*
J Soc H - v38 - i2 - Winter 2004 - p539(3) [501+]

Branston, Julian - *Tilting at Windmills: A Novel of Cervantes and the Errant Knight*
BL - v101 - i9-10 - Jan 1 2005 - p811(1) [1-50]
KR - v72 - i23 - Dec 1 2004 - p1101(1) [501+]
LJ - v130 - i1 - Jan 1 2005 - p94(1) [501+]
PW - v252 - i5 - Jan 31 2005 - p50(1) [501+]

Brant, Sandra J. - *Andy Warhol's Interview: Best of the First Decade, 1969-1979.*
PW - v251 - i50 - Dec 13 2004 - p54(1) [501+]

Brantlinger, Ellen - *Dividing Classes: How the Middle Class Negotiates and Rationalizes School Advantage*
JEL - v41 - i4 - Dec 2003 - p1376(2) [501+]
Middle Class Identity and Education: A Review Essay
TCR - v106 - i2 - Feb 2004 - pNA [51-500]

Brantlinger, Patrick - *A Companion to the Victorian Novel*
VS - v46 - i4 - Summer 2004 - p679(4) [501+]
Dark Vanishings: Discourse on the Extinction of Primitive Races, 1800-1930
AHR - v109 - i2 - April 2004 - p482(2) [501+]
Clio - v33 - i3 - Spring 2004 - p341(5) [501+]
ELT - v48 - i1 - Wntr 2005 - p227(3) [501+]
JAH - v91 - i3 - Dec 2004 - p1007(2) [501+]

Brashares, Ann - *Girls in Pants: The Third Summer of the Sisterhood*
y BL - v101 - i8 - Dec 15 2004 - p738(1) [51-500]
Ent W - i803 - Jan 28 2005 - p87 [51-500]
y HB - v81 - i2 - March-April 2005 - p198(1) [51-500]
y Kliatt - v39 - i1 - Jan 2005 - p6(1) [51-500]
KR - v72 - i24 - Dec 15 2004 - p1199(1) [501+]
y PW - v251 - i51 - Dec 20 2004 - p61(1) [501+]
y SLJ - v51 - i1 - Jan 2005 - p122(2) [51-500]
The Second Summer of the Sisterhood
c CH Bwatch - v14 - i7 - July 2004 - p7(2) [51-500]
y Kliatt - v39 - i1 - Jan 2005 - p12(1) [501+]
PW - v251 - i51 - Dec 20 2004 - p62(1) [501+]
The Sisterhood of the Traveling Pants
y Kliatt - v38 - i4 - July 2004 - p14(1) [51-500]

Brashier, Ralph C. - *Inheritance Law and the Evolving Family*
Law&PolBR - August 2004 - p645(3) [501+]

Brasme, Anne Sophie - *Breathe*
BL - v101 - i1 - Sept 1 2004 - p59(1) [51-500]

Brass, Paul R. - *The Production of Hindu-Muslim Violence in Contemporary India*
CS - v33 - i4 - July 2004 - p483(2) [501+]

Brass, Perry - *The Substance of God: A Spiritual Thriller*
Lam Bk Rpt - v13 - i3 - Oct 2004 - p37(2) [501+]

Brassey, Richard - *The Story of London*
Sch Lib - v52 - i3 - Autumn 2004 - p149(2) [501+]

Braswell, Geoffrey E. - *The Maya and Teotihuacan: Reinterpreting Early Classic Interaction*
Choice - v41 - i7 - March 2004 - p1337(1) [501+]
JRAI - v10 - i3 - Sept 2004 - p711(2) [501+]

Brathwaite, Kamau - *Words Need Love Too*
Poet - v185 - i6 - March 2005 - p463(13) [501+]

Bratlinger, Ellen A. - *Dividing Classes: How the Middle Class Negotiates and Rationalizes School Advantage*
CS - v33 - i5 - Sept 2004 - p604-605 [501+]

Bratman, Steven - *Mosby's Handbook of Herbs and Supplements and Their Therapeutic Uses*
SciTech - v28 - i1 - March 2004 - p122(1) [51-500]

Bratteli, Ola - *Wavelets through a Looking Glass: The World of the Spectrum*
SIAM Rev - v46 - i2 - June 2004 - p368-372 [501+]

Bratton, J.S. - *New Readings in Theatre History*
Theat J - v56 - i4 - Dec 2004 - p710-712 [501+]
TimHES - v0 - i1655 - August 27 2004 - p26(1) [501+]

Bratton, John - *Organizational Leadership*
SciTech - v28 - i1 - March 2004 - p89(1) [501+]

Bratton, William J. - *Scene of the Crime (Illus. by Ellroy, James)*
PW - v251 - i41 - Oct 11 2004 - p73(1) [51-500]

Braude, Ann - *Transforming the Faiths of Our Fathers: The Women Who Changed American Religion*
Choice - v42 - i4 - Dec 2004 - p681(1) [1-50]
Transforming the Faiths of Our Fathers: Women Who Changed American Religion
CC - v122 - i2 - Jan 25 2005 - p38(2) [501+]
R&R Bk N - v20 - i1 - Feb 2005 - p11(1) [51-500]

Braudeau, Michel - *The Flight of the Monarch and Other Reflections*
SciTech - v28 - i3 - Sept 2004 - p64(1) [51-500]

Braudy, Leo - *From Chivalry to Terrorism: War and the Changing Nature of Masculinity*
Choice - v41 - i11-12 - July-August 2004 - p2084(1) [501+]

Braudy, Susan - *Family Circle: The Boudins and the Aristocracy of the Left*
ABR - v25 - i5 - July-August 2004 - p11(2) [501+]
HNet - Sept 2004 - pNA [501+]

Brauer, Holger - *The Real Exchange Rate and Prices of Traded Goods in OECD Countries*
JEL - v42 - i1 - March 2004 - p265(1) [501+]

Brauer, Jurgen - *The Economics of Regional Security: NATO, the Mediterranean, and Southern Africa*
JEL - v41 - i4 - Dec 2003 - p1299(2) [501+]

Brauers, Willem K. - *Optimization Methods for a Stakeholder Society: A Revolution in Economic Thinking by Multi-Objective Optimization*
R&R Bk N - v19 - i1 - Feb 2004 - p94(1) [51-500]

Braught, Mark - *Cosmo's Moon*
LibMed - v22 - i5 - Feb 2004 - p66(1) [501+]

Braun, Bev - *New Ideas for Crafting Heritage Albums*
EFHM - v58 - i2 - March-April 2004 - p88(1) [51-500]

Braun, Dietmar - *Fiscal Policies in Federal States*
JEL - v42 - i1 - March 2004 - p258(1) [501+]

Braun, Hans - *Giving Voice: Canadian and German Perspectives*
Can Lit - i181 - Summer 2004 - p112-113 [501+]

Braun, Lilian Jackson - *The Cat Who Went Bananas*
BL - v101 - i8 - Dec 15 2004 - p710(1) [51-500]
Globe & Mail - Feb 5 2005 - pD15 [51-500]
KR - v72 - i20 - Oct 15 2004 - p985(1) [51-500]
PW - v251 - i47 - Nov 22 2004 - p41(1) [51-500]

Braun, Linda W. - *Technically Involved: Technology-Based Youth Participation Activities for Your Library*
VOYA - v27 - i4 - Oct 2004 - p266(1) [51-500]

Braun, Mary Beth - *Introduction to Massage Therapy*
SciTech - v28 - i3 - Sept 2004 - p123(1) [51-500]

Braun, Stefan - *Democracy Off Balance: Freedom of Expression and Hate Propaganda Law in Canada*
R&R Bk N - v19 - i3 - August 2004 - p145(1) [51-500]

The Last Refuge: Patriotism, Politics, and the Environment in an Age of Terror
Choice - v42 - i3 - Nov 2004 - p556(1) [1-50]
Braun, Suzanne - *Inventing the Rest of Our Lives*
People - v63 - i2 - Jan 17 2005 - p57 [51-500]
Braun, Thom - *The Philosophy of Branding: Great Philosophers Think Brands*
R&R Bk N - v19 - i3 - August 2004 - p109(1) [51-500]
Brauninger, Michael - *Public Debt and Endogenous Growth*
JEL - v42 - i1 - March 2004 - p258(1) [501+]
Braunstein, Peter - *The Sixties Chronicle*
Choice - v42 - i7 - March 2005 - p1210(1) [51-500]
Braver, Adam - *Divine Sarah*
BL - v100 - i21 - July 2004 - p1815(1) [51-500]
Braver, Vanita - *Pinky Promise: A Book about Telling the Truth (Illus. by Pillo, Cary)*
c SLJ - v50 - i12 - Dec 2004 - p98(1) [501+]
Brawley, Mark R. - *The Politics of Globalization: Gaining Perspective, Assessing Consequences*
CBRA - Annual 2003 - p303(1) [51-500]
R&R Bk N - v19 - i3 - August 2004 - p187(1) [501+]
Bray, Abigail - *Helene Cixous: Writing and Sexual Difference*
Choice - v42 - i2 - Oct 2004 - p297(2) [501+]
Bray, Alan - *The Friend*
AHR - v109 - i3 - June 2004 - p865(2) [501+]
Bray, George A. - *Handbook of Obesity: Clinical Applications. 2nd Ed.*
E-Streams - June 2004 - pNA [501+]
SciTech - v28 - i1 - March 2004 - p103(1) [51-500]
Handbook of Obesity: Etiology and Pathophysiology. 2nd Ed.
E-Streams - June 2004 - pNA [501+]
SciTech - v28 - i1 - March 2004 - p103(1) [51-500]
Bray, Libba - *A Great and Terrible Beauty (Read by Bailey, Josephine). Audiobook Review*
c BL - v100 - i22 - August 2004 - p1954(1) [51-500]
A Great and Terrible Beauty
c HB - v80 - i5 - Sept-Oct 2004 - p609(2) [51-500]
c LibMed - v22 - i6 - March 2004 - p66(1) [501+]
Bray, Mark - *Comparative Education: Continuing Traditions, New Challenges, and New Paradigms*
R&R Bk N - v19 - i1 - Feb 2004 - pNA [51-500]
Bray-Moffatt, Naia - *Ice Skating School (Illus. by Handley, David)*
c BL - v101 - i1 - Sept 1 2004 - p115(1) [501+]
c SLJ - v50 - i7 - July 2004 - p90(2) [51-500]
Bray, Robin - *Thura's Diary: My Life in Wartime Iraq*
c CCB-B - v57 - i11 - July-August 2004 - p452(2) [501+]
Bray, Tamara L. - *The Archaeology and Politics of Food and Feasting in Early States and Empires*
R&R Bk N - v19 - i1 - Feb 2004 - p73(1) [51-500]
Bray, Xavier - *El Greco*
Choice - v42 - i1 - Sept 2004 - p88(1) [501+]
Braybrooke, David - *Utilitarianism: Restorations, Repairs, Renovations, Variations on Bentham's Master-Idea, That Disputes about Social Policy Should Be Settled by Statistical Evidence about the Comparative Consequences...*
R&R Bk N - v20 - i1 - Feb 2005 - p3(1) [51-500]
Braybrooke, Neville - *Olivia Manning*
Spec - v296 - i9195 - Oct 30 2004 - p46(2) [501+]
Braysmith, Tara - *West of Then: A Mother, a Daughter, and a Journey Past Paradise*
PW - v251 - i29 - July 19 2004 - p151(2) [51-500]
Braz, Albert Raimundo - *The False Traitor: Louis Riel in Canadian Culture*
AHR - v109 - i4 - Oct 2004 - p1216-1217 [501+]
Can Hist R - v85 - i4 - Dec 2004 - p832(3) [501+]
CBRA - Annual 2003 - p253(1) [501+]
Brazaitis, Peter - *You Belong in a Zoo! Tales from a Lifetime Spent with Cobras, Crocs, and Other Creatures*
y Kliatt - v39 - i2 - March 2005 - p42(1) [51-500]
y SB - v40 - i3 - May-June 2004 - p124(1) [501+]
Brazelton, Katie - *Pathway to Purpose for Women*
PW - v252 - i11 - March 14 2005 - p64(1) [51-500]
Braziel, Jana Evans - *Bodies out of Bounds: Fatness and Transgression*
Am Q - v56 - i4 - Dec 2004 - p1115(10) [501+]
J Am St - v38 - i2 - August 2004 - p360(2) [501+]
Brazil: Equitable, Competitive, Sustainable
R&R Bk N - v19 - i1 - Feb 2004 - p82(1) [1-50]
Brazile, Donna - *Cooking with Grease: Stirring the Pots in American Politics*
Black Iss - v6 - i4 - July-August 2004 - p52(1) [501+]
LJ - v129 - i12 - July 2004 - p102(2) [51-500]
Brazilian Association of Researches in Economic History - *Historia Economica e Historia De Empresas*
JEL - v41 - i4 - Dec 2003 - p1446(1) [501+]
Brazin, Lillian R. - *Guide to Complementary and Alternative Medicine on the Internet*
SciTech - v28 - i1 - March 2004 - p79(1) [51-500]
BRB Publications - *The Sourcebook to Public Record Information: The Comprehensive Guide to County, State, and Federal Public Records Sources, 5th Ed.*
R&R Bk N - v19 - i1 - Feb 2004 - pNA [51-500]
Brea, L. Bernabo - *Gli scavi nella necropoli greca e romana di Lipari nell'area del Terreno Vescovile*
Class R - v54 - i1 - May 2004 - p214(2) [501+]
Breakwell, Glynis M. - *Doing Social Psychology Research*
R&R Bk N - v19 - i2 - May 2004 - p129 [51-500]
Breazeal, Cynthia L. - *Designing Sociable Robots*
Fut - v39 - i1 - Jan-Feb 2005 - p48(1) [51-500]
Brebbia, C.A. - *Boundary Elements XXVI: Proceedings*
SciTech - v28 - i4 - Dec 2004 - p132 [51-500]
Damage and Fracture Mechanics VIII: Computer Aided Assessment and Control: Proceedings
SciTech - v28 - i4 - Dec 2004 - p134 [51-500]
Urban Transport X: Urban Transport and the Environment in the 21st Century: Proceedings
SciTech - v28 - i4 - Dec 2004 - p8(1) [1-50]
Brecher, Erwin - *Focus on Hocus-Pocus*
Spec - v296 - i9188 - Sept 11 2004 - p61(1) [501+]
Brecher, Frank W. - *Securing American Independence: John Jay and the French Alliance*
JAH - v91 - i3 - Dec 2004 - p995(1) [501+]
Brechin, Steven R. - *Contested Nature: Promoting International Biodiversity with Social Justice in the Twenty- First Century*
CS - v33 - i5 - Sept 2004 - p622-622 [501+]
Breck, Judy - *Connectivity, the Answer to Ending Ignorance and Separation: Can You Hear Me Yet?*
R&R Bk N - v19 - i3 - August 2004 - p217(1) [1-50]
Brecon, Connah - *Tomorrow*
y Magpies - v19 - i5 - Nov 2004 - p32(1) [501+]
Bredbenner, Candice Lewis - *A Nationality of Her Own: Women, Marriage, and the Law of Citizenship*
Signs - v30 - i2 - Wntr 2005 - p1659(12) [501+]
Bredehoft, Tom - *Glass Tumblers: Identification and Value Guide 1860s to 1920s*
Ant&CM - v108 - i11 - Jan 2004 - p16(1) [501+]
Bredel, Ralf - *Long-Term Conflict Prevention and Industrial Development: The United Nations and its Specialized Agency, UNIDO*
R&R Bk N - v19 - i3 - August 2004 - p188(1) [501+]
Bredes, Don - *The Fifth Season*
KR - v73 - i5 - March 1 2005 - p260(1) [51-500]
PW - v252 - i10 - March 7 2005 - p49(1) [51-500]
Bredeson, Carmen - *After the Last Dog Died: The True-Life, Hair-Raising Adventure of Douglas Mawson and His 1911-1914 Antarctic Expedition*
SLJ - v50 - i10 - Oct 2004 - pS40(1) [51-500]
Bredsdorff, Bodil - *The Crow-Girl: The Children of Crow Cove*
c BL - v101 - i9-10 - Jan 1 2005 - p773(1) [1-50]
c SLJ - v50 - i10 - Oct 2004 - pS53(1) [51-500]
Bredsdorff, Thomas - *Enlightened Networking: Import and Export of Enlightenment in 18th Century Denmark*
R&R Bk N - v19 - i4 - Nov 2004 - p41(1) [51-500]
Breen, Ann - *Intown Living: A Different American Dream*
R&R Bk N - v19 - i4 - Nov 2004 - p135(1) [1-50]
Breen, Christopher - *Secrets of the iPod. 4th Ed.*
LJ - v129 - i13 - August 2004 - p114(1) [501+]
Breen, Margaret Sonser - *Truth, Reconciliation, and Evil*
R&R Bk N - v20 - i1 - Feb 2005 - p10(1) [51-500]
Understanding Evil: An Interdisciplinary Approach
R&R Bk N - v19 - i1 - Feb 2004 - p10(1) [1-50]
Breen, Mark - *Kid's Book of Weather Forecasting*
c SB - v40 - i5 - Sept-Oct 2004 - p194 [51-500]
Breen, T.H. - *The Marketplace of Revolution: How Consumer Politics Shaped American Independence*
HRNB - v33 - i1 - Fall 2004 - p16(1) [501+]
RAH - v32 - i3 - Sept 2004 - p329-340 [501+]
TLS - i5299 - Oct 22 2004 - p3-4 [501+]
W&M Q - v61 - i4 - Oct 2004 - p765-769 [501+]
Breene, Robert G., Jr. - *Latin American Political Yearbook 2001. Vol. 4*
JEL - v41 - i4 - Dec 2003 - p1407(1) [501+]
Breger, Marshall J. - *The Vatican-Israel Accords: Political, Legal, and Theological Contexts*
Choice - v42 - i3 - Nov 2004 - p502(1) [51-500]
Pers PS - v33 - i4 - Fall 2004 - p240(1) [501+]
Bregman, Lucy - *Death and Dying, Spirituality, and Religions: A Study of the Death Awareness Movement*
Choice - v41 - i11-12 - July-August 2004 - p2060(1) [501+]
Brehm, Barbara A. - *Successful Fitness Motivation Strategies*
R&R Bk N - v19 - i3 - August 2004 - p87(1) [51-500]
Breidbach, Olaf - *Naturwissenschaften um 1800: Wissenschaftskultur in Jena-Weimar*
Isis - v95 - i2 - June 2004 - p305(2) [501+]
Breier, Davida Gypsy - *Vegan and Vegetarian FAQ--Answers to Your Frequently Asked Questions*
Veg J - v24 - i1 - Jan-Feb 2005 - p34(1) [501+]
Breiger, Ronald - *Dynamic Social Network Modeling and Analysis: Workshop Summary and Papers, Proceedings*
R&R Bk N - v19 - i4 - Nov 2004 - p122(1) [51-500]
Breisach, Ernst - *On the Future of History: The Postmodernist Challenge and Its Afternoon*
JAH - v91 - i3 - Dec 2004 - p1112(2) [501+]
Breit, William - *Lives of the Laureates: Eighteen Nobel Economists*
Choice - v42 - i4 - Dec 2004 - p708(1) [1-50]
TimHES - v0 - i1659 - Sept 24 2004 - p25(1) [501+]
Breitbart, Andrew - *Hollywood, Interrupted: Insanity Chic in Babylon--the Case Against Celebrity*
Am Spect - v37 - i4 - May 2004 - p60(2) [501+]
Breithaupt, Fritz - *Goethe and Wittgenstein: Seeing the World's Unity in its Variety*
R&R Bk N - v19 - i1 - Feb 2004 - p5(1) [51-500]
Breitman, Richard - *U.S. Intelligence and the Nazis*
Choice - v42 - i5 - Jan 2005 - p919(1) [1-50]
Brekhus, Wayne - *Peacocks, Chameleons, Centaurs: Gay Suburbia and the Grammar of Social Identity*
AJS - v110 - i1 - July 2004 - p250(3) [501+]
SF - v83 - i1 - Sept 2004 - p453(3) [501+]
Bremer, Francis J. - *John Winthrop: America's Forgotten Founding Father*
AHR - v109 - i4 - Oct 2004 - p1221(2) [501+]
NEQ - v77 - i2 - June 2004 - p320-322 [501+]
RAH - v32 - i2 - June 2004 - p137-6 [501+]
Bremmer, Rolf H., Jr. - *Rome and the North: The Early Reception of Gregory the Great in Germanic Europe*
Specu - v79 - i3 - July 2004 - p742-744 [501+]
Bremner, Gavin - *Theories of Infant Development*
Soc Ser R - v78 - i4 - Dec 2004 - p691(3) [501+]
Bremner, Robert P. - *Chairman of the Fed: William McChesney Martin, Jr., and the Creation of the Modern American Financial System*
PW - v251 - i44 - Nov 1 2004 - p57(2) [501+]
Brende, Eric - *Better Off: Flipping the Switch on Technology*
BL - v100 - i21 - July 2004 - p1804(1) [51-500]
Globe & Mail - July 24 2004 - pF6 [51-500]
KR - v72 - i13 - July 1 2004 - p611(1) [501+]
y SLJ - v50 - i11 - Nov 2004 - p178(1) [51-500]
Brendecke, Arndt - *Wege in die Fruehe Neuzeit: Werkstattberichte, eine Linksammlung sowie Bildmaterialien zu Muenchen in Dreissigjaehrigen Krieg und zur Hexenverfolgung auf CD-ROM*
HNet - Dec 2004 - pNA [501+]
Brendemoen, Bernt - *The Turkish Dialects of Trabzon: Their Phonology and Historical Development, Vols. 1-2.*
R&R Bk N - v19 - i3 - August 2004 - p255(1) [51-500]
Brener, Milton E. - *Vanishing Points: Three Dimensional Perspective in Art and History*
R&R Bk N - v19 - i3 - August 2004 - p242(1) [51-500]
Brenholdt, Jorgen Ole - *Performing Tourist Places*
R&R Bk N - v19 - i4 - Nov 2004 - p72(1) [51-500]
Brennan, Christine - *Edge of Glory*
BL - v101 - i1 - Sept 1 2004 - p53(1) [51-500]
Brennan, David J. - *Retransmission and U.S. Compliance with TRIPS*
R&R Bk N - v19 - i1 - Feb 2004 - pNA [51-500]
Brennan, Denise - *What's Love Got to Do With It?: Transnational Desires and Sex Tourism in the Dominican Republic*
CS - v33 - i6 - Nov 2004 - p742(1) [1-50]
Wom R Bks - v21 - i10-11 - July 2004 - p27(1) [51-500]
Brennan, Geoffrey - *The Economy of Esteem: An Essay on Civil and Political Society*
Choice - v42 - i6 - Feb 2005 - p1062(1) [51-500]

Brennan, Gillian E. - *Patriotism, Power and Print: National Consciousness in Tudor England*
R&R Bk N - v19 - i1 - Feb 2004 - p234(1) [51-500]

Brennan, Herbie - *Faerie Wars (Read by Doyle, Gerard). Audiobook Review*
c Kliatt - v38 - i6 - Nov 2004 - p46(1) [51-500]
c SLJ - v50 - i7 - July 2004 - p58(1) [51-500]
Faerie Wars
c Kliatt - v38 - i6 - Nov 2004 - p21(2) [51-500]
y PW - v251 - i42 - Oct 18 2004 - p66(1) [1-50]
The Purple Emperor
y BL - v101 - i2 - Sept 15 2004 - p229(1) [51-500]
y CCB-B - v58 - i3 - Nov 2004 - p115(2) [501+]
c KR - v72 - i18 - Sept 15 2004 - p911(1) [501+]
c PW - v251 - i50 - Dec 13 2004 - p70(1) [501+]
c SLJ - v50 - i12 - Dec 2004 - p140(1) [501+]

Brennan, Jonathan - *When Brer Rabbit Meets Coyote*
Am Ind CRJ - v27 - i4 - Fall 2003 - p189-191 [501+]

Brennan, Linda Crotta - *The Black Regiment of the American Revolution (Illus. by Noll, Cheryl Kirk)*
c BL - v101 - i4 - Oct 15 2004 - p400(1) [51-500]
c CH Bwatch - v14 - i12 - Dec 2004 - pNA [501+]
y SLJ - v51 - i1 - Jan 2005 - p142(1) [51-500]

Brennan, Linda L. - *Social, Ethical, and Policy Implications of Information Technology*
R&R Bk N - v19 - i1 - Feb 2004 - p123(1) [51-500]

Brennan, Marcia - *Modernism's Masculine Subjects: Matisse, the New York School, and Post-Painterly Abstraction*
Afterimage - v32 - i4 - Jan-Feb 2005 - p15(1) [51-500]

Brennan, Michael G. - *A Sidney Chronology, 1554-1654*
Choice - v42 - i3 - Nov 2004 - p448-1 [1-50]

Brennan-Nelson, Denise - *Penny: The Forgotten Coin (Illus. by Monroe, Michael Glenn)*
c LibMed - v22 - i6 - March 2004 - p56(1) [501+]

Brennan, Noel-Anne - *The Blood of the Land*
y Kliatt - v38 - i4 - July 2004 - p26(2) [51-500]

Brennan, Samantha - *Feminist Moral Philosophy*
CBRA - Annual 2003 - p382(1) [501+]
R&R Bk N - v19 - i1 - Feb 2004 - p132(1) [51-500]

Brennan, Stephen - *Classic Adventure Stores; Twenty-One Tales of People Pushed to the Limit*
y Kliatt - v38 - i4 - July 2004 - p36(1) [51-500]

Brennan, Teresa - *Globalisation and Its Terror: Daily Life in the West*
Arena - i72 - August-Sept 2004 - p49(3) [501+]
The Transmission of Affect
Choice - v42 - i1 - Sept 2004 - p191(1) [501+]

Brennan, Thomas - *The Debt*
KR - v72 - i23 - Dec 1 2004 - p1118(1) [51-500]
LJ - v130 - i1 - Jan 1 2005 - p83(1) [51-500]

Brenner, Barbara - *Bunny Tails (Illus. by Munsinger, Lynn)*
c PW - v252 - i7 - Feb 14 2005 - p76(1) [51-500]
One Small Place by the Sea (Illus. by Leonard, Tom)
c SB - v40 - i4 - July-August 2004 - p175(1) [51-500]
c SLJ - v50 - i10 - Oct 2004 - pS23(1) [51-500]
One Small Place in a Tree (Illus. by Leonard, Tom)
c SB - v40 - i5 - Sept-Oct 2004 - p221(1) [51-500]
c SLJ - v50 - i10 - Oct 2004 - pS23(1) [51-500]

Brenner, Barry M. - *Brenner and Rector's The Kidney. 7th Ed. Vols. 1-2*
SciTech - v28 - i1 - March 2004 - p107(1) [51-500]

Brenner, David - *I Think There's Another Terrorist in My Soup (Read by Brenner, David). Audiobook Review*
LJ - v129 - i18 - Nov 1 2004 - p130(1) [51-500]

Brenner, Emily - *On the First Day of Grade School (Illus. by Whatley, Bruce)*
c BL - v100 - i22 - August 2004 - p1947(1) [51-500]
c SLJ - v50 - i7 - July 2004 - p68(1) [51-500]

Brenner, Frederic - *Diaspora: Homelands in Exile, Vols. 1-2*
ABR - v25 - i5 - July-August 2004 - p21(2) [501+]
Globe & Mail - Nov 27 2004 - pD3 [51-500]
R&R Bk N - v19 - i1 - Feb 2004 - p44(1) [51-500]

Brenner, Gerry - *Performative Criticism: Experiments in Reader Response*
Choice - v42 - i1 - Sept 2004 - p94(1) [501+]

Brenner, Ira - *Psychic Trauma: Dynamics, Symptoms, and Treatment*
SciTech - v28 - i4 - Dec 2004 - p100(1) [51-500]

Brenner, John C. - *Forensic Science: An Illustrated Dictionary*
Choice - v41 - i11-12 - July-August 2004 - p2020(3) [501+]

Brenner, Mary E. - *Everyday and Academic Mathematics in the Classroom*
SciTech - v28 - i4 - Dec 2004 - p15(1) [1-50]

Brenner, Michael - *Jewish Emancipation Reconsidered: The French and German Models*
R&R Bk N - v19 - i3 - August 2004 - p51(1) [51-500]

Brenner, Neil - *Spaces of Neoliberalism: Urban Restructuring in North America and Western Europe*
PG - v23 - i2 - Feb 2004 - p226 [501+]

Brenner, Robert - *The Boom and the Bubble: The US in the World Economy*
JEL - v41 - i4 - Dec 2003 - p1282(3) [501+]

Brennfleck, Joyce - *Sports Injuries Information for Teens*
y VOYA - v27 - i4 - Oct 2004 - p335(1) [51-500]

Brenson, Michael - *Acts of Engagement: Writings on Art, Criticism, and Institutions, 1993-2002*
PW - v251 - i35 - August 30 2004 - p39(1) [501+]
R&R Bk N - v19 - i4 - Nov 2004 - p199(1) [501+]

Brent, Robert J. - *Cost-Benefit Analysis and Health Care Evaluations*
JEL - v41 - i4 - Dec 2003 - p1373(1) [501+]

Breon, Emmanuel - *Jacques-Emile Ruhlmann: The Designer's Archives, Vol. 1*
Choice - v42 - i3 - Nov 2004 - p475(1) [1-50]
Jacques-Emile Ruhlmann: The Designer's Archives, Vol. 2
Choice - v42 - i3 - Nov 2004 - p475(1) [1-50]
Jacques-Emile Ruhlmann: The Designer's Archives. Vol. 2
LJ - v129 - i14 - Sept 1 2004 - p146(1) [501+]

Bresler, Robert J. - *Freedom of Association: Rights and Liberties under the Law*
Choice - v42 - i3 - Nov 2004 - p564(1) [1-50]
y Ref Rev - Sept 2004 - pNA [501+]
R&R Bk N - v19 - i3 - August 2004 - p203(1) [1-50]

Breslin, Beau - *The Communitarian Constitution*
Choice - v42 - i4 - Dec 2004 - p735(1) [1-50]
Law&PolBR - Sept 2004 - pNA [501+]
R&R Bk N - v19 - i3 - August 2004 - p191(1) [501+]

Breslin, Herbert - *The King and I: The Uncensored Tale of Luciano Pavarotti's Rise to Fame by His Manager, Friend, and Sometime Adversary*
BL - v101 - i3 - Oct 1 2004 - p293(1) [51-500]
BW - v34 - i42 - Oct 17 2004 - p4(1) [501+]
KR - v72 - i16 - August 15 2004 - p784(1) [51-500]
LJ - v129 - i14 - Sept 1 2004 - p152(1) [51-500]
NYTBR - Dec 12 2004 - p9 [501+]
People - v62 - i18 - Nov 1 2004 - p49 [51-500]
PW - v251 - i30 - July 26 2004 - p45(1) [501+]

Breslin, Jimmy - *The Church That Forgot Christ*
BL - v100 - i21 - July 2004 - p1795(1) [51-500]
BW - v34 - i31 - August 1 2004 - p4(1) [501+]
CC - v121 - i19 - Sept 21 2004 - p50(3) [501+]
LJ - v129 - i12 - July 2004 - p86(1) [51-500]
NYTBR - August 15 2004 - p7 [501+]
R&R Bk N - v19 - i4 - Nov 2004 - p27(1) [501+]

Breslin, Susannah - *You're a Bad Man, Aren't You?*
ABR - v25 - i5 - July-August 2004 - p29(1) [501+]

Breslin, Theresa - *Whispers in the Graveyard*
y Kliatt - v38 - i5 - Sept 2004 - p18(3) [51-500]

Brestler, Don - *Young Adult's Guide to the Canadian West*
y CBRA - Annual 2003 - p533(1) [51-500]

Bretell, Caroline - *Anthropology and Migration: Essays on Transnationalism, Ethnicity, and Identity*
R&R Bk N - v19 - i1 - Feb 2004 - p40(1) [1-50]

Breton, Albert - *Rational Foundations of Democratic Politics*
JEL - v42 - i1 - March 2004 - p249(1) [501+]

Breton, Marcos - *Home Is Everything: The Latino Baseball Story*
SLJ - v50 - i10 - Oct 2004 - pS65(2) [501+]

Breton, Raymond - *Globalization and Society: Processes of Differentiation Examined*
R&R Bk N - v19 - i2 - May 2004 - p110(1) [51-500]

Brett, Alex - *Cold Dark Matter*
Globe & Mail - Feb 19 2005 - pD15 [501+]
Dead Water Creek: A Morgan O'Brien Mystery
CBRA - Annual 2003 - p154(2) [501+]

Brett, Brian - *Coyote*
BIC - v33 - i7 - Oct 2004 - p17(2) [501+]
CBRA - Annual 2003 - p155(1) [51-500]
Uproar's Your Only Music
Globe & Mail - Dec 24 2004 - pD3 [1-50]
Globe & Mail - March 5 2005 - pD4 [501+]

Brett, Dan - *Tales from the Blue Ox: A Hands-On Manual of Traditional Skills from the Blue Ox Millworks Historic Park*
R&R Bk N - v19 - i4 - Nov 2004 - p250(1) [501+]

Brett, Edward T. - *The U.S. Catholic Press on Central America: From Cold War Anticommunism to Social Justice*
AHR - v109 - i3 - June 2004 - p941(2) [501+]
JAH - v91 - i1 - June 2004 - p299-300 [501+]
Theol St - v66 - i1 - March 2005 - p233(2) [501+]

Brett, Jan - *Daisy Comes Home*
c PW - v252 - i2 - Jan 10 2005 - p58(1) [1-50]
On Noah's Ark (Illus. by Brett, Jan)
LibMed - v22 - i7 - April-May 2004 - p56(1) [501+]
The Umbrella (Illus. by Brett, Jan)
c BL - v101 - i7 - Dec 1 2004 - p658(1) [51-500]
c KR - v72 - i16 - August 15 2004 - p802(1) [51-500]
c PW - v251 - i31 - August 2 2004 - p69(1) [51-500]
c SLJ - v50 - i11 - Nov 2004 - p91(2) [51-500]

Brett, Judith - *Australian Liberals and the Moral Middle Class: From Alfred Deakin to John Howard*
Quad - v48 - i12 - Dec 2004 - p86(2) [501+]
TLS - i5263 - Feb 13 2004 - p26-26 [501+]

Brett, Leo - *March of the Robots*
MFSF - v107 - i4-5 - Oct-Nov 2004 - p242(1) [51-500]

Brett, Michael - *New Collected Poems*
CR - v285 - i1665 - Oct 2004 - p245(3) [501+]

Brett, Simon - *The Hanging in the Hotel: A Fethering Mystery*
BL - v100 - i21 - July 2004 - p1823(1) [1-50]
PW - v251 - i29 - July 19 2004 - p148(1) [51-500]
Murder in the Museum (Read by Brett, Simon). Audiobook Review
BL - v101 - i8 - Dec 15 2004 - p752(1) [1-50]

Bretton, Barbara - *Chances Are*
y BL - v101 - i3 - Oct 1 2004 - p315(1) [51-500]
PW - v251 - i33 - August 16 2004 - p48(1) [51-500]

Breuss, Fritz - *The Banana Dispute: An Economic and Legal Analysis*
JEL - v41 - i4 - Dec 2003 - p1352(1) [501+]

The Brevard Rosenwald School: Black Education and Community Building in a Southern Appalachian Town, 1920-1966
Black Iss - v6 - i5 - Sept-Oct 2004 - p42(2) [501+]

Breverton, Terry - *Black Bart Roberts*
Bwatch - v26 - i7 - July 2004 - p11(1) [51-500]

Brewer, D.S. - *Medieval Allegory and the Building of the New Jerusalem*
HER - v119 - i483 - Sept 2004 - p1041(2) [501+]

Brewer, John - *A Sentimental Murder: Love and Madness in the Eighteenth Century*
Lon R Bks - v26 - i19 - Oct 7 2004 - p16(2) [501+]
TLS - i5264 - Feb 20 2004 - p36-36 [501+]

Brewer, Marilynn - *Self and Social Identity*
Choice - v42 - i1 - Sept 2004 - p193(1) [501+]
Social Cognition
Choice - v42 - i1 - Sept 2004 - p193(1) [501+]

Brewer, Marilynn B. - *Applied Social Psychology*
R&R Bk N - v19 - i2 - May 2004 - p129 [51-500]
TimHES - v0 - i1684 - March 25 2005 - p31(1) [501+]
Emotion and Motivation
TimHES - v0 - i1684 - March 25 2005 - p31(1) [501+]
Self and Social Identity
TimHES - v0 - i1684 - March 25 2005 - p31(1) [501+]
Social Cognition
TimHES - v0 - i1684 - March 25 2005 - p31(1) [501+]

Brewer, Mark D. - *Relevant No More? The Catholic/Protestant Divide in American Electoral Politics*
Choice - v41 - i7 - March 2004 - p1371(1) [501+]
HNet - Sept 2004 - pNA [501+]

Brewer, Michael - *Who Needs a Superhero?: Finding Virtue, Vice, and What's Holy in the Comics*
PW - v251 - i37 - Sept 13 2004 - p75(1) [501+]

Brewer, Richard - *Conservancy: The Land Trust Movement in America*
NRJ - v44 - i2 - Spring 2004 - p621-651 [501+]

Brewer, Sarah - *1,001 Facts about the Human Body*
c SB - v40 - i4 - July-August 2004 - p148(1) [51-500]

Brewer, Sonny - *The Poet of Tolstoy Park*
KR - v72 - i24 - Dec 15 2004 - p1153(2) [501+]
LJ - v129 - i20 - Dec 1 2004 - p97(2) [51-500]
PW - v252 - i7 - Feb 14 2005 - p53(1) [51-500]

Stories from the Blue Moon Cafe III: Anthology of Southern Writers
   BL - v101 - i4 - Oct 15 2004 - p380(1) [51-500]
Brewer, Thomas L. - *The New Economic Analysis of Multinationals: An Agenda for Management, Policy and Research*
   JEL - v41 - i4 - Dec 2003 - p1356(1) [501+]
Brewerton, Timothy D. - *Clinical Handbook of Eating Disorders: An Integrated Approach*
   E-Streams - Nov 2004 - pNA [501+]
   SciTech - v28 - i3 - Sept 2004 - p101(1) [51-500]
Brewster, David - *Poems from the Coffee Lands*
   LJ - v129 - i15 - Sept 15 2004 - p62(1) [51-500]
Brewster, Hugh - *Le Debarquement A Juno: Des Heros Du Jour J*
   Res Links - v10 - i1 - Oct 2004 - p51(1) [51-500]
Brewster, Ian - *Simple Universe*
   y   SB - v40 - i4 - July-August 2004 - p163(1) [51-500]
Brian Dolan - *Josiah Wedgwood: Entrepreneur to the Enlightenment*
   Spec - v296 - i9197 - Nov 13 2004 - p44(1) [501+]
Brian, James - *Perfect World*
   SLJ - v51 - i1 - Jan 2005 - p132(1) [51-500]
Brian, Kate - *The V Club*
   y   VOYA - v27 - i3 - August 2004 - p207(1) [1-50]
Briand, Kevin - *The Baseball Book: A Young Player's Guide to Baseball*
   SLJ - v50 - i10 - Oct 2004 - pS48(1) [51-500]
Brians, Paul - *Modern South Asian Literature in English*
   R&R Bk N - v19 - i1 - Feb 2004 - p241(1) [501+]
Brick, John - *Handbook of the Medical Consequences of Alcohol and Drug Abuse*
   SciTech - v28 - i1 - March 2004 - p102(1) [51-500]
Brickell, Christopher - *The American Horticultural Society A-Z Encyclopedia of Garden Plants*
   LJ - v129 - i20 - Dec 1 2004 - p161(1) [51-500]
Bricker, Victoria R. - *An Encounter of Two Worlds: The Book of Chilam Balam of Kaua*
   HAHR - v84 - i4 - Nov 2004 - p725(2) [501+]
Bridal, Tessa - *Exploring Museum Theatre*
   R&R Bk N - v20 - i1 - Feb 2005 - p1(1) [51-500]
Bridge, Carl - *The British World: Diaspora, Culture and Identity*
   AHS - v35 - i124 - Oct 2004 - p414(3) [501+]
Bridge, F.R. - *Great Powers and the European States System 1814-1914, 2nd Ed.*
   R&R Bk N - v20 - i1 - Feb 2005 - p31(1) [51-500]
Bridge, Helen - *Women's Writing and Historiography in the GDR*
   GSR - v27 - i3 - Oct 2004 - p671(2) [501+]
Bridge, Kathryn Anne - *Extraordinary Accounts of Native Life on the West Coast*
   Res Links - v10 - i3 - Feb 2005 - p44(2) [501+]
Bridge, Steven L. - *Getting the Gospels: Understanding the New Testament Accounts of Jesus' Life*
   LJ - v129 - i16 - Oct 1 2004 - p86(1) [51-500]
   PW - v251 - i46 - Nov 15 2004 - pS17(1) [51-500]
Bridgeford, Andrew - *1066: The Hidden History in the Bayeux Tapestry*
   KR - v73 - i3 - Feb 1 2005 - p159(1) [501+]
   PW - v252 - i9 - Feb 28 2005 - p56(1) [51-500]
Bridger, Bobby - *Buffalo Bill and Sitting Bull: Inventing the Wild West*
   Am Ind CRJ - v28 - i2 - Spring 2004 - p145(3) [501+]
   WHQ - v35 - i1 - Spring 2004 - p101-102 [501+]
Bridger, Christopher J. - *Open Ocean Aquaculture: From Research to Commercial Reality*
   SciTech - v28 - i4 - Dec 2004 - p127 [51-500]
Bridges, Kate - *The Proposition*
   BL - v101 - i1 - Sept 1 2004 - p71(1) [51-500]
Bridges, Ruby - *Through My Eyes*
   c   SLJ - v50 - i10 - Oct 2004 - p67(1) [51-500]
Bridges, William - *Managing Transitions: Making the Most of Change*
   NACEJou - v64 - i2 - Wntr 2004 - p14(1) [501+]
Bridgman, Rae - *Safe Haven: The Story of a Shelter for Homeless Women*
   CBRA - Annual 2003 - p379(2) [501+]
Bridgman, Roger - *Robot*
   y   SB - v40 - i3 - May-June 2004 - p128(1) [501+]
Briere, John - *Psychological Assessment of Adult Posttraumatic States: Phenomenology, Diagnosis, and Measurement. 2nd Ed.*
   SciTech - v28 - i3 - Sept 2004 - p102(1) [51-500]
Briggs, Asa - *Modern Europe: 1789-Present. 2nd Ed.*
   TimHES - v0 - i1668 - Nov 26 2004 - pV(1) [501+]

Briggs, Charles L. - *Stories in the Time of Cholera: Racial Profiling During a Medical Nightmare*
   CS - v33 - i1 - Jan 2004 - p109-110 [501+]
Briggs, Harold E. - *Using Evidence in Social Work Practice: Behavioral Perspectives*
   R&R Bk N - v19 - i3 - August 2004 - p159(1) [51-500]
Briggs, Vernon M., Jr. - *Mass Immigration and the National Interest: Policy Directions for the New Century*
   JEL - v42 - i1 - March 2004 - p278(2) [501+]
Briggs, William L. - *A Multigrid Tutorial, 2nd Ed.*
   SIAM Rev - v46 - i4 - Dec 2004 - p746-746 [501+]
Brigham, Eugene F. - *Financial Management, Theory and Practice, 11th Ed.*
   R&R Bk N - v19 - i3 - August 2004 - p136(1) [51-500]
Bright, Elise M. - *Reviving America's Forgotten Neighborhoods: An Investigation of Inner City Revitalization Efforts*
   JEL - v41 - i4 - Dec 2003 - p1440(2) [501+]
Bright, Paul - *Under the Bed (Illus. by Curt, Ben)*
   c   SLJ - v50 - i8 - August 2004 - p84(1) [51-500]
Bright, Robin - *Write from the Start: Writers Workshop for the Primary Grades*
   CBRA - Annual 2003 - p392(2) [51-500]
Bright, Susie - *The Best American Erotica 2005*
   KR - v72 - i22 - Nov 15 2004 - p1069(1) [51-500]
Brightman, Carol - *Total Insecurity: The Myth of American Omnipotence*
   BL - v101 - i2 - Sept 15 2004 - p181(2) [51-500]
Brighton, Terry - *Hell Riders: The True Story of the Charge of the Light Brigade*
   BL - v101 - i5 - Nov 1 2004 - p456(1) [51-500]
   PW - v251 - i38 - Sept 20 2004 - p53(1) [51-500]
   Spec - v296 - i9192 - Oct 9 2004 - p43(1) [501+]
Briginshaw, Valerie - *Dance, Space and Subjectivity*
   Dance RJ - v35 - i2 - Winter 2003 - p181-183 [501+]
Brignon, Arnaud - *Phase Conjugate Laser Optics*
   E-Streams - June 2004 - pNA [501+]
   SciTech - v28 - i1 - March 2004 - p146(1) [51-500]
Brigs, Raymond - *The Puddleman*
   c   Sch Lib - v52 - i4 - Winter 2004 - p192(1) [51-500]
Brill, Marlene Targ - *Bronco Charlie and the Pony Express (Illus. by Orback, Craig)*
   c   SLJ - v50 - i8 - August 2004 - p106(1) [51-500]
   Doctors
   c   BL - v101 - i4 - Oct 15 2004 - p426(1) [51-500]
Brill, Patricia A. - *Functional Fitness for Older Adults*
   SciTech - v28 - i3 - Sept 2004 - p109(1) [51-500]
Brilliantov, Nikolai V. - *Kinetic Theory of Granular Gases*
   SciTech - v28 - i4 - Dec 2004 - p47(1) [51-500]
Brillouin, Leon - *Science and Information Theory, 2nd Ed.*
   SciTech - v28 - i4 - Dec 2004 - p14(1) [1-50]
Brim, Orville Gilbert - *How Healthy Are We? A National Study of Well-Being at Midlife*
   Choice - v41 - i11-12 - July-August 2004 - p2127(1) [501+]
Brimer, Stephen - *The Screenwriter's Legal Guide*
   Bwatch - Feb 2005 - pNA [51-500]
Brimley, Vern - *Financing Education in a Climate of Change, 9th Ed.*
   R&R Bk N - v19 - i3 - August 2004 - p223(1) [1-50]
Brimner, Larry Dane - *Captain Stormalong (Illus. by Chung, Chi)*
   c   SLJ - v50 - i7 - July 2004 - p91(1) [51-500]
   Le Chien a Garde Partagee
   c   Res Links - v10 - i3 - Feb 2005 - p58(1) [501+]
   Le Chien Savant
   c   Res Links - v10 - i3 - Feb 2005 - p58(1) [501+]
   Le Manteau Cool
   c   Res Links - v10 - i3 - Feb 2005 - p58(1) [501+]
   Le Truc qui Brille
   c   Res Links - v10 - i3 - Feb 2005 - p58(1) [501+]
   The Littlest Wolf (Illus. by Aruego, Jose)
   c   RT - v57 - Oct 2003 - p170 [1-50]
   Molly Pitcher (Illus. by Girouard, Patrick)
   c   SLJ - v50 - i7 - July 2004 - p91(1) [51-500]
   Ou est l'argent?
   c   Res Links - v10 - i3 - Feb 2005 - p58(1) [501+]
   Subway: The Story of Tunnels, Tubes, and Tracks (Illus. by Waldman, Neil)
   c   BL - v101 - i4 - Oct 15 2004 - p400(1) [51-500]
   c   KR - v72 - i19 - Oct 1 2004 - p957(1) [51-500]
   Tout le Monde a l'eau!
   c   Res Links - v10 - i3 - Feb 2005 - p58(1) [501+]
Brindley, John - *Amy Peppercorn: Living the Dream*
   y   Sch Lib - v52 - i3 - Autumn 2004 - p155(1) [501+]

Bringhurst, Newell G. - *Black and Mormon*
   PW - v251 - i46 - Nov 15 2004 - pS17(1) [51-500]
   Excavating Mormon Pasts: The New Historiography of the Last Half Century
   Bwatch - v26 - i8 - August 2004 - p11(1) [51-500]
Bringhurst, Robert - *The Solid Form of Language*
   Globe & Mail - Oct 16 2004 - pD12 [501+]
   Ursa Major: A Polyphonic Masque for Speakers and Dancers
   BIC - v33 - i2 - March 2004 - p42(1) [501+]
   CBRA - Annual 2003 - p239(1) [51-500]
Brink, Andre - *Before I Forget*
   Spec - v296 - i9195 - Oct 30 2004 - p55(2) [501+]
   TLS - i5293 - Sept 10 2004 - p21(1) [501+]
Brink, David - *Perfectionism and the Common Good: Themes in the Philosophy of T.H. Green*
   RM - v58 - i2 - Dec 2004 - p425(2) [501+]
Brink, David O. - *Prudence and Authenticity: Intrapersonal Conflicts of Value*
   RM - v58 - i1 - Sept 2004 - p229(1) [501+]
Brinkerhoff, Robert O. - *The Success Case Method: Find out Quickly What's Working and What's Not*
   Per Psy - v57 - i4 - Winter 2004 - p1107(4) [501+]
Brinkerhoff, Shirley - *Drug Therapy and Anxiety Disorders*
   LibMed - v23 - i1 - August-Sept 2004 - p74(1) [51-500]
   Drug Therapy and Childhood and Adolescent Disorders
   y   VOYA - v27 - i4 - Oct 2004 - p334(2) [51-500]
   Drug Therapy and Eating Disorders
   y   VOYA - v27 - i4 - Oct 2004 - p334(2) [51-500]
   Why Can't I Learn Like Everyone Else?: Youth with Learning Disabilities
   y   SLJ - v50 - i11 - Nov 2004 - p160(1) [51-500]
   y   VOYA - v27 - i4 - Oct 2004 - p335(2) [51-500]
Brinkley, Alan - *The American Presidency*
   Choice - v42 - i1 - Sept 2004 - p76(1) [501+]
   R&R Bk N - v19 - i4 - Nov 2004 - p56(1) [51-500]
Brinkley, Douglas - *Tour of Duty: John Kerry and the Vietnam War*
   BW - v34 - i38 - Sept 19 2004 - p11(1) [51-500]
   NYTBR - Oct 24 2004 - p30 [501+]
   Wheels for the World: Henry Ford, His Company, and a Century of Progress, 1903-2003
   BHR - v77 - i4 - Winter 2003 - p725(730) [501+]
   T&C - v45 - i4 - Oct 2004 - p856(2) [501+]
   The World War II Memorial: A Grateful Nation Remembers
   y   BL - v101 - i1 - Sept 1 2004 - p44(1) [51-500]
   LJ - v129 - i13 - August 2004 - p97(1) [501+]
Brinley, Maryann Bucknum - *Oh Boy! Mothers Tell the Truth about Raising Teen Sons*
   BL - v101 - i5 - Nov 1 2004 - p452(1) [51-500]
Brinsfield, John W. - *Faith in the Fight: Civil War Chaplains*
   HNet - Oct 2004 - pNA [501+]
   JSH - v70 - i3 - August 2004 - p682(2) [501+]
Brinson, Susan L. - *The Red Scare, Politics, and the Federal Communications Commission, 1941-1960*
   Choice - v42 - i6 - Feb 2005 - p1080(1) [51-500]
   R&R Bk N - v19 - i3 - August 2004 - p69(1) [51-500]
Briody, Dan - *The Halliburton Agenda: The Politics of Oil and Money*
   R&R Bk N - v19 - i3 - August 2004 - pNA [51-500]
Brisbian, Richard A. - *A Strike Like No Other Strike: Law & Resistance During the Pittston Coal Strike of 1989-1990*
   JAH - v91 - i1 - June 2004 - p342-343 [501+]
Brisbin, Terri - *The King's Mistress*
   BL - v101 - i8 - Dec 15 2004 - p714(1) [51-500]
Briscoe, Connie - *Can't Get Enough*
   LJ - v129 - i20 - Dec 1 2004 - p86(1) [1-50]
Briscoe, James R. - *New Historical Anthology of Music by Women*
   Am MT - v54 - i4 - Feb-March 2005 - p115(1) [501+]
   LJ - v129 - i20 - Dec 1 2004 - p168(2) [51-500]
Briscoe, Jill - *Here Am I Lord ... Send Somebody Else!: How God Uses Ordinary People to do Extraordinary Things*
   Ch Today - v48 - i8 - August 2004 - p59(1) [51-500]
Brisick, Jamie - *Have Board, Will Travel: The Definitive History of Surf, Skate, and Snow*
   SLJ - v50 - i12 - Dec 2004 - p175(1) [51-500]

Brisson, Pat - *Beach Is to Fun: A Book of Relationships* (Illus. by Yoshikawa, Sachiko)
  c BL - v100 - i22 - August 2004 - p1940(2) [51-500]
  c CCB-B - v57 - i11 - July-August 2004 - p456(1) [501+]
  c SLJ - v50 - i7 - July 2004 - p68(1) [51-500]
Mama Loves Me from Away (Illus. by Caple, Laurie)
  c BL - v101 - i8 - Dec 15 2004 - p746(1) [51-500]
  c KR - v72 - i20 - Oct 15 2004 - p1002(1) [51-500]
  c PW - v251 - i49 - Dec 6 2004 - p60(1) [51-500]
  c SLJ - v51 - i2 - Feb 2005 - p94(1) [51-500]
Tap-Dance Fever (Illus. by Mills, Nancy Cote Boyds)
  c KR - v73 - i3 - Feb 1 2005 - p174(1) [51-500]

Brissoni, Armando - *Saggio su Galileo Galilei: Discorsi di dottrina*
  Isis - v95 - i3 - Sept 2004 - p537(2) [501+]

Bristow, Joseph - *Wilde Writings: Contextual Conditions*
  RES - v55 - i220 - June 2004 - p476-478 [501+]
  R&R Bk N - v19 - i1 - Feb 2004 - p239(1) [51-500]

Brite, Poppy Z. - *Prime*
  KR - v73 - i2 - Jan 15 2005 - p66(1) [501+]

British Press Photographer's Association - *Five Thousand Days: Press Photography in a Changing World*
  NS - v133 - i4711 - Oct 25 2004 - p38(3) [501+]

Britnell, Jennifer Joan - *Jean Bouchet: Traverseur des voies perilleuses (1476-1557).*
  Ren Q - v57 - i4 - Winter 2004 - p1424(2) [501+]

Britt, John - *The Complete Guide to High-Fire Glazes: Glazing and Firing at Cone 10*
  Ceram Mo - v53 - i1 - Jan 2005 - p74(2) [501+]

Brittain, Charles - *Philo of Larissa: The Last of the Academic Sceptics*
  Class R - v53 - i2 - Nov 2003 - p314-316 [501+]

Brittan, Samuel - *Against the Flow*
  Econ - v374 - i8416 - March 5 2005 - p83US [501+]

Britten, Benjamin - *Britten on Music*
  Choice - v41 - i11-12 - July-August 2004 - p2052(2) [501+]
Plymouth Town
  TLS - i5263 - Feb 13 2004 - p20-20 [501+]

Britting, Jeff - *Ayn Rand*
  Cur R - v44 - i7 - March 2005 - p12(1) [51-500]
  KR - v72 - i21 - Nov 1 2004 - p1034(1) [501+]
  LJ - v130 - i1 - Jan 1 2005 - p110(1) [51-500]

Britton, Celia - *Race and the Unconscious: Freudianism in French Caribbean Thought*
  FS - v58 - i3 - July 2004 - p439-440 [501+]

Britton, Nicholas F. - *Essential Mathematical Biology*
  Phys Today - v57 - i3 - March 2004 - p80-82 [501+]

Britton, Pamela - *Scandal*
  BL - v100 - i21 - July 2004 - p1826(1) [1-50]

Britton, Tamara L. - *Air Force One*
  c SLJ - v50 - i11 - Nov 2004 - p122(1) [51-500]
The Alamo
  c SLJ - v50 - i11 - Nov 2004 - p122(1) [51-500]
The Smithsonian Institution
  c SLJ - v50 - i11 - Nov 2004 - p122(1) [51-500]
South Africa
  c SLJ - v50 - i10 - Oct 2004 - p138(1) [51-500]

Britton, Wesley - *Spy Television*
  Choice - v42 - i1 - Sept 2004 - p94(1) [501+]
  TV Q - v35 - i1 - Fall 2004 - p71(3) [501+]

Brix, Michel - *L'Heritage de Fourier: Utopie Amoureuse et Liberation Sexuelle*
  NCFS - v32 - i3-4 - Spring-Summer 2004 - p359(3) [501+]
Sainte-Beuve, ou, la Liberte Critique
  FS - v58 - i2 - April 2004 - p273(3) [501+]

Brizuela, Barbara M. - *Mathematical Development in Young Children: Exploring Notations*
  Choice - v42 - i4 - Dec 2004 - p710(1) [1-50]

Brkic, Courtney Angela - *Stillness and Other Stories*
  NYTBR - Sept 19 2004 - p24 [501+]
The Stone Fields: An Epitaph for the Living
  y BL - v100 - i22 - August 2004 - p1892(1) [51-500]
  BW - v34 - i32 - August 8 2004 - p2(1) [501+]
  LJ - v129 - i12 - July 2004 - p82(1) [51-500]
  PW - v251 - i27 - July 5 2004 - p48(1) [51-500]
  Wom R Bks - v21 - i12 - Sept 2004 - p27(1) [501+]

Bro, Ruth Hill - *The E-Business Legal Arsenal: Practioner Agreements and Checklists*
  SciTech - v28 - i4 - Dec 2004 - p10(1) [1-50]

Broadband Networks; Proceedings
  SciTech - v28 - i4 - Dec 2004 - p148(1) [501+]

Broadbent, Marianne - *The New CIO Leader: Setting the Agenda and Delivering Results*
  ALJ - v53 - i4 - Nov 2004 - p431(2) [501+]

Broaddus, Cindi - *A Random Act: An Inspiring True Story of Fighting to Survive and Choosing to Forgive*
  PW - v252 - i9 - Feb 28 2005 - p53(1) [501+]

Broberg, Catherine - *Kenya in Pictures*
  c HNet - Sept 2004 - pNA [501+]

Broberg, Morten P. - *The European Commission's Jurisdiction to Scrutinise Mergers, 2nd Ed.*
  R&R Bk N - v19 - i1 - Feb 2004 - pNA [51-500]

Broch, Hermann - *Geist and Zeitgeist: Six Essays by Hermann Broch: The Spirit in an Unspiritual Age*
  R&R Bk N - v19 - i1 - Feb 2004 - p247(1) [51-500]

Brochert, Adam - *Surgery and Trauma*
  SciTech - v28 - i3 - Sept 2004 - p110(1) [51-500]
USMLE Step 2 Muck Exam, 2nd Ed.
  SciTech - v28 - i4 - Dec 2004 - p78(1) [51-500]

Brochu, Andre - *Devil's Paintbrush*
  CBRA - Annual 2003 - p155(1) [51-500]

Brochu, Serge - *Drugs and Crime Deviant Pathways*
  CS - v33 - i1 - Jan 2004 - p125-125 [501+]

Brock, Ann Graham - *Mary Magdalene, the First Apostle: The Struggle for Authority*
  Theol St - v65 - i3 - Sept 2004 - p673(2) [501+]

Brock-Broido, Lucie - *Trouble in Mind*
  Ga R - v58 - i2 - Summer 2004 - p502(1) [501+]
  VQR - v80 - i3 - Summer 2004 - p263(2) [1-50]
  ABR - v25 - i6 - Sept-Oct 2004 - p23(2) [501+]

Brock, Cole - *Fair Monaco*
  c HB - v81 - i1 - Jan-Feb 2005 - p73(2) [51-500]

Brock, David - *The Republican Noise Machine: Right-Wing Media and How It Corrupts Democracy (Read by Kramer, Michael). Audiobook Review*
  LJ - v130 - i2 - Feb 1 2005 - p124(1) [51-500]
The Republican Noise Machine: Right-Wing Media and How It Corrupts Democracy
  BW - v34 - i29 - July 18 2004 - p4(1) [1-50]
  Globe & Mail - Nov 13 2004 - pD23 [501+]
  Reason - v36 - i6 - Nov 2004 - p62(5) [501+]

Brock, Fred - *Live Well on Less Than You Think: The New York Times Guide to Achieving Your Financial Freedom*
  BL - v101 - i8 - Dec 15 2004 - p695(1) [51-500]

Brock, Geoffrey - K.
  Globe & Mail - Feb 19 2005 - pD12 [501+]

Brock, Gerald W. - *The Second Information Revolution*
  BHR - v78 - i2 - Summer 2004 - p316(4) [501+]
  JEL - v41 - i4 - Dec 2003 - p1417(1) [501+]
  JEL - v42 - i4 - Dec 2004 - p1157(2) [501+]

Brock, Peter - *'These Strange Criminals': An Anthology of Prison Memoirs by Conscientious Objectors from the Great War to the Cold War*
  Choice - v42 - i5 - Jan 2005 - p940(1) [51-500]

Brock, Steen - *Niels Bohr's Philosophy of Quantum Physics in the Light of the Helmholtzian Tradition of Theoretical Physics*
  Isis - v95 - i2 - June 2004 - p334(2) [501+]

Brock, Stuart - *The Ubiquitous Problem of Empty Names*
  RM - v58 - i1 - Sept 2004 - p220(1) [501+]

Brocken, Michael - *The British Folk Revival, 1944-2002*
  Notes - v61 - i3 - March 2005 - p734(4) [501+]
  R&R Bk N - v19 - i2 - May 2004 - p192(1) [51-500]

Brocker, Johannes - *Innovation Clusters and Interregional Competition*
  JEL - v41 - i4 - Dec 2003 - p1439(1) [501+]

Brockett, Ralph Grover - *Toward Ethical Practice*
  R&R Bk N - v19 - i4 - Nov 2004 - p183(1) [501+]

Brocklebank, John C. - *SAS for Forecasting Time Series*
  JEL - v42 - i1 - March 2004 - p246(1) [501+]

Brocklehurst, Marianne - *Miss Brocklehurst on the Nile: Diary of a Victorian Traveller in Egypt*
  Spec - v296 - Dec 18 2004 - p94(1) [501+]

Brocklehurst, Ruth - *Victorians*
  HT - v55 - i3 - March 2005 - p5(1) [501+]

Brockliss, L.W.B. - *Calvet's Web: Enlightenment and the Republic of Letters in Eighteenth-Century France*
  AHR - v109 - i2 - April 2004 - p628(2) [501+]
  JMH - v76 - i3 - Sept 2004 - p691(3) [501+]

Brockman, John - *Curious Minds: How a Child Becomes a Scientist*
  y BL - v101 - i2 - Sept 15 2004 - p187(1) [51-500]
  BW - v34 - i38 - Sept 19 2004 - p13(1) [501+]
  CH Bwatch - Feb 2005 - pNA [1-50]
  Choice - v42 - i5 - Jan 2005 - p873(1) [1-50]
  Globe & Mail - August 28 2004 - pD10 [501+]
  LJ - v129 - i14 - Sept 1 2004 - p183(1) [51-500]
  Nature - v431 - i7011 - Oct 21 2004 - p904(2) [501+]
  New Sci - v183 - i2462 - August 28 2004 - p50(1) [501+]
  PW - v251 - i29 - July 19 2004 - p153(1) [501+]
  y SB - v41 - i1 - Jan-Feb 2005 - p24(1) [501+]
Science at the Edge
  TimHES - v0 - i1672 - Dec 24 2004 - p24(1) [501+]

Brockmann, Suzanne - *The Defiant Hero (Read by MacDuffie, Carrington). Audiobook Review*
  y Kliatt - v39 - i1 - Jan 2005 - p40(1) [51-500]
Flashpoint (Read by Ewbank, Melanie). Audiobook Review
  Kliatt - v38 - i6 - Nov 2004 - p46(2) [51-500]
Hot Target
  BL - v101 - i8 - Dec 15 2004 - p713(1) [51-500]
  KR - v72 - i21 - Nov 1 2004 - p1021(1) [501+]
  LJ - v130 - i1 - Jan 1 2005 - p91(1) [501+]
  PW - v251 - i51 - Dec 20 2004 - p37(1) [51-500]

Brockmeier, Kevin - *The Truth About Cella*
  Ent W - i803 - Jan 28 2005 - p89 [51-500]

Brockoff, Evamaria - *Kaiser Heinrich II, 1002-1024*
  Med R - July 2004 - pNA [501+]

Brockway, Connie - *My Pleasure*
  BL - v101 - i5 - Nov 1 2004 - p469(1) [51-500]
  PW - v251 - i39 - Sept 27 2004 - p43(1) [51-500]
My Seduction
  y BL - v101 - i2 - Sept 15 2004 - p222(1) [51-500]

Broda, Krysia - *Compiled Labelled Deductive Systems: A Uniform Presentation of Non-Classical Logics*
  SciTech - v28 - i4 - Dec 2004 - p30(1) [51-500]

Brodax, Al - *Up Periscope Yellow: The Making of the Beatles Yellow Submarine*
  R&R Bk N - v19 - i3 - August 2004 - p263(1) [51-500]

Brode, Patrick - *Courted and Abandoned: Seduction in Canadian Law*
  AHR - v109 - i2 - April 2004 - p508(2) [501+]

Broder, Henryk M. - *A Jew in the New Germany*
  Choice - v42 - i1 - Sept 2004 - p179(1) [501+]
  HNet - Nov 2004 - pNA [501+]

Broderick, John - *The Pilgrimage*
  TLS - i5307 - Dec 17 2004 - p21-22 [501+]
The Waking of Willie Ryan
  TLS - i5307 - Dec 17 2004 - p21-22 [501+]

Broderick, Marian - *Wild Irish Women: Extraordinary Lives from History*
  ILS - v24 - i1 - Fall 2004 - p32(1) [51-500]

Brodersen, Soren - *Do-It-Yourself Work in North-Western Europe: Maintenance and Improvement of Homes*
  JEL - v42 - i1 - March 2004 - p247(1) [501+]

Brodeur, Raymond - *Femme, mystique et missionnaire. Marie Guyart de l'Incarnation*
  Can Lit - i181 - Summer 2004 - p94-95 [501+]

Brodhead, Michael J. - *Isaac C. Parker: Federal Justice on the Frontier*
  Roundup M - v11 - i6 - August 2004 - p23(1) [501+]

Brodie, Douglas - *A History of British Labour Law, 1867-1945*
  R&R Bk N - v19 - i1 - Feb 2004 - pNA [51-500]

Brodie, Marc - *The Politics of the Poor: The East End of London, 1885-1914*
  Choice - v42 - i3 - Nov 2004 - p553(1) [1-50]
  TLS - i5288 - August 6 2004 - p29(1) [51-500]

Brodsgaard, Kjeld Erik - *Bringing the Party Back In: How China Is Governed*
  R&R Bk N - v19 - i3 - August 2004 - p183(1) [501+]

Brodsgaard, Shel - *Soccer: Guarding the Goal*
  CBRA - Annual 2003 - p141(2) [51-500]

Brodsky, Allen - *Public Protection from Nuclear, Chemical, and Biological Terrorism: Health Physics Society 2004 Summer School*
  SciTech - v28 - i4 - Dec 2004 - p91(1) [51-500]

Brodsky, Anne E. - *With All Our Strength: The Revolutionary Association of the Women of Afghanistan*
  Choice - v41 - i7 - March 2004 - p1349(2) [501+]
  R&R Bk N - v19 - i4 - Nov 2004 - p133(1) [1-50]

Brodsky, Jenny - *Long-Term Care in Developing Countries: Ten Case-Studies*
  SciTech - v28 - i3 - Sept 2004 - p87(1) [51-500]

Brodsky, Joseph - *Conversations*
  WLT - v78 - i3-4 - Sept-Dec 2004 - p136(1) [501+]

Brody, Baruch A. - *Taking Issue: Pluralism and Casuistry in Bioethics*
  SciTech - v28 - i1 - March 2004 - p78(1) [51-500]

Brody, Evelyn - *Property-Tax Exemption for Charities: Mapping the Battlefield*
  JEL - v41 - i4 - Dec 2003 - p1311(2) [501+]

Brody, Larry - *Television Writing from the Inside Out: Your Channel to Success*
  R&R Bk N - v19 - i1 - Feb 2004 - p224(1) [1-50]

Brody, Miriam - *Victoria Woodhull: Free Spirit for Women's Rights*
  y Cur R - v44 - i7 - March 2005 - p12(1) [51-500]
  c SLJ - v51 - i2 - Feb 2005 - p145(2) [501+]

Broedel, Hans Peter - *The Malleus Maleficarum and the Construction of Witchcraft: Theology and Popular Belief*
Choice - v41 - i11-12 - July-August 2004 - p2084(1) [501+]

Broekmeyer, M. J. - *Stalin, the Russians, and Their War*
R&R Bk N - v20 - i1 - Feb 2005 - p32(1) [51-500]

Broelmann, Jobst - *Intuition und Wissenschaft in der Kreiseltechnik, 1750 bis 1930.*
Isis - v95 - i3 - Sept 2004 - p500(1) [501+]

Brogan, Jacqueline Vaught - *Violence Within/The Violence Without: Wallace Stevens and the Emergence of a Revolutionary Poetics*
R&R Bk N - v19 - i1 - Feb 2004 - p246(1) [51-500]

Brogan, Jan - *A Confidential Source*
KR - v73 - i5 - March 1 2005 - p260(1) [51-500]
LJ - v129 - i20 - Dec 1 2004 - p96(1) [51-500]

Brogan, Kathryn Struckel - *2005 Guide to Literary Agents*
Bwatch - Dec 2004 - pNA [51-500]
2005 Writer's Market
Bwatch - Dec 2004 - pNA [51-500]

Brogger, Suzanne - *The Jade Cat*
Globe & Mail - Oct 23 2004 - pD5 [501+]

Brogi, Alessandro - *A Question of Self-Esteem : The United States and the Cold War Choices in France and Italy, 1944-1958*
JAH - v91 - i3 - Dec 2004 - p1078(2) [501+]

Brogiolo, Gian Pietro - *Towns and Their Territories between Late Antiquity and the Early Middle Ages*
Class R - v53 - i2 - Nov 2003 - p444-446 [51+]

Broida, Rick - *101 Killer Apps for Your Pocket PC*
LJ - v129 - i14 - Sept 1 2004 - p182(1) [501+]

Broks, Paul - *Into the Silent Land: Travels in Neuropsychology*
y   Kliatt - v38 - i4 - July 2004 - p36(2) [51-500]

Bromberg, Alan R. - *Bromberg and Ribstein on Limited Liability Partnerships, the Revised Uniform Partnership Act, and the Uniform Limited Partnership Act, 2003 Ed.*
R&R Bk N - v19 - i1 - Feb 2004 - pNA [51-500]

Bromfield, Andrew - *Murder of the Leviathan*
BooChiTr - May 23 2004 - p2(1) [501+]
The Turkish Gambit
PW - v252 - i8 - Feb 21 2005 - p161(1) [51-500]

Bromhead, Geoffrey - *Struck*
CBRA - Annual 2003 - p155(2) [51-500]

Bromley, Michael L. - *Stretching It: The Story of the Limousine*
SciTech - v28 - i1 - March 2004 - p167(1) [51-500]

Bronchud, Miguel H. - *Principles of Molecular Oncology. 2nd Ed.*
SciTech - v28 - i1 - March 2004 - p91(1) [51-500]

Bronfen, Elisabeth - *Home in Hollywood: The Imaginary Geography of Cinema*
Choice - v42 - i7 - March 2005 - p1234(1) [51-500]
PW - v251 - i36 - Sept 6 2004 - p54(1) [51-500]

Bronfenbrenner, Urie - *Making Human Beings Human: Bioecological Perspectives on Human Development*
SciTech - v28 - i4 - Dec 2004 - p3(1) [1-50]

Brongers, E.H. - *Battle for the Hague, 1940: The First Great Airborne Operation in History*
R&R Bk N - v20 - i1 - Feb 2005 - p33(1) [51-500]

Bronner, Eric Stephen - *A Rumor about the Jews, Antisemitism, Conspiracy, and the Protocols of Zion*
IJMES - v36 - i4 - Nov 2004 - p697(2) [501+]

Bronner, Leila Leah - *Stories of Biblical Mothers: Maternal Power in the Hebrew Bible*
R&R Bk N - v19 - i3 - August 2004 - p22(1) [1-50]

Bronner, Stephen Eric - *Reclaiming the Enlightenment*
LJ - v129 - i14 - Sept 1 2004 - p166(2) [501+]
TLS - i5296 - Oct 1 2004 - p31(1) [501+]

Bronshtein, I.N. - *Handbook of Mathematics*
Choice - v42 - i3 - Nov 2004 - p521(1) [1-50]

Bronson, Eric - *Baseball and Philosophy: Thinking Outside the Batter's Box*
Choice - v42 - i1 - Sept 2004 - p143(1) [501+]
R&R Bk N - v19 - i3 - August 2004 - p88(1) [51-500]

Bronson, Tammy Carter - *Pillong*
LibMed - v23 - i1 - August-Sept 2004 - p79(1) [51-500]

Bronte, Charlotte - *Jane Eyre (Read by Stevenson, Juliet). Audiobook Review*
y   Kliatt - v39 - i1 - Jan 2005 - p45(1) [51-500]
The Letters of Charlotte Bronte: With a Selection of Letters by Family and Friends, Vol. 3.
Choice - v42 - i5 - Jan 2005 - p850(1) [1-50]

Broodbank, Cyprian - *An Island Archaeology of the Early Cyclades*
Am Ant - v69 - i3 - July 2004 - p588(2) [501+]

Brook, Peter - *Open Door: Thoughts on Acting and Theatre*
Econ - v374 - i8418 - March 19 2005 - p89US [501+]

Brook Stephen - *Hugh Johnson's Wine Companion: The Encyclopedia of Wines, Vineyards, and Winemakers, Rev. Ed.*
E-Streams - Nov 2004 - pNA [501+]

Brook, Timothy - *Opium Regimes: China, Britain, and Japan, 1839-1952*
Ch Rev Int - v10 - i2 - Fall 2003 - p307(20) [501+]

Brooke, Alan - *Tyburn: London's Fatal Tree*
CR - v285 - i1664 - Sept 2004 - p189(2) [501+]

Brooke, Iris - *English Children's Costume*
Bwatch - v26 - i9 - Sept 2004 - p2(1) [51-500]
English Costume of the Later Middle Ages: Fourteenth-Fifteenth Century, Rev. 3rd Ed.
R&R Bk N - v19 - i4 - Nov 2004 - p77(1) [51-500]

Brooke, Martha - *True Confessions of a Heartless Girl*
Kliatt - v38 - i6 - Nov 2004 - p14(1) [501+]

Brooke, Michael Z. - *New Product Development: Successful Innovation in the Marketplace*
JEL - v41 - i4 - Dec 2003 - p1398(1) [501+]

Brooke, Robert E. - *Rural Voices: Place-Conscious Education and the Teaching of Writing*
TCR - v106 - i5 - May 2004 - p973(4) [501+]

Brooke, Simon - *Upgrading*
BL - v100 - i21 - July 2004 - p1815(2) [51-500]
KR - v72 - i13 - July 1 2004 - p588(2) [501+]

Brooke-Smith, Robin - *Leading Learners, Leading Schools*
TCR - v106 - i5 - May 2004 - p880(4) [501+]

Brooker, Geoffrey - *Modern Classical Optics*
SciTech - v28 - i1 - March 2004 - p145(1) [51-500]
TimHES - v0 - i1668 - Nov 26 2004 - pXIV(1) [501+]

Brooker, Jewel Spears - *T.S. Eliot: The Contemporary Reviews*
Lon R Bks - v26 - i21 - Nov 4 2004 - p30(3) [501+]
TLS - i5299 - Oct 22 2004 - p24(1) [501+]

Brooker, Will - *Alice's Adventures: Lewis Carroll In Popular Culture*
Bwatch - Feb 2005 - pNA [51-500]
Choice - v42 - i2 - Oct 2004 - p290(1) [501+]

Brookes, Martin - *Extreme Measures: The Dark Visions and Bright Ideas of Francis Galton*
NY - v80 - i44 - Jan 24 2005 - p084 [501+]
KR - v72 - i16 - August 15 2004 - p784(1) [501+]
New Sci - v184 - i2476 - Dec 4 2004 - p54(1) [501+]
NYTBR - Oct 24 2004 - p34 [501+]
PW - v251 - i31 - August 2 2004 - p58(1) [501+]
SciTech - v28 - i4 - Dec 2004 - p61(1) [51-500]
TimHES - v0 - i1674 - Jan 14 2005 - p26(1) [501+]

Brookes, Tim - *Guitar: An American Life*
KR - v73 - i4 - Feb 15 2005 - p206(1) [501+]

Brookfield, Harold - *Agrodiversity: Learning from Farmers Across the World*
Choice - v42 - i1 - Sept 2004 - p127(2) [501+]
SciTech - v28 - i1 - March 2004 - p127(1) [51-500]

Brookfield, Michael E. - *Principles of Stratigraphy*
Choice - v42 - i1 - Sept 2004 - p134(1) [501+]

Brookhiser, Richard - *Gentleman Revolutionary: Gouverneur Morris, the Rake Who Wrote the Constitution*
Reason - v36 - i3 - July 2004 - p59(5) [501+]
NYTBR - Sept 19 2004 - p24 [501+]

Brooking, Tom - *History of New Zealand*
R&R Bk N - v19 - i4 - Nov 2004 - p52(1) [51-500]

Brookman, Philip - *Common Ground: Discovering Community in 150 Years of Art*
Black Iss - v7 - i1 - Jan-Feb 2005 - p44(1) [51-500]
LJ - v130 - i2 - Feb 1 2005 - p74(2) [51-500]

Brookner, Anita - *Leaving Home*
Globe & Mail - March 19 2005 - pD9 [501+]
Spec - v297 - i9211 - Feb 19 2005 - p37(2) [501+]
NS - v134 - i4727 - Feb 14 2005 - p53(1) [501+]
The Rules of Engagement
BooChiTr - Jan 4 2004 - p2(1) [501+]

Brookner, Janine M. - *Piercing the Veil of Secrecy: Litigation Against U.S. Intelligence*
R&R Bk N - v19 - i3 - August 2004 - p199(1) [1-50]

Brooks, Andree Aelion - *Russian Dance: A True Story of Intrigue and Passion in Stalinist Moscow*
TLS - i5296 - Oct 1 2004 - p27(1) [501+]

Brooks, Bill - *Law for Hire: Saving Masterson*
Roundup M - v11 - i6 - August 2004 - p26 [501+]

Brooks, Brenda - *Gotta Find Me an Angel*
Globe & Mail - March 12 2005 - pD8 [501+]

Brooks, Brian S. - *The Art of Editing in the Age of Convergence, 8th Ed.*
R&R Bk N - v19 - i4 - Nov 2004 - p227(1) [501+]

Brooks, Charles - *Best Editorial Cartoons of the Year, 2004 Ed.*
Bwatch - v26 - i9 - Sept 2004 - p1(1) [51-500]
R&R Bk N - v19 - i3 - August 2004 - p70(1) [51-500]

Brooks, Dana Marie - *Cut and Carve Candles: Beautiful Candles to Dip, Carve, Twist and Curl*
LJ - v130 - i3 - Feb 15 2005 - p126(1) [51-500]

Brooks, David - *On Paradise Drive: How We Live Now (and Always Have) in the Future Tense*
Bus W - i3890 - July 5 2004 - p26 [501+]
CC - v121 - i22 - Nov 2 2004 - p39(2) [501+]
Comw - v131 - i18 - Oct 22 2004 - p7(2) [501+]
Dis - v51 - i4 - Fall 2004 - p107(3) [501+]
Har Bus R - v82 - i6 - June 2004 - p28(1) [501+]
New R - August 2 2004 - p27 [501+]

Brooks, Douglas S. - *The Complete Book of Personal Training*
R&R Bk N - v19 - i3 - August 2004 - p87(1) [51-500]

Brooks, George E. - *Eurafricans in Western Africa: Commerce, Social Status, Gender, and Religious Observance from the Sixteenth to the Eighteenth Century*
AHR - v109 - i3 - June 2004 - p1020(2) [501+]
IJAHS - v37 - i1 - Wntr 2004 - p135-136 [501+]
JEL - v42 - i1 - March 2004 - p300(1) [501+]

Brooks, Geraldine - *March*
KR - v73 - i1 - Jan 1 2005 - p5(1) [501+]
PW - v251 - i51 - Dec 20 2004 - p34(1) [51-500]
Atl - v295 - i3 - April 2005 - p115(1) [501+]

Brooks, Ian - *Chambers Concise Dictionary*
TLS - i5294 - Sept 17 2004 - p24(1) [501+]

Brooks, Jacqueline Grennon - *Schooling for Life: Reclaiming the Essence of Learning*
TCR - v106 - i2 - Feb 2004 - p308-310 [501+]

Brooks, James F. - *Captives and Cousins: Slavery, Kinship, and Community in the Southwest Borderlands*
Am Ind CRJ - v28 - i1 - Winter 2004 - p85-90 [501+]
JSH - v70 - i3 - August 2004 - p639(3) [501+]

Brooks, James L. - *Spanglish*
LJ - v130 - i3 - Feb 15 2005 - p132(1) [51-500]

Brooks, Joanna - *American Lazarus: Religion and the Rise of African-American and Native American Literature*
Choice - v41 - i7 - March 2004 - p1294(1) [501+]
American Lazarus: Religion and the Rise of African-American and Native American Literatures
JAH - v91 - i3 - Dec 2004 - p998(2) [501+]

Brooks, Joe - *Joe Brooks on Fishing*
BL - v101 - i4 - Oct 15 2004 - p375(1) [51-500]

Brooks, Kevin - *Candy*
y   CCB-B - v58 - i6 - Feb 2005 - p245(2) [51-500]
y   Kliatt - v39 - i2 - March 2005 - p6(2) [51-500]
y   KR - v73 - i2 - Jan 15 2005 - p117(1) [51-500]
y   PW - v252 - i5 - Jan 31 2005 - p69(1) [51-500]
Kissing the Rain
c   LibMed - v23 - i1 - August-Sept 2004 - p68(1) [51-500]
Lucas (Read by Nielsen, Stina). Audiobook Review
y   BL - v101 - i9-10 - Jan 1 2005 - p887(1) [51-500]
y   Kliatt - v39 - i1 - Jan 2005 - p47(1) [51-500]
Lucas (Read by Nielson, Stina). Audiobook Review
c   SLJ - v51 - i2 - Feb 2005 - p77(1) [501+]

Brooks, Larry - *Bait and Switch*
PW - v251 - i49 - Dec 6 2004 - p32(2) [51-500]

Brooks, Leonard J. - *Business and Professional Ethics for Directors, Executives and Accountants*
R&R Bk N - v19 - i1 - Feb 2004 - p112(1) [51-500]

Brooks, Martha - *True Confessions of a Heartless Girl*
y   Can CL - i111-112 - Fall-Winter 2003 - p153(6) [501+]

Brooks, Robin - *The Mystery of the Portland Vase*
Spec - v295 - i9184 - August 14 2004 - p34(1) [501+]
The Portland Vase: The Extraordinary Odyssey of a Mysterious Roman Treasure
BL - v100 - i22 - August 2004 - p1887(2) [51-500]
KR - v72 - i13 - July 1 2004 - p611(2) [501+]

Brooks, Sheldon - *Life in the Arctic*
VOYA - v27 - i5 - Dec 2004 - p420(1) [51-500]

Brooks, Terry - *High Druid of Shannara: Jarka Ruis (Read by Brick, Scott). Audiobook Review*
c Kliatt - v38 - i4 - July 2004 - p51(1) [51-500]
High Druid of Shannara: Tanequil (Read by Boehmer, Paul). Audiobook Review
y Kliatt - v39 - i2 - March 2005 - p53(1) [51-500]
High Druid of Shannara: Tanequil
LJ - v129 - i12 - July 2004 - p75(1) [51-500]
PW - v251 - i31 - August 2 2004 - p56(1) [501+]

Brooks, Tim - *Lost Sounds: Blacks and the Birth of the Recording Industry, 1890-1919*
Choice - v42 - i2 - Oct 2004 - p301(2) [51-500]
NYTBR - Oct 31 2004 - p31 [501+]

Brooks, Walter R. - *Freddy and the Space Ship (Read by McDonough, John). Audiobook Review*
c SLJ - v50 - i12 - Dec 2004 - p73(2) [501+]

Brooks, William T. - *The New Science of Selling and Persuasion: How Smart Companies and Great Salespeople Sell*
R&R Bk N - v19 - i3 - August 2004 - p128(1) [51-500]

Brooks-Young, Susan - *101 Best Web Sites for District Leaders*
c LibMed - v23 - i3 - Nov-Dec 2004 - p90(1) [51-500]

Brooman, Josh - *Germany 1918-1945: Democracy and Dictatorship*
y TES - v0 - i4586 - June 4 2004 - pssss14(2) [501+]

Broome, Errol - *Drusilla the Lucky Duck (Illus. by Thompson, Sharon)*
c CBRA - Annual 2003 - p476(1) [51-500]
What A Goat! (Illus. by Thompson, Sharon)
c Res Links - v10 - i3 - Feb 2005 - p11(2) [51-500]

Broome, John - *All Star Comics Archives, Vol. 10*
y BL - v101 - i4 - Oct 15 2004 - p395(2) [51-500]

Broomfield, Samuel - *Congregation-to-Congregation Relationship: A Case Study of the Partnership Between a Liberian Church and a North American Church*
R&R Bk N - v19 - i4 - Nov 2004 - p28(1) [501+]

Broomhall, Susan - *Women and the Book Trade in Sixteenth-Century France*
FS - v58 - i1 - Jan 2004 - p84(3) [501+]
Six Ct J - v34 - i4 - Winter 2003 - p1120-1121 [501+]

Brophy, Alfred L. - *Reconstructing the Dreamland: The Tulsa Riot of 1921, Race, Reparations, and Reconciliation*
RAH - v32 - i1 - March 2004 - p76(8) [501+]

Brophy, Jere - *Motivating Students to Learn*
R&R Bk N - v19 - i3 - August 2004 - p218(1) [1-50]

Brophy, Peter - *Libraries Without Walls 4: The Delivery of Library Services to Distant Users*
Lib & Cul - v39 - i3 - Summer 2004 - p338(3) [501+]
Libraries Without Walls 5: The Distributed Delivery of Library and Information Services
R&R Bk N - v19 - i4 - Nov 2004 - p256(1) [501+]

Brophy, Philip - *100 Modern Soundtracks*
NS - v133 - i4716 - Nov 29 2004 - p48(1) [51-500]

Brophy, Sarah - *Witnessing AIDS: Writing, Testimony, and the Work of Mourning*
R&R Bk N - v19 - i3 - August 2004 - p258(1) [51-500]

Brose, Eric Dorn - *The Kaiser's Army: The Politics of Military Technology in Germany During the Machine Age, 1870-1918*
CEH - v37 - i3 - Summer 2004 - p444(3) [501+]

Brosnan, John - *Mothership*
KR - v73 - i5 - March 1 2005 - p265(2) [51-500]

Brosnan, Kathleen A. - *Uniting Mountain and Plan: Cities, Law and Environmental Change along the Front Range*
WHQ - v35 - i1 - Spring 2004 - p76-77 [501+]

Brosnan, Meredith - *Mr. Dynamite*
PW - v251 - i31 - August 2 2004 - p53(1) [501+]

Bross, Kristina - *Dry Bones and Indian Sermons: Praying Indians and Colonial American Identity*
W&M Q - v61 - i4 - Oct 2004 - p747-750 [501+]

Brossler, Adam - *Green Park (Reading Business Park): Phase 2 Excavations 1995, Neolitich and Bronze Age Sites*
R&R Bk N - v19 - i3 - August 2004 - p39(1) [51-500]

Brotak, Ed - *Wild about Weather: 50 Wet, Windy and Wonderful Activities*
c BL - v101 - i7 - Dec 1 2004 - p665(1) [51-500]

Broth, Ed - *Stories from a Moron: Real Stories Rejected by Real Magazines*
BL - v101 - i7 - Dec 1 2004 - p626(1) [51-500]

Brotherton, David C. - *The Almighty Latin King and Queen Nation: Street Politics and the Transformation of a New York City Gang*
Choice - v42 - i2 - Oct 2004 - p375(2) [51-500]
R&R Bk N - v19 - i3 - August 2004 - p165(1) [501+]

Brotherton, Mike - *Star Dragon*
y Analog - v124 - i6 - June 2004 - p132(6) [501+]

Brottman, Mikita - *Funny Peculiar: Gershon Legman and the Psychopathology of Humor*
Choice - v42 - i4 - Dec 2004 - p644(1) [1-50]

Brotton, Jerry - *The Renaissance Bazaar: From the Silk Road to Michelangelo*
J Hist G - v30 - i1 - Jan 2004 - p196(3) [501+]

Broughton, Janet - *Descartes's Method of Doubt*
Phil R - v113 - i1 - Jan 2004 - p101(25) [501+]

Broughton, Vanda - *Essential Classification*
LJ - v130 - i3 - Feb 15 2005 - p164(1) [51-500]

Brouwer, Floor - *Governance of Water-Related Conflicts in Agriculture: New Directions in Agri-Environmental and Water Policies in the EU*
R&R Bk N - v19 - i1 - Feb 2004 - p96(1) [1-50]

Brouwer, Ruth Compton - *Modern Women Modernizing Men: The Changing Missions of Three Professional Women in Asia and Africa*
Can Lit - i182 - Autumn 2004 - p98(3) [501+]

Browdy de Hernandez, Jennifer - *Women Writing Resistance: Essays on Latin America and the Caribbean*
ABR - v25 - i6 - Sept-Oct 2004 - p5(2) [51-500]

Brower, Brock - *Blue Dog, Green River (Illus. by Lawton, Nancy)*
BL - v101 - i9-10 - Jan 1 2005 - p811(2) [1-50]
KR - v72 - i23 - Dec 1 2004 - p1101(1) [501+]
The Late Great Creature
MFSF - v107 - i6 - Dec 2004 - p162(1) [51-500]

Brower, Daniel - *Turkestan and the Fate of the Russian Empire*
Slav R - v63 - i3 - Fall 2004 - p643-645 [501+]

Brower, Harry - *Whales, They Give Themselves: Conversations with Harry Brower, Sr.*
R&R Bk N - v19 - i4 - Nov 2004 - p55(1) [51-500]

Browing, Christopher - *The Origins of the Final Solution: The Evolution of Nazi Jewish Policy, September 1939-March 1942*
Choice - v42 - i2 - Oct 2004 - p361(1) [51-500]

Brown, A. Duncan - *Feed or Feedback: Agriculture, Population Dynamics and the State of the Planet*
Choice - v41 - i7 - March 2004 - p1319(2) [501+]
JEL - v41 - i4 - Dec 2003 - p1435(2) [501+]

Brown, A. Peter - *The Second Golden Age of the Viennese Symphony: Brahms, Bruckner, Dvorak, Mahler, and Selected Contemporaries*
Choice - v41 - i7 - March 2004 - p1305(1) [501+]

Brown, Adrienne Maree - *How to Get Stupid White Men Out of Office: The Anti-Politics, Un-Boring Guide to Power*
R&R Bk N - v19 - i3 - August 2004 - p179(1) [501+]

Brown, Allan - *Digital Terrestrial Television in Europe*
SciTech - v28 - i4 - Dec 2004 - p9(1) [1-50]

Brown, Alyson - *English Society and the Prison: Time, Culture, and Politics in the Development of the Modern Prison, 1850-1920*
Choice - v41 - i11-12 - July-August 2004 - p2111(1) [501+]

Brown, Amanda - *Family Trust*
y Kliatt - v38 - i5 - Sept 2004 - p19(2) [51-500]

Brown, Andrew (b. 1955 -) - *In the Beginning Was the Worm: Finding the Secrets of Life in a Tiny Hermaphrodite*
SciTech - v28 - i1 - March 2004 - p68(1) [51-500]

Brown, Andrew (b. 1964 -) - *Church and Society in England, 1000-1500*
R&R Bk N - v19 - i1 - Feb 2004 - p17(1) [51-500]

Brown, Anita - *27 East*
Dbt - v71 - i12 - Dec 2004 - p83(1) [501+]

Brown, Ann Eckert - *American Wall Stenciling, 1790-1840*
Ant&CM - v108 - i6 - August 2003 - p16(1) [501+]

Brown-Azarowicz, Marjory Frances - *The Hobbyist's Guide to Playing the Piano*
M Ed J - v91 - i4 - March 2005 - p67(1) [501+]

Brown, Barbara - *My Breasts, My Choice: Journeys through Surgery*
CBRA - Annual 2003 - p428(1) [51-500]

Brown, Barbara W. - *Black Roots in Southeastern Connecticut, 1650-1900*
EFHM - v58 - i3 - May-June 2004 - p58(1) [51-500]

Tapestry: A Living History of the Black Family in Southeastern Connecticut
EFHM - v58 - i3 - May-June 2004 - p58(1) [51-500]

Brown, Ben - *Fifty-Five Feathers (Illus. by Taylor, Helen)*
c Magpies - v19 - i5 - Nov 2004 - p6S(1) [501+]

Brown, Bern Will - *Arctic Journal: A Fifty-Year Adventure in Canada's North*
CBRA - Annual 2003 - p35(1) [51-500]

Brown, Beverly Louise - *The Genius of Rome, 1592-1623*
Ren Q - v57 - i3 - Fall 2004 - p995(3) [501+]

Brown, Bill - *A Sense of Things: The Object Matter of American Literature*
T&C - v45 - i3 - July 2004 - p672-673 [501+]

Brown, Brendan - *Euro on Trial: To Reform or Split Up?*
Choice - v42 - i2 - Oct 2004 - p338(1) [51-500]

Brown, Bryson - *The Pragmatics of Empirical Adequacy*
RM - v58 - i1 - Sept 2004 - p213(3) [501+]

Brown, Campbell - *Campbell Brown's Civil War: With Ewell and the Army of Northern Virginia*
HNet - July 2004 - pNA [501+]

Brown, Candy Gunther - *The Word in the World: Evangelical Writing, Publishing, and Reading in America, !789-1880.*
BHR - v78 - i3 - Autumn 2004 - p532(3) [501+]
The Word in the World: Evangelical Writing, Publishing, and Reading in America, 1789-1880
Choice - v42 - i2 - Oct 2004 - p308(2) [51-500]

Brown, Carolyn - *Augusta*
BL - v101 - i8 - Dec 15 2004 - p713(1) [51-500]
Garnet
BL - v101 - i1 - Sept 1 2004 - p71(2) [51-500]

Brown, Carrie - *Confinement*
CQ - v56 - i2-3 - Spring-Summer 2004 - p101(3) [501+]
y SLJ - v50 - i11 - Nov 2004 - p176(1) [51-500]

Brown, Cecil - *Stagolee Shot Billy*
NYTBR - Oct 24 2004 - p30 [501+]

Brown, Charles E. - *Beginning Dreamweaver MX 2004*
SciTech - v28 - i3 - Sept 2004 - p155(1) [51-500]
SciTech - v28 - i3 - Sept 2004 - p155(1) [51-500]

Brown, Charles N. - *The Locus Awards: Thirty Years of the Best in Science Fiction and Fantasy*
BL - v100 - i21 - July 2004 - p1828(1) [1-50]
ChrSFF&H - v26 - i10 - Oct 2004 - p50(1) [501+]

Brown, Christy - *My Left Foot (Read by Mullen, Conor). Audiobook Review*
y Kliatt - v39 - i2 - March 2005 - p60(1) [51-500]

Brown, Clive - *A Portrait of Mendelssohn*
NYRB - v51 - i17 - Nov 4 2004 - p44(3) [501+]

Brown, Colin - *A Short Story of Indonesia: The Unlikely Nation?*
Choice - v42 - i2 - Oct 2004 - p349(1) [51-500]

Brown, Craig - *How Do You Raise a Raisin?*
c LibMed - v22 - i5 - Feb 2004 - p61(1) [501+]

Brown, Curtis M. - *Brown's Boundary Control and Legal Principles, 5th Ed.*
R&R Bk N - v19 - i1 - Feb 2004 - pNA [51-500]

Brown, Cynthia - *Lost Liberties: Ashcroft and the Assault on Personal Freedom*
ABR - v25 - i6 - Sept-Oct 2004 - p9(2) [501+]

Brown, D.J. - *Quinoxalines: Supplement 2*
SciTech - v28 - i1 - March 2004 - p55(1) [51-500]

Brown, Dale - *Plan of Attack (Read by Dufris, William). Audiobook Review*
y Kliatt - v39 - i2 - March 2005 - p55(1) [51-500]

Brown, Dan - *Angels and Demons (Read by Poe, Richard). Audiobook Review*
LJ - v129 - i14 - Sept 1 2004 - p200(1) [51-500]
The Da Vinci Code
Globe & Mail - Dec 18 2004 - pD14 [1-50]
Quad - v48 - i9 - Sept 2004 - p93(2) [501+]
New R - v231 - August 16 2004 - p21 [501+]
Digital Fortress (Read by Michael, Paul). Audiobook Review
BL - v100 - i21 - July 2004 - p1855(1) [1-50]
Kliatt - v38 - i6 - Nov 2004 - p44(1) [51-500]

Brown, David (1972-) - *Palmerston and the Politics of Foreign Policy: 1846-55*
HNet - July 2004 - pNA [501+]

Brown, David Alan - *Virtue and Beauty: Leonardo's 'Geneva de' Benci' and Renaissance Portraits of Women*
Six Ct J - v35 - i3 - Fall 2004 - p923-924 [501+]

Brown, David E. - *Orthopedic Secrets, 3rd Ed.*
SciTech - v28 - i1 - March 2004 - p112(1) [51-500]

Brown, David H. - *Santeria Enthroned: Art, Ritual, and Innovation in an Afro-Cuban Religion*
Choice - v41 - i11-12 - July-August 2004 - p2086(1) [501+]
IJAHS - v37 - i2 - Spring 2004 - p385-387 [501+]
JR - v85 - i1 - Jan 2005 - p177(2) [501+]

Brown, David L. - *Challenges of Rural America in the Twenty-First Century*
    Choice - v42 - i3 - Nov 2004 - p571(1) [1-50]
Brown, Dee - *Showdown at Little Big Horn*
    Roundup M - v12 - i1 - Oct 2004 - p21(1) [51-500]
Brown, Diane R. - *In and out of Our Right Minds: The Mental Health of African American Women*
    SciTech - v28 - i1 - March 2004 - p95(1) [51-500]
Brown, Don - *Kid Blink Beats the World (Illus. by Brown, Don)*
  c BL - v101 - i2 - Sept 15 2004 - p240(1) [51-500]
  c BW - v34 - i50 - Dec 12 2004 - p8(1) [501+]
  c CCB-B - v58 - i4 - Dec 2004 - p162(1) [51-500]
  c HB - v80 - i6 - Nov-Dec 2004 - p724(2) [501+]
  c KR - v72 - i17 - Sept 1 2004 - p861(1) [51-500]
  c PW - v251 - i42 - Oct 18 2004 - p64(1) [51-500]
    SLJ - v50 - i12 - Dec 2004 - p98(1) [501+]
Mack Made Movies (Illus. by Brown, Don)
  c SLJ - v50 - i11 - Nov 2004 - p65(1) [51-500]
Odd Boy Out: Young Albert Einstein (Illus. by Brown, Don)
  c BL - v101 - i1 - Sept 1 2004 - p116(1) [501+]
  c BW - v34 - i37 - Sept 12 2004 - p12(1) [51-500]
  c CCB-B - v58 - i2 - Oct 2004 - p61(1) [51-500]
  c Globe & Mail - Nov 20 2004 - pD26 [51-500]
  c HB - v80 - i5 - Sept-Oct 2004 - p604(2) [51-500]
  c Inst - v114 - i5 - Jan-Feb 2005 - p73(2) [501+]
  c KR - v72 - i17 - Sept 1 2004 - p861(1) [51-500]
  c PW - v251 - i42 - Oct 18 2004 - p63(1) [51-500]
  c SLJ - v50 - i10 - Oct 2004 - p138(2) [51-500]
Odd Boy Out: Young Albert Einstein
  c NH - v113 - i10 - Dec 2004 - p50 [501+]
Brown, E.S. - *Asthma: Social and Psychological Factors and Psychosomatic Syndromes*
    SciTech - v28 - i1 - March 2004 - p102(1) [51-500]
Brown, Earl J. - *Pathology: PreTest Self-Assessment and Review, 11th Ed.*
    SciTech - v28 - i4 - Dec 2004 - p87(1) [1-50]
Brown, Elaine Meryl - *Lemon City*
    BL - v100 - i21 - July 2004 - p1816(1) [1-50]
    DroRevMy - v24 - i4 - July-August 2004 - p6(1) [501+]
    PW - v251 - i29 - July 19 2004 - p144(1) [51-500]
Brown, Elizabeth - *Ferguson Coal Country Christmas*
    CE - v81 - i2 - Winter 2004 - p107(1) [51-500]
Brown, Fleda - *The Women Who Loved Elvis All Their Lives*
  y Kliatt - v38 - i5 - Sept 2004 - p38(2) [51-500]
Brown, Frank Burch - *Good Taste, Bad Taste and Christian Taste: Aesthetics in Religious Life*
    JAAR - v72 - i4 - Dec 2004 - p1026(3) [501+]
Brown, George E. - *The Pruning of Trees, Shrubs, and Conifers. 2nd Ed.*
    Ref Rev - August 2004 - pNA [501+]
    SciTech - v28 - i1 - March 2004 - p129(1) [51-500]
Brown, Gregory S. - *Cultures in Conflict: The French Revolution*
    R&R Bk N - v19 - i1 - Feb 2004 - p35(1) [1-50]
Brown, Harry J. - *Injun Joe's Ghost: The Indian Mixed-Blood in American Writing*
    Choice - v42 - i5 - Jan 2005 - p850(1) [1-50]
Brown, Helen Gurley - *Dear Pussycat*
    CJR - v43 - i4 - Nov-Dec 2004 - p67(2) [501+]
Brown, Howard H. - *Breakthrough Management for Not-for-Profit Organizations: Beyond Survival in the 21st Century*
    R&R Bk N - v19 - i1 - Feb 2004 - p92(1) [1-50]
Brown, Ian - *Journey's Beginning: The Gateway Theatre Building and Company, 1884-1965*
    R&R Bk N - v19 - i4 - Nov 2004 - p238(1) [501+]
Brown, Ian W. - *Bottle Creek. A Pensacola Culture Site in South Alabama*
    Am Ant - v70 - i1 - Jan 2005 - p201(2) [501+]
Brown, Irene Quenzler - *The Hanging of Ephraim Wheeler: A Story of Rape, Incest, and Justice in Early America*
    AHR - v109 - i2 - April 2004 - p520(2) [501+]
    J Soc H - v38 - i2 - Winter 2004 - p545(2) [501+]
    JAH - v91 - i1 - June 2004 - p225-226 [501+]
    RAH - v32 - i4 - Dec 2004 - p499-505 [501+]
Brown, Jackie - *Little Cricket*
  c BL - v100 - i21 - July 2004 - p1841(2) [1-50]
  c CCB-B - v57 - i11 - July-August 2004 - p456(2) [501+]
  c LibMed - v23 - i1 - August-Sept 2004 - p67(1) [51-500]
  c PW - v251 - i28 - July 12 2004 - p64(1) [51-500]
  c SLJ - v50 - i7 - July 2004 - p98(2) [51-500]
  y VOYA - v27 - i3 - August 2004 - p207(1) [1-50]

Brown, James - *I Feel Good: A Memoir of a Life of Soul People* - v63 - i3 - Jan 24 2005 - p52 [51-500]
    BL - v101 - i7 - Dec 1 2004 - p618(1) [51-500]
    Globe & Mail - March 12 2005 - pD17 [501+]
    LJ - v130 - i1 - Jan 1 2005 - p114(1) [51-500]
Brown, James (American musician) - *I Feel Good: A Memoir of a Life of Soul*
    NYTBR - Feb 20 2005 - p30 [501+]
Brown, Jane - *The Garden at Buckingham Palace: An Illustrated History*
    BL - v101 - i7 - Dec 1 2004 - p626(1) [51-500]
Tales of the Rose Tree: Ravishing Rhododendrons and Their Travels around the World
    TimHES - v0 - i1649 - July 16 2004 - p28(1) [501+]
Brown, Jason C. - *Motor Vehicle Structures: Concepts and Fundamentals*
    SciTech - v28 - i1 - March 2004 - p168(1) [51-500]
Brown, Jeff - *Flat Stanley Audio Collection (Read by Pinkwater, Daniel). Audiobook Review*
  c SLJ - v50 - i10 - Oct 2004 - pS30(1) [51-500]
Brown, Jeffrey - *Drawn and Quarterly Showcase: Book Two*
    BL - v101 - i1 - Sept 1 2004 - p76(1) [501+]
Drawn and Quarterly Showcase, Vol. 2
    LJ - v130 - i1 - Jan 1 2005 - p88(1) [51-500]
Brown, Jeremy - *Dementia: Your Questions Answered*
    SciTech - v28 - i1 - March 2004 - p100(1) [51-500]
Brown, Jerry - *Bighead*
    PW - v251 - i51 - Dec 20 2004 - p39(1) [51-500]
Brown, Jo - *Hoppity Skip Little Chick (Illus. by Brown, Jo)*
  c KR - v73 - i5 - March 1 2005 - p284(1) [51-500]
Brown, Joanne - *Declarations of Independence: Empowered Girls in Young Adult Literature, 1990-2001*
    SFS - v31 - i1 - March 2004 - p138-138 [501+]
Brown, John L. - *Making the Most of Understanding by Design*
    R&R Bk N - v19 - i4 - Nov 2004 - p186(1) [501+]
Brown, John M. - *Rotational Spectroscopy of Diatomic Molecules*
    Phys Today - v57 - i12 - Dec 2004 - p68-69 [501+]
Brown, John Robert - *A Concise History of Jazz*
    Teach Mus - v12 - i4 - Feb 2005 - p79(1) [51-500]
Brown, Jonatha A. - *Cesar Chavez*
  c SLJ - v50 - i7 - July 2004 - p118(1) [51-500]
Brown, Joshua - *Beyond the Lines: Pictorial Reporting, Everyday Life, and the Crisis of Gilded Age America*
    JIH - v34 - i3 - Wntr 2004 - p478(3) [501+]
    RAH - v32 - i2 - June 2004 - p204-10 [501+]
A Good Idea of Hell: Letters from a Chasseur-a-Pied
    J Mil H - v68 - i3 - April 2004 - p618-619 [501+]
Brown, Judith E. - *Nutrition Through the Life Cycle, 2nd Ed.*
    SciTech - v28 - i3 - Sept 2004 - p68(1) [51-500]
Brown, Judith M. - *Christians, Cultural Interactions, and India's Religious Traditions*
    CH - v73 - i4 - Dec 2004 - p903(3) [501+]
Nehru: A Political Life
    A Aff - v35 - i2 - July 2004 - p238-239 [501+]
    BW - v34 - i1 - Jan 4 2004 - p2(1) [501+]
    Lon R Bks - v26 - i13 - July 8 2004 - p6(3) [501+]
    New R - Feb 14 2005 - p25 [501+]
    TimHES - v0 - i1657 - Sept 10 2004 - p33(1) [501+]
Brown, Kate - *A Biography of No Place: From Ethnic Borderland to Soviet Heartland*
    TLS - i5295 - Sept 24 2004 - p10-11 [501+]
Brown, Kathleen M. Pelletier - *Management Guidelines for Nurse Practitioners Working with Women, 2nd Ed.*
    SciTech - v28 - i1 - March 2004 - p115(1) [51-500]
Brown, Keith - *The Past in Question: Modern Macedonia and the Uncertainties of Nation*
    AHR - v109 - i3 - June 2004 - p1002(2) [501+]
    Slav R - v63 - i4 - Winter 2004 - p869(2) [501+]
Brown, Keven - *Evolution and Baha'i Belief Abdul-baha Response to Nineteenth Century Darwinism, Studies in Babi and Baha'i Religions*
    IJMES - v36 - i1 - Feb 2004 - p148-149 [501+]
Brown, Laura - *Project Management for the Pharmaceutical Industry*
    SciTech - v28 - i4 - Dec 2004 - p8(1) [1-50]
Brown, Leo M. - *Media Relations for Public Safety Professionals*
    R&R Bk N - v19 - i3 - August 2004 - p167(1) [501+]

Brown, Liam D'Arcy - *Green Dragon, Sombre Warrior: A Journey Around China's Symbolic Frontiers*
    LJ - v129 - i16 - Oct 1 2004 - p102(1) [51-500]
Brown, Lillian - *Your Public Best: The Complete Guide to Making Successful Public Appearances in the Meeting Room, on the Platform, and on TV, 2nd Ed.*
    R&R Bk N - v19 - i2 - May 2004 - p129 [51-500]
Brown, Lloyd J. - *Pediatrics*
    SciTech - v28 - i4 - Dec 2004 - p111(1) [1-50]
Brown, Lyn Mike - *Girlfighting: Betrayal and Rejection Among Girls*
    CS - v33 - i5 - Sept 2004 - p622-622 [501+]
Brown, M. Christopher - *Black Colleges: New Perspectives on Policy and Practice*
    R&R Bk N - v19 - i4 - Nov 2004 - p192(1) [501+]
Brown, M. Kathryn - *Ancient Mesoamerican Warfare*
    HNet - August 2004 - pNA [501+]
    R&R Bk N - v19 - i1 - Feb 2004 - p66(1) [51-500]
Brown, Malcolm - *After the Market: Economics, Moral Agreement, and the Churches' Mission*
    R&R Bk N - v19 - i4 - Nov 2004 - p19(1) [51-500]
Brown, Malcolm Hamrick - *A Shostakovich Casebook*
    Choice - v42 - i2 - Oct 2004 - p303(2) [51-500]
Brown, Malcolm Kenneth - *The Narratives of Konon*
    Class R - v54 - i1 - May 2004 - p56(1) [501+]
Brown, Marc - *Arthur, It's Only Rock 'n' Roll (Illus. by Brown, Marc)*
  c RT - v57 - Oct 2003 - p168 [1-50]
Brown, Marcia - *Stone Soup*
  c Globe & Mail - March 12 2005 - pD14 [51-500]
Brown, Margaret Wise - *Christmas in the Barn (Illus. by Goode, Diane)*
  c BL - v101 - i3 - Oct 1 2004 - p332(1) [51-500]
  c BW - v34 - i50 - Dec 12 2004 - p9(1) [501+]
  c KR - v72 - i21 - Nov 1 2004 - p1048(1) [51-500]
The Golden Egg Book (Illus. by Weisgard, Leonard)
  c CH Bwatch - v14 - i7 - July 2004 - p4(1) [51-500]
Good Night, Moon
  c RT - v57 - Sept 2003 - p100 [51-500]
Brown, Matthew - *Debussy's 'Iberia'*
    MT - v145 - i1887 - Summer 2004 - p118(2) [501+]
    Notes - v61 - i2 - Dec 2004 - p419(3) [501+]
Brown, Melissa J. - *Is Taiwan Chinese?: The Impact of Culture, Power, and Migration on Changing Identities*
    Ch Rev Int - v11 - i1 - Spring 2004 - p30(5) [501+]
    Choice - v42 - i2 - Oct 2004 - p349(1) [51-500]
Brown, Meta - *Drug Calculations: Process and Problems for Clinical Practice, 7th Ed.*
    SciTech - v28 - i1 - March 2004 - p123(1) [51-500]
Brown, Michael E. - *Grave New World: Security Challenges in the 21st Century*
    R&R Bk N - v19 - i1 - Feb 2004 - pNA [51-500]
Brown, Michael F. - *Who Owns Native Culture?*
    JAH - v91 - i3 - Dec 2004 - p1111(2) [501+]
    JEL - v41 - i4 - Dec 2003 - p1442(1) [501+]
  y Kliatt - v39 - i1 - Jan 2005 - p32(1) [51-500]
Brown, Michael K. - *White Washing Race: The Myth of a Color-Blind Society*
    PSQ - v119 - i4 - Winter 2004 - p699(2) [501+]
Whitewashing Race: The Myth of a Color-Blind Society
    Dis - v51 - i3 - Summer 2004 - p91(4) [501+]
    JAH - v91 - i3 - Dec 2004 - p1109(2) [501+]
    JEL - v41 - i4 - Dec 2003 - p1382(1) [501+]
    NYRB - v51 - i19 - Dec 2 2004 - p29(4) [501+]
    Soc Ser R - v79 - i1 - March 2005 - p208(1) [51-500]
Brown, Michael V. - *Audel Managing Maintenance Planning and Scheduling*
    SciTech - v28 - i3 - Sept 2004 - p171(1) [51-500]
Brown, Michelle P. - *The Lindisfarne Gospels: Society, Spirituality and the Scribe*
    CH - v73 - i3 - Sept 2004 - p685(2) [501+]
Brown, Monica - *Gang Nation: Delinquent Citizens in Puerto Rican, Chicano, and Chicana Narratives*
    Am Q - v56 - i4 - Dec 2004 - p1135(10) [501+]
My Name Is Celia/Me llamo Celia: The Life of Celia Cruz/la vida de Celia Cruz (Illus. by Lopez, Rafael)
  c SLJ - v51 - i1 - Jan 2005 - p120(1) [51-500]
Brown, Oral Lee - *The Promise: How One Woman Made Good on Her Extraordinary Pact to Send a Classroom of First Graders to College*
    KR - v73 - i2 - Jan 15 2005 - p96(1) [501+]
    LJ - v129 - i20 - Dec 1 2004 - p90(1) [51-500]
    PW - v252 - i9 - Feb 28 2005 - p52(2) [51-500]

Brown, Pamela Allen - *Better a Shrew than a Sheep: Women, Drama and the Culture of Jest in Early Modern England*
Critm - v46 - i2 - Spring 2004 - p281(18) [501+]
Better a Shrew than a Sheep: Women, Drama, and the Culture of Jest in Early Modern England
Ren Q - v57 - i3 - Fall 2004 - p1145(3) [501+]
Six Ct J - v35 - i3 - Fall 2004 - p869-870 [501+]

Brown, Patricia Fortini - *Private Lives in Renaissance Venice: Art, Architecture, and the Family*
Apo - v160 - i514 - Dec 2004 - p86(2) [501+]
Choice - v42 - i5 - Jan 2005 - p840(1) [1-50]
NYTBR - Dec 5 2004 - p86 [501+]
TLS - i5291 - August 27 2004 - p23(1) [501+]

Brown, Paul B. - *Publishing Confidential*
Bwatch - v26 - i7 - July 2004 - p11(1) [51-500]

Brown, Phyllis R. - *Hrotsvit of Gandersheim: Contexts, Identities, Affinities, and Performances*
Choice - v42 - i4 - Dec 2004 - p665(1) [1-50]

Brown, R. Harold - *The Greening of Georgia: The Improvement of the Environment in the Twentieth Century*
JSH - v70 - i3 - August 2004 - p710(2) [501+]

Brown, Raymond E. - *An Introduction to the Gospel of John*
CC - v121 - i21 - Oct 19 2004 - p32(2) [501+]
TT - v61 - i2 - July 2004 - p232(4) [501+]

Brown, Rebecca - *Excerpts from a Family Medical Dictionary*
SciTech - v28 - i4 - Dec 2004 - p92(1) [51-500]

Brown, Rita Mae - *Cat's Eyewitness: A Mrs. Murphy Mystery*
PW - v252 - i5 - Jan 31 2005 - p52(1) [51-500]
Whisker of Evil (Read by Forbes, Kate). Audiobook Review
BL - v101 - i7 - Dec 1 2004 - p678(1) [51-500]
Kliatt - v38 - i6 - Nov 2004 - p53(1) [51-500]
Whisker of Evil (Illus. by Gellatly, Michael)
y SLJ - v50 - i9 - Sept 2004 - p234(1) [51-500]

Brown, Robert D. - *Canadian Conundrums: View from the Clifford Clark Visiting Economists*
CBRA - Annual 2003 - p323(1) [501+]

Brown, Robert E. - *Jonathan Edwards and the Bible*
NEQ - v77 - i2 - June 2004 - p333-334 [501+]

Brown, Robert S. - *Case Studies in Sport Communication*
Choice - v42 - i1 - Sept 2004 - p143(1) [501+]

Brown, Roger - *William Stott of Oldham, 1857-1900: "A Comet Rushing to the Sun."*
Choice - v42 - i4 - Dec 2004 - p648(1) [1-50]

Brown, Ronald J. - *A Few Good Men: The Story of the Fighting Fifth Marines*
Mar Crp G - v88 - i2 - Feb 2004 - p56(1) [501+]

Brown, Russell - *Photoshop Show*
Bwatch - v26 - i8 - August 2004 - p6(2) [51-500]

Brown, Ruth - *Lion in the Grass*
c Sch Lib - v52 - i4 - Winter 2004 - p186(1) [51-500]

Brown, Sam - *Rainbows and Worms: Science Experiments for Preschool Children. Rev. Ed.*
SLJ - v50 - i10 - Oct 2004 - pS71(2) [51-500]

Brown, Sandra - *Hello, Darkness (Read by Slezak, Victor). Audiobook Review*
LJ - v129 - i14 - Sept 1 2004 - p200(1) [51-500]
Sunny Chandler's Return (Read by MacDonald, Beth). Audiobook Review
LJ - v129 - i16 - Oct 1 2004 - p118(1) [51-500]
White Hot
BL - v100 - i21 - July 2004 - p1796(2) [51-500]
KR - v72 - i13 - July 1 2004 - p589(1) [501+]
LJ - v129 - i12 - July 2004 - p67(1) [51-500]
Words of Silk (Read by Ferrone, Richard). Audiobook Review
LJ - v129 - i19 - Nov 15 2004 - p97(1) [51-500]

Brown, Sandra L. - *The Moody Pews: A 52 Week Devotional for the Flower Child/Baby Boomer*
LJ - v130 - i4 - March 1 2005 - p92(1) [51-500]

Brown, Scot - *Fighting for US: Maulana Karenga, the US Organization, and Black Cultural Nationalism*
Choice - v41 - i7 - March 2004 - p1354(1) [501+]
Fighting for US: Maulana Karenga, the US Organization, and Black Cultural Nationalism
HNet - Sept 2004 - pNA [501+]
JAH - v91 - i2 - Sept 2004 - p715(1) [501+]

Brown, Scott - *Fighting For US: Maulana Karenga, the US Organization, and Black Cultural Nationalism*
Am St - v45 - i1 - Spring 2004 - p172-172 [501+]

Brown, Seymon - *The Illusion of Control: Force and Foreign Policy in the Twenty-First Century*
Choice - v42 - i4 - Dec 2004 - p732(1) [1-50]

Brown, Sid - *The Journey of One Buddhist Nun: Even Against the Wind*
HNet - June 2004 - pNA [501+]
HNet - June 2004 - pNA [501+]

Brown, Stephen E. - *Criminology: Explaining Crime and Its Context, 5th Ed.*
R&R Bk N - v19 - i3 - August 2004 - p163(1) [501+]

Brown, Stephen Gilbert - *The Gardens of Desire: Marcel Proust and the Fugitive Sublime*
Choice - v42 - i4 - Dec 2004 - p666(1) [1-50]

Brown, Steve - *A Scandalous Freedom: Exploring Christian Liberty*
LJ - v129 - i13 - August 2004 - p87(1) [501+]

Brown, Steven - *Trumping Religion: The New Christian Right, the Free Speech Clause, and the Courts*
AHR - v109 - i4 - Oct 2004 - p1270-1270 [501+]

Brown, Stuart E., Jr. - *Virginia Baron: The Story of Thomas 6th Lord Fairfax*
EFHM - v58 - i2 - March-April 2004 - p91(1) [51-500]

Brown, Terrence E. - *Innovation, Enterpreneurship and Culture: The Interaction between Technology Progress and Economic Growth*
R&R Bk N - v19 - i3 - August 2004 - p104(1) [1-50]

Brown, Toby - *Spartacus and His Glorious Gladiators (Illus. by Goddard, Clive)*
c Sch Lib - v52 - i4 - Winter 2004 - p206(1) [51-500]

Brown, Tom - *Best Practice: Ideas and Insights from the World's Foremost Business Thinkers*
Choice - v42 - i1 - Sept 2004 - p149(1) [501+]

Brown, Victoria Bissell - *The Education of Jane Addams*
HNet - Nov 2004 - pNA [501+]
Soc Ser R - v78 - i4 - Dec 2004 - p677(5) [501+]
Wom R Bks - v22 - i1 - Oct 2004 - p6(1) [501+]

Brown, Virginia - *Momus*
Ren Q - v57 - i4 - Winter 2004 - p1354(4) [501+]

Brown, Warren C. - *Conflict in Medieval Europe: Changing Perspectives on Society and Culture*
Med R - Nov 2004 - pNA [501+]
R&R Bk N - v19 - i1 - Feb 2004 - pNA [51-500]

Brown, Wendy - *Left Legalism/ Left Critique*
S&S - v68 - i2 - Summer 2004 - p252-255 [501+]

Brown, William P. - *Character & Scripture: Moral Formation, Community, and Biblical Interpretation*
Intpr - v58 - i4 - Oct 2004 - p420(1) [501+]
Seeing the Psalms: A Theology of Metaphor
Theol St - v66 - i1 - March 2005 - p179(3) [501+]

Brown, William Wells - *The Negro in the American Rebellion: His Heroism and His Fidelity*
Choice - v42 - i1 - Sept 2004 - p172(1) [501+]

Browne, Anthony - *Changes (Illus. by Browne, Anthony)*
c SLJ - v50 - i11 - Nov 2004 - p64(1) [51-500]
I Like Books
c PW - v251 - i36 - Sept 6 2004 - p65(1) [51-500]
Into the Forest (Illus. by Browne, Anthony)
c BL - v101 - i6 - Nov 15 2004 - p580(1) [51-500]
c CCB-B - v58 - i4 - Dec 2004 - p163(1) [51-500]
c HB - v81 - i1 - Jan-Feb 2005 - p71(1) [51-500]
c KR - v72 - i18 - Sept 15 2004 - p911(1) [501+]
c PW - v251 - i42 - Oct 18 2004 - p64(1) [51-500]
c SLJ - v50 - i11 - Nov 2004 - p92(1) [51-500]
The Shape Game (Illus. by Browne, Anthony)
c HB - v81 - i1 - Jan-Feb 2005 - p18(1) [51-500]
c SLJ - v50 - i11 - Nov 2004 - p64(1) [51-500]

Browne, David - *Amped: How Big Air, Big Dollars, and a New Generation Took Sports to the Extreme*
LJ - v129 - i16 - Oct 1 2004 - p89(1) [51-500]

Browne, Jill Conner - *The Sweet Potato Queens' Field Guide to Men: Every Man I Love Is Either Married, Gay, or Dead (Read by Brown, Jill Conner). Audiobook Review*
PW - v251 - i44 - Nov 1 2004 - p28(1) [501+]
The Sweet Potato Queens' Field Guide to Men: Every Man I Love Is Either Married, Gay, or Dead
BL - v101 - i2 - Sept 15 2004 - p193(1) [501+]
PW - v251 - i28 - July 12 2004 - p64(2) [501+]

Browne, Michael Dennis - *Give Her the River: A Father's Wish for His Daughter (Illus. by Wendell Minor)*
c SLJ - v50 - i7 - July 2004 - p91(1) [51-500]

Browne, N.M. - *Basilisk*
y CCB-B - v57 - i11 - July-August 2004 - p457(1) [501+]
y Sch Lib - v52 - i3 - Autumn 2004 - p155(1) [501+]
y VOYA - v27 - i3 - August 2004 - p227(1) [1-50]

Browne, Ray Broadus - *Murder on the Reservation: American Indian Crime Fiction: Aims and Achievements*
Choice - v42 - i5 - Jan 2005 - p850(1) [1-50]
R&R Bk N - v19 - i3 - August 2004 - p240(1) [501+]

Browne, Stephen Howard - *Jefferson's Call for Nationhood: The First Inaugural Address*
JAH - v91 - i2 - Sept 2004 - p610(2) [501+]
JSH - v70 - i4 - Nov 2004 - p901(2) [501+]

Browne, Susan - *Buddha's Dogs*
Wom R Bks - v22 - i3 - Dec 2004 - p26(2) [501+]

Browne, Susan Chalker - *At Ocean's Edge (Illus. by D'Souza, Mel)*
c CBRA - Annual 2003 - p476(2) [51-500]

Browne, Sylvia - *Prophecy: What the Future Holds for You*
PW - v251 - i27 - July 5 2004 - p50(1) [51-500]

Browne, Valerie - *Phiz*
Spec - v296 - i9199 - Nov 27 2004 - p42(1) [501+]

Browning, Charles H. - *Welsh Settlement of Pennsylvania*
EFHM - v58 - i3 - May-June 2004 - p60(1) [51-500]

Browning, Christopher - *The Origins of the Final Solution: The Evolution of Nazi Jewish Policy, September 1939-March 1942*
CR - v285 - i1666 - Nov 2004 - p317(2) [501+]
NYRB - v51 - i14 - Sept 23 2004 - p78(4) [501+]

Browning, Christopher R. - *Collected Memories: Holocaust History and Postwar Testimony*
TLS - i5305 - Dec 3 2004 - p4(2) [501+]
The Origins of the Final Solution
Atl - v294 - i5 - Dec 2004 - p123(1) [501+]
TLS - i5305 - Dec 3 2004 - p4(2) [501+]

Browning, Don S. - *Marriage and Modernization: How Globalization Threatens Marriage and What to Do About It*
Theol St - v65 - i4 - Dec 2004 - p883(3) [501+]
TT - v61 - i3 - Oct 2004 - p365(3) [501+]

Browning, Gary K. - *Rethinking R.G. Collingwood: Philosophy, Politics, and the Unity of Theory and Practice*
Choice - v42 - i3 - Nov 2004 - p495(2) [51-500]

Browning, Marie - *Totally Cool Soapmaking for Kids*
c BL - v100 - i22 - August 2004 - p1921(1) [51-500]

Browning, Reed - *Baseball's Greatest Season, 1924*
JouAmCul - v27 - i3 - Sept 2004 - p336(2) [501+]

Browning, Robert M., Jr. - *Success Is All That Was Expected: The South Atlantic Blockading Squadron during the Civil War*
JSH - v71 - i1 - Feb 2005 - p164(2) [501+]

Brownlee, W. Elliot - *Federal Taxation in America: A Short History, 2nd Ed.*
Choice - v42 - i4 - Dec 2004 - p706(1) [1-50]
The Reagan Presidency: Pragmatic Conservatism and Its Legacies
JAH - v91 - i3 - Dec 2004 - p1105(2) [501+]
Pres St Q - v34 - i4 - Dec 2004 - p907(4) [501+]
R&R Bk N - v19 - i1 - Feb 2004 - p62(1) [501+]
R&R Bk N - v19 - i1 - Feb 2004 - p62(1) [501+]

Brownlie, Robin Jarvis - *A Fatherly Eye: Indian Agents, Government Power, and Aboriginal Resistance in Ontario, 1918-1939.*
Can Hist R - v85 - i4 - Dec 2004 - p796(3) [501+]
CBRA - Annual 2003 - p362(2) [501+]

Brox, Jane - *Clearing Land: Legacies of the American Farm*
BL - v101 - i2 - Sept 15 2004 - p196(1) [501+]
KR - v72 - i14 - July 15 2004 - p668(2) [501+]
PW - v251 - i33 - August 16 2004 - p54(1) [51-500]
Wom R Bks - v22 - i2 - Nov 2004 - p5(2) [501+]

Broxmeyer, Hal E. - *Cord Blood: Biology, Immunology, Banking, and Clinical Transplantation*
SciTech - v28 - i4 - Dec 2004 - p115(1) [1-50]

Broyard, Sandy - *Standby*
KR - v72 - i24 - Dec 15 2004 - p1174(1) [501+]
PW - v251 - i51 - Dec 20 2004 - p46(1) [501+]

Broyles, Janell - *The Triangle Shirtwaist Factory Fire of 1911*
y SLJ - v51 - i1 - Jan 2005 - p140(1) [51-500]

Broyles, Matthew - *The Six-Day War*
y SLJ - v51 - i1 - Jan 2005 - p142(1) [51-500]

Broyles, Michael - *Mavericks and Other Traditions in American Music*
Choice - v42 - i2 - Oct 2004 - p302(1) [51-500]
Notes - v61 - i3 - March 2005 - p754(4) [501+]

Bruand, Olivier - *Voyageurs et marchandises aux temps carolingiens: Les reseaux de communication entre Loire et Meuse aux VIIIe et IXe siecles*
Specu - v79 - i4 - Oct 2004 - p1043(3) [501+]

Brubaker, Ed - *All False Moves*
BL - v101 - i1 - Sept 1 2004 - p76(1) [501+]
Gotham Central: In the Line of Duty. (Illus. by Michael, Lark)
LJ - v129 - i18 - Nov 1 2004 - p64(2) [501+]

Bruccoli, Matthew J. - *The Sons of Maxwell Perkins: Letters of F. Scott Fitzgerald, Ernest Hemingway, Thomas Wolfe, and Their Editor*
Choice - v42 - i4 - Dec 2004 - p663(1) [1-50]
R&R Bk N - v19 - i4 - Nov 2004 - p239(1) [501+]
TLS - i5305 - Dec 3 2004 - p24(1) [501+]

Bruce, Alexander M. - *Scyld and Scef: Expanding the Analouges*
    Specu - v79 - i4 - Oct 2004 - p1045(3) [501+]
Bruce, Colin - *Conned Again, Watson! Cautionary Tales of Logic, Math, and Probability*
    y SLJ - v50 - i9 - Sept 2004 - p59(1) [51-500]
Schrodinger's Rabbits: The Many Worlds of Quantum
    PW - v251 - i42 - Oct 18 2004 - p59(1) [51-500]
Bruce, Duncan A. - *The Great Scot: A Novel of Robert the Bruce, Scotland's Legendary Warrior King*
    BL - v100 - i21 - July 2004 - p1816(1) [1-50]
Bruce, Harry - *Never Content: How Mavericks Outsiders Made a Surprise Winner of Maritime Life*
    CBRA - Annual 2003 - p322(1) [51-500]
Bruce, Leo - *Death in the Middle Watch*
    BL - v101 - i1 - Sept 1 2004 - p68(1) [51-500]
    LJ - v129 - i14 - Sept 1 2004 - p121(1) [51-500]
Bruce, Robert A. - *A Fraternity of Arms: America and France in the Great War*
    J Mil H - v68 - i3 - April 2004 - p620-621 [501+]
Bruce, Robert B. - *A Fraternity of Arms: America and France in the Great War*
    JAH - v91 - i1 - June 2004 - p289-291 [501+]
Bruce, Stephen D. - *How to Write an Affirmative Action Plan*
    HR Mag - v50 - i2 - Feb 2005 - pS6(1) [501+]
Bruce, Steve - *Politics and Religion*
    Choice - v41 - i7 - March 2004 - p1312(1) [501+]
    CS - v33 - i4 - July 2004 - p478(2) [501+]
    PSQ - v119 - i2 - Summer 2004 - p357(2) [501+]
    TimHES - v0 - i1673 - Jan 7 2005 - p23(1) [501+]
Bruce, Tina - *Developing Learning in Early Childhood*
    Choice - v42 - i4 - Dec 2004 - p710(1) [1-50]
    R&R Bk N - v19 - i3 - August 2004 - p218(1) [1-50]
Bruch, Heike - *A Bias for Action: How Effective Managers Harness Their Willpower, Achieve Results, and Stop Wasting Time*
    HR Mag - v49 - i9 - Sept 2004 - p177(1) [501+]
    R&R Bk N - v19 - i3 - August 2004 - p103(1) [1-50]
Bruchac, Joseph - *Code Talker: A Novel About the Navajo Marines of World War Two*
    y CCB-B - v58 - i6 - Feb 2005 - p246(1) [51-500]
    y Kliatt - v39 - i2 - March 2005 - p8(1) [51-500]
    c KR - v73 - i2 - Jan 15 2005 - p117(1) [51-500]
The Dark Pond (Illus. by Comport, Sally Wern)
    c BL - v100 - i22 - August 2004 - p1932(1) [51-500]
    y CCB-B - v58 - i2 - Oct 2004 - p62(1) [51-500]
    c Kliatt - v38 - i4 - July 2004 - p7(1) [51-500]
    c SLJ - v50 - i8 - August 2004 - p115(2) [51-500]
    c VOYA - v27 - i5 - Dec 2004 - p400(1) [51-500]
Hidden Roots
    LibMed - v22 - i7 - April-May 2004 - p60(60) [501+]
    c SLJ - v50 - i10 - Oct 2004 - pS37(1) [1-50]
    y VOYA - v27 - i3 - August 2004 - p208(1) [1-50]
Jim Thorpe's Bright Path (Illus. by Nelson, S.D.)
    c BL - v100 - i22 - August 2004 - p1938(1) [51-500]
    c CCB-B - v58 - i1 - Sept 2004 - p8(2) [51-500]
Journal of Jesse Smoke: A Cherokee Boy, Trail of Tears, 1838.
    y Teach Lib - v32 - i3 - Feb 2005 - p14(1) [51-500]
Ndakinna (Our Land): New and Selected Peoms
    Am Ind CRJ - v28 - i2 - Spring 2004 - p171(3) [501+]
Our Stories Remember: American Indian History, Culture, and Values through Storytelling
    Am Ind CRJ - v28 - i2 - Spring 2004 - p174(3) [501+]
Raccoon's Last Race: A Traditional Abenaki Story (Illus. by Aruego, Jose)
    c CCB-B - v58 - i3 - Nov 2004 - p116(1) [501+]
    c HB - v81 - i1 - Jan-Feb 2005 - p102(2) [51-500]
    c KR - v72 - i20 - Oct 15 2004 - p1002(1) [51-500]
    c SLJ - v50 - i12 - Dec 2004 - p127(1) [51-500]
Rachel Carson: Preserving a Sense of Wonder
    y BL - v100 - i21 - July 2004 - p1838(1) [1-50]
Sacajawea: The Story of Bird Woman and the Lewis and Clark Expedition (Read by Littrell, Nicole). Audiobook Review
    c Kliatt - v38 - i4 - July 2004 - p56(1) [51-500]
Skeleton Man (Read by Montbertrand, Carine). Audiobook Review
    y Kliatt - v39 - i2 - March 2005 - p56(1) [51-500]
    c SLJ - v51 - i2 - Feb 2005 - p76(1) [501+]
The Warriors
    c BL - v101 - i1 - Sept 1 2004 - p115(1) [501+]
    c RT - v58 - i3 - Nov 2004 - p289(1) [1-50]

Bruck, Connie - *When Hollywood Had a King: The Reign of Lew Wasserman, Who Leveraged Talent into Power and Influence*
    NYTBR - July 25 2004 - p20 [501+]
Brucks, Karen M. - *Topics from One-Dimensional Dynamics*
    SciTech - v28 - i4 - Dec 2004 - p43(1) [51-500]
Bruegel, Martin - *Farm, Shop, Landing: The Rise of a Market Society in the Hudson Valley, 1780-1806*
    JIH - v34 - i3 - Wntr 2004 - p470(2) [501+]
Brueggemann, Walter - *Inscribing the Text: Sermons and Prayers of Walter Brueggemann*
    Intpr - v58 - i3 - July 2004 - p336(1) [51-500]
Bruel, Nick - *Boing! (Illus. by Bruel, Nick)*
    c HB - v81 - i1 - Jan-Feb 2005 - p72(1) [51-500]
    c KR - v72 - i20 - Oct 15 2004 - p1002(1) [51-500]
    c PW - v251 - i35 - August 30 2004 - p53(1) [51-500]
Bruen, Ken - *The Magdalen Martyrs*
    BL - v101 - i9-10 - Jan 1 2005 - p826(1) [1-50]
    KR - v73 - i4 - Feb 15 2005 - p198(2) [51-500]
    LJ - v130 - i1 - Jan 1 2005 - p85(1) [51-500]
    PW - v252 - i7 - Feb 14 2005 - p57(1) [51-500]
Bruess, Clint E. - *Sexuality Education: Theory and Practice, 4th Ed.*
    R&R Bk N - v19 - i4 - Nov 2004 - p128(1) [1-50]
Bruges, James - *The Little Earth Book*
    E Mag - v15 - i5 - Sept-Oct 2004 - p61(1) [51-500]
Brugess, Ann Carroll - *Secret Portland, Oregon: The Unique Guidebook to Portland's Hidden Sites, Sounds, and Tastes*
    R&R Bk N - v19 - i1 - Feb 2004 - p68(1) [501+]
Bruggemann, Karsten - *Die Grundung der Republik Estland und das "Einen und unteilbaren Rubland": Die Petrograder FRront des Russischen Burgerkrieges, 1918-1920*
    Slav R - v63 - i3 - Fall 2004 - p639-640 [501+]
Brugger, Christian E. - *Captial Punishment and Roman Catholic Moral Tradition*
    TT - v61 - i3 - Oct 2004 - p367(3) [501+]
Brugger, E. Christian - *Capital Punishment and Roman Catholic Moral Tradition*
    Comw - v131 - i16 - Sept 24 2004 - p29(2) [501+]
    Theol St - v66 - i1 - March 2005 - p215(3) [501+]
Brugman, Alyssa - *Finding Grace*
    y BL - v101 - i2 - Sept 15 2004 - p229(2) [51-500]
    y CCB-B - v58 - i5 - Jan 2005 - p201(2) [51-500]
    c CH Bwatch - Feb 2005 - pNA [51-500]
    y HB - v81 - i1 - Jan-Feb 2005 - p89(1) [51-500]
    y Kliatt - v38 - i6 - Nov 2004 - p6(1) [51-500]
    y KR - v72 - i22 - Nov 15 2004 - p1088(1) [51-500]
    y SLJ - v50 - i11 - Nov 2004 - p134(1) [51-500]
    y VOYA - v27 - i5 - Dec 2004 - p378(1) [51-500]
Walking Naked
    c HB - v80 - i4 - July-August 2004 - p447(2) [51-500]
    c SLJ - v50 - i7 - July 2004 - p102(1) [51-500]
Bruhn, John G. - *Trust and the Health of Organizations*
    CS - v33 - i2 - March 2004 - p189-190 [501+]
Bruhns, Maike - *Kunst in der Krise*
    GSR - v27 - i1 - Feb 2004 - p171-172 [501+]
Bruinsma, Gerben - *Punishment, Places and Perpetrators: Developments in Criminology and Criminal Justice Research*
    Law&PolBR - Sept 2004 - pNA [501+]
    R&R Bk N - v19 - i4 - Nov 2004 - p143(1) [501+]
Bruinsma, Jelle - *World Agriculture: Towards 2015/2030: An FAO Perspective*
    R&R Bk N - v19 - i3 - August 2004 - p111(1) [51-500]
Bruinsma, Max - *Deep Sites: Intelligent Innovation in Contemporary Web Design*
    SciTech - v28 - i1 - March 2004 - p156(1) [51-500]
Bruisov, Valery - *The Fiery Angel*
    LJ - v130 - i3 - Feb 15 2005 - p172(1) [1-50]
Brukner, Peter - *The Encyclopedia of Exercise, Sport and Health*
    Choice - v42 - i5 - Jan 2005 - p823(1) [51-500]
Brule, Pierre - *Women of Ancient Greece*
    Choice - v42 - i5 - Jan 2005 - p909(1) [1-50]
Brumbaugh, Douglas K. - *Mathematics Content for Elementary Teachers*
    SciTech - v28 - i4 - Dec 2004 - p34(1) [51-500]
Brumbaugh, Gaius M. - *Revolutionary Records of Maryland*
    EFHM - v58 - i2 - March-April 2004 - p90(1) [1-50]
Brumbaugh, Sam - *Goodbye, Goodness*
    KR - v73 - i2 - Jan 15 2005 - p66(2) [501+]

Brumbeau, Jeff - *The Quiltmaker's Journey (Illus. by de Marcken, Gail)*
    c PW - v252 - i11 - March 14 2005 - p69(1) [501+]
Brumberg, Joan Jacobs - *Kansas Charley: The Story of a Nineteenth-Century Boy Murderer*
    JAH - v91 - i3 - Dec 2004 - p1037(2) [501+]
Brumfield, William Craft - *A History of Russian Architecture*
    LJ - v129 - i12 - July 2004 - p77(1) [51-500]
Brumley, Rebecca - *The Public Library Manager's Forms, Policies, and Procedures Handbook with CD-ROM*
    R&R Bk N - v19 - i4 - Nov 2004 - p257(1) [501+]
The Public Library Manager's Forms, Policies, and Procedures Manual with CD-ROM
    LJ - v129 - i13 - August 2004 - p124(1) [51-500]
Brumpton, Paul R. - *Security and Progress: Lord Salisbury at the India Office*
    Albion - v36 - i2 - Summer 2004 - p336(1) [501+]
    HER - v119 - i483 - Sept 2004 - p1084(2) [501+]
Brumwell, Stephen - *Redcoats: The British Soldier and War in the Americas, 1755-1763*
    Can Hist R - v85 - i3 - Sept 2004 - p590(2) [501+]
White Devil: A True Story of War, Savagery, and Vengeance in Colonial America
    LJ - v130 - i4 - March 1 2005 - p97(1) [51-500]
White Devil: An Epic Story of Revenge from the Savage War That Inspired the Last of the Mohicans
    CR - v285 - i1665 - Oct 2004 - p254(1) [501+]
    Globe & Mail - July 24 2004 - pD14 [51-500]
    TLS - i5284 - July 9 2004 - p29(1) [501+]
Brun-Cosme, Nadine - *No, I Want Daddy! (Illus. by Backes, Michel)*
    c HB - v81 - i1 - Jan-Feb 2005 - p72(1) [51-500]
    c KR - v72 - i19 - Oct 1 2004 - p957(1) [51-500]
    c SLJ - v50 - i12 - Dec 2004 - p99(1) [501+]
Brun, Herbert - *When Music Resists Meaning: The Major Writings of Herbert Brun*
    Am MT - v54 - i2 - Oct-Nov 2004 - p78(2) [501+]
Bruna, Dick - *Miffy's Happy New Year!*
    c PW - v251 - i51 - Dec 20 2004 - p61(1) [501+]
Brundage, Elizabeth - *The Doctor's Wife*
    BL - v100 - i21 - July 2004 - p1816(1) [1-50]
    DroRevMy - v24 - i3 - May-June 2004 - p6(2) [501+]
Brundage, James A. - *The Profession and Practice of Medieval Canon Law*
    R&R Bk N - v19 - i4 - Nov 2004 - p174(1) [501+]
Brundage, W. Fitzhugh - *Booker T. Washington and Black Progress: Up from Slavery 100 Years Later*
    Black Iss - v6 - i4 - July-August 2004 - p55(1) [51-500]
    JSH - v71 - i1 - Feb 2005 - p193(3) [501+]
Brundenius, Claes - *Technological Change and the Environmental Imperative: Challenges to the Copper Industry*
    R&R Bk N - v19 - i2 - May 2004 - p107(1) [51-500]
Brune, Kay - *Hyperalgesia: Molecular Mechanisms and Clinical Implications*
    SciTech - v28 - i4 - Dec 2004 - p88(1) [51-500]
Brunelle, Lynn - *Pop Bottle Science (Illus. by Meisel, Paul)*
    c PW - v251 - i37 - Sept 13 2004 - p81(1) [501+]
Brunelli, Giampiero - *Soldati del papa: Politica militare e nobilta nello Stato della Chiesa*
    Ren Q - v57 - i4 - Winter 2004 - p1378(2) [501+]
Bruner, Edward M. - *Culture on Tour: Ethnographies of Travel*
    CHE - v51 - i19 - Jan 14 2005 - pB13-B14 [501+]
Brunet, Bert - *Australian Insects: Natural History*
    QRB - v79 - i4 - Dec 2004 - p433(1) [501+]
Brunhoff, Jean de - *Babar Family Time and Babar Bedtime*
    PW - v251 - i47 - Nov 22 2004 - p62(1) [501+]
My First Book: A Babar Baby Journal
    PW - v251 - i47 - Nov 22 2004 - p62(1) [501+]
Brunhoff, Laurent de - *Babar's Museum of Art*
    LibMed - v22 - i5 - Feb 2004 - p62(2) [501+]
Brunicardi, F. Charles - *Schwartz's Principles of Surgery, 8th Ed.*
    SciTech - v28 - i4 - Dec 2004 - p107(1) [51-500]
Brunkhorst, Alex - *The Mating Season*
    LJ - v129 - i13 - August 2004 - p64(1) [51-500]
Brunn, Joanne E. - *Awakening Your Psychic Skills*
    Bwatch - Feb 2005 - pNA [51-500]
Brunn, Stanley D. - *11 September and Its Aftermath: The Geopolitics of Terror*
    R&R Bk N - v19 - i1 - Feb 2004 - p141(1) [51-500]
    Choice - v42 - i3 - Nov 2004 - p559(1) [1-50]

Brunner, Paul H. - *Practical Handbook of Material Flow Analysis*
　　SciTech - v28 - i1 - March 2004 - p177(1) [51-500]

Brunnholzl, Karl - *The Center of the Sunlit Sky: Madhyamaka in the Kagyu Tradition*
　　LJ - v129 - i20 - Dec 1 2004 - p123(2) [51-500]

Bruno, A. Anthony - *CCDA Sel-Study: CCDA Exam Certification Guide, 2nd Ed.*
　　SciTech - v28 - i3 - Sept 2004 - p19(1) [501+]

Bruno, Thomas J. - *Handbook of Basic Tables for Chemical Analysis*
　　Choice - v42 - i1 - Sept 2004 - p133(1) [501+]

Brunori, David - *Local Tax Policy: A Federalist Perspective*
　　R&R Bk N - v19 - i2 - May 2004 - p125 [51-500]

Bruns, Barbara - *Achieving Universal Primary Education by 2015: A Chance for Every Child*
　　JEL - v42 - i1 - March 2004 - p275(1) [501+]

Bruns, Roger - *Billy Graham: A Biography*
　　R&R Bk N - v19 - i3 - August 2004 - p27(1) [1-50]

Brunsma, David L. - *The School Uniform and What It Tells Us About American Education: A Symbolic Crusade*
　　R&R Bk N - v19 - i4 - Nov 2004 - p188(1) [501+]

Brunstrom, Conard - *William Cowper: Religion, Satire, Society*
　　Choice - v42 - i2 - Oct 2004 - p290(2) [501+]

Brunt, Bruce Van - *The Calculus of Variations*
　　Choice - v41 - i11-12 - July-August 2004 - p2081(1) [501+]

Brunt, Maureen - *Economic Essays on Australian and New Zealand Competition Law*
　　JEL - v41 - i4 - Dec 2003 - p1390(1) [501+]

Brunt, Stephen - *The Way It Looks from Here: Contemporary Canadian Writing on Sports*
　　Globe & Mail - Nov 20 2004 - pD30 [51-500]

Brunton, Deborah - *Health, Disease and Society in Europe 1800-1930: A Source Book, 1st ed.*
　　TimHES - v0 - i1680 - Feb 25 2005 - pXV(1) [501+]
Medicine Transformed: Health, Disease and Society in Europe 1800-1930, 1st ed.
　　TimHES - v0 - i1680 - Feb 25 2005 - pXV(1) [501+]

Brusatte, Stephen - *Stately Fossils: A Comprehensive Look at the State Fossils and Other Official Fossils*
　　R&R Bk N - v19 - i1 - Feb 2004 - p248(1) [1-50]

Bruschi, Caterina - *Texts and the Repression of Medieval Heresy*
　　Specu - v79 - i4 - Oct 2004 - p1047(2) [501+]

Bruschke, Jon - *Free Press vs. Fair Trials: Examining Publicity's Role in Trial Outcomes*
　　Choice - v42 - i2 - Oct 2004 - p371(1) [51-500]
　　R&R Bk N - v19 - i1 - Feb 2004 - pNA [51-500]

Bruseth, James E. - *From a Watery Grave: The Discovery and Excavation of La Salle's Shipwreck*
　　LJ - v130 - i2 - Feb 1 2005 - p95(2) [51-500]

Brush, Candida G. - *Clearing the Hurdles: Women Building High-Growth Businesses*
　　Choice - v42 - i6 - Feb 2005 - p1066(1) [51-500]

Brush, Stephen B. - *Farmers' Bounty: Locating Crop Diversity in the Contemporary World*
　　Choice - v42 - i4 - Dec 2004 - p686(1) [1-50]
　　Nature - v430 - i7003 - August 26 2004 - p967(2) [501+]
　　SciTech - v28 - i3 - Sept 2004 - p128(1) [51-500]

Brush, Stephen G. - *Kinetic Theory of Gases: An Anthology of Classic Papers with Historical Commentary*
　　SciTech - v28 - i4 - Dec 2004 - p49(1) [51-500]

Brust, Steven - *The Lord of Castle Black*
　　y VOYA - v27 - i3 - August 2004 - p227(1) [1-50]

Brustein, Robert - *Letters to a Young Actor: A Universal Guide to Performance*
　　LJ - v130 - i4 - March 1 2005 - p86(2) [51-500]

Bruster, Douglas - *Shakespeare and the Question of Culture: Early Modern Literature and the Cultural Turn*
　　Shakes Q - v55 - i2 - Summer 2004 - p228-232 [501+]

Bruton, James H. - *The Big House: Life Inside a Supermax Security Prison*
　　R&R Bk N - v19 - i3 - August 2004 - p170(1) [51-500]

Bruun, Ole - *Fengshui in China: Geomantic Divination between State Orthodoxy and Popular Religion*
　　Ch Rev Int - v11 - i1 - Spring 2004 - p35(7) [501+]

Bruzelius, Caroline - *The Stones of Naples: Church Building in Angevin Italy, 1266-1343*
　　Choice - v42 - i5 - Jan 2005 - p845(1) [1-50]
　　R&R Bk N - v19 - i4 - Nov 2004 - p204(1) [501+]

Bryan, Appleyard - *Understanding the Present: An Alternative History of Science*
　　SB - v40 - i5 - Sept-Oct 2004 - p201(1) [51-500]

Bryan, Ashley - *Ashley Bryan's Beautiful Blackbird and Other Folktales (Read by Bryan, Ashley). Audiobook Review*
　　c SLJ - v50 - i10 - Oct 2004 - pS28(1) [51-500]

Bryan, Nichol - *Cuban Americans*
　　c SLJ - v50 - i9 - Sept 2004 - p184(1) [1-50]
Filipino Americans
　　c SLJ - v50 - i9 - Sept 2004 - p184(1) [1-50]
Hmong Americans
　　c SLJ - v50 - i9 - Sept 2004 - p184(1) [1-50]

Bryan, Nora - *Prairie Gardener's Book of Bugs: A Guide to Living with Common Garden Insects*
　　CBRA - Annual 2003 - p416(1) [51-500]

Bryan, Patricia L. - *Midnight Assassin: A Murder in America's Heartland*
　　PW - v252 - i7 - Feb 14 2005 - p64(1) [51-500]
Midnight Assassin: Murder in America's Heartland
　　KR - v73 - i3 - Feb 1 2005 - p159(1) [501+]

Bryan, Sean - *A Boy and His Bunny*
　　KR - v73 - i1 - Jan 1 2005 - p49(1) [51-500]
　　PW - v252 - i5 - Jan 31 2005 - p66(1) [501+]

Bryan, Sharon - *Planet on the Table: Poets on the Reading Life*
　　Ga R - v58 - i2 - Summer 2004 - p471-483 [501+]

Bryant, Andrew - *Flirting 101: How to Charm Your Way to Love, Friendship, and Success*
　　LJ - v130 - i3 - Feb 15 2005 - p142(1) [51-500]

Bryant, Annie - *Worst Enemies, Best Friends*
　　Kliatt - v38 - i6 - Nov 2004 - p14(1) [501+]

Bryant, Clifton D. - *Handbook of Death and Dying*
　　R&R Bk N - v19 - i1 - Feb 2004 - p131(1) [51-500]

Bryant, Edwin F. - *The Hare Krishna Movement: The Postcharismatic Fate of a Religious Transplant*
　　Choice - v42 - i5 - Jan 2005 - p871(1) [1-50]
　　R&R Bk N - v19 - i3 - August 2004 - p14(1) [1-50]

Bryant, Emma Frances Spaulding - *Emma Spaulding Bryant: Civil War Bride, Carpetbagger's Wife, Ardent Feminist: Letters and Diaries, 1860-1900*
　　R&R Bk N - v19 - i3 - August 2004 - p74(1) [501+]

Bryant, Howard - *Shut Out: A Story of Race and Baseball in Boston*
　　NEQ - v77 - i3 - Sept 2004 - p503-505 [501+]

Bryant-Jefferies, Richard - *Relationship Counselling: Sons and Their Mothers, a Person-Centred Dialogue*
　　R&R Bk N - v20 - i1 - Feb 2005 - p8(1) [51-500]

Bryant, Jen - *Georgia's Bones (Illus. by Andersen, Bethanne)*
　　c KR - v73 - i2 - Jan 15 2005 - p117(1) [51-500]
　　c PW - v252 - i11 - March 14 2005 - p67(1) [51-500]
Millions
　　y VOYA - v27 - i4 - Oct 2004 - p291(1) [51-500]

Bryant, John - *Bioethics for Scientists*
　　QRB - v79 - i3 - Sept 2004 - p295(2) [501+]

Bryant, Kobe - *The Last Season*
　　Time - v164 - i17 - Oct 25 2004 - p104 [501+]

Bryant, Rachel - *Eating Disorders*
　　Bwatch - Dec 2004 - pNA [51-500]

Bryant, Ralph C. - *Turbulent Waters: Cross-Border Finance and International Governance*
　　JEL - v41 - i4 - Dec 2003 - p1359(1) [501+]

Bryant, Robert - *Exterior Differential Systems: Euler-Lagrange Partial Differential Equations*
　　JEL - v41 - i4 - Dec 2003 - p1444(1) [501+]

Bryce, Robert - *Pipe Dreams: Greed, Ego, and the Death of Enron*
　　En Jnl - v25 - i4 - Oct 2004 - p115(20) [501+]
　　R&R Bk N - v19 - i3 - August 2004 - p119(1) [501+]

Bryce, Trevor - *Life and Society in the Hittite World*
　　JNES - v63 - i4 - Oct 2004 - p305(3) [501+]

Bryden, J.M. - *A New Approach to Rural Development in Europe: Germany, Greece, Scotland and Sweden*
　　R&R Bk N - v19 - i3 - August 2004 - p147(1) [51-500]

Bryder, Linda - *A Voice for Mothers: The Plunket Society and Infant Welfare 1907-2000*
　　AHS - v35 - i124 - Oct 2004 - p407(2) [501+]

Brydon, Diana - *Shakespeare in Canada: A World Elsewhere?*
　　CBRA - Annual 2003 - p263(1) [51-500]

Brydon-Miller, Mary - *Traveling Companions: Feminism, Teaching, and Action Research*
　　R&R Bk N - v19 - i3 - August 2004 - p153(1) [51-500]

Bryer, Jackson R. - *The Facts on File Companion to American Drama*
　　LibMed - v23 - i1 - August-Sept 2004 - p77(1) [51-500]
　　LJ - v129 - i12 - July 2004 - p115(1) [51-500]
　　R&R Bk N - v19 - i1 - Feb 2004 - p242(1) [501+]
Resources for American Literary Study: Vol. 28
　　R&R Bk N - v19 - i1 - Feb 2004 - p243(1) [51-500]

Bryher - *Visa for Avalon*
　　y BL - v101 - i4 - Oct 15 2004 - p388(1) [51-500]
　　LJ - v129 - i19 - Nov 15 2004 - p103(1) [51-500]
　　Wom R Bks - v22 - i2 - Nov 2004 - p20(1) [501+]

Bryk, Anthony S. - *Trust in Schools: A Core Resource for Improvement*
　　AJE - v111 - i1 - Nov 2004 - p132(3) [501+]

Brym, Robert J. - *Sociology: Your Compass for a New World, 2nd Ed.*
　　R&R Bk N - v19 - i2 - May 2004 - p126 [51-500]

Brynie, Faith Hickman - *101 Questions about Sex and Sexuality-- :With Answers for the Curious, Cautious, and Confused*
　　c Sci Teach - v71 - i3 - March 2004 - p57-64 [501+]
　　Sci Teach - v71 - i4 - April 2004 - p73-74 [501+]

Brysk, Alison - *People out of Place: Globalization, Human Rights, and the Citizenship Gap*
　　Pers PS - v33 - i4 - Fall 2004 - p245(2) [501+]

Bryson, Christopher - *The Flouride Deception*
　　Choice - v42 - i7 - March 2005 - p1258(1) [51-500]

Bryson, Michael A. - *Visions of the Land: Science, Literature, and the American Environment from the Era of Exploration to the Age of Ecology*
　　HNet - June 2004 - pNA [501+]

Brzezinski, Matthew - *Fortress America: On the Front Lines of Homeland Security, an Inside Look at the Coming Surveillance State*
　　y BL - v100 - i22 - August 2004 - p1879(1) [51-500]
　　BW - v34 - i37 - Sept 12 2004 - p3(1) [501+]
　　KR - v72 - i14 - July 15 2004 - p669(1) [501+]
　　LJ - v129 - i14 - Sept 1 2004 - p170(2) [51-500]
　　NYTBR - Nov 7 2004 - p9 [501+]
　　PW - v251 - i28 - July 12 2004 - p53(1) [51-500]

Brzezinski, Zbigniew - *The Choice: Global Domination or Global Leadership*
　　Choice - v42 - i3 - Nov 2004 - p560(1) [1-50]
　　PSQ - v119 - i4 - Winter 2004 - p686(2) [501+]

Bstan-'dzin-rgya-mtsho, Dalai Lama XIV - *The New Physics and Cosmology: Dialogues with the Dalai Lama*
　　R&R Bk N - v19 - i3 - August 2004 - p18(1) [1-50]
The Wisdom of Forgiveness: Intimate Conversations and Journeys
　　LJ - v129 - i16 - Oct 1 2004 - p86(1) [51-500]
　　PW - v251 - i33 - August 16 2004 - p61(1) [51-500]
　　SLJ - v50 - i12 - Dec 2004 - p54(4) [501+]

Bu, Liping - *Making the World Like Us: Education, Cultural Expansion, and the American Century*
　　JAH - v91 - i2 - Sept 2004 - p693(2) [501+]

Buamol, William, J. - *Growth, Industrial Organization and Economic Generalities*
　　R&R Bk N - v19 - i1 - Feb 2004 - p89(1) [51-500]

Buarque, Chico - *Budapest*
　　BL - v101 - i2 - Sept 15 2004 - p206(1) [501+]
　　KR - v72 - i15 - August 1 2004 - p701(2) [501+]
　　LJ - v129 - i17 - Oct 15 2004 - p52(2) [51-500]
　　PW - v251 - i35 - August 30 2004 - p29(2) [501+]
　　TLS - i5288 - August 6 2004 - p20(1) [51-500]

Buber, Martin - *Two Types of Faith*
　　R&R Bk N - v19 - i1 - Feb 2004 - p14(1) [1-50]

Bubley, Glenn J. - *What Your Doctor May Not Tell You about Prostate Cancer: The Breakthrough Information and Treatments That Can Help Save Your Life*
　　LJ - v129 - i19 - Nov 15 2004 - p79(1) [501+]

Bucaille, Laetitia - *Growing Up Palestinian: Israeli Occupation and the Intifada Generation*
　　CC - v121 - i19 - Sept 21 2004 - p44(3) [501+]

Bucco, Martin - *Sinclair Lewis as Reader and Critic*
　　R&R Bk N - v19 - i4 - Nov 2004 - p243(1) [501+]

Buchan, Elizabeth - *Everything She Thought She Wanted*
　　KR - v73 - i1 - Jan 1 2005 - p5(2) [501+]
　　LJ - v129 - i19 - Nov 15 2004 - p42(2) [501+]
　　PW - v252 - i6 - Feb 7 2005 - p42(1) [51-500]

Buchanan, Angus - *Brunel: The Life and Times of Isambard Kingdom Brunel*
　　CT - v45 - i1 - Jan 2004 - p183(2) [501+]

Buchanan, Carl Jay - *Poetry of Contemporary American Poet Jonathan Holden*
　　R&R Bk N - v19 - i1 - Feb 2004 - p246(1) [51-500]

Buchanan, Edna - *Cold Case Squad (Read by Dean, Robertson). Audiobook Review*
  y Kliatt - v39 - i1 - Jan 2005 - p40(1) [51-500]
The Corpse Had a Familiar Face: Covering Miami
  NYTBR - August 8 2004 - p20 [501+]
Buchanan, Elizabeth A. - *Readings in Virtual Research Ethics: Issues and Controversies*
  R&R Bk N - v19 - i1 - Feb 2004 - p262(1) [51-500]
Buchanan, George - *A Dialogue on the Law of Kingship among the Scots: A Critical Edition and Translation of George Buchanan's De jure regni apud Scotos dialogus*
  R&R Bk N - v19 - i3 - August 2004 - p195(1) [1-50]
Buchanan, James L. - *Marine Acoustics: Direct and Inverse Problems*
  SciTech - v28 - i3 - Sept 2004 - p47(1) [1-50]
Buchanan, Jane - *Goodbye, Charley*
  c BL - v100 - i22 - August 2004 - p1932(2) [51-500]
  c CCB-B - v58 - i2 - Oct 2004 - p62(2) [51-500]
  c KR - v72 - i14 - July 15 2004 - p682(1) [51-500]
  c SLJ - v50 - i8 - August 2004 - p116(1) [51-500]
Buchanan, John M. - *The Road to Valley Forge: How Washington Built the Army That Won the Revolution*
  BL - v101 - i3 - Oct 1 2004 - p296(1) [51-500]
Buchanan, Michael. - *Prefab Home*
  LJ - v130 - i1 - Jan 1 2005 - p106(1) [51-500]
Buchanan, Patrick - *The Death of the West: How Dying Populations and Immigrant Invasions Imperil Our Country and Civilization*
  CI - v13 - i2 - Feb 2005 - p40(2) [501+]
Where the Right Went Wrong: How Neoconservatives Subverted the Reagan Revolution and Hijacked the Bush Presidency
  Bus W - i3902 - Oct 4 2004 - p24 [501+]
  NYTBR - Sept 12 2004 - p21 [501+]
Buchanan, Relva C. - *Ceramic Materials for Electronics, 3rd Rev. Ed.*
  SciTech - v28 - i4 - Dec 2004 - p156(1) [51-500]
Buchanan, Robert W. - *Tuning Microsoft Server Clusters: Guaranteeing High Availability*
  SciTech - v28 - i4 - Dec 2004 - p33(1) [51-500]
Buchanan-Smith, Peter - *The Wilco Book*
  PW - v251 - i48 - Nov 29 2004 - p36(1) [51-500]
Buchanan, William J. - *Diablo, the Devil Steer*
  Roundup M - v12 - i1 - Oct 2004 - p28(1) [51-500]
Buchanan, William L. - *A Marine Rifle Company in Vietnam*
  Mar Crp G - v88 - i5 - May 2004 - p87(1) [501+]
Buchar, Robert - *Czech New Wave Filmmakers in Interviews*
  R&R Bk N - v19 - i1 - Feb 2004 - p224(1) [51-500]
Buchen, Irving H. - *The Future of the American School System*
  Fut - v39 - i1 - Jan-Feb 2005 - p48(1) [51-500]
  R&R Bk N - v19 - i4 - Nov 2004 - p176(1) [501+]
Parent's Guide to Student Success: Home and School Partners in the Twenty-First Century
  R&R Bk N - v19 - i4 - Nov 2004 - p180(1) [501+]
Bucher, Andreas - *La famille en droit international prive and Evolution of Principles for Resolving Conflicts in the Field of Contracts and Torts*
  R&R Bk N - v19 - i4 - Nov 2004 - p159(1) [501+]
Bucher, Jay L. - *The Metrology Handbook*
  Bwatch - v26 - i9 - Sept 2004 - p8(1) [51-500]
  SciTech - v28 - i3 - Sept 2004 - p134(1) [51-500]
Buchheit, R.G. - *Corrosion and Protection of Light Metal Alloys: Proceedings of the International Symposium*
  SciTech - v28 - i3 - Sept 2004 - p165(1) [51-500]
Buchler, Markus - *Diseases of the Pancreas: Acute Pancreatitis, Chronic Pancreatitis, Neoplasms of the Pancreas. 2nd Ed.*
  SciTech - v28 - i3 - Sept 2004 - p107(1) [51-500]
Buchloh, Benjamin H.D. - *Thomas Hirschhorn*
  LJ - v129 - i20 - Dec 1 2004 - p112(1) [51-500]
Buchman, Alan L. - *Practical Nutritional Support Techniques. 2nd Ed.*
  SciTech - v28 - i1 - March 2004 - p121(1) [51-500]
Buchman, Jeremy - *Drawing Lines in Quicksand: Courts, Legislatures, and Redistricting*
  R&R Bk N - v19 - i1 - Feb 2004 - pNA [51-500]
Buchmann, Stephen - *Letters from the Hive: An Intimate History of Bees, Honey, and Humankind*
  KR - v73 - i4 - Feb 15 2005 - p206(1) [501+]
Buchsel, Patricia C. - *Oncology Nursing in the Ambulatory Setting: Issues and Models of Care, 2nd Ed.*
  SciTech - v28 - i4 - Dec 2004 - p92(1) [51-500]

Buchstaber, V.M. - *Geometry, Topology, and Mathematical Physics: S.P. Novikov's Seminar, 2002-2003*
  SciTech - v28 - i3 - Sept 2004 - p45(1) [1-50]
Buchta, Wilfried - *Who Rules Iran? The Structure of Power in the Islamic Republic*
  MEQ - v11 - i4 - Fall 2004 - p87(1) [501+]
Buck, Carol J. - *Step-by-Step Medical Coding. 5th Ed.*
  SciTech - v28 - i1 - March 2004 - p87(1) [51-500]
Buck, Gordon H. - *Drafting Rules: How Community Association Maintain Peace & Harmony, A Guide for Association Practitioners*
  R&R Bk N - v19 - i4 - Nov 2004 - p166(1) [501+]
Buck-Morss, Susan - *Thinking Past Terror: Islamism and Critical Theory on the Left*
  R&R Bk N - v19 - i1 - Feb 2004 - p126(1) [51-500]
Buck, Stephanie - *Hans Holbein the Younger: Painter at the Court of Henry VIII*
  Choice - v42 - i2 - Oct 2004 - pNA [501+]
  LJ - v129 - i12 - July 2004 - p78(1) [51-500]
  R&R Bk N - v19 - i2 - May 2004 - p196(1) [51-500]
Buck, Trevor - *Poor Relief or Poor Deal? The Social Fund, Safety Nets, and Social Security*
  Soc Ser R - v78 - i3 - Sept 2004 - p519(2) [501+]
Buckely, Bruce - *Weather: A Visual Guide*
  SciTech - v28 - i4 - Dec 2004 - p53(1) [51-500]
Buckhanon, Kalisha - *Upstate*
  BL - v101 - i8 - Dec 15 2004 - p707(1) [51-500]
  Black Iss - v7 - i1 - Jan-Feb 2005 - p63(1) [51-500]
  LJ - v130 - i1 - Jan 1 2005 - p94(1) [51-500]
  People - v63 - i7 - Feb 21 2005 - p48 [501+]
  PW - v251 - i47 - Nov 22 2004 - p37(2) [51-500]
  Ent W - i803 - Jan 28 2005 - p88 [51-500]
Buckie, Catherine - *Lobster Kids's Guide to Exploring Halifax*
  CBRA - Annual 2003 - p21(1) [51-500]
Buckingham, Jane - *Leprosy in Colonial South India: Medicine and Confinement*
  HNet - June 2004 - pNA [501+]
Buckingham, John - *Chasing the Molecule*
  CR - v285 - i1665 - Oct 2004 - p251(1) [501+]
  Nature - v430 - i6997 - July 15 2004 - p295(1) [501+]
Buckingham, Linda - *Projection Art for Kids: Murals and Painting Projects for Kids of All Ages*
  c CBRA - Annual 2003 - p551(1) [51-500]
Buckingham, Marcus - *The One Thing You Need to Know: about Great Managing, Great Leading, and Sustained Individual Success*
  Har Bus R - v83 - i2 - Feb 2005 - p56(1) [1-50]
  LJ - v130 - i4 - March 1 2005 - p96(1) [51-500]
Buckingham, Mark - *Fables: Animal Farm*
  LibMed - v22 - i6 - March 2004 - p70(1) [501+]
Buckland, Raymond - *Book of Spirit Communications*
  Bwatch - Feb 2005 - pNA [51-500]
The Fortune-Telling Book: The Encyclopedia of Divination And Soothsaying
  Bwatch - Feb 2005 - pNA [51-500]
Practical Candleburning Rituals
  Bwatch - March 2005 - pNA [51-500]
Buckler, Ernest - *Thanks for Listening: Stories and Short Fictions*
  Globe & Mail - August 7 2004 - pD11 [501+]
Buckler, John - *Aegean Greece in the Fourth Century BC*
  Choice - v41 - i7 - March 2004 - p1349(1) [501+]
  Class R - v54 - i2 - Nov 2004 - p467(3) [501+]
Buckler, Julie A. - *The Literary Lorgnette: Attending Opera in Imperial Russia*
  Notes - v61 - i1 - Sept 2004 - p137(4) [501+]
Buckley, Bruce - *Weather: A Visual Guide*
  y BL - v101 - i4 - Oct 15 2004 - p370(1) [51-500]
  y SB - v41 - i1 - Jan-Feb 2005 - p26(1) [501+]
  SLJ - v50 - i12 - Dec 2004 - p176(1) [51-500]
Buckley, Christopher - *Florence of Arabia (Read by Kalember, Patricia). Audiobook Review*
  PW - v251 - i44 - Nov 1 2004 - p26(1) [501+]
Florence of Arabia
  BW - v34 - i39 - Sept 26 2004 - p7(1) [501+]
  Ent W - i784 - Sept 17 2004 - p86 [501+]
  KR - v72 - i17 - Sept 1 2004 - p819(2) [501+]
  NYTBR - Oct 10 2004 - p21 [501+]
  PW - v251 - i34 - August 23 2004 - p38(1) [501+]
Buckley, D.N. - *State-of-the-Art Program on Compound Semiconductors XL: (SOTAPOCS XL) and Narrow Bandgap Optoelectronic Materials and Devices II: Proceedings of the International Symposia*
  SciTech - v28 - i3 - Sept 2004 - p161(1) [51-500]

Buckley, Fiona - *The Siren Queen: An Ursula Blanchard Mystery at Queen Elizabeth I's Court*
  BL - v101 - i5 - Nov 1 2004 - p466(1) [51-500]
  KR - v72 - i17 - Sept 1 2004 - p838(1) [501+]
  LJ - v129 - i18 - Nov 1 2004 - p62(1) [51-500]
  PW - v251 - i40 - Oct 4 2004 - p73(1) [51-500]
Buckley, Geoffrey L. - *Extracting Appalachia: Images of the Consolidation Coal Company, 1910-1945*
  Choice - v42 - i5 - Jan 2005 - p914(1) [1-50]
Buckley, James - *Baseball Top 10*
  c RT - v57 - Oct 2003 - p176 [1-50]
Great Moments in Football
  c LibMed - v22 - i4 - Jan 2004 - p82(1) [51-500]
Scholastic Book of Lists
  c LibMed - v22 - i6 - March 2004 - p83(1) [51-500]
Sports in America
  c SLJ - v51 - i2 - Feb 2005 - p82(1) [51-500]
Unhittable: Reliving the Magic and Drama of Baseball's Best-Pitched Games
  BL - v101 - i1 - Sept 1 2004 - p45(1) [501+]
Buckley, James J. - *Fuzzy Statistics*
  Choice - v42 - i5 - Jan 2005 - p889(1) [1-50]
Buckley, John F. - *2004 State by State Guide to Workplace Safety Regulation*
  R&R Bk N - v19 - i1 - Feb 2004 - pNA [51-500]
2005 State by State Guide to Workplace Safety Regulation
  R&R Bk N - v19 - i4 - Nov 2004 - p170(1) [501+]
Equal Employment Opportunity 2004 Compliance guide
  R&R Bk N - v19 - i3 - August 2004 - p198(1) [1-50]
Buckley, Roger - *Theory and Practice of Training, 5th Ed.*
  R&R Bk N - v19 - i4 - Nov 2004 - p113(1) [51-500]
Buckley, Ross P. - *The WTO and the Doha Round: The Changing Face of World Trade*
  R&R Bk N - v19 - i2 - May 2004 - p111(1) [51-500]
Buckley, Thomas - *Standing Ground: Yurok Indian Spirituality, 1850-1990*
  Am Ind CRJ - v28 - i2 - Spring 2004 - p182(3) [501+]
  JRAI - v10 - i4 - Dec 2004 - p938(1) [501+]
Buckley, Thomas E. - *The Great Catastrophe of My Life: Divorce in the Old Dominion*
  HNet - Sept 2004 - pNA [501+]
  JIH - v34 - i3 - Wntr 2004 - p471(2) [501+]
  JSH - v70 - i4 - Nov 2004 - p914(2) [501+]
Buckley, Veronica - *Christina, Queen of Sweden: The Restless Life of a European Eccentric*
  BL - v101 - i4 - Oct 15 2004 - p382(2) [51-500]
  KR - v72 - i16 - August 15 2004 - p784(1) [501+]
  NYTBR - Nov 7 2004 - p34 [501+]
  PW - v251 - i36 - Sept 6 2004 - p55(2) [501+]
Christina ,Queen of Sweden: The Restless Life of
  CR - v285 - i1666 - Nov 2004 - p314(2) [501+]
Buckley, William F., Jr. - *The Fall of the Berlin Wall*
  Am Spect - v37 - i4 - May 2004 - p63(2) [501+]
Miles Gone By: A Literary Autobiography
  Am Spect - v37 - i7 - Sept 2004 - p62(2) [501+]
  NYTBR - Oct 17 2004 - p28 [501+]
Bucklin, Stephen J. - *From Cold War to Gulf War: The South Dakota National Guard, 1945 to the Millennium*
  J Mil H - v68 - i4 - Oct 2004 - p1311-1312 [501+]
Bucknam, Mark A. - *Responsibility of Command: How UN and NATO Commanders Influenced Airpower over Bosnia*
  J Mil H - v68 - i3 - July 2004 - p1020-1021 [501+]
Bucknell, Katherine - *Canarino*
  Econ - v372 - i8384 - July 17 2004 - p81US [501+]
  Spec - v295 - i9178 - July 3 2004 - p38(1) [501+]
  TLS - i5284 - July 9 2004 - p21(1) [501+]
Buckow, Anjana - *Zwischen Propaganda und Realpolitik: Die USA und der sowjetisch besetzte Teil Deutschlands 1945-1955*
  HNet - Oct 2004 - pNA [501+]
Buckridge, Steeve O. - *The Language of Dress: Resistance and Accomodation in Jamaica, 1760-1890*
  Choice - v42 - i5 - Jan 2005 - p912(1) [1-50]
Buckser, Andrew - *After the Rescue: Jewish Identity and Community in Contemporary Denmark*
  JRAI - v10 - i3 - Sept 2004 - p739(2) [501+]
Anthropology of Religious Conversion
  R&R Bk N - v19 - i1 - Feb 2004 - p12(1) [1-50]
Buckup, Klaus - *Clinical Tests for the Musculoskeletal System: Examinations, Signs, Phenomena*
  SciTech - v28 - i4 - Dec 2004 - p109(1) [51-500]
Bucur, Maria - *Eugenics and Modernization in Interwar Romania*
  HNet - Sept 2004 - pNA [501+]

Bucy, Erik P. - *Media Access: Social and Psychological Dimensions of New Technology Use*
 R&R Bk N - v19 - i1 - Feb 2004 - p210(1) [51-500]

Buczinsky, Bill - *Kiss the Fish: Poetry from a Child's Voice (Read by Buczinsky, Bill). Audiobook Review*
 c SLJ - v50 - i11 - Nov 2004 - p81(2) [51-500]

Buday, Grant - *Sack of Teeth*
 CBRA - Annual 2003 - p156(1) [501+]

Budd, Ann - *The Knitter's Handy Book of Sweater Patterns: Basic Designs in Multiple Sizes & Gauges*
 LJ - v129 - i20 - Dec 1 2004 - p108(1) [51-500]

Budd, John W. - *Employment with a Human Face: Balancing Efficiency, Equity, and Voice*
 Choice - v42 - i1 - Sept 2004 - p149(1) [501+]

Budd, Malcolm - *The Aesthetic Appreciation of Nature*
 TLS - i5266 - March 5 2004 - p32-32 [501+]

Budd, Richard - *Serving Two Masters: The Development of the American Military Chaplaincy, 1860-1920*
 CH - v73 - i4 - Dec 2004 - p884(2) [501+]

Budgeon, Shelley - *Choosing a Self: Young Women and the Individualization of Identity*
 AJS - v110 - i3 - Nov 2004 - p844(3) [501+]
 CS - v33 - i2 - March 2005 - p194-195 [501+]

Budget Living Magazine - *Home Cheap Home: A Room-by-Room Guide to Great Decorating*
 LJ - v129 - i15 - Sept 15 2004 - p56(1) [51-500]

Budiansky, Stephen - *Air Power: The Men, Machines, and Ideas That Revolutionized War, from Kitty Hawk to Gulf War II*
 Choice - v42 - i5 - Jan 2005 - p906(1) [1-50]
 J Mil H - v68 - i4 - Oct 2004 - p1321-1322 [501+]

Budin, Stephanie Lynn - *The Ancient Greeks: New Perspectives*
 LJ - v130 - i2 - Feb 1 2005 - p114(1) [51-500]

Budker, Dmitry - *Atomic Physics: An Exploration through Problems and Solutions*
 Choice - v42 - i2 - Oct 2004 - p330(1) [51-500]

Budnick, Dean - *Jambands: The Complete Guide to the Players, Music & Scene*
 JPC - v38 - i3 - Feb 2005 - p574(2) [501+]

Budnitz, Judy - *Nice Big American Baby*
 Ent W - i806 - Feb 11 2005 - p69 [51-500]
 KR - v72 - i23 - Dec 1 2004 - p1101(2) [501+]
 NW - March 28 2005 - p53 [501+]
 NYTBR - Feb 20 2005 - p8 [501+]
 PW - v251 - i49 - Dec 6 2004 - p41(1) [51-500]

Budrys, Grace - *Unequal Health: How Inequality Contributes to Health or Illness*
 Choice - v41 - i7 - March 2004 - p1326(1) [501+]
 CS - v33 - i4 - July 2004 - p486(2) [501+]

Budz, Mark - *Crache*
 BL - v101 - i6 - Nov 15 2004 - p570(1) [51-500]
 Ent W - i795 - Dec 3 2004 - p94 [501+]
 PW - v251 - i42 - Oct 18 2004 - p53(1) [51-500]

Budziszewski, J. - *What We Can't Not Know: A Guide*
 Choice - v42 - i1 - Sept 2004 - p114(1) [501+]

Bueche, Shelley - *The Ebola Virus*
 c SB - v40 - i5 - Sept-Oct 2004 - p224(1) [501+]

Buechler, John - *Microsoft Windows Movie Maker 2: Do Amazing Things*
 SciTech - v28 - i1 - March 2004 - p176(1) [51-500]

Buecker, Thomas R. - *Fort Robinson and the American West, 1874-1899*
 Am Ind CRJ - v27 - i4 - Fall 2003 - p151-153 [501+]

Buehner, Mark - *Superdog: The Heart of a Hero*
 c BooChiTr - March 14 2004 - p2(1) [501+]

Buell, Emmett H. - *Enduring Controversies in Presidential Nominating Politics*
 Pers PS - v34 - i1 - Wntr 2005 - p49(2) [501+]

Buell, Frederick - *From Apocalypse to Way of Life: Environmental Crisis in the American Century*
 R&R Bk N - v20 - i1 - Feb 2005 - p83(1) [51-500]
 T&C - v45 - i3 - July 2004 - p638-639 [501+]

Buell, Lawrence - *Emerson*
 AL - v76 - i2 - June 2004 - p391(3) [501+]

Bueno, Eva P. - *I Wouldn't Want Anybody to Know: Native English Teaching in Japan*
 HNet - Sept 2004 - pNA [501+]

Buenstorf, Guido - *The Economics of Energy and the Production Process: An Evolutionary Approach*
 R&R Bk N - v19 - i3 - August 2004 - p118(1) [51-500]

Buerk, Michael - *The Road Taken: An Autobiography*
 NS - v133 - i4707 - Sept 27 2004 - p81(2) [501+]

Buettner, Elizabeth - *Empire Families: Britons and Late Imperial India*
 CR - v286 - i1668 - Jan 2005 - p57(1) [51-500]
 HT - v54 - i12 - Dec 2004 - p54(2) [501+]
 TLS - i5296 - Oct 1 2004 - p36(1) [501+]

Buff, Rachel - *Immigration and Political Economy of Home: West Indian Brooklyn and American Indian Minneapolis, 1945-1992*
 Am St - v45 - i1 - Spring 2004 - p165-166 [501+]

Buffa, D.W. - *Trial by Fire*
 KR - v73 - i5 - March 1 2005 - p243(1) [501+]
 PW - v252 - i10 - March 7 2005 - p50(1) [51-500]

Buffet, Annabel - *Bernard Buffet, the Secret Studio (Illus. by Fournol, Luc)*
 Choice - v42 - i2 - Oct 2004 - p284(1) [501+]
 LJ - v129 - i17 - Oct 15 2004 - p59(1) [501+]

Buffett, Jimmy - *A Salty Piece of Land*
 BL - v101 - i6 - Nov 15 2004 - p531(1) [51-500]
 Ent W - i797 - Dec 17 2004 - p91 [501+]
 KR - v72 - i20 - Oct 15 2004 - p975(1) [501+]
 NYTBR - Nov 28 2004 - p19 [501+]
 People - v62 - i24 - Dec 13 2004 - p54 [51-500]
 PW - v251 - i42 - Oct 18 2004 - p47(1) [51-500]
 S Liv - v40 - i2 - Feb 2005 - p151(1) [501+]

Buffie, Margaret - *The Finder*
 y BL - v101 - i4 - Oct 15 2004 - p397(1) [51-500]
 KR - v72 - i17 - Sept 1 2004 - p861(1) [501+]
 y SLJ - v51 - i1 - Jan 2005 - p126(1) [51-500]

Bufwack, Mary A. - *Finding Her Voice: Women in Country Music, 1800-2000*
 Choice - v41 - i7 - March 2004 - p1305(1) [501+]

Bugajski, Janusz - *Cold Peace: Russia's New Imperialism*
 NYRB - v52 - i2 - Feb 10 2005 - p19(4) [501+]

Buggelin, Gretchen - *Temples of Grace: The Material Transformation of Connecticut's Churches, 1790-1840.*
 W&M Q - v61 - i4 - Oct 2004 - p780-783 [51+]

Buggeln, Gretchen Townsend - *Temples of Grace: The Material Transformation of Connecticut's Churches, 1790-1840*
 JAH - v91 - i3 - Dec 2004 - p1003(2) [501+]
 JR - v85 - i1 - Jan 2005 - p134(3) [501+]
 Pub Hist - v26 - i3 - Summer 2004 - p84(86) [501+]

Buhle, Paul - *From the Lower East Side to Hollywood: Jews in American Popular Culture*
 Choice - v42 - i7 - March 2005 - p1267(1) [51-500]
 NS - v133 - i4697 - July 19 2004 - p53(2) [501+]
 R&R Bk N - v19 - i3 - August 2004 - p260(1) [51-500]
 Spec - v295 - i9183 - August 7 2004 - p35(1) [501+]

Hide in Plain Sight: The Hollywood Blacklistees in Film and Television, 1950-2002
 JAH - v91 - i3 - Dec 2004 - p1082(1) [501+]
 PHR - v73 - i3 - August 2004 - p522(523) [501+]
 R&R Bk N - v19 - i1 - Feb 2004 - p223(1) [51-500]
 Tikkun - v19 - i5 - Sept-Oct 2004 - p72(2) [501+]
 TV Q - v34 - i2 - Wntr 2004 - p73-76 [501+]

Radical Hollywood: The Untold Story Behind America's Favorite Movies
 S&S - v68 - i2 - Summer 2004 - p239-242 [501+]

Buhner, Stephen Harrod - *The Secret Teachings of Plants: The Intelligence of the Heart in the Direct Perception of Nature*
 Bwatch - March 2005 - pNA [51-500]
 PW - v251 - i45 - Nov 8 2004 - p44(1) [501+]

Buignes, Pierre A. - *Economics of Antitrust and Regulation in Telecommunications: Perspectives for the New European Regulatory Framework*
 SciTech - v28 - i3 - Sept 2004 - p8(1) [501+]

Buira, Ariel - *Challenges to the World Bank and IMF: Developing Country Perspectives*
 Choice - v41 - i11-12 - July-August 2004 - p2091(1) [501+]

Buis, Kellie - *Writing Every Day: Reading, Writing, and Conferencing Using Student-Led Language Experiences*
 Res Links - v10 - i1 - Oct 2004 - p42(2) [501+]

Buisseret, David - *The Mpamaker's Quest: Depicting New Worlds in Renaissance Europe*
 HNet - Nov 2004 - pNA [501+]

Buist, Ron - *Tales from Under the Rim: The Marketing of Tim Hortons*
 CBRA - Annual 2003 - p322(2) [51-500]

Bujold, Lois McMaster - *The Curse of Chalion (Read by James, Lloyd). Audiobook Review*
 y Kliatt - v39 - i1 - Jan 2005 - p40(1) [501+]

Bujor, Flavia - *The Prophecy of the Stones (Read by Ikeda, Jennifer). Audiobook Review*
 SLJ - v50 - i12 - Dec 2004 - p75(1) [501+]

The Prophecy of the Stones
 Globe & Mail - July 24 2004 - pD6 [501+]

Bukatman, Scott - *Matters of Gravity: Special Effects and Supermen in the 20th Century*
 Col Lit - v32 - i1 - Wntr 2005 - p166(11) [501+]
 JAAC - v62 - i3 - Summer 2004 - p307-309 [501+]
 JPC - v38 - i1 - August 2004 - p216(2) [501+]
 SFS - v31 - i2 - July 2004 - p302-306 [501+]

Bukdahl, Jorgen - *Soren Kierkegaard and the Common Man*
 Dialogue - v43 - i1 - Wntr 2004 - p175-177 [501+]

Bukhari, Zahid H. - *Muslims' Place in the American Public Square: Hope, Fears, and Aspirations*
 R&R Bk N - v19 - i3 - August 2004 - p65(1) [51-500]

Bukowski, Charles - *Selected Letters. Vol. 1: 1958-1965*
 TLS - i5293 - Sept 10 2004 - p26(1) [501+]

Sifting through the Madness for the Word, the Line, the Way: New Poems
 WLT - v78 - i3-4 - Sept-Dec 2004 - p97(2) [501+]

Slouching Toward Nirvana: New Poems
 BL - v101 - i9-10 - Jan 1 2005 - p803(1) [51-500]
 LJ - v130 - i3 - Feb 15 2005 - p134(1) [51-500]

Bulfoni, Clara - *Lost China: The Photographs of Leone Nani*
 Choice - v42 - i1 - Sept 2004 - p93(1) [501+]

Bulgakowa, Oksana - *Sergei Eisenstein: A Biography*
 Slav R - v63 - i4 - Winter 2004 - p911(2) [501+]

Bulger, Brad - *MySQL/PHP Database Applications. 2nd Ed.*
 SciTech - v28 - i3 - Sept 2004 - p23(1) [51-500]

Bulik, Cynthia M. - *Runaway Eating: The 8-Point Plan to Conquer Adult Food and Weight Obsessions*
 LJ - v130 - i2 - Feb 1 2005 - p108(1) [51-500]

Bull, Alan T. - *Microbial Diversity and Bioprospecting*
 E-Streams - July 2004 - pNA [501+]
 QRB - v79 - i3 - Sept 2004 - p309(2) [501+]
 SciTech - v28 - i1 - March 2004 - p75(1) [51-500]

Bull, Emma - *War for the Oaks*
 Cur R - v44 - i6 - Feb 2005 - p13(1) [501+]

Bull, Jane - *The Crafty Art Book*
 c BL - v101 - i8 - Dec 15 2004 - p748(1) [1-50]

Bull, John W. - *Numerical Analysis and Modelling in Geomechanics*
 E-Streams - August 2004 - pNA [501+]

Bull, Malcolm - *The Mirror of the Gods: How the Renaissance Artists Rediscovered the Pagan Gods*
 PW - v251 - i51 - Dec 20 2004 - p50(1) [501+]

Bull, Michael - *The Auditory Culture Reader*
 Choice - v42 - i3 - Nov 2004 - p524(1) [501+]

Bull, Stephen - *Encyclopedia of Military Technology and Innovation*
 SciTech - v28 - i4 - Dec 2004 - p171(1) [51-500]
 BL - v101 - i8 - Dec 15 2004 - p756(2) [501+]

Bullard, Carol - *Lungs: Injury, Illness and Health*
 c LibMed - v22 - i5 - Feb 2004 - p54(1) [501+]

Bullard, Robert D. - *Highway Robbery: Transportation Racism and New Routes to Equity*
 R&R Bk N - v19 - i3 - August 2004 - p121(1) [51-500]

Bullard, Stephan G. - *Larvae of Anomuran and Brachyuran Crabs of North Carolina: A Guide to the Described Larval Stages*
 SciTech - v28 - i1 - March 2004 - p69(1) [51-500]

Bullen, J.B. - *Byzantium Rediscovered: The Byzantine Revival in Europe and America*
 TimHES - v0 - i1664 - Oct 29 2004 - p26(1) [501+]

Buller, Jon - *Smart about the Fifty States*
 c LibMed - v22 - i4 - Jan 2004 - p74(1) [501+]

Smart about the Presidents
 c BL - v101 - i1 - Sept 1 2004 - p116(1) [501+]
 c BL - v101 - i3 - Oct 1 2004 - p327(1) [51-500]
 c PW - v251 - i28 - July 12 2004 - p66(1) [51-500]

The Wright Brothers Take Off (Illus. by Buller, Jon)
 c LibMed - v22 - i6 - March 2004 - p80(1) [501+]

Buller, Nickey B. - *Bacteria from Fish and Other Aquatic Animals: A Practical Identification Manual*
 SciTech - v28 - i3 - Sept 2004 - p74(1) [51-500]

Bulliet, Richard W. - *The Case for Islamo-Christian Civilization*
 LJ - v129 - i14 - Sept 1 2004 - p167(2) [51-500]
 MEP - v11 - i4 - Winter 2004 - p150(3) [501+]
 PW - v251 - i30 - July 26 2004 - p52(1) [501+]

Bullivant, Lucy - *Home Front: New Deveopment in Housing*
 R&R Bk N - v19 - i1 - Feb 2004 - p102(1) [51-500]

Bullock, August - *The Secret Sales Pitch: An Overview of Subliminal Advertising*
 Choice - v42 - i3 - Nov 2004 - p528(2) [1-50]

Bullock, Linda - *Looking through a Microscope*
   c SB - v40 - i3 - May-June 2004 - p130(1) [501+]
Looking through a Telescope
   c SB - v40 - i3 - May-June 2004 - p130(1) [501+]
Bullock, Steven R. - *Playing for Their Nation: Baseball and the American Military During the World War II*
   Choice - v42 - i2 - Oct 2004 - p331(1) [51-500]
Bullough, Peter G. - *Orthopaedic Pathology. 4th Ed.*
   SciTech - v28 - i3 - Sept 2004 - p108(1) [51-500]
Bulmer, Michael G. - *Francis Galton: Pioneer of Heredity and Biometry*
   SciTech - v28 - i3 - Sept 2004 - p59(1) [1-50]
Bultinck, Patrick - *Computational Medicinal Chemistry for Drug Discovery*
   SciTech - v28 - i1 - March 2004 - p125(1) [51-500]
Bulwer-Lytton, Edward - *Athens: Its Rise and Fall*
   TimHES - v0 - i1683 - March 18 2005 - p24(2) [501+]
Bulychev, Kir - *Those Who Survive*
   ChrSFF&H - v26 - i9 - Sept 2004 - p34(1) [51-500]
Bumgarner, Jeffery B. - *Profiling and Criminal Justice in America: A Reference Handbook*
   Choice - v42 - i7 - March 2005 - p1203(1) [51-500]
Bumgarner, John R. - *Parade of the Dead: A United States Army Physician's Memoir of Imprisonment by the Japanese, 1942-1945*
   R&R Bk N - v19 - i3 - August 2004 - p35(1) [51-500]
Bumstead, Pat E. - *Canadian Skin and Scales (Illus. by Worsley, Norman H.)*
   c CBRA - Annual 2003 - p563(2) [51-500]
Bumsted, J.M. - *Reporting the Resistance: Alexander Begg and Joseph Hargarve on the Red River Resistance*
   Beav - v84 - i6 - Dec 2004 - p47(2) [501+]
Trials and Tribulations: The Red River Settlement and the Emergence of Manitoba, 1811-1870
   CBRA - Annual 2003 - p337(1) [51-500]
Bunanta, Murti - *Indonesian Folktales (Illus. by Sudarta, G.M.)*
   R&R Bk N - v19 - i1 - Feb 2004 - p72(1) [1-50]
Buncel, E. - *Role of the Solvent in Chemical Reactions*
   SciTech - v28 - i1 - March 2004 - p57(1) [51-500]
Bunch, Bryan H. - *The History of Science and Technology: A Browser's Guide to the Great Discoveries, Inventions, and the People Who Made Them from the Dawn of Time to Today*
   Choice - v42 - i1 - Sept 2004 - p124(1) [501+]
   LJ - v129 - i12 - July 2004 - p115(1) [51-500]
   SciTech - v28 - i4 - Dec 2004 - p12(1) [1-50]
   y SLJ - v50 - i10 - Oct 2004 - p91(1) [51-500]
Bunch, Chris - *The Doublecross Program*
   ChrSFF&H - v26 - i9 - Sept 2004 - p34(1) [51-500]
Bunch, Meribeth - *The Singing Book. Audiobook Review*
   Teach Mus - v12 - i2 - Oct 2004 - p72(2) [51-500]
The Singing Book
   R&R Bk N - v19 - i2 - May 2004 - p193(1) [51-500]
Bunche, Ralph J. - *A Brief and Tentative Analysis of Negro Leadership*
   BL - v101 - i7 - Dec 1 2004 - p622(1) [51-500]
   Black Iss - v7 - i2 - March-April 2005 - p56(2) [501+]
Bundy, Carol - *The Nature of Sacrifice: A Biography of Charles Russell Lowell. Jr., 1835-64*
   KR - v73 - i1 - Jan 1 2005 - p28(2) [501+]
The Nature of Sacrifice: A Biography of Charles Russell Lowell, Jr., 1835-64
   LJ - v130 - i2 - Feb 1 2005 - p93(1) [51-500]
   PW - v252 - i5 - Jan 31 2005 - p59(1) [501+]
Bungartz, Hans-Joachim - *Introduction to Computer Graphics. 2nd Ed.*
   SciTech - v28 - i3 - Sept 2004 - p136(1) [51-500]
Bunge, Wiep van - *The Early Enlightenment in the Dutch Republic, 1650-1750: Selected Papers of a Conference Held at the Herzog August Bibliothek, Wolfenbuttel, 22-23 March 2001*
   R&R Bk N - v19 - i1 - Feb 2004 - p38(1) [1-50]
Bunkse, Edmunds Valdemars - *Geography and the Art of Life*
   R&R Bk N - v19 - i4 - Nov 2004 - p75(1) [501+]
Bunn, Davis - *Elixer (Read by Colacci, David). Audiobook Review*
   Kliatt - v38 - i6 - Nov 2004 - p46(1) [51-500]
Bunnett, Rochelle - *Friends at School*
   c SLJ - v50 - i7 - July 2004 - p45(1) [51-500]

Bunnin, Nicholas - *The Blackwell Dictionary of Western Philosophy*
   Choice - v42 - i7 - March 2005 - p1194(1) [51-500]
   LJ - v130 - i1 - Jan 1 2005 - p116(1) [51-500]
Bunting, Basil - *Basil Bunting on Poetry*
   Poet - v185 - i6 - March 2005 - p454(9) [501+]
Complete Poems
   Nation - v280 - i1 - Jan 3 2005 - p38 [501+]
   ABR - v25 - i6 - Sept-Oct 2004 - p15(2) [501+]
   Poet - v185 - i6 - March 2005 - p454(9) [501+]
Bunting, Eve - *Christmas Cricket (Illus. by Bush, Timothy)*
   c RT - v57 - Oct 2003 - p165 [1-50]
A Day's Work (Read by Fox, Joe). Audiobook Review
   c SLJ - v51 - i2 - Feb 2005 - p74(1) [51-500]
Gleam and Glow
   c RT - v57 - Dec 2003 - p394 [51-500]
The Presence (Read by Bresnahan, Alyssa). Audiobook Review
   c BL - v101 - i1 - Sept 1 2004 - p148(1) [51-500]
   c Kliatt - v38 - i4 - July 2004 - p54(2) [51-500]
   c SLJ - v50 - i7 - July 2004 - p60(1) [51-500]
The Presence
   c JAAL - v48 - i1 - Sept 2004 - p75(1) [501+]
   LibMed - v22 - i5 - Feb 2004 - p71(1) [501+]
Bunting, Josiah - *Ulysses S. Grant*
   NYTBR - Nov 14 2004 - p13 [501+]
   BL - v101 - i1 - Sept 1 2004 - p41(1) [51-500]
   BW - v34 - i38 - Sept 19 2004 - p2(1) [501+]
   KR - v72 - i13 - July 1 2004 - p612(1) [501+]
Bunting, Josiah, III - *Ulysses S. Grant*
   Am Spect - v38 - i1 - Feb 2005 - p58(3) [501+]
Bunting, Madeleine - *Willing Slaves: How the Overwork Culture Is Ruling Our Lives*
   TLS - i5299 - Oct 22 2004 - p28(1) [501+]
Buntman, Fran Lisa - *Robben Island and Prisoner Resistance to Apartheid*
   HNet - Dec 2004 - pNA [501+]
   Law&PolBR - June 2004 - p398(4) [501+]
Bunyak, Dawn Trimble - *Our Last Mission: A World War II Prisoner in Germany*
   HNet - Oct 2004 - pNA [501+]
Bunzel, Tom - *Make the Most of Your Digital Photos, Videos and Music*
   SciTech - v28 - i1 - March 2004 - p175(1) [1-50]
Bunzl, John - *Islam, Judaism, and the Political Role of Religions in the Middle East*
   Choice - v42 - i4 - Dec 2004 - p733(1) [1-50]
Buonaventura, Wendy - *Something in the Way She Moves: Dancing Women from Salome to Madonna*
   Choice - v42 - i5 - Jan 2005 - p863(1) [1-50]
Buppert, Carolyn - *Nurse Practitioner's Business Practice and Legal Guide, 2nd Ed.*
   E-Streams - Sept 2004 - pNA [501+]
Buracas, Giedrius T. - *Modulation of Neuronal Responses: Implications for Active Vision*
   SciTech - v28 - i4 - Dec 2004 - p71(1) [51-500]
Burack, Cynthia - *Healing Identities: Black Feminist Thought and the Politics of Groups*
   Bl S - v34 - i3 - Fall 2004 - p70-70 [501+]
Burana, Lily - *Strip City: A Stripper's Farewell Journey Across America*
   NY - v81 - i2 - Feb 28 2005 - p086 [501+]
Burant, Jim - *Drawing on the Land: The New World Travel Diaries and Watercolours of Millicent Mary Chaplin, 1838-1842*
   R&R Bk N - v19 - i4 - Nov 2004 - p70(1) [51-500]
Burch, Beverly - *Sweet to Burn*
   Lam Bk Rpt - v13 - i4-5 - Nov-Dec 2004 - p17(1) [501+]
Burch, Brian - *Resources for Radicals, 5th Ed.*
   CBRA - Annual 2003 - p10(2) [51-500]
Burch, Claire - *Tales of Young Urban Squatters Plus How to Squat*
   y Kliatt - v38 - i4 - July 2004 - p40(1) [51-500]
   R&R Bk N - v19 - i3 - August 2004 - p162(1) [501+]
Burchardt, Jeremy - *The Allotment Movement in England, 1793-1873*
   Albion - v36 - i1 - Spring 2004 - p150(2) [501+]
Paradise Lost: Rural Idyll and Social Change Since 1800
   Albion - v36 - i1 - Spring 2004 - p160(3) [501+]
Burchell, Brendan - *Systems of Production: Markets, Organisations and Performance*
   JEL - v41 - i4 - Dec 2003 - p1426(1) [501+]
Burchell, David - *Australian and New Zealand Politics*
   AJPS - v39 - i2 - July 2004 - p441(441) [501+]
Burckhart, Lewis - *Arabic Proverbs*
   Bwatch - v26 - i9 - Sept 2004 - p2(1) [51-500]

Burdekin, Richard C.K. - *Deflation: Current and Historical Perspectives*
   Choice - v42 - i7 - March 2005 - p1275(2) [51-500]
Burden, Ernest - *Illustrated Dictionary of Architectural Preservation*
   Choice - v41 - i11-12 - July-August 2004 - p2014(1) [501+]
Burden, George - *Amazing Medical Stories*
   CBRA - Annual 2003 - p428(2) [51-500]
Burdett, Carolyn - *Olive Schreiner and the Progress of Feminism: Evolution, Gender, Empire*
   Wom HR - v13 - i1 - Spring 2004 - p144(3) [501+]
Burdett, John - *Bangkok 8*
   NYTBR - August 8 2004 - p20 [501+]
Burdman, Anita - *Alfred Tarski: Life and Logic*
   Am Sci - v93 - i2 - March-April 2005 - p175(3) [501+]
Burdon, R.H. - *Suffering Gene: Environmental Threats to Our Health*
   SciTech - v28 - i1 - March 2004 - p86(1) [51-500]
Bureau of National Affairs - *Grievance Guide, 11th Ed.*
   HR Mag - v49 - i7 - July 2004 - pS20(1) [51-500]
   R&R Bk N - v19 - i1 - Feb 2004 - p101(1) [51-500]
Bureau of Transport and Regional Economics (Australia) - *Rail Infrastructure Pricing: Principles and Practice*
   JEL - v42 - i1 - March 2004 - p291(2) [501+]
Buresh, Bernice - *From Silence to Voice: What Nurses Know and Must Communicate to the Public*
   SciTech - v28 - i1 - March 2004 - p125(1) [1-50]
Burfield, Diana - *Edward Cresy, 1792-1858: Architect and Civil Engineer*
   HER - v119 - i483 - Sept 2004 - p1073(2) [501+]
   HER - v119 - i483 - Sept 2004 - p1073(2) [501+]
Burg, David F. - *A World History of Tax Rebellions: An Encyclopedia of Tax Rebels, Revolts, and Riots from Antiquity to the Present*
   R&R Bk N - v19 - i2 - May 2004 - p125 [501+]
Burgan, Michael - *Connecticut*
   c SLJ - v51 - i2 - Feb 2005 - p114(2) [51-500]
Burgard, Anna Marlis - *Flying Feet: A Story of Irish Dance (Illus. by Dees, Leighanne)*
   c PW - v252 - i11 - March 14 2005 - p66(1) [51-500]
Burgat, Francois - *Face to Face with Political Islam*
   JPR - v41 - i4 - July 2004 - p517-517 [501+]
Burge, James - *Heloise & Abelard : A New Biography*
   NYTBR - Feb 13 2005 - p8 [501+]
Heloise & Abelard: A Twelfth-Century Love Story
   Atl - v294 - i2 - Sept 2004 - p125(1) [501+]
   Bks & Cult - v11 - i1 - Jan-Feb 2005 - p15(1) [501+]
   BL - v101 - i4 - Oct 15 2004 - p364(1) [51-500]
   CR - v285 - i1663 - August 2004 - p120(2) [501+]
   KR - v72 - i17 - Sept 1 2004 - p845(1) [501+]
   LJ - v129 - i16 - Oct 1 2004 - p79(1) [51-500]
   PW - v251 - i42 - Oct 18 2004 - p56(1) [51-500]
Burge, Tyler - *Memory and Persons*
   RM - v58 - i1 - Sept 2004 - p230(1) [501+]
Burger, Philippe - *Sustainable Fiscal Policy and Economic Stability: Theory and Practice*
   R&R Bk N - v19 - i2 - May 2004 - p125 [501+]
Burger, Richard L. - *Machu Picchu: Unveiling the Mystery of the Incas*
   Choice - v42 - i2 - Oct 2004 - p335(1) [51-500]
Burgess, Adam - *Cellular Phones, Public Fears, and a Culture of Precaution*
   AJS - v110 - i3 - Nov 2004 - p840(3) [501+]
   TimHES - v0 - i1665 - Nov 5 2004 - p26(2) [501+]
Burgess, Andrew - *The Ascension of Karl Barth*
   R&R Bk N - v19 - i4 - Nov 2004 - p24(1) [51-500]
Burgess, Colin - *Fallen Astronauts: Heroes Who Died Reaching for the Moon*
   Choice - v41 - i7 - March 2004 - p1318(1) [501+]
Burgess, Geoffrey - *The Oboe*
   Choice - v42 - i1 - Sept 2004 - p110(1) [501+]
"The Premier Oboist of Europe": A Portrait of Gustave Vogt
   R&R Bk N - v19 - i1 - Feb 2004 - p197(1) [51-500]
Burgess, Helen - *Red Planet: Scientific and Cultural Encounters with Mars*
   SFS - v31 - i2 - July 2004 - p311-315 [501+]
Burgess, J.S. - *The Tradition of the War in Homer and the Epic Cycle*
   Class R - v53 - i2 - Nov 2003 - p276-278 [501+]

Book Review Index 2005 Cumulation **BURNS • 83**

Burgess, Melvin - *Doing It (Read by Gilby, James). Audiobook Review*
y Kliatt - v38 - i6 - Nov 2004 - p44(2) [51-500]
Doing It (Read by Flemyng, Jason). Audiobook Review
y PW - v251 - i41 - Oct 11 2004 - p27(1) [51-500]
Doing It
y CCB-B - v57 - i11 - July-August 2004 - p457(1) [501+]
y HB - v80 - i4 - July-August 2004 - p448(1) [51-500]
c LibMed - v23 - i3 - Nov-Dec 2004 - p71(1) [51-500]
Burgess, Michael C. - *Reference Guide to Science Fiction, Fantasy, and Horror*
SFS - v31 - i1 - March 2004 - p138-141 [501+]
Burgess, Robert - *Evolutionary Perspectives on Human Development, 2nd Ed.*
R&R Bk N - v19 - i4 - Nov 2004 - p11(1) [51-500]
Burgess, William A. - *Ventilation for Control of the Work Environment. 2nd Ed.*
SciTech - v28 - i3 - Sept 2004 - p149(1) [51-500]
Burgett, James - *Collaborative Collection Development: A Practical Guide for Your Library*
R&R Bk N - v19 - i4 - Nov 2004 - p256(1) [501+]
Burggraeve, Roger - *The Wisdom of Love in the Service of Love: Emmanuel Levinas on Justice, Peace, and Human Rights*
Theol St - v66 - i1 - March 2005 - p239(2) [501+]
Burgio, Santo - *Studia Borromaica, Saggi e documenti di storia religiosa e civile della prima eta moderna. Vols. 1-16*
Six Ct J - v35 - i3 - Fall 2004 - p838-840 [501+]
Burgmann, Verity - *Power, Profit and Protest: Australian Social Movements and Globalisation*
JEL - v42 - i1 - March 2004 - p322(1) [501+]
Burgoyne, John - *The New Best Recipe (Illus. by Burgoyne, John)*
LJ - v129 - i17 - Oct 15 2004 - p82(1) [51-500]
The Burial at Thebes
Am Theat - v21 - i8 - Oct 2004 - p139(4) [51-500]
Burian, Peter - *Sophocles: Electra*
Can Lit - i182 - Autumn 2004 - p176(2) [501+]
Buridge, Richard A. - *Jesus Now andTthen*
Choice - v42 - i5 - Jan 2005 - p869(1) [1-50]
Burk, Martha - *Cult of Power: Sex Discrimination in Corporate America and What Can Be Done About It*
KR - v73 - i1 - Jan 1 2005 - p29(1) [501+]
Burk, Ronald L. - *Small Animal Radiology and Ultrasonography: A Diagnostic Atlas and Text. 3rd Ed.*
SciTech - v28 - i1 - March 2004 - p132(1) [51-500]
Burke, Alafair - *Missing Justice*
Globe & Mail - July 10 2004 - pD12 [501+]
Burke, Anthony - *In Fear of Security: Australia's Invasion Anxiety*
AJPS - v39 - i3 - Nov 2004 - p661(1) [501+]
Burke, Bill - *Autrefois Maison Privee.*
LJ - v129 - i19 - Nov 15 2004 - p56(1) [51-500]
Burke, Carol - *Camp All-American, Hanoi Jane, and the High-and-Tight: Gender, Folklore, and Changing Military Culture*
HNet - Oct 2004 - pNA [501+]
R&R Bk N - v19 - i4 - Nov 2004 - p251(1) [501+]
Burke, Declan - *Eight-Ball Boogie*
BL - v101 - i5 - Nov 1 2004 - p466(1) [51-500]
Burke, Dorothy - *How to Use Lotus Notes 6*
R&R Bk N - v19 - i1 - Feb 2004 - p110(1) [1-50]
Burke, Edmund R. - *High-Tech Cycling. 2nd Ed.*
E-Streams - July 2004 - pNA [501+]
SciTech - v28 - i1 - March 2004 - p109(1) [51-500]
Burke, James Lee - *In the Moon of Red Ponies (Read by Stechschulte, Tom). Audiobook Review*
PW - v251 - i31 - August 2 2004 - p20(1) [501+]
In the Moon of Red Ponies
Globe & Mail - July 10 2004 - pD12 [501+]
People - v62 - i1 - July 5 2004 - p49 [51-500]
Burke, Jan - *Bloodlines: An Irene Kelly Novel*
KR - v72 - i21 - Nov 1 2004 - p1029(1) [51-500]
LJ - v129 - i20 - Dec 1 2004 - p94(1) [51-500]
Burke, Jason - *Al-Qaeda: Casting a Shadow of Terror*
ABR - v25 - i5 - July-August 2004 - p9(2) [501+]
Choice - v42 - i2 - Oct 2004 - p367(2) [51-500]
Burke, Jill - *Changing Patrons: Social Identity and the Visual Arts in Renaissance Florence*
Choice - v42 - i4 - Dec 2004 - p648(1) [1-50]
Burke, John Francis - *Mestizo Democracy: The Politics of Crossing Borders*
SHQ - v107 - i3 - Jan 2004 - p472(1) [501+]
WHQ - v35 - i4 - Winter 2004 - p510-511 [501+]
Burke, John P. - *Becoming President: The Bush Transition, 2000-2003*
Choice - v42 - i5 - Jan 2005 - p933(2) [51-500]
R&R Bk N - v19 - i4 - Nov 2004 - p64(1) [51-500]
Burke, Kealan Patrick - *Taverns of the Dead*
PW - v251 - i47 - Nov 22 2004 - p42(2) [51-500]
Burke, Mary M. - *Primary Care of the Older Adult: A Multidisciplinary Approach. 2nd Ed.*
SciTech - v28 - i1 - March 2004 - p108(1) [51-500]
Burke, Monte - *Sowbelly: The Obsessive Quest for the World-Record Largemouth Bass*
LJ - v130 - i4 - March 1 2005 - p94(1) [51-500]
PW - v252 - i6 - Feb 7 2005 - p56(1) [51-500]
Burke, Morgan - *The Party Room #1: Get It Started*
y PW - v252 - i9 - Feb 28 2005 - p68(1) [51-500]
Burke, Peter - *History and Historians in the Twentieth Century*
JIH - v35 - i2 - Autumn 2004 - p297(2) [501+]
Burke, Roger Hopkins - *Hard Cop, Soft Cop: Dilemmas and Debates in Contemporary Policing*
R&R Bk N - v19 - i3 - August 2004 - p167(1) [501+]
Burke, Scott - *Maiden Voyage: Ship's Company Theatre Premieres*
CBRA - Annual 2003 - p247(1) [51-500]
Burke, Shannon - *Safelight*
BL - v100 - i22 - August 2004 - p1896(1) [51-500]
KR - v72 - i24 - Dec 15 2004 - pS10(1) [501+]
LJ - v129 - i15 - Sept 15 2004 - p47(1) [51-500]
NYTBR - Oct 10 2004 - p20 [501+]
PW - v251 - i28 - July 12 2004 - p41(1) [51-500]
Burke, W. Lewis - *Matthew J. Perry: The Man, His Times, and His Legacy*
Law&PolBR - Sept 2004 - pNA [501+]
Burkett, B.G. - *Stolen Valor: How the Vietnam Generation Was Robbed of Its Heroes and Its History*
Mar Crp G - v88 - i8 - August 2004 - p58(1) [501+]
Burkey, John M. - *Overcoming Hearing Aid Fears: The Road to Better Hearing*
SciTech - v28 - i1 - March 2004 - p115(1) [51-500]
Burkhardt, Barbara - *William Maxwell: A Literary Life*
LJ - v130 - i4 - March 1 2005 - p84(1) [51-500]
Burkhardt, Johannes - *Das Reformations-Jahhundert*
Six Ct J - v34 - i4 - Winter 2003 - p1200-1201 [501+]
Burkhardt, Ross M. - *Refiguring History: New Thoughts on an Old Discipline*
TCR - v106 - i2 - Feb 2004 - p257-261 [501+]
Burkhart, William H. - *Shippensburg, Pennsylvania in the Civil War, 2nd Rev. Ed.*
R&R Bk N - v19 - i4 - Nov 2004 - p65(1) [51-500]
Burkholder, Nicholas - *On Staffing: Advice and Perspectives from HR Leaders*
NACEJou - v64 - i4 - Summer 2004 - p11-11 [501+]
Burks, Alice Rowe - *Who Invented the Computer? The Legal Battle That Changed Computing History*
T&C - v45 - i2 - April 2004 - p449-450 [501+]
Burleigh, Robert - *American Moments: Scenes from American History*
c BL - v100 - i21 - July 2004 - p1838(2) [1-50]
Into the Air (Illus. by Wylie, Bill)
c RT - v57 - Oct 2003 - p173 [1-50]
Langston's Train Ride (Illus. by Jenkins, Leonard)
c BL - v101 - i2 - Sept 15 2004 - p238(1) [51-500]
c KR - v72 - i18 - Sept 15 2004 - p911(1) [501+]
c PW - v252 - i1 - Jan 3 2005 - p54(1) [51-500]
c SLJ - v50 - i12 - Dec 2004 - p127(1) [51-500]
Seurat and La Grande Jatte
y Sch Lib - v52 - i3 - Autumn 2004 - p164(1) [501+]
Burleson, Donald K. - *Physical Database Design Using Oracle*
SciTech - v28 - i4 - Dec 2004 - p32(1) [51-500]
Burley, Jeffery - *Encyclopedia of Forest Sciences*
Choice - v42 - i4 - Dec 2004 - p632(2) [1-50]
Nature - v431 - i7004 - Sept 2 2004 - p23(1) [501+]
Burley, Justice - *Dworkin and His Critics: With Replies by Dworkin*
Choice - v42 - i7 - March 2005 - p1240(1) [51-500]
Burlingame, Dwight F. - *Philanthropy in America: A Comprehensive Historical Encyclopedia, Vols. 1-3*
Choice - v42 - i5 - Jan 2005 - p838(2) [1-50]
BL - v101 - i8 - Dec 15 2004 - p759(1) [501+]
Burman, Barbara - *Material Strategies: Dress and Gender in Historical Perspective*
Choice - v41 - i7 - March 2004 - p1346(2) [501+]
Burn, Amos - *A Chess Biography by Richard Forster*
Spec - v297 - i9206 - Jan 15 2005 - p62(1) [501+]
Burnard, Trevor - *Creole Gentlemen: The Maryland Elite, 1691-1776*
HNet - Sept 2004 - pNA [501+]
Mastery, Tyranny, and Desire: Thomas Thistlewood and His Slaves in the Anglo-Jamaican World
Choice - v42 - i5 - Jan 2005 - p912(1) [1-50]
Nation - v279 - i18 - Nov 29 2004 - p23 [501+]
NYRB - v51 - i18 - Nov 18 2004 - p43(5) [501+]
Burner, David - *John F. Kennedy and a New Generation, 2nd Ed.*
R&R Bk N - v19 - i4 - Nov 2004 - p64(1) [51-500]
Burnett, Betty - *Delta Force: Counterterrorism Unit of the U.S. Army*
y VOYA - v27 - i4 - Oct 2004 - p333(1) [51-500]
The Trial of Julius and Ethel Rosenberg: A Primary Source Account
c SLJ - v50 - i10 - Oct 2004 - p187(2) [51-500]
Burnett, D. Graham - *Masters of All They Surveyed: Exploration, Geography, and a British El Dorado*
Ams - v61 - i2 - Oct 2004 - p270(2) [501+]
Burnett, Frances Hodgson - *The Secret Garden*
c RT - v57 - Sept 2003 - p98 [1-50]
c Storyworks - v12 - i2 - Oct 2004 - p6(1) [501+]
Burnett, J. Alexander - *Passion for Wildlife: The History of the Canadian Wildlife Service*
CBRA - Annual 2003 - p408(1) [501+]
Burnett, John - *England Eats Out: A Social History of Eating Out in England From 1830 to the Present*
R&R Bk N - v19 - i4 - Nov 2004 - p79(1) [51-500]
Burnett, Mark - *Jump In! Even If You Don't Know How to Swim*
Ent W - Feb 4 2005 - p139 [51-500]
NW - Feb 21 2005 - p32 [51-500]
Burnett, Mark M. - *Hacking the Code: ASP.NET Web Application Security*
SciTech - v28 - i3 - Sept 2004 - p156(1) [51-500]
Burnett, Mark Thornton - *Constructing 'Monsters' in Shakespearean Drama and Early Modern Culture*
Shakes Q - v55 - i1 - Spring 2004 - p98-100 [501+]
Burnett, Paula - *The EmLit Project: European Minority Literatures in Translation*
TimHES - v0 - i1666 - Nov 12 2004 - p31(1) [501+]
Burnett, Ron - *How Images Think*
Afterimage - v32 - i1 - July-August 2004 - p18(1) [501+]
Choice - v42 - i1 - Sept 2004 - p191(1) [501+]
Burnett, Ros - *What Works in Probation and Youth Justice: Developing Evidence-Based Practice*
R&R Bk N - v19 - i4 - Nov 2004 - p149(1) [501+]
Burney, Charles - *Historical Dictionary of the Hittites*
Choice - v42 - i3 - Nov 2004 - p462(1) [1-50]
R&R Bk N - v19 - i3 - August 2004 - p49(1) [51-500]
Burnford, Sheila Every - *The Incredible Journey*
c Storyworks - v12 - i3 - Nov-Dec 2004 - p6(1) [51-500]
Burnham, Gracia - *To Fly Again: Surviving the Tailspins of Life*
PW - v252 - i7 - Feb 14 2005 - p72(1) [51-500]
Burnham, Niki - *Spin Control*
y SLJ - v51 - i2 - Feb 2005 - p132(1) [51-500]
Burnham, Robert - *Exploring the Starry Sky*
Astron - v32 - i10 - Oct 2004 - p90 [51-500]
Burnham, William - *Return of the Peregrine: A North American Saga of Tenacity and Teamwork*
SciTech - v28 - i3 - Sept 2004 - p65(1) [51-500]
Burnie, David - *Endangered Planet.*
y SLJ - v51 - i1 - Jan 2005 - p142(1) [51-500]
The Kingfisher Illustrated Nature Encyclopedia
c SB - v40 - i6 - Nov-Dec 2004 - p264(2) [51-500]
c Sch Lib - v52 - i3 - Autumn 2004 - p150(1) [501+]
c SLJ - v50 - i8 - August 2004 - p55(2) [51-500]
Burns, Catherine M. - *Ecological Interface Design*
SciTech - v28 - i4 - Dec 2004 - p131 [51-500]
Burns, Chester R. - *Saving Lives, Training Caregivers, Making Discoveries: A Centennial History of the University of Texas Medical Branch at Galveston*
SHQ - v108 - i1 - July 2004 - p118-119 [501+]
Burns, David - *Feeling Good: The New Mood Therapy*
Globe & Mail - August 21 2004 - pD15 [501+]
Stark's Conjectures: Recent Work and New Directions, Proceedings
SciTech - v28 - i4 - Dec 2004 - p35(1) [51-500]

Burton, Jessica - *Death Goes Shopping: A Jenny Turnbull Mystery*
　CBRA - Annual 2003 - p156(1) [51-500]
Burton, Lloyd - *Worship and Wilderness: Culture, Religion, and Law in the Management of Public Lands and Resources*
　WHQ - v35 - i1 - Spring 2004 - p77-78 [501+]
Burton, Michael G. - *Star Formation at High Angular Resolution: Proceedings*
　SciTech - v28 - i4 - Dec 2004 - p46(1) [51-500]
Burton, Richard D.E. - *Holy Tears, Holy Blood: Women, Catholicism, and the Culture of Suffering in France, 1840-1970*
　Choice - v42 - i6 - Feb 2005 - p1088(1) [51-500]
　Comw - v131 - i16 - Sept 24 2004 - p24(3) [501+]
　TLS - i5298 - Oct 15 2004 - p30(1) [51-500]
Burton, Richard Francis, Sir - *The Thousand and One Nights*
　Globe & Mail - July 24 2004 - pD15 [501+]
Burton, Sarah - *A Double Life: A Biography of Charles and Mary Lamb*
　NYRB - v51 - i16 - Oct 21 2004 - p54(4) [501+]
Burton, Sharon - *Business Math Using Excel*
　R&R Bk N - v19 - i3 - August 2004 - p132(1) [51-500]
Burton, Thomas - *The Serpent and the Spirit; Glenn Summerford's Story*
　R&R Bk N - v19 - i3 - August 2004 - p195(1) [501+]
Burton, Virginia Lee - *Mike Mulligan and His Steam Shovel (Read by Ross, Rod). Audiobook Review*
　c BL - v101 - i5 - Nov 1 2004 - p508(1) [51-500]
　Mike Mulligan and His Steam Shovel (Read by Simon, Stephen). Audiobook Review
　c BL - v101 - i9-10 - Jan 1 2005 - p778(1) [1-50]
　Mike Mulligan and His Steam Shovel (Read by Ross, Rod). Audiobook Review
　c PW - v251 - i37 - Sept 13 2004 - p36(1) [51-500]
Burton, Wendy - *Joy Is a Plum Colored Acrobat: 45 Life-Affirming Visualizations for Breast Cancer Treatment and Aftercare (Illus. by Mulazzani, Simona)*
　LJ - v129 - i14 - Sept 1 2004 - p184(2) [501+]
Burud, Sandra - *Leveraging the New Human Capital: Adaptive Strategies, Results Achieved, and Stories of Transformation*
　Choice - v42 - i7 - March 2005 - p1273(1) [51-500]
Buruma, Ian - *Occidentalism: A Short History of Anti-Westernism*
　NS - v133 - i4708 - Oct 4 2004 - p48(3) [501+]
　TimHES - v0 - i1673 - Jan 7 2005 - p22(1) [501+]
　TLS - i5297 - Oct 8 2004 - p25(1) [501+]
　Occidentalism: The West in the Eyes of Its Enemies
　Choice - v42 - i1 - Sept 2004 - p162(1) [501+]
　Globe & Mail - Nov 27 2004 - pD3 [51-500]
　IBMR - v28 - i3 - July 2004 - p97(1) [501+]
　R&R Bk N - v19 - i3 - August 2004 - p28(1) [1-50]
Bury, Laurent - *Seductive Strategies in the Novels of Anthony Trollope*
　R&R Bk N - v19 - i4 - Nov 2004 - p237(1) [501+]
Busby, Ailie - *Drat the Fat Cat!*
　LibMed - v22 - i4 - Jan 2004 - p61(1) [501+]
Busby, Brian - *Character Parts: Who's Really Who in CanLit*
　CBRA - Annual 2003 - p253(2) [51-500]
　Character Parts: Who's Really Who in CanLit. Audiobook Review
　Globe & Mail - Dec 18 2004 - pD25 [1-50]
Busby, Horace - *The Thirty-First of March: An Intimate Portrait of Lyndon Johnson's Final Days in Office*
　KR - v72 - i24 - Dec 15 2004 - p1175(1) [501+]
　LJ - v130 - i1 - Jan 1 2005 - p131(1) [51-500]
　PW - v252 - i5 - Jan 31 2005 - p58(1) [501+]
Busby, Jason - *Mastering Unreal Technology: The Art of Level Design*
　Bwatch - Feb 2005 - pNA [51-500]
　Bwatch - March 2005 - pNA [51-500]
Busby, Peter - *First to Fly (Illus. by Craig, David)*
　c RT - v58 - i3 - Nov 2004 - p288(1) [1-50]
Busby, Sian - *A Wonderful Little Girl*
　y Sch Lib - v52 - i4 - Winter 2004 - p217(1) [51-500]
Buscaglia-Salgado, Jose F. - *Undoing Empire: Race and Nation in the Mulatto Carribbean*
　Ams - v61 - i2 - Oct 2004 - p307(2) [501+]
Busch, Briton C. - *Canada and the Great War: Western Front Association Papers*
　Can Hist R - v85 - i3 - Sept 2004 - p643(3) [501+]
　J Mil H - v68 - i4 - Oct 2004 - p1275-1276 [501+]

Busch, Fredric N. - *Psychodynamic Treatment of Depression*
　SciTech - v28 - i3 - Sept 2004 - p101(1) [51-500]
Busch, Peter - *All the Way with JFK?: Britain, the US and the Vietnam War*
　JAH - v91 - i1 - June 2004 - p324-325 [501+]
Busch, Robert H. - *The Grizzly Almanac*
　Kliatt - v38 - i6 - Nov 2004 - p38(2) [51-500]
Buscombe, Edward - *Cinema Today*
　Choice - v41 - i11-12 - March 2004 - p1303(1) [501+]
　TimHES - v0 - i1647 - July 2 2004 - p28(2) [501+]
Buser, Thomas - *Religious Art in the Nineteenth Century in Europe and America*
　CHR - v90 - i3 - July 2004 - p519(2) [501+]
Bush, Barbara (American first lady) - *Courting the Countess*
　BL - v101 - i6 - Nov 15 2004 - p569(1) [51-500]
Bush, Catherine - *Claire's Head*
　BIC - v33 - i9 - Dec 2004 - p7(2) [501+]
　Globe & Mail - Sept 18 2004 - pD3 [501+]
　Globe & Mail - Nov 27 2004 - pD3 [51-500]
Bush, David M. - *Living with Florida's Atlantic Beaches: Coastal Hazards from Amelia Island to Key West*
　Choice - v42 - i3 - Nov 2004 - p512(2) [1-50]
Bush, Gail - *The School Buddy System: The Practice of Collaboration*
　SLJ - v50 - i10 - Oct 2004 - pS72(1) [51-500]
Bush, George W. - *We Will Prevail: President George W. Bush on War, Terrorism, and Freedom*
　R&R Bk N - v19 - i1 - Feb 2004 - p61(1) [501+]
Bush, Karen - *The Complete Equine Emergency Bible: The Comprehensive Guide to Coping with Every Horse-Related Emergency from First Aid to Road Safety*
　LJ - v129 - i15 - Sept 15 2004 - p74(1) [51-500]
Bush, Melanie E. L. - *Breaking the Code of Good Intentions: Everyday Forms of Whiteness*
　R&R Bk N - v19 - i4 - Nov 2004 - p57(1) [51-500]
Bush, Richard C. - *At Cross Purposes: U.S.-Taiwan Relations Since 1942*
　Choice - v42 - i5 - Jan 2005 - p929(1) [51-500]
　R&R Bk N - v19 - i3 - August 2004 - p64(1) [51-500]
Bush, Tony - *Theories of Educational Leadership and Management, 3rd Ed.*
　R&R Bk N - v19 - i1 - Feb 2004 - p187(1) [51-500]
Bushey, Jeanne - *Orphans in the Sky (Illus. by Krykorka, Vladyana)*
　c Globe & Mail - Dec 11 2004 - pD28 [51-500]
Bushill-Matthews, Philip - *The Gravy Train.*
　CR - v285 - i1662 - July 2004 - p49(2) [501+]
Bushko, Renata G. - *Future of Health Technology*
　SciTech - v28 - i3 - Sept 2004 - p79(1) [51-500]
Bushman, Richard Lyman - *Believing History: Latter-Day Saint Essays*
　Bks & Cult - v10 - i6 - Nov-Dec 2004 - p38(2) [501+]
　R&R Bk N - v19 - i3 - August 2004 - p28(1) [1-50]
Bushnell, David - *Simon Bolivar: Liberation and Disappointment*
　Ams - v61 - i2 - Oct 2004 - p261(1) [1-50]
Bushnell, Rebecca - *Green Desire: Imagining Early Modern English Gardens*
　Choice - v41 - i7 - March 2004 - p1321(1) [501+]
Busick, Jennifer - *OSHA Compliance Guide for Medical Employers, 2nd Ed.*
　SciTech - v28 - i3 - Sept 2004 - p87(1) [51-500]
Busiek, Kurt - *Arrowsmith: So Smart in Their Fine Uniforms (Illus. by Pacheco, Carlos)*
　LJ - v130 - i1 - Jan 1 2005 - p87(2) [51-500]
　PW - v251 - i39 - Sept 27 2004 - p39(2) [51-500]
　Shockrockets
　y BL - v101 - i5 - Nov 1 2004 - p474(1) [51-500]
Business and Legal Reports - *How to Write an Affirmative Action Plan*
　HR Mag - v49 - i7 - July 2004 - pS12(1) [51-500]
Business and Research Associates - *The UK Market for Office Furniture*
　R&R Bk N - v19 - i3 - August 2004 - p121(1) [51-500]
Buskirk, Judith L. Van - *Generous Enemies: Patriots and Loyalists in Revolutionary New York*
　Am St - v45 - i2 - Spring 2004 - p143-144 [501+]
　J Am St - v38 - i1 - April 2004 - p172-172 [501+]
Busquet, Carisse - *Impressions of Rajasthan*
　R&R Bk N - v19 - i3 - August 2004 - p54(1) [51-500]

Buss, Andreas E. - *Russian-Orthodox Tradition and Modernity*
　R&R Bk N - v19 - i1 - Feb 2004 - p24(1) [51-500]
Buss, David - *The Murderer Next Door: Why the Mind Is Designed to Kill*
　LJ - v129 - i20 - Dec 1 2004 - p90(1) [51-500]
Buss, Doris - *Globalizing Family Values: The Christian Right in International Politics*
　AJS - v110 - i1 - July 2004 - p257(3) [501+]
Buss, Samuel R. - *3-D Computer Graphics: A Mathematical Introduction with OpenGL*
　SIAM Rev - v46 - i2 - June 2004 - p364-365 [501+]
Buss, Sarah - *Contours of Agency: Essays on Themes from Harry Frankfurt*
　Ethics - v114 - i4 - July 2004 - p810(6) [501+]
Bussagli, Marco - *Understanding Architecture. Vols. 1-2*
　LJ - v130 - i1 - Jan 1 2005 - p105(2) [51-500]
　Understanding Architecture, Vols. 1-2
　Ref Rev - Oct 2004 - pNA [501+]
　R&R Bk N - v19 - i4 - Nov 2004 - p202(1) [501+]
　Understanding Architecture. Vols. 1-2
　SLJ - v50 - i12 - Dec 2004 - p83(1) [501+]
Bussani, Mauro - *Pure Economic Loss in Europe*
　Law Q Rev - v120 - July 2004 - p524-528 [501+]
Busse, Richard C. - *Fired, Laid Off or Forced Out: A Complete Guide to Severance, Benefits and Your Rights When You're Starting Over*
　LJ - v130 - i4 - March 1 2005 - p99(1) [51-500]
Bussey, Ben - *The Clementine Atlas of the Moon*
　Astron - v32 - i10 - Oct 2004 - p90 [51-500]
　Choice - v42 - i3 - Nov 2004 - p506(1) [1-50]
Bussing-Burks, Marie - *Influential Economists*
　SLJ - v50 - i10 - Oct 2004 - pS58(1) [51-500]
Bustard, Anne - *Buddy: The Story of Buddy Holly (Illus. by Cyrus, Kurt)*
　c KR - v73 - i1 - Jan 1 2005 - p49(1) [51-500]
　c PW - v252 - i8 - Feb 21 2005 - p175(1) [51-500]
　c SLJ - v51 - i2 - Feb 2005 - p115(1) [51-500]
Bustin, Stephen A. - *A-Z of Quantitative PCR*
　SciTech - v28 - i4 - Dec 2004 - p73(1) [51-500]
Buswell, Robert - *The Encyclopedia of Buddhism, Vols. 1-2.*
　HNet - Oct 2004 - pNA [501+]
Buswell, Robert E. - *Encyclopaedia of Buddhism, Vols. 1-2*
　R&R Bk N - v19 - i1 - Feb 2004 - p15(1) [51-500]
Butala, Sharon - *Old Man on His Back: Portrait of a Prairie Landscape*
　CBRA - Annual 2003 - p112(1) [501+]
Butalia, Tarunjit Singh - *Religion in Ohio: Profiles of Faith Communities*
　R&R Bk N - v19 - i3 - August 2004 - p15(1) [1-50]
Butalia, Urvashi - *Speaking Peace: Women's Voices from Kashmir*
　JGS - v13 - i3 - Nov 2004 - p290-291 [501+]
Butcher, A.J. - *Spy High: Mission One*
　ChrSFF&H - v26 - i9 - Sept 2004 - p34(1) [51-500]
　y PW - v251 - i27 - July 5 2004 - p57(1) [51-500]
　y SLJ - v50 - i7 - July 2004 - p102(1) [51-500]
　Spy High: Mission Three: The Serpent Scenario.
　SLJ - v50 - i12 - Dec 2004 - p140(1) [501+]
　Spy High: Mission Two: Chaos Rising
　ChrSFF&H - v26 - i9 - Sept 2004 - p34(1) [51-500]
Butcher, James Neal - *A Beginner's Guide to the MMPI-2, 2nd Ed.*
　R&R Bk N - v19 - i4 - Nov 2004 - p11(1) [51-500]
Butcher, Jim - *Blood Rites*
　BL - v100 - i22 - August 2004 - p1912(1) [51-500]
　The Dead Beat
　KR - v73 - i5 - March 1 2005 - p266(1) [501+]
　Furies of Calderon
　y BL - v101 - i3 - Oct 1 2004 - p318(1) [51-500]
　Bwatch - Dec 2004 - pNA [501+]
　LJ - v129 - i15 - Sept 15 2004 - p52(1) [51-500]
　PW - v251 - i39 - Sept 27 2004 - p42(2) [51-500]
Butcher, Kevin - *Roman Syria and the Near East*
　Choice - v42 - i5 - Jan 2005 - p909(1) [1-50]
Butcher, Kristin - *Trouble with Liberty*
　c CBRA - Annual 2003 - p476(2) [51-500]
Butcher, Melissa - *Transnational Television, Cultural Identity and Change: When STAR Came to India*
　R&R Bk N - v19 - i2 - May 2004 - p109(1) [1-50]
Butcher, Nancy - *Beauty*
　y Kliatt - v39 - i2 - March 2005 - p24(1) [51-500]

Butcher, Pat - *The Perfect Distance: Ovett and Coe: The Record Breaking Rivalry*
Econ - v372 - i8386 - July 31 2004 - p70US [501+]
Lon R Bks - v26 - i17 - Sept 2 2004 - p20(1) [501+]

Buten, Howard - *Through the Glass Wall: Journeys into the Closed-Off Worlds of the Autistic*
NYT - August 10 2004 - pF7(L) [501+]

Butler, Andrew - *The True Knowledge of Ken MacLeod*
SFS - v31 - i2 - July 2004 - p294-298 [501+]

Butler, Anne - *Our Wonderful World! (Illus. by Munro, Moira)*
c Sch Lib - v52 - i3 - Autumn 2004 - p129(1) [51-500]

Butler, Anthony - *Contemporary South Africa*
Choice - v42 - i3 - Nov 2004 - p539(2) [1-50]

Butler, Daniel Allen - *The Age of Cunard: A Transatlantic History 1839-2003*
R&R Bk N - v19 - i3 - August 2004 - p122(1) [51-500]

Butler, Dom Cuthbert - *Western Mysticism: Augustine, Gregory, and Bernard on Comtemplation and the Contemplative Life, 2nd Ed.*
R&R Bk N - v19 - i1 - Feb 2004 - p24(1) [1-50]

Butler, Dori Hillestad - *My Mom's Having a Baby! (Illus. by Thompson, Whitman)*
c KR - v73 - i5 - March 1 2005 - p284(1) [51-500]

Butler, Elizabeth - *Yankee Doodle Riddles: American History Fun*
LibMed - v22 - i4 - Jan 2004 - p75(1) [501+]
LibMed - v22 - i4 - Jan 2004 - p75(2) [501+]

Butler, John E. - *New Perspectives on Women Entrepreneurs*
R&R Bk N - v19 - i1 - Feb 2004 - p100(1) [1-50]
Opportunity Identification and Entrepreneurial Behavior
R&R Bk N - v19 - i4 - Nov 2004 - p85(1) [51-500]

Butler, Judith - *Antigone's Claim: Kinship between Life and Death*
Signs - v30 - i2 - Wntr 2005 - p1711(4) [501+]
The Judith Butler Reader
Wom R Bks - v22 - i2 - Nov 2004 - p18(2) [501+]
Precarious Life: The Power of Mourning and Violence
Wom R Bks - v22 - i2 - Nov 2004 - p18(2) [501+]
Undoing Gender
Wom R Bks - v22 - i2 - Nov 2004 - p18(2) [501+]

Butler, Lee - *Emperor and Aristocracy in Japan, 1467-1680: Resilience and Renewal*
HJAS - v64 - i1 - June 2004 - p176-184 [501+]

Butler, Linda - *Yangtze Remembered: The River Beneath the Lake*
E Mag - v16 - i2 - March-April 2005 - p62(1) [501+]
LJ - v130 - i1 - Jan 1 2005 - p107(2) [51-500]

Butler, M. - *Animal Cell Culture and Technology, 2nd ed.*
E-Streams - Dec 2004 - pNA [501+]
QRB - v79 - i4 - Dec 2004 - p417(1) [501+]
SciTech - v28 - i3 - Sept 2004 - p167(1) [51-500]

Butler, M. Christina - *Who's Been Eating My Porridge? (Illus. by Howarth, Daniel)*
c KR - v72 - i15 - August 1 2004 - p738(1) [51-500]
c SLJ - v51 - i1 - Jan 2005 - p88(1) [51-500]

Butler, Marilyn - *The Novels and Selected Works of Maria Edgeworth, Vols. 1-12*
R&R Bk N - v19 - i4 - Nov 2004 - p236(1) [501+]

Butler, Nancy - *The Kindness of a Rogue*
BL - v101 - i5 - Nov 1 2004 - p469(1) [51-500]

Butler, Rachel - *The Assassin*
PW - v252 - i10 - March 7 2005 - p55(1) [51-500]

Butler, Rebecca P. - *Copyright for Teachers and Librarians*
R&R Bk N - v19 - i4 - Nov 2004 - p169(1) [501+]
SLJ - v50 - i12 - Dec 2004 - p178(1) [51-500]

Butler, Robert - *Jade Coast: The Ecology of the North Pacific Ocean*
CBRA - Annual 2003 - p400(1) [51-500]

Butler, Robert Olen - *Had a Good Time: Stories from American Postcards*
BW - v34 - i32 - August 8 2004 - p7(1) [501+]
Ent W - i779 - August 20 2004 - p130 [51-500]
NYTBR - August 15 2004 - p6 [501+]

Butler, Roger - *Place Made: Australian Print Workshop*
Choice - v42 - i5 - Jan 2005 - p844(2) [1-50]

Butler, Shane - *The Hand of Cicero*
Class R - v53 - i2 - Nov 2003 - p346-347 [501+]

Butler, Smedley D. - *War Is a Racket*
NS - v133 - i4697 - July 19 2004 - p48(2) [501+]

Butler, Tajuana - *Just My Luck*
PW - v252 - i5 - Jan 31 2005 - p49(1) [51-500]

Butlin, R. A. - *Historical Atlas of North Yorkshire*
HER - v119 - i483 - Sept 2004 - p972(3) [501+]

Butlin, Ron - *Vivaldi and the Number 3 and Other Impossible Stories*
LJ - v130 - i2 - Feb 1 2005 - p73(1) [51-500]
TLS - i5287 - July 30 2004 - p20(1) [501+]

Butor, Michel - *Degrees*
LJ - v130 - i3 - Feb 15 2005 - p172(1) [51-500]

Butricia, Andrew J. - *Single Stage to Orbit: Politics, Space Technology and the Quest for Reusable Rocketry*
SciTech - v28 - i3 - Sept 2004 - p164(1) [51-500]
T&C - v45 - i3 - July 2004 - p633-635 [501+]
TLS - i5284 - July 9 2004 - p11(1) [501+]

Butt, Hans-Jurgen - *Physics and Chemistry of Interfaces*
SciTech - v28 - i1 - March 2004 - p55(1) [51-500]

Butt, Howard E. - *Who Can You Trust? Overcoming Betrayal and Fear*
Ch Today - v48 - i11 - Nov 2004 - p86(1) [501+]

Butt, Tony - *Surf Science: An Introduction to Waves for Surfing*
SciTech - v28 - i3 - Sept 2004 - p6(1) [501+]

Butte, George - *I Know That You Know That I Know: Narrating Subjects from Moll Flanders to Marnie*
Choice - v41 - i11-12 - July-August 2004 - p2042(1) [501+]

Butterfield, Ardis - *Poetry and Music in Medievel France: From Jean Renart to Guillaume de Machant*
FS - v58 - i2 - April 2004 - p240(2) [501+]

Butterfield, Samuel Hale - *U.S. Development Aid--an Historic First: Achievements and Failures in the Twentieth Century*
Choice - v42 - i6 - Feb 2004 - p1068(2) [501+]

Buttino, Marco - *La rivoluzione capovolta: L'Asia centrale tra il crollo dell'Impero zarista e la formazione dell'URSS*
Russ Rev - v63 - i3 - July 2004 - pNA [501+]
Slav R - v63 - i4 - Winter 2004 - p876(2) [501+]

Button, Kenneth - *Defining Aerospace Policy: Essays in Honor of Francis T. Hoban*
SciTech - v28 - i3 - Sept 2004 - p8(1) [501+]
Recent Developments in Transport Economics
JEL - v42 - i1 - March 2004 - p341(2) [501+]
R&R Bk N - v19 - i1 - Feb 2004 - p103(1) [51-500]

Buttrick, David - *Speaking Jesus: Homiletic Theology and the Sermon on the Mount*
Intpr - v58 - i4 - Oct 2004 - p424(1) [501+]

Butts, Michele Tucker - *Galvanized Yankees on the Upper Missouri: The Face of Loyalty*
AHR - v109 - i2 - April 2004 - p528(2) [501+]
JAH - v91 - i3 - Dec 2004 - p1023(1) [501+]
WHQ - v35 - i3 - Autumn 2004 - p401(2) [501+]

Butz, Bob - *Beast of Never, Cat of God: The Hunt for the Mountain Lion East of the Mississippi*
BL - v101 - i9-10 - Jan 1 2005 - p794(1) [51-500]
PW - v251 - i49 - Dec 6 2004 - p52(1) [51-500]

Butz, Jeffrey J. - *The Brother of Jesus and the Lost Teachings of Christianity*
LJ - v130 - i3 - Feb 15 2005 - p135(1) [51-500]

Butz, Jewrey - *The Brother of Jesus and the Lost Teachings of Christianity*
c PW - v252 - i7 - Feb 14 2005 - p73(1) [51-500]

Butz, William P. - *Will the Scientific and Technical Workforce Meet the Requirements of the Federal Government?*
SciTech - v28 - i4 - Dec 2004 - p13(1) [1-50]

Butzen, Paul - *Firms' Investment and Finance Decisions: Theory and Empirical Methodology, Proceedings*
R&R Bk N - v19 - i1 - Feb 2004 - p117(1) [51-500]

Buvelot, Quentin - *Albert Eckhout: A Dutch Artist in Brazil*
NYRB - v51 - i13 - August 12 2004 - p8(4) [501+]

Buxton, Richard - *The Complete World of Greek Mythology*
CR - v285 - i1666 - Nov 2004 - p316(1) [501+]
LJ - v129 - i12 - July 2004 - p92(1) [51-500]

Buyer, Laurie Wagner - *Side Canyons*
BL - v101 - i3 - Oct 1 2004 - p307(1) [51-500]
Roundup M - v12 - i3 - Feb 2005 - p25(1) [51-500]

Buys, Christian J. - *Quick History of Leadville*
Bwatch - v26 - i8 - August 2004 - p10(1) [51-500]

Buysse, Virginia - *Consultation in Early Childhood Settings*
R&R Bk N - v20 - i1 - Feb 2005 - p7(1) [51-500]

Buzan, Barry - *From International to World Society?: English School Theory and the Social Structure of Globalisation*
Choice - v42 - i4 - Dec 2004 - p732(1) [1-50]

Buzzanell, Patrice M. - *Gender in Applied Communication Contexts*
R&R Bk N - v19 - i1 - Feb 2004 - p124(1) [51-500]

Buzzatti, Dino - *The Bears' Famous Invasion of Sicily*
People - v62 - i25 - Dec 20 2004 - p58 [51-500]

Buzzeo, Toni - *Dawdle Duckling*
c PW - v252 - i5 - Jan 31 2005 - p69(2) [51-500]
Ready or Not, Dawdle Duckling
c KR - v73 - i1 - Jan 1 2005 - p49(1) [51-500]

By the Great Horn Spoon!
c PW - v251 - i45 - Nov 8 2004 - p25(1) [501+]

By the Great Spoon!
c PW - v251 - i45 - Nov 8 2004 - p25(1) [501+]

Byars, Betsy - *Keeper of the Doves (Read by Campbell, Cassandra). Audiobook Review*
c BL - v100 - i21 - July 2004 - p1857(1) [1-50]
Little Horse on His Own (Illus. by McPhail, David)
c BL - v101 - i1 - Sept 1 2004 - p120(1) [1-50]
c KR - v72 - i16 - August 15 2004 - p803(1) [51-500]
c SLJ - v50 - i9 - Sept 2004 - p154(1) [51-500]

Byars, Mel - *The Design Encyclopedia*
Choice - v42 - i5 - Jan 2005 - p824(2) [51-500]

Byatt, A.S. - *Essential Guide*
Bwatch - v26 - i9 - Sept 2004 - p1(1) [51-500]
Little Black Book of Stories
AM - v191 - i9 - Oct 4 2004 - p17 [501+]
Little Black Book of Stories. Audiobook Review
Globe & Mail - Dec 18 2004 - pD25 [1-50]
Little Black Book of Stories
Wom R Bks - v21 - i10-11 - July 2004 - p12(1) [501+]

Bybee, Rodger W. - *Evolution in Perspective: The Science Teacher's Compendium*
SB - v40 - i4 - July-August 2004 - p158(2) [51-500]
Sci Teach - v71 - i4 - April 2004 - p79-80 [501+]

Byers, Ann - *African-American History from Emancipation to Today: Rising Above the Ashes of Slavery*
y SLJ - v50 - i12 - Dec 2004 - p156(1) [51-500]
Neil Armstrong: The First Man on the Moon
y SLJ - v51 - i1 - Jan 2005 - p142(1) [51-500]
The Trail of Tears: A Primary Source History of the Forced Relocation of the Cherokee Nation
y SLJ - v50 - i10 - Oct 2004 - p188(1) [51-500]

Byers, Jacqueline Fowler - *Patient Safety: Principles and Practice*
SciTech - v28 - i3 - Sept 2004 - p78(1) [51-500]

Byers, Julia J. Gentleman - *Educators, Therapists, and Artists on Reflective Practice*
R&R Bk N - v19 - i1 - Feb 2004 - p249(1) [51-500]

Byers, Michael - *Long for This World*
VQR - v80 - i1 - Wntr 2004 - p272-272 [501+]

Byham-Gray, Laura - *A Clinical Guide to Nutrition Care in Kidney Disease*
SciTech - v28 - i4 - Dec 2004 - p105(1) [51-500]

Byman, Daniel L. - *Keeping the Peace: Lasting Solutions to Ethnic Conflict*
JPR - v41 - i6 - Nov 2004 - p752-753 [501+]

Byman, Jeremy - *Showdown at High Noon: Witch-Hunts, Critics, and the End of the Western*
Choice - v42 - i6 - Feb 2005 - p1028(2) [51-500]
R&R Bk N - v19 - i4 - Nov 2004 - p224(1) [501+]

Byng, Georgia - *Molly Moon Stops the World (Read by Higgins, Clare). Audiobook Review*
c BL - v101 - i2 - Sept 15 2004 - p261(1) [51-500]

Bynum, Eboni - *Jamari's Drum (Illus. by Diakite, Baba Wague)*
c Globe & Mail - Jan 29 2005 - pD10 [51-500]
y HB - v81 - i1 - Jan-Feb 2005 - p72(2) [51-500]
c KR - v72 - i20 - Oct 15 2004 - p1002(1) [51-500]
c SLJ - v50 - i11 - Nov 2004 - p92(1) [51-500]

Bynum, Richard T. - *Archi-Toons: Funniness, Comedy & Delight*
R&R Bk N - v19 - i4 - Nov 2004 - p206(1) [501+]

Bynum, Sarah Shun-lien - *Madeleine Is Sleeping*
BW - v34 - i40 - Oct 3 2004 - p11(1) [501+]
KR - v72 - i13 - July 1 2004 - p589(1) [501+]
LJ - v129 - i12 - July 2004 - p67(1) [51-500]
People - Sept 20 2004 - p61 [51-500]

Byrd, Adrianne - *Measure of a Man*
BL - v101 - i6 - Nov 15 2004 - p567(1) [51-500]
LJ - v130 - i1 - Jan 1 2005 - p91(1) [51-500]

Byrd, Max - *Shooting the Sun*
NYTBR - Jan 30 2005 - p24 [501+]

Byrd, Robert C. - *Leonardo, Beautiful Dreamer*
 c LibMed - v22 - i6 - March 2004 - p74(1) [501+]
 c LibMed - v22 - i6 - March 2004 - p74(1) [501+]
 Losing America: Confronting a Reckless and Arrogant
 Presidency
  BW - v34 - i29 - July 18 2004 - p2(1) [501+]
  NYRB - v51 - i13 - August 12 2004 - p4(3)
  [501+]
  NYTBR - Sept 12 2004 - p24 [501+]
Byrne, Dana N. - *The Unfinished Agenda of the*
 Selma-Montgomery Voting Rights March
  Black Iss - v7 - i2 - March-April 2005 - p36(2)
  [501+]
Byrne, Ed - *Game Level Design*
  Bwatch - March 2005 - pNA [501+]
Byrne, Geraldine - *Tom & Jack: A Frontier Story*
  Quad - v48 - i7-8 - July-August 2004 - p42(4)
  [501+]
Byrne, Jane M. - *My Chicago*
  R&R Bk N - v19 - i3 - August 2004 - p74(1) [51-
  500]

Byrne, Joseph Patrick - *The Black Death*
  SciTech - v28 - i4 - Dec 2004 - p91(1) [51-500]
Byrne, Julie - *O God of Players: The Story of the*
 Immaculata Mighty Macs
  CH - v73 - i4 - Dec 2004 - p892(2) [501+]
  Choice - v41 - i7 - March 2004 - p1332(1) [501+]
  JAH - v91 - i3 - Dec 2004 - p1099(2) [501+]
  R&R Bk N - v19 - i1 - Feb 2004 - p75(1) [51-500]
  CHR - v90 - i3 - July 2004 - p588(1) [501+]
Byrne, Paula - *Perdita: The Life of Mary Robinson*
  NS - v133 - i4714 - Nov 15 2004 - p51(1) [501+]
  Spec - v297 - i9207 - Jan 22 2005 - p37(1) [501+]
Byrnes, Dolores M. - *Driving the State: Families and*
 Public Policy in Central Mexico
  JEL - v42 - i1 - March 2004 - p315(2) [501+]
  JRAI - v10 - i3 - Sept 2004 - p740(3) [501+]
Byrnes, Mark E. - *Nuclear, Chemical, and Biological*
 Terrorism: Emergency Response and Public Protection
  E-Streams - June 2004 - pNA [501+]

Byron, Christopher - *Testosterone, Inc.: Tales of CEOs*
 Gone Wild
  BL - v101 - i4 - Oct 15 2004 - p387(1) [51-500]
 Testosterone Inc.: Tales of CEOs Gone Wild
  NYT - July 11 2004 - pBU8 [501+]
Byron, Gay, L. - *Symbolic Blackness and Ethnic Difference*
 in Early Christian Literature
  JAAR - v72 - i3 - Sept 2004 - p765-768 [501+]
Byron, Reginald - *Regional Development on the North*
 American Margin
  R&R Bk N - v19 - i4 - Nov 2004 - p137(1) [1-50]
 Retrenchment and Regeneration in Rural Newfoundland
  CBRA - Annual 2003 - p348(2) [501+]
  CS - v33 - i6 - Nov 2004 - p696(2) [501+]
Bytwerk, Randall L. - *Bending Spines: The Propagandas*
 of Nazi Germany and the German Democratic Republic
  Bwatch - Dec 2004 - pNA [51-500]
  Choice - v42 - i6 - Feb 2005 - p1017(1) [51-500]
  R&R Bk N - v19 - i4 - Nov 2004 - p156(1) [501+]

C

Caban, Geoffrey - *World Graphic Design: Contemporary Graphics from Africa, the Far East, Latin America and the Middle East*
Choice - v42 - i1 - Sept 2004 - p85(1) [501+]
LJ - v129 - i12 - July 2004 - p77(2) [51-500]

Cabantous, Alain - *Blasphemy: Impious Speech in the West from the Seventeenth to the Nineteenth Century*
HER - v119 - i483 - Sept 2004 - p1060(2) [501+]
HER - v119 - i483 - Sept 2004 - p1060(2) [501+]
JIH - v35 - i1 - Summer 2004 - p122-123 [501+]

Cabet, Etienne - *Travels in Icaria*
R&R Bk N - v19 - i1 - Feb 2004 - p147(1) [51-500]

Cabibbo, Andrea - *The Internet for Cell and Molecular Biologists, 2nd Ed.*
SciTech - v28 - i3 - Sept 2004 - p58(1) [1-50]

Cabot, Meg - *Every Boy's Got One*
BL - v101 - i6 - Nov 15 2004 - p560(1) [51-500]
Globe & Mail - Feb 12 2005 - pD6 [501+]
KR - v72 - i17 - Sept 1 2004 - p820(1) [51-500]
PW - v251 - i45 - Nov 8 2004 - p33(1) [501+]
The Highs and Lows of Being Mia.
Kliatt - v38 - i6 - Nov 2004 - p14(1) [501+]
Mia Tells It Like It Is
PW - v251 - i34 - August 23 2004 - p56(1) [51-500]
Princess in Pink (Read by Lewis, Clea). Audiobook Review
c BL - v101 - i1 - Sept 1 2004 - p148(1) [51-500]
y Kliatt - v38 - i5 - Sept 2004 - p63(3) [51-500]
SLJ - v50 - i10 - Oct 2004 - p84(2) [51-500]
Princess in Pink
c SLJ - v50 - i8 - August 2004 - p116(1) [51-500]
y VOYA - v27 - i4 - Oct 2004 - p292(1) [51-500]
The Princess Present: A Princess Diaries Book.
y Kliatt - v38 - i6 - Nov 2004 - p6(1) [51-500]
y PW - v251 - i42 - Oct 18 2004 - p66(1) [501+]
Teen Idol
y BL - v101 - i3 - Oct 1 2004 - p321(1) [51-500]
y CCB-B - v57 - i11 - July-August 2004 - p458(1) [501+]
y Kliatt - v38 - i4 - July 2004 - p7(1) [51-500]
c KR - v72 - i14 - July 15 2004 - p682(1) [51-500]
y PW - v251 - i35 - August 30 2004 - p56(1) [51-500]
c SLJ - v50 - i8 - August 2004 - p116(1) [51-500]
y VOYA - v27 - i4 - Oct 2004 - p292(1) [51-500]
Twilight
y SLJ - v51 - i2 - Feb 2005 - p132(1) [51-500]

Cabrera, Jane - *If You're Happy and You Know It! (Illus. by Cabrera, Jane)*
c KR - v73 - i3 - Feb 1 2005 - p174(1) [51-500]
c PW - v252 - i11 - March 14 2005 - p70(1) [501+]

Cach, Lisa - *Dream of Me*
BL - v101 - i2 - Sept 15 2004 - p218(1) [51-500]

Cachin, Francoise - *Gauguin*
Choice - v41 - i11-12 - July-August 2004 - p2033(2) [501+]
R&R Bk N - v19 - i2 - May 2004 - p196(1) [51-500]

Caciola, Nancy - *Discerning Spirits: Divine and Demonic Possession in the Middle Ages*
AHR - v109 - i3 - June 2004 - p964(2) [501+]
Ren Q - v57 - i4 - Winter 2004 - p1460(3) [501+]

The Caddie Was a Reindeer: And Other Tales of Extreme Recreation (Book) - *The Caddie Was a Reindeer: And Other Tales of Extreme Recreation*
BL - v101 - i7 - Dec 1 2004 - p626(1) [51-500]

Cade, Jack - *Rumpole and the Penge Bungalow Murders*
BL - v101 - i4 - Oct 15 2004 - p362(1) [51-500]
Globe & Mail - Nov 27 2004 - pD30 [501+]
KR - v72 - i19 - Oct 1 2004 - p942(2) [501+]
PW - v251 - i44 - Nov 1 2004 - p47(1) [501+]

Cade, Tom J. - *Return of the Peregrine: A North American Saga of Tenacity and Teamwork*
Choice - v42 - i1 - Sept 2004 - p132(1) [501+]
y SB - v40 - i5 - Sept-Oct 2004 - p213(1) [51-500]
SB - v40 - i6 - Nov-Dec 2004 - p244(1) [51-500]

Cadenhead, Rogers - *How to Use the Internet. 8th Ed.*
SciTech - v28 - i1 - March 2004 - p156(1) [51-500]

Cadge, Wendy - *God in Chinatown: Religion and Survival in New York's Evolving Immigrant Community*
CS - v33 - i5 - Sept 2004 - p564-566 [501+]
Heartwood: The First Generation of Theravada Buddhism in America
LJ - v130 - i2 - Feb 1 2005 - p84(1) [51-500]
PW - v251 - i50 - Dec 13 2004 - p63(1) [51-500]

Cadier, Florence - *My Parents Are Getting Divorced: How to Keep It Together When Your Mom and Dad Are Splitting Up (Illus. by Gandini, Claire)*
y BL - v101 - i7 - Dec 1 2004 - p645(1) [51-500]
y SLJ - v50 - i9 - Sept 2004 - p223(1) [51-500]
y TES - v0 - i4586 - June 4 2004 - psssss18(2) [501+]
y VOYA - v27 - i4 - Oct 2004 - p335(1) [501+]

Cadili, L. - *Viamque Adfectat Olympo. Memoria Ellenistica Nelle 'Georgiche' di Virgilio*
Class R - v53 - i2 - Nov 2003 - p359-360 [501+]

Cadnum, Michael - *Blood Gold*
y HB - v80 - i4 - July-August 2004 - p448(2) [51-500]
c Teach Lib - v32 - i3 - Feb 2005 - p10(1) [51-500]
y VOYA - v27 - i3 - August 2004 - p208(1) [1-50]
Daughter of the Wind
y LibMed - v22 - i6 - March 2004 - p66(1) [501+]
Starfall: Phaeton and the Chariot of the Sun.
y BL - v101 - i3 - Oct 1 2004 - p321(1) [51-500]
c CCB-B - v58 - i4 - Dec 2004 - p163(1) [51-500]
y Kliatt - v38 - i5 - Sept 2004 - p6(2) [51-500]
c KR - v72 - i17 - Sept 1 2004 - p861(1) [51-500]
c PW - v251 - i42 - Oct 18 2004 - p64(2) [51-500]
y SLJ - v50 - i10 - Oct 2004 - p158(1) [51-500]

Cadwalladr, Carole - *The Family Tree*
BL - v101 - i7 - Dec 1 2004 - p634(1) [51-500]
KR - v72 - i18 - Sept 15 2004 - p881(2) [501+]
LJ - v129 - i16 - Oct 1 2004 - p66(1) [51-500]
People - v63 - i6 - Feb 14 2005 - p59 [501+]
PW - v251 - i45 - Nov 8 2004 - p33(1) [501+]
Ent W - i798 - Dec 24 2004 - p72 [501+]
Genealogy Is Destiny
NYTBR - Jan 23 2005 - p13 [501+]

Cadwell, Karin - *Case Studies in Breastfeeding: Problem-Solving Skills and Strategies*
SciTech - v28 - i1 - March 2004 - p117(1) [51-500]

Cadwell, L.B. - *Bringing Learning to Life: The Reggio Approach to Early Childhood Education*
CE - v80 - i5 - Mid-Summer 2004 - p277(1) [51-500]

Caesar, Sid - *Caesar's Hours: My Life in Comedy, with Love and Laughter*
R&R Bk N - v19 - i1 - Feb 2004 - p227(1) [51-500]
TV Q - v34 - i2 - Wntr 2004 - p70-72 [501+]

Caestecker, Frank - *Alien Policy in Belgium, 1840-1940: The Creation of Guest Workers, Refugees, and Illegal Aliens*
JMH - v76 - i3 - Sept 2004 - p700(3) [501+]

Cafaro, Philip - *Thoreau's Living Ethics: Walden and the Pursuit of Virtue*
R&R Bk N - v20 - i1 - Feb 2005 - p3(1) [51-500]

Cagle, Eldon, Jr. - *Fort Sam: The Story of Fort Sam Houston, Texas*
SHQ - v107 - i4 - April 2004 - p625(2) [501+]

Cahan, David - *From Natural Philosophy to the Sciences: Writing the History of Nineteenth-Century Science*
Choice - v41 - i7 - March 2004 - p1317(1) [501+]

Cahay, M. - *Cold Cathodes II: Proceedings*
SciTech - v28 - i1 - March 2004 - p161(1) [51-500]

Cahiers Patrice de La Tour du Pin, 18: Correspondance
FS - v58 - i1 - Jan 2004 - p136(1) [501+]

Cahill, Christopher - *Gather Round Me*
ILS - v24 - i1 - Fall 2004 - p32(1) [51-500]

Cahill, Lisa Sowle - *Bioethics and the Common Good*
SciTech - v28 - i3 - Sept 2004 - p58(1) [1-50]

Cahill, Sean - *Same-Sex Marriage in the United States: Focus on the Facts*
LJ - v129 - i13 - August 2004 - p103(2) [501+]
R&R Bk N - v19 - i4 - Nov 2004 - p131(1) [1-50]

Cahill, Spencer E. - *Inside Social Life: Readings in Sociological Psychology and Microsociology, 4th Ed.*
R&R Bk N - v19 - i3 - August 2004 - p144(1) [51-500]

Cahill, Susan - *The Smiles of Rome: A Literary Companion for Readers and Travelers*
LJ - v130 - i2 - Feb 1 2005 - p106(2) [51-500]
Women Write: A Mosaic of Women's Voices in Fiction, Poetry, Memoir, and Essay
y Kliatt - v38 - i5 - Sept 2004 - p40(2) [51-500]

Cahill, Thomas - *Sailing the Wine-Dark Sea: Why the Greeks Matter. Audiobook Review*
Globe & Mail - August 14 2004 - pD13 [1-50]
Sailing the Wine-Dark Sea: Why the Greeks Matter
NYTBR - Oct 17 2004 - p26 [501+]

Cahill, Tim - *Lost in My Own Backyard: A Walk in Yellowstone National Park (Read by Prichard, Michael). Audiobook Review*
Kliatt - v38 - i6 - Nov 2004 - p56(1) [51-500]
Lost in My Own Backyard: A Walk in Yellowstone National Park
BW - v34 - i39 - Sept 26 2004 - p8(1) [501+]

Cahn, Isabelle - *The Little Book of Gauguin*
R&R Bk N - v19 - i2 - May 2004 - p196(1) [1-50]

Cahn, Naomi R. - *Families by Law: An Adoption Reader*
Choice - v42 - i2 - Oct 2004 - p376(1) [51-500]
Law&PolBR - July 2004 - p546(2) [501+]

Cahnman, Werner J. - *Jews and Gentiles: A Historical Sociology of Their Relations*
Choice - v42 - i5 - Jan 2005 - p938(2) [51-500]

Cai, Rong - *The Subject in Crisis in Contemporary Chinese Literature*
R&R Bk N - v19 - i3 - August 2004 - p256(1) [51-500]

Cai, Zong-qi - *Chinese Aesthetics: The Ordering of Literature, the Arts, and the Universe in the Six Dynasties*
R&R Bk N - v19 - i4 - Nov 2004 - p12(1) [1-50]

Caiazza, G. - *Ricerche su Dione di Prusa*
Class R - v54 - i1 - May 2004 - p53(2) [501+]

Caiazzo, Irene - *Lectures medievales de Macrobe: Les Glosae Colonienses super Macrobium: Etude et edition*
Isis - v95 - i3 - Sept 2004 - p486(2) [501+]

Caillault, Jean-Pierre - *A Tale of Four Cities: Nineteenth Century Baseball's Most Exciting Season, 1889, in Contemporary Accounts*
R&R Bk N - v19 - i1 - Feb 2004 - p74(1) [1-50]

Cailleteau, Sylvie Thorel - *Anamorphoses Decadentes: L'Art De La Defiguration 1880-1914-Etudes Offertes A Jean De Palacole:.*
FS - v58 - i3 - July 2004 - p425-426 [501+]

Cailliet, Rene - *Illustrated Guide to Functional Anatomy of the Musculoskeletal System*
E-Streams - July 2004 - pNA [501+]

Caima, Neil - *The Neil Caiman Audio Collection (Read by Caiman, Neil). Audiobook Review*
c PW - v252 - i2 - Jan 10 2005 - p24(1) [51-500]

Cain, Chelsea - *Confessions of a Teen Sleuth! (Illus. by Lia, Miternique)*
LJ - v129 - i18 - Nov 1 2004 - p72(1) [501+]
Confessions of a Teen Sleuth. (Illus. by Miternique, Lia)
KR - v72 - i17 - Sept 1 2004 - p837(1) [51-500]

Cain, Clive Thomas - *Building Down Barriers: A Guide to Construction Best Practice*
R&R Bk N - v19 - i1 - Feb 2004 - p103(1) [51-500]

Cain, David - *Nature's Art Box: From T-Shirts to Twig Baskets, 65 Cool Projects for Crafty Kids to Make*
LibMed - v22 - i4 - Jan 2004 - p73(1) [501+]
LibMed - v22 - i4 - Jan 2004 - p73(2) [501+]

Cain, Glenye - *The Home Run Horse: Inside America's Billion-Dollar Racehorse Industry and the High-Stakes Dreams That Fuel It*
PW - v251 - i34 - August 23 2004 - p46(1) [51-500]

Cain, M.J. - *Fodor: Language, Mind and Philosophy*
Dialogue - v43 - i2 - Spring 2004 - p395(3) [501+]

Cain, P.J. - *Hobson and Imperialism: Radicalism, New Liberalism, and the Finance 1887-1938*
AHR - v109 - i2 - April 2004 - p612(2) [501+]

Caine, Leslie - *Death by Inferior Design: A Domestic Bliss Mystery*
PW - v251 - i37 - Sept 13 2004 - p64(1) [51-500]

Caine, Rachel - *Chill Factor*
BL - v101 - i7 - Dec 1 2004 - p624(2) [51-500]
PW - v251 - i50 - Dec 13 2004 - p51(1) [51-500]
Heat Stroke
Bwatch - Dec 2004 - pNA [51-500]

Caines, Michael - *Major Voices: Eighteenth-Century Women Playwrights*
TLS - i5300 - Oct 29 2004 - p31(1) [51-500]

Cairncross, Frances - *The Company of the Future: Meeting the Management Challenges of the Communications Revolutions*
JPR - v41 - i5 - Sept 2004 - p638-638 [501+]
The Death of Distance: 2.0. How the Communications Revolution Will Change Our Lives
JPR - v41 - i5 - Sept 2004 - p638-638 [501+]

Cairns, Francis - *Caesar Against Liberty? Perspectives on His Autocracy*
R&R Bk N - v19 - i1 - Feb 2004 - p147(1) [51-500]

Cairns, Kathleen V. - *Treasures: The Stories Women Tell About the Things They Keep*
R&R Bk N - v19 - i4 - Nov 2004 - p1(1) [51-500]

Cajani, G. - *L'Antico Degli Antichi*
Class R - v53 - i2 - Nov 2003 - p470-472 [501+]

Cajita Musica de Crayola!
c SLJ - v50 - i11 - Nov 2004 - p80(1) [51-500]

Calabrese, Andrew - *Toward a Political Economy of Culture: Capitalism and Communication in the Twenty-First Century*
Choice - v41 - i11-12 - July-August 2004 - p2038(1) [501+]
R&R Bk N - v19 - i2 - May 2004 - p129 [51-500]

Calame, Claude - *Myth and History in Ancient Greece: The Symbolic Creation of a Colony*
AHR - v109 - i4 - Oct 2004 - p1285-1286 [501+]

Calaprice, Alice - *The Einstein Almanac*
AS - v74 - i1 - Wntr 2005 - p127(3) [501+]

Calarco, Matthew - *Animal Philosophy: Essential Readings in Continental Thought*
R&R Bk N - v19 - i4 - Nov 2004 - p2(1) [51-500]

Calasso, Roberto - *K*
LJ - v130 - i4 - March 1 2005 - p84(1) [51-500]
NY - v81 - i3 - March 7 2005 - p078 [51-500]
NYRB - v52 - i2 - Feb 10 2005 - p4(4) [501+]
PW - v252 - i2 - Jan 10 2005 - p53(1) [51-500]

Caldecott, Keith W. - *Eukaryotic DNA Damage Surveillance and Repair*
SciTech - v28 - i3 - Sept 2004 - p60(1) [1-50]

Calder, Alan - *James Maclaren: Arts and Crafts Pioneer*
Apo - v160 - i511 - Sept 2004 - p102(2) [501+]

Calder, Alexander - *Calder, Miro*
LJ - v130 - i3 - Feb 15 2005 - p125(1) [51-500]

Calder, Angus - *Disasters and Heroes: On War, Memory and Representation*
TLS - i5291 - August 27 2004 - p28(1) [51-500]

Calder, Iain - *The Untold Story: My 20 Years Running The National Enquirer*
CJR - v43 - i2 - July-August 2004 - p48(4) [501+]
Mac - Sept 20 2004 - p78(1) [51-500]
NYT - July 26 2004 - pE6 [501+]
NYTBR - August 1 2004 - p6 [501+]

Calder, K.E. - *How to Be a Frog Millionaire*
c CBRA - Annual 2003 - p477(1) [51-500]
Prank
c CBRA - Annual 2003 - p477(1) [51-500]

Calder, Nigel - *Magic Universe*
TLS - i5263 - Feb 13 2004 - p9-9 [501+]

Calder, Robert L. - *Beware the British Serpent: The Role of Writers in British Propoganda in the United States, 1939-1945*
R&R Bk N - v19 - i3 - August 2004 - p35(1) [51-500]

Calderazzo, John - *Rising Fire: Volcanoes and Our Inner Lives*
BL - v100 - i22 - August 2004 - p1884(1) [51-500]
BL - v101 - i7 - Dec 1 2004 - p632(1) [51-500]

Calderon-Benavides, H.A. - *Advanced Structural Materials: Proceedings*
SciTech - v28 - i1 - March 2004 - p139(1) [51-500]

Calderon, Gloria - *Argueta, Jorge: Zipitio*
CE - v81 - i1 - Fall 2004 - p46(1) [51-500]

Calderone, Richard A. - *Pathogenic Fungi: Host Interactions and Emerging Strategies for Control*
SciTech - v28 - i3 - Sept 2004 - p76(1) [51-500]

Caldicott, Edric - *Cultural Memory: Essays on European Literature and History*
R&R Bk N - v19 - i1 - Feb 2004 - p222(1) [51-500]

Caldwell, Ben - *Action! Cartooning*
LJ - v129 - i12 - July 2004 - p80(1) [51-500]

Caldwell, Bruce - *Hayek's Challenge: An Intellectual Biography of F.A. Hayek*
JEL - v42 - i1 - March 2004 - p240(1) [501+]
JEL - v42 - i3 - Sept 2004 - p840(2) [501+]
RM - v58 - i2 - Dec 2004 - p427(2) [501+]

Caldwell, Ian - *The Rule of Four (Read by Woodman, Jeff). Audiobook Review*
Globe & Mail - Jan 15 2005 - pD13 [1-50]
PW - v251 - i27 - July 5 2004 - p17(1) [51-500]
The Rule of Four
BooChiTr - May 23 2004 - p2(1) [501+]
NYRB - v51 - i14 - Sept 23 2004 - p66(4) [501+]
y SLJ - v50 - i10 - Oct 2004 - p198(1) [51-500]
CC - v122 - i4 - Feb 22 2005 - p62(2) [51-500]

Caldwell, J. Paul - *Sleep: The Complete Guide to Sleep Disorders and a Better Night's Sleep. Rev. Ed.*
SciTech - v28 - i1 - March 2004 - p101(1) [51-500]

Caldwell, John A. - *Fatigue in Aviation: A Guide to Staying Awake at the Stick*
SciTech - v28 - i1 - March 2004 - p108(1) [51-500]

Caldwell, Kirbyjon - *Entrepreneurial Faith: Launching Bold Initiatives to Expand God's Kingdom*
Black Iss - v7 - i2 - March-April 2005 - p61(1) [501+]

Caldwell, Linda - *The Year of Living Famously*
y BL - v101 - i3 - Oct 1 2004 - p315(2) [51-500]

Caldwell, Melissa L. - *Not by Bread Alone: Social Support in the New Russia*
Choice - v42 - i4 - Dec 2004 - p717(1) [1-50]

Caldwell, Sarah - *Oh Terrifying Mother: Sexuality, Violence and Worship of the Goddess Kali*
JRAI - v10 - i3 - Sept 2004 - p731(2) [501+]

Caldwell, Wendy - *Narrative Voices and the Liberation Movement in the Mexican State of Chiapas*
R&R Bk N - v19 - i4 - Nov 2004 - p232(1) [501+]

Caldwell, Wilma R. - *Cancer Information for Teens: Health Tips about Cancer Awareness, Prevention, Diagnosis, and Treatment: Including Facts about Frequently Occurring Cancers, Cancer Risk Factors, and Coping Strategies....*
y CH Bwatch - Feb 2005 - pNA [51-500]
SciTech - v28 - i4 - Dec 2004 - p92(1) [51-500]
y SLJ - v50 - i12 - Dec 2004 - p158(2) [51-500]

Caleshu, Anthony - *The Siege of the Body and a Brief Respite*
South CR - v37 - i1 - Fall 2004 - p191-192 [501+]

Caletti, Deb - *Honey, Baby, Sweetheart*
y BL - v101 - i2 - Sept 15 2004 - p236(1) [51-500]
y SLJ - v50 - i7 - July 2004 - p102(1) [51-500]
y Teach Lib - v32 - i3 - Feb 2005 - p18(1) [51-500]
y VOYA - v27 - i3 - August 2004 - p208(1) [1-50]

Calhoun, Arthur W. - *The American Family in the Colonial Period*
R&R Bk N - v19 - i4 - Nov 2004 - p128(1) [51-500]

Calhoun, Charles C. - *Longfellow: A Rediscovered Life*
Choice - v42 - i5 - Jan 2005 - p850(1) [1-50]
R&R Bk N - v19 - i4 - Nov 2004 - p241(1) [501+]

Calhoun, Craig - *Understanding September 11*
WP - v56 - i2 - Jan 2004 - p303-325 [501+]

Calhoun, Dia - *White Midnight*
LibMed - v22 - i6 - March 2004 - p66(1) [501+]

Calhoun, Noel - *Dilemmas of Justice in Eastern Europe's Democratic Transitions*
Choice - v42 - i6 - Feb 2005 - p1091(1) [51-500]

Calhoun, Scott - *Yard Full of Sun: The Story of a Gardener's Obsession That Got a Little out of Hand*
PW - v252 - i3 - Jan 17 2005 - p50(1) [51-500]

Calian, Carnegie Samuel - *The Gospel According to The Wall Street Journal*
Bks & Cult - v11 - i1 - Jan-Feb 2005 - p16(2) [501+]

Califano, Joseph A. - *Inside: A Public and Private Life*
AM - v191 - i4 - August 16 2004 - p23 [501+]
Comw - v131 - i13 - July 16 2004 - p27(3) [501+]
R&R Bk N - v19 - i3 - August 2004 - p70(1) [51-500]

Calisher, Hortense - *Tattoo for a Slave*
BL - v101 - i4 - Oct 15 2004 - p377(1) [51-500]
Ent W - i790 - Oct 29 2004 - p71 [51-500]
KR - v72 - i13 - July 1 2004 - p612(2) [501+]
LJ - v129 - i15 - Sept 15 2004 - p56(1) [51-500]
NL - v87 - i6 - Nov-Dec 2004 - p35(2) [501+]
NYTBR - Jan 30 2005 - p23 [501+]

Call, Michael J. - *Infertility and the Novels of Sophie Cottin*
FS - v58 - i2 - April 2004 - p268(2) [501+]
NCFS - v32 - i3-4 - Spring-Summer 2004 - p405(3) [501+]

Callahan, Avid - *The Cheating Culture*
Bwatch - v26 - i9 - Sept 2004 - p12(1) [51-500]

Callahan, Bob - *The New Smithsonian Book of Comic-Book Stories: From Crumb to Clowes*
LJ - v130 - i1 - Jan 1 2005 - p88(1) [51-500]
PW - v251 - i46 - Nov 15 2004 - p42(2) [51-500]

Callahan, Daniel - *What Price Better Health? Hazards of the Research Imperative*
Hast Cen R - v34 - i4 - July-August 2004 - p50(2) [501+]

Callahan, David - *Anything to Get Ahead: The New American Norm?*
Fut - v38 - i5 - Sept-Oct 2004 - p60(2) [501+]
The Cheating Culture: Why More Americans Are Doing Wrong to Get Ahead
Fut - v38 - i5 - Sept-Oct 2004 - p62(1) [501+]
Har Bus R - v82 - i5 - May 2004 - p30(1) [501+]
Reason - v36 - i3 - July 2004 - p56(3) [501+]
R&R Bk N - v19 - i2 - May 2004 - p113(1) [51-500]
SLJ - v50 - i12 - Dec 2004 - p54(4) [501+]
y VOYA - v27 - i3 - August 2004 - p236(1) [1-50]
VQR - v80 - i3 - Summer 2004 - p266(2) [1-50]

Callahan, Mary P. - *Making Enemies: War and State Building in Burma*
Choice - v42 - i1 - Sept 2004 - p165(1) [501+]
Pac A - v77 - i3 - Fall 2004 - p602(2) [501+]

Callahan, Patrick - *Logics of American Foreign Policy: Theories of America's World Role*
R&R Bk N - v19 - i3 - August 2004 - p187(1) [501+]

Callahan, Tamara L. - *Blueprints in Obstetrics and Gynecology, 3rd Ed.*
SciTech - v28 - i1 - March 2004 - p115(1) [51-500]

Callan, Michael Feeney - *Sex, Death & the Movies: An Intimate Biography*
KR - v73 - i5 - March 1 2005 - p270(2) [51-500]

Callanan, Liam - *The Cloud Atlas*
NYTBR - Dec 19 2004 - p30 [501+]

Callies, David L. - *Bargaining for Development: A Handbook on Development Agreements, Annexation Agreements, Land Development Conditions, Vested Rights, and the Provision of Public Facilities*
NRJ - v44 - i3 - Summer 2004 - p907-916 [501+]

Callihan, Joanna - *Creative Activities for the School Year*
LibMed - v22 - i6 - March 2004 - p88(1) [501+]
Holiday & Everyday Projects: Festive and Fun Creation
y LibMed - v22 - i5 - Feb 2004 - pNA [501+]
Music Makers & Toys
y LibMed - v22 - i5 - Feb 2004 - pNA [501+]

Callingham, Martin - *Market Intelligence: How and Why Organisations Use Market Research*
R&R Bk N - v19 - i3 - August 2004 - pNA [51-500]

Callinicos, Alex - *Against the Third Way: An Anti-Capitalist Critique*
AJES - v63 - i3 - July 2004 - p747(7) [501+]
Making History: Agency, Structure, and Change in Social Theory, 2nd Ed.
R&R Bk N - v19 - i4 - Nov 2004 - p8(1) [51-500]

Callison, William L. - *Raising Test Scores Using Parent Involvement*
R&R Bk N - v19 - i3 - August 2004 - p217(1) [1-50]

Callow, Philip - *Body of Truth: D.H. Lawrence, the Nomadic Years, 1919-1930*
R&R Bk N - v19 - i1 - Feb 2004 - p239(1) [51-500]

Calloway, Colin G. - *Germans and Indians: Fantasies, Encounters, Projections*
Am Ind CRJ - v27 - i2 - Spring 2003 - p121-123 [501+]
One Vast Winter Count: The Native American West Before Lewis and Clark
JAH - v91 - i2 - Sept 2004 - p594(2) [501+]
NYRB - v51 - i12 - July 15 2004 - p47(3) [501+]
PHR - v73 - i3 - August 2004 - p504(505) [501+]
Reinterpreting New England Indians and the Colonial Experience
R&R Bk N - v19 - i3 - August 2004 - p60(1) [51-500]

Calloway, Licia Morrow - *Black Family (Dys)Function in Novels*
JGS - v13 - i3 - Nov 2004 - p287-288 [501+]
Fannie Hurst
JGS - v13 - i3 - Nov 2004 - p287-288 [501+]

Calloway, Stephen - *Obsessions*
Spec - v296 - i9194 - Oct 23 2004 - p45(2) [501+]

Caloghirou, Yannis - *European Collaboration in Research and Development: Business Strategy and Public Policy*
SciTech - v28 - i4 - Dec 2004 - p130 [51-500]

Caloyannides, Michael A. - *Privacy Protection and Computer Forensics, 2nd Ed.*
SciTech - v28 - i4 - Dec 2004 - p32(1) [51-500]

Calvert, Gemma - *The Handbook of Multisensory Processes*
Choice - v42 - i7 - March 2005 - p1251(1) [51-500]

Calvin, William A. - *A Brief History of the Mind: From Apes to Intellect and Beyond*
SB - v40 - i5 - Sept-Oct 2004 - p199(1) [51-500]

Calvin, William H. - *A Brief History of the Mind: From Apes to Intellect and Beyond*
Bwatch - Dec 2004 - pNA [51-500]
QRB - v79 - i4 - Dec 2004 - p454(1) [501+]

Calvino, Italo - *Hermit in Paris: Autobiographical Writings*
NYTBR - August 22 2004 - p20 [501+]
If on a Winter's Night a Traveler
Globe & Mail - Sept 25 2004 - pD31 [501+]

Camacho, Jose - *The Structure of Coordination: Conjunction and Agreement Phenomena in Spanish and Other Languages*
R&R Bk N - v19 - i1 - Feb 2004 - p213 [51-500]

Cambell, Geoffrey - *A Vulnerable America: An Overview of National Security*
LibMed - v23 - i1 - August-Sept 2004 - p83(1) [51-500]

Cambray, Joseph - *Analytical Psychology: Contemporary Perspectives in Jungian Analysis*
SciTech - v28 - i4 - Dec 2004 - p2(1) [1-50]

The Cambridge Companion to the Modern German Novel
CR - v285 - i1662 - July 2004 - p55(3) [501+]

The Cambridge Companion to Victorian and Edwardian Theatre
CR - v285 - i1662 - July 2004 - p55(3) [501+]

Camden Hotten, John - *The Original Lists of Persons of Quality Who Went from Britain to the American Plantations, 1660-1700: Localities Where They Formerly Lived in the Mother Country, the Names of the Ships in Which They Embarked, and Other Interesting Particulars*
EFHM - v58 - i2 - March-April 2004 - p89(1) [51-500]

Camelin, Colette - *La 'Rhetorique profonde' de Saint-John Perse*
FS - v58 - i2 - April 2004 - p281(2) [501+]

Cameran, W. Bruce - *How to Remodel a Man*
PW - v251 - i36 - Sept 6 2004 - p56(2) [51-500]

Camerer, Colin F. - *Behavioral Game Theory: Experiments in Strategic Interaction*
JEL - v42 - i3 - Sept 2004 - p841(2) [501+]

Cameron, A. - *The Cambridge Ancient History. 2nd Ed.*
Class R - v54 - i1 - May 2004 - p185(2) [501+]

Cameron, Amy - *Playing with Matches: Misadventures in Dating*
Globe & Mail - Feb 12 2005 - pD8 [501+]

Cameron, Ann - *Colibri (Read by Kim, Jacqui). Audiobook Review*
c BL - v101 - i5 - Nov 1 2004 - p508(1) [51-500]
Colibri (Read by Kim, Jacqui)
c HB - v80 - i6 - Nov-Dec 2004 - p733(1) [501+]
Colibri
c LibMed - v22 - i6 - March 2004 - p66(1) [501+]

Cameron, Anne - *Dahlia Cassidy*
Globe & Mail - Jan 1 2005 - pD12 [501+]
Hardscratch Row
CBRA - Annual 2003 - p157(1) [51-500]

Cameron, Bill - *Cat's Crossing*
CBRA - Annual 2003 - p157(1) [51-500]

Cameron, Cooke - *Pride Runs Deep*
PW - v252 - i9 - Feb 28 2005 - p47(1) [51-500]

Cameron, David W. - *Bones, Stones, and Molecules: "Out of Africa" and Human Rights*
Choice - v42 - i5 - Jan 2005 - p895(1) [1-50]

Cameron, Deborah - *Language and Sexuality*
Choice - v41 - i7 - March 2004 - p1334(1) [501+]
JRAI - v10 - i4 - Dec 2004 - p928(2) [501+]

Cameron, Esther - *Making Sense of Change Management: A Complete Guide to the Models, Tools and Techniques of Organizational Change*
R&R Bk N - v19 - i3 - August 2004 - p106(1) [51-500]

Cameron, John L. - *Current Surgical Therapy. 8th Ed.*
SciTech - v28 - i3 - Sept 2004 - p110(1) [51-500]

Cameron, Julia - *Answered Prayers: Love Letters from the Divine*
LJ - v129 - i16 - Oct 1 2004 - p86(1) [51-500]
PW - v251 - i37 - Sept 13 2004 - p74(1) [501+]
Letters to a Young Artist: Building a Life in Art
PW - v252 - i11 - March 14 2005 - p58(1) [51-500]

Cameron, Keith - *Le Visage changeant de Montaigne/The Changing Face of Montaigne*
Ren Q - v57 - i4 - Winter 2004 - p1428(2) [501+]

Cameron, Kim S. - *Positive Organizational Scholarship: Foundations of a New Discipline*
Per Psy - v57 - i4 - Winter 2004 - p1059(4) [501+]

Cameron, Layne Scott - *Geocaching Handbook*
R&R Bk N - v19 - i4 - Nov 2004 - p81(1) [51-500]

Cameron, Stella - *Now You See Him*
BL - v101 - i5 - Nov 1 2004 - p469(1) [51-500]
PW - v251 - i44 - Nov 1 2004 - p42(1) [501+]
Testing Miss Toogood
PW - v252 - i6 - Feb 7 2005 - p47(1) [51-500]

Camic, Charles - *The Dialogical Turn: New Roles for Sociology in the Postdisciplinary Age: Essays in Honor of Donald N. Levine*
R&R Bk N - v19 - i1 - Feb 2004 - p122(1) [51-500]

Camic, Paul M. - *Clinical Handbook of Health Psychology: A Practical Guide to Effective Interventions. 2nd Ed.*
SciTech - v28 - i3 - Sept 2004 - p77(1) [51-500]

Camille, Alice - *A Faith Interrupted: An Honest Conversation with Alienated Catholics*
PW - v251 - i35 - August 30 2004 - p50(2) [51-500]

Camilleri, Andrea - *Excursion to Tindari*
KR - v72 - i23 - Dec 1 2004 - p1118(1) [51-500]

Camilleri, Anna - *I Am a Red Dress: Incantations on a Grandmother, a Mother, and a Daughter*
Globe & Mail - Dec 18 2004 - pD5 [501+]

Camilleri, Joseph A. - *Regionalism in the New Asia-Pacific Order: The Political Economy of the Asia-Pacific Region, Vol. 2*
R&R Bk N - v19 - i1 - Feb 2004 - p85(1) [51-500]

Camp, Elizabeth - *The Generality Constraint and Categorial Restrictions*
RM - v58 - i1 - Sept 2004 - p224(2) [501+]

Camp, J.M. - *The Archaeology of Athens*
Class R - v53 - i2 - Nov 2003 - p449-450 [501+]

Campa, Laurence - *Apollinaire: Critique Litteraire*
FS - v58 - i3 - July 2004 - p429-430 [501+]

Campager, R. - *Lessico Agonistico Di Aristofane*
Class R - v53 - i2 - Nov 2003 - p465-467 [501+]

Campagna, Palmiro - *Requiem for a Giant: A.V. Roe Canada and the Avro Arrow*
CBRA - Annual 2003 - p438(1) [51-500]

Campanella, Miriam L. - *EU Economic Governance and Globalization*
R&R Bk N - v19 - i1 - Feb 2004 - p83(1) [51-500]

Campanella, Thomas J. - *Republic of Shade: New England and the American Elm*
J Hist G - v30 - i3 - July 2004 - p582(2) [501+]
NEQ - v77 - i3 - Sept 2004 - p515-517 [501+]

Campanella, Tommaso - *Opuscoli astrologici: Come evitare il fato astrale, Apologetico, Disputa sulle Bolle*
Ren Q - v57 - i4 - Winter 2004 - p1473(2) [501+]

Company, Robert Ford - *To Live as Long as Heaven and Earth: A Translation and Study of Ge Hong's Traditions of Divine Transcendents*
HJAS - v64 - i2 - Dec 2004 - p479-487 [501+]
HJAS - v64 - i2 - Dec 2004 - p479-487 [501+]
JAS - v63 - i2 - May 2004 - p488(3) [501+]

Campbel, Jonathan A. - *The Venomous Reptiles of the Western Hemisphere*
Choice - v42 - i7 - March 2005 - p1253(1) [51-500]

Campbell Adair, Vivian - *Reclaiming Class: Women, Poverty, and the Promise of Higher Education in America*
CS - v33 - i2 - March 2004 - p171-172 [501+]

Campbell, Allan - *Annual Review of Genetics. Vol. 37, 2003*
QRB - v79 - i3 - Sept 2004 - p306(2) [501+]
SciTech - v28 - i1 - March 2004 - p62(1) [51-500]

Campbell, Andrea Louise - *How Policies Make Citizens: Senior Political Activism and the American Welfare State*
AJS - v110 - i1 - July 2004 - p247(2) [501+]

Campbell, Ann-Jeannette - *New York Public Library Incredible Earth: A Book of Answers for Kids*
c SB - v40 - i5 - Sept-Oct 2004 - p196(1) [51-500]

Campbell, Anne - *Practitioner Research and Professional Development in Education*
R&R Bk N - v19 - i3 - August 2004 - p220(1) [1-50]

Campbell, Anneke - *Mary of Bellingham*
y SLJ - v50 - i7 - July 2004 - p131(1) [51-500]

Campbell, Antony F. - *1 Samuel*
Intpr - v58 - i4 - Oct 2004 - p404(3) [501+]

Campbell, B. - *War and Society in Imperial Rome 31 BC-AD 284*
Class R - v53 - i2 - Nov 2003 - p416-417 [501+]

Campbell, Bonnie Jo - *Q Road*
South R - v39 - i1 - Winter 2003 - p209 [501+]

Campbell, Bruce - *Make Love the Bruce Campbell Way*
PW - v252 - i4 - Jan 24 2005 - p114(1) [501+]

Campbell, Cameron - *Life under Pressure: Mortality and Living Standards in Europe and Asia, 1700-1900*
HRNB - v33 - i1 - Fall 2004 - p26(2) [501+]

Campbell, Catherine - *Letting Them Die: Why HIV/AIDS Programmes Fail*
TLS - i5288 - August 6 2004 - p5-6 [501+]

Campbell, Charles C. - *The Word Before the Powers: An Ethic of Preaching*
TT - v61 - i1 - April 2004 - p90-92 [501+]

Campbell, Christy - *The Botanist and the Vintner: How Wine Was Saved for the World*
BL - v101 - i7 - Dec 1 2004 - p629(1) [51-500]
KR - v73 - i1 - Jan 1 2005 - p29(1) [501+]
PW - v251 - i50 - Dec 13 2004 - p52(1) [51-500]
Phylloxera: How Wine was Saved for the World. Audiobook Review
Globe & Mail - Feb 5 2005 - pD17 [1-50]

Campbell, Colin - *The Art of William Nicholson*
Lon R Bks - v26 - i22 - Nov 18 2004 - p23(1) [501+]
George W. Bush Presidency: Appraisals and Prospects
R&R Bk N - v19 - i3 - August 2004 - p71(1) [51-500]

Campbell, David - *A Land of Ghosts*
New Sci - v185 - i2483 - Jan 22 2005 - p50(1) [501+]

Campbell, Deborah - *This Heated Place: Encounters in the Promised Land*
R&R Bk N - v19 - i3 - August 2004 - p50(1) [51-500]

Campbell, Debra - *Graceful Exits: Catholic Women and the Art of Departure*
Choice - v41 - i11-12 - July-August 2004 - p2060(1) [501+]

Campbell, Donald - *Edinburgh: A Cultural and Literary History*
R&R Bk N - v19 - i1 - Feb 2004 - p34(1) [1-50]

Campbell, Douglas N. - *The Warthog and the Close Air Support Debate*
APH - v51 - i3 - Fall 2004 - p46(2) [501+]
Mar Crp G - v88 - i3 - March 2004 - p64(1) [501+]

Campbell, Drew - *Technical Theater for Nontechnical People, 2nd Ed.*
R&R Bk N - v19 - i3 - August 2004 - p264(1) [51-500]

Campbell, Duncan Andrew - *English Public Opinion and the American Civil War*
   AHR - v109 - i3 - June 2004 - p978(2) [501+]
   J Mil H - v68 - i4 - Oct 2004 - p1260-1261 [501+]
   JAH - v91 - i2 - Sept 2004 - p637(2) [501+]
   JSH - v71 - i1 - Feb 2005 - p162(3) [501+]

Campbell, Eddy H.E.A. - *Invariant Theory in All Characteristics*
   SciTech - v28 - i3 - Sept 2004 - p35(1) [51-500]

Campbell, Elizabeth - *The Ethical Teacher*
   AJE - v111 - i1 - Nov 2004 - p122(5) [501+]

Campbell, Elizabeth A. - *Fortune's Wheel: Dickens and the Iconography of Women's Time*
   Choice - v41 - i11-12 - July-August 2004 - p2043(1) [501+]
   VS - v46 - i4 - Summer 2004 - p687(2) [501+]

Campbell, Geoffrey - *A Vulnerable America: An Overview of National Security*
   c SLJ - v50 - i10 - Oct 2004 - pS36(1) [51-500]

Campbell, Gwyn - *The Indian Ocean Rim: Southern Africa and Regional Cooperation.*
   HNet - Oct 2004 - pNA [501+]
   The Structure of Slavery in Indian Ocean Africa and Asia
   Choice - v42 - i2 - Oct 2004 - p347(1) [51-500]

Campbell, Harry F. - *Benefit-Cost Analysis: Financial and Economic Appraisal Using Spreadsheets*
   JEL - v41 - i4 - Dec 2003 - p1341(1) [501+]

Campbell, Ian - *Ancient Roman Topography and Architecture, Vols. 1-3*
   R&R Bk N - v19 - i4 - Nov 2004 - p202(1) [501+]

Campbell, Jacqueline Glass - *When Sherman Marched North from the Sea: Resistance on the Confederate Home Front*
   HNet - August 2004 - pNA [501+]
   JAH - v91 - i3 - Dec 2004 - p1025(2) [501+]
   JSH - v70 - i4 - Nov 2004 - p928(2) [501+]

Campbell, James D. - *Mr. Chilehead: Adventures in the Taste of Pain*
   CBRA - Annual 2003 - p127(1) [51-500]

Campbell, James W.P. - *Brick: A World History*
   Sci - v305 - i5690 - Sept 10 2004 - p1570(1) [51-500]
   TimHES - v0 - i1671 - Dec 17 2004 - p22(2) [501+]
   TLS - i5288 - August 6 2004 - p24(1) [501+]

Campbell, Jane - *A.S. Byatt and the Heliotropic Imagination*
   Choice - v42 - i7 - March 2005 - p1226(1) [51-500]
   R&R Bk N - v19 - i4 - Nov 2004 - p238(1) [501+]

Campbell, Jean - *Beadwork Creates Beaded Rings: 30 Designs*
   BL - v100 - i22 - August 2004 - p1889(1) [51-500]

Campbell, John - *Margaret Thatcher, Vol. II*
   Lon R Bks - v26 - i6 - March 18 2004 - pNA [501+]

Campbell, John Angus - *Darwinism, Design, and Public Education*
   SciTech - v28 - i1 - March 2004 - p62(1) [51-500]

Campbell, John Edward - *Getting in on Online: Cyberspace, Gay Male Sexuality, and Embodied Identity*
   R&R Bk N - v19 - i3 - August 2004 - p148(1) [51-500]

Campbell, John H. - *Profilers: Leading Investigators Take You Inside the Criminal Mind*
   PW - v251 - i46 - Nov 15 2004 - p55(2) [501+]

Campbell, Jonathan - *Tarcadia*
   BIC - v33 - i9 - Dec 2004 - p38(2) [51-500]
   Globe & Mail - Nov 13 2004 - pD10 [501+]

Campbell, Jonathan A. - *The Venomous Reptiles of the Western Hemisphere, Vols. 1-2*
   LJ - v129 - i13 - August 2004 - p116(1) [51-500]
   Sci - v305 - i5681 - July 9 2004 - p182(1) [501+]

Campbell, Joseph - *Baksheesh & Brahman: Asian Journals, India*
   Parabola - v28 - i3 - Fall 2003 - p117(3) [501+]
   Hero's Journey: Joseph Campbell on His Life and Work, Centennial Ed.
   R&R Bk N - v19 - i1 - Feb 2004 - p12(1) [1-50]
   Pathways to Bliss: Mythology and Personal Transformation
   Bwatch - Jan 2005 - pNA [51-500]
   PW - v251 - i39 - Sept 27 2004 - p56(2) [51-500]
   R&R Bk N - v20 - i1 - Feb 2005 - p11(1) [51-500]

Campbell, Julie - *The Secret of the Mansion (Read by Meyers, Ari). Audiobook Review*
   c SLJ - v50 - i12 - Dec 2004 - p75(1) [501+]

Campbell, Kathy Kuhtz - *Let's Draw a Fish with Triangles/Vamos a dibujar un pez usando triangulos (Illus. by Muschinske, Emily)*
   c SLJ - v50 - i9 - Sept 2004 - p195(1) [1-50]
   Let's Draw a Frog with Ovals/Vamos a dibujar una rana usando ovalos (Illus. by Muschinske, Emily)
   c SLJ - v50 - i9 - Sept 2004 - p195(1) [1-50]

Campbell, Katy - *E-ffective Writing for E-Learning Environments*
   R&R Bk N - v19 - i1 - Feb 2004 - p186(1) [501+]

Campbell-Kelly, Martin - *Computer: A History of the Information Machine, 2nd Ed.*
   SciTech - v28 - i4 - Dec 2004 - p17(1) [1-50]
   From Airline Reservations to Sonic the Hedgehog: A History of the Software Industry
   T&C - v45 - i2 - April 2004 - p447-448 [501+]
   A History of Mathematical Tables: From Sumer to spreadsheets
   T&C - v45 - i3 - July 2004 - p662-664 [501+]

Campbell Kids Alphabet Soup: An ABC Book
   c PW - v251 - i44 - Nov 1 2004 - p65(1) [501+]
   c SLJ - v50 - i12 - Dec 2004 - p99(2) [501+]

Campbell, Kurt M. - *The Nuclear Tipping Point: Why States May Reconsider Their Nuclear Choices*
   R&R Bk N - v19 - i4 - Nov 2004 - p161(1) [501+]

Campbell, Linda - *Mindful Learning: 101 Proven Strategies for Student and Teacher Success*
   R&R Bk N - v19 - i1 - Feb 2004 - pNA [51-500]

Campbell, Lyle - *Historical Linguistics: An Introduction. 2nd Ed.*
   TimHES - v0 - i1668 - Nov 26 2004 - pIX(1) [501+]

Campbell, Neil - *Napoleon on Elba: Diary of an Eyewitness to Exile*
   NS - v133 - i4716 - Nov 29 2004 - p46(1) [51-500]

Campbell, Neil (b. 1957-) - *American Youth Cultures*
   R&R Bk N - v19 - i3 - August 2004 - p62(1) [51-500]

Campbell, Nina - *Nina Campbell's Decorating Notebook*
   BL - v101 - i8 - Dec 15 2004 - p704(1) [51-500]

Campbell, Patricia Shehan - *Teaching Music Globally: Experiencing Music, Expressing Culture*
   Am MT - v54 - i2 - Oct-Nov 2004 - p76(1) [501+]
   M Ed J - v91 - i2 - Nov 2004 - p52(2) [501+]

Campbell, Ramsey - *The Overnight*
   KR - v73 - i5 - March 1 2005 - p243(2) [501+]
   PW - v252 - i11 - March 14 2005 - p50(1) [51-500]

Campbell, Randolph B. - *Gone to Texas: A History of the Lone Star State*
   Choice - v41 - i7 - March 2004 - p1354(1) [501+]
   JSH - v70 - i4 - Nov 2004 - p980(2) [501+]
   SHQ - v108 - i1 - July 2004 - p101-102 [501+]

Campbell, Robert - *Why Don't the Rest of Us Like the Buildings the Architects Like?*
   Wil Q - v29 - i1 - Wntr 2005 - p104(1) [501+]

Campbell, Robert Jean - *Campbell's Psychiatric Dictionary. 8th Ed.*
   SciTech - v28 - i1 - March 2004 - p95(1) [51-500]

Campbell, Sean - *Introducing Microsoft Visual Basic 2005 for Developers*
   SciTech - v28 - i4 - Dec 2004 - p20(1) [1-50]

Campbell, Stephen K. - *Flaws and Fallacies in Statistical Thinking*
   SciTech - v28 - i3 - Sept 2004 - p37(1) [1-50]

Campbell, Sue - *Relational Remembering: Rethinking the Memory Wars*
   Choice - v42 - i1 - Sept 2004 - p114(1) [501+]

Campbell, Susan - *Saying What's Real: Seven Keys to Authentic Communication and Relationship Success*
   LJ - v130 - i3 - Feb 15 2005 - p142(1) [51-500]

Campbell, T. Colin - *The China Study: Startling Implications for Diet, Weight Loss and Long-Term Health*
   LJ - v129 - i20 - Dec 1 2004 - p148(1) [51-500]

Campbell, Thomas - *Separation of Powers in Practice*
   Law&PolBR - Nov 2004 - p929(4) [501+]
   Pers PS - v34 - i1 - Wntr 2005 - p51(2) [501+]
   R&R Bk N - v19 - i4 - Nov 2004 - p171(1) [501+]

Campbell, Tom - *Separation of Powers in Practice*
   Choice - v42 - i6 - Feb 2005 - p1097(1) [51-500]

Campen, Rebecca B. - *Blueprints Dermatology*
   SciTech - v28 - i3 - Sept 2004 - p120(1) [51-500]

Camper, Jennifer - *Juicy Mother*
   PW - v251 - i51 - Dec 20 2004 - p38(2) [51-500]

Campey, Lucille H. - *Silver Chief: Lord Selkirk and the Scottish Pioneers of Belfast, Baldoon and Red River*
   CBRA - Annual 2003 - p35(2) [501+]

Campiglia, Maddalena - *Flori, a Pastoral Drama*
   Choice - v42 - i7 - March 2005 - p1233(1) [51-500]

Campion, Nardi Reeder - *Everyday Matters: A Love Story*
   KR - v72 - i15 - August 1 2004 - p720(1) [501+]
   PW - v251 - i32 - August 9 2004 - p240(1) [51-500]

Campion, Thomas - *A New Way of Making Fowre Parts in Counterpoint*
   R&R Bk N - v19 - i1 - Feb 2004 - p198(1) [51-500]

Campling, Penelope - *From Toxic Institutions to Therapeutic Environments: Residential Settings in Mental Health Services*
   SciTech - v28 - i4 - Dec 2004 - p85(1) [51-500]

Campo, Rafael - *The Healing Art: A Doctor's Black Bag of Poetry*
   Ga R - v58 - i2 - Summer 2004 - p471-483 [501+]

Campolo, Tony - *Speaking My Mind*
   LJ - v129 - i13 - August 2004 - p87(1) [501+]

Campos, David - *Diverse Sexuality and Schools: A Reference Handbook*
   LibMed - v22 - i7 - April-May 2004 - p86(1) [501+]

Campos, Nauro F. - *Political Economy of Transition and Development: Institutions, Politics, and Policies*
   R&R Bk N - v19 - i1 - Feb 2004 - p83(1) [51-500]

Campos, Paul F. - *The Obesity Myth*
   Bwatch - Nov 2004 - pNA [51-500]

Campt, Tina - *Other Germans: Black Germans and the Politics of Race, Gender, and Memory in the Third Reich*
   Choice - v42 - i1 - Sept 2004 - p180(1) [501+]

Camus, Albert - *The Rebel*
   Globe & Mail - Sept 11 2004 - pD23 [501+]

Camus, Marianne - *Gender and Madness in the Novels of Charles Dickens*
   R&R Bk N - v19 - i4 - Nov 2004 - p236(1) [501+]

Can Saudi Arabia Reform Itself?
   NYRB - v51 - i16 - Oct 21 2004 - p22(4) [501+]

Canada, 5th ed.
   CBRA - Annual 2003 - p21(1) [51-500]

Canadian Accounting Perspectives/Perspectives Comptables Canadienne
   JEL - v42 - i1 - March 2004 - p345(1) [501+]

Canadian Council - *The Measure of International Law: Effectiveness, Fairness and Validity*
   R&R Bk N - v19 - i3 - August 2004 - p192(1) [501+]

Canadian Hurricane Centre: Just for Kids
   LibMed - v22 - i7 - April-May 2004 - p90(1) [501+]

Canadian World Atlas
   Globe & Mail - Jan 15 2005 - pD14 [1-50]

Canan, Penelope - *Ozone Connections: Expert Networks in Global Environmental Governance*
   CS - v33 - i1 - Jan 2004 - p67-69 [501+]

Canarina, John - *Pierre Monteux, Maitre*
   Choice - v42 - i1 - Sept 2004 - p111(1) [501+]
   R&R Bk N - v19 - i1 - Feb 2004 - p197(1) [51-500]

Cancian, Francesca M. - *Child Care & Inequality: Rethinking Carework for Children and Youth*
   CE - v81 - i1 - Fall 2004 - p49(1) [501+]

Cancik, Hubert - *Brill's New Pauly: Encyclopaedia of the Ancient World: Antiquity, Vol. 2*
   R&R Bk N - v19 - i1 - Feb 2004 - p37(1) [1-50]
   R&R Bk N - v19 - i1 - Feb 2004 - p37(1) [1-50]
   Brill's New Pauly: Encyclopaedia of the Ancient World: Antiquity, Vol. 4
   R&R Bk N - v19 - i4 - Nov 2004 - p39(1) [51-500]

Candian Egg Marketing Agency - *Omelettes: Perfect Anytime*
   CBRA - Annual 2003 - p135(1) [51-500]

Candis, Judy - *All Things Hidden*
   Black Iss - v6 - i6 - Nov-Dec 2004 - p73(2) [501+]
   KR - v72 - i15 - August 1 2004 - p714(2) [51-500]
   LJ - v129 - i14 - Sept 1 2004 - p130(1) [51-500]
   PW - v251 - i29 - July 19 2004 - p143(1) [51-500]

Candy, Paolo - *Atlas of the Constellations*
   Astron - v32 - i12 - Dec 2004 - p104 [51-500]

Cane, Peter - *Responsibility in Law and Morality*
   Phil R - v113 - i1 - Jan 2004 - p133(3) [501+]

Caner, D. - *Wandering, Begging Monks. Spiritual Authority and the Promotion of Monasticism in Late Antiquity*
   Class R - v54 - i1 - May 2004 - p208(3) [501+]

Caner, Ergun Mehmet - *Christian Jihad: Two Former Muslims Look at the Crusades and Killing in the Name of Christ*
   LJ - v129 - i12 - July 2004 - p86(2) [51-500]

Canfield, Jack - *Chicken Soup for the African American Soul: Celebrating and Sharing Our Culture One Story at a Time*
LJ - v129 - i15 - Sept 15 2004 - p62(2) [51-500]
Chicken Soup for the Girlfriend's Soul: Stories Celebrating the Magic of Friendship
PW - v251 - i41 - Oct 11 2004 - p66(2) [51-500]
Chicken Soup for the Recovering Soul: Your Personal, Portable Support Group with Stories of Healing, Hope, Love and Resilience
PW - v251 - i49 - Dec 6 2004 - p55(2) [501+]
The Success Principles: How to Get from Where You Are to Where You Want to Be
BL - v101 - i5 - Nov 1 2004 - p442(1) [51-500]
LJ - v129 - i20 - Dec 1 2004 - p142(2) [51-500]
People - v63 - i1 - Jan 10 2005 - p49 [51-500]
PW - v251 - i46 - Nov 15 2004 - p52(1) [51-500]
Canham, Charles D. - *Models in Ecosystem Science*
Choice - v41 - i11-12 - July-August 2004 - p2070(1) [501+]
QRB - v79 - i3 - Sept 2004 - p330(2) [501+]
Canham, Marsha - *My Forever Love*
BL - v100 - i21 - July 2004 - p1826(1) [51-500]
Caniff, Milton - *Milton Caniff's Steve Canyon: 1949*
BL - v100 - i22 - August 2004 - p1915(1) [501+]
Canino, Ian A. - *Culturally Diverse Children and Adolescents: Assessment, Diagnosis, and Treatment*
Adoles - v39 - i154 - Summer 2004 - p398(1) [51-500]
Canizares-Esguerra, Jorge - *How to Write the History of the New World: Histories, Epistemologies, and Identities in the Eighteenth-Century Atlantic World*
HAHR - v84 - i3 - August 2004 - p515(2) [501+]
Cann, Kate - *Shacked Up*
y SLJ - v50 - i7 - July 2004 - p102(1) [51-500]
Speeding
y SLJ - v50 - i11 - Nov 2004 - p138(1) [51-500]
Cannadine, David - *History and the Media*
HT - v54 - i8 - August 2004 - p59(1) [501+]
Spec - v295 - i9183 - August 7 2004 - p32(1) [501+]
Ornamentalism: How the British Saw Their Empire
Dal R - v83 - i3 - Autumn 2003 - p369-390 [501+]
Cannarella, Deborah - *James Baldwin: African-American Writer and Activist*
LibMed - v22 - i6 - March 2004 - p75(1) [501+]
Cannata Fera, Maria - *I lirici greci. Forme della communicazione e storia del testo. Atti dell'Incontro di Studi, Messina, 5-6 novembre 1999*
Class R - v54 - i1 - May 2004 - p23(2) [501+]
Cannell, Stephen J. - *Vertical Coffin (Read by Brick, Scott). Audiobook Review*
c Kliatt - v38 - i4 - July 2004 - p58(1) [51-500]
LJ - v129 - i16 - Oct 1 2004 - p118(1) [51-500]
Canning, Joseph - *Power, Violence, and Mass Death in Pre-Modern and Modern Times*
J Mil H - v68 - i4 - Oct 2004 - p1244-1245 [501+]
R&R Bk N - v19 - i2 - May 2004 - p131 [51-500]
Canning, Richard - *Hear Us Out: Conversations with Gay Novelists*
G&L Rev W - v11 - i6 - Nov-Dec 2004 - p46(2) [501+]
Cannistraro, Philip V. - *The Lost World of Italian American Radicalism: Politics, Labor, and Culture*
Choice - v42 - i1 - Sept 2004 - p175(1) [501+]
Cannon, A.E. - *Charlotte's Rose*
y Kliatt - v38 - i4 - July 2004 - p14(1) [51-500]
Let the Good Times Roll with Pirate Pete and Pirate Joe (Illus. by Smith, Elwood H.)
c SLJ - v50 - i10 - Oct 2004 - pS29(1) [1-50]
Cannon, Janell - *Little Yau (Illus. by Cannon, Janell)*
c RT - v57 - Oct 2003 - p174 [1-50]
Pinduli (Illus. by Cannon, Janell)
c BL - v101 - i1 - Sept 1 2004 - p129(2) [1-50]
c HB - v80 - i5 - Sept-Oct 2004 - p565(1) [51-500]
c KR - v72 - i15 - August 1 2004 - p738(1) [51-500]
c PW - v251 - i31 - August 2 2004 - p69(1) [51-500]
c SLJ - v50 - i10 - Oct 2004 - p110(1) [51-500]
Cannon, Lou - *Governor Reagan: His Rise to Power*
PSQ - v119 - i2 - Summer 2004 - p339(2) [501+]
Ronald Reagan: A Life in Politics
LJ - v129 - i14 - Sept 1 2004 - p204(1) [51-500]
y NYTBR - August 1 2004 - p16 [501+]
Cannon, Peter - *The Lovecraft Chronicles*
PW - v251 - i33 - August 16 2004 - p48(1) [51-500]
Cannon, Robert H., Jr. - *Dynamics of Physical Systems*
SciTech - v28 - i1 - March 2004 - p136(1) [51-500]
Canon, David T. - *Faultlines: Debating the Issues in American Politics*
R&R Bk N - v19 - i4 - Nov 2004 - p154(1) [501+]
Canone, Eugenio - *La filosofia di Giordano Bruno: Problemi ermeneutici e storiografici*
Ren Q - v57 - i3 - Fall 2004 - p1101(2) [501+]
Canongate, David Maine - *The Flood*
Spec - v296 - i9201 - Dec 11 2004 - p44(2) [501+]
Canonica-Walangitang, Resy - *The End of Suharto's New Order in Indonesia*
R&R Bk N - v19 - i1 - Feb 2004 - pNA [501+]
Canova, Mauro - *Le Lacrime di Minerva: Lungo i sentieri della commedia e della tragedia a Padova, Venezia e Ferrara tra il 1540 e il 1550*
Ren Q - v57 - i3 - Fall 2004 - p974(2) [501+]
Canseco, Jose - *Juiced: Wild Times, Rampant 'Roids, Smash Hits, and How Baseball Got Big*
NW - Feb 28 2005 - p57 [501+]
NY - v81 - i3 - March 7 2005 - p028 [501+]
Juiced: Wild Times, Rampant 'Roids, Smash Hits and How Baseball Got Big
People - v63 - i9 - March 7 2005 - p54 [501+]
Canter, Jonathan D. - *Lucky Leonardo*
KR - v72 - i14 - July 15 2004 - p644(2) [51-500]
PW - v251 - i33 - August 16 2004 - p42(2) [51-500]
Cantor, Brian - *Metal and Ceramic Matrix Composites*
E-Streams - August 2004 - pNA [501+]
Cantor, Dorothy - *Finding Your Voice: A Woman's Guide to Using Self Talk for Fulfilling Relationships, Work, and Life*
R&R Bk N - v19 - i3 - August 2004 - p153(1) [51-500]
Cantor, Erick Werner - *Ni aniquilados ni vencidos: Los Embera y la gente negra del Atrato bajo el dominio espanol, siglo XVIII*
HAHR - v84 - i4 - Nov 2004 - p740(2) [501+]
Cantor, Geoffrey - *Science Serialized: Representation of the Sciences in Nineteenth-Century Periodicals*
TLS - i5297 - Oct 8 2004 - p30(1) [51-500]
Cantor, Jay - *Great Neck*
NYTBR - August 22 2004 - p20 [501+]
Cantor, Jay E. - *Art in a Mirror: The Counterproofs of Mary Cassatt*
Mag Antiq - v167 - i1 - Jan 2005 - p129(1) [51-500]
Mag Antiq - v167 - i2 - Feb 2005 - p55(1) [51-500]
Cantor, Jeremy - *Inspired 3D Short Film Production*
R&R Bk N - v19 - i4 - Nov 2004 - p249(1) [501+]
Cantor, Joanne - *Teddy's TV Troubles (Illus. by Lowes, Tom)*
c CH Bwatch - v14 - i12 - Dec 2004 - pNA [51-500]
c SLJ - v50 - i11 - Nov 2004 - p92(1) [51-500]
Cantor, Paul A. - *Gilligan Unbound: Popular Culture in the Age of Globalization*
R&R Bk N - v19 - i1 - Feb 2004 - p223(1) [51-500]
Cantor, Rachel - *Slave for a Day*
New ER - v24 - i4 - Fall 2003 - p159-166 [501+]
Cantrell, John - *Henry Maudslay and the Pioneers of the Machine Age*
BHR - v77 - i4 - Winter 2003 - p782(785) [501+]
Cantu, D. Antonio - *Teaching History in the Digital Classroom*
JAH - v91 - i1 - June 2004 - p344-345 [501+]
Canty, Kevin - *Winslow in Love*
BL - v101 - i7 - Dec 1 2004 - p634(1) [51-500]
KR - v72 - i23 - Dec 1 2004 - p1102(1) [501+]
LJ - v129 - i20 - Dec 1 2004 - p98(1) [51-500]
PW - v251 - i45 - Nov 8 2004 - p32(1) [501+]
Canyon, Christopher - *John Denver's Ancient Rhymes: A Dolphin Lullaby (Read by Denver, John)*
c PW - v251 - i37 - Sept 13 2004 - p38(1) [51-500]
John Denver's Ancient Rhymes: A Dolphin Lullaby (Illus. by Canyon, Christopher)
c KR - v72 - i18 - Sept 15 2004 - p911(1) [501+]
c SLJ - v50 - i11 - Nov 2004 - p122(1) [51-500]
Cao, Guozhong - *Nanostructures and Nanomaterials: Synthesis, Properties and Applications*
Choice - v42 - i4 - Dec 2004 - p698(1) [1-50]
Nanostructures and Nanomaterials; Synthesis, Properties and Applications
SciTech - v28 - i3 - Sept 2004 - p47(1) [1-50]
Capaldi, Nicholas - *John Stuart Mill: A Biography*
BW - v34 - i5 - Feb 1 2004 - p3(1) [501+]
Choice - v42 - i2 - Oct 2004 - p305(2) [51-500]
CR - v285 - i1664 - Sept 2004 - p190(1) [51-500]
Capatti, Alberto - *Italian Cuisine: A Cultural History*
R&R Bk N - v19 - i1 - Feb 2004 - p253(1) [51-500]
Capatti, Berenice - *Klimt and His Cat (Illus. by Monaco, Octavia)*
c KR - v73 - i1 - Jan 1 2005 - p49(1) [51-500]
c PW - v252 - i2 - Jan 10 2005 - p54(1) [51-500]
Cape, Norman Rose - *Harold Nicolson*
Spec - v297 - i9208 - Jan 29 2005 - p36(1) [501+]
Capeci, Anne - *Danger, Dynamite!*
c LibMed - v22 - i5 - Feb 2004 - p66(1) [501+]
Daredevils (Illus. by Casale, Paul)
c BL - v100 - i21 - July 2004 - p1844(1) [501+]
c SLJ - v50 - i9 - Sept 2004 - p156(1) [51-500]
Ghost Train (Illus. by Capeci, Anne)
c SLJ - v51 - i1 - Jan 2005 - p88(1) [51-500]
Capehart, Barney L. - *Information Technology for Energy Managers*
SciTech - v28 - i3 - Sept 2004 - p148(1) [51-500]
Capek, Karel - *The Gardener's Year*
TLS - i5265 - Feb 27 2004 - p36-36 [501+]
Capela, John J. - *Dictionary of International Business Terms*
R&R Bk N - v19 - i3 - August 2004 - p107(1) [51-500]
Capella, Anthony - *The Food of Love*
BW - v34 - i29 - July 18 2004 - p10(1) [501+]
Ent W - i777 - August 6 2004 - p85 [51-500]
LJ - v129 - i12 - July 2004 - p67(1) [51-500]
NYTBR - July 25 2004 - p8 [501+]
People - v62 - i6 - August 9 2004 - p47 [51-500]
Capetz, Paul E. - *God: A Brief History*
Intpr - v58 - i4 - Oct 2004 - p439(1) [501+]
Capie, David - *Under the Gun: The Small Arms Challenge in the Pacific*
Cont Pac - v17 - i1 - Spring 2005 - p245(4) [501+]
Capie, Forrest H. - *Policy Makers on Policy: The Mais Lectures*
JEL - v42 - i4 - Dec 2004 - p1127(3) [501+]
Caplan, Ben - *Creatures of Fiction, Myth, and Imagination*
RM - v58 - i1 - Sept 2004 - p211(3) [501+]
Caple, Kathy - *Worm Gets a Job (Illus. by Caple, Kathy)*
c SLJ - v50 - i7 - July 2004 - p68(1) [51-500]
Caple, Natalee - *Mackerel Sky*
BW - v34 - i39 - Sept 26 2004 - p10(1) [501+]
KR - v72 - i15 - August 1 2004 - p702(1) [51-500]
PW - v251 - i35 - August 30 2004 - p32(1) [501+]
Caplin, Steve - *How to Cheat in Photoshop*
PetPho - v33 - i3 - July 2004 - p47(1) [51-500]
Caponigro, John Paul - *Adobe Photoshop Master Class: The Essential Guide to Revisioning Photography. 2nd Ed.*
SciTech - v28 - i1 - March 2004 - p135(1) [51-500]
Capossela, Cappy - *Share the Care: How to Organize a Group to Care for Someone Who Is Seriously Ill*
LJ - v129 - i17 - Oct 15 2004 - p80(1) [51-500]
Capote, Truman - *The Bargain*
NYTBR - Sept 12 2004 - p10 [501+]
The Collected Stories of Truman Capote
BL - v101 - i1 - Sept 1 2004 - p59(1) [51-500]
KR - v72 - i16 - August 15 2004 - p777(1) [51-500]
The Complete Short Stories of Truman Capote
Globe & Mail - Nov 27 2004 - pD36 [501+]
The Complete Stories of Truman Capote
TLS - i5301 - Nov 5 2004 - p3-4 [501+]
Too Brief a Treat: The Letters of Truman Capote
Choice - v42 - i6 - Feb 2005 - p1020(1) [51-500]
Globe & Mail - Nov 27 2004 - pD36 [501+]
Capote, Truman (b. 1924 -) - *Too Brief a Treat: The Letters of Truman Capote*
LJ - v129 - i19 - Nov 15 2004 - p61(1) [501+]
Capp, Al - *Al Capp's Li'l Abner: The Frazetta Years. Vol. 4: 1960-1961 (Illus. by Frazetta, Frank)*
LJ - v129 - i12 - July 2004 - p60(1) [51-500]
Cappelorn, Niels Jorgen - *Kierkegaard Studies: Yearbook 2003.*
Scan St - v76 - i3 - Fall 2004 - p425(5) [501+]
Capponi, Pat - *Beyond the Crazy House: Changing the Future of Madness*
CBRA - Annual 2003 - p429(1) [51-500]
Capps, Patrick - *Asserting Jurisdiction: International and European Legal Perspectives*
R&R Bk N - v19 - i1 - Feb 2004 - pNA [51-500]
Capps, Randall - *Entrepreneurship and Innovation in Quebec: How the Province Became a World-Class Player*
R&R Bk N - v19 - i3 - August 2004 - p94(1) [51-500]
Capps, Ronald Everett - *Off Magazine Street*
BL - v101 - i6 - Nov 15 2004 - p553(1) [51-500]
Capra, Fritjof - *The Hidden Connections; A Science for Sustainable Living*
Kliatt - v38 - i4 - July 2004 - p44(1) [51-500]
Caprara, Giovanni - *Solar System*
CBRA - Annual 2003 - p424(1) [51-500]
E-Streams - July 2004 - pNA [501+]
SciTech - v28 - i1 - March 2004 - p44(1) [51-500]

Capshaw, Jeffrey L. - *A Textlinguistic Analysis of Selected Old Testament Texts in Matthew 1-4*
R&R Bk N - v19 - i3 - August 2004 - p24(1) [1-50]

Capstick, Peter - *Death in the Long Grass*
BL - v101 - i1 - Sept 1 2004 - p52(1) [501+]

Caputo, Philip - *Acts of Faith*
KR - v73 - i4 - Feb 15 2005 - p189(1) [501+]
LJ - v130 - i3 - Feb 15 2005 - p114(1) [51-500]
PW - v252 - i9 - Feb 28 2005 - p39(1) [51-500]

Caputo, Tony C. - *Vespers*
PW - v251 - i51 - Dec 20 2004 - p39(1) [51-500]

Capuzzi, David - *Introduction to the Counseling Profession, 4th Ed.*
R&R Bk N - v20 - i1 - Feb 2005 - p7(1) [51-500]

Capuzzio, Michael - *Close to Shore*
c Five Owls - v18 - i1 - Fall 2004 - p21(2) [51-500]

Caraballo, Samuel - *My Grandparents and I/Mis Abuelos y Yo (Illus. by Cruz, Nina D.)*
c KR - v72 - i22 - Nov 15 2004 - p1088(1) [51-500]

Carabott, Philip - *The Greek Civil War: Essays on a Conflict of Exceptionalism and Silences*
R&R Bk N - v19 - i3 - August 2004 - p44(1) [51-500]

Carafano, James Jay - *Waltzing into the Cold war: The Struggle for Occupied Austria*
JAH - v91 - i1 - June 2004 - p296-296 [501+]

Caraganis, Joan - *And One More Thing ...: A Mother's Advice on Life, Love, and Lipstick*
PW - v252 - i9 - Feb 28 2005 - p50(2) [51-500]

Caraher, Denise Page - *The End of Forever: The Story of Mekinges and William Conner.*
y CH Bwatch - Oct 2004 - pNA [51-500]

Caraley, Demetrios James - *American Hegemony: Preventive War, Iraq, and Imposing Democracy*
R&R Bk N - v19 - i3 - August 2004 - p71(1) [51-500]
September 11, Terrorist Attacks and U.S. Foreign Policy
WP - v56 - i2 - Jan 2004 - p303-325 [501+]

Caravale, Giorgio - *L'orazione proibita. Censura ecclesiastica e letteratura devozionale nella prima eta moderna*
CHR - v90 - i4 - Oct 2004 - p790(2) [501+]

Caravantes, Peggy - *Waging Peace: The Story of Jane Addams*
SLJ - v51 - i2 - Feb 2005 - p146(1) [51-500]

Carbado, Devon W. - *Time on Two Crosses: The Collected Writings of Bayard Rustin*
Dis - v51 - i1 - Wntr 2004 - p126(6) [501+]

Carbone, Elisa - *Last Dance on Holladay Street*
y Kliatt - v39 - i2 - March 2005 - p8(1) [51-500]
KR - v73 - i3 - Feb 1 2005 - p174(1) [51-500]

Carbone, G. - *Il centone De Alea.*
Class R - v54 - i1 - May 2004 - p133(2) [501+]

Carbone, Larry - *What Animals Want: Expertise and Advocacy in Laboratory Animal Welfare Policy*
Am Sci - v93 - i1 - Jan-Feb 2005 - p87(3) [501+]
Choice - v42 - i4 - Dec 2004 - p690(1) [1-50]

Carbone, Mauro - *The Thinking of the Sensible: Merleau-Ponty's A-Philosophy*
R&R Bk N - v19 - i4 - Nov 2004 - p5(1) [51-500]

Carbonell, Bettina Messias - *Museum Studies: An Anthology of Contexts*
Apo - v159 - i510 - August 2004 - p76(2) [501+]
R&R Bk N - v20 - i1 - Feb 2005 - p1(1) [51-500]

Carbyn, Lu - *The Buffalo Wolf: Predators, Prey, and the Politics of Nature*
CG - v124 - i3 - May-June 2004 - p127(1) [501+]
QRB - v79 - i4 - Dec 2004 - p439(2) [501+]
A Dance of Life and Death
CG - v124 - i2 - March-April 2004 - p95(1) [501+]

Carcaterra, Lorenzo - *Paradise City*
BL - v100 - i22 - August 2004 - p1868(1) [51-500]
DroRevMy - v24 - i4 - July-August 2004 - p3(2) [501+]
Globe & Mail - Dec 4 2004 - pD35 [51-500]
KR - v72 - i13 - July 1 2004 - p589(2) [501+]
PW - v251 - i27 - July 5 2004 - p34(2) [51-500]

Card, Claudia - *The Cambridge Companion to Simone de Beauvoir*
Ethics - v115 - i2 - Jan 2005 - p389(5) [501+]

Card, Michael - *Sacred Sorrow: Reaching Out to God in the Lost Language of Lament*
PW - v252 - i4 - Jan 24 2005 - p240(1) [501+]

Card, Orson Scott - *The Crystal City*
Analog - v124 - i5 - May 2004 - p132(142) [501+]
y Kliatt - v39 - i2 - March 2005 - p24(2) [51-500]
Ender's Game (Read by Rudnicki, Stephan). Audiobook Review
PW - v251 - i49 - Dec 6 2004 - p19(1) [51-500]
Posing as People: Three Stories, Three Plays
PW - v252 - i11 - March 14 2005 - p51(1) [51-500]

Shadow of the Giant
KR - v73 - i5 - March 1 2005 - p266(1) [51-500]
PW - v252 - i8 - Feb 21 2005 - p162(1) [51-500]
Ent W - i810 - March 11 2005 - p108 [51-500]

Cardelle, Alberto Jose Frick - *Health Care Reform in Central America: NGO-Government Collaboration in Guatemala and El Salvador*
SciTech - v28 - i1 - March 2004 - p81(1) [51-500]

Cardenas, Gilberto - *La Causa: Civil Rights, Social Justice, and the Struggle for Equality in the Midwest*
Choice - v42 - i6 - Feb 2005 - p1103(1) [51-500]
R&R Bk N - v19 - i4 - Nov 2004 - p62(1) [51-500]

Cardinal, Linda - *Shaping Nations: Constitutionalism and Society in Australia and Canada*
R&R Bk N - v19 - i1 - Feb 2004 - pNA [51-500]

Cardinal, Tantoo - *Our Story: Aboriginal Voices on Canada's Past*
Globe & Mail - Dec 24 2004 - pD2 [501+]

Cardiovascular Care Made Incredibly Easy
SciTech - v28 - i3 - Sept 2004 - p105(1) [51-500]

Cardona, George - *The Indo-Aryan Languages*
TimHES - v0 - i1661 - Oct 8 2004 - p26(2) [501+]

Cardone, Fabio - *Energy and Geometry: An Introduction to Deformed Special Relativity*
SciTech - v28 - i4 - Dec 2004 - p48(1) [51-500]

Cardullo, Robert James - *In Search of Cinema: Writings on International Film Art*
R&R Bk N - v19 - i3 - August 2004 - p262(1) [51-500]

Cardwell, M. John - *Arts and Arms: Literature, Politics and Patriotism During the Seven Years War*
Choice - v42 - i6 - Feb 2005 - p1085(1) [51-500]
HNet - Dec 2004 - pNA [501+]

Cardy, Robert L. - *Performance Management: Concepts, Skills, and Excercises*
R&R Bk N - v19 - i1 - Feb 2004 - p111(1) [51-500]
Performance Management: Concepts, Skills, and Exercises
Per Psy - v57 - i4 - Winter 2004 - p1094(4) [501+]

Cardy, Sandy - *Cottage, the Spider Brooch, and the Second Wife: How to Overcome the Challenges of Estate Planning*
CBRA - Annual 2003 - p28(2) [501+]

Care, Curtis - *Friedrich Nietzsche*
LJ - v130 - i4 - March 1 2005 - p89(1) [51-500]

Career Discovery Encyclopedia. 5th Ed.
y LibMed - v22 - i6 - March 2004 - p76(1) [501+]

'Career Skills Library. 2nd Ed., Vols. 1-8
y VOYA - v27 - i4 - Oct 2004 - p332(2) [51-500]

Careers in Focus: Art
BL - v100 - i21 - July 2004 - p1832(1) [1-50]
y SLJ - v50 - i11 - Nov 2004 - p160(1) [51-500]

Careers in Focus: Coaches and Fitness Professionals
BL - v100 - i21 - July 2004 - p1832(1) [1-50]
y SLJ - v50 - i11 - Nov 2004 - p160(1) [51-500]

Careers In Focus: Computers, 4th Ed.
y SLJ - v51 - i1 - Jan 2005 - p142(2) [51-500]

Careers in Focus: Entrepreneurs
y SLJ - v50 - i11 - Nov 2004 - p160(1) [51-500]

Careers in Focus: Environment
y SLJ - v50 - i11 - Nov 2004 - p160(1) [51-500]

Careers in Focus: Law, 2nd Ed.
R&R Bk N - v19 - i1 - Feb 2004 - pNA [1-50]

Careers in Focus: Mathematics & Physics
NACEJou - v64 - i2 - Wntr 2004 - p12(1) [501+]

Careers In Focus: Music
y SLJ - v51 - i1 - Jan 2005 - p142(2) [51-500]

Careers in Focus: Sports
SLJ - v50 - i10 - Oct 2004 - pS66(1) [501+]

Carel, Havi - *What Philosophy Is: Contemporary Philosophy in Action*
R&R Bk N - v19 - i3 - August 2004 - p2(1) [1-50]

Careless, Sue - *Discovering the Book of Common Prayer: A Hands-On Approach*
CBRA - Annual 2003 - p88(2) [51-500]

Carelli, Anne O'Brien - *The Truth about Supervision: Coaching, Teamwork, Interviewing, Appraisals, 360 Degree Assessments, and Recognition*
R&R Bk N - v19 - i3 - August 2004 - p131(1) [51-500]

Carelli, O'Brien Anne - *The Truth about Supervison: Coaching, Teamwork, Interviewing, Appraisals, 360 Degree Assessments, and Recognition*
TCR - v106 - i12 - Dec 2004 - p2256(4) [501+]

Carens, Joseph H. - *Is Quebec Nationalism Just? Perspectives from Anglophone Canada*
Globe & Mail - Oct 2 2004 - pD23 [501+]

Careri, Giovanni - *Baroques (Illus. by Ferranti, Ferrante)*
Ren Q - v57 - i4 - Winter 2004 - p1462(2) [501+]

Carew, Mairead - *Tara and the Ark of the Covenant: A Search for the Ark of the Covenant by British-Israelites on the Hill of Tara*
R&R Bk N - v19 - i4 - Nov 2004 - p17(1) [51-500]

Carew-Miller, Anna - *Jordan*
y LibMed - v22 - i4 - Jan 2004 - p74(1) [501+]

Carey, Charles W. - *African-American Political Leaders*
BL - v100 - i21 - July 2004 - p1860(1) [501+]
Choice - v41 - i11-12 - July-August 2004 - p2024(1) [501+]
Castro's Cuba
y SLJ - v50 - i11 - Nov 2004 - p160(1) [51-500]

Carey, Charles W. Jr. - *African-American Political Leaders*
VOYA - v27 - i5 - Dec 2004 - p421(1) [501+]

Carey, George - *Know the Truth: A Memoir*
CR - v285 - i1665 - Oct 2004 - p235(4) [501+]
TLS - i5283 - July 2 2004 - p10-11 [501+]

Carey, Henry F. - *Romania Since 1989: Politics, Economics, and Society*
Choice - v42 - i6 - Feb 2005 - p1093(1) [51-500]
R&R Bk N - v19 - i3 - August 2004 - p182(1) [501+]

Carey, Jacqueline - *Banewreaker*
BL - v101 - i6 - Nov 15 2004 - p570(1) [51-500]
KR - v72 - i17 - Sept 1 2004 - p842(1) [51-500]
LJ - v129 - i17 - Oct 15 2004 - p57(1) [51-500]
PW - v251 - i37 - Sept 13 2004 - p63(1) [501+]
The Crossley Baby
y Kliatt - v38 - i5 - Sept 2004 - p19(2) [51-500]
NYTBR - July 25 2004 - p20 [501+]

Carey, James R. - *Life Span: Evolutionary, Ecological and Demographic Perspectives.*
JEL - v41 - i4 - Dec 2003 - p1382(1) [501+]

Carey, Janet Lee - *The Double Life of Zoe Flynn*
c BL - v101 - i1 - Sept 1 2004 - p120(1) [1-50]
c CCB-B - v58 - i1 - Sept 2004 - p9(1) [51-500]
c SLJ - v50 - i8 - August 2004 - p116(1) [51-500]

Carey, Joseph - *Creole Nouvelle: Contemporary Creole Cookery*
LJ - v129 - i19 - Nov 15 2004 - p82(1) [501+]

Carey, Mike - *Inferno*
y Kliatt - v38 - i4 - July 2004 - p33(1) [51-500]
John Constantine Hellblazer: All His Engines
PW - v252 - i5 - Jan 31 2005 - p51(1) [51-500]
My Faith in Frankie (Illus. by Liew, Sonny)
y BL - v101 - i9-10 - Jan 1 2005 - p844(1) [1-50]
PW - v252 - i1 - Jan 3 2005 - p38(1) [51-500]

Carey, Patrick W. - *Catholics in America: A History*
LJ - v130 - i3 - Feb 15 2005 - p156(1) [51-500]

Carey, Peter - *My Life as a Fake*
BooChiTr - Jan 18 2004 - p2(1) [501+]
My Life as a Fake. Audiobook Review
Globe & Mail - Feb 5 2005 - pD17 [1-50]
My Life as a Fake
HR - v57 - i2 - Summer 2004 - p311-316 [501+]
WLT - v78 - i3-4 - Sept-Dec 2004 - p84(2) [501+]
Wrong about Japan: A Father's Journey with His Son
Econ - v374 - i8411 - Jan 29 2005 - p82US [501+]
Globe & Mail - Jan 22 2005 - pD4 [501+]
KR - v72 - i22 - Nov 15 2004 - p1074(1) [501+]
NS - v134 - i4721 - Jan 10 2005 - p51(2) [501+]
NYTBR - Jan 30 2005 - p8 [501+]
PW - v251 - i47 - Nov 22 2004 - p49(2) [51-500]

Carey, Raymond G. - *Improving Healthcare with Control Charts: Basic and Advanced SPC Methods and Case Studies*
R&R Bk N - v19 - i1 - Feb 2004 - p249(1) [51-500]

Carey, Richard Adams - *The Philosopher Fish: Sturgeon, Caviar, and the Geography of Desire*
Econ - v374 - i8415 - Feb 26 2005 - p85US [501+]
Ent W - i809 - March 4 2005 - p79 [51-500]
KR - v73 - i1 - Jan 1 2005 - p29(2) [501+]
PW - v252 - i5 - Jan 31 2005 - p58(1) [51-500]

Carey, Sabine C. - *Understanding Human Rights Violations: New Systematic Studies*
R&R Bk N - v19 - i3 - August 2004 - p172(1) [501+]

Carey, Sorcha - *Pliny's Catalogue of Culture: Art and Empire in the Natural History*
TLS - i5304 - Nov 26 2004 - p28(1) [501+]

Carey, Vincent P. - *Taking Sides? Colonial and Confessional Mentalites in Early Modern Ireland: Essays in Honor of Karl S. Bottigheimer*
Ren Q - v57 - i4 - Winter 2004 - p1545(2) [501+]

Caring for Your Pet
c LibMed - v23 - i3 - Nov-Dec 2004 - p76(1) [51-500]

Carroll, James - *Crusade: Chronicles of an Unjust War*
LJ - v129 - i12 - July 2004 - p103(1) [51-500]
Secret Father
WLT - v78 - i3-4 - Sept-Dec 2004 - p92(2) [501+]
Carroll, Jane L. - *Saints, Sinners, and Sisters: Gender and Northern Art in Medieval and Early Modern Europe*
Ren Q - v57 - i4 - Winter 2004 - p1487(3) [501+]
Carroll, Janell L. - *Sexuality Now: Embracing Diversity*
R&R Bk N - v19 - i2 - May 2004 - p132 [51-500]
Carroll, Joy - *Wolfe and Montcalm: Their Lives, Their Times, and the Fate of a Continent*
Globe & Mail - Oct 16 2004 - pD15 [501+]
R&R Bk N - v19 - i4 - Nov 2004 - p70(1) [51-500]
Carroll, Lewis - *Alice's Adventures in Wonderland (Illus. by Foreman, Michael)*
y Magpies - v19 - i5 - Nov 2004 - p20(4) [501+]
c SLJ - v50 - i11 - Nov 2004 - p92(2) [51-500]
Jabberwocky (Illus. by Jorisch, Stephane)
c BL - v101 - i4 - Oct 15 2004 - p397(1) [51-500]
c Globe & Mail - Nov 6 2004 - pD22 [1-50]
y Res Links - v10 - i2 - Dec 2004 - p35(1) [501+]
c SLJ - v50 - i9 - Sept 2004 - p223(2) [51-500]
Nonsense Verse
c KR - v73 - i1 - Jan 1 2005 - p50(1) [51-500]
c Sch Lib - v52 - i4 - Winter 2004 - p210(1) [51-500]
The Political Pamphlets and Letters of Charles Lutwidge Dodgson and Related Pieces: A Mathematical Approach
Isis - v95 - i3 - Sept 2004 - p520(2) [501+]
Carroll, Mark - *Music and Ideology in Cold War Europe*
MT - v145 - i1886 - Spring 2004 - p91-96 [501+]
Carroll, Maureen - *Earthly Paradises*
Arch - v57 - i4 - July-August 2004 - p58-58 [501+]
Carroll, Michael - *Awake at Work: Facing the Challenges of Life on the Job*
PW - v251 - i33 - August 16 2004 - p61(1) [51-500]
Carroll, Michael Christopher - *Lab 257: The Disturbing Story of the Government's Secret Plum Island Germ Laboratory*
SciTech - v28 - i3 - Sept 2004 - p76(1) [51-500]
Carroll, Michael P. - *The Penitente Brotherhood: Patriarchy and Hispano-Catholicism in New Mexico*
CS - v33 - i5 - Sept 2004 - p562-563 [501+]
The Penitente Brotherhood: Patriarchy and Hispano-Catholicism in New Mexico
Ams - v61 - i2 - Oct 2004 - p315(2) [501+]
Carroll, Pamela M. - *Model Organisms in Drug Discovery*
SciTech - v28 - i1 - March 2004 - p121(1) [51-500]
Carroll, Pamela Sissi - *Integrated Literacy Instruction in the Middle Grades: Channeling Young Adolescents' Spontaneous Overflow of Energy*
R&R Bk N - v19 - i1 - Feb 2004 - p184(1) [51-500]
Carroll, Patricia - *What Nurses Know And Doctors Don't Have Time To Tell You*
Bwatch - Nov 2004 - pNA [51-500]
Carroll, Patrick J. - *Felix Longoria's Wake: Bereavement, Racism, and the Rise of Mexican American Activism*
SHQ - v107 - i3 - Jan 2004 - p472(2) [501+]
WHQ - v35 - i2 - Summer 2004 - p234-234 [501+]
Carroll, Patrick James - *Felix Longoria's Wake: Bereavement, Racism, and the Rise of Mexican American Activism*
AHR - v109 - i3 - June 2004 - p939(2) [501+]
Felix Longoria's wake: Bereavement, Racism and the Rise of Mexican American Activism
JAH - v91 - i1 - June 2004 - p313-314 [501+]
Carroll, Sean B. - *Endless Forms Most Beautiful: The New Science of Evo Devo and the Making of the Animal Kingdom*
KR - v73 - i3 - Feb 1 2005 - p159(2) [501+]
LJ - v129 - i20 - Dec 1 2004 - p90(1) [51-500]
LJ - v130 - i4 - March 1 2005 - p105(1) [51-500]
PW - v252 - i9 - Feb 28 2005 - p55(1) [501+]
Carroll, Sean M. - *Spacetime and Geometry; An Introduction to General Relativity*
SciTech - v28 - i3 - Sept 2004 - p46(1) [1-50]
Carroll, Steven B. - *Ecology for Gardeners*
SciTech - v28 - i4 - Dec 2004 - p63(1) [51-500]
Carroll, Susan - *The Dark Queen*
KR - v73 - i3 - Feb 1 2005 - p133(1) [501+]
Carroll, Will - *Saving the Pitcher: Preventing Pitching Injuries in Modern Baseball*
Bwatch - March 2005 - pNA [51-500]
SciTech - v28 - i3 - Sept 2004 - p109(1) [51-500]

Carroll, William L. Taylor - *The Passion of My Times: An Advocate's Fifty-Year Journey in the Civil Rights Movement*
NL - v87 - i6 - Nov-Dec 2004 - p23(3) [501+]
Carroll, Yvonne - *Irish Legends for Children*
c CH Bwatch - v14 - i12 - Dec 2004 - pNA [51-500]
Carruth, Hayden - *Letters to Jane*
BL - v101 - i1 - Sept 2004 - p33(2) [51-500]
BW - v34 - i42 - Oct 17 2004 - p13(1) [501+]
Carruthers, Gerard - *English Romanticism and the Celtic World*
ILS - v24 - i1 - Fall 2004 - p32(1) [51-500]
Carryl, Charles E. - *The Camel's Lament (Illus. by Santore, Charles)*
c BL - v100 - i21 - July 2004 - p1842(1) [1-50]
The Camel's Lament. (Illus. by Santore, Charles)
c KR - v72 - i17 - Sept 1 2004 - p861(1) [51-500]
The Camel's Lament (Illus. by Santore, Charles)
c PW - v251 - i42 - Oct 18 2004 - p63(1) [51-500]
Carryl, Charles E, - *The Camel's Lament (Illus. by Santore, Charles)*
c SLJ - v50 - i10 - Oct 2004 - p139(1) [51-500]
Carryl, Charles Edward - *The Camel's Lament (Illus. by Santore, Charles)*
c CCB-B - v58 - i2 - Oct 2004 - p63(1) [51-500]
Cars
c SB - v40 - i3 - May-June 2004 - p135(1) [501+]
Carson, Anne - *Economy of the Unlost*
Dal R - v83 - i3 - Autumn 2003 - p460-462 [501+]
If Not, Winter: Fragments of Sappho
BIC - v33 - i7 - Oct 2004 - p31(2) [501+]
Lon R Bks - v26 - i1 - Jan 8 2004 - pNA [501+]
Carson, Ciaran - *Selected Poems*
Sew R - v111 - i3 - Summer 2003 - p486-492 [501+]
Carson, Clayborne - *The Papers of Martin Luther King, Jr., Vol. 5*
Soc Ser R - v79 - i1 - March 2005 - p207(1) [51-500]
Carson, David K. - *Creativity in Psychotherapy: Reaching New Heights with Individuals, Couples, and Families*
SciTech - v28 - i1 - March 2004 - p98(1) [51-500]
Carson, Donald - *Mo: The Life and Times of Morris K. Udall*
Bwatch - Oct 2004 - pNA [51-500]
Carson, Jo Ann S. - *Cardiovascular Nutrition: Disease Management and Prevention*
SciTech - v28 - i4 - Dec 2004 - p102(1) [51-500]
Carson, Mina - *Girls Rock!: Fifty Years of Women Making Music*
Choice - v42 - i4 - Dec 2004 - p670(1) [1-50]
Carson, Rachel - *The Sea Around Us*
SB - v40 - i6 - Nov-Dec 2004 - p244(1) [51-500]
Carson, Tom - *Elementary and Intermediate Algebra*
SciTech - v28 - i3 - Sept 2004 - p34(1) [51-500]
Carstens, R.W. - *Notes on Humanity: Faith, Reason, Certainty, 2nd Ed.*
R&R Bk N - v19 - i1 - Feb 2004 - p26(1) [1-50]
Carswell, Sue - *Faded Pictures from My Backyard: A Memoir*
KR - v73 - i5 - March 1 2005 - p271(1) [501+]
PW - v252 - i9 - Feb 28 2005 - p51(1) [501+]
Cart, Michael - *Bad Boys: A Journal of Contemporary Voices*
y KR - v72 - i17 - Sept 1 2004 - p862(1) [51-500]
c SLJ - v50 - i9 - Sept 2004 - p198(1) [51-500]
In the Stacks: Short Stories about Libraries and Librarians
LQ - v74 - i3 - July 2004 - p382(3) [501+]
Rush Hour: A Journal of Contemporary Voices
y Kliatt - v38 - i6 - Nov 2004 - p30(2) [501+]
Cartano, David J. - *Federal and State Taxation of Limited Liability Companies, 2004 Ed.*
R&R Bk N - v19 - i1 - Feb 2004 - pNA [51-500]
Carte, Penny - *Bridging the Culture Gap: A Practical Guide to International Business Communications*
Choice - v42 - i4 - Dec 2004 - p704(1) [1-50]
R&R Bk N - v19 - i4 - Nov 2004 - p110(1) [51-500]
Carter, Alden R. - *Bright Starry Banner: A Novel of the Civil War*
BW - v34 - i29 - July 18 2004 - p13(1) [501+]
Carter, Allene G. - *Honoring Sergeant Carter*
S&S - v68 - i3 - Fall 2004 - p377-378 [501+]
Carter, Anne Laurel - *Bless This House: Elizabeth*
y Can CL - i111-112 - Fall-Winter 2003 - p128(7) [501+]
F Team (Illus. by Cowles, Rose)
c CBRA - Annual 2003 - p449(1) [51-500]
Last Chance Bay
c Globe & Mail - Sept 25 2004 - pD26 [51-500]
c Res Links - v10 - i1 - Oct 2004 - p28(1) [501+]
My Home Bay (Illus. by Daniel, Alan)
c CBRA - Annual 2003 - p449(2) [51-500]
c SLJ - v50 - i8 - August 2004 - p84(1) [501+]

Carter, Barry E. - *International Law: Selected Documents, 2003-2004 Ed.*
R&R Bk N - v19 - i1 - Feb 2004 - pNA [501+]
Carter, Brian - *Saucier + Perrotte Architectes, 1995-2002*
R&R Bk N - v19 - i4 - Nov 2004 - p203(1) [501+]
Carter, Charlotte - *Trip Wire: A Cook County Mystery*
KR - v73 - i3 - Feb 1 2005 - p150(1) [51-500]
LJ - v130 - i2 - Feb 1 2005 - p56(1) [51-500]
PW - v252 - i8 - Feb 21 2005 - p161(2) [501+]
Carter, Colin B. - *Back to the Drawing Board: Designing Corporate Boards for a Complex World*
JEL - v42 - i1 - March 2004 - p269(2) [501+]
R&R Bk N - v19 - i1 - Feb 2004 - p97(1) [1-50]
Carter, David - *Stonewall: The Riots That Sparked the Gay Revolution*
G&L Rev W - v11 - i6 - Nov-Dec 2004 - p37(2) [501+]
Lam Bk Rpt - v13 - i1-2 - August-Sept 2004 - p14(2) [501+]
Carter, Don - *Send It! (Illus. by Carter, Don)*
c LibMed - v22 - i7 - April-May 2004 - p80(1) [501+]
c SLJ - v50 - i10 - Oct 2004 - pS22(1) [1-50]
Carter, Dorothy - *Grandma's General Store: The Ark (Illus. by Allen, Thomas B.)*
c KR - v73 - i4 - Feb 15 2005 - p226(1) [51-500]
Carter, Graydon - *Oscar Night: 75 Years of Hollywood Parties from the Editors of Vanity Fair*
LJ - v129 - i17 - Oct 15 2004 - p64(1) [51-500]
What We've Lost
BW - v34 - i38 - Sept 19 2004 - p4(1) [501+]
Globe & Mail - Sept 18 2004 - pD25 [501+]
LJ - v129 - i18 - Nov 1 2004 - p108(2) [51-500]
Nation - v279 - i11 - Oct 11 2004 - p36 [501+]
NYTBR - August 29 2004 - p13 [501+]
What We've Lost: Bush's War on Democracy and Freedom
PW - v251 - i34 - August 23 2004 - p48(2) [51-500]
Carter, Holly R. - *The Essential Guide for Study Abroad in the United Kingdom*
R&R Bk N - v19 - i3 - August 2004 - p213(1) [1-50]
Carter, J.D. - *Mathematica 5.0*
SIAM Rev - v46 - i3 - Sept 2004 - p564(5) [501+]
Carter, Jack L. - *Common Southwestern Native Plants: An Identification Guide*
SciTech - v28 - i3 - Sept 2004 - p62(1) [51-500]
Carter, James H. - *Creating a Chinese Harbin: Nationalism in an International City, 1916-1932*
JIH - v35 - i1 - Summer 2004 - p179-180 [501+]
Carter, Jimmy - *The Hornet's Nest (Read by McDonough, John). Audiobook Review*
LJ - v130 - i1 - Jan 1 2005 - p167(1) [51-500]
The Hornet's Nest
TLS - i5297 - Oct 8 2004 - p22(1) [501+]
Sharing Good Times
BL - v101 - i6 - Nov 15 2004 - p530(1) [51-500]
PW - v251 - i43 - Oct 25 2004 - p37(2) [51-500]
Carter, John D. - *Western Humanism: A Christian Perspective*
LJ - v130 - i1 - Jan 1 2005 - p118(1) [51-500]
Carter, K. Codell - *First Course in Logic*
R&R Bk N - v19 - i1 - Feb 2004 - p5(1) [51-500]
Carter, Les - *Grace and Divorce: God's Healing Gift to Those Whose Marriages Fall Short*
PW - v251 - i45 - Nov 8 2004 - p52(1) [51-500]
Carter, Matt - *T.H. Green and the Development of Ethical Socialism*
Ethics - v115 - i2 - Jan 2005 - p436(2) [501+]
Carter, Philip - *IQ and Psychometric Tests: Assess Your Personality, Aptitude, and Intelligence*
R&R Bk N - v19 - i3 - August 2004 - p8(1) [1-50]
Carter, R.J. - *Materials, Technology and Reliability for Advanced Interconnects and Low-K Dielectrics -- 2004: Proceedings*
SciTech - v28 - i4 - Dec 2004 - p156(1) [51-500]
Carter, Rebecca - *Scrapbooking Baby's Cherished Moments: 200 Page Designs*
BL - v101 - i8 - Dec 15 2004 - p704(1) [51-500]
Carter, Ronald - *Language and Creativity: The Art of Common Talk*
TimHES - v0 - i1678 - Feb 11 2005 - p24(1) [501+]
Carter, Sophie - *Purchasing Power: Representing Prostitution in Eighteenth-Century English Popular Print Culture*
R&R Bk N - v19 - i4 - Nov 2004 - p208(1) [501+]
Carter, Steven - *Help! I'm in Love with a Narcissist*
PW - v251 - i51 - Dec 20 2004 - p49(1) [51-500]

Cashman, Patricia - *Guide to Criminal Law for Florida, 3rd Ed.*
R&R Bk N - v19 - i4 - Nov 2004 - p173(1) [501+]

Cashmore, Ernest - *Encyclopedia of Race and Ethnic Studies*
R&R Bk N - v19 - i3 - August 2004 - p83(1) [51-500]

Cashwell, Craig S. - *Integrating Spirituality and Religion into Counseling: A Guide to Competent Practice*
R&R Bk N - v20 - i1 - Feb 2005 - p7(1) [51-500]

Casil, Amy Sterling - *50 Reasons Not to Vote for Bush*
R&R Bk N - v19 - i4 - Nov 2004 - p64(1) [51-500]

Caskie, Kathryn - *Lady in Waiting*
BL - v101 - i7 - Dec 1 2004 - p640(2) [51-500]
PW - v251 - i48 - Nov 29 2004 - p28(1) [51-500]

Casmer, Tom - *Henry and Pawl and the Round Yellow Ball*
c KR - v73 - i2 - Jan 15 2005 - p118(1) [51-500]

Casner, A. James - *Cases and Text on Property, 5th Ed.*
R&R Bk N - v19 - i3 - August 2004 - p197(1) [1-50]

Caspari, John A. - *Management Dynamics: Merging Constraints Accounting to Drive Improvement*
R&R Bk N - v19 - i4 - Nov 2004 - p114(1) [51-500]

Casper, Lionel I. - *The Rape of Palestine and the Struggle for Jerusalem*
R&R Bk N - v19 - i1 - Feb 2004 - p43(1) [51-500]

Casper, Monica J. - *Synthetic Planet: Chemicals, Politics and the Hazards of Modern Life*
T&C - v45 - i3 - July 2004 - p643-645 [501+]

Caspi, Mishael - *Eve in Three Traditions and Literatures: Judaism, Christianity, and Islam*
R&R Bk N - v19 - i3 - August 2004 - p22(1) [1-50]

Cass, Deborah Z. - *China and the World Trading System: Entering the New Millennium*
Pac A - v77 - i2 - Summer 2004 - p313(3) [501+]

Cass, Frank - *SOE in France: An Account of the Work of the British Special Operations Executive in France 1940-1944*
CR - v285 - i1666 - Nov 2004 - p319(2) [501+]

Cass, Ronald A. - *International Trade Law*
R&R Bk N - v19 - i1 - Feb 2004 - pNA [51-500]
The Rule of Law in America
Law&PolBR - July 2004 - p563(4) [501+]

Cassanos, Lynda Cohen - *Morocco*
y LibMed - v22 - i4 - Jan 2004 - p74(1) [501+]

Cassar, George H. - *Kitchener's War: British Strategy from 1914 to 1916*
R&R Bk N - v19 - i4 - Nov 2004 - p32(1) [51-500]

Cassar, Mario-Paul - *Handbook of Clinical Massage: A Complete Guide for Students and Professionals, 2d ed.*
SciTech - v28 - i1 - March 2004 - p122(1) [51-500]

Cassara, Lou - *From Selling to Serving: The Essence of Client Creation*
R&R Bk N - v19 - i3 - August 2004 - p126(1) [51-500]

Casse, Michel - *Stellar Alchemy: The Celestial Origin of Atoms*
Phys Today - v57 - i12 - Dec 2004 - p69-70 [501+]

Cassedy, Patrice - *Computer Technology*
y SLJ - v50 - i11 - Nov 2004 - p160(1) [51-500]

Cassell, Anthony K. - *The Monarchia Controversy: An Historical Study with Accompanying Translations of Dante Alighieri's Monarchia, Guido Vernani's Refutation of the Monarchia Composed by Dante, and Pope John XXII's Bull, Si Fratrum*
Choice - v41 - i11-12 - July-August 2004 - p2049(1) [501+]
The Monarchia Controversy: An Historical Study with Accompanying Translations of Dante Alighieri's Monarchia, Guido Vernani's Refutation of the Monarchia Composed by Dante, and Pope John XXII's Bull Si Fratrum
CHR - v90 - i4 - Oct 2004 - p772(2) [501+]

Cassell, Catherine - *Essential Guide to Qualitative Methods in Organizational Research*
Choice - v42 - i6 - Feb 2005 - p1062(1) [51-500]
R&R Bk N - v19 - i3 - August 2004 - p105(1) [1-50]

Cassella-Blackburn, Michael - *The Donkey, the Carrot, and the Club: William C. Bullitt and Soviet-American Relations, 1917-1948*
Choice - v42 - i6 - Feb 2005 - p1080(1) [51-500]
R&R Bk N - v19 - i3 - August 2004 - p69(1) [51-500]

Cassells, Cyrus - *More than Peace and Cypresses*
LJ - v129 - i15 - Sept 15 2004 - p60(2) [51-500]

Casselman, Grace - *Hole in the Hedge*
y CBRA - Annual 2003 - p477(2) [51-500]

Cassels, Jean - *The Mysterious Collection of Dr. David Harleyson*
c BL - v101 - i5 - Nov 1 2004 - p498(1) [51-500]
c KR - v72 - i17 - Sept 1 2004 - p862(1) [51-500]
c PW - v251 - i41 - Oct 11 2004 - p79(1) [51-500]
c SLJ - v50 - i12 - Dec 2004 - p105(1) [501+]

Cassidi, Deborah - *Favourite Wisdom*
A Aff - v35 - i2 - July 2004 - p210-211 [501+]

Cassidy, Anne - *Naughty Nancy (Illus. by Guicciardini, Desideria)*
c SLJ - v50 - i11 - Nov 2004 - p94(1) [51-500]
The Queen's Dragon (Illus. by Williamson, Gwyneth)
c SLJ - v51 - i2 - Feb 2005 - p94(1) [51-500]

Cassidy, Carla - *The Perfect Family*
LJ - v130 - i1 - Jan 1 2005 - p91(1) [51-500]

Cassidy, Cathy - *Dizzy: A Novel*
y BL - v101 - i3 - Oct 1 2004 - p321(2) [51-500]
c CCB-B - v58 - i5 - Jan 2005 - p203(1) [51-500]
c KR - v72 - i15 - August 1 2004 - p738(1) [51-500]
c PW - v251 - i41 - Oct 11 2004 - p80(1) [51-500]
y SLJ - v50 - i9 - Sept 2004 - p198(2) [51-500]

Cassidy, Daniel J. - *The Scholarship Book: The Complete Guide to Private-Sector Scholarships, Fellowships, Grants, and Loans for the Undergraduate*
Choice - v42 - i6 - Feb 2005 - p1006(1) [51-500]

Cassidy, David C. - *J. Robert Oppenheimer and the American Century*
LJ - v129 - i16 - Oct 1 2004 - p108(1) [51-500]
PW - v251 - i35 - August 30 2004 - p44(2) [51-500]
SB - v40 - i6 - Nov-Dec 2004 - p249(1) [501+]
Sci - v306 - i5699 - Nov 12 2004 - p1137(1) [501+]
TimHES - v0 - i1668 - Nov 26 2004 - p22(2) [501+]

Cassidy, Margaret - *Bookends: The Changing Media Environment of American Classrooms*
R&R Bk N - v19 - i3 - August 2004 - p215(1) [1-50]

Cassidy, Rebecca - *The Sport of Kings: Kinship, Class and Thoroughbred Breeding in Newmarket*
BHR - v77 - i4 - Winter 2003 - p790(793) [501+]
JRAI - v10 - i3 - Sept 2004 - p742(2) [501+]

Cassidy, Robert M. - *Peacekeeping in the Abyss: British and American Peacekeeping Doctrine and Practice After the Cold War*
Choice - v42 - i5 - Jan 2005 - p929(2) [51-500]
R&R Bk N - v19 - i3 - August 2004 - p189(1) [501+]

Cassidy, Sean - *Gummytoes*
c Globe & Mail - Jan 29 2005 - pD10 [51-500]
c Res Links - v10 - i2 - Dec 2004 - p2(1) [51-500]
c SLJ - v51 - i2 - Feb 2005 - p94(2) [51-500]

Cassidy, W.A. - *Meteorites, Ice, and Antarctica*
LibMed - v22 - i7 - April-May 2004 - p77(1) [501+]

Cassiolato, Jose E. - *Systems of Innovation and Development: Evidence From Brazil*
R&R Bk N - v19 - i1 - Feb 2004 - p83(1) [1-50]

Cassuto, Leonard - *The Cambridge Companion to Theodore Dreiser*
Choice - v42 - i2 - Oct 2004 - p291(1) [501+]

Casta, Isabelle - *La Litterature dans les ombres: Gaston Leroux les ceuvres noires*
FS - v58 - i3 - July 2004 - p426-427 [501+]

Castagno, Dario - *Too Much Tuscan Sun: Confessions of a Chianti Tour Guide*
LJ - v129 - i17 - Oct 15 2004 - p78(1) [51-500]
PW - v251 - i29 - July 19 2004 - p153(1) [51-500]

Castaldo, Nancy F. - *Deserts: An Activity Guide for Ages 6-9*
c Cur R - v44 - i5 - Jan 2005 - p12(1) [51-500]
c SB - v40 - i5 - Sept-Oct 2004 - p221(1) [51-500]
c SLJ - v50 - i8 - August 2004 - p133(1) [51-500]

Castaneda, Claudia - *Figurations: Child, Bodies, Worlds*
T&C - v45 - i1 - Jan 2004 - p224(2) [501+]
Uprootings/Regroundings: Questions of Home and Migration
JRAI - v10 - i4 - Dec 2004 - p914(2) [501+]

Castel-Bloom, Orly - *Human Parts*
BIC - v33 - i2 - March 2004 - p14(2) [501+]

Castellani, Christopher - *A Kiss from Maddalena: A Novel*
Kliatt - v38 - i6 - Nov 2004 - p14(1) [51-500]

Castellano, Marie - *Simply Super Storytimes, Programming Ideas for Ages 3-6*
R&R Bk N - v19 - i2 - Jan 2004 - p83(1) [501+]

Castelli, Elizabeth A. - *Martyrdom and Economy: Early Christian Culture Making*
Choice - v42 - i6 - Feb 2005 - p1036(1) [51-500]

Castellino, Onorato - *Pension Policy in an Integrating Europe*
JEL - v42 - i1 - March 2004 - p272(1) [501+]
R&R Bk N - v19 - i1 - Feb 2004 - p101(1) [51-500]

Castells, Manuel - *Conversations with Manuel Castells*
JEL - v42 - i1 - March 2004 - p344(1) [501+]
The Power of Identity, 2nd Ed.
R&R Bk N - v19 - i1 - Feb 2004 - p124(1) [51-500]

Castellucci, Cecil - *Boy Proof*
y CCB-B - v58 - i6 - Feb 2005 - p246(2) [51-500]
y Kliatt - v39 - i2 - March 2005 - p8(1) [51-500]
y KR - v73 - i3 - Feb 1 2005 - p175(1) [51-500]
y PW - v252 - i8 - Feb 21 2005 - p176(1) [51-500]

Casterline, C.L. - *The Sounds of Music (Illus. by Yerkes, Lane)*
c SLJ - v50 - i9 - Sept 2004 - p156(1) [51-500]

Casterline, John B. - *Reproduction and Social Context in Sub-Saharan Africa: A Collection of Micro-Demographic Studies*
IJAHS - v37 - i1 - Wntr 2004 - p187-189 [501+]

Casterline, Linda - *Natural-Born Killers: A Chapter Book*
c SLJ - v51 - i2 - Feb 2005 - p146(1) [51-500]

Castiglione, Dario - *Toleration, Neutrality, and Democracy*
R&R Bk N - v19 - i2 - May 2004 - p130 [51-500]

Castillo, Ana - *Peel My Love Like An Onion*
LJ - v129 - i20 - Dec 1 2004 - p186(1) [501+]

Castle, Caroline - *Funny!*
c Sch Lib - v52 - i4 - Winter 2004 - p186(1) [51-500]

Castle Connolly Medical Ltd. - *America's Top Doctors, 4th Ed.*
BL - v101 - i7 - Dec 1 2004 - p684(1) [501+]

Castle, Marjorie - *Triggering Communism's Collapse: Perceptions and Power in Poland's Transition*
Slav R - v63 - i3 - Fall 2004 - p627-628 [501+]

Castleberry, May - *The New World's Old World: Photographic Views of Ancient America*
Ams - v61 - i2 - Oct 2004 - p263(1) [501+]

Castor, Helen - *Blood and Roses*
HT - v54 - i11 - Nov 2004 - p65(1) [501+]

Castor, Stephen B. - *Minerals of Nevada*
RocksMiner - v79 - i4 - July-August 2004 - p275(1) [501+]

Castrigiano, Domenico P.L. - *Catastrophe Theory, 2nd Ed.*
SciTech - v28 - i1 - March 2004 - p41(1) [51-500]

Castro, Arachu - *Unhealthy Health Policy: A Critical Anthropological Examination*
SciTech - v28 - i4 - Dec 2004 - p83(1) [51-500]

Castro, Candida - *Human Factors of Transport Signs*
SciTech - v28 - i3 - Sept 2004 - p148(1) [51-500]

Castro, Elizabeth - *HTML for the World Wide Web, 5th Ed.*
LibMed - v22 - i5 - Feb 2004 - p77(1) [501+]

Castro, Fidel - *Cold War: Warnings for a Unipolar World*
R&R Bk N - v19 - i4 - Nov 2004 - p35(1) [51-500]
On Imperialist Globalization: Two Speeches
R&R Bk N - v19 - i2 - May 2004 - p110(1) [51-500]

Castro, Juan E, De - *Mestizo Nations: Culture, Race and Conformity in Latin American Literature*
MFSF - v50 - i2 - Summer 2004 - p495-496 [501+]

Castro, Ruy - *Garrincha: The Triumph and Tragedy of Brazil's Forgotten Football Hero*
TLS - i5303 - Nov 19 2004 - p35(1) [51-500]
Rio de Janeiro: Carnival under Fire
BL - v101 - i2 - Sept 15 2004 - p200(1) [501+]
LJ - v129 - i13 - August 2004 - p105(1) [51-500]
PW - v251 - i30 - July 26 2004 - p49(1) [501+]

Castronovo, David - *Beyond the Gray Flannel Suit: Books from The 1950s That Made American Culture*
AM - v192 - i3 - Jan 31 2005 - p16 [501+]
BL - v101 - i1 - Sept 1 2004 - p39(1) [51-500]
LJ - v129 - i19 - Nov 15 2004 - p60(1) [501+]

Castronovo, Russ - *Necro Citizenship: Death, Eroticism and the Public Sphere in the Nineteenth Century United States*
JIH - v35 - i1 - Summer 2004 - p149-151 [501+]

Casway, Jerrold - *Ed Delahanty in the Emerald Age of Baseball*
Choice - v41 - i11-12 - July-August 2004 - p2083(1) [501+]
HRNB - v33 - i1 - Fall 2004 - p14(1) [501+]
ILS - v24 - i1 - Fall 2004 - p10(1) [51-500]

The Cat in the Hat's Learning Library
LibMed - v22 - i7 - April-May 2004 - p77(1) [501+]

Catala, Rafael - *Index of American Periodical Verse, 2001*
    R&R Bk N - v19 - i1 - Feb 2004 - p262(1) [51-500]

Catalanotto, Peter - *Kitten Red, Yellow, Blue*
    c KR - v73 - i1 - Jan 1 2005 - p50(1) [51-500]
    c PW - v252 - i6 - Feb 7 2005 - p61(2) [501+]

Catani, Damian - *The Poet in Society: Art, Consumerism, and Politics in Mallarme*
    NCFS - v33 - i1-2 - Fall-Winter 2004 - p213(2) [501+]
    R&R Bk N - v19 - i1 - Feb 2004 - p231(1) [51-500]

Cate-Arries, Francie - *Spanish Culture Behind Barbed Wire: Memory and Representation of the French Concentration Camps, 1939-1945*
    Choice - v42 - i4 - Dec 2004 - p727(1) [1-50]
    R&R Bk N - v19 - i3 - August 2004 - p47(1) [51-500]

Cate, Curtis - *Friedrich Nietzsche*
    KR - v73 - i1 - Jan 1 2005 - p30(1) [501+]

Cate, Hugo ten - *Molecular Mechanisms of Disseminated Intravascular Coagulation*
    SciTech - v28 - i3 - Sept 2004 - p104(1) [51-500]

Cate, Sandra - *Making Merit, Making Art: A Thai Temple in Wimbledon*
    HNet - Sept 2004 - pNA [501+]

Cates, Jo A. - *Journalism: A Guide to the Reference Literature, 3rd Ed.*
    Choice - v42 - i3 - Nov 2004 - p448(1) [1-50]

Cates, Kimberly - *Picket Fence*
    BL - v101 - i9-10 - Jan 1 2005 - p830(1) [1-50]

Cathcart, Brian - *The Fly in the Cathedral*
    y BL - v101 - i7 - Dec 1 2004 - p629(1) [51-500]
    CR - v285 - i1663 - August 2004 - p126(1) [501+]
    KR - v72 - i20 - Oct 15 2004 - p991(2) [501+]
    Nature - v429 - i6993 - June 17 2004 - p702(1) [501+]
    NYTBR - Jan 9 2005 - p9 [501+]
    PW - v251 - i43 - Oct 25 2004 - p34(1) [51-500]
    SB - v41 - i1 - Jan-Feb 2005 - p19(1) [501+]

Cathcart, James - *Gravity*
    R&R Bk N - v19 - i1 - Feb 2004 - p203(1) [51-500]

Cather, Willa - *The Professor's House*
    Globe & Mail - Dec 24 2004 - pD3 [1-50]

Catherall, Don R. - *Handbook of Stress, Trauma, and the Family*
    Adoles - v39 - i154 - Summer 2004 - p398(1) [51-500]

Catherine II, Queen of Russia - *Love and Conquest: Personal Correspondence of Catherine the Great and Prince Grigory Potemkin*
    R&R Bk N - v19 - i3 - August 2004 - p45(1) [51-500]

Cathers, David - *Gustav Stickley*
    Am Craft - v64 - i1 - Feb-March 2004 - p24(1) [501+]

Catherwood, Christopher - *Churchill's Folly: How Winston Churchill Created Modern Iraq*
    MEJ - v58 - i4 - Autumn 2004 - p705(1) [501+]
Winston's Folly: Imperialism and the Creation of Modern Iraq
    CR - v286 - i1668 - Jan 2005 - p59(1) [51-500]
    NS - v133 - i4698 - July 26 2004 - p51(2) [501+]

Catherwood, Dianne - *Developmental Psychology*
    TimHES - v0 - i1684 - March 25 2005 - p28(1) [501+]

Cato, Vivienne - *The Torah and Judaism*
    c CH Bwatch - v14 - i7 - July 2004 - p2(1) [51-500]

Catran, Ken - *Bloody Liggie*
    c SLJ - v50 - i8 - August 2004 - p116(1) [51-500]

Cattell, John - *The Birmingham Jewellery Quarter: An Architectural Survey of the Manufactories*
    R&R Bk N - v19 - i1 - Feb 2004 - p202(1) [51-500]

Catullus - *Poems of Love and Hate*
    Quad - v49 - i1-2 - Jan-Feb 2005 - p122(3) [501+]

Catwoman: Nine Lives of a Feline Fatale
    BL - v101 - i1 - Sept 1 2004 - p76(1) [501+]

Caudill, Rebecca - *A Pocketful of Cricket (Illus. by Ness, Evaline)*
    c PW - v251 - i37 - Sept 13 2004 - p80(1) [51-500]

Caulkins, Jonathan P. - *Intelligent Giving: Insights and Strategies for Higher Education Donors*
    R&R Bk N - v19 - i1 - Feb 2004 - p185(1) [51-500]

Causey, Andrew - *Hard Bargaining in Sumatra: Western Travelers and Toba Bataks in the Marketplace of Souvenirs*
    R&R Bk N - v19 - i1 - Feb 2004 - p48(1) [51-500]

Causton, Helen C. - *Microarray Gene Expression Data Analysis: A Beginner's Guide*
    QRB - v79 - i3 - Sept 2004 - p308(2) [501+]

Caute, David - *The Dancer Defects: The Struggle for Cultural Supremacy During the Cold War*
    Lon R Bks - v26 - i19 - Oct 7 2004 - p31(3) [501+]
    NS - v133 - i4716 - Nov 29 2004 - p44(1) [51-500]

Cauwelaert, Didier van - *Out of My Head*
    Ent W - i797 - Dec 17 2004 - p89 [501+]
    NYTBR - Jan 23 2005 - p23 [501+]

Cavaco-Paulo, A. - *Textile Processing with Enzymes*
    E-Streams - Sept 2004 - pNA [501+]

Cavadini, John C. - *Who Do You Say That I Am? Confessing the Mystery of Christ*
    Comw - v132 - i2 - Jan 28 2005 - p42(3) [501+]

Cavafy, C.P. - *154 Poems*
    TLS - i5288 - August 6 2004 - p30(1) [501+]
I've Gazed So Much
    WLT - v78 - i3-4 - Sept-Dec 2004 - p150(1) [501+]

Cavalieri, Joey - *Bizarro World*
    PW - v252 - i4 - Jan 24 2005 - p223(1) [501+]

Cavalli-Sforza, L.L. - *Consanguinity Inbreeding and Genetic Drift in Italy*
    Nature - v432 - i7017 - Dec 2 2004 - p554(1) [501+]

Cavallo, Guglielmo - *History of Reading in the West*
    JMH - v76 - i4 - Dec 2004 - p934(3) [501+]

Cavanagh, Catherine - *Development and Management of Virtual Schools: Issues and Trends*
    R&R Bk N - v19 - i1 - Feb 2004 - p182(1) [51-500]

Cavanaugh, Willia T. - *Theopolitical Imagination: Discovering the Liturgy as a Political Act in an Age of Global Consumerism*
    TT - v60 - i4 - Jan 2004 - p562-566 [501+]

Cavaness, Chuck - *Programming Jakarta Struts. 2nd Ed.*
    SciTech - v28 - i3 - Sept 2004 - p28(1) [51-500]

Cavarzere, A. - *Iambic Ideas: Essays on a Poetic Tradition from Archaic Greece to the Late Roman Empire*
    Class R - v53 - i2 - Nov 2003 - p279-281 [501+]

Cave, Emma - *The Mother of All Crimes: Human Rights, Criminalization, and the Child Born Alive*
    Law&PolBR - Nov 2004 - p889(3) [501+]
    R&R Bk N - v19 - i4 - Nov 2004 - p164(1) [501+]

Cave, Kathryn - *That's What Friends Do (Illus. by Maland, Nick)*
    c SLJ - v50 - i11 - Nov 2004 - p94(1) [51-500]

Cave, Patrick - *Sharp North*
    y Sch Lib - v52 - i4 - Winter 2004 - p212(1) [51-500]

Cave, Roderick - *A History of the Golden Cockerel Press 1920-1960*
    Lib & Cul - v39 - i3 - Summer 2004 - p327(2) [501+]

Cave, Terence - *Pre-histories II: Langues etrangeres et troubles economiques au XVIe siecle*
    Six Ct J - v35 - i1 - Spring 2004 - p224(2) [501+]

Cavelier, M. - *In memoria di Luigi Bernabo Brea*
    Class R - v54 - i1 - May 2004 - p214(2) [501+]

Cavell, Colin S. - *Exporting 'Made-in-America' Democracy: The National Endowment for Democracy and U.S. Foreign Policy*
    AJPS - v39 - i2 - July 2004 - p448(448) [501+]

Cavell, Richard - *Love, Hate, and Fear in Canada's Cold War*
    HNet - Sept 2004 - pNA [501+]
    R&R Bk N - v19 - i3 - August 2004 - p76(1) [51-500]

Cavell, Stanley - *Cities of Words: Pedagogical Letters on a Register of the Moral Life*
    Choice - v42 - i3 - Nov 2004 - p496(1) [51-500]
    Wil Q - v28 - i4 - Autumn 2004 - p125(2) [501+]
Philosophy the Day After Tomorrow
    LJ - v130 - i2 - Feb 1 2005 - p82(1) [51-500]

Cavelos, Jeanne - *The Many Faces of Van Helsing*
    y Kliatt - v38 - i4 - July 2004 - p28(1) [501+]
    y VOYA - v27 - i3 - August 2004 - p230(1) [1-50]

Cavelti, Peter C. - *A Dangerous Remedy*
    Globe & Mail - Jan 8 2005 - pD11 [51-500]

Cavender, Anthony P. - *Folk Medicine in Southern Appalachia*
    Choice - v41 - i11-12 - July-August 2004 - p2086(2) [501+]
    JAH - v91 - i3 - Dec 2004 - p1028(2) [501+]
    JSH - v71 - i1 - Feb 2005 - p179(3) [501+]

Cavendish, Grace - *Assassin*
    c BL - v101 - i2 - Sept 15 2004 - p242(1) [51-500]
Betrayal
    c BL - v101 - i2 - Sept 15 2004 - p242(1) [51-500]
    y SLJ - v50 - i10 - Oct 2004 - p158(1) [51-500]

Caver, Larry E., Jr. - *Death and Marriage Notices from Jefferson County, Alabama Newspapers. Vol. 1*
    EFHM - v58 - i2 - March-April 2004 - p89(1) [51-500]

Cawood, Ian - *Britain in the Twentieth Century*
    R&R Bk N - v19 - i4 - Nov 2004 - p36(1) [51-500]

Caws, Mary Ann - *Maria Jolas: Woman of Action: A Memoir and Other Writings*
    TLS - i5301 - Nov 5 2004 - p34(1) [51-500]
The Reception of Virginia Woolf in Europe
    TSWL - v23 - i1 - Spring 2004 - p141-143 [501+]
Surrealism
    LJ - v130 - i2 - Feb 1 2005 - p78(1) [51-500]
The Yale Anthology of Twentieth-Century French Poetry
    Nation - v279 - i22 - Dec 27 2004 - p34 [501+]

Cawsey, Suzanne F. - *Kingship and Propaganda: Royal Eloquence and the Crown of Aragon, c. 1200-1450*
    HER - v119 - i483 - Sept 2004 - p1037(2) [501+]
    HER - v119 - i483 - Sept 2004 - p1037(2) [501+]

Cawthon, Charles R. - *Other Clay: A Remembrance of World War II Infantry*
    LJ - v129 - i13 - August 2004 - p131(1) [51-500]

Cawthon, Elisabeth A. - *Medicine on Trial: A Handbook with Cases, Laws, and Documents*
    y Ref Rev - June 2004 - pNA [501+]
    SciTech - v28 - i3 - Sept 2004 - p12(1) [501+]

Cawthorne, Nigel - *Military Commanders: The 100 Greatest Throughout History*
    LibMed - v22 - i7 - April-May 2004 - p65(1) [501+]

Cawthra, Gavin - *Governing Insecurity: Democratic Control of Military and Security Establishments in Transitional Democracies*
    Choice - v41 - i7 - March 2004 - p1368(1) [501+]
    R&R Bk N - v19 - i1 - Feb 2004 - p150(1) [51-500]

Caymax, Matty - *High-Mobility Group-IV Materials and Devices: Proceedings*
    SciTech - v28 - i4 - Dec 2004 - p156(1) [51-500]

Cazaux, Christelle - *La musique a la cour de Francois Ier*
    AHR - v109 - i2 - April 2004 - p625(2) [501+]
    Ren Q - v57 - i3 - Fall 2004 - p1094(3) [501+]
    Six Ct J - v35 - i3 - Fall 2004 - p880-881 [501+]

Cazdyn, Eric M. - *The Flash of Capital*
    FQ - v57 - i4 - Summer 2004 - p55(3) [501+]

Cazet, Denys - *Minnie and Moo and the Potato from Planet X (Read by Caruso, Barbara). Audiobook Review*
    c SLJ - v50 - i7 - July 2004 - p59(1) [51-500]
Minnie and Moo and the Seven Wonders of the World
    c BooChiTr - Feb 1 2004 - p5(1) [501+]
Minnie and Moo: The Attack of the Easter Bunnies
    c PW - v252 - i7 - Feb 14 2005 - p79(2) [501+]
Minnie and Moo: The Night Before Christmas (Read by Caruso, Barbara). Audiobook Review
    c SLJ - v50 - i9 - Sept 2004 - p78(1) [51-500]
Minnie and Moo: Will You Be My Valentine? (Read by Caruso, Barbara). Audiobook Review
    c SLJ - v50 - i7 - July 2004 - p59(1) [51-500]
The Octopus (Illus. by Cazet, Denys)
    c BL - v101 - i9-10 - Jan 1 2005 - p868(1) [501+]
    c KR - v72 - i24 - Dec 15 2004 - p1199(1) [501+]
    c SLJ - v51 - i1 - Jan 2005 - p88(1) [51-500]
    c HB - v81 - i1 - Jan-Feb 2005 - p89(2) [51-500]

Cebula, Larry - *Plateau Indians and the Quest for Spiritual Power, 1700-1850*
    WHQ - v35 - i3 - Autumn 2004 - p393(2) [501+]

Ceccarelli, Leah - *Shaping Science with Rhetoric: The Cases of Dobzhansky, Schrodinger, and Wilson*
    Isis - v95 - i3 - Sept 2004 - p470(2) [501+]

Ceccoli, Stephen J. - *Pill Politics: Drugs and the FDA*
    SciTech - v28 - i1 - March 2004 - p82(1) [51-500]

Cecconi, G.A. - *Commento storica al libro II dell' epistolario di Q. Aurelio Simmaco: Con introduzione, testo, traduzione e indici*
    Class R - v54 - i2 - Nov 2004 - p415(3) [501+]

Cecelski, David S. - *The Waterman's Song: Slavery and Freedom in Maritime North Carolina*
    AHR - v109 - i2 - April 2004 - p526(2) [501+]

Cecil, Nancy Lee - *Activities for a Comprehensive Approach to Literacy*
    R&R Bk N - v19 - i3 - August 2004 - p218(1) [1-50]

Cecil, Randy - *One Dark and Dreadful Night (Illus. by Cecil, Randy)*
  c CCB-B - v58 - i2 - Oct 2004 - p63(1) [51-500]
  c KR - v72 - i14 - July 15 2004 - p682(1) [51-500]
  c PW - v251 - i32 - August 9 2004 - p250(1) [51-500]
  c SLJ - v50 - i8 - August 2004 - p84(1) [51-500]

Cedro, Isabella - *Georges De Schudery: La Comdedie des comediens*
  FS - v58 - i1 - Jan 2004 - p96(2) [501+]

Cefrey, Holly - *The Interstate Commerce Act: The Government Takes Control of Trade between States*
  y SLJ - v50 - i11 - Nov 2004 - p160(1) [501+]
  The Pinckney Treaty: America Wins the Right to Travel the Mississippi River
  c SLJ - v50 - i8 - August 2004 - p132(1) [501+]
  The Sherman Antitrust Act: Getting Big Business under Control
  y SLJ - v50 - i11 - Nov 2004 - p160(1) [501+]

Cejka, Mary Ann - *Artisans of Peace: Grassroots Peacemaking among Christian Communities*
  IBMR - v28 - i3 - July 2004 - p136(2) [501+]

Cela, Camilo Jose - *The Family of Pascual Duarte*
  LJ - v129 - i14 - Sept 1 2004 - p204(1) [51-500]

Cela Conde, Camilo Jose - *Como bestia que duerme*
  WLT - v78 - i3-4 - Sept-Dec 2004 - p143(2) [501+]

Celan, Paul - *Poemes*
  TLS - i5296 - Oct 1 2004 - p4-6 [501+]

Celani, David P. - *Leaving Home: The Art of Separating from Your Difficult Family*
  LJ - v130 - i3 - Feb 15 2005 - p142(1) [51-500]

Celant, Germano - *Architecture and Arts 1900/2004: A Century of Creative Projects in Building, Design, Cinema, Painting, Sculpture*
  LJ - v130 - i4 - March 1 2005 - p82(1) [51-500]

Celebrating Cultures
  LibMed - v23 - i1 - August-Sept 2004 - p81(1) [51-500]

Celebrating Holidays Scrapbook-Style: 250 Sensational Pages That You Can Create
  BL - v101 - i4 - Oct 15 2004 - p375(1) [51-500]

Celebrating the Seasons of Life: Samhain to Ostara
  Bwatch - Feb 2005 - pNA [501+]

Celenza, Christopher S. - *The Lost Italian Renaissance: Humanists, Historians, and Latin's Legacy*
  Choice - v42 - i5 - Jan 2005 - p922(1) [1-50]
  R&R Bk N - v19 - i3 - August 2004 - p44(1) [51-500]

Celine, Marie - *Dishing Up Death: Gourmet Pet Chef Mystery Featuring Kitty Karlyle*
  LJ - v130 - i1 - Jan 1 2005 - p83(1) [51-500]

Celli, Bartolome R. - *Pharmacotherapy in Chronic Obstructive Pulmonary Disease*
  SciTech - v28 - i1 - March 2004 - p106(1) [51-500]

Cellich, Claude - *Global Business Negotiations: A Practical Guide*
  Choice - v41 - i7 - March 2004 - p1338(1) [501+]

Cells
  y SB - v40 - i4 - July-August 2004 - p167(1) [51-500]

Cennamo, Katherine - *Real World Instructional Design*
  R&R Bk N - v19 - i4 - Nov 2004 - p179(1) [501+]

Cenoz, Jasone - *The Multilingual Lexicon*
  R&R Bk N - v19 - i1 - Feb 2004 - p212 [51-500]

Censer, Jane Turner - *The Reconstruction of White Southern Womanhood, 1865-1895.*
  JSH - v71 - i1 - Feb 2005 - p175(3) [501+]
  RAH - v32 - i3 - Sept 2004 - p392-398 [501+]
  VQR - v80 - i2 - Spring 2004 - p257-257 [501+]

Centeno, Miguel Angel - *Blood and Debt: War and the Nation State in Latin America*
  HAHR - v84 - i2 - May 2004 - p327(2) [501+]

Center for Lesbian and Gay Studies - *Queer Ideas: The David R. Kessler Lectures in Lesbian and Gay Studies*
  R&R Bk N - v19 - i3 - August 2004 - p148(1) [501+]

Centner, Terence J. - *Empty Pastures: Confined Animals and the Transformation of the Rural Landscape*
  Choice - v42 - i2 - Oct 2004 - p316(1) [51-500]

Centore, F.F. - *Theism or Atheism: The Eternal Debate*
  R&R Bk N - v19 - i4 - Nov 2004 - p25(1) [501+]

Central Government Debt: Statistical Yearbook/Dette de L'Administration Centrale: Annuaire Statistique: 1992-2001
  JEL - v42 - i1 - March 2004 - p274(1) [501+]

Centre d'Etudes Medievales d'Auxerre - *Avant-nNefs et Espaces d'Accueil dans l'Eglise entre le IVe et le XIIe Siecle*
  Specu - v79 - i4 - Oct 2004 - pNA [501+]

Centrella, Joan M. - *The Astrophysics of Gravitational Wave Souces: College Park, Maryland, 24-26 April, 2003*
  SciTech - v28 - i1 - March 2004 - p45(1) [51-500]

Centrie, Craig - *Identity Formation of Vietnamese Immigrant Youth in an American High School*
  R&R Bk N - v19 - i3 - August 2004 - p229(1) [1-50]

Cepeda, Raquel - *And It Don't Stop: The Best American Hip-Hip Journalism of the Last 25 Years*
  Black Iss - v6 - i5 - Sept-Oct 2004 - p47(2) [51-500]
  And It Don't Stop: The Best American Hip-Hop Journalism of the Last 25 Years
  y BL - v101 - i1 - Sept 1 2004 - p36(1) [51-500]
  LJ - v129 - i13 - August 2004 - p82(1) [501+]

Cerami, Charles A. - *Jefferson's Great Gamble*
  TLS - i5264 - Feb 20 2004 - p9-10 [501+]

Cerasini, Marc - *Wolverine: Weapon X*
  PW - v251 - i48 - Nov 29 2004 - p28(1) [51-500]

Cercas, Javier - *Soldiers of Salamis*
  NYRB - v51 - i15 - Oct 7 2004 - p36(4) [501+]

Cerin, Christopher - *Parallel I/O for Cluster Computing*
  E-Streams - Oct 2004 - pNA [501+]

Cernuschi, Alain - *Penser la Musique dans l'Encyclopedie*
  Eight-C St - v37 - i3 - Spring 2004 - p497-500 [501+]

Cerulean, Susan - *Tracking Desire: A Journey After Swallow-Tailed Kites*
  LJ - v130 - i3 - Feb 15 2005 - p154(1) [51-500]
  PW - v252 - i5 - Jan 31 2005 - p60(1) [501+]

Cerullo, Mary M. - *Sea Turtles: Ocean Nomads (Illus. by Rotman, Jeffrey L.)*
  c CE - v80 - i5 - Mid-Summer 2004 - p275(1) [51-500]
  c LibMed - v22 - i5 - Feb 2004 - p54(1) [501+]

Cervantes Saavedra, Miguel de - *Don Quixote*
  VQR - v80 - i2 - Spring 2004 - p260-260 [501+]

Cerwonka, Allaine - *Native to the Nation: Disciplining Landscapes and Bodies in Australia*
  R&R Bk N - v19 - i4 - Nov 2004 - p52(1) [51-500]

Cesarani, David - *Eichmann: His Life and Crimes*
  CR - v286 - i1668 - Jan 2005 - p62(1) [51-500]
  Lon R Bks - v26 - i21 - Nov 4 2004 - p7(6) [501+]
  TLS - i5290 - August 20 2004 - p10(1) [501+]

Cesaretti, Paolo - *Theodora: Empress of Byzantium*
  Choice - v42 - i3 - Nov 2004 - p544(1) [1-50]
  R&R Bk N - v19 - i3 - August 2004 - p43(1) [51-500]

Cesereanu, Ruxandra - *Lunacies*
  WLT - v79 - i1 - Jan-April 2005 - p110(1) [501+]

Cestaro, Gary P. - *Queer Italia: Same-Sex Desire in Italian Literature and Film*
  Choice - v42 - i6 - Feb 2005 - p1027(1) [51-500]

Cetron, Marvin J. - *Hospitality 2010*
  Fut - v39 - i2 - March-April 2005 - pNA [501+]

Cha, Victor D. - *Asia-Pacific Security: Policy Challenges*
  R&R Bk N - v19 - i1 - Feb 2004 - p256(1) [51-500]
  Nuclear North Korea: A Debate on Engagement Strategies
  NYRB - v52 - i2 - Feb 10 2005 - p25(3) [501+]
  TimHES - v0 - i1659 - Sept 24 2004 - p27(1) [501+]

Chabal, Patrick - *A History of Postcolonial Lusophone Africa*
  IJAHS - v37 - i1 - Wntr 2004 - p167-169 [501+]

Chabbot, Colette - *Understanding Others, Educating Ourselves: Getting More from International Comparative Studies in Education*
  Sci Teach - v71 - i7 - Sept 2004 - p94-95 [501+]

Chabon, Michael - *The Amazing Adventures of the Escapist. Vol. 1*
  y BL - v100 - i22 - August 2004 - p1915(1) [51-500]
  KR - v72 - i14 - July 15 2004 - pNA [501+]
  PhiKapP - v84 - i3 - Summer 2004 - p45(2) [501+]
  The Final Solution: A Story of Detection
  Globe & Mail - March 12 2005 - pD17 [1-50]
  BL - v101 - i3 - Oct 1 2004 - p282(1) [51-500]
  BW - v34 - i46 - Nov 14 2004 - p7(1) [501+]
  Globe & Mail - Jan 8 2005 - pD11 [51-500]
  HM - v309 - i1855 - Dec 2004 - p87(2) [501+]
  KR - v72 - i19 - Oct 1 2004 - p928(1) [501+]
  NS - v134 - i4722 - Jan 17 2005 - p55(1) [501+]
  NYTBR - Nov 14 2004 - p57 [501+]
  People - v62 - i24 - Dec 13 2004 - p58 [51-500]
  PW - v251 - i44 - Nov 1 2004 - p43(1) [501+]
  Spec - v297 - i9209 - Feb 5 2005 - p42(2) [501+]
  Ent W - i792 - Nov 12 2004 - p128 [51-500]

McSweeney's Enchanted Chamber of Astonishing Stories
  KR - v72 - i19 - Oct 1 2004 - p928(1) [1-50]
  PW - v251 - i44 - Nov 1 2004 - p45(1) [501+]

Chace, James - *1912: Wilson, Roosevelt, Taft and Debs--the Election That Changed the Country*
  CC - v121 - i25 - Dec 14 2004 - p20(1) [1-50]
  Choice - v42 - i6 - Feb 2005 - p1080(1) [51-500]
  For Aff - v83 - i5 - Sept-Oct 2004 - p164 [501+]
  NYRB - v51 - i14 - Sept 23 2004 - p58(4) [501+]
  y SLJ - v50 - i11 - Nov 2004 - p178(1) [51-500]

Chacham, Ronit - *Breaking Ranks*
  MEP - v11 - i4 - Winter 2004 - p138(4) [501+]

Chaconas, Dori - *Cork and Fuzz (Illus. by McCue, Lisa)*
  c KR - v73 - i5 - March 1 2005 - p284(1) [51-500]

Chaconas, Doris - *Momma, Will You? (Illus. by Johnson, Steve)*
  c BL - v101 - i5 - Nov 1 2004 - p487(2) [51-500]
  c SLJ - v50 - i11 - Nov 2004 - p94(1) [51-500]

Chadarevian, Soraya de - *Models: The Third Dimension of Science*
  Choice - v42 - i5 - Jan 2005 - p873(1) [1-50]
  Sci - v306 - i5699 - Nov 12 2004 - p1136(2) [501+]
  SciTech - v28 - i4 - Dec 2004 - p14(1) [1-50]

Chadwick, Bruce - *George Washington's War: The Forging of a Revolutionary Leader and the American Presidency*
  BW - v34 - i27 - July 4 2004 - p4(1) [501+]
  R&R Bk N - v19 - i3 - August 2004 - p67(1) [51-500]

Chadwick, Charles - *It's All Right Now*
  PW - v252 - i11 - March 14 2005 - p42(2) [51-500]

Chadwick, Daniel R. - *Tables for Students of Moral Philosophy: A Supplement to Philosophical Discussion about Ethics*
  R&R Bk N - v19 - i3 - August 2004 - p2(1) [1-50]

Chadwick, Derek J. - *Development of the Cardiac Conduction System: Proceedings*
  SciTech - v28 - i1 - March 2004 - p72(1) [51-500]
  Molecular Clocks and Light Signalling
  SciTech - v28 - i1 - March 2004 - p71(1) [51-500]

Chadwick, Henry - *East and West: The Making of a Rift in the Church: From Apostolic Times Until the Council of Florence*
  HER - v119 - i483 - Sept 2004 - p970(972) [501+]
  TLS - i5292 - Sept 3 2004 - p22(1) [501+]

Chadwick, Kay - *Jean Dutourd: 'Au Bon Beurre'*
  FS - v58 - i1 - Jan 2004 - p140(2) [501+]

Chadwick, Whitney - *The Modern Woman Revisited: Paris between the Wars*
  R&R Bk N - v19 - i1 - Feb 2004 - p36(1) [1-50]

Chafe, William H. - *The Achievement of American Liberalism: The New Deal and Its Legacies*
  JAH - v91 - i1 - June 2004 - p304-305 [501+]

Chafer, Tony - *The End of Empire in French West Africa: France's Successful Decolonization?*
  AHR - v109 - i2 - April 2004 - p661(1) [501+]

Chaffin, J. Thomas - *Pathfinder: John Charles Fremont and the Course of American Empire*
  J Mil H - v68 - i2 - April 2004 - p575-576 [501+]
  J Mil H - v68 - i2 - April 2004 - p576-577 [501+]
  R&R Bk N - v19 - i3 - August 2004 - p67(1) [51-500]

Chafuen, Alejandro A. - *Faith and Liberty: The Economic Thought of the Late Scholastics*
  JEL - v42 - i1 - March 2004 - p239(1) [501+]
  Theol St - v65 - i3 - Sept 2004 - p682(1) [501+]

Chah, Ajahn - *Everything Arises, Everything Falls Away: Teachings on Impermanence and the End of Suffering*
  LJ - v130 - i4 - March 1 2005 - p92(1) [51-500]

Chai, Arlene - *Eating Fire and Drinking Water*
  Critq - v44 - Winter 2003 - p185 [501+]

Chai, Sun-Ki - *Choosing an Identity: A General Model of Preference and Belief Formation*
  JEL - v42 - i4 - Dec 2004 - p1166(3) [501+]

Chaikin, Andrew - *Space: A History of Space Exploration in Photographs*
  Bwatch - Jan 2005 - pNA [51-500]
  Globe & Mail - Dec 18 2004 - pD14 [1-50]
  SB - v40 - i6 - Nov-Dec 2004 - p244(1) [51-500]
  SciTech - v28 - i4 - Dec 2004 - p45(1) [1-50]

Chaikin, Linda Lee - *Today's Embrace*
  LJ - v130 - i2 - Feb 1 2005 - p64(1) [51-500]

Chaitow, Leon - *Fibromyalgia Syndrome: A Practitioner's Guide to Treatment, with Accompanying CD-ROM. 2nd Ed.*
  SciTech - v28 - i1 - March 2004 - p107(1) [1-50]

Chajes, J.H. - *Between Worlds: Dybbuks, Exorcists, and Early Modern Judaism*
  Choice - v41 - i7 - March 2004 - p1 [501+]

Chakrabarthy, K. - *Cisco IP Routing Protocols: Troubleshooting Techniques*
Bwatch - v26 - i9 - Sept 2004 - p5(1) [51-500]

Chakrabarti, G.S. - *Pressure Vessel and Piping Codes and Standards: Proceedings*
SciTech - v28 - i4 - Dec 2004 - p163(1) [51-500]

Chakrabarti, Subrata - *OMAE 2003, Vol. 1*
SciTech - v28 - i1 - March 2004 - p171(1) [51-500]

Chakrabarty, Dipesh - *Habitations of Modernity: Essays in the Wake of Subaltern Studies*
JIH - v35 - i2 - Autumn 2004 - p343(3) [501+]

Chakravorti, Bhaskar - *The Slow Pace of Fast Change: Bringing Innovations to Market in a Connected World*
JEL - v41 - i4 - Dec 2003 - p1417(2) [501+]
R&R Bk N - v19 - i1 - Feb 2004 - p81(1) [51-500]

Chalcraft, Edwin L. - *Assimilation's Agent: My Life as a Superintendent in the Indian Boarding School System*
Roundup M - v12 - i3 - Feb 2005 - p16(1) [51-500]

Chalcraft, John T. - *The Striking Cabbies of Cairo and Other Stories: Crafts and Guilds in Egypt, 1863-1914*
MEJ - v59 - i1 - Wntr 2005 - p141(2) [501+]

Chaliand, Gerard - *Nomadic Empires: From Mongolia to the Danube*
Choice - v41 - i11-12 - July-August 2004 - p2098(1) [501+]

Chalk, Peter - *Confronting the "Enemy Within": Security Intelligence, the Police, and Counterterrorism in Four Democracies*
R&R Bk N - v19 - i3 - August 2004 - p164(1) [501+]

Chalker, Jack L. - *Kaspar's Box*
y Kliatt - v39 - i1 - Jan 2005 - p19(1) [501+]

Chall, Marsha Wilson - *Prairie Train (Illus. by Thompson, John)*
c LibMed - v22 - i6 - March 2004 - p56(1) [501+]

Challem, Jack - *Prevent and Reverse Heart Disease, Arthritis, Diabetes, Allergies, and Asthma*
E-Streams - Sept 2004 - pNA [501+]

Challenges of Large Applications in Distributed Environments (CLADE 2004): Proceedings
SciTech - v28 - i3 - Sept 2004 - p30(1) [51-500]

Challis, Lawrence - *Electron-Phonon Interaction in Low-Dimensional Structures*
SciTech - v28 - i1 - March 2004 - p52(1) [51-500]

Challis, Sarah - *Blackthorn Winter (Read by Haddon, Eva). Audiobook Review*
BL - v101 - i7 - Dec 1 2004 - p676(2) [51-500]
Blackthorn Winter
BL - v101 - i2 - Sept 15 2004 - p206(1) [501+]

Chalmers, David - *Backfire: How the Ku Klux Klan Helped the Civil Rights Movement*
JSH - v70 - i4 - Nov 2004 - p951(2) [501+]
TimHES - v0 - i1659 - Sept 24 2004 - p28(2) [501+]

Chalmers, Robert - *Fortune's Bastard*
BL - v101 - i1 - Sept 1 2004 - p59(1) [51-500]
KR - v72 - i15 - August 1 2004 - p702(1) [501+]
LJ - v129 - i15 - Sept 15 2004 - p47(1) [51-500]
PW - v251 - i32 - August 9 2004 - p231(1) [51-500]

Chalupa, Leo M. - *The Visual Neurosciences, Vol. I*
TimHES - v0 - i1684 - March 25 2005 - p28(1) [501+]
The Visual Neurosciences, Vol. II
TimHES - v0 - i1684 - March 25 2005 - p28(1) [501+]
The Visual Neurosciences, Vols. 1-2
QRB - v79 - i3 - Sept 2004 - p332(2) [501+]

Chamberlain, Diane - *The Bay at Midnight*
y BL - v101 - i8 - Dec 15 2004 - p690(1) [51-500]
PW - v252 - i2 - Jan 10 2005 - p37(2) [51-500]

Chamberlain, Franc - *Michael Chekhov*
TimHES - v0 - i1655 - August 27 2004 - p26(1) [501+]

Chamberlain, Lesley - *Motherland: A Philosophical History of Russia*
NS - v133 - i4701 - August 16 2004 - p36(2) [501+]

Chamberlain, Penny - *Olden Days Locket*
y Can CL - i111-112 - Fall-Winter 2003 - p139(8) [501+]
c CBRA - Annual 2003 - p478(1) [51-500]

Chamberlayne, Prue - *Biographical Methods and Professional Practice: An International Perspective*
R&R Bk N - v19 - i3 - August 2004 - p89(1) [51-500]

Chamberlin, J. Edward - *If This Is Your Land, Where Are Your Stories?: Finding Common Ground*
BIC - v33 - i5 - August 2004 - p13(1) [501+]
CBRA - Annual 2003 - p267(1) [501+]

Chamberlin, Mary - *Mama Panya's Pancakes: A Village Tale from Kenya (Illus. by Cairns, Julia)*
c KR - v73 - i5 - March 1 2005 - p285(1) [51-500]

Chambers, Aidan - *Postcards from No Man's Land*
c WLT - v79 - i1 - Jan-April 2005 - p69(4) [501+]

Chambers, Allen S., Jr. - *Buildings of West Virginia*
Choice - v42 - i4 - Dec 2004 - p651(1) [1-50]

Chambers, Austin - *Modern Vacuum Physics*
SciTech - v28 - i4 - Dec 2004 - p47(1) [51-500]

Chambers, Carole - *Echolocation*
CBRA - Annual 2003 - p210(1) [51-500]

Chambers, Colin - *Inside the Royal Shakespeare Company: Creativity and the Institution*
TimHES - v0 - i1655 - August 27 2004 - p28(1) [501+]

Chambers, Edward J. - *NAFTA in the New Millennium*
CBRA - Annual 2003 - p331(2) [51-500]

Chambers, Edward T. - *Roots for Radicals: Organizing for Power, Action, and Justice*
R&R Bk N - v19 - i1 - Feb 2004 - p127(1) [51-500]
Tikkun - v19 - i6 - Nov-Dec 2004 - p69(3) [501+]

Chambers, Jack - *Bouncing with Bartok*
LJ - v129 - i14 - Sept 1 2004 - p152(1) [51-500]

Chambers, James - *Palmerston: "The People's Darling"*
HT - v54 - i11 - Nov 2004 - p71(1) [501+]
TLS - i5291 - August 27 2004 - p6-7 [501+]

Chambers, Jeanne C. - *Great Basin Riparian Area: Ecology, Management, and Restoration*
SciTech - v28 - i3 - Sept 2004 - p57(1) [1-50]

Chambers, Paul - *A Sheltered Life: The Unexpected History of the Giant Tortoise*
Globe & Mail - Nov 20 2004 - pD30 [51-500]
TLS - i5298 - Oct 15 2004 - p32(1) [501+]

Chambers, Sally - *Wilbie Finds a Friend*
c Sch Lib - v52 - i4 - Winter 2004 - p186(1) [51-500]

Chambers, Thomas A. - *Drinking the Waters: Creating an American Leisure Class at Nineteenth-Century Mineral Springs*
JAH - v91 - i2 - Sept 2004 - p631(1) [501+]

Chambers, Tod - *Prozac as a Way of Life*
CHE - v50 - i48 - August 6 2004 - pA17(1) [501+]

Chambers, Veronica - *When Did You Stop Loving Me*
Black Iss - v6 - i4 - July-August 2004 - p44(2) [501+]
NW - July 12 2004 - p64 [501+]

Chamings, Matt - *Time Switch*
c Sch Lib - v52 - i3 - Autumn 2004 - p135(1) [501+]

Chamoiseau, Patrick - *Chronicle of the Seven Sorrows*
Callaloo - v26 - Winter 2003 - p219 [501+]

Chamoux, F. - *Hellenistic Civilization*
Class R - v54 - i1 - May 2004 - p154(2) [501+]

Champagne, Duane - *The Future of Indigenous Peoples: Strategies for Survival and Development*
Am Ind CRJ - v28 - i2 - Spring 2004 - p150(4) [501+]

Champe, Pamela C. - *Lippincott's Illustrated Reviews: Biochemistry*
SciTech - v28 - i4 - Dec 2004 - p74(1) [51-500]

Champeau, Nicole V. - *Moulinette*
Can Lit - i181 - Summer 2004 - p114-116 [501+]

Champion, Daryl - *The Paradoxical Kingdom: Saudi Arabia and the Momentum of Reform*
MEQ - v11 - i3 - Summer 2004 - p92(1) [501+]
R&R Bk N - v19 - i1 - Feb 2004 - p84(1) [1-50]

Champion, Justin - *Republican Learning: John Toland and Crises of Christian Culture, 1696-1722*
RES - v55 - i219 - April 2004 - pNA [501+]

Champlin, Dell P. - *The Institutionalist Tradition in Labor Economics*
Choice - v42 - i7 - March 2005 - p1277(1) [51-500]

Champlin, Edward - *Nero*
Lon R Bks - v26 - i17 - Sept 2 2004 - p17(1) [501+]

Champod, Christophe - *Fingerprints and Other Ridge Skin Impressions*
R&R Bk N - v19 - i3 - August 2004 - p163(1) [501+]

Champollion, Herve - *Egypt: Stones of Light*
Choice - v41 - i11-12 - July-August 2004 - p2031(1) [501+]

Champton, Justin - *Republican Learning: John Toland and the Crisis of Christian Culture, 1696-1722*
R&R Bk N - v19 - i1 - Feb 2004 - p3(1) [51-500]

Chan, Albert - *Chinese Books and Documents in the Jesuit Archives in Rome: A Descriptive Catalogue: Japonica-Sinica I-IV*
Ch Rev Int - v10 - i2 - Fall 2003 - p326(12) [501+]
CHR - v90 - i3 - July 2004 - p586(2) [501+]

Chan, Anthony B. - *Perpetually Cool: The Many Lives of Anna May Wong, 1905-1961*
NYRB - v52 - i1 - Jan 13 2005 - p40(2) [501+]
R&R Bk N - v19 - i1 - Feb 2004 - p227(1) [1-50]

Chan, Arlene - *Awakening the Dragon: The Dragon Boat Festival (Illus. by Song Nan Zhang)*
c BL - v100 - i22 - August 2004 - p1921(1) [51-500]

Chan, Cassandra - *The Young Widow*
KR - v73 - i5 - March 1 2005 - p261(1) [51-500]

Chan, Christine - *Cognitive Informatics: Proceedings*
SciTech - v28 - i4 - Dec 2004 - p24(1) [51-500]

Chan, Gillian - *The Carved Box*
y Kliatt - v38 - i4 - July 2004 - p14(2) [51-500]
A Foreign Field
y Kliatt - v38 - i4 - July 2004 - p16(1) [51-500]

Chan, Janet B.L. - *Fair Cop: Learning the Art of Policing*
R&R Bk N - v19 - i1 - Feb 2004 - p143(1) [51-500]

Chan, Jeffery Paul - *Eat Everything Before You Die: A Chinaman in the Counterculture*
BL - v101 - i2 - Sept 15 2004 - p206(1) [501+]
LJ - v129 - i14 - Sept 1 2004 - p136(1) [51-500]
PW - v251 - i38 - Sept 20 2004 - p45(1) [51-500]

Chan, Kara K.W. - *Advertising to Children in China*
Ch Rev Int - v11 - i1 - Spring 2004 - p41(4) [501+]
Choice - v42 - i3 - Nov 2004 - p529(1) [1-50]

Chan, Marty - *The Mystery of the Frozen Brains*
c Res Links - v10 - i1 - Oct 2004 - p12(1) [501+]

Chan, Mary - *Roger North's "Of Sounds" and Prendcourt Tracts, c. 1710-c. 1716*
Isis - v95 - i2 - June 2004 - p291(3) [501+]
Roger North's Writings on Music, c. 1704-c. 1709
Isis - v95 - i2 - June 2004 - p291(3) [501+]

Chan, Peter T. - *Reproductive Medicine Secrets*
SciTech - v28 - i4 - Dec 2004 - p110(1) [51-500]

Chan, Russell - *Red Dust: Ten Intriguing, Sensuous Stories*
Globe & Mail - Feb 12 2005 - pD13 [1-50]

Chan, Steve - *Coping with Globalization: Cross-National Patterns in Domestic Governance and Policy Performance*
JPR - v41 - i6 - Nov 2004 - p753-753 [501+]

Chan, Sucheng - *Remapping Asian American History*
R&R Bk N - v19 - i1 - Feb 2004 - p57(1) [51-500]

Chan, Theodore C. - *ECG in Emergency Medicine and Acute Care*
SciTech - v28 - i4 - Dec 2004 - p103(1) [51-500]

Chan-Tiberghien, Jennifer - *Gender and Human Rights Politics in Japan: Global Norms and Domestic Networks*
R&R Bk N - v19 - i4 - Nov 2004 - p133(1) [51-500]

Chanan, Michael - *Cuban Cinema*
Choice - v42 - i1 - Sept 2004 - p108(1) [501+]

Chance, Jane - *Tolkien and the Invention of Myth: A Reader*
Choice - v42 - i3 - Nov 2004 - p488(1) [1-50]
CR - v285 - i1667 - Dec 2004 - p379(1) [51-500]
Med R - July 2004 - pNA [501+]
Tolkien the Medievalist
TLS - i5296 - Oct 1 2004 - p32-33 [501+]

Chance, Megan - *An Inconvenient Wife (Read by Mazur, Kathe). Audiobook Review*
Kliatt - v38 - i6 - Nov 2004 - p48(1) [51-500]

Chancellor, Deborah - *Maps and Mapping*
c BL - v101 - i1 - Sept 1 2004 - p126(1) [1-50]

Chancellor, Edward - *Capital Account: A Money Manager's Reports from a Turbulent Decade*
Choice - v42 - i4 - Dec 2004 - p706(1) [1-50]
R&R Bk N - v19 - i3 - August 2004 - p138(1) [1-50]

Chandler, Alfred D., Jr. - *The Visible Hand*
Har Bus R - v82 - i7-8 - July-August 2004 - p35(5) [501+]

Chandler, Charlotte - *It's Only a Movie: Alfred Hitchcock: A Personal Biography*
KR - v72 - i24 - Dec 15 2004 - p1175(1) [501+]
LJ - v130 - i2 - Feb 1 2005 - p80(1) [51-500]
PW - v252 - i2 - Jan 10 2005 - p47(1) [51-500]

Chandler, David G. - *Blenheim Preparation: The English Army on the March to the Danube, Collected Essays*
TLS - i5299 - Oct 22 2004 - p7 [501+]

Chandler, E.A. - *Feline Medicine and Therapeutics, 3rd Ed.*
E-Streams - Oct 2004 - pNA [501+]

Chandler, Jennifer - *Shrinking Violets and Caspar Milequetoasts: Shyness, Power, and Intimacy in the United States*
CS - v33 - i5 - Sept 2004 - p554-555 [501+]

Chandler, Katherine R. - *Surveying the Literary Landscapes of Terry Tempest Williams: New Critical Essays*
R&R Bk N - v19 - i1 - Feb 2004 - p247(1) [1-50]

Chandler, Stuart - *Establishing a Pure Land on Earth: The Foguang Buddhist Perspective on Modernization and Globalization*
R&R Bk N - v19 - i4 - Nov 2004 - p18(1) [51-500]

Chandler, Wilma Marcus - *Ultimate Scene Study Series for Teens*
LibMed - v22 - i6 - March 2004 - p88(1) [501+]

Chandra, A.M. - *Engineering Graphics, 2nd Ed.*
SciTech - v28 - i4 - Dec 2004 - p130 [51-500]

Chandra, Kanchan - *Why Ethnic Parties Succeed: Patronage and Ethnic Headcounts in India*
Pers PS - v33 - i4 - Fall 2004 - p241(2) [501+]

Chaney, Edward - *Richard Eurich, 1903-1992: Visionary Artist*
Choice - v41 - i11-12 - July-August 2004 - p2034(1) [501+]

Chang, Ching-Cheng - *Global Warming and the Asian Pacific*
SciTech - v28 - i1 - March 2004 - p53(1) [51-500]

Chang, David F. - *Phaco Chop: Mastering Techniques, Optimizing Technology, and Avoiding Complications*
SciTech - v28 - i3 - Sept 2004 - p115(1) [51-500]

Chang, Edward C. - *Social Problem Solving: Theory, Research, and Training*
Choice - v42 - i5 - Jan 2005 - p938(1) [51-500]
SciTech - v28 - i4 - Dec 2004 - p2(1) [51-500]

Chang, Eileen - *Written on Water*
KR - v73 - i3 - Feb 1 2005 - p160(1) [501+]

Chang, Gordon H. - *Asian Americans and Politics: Perspectives, Experiences, Prospects*
J Urban H - v30 - i4 - May 2004 - p604-615 [501+]

Chang, Ha-Joon - *Rethinking Development Economics*
Choice - v41 - i7 - March 2004 - p1342(1) [501+]

Chang, Jeff - *Can't Stop Won't Stop: A History of the Hip-Hop Generation*
Ent W - Feb 4 2005 - p141 [51-500]
PW - v252 - i5 - Jan 31 2005 - p61(2) [501+]

Chang, Kai - *Microwave Ring Circuits and Related Structures. 2nd Ed.*
SciTech - v28 - i3 - Sept 2004 - p162(1) [51-500]

Chang, Kang-Tsung - *Programming ArcObjects with VBA: A Task-Oriented Approach*
SciTech - v28 - i4 - Dec 2004 - p129 [51-500]

Chang, Kelly H. - *Appointing Central Bankers: The Politics of Monetary Policy in the United States and the European Monetary Union*
JEL - v42 - i1 - March 2004 - p256(2) [501+]

Chang, Kwen-Jen - *Delta Receptor*
SciTech - v28 - i1 - March 2004 - p74(1) [51-500]

Chang, Lan Samantha - *Inheritance*
BL - v100 - i21 - July 2004 - p1816(1) [1-50]

Chang, Maria Hsia - *Falun Gong: The End of Days*
Choice - v42 - i2 - Oct 2004 - p309(1) [51-500]
For Aff - v83 - i5 - Sept-Oct 2004 - p164 [501+]
TimHES - v0 - i1676 - Jan 28 2005 - p28(2) [501+]

Chang, Michael - *Racial Politics in an Era of Transnational Citizenship: The 1996 "Asian Donorgate" Controversy in Perspective*
Choice - v42 - i6 - Feb 2005 - p1097(1) [51-500]
R&R Bk N - v19 - i4 - Nov 2004 - p59(1) [51-500]

Chang, Miman - *The Jehol Biota: The Emergence of Feathered Dinosaurs, Beaked Birds and Flowering Plants*
Sci - v306 - i5702 - Dec 3 2004 - p1685(1) [1-50]

Chang, Samantha - *Inheritance*
PW - v251 - i27 - July 5 2004 - p36(1) [51-500]

Chang, Sea-Jin - *Financial Crisis and Transformation of Korean Business Groups: The Rise and Fall of Chaebols*
JEL - v41 - i4 - Dec 2003 - p1408(1) [501+]

Chang, Shu-Ting - *Mushrooms: Cultivation, Nutritional Value, Medicinal Effect, and Environmental Impact. 2nd Ed.*
SciTech - v28 - i3 - Sept 2004 - p129(1) [51-500]

Chang, Victoria - *Asian American Poetry: The Next Generation*
Choice - v42 - i6 - Feb 2005 - p1020(1) [51-500]

Change Your Job, Change Your Life: Careering and Re-Careering in the New Boom/Bust Economy, 9th Ed.
Bwatch - Feb 2005 - pNA [51-500]

Changeux, Jean-Pierre - *The Physiology of Truth: Neuroscience and Human Knowledge*
Choice - v42 - i3 - Nov 2004 - p507(1) [1-50]
Nature - v429 - i6991 - June 3 2004 - p505(2) [501+]
Sci - v306 - i5702 - Dec 3 2004 - p1684(1) [501+]

Chaniotis, A. - *Army and Power in the Ancient World*
Class R - v54 - i2 - Nov 2004 - p478(3) [501+]

Channell, James E.T. - *Timescales of the Paleomagnetic Field*
SciTech - v28 - i4 - Dec 2004 - p57(1) [51-500]

Channer, Colin - *Passing Through*
Black Iss - v6 - i5 - Sept-Oct 2004 - p50(1) [501+]

Channon, Geoffrey - *Railways in Britain and the United States, 1830-1940*
BHR - v77 - i4 - Winter 2003 - p785(787) [501+]

Chansky, Dorothy - *Composing Ourselves: The Little Theatre Movement and the American Audience*
Choice - v42 - i5 - Jan 2005 - p863(1) [1-50]

Chanteraud, Annabel R. - *La Saga du kava, du Vanuatu a la Nouvelle-Caledonie*
Cont Pac - v16 - i2 - Fall 2004 - p459(2) [501+]

Chao, Evelina - *Yeh Yeh's House*
y   BL - v101 - i5 - Nov 1 2004 - p454(1) [51-500]
LJ - v130 - i2 - Feb 1 2005 - p93(1) [51-500]

Chao, Lien - *Strike the Wok: An Anthology of Contemporary Chinese Canadian Fiction*
WLT - v79 - i1 - Jan-April 2005 - p92(1) [501+]

Chao, Patricia - *Mambo Peligroso*
KR - v73 - i5 - March 1 2005 - p244(1) [501+]

Chaon, Dan - *You Remind Me of Me*
NYTBR - July 11 2004 - p9 [501+]
NYTBR - July 18 2004 - p18 [501+]
NYTBR - July 25 2004 - p18 [501+]
y   SLJ - v50 - i9 - Sept 2004 - p241(1) [51-500]

Chaouli, Michel - *The Laboratory of Poetry: Chemistry and Poetics in the Work of Friedrich Schlegel*
Clio - v33 - i2 - Wntr 2004 - p220(6) [501+]
Comp L - v56 - i2 - Spring 2004 - p201-203 [501+]

Chapais, Bernard - *Kinship and Behavior in Primates*
Choice - v42 - i2 - Oct 2004 - p320(1) [51-500]

Chapam, Graham - *The Pythons: Autobiography by the Pythons*
TV Q - v34 - i3-4 - Spring-Summer 2004 - p69-70 [501+]

Chapel, Jim D. - *Guidance and Control 2004: Proceedings*
SciTech - v28 - i4 - Dec 2004 - p161(1) [51-500]

Chapin, Anne P. - *Charis: Essays in Honor of Sara A. Immerwahr*
R&R Bk N - v19 - i2 - May 2004 - p194(1) [51-500]

Chapin, Paul G. - *Research Projects and Research Proposals*
Bwatch - Nov 2004 - pNA [51-500]

Chapin, Ted - *Everything Was Possible: The Birth of the Musical Follies*
Am Theat - v21 - i6 - July-August 2004 - p79(3) [501+]

Chapius, Julien - *Stefan Lochner: Image Making in Fifteenth-Century Cologne*
R&R Bk N - v19 - i4 - Nov 2004 - p199(1) [501+]

Chaplais, Pierre - *English Diplomatic Practice in the Middle Ages*
AHR - v109 - i2 - April 2004 - p591(2) [501+]

Chaplan, Michael - *The Urban Treasure Hunter: A Practical Handbook for Beginners*
PW - v251 - i51 - Dec 20 2004 - p45(1) [51-500]

Chapleau, Marc - *Let's Talk Wine!: An Expert Takes on Your Questions*
CBRA - Annual 2003 - p127(1) [51-500]

Chaplin, A. - *Terror: The New Theater of War. Mao's Legacy: Selected Cases of Terrorism in the 20th and 21st Centuries*
R&R Bk N - v19 - i1 - Feb 2004 - p141(1) [51-500]

Chaplin, Joyce E. - *Subject Matter: Technology, the Body and Science on the Anglo-American Frontier, 1500-1676*
Isis - v95 - i2 - June 2004 - p298(2) [501+]
Six Ct J - v34 - i4 - Winter 2003 - p1197-1198 [501+]

Chaplin, Sid - *The Day of the Sardine*
TLS - i5306 - Dec 10 2004 - p21-22 [501+]
The Watchers and the Watched
TLS - i5306 - Dec 10 2004 - p21-22 [501+]

Chapman, Alison - *Unfolding the South: Nineteenth-Century British Women Writers and Artists in Italy*
JGS - v13 - i1 - March 2004 - p90-91 [501+]
Nine-C Lit - v58 - i4 - March 2004 - p555(559) [501+]

Chapman, Allan - *Mary Somerville and the World of Science*
Nature - v432 - i7017 - Dec 2 2004 - p553(1) [501+]
New Sci - v184 - i2476 - Dec 4 2004 - p55(1) [501+]

Chapman, Audrey R. - *Religion and Reconciliation in South Africa: Voices of Religious Leaders*
HNet - June 2004 - pNA [501+]

Chapman, C. Stuart - *Shelby Foote: A Writer's Life*
JSH - v70 - i3 - August 2004 - p715(2) [501+]

Chapman, Edgar L. - *Classic and Iconoclastic Alternate History Science Fiction*
R&R Bk N - v19 - i1 - Feb 2004 - p242(1) [501+]

Chapman, Graham - *The Geopolitics of South Asia: From Early Empires to the Nuclear Age*
PG - v23 - i4 - May 2004 - p493-495 [501+]

Chapman, Jane - *Sing a Song of Sixpence: A Pocketful of Nursery Rhymes and Tales (Illus. by Chapman, Jane)*
c   BL - v101 - i1 - Sept 1 2004 - p126(1) [1-50]
c   KR - v72 - i13 - July 1 2004 - p626(1) [51-500]
c   PW - v251 - i36 - Sept 6 2004 - p65(1) [51-500]
c   SLJ - v50 - i10 - Oct 2004 - p139(1) [51-500]

Chapman, Janet - *Tempting the Highlander*
y   BL - v101 - i1 - Sept 1 2004 - p72(1) [51-500]

Chapman, Lee - *Eight Animals Play Ball*
LibMed - v22 - i4 - Jan 2004 - p56(1) [501+]

Chapman, Mark D. - *Ambassadors of Christ: Commemorating 150 Years of Theological Education in Cuddesdon, 1854-2004*
R&R Bk N - v19 - i4 - Nov 2004 - p25(1) [501+]

Chapman, Mary Beth - *Shaoey and Dot: Bug Meets Bundle (Illus. by Chapman, Jim)*
c   SLJ - v50 - i12 - Dec 2004 - p105(1) [501+]

Chapman, Sarah Bahnson - *Bright and Gloomy Days: The Civil War Correspondence of Captain Charles Frederic Bahnson, a Moravian Confederate*
JSH - v70 - i4 - Nov 2004 - p938(2) [501+]

Chapman, Serle L. - *Promise: Bozeman's Trail to Destiny*
Bwatch - Feb 2005 - pNA [51-500]

Chapman, Simon - *Explorers Wanted on the South Sea Islands*
y   Sch Lib - v52 - i4 - Winter 2004 - p217(1) [51-500]

Chapman, Stanley D. - *Hosiery and Knitwear: Four Centuries of Small-Scale Industry in Britain, c. 1589-2000*
Albion - v36 - i2 - Summer 2004 - p332(2) [501+]
BHR - v77 - i4 - Winter 2003 - p780(782) [501+]

Chapman, Victoria L. - *World History on File: The 20th Century, Updated Ed.*
c   LibMed - v23 - i3 - Nov-Dec 2004 - p81(1) [51-500]

Chapman, Wayne K. - *Yeat's Collaborations*
ILS - v24 - i1 - Fall 2004 - p23(2) [501+]

Chapman, Woodrow W. - *Modern Machine Shop's Guide to Engineering Materials*
Choice - v42 - i2 - Oct 2004 - p323(1) [51-500]
Modern Machine Shop's Guide to Machining Operations
SciTech - v28 - i3 - Sept 2004 - p150(1) [51-500]
Modern Machine Shop's Guide to Threads, Threading and Threaded Fasteners
Choice - v42 - i4 - Dec 2004 - p693(1) [1-50]
Modern Machine Shop's Guide to Threads, Threading, and Threaded Fasteners
SciTech - v28 - i3 - Sept 2004 - p151(1) [51-500]

Chappell, David L. - *A Stone of Hope: Prophetic Religion and the Death of Jim Crow*
Bks & Cult - v10 - i4 - July-August 2004 - p8(2) [501+]
CH - v73 - i4 - Dec 2004 - p828(6) [501+]
Choice - v42 - i1 - Sept 2004 - p172(1) [501+]
HNet - Oct 2004 - pNA [501+]

Chappell, Fred - *Backsass: Poems*
LJ - v129 - i12 - July 2004 - p87(1) [51-500]

Chappell, Henry - *Blood Kin: A Haunting Novel of Early Texas*
Roundup M - v12 - i1 - Oct 2004 - p29(1) [51-500]

Chappell, Michaele F. - *Empowering the Beginning Teacher of Mathematics: Elementary School*
SciTech - v28 - i4 - Dec 2004 - p33(1) [51-500]

Chappuis, Pierre - *Traces d'incertitude*
WLT - v78 - i3-4 - Sept-Dec 2004 - p121(1) [501+]

Chappuys, Gabriel - *Les Facetieuses Journees*
Ren Q - v57 - i4 - Winter 2004 - p1433(2) [501+]

Chapra, Mimi - *Amelia's Show-and-Tell Fiesta/Amelia y la fiesta de "muestra y cuenta." (Illus. by Aviles, Martha)*
c   SLJ - v50 - i9 - Sept 2004 - p195(2) [51-500]

Chapuis, Julien - *Stefan Lochner: Image Making in Fifteenth-Century Cologne*
Apo - v159 - i510 - August 2004 - p77(2) [501+]
Tilman Riemenschneider, c. 1460-1531
Choice - v42 - i3 - Nov 2004 - p474(1) [1-50]
LJ - v129 - i15 - Sept 15 2004 - p55(1) [51-500]

Characterization and Failure Analysis of Plastics
SciTech - v28 - i3 - Sept 2004 - p140(1) [51-500]

Charalambis, Dimitris - *Recent Social Trends in Greece, 1960-2000*
R&R Bk N - v19 - i3 - August 2004 - p147(1) [51-500]

Charan, Ram - *Profitable Growth Is Everyone's Business*
Har Bus R - v82 - i7-8 - July-August 2004 - p35(5) [501+]

Charap, John M. - *Explaining the Universe: The New Age of Physics*
Isis - v95 - i3 - Sept 2004 - p526(2) [501+]

Charbonnel, Corinne - *CNO in the Universe: Proceedings*
SciTech - v28 - i1 - March 2004 - p61(1) [51-500]

Chardin, Pierre Teilhard De - *Christianity and Evolution*
AS - v74 - i1 - Wntr 2005 - p10(2) [501+]

Charen, Mona - *Do-Gooders: How Liberals Hurt Those They Claim to Help*
PW - v252 - i1 - Jan 3 2005 - p50(1) [51-500]

Chari, Sharad - *Fraternal Capital: Peasant-Workers, Self-Made, and Globalization in Provincial India*
Choice - v42 - i5 - Jan 2005 - p900(1) [1-50]

Charite, Claude La - *La rhetorique epistolaire de Rabelais*
Ren Q - v57 - i3 - Fall 2004 - p1015(2) [501+]

Charitonenko, Stephanie - *Commercialization of Microfinance: Sri Lanka*
JEL - v41 - i4 - Dec 2003 - p1408(1) [501+]

Charles, C.M. - *Building Classroom Discipline, 8th Ed.*
R&R Bk N - v19 - i3 - August 2004 - p225(1) [1-50]

Charles, David - *Aristotle on Meaning and Essence*
Dialogue - v43 - i1 - Wntr 2004 - p171-173 [501+]

Charles Dickens. Vol. 3
LJ - v129 - i14 - Sept 1 2004 - p198(1) [51-500]

Charles, Maria - *Occupational Ghettos: The Worldwide Segregation of Women and Men*
Choice - v42 - i7 - March 2005 - p1273(1) [51-500]

Charles, Norma - *All the Way to Mexico*
c CBRA - Annual 2003 - p478(1) [51-500]
Criss Cross, Double Cross: Sophie, Alias Star Girl, to the Rescue
y Can CL - i111-112 - Fall-Winter 2003 - p128(7) [501+]

Charles, Paul - *I Love the Sound of Breaking Glass*
PW - v251 - i42 - Oct 18 2004 - p51(1) [501+]

Charles, Randall I. - *Teaching Mathematics through Problem Solving: Grades 6-12*
Math T - v98 - i1 - August 2004 - p62-62 [501+]

Charles, Ronald - *Trade, Aid, and Arbitrate: The Globalization of Western Law*
R&R Bk N - v19 - i3 - August 2004 - p193(1) [501+]

Charlesworth, Monique - *The Children's War*
y BL - v100 - i22 - August 2004 - p1896(1) [51-500]
BW - v34 - i50 - Dec 12 2004 - p4(1) [501+]
Globe & Mail - Nov 27 2004 - pD29 [501+]
KR - v72 - i13 - July 1 2004 - p590(1) [501+]
NYTBR - Oct 24 2004 - p20 [501+]
PW - v251 - i33 - August 16 2004 - p43(1) [51-500]

Charlip, Julie A. - *Cultivating Coffee: The Farmers of Carazo, Nicaragua, 1880-1930*
AHR - v109 - i2 - April 2004 - p576(2) [501+]
Ams - v61 - i2 - Oct 2004 - p265(3) [501+]
BHR - v78 - i2 - Summer 2004 - p336(3) [501+]

Charlotte Elizabeth - *Irish Recollections*
LJ - v129 - i15 - Sept 15 2004 - p91(1) [1-50]

Charlton, David - *The Cambridge Companion to Grand Opera*
MT - v145 - i1886 - Spring 2004 - p101-105 [501+]
Notes - v61 - i2 - Dec 2004 - p415(3) [501+]

Charmatz, Konrad - *Nightmares: Memoirs of the Years of Horror Under Nazi Rule in Europe, 1939-1945*
R&R Bk N - v19 - i1 - Feb 2004 - p44(1) [51-500]

Charnas, Suzy McKee - *Stagestruck Vampires and Other Phantasms*
BL - v101 - i8 - Dec 15 2004 - p715(1) [51-500]

Charner, Kathy - *The Giant Encyclopedia of Kindergarten Activities: Over 600 Activities Created by Teachers for Teachers*
R&R Bk N - v19 - i4 - Nov 2004 - p181(1) [501+]

Charney, Cy - *Trainer's Tool Kit*
HR Mag - v50 - i2 - Feb 2005 - pS17(1) [501+]

Charney, Dennis S. - *The Peace of Mind Prescription: An Authoritative Guide to Finding the Most Effective Treatment for Anxiety and Depression*
SciTech - v28 - i4 - Dec 2004 - p99(1) [51-500]

Charney, Pamela - *ADA Pocket Guide to Nutrition Assessment*
SciTech - v28 - i1 - March 2004 - p103(1) [51-500]

Charnley, Joy - *Living with Languages: The Contemporary Swiss Model*
R&R Bk N - v19 - i1 - Feb 2004 - p213 [501+]

Charnov, Bruce H. - *From Autogiro to Gyroplane: The Amazing Survival of an Aviation Technology*
APH - v51 - i3 - Fall 2004 - p47(2) [501+]
Choice - v41 - i7 - March 2004 - p1316(1) [501+]

Charpak, Georges - *Debunked: ESP, Telekinesis, and Other Pseudoscience*
R&R Bk N - v20 - i1 - Feb 2005 - p8(1) [51-500]

Charters, David - *The Insiders: A Portfolio of Stories from High Finance*
KR - v72 - i16 - August 15 2004 - p758(1) [501+]

Chartier, JoAnn - *She Wore a Yellow Ribbon: Women Soldiers and Patriots of the Western Frontier*
y Kliatt - v39 - i1 - Jan 2005 - p33(1) [51-500]
R&R Bk N - v19 - i4 - Nov 2004 - p67(1) [51-500]

Chartrand, David - *A View from the Heartland: Everyday Life in America*
R&R Bk N - v19 - i1 - Feb 2004 - p64(1) [501+]

Chartrand, Mark R. - *Satellite Communications for the Nonspecialist*
Choice - v42 - i3 - Nov 2004 - p514(1) [1-50]
SciTech - v28 - i3 - Sept 2004 - p154(1) [51-500]

Chartterton, Paul - *Urban Nightscapes: Youth Cultures, Pleasure Spaces, and Corporate Power*
CS - v33 - i6 - Nov 2004 - p693(2) [501+]

Charvat, Robert A. - *Coloring of Plastics: Fundamentals. 2nd Ed.*
E-Streams - July 2004 - pNA [501+]
SciTech - v28 - i1 - March 2004 - p174(1) [1-50]

Charyn, Jerome - *Gangsters and Gold Diggers: Old New York, the Jazz Age, and the Birth of Broadway*
Choice - v41 - i11-12 - July-August 2004 - p2105(1) [501+]
The Green Lantern: A Romance of Stalinist Russia
BL - v101 - i6 - Nov 15 2004 - p560(1) [51-500]
BW - v34 - i48 - Nov 28 2004 - p6(1) [501+]
KR - v72 - i17 - Sept 1 2004 - p820(2) [501+]
LJ - v129 - i18 - Nov 1 2004 - p72(1) [501+]
PW - v251 - i42 - Oct 18 2004 - p48(1) [501+]

Chase, Andra - *Ludmila's Way*
c CH Bwatch - v14 - i7 - July 2004 - p1(1) [51-500]

Chase, Diana - *The Lighthouse Kids*
c SLJ - v50 - i11 - Nov 2004 - p138(1) [51-500]

Chase, John - *Glitter Stucco and Dumpster Diving*
JAAC - v61 - Winter 2003 - p92 [501+]

Chase, Karen - *The Spectacle of Intimacy*
VS - v45 - i2 - Winter 2003 - p377 [501+]

Chase, Kate J. - *PC Hardware and A+ Handbook*
SciTech - v28 - i3 - Sept 2004 - p19(1) [501+]

Chase, Kenneth B. - *Must Christianity Be Violent? Reflections on History, Practice, and Theology*
CC - v121 - i26 - Dec 28 2004 - p33(2) [501+]

Chase, Loreta - *Mr. Impossible*
PW - v252 - i7 - Feb 14 2005 - p59(1) [51-500]

Chase, Philander D. - *The Papers of George Washington: Revolutionary War Series*
R&R Bk N - v19 - i4 - Nov 2004 - p60(1) [51-500]

Chase, Susan K. - *Clinical Judgement and Communication in Nurse Practitioner Practice*
SciTech - v28 - i3 - Sept 2004 - p126(1) [51-500]

Chaskey, Scott - *This Common Ground: Seasons on an Organic Farm*
KR - v73 - i4 - Feb 15 2005 - p206(2) [51-500]

Chastain, Bill - *Payne at Pinehurst: The Greatest US Open Ever*
y BW - v34 - i34 - August 22 2004 - p8(2) [501+]

Chastang, Pierre - *Lire, ecrire, transcrire: Le travail des redacteurs de cartulaires en Bas-Languedoc, XI-XIII siecles*
Med R - Dec 2004 - pNA [501+]

Chasteen, John Charles - *National Rythms, African Roots: The Deep History of Latin American Popular Dance*
Choice - v41 - i11-12 - July-August 2004 - p2055(1) [501+]
Problems in Modern Latin American History: Sources and Interpretations
R&R Bk N - v19 - i1 - Feb 2004 - p66(1) [501+]
Ams - v61 - i2 - Oct 2004 - p261(2) [501+]

Chastelain, Georges - *Les Douze Dames de rhetorique*
FS - v58 - i2 - April 2004 - p241(2) [501+]

Chaston, Ian - *Knowledge-Based Marketing: The Twenty-First Century Competitive Edge*
R&R Bk N - v19 - i3 - August 2004 - p127(1) [51-500]

Chataway, Carol - *Wings (Illus. by Lee, Declan)*
y Magpies - v19 - i5 - Nov 2004 - p31(2) [501+]

Chatel, Vivianne - *Coping and Pulling Through: Action Processes in Vulnerable Situtations*
R&R Bk N - v19 - i4 - Nov 2004 - p123(1) [51-500]

Chatelain, Jean-Marc - *La Bibliotheque de l'Honnete Homme: Livres, Lecture et Collections en France a l'Age Classique*
BSA-P - v98 - i3 - Sept 2004 - p370-374 [501+]

Chater, James - *Luca Marenzio: The Career of a Musician between the Renaissance and the Counter-Reformation*
R&R Bk N - v19 - i1 - Feb 2004 - p196(1) [51-500]

Chatgilialoglu, Chryssostomos - *Organosilanes in Radical Chemistry*
SciTech - v28 - i3 - Sept 2004 - p51(1) [1-50]

Chatterjea, Tara - *Knowledge and Freedom in Indian Philosophy*
R&R Bk N - v19 - i1 - Feb 2004 - p1(1) [51-500]

Chatterjee, Choi - *Celebrating Women: Gender, Festival Culture, and Bolshevik Ideology, 1910-1939.*
JMH - v77 - i1 - March 2005 - p260(3) [501+]

Chatterjee, Deen K. - *Ethics and Foreign Intervention*
JPR - v41 - i4 - July 2004 - p518-518 [501+]
The Ethics of Assistance: Morality and the Distant Needy
Choice - v42 - i5 - Jan 2005 - p865(2) [1-50]
Pers PS - v34 - i1 - Wntr 2005 - p61(1) [501+]

Chatterjee, Partha - *The Politics of the Governed: Reflections on Popular Politics in Most of the World*
Nation - v279 - i22 - Dec 27 2004 - p25 [501+]

Chatterjee, Piya - *A Time for Tea: Women, Labor and Post/Colonial Politics on an Indian Plantation*
R&R Bk N - v19 - i4 - Nov 2004 - p104(1) [51-500]

Chatterjee, Ranjit - *Wittgenstein and Judaism: A Triumph of Concealment*
R&R Bk N - v20 - i1 - Feb 2005 - p5(1) [51-500]

Chatterjee, Sayan - *Failsafe Strategies: Profit and Grow from Risks That Others Avoid*
LJ - v129 - i17 - Oct 15 2004 - p70(1) [501+]

Chatterjee, Shoutir Kishore - *Statistical Thought: A Perspective and History*
Choice - v41 - i7 - March 2004 - p1329(1) [501+]

Chatterton, Martin - *The Kingfisher First Thesaurus*
c SLJ - v50 - i8 - August 2004 - p55(1) [501+]

Chatterton, Paul - *Urban Nightscapes: Youth Cultures, Pleasure Spaces and Corporate Power*
AJS - v110 - i1 - July 2004 - p267(3) [501+]

Chatto, James - *The Greek for Love: A Memoir of Corfu*
Globe & Mail - March 19 2005 - pD6 [501+]

Chatzky, Jean - *Pay It Down!: From Debt to Wealth on $10 a Day*
LJ - v129 - i14 - Sept 1 2004 - p164(1) [51-500]
PW - v251 - i33 - August 16 2004 - p50(1) [501+]

Chau, Foo-Tim - *Chemometrics from Basics to Wavelet Transform*
E-Streams - Oct 2004 - pNA [501+]

Chaucer, Geoffrey - *Canterbury Tales, vol. 2. Audiobook Review*
y Kliatt - v39 - i2 - March 2005 - p58(1) [51-500]

Chaudhuri, B.B. - *Tribes, Forest and Social Formation in Indian History*
R&R Bk N - v19 - i4 - Nov 2004 - p47(1) [51-500]

Chauncey, George - *Why Marriage? The History Shaping Today's Debate over Gay Equality*
BL - v101 - i1 - Sept 1 2004 - p26(1) [51-500]

Chauveau, Michel - *Cleopatra: Beyond the Myth*
Globe & Mail - Nov 20 2004 - pD29 [1-50]

Chauvin, Pierre - *Prevention and Health Promotion for the Excluded and the Destitute in Europe*
SciTech - v28 - i3 - Sept 2004 - p82(1) [501+]

Chavalas, Mark W. - *Great Events from History: The Ancient World, Prehistory-476 C.E., Vols. 1-2*
BL - v101 - i4 - Oct 15 2004 - p438(1) [501+]
Ref Rev - July 2004 - pNA [501+]
y Ref Rev - Sept 2004 - pNA [501+]
R&R Bk N - v19 - i3 - August 2004 - p31(1) [51-500]

Chaves, Mark - *Congregations in America*
CC - v121 - i24 - Nov 30 2004 - p40(5) [501+]
Choice - v42 - i4 - Dec 2004 - p741(1) [1-50]
Comw - v132 - i3 - Feb 11 2005 - p26(2) [501+]
TLS - i5303 - Nov 19 2004 - p12-13 [501+]

Chavez, Angelico - *Wake for a Fat Vicar: Father Juan Felipe Ortiz, Archbishop Lamy, and the New Mexican Catholic Church in the Middle of the Nineteenth Century*
Choice - v42 - i4 - Dec 2004 - p741(1) [1-50]
CHR - v90 - i4 - Oct 2004 - p824(2) [501+]

Chavez, Cordelia - *Encyclopedia of Latino Popular Culture, Vols. 1-2*
LJ - v130 - i2 - Feb 1 2005 - p114(1) [51-500]

Chavez, Denise - *The Last of the Menu Girls*
  y   Kliatt - v38 - i5 - Sept 2004 - p37(2) [51-500]
Chavez, Edgar - *Computer Science: Proceedings*
  SciTech - v28 - i4 - Dec 2004 - p168(1) [51-500]
Chavez, Ernesto - *"Mi Raza Primero" (My People First): Nationalism, Identity and Insurgency in the Chicano Movement in Los Angeles--1966-1978*
  WHQ - v35 - i1 - Spring 2004 - p94-95 [501+]
Chavez-Garcia, Miroslava - *Negotiating Conquest: Gender and Power in California, 1770s to 1880s*
  R&R Bk N - v19 - i4 - Nov 2004 - p68(1) [51-500]
Chavez, Linda - *Betrayal: How Union Bosses Shake Down Their Members and Corrupt American Politics*
  BL - v100 - i22 - August 2004 - p1883(1) [51-500]
  Nation - v279 - i17 - Nov 22 2004 - p28 [501+]
  An Unlikely Conservative: The Transformation of an Ex-Liberal
  Nation - v279 - i17 - Nov 22 2004 - p28 [501+]
Chavez, Rebecca Bill - *The Rule of Law in Nascent Democracies: Judicial Politics in Argentina*
  Choice - v42 - i4 - Dec 2004 - p730(1) [1-50]
  R&R Bk N - v19 - i3 - August 2004 - p192(1) [501+]
Chavez-Silverman, Susana - *Killer Cronicas: Bilingual Memories*
  Advocate - March 1 2005 - pS34(1) [501+]
  PW - v251 - i39 - Sept 27 2004 - p48(1) [51-500]
Chavez, Thomas E. - *Spain and the Independence of the United States*
  Roundup M - v12 - i1 - Oct 2004 - p23(1) [51-500]
Chavis, Melody Ermachild - *Meena, Heroine of Afghanistan: The Martyr Who Founded RAWA, the Revolutionary Association of the Women of Afghanistan*
  BW - v34 - i1 - Jan 4 2004 - p6(1) [501+]
  OOB - v34 - i7-8 - July-August 2004 - p48(4) [501+]
Chavous, Kevin P. - *Serving Our Children: Charter Schools and the Reform of American Public Education*
  CE - v81 - i2 - Winter 2004 - p111(1) [51-500]
  R&R Bk N - v19 - i4 - Nov 2004 - p187(1) [501+]
Chawla, H.S. - *Plant Biotechnology: A Practical Approach*
  SciTech - v28 - i1 - March 2004 - p173(1) [1-50]
Chaykin, Howard - *American Flagg!*
  Ent W - i794 - Nov 26 2004 - p125 [51-500]
Chazan, Robert - *Fashioning Jewish Identity in Medieval Western Christendom*
  Med R - Nov 2004 - pNA [501+]
Chazelle, Celia - *The Crucified God in the Carolingian Era*
  CH - v73 - i4 - Dec 2004 - p842(3) [501+]
  The Study of the Bible in the Carolingian Era
  Med R - Nov 2004 - pNA [501+]
Che, Chien-Hsun - *Banking and Insurance in the New China: Competition and the Challenge of Accession to the WTO*
  R&R Bk N - v19 - i2 - May 2004 - p122 [51-500]
Cheadle, Chris - *Canada's West Coast*
  CBRA - Annual 2003 - p112(2) [51-500]
Cheal, David - *Aging and Demographic Change in Canadian Context*
  CBRA - Annual 2003 - p371(2) [51-500]
Check, Laura - *Create Your Own Candles: 30 Easy-to-Make Designs (Illus. by Martin-Jourdenais, Norma Jean)*
  y   SLJ - v50 - i11 - Nov 2004 - p160(2) [51-500]
Checker, Melissa - *Local Actions: Cultural Activism, Power, and Public Life in America*
  Choice - v42 - i3 - Nov 2004 - p573(1) [1-50]
  R&R Bk N - v19 - i2 - May 2004 - p131 [51-500]
Cheek, Gene - *The Color of Love: A Mother's Choice in the Jim Crow South*
  KR - v73 - i3 - Feb 1 2005 - p160(1) [501+]
  LJ - v130 - i3 - Feb 15 2005 - p138(1) [51-500]
Cheek, Roland - *Crisis on the Stinking Water*
  Roundup M - v12 - i1 - Oct 2004 - p29(1) [51-500]
Cheek, Timothy - *Mao Zedong and China's Revolutions: A Brief History with Documents*
  Ch Rev Int - v11 - i1 - Spring 2004 - p1(8) [501+]
Cheeke, Stephen - *Byron and Place: History, Translation, Nostalgia*
  Choice - v41 - i7 - March 2004 - p1294(1) [501+]
Cheetham, David - *John Hick: A Critical Introduction and Reflection*
  Rel St - v40 - i3 - Sept 2004 - p378(4) [501+]

Cheever, Benjamin - *The Good Nanny*
  BL - v100 - i22 - August 2004 - p1896(1) [51-500]
  Globe & Mail - Nov 6 2004 - pD21 [501+]
  LJ - v129 - i12 - July 2004 - p67(1) [51-500]
  NYT - July 16 2004 - pE34 [501+]
  NYTBR - July 18 2004 - p22 [501+]
  NYTBR - July 25 2004 - p18 [501+]
Cheever, John - *The John Cheever Audio Collection (Read by Streep, Meryl). Audiobook Review*
  BL - v101 - i9-10 - Jan 1 2005 - p778(1) [1-50]
Cheever, Susan - *My Name Is Bill*
  New York - v37 - i6 - Feb 23 2004 - p45(1) [501+]
  Note Found in a Bottle: My Life as a Drinker
  Globe & Mail - Jan 8 2005 - pD15 [51-500]
Chekhov, Anton - *Anton Chekhov at the Moscow Art Theatre*
  Am Theat - v21 - i8 - Oct 2004 - p139(4) [51-500]
  The Complete Short Novels
  KR - v72 - i13 - July 1 2004 - p590(1) [501+]
  Nation - v279 - i20 - Dec 13 2004 - p34 [501+]
  The Shooting Party
  Spec - v295 - i9182 - July 31 2004 - p31(1) [501+]
  Three Years
  LJ - v129 - i14 - Sept 1 2004 - p204(1) [51-500]
Chelly, Jacques E. - *Peripheral Nerve Blocks: A Color Atlas. 2nd Ed.*
  SciTech - v28 - i1 - March 2004 - p110(1) [51-500]
Chelminski, Rudolph - *The Perfectionist: Life and Death in Haute Cuisine*
  NS - v134 - i4727 - Feb 14 2005 - p52(2) [501+]
Chelton, Mary K. - *Youth Information-Seeking Behavior: Theories, Models, and Issues*
  SLJ - v50 - i12 - Dec 2004 - p178(1) [51-500]
Chemeche, George - *Ibeji: The Cult of Yoruba Twins*
  R&R Bk N - v19 - i1 - Feb 2004 - p204(1) [51-500]
Chemistry! Best Science Projects
  LibMed - v23 - i3 - Nov-Dec 2004 - p86(1) [51-500]
Chemistry: Foundation and Applications. Vol. 4
  LJ - v129 - i14 - Sept 1 2004 - p186(1) [51-500]
Chen, Aimin - *Urban Transformation in China*
  R&R Bk N - v19 - i4 - Nov 2004 - p136(1) [1-50]
  Urbanization and Social Welfare in China
  R&R Bk N - v19 - i4 - Nov 2004 - p137(1) [51-500]
Chen, Chaomei - *Mapping Scientific Frontiers: The Quest for Knowledge Visualization*
  Isis - v95 - i2 - June 2004 - p325(1) [501+]
Chen, Chi-Tsong - *Signals and Systems. 3rd Ed.*
  TimHES - v0 - i1668 - Nov 26 2004 - pXV(1) [501+]
Chen, Chien-Hsun - *Inside the World's Development Finance Institutions*
  R&R Bk N - v19 - i2 - May 2004 - p122 [51-500]
Chen, Chih-Yuan - *Guji Guji (Illus. by Chen, Chih-Yuan)*
  c   BW - v34 - i35 - August 2004 - p12(1) [51-500]
  c   CCB-B - v58 - i1 - Sept 2004 - p9(2) [51-500]
  c   PW - v251 - i45 - Nov 8 2004 - p55(1) [51-500]
  c   SLJ - v50 - i11 - Nov 2004 - p94(1) [51-500]
Chen, Chiung Hwang - *Mormon and Asian American Model Minority Discourses in News and Popular Magazines*
  R&R Bk N - v19 - i4 - Nov 2004 - p59(1) [51-500]
Chen, Da - *Wandering Warrior*
  y   Kliatt - v39 - i2 - March 2005 - p17(1) [51-500]
Chen, Dechang - *Pattern Recognition and String Matching*
  SciTech - v28 - i1 - March 2004 - p145(1) [51-500]
Chen, E.C.M. - *Electron Capture Detector and the Study of Reactions with Thermal Electrons*
  E-Streams - Oct 2004 - pNA [501+]
Chen Hongmin - *Handian li de renjiguanxi yu zhengzhi--Du Hafo-Yanjing Tushuguan cang "Hu Hanmin wanglai handiangao"*
  Ch Rev Int - v11 - i1 - Spring 2004 - p44(4) [501+]
Chen, Huan - *Radio Resource Management for Multimedia QoS Support in Wireless Networks*
  SciTech - v28 - i1 - March 2004 - p154(1) [51-500]
Chen, Jie - *Popular Political Support in Urban China*
  Choice - v42 - i1 - Sept 2004 - p182(1) [501+]
Chen, Jie-Qi - *Effective Partnering for School Change: Improving Early Childhood Education in Urban Classrooms*
  TCR - v106 - i5 - May 2004 - p925(4) [501+]

Chen, John K. - *Chinese Medical Herbology and Pharmacology*
  SciTech - v28 - i1 - March 2004 - p124(1) [51-500]
Chen, John-ren - *The Role of International Institutions in Globalisation: The Challenges of Reform*
  R&R Bk N - v19 - i2 - May 2004 - p111(1) [1-50]
Chen, Lieping - *B7-CD28 Family Molecules*
  SciTech - v28 - i1 - March 2004 - p76(1) [51-500]
Chen, Lingen - *Advances in Finite Time Thermodynamics; Analysis and Optimization*
  SciTech - v28 - i3 - Sept 2004 - p150(1) [51-500]
Chen, Ping - *Diagnosis in Traditional Chinese Medicine*
  SciTech - v28 - i4 - Dec 2004 - p89(1) [51-500]
  Modern Chinese Ear Acupuncture
  SciTech - v28 - i4 - Dec 2004 - p115(1) [1-50]
Chen, Ran - *A Private Life*
  Choice - v42 - i6 - Feb 2005 - p1019(1) [51-500]
  LJ - v129 - i13 - August 2004 - p64(1) [51-500]
Chen, Ruoxi - *The Execution of Mayor Yin and Other Stories from the Great Proletarian Cultural Revolution*
  Choice - v42 - i7 - March 2005 - p1225(1) [51-500]
Chen, Shih-Ann - *Thoracic Vein Arrhythmias: Mechanisms and Treatment*
  SciTech - v28 - i4 - Dec 2004 - p103(1) [51-500]
Chen, Tain-Jy - *The New Knowledge Economy of Taiwan*
  R&R Bk N - v19 - i4 - Nov 2004 - p91(1) [501+]
Chen, Wenfang - *Advanced Mathematics for Engineering and Science*
  SIAM Rev - v46 - i3 - Sept 2004 - p549(13) [501+]
Chen, Xiaomei - *Occidentalism: A Theory Counter-Discourse in Post-Mao China, 2nd Ed., Rev. and Expanded*
  Pac A - v77 - i2 - Summer 2004 - p321(2) [501+]
  Reading the Right Text: An Anthology of Contemporary Chinese Drama
  Ch Rev Int - v11 - i1 - Spring 2004 - p47(4) [501+]
Chen, Yi-Ping Phoebe - *Multimedia Modelling (MMM 2004): Proceedings*
  SciTech - v28 - i1 - March 2004 - p175(1) [51-500]
Chen, Zhi Yuan - *On My Way to Buy Eggs*
  LibMed - v22 - i5 - Feb 2004 - p62(1) [501+]
Cheney, Liana de Girolami - *Neoplatonic Aesthetics: Music, Literature, and the Visual Arts*
  R&R Bk N - v19 - i3 - August 2004 - p3(1) [1-50]
Cheney, Lynne - *America: A Patriotic Primer (Illus. by Glasser, Robin Preiss)*
  c   RT - v57 - Nov 2003 - p274 [51-500]
  When Washington Crossed the Delaware: A Wintertime Story for Young Patriots (Illus. by Fiore, Peter M.)
  c   BL - v101 - i3 - Oct 1 2004 - p330(1) [51-500]
  c   HB - v81 - i1 - Jan-Feb 2005 - p107(2) [51-500]
  c   PW - v251 - i37 - Sept 13 2004 - p77(1) [501+]
  c   SLJ - v50 - i11 - Nov 2004 - p122(2) [51-500]
Cheney, Patrick - *The Cambridge Companion to Christopher Marlowe*
  Choice - v42 - i7 - March 2005 - p1226(1) [51-500]
  CR - v285 - i1665 - Oct 2004 - p245(3) [501+]
Cheng, Andrea - *Honeysuckle House*
  c   CCB-B - v58 - i2 - Oct 2004 - p63(2) [51-500]
  c   CH Bwatch - v14 - i7 - July 2004 - p6(1) [51-500]
  c   CH Bwatch - v14 - i8 - August 2004 - p2(2) [51-500]
  c   HB - v80 - i4 - July-August 2004 - p449(1) [51-500]
  c   VOYA - v27 - i5 - Dec 2004 - p379(1) [501+]
Cheng, Joseph Y.S. - *China's Challenges in the Twenty-First Century*
  Pac A - v77 - i2 - Summer 2004 - p315(2) [501+]
Cheng, K. - *Advances in E-Engineering and Digital Enterprise Technology: Proceedings*
  SciTech - v28 - i4 - Dec 2004 - p167(1) [51-500]
Cheng, Linsun - *Banking in Modern China: Entrepreneurs, Professional Managers, and the Development of Chinese Banks, 1897-1937*
  AHR - v109 - i3 - June 2004 - p880(2) [501+]
Cheng, Vincent J. - *Inauthentic: The Anxiety over Culture and Identity*
  Choice - v42 - i6 - Feb 2005 - p1062(1) [51-500]
Cheng, Wing L. - *Emerging Technology in Fluids, Structures, and Fluid-Structure Interactions, Vols. 1-2*
  SciTech - v28 - i4 - Dec 2004 - p133(1) [51-500]
Cheng, Xiuzhen - *Ad Hoc Wireless Networking*
  SciTech - v28 - i1 - March 2004 - p153(1) [51-500]
Chenoune, Farid - *Carried Away: All about Bags*
  PW - v252 - i9 - Feb 28 2005 - p57(2) [51-500]

Chien, Evelyn Nien-Ming - *Weird English*
Choice - v42 - i4 - Dec 2004 - p655(2) [1-50]
Chieng, Chieh - *A Long Stay in a Distant Land*
KR - v73 - i1 - Jan 1 2005 - p6(1) [501+]
Chiesara, M.L. - *Aristocles of Messene: Testimonies and Fragments*
Class R - v54 - i1 - May 2004 - p57(3) [501+]
Chigara, Ben - *Land Reform Policy: The Challenge of Human Rights Law*
R&R Bk N - v19 - i3 - August 2004 - p111(1) [51-500]
Chihara, Charles S. - *A Structural Account of Mathematics*
Choice - v42 - i4 - Dec 2004 - p674(1) [501+]
Chikuhwa, Jacob - *A Crisis of Governance: Zimbabwe*
Choice - v42 - i5 - Jan 2005 - p926(1) [1-50]
PW - v251 - i27 - July 5 2004 - p44(1) [51-500]
Child, Dennis - *Psychology and the Teacher, 7th Ed.*
R&R Bk N - v19 - i3 - August 2004 - p217(1) [1-50]
Child, Francis James - *The English and Scottish Popular Ballads: In Five Volumes, Vol. 1*
R&R Bk N - v19 - i1 - Feb 2004 - p236(1) [51-500]
The English and Scottish Popular Ballads: In Five Volumes, Vol. 3
R&R Bk N - v19 - i1 - Feb 2004 - p236(1) [51-500]
The English and Scottish Popular Ballads: In Five Volumes, Vol. 4
R&R Bk N - v19 - i1 - Feb 2004 - p236(1) [51-500]
Child, Lauren - *Clarice Bean Spells Trouble*
c Magpies - v19 - i5 - Nov 2004 - p33(1) [501+]
Hubert Horatio Bartle Bobton-Trent
c Magpies - v19 - i5 - Nov 2004 - p30(1) [501+]
I Am Too Absolutely Small for School (Illus. by Child, Lauren)
c BL - v101 - i3 - Oct 1 2004 - p332(2) [51-500]
c CCB-B - v58 - i1 - Sept 2004 - p10(1) [51-500]
c KR - v72 - i13 - July 1 2004 - p626(1) [51-500]
c SLJ - v50 - i8 - August 2004 - p84(2) [51-500]
Nunca jamas comere tomates/I Will Never Not Ever Eat a Tomato
c BL - v100 - i22 - August 2004 - p1950(1) [501+]
Utterly Me, Clarice Bean (Illus. by Child, Lauren)
c SLJ - v50 - i10 - Oct 2004 - pS30(1) [1-50]
What Planet Are You From, Clarice Bean? (Illus. by Child, Lauren)
c RT - v57 - Oct 2003 - p175 [1-50]
Who's Afraid of the Big Bad Book?
c LibMed - v22 - i5 - Feb 2004 - p62(1) [501+]
Child, Lee - *The Enemy (Read by Hill, Dick). Audiobook Review*
PW - v251 - i27 - July 5 2004 - p17(1) [51-500]
The Enemy
BooChiTr - June 6 2004 - p4(1) [501+]
Child, Lincoln - *Death Match (Read by Whitener, Barrett). Audiobook Review*
BL - v101 - i5 - Nov 1 2004 - p502(1) [51-500]
y Kliatt - v39 - i1 - Jan 2005 - p40(1) [51-500]
LJ - v130 - i4 - March 1 2005 - p122(1) [51-500]
Death Match
NYT - August 8 2004 - p10 [501+]
Child, Maureen - *And Then Came You*
BL - v100 - i21 - July 2004 - p1826(1) [51-500]
A Crazy Kind of Love: Mike's Story
BL - v101 - i8 - Dec 15 2004 - p713(1) [51-500]
PW - v252 - i1 - Jan 3 2005 - p41(2) [51-500]
Childers, Mary - *Welfare Brat: A Memoir*
KR - v73 - i4 - Feb 15 2005 - p207(1) [51-500]
Children's Catalog. 18th Ed.
c SLJ - v50 - i8 - August 2004 - p62(1) [501+]
Children's World Atlas: The Atlas That Brings the World and Its People to Life
LibMed - v22 - i6 - March 2004 - p77(1) [501+]
Childress, Diana - *The War of 1812*
c SLJ - v50 - i10 - Oct 2004 - p189(1) [51-500]
Childs, Alan - *The Dragon's Head Company (Illus. by Laurie, Robin)*
c Sch Lib - v52 - i4 - Winter 2004 - p192(1) [51-500]
Childs, Craig - *The Elements: Earth, Air, Fire, Water (Illus. by Art Wolfe)*
Sci - v307 - i5710 - Feb 4 2005 - p678(1) [51-500]
Childs, Elizabeth C. - *Daumier and Exoticism: Satirizing the French and the Foreign*
R&R Bk N - v19 - i4 - Nov 2004 - p206(1) [501+]
Childs, John Brown - *Transcommunality: From the Politics of Conversion to the Ethics of Respect*
CS - v33 - i1 - Jan 2004 - p125-125 [501+]

Childs, Laura - *The Jasmine Moon Murder: A Tea Shop Mystery*
LJ - v129 - i14 - Sept 1 2004 - p121(1) [51-500]
PW - v251 - i34 - August 23 2004 - p40(1) [51-500]
Childs, P.R.N. - *Total Vehicle Technology: Finding the Radical, Implementing the Practical; Proceedings*
SciTech - v28 - i3 - Sept 2004 - p140(1) [51-500]
Childs, William R. - *Business and Industry, Vols. 1-11*
LibMed - v23 - i1 - August-Sept 2004 - p81(1) [51-500]
y Ref Rev - June 2004 - pNA [501+]
R&R Bk N - v19 - i2 - May 2004 - p110(1) [51-500]
R&USQ - v44 - i2 - Winter 2004 - p130(2) [501+]
Chile
R&R Bk N - v19 - i4 - Nov 2004 - p70(1) [51-500]
Chilean Computer Science Society (SCCC 2004); proceedings
SciTech - v28 - i4 - Dec 2004 - p18(1) [1-50]
Chiles, John A. - *Clinical Manual for Assessment and Treatment of Suicidal Patients*
SciTech - v28 - i4 - Dec 2004 - p101(1) [51-500]
Chilson, Clark - *Shamans in Asia*
JAS - v63 - i2 - May 2004 - p472(2) [501+]
Chilton, Bruce - *Classical Christianity and Rabbinic Judaism: Comparing Theologies*
LJ - v130 - i1 - Jan 1 2005 - p118(1) [51-500]
Rabbi Paul: An Intellectual Biography
LJ - v129 - i13 - August 2004 - p87(1) [501+]
AM - v191 - i11 - Oct 18 2004 - p22 [501+]
BL - v100 - i22 - August 2004 - p1878(1) [51-500]
KR - v72 - i13 - July 1 2004 - p613(1) [501+]
NYTBR - Sept 26 2004 - p20 [501+]
PW - v251 - i28 - July 12 2004 - p61(1) [51-500]
Chilton, Floyd H. - *Inflammation Nation: The First Clinically Proven Eating Plan to End Our Nation's Secret Epidemic*
PW - v252 - i1 - Jan 3 2005 - p52(1) [51-500]
Chilton, John - *Who's Who of British Jazz, 2nd Ed.*
R&R Bk N - v19 - i4 - Nov 2004 - p194(1) [501+]
Chilvers, Ian - *The Concise Oxford Dictionary of Art and Artists, 3rd Ed.*
R&R Bk N - v19 - i1 - Feb 2004 - p199(1) [51-500]
The Oxford Dictionary of Art, 3rd Ed.
LJ - v129 - i13 - August 2004 - p120(1) [51-500]
The Oxford Dictionary of Art
CR - v285 - i1663 - August 2004 - p124(1) [501+]
SLJ - v50 - i12 - Dec 2004 - p83(2) [501+]
BL - v101 - i5 - Nov 1 2004 - p524(1) [501+]
Chimisso, Cristina - *Gaston Bachelard: Critic of Science and the Imagination*
FS - v58 - i2 - April 2004 - p280(2) [501+]
Chimni, B.S. - *Asian Yearbook of International Law, Vol. 8*
R&R Bk N - v19 - i3 - August 2004 - p186(1) [501+]
Chin, Ko-lin - *Heijin: Organized Crime, Business and Politics in Taiwan*
Pac A - v77 - i3 - Fall 2004 - p572(2) [501+]
Chin, Lily M. - *Knit and Crochet with Beads*
LJ - v129 - i13 - August 2004 - p77(1) [501+]
Chin, Tiffani - *School Sense: How to Help Your Child Succeed in Elementary School*
LJ - v129 - i18 - Nov 1 2004 - p116(1) [51-500]
PW - v251 - i37 - Sept 13 2004 - p73(1) [501+]
Chin, Warren A. - *British Weapons Acquisition Policy and the Futility of Reform*
R&R Bk N - v19 - i4 - Nov 2004 - p252(1) [501+]
China: An Economics Research Study Series, Vol. 1
R&R Bk N - v19 - i3 - August 2004 - p99(1) [51-500]
R&R Bk N - v19 - i3 - August 2004 - p99(1) [51-500]
China: An Economics Research Study Series, Vol. 2
R&R Bk N - v19 - i4 - Nov 2004 - p90(1) [51-500]
China: An Economics Research Study Series, Vol. 3
R&R Bk N - v19 - i4 - Nov 2004 - p91(1) [51-500]
China in the World Economy: An OECD Economic and Statistical Survey
R&R Bk N - v19 - i1 - Feb 2004 - p85(1) [51-500]
China: Progress and Reform Challenges
R&R Bk N - v19 - i2 - May 2004 - p124 [51-500]
China Review
JEL - v41 - i4 - Dec 2003 - p1445(2) [501+]
Ching-hwang, Yen - *The Ethnic Chinese in East and Southeast Asia: Business, Culture and Politics*
R&R Bk N - v19 - i1 - Feb 2004 - p47(1) [51-500]

Chingos, Peter T. - *Paying for Performance: A Guide to Compensation Management. 2nd Ed.*
HR Mag - v49 - i7 - July 2004 - pS8(1) [51-500]
Responsible Executive Compensation for a New Era of Accountability
HR Mag - v49 - i9 - Sept 2004 - p178(2) [501+]
Chingy - *Powerballin'*
People - v62 - i21 - Nov 22 2004 - p48 [501+]
Chinn, Carl - *Birmingham: Bibliography of a City*
R&R Bk N - v19 - i4 - Nov 2004 - p37(1) [51-500]
Chinn, Peggy L. - *Peace and Power: Creative Leadership for Building Communities, 6th Ed.*
R&R Bk N - v19 - i4 - Nov 2004 - p134(1) [51-500]
Chintapalli, Meena - *Brain Mind SAI Educare: A Transformational Program Integrating Experiential Neurodevelopment and Biosocial Behaviors with the Spiritual Health for Parents, Counselors, Educators and Children*
SciTech - v28 - i4 - Dec 2004 - p10(1) [1-50]
Chiodi, Maurizio - *Tra Terra E Cielo: Il Senso Della Vite a Partire dal Dibattito Bioetico*
Theol St - v65 - i3 - Sept 2004 - p682(2) [501+]
Chion, Michel - *Films of Jacques Tati*
CBRA - Annual 2003 - p104(1) [51-500]
Chioni, Georgia - *The Rise and Fall of Satellite Personal Communication Systems: Business and Legal Issues*
R&R Bk N - v19 - i4 - Nov 2004 - p106(1) [51-500]
Chipley, Robert M. - *American Bird Conservancy Guide to the 500 Most Important Bird Areas in the United States: Key Sites for Birds and Birding in All 50 States*
E-Streams - Sept 2004 - pNA [501+]
Chipman, Liz - *From the Lighthouse*
c BL - v101 - i6 - Nov 15 2004 - p601(1) [51-500]
y CCB-B - v58 - i5 - Jan 2005 - p204(1) [51-500]
c KR - v72 - i20 - Oct 15 2004 - p1002(1) [51-500]
c SLJ - v50 - i12 - Dec 2004 - p140(1) [501+]
Chippendale, Lisa A. - *Yo-Yo Ma: A Cello Superstar Brings Music to the World*
c BL - v101 - i5 - Nov 1 2004 - p495(1) [51-500]
c SLJ - v51 - i2 - Feb 2005 - p146(1) [51-500]
Chippindale, Christopher - *Pictures in Place: The Figured Landscapes of Rock-Art*
Choice - v42 - i5 - Jan 2005 - p896(2) [1-50]
Chiras, Daniel D. - *The New Ecological Home: A Complete Guide to Green Building Options*
Bwatch - v26 - i9 - Sept 2004 - p11(1) [51-500]
R&R Bk N - v19 - i4 - Nov 2004 - p247(1) [501+]
Chirazi, Steffan - *So What! The Good, the Mad and the Ugly*
y BL - v100 - i22 - August 2004 - p1889(1) [51-500]
LJ - v129 - i12 - July 2004 - p84(2) [51-500]
Chireau, Yvonne P. - *Black Magic: Religion and the African American Conjuring Tradition*
Choice - v41 - i11-12 - July-August 2004 - p2061(1) [501+]
Chirkova, Ekaterina Yurievna - *In Search of Time in Peking Mandarin*
Ch Rev Int - v11 - i1 - Spring 2004 - p50(4) [501+]
Chisholm, Clive Scott - *Following the Wrong God Home: Footloose in an American Dream*
WHQ - v35 - i1 - Spring 2004 - p100-101 [501+]
Chittenden, David - *Creating Connections: Museums and the Public Understanding of Current Research*
Nature - v431 - i7010 - Oct 14 2004 - p743(1) [501+]
R&R Bk N - v19 - i4 - Nov 2004 - p1(1) [51-500]
Chittister, Joan - *Becoming Fully Human: The Greatest Glory of God*
LJ - v130 - i4 - March 1 2005 - p92(1) [51-500]
In the Heart of the Temple: My Spiritual Vision for Today's World
PW - v251 - i39 - Sept 27 2004 - p56(1) [51-500]
Chittolini, Giorgio - *Ordini religiosi e societa politica in Italia e Germania nei secoli XIV e XV*
Specu - v79 - i4 - Oct 2004 - p1048(3) [501+]
Chiu, Monica - *Filthy Fictions: Asian American Literature by Women*
Choice - v42 - i2 - Oct 2004 - p291(1) [501+]
Chizmar, Richard - *Shivers III*
PW - v251 - i42 - Oct 18 2004 - p52(1) [51-500]
Chkhartishvili, Grigory - *Murder on the Leviathan (Read by Kramer, Michael). Audiobook Review*
y Kliatt - v39 - i1 - Jan 2005 - p48(1) [51-500]
Murder on the Leviathan
y SLJ - v50 - i7 - July 2004 - p131(1) [51-500]
The Turkish Gambit: A Novel
Ent W - i810 - March 11 2005 - p109 [501+]
KR - v73 - i2 - Jan 15 2005 - p83(1) [51-500]
LJ - v130 - i4 - March 1 2005 - p74(1) [51-500]
Spec - v297 - i9206 - Jan 15 2005 - p46(1) [501+]

The Winter Queen: The First Erast Fandorin Mystery (Read by Kramer, Michael). Audiobook Review
c Kliatt - v38 - i4 - July 2004 - p58(1) [51-500]

Cho, Arthur K. - *Annual Review of Pharmacology and Toxicology. Vol. 44*
QRB - v79 - i3 - Sept 2004 - p345(1) [501+]

Choate, Joyce S. - *Successful Inclusive Teaching: Proven Ways to Detect and Correct Special Needs, 4th Ed.*
R&R Bk N - v19 - i1 - Feb 2004 - p191(1) [51-500]

Choate, Judd - *Torn and Frayed: Congressional Norms and Party Switching in an Era of Reform*
PSQ - v119 - i3 - Fall 2004 - p535(2) [501+]
R&R Bk N - v19 - i1 - Feb 2004 - pNA [51-500]

Choate, Pat - *Hot Property: The Stealing of Ideas in an Age of Globalization*
Har Bus R - v83 - i2 - Feb 2005 - p56(1) [1-50]
KR - v73 - i3 - Feb 1 2005 - p160(2) [501+]
LJ - v129 - i20 - Dec 1 2004 - p90(1) [1-50]
PW - v252 - i7 - Feb 14 2005 - p64(1) [51-500]

Choca, James P. - *Interpretive Guide to the Millon Clinical Multiaxial Inventory. 3rd Ed.*
SciTech - v28 - i3 - Sept 2004 - p97(1) [51-500]

Chodakiewicz, Marek Jan - *After the Holocaust: Polish-Jewish Conflict in the Wake of World War II*
AHR - v109 - i3 - June 2004 - p1000(2) [501+]
Between Nazis and Soviets: Occupation Politics in Poland, 1939-1947
Choice - v42 - i6 - Feb 2005 - p1077(2) [51-500]
R&R Bk N - v19 - i3 - August 2004 - p46(1) [51-500]

Chodas, Nadine - *Queen*
Bwatch - Jan 2005 - pNA [51-500]

Chodos, Bob - *Faith and Freedom: The Life and Times of Bill Ryan SJ*
CBRA - Annual 2003 - p37(2) [51-500]

Choi, Alfred - *Fighting Youth Crime: A Comparative Study of Two Little Dragons in Asia, 2nd Ed.*
R&R Bk N - v19 - i3 - August 2004 - p170(1) [501+]

Choi, E. Kwan - *North Korea in the World Economy*
JAS - v63 - i3 - August 2004 - p810-812 [501+]
JEL - v41 - i4 - Dec 2003 - p1423(1) [501+]

Choi, Seok-ki - *Synthetic Multivalent Molecules: Concepts and Biomedical Applications*
SciTech - v28 - i4 - Dec 2004 - p120(1) [51-500]

Choi, Susan - *American Woman*
NYTBR - Sept 19 2004 - p24 [501+]

Choi, Yangsook - *The Name Jar*
c RT - v57 - Dec 2003 - p398 [51-500]

Choi, Ying-Kit - *Principles of Applied Civil Engineering Design*
SciTech - v28 - i3 - Sept 2004 - p148(1) [51-500]

Choldenko, Gennifer - *Al Capone Does My Shirts (Read by Heller, Johnny). Audiobook Review*
c Kliatt - v38 - i6 - Nov 2004 - p41(1) [51-500]
y SLJ - v50 - i9 - Sept 2004 - p76(2) [51-500]
Al Capone Does My Shirts
c BooChiTr - April 4 2004 - p2(1) [501+]
c SLJ - v50 - i10 - Oct 2004 - pS53(1) [51-500]
c Teach Lib - v32 - i3 - Feb 2005 - p10(1) [51-500]
Never Mind!: A Twin Novel
c LibMed - v23 - i3 - Nov-Dec 2004 - p69(1) [51-500]

Cholidis, Nadja - *Der Tell Halaf und sein Ausgraber Max Freiherr von Oppenheim: Kopf hoch! Mut hoch! und Humor hoch?*
JNES - v63 - i4 - Oct 2004 - p312(2) [501+]

Cholij, Roman - *Theodore the Stoudite: The Ordering of Holiness*
CH - v73 - i3 - Sept 2004 - p683(2) [501+]

Chomatenos, Demetrios - *Demetrii Chomateni Ponemata diaphora*
Specu - v79 - i4 - Oct 2004 - p1050(2) [501+]

Chomsky, Aviva - *The Cuba Reader: History, Culture, Politics*
Ams - v61 - i2 - Oct 2004 - p311(2) [501+]
Choice - v42 - i1 - Sept 2004 - p170(1) [501+]

Chomsky, Noam - *Chomsky on Democracy and Education*
TCR - v106 - i2 - Feb 2004 - p365-374 [501+]
Hegemony or Survival: America's Quest for Global Dominance
BW - v34 - i1 - Jan 4 2004 - p3(2) [501+]
Language and Politics
LJ - v129 - i18 - Nov 1 2004 - p134(1) [1-50]
Letters from Lexington: Reflections on Propaganda, New Updated Ed.
R&R Bk N - v19 - i3 - August 2004 - p144(1) [51-500]

Middle East Illusions: Including Peace in the Middle East?, Reflections on Justice and Nationhood
R&R Bk N - v19 - i3 - August 2004 - p51(1) [51-500]
Pirates and Emperors, Old and New: International Terrorism in the Real World
PG - v23 - i8 - Nov 2004 - p1065-1067 [501+]
Syntactic Structures
CHE - v51 - i14 - Nov 26 2004 - pB4-B4 [501+]

Chong, Alan - *Raphael, Callini, and a Renaissance Banker: The Patronage of Bindo Altoviti*
Choice - v42 - i4 - Dec 2004 - p651(1) [1-50]

Chong, Kim Chong - *The Moral Circle and the Self: Chinese and Western Approaches*
Ch Rev Int - v11 - i1 - Spring 2004 - p54(5) [501+]
Moral Circle and the Self: Chinese and Western Approaches
R&R Bk N - v19 - i1 - Feb 2004 - p9(1) [1-50]

Choo, Miho - *The Sounds of Korean: A Pronunciation Guide*
R&R Bk N - v19 - i1 - Feb 2004 - p219(1) [51-500]

Chopra, Deepak - *The Book of Secrets: Unlocking the Hidden Dimensions of Your Life*
LJ - v129 - i16 - Oct 1 2004 - p100(1) [51-500]
PW - v251 - i36 - Sept 6 2004 - p59(1) [51-500]
Fire in the Heart: A Spiritual Guide for Teens
c SLJ - v50 - i8 - August 2004 - p133(1) [51-500]
y VOYA - v27 - i3 - August 2004 - p208(1) [1-50]
Magical Beginnings, Enchanted Lives: A Holistic Guide to Pregnancy and Childbirth
PW - v252 - i5 - Jan 31 2005 - p65(1) [501+]
Peace Is the Way: Bringing War and Violence to an End
LJ - v130 - i4 - March 1 2005 - p92(1) [51-500]
PW - v252 - i2 - Jan 10 2005 - p50(1) [51-500]
The Seven Spiritual Laws of Yoga: A Practical Guide to Healing Body, Mind, and Spirit
LJ - v129 - i12 - July 2004 - p109(1) [51-500]

Chopra, Vivek - *Professional Apache Tomcat 5*
SciTech - v28 - i3 - Sept 2004 - p158(1) [51-500]

Choquette, Robert - *Canada's Religions: An Historical Introduction*
Choice - v42 - i3 - Nov 2004 - p498(1) [1-50]
R&R Bk N - v19 - i3 - August 2004 - p15(1) [1-50]

Chorafas, Dimitris N. - *Alternative Investments and the Mismanagement of Risk*
JEL - v41 - i4 - Dec 2003 - p1363(1) [501+]
Management Risk: The Bottleneck Is at the Top of the Bottle
Choice - v41 - i11-12 - July-August 2004 - p2088(1) [501+]

Chorao, Kay - *D Is for Drums: A Colonial Williamsburg ABC (Illus. by Chorao, Kay)*
c KR - v72 - i15 - August 1 2004 - p739(1) [51-500]
c PW - v251 - i44 - Nov 1 2004 - p65(1) [501+]
c SLJ - v50 - i11 - Nov 2004 - p123(1) [51-500]

Chorkendorff, I. - *Concepts of Modern Catalysis and Kinetics*
Choice - v41 - i11-12 - July-August 2004 - p2073(1) [501+]
SciTech - v28 - i1 - March 2004 - p56(1) [51-500]

Chossudovsky, Michel - *Globalization of Poverty and the New World Order, 2nd Ed.*
CBRA - Annual 2003 - p324(1) [501+]
War and Globalization: The Truth Behind September
CBRA - Annual 2003 - p282(2) [501+]

Chotjewitz, David - *Daniel Half Human: And the Good Nazi*
y BL - v101 - i2 - Sept 15 2004 - p231(1) [51-500]
y CCB-B - v58 - i4 - Dec 2004 - p164(1) [51-500]
y HB - v80 - i6 - Nov-Dec 2004 - p705(1) [51-500]
y KR - v72 - i18 - Sept 15 2004 - p912(1) [501+]
c PW - v251 - i48 - Nov 29 2004 - p41(1) [51-500]
y SLJ - v50 - i12 - Dec 2004 - p140(2) [501+]
y VOYA - v27 - i5 - Dec 2004 - p379(1) [501+]

Chouaki, Aziz - *The Star of Algiers*
BL - v101 - i8 - Dec 15 2004 - p707(1) [51-500]
KR - v72 - i22 - Nov 15 2004 - p1060(1) [501+]
LJ - v129 - i20 - Dec 1 2004 - p98(1) [51-500]
PW - v251 - i48 - Nov 29 2004 - p23(1) [51-500]

Choudhri, Nihara K. - *What to Do Before "I Do": The Modern Couple's Guide to Marriage, Money and Prenups*
LJ - v129 - i20 - Dec 1 2004 - p140(1) [51-500]

Chouillet, Anne-Marie - *Science, Musiques, Lumieres: Melanges Offerts a Anne-Marie Chouillet*
Eight-C St - v37 - i3 - Spring 2004 - p500-504 [501+]

Choukas-Bradley, Melanie - *An Illustrated Guide to Eastern Woodland Wildflowers and Trees: 350 Plants Observed at Sugarloaf Mountain, Maryland (Illus. by Brown, Tina Thieme)*
SciTech - v28 - i3 - Sept 2004 - p62(1) [51-500]

Chouliaraki, Lilie - *Discourse in Late Modernity: Rethinking Critical Discourse Analysis*
Lang Soc - v33 - i3 - June 2004 - p433-437 [501+]

Chow, Bennett - *The Ricci Flow: An Introduction*
SciTech - v28 - i3 - Sept 2004 - p42(1) [1-50]

Chow, Daniel C.K. - *The Legal System of the People's Republic of China: In a Nutshell*
R&R Bk N - v19 - i1 - Feb 2004 - pNA [51-500]

Chow, Esther Ngan-ling - *Transforming Gender and Development in East Asia*
Pac A - v77 - i2 - Summer 2004 - p310(2) [501+]

Chow, Garrick - *Mac OS X Panther: Hands-on Training*
SciTech - v28 - i3 - Sept 2004 - p26(1) [51-500]

Chow, Kai-wing - *Publishing, Culture, and Power in Early Modern China*
HRNB - v33 - i1 - Fall 2004 - p35(2) [501+]

Chow, Kam Thye - *Thai Yoga Massage*
Bwatch - v26 - i9 - Sept 2004 - p2(1) [51-500]

Chow, Shei-Chung - *Design and Analysis of Clinical Trials: Concepts and Methodologies. 2nd Ed.*
SciTech - v28 - i1 - March 2004 - p80(1) [51-500]

Chowdhury, Mamta Banu - *Resources Booms and Macroeconomic Adjustments in Developing Countries*
R&R Bk N - v19 - i3 - August 2004 - p100(1) [51-500]

Chown, John - *A History of Monetary Unions*
Choice - v41 - i7 - March 2004 - p1341(1) [501+]
JEL - v41 - i4 - Dec 2003 - p1359(1) [501+]

Chown, Marcus - *Time's Eye*
New Sci - v183 - i2458 - July 31 2004 - p52(1) [51-500]

Chowning, Larry S. - *Chesapeake Bay Buyboats*
Bwatch - v26 - i7 - July 2004 - p12(1) [51-500]

Choy, Wayson - *All That Matters*
BIC - v33 - i9 - Dec 2004 - p5(2) [501+]
Globe & Mail - Oct 9 2004 - pD3 [501+]
Globe & Mail - Nov 27 2004 - pD3 [501+]
The Jade Peony
Essays CW - Winter 2003 - p61 [501+]

Choyce, Lesley - *Cold Clear Morning*
CBRA - Annual 2003 - p157(2) [51-500]

Chretien, Jean-Pierre - *The Great Lakes of Africa: Two Thousand Years of History*
HNet - June 2004 - pNA [501+]

Chrisler, Joan C. - *From Menarche to Menopause: The Female Body in Feminist Therapy*
SciTech - v28 - i3 - Sept 2004 - p99(1) [51-500]

Chrisman, James J. - *Innovation and Entrepreneurship in Western Canada: From Family Businesses to Multinationals*
CBRA - Annual 2003 - p328(2) [501+]

Chrisman, Laura - *Postcolonial Contraventions: Cultural Readings of Race, Imperialism and Transnationalism*
HNet - June 2004 - pNA [501+]

Chrisp, Peter - *Daily Life*
y Sch Lib - v52 - i4 - Winter 2004 - p217(1) [51-500]
Mesopotamia: Iraq in Ancient Times
c BL - v101 - i4 - Oct 15 2004 - p415(1) [51-500]
c SLJ - v50 - i11 - Nov 2004 - p123(1) [51-500]

Chrispeels, Janet - *Learning to Lead Together: The Promise and Challenge of Sharing Leadership*
R&R Bk N - v19 - i3 - August 2004 - p223(1) [1-50]

Christ, Carol P. - *She Who Changes: Re-Imaging the Divine in the World*
CWS - v23 - i3-4 - Spring-Summer 2004 - p219(2) [501+]
R&R Bk N - v19 - i1 - Feb 2004 - p6(1) [51-500]

Christ, Mark K. - *"All Cut to Pieces and Gone to Hell": The Civil War, Race Relations, and the Battle of Poison Spring*
JSH - v71 - i1 - Feb 2005 - p166(2) [501+]
Getting Used to Being Shot At: The Spence Family Civil War Letters
HNet - Oct 2004 - pNA [501+]

Christelow, Eileen - *Five Little Monkeys Play Hide-and-Seek (Illus. by Christelow, Eileen)*
c BL - v100 - i22 - August 2004 - p1941(1) [51-500]
c SLJ - v50 - i9 - Sept 2004 - p156(1) [51-500]
The Great Pig Escape
c SLJ - v50 - i10 - Oct 2004 - pS29(1) [51-500]
Vote!
c BL - v101 - i3 - Oct 1 2004 - p327(1) [51-500]
c SLJ - v50 - i8 - August 2004 - p47(1) [51-500]

Christensen, Alan J. - *Patient Adherence to Medical Treatment Regimens.*
Choice - v42 - i6 - Feb 2005 - p1054(1) [51-500]

Christensen, Allan Conrad - *The Subverting Vision of Bulwer Lytton: Bicentenary Reflections*
Choice - v42 - i2 - Oct 2004 - p296(1) [501+]

Christensen, Bonnie - *The Daring Nellie Bly: America's Star Reporter*
LibMed - v22 - i6 - March 2004 - p74(1) [501+]
Red Lodge and the Mythic West: Coal Miners to Cowboys
AHR - v109 - i2 - April 2004 - p536(2) [501+]
WHQ - v35 - i2 - Summer 2004 - p225-225 [501+]

Christensen, Clayton M. - *The Innovator's Solution: Creating and Sustaining Successful Growth*
JEL - v42 - i1 - March 2004 - p295(1) [501+]
R&R Bk N - v19 - i3 - August 2004 - p104(1) [1-50]

Christensen, Hilda Romer - *Crossing Borders: Re-Mapping Women's Movements at the Turn of the 21st Century*
R&R Bk N - v19 - i4 - Nov 2004 - p156(1) [501+]

Christensen, Jo-Anne - *Haunted Halloween Stories: 13 Chilling Read-Aloud Tales*
y CBRA - Annual 2003 - p479(1) [51-500]

Christensen, Karen - *Encyclopedia of Community: From the Village to the Virtual World*
Ref Rev - May 2004 - pNA [501+]

Christensen, Lisa - *Clueless about Cars: An Easy Guide to Car Maintenance and Repair*
Bwatch - Feb 2005 - pNA [51-500]
SLJ - v50 - i12 - Dec 2004 - p176(1) [51-500]

Christgau, John - *Tricksters in the Madhouse: Lakers vs. Globetrotters*
LJ - v129 - i17 - Oct 15 2004 - p68(1) [51-500]

Christian, David - *Maps of Time: An Introduction to Big History*
Am Sci - v92 - i4 - July-August 2004 - p379(3) [501+]
Choice - v42 - i3 - Nov 2004 - p537(2) [1-50]

Christian, Paula - *The Other Side of Desire*
LJ - v129 - i17 - Oct 15 2004 - p99(1) [51-500]

Christian, Peter - *Genealogist's Internet*
CBRA - Annual 2003 - p13(1) [51-500]

Christian, Shirley - *Before Lewis and Clark: The Story of the Chouteaus, the French Dynasty That Ruled America's Frontier*
Choice - v42 - i4 - Dec 2004 - p720(1) [1-50]
NYRB - v51 - i12 - July 15 2004 - p47(3) [501+]

Christian, Vicki - *Girls Just Wanna Have Clean!*
Globe & Mail - March 19 2005 - pL6 [51-500]

Christiansen, Eric - *The Norsemen in the Viking Age*
Specu - v79 - i4 - Oct 2004 - p1051-3 [501+]

Christiansen, Flemming - *The Politics of Multiple Belonging: Ethnicity and Nationalism in Europe and East Asia*
R&R Bk N - v19 - i4 - Nov 2004 - p122(1) [501+]

Christiansen, Morten H. - *Language Evolution*
JRAI - v10 - i4 - Dec 2004 - p929(2) [501+]

Christiansen, Richard - *A Theater of Our Own: A History and a Memoir of 1,001 Nights in Chicago*
BL - v101 - i6 - Nov 15 2004 - p541(1) [51-500]
LJ - v130 - i1 - Jan 1 2005 - p114(1) [51-500]

Christiansen, Thomas - *Informal Governance in the European Union*
R&R Bk N - v19 - i3 - August 2004 - p181(1) [501+]

Christiansen, Tom - *Perl Cookbook, 2nd Ed.*
SciTech - v28 - i4 - Dec 2004 - p22(1) [51-500]

Christianson, Stephen G. - *The International Book of Days*
LJ - v130 - i4 - March 1 2005 - p114(1) [51-500]

Christie, Agatha - *Agatha Christie Boxed Set*
Globe & Mail - March 19 2005 - pD17 [1-50]
The Big Four: A Hercule Poirot Mystery (Read by Fraser, Hugh). Audiobook Review
PW - v252 - i10 - March 7 2005 - p26(1) [51-500]
Destination Unknown (Read by Fox, Emilia). Audiobook Review
Globe & Mail - Nov 27 2004 - pD49 [1-50]
The Golden Ball
y VOYA - v26 - Dec 2003 - p362 [51-500]
One, Two, Buckle My Shoe (Read by Hugh, Fraser). Audiobook Review
LJ - v129 - i20 - Dec 1 2004 - p180(1) [51-500]
The Secret of Chimneys (Read by Hugh, Fraser). Audiobook Review
LJ - v129 - i20 - Dec 1 2004 - p180(1) [51-500]

Christie-Brown, Margaret - *Beyond the Disappointment of Sex: Understanding the Roots of Partnership Conflict*
Choice - v42 - i6 - Feb 2005 - p1100(1) [51-500]
R&R Bk N - v19 - i4 - Nov 2004 - p129(1) [1-50]

Christie, Dolores L. - *Last Rights: A Catholic Perspective on End-of-Life Decisions*
SciTech - v28 - i1 - March 2004 - p78(1) [51-500]

Christie, Frances - *Classroom Discourse Analysis: A Functional Perspective*
Lang Soc - v33 - i3 - June 2004 - p443-446 [501+]

Christie, Gregory - *Ruler of the Courtyard*
LibMed - v22 - i4 - Jan 2004 - p58(1) [501+]

Christie, Jessica Joyce - *Maya Palaces and Elite Residences: An Interdisciplinary Approach*
Ams - v61 - i2 - Oct 2004 - p343(3) [501+]

Christie, Nancy - *Mapping the Margins: The Family and Social Discipline in Canada, 1700-1975*
R&R Bk N - v19 - i3 - August 2004 - p154(1) [51-500]

Christie, Neil - *Landscapes of Change: Rural Evolutions in Late Antiquity and the Early Middle Ages*
R&R Bk N - v20 - i1 - Feb 2005 - p83(1) [51-500]

Christie, Stuart - *Granny Made Me an Anarchist*
Lon R Bks - v26 - i24 - Dec 16 2004 - p9(2) [501+]
TLS - i5300 - Oct 29 2004 - p30(1) [51-500]

Christin, Pierre - *The Chaos Effect (Illus. by Bilal, Enki)*
PW - v252 - i11 - March 14 2005 - p48(1) [51-500]
Townscapes
BL - v101 - i5 - Nov 1 2004 - p472(1) [51-500]

Christmas, Jane - *Pelee Project: One Woman's Escape from Urban Madness*
CBRA - Annual 2003 - p38(1) [51-500]

Christmas, William - *The Lab'ring Muses: Work, Writing and the Social Order in English Plebeian Poetry*
RES - v55 - i219 - April 2004 - p286-287 [501+]

Christofferson, April - *Buffalo Medicine*
Kliatt - v38 - i6 - Nov 2004 - p15(1) [51-500]

Christofferson, Bill - *The Man from Clear Lake: Earth Day Founder Gaylord Nelson*
Choice - v42 - i5 - Jan 2005 - p914(1) [1-50]
E Mag - v15 - i5 - Sept-Oct 2004 - p62(1) [51-500]
R&R Bk N - v19 - i3 - August 2004 - p69(1) [51-500]
SB - v40 - i4 - July-August 2004 - p156(1) [51-500]

Christophe, Lambert - *Cuentos y leyendas de lugares misteriosos/Tales and Legends from Mysterious Places*
c BL - v100 - i22 - August 2004 - p1950(1) [501+]

Christopher, Matt - *Snowboard Champ*
SLJ - v50 - i12 - Dec 2004 - p144(1) [501+]

Christopher, Nicholas - *Crossing the Equator: New and Selected Poems, 1972-2004*
LJ - v129 - i12 - July 2004 - p87(1) [501+]

Christopher, Paul Curtis - *Bucking the Sarge (Read by Boatman, Michael). Audiobook Review*
y HB - v81 - i2 - March-April 2005 - p220(1) [51-500]

Christopher, Victoria - *Truth Be Told*
Black Iss - v6 - i5 - Sept-Oct 2004 - p51(1) [51-500]

Christou, Paul - *Handbook of Plant Biotechnology, Vols. 1-2*
Choice - v42 - i6 - Feb 2005 - p1045(2) [51-500]
E-Streams - Nov 2004 - pNA [501+]
SciTech - v28 - i3 - Sept 2004 - p167(1) [51-500]

Christy, Jim - *Terminal Avenue*
CBRA - Annual 2003 - p158(1) [51-500]
Tight Like That
CBRA - Annual 2003 - p197(1) [51-500]

Chronicles of America Wars
LibMed - v22 - i7 - April-May 2004 - p70(1) [501+]

Chrono, Nanae - *Peacemaker, Vol. 1*
PW - v251 - i45 - Nov 8 2004 - p37(1) [501+]

Chrustowski, Rick - *Blue Sky Bluebird*
c BL - v100 - i22 - August 2004 - p1938(1) [51-500]

Chryssochoou, Xenia - *Cultural Diversity: Its Social Psychology*
R&R Bk N - v19 - i2 - May 2004 - p130 [51-500]

Chu, Judy - *Junzi, a Man of Virtue: The Biography of Yuan-li Wu*
R&R Bk N - v19 - i1 - Feb 2004 - p56(1) [51-500]

Chu, Stephen J. - *Fundamentals of Color: Shade Matching and Communication in Esthetic Dentistry*
SciTech - v28 - i4 - Dec 2004 - p114(1) [1-50]

Chua, Amy - *World on Fire: How Exporting Free Market Democracy Breeds Ethnic Hatred and Global Instability*
TimHES - v0 - i1657 - Sept 10 2004 - p28(2) [501+]

Chubarian, A.O. - *The Russian Discovery of America: Collected Articles, Devoted to the Seventieth Birthday of the Academician Nikolai Nikolaevich Bolkhovitinov*
JAH - v91 - i3 - Dec 2004 - p987(2) [501+]

Chulos, Chris J. - *Converging Worlds: Religion and Community in Peasant Russia, 1861-1917*
R&R Bk N - v19 - i1 - Feb 2004 - p96(1) [51-500]
Slav R - v63 - i4 - Winter 2004 - p891(2) [501+]

Chumachenko, Tatiana A. - *Church and State in Soviet Russia: Russian Orthodoxy from World War II to the Khrushchev Years*
Slav R - v63 - i2 - Summer 2004 - p418(2) [501+]

Chun, Pam - *Night Whispers*
BL - v101 - i2 - Sept 15 2004 - p206(1) [51-500]
When Strange Gods Call
KR - v72 - i16 - August 15 2004 - p758(2) [501+]
PW - v251 - i43 - Oct 25 2004 - p29(1) [51-500]

Chung, Anita - *Drawing Boundaries: Architectural Images in Qing China*
Choice - v42 - i7 - March 2005 - p1220(1) [51-500]

Chung, Christopher A. - *Simulation Modeling Handbook: A Practical Approach*
E-Streams - Oct 2004 - pNA [501+]

Chung, Duck-Koo - *The Korean Economy Beyond the Crisis*
R&R Bk N - v19 - i3 - August 2004 - p100(1) [51-500]

Chung, Man Cheung - *Psychoanalytic Knowledge*
SciTech - v28 - i3 - Sept 2004 - p1(1) [501+]

Chung, Ook - *L'Experience interdite*
WLT - v78 - i3-4 - Sept-Dec 2004 - p116(2) [501+]

Chung, Sung Wook - *Admiration and Challenge: Karl Barth's Theological Relationship with John Calvin*
TT - v61 - i1 - April 2004 - p94-97 [501+]

Chunlai, Chen - *China's Domestic Grain Marketing Reform and Integration*
R&R Bk N - v19 - i3 - August 2004 - p112(1) [51-500]

Chunshu - *Beijing Doll: A Novel*
PW - v251 - i34 - August 23 2004 - p39(1) [51-500]

Church, Audrey P. - *Leverage Your Library Program to Raise Test Scores: A Guide for Library Media Specialists, Principals, Teachers, and Parents*
LibMed - v22 - i4 - Jan 2004 - p83(1) [501+]
y Teach Lib - v32 - i1 - Oct 2004 - p38(2) [501+]

Church, Caroline Jayne - *Do Your Ears Hang Low? (Illus. by Church, Caroline Jayne)*
c RT - v57 - Oct 2003 - p168 [51-500]

Church, Steven - *The Guinness Book of Me: A Memoir of Record*
KR - v73 - i2 - Jan 15 2005 - p96(1) [501+]
PW - v252 - i9 - Feb 28 2005 - p51(2) [51-500]

Churchill, J. - *Woodworker's Complete Shop Reference*
R&R Bk N - v19 - i1 - Feb 2004 - p252(1) [501+]

Churchill, Jill - *A Midsummer Night's Scream: A Jane Jeffry Mystery*
BL - v101 - i6 - Nov 15 2004 - p564(1) [51-500]
PW - v251 - i42 - Oct 18 2004 - p51(1) [51-500]

Churchill, Ward - *Kill the Indian, Save the Man: The Genocidal Impact of American Indian Residential Schools*
BL - v101 - i5 - Nov 1 2004 - p447(1) [51-500]
y Kliatt - v39 - i2 - March 2005 - p38(1) [51-500]
On the Justice of Roosting Chickens: Reflections on the Consequences of U.S. Imperial Arrogance and Criminality
R&R Bk N - v19 - i3 - August 2004 - p65(1) [51-500]

Churchwell, Sarah - *The Many Lives of Marilyn Monroe*
NYTBR - March 6 2005 - p16 [501+]
KR - v72 - i20 - Oct 15 2004 - p992(1) [501+]
PW - v251 - i46 - Nov 15 2004 - p50(1) [51-500]
TimHES - v0 - i1672 - Dec 24 2004 - p27(1) [501+]

Churton, Tobias - *Gnostic Philosophy: From Ancient Persia to Modern Times*
LJ - v130 - i1 - Feb 1 2005 - p84(1) [51-500]
PW - v252 - i4 - Jan 24 2005 - p237(2) [501+]

Chuvin, Pierre - *Samarkand, Bukhara, Khiva*
R&R Bk N - v19 - i1 - Feb 2004 - p49(1) [51-500]

Chuwkwu, E.N. - *Optimal Control of the Growth of Wealth and Nations*
R&R Bk N - v19 - i1 - Feb 2004 - p78(1) [1-50]

Chvojka, Erhard - *Geschichte der Grosselternrollen vom 16 bis zum 20*
HNet - Nov 2004 - pNA [501+]

Clark, Beverly Lyon - *Kiddie Lit: The Cultural Construction of Children's Literature in America*
HB - v80 - i4 - July-August 2004 - p472(1) [51-500]
R&R Bk N - v19 - i1 - Feb 2004 - p243(1) [51-500]
Wom R Bks - v22 - i1 - Oct 2004 - p15(1) [501+]

Clark-Carter, David - *Quantitative Psychological Research: A Students Handbook. 2nd Ed.*
TimHES - v0 - i1668 - Nov 26 2004 - pXVIII(2) [501+]

Clark, Catherine - *The Alison Rules*
y BL - v101 - i4 - Oct 15 2004 - p398(1) [51-500]
y CCB-B - v58 - i2 - Oct 2004 - p64(1) [51-500]
y Kliatt - v38 - i4 - July 2004 - p7(1) [51-500]
y KR - v72 - i13 - July 1 2004 - p626(1) [51-500]
y PW - v251 - i36 - Sept 6 2004 - p64(1) [51-500]
c SLJ - v50 - i8 - August 2004 - p120(1) [51-500]
y VOYA - v27 - i5 - Dec 2004 - p379(1) [501+]
Maine Squeeze
y Kliatt - v38 - i5 - Sept 2004 - p19(2) [51-500]
c SLJ - v50 - i8 - August 2004 - p120(1) [51-500]

Clark, Christopher - *The Communitarian Moment: The Radical Challenge of the Northampton Association*
R&R Bk N - v19 - i4 - Nov 2004 - p150(1) [501+]
Letters from an American Utopia: The Stetson Family and the Northampton Association
NEQ - v77 - i4 - Dec 2004 - p666-667 [501+]

Clark, Clara Gillow - *Hill Hawk Hattie*
LibMed - v22 - i4 - Jan 2004 - p64(1) [501+]

Clark, Dana - *Demanding Accountability: Civil-Society Claims and the World Bank Inspection Panel*
R&R Bk N - v19 - i1 - Feb 2004 - p116(1) [51-500]

Clark, David - *Grumblebunny (Illus. by Clark, David)*
c LibMed - v22 - i4 - Jan 2004 - p58(1) [501+]

Clark, David A. - *Cognitive-Behavioral Therapy for OCD*
SciTech - v28 - i4 - Dec 2004 - p97(1) [51-500]

Clark, David H. - *Measuring the Cosmos: How Scientists Discovered the Dimensions of the Universe*
Astron - v32 - i12 - Dec 2004 - p104 [51-500]
Choice - v42 - i5 - Jan 2005 - p876(1) [1-50]
SciTech - v28 - i3 - Sept 2004 - p45(1) [1-50]
S&T - v109 - i2 - Feb 2005 - p110(3) [501+]

Clark, David K. - *Empirical Realism: Meaning and the Generative Foundation of Morality*
R&R Bk N - v19 - i3 - August 2004 - p12(1) [1-50]
To Know and Love God: Method for Theology
TT - v61 - i2 - July 2004 - p283(1) [501+]

Clark, Delia - *Questing: A Guide to Creating Community Treasure Hunts*
R&R Bk N - v19 - i4 - Nov 2004 - p190(1) [501+]

Clark, Donald N. - *Living Dangerously in Korea: The Western Experience, 1900-1950*
A Aff - v35 - i2 - July 2004 - p257-258 [501+]
Pac A - v77 - i2 - Summer 2004 - p354(2) [501+]

Clark, Douglas R. - *One Hundred Years of American Archaeology in the Middle East: Proceedings*
R&R Bk N - v19 - i4 - Nov 2004 - p44(1) [51-500]

Clark, Ephraim - *Arbitrage, Hedging, and Speculation: The Foreign Exchange Market*
R&R Bk N - v19 - i3 - August 2004 - p139(1) [51-500]

Clark, Francis - *The "Gregorian" Dialogues and the Origins of Benedictine Monasticism*
Med R - Oct 2004 - pNA [501+]
Specu - v79 - i3 - July 2004 - p748-750 [501+]

Clark, G. - *Philosophy and Power in the Graeco-Roman World: Essays in Honour of Miriam Griffin*
Class R - v54 - i1 - May 2004 - p73(4) [501+]

Clark, Gracia - *Gender at Work in Economic Life*
R&R Bk N - v19 - i1 - Feb 2004 - p100(1) [51-500]

Clark, Graeme - *Cochlear Implants: Fundamentals and Applications*
Phys Today - v57 - i11 - Nov 2004 - p66-68 [501+]

Clark, Gregory T. - *The Spitz Master: A Parisian Book of Hours*
Med R - Oct 2004 - pNA [501+]

Clark, Hilary - *Dwelling of Weather*
CBRA - Annual 2003 - p210(2) [51-500]

Clark, Ira - *Comedy, Youth, Manhood in Early Modern England*
Ren Q - v57 - i3 - Fall 2004 - p1139(2) [501+]

Clark, J.C.D. - *Our Shadowed Present: Modernism, Postmodernism, and History*
R&R Bk N - v20 - i1 - Feb 2005 - p31(1) [51-500]

Clark, James G. - *The Religious Orders in Pre-Reformation England*
Albion - v36 - i1 - Spring 2004 - p103(3) [501+]

Clark, Janine A. - *Islam, Charity, and Activism: Middle-Class Networks and Social Welfare in Egypt, Jordan, and Yemen*
Choice - v41 - i11-12 - July-August 2004 - p2116(1) [501+]
MEJ - v58 - i4 - Autumn 2004 - p701(2) [501+]

Clark, Jeanne L. - *America's Wildlife Refuges: Lands of Promise*
SciTech - v28 - i1 - March 2004 - p68(1) [51-500]

Clark, Jeff - *Music and Suicide*
Poet - v185 - i2 - Nov 2004 - p138(1) [501+]

Clark, Joan - *From a High Thin Wire*
Globe & Mail - August 28 2004 - pD13 [51-500]
Word for Home
y Can CL - i111-112 - Fall-Winter 2003 - p128(7) [501+]

Clark, John - *The Money Is the Gravy: Finding the Career That Nourishes You*
NACEJou - v64 - i2 - Wntr 2004 - p13(1) [501+]

Clark, John A. - *Southern Political Party Activists: Patterns of Conflict and Change, 1991-2001*
Pers PS - v34 - i1 - Wntr 2005 - p47(2) [501+]

Clark, John D. - *Worlds Apart: Civil Society and the Battle for Ethical Globalization*
PSQ - v119 - i3 - Fall 2004 - p561(2) [501+]

Clark, Johnnie M. - *Gunner's Glory: Untold Stories of Marine Machine Gunners*
y Kliatt - v39 - i2 - March 2005 - p38(2) [51-500]

Clark, Juan Manuel - *Collectible Lighters*
Ant&CM - v108 - i9 - Nov 2003 - p16(1) [501+]

Clark, Kenneth B. - *Toward Humanity and Justice: The Writings of Kenneth B. Clark, Scholar of the 1954 Brown v. Board of Education Decision*
Choice - v42 - i4 - Dec 2004 - p720(1) [1-50]

Clark, Lewis J. - *Lewis Clark's Field Guide to Wild Flowers of Field and Slope in the Pacific Northwest, Rev. Ed.*
CBRA - Annual 2003 - p400(1) [51-500]
Lewis Clark's Field Guide to Wild Flowers of Forest and Woodland in the Pacific Northwest
CBRA - Annual 2003 - p400(2) [51-500]
Lewis Clark's Field Guide to Wild Flowers of the Mountains in the Pacific Northwest
CBRA - Annual 2003 - p400(2) [51-500]

Clark, Linda - *The Fifteenth Century: Authority and Subversion*
Med R - Dec 2004 - pNA [501+]

Clark, Lynn Schofield - *From Angels to Aliens: Teenagers, the Media, and the Supernatural*
JPC - v38 - i1 - August 2004 - p231(3) [501+]

Clark, Mary Higgins - *The Christmas Thief*
Ent W - i796 - Dec 10 2004 - p98 [51-500]
People - v62 - i23 - Dec 6 2004 - p58 [51-500]
PW - v251 - i43 - Oct 25 2004 - p31(1) [51-500]
I'll Be Seeing You (Read by Skinner, Kate). Audiobook Review
LJ - v130 - i4 - March 1 2005 - p122(1) [51-500]
No Place Like Home (Read by Maxwell, Jan). Audiobook Review
LJ - v129 - i20 - Dec 1 2004 - p86(1) [51-500]

Clark, Mary Jane - *Hide Yourself Away*
Globe & Mail - August 7 2004 - pD12 [51-500]
PW - v251 - i28 - July 12 2004 - p46(1) [51-500]

Clark, Melissa - *Find Courtney*
DroRevMy - v24 - i4 - July-August 2004 - p11(1) [51-500]
KR - v72 - i16 - August 15 2004 - p779(1) [51-500]

Clark, Michael P. - *The Eliot Tracts: With Letters from John Eliot to Thomas Thorowgood and Richard Baxter*
Choice - v41 - i11-12 - July-August 2004 - p2106(1) [501+]
R&R Bk N - v19 - i1 - Feb 2004 - p52(1) [51-500]

Clark, Mike - *Pragmatic Project Automation: How to Build, Deploy, and Monitor Java Applications*
SciTech - v28 - i4 - Dec 2004 - p22(1) [51-500]

Clark, Murtie June - *American Militia in the Frontier Wars, 1790-1796*
EFHM - v58 - i3 - May-June 2004 - p57(1) [51-500]

Clark, Nancy L. - *South Africa: The Rise and Fall of Apartheid*
y HNet - Sept 2004 - pNA [501+]

Clark, Nora Joan - *The Story of the Irish Harp: Its History and Influence*
R&R Bk N - v19 - i4 - Nov 2004 - p196(1) [501+]

Clark, Peter - *The Cambridge Urban History of Britain. Vols. 2-3*
VS - v45 - i2 - Winter 2003 - p360 [501+]

Clark, Peter A. - *To Treat or Not to Treat: The Ethical Methodology of Richard A. McCormick, S.J., as Applied to Treatment Decisions for Handicapped Newborns*
Theol St - v66 - i1 - March 2005 - p230(2) [501+]

Clark, Phillip - *Haematology of Australian Mammals*
SciTech - v28 - i3 - Sept 2004 - p66(1) [51-500]

Clark, Rebecca A. - *A Woman's Guide to Living with HIV Infection*
SciTech - v28 - i4 - Dec 2004 - p102(1) [51-500]

Clark, Richard E. - *Turning Research into Results*
HR Mag - v49 - i7 - July 2004 - pS52(1) [51-500]

Clark, Robert L. - *A History of Public Sector Pensions in the United States*
BHR - v77 - i4 - Winter 2003 - p750(752) [501+]
JEH - v64 - i1 - March 2004 - p267(2) [501+]
JEL - v42 - i4 - Dec 2004 - p1155(2) [501+]
Soc Ser R - v78 - i2 - June 2004 - p338(1) [51-500]

Clark, Ron - *The Excellent 11: Qualities Teachers and Parents Use to Motivate, Inspire, and Educate Children*
JAAL - v48 - i1 - Sept 2004 - p87(1) [501+]

Clark, Ronald W. - *Benjamin Franklin*
LJ - v129 - i13 - August 2004 - p131(1) [51-500]

Clark, Steve - *Something We Have That They Don't: British and American Poetic Relations Since 1925*
Choice - v42 - i4 - Dec 2004 - p663(1) [1-50]

Clark, T.J. - *Farewell to an Idea: Episodes from a History of Modernism*
JAAC - v62 - i3 - Summer 2004 - p297-298 [501+]
MA - v46 - i4 - Fall 2004 - p359(4) [501+]

Clark, Terry D. - *Changing Attitudes Toward Economic Reform During the Yeltsin Era*
Russ Rev - v63 - i3 - July 2004 - pNA [501+]

Clark, Thomas Ralph - *Defending Rights: Law, Labor, Politics, and the State in California, 1890-1925*
AHR - v109 - i3 - June 2004 - p933(2) [501+]

Clark, Wallace - *Brave Men and True*
ILS - v24 - i1 - Fall 2004 - p32(1) [51-500]

Clark, Wesley K. - *Winning Modern Wars: Iraq, Terrorism, and the American Empire*
R&R Bk N - v19 - i1 - Feb 2004 - p42(1) [51-500]

Clark, Willard F. - *Remembering Santa Fe*
R&R Bk N - v19 - i3 - August 2004 - p244(1) [51-500]

Clark, William A.V. - *Immigrants and the American Dream: Remaking the Middle Class*
Choice - v42 - i2 - Oct 2004 - p376(1) [51-500]

Clark, William Roberts - *Capitalism, Not Globalism: Capital Mobility, Central Bank Independence, and the Political Control of the Economy*
JEL - v41 - i4 - Dec 2003 - p1347(1) [501+]

Clarke, Arthur C. - *Christmas Stars*
Ent W - i796 - Dec 10 2004 - p98 [51-500]
Sunstorm
y BL - v101 - i8 - Dec 15 2004 - p690(1) [51-500]
KR - v73 - i1 - Jan 1 2005 - p25(1) [501+]
PW - v252 - i3 - Jan 17 2005 - p39(1) [51-500]
Time's Eye
BooChiTr - Jan 11 2004 - p3(1) [501+]
y VOYA - v27 - i4 - Oct 2004 - p312(1) [51-500]

Clarke, Austin - *Love and Sweet Food: A Culinary Memoir*
BIC - v33 - i9 - Dec 2004 - p26(2) [501+]

Clarke, Averil Y. - *Race Mixing: Black-White Marriage in Postwar America*
CS - v33 - i5 - Sept 2004 - p534-535 [501+]

Clarke, Bob - *From Grub Street to Fleet Street: An Illustrated History of English Newspapers to 1899*
Choice - v42 - i6 - Feb 2005 - p1017(1) [51-500]
CR - v286 - i1669 - Feb 2005 - p128(1) [51-500]

Clarke, Brian - *The Stream*
y BL - v100 - i21 - July 2004 - p1816(1) [51-500]
LJ - v129 - i12 - July 2004 - p67(2) [51-500]

Clarke, Bruce - *From Energy to Information: Representation in Science and Technology, Art, and Literature*
T&C - v45 - i1 - Jan 2004 - p227(3) [501+]

Clarke, David B. - *The Consumption Reader*
TimHES - v0 - i1677 - Feb 4 2005 - p32(1) [501+]

Clarke, David James, IV - *CNE for NetWare 6: Study Guide*
SciTech - v28 - i4 - Dec 2004 - p150(1) [51-500]

Clarke, Desmond M. - *Descartes's Theory of Mind*
Choice - v41 - i11-12 - July-August 2004 - p2056(1) [501+]
RM - v58 - i2 - Dec 2004 - p430(4) [501+]

Clarke, Emma C. - *Iamblichus, De mysteriis*
Class R - v54 - i2 - Nov 2004 - p349(3) [501+]
R&R Bk N - v19 - i3 - August 2004 - p14(1) [1-50]

Cleage, Pearl - *Babylon Sisters*
KR - v73 - i2 - Jan 15 2005 - p67(1) [501+]
LJ - v130 - i2 - Feb 1 2005 - p66(1) [51-500]
PW - v252 - i11 - March 14 2005 - p45(1) [51-500]
Black Iss - v7 - i2 - March-April 2005 - p49(1) [51-500]
Some Things I Never Thought I'd Do (Read by Forrest, Angela). Audiobook Review
LJ - v129 - i15 - Sept 15 2004 - p88(1) [51-500]

Clear, Richard E. - *Old Magazines: Identification & Value Guide*
R&R Bk N - v19 - i4 - Nov 2004 - p229(1) [501+]
Price Guide to Old Magazines
Ant&CM - v108 - i5 - July 2003 - p16(1) [501+]

Clearwater, Rachael - *Dreamwalk*
Bwatch - Nov 2004 - pNA [51-500]

Cleary, Brenda Lewis - *Conducting Research in Long-Term Care Settings*
SciTech - v28 - i3 - Sept 2004 - p85(1) [501+]

Cleary, Brian P. - *I and You and Don't Forget Who: What Is a Pronoun? (Illus. by Gable, Brian)*
c SLJ - v50 - i7 - July 2004 - p91(2) [51-500]

Cleary, J.J. - *Proceedings of the Boston Area Colloquium in Ancient Philosophy. Volume XVII, 2001*
Class R - v54 - i1 - May 2004 - p243(2) [501+]

Cleary, Thomas - *The Counsels of Cormac: An Ancient Irish Guide to Leadership*
BW - v34 - i46 - Nov 14 2004 - p9(2) [501+]

Cleaveland, Clif - *Healers and Heroes: Ordinary People in Extraordinary Times*
SciTech - v28 - i4 - Dec 2004 - p76(1) [51-500]

Cleaves, Cheryl S. - *College Mathematics for Technology. 6th Ed.*
SciTech - v28 - i3 - Sept 2004 - p18(1) [501+]

Clee, Paul - *Photography, and the Making of the American West*
LibMed - v22 - i7 - April-May 2004 - p71(1) [501+]
SLJ - v50 - i10 - Oct 2004 - pS66(1) [501+]

Cleef, Alfred van - *The Lost Island: Alone among the Fruitful and Multiplying.*
BL - v100 - i22 - August 2004 - p1892(1) [51-500]
KR - v72 - i13 - July 1 2004 - p624(1) [501+]

Clegg, Brian - *A Brief History of Infinity: The Quest to Think the Unthinkable*
TimHES - v0 - i1653 - August 13 2004 - p25(1) [501+]
Infinity: The Quest to Think the Unthinkable
Math T - v98 - i1 - August 2004 - p63-63 [501+]

Clegg, Claude Andrew - *The Price of Liberty: African Americans and the Making of Liberia*
Choice - v42 - i4 - Dec 2004 - p713(2) [1-50]
For Aff - v83 - i5 - Sept-Oct 2004 - p164 [501+]

Clegg, Cyndia Susan - *Press Censorship in Jacobean England*
RES - v55 - i218 - Feb 2004 - p131-134 [501+]

Clegg, Douglas - *Afterlife*
PW - v251 - i47 - Nov 22 2004 - p44(1) [51-500]
LJ - v129 - i20 - Dec 1 2004 - p105(1) [51-500]
The Machinery of Night
PW - v252 - i2 - Jan 10 2005 - p43(1) [51-500]

Clegg, Justin - *The Medieval Church in Manuscripts*
R&R Bk N - v19 - i1 - Feb 2004 - p207(1) [51-500]

Cleirigh, Nellie O - *Hardship and High Living: Irish Women's Lives 1808-1923*
ILS - v24 - i1 - Fall 2004 - p13(1) [501+]

Clemens, Frank A. - *Conflict in Afghanistan: An Encyclopedia*
J Mil H - v68 - i3 - July 2004 - p1023-1024 [501+]

Clemens, Judy - *Till the Cows Come Home*
BooChiTr - April 18 2004 - p6(1) [501+]
Bwatch - v26 - i7 - July 2004 - p7(1) [51-500]

Clemens, Justin - *The Romanticism of Contemporary Theory: Institutions, Aesthetics, Nihilism*
R&R Bk N - v19 - i1 - Feb 2004 - p220(1) [51-500]

Clemens, Theo - *The Pastor Bonus: Proceedings*
R&R Bk N - v19 - i3 - August 2004 - p25(1) [1-50]

Clemens, Walter C. - *Dynamics of International Relations: Conflict and Mutual Gain in an Era of Global Interdependence, 2nd Ed.*
R&R Bk N - v19 - i3 - August 2004 - p186(1) [501+]

Clemensoon, Per - *Directory of Scots Banished to the American Plantations, 1650-1775*
EFHM - v58 - i2 - March-April 2004 - p88(1) [51-500]

Clement-Davies, David - *Fire Bringer*
c Teach Lib - v32 - i3 - Feb 2005 - p54(1) [1-50]

Clement, Gilles - *Fundamentals of Space Medicine*
SciTech - v28 - i1 - March 2004 - p108(1) [51-500]

Clement, Hal - *Noise*
Analog - v124 - i3 - March 2004 - p133(2) [501+]

Clement, Peter - *The Inquisitor*
Globe & Mail - Jan 22 2005 - pD12 [51-500]
KR - v72 - i21 - Nov 1 2004 - p1021(1) [51-500]
PW - v251 - i48 - Nov 29 2004 - p25(1) [51-500]

Clement, Richard W. - *Books on the Frontier: Print Culture in the American West, 1763-1875*
SHQ - v108 - i1 - July 2004 - p113-114 [501+]

Clements, Andrew - *The Last Holiday Concert*
c BL - v101 - i4 - Oct 15 2004 - p403(1) [51-500]
y HB - v80 - i6 - Nov-Dec 2004 - p657(1) [51-500]
y KR - v72 - i21 - Nov 1 2004 - p1048(1) [51-500]
c PW - v251 - i41 - Oct 11 2004 - p80(1) [51-500]
c SLJ - v50 - i10 - Oct 2004 - p159(1) [51-500]
Naptime for Slippers (Illus. by Bynum, Janie)
c KR - v73 - i3 - Feb 1 2005 - p175(1) [51-500]
c SLJ - v51 - i2 - Feb 2005 - p96(1) [51-500]
The Report Card
c LibMed - v23 - i3 - Nov-Dec 2004 - p68(2) [51-500]
Slippers at Home (Illus. by Bynum, Janie)
c SLJ - v51 - i1 - Jan 2005 - p88(1) [51-500]
A Week in the Woods (Illus. by Selznick, Brian)
c RT - v57 - Oct 2003 - p175 [1-50]

Clements, Douglas H. - *Engaging Young Children in Mathematics: Standards for Early Childhood Mathematics Education*
TC Math - v11 - i1 - August 2004 - p46(1) [501+]

Clements, Eric L. - *After the Boom in Tombstone and Jerome, Arizona: Decline in Western Resource Towns*
JAH - v91 - i3 - Dec 2004 - p1040(1) [501+]
PHR - v73 - i4 - Nov 2004 - p668(2) [501+]

Clements, Gillian - *Egyptian Pyramid*
c TES - v0 - i4587 - June 11 2004 - psss29(1) [501+]
Roman Villa
y Sch Lib - v52 - i4 - Winter 2004 - p206(1) [51-500]

Clements, Marie - *Burning Vision*
CBRA - Annual 2003 - p239(1) [51-500]

Clements, Philip J. - *Systemic Sclerosis. 2nd Ed.*
SciTech - v28 - i1 - March 2004 - p107(1) [51-500]

Clements, Rhonda L. - *The Child's Right to Play: A Global Approach*
Choice - v42 - i6 - Feb 2005 - p1071(2) [51-500]
R&R Bk N - v19 - i3 - August 2004 - p10(1) [1-50]

Clements, Warren - *Full Mountie: And Other Highlights from the Global Challenge*
CBRA - Annual 2003 - p82(2) [51-500]

Clements, William M. - *Oratory in Native North America*
WestFolk - v62 - i4 - Fall 2003 - p310(3) [501+]

Clendenin, Daniel B. - *Eastern Orthodox Christianity: A Western Perspective*
IBMR - v29 - i1 - Jan 2005 - p52(2) [501+]
Eastern Orthodox Theology: A Contemporary Reader
IBMR - v29 - i1 - Jan 2005 - p52(2) [501+]

Clendinnen, Inga - *Dancing with Strangers*
Quad - v48 - i7-8 - July-August 2004 - p42(4) [501+]

Clermont-Ferrand, Meredith - *Anglo-Saxon Propaganda in the Bayeux Tapestry*
R&R Bk N - v19 - i4 - Nov 2004 - p35(1) [51-500]

Clery, Arthur - *The Idea of a Nation*
ILS - v24 - i1 - Fall 2004 - p4(1) [501+]

Clery, E.J. - *The Feminization Debate in Eighteenth-Century England: Literature, Commerce and Luxury*
Choice - v42 - i5 - Jan 2005 - p851(1) [1-50]

Clesse, Armand - *The Vitality of China and the Chinese*
For Aff - v83 - i5 - Sept-Oct 2004 - p164 [501+]
The Vitality of Russia
For Aff - v83 - i5 - Sept-Oct 2004 - p164 [501+]

Cleveland, Chris Boone - *Welcome to My World: A Strategy Guide for New Teachers*
R&R Bk N - v19 - i4 - Nov 2004 - p188(1) [501+]

Cleveland, Cutler J. - *Encyclopedia of Energy, Vols. 1-6*
Choice - v42 - i2 - Oct 2004 - p271(1) [501+]
En Jnl - v26 - i1 - Jan 2005 - p147(7) [501+]
LJ - v129 - i18 - Nov 1 2004 - p120(1) [51-500]

Cleveland, Darrell - *A Long Way to Go: Conversations about Race by African American Faculty and Graduate Students*
R&R Bk N - v19 - i3 - August 2004 - p229(1) [1-50]

Cleverly, Barbara - *The Damascened Blade*
BL - v100 - i21 - July 2004 - p1823(2) [1-50]
DroRevMy - v24 - i4 - July-August 2004 - p2(1) [501+]
LJ - v129 - i12 - July 2004 - p63(1) [51-500]
NYTBR - August 8 2004 - p15 [501+]

Cliff, Michelle - *Free Enterprise: A Novel of Mary Ellen Pleasant*
LJ - v129 - i17 - Oct 15 2004 - p53(1) [51-500]

Cliffe, Susan - *Thread of Deceit: A Tale of Crime and Betrayal in Upper Canada*
y Kliatt - v39 - i2 - March 2005 - p17(1) [51-500]

Clifford, David - *Outsiders Looking In: The Rossettis Then and Now*
TLS - i5283 - July 2 2004 - p27(1) [501+]

Clifford, Deborah Pickman - *The Passion of Abby Hemenway: Memory, Spirit, and the Making of History*
CHR - v90 - i3 - July 2004 - p580(2) [501+]

Clifford, Frith B. - *The Bowerbirds: Ptilnorhynchiadae*
Choice - v42 - i3 - Nov 2004 - p511(1) [1-50]

Clifford, Helen - *Silver in London: The Parker and Wakelin Partnership*
Apo - v161 - i516 - Feb 2005 - p77(2) [501+]

Clifford, Richard J. - *Psalms 1-72*
Intpr - v59 - i1 - Jan 2005 - p86(1) [501+]

Clift, Eleanor - *Founding Sisters and the Nineteenth Amendment*
R&R Bk N - v19 - i1 - Feb 2004 - pNA [51-500]

Clift, Peter - *Continent-Ocean Interactions Within East Asian Marginal Seas*
SciTech - v28 - i4 - Dec 2004 - p57(1) [51-500]

Clifton, Judith - *Privatisation in the European Union: Public Enterprises and Integration*
R&R Bk N - v19 - i1 - Feb 2004 - p98(1) [51-500]

Clifton, Lucille - *Mercy*
BL - v101 - i1 - Sept 15 2004 - p195(1) [501+]
LJ - v129 - i14 - Sept 1 2004 - p154(1) [51-500]

Clifton-Mogg, Caroline - *Secret Gardens of London (Illus. by Majerus, Marianne)*
Bwatch - v26 - i9 - Sept 2004 - p2(1) [51-500]

Clifton, Rita - *Brands and Branding*
R&R Bk N - v19 - i3 - August 2004 - p109(1) [51-500]

Clin-Lalande, Anne-Marie - *Satyres nouvelles*
FS - v58 - i1 - Jan 2004 - p106(2) [501+]

Clinard, Marshall B. - *Sociology of Deviant Behavior, 12th Ed.*
R&R Bk N - v19 - i1 - Feb 2004 - p123(1) [51-500]

Cline, Edward - *Sparrowhawk. Bk. 4, Empire*
PW - v251 - i46 - Nov 15 2004 - p41(1) [51-500]

Cline, Elizabeth - *Bargain Buyer's Guide 2004: The Consumer's Bible to Big Savings Online and by Mail*
R&R Bk N - v19 - i1 - Feb 2004 - p252(1) [51-500]

Cline, Rachel - *What to Keep*
KR - v72 - i24 - Dec 15 2004 - pS6(2) [501+]

Cline-Ransome, Lesa - *Major Taylor: Champion Cyclist (Illus. by Ransome, James)*
c BL - v101 - i1 - Sept 1 2004 - p115(1) [501+]
c SLJ - v50 - i10 - Oct 2004 - pS26(1) [1-50]

Cling, Jean-Pierre - *The Dynamics of Social Exclusion in Europe: Comparing Austria, Germany, Portugal and the UK*
JEL - v41 - i4 - Dec 2003 - p1380(1) [501+]

Clingman, Dustin - *Practical Java Game Programming*
Bwatch - v26 - i9 - Sept 2004 - p5(1) [51-500]
SciTech - v28 - i3 - Sept 2004 - p23(1) [51-500]

Clinical Pharmacology Made Incredibly Easy. 2nd Ed.
SciTech - v28 - i3 - Sept 2004 - p121(1) [51-500]

Clinkskill, James - *Prairie Memoir: The Life and Times of James Clinkskill, 1853-1936*
CBRA - Annual 2003 - p39(2) [501+]

Clinton, Bill - *My Life (Read by Clinton, Bill). Audiobook Review*
BL - v100 - i22 - August 2004 - p1866(1) [51-500]
BL - v101 - i9-10 - Jan 1 2005 - p778(1) [1-50]
People - v62 - i4 - July 26 2004 - p48 [51-500]
PW - v251 - i27 - July 5 2004 - p18(1) [501+]
LJ - v129 - i20 - Dec 1 2004 - p183(1) [51-500]

Cochran-Smith, Marilyn - *Walking the Road: Race, Diversity, and Social Justice in Teacher Education*
TCR - v106 - i8 - August 2004 - p1654(4) [501+]

Cochrane, Becky - *I'm Your Man*
BL - v101 - i5 - Nov 1 2004 - p469(1) [51-500]

Cochrane, Michelle - *When AIDS Began: San Francisco and the Making of an Epidemic*
SciTech - v28 - i4 - Dec 2004 - p84(1) [51-500]

Cochrane, Peter - *Uncommon Sense: Out of the Box Thinking for an in the Box World*
New Sci - v183 - i2463 - Sept 4 2004 - p47(1) [51-500]

Cockburn, Alexander - *The Politics of Anti-Semitism*
BIC - v33 - i9 - Dec 2004 - pNA [501+]
R&R Bk N - v19 - i1 - Feb 2004 - p45(1) [51-500]

Cockburn, Cynthia - *The Line: Women, Partition and the Gender Order in Cyprus*
Wom R Bks - v21 - i12 - Sept 2004 - p1(2) [501+]

Cockcroft, Robert - *Rhetorical Affect in Early Modern Writing: Renaissance Passions Reconsidered*
RES - v55 - i220 - June 2004 - p453-455 [501+]

Cockett, Martin - *Maths for Chemists, Vol. 1*
TimHES - v0 - i1680 - Feb 25 2005 - pXIV(1) [501+]

Maths for Chemists, Vol. 2
TimHES - v0 - i1680 - Feb 25 2005 - pXIV(1) [501+]

Cockey, Tim - *Backstabber (Read by Lawlor, Patrick Girard). Audiobook Review*
BL - v101 - i7 - Dec 1 2004 - p676(1) [51-500]
y Kliatt - v39 - i1 - Jan 2005 - p38(1) [51-500]
PW - v251 - i36 - Sept 6 2004 - p25(1) [51-500]

Cockfield, Jamie H. - *White Crow:The Life and Times of the Grand Duke Nicholas Mikhailovich Romanov, 1859-1919*
Slav R - v63 - i4 - Winter 2004 - p892(2) [501+]

Cocks, Doug - *Deep Futures: Our Prospects for Survival*
Fut - v39 - i2 - March-April 2005 - p60(1) [51-500]

Cocks, Geoffrey - *The Wolf at the Door: Stanley Kubrick, History, and the Holocaust*
R&R Bk N - v19 - i4 - Nov 2004 - p225(1) [501+]

Cocks, H.G. - *Nameless Offences: Homosexual Desire in the 19th Century*
ELT - v48 - i1 - Wntr 2005 - p209(6) [501+]

Coconut Photo Journal (Illus. by Lukatz, Casey)
c PW - v252 - i8 - Feb 21 2005 - p177(1) [501+]

Coconut's Cookbook: Fun and Fluffy Treats to Eat (Illus. by Lukatz, Casey)
c PW - v251 - i37 - Sept 13 2004 - p81(1) [51-500]

Cocroft, Wayne D. - *Cold War: Building for Nuclear Confrontation 1946-1989*
TimHES - v0 - i1681 - March 4 2005 - p28(2) [501+]

Coddington, Ron S. - *Faces of the Civil War: An Album of Union Soldiers and Their Stories*
R&R Bk N - v19 - i4 - Nov 2004 - p61(1) [51-500]

Coddon, Karin S. - *Black Women Activists*
y SLJ - v50 - i11 - Nov 2004 - p162(1) [51-500]

Codell, Esme Raji - *How to Get Your Child to Love Reading*
R&R Bk N - v19 - i1 - Feb 2004 - p261(1) [51-500]

Sahara Special
y Sch Lib - v52 - i4 - Winter 2004 - p212(1) [51-500]

Sing a Song of Tuna Fish: Hard-to-Swallow Stories from Fifth Grade (Read by Codell, Esme Raji). Audiobook Review
c PW - v252 - i7 - Feb 14 2005 - p20(1) [51-500]

Sing a Song of Tuna Fish: Hard-to-Swallow Stories from Fifth Grade
c BL - v101 - i5 - Nov 1 2004 - p480(1) [51-500]
c KR - v72 - i24 - Dec 15 2004 - p1199(1) [501+]
c PW - v251 - i50 - Dec 13 2004 - p69(1) [51-500]
c SLJ - v51 - i1 - Jan 2005 - p144(1) [51-500]

Codell, Julie F. - *Imperial Co-Histories: National Identities and the British and Colonial Press*
ELT - v47 - i3 - Summer 2004 - p335(5) [501+]

The Victorian Artist: Artists' Lifewritings in Britain, ca. 1870-1910
ELT - v48 - i2 - Spring 2005 - p85(3) [501+]
VS - v46 - i4 - Summer 2004 - p711(3) [501+]

Codrescu, Andrei - *Wakefield (Read by Woodman, Jeff). Audiobook Review*
LJ - v130 - i4 - March 1 2005 - p122(1) [51-500]

Wakefield
BIC - v33 - i6 - Sept 2004 - p3(1) [501+]
y SLJ - v50 - i8 - August 2004 - p146(1) [501+]

Cody, H.A. - *An Apostle of the North: Memoirs of the Right Reverend William Carpenter Bompas*
Can Hist R - v85 - i3 - Sept 2004 - p622(3) [501+]
CBRA - Annual 2003 - p40(2) [51-500]

Coe, Angela L. - *The Sedimentary Record of Sea-Level Change*
Choice - v41 - i7 - March 2004 - p1324(1) [501+]

Coe, David G. - *Kaunda's Gaoler: Memoirs of a District Officer in Northern Rhodesia and Zambia*
IJAHS - v37 - i1 - Wntr 2004 - p139-141 [501+]

Coe, Harrie B. - *Maine Biographies Excerpted from Maine Resources, Attractions, and It's People: A History. Vols. 1-2*
EFHM - v58 - i2 - March-April 2004 - p89(1) [51-500]

Coe, Jonathan - *The Closed Circle*
KR - v73 - i5 - March 1 2005 - p244(2) [501+]
LJ - v130 - i4 - March 1 2005 - p76(1) [51-500]
Lon R Bks - v26 - i20 - Oct 21 2004 - p12(1) [501+]
NS - v133 - i4708 - Oct 4 2004 - p55(1) [501+]
y NS - v133 - i4716 - Nov 29 2004 - p46(1) [51-500]
Spec - v296 - i9187 - Sept 4 2004 - p42(2) [501+]
TLS - i5293 - Sept 10 2004 - p19(1) [501+]

Like a Fiery Elephant: The Story of B.S. Johnson
Lon R Bks - v26 - i15 - August 5 2004 - p11(3) [501+]
NS - v133 - i4716 - Nov 29 2004 - p43(1) [51-500]

The Rotter's Club (Read by Buchanan, Colin). Audiobook Review
BL - v101 - i7 - Dec 1 2004 - p677(1) [51-500]

Coe, Ralph T. - *The Responsive Eye: Ralph T. Coe and the Collecting of American Indian Art*
Am Craft - v64 - i1 - Feb-March 2004 - p47(1) [501+]

Coeckelbergh, Mark - *The Metaphysics of Autonomy: The Reconciliation of Ancient and Modern Ideals of the Person*
R&R Bk N - v20 - i1 - Feb 2005 - p2(1) [51-500]

Coel, Margaret - *Killing Raven (Read by Brush, Stephanie). Audiobook Review*
LJ - v130 - i2 - Feb 1 2005 - p122(1) [51-500]

Killing Raven
Kliatt - v38 - i6 - Nov 2004 - p15(1) [51-500]

Wife of Moon
BL - v101 - i1 - Sept 1 2004 - p68(1) [51-500]
LJ - v129 - i14 - Sept 1 2004 - p122(1) [51-500]
PW - v251 - i32 - August 9 2004 - p234(1) [51-500]
Roundup M - v12 - i3 - Feb 2005 - p26(1) [51-500]

Coelho, Paolo - *The Alchemist*
LJ - v129 - i20 - Dec 1 2004 - p186(1) [501+]

Coerver, Don M. - *Mexico: An Encyclopedia of Contemporary Culture and History*
Choice - v42 - i7 - March 2005 - p1206(1) [51-500]
BL - v101 - i9-10 - Jan 1 2005 - p903(2) [501+]

Coetzee, J.M. - *Elizabeth Costello*
Ant R - v63 - i1 - Wntr 2005 - p189(1) [51-500]
BIC - v33 - i5 - August 2004 - p10(2) [501+]
Globe & Mail - July 10 2004 - pD15 [501+]
Globe & Mail - Oct 30 2004 - pD29 [51-500]
HM - v309 - i1850 - July 2004 - p85(5) [501+]
Ken R - v27 - i1 - Wntr 2005 - p124(10) [501+]
Sew R - v112 - i2 - Spring 2004 - pXLVII-L [501+]
VQR - v80 - i2 - Spring 2004 - p259-259 [501+]

Coffelt, Nancy - *What's Cookin'?: A Happy Birthday Counting Book*
y SLJ - v51 - i2 - Feb 2005 - p57(1) [51-500]

Coffey, Colleen - *Papier-Mache*
c SLJ - v50 - i11 - Nov 2004 - p172(1) [51-500]

Recyclables
c SLJ - v50 - i11 - Nov 2004 - p172(1) [51-500]

Coffey, Dennis - *Guitars, Bars, and Motown Superstars*
Bwatch - v26 - i9 - Sept 2004 - p9(1) [51-500]

Coffey, Joan L. - *Leon Harmel: Entrepreneur as Catholic Social Reformer*
CHR - v90 - i4 - Oct 2004 - p807(2) [501+]
JEL - v42 - i1 - March 2004 - p300(1) [51-500]

Coffey, Kathy - *Dancing in the Margins: Meditations for People Who Struggle with Their Churches*
Comw - v131 - i21 - Dec 3 2004 - p32(1) [501+]

Coffey, Wayne - *The Boys of Winter: The Untold Story of a Coach, a Dream, and the 1980 U.S. Olympic Hockey Team*
y BL - v101 - i6 - Nov 15 2004 - p545(1) [51-500]
KR - v72 - i21 - Nov 1 2004 - p1034(1) [501+]
NYTBR - Jan 9 2005 - p8 [501+]
PW - v251 - i51 - Dec 20 2004 - p47(1) [501+]

Coffin, Caroline - *Applying English Grammar: Functional and Corpus Approaches. 1st Ed.*
TimHES - v0 - i1668 - Nov 26 2004 - pX(2) [501+]

Coffin, David R. - *Pirro Ligorio: The Renaissance Artist, Architect, and Antiquarian*
Choice - v42 - i6 - Feb 2005 - p1010(2) [51-500]

Coffman, Edward M. - *The Regulars: The American Army, 1898-1941*
Choice - v42 - i4 - Dec 2004 - p720(1) [1-50]
HRNB - v33 - i1 - Fall 2004 - p12(1) [501+]
J Mil H - v68 - i4 - Oct 2004 - p1272-1274 [501+]
Parameters - v34 - i4 - Winter 2004 - p135(3) [501+]
PSQ - v119 - i4 - Winter 2004 - p723(2) [501+]

Coffman, Tom - *The Island Edge of America: A Political History of Hawai'i*
AHR - v109 - i2 - April 2004 - p542(2) [501+]

Cogan, Charles - *French Negotiating Behavior: Dealing with La Grande Nation*
Choice - v41 - i11-12 - July-August 2004 - p2119(1) [501+]

Smart Sanctions: Targeting Economic Statecraft
JPR - v41 - i5 - Sept 2004 - p639-639 [501+]

Cogdell, James W. - *Lectures on Automorphic L-Functions*
SciTech - v28 - i3 - Sept 2004 - p36(1) [51-500]

Coggan, D.A. - *Fundamentals of Industrial Control, 2nd Ed.*
SciTech - v28 - i4 - Dec 2004 - p168(1) [51-500]

Coggin, Joan - *Dancing with Death*
LJ - v129 - i13 - August 2004 - p131(1) [51-500]

Coggins, Jack - *Arms and Equipment of the Civil War*
LJ - v129 - i12 - July 2004 - p127(1) [1-50]

Cogswell, Michael - *Louis Armstrong: The Offstage Story of Satchmo*
Notes - v61 - i2 - Dec 2004 - p460(3) [501+]

Cogswell, Thomas - *Politics, Religion and Popularity in Early Stuart Britain: Essays in Honour of Conrad Russell*
Albion - v36 - i1 - Spring 2004 - p124(2) [501+]
Ren Q - v57 - i3 - Fall 2004 - p1124(2) [501+]

Cohan, Peter S. - *Value Leadership: The Seven Principles That Drive Corporate Value in Any Economy*
R&R Bk N - v19 - i1 - Feb 2004 - p90(1) [1-50]

Cohan, Steven - *Hollywood Musicals, the Film Reader*
Am M - v22 - i1 - Spring 2004 - p187-189 [501+]

Cohee, Allison - *Your Child in Film and Television*
CBRA - Annual 2003 - p104(2) [51-500]

Cohen, Adam - *American Pharaoh: Mayor Richard J. Daley: His Battle for Chicago and the Nation*
J Urban H - v30 - i4 - May 2004 - p616-626 [501+]

Cohen, Alan B. - *Technology in American Health Care: Policy Directions for Effective Evaluation and Management*
Choice - v42 - i4 - Dec 2004 - p694(1) [1-50]

Cohen, Allen - *Howard Hanson in Theory and Practice*
Choice - v41 - i11-12 - July-August 2004 - p2053(1) [501+]

Cohen, Allen Carson - *Insect Diets: Science and Technology*
SciTech - v28 - i1 - March 2004 - p131(1) [51-500]

Cohen, Andrew - *While Canada Slept: How We Lost Our Place in the World*
CBRA - Annual 2003 - p304(2) [501+]

Cohen, Andrew Wender - *The Racketeer's Progress: Chicago and the Struggle for the Modern American Economy, 1900-1940*
Choice - v42 - i4 - Dec 2004 - p704(1) [1-50]

Cohen, Bronwen - *A New Deal for Children?: Reforming Education and Care in England, Scotland and Sweden*
R&R Bk N - v19 - i4 - Nov 2004 - p177(1) [501+]
TES - v0 - i4587 - June 11 2004 - psss17(1) [501+]

Cohen, Bruce - *Pension Puzzle: Your Complete Guide to Government Benefits, RRSPs and Employer Plans*
CBRA - Annual 2003 - p29(1) [51-500]

Cohen, Charles D. - *Seuss, the Whole Seuss, and Nothing but the Seuss: A Visual Biography of Theodor Seuss Geisel*
c LibMed - v23 - i3 - Nov-Dec 2004 - p78(1) [51-500]

Cohen, Daniel - *Arguments and Metaphors in Philosophy*
R&R Bk N - v19 - i3 - August 2004 - p259(1) [51-500]

Our Modern Times: The New Nature of Capitalism in the Information Age
Econ J - v114 - i499 - Nov 2004 - pF537-F538 [501+]

Cohen, David B. - *American National Security and Civil Liberties in an Era of Terrorism*
Choice - v42 - i5 - Jan 2005 - p933(1) [51-500]

Cohen, Deborah Bodin - *The Seventh Day (Illus. by Hall, Melanie)*
c PW - v252 - i7 - Feb 14 2005 - p78(1) [51-500]

Cohen, Derek - *Searching Shakespeare: Studies in Culture and Authority*
Ren Q - v57 - i4 - Winter 2004 - p1521(2) [501+]

Cohen, Eliot A. - *Supreme Command: Soldiers, Statesmen and Leadership in Wartime*
Soc - v41 - i3 - March-April 2004 - p87(4) [501+]

Cohen, Elizabeth - *The House on Beartown Road: A Memoir of Learning and Forgetting (Read by Dunne, Bernadette). Audiobook Review*
PW - v251 - i31 - August 2 2004 - p21(1) [501+]

Cohen, Elizabeth G. - *Teaching Cooperative Learning: The Challenge for Teacher Education*
Choice - v42 - i6 - Feb 2005 - p1074(1) [51-500]

Cohen, Elliot D. - *News Incorporated: Corporate Media Ownership and Its Threat to Democracy*
PW - v251 - i44 - Nov 1 2004 - p53(1) [501+]
PW - v251 - i50 - Dec 13 2004 - p57(1) [501+]

Cohen, Esther - *Book Doctor*
BL - v101 - i8 - Dec 15 2004 - p707(1) [51-500]
KR - v72 - i23 - Dec 1 2004 - p1102(1) [51-500]
LJ - v130 - i2 - Feb 1 2005 - p66(2) [51-500]
PW - v251 - i50 - Dec 13 2004 - p43(1) [51-500]

Cohen, Etty - *Playing Hard at Life: A Relational Approach to Treating Multiply Traumatized Adolescents*
Adoles - v39 - i156 - Winter 2004 - p828(2) [501+]

Cohen, Getzel M. - *Breaking Ground: Pioneering Women Archeologists*
Choice - v42 - i7 - March 2005 - p1269(1) [51-500]

Cohen, Hermann - *Ethics of Maimonides*
R&R Bk N - v19 - i3 - August 2004 - p12(1) [1-50]

Cohen, I. Bernard - *Triumph of Numbers: How They Shaped Modern Life*
PW - v252 - i6 - Feb 7 2005 - p53(1) [51-500]

Cohen, Janet Langhart - *From Rage to Reason: My Life in Two Americas*
Black Iss - v6 - i5 - Sept-Oct 2004 - p48(1) [51-500]

Cohen, Jayne - *The Ultimate Bar/Bat Mitzvah Celebration Book: A Guide to Inspiring Ceremonies and Joyous Festivities*
LJ - v129 - i12 - July 2004 - p92(1) [51-500]

Cohen, Jennifer Beth - *Lying Together: My Russian Affair*
BW - v34 - i40 - Oct 3 2004 - p14(1) [501+]
KR - v72 - i13 - July 1 2004 - p613(2) [501+]
LJ - v129 - i19 - Nov 15 2004 - p68(1) [501+]
NYTBR - Sept 26 2004 - p12 [501+]
PW - v251 - i28 - July 12 2004 - p53(1) [501+]
R&R Bk N - v19 - i4 - Nov 2004 - p229(1) [501+]

Cohen, Jere - *Protestantism and Capitalism: The Mechanisms of Influence*
CS - v33 - i1 - Jan 2004 - p110-112 [501+]

Cohen, Jeremy - *Sanctifying the Name of God: Jewish Martys and Jewish Memories of the First Crusade*
Choice - v42 - i6 - Feb 2005 - p1088(1) [51-500]

Cohen, John - *Young Bob*
TLS - i5302 - Nov 12 2004 - p8-9 [501+]

Cohen, Jon - *Coming to Term: Uncovering the Truth about Miscarriage*
BL - v101 - i9-10 - Jan 1 2005 - p796(1) [51-500]
KR - v72 - i20 - Oct 15 2004 - p992(1) [501+]
LJ - v129 - i20 - Dec 1 2004 - p148(2) [51-500]
PW - v251 - i47 - Nov 22 2004 - p51(1) [51-500]

Cohen, Julie E. - *Copyright in a Global Information Economy: 2004 Case and Statutory Supplement*
R&R Bk N - v19 - i4 - Nov 2004 - p168(1) [501+]

Cohen, Karl F. - *Forbidden Animation: Censored Cartoons and Blacklisted Animators in America*
R&R Bk N - v19 - i3 - August 2004 - p242(1) [51-500]

Cohen, Lazaro Issi - *Web Programmer's Desk Reference*
Bwatch - Dec 2004 - pNA [51-500]

Cohen, Leah Hager - *Without Apology: Girls, Women, and the Desire to Fight.*
KR - v72 - i24 - Dec 15 2004 - p1176(1) [501+]
LJ - v130 - i1 - Jan 1 2005 - p87(1) [51-500]
PW - v251 - i51 - Dec 20 2004 - p46(1) [501+]

Cohen, Lee M. - *Health Psychology Handbook: Practical Issues for the Behavioral Medicine Specialist*
E-Streams - June 2004 - pNA [501+]

Cohen, Leonard - *Beautiful Losers*
Essays CW - Winter 2003 - p42 [501+]
Stranger Music: Selected Poems and Songs
Globe & Mail - Feb 12 2005 - pD15 [501+]

Cohen, Lizabeth - *A Consumers' Republic: The Politics of Mass Consumption in Postwar America*
JIH - v35 - i1 - Summer 2004 - p166-167 [501+]
T&C - v45 - i2 - April 2004 - p454-455 [501+]

Cohen, Luanne Seymour - *Adobe Illustrator CS: Creative Studio, Techniques for Digital Artists*
SciTech - v28 - i3 - Sept 2004 - p135(1) [51-500]

Cohen, Lucy M. - *Colombianas en la Vanguardia*
HAHR - v84 - i2 - May 2004 - p370(2) [501+]

Cohen, M.J. - *History in Quotations*
CR - v285 - i1662 - July 2004 - p63(2) [51-500]
TimHES - v0 - i1651 - July 30 2004 - p25(1) [501+]

Cohen, Mark - *The Fractal Murders*
DroRevMy - v24 - i3 - May-June 2004 - p11(1) [1-50]

Cohen, Martin - *101 Ethical Dilemmas*
TimHES - v0 - i1663 - Oct 22 2004 - p27(1) [501+]

Cohen, Milton A. - *Movement, Manifesto, Melee: The Modernist Group 1910-1914*
R&R Bk N - v19 - i4 - Nov 2004 - p210(1) [501+]

Cohen, Miriam - *Mimmy and Sophie All around the Town (Illus. by Yezerski, Thomas F.)*
c SLJ - v50 - i10 - Oct 2004 - pS30(1) [1-50]
My Big Brother (Illus. by Himler, Ronald)
c BL - v101 - i9-10 - Jan 1 2005 - p852(1) [1-50]
c KR - v73 - i2 - Jan 15 2005 - p118(1) [51-500]

Cohen-Mor, Dalya - *A Matter of Fate: The Concept of Fate in the Arab World as Reflected in Modern Arabic Literature*
IJMES - v36 - i1 - Feb 2004 - p140-141 [501+]

Cohen, Morton N. - *Lewis Carroll and His Illustrators: Collaborations and Correspondence, 1865-1898*
BSA-P - v98 - i2 - June 2004 - p231-233 [501+]
Choice - v41 - i7 - March 2004 - p1297(1) [501+]

Cohen, Nancy J. - *Died Blonde: A Bad Hair Day Mystery*
LJ - v129 - i16 - Oct 1 2004 - p64(1) [1-50]
PW - v251 - i45 - Nov 8 2004 - p39(2) [501+]

Cohen, Naomi W. - *The Americanization of Zionism, 1897-1948*
Choice - v42 - i2 - Oct 2004 - p345(2) [501+]

Cohen, Paul A. - *China Unbound: Evolving Perspectives on the Chinese Past*
Ch Rev Int - v11 - i1 - Spring 2004 - p59(4) [501+]

Cohen, Rachel - *A Chance Meeting: Intertwined Lives of American Writers and Artists, 1854-1967*
Choice - v42 - i2 - Oct 2004 - p291(2) [501+]
TLS - i5284 - July 9 2004 - p8(1) [501+]

Cohen, Rich - *Machers and Rockers: Chess Records and the Business of Rock & Roll*
BL - v101 - i2 - Sept 15 2004 - p190(1) [51-500]
Bus W - i3914 - Dec 27 2004 - p16 [501+]
Bwatch - Jan 2005 - pNA [51-500]
Globe & Mail - March 12 2005 - pD17 [501+]
LJ - v129 - i16 - Oct 1 2004 - p82(1) [51-500]
PW - v251 - i34 - August 23 2004 - p50(2) [51-500]

Cohen, Rip - *500 Cantigas d'Amigo*
TLS - i5294 - Sept 17 2004 - p32(1) [501+]

Cohen, Robert - *The Free Speech Movement: Reflections on Berkley in the 1960s*
WHQ - v35 - i1 - Spring 2004 - p93-94 [501+]

Cohen, Roger - *Soldiers and Slaves: American POWs Trapped by the Nazis' Final Gamble*
KR - v73 - i2 - Jan 15 2005 - p96(2) [501+]
LJ - v129 - i20 - Dec 1 2004 - p90(1) [501+]
LJ - v130 - i2 - Feb 1 2005 - p96(1) [51-500]
PW - v252 - i6 - Feb 7 2005 - p49(1) [501+]

Cohen, Ronald D. - *Rainbow Quest: The Folk Music Revival and American Society*
S&S - v68 - i4 - Winter 2004 - p507-4 [501+]

Cohen, Santiago - *This Is Passover (Illus. by Cohen, Santiago)*
c SLJ - v51 - i2 - Feb 2005 - p115(1) [51-500]

Cohen, Saul B. - *Geopolitics of the World System*
PG - v23 - i6 - August 2004 - p801-804 [501+]

Cohen, Shaul E. - *Planting Nature: Trees and the Manipulation of Environmental Stewardship in America*
Choice - v42 - i4 - Dec 2004 - p689(1) [1-50]

Cohen, Stephanie - *The Perennial Gardener's Design Primer*
BL - v101 - i9-10 - Jan 1 2005 - p796(1) [51-500]
Bwatch - March 2005 - pNA [51-500]
LJ - v130 - i1 - Jan 1 2005 - p138(1) [51-500]
PW - v251 - i51 - Dec 20 2004 - p54(1) [501+]

Cohen, Stephen Philip - *The Idea of Pakistan*
MEJ - v59 - i1 - Wntr 2005 - p148(2) [501+]

Cohen, Steven M. (b. 1974 -) - *Keeping Current: Advanced Internet Strategies to Meet Librarian and Patron Needs*
LHT - v22 - i2 - Spring 2004 - p238(1) [501+]
Keeping Current: Advanced Internet Strategies to Meet Librarians and Patron Needs
LibMed - v22 - i7 - April-May 2004 - p86(1) [501+]

Cohen, Susan L. - *Canaanites, Chronologies, and Connections: The Relationship of Middle Bronze Age IIA Canaan to Middle Kingdom Egypt*
JNES - v63 - i4 - Oct 2004 - p317(3) [501+]

Cohen-Tanugi, Laurent - *An Alliance at Risk: The United States and Europe Since September 11*
R&R Bk N - v19 - i3 - August 2004 - p36(1) [51-500]
VQR - v80 - i2 - Spring 2004 - p256-256 [501+]

Cohen, Thomas V. - *Love and Death in Renaissance Italy*
Globe & Mail - Jan 29 2005 - pD6 [501+]
HT - v54 - i11 - Nov 2004 - p67(2) [501+]
TLS - i5303 - Nov 19 2004 - p26(1) [501+]

Cohen, William A. - *The Art of the Strategist: 10 Essential Principles for Leading Your Company to Victory*
Choice - v42 - i3 - Nov 2004 - p529(1) [1-50]
R&R Bk N - v19 - i3 - August 2004 - p104(1) [1-50]

Cohen, Zafrira Lidvosky - *"Loosen the Fetters of Thy Tongue, Woman": The Poetry and Poetics of Yona Wallach*
WLT - v78 - i3-4 - Sept-Dec 2004 - p151(1) [501+]

Cohn, Mike - *User Stories Applied: For Agile Software Development*
SciTech - v28 - i3 - Sept 2004 - p28(1) [1-50]

Cohn, Rachel - *Pop Princess (Read by Romano, Christy Carlson). Audiobook Review*
Kliatt - v38 - i6 - Nov 2004 - p49(1) [51-500]
Pop Princess
y VOYA - v27 - i3 - August 2004 - p210(1) [1-50]
Shrimp
y CCB-B - v58 - i6 - Feb 2005 - p247(2) [51-500]
y HB - v81 - i2 - March-April 2005 - p198(1) [51-500]
y Kliatt - v39 - i2 - March 2005 - p9(1) [51-500]
KR - v73 - i4 - Feb 15 2005 - p227(1) [51-500]
y PW - v252 - i4 - Jan 24 2005 - p245(1) [51-500]
y SLJ - v51 - i2 - Feb 2005 - p136(1) [51-500]
The Steps
y Sch Lib - v52 - i4 - Winter 2004 - p214(1) [51-500]

Cohn, Samuel K., Jr. - *The Black Death Transformed: Disease and Culture in Early Renaissance Europe*
J Soc H - v38 - i2 - Winter 2004 - p543(3) [501+]
JIH - v34 - i4 - Spring 2004 - p622-623 [501+]
Specu - v79 - i4 - Oct 2004 - p1053(3) [501+]

Cohn, Scotti - *Liberty's Children: Stories of Eleven Revolutionary War Children*
y Kliatt - v39 - i1 - Jan 2005 - p33(1) [51-500]

Cohn, Theodore H. - *Global Political Economy: Theory and Practice, 3rd Ed.*
R&R Bk N - v19 - i4 - Nov 2004 - p108(1) [51-500]

Cohodas, Nadine - *Queen: The Life and Music of Dinah Washington*
BL - v100 - i22 - August 2004 - p1888(1) [51-500]
Black Iss - v6 - i6 - Nov-Dec 2004 - p40(2) [501+]
BW - v34 - i36 - Sept 5 2004 - p8(1) [501+]
KR - v72 - i13 - July 1 2004 - p614(1) [501+]
LJ - v129 - i13 - August 2004 - p82(1) [501+]
PW - v251 - i27 - July 5 2004 - p47(1) [51-500]

Coicaud, Jean-Marc - *The Globalization of Human Rights*
JPR - v41 - i4 - July 2004 - p518-518 [501+]

Coifer, Eoin - *Artemis Fowl (Read by Parker, Nathaniel). Audiobook Review*
c SLJ - v50 - i12 - Dec 2004 - p73(1) [501+]

Coil, Susan - *Rockville Pike*
KR - v72 - i19 - Oct 1 2004 - p928(2) [501+]

Cojean, Annick - *Marc Riboud: 50 Years of Photography*
Choice - v42 - i1 - Sept 2004 - p93(1) [501+]
TimHES - v0 - i1651 - July 30 2004 - p26(2) [501+]

Cokal, Susann - *Breath and Bones*
KR - v73 - i4 - Feb 15 2005 - p189(1) [501+]
LJ - v130 - i4 - March 1 2005 - p76(2) [51-500]
PW - v252 - i10 - March 7 2005 - p49(1) [51-500]

Coker, Niyi - *A Study of the Music and Social Criticism of African Musician Fela Anikulapo-Kuti*
Choice - v41 - i11-12 - July-August 2004 - p2053(2) [501+]

Colacello, Bob - *Ronnie and Nancy: Their Path to the White House, 1911 to 1980*
    BL - v101 - i3 - Oct 1 2004 - p282(1) [51-500]
    NYTBR - Oct 31 2004 - p9 [501+]
    PW - v251 - i40 - Oct 4 2004 - p84(2) [51-500]

Colander, David - *Race, Liberalism, and Economics*
    Choice - v42 - i3 - Nov 2004 - p533(1) [1-50]

Colarelli, Stephen M. - *No Best Way: An Evolutionary Perspective on Human Resource Management*
    Per Psy - v57 - i4 - Winter 2004 - p1097(3) [501+]

Colato Lainez, Rene - *Waiting for Papa/Esperando a Papa (Illus. by Accardo, Anthony)*
    c Cur R - v44 - i7 - March 2005 - p12(2) [51-500]
    c SLJ - v51 - i1 - Jan 2005 - p120(1) [51-500]

Colavincenzo, Marc - *'Trading Magic for Fact,' Fact for Magic: Myth and Mythologizing in Postmodern Canadian Historical Fiction*
    R&R Bk N - v19 - i1 - Feb 2004 - p247(1) [51-500]

Colbert, David - *The Magical Worlds of Harry Potter*
    c CH Bwatch - v14 - i9 - Sept 2004 - p3(1) [51-500]

Colbert, Jan - *Dear Dr. King: Letters from Today's Children to Dr. Martin Luther King, Jr.*
    y SLJ - v50 - i10 - Oct 2004 - p67(1) [51-500]

Colbert, Judy - *Career Opportunities in the Travel Industry*
    Choice - v42 - i2 - Oct 2004 - p272(2) [501+]
    R&R Bk N - v19 - i3 - August 2004 - p79(1) [51-500]
    SLJ - v50 - i7 - July 2004 - p118(1) [51-500]

Colburn, Kerry - *So You Want to Be a Canadian: All about the Most Fascinating People in the World and the Magical Place We Call Home*
    Globe & Mail - Nov 13 2004 - pD21 [501+]

Colby, Cliff - *The Mac Panther Bible. 9th Ed.*
    SciTech - v28 - i3 - Sept 2004 - p26(1) [51-500]

Colby, Vineta - *Vernon Lee: A Literary Biography*
    Lon R Bks - v26 - i2 - Jan 22 2004 - p26(1) [501+]

Colchester, Chloe - *Clothing the Pacific*
    JRAI - v10 - i3 - Sept 2004 - p717(3) [501+]

Coldewey, Gaby - *Zwischen Pruth und Jordan: Lebenserinnerungen Czernowitzer Juden*
    HNet - Oct 2004 - pNA [501+]

Coldiron, A.E.B. - *Canon, Period, and the Poetry of Charles of Orleans: Found in Translation*
    JEGP - v103 - i3 - July 2004 - p395-398 [501+]
    Specu - v79 - i3 - July 2004 - p,752-754 [501+]

Coldiron, Margaret - *Trance and Transformation of the Actor in Japanese Noh and Balinese Masked Dance-Drama*
    R&R Bk N - v19 - i4 - Nov 2004 - p225(1) [501+]

Colditz, Graham A. - *Handbook of Cancer Risk Assessment and Prevention*
    E-Streams - August 2004 - pNA [501+]
    SciTech - v28 - i1 - March 2004 - p91(1) [51-500]

Coldren, James R. - *Patuxent Institution: An American Experiment in Corrections*
    R&R Bk N - v19 - i4 - Nov 2004 - p149(1) [501+]

Coldsmith, Don - *Pipestone Quest*
    Roundup M - v12 - i1 - Oct 2004 - p29(1) [51-500]

Coldstream, John - *Dirk Bogarde: The Authorised Biography*
    Globe & Mail - Feb 26 2005 - pD13 [51-500]
    NS - v133 - i4708 - Oct 4 2004 - p51(2) [501+]
    TimHES - v0 - i1684 - March 25 2005 - p24(1) [501+]
    TLS - i5303 - Nov 19 2004 - p14-15 [501+]

Cole, Andrew J. - *Comprehensive Aquatic Therapy. 2nd Ed.*
    SciTech - v28 - i1 - March 2004 - p123(1) [51-500]

Cole, Babette - *Princess Smartypants Rules*
    c KR - v73 - i3 - Feb 1 2005 - p175(1) [51-500]
    c PW - v252 - i6 - Feb 7 2005 - p61(2) [501+]
    Truelove (Illus. by Cole, Babette)
    c RT - v57 - Oct 2003 - p172 [1-50]

Cole, Barbara H. - *Wash Day (Illus. by Himler, Ronald)*
    c BL - v101 - i1 - Sept 1 2004 - p130(1) [1-50]
    c CH Bwatch - v14 - i8 - August 2004 - p8(1) [51-500]
    c SLJ - v50 - i10 - Oct 2004 - p110(1) [51-500]

Cole, Benjamin Mark - *The New Investor Relations: Expert Perspectives on the State of the Art*
    R&R Bk N - v19 - i3 - August 2004 - p113(1) [51-500]

Cole, Brock - *Fair Monaco (Illus. by Cole, Brock)*
    c BL - v101 - i5 - Nov 1 2004 - p488(1) [51-500]
    c CCB-B - v58 - i3 - Nov 2004 - p117(1) [501+]
    c KR - v72 - i18 - Sept 15 2004 - p912(1) [501+]
    c PW - v251 - i42 - Oct 18 2004 - p62(1) [51-500]
    c SLJ - v51 - i1 - Jan 2005 - p88(2) [51-500]

Cole, Daniel J. - *Adult Perioperative Anesthesia: The Requisites in Anesthesiology*
    SciTech - v28 - i3 - Sept 2004 - p110(1) [51-500]

Cole, David John - *Encyclopedia of Modern Everyday Inventions*
    LibMed - v22 - i4 - Jan 2004 - p80(1) [501+]

Cole, Donald B. - *A Jackson Man: Amos Kendall and the Rise of American Democracy*
    Choice - v42 - i6 - Feb 2005 - p1080(2) [51-500]

Cole, Edwina - *Walk in Their Shoes*
    Sch Lib - v52 - i3 - Autumn 2004 - p167(1) [501+]

Cole, Henri - *Middle Earth*
    Poet - v184 - i5 - Sept 2004 - p375(3) [501+]

Cole, James H. - *Twentieth-Century China: An Annotated Bibliography of Reference Works in Chinese, Japanese, and Western Languages*
    Choice - v42 - i2 - Oct 2004 - p277(1) [501+]

Cole, Jim - *E-Serials Cataloging: Access to Continuing and Integrating Resources via the Catalog and the Web*
    LRTS - v48 - i4 - Oct 2004 - p305(2) [501+]

Cole, Joanna - *Ms. Frizzle's Adventures: Medieval Castle (Illus. by Degen, Bruce)*
    c CH Bwatch - v14 - i7 - July 2004 - p4(2) [51-500]
    c LibMed - v22 - i6 - March 2004 - p78(1) [501+]
    Sharing Is Fun (Illus. by Chambliss, Maxie)
    c PW - v251 - i34 - August 23 2004 - p56(2) [501+]
    c SLJ - v50 - i8 - August 2004 - p85(1) [51-500]

Cole, John Y. - *The Encyclopedia of the Library of Congress: For Congress, the Nation & the World*
    LJ - v129 - i20 - Dec 1 2004 - p174(1) [51-500]

Cole, Jonathan - *Still Lives: Narratives of Spinal Cord Injury*
    SB - v40 - i4 - July-August 2004 - p156(1) [51-500]
    TLS - i5293 - Sept 10 2004 - p26(1) [501+]

Cole, Juan - *Sacred Space and Holy War: The Politics, Culture and History of Shi'ite Islam*
    Globe & Mail - Feb 26 2005 - pD15 [501+]
    IJMES - v36 - i4 - Nov 2004 - p690(3) [501+]

Cole, Kenneth - *Footnotes*
    Esq - v140 - i3 - Sept 2003 - p66 [51-500]

Cole, Michael D. - *The Columbia Space Shuttle Disaster from First Liftoff to Tragic Final Flight*
    c LibMed - v22 - i5 - Feb 2004 - p55(1) [501+]
    Comets and Asteroids: Ice and Rocks in Space
    c LibMed - v22 - i5 - Feb 2004 - p55(1) [501+]

Cole, Peter H. - *Mastering the Financial Dimension of Your Practice: The Definitive Resource for Private Practice Development and Financial Planning*
    SciTech - v28 - i4 - Dec 2004 - p96(1) [51-500]

Cole, Robert - *A Traveller's History of Germany*
    R&R Bk N - v19 - i4 - Nov 2004 - p38(1) [51-500]

Cole, Stephen (b. 1941 -) - *Increasing Faculty Diversity: The Occupational Choices of High-Achieving Minority Students*
    JEL - v42 - i1 - March 2004 - p197(2) [501+]

Cole, Stephen (b. 1971 -) - *Prey*
    y Sch Lib - v52 - i4 - Winter 2004 - p212(1) [51-500]

Cole, Susan Guettel - *Landscapes, Gender, and Ritual Space: The Ancient Greek Experience*
    Choice - v42 - i3 - Nov 2004 - p498(1) [1-50]

Cole, Terry W. - *Communication Law: Cases and Materials*
    R&R Bk N - v19 - i3 - August 2004 - p203(1) [1-50]

Cole, Tim - *Holocaust City: The Making of a Jewish Ghetto*
    AHR - v109 - i3 - June 2004 - p999(2) [501+]
    CS - v33 - i6 - Nov 2004 - p712(2) [501+]

Cole, Trevor - *Norman Bray in the Performance of His Life*
    BIC - v33 - i9 - Dec 2004 - p6(2) [501+]
    Globe & Mail - Nov 27 2004 - pD3 [51-500]
    Globe & Mail - Jan 29 2005 - pD13 [1-50]

Colebatch, Hal - *Man-Kzin Wars X: The Wunder War*
    Quad - v48 - i12 - Dec 2004 - p90(2) [501+]

Coleborne, Catharine - *Madness in Australia: Histories, Heritage and the Asylum*
    AHS - v35 - i124 - Oct 2004 - p397(3) [501+]

Colegate, Isabel - *A Pelican in the Wilderness: Hermits, Solitaries and Recluses*
    Parabola - v29 - i2 - Summer 2004 - p114-117 [501+]

Coleman, Anne - *I'll Tell You a Secret: A Memory of Seven Summers*
    Globe & Mail - Sept 4 2004 - pD3 [501+]
    Globe & Mail - Nov 27 2004 - pD3 [51-500]
    Globe & Mail - Dec 24 2004 - pD3 [1-50]

Coleman, Brian - *Classic Cottages: Simple, Romantic Homes*
    R&R Bk N - v19 - i3 - August 2004 - p242(1) [51-500]

Coleman, Carter - *Cage's Bend*
    BL - v101 - i5 - Nov 1 2004 - p462(1) [51-500]
    KR - v72 - i23 - Dec 1 2004 - p1102(2) [51-500]
    PW - v251 - i42 - Oct 18 2004 - p45(2) [51-500]
    People - v63 - i3 - Jan 24 2005 - p52(1) [51-500]

Coleman, Christopher - *An Introduction to Radio Frequency Engineering*
    Choice - v42 - i5 - Jan 2005 - p883(1) [1-50]

Coleman, Daniel - *Scent of Eucalyptus*
    CBRA - Annual 2003 - p41(1) [51-500]

Coleman, David - *Creating Christian Granada: Society & Religious Culture in an Old-World Frontier City, 1492-1600*
    CHR - v90 - i3 - July 2004 - p541(3) [501+]

Coleman, Jane Candia - *Tombstone Travesty: Allie Earp Remembers*
    Roundup M - v12 - i3 - Feb 2005 - p26(1) [51-500]

Coleman, Jon T. - *Vicious: Wolves and Men in America*
    Atl - v294 - i2 - Sept 2004 - p121(2) [501+]
    BL - v101 - i2 - Sept 15 2004 - p186(2) [51-500]
    LJ - v129 - i14 - Sept 1 2004 - p183(1) [51-500]

Coleman, Larry - *Dictionary of Physics*
    E-Streams - Dec 2004 - pNA [501+]

Coleman, Loren - *The Copycat Effect: How the Media and Popular Culture Trigger the Mayhem in Tomorrow's Headlines*
    KR - v72 - i14 - July 15 2004 - p669(1) [501+]
    LJ - v129 - i16 - Oct 1 2004 - p91(1) [51-500]

Coleman, Mark - *Playback; From the Victrola to MP3, 100 Years of Music, Machines, and Money*
    R&R Bk N - v19 - i2 - May 2004 - p192(1) [51-500]

Coleman, Michael - *On the Run*
    y VOYA - v27 - i3 - August 2004 - p210(1) [1-50]

Coleman, Monica A. - *The Dinah Project: A Handbook for Congregational Response to Sexual Violence*
    Black Iss - v6 - i5 - Sept-Oct 2004 - p37(2) [501+]

Coleman, Reed Farrel - *The James Deans: A Moe Prager Mystery*
    PW - v251 - i46 - Nov 15 2004 - p44(1) [51-500]

Coleman, Simon - *The Cultures of Creationism: Anti-Evolution in English-Speaking Countries*
    New Sci - v183 - i2456 - July 17 2004 - p47(1) [501+]
    R&R Bk N - v19 - i4 - Nov 2004 - p21(1) [51-500]
    Religion, Identity, and Change: Perspectives on Global Transformations
    R&R Bk N - v19 - i3 - August 2004 - p13(1) [1-50]

Coleman, Stephen - *The e-Connected World: Risks and Opportunities*
    PSQ - v119 - i2 - Summer 2004 - p392(4) [501+]

Coleman, Wanda - *Ostinato Vamps*
    Black Iss - v6 - i6 - Nov-Dec 2004 - p46(1) [51-500]

Coleman, Will - *Tribal Talk: Black Theology, Hermeneutics, and African/American Ways of "Telling the Story"*
    TT - v60 - i4 - Jan 2004 - p566-568 [501+]

Coleman, William Oliver - *Economics and Its Enemies: Two Centuries of Anti-Economics*
    JEL - v41 - i4 - Dec 2003 - p1275(2) [501+]

Coles, Don - *Doctor Bloom's Story: A Novel 1st Ed.*
    Globe & Mail - Nov 27 2004 - pD3 [51-500]
    Doctor Bloom's Story: A Novel
    BIC - v33 - i5 - August 2004 - p03(1) [501+]
    Doctor Bloom's Story: A Novel. Audiobook Review
    Globe & Mail - Jan 8 2005 - pD13 [1-50]

Coles, Gerald - *Reading the Naked Truth: Literacy, Legislation, and Lies*
    TCR - v106 - i5 - May 2004 - p961(4) [501+]

Coles, Robert - *Bruce Springsteen's America: The People Listening, a Poet Singing*
    RAH - v32 - i2 - June 2004 - p274-281 [501+]
    Teaching Stories: An Anthology on the Power of Learning and Literature
    BL - v101 - i2 - Sept 15 2004 - p195(1) [501+]
    LJ - v129 - i18 - Nov 1 2004 - p83(1) [501+]

Coles, Tim - *Isolation Technology: A Practical Guide. 2nd Ed.*
    SciTech - v28 - i3 - Sept 2004 - p124(1) [51-500]

Coles, Tim Edward - *Tourism, Diasporas, and Space*
R&R Bk N - v19 - i4 - Nov 2004 - p72(1) [51-500]

Coletti, Theresa - *Mary Magdalene and the Drama of Saints: Theater, Gender, and Religion in Late Medieval England*
Choice - v42 - i6 - Feb 2005 - p1021(1) [51-500]

Colfer, Billy - *The Hoof Peninsula, County Wexford*
ILS - v24 - i1 - Fall 2004 - p32(1) [51-500]

Colfer, Eoin - *Artemis Fowl (Read by Parker, Nathaniel). Audiobook Review*
c BL - v101 - i1 - Sept 1 2004 - p148(1) [51-500]
c HB - v80 - i4 - July-August 2004 - p474(1) [51-500]
y Kliatt - v39 - i1 - Jan 2005 - p37(2) [501+]
c SLJ - v50 - i11 - Nov 2004 - p80(1) [51-500]
Artemis Fowl
y Analog - v124 - i6 - June 2004 - p132(6) [501+]
The Artemis Fowl Files
y PW - v251 - i42 - Oct 18 2004 - p66(1) [501+]
SLJ - v50 - i12 - Dec 2004 - p144(1) [501+]
Artemis Fowl: The Arctic Incident (Read by Parker, Nathaniel). Audiobook Review
y Kliatt - v39 - i1 - Jan 2005 - p37(2) [501+]
Artemis Fowl: The Eternity Code (Read by Parker, Nathaniel). Audiobook Review
y Kliatt - v39 - i1 - Jan 2005 - p37(2) [501+]
Artemis Fowl: The Eternity Code
y Kliatt - v38 - i5 - Sept 2004 - p27(2) [51-500]
The Legend of Spud Murphy (Illus. by McCoy, Glenn)
c KR - v72 - i16 - August 15 2004 - p803(1) [51-500]
c PW - v251 - i37 - Sept 13 2004 - p79(1) [51-500]
c SLJ - v50 - i10 - Oct 2004 - p110(2) [51-500]
The Supernaturalist (Read by Ejiofor, Chiwetel). Audiobook Review
y Kliatt - v39 - i1 - Jan 2005 - p50(1) [51-500]
The Supernaturalist (Read by Davenport, Jack). Audiobook Review
y Magpies - v19 - i5 - Nov 2004 - p43(1) [501+]
The Supernaturalist
y BL - v100 - i22 - August 2004 - p1918(1) [51-500]
y CCB-B - v58 - i1 - Sept 2004 - p10(2) [51-500]
c CH Bwatch - v14 - i7 - July 2004 - p6(2) [51-500]
c LibMed - v23 - i3 - Nov-Dec 2004 - p69(2) [51-500]
y Magpies - v19 - i5 - Nov 2004 - p33(2) [501+]
y Sch Lib - v52 - i4 - Winter 2004 - p214(1) [51-500]
c SLJ - v50 - i7 - July 2004 - p102(1) [51-500]
y VOYA - v27 - i3 - August 2004 - p227(1) [1-50]
The Wish List (Read by Wilby, James). Audiobook Review
y Magpies - v19 - i5 - Nov 2004 - p42(1) [501+]
SLJ - v50 - i10 - Oct 2004 - pS68(1) [51-500]
The Wish List
y Kliatt - v38 - i5 - Sept 2004 - p27(2) [51-500]

Colgan, Jenny - *The Boy I Loved Before*
Ent W - i809 - March 4 2005 - p77 [501+]
KR - v73 - i1 - Jan 1 2005 - p6(1) [51-500]
PW - v252 - i8 - Feb 21 2005 - p157(1) [51-500]

Colignon, Richard A. - *Amakudari: The Hidden Fabric of Japan's Economy*
CS - v33 - i4 - July 2004 - p474(3) [501+]
JEL - v41 - i4 - Dec 2003 - p1342(1) [501+]

Colin, Chris - *What Really Happened to the Class of '93: Start-ups, Dropouts, and Other Navigations through an Untidy Decade*
y SLJ - v50 - i7 - July 2004 - p133(1) [51-500]

Colin, F. - *Les peuples libyens de la Cyrenaique a l'Egypte: d'apres les sources de l'Antiquite classique*
Class R - v53 - i2 - Nov 2003 - p437-438 [501+]

Coll, Steve - *Ghost Wars: The Secret History of the CIA, Afghanistan, and bin Laden, from the Soviet Invasion to September 10, 2001*
Choice - v42 - i2 - Oct 2004 - p346(1) [51-500]
For Aff - v83 - i5 - Sept-Oct 2004 - p164 [501+]
Globe & Mail - Nov 27 2004 - pD3 [51-500]
Lon R Bks - v26 - i20 - Oct 21 2004 - p25(4) [501+]

Coll, Susan - *Rockville Pike: A Suburban Comedy of Manners*
BL - v101 - i9-10 - Jan 1 2005 - p813(1) [1-50]
People - v63 - i2 - Jan 17 2005 - p61 [51-500]
PW - v251 - i50 - Dec 13 2004 - p46(1) [51-500]

Collard, Sneed B. - *Beaks! (Illus. by Brickman, Robin)*
c RT - v57 - Nov 2003 - p272 [51-500]

Colle, Enrico - *Il Mobile Rococo in Italia. Arredi e decorazioni d'interni dal 1738 al 1775*
Apo - v159 - i509 - July 2004 - p68(3) [501+]

The Collector of Bedford Street
LibMed - v22 - i6 - March 2004 - p92(1) [501+]

College of Business - *International Journal of Business and Economics*
JEL - v41 - i4 - Dec 2003 - p1446(2) [501+]

Colley, Ann C. - *Robert Louis Stevenson and the Colonial Imagination*
Choice - v42 - i7 - March 2005 - p1226(2) [51-500]
R&R Bk N - v19 - i4 - Nov 2004 - p237(1) [501+]

Colley, Barbara - *Wiped Out: A Charlotte LaRue Mystery*
KR - v72 - i23 - Dec 1 2004 - p1118(1) [51-500]
LJ - v130 - i2 - Feb 1 2005 - p57(1) [1-50]
PW - v252 - i4 - Jan 24 2005 - p226(1) [51-500]

Colley, David P. - *Safely Rest*
LJ - v129 - i19 - Nov 15 2004 - p69(2) [501+]
PW - v251 - i44 - Nov 1 2004 - p55(2) [501+]

Colli, Andrea - *The History of Family Business, 1850-2000*
BHR - v78 - i1 - Spring 2004 - p172(4) [501+]

Collicutt, Paul - *This Truck (Illus. by Collicutt, Paul)*
c SLJ - v50 - i7 - July 2004 - p92(1) [51-500]

Collie, Michael - *Murchison's Wanderings in Russia*
Nature - v430 - i7001 - August 12 2004 - p728(2) [501+]

Collier, Christopher - *All Politics Is Local: Family, Friends, and Provincial Interests in the Creation of the Constitution*
Choice - v41 - i11-12 - July-August 2004 - p2105(1) [501+]
JAH - v91 - i3 - Dec 2004 - p996(2) [501+]
W&M Q - v61 - i3 - July 2004 - p578-581 [501+]

Collier, Gaydell M. - *Crazy Woman Creek: Women Rewrite the American West*
Roundup M - v11 - i6 - August 2004 - p24(2) [501+]

Collier, James Lincoln - *The Empty Mirror*
c BL - v101 - i4 - Oct 15 2004 - p403(1) [51-500]
c CCB-B - v58 - i2 - Oct 2004 - p64(2) [51-500]
y CH Bwatch - v14 - i11 - Nov 2004 - pNA [51-500]
c KR - v72 - i16 - August 15 2004 - p803(1) [51-500]
y SLJ - v50 - i10 - Oct 2004 - p159(2) [51-500]
y VOYA - v27 - i5 - Dec 2004 - p400(1) [51-500]
Me and Billy
y BL - v101 - i2 - Sept 15 2004 - p231(1) [51-500]
KR - v72 - i18 - Sept 15 2004 - p912(1) [51-500]
y SLJ - v51 - i1 - Jan 2005 - p126(1) [51-500]
The Sitting Bull You Never Knew
LibMed - v22 - i6 - March 2004 - p75(1) [501+]
LibMed - v22 - i6 - March 2004 - p75(1) [501+]
Vaccines
Sci Teach - v71 - i6 - July 2004 - p64-64 [501+]

Collier, Marsha - *eBay for Dummies, 4th Ed.*
Bwatch - March 2005 - pNA [51-500]
LJ - v129 - i14 - Sept 1 2004 - p182(1) [501+]
eBay Timesaving Techniques for Dummies
LJ - v129 - i14 - Sept 1 2004 - p182(1) [501+]

Collier, Michael - *The Ledge*
Sew R - v111 - i3 - Summer 2003 - p470-479 [501+]

Collier, Paul - *Breaking the Conflict Trap: Civil War and Development Policy*
JEL - v41 - i4 - Dec 2003 - p1342(2) [501+]
R&R Bk N - v19 - i1 - Feb 2004 - p80(1) [501+]

Collier, Peter - *The Anti-Chomsky Reader*
R&R Bk N - v19 - i4 - Nov 2004 - p211(1) [501+]
The Fords: An American Epic
Atl - v294 - i5 - Dec 2004 - p137(1) [501+]

Collier, Simon - *Chile: The Making of a Republic, 1830-1865: Politics and Ideas*
HAHR - v84 - i4 - Nov 2004 - p768(3) [501+]

Collier, T.O., Jr. - *Supervisor's Guide to Labor Relations*
HR Mag - v49 - i12 - Dec 2004 - p59(1) [501+]

Colligan, Mimi - *Canvas Documentaries: Panoramic Entertainments in Nineteenth-Century Australia and New Zealand*
AHS - v35 - i123 - April 2004 - p188-189 [501+]

Colling, Herb - *Turning Points: The Detroit Riot of 1967, a Canadian Perspective*
CBRA - Annual 2003 - p283(1) [501+]

Collins, Aileen - *Eternal Conversations: Remember Louis Dudek*
CBRA - Annual 2003 - p245(1) [501+]

Collins, Amy Fine - *The God of Driving: How I Overcame Fear and Put Myself in the Driver's Seat*
NYTBR - Oct 3 2004 - p29 [501+]
The God of Driving: How I Overcame Fear and Put Myself in the Driver's Seat with the Help of a Good and Mysterious Man
BL - v100 - i22 - August 2004 - p1884(2) [51-500]
PW - v251 - i27 - July 5 2004 - p46(1) [51-500]

Collins, Billy - *The Art of Drowning*
BW - v34 - i5 - Feb 1 2004 - p12(1) [501+]

Collins, Bradley - *Van Gogh and Gauguin: Electric Arguments and Utopian Dreams*
R&R Bk N - v19 - i2 - May 2004 - p196(1) [51-500]

Collins, Brandilyn - *Stain of Guilt*
LJ - v129 - i18 - Nov 1 2004 - p70(1) [501+]

Collins, Gail - *America's Women: Four Hundred Years of Dolls, Drudges, Helpmates, and Heroines*
NYTBR - Sept 26 2004 - p28 [501+]

Collins-Gates, Carolyn - *Medical Transcriptionist's Desk Reference*
E-Streams - June 2004 - pNA [501+]

Collins, Gregory B. - *Mental Illness and Psychiatric Treatment: A Guide for Pastoral Counselors*
R&R Bk N - v19 - i1 - Feb 2004 - p23(1) [1-50]

Collins, Harry - *Gravity's Shadow: The Search for Gravitational Waves*
New Sci - v184 - i2469 - Oct 16 2004 - p52(1) [501+]
TimHES - v0 - i1681 - March 4 2005 - p30(1) [501+]

Collins, Heather - *Hey Diddle Diddle*
c CBRA - Annual 2003 - p528(1) [51-500]
Jack and Jill
c CBRA - Annual 2003 - p528(1) [51-500]
Little Miss Muffet
c CBRA - Annual 2003 - p528(1) [51-500]
Pat-a-Cake
c CBRA - Annual 2003 - p528(1) [51-500]

Collins, Helen - *Edward Jerman, 1605-1668: The Metamorphosis of a Master-Craftsman*
TLS - i5285 - July 16 2004 - p29(1) [501+]

Collins, John J. - *Does the Bible Justify Violence*
Intpr - v58 - i4 - Oct 2004 - p439(1) [501+]

Collins, John W., III - *The Greenwood Dictionary of Education*
Ref Rev - May 2004 - pNA [501+]
R&R Bk N - v19 - i1 - Feb 2004 - pNA [51-500]

Collins, Julia - *My Father's War: A Memoir*
Sew R - v112 - i1 - Wntr 2004 - pXIV-XVI [501+]

Collins, Kathleen - *Jesse James: Western Bank Robber*
c BL - v101 - i2 - Sept 15 2004 - p238(1) [51-500]
c SLJ - v50 - i12 - Dec 2004 - p126(1) [51-500]

Collins, Kaye Carver - *Angle and Foxfire Students*
Kliatt - v38 - i6 - Nov 2004 - p36(1) [51-500]
Foxfire 12
PW - v251 - i35 - August 30 2004 - p45(1) [51-500]

Collins, Larry - *The Road to Armageddon (Read by Brick, Scott). Audiobook Review*
c Kliatt - v38 - i4 - July 2004 - p55(1) [51-500]

Collins, Laura - *Eating with Your Anorexic: How My Child Recovered through Family-Based Treatment and Yours Can Too*
LJ - v130 - i2 - Feb 1 2005 - p103(1) [501+]

Collins, Lowery - *The Fattening Hut*
y LibMed - v22 - i6 - March 2004 - p66(1) [501+]

Collins, M. - *Design and Nature II: Comparing Design in Nature with Science and Engineering: Proceedings*
SciTech - v28 - i4 - Dec 2004 - p132 [51-500]

Collins, M.W. - *Optimisation Mechanics in Nature*
SciTech - v28 - i3 - Sept 2004 - p141(1) [51-500]
Wall-Fluid Interactions in Physiological Flows
SciTech - v28 - i3 - Sept 2004 - p68(1) [51-500]

Collins, Martin J. - *Cold War Laboratory: RAND, the Air Force, and the American State 1945-1950*
T&C - v45 - i4 - Oct 2004 - p886(3) [501+]

Collins, Max Allan - *CSI: Crime Scene Investigation: Bad Rap*
y Teach Lib - v32 - i1 - Oct 2004 - p17(2) [501+]
Dick Tracy: The Collins Casefiles. Vol. 2
BL - v100 - i22 - August 2004 - p1915(1) [501+]
On the Road to Perdition: Detour
BL - v101 - i1 - Sept 1 2004 - p76(2) [501+]
Road to Purgatory
BL - v101 - i7 - Dec 1 2004 - p638(1) [51-500]
Ent W - i794 - Nov 26 2004 - p125 [501+]
KR - v72 - i21 - Nov 1 2004 - p1021(1) [501+]
LJ - v130 - i1 - Jan 1 2005 - p95(1) [51-500]
PW - v251 - i47 - Nov 22 2004 - p39(1) [51-500]

Collins, Michael (b. 1960 -) - *The Fisherman's Net: The Influence of the Popes on History*
CI - v12 - i10 - Nov 2004 - p28(1) [51-500]

Collins, Michael (b. 1964 -) - *The Likes of Us: A Biography of the White Working Class*
NS - v133 - i4702 - August 23 2004 - p36(2) [501+]
Spec - v295 - i9181 - July 24 2004 - p34(2) [501+]
TLS - i5293 - Sept 10 2004 - p24(1) [501+]

Collins, Michael (b. 1964 -) - *Lost Souls*
BL - v100 - i21 - July 2004 - p1824(1) [1-50]
Ent W - i779 - August 20 2004 - p131 [51-500]
PW - v251 - i30 - July 26 2004 - p40(1) [501+]

Collins, Michael J. - *Hot Lights, Cold Steel: Life, Death and Sleepless Nights in a Surgeon's First Year*
BL - v101 - i7 - Dec 1 2004 - p625(1) [51-500]
LJ - v129 - i19 - Nov 15 2004 - p79(2) [501+]
PW - v251 - i49 - Dec 6 2004 - p52(1) [51-500]
Hot Lights, Cold Steel: Life, Death and Sleepness Nights in a Surgeon's First Year
KR - v72 - i21 - Nov 1 2004 - p1034(2) [501+]

Collins, Natalie R. - *Wives and Sisters*
KR - v72 - i16 - August 15 2004 - p759(1) [501+]

Collins, Patricia Hill - *Black Sexual Politics: African Americans, Gender, and the New Racism*
Choice - v42 - i6 - Feb 2005 - p1103(1) [51-500]

Collins, Paul - *Not Even Wrong: Adventures in Autism*
TLS - i5291 - August 27 2004 - p10-11 [501+]

Collins, Peter - *Concrete: The Vision of a New Architecture, 2nd Ed.*
R&R Bk N - v19 - i3 - August 2004 - p241(1) [51-500]

Collins, Randall - *Interaction Ritual Chains*
CC - v121 - i15 - July 27 2004 - p38(2) [501+]
Choice - v42 - i2 - Oct 2004 - p376(1) [51-500]

Collins, Raymond E. - *I & II Timothy and Titus: A Commentary*
Intpr - v59 - i1 - Jan 2005 - p74(2) [501+]

Collins, Raymond F. - *I & II Timothy and Titus: A Commentary*
TT - v61 - i1 - April 2004 - p97-98 [501+]
The Many Faces of the Church A Study in New Testament Ecclesiology
AM - v191 - i4 - August 16 2004 - p24 [501+]

Collins, Robert - *Prairie People: A Celebration of My Homeland*
CBRA - Annual 2003 - p337(2) [51-500]

Collins, Roger - *Visigothic Spain, 409-711*
Choice - v42 - i5 - Jan 2005 - p922(1) [1-50]

Collins, Ross - *Germs*
c KR - v72 - i20 - Oct 15 2004 - p1003(1) [51-500]
c PW - v251 - i50 - Dec 13 2004 - p67(1) [51-500]
c SLJ - v51 - i2 - Feb 2005 - p96(1) [51-500]

Collins, Sally - *Border, Bindings & Edges*
Bwatch - v26 - i7 - July 2004 - p7(1) [51-500]

Collins, Sarah - *The Foundation Center's Guide to Winning Proposals*
R&R Bk N - v19 - i3 - August 2004 - p159(1) [51-500]

Collins, Scott - *Crazy Like a Fox: The Inside Story of How Fox News Beat CNN*
Choice - v42 - i4 - Dec 2004 - p654(1) [1-50]
CJR - v43 - i2 - July-August 2004 - p56(1) [51-500]
TV Q - v35 - i1 - Fall 2004 - p74(3) [501+]

Collins-Sussman, Ben - *Version Control with Subversion*
SciTech - v28 - i3 - Sept 2004 - p173(1) [51-500]

Collins, Suzanne - *Gregor and the Prophecy of Bane*
c BL - v101 - i1 - Sept 1 2004 - p120(1) [1-50]
c CCB-B - v58 - i2 - Oct 2004 - p65(1) [51-500]
c HB - v80 - i5 - Sept-Oct 2004 - p578(1) [51-500]
y KR - v72 - i15 - August 1 2004 - p739(1) [51-500]
y SLJ - v50 - i10 - Oct 2004 - p160(1) [51-500]
c VOYA - v27 - i5 - Dec 2004 - p402(1) [51-500]
Gregor the Overlander
c BL - v101 - i6 - Nov 15 2004 - p599(1) [501+]

Collins, Wilkie - *Sensation Stories*
LJ - v129 - i16 - Oct 1 2004 - p121(1) [1-50]

Collinson, Patrick - *The Reformation*
BL - v101 - i4 - Oct 15 2004 - p364(2) [51-500]
NYTBR - Dec 5 2004 - p70 [501+]
Ren Q - v57 - i4 - Winter 2004 - p1482(2) [501+]
Six Ct J - v35 - i3 - Fall 2004 - p953-954 [501+]

Collinwood, Dean W. - *Samurais in Salt Lake: Diary of the First Diplomatic Japanese Delegation to Visit Utah, 1872*
HNet - August 2004 - pNA [501+]

Collodi, Carlo - *Pinocchio (Illus. by Fanelli, Sara)*
c SLJ - v50 - i10 - Oct 2004 - pS50(1) [1-50]

Colls, Robert - *Cities of Ideas: Civil Society and Urban Governance in Britain 1800-2000, Essays in Honour of David Reader (i.e. Reeder).*
R&R Bk N - v19 - i3 - August 2004 - p155(1) [51-500]

Collste, Goran - *Is Human Life Special?: Religious and Philosophical Perspectives on the Principle of Human Dignity*
R&R Bk N - v19 - i1 - Feb 2004 - p7(1) [51-500]

Collum, Jason Paul - *Assault of the Killer B's: Interviews with 20 Cult Film Actresses*
R&R Bk N - v19 - i4 - Nov 2004 - p225(1) [501+]

Collyn, Joan - *Misfortune's Daughters*
PW - v252 - i7 - Feb 14 2005 - p55(1) [51-500]

Colmes, Alan - *Red, White & Liberal: How Left Is Right & Right Is Wrong*
R&R Bk N - v19 - i1 - Feb 2004 - p149(1) [51-500]

Colnett, James - *Earthbound and Heavenbent: The Life of Elizabeth Porter Phelps and the Life at Forty Acres, 1747-1817*
Choice - v42 - i3 - Nov 2004 - p545(1) [1-50]
A Voyage to the North West Side of America: The Journals of James Colnett, 1786-89
Choice - v42 - i3 - Nov 2004 - p545(1) [1-50]

Coloma, German - *Defensa de la Competencia: Analisis Economico Comparado*
JEL - v42 - i1 - March 2004 - p288(1) [501+]

Colombo, John Robert - *The Monster Book of Canadian Monsters*
Globe & Mail - July 17 2004 - pD14 [1-50]
Penguin Book of More Canadian Jokes
CBRA - Annual 2003 - p83(1) [51-500]

Colon, Raul - *Orson Blasts Off!*
c Sch Lib - v52 - i3 - Autumn 2004 - p130(1) [501+]

Colonial America
c LibMed - v23 - i3 - Nov-Dec 2004 - p81(1) [51-500]

Colonnello, A. - *Uno Storico, Un mugnaio un Libro: Carlo Ginzburg, 'll Formaggio e i Vermi, 1976-2002*
HER - v119 - i483 - Sept 2004 - p1056(2) [501+]

Color Correction for Avid Xpress DV 3.5
SciTech - v28 - i3 - Sept 2004 - p169(1) [51-500]

Coloroso, Barbara - *Bully, the Bullied, and the Bystander*
CBRA - Annual 2003 - p393(1) [501+]

Colpitts, George - *Game in the Garden: A Human History of Wildlife in Western Canada to 1940*
CBRA - Annual 2003 - p273(1) [51-500]
Hist Geo - v32 - Annual 2004 - p215(2) [501+]
WHQ - v35 - i4 - Winter 2004 - p533-534 [501+]

Colson, Charles W. - *Human Dignity in the Biotech Century: A Christian Vision for Public Policy*
PW - v251 - i28 - July 12 2004 - p61(1) [51-500]

Coltman, Leycester - *The Real Fidel Castro*
Lon R Bks - v26 - i16 - August 19 2004 - p24(2) [501+]

Colton, Kent W. - *Housing in the Twenty-First Century: Achieving Common Ground*
JEL - v41 - i4 - Dec 2003 - p1440(1) [501+]
Soc Ser R - v78 - i3 - Sept 2004 - p508(3) [501+]

Coluccia, Pina - *Belly Dancing: The Sensual Art of Energy and Spirit*
LJ - v130 - i4 - March 1 2005 - p87(1) [51-500]

Columbia American History Online
LibMed - v22 - i4 - Jan 2004 - p88(1) [501+]

Columbia Gazetteer of the World Online
LJ - v129 - i16 - Oct 1 2004 - p109(1) [51-500]

Colville, John - *The Fringes of Power: Downing Street Diaries 1939-1955*
CR - v286 - i1668 - Jan 2005 - p63(1) [51-500]

Colvin, Sarah - *Women and German Drama: Playwrights and Their Texts, 1860-1945*
GSR - v27 - i2 - May 2004 - p372-374 [501+]

Colyar, Margaret R. - *Ambulatory Care Procedures for the Nurse Practitioner, 2nd Ed.*
E-Streams - Sept 2004 - pNA [501+]
SciTech - v28 - i1 - March 2004 - p126(1) [51-500]

Coman, Carolyn - *The Big House (Illus. by Shepperson, Rob)*
c BL - v101 - i2 - Sept 15 2004 - p242(1) [51-500]
c CCB-B - v58 - i2 - Oct 2004 - p65(2) [51-500]
y HB - v81 - i1 - Jan-Feb 2005 - p91(1) [51-500]
c KR - v72 - i17 - Sept 1 2004 - p862(1) [51-500]
c PW - v251 - i36 - Sept 6 2004 - p63(1) [51-500]
c SLJ - v50 - i11 - Nov 2004 - p138(1) [51-500]

Comaneci, Nadia - *Letters to a Young Gymnast*
Globe & Mail - August 14 2004 - pD15 [501+]
R&R Bk N - v19 - i3 - August 2004 - p87(1) [51-500]
TLS - i5286 - July 23 2004 - p24-25 [501+]

Combating Child Labour: A Review of Policies
JEL - v42 - i1 - March 2004 - p284(1) [501+]

Combettes, Bernard - *Evolution et variation en francais preclassique: etudes de syntaxe*
FS - v58 - i2 - April 2004 - p298(2) [501+]

Combi, Carlo - *Temporal Representation and Reasoning (TIME 2004): Proceedings*
SciTech - v28 - i3 - Sept 2004 - p15(1) [501+]

Combs, Allan - *Mind in Time: The Dynamics of Thought, Reality, and Consciousness*
R&R Bk N - v19 - i1 - Feb 2004 - p6(1) [51-500]

Combs, Diedre - *Way of Conflict*
Bwatch - v26 - i8 - August 2004 - p1(1) [51-500]

Comden, Betty - *The House on Beartown Road (Read by Dunne, Bernadette). Audiobook Review*
y Kliatt - v38 - i5 - Sept 2004 - p68(2) [51-500]

Come and Make a Circle: 20 Terrific Tunes for Kids and Teachers
BL - v100 - i21 - July 2004 - p1856(1) [1-50]

Come On Rain!
LibMed - v22 - i4 - Jan 2004 - p91(1) [501+]

Comer, James P. - *Leave No Child Behind: Preparing Today's Youth for Tomorrow's World*
BL - v101 - i1 - Sept 1 2004 - p26(2) [51-500]
BW - v34 - i38 - Sept 19 2004 - p13(1) [501+]
Choice - v42 - i6 - Feb 2005 - p1072(1) [51-500]
LJ - v129 - i18 - Nov 1 2004 - p99(1) [51-500]
NYT - Nov 7 2004 - p10 [501+]

Comer, Michael J. - *An HR Guide to Workplace Fraud and Criminal Behaviour: Recognition, Prevention, and Management*
R&R Bk N - v19 - i3 - August 2004 - p166(1) [501+]

Comer, Ronald J. - *Abnormal Psychology, 5th Ed.*
SciTech - v28 - i4 - Dec 2004 - p95(1) [51-500]

Comer, Sheree - *Delmar's Critical Care Nursing Care Plans, 2nd Ed.*
SciTech - v28 - i4 - Dec 2004 - p122 [51-500]

Cometti, J.-P. - *Questions D'Esthetique*
JAAC - v61 - Winter 2003 - p91 [501+]

Comey, Henry Newton - *A Legacy of Valor: The Memoirs and Letters of Captain Henry Newton Comey, 2nd Massachusetts Infantry*
R&R Bk N - v19 - i3 - August 2004 - p68(1) [51-500]

Coming Home: American Paintings 1930-1950, from the Schoen Collection
R&R Bk N - v19 - i1 - Feb 2004 - p205(1) [51-500]

Coming to Terms with Security: A Handbook on Verification and Compliance
R&R Bk N - v19 - i1 - Feb 2004 - pNA [501+]

Comingore, Dorothy - *My Teacher for President (Illus. by Brunkus, Denise)*
c BL - v101 - i1 - Sept 1 2004 - p137(1) [1-50]
c KR - v72 - i15 - August 1 2004 - p751(1) [51-500]
c PW - v251 - i31 - August 2 2004 - p69(2) [51-500]
c SLJ - v50 - i8 - August 2004 - p104(1) [51-500]
The Teeny Tiny Ghost and the Monster (Illus. by Munsinger, Lynn)
c CCB-B - v58 - i1 - Sept 2004 - p46(1) [51-500]
c SLJ - v50 - i8 - August 2004 - p104(1) [51-500]

Comini, Alessandra - *In Passionate Pursuit: A Memoir*
BL - v101 - i4 - Oct 15 2004 - p373(1) [51-500]
Choice - v42 - i6 - Feb 2005 - p1010(1) [51-500]

Comins, Neil F. - *Discovering the Essential Universe. 2nd Ed.*
SciTech - v28 - i3 - Sept 2004 - p43(1) [1-50]
Heavenly Errors
Bwatch - Nov 2004 - pNA [51-500]

Comiskey, Michael - *Seeking Justices: The Judging of Supreme Court Nominees*
Pers PS - v34 - i1 - Wntr 2005 - p48(1) [501+]

Commager, Henry Steele - *The Story of the Second World War*
R&R Bk N - v19 - i4 - Nov 2004 - p32(1) [51-500]

Commeyras, Michelle - *Teachers as Readers: Perspectives on the Importance of Reading in Teacher's Classrooms and Lives*
y VOYA - v27 - i3 - August 2004 - p252(1) [1-50]

Commins, David Dean - *Historical Dictionary of Syria, 2nd Ed.*
Choice - v42 - i3 - Nov 2004 - pNA [1-50]
Historical Dictionary of Syria. 2nd Ed.
R&R Bk N - v19 - i3 - August 2004 - p50(1) [51-500]
Historical Dictionary of Syria, 2nd Ed.
BL - v101 - i5 - Nov 1 2004 - p520(1) [501+]

Commission on Human Security - *Human Security Now*
R&R Bk N - v19 - i1 - Feb 2004 - pNA [501+]

Committee on Biological Confinement of Genetically Engineered Organisms - *Biological Confinement of Genetically Engineered Organisms*
SciTech - v28 - i3 - Sept 2004 - p60(1) [1-50]

Committee on Restoration of the Greater Everglades Ecosystem - *Adaptive Monitoring and Assessment for the Comprehensive Everglades Restoration Plan*
SciTech - v28 - i4 - Dec 2004 - p58(1) [51-500]

Committee on Review of Geographic Information Systems Research and Applications at HUD - *GIS for Housing and Urban Development*
R&R Bk N - v19 - i4 - Nov 2004 - p104(1) [51-500]

Committee on the Review of the Use of Scientific Criteria and Performance Standards for Safe Food - *Scientific Criteria to Ensure Safe Food*
Choice - v41 - i11-12 - July-August 2004 - p2077(2) [501+]
SciTech - v28 - i1 - March 2004 - p179(1) [51-500]

Common Sense ... and Uncommon Fun!
BL - v100 - i21 - July 2004 - p1856(1) [1-50]

Communication Skills, 2nd Ed.
y SLJ - v51 - i1 - Jan 2005 - p144(1) [51-500]

Como, David - *Blown by the Spirit: Puritanism and the Emergence of an Antinomian Underground in Pre-Civil-War England*
Choice - v42 - i1 - Sept 2004 - p117(2) [501+]
HNet - Sept 2004 - pNA [501+]

Comodromos, Eliza A. - *Teacher's Guide to the Bluford Series*
JAAL - v48 - i4 - Dec 2004 - p354(3) [501+]

Compagnon, Antoine - *Baudelaire devant l'innombrable*
FS - v58 - i3 - July 2004 - p421-422 [501+]
NCFS - v33 - i1-2 - Fall-Winter 2004 - p194(2) [501+]

Comparato, Scott A. - *Amici Curiae and Strategic Behavior in the State Supreme Courts*
R&R Bk N - v19 - i1 - Feb 2004 - pNA [51-500]

Compensation and Benefits: Vital Statistics for Your Veterinary Practice. 3rd Ed.
SciTech - v28 - i3 - Sept 2004 - p132(1) [51-500]

The Complete Directory for People with Disabilities: A Comprehensive Source Book for Individuals and Professionals, 12th Ed.
R&R Bk N - v19 - i1 - Feb 2004 - p138(1) [51-500]

The Complete Learning Disabilities Directory 2004/05: Associations, Products, Resources, Magazines, Books, Services, Conferences, Web Sites, 11th Ed.
R&R Bk N - v19 - i3 - August 2004 - p230(1) [1-50]

Compton, Ann - *The Sculpture of Charles Sargeant Jagger*
CR - v286 - i1669 - Feb 2005 - p124(2) [51-500]

Compton, Anne - *Coastlines: The Poetry of Atlantic Canada*
CBRA - Annual 2003 - p243(1) [51-500]

Compton, Jennifer - *Parker & Quink*
Quad - v48 - i12 - Dec 2004 - p89(2) [501+]

Compton, Jodi - *Sympathy between Humans*
KR - v73 - i2 - Jan 15 2005 - p84(2) [51-500]
LJ - v130 - i3 - Feb 15 2005 - p114(1) [51-500]
PW - v252 - i7 - Feb 14 2005 - p54(1) [51-500]

Compton-Lilly, Catherine - *Confronting Racism, Poverty and Power: Classroom Strategies to Change the World*
R&R Bk N - v19 - i3 - August 2004 - p227(1) [1-50]

Compton, Shanna - *Gamers: Writers, Artists, and Programmers on the Pleasures of Pixels*
LJ - v129 - i18 - Nov 1 2004 - p112(1) [51-500]

Compton, Wayde - *49th Parallel Psalm*
Can Lit - i182 - Autumn 2004 - p103(3) [501+]
Blueprint: Black British Columbian Literature and Orature
Can Lit - i182 - Autumn 2004 - p105(2) [501+]

Compton, William C. - *Introduction to Positive Psychology*
R&R Bk N - v19 - i4 - Nov 2004 - p9(1) [51-500]

Compton's Encyclopedia and Fact-Index
BL - v101 - i2 - Sept 15 2004 - p264(1) [501+]

Computational Systems Bioinformatics Conference - *Computational Systems Bioinformatics (CSB 2004): Proceedings*
SciTech - v28 - i4 - Dec 2004 - p73(1) [501+]

Computer and Robot Vision: Proceedings
SciTech - v28 - i3 - Sept 2004 - p143(1) [51-500]

Computer Architecture: Proceedings
SciTech - v28 - i3 - Sept 2004 - p30(1) [51-500]

Computer Design: VLSI in Computers and Processors: Proceedings
SciTech - v28 - i4 - Dec 2004 - p158(1) [51-500]

Computer Graphics and Applications (PG-2004): Proceeedings
SciTech - v28 - i4 - Dec 2004 - p130 [51-500]

Computer Graphics International: Proceedings
SciTech - v28 - i3 - Sept 2004 - p136(1) [51-500]

Computer Security Foundations Workshop: Proceedings
SciTech - v28 - i3 - Sept 2004 - p30(1) [51-500]

Computer Security Sourcebook: Basic Information for General Readers about Computers, Internet and E-Mail Security
LibMed - v22 - i6 - March 2004 - p88(1) [501+]

Computer Software and Applications Conference: Procedings, Vols. 1-2
SciTech - v28 - i4 - Dec 2004 - p17(1) [1-50]

Computer Vision and Pattern Recognition: CVPR 2004, Proceedings. 2nd Ed.
SciTech - v28 - i3 - Sept 2004 - p142(1) [51-500]

Computers
LibMed - v22 - i4 - Jan 2004 - p73(1) [501+]

Comstock, Dana - *Diversity and Development: Critical Contexts That Shape Our Lives and Relationships*
R&R Bk N - v19 - i4 - Nov 2004 - p10(1) [51-500]

Conaghan, Joanne - *Labour Law in an Era of Globalization: Transformative Practices and Possibilities*
Law&PolBR - August 2004 - p662(4) [501+]

Conant, Jennet - *109 East Palace: Robert Oppenheimer and the Secret City of Los Alamos*
PW - v252 - i10 - March 7 2005 - p59(1) [51-500]
Tuxedo Park: A Wall Street Tycoon and the Secret Palace of Science That Changed the Course of World War II
T&C - v45 - i2 - April 2004 - p456-457 [501+]

Conard, Mark T. - *Woody Allen and Philosophy: You Mean My Whole Fallacy Is Wrong?*
Choice - v42 - i6 - Feb 2005 - p1030(1) [51-500]
R&R Bk N - v19 - i4 - Nov 2004 - p225(1) [501+]

Conard, Nicholas J. - *Settlement Dynamics of the Middle Paleolithic and Middle Stone Age*
Am Ant - v69 - i4 - Oct 2004 - p787(2) [501+]

Conaty, Gerlad T. - *Reindeer Herders of the Mackenzie Delta*
CBRA - Annual 2003 - p355(1) [501+]

Conboy, Kenneth - *The CIA's Secret War in Tibet*
HRNB - v31 - i2 - Winter 2003 - p85 [51-500]

Conca, C. - *Partial Differential Equations and Inverse Problems: Proceedings*
SciTech - v28 - i4 - Dec 2004 - p40(1) [501+]

Conceicao, Pedro - *Innovation, Competence Building, and Social Cohesion in Europe: Towards a Learning Society*
JEL - v42 - i1 - March 2004 - p317(2) [501+]
R&R Bk N - v19 - i1 - Feb 2004 - p83(1) [501+]

Conceison, Claire - *Significant Other: Staging the American in China*
Choice - v42 - i7 - March 2005 - p1238(1) [51-500]
R&R Bk N - v19 - i4 - Nov 2004 - p57(1) [51-500]

Concilio, C. - *La tradizione metrica della tragedia*
Class R - v54 - i1 - May 2004 - p240(1) [501+]

Concise Oxford English Dictionary. 11th Ed.
LJ - v129 - i17 - Oct 15 2004 - p90(1) [51-500]

Conde, Maryse - *Who Slashed Celanire's Throat? A Fantastical Tale*
Black Iss - v6 - i6 - Nov-Dec 2004 - p70(2) [51-500]
BW - v34 - i39 - Sept 26 2004 - p6(1) [501+]
KR - v72 - i13 - July 1 2004 - p591(1) [501+]
LJ - v129 - i14 - Sept 1 2004 - p136(2) [51-500]
PW - v251 - i29 - July 19 2004 - p143(1) [501+]

Condon, Bill - *Kinsey: Public and Private*
LJ - v130 - i3 - Feb 15 2005 - p132(1) [51-500]

Condon, Bradley J. - *Insurance Regulation in North America: Integrating American, Canadian, and Mexican Markets*
R&R Bk N - v19 - i2 - May 2004 - p124 [51-500]

Condon, Phil - *Clay Center*
BL - v101 - i6 - Nov 15 2004 - p558(1) [51-500]

Condon, Sean - *Sean and David's Long Drive*
BL - v101 - i2 - Sept 15 2004 - p201(1) [501+]

Condrey, Stephen E. - *Handbook of Human Resource Management in Government*
HR Mag - v49 - i7 - July 2004 - pS32(1) [501+]

Cone, Marla - *Silent Snow: The Slow Poisoning of the Arctic*
KR - v73 - i3 - Feb 1 2005 - p161(1) [501+]
PW - v252 - i9 - Feb 28 2005 - p49(1) [501+]

Cone, Molly - *Family of Strangers: Building a Jewish Community in Washington State*
PHR - v73 - i4 - Nov 2004 - p683(4) [501+]
WHQ - v35 - i4 - Winter 2004 - p514-515 [501+]

Conejo, Carlos A. - *Motivating Hispanic Employees: A Practical Guide to Understanding & Managing Hispanic Employees*
HR Mag - v50 - i2 - Feb 2005 - pS7(1) [501+]

Conekin, Becky E. - *"The Autobiography of a Nation": The 1951 Festival of Britain*
AHR - v109 - i4 - Oct 2004 - p1315(2) [501+]
J Hist S - v30 - i1 - Jan 2004 - p190(2) [501+]

Conference Hosted by the Center for Research Libraries (2002: Atlanta, Georgia) - *The New Dynamics and Economics of Cooperative Collection Development: Proceedings*
R&R Bk N - v19 - i4 - Nov 2004 - p256(1) [501+]

Conference of the International Council for Archaeology - *Behaviour Behind Bone: The Zooarchaeology of Ritual, Religion, Status and Identity: Proceedings*
R&R Bk N - v19 - i4 - Nov 2004 - p29(1) [501+]

Conference of the International Council for Archaeozoology - *The Future from the Past: Zooarchaeology in Wildlife Conservation and Heritage Management: Proceedings*
R&R Bk N - v19 - i4 - Nov 2004 - p30(1) [501+]

Conference on Challenge and Change for the Military (2002: Kingston, Ontario) - *Challenge and Change for the Military: Social and Cultural Change; Proceedings*
R&R Bk N - v19 - i4 - Nov 2004 - p251(1) [501+]

Confessions of a Backup Dancer
y BL - v101 - i2 - Sept 15 2004 - p229(1) [51-500]
Kliatt - v38 - i6 - Nov 2004 - p13(1) [51-500]
y VOYA - v27 - i4 - Oct 2004 - p291(1) [51-500]

Conforti, Benedetto - *The Italian Yearbook of International Law, Vol.12*
R&R Bk N - v19 - i3 - August 2004 - p210(1) [1-50]

Confronting Cruel Historical Perspectives on Child Protection in Australia
CS - v33 - i5 - Sept 2004 - p626-626 [501+]

Congdon, Howard K. - *Philosophies of Space and Time*
R&R Bk N - v19 - i4 - Nov 2004 - p7(1) [51-500]

Congressional Districts in the 2000s: A Portrait of America
Choice - v41 - i11-12 - July-August 2004 - p2024(1) [501+]

Congressional Quarterly Almanac Plus, 2002: 107th Congress, 2nd Session
Choice - v41 - i11-12 - July-August 2004 - p2024(1) [501+]

Congressional Quarterly's Desk Reference on the Presidency
BL - v101 - i3 - Oct 1 2004 - p358(1) [501+]

Congressional Role Call 2003: A Chronology and Analysis of Votes in the House and Senate 108th Congress, First Session
R&R Bk N - v19 - i4 - Nov 2004 - p154(1) [501+]

Congressional Staff Directory, 2004 Summer Edition, 108th Congress, 2d Session: Members, Committees, Staffs, Biographies, 70th ed.
R&R Bk N - v19 - i4 - Nov 2004 - p154(1) [501+]

Coniglione, Francesco - *Idealization XI: Historical Studies on Abstraction and Idealization*
R&R Bk N - v20 - i1 - Feb 2005 - p2(1) [51-500]

Conkin, Paul K. - *Peabody College: From a Frontier Academy to the Frontiers of Teaching and Learning*
JSH - v70 - i4 - Nov 2004 - p947(2) [501+]

Conkle, David O. - *Constitutional Law: The Religion Clauses*
J Ch St - v46 - i4 - Autumn 2004 - p906(2) [501+]

Conklin, Alfred R. - *Field Sampling: Principles and Practices in Environmental Analysis*
E-Streams - Nov 2004 - pNA [501+]
SciTech - v28 - i3 - Sept 2004 - p144(1) [51-500]

Conkling, Roger L. - *Marginal Cost in the New Economy: A Proposal for a Uniform Approach to Policy Evaluations*
R&R Bk N - v19 - i2 - May 2004 - p120 [51-500]

Conlan, Kathy - *Under the Ice*
c RT - v57 - Oct 2003 - p178 [1-50]

Conlan, Thomas Donald - *State of War: The Violent Order of Fourteenth-Century Japan*
Choice - v42 - i1 - Sept 2004 - p165(1) [51-500]

Conley, Dalton - *The Pecking Order: Which Siblings Succeed and Why*
Am Spect - v37 - i4 - May 2004 - p61(3) [501+]
The Starting Gate: Birth Weight and Life Chances
CS - v33 - i6 - Nov 2004 - p667(2) [501+]

Conley, David T. - *Who Governs Our Schools?: Changing Roles and Responsibilities*
TCR - v106 - i2 - Feb 2004 - p317-320 [501+]

Conley, John J. - *The Suspicion of Virtue: Women Philosophers in Neoclassical France*
Ren Q - v57 - i3 - Fall 2004 - p1023(3) [501+]

Conley, Katharine - *Robert Desnos, Surrealism, and the Marvelous in Everyday Life*
Choice - v41 - i11-12 - July-August 2004 - p2049(1) [501+]
TLS - i5292 - Sept 3 2004 - p8-9 [501+]

Conley, Richard S. - *The Presidency, Congress, and Divided Government: A Postwar Assessment*
Pres St Q - v34 - i4 - Dec 2004 - p891(3) [501+]
Reassessing the Reagan Presidency
Bwatch - Jan 2005 - pNA [51-500]

Conlin, Christy Ann - *Heave*
CBRA - Annual 2003 - p158(2) [51-500]

Conroy, Frank - *Time and Tide: A Walk through Nantucket (Read by Conroy, Frank). Audiobook Review*
 y   Kliatt - v38 - i5 - Sept 2004 - p69(2) [51-500]
Time and Tide: A Walk through Nantucket (Read by Gardner, Grover). Audiobook Review
     LJ - v129 - i13 - August 2004 - p129(1) [51-500]
Conroy, James C. - *Betwixt and Between: The Liminal Imagination, Education, and Democracy*
     R&R Bk N - v19 - i4 - Nov 2004 - p177(1) [501+]
Conroy, Jane - *Cross-Cultural Travel: Papers from the Royal Irish Academy International Symposium on Literature and Travel; Proceedings*
     R&R Bk N - v19 - i1 - Feb 2004 - p68(1) [501+]
Conroy, Mark - *Muse in the Machine: American Fiction and Publicity*
     Choice - v42 - i5 - Jan 2005 - p851(1) [1-50]
Conroy, Pat - *The Pat Conroy Cookbook: Recipes of My Life*
     BL - v101 - i4 - Oct 15 2004 - p372(1) [51-500]
     LJ - v129 - i15 - Sept 15 2004 - p78(1) [51-500]
     PW - v251 - i35 - August 30 2004 - p49(1) [501+]
Recipes from My Life (Read by Conroy, Pat). Audiobook Review
     PW - v251 - i40 - Oct 4 2004 - p29(1) [501+]
Consalvo, Mia - *Internet Research Annual: Selected Papers from the Association of Internet Researchers Conference 2000-2002, Vol. 1*
     R&R Bk N - v19 - i4 - Nov 2004 - p260(1) [501+]
Consigny, S. - *Gorgias, Sophist and Artist*
     Class R - v53 - i2 - Nov 2003 - p293-295 [501+]
Consortium on Revolutionary Europe 1750-1850: Selected Papers 1999
     J Mil H - v68 - i3 - July 2004 - p598-599 [501+]
Constable, George - *A Century of Innovation: Twenty Engineering Achievements That Transformed Our Lives*
     Choice - v42 - i1 - Sept 2004 - p124(1) [501+]
     Phys Today - v57 - i12 - Dec 2004 - p63-63 [501+]
     SciTech - v28 - i1 - March 2004 - p134(1) [51-500]
Constable, Kate - *The Singer of All Songs (Read by Ziemba, Karen). Audiobook Review*
 y   BL - v101 - i3 - Oct 1 2004 - p352(1) [51-500]
 c   BL - v101 - i9-10 - Jan 1 2005 - p778(1) [1-50]
 c   Kliatt - v38 - i6 - Nov 2004 - p51(1) [51-500]
 c   SLJ - v50 - i10 - Oct 2004 - p85(2) [51-500]
The Singer of All Songs
 c   BL - v101 - i6 - Nov 15 2004 - p599(1) [501+]
 y   BL - v101 - i9-10 - Jan 1 2005 - p772(1) [51-500]
Constable, Pamela - *Fragments of Grace: My Search for Meaning in the Strife of South Asia*
     BW - v34 - i33 - August 15 2004 - p4(1) [501+]
     For Aff - v83 - i5 - Sept-Oct 2004 - p164 [501+]
     R&R Bk N - v19 - i3 - August 2004 - p54(1) [51-500]
Constance, Debrah - *Fat, Stupid, Ugly: One Woman's Courage to Survive*
     PW - v251 - i28 - July 12 2004 - p52(2) [51-500]
Constant, Benjamin - *Principles of Politics Applicable to All Governments*
     R&R Bk N - v19 - i1 - Feb 2004 - pNA [501+]
Constantine, Helen - *Paris Tales: A Literary Tour of the City*
     LJ - v129 - i19 - Nov 15 2004 - p55(1) [501+]
Constantine, Storm - *The Shades of Time and Memory*
     KR - v72 - i20 - Oct 15 2004 - p989(1) [501+]
     LJ - v129 - i19 - Nov 15 2004 - p55(1) [501+]
     PW - v251 - i43 - Oct 25 2004 - p32(1) [51-500]
Constantinescu, Gheorghe M. - *Clinical Dissection Guide for Large Animals: Horse and Large Ruminants. 2nd Ed.*
     SciTech - v28 - i1 - March 2004 - p132(1) [51-500]
Constantinides, George M. - *Handbook of the Economics of Finance, Volume 1A*
     JEL - v42 - i1 - March 2004 - p270(1) [501+]
Handbook of the Economics of Finance, Volume 1B
     JEL - v42 - i1 - March 2004 - p267(1) [501+]
Constitutions of Europe: Texts Collected by the Council of Europe Venice Commission
     R&R Bk N - v19 - i3 - August 2004 - p207(1) [1-50]
Cont, Rama - *Financing Modelling with Jump Processes*
     R&R Bk N - v19 - i2 - May 2004 - p121 [51-500]
Contamine, Philippe - *Louis XII en Milanais: Guerre et politique, art et culture*
     Ren Q - v57 - i4 - Winter 2004 - p1381(2) [501+]
Contardi, Simone - *La casa di Salomone a Firenze: L'Imperiale e Reale Museo di Fisico e Storia Naturale (1755-1801).*
     Isis - v95 - i3 - Sept 2004 - p488(2) [501+]
Contarini, Gasparo - *The Office of a Bishop*
     CHR - v90 - i3 - July 2004 - p589(1) [51-500]

Conte, Christopher Allan - *Highland Sanctuary: Environmental History in Tanzania's Usambara Mountains*
     Choice - v42 - i6 - Feb 2005 - p1076(1) [51-500]
     R&R Bk N - v19 - i4 - Nov 2004 - p75(1) [51-500]
Conteh-Morgan, Earl - *Collective Political Violence: An Introduction to the Theories and Cases of Violent Conflicts*
     PSQ - v119 - i4 - Winter 2004 - p719(2) [501+]
Contemporary Arts Museum & Gallery (Portland, Or.) - *The Soul of a Bowl*
     Ceram Mo - v52 - i3 - March 2004 - p38(1) [501+]
Contemporary Hispanic Biographies. Vol. 3
     LibMed - v22 - i6 - March 2004 - p74(1) [501+]
Continents of the World
 c   LibMed - v23 - i3 - Nov-Dec 2004 - p80(1) [51-500]
Contreras, Bonifacio - *Salud: Medical Spanish Dictionary and Phrase Book. 2nd Ed.*
     R&USQ - v44 - i1 - Fall 2004 - p95(1) [501+]
Contributions to the Study of World Literature: The Presence of the Past in Children's Literature
     LibMed - v22 - i7 - April-May 2004 - p86(1) [501+]
Controvich, James T. - *United States Air Force and Its Antecedents: Published and Printed Unit Histories, a Bibliography, Rev. Ed.*
     R&R Bk N - v19 - i4 - Nov 2004 - p252(1) [501+]
Conway, Andrew J. - *Introduction to Astrobiology*
     SciTech - v28 - i4 - Dec 2004 - p45(1) [51-500]
Conway, Flo - *Dark Hero of the Information Age: In Search of Norbert Wiener, the Father of Cybernetics*
     BL - v101 - i9-10 - Jan 1 2005 - p794(1) [51-500]
     New Sci - v185 - i2485 - Feb 5 2005 - p52(1) [501+]
     PW - v252 - i1 - Jan 3 2005 - p48(1) [51-500]
Conway, John F. - *Canadian Family in Crisis*
     CBRA - Annual 2003 - p380(1) [501+]
Conway, Kelley - *Chanteuse in the City: The Realist Singer in French Film*
     Choice - v42 - i5 - Jan 2005 - p859(2) [51-500]
     Choice - v42 - i5 - Jan 2005 - p860(2) [1-50]
Conway, Kevin - *After the Rain (Read by Conway, Kevin). Audiobook Review*
     PW - v251 - i40 - Oct 4 2004 - p31(1) [51-500]
Conway, Richard - *Code Hacking: A Developer's Guide to Network Security*
     Bwatch - v26 - i8 - August 2004 - p7(1) [51-500]
     Choice - v42 - i3 - Nov 2004 - p519(1) [1-50]
     SciTech - v28 - i3 - Sept 2004 - p156(1) [51-500]
Conway, Russ - *Game Misconduct*
     Globe & Mail - Sept 18 2004 - pD27 [501+]
Conyers, John G. - *Charting Your Course: Lessons Learned During the Journey Toward Performance Excellence*
     R&R Bk N - v19 - i3 - August 2004 - p222(1) [1-50]
Coogan, Tim Pat - *Ireland in the Twentieth Century*
     BooChiTr - March 14 2004 - p1(2) [501+]
     Choice - v42 - i4 - Dec 2004 - p727(1) [1-50]
Cook, Billie Montgomery - *The Real Deal: A Spiritual Guide for Black Teen Girls*
     Black Iss - v6 - i6 - Nov-Dec 2004 - p18(1) [51-500]
Cook, Bruce - *Young Will: The Confessions of William Shakespeare*
     BL - v101 - i1 - Sept 1 2004 - p59(1) [51-500]
     KR - v72 - i17 - Sept 1 2004 - p821(1) [501+]
     LJ - v129 - i14 - Sept 1 2004 - p138(1) [51-500]
     PW - v251 - i38 - Sept 20 2004 - p47(1) [51-500]
Cook, Christopher - *Pears Cyclopaedia 2004-2005: A Book of Reference and Background Information for All the Family*
     CR - v286 - i1669 - Feb 2005 - p124(1) [51-500]
Cook, Christopher D. - *Diet for a Dead Planet: How the Food Industry Is Killing Us*
     E Mag - v16 - i1 - Jan-Feb 2005 - p57(2) [51-500]
     PW - v251 - i44 - Nov 1 2004 - p59(1) [501+]
Cook, Claire - *Multiple Choice*
     BL - v100 - i21 - July 2004 - p1816(1) [51-500]
Cook, Daniel Thomas - *The Commodification of Childhood: The Children's Clothing Industry and the Rise of the Child Consumer*
     HRNB - v33 - i1 - Fall 2004 - p13(1) [501+]
Cook, David A. - *A History of Narrative Film*
     HNet - Oct 2004 - pNA [501+]
     TimHES - v0 - i1647 - July 2 2004 - p28(1) [501+]
Cook, Dawn - *Lost Truth*
     BL - v101 - i8 - Dec 15 2004 - p715(1) [51-500]

Cook, Frank - *You're Not Buying That House Are You? Everything You May Forget to Do, or Think about Before Signing on the Dotted Line*
     R&R Bk N - v19 - i3 - August 2004 - p111(1) [51-500]
Cook, Gloria - *Pengarron Rivalry*
 y   BL - v101 - i6 - Nov 15 2004 - p560(1) [51-500]
Cook, Hera - *The Long Sexual Revolution: English Women, Sex, and Contraception 1800-1975*
     CR - v285 - i1663 - August 2004 - p123(1) [501+]
Cook, Ian - *Government and Democracy in Australia*
     AJPS - v39 - i3 - Nov 2004 - p662(1) [501+]
Cook, James F. - *Carl Vinson: Patriarch of Armed Forces*
     R&R Bk N - v19 - i3 - August 2004 - p69(1) [51-500]
Cook, Judith - *Keeper's Gold*
     BL - v101 - i4 - Oct 15 2004 - p392(1) [51-500]
     KR - v72 - i24 - Dec 15 2004 - p1165(1) [501+]
Cook, K.L. - *Last Call*
     BL - v101 - i3 - Oct 1 2004 - p307(1) [51-500]
     KR - v72 - i17 - Sept 1 2004 - p821(2) [501+]
     LJ - v129 - i17 - Oct 15 2004 - p58(1) [51-500]
Cook, Karen S. - *Annual Review of Sociology, Vol. 29*
     R&R Bk N - v19 - i1 - Feb 2004 - p121(1) [51-500]
Annual Review of Sociology, Vol. 30
     R&R Bk N - v19 - i4 - Nov 2004 - p120(1) [51-500]
Cook, Kristina - *Unlaced*
     BL - v101 - i5 - Nov 1 2004 - p470(1) [51-500]
Cook, Lorna J. - *Departures*
     BL - v101 - i9-10 - Jan 1 2005 - p771(1) [1-50]
 y   Kliatt - v39 - i2 - March 2005 - p17(2) [501+]
Home Away from Home
     KR - v72 - i21 - Nov 1 2004 - p1022(1) [501+]
     LJ - v129 - i20 - Dec 1 2004 - p98(1) [51-500]
     PW - v252 - i1 - Jan 3 2005 - p36(2) [51-500]
Cook, Lyn - *Bells on Finland Street*
 c   CBRA - Annual 2003 - p480(1) [51-500]
Flight from the Fortress
 c   Res Links - v10 - i1 - Oct 2004 - p28(1) [51-500]
 y   SLJ - v50 - i9 - Sept 2004 - p202(1) [51-500]
Pegeen and the Pilgrim
 y   Can CL - i111-112 - Fall-Winter 2003 - p153(6) [501+]
Cook-Lynn, Elizabeth - *Anti-Indianism in Modern America: A Voice from Tatekeya's Earth*
     AIQ - v28 - i1-2 - Wntr-Spring 2004 - p130(12) [501+]
     Can Lit - i181 - Summer 2004 - p116-118 [501+]
Cook, Malcolm - *Reecritures: 1700-1820*
     FS - v58 - i1 - Jan 2004 - p108(2) [501+]
Cook, Martin L. - *The Moral Warrior: Ethics and Service in the U.S. Military*
     Choice - v42 - i4 - Dec 2004 - p674(1) [1-50]
Cook, Mary F. - *Complete Do-It-Yourself Human Resources Department, 2004 Ed.*
     R&R Bk N - v19 - i2 - May 2004 - p117 [51-500]
Cook, Matt - *London and the Culture of Homosexuality, 1885-1914.*
     ELT - v48 - i1 - Wntr 2005 - p209(6) [501+]
     TimHES - v0 - i1656 - Sept 3 2004 - p27(1) [501+]
Cook, Michael - *A Brief History of the Human Race*
     NS - v133 - i4674 - Feb 9 2004 - p49(2) [501+]
     R&R Bk N - v19 - i1 - Feb 2004 - p72(1) [51-500]
Studies in the Origins of Early Islamic Culture and Tradition
     R&R Bk N - v19 - i3 - August 2004 - p48(1) [51-500]
Cook, Michael L. - *Justice, Jesus and the Jews: A Proposal for Jewish-Christian Relations*
     Intpr - v58 - i3 - July 2004 - p328(2) [51-500]
Cook, R.C. - *Nematology: Proceedings*
     SciTech - v28 - i1 - March 2004 - p130(1) [51-500]
Cook, Rhodes - *How Congress Gets Elected.*
 c   SLJ - v50 - i8 - August 2004 - p49(1) [51-500]
The Presidential Nominating Process: A Place for Us?
     PSQ - v119 - i3 - Fall 2004 - p565(2) [501+]
     R&R Bk N - v19 - i1 - Feb 2004 - pNA [51-500]
Race for the Presidency: Winning the 2004 Nomination
     R&R Bk N - v19 - i3 - August 2004 - p178(1) [501+]
Cook, Richard - *The Penguin Guide to Jazz on CD*
     LJ - v129 - i19 - Nov 15 2004 - p86(1) [51-500]
Cook, Robert - *Civil War America: Making a Nation, 1848-1877*
     JSH - v70 - i4 - Nov 2004 - p919(2) [501+]
Cook, Roger F. - *A Companion to the Works of Heinrich Heine*
     GSR - v27 - i1 - Feb 2004 - p147-148 [501+]

Cook, Sally - *Good Night Pillow Fight (Illus. by Cornell, Laura)*
  c SLJ - v50 - i7 - July 2004 - p68(2) [51-500]
Cook, Sarah - *Compendium of Learning and Development Quizzes*
  R&R Bk N - v19 - i2 - May 2004 - p117 [51-500]
Cook, Scott - *Understanding Commodity Cultures: Explorations in Economic Anthropology with Case Studies from Mexico*
  R&R Bk N - v19 - i4 - Nov 2004 - p77(1) [51-500]
Cook, Simon - *Clinical Studies Management: A Practical Guide to Success*
  SciTech - v28 - i3 - Sept 2004 - p121(1) [51-500]
Cook, Terrence E. - *Separation, Assimilation, or Accomodation: Contrasting Ethnic Minority Policies*
  R&R Bk N - v19 - i1 - Feb 2004 - p71(1) [1-50]
Cook, Thomas A. - *Mastering Import and Export Management*
  R&R Bk N - v19 - i4 - Nov 2004 - p108(1) [51-500]
Cook, Thomas H. - *Best American Crime Writing. 2004 Ed.*
  AJR - v26 - i4 - August-Sept 2004 - p79(1) [501+]
Cook, Vivian - *Accomodating Brocolli in the Cemetary, or Why Can't Anybody Spell English?*
  NS - v133 - i4706 - Sept 20 2004 - p51(2) [501+]
  TimHES - v0 - i1678 - Feb 11 2005 - p25(1) [501+]
Cook, William - *25 Years of Viz*
  NS - v133 - i4715 - Nov 22 2004 - p52(2) [501+]
  Spec - v297 - i9206 - Jan 15 2005 - p47(1) [501+]
Cook, William J. - *The Best of Amateur Telescope Making Journal*
  S&T - v107 - i3 - March 2004 - p74(2) [501+]
Cook, William R. - *The Medieval World View: An Introduction*
  Specu - v79 - i3 - July 2004 - p754-755 [501+]
Cooke, Alistair - *Letter from America, 1946-2004*
  BL - v101 - i6 - Nov 15 2004 - p530(1) [51-500]
  PW - v251 - i46 - Nov 15 2004 - p54(2) [501+]
  Spec - v296 - i9196 - Nov 6 2004 - p68(1) [501+]
Cooke, Anthony - *Visual Astronomy in the Suburbs*
  Astron - v32 - i9 - Sept 2004 - p92 [51-500]
Cooke, Bill - *A Rebel to His Last Breath: Joseph McCabe and Rationalism*
  Isis - v95 - i2 - June 2004 - p309(2) [501+]
Cooke, Edward S., Jr. - *The Maker's Hand: American Studio Furniture, 1940-1990*
  R&R Bk N - v19 - i1 - Feb 2004 - p207(1) [51-500]
Cooke, Lez - *British Television Drama: A History*
  TLS - i5291 - August 27 2004 - p29(1) [501+]
Cooke, Nola - *Water Frontier: Commerce and the Chinese in the Lower Mekong Region, 1750-1880*
  R&R Bk N - v19 - i4 - Nov 2004 - p109(1) [51-500]
Cooke, Paul - *German Writers and the Politics of Culture: Dealing with the Stasi*
  Choice - v41 - i11-12 - July-August 2004 - p2048(1) [501+]
Cooke, Peter - *Ecrits sur l'art*
  NCFS - v32 - i3-4 - Spring-Summer 2004 - p377(2) [501+]
Cooke, Richard - *Coastline UK: Amazing Views from the Air*
  R&R Bk N - v19 - i4 - Nov 2004 - p249(1) [501+]
  y Sch Lib - v52 - i4 - Winter 2004 - p218(1) [51-500]
Cooke, Robin A. - *Colour Atlas of Anatomical Pathology. 3rd Ed.*
  SciTech - v28 - i1 - March 2004 - p86(1) [51-500]
Cooke, Roger - *Mathematical Analysis I*
  Choice - v42 - i2 - Oct 2004 - p329(1) [501+]
  Mathematical Analysis II
  Choice - v42 - i2 - Oct 2004 - p329(1) [501+]
Cookies: 1,001 Mouthwatering Recipes from around the World
  BL - v101 - i5 - Nov 1 2004 - p452(2) [51-500]
  PW - v251 - i41 - Oct 11 2004 - p70(2) [51-500]
Cook's Illustrated - *The New Best Recipe*
  Globe & Mail - Nov 27 2004 - pD26 [51-500]
Cookshaw, Marlene - *Shameless*
  Can Lit - i182 - Autumn 2004 - p107(2) [501+]
Cookson, Catherine - *The Glass Virgin*
  BL - v101 - i5 - Nov 1 2004 - p470(1) [51-500]
  KR - v72 - i20 - Oct 15 2004 - p983(1) [51-500]
  PW - v251 - i42 - Oct 18 2004 - p47(1) [51-500]
Cookson, Gillian - *A Victorian Scientist and Engineer: Fleeming Jenkin and the Birth of Electrical Engineering*
  Isis - v95 - i2 - June 2004 - p319(2) [501+]

Cooley, A.E. - *Pompeii*
  Class R - v54 - i2 - Nov 2004 - p499-501 [501+]
Cooley, Dennis - *Bloody Jack*
  CBRA - Annual 2003 - p211(1) [51-500]
  Shameless
  CBRA - Annual 2003 - p211(1) [501+]
Cooley, Karen - *Legendary Away Days: The Complete Guide to Running Successful Team Events*
  R&R Bk N - v19 - i3 - August 2004 - p117(1) [51-500]
Cooley, Martha - *Thirty-Three Swoons*
  KR - v73 - i3 - Feb 1 2005 - p133(1) [501+]
  LJ - v130 - i4 - March 1 2005 - p77(2) [51-500]
  PW - v252 - i10 - March 7 2005 - p47(1) [51-500]
Cooley, Nicole - *Afflicted Girls: Poems*
  LJ - v129 - i12 - July 2004 - p87(1) [51-500]
Cooley, Robert - *When Corruption Was King: How I Helped the Mob Rule Chicago, Then Brought the Outfit Down*
  BL - v101 - i2 - Sept 15 2004 - p183(1) [51-500]
  PW - v251 - i32 - August 9 2004 - p237(1) [51-500]
Cooling, Wendy - *All the Colours of the Earth*
  c Sch Lib - v52 - i3 - Autumn 2004 - p154(1) [501+]
  With Love: A Celebration of Words and Pictures for the Very Young
  c Magpies - v19 - i5 - Nov 2004 - p26(1) [501+]
  c Sch Lib - v52 - i4 - Winter 2004 - p185(1) [51-500]
Coolman, Boyd Taylor - *Knowing God by Experience: The Spiritual Senses in the Theology of William of Auxerre*
  Choice - v42 - i5 - Jan 2005 - p869(1) [1-50]
Cooman, G. - *Zeger-Bernard van Espen at the Crossroads of Canon Law, History, Theology, and Church-State Relations*
  R&R Bk N - v19 - i4 - Nov 2004 - p164(1) [501+]
Coomber, Ross - *Drug Use and Cultural Contexts 'Beyond the West': Tradition, Change and Post-Colonialism*
  R&R Bk N - v19 - i4 - Nov 2004 - p143(1) [501+]
Coombes, Annie E. - *History After Apartheid: Visual Culture and Public Memory in a Democratic South Africa*
  Choice - v42 - i1 - Sept 2004 - p164(1) [501+]
  JRAI - v10 - i4 - Dec 2004 - p907(2) [501+]
  Pub Hist - v26 - i4 - Fall 2004 - p115(4) [501+]
Coombes, Robert Holman - *Handbook of Addictive Disorders: A Practical Guide to Diagnosis and Treatment*
  Choice - v42 - i4 - Dec 2004 - p694(1) [1-50]
Coombs, David - *Sir Winston Churchill: His Life and His Paintings*
  BL - v101 - i1 - Sept 1 2004 - p37(1) [51-500]
  LJ - v129 - i17 - Oct 15 2004 - p59(1) [51-500]
Coombs, Jan Gregoire - *Rise and Fall of HMOs: An American Health Care Revolution*
  PW - v252 - i6 - Feb 7 2005 - p52(1) [51-500]
Coombs, Robert H. - *Family Therapy Review: Preparing for Comprehensive and Licensing Examinations*
  SciTech - v28 - i4 - Dec 2004 - p97(1) [51-500]
Coon, Carleton - *One Planet, One People: Beyond "Us vs. Them"*
  R&R Bk N - v19 - i4 - Nov 2004 - p121(1) [51-500]
Coon, Cheryl F. - *Books to Grow With: A Guide to Using the Best Children's Fiction for Everyday Issues and Tough Challenges*
  SLJ - v50 - i10 - Oct 2004 - p202(1) [51-500]
Coon, Dennis - *Psychology: A Journey, 2nd Ed.*
  SciTech - v28 - i4 - Dec 2004 - p1(1) [1-50]
Cooney, Brian - *Posthumanity: Thinking Philosophically about the Future*
  Choice - v42 - i7 - March 2005 - p1240(1) [51-500]
  SciTech - v28 - i3 - Sept 2004 - p133(1) [51-500]
Cooney, Caroline - *Family Reunion*
  c CH Bwatch - v14 - i7 - July 2004 - p7(2) [501+]
Cooney, Doug - *I Know Who Likes You*
  c BooChiTr - April 4 2004 - p2(1) [501+]
Cooney, Ellen - *Gun Ball Hill*
  BL - v100 - i22 - August 2004 - p1897(1) [51-500]
Cooney, Helen - *Nation, Court and Culture: New Essays on Fifteenth-Century English Poetry*
  Specu - v79 - i4 - Oct 2004 - p1055(3) [501+]
Cooney, Mark - *Homocide: A Sociological Explanation*
  CS - v33 - i5 - Sept 2004 - p601-602 [501+]
Cooney, Timothy - *Teaching Science in the Two-Year College*
  SB - v40 - i5 - Sept-Oct 2004 - p201(1) [501+]
Coons, Lorraine - *Tourist Third Cabin: Steamship Travel in the Interwar Years*
  AHR - v109 - i3 - June 2004 - p874(2) [501+]

Coonts, Stephen - *Dark Zone*
  BL - v101 - i6 - Nov 15 2004 - p560(1) [51-500]
  Saucer: The Conquest (Read by Conger, Eric). Audiobook Review
  y Kliatt - v39 - i2 - March 2005 - p56(1) [51-500]
  Saucer: The Conquest
  BL - v100 - i22 - August 2004 - p1868(1) [51-500]
  Ent W - i790 - Oct 29 2004 - p71 [501+]
  PW - v251 - i32 - August 9 2004 - p230(1) [51-500]
Coontz, Stephanie - *Marriage, a History: From Obedience to Intimacy, or How Love Conquered Marriage*
  KR - v73 - i5 - March 1 2005 - p271(1) [501+]
  PW - v252 - i11 - March 14 2005 - p56(1) [51-500]
Cooper, Andre R. - *Air CRFs Made Easy, 2nd Ed.*
  SciTech - v28 - i4 - Dec 2004 - p11(1) [1-50]
Cooper, Andrew Fenton - *Tests of Global Governance: Canadian Diplomacy and United Nations World Conferences*
  R&R Bk N - v19 - i3 - August 2004 - p160(1) [501+]
Cooper, B. Lee - *The Popular Music Teaching Handbook: An Educator's Guide to Music-Related Print Resources*
  Teach Lib - v32 - i2 - Dec 2004 - p39(1) [501+]
Cooper, Barbara - *Ethel Exclamation Mark (Illus. by Raynor, Maggie)*
  c Sch Lib - v52 - i4 - Winter 2004 - p206(2) [51-500]
  An Introduction to the Story of Punctuation (Illus. by Raynor, Maggie)
  c Sch Lib - v52 - i4 - Winter 2004 - p206(2) [51-500]
Cooper, Barry - *New Political Religions, or an Analysis of Modern Terrorism*
  R&R Bk N - v19 - i4 - Nov 2004 - p144(1) [501+]
  Wil Q - v28 - i4 - Autumn 2004 - p124(2) [501+]
Cooper, Bruce S. - *Better Policies, Better Schools: Theories and Applications*
  R&R Bk N - v19 - i1 - Feb 2004 - p189(1) [51-500]
Cooper, Cary - *Advances in Mergers and Acquisitions*
  JEL - v41 - i4 - Dec 2003 - p1368(1) [501+]
Cooper, Cary L. - *Stress: A Brief History*
  Choice - v42 - i3 - Nov 2004 - p567(1) [1-50]
Cooper, Dave - *Underbelly: Additional Observations on the Beauty/Ugliness of Mostly Pillowy Girls*
  PW - v252 - i9 - Feb 28 2005 - p58(1) [51-500]
Cooper, Edward S. - *Vinnie Ream: An American Sculptor*
  Choice - v42 - i4 - Oct 2004 - p284(1) [501+]
Cooper, Emmanuel - *Bernard Leach: Life and Work*
  Ceram Mo - v52 - i3 - March 2004 - p38(1) [501+]
  David Leach: A Biography
  Ceram Mo - v52 - i5 - May 2004 - p32(1) [501+]
  Male Bodies: A Photographic History of the Nude
  Choice - v42 - i4 - Dec 2004 - p653(2) [1-50]
  Lam Bk Rpt - v13 - i4-5 - Nov-Dec 2004 - p50(2) [501+]
  Ten Thousand Years of Pottery
  JAAC - v61 - Winter 2003 - p95 [501+]
Cooper, Floyd - *Jump!: From the Life of Michael Jordan (Illus. by Cooper, Floyd)*
  c BL - v101 - i1 - Sept 1 2004 - p114(1) [501+]
  c Black Iss - v7 - i1 - Jan-Feb 2005 - p70(2) [501+]
  c CCB-B - v58 - i5 - Jan 2005 - p205(1) [51-500]
  c HB - v80 - i6 - Nov-Dec 2004 - p725(2) [501+]
  c KR - v72 - i20 - Oct 15 2004 - p1003(1) [51-500]
  c PW - v251 - i48 - Nov 29 2004 - p40(1) [51-500]
  c SLJ - v50 - i12 - Dec 2004 - p127(1) [51-500]
Cooper, Fredrick - *Africa Since 1940: The Past of the Present*
  IJAHS - v37 - i2 - Spring 2004 - p356-357 [501+]
Cooper, Geoffrey M. - *The Cell: A Molecular Approach*
  QRB - v79 - i4 - Dec 2004 - p418(2) [501+]
Cooper, Harris - *The Battle over Homework: Common Ground for Administrators, Teachers, and Parents*
  CE - v81 - i1 - Fall 2004 - p56(1) [51-500]
Cooper, Helen - *Tatty Ratty (Illus. by Cooper, Helen)*
  c RT - v57 - Oct 2003 - p167 [1-50]
Cooper, Helen (b. 1947 -) - *The English Romance in Time: Transforming Motifs from Geoffrey of Monmouth to the Death of Shakespeare*
  Choice - v42 - i6 - Feb 2005 - p1022(1) [51-500]
  Lon R Bks - v26 - i23 - Dec 2 2004 - p32(1) [501+]
  TLS - i5297 - Oct 8 2004 - p3-4 [501+]
Cooper, Hilary - *Teaching Across the Early Years 3-7: Curriculum Coherence and Continuity*
  CE - v80 - i5 - Mid-Summer 2004 - p276(1) [501+]

Cooper, Ilene - *Sam I Am*
c CCB-B - v58 - i6 - Feb 2005 - p248(1) [51-500]
c HB - v80 - i6 - Nov-Dec 2004 - p705(2) [51-500]
y KR - v72 - i21 - Nov 1 2004 - p1048(1) [51-500]
y PW - v251 - i51 - Dec 20 2004 - p60(1) [51-500]
c SLJ - v50 - i10 - Oct 2004 - p160(1) [51-500]

Cooper, J. California - *Some People, Some Other Place*
y BL - v101 - i3 - Oct 1 2004 - p307(1) [51-500]
   KR - v72 - i17 - Sept 1 2004 - p822(1) [51-500]
   LJ - v129 - i15 - Sept 15 2004 - p48(1) [51-500]
   PW - v251 - i37 - Sept 13 2004 - p57(1) [51-500]

Cooper, J.P.D. - *Propaganda and the Tudor State: Political Culture in the Westcountry*
   Choice - v41 - i11-12 - July-August 2004 - p2112(1) [501+]

Cooper, Jason - *Life Cycle of a Pine Tree*
c SB - v40 - i4 - July-August 2004 - p176(1) [51-500]
   Life Cycle of a Sunflower
c SB - v40 - i4 - July-August 2004 - p176(1) [51-500]

Cooper, John (b. 1958 -) - *Season of Rage: Racial Conflict in a Small Town*
c Globe & Mail - Jan 29 2005 - pD10 [51-500]

Cooper, John Xiros - *Modernism and the Culture of Market Society*
   Choice - v42 - i7 - March 2005 - p1227(1) [51-500]

Cooper, Karyn - *Burning Issues: Foundations of Education*
   R&R Bk N - v19 - i4 - Nov 2004 - p180(1) [501+]

Cooper, Kim - *Lost in the Grooves: Scram's Capricious Guide to the Music You Missed*
   LJ - v129 - i17 - Oct 15 2004 - p65(1) [51-500]

Cooper, Laura A. - *Belly Dancing Basics*
   LJ - v129 - i13 - August 2004 - p82(2) [501+]

Cooper, Leon - *Theory of Plasticity*
   SciTech - v28 - i4 - Dec 2004 - p70(1) [51-500]

Cooper, Lynn G. - *Teaching Band and Orchestra: Methods and Materials*
   M Ed J - v91 - i2 - Nov 2004 - p55(1) [501+]

Cooper, Mark Garett - *Love Rules: Silent Hollywood and the Rise of the Professional Managerial Class*
   Film Cr - v29 - i1 - Fall 2004 - p82(5) [501+]

Cooper, Michael - *'A More Beautiful City': Robert Hooke and the Rebuilding of London after the Great Fire*
   TimHES - v0 - i1671 - Dec 17 2004 - p21(2) [501+]

Cooper, Michael L. - *Dust to Eat: Drought and Depression in the 1930s*
c BL - v100 - i21 - July 2004 - p1839(1) [1-50]
y CCB-B - v58 - i1 - Sept 2004 - p11(1) [51-500]
c SLJ - v50 - i9 - Sept 2004 - p224(1) [51-500]
y VOYA - v27 - i4 - Oct 2004 - p323(1) [51-500]

Cooper, Mick - *Existential Therapies*
   SciTech - v28 - i4 - Dec 2004 - p98(1) [51-500]

Cooper, Natasha - *Keep Me Alive: A Trish Maguire Mystery*
   BL - v101 - i6 - Nov 15 2004 - p564(1) [51-500]
   Globe & Mail - Nov 27 2004 - pD16 [51-500]
   KR - v72 - i18 - Sept 15 2004 - p892(1) [51-500]
   LJ - v129 - i16 - Oct 1 2004 - p64(1) [51-500]
   PW - v251 - i37 - Sept 13 2004 - p62(1) [501+]

Cooper, Page - *Man O' War*
   LJ - v129 - i16 - Oct 1 2004 - p121(1) [1-50]

Cooper, Phillip J. - *Implementing Sustainable Development: From Global Policy to Local Action*
   R&R Bk N - v19 - i3 - August 2004 - p96(1) [51-500]

Cooper, Randolf G.S. - *The Anglo-Maratha Campaigns and the Contest for India: The Struggle for Control of the South Asian Military Economy*
   J Mil H - v68 - i4 - Oct 2004 - p1257-1258 [501+]

Cooper, Robert - *The Breaking of Nations*
   Globe & Mail - Dec 24 2004 - pD3 [1-50]
   Nation - v279 - i1 - July 5 2004 - p56 [501+]

Cooper, Sally - *Love Object*
   CBRA - Annual 2003 - p159(1) [51-500]

Cooper, Sarah E. - *The Ties That Bind: Questioning Family Dynamics and Family Discourse in Hispanic Literature*
   Choice - v42 - i4 - Dec 2004 - p667(1) [1-50]

Cooper, Susan - *The Magician's Boy (Illus. by Riglietti, Serena)*
   BL - v101 - i9-10 - Jan 1 2005 - p858(1) [1-50]
   KR - v73 - i2 - Jan 15 2005 - p118(1) [51-500]
y PW - v252 - i7 - Feb 14 2005 - p76(2) [51-500]

Cooper, Victoria L. - *The House of Novello: The Practice and Policy of a Victorian Music Publisher, 1829-1866*
   R&R Bk N - v19 - i1 - Feb 2004 - p197(1) [51-500]

Cooper, W.R. - *Wycliffe New Testament (1388): An Edition in Modern Spelling with an Introduction, the Original Prologues and the Epistle to the Laodiceans*
   R&R Bk N - v19 - i1 - Feb 2004 - p18(1) [51-500]

Cooper, Zarine - *Archaeology and History: Early Settlements in the Andaman Islands*
   JAS - v63 - i3 - August 2004 - p820-822 [501+]

Cooperman, Stephanie H. - *Gertrude Elion: Nobel Prize Winner in Physiology and Medicine*
c SLJ - v50 - i9 - Sept 2004 - p220(2) [51-500]

Coote, Stephen - *Napoleon and the Hundred Days*
   LJ - v130 - i3 - Feb 15 2005 - p144(1) [51-500]

Cooter, Robert B., Jr. - *Perspectives on Rescuing Urban Literacy Education: Spies, Saboteurs, and Saints*
   R&R Bk N - v19 - i1 - Feb 2004 - p193(1) [51-500]

Coots, J. Fred - *O Holy Night: Christmas with the Boys' Choir of Harlem (Illus. by Ringgold, Faith)*
c BL - v101 - i1 - Sept 1 2004 - p130(1) [501+]
   Santa Claus Is Comin' to Town (Illus. by Kellogg, Steven)
c BL - v101 - i1 - Sept 1 2004 - p130(1) [501+]
c HB - v80 - i6 - Nov-Dec 2004 - p657(1) [51-500]
c KR - v72 - i21 - Nov 1 2004 - p1048(1) [51-500]
c PW - v251 - i39 - Sept 27 2004 - p62(1) [51-500]

Copan, Paul - *Creation out of Nothing: A Biblical, Philosophical, and Scientific Exploration*
   LJ - v129 - i12 - July 2004 - p88(1) [51-500]

Cope, Kevin L. - *1650-1850: Ideas, Aesthetics, and Inquiries in the Early Modern Era, Vol. 9*
   R&R Bk N - v19 - i1 - Feb 2004 - p215(1) [51-500]

Copeland, Brenda S. - *Linking Picture Books to Standards*
   LibMed - v23 - i1 - August-Sept 2004 - p84(1) [51-500]

Copeland, Brian R. - *Trade and the Environment: Theory and Evidence*
   Env - v46 - i6 - July-August 2004 - p45(1) [51-500]
   JEL - v41 - i4 - Dec 2003 - p1352(1) [501+]

Copeland, Cynthia - *Fun on the Run for Kids (Illus. by Hoffman, Sanford)*
c PW - v251 - i28 - July 12 2004 - p66(1) [501+]

Copeland, David A. - *The Antebellum Era: Primary Documents on Events from 1820 to 1860*
c SLJ - v50 - i8 - August 2004 - p56(1) [501+]

Copeland, Lori - *A Case of Nosy Neighbors: A Morning Shade Mystery*
   LJ - v129 - i14 - Sept 1 2004 - p134(1) [51-500]

Copeland, Marion - *Cockroach*
   Choice - v41 - i11-12 - July-August 2004 - p2064(1) [501+]

Copeland, Roger - *Merce Cunningham: The Modernizing of Modern Dance*
   Choice - v42 - i2 - Oct 2004 - p304(1) [51-500]

Copeland, Tom - *Real Options: A Practitioner's Guide*
   R&R Bk N - v19 - i1 - Feb 2004 - p118(1) [51-500]

Copernicus, Nicolaus - *De Revolutionibus orbium coelestium*
   New Sci - v184 - i2475 - Nov 27 2004 - p50(1) [501+]
   Three Copernican Treatises
   SciTech - v28 - i3 - Sept 2004 - p42(1) [1-50]

Copestake, Ian D. - *Rigor of Beauty: Essays in Commemoration of William Carlos Williams*
   R&R Bk N - v19 - i4 - Nov 2004 - p243(1) [501+]

Coplestone, Lis - *Noah's Bed*
c Sch Lib - v52 - i3 - Autumn 2004 - p130(1) [501+]

Copp, Rick - *The Actor's Guide to Adultery*
   PW - v251 - i40 - Oct 4 2004 - p73(1) [51-500]

Copp, Terry - *Fields of Fire: The Canadians in Normandy*
   Can Hist R - v85 - i3 - Sept 2004 - p569(4) [501+]
   CBRA - Annual 2003 - p284(2) [501+]

Coppa, Francesca - *Joe Orton: A Casebook*
   Theat J - v56 - i3 - Oct 2004 - p529-530 [501+]

Coppard, A.E. - *Dusky Ruth and Other Stories*
   NS - v133 - i4716 - Nov 29 2004 - p53(2) [501+]

Coppola, A. - *Il re, il barbaro, il tiranno. Poesia e ideologia in eta ellenistica*
   Class R - v53 - i2 - Nov 2003 - p312-313 [501+]

Copps, Sheila - *Worth Fighting For*
   Globe & Mail - Oct 30 2004 - pD16 [501+]

Corba, Anna - *Vintage Paper Crafts*
   LJ - v129 - i17 - Oct 15 2004 - p62(1) [51-500]

Corbeil, Jean-Claude - *The Firefly Five Language Visual Dictionary*
   LJ - v130 - i3 - Feb 15 2005 - p158(1) [51-500]
   The Firefly French/English Visual Dictionary
c Globe & Mail - Jan 15 2005 - pD16 [51-500]

Corbett, Ben - *This Is Cuba: An Outlaw Culture Survives*
   R&R Bk N - v19 - i3 - August 2004 - p146(1) [1-50]

Corbett, Bernard - *The Only Game That Matters: The Harvard/Yale Rivalry*
   KR - v72 - i17 - Sept 1 2004 - p845(2) [501+]
   PW - v251 - i36 - Sept 6 2004 - p54(2) [51-500]

Corbett, Bill - *Best of Alberta: Day Trips from Calgary, Rev. Ed.*
   CBRA - Annual 2003 - p22(1) [51-500]

Corbett, Claire - *Car Crime*
   R&R Bk N - v19 - i2 - May 2004 - p109(1) [1-50]

Corbett, David - *Done for a Dime*
   TLS - i5304 - Nov 26 2004 - p23(1) [501+]

Corbett, John - *An Intercultural Approach to English Language Teaching*
   R&R Bk N - v19 - i1 - Feb 2004 - p215(1) [51-500]

Corbett, William - *Just the Thing: Selected Letters of James Schuyler, 1951-1991*
   BW - v34 - i42 - Oct 17 2004 - p15(1) [501+]
   Lam Bk Rpt - v13 - i4-5 - Nov-Dec 2004 - p24(1) [501+]
   PW - v251 - i39 - Sept 27 2004 - p47(1) [51-500]

Corbin, Carol - *Northwest Montana's Environmental Debates*
   R&R Bk N - v19 - i3 - August 2004 - p82(1) [51-500]

Corbishley, Mike - *Ancient Egypt. Rev. Ed.*
c LibMed - v22 - i5 - Feb 2004 - p79(1) [501+]

Corbitt, Brian J. - *eBusiness, eGovernment and Small and Medium-Size Enterprises: Opportunities and Challenges*
   R&R Bk N - v19 - i3 - August 2004 - p128(1) [51-500]

Corcoran, Michael - *The Game of the Century: Nebraska vs. Oklahoma in College Football's Ultimate Battle*
   BL - v101 - i1 - Sept 1 2004 - p45(2) [51-500]
   LJ - v129 - i17 - Oct 15 2004 - p68(1) [51-500]
   PW - v251 - i35 - August 30 2004 - p42(1) [51-500]

Corcoran, Neil - *Elizabeth Bowen: The Enforced Return*
   NYTBR - Feb 20 2005 - p22 [501+]
   TLS - i5305 - Dec 3 2004 - p31(1) [51-500]

Corcuff, Stephane - *Memories of the Future: National Identity Issues and the Search for a New Taiwan*
   Ch Rev Int - v10 - i2 - Fall 2003 - p382(4) [501+]

Cordell, Karl - *The Ethnopolitical Encyclopedia of Europe*
   Choice - v42 - i6 - Feb 2005 - p1002(2) [51-500]

Corden, W. Max - *Too Sensational: On the Choice of Exchange Rate Regimes*
   JEL - v41 - i4 - Dec 2003 - p1289(2) [501+]

Corder, Zizou - *Lion Boy (Read by Jones, Simon). Audiobook Review*
c BL - v101 - i9-10 - Jan 1 2005 - p778(1) [1-50]
c Kliatt - v38 - i4 - July 2004 - p53(1) [51-500]
y Magpies - v19 - i5 - Nov 2004 - p43(1) [501+]
   Lion Boy
c BooChiTr - Jan 11 2004 - p5(1) [51-500]
c PW - v251 - i40 - Oct 4 2004 - p90(1) [1-50]
   Lion Boy: The Chase (Read by Jones, Simon). Audiobook Review
y Kliatt - v39 - i2 - March 2005 - p54(1) [51-500]
   Lion Boy: The Chase
c BL - v101 - i1 - Sept 1 2004 - p120(1) [1-50]
c CCB-B - v58 - i2 - Oct 2004 - p66(1) [51-500]
y Kliatt - v38 - i5 - Sept 2004 - p6(2) [51-500]
c KR - v72 - i17 - Sept 1 2004 - p862(1) [51-500]
y Magpies - v19 - i5 - Nov 2004 - p38(1) [501+]
y SLJ - v50 - i11 - Nov 2004 - p139(1) [51-500]
y VOYA - v27 - i4 - Oct 2004 - p312(1) [51-500]

Cordesman, Anthony H. - *The Iraq War: Strategy, Tactics, and Military Lessons*
   J Mil H - v68 - i2 - April 2004 - p661(2) [501+]
   R&R Bk N - v19 - i1 - Feb 2004 - p141(1) [51-500]
   Saudi Arabia Enters the Twenty-First Century, Vol. 2
   MEQ - v11 - i3 - Summer 2004 - p93(2) [501+]
   Saudi Arabia Enters the Twenty-First Century, Vols. 1-2
   A Aff - v35 - i2 - July 2004 - p215-218 [501+]
   War After the War: Strategic Lessons of Iraq and Afghanistan
   R&R Bk N - v19 - i4 - Nov 2004 - p44(1) [51-500]

Cording, Robert - *Against Consolation*
   Sew R - v111 - i3 - Summer 2003 - pLXXXIV-LXXXVI [501+]

Cordingley, Julian - *Code Hacking: A Developer's Guide to Network Security*
   Bwatch - v26 - i8 - August 2004 - p7(1) [51-500]

Cordner, Gary W. - *Police Administration, 4th Ed.*
   R&R Bk N - v19 - i1 - Feb 2004 - p143(1) [51-500]

Coren, Stanley - *How Dogs Think: Understanding the Canine Mind*
y   BL - v101 - i1 - Sept 1 2004 - p33(1) [51-500]
    Bwatch - Oct 2004 - pNA [51-500]
    Globe & Mail - Oct 16 2004 - pD14 [501+]
    LJ - v129 - i13 - August 2004 - p107(1) [51-500]
    SciTech - v28 - i3 - Sept 2004 - p132(1) [51-500]

Cores, Lucy - *Corpse de Ballet*
    LJ - v129 - i14 - Sept 1 2004 - p204(1) [51-500]
    Painted for the Kill
    LJ - v129 - i14 - Sept 1 2004 - p204(1) [51-500]

Coreth, Anna - *Pietas Austriaca*
    CHR - v90 - i4 - Oct 2004 - p798(3) [501+]

Corey, Deborah Joy - *The Skating Pond*
y   Kliatt - v38 - i4 - July 2004 - p16(1) [51-500]

Corey, Shana - *Players in Pigtails (Illus. by Gibbon, Rebecca)*
c   CE - v80 - i5 - Mid-Summer 2004 - p273(1) [51-500]

Corfield, David - *Towards a Philosophy of Real Mathematics*
    SIAM Rev - v46 - i2 - June 2004 - p365-367 [501+]

Corfield, Justin - *Bibliography of the First World War in the Far East and Southeast Asia*
    R&R Bk N - v19 - i1 - Feb 2004 - p262(1) [51-500]
    Historical Dictionary of Cambodia
    JAS - v63 - i3 - August 2004 - p842-845 [501+]

Corfield, Richard - *The Silent Landscape: In the Wake of HMS Challenger 1872-1876*
    TimHES - v0 - i1674 - Jan 14 2005 - p26(1) [501+]
    The Silent Landscape: The Scientific Voyage of HMS Challenger
    Choice - v41 - i7 - March 2004 - p1316(1) [501+]

Corgan, Billy - *Blinking with Fists*
    Ent W - i784 - Sept 17 2004 - p87 [51-500]
    LJ - v129 - i14 - Sept 1 2004 - p154(2) [51-500]
    NYTBR - Nov 21 2004 - p34(L) [501+]

Corin, Lucy - *Everyday Psychokillers: A History for Girls*
    ABR - v26 - i2 - Jan-Feb 2005 - p31(1) [501+]

Corino, Karl - *Robert Musil: Eine Biographie*
    TLS - i5288 - August 6 2004 - p9(1) [501+]

Corio, David - *Megaliths: The Ancient Stone Monuments of England and Wales*
    Choice - v42 - i3 - Nov 2004 - p527(1) [1-50]

Cork, Daniel C. - *Reengineering the 2010 Census: Risks and Challenges*
    R&R Bk N - v19 - i3 - August 2004 - p92(1) [51-500]

Corkin, Stanley - *Cowboys as Cold Warriors: The Western and U.S. History*
    Choice - v42 - i6 - Feb 2005 - p1029(1) [51-500]

Corlett, J. Angelo - *Race, Racism & Reparations*
    Choice - v41 - i7 - March 2004 - p1309(1) [501+]
    Terrorism: A Philosophical Analysis
    Choice - v42 - i2 - Oct 2004 - p306(1) [51-500]
    R&R Bk N - v19 - i1 - Feb 2004 - p141(1) [51-500]

Corlett, William - *Kitty*
c   Sch Lib - v52 - i3 - Autumn 2004 - p135(2) [501+]

Corley, Kathleen E. - *Jesus and Mel Gibson's The Passion of the Christ: The Film, the Gospels and the Claims of History*
    LJ - v129 - i19 - Nov 15 2004 - p65(1) [501+]
    PW - v251 - i28 - July 12 2004 - p60(1) [51-500]
    Women and the Historical Jesus: Feminist Myths of Christian Origins
    Theol St - v65 - i3 - Sept 2004 - p671(2) [501+]

Corley, Troy - *Free L.A.*
    Bwatch - Dec 2004 - pNA [51-500]

Cormack, Patricia - *Sociology and Mass Culture: Durkheim, Mills, and Baudrillard*
    CS - v33 - i2 - March 2004 - p200-201 [501+]

Corman, Avery - *A Perfect Divorce*
    KR - v72 - i14 - July 15 2004 - p645(2) [501+]
    PW - v251 - i40 - Oct 4 2004 - p72(1) [51-500]

Corman, Ed - *Everybody's Somebody's Fool*
    DroRevMy - v24 - i3 - May-June 2004 - p7(2) [501+]

Cormier, Jeffrey - *The Canadianization Movement: Emergence, Survival, and Success*
    Choice - v42 - i5 - Jan 2005 - p915(1) [1-50]
    R&R Bk N - v19 - i3 - August 2004 - p89(1) [51-500]

Cormier, Loretta A. - *Kinship with Monkeys: The Guaja Foragers of Eastern Amazonia*
    R&R Bk N - v19 - i1 - Feb 2004 - p67(1) [501+]

Cornbleth, Catherine - *Hearing America's Youth: Social Identities in Uncertain Times*
    Adoles - v39 - i156 - Winter 2004 - p829(1) [51-500]

Cornelis, Rita - *Handbook of Elemental Speciation: Techniques and Methodology*
    SciTech - v28 - i1 - March 2004 - p54(1) [51-500]

Cornelison, Pam - *The Great American History Fact-Finder: The Who, What, Where, When and Why of American History, 2nd Ed.*
    Choice - v42 - i5 - Jan 2005 - p836(1) [1-50]
y   Kliatt - v38 - i5 - Sept 2004 - p46(2) [51-500]

Cornelissen, Christoph - *Erinnerungskulturen: Deutschland, Italien und Japan seit 1945*
    HNet - June 2004 - pNA [501+]

Cornelius, Steven H. - *Music of the Civil War Era*
    R&R Bk N - v19 - i4 - Nov 2004 - p198(1) [51-500]

Cornelius, Wayne A. - *Controlling Immigration: A Global Perspective, Rev. Ed.*
    R&R Bk N - v19 - i4 - Nov 2004 - p158(1) [51-500]

Cornell, Deirdre - *A Priceless View: My Spiritual Homecoming*
    AM - v191 - i7 - Sept 20 2004 - p29 [51-500]

Cornell, George L. - *Ojibwa*
    SLJ - v50 - i10 - Oct 2004 - pS60(2) [51-500]

Cornell, Kari A. - *For the Love of Knitting: A Celebration of the Knitter's Art*
    LJ - v129 - i20 - Dec 1 2004 - p108(2) [51-500]
    Holiday Cooking around the World
y   LJ - v51 - i2 - Feb 2005 - p59(1) [51-500]
    Our Texas
    R&R Bk N - v19 - i4 - Nov 2004 - p62(1) [51-500]

Corneloup, Jean - *Les Theories Sociologiques de la Pratique Sportive*
    SSJ - v21 - i1 - March 2004 - p101-103 [501+]

Corner, John - *Media and the Restyling of Politics: Consumerism, Celebrity and Cynicism*
    Choice - v41 - i7 - March 2004 - p1335(1) [501+]

Cornes, Alan - *Culture from the Inside Out: Travel and Meet Yourself*
    R&R Bk N - v19 - i3 - August 2004 - p144(1) [51-500]

Cornfield, Daniel B. - *Research in the Sociology of Work, Vol.11*
    CS - v33 - i6 - Nov 2004 - p671(2) [501+]

Cornford, F.M. - *From Religion to Philosophy: A Study in the Origins of Western Speculation*
    LJ - v129 - i15 - Sept 15 2004 - p91(1) [1-50]
    R&R Bk N - v19 - i4 - Nov 2004 - p3(1) [51-500]

Cornforth, Trevor - *Chinese Snuff Bottles: A Guide to Addictive Miniatures*
    R&R Bk N - v19 - i1 - Feb 2004 - p208(1) [51-500]

Corngold, Stanley - *Franz Kafka: The Necessity of Form*
    NYRB - v52 - i2 - Feb 10 2005 - p4(4) [501+]
    Lambent Traces: Franz Kafka
    Choice - v42 - i5 - Jan 2005 - p857(1) [1-50]
    NYRB - v52 - i2 - Feb 10 2005 - p4(4) [501+]

Cornils, Boy - *Catalysis from A to Z: A Concise Encyclopedia. 2nd Ed.*
    SciTech - v28 - i1 - March 2004 - p56(1) [51-500]

Corning, Gregory P. - *Japan and the Politics of Techno-Globalism*
    Choice - v42 - i3 - Nov 2004 - p532(1) [1-50]
    R&R Bk N - v19 - i3 - August 2004 - p100(1) [51-500]

Corning, Howard McKinley - *Willamette Landings, 3rd Ed.*
    R&R Bk N - v19 - i3 - August 2004 - p75(1) [51-500]

Corning, Peter - *Nature's Magic: Synergy in Evolution and the Fate of Humankind*
    JEL - v41 - i4 - Dec 2003 - p1444(1) [501+]
    SB - v40 - i3 - May-June 2004 - p114(2) [501+]

Cornish, Edward - *Futuring: The Exploration of the Future*
    Choice - v42 - i2 - Oct 2004 - p332(1) [51-500]
    Fut - v38 - i6 - Nov-Dec 2004 - p56(2) [501+]

Cornish, Geoff - *Battlefield Support*
c   SLJ - v50 - i7 - July 2004 - p118(2) [501+]

Cornish, Joe - *Light and the Art of Landscape Photography*
    R&R Bk N - v19 - i4 - Nov 2004 - p248(1) [501+]

Corno, Lyn - *Looking at Homework Differently*
    CE - v81 - i1 - Fall 2004 - p57(1) [51-500]

Cornog, Evan - *The Power and the Story: How the Crafted Presidential Narrative Has Determined Political Success from George Washington to George W. Bush*
    LJ - v129 - i13 - August 2004 - p99(1) [501+]
    NYT - July 29 2004 - pE8 [501+]

Cornwell, Bernard - *The Last Kingdom*
    BL - v101 - i6 - Nov 15 2004 - p531(1) [51-500]
    BW - v35 - i4 - Jan 30 2005 - p7(1) [501+]
    KR - v72 - i21 - Nov 1 2004 - p1022(1) [51-500]
    LJ - v129 - i20 - Dec 1 2004 - p98(1) [51-500]
    PW - v251 - i49 - Dec 6 2004 - p41(2) [51-500]
    TLS - i5300 - Oct 29 2004 - p23(1) [501+]
    Ent W - i803 - Jan 28 2005 - p87 [51-500]
    Sharpe's Escape (Read by Tull, Patrick). Audiobook Review
y   Kliatt - v39 - i1 - Jan 2005 - p50(1) [51-500]

Cornwell, John - *Explanations: Styles of Explanation in Science*
    TimHES - v0 - i1673 - Jan 7 2005 - p20(2) [501+]
    Hitler's Scientists: Science, War, and the Devil's Pact
    New Sci - v184 - i2469 - Oct 16 2004 - p53(1) [51-500]
    SciTech - v28 - i3 - Sept 2004 - p13(1) [501+]
    VQR - v80 - i2 - Spring 2004 - p266-266 [501+]
    The Pontiff in Winter: Triumph and Conflict in the Reign of John Paul II
    BW - v35 - i4 - Jan 30 2005 - p1(2) [501+]
    Econ - v373 - i8405 - Dec 11 2004 - p83US [501+]
    Globe & Mail - Jan 1 2005 - pD10 [501+]
    The Pope in Winter: The Dark Face of John Paul's Papacy
    Lon R Bks - v27 - i3 - Feb 3 2005 - p19(2) [501+]
    Spec - v296 - i9199 - Nov 27 2004 - p46(1) [501+]
    TLS - i5306 - Dec 10 2004 - p32-33 [51-500]

Cornwell, Patricia D. - *Blow Fly*
    Globe & Mail - Sept 25 2004 - pD30 [1-50]
    Trace (Read by Reading, Kate). Audiobook Review
    BL - v101 - i8 - Dec 15 2004 - p752(1) [1-50]
    Trace
    BL - v100 - i22 - August 2004 - p1868(1) [51-500]
    Ent W - Sept 10 2004 - p167 [501+]
    Globe & Mail - Oct 16 2004 - pD26 [501+]
    KR - v72 - i15 - August 1 2004 - p715(1) [51-500]
    LJ - v129 - i15 - Sept 15 2004 - p48(1) [51-500]
    People - v62 - i11 - Sept 13 2004 - p56 [51-500]
    PW - v251 - i31 - August 2 2004 - p50(2) [501+]

Corona, Laurel - *War within a War: Vietnam and the Cold War*
y   SLJ - v50 - i10 - Oct 2004 - p189(1) [51-500]

Coronato, Rocco - *Jonson versus Bakhtin: Carnival and the Grotesque*
    Ren Q - v57 - i4 - Winter 2004 - p1535(3) [501+]
    R&R Bk N - v19 - i1 - Feb 2004 - p228(1) [51-500]

Coroneos, Con - *Space, Conrad and Modernity*
    RES - v55 - i220 - June 2004 - p480-482 [501+]

Corp, Edward - *A Court in Exile: The Stuarts in France, 1689-1718*
    HNet - Dec 2004 - pNA [501+]

Corpus na Gaeilge, 1600-1882: Focloir na Nua-Ghaeilge/The Irish Language Corpus
    R&R Bk N - v19 - i4 - Nov 2004 - p215(1) [501+]

Corrado, Anthony - *Inside the Campaign Finance Battle: Court Testimony on the New Reforms*
    Choice - v42 - i4 - Dec 2004 - p737(1) [1-50]

Correa, Arnaldo - *Cold Havana Ground*
    WLT - v79 - i1 - Jan-April 2005 - p107(1) [501+]

Correale, Robert M. - *Sources and Analogues of the Canterbury Tales*
    Specu - v79 - i4 - Oct 2004 - p1057(3) [501+]

Correspondance de Pierre Bayle, Vol. 1
    Eight-C St - v37 - i3 - Spring 2004 - p504-507 [501+]

Correspondance de Pierre Bayle, Vol. 2
    Eight-C St - v37 - i3 - Spring 2004 - p504-507 [501+]

Correspondence and Epistolary Fiction: La Fete, Science and Medicine: Voltaire
    FS - v58 - i3 - July 2004 - p411-412 [501+]

Corrett, Christopher - *Orphans Preferred: The Twisted Truth and Lasting Legend of the Pony Express*
    JouAmCul - v27 - i3 - Sept 2004 - p348(2) [501+]

Corrigan, Ann - *Core Curriculum for Infusion Nursing, 3rd Ed.*
    SciTech - v28 - i4 - Dec 2004 - p115(1) [1-50]

Corrigan, Brian Jay - *Playhouse Law in Shakespeare's World*
    Choice - v42 - i6 - Feb 2005 - p1022(1) [51-500]

Corrigan, Eireann - *Splintering*
y   SLJ - v50 - i7 - July 2004 - p102(2) [51-500]
y   VOYA - v27 - i3 - August 2004 - p210(1) [1-50]

Corrigan, John - *Business of the Heart: Religion and Emotion in the Nineteenth Century*
    Am St - v45 - i1 - Spring 2004 - p149-150 [501+]

Corrigan, John R. - *Center Cut*
  BL - v101 - i4 - Oct 15 2004 - p392(1) [51-500]
  DroRevMy - v24 - i4 - July-August 2004 - p11(1) [51-500]
  LJ - v129 - i12 - July 2004 - p64(1) [51-500]

Corry, Emmett - *The History of the Franciscan Brothers of Brooklyn in Ireland and America*
  CHR - v90 - i3 - July 2004 - p578(2) [501+]

Corry, John A. - *Lincoln at Cooper Union: The Speech That Made Him President*
  NYRB - v51 - i13 - August 12 2004 - p20(3) [501+]

Corry, Michael - *Distance Education: What Works Well*
  ALJ - v53 - i3 - August 2004 - p307(2) [501+]

Corrywright, Dominic - *Theoretical and Empirical Investigations into New Age Spiritualities*
  R&R Bk N - v19 - i1 - Feb 2004 - p15(1) [51-500]

Corsaro, William A. - *The Sociology of Childhood, 2nd Ed.*
  R&R Bk N - v19 - i4 - Nov 2004 - p130(1) [51-500]
  We're Friends, Right?: Inside Kids' Culture
  CE - v81 - i1 - Fall 2004 - p50(2) [51-500]
  CS - v33 - i6 - Nov 2004 - p670(2) [501+]
  R&R Bk N - v19 - i2 - May 2004 - p134 [51-500]

Corson, Trevor - *The Secret Life of Lobsters: How Fishermen and Scientists Are Unraveling the Mysteries of Our Favorite Crustacean*
  Am Sci - v93 - i1 - Jan-Feb 2005 - p74(1) [501+]
  Econ - v372 - i8382 - July 3 2004 - p71US [501+]
  Globe & Mail - August 21 2004 - pD11 [51-500]
  Sci - v305 - i5692 - Sept 24 2004 - p1914(1) [501+]

Cort, Robert - *Action*
  NYTBR - Oct 24 2004 - p30 [501+]

Cortada, James W. - *The Digital Hand: How Computers Changed the Work of American Manufacturing, Transportation, and Retail Industries.*
  BHR - v78 - i3 - Autumn 2004 - p566(3) [501+]
  Choice - v41 - i11-12 - July-August 2004 - p2091(1) [501+]

Cortazzi, Hugh - *British Envoys in Japan, 1859-1972*
  A Aff - v35 - i2 - July 2004 - p260-261 [501+]

Corteguera, Luis R. - *For the Common Good: Popular Politics in Barcelona, 1580-1640*
  JIH - v34 - i4 - Spring 2004 - p644-645 [501+]
  Six Ct J - v34 - i4 - Winter 2003 - p1180-1180 [501+]

Cortelazzo, G. - *3D Data Processing Visualization and Transmission: Proceedings*
  SciTech - v28 - i4 - Dec 2004 - p29(1) [51-500]

Cortes, Eladio - *Encyclopedia of Latin American Theater*
  Choice - v41 - i11-12 - July-August 2004 - p2016(1) [501+]

Cortes, Ricardo - *It's Just A Plant (Illus. by Cortes, Ricardo)*
  c Ent W - i801 - Jan 14 2005 - p91 [1-50]

Cortese, Anthony Joseph Paul - *Provocateur: Images of Women and Minorities in Advertising, 2nd Ed.*
  R&R Bk N - v19 - i3 - August 2004 - p133(1) [1-50]
  Provocateur: Images of Women and Minorities in Advertising
  Choice - v42 - i2 - Oct 2004 - p335(2) [51-500]

Cortesi, Gerald R. - *Mastering Real Estate Principles*
  R&R Bk N - v19 - i3 - August 2004 - p111(1) [51-500]

Corti, Angelo - *Tumor Necrosis Factor: Methods and Protocols*
  SciTech - v28 - i3 - Sept 2004 - p75(1) [51-500]

Cortina Orts, Adela - *Covenant and Contract: Politics, Ethics, and Religion*
  R&R Bk N - v19 - i3 - August 2004 - p174(1) [501+]
  Theol St - v66 - i1 - March 2005 - p231(1) [501+]

Cortright, David - *Smart Sanctions: Targeting Economic Statecraft*
  JPR - v41 - i5 - Sept 2004 - p639-639 [501+]

Corveleyn, Jozef - *Psychosis: Phenomenological and Psychoanalytical Approaches*
  SciTech - v28 - i1 - March 2004 - p100(1) [51-500]

Corwin, Miles - *Homicide Special*
  VQR - v80 - i3 - Summer 2004 - p267(1) [1-50]

Cory, Gerald A., Jr. - *The Consilient Brain: The Bioneurological Basis of Economics, Society, and Politics*
  JEL - v42 - i1 - March 2004 - p232(1) [501+]

Cory, Kathleen B. - *Tracing Your Scottish Ancestry*
  LJ - v129 - i17 - Oct 15 2004 - p99(1) [51-500]

Cory, Steve - *Decks: Plan, Design, Build*
  LJ - v130 - i4 - March 1 2005 - p108(1) [51-500]

Corzo, Gabino La Rosa - *Runaway Slave Settlements in Cuba: Resistance and Repression*
  Ams - v61 - i2 - Oct 2004 - p318(2) [501+]

Coscia, Joseph - *Light on Stone: Greek and Roman Sculpture in the Metropolitan Museum of Art: A Photographic Essay*
  Choice - v41 - i11-12 - July-August 2004 - p2034(1) [501+]

Cose, Ellis - *Bone to Pick: Of Forgiveness, Reconciliation, Reparation, and Revenge*
  Black Iss - v6 - i4 - July-August 2004 - p51(1) [501+]

Cosentino, Ralph - *The Story of Honk-Honk-Ashoo and Swella-Bow-Wow.*
  c KR - v72 - i24 - Dec 15 2004 - p1199(1) [501+]
  c PW - v252 - i5 - Jan 31 2005 - p66(2) [501+]
  c SLJ - v51 - i2 - Feb 2005 - p96(1) [51-500]

CosmoGIRL! Quiz Books
  y PW - v251 - i31 - August 2 2004 - p73(1) [51-500]

Coss, Peter - *The Origins of the English Gentry*
  Med R - June 2004 - pNA [501+]

Cossons, Neil - *The Iron Bridge: Symbol of the Industrial Revolution*
  T&C - v45 - i3 - July 2004 - p649-650 [501+]

Costa, C.D.N. - *Greek Fictional Letters*
  Class R - v53 - i2 - Nov 2003 - p313-314 [501+]

Costa, Dora L. - *Health and Labor Force Participation over the Life Cycle: Evidence from the Past*
  JEH - v64 - i1 - March 2004 - p271(2) [501+]
  JEL - v41 - i4 - Dec 2003 - p1403(2) [501+]

Costabile-Heming, Carol Anne - *Berlin, the Symphony Continues: Orchestrating Architectural, Social, and Artistic Change in Germany's New Capital*
  HNet - Nov 2004 - pNA [501+]

Costanza, Stephen - *Mozart Finds a Melody (Illus. by Costanza, Stephen)*
  c BL - v101 - i5 - Nov 1 2004 - p498(1) [51-500]
  c KR - v72 - i16 - August 15 2004 - p803(1) [51-500]
  c PW - v251 - i45 - Nov 8 2004 - p55(1) [51-500]
  c SLJ - v50 - i11 - Nov 2004 - p94(1) [51-500]

Costas - *Balanchine: Celebrating a Life in Dance (Illus. by Costas)*
  Choice - v42 - i3 - Nov 2004 - p494(2) [51-500]

Coste, Joanne Koenig - *Learning to Speak Alzheimer's; A Groundbreaking Approach for Everyone Dealing with the Disease*
  SciTech - v28 - i3 - Sept 2004 - p100(1) [51-500]

Coste, Rene - *Les fondements theologiques de l'Evangile social: la Pertinence de la theologie contemporaine pour l'ethique sociale*
  Theol St - v65 - i4 - Dec 2004 - p877(2) [501+]

Costell, Josh - *The Science of Sales Success: A Proven System for High-Profit, Repeatable Results*
  R&R Bk N - v19 - i2 - May 2004 - p115(1) [1-50]

Costello, David - *Here They Come! (Illus. by Costello, David)*
  c KR - v72 - i19 - Oct 1 2004 - p958(1) [51-500]
  c PW - v251 - i41 - Oct 11 2004 - p78(1) [51-500]
  c SLJ - v50 - i11 - Nov 2004 - p94(2) [51-500]

Costello, Mark - *Big If*
  Lon R Bks - v26 - i15 - August 5 2004 - p33(1) [501+]

Costeloe, Michael P. - *Bonds and Bondholders: British Investors and Mexico's Foreign Debt, 1824-1888*
  AHR - v109 - i4 - Oct 2004 - p1278-1279 [501+]
  Albion - v36 - i2 - Summer 2004 - p320(3) [501+]

Coster-Mullen, John - *Atom Bombs: The Top Secret Inside Story of Little Boy and Fat Man*
  SPA - v60 - i6 - Nov-Dec 2004 - p74(2) [501+]

Coster, Will - *Baptism and Spiritual Kinship in Early Modern England*
  CHR - v90 - i4 - Oct 2004 - p787(2) [501+]

Costigan, Arthur T. - *Learning to Teach in an Age of Accountability*
  Choice - v42 - i6 - Feb 2005 - p1072(1) [51-500]
  R&R Bk N - v19 - i4 - Nov 2004 - p186(1) [501+]

Coston, Charisse Tia Maria - *Victimizing Vulnerable Groups: Images of Uniquely High-Risk Crime Targets.*
  R&R Bk N - v19 - i4 - Nov 2004 - p143(1) [501+]

Costopoulos, William C. - *Murder Is the Charge: The True Story of Mayor Charlie Robertson and the York, Pennsylvania, Race Riots*
  Bwatch - v26 - i8 - August 2004 - p4(2) [51-500]

Cotarca, L. - *Phosgenations: A Handbook*
  E-Streams - Dec 2004 - pNA [501+]

Cote, Richard - *Lazarus! Come Out!: Why Faith Needs Imagination*
  CBRA - Annual 2003 - p89(1) [51-500]
  CI - v12 - i9 - Oct 2004 - p48(2) [501+]

Cote, Richard N. - *Strength and Honor: The Life of Dolley Madison*
  BL - v101 - i9-10 - Jan 1 2005 - p805(2) [51-500]
  LJ - v130 - i1 - Jan 1 2005 - p123(1) [51-500]

Cothran, James R. - *Gardens and Historic Plants of the Antebellum South*
  SciTech - v28 - i1 - March 2004 - p130(1) [51-500]

Cotkin, George - *Existential America*
  AHR - v109 - i2 - April 2004 - p557(2) [501+]

Cotler, Joanna - *Abarat: Days of Magic, Nights of War*
  MFSF - v108 - i2 - Feb 2005 - p44(6) [501+]

Cotran, Eugene - *Democracy: The Rule of Law and Islam*
  R&R Bk N - v19 - i3 - August 2004 - p191(1) [501+]
  Yearbook of Islamic and Middle Eastern Law, Vol. 2
  R&R Bk N - v19 - i4 - Nov 2004 - p161(1) [501+]
  Yearbook of Islamic and Middle Eastern Law, Vol. 7
  R&R Bk N - v19 - i4 - Nov 2004 - p161(1) [501+]
  Yearbook of Islamic and Middle Eastern Law, Vol. 8
  R&R Bk N - v19 - i1 - Feb 2004 - pNA [501+]

Cotsen, Lloyd - *The Bamboo Basket Art of Higashi Takesonosai*
  Am Craft - v64 - i1 - Feb-March 2004 - p49(1) [501+]

Cott, Nancy F. - *Public Vows: A History of Marriage and the Nation*
  Signs - v30 - i2 - Wntr 2005 - p1659(12) [501+]

Cottam, Martha L. - *Introduction to Political Psychology*
  R&R Bk N - v19 - i3 - August 2004 - p172(1) [501+]

Cotter, Charis - *Toronto between the Wars: Life in the City, 1919-1939*
  BIC - v33 - i8 - Nov 2004 - p33(2) [501+]

Cotter, David W. - *Genesis*
  Intpr - v58 - i4 - Oct 2004 - p422(1) [501+]

Cotter, Matthew J. - *Sidney Hook Reconsidered*
  R&R Bk N - v20 - i1 - Feb 2005 - p3(1) [501+]

Cotter, T.G. - *Programmed Cell Death*
  QRB - v79 - i4 - Dec 2004 - p417(1) [501+]
  SciTech - v28 - i1 - March 2004 - p63(1) [51-500]

Cotterill, Colin - *The Coroner's Lunch*
  BL - v101 - i3 - Oct 1 2004 - p313(1) [51-500]
  KR - v72 - i16 - August 15 2004 - p779(1) [51-500]
  LJ - v129 - i20 - Dec 1 2004 - p94(2) [51-500]
  NYTBR - Dec 26 2004 - p22 [501+]
  PW - v251 - i47 - Nov 22 2004 - p42(1) [51-500]

Cotterill, Rodney - *Biophysics: An Introduction*
  QRB - v79 - i3 - Sept 2004 - p297(1) [501+]

Cottier, Thomas - *The Role of the Judge in International Trade Regulation: Experience and Lessons for the WTO*
  JEL - v42 - i1 - March 2004 - p286(1) [501+]

Cottle, Drew - *The Brisbane Line: A Reappraisal*
  AHS - v35 - i123 - April 2004 - p192-193 [501+]

Cottle, Richard W. - *The Basic George B. Dantzig*
  SIAM Rev - v46 - i3 - Sept 2004 - p584(3) [501+]

Cottle, Simon - *News, Public Relations and Power*
  R&R Bk N - v19 - i4 - Nov 2004 - p227(1) [501+]

Cottle, Thomas J. - *A Sense of Self: The Work of Affirmation*
  TCR - v106 - i2 - Feb 2004 - p378-381 [501+]

Cottom, Daniel - *Why Education Is Useless*
  Sew R - v112 - i3 - Summer 2004 - p427-438 [501+]

Cotton, Charlotte - *The Photograph in Contemporary Art*
  Afterimage - v32 - i4 - Jan-Feb 2005 - p14(1) [501+]

Cotton, Gordon A. - *Vicksburg and the War*
  R&R Bk N - v19 - i3 - August 2004 - p74(1) [51-500]

Cotton, Kathleen - *Principals and Student Achievement: What the Research Says*
  TCR - v106 - i8 - August 2004 - p1521(4) [501+]

Cotton, Ralph - *Between Hell and Texas*
  Roundup M - v11 - i6 - August 2004 - p27 [501+]
  Dead Man's Canyon
  Roundup M - v12 - i3 - Feb 2005 - p26(1) [51-500]
  Hell's Riders
  Roundup M - v12 - i1 - Oct 2004 - p29(1) [51-500]

Cottrell Boyce, Frank - *Millions (Read by Jones, Simon). Audiobook Review*
  y BL - v101 - i8 - Dec 15 2004 - p754(1) [1-50]
  y PW - v251 - i41 - Oct 11 2004 - p27(1) [51-500]
  Millions
  c BL - v100 - i22 - August 2004 - p1932(1) [51-500]
  c CC - v121 - i25 - Dec 14 2004 - p24(1) [501+]
  y CCB-B - v57 - i11 - July-August 2004 - p455(1) [501+]
  y KR - v72 - i13 - July 1 2004 - p626(1) [51-500]
  y PW - v251 - i34 - August 23 2004 - p55(1) [501+]
  c SLJ - v50 - i10 - Oct 2004 - p158(1) [51-500]

Cottrell, Robert C. - *Vietnam: The 17th Parallel*
  y BL - v100 - i22 - August 2004 - p1917(1) [51-500]
  c SLJ - v50 - i7 - July 2004 - p118(1) [51-500]
Cottrell, William H. - *The Book of Fire, 2nd Ed.*
  Bwatch - Feb 2005 - pNA [51-500]
  Sci Teach - v71 - i8 - Oct 2004 - p74-76 [501+]
Cottringer, Anne - *Bruna (Illus. by McClure, Gillian)*
  c Sch Lib - v52 - i4 - Winter 2004 - p186(1) [51-500]
Cottrol, Robert J. - *Brown v. Board of Education: Caste, Culture, and the Constitution*
  HNet - Sept 2004 - pNA [501+]
  Law&PolBR - July 2004 - p525(5) [501+]
  Pers PS - v33 - i4 - Fall 2004 - p233(2) [501+]
Cotts, David G. - *Facility Managers Guide to Finance and Budgeting*
  R&R Bk N - v19 - i1 - Feb 2004 - p252(1) [51-500]
Couchman, Bob - *Reflections on Canadian Character: From Monarch Park to Monarch Mountain*
  CBRA - Annual 2003 - p374(2) [501+]
Coudert, Allison P. - *Hebraica Veritas?: Christian Hebraists and the Study of Judaism in Early Modern Europe*
  Choice - v42 - i6 - Feb 2005 - p1038(1) [51-500]
Coughlin, Amy - *Cross-Cultural Adoption: How to Answer Questions from Family, Friends, and Community*
  LJ - v129 - i13 - August 2004 - p101(2) [501+]
Couldry, Nick - *Contesting Media Power: Alternative Media in a Networked World*
  R&R Bk N - v19 - i1 - Feb 2004 - p211 [51-500]
Coulehan, J. - *Chekhov's Doctors: A Collection of Chekhov's Medical Tales*
  MHR - v30 - i2 - Dec 2004 - p106(2) [501+]
Coulet, Henri - *Nouvelles du XVIII siecle*
  FS - v58 - i1 - Jan 2004 - p107(2) [501+]
Coulman, Valerie - *I Am a Ballerina (Illus. by Lamb, Sandra)*
  c Res Links - v10 - i3 - Feb 2005 - p3(1) [51-500]
Coulmas, Florian - *Writing Systems: An Introduction to their Linguistic Analysis*
  Lang Soc - v33 - i3 - June 2004 - p425-429 [501+]
Coulter, Ann - *How to Talk to a Liberal (If You Must): The World According to Ann Coulter*
  NYTBR - Oct 31 2004 - p11 [501+]
Coulter, Catherine - *Blow Out (Read by Burr, Sandra). Audiobook Review*
  y Kliatt - v39 - i2 - March 2005 - p48(1) [51-500]
Coulter, Catherine Ann - *Winging It: A Beginner's Guide to Birds of the Southwest*
  Bwatch - March 2005 - pNA [51-500]
  Roundup M - v12 - i3 - Feb 2005 - p16(1) [51-500]
Coulter, Lane - *Navajo Saddle Blankets: Textiles to Ride in the American West*
  Am Ind CRJ - v28 - i2 - Spring 2004 - p167(4) [501+]
  New Mexican Tinwork 1840-1940
  Bwatch - Dec 2004 - pNA [51-500]
The Council of Europe - *European Yearbook, 2002, Vol. 50*
  R&R Bk N - v19 - i3 - August 2004 - p181(1) [501+]
Council on Library and Information Resources - *Access in the Future Tense*
  A Lib - v35 - i8 - Sept 2004 - p79(1) [51-500]
Counter, Ben - *Grey Knights*
  ChrSFF&H - v26 - i9 - Sept 2004 - p34(1) [51-500]
Countinho, John - *Touching the Moon*
  Bwatch - v26 - i9 - Sept 2004 - p9(1) [51-500]
Country Music Hall of Fame - *The Country Music Pop-Up Book*
  S Liv - v39 - i3 - March 2004 - p121(1) [501+]
Couper, Mary R. - *WHO Model Formulary 2002*
  SciTech - v28 - i1 - March 2004 - p122(1) [51-500]
Coupland, Douglas - *Eleanor Rigby*
  y BL - v101 - i6 - Nov 15 2004 - p560(1) [51-500]
  Globe & Mail - Nov 13 2004 - pD15 [501+]
  KR - v72 - i20 - Oct 15 2004 - p975(2) [51-500]
  LJ - v129 - i20 - Dec 1 2004 - p98(1) [51-500]
  NYTBR - Jan 2 2005 - p11 [501+]
  PW - v251 - i46 - Nov 15 2004 - p38(2) [51-500]
  Spec - v296 - i9192 - Oct 9 2004 - p48(1) [501+]
  TLS - i5294 - Sept 17 2004 - p23(1) [501+]
  People - v63 - i3 - Jan 24 2005 - p49 [51-500]

Hey Nostradamus!
  Globe & Mail - July 17 2004 - pD13 [1-50]
Souvenir of Canada 2
  Globe & Mail - Nov 27 2004 - pD3 [51-500]
Souvenir of Canada
  CBRA - Annual 2003 - p274(1) [51-500]
  R&R Bk N - v54 - i2 - Nov 2004 - p68(1) [51-500]
Couppie, Thomas - *Des bancs de l'ecole aux postes de travail ... Chronique d'une segregation annoncee*
  ILR - v143 - i3 - Autumn 2004 - p282(2) [501+]
Couprie, Dirk L. - *Anaximander in Context: New Studies in the Origins of Greek Philosophy*
  Class R - v54 - i2 - Nov 2004 - p288-289 [501+]
Courcelles, Dominique de - *La Confession d'un pecheur devant Jesus Christ redempteur et juge des hommes, 1547*
  Six Ct J - v34 - i4 - Winter 2003 - p1206-1207 [501+]
  La Varietas a la Renaissance: Actes de la journee d'etude organisee par l'Ecole nationale des Chartes, Paris, 27 Avril 2000
  Six Ct J - v34 - i4 - Winter 2003 - p1184-1185 [501+]
  Langages mystiques et avenement de la modernite
  FS - v58 - i3 - July 2004 - p399-399 [501+]
  Ouvrages Miscellanees et Theories de la Connaissance a la Renaissance
  FS - v58 - i3 - July 2004 - p400-400 [501+]
Courchene, Thomas J. - *Framing Financial Structure in an Information Environment*
  JEL - v41 - i4 - Dec 2003 - p1366(1) [501+]
Couric, Katie (b. 1957 -) - *Blue Planet: Frozen Seas*
  y LibMed - v22 - i6 - March 2004 - p92(1) [501+]
  The Blue Ribbon Day (Illus. by Priceman, Marjorie)
  c PW - v251 - i44 - Nov 1 2004 - p60(1) [51-500]
  c SLJ - v51 - i1 - Jan 2005 - p89(1) [51-500]
Court, John M. - *Biblical Interpretation: The Meanings of Scripture--Past and Present*
  Intpr - v58 - i4 - Oct 2004 - p440(1) [501+]
Court, Margaret Smith - *The Oxford Companion to the Brontes*
  TLS - i5263 - Feb 13 2004 - p29-29 [501+]
Courtemanche, Gil - *A Sunday at the Pool in Kigali*
  Can Lit - i182 - Autumn 2004 - p108(2) [501+]
  CBRA - Annual 2003 - p159(1) [501+]
  World&I - v19 - i9 - Sept 2004 - pNA [501+]
Courten, Manon de - *History, Sophia and the Russian Nation: A Reassessment of Vladimir Solov'ev's View on History and His Social Commitment*
  R&R Bk N - v19 - i4 - Nov 2004 - p31(1) [51-500]
Courtenay, William J. - *Rotuli Parisienses: Supplications to the Pope from the University of Paris, Vol. I*
  CHR - v90 - i4 - Oct 2004 - p770(3) [501+]
  Rotuli Parisienses: Supplications to the Pope from the University of Paris, Vol. II
  CHR - v90 - i4 - Oct 2004 - p770(3) [501+]
Courtney, E. - *A Companion to Petronius*
  Class R - v53 - i2 - Nov 2003 - p372-374 [501+]
Courtney, John C. - *Elections*
  R&R Bk N - v19 - i3 - August 2004 - p180(1) [501+]
Courtney, Tim - *Virtual LEGO: The Official LDraw.Org Guide to LDraw Tools for Windows*
  R&R Bk N - v19 - i1 - Feb 2004 - p252(1) [51-500]
Courville, Serge - *Immigration, Colonisation et Propagande: Du Reve American au Reve Colonial*
  J Hist G - v30 - i1 - Jan 2004 - p185(3) [501+]
Coury, David N. - *The Return of Storytelling in Contemporary German Literature and Film: Peter Handke and Wim Wenders*
  R&R Bk N - v19 - i4 - Nov 2004 - p244(1) [501+]
Cousens, Gabriel - *Rainbow Green Live-Food Cuisine*
  Veg J - v24 - i1 - Jan-Feb 2005 - p32(1) [501+]
Cousineau-Levine, Penny - *Faking Death: Canadian Art Photography and the Canadian Imagination*
  CBRA - Annual 2003 - p113(1) [51-500]
Cousineau, Phil - *The Olympic Odyssey: Rekindling the True Spirit of the Great Games*
  Parabola - v29 - i3 - Fall 2004 - p138(2) [501+]
  The Way Things Are: Conversations with Huston Smith on the Religious Life
  Parabola - v29 - i4 - Winter 2004 - p118-121 [501+]
Cousineau, Thomas J. - *Ritual Unbound: Reading Sacrifice in Modernist Fiction*
  Choice - v42 - i3 - Nov 2004 - p481(1) [1-50]

Cousins, Lucy - *How Will You Get There, Maisy?*
  c SLJ - v51 - i2 - Feb 2005 - p96(1) [51-500]
  Is This Maisy's House?
  c SLJ - v51 - i2 - Feb 2005 - p96(1) [51-500]
  Maisy Goes Camping (Illus. by Cousins, Lucy)
  c HB - v80 - i4 - July-August 2004 - p434(1) [51-500]
  Maisy Loves You Book and Toy Gift Set
  c PW - v251 - i49 - Dec 6 2004 - p61(2) [501+]
  Maisy's Pirate Treasure Hunt
  c PW - v251 - i31 - August 2 2004 - p72(2) [501+]
  With Love from Maisy
  c PW - v251 - i49 - Dec 6 2004 - p61(2) [501+]
Cousins, Mark - *The Story of Film*
  Globe & Mail - Dec 18 2004 - pD25 [51-500]
  Spec - v296 - i9200 - Oct 24 2004 - p41(2) [501+]
Cousins, Suss - *Hollywood Knits Style: A Guide to Good Knitting and Good Living*
  BL - v101 - i8 - Dec 15 2004 - p704(1) [51-500]
Coutinho, Steve - *Zhuangzi and Early Chinese Philosophy: Vagueness, Transformation and Paradox*
  R&R Bk N - v20 - i1 - Feb 2005 - p12(1) [51-500]
Couture, Pauline - *Ice: Beauty, Danger, History*
  Globe & Mail - Dec 4 2004 - pD32 [501+]
Couturier, Edith Boorstein - *The Silver King: The Remarkable Life of the Count of Regla in Colonial Mexico*
  BHR - v78 - i2 - Summer 2004 - p334(3) [501+]
Couturier, Lisa - *The Hopes of Snakes: And Other Tales from the Urban Landscape*
  y BL - v101 - i7 - Dec 1 2004 - p629(1) [51-500]
  KR - v72 - i21 - Nov 1 2004 - p1035(1) [501+]
  LJ - v130 - i2 - Feb 1 2005 - p112(1) [51-500]
  PW - v251 - i48 - Nov 29 2004 - p29(1) [51-500]
Cova, Antonio Rafael de la - *Cuban Confederate Colonel: The Life of Ambrosio Jose Gonzales*
  JAH - v91 - i3 - Dec 2004 - p1024(2) [501+]
Cover, J.A. - *Substance and Individuation in Leibniz*
  Phil R - v113 - i1 - Jan 2004 - p136(4) [501+]
Coverly, Dave - *Speed Bump: Cartoons for Idea People*
  Bwatch - Feb 2005 - pNA [51-500]
  SEP - v277 - i2 - March-April 2005 - p40(2) [501+]
Covert, James - *A Victorian Marriage*
  VS - v45 - i2 - Winter 2003 - p378 [501+]
Covey, Anne - *The Workplace Law Advisor*
  HR Mag - v49 - i7 - July 2004 - pS31(1) [501+]
Covey, Stephen - *The 8th Habit: From Effectiveness to Greatness*
  BL - v101 - i9-10 - Jan 1 2005 - p786(1) [1-50]
  Har Bus R - v82 - i12 - Dec 2004 - p28(1) [1-50]
  LJ - v129 - i16 - Oct 1 2004 - p100(1) [51-500]
  NW - Nov 29 2004 - p36 [501+]
  PW - v251 - i43 - Oct 25 2004 - p40(1) [51-500]
Coville, Bruce - *The Dragon of Doom. Audiobook Review*
  c BL - v101 - i4 - Oct 15 2004 - p433(1) [51-500]
  c SLJ - v50 - i10 - Oct 2004 - p84(1) [51-500]
  Juliet Dove, Queen of Love. Audiobook Review
  y Kliatt - v38 - i5 - Sept 2004 - p62(2) [51-500]
  c SLJ - v50 - i7 - July 2004 - p58(2) [51-500]
  The Weeping Werewolf (Illus. by Coville, Katherine)
  c SLJ - v50 - i10 - Oct 2004 - p111(2) [51-500]
  William Shakespeare's Hamlet (Illus. by Gore, Leonid)
  c SLJ - v50 - i10 - Oct 2004 - pS50(1) [51-500]
  c Teach Lib - v32 - i3 - Feb 2005 - p21(1) [51-500]
Covington, Howard E., Jr. - *The North Carolina Century: Tar Heels Who Made a Difference, 1900-2000.*
  JSH - v71 - i1 - Feb 2005 - p191(2) [501+]
Covington, Sarah - *The Trail of Martyrdom: Persecution and Resistance in Sixteenth-Century England*
  Choice - v42 - i1 - Sept 2004 - p178(1) [501+]
  Ren Q - v57 - i4 - Winter 2004 - p1498(2) [501+]
Covington, Tim R. - *Nonprescription Drug Therapy: Guiding Patient Self-Care, 3rd Ed.*
  SciTech - v28 - i4 - Dec 2004 - p117(1) [1-50]
Cowan, Carrie - *Urban Development in North-West Roman Southwark: Excavations 1974-1990*
  R&R Bk N - v19 - i3 - August 2004 - p39(1) [51-500]
Cowan, Douglas E. - *Bearing False Witness? An Introduction to the Christian Countercult*
  AJS - v110 - i3 - Nov 2004 - p831(3) [501+]
  The Remnant Spirit: Conservative Reform in Mainline Protestantism
  Choice - v42 - i1 - Sept 2004 - p118(1) [51-500]
  CS - v33 - i6 - Nov 2004 - p688(2) [501+]
  R&R Bk N - v19 - i1 - Feb 2005 - p16(1) [51-500]
Cowan, Edward J. - *"For Freedom Alone": The Declaration of Arbroath, 1320*
  Albion - v36 - i1 - Spring 2004 - p184(3) [501+]
  TLS - i5268 - March 19 2004 - p24-25 [501+]

Please Pass the Biscuits, Pappy: Pictures of Governor W. Lee "Pappy" O'Daniel
    Roundup M - v12 - i3 - Feb 2005 - p16(1) [51-500]

Crawford, Colin - *Inside the UDA*
    ILS - v24 - i1 - Fall 2004 - p32(1) [51-500]

Crawford, Isis - *A Catered Murder*
    LJ - v129 - i18 - Nov 1 2004 - p58(1) [51-500]
A Catered Wedding: A Mystery with Recipes
    PW - v251 - i45 - Nov 8 2004 - p39(2) [501+]

Crawford, John - *One Flag, One Queen, One Tongue: New Zealand, the British Empire and the South African War, 1899-1902*
    HNet - Sept 2004 - pNA [501+]

Crawford, Karin - *Social Work and Human Development, 1st Ed.*
    TimHES - v0 - i1680 - Feb 25 2005 - pIV(1) [501+]
Social Work with Older People, 1st Ed.
    TimHES - v0 - i1680 - Feb 25 2005 - pIV(1) [501+]

Crawford, Michael H. - *Essentials of Diagnosis and Treatment in Cardiology*
    SciTech - v28 - i1 - March 2004 - p104(1) [51-500]

Crawford, Michael J. - *The Naval War of 1812: A Documentary History. Vol. 3*
    JSH - v70 - i3 - August 2004 - p663(2) [501+]

Crawford, Patricia - *Contested Country: A History of the Northcliffe Area, Western Australia*
    R&R Bk N - v19 - i1 - Feb 2004 - p51(1) [51-500]

Crawford, Paul - *Templar of Tyre: Part III of the 'Deeds of the Cypriots'*
    R&R Bk N - v19 - i1 - Feb 2004 - p28(1) [51-500]

Crawford, Philip Charles - *Graphic Novels 101: Selecting and Using Graphic Novels to Promote Literacy for Children and Young Adults, A Resource Guide for School Librarians and Educators*
    LibMed - v23 - i1 - August-Sept 2004 - p84(1) [51-500]

Crawford, Rachel - *Poetry, Enclosure and the Vernacular Landscape, 1700-1830*
    Dal R - v83 - i3 - Autumn 2003 - p453-455 [501+]

Crawford, Rhiannon - *Storytelling in Therapy*
    SciTech - v28 - i3 - Sept 2004 - p9(1) [501+]

Crawford, S. Cromwell - *Hindu Bioethics for the Twenty-First Century*
    Choice - v42 - i1 - Sept 2004 - p137(1) [501+]

Crawford, Stanley - *Petroleum Man*
    KR - v72 - i24 - Dec 15 2004 - p1154(1) [501+]

Crawford, Tad - *Business and Legal Forms for Authors and Self-Publishers*
    Bwatch - Feb 2005 - pNA [51-500]
Starting Your Career as a Freelance Photographer
    R&R Bk N - v19 - i1 - Feb 2004 - p251(1) [51-500]

Crawford, Timothy W. - *Pivotal Deterrence: Third-Party Statecraft and the Pursuit of Peace*
    VQR - v80 - i2 - Spring 2004 - p255-256 [501+]

Crawley, Dave - *Cat Poems (Illus. by Petrosino, Tamara)*
c PW - v252 - i11 - March 14 2005 - p67(1) [51-500]

Crawley, Elaine - *Doing Prison Work: The Public and Private Lives of Prison Officers*
    R&R Bk N - v19 - i4 - Nov 2004 - p149(1) [501+]

Crawshaw, Ralph - *Human rights and policing; standards for good behaviour and a strategy for change*
    R&R Bk N - v19 - i3 - August 2004 - p192(1) [501+]

Crawshaw, Ralph (b. 1921 -) - *Compassion's Way: A Doctor's Quest into the Soul of Medicine*
    MHR - v30 - i2 - Dec 2004 - p107(1) [501+]

Cray, David - *Dead Is Forever: A Novel of Crime*
    BL - v101 - i9-10 - Jan 1 2005 - p826(1) [1-50]
    KR - v72 - i24 - Dec 15 2004 - p1166(1) [501+]
    LJ - v130 - i2 - Feb 1 2005 - p56(1) [51-500]

Cray, Ed - *Ramblin' Man: The Life and Times of Woody Guthrie*
    BooChiTr - Jan 18 2004 - p3(1) [501+]
    Choice - v41 - i11-12 - July-August 2004 - p2054(1) [501+]
    R&R Bk N - v19 - i4 - Nov 2004 - p196(1) [501+]

Crayton, Christopher A. - *A+ Certification and PC Repair Handbook*
    SciTech - v28 - i3 - Sept 2004 - p19(1) [501+]

Crazy Talk
    LibMed - v22 - i4 - Jan 2004 - p89(1) [501+]

Creach, Jerome F.D. - *Joshua*
    Intpr - v58 - i4 - Oct 2004 - p418(2) [501+]

Creager, Angela N.H. - *The Animal/Human Boundary: Historical Perspectives*
    TLS - i5287 - July 30 2004 - p23(1) [501+]
The Life of a Virus: Tobacco Mosaic Virus as an Experimental Model, 1930-1965
    JIH - v34 - i3 - Wntr 2004 - p485(7) [501+]

Crease, Robert P. - *Prism and the Pendulum: The Ten Most Beautiful Experiments in Science*
    SB - v40 - i6 - Nov-Dec 2004 - p241(1) [51-500]

Creating Graphics for Avid Xpress DV 3.5 with Adobe Photoshop 7
    SciTech - v28 - i1 - March 2004 - p135(1) [51-500]

Creation
    LibMed - v22 - i7 - April-May 2004 - p57(1) [501+]

Creative Arts and Activities
c LibMed - v23 - i1 - August-Sept 2004 - p71(1) [51-500]

Creative Media Applications - *American Presidents in World History*
y LibMed - v22 - i4 - Jan 2004 - p74(1) [501+]
y VOYA - v27 - i4 - Oct 2004 - p336(1) [51-500]
Debatable Issues
y SB - v40 - i6 - Nov-Dec 2004 - p259(1) [51-500]
Debatable Issues. Vol. 4
y SB - v40 - i5 - Sept-Oct 2004 - p195(1) [51-500]
The Middle East, Vol. 5
    R&R Bk N - v19 - i3 - August 2004 - p85(1) [51-500]
A Student's Guide to Earth Science, Vols. 1-4
c BL - v101 - i1 - Sept 1 2004 - p175(1) [51-500]
y Ref Rev - August 2004 - pNA [501+]
y VOYA - v27 - i5 - Dec 2004 - p423(1) [51-500]
A Student's Guide to Mental Health & Wellness
    LibMed - v22 - i6 - March 2004 - p78(1) [501+]
    LibMed - v22 - i6 - March 2004 - p78(1) [501+]
y VOYA - v27 - i3 - August 2004 - p247(1) [1-50]

Creatsas, George - *Women's Health and Disease: Gynecologic and Reproductive Issues, Proceedings*
    SciTech - v28 - i3 - Sept 2004 - p86(1) [501+]

Crebbin, June - *Hal the Pirate*
c Sch Lib - v52 - i4 - Winter 2004 - p186(1) [51-500]

Crebbin, Wendy - *Quality Teaching and Learning: Challenging Orthodoxies*
    R&R Bk N - v19 - i3 - August 2004 - p215(1) [1-50]

Crecraft, D.E. - *Electronics, 2nd Ed.*
    SciTech - v28 - i4 - Dec 2004 - p155(1) [51-500]

Creech, Sharon - *Granny Torrelli Makes Soup (Read by Murphy, Donna). Audiobook Review*
c BL - v101 - i9-10 - Jan 1 2005 - p778(1) [1-50]
Granny Torrelli Makes Soup
c Five Owls - v18 - i1 - Fall 2004 - p22(1) [51-500]
y Kliatt - v39 - i2 - March 2005 - p18(1) [51-500]
c LibMed - v22 - i5 - Feb 2004 - p67(1) [501+]
y PW - v252 - i2 - Jan 10 2005 - p58(1) [1-50]
c SLJ - v51 - i2 - Feb 2005 - p58(1) [51-500]
Heartbeat (Read by Siegfried, Mandy). Audiobook Review
c BL - v100 - i21 - July 2004 - p1857(1) [1-50]
y Kliatt - v38 - i5 - Sept 2004 - p61(2) [501+]
c SLJ - v50 - i9 - Sept 2004 - p77(1) [51-500]
Heartbeat
c Sch Lib - v52 - i3 - Autumn 2004 - p136(1) [501+]
Love That Dog
c SLJ - v50 - i11 - Nov 2004 - p65(1) [51-500]
Walk Two Moons
c Teach Lib - v32 - i1 - Oct 2004 - p14(1) [51-500]

Creek, Roland - *The Silver Yoke*
    Roundup M - v12 - i3 - Feb 2005 - p26(1) [51-500]

Creeley, Robert - *George Oppen: Selected Poems*
    BIC - v33 - i7 - Oct 2004 - pNA [501+]

Creese, Angela - *Multilingual Classroom Ecologies: Inter-Relationships, Interactions and Ideologies*
    R&R Bk N - v19 - i1 - Feb 2004 - p192(1) [501+]

Creese, Mary R.S. - *Ladies in the Laboratory II: West European Women in Science, 1800-1900: A Survey of Their Contributions to Research*
    Choice - v42 - i3 - Nov 2004 - p504(1) [1-50]
    SciTech - v28 - i3 - Sept 2004 - p13(1) [501+]

Creeser, Rosemary - *Wildlife-Friendly Plants: Make Your Garden a Haven for Beneficial Insects, Amphibians and Birds*
    BL - v101 - i3 - Oct 1 2004 - p290(1) [51-500]
    Bwatch - Feb 2005 - pNA [51-500]
    LJ - v129 - i18 - Nov 1 2004 - p111(1) [501+]
    PW - v251 - i37 - Sept 13 2004 - p73(1) [1-50]
    SciTech - v28 - i4 - Dec 2004 - p66(1) [501+]

Crehan, Kate - *Gramsci, Culture and Anthropology*
    IJAHS - v37 - i1 - Wntr 2004 - p181-183 [501+]

Creighton, Donald - *The Empire of the St. Lawrence: A Study in Commerce and Politics*
    Can Hist R - v85 - i3 - Sept 2004 - p555(4) [501+]
    CBRA - Annual 2003 - p274(1) [501+]

Creighton, Margaret - *The Colors of Courage: Gettysburg's Forgotten History: Immigrants, Women, and African Americans in the Civil War's Defining Battle*
    KR - v72 - i22 - Nov 15 2004 - p1075(1) [501+]
    LJ - v130 - i1 - Jan 1 2005 - p127(1) [51-500]

Crellin, John K. - *A Social History of Medicines in the Twentieth Century: To Be Taken Three Times a Day*
    Choice - v42 - i3 - Nov 2004 - p516(1) [1-50]
    E-Streams - Nov 2004 - pNA [501+]
    SciTech - v28 - i3 - Sept 2004 - p121(1) [51-500]

Cresciani, Gianfranco - *The Italians in Australia*
    AHS - v35 - i124 - Oct 2004 - p391(2) [501+]

Crespi, Juan - *A Description of Distant Roads: Original Journals of the First Expedition into California, 1769-1770*
    CHR - v90 - i4 - Oct 2004 - p814(3) [501+]

Crespy, David A. - *Off-Off Broadway Explosion: How Playwrights of the 1960s Ignited a New American Theater*
    Am Theat - v21 - i9 - Nov 2004 - p81(3) [501+]

Cressler, W.L., III - *Catastrophes and Lesser Calamities: The Causes of Mass Extinctions*
    Choice - v42 - i7 - March 2005 - p1255(2) [51-500]

Cressman, Robert J. - *USS Ranger: The Navy's First Flattop from Keel to Mast, 1934-1946*
    J Mil H - v68 - i4 - Oct 2004 - p1280-1281 [501+]

Cressman, Ross - *Evolutionary Dynamics and Extensive Form Games*
    JEL - v42 - i1 - March 2004 - p246(1) [501+]
    JEL - v42 - i4 - Dec 2004 - p1118(2) [501+]
    QRB - v79 - i4 - Dec 2004 - p419(2) [501+]

Cresswell, Clio - *Mathematics and Sex*
    Esq - v142 - i5 - Nov 2004 - p48(1) [51-500]

Cresswell, Helen - *Rumpelstiltskin (Illus. by Player, Stephen)*
c SLJ - v51 - i1 - Jan 2005 - p107(2) [51-500]

Cressy, Judith - *Can You Find It, Too?*
c BL - v101 - i5 - Nov 1 2004 - p495(1) [51-500]
c KR - v72 - i22 - Nov 15 2004 - p1088(1) [51-500]
c PW - v251 - i49 - Dec 6 2004 - p62(1) [51-500]
c SLJ - v50 - i12 - Dec 2004 - p128(1) [51-500]

Cresti, Carlo - *Villas of Tuscany*
    R&R Bk N - v19 - i1 - Feb 2004 - p204(1) [51-500]

Crestin-Billet, Frederique - *Collectible Eyeglasses*
    Ant&CM - v109 - i3 - May 2004 - p16(1) [501+]

Crete-Protin, Isabelle - *Eglise et vie chretienne dans le diocese de Troyes du IVe au IXe siecle*
    Specu - v79 - i4 - Oct 2004 - p1062(2) [501+]

Cretney, Stephen - *Family Law in the Twentieth Century: A History*
    Law Q Rev - v120 - July 2004 - p510-513 [501+]

Crew, Cheryl Howard - *In the Face of Jinn*
    KR - v73 - i2 - Jan 15 2005 - p74(1) [501+]

Crew, Frederick - *Postmodern Pooh*
    NS - v133 - i4716 - Nov 29 2004 - p48(1) [501+]

Crew, Gary - *I Said Nothing: The Extinction of the Paradise Parrot*
c Sch Lib - v52 - i3 - Autumn 2004 - p136(1) [501+]
In the Wake of the Mary Celeste (Illus. by Ingpen, Robert)
y Magpies - v19 - i5 - Nov 2004 - p31(1) [501+]
Memorial (Illus. by Tan, Shaun)
c SLJ - v50 - i12 - Dec 2004 - p144(1) [501+]
Memorial (Illus. by Tan, Shuan)
c Res Links - v10 - i1 - Oct 2004 - p3(2) [501+]
Pig on the Titanic: A True Story (Illus. by Whatley, Bruce)
c KR - v73 - i5 - March 1 2005 - p285(1) [51-500]

Crewe, Ben - *Representing Men: Cultural Production and Producers in the Men's Magazine Market*
    JGS - v13 - i3 - Nov 2004 - p277-280 [501+]

Crewe, Sabrina - *The First Moon Landing*
c SLJ - v50 - i8 - August 2004 - p134(1) [51-500]
Lexington and Concord
c SLJ - v50 - i8 - August 2004 - p134(1) [51-500]
Los Angeles
c SLJ - v50 - i7 - July 2004 - p116(1) [1-50]
The Scottsboro Case
y BL - v101 - i9-10 - Jan 1 2005 - p848(1) [1-50]
The Triangle Shirtwaist Factory Fire
c SLJ - v50 - i8 - August 2004 - p134(1) [51-500]

Crews, Harry - *The Knockout Artist*
    BL - v101 - i1 - Sept 1 2004 - p52(1) [501+]

Crews, Nina - *The Neighborhood Mother Goose (Illus. by Crews, Nina)*
  c NYTBR - July 11 2004 - p18 [501+]
  c SLJ - v50 - i10 - Oct 2004 - pS28(1) [1-50]
Crews, Stephen T. - *PAS Proteins: Regulators and Sensors of Development and Physiology*
  SciTech - v28 - i1 - March 2004 - p75(1) [51-500]
Cribb, R.B. - *Historical Dictionary of Indonesia, 2nd Ed.*
  Bwatch - v26 - i9 - Sept 2004 - p11(1) [51-500]
  Choice - v42 - i4 - Dec 2004 - p636(1) [1-50]
  R&R Bk N - v19 - i3 - August 2004 - p55(1) [51-500]
Cribiore, Raffaella - *Gymnastics of the Mind: Greek Education in Hellenistic and Roman Egypt*
  CJ - v100 - i1 - Oct-Nov 2004 - p107-110 [501+]
Crichlow, Wesley - *Buller Men and Batty Bwoys: Hidden Men in Toronto and Halifax Black Communities*
  AJS - v110 - i3 - Nov 2004 - p846(2) [501+]
  Lam Bk Rpt - v13 - i1-2 - August-Sept 2004 - p22(2) [501+]
Crichton, Michael - *State of Fear*
  Am Spect - v38 - i1 - Feb 2005 - p64(2) [501+]
  BL - v101 - i9-10 - Jan 1 2005 - p783(1) [1-50]
  Ent W - i797 - Dec 17 2004 - p87 [501+]
  Globe & Mail - Dec 11 2004 - pD8 [501+]
  NYTBR - Jan 30 2005 - p12 [501+]
  People - v63 - i1 - Jan 10 2005 - p48 [51-500]
  PW - v252 - i6 - Feb 7 2005 - p34(1) [51-500]
Crick, Francis - *Of Molecules and Men*
  SciTech - v28 - i4 - Dec 2004 - p63(1) [51-500]
Crick, Julia - *The Uses of Script and Print, 1300-1700*
  Clio - v33 - i4 - Summer 2004 - p427(12) [501+]
Crickmore, Paul - *Combat Legend: F-117 Nighthawk*
  APH - v51 - i4 - Winter 2004 - p56(1) [501+]
Crider, Bill - *A Bond with Death*
  BL - v101 - i4 - Oct 15 2004 - p392(1) [51-500]
  PW - v251 - i44 - Nov 1 2004 - p47(1) [501+]
Dead Soldiers
  BL - v100 - i21 - July 2004 - p1824(1) [1-50]
Crile, George - *Charlie Wilson's War: The Extraordinary Story of How the Wildest Man in Congress and a Rogue CIA Agent Changed the History of Our Times*
  y Kliatt - v38 - i5 - Sept 2004 - p46(2) [51-500]
Crill, Rosemary - *Arts of Mughal India: Studies in Honour of Robert Skelton*
  TimHES - v0 - i1680 - Feb 25 2005 - p32(1) [501+]
Crilley, Mark - *Billy Clikk: Creach Battler (Illus. by Crilley, Mark)*
  c CCB-B - v58 - i1 - Sept 2004 - p11(2) [51-500]
  c SLJ - v50 - i7 - July 2004 - p104(1) [51-500]
Crim, A. Carolina Castillo - *Turn-of-the-Century Photographs from San Diego, Texas*
  SHQ - v108 - i1 - July 2004 - p117-118 [501+]
Crimi, Carolyn - *Boris and Bella (Illus. by Grimly, Gris)*
  c BL - v101 - i9-10 - Jan 1 2005 - p868(1) [51-500]
  c KR - v72 - i16 - August 15 2004 - p804(1) [51-500]
  c PW - v251 - i32 - August 9 2004 - p248(1) [51-500]
  c SLJ - v50 - i9 - Sept 2004 - p156(2) [51-500]
Get Busy, Beaver! (Illus. by Bynum, Janie)
  c KR - v72 - i19 - Oct 1 2004 - p958(1) [51-500]
  c SLJ - v50 - i11 - Nov 2004 - p96(1) [51-500]
Crimmins, Barry - *Never Shake Hands with a War Criminal*
  PW - v251 - i45 - Nov 8 2004 - p45(1) [501+]
Crimmins, Cathy - *How the Homosexuals Saved Civilization: The True and Heroic Story of How Gay Men Shaped the Modern World*
  LJ - v129 - i16 - Oct 1 2004 - p101(1) [51-500]
  PW - v251 - i33 - August 16 2004 - p55(1) [51-500]
Crimp, Daryl - *Crimpy's Fishing for Kids*
  y Magpies - v19 - i5 - Nov 2004 - p8S(1) [501+]
Crinson, Mark - *Modern Architecture and the End of Empire*
  R&R Bk N - v19 - i1 - Feb 2004 - p202(1) [51-500]
Cripe, Edward J. - *Value-Added Employee: 31 Competencies to Make Yourself Irresistible to Any Company*
  HR Mag - v50 - i2 - Feb 2005 - pS4(1) [501+]
Cripps, Cathy L. - *Fungi in Forest Ecosystems: Systematics, Diversity, and Ecology*
  SciTech - v28 - i4 - Dec 2004 - p64(1) [51-500]
Criscuolo, Vincenzo - *I Cappuccini nell'Umbria del Cinquecento*
  CHR - v90 - i4 - Oct 2004 - p788(2) [501+]
Crisler, Jesse S. - *An Exemplary Citizen: Letters of Charles W. Chesnutt, 1906-1932*
  Afr Am R - v38 - i3 - Fall 2004 - p525(2) [501+]

Crisp, Colin - *Genre, Myth and Convention in the French Cinema: 1929-1939*
  FS - v58 - i3 - July 2004 - p431-432 [501+]
Crisp, James E. - *Sleuthing the Alamo: Davy Crockett's Last Stand and Other Mysteries of the Texas Revolution*
  LJ - v129 - i19 - Nov 15 2004 - p70(1) [501+]
Crisp, Marty - *Everything Dolphin: What Kids Really Want to Know about Dolphins*
  c PW - v251 - i38 - Sept 20 2004 - p64(2) [51-500]
  c SLJ - v50 - i11 - Nov 2004 - p123(1) [51-500]
Crisp, Peter - *Ancient Egypt Revealed*
  c RT - v57 - Oct 2003 - p175 [1-50]
Crispin, Avi - *The End of the Beginning: Being the Adventures of a Small Snail (Illus. by Tusa, Tricia)*
  c PW - v251 - i43 - Oct 25 2004 - p48(1) [51-500]
Crist-Evans, Craig - *Amaryllis*
  y LibMed - v22 - i4 - Jan 2004 - p67(1) [51-500]
North of Everything
  c BL - v101 - i9-10 - Jan 1 2005 - p858(1) [1-50]
  y Kliatt - v38 - i5 - Sept 2004 - p6(2) [51-500]
  c KR - v72 - i20 - Oct 15 2004 - p1003(1) [51-500]
  y SLJ - v50 - i11 - Nov 2004 - p139(1) [51-500]
Crist, James J. - *What to Do When You're Scared & Worried: A Guide for Kids (Illus. by Chesworth, Michael)*
  c SLJ - v50 - i7 - July 2004 - p119(1) [51-500]
Crist, Lynda Lasswell - *The Papers of Jefferson Davis, Vol. 11*
  JSH - v71 - i1 - Feb 2005 - p168(2) [501+]
The Papers of Jefferson Davis, Vol. 11
  VQR - v80 - i3 - Summer 2004 - p255(2) [501+]
Crist, Patricia - *Best Practices in Occupational Therapy Education*
  SciTech - v28 - i4 - Dec 2004 - p118(1) [1-50]
Cristescu, N. - *Mechanics of Elastic Composites*
  SciTech - v28 - i1 - March 2004 - p141(1) [51-500]
Cristian, Adrian - *Living with Spinal Cord Injury: A Wellness Approach*
  SciTech - v28 - i4 - Dec 2004 - p109(1) [51-500]
Cristoloveanu, S. - *Silicon-on-Insulator Technology and Devices XI: Proceedings*
  SciTech - v28 - i1 - March 2004 - p162(1) [51-500]
Cristy, Raphael James - *Charles M. Russell: The Storyteller's Art*
  Choice - v42 - i7 - March 2005 - p1227(1) [51-500]
Critchfield, James H. - *Partners at the Creation: The Men Behind Postwar Germany's Defense and Intelligence Establishments*
  Choice - v41 - i11-12 - July-August 2004 - p2113(1) [501+]
  For Aff - v83 - i4 - July-August 2004 - p126 [501+]
  HT - v54 - i8 - August 2004 - p57(1) [501+]
  J Mil H - v68 - i3 - July 2004 - p1010-1011 [501+]
Critchlow, Donald T. - *Enemies of the State: Personal Stories from the Gulag*
  Russ Rev - v63 - i2 - April 2004 - pNA [501+]
Critical Issues in Weather Modification Research
  Choice - v41 - i11-12 - July-August 2004 - p2082(1) [501+]
Critser, Greg - *Fat Land; How Americans Became the Fattest People in the World*
  Kliatt - v38 - i4 - July 2004 - p40(1) [51-500]
Crittenden, Ann - *If You've Raised Kids, You Can Manage Anything: Leadership Begins at Home*
  BL - v101 - i1 - Sept 1 2004 - p27(1) [51-500]
  BW - v34 - i38 - Sept 19 2004 - p13(1) [501+]
  People - v62 - i9 - August 30 2004 - p49 [501+]
  PW - v251 - i27 - July 5 2004 - p49(1) [51-500]
  Wom R Bks - v21 - i12 - Sept 2004 - p27(1) [501+]
If You've Raised Kids, You Can Manage Anything: Leadership Beings at Home
  HR Mag - v50 - i1 - Jan 2005 - p105(1) [501+]
Crivelli, Carlo - *Ronald Lightbown*
  Apo - v161 - i517 - March 2005 - p98(2) [501+]
Croce, Arlene - *Writing in the Dark, Dancing in The New Yorker*
  BL - v101 - i5 - Nov 1 2004 - p458(1) [51-500]
Crochet, Treena - *Colonial Style*
  PW - v251 - i51 - Dec 20 2004 - p54(1) [51-500]
Crocheting School: A Complete Course
  BL - v100 - i22 - August 2004 - p1889(2) [51-500]
  LJ - v129 - i13 - August 2004 - p77(1) [51-500]
Croci, Pascal - *Auschwitz*
  LJ - v129 - i12 - July 2004 - p60(2) [51-500]

Crocker, Betty - *Betty Crocker's Diabetes Cookbook: Everyday Meals, Easy as 1-2-3*
  SEP - v276 - i4 - July-August 2004 - p50(2) [501+]
Crocker, Carter - *The Tale of the Swamp Rat*
  LibMed - v22 - i7 - April-May 2004 - p60(60) [501+]
Crocker, Chester A. - *Herding Cats: Multiparty Mediation in a Complex World*
  JTWS - v21 - i1 - Spring 2004 - p339(5) [501+]
Taming Intractable Conflicts" Mediation in the Hardest Cases
  Pers PS - v34 - i1 - Wntr 2005 - p57(1) [501+]
Crocker, Cornelia Cyss - *Reading 1 Corinthians in the Twenty-First Century*
  R&R Bk N - v19 - i4 - Nov 2004 - p23(1) [51-500]
Crocker, Pat - *The Smoothies Bible*
  BIC - v33 - i8 - Nov 2004 - p26(2) [501+]
Crockett, Alasdair - *Patterns and Processes of Religious Change in Modern Industrial Societies: Europe and the United States*
  R&R Bk N - v19 - i4 - Nov 2004 - p15(1) [51-500]
Crockett, James R. - *Operation Pretense: The FBI's Sting on County Corruption in Mississippi*
  JSH - v70 - i3 - August 2004 - p728(1) [501+]
Crockett, Rigel - *Fair Wind and Plenty of It: A Modern-Day Tall Ship Adventure*
  KR - v73 - i2 - Jan 15 2005 - p97(1) [501+]
  LJ - v130 - i2 - Feb 15 2005 - p106(1) [51-500]
  PW - v252 - i8 - Feb 21 2005 - p166(1) [51-500]
Crocombe, Ron - *Akono'anga Maori: Cook Islands Culture*
  Cont Pac - v17 - i1 - Spring 2005 - p248(3) [501+]
Croft, Anthony - *Mathematics for Engineers. 2nd Ed.*
  TimHES - v0 - i1668 - Nov 26 2004 - pXVI(1) [501+]
Croft, Janet Brennan - *War and the Works of J.R.R. Tolkien*
  Choice - v42 - i5 - Jan 2005 - p851(1) [1-50]
  TLS - i5300 - Oct 29 2004 - p30(1) [51-500]
Croft, Pauline - *King James*
  Albion - v36 - i2 - Summer 2004 - p300(4) [501+]
Patronage, Culture and Power: The Early Cecils
  HNet - July 2004 - pNA [501+]
  Six Ct J - v35 - i3 - Fall 2004 - p954-955 [501+]
Croft, Susan - *She Also Wrote Plays: An International Guide to Women Playwrights from the 10th to the 21st Century*
  Theat J - v56 - i1 - March 2004 - p151(3) [501+]
Crofton, Christine - *Nursing Documentation in Aged Care: A Guide to Practice*
  SciTech - v28 - i4 - Dec 2004 - p120(1) [51-500]
Croggon, Alison - *The Gift*
  y Sch Lib - v52 - i4 - Winter 2004 - p214(1) [51-500]
Croisille, Christian - *Correspondance d'Alphonse de Lamartine (1830-1867), Vol. 6*
  FS - v58 - i1 - Jan 2004 - p123(2) [501+]
Croke, B. - *Count Marcellinus and His Chronicle*
  Class R - v53 - i2 - Nov 2003 - p394-395 [501+]
Cromartie, Michael - *A Public Faith: Evangelicals and Civic Engagement*
  J Ch St - v46 - i4 - Autumn 2004 - p902(3) [501+]
  R&R Bk N - v19 - i1 - Feb 2004 - p17(1) [51-500]
Crombie, Deborah - *In a Dark House (Read by Deehy, Michael). Audiobook Review*
  y Kliatt - v39 - i2 - March 2005 - p53(1) [51-500]
In a Dark House
  PW - v251 - i40 - Oct 4 2004 - p74(1) [51-500]
A Share in Death (Read by Deehy, Michael). Audiobook Review
  y Kliatt - v39 - i1 - Jan 2005 - p50(1) [51-500]
Crombie, John - *Chez Charlotte and Fin-De-Siecle Montparnasse*
  TLS - i5300 - Oct 29 2004 - p31(1) [51-500]
Crome, Keith - *Lyotard and Greek Thought: Sophistry*
  R&R Bk N - v20 - i1 - Feb 2005 - p4(1) [51-500]
Crompton, Louis - *Homosexuality & Civilization*
  Choice - v41 - i7 - March 2004 - p1376(1) [501+]
  G&L Rev W - v11 - i4 - July-August 2004 - p36(2) [501+]
  TimHES - v0 - i1656 - Sept 3 2004 - p27(1) [501+]
Crompton, Samuel Willard - *Gouverneur Morris: Creating a Nation*
  c SLJ - v50 - i7 - July 2004 - p119(1) [51-500]

Crompton, T.R. - *Preconcentration Techniques for Natural and Treated Waters: High Sensitivity Determination of Organic and Organometallic Compounds, Cations and Anions*
E-Streams - Oct 2004 - pNA [501+]

Cronberg, Tarja - *Transforming Russia: From a Military to a Peace Economy*
JPR - v41 - i5 - Sept 2004 - p639-640 [501+]
Russ Rev - v63 - i2 - April 2004 - pNA [501+]

Crone, Deanne A. - *Responding to Problem Behavior in Schools: The Behavior Education Program*
R&R Bk N - v19 - i4 - Nov 2004 - p180(1) [501+]

Crone-Findlay, Noreen - *Creative Crocheted Dolls: 50 Whimsical Designs*
LJ - v129 - i13 - August 2004 - p77(2) [501+]

Crone, Patricia - *God's Rule: Government and Islam*
MEJ - v59 - i1 - Wntr 2005 - p163(2) [501+]
R&R Bk N - v19 - i3 - August 2004 - p48(1) [51-500]

Crone, Robert A. - *Seeing Space*
E-Streams - Oct 2004 - pNA [501+]
SciTech - v28 - i1 - March 2004 - p74(1) [51-500]

Cronin, Anne - *Human Development and Performance, Throughout the Lifespan*
SciTech - v28 - i4 - Dec 2004 - p118(1) [1-50]

Cronin, Doreen - *Duck for President (Illus. by Lewin, Betsy)*
c BooChiTr - March 14 2004 - p2(1) [501+]
y NYTBR - Sept 19 2004 - p16 [501+]
c SLJ - v50 - i10 - Oct 2004 - pS28(1) [1-50]

Cronin-Golumb, Alice - *Vision in Alzheimer's Disease*
SciTech - v28 - i4 - Dec 2004 - p9(1) [1-50]

Cronin, James E. - *New Labour's Past*
CR - v285 - i1666 - Nov 2004 - p306(2) [501+]

Cronin, James W. - *Fermi Remembered*
Am Sci - v92 - i6 - Nov-Dec 2004 - p569(2) [501+]
New Sci - v184 - i2470 - Oct 23 2004 - p55(1) [51-500]
TimHES - v0 - i1682 - March 11 2005 - p27(1) [501+]

Cronin, Justin - *The Summer Guest*
BW - v34 - i34 - August 22 2004 - p4(1) [501+]
LJ - v129 - i13 - August 2004 - p66(1) [501+]
NYTBR - August 29 2004 - p8 [501+]

Cronin, Mark T.D. - *Predicting Chemical Toxicity and Fate*
SciTech - v28 - i3 - Sept 2004 - p88(1) [51-500]

Cronin, Michael - *The Languages of Ireland*
R&R Bk N - v19 - i1 - Feb 2004 - p34(1) [1-50]

Cronin, Richard - *Romantic Victorians: English Literature, 1824-1840*
Nine-C Lit - v59 - i1 - June 2004 - p126(129) [501+]
VS - v46 - i4 - Summer 2004 - p684(3) [501+]

Cronk, Judith B. - *Intestates and Others from the Orphans Court Books of Manmouth County, New Jersey, 1785-1906*
EFHM - v58 - i3 - May-June 2004 - p59(1) [51-500]

Cronk, Nicholas - *The Classical Sublime: French Neoclassicism and the Language of Literature*
FS - v58 - i2 - April 2004 - p254(2) [501+]
Les Oeuvres Completes de Voltaire. IB, Oeuvres de 1707-1722
FS - v58 - i2 - April 2004 - p260(1) [501+]

Cronon, William - *The Rhine: An Eco-Biography, 1815-2000*
Pub Hist - v26 - i1 - Wntr 2004 - p163(2) [501+]

Crook, Connie Brummel - *The Perilous Year*
c Can CL - i113/114 - Spring-Summer 2004 - p136(3) [501+]
y VOYA - v27 - i3 - August 2004 - p215(1) [1-50]

Crook, David - *Curis Regis Rolls of the Reign of Henry III Preserved in the Public Record Office*
HER - v119 - i483 - Sept 2004 - p1035(2) [501+]

Crook, Malcolm - *Enlightenment and Revolution: Essays in Honour of Norman Hampson*
R&R Bk N - v19 - i3 - August 2004 - p42(1) [51-500]

Crooker, Constance Emerson - *Gun Control and Gun Rights*
LibMed - v22 - i6 - March 2004 - p86(1) [501+]

Crooks, Clayton E. - *Awesome 3D Game Development: No Programming Required*
SciTech - v28 - i4 - Dec 2004 - p23(1) [51-500]

Crooks, James B. - *Jacksonville: The Consolidation Story, from Civil Rights to the Jaguars*
Choice - v42 - i3 - Nov 2004 - p546(1) [1-50]
HNet - Sept 2004 - pNA [501+]

Crooks, Robert - *Our Sexuality, 9th Ed.*
R&R Bk N - v19 - i4 - Nov 2004 - p127(1) [1-50]
R&R Bk N - v19 - i4 - Nov 2004 - p127(1) [1-50]

Crosa, Jorge H. - *Iron Transport in Bacteria*
SciTech - v28 - i4 - Dec 2004 - p74(1) [51-500]

Crosby, Alfred W. - *Throwing Fire: Projectile Technology through History*
Isis - v95 - i3 - Sept 2004 - p471(2) [501+]

Crosby, Donald G. - *The Poisoned Weed: Plants Toxic to Skin*
Choice - v42 - i3 - Nov 2004 - p510(1) [1-50]

Crosby, Faye J. - *Affirmative Action Is Dead: Long Live Affirmative Action*
Choice - v42 - i4 - Dec 2004 - p741(1) [1-50]
Econ - v371 - i8380 - June 19 2004 - p80US [501+]
HLR - v118 - i3 - Jan 2005 - p1095-1096 [1-50]
R&R Bk N - v19 - i3 - August 2004 - p129(1) [51-500]

Cross, Anthony - *St. Petersburg, 1703-1825*
HER - v119 - i483 - Sept 2004 - p1066(2) [501+]
Slav R - v63 - i4 - Winter 2004 - p878(2) [501+]

Cross, Anthony Glenn - *St Petersburg, 1703-1825*
HER - v119 - i483 - Sept 2004 - p1066(2) [501+]

Cross, Christopher T. - *Political Education: National Policy Comes of Age*
TCR - v106 - i5 - May 2004 - p949(4) [501+]
TCR - v106 - i8 - August 2004 - p1602(3) [501+]

Cross, Gary S. - *The Cute and the Cool: Wondrous Innocence and Modern American Children's Culture*
CC - v122 - i1 - Jan 11 2005 - p22(4) [501+]
Choice - v42 - i5 - Jan 2005 - p939(1) [51-500]
Encyclopedia of Recreation and Leisure in America, Vols. 1-2
BL - v101 - i9-10 - Jan 1 2005 - p902(1) [501+]
LJ - v130 - i2 - Feb 1 2005 - p114(2) [51-500]

Cross, Gillian - *The Dark Ground: Book One of the Dark Ground Trilogy*
y BL - v101 - i1 - Sept 1 2004 - p106(1) [1-50]
c CCB-B - v58 - i5 - Jan 2005 - p205(2) [501+]
c HB - v80 - i5 - Sept-Oct 2004 - p579(1) [51-500]
c KR - v72 - i15 - August 1 2004 - p739(1) [501+]
y SLJ - v50 - i9 - Sept 2004 - p202(1) [51-500]

Cross, Jonathan - *The Cambridge Companion to Stravinsky*
Choice - v41 - i7 - March 2004 - p1305(2) [501+]
MT - v145 - i1887 - Summer 2004 - p111(6) [501+]

Cross, Kathleen - *Schooling Carmen*
KR - v72 - i16 - August 15 2004 - p759(1) [51-500]

Cross, Kelvin F. - *Quick Hits: Ten Key Surgical Strike Actions to Improve Business Process Performance*
R&R Bk N - v19 - i4 - Nov 2004 - p91(') [1-50]

Cross, Mary - *A Century of American Icons: 100 Products and Slogans from the Twentieth Century Consumer Culture*
TLS - i5284 - July 9 2004 - p10(1) [501+]

Cross, Richard - *The Metaphysics of the Incarnation: Thomas Aquinas to Duns Scotus*
JR - v84 - i4 - Oct 2004 - p641(2) [501+]

Cross, Robert L. - *The Hidden Power of Social Networks: Understanding How Work Really Gets Done in Organizations*
Choice - v42 - i1 - Sept 2004 - p150(1) [501+]
HR Mag - v49 - i10 - Oct 2004 - p142(2) [501+]
R&R Bk N - v19 - i3 - August 2004 - p109(1) [51-500]

Cross, Roger - *A Vision for Science Education: Responding to the Work of Peter Fensham*
TCR - v106 - i2 - Feb 2004 - p248-251 [501+]

Cross, William - *Political Parties*
Choice - v42 - i5 - Jan 2005 - p926(1) [1-50]
R&R Bk N - v19 - i3 - August 2004 - p181(1) [501+]

Crossan, John Dominic - *In Search of Paul: How Jesus's Apostle Opposed Rome's Empire with God's Kingdom*
BL - v101 - i6 - Nov 15 2004 - p534(1) [51-500]
PW - v251 - i41 - Oct 11 2004 - p75(1) [51-500]

Crosscurrents at Century's End: Selections from the Neuberger Berman Art Collection
Choice - v42 - i3 - Nov 2004 - p474(1) [1-50]

Crossen, Craig - *Sky Vistas: Astronomy for Binoculars and Richest-Field Telescopes*
Astron - v32 - i7 - July 2004 - p98 [51-500]
Choice - v42 - i1 - Sept 2004 - p127(1) [501+]
S&T - v107 - i6 - June 2004 - p109(2) [501+]

Crossing Philip Booth
c PW - v251 - i31 - August 2 2004 - p73(1) [51-500]

Crossingham, John - *Cheerleading in Action (Illus. by Rouse, Bonna)*
c CBRA - Annual 2003 - p557(2) [501+]
Extreme Climbing
BL - v101 - i1 - Sept 1 2004 - p110(2) [1-50]
Extreme Sports
BL - v101 - i1 - Sept 1 2004 - p110(2) [1-50]
Gymnastics in Action (Illus. by Rouse, Bonna)
c CBRA - Annual 2003 - p557(2) [501+]
In-line Skating in Action (Illus. by Rouse, Bonna)
c CBRA - Annual 2003 - p557(2) [501+]
Lacrosse in Action (Illus. by Rouse, Bonna)
c CBRA - Annual 2003 - p557(2) [501+]
Swimming in Action (Illus. by Rouse, Bonna)
c CBRA - Annual 2003 - p557(2) [501+]
Wrestling in Action (Illus. by Rouse, Bonna)
c CBRA - Annual 2003 - p557(2) [501+]

Crossley-Holland, Kevin - *At the Crossing Places*
y PW - v251 - i46 - Nov 15 2004 - p62(1) [501+]
How Many Miles to Bethlehem? (Illus. by Malone, Peter)
c BL - v101 - i3 - Oct 1 2004 - p331(1) [51-500]
c CCB-B - v58 - i4 - Dec 2004 - p164(1) [51-500]
HB - v80 - i6 - Nov-Dec 2004 - p658(1) [51-500]
c KR - v72 - i21 - Nov 1 2004 - p1048(1) [51-500]
c PW - v251 - i39 - Sept 27 2004 - p62(1) [501+]
King of the Middle March
y BL - v101 - i1 - Sept 1 2004 - p122(1) [1-50]
y CCB-B - v58 - i6 - Feb 2005 - p248(2) [501+]
y HB - v81 - i1 - Jan-Feb 2005 - p15(1) [51-500]
y HB - v81 - i1 - Jan-Feb 2005 - p91(2) [51-500]
y Kliatt - v38 - i5 - Sept 2004 - p6(2) [51-500]
y KR - v72 - i18 - Sept 15 2004 - p912(1) [501+]
y PW - v251 - i42 - Oct 18 2004 - p66(1) [501+]
y Sch Lib - v52 - i4 - Winter 2004 - p211(1) [51-500]
y SLJ - v50 - i11 - Nov 2004 - p139(2) [51-500]
The King Who Was and Will Be
y Sch Lib - v52 - i4 - Winter 2004 - p211(1) [51-500]
The Old Stories (Illus. by Lawrence, John)
c Sch Lib - v52 - i4 - Winter 2004 - p203(1) [51-500]
Once upon a Poem: Favorite Poems That Tell Stories (Illus. by Bailey, Peter)
KR - v72 - i24 - Dec 15 2004 - p1199(1) [501+]
c SLJ - v51 - i1 - Jan 2005 - p108(1) [51-500]

Crossley, Nick - *After Habermas: New Perspectives on the Public Sphere*
Choice - v42 - i7 - March 2005 - p1238(1) [51-500]

Crossman, William - *VIVO [Voice-In/Voice-Out]: The Coming Age of Talking Computers*
Fut - v38 - i6 - Nov-Dec 2004 - p57(3) [501+]
Fut - v38 - i6 - Nov-Dec 2004 - p61(1) [51-500]
R&R Bk N - v19 - i4 - Nov 2004 - p122(1) [51-500]

Crosson-Tower, Cynthia - *Understanding Child Abuse and Neglect, 6th Ed.*
R&R Bk N - v19 - i4 - Nov 2004 - p146(1) [501+]

Crosthwaite, Luis Humberto - *Puro Border: Dispatches, Snapshots and Graffiti*
WLT - v78 - i3-4 - Sept-Dec 2004 - p158(1) [501+]

Croswell, Ken - *Magnificent Mars*
S&T - v107 - i1 - Jan 2004 - p72(2) [501+]

Croteau, James M. - *Deconstructing Heterosexism in the Counseling Professions: A Narrative Approach*
R&R Bk N - v19 - i4 - Nov 2004 - p10(1) [51-500]

Croteau, Marie-Danielle - *Fred's Halloween Adventure (Illus. by St-Aubin, Bruno)*
y Can CL - i111-112 - Fall-Winter 2003 - p134(6) [501+]

Crotty, Raymond D. - *When Histories Collide: The Development and Impact of Individualistic Capitalism*
AHR - v109 - i4 - Oct 2004 - p1193-1194 [501+]
CS - v33 - i2 - March 2004 - p190-192 [501+]

Crotty, William - *The Politics of Terror: The U.S. Response to 9/11*
Choice - v41 - i11-12 - July-August 2004 - p2122(1) [501+]
R&R Bk N - v19 - i1 - Feb 2004 - p63(1) [501+]

Crouch, Geoffrey I. - *Consumer Psychology of Tourism, Hospitality and Leisure, Vol. 3*
R&R Bk N - v19 - i3 - August 2004 - p79(1) [51-500]

Crouch, Stanley - *The Artificial White Man: Essays on Authenticity*
BL - v101 - i5 - Nov 1 2004 - p447(2) [51-500]
Black Iss - v6 - i6 - Nov-Dec 2004 - p63(2) [501+]
NYTBR - Jan 16 2005 - p7 [501+]
PW - v251 - i38 - Sept 20 2004 - p55(1) [51-500]

Crouch, Tom D. - *Wings: A History of Aviation from Kites to the Space Age*
E-Streams - July 2004 - pNA [501+]
y   Kliatt - v39 - i2 - March 2005 - p39(1) [51-500]
VQR - v80 - i2 - Spring 2004 - p254-254 [501+]

Croucher, Sheila L. - *Globalization and Belonging: The Politics of Identity in a Changing World*
Choice - v41 - i11-12 - July-August 2004 - p2120(1) [501+]

Crouse, Richard - *100 Best Movies You've Never Seen*
CBRA - Annual 2003 - p13(2) [51-500]

Crouzet, Denis - *"Practiques" et "practiqueurs": La vie politique a la fin du regne de Henri III, 1584-1589*
JMH - v76 - i4 - Dec 2004 - p959(2) [501+]

Crow, Carl - *400 Million Customers: The Experiences--Some Happy, Some Sad of an American in China and What They Taught Him*
Pac A - v77 - i3 - Fall 2004 - p568(3) [501+]

Crow, Charles L. - *A Companion to the Regional Literatures of America*
NEQ - v77 - i2 - June 2004 - p300-307 [501+]

Crow, Linda W. - *Teaching Tips: Innovations in Undergraduate Science Instruction*
SB - v40 - i6 - Nov-Dec 2004 - p246(2) [501+]

Crowder, A.B. - *Wakeful Anguish: A Literary Biography of William Humphrey*
Choice - v41 - i11-12 - July-August 2004 - p2043(1) [501+]
Sew R - v112 - i2 - Spring 2004 - pLIII-LIV [501+]

Crowder, David - *Building a Web Site for Dummies*
LJ - v129 - i20 - Dec 1 2004 - p152(1) [51-500]

Crowder, Ralph L. - *John Edward Bruce: Politician, Journalist, and Self-Trained Historian of the African Diaspora*
Choice - v42 - i3 - Nov 2004 - p546(1) [1-50]

Crowe, Chris - *Getting Away with Murder: The True Story of the Emmett Till Case*
LibMed - v22 - i4 - Jan 2004 - p75(1) [501+]
More than a Game: Sports Literature for Young Adults
y   VOYA - v27 - i4 - Oct 2004 - p337(1) [51-500]

Crowe, David M. - *Oskar Schindler: The Untold Account of His Life, Wartime Activities, and the True Story Behind the List*
LJ - v129 - i20 - Dec 1 2004 - p129(2) [51-500]
Spec - v297 - i9212 - Feb 26 2005 - p43(1) [501+]
BL - v101 - i4 - Oct 15 2004 - p383(1) [51-500]

Crowe, Yolande - *Persia and China: Safavid Blue and White Ceramics in the Victoria & Albert Museum, 1501-1738*
A Aff - v35 - i2 - July 2004 - p224-225 [501+]

Crowley, Chris - *Younger Next Year: A Guide to Living Like 50 Until You're 80 and Beyond*
LJ - v130 - i2 - Feb 1 2005 - p108(1) [51-500]
PW - v251 - i47 - Nov 22 2004 - p55(1) [51-500]

Crowley, Jocelyn Elise - *The Politics of Child Support in America*
Choice - v42 - i1 - Sept 2004 - pNA [501+]

Crowley, John - *Novelties and Souvenirs: Collected Short Fiction*
c   MFSF - v107 - i2 - August 2004 - p35(6) [501+]

Crowley, Kieran - *Almost Paradise: The East Hampton Murder of Ted Ammon*
KR - v72 - i23 - Dec 1 2004 - p1128(1) [501+]
PW - v251 - i50 - Dec 13 2004 - p59(1) [51-500]

Crowley, M. Sue - *The Search for Autonomous Intimacy: Sexual Abuse and Young Women's Identity Development*
Adoles - v39 - i156 - Winter 2004 - p830(1) [51-500]

Crowley, Stephen - *Explaining Labor Quiescence in Post-Communist Europe: Historical Legacies and Comparative Perspective*
Wil Q - v28 - i4 - Autumn 2004 - p110(1) [501+]

Crowley, Terry - *Bislama Reference Grammar*
R&R Bk N - v19 - i4 - Nov 2004 - p220(1) [501+]

Crowley, Terry A. - *Marriage of Minds: Isabel and Oscar Skelton Reinventing Canada*
CBRA - Annual 2003 - p41(2) [51-500]

Crowley, Tony - *Lo-Tech Navigator*
SciTech - v28 - i3 - Sept 2004 - p172(1) [51-500]

The Crown of the Continent: Glacier National Park
LJ - v129 - i19 - Nov 15 2004 - p96(1) [51-500]

Crown, Susan Rubin - *Art Against the Odds: From Slave Quilts to Prison Paintings*
y   Teach Lib - v32 - i1 - Oct 2004 - p30(1) [51-500]

Crowner, David - *The Spirituality of the German Awakening*
HNet - Nov 2004 - pNA [501+]

Crowston, Clare Haru - *Fabricating Women: The Seamstresses of Old Regime France, 1675-1791*
JWH - v16 - i4 - Winter 2004 - p226(8) [501+]

Crowther, David - *Perspectives on Corporate Social Responsibility*
R&R Bk N - v19 - i3 - August 2004 - p107(1) [1-50]

Crowther, Peter - *Cities*
Bwatch - v26 - i7 - July 2004 - p6(1) [51-500]
Constellations
LJ - v130 - i1 - Jan 1 2005 - p103(1) [51-500]
Fourbodings
PW - v252 - i1 - Jan 3 2005 - p41(1) [51-500]
Postscripts 1
ChrSFF&H - v26 - i9 - Sept 2004 - p34(1) [51-500]
Songs of Leaving
y   BL - v100 - i21 - July 2004 - p1828(1) [51-500]

Crowther, Robert - *Let's Cook! A Press-Out-and-Play Book*
c   PW - v252 - i2 - Jan 10 2005 - p58(1) [51-500]

Croxton, Derek - *The Peace of Westphalia: A Historical Dictionary*
GSR - v27 - i3 - Oct 2004 - p607(1) [501+]
Six Ct J - v35 - i1 - Spring 2004 - p242(2) [501+]

Croydem, Margaret - *Conversations with Peter Brook, 1970-2000*
Parabola - v28 - i3 - Fall 2003 - p111(3) [501+]

Crozier, Lorna - *Breathing Fire 2: Canada's New Poets*
Globe & Mail - Nov 6 2004 - pD13 [501+]

Cruickshank, Tom - *Old Toronto Houses*
BIC - v33 - i6 - Sept 2004 - p38(2) [501+]
CBRA - Annual 2003 - p113(1) [501+]

Cruikshank, Jeffrey - *Murder at the B-School*
BL - v101 - i3 - Oct 1 2004 - p312(1) [51-500]
BW - v34 - i44 - Oct 31 2004 - p13(1) [501+]
DroRevMy - v24 - i4 - July-August 2004 - p11(1) [51-500]
KR - v72 - i17 - Sept 1 2004 - p838(1) [51-500]
LJ - v129 - i14 - Sept 1 2004 - p122(1) [51-500]
PW - v251 - i36 - Sept 6 2004 - p48(2) [51-500]

Crum, Shutta - *The Bravest of the Brave*
KR - v72 - i24 - Dec 15 2004 - p1200(1) [501+]
Spitting Image (Read by Gibson, Julia). Audiobook Review
c   Kliatt - v38 - i6 - Nov 2004 - p51(1) [51-500]
c   SLJ - v50 - i7 - July 2004 - p60(1) [51-500]

Crumey, Andrew - *Mobius Dick*
NS - v133 - i4716 - Nov 29 2004 - p45(1) [51-500]
TLS - i5285 - July 16 2004 - p23(1) [501+]

Crumlish, Christian - *The Power of Many: How the Living Web Is Transforming Politics, Business, and Everday Life*
Choice - v42 - i6 - Feb 2005 - p1062(1) [501+]

Crump, Jennifer - *The War of 1812 Against the States: Heroes of a Great Canadian Victory*
y   Res Links - v10 - i3 - Feb 2005 - p45(2) [501+]

Crumpacker, Bunny - *Alexander's Pretending Day (Illus. by Andreasen, Dan)*
c   PW - v252 - i6 - Feb 7 2005 - p58(1) [51-500]

Cruse, Julius M. - *Atlas of Immunology*
Choice - v42 - i2 - Oct 2004 - p270-2 [501+]

Crushshon, Theresa - *Malcolm X*
c   SLJ - v51 - i1 - Jan 2005 - p57(1) [51-500]

Crusius, Irene - *Studien zum Pramonstratenserorden*
HNet - Nov 2004 - pNA [501+]

Crutcher, Chris - *King of the Mild Frontier: An Ill-Advised Autobiography*
PW - v251 - i45 - Nov 8 2004 - p58(1) [51-500]
y   Teach Lib - v32 - i1 - Oct 2004 - p51(1) [51-500]
y   Kliatt - v39 - i2 - March 2005 - p33(1) [51-500]

Cruver, Brian - *Anatomy of Greed: Unshredded Truth from an Enron Insider*
En Jnl - v25 - i4 - Oct 2004 - p115(20) [501+]

Cruysberghs, Paul - *Immediacy and Reflection in Kierkegaard's Thought*
R&R Bk N - v19 - i3 - August 2004 - p6(1) [1-50]

Cruysse, Dirk Van der - *Noble desir de courir le monde: Voyager en Asie au XVII siecle*
JMH - v76 - i4 - Dec 2004 - p960(3) [501+]

Cruz, Angie - *Let It Rain Coffee*
KR - v73 - i5 - March 1 2005 - p245(1) [501+]
PW - v252 - i10 - March 7 2005 - p48(1) [51-500]

Cruz, Barbara C. - *Alvin Ailey: Celebrating African-American Culture in Dance*
y   SLJ - v51 - i1 - Jan 2005 - p144(1) [51-500]

Cruz, Celia - *Celia: My Life*
Black Iss - v6 - i6 - Nov-Dec 2004 - p40(2) [501+]
Ent W - i773 - July 9 2004 - p94 [1-50]

Cruz, J. Micheal - *Sociological Analysis of Aging: The Gay Male Perspective*
R&R Bk N - v19 - i2 - May 2004 - p133 [51-500]

Cruz, Robyn Flaum - *Dance/Movement Therapists in Action: A Working Guide to Research Options*
SciTech - v28 - i4 - Dec 2004 - p97(1) [51-500]

Crystal, David - *The New Penguin Factfinder*
Choice - v42 - i5 - Jan 2005 - p824(1) [51-500]
Shakespeare's Words: A Glossary and Language Companion
R&R Bk N - v19 - i1 - Feb 2004 - p237(1) [51-500]
The Stories of English
BL - v101 - i3 - Oct 1 2004 - p288(1) [51-500]
CR - v285 - i1666 - Nov 2004 - p319(1) [501+]
KR - v72 - i15 - August 1 2004 - p721(1) [51-500]
LJ - v129 - i19 - Nov 15 2004 - p60(1) [501+]
PW - v251 - i32 - August 9 2004 - p240(1) [51-500]
TES - v0 - i4587 - June 11 2004 - psss18(2) [501+]
TLS - i5290 - August 20 2004 - p11(1) [501+]

Crystal, Jonathan - *Unwanted Company: Foreign Investment in American Industries*
JEL - v41 - i4 - Dec 2003 - p1356(1) [501+]

Csaki, Csaba - *Reaching the Rural Poor: A Renewed Strategy for Rural Development*
JEL - v42 - i1 - March 2004 - p314(1) [501+]

Csanyi, Vilmos - *If Dogs Could Talk: Exploring the Canine Mind*
LJ - v130 - i1 - Jan 1 2005 - p138(1) [51-500]
PW - v251 - i48 - Nov 29 2004 - p32(1) [51-500]

Csapo, Eric - *Poetry, Theory, Praxis: The Social Life of Myth, Word and Image in Ancient Greece: Essays in Honour of William J. Slater*
Class R - v54 - i2 - Nov 2004 - p564-565 [501+]

Csele, Mark - *Fundamentals of Lights and Lasers*
SciTech - v28 - i4 - Dec 2004 - p50(1) [51-500]

Csendes, Peter - *Philipp Von Schwaben: Ein Staufer in Kampf um Die Macht*
HER - v119 - i483 - Sept 2004 - p1030(2) [501+]

Csermely, Peter - *Science Education: Talent Recruitment and Public Understanding*
SciTech - v28 - i3 - Sept 2004 - p14(1) [501+]

Csikszentmihalyi, Mark - *Material Virtue: Ethics and the Body in Early China*
R&R Bk N - v20 - i1 - Feb 2005 - p12(1) [51-500]

Csikszentmihalyi, Mihaly - *Good Business: Leadership, Flow, and the Making of Meaning*
HR Mag - v49 - i7 - July 2004 - pS3(1) [51-500]

CSIS Commission on Spectrum Management - *Spectrum Management for the 21st Century: A Report of the CSIS Commission on Spectrum Management*
R&R Bk N - v19 - i2 - May 2004 - p109(1) [51-500]

Cua, Antonio S. - *Encyclopedia of Chinese Philosophy*
Ch Rev Int - v11 - i1 - Spring 2004 - p62(8) [501+]

Cuban, Larry - *The Blackboard and the Bottom Line: Why Schools Can't Be Businesses*
LJ - v129 - i20 - Dec 1 2004 - p133(1) [51-500]
Powerful Reforms with Shallow Roots: Improving America's Urban Schools
TCR - v106 - i2 - Feb 2004 - p323-326 [501+]
Why is it So Hard to Get Good Schools?
HER - v74 - i4 - Winter 2004 - p454-456 [501+]
TCR - v106 - i2 - Feb 2004 - p320-322 [501+]

The Cuban Missile Crises
LibMed - v22 - i6 - March 2004 - p92(1) [501+]

Cubbage, Norman Brian - *Nothingness and the Quarrel between Faith and Reason*
RM - v58 - i1 - Sept 2004 - p209(3) [501+]

Cubberley, William - *Round about the Ballet*
Dance - v79 - i3 - March 2005 - p71(2) [501+]

Cubitt, Sean - *The Cinema Effect*
TimHES - v0 - i1647 - July 2 2004 - p29(1) [501+]

Cuccurullo, Sara J. - *Physical Medicine and Rehabilitation Board Review*
SciTech - v28 - i4 - Dec 2004 - p118(1) [1-50]

Cucullu, Gordon - *Separated at Birth*
Bwatch - Dec 2004 - pNA [501+]

Cudahy, Brian J. - *A Century of Subways: Celebrating 100 Years of New York's Underground Railways*
AM - v191 - i5 - August 30 2004 - p2 [501+]
JAH - v91 - i3 - Dec 2004 - p1053(2) [501+]

Cuddy-Keane, Melba - *Virginia Woolf, the Intellectual, and the Public Sphere*
Choice - v41 - i7 - March 2004 - p1294(2) [501+]
ELT - v48 - i2 - Spring 2005 - p118(4) [501+]

Cuddy, Lois A. - *Evolution and Eugenics in American Literature and Culture, 1880-1940: Essays on Ideological Conflict and Complicity*
Am St - v45 - i1 - Spring 2004 - p154-155 [501+]

Cudjoe, Selwyn R. - *Beyond Boundaries: The Intellectual Tradition of Trinidad and Tobago in the Nineteenth-Century*
AHR - v109 - i3 - June 2004 - p945(1) [501+]

Cuellar, Carlos E. - *Stories from the Barrio: A History of Mexican Fort Worth*
SHQ - v107 - i3 - Jan 2004 - p471(2) [501+]

Cuentas Financieras de la Economia Espanola: 1990-2002
JEL - v42 - i1 - March 2004 - p253(1) [501+]

Cuerda, Josep - *The Essential Atlas of Botany*
y SB - v40 - i5 - Sept-Oct 2004 - p212(2) [51-500]

Culhane-Pera, Kathleen A. - *Healing by Heart: Clinical and Ethical Case Stories of Hmong Families and Western Providers*
MAQ - v18 - i4 - Dec 2004 - p511(5) [501+]

Culinary Institute of America - *Baking at Home with the Culinary Institute of America*
LJ - v129 - i14 - Sept 1 2004 - p181(1) [501+]
Gourmet Meals in Minutes
People - v62 - i21 - Nov 22 2004 - p58 [51-500]

Cull, Nicholas - *Propaganda and Mass Persuasion: A Historical Encyclopedia 1500 to the Present*
LibMed - v23 - i1 - August-Sept 2004 - p82(1) [51-500]

Cullen, David - *The First Man in Space*
c SLJ - v50 - i7 - July 2004 - p116(1) [51-500]

Cullen, Fintan - *The Irish Face: Redefining the Irish Portrait*
Apo - v160 - i512 - Oct 2004 - p86(2) [501+]

Cullen, Mark - *Mark Cullen's Ontario Gardening*
CBRA - Annual 2003 - p417(1) [501+]

Cullet, Philippe - *Differential Treatment in International Environmental Law*
R&R Bk N - v19 - i1 - Feb 2004 - pNA [51-500]

Culleton, Claire A. - *Joyce and the G-Men: J. Edgar Hoover's Manipulation of Modernism*
Choice - v42 - i4 - Dec 2004 - p659(1) [1-50]
LJ - v129 - i14 - Sept 1 2004 - p149(1) [51-500]

Cullin, Mitch - *A Slight Trick of the Mind (Read by Jones, Simon). Audiobook Review*
LJ - v130 - i3 - Feb 15 2005 - p171(1) [1-50]
A Slight Trick of the Mind
KR - v73 - i3 - Feb 1 2005 - p133(2) [501+]
PW - v252 - i7 - Feb 14 2005 - p50(1) [51-500]

Cullina, William - *Understanding Orchids: An Uncomplicated Guide to Growing the World's Most Exotic Plants*
BL - v101 - i4 - Oct 15 2004 - p372(1) [51-500]
LJ - v129 - i19 - Nov 15 2004 - p79(1) [501+]
PW - v251 - i39 - Sept 27 2004 - p52(1) [51-500]

Cullinan, Colleen Carpenter - *Redeeming the Story: Women, Suffering, and Christ*
LJ - v129 - i16 - Oct 1 2004 - p87(1) [51-500]

Cullinane, Jan - *The New Retirement: The Ultimate Guide to the Rest of Your Life*
BL - v100 - i21 - July 2004 - p1806(1) [51-500]
BL - v101 - i4 - Oct 15 2004 - p387(1) [51-500]
LJ - v129 - i13 - August 2004 - p91(1) [501+]

Cullis, Christopher A. - *Plant Genomics and Proteomics*
Choice - v42 - i1 - Sept 2004 - p130(2) [51-500]
E-Streams - July 2004 - pNA [501+]

Cullum, Linda E. - *Contemporary American Ethnic Poets: Lives, Works, Sources*
Choice - v42 - i3 - Nov 2004 - p448(1) [1-50]
LJ - v129 - i12 - July 2004 - p118(1) [51-500]

Culpepper, Marilyn Mayer - *Women of the Civil War South: Personal Accounts from Diaries, Letters, and Postwar Reminiscences*
R&R Bk N - v19 - i1 - Feb 2004 - p59(1) [51-500]

Culpepper, Pepper D. - *Creating Cooperation: How States Develop Human Capital in Europe*
Soc Ser R - v79 - i1 - March 2005 - p210(2) [51-500]

Cultraro, M. - *L'anello di Minosse. Archaeologia della regalita nell'egeo minoico*
Class R - v53 - i2 - Nov 2003 - p448-449 [501+]

Cultural Trends
TLS - i5267 - March 12 2004 - p27-27 [501+]

Culture In Series
LibMed - v23 - i1 - August-Sept 2004 - p73(1) [51-500]

CultureGrams 2004 World Edition
LibMed - v23 - i1 - August-Sept 2004 - p73(1) [51-500]

Cultures on the Edge - *African Ceremonies*
y SLJ - v50 - i12 - Dec 2004 - p62(1) [501+]

Culver, Leigh - *Adapting Police Services to New Immigration*
R&R Bk N - v19 - i4 - Nov 2004 - p147(1) [501+]

Cumings, Bruce - *North Korea: Another Country*
R&R Bk N - v19 - i3 - August 2004 - p57(1) [51-500]
North Korea: The Hermit Kingdom
TimHES - v0 - i1659 - Sept 24 2004 - p27(1) [501+]

Cumming, David - *Letters from around the World: Pakistan*
c CH Bwatch - v14 - i11 - Nov 2004 - pNA [51-500]

Cumming, Mark - *The Carlyle Encyclopedia*
Choice - v42 - i2 - Oct 2004 - p266(1) [51-500]

Cumming, Peter - *Out on the Ice in the Middle of the Bay (Illus. by Priestley, Alice)*
c PW - v252 - i2 - Jan 10 2005 - p58(1) [1-50]
c Res Links - v10 - i3 - Feb 2005 - p3(2) [51-500]

Cummings, Anne L. - *Research and Treatment for Aggression with Adolescent Girls*
Adoles - v39 - i155 - Fall 2004 - p623(1) [51-500]

Cummings, Brian - *The Literary Culture of the Reformation: Grammar and Grace*
CH - v73 - i4 - Dec 2004 - p858(2) [501+]

Cummings, Nicholas A. - *Early Detection and Treatment of Substance Abuse Within Integrated Primary Care: Proceedings*
SciTech - v28 - i4 - Dec 2004 - p101(1) [51-500]

Cummings, Pat - *Talking with Artists. Vol. 2*
c SLJ - v50 - i11 - Nov 2004 - p65(1) [51-500]

Cummings, Priscilla - *Red Kayak*
y BL - v101 - i1 - Sept 1 2004 - p106(1) [1-50]
c CCB-B - v58 - i2 - Oct 2004 - p66(2) [51-500]
y Kliatt - v38 - i5 - Sept 2004 - p6(2) [51-500]
y KR - v72 - i17 - Sept 1 2004 - p862(1) [51-500]
y SLJ - v50 - i9 - Sept 2004 - p202(1) [51-500]
y VOYA - v27 - i4 - Oct 2004 - p293(1) [51-500]

Cummins, Bryan D. - *Colonel Richardson's Airedales: The Making of the British War Dog School, 1900-1918*
CBRA - Annual 2003 - p338(1) [51-500]

Cummins, Juliet - *Milton and the Ends of Time*
Ren Q - v57 - i3 - Fall 2004 - p1170(2) [501+]
RES - v55 - i220 - June 2004 - p461-462 [501+]

Cumpsty, N.A. - *Compressor Aerodynamics*
SciTech - v28 - i3 - Sept 2004 - p150(1) [51-500]

Cumyn, Alan - *After Sylvia*
Globe & Mail - Sept 11 2004 - pD12 [501+]
Res Links - v10 - i3 - Feb 2005 - p14(1) [501+]
Secret Life of Owen Skye
y Can CL - i111-112 - Fall-Winter 2003 - p134(6) [501+]
The Sojourn
CBRA - Annual 2003 - p160(1) [51-500]
Mac - v117 - i45 - Nov 8 2004 - p50(1) [1-50]

Cumyn, Richard - *Obstacle Course*
CBRA - Annual 2003 - p197(1) [51-500]
View from Tamischeira
CBRA - Annual 2003 - p160(1) [51-500]

Cuneen, Joseph - *Robert Bresson: A Spiritual Style in Film*
FS - v58 - i2 - April 2004 - p291(2) [501+]

Cunningham, Andrew - *The Four Horsemen of the Apocalypse: Religion, War, Famine and Death in Reformation Europe*
S&S - v68 - i1 - Spring 2004 - p117-120 [501+]

Cunningham, Bernadette - *Stories from Gaelic Ireland: Microhistories from the Sixteenth-Century Irish Annals*
Ren Q - v57 - i4 - Winter 2004 - p1543(2) [501+]
R&R Bk N - v19 - i1 - Feb 2004 - p34(1) [1-50]

Cunningham, David - *There's Something Happening Here: The New Left, the Klan, and FBI Counterintelligence*
Choice - v42 - i4 - Dec 2004 - p702(1) [1-50]

Cunningham, David S. - *To Teach, to Delight, and to Move: Theological Education in a Post-Christian World*
CC - v122 - i4 - Feb 22 2005 - p48(2) [501+]

Cunningham, Don - *Taiho-jutsu: Law and Order in the Age of the Samurai*
R&R Bk N - v19 - i3 - August 2004 - p169(1) [501+]

Cunningham, Donald H. - *How to Write for the World of Work, 7th ed.*
R&R Bk N - v19 - i4 - Nov 2004 - p115(1) [51-500]

Cunningham, E.P. - *After BSE: A Future for the European Livestock Sector*
SciTech - v28 - i1 - March 2004 - p84(1) [51-500]

Cunningham, Elaine - *Shadows in the Darkness*
BL - v101 - i4 - Oct 15 2004 - p394(2) [51-500]
ChrSFF&H - v26 - i10 - Oct 2004 - p25(1) [51-500]
LJ - v129 - i15 - Sept 15 2004 - p52(1) [51-500]
PW - v251 - i37 - Sept 13 2004 - p63(1) [51-500]

Cunningham, Ian - *The Handbook of Work Based Learning*
R&R Bk N - v19 - i3 - August 2004 - p129(1) [51-500]

Cunningham, John - *Hungarian Cinema: From Coffee House to Multiplex*
Choice - v42 - i3 - Nov 2004 - p490(2) [51-500]
TimHES - v0 - i1674 - Jan 14 2005 - p28(1) [501+]

Cunningham, John C. - *The Last Man: The Life and Times of Surgeon Major William Brydon CB*
A Aff - v35 - i2 - July 2004 - p228-229 [501+]

Cunningham, Kevin - *The Declaration of Independence*
c SLJ - v51 - i1 - Jan 2005 - p144(1) [51-500]
Power to the People: How We Elect the President and Other Officials
c BL - v101 - i4 - Oct 15 2004 - p415(2) [51-500]
c SLJ - v51 - i1 - Jan 2005 - p144(1) [51-500]

Cunningham, Lawrence S. - *Francis of Assisi: Performing the Gospel Life*
Comw - v131 - i21 - Dec 3 2004 - p29(2) [501+]

Cunningham, M. Allen - *The Green Age of Asher Witherow*
BL - v101 - i1 - Sept 1 2004 - p59(2) [51-500]
KR - v72 - i15 - August 1 2004 - p703(1) [51-500]
LJ - v129 - i13 - August 2004 - p66(1) [51-500]
PW - v251 - i37 - Sept 13 2004 - p56(1) [51-500]

Cunningham, Mary Kay - *The Interpreter's Training Manual for Museums*
R&R Bk N - v19 - i4 - Nov 2004 - p1(1) [51-500]

Cunningham, Michael - *A Home at the End of the World. Audiobook Review*
BL - v101 - i7 - Dec 1 2004 - p677(1) [1-50]
A Home at the End of the World (Read by Farrell, Colin). Audiobook Review
y Kliatt - v39 - i1 - Jan 2005 - p44(1) [51-500]
PW - v251 - i36 - Sept 6 2004 - p26(1) [51-500]
A Home at the End of the World
Globe & Mail - Sept 4 2004 - pD18 [1-50]
The Hours (Read by Cunningham, Michael). Audiobook Review
LJ - v129 - i12 - July 2004 - p124(1) [51-500]
The Hours
BW - v34 - i1 - Jan 4 2004 - p13(1) [501+]
Land's End: A Walk in Provincetown (Read by Brick, Scott). Audiobook Review
BL - v101 - i2 - Sept 15 2004 - p258(2) [51-500]
LJ - v129 - i19 - Nov 15 2004 - p98(1) [51-500]
Specimen Days
Time - v164 - i15 - Oct 11 2004 - p97 [51-500]

Cunningham, Nancy Brady - *Snow Melting in a Silver Bowl: A Book of Active Meditations*
LJ - v129 - i16 - Oct 1 2004 - p86(1) [51-500]

Cunningham, Patricia A. - *Reforming Women's Fashion 1850-1920: Politics, Health, and Art*
JAH - v91 - i2 - Sept 2004 - p655(2) [501+]

Cunningham, Patricia Marr - *Phonics They Use: Words for Reading and Writing, 4th Ed.*
R&R Bk N - v19 - i3 - August 2004 - p218(1) [1-50]

Cunningham, Paul - *Building the Knowledge Economy: Issues, Applications, Case Studies. Vols. 1-2*
SciTech - v28 - i3 - Sept 2004 - p6(1) [501+]

Cunningham, Philip A. - *Pondering the Passion: What's at Stake for Christians and Jews?*
LJ - v130 - i1 - Jan 1 2005 - p119(1) [51-500]
PW - v251 - i45 - Nov 8 2004 - p51(2) [51-500]

Cunningham, Sean - *Richard III: A Royal Enigma*
Six Ct J - v35 - i3 - Fall 2004 - p905-906 [501+]

Cuomo, Mario M. - *Why Lincoln Matters: Today More than Ever*
Comw - v131 - i15 - Sept 10 2004 - p27(3) [501+]
NYRB - v51 - i13 - August 12 2004 - p20(3) [501+]
R&R Bk N - v19 - i3 - August 2004 - p68(1) [51-500]
NYTBR - July 18 2004 - p8 [501+]

Curcio-Nagy, Linda Ann - *The Great Festivals of Colonial Mexico City: Performing Power and Identity*
Choice - v42 - i5 - Jan 2005 - p912(1) [1-50]
R&R Bk N - v19 - i3 - August 2004 - p86(1) [51-500]

Curiel, David T. - *Cancer Gene Therapy*
SciTech - v28 - i4 - Dec 2004 - p92(1) [51-500]

Curlee, Lynn - *Ballpark: The Story of America's Baseball Fields (Illus. by Curlee, Lynn)*
c HB - v81 - i2 - March-April 2005 - p212(2) [51-500]
c KR - v73 - i2 - Jan 15 2005 - p118(1) [51-500]
c PW - v252 - i6 - Feb 7 2005 - p58(1) [51-500]
Parthenon (Illus. by Curlee, Lynn)
c BL - v101 - i2 - Sept 15 2004 - p240(1) [51-500]
y BW - v34 - i31 - August 1 2004 - p11(1) [51-500]
c CCB-B - v58 - i2 - Oct 2004 - p67(1) [51-500]
c HB - v80 - i4 - July-August 2004 - p465(2) [51-500]
c NYTBR - August 8 2004 - p16 [501+]
c PW - v251 - i30 - July 26 2004 - p53(1) [51-500]

Curnow, Barry - *The International Guide to Management Consultancy, 2nd Ed.*
R&R Bk N - v19 - i1 - Feb 2004 - p94(1) [51-500]

Curnutt, Kirk - *A Historical Guide to F. Scott Fitzgerald*
CR - v286 - i1669 - Feb 2005 - p127(1) [51-500]

Curott, Phyllis - *The Love Spell: An Erotic Memoir of Spiritual Awakening*
BL - v101 - i9-10 - Jan 1 2005 - p786(1) [1-50]
PW - v251 - i47 - Nov 22 2004 - p49(1) [51-500]

Curran, Bob - *The Dark Spirit: Sinister Portraits from Celtic Folklore*
Folkl - v115 - i3 - Dec 2004 - p370(2) [501+]

Curran, Brendan - *Terrible Beauty Is Born: Clones, Genes and the Future of Mankind*
SciTech - v28 - i4 - Dec 2004 - p61(1) [51-500]

Curran, Charles E. - *Catholic Social Teaching 1891-Present: A Historical, Theological, and Ethical Analysis*
ER - v56 - i3 - July 2004 - p378(2) [501+]

Curran, Colleen - *Whores on the Hill*
KR - v73 - i5 - March 1 2005 - p245(1) [501+]
PW - v252 - i4 - Jan 24 2005 - p114(1) [501+]

Curran, Jane V. - *Goethe's Wilhelm Meister's Apprenticeship: A Reader's Commentary*
GSR - v27 - i3 - Oct 2004 - p610(1) [501+]

Curran, Thomas F. - *Soldiers of Peace: Civil War Pacifism and the Postwar Radical Peace Movement*
JAH - v91 - i2 - Sept 2004 - p639(2) [501+]
JSH - v71 - i1 - Feb 2005 - p174(2) [501+]

Currell, Fred J. - *The Physics of Multiply and Highly Charged Ions. Vols. 1-2*
Choice - v42 - i1 - Sept 2004 - pNA [501+]
SciTech - v28 - i1 - March 2004 - p50(1) [51-500]

Current Controversies
LibMed - v23 - i1 - August-Sept 2004 - p82(1) [51-500]

Currie, Elliott - *The Road to Whatever: Middle-Class Culture and the Crisis of Adolescence*
BL - v101 - i9-10 - Jan 1 2005 - p789(1) [1-50]
KR - v72 - i24 - Dec 15 2004 - p1176(1) [501+]
LJ - v130 - i1 - Jan 1 2005 - p136(1) [51-500]
PW - v252 - i1 - Jan 3 2005 - p47(2) [51-500]

Currie, Jan - *Globalizing Practices and University Responses*
AJPS - v39 - i2 - July 2004 - p463(464) [501+]

Currie, Philip J. - *Feathered Dragons: Studies on the Transition from Dinosaurs to Birds*
Choice - v42 - i3 - Nov 2004 - p512(1) [1-50]
New Sci - v183 - i2460 - August 14 2004 - p46(1) [51-500]
SB - v41 - i1 - Jan-Feb 2005 - p20(1) [501+]

Currie, Robert - *Teaching Mr. Cutler*
CBRA - Annual 2003 - p160(2) [501+]

Currie, Robin - *Baby Bible ABC*
c CH Bwatch - Oct 2004 - pNA [51-500]

Currie, Sheldon - *Down the Coaltown Road*
Can Lit - i182 - Autumn 2004 - p109(3) [501+]

Currie, Stephen - *Antarctica*
y BL - v101 - i4 - Oct 15 2004 - p412(1) [51-500]
Escapes from Religious Oppression
c LibMed - v23 - i1 - August-Sept 2004 - p75(1) [51-500]

Currier, Jameson - *Desire, Lust, Passion, Sex*
G&L Rev W - v11 - i6 - Nov-Dec 2004 - p47(1) [501+]

Curry, Constance - *Deep in Our Hearts: Nine White Women in the Freedom Movement*
Signs - v30 - i2 - Wntr 2005 - p1670(4) [501+]

Curry, Don L. - *How Do Your Lungs Work?*
c SB - v40 - i3 - May-June 2004 - p134(1) [501+]
How Does Your Brain Work?
c SB - v40 - i3 - May-June 2004 - p134(1) [501+]
How Does Your Heart Work?
c SB - v40 - i3 - May-June 2004 - p134(1) [501+]

Curry, Jane Leftwich - *The Left Transformed in Post-Communist Societies: The Cases of East-Central Europe, Russia, and Ukraine*
Slav R - v63 - i4 - Winter 2004 - p853(2) [501+]

Curry, Jane Louise - *The Black Canary*
y HB - v81 - i2 - March-April 2005 - p199(1) [51-500]
Brave Cloelia (Illus. by Crosby, Jeff)
c BL - v101 - i6 - Nov 15 2004 - p587(2) [501+]
c SLJ - v51 - i2 - Feb 2005 - p115(2) [501+]

Curtin, Jeremiah - *Native American Creation Myths*
LJ - v130 - i3 - Feb 15 2005 - p172(1) [51-500]

Curtis, Andrea - *Into the Blue: Family Secrets and the Search for a Great Lakes Shipwreck*
CBRA - Annual 2003 - p439(1) [51-500]

Curtis, Brian - *Every Week a Season: A Journey Inside Big-Time College Football*
BL - v101 - i1 - Sept 1 2004 - p46(1) [51-500]
PW - v251 - i30 - July 26 2004 - p49(1) [501+]

Curtis, C. Michael - *Faith: Stories*
BL - v101 - i3 - Oct 1 2004 - p303(1) [51-500]

Curtis, Carolyn - *I Took the Moon for a Walk (Illus. by Jay, Alison)*
c TES - v0 - i4586 - June 4 2004 - p21(1) [501+]

Curtis, Christopher Paul - *Bucking the Sarge (Read by Boatman, Michael). Audiobook Review*
y BL - v101 - i8 - Dec 15 2004 - p754(1) [1-50]
y BL - v101 - i9-10 - Jan 1 2005 - p778(1) [1-50]
y PW - v251 - i50 - Dec 13 2004 - p24(1) [51-500]
Bucking the Sarge
c BL - v100 - i21 - July 2004 - p1842(1) [1-50]
y BL - v101 - i9-10 - Jan 1 2005 - p772(1) [51-500]
y CCB-B - v58 - i2 - Oct 2004 - p67(2) [51-500]
y Globe & Mail - Dec 11 2004 - pD38 [501+]
y HB - v80 - i5 - Sept-Oct 2004 - p579(1) [51-500]
c Inst - v114 - i5 - Jan-Feb 2005 - p73(2) [501+]
y Kliatt - v38 - i5 - Sept 2004 - p6(3) [501+]
y KR - v72 - i15 - August 1 2004 - p739(1) [51-500]
c PW - v251 - i29 - July 19 2004 - p162(2) [501+]
y Res Links - v10 - i2 - Dec 2004 - p35(2) [501+]
y SLJ - v50 - i9 - Sept 2004 - p202(1) [51-500]
y VOYA - v27 - i4 - Oct 2004 - p293(1) [51-500]
y NYTBR - Nov 14 2004 - p34(L) [501+]

Curtis, Dorris - *Come Walk with Me: The Art of Dorris Curtis*
Choice - v42 - i4 - Dec 2004 - p648(2) [1-50]
LJ - v129 - i17 - Oct 15 2004 - p59(1) [51-500]

Curtis, Edward, E., IV - *Islam in Black America: Identity, Liberation, and Difference in African-American Islamic Thought*
JAAR - v72 - i3 - Sept 2004 - p768-771 [501+]

Curtis, Emily Byrne - *The Glass of China: Pure Brightness Shines Everywhere*
Choice - v41 - i11-12 - July-August 2004 - p2032(1) [501+]

Curtis, Gareth - *Early Masses and Mass-Pairs*
Notes - v61 - i1 - Sept 2004 - p219(4) [501+]

Curtis, Gregory - *Disarmed: The Story of the Venus de Milo*
R&R Bk N - v19 - i1 - Feb 2004 - p204(1) [51-500]

Curtis, James - *W.C. Fields: A Biography*
NYTBR - Oct 17 2004 - p26 [501+]
R&R Bk N - v19 - i4 - Nov 2004 - p226(1) [501+]

Curtis, Jamie Lee - *It's Hard to Be Five: Learning How to Work My Control Panel (Illus. by Cornell, Laura)*
c BIC - v33 - i7 - Oct 2004 - p40(1) [501+]
c BL - v101 - i4 - Oct 15 2004 - p410(1) [51-500]
c KR - v72 - i15 - August 1 2004 - p740(1) [51-500]
c PW - v251 - i36 - Sept 6 2004 - p62(1) [51-500]
c SLJ - v50 - i12 - Dec 2004 - p105(1) [501+]

Curtis, L. Perry, Jr. - *Jack the Ripper and the London Press*
JMH - v76 - i3 - Sept 2004 - p685(2) [501+]

Curtis, Marci - *Big Brother, Little Brother (Illus. by Curtis, Marci)*
c SLJ - v50 - i7 - July 2004 - p69(1) [51-500]

Curtis, Mark - *Web of Deceit: Britain's Real Role in the World*
A Aff - v35 - i2 - July 2004 - p206-209 [501+]

Curtis, Michael - *Verdict on Vichy: Power and Prejudice in the Vichy France Regime*
Choice - v41 - i7 - March 2004 - p1361(1) [501+]

Curtis-Prior, Peter - *The Eicosanoids*
E-Streams - Sept 2004 - pNA [501+]
SciTech - v28 - i3 - Sept 2004 - p72(1) [51-500]

Curtis, Vanessa - *Virginia Woolf's Women*
ELT - v48 - i2 - Spring 2005 - p122(3) [501+]

Curtler, Hugh Mercer - *The Inversion of Consciousness from Dante to Derrida: A Study of Intellectual History*
R&R Bk N - v19 - i4 - Nov 2004 - p4(1) [51-500]

Curto, Jose C. - *Enslaving Connections: Changing Cultures of Africa and Brazil During the Era of Slavery*
R&R Bk N - v19 - i1 - Feb 2004 - p135(1) [51-500]
Enslaving Spirits: The Portuguese-Brazilian Alcohol Trade at Luanda and Its Hinterland, c. 1550-1830
R&R Bk N - v19 - i2 - May 2004 - p107(1) [51-500]

Curwen, Peter J. - *Telecommunications Strategy: Cases, Theory and Applications*
SciTech - v28 - i4 - Dec 2004 - p9(1) [1-50]

Curwood, James Oliver - *Baree: The Wolf-Dog (Read by Lawlor, Patrick). Audiobook Review*
BL - v101 - i2 - Sept 15 2004 - p261(1) [501+]

Curzon, Clare - *A Meeting of Minds: A Thames Valley Mystery*
KR - v72 - i16 - August 15 2004 - p779(1) [51-500]
PW - v251 - i34 - August 23 2004 - p40(1) [51-500]

Cusack, Thomas R. - *A National Challenge at the Local Level: Citizens, Elites and Institutions in Reunified Germany*
R&R Bk N - v19 - i1 - Feb 2004 - pNA [501+]

Cushing, Dana - *A Middle English Chronicle of the First Crusade: The Caxton Eracles*
Med R - Nov 2004 - pNA [501+]

Cushing, J.M. - *Differential Equations*
SciTech - v28 - i3 - Sept 2004 - p39(1) [51-500]

Cushing, Lincoln - *Revolucion!: Cuban Poster Art*
R&R Bk N - v19 - i1 - Feb 2004 - p205(1) [51-500]

Cushman, Clare - *Black, White and Brown: The Landmark School Desegregation Case in Retrospect*
R&R Bk N - v19 - i3 - August 2004 - p196(1) [1-50]

Cushman, Doug - *Mystery at the Club Sandwich (Illus. by Cushman, Doug)*
c CH Bwatch - Feb 2005 - pNA [51-500]
c KR - v72 - i17 - Sept 1 2004 - p863(1) [51-500]
c PW - v251 - i50 - Dec 13 2004 - p68(1) [51-500]
c SLJ - v51 - i1 - Jan 2005 - p89(1) [51-500]
Space Cat (Illus. by Cushman, Doug)
c BL - v100 - i21 - July 2004 - p1850(1) [1-50]

Cushman, Jean - *Do You Wanna Bet? Your Chance to Find Out about Probability*
c SLJ - v50 - i9 - Sept 2004 - p58(1) [51-500]

Cushman, Karen - *Rodzina*
LibMed - v22 - i5 - Feb 2004 - p68(1) [501+]

Cushman, Peter - *Fires in the Bathroom: Advice for Teachers from High School Students*
TCR - v106 - i2 - Feb 2004 - p401-403 [501+]

Cusic, Don - *Baseball and Country Music*
Choice - v41 - i11-12 - July-August 2004 - p2083(1) [501+]
It's the Cowboy Way: The Amazing True Adventures of Riders in the Sky
JPC - v38 - i1 - August 2004 - p209(2) [501+]

Cusick, James G. - *The Other War of 1812: The Patriot War and the American Invasion of Spanish East Florida*
HNet - August 2004 - pNA [501+]
J Mil H - v68 - i3 - July 2004 - p599-601 [501+]
JAH - v91 - i3 - Dec 2004 - p1001(1) [501+]
JSH - v71 - i1 - Feb 2005 - p147(3) [501+]

Cusik, Dawn - *The Michaels Book of Arts and Crafts*
BL - v101 - i8 - Dec 15 2004 - p706(1) [501+]

Cusimano, Richard - *Translation of the Chronicle of the Abbey of Morigny, France, c.1100-1150*
R&R Bk N - v19 - i1 - Feb 2004 - p25(1) [51-500]

Cusk, Rachel - *The Lucky Ones*
BooChiTr - May 9 2004 - p2(1) [501+]

Cussler, Clive - *Black Wind*
BL - v101 - i6 - Nov 15 2004 - p564(1) [51-500]
KR - v72 - i20 - Oct 15 2004 - p984(1) [51-500]
NYTBR - Dec 26 2004 - p11 [501+]
PW - v251 - i41 - Oct 11 2004 - p53(1) [51-500]
Lost City (Read by Brick, Scott). Audiobook Review
y Kliatt - v39 - i1 - Jan 2005 - p47(1) [501+]
Lost City
BL - v101 - i1 - Sept 1 2004 - p60(1) [51-500]
PW - v251 - i29 - July 19 2004 - p145(1) [51-500]
y SLJ - v50 - i11 - Nov 2004 - p176(1) [51-500]
Sacred Stone
BL - v101 - i4 - Oct 15 2004 - p392(1) [51-500]
y Kliatt - v39 - i1 - Jan 2005 - p12(1) [51-500]
KR - v72 - i15 - August 1 2004 - p714(1) [51-500]
PW - v251 - i35 - August 30 2004 - p30(1) [501+]

Custer, Jay F. - *Classification Guide for Arrowheads and Spearpoints of Eastern Pennsylvania and the Central Middle Atlantic*
Am Ant - v69 - i3 - July 2004 - p589(2) [501+]

Cusumano, Camille - *France, a Love Story: Women Write about the French Experience*
Globe & Mail - Nov 3 2004 - pT1 [501+]

Cuthbert, John A. - *Richard Kidwell Miller*
Choice - v42 - i7 - March 2005 - p1216(1) [51-500]

Cutkosky, Steven Dale - *Resolution of Singularities*
SciTech - v28 - i3 - Sept 2004 - p42(1) [1-50]

Cutler, Alan - *The Seashell on the Mountaintop: A Story of Science, Sainthood, and the Humble Genius Who Discovered a New History of the Earth*
Isis - v95 - i3 - Sept 2004 - p489(2) [501+]
The Seashell on the Mountaintop; How Nicolaus Steno Solved an Ancient Mystery and Created a Science of the Earth
Kliatt - v38 - i4 - July 2004 - p44(2) [51-500]

Cutler, David M. - *Frontiers in Health Policy Research*
JEL - v41 - i4 - Dec 2003 - p1373(2) [501+]
Your Money or Your Life: Strong Medicine for America's Health Care System
Choice - v41 - i11-12 - July-August 2004 - p2077(1) [501+]

Cutler, Jane - *Common Sense and Fowls (Illus. by Barasch, Lynne)*
c KR - v73 - i5 - March 1 2005 - p285(1) [51-500]
Rose and Riley (Illus. by Yezerski, Thomas F.)
c KR - v73 - i4 - Feb 15 2005 - p227(1) [51-500]

Cutler, Jessica - *The Washingtonienne (Read by Shepardson, Dia). Audiobook Review*
LJ - v130 - i3 - Feb 15 2005 - p171(1) [1-50]
The Washingtonienne
PW - v252 - i4 - Jan 24 2005 - p114(1) [501+]

Cutler, Jonathan - *Labor's Time: Shorter Hours, the UAW, and the Struggle for American Unionism*
Choice - v42 - i5 - Jan 2005 - p898(1) [1-50]
Dis - v51 - i4 - Fall 2004 - p97(5) [501+]

Cutler, Karan Davis - *Pruning Trees, Shrubs & Vines*
SciTech - v28 - i3 - Sept 2004 - p128(1) [51-500]

Cutler, Paul - *Protein Purification Protocols. 2nd Ed.*
SciTech - v28 - i1 - March 2004 - p74(1) [51-500]

Cutler, Robert W.P. - *The Mysterious Death of Jane Stanford*
JIH - v35 - i1 - Summer 2004 - p159-160 [501+]

Cutter, Barbara - *Domestic Devils, Battlefield Angels: The Radicalism of American Womanhood, 1830-1865*
CWS - v23 - i3-4 - Spring-Summer 2004 - p220(2) [501+]
JAH - v91 - i2 - Sept 2004 - p628(2) [501+]
R&R Bk N - v19 - i1 - Feb 2004 - p132(1) [51-500]

Cutter, Charles - *Judiaca Reference Sources: A Selective, Annotated Bibliographic Guide*
Choice - v41 - i11-12 - July-August 2004 - p2104(1) [501+]

Cutter, Leah R. - *The Caves of Buda*
y Kliatt - v38 - i5 - Sept 2004 - p27(3) [51-500]

Cuyler, Margery - *100th Day Worries (Illus. by Arthur Howard)*
c SLJ - v50 - i7 - July 2004 - p42(1) [51-500]
Big Friends (Illus. by Tucker, Esra)
c LibMed - v23 - i1 - August-Sept 2004 - p64(1) [51-500]

Cvetkovich, Ann - *An Archive of Feelings: Trauma, Sexuality, and Lesbian Public Cultures*
Am Q - v56 - i4 - Dec 2004 - p1099(7) [501+]
NWSA Jnl - v16 - i3 - Fall 2004 - p224(2) [501+]

Cvijetic, Milorad - *Optical Transmission Systems Engineering*
SciTech - v28 - i1 - March 2004 - p154(1) [51-500]

Cybinski, P.J. - *Doomed Firms: An Economic Analysis of the Path to Failure*
R&R Bk N - v19 - i1 - Feb 2004 - p115(1) [51-500]

Cynober, Luc A. - *Metabolic and Therapeutic Aspects of Amino Acids in Clinical Nutrition. 2nd Ed.*
SciTech - v28 - i3 - Sept 2004 - p71(1) [51-500]

Czajkowski, Chris - *Snowshoes and Spotted Dick: Letters from a Wilderness Dweller*
CBRA - Annual 2003 - p42(1) [51-500]

Czaplicka, John - *Composing Urban History and the Constitution of Civic Identities*
Choice - v42 - i1 - Sept 2004 - p162(1) [501+]
Lviv: A City in the Crosscurrents of Culture
Slav R - v63 - i2 - Summer 2004 - p395(2) [501+]

Czarniawska, Barbara - *Narratives in Social Science Research*
R&R Bk N - v19 - i3 - August 2004 - p90(1) [51-500]

Czekaj, Jef - *Grampa and Julie: Shark Hunters*
c BL - v101 - i5 - Nov 1 2004 - p478(2) [51-500]
c PW - v251 - i38 - Sept 20 2004 - p48(2) [51-500]

Czernecki, Stefan - *Ride 'Em, Cowboy*
c Res Links - v10 - i2 - Dec 2004 - p2(1) [51-500]
c SLJ - v50 - i12 - Dec 2004 - p105(2) [501+]

Czerneda, Julie - *ReVisions*
BL - v100 - i22 - August 2004 - p1914(1) [501+]
Space, Inc.
Analog - v124 - i1-2 - Jan-Feb 2004 - p234(1) [51-500]
Survival
y VOYA - v27 - i4 - Oct 2004 - p312(1) [51-500]

Czernis-Ryl, Eva - *Contemporary Silver: Made in Itlay*
Choice - v42 - i4 - Dec 2004 - p646(1) [1-50]

Czinkota, Michael R. - *Internal Business, 7th Ed.*
R&R Bk N - v19 - i2 - May 2004 - p121 [51-500]

Czitrom, Nina - *Take a Bow!: Lesson Plans for Preschool Drama*
y SLJ - v50 - i10 - Oct 2004 - p202(1) [51-500]

D

Dale, Anna - *Whispering to Witches (Read by Curless, John). Audiobook Review*
  y Kliatt - v39 - i2 - March 2005 - p58(1) [51-500]
  c PW - v252 - i2 - Jan 10 2005 - p24(1) [51-500]
  c SLJ - v51 - i2 - Feb 2005 - p76(1) [501+]
  Whispering to Witches
  c BL - v101 - i6 - Nov 15 2004 - p601(2) [51-500]
  c CCB-B - v58 - i3 - Nov 2004 - p117(2) [501+]
  c KR - v72 - i19 - Oct 1 2004 - p958(1) [51-500]
  c PW - v251 - i40 - Oct 4 2004 - p88(1) [51-500]
  y SLJ - v50 - i11 - Nov 2004 - p140(1) [51-500]

Dale, Catherine - *Music Analysis in Britain in the Nineteenth and Early Twentieth Centuries*
  R&R Bk N - v19 - i1 - Feb 2004 - p195(1) [51-500]

Dale, Gareth - *Between State Capitalism and Globalisation: The Collapse of the East German Economy*
  R&R Bk N - v19 - i4 - Nov 2004 - p90(1) [51-500]

Dale, Iain - *The Times House of Commons: 1929, 1931, 1935*
  R&R Bk N - v19 - i1 - Feb 2004 - pNA [501+]

Dale, Kim - *Bush Babies*
  c Sch Lib - v52 - i3 - Autumn 2004 - p130(1) [1-50]

Dale, Nell B. - *Programming and Problem Solving with C++. 4th Ed.*
  SciTech - v28 - i3 - Sept 2004 - p23(1) [51-500]

Dale, Richard - *The First Crash: Lessons from the South Sea Bubble*
  Choice - v42 - i7 - March 2005 - p1275(1) [51-500]

Dale, Stephen Frederic - *The Garden of the Eight Paradises: Babur and the Culture of Empire in Central Asia, Afghanistan and India, 1483-1530*
  R&R Bk N - v19 - i3 - August 2004 - p54(1) [51-500]

D'Alessandro, Jacquie - *Love and the Single Heiress*
  PW - v251 - i32 - August 9 2004 - p236(1) [51-500]

D'Alessandro, Stephanie - *German Expressionist Prints*
  Bwatch - Jan 2005 - pNA [51-500]

Daley, Caroline - *Leisure and Pleasure: Reshaping & Revealing the New Zealand Body 1900-1960*
  AHS - v35 - i124 - Oct 2004 - p396(2) [501+]

Daley, Patrick J. - *Cultural Politics and the Mass Media: Alaska Native*
  Choice - v42 - i7 - March 2005 - p1221(2) [51-500]

Dalke, Anne - *Minding the Light: Essays in Friendly Pedagogy*
  R&R Bk N - v19 - i4 - Nov 2004 - p191(1) [501+]

Dall, Mary Doerfler - *Little Hands Create!: Art & Activities for Kids Ages 3 to 6*
  c BL - v101 - i9-10 - Jan 1 2005 - p865(2) [51-500]
  c SLJ - v50 - i12 - Dec 2004 - p128(1) [51-500]

Dallaire, Romeo - *Shake Hands with the Devil: The Failure of Humanity in Rwanda*
  BIC - v33 - i9 - Dec 2004 - p11(1) [501+]
  BL - v101 - i9-10 - Jan 1 2005 - p808(1) [1-50]
  CBRA - Annual 2003 - p285(2) [501+]
  Comw - v131 - i15 - Sept 10 2004 - p32(2) [501+]
  Globe & Mail - Oct 16 2004 - pD29 [501+]
  KR - v72 - i22 - Nov 15 2004 - p1075(1) [501+]
  LJ - v130 - i2 - Feb 1 2005 - p96(1) [51-500]
  PW - v251 - i51 - Dec 20 2004 - p48(2) [51-500]

Dallapiccola, Anna L. - *Sculpture at Vijayanagara: Iconography and Style*
  JAS - v63 - i3 - August 2004 - p822-823 [501+]

Dallas-Conte, Juliet - *Cock-a-Moo-Moo (Illus. by Bartlett, Alison)*
  c RT - v57 - Oct 2003 - p165 [1-50]

Dallas, George - *Standard & Poor's Handbook of Governance and Risk*
  HR Mag - v49 - i7 - July 2004 - pS52(1) [51-500]

Dallas, Gregor - *Poisoned Peace, 1945:The War That Never Ended*
  Spec - v297 - i9210 - Feb 12 2005 - p34(1) [501+]

Dallas, Sandra - *The Quilt That Walked to Golden: Women and Quilts in the Mountain West from the Overland Trail to Contemporary Colorado*
  Roundup M - v12 - i3 - Feb 2005 - p17(1) [51-500]

Dallek, Robert - *John F. Kennedy: An Unfinished Life 1917-1963*
  CR - v285 - i1664 - Sept 2004 - p178(3) [51-500]

Daller, Morton F. - *Product Liability Desk Reference: A Fifty-State Compendium, 2004 Ed.*
  R&R Bk N - v19 - i3 - August 2004 - pNA [1-50]
  Tort Law Desk Reference: A Fifty-State Compendium, 2004 Ed.
  R&R Bk N - v19 - i4 - Nov 2004 - p167(1) [501+]

Dalley, Bronwyn - *Past Judgement: Social Policy in New Zealand History*
  R&R Bk N - v19 - i4 - Nov 2004 - p52(1) [1-50]

Dallison, Robert L. - *Hope Restored: The American Revolution and the Founding of New Brunswick*
  Can Hist R - v85 - i4 - Dec 2004 - p816(3) [501+]
  CBRA - Annual 2003 - p338(2) [51-500]

Dalmas, John - *Regiment: A Trilogy*
  Bwatch - v26 - i7 - July 2004 - p5(1) [51-500]

Dalpiaz, Christina M. - *Breaking Free, Starting Over: Parenting in the Aftermath of Family Violence.*
  LJ - v129 - i13 - August 2004 - p108(1) [51-500]
  R&R Bk N - v19 - i3 - August 2004 - p166(1) [501+]

Dalrymple, G. Brent - *Ancient Earth, Ancient Skies: The Age of Earth and Its Cosmic Surroundings*
  Choice - v42 - i4 - Dec 2004 - p685(1) [1-50]

Dalrymple, Theodore - *Little Done: The Testament of a Serial Killer*
  Spec - v297 - i9206 - Jan 15 2005 - p23(1) [501+]

Dalsgaard, Anne Line - *Matters of Life and Longing: Female Sterilisation in Northeast Brazil*
  R&R Bk N - v19 - i4 - Nov 2004 - p129(1) [51-500]

Dalton, Annie - *Invisible Threads*
  y Sch Lib - v52 - i4 - Winter 2004 - p214(1) [51-500]
  Lilac Peabody and Bella Bright
  c Sch Lib - v52 - i3 - Autumn 2004 - p136(1) [501+]

Dalton, John - *Heaven Lake*
  BooChiTr - May 23 2004 - p1(2) [501+]
  PW - v251 - i49 - Dec 6 2004 - p32(2) [51-500]

Dalton, Kathleen - *Theodore Roosevelt: A Strenuous Life*
  y Kliatt - v38 - i4 - July 2004 - p37(1) [51-500]

Dalton, Mary - *Merrybegot*
  CBRA - Annual 2003 - p212(1) [51-500]
  Globe & Mail - July 3 2004 - pD6 [501+]

Dalton, Quinn - *Bulletproof Girl: Stories*
  KR - v73 - i5 - March 1 2005 - p245(2) [501+]

Dalton, Sharron - *Our Overweight Children: What Parents, Schools, and Communities Can Do to Control the Fatness Epidemic*
  Choice - v42 - i3 - Nov 2004 - p516(1) [1-50]
  TES - v0 - i4587 - June 11 2004 - psss19(1) [501+]

Daly, Herman - *Ecological Economics: Principles and Applications*
  R&R Bk N - v19 - i1 - Feb 2004 - p94(1) [1-50]

Daly, John - *When Slavery Was Called Freedom: Evangelicalism, Proslavery, and the Causes of the Civil War*
  AHR - v109 - i3 - June 2004 - p907(2) [501+]

Daly, Kathleen N. - *Greek and Roman Mythology A to Z*
  SLJ - v50 - i10 - Oct 2004 - pS62(1) [51-500]
  Norse Mythology A to Z
  SLJ - v50 - i10 - Oct 2004 - pS62(1) [51-500]

Daly, Niki - *Once upon a Time*
  c Sch Lib - v52 - i4 - Winter 2004 - p186(1) [51-500]
  Where's Jamela? (Illus. by Daly, Niki)
  c BL - v101 - i1 - Sept 1 2004 - p122(1) [1-50]
  c HB - v80 - i5 - Sept-Oct 2004 - p565(2) [51-500]
  c KR - v72 - i14 - July 15 2004 - p682(1) [51-500]
  c Sch Lib - v52 - i3 - Autumn 2004 - p130(1) [1-50]
  c SLJ - v50 - i9 - Sept 2004 - p157(1) [51-500]

Daly, Peter M. - *Why Weimar?; Questioning the Legacy of Weimar from Goethe to 1999*
  R&R Bk N - v19 - i1 - Feb 2004 - p36(1) [1-50]

Daly, Tim - *The Digital Photography Handbook: An Easy-to-Use Basic Guide for Everybody*
  SciTech - v28 - i4 - Dec 2004 - p167(1) [51-500]

Dalziell, Tanya - *Settler Romances and the Australian Girl*
  Choice - v42 - i6 - Feb 2005 - p1022(1) [51-500]

Damas, David - *Arctic Migrants/Arctic Villagers: The Transformation of Inuit Settlement in the Central Arctic*
  R&R Bk N - v19 - i4 - Nov 2004 - p54(1) [51-500]

Damasio, Antonio - *Looking for Spinoza: Joy, Sorrow and the Feeling Brain*
  Lon R Bks - v26 - i2 - Jan 22 2004 - p22(1) [501+]

D'Amato, Anthony - *International Law Sources: Collected Papers; Vol. 3*
  R&R Bk N - v19 - i3 - August 2004 - p211(1) [1-50]

Damberg, Cheryl L. - *Evaluating the Feasibility of Developing National Outcomes Data Bases to Assist Patients with Making Treatement Decisions*
  SciTech - v28 - i1 - March 2004 - p80(1) [51-500]

D'Ambrosio, Antonino - *Let Fury Have the Hour: The Punk Rock Politics of Joe*
  PW - v251 - i45 - Nov 8 2004 - p43(2) [501+]

D'Ambrosio, Charles - *Cooking and Stealing: The Tin House Nonfiction Reader*
  PW - v251 - i35 - August 30 2004 - p45(1) [51-500]
  Orphans
  BL - v101 - i7 - Dec 1 2004 - p626(1) [51-500]
  PW - v251 - i47 - Nov 22 2004 - p52(1) [51-500]

D'Ambrosio, Jay - *E-Teaching: Creating Web Sites and Student Web Portfolios Using Microsoft Powerpoint*
  LibMed - v22 - i7 - April-May 2004 - p86(1) [501+]
  SciTech - v28 - i3 - Sept 2004 - p156(1) [51-500]
  SLJ - v50 - i7 - July 2004 - p135(1) [51-500]

D'Amico, Carmela - *Ella the Elegant Elephant (Illus. by D'Amico, Steven)*
  c BL - v101 - i5 - Nov 1 2004 - p488(1) [51-500]
  c KR - v72 - i16 - August 15 2004 - p804(1) [51-500]
  c PW - v251 - i40 - Oct 4 2004 - p87(1) [51-500]
  c SLJ - v50 - i11 - Nov 2004 - p96(1) [51-500]

D'Amico, Joan - *The Coming to America Cookbook: Delicious Recipes and Fascinating Stories from America's Many Cultures (Illus. by Rockwell, Lizzy)*
  c PW - v252 - i6 - Feb 7 2005 - p62(1) [51-500]
  The Healthy Body Cookbook: Over 50 Fun Activities and Delicious Recipes for Kids (Illus. by Cash-Walsh, Tina)
  y SLJ - v51 - i2 - Feb 2005 - p59(1) [51-500]
  The Science Chef: 100 Fun Food Experiments and Recipes for Kids (Illus. by Cash-Walsh, Tina)
  y SLJ - v51 - i2 - Feb 2005 - p59(1) [51-500]

Damm, E. Buddy - *Austenite Formation and Decomposition: Proceedings*
  SciTech - v28 - i1 - March 2004 - p171(1) [51-500]

D'Ammassa, Don - *Haven*
  LJ - v129 - i20 - Dec 1 2004 - p105(1) [51-500]
  Murder in Silverplate
  KR - v72 - i18 - Sept 15 2004 - p892(1) [51-500]
  PW - v251 - i44 - Nov 1 2004 - p47(1) [501+]

Damms, Richard V. - *The Eisenhower Presidency, 1953-1961*
  HNet - Oct 2004 - pNA [501+]
  J Am St - v38 - i2 - August 2004 - p354(2) [501+]
  J Am St - v38 - i2 - August 2004 - p354-355 [501+]

Damon-Bach, Lucinda L. - *Catharine Maria Sedgwick: Critical Perspectives*
  Legacy - v21 - i2 - June 2004 - p246(2) [501+]

Damon, Cynthia - *Histories. Book 1*
  Class R - v54 - i1 - May 2004 - p111(2) [501+]
  Lon R Bks - v26 - i2 - Jan 22 2004 - p16(3)

Damon, John Edward - *Soldier Saints and Holy Warriors: Warfare and Sanctity in the Literature of Early England*
  R&R Bk N - v19 - i1 - Feb 2004 - p233(1) [51-500]

Damon, Richard A., Jr. - *Damon Family of Scituate, Massachusetts. Genealogy, 2000, One of 3 Separate Colonial Families Massachusetts Damon Families*
  EFHM - v58 - i3 - May-June 2004 - p57(1) [1-50]

Damon, William - *The Moral Advantage: How to Succeed in Business by Doing the Right Thing*
  R&R Bk N - v19 - i4 - Nov 2004 - p110(1) [51-500]

Damousi, Joy - *Living with the Aftermath: Trauma, Nostalgia and Grief in Post-War Australia*
  J Soc H - v38 - i2 - Winter 2004 - p517(4) [501+]
  JIH - v34 - i4 - Spring 2004 - p672-674 [501+]

Damp, Dennis V. - *Post Office Jobs: How to Get a Job with the U.S. Postal Service*
  JEL - v41 - i4 - Dec 2003 - p1385(2) [501+]

Damrosch, David - *The Longman Anthology of English Literature, 2nd Compact Ed., Vol. A*
  R&R Bk N - v19 - i1 - Feb 2004 - p235(1) [51-500]

Dams, Jeanne M. - *Winter of Discontent: A Dorothy Martin Mystery*
  BL - v101 - i7 - Dec 1 2004 - p639(1) [51-500]
  KR - v72 - i21 - Nov 1 2004 - p1029(1) [51-500]
  PW - v251 - i44 - Nov 1 2004 - p47(1) [501+]

Dan, Ramsey - *The Complete Idiot's Guide to Remodeling Your Bathroom*
  LJ - v129 - i14 - Sept 1 2004 - p180(1) [51-500]

Dana Foundation - *Neuroscience and the Law: Brain, Mind and the Scales of Justice*
  Sci - v305 - i5692 - Sept 24 2004 - p1925(1) [51-500]

Dana, Nissim - *The Druze in the Middle East: Their Faith, Leadership, Identity and Status*
  Choice - v42 - i2 - Oct 2004 - p352(1) [51-500]

Darian, Steven - *Understanding the Language of Science*
VQR - v80 - i2 - Spring 2004 - p267-267 [501+]
Dario, Ruben - *Songs of Life and Hope=Cantos de Vida y Esperanza*
Choice - v42 - i1 - Sept 2004 - p106(1) [501+]
Dark, David - *The Gospel According to America: A Meditation on a God-Blessed, Christ-Haunted Idea*
PW - v252 - i4 - Jan 24 2005 - p239(1) [501+]
Darke, Rick - *Pocket Guide to Ornamental Grasses*
BL - v100 - i22 - August 2004 - p1886(1) [51-500]
SciTech - v28 - i4 - Dec 2004 - p125 [51-500]
Darling, Andrew - *Thunderbirds: The Making of the Movie*
ChrSFF&H - v26 - i10 - Oct 2004 - p28(1) [51-500]
Darling, David - *Complete Book of Spaceflight: From Apollo 1 to Zero Gravity*
SciTech - v28 - i1 - March 2004 - p170(1) [51-500]
The Universal Book of Astronomy: From the Andromeda Galaxy to the Zone of Avoidance
Choice - v41 - i11-12 - July-August 2004 - p2022(1) [501+]
E-Streams - Oct 2004 - pNA [501+]
SciTech - v28 - i1 - March 2004 - p42(1) [51-500]
The Universal Book of Mathematics: From Abracadabra to Zeno's Paradoxes
BL - v101 - i7 - Dec 1 2004 - p687(1) [1-50]
Choice - v42 - i6 - Feb 2005 - p1058(1) [51-500]
Darling, Janina K. - *Architecture of Greece*
R&R Bk N - v19 - i4 - Nov 2004 - p203(1) [501+]
Darling, Julia - *The Taxi Driver's Daughter*
Globe & Mail - Nov 6 2004 - pD11 [501+]
Darlington, Tenaya - *Maybe Baby*
BL - v100 - i22 - August 2004 - p1897(1) [51-500]
Ent W - Sept 10 2004 - p167 [51-500]
KR - v72 - i13 - July 1 2004 - p591(2) [501+]
Darmon, Henri - *Rational Points on Modular Elliptic Curves*
SciTech - v28 - i1 - March 2004 - p41(1) [51-500]
Darnton, Robert - *George Washington's False Teeth: An Unconventional Guide to the Eighteenth Century*
R&R Bk N - v19 - i1 - Feb 2004 - p35(1) [1-50]
Darraj, Susan Muaddi - *Scheherazade's Legacy: Arab and Arab-American Women on Writing*
Choice - v42 - i7 - March 2005 - p1231(2) [51-500]
Darrell, Elizabeth - *Shadows Over the Sun*
BL - v101 - i7 - Dec 1 2004 - p634(1) [51-500]
Darrow, Sharon - *The Painters of Lexieville*
y LibMed - v22 - i4 - Jan 2004 - p67(1) [501+]
Darsie, Richard F. Jr. - *Identification and Geographical Distribution of the Mosquitoes of North America (Illus. by Chang, Chien C.)*
LJ - v129 - i20 - Dec 1 2004 - p161(2) [501+]
Dart, Iris Rainer - *Some Kind of Miracle (Read by Driscoll, Moira). Audiobook Review*
LJ - v129 - i16 - Oct 1 2004 - p118(1) [501+]
Dart, Rebecca - *Rabbithead*
PW - v251 - i37 - Sept 13 2004 - p60(2) [501+]
d'Artali, Gino - *I Love You*
CBRA - Annual 2003 - p245(2) [51-500]
Dartford, Mark - *Warships*
c SLJ - v50 - i7 - July 2004 - p118(2) [51-500]
Darty, Linda - *The Art of Enameling: Techniques, Projects, Inspiration*
BL - v101 - i8 - Dec 15 2004 - p704(2) [51-500]
LJ - v130 - i3 - Feb 15 2005 - p126(1) [51-500]
Darvas, Ferenc - *Chemical Genomics*
E-Streams - Nov 2004 - pNA [501+]
SciTech - v28 - i3 - Sept 2004 - p60(1) [1-50]
Darwall, Stephen - *Welfare and Rational Care*
Ethics - v114 - i4 - July 2004 - p815(5) [501+]
Darwin, Charles - *Origin of Species: and, Voyage of the Beagle*
SciTech - v28 - i1 - March 2004 - p62(1) [51-500]
Darwin, Ian F. - *Java Cookbook. 2nd Ed.*
SciTech - v28 - i3 - Sept 2004 - p22(1) [1-50]
Dary, David - *The Oregon Trail: An American Saga*
y BL - v101 - i4 - Oct 15 2004 - p384(1) [51-500]
BL - v101 - i9-10 - Jan 1 2005 - p767(1) [51-500]
KR - v72 - i18 - Sept 15 2004 - p898(2) [501+]
LJ - v129 - i18 - Nov 1 2004 - p101(1) [51-500]
PW - v251 - i43 - Oct 25 2004 - p39(1) [501+]
Das, A. - *Introduction to Nuclear and Particle Physics*
Choice - v42 - i1 - Sept 2004 - p142(1) [501+]
Das, A. Andrew - *Paul and the Jews*
Intpr - v58 - i3 - July 2004 - p321(1) [501+]
Paul, the Law, and the Covenant
Intpr - v58 - i3 - July 2004 - p319(2) [501+]
Theol St - v65 - i4 - Dec 2004 - p853(2) [501+]
Das, Dilip K. - *The Economic Dimensions of Globalization*
Choice - v42 - i2 - Oct 2004 - p338(1) [51-500]

Das, R. - *Enabling IP Routing with Cisco Routers*
Bwatch - v26 - i9 - Sept 2004 - p5(1) [51-500]
SciTech - v28 - i3 - Sept 2004 - p156(1) [51-500]
Das, Surya - *Where There's Life, There's Lawsuits: Not Altogether Serious Ruminations on Law and Life*
CBRA - Annual 2003 - p317(1) [51-500]
Das, V.S. Rama - *Photosynthesis: Regulation under Varying Light Regimes*
SciTech - v28 - i3 - Sept 2004 - p63(1) [51-500]
Dasch, Pat - *Icy Worlds of the Solar System*
Astron - v33 - i2 - Feb 2005 - p98 [51-500]
Dasgupta, Rana - *Tokyo Cancelled*
KR - v73 - i5 - March 1 2005 - p246(1) [501+]
Dash, Samuel - *The Intruders: Unreasonable Searches and Seizures from King John to John Ashcroft*
Choice - v42 - i5 - Jan 2005 - p934(1) [51-500]
Law&PolBR - August 2004 - p673(3) [501+]
NYRB - v51 - i18 - Nov 18 2004 - p56(5) [501+]
DaSilva, Zenia Sacks - *The Hispanic Connection: Spanish and Spanish-American Literature in the Arts of the World*
R&R Bk N - v19 - i4 - Nov 2004 - p231(1) [501+]
Daskalov, Roumen - *The Making of a Nation in the Balkans: Historiography of the Bulgarian Revival*
R&R Bk N - v19 - i3 - August 2004 - p47(1) [51-500]
d'Astier, Martine - *Lartigue: Album of a Century*
Apo - v160 - i514 - Dec 2004 - p87(2) [501+]
Daswani, Kavita - *The Village Bride of Beverly Hills*
y BL - v100 - i22 - August 2004 - p1897(1) [51-500]
Ent W - i777 - August 6 2004 - p85 [51-500]
LJ - v129 - i12 - July 2004 - p69(1) [51-500]
Datar, Chhaya - *The Struggle Against Violence*
CS - v33 - i6 - Nov 2004 - p651(4) [501+]
Date-Bah, Eugenia - *Jobs After War: A Critical Challenge in the Peace and Reconstruction Puzzle*
ILR - v143 - i3 - Autumn 2004 - p289(1) [51-500]
Dating and Sexuality in America
LibMed - v22 - i7 - April-May 2004 - p84(1) [501+]
Datlow, Ellen - *The Faery Reel: Tales from the Twilight Realm (Illus. by Vess, Charles)*
Bwatch - Nov 2004 - pNA [51-500]
The Faery Reel: Tales from the Twilight Realm (Illus. by Vess, Charles)
y CCB-B - v58 - i1 - Sept 2004 - p12(1) [51-500]
The Faery Reel: Tales from the Twilight Realm (Illus. by Vess, Charles)
c PW - v251 - i28 - July 12 2004 - p65(2) [501+]
y SLJ - v50 - i7 - July 2004 - p104(1) [51-500]
The Year's Best Fantasy and Horror: Seventeenth Annual Collection
BL - v100 - i22 - August 2004 - p1914(2) [501+]
ChrSFF&H - v26 - i9 - Sept 2004 - p31(2) [51-500]
PW - v251 - i31 - August 2 2004 - p56(1) [501+]
Datta, Satya - *Women and Men in early Modern Venice: Reassessing History*
R&R Bk N - v19 - i1 - Feb 2004 - p37(1) [1-50]
Daum, Andreas W. - *America, the Vietnam War, and the World: Comparative and International Perspectives*
Am St - v45 - i1 - Spring 2004 - p170-171 [501+]
HNet - Sept 2004 - pNA [501+]
JAH - v91 - i3 - Dec 2004 - p1092(2) [501+]
Daun, Holger - *Educational Strategies Among Muslims in the Context of Globalization: Some National Case Studies*
R&R Bk N - v19 - i3 - August 2004 - p228(1) [1-50]
Dauncey, Hugh - *French Popular Culture: An Introduction*
R&R Bk N - v19 - i4 - Nov 2004 - p38(1) [51-500]
Popular Music in France from Chanson to Techno: Culture, Identity, and Society
R&R Bk N - v19 - i1 - Feb 2004 - p197(1) [51-500]
The Tour de France, 1903-2003: A Century of Sporting Structures, Meanings, and Values
Choice - v41 - i7 - March 2004 - p1333(1) [501+]
Daunton, Martin - *Just Taxes: The Politics of Taxation in Britain, 1914-1979*
AHR - v109 - i2 - April 2004 - p617(2) [501+]
Albion - v36 - i1 - Spring 2004 - p181(2) [501+]
Dauphin, Cecile - *Correspondence: Models of Letter-Writing from the Middle Ages to the Nineteenth Century*
JMH - v76 - i4 - Dec 2004 - p934(3) [501+]
Dauphin, Claude - *La Musique au Temps des Encyclopedistes*
Eight-C St - v37 - i3 - Spring 2004 - p497-500 [501+]
Davalos, Karen Mary - *Exhibiting Mestizaje: Mexican (American) Museums in the Diaspora*
Aztlan - v29 - i2 - Fall 2004 - p219-221 [501+]

Davenport, Hester - *The Prince's Mistress: A Life of Mary Robinson*
CR - v286 - i1668 - Jan 2005 - p57(2) [51-500]
Spec - v297 - i9207 - Jan 22 2005 - p37(1) [501+]
Davenport, John C. - *The Mason-Dixon Line*
y BL - v100 - i22 - August 2004 - p1917(1) [51-500]
y SLJ - v50 - i9 - Sept 2004 - p224(1) [51-500]
Davenport, Thomas H. - *The Care and Feeding of the Knowledge Worker*
Har Bus R - v83 - i2 - Feb 2005 - p57(1) [1-50]
Davenport, W.G. - *Flash Smelting: Analysis, Control and Optimization. 2nd Ed.*
SciTech - v28 - i3 - Sept 2004 - p165(1) [51-500]
Davenport, Will - *The Sinner's Tale*
KR - v73 - i3 - Feb 1 2005 - p134(1) [501+]
Daves, Philip R. - *Corporate Valuation: A Guide for Managers and Investors*
R&R Bk N - v19 - i1 - Feb 2004 - p117(1) [51-500]
Davey, Charles - *The Complete Guide to Buying Property in France*
R&R Bk N - v19 - i3 - August 2004 - p197(1) [1-50]
The Complete Guide to Buying Property in Spain
R&R Bk N - v19 - i4 - Nov 2004 - p42(1) [51-500]
Davey, Frank - *Mr. and Mrs. G.G.: The Media Princess and the Court Philosopher*
CBRA - Annual 2003 - p42(2) [51-500]
Davey, Graham - *Complete Psychology. 1st Ed.*
TimHES - v0 - i1668 - Nov 26 2004 - pXVIII(2) [501+]
Davey, Janet - *First Aid*
TLS - i5289 - August 13 2004 - p21(1) [501+]
Davey, Patrick - *The ECG in Clinical Decision-Making*
SciTech - v28 - i4 - Dec 2004 - p103(1) [51-500]
Davey, Steve - *Unforgettable Places to See Before You Die*
Bwatch - Dec 2004 - pNA [501+]
Globe & Mail - August 14 2004 - pD12 [1-50]
LJ - v129 - i14 - Sept 1 2004 - p174(2) [51-500]
R&R Bk N - v19 - i4 - Nov 2004 - p72(1) [51-500]
Davich, Victor - *8 Minute Meditation*
LJ - v129 - i12 - July 2004 - p89(1) [51-500]
David, Andrew - *The Malaspina Expedition 1789-1794: Journal of the Voyage by Aleyandro Malaspina, Vol. 2*
R&R Bk N - v19 - i3 - August 2004 - p79(1) [51-500]
David, Anthony - *The Patron: A Life of Salman Schocken 1877-1959*
TLS - i5265 - Feb 27 2004 - p6-6 [501+]
David, Deirdre - *The Cambridge Companion to the Victorian Novel*
VS - v45 - i2 - Winter 2003 - p353 [501+]
David, Jennifer - *Canadian Country Style*
Globe & Mail - Nov 6 2004 - pL6 [51-500]
Globe & Mail - Dec 18 2004 - pD14 [1-50]
David, Lawrence - *Pickle and Penguin (Illus. by Nash, Scott)*
c CCB-B - v58 - i6 - Feb 2005 - p249(1) [51-500]
c KR - v72 - i20 - Oct 15 2004 - p1003(1) [51-500]
c PW - v251 - i50 - Dec 13 2004 - p67(2) [51-500]
c SLJ - v51 - i1 - Jan 2005 - p90(1) [51-500]
David, Matthew - *Social Research: The Basics*
R&R Bk N - v19 - i3 - August 2004 - p91(1) [51-500]
TimHES - v0 - i1680 - Feb 25 2005 - pVI(1) [501+]
David, Norman - *The Ella Fitzgerald Companion*
Choice - v42 - i3 - Nov 2004 - p491(2) [51-500]
David, Peter - *Fallen Angel (Illus. by Lopez, David)*
LJ - v130 - i1 - Jan 1 2005 - p88(1) [51-500]
Negima. Vol. 1
LJ - v129 - i14 - Sept 1 2004 - p127(1) [51-500]
One Knight Only
Analog - v124 - i3 - March 2004 - p133(1) [501+]
Stone and Anvil
y Kliatt - v39 - i2 - March 2005 - p26(1) [51-500]
Supergirl: Many Happy Returns
LibMed - v22 - i6 - March 2004 - p69(1) [501+]
LibMed - v22 - i6 - March 2004 - p69(1) [501+]
David, Price - *Let It Go Among Our People: An Illustrated History of the English Bible from John Wyclif to the King James Version*
Choice - v42 - i6 - Feb 2005 - p1040(1) [51-500]
David, Robert C. - *Venice, the Tourist Maze: A Cultural Critique and the World's Most Touristed City*
Choice - v42 - i6 - Feb 2005 - p1088(1) [51-500]

David, Saul - *Zulu: The Heroism and Tragedy of the Zulu War of 1879*
    CR - v286 - i1669 - Feb 2005 - p123(1) [51-500]
    HT - v55 - i1 - Jan 2005 - p56(2) [501+]
    Spec - v296 - i9192 - Oct 9 2004 - p45(2) [501+]

David, Sue - *Understanding the Constitution, 16th Ed.*
    R&R Bk N - v19 - i1 - Feb 2004 - pNA [51-500]

David, Todd - *The New Big Book of U.S. Presidents*
    c CH Bwatch - March 2005 - pNA [51-500]

David, Zdenek V. - *Finding the Middle Way: The Utraquists' Liberal Challenge to Rome and Luther*
    CHR - v90 - i4 - Oct 2004 - p782(3) [501+]
    R&R Bk N - v19 - i1 - Feb 2004 - p25(1) [51-500]

Davidova, Sophia - *Romanian Agriculture and Transition Toward the EU*
    JEL - v42 - i1 - March 2004 - p325(1) [501+]

Davidow, Jeffrey - *The U.S. and Mexico: The Bear and the Porcupine*
    Choice - v42 - i5 - Jan 2005 - p930(1) [51-500]
    Econ - v372 - i8385 - July 24 2004 - p78US [501+]
    R&R Bk N - v19 - i3 - August 2004 - p65(1) [51-500]

Davidow, Shelley - *Spirit of the Mountain*
    y Sch Lib - v52 - i3 - Autumn 2004 - p156(1) [501+]

Davidsen, Susanna - *Web Site Design with the Patron in Mind: A Step-by-Step Guide for Libraries*
    BL - v101 - i1 - Sept 1 2004 - p165(1) [1-50]
    LibMed - v23 - i3 - Nov-Dec 2004 - p90(1) [51-500]
    VOYA - v27 - i5 - Dec 2004 - p424(1) [51-500]

Davidson, Alan - *Fish and Fish Dishes of Laos*
    SciTech - v28 - i1 - March 2004 - p69(1) [51-500]
    Food History Comes of Age
    TLS - i5264 - Feb 20 2004 - p30-30 [501+]

Davidson, Alexander - *How to Win as a Stock Market Speculator*
    R&R Bk N - v19 - i4 - Nov 2004 - p118(1) [51-500]

Davidson, Andrew P. - *Privatization and the Crisis of Agricultural Extension: The Case of Pakistan*
    JEL - v42 - i1 - March 2004 - p306(1) [501+]

Davidson, Apollon - *South Africa and the Communist International: A Documentary History. Vols. 1-2*
    Choice - v41 - i7 - March 2004 - p1348(1) [501+]

Davidson, D. Kirk - *Selling Sin: The Marketing of Socially Unacceptable Products. 2nd Ed.*
    Choice - v41 - i11-12 - July-August 2004 - p2088(1) [501+]
    R&R Bk N - v19 - i2 - May 2004 - p115(1) [51-500]

Davidson, Dana - *Jason & Kyra*
    y Black Iss - v6 - i4 - July-August 2004 - p60(1) [51-500]
    y CCB-B - v58 - i1 - Sept 2004 - p12(2) [51-500]
    y SLJ - v50 - i7 - July 2004 - p104(1) [51-500]

Davidson, Diane Mott - *Double Shot*
    NYTBR - Nov 7 2004 - p28 [501+]
    BL - v101 - i6 - Nov 15 2004 - p564(1) [51-500]
    Globe & Mail - Nov 27 2004 - pD16 [51-500]
    KR - v72 - i19 - Oct 1 2004 - p941(1) [501+]
    LJ - v129 - i16 - Oct 1 2004 - p65(1) [51-500]
    People - v62 - i19 - Nov 8 2004 - p59 [51-500]
    PW - v251 - i37 - Sept 13 2004 - p61(2) [501+]

Davidson, Hilda Ellis - *A Companion to the Fairy Tale*
    Choice - v41 - i11-12 - July-August 2004 - p2029(2) [501+]
    Med R - June 2004 - pNA [501+]

Davidson, Ian - *Voltaire in Exile: The Last Years*
    BL - v101 - i7 - Dec 1 2004 - p626(2) [51-500]
    KR - v72 - i20 - Oct 15 2004 - p992(2) [501+]
    LJ - v130 - i1 - Jan 1 2005 - p111(1) [51-500]
    NY - v81 - i3 - March 7 2005 - p074 [501+]
    Spec - v295 - i9180 - July 17 2004 - p34(1) [501+]
    TLS - i5305 - Dec 3 2004 - p25(1) [501+]

Davidson, J. Kenneth - *Speaking of Sexuality: Interdisciplinary Readings, 2nd Ed.*
    R&R Bk N - v19 - i4 - Nov 2004 - p127(1) [51-500]

Davidson, Janet E. - *The Psychology of Problem Solving*
    Per Psy - v57 - i4 - Winter 2004 - p1076(4) [501+]
    TCR - v106 - i5 - May 2004 - p944(5) [501+]

Davidson, Jean - *My Daddy Makes the Best Motorcycle in the Whole Wide World--the Harley-Davidson*
    c CH Bwatch - v14 - i8 - August 2004 - p8(1) [51-500]

Davidson, Jenny - *Hypocrisy and the Politics of Politeness: Manners and Morals from Locke to Austen*
    Choice - v42 - i3 - Nov 2004 - p481(1) [1-50]

Davidson, Joseph - *Robots and Screw Theory: Applications of Kinematics and Statics to Robotics*
    SciTech - v28 - i3 - Sept 2004 - p117(1) [51-500]

Davidson, Lawrence - *America's Palestine: Popular and Official Perceptions from Balfour to Israeli Statehood*
    IJMES - v36 - i3 - August 2004 - p487-488 [501+]

Davidson, Leif - *I Spejlet: Roman om Johanne Luise Heiberg*
    WLT - v78 - i3-4 - Sept-Dec 2004 - p129(1) [501+]

Davidson, Marilyn J. - *Women in Management Worldwide: Facts, Figures and Analysis*
    Choice - v42 - i2 - Oct 2004 - p337(2) [51-500]
    R&R Bk N - v19 - i3 - August 2004 - p115(1) [51-500]

Davidson, Martin - *Spitfire Ace*
    CR - v285 - i1663 - August 2004 - p123(1) [501+]

Davidson, MaryJanice - *Derik's Bane*
    BL - v101 - i7 - Dec 1 2004 - p641(1) [51-500]
    Undead and Unemployed
    BL - v100 - i22 - August 2004 - p1908(1) [51-500]
    Undead and Unwed
    y BL - v101 - i2 - Sept 15 2004 - p222(1) [51-500]

Davidson, Michael - *Guys Like Us: Citing Masculinity in Cold War Poetics*
    Choice - v41 - i11-12 - July-August 2004 - p2043(1) [501+]

Davidson, Norman - *Statistical Mechanics*
    SciTech - v28 - i1 - March 2004 - p48(1) [51-500]

Davidson, Osha Gray - *Fire in the Turtle House: The Green Sea Turtle and the Fate of the Ocean*
    QRB - v79 - i4 - Dec 2004 - p445(2) [501+]

Davidson, P.A. - *Turbulence: An Introduction for Scientists and Engineers*
    Choice - v42 - i6 - Feb 2005 - p1052(1) [51-500]
    SciTech - v28 - i4 - Dec 2004 - p44(1) [51-500]

Davidson, Roger H. - *Workways of Governance: Monitoring Our Government's Health*
    Pres St Q - v34 - i3 - Sept 2004 - p702(3) [501+]

Davidson, Russell - *Econometric Theory and Methods*
    JEL - v42 - i1 - March 2004 - p234(1) [501+]

Davie, Doreen - *A Travelling Man: Eighteenth-Century Bearings*
    TLS - i5264 - Feb 20 2004 - p27-27 [501+]

Davies, Alan - *The Handbook of Applied Linguistics*
    Choice - v42 - i1 - Sept 2004 - p95(1) [501+]

Davies, Alun H. - *Vascular Surgery Highlights 2003-04*
    SciTech - v28 - i3 - Sept 2004 - p113(1) [51-500]

Davies, Ann - *The Metamorphoses of Don Juan's Women: Early Parity to Late Modern Pathology*
    R&R Bk N - v19 - i4 - Nov 2004 - p221(1) [501+]

Davies, B. - *Exploring Chaos: Theory and Experiment*
    SciTech - v28 - i1 - March 2004 - p47(1) [51-500]

Davies, Brian - *Thomas Aquinas: Contemporary Philosophical Perspectives*
    Med R - July 2004 - pNA [501+]

Davies, Celia - *Future Health Workforce*
    SciTech - v28 - i3 - Sept 2004 - p82(1) [51-500]

Davies, David - *Art of Performance*
    Choice - v41 - i11-12 - July-August 2004 - p2056(1) [501+]

Davies, David Twiston - *The Daily Telegraph Book of Naval Obituaries*
    CR - v286 - i1669 - Feb 2005 - p125(1) [51-500]

Davies, Douglas J. - *Anthropology and Theology*
    Theol St - v65 - i3 - Sept 2004 - p685(2) [501+]
    An Introduction to Mormonism
    Choice - v42 - i1 - Sept 2004 - p118(1) [501+]

Davies, E.B. - *Science in the Looking Glass: What Do Scientists Really Know?*
    Phys Today - v57 - i7 - July 2004 - p60-60 [501+]
    SB - v40 - i6 - Nov-Dec 2004 - p246(1) [501+]
    TimHES - v0 - i1659 - Sept 24 2004 - p26(1) [501+]

Davies, Gill - *Critical Essays on Ronald Firbank, English Novelist, 1886-1926*
    Choice - v42 - i2 - Oct 2004 - p292(1) [501+]

Davies, Gloria - *Globalization in the Asian Region: Impact and Consequences*
    R&R Bk N - v19 - i3 - August 2004 - p99(1) [51-500]

Davies, Jacqueline - *The Boy Who Drew Birds: A Story of John James Audubon (Illus. by Sweet, Melissa)*
    c BL - v101 - i5 - Nov 1 2004 - p477(1) [51-500]
    c BW - v34 - i37 - Sept 12 2004 - p12(1) [51-500]
    c CCB-B - v58 - i2 - Oct 2004 - p68(2) [51-500]
    c CH Bwatch - Jan 2005 - pNA [51-500]
    c HB - v80 - i6 - Nov-Dec 2004 - p726(1) [501+]
    c KR - v72 - i17 - Sept 1 2004 - p863(1) [501+]
    c PW - v251 - i37 - Sept 13 2004 - p81(1) [501+]
    c SLJ - v50 - i12 - Dec 2004 - p128(1) [51-500]
    c USNews & Wrld Rpt - v137 - i10 - Sept 27 2004 - pd16 [501+]

Davies, Jane - *A Glaze of Color: Creating Color and Design on Ceramics*
    Ceram Mo - v52 - i7 - Sept 2004 - p82(1) [501+]

Davies, John - *Safety Management: A Qualitative Systems Approach*
    E-Streams - June 2004 - pNA [501+]
    R&R Bk N - v19 - i1 - Feb 2004 - p137(1) [51-500]

Davies, Karen - *Understanding EU Law, 2nd Ed.*
    R&R Bk N - v19 - i1 - Feb 2004 - pNA [501+]

Davies, Katharine - *The Madness of Love*
    KR - v72 - i24 - Dec 15 2004 - p1154(2) [501+]
    LJ - v130 - i1 - Jan 1 2005 - p95(1) [51-500]
    PW - v251 - i50 - Dec 13 2004 - p46(1) [51-500]
    BL - v101 - i9-10 - Jan 1 2005 - p813(1) [1-50]

Davies, Mark - *Standard Handbook for Aeronautical and Astronautical Engineers*
    SciTech - v28 - i1 - March 2004 - p168(1) [51-500]

Davies, Martin - *Mrs. Hudson and the Spirits' Curse*
    KR - v72 - i23 - Dec 1 2004 - p1119(1) [51-500]
    PW - v251 - i45 - Nov 8 2004 - p39(1) [501+]

Davies, Matthew - *The History of the Merchant Taylors' Company*
    R&R Bk N - v19 - i4 - Nov 2004 - p105(1) [51-500]

Davies, Michael - *Graceful Reading: Theology and Narrative in the Works of John Bunyan*
    Lon R Bks - v26 - i24 - Dec 16 2004 - p11(4) [501+]
    Six Ct J - v35 - i3 - Fall 2004 - p916-917 [501+]
    Guide to the Use of Materials in Waters
    SciTech - v28 - i3 - Sept 2004 - p138(1) [51-500]

Davies, Nicola - *Oceans and Seas*
    c BL - v101 - i1 - Sept 1 2004 - p126(1) [1-50]
    Poop: A Natural History of the Unmentionable (Illus. by Layton, Neal)
    c BL - v101 - i4 - Oct 15 2004 - p400(2) [51-500]
    c CCB-B - v58 - i3 - Nov 2004 - p118(1) [501+]
    c Globe & Mail - August 14 2004 - pD16 [51-500]
    c HB - v80 - i5 - Sept-Oct 2004 - p605(1) [51-500]
    c KR - v72 - i16 - August 15 2004 - p804(1) [51-500]
    c PW - v251 - i35 - August 30 2004 - p55(1) [51-500]
    c Sch Lib - v52 - i4 - Winter 2004 - p207(1) [51-500]
    c SLJ - v50 - i12 - Dec 2004 - p128(1) [51-500]
    Star in the Custard
    c Sch Lib - v52 - i4 - Winter 2004 - p210(1) [51-500]
    Surprising Sharks (Illus. by Croft, James)
    c HB - v81 - i1 - Jan-Feb 2005 - p24(1) [51-500]
    c LibMed - v22 - i6 - March 2004 - p71(1) [501+]

Davies, Norman - *Rising '44: The Battle for Warsaw*
    Globe & Mail - Nov 27 2004 - pD3 [51-500]
    NYRB - v51 - i12 - July 15 2004 - p14(4) [501+]
    NYTBR - July 25 2004 - p14 [501+]
    NYTBR - August 1 2004 - p14 [501+]
    R&R Bk N - v19 - i3 - August 2004 - p33(1) [51-500]
    TLS - i5264 - Feb 20 2004 - p13-13 [501+]

Davies, Paul - *What's This India Business?: Offshoring, Outsourcing and the Global Services Revolution*
    R&R Bk N - v19 - i3 - August 2004 - p113(1) [51-500]

Davies, Peter - *Dangerous Liaisons: Collaborations and World War Two*
    Choice - v42 - i4 - Dec 2004 - p728(1) [1-50]

Davies, Peter G.G. - *European Union Environmental Law: An Introduction to Key Selected Issues*
    R&R Bk N - v19 - i4 - Nov 2004 - p174(1) [501+]

Davies, R.W. - *The Stalin-Kaganovich Correspondence 1931-1936*
    E-A St - v56 - i6 - Sept 2004 - p907(919) [501+]
    The Years of Hunger: Soviet Agriculture, 1931-1933
    Choice - v42 - i4 - Dec 2004 - p717(1) [51-500]

Davies, Sean - *Welsh Military Institutions, 633-1283*
    HER - v119 - i483 - Sept 2004 - p1026(2) [501+]

Davies, Stephen - *Art and Essence*
    R&R Bk N - v19 - i1 - Feb 2004 - p9(1) [1-50]

Davies, Stevie - *Kith and Kin*
    TLS - i5264 - Feb 20 2004 - p23-23 [501+]

Davies, Tansy - *Keep On Keepin' On [for] Brass Quintet*
    Notes - v61 - i3 - March 2005 - p870(5) [501+]

Davies, Wayne Kenneth David - *Writing Geographical Exploration: James and the Northwest Passage, 1631-33*
    Bwatch - v26 - i8 - August 2004 - p11(1) [51-500]
    CBRA - Annual 2003 - p286(1) [501+]
    Choice - v42 - i6 - Feb 2005 - p1081(1) [51-500]

Davila, Jerry - *Diploma of Whiteness: Race and Social Policy in Brazil, 1917-1945*
AHR - v109 - i2 - April 2004 - p581(2) [501+]
HAHR - v84 - i2 - May 2004 - p379(2) [501+]
JIH - v35 - i2 - Autumn 2004 - p329(2) [501+]

Davila, Lori - *How to Choose the Right Person for the Right Job Every Time*
HR Mag - v50 - i2 - Feb 2005 - pS10(1) [501+]

Davis, Alan M. - *Great Software Debates*
SciTech - v28 - i4 - Dec 2004 - p31(1) [51-500]

Davis, Alex - *Chivalry and Romance in the English Renaissance*
Ren Q - v57 - i3 - Fall 2004 - p1141(2) [501+]

Davis, Angela Y. - *Women, Race, and Class*
OOB - v35 - Jan-Feb 2005 - p48(2) [501+]

Davis, Aubrey - *Bagels from Benny (Illus. by Petricic, Dusan)*
c CBRA - Annual 2003 - p528(1) [51-500]

Davis, Audrey Craft - *Metaphysical Techniques That Really Work*
Bwatch - Jan 2005 - pNA [51-500]

Davis, Bridgett M. - *Shifting through Neutral: A Novel*
y VOYA - v27 - i5 - Dec 2004 - p380(1) [501+]

Davis, Carol M. - *Complementary Therapies in Rehabilitation*
Choice - v41 - i11-12 - July-August 2004 - p2077(1) [501+]

Davis, Caroline - *Essential Cat: The Ultimate Guide to Caring for Your Cat*
y BL - v101 - i5 - Nov 1 2004 - p451(1) [51-500]
LJ - v129 - i18 - Nov 1 2004 - p111(1) [51-500]

Davis, Charles G. - *Around Cape Horn*
Bwatch - v26 - i8 - August 2004 - p12(1) [51-500]

Davis, Christina L. - *Food Fights over Free Trade: How International Institutions Promote Agricultural Trade Liberalization*
Choice - v41 - i7 - March 2004 - p1341(1) [501+]

Davis, Claire - *Season of the Snake*
KR - v72 - i24 - Dec 15 2004 - p1155(1) [501+]
LJ - v130 - i2 - Feb 1 2005 - p67(1) [51-500]

Davis, Clark - *The Human Tradition in California*
WHQ - v35 - i1 - Spring 2004 - p91-91 [501+]

Davis, Colin J. - *Waterfront Revolts: New York and London Dockworkers, 1946-61*
BHR - v78 - i2 - Summer 2004 - p324(3) [501+]

Davis, Cynthia J. - *Charlotte Perkins Gilman and Her Contemporaries: Literary and Intellectual Contexts*
Choice - v42 - i4 - Dec 2004 - p658(1) [51-50]

Davis, Daniel Leifeld - *Your Angry Child: A Guide for Parents*
R&R Bk N - v19 - i3 - August 2004 - p10(1) [1-50]

Davis, Dave - *Continuing Professional Development of Physicians from Research to Practice*
SciTech - v28 - i1 - March 2004 - p79(1) [51-500]

Davis, David (b. 1948 -) - *Ten Redneck Babies (Illus. by Ward, Sue Marshall)*
c KR - v72 - i18 - Sept 15 2004 - p913(1) [501+]
c PW - v252 - i2 - Jan 10 2005 - p56(1) [51-500]
c SLJ - v51 - i1 - Jan 2005 - p90(1) [51-500]

Davis, David Brion - *Challenging the Boundaries of Slavery*
Afr Am R - v38 - i3 - Fall 2004 - p530(3) [501+]
Black Iss - v7 - i1 - Jan-Feb 2005 - p28(2) [501+]
JAH - v91 - i2 - Sept 2004 - p598(3) [501+]

Davis, Deborah (b. 1952 -) - *Strapless: John Singer Sargent and the Fall of Madame X*
Art N - v103 - i1 - Jan 2004 - p98(1) [501+]
NYTBR - Sept 5 2004 - p20 [501+]

Davis, Deborah L. - *Parenting Your Premature Baby and Child: The Emotional Journey*
LJ - v129 - i13 - August 2004 - p109(1) [51-500]

Davis, Denise - *Childish Things*
Globe & Mail - Sept 11 2004 - pD22 [1-50]

Davis, Devra - *When Smoke Ran Like Water: Tales of Environmental Deception and the Battle Against Pollution*
Kliatt - v38 - i4 - July 2004 - p44(1) [51-500]

Davis, Diane E. - *Irregular Armed Forces and Their Role in Politics and State Formation*
JPR - v41 - i6 - Nov 2004 - p755-755 [501+]

Davis, Don - *Lightning Strike: The Secret Mission to Kill Admiral Yamamoto and Avenge Pearl Harbor*
KR - v72 - i22 - Nov 15 2004 - p1075(2) [501+]

Davis, Donald - *The Pig Who Went Home on Sunday: An Appalachian Folktale (Illus. by Mazzucco, Jennifer)*
c CH Bwatch - v14 - i8 - August 2004 - p4(1) [51-500]
c KR - v72 - i13 - July 1 2004 - p626(1) [51-500]
c PW - v251 - i28 - July 12 2004 - p62(2) [51-500]
c SLJ - v50 - i8 - August 2004 - p106(1) [51-500]

Davis, Donald Edward - *Where There Are Mountains: An Environmental History of the Southern Appalachians*
JIH - v35 - i1 - Summer 2004 - p141-142 [501+]

Davis, Duane - *Business Research for Decision Making, 6th Ed.*
R&R Bk N - v19 - i4 - Nov 2004 - p92(1) [501+]

Davis, Elena - *Where Do the Balloons Go?*
c CH Bwatch - v14 - i8 - August 2004 - p7(1) [51-500]

Davis, Ellen F. - *The Art of Reading Scripture*
Intpr - v58 - i4 - Oct 2004 - p439(1) [501+]

Davis, Frances - *Afterglow: A Last Conversation with Pauline Kael*
NYRB - v51 - i17 - Nov 4 2004 - p52(1) [501+]

Davis, Geoffrey V. - *Voices of Justice and Reason: Apartheid and Beyond in South African Literature*
HNet - Oct 2004 - pNA [501+]
R&R Bk N - v19 - i1 - Feb 2004 - p241(1) [501+]

Davis, Gibbs - *Wackiest White House Pets (Illus. by Johnson, David A.)*
c BL - v101 - i3 - Oct 1 2004 - p331(1) [51-500]
c KR - v72 - i20 - Oct 15 2004 - p1004(1) [51-500]
c SLJ - v50 - i11 - Nov 2004 - p123(2) [51-500]

Davis, Glyn - *Teen TV: Genre, Consumption and Identity*
Atl - v294 - i1 - July-August 2004 - p147(4) [501+]

Davis-Goff, Annabel - *The Fox's Walk*
BW - v34 - i5 - Feb 1 2004 - p7(1) [501+]
NYTBR - Oct 10 2004 - p26 [501+]

Davis, Helen - *Understanding Stuart Hall*
R&R Bk N - v19 - i3 - August 2004 - p141(1) [51-500]

Davis, Isabel - *Love, Marriage, and Family Ties in the Later Middle Ages*
R&R Bk N - v19 - i2 - May 2004 - p134 [51-500]

Davis, J.H. - *Methods of Applied Mathematics with a MATLAB Overview*
SIAM Rev - v46 - i2 - June 2004 - p367-368 [501+]

Davis, J.R. - *Handbook of Materials for Medical Devices*
SciTech - v28 - i3 - Sept 2004 - p79(1) [51-500]
Handbook of Thermal Spray Technology
SciTech - v28 - i4 - Dec 2004 - p169(1) [51-500]

Davis, Jack - *Adobe Photoshop 7: One-Click Wow!*
SciTech - v28 - i1 - March 2004 - p135(1) [51-500]
How to Wow: Photoshop Photography
Bwatch - v26 - i9 - Sept 2004 - p5(2) [501+]

Davis, Jack E. - *Making Waves: Female Activists in Twentieth-Century Florida*
JSH - v70 - i3 - August 2004 - p712(2) [501+]
They'll Believe Me When I'm Gone
LibMed - v22 - i5 - Feb 2004 - p62(1) [501+]

Davis, Jacqueline - *The Language Teacher's Portfolio: A Guide for Professional Development*
R&R Bk N - v19 - i1 - Feb 2004 - p210(1) [51-500]

Davis, James C. - *The Human Story: Our History, from the Stone Age to Today*
LJ - v129 - i15 - Sept 15 2004 - p67(1) [51-500]
R&R Bk N - v20 - i1 - Feb 2005 - p31(1) [501+]

Davis, Jan - *Introduction to Online Investment Research: Search Strategies, Research Case Study, Research Problems, and Data Source Evaluations and Reviews*
R&R Bk N - v19 - i3 - August 2004 - p136(1) [51-500]

Davis, Jeff - *Papa Bear: The Life and Legacy of George Halas*
LJ - v129 - i19 - Nov 15 2004 - p66(1) [501+]
BL - v101 - i5 - Nov 1 2004 - p453(1) [51-500]
Choice - v42 - i7 - March 2005 - p1265(1) [51-500]
PW - v251 - i43 - Oct 25 2004 - p36(1) [501+]

Davis, Jill - *My Busy Day (Illus. by Kastner, Jill)*
c BL - v101 - i5 - Nov 1 2004 - p488(1) [51-500]
c KR - v72 - i16 - August 15 2004 - p804(1) [51-500]
c SLJ - v50 - i12 - Dec 2004 - p106(1) [501+]

Davis, Jim A. - *The Gathering Biological Warfare Storm*
Choice - v42 - i4 - Dec 2004 - p686(2) [1-50]

Davis, John - *Sacco and Vanzetti*
Kliatt - v38 - i6 - Nov 2004 - p32(1) [51-500]

Davis, John (b. 1962 -) - *The Global War on Terrorism: Assessing the American Response*
R&R Bk N - v19 - i3 - August 2004 - p164(1) [501+]

Davis, John D. - *Pewter at Colonial Williamsburg*
Ant&CM - v108 - i7 - Sept 2003 - p16(1) [501+]

Davis, Jordan - *Free Radicals: American Poets Before Their First Books*
ABR - v26 - i2 - Jan-Feb 2005 - p11(1) [501+]

Davis, Joyce M. - *Between Jihad and Saalm: Profiles in Islam*
JTWS - v21 - i1 - Spring 2004 - p334(3) [501+]
Martyrs: Innocence, Vengeance, and Despair in the Middle East
R&R Bk N - v19 - i1 - Feb 2004 - p15(1) [51-500]

Davis, Judy - *The No-Nonsense Guide to Teaching Writing: Strategies, Structures, and Solutions*
R&R Bk N - v19 - i1 - Feb 2004 - p184(1) [51-500]
VOYA - v27 - i5 - Dec 2004 - p425(1) [51-500]

Davis, Keir - *Definitive Guide to Linux Network Programming*
SciTech - v28 - i4 - Dec 2004 - p24(1) [51-500]

Davis, Kenneth - *Reconstructing the Sacred Tower: Challenge and Promise of Latino/a Theological Education*
Theol St - v66 - i1 - March 2005 - p233(1) [501+]

Davis, Kenneth C. - *Don't Know Much about Dinosaurs*
c SB - v40 - i5 - Sept-Oct 2004 - p220(1) [51-500]
Don't Know Much about Thomas Jefferson
y Kliatt - v39 - i2 - March 2005 - p33(2) [51-500]

Davis, L.J. - *Fleet Fire: Thomas Edison and the Pioneers of the Electric Revolution*
Bwatch - v26 - i8 - August 2004 - p3(1) [51-500]

Davis, Lambert - *Swimming with Dolphins (Illus. by Davis, Lambert)*
c BL - v100 - i21 - July 2004 - p1848(1) [1-50]
c KR - v72 - i13 - July 1 2004 - p627(1) [51-500]
c SLJ - v50 - i8 - August 2004 - p85(1) [51-500]

Davis, Lauren B. - *The Radiant City*
Globe & Mail - March 12 2005 - pD7 [501+]

Davis, Leith - *Scotland and the Borders of Romanticism*
TLS - i5290 - August 20 2004 - p7-8 [501+]

Davis, Leslie Dorfman - *Serapion Sister: The Poetry of Elizaveta Polonskaja*
Slav R - v63 - i2 - Summer 2004 - p440(2) [501+]

Davis, Lindsey - *The Jupiter Myth (Read by Rodska, Christian). Audiobook Review*
y Kliatt - v39 - i2 - March 2005 - p54(1) [51-500]
Scandal Takes a Holiday
BL - v101 - i1 - Sept 1 2004 - p68(1) [51-500]
Globe & Mail - Oct 2 2004 - pD18 [51-500]
PW - v251 - i28 - July 12 2004 - p47(1) [51-500]
TLS - i5283 - July 2 2004 - p21(1) [501+]

Davis, Lloyd S. - *Penguins*
Choice - v42 - i1 - Sept 2004 - p131(1) [501+]

Davis, Lydia - *Swann's Way*
Sew R - v112 - i2 - Spring 2004 - p285-294 [501+]

Davis, Lynn E. - *Individual Preparedness and Response to Chemical, Radiological, Nuclear, and Biological Terrorist Attacks*
R&R Bk N - v19 - i1 - Feb 2004 - p254(1) [51-500]

Davis, Margo Baumgarten - *Under One Sky*
Choice - v42 - i7 - March 2005 - p1221(1) [51-500]
R&R Bk N - v19 - i4 - Nov 2004 - p248(1) [501+]

Davis, Martin - *Undecidable: Basic Papers on Undecidable Propositions, Unsolvable Problems, and Computable Functions*
SciTech - v28 - i3 - Sept 2004 - p16(1) [501+]

Davis, Michael C. - *International Intervention in the Post-Cold War World: Moral Responsibility and Power Politics*
R&R Bk N - v19 - i1 - Feb 2004 - pNA [501+]

Davis, Michele Ivy - *Evangeline Brown and the Cadillac Motel*
c CCB-B - v58 - i1 - Sept 2004 - p13(1) [51-500]

Davis, Natalie Zemon - *Gift in Sixteenth-Century France*
JMH - v76 - i4 - Dec 2004 - p957(2) [501+]

Davis, Olena Kalytiak - *Shattered Sonnets, Love Cards, and Other Off and Back Handed Importunities*
Poet - v184 - i5 - Sept 2004 - p389(3) [501+]

Davis, Olga Samples - *Things My Mama Told Me: The Wisdom That Shapes Our Lives*
Black Iss - v6 - i5 - Sept-Oct 2004 - p36(2) [501+]

Davis, Ossie - *Just Like Martin*
c SLJ - v50 - i10 - Oct 2004 - p66(1) [51-500]

Davis, Patti - *The Long Goodbye*
BL - v101 - i6 - Nov 15 2004 - p530(1) [51-500]
LJ - v129 - i20 - Dec 1 2004 - p150(2) [51-500]
PW - v251 - i45 - Nov 8 2004 - p44(2) [501+]

Davis, R. Deborah - *Black Students' Perceptions: The Complexity of Persistence to Graduation at an American University*
R&R Bk N - v19 - i4 - Nov 2004 - p192(1) [501+]

Davis, Richard - *Woven Histories, Dancing Lives: Torres Strait Islander Identity, Culture and History*
R&R Bk N - v19 - i4 - Nov 2004 - p52(1) [1-50]

Davis, Richard G. - *Anatomy of a Reform: The Expeditionary Aerospace Force*
APH - v51 - i3 - Fall 2004 - p48(1) [501+]
Davis, Robert H. - *Jung, Freud, and Hillman: Three Depth Psychologies in Context*
R&R Bk N - v19 - i1 - Feb 2004 - p7(1) [1-50]
Davis, Rocio - *Transcultural Reinventions: Asian American and Asian Canadian Short Story Cycles*
Can Lit - i182 - Autumn 2004 - p111(2) [501+]
Davis, Ronald L. - *Just Making Movies: Company Directors on the Studio System*
Globe & Mail - Feb 26 2005 - pD13 [51-500]
William S. Hart: Projecting the American West
Roundup M - v11 - i6 - August 2004 - p23(1) [501+]
SHQ - v107 - i4 - April 2004 - p621(2) [501+]
Davis, Rowland H. - *The Microbial Models of Molecular Biology: From Genes to Genomes*
QRB - v79 - i3 - Sept 2004 - p301(2) [501+]
Davis, Sam - *Designing for the Homeless: Architecture That Works*
Choice - v42 - i7 - March 2005 - p1220(1) [51-500]
Davis, Stan - *The Art Of Business: Make All Your Work a Work of Art*
Bwatch - March 2005 - pNA [51-500]
Davis, Stephen (b. 1947 -) - *Jim Morrison: Life, Death, Legend*
Globe & Mail - July 24 2004 - pD10 [501+]
Davis, Stephen Randy - *C++ for Dummies*
LJ - v129 - i16 - Oct 1 2004 - p104(1) [51-500]
Davis, Stephen T. - *The Incarnation*
JR - v85 - i1 - Jan 2005 - p142(2) [501+]
Davis, Steven L. - *Texas Literary Outlaws: Six Writers in the Sixties and Beyond*
Choice - v42 - i3 - Nov 2004 - p481(1) [1-50]
Davis, Sue - *The Russian Far East: The Last Frontier?*
Russ Rev - v63 - i2 - April 2004 - pNA [501+]
Davis, Thadious M. - *Games of Property: Law, Race, Gender, and Faulkner's Go Down, Moses*
JSH - v71 - i1 - Feb 2005 - p210(2) [501+]
Davis, Therese - *The Face on the Screen: Death, Recognition and Spectatorship*
R&R Bk N - v19 - i3 - August 2004 - p261(1) [51-500]
Davis, Thomas W. - *Shifting Sands: The Rise and Fall of Biblical Archaeology*
Choice - v42 - i3 - Nov 2004 - p499(1) [51-500]
Davis, Tina - *Look and Cook: A Cookbook for Children*
y SLJ - v50 - i9 - Sept 2004 - p224(2) [51-500]
Davis, Todd F. - *The Critical Response to John Irving*
R&R Bk N - v19 - i4 - Nov 2004 - p243(1) [501+]
Davis, Uri - *Apartheid Israel: Possibilities for the Struggle Within*
Choice - v42 - i6 - Feb 2005 - p1091(1) [51-500]
Davis, Wade - *The Lost Amazon: The Photographic Journey of Richard Evans Schultes*
Am Sci - v93 - i1 - Jan-Feb 2005 - p78(2) [501+]
Davis, William C. - *Lone Star Rising: The Revolutionary Birth of the Texas Republic*
Choice - v42 - i2 - Oct 2004 - p353(1) [501+]
JAH - v91 - i3 - Dec 2004 - p1002(2) [501+]
SHQ - v108 - i1 - July 2004 - p102-105 [501+]
A Taste for War: A Culinary History of the Blue and the Gray
JPC - v38 - i2 - Nov 2004 - p448(3) [501+]
Davis, William S. - *Operating Systems: A Systematic View, 6th Ed.*
SciTech - v28 - i4 - Dec 2004 - p27(1) [51-500]
SciTech - v28 - i4 - Dec 2004 - p27(1) [51-500]
Davison, Annette - *Hollywood Theory, Non-Hollywood Practice: Cinema Soundtracks in the 1980s and 1990s*
Choice - v42 - i2 - Oct 2004 - p299(2) [51-500]
Davison, Carol Margaret - *Anti-Semitism and British Gothic Literature*
Choice - v42 - i5 - Jan 2005 - p852(1) [1-50]
Davison, Gary Marvin - *A Short History of Taiwan: The Case for Independence*
R&R Bk N - v19 - i1 - Feb 2004 - p49(1) [51-500]
Davoine, Francoise - *History Beyond Trauma: Whereof One Cannot Speak, Thereof One Cannot Stay Silent*
SciTech - v28 - i3 - Sept 2004 - p102(1) [1-50]
Dawes, Kwame Senu Neville - *I Saw Your Face (Illus. by Feelings, Tom)*
c HB - v81 - i1 - Jan-Feb 2005 - p74(2) [51-500]
c PW - v252 - i4 - Jan 24 2005 - p243(2) [51-500]
A Place to Hide
WLT - v78 - i3-4 - Sept-Dec 2004 - p82(2) [501+]
Dawesar, Abha - *Babyji*
PW - v252 - i4 - Jan 24 2005 - p222(1) [501+]
G&L Rev W - v12 - i2 - March-April 2005 - p44(1) [501+]

Daweson, Leslie - *How to Save Up to $3000 a Year on Your Diabetes Costs*
Choice - v26 - i7 - July 2004 - p3(1) [51-500]
Dawisha, Adeed - *Arab Nationalism in the Twentieth Century: From Triumph to Despair*
PSQ - v119 - i2 - Summer 2004 - p359(2) [501+]
Dawkins, Heather - *The Nude in French Art and Culture, 1870-1910*
NCFS - v32 - i3-4 - Spring-Summer 2004 - p361(2) [501+]
Dawkins, Pete - *Hard Heads, Soft Hearts: A New Reform Agenda for Australia*
JEL - v41 - i4 - Dec 2003 - p1423(1) [501+]
Dawkins, Richard - *The Ancestor's Tale: A Pilgrimage to the Dawn of Evolution*
Am Sci - v93 - i2 - March-April 2005 - p168(4) [501+]
BL - v101 - i3 - Oct 1 2004 - p289(1) [51-500]
BL - v101 - i7 - Dec 1 2004 - p632(1) [51-500]
BW - v34 - i46 - Nov 14 2004 - p10(1) [501+]
Ent W - i790 - Oct 29 2004 - p75 [51-500]
KR - v72 - i17 - Sept 1 2004 - p846(1) [501+]
LJ - v129 - i15 - Sept 15 2004 - p80(1) [51-500]
NYTBR - Oct 17 2004 - p13 [501+]
PW - v251 - i34 - August 23 2004 - p45(2) [51-500]
The Ancestor's Tale: A Pilgrimage to the Dawn of Life
Globe & Mail - Oct 16 2004 - pD19 [501+]
Nature - v431 - i7011 - Oct 21 2004 - p903(2) [501+]
New Sci - v184 - i2472 - Nov 6 2004 - p52(1) [501+]
New Sci - v184 - i2476 - Dec 4 2004 - p55(1) [501+]
Sci - v307 - i5710 - Feb 4 2005 - p676(2) [501+]
Spec - v296 - i9190 - Sept 25 2004 - p58(2) [501+]
TLS - i5303 - Nov 19 2004 - p3-4 [501+]
Dawley, Alan - *Changing the World: American Progressive in War and Revolution*
JAH - v91 - i1 - June 2004 - p277-278 [501+]
Dawn, Marva J. - *Unfettered Hope: A Call to Faithful Living in an Affluent Society*
CC - v121 - i21 - Oct 19 2004 - p35(1) [501+]
TT - v61 - i2 - July 2004 - p238(3) [501+]
Daws, Gavan - *Prisoners of the Japanese: POWs of World War II in the Pacific*
TLS - i5285 - July 16 2004 - p29(1) [501+]
Dawson, Andrew - *Lives of the Philadelphia Engineers: Capital, Class and Revolution, 1830-1890*
R&R Bk N - v19 - i3 - August 2004 - p119(1) [51-500]
Dawson, Anna - *Studying The Matrix*
TES - v0 - i4587 - June 11 2004 - pssss19(1) [501+]
Dawson, Jane E.A. - *The Politics of Religion in the Age of Mary, Queen of Scots, the Earl of Argyll and the Struggle for Britain and Ireland*
CHR - v90 - i3 - July 2004 - p553(3) [501+]
Dawson, John David - *Christian Figural Reading and the Fashioning of Identity*
JR - v84 - i3 - July 2004 - p477(3) [501+]
Dawson, John R. - *Their Roles Remembered: Farmer City Veterans in World War II*
EFHM - v58 - i2 - March-April 2004 - p88(1) [51-500]
EFHM - v58 - i2 - March-April 2004 - p89(1) [51-500]
Dawson, Michael - *The Consumer Trap: Big Business Marketing in American Life*
CC - v122 - i1 - Jan 11 2005 - p38(2) [501+]
JEL - v41 - i4 - Dec 2003 - p1400(1) [501+]
Dawson, Peg - *Executive Skills in Children and Adolescents: A Practical Guide to Assessment and Intervention*
SciTech - v28 - i3 - Sept 2004 - p3(1) [501+]
Dawson, Ruth P. - *The Contested Quill: Literature by Women in Germany, 1770-1800*
GSR - v27 - i3 - Oct 2004 - p608(2) [501+]
Dawson, Ted - *Spooner: Love Is Strange*
y Kliatt - v39 - i2 - March 2005 - p30(1) [51-500]
Day, Alexandra - *The Flight of a Dove (Illus. by Day, Alexandra)*
c BL - v101 - i6 - Nov 15 2004 - p580(2) [51-500]
c PW - v251 - i37 - Sept 13 2004 - p78(1) [51-500]
c SLJ - v50 - i9 - Sept 2004 - p157(1) [51-500]
Day, Cathy - *The Circus in Winter*
BL - v100 - i21 - July 2004 - p1817(1) [51-500]
NYTBR - July 18 2004 - p21 [501+]
People - v62 - i4 - July 26 2004 - p48 [51-500]

Day, Graham - *Making Sense of Wales: A Sociological Perspective*
Choice - v41 - i7 - March 2004 - p1360(1) [501+]
Day, James M. - *Oilmen and Other Scoundrels*
R&R Bk N - v19 - i3 - August 2004 - p119(1) [51-500]
Day, Jeni Pollack - *Moving Forward with Literature Circles*
RT - v57 - Nov 2003 - p296 [501+]
Day, John A. - *Book of Clouds*
SB - v40 - i6 - Nov-Dec 2004 - p244(2) [51-500]
Day-Lewis, Tamasin - *Good Tempered Food: Recipes to Love, Leave and Linger Over*
PW - v251 - i41 - Oct 11 2004 - p72(1) [51-500]
Day, Nancy Raines - *Double Those Wheels*
c TC Math - v11 - i2 - Sept 2004 - p109(1) [51-500]
Piecing Earth and Sky Together: A Creation Story from the Mien Tribe of Laos
c Teach Lib - v32 - i1 - Oct 2004 - p22(1) [51-500]
Day, Peter - *Dictionary of Christian Denominations*
IBMR - v28 - i3 - July 2004 - p137(2) [501+]
Day, Preston Leslie - *Crete Beyond the Palaces: Proceedings*
R&R Bk N - v19 - i4 - Nov 2004 - p40(1) [51-500]
Day, Randal D. - *Conceptualizing and Measuring Father Involvement*
R&R Bk N - v19 - i1 - Feb 2004 - p129(1) [51-500]
Day, Roger - *Playground Survival (Illus. by Allwright, Deborah)*
c SLJ - v51 - i1 - Jan 2005 - p107(1) [51-500]
Day, S. Ye - *Microarrays and Microplates: Applications in Biomedical Sciences*
E-Streams - Oct 2004 - pNA [501+]
Day, Sonia - *Urban Gardener: How to Grow Things Successfully on Balconies, Terraces, Decks and Rooftops*
CBRA - v2003 - April 2003 - p417(1) [501+]
Day, Susan - *Art Deco and Modernist Carpets*
Ant&CM - v109 - i1 - March 2004 - p16(1) [501+]
Day, Susie - *Whump!*
c Sch Lib - v52 - i3 - Autumn 2004 - p136(1) [501+]
A Day That Changed America
LibMed - v22 - i6 - March 2004 - p79(1) [501+]
The Day the Babies Crawled Away (Illus. by Rathmann, Peggy)
c LibMed - v22 - i7 - April-May 2004 - p58(1) [501+]
Day, William H.E. - *Axiomatic Consensus Theory in Group Choice and Biomathematics*
SciTech - v28 - i1 - March 2004 - p61(1) [51-500]
Daybell, Chad - *Through the Eyes of John (Illus. by Murray, Rhett E.)*
y PW - v252 - i7 - Feb 14 2005 - p79(1) [51-500]
Daybell, James - *Early Modern Women's Letter Writing, 1450-1700*
JWH - v16 - i4 - Winter 2004 - p207(8) [501+]
Women and Politics in Early Modern England, 1450-1700
R&R Bk N - v19 - i3 - August 2004 - p153(1) [51-500]
Daymond, M.J. - *Women Writing Africa: The Southern Region*
Biomag - v27 - i3 - Summer 2004 - p665(8) [501+]
IJAHS - v37 - i2 - Spring 2004 - p347-349 [501+]
NYRB - v52 - i2 - Feb 10 2005 - p28(2) [501+]
Days That Shook the World
LibMed - v22 - i7 - April-May 2004 - p71(1) [501+]
Dayton, Tim - *Muriel Rukeyser's "The Book of the Dead"*
TSWL - v23 - i1 - Spring 2004 - p146-148 [501+]
de Acosta, Jose - *Natural and Moral History of the Indies*
Six Ct J - v35 - i1 - Spring 2004 - p231(2) [501+]
De Acosta, Mercedes - *Women in Turmoil: Six Plays*
TLS - i5293 - Sept 10 2004 - p18(1) [501+]
De Anda, Diane - *Kikiriki (Illus. by Lechon, Daniel)*
c SLJ - v50 - i9 - Sept 2004 - p196(1) [51-500]
Social Work with Multicultural Youth
R&R Bk N - v19 - i1 - Feb 2004 - p137(1) [51-500]
De Angelis, Franco - *Megara Hyblaia and Selinous: The Development of Two Greek City-States in Archaic Sicily*
R&R Bk N - v19 - i3 - August 2004 - p44(1) [51-500]
De Angelis, Gina - *It Happened in Washington, D.C.*
Kliatt - v38 - i4 - July 2004 - p42(1) [51-500]
Motion Pictures: Making Cinema Magic
c SLJ - v50 - i9 - Sept 2004 - p225(1) [51-500]
De Angelis, Rose - *Between Anthropology and Literature: Interdisciplinary Discourse*
JRAI - v10 - i4 - Dec 2004 - p930(3) [501+]

De Armas, Fredrick A. - *Writing for the Eyes in the Spanish Golden Age*
Choice - v42 - i7 - March 2005 - p1233(2) [51-500]

de Banville, Theodore - *Oeuvres poetiques completes*
NCFS - v32 - i3-4 - Spring-Summer 2004 - p397(3) [501+]

De Barros, Juanita - *Order and Place in a Colonial City: Patterns of Struggle and Resistance in Georgetown, British Guiana, 1889-1924*
AHR - v109 - i2 - April 2004 - p578(2) [501+]

De Beer, Hans - *Leonardo's Dream*
c   SLJ - v51 - i2 - Feb 2005 - p96(1) [51-500]
Oh No, Ono! (Illus. by De Beer, Hans)
c   LibMed - v23 - i3 - Nov-Dec 2004 - p66(1) [51-500]
c   Sch Lib - v52 - i3 - Autumn 2004 - p130(1) [501+]
c   SLJ - v50 - i9 - Sept 2004 - p158(1) [51-500]

De Bellaigue, Christopher - *In the Rose Garden of the Martyrs: A Memoir of Iran*
BL - v101 - i9-10 - Jan 1 2005 - p808(1) [51-500]
Bus W - i3915 - Jan 10 2005 - p22 [501+]
KR - v72 - i23 - Dec 1 2004 - p1128(2) [501+]
NYTBR - Feb 13 2005 - p1 [501+]

De Berg, Henk - *Freud's Theory and Its Use in Literary and Cultural Studies: An Introduction*
Ger Q - v77 - i1 - Wntr 2004 - p115(2) [501+]

De Bernieres, Louis - *Birds Without Wings (Read by Lee, John). Audiobook Review*
BL - v101 - i7 - Dec 1 2004 - p676(1) [51-500]
Birds Without Wings (Read by Bonneville, Hugh). Audiobook Review
Globe & Mail - Jan 8 2005 - pD13 [1-50]
Birds Without Wings (Read by Lee, John). Audiobook Review
y   Kliatt - v39 - i2 - March 2005 - p48(1) [51-500]

de Bernieres, Louis - *Birds Without Wings*
BIC - v33 - i8 - Nov 2004 - p7(2) [501+]

De Bernieres, Louis - *Birds Without Wings*
BL - v101 - i2 - Sept 15 2004 - p205(1) [501+]
BL - v101 - i9-10 - Jan 1 2005 - p769(1) [51-500]
BW - v34 - i42 - Oct 17 2004 - p6(2) [501+]
Econ - v372 - i8384 - July 17 2004 - p79US [501+]
KR - v72 - i16 - August 15 2004 - p759(2) [501+]
LJ - v129 - i15 - Sept 15 2004 - p48(1) [501+]
NW - Sept 6 2004 - p69 [501+]
Spec - v295 - i9178 - July 3 2004 - p33(2) [501+]
TLS - i5284 - July 9 2004 - p19-20 [501+]

De Beyer, Joy - *Tobacco Control Policy: Strategies, Success, and Setbacks*
JEL - v41 - i4 - Dec 2003 - p1373(1) [501+]

De Blasi, Marlena - *A Thousand Days in Tuscany: A Bittersweet Adventure*
BL - v101 - i3 - Oct 1 2004 - p291(1) [51-500]
KR - v72 - i16 - August 15 2004 - p785(1) [51-500]
LJ - v129 - i15 - Sept 15 2004 - p72(1) [51-500]
PW - v251 - i30 - July 26 2004 - p44(1) [501+]

De Boef, Suzanna - *The Political (and Economic) Origins of Consumer Confidence*
Wil Q - v29 - i1 - Wntr 2005 - p92(1) [501+]

de Boer, E.A. - *John Calvin on the Visions of Ezekiel: Historical, Hermeneutical, and Exegetical Studies in Calvin's 'Sermons Inedits', Especially on Ezek. 36-48*
R&R Bk N - v19 - i1 - Feb 2004 - p20(1) [51-500]

De Boer, Jelle Zelinga - *Earthquakes in Human History: The Far-Reaching Effects of Seismic Disruptions*
PW - v251 - i46 - Nov 15 2004 - p49(1) [51-500]

De Boer, Trent - *Shovel Bum: Comix of Archaeological Field Life*
R&R Bk N - v19 - i4 - Nov 2004 - p29(1) [501+]

De Borbone, Stephanus - *Tractatus de Diversis Materiis Predicabilibus: Prologus; Prima Pars: De Dono Trimoris*
Specu - v79 - i4 - Oct 2004 - p1153(3) [501+]

de Botton, Alain - *Status Anxiety*
CC - v121 - i22 - Nov 2 2004 - p34(3) [501+]
NYTBR - August 22 2004 - p16 [501+]
SLJ - v50 - i12 - Dec 2004 - p54(4) [501+]

De Bruin, Anne - *Entrepreneurship: New Perpective in a Global Age*
JEL - v41 - i4 - Dec 2003 - p1398(1) [501+]

De Capoa, Chiara - *Old Testament Figures in Art*
Choice - v42 - i4 - Dec 2004 - p649(1) [1-50]

De Capua, Sarah - *How People Immigrate*
c   SLJ - v50 - i8 - August 2004 - p106(1) [501+]
Running for Public Office
c   SLJ - v50 - i8 - August 2004 - p47(1) [51-500]
Voting
c   SLJ - v50 - i8 - August 2004 - p47(1) [51-500]

De Caro, Frank - *Re-Situating Folklore: Folk Contexts and Twentieth-Century Literature and Art*
JouAmCul - v27 - i3 - Sept 2004 - p354(1) [501+]

De Caso, Jacques - *The Drawing Speaks: Theophile Bra: Works 1826-1855*
NCFS - v32 - i3-4 - Spring-Summer 2004 - p358(2) [501+]

De Castro, Leandro Nunes - *Recent Developments in Biologically Inspired Computing*
Choice - v42 - i7 - March 2005 - p1261(1) [51-500]

de Chesnay, Mary - *Caring for the Vulnerable: Perspectives in Nursing Theory, Practice, and Research*
SciTech - v28 - i4 - Dec 2004 - p122 [51-500]

De Clerq, Peter - *Scientific Instruments: Originals and Imitations*
Isis - v95 - i3 - Sept 2004 - p472(2) [501+]

De Cock, Nicole - *The Girl and the Elephant (Illus. by De Cock, Nicole)*
c   PW - v251 - i29 - July 19 2004 - p160(1) [51-500]
c   SLJ - v50 - i11 - Nov 2004 - p96(1) [51-500]

De Courcelles, Dominique - *Philologie et subjectivite: actes de la journee d'etude organisee par l'Ecole nationale des chartes*
FS - v58 - i1 - Jan 2004 - p82(2) [501+]

De Cunzo, Lu Ann - *A Historical Archaeology of Delaware: People, Contexts, and the Cultures of Agriculture*
Choice - v42 - i6 - Feb 2005 - p1081(1) [51-500]
R&R Bk N - v19 - i3 - August 2004 - p73(1) [51-500]

de Ferranti, David - *Inequality in Latin America: Breaking with History*
R&R Bk N - v19 - i3 - August 2004 - p146(1) [51-500]

De Filippo, Eduardo - *Theater Neapolitan Style: Five One-Act Plays*
R&R Bk N - v19 - i4 - Nov 2004 - p231(1) [501+]

De Goey, John J. - *Professional Financial Advisor: Ethics, Unbundling and Other Things to Ask Your Financial Advisor*
CBRA - Annual 2003 - p29(1) [51-500]

de Gournay, Marie le Jars - *Apology for the Woman Writing and Other Works*
Six Ct J - v35 - i1 - Spring 2004 - p295(2) [501+]

De Grauwe, Paul - *Economics of Monetary Union*
TimHES - v0 - i1675 - Jan 21 2005 - p25(1) [501+]

de Grazia, Victoria - *Irresistible Empire: America's Advance through 20th Century Europe*
KR - v73 - i2 - Jan 15 2005 - p97(1) [501+]

de Grenaille, Francois - *L'honnete fille ou dans le premier livre il est traite de l'esprit des filles*
Ren Q - v57 - i4 - Winter 2004 - p1434(3) [501+]

De Guzman, Michael - *Beekman's Big Deal*
c   BL - v101 - i3 - Oct 1 2004 - p329(1) [51-500]
c   CCB-B - v58 - i5 - Jan 2005 - p206(2) [51-500]
c   KR - v72 - i19 - Oct 1 2004 - p958(1) [51-500]
c   PW - v251 - i48 - Nov 29 2004 - p40(2) [51-500]
y   SLJ - v50 - i11 - Nov 2004 - p141(1) [51-500]
c   VOYA - v27 - i5 - Dec 2004 - p380(1) [51-500]

De Hamel, Christopher - *Horae Beatae Mariae ad usum Romanum (Hours of the Blessed Virgin Mary Following the Roman Use), France, 1524*
Lib & Cul - v39 - i3 - Summer 2004 - p323(2) [501+]

de Hoyos, Arturo - *Freemasonry in Context: History, Ritual, Controversy*
R&R Bk N - v19 - i3 - August 2004 - p155(1) [51-500]

de Jonge, Eccy - *Spinoza and Deep Ecology: Challenging Traditional Approaches to Environmentalism*
R&R Bk N - v19 - i4 - Nov 2004 - p75(1) [51-500]

De Jonge, Piet - *Van Gogh to Mondrian: Modern Art from the Kroller-Muller Museum*
LJ - v129 - i19 - Nov 15 2004 - p57(1) [51-500]

De Kretser, Michelle - *The Hamilton Case*
NYRB - v51 - i19 - Dec 2 2004 - p25(4) [501+]

de La Beaumelle, Agnes - *Joan Miro, 1917-1934*
Choice - v42 - i5 - Jan 2005 - p844(1) [1-50]
LJ - v129 - i17 - Oct 15 2004 - p59(2) [51-500]

De La Bedoyere, Guy - *Defying Rome: The Rebels of Roman Britain*
Choice - v42 - i6 - Feb 2005 - p1085(2) [51-500]

De la Billiere, Peter - *Supreme Courage*
Spec - v296 - i9190 - Sept 25 2004 - p51(2) [501+]

De la Cova, Antonio Rafael - *Cuban Confederate Colonel: The Life of Ambrosio Jose Gonzales*
Choice - v41 - i7 - March 2004 - p1346(1) [501+]

De La Cruz, Melissa - *The Au Pairs*
BL - v100 - i21 - July 2004 - p1833(1) [1-50]
y   CCB-B - v58 - i1 - Sept 2004 - p14(1) [51-500]
y   VOYA - v27 - i4 - Oct 2004 - p293(2) [51-500]
The Fashionista Files: Adventures in Four-Inch Heels and Faux Pas
Time - v164 - i12 - Sept 20 2004 - p80 [51-500]

de la Flor, Mike - *Digital Biomedical Illustration Handbook*
SciTech - v28 - i4 - Dec 2004 - p79(1) [51-500]

De La Fontaine, Jean - *Les Fables De La Fontaine*
Res Links - v10 - i1 - Oct 2004 - p51(2) [51-500]

de la Garza, Rodolfo O. - *Muted Voices: Latinos and the 2000 Elections*
R&R Bk N - v19 - i4 - Nov 2004 - p59(1) [51-500]

De La Gueriviere, Jean - *The Exploration of Africa*
LJ - v129 - i15 - Sept 15 2004 - p67(2) [51-500]

De La Haye, Amy - *Defining Dress*
JAAC - v61 - Winter 2003 - p94 [501+]

de la Maza, Luis M. - *Color Atlas of Medical Bacteriology*
SB - v40 - i6 - Nov-Dec 2004 - p252(1) [51-500]
SciTech - v28 - i3 - Sept 2004 - p73(1) [51-500]

De La Roque, Jean - *A Voyage to Arabia Felix*
A Aff - v35 - i2 - July 2004 - p219-220 [501+]

De La Torre, Miguel A. - *The Quest for the Cuban Christ: A Historical Search*
JAAR - v72 - i3 - Sept 2004 - p771-773 [501+]
Santeria: The Beliefs and Rituals of a Growing Religion in America
BL - v101 - i1 - Sept 1 2004 - p22(1) [51-500]
Bwatch - Feb 2005 - pNA [51-500]
LJ - v129 - i19 - Nov 15 2004 - p64(2) [51-500]
PW - v251 - i33 - August 16 2004 - p61(1) [501+]

De Lacheisserie, Etienne du Tremolet - *Magnetism: Fundamentals*
Choice - v42 - i6 - Feb 2005 - p1059(2) [51-500]
Magnetism: Materials and Applications
Choice - v42 - i6 - Feb 2005 - p1059(2) [51-500]

De las Casas, Bartolome - *An Account, Much Abbreviated, of the Destruction of the Indies, with Related Texts*
R&R Bk N - v19 - i1 - Feb 2004 - p66(1) [501+]

De Laurentiis, Giada - *Everyday Italian: 125 Simple and Delicious Recipes*
LJ - v130 - i3 - Feb 15 2005 - p152(1) [51-500]
PW - v252 - i5 - Jan 31 2005 - p64(2) [501+]

De Leon, Arnoldo - *Racial Frontiers: Africans, Chinese, and Mexicans in Western America, 1848-1890*
Ams - v61 - i2 - Oct 2004 - p306(2) [501+]

De Leon, Sonia Vuson - *Global Handbook on Food and Water Safety: For the Education of Food Industry Management, Food Handlers, and Consumers*
SciTech - v28 - i1 - March 2004 - p86(1) [51-500]

de Ley, Marc - *Cytokine Protocols*
SciTech - v28 - i1 - March 2004 - p76(1) [51-500]

De Lillo, Don - *The Body Artist*
PSQ - v78 - i3 - Fall 2004 - p183(3) [501+]

De Lint, Charles - *The Blue Girl*
y   BL - v101 - i6 - Nov 15 2004 - p573(2) [51-500]
y   CCB-B - v58 - i4 - Dec 2004 - p164(2) [51-500]
y   Globe & Mail - Dec 11 2004 - pD26 [501+]
Kliatt - v38 - i6 - Nov 2004 - p6(2) [51-500]
y   KR - v72 - i19 - Oct 1 2004 - p959(1) [51-500]
y   PW - v251 - i51 - Dec 20 2004 - p60(2) [51-500]
y   SLJ - v50 - i11 - Nov 2004 - p141(1) [51-500]
VOYA - v27 - i5 - Dec 2004 - p402(1) [51-500]
A Circle of Cats (Illus. by Vess, Charles)
c   LibMed - v22 - i5 - Feb 2004 - p63(1) [501+]
Quicksilver and Shadow
PW - v251 - i47 - Nov 22 2004 - p43(1) [51-500]
Quicksilver & Shadow: Collected Early Stories, Vol. 2
y   BL - v101 - i8 - Dec 15 2004 - p715(1) [51-500]
Quicksilver & Shadow: Collected Early Stories, Vol. 2
LJ - v129 - i20 - Dec 1 2004 - p105(1) [51-500]

De Lizardi, Fernandez - *The Mangy Parrot: The Life and Times of Periquillo Sarniento; Written by Himself for His Children*
R&R Bk N - v19 - i4 - Nov 2004 - p232(1) [501+]

de Lope, Manuel - *Iberia: La puerta iluminada*
TLS - i5268 - March 19 2004 - p26-26 [501+]

De Los Santos, Hector J. - *Introduction to Microelectromechanical Microwave Systems, 2nd Ed.*
SciTech - v28 - i4 - Dec 2004 - p158(1) [51-500]

De Luca, Tony - *Recipes from Wine Country*
Globe & Mail - Nov 27 2004 - pD26 [51-500]

De Marneffe, Daphne - *Maternal Desire: On Children, Love, and the Inner Life*
Choice - v42 - i2 - Oct 2004 - p374(1) [51-500]
NYTBR - Oct 24 2004 - p26 [501+]

Dearen, Patrick - *When the Sky Rained Dust*
  Roundup M - v12 - i3 - Feb 2005 - p27(1) [51-500]
Dearing, Ramona - *So Beautiful*
  Globe & Mail - Nov 27 2004 - pD3 [51-500]
Dearinger, David B. - *Painting and Sculpture in the Collection of the National Academy of Design, Vol. 1*
  Mag Antiq - v167 - i1 - Jan 2005 - p129(1) [51-500]
  Mag Antiq - v167 - i2 - Feb 2005 - p55(1) [51-500]
  Mag Antiq - v167 - i3 - March 2005 - p59(1) [501+]
  R&R Bk N - v19 - i4 - Nov 2004 - p200(1) [501+]
DeArment, Robert K. - *Jim Courtright of Fort Worth: His Life and Legend*
  Roundup M - v12 - i2 - Dec 2004 - p21(2) [501+]
Dearstyne, Bruce W. - *Effective Approaches for Managing Electronic Records and Archives*
  Archiv - i56 - Fall 2003 - p408(4) [501+]
Deary, Terry - *The Boy Who Haunted Himself*
  y Sch Lib - v52 - i4 - Winter 2004 - p215(1) [51-500]
  Classified: Vanished!
  PW - v251 - i46 - Nov 15 2004 - p60(2) [501+]
Deater-Deckard, Kirby D. - *Parenting Stress*
  R&R Bk N - v19 - i4 - Nov 2004 - p129(1) [1-50]
Deaver, Jeffery - *Garden of Beasts: A Novel of Berlin 1936*
  BIC - v33 - i8 - Nov 2004 - p16(3) [501+]
  y SLJ - v51 - i1 - Jan 2005 - p158(2) [51-500]
  Garden of Beasts (Read by Mays, Jefferson). Audiobook Review
  y Kliatt - v39 - i2 - March 2005 - p52(1) [51-500]
  LJ - v130 - i1 - Jan 1 2005 - p167(1) [51-500]
  Garden of Beasts
  Ent W - i775 - July 23 2004 - p83 [51-500]
  Globe & Mail - July 24 2004 - pD11 [51-500]
  Twisted. Audiobook Review
  LJ - v129 - i19 - Nov 15 2004 - p97(1) [51-500]
  The Vanished Man. Audiobook Review
  Globe & Mail - July 24 2004 - pD13 [51-500]
Deb, Sagarmay - *Multimedia Systems and Content-Based Image Retrieval*
  Choice - v42 - i3 - Nov 2004 - p520(1) [1-50]
Deb, Siddhartha - *An Outline of the Republic*
  KR - v73 - i5 - March 1 2005 - p246(1) [51-500]
  PW - v252 - i6 - Feb 7 2005 - p38(1) [51-500]
DeBare, Ilana - *Where Girls Come First: The Rise, Fall, and Surprising Revival of Girls' Schools*
  HER - v74 - i3 - Fall 2004 - p354(3) [501+]
Debatable Issues in U.S. History, Vol. 5
  R&R Bk N - v19 - i3 - August 2004 - p64(1) [51-500]
Debatable Issues in U.S. History, Vols. 1-5
  SLJ - v50 - i12 - Dec 2004 - p84(1) [501+]
  BL - v101 - i7 - Dec 1 2004 - p684(2) [501+]
Debax, Helene - *La feodalite languedocienne XI-XII siecles: serments, sommages et fiefs dans le Languedoc des Trencavel*
  Med R - Dec 2004 - pNA [501+]
Debevec, Anton - *United States Documents in the Propaganda Fide Archives: A Calendar, Vol. 12*
  CHR - v90 - i4 - Oct 2004 - p827(2) [501+]
DeBlack, Thomas A. - *With Fire and Sword: Arkansas, 1861-1874*
  SHQ - v107 - i4 - April 2004 - p639(2) [501+]
DeBlasih, Anthony - *Reform in the Balance: The Defense of Literary Culture in Mid-Tang China*
  AHR - v109 - i3 - June 2004 - p877(2) [501+]
DeBlieu, Jan - *Year of the Comets: A Journey from Sadness to the Stars*
  PW - v252 - i10 - March 7 2005 - p58(2) [51-500]
Deblieux, Mike - *Performance Appraisal Source Book: A Collection of Practical Samples*
  HR Mag - v50 - i2 - Feb 2005 - pNA [501+]
  HR Mag - v50 - i2 - Feb 2005 - pS15(1) [501+]
Debnath, Lokenath - *Partial Differential Equations: Methods and Applications*
  SIAM Rev - v46 - i1 - March 2004 - p162-163 [501+]
Debon, Nicolas - *Four Pictures by Emily Carr*
  c CBRA - Annual 2003 - p534(2) [51-500]
Debray, Regis - *God: An Itinerary*
  Choice - v42 - i4 - Dec 2004 - p676(1) [1-50]
  Lon R Bks - v27 - i4 - Feb 17 2005 - p29(2) [501+]
Debreu, Gerard - *Economic Essays: A Festschrift for Werner Hildenbrand*
  JEL - v41 - i4 - Dec 2003 - p1272(3) [501+]

Debris, Carrie - *Suspense and Sensibility, or, First Impressions Revisited: A Mr. and Mrs. Darcy Mystery*
  KR - v73 - i2 - Jan 15 2005 - p84(1) [51-500]
Debrock, Guy - *Process Pragmatism: Essays on a Quiet Philosophical Revolution*
  R&R Bk N - v19 - i1 - Feb 2004 - p3(1) [1-50]
Debroux, Philippe - *Human Resource Management in Japan: Changes and Uncertainties: A New Human Resource Management System Fitting to the Global Economy*
  R&R Bk N - v19 - i1 - Feb 2004 - p111(1) [51-500]
Debru, A. - *Docente natura. Melanges de medecine ancienne et medievale offerts a Guy Sabbah*
  Class R - v53 - i2 - Nov 2003 - p339-340 [501+]
Debry, Gerard - *Dietary Proteins and Atherosclerosis*
  SciTech - v28 - i3 - Sept 2004 - p106(1) [51-500]
Debs, Victor, Jr. - *"That Was Part of Baseball Then": Interviews with 24 Major League Players, Coaches and Managers*
  SSJ - v21 - i2 - June 2004 - p230-237 [501+]
Debus, Allen A. - *Dinosaur Memories: Dino-Trekking for Beasts of Thunder, Fantastic Suarians, 'Paleo-People,' Dinosaurabilia, and Other 'Prehistoria*
  R&R Bk N - v19 - i1 - Feb 2004 - p248(1) [1-50]
Debussy, Claude - *Rodrigue et Chimene. Edition de Richard Langham Smith*
  Notes - v61 - i2 - Dec 2004 - p537(4) [501+]
Debut, Kallos - *Broken for You*
  Ent W - i789 - Oct 22 2004 - p100 [501+]
deBuys, William - *Seeing Things Whole: The Essential John Wesley Powell*
  NRJ - v44 - i1 - Wntr 2004 - p319-332 [501+]
DeCandido, Keith R.A. - *Dragon Precinct*
  BL - v100 - i22 - August 2004 - p1912(1) [51-500]
  LJ - v129 - i15 - Sept 15 2004 - p53(1) [51-500]
  A Time for War, a Time for Peace
  y Kliatt - v39 - i2 - March 2005 - p26(1) [51-500]
DeCaro, Louis A., Jr. - *"Fire from the Midst of You": A Religious Life of John Brown*
  HNet - Oct 2004 - pNA [501+]
  JAH - v91 - i1 - June 2004 - p244-245 [501+]
Decharne, Max - *Hardboiled Hollywood: The Origins of the Great Crime Films*
  Bwatch - Oct 2004 - pNA [51-500]
Decker, Jochen - *Molecular Diagnosis of Infectious Diseases. 2nd Ed.*
  SciTech - v28 - i1 - March 2004 - p89(1) [51-500]
Decker, Peter R. - *"The Utes Must Go!": American Expansion and the Removal of a People*
  Choice - v42 - i5 - Jan 2005 - p915(1) [1-50]
Decommissioning Nuclear Power Plants: Policies, Strategies and Costs
  SciTech - v28 - i3 - Sept 2004 - p163(1) [51-500]
DeConde, Alexander - *Gun Violence in America: The Struggle for Control*
  R&R Bk N - v19 - i1 - Feb 2004 - pNA [51-500]
DeCosta-Willis, Miriam - *Daughters of the Diaspora: Afra-Hispanic Writers*
  Afr Am R - v38 - i2 - Summer 2004 - p341(3) [501+]
Decoste, F.C. - *The Holocaust's Ghost: Writing on Art, Politics, Law and Education*
  GSR - v27 - i2 - May 2004 - p437-438 [501+]
DeCristofano, Carolyn Cinami - *Big Bang!: The Tongue-Tickling Tale of a Speck That Became Spectacular*
  KR - v73 - i1 - Jan 1 2005 - p50(1) [51-500]
Dederick, Paul - *Looking Back: True Tales from Saskatchewan's Past*
  CBRA - Annual 2003 - p339(1) [51-500]
DeDonato, Colette - *City of One: Young Writers Speak to the World*
  y BL - v100 - i22 - August 2004 - p1917(1) [51-500]
  y Kliatt - v39 - i1 - Jan 2005 - p28(1) [51-500]
  c SLJ - v50 - i8 - August 2004 - p134(1) [51-500]
  y VOYA - v27 - i4 - Oct 2004 - p322(1) [51-500]
Dee, J.H. - *Epitheta rerum et locorum apud Homerum: A Repertory of Descriptive Expressions for Things and Places in the Iliad and the Odyssey*
  Class R - v54 - i1 - May 2004 - p239(1) [501+]
Dee, Kay C. - *An Introduction to Tissue-Biomaterial Interactions*
  QRB - v79 - i3 - Sept 2004 - p345(1) [501+]
Deedes, W.F. - *Brief Lives*
  NS - v133 - i4698 - July 26 2004 - p53(2) [501+]
  Spec - v295 - i9179 - July 10 2004 - p35(1) [501+]

Deeds, Susan M. - *Defiance and Deference in Mexico's Colonial North: Indians under Spanish Rule in Nueva Vizcaya*
  HAHR - v84 - i3 - August 2004 - p527(2) [501+]
  SHQ - v108 - i1 - July 2004 - p112-113 [501+]
  Six Ct J - v35 - i3 - Fall 2004 - p945-947 [501+]
  WHQ - v35 - i4 - Winter 2004 - p519-520 [501+]
Deely, John N. - *The Impact on Philosophy of Semiotics: The Quasi-Error of the External World with a Dialogue between a 'Semiotist' and a 'Realist'*
  Choice - v41 - i11-12 - July-August 2004 - p2056(2) [501+]
  R&R Bk N - v20 - i1 - Feb 2005 - p3(1) [51-500]
Deem, George - *How to Paint a Vermeer: A Painter's History of Art*
  A Art - v69 - i750 - Jan 2005 - p76(1) [501+]
Deem, James M. - *3 NBs of Julian Drew*
  y Kliatt - v38 - i5 - Sept 2004 - p19(2) [51-500]
Deen, Hanifa - *Caravanserai: Journey Among Australian Muslims, 2nd Ed.*
  R&R Bk N - v19 - i1 - Feb 2004 - p46(1) [51-500]
Deen, M. Jamal - *CMOS RF Modelling, Characterization and Applications*
  SciTech - v28 - i1 - March 2004 - p161(1) [51-500]
Deen, Paula - *Paula Deen and Friends: Living It Up, Southern Style*
  PW - v252 - i9 - Feb 28 2005 - p58(2) [51-500]
Deena, Seodial F.H. - *Canonization, Colonization, Decolonization: A Comparative Study of Political and Critical Works by Minority Writers*
  Can Lit - i182 - Autumn 2004 - p112(3) [501+]
The Deep: and Other Stories
  NYTBR - July 18 2004 - p20 [51-500]
Deep
  LibMed - v22 - i5 - Feb 2004 - p73(1) [501+]
Deere, Carmen Diana - *Empowering Women: Land and Property Rights in Latin America*
  Signs - v30 - i2 - Wntr 2005 - p1689(6) [501+]
Dees-Thomases, Donna - *Looking for a Few Good Moms: How One Mother Rallied a Million Others Against the Gun Lobby*
  R&R Bk N - v19 - i3 - August 2004 - p167(1) [501+]
DeFalco, Tom - *Spider-Girl, Vol. 1*
  c Teach Lib - v32 - i3 - Feb 2005 - p24(1) [51-500]
DeFelice, Cynthia C. - *The Ghost of Cutler Creek*
  BL - v100 - i21 - July 2004 - p1844(1) [1-50]
  The Missing Manatee
  y Kliatt - v39 - i2 - March 2005 - p9(2) [51-500]
Deffeyes, Kenneth S. - *Beyond Oil: The View from Hubbert's Peak.*
  KR - v73 - i1 - Jan 1 2005 - p31(1) [51-500]
Defoe, Daniel - *The Life and Strange Surprising Adventures of Robinson Crusoe*
  c RT - v57 - Sept 2003 - p97 [51-500]
Defoe, Gideon - *The Pirates! In an Adventure with Scientists*
  BL - v101 - i4 - Oct 15 2004 - p389(1) [51-500]
  Ent W - i789 - Oct 22 2004 - p100 [51-500]
  KR - v72 - i16 - August 15 2004 - p760(1) [51-500]
Deford, Frank - *The Old Ball Game: How John McGraw, Christy Mathewson, and the New York Giants Created Modern Baseball*
  KR - v73 - i2 - Jan 15 2005 - p97(2) [501+]
  PW - v252 - i6 - Feb 7 2005 - p51(2) [51-500]
DeForest, Tim - *Storytelling in the Pulps, Comics, and Radio*
  ChrSFF&H - v26 - i9 - Sept 2004 - p37(1) [51-500]
DeFrancis, John - *ABC Chinese-English Comprehensive Dictionary*
  R&R Bk N - v19 - i3 - August 2004 - p256(1) [51-500]
DeFrantz, Thomas - *Dancing Many Drums: Excavations in African American Dance*
  Dance RJ - v35 - i2 - Winter 2003 - p183-187 [501+]
  Dancing Revelations: Alvin Ailey's Embodiment of African American Culture
  Choice - v42 - i2 - Oct 2004 - p304(1) [51-500]
  Dance - v78 - i12 - Dec 2004 - p46(1) [501+]
Degani, Asaf - *Taming Hal: Designing Interfaces Beyond 2001*
  Choice - v41 - i11-12 - July-August 2004 - p2080(1) [501+]
  SciTech - v28 - i3 - Sept 2004 - p33(1) [51-500]

Dege, Wilhelm - *War North of 80: The Last German Arctic Weather Station of World War II*
Choice - v42 - i6 - Feb 2005 - p1043(1) [51-500]
R&R Bk N - v19 - i4 - Nov 2004 - p34(1) [51-500]

Degeling, Simone - *Restitutionary Rights to Share in Damages: Carers' Claims*
Law Q Rev - v120 - April 2004 - p351-355 [501+]

DeGennaro, Matt - *Tupelo: The World's Forgotten Boy*
BL - v100 - i22 - August 2004 - p1915(2) [501+]

DeGezelle, Terri - *Manners at a Friend's Home*
c   SLJ - v51 - i1 - Jan 2005 - p108(1) [51-500]
Manners at a Restaurant
c   SLJ - v51 - i1 - Jan 2005 - p108(1) [51-500]
Manners at the Library
c   SLJ - v51 - i1 - Jan 2005 - p108(1) [51-500]
Manners in the Classroom
c   SLJ - v51 - i1 - Jan 2005 - p108(1) [51-500]
Manners on the Telephone
c   SLJ - v51 - i1 - Jan 2005 - p108(1) [51-500]
Your Bones
c   SB - v40 - i4 - July-August 2004 - p148(1) [51-500]
Your Brain
c   SB - v40 - i4 - July-August 2004 - p148(1) [51-500]
Your Heart
c   SB - v40 - i4 - July-August 2004 - p148(1) [51-500]
Your Muscles
c   SB - v40 - i4 - July-August 2004 - p148(1) [51-500]
Your Stomach
c   SB - v40 - i4 - July-August 2004 - p148(1) [51-500]

Degnbol-Martinussen, John - *Aid: Understanding International Development Cooperation*
R&R Bk N - v19 - i1 - Feb 2004 - p80(1) [51-500]
Understanding International Development Cooperation
JEL - v42 - i1 - March 2004 - p265(1) [501+]

Degregori, Luis Nieto - *Cuzco despues del amor*
WLT - v79 - i1 - Jan-April 2005 - p107(1) [501+]

DeGregori, Thomas R. - *Origins of the Organic Agriculture Debate*
SciTech - v28 - i1 - March 2004 - p128(1) [51-500]

DeGroot, Gerard J. - *The Bomb: A Life*
KR - v73 - i1 - Jan 1 2005 - p31(1) [501+]
LJ - v130 - i1 - Jan 1 2005 - p127(1) [51-500]
PW - v252 - i1 - Jan 3 2005 - p46(1) [51-500]
TimHES - v0 - i1668 - Nov 26 2004 - p22(2) [501+]

Dehne, Klaus - *German Immigration in Rural Southern Indiana [USA]: A Historical-Geographical Analysis*
JAH - v91 - i3 - Dec 2004 - p1009(2) [501+]

Dei, George J. Sefa - *Playing the Race Card: Exposing White Power and Privilege*
R&R Bk N - v19 - i1 - Feb 2004 - p57(1) [51-500]

Dei, H. Daniel - *Human Being in History: Freedom, Power, and Shared Ontological Meaning*
R&R Bk N - v19 - i1 - Feb 2004 - p7(1) [51-500]

Deibler, Tim - *Land & Light Workshop: Capturing the Seasons in Oils*
LJ - v129 - i19 - Nov 15 2004 - p58(1) [501+]

Dein, Simon - *Religion and Healing Among the Lubavitch Community in Stamford Hill, North London: A Case Study of Hasidism*
R&R Bk N - v19 - i4 - Nov 2004 - p16(1) [51-500]

Deininger, Klaus - *Land Policies for Growth and Poverty Reduction*
JEL - v41 - i4 - Dec 2003 - p1408(1) [501+]

Deitch, Robert - *Hemp: American History Revisited: The Plant with a Divided History*
R&R Bk N - v19 - i1 - Feb 2004 - p140(1) [51-500]

DeJean, Joan E. - *Against Marriage: The Correspondence of La Grande Mademoiselle*
Ren Q - v57 - i3 - Fall 2004 - p1025(3) [501+]
The Reinvention of Obscenity: Sex, Lies, and Tabloids in Early Modern France
Comp L - v56 - i3 - Summer 2004 - p266-269 [501+]

DeJohn, Jacqueline - *Antonio's Wife*
BL - v101 - i6 - Nov 15 2004 - p558(1) [51-500]

Dekker, Henri A.L. - *Property Regimes in Transition, Land Reform, Food Security and Economic Development: A Case Study in the Kyrgyz Republic*
R&R Bk N - v19 - i1 - Feb 2004 - p96(1) [1-50]

Dekker, Ted - *Black (Read by Lamont, Rob). Audiobook Review*
BL - v101 - i5 - Nov 1 2004 - p502(1) [51-500]
Obsessed
LJ - v130 - i2 - Feb 1 2005 - p60(1) [51-500]
PW - v251 - i44 - Nov 1 2004 - p41(1) [51-500]
White
LJ - v129 - i18 - Nov 1 2004 - p70(1) [501+]

DeKoven, Marianne - *Utopia Limited: The Sixties and the Emergence of the Postmodern*
Choice - v42 - i3 - Nov 2004 - p481(1) [1-50]

Del Carmen, Rolando V. - *Briefs of Leading Cases in Law Enforcement, 5th Ed.*
R&R Bk N - v19 - i1 - Feb 2004 - pNA [51-500]

Del Col, Andrea - *L'Inquisizione Romana: Metodologia delle fonti e storia istituzionale*
Six Ct J - v35 - i3 - Fall 2004 - p930-932 [501+]

Del Negro, Giovanni P. - *The Passeggiata and Popular Culture in an Italian Town: Folklore and the Performance of Modernity*
R&R Bk N - v19 - i3 - August 2004 - p147(1) [51-500]

Del Rio, Martin Antoine - *Die Chronik ueber Don Juan de Austria*
HNet - August 2004 - pNA [501+]

del Sarto, Ana - *Pleasure and Change: The Aesthetics of Canon*
Choice - v42 - i6 - Feb 2005 - p1008(1) [51-500]

Del Testa, David W. - *Global History: Cultural Encounters from Antiquity to the Present Vols. 1-4*
BL - v100 - i21 - July 2004 - p1863(1) [501+]
Global History: Cultural Encounters from Antiquity to the Present, Vols. 1-4
R&R Bk N - v19 - i3 - August 2004 - p31(1) [51-500]
Global History: Cultural Encounters from Antiquity to the Present Vols. 1-4
R&USQ - v44 - i2 - Winter 2004 - p171(2) [501+]
c   SLJ - v50 - i8 - August 2004 - p57(1) [501+]

Del Vecchio, Gene - *The Blockbuster Toy: How to Invent the Next Big Thing*
R&R Bk N - v19 - i2 - May 2004 - p108(1) [51-500]
The Pearl of Anton
y   VOYA - v27 - i4 - Oct 2004 - p312(2) [51-500]

Delacorte, David Almond - *Life-Eaters*
c   Teach Lib - v32 - i3 - Feb 2005 - p10(1) [51-500]

Delacourt, Susan - *Juggernaut: Paul Martin's Campaign for Chretien's Crown*
CBRA - Annual 2003 - p305(1) [51-500]

Delacre, Lulu - *Arrorro, Mi Nino: Latino Lullabies and Gentle Games*
c   CH Bwatch - v14 - i12 - Dec 2004 - pNA [51-500]
Arrorro Mi Nino: Latino Lullabies and Gentle Games (Illus. by Delacre, Lulu)
BL - v100 - i21 - July 2004 - p1846(1) [1-50]
c   HB - v80 - i4 - July-August 2004 - p463(2) [51-500]
Arroz Con Leche: Popular Songs and Rhymes from Latin America
SLJ - v50 - i12 - Dec 2004 - p59(1) [501+]

Delacroix, Claire - *The Beauty Bride*
BL - v101 - i7 - Dec 1 2004 - p641(1) [51-500]
PW - v251 - i47 - Nov 22 2004 - p43(2) [51-500]
To Weave a Web of Magic
y   Kliatt - v38 - i5 - Sept 2004 - p28(2) [51-500]

Delaet, Marianne - *Research in Science and Technology Studies: Knowledge and Technology Transfer*
T&C - v45 - i1 - Jan 2004 - p229(2) [501+]

Delafield, E.M. - *Diary of a Provincial Lady*
Ent W - i774 - July 16 2004 - p83 [501+]

Delahunty, Andrew - *Oxford Dictionary of Nicknames*
Choice - v42 - i1 - Sept 2004 - p59(1) [501+]
BL - v101 - i2 - Sept 15 2004 - p276(1) [51-500]

Delamater, John - *Handbook of Social Psychology*
CS - v33 - i6 - Nov 2004 - p679(2) [501+]

Delamont, Sara - *Feminist Sociology*
R&R Bk N - v19 - i3 - August 2004 - p153(1) [51-500]

Delaney, Frank - *Ireland: A Novel*
Ent W - i808 - Feb 25 2005 - p105 [51-500]
KR - v72 - i22 - Nov 15 2004 - p1060(2) [501+]
LJ - v129 - i20 - Dec 1 2004 - p98(2) [51-500]
PW - v251 - i50 - Dec 13 2004 - p43(1) [51-500]
TLS - i5298 - Oct 15 2004 - p23(1) [501+]

Delaney, John D. - *Dictionary of Saints*
CI - v33 - i8 - Sept 2004 - p42(1) [501+]

Delaney, M.C. - *The Great Sockathon*
c   BL - v100 - i22 - August 2004 - p1933(1) [51-500]
c   KR - v72 - i14 - July 15 2004 - p683(1) [51-500]
c   SLJ - v50 - i8 - August 2004 - p120(1) [51-500]

Delaney, Mark - *Pepperland*
y   BL - v101 - i7 - Dec 1 2004 - p646(1) [51-500]
    Kliatt - v38 - i6 - Nov 2004 - p6(1) [51-500]
y   SLJ - v50 - i11 - Nov 2004 - p141(2) [51-500]
y   VOYA - v27 - i4 - Oct 2004 - p294(1) [51-500]

Delang, Claudio O. - *Living at the Edge of Thai Society: The Karen in the Highlands of Northern Thailand*
A Aff - v35 - i2 - July 2004 - p244-245 [501+]

Delange, Francois M. - *Micronutrient Deficiencies in the First Months of Life: Proceedings*
SciTech - v28 - i1 - March 2004 - p118(1) [51-500]

Delano, Sterling F. - *Brook Farm: The Dark Side of Utopia*
NEQ - v77 - i3 - Sept 2004 - p513-515 [501+]
Pub Int - i157 - Fall 2004 - p126(5) [501+]

Delanty, Gerard - *Community*
Choice - v41 - i7 - March 2004 - p1376(1) [501+]

Delany, Paul - *Bill Brandt: A Life*
Afterimage - v32 - i2 - Sept-Oct 2004 - p12(1) [501+]
Choice - v42 - i1 - Sept 2004 - p92(1) [501+]
Lon R Bks - v26 - i13 - July 8 2004 - p25(3) [501+]

Delany, Sheila - *Chaucer and the Jews: Sources, Contexts, Meanings*
Med R - Dec 2004 - pNA [501+]

Delany, Vicki - *Scare the Light Away*
KR - v73 - i3 - Feb 1 2005 - p150(1) [51-500]
PW - v252 - i8 - Feb 21 2005 - p161(1) [51-500]

Delaporte, Guillemette - *Rene Herbst: Pioneer of Modernism*
Choice - v42 - i6 - Feb 2005 - p1010(1) [51-500]
LJ - v130 - i1 - Jan 1 2005 - p108(1) [51-500]

Delattre, Lucas - *A Spy at the Heart of the Third Reich: The Extraordinary Story of Fritz Kolbe, America's Most Important Spy in World War II*
KR - v72 - i23 - Dec 1 2004 - p1129(1) [501+]
LJ - v130 - i4 - March 1 2005 - p97(1) [51-500]
PW - v252 - i2 - Jan 10 2005 - p50(1) [51-500]

Delbanco, Nicholas - *Anywhere out of the World: Travel, Writing, Death*
KR - v73 - i2 - Jan 15 2005 - p98(1) [501+]
The Vagabonds
BL - v101 - i3 - Oct 1 2004 - p307(1) [51-500]
BW - v34 - i50 - Dec 12 2004 - p4(1) [501+]
KR - v72 - i17 - Sept 1 2004 - p822(1) [51-500]
LJ - v129 - i16 - Oct 1 2004 - p66(2) [501+]
PW - v251 - i45 - Nov 8 2004 - p36(2) [501+]

DeLeo, Peter - *Survive!: My Fight for Life in the High Sierras*
LJ - v130 - i1 - Jan 1 2005 - p121(1) [51-500]
PW - v251 - i48 - Nov 29 2004 - p31(1) [51-500]

Delessert, Etienne - *Who Killed Cock Robin?*
c   CH Bwatch - Feb 2005 - pNA [51-500]

Deleuze, Gilles - *Desert Islands and Other Texts, 1953-1974*
Choice - v42 - i1 - Sept 2004 - p114(1) [501+]
Francis Bacon: The Logic of Sensation
Lon R Bks - v26 - i18 - Sept 23 2004 - p19(2) [501+]

DelFattore, Joan - *The Fourth R: Conflicts over Religion in America's Public Schools*
Choice - v42 - i4 - Dec 2004 - p735(1) [1-50]
JR - v85 - i1 - Jan 2005 - p169(2) [501+]

Delfini, Luca Dosi - *The Furniture Collection, Stedelijk Museum Amsterdam, 1850-2000/From Michael Thonet to Marcel Wanders*
Mag Antiq - v167 - i1 - Jan 2005 - p129(1) [51-500]
Mag Antiq - v167 - i2 - Feb 2005 - p55(1) [1-50]
Mag Antiq - v167 - i3 - March 2005 - p59(1) [501+]

Delgado, Jaime - *Proceeding of the Fourth International Conference on Web Delivering of Music Wedelmusic 2004: 13-14 September 2004, Barcelona, Spain*
SciTech - v28 - i4 - Dec 2004 - p11(1) [1-50]
WEB Delivering of Music: WEDELMUSIC 2004
SciTech - v28 - i4 - Dec 2004 - p11(1) [1-50]

Delgado, James P. - *Adventures of a Sea Hunter: In Search of Famous Shipwrecks*
Globe & Mail - Oct 30 2004 - pD24 [501+]
R&R Bk N - v20 - i1 - Feb 2005 - p81(1) [51-500]
Arctic Workhorse: The RCMP Schooner St. Roch
CBRA - Annual 2003 - p439(2) [51-500]

Delgado, Manuela Canton - *Bautizados en Fuego: Protestantes, Discursos de Conversion y Politica en Guatemala*
Ams - v61 - i2 - Oct 2004 - p330(2) [501+]

Delgado, Melvin - *Social Youth Entrepreneurship: The Potential for Youth and Community Transformation*
R&R Bk N - v19 - i3 - August 2004 - p161(1) [501+]

Delgado, Richard - *Justice at War: Civil Liberties and Civil Rights During Times of Crisis*
CS - v33 - i6 - Nov 2004 - p715(2) [501+]
Understanding Words That Wound
Choice - v42 - i2 - Oct 2004 - p343(1) [51-500]

Delhaes, Pierre - *Fibers and Composites*
SciTech - v28 - i1 - March 2004 - p140(1) [51-500]

Delillo, Don - *Cosmopolis*
Dal R - v84 - i1 - Spring 2004 - p177-179 [501+]

Dell, Marion - *Virginia Woolf and Vanessa Bell: Remembering St. Ives*
TLS - i5286 - July 23 2004 - p33(1) [501+]

Dell, Pamela - *The Plymouth Colony*
c SLJ - v50 - i8 - August 2004 - p133(1) [501+]

Dell, Ronald - *Clean Energy*
Choice - v42 - i7 - March 2005 - p1257(1) [51-500]

Della-Giustina, Daniel E. - *Motor Fleet Safety and Security Management*
R&R Bk N - v19 - i4 - Nov 2004 - p106(1) [51-500]

Della Porta, Donatella - *Transnational Protest and Global Activism*
R&R Bk N - v19 - i4 - Nov 2004 - p122(1) [51-500]

Dellasega, Cheryl - *Girl Wars: 12 strategies That Will End Female Bullying*
VOYA - v27 - i5 - Dec 2004 - p425(1) [51-500]
The Starving Family: Caregiving Mothers and Fathers Share Their Eating Disorder Wisdom
LJ - v130 - i2 - Feb 1 2005 - p103(1) [501+]

Delleman, Nico J. - *Working Postures and Movements: Tools for Evaluation and Engineering*
SciTech - v28 - i4 - Dec 2004 - p131 [51-500]

Delli Carpini, John - *History, Religion, and Politics in William Wordsworth's Ecclesiastical Sonnets*
R&R Bk N - v19 - i4 - Nov 2004 - p237(1) [501+]

Dell'Orto, Alessandro - *Place and Spirit in Taiwan: Tudi Gong in the Stories, Strategies, and Memories of Everyday Life*
JAS - v63 - i2 - May 2004 - p492(2) [501+]

Dellutri, Laura - *Speed Cleaning 101*
Globe & Mail - March 19 2005 - pL6 [51-500]

Delmendo, Sharon - *The Star-Entangled Banner: One Hundrerd Years of American in the Philippines*
Choice - v42 - i5 - Jan 2005 - p906(1) [1-50]

Delmer, Deborah P. - *Annual Review of Plant Biology Vol. 55*
QRB - v79 - i4 - Dec 2004 - p429(1) [501+]
Annual Review of Plant Biology. Vol. 55
SciTech - v28 - i3 - Sept 2004 - p63(1) [51-500]

Delogu, Paolo - *An Introduction to Medieval History*
Specu - v79 - i4 - Oct 2004 - p1063(3) [501+]

Deloince-Louette, Christiane - *Sponde: Commentateur d'Homere*
Six Ct J - v35 - i1 - Spring 2004 - p220(3) [501+]

DeLong-Bas, Natana J. - *Wahhabi Islam: From Revival and Reform to Global Jihad*
Choice - v42 - i6 - Feb 2005 - p1036(2) [51-500]
LJ - v129 - i13 - August 2004 - p87(1) [501+]
MEQ - v12 - i1 - Wntr 2005 - p95(1) [501+]
Spec - v296 - i9201 - Dec 11 2004 - p43(2) [501+]

DeLong, David W. - *Lost Knowledge: Confronting the Threat of an Aging Workforce*
HR Mag - v50 - i3 - March 2005 - p127(1) [501+]
LJ - v129 - i17 - Oct 15 2004 - p70(1) [501+]
NYT - Sept 5 2004 - pBU8 [501+]

DeLong, Howard - *A Profile of Mathematical Llogic*
SciTech - v28 - i4 - Dec 2004 - p15(1) [1-50]

DeLong, J. Bradford - *Should We Still Support Untrammeled International Capital Mobility? or Are Capital Controls Less Evil than We Once Believed?*
Wil Q - v29 - i1 - Wntr 2005 - p91(1) [501+]

Deloria, Philip J. - *Indians in Unexpected Places*
BL - v101 - i2 - Sept 15 2004 - p196(1) [501+]
LJ - v129 - i15 - Sept 15 2004 - p68(1) [501+]

Deloria, Vine - *Evolution, Creationism, and Other Modern Myths: A Critical Inquiry*
Am Ind CRJ - v28 - i1 - Winter 2004 - p92-96 [501+]
Kliatt - v38 - i6 - Nov 2004 - p38(1) [501+]
God Is Red: A Native View of Religion, 3rd Ed.
R&R Bk N - v19 - i1 - Feb 2004 - p13(1) [501+]

DeLoughery, Thomas G. - *Hemostasis and Thrombosis. 2nd Ed.*
SciTech - v28 - i3 - Sept 2004 - p106(1) [51-500]

Delphos, William A. - *Inside Washington: Government Resources for International Business*
R&R Bk N - v19 - i3 - August 2004 - p113(1) [51-500]

DelPlato, Joan - *Multiple Wives, Multiple Pleasures: Representing the Harem, 1800-1875*
NCFS - v32 - i3-4 - Spring-Summer 2004 - p362(4) [501+]

DelPo, Amy - *Create Your Own Employee Handbook: A Legal & Practical Guide*
HR Mag - v50 - i2 - Feb 2005 - pS8(1) [501+]

Delsohn, Gary - *The Prosecutors: Kidnap, Rape, Murder, Justice: One Year Behind the Scenes in a Big-City DA's Office*
R&R Bk N - v19 - i4 - Nov 2004 - p174(1) [501+]

Delsol, Chantal - *Icarus Fallen: The Search for Meaning in an Uncertain World*
Choice - v41 - i11-12 - July-August 2004 - p2057(1) [501+]

DeLucia-Waack, Janice L. - *Handbook of Group Counseling and Psychotherapy*
Choice - v42 - i1 - Sept 2004 - p192(1) [501+]
SciTech - v28 - i1 - March 2004 - p99(1) [51-500]

DelVecchio, Vito G. - *Applications of Genomics and Proteomics for Analysis of Bacterial Biological Warfare Agents*
SciTech - v28 - i4 - Dec 2004 - p61(1) [51-500]

Demarais, Ann - *First Impressions: What You Don't Know about How Others See You*
Bus W - i3890 - July 5 2004 - p86 [501+]
y SLJ - v50 - i7 - July 2004 - p133(1) [51-500]

DeMarco-Barrett, Barbara - *Pen on Fire: A Busy Woman's Guide to Igniting the Writer Within*
BL - v101 - i2 - Sept 15 2004 - p194(1) [501+]
LJ - v129 - i14 - Sept 1 2004 - p164(2) [501+]

Demarest, Arthur A. - *The Terminal Classic in the Maya Lowlands: Collapse, Transition, and Transformation*
Choice - v42 - i1 - Sept 2004 - p148(1) [51-500]

Demarest, Chris L. - *I Invited a Dragon to Dinner and Other Poems to Make You Laugh out Loud (Illus. by Demarest, Chris L.)*
c RT - v57 - Oct 2003 - p169 [1-50]
Mayday! Mayday! A Coast Guard Rescue (Illus. by Demarest, Chris L.)
c BL - v101 - i1 - Sept 1 2004 - p126(2) [1-50]
c SLJ - v50 - i7 - July 2004 - p92(1) [51-500]

DeMarinis, Rick - *Apocalypse Then: Stories*
BL - v101 - i3 - Oct 1 2004 - p310(1) [51-500]
KR - v72 - i17 - Sept 1 2004 - p822(1) [501+]
The Year of the Zinc Penny
LJ - v130 - i2 - Feb 1 2005 - p126(1) [1-50]

deMarrais, Kathleen - *Foundations for Research: Methods of Inquiry in Education and the Social Sciences*
R&R Bk N - v19 - i1 - Feb 2004 - pNA [51-500]

Demas, Corinne - *Saying Goodbye to Lulu (Illus. by Hoyt, Ard)*
c BL - v101 - i9-10 - Jan 1 2005 - p775(1) [1-50]
c CH Bwatch - v14 - i7 - July 2004 - p4(1) [51-500]
c PW - v251 - i28 - July 12 2004 - p63(1) [51-500]
c SLJ - v50 - i7 - July 2004 - p69(1) [51-500]

Demastes, William W. - *Staging Consciousness: Theater and the Materialization of Mind*
Theat J - v56 - i1 - March 2004 - p140(2) [501+]

Dematons, Charlotte - *The Yellow Balloon (Illus. by Dematons, Charlotte)*
c HB - v80 - i4 - July-August 2004 - p435(2) [51-500]

DeMatteis, J.M. - *Abadazad*
MFSF - v107 - i3 - Sept 2004 - p32(2) [501+]

DeMauro, Lisa - *Theodore Roosevelt: The Adventurous President*
c SLJ - v51 - i2 - Feb 2005 - p130(1) [501+]
c KR - v73 - i1 - Jan 1 2005 - p51(1) [51-500]

Dembo, Myron H. - *Motivation and Learning Strategies for College Success: A Self-Management Approach, 2nd Ed.*
R&R Bk N - v19 - i3 - August 2004 - p221(1) [1-50]

DeMello, Margo - *Low-Carb Vegetarian*
Bwatch - v26 - i8 - August 2004 - p3(1) [51-500]

Demerson, Velma - *Incorrigible*
Globe & Mail - Feb 5 2005 - pD3 [501+]

Demeter, Tamas - *Essays on Wittgenstein and Austrian Philosophy: In Honour of J.C. Nyiri*
R&R Bk N - v19 - i3 - August 2004 - p6(1) [1-50]

Demi - *The Hungry Coat: A Tale from Turkey*
c SLJ - v50 - i7 - July 2004 - p92(1) [51-500]
The Hungry Coat (Illus. by Demi)
c BL - v100 - i22 - August 2004 - p1938(1) [51-500]
Mother Teresa
c BL - v101 - i9-10 - Jan 1 2005 - p848(1) [1-50]
c HB - v81 - i2 - March-April 2005 - p213(1) [51-500]
c KR - v73 - i1 - Jan 1 2005 - p51(1) [51-500]
c PW - v252 - i7 - Feb 14 2005 - p78(2) [501+]
c SLJ - v51 - i2 - Feb 2005 - p116(1) [51-500]
Muhammad (Illus. by Demi)
c SLJ - v51 - i1 - Jan 2005 - p55(1) [51-500]

Demick, Jack - *Handbook of Adult Development*
Choice - v41 - i7 - March 2004 - p1374(1) [501+]

Demidenko, Eugene Z. - *Mixed Models: Theory and Applications*
SciTech - v28 - i4 - Dec 2004 - p38(1) [51-500]

Demidov, Vadim V. - *DNA Amplification: Current Technologies and Applications*
SciTech - v28 - i3 - Sept 2004 - p72(1) [51-500]

D'Emilio, John - *Lost Prophet: The Life and Times of Bayard Rustin*
Dis - v51 - i1 - Wntr 2004 - p126(6) [501+]
JAH - v91 - i2 - Sept 2004 - p707(2) [501+]

DeMille, Nelson - *The Best American Mystery Stories 2004*
BL - v101 - i2 - Sept 15 2004 - p211(1) [51-500]
PW - v251 - i35 - August 30 2004 - p35(1) [501+]
Night Fall
BL - v101 - i1 - Sept 1 2004 - p4(1) [51-500]
Globe & Mail - Nov 27 2004 - pD16 [51-500]
KR - v72 - i18 - Sept 15 2004 - p882(1) [501+]
LJ - v129 - i16 - Oct 1 2004 - p68(1) [51-500]
PW - v251 - i38 - Sept 20 2004 - p43(1) [501+]
Ent W - i795 - Dec 3 2004 - p97 [501+]

Demissew, Sebsebe - *Flowers of Ethiopia and Eritrea: Aloes and Other Lilies*
Nature - v431 - i7010 - Oct 14 2004 - p742(1) [501+]

Demkin, Joseph A. - *The Architect's Handbook of Professional Practice: Update 2004*
R&R Bk N - v19 - i3 - August 2004 - p241(1) [51-500]
Security Planning and Design: A Guide for Architects and Building Design Professionals
SciTech - v28 - i1 - March 2004 - p150(1) [51-500]

Demmer, Klaus - *Angewandte Theologie des Ethischen*
Theol St - v65 - i4 - Dec 2004 - p873(3) [501+]

Demon Wars: Trial by Fire
LibMed - v22 - i5 - Feb 2004 - p74(1) [501+]

Demonet, Marie-Luce - *"A plaisir": Semiotique et scepticisme chez Montaigne*
Six Ct J - v35 - i1 - Spring 2004 - p272(3) [501+]

deMontravel, Jacqueline - *Escape from Bridezilla*
BL - v101 - i7 - Dec 1 2004 - p641(1) [501+]

Demoor, Marysa - *Marketing the Author: Aithorial Personae, Narrative Selves and Self-Fashioning, 1880-1930*
Choice - v42 - i4 - Dec 2004 - p661(1) [1-50]

Demorest, Amy - *Psychology's Grand Theorists: How Personal Experiences Shaped Professional Ideals*
Choice - v42 - i5 - Jan 2005 - p937(1) [51-500]
SciTech - v28 - i4 - Dec 2004 - p1(1) [1-50]

Demoris, Rene - *Le Roman a la premiere personne: du classicisme aux Lumieres*
FS - v58 - i1 - Jan 2004 - p102(2) [501+]

Demos, John - *Circles and Lines: The Shape of Life in Early America*
HRNB - v33 - i1 - Fall 2004 - p17(1) [501+]

DeMoss, Gary - *Making the Client Connection: Maximizing the Power of Your Personality, Presentations, Presence*
R&R Bk N - v19 - i3 - August 2004 - p134(1) [1-50]

DeMoura, Denise - *Break the Silence*
CBRA - Annual 2003 - p212(1) [51-500]

Dempsey, Dave - *On the Brink: The Great Lakes in the 21st Century*
Choice - v42 - i4 - Dec 2004 - p686(1) [1-50]

Dempsey, Diana - *Too Close to the Sun*
BL - v100 - i22 - August 2004 - p1908(1) [51-500]

Dempsey, Hugh A. - *The Vengeful Wife and Other Blackfoot Stories*
Am Ind CRJ - v28 - i1 - Winter 2004 - p110-114 [501+]
Can Hist R - v85 - i3 - Sept 2004 - p578(2) [501+]

Dempsey, John Mark - *The Light Crust Doughboys Are on the Air: Celebrating Seventy Years of Texas Music*
JSH - v70 - i4 - Nov 2004 - p956(2) [501+]

Dempsey, John S. - *An Introduction to Policing, 3rd Ed.*
R&R Bk N - v19 - i4 - Nov 2004 - p148(1) [501+]

Dempsey, Paul Stephen - *European Aviation Law*
R&R Bk N - v19 - i4 - Nov 2004 - p168(1) [501+]

Dempsey, Terrell - *Searching for Jim: Slavery in Sam Clemens's World*
Choice - v41 - i7 - March 2004 - p1295(1) [501+]
Searching for Jim: Slavery in Sam Clemens's World
R&R Bk N - v19 - i1 - Feb 2004 - p244(1) [51-500]

Demurger, Alain - *The Last Templar: The Tragedy of Jacques de Molay*
TLS - i5289 - August 13 2004 - p22(1) [501+]

Denby, David - *American Sucker*
New York - v37 - i3 - Feb 2 2004 - p47(2) [501+]

Denckla, Tanya - *The Gardener's A-Z Guide to Growing Organic Food*
    Bwatch - v26 - i8 - August 2004 - p10(1) [51-500]
    SciTech - v28 - i1 - March 2004 - p129(1) [51-500]

Dendup, Tshewang - *Travellers & Magicians*
    Ent W - Feb 4 2005 - p114 [51-500]

Denenberg, Barry - *Atticus of Rome: 30 B.C.*
    c BL - v101 - i5 - Nov 1 2004 - p482(1) [51-500]
    y SLJ - v50 - i11 - Nov 2004 - p142(1) [501+]
    Atticus of Rome
    y CH Bwatch - Feb 2005 - pNA [51-500]
    Pandora of Athens: 399 B.C.
    c BL - v101 - i5 - Nov 1 2004 - p482(1) [51-500]
    y SLJ - v50 - i11 - Nov 2004 - p142(1) [501+]
    Pandora of Athens
    y CH Bwatch - Feb 2005 - pNA [51-500]
    Shadow Life: A Portrait of Anne Frank and Her Family
    y HB - v81 - i2 - March-April 2005 - p214(1) [501+]
    y Kliatt - v39 - i2 - March 2005 - p10(1) [51-500]
    y KR - v73 - i2 - Jan 15 2005 - p119(1) [51-500]

Denenberg, Thomas Andrew - *Wallace Nutting and the Invention of Old America*
    Ant&CM - v108 - i12 - Feb 2004 - p16(1) [501+]
    JAH - v91 - i1 - June 2004 - p282-282 [501+]

Denes, Magda - *Castles Burning: A Child's Life in War*
    y Can CL - i111-112 - Fall-Winter 2003 - p146(6) [501+]

DeNevi, Don - *Into the Minds of Madmen: How the FBI's Behavioral Science Unit Revolutionized Crime Investigation*
    R&R Bk N - v19 - i1 - Feb 2004 - p141(1) [51-500]
    TLS - i5290 - August 20 2004 - p27(1) [501+]

Denezhkina, Irina - *Give Me*
    BL - v101 - i9-10 - Jan 1 2005 - p813(1) [1-50]
    KR - v72 - i23 - Dec 1 2004 - p1103(1) [501+]
    LJ - v130 - i1 - Jan 1 2005 - p94(1) [51-500]
    PW - v252 - i2 - Jan 10 2005 - p38(1) [51-500]

Deng, Benson - *They Poured Fire on Us from the Sky: The True Story of Three Lost Boys from Sudan*
    KR - v73 - i5 - March 1 2005 - p272(1) [501+]

Denham, Joe - *Flux*
    BIC - v33 - i5 - August 2004 - p34(3) [501+]
    CBRA - Annual 2003 - p212(2) [51-500]

Denham, Robert D. - *The Diaries of Northrop Frye*
    South HR - v38 - i1 - Wntr 2004 - p95-99 [501+]

Denham, Susanne A. - *Social and Emotional Prevention and Intervention Programming for Preschoolers*
    R&R Bk N - v19 - i2 - May 2004 - p134 [51-500]

Denizot, Veronique - *"Comme un souci aux rayons du soleil": Ronsard et l'invention d'une poetique de la merveille 1550-1556*
    Ren Q - v57 - i3 - Fall 2004 - p1017(2) [501+]

Denker, Alfred - *Hegel's Phenomenology of Spirit: New Critical Essays*
    R&R Bk N - v19 - i4 - Nov 2004 - p6(1) [51-500]

Denker, Ellen Paul - *Byrdcliffe: An American Arts and Crafts Colony*
    Choice - v42 - i6 - Feb 2005 - p1009(1) [51-500]

Denman, Terence - *Ireland's Unknown Soldiers: The 16th (Irish) Division in the Great War*
    HER - v119 - i483 - Sept 2004 - p1089(3) [501+]

Denmark, Florence - *Engendering Psychology: Women and Gender Revisted, 2nd Ed.*
    R&R Bk N - v19 - i4 - Nov 2004 - p133(1) [1-50]

Dennard, Deborah - *Reptiles (Illus. by Dewey, Jennifer Owings)*
    c SLJ - v50 - i8 - August 2004 - p134(1) [51-500]

Denning, Lee - *Monkey Trap*
    LJ - v129 - i19 - Nov 15 2004 - p54(1) [501+]

Denning, Michael - *Culture in the Age of Three Worlds*
    JouAmCul - v27 - i4 - Dec 2004 - p440(2) [501+]
    R&R Bk N - v19 - i3 - August 2004 - p142(1) [51-500]

Denning, Patt - *Over the Influence: The Harm Reduction Guide for Managing Drugs and Alcohol*
    SciTech - v28 - i3 - Sept 2004 - p103(1) [51-500]

Denning, Stephen - *Squirrel Inc.: A Fable of Leadership through Storytelling*
    Econ - v371 - i8380 - June 19 2004 - p81US [501+]

Dennis, Charles - *E-Retailing, 1st Ed.*
    TimHES - v0 - i1680 - Feb 25 2005 - pVII(1) [501+]

Dennis, Felix - *In a Glass Half Full*
    Ent W - i784 - Sept 17 2004 - p87 [51-500]

Dennis, Jeanne Gowen - *Homeschooling High School: Planning Ahead for College Admission, 2nd Ed.*
    R&R Bk N - v19 - i3 - August 2004 - p226(1) [1-50]

Dennis, Michael - *Luther P. Jackson and a Life for Civil Rights*
    Bl S - v34 - i3 - Fall 2004 - p70-70 [501+]

Dennis, Mike - *United and Divided: Germany Since 1990*
    R&R Bk N - v19 - i3 - August 2004 - p43(1) [51-500]

Dennis, Yvonne Wakim - *Sequoyah, 1770?-1843*
    c SLJ - v50 - i7 - July 2004 - p92(1) [51-500]

Dennish, Michael - *This Day Full of Promise: Poems Selected and New*
    CBRA - Annual 2003 - p213(1) [51-500]

Dennison, Amy - *Our Dad Died: The True Story of Three Kids Whose Lives Changed*
    SLJ - v50 - i10 - Oct 2004 - pS47(1) [51-500]

Dennison, E. Patricia - *Aberdeen Before 1800: A New History*
    Six Ct J - v35 - i3 - Fall 2004 - p934-936 [501+]

Dennison, Louise - *Away Laughing on a Fast Camel (Read by Dennison, Louise). Audiobook Review*
    y SLJ - v51 - i1 - Jan 2005 - p78(1) [51-500]

Dennison, Robert - *Helen Breaks Bones and Other Stories*
    CBRA - Annual 2003 - p197(2) [51-500]

Denny, Hebson - *Robots Everywhere (Illus. by Hoffman, Todd)*
    c LibMed - v23 - i1 - August-Sept 2004 - p65(1) [51-500]

Denny, Joanna - *Anne Boleyn: A New Life of England's Tragic Queen*
    TLS - i5294 - Sept 17 2004 - p12(1) [501+]

Denny, Walter B. - *Iznik: The Artistry of Ottoman Ceramics*
    Ceram Mo - v53 - i2 - Feb 2005 - p64(1) [501+]

Denoon, Anne - *Back Flip*
    Can Lit - i182 - Autumn 2004 - p114(3) [501+]
    CBRA - Annual 2003 - p161(1) [51-500]

Denslow, Sharon Phillips - *All Their Names Were Courage: A Novel of the Civil War*
    LibMed - v22 - i6 - March 2004 - p63(1) [501+]

Dent, Alxander W. - *User's Guide to Cryptography and Standards*
    Choice - v42 - i7 - March 2005 - p1261(2) [51-500]

Dent, David W. - *Encyclopedia of Modern Mexico*
    BL - v101 - i9-10 - Jan 1 2005 - p903(2) [501+]

Dent, Grace - *LBD: Live and Fabulous*
    y HB - v81 - i2 - March-April 2005 - p199(2) [51-500]
    y Kliatt - v39 - i2 - March 2005 - p10(1) [51-500]
    y KR - v73 - i3 - Feb 1 2005 - p176(1) [51-500]

Dent, Martin J. - *Identity Politics: Filling the Gap between Federalism and Independence*
    R&R Bk N - v19 - i4 - Nov 2004 - p124(1) [51-500]

Dent, Mike - *Questioning the New Public Management*
    R&R Bk N - v19 - i4 - Nov 2004 - p156(1) [501+]

Dent, Stephen M. - *Partnering Intelligence: Creating Value for Your Business by Building Strong Alliances*
    R&R Bk N - v19 - i3 - August 2004 - p109(1) [51-500]

Dent, Susie - *The Language Report*
    Globe & Mail - July 31 2004 - pD13 [51-500]

Denton, Diana - *Spirituality, Action, & Pedagogy: Teaching from the Heart*
    R&R Bk N - v19 - i4 - Nov 2004 - p178(1) [501+]

Denton, Robert E., Jr. - *Languages, Symbols and the Media: Communication in the Aftermath of the World Trade Center Attack*
    Choice - v42 - i6 - Feb 2005 - p1017(1) [51-500]
    R&R Bk N - v19 - i4 - Nov 2004 - p212(1) [501+]

Denton, Sally - *American Massacre: The Tragedy at Mountain Meadows, September 1857*
    JAH - v91 - i2 - Sept 2004 - p632(2) [501+]
    Faith and Betrayal: A Pioneer Woman's Passage in the American West
    KR - v73 - i4 - Feb 15 2005 - p208(1) [501+]

Denton, Terry - *The Obelisk of Eeno*
    y Sch Lib - v52 - i4 - Winter 2004 - p214(1) [51-500]

Denver, John - *Ancient Rhymes: A Dolphin's Lullaby*
    CH Bwatch - v14 - i11 - Nov 2004 - pNA [51-500]

Denver Museum of Nature and Science
    c LibMed - v23 - i3 - Nov-Dec 2004 - p86(2) [51-500]

Denyer, N. - *Alcibiades*
    Class R - v53 - i2 - Nov 2003 - p296-298 [501+]

Denyer, Stephen - *Hugo and Russell's Pharmaceutical Microbiology, 7th Ed.*
    SciTech - v28 - i4 - Dec 2004 - p74(1) [51-500]

Denzin, Norman K. - *Studies in Symbolic Interaction. Vol. 25*
    CS - v33 - i1 - Jan 2004 - p119-120 [501+]

DePaola, Tomie - *Four Friends in Autumn (Illus. by DePaola, Tomie)*
    c SLJ - v50 - i11 - Nov 2004 - p96(1) [51-500]
    Guess Who's Coming to Santa's for Dinner?
    c BL - v101 - i2 - Sept 15 2004 - p247(1) [51-500]
    Guess Who's Coming to Santa's for Dinner? (Illus. by DePaola, Tomie)
    c BW - v34 - i50 - Dec 12 2004 - p9(1) [501+]
    HB - v80 - i6 - Nov-Dec 2004 - p658(1) [51-500]
    c PW - v251 - i39 - Sept 27 2004 - p62(1) [51-500]
    Pascual and the Kitchen Angels (Illus. by DePaola, Tomie)
    c SLJ - v50 - i10 - Oct 2004 - pS23(1) [1-50]

DeParle, Jason - *American Dream: Three Women, Ten Kids, and a Nation's Drive to End Welfare*
    BL - v101 - i2 - Sept 15 2004 - p182(1) [51-500]
    Bus W - i3910 - Nov 29 2004 - p24 [501+]
    BW - v34 - i47 - Nov 21 2004 - p10(1) [501+]
    Dis - v51 - i4 - Fall 2004 - p89(4) [501+]
    Nation - v279 - i21 - Dec 20 2004 - p36 [501+]
    New R - Oct 11 2004 - p41 [501+]
    NW - Jan 10 2005 - p54 [501+]
    NY - v80 - i26 - Sept 13 2004 - p89(1) [1-50]
    NYTBR - Sept 26 2004 - p16 [501+]
    PW - v251 - i30 - July 26 2004 - p47(1) [501+]

DePastino, Todd - *Citizen Hobo: How a Century of Homelessness Shaped America.*
    BHR - v78 - i2 - Summer 2004 - p308(4) [501+]
    JAH - v91 - i3 - Dec 2004 - p1070(2) [501+]
    JEL - v42 - i1 - March 2004 - p300(1) [501+]
    JPC - v38 - i2 - Nov 2004 - p434(3) [501+]

DePaul, Michael - *Intellectual Virtue: Perspectives from Ethics and Epistemology*
    Ethics - v115 - i2 - Jan 2005 - p437(2) [501+]

Depue, Roger L. - *Between Good and Evil: A Master Profiler's Hunt for Society's Most Violent Predators*
    KR - v72 - i24 - Dec 15 2004 - p1177(1) [501+]

der Kiureghian, Armen - *Applications of Statistics and Probability in Civil Engineering: Proceedings*
    SciTech - v28 - i1 - March 2004 - p137(1) [51-500]

Deraison, Renaud - *Nessus Network Auditing*
    SciTech - v28 - i4 - Dec 2004 - p32(1) [51-500]

D'Eramo, Marco - *The Pig and the Skyscraper: Chicago, a History of Our Future*
    Am St - v45 - i1 - Spring 2004 - p151-152 [501+]

Deramus, Betit - *Forbidden Fruit: Love Stories from the Underground Railroad and Beyond*
    PW - v252 - i4 - Jan 24 2005 - p235(1) [501+]

D'Erasmo, Stacey - *A Seahorse Year*
    BW - v34 - i38 - Sept 19 2004 - p10(1) [501+]
    Lam Bk Rpt - v13 - i1-2 - August-Sept 2004 - p26(2) [501+]
    NYTBR - August 15 2004 - p18 [501+]
    NYTBR - August 22 2004 - p18 [501+]
    Wom R Bks - v21 - i10-11 - July 2004 - p23(2) [501+]

Derber, Charles - *Regime Change Begins at Home: Freeing America from Corporate Rule*
    R&R Bk N - v19 - i3 - August 2004 - p177(1) [501+]

Derby, Ken - *The Top 10 Ways to Ruin the First Day of 5th Grade.*
    c KR - v72 - i24 - Dec 15 2004 - p1200(1) [501+]
    c SLJ - v51 - i1 - Jan 2005 - p90(1) [51-500]

Derby, Pat - *Away to the Goldfields!*
    c BL - v101 - i5 - Nov 1 2004 - p482(1) [51-500]
    c KR - v72 - i19 - Oct 1 2004 - p959(1) [51-500]
    y SLJ - v50 - i11 - Nov 2004 - p142(1) [51-500]

Derbyshire, John - *Prime Obsession: Bernhard Riemann and the Greatest Unsolved Problem in Mathematics*
    Math T - v97 - i4 - April 2004 - p301-302 [501+]
    SciTech - v28 - i3 - Sept 2004 - p36(1) [51-500]

Derek, Attridge - *The Singularity of Literature*
    Choice - v42 - i6 - Feb 2005 - p1018(1) [51-500]

Dereske, Jo - *Miss Zukas and the Library Murders*
    LJ - v129 - i14 - Sept 1 2004 - p207(1) [501+]

Derfler, Frank, Jr. - *How Networks Work*
    LJ - v130 - i2 - Feb 1 2005 - p110(1) [501+]

Derks, Scott - *Working Americans, 1880-2003, Vol. 5*
    R&R Bk N - v19 - i2 - May 2004 - p106(1) [51-500]

Derlega, Valerian A. - *Personality: Contemporary Theory and Research, 3rd Ed.*
    R&R Bk N - v19 - i3 - August 2004 - p10(1) [1-50]

Derman, Emanuel - *My Life as a Quant: Reflections on Physics and Finance*
    Bus W - i3908 - Nov 15 2004 - p26 [501+]
    R&R Bk N - v19 - i4 - Nov 2004 - p118(1) [51-500]

Detering, Heinrich - *Das offene Geheimnis: Zur literarischen Produktivität eines Tabus von Winckelmann bis zu Thomas Mann*
Ger Q - v77 - i4 - Fall 2004 - p512-514 [501+]

Detmer, David - *Challenging Postmodernism: Philosophy and the Politics of Truth*
R&R Bk N - v19 - i1 - Feb 2004 - p2(1) [1-50]

Dettenhoffer, M.H. - *Herrschaft und Widerstand im augusteischen Principat. Die Konkurrenz zwischen res publica und und domus Augusta*
Class R - v53 - i2 - Nov 2003 - p417-419 [501+]

Dettori, Frankie - *Frankie*
Spec - i9192 - Oct 9 2004 - p74(1) [501+]

Detweiler, Craig - *A Matrix of Meanings: Finding God in Pop Culture*
Choice - v42 - i1 - Sept 2004 - p118(1) [501+]

Detzer, David - *Donnybrook: The Battle of Bull Run, 1861*
BL - v100 - i22 - August 2004 - p1893(1) [51-500]
KR - v72 - i13 - July 1 2004 - p615(1) [501+]

Detzner, Daniel F. - *Elder Voices: Southeast Asian Families in the United States*
R&R Bk N - v19 - i4 - Nov 2004 - p58(1) [51-500]

Deutsch, Eliot - *The Essential Vedanta: A New Source Book of Advaita Vedanta*
LJ - v129 - i20 - Dec 1 2004 - p124(1) [51-500]

Deutsch, Helen - *Defects: Engendering the Modern Body*
Eight-C St - v36 - i2 - Winter 2003 - p259 [501+]

Deutsch, Nathaniel - *The Maiden of Ludmir: A Jewish Holy Woman and Her World*
Choice - v42 - i2 - Oct 2004 - p309(1) [51-500]

Deutsch, Sid - *Are You Conscious, and Can You Prove It? Short Science Essays*
y SB - v40 - i4 - July-August 2004 - p162(1) [51-500]

Deutsch, Stacia - *Lincoln's Legacy (Illus. by Wnezel, David)*
y PW - v252 - i3 - Jan 17 2005 - p56(1) [51-500]

Deutscher, Guy - *The Unfolding of Language: An Evolutionary Tour of Mankind's Greatest Invention*
KR - v73 - i4 - Feb 15 2005 - p208(2) [501+]

Deutscher, Irwin - *Accomodating Diversity: National Policies That Prevent Ethnic Conflict*
CS - v33 - i2 - March 2004 - p206-208 [501+]

Deutscher, Isaac - *The Prophet Armed: Trotsky 1879-1921*
Atl - v294 - i1 - July-August 2004 - p152(7) [501+]
Lon R Bks - v26 - i23 - Dec 2 2004 - p3(3) [501+]
The Prophet Outcast: Trotsky 1929-1940
Atl - v294 - i1 - July-August 2004 - p152(7) [501+]
R&R Bk N - v19 - i4 - Nov 2004 - p41(1) [51-500]
The Prophet Unarmed: Trotsky 1921-1929
Atl - v294 - i1 - July-August 2004 - p152(7) [501+]
Lon R Bks - v26 - i23 - Dec 2 2004 - p3(3) [501+]

Deux essais: Michel Leiris Andre du Bouchet
WLT - v78 - i3-4 - Sept-Dec 2004 - p121(1) [501+]

Devane, Tom - *Integrating Lean Six Sigma and High-Performance Organizations: Leading the Charge Toward Dramatic, Rapid and Sustainable Improvement*
R&R Bk N - v19 - i3 - August 2004 - p105(1) [1-50]

Deveau, Sarah - *Sink or Swim: Get Your Degree Without Drowning in Debt*
CBRA - Annual 2003 - p29(1) [51-500]

Deveaud, B. - *Electron and Photon Confinement in Semiconductor Nanostructures: Proceedings*
SciTech - v28 - i3 - Sept 2004 - p48(1) [1-50]

de'Velliers, Mark - *A Dune Adrift: The Strange Origins and Curious History of Sable Island*
CG - v124 - i5 - Sept-Oct 2004 - p111(1) [501+]

Developing Rates for Small Systems 1st Ed.
SciTech - v28 - i3 - Sept 2004 - p146(1) [51-500]

Developments and Discoveries, Vol. 3
y SB - v40 - i6 - Nov-Dec 2004 - p259(1) [51-500]

DeVenney, David P. - *Forging America: New Lands and High Culture*
R&R Bk N - v19 - i1 - Feb 2004 - p208(1) [51-500]

Deveny, Thomas G. - *Contemporary Spanish Film from Fiction*
R&R Bk N - v19 - i1 - Feb 2004 - p224(1) [51-500]

Dever, Carolyn - *Skeptical Feminism: Activist Theory, Activist Practice*
Wom R Bks - v22 - i3 - Dec 2004 - p21(2) [501+]

Deveraux, Jude - *Always*
PW - v251 - i41 - Oct 11 2004 - p62(1) [51-500]

Deverell, William - *Mind Games*
Globe & Mail - Oct 30 2004 - pD29 [501+]

Devi, Gayatri - *What Your Doctor May Not Tell You about Alzheimer's Disease*
SEP - v277 - i1 - Jan-Feb 2005 - p36(2) [501+]

The Devil Kissed Her: The Story of Maty Lamb
Ent W - i785 - Sept 24 2004 - p114 [51-500]

Deville, Michel - *Almost Peaceful*
New York - v37 - i29 - August 23 2004 - p138(1) [501+]

DeVillers, Julia - *How My Private, Personal Journal Became a Bestseller*
c BL - v100 - i22 - August 2004 - p1918(2) [51-500]

Devine, Carrick - *Encyclopedia of Meat Sciences*
Choice - v42 - i7 - March 2005 - p1200(1) [51-500]

Devine, Donald J. - *In Defense of the West: American Values Under Seige*
R&R Bk N - v19 - i4 - Nov 2004 - p126(1) [1-50]

Devine, Fiona - *Social Inequalities in Comparative Perspective*
Choice - v42 - i2 - Oct 2004 - p378(1) [501+]

Devine, Heather - *People Who Own Themselves: Aboriginal Ethnogenesis in a Canadian Family, 1660-1900*
R&R Bk N - v19 - i4 - Nov 2004 - p55(1) [1-50]

Devine, Robert S. - *Bush versus the Environment*
y Kliatt - v39 - i1 - Jan 2005 - p32(1) [501+]

Devins, Neal - *The Democratic Constitution*
Law&PolBR - Dec 2004 - p969(7) [501+]

DeVita Raeburn, Elizabeth - *The Empty Room: Surviving the Loss of a Brother or Sister at Any Age*
Globe & Mail - Sept 11 2004 - pD22 [1-50]

Devitt, Amy J. - *Writing Genres*
Choice - v42 - i2 - Oct 2004 - p288(1) [51-500]

Devlin, Albert J. - *The Selected Letters of Tennessee Williams*
NYTBR - Dec 26 2004 - p8 [501+]

Devlin, F. Roger - *Alexandre Kojeve and the Outcome of Modern Thought*
R&R Bk N - v20 - i1 - Feb 2005 - p5(1) [51-500]

Devlin, Frank - *Love in All the Wrong Places*
BL - v101 - i1 - Sept 1 2004 - p68(1) [51-500]
KR - v72 - i14 - July 15 2004 - p661(1) [51-500]
PW - v251 - i34 - August 23 2004 - p38(1) [51-500]

Devlin, Keith J. - *The Millennium Problems: The Seven Greatest Unsolved Mathematical Puzzles of Our Time*
Lon R Bks - v26 - i14 - July 22 2004 - p22(3) [501+]
TimHES - v0 - i1658 - Sept 17 2004 - p28(2) [501+]
Sets, Functions, and Logic: An Introduction to Abstract Mathematics 3d Ed.
SciTech - v28 - i3 - Sept 2004 - p17(1) [501+]

DeVoe, Forrest - *Into the Volcano*
BL - v101 - i2 - Sept 15 2004 - p211(2) [51-500]

Devonshire, Andrew - *Accidents of Fortune*
Spec - v295 - i9178 - July 3 2004 - p38(1) [501+]

DeVos, Janie - *The Path Winds Home*
c CH Bwatch - v14 - i8 - August 2004 - p6(1) [51-500]

DeVoto, Mark - *Debussy and the Veil of Tonality: Essays on His Music*
R&R Bk N - v19 - i4 - Nov 2004 - p198(1) [501+]

DeVotta, Neil - *Blowback: Linguistic Nationalism, Institutional Decay, and Ethnic Conflict in Sri Lanka*
R&R Bk N - v19 - i4 - Nov 2004 - p47(1) [51-500]

DeVries, Duane - *General Studies of Charles Dickens and His Writings and Collected Editions of His Works: An Annotated Bibliography*
Choice - v42 - i2 - Oct 2004 - p266(1) [51-500]

DeVries, Kelly - *Joan of Arc, a Military Leader*
J Mil H - v68 - i3 - July 2004 - p952(1) [501+]

Dew, John Robert - *Continuous Quality Improvement in Higher Education*
R&R Bk N - v19 - i4 - Nov 2004 - p184(1) [501+]

Dew, Philip - *Doing Business with Jordan*
R&R Bk N - v19 - i4 - Nov 2004 - p90(1) [51-500]
Doing Business with the Republic of Cyprus
R&R Bk N - v19 - i2 - May 2004 - p112(1) [1-50]

Dewald, Jonathan - *Europe 1450 to 1789: Encyclopedia of the Early Modern World*
Choice - v41 - i11-12 - July-August 2004 - p2026(1) [501+]
y Ref Rev - May 2004 - pNA [501+]
Europe 1450 to 1789: Encyclopedia of the Early Modern World Vols. 1-4
BL - v101 - i9-10 - Jan 1 2005 - p780(1) [1-50]
Europe 1450 to 1789: Encyclopedia of the Early Modern World Vols. 1-6
R&R Bk N - v19 - i1 - Feb 2004 - p28(1) [51-500]
R&USQ - v44 - i1 - Fall 2004 - p88(2) [501+]

Dewan, Mantosh J. - *The Art and Science of Brief Psychotherapies: A Practitioner's Guide*
SciTech - v28 - i3 - Sept 2004 - p97(1) [51-500]

Dewan, Ted - *Bing: Get Dressed (Illus. by Dewan, Ted)*
c SLJ - v50 - i7 - July 2004 - p69(1) [51-500]
Bing: Go Picnic (Illus. by Dewan, Ted)
c SLJ - v51 - i2 - Feb 2005 - p96(1) [51-500]
Bing Make Music
c SLJ - v51 - i2 - Feb 2005 - p96(1) [51-500]
Bing: Paint Day (Illus. by Dewan, Ted)
c SLJ - v50 - i7 - July 2004 - p69(1) [51-500]

Dewar, David - *Rethinking Urban Transport after Modernism: Lessons from South Africa*
R&R Bk N - v19 - i4 - Nov 2004 - p106(1) [51-500]

Dewar, Elaine - *The Second Tree: Of Clones, Chimeras and Quests for Immortality*
Globe & Mail - Oct 16 2004 - pD20 [501+]
The Second Tree: Stem Cells, Clones, Chimeras, and Quests for Immortality
KR - v72 - i22 - Nov 15 2004 - p1076(1) [501+]
LJ - v130 - i1 - Jan 1 2005 - p142(1) [51-500]
PW - v251 - i47 - Nov 22 2004 - p51(1) [51-500]

Dewar, James A. - *To the End of the Solar System: The Story of the Nuclear Rocket*
APH - v51 - i3 - Fall 2004 - p48(2) [501+]

Dewar, Kenneth C. - *Charles Clarke, Pen and Ink Warrior*
CBRA - Annual 2003 - p43(1) [51-500]
HNet - June 2004 - pNA [501+]

Dewdney, A.K. - *Beyond Reason: Eight Great Problems That Reveal the Limits of Science*
Globe & Mail - July 3 2004 - pD10 [501+]
SciTech - v28 - i3 - Sept 2004 - p14(1) [501+]

Dewdney, Christopher - *Acquainted with the Night: An Intimate Journey through the World After Dark*
Econ - v372 - i8388 - August 14 2004 - p76US [501+]
Acquainted with the Night: Excursions through the World after Dark
Globe & Mail - Nov 27 2004 - pD3 [51-500]
R&R Bk N - v19 - i4 - Nov 2004 - p239(1) [501+]
TLS - i5294 - Sept 17 2004 - p31(1) [501+]

Deweese, Garrett J. - *God and the Nature of Time*
R&R Bk N - v19 - i4 - Nov 2004 - p24(1) [51-500]

Dewey, Donald - *The 10th Man: The Fan in Baseball History*
Choice - v42 - i5 - Jan 2005 - p891(2) [1-50]

Dewey, John - *Democracy and Education*
R&R Bk N - v19 - i3 - August 2004 - p215(1) [1-50]

Dewey, Larry - *War and Redemption: Treatment and Recovery in Combat-Related Posttraumatic Stress Disorder*
SciTech - v28 - i3 - Sept 2004 - p102(1) [51-500]

Dewhurst, Rick - *Bye Bye Bertie: A Joe LaFlam Mystery*
Globe & Mail - Feb 5 2005 - pD15 [51-500]
LJ - v130 - i2 - Feb 1 2005 - p62(1) [51-500]
PW - v251 - i50 - Dec 13 2004 - p49(1) [51-500]

Dewinetz, Jason - *Moving to the Clear*
Can Lit - i182 - Autumn 2004 - p116(3) [501+]
CBRA - Annual 2003 - p214(1) [51-500]

DeWitt, Bryce - *The Global Approach to Quantum Field Theory*
Phys Today - v57 - i3 - March 2004 - p77-78 [501+]

DeWitt, Richard - *Worldviews: An Introduction to the History and Philosophy of Science*
Choice - v42 - i2 - Oct 2004 - p306(1) [51-500]

DeWitt, Thomas J. - *Phenotypic Plasticity: Functional and Conceptual Approaches*
QRB - v79 - i4 - Dec 2004 - p421(2) [501+]

DeWoskin, Rachel - *Foreign Babes in Beijing: Behind the Scenes of a New China*
KR - v73 - i4 - Feb 15 2005 - p209(1) [501+]

Dewson, David - *Lucifer's Shadow*
DroRevMy - v24 - i4 - July-August 2004 - p12(1) [51-500]

Dey, Claudia - *The Gwendolyn Poems*
Can Lit - i181 - Summer 2004 - p118-119 [501+]

Deysine, Maximo - *Hernia Infections: Pathophysiology, Diagnosis, Treatment, Prevention*
SciTech - v28 - i1 - March 2004 - p112(1) [51-500]

Dhaen, Theo - *Configuring Romanticism: Essays Offered to C.C. Barfoot*
R&R Bk N - v19 - i1 - Feb 2004 - p222(1) [51-500]

Dhagamwar, Vasudha - *Industrial Development and Displacement: The People of Korba*
R&R Bk N - v19 - i2 - May 2004 - p132 [51-500]

Dhalla, Naranjan S. - *Pathophysiology of Cardiovascular Diseases: Proceedings*
SciTech - v28 - i1 - March 2004 - p104(1) [51-500]

Dhami, Narinder - *Bindi Babes (Read by Wadia, Nina). Audiobook Review*
y   BL - v101 - i8 - Dec 15 2004 - p752(1) [1-50]
c   HB - v80 - i6 - Nov-Dec 2004 - p734(1) [501+]
c   PW - v251 - i41 - Oct 11 2004 - p27(1) [51-500]
c   SLJ - v50 - i12 - Dec 2004 - p73(1) [501+]
Bindi Babes
c   BL - v101 - i2 - Sept 15 2004 - p244(1) [51-500]
y   KR - v72 - i16 - August 15 2004 - p804(1) [51-500]
c   PW - v251 - i34 - August 23 2004 - p55(1) [501+]
c   SLJ - v50 - i8 - August 2004 - p120(1) [51-500]
Bollywood Babes
y   KR - v73 - i4 - Feb 15 2005 - p227(1) [51-500]
y   Sch Lib - v52 - i3 - Autumn 2004 - p156(1) [51+]

D'Hancarville, Pierre Francois Hugues - *The Complete Collection of Antiquities from the Cabinet of Sir William Hamilton*
Mag Antiq - v167 - i2 - Feb 2005 - p42(1) [501+]

Dhaquadi, Mahmoud - *Globalization of the Other Underdevelopment: Third World Cultural Identities*
JTWS - v21 - i1 - Spring 2004 - p330(2) [501+]

Dherbier, Yann-Brice - *John Fitzgerald Kennedy: A Life in Pictures*
Globe & Mail - Dec 18 2004 - pD14 [1-50]

Dhillon, B.S. - *Human Reliability and Error in Medical System*
SciTech - v28 - i1 - March 2004 - p80(1) [51-500]

Di Bacco, M. - *Applied Bayesian Statistical Studies in Biology and Medicine*
SciTech - v28 - i1 - March 2004 - p80(1) [51-500]

Di Cicco, Pier Giorgio - *Honeymoon Wilderness*
CBRA - Annual 2003 - p214(1) [51-500]

Di Filippo, Paul - *Harp, Pipe, and Symphony*
PW - v252 - i2 - Jan 10 2005 - p44(1) [51-500]

Di Giovanni, Jannine - *Madness Visible: A Memoir of War*
R&R Bk N - v19 - i1 - Feb 2004 - p40(1) [1-50]

Di Gropello, Emanuela - *Monitoring Educational Performance in the Caribbean*
JEL - v42 - i1 - March 2004 - p307(2) [501+]

Di Leo, Jeffrey R. - *Affiliations: Identity in Academic Culture*
Sew R - v112 - i3 - Summer 2004 - p427-438 [501+]
If Classrooms Matter: Progressive Visions of Educational Environments
R&R Bk N - v19 - i4 - Nov 2004 - p188(1) [501+]

Di Liscia, Maria Silvia - *Saberes, terapias y practicas medicas en Argentina*
HAHR - v84 - i4 - Nov 2004 - p764(2) [501+]

Di Marco, M. - *Poiesis. Bibliografia della poesia greca 2000. I*
Class R - v54 - i1 - May 2004 - p241(1) [501+]

Di Matteo, Massimo - *The Italian Economy at the Dawn of the 21st Century*
R&R Bk N - v19 - i1 - Feb 2004 - p84(1) [501+]

Di Michele, Mary - *Tenor of Love*
Globe & Mail - Feb 5 2005 - pD5 [501+]
PW - v252 - i1 - Jan 3 2005 - p37(1) [51-500]

Di Piero, W.S. - *Brother Fire*
BL - v101 - i2 - Sept 15 2004 - p195(1) [501+]
Poet - v185 - i4 - Jan 2005 - p325(4) [501+]
PW - v251 - i47 - Nov 22 2004 - p56(1) [501+]

Di Prima, Diane - *Recollections of My Life as a Woman: The New York Years*
Can Lit - i181 - Summer 2004 - p120-121 [501+]

Di Tella, Torcuato S. - *History of Political Parties in Twentieth-Century Latin America*
R&R Bk N - v19 - i1 - Feb 2004 - pNA [501+]

di Toppi, Luigi Sanita - *Abiotic Stresses in Plants*
SciTech - v28 - i1 - March 2004 - p129(1) [51-500]

Diacon, Todd A. - *Stringing Together a Nation: Candido Mariano da Silva Rondon and the Construction of a Modern Brazil, 1906-1930*
Choice - v42 - i2 - Oct 2004 - p351(1) [51-500]

Diagnostic Study of Accounting and Auditing Practices in Selected Developing Member Countries: Azerbaijan, Fiji Islands, Republic of the Marshall Islands, Philippines, Sri Lanka
JEL - v42 - i1 - March 2004 - p297(2) [501+]

Diagram Group - *African History on File*
c   LibMed - v22 - i5 - Feb 2004 - p85(1) [501+]
Biology Experiments on File
y   LibMed - v23 - i3 - Nov-Dec 2004 - p87(1) [501+]
SciTech - v28 - i1 - March 2004 - p61(1) [501+]
The First Humans
y   VOYA - v27 - i4 - Oct 2004 - p334(1) [51-500]
History of Southern Africa
y   HNet - Nov 2004 - pNA [501+]

The Diagram Group - *How to Hold a Crocodile*
R&R Bk N - v19 - i1 - Feb 2004 - p1(1) [51-500]

Diagram Group - *Human Anatomy on File*
c   LibMed - v22 - i5 - Feb 2004 - p85(1) [501+]
Human Physiology on File
c   LibMed - v22 - i5 - Feb 2004 - p85(1) [501+]

Dial, Raymond - *Where Washington Walked*
c   PW - v252 - i5 - Jan 31 2005 - p70(1) [501+]

Diallo, Alfa Omar - *Microbiology Recall*
SciTech - v28 - i4 - Dec 2004 - p74(1) [51-500]

Diamant, Lincoln - *Chaining the Hudson: The Fight for the River in the American Revolution*
Bwatch - v26 - i7 - July 2004 - p10(1) [51-500]

Diamond, Etan - *Souls of the City: Religion and the Search for Community in Postwar America*
AHR - v109 - i4 - Oct 2004 - p1268-1269 [501+]

Diamond, Jared - *Collapse (Read by Murney, Christopher). Audiobook Review*
PW - v252 - i6 - Feb 7 2005 - p35(1) [501+]
Collapse: How Societies Choose to Fail or Succeed
Am Sci - v93 - i2 - March-April 2005 - p172(4) [501+]
BL - v101 - i5 - Nov 1 2004 - p442(1) [51-500]
Bus W - i3913 - Dec 20 2004 - p26 [501+]
Ent W - i801 - Jan 14 2005 - p95 [51-500]
For Aff - v84 - i2 - March-April 2005 - p134 [501+]
Globe & Mail - Jan 15 2005 - pD3 [501+]
LJ - v130 - i3 - Feb 15 2005 - p154(1) [51-500]
NW - Jan 17 2005 - p12 [501+]
NYTBR - Jan 30 2005 - p10 [501+]
People - v63 - i5 - Feb 7 2005 - p52 [501+]
PW - v251 - i46 - Nov 15 2004 - p49(1) [51-500]
Sci - v307 - i5706 - Jan 7 2005 - p45(1) [501+]
Time - v165 - i7 - Feb 14 2005 - p62 [501+]
Collapse: How Societies Choose to Fail or Survive
NS - v134 - i4726 - Feb 7 2005 - p50(2) [501+]
Spec - v297 - i9212 - Feb 26 2005 - p34(2) [501+]
TimHES - v0 - i1676 - Jan 28 2005 - p24(2) [501+]
Guns, Germs, and Steel
Globe & Mail - Dec 24 2004 - pD3 [1-50]

Diamond, Jed - *The Irritable Male Syndrome: Managing the 4 Key Causes of Depression and Aggression*
Globe & Mail - Oct 9 2004 - pF6 [501+]
LJ - v129 - i14 - Sept 1 2004 - p172(1) [51-500]
PW - v251 - i29 - July 19 2004 - p151(1) [51-500]

Diamond, Larry - *Islam and Democracy in the Middle East*
R&R Bk N - v19 - i1 - Feb 2004 - pNA [501+]

Diamond, Marie Josephine - *Encyclopedia of World Writers, 19th and 20th Centuries*
R&R Bk N - v19 - i1 - Feb 2004 - p221(1) [51-500]

Diamond, Michael - *Victorian Sensation, or, The Spectacular, the Shocking and the Scandalous in Nineteenth-Century Britain*
Albion - v36 - i2 - Summer 2004 - p324(3) [501+]

Diamond, Patrick - *New Labour's Old Roots: Revisionist Thinkers in Labour's History*
NS - v133 - i4717 - Dec 6 2004 - p54(2) [501+]

Diamond, Peter A. - *Taxation, Incomplete Markets, and Social Security: Munich Lectures in Economics*
Econ J - v114 - i499 - Nov 2004 - pF536(1) [501+]

Diana, James S. - *Biology and Ecology of Fishes*
QRB - v79 - i4 - Dec 2004 - p443(1) [501+]

Diaz, Arlene J. - *Female Citizens, Patriarchs, and the Law in Venezuela, 1786-1904*
Choice - v42 - i4 - Dec 2004 - p717(2) [1-50]

Diaz, Brigitte - *Stendhal en sa correspondance ou "L'Histoire d'un esprit"*
NCFS - v33 - i1-2 - Fall-Winter 2004 - p221(3) [501+]

Diaz, Harry P. - *Farm Communities at the Crossroads: Challenge and Resistance*
Can Hist R - v85 - i4 - Dec 2004 - p885(2) [501+]

Diaz, Henry F. - *Climate and Water: Transboundary Challenges in the Americas*
SciTech - v28 - i1 - March 2004 - p147(1) [51-500]

Diaz, Karen R. - *IssueWeb: A Guide and Sourcebook for Researching Controversial Issues on the Web*
Choice - v42 - i3 - Nov 2004 - p445(1) [1-50]
R&R Bk N - v19 - i4 - Nov 2004 - p260(1) [501+]
SLJ - v50 - i9 - Sept 2004 - p238(1) [51-500]

Diaz-Maggioli, Gabriel - *Teacher-Centered Professional Development*
R&R Bk N - v19 - i4 - Nov 2004 - p182(1) [501+]

Diaz, Tom - *Making a Killing: The Business of Guns in America*
Globe & Mail - Dec 4 2004 - pD39 [501+]

Dib, Kamal - *Warlords and Merchants: The Lebanese Business and Political Establishment*
R&R Bk N - v19 - i3 - August 2004 - p50(1) [51-500]

DiBacco, Thomas V. - *Made in the USA: The History of American Business*
R&R Bk N - v19 - i1 - Feb 2004 - p81(1) [1-50]

DiCamillo, Kate - *The Tale of Despereaux*
c   Five Owls - v18 - i1 - Fall 2004 - p26(2) [51-500]
c   Storyworks - v12 - i4 - Jan 2005 - p7(1) [51-500]

Dick, Bernard F. - *Hal Wallis: Producer to the Stars*
Choice - v42 - i3 - Nov 2004 - p491(1) [51-500]

Dick, H.W. - *Surabaya, City of Work: A Socioeconomic History, 1900-2000*
JTWS - v21 - i1 - Spring 2004 - p271(3) [501+]

Dick, John S. - *Basic Rubber Testing: Selecting Methods for a Rubber Test Program*
SciTech - v28 - i1 - March 2004 - p142(1) [51-500]

Dick, Lyle - *Muskox Land: Ellesmere Island in the Age of Contact*
Can Hist R - v85 - i4 - Dec 2004 - p791(3) [501+]

Dick, Ron - *Aviation Century: The Early Years*
E-Streams - July 2004 - pNA [501+]
Aviation Century: The Golden Age
y   BL - v101 - i7 - Dec 1 2004 - p627(2) [51-500]
LJ - v130 - i2 - Feb 1 2005 - p96(1) [501+]
Aviation Century: World War II
y   BL - v101 - i7 - Dec 1 2004 - p627(2) [51-500]
LJ - v130 - i2 - Feb 1 2005 - p96(1) [501+]
Flight: A History of Aviation in Photographs
LJ - v130 - i2 - Feb 1 2005 - p96(1) [501+]

Dick, Steven J. - *The Living Universe: NASA and the Development of Astrobiology*
Sci - v307 - i5706 - Jan 7 2005 - p46(1) [501+]
Sky and Ocean Joined: The U.S. Naval Observatory, 1830-2000
NWCR - v57 - Autumn 2004 - p171(2) [501+]

Dickens, Charles - *The Annotated 'Christmas Carol': 'A Christmas Carol' in Prose (Illus. by Leech, John)*
R&R Bk N - v19 - i1 - Feb 2004 - p238(1) [51-500]
A Christmas Carol (Read by Dale, Jim). Audiobook Review
c   CH Bwatch - Feb 2005 - pNA [51-500]
A House to Let
BW - v34 - i32 - August 8 2004 - p11(1) [501+]
LJ - v129 - i13 - August 2004 - p131(1) [51-500]

Dicker, Susan J. - *Languages in America: A Pluralist View, 2nd Ed.*
R&R Bk N - v19 - i1 - Feb 2004 - p212 [501+]

Dickerson, Constance B. - *Teen Book Discussion Groups @ the Library*
BL - v101 - i1 - Sept 1 2004 - p165(1) [1-50]

Dickerson, Debra J. - *The End of Blackness: Returning the Souls of Black Folk to Their Rightful Owners*
BooChiTr - March 28 2004 - p3(1) [501+]
BW - v34 - i3 - Jan 18 2004 - p6(1) [501+]
Choice - v42 - i2 - Oct 2004 - p376(1) [51-500]

Dickerson, Donna L. - *The Reconstruction Era: Primary Documents on Events from 1865 to 1877*
c   SLJ - v50 - i8 - August 2004 - p56(1) [51-500]

Dickey, Christopher - *The Sleeper*
BW - v34 - i37 - Sept 12 2004 - p10(1) [501+]
KR - v72 - i13 - July 1 2004 - p592(1) [501+]
LJ - v129 - i14 - Sept 1 2004 - p138(1) [51-500]

Dickey, E. - *Latin Forms of Address: From Plautus to Apuleius*
Class R - v54 - i1 - May 2004 - p136(2) [501+]

Dickey, Eric Jerome - *Drive Me Crazy*
BL - v100 - i21 - July 2004 - p1797(1) [51-500]
Ent W - i775 - July 23 2004 - p81 [51-500]
Genevieve (Read by Allen, Richard). Audiobook Review
LJ - v129 - i20 - Dec 1 2004 - p182(1) [51-500]

Dickey, James - *Classes of Modren Poets and the Art of Poetry*
Choice - v42 - i3 - Nov 2004 - p482(1) [1-50]

Dickey, Stephanie S. - *Rembrandt: Portraits in Print*
Choice - v42 - i4 - Dec 2004 - p649(1) [1-50]

Dickie, John - *Cosa Nostra: A History of the Sicilian Mafia*
LJ - v129 - i17 - Oct 15 2004 - p72(1) [51-500]
NYTBR - Oct 31 2004 - p20 [501+]
TLS - i5265 - Feb 27 2004 - p10-10 [501+]
The New Mandarins: How British Foreign Policy Works
CR - v286 - i1668 - Jan 2005 - p50(2) [501+]
TimHES - v0 - i1682 - March 11 2005 - p24(2) [501+]

Dickinson, Adam - *Cartography and Walking*
CBRA - Annual 2003 - p214(2) [51-500]

Dikotter, Frank - *Narcotic Culture: A History of Drugs in China*
  HT - v54 - i11 - Nov 2004 - p83(1) [501+]
Dilevko, Juris - *Reading and the Reference Librarian: The Importance to Library Service of Staff Reading Habits*
  A Lib - v35 - i7 - August 2004 - p86(2) [501+]
Diliberto, Gioia - *I Am Madame X*
  TLS - i5289 - August 13 2004 - p20(1) [501+]
Dilke, Annabel - *The Inheritance*
  TLS - i5292 - Sept 3 2004 - p32(1) [501+]
Dillane, Fionnuala - *New Voices in Irish Criticism 4*
  R&R Bk N - v19 - i1 - Feb 2004 - p240(1) [51-500]
Dillard, Annie - *An American Childhood*
  BW - v34 - i31 - August 1 2004 - p13(1) [501+]
Diller, Frank - *The Geese of Beaver Bog*
  Am Sci - v92 - i4 - July-August 2004 - p379(1) [501+]
Diller, Phyllis - *Like a Lampshade in a Whorehouse: My Life in Comedy*
  NYTBR - March 13 2005 - p7 [501+]
  PW - v252 - i6 - Feb 7 2005 - p57(1) [51-500]
Dillon, Anne - *The Construction of Martyrdom in the English Catholic Community, 1535-1603*
  Albion - v36 - i2 - Summer 2004 - p294(2) [501+]
The Construction of Martyrdom in the English Catholic Community, 1553-1603
  Six Ct J - v35 - i3 - Fall 2004 - p831-832 [501+]
Dillon, Elizabeth Maddock - *The Gender of Freedom: Fictions of Liberalism and the Literary Public Sphere*
  Choice - v42 - i3 - Nov 2004 - p482(1) [1-50]
Dillon, Ellis - *The Island of Horses*
  c Sch Lib - v52 - i4 - Winter 2004 - p201(1) [51-500]
Dillon, Emma - *Medieval Music-Making and the Roman de Fauvel*
  FS - v58 - i1 - Jan 2004 - p79(2) [501+]
  Specu - v79 - i4 - Oct 2004 - p1065(2) [501+]
Dillon, John - *The Heirs of Plato: A Study of the Old Academy*
  AJP - v125 - i3 - Fall 2004 - p459-462 [501+]
Neoplatonic Philosophy: Introductory Readings
  R&R Bk N - v19 - i4 - Nov 2004 - p3(1) [51-500]
Dillon, Martin - *ARBA In-Depth: Economics and Business*
  Choice - v42 - i2 - Oct 2004 - p272(1) [501+]
ARBA In-Depth: Health and Medicine
  Choice - v42 - i1 - Sept 2004 - p68(1) [501+]
  LJ - v129 - i13 - August 2004 - p124(1) [51-500]
ARBA In-Depth: Philosophy and Religion
  Choice - v42 - i2 - Oct 2004 - p264(1) [51-500]
Index to American Reference Books Annual: 2002-2004, A Cumulative Index to Subjects, Authors, and Titles
  R&R Bk N - v19 - i4 - Nov 2004 - p258(1) [501+]
Dillon, Michael - *The Life and Times of Edward H. Butler, Founder of the 'Buffalo News' (1850-1914): A Crusading Journalist Navigates the Gilded Age*
  R&R Bk N - v19 - i1 - Feb 2004 - p229(1) [51-500]
Xinjiang--China's Muslim Far Northwest
  For Aff - v83 - i4 - July-August 2004 - p136 [501+]
  TLS - i5306 - Dec 10 2004 - p30-31 [501+]
Dillon, Michele - *Handbook of the Sociology of Religion*
  CS - v33 - i6 - Nov 2004 - p694(3) [501+]
They Call Him Pastor: Married Men in Charge of Catholic Parishes
  CS - v33 - i5 - Sept 2004 - p559-560 [501+]
Dillon, Patricia M. - *Nursing Health Assessment: Student Applications*
  SciTech - v28 - i4 - Dec 2004 - p120(1) [51-500]
DiLorenzo, Thomas J. - *How Capitalism Saved America: The Untold History of Our Country, from the Pilgrims to the Present*
  LJ - v129 - i12 - July 2004 - p95(1) [51-500]
The Real Lincoln: A New Look at Abraham Lincoln, His Agenda, and an Unnecessary War
  RAH - v32 - i2 - June 2004 - p184-12 [501+]
Dilsaver, Larry M. - *Cumberland Island National Seashore: A History of Conservation Conflict*
  R&R Bk N - v19 - i3 - August 2004 - p74(1) [51-500]
Dilthey, Wilhelm - *Oeuvres. Vol. 4*
  Dialogue - v42 - i1 - Winter 2003 - p162 [501+]
Dilveko, Juris - *Reading and the Reference Librarian: The Importance to Library Service of Staff Reading Habits*
  R&R Bk N - v19 - i1 - Feb 2004 - p260(1) [51-500]
Dilworth, Leah - *Acts of Possession: Collecting in America*
  Choice - v41 - i7 - March 2004 - p1333(1) [501+]
DiMaggio, Jerry A. - *Current Practices and Future Trends in Deep Foundations*
  SciTech - v28 - i3 - Sept 2004 - p142(1) [51-500]

Dimand, Robert - *The Status of Women in Classical Economic Thought*
  Choice - v42 - i1 - Sept 2004 - p157(1) [501+]
  R&R Bk N - v19 - i3 - August 2004 - p154(1) [51-500]
DiMarco, John - *Computer Graphics and Multimedia: Applications, Problems and Solutions*
  Choice - v42 - i1 - Sept 2004 - p139(1) [501+]
Dimbleby, Josceline - *May and Amy: A True Story of Family, Forbidden Love, and the Secret Lives of May Gaskell, Her Daughter Amy, and Sir Edward Burne-Jones*
  KR - v72 - i22 - Nov 15 2004 - p1076(1) [501+]
  LJ - v130 - i3 - Feb 15 2005 - p140(1) [51-500]
  PW - v251 - i47 - Nov 22 2004 - p48(1) [51-500]
A Profound Secret: Mary Gaskell, Her Daughter Amy, and Edward Burne-Jones
  TLS - i5268 - March 19 2004 - p11-11 [501+]
Dimendberg, Edward - *Film Noir and the Spaces of Modernity*
  Choice - v42 - i2 - Oct 2004 - p300(1) [51-500]
  TimHES - v0 - i1681 - March 4 2005 - p24(1) [501+]
Dimitri, Nicola - *Cognitive Processes and Economic Behaviour*
  JEL - v42 - i1 - March 2004 - p251(1) [501+]
Dimitriadis, Greg - *Friendship, Cliques, and Gangs: Young Black Men Coming of Age in Urban America*
  TCR - v106 - i5 - May 2004 - p907(3) [501+]
  VOYA - v27 - i5 - Dec 2004 - p426(1) [51-500]
Promises to Keep: Cultural Studies, Democratic Education, and Public Life
  CS - v33 - i6 - Nov 2004 - p743(1) [1-50]
  JEL - v41 - i4 - Dec 2003 - p1377(1) [501+]
Dimitrova, Blaga - *Scars*
  South CR - v36 - i2 - Spring 2004 - p169-171 [501+]
Dimitrova, Diana - *Western Tradition and Naturalistic Hindi Theatre*
  R&R Bk N - v19 - i4 - Nov 2004 - p219(1) [501+]
Dimnik, Martin - *The Dynasty of Chernigov, 1146-1246*
  AHR - v109 - i4 - Oct 2004 - p1291-1292 [501+]
  Russ Rev - v63 - i3 - July 2004 - pNA [501+]
Dimock, Peter - *A Short Rhetoric for Leaving the Family*
  Spec - v295 - i9186 - August 28 2004 - p29(2) [501+]
  TLS - i5289 - August 13 2004 - p20(1) [501+]
DiMucci, Dion - *Fishing with Balloons*
  c CH Bwatch - Oct 2004 - pNA [51-500]
Dinan, Desmond - *Europe Recast: A History of European Union*
  Choice - v42 - i4 - Dec 2004 - p730(1) [1-50]
  TimHES - v0 - i1668 - Nov 26 2004 - pIV(1) [501+]
Dincauze, Dena F. - *Environmental Archaeology: Principles and Practice*
  Am Ant - v70 - i1 - Jan 2005 - p206(2) [501+]
Dinega, Alyssa W. - *A Russian Psyche: The Poetic Mind of Marina Tsvetaeva*
  JGS - v13 - i1 - March 2004 - p78-80 [501+]
Diner, Hasia R - *The Jews of the United States: 1654 to 2000*
  LJ - v129 - i13 - August 2004 - p93(1) [501+]
Diner, Hasia R. - *The Jews of the United States*
  Bwatch - Jan 2005 - pNA [51-500]
Dinerstein, Joel - *Swinging the Machine: Modernity, Technology, and African American Culture between the World Wars*
  AHR - v109 - i4 - Oct 2004 - p1252(2) [501+]
  Am Q - v56 - i2 - June 2004 - p449(12) [501+]
  JAH - v91 - i1 - June 2004 - p279-280 [501+]
  JPC - v38 - i3 - Feb 2005 - p579(3) [501+]
Ding Xiang Warner - *A Wild Deer Amid Soaring Phoenixes: The Opposition Poetics of Wang Ji*
  Ch Rev Int - v11 - i1 - Spring 2004 - p189(5) [501+]
Dinger, Felix - *The Future of Liner Conferences in Europe: A Critical Analysis of Agreements in Liner Shipping under Current European Competition Law*
  R&R Bk N - v19 - i3 - August 2004 - p208(1) [1-50]
Dingermann, Th. - *Molecular Biology in Medicinal Chemistry*
  SciTech - v28 - i3 - Sept 2004 - p125(1) [51-500]
Dinges, John - *The Condor Years: How Pinochet and His Allies Brought Terrorism to Three Continents*
  CC - v122 - i1 - Jan 11 2005 - p28(7) [501+]
  HRNB - v33 - i1 - Fall 2004 - p18(1) [501+]
Dingus, Lowell - *Hell Creek, Montana: America's Key to the Prehistoric Past*
  LJ - v129 - i12 - July 2004 - p113(1) [51-500]

Dinnage, Rosemary - *Alone! Alone! Lives of Some Outsider Women*
  NYRB - v51 - i13 - August 12 2004 - p38(2) [501+]
  Spec - v296 - i9193 - Oct 16 2004 - p66(2) [501+]
  TLS - i5307 - Dec 17 2004 - p25(1) [501+]
  Wom R Bks - v22 - i1 - Oct 2004 - p12(1) [501+]
  NYTBR - July 11 2004 - p20 [51-500]
Dinosaur World
  LibMed - v22 - i7 - April-May 2004 - p78(1) [501+]
Dinsdale, Christopher - *Broken Circle*
  Res Links - v10 - i3 - Feb 2005 - p15(1) [501+]
Dinshaw, Carolyn - *The Cambridge Companion to Medieval Women's Writing*
  Med R - June 2004 - pNA [501+]
Dinstein, Yoram - *The Conduct of Hostilities under the Law of International Armed Forces*
  Choice - v42 - i3 - Nov 2004 - p560(1) [1-50]
Israel Yearbook on Human Rights Vol. 32
  R&R Bk N - v19 - i3 - August 2004 - p51(1) [51-500]
Israel Yearbook on Human Rights Vol. 33
  R&R Bk N - v19 - i4 - Nov 2004 - p45(1) [51-500]
Israeli Yearbook on Human Rights Vol. 34
  R&R Bk N - v19 - i4 - Nov 2004 - p45(1) [51-500]
Dinteman, Walter A. - *Zero Defect Hiring: A Quick Guide to the Most Important Decisions Managers Have to Make*
  HR Mag - v50 - i2 - Feb 2005 - pS11(1) [501+]
Dinwoodie, David W. - *Reserve Memories: The Power of the Past in a Chilcotin Community*
  Can Hist R - v85 - i3 - Sept 2004 - p582(2) [501+]
Dinwoodie, Graeme B. - *Trademarks and Unfair Competition: Law & Policy*
  R&R Bk N - v19 - i4 - Nov 2004 - p169(1) [501+]
Diochon, Monica C. - *Entrepreneurship and Community Economic Development*
  R&R Bk N - v19 - i3 - August 2004 - p95(1) [51-500]
Diome, Fatou - *Le ventre de l'Atlantique*
  WLT - v78 - i3-4 - Sept-Dec 2004 - p83(1) [501+]
Dionisio, Daniele - *Textbook-Atlas of Intestinal Infections in AIDS*
  SciTech - v28 - i3 - Sept 2004 - p107(1) [51-500]
Dionne, Criag - *Rogues and Early Modern Culture*
  Choice - v42 - i3 - Nov 2004 - p486(2) [1-50]
Dionne, E.J. - *One Electorate under God?: A Dialogue on Religion and American Politics*
  Choice - v42 - i6 - Feb 2005 - p1039(1) [51-500]
  NYT - August 21 2004 - pA12 [501+]
  R&R Bk N - v19 - i3 - August 2004 - pNA [1-50]
Stand Up, Fight Back: Republican Toughs, Democratic Wimps, and the Politics of Revenge
  BW - v34 - i29 - July 18 2004 - p4(1) [1-50]
  NYTBR - July 18 2004 - p9 [501+]
Diorio, Mary Ann L. - *A Student's Guide to Nathaniel Hawthorne*
  y Teach Lib - v32 - i1 - Oct 2004 - p51(1) [51-500]
  VOYA - v27 - i5 - Dec 2004 - p420(1) [51-500]
Diouf, Sylviane A. - *Bintou's Braids (Illus. by Evans, Shane W.)*
  c HNet - June 2004 - pNA [501+]
Fighting the Slave Trade: West African Strategies
  Choice - v41 - i11-12 - July-August 2004 - p2099(1) [501+]
DiPucchio, Kelly - *Liberty's Journey (Illus. by Egielski, Richard)*
  c BL - v101 - i2 - Sept 15 2004 - p247(2) [51-500]
  c KR - v72 - i16 - August 15 2004 - p805(1) [51-500]
  c NYTBR - Nov 14 2004 - p40 [501+]
  c PW - v251 - i29 - July 19 2004 - p160(1) [51-500]
  c SLJ - v50 - i11 - Nov 2004 - p97(1) [51-500]
What's the Magic Word? (Illus. by Winborn, Marsha)
  c KR - v72 - i24 - Dec 15 2004 - p1200(1) [501+]
Dirda, Michael - *Bound to Please: An Extraordinary One-Volume Literary Education*
  BL - v101 - i7 - Dec 1 2004 - p620(1) [51-500]
  Globe & Mail - Feb 5 2005 - pD10 [501+]
  KR - v72 - i19 - Oct 1 2004 - p946(2) [501+]
An Open Book: Coming of Age in the Heartland
  VQR - v80 - i2 - Spring 2004 - p263-263 [501+]
Directory: Non-Governmental Organizations and Drug Abuse Prevention, Treatment and Rehabilitation
  R&R Bk N - v19 - i1 - Feb 2004 - p140(1) [51-500]

The Directory of Business to Business Catalogs: A
Comprehensive Source to Meet Most Day-to-day
Business Needs 12th Ed.
  R&R Bk N - v19 - i2 - May 2004 - p115(1) [51-
  500]
Directory of Distance Learning Opportunities
  LibMed - v22 - i4 - Jan 2004 - p83(1) [501+]
Directory of Drug and Alcohol Residential Rehabilitation
Facilities 2004
  SciTech - v28 - i1 - March 2004 - p101(1) [51-
  500]
Directory of Hospital Personnel: U.S. Hospitals and Key
Decision Makers 16th Ed.
  SciTech - v28 - i1 - March 2004 - p85(1) [51-500]
Dirlik, Arif - *Chinese on the American Frontier*
  R&R Bk N - v19 - i1 - Feb 2004 - p55(1) [51-500]
  Postmodernism and China
  Can Lit - i181 - Summer 2004 - p122-123 [501+]
Disabilities Studies
  CS - v33 - i5 - Sept 2004 - p621-621 [501+]
Discover the Life of an American Legend II
  LibMed - v23 - i1 - August-Sept 2004 - p72(1)
  [51-500]
Discovering Dinosaurs
  LibMed - v23 - i3 - Nov-Dec 2004 - p62(1) [51-
  500]
Discovering World Cultures: The Middle East
  y BL - v101 - i1 - Sept 1 2004 - p166(1) [501+]
  y Ref Rev - Sept 2004 - pNA [501+]
  y SLJ - v50 - i10 - Oct 2004 - p91(2) [51-500]
Discovery Channel Science: Our Planet Earth
  c LibMed - v23 - i3 - Nov-Dec 2004 - p87(1) [51-
  500]
A Disease-Based Comparison of Health Systems: What Is
Best and at What Cost?
  JEL - v41 - i4 - Dec 2003 - p1374(2) [501+]
Disher, Garry - *The Divine Wind*
  y Kliatt - v38 - i5 - Sept 2004 - p19(2) [501+]
  The Dragon Man
  BW - v34 - i36 - Sept 5 2004 - p10(1) [501+]
Disheroon-Green, Suzanne - *Voices of the American South*
  R&R Bk N - v19 - i4 - Nov 2004 - p241(1) [501+]
Dishman, Rod K. - *Physical Activity Epidemiology*
  SciTech - v28 - i1 - March 2004 - p84(1) [51-500]
DiSilvestro, Robert A. - *Handbook of Minerals as
Nutritional Supplements*
  SciTech - v28 - i4 - Dec 2004 - p71(1) [51-500]
DiSpezio, Michael A. - *Weather Mania: Discovering
What's Up and What's Coming Down*
  c SB - v40 - i5 - Sept-Oct 2004 - p194(1) [51-500]
Dispirito, Rocco - *Rocco's Italian-American*
  BL - v101 - i5 - Nov 1 2004 - p453(1) [51-500]
  PW - v251 - i41 - Oct 11 2004 - p71(1) [51-500]
Dispute Settlement: Investor--State
  JEL - v42 - i1 - March 2004 - p263(2) [501+]
Dispute Settlement: State--State
  JEL - v42 - i1 - March 2004 - p264(1) [501+]
Disraeli, Benjamin - *Coningsby*
  Globe & Mail - Dec 18 2004 - pD27 [51-500]
  Sybil
  Globe & Mail - Dec 18 2004 - pD27 [51-500]
Disraeli, Isaac - *Isaac D'Israeli on Books*
  TLS - i5286 - July 23 2004 - p32(1) [501+]
Dissertori, Gunther - *Quantum Chromodynamics: High
Energy Experiments and Theory*
  Phys Today - v57 - i8 - August 2004 - p57-58
  [501+]
Distad, Linda Schaak - *Talking Teaching: Implementing
Reflective Practice in Groups*
  R&R Bk N - v19 - i4 - Nov 2004 - p178(1) [501+]
DiStefano, Anna - *Encyclopedia of Distributed Learning*
  R&R Bk N - v19 - i1 - Feb 2004 - p193(1) [51-
  500]
  R&USQ - v44 - i1 - Fall 2004 - p84(1) [501+]
Distributed Public Governance: Agencies, Authorities
and Other Government Bodies
  R&R Bk N - v19 - i3 - August 2004 - p176(1)
  [501+]
Ditchfield, G.M. - *George III: An Essay in Monarchy*
  HNet - June 2004 - pNA [501+]
DiTerlizzi, Tony - *The Ironwood Tree*
  MFSF - v107 - i2 - August 2004 - p32(2) [51-500]
  *Lucinda's Secret and The Ironwood Tree (Read by
Hamill, Mark). Audiobook Review*
  c SLJ - v50 - i9 - Sept 2004 - p78(1) [51-500]
  The Spiderwick Chronicles, Bk. 5
  y MFSF - v108 - i3 - March 2005 - p27(2) [51-500]
Diterlizzi, Tony - *The Wrath of Mulgarath (Read by
Hamill, Hark). Audiobook Review*
  c SLJ - v51 - i1 - Jan 2005 - p77(1) [51-500]

Ditghfield, Christin - *Knowing Your Civil Rights*
  c SLJ - v50 - i8 - August 2004 - p106(1) [501+]
  Serving Your Community
  c SLJ - v50 - i8 - August 2004 - p106(1) [501+]
Ditt, Karl - *Agrarmodernisierung und okologische Folgen:
Westfalen vom 18*
  T&C - v45 - i1 - Jan 2004 - p197(3) [501+]
Dittmar, Hank - *The New Transit Town: Best Practices in
Transit-Oriented Development*
  Choice - v42 - i1 - Sept 2004 - p156(1) [501+]
  Env - v46 - i7 - Sept 2004 - p41(1) [501+]
  NRJ - v44 - i3 - Summer 2004 - p907-916 [501+]
  R&R Bk N - v19 - i2 - May 2004 - p109(1) [1-50]
  SciTech - v28 - i3 - Sept 2004 - p8(1) [501+]
Dittrich, Lothar - *Die Kulturgeschichte des Zoos*
  Isis - v95 - i2 - June 2004 - p281(2) [501+]
Divakaruni, Chitra Banerjee - *The Conch Bearer*
  c CE - v80 - i5 - Mid-Summer 2004 - p273(1) [51-
  500]
  LibMed - v22 - i4 - Jan 2004 - p64(1) [501+]
  c PW - v252 - i6 - Feb 7 2005 - p62(1) [51-500]
  y Sch Lib - v52 - i4 - Winter 2004 - p215(1) [51-
  500]
  Queen of Dreams: A Novel
  Ent W - i785 - Sept 24 2004 - p117 [51-500]
  Queen of Dreams
  BL - v100 - i21 - July 2004 - p1798(1) [51-500]
  BW - v34 - i37 - Sept 12 2004 - p10(1) [501+]
  KR - v72 - i14 - July 15 2004 - p646(2) [51-500]
  LJ - v129 - i13 - August 2004 - p66(1) [51-500]
  PW - v251 - i32 - August 9 2004 - p229(1) [51-
  500]
Divall, Colin - *Making Histories in Transport Museums*
  T&C - v45 - i1 - Jan 2004 - p234(2) [501+]
  *Suburbanising the Masses: Public Transport and Urban
Development in Historical Perspective*
  R&R Bk N - v19 - i1 - Feb 2004 - p103(1) [51-
  500]
Divina, Fernando - *Foods of the Americas: Native Recipes
and Traditions*
  BL - v101 - i1 - Sept 1 2004 - p35(1) [51-500]
  LJ - v129 - i13 - August 2004 - p113(1) [51-500]
Diwekar, Urmila M. - *Introduction to Applied Optimization*
  Choice - v42 - i1 - Sept 2004 - p139(2) [501+]
Dix, Mark - *Discovering AutoCAD 2004*
  SciTech - v28 - i3 - Sept 2004 - p136(1) [51-500]
Dixit, Avinash K. - *Lawlessness and Economics:
Alternative Modes of Governance*
  Law&PolBR - Dec 2004 - p961(3) [501+]
Dixon, Bill - *Justice Gained? Crime and Crime Control in
South Africa's Transition*
  R&R Bk N - v19 - i4 - Nov 2004 - p148(1) [501+]
Dixon, Dougal - *Ankylosaurus and Other Mountain
Dinosaurs (Illus. by Weston, Steve)*
  c SLJ - v51 - i2 - Feb 2005 - p116(1) [51-500]
  Big Cat Summer
  c SLJ - v51 - i1 - Jan 2005 - p146(1) [51-500]
  City Bear
  c SLJ - v51 - i1 - Jan 2005 - p146(1) [51-500]
  *Deltadromeus and Other Shoreline Dinosaurs (Illus. by
Weston, Steve)*
  c SLJ - v51 - i2 - Feb 2005 - p116(1) [51-500]
  Dinosaur
  y BL - v101 - i7 - Dec 1 2004 - p665(1) [51-500]
  y Sci Teach - v72 - i3 - March 2005 - p81(1) [501+]
  Gorilla Mountain
  c SLJ - v51 - i1 - Jan 2005 - p146(1) [51-500]
  Orangutan Rescue
  c SLJ - v51 - i1 - Jan 2005 - p146(1) [51-500]
  Stegosaurus and Other Plains Dinosaurs
  c BL - v101 - i4 - Oct 15 2004 - p426(1) [51-500]
  Triceratops and Other Forest Dinosaurs
  c BL - v101 - i4 - Oct 15 2004 - p426(1) [51-500]
  *Triceratops and Other Forest Dinosaurs (Illus. by
Weston, Steve)*
  c SLJ - v51 - i2 - Feb 2005 - p116(1) [51-500]
Dixon, Douglas A. - *Biology, Management, and Protection
of Catadromous Eels*
  QRB - v79 - i4 - Dec 2004 - p442(2) [501+]
Dixon, J.E.G. - *The Battle of Britain in Victory and Defeat:
The Achievements of Air Chief Marshal Dowding and the
Scandal of His Dismissal from Office*
  APH - v51 - i4 - Winter 2004 - p56(2) [501+]
  The Battle of Britain: Victory and Defeat
  Spec - v297 - i9207 - Jan 22 2005 - p39(1) [501+]
Dixon, Philip - *Nice and Hot Disputes: The Doctrine of the
Trinity in the Seventeenth Century*
  TT - v61 - i1 - April 2004 - p103-104 [501+]
Dixon, Roger A. - *New Frontiers in Cognitive Aging*
  Nature - v431 - i7006 - Sept 16 2004 - pNA
  [501+]

Dixon, Scott - *The Protestant Clergy of Early Modern
Europe*
  Choice - v41 - i11-12 - July-August 2004 -
  p2115(1) [501+]
Dixon, Stephen - *The Old Friends*
  PW - v251 - i41 - Oct 11 2004 - p56(2) [51-500]
Dixon, Thomas - *From Passions to Emotions: The
Creation of a Secular Psychological Category*
  TLS - i5266 - March 5 2004 - p32-32 [501+]
Dixon, Tony - *The Performance Coach: Seeking Coaching
Excellence*
  R&R Bk N - v19 - i3 - August 2004 - p130(1)
  [501+]
Dixon, Wheeler Winston - *Film and Television After 9/11*
  Choice - v42 - i1 - Sept 2004 - p107(1) [501+]
Dixsaut, Monique - *Metamorphoses de la dialectique dans
les dialogues de Platon*
  Dialogue - v43 - i1 - Wntr 2004 - p167-171 [501+]
Dizard, Wilson P. - *Inventing Public Diplomacy: The Story
of the U.S. Information Agency*
  HRNB - v33 - i1 - Fall 2004 - p10(2) [501+]
  R&R Bk N - v19 - i3 - August 2004 - p70(1) [51-
  500]
Dizon, Don S. - *100 Questions and Answers about Ovarian
Cancer*
  SciTech - v28 - i1 - March 2004 - p91(1) [51-500]
Djelic, Marie-Laure - *Globalization and Institutions:
Redefining the Rules of the Economic Game*
  JEL - v41 - i4 - Dec 2003 - p1349(1) [501+]
Djokic, Dejan - *Yugoslavism: Histories of a Failed Idea,
1918-1992*
  Slav R - v63 - i3 - Fall 2004 - p631-633 [501+]
Djordjevic, Ksenija - *The Seeds of Neoplanta*
  WLT - v78 - i3-4 - Sept-Dec 2004 - p139(1)
  [501+]
Djwa, Sandra - *Professing English: A Life of Roy Daniells*
  Can Lit - i182 - Autumn 2004 - p120(3) [501+]
d'Lacey, Chris - *Horace*
  y Sch Lib - v52 - i4 - Winter 2004 - p214(1) [51-
  500]
Dnes, Antony W. - *The Economics of Law: Property,
Contracts, and Obligations*
  R&R Bk N - v19 - i4 - Nov 2004 - p166(1) [501+]
  The Law and Economics of Marriage and Divorce
  JEL - v41 - i4 - Dec 2003 - p1309(3) [501+]
Do, Trinh Quang - *Saigon to San Diego: Memoir of a Boy
Who Escaped from Communist Vietnam*
  R&R Bk N - v19 - i4 - Nov 2004 - p48(1) [1-50]
Do Your ABC's, Little Brown Bear
  c PW - v252 - i5 - Jan 31 2005 - p69(2) [51-500]
Doak, Robin S. - *Cuba*
  c SLJ - v51 - i1 - Jan 2005 - p108(1) [51-500]
  Georgia
  c SLJ - v51 - i2 - Feb 2005 - p114(2) [51-500]
  Iran
  c SLJ - v51 - i1 - Jan 2005 - p108(1) [51-500]
  The United States
  c SLJ - v51 - i1 - Jan 2005 - p108(1) [51-500]
Doan Le - *The Cemetery of Chua Village and Other Stories
1st Ed.*
  KR - v72 - i23 - Dec 1 2004 - p1104(1) [501+]
Dobak, William A. - *The Black Regulars, 1866-1898*
  JAH - v91 - i1 - June 2004 - p259-260 [501+]
Dobbert, Duane L. - *Halting the Sexual Predators among
Us: Preventing Attack, Rape, and Lust Homicide*
  Bwatch - Feb 2005 - pNA [51-500]
  R&R Bk N - v19 - i4 - Nov 2004 - p145(1) [501+]
Dobbin, Murray - *Paul Martin: CEO for Canada?*
  CBRA - Annual 2003 - p43(1) [51-500]
Dobbins, James - *America's Role in Nation-Building:
From Germany to Iraq*
  R&R Bk N - v19 - i1 - Feb 2004 - p61(1) [501+]
Dobbins, James C. - *Letters of the Nun Eshinni: Images of
Pure Land Buddhism in Medieval Japan*
  R&R Bk N - v19 - i4 - Nov 2004 - p18(1) [51-
  500]
Dobbs, David - *Reef Madness: Charles Darwin, Alexander
Agassiz, and the Meaning of Coral*
  Am Sci - v93 - i2 - March-April 2005 - p177(1)
  [51-500]
  BL - v101 - i9-10 - Jan 1 2005 - p794(1) [51-500]
  KR - v72 - i23 - Dec 1 2004 - p1129(1) [51-500]
  PW - v251 - i47 - Nov 22 2004 - p47(1) [51-500]
Dobbs, Lou - *Exporting America: Why Corporate Greed Is
Shipping American Jobs Overseas*
  BL - v101 - i4 - Oct 15 2004 - p385(1) [51-500]
  NW - Oct 4 2004 - p38 [51-500]
Dobke, Dirk - *Dieter Roth: Books + Multiples: Catalogue
Raisonne*
  Choice - v42 - i3 - Nov 2004 - p471(1) [1-50]

Dobkin, Matt - *I Never Loved a Man the Way I Love You: Aretha Franklin, Respect, and the Making of a Soul Music Masterpiece*
   BL - v101 - i5 - Nov 1 2004 - p457(1) [51-500]
   PW - v251 - i41 - Oct 11 2004 - p66(1) [51-500]

Dobozy, Tamas - *When X Equals Marylou*
   CBRA - Annual 2003 - p198(1) [51-500]

Dobratz, Betty A. - *Research in Political Sociology, Vol. 12*
   CS - v33 - i5 - Sept 2004 - p587-589 [501+]
   Theoretical Directions in Political Sociology for the Twenty-First Century
   CS - v33 - i2 - March 2004 - p228-229 [501+]

Dobrenko, Evgeny - *The Landscape of Stalinism; The Art and Odeology of Soviet Space*
   Slav R - v63 - i4 - Winter 2004 - p907(2) [501+]
   The Making of the State Writer: Social and Aesthetic Origins of Soviet Literary Culture
   HNet - June 2004 - pNA [501+]
   Slav R - v63 - i2 - Summer 2004 - p445(1) [501+]

Dobres, Marcia-Anne - *Technology and Social Agency*
   T&C - v45 - i1 - Jan 2004 - p231(2) [501+]

Dobrow, Larry - *When Advertising Tried Harder*
   Globe & Mail - March 19 2005 - pD19 [51-500]

Dobrowolsky, Alexandra - *Women Making Constitutions: New Politics and Comparative Perspectives*
   Choice - v42 - i1 - Sept 2004 - p184(1) [501+]

Dobson, Alan P. - *US Economic Statecraft for Survival, 1933-1991: Of Sanction, Embargoes, and Economic Warfare*
   J Am St - v38 - i2 - August 2004 - p356(1) [501+]
   US Economic Statecraft for Survival, 1933-1991: Of Sanctions, Embargoes, and Economic Warfare
   J Am St - v38 - i2 - August 2004 - p356-357 [501+]
   JAH - v91 - i2 - Sept 2004 - p726(2) [501+]

Dobson, Andrew - *Citizenship and the Environment*
   PSQ - v119 - i2 - Summer 2004 - p396(2) [501+]

Dobson, Chris - *An Introduction to Online Company Research: Search Strategies, Case Study, Problems and Data Source Evaluations*
   Choice - v42 - i1 - Sept 2004 - p80(1) [501+]

Dobson, Christina - *Pizza Counting*
  c TC Math - v11 - i2 - Sept 2004 - p109(2) [51-500]

Dobson, David - *Irish Immigrants in North America, Pt. 6*
   EFHM - v58 - i3 - May-June 2004 - p57(1) [51-500]
   Scots in Poland, Russia, and the Baltic States
   EFHM - v58 - i2 - March-April 2004 - p89(1) [51-500]
   Scots in the Mid-Atlantic Colonies, 1635-1783
   EFHM - v58 - i3 - May-June 2004 - p57(1) [51-500]

Dobson, Michael - *England's Elizabeth: An Afterlife in Fame and Fantasy*
   AHR - v109 - i2 - April 2004 - p604(2) [501+]

Dobson, Ryan - *2Die4*
   PW - v251 - i28 - July 12 2004 - p59(1) [51-500]

Dobson, Sean - *Authority and Upheaval in Leipzig, 1910-1920: The Story of a Relationship*
   JMH - v76 - i3 - Sept 2004 - p719(3) [501+]

Dobson, Sebastian - *Art and Artifice: Japanese Photographs of the Meiji Era: Selections from the Jean S. and Fredrick A. Sharf Collection at the Museum of Fine Arts, Boston*
   Choice - v42 - i4 - Dec 2004 - p654(1) [1-50]

Dobson, Wendy - *World Capital Markets: Challenge to the G-10*
   JEL - v41 - i4 - Dec 2003 - p1293(2) [501+]

Dochartaigh, Pol O. - *Julius Pokorny, 1887-1970: Germans, Celts and nationalism*
   R&R Bk N - v19 - i1 - Feb 2004 - p34(1) [1-50]

Docherty, Iain - *A New Deal for Transport? The UK's Struggle with the Sustainable Transport Agenda*
   R&R Bk N - v19 - i1 - Feb 2004 - p104(1) [51-500]

Docherty, James C - *Historical Dictionary of Organized Labor 2nd Ed.*
   Choice - v42 - i2 - Oct 2004 - p274(1) [501+]

Dochterman, Joanne McCloskey - *Nursing Interventions Classification (NIC) 4th Ed.*
   SciTech - v28 - i1 - March 2004 - p125(1) [1-50]

Dockery, Kevin - *Navy SEALs: A History*
   Kliatt - v38 - i6 - Nov 2004 - p37(1) [51-500]

Doctorow, Cory - *Someone Comes to Town, Someone Leaves Town*
   KR - v73 - i5 - March 1 2005 - p266(2) [51-500]
   PW - v252 - i10 - March 7 2005 - p54(1) [51-500]

Doctorow, E.L. - *Sweet Land Stories*
   NYTBR - July 4 2004 - p18 [501+]

Docx, Edward - *The Calligrapher*
   NYTBR - March 13 2005 - p32 [501+]

Dodd, C. Kenneth - *The Amphibians of Great Smoky Mountains National Park*
   Choice - v42 - i5 - Jan 2005 - p880(1) [1-50]
   SciTech - v28 - i3 - Sept 2004 - p65(1) [51-500]

Dodd, Clement - *Storm Clouds over Cyprus: A Briefing*
   IJMES - v36 - i1 - Feb 2004 - p147-148 [501+]

Dodd, Gwilym - *Henry IV: The Establishment of the Regime, 1399-1406*
   Albion - v36 - i2 - Summer 2004 - p284(3) [501+]

Dodd, Mike - *An Autobiography of Sorts*
   Ceram Mo - v52 - i10 - Dec 2004 - p66(1) [501+]

Dodd, Patton - *My Faith So Far: A Story of Conversion and Confusion*
   BL - v101 - i5 - Nov 1 2004 - p445(1) [51-500]
   Ch Today - v49 - i1 - Jan 2005 - p71(3) [501+]
   LJ - v129 - i20 - Dec 1 2004 - p124(1) [51-500]
   PW - v251 - i41 - Oct 11 2004 - p76(1) [51-500]

Dodd, Quentin - *The Princess of Neptune*
  c BL - v101 - i5 - Nov 1 2004 - p482(2) [51-500]
  c CCB-B - v58 - i2 - Oct 2004 - p69(1) [51-500]
  y Kliatt - v38 - i5 - Sept 2004 - p7(3) [51-500]
  c KR - v72 - i16 - August 15 2004 - p805(1) [51-500]
  c PW - v251 - i41 - Oct 11 2004 - p80(1) [51-500]
  c SLJ - v50 - i10 - Oct 2004 - p161(1) [51-500]

Dodd, Wayne - *Is: Poems*
   ABR - v25 - i5 - July-August 2004 - p17(2) [501+]

Dodds, Bill - *Managing Customer Value: Essentials of Product Quality, Customer Service, and Price Decisions*
   R&R Bk N - v19 - i1 - Feb 2004 - p108(1) [51-500]

Dodds, Dayle Ann - *The Great Divide: A Mathematical Marathon (Illus. by Mitchell, Tracy)*
  c PW - v252 - i6 - Feb 7 2005 - p62(1) [51-500]
   Henry's Amazing Machine (Illus. by Brooker, Kyrsten)
  c BL - v101 - i1 - Sept 1 2004 - p130(1) [1-50]
  c CCB-B - v58 - i2 - Oct 2004 - p69(2) [51-500]
  c HB - v80 - i4 - July-August 2004 - p436(1) [51-500]
  c KR - v72 - i13 - July 1 2004 - p627(1) [51-500]
  c PW - v251 - i35 - August 30 2004 - p53(2) [51-500]
  c SLJ - v50 - i9 - Sept 2004 - p158(1) [51-500]
   Minnie's Diner: A Multiplying Menu (Illus. by Manders, John)
  c BL - v100 - i22 - August 2004 - p1941(1) [51-500]
  c HB - v81 - i1 - Jan-Feb 2005 - p75(1) [51-500]
  c KR - v72 - i14 - July 15 2004 - p683(1) [51-500]
  c PW - v251 - i36 - Sept 6 2004 - p62(1) [51-500]
  c SLJ - v50 - i8 - August 2004 - p85(1) [51-500]

dodds, Dayle Ann - *Where's Pup (Illus. by Pratt, Pierre)*
  c CBRA - Annual 2003 - p450(1) [51-500]

Dodds, Felix - *How to Lobby at Intergovernmental Meetings: Mine's a Caffe Latte*
   R&R Bk N - v19 - i3 - August 2004 - p188(1) [501+]

Dodds, Klaus - *Pink Ice: Britain and the South Atlantic Empire*
   Albion - v36 - i2 - Summer 2004 - p391(2) [501+]

Dodds, Linda J. - *Drugs in Use: Clinical Case Studies for Pharmacists, 3rd Ed.*
   E-Streams - Sept 2004 - pNA [501+]

Dodds, Robert - *The Secret of Iguando*
  c Sch Lib - v52 - i3 - Autumn 2004 - p136(2) [501+]

Dodelson, Scott - *Modern Cosmology*
   Phys Today - v57 - i7 - July 2004 - p60-61 [501+]

Dodge, Abigail Johnson - *The Weekend Baker: Irresistible Recipes, Simple Techniques, and Stress-Free Stragegies for Busy People*
   PW - v251 - i41 - Oct 11 2004 - p70(1) [51-500]

Dodge, Clayton W. - *Euclidean Geometry and Transformations*
   SciTech - v28 - i3 - Sept 2004 - p41(1) [1-50]

Dodge, Mary - *Stealing Dreams: A Fertility Clinic Scandal*
   Choice - v41 - i7 - March 2004 - p1326(2) [501+]

Dodge, Toby - *Globalisation and the Middle East: Islam, Economy, Society and Politics*
   AJPS - v39 - i3 - Nov 2004 - p670(2) [501+]
   Inventing Iraq: The Failure of Nation-Building and a History Denied
   AHR - v109 - i4 - Oct 2004 - p1346-1347 [501+]
   APJ - v18 - i3 - Fall 2004 - p119(3) [501+]
   R&R Bk N - v19 - i1 - Feb 2004 - p41(1) [51-500]
   TLS - i5263 - Feb 13 2004 - p6-6 [501+]

Dodge, Yadolah - *The Oxford Dictionary of Statistical Terms*
   R&R Bk N - v19 - i1 - Feb 2004 - p77(1) [1-50]

Dodonov, V.V. - *Theory of Nonclassical States of Light*
   E-Streams - Nov 2004 - pNA [501+]
   SciTech - v28 - i1 - March 2004 - p49(1) [51-500]

Dodson, Aidan - *The Complete Royal Families of Ancient Egypt*
   Choice - v42 - i5 - Jan 2005 - p834(1) [1-50]

Dodson, James - *Ben Hogan: A Life*
   Spec - v296 - Dec 18 2004 - p86(2) [501+]
   Ben Hogan: An American Life
   BL - v101 - i1 - Sept 1 2004 - p46(1) [51-500]
   Choice - v42 - i4 - Dec 2004 - p698(2) [1-50]

Dodson, Peter - *The Dinosauria 2nd Ed.*
   Sci - v307 - i5709 - Jan 28 2005 - p520(1) [501+]

Doe, Mimi - *Nurturing Your Teenager's Soul: A Practical Approach to Raising a Kind, Honorable, Compassionate Teen*
   LJ - v129 - i20 - Dec 1 2004 - p153(1) [51-500]

Doeringer, Peter R. - *Start-Up Factories: High Performance Management, Job Quality, and Regional Advantage*
   JEL - v42 - i1 - March 2004 - p209(2) [501+]

Doerksen, Daniel W. - *Centered on the Word: Literature, Scripture, and the Tudor-Stuart Middle Way*
   Choice - v42 - i1 - Sept 2004 - p99(1) [501+]

Doern, G. Bruce - *Power Switch: Energy Regulatory Governance in the Twenty-First Century*
   CBRA - Annual 2003 - p412(2) [501+]
   Choice - v41 - i11-12 - July-August 2004 - p2091(1) [501+]
   R&R Bk N - v19 - i2 - May 2004 - p107(1) [51-500]

Doerr, Anthony - *About Grace*
   BL - v100 - i22 - August 2004 - p1897(1) [51-500]
   BW - v34 - i42 - Oct 17 2004 - p6(1) [501+]
   Ent W - i785 - Sept 24 2004 - p114 [51-500]
   KR - v72 - i16 - August 15 2004 - p760(1) [51-500]
   LJ - v129 - i17 - Oct 15 2004 - p53(1) [51-500]
   NYTBR - Nov 7 2004 - p29 [501+]
   PW - v251 - i35 - August 30 2004 - p29(1) [501+]
   Spec - v297 - i9208 - Jan 29 2005 - p35(2) [501+]

Doerr, Marilyn N. - *Currere and the Environmental Autobiography: A Phenomenological Approach to the Teaching of Ecology*
   SciTech - v28 - i3 - Sept 2004 - p60(1) [1-50]

Doerries, Reinhard R. - *Diplomaten und Agenten: Nachrichtendienste in der Geschichte der Deutsch-Amerikanischen Beziehungen*
   GSR - v27 - i3 - Oct 2004 - p630(2) [501+]
   Hitler's Last Chief of Foreign Intelligence: Allied Interrogations of Walter Schellenberg
   R&R Bk N - v19 - i1 - Feb 2004 - p36(1) [1-50]

Does, Willem van der - *Storms, Ice, and Whales: The Antarctic Adventures of a Dutch Artist on a Norwegian Whaler*
   R&R Bk N - v19 - i1 - Feb 2004 - p69(1) [501+]

Dog Artist Collection (Firm) (Book) - *The Dog from Arf! Arf! to Zzzzzz*
  c SLJ - v50 - i7 - July 2004 - p92(1) [51-500]

Dogantan, Mine - *Mathis Lussy: A Pioneer in Studies of Expressive Performance*
   R&R Bk N - v19 - i2 - May 2004 - p191(1) [51-500]

Dohan, Daniel - *The Price of Poverty: Money, Work, and Culture in the Mexican American Barrio*
   Choice - v42 - i1 - Sept 2004 - p193(2) [501+]

Dohaney, M.T. - *The Corrigan Women. Audiobook Review*
   Globe & Mail - Dec 4 2004 - pD38 [1-50]

Doherty, Berlie - *The Nutcracker (Illus. by Beck, Ian)*
  c KR - v72 - i21 - Nov 1 2004 - p1049(1) [51-500]
   The Star Burster
  c Sch Lib - v52 - i4 - Winter 2004 - p201(1) [51-500]

Doherty, Brian - *This Is Burning Man: The Rise of a New American Underground*
   BL - v100 - i22 - August 2004 - p1879(1) [51-500]
   KR - v72 - i13 - July 1 2004 - p615(1) [501+]
   NYTBR - Sept 19 2004 - p14 [501+]
   PW - v251 - i27 - July 5 2004 - p49(1) [51-500]

Doherty, Daniel - *Voluntary Simplicity: Responding to Consumer Culture*
   Choice - v42 - i2 - Oct 2004 - p308(1) [501+]

Doherty, Gerrard - *Current Consult Surgery*
   SciTech - v28 - i4 - Dec 2004 - p107(1) [501+]

Doherty, Gillian M. - *Irish Ordnance Survey: History, Culture and Memory*
   R&R Bk N - v19 - i4 - Nov 2004 - p74(1) [51-500]

Doherty, Kieran - *Voyageurs, Lumberjacks, and Farmers: Pioneers of the Midwest*
  c SLJ - v50 - i9 - Sept 2004 - p225(1) [51-500]

Doherty, Michael - *Those Tender Mayfly Childhood Sweetheart Games*
   South CR - v36 - i2 - Spring 2004 - p47-59 [501+]

Doherty, P.C. - *Alexander the Great: The Death of a God*
TLS - i5297 - Oct 8 2004 - p4-5 [501+]
The Death of Alexander the Great
BL - v101 - i3 - Oct 1 2004 - p296(1) [51-500]
Globe & Mail - Nov 20 2004 - pD5 [501+]
KR - v72 - i17 - Sept 1 2004 - p846(2) [501+]
The Hangman's Hymn: The Carpenter's Tale of Mystery and Murder as He Goes on a Pilgrimage from London to Canterbury
BL - v101 - i8 - Dec 15 2004 - p710(1) [51-500]
KR - v72 - i24 - Dec 15 2004 - p1166(1) [501+]
PW - v251 - i46 - Nov 15 2004 - p44(1) [51-500]

Doherty, Richard - *Ireland's Generals in the Second World War.*
R&R Bk N - v20 - i1 - Feb 2005 - p32(1) [51-500]

Doherty, Robert - *Bodyguard of Lies*
KR - v73 - i2 - Jan 15 2005 - p68(1) [51-500]

Doherty, Thomas - *Cold War, Cool Medium: Television, McCarthism, and American Culture*
T&C - v45 - i4 - Oct 2004 - p888(2) [501+]
Cold War, Cool Medium: Television, McCarthyism, and American Culture
JAH - v91 - i2 - Sept 2004 - p701(1) [501+]
R&R Bk N - v19 - i1 - Feb 2004 - p223(1) [51-500]
TV Q - v34 - i2 - Wntr 2004 - p73-76 [501+]

Doherty-Wayne, C.H. - *The Book of Broken Hours*
y Res Links - v10 - i3 - Feb 2005 - p34(2) [51-500]

Doig, Ivan - *This House of Sky: Landscapes of a Western Mind*
A Lib - v35 - i7 - August 2004 - p88(1) [501+]
The Writing Life
BW - v34 - i3 - Jan 18 2004 - p10(1) [501+]

Doin, Sophie - *La Famille noire, suivie de trois nouvelles blanches et noires*
NCFS - v32 - i3-4 - Spring-Summer 2004 - p365(3) [501+]

Doing Business in 2004: Understanding Regulation
JEL - v42 - i1 - March 2004 - p289(1) [501+]

Doka, Kenneth J. - *Alzheimer's Disease*
Choice - v42 - i2 - Oct 2004 - p324(1) [51-500]

Dokecki, Paul R. - *The Clergy Sexual Abuse Crisis: Reform and Renewal in the Catholic Community.*
Choice - v42 - i3 - Nov 2004 - p499(1) [51-500]

Dokey, Cameron - *Sunlight and Shadow*
y Kliatt - v38 - i5 - Sept 2004 - p28(2) [51-500]
y SLJ - v50 - i11 - Nov 2004 - p142(1) [51-500]
VOYA - v27 - i5 - Dec 2004 - p402(1) [51-500]

Dolan, Anne - *Commemorating the Irish Civil War: History and Memory, 1923-2000*
ILS - v24 - i1 - Fall 2004 - p9(1) [501+]
J Mil H - v68 - i4 - Oct 2004 - p1278-1280 [501+]

Dolan, Brian - *Josiah Wedgwood: Entrepreneur to the Enlightenment*
New Sci - v184 - Dec 25 2004 - p77(1) [501+]
Wedgwood: The First Tycoon
BL - v101 - i4 - Oct 15 2004 - p385(1) [501+]
BW - v34 - i43 - Oct 24 2004 - p9(1) [501+]
KR - v72 - i16 - August 15 2004 - p785(1) [501+]
NYTBR - Nov 14 2004 - p53(L) [501+]
PW - v251 - i33 - August 16 2004 - p53(1) [51-500]

Dolan, Edward F. - *The American Indian Wars*
LibMed - v22 - i7 - April-May 2004 - p71(1) [501+]

Dolan, Jay P. - *In Search of an American Catholicism: A History of Religion and Culture in Tension*
J Am St - v38 - i1 - April 2004 - p141-142 [501+]

Dolan, Kathleen A. - *Voting for Women: How the Public Evaluates Women Candidates*
R&R Bk N - v19 - i1 - Feb 2004 - p132(1) [51-500]

Dolan, Penny - *Moo! (Illus. by Sharp, Melanie)*
c SLJ - v51 - i1 - Jan 2005 - p90(1) [51-500]

Dolan, Robert W. - *Facial Plastic, Reconstructive, and Trauma Surgery*
SciTech - v28 - i1 - March 2004 - p111(1) [51-500]

Dolbeare, Kenneth M. - *American Political Thought, 5th Ed.*
R&R Bk N - v19 - i3 - August 2004 - p173(1) [501+]

Dole, Bob - *One Soldier's Story (Read by Hecht, Paul). Audiobook Review*
LJ - v129 - i20 - Dec 1 2004 - p90(2) [1-50]

Dole, John M. - *Butterflies of Oklahoma, Kansas, and North Texas*
E-Streams - Nov 2004 - pNA [501+]

Dole, Mayra L. - *Birthday in the Barrio (Illus. by Tonel)*
c BL - v101 - i2 - Sept 15 2004 - p248(1) [51-500]
c CH Bwatch - v14 - i12 - Dec 2004 - pNA [51-500]
c CH Bwatch - Jan 2005 - pNA [51-500]
c KR - v72 - i13 - July 1 2004 - p627(1) [51-500]
c SLJ - v50 - i9 - Sept 2004 - p196(1) [51-500]

Dolezal, Robert J. - *Birds in Your Backyard: A Bird Lover's Guide to Creating a Garden Sanctuary*
LJ - v129 - i18 - Nov 1 2004 - p111(1) [51-500]
PW - v251 - i39 - Sept 27 2004 - p52(1) [51-500]

Dolfsma, Wilfred - *Globalization, Social Capital and Inequality: Contested Concepts, Contested Experiences*
JEL - v41 - i4 - Dec 2003 - p1442(1) [501+]
Institutional Economics and the Formation of Preferences: The Advent of Pop Music
Choice - v42 - i5 - Jan 2005 - p901(1) [1-50]
R&R Bk N - v19 - i4 - Nov 2004 - p197(1) [501+]

Dolin, Eric Jay - *Political Waters: The Long, Dirty, Contentious, Incredibly Expensive, but Eventually Triumphant History of Boston Harbor A Unique Environmental Success Story*
Bwatch - Feb 2005 - pNA [51-500]
Political Waters: The Long, Dirty, Contentious, Incredibly Expensive, but Eventually Triumphant History of Boston Harbor--A Unique Environmental Success Story
SciTech - v28 - i3 - Sept 2004 - p145(1) [51-500]

Doll, Beth - *Resilient Classrooms: Creating Healthy Environments for Learning*
R&R Bk N - v19 - i4 - Nov 2004 - p193(1) [501+]

Doll Jewelry
c PW - v252 - i8 - Feb 21 2005 - p177(1) [501+]

Doll, William E., Jr. - *Curriculum Visions*
TCR - v106 - i5 - May 2004 - p895(3) [501+]

Dolman, Claude E. - *Suppressing the Diseases of Animals and Man: Theobald Smith, Microbiologist*
Choice - v41 - i7 - March 2004 - p1316(1) [501+]
Isis - v95 - i3 - Sept 2004 - p527(1) [501+]

Dolnick, Edward - *Down the Great Unknown: John Wesley Powell's 1869 Journey of Discovery and Tragedy through the Grand Canyon*
NRJ - v44 - i1 - Wntr 2004 - p319-332 [501+]

Dolnick, Sandy - *The Essential Friends of Libraries: Fast Facts, Forms, and Tips*
LJ - v130 - i1 - Jan 1 2005 - p160(1) [51-500]

Dolphin, Paul - *Bend in the Willows: The Art of Making Rustic Furniture*
CBRA - Annual 2003 - p124(1) [51-500]

Dolphins
c SB - v40 - i4 - July-August 2004 - p176(2) [51-500]

Doltsinis, Ioannis - *Large Deformation Processes of Solids: From Fundamentals to Numerical Simulation and Engineering Applications*
SciTech - v28 - i3 - Sept 2004 - p139(1) [51-500]

Dolzani, Michael - *The "Third Book" Notebooks of Northrop Frye: 1964-1972*
Can Lit - i181 - Summer 2004 - p123-124 [501+]

Domach, Michael M. - *Introduction to Biomedical Engineering*
SciTech - v28 - i1 - March 2004 - p80(1) [51-500]

Domaradskij, Igor V. - *Biowarrior: Inside the Soviet/Russian Biological War Machine*
Choice - v41 - i7 - March 2004 - p1316(2) [501+]
Isis - v95 - i3 - Sept 2004 - p527(2) [501+]

Domarus, Max - *Hitler: Speeches and Proclamations, 1932-1945 and Commentary by a Contemporary, Vol. 4*
R&R Bk N - v19 - i3 - August 2004 - p43(1) [51-500]

Dombek, George - *Airbrush Illustration for Architecture*
R&R Bk N - v19 - i1 - Feb 2004 - p203(1) [51-500]

Dombrowski, Daniel A. - *Divine Beauty:The Aesthetics of Charles Hartshorne*
R&R Bk N - v19 - i3 - August 2004 - p5(1) [1-50]

Domenicani, David - *M Is for Majestic: A National Parks Alphabet (Illus. by Carroll, Pamela)*
c LibMed - v22 - i5 - Feb 2004 - p63(1) [501+]

Domenici, Pete V. - *A Brighter Tomorrow: Fulfilling the Promise of Nuclear Energy*
Choice - v42 - i6 - Feb 2005 - p1052(2) [51-500]

Domhoff, William G. - *Changing the Powers That Be, How the Left Can Stop Losing and Win*
Dis - v51 - i1 - Wntr 2004 - p132(2) [501+]

Dominelli, Lena - *Broadening Horizons: International Exchanges in Social Work*
R&R Bk N - v19 - i1 - Feb 2004 - p135(1) [51-500]
Social Work: Theory and Practice for a Changing Profession, 1st Ed.
TimHES - v0 - i1680 - Feb 25 2005 - pV(1) [501+]

Dominguez, Jorge I. - *Mexico's Pivotal Democracy Election: Candidates, Voters, Campaign Effects, and the Presidential Campaign of 2000*
R&R Bk N - v19 - i1 - Feb 2004 - pNA [501+]

Domiteaux, Diane - *Washoe Seasons of Life: A Native American Story (Illus. by Saling, Lea)*
c CH Bwatch - v14 - i7 - July 2004 - p4(1) [51-500]

Domjan, Michael - *The Essentials of Conditioning and Learning, 3rd Ed.*
SciTech - v28 - i4 - Dec 2004 - p3(1) [1-50]

Domke, David - *God Willing*
Tikkun - v20 - i1 - Jan-Feb 2005 - p73(2) [501+]

Domm, Kristin Bieber - *Hatchling's Journey*
c CBRA - Annual 2003 - p564(1) [51-500]

Dommen, Arthur J. - *The Indochinese Experience of the French and the Americans: Nationalism and Communism in Cambodia, Laos, and Vietnam*
APH - v51 - i3 - Fall 2004 - p49(1) [501+]

Donabedian, Martin - *Spacecraft Thermal Control Handbook Vol. 2*
SciTech - v28 - i1 - March 2004 - p170(1) [51-500]

Donaghy, Greg - *Tolerant Allies: Canada and the United States, 1963-1968*
HNet - Sept 2004 - pNA [501+]

Donahue, Brenda - *C.G. Jung's Complex Dynamics and the Clinical Relationship: One Map for Mystery*
SciTech - v28 - i1 - March 2004 - p102(1) [51-500]

Donahue, Brian - *The Great Meadow: Farmers and the Land in Colonial Concord*
Choice - v42 - i2 - Oct 2004 - p354(1) [51-500]
W&M Q - v62 - i1 - Jan 2005 - p123-3 [501+]

Donahue, David M. - *Teaching as Principled Practice: Managing Complexity for Social Justice*
R&R Bk N - v19 - i4 - Nov 2004 - p182(1) [501+]

Donahue, Neil H. - *Karl Krolow and the Poetics of Amnesia in Postwar Germany*
Ger Q - v77 - i1 - Wntr 2004 - p110(2) [501+]
GSR - v27 - i1 - Feb 2004 - p214-215 [501+]

Donald, Benson C. - *A Smoother Pebble: Mathematical Explorations*
Choice - v42 - i1 - Sept 2004 - p141(1) [501+]

Donald, Chris - *Rude Kids: The Unfeasible Story of Viz*
NS - v133 - i4715 - Nov 22 2004 - p52(2) [501+]
NS - v133 - i4716 - Nov 29 2004 - p43(1) [51-500]
Spec - v297 - i9206 - Jan 15 2005 - p47(1) [501+]

Donald, David Herbert - *"We Are Lincoln Men": Abraham Lincoln and His Friends*
JAH - v91 - i3 - Dec 2004 - p1022(2) [501+]

Donald, Janet Gail - *Learning to Think: Disciplinary Perspectives*
J Hi E - v75 - i4 - July-August 2004 - p476(5) [501+]

Donaldson, Dave - *A Revolution of Compassion: Faith-Based Groups as Full Partners in Fighting America's Social Problems*
Bks & Cult - v10 - i5 - Sept-Oct 2004 - p32(1) [501+]
CC - v121 - i17 - August 24 2004 - p27(7) [501+]

Donaldson, Gary - *Liberalism's Last Hurrah: The Presidential Campaign of 1964*
JSH - v70 - i3 - August 2004 - p723(2) [501+]

Donaldson, Julia - *The Gruffalo's Child (Illus. by Scheffler, Axel)*
c HB - v81 - i1 - Jan-Feb 2005 - p75(2) [51-500]
c PW - v251 - i50 - Dec 13 2004 - p68(1) [51-500]
Sharing a Shell
c Sch Lib - v52 - i4 - Winter 2004 - p186(1) [51-500]
The Snail and the Whale
c BooChiTr - March 28 2004 - p2(1) [501+]
The Spiffiest Giant in Town (Illus. by Scheffler, Axel)
c PW - v252 - i2 - Jan 10 2005 - p58(1) [1-50]

Donaldson, Madeline - *Africa*
c SLJ - v51 - i1 - Jan 2005 - p108(1) [51-500]
Australia
c SLJ - v51 - i1 - Jan 2005 - p108(1) [51-500]
North America
c SLJ - v51 - i1 - Jan 2005 - p108(1) [51-500]

Donaldson, Michael C. - *Clearance and Copyright: Everything the Independent Filmmaker Needs to Know, 2nd Ed.*
R&R Bk N - v19 - i1 - Feb 2004 - pNA [51-500]

Donaldson, Stephen R. - *The Last Chronicles of Thomas Covenant: The Runes of Earth*
MFSF - v108 - i2 - Feb 2005 - p44(6) [501+]
The Man Who Tried to Get Away
LJ - v129 - i18 - Nov 1 2004 - p60(1) [51-500]
PW - v251 - i43 - Oct 25 2004 - p31(1) [51-500]

The Runes of the Earth (Read by Brick, Scott).
Audiobook Review
    BL - v101 - i9-10 - Jan 1 2005 - p886(1) [51-500]
The Runes of the Earth
    BL - v101 - i1 - Sept 1 2004 - p4(1) [51-500]
    Ent W - i788 - Oct 15 2004 - p80 [51-500]
    LJ - v129 - i17 - Oct 15 2004 - p57(1) [51-500]
    PW - v251 - i39 - Sept 27 2004 - p42(1) [51-500]
Donaldson, Thomas E. - *Konark*
    JAS - v63 - i3 - August 2004 - p823-825 [501+]
Donat, Sebastian - *"Es klang aber fast wie deine Lieder..."*
Die russischen Nachdichtungen aus Goethes
"Westostlichem Divan"
    Slav R - v63 - i2 - Summer 2004 - p431(2) [501+]
Donatelli, Robert A. - *Physical Therapy of the Shoulder*
4th Ed.
    SciTech - v28 - i1 - March 2004 - p112(1) [51-500]
Donati, Sara - *Fire Along the Sky*
    BL - v100 - i22 - August 2004 - p1868(1) [51-500]
    LJ - v129 - i16 - Oct 1 2004 - p68(1) [51-500]
    PW - v251 - i33 - August 16 2004 - p44(2) [51-500]
Donatich, John - *Ambivalence, a Love Story: Portrait of a Marriage*
    BL - v101 - i6 - Nov 15 2004 - p536(1) [51-500]
    KR - v72 - i21 - Nov 1 2004 - p1036(1) [501+]
    NYTBR - Jan 23 2005 - p30 [501+]
Donegan, Patricia - *Haiku*
    c SLJ - v50 - i8 - August 2004 - p134(2) [51-500]
Dongala, Emmanuel - *Johnny Mad Dog*
    PW - v252 - i11 - March 14 2005 - p43(1) [51-500]
Dongman, Debbie Guice - *College Learning and Study Skills, 7th Ed.*
    R&R Bk N - v19 - i3 - August 2004 - p222(1) [1-50]
Dongsu, Kim - *An Exegesis of Apostasy Embedded in John's Narratives of Peter and Judas Against the Synoptic parallels*
    R&R Bk N - v19 - i3 - August 2004 - p25(1) [1-50]
Donini, Antonio - *Nation-Building Unraveled? Aid, Peace and Justice in Afghanistan*
    R&R Bk N - v19 - i1 - Feb 2004 - p46(1) [51-500]
Nation-Building Unravelled? Aid, Peace and Justice in Afghanistan
    JPR - v41 - i6 - Nov 2004 - p755-756 [501+]
Donkin, Andrew - *William Shakespeare and His Dramatic Acts*
    Sch Lib - v52 - i3 - Autumn 2004 - p150(1) [501+]
Donkin, R.A. - *Between East and West: The Moluccas and the Traffic in Spices up to the Arrival of the Europeans*
    R&R Bk N - v19 - i3 - August 2004 - p118(1) [51-500]
Donlon, Diane Y. - *Balancing on a Rock*
    CH Bwatch - v14 - i8 - August 2004 - p8(1) [51-500]
Donnan, Christopher B. - *Moche Portraits from Ancient Peru*
    Choice - v42 - i5 - Jan 2005 - p895(1) [1-50]
Donnell, Sidney - *Feminizing the Enemy: Imperial Spain, Transvestite Drama, and the Crisis of Masculinity*
    Ren Q - v57 - i4 - Winter 2004 - p1411(3) [501+]
    R&R Bk N - v19 - i1 - Feb 2004 - p228(1) [51-500]
Donnelly, Brian - *Socialist Emigre: Marxism and the Later Tillich*
    R&R Bk N - v19 - i1 - Feb 2004 - p25(1) [1-50]
Donnelly, Denise A. - *Culture of Prejudice: Arguments in Critical Social Science*
    CS - v33 - i5 - Sept 2004 - p535-536 [501+]
Donnelly, Gerard - *Technological Issues in Broadcast Education: Critical Challenges*
    R&R Bk N - v19 - i1 - Feb 2004 - p223(1) [51-500]
Donnelly, Ignatius - *Destruction of Atlantis*
    Bwatch - v26 - i9 - Sept 2004 - p2(1) [51-500]
Donnelly, James S., Jr. - *Encyclopedia of Irish History and Culture*
    LJ - v130 - i1 - Jan 1 2005 - p154(1) [51-500]
Donnelly, Jennifer - *A Northern Light*
    Kliatt - v38 - i6 - Nov 2004 - p16(1) [51-500]
    y PW - v251 - i40 - Oct 4 2004 - p90(1) [51-500]
    y SLJ - v50 - i11 - Nov 2004 - p66(2) [51-500]
Donnelly, John Patrick - *The Office of a Bishop*
    Six Ct J - v34 - i4 - Winter 2003 - p1204-1205 [501+]
Donnelly, K.J. - *Film Music*
    FQ - v57 - i4 - Summer 2004 - p54(2) [51-500]

Donnelly, Marcos - *Letters from the Flesh*
    BIC - v33 - i7 - Oct 2004 - p17(1) [501+]
    BL - v101 - i3 - Oct 1 2004 - p318(1) [51-500]
Donnelly, Mary Queen - *Skills for Consumer Success 5th Ed.*
    R&R Bk N - v19 - i2 - May 2004 - p116(1) [51-500]
Donnelly, Patrick - *The Charge*
    Ant R - v63 - i1 - Wntr 2005 - p193(1) [501+]
Donninghaus, Victor - *Die Deutschen in der Moskauer Gesellschaft. Symbiose und Konflikte*
    JMH - v77 - i1 - March 2005 - p246(3) [501+]
Revolution, Reform und Krieg: Die Deutschen an der Wolga im ausgehenden Zarenreich
    Slav R - v63 - i2 - Summer 2004 - p406(2) [501+]
Donoghue, Daniel - *Lady Godiva: A Literary History of the Legend*
    Albion - v36 - i1 - Spring 2004 - p90(2) [501+]
Old English Literature: A Short Introduction
    Choice - v42 - i2 - Oct 2004 - p292(1) [501+]
Donoghue, Denis - *Speaking of Beauty*
    Sew R - v111 - i4 - Fall 2003 - pcxxvii-cxxix [501+]
Donoghue, Emma - *Life Mask*
    BL - v101 - i1 - Sept 1 2004 - p60(1) [51-500]
    BW - v34 - i41 - Oct 10 2004 - p10(1) [501+]
    Ent W - i778 - August 13 2004 - p92 [51-500]
    Globe & Mail - July 31 2004 - pD3 [501+]
    KR - v72 - i13 - July 1 2004 - p592(1) [501+]
    Lam Bk Rpt - v13 - i4-5 - Nov-Dec 2004 - p36(2) [501+]
    LJ - v129 - i15 - Sept 15 2004 - p48(1) [51-500]
    NYTBR - Sept 26 2004 - p22 [501+]
    PW - v251 - i30 - July 26 2004 - p38(1) [501+]
    Advocate - Nov 23 2004 - p95(1) [501+]
Donoghue, Philip C.J. - *Telling the Evolutionary Time: Molecular Clocks and the Fossil Record*
    Choice - v41 - i11-12 - July-August 2004 - p2071(1) [501+]
    QRB - v79 - i4 - Dec 2004 - p413(2) [501+]
Donohue, John J. - *The Buwayhid Dynasty in Iraq 334 H./945 to 403 H./1012: Shaping Institutions for the Future*
    IJMES - v36 - i3 - August 2004 - p474-475 [501+]
Deshi
    KR - v73 - i1 - Jan 1 2005 - p22(1) [51-500]
    PW - v252 - i4 - Jan 24 2005 - p224(2) [501+]
Donohue, Kathleen G. - *Freedom from Want: American Liberalism and the Idea of the Consumer*
    Choice - v42 - i1 - Sept 2004 - p187(1) [501+]
Donovan, Chris - *Difficult Consultations with Adolescents*
    SciTech - v28 - i3 - Sept 2004 - p119(1) [51-500]
Donovan, Fiona - *Rubens and England*
    Choice - v42 - i7 - March 2005 - p1217(1) [51-500]
    LJ - v129 - i20 - Dec 1 2004 - p112(1) [51-500]
Donovan, Karen - *V. Goliath: The Trials of David Boies.*
    KR - v72 - i24 - Dec 15 2004 - p1178(1) [501+]
    LJ - v130 - i3 - Feb 15 2005 - p146(1) [51-500]
V. Goliath : The Trials of David Boies
    PW - v252 - i5 - Jan 31 2005 - p60(1) [501+]
Donovan, Sandy - *The Channel Tunnel*
    c TES - v0 - i4587 - June 11 2004 - pssss29(1) [501+]
Making Laws: A Look at How a Bill Becomes a Law
    c SLJ - v50 - i8 - August 2004 - p48(2) [51-500]
Running for Office: A Look at Political Campaigns
    y Teach Lib - v32 - i1 - Oct 2004 - p20(1) [51-500]
Donovan, Sierra - *Love on the Air*
    BL - v101 - i7 - Dec 1 2004 - p641(1) [51-500]
Donovan, Therese M. - *Spreadsheet Exercises in Ecology and Evolution*
    Am Bio T - v66 - i4 - April 2004 - p305(306) [501+]
Donskis, Leonidas - *Forms of Hatred: The Troubled Imagination in Modern Philosophy and Literature*
    RM - v58 - i1 - Sept 2004 - p175(2) [501+]
Don't Fret Finger Position Decals. Audiobook Review
    Teach Mus - v12 - i2 - Oct 2004 - p70(1) [51-500]
Doob, Anthony N. - *Responding to Youth Crime in Canada*
    R&R Bk N - v19 - i3 - August 2004 - p170(1) [501+]
Dood, Gwilym - *Henry IV: The Establishment of the Regime, 1399-1406*
    HER - v119 - i483 - Sept 2004 - p989(991) [501+]
Dooge, James C.I. - *Deterministic Methods in Systems Hydrology*
    E-Streams - Dec 2004 - pNA [501+]
Doole, Isobel - *International Marketing Strategy: Analysis, Development and Implementation, 4th Ed.*
    TimHES - v0 - i1680 - Feb 25 2005 - pIX(1) [501+]

Strategic Marketing Decisions in Global Markets, 1st Ed.
    TimHES - v0 - i1680 - Feb 25 2005 - pIX(1) [501+]
Dooley, Edwin L., Jr. - *The Soldier at the Crossroad: The 726th MP Battalion in World War II*
    J Mil H - v68 - i3 - July 2004 - p1002-1003 [501+]
Dooley, Kevin - *Cisco Cookbook*
    SciTech - v28 - i1 - March 2004 - p156(1) [51-500]
Dooley, Mark - *A Passion for the Impossible: John D. Caputo in Focus*
    JAAR - v72 - i3 - Sept 2004 - p774-780 [501+]
Dooley, Michael P. - *Managing Currency Crises in Emerging Markets*
    JEL - v42 - i4 - Dec 2004 - p1132(3) [501+]
Doonan, Owen P. - *Sinop Lnadscapes: Exploring Connection in a Black Sea Hinterland*
    Choice - v42 - i4 - Dec 2004 - p702(1) [1-50]
Dooyeweerd, Herman - *Reformation and Scholasticism in Philosophy Vol. 1*
    R&R Bk N - v19 - i4 - Nov 2004 - p7(1) [51-500]
Dor, Daniel - *Intifada Hits the Headlines: How the Israeli Press Misreported the Outbreak of the Second Palestinian Uprising*
    Choice - v42 - i2 - Oct 2004 - p287(1) [51-500]
    MEJ - v58 - i4 - Autumn 2004 - p706(1) [501+]
Dorais, Michel - *Dead Boys Can't Dance: Sexual Orientation, Masculinity, and Suicide*
    R&R Bk N - v19 - i3 - August 2004 - p166(1) [501+]
Doran, Phil - *The Reluctant Tuscan: How I Discovered My Inner Italian*
    BL - v101 - i9-10 - Jan 1 2005 - p808(1) [51-500]
    KR - v72 - i24 - Dec 15 2004 - p1178(1) [501+]
    LJ - v130 - i1 - Jan 1 2005 - p137(1) [51-500]
    PW - v252 - i8 - Feb 21 2005 - p166(1) [51-500]
Doran, Sally - *Fair Cop: Learning the Art of Policing*
    CS - v33 - i2 - March 2004 - p237-238 [501+]
Doran, Susan - *The Myth of Elizabeth*
    Ren Q - v57 - i3 - Fall 2004 - p1119(2) [501+]
Queen Elizabeth I
    HNet - June 2004 - pNA [501+]
Dore, Gustave - *London*
    Bwatch - v26 - i8 - August 2004 - p1(1) [51-500]
Doren, Kim - *You Go Girl: The Winning Way*
    Choice - v41 - i7 - March 2004 - p1333(1) [501+]
Dorf, Michael C. - *Constitutional Law Stories*
    Choice - v42 - i2 - Oct 2004 - p371(1) [51-500]
Dorf, Richard C. - *CRC Handbook of Engineering Tables*
    E-Streams - Sept 2004 - pNA [501+]
    SciTech - v28 - i3 - Sept 2004 - p137(1) [51-500]
The Engineering Handbook, 2nd Ed.
    Choice - v42 - i6 - Feb 2005 - p1053(1) [51-500]
    SciTech - v28 - i4 - Dec 2004 - p131 [51-500]
Traffic Safety
    Choice - v42 - i6 - Feb 2005 - p1053(1) [51-500]
Dorfman, Ariel - *Desert Memories: Journeys through the Chilean North*
    Globe & Mail - July 10 2004 - pT7 [501+]
Dorhojowasa-Philp, Hunter - *Full Bloom: The Art and Life of Georgia O'Keeffe*
    Choice - v42 - i6 - Feb 2005 - p1012(2) [51-500]
Doring, Herbert - *Patterns of Parliamentary behavior: Passage of Legislation Across Western Europe*
    R&R Bk N - v19 - i3 - August 2004 - p208(1) [1-50]
Doring, Tobius - *African Cultures, Visual Arts, and the Museums: Sights/Sites of Creativity and Conflict*
    R&R Bk N - v19 - i1 - Feb 2004 - p49(1) [51-500]
Dorland, Michael - *The Captors' Narrative: Catholic Women and Their Puritan Men on the Early American Frontier*
    AHR - v109 - i2 - April 2004 - p506(2) [501+]
Law, Rhetoric and Irony in the Formation of Canadian Civic Culture
    AHR - v109 - i2 - April 2004 - p507(2) [501+]
Law, Rhetoric and Irony in the Formation of Canadian Civil Culture
    R&R Bk N - v19 - i1 - Feb 2004 - pNA [501+]
Dorland's Pocket Medical Dictionary, 27th Ed.
    SciTech - v28 - i4 - Dec 2004 - p75(1) [51-500]
Dorleijn, Gillis J. - *Cultural Repertoires: Structure, Function and Dynamics*
    R&R Bk N - v19 - i1 - Feb 2004 - p222(1) [51-500]
Dorling, Daniel - *People and Places: A 2001 Census Atlas of the UK*
    Choice - v42 - i6 - Feb 2005 - p1000(2) [51-500]
    R&R Bk N - v19 - i4 - Nov 2004 - p86(1) [51-500]

Douglass, Sara - *The Nameless Day*
  BL - v100 - i21 - July 2004 - p1828(1) [51-500]
Sinner
  y BL - v101 - i2 - Sept 15 2004 - p215(1) [51-500]
  ChrSFF&H - v26 - i9 - Sept 2004 - p30(1) [51-500]
  PW - v251 - i30 - July 26 2004 - p42(1) [501+]
The Wounded Hawk
  BL - v101 - i9-10 - Jan 1 2005 - p833(1) [1-50]
  PW - v251 - i51 - Dec 20 2004 - p41(1) [51-500]

Douglass, Sarah - *The Nameless Day*
  y VOYA - v27 - i5 - Dec 2004 - p402(1) [51-500]

Doukidis, Georgios - *Social and Economic Transformation in the Digital Era*
  R&R Bk N - v19 - i1 - Feb 2004 - p123(1) [51-500]

Doumani, Beshara - *Family History in the Middle East: Household, Property, and Gender*
  AHR - v109 - i4 - Oct 2004 - p1343-1344 [501+]

Doumbia, Adama - *The Way of the Elders*
  LJ - v130 - i1 - Jan 1 2005 - p120(1) [51-500]

Dounton, Martin - *Trusting Leviathan: The Politics of Taxation in Britain, 1799-1914*
  BHR - v77 - i4 - Winter 2003 - p737(741) [501+]

Douoghty, Harold R. - *Guide to American Graduates Schools, 9th Ed.*
  Choice - v42 - i6 - Feb 2005 - p1002(1) [51-500]

Douthat, Ross Gregory - *Privilege: Harvard and the Education of the Ruling Class*
  KR - v73 - i1 - Jan 1 2005 - p31(2) [51-500]
  LJ - v130 - i3 - Feb 15 2005 - p142(2) [51-500]
  PW - v252 - i7 - Feb 14 2005 - p67(1) [51-500]

Douthit, Nathan - *Uncertain Encounters: Indians and Whites at Peace and War in Southern Oregon, 1820s-1860s*
  JAH - v91 - i1 - June 2004 - p236-237 [501+]
  WHQ - v35 - i2 - Summer 2004 - p242-243 [501+]

Douthwaite, Julia V. - *The Wild Girl, Natural Man, and the Monster: Dangerous Experiments in the Age of Enlightenment*
  Clio - v33 - i4 - Summer 2004 - p477(6) [501+]

Doutrich, Paul E. - *Shapers of the Great Debate on Jacksonion Democracy: A Biographical Dictionary*
  R&R Bk N - v19 - i3 - August 2004 - p67(1) [51-500]

Doval, Alexis James - *Cyril of Jerusalem, Mystagogue: The Authorship of the Mystagogic Catecheses*
  JR - v84 - i3 - July 2004 - p471(2) [501+]

Dove, Mary - *The 'Glossa Ordinaria' on the 'Song of Songs'*
  R&R Bk N - v19 - i4 - Nov 2004 - p22(1) [51-500]

Dove, Patricia M. - *Biomineralization*
  Sci - v305 - i5683 - July 23 2004 - p480(1) [501+]

Dove, Patrick - *The Catastrophe of Modernity: Tragedy and the Nation in Latin American Literature*
  Choice - v42 - i2 - Oct 2004 - p298(1) [501+]

Dove, Rita - *American Smooth: Poems*
  BL - v101 - i2 - Sept 15 2004 - p195(1) [501+]
  Black Iss - v7 - i2 - March-April 2005 - p31(1) [501+]
  LJ - v129 - i15 - Sept 15 2004 - p61(1) [51-500]
  NYTBR - Nov 21 2004 - p9 [501+]
  Prog - v69 - i2 - Feb 2005 - p46(3) [501+]
  PW - v251 - i38 - Sept 20 2004 - p60(1) [51-500]
  SLJ - v51 - i2 - Feb 2005 - p158(1) [51-500]
Conversations with Rita Dove
  WLT - v79 - i1 - Jan-April 2005 - p92(2) [501+]

Dove, Sue - *Painting with Stitches*
  Bwatch - v26 - i7 - July 2004 - p6(2) [51-500]

Dover, Carol - *A Companion to the Lancelot-Grail Cycle*
  Med R - Nov 2004 - pNA [501+]

Dover, E.D. - *The Disputed Presidential Election of 2000: A History and Reference Guide*
  LibMed - v22 - i5 - Feb 2004 - p86(1) [501+]

Dovers, Stephen - *New Dimensions in Ecological Economics: Integrated Approaches to People and Nature*
  R&R Bk N - v19 - i1 - Feb 2004 - p94(1) [51-500]
South Africa's Environmental History: Cases and Comparisons
  IJAHS - v37 - i1 - Wntr 2004 - p185-187 [501+]

Dow, David R. - *Executed on a Technicality: Lethal Injustice on America's Death Row*
  KR - v73 - i4 - Feb 15 2005 - p209(1) [501+]

Dow, Gregory K. - *Governing the Firm: Workers' Control in Theory and Practice*
  Econ J - v114 - i499 - Nov 2004 - pF555(1) [501+]

Dow, James R. - *The Study of European Ethnology in Austria*
  R&R Bk N - v19 - i3 - August 2004 - p41(1) [51-500]

Dow, Mark - *American Gulag: Inside U.S. Immigration Prisons*
  Choice - v42 - i4 - Dec 2004 - p736(1) [1-50]

Dowbiggin, Ian Robert - *Keeping America Sane: Psychiatry and Eugenics in the United States and Canada, 1880-1940*
  SciTech - v28 - i4 - Dec 2004 - p85(1) [51-500]
A Merciful End: The Euthanasia Movement in Modern America
  CBRA - Annual 2003 - p89(2) [51-500]
  JAH - v91 - i1 - June 2004 - p307-307 [501+]

Dowd, Gregory Evans - *War under Heaven: Pontiac, the Indian Nations, and the British Empire*
  AHR - v109 - i3 - June 2004 - p891(1) [501+]
  Am Ind CRJ - v27 - i4 - Fall 2003 - p184-186 [501+]
  Atl - v294 - i1 - July-August 2004 - p144(2) [501+]
  WHQ - v35 - i2 - Summer 2004 - p240-241 [501+]

Dowd, John - *Sea Kayaking: A Manual for Long-Distance Touring, Rev. 5th Ed.*
  R&R Bk N - v19 - i4 - Nov 2004 - p81(1) [51-500]

Dowd, Kevin - *Money and the Nation State: The Financial Revolution, Government and the World Monetary System*
  Econ J - v114 - i499 - Nov 2004 - pF546(1) [501+]

Dowd, Maureen - *Bushworld: Enter at Your Own Risk (Read by Mazur, Kathe). Audiobook Review*
  BL - v101 - i5 - Nov 1 2004 - p502(1) [51-500]
  PW - v251 - i40 - Oct 4 2004 - p31(2) [51-500]
Bushworld: Enter at Your Own Risk
  BL - v101 - i1 - Sept 1 2004 - p2(1) [51-500]
  Globe & Mail - Oct 30 2004 - pD3 [501+]
  LJ - v129 - i16 - Oct 1 2004 - p98(1) [51-500]
  NYTBR - August 29 2004 - p13 [501+]
  Prog - v68 - i10 - Oct 2004 - p45(4) [501+]
  PW - v251 - i31 - August 2 2004 - p65(1) [51-500]
  Spec - v296 - i9195 - Oct 30 2004 - p50(3) [501+]

Dowdeswell, Julian - *Islands of the Arctic*
  GJ - v170 - i3 - Sept 2004 - p285(1) [501+]

Dowell, Earl H. - *Dynamics of Very High Dimensional Systems*
  SciTech - v28 - i1 - March 2004 - p42(1) [51-500]

Dowell, Frances O'Roark - *The Secret Language of Girls (Read by Santopietro, Michele). Audiobook Review*
  c Kliatt - v38 - i6 - Nov 2004 - p50(1) [51-500]
  c SLJ - v50 - i10 - Oct 2004 - p85(1) [51-500]
The Secret Language of Girls
  c CCB-B - v57 - i11 - July-August 2004 - p460(1) [501+]
  c HB - v80 - i4 - July-August 2004 - p450(1) [51-500]
Where I'd Like to Be
  y PW - v251 - i36 - Sept 6 2004 - p65(1) [501+]

Dowers, Kenroy - *Focus on Capital: New Approaches to Developing Latin American Capital Markets*
  R&R Bk N - v19 - i1 - Feb 2004 - p64(1) [501+]

Dowling, C. - *Information and Communication Technology and the Teacher of the Future: Proceedings*
  R&R Bk N - v19 - i1 - Feb 2004 - pNA [501+]

Dowling, Helen - *Encyclopedia: Science*
  y SB - v40 - i6 - Nov-Dec 2004 - p254(2) [51-500]

Dowling, Peter J. - *International Human Resources Management: Managing People in a Multinational Context*
  R&R Bk N - v19 - i3 - August 2004 - p130(1) [51-500]

Downe, Lise - *Disturbance of Progress*
  Can Lit - i182 - Autumn 2004 - p118(2) [501+]

Downer, Martyn - *Nelson's Purse: An Extraordinary Historical Detective Story Shedding New Light on the Life of Britain's Greatest Naval Hero*
  Globe & Mail - Feb 5 2005 - pD8 [501+]

Downes, Paul - *Democracy, Revolution, and Monarchism in Early American Literature*
  NEQ - v77 - i3 - Sept 2004 - p522-524 [501+]

Downey, Carolyn J. - *The Three-Minute Classroom Walk-Through: Changing School Supervisory Practice One Teacher at a Time*
  R&R Bk N - v19 - i3 - August 2004 - p219(1) [1-50]

Downey, Lynn - *Most Loved Monster (Illus. by Davis, Jack E.)*
  c KR - v72 - i14 - July 15 2004 - p683(1) [51-500]
  c PW - v251 - i32 - August 9 2004 - p250(1) [51-500]
  c SLJ - v50 - i8 - August 2004 - p85(2) [51-500]

Downey, Myles - *Effective Coaching: Lessons from the Coach's Coach*
  HR Mag - v50 - i2 - Feb 2005 - pS16(1) [501+]

Downie, Glen - *Desire Lines*
  CBRA - Annual 2003 - p215(1) [51-500]

Downie, Jocelyn - *Dying Justice: A Case for Decriminalizing Euthanasia and Assisted Suicide in Canada*
  Choice - v42 - i6 - Feb 2005 - p1091(1) [51-500]

Downie, Mary Alice - *Scared Sarah (Illus. by Wood, Muriel)*
  y Can CL - i111-112 - Fall-Winter 2003 - p128(7) [501+]
  c Can Lit - i182 - Autumn 2004 - p166(2) [501+]
A Song for Acadia
  c Res Links - v10 - i1 - Oct 2004 - p12(1) [501+]
Une chanson pour l'Acadie
  Res Links - v10 - i2 - Dec 2004 - p54(1) [501+]

Downie, Neil A. - *Ink Sandwiches, Electric Worms and 37 Other Experiments for Saturday Science*
  Phys Today - v57 - i9 - Sept 2004 - p60-62 [501+]

Downing, Ben - *The Calligraphy Shop*
  BIC - v33 - i5 - August 2004 - p38(2) [501+]

Downing, Beth - *The Hatbox Letters*
  PW - v252 - i7 - Feb 14 2005 - p53(1) [51-500]

Downing, Bonnie - *Peculiar Beauty: Three Centuries of Charmingly Absurd Advice*
  PW - v251 - i40 - Oct 4 2004 - p83(1) [51-500]

Downing, Crystal - *Writing Performance: The Stages of Dorothy L. Sayers*
  Choice - v42 - i5 - Jan 2005 - p852(1) [1-50]

Downing, David - *Afghanistan*
  y SLJ - v50 - i12 - Dec 2004 - p155(2) [51-500]
Apartheid in South Africa
  y BL - v101 - i9-10 - Jan 1 2005 - p837(2) [51-500]

Downing, Kristina A. - *Protein NMR Techniques, 2nd Ed.*
  SciTech - v28 - i4 - Dec 2004 - p72(1) [51-500]

Downing, Lisa - *Desiring the Dead: Necrophilia and Nineteenth-Century French Literature*
  NCFS - v33 - i1-2 - Fall-Winter 2004 - p176(2) [501+]

Downing, Michael - *Spring Forward: The Annual Madness of Daylight Saving Time*
  PW - v252 - i11 - March 14 2005 - p57(2) [51-500]

Downs, Cal W. - *Assessing Organizational Communication: Strategic Communication Audits*
  R&R Bk N - v19 - i4 - Nov 2004 - p92(1) [501+]

Downs, Chuck - *Over the Line: North Korea's Negotiating Strategy*
  APJ - v18 - i3 - Fall 2004 - p114(2) [501+]

Downs, Laura Lee - *Childhood in the Promised Land: Working-Class Movements and the Colonies de Vacances in France, 1880-1960*
  JIH - v35 - i1 - Summer 2004 - p132-133 [501+]
  JMH - v76 - i4 - Dec 2004 - p970(3) [501+]
  NCFS - v32 - i3-4 - Spring-Summer 2004 - p367(3) [501+]

Downs, Mike - *You See a Circus. I See ... (Illus. by McGrory, Anik)*
  c PW - v252 - i9 - Feb 28 2005 - p65(1) [51-500]

Downs, Susan Whitelaw - *Child Welfare and Family Services: Policies and Practice, 7th Ed.*
  R&R Bk N - v19 - i1 - Feb 2004 - p137(1) [51-500]

Downs, Tim - *Bug Man*
  PW - v251 - i34 - August 23 2004 - pS17(3) [501+]

Dowson, Jane - *Women, Modernism and British Poetry, 1910-1939: Resisting Femininity*
  ELT - v47 - i4 - Fall 2004 - p463(4) [501+]

Dowson, Nick - *Tigress (Illus. by Chapman, Jane)*
  c CCB-B - v57 - i11 - July-August 2004 - p460(2) [501+]
  c HB - v80 - i4 - July-August 2004 - p466(2) [51-500]
  c PW - v251 - i27 - July 5 2004 - p55(2) [51-500]
  c Sch Lib - v52 - i3 - Autumn 2004 - p150(1) [501+]
  c SLJ - v50 - i7 - July 2004 - p69(1) [51-500]

Dowswell, Paul - *Investigating Murder Mysteries*
  c SLJ - v50 - i10 - Oct 2004 - p189(1) [51-500]
Tiananmen Square: June 4, 1989
  y SLJ - v50 - i10 - Oct 2004 - p186(1) [51-500]

Doxey, W.S. - *Bear*
  South CR - v36 - i2 - Spring 2004 - p111-114 [501+]

Doyle, Aaron - *Arresting Images: Crime and Policing in Front of the Television Camera*
  Choice - v42 - i1 - Sept 2004 - p145(1) [501+]
Arresting Images: Crime and Policing in Front of the Television Camera
  CBRA - Annual 2003 - p78(1) [51-500]

Doyle, Arthur Conan - *The New Annotated Sherlock Holmes, Vols. 1-2*
> BW - v34 - i49 - Dec 5 2004 - p8(1) [501+]
> Globe & Mail - Dec 18 2004 - pD6 [501+]
> LJ - v129 - i19 - Nov 15 2004 - p60(1) [501+]
> New R - Oct 11 2004 - p47 [501+]
> NYRB - v52 - i2 - Feb 10 2005 - p17(2) [501+]
> PW - v251 - i36 - Sept 6 2004 - p48(1) [51-500]

The Sign of Four (Read by Timson, David). Audiobook Review
> Kliatt - v38 - i4 - July 2004 - p56(1) [51-500]
> LJ - v129 - i16 - Oct 1 2004 - p118(1) [51-500]

The White Company (Read by Rawlinson, Nick). Audiobook Review
> y Kliatt - v39 - i2 - March 2005 - p58(1) [51-500]

Doyle, Arthur Conan, Sir - *The Best of Sherlock Holmes, Vols. 1-4 (Read by Gielgud, John). Audiobook Review*
> Globe & Mail - Dec 18 2004 - pD25 [1-50]

Doyle, Brian - *The Best Catholic Writing 2004*
> LJ - v129 - i19 - Nov 15 2004 - p64(1) [501+]
> PW - v251 - i37 - Sept 13 2004 - p74(1) [501+]

Boy O'Boy
> c Can CL - i113/114 - Spring-Summer 2004 - p136(3) [501+]
> y CBRA - Annual 2003 - p480(2) [501+]
> c CC - v121 - i25 - Dec 14 2004 - p24(1) [51-500]

Leaping: Revelations and Epiphanies
> ABR - v25 - i5 - July-August 2004 - p23(1) [501+]

Doyle, Charlotte - *Supermarket! (Illus. by Westcott, Nadine Bernard)*
> c KR - v72 - i13 - July 1 2004 - p627(1) [51-500]
> c PW - v251 - i36 - Sept 6 2004 - p65(1) [51-500]

Doyle, F.M. - *Electrochemistry in Mineral and Metal Processing VI: Proceedings*
> SciTech - v28 - i1 - March 2004 - p170(1) [51-500]

Doyle, Georgina - *Out of the Shadows: The Untold Story of Arthur Conan Doyle's First Family*
> TLS - i5301 - Nov 5 2004 - p34-35 [51-500]

Doyle, Jack - *Trespass Against Us*
> E Mag - v16 - i2 - March-April 2005 - p63(1) [501+]

Doyle, James - *Progressive Heritage: The Evolution of a Politically Radical Literary Tradition in Canada*
> CBRA - Annual 2003 - p254(2) [51-500]

True Witness: Cops, Courts, Science and the Battle Against Misidentification
> LJ - v130 - i2 - Feb 1 2005 - p100(1) [51-500]

Doyle, Kevin - *Aircraft Carriers*
> c SLJ - v50 - i7 - July 2004 - p118(2) [51-500]

Submarines
> c SLJ - v50 - i7 - July 2004 - p118(2) [51-500]

Doyle, Malachy - *The Great Castle of Marshmangle*
> c KR - v72 - i20 - Oct 15 2004 - p1004(1) [51-500]

One, Two, Three O'Leary (Illus. by Hillenbrand, Will)
> c KR - v72 - i15 - August 1 2004 - p740(1) [51-500]
> c PW - v251 - i40 - Oct 4 2004 - p86(2) [51-500]
> c SLJ - v50 - i11 - Nov 2004 - p97(1) [51-500]
> c HB - v81 - i1 - Jan-Feb 2005 - p76(1) [51-500]

Splash, Joshua, Splash! (Illus. by Wilson-Max, Ken)
> c BL - v100 - i22 - August 2004 - p1941(1) [51-500]
> c CCB-B - v58 - i3 - Nov 2004 - p119(1) [501+]
> c Sch Lib - v52 - i4 - Winter 2004 - p186(1) [51-500]
> c SLJ - v50 - i9 - Sept 2004 - p158(1) [51-500]

Tales from Old Ireland
> c CH Bwatch - v14 - i8 - August 2004 - p4(1) [51-500]

Who Is Jesse Flood?
> c Kliatt - v38 - i6 - Nov 2004 - p15(1) [51-500]

Doyle, Marian I. - *An Illustrated History of Hairstyles: 1830-1930*
> Ant&CM - v108 - i8 - Oct 2003 - p16(1) [501+]

Doyle, Mary Ellen - *Voices from the Quarters: The Fiction of Ernest J. Gaines*
> Afr Am R - v38 - i2 - Summer 2004 - p348(3) [501+]
> Afr Am R - v38 - i2 - Summer 2004 - p350(2) [501+]

Doyle, Michael (b. 1956 -) - *The Forestport Breaks: A Nineteenth-Century Conspiracy Along the Black River Canal*
> R&R Bk N - v19 - i3 - August 2004 - p73(1) [51-500]

Doyle, Michael (b. 1957 -) - *Maximum Dreamweaver: 85 Add-Ons to Supercharge Your Development*
> SciTech - v28 - i1 - March 2004 - p157(1) [51-500]

Doyle, Paul E. - *Hot Shots and Heavy Hits: Tales of an Undercover Drug Agent*
> R&R Bk N - v19 - i3 - August 2004 - p168(1) [501+]

Doyle, Peter - *Get Rich Quick*
> KR - v72 - i14 - July 15 2004 - p661(2) [501+]
> LJ - v129 - i16 - Oct 1 2004 - p65(1) [51-500]

Doyle, Roddy - *The Giggler Treatment (Illus. by Ajhar, Brian)*
> c PW - v251 - i44 - Nov 1 2004 - p64(1) [501+]

The Meanwhile Adventures (Illus. by Ajhar, Brian)
> c BL - v101 - i5 - Nov 1 2004 - p484(1) [51-500]
> c Globe & Mail - Dec 11 2004 - pD22 [501+]
> c KR - v72 - i20 - Oct 15 2004 - p1004(1) [51-500]
> y PW - v251 - i42 - Oct 18 2004 - p66(1) [501+]
> c SLJ - v50 - i12 - Dec 2004 - p106(1) [501+]

Oh, Play That Thing
> BL - v101 - i1 - Sept 1 2004 - p4(1) [51-500]
> BW - v34 - i51 - Dec 19 2004 - p3(1) [501+]
> Ent W - i793 - Nov 19 2004 - p89 [501+]
> Globe & Mail - Sept 18 2004 - pD12 [501+]
> KR - v72 - i17 - Sept 1 2004 - p823(1) [501+]
> NYTBR - Nov 14 2004 - p62(L) [501+]
> People - Nov 29 2004 - p58 [51-500]
> PW - v251 - i38 - Sept 20 2004 - p43(1) [51-500]
> Spec - v296 - i9191 - Oct 2 2004 - p49(1) [501+]
> TLS - i5292 - Sept 3 2004 - p13(1) [501+]

Doyle, Susan Badger - *Bound for Montana: Diaries from the Bozeman Trail*
> Roundup M - v12 - i2 - Dec 2004 - p22 [501+]
> R&R Bk N - v19 - i4 - Nov 2004 - p67(1) [51-500]

Doyle, Tara - *Mini Egg (Illus. by McQueen, Lucinda)*
> c PW - v252 - i7 - Feb 14 2005 - p79(2) [501+]

Doyon, Jaunita - *Not with Our Kids You Don't: 10 Strategies to Save Our Schools*
> TCR - v106 - i5 - May 2004 - p970(3) [501+]

Dozois, David J.A. - *Prevention of Anxiety and Depression: Theory, Research, and Practice*
> SciTech - v28 - i1 - March 2004 - p101(1) [51-500]

Dozois, Gardner R. - *Best of the Best: 20 Years of the Year's Best Science Fiction*
> KR - v73 - i2 - Jan 15 2005 - p89(1) [51-500]

The Year's Best Science Fiction: Twenty-First Annual Collection
> BL - v100 - i21 - July 2004 - p1830(1) [1-50]
> ChrSFF&H - v26 - i10 - Oct 2004 - p49(2) [501+]

Dr. Atkins' New Diet Revolution: The No-Hunger, Luxurious Weight Loss Plan hat Really Works
> Lon R Bks - v26 - i15 - August 5 2004 - p16(3) [501+]

Draanen, Wendelin Van - *Sammy Keyes and the Psycho Kitty Queen*
> c CH Bwatch - Feb 2005 - pNA [501+]

Drabble, Margaret - *The Radiant Way*
> Critq - v44 - Winter 2003 - p136 [501+]

The Red Queen: A Transcultural Tragicomedy
> BL - v101 - i1 - Sept 1 2004 - p4(1) [51-500]
> Globe & Mail - Oct 23 2004 - pD19 [501+]
> KR - v72 - i16 - August 15 2004 - p761(1) [501+]
> LJ - v129 - i14 - Sept 1 2004 - p138(1) [51-500]
> NYTBR - Oct 10 2004 - p15 [501+]
> PW - v251 - i36 - Sept 6 2004 - p44(1) [501+]
> Spec - v295 - i9185 - August 21 2004 - p34(1) [501+]
> TLS - i5290 - August 20 2004 - p21(1) [501+]
> Ent W - i787 - Oct 8 2004 - p119 [501+]

The Seven Sisters
> HR - v55 - i4 - Winter 2003 - p685 [501+]

Drache, Sharon Abron - *Magic Pot (Illus. by Schowalter, Ellen)*
> c CBRA - Annual 2003 - p450(1) [51-500]

Drachman, Eric - *It's Me! (Illus. by Decenciere, Isabelle) (Read by Drachman, Eric). Audiobook Review*
> c PW - v252 - i2 - Jan 10 2005 - p71(1) [51-500]

Drackle, Dorle - *Current Policies and Practices in European Social Anthropology Education*
> Choice - v42 - i5 - Jan 2005 - p895(1) [1-50]
> R&R Bk N - v19 - i3 - August 2004 - p82(1) [51-500]

Dracos, Ted - *Ungodly: The Passions, Torments, and Murder of Atheist Madalyn Murray O'Hair*
> BL - v101 - i3 - Oct 1 2004 - p302(1) [51-500]

Drader, Brian - *Breakout*
> BIC - v33 - i9 - Dec 2004 - p24(3) [501+]

Liar
> BIC - v33 - i9 - Dec 2004 - p24(3) [501+]

Prok
> Lam Bk Rpt - v13 - i4-5 - Nov-Dec 2004 - p22(3) [501+]

Drafahl, Jack - *Advanced Digital Camera Techniques*
> SciTech - v28 - i4 - Dec 2004 - p166(1) [51-500]

Step-by-Step Digital Photography: A Guide for Beginners, 2nd Ed.
> SciTech - v28 - i4 - Dec 2004 - p167(1) [51-500]

Drager, P. - *Die Argonautika des Apollonios Rhodios. Das zweite Zorn-Epos der griechischen Literatur*
> Class R - v54 - i1 - May 2004 - p44(2) [501+]

Mosella
> Class R - v53 - i2 - Nov 2003 - p383-384 [501+]

Dragland, Stan - *Apocrypha: Further Journeys*
> Can Lit - i182 - Autumn 2004 - p119(2) [501+]

Drago-Severson, Eleanor - *Becoming Adult Learners: Principle and Practices for Effective Development*
> Choice - v42 - i5 - Jan 2005 - p905(1) [1-50]

Helping Teachers Learn: Principal Leadership for Adult Growth and Development
> TCR - v107 - i2 - Feb 2005 - p241(3) [501+]

Dragojlovic, Dragan - *Pod juznim krstom. 2nd Ed.*
> WLT - v78 - i3-4 - Sept-Dec 2004 - p139(2) [501+]

Dragomir, Sever Silvestru - *Some Gronwall Type Inequalities and Applications*
> SciTech - v28 - i1 - March 2004 - p40(1) [51-500]

Dragon's Breath
> LibMed - v22 - i7 - April-May 2004 - p60(60) [501+]

Dragons in the Archives: The Best of Weis and Hickman Anthology
> y Kliatt - v39 - i2 - March 2005 - p26(1) [51-500]

Dragovic-Soso, Jasna - *"Saviours of the Nation": Serbia's Intellectual Opposition and the Revival of Nationalism*
> AHR - v109 - i3 - June 2004 - p1002(1) [501+]
> Slav R - v63 - i4 - Winter 2004 - p866(1) [501+]

Draho, Jason - *The IPO Decision: Why and How Companies Go Public*
> Choice - v42 - i3 - Nov 2004 - p532(1) [1-50]

The IPO Decision: Why and How Firms Go Public
> R&R Bk N - v19 - i3 - August 2004 - p136(1) [51-500]

Drahozal, Christopher R. - *The Supremacy Clause: A Reference Guide to the United States Constitution*
> R&R Bk N - v19 - i3 - August 2004 - p202(1) [1-50]

Draitser, Emil - *Kto ty takoi: Odessa, 1945-1953*
> WLT - v78 - i3-4 - Sept-Dec 2004 - p136(2) [501+]

Drake, David - *Master of the Cauldron*
> y BL - v101 - i4 - Oct 15 2004 - p395(1) [51-500]
> LJ - v129 - i17 - Oct 15 2004 - p58(1) [51-500]
> PW - v251 - i42 - Oct 18 2004 - p52(2) [501+]

The World Turned Upside Down
> y BL - v101 - i7 - Dec 1 2004 - p643(1) [51-500]

Drake, Emily - *The Gate of Bones*
> Bwatch - Dec 2004 - pNA [51-500]

Drake, Ernest - *Dr. Ernest Drake's Dragonology: The Complete Book of Dragons*
> y VOYA - v27 - i3 - August 2004 - p228(1) [1-50]

The Dragonology Handbook: A Practical Course in Dragons (Illus. by Anderson, Wayne)
> c PW - v252 - i11 - March 14 2005 - p69(1) [501+]

Drake, Jane - *Cool Woods: A Trip around the World's Boreal Forest (Illus. by Kiss, Andrew)*
> c CBRA - Annual 2003 - p564(1) [51-500]

Snow Amazing: Cool Facts and Warm Tales (Illus. by Thurman, Mark)
> c CCB-B - v58 - i4 - Dec 2004 - p165(1) [51-500]
> c Globe & Mail - Dec 11 2004 - pD28 [51-500]
> c KR - v72 - i20 - Oct 15 2004 - p1004(1) [51-500]
> c Res Links - v10 - i2 - Dec 2004 - p26(1) [51-500]
> y SLJ - v50 - i12 - Dec 2004 - p160(1) [51-500]
> c VOYA - v27 - i5 - Dec 2004 - p414(1) [51-500]

Drake, Michael S. - *Problematics of Military Power: Government, Discipline and the Subject of Violence*
> JIH - v35 - i2 - Autumn 2004 - p285(3) [501+]
> JIH - v35 - i2 - Autumn 2004 - p287(2) [501+]

Drake, Miriam A. - *Encyclopedia of Library and Information Science, 2nd Ed.*
> LQ - v74 - i3 - July 2004 - p384(3) [501+]
> SciTech - v28 - i1 - March 2004 - p180(1) [51-500]

Drake, P.J. - *Currency, Credit and Commerce: Early Growth in Southeast Asia*
> R&R Bk N - v19 - i3 - August 2004 - p135(1) [51-500]

Drake, Richard - *Apostles and Agitators: Italy's Marxist Revolutionary Tradition*
> AHR - v109 - i3 - June 2004 - p995(2) [501+]
> Choice - v41 - i7 - March 2004 - p1361(1) [501+]

Drakulic, Slavenka - *They Would Never Hurt a Fly: War Criminals on Trial in the Hague*
> CR - v285 - i1665 - Oct 2004 - p243(2) [501+]
> LJ - v129 - i12 - July 2004 - p103(1) [51-500]

Drane, James F. - *More Humane Medicine: A Liberal Catholic Bioethics*
Choice - v41 - i7 - March 2004 - p1313(1) [501+]
Hast Cen R - v34 - i5 - Sept-Oct 2004 - p46(2) [501+]

Draper, Elaine - *The Company Doctor: Risk, Responsibility, and Corporate Professionalism*
AJS - v110 - i3 - Nov 2004 - p820(3) [501+]
CS - v33 - i5 - Sept 2004 - p608-609 [501+]

Draper, James David - *Playing with Fire: European Terracotta Models, 1740-1840*
Choice - v41 - i11-12 - July-August 2004 - p2031(1) [501+]

Draper, Jonathan A. - *Orality, Literacy, and Colonialism in Antiquity*
R&R Bk N - v19 - i4 - Nov 2004 - p15(1) [51-500]

Draper, Melissa - *Holly the Christmas Collie*
c CH Bwatch - v14 - i9 - Sept 2004 - p2(1) [51-500]

Draper, Paul - *Cosmic Fine-Tuning and Terrestrial Suffering: Parallel Problems for Naturalism and Theism*
RM - v58 - i1 - Sept 2004 - p211(3) [501+]

Draper, Peter - *Reassessing Nikolaus Pevsner*
Apo - v159 - i510 - August 2004 - p78(2) [501+]
R&R Bk N - v19 - i4 - Nov 2004 - p203(1) [501+]

Draper, Sharon M. - *The Battle of Jericho (Read by Jackson, J.D.). Audiobook Review*
y Kliatt - v38 - i5 - Sept 2004 - p54(2) [51-500]
y VOYA - v27 - i5 - Dec 2004 - p371(1) [501+]
The Battle of Jericho
y Kliatt - v39 - i2 - March 2005 - p18(1) [51-500]
PW - v251 - i51 - Dec 20 2004 - p62(1) [501+]

Drasher, Norm - *Index of Surnames Appearing in the Hazelton Semi-Weekly, Hazelton, Pennsylvania, Pt. 4*
EFHM - v58 - i2 - March-April 2004 - p91(1) [1-50]

Draves, William A. - *Nine Shift: Work, Life, and Education in the 21st Century*
Fut - v38 - i6 - Nov-Dec 2004 - p61(1) [51-500]

Draycott, Jane - *The Night Tree*
TLS - i5297 - Oct 8 2004 - p29(1) [501+]

Dreaming on a Sunday in the Alameda and Other Plays
Am Theat - v21 - i8 - Oct 2004 - p139(4) [51-500]

Drebenstedt, Carsten - *Resources in Our Day-to-Day Life*
R&R Bk N - v19 - i3 - August 2004 - p97(1) [51-500]

Dreger, Alice Domurat - *Disaster Psychiatry: Intervening when Nightmares Come True*
Choice - v42 - i3 - Nov 2004 - p516(1) [1-50]
One of Us: Conjoined Twins and the Future of Normal
Lon R Bks - v26 - i14 - July 22 2004 - p3(2) [501+]
Nature - v429 - i6987 - May 6 2004 - p26(1) [501+]

Dregni, Michael - *Django: The Life and Music of a Gypsy Legend*
BL - v101 - i6 - Nov 15 2004 - p540(1) [51-500]
Globe & Mail - Nov 20 2004 - pD12 [501+]
LJ - v129 - i15 - Sept 15 2004 - p59(1) [51-500]
NYTBR - Nov 28 2004 - p25 [501+]
PW - v251 - i36 - Sept 6 2004 - p57(1) [51-500]
Mustang Legends: The Power, the Performance, the Passion
Ant&CM - v109 - i3 - May 2004 - p16(1) [501+]

Dreikurs, Rudolf - *Discipline Without Tears: How to Reduce Conflict and Establish Cooperation in the Classroom*
Res Links - v10 - i2 - Dec 2004 - p52(1) [51-500]

Dreisbach, Daniel L. - *Thomas Jefferson and the Wall of Separation between Church and State*
JSH - v70 - i3 - August 2004 - p652(2) [501+]
W&M Q - v61 - i4 - Oct 2004 - p776-780 [501+]

Dreiser, Theodore - *A Book about Myself: Newspaper Days*
AS - v74 - i1 - Wntr 2005 - p10(2) [501+]
Sister Carrie
Ent W - i778 - August 13 2004 - p93 [501+]

Drennan, James C. - *Pediatrics*
SciTech - v28 - i1 - March 2004 - p112(1) [51-500]

Drennan, Matthew P. - *The Information Economy and American Cities*
CS - v33 - i1 - Jan 2004 - p126-126 [501+]

Drennen, William M. - *Red, White, Black & Blue: A Dual Memoir of Race and Class in Appalachia*
Choice - v42 - i1 - Sept 2004 - p194(1) [501+]

Dresch, Paula A. - *A History of Modern Yemen*
JRAI - v10 - i4 - Dec 2004 - p908(2) [51-500]

Drescher, Seymour - *The Mighty Experiment: Free Labor versus Slavery in British Emancipation*
JIH - v34 - i4 - Spring 2004 - p634-636 [501+]

Dresner, Steven - *PIPE's: A Guide to Private Investments in Public Equity*
R&R Bk N - v19 - i3 - August 2004 - p138(1) [51-500]

Dressier, Rachel - *Of Armour and Men in Medieval England: The Chivalric Rhetoric of Three English Knights*
Apo - v161 - i515 - Jan 2005 - p64(2) [501+]

Dressler, Markus - *Die alevitische Religion: Traditionslinien und Neubestimmungen*
IJMES - v36 - i1 - Feb 2004 - p149-151 [501+]

Drew, A.J. - *A Wiccan Formulary and Herbal*
Bwatch - March 2005 - pNA [51-500]

Drew, Naomi - *The Kids' Guide to Working Out Conflicts: How to Keep Cool, Stay Safe, and Get Along*
c CH Bwatch - v14 - i7 - July 2004 - p1(1) [51-500]
c SLJ - v50 - i9 - Sept 2004 - p225(2) [51-500]
y VOYA - v27 - i4 - Oct 2004 - p323(2) [51-500]

Drewe, Robert - *Our Sunshine (Read by Veitch, Michael). Audiobook Review*
y Kliatt - v38 - i5 - Sept 2004 - p65(2) [51-500]

Drewe, Sheryle Bergmann - *Why Sport? An Introduction to the Philosophy of Sport*
SSJ - v21 - i2 - June 2004 - p239-240 [501+]

Drewery, Melanie - *Nanny Mihi's Treasure Hunt (Illus. by Duncan, Tracey)*
c Magpies - v19 - i5 - Nov 2004 - p6S(1) [501+]

Drewry, Henry N. - *Stand and prosper: Private Black Colleges and their Students*
J Hi E - v75 - i6 - Nov-Dec 2004 - p704(4) [501+]
TCR - v106 - i5 - May 2004 - p935(4) [501+]

Drews, Robert - *Greater Anatolia and the Indo-Hittite Language Family: Papers Presented at a Colloquium Hosted by the University of Richmond, March 18-19, 2000*
JNES - v63 - i3 - July 2004 - p228(3) [501+]

Dreyer, B. - *Untersuchungen zur Geschichte des spatklassischen Athen: 322-ca. 230 v. Chr.*
Class R - v54 - i1 - May 2004 - p159(2) [501+]

Dreyer, Elizabeth A. - *Passionate Spirituality: Hildegard of Bingen and Hadewijch of Brabant*
PW - v252 - i11 - March 14 2005 - p65(1) [51-500]

Dreyer, June Teufel - *China's Political System: Modernization and Tradition, 4th Ed.*
R&R Bk N - v19 - i4 - Nov 2004 - p156(1) [501+]

Dreyfus, Francois-Georges - *Unrecognized Resistance: The Franco-American Experience in World War Two: Proceedings*
R&R Bk N - v19 - i4 - Nov 2004 - p34(1) [51-500]

Dreyfus, Georges B.J. - *The Sound of Two Hands Clapping: The Education of a Tibetan Buddhist Monk*
JAAR - v72 - i4 - Dec 2004 - p1028(3) [501+]

Dreyfus, Jean-Marc - *Pillages sur ordonnances: Aryanisation et restitution des banques en France 1940-1953*
AHR - v109 - i3 - June 2004 - p989(1) [501+]

Dreyfuss, Henry - *Desiging for People*
SciTech - v28 - i1 - March 2004 - p177(1) [51-500]

Drez, Ronald J. - *Remember D-Day: The Plan, the Invasion, Survivor Stories*
c BL - v100 - i21 - July 2004 - p1839(1) [1-50]
c SLJ - v50 - i7 - July 2004 - p120(1) [51-500]

Drielak, Steven C. - *Hot Zone Forensics: Chemical, Biological, and Radiological Evidence Collection*
SciTech - v28 - i3 - Sept 2004 - p10(1) [501+]

Driels, Morris R. - *Weaponeering: Conventional Weapon System Effectiveness*
SciTech - v28 - i3 - Sept 2004 - p172(1) [501+]

Driess, Matthias - *Molecular Clusters of the Main Group Elements*
E-Streams - Nov 2004 - pNA [501+]

Driessen, Elizabeth - *On the Banks of the Amazon/En Las Orillas del Amazonas (Illus. by Driessen, Elizabeth)*
LibMed - v22 - i7 - April-May 2004 - p64(1) [501+]

Drill, Esther - *Where Do I Go from Here? Getting a Life After High School*
y Kliatt - v38 - i4 - July 2004 - p39(1) [51-500]

Drinan, Robert F. - *Can God and Caesar Coexist? Balancing Religious Freedom and International Law*
BL - v101 - i4 - Oct 15 2004 - p365(1) [51-500]
NYTBR - March 13 2005 - p24 [501+]

Dris, Ramdane - *Crop Management and Postharvest Handling of Horticultural Products, Vol. 4*
SciTech - v28 - i3 - Sept 2004 - p128(1) [51-500]

Driscoll, Lori - *Electronic Reserve: A Manual and Guide for Library Staff Members*
LJ - v129 - i16 - Oct 1 2004 - p114(1) [51-500]

Driscoll, Michael - *A Child's Introduction to Poetry*
c LibMed - v22 - i6 - March 2004 - p70(1) [501+]
A Child's Introduction to Poetry (Illus. by Hamilton, Meredith)
SLJ - v50 - i10 - Oct 2004 - pS50(2) [51-500]
A Child's Introduction to the Night Sky: The Story of the Stars, Planets and Constellations--and How You Can Find Them in the Sky (Illus. by Hamilton, Meredith)
c SB - v40 - i6 - Nov-Dec 2004 - p265(2) [51-500]
c SLJ - v50 - i9 - Sept 2004 - p226(1) [51-500]

Driver, Elizabeth - *Five Roses: Guide to Good Cooking*
CBRA - Annual 2003 - p128(2) [51-500]

Driver, Felix - *Geography Militant: Cultures of Exploration and Empire*
Hist Geo - v32 - Annual 2004 - p224(3) [501+]
Imperial Cities
VS - v45 - i2 - Winter 2003 - p319 [501+]

Driver, Martha W. - *The Medieval Hero on Screen: Representations from Beowulf to Buffy*
Choice - v42 - i7 - March 2005 - p1235(1) [51-500]

Driver, Stephanie Schwartz - *Words Changed the World: The Declaration of Independence*
y Kliatt - v39 - i1 - Jan 2005 - p33(2) [51-500]

Drobot, Eve - *Money, Money, Money: Where It Comes from, How to Save It, Spend It, and Make It (Illus. by Davila, Claudia)*
c BL - v101 - i9-10 - Jan 1 2005 - p848(1) [1-50]
c Res Links - v10 - i2 - Dec 2004 - p26(1) [51-500]
y SLJ - v51 - i1 - Jan 2005 - p146(1) [51-500]

Drogin, Eric York - *Law and Mental Health Professionals: Kentucky*
SciTech - v28 - i3 - Sept 2004 - p12(1) [501+]

Drohan, Madelaine - *Making a Killing: How and Why Corporations Use Armed Force to Do Business*
Bwatch - Feb 2005 - pNA [51-500]
CBRA - Annual 2003 - p325(1) [501+]
PW - v251 - i40 - Oct 4 2004 - p85(1) [51-500]

Drohojowska-Philp, Hunter - *Full Bloom: The Art and Life of Georgia O'Keeffe*
Art N - v104 - i2 - Feb 2005 - p106(1) [501+]
BL - v101 - i1 - Sept 1 2004 - p37(1) [51-500]
BW - v34 - i41 - Oct 10 2004 - p8(1) [501+]
Globe & Mail - Oct 23 2004 - pD21 [501+]
KR - v72 - i15 - August 1 2004 - p722(1) [501+]
LJ - v129 - i20 - Dec 1 2004 - p107(1) [51-500]
NYTBR - Sept 26 2004 - p10 [501+]
PW - v251 - i30 - July 26 2004 - p48(1) [51-500]

Droit, Roger-Pol - *The Cult of Nothingness: The Philosophers and the Buddha*
JR - v85 - i1 - Jan 2005 - p158(3) [501+]

Drolet, Michael - *Tocqueville, Democracy, and Social Reform*
Choice - v42 - i1 - Sept 2004 - p187(1) [501+]

Dromgoole, Glenn - *A Small Town in Texas: Reflections on Growing Up in the '50s and '60s*
Roundup M - v12 - i3 - Feb 2005 - p17(1) [501+]

Dronamraju, Krishna R. - *Infectious Disease and Host-Pathogen Evolution*
Nature - v432 - i7013 - Nov 4 2004 - p19(1) [501+]
QRB - v79 - i4 - Dec 2004 - p463(1) [501+]

Droney, Maureen - *Mix Masters: Platinum Engineers Reveal Their Secrets for Success*
R&R Bk N - v19 - i2 - May 2004 - p193(1) [51-500]

Drooz, Daniel B. - *American Prisoners of War in German Death, Concentration, and Slave Labor Camps: Germany's Lethal Policy in the Second World War*
Bwatch - v26 - i9 - Sept 2004 - p6(1) [51-500]
R&R Bk N - v19 - i3 - August 2004 - p34(1) [51-500]

Drower, Margaret - *Letters from the Desert: The Correspondence of Flinders and Hilda Petrie*
Apo - v161 - i517 - March 2005 - p103(1) [501+]
R&R Bk N - v19 - i4 - Nov 2004 - p218(1) [501+]
TimHES - v0 - i1681 - March 4 2005 - p27(1) [501+]

Drowne, Karhleen - *The 1920's*
R&R Bk N - v19 - i3 - August 2004 - p62(1) [51-500]

Drozdeck, Steven R. - *The Mega Producers: Secrets of Financial Services Superstars to Lead You to the Top*
R&R Bk N - v19 - i3 - August 2004 - p138(1) [51-500]

Druchunas, Donna - *The Knitted Rug: 21 Fantastic Designs*
LJ - v129 - i20 - Dec 1 2004 - p108(1) [51-500]

Drucker, Doris - *Invent Radium or I'll Pull Your Hair: A Memoir*
Globe & Mail - July 31 2004 - pD12 [1-50]

Drucker, Joel - *Jimmy Connors Saved My Life*
  BL - v101 - i2 - Sept 15 2004 - p192(1) [51-500]
  LJ - v129 - i15 - Sept 15 2004 - p64(1) [51-500]
Drucker, Peter F. - *The Daily Drucker: 365 Days of
  Insight and Motivation for Getting the Right Things Done*
  LJ - v129 - i20 - Dec 1 2004 - p132(1) [51-500]
  NW - Dec 20 2004 - p38 [501+]
Druckman, Nancy - *American Flags: Designs for a Young
  Nation (Illus. by Druckman, Nancy)*
  y LibMed - v22 - i6 - March 2004 - p79(1) [501+]
Druett, Joan - *In the Wake of Madness: The Murderous
  Voyage of the Whaleship Sharon*
  R&R Bk N - v19 - i3 - August 2004 - p79(1) [51-
  500]
  A Watery Grave
  BL - v101 - i1 - Sept 1 2004 - p68(1) [51-500]
  DroRevMy - v24 - i4 - July-August 2004 - p11(1)
  [51-500]
  KR - v72 - i15 - August 1 2004 - p715(1) [51-500]
  LJ - v129 - i13 - August 2004 - p59(1) [501+]
  PW - v251 - i30 - July 26 2004 - p41(1) [501+]
**Drug Facts and Comparisons 2005: Pocket Version, 9th
  ed**
  SciTech - v28 - i4 - Dec 2004 - p116(1) [1-50]
Druger, Marvin - *Teaching Tips: Innovations in
  Undergraduate Science Instruction*
  SciTech - v28 - i3 - Sept 2004 - p15(1) [501+]
Druick, Douglas W. - *Graphic Modernism: Selections from
  the Francey and Dr. Martin L. Gecht Collection at the
  Art Institute of Chicago*
  R&R Bk N - v19 - i2 - May 2004 - p195(1) [51-
  500]
Drummond, Allan - *The Flyers*
  c LibMed - v22 - i5 - Feb 2004 - p63(1) [501+]
Drummond, Andrew - *The Abridged History*
  TLS - i5303 - Nov 19 2004 - p24(1) [501+]
Drury, Nevill - *The New Age: The History of a Movement*
  PW - v251 - i43 - Oct 25 2004 - p44(1) [51-500]
Drury, Shadia B. - *Terror and Civilization: Christianity,
  Politics, and the Western Psyche*
  Choice - v42 - i2 - Oct 2004 - p309(1) [51-500]
Druse, Eleanor - *The Journals of Eleanor Druse (Read by
  Druse, Eleanor). Audiobook Review*
  y Kliatt - v39 - i1 - Jan 2005 - p45(1) [51-500]
Druse, Kenneth - *Natural Habitat Garden*
  SciTech - v28 - i3 - Sept 2004 - p129(1) [51-500]
Druzhnikov, Yuri - *Angels on the Head of a Pin*
  NYRB - v51 - i20 - Dec 16 2004 - p65(6) [501+]
Dryden, Edgar A. - *Monumental Melville: The Formation
  of a Literary Career*
  ABR - v26 - i2 - Jan-Feb 2005 - p26(1) [501+]
Dryden, John - *The Spanish Fryar*
  Clio - v32 - i2 - Winter 2003 - p177 [501+]
Dryden, Ken - *The Game*
  Globe & Mail - Sept 18 2004 - pD27 [501+]
Drysdale, John D. - *Louis Veron and the Finances of the
  Academie Royale de Musique*
  R&R Bk N - v19 - i1 - Feb 2004 - p198(1) [51-
  500]
D'Souza, Carmo - *Portugal: In Search of Identity*
  WLT - v78 - i3-4 - Sept-Dec 2004 - p86(2) [501+]
Du Bellay, Joachim - *La Deffence, et illustration de la
  langue francoyse*
  Six Ct J - v35 - i1 - Spring 2004 - p228(1) [501+]
Du Bois, W.E.B. - *The Negro Church: Report of a Social
  Study Made under the Direction of Atlanta University*
  HNet - Sept 2004 - pNA [501+]
  The Quest of the Silver Fleece
  LJ - v129 - i16 - Oct 1 2004 - p121(1) [1-50]
  The Social Theory of W.E.B. Du Bois
  Choice - v42 - i3 - Nov 2004 - p571(1) [1-50]
Du Bouchet, Paule - *Prince Orpheus (Illus. by Negrin,
  Fabian)*
  c SLJ - v50 - i9 - Sept 2004 - p186(1) [51-500]
Du Boulay, Shirley - *Teresa of Avila: An Extraordinary
  Life*
  LJ - v129 - i17 - Oct 15 2004 - p68(1) [51-500]
du Pont De Bie, Natacha - *Ant Egg Soup*
  Globe & Mail - July 24 2004 - pT7 [501+]
du Pont, Pennie - *Uta Hagen's Acting Class*
  Am Theat - v21 - i8 - Oct 2004 - p139(4) [51-500]
Du Sautoy, Marcus - *Music of the Primes: Searching to
  Solve the Greatest Mystery in Mathematics*
  SciTech - v28 - i4 - Dec 2004 - p35(1) [51-500]
du Toit, Johan T. - *Kruger Experience: Ecology and
  Management of Savanna Heterogeneity*
  SciTech - v28 - i1 - March 2004 - p60(1) [51-500]
Dua, Ashok Kumar - *Diamond Thin Films: An Emerging
  Technology: Past, Present and Future*
  SciTech - v28 - i4 - Dec 2004 - p165(1) [51-500]

Duany, Andres - *The New Civic Art: Elements of Town
  Planning*
  R&R Bk N - v19 - i3 - August 2004 - p156(1)
  [51-500]
Duara, Prasenjit - *Sovereignty and Authenticity:
  Manchukuo and the East Asian Modern*
  AHR - v109 - i4 - Oct 2004 - p1208-1209 [501+]
  JAS - v63 - i2 - May 2004 - p473(3) [501+]
Dubal, David - *Art of the Piano*
  Bwatch - Jan 2005 - pNA [51-500]
Dubber, Markus Dirk - *Victims in the War on Crime: The
  Use and Abuse of Victims' Rights*
  CS - v33 - i2 - March 2004 - p238-239 [501+]
Dubbink, W. - *Assisting the Invisible Hand: Contested
  Relations between Market, State, and Civil Society*
  R&R Bk N - v19 - i1 - Feb 2004 - p77(1) [51-500]
Dube, Pierre H. - *Nouvelle Bibliographie refondue et
  augmentee de la critique sur Francois-Rene de
  Chateaubriand: 1801-1999*
  FS - v58 - i2 - April 2004 - p267(2) [501+]
Duberman, Martin - *Haymarket*
  BooChiTr - Jan 11 2004 - p1(2) [501+]
Dubie, Norman - *The Mercy Seat: Collected and New
  Poems, 1967-2001*
  Ga R - v58 - i1 - Spring 2004 - p179-184 [501+]
  Ordinary Mornings of a Coliseum
  BL - v101 - i4 - Oct 15 2004 - p381(1) [51-500]
  LJ - v129 - i13 - August 2004 - p85(1) [501+]
Dubin, Daniel - *Numerical and Analytical Methods for
  Scientists and Engineers Using Mathematica*
  Phys Today - v57 - i6 - June 2004 - p62-63 [501+]
Duble, Kathleen Benner - *Pilot Mom (Illus. by Marks,
  Alan)*
  LibMed - v22 - i5 - Feb 2004 - p63(1) [501+]
Dubler, Nancy Neveloff - *Bioethics Medication: A Guide to
  Shaping Shared Solutions*
  Choice - v42 - i3 - Nov 2004 - p516(1) [1-50]
Dublin, Anne - *Bobbie Rosenfeld: The Olympian Who
  Could Do Everything*
  BL - v101 - i1 - Sept 1 2004 - p111(1) [1-50]
DuBoff, Leonard D. - *The Law (in Plain English) for
  Small Businesses, 3rd Ed.*
  R&R Bk N - v19 - i3 - August 2004 - p197(1)
  [1-50]
Dubofsky, Melvyn - *Labor in America: A History, 7th Ed.*
  R&R Bk N - v19 - i2 - May 2004 - p106(1) [51-
  500]
DuBois, Brenda - *Social Work: An Empowering Profession,
  5th Ed.*
  R&R Bk N - v19 - i3 - August 2004 - p158(1)
  [51-500]
Dubois, Brendan - *Buried Dreams: A Lewis Cole Mystery*
  LJ - v129 - i12 - July 2004 - p64(1) [51-500]
Dubois, Daniel M. - *Computing Anticipatory Systems:
  Proceedings*
  SciTech - v28 - i4 - Dec 2004 - p16(1) [1-50]
Dubois, David D. - *Competency-Based Human Resource
  Management*
  Choice - v42 - i1 - Sept 2004 - p150(1) [501+]
  HR Mag - v49 - i7 - July 2004 - p139(2) [501+]
  HR Mag - v49 - i7 - July 2004 - pS32(1) [501+]
  HR Mag - v50 - i2 - Feb 2005 - pS14(1) [501+]
Dubois, Laurent - *Avengers of the New World: The Story
  of the Haitian Revolution*
  Choice - v42 - i3 - Nov 2004 - p543(2) [1-50]
  Nation - v279 - i10 - Oct 4 2004 - p26 [501+]
  *A Colony of Citizens: Revolution and Slave Emancipation
  in the French Caribbean, 1787-1804*
  Choice - v42 - i3 - Nov 2004 - p543(1) [1-50]
  Nation - v279 - i10 - Oct 4 2004 - p26 [501+]
DuBois, Page - *Slaves and Other Objects*
  AHR - v109 - i4 - Oct 2004 - p1286-1287 [501+]
  Choice - v41 - i7 - March 2004 - p1349(1) [501+]
  Class R - v54 - i2 - Nov 2004 - p480(2) [501+]
  TLS - i5262 - Feb 6 2004 - p28(1) [501+]
DuBois, Paul - *MySQL Cookbook*
  SciTech - v28 - i4 - Dec 2004 - p22(1) [51-500]
Dubois, Philippe - *The Future of the Earth: An
  Introduction to Sustainable Development for Young
  Readers*
  y Sch Lib - v52 - i4 - Winter 2004 - p206(1) [51-
  500]
DuBois, W.E.B. - *The Souls of Black Folk (Read by
  Hazlett, Warren). Audiobook Review*
  BL - v101 - i8 - Dec 15 2004 - p751(1) [1-50]
  BL - v101 - i9-10 - Jan 1 2005 - p778(1) [1-50]
Dubose, Lou - *The Hammer: Tom DeLay, God, Money, and
  the Rise of the Republican Congress*
  LJ - v129 - i17 - Oct 15 2004 - p76(1) [51-500]
  NYTBR - Oct 10 2004 - p11 [501+]
  PW - v251 - i37 - Sept 13 2004 - p71(1) [501+]

Dubris, Maggie - *Skels*
  NYTBR - August 22 2004 - p23 [501+]
  NYTBR - August 29 2004 - p18 [501+]
Dubrow, Gail Lee - *Restoring Women's History through
  Historic Preservation*
  Wom R Bks - v21 - i12 - Sept 2004 - p23(2)
  [501+]
  Restoring Women's History through History Preservation
  Pub Hist - v26 - i4 - Fall 2004 - p119(3) [501+]
  *Sento at Sixth and Main: Preserving Landmarks of
  Japanese American Heritage*
  HNet - Oct 2004 - pNA [501+]
Dubrow, Heather - *Shakespeare and Domestic Loss:
  Forms of Deprivation, Mourning, and Recuperation*
  Shakes Q - v55 - i1 - Spring 2004 - p83-84 [501+]
Dubuisson, Daniel - *The Western Construction of Religion:
  Myths, Knowledge and Ideology*
  Choice - v41 - i7 - March 2004 - p1313(1) [501+]
Duc, Pierre-Alain - *Recycling Intergalactic and Interstellar
  Matter: Proceedings*
  SciTech - v28 - i3 - Sept 2004 - p44(1) [1-50]
Ducat, Stephen J. - *The Wimp Factor: Gender Gaps, Holy
  Wars, and the Politics of Anxious Masculinity*
  Choice - v42 - i6 - Feb 2005 - p1100(1) [51-500]
  R&R Bk N - v19 - i4 - Nov 2004 - p132(1) [51-
  500]
Ducey, Michael Thomas - *A Nation of Villates: Riot and
  Rebellion in the Mexican Huasteca, 1750-1850*
  R&R Bk N - v19 - i4 - Nov 2004 - p126(1) [51-
  500]
Duchan, Judith Felson - *Frame Work in Language and
  Literacy: How Theory Informs Practice*
  TCR - v106 - i12 - Dec 2004 - p2277(4) [501+]
Ducharme, Rejean - *Go Figure*
  CBRA - Annual 2003 - p161(1) [51-500]
Duchhardt, Heinz - *Krieg und Frieden im Ubergang vom
  Mittelalter zur Neuzeit: Theorie, Praxis, Bilder*
  Six Ct J - v34 - i4 - Winter 2003 - p1274-1275
  [501+]
Duckenfield, Mark - *The Monetary History of Gold: A
  Documentary History, 1660-1999*
  Choice - v42 - i6 - Feb 2005 - p1070(1) [51-500]
  R&R Bk N - v19 - i4 - Nov 2004 - p116(1) [51-
  500]
Duckworth, Jeannie - *Fagin's Children: Criminal Children
  in Victorian England*
  Albion - v36 - i2 - Summer 2004 - p326(3) [501+]
Ducornet, Rikki - *Gazelle*
  y Kliatt - v39 - i1 - Jan 2005 - p12(1) [51-500]
Duczko, Wladyslaw - *Viking Rus: Studies on the Presence
  of Scandinavians in Eastern Europe*
  R&R Bk N - v19 - i3 - August 2004 - p45(1) [51-
  500]
Dudden, Arthur Power - *American Empire in the Pacific:
  From Trade to Strategic Balance, 1700-1922*
  R&R Bk N - v19 - i3 - August 2004 - p60(1) [51-
  500]
Dudertadt, James J. - *The Future of the Public University
  in America: Beyond the Crossroads*
  JEL - v41 - i4 - Dec 2003 - p1377(1) [501+]
Dudewicz, Edward J. - *Modern Mathematical,
  Management, and Statistical Sciences, III*
  SciTech - v28 - i3 - Sept 2004 - p17(1) [501+]
Dudley, John - *A Man's Game: Masculinity and the
  Anti-Aesthetics of American Literary Naturalism*
  Choice - v42 - i2 - Oct 2004 - p292(1) [501+]
Dudley, Michael - *Silicon Carbide 2004 -- Materials,
  Processing and Devices: Proceedings*
  SciTech - v28 - i4 - Dec 2004 - p157(1) [51-500]
Dudley, Steven - *Walking Ghosts: Murder and Guerrilla
  Politics in Colombia*
  BW - v34 - i3 - Jan 18 2004 - p8(1) [51-500]
  Nation - v279 - i5 - August 16 2004 - p31 [501+]
Dudley, Wendy - *Don't Name the Ducks and Other Truths
  about Life in the Country*
  CBRA - Annual 2003 - p84(1) [51-500]
Dudley, William - *Iraq*
  c SLJ - v50 - i8 - August 2004 - p135(1) [51-500]
  Islam
  y BL - v101 - i3 - Oct 1 2004 - p340(1) [51-500]
  y SLJ - v50 - i12 - Dec 2004 - p160(1) [51-500]
  Reconstruction
  SLJ - v50 - i10 - Oct 2004 - pS57(1) [51-500]
Dudman, Clare - *98 Reasons for Being*
  TLS - i5301 - Nov 5 2004 - p25(1) [501+]
Dudney, Bill - *Mastering JavaServer Faces*
  SciTech - v28 - i4 - Dec 2004 - p152(1) [51-500]
Dudziak, Mary L. - *September 11 in History: A Watershed
  Moment?*
  JAH - v91 - i3 - Dec 2004 - p1117(2) [501+]
Due, Tananarive - *The Good House*
  NYTBR - Oct 31 2004 - p18 [501+]

Duelt, Daniel Duran i - *Manual del Viatge fet per Berenguer Benet a Romania, 1341-1342*
HER - v119 - i483 - Sept 2004 - p1039(2) [501+]

Duerden, R. Chamberlain - *The Choreography of Antony Tudor: Focus on Four Ballets*
Choice - v42 - i2 - Oct 2004 - p304(1) [51-500]

Duerksen, Christopher J. - *True West: Authentic Development Patterns for Small Towns and Rural Planning Areas*
NRJ - v44 - i3 - Summer 2004 - p907-916 [501+]

Duesterberg, Thomas J. - *U.S. Manufacturing: The Engine for Growth in a Global Economy*
Choice - v41 - i7 - March 2004 - p1343(1) [501+]
R&R Bk N - v19 - i1 - Feb 2004 - p103(1) [51-500]

Duey, Kathleen - *Arthur (Illus. by Gould, Robert)*
c SLJ - v50 - i10 - Oct 2004 - p112(1) [51-500]

Duff, Andrew - *Mammals of the World: A Checklist*
Choice - v42 - i5 - Jan 2005 - p880(1) [1-50]

Duff, Patrick - *Obstetrics and Gynecology: Just the Facts*
SciTech - v28 - i3 - Sept 2004 - p116(1) [51-500]

Duff, T.E - *The Greek and Roman Historians*
Class R - v54 - i2 - Nov 2004 - p447(3) [501+]

Duffek, Karen - *Bill Reid and Beyond: Expanding on Modern Native Art*
R&R Bk N - v19 - i3 - August 2004 - p71(1) [51-500]

Duffey, Betsy - *How to Be Cool in the Third Grade*
c SLJ - v50 - i7 - July 2004 - p42(1) [51-500]

Duffin, Ross - *Shakespeare's Songbook*
Choice - v42 - i2 - Oct 2004 - p302(1) [51-500]

Duffy, Chris - *Scooby-Doo, Vol. 1*
y Teach Lib - v32 - i1 - Oct 2004 - p17(2) [501+]

Duffy, Christopher - *The '45: Bonnie Prince Charlie and the Untold Story of the Jacobite Rising*
Lon R Bks - v26 - i2 - Jan 22 2004 - p19(3) [501+]
Prussia's Glory: Rossbach and Leuthen 1757
J Mil H - v68 - i3 - July 2004 - p954-955 [501+]

Duffy, Dean G. - *Advanced Engineering Mathematics with MATLAB*
SIAM Rev - v46 - i3 - Sept 2004 - p549(13) [501+]
Transform Methods for Solving Partial Differential Equations, 2nd Ed.
SciTech - v28 - i4 - Dec 2004 - p42(1) [51-500]

Duffy, Eamon - *Faith of Our Fathers: Reflections on Catholic Tradition*
TLS - i5306 - Dec 10 2004 - p26(1) [501+]

Duffy, Francis M. - *Moving Upward Together: Creating Strategic Alignment to Sustain Systemic School Improvement*
R&R Bk N - v19 - i3 - August 2004 - p223(1) [1-50]

Duffy, Gerald G. - *Explaining Reading: A Reading for Teaching Concepts*
Choice - v41 - i11-12 - July-August 2004 - p2096(1) [501+]

Duffy, James P. - *Target America: Hitler's Plan to Attack the United States*
R&R Bk N - v19 - i3 - August 2004 - p33(1) [51-500]

Duffy, Jean H. - *Signs and Designs: Art and Architecture in the Work of Michel Butor*
R&R Bk N - v19 - i1 - Feb 2004 - p231(1) [51-500]

Duffy, John - *Fights of Our Lives: Elections, Leadership, and the Making of Canada*
BIC - v33 - i2 - March 2004 - p34(3) [501+]

Duffy, Maureen - *Alchemy*
Spec - v295 - i9183 - August 7 2004 - p31(1) [501+]
TLS - i5287 - July 30 2004 - p20(1) [501+]

Duffy, Maureen P. - *Teen Gangs: A Global View*
R&R Bk N - v19 - i3 - August 2004 - p165(1) [501+]
VOYA - v27 - i5 - Dec 2004 - p423(1) [51-500]

Duffy, Michael - *First World War.com*
LibMed - v22 - i4 - Jan 2004 - p87(1) [501+]
Latham and Abbott: The Lives and Rivalry of the Two Finest Politicians of Their Generation
Quad - v48 - i10 - Oct 2004 - p87(2) [501+]

Duffy, Robert J. - *The Green Agenda in American Politics: New Strategies for the Twenty-First Century*
PSQ - v119 - i3 - Fall 2004 - p559(3) [501+]

Duffy, Rosaleen - *A Trip Too Far: Ecotourism, Politics and Exploitation*
GJ - v170 - i3 - Sept 2004 - p284(2) [501+]

Duffy, Sean - *Medieval Dublin V: Proceedings*
R&R Bk N - v19 - i4 - Nov 2004 - p37(1) [51-500]

Duffy, Stella - *State of Happiness*
BL - v101 - i5 - Nov 1 2004 - p462(1) [51-500]
KR - v72 - i21 - Nov 1 2004 - p1022(1) [51-500]
PW - v251 - i47 - Nov 22 2004 - p40(1) [51-500]

Duffy, Thomas M. - *Learner-Centered Theory and Practice in Distance Education: Cases from Higher Education*
R&R Bk N - v19 - i1 - Feb 2004 - p193(1) [51-500]

Duffy, Timothy - *Music Makers: Portraits and Songs from the Roots of America*
Notes - v61 - i2 - Dec 2004 - p469(3) [501+]

Dufour, Alain - *Correspondence de Theodore de Beze*
Six Ct J - v35 - i1 - Spring 2004 - p225(2) [501+]

Dufour, Rose - *Naitre rien: Des orphelins de Duplessis, de la creche a l'asile*
Can Hist R - v85 - i4 - Dec 2004 - p854(3) [501+]

Dufresne, John - *Johnny Too Bad: Stories*
KR - v73 - i2 - Jan 15 2005 - p69(1) [501+]
LJ - v130 - i1 - Jan 1 2005 - p104(1) [51-500]
PW - v251 - i48 - Nov 29 2004 - p21(1) [51-500]

Dufresne, Todd - *Killing Freud: Twentieth Century Culture and the Death of Psychoanalysis*
TLS - i5264 - Feb 20 2004 - p30-30 [501+]

Dugan, Ellen - *Cottage Witchery: Natural Magick for Hearth and Home*
PW - v252 - i7 - Feb 14 2005 - p72(2) [501+]

Dugan, Melanie - *Revising Romance*
Globe & Mail - Sept 11 2004 - pD18 [501+]

Dugan, Mike - *Men Fake Foreplay: And Other Lies That Are True*
LJ - v129 - i19 - Nov 15 2004 - p76(1) [501+]
PW - v251 - i40 - Oct 4 2004 - p81(1) [51-500]

Dugas, Marcel - *Psyche au cinema: poems en prose*
Can Lit - i181 - Summer 2004 - p125-127 [501+]

Duggal, Krishan L. - *Recent Advances in Riemannian and Lorentzian Geometries*
SciTech - v28 - i1 - March 2004 - p42(1) [51-500]

Duggan, Lisa - *Sapphic Slashers: Sex, Violence, and American Modernity*
AHR - v109 - i2 - April 2004 - p540(2) [501+]
The Twilight of Equality? Neoliberalism, Cultural Politics, and the Attack on Democracy
Choice - v41 - i11-12 - July-August 2004 - p2123(1) [501+]

Duhbaum, Gary - *My Teacher Rides a Harley: Enhancing K-5 Literacy through Songwriting*
LibMed - v22 - i4 - Jan 2004 - p84(1) [501+]

Duhon-Sells, Rose - *International Perspectives on Methods of Improving Education Focusing on the Quality of Diversity*
R&R Bk N - v19 - i1 - Feb 2004 - p191(1) [51-500]

Duiker, William J. - *The World Since World War II*
R&R Bk N - v19 - i3 - August 2004 - p31(1) [51-500]

Duindam, Jeroen - *Vienna and Versailles: The Courts of Europe's Dynastic Rivals, 1550-1780*
AHR - v109 - i3 - June 2004 - p967(2) [501+]
HNet - Oct 2004 - pNA [501+]
Ren Q - v57 - i4 - Winter 2004 - p1465(2) [501+]

Duke, Daniel L. - *The Challenges of Educational Change*
R&R Bk N - v19 - i1 - Feb 2004 - p186(1) [51-500]

Duke Ellington
SLJ - v50 - i12 - Dec 2004 - p61(1) [501+]

Dukes, H.H. - *Dukes' Physiology of Domestic Animals, 12th Ed.*
SciTech - v28 - i4 - Dec 2004 - p126 [51-500]

Dulio, David A. - *For Better or Worse?: How Political Consultants Are Changing Elections in the United States*
Choice - v42 - i2 - Oct 2004 - p371(1) [51-500]

Dulisse, Richard A. - *Essentials of Long-Term Care Insurance*
R&R Bk N - v19 - i4 - Nov 2004 - p119(1) [51-500]

Dulken, Stephen van - *Inventing the American Dream: A History of Curious, Extraordinary and Just Plain Useful Patents*
TLS - i5288 - August 6 2004 - p27(1) [501+]

Dumas, Alexandre - *One Thousand and One Ghosts*
TLS - i5303 - Nov 19 2004 - p37(1) [51-500]

Dumas, Margaret - *Speak Now*
BL - v101 - i1 - Sept 1 2004 - p68(1) [51-500]
Bwatch - Dec 2004 - pNA [501+]
PW - v251 - i36 - Sept 6 2004 - p50(1) [51-500]
y SLJ - v51 - i1 - Jan 2005 - p159(1) [51-500]

Dumbill, Edd - *Mono: A Developer's Notebook*
SciTech - v28 - i4 - Dec 2004 - p26(1) [51-500]

Dumbleton, Mike - *Watch out for Jamie Joel*
Kliatt - v38 - i6 - Nov 2004 - p16(1) [51-500]
y VOYA - v27 - i3 - August 2004 - p215(1) [1-50]

Dumenil, Gerard - *Capital Resurgent: Roots of the Neoliberal Revolution*
Choice - v42 - i5 - Jan 2005 - p901(1) [1-50]

Dummett, Michael - *History of Games Played with the Tarot Pack: The Game of Triumphs, Vol. 1*
R&R Bk N - v19 - i4 - Nov 2004 - p81(1) [51-500]
History of Games Played with the Tarot Pack: The Game of Triumphs, Vol. 2
R&R Bk N - v19 - i4 - Nov 2004 - p81(1) [51-500]
Truth and the Past
Choice - v42 - i2 - Oct 2004 - p306(1) [51-500]

Dumont, Micheline - *Decouvrir la memoire des femmes. Une historienne face a l'histoire des femmes*
Can Hist R - v85 - i3 - Sept 2004 - p628(3) [501+]

Dumouchel, J. Robert - *Government Assistance Almanac, 2004-2005, 18th Ed.*
R&R Bk N - v19 - i3 - August 2004 - p98(1) [51-500]

Dumoulin, Olivier - *Le role social de L'historien: De la chaire au pretoire*
JIH - v35 - i2 - Autumn 2004 - p280(3) [501+]

Dunand, Francoise - *Gods and Men in Egypt: 3000 BCE to 395 CE*
Choice - v42 - i5 - Jan 2005 - p869(2) [1-50]

Dunant, Sarah - *The Birth of Venus (Read by Mazur, Kathe). Audiobook Review*
Kliatt - v38 - i4 - July 2004 - p48(1) [51-500]
LJ - v129 - i16 - Oct 1 2004 - p118(2) [51-500]
The Birth of Venus
NYTBR - Dec 19 2004 - p30 [501+]

Dunaway, David King - *Writing the Southwest, Rev. Ed.*
R&R Bk N - v19 - i1 - Feb 2004 - p244(1) [51-500]

Dunaway, Wilma A. - *The African-American Family in Slavery and Emancipation*
JAH - v91 - i2 - Sept 2004 - p642(2) [501+]
Slavery in the American Mountain South
AJS - v110 - i2 - Sept 2004 - p531(3) [501+]
JAH - v91 - i2 - Sept 2004 - p618(2) [501+]

Dunay, Pal - *Open Skies: A Cooperative Approach to Military Transparency and Confidence Building*
SciTech - v28 - i4 - Dec 2004 - p171(1) [51-500]

Dunayevskaya, Raya - *The Power of Negativity: Selected Writings on the Dialectic in Hegel and Marx*
S&S - v68 - i1 - Spring 2004 - p123-125 [501+]

Dunbar, Anthony P. - *Where We Stand: Voices of Southern Dissent*
BW - v34 - i35 - August 2004 - p3(2) [501+]
LJ - v129 - i16 - Oct 1 2004 - p99(2) [51-500]
NYRB - v51 - i16 - Oct 21 2004 - p48(3) [501+]

Dunbar, Fiona - *The Truth Cookie*
c Sch Lib - v52 - i3 - Autumn 2004 - p145(1) [501+]

Dunbar, Gary S. - *Geography: Discipline, Profession and Subject since 1870: An International Survey*
Hist Geo - v32 - Annual 2004 - p186(2) [501+]

Dunbar, Ian - *Before and After Getting Your Puppy: A Guide to Positive Puppy Raising*
Bwatch - Oct 2004 - pNA [51-500]

Dunbar, Linda J. - *Reforming the Scottish Church: John Winram, c. 1492-1582, and the Example of Fife*
Six Ct J - v35 - i3 - Fall 2004 - p829-831 [501+]

Dunbar, Paul Laurence - *Dunbar Out Loud (Read by Norfolk, Bobby). Audiobook Review*
c SLJ - v50 - i11 - Nov 2004 - p81(1) [51-500]
Selected Poems
Bl S - v34 - i3 - Fall 2004 - p70-70 [501+]

Dunbar, Polly - *Dog Blue (Illus. by Dunbar, Polly)*
c BL - v100 - i21 - July 2004 - p1846(2) [51-500]
c HB - v80 - i5 - Sept-Oct 2004 - p566(1) [51-500]
c KR - v72 - i13 - July 1 2004 - p627(1) [51-500]
c PW - v251 - i35 - August 30 2004 - p53(1) [51-500]
c SLJ - v50 - i9 - Sept 2004 - p158(1) [51-500]
Flyaway Katie (Illus. by Dunbar, Polly)
c NYTBR - Oct 17 2004 - p21 [501+]
c PW - v251 - i27 - July 5 2004 - p54(1) [51-500]
c SLJ - v50 - i9 - Sept 2004 - p158(1) [51-500]
c TES - v0 - i4577 - April 2 2004 - p35(1) [501+]

Dunbar, Robin - *The Human Story: A New History of Mankind's Evolution*
Nature - v429 - i6987 - May 6 2004 - p17(2) [501+]

Duncan, A.A.M. - *The Kingship of the Scots, 842-1292: Succession and Independence*
Albion - v36 - i2 - Summer 2004 - p374(2) [501+]

Duncan, A.A.M - *The Kingship of the Scots, 842-1292: Succession and Independence*
HER - v119 - i483 - Sept 2004 - p980(2) [501+]

Duncan, A.A.M. - *The Kingship of the Scots, 842-1292: Succession and Independence*
  TLS - i5268 - March 19 2004 - p24-25 [501+]
Duncan, Alasdair - *Sushi Central*
  Lam Bk Rpt - v13 - i3 - Oct 2004 - p13(2) [501+]
Duncan, Alice Faye - *Honey Baby Sugar Child*
  c Black Iss - v7 - i2 - March-April 2005 - p66(2) [501+]
  c KR - v72 - i24 - Dec 15 2004 - p1200(1) [501+]
Duncan, Andrew - *Secret London: Exploring the Hidden City, with Original Walks, and Unusual Places to Visit*
  R&R Bk N - v19 - i1 - Feb 2004 - p33(1) [1-50]
Duncan, Bill - *The Wee Book of Calvin: Air-Kissing in the North-East*
  Econ - v373 - i8400 - Nov 6 2004 - p58US [501+]
  TLS - i5304 - Nov 26 2004 - p7(1) [501+]
Duncan, Dave - *The Jaguar Knights: A Chronicle of the King's Blades*
  BL - v101 - i1 - Sept 1 2004 - p74(1) [51-500]
  ChrSFF&H - v26 - i9 - Sept 2004 - p30(1) [51-500]
  KR - v72 - i14 - July 15 2004 - p665(1) [51-500]
  LJ - v129 - i17 - Oct 15 2004 - p58(1) [51-500]
  PW - v251 - i28 - July 12 2004 - p48(1) [51-500]
West of January
  CBRA - Annual 2003 - p161(2) [51-500]
Duncan, Dayton - *Horatio's Drive: America's First Road Trip*
  JPC - v38 - i2 - Nov 2004 - p430(2) [501+]
Scenes of Visionary Enchantment: Reflections on Lewis and Clark
  Bwatch - March 2005 - pNA [51-500]
  Roundup M - v11 - i6 - August 2004 - p23(1) [501+]
Duncan, Glen - *Death of an Ordinary Man*
  BL - v101 - i5 - Nov 1 2004 - p462(1) [51-500]
  KR - v72 - i19 - Oct 1 2004 - p929(1) [501+]
  NYTBR - Feb 6 2005 - p14 [501+]
  PW - v251 - i50 - Dec 13 2004 - p44(1) [51-500]
  TLS - i5287 - July 30 2004 - p21(1) [501+]
  Ent W - i802 - Jan 21 2005 - p95 [501+]
  LJ - v129 - i19 - Nov 15 2004 - p49(1) [501+]
Duncan, James R. - *Owls of the World: Their Lives, Behavior, and Survival*
  CBRA - Annual 2003 - p401(2) [51-500]
  CG - v124 - i2 - March-April 2004 - p101(1) [501+]
  y SB - v40 - i3 - May-June 2004 - p124(2) [501+]
Duncan, James S. - *A Companion to Cultural Geography*
  Choice - v42 - i3 - Nov 2004 - p538(1) [1-50]
Duncan, Jennifer - *Frontier Spirit: The Brave Women of the Klondike*
  CBRA - Annual 2003 - p381(1) [51-500]
  Globe & Mail - Oct 30 2004 - pD29 [51-500]
Duncan, Joyce - *Sport in American Culture: From Ali to X-Games*
  LJ - v130 - i4 - March 1 2005 - p116(1) [51-500]
Duncan, Karen A. - *Healing from the Trauma of Childhood Sexual Abuse: The Journey for Women*
  R&R Bk N - v19 - i4 - Nov 2004 - p145(1) [501+]
Duncan, Kirsty - *Hunting the 1918 Flu: One Scientist's Search for a Killer Virus*
  CBRA - Annual 2003 - p429(1) [501+]
Duncan, Paul - *Alfred Hitchcock: The Complete Films*
  TimHES - v0 - i1647 - July 2 2004 - p26(1) [501+]
Stanley Kubrick: The Complete Films
  TimHES - v0 - i1647 - July 2 2004 - p26(1) [501+]
Duncan, Robert - *The Letters of Robert Duncan and Denise Levertov*
  NYRB - v51 - i17 - Nov 4 2004 - p18(3) [501+]
  R&R Bk N - v19 - i1 - Feb 2004 - p245(1) [51-500]
Duncan, Russell - *Contemporary America*
  R&R Bk N - v19 - i1 - Feb 2004 - p54(1) [51-500]
Duncan, Shannon - *Present Moment Awareness: A Simple, Step-by-Step Guide to Living in the Now*
  Bwatch - Feb 2005 - pNA [501+]
Duncan, Stephen F. - *A History of the Sacred Musical Life of an Orthodox Church in America*
  R&R Bk N - v19 - i4 - Nov 2004 - p197(1) [501+]
Duncan, Stephen M. - *A War of a Different Kind: Military Force and America's Search for Homeland Security*
  Choice - v42 - i3 - Nov 2004 - p564(1) [1-50]
  Mar Crp G - v88 - i12 - Dec 2004 - p48(1) [501+]
Dundee, Wayne D. - *The Fight in the Dog*
  KR - v73 - i3 - Feb 1 2005 - p150(1) [51-500]
Dundon, M.D. - *Macromedia Flash MX Production Techniques*
  SciTech - v28 - i1 - March 2004 - p175(1) [51-500]

Dung, Houchi - *Acupuncture: An Anatomical Approach*
  SciTech - v28 - i3 - Sept 2004 - p121(1) [51-500]
Dunham, Mikel - *Buddha's Warriors*
  LJ - v130 - i1 - Jan 1 2005 - p127(1) [51-500]
Duning, David - *Afghanistan*
  y Sch Lib - v52 - i4 - Winter 2004 - p218(1) [51-500]
Dunkerley, James - *Studies in the Formation of the Nation-State in Latin America*
  HAHR - v84 - i3 - August 2004 - p517(2) [501+]
Dunkle, Clare B. - *Close Kin*
  y BL - v101 - i3 - Oct 1 2004 - p322(1) [51-500]
  y CCB-B - v58 - i4 - Dec 2004 - p165(2) [51-500]
     KR - v72 - i18 - Sept 15 2004 - p913(1) [501+]
  y SLJ - v50 - i10 - Oct 2004 - p161(1) [51-500]
     VOYA - v27 - i5 - Dec 2004 - p402(1) [51-500]
The Hollow Kingdom (Read by Sterlin, Jenny). Audiobook Review
  c Kliatt - v38 - i4 - July 2004 - p51(2) [51-500]
Dunlap, David W. - *From Abyssinian to Zion: A Guide to Manhattan's Houses of Worship*
  Black Iss - v6 - i5 - Sept-Oct 2004 - p38(1) [501+]
  R&R Bk N - v19 - i3 - August 2004 - p15(1) [1-50]
Dunlap, Julie - *John Muir and Stickeen: An Icy Adventure with a No-Good Dog (Illus. by Farnsworth, Bill)*
  c BL - v101 - i6 - Nov 15 2004 - p588(1) [51-500]
  c CH Bwatch - v14 - i12 - Dec 2004 - pNA [51-500]
  c Inst - v114 - i5 - Jan-Feb 2005 - p73(2) [501+]
  c KR - v72 - i20 - Oct 15 2004 - p1005(1) [51-500]
  c SLJ - v50 - i12 - Dec 2004 - p106(1) [501+]
Dunlap, Linda L. - *What All Children Need: Theory and Application, 2nd Ed.*
  R&R Bk N - v19 - i4 - Nov 2004 - p130(1) [51-500]
Dunlap, Riley E. - *Sociological Theory and the Environment: Classical Foundations, Contemporary Insights*
  CS - v33 - i1 - Jan 2004 - p66-67 [501+]
Dunlap, Susan - *Fast Friends.*
  KR - v72 - i18 - Sept 15 2004 - p892(2) [51-500]
Dunlap, Susanne Emily - *Emilie's Voice*
  KR - v73 - i4 - Feb 15 2005 - p190(1) [51-500]
Dunlap, Thomas R. - *Faith in Nature: Environmentalism as Religious Quest*
  Aud - v106 - i3 - July-August 2004 - p66(3) [501+]
  Choice - v42 - i2 - Oct 2004 - p309(1) [51-500]
  E-Streams - Oct 2004 - pNA [501+]
  HNet - Oct 2004 - pNA [501+]
  PHR - v73 - i4 - Nov 2004 - p663(2) [501+]
  RAH - v32 - i3 - Sept 2004 - p380-387 [501+]
Nature and the English Diaspora: Environment and History in the United States, Canada, Australia, and New Zealand
  Isis - v95 - i3 - Sept 2004 - p501(2) [501+]
Dunlop, Beth - *Arquitectonica*
  Choice - v42 - i6 - Feb 2005 - p1015(1) [51-500]
Dunlop, Bonnie - *The Beauty Box*
  Globe & Mail - July 17 2004 - pD7 [501+]
Dunlop, Ian - *Edward VII and the Entente Cordiale*
  CR - v285 - i1666 - Nov 2004 - p318(1) [51-500]
  TLS - i5286 - July 23 2004 - p28(1) [501+]
Dunlop, Storm - *Firefly Practical Astronomy*
  E-Streams - August 2004 - pNA [501+]
  y VOYA - v27 - i4 - Oct 2004 - p324(1) [51-500]
Dunmore, 4th Earl of - *Encyclopedia of Modern French Thought*
  R&R Bk N - v19 - i3 - August 2004 - p41(1) [51-500]
London 1945: Life in the Debris of War
  CR - v285 - i1665 - Oct 2004 - p250(1) [501+]
London's Thames. Gavin Weightman
  CR - v285 - i1666 - Nov 2004 - p318(1) [501+]
Murphy's Favorite Channels
  TLS - i5292 - Sept 3 2004 - p32(1) [501+]
Dunmore, Helen - *Mourning Ruby*
  BooChiTr - May 2 2004 - p5(1) [501+]
  NYTBR - August 8 2004 - p14 [501+]
Dunn, Brad - *New York: The Unknown City*
  LJ - v129 - i18 - Nov 1 2004 - p110(1) [51-500]
Dunn, Carola - *A Mourning Wedding*
  BL - v101 - i3 - Oct 1 2004 - p312(2) [51-500]
  KR - v72 - i18 - Sept 15 2004 - p893(1) [51-500]
  LJ - v129 - i18 - Nov 1 2004 - p60(1) [51-500]
Dunn, Charles W. - *Faith, Freedom, and the Future: Religion in American Political Culture*
  HNet - August 2004 - pNA [501+]
Dunn, Christian - *Inferno!*
  ChrSFF&H - v26 - i10 - Oct 2004 - p28(1) [51-500]

Dunn, Dana S. - *Measuring Up: Educational Assessment Challenges and Practices for Psychology*
  Choice - v42 - i6 - Feb 2005 - p1102(1) [51-500]
  R&R Bk N - v19 - i3 - August 2004 - p8(1) [1-50]
Dunn, Dennis J. - *The Catholic Church and Russia: Popes, Patriarchs, Tsars, and Commissars*
  Choice - v42 - i6 - Feb 2005 - p1078(1) [51-500]
  R&R Bk N - v19 - i4 - Nov 2004 - p27(1) [501+]
  TLS - i5294 - Sept 17 2004 - p30(1) [501+]
Dunn, Elizabeth C. - *Privatizing Poland: Baby Food, Big Business and the Remaking of Labor*
  CHE - v50 - i47 - July 30 2004 - pA14-A14 [501+]
Dunn, I.J. - *Biological Reaction Engineering: Dynamic Modelling Fundamentals with Simulation Examples, 2nd Ed.*
  SciTech - v28 - i1 - March 2004 - p172(1) [51-500]
Dunn, James D.G. - *The Cambridge Companion to St. Paul*
  Intpr - v58 - i3 - July 2004 - p334(1) [51-500]
  TT - v61 - i3 - Oct 2004 - p423(1) [501+]
Eerdmans Commentary on the Bible
  Intpr - v58 - i3 - July 2004 - p334(1) [51-500]
  TT - v61 - i3 - Oct 2004 - p423(2) [501+]
Jesus Remembered
  Choice - v41 - i7 - March 2004 - p1313(1) [501+]
  Intpr - v58 - i4 - Oct 2004 - p410(3) [501+]
Dunn, Jane - *Elizabeth and Mary: Cousins, Rivals, Queens (Read by Peters, Donada). Audiobook Review*
  LJ - v129 - i18 - Nov 1 2004 - p130(2) [51-500]
Elizabeth and Mary: Cousins, Rivals, Queens
  Choice - v42 - i1 - Sept 2004 - p178(1) [501+]
  y Kliatt - v39 - i2 - March 2005 - p34(1) [51-500]
  Lon R Bks - v26 - i20 - Oct 21 2004 - p1(3) [501+]
Dunn, John M. - *The Civil Rights Movement*
  y SLJ - v50 - i10 - Oct 2004 - p167(1) [51-500]
Dunn, Mark - *Ella Minnow Pea: A Novel in Letters*
  LJ - v130 - i1 - Jan 1 2005 - p174(1) [501+]
United States Counties
  Ref Rev - August 2004 - pNA [501+]
  R&R Bk N - v19 - i1 - Feb 2004 - p55(1) [51-500]
Welcome to Higby
  TLS - i5305 - Dec 3 2004 - p22(1) [51-500]
Dunn, Opal - *Number Rhymes to Say and Play! (Illus. by Gon, Adriano)*
  c SLJ - v51 - i2 - Feb 2005 - p116(1) [51-500]
Dunn-Rankin, Peter - *Scaling methods, 2nd Ed.*
  SciTech - v28 - i4 - Dec 2004 - p1(1) [1-50]
Dunn, Ross E. - *The Adventures of Ibn Battuta: A Muslim Traveler of the 14th Century. Audiobook Review*
  Globe & Mail - Nov 27 2004 - pD49 [1-50]
Dunn, Sarah - *The Big Love (Read by Foss, Eliza). Audiobook Review*
  BL - v101 - i5 - Nov 1 2004 - p502(1) [51-500]
  y Kliatt - v39 - i1 - Jan 2005 - p38(1) [51-500]
  PW - v251 - i31 - August 2 2004 - p20(1) [501+]
The Big Love
  BL - v100 - i21 - July 2004 - p1817(1) [51-500]
  Ent W - i773 - July 9 2004 - p95 [1-50]
  KR - v72 - i13 - July 1 2004 - p592(2) [51-500]
  LJ - v129 - i12 - July 2004 - p69(1) [51-500]
Dunn, Stephen - *The Insistence of Beauty*
  BL - v101 - i1 - Sept 1 2004 - p40(1) [51-500]
  LJ - v129 - i18 - Nov 1 2004 - p88(2) [51-500]
  Poet - v185 - i2 - Nov 2004 - p133(3) [501+]
Local Visitations: Poems
  y Kliatt - v39 - i2 - March 2005 - p32(1) [51-500]
Dunn, Susan - *Jefferson's Second Revolution: The Election Crisis of 1800 and the Triumph of Republicanism*
  BL - v101 - i2 - Sept 15 2004 - p182(1) [51-500]
  BW - v34 - i44 - Oct 31 2004 - p3(1) [501+]
  Ent W - Sept 10 2004 - p168 [51-500]
  KR - v72 - i14 - July 15 2004 - p670(1) [51-500]
  NL - v87 - i5 - Sept-Oct 2004 - p26(2) [501+]
  PW - v251 - i31 - August 2 2004 - p61(1) [501+]
Dunn, Suzannah - *O Henry!*
  BW - v34 - i44 - Oct 31 2004 - p12(1) [501+]
The Queen of Subtleties
  BL - v101 - i4 - Oct 15 2004 - p389(1) [51-500]
  KR - v72 - i16 - August 15 2004 - p761(1) [501+]
  LJ - v129 - i14 - Sept 1 2004 - p138(2) [51-500]
  PW - v251 - i38 - Sept 20 2004 - p44(1) [51-500]
Dunn, Walter S., Jr. - *Heroes or Traitors: The German Replacement Army, the July Plot, and Adolf Hitler*
  HNet - Sept 2004 - pNA [501+]
Dunne, Dominick - *Oscar Night: 75 Years of Hollywood Parties*
  PW - v251 - i45 - Nov 8 2004 - p49(1) [501+]

Dunne, John Gregory - *Nothing Lost*
AM - v192 - i6 - Feb 21 2005 - p23 [501+]
BooChiTr - May 2 2004 - p1(1) [501+]
Globe & Mail - July 10 2004 - pD6 [501+]
KR - v72 - i24 - Dec 15 2004 - pS9(1) [501+]

Dunne, John S. - *The Road of the Heart's Desire: An Essay on the Cycles of Story and Song*
Theol St - v65 - i4 - Dec 2004 - p906(1) [501+]

Dunne, Patrick M. - *Retailing. 5th Ed.*
R&R Bk N - v19 - i2 - May 2004 - p115(1) [51-500]

Dunnett, Nigel - *Planting Green Roofs and Living Walls*
Bwatch - v26 - i9 - Sept 2004 - p2(2) [51-500]
E Mag - v15 - i5 - Sept-Oct 2004 - p61(2) [51-500]
R&R Bk N - v19 - i4 - Nov 2004 - p246(1) [501+]

Dunning, Donna - *TLC at Work: Training, Leading, Coaching All Types for Star Performance*
Bwatch - v26 - i7 - July 2004 - p4(1) [51-500]
HR Mag - v49 - i8 - August 2004 - p142(2) [501+]
R&R Bk N - v19 - i4 - Nov 2004 - p113(1) [51-500]

Dunning, Eric - *Fighting Fans: Football Hooliganism as a World Phenomenon*
SSJ - v21 - i1 - March 2004 - p105-108 [501+]

Dunning, John - *Booked to Die*
LJ - v129 - i14 - Sept 1 2004 - p207(1) [501+]
The Bookman's Promise (Read by Guidall, George). Audiobook Review
BL - v101 - i4 - Oct 15 2004 - p432(1) [51-500]
LJ - v129 - i15 - Sept 15 2004 - p88(1) [51-500]
The Sign of the Book: A Cliff Janeway Novel
BL - v101 - i9-10 - Jan 1 2005 - p825(1) [1-50]
KR - v73 - i1 - Jan 1 2005 - p22(1) [51-500]
NYTBR - March 13 2005 - p28 [501+]
PW - v252 - i1 - Jan 3 2005 - p39(1) [501+]

Dunningan, Sarah M. - *Woman and Feminine in Medieval and Early Modern Scottish Writing*
Choice - v42 - i4 - Dec 2004 - p644(1) [1-50]

Dunninton, G. Waldo - *Carl Friedrich Gauss: Titan of Science*
SciTech - v28 - i1 - March 2004 - p41(1) [51-500]

Dunnion, Kristyn - *Missing Matthew*
c CBRA - Annual 2003 - p481(1) [51-500]
y VOYA - v27 - i3 - August 2004 - p215(1) [1-50]
Mosh Pit
y BIC - v33 - i9 - Dec 2004 - p39(2) [51-500]

Dunnivant, Frank M. - *Environmental Laboratory Exercises for Instrumnetal Analysis and Environmental Chemistry*
Choice - v42 - i6 - Feb 2005 - p1050(1) [51-500]

Dunphy, Lynne M. Hektor - *Management Guidelines for Nurse Practitioners Working with Adults, 2nd Ed.*
SciTech - v28 - i1 - March 2004 - p126(1) [1-50]

Dunrea, Olivier - *BooBoo (Illus. by Dunrea, Olivier)*
c BL - v100 - i22 - August 2004 - p1941(1) [51-500]
c CCB-B - v58 - i2 - Oct 2004 - p70(1) [51-500]
c KR - v72 - i14 - July 15 2004 - p683(1) [51-500]
c SLJ - v50 - i10 - Oct 2004 - p112(1) [51-500]
Ollie the Stomper
c LibMed - v22 - i6 - March 2004 - p56(1) [501+]
Peedie (Illus. by Dunrea, Olivier)
c BL - v100 - i22 - August 2004 - p1941(1) [51-500]
c PW - v251 - i28 - July 12 2004 - p62(1) [51-500]
c SLJ - v50 - i10 - Oct 2004 - p112(1) [51-500]

Duns Scotus, John - *Duns Scotus on Divine Love: Texts and Commentary on Goodness and Freedom, God and Humans*
R&R Bk N - v19 - i1 - Feb 2004 - p21(1) [51-500]

Dunsby, Jonathan - *Making Words Sing: Nineteenth-and Twentieth- Century Song*
Choice - v42 - i5 - Jan 2005 - p861(1) [1-50]

Duntemann, Jeff - *Degunking Your Email, Spam, and Viruses*
LJ - v130 - i4 - March 1 2005 - p106(1) [501+]
Jeff Duntemann's Wi-Fi Guide, 2nd Ed.
SciTech - v28 - i3 - Sept 2004 - p157(1) [51-500]

Dunton-Downer, Leslie - *Essential Shakespeare Handbook*
NYTBR - Oct 3 2004 - p23 [501+]
R&R Bk N - v19 - i4 - Nov 2004 - p235(1) [501+]

Dunton, John - *Teague Land, or A Merry Ramble to the Wild Irish*
Choice - v42 - i1 - Sept 2004 - p100(1) [501+]

Duong, Thu Huong - *No Man's Land*
KR - v73 - i4 - Feb 15 2005 - p196(1) [501+]

Dupee, Jeffrey N. - *British Travel Writers in China - Writing Home to a British Public, 1890-1914*
R&R Bk N - v19 - i3 - August 2004 - p56(1) [51-500]

Dupin, Jacques - *Miro*
R&R Bk N - v19 - i2 - May 2004 - p193(1) [51-500]

Duport, Daniele - *Le Jardin et la Nature: Ordre et Variete dans la litterature de la Renaissance*
Six Ct J - v34 - i4 - Winter 2003 - p1188-1190 [501+]

DuPrau, Jeanne - *The City of Ember. Audiobook Review*
c Kliatt - v38 - i6 - Nov 2004 - p42(2) [51-500]
c SLJ - v50 - i10 - Oct 2004 - p84(1) [51-500]
The City of Ember
c SLJ - v50 - i10 - Oct 2004 - pS53(1) [51-500]
The People of Sparks (Read by Dillon, Wendy). Audiobook Review
y Kliatt - v39 - i1 - Jan 2005 - p48(2) [51-500]
c SLJ - v50 - i10 - Oct 2004 - p84(1) [51-500]
The People of Sparks
c CCB-B - v57 - i11 - July-August 2004 - p461(1) [501+]
c CH Bwatch - v14 - i7 - July 2004 - p7(2) [501+]
c HB - v80 - i4 - July-August 2004 - p450(2) [51-500]
c NYTBR - Sept 19 2004 - p16 [51-500]
c SLJ - v50 - i10 - Oct 2004 - pS53(1) [51-500]
c VOYA - v27 - i5 - Dec 2004 - p402(1) [51-500]

Dupre, John - *Darwin's Legacy: What Evolution Means Today*
QRB - v79 - i3 - Sept 2004 - p304(1) [501+]
SciTech - v28 - i1 - March 2004 - p62(1) [51-500]

Dupre, Louis - *The Enlightenment and the Intellectual Foundations of Modern Culture*
Choice - v42 - i3 - Nov 2004 - p496(1) [51-500]
R&R Bk N - v19 - i4 - Nov 2004 - p4(1) [51-500]

DuPuis, E. Melanie - *Nature's Perfect Food: How Milk Became America's Drink*
Am St - v45 - i1 - Spring 2004 - p140-140 [501+]
Smoke and Mirrors: The Politics and Culture of Air Pollution
Choice - v42 - i5 - Jan 2005 - p883(2) [1-50]

Dupuis, Jacques - *Christianity and the Religions: From Confrontation to Dialogue*
TLS - i5266 - March 5 2004 - p25-25 [501+]

DuQuette, Keith - *They Call Me Woolly (Illus. by DuQuette, Keith)*
c RT - v57 - Nov 2003 - p273 [51-500]

Duran, Daniel - *Manual del Viatge fet per Bergenuer Benet a Romania, 1341-1342: Estudi i Edicio*
HER - v119 - i483 - Sept 2004 - p1039(2) [501+]

Duranceau, Steven J. - *Optimizing Corrosion Control in Water Distribution Systems*
SciTech - v28 - i3 - Sept 2004 - p146(1) [51-500]

Durand, Alain-Philippe - *Black, Blanc, Beur: Rap Music and Hip-Hop Culture in the Francophone World*
FS - v58 - i3 - July 2004 - p444-445 [51-500]
Lang Soc - v33 - i3 - June 2004 - p459-461 [501+]

Durand, Jean-Francois - *Giono dans sa culture*
FS - v58 - i3 - July 2004 - p434-535 [51-500]

Durand, Kevin K.J. - *Virtue: Essays in Ancient Philosophy*
R&R Bk N - v19 - i4 - Nov 2004 - p3(1) [51-500]

Durand, Stephane - *Winged Migration: The Junior Edition*
c PW - v251 - i37 - Sept 13 2004 - p36(2) [51-500]
c SB - v40 - i5 - Sept-Oct 2004 - p223(1) [51-500]
c SLJ - v50 - i10 - Oct 2004 - p189(2) [51-500]

Durant, Alan - *Always and Forever*
c BL - v100 - i21 - July 2004 - p1847(1) [51-500]
Brown Bear Gets in Shape (Illus. by Hudson, Annabel)
c SLJ - v50 - i8 - August 2004 - p86(1) [51-500]
Happy Birthday Spider McDrew
c Sch Lib - v52 - i4 - Winter 2004 - p203(1) [51-500]
That's Not Right! (Illus. by McEwen, Katharine)
c SLJ - v50 - i8 - August 2004 - p85(1) [501+]

Durant, Michael J - *In the Company of Heroes*
y Kliatt - v38 - i5 - Sept 2004 - p41(2) [51-500]

Durant, Will - *The Story of Philosophy: From Plato to the American Pragmatists (Read by Gardner, Grover)*
Globe & Mail - Jan 1 2005 - pD14 [1-50]

Duranti, Alessandro - *An Companion to Linguistic Anthropology*
Choice - v42 - i3 - Nov 2004 - p527(1) [1-50]

Durbin, Christopher - *Islands*
Sch Lib - v52 - i3 - Autumn 2004 - p150(1) [501+]

Durbin, William - *The Darkest Evening*
c BL - v101 - i6 - Nov 15 2004 - p582(1) [51-500]
y CCB-B - v58 - i5 - Jan 2005 - p207(2) [51-500]
y Kliatt - v38 - i6 - Nov 2004 - p7(1) [51-500]
y KR - v72 - i22 - Nov 15 2004 - p1088(1) [51-500]
y SLJ - v51 - i1 - Jan 2005 - p126(1) [51-500]

Durcan, Liam - *A Short Journey by Car*
Globe & Mail - Oct 23 2004 - pD23 [501+]
Globe & Mail - Nov 27 2004 - pD3 [501+]

Durden, Robert F. - *Bold Entrepreneur: A Life of James B. Duke*
JSH - v70 - i3 - August 2004 - p675(2) [501+]

Durham, Alan L. - *Patent Law Essentials: A Concise Guide, 2nd Ed.*
SciTech - v28 - i4 - Dec 2004 - p10(1) [1-50]

Durham, David Anthony - *Pride of Carthage*
BL - v101 - i9-10 - Jan 1 2005 - p813(1) [1-50]
LJ - v129 - i18 - Nov 1 2004 - p72(1) [501+]
PW - v251 - i42 - Oct 18 2004 - p45(1) [51-500]
NYTBR - Feb 6 2005 - p23 [501+]

Durham, John - *Mass Communications and American Social Thought: Key Texts, 1919-1968*
Choice - v42 - i7 - March 2005 - p1222(1) [51-500]

Durham, Laura - *Better Off Wed: An Annabelle Archer Mystery*
LJ - v129 - i16 - Oct 1 2004 - p64(1) [501+]

Durham, William H. - *Annual Review of Anthropology, Vol. 32*
R&R Bk N - v19 - i1 - Feb 2004 - p71(1) [1-50]

Durie, Alastair J. - *Scotland for the Holidays: Tourism in Scotland c. 1780-1939*
Albion - v36 - i2 - Summer 2004 - p380(2) [501+]

During, Simon - *Modern Enchantments: The Cultural Power of Secular Magic*
T&C - v45 - i4 - Oct 2004 - p895(3) [501+]
TDR - v48 - i3 - Fall 2004 - p192(3) [501+]

Durnford, Hugh - *Tunnelling to Freedom and Other Escape Narratives from World War I*
LJ - v129 - i17 - Oct 15 2004 - p99(1) [51-500]

Duroselle, Jean-Baptiste - *France and the Nazi Threat: The Collapse of French Diplomacy, 1932-1939*
Choice - v42 - i4 - Dec 2004 - p728(1) [1-50]

Durr, Kenneth D. - *Behind the Backlash: White Working-Class Politics in Baltimore, 1940-1980*
AHR - v109 - i4 - Oct 2004 - p1255(2) [501+]
JAH - v91 - i1 - June 2004 - p317-318 [501+]

Durr, Marlese - *The New Politics of Race: From Du Bois to the Twenty-First Century*
CS - v33 - i1 - Jan 2004 - p28-29 [501+]

Durr, Virginia Foster - *Freedom Writer: Virginia Foster Durr, Letters from the Civil Rights Years*
Choice - v41 - i7 - March 2004 - p1355(1) [501+]

Durr, Volker - *Flaubert's 'Salammbo': The Ancient Orient as a Political Allegory of Nineteenth-Century France*
FS - v58 - i1 - Jan 2004 - p124(2) [501+]

Durrani, Osman - *Travellers in Time and Space: The German Historical Novel*
GSR - v27 - i1 - Feb 2004 - p157-158 [501+]

Durrant, Lynde - *The Sun, the Rain, and the Apple Seed: A Novel of Johnny Appleseed's Life*
LibMed - v22 - i4 - June 2004 - p64(1) [501+]

Durrant, Sabine - *The Great Indoors*
BL - v101 - i7 - Dec 1 2004 - p634(1) [51-500]
KR - v72 - i21 - Nov 1 2004 - p1023(1) [501+]
LJ - v129 - i20 - Dec 1 2004 - p99(1) [501+]
NYTBR - Jan 30 2005 - p21 [501+]
PW - v251 - i50 - Dec 13 2004 - p45(2) [501+]

Durrant, Sam - *Postcolonial Narrative and the Work of Mourning: J.M. Coetzee, Wilson Harris, and Toni Morrison*
Choice - v42 - i1 - Sept 2004 - p100(1) [501+]

Durrett, Deanne - *The 1950s*
y CH Bwatch - v14 - i7 - July 2004 - p5(1) [51-500]

Durso, Pamela R. - *The Power of Woman: The Life and Writings of Sarah Moore Grimke*
R&R Bk N - v19 - i3 - August 2004 - p26(1) [1-50]

Durst, David C. - *Weimar Modernism: Philosophy, Politics, and Culture in Germany, 1918-1933*
R&R Bk N - v20 - i1 - Feb 2005 - p9(1) [51-500]

Duruigbo, Emeka A. - *Multinational Corporations and International Law: Accountability and Compliance Issues in the Petroleum Industry*
R&R Bk N - v19 - i1 - Feb 2004 - pNA [51-500]

Duskin, Gerald L. - *If the Gods Are Good: The Epic Sacrifice of HMS Jervis Bay*
R&R Bk N - v20 - i1 - Feb 2005 - p33(1) [51-500]

Dussel, Enrique D. - *Beyond Philosophy: Ethics, History, Marxism, and Liberation Theology*
R&R Bk N - v19 - i1 - Feb 2004 - p3(1) [51-500]

Dust
LibMed - v22 - i5 - Feb 2004 - p73(1) [501+]

DuTemple, Leslie A. - *The Colosseum*
c TES - v0 - i4587 - June 11 2004 - psssss29(1) [501+]
The Hoover Dam
c TES - v0 - i4587 - June 11 2004 - psssss29(1) [501+]
The Panama Canal
c TES - v0 - i4587 - June 11 2004 - psssss29(1) [501+]

Duthie, G. Andrew - *ASP.NET in a Nutshell, 2nd Ed.*
SciTech - v28 - i1 - March 2004 - p155(1) [51-500]

Dutilleux, Henri - *Music: Mystery and Memory: Conversations with Claude Glayman*
MT - v145 - i1886 - Spring 2004 - p91-96 [501+]

Dutschke, Gretchen - *Jeder hat sein Leben ganz zu leben: Die Tagebucher 1963-1979*
  HNet - July 2004 - pNA [501+]
  TLS - i5264 - Feb 20 2004 - p29-29 [501+]

Dutt, Michael Madhusudan - *The Slaying of Meghanada: A Ramayana from Colonial Bengal*
  Choice - v42 - i1 - Sept 2004 - p97(1) [501+]

Dutta, Paresh C. - *Phytosterols as Functional Food Components and Nutraceuticals*
  E-Streams - Dec 2004 - pNA [501+]
  SciTech - v28 - i1 - March 2004 - p72(1) [51-500]

Dutton, Benjamin - *Dutton's Nautical Navigation, 15th Ed.*
  R&R Bk N - v19 - i1 - Feb 2004 - p257(1) [51-500]
  SciTech - v28 - i1 - March 2004 - p180(1) [51-500]

Dutton, Paul (b. 1943 -) - *Several Women Dancing*
  CBRA - Annual 2003 - p162(1) [501+]

Dutton, Paul Edward - *Charlemagne's Mustache: And Other Cultural Clusters of the Dark Ages*
  Choice - v42 - i3 - Nov 2004 - p555(1) [1-50]

Dutton, Paul V. - *Origins of the French Welfare State: The Struggle for Social Reform in France, 1914-1947*
  JMH - v76 - i3 - Sept 2004 - p706(3) [501+]

Dutton, Richard - *A Companion to Shakespeare's Works*
  Ren Q - v57 - i4 - Winter 2004 - p1516(3) [501+]
  Theatre and Religion: Lancastrian Shakespeare
  Choice - v42 - i3 - Nov 2004 - p487(2) [1-50]

Dutzler, Barbara - *The European System of Central Banks: An Autonomous Actor? The Quest for an Institutional Balance in EMU*
  JEL - v41 - i4 - Dec 2003 - p1347(1) [501+]

Duus, Masayo - *The Life of Isamu Noguchi: Journey Without Borders*
  BL - v101 - i3 - Oct 1 2004 - p291(1) [51-500]
  Choice - v42 - i6 - Feb 2005 - p1010(1) [51-500]
  TimHES - v0 - i1680 - Feb 25 2005 - p30(1) [501+]

Duval, David Timothy - *Tourism in the Caribbean: Trends, Development, Prospects*
  R&R Bk N - v19 - i3 - August 2004 - p79(1) [51-500]

DuVal, Elizabeth - *Mosaics*
  LJ - v130 - i3 - Feb 15 2005 - p126(1) [51-500]

Duval, Pete - *Rear View: Stories*
  BL - v100 - i21 - July 2004 - p1817(1) [51-500]
  y Kliatt - v39 - i2 - March 2005 - p31(1) [51-500]

Duvall, Deborah L. - *Rabbit and the Bears*
  c Roundup M - v12 - i1 - Oct 2004 - p30(1) [51-500]
  Rabbit Goes Duck Hunting: A Traditional Cherokee Legend (Illus. by Jacob, Murv)
  c CCB-B - v58 - i5 - Jan 2005 - p208(1) [51-500]

Duvall, Jill - *Congressional Committees*
  c SLJ - v50 - i8 - August 2004 - p49(1) [51-500]

Duvall, John N. - *The Identifying Fiction of Toni Morrison: Modernist Authenticity and Postmodern Blackness*
  Callaloo - v27 - i2 - Spring 2004 - p572(575) [501+]

Duvoisin, Roger - *Petunia's Christmas (Illus. by Duvoisin, Roger)*
  c BW - v34 - i50 - Dec 12 2004 - p9(1) [501+]

Duwell, Martin - *The Best Australian Poetry 2003*
  WLT - v78 - i3-4 - Sept-Dec 2004 - p84(1) [501+]

Duyker, Edward - *Citizen Labillardiere: A Naturalist's Life in Revolution and Exploration*
  Quad - v48 - i11 - Nov 2004 - p87(3) [501+]

Duzhin, S.V. - *Transformation Groups for Beginners*
  SciTech - v28 - i1 - March 2004 - p41(1) [51-500]

Duzinkiewicz, Janusz - *States, Societies, Cultures: East and West, Essays in Honor of Jaroslaw Pelenski*
  R&R Bk N - v19 - i3 - August 2004 - p45(1) [51-500]

DVD Delirium
  Globe & Mail - Dec 10 2004 - pR21 [1-50]

Dvorak in America
  LibMed - v22 - i5 - Feb 2004 - p81(1) [501+]

Dvorak, John - *Online!: The Book*
  SciTech - v28 - i1 - March 2004 - p158(1) [51-500]

Dvorak, V. - *Engineering of Computer-Based Systems (ECBS 2004): Proceedings*
  SciTech - v28 - i3 - Sept 2004 - p151(1) [51-500]

Dwan, Renata - *Executive Policing: Enforcing the Law in Peace Operations*
  JPR - v41 - i6 - Nov 2004 - p756-756 [501+]

Dworkin, Joan - *Advanced Social Work Practice: An Integrative, Multilevel Approach*
  R&R Bk N - v19 - i3 - August 2004 - p158(1) [51-500]

Dworkin, Robert H. - *Psychosocial Aspects of Pain: A Handbook for Health Care Providers*
  SciTech - v28 - i1 - March 2004 - p87(1) [51-500]

Dworkin, Ronald William - *From Liberal Values to Democratic Transition: Essays in Honor of Janos Kis*
  Choice - v41 - i11-12 - July-August 2004 - p2124(1) [501+]
  R&R Bk N - v19 - i1 - Feb 2004 - p148(1) [51-500]

Dworkin, Shari L. - *Built to Win: The Female Athlete as Cultural Icon*
  SSJ - v21 - i2 - June 2004 - p244-247 [501+]

Dworschak, Helmut - *Milch und Acker. Koperliche und Sexuelle Aspekte der Religiosen Erfahrung. Am Besipiel der Bussdidaxe des Strickers*
  GSR - v27 - i3 - Oct 2004 - p602(2) [501+]

Dwyer, Deidre - *Going to the Eyestone*
  CBRA - Annual 2003 - p215(2) [501+]

Dwyer, Jim - *102 Minutes: The Untold Story of the Fight to Survive Inside the Twin Towers*
  y BL - v101 - i6 - Nov 15 2004 - p548(1) [51-500]
  Ent W - i801 - Jan 14 2005 - p94 [51-500]
  KR - v72 - i20 - Oct 15 2004 - p993(1) [501+]
  LJ - v129 - i20 - Dec 1 2004 - p134(2) [51-500]
  NW - Nov 14 2005 - p7 [501+]
  NYTBR - Jan 9 2005 - p15 [501+]
  People - v63 - i4 - Jan 31 2005 - p53 [51-500]
  PW - v251 - i45 - Nov 8 2004 - p42(1) [501+]

Dwyer, Karen Kangas - *Conquer Your Speech Anxiety: Learn How to Overcome Your Nervousness about Public Speaking, 2nd Ed.*
  R&R Bk N - v19 - i4 - Nov 2004 - p227(1) [501+]

Dwyer, Mindy - *Sweet Dreams, Polar Bear*
  c SLJ - v51 - i2 - Feb 2005 - p97(1) [51-500]

Dwyer, Peter - *Understanding Social Citizenship: Themes and Perspectives for Policy and Practice*
  R&R Bk N - v19 - i4 - Nov 2004 - p153(1) [501+]

Dybek, Stuart - *I Sailed with Magellan*
  Ant R - v62 - i4 - Fall 2004 - p774(2) [501+]
  Streets in Their Own Ink
  AM - v192 - i4 - Feb 7 2005 - p39 [501+]
  BL - v101 - i5 - Nov 1 2004 - p455(1) [51-500]
  LJ - v129 - i18 - Nov 1 2004 - p89(1) [51-500]

Dyck, Andrew R. - *De natura deorum, Bk. 1*
  Class R - v54 - i2 - Nov 2004 - p364(2) [501+]

Dyck, Arthur J. - *Life's Worth: The Case Against Assisted Suicide*
  Theol St - v65 - i4 - Dec 2004 - p901(2) [501+]

Dyck, Noel - *Sport, Dance and Embodied Identities*
  JRAI - v10 - i4 - Dec 2004 - p943(2) [501+]

Dyckman, John M. - *Scapegoats at Work: Taking the Bull's-Eye Off Your Back*
  R&R Bk N - v19 - i1 - Feb 2004 - p91(1) [1-50]

Dyer, Davis - *Rising Tide: Lessons from 165 Years of Brand Building at Procter & Gamble*
  BHR - v78 - i3 - Autumn 2004 - p559(3) [501+]
  Econ - v372 - i8385 - July 24 2004 - p76US [501+]

Dyer, Geoff - *Yoga for People Who Can't Be Bothered to Do It*
  Globe & Mail - August 7 2004 - pD14 [1-50]

Dyer, Gwynne - *Future Tense: The Coming World Order*
  Globe & Mail - Nov 27 2004 - pD22 [501+]
  Ignorant Armies: Sliding into War in Iraq
  CBRA - Annual 2003 - p305(2) [501+]
  War, New Ed.
  BIC - v33 - i8 - Nov 2004 - p20(2) [501+]
  Globe & Mail - Nov 27 2004 - pD22 [501+]

Dyer, Heather - *The Fish in Room 11*
  c CH Bwatch - v14 - i9 - Sept 2004 - p4(1) [51-500]
  c Sch Lib - v52 - i3 - Autumn 2004 - p130(1) [501+]

Dyer, J. Franklin - *The Journal of a Civil War Surgeon*
  JSH - v70 - i3 - August 2004 - p695(2) [501+]

Dyer, Jane - *Little Brown Bear and the Bundle of Joy (Illus. by Dyer, Jane)*
  c BL - v101 - i8 - Dec 15 2004 - p746(1) [1-50]
  c KR - v72 - i22 - Nov 15 2004 - p1089(1) [51-500]
  c SLJ - v51 - i1 - Jan 2005 - p90(2) [51-500]
  Little Brown Bear Won't Take a Nap! (Illus. by Dyer, Jane)
  c RT - v57 - Oct 2003 - p167 [1-50]

dyer, kc - *Secret of Light*
  y BIC - v33 - i2 - March 2004 - p44(1) [501+]
  y CBRA - Annual 2003 - p481(1) [51-500]

Dyer, Richard - *The Culture of Queers*
  JGS - v13 - i1 - March 2004 - p77-78 [501+]

Dyer, Sarah - *Clementine and Mungo (Illus. by Dyer, Sarah)*
  c BL - v100 - i22 - August 2004 - p1941(1) [51-500]
  c KR - v72 - i14 - July 15 2004 - p684(1) [51-500]
  c PW - v251 - i30 - July 26 2004 - p53(1) [51-500]
  c SLJ - v50 - i9 - Sept 2004 - p158(2) [51-500]

Dyja, Thomas - *The Moon in Our Hands*
  KR - v72 - i23 - Dec 1 2004 - p1104(1) [501+]
  PW - v252 - i3 - Jan 17 2005 - p35(1) [51-500]

Dyke, Greg - *Inside Story*
  CR - v286 - i1669 - Feb 2005 - p115(2) [501+]
  NS - v133 - i4711 - Oct 25 2004 - p50(2) [501+]
  Spec - v296 - i9190 - Sept 25 2004 - p55(1) [501+]

Dyke, Tom Hart - *The Cloud Garden: A True Story of Adventure, Survival, and Extreme Horticulture*
  Ent W - i779 - August 20 2004 - p130 [51-500]
  LJ - v129 - i13 - August 2004 - p105(1) [51-500]

Dykstra, Michael J. - *Biological Electron Microscopy: Theory, Techniques, and Troubleshooting, 2nd Ed.*
  SciTech - v28 - i1 - March 2004 - p60(1) [51-500]

Dylan, Bob - *Chronicles, Vol. 1 (Read by Penn, Sean). Audiobook Review*
  PW - v251 - i40 - Oct 4 2004 - p30(1) [51-500]
  PW - v251 - i49 - Dec 6 2004 - p20(1) [51-500]
  Chronicles, Vol. 1
  Am Spect - v37 - i9 - Nov 2004 - p55(2) [501+]
  BIC - v33 - i8 - Nov 2004 - p19(1) [501+]
  BL - v101 - i6 - Nov 15 2004 - p530(1) [51-500]
  BW - v34 - i41 - Oct 10 2004 - p5(1) [501+]
  Choice - v42 - i7 - March 2005 - p1236(1) [51-500]
  Comw - v132 - i1 - Jan 14 2005 - p24(2) [501+]
  CR - v286 - i1669 - Feb 2005 - p113(2) [501+]
  Ent W - Sept 10 2004 - p166 [1-50]
  Ent W - i788 - Oct 15 2004 - p77 [501+]
  Globe & Mail - Oct 7 2004 - pR4 [501+]
  Globe & Mail - Oct 23 2004 - pD3 [501+]
  Globe & Mail - Nov 27 2004 - pD3 [51-500]
  Lon R Bks - v26 - i20 - Oct 21 2004 - p22(1) [501+]
  NS - v133 - i4716 - Nov 29 2004 - p46(1) [51-500]
  NS - v133 - i4718 - Dec 13 2004 - p74(2) [501+]
  NY - v80 - i32 - Oct 25 2004 - p91(1) [51-500]
  NYTBR - Oct 24 2004 - p14 [501+]
  People - v62 - i17 - Oct 25 2004 - p51 [501+]
  People - Dec 27 2004 - p63 [501+]
  PW - v251 - i49 - Dec 6 2004 - p39(1) [1-50]
  Spec - v296 - i9197 - Nov 13 2004 - p50(2) [501+]
  TLS - i5302 - Nov 12 2004 - p8-9 [501+]
  Lyrics, 1962-2001
  BL - v101 - i6 - Nov 15 2004 - p530(1) [51-500]
  BW - v34 - i41 - Oct 10 2004 - p5(1) [501+]
  NYTBR - Oct 24 2004 - p15 [501+]
  TLS - i5302 - Nov 12 2004 - p8-9 [501+]
  Memoir
  Ent W - i788 - Oct 15 2004 - p77 [501+]
  Tarantula
  LJ - v129 - i16 - Oct 1 2004 - p121(1) [1-50]
  NYTBR - Oct 24 2004 - p15 [501+]

Dymmoch, Michael Allen - *The Fall*
  BL - v100 - i22 - August 2004 - p1904(1) [501+]
  DroRevMy - v24 - i3 - May-June 2004 - p11(1) [1-50]
  KR - v72 - i13 - July 1 2004 - p606(1) [51-500]
  PW - v251 - i28 - July 12 2004 - p47(1) [51-500]

Dynkin, E.B. - *Superdiffusions and Positive Solutions of Nonlinear Partial Differential Equations*
  SciTech - v28 - i4 - Dec 2004 - p40(1) [51-500]

Dyrness, William A. - *Reformed Theology and Visual Culture: The Protestant Imagination from Calvin to Edwards*
  Choice - v42 - i6 - Feb 2005 - p1037(1) [51-500]

Dyson, Kenneth - *Germany, Europe, and the Politics of Constraint*
  Pers PS - v33 - i4 - Fall 2004 - p239(1) [501+]

Dyson, Michael Eric - *Mercy, Mercy Me: The Art, Loves and Demons of Marvin Gaye*
  Black Iss - v6 - i4 - July-August 2004 - p35(1) [501+]
  Globe & Mail - July 10 2004 - pD10 [501+]
  The Michael Eric Dyson Reader
  Choice - v42 - i1 - Sept 2004 - p173(1) [501+]
  Pride
  HM - v310 - i1856 - Jan 2005 - p96(6) [501+]
  Why I Love Black Women
  Kliatt - v38 - i6 - Nov 2004 - p36(1) [51-500]

Dyson, Stephen L. - *Eugenie Sellers Strong: Portrait of an Archaeologist*
  Arch - v57 - i5 - Sept-Oct 2004 - p58-58 [501+]
  R&R Bk N - v19 - i3 - August 2004 - p29(1) [1-50]
  The Roman Countryside
  R&R Bk N - v19 - i3 - August 2004 - p44(1) [51-500]

E

E-Commerce and Development Report 2003
    JEL - v42 - i1 - March 2004 - p291(1) [501+]
    R&R Bk N - v19 - i2 - May 2004 - p116(1) [1-50]
E.Encyclopedia Science
    c SLJ - v50 - i12 - Dec 2004 - p84(1) [501+]
    c BL - v101 - i7 - Dec 1 2004 - p685(1) [501+]
Each One Believing: Paul McCartney on Stage, Off Stage, and Backstage
    Globe & Mail - Dec 18 2004 - pD14 [1-50]
Eades, J.S. - *Globalization in Southeast Asia: Local, National, and Transnational Perspectives*
    Pac A - v77 - i2 - Summer 2004 - p366(2) [501+]
Eager, Edward - *Half Magic*
    People - v62 - i25 - Dec 20 2004 - p58 [51-500]
Eager, Paige Whaley - *Global Population Policy: From Population Control to Reproductive Rights*
    R&R Bk N - v19 - i4 - Nov 2004 - p86(1) [51-500]
Eagleton, Terry - *After Theory*
    ABR - v25 - i5 - July-August 2004 - p16(1) [501+]
    Arena - i74 - Dec 2004 - p42(2) [501+]
    CHE - v50 - i20 - Jan 23 2004 - pB9(1) [501+]
    CR - v285 - i1662 - July 2004 - p59(1) [51-500]
    JouAmCul - v27 - i3 - Sept 2004 - p334(1) [501+]
    The English Novel: An Introduction
    R&R Bk N - v19 - i4 - Nov 2004 - p234(1) [501+]
    TimHES - v0 - i1652 - August 6 2004 - p26(2) [501+]
    TLS - i5305 - Dec 3 2004 - p13(1) [501+]
    Figures of Dissent: Critical Essays on Fish, Spivak, Zizek and Others
    R&R Bk N - v19 - i1 - Feb 2004 - p240(1) [51-500]
    WLT - v78 - i3-4 - Sept-Dec 2004 - p156(2) [501+]
    Sweet Violence: The Idea of the Tragic
    RES - v55 - i218 - Feb 2004 - p106-107 [501+]
    Theat J - v56 - i1 - March 2004 - p129(2) [501+]
Eagly, Alice H. - *Psychology of Gender. 2nd Ed.*
    SciTech - v28 - i3 - Sept 2004 - p3(1) [501+]
Eaker, Sherry - *The Back Stage Actor's Handbook: The How-to and Who-to-Contact Reference for Actors, Singers, and Dancers, 4th Ed.*
    R&R Bk N - v19 - i3 - August 2004 - p264(1) [51-500]
Eakin, Paul John - *The Ethics of Life Writing*
    Choice - v42 - i4 - Dec 2004 - p656(1) [1-50]
Earl, Chris - *Gotcha Down*
    BL - v101 - i1 - Sept 1 2004 - p53(1) [51-500]
Earl, Robert - *The Burning Shore*
    ChrSFF&H - v26 - i9 - Sept 2004 - p34(1) [51-500]
Earl, Windsor George - *Enterprise in Tropical Australia*
    AHS - v35 - i123 - April 2004 - p197-197 [501+]
Earle, Carville - *The American Way: A Geographical History of Crisis and Recovery*
    AHR - v109 - i4 - Oct 2004 - p1219(2) [501+]
    HNet - July 2004 - pNA [501+]
    W&M Q - v61 - i3 - July 2004 - p556-559 [501+]
Earle, Joe - *Lethal Elegance*
    Bwatch - Dec 2004 - pNA [51-500]
Earle, Peter - *The Pirate Wars*
    KR - v73 - i1 - Jan 1 2005 - p32(1) [501+]
    LJ - v130 - i2 - Feb 1 2005 - p96(2) [51-500]
Earley, Chris G. - *Hawks and Owls of the Great Lakes Region and Eastern North America*
    Choice - v42 - i2 - Oct 2004 - p319(2) [501+]
    E-Streams - v35 - i5 - April 2004 - p197-197 [51-500]
    y SB - v40 - i5 - Sept-Oct 2004 - p214(2) [51-500]
    Sparrows and Finches of the Great Lakes Region and Eastern North America
    CBRA - Annual 2003 - p402(2) [51-500]
    Warblers of the Great Lakes Region and Eastern North America
    CBRA - Annual 2003 - p402(2) [51-500]

Earley, Christopher - *Cultural Intelligence: Individual Interactions Across Cultures*
    Per Psy - v57 - i3 - Autumn 2004 - p792(3) [501+]
Earley, Lawrence S. - *Looking for Longleaf: The Fall and Rise of an American Forest*
    BL - v100 - i22 - August 2004 - p1887(1) [51-500]
    Choice - v42 - i6 - Feb 2005 - p1048(1) [51-500]
    Wil Q - v28 - i4 - Autumn 2004 - p115(1) [501+]
Earley, Peter - *Leading and Managing Continuing Professional Development: Developing People, Developing Schools*
    R&R Bk N - v19 - i3 - August 2004 - p219(1) [1-50]
    TES - v0 - i4576 - March 26 2004 - psss17(1) [501+]
Earls, Irene - *Artists of the Renaissance*
    LJ - v129 - i18 - Nov 1 2004 - p122(1) [51-500]
    VOYA - v27 - i5 - Dec 2004 - p422(1) [51-500]
Earls, Nick - *48 Shades of Brown*
    BL - v100 - i21 - July 2004 - p1833(2) [1-50]
    y BL - v101 - i2 - Sept 15 2004 - p236(1) [51-500]
    y CCB-B - v57 - i11 - July-August 2004 - p461(2) [501+]
    HB - v80 - i5 - Sept-Oct 2004 - p580(2) [501+]
    After Summer
    y Sch Lib - v52 - i4 - Winter 2004 - p215(1) [51-500]
Early American Imprints, 1639-1800
    BL - v101 - i5 - Nov 1 2004 - p518(2) [501+]
Early, Ann M. - *Forest Farmsteads: A Millennium of Human Occupation at Winding Stair in the Ouachita Mountains*
    Am Ant - v69 - i3 - July 2004 - p589(2) [501+]
Early Civilizations
    c LibMed - v23 - i3 - Nov-Dec 2004 - p81(1) [51-500]
Early, Frances - *Athena's Daughters: Television's New Women Warriors*
    HNet - Sept 2004 - pNA [501+]
Early, James - *Presidio, Mission, and Pueblo: Spanish Architecture and Urbanism in the United States*
    Choice - v42 - i1 - Sept 2004 - p91(1) [501+]
Early, Joseph E. - *A Texas Baptist History Sourcebook: A Companion to McBeth's Texas Baptists*
    R&R Bk N - v19 - i4 - Nov 2004 - p28(1) [501+]
Early, R.H. - *Campbell Chronicles and Family Sketches Embracing the History of Campbell County, Virginia 1782-1926*
    EFHM - v58 - i2 - March-April 2004 - p91(1) [501+]
Earnest, John Guilford - *All Right Let Them Come: The Civil War Diary of an East Tennessee Confederate*
    R&R Bk N - v19 - i1 - Feb 2004 - p59(1) [51-500]
Earth Calendar
    SLJ - v50 - i12 - Dec 2004 - p62(1) [501+]
Earth Friends
    c LibMed - v23 - i3 - Nov-Dec 2004 - p88(1) [51-500]
Earthsong
    Globe & Mail - Dec 18 2004 - pD14 [1-50]
Eason, Andrew Mark - *Women in God's Army: Gender and Equality in the Early Salvation Army*
    AHR - v109 - i3 - June 2004 - p976(1) [501+]
    CBRA - Annual 2003 - p382(1) [501+]
Easterbrook, Gregg - *The Progress Paradox (Read by Marosz, Jonathan). Audiobook Review*
    Kliatt - v38 - i6 - Nov 2004 - p57(1) [51-500]
    The Progress Paradox: How Life Gets Better while People Feel Worse
    Am Spect - v37 - i1 - Feb 2004 - p60(2) [501+]
    Choice - v42 - i2 - Oct 2004 - p332(1) [51-500]
    SEP - v277 - i1 - Jan-Feb 2005 - p41(2) [501+]
    Soc - v42 - i2 - Jan-Feb 2005 - p76(7) [501+]

Easterlin, Richard - *The Reluctant Economist: Perspectives on Economics, Economic History, and Demography*
    Choice - v42 - i3 - Nov 2004 - p532(1) [1-50]
Easterling, P. - *Greek and Roman Actors. Aspects of an Ancient Profession*
    Class R - v54 - i2 - Nov 2004 - p445(3) [501+]
Easterly, William - *The Limits of Stabilization: Infrastructure, Public Deficits, and Growth in Latin America*
    JEL - v42 - i1 - March 2004 - p272(1) [501+]
    JEL - v42 - i4 - Dec 2004 - p1139(2) [501+]
    R&R Bk N - v19 - i1 - Feb 2004 - p82(1) [51-500]
Eastman Kodak Company - *Kodak's Ergonomic Design for People at Work, 2nd Ed.*
    E-Streams - Sept 2004 - pNA [501+]
Eastmond, Antony - *Icon and Word: The Power of Images in Byzantium: Studies Presented to Robin Cormack*
    R&R Bk N - v19 - i1 - Feb 2004 - p201(1) [51-500]
Easton, Kelly - *Walking on Air*
    c CCB-B - v57 - i11 - July-August 2004 - p462(2) [501+]
    c SLJ - v50 - i7 - July 2004 - p104(1) [51-500]
Easton, Laird McLeod - *The Red Count: The Life and Times of Harry Kessler*
    GSR - v27 - i3 - Oct 2004 - p632(2) [501+]
    HNet - June 2004 - pNA [501+]
    JMH - v76 - i3 - Sept 2004 - p714(3) [501+]
Easton, M.J. - *Cross-Platform .NET Development*
    Bwatch - Dec 2004 - pNA [51-500]
Eaton, Chris - *Inactivist*
    CBRA - Annual 2003 - p162(2) [501+]
Eaton, Douglas C. - *Vander's Renal Physiology, 6th Ed.*
    SciTech - v28 - i3 - Sept 2004 - p69(1) [51-500]
Eaton, Heather - *Ecofeminism and Globalization: Exploring Culture, Context, and Religion*
    R&R Bk N - v19 - i1 - Feb 2004 - p132(1) [51-500]
Eaton, Jan - *200 Crochet Blocks for Blankets, Throws, and Afghans*
    LJ - v129 - i20 - Dec 1 2004 - p108(1) [51-500]
Eaton, Kent - *Politics Beyond the Capital: The Design of Subnational Institutions in South America*
    R&R Bk N - v19 - i4 - Nov 2004 - p155(1) [501+]
Eaton, Margaret L. - *Ethics and the Business of Bioscience*
    Choice - v42 - i3 - Nov 2004 - p517(1) [1-50]
    SciTech - v28 - i3 - Sept 2004 - p77(1) [51-500]
Eaton, Susan E. - *The Other Boston Busing Story*
    TCR - v106 - i5 - May 2004 - p985(10) [501+]
Eaves, David - *Handbook of Polymer Foams*
    Choice - v42 - i2 - Oct 2004 - p323(1) [51-500]
Eaves, Ian - *Catalogue of European Armour at the Fitzwilliam Museum*
    Six Ct J - v34 - i4 - Winter 2003 - p1140-1140 [501+]
Eaves, Jon - *Apache Tomcat Bible*
    SciTech - v28 - i3 - Sept 2004 - p155(1) [51-500]
Eban, Katherine - *Dangerous Doses: How Counterfeiters Are Contaminating America's Drug Supply*
    PW - v252 - i11 - March 14 2005 - p54(2) [51-500]
Ebbinghaus, Angelika - *Vernichten und Heilen: Der Nürnberger Ärzteprozess und seine Folgen*
    CEH - v37 - i3 - Summer 2004 - p489(4) [501+]
Ebbinghaus, Bernhard - *Comparing Welfare Capitalism: Social Policy and Political Economy in Europe, Japan, and the United States*
    CS - v33 - i6 - Nov 2004 - p698(3) [501+]

Ebel, Hans F. - *Art of Scientific Writing: From Student Reports to Professional Publications in Chemistry and Related Fields, 2nd Ed.*
E-Streams - Nov 2004 - pNA [501+]

Ebeling, Richard - *Austrian Economics and the Political Economy of Freedom*
JEL - v42 - i1 - March 2004 - p242(2) [501+]

Ebenstein, Alan - *Hayek's Journey: The Mind of Friedrich Hayek*
AJES - v63 - i4 - Oct 2004 - p943(4) [501+]
Choice - v41 - i7 - March 2004 - p1341(1) [501+]

Ebensten, Hanns - *The Seals on the Icepack and More Gay Travel Adventures*
Advocate - Oct 26 2004 - pS31(1) [501+]

Eber, Irene - *The Choice: Poland, 1939-1945*
KR - v72 - i13 - July 1 2004 - p615(2) [501+]
R&R Bk N - v19 - i4 - Nov 2004 - p45(1) [51-500]

Eberl, Hans-Christian - *Museum und Film*
HNet - Sept 2004 - pNA [501+]

Eberle, Christopher J. - *Religious Conviction in Liberal Politics*
JR - v84 - i3 - July 2004 - p485(3) [501+]
Soc - v41 - i3 - March-April 2004 - p75(5) [501+]

Ebersole, Priscilla - *Toward Healthy Aging: Human Needs and Nursing Response, 6th Ed.*
SciTech - v28 - i1 - March 2004 - p108(1) [51-500]

Eberstadt, Mary - *Home-Alone America: The Hidden Toll of Day Care, Behavioral Drugs, and Other Parent Substitutes*
BL - v101 - i4 - Oct 15 2004 - p365(1) [51-500]
BW - v34 - i47 - Nov 21 2004 - p10(1) [501+]
NYTBR - Oct 24 2004 - p26 [501+]

Eberstadt, Nicholas - *Four Surprises in Global Demography*
Fut - v39 - i1 - Jan-Feb 2005 - p9(1) [501+]

Ebert, Berthold - *Hans und Rosemarie Ahrbeck: den Lehrern vieler Lehrer*
HNet - Nov 2004 - pNA [501+]

Ebert, David A. - *Sharks, Rays, and Chimaeras of California*
Choice - v41 - i7 - March 2004 - p1322(1) [501+]

Ebert, Hans-Holger - *Easy ECGs: Interpretation, Differential Diagnoses*
SciTech - v28 - i4 - Dec 2004 - p103(1) [51-500]

Ebert, Roger - *The Great Movies*
Globe & Mail - Feb 26 2005 - pD13 [51-500]
The Great Movies II
BL - v101 - i9-10 - Jan 1 2005 - p798(1) [51-500]
Globe & Mail - Feb 26 2005 - pD13 [51-500]
LJ - v130 - i1 - Jan 1 2005 - p114(1) [51-500]
PW - v252 - i2 - Jan 10 2005 - p49(1) [51-500]
Roger Ebert's Movie Yearbook 2005
Globe & Mail - Dec 10 2004 - pR21 [1-50]

Ebrahim, Alnoor - *NGO's and Organizational Change: Discourse, Reporting, and Learning*
JEL - v42 - i1 - March 2004 - p306(1) [501+]

Ebrahimian, Babak A. - *The Cinematic Theater*
Choice - v42 - i6 - Feb 2005 - p1027(2) [51-500]

EBRI - *Fundamentals of Employee Benefit Programs, 5th Ed.*
HR Mag - v49 - i7 - July 2004 - pS7(1) [51-500]

Ebury, Max Arthur - *Forgotten Voices of the Second World War*
Spec - v296 - i9193 - Oct 16 2004 - p63(1) [501+]

Eccles, Marjorie - *Killing a Unicorn*
KR - v73 - i2 - Jan 15 2005 - p85(1) [51-500]
PW - v252 - i1 - Jan 3 2005 - p49(1) [51-500]

ECG Interpretation Made Incredibly Easy, 3rd Ed.
SciTech - v28 - i4 - Dec 2004 - p103(1) [51-500]

Echard, Sian - *A Companion to Gower*
Choice - v42 - i2 - Oct 2004 - p292(1) [501+]

Echenoz, Jean - *Chopin's Move*
WLT - v78 - i3-4 - Sept-Dec 2004 - p115(1) [501+]
Piano
Spec - v297 - i9204 - Jan 1 2005 - p29(1) [501+]
TLS - i5305 - Dec 3 2004 - p23(1) [501+]

Echevarria, Jana - *Making Content Comprehensible for English Language Learners: The SIOP Model, 2nd Ed.*
R&R Bk N - v19 - i1 - Feb 2004 - p215(1) [51-500]

Echikson, William - *Noble Rot: A Bordeaux Wine Revolution*
Bwatch - Dec 2004 - pNA [51-500]
NY - v80 - i25 - Sept 6 2004 - p157(6) [501+]
R&R Bk N - v19 - i3 - August 2004 - p118(1) [51-500]

Echlin, Kim - *Elizabeth Smart: A Fugue Essay on Women and Creativity*
BIC - v33 - i7 - Oct 2004 - p23(1) [501+]
Globe & Mail - August 14 2004 - pD12 [1-50]
Inanna (Illus. by Wolfsgruber, Linda)
y CBRA - Annual 2003 - p525(2) [51-500]

Echols, James - *I Have a Dream: Martin Luther King, Jr. and the Future of Multicultural America*
Intpr - v59 - i1 - Jan 2005 - p111(1) [51-500]

Eck, W. - *The Age of Augustus*
Class R - v54 - i1 - May 2004 - p175(2) [501+]

Eckard, Paula Gallant - *Maternal Body and Voice in Toni Morrison, Bobbie Ann Mason and Lee Smith*
TSWL - v22 - i2 - Fall 2003 - p419-423 [501+]

Eckardt, Frank - *Consumption and the Post-Industrial City*
R&R Bk N - v19 - i1 - Feb 2004 - p134(1) [51-500]

Eckart, Edana - *Watching the Moon*
c SLJ - v51 - i2 - Feb 2005 - p116(1) [51-500]
Watching the Seasons
c SLJ - v51 - i2 - Feb 2005 - p116(1) [51-500]
Watching the Sun
c SLJ - v51 - i2 - Feb 2005 - p116(1) [51-500]

Eckart, Karl - *Deutschland auf dem Weg zur inneren Einheit*
HNet - June 2004 - pNA [501+]

Eckel, Peter D. - *Changing Course: Making the Hard Decisions to Eliminate Academic Programs*
R&R Bk N - v19 - i1 - Feb 2004 - p186(1) [51-500]

Ecker, Heather - *Caliphs and Kings: The Art and Influence of Islamic Spain*
Choice - v42 - i5 - Jan 2005 - p840(1) [1-50]
LJ - v129 - i17 - Oct 15 2004 - p59(1) [51-500]

Ecker, Klaus - *Regularity Theory for Mean Curvature Flow*
SIAM Rev - v46 - i4 - Dec 2004 - p759-762 [501+]

Eckersall, Peter - *Alternatives: Debating Theatre Culture in the Age of Confusion*
R&R Bk N - v19 - i4 - Nov 2004 - p225(1) [501+]

Eckersley, Glennyce S. - *Teen Angel: True Stories of Teenage Experiences of Angels*
y SLJ - v51 - i1 - Jan 2005 - p146(1) [51-500]

Eckersley, Richard - *Well and Good: How We Feel and Why It Matters*
Fut - v38 - i5 - Sept-Oct 2004 - p63(1) [51-500]

Eckersley, Robyn - *The Green State: Rethinking Democracy and Sovereignty*
Choice - v42 - i6 - Feb 2005 - p1093(2) [51-500]
Pers PS - v33 - i4 - Fall 2004 - p248(2) [501+]

Eckert, Allan W. - *Twilight of Empire: A Narrative*
R&R Bk N - v19 - i4 - Nov 2004 - p67(1) [1-50]

Eckler, Rebecca - *Knocked Up: Confessions of a Hip Mother-to-Be*
KR - v73 - i4 - Feb 15 2005 - p210(1) [501+]
PW - v252 - i8 - Feb 21 2005 - p168(1) [51-500]

Eckstein, Jutta - *Agile Software Development in the Large: Diving into the Deep*
SciTech - v28 - i3 - Sept 2004 - p24(1) [51-500]

Eckstein, Susan Eva - *Struggles for Social Rights in Latin America*
CS - v33 - i2 - March 2004 - p234-235 [501+]
What Justice? Whose Justice? Fighting for Fairness in Latin America
Ams - v61 - i2 - Oct 2004 - p280(1) [501+]

Eclair, Jenny - *Having a Lovely Time*
Globe & Mail - Feb 12 2005 - pD6 [501+]

Eco, Umberto - *Baudolino*
HR - v55 - i4 - Winter 2003 - p685 [501+]
History of Beauty
BL - v101 - i4 - Oct 15 2004 - p374(1) [51-500]
Globe & Mail - Jan 1 2005 - pD16 [501+]
LJ - v130 - i3 - Feb 15 2005 - p125(1) [51-500]
PW - v251 - i48 - Nov 29 2004 - p35(1) [51-500]
The Mysterious Flame of Queen Loana
KR - v73 - i4 - Feb 15 2005 - p190(1) [501+]
On Beauty
CR - v286 - i1669 - Feb 2005 - p121(2) [51-500]
Spec - v296 - i9198 - Nov 20 2004 - p48(3) [501+]

Economic and Social Commission for Asia and the Pacific - *Atlas of Mineral Resources of the ESCAP Region: Vol. 17, Geology and Mineral Resources of Timor-Leste*
SciTech - v28 - i3 - Sept 2004 - p165(1) [51-500]
Combating Commercial Sexual Exploitation of Children and Youth in Asia: Directory of Organizations
R&R Bk N - v19 - i3 - August 2004 - p166(1) [501+]

Combating Human Trafficking in Asia: A Resource Guide to International and Regional Legal Instruments, Political Commitments and Recommended Practices
R&R Bk N - v19 - i4 - Nov 2004 - p175(1) [501+]
Commercial Development of Regional Ports as Logistics Centres
R&R Bk N - v19 - i3 - August 2004 - p122(1) [51-500]
Electric Power in Asia and the Pacific, 1999 and 2000
SciTech - v28 - i3 - Sept 2004 - p151(1) [51-500]
ESCAP Towards 2020
R&R Bk N - v19 - i4 - Nov 2004 - p108(1) [51-500]
Fifth Asian and Pacific Population Conference: Selected Papers
R&R Bk N - v19 - i1 - Feb 2004 - p79(1) [51-500]
Focus on Ability, Celebrate Diversity: Highlights of the Asian and Pacific Decade of Disabled Persons, 1993-2002
R&R Bk N - v19 - i3 - August 2004 - p161(1) [501+]
Gender Indicators for Monitoring the Implementation of the Beijing Platform for Action on Women in the ESCAP Region
R&R Bk N - v19 - i3 - August 2004 - p153(1) [51-500]
Guidelines on Participatory Planning and Management for Flood Mitigation and Preparedness
SciTech - v28 - i1 - March 2004 - p146(1) [51-500]
Integrating Unpaid Work into National Policies
R&R Bk N - v19 - i3 - August 2004 - p116(1) [51-500]
Investment Promotion and Enterprise Development: Bulletin for Asia and Pacific
R&R Bk N - v19 - i3 - August 2004 - p124(1) [51-500]
Policies, Regulatory Regimes and Management Practices for Investment Promotion...Mineral Resources Sector...of East and South-East Asia
R&R Bk N - v19 - i1 - Feb 2004 - p80(1) [51-500]

Economic and Social Commission for Asia and the Pacific and the United Nations Development Programme - *Promoting the Millennium Development Goals in Asia and the Pacific: Meeting the Challenges of Poverty Reduction*
R&R Bk N - v19 - i1 - Feb 2004 - p85(1) [1-50]

Economic and Social Survey of Asia and the Pacific 2004
R&R Bk N - v19 - i3 - August 2004 - p47(1) [51-500]

Economic Commision for Latin America and the Caribbean - *Decade of Social Development in Latin America, 1990-1999*
R&R Bk N - v19 - i4 - Nov 2004 - p89(1) [51-500]

Economic Commission for Africa - *Compendium of Intra-African and Related Foreign Trade Statistics, 2003 ed*
R&R Bk N - v19 - i4 - Nov 2004 - p91(1) [501+]

Economic Commission for Europe - *Carbon Emissions Trading Handbook*
R&R Bk N - v19 - i3 - August 2004 - p96(1) [51-500]
Economic Survey of Europe, 2004, No. 1
R&R Bk N - v19 - i4 - Nov 2004 - p89(1) [51-500]
Environmental Performance Reviews: Azerbaijan
R&R Bk N - v19 - i3 - August 2004 - p80(1) [51-500]

Economic Commission for Europe, Geneva - *Annual Bulletin of Transport Statistics for Europe and North America 2004, Vol. 52*
R&R Bk N - v19 - i4 - Nov 2004 - p106(1) [51-500]

Economic Indicators, North American Ed.
R&R Bk N - v19 - i4 - Nov 2004 - p107(1) [51-500]

Economy, Elizabeth C. - *The River Runs Black: The Environmental Challenge to China's Future*
Am Sci - v92 - i6 - Nov-Dec 2004 - p564(2) [501+]
Choice - v42 - i3 - Nov 2004 - p532(1) [1-50]
For Aff - v83 - i5 - Sept-Oct 2004 - p164 [501+]

Ecosystems
c LibMed - v23 - i3 - Nov-Dec 2004 - p85(1) [51-500]

Ecott, Tim - *Vanilla: Travels in Search of the Ice Cream Orchid*
Globe & Mail - August 28 2004 - pD10 [501+]
NH - v113 - i7 - Sept 2004 - p68(2) [501+]

Ecstasy and Amphetamines: Global Survey 2003
  R&R Bk N - v19 - i1 - Feb 2004 - p140(1) [51-500]

Edbury, P.W. - *The Experience of Crusading, Vol. 2*
  CH - v73 - i4 - Dec 2004 - p849(3) [501+]
  John of Ibelin: Le Livre des Assises
  R&R Bk N - v19 - i1 - Feb 2004 - pNA [51-500]

Edders, Dave - *Created in Darkness by Troubled Americans: The Best of McSweeney's Humor Category: 1998-2003*
  PW - v251 - i32 - August 9 2004 - p246(1) [51-500]

Eddings, David - *The Treasured One*
  LJ - v129 - i19 - Nov 15 2004 - p54(1) [501+]
  PW - v251 - i39 - Sept 27 2004 - p42(1) [51-500]

Eddy, Beth - *The Rites of Identity: The Religious Naturalism and Cultural Criticism of Kenneth Burke and Ralph Ellison*
  Choice - v41 - i11-12 - July-August 2004 - p2061(1) [501+]
  JR - v85 - i1 - Jan 2005 - p186(3) [501+]

Ede, Andrew - *A History of Science in Society: From Philosophy to Utility*
  Choice - v42 - i4 - Dec 2004 - p683(1) [1-50]

Edelman, Charles - *The Merchant of Venice*
  Shakes Q - v55 - i2 - Summer 2004 - p214-217 [501+]
  Shakespeare's Military Language: A Dictionary
  Shakes Q - v55 - i2 - Summer 2004 - p217-219 [501+]

Edelman, Gerald M. - *Wider than the Sky: The Phenomenal Gift of Consciousness*
  E-Streams - Oct 2004 - pNA [501+]
  TimHES - v0 - i1660 - Oct 4 2004 - p26(1) [501+]

Edelson, Edward. - *Gregor Mendel and the Roots of Genetics*
  Am Bio T - v66 - i4 - April 2004 - p310(2) [501+]

Edelstein, Jillian - *Truth and Lies: Stories from the Truth and Reconciliation Commission in South Africa*
  R&R Bk N - v19 - i3 - August 2004 - p60(1) [51-500]

Edelstein, Michael R. - *Contaminated Communities: Coping with Residential Toxic Exposure, 2nd Ed.*
  SciTech - v28 - i1 - March 2004 - p148(1) [51-500]

Edelstein, Robert - *Full Throttle: The Life and Fast Times of NASCAR Legend Curtis Turner*
  BL - v101 - i9-10 - Jan 1 2005 - p801(1) [51-500]
  LJ - v130 - i1 - Jan 1 2005 - p121(2) [51-500]
  PW - v252 - i2 - Jan 10 2005 - p46(1) [51-500]

Eden, Bradford Lee - *Innovative Redesign and Reorganization of Library Technical Services: Paths for the Future and Case Studies*
  A Lib - v35 - i8 - Sept 2004 - p78(1) [51-500]
  LJ - v129 - i16 - Oct 1 2004 - p114(1) [51-500]

Eden, Diana - *Retro Chic*
  Ant&CM - v108 - i5 - July 2003 - p16(1) [501+]

Eden, Edward - *Carol Shields, Narrative Hunger, and the Possibilities of Fiction*
  Can Lit - i182 - Autumn 2004 - p171(3) [501+]
  CBRA - Annual 2003 - p254(1) [501+]
  Dal R - v84 - i1 - Spring 2004 - p180-182 [501+]

Eden, Kathy - *Friends Hold All Things in Common: Tradition, Intellectual Property, and the Adages of Erasmus*
  MP - v102 - i1 - August 2004 - p105(3) [501+]

Eden, Lynn - *Whole World on Fire: Organizations, Knowledge, and Nuclear Weapons Devastation*
  Choice - v42 - i1 - Sept 2004 - p145(1) [501+]
  VQR - v80 - i3 - Summer 2004 - p258(1) [501+]

Eden, Philip - *The 'Daily Telegraph' Book of the Weather: Past and Future Climate Changes Explained*
  SciTech - v28 - i3 - Sept 2004 - p50(1) [1-50]

Edens, Cooper - *Princess Stories, A Classic Illustrated Ed.*
  c BL - v101 - i4 - Oct 15 2004 - p402(1) [51-500]
  c PW - v251 - i38 - Sept 20 2004 - p65(1) [51-500]
  c SLJ - v51 - i1 - Jan 2005 - p109(1) [51-500]

Eder, Elizabeth K. - *Constructing Opportunity: American Women Educators in Early Meiji Japan*
  JAH - v91 - i3 - Dec 2004 - p1031(2) [501+]
  R&R Bk N - v19 - i1 - Feb 2004 - pNA [51-500]

Eder, Marcus - *Crime and Punishment in the Royal Navy of the Seven Years' War, 1755-1763*
  HER - v119 - i483 - Sept 2004 - p1069(1) [501+]

Edgar Allen Poe: A Biography
  LibMed - v22 - i7 - April-May 2004 - p67(1) [501+]

Edgar, Gerald A. - *Classics on Fractals*
  SciTech - v28 - i1 - March 2004 - p41(1) [51-500]

Edge, John T. - *Apple Pie: An American Story*
  LJ - v129 - i17 - Oct 15 2004 - p81(1) [51-500]
  NYTBR - Dec 19 2004 - p31 [501+]

Fried Chicken: An American Story
  BL - v101 - i2 - Sept 15 2004 - p189(1) [51-500]
  LJ - v129 - i17 - Oct 15 2004 - p81(1) [51-500]
  NYTBR - Dec 19 2004 - p31 [501+]
  PW - v251 - i30 - July 26 2004 - p45(1) [51-500]

Edgerton, Gary R. - *Television Histories: Shaping Collective Memory in the Media Age*
  Can Lit - i181 - Summer 2004 - p127-128 [501+]
  HNet - Sept 2004 - pNA [501+]

Edgeworth, Francis Ysidro - *Edgeworth: Mathematical Psychics and Further Papers on Political Economy*
  JEL - v41 - i4 - Dec 2003 - p1337(1) [501+]

Edghill, India - *File M for Murder*
  KR - v72 - i20 - Oct 15 2004 - p985(1) [51-500]
  Wisdom's Daughter: A Novel of Solomon and Sheba
  BL - v101 - i2 - Sept 15 2004 - p207(1) [501+]
  KR - v72 - i16 - August 15 2004 - p761(1) [51-500]

Edghill, Rosemary - *Murder by Magic: Twenty Tales of Crime and the Supernatural*
  BL - v101 - i3 - Oct 1 2004 - p314(1) [51-500]
  LJ - v129 - i15 - Sept 15 2004 - p52(1) [51-500]
  PW - v251 - i36 - Sept 6 2004 - p50(2) [51-500]

Edgington, David W. - *Japan at the Millennium: Joining Past and Future*
  R&R Bk N - v19 - i3 - August 2004 - p57(1) [51-500]

Edin, Kathryn - *Promises I Can Keep: Why Poor Women Put Motherhood Before Marriage*
  LJ - v130 - i2 - Feb 1 2005 - p105(1) [51-500]

Edinger, Ray - *Fury Beach: The Four-Year Odyssey of Captain John Ross and the Victory*
  y Kliatt - v38 - i5 - Sept 2004 - p46(2) [501+]

Editors of Life - *Great Inventions*
  LibMed - v23 - i1 - August-Sept 2004 - p75(1) [51-500]
  The Great Life Photographers
  TimHES - v0 - i1683 - March 18 2005 - p27(1) [501+]
  Great Mountain Ranges of the World
  c LibMed - v23 - i3 - Nov-Dec 2004 - p80(1) [51-500]

Editors of YM - *YM the Best of Say Anything (Illus. by Krall, Daniel)*
  c SLJ - v50 - i8 - August 2004 - p145(1) [51-500]

Edizioni Dedalo - *New Medit: Mediterranean Journal of Economics, Agriculture and Environment*
  JEL - v41 - i4 - Dec 2003 - p1447(1) [501+]

Edkins, Graham - *Innovation and Consolidation in Aviation: Selected Contributions to the Australian Aviation Psychology Symposium 2000*
  SciTech - v28 - i1 - March 2004 - p169(1) [51-500]

Edling, Max M. - *A Revolution in Favor of Government: Origins of the U.S. Constitution and the Making of the American State*
  BHR - v78 - i1 - Spring 2004 - p99(3) [501+]

Edmonds, Christopher M. - *Reducing Poverty in Asia: Emerging Issues in Growth, Targeting, and Measurement*
  JEL - v42 - i1 - March 2004 - p307(1) [501+]
  R&R Bk N - v19 - i1 - Feb 2004 - p84(1) [51-500]

Edmonds, David - *Bobby Fischer Goes to War: How the Soviets Lost the Most Extraordinary Chess Match of All Time*
  Am Spect - v37 - i5 - June 2004 - p60(2) [501+]
  BW - v34 - i12 - March 21 2004 - p3(1) [501+]
  Choice - v42 - i6 - Feb 2005 - p1060(1) [51-500]

Edmonds, Ennis Barrington - *Rastafari: From Outcasts to Culture Bearers*
  JR - v84 - i3 - July 2004 - p500(3) [501+]

Edmonds, Lyra - *An African Princess (Illus. by Wilson, Anne)*
  c BL - v100 - i22 - August 2004 - p1941(2) [51-500]
  c KR - v72 - i15 - August 1 2004 - p740(1) [51-500]
  c Sch Lib - v52 - i4 - Winter 2004 - p186(1) [51-500]
  c SLJ - v50 - i11 - Nov 2004 - p97(2) [51-500]

Edmondson, Jacqueline - *Prairie Town: Redefining Rural Life in the Age of Globalization*
  CS - v33 - i1 - Jan 2004 - p126-126 [501+]

Edmonston, Phil - *Car Smarts: Hot Tips for the Car Crazy (Illus. by Sauve, Gordon)*
  c SLJ - v50 - i7 - July 2004 - p120(1) [51-500]
  y VOYA - v27 - i4 - Oct 2004 - p324(1) [51-500]

Edmund, King - *Victorian Decorated Trade Bindings, 1830-1880: A Descriptive Bibliography*
  BSA-P - v98 - i1 - March 2004 - p115-118 [501+]

Edmunds, David - *Local Forest Management: The Impacts of Devolution Policies*
  SciTech - v28 - i3 - Sept 2004 - p131(1) [51-500]

Edmundson, Mark - *Why Read?*
  AS - v73 - i4 - Autumn 2004 - p167(3) [501+]
  BL - v101 - i1 - Sept 1 2004 - p39(1) [51-500]
  BW - v34 - i35 - August 2004 - p2(1) [501+]
  LJ - v129 - i16 - Oct 1 2004 - p80(1) [51-500]
  SLJ - v50 - i12 - Dec 2004 - p54(4) [501+]

Edmundson, William A. - *An Introduction to Rights*
  Law&PolBR - Sept 2004 - pNA [501+]

Edner, Klaus - *Collective Identities in Action: A Sociological Approach to Ethnicity*
  CS - v33 - i1 - Jan 2004 - p49-50 [501+]

Edouard Vuillard
  TLS - i5263 - Feb 13 2004 - p18-19 [501+]

Edric, Robert - *Cradle Song*
  KR - v72 - i18 - Sept 15 2004 - p882(1) [51-500]
  Siren Song
  TLS - i5289 - August 13 2004 - p21(1) [501+]

Eds. of YES Mag - *Fantastic Feats and Failures*
  KR - v72 - i17 - Sept 1 2004 - p863(1) [51-500]

Edsall, Nicholas C. - *Toward Stonewall: Homosexuality and Society in the Modern Western World*
  Lam Bk Rpt - v13 - i1-2 - August-Sept 2004 - p15(1) [501+]
  R&R Bk N - v19 - i1 - Feb 2004 - p128(1) [51-500]

Education at a Glance: OECD Indicators 2003
  R&R Bk N - v19 - i1 - Feb 2004 - pNA [501+]

Edugyan, Esi - *The Second Life of Samuel Tyne*
  BIC - v33 - i5 - August 2004 - p42(1) [501+]
  BL - v100 - i22 - August 2004 - p1897(1) [51-500]
  Black Iss - v6 - i5 - Sept-Oct 2004 - p50(1) [51-500]
  Globe & Mail - March 19 2005 - pD17 [1-50]
  LJ - v129 - i12 - July 2004 - p69(1) [51-500]
  PW - v251 - i28 - July 12 2004 - p45(1) [51-500]

Edvall, Lilian - *The Rabbit Who Didn't Want to Go to Sleep*
  c BooChiTr - June 6 2004 - p2(1) [501+]

Edward, Duyker - *Citizen Labillardiere: A Naturalist's Life in Revolution and Exploration*
  Choice - v41 - i7 - March 2004 - p1317(1) [501+]

Edward Hopper
  LibMed - v22 - i4 - Jan 2004 - p72(1) [501+]

Edwards, A.S.G - *Decoration and Illustration in Medieval English Manuscripts*
  RES - v55 - i220 - June 2004 - p450-451 [501+]

Edwards, A.W.F. - *Cogwheels of the Mind: The Story of Venn Diagrams*
  Am Sci - v93 - i1 - Jan-Feb 2005 - p84(2) [501+]
  Bwatch - March 2005 - pNA [51-500]
  Choice - v42 - i3 - Nov 2004 - p520(2) [1-50]
  Nature - v430 - i6998 - July 22 2004 - p405(2) [501+]
  SciTech - v28 - i3 - Sept 2004 - p36(1) [51-500]
  SLJ - v50 - i9 - Sept 2004 - p235(2) [51-500]

Edwards, Anne - *Rethinking Teacher Education: Collaborative Responses to Uncertainty*
  TCR - v106 - i2 - Feb 2004 - p393-396 [501+]

Edwards, Anthony T. - *Hesiod's Ascra*
  Choice - v41 - i11-12 - July-August 2004 - p2041(1) [501+]
  TLS - i5303 - Nov 19 2004 - p30(1) [501+]

Edwards, B.K. (b. 1954 -) - *The Economics of Hydroelectric Power*
  R&R Bk N - v19 - i1 - Feb 2004 - p102(1) [51-500]

Edwards, Becky - *My First Day at Nursery School (Illus. by Flintoft, Anthony)*
  c SLJ - v50 - i7 - July 2004 - p43(1) [51-500]

Edwards, Betty - *Color: A Course in Mastering the Art of Mixing Colors*
  A Art - v69 - i751 - Feb 2005 - p76(1) [51-500]

Edwards, Bill - *Carnival Glass: The Best of the Best*
  Ant&CM - v108 - i10 - Dec 2003 - p16(1) [501+]

Edwards, Bob - *Edward R. Murrow and the Birth of Broadcast Journalism*
  BW - v34 - i41 - Oct 10 2004 - p13(1) [501+]
  Choice - v42 - i2 - Oct 2004 - p287(1) [501+]
  Edward R. Murrow and the Birth of Broadcast Television
  TV Q - v35 - i1 - Fall 2004 - p65(3) [501+]

Edwards, Brent Hayes - *The Practice of Diaspora: Literature, Tranlation and the Rise of Black Internationalism*
  MFSF - v50 - i3 - Fall 2004 - p792-794 [501+]

Edwards, Brian (b. 1944 -) - *Green Buildings Pay, 2nd Ed.*
  R&R Bk N - v19 - i1 - Feb 2004 - p203(1) [51-500]

Edwards, Burt - *Credit Management Handbook, 5th Ed.*
  R&R Bk N - v19 - i4 - Nov 2004 - p117(1) [51-500]

Edwards, C. Henry - *Differential Equations and Boundary Value Problems: Computing and Modeling, 3rd Ed.*
SciTech - v28 - i3 - Sept 2004 - p39(1) [51-500]

Edwards, Catharine - *Rome the Cosmopolis*
Class R - v54 - i2 - Nov 2004 - p492(2) [501+]

Edwards, Cheri Paris - *Plenty Good Room*
PW - v252 - i11 - March 14 2005 - p46(1) [51-500]

Edwards, Cliff - *The Shoes of van Gogh: A Spiritual and Artistic Journey to the Ordinary*
CC - v121 - i24 - Nov 30 2004 - p45(2) [501+]

Edwards, Clive A. - *Earthworm Ecology: Proceedings, 2nd Ed.*
SciTech - v28 - i3 - Sept 2004 - p64(1) [51-500]

Edwards, Curtis L. - *Zemmouri Algeria: Mw 6.8 Earthquake of May 21, 2003*
SciTech - v28 - i4 - Dec 2004 - p58(1) [51-500]

Edwards, David - *Art Therapy*
SciTech - v28 - i4 - Dec 2004 - p97(1) [51-500]

Edwards, David (b. 1963 -) - *The Ormond Lordship in County Kilkenny, 1515-1642: The Rise and Fall of Butler Feudal Power*
AHR - v109 - i4 - Oct 2004 - p1309-1309 [501+]

Edwards, David (b. 1963 -) - *The Ormond Lordship in County Kilkenny, 1515-1642: The Rise and Fall of Butler Feudal Power*
R&R Bk N - v19 - i1 - Feb 2004 - p34(1) [1-50]

Edwards, David J. - *Management of Off-Highway Plant and Equipment*
SciTech - v28 - i1 - March 2004 - p136(1) [51-500]

Edwards, David L. - *John Donne: Man of Flesh and Spirit*
Six Ct J - v35 - i1 - Spring 2004 - p234(2) [501+]

Edwards, Denis - *Breath of Life: A Theology of the Creator Spirit*
Theol St - v66 - i1 - March 2005 - p227(2) [501+]

Edwards, Elizabeth - *Lucy and Desi: A Real-Life Scrapbook of America's Favorite TV Couple*
PW - v251 - i41 - Oct 11 2004 - p74(2) [501+]

Edwards, Francis - *Plots and Plotters of the Reign of Elizabeth I*
Six Ct J - v35 - i3 - Fall 2004 - p883-884 [501+]

Edwards, Garry - *Hiking the Cariboo Goldfields*
CBRA - Annual 2003 - p22(2) [51-500]

Edwards, George C. - *On Deaf Ears: The Limits of the Bully Pulpit*
Choice - v41 - i11-12 - July-August 2004 - p2124(2) [501+]
Pres St Q - v34 - i3 - Sept 2004 - p695(2) [501+]
Why the Electoral College Is Bad for America
NY - v80 - i31 - Oct 18 2004 - p203(1) [51-500]

Edwards, John - *Telecosmos: The Next Great Telecom Revolution*
Choice - v42 - i7 - March 2005 - p1257(1) [51-500]

Edwards, John (b. 1953 -) - *Four Trials*
Barron's - v84 - i44 - Nov 1 2004 - p41(1) [501+]

Edwards, John (b. 1953 -) - *Four Trials*
NYTBR - August 22 2004 - p20 [501+]

Edwards-Jones, Imogen - *Hotel Babylon: Inside the Extravagance and Mayhem of a Luxury Five-Star Hotel*
Econ - v372 - i8388 - August 14 2004 - p74US [501+]
NYTBR - Feb 20 2005 - p23 [501+]
PW - v251 - i45 - Nov 8 2004 - p44(1) [51-500]
Tuscany for Beginners
KR - v73 - i5 - March 1 2005 - p246(2) [501+]

Edwards, Judith - *Abolitionists and Slave Resistance: Breaking the Chains of Slavery*
c   CH Bwatch - v14 - i7 - July 2004 - p5(1) [51-500]
c   CH Bwatch - v14 - i11 - Nov 2004 - pNA [51-500]
c   SLJ - v50 - i8 - August 2004 - p135(1) [501+]
The Great Expedition of Lewis and Clark by Private Rubin Field, Member of the Corps of Discovery
LibMed - v22 - i6 - March 2004 - p79(1) [501+]

Edwards, Julie Andrews - *Dragon: Hound of Honor*
c   BL - v101 - i1 - Sept 1 2004 - p120(1) [1-50]
c   SLJ - v50 - i9 - Sept 2004 - p204(1) [51-500]
The Last of the Really Great Whangdoodles
c   Storyworks - v12 - i1 - Sept 2004 - p8(1) [51-500]

Edwards, Kathryn A. - *Families and Frontiers: Re-Creating Communities and Boundaries in the Early Modern Burgundies*
Six Ct J - v34 - i4 - Winter 2003 - p1141-1142 [501+]
Werewolves, Witches, and Wandering Spirits: Traditional Belief and Folklore in Early Modern Europe
Six Ct J - v35 - i1 - Spring 2004 - p289(2) [501+]

Edwards, Katie - *Myths and Monsters: Secrets Revealed (Illus. by Mendez, Simon)*
c   SLJ - v51 - i2 - Feb 2005 - p116(1) [51-500]

Edwards, Kirsten - *Real-time PCR: An Essential Guide*
SciTech - v28 - i3 - Sept 2004 - p72(1) [51-500]

Edwards, Libby - *Genital Dermatology Atlas*
SciTech - v28 - i3 - Sept 2004 - p108(1) [51-500]

Edwards, M.J. - *Origen Against Plato*
Theol St - v65 - i4 - Dec 2004 - p895(2) [501+]

Edwards, Mark - *John*
TLS - i5289 - August 13 2004 - p24(1) [501+]

Edwards, Martin - *The Coffin Trail*
BL - v101 - i2 - Sept 15 2004 - p212(1) [51-500]
LJ - v129 - i14 - Sept 1 2004 - p122(1) [51-500]
PW - v251 - i31 - August 2 2004 - p55(1) [501+]

Edwards, Michael - *Global Citizen Action*
PG - v23 - i5 - June 2004 - p625-636 [501+]

Edwards, Michelle - *Papa's Latkes (Illus. by Schuett, Stacey)*
c   BL - v101 - i2 - Sept 15 2004 - p248(1) [51-500]
c   CH Bwatch - v14 - i11 - Nov 2004 - pNA [51-500]
c   HB - v80 - i6 - Nov-Dec 2004 - p659(1) [51-500]
c   KR - v72 - i21 - Nov 1 2004 - p1049(1) [51-500]
c   PW - v251 - i39 - Sept 27 2004 - p59(1) [51-500]

Edwards, Nicola - *My Friend Has Dyspraxia*
c   SLJ - v51 - i2 - Feb 2005 - p116(2) [501+]
My Friend Is Blind
c   SLJ - v51 - i2 - Feb 2005 - p116(2) [501+]

Edwards, Pamela (b. 1956 -) - *The Statesman's Science: History, Nature, and Law in the Political Thought of Samuel Taylor Coleridge*
Pers PS - v34 - i1 - Wntr 2005 - p60(1) [501+]

Edwards, Pamela Duncan - *Gigi and Lulu's Gigantic Fight (Illus. by Cole, Henry)*
c   BL - v101 - i1 - Sept 1 2004 - p130(1) [1-50]
c   KR - v72 - i16 - August 15 2004 - p805(1) [51-500]
c   PW - v251 - i44 - Nov 1 2004 - p60(1) [501+]
c   SLJ - v50 - i11 - Nov 2004 - p103(1) [51-500]
The Leprechaun's Gold (Illus. by Cole, Henry)
c   CE - v81 - i1 - Fall 2004 - p46(1) [51-500]
McGillycuddy Could! (Illus. by Porter, Sue)
c   CCB-B - v58 - i6 - Feb 2005 - p250(2) [51-500]
c   HB - v81 - i2 - March-April 2005 - p187(2) [51-500]
c   KR - v73 - i2 - Jan 15 2005 - p119(1) [51-500]

Edwards, Patricia A. - *Children's Literacy Development: Making It Happen through School, Family, and Community Involvement*
R&R Bk N - v19 - i1 - Feb 2004 - p182(1) [51-500]

Edwards, Paul (b. 1923 -) - *Heidegger's Confusions*
R&R Bk N - v20 - i1 - Feb 2005 - p5(1) [51-500]

Edwards, Paul M. - *To Acknowledge a War*
NWCR - v56 - i1 - Winter 2003 - p159 [501+]

Edwards, Peter - *The Encyclopedia of Canadian Organized Crime: From Captain Kidd to Mom Boucher*
Globe & Mail - Oct 2 2004 - pD17 [501+]
Night Justice: The True Story of the Black Donnellys
Globe & Mail - Dec 24 2004 - pD13 [1-50]

Edwards, Robert R. - *Chaucer and Boccaccio: Antiquity and Modernity*
MP - v102 - i1 - August 2004 - p95(3) [501+]
RES - v55 - i218 - Feb 2004 - p115-117 [501+]

Edwards, Roberta - *Funny Bunny Feet (Illus. by Gevry, Claudine)*
c   PW - v252 - i7 - Feb 14 2005 - p80(2) [501+]

Edwards, Ron - *Rocks, Minerals, and Resources Series*
c   Res Links - v10 - i1 - Oct 2004 - p26(2) [51-500]

Edwards, Ruth Dudley - *Carnage on the Committee*
Bwatch - Feb 2005 - pNA [51-500]
PW - v251 - i43 - Oct 25 2004 - p31(1) [51-500]
Newspapermen: Hugh Cudlipp, Cecil Harmsworth King and the Glory Days of Fleet Street
CJR - v43 - i5 - Jan-Feb 2005 - p62(1) [51-500]
LJ - v129 - i18 - Nov 1 2004 - p98(1) [51-500]

Edwards, Sebastian - *Preventing Currency Crises in Emerging Markets*
JEL - v42 - i1 - March 2004 - p'79(3) [501+]

Edwards, Steve - *Art of the Avant-Gardes*
LJ - v130 - i1 - Jan 1 2005 - p105(1) [51-500]

Edwards, Vincent - *The Russian Province After Communism: Enterprise, Continuity, and Change*
Russ Rev - v63 - i2 - April 2004 - pNA [501+]

Edwards, Wallace - *Alphabeasts*
c   Can Lit - i182 - Autumn 2004 - p122(3) [501+]
Alphabeasts (Illus. by Edwards, Wallace)
c   RT - v57 - Oct 2003 - p168 [1-50]
Monkey Business
c   BL - v101 - i5 - Nov 1 2004 - p477(1) [51-500]
c   BW - v34 - i41 - Oct 10 2004 - p12(1) [501+]
c   Globe & Mail - Sept 11 2004 - pD13 [51-500]
c   KR - v72 - i17 - Sept 1 2004 - p863(1) [51-500]
c   PW - v251 - i40 - Oct 4 2004 - p86(1) [51-500]
c   SLJ - v50 - i9 - Sept 2004 - p186(1) [51-500]

Edwards, Wendy J. Deichmann - *Gender and the Social Gospel*
HNet - June 2004 - pNA [501+]

Edwards, William Pearson - *The Festival of Nine Lessons and Carols: As Celebrated on Christmas Eve in the Chapel of King's College, Cambridge*
Globe & Mail - Dec 18 2004 - pD14 [1-50]

Eels, Emily - *Proust's Cup of Tea*
FS - v58 - i3 - July 2004 - p427-428 [501+]

Eemeren, Frans H. van - *Anyone Who Has a View: Theoretical Contributions to the Study of Argumentation*
R&R Bk N - v19 - i1 - Feb 2004 - p6(1) [51-500]

Eerdmans, Jeffrey John - *The Meaning in the Miracles*
CC - v121 - i25 - Dec 14 2004 - p21(1) [501+]

Eerikainen, Atso A. - *Two Dimensions of Time: The Dimensional Theory of Karl Helm, an Ontological Solution to the Problems of Science, Philosophy, and Theology*
R&R Bk N - v19 - i1 - Feb 2004 - p7(1) [51-500]

Effect 3 D Studio
LibMed - v22 - i4 - Jan 2004 - p89(1) [501+]

Effinger, George Alec - *Budayeen Nights*
Analog - v124 - i1-2 - Jan-Feb 2004 - p234(1) [501+]

Effros, Bonnie - *Creating Community with Food and Drink in Merovingian Gaul*
AHR - v109 - i2 - April 2004 - p586(1) [501+]
Merovingian Mortuary Archaeology and the Making of the Early Middle Ages
AHR - v109 - i3 - June 2004 - p959(2) [501+]

Efimov, Igor Markovich - *Five Talents or One? The Shocking Secret of Inequality*
R&R Bk N - v19 - i4 - Nov 2004 - p152(1) [51-500]

Efremovich, G.E. - *Quantitative Level of Chemical Reactions*
SciTech - v28 - i1 - March 2004 - p56(1) [51-500]

Egan, Bill - *Florence Mills: Harlem Jazz Queen*
Bwatch - Feb 2005 - pNA [51-500]

Egan, Jeanette - *The Book of Roasting*
Kliatt - v38 - i4 - July 2004 - p45(1) [51-500]

Egan, Ken - *Hope and Dread in Montana Literature*
PHR - v73 - i3 - August 2004 - p499(500) [501+]
WHQ - v35 - i4 - Winter 2004 - p532-533 [501+]

Egan, Kerry - *Fumbling: A Pilgrimage Tale of Love, Grief, and Spiritual Renewal on the Camino de Santiago*
BL - v101 - i2 - Sept 15 2004 - p200(1) [51-500]
BW - v34 - i40 - Oct 3 2004 - p14(1) [501+]
LJ - v129 - i15 - Sept 15 2004 - p72(1) [51-500]
PW - v251 - i30 - July 26 2004 - p50(1) [501+]

Egan, Tim - *Serious Farm*
c   BooChiTr - Jan 25 2004 - p5(1) [501+]
c   Five Owls - v18 - i1 - Fall 2004 - p19(1) [51-500]
c   LibMed - v22 - i7 - April-May 2004 - p56(1) [501+]
The Trial of Cardigan Jones (Illus. by Egan, Tim)
c   CCB-B - v58 - i2 - Oct 2004 - p70(2) [51-500]
c   KR - v72 - i13 - July 1 2004 - p628(1) [51-500]
c   PW - v251 - i33 - August 16 2004 - p62(2) [51-500]
c   SLJ - v50 - i9 - Sept 2004 - p160(1) [51-500]

Egan, Tracie - *Francisca Alvarez: The Angel of Goliad/El angel de Goliad*
c   SLJ - v50 - i9 - Sept 2004 - p195(1) [51-500]
How a Bill Becomes a Law
c   SLJ - v51 - i2 - Feb 2005 - p118(1) [51-500]
Voting
c   SLJ - v51 - i2 - Feb 2005 - p118(1) [51-500]

Egelhaff-Gaiser, U. - *Religiose Vereine in der romischen Antike. Untersuchungen zu Organisation, Ritual und Raumordnung*
Class R - v54 - i1 - May 2004 - p205(2) [501+]

Egendorf, Laura K. - *The Information Revolution: Opposing Viewpoints*
SLJ - v50 - i10 - Oct 2004 - pS59(1) [51-500]
Terrorism
y   SLJ - v51 - i2 - Feb 2005 - p146(1) [51-500]

Eger, Joseph - *Einstein's Violin: a Conductor's Notes on Music, Physics, and Social Change*
KR - v73 - i2 - Jan 15 2005 - p98(1) [501+]
LJ - v130 - i3 - Feb 15 2005 - p131(1) [51-500]

Egerton, Douglas R. - *Rebels, Reformers, and Revolutionaries: Collected Essays and Second Thoughts*
JSH - v70 - i4 - Nov 2004 - p902(3) [501+]

Egerton, Frank N. - *Hewett Cottrell Watson: Victorian Plant Ecologist and Evolutionist*
Isis - v95 - i2 - June 2004 - p311(2) [501+]

Eggener, Keith L. - *American Architectural History: A Contemporary Reader*
R&R Bk N - v19 - i4 - Nov 2004 - p202(1) [501+]

Eijk, Ph. J. van der - *Diocles of Carystus. A Collection of the Fragments with Translation and Commentary, Vol. 1*
Class R - v53 - i2 - Nov 2003 - p334-337 [501+]

Eilan, Naomi - *Agency and Self-Awareness*
TLS - i5298 - Oct 15 2004 - p10(1) [501+]

Eileen, Cleere - *Avuncuralism: Capitalism, Patriarchy, and Nineteenth-Century English Culture*
Choice - v42 - i3 - Nov 2004 - p480(2) [1-50]

Einarsen, Stale - *Bullying and Emotional Abuse in the Workplace: International Perspectives in Research and Practice*
Per Psy - v57 - i4 - Winter 2004 - p1088(4) [501+]

Einarson, John - *Mr. Tambourine Man*
Ent W - i812 - March 25 2005 - p78 [51-500]

Einhorn, Michael A. - *Media, Technology, and Copyright: Integrating Law and Economics*
SciTech - v28 - i3 - Sept 2004 - p11(1) [501+]

Einstein, Albert - *The Born-Einstein Letters 1916-1955: Friendship, Politics and Physics in Uncertain Times*
LJ - v130 - i3 - Feb 15 2005 - p172(1) [51-500]
The Collected Papers of Albert Einstein
New Sci - v185 - i2484 - Jan 29 2005 - p50(2) [501+]
The Meaning of Relativity. Audiobook Review
Globe & Mail - Dec 18 2004 - pD25 [1-50]

Eisenach, Emlyn - *Husbands, Wives, and Concubines: Marriage, Family, and Social Order in Sixteenth-Century Verona*
R&R Bk N - v19 - i4 - Nov 2004 - pNA [51-500]

Eisenberg, James R. - *Law, Pyschology, and Death Penalty Litigation*
Choice - v42 - i6 - Feb 2005 - p1097(1) [51-500]

Eisenberg, Michael - *Information Literacy: Essential Skills for the Information Age. 2nd Ed.*
BL - v100 - i21 - July 2004 - p1859(1) [1-50]
Information Literacy: Essential Skills for the Information Age, 2nd Ed.
LibMed - v23 - i1 - August-Sept 2004 - p84(1) [51-500]
Information Literacy: Essential Skills for the Information Age, 2nd Ed.
R&USQ - v44 - i1 - Fall 2004 - p99(2) [501+]
Information Literacy: Essential Skills for the Information Age, 2nd Ed.
Teach Lib - v32 - i2 - Dec 2004 - p36(2) [501+]

Eisenberg, Ronald L. - *The JPS Guide to Jewish Traditions*
PW - v251 - i41 - Oct 11 2004 - p75(1) [51-500]

Eisenbichler, Konrad - *The Cultural World of Eleonora di Toledo: Duchess of Florence and Siena*
R&R Bk N - v19 - i4 - Nov 2004 - p40(1) [51-500]
The Premodern Teenager: Youth in Society, 1150-1650
Six Ct J - v35 - i1 - Spring 2004 - p219(2) [501+]

Eisendle, Helmut - *Ein Stuck des blauen Himmels*
WLT - v78 - i3-4 - Sept-Dec 2004 - p125(1) [501+]

Eisendrath, Craig R. - *Bush League Diplomacy: How the Neoconservatives Are Putting the World at Risk*
Choice - v42 - i4 - Dec 2004 - p736(1) [1-50]
R&R Bk N - v19 - i3 - August 2004 - p71(1) [51-500]

Eisenhauer, Robert - *Mythic Paradigms in Literature, Philosophy, and the Arts*
R&R Bk N - v19 - i3 - August 2004 - p259(1) [51-500]

Eisenhour, Jerry D. - *Joe Leblang's Cut-Rate Ticket Empire and the Broadway Theatre, 1984-1931*
R&R Bk N - v19 - i1 - Feb 2004 - p103(1) [51-500]

Eisenhower, John S.D. - *General Ike: A Personal Reminiscence*
J Mil H - v68 - i2 - April 2004 - p639(3) [501+]

Eisenman, Peter - *Eisenman Inside Out: Selected Writings, 1963-1988*
Choice - v42 - i3 - Nov 2004 - p475(1) [1-50]

Eisenstadt, S.N. - *Explorations in Jewish Historical Experience: The Civilizational Dimension*
R&R Bk N - v19 - i3 - August 2004 - p51(1) [51-500]

Eisenstadt, Todd A. - *Courting Democracy in Mexico: Party Strategies and Electoral Institutions*
Choice - v42 - i3 - Nov 2004 - p557(1) [1-50]

Eisinger, Robert M. - *The Evolution of Presidential Polling*
JAH - v91 - i2 - Sept 2004 - p721(3) [501+]
Pub Op Q - v68 - i3 - Fall 2004 - p426(5) [501+]

Eisler, Barry - *Rain Storm*
BL - v100 - i21 - July 2004 - p1824(1) [1-50]
Ent W - i777 - August 6 2004 - p87 [51-500]
PW - v251 - i27 - July 5 2004 - p39(1) [51-500]

Eisler, Benita - *Chopin's Funeral*
NYTBR - July 11 2004 - p24 [501+]

Eismann, Katrin - *Digital Photography. 2nd Ed.*
Bwatch - v26 - i8 - August 2004 - p6(2) [51-500]
Photoshop Masking and Compositing
Bwatch - March 2005 - pNA [501+]
Real World Digital Photography, 2nd Ed.
SciTech - v28 - i4 - Dec 2004 - p167(1) [51-500]

Eisner, Elliot W. - *The Arts and the Creation of Mind*
Adoles - v39 - i156 - Winter 2004 - p830(1) [51-500]
TCR - v106 - i2 - Feb 2004 - p403-406 [501+]

Eisner, Jane - *Taking Back the Vote: Getting American Youth Involved in Our Democracy*
R&R Bk N - v19 - i4 - Nov 2004 - p130(1) [1-50]

Eisner, Thomas - *For Love of Insects*
Am Sci - v92 - i4 - July-August 2004 - p382(2) [501+]
Isis - v95 - i3 - Sept 2004 - p502(2) [501+]
QRB - v79 - i3 - Sept 2004 - p314(2) [501+]
SB - v40 - i6 - Nov-Dec 2004 - p243(1) [51-500]
TimHES - v0 - i1668 - Nov 26 2004 - p24(1) [501+]
TLS - i5287 - July 30 2004 - p3-4 [501+]

Eisner, Will - *John Law, Detective: Dead Man Walking*
Ent W - i797 - Dec 17 2004 - p88 [501+]
Will Eisner's The Spirit Archives, Vol. 13
y BL - v100 - i22 - August 2004 - p1916(1) [51-500]
Will Eisner's The Spirit Archives, Vol. 14 (Illus. by Eisner, Will)
y BL - v101 - i4 - Oct 15 2004 - p396(1) [51-500]

Eitan, Ora - *A-Tisket, A-Tasket*
LibMed - v22 - i5 - Feb 2004 - p64(1) [51-500]

Eitenmiller, Ronald - *Vitamin E: Food Chemistry, Composition and Analysis*
SciTech - v28 - i3 - Sept 2004 - p73(1) [51-500]

Eitzen, D. Stanley - *Fair and Foul: Beyond the Myths and Paradoxes of Sport*
SSJ - v21 - i1 - March 2004 - p112-113 [501+]

Ejersbo, Jakob - *Nordkraft*
Globe & Mail - Oct 30 2004 - pD15 [501+]

eJournal of Tax Research
JEL - v42 - i1 - March 2004 - p345(1) [501+]

Ekberg, Carl J. - *Francois Valle and His World: Upper Louisiania before Lewis and Clark*
WHQ - v35 - i3 - Autumn 2004 - p382(2) [501+]

Eker, T. Harv - *Secrets of the Millionaire Mind: Mastering the Inner Game of Wealth*
NW - March 21 2005 - p36 [501+]
PW - v252 - i7 - Feb 14 2005 - p66(1) [51-500]

Ekuni, Kaori - *Twinkle Twinkle*
Lam Bk Rpt - v13 - i1-2 - August-Sept 2004 - p46(2) [501+]

Ekvall, Robert - *Fields on the Hoof: Nexus of Tibetan Nomadic Pastoralism*
Globe & Mail - Dec 24 2004 - pD15 [51-500]

El-Ali, Taan S. - *Discrete Systems and Digital Signal Processing with MATLAB*
SciTech - v28 - i1 - March 2004 - p153(1) [51-500]

El-Ayouty, Yassin - *Perspectives on 9/11*
R&R Bk N - v19 - i4 - Nov 2004 - p145(1) [501+]

El-Dine, Dani Saad - *Control Self-Assessment: Concepts and Applications*
R&R Bk N - v19 - i4 - Nov 2004 - p114(1) [51-500]

El Fadl, Khaled Abou - *The Place of Tolerance in Islam*
JPR - v41 - i6 - Nov 2004 - p756-757 [501+]
Rebellion and Violence in Islamic Law
AHR - v109 - i2 - April 2004 - p651(2) [501+]

El-Hai, Jack - *The Lobotomist: A Maverick Medical Genius and His Tragic Quest to Rid the World of Mental Illness*
LJ - v130 - i1 - Jan 1 2005 - p139(1) [51-500]

El Islam y Occidente - *Islam and the West*
y VOYA - v27 - i3 - August 2004 - p181(1) [51-500]

El Koudia, Jilali - *Moroccan Folktales*
R&R Bk N - v19 - i1 - Feb 2004 - p72(1) [51-500]

El-Shafai, Saber Abdel-Aziz Abdel Salam Mohamed - *Nutrients Valorisation via Duckweed-Based Wastewater Treatment and Aquaculture*
SciTech - v28 - i1 - March 2004 - p148(1) [51-500]

Elaissari, Abdelhamid - *Colloidal Biomolecules, Biomaterials, and Biomedical Applications*
SciTech - v28 - i1 - March 2004 - p58(1) [51-500]

Eland, Ivan - *Putting Defense Back into U.S. Defense Policy*
IndRev - v7 - i3 - Winter 2003 - p469 [501+]

Elasmar, M. - *The Impact of International Television: A Paradigm Shift*
J Broadcst - v48 - i3 - Sept 2004 - p518(7) [501+]

Elbaum, Max - *Revolution in the Air: Sixties Radicals Turn to Lenin, Mao and Che*
J Soc H - v38 - i1 - Fall 2004 - p226(4) [501+]
S&S - v68 - i2 - Summer 2004 - p231-233 [501+]

Elbert, Bruce R. - *Satellite Communication Applications Handbook, 2nd Ed.*
SciTech - v28 - i1 - March 2004 - p155(1) [51-500]

Elbom, Gilad - *Scream Queens of the Dead Sea*
BL - v101 - i1 - Sept 1 2004 - p60(1) [51-500]
KR - v72 - i19 - Oct 1 2004 - p929(1) [501+]
PW - v251 - i40 - Oct 4 2004 - p69(1) [51-500]
Tikkun - v20 - i1 - Jan-Feb 2005 - p73(1) [501+]

Elbourne, Elizabeth - *Blood Ground: Colonialism, Missions, and the Contest for Christianity in the Cape Colony and Britain, 1799-1853*
AHR - v109 - i2 - April 2004 - p482(1) [501+]
IBMR - v28 - i3 - July 2004 - p133(2) [501+]
JIH - v35 - i2 - Autumn 2004 - p333(2) [501+]

Eldash, Khaled - *In an Egyptian City*
c SLJ - v51 - i1 - Jan 2005 - p56(1) [51-500]

Elden, Stuart - *Understanding Henri Lefebvre: Theory and the Possible*
Choice - v42 - i6 - Feb 2005 - p1034(1) [51-500]

Elder, Chet H. - *Dismissal Doesn't Have to Be Difficult: What Every Administrator and Supervisor Should Know*
R&R Bk N - v19 - i4 - Nov 2004 - p187(1) [51-500]

Elder, Crawford L. - *Real Natures and Familiar Objects*
Choice - v42 - i4 - Dec 2004 - p674(1) [1-50]

Elder, Donald C. - *Love Amid the Turmoil: The Civil War Letters of William and Mary Vermilion*
JSH - v70 - i4 - Nov 2004 - p939(2) [501+]

Elderkin, Susan - *The Voices*
y Kliatt - v39 - i2 - March 2005 - p18(1) [51-500]

Eldin, Mohie Eldin I. Alam - *Arbitral Awards of the Cairo Regional Centre for International Commercial Arbitration 2, 1997-2000*
R&R Bk N - v19 - i4 - Nov 2004 - p163(1) [501+]

Eldredge, Charles C. - *Tales from the Easel: American Narrative Paintings from Southeastern Museums, Circa 1800-1950*
R&R Bk N - v19 - i3 - August 2004 - p243(1) [51-500]

Eldredge, John - *Epic: The Story God Is Telling and the Role That Is Yours to Play*
PW - v251 - i33 - August 16 2004 - p60(1) [51-500]

Eldredge, Niles - *Why We Do It: Rethinking Sex and the Selfish Gene*
Choice - v42 - i3 - Nov 2004 - p507(1) [1-50]
Nature - v430 - i7000 - August 5 2004 - p613(2) [501+]
NYTBR - July 4 2004 - p18 [501+]
SB - v40 - i6 - Nov-Dec 2004 - p246(1) [501+]
SciTech - v28 - i3 - Sept 2004 - p69(1) [51-500]

Eldridge, Bruce F. - *Medical Entomology: A Textbook on Public Health and Veterinary Problems Caused by Arthropods, Rev. Ed.*
SciTech - v28 - i1 - March 2004 - p83(1) [51-500]

Eldridge, Courtney - *Unkempt*
NYTBR - Sept 12 2004 - p26 [501+]
PW - v251 - i28 - July 12 2004 - p43(1) [51-500]

Eldridge, Jim - *Desert Duel*
y Sch Lib - v52 - i3 - Autumn 2004 - p164(1) [501+]

Eldridge, Richard - *An Introduction to the Philosophy of Art*
Choice - v41 - i11-12 - July-August 2004 - p2057(1) [501+]

Eldridge, Robert D. - *The Return of the Amami Islands: The Reversion Movement and U.S.-Japan Relations*
Choice - v42 - i2 - Oct 2004 - p349(1) [51-500]

Elementary Themes: Maps And Map Skills
LibMed - v22 - i7 - April-May 2004 - p90(1) [501+]

Elena, Alberto - *The Cinema of Latin America*
Choice - v42 - i3 - Nov 2004 - p490(1) [51-500]
Si & So - v14 - i8 - August 2004 - p36(2) [501+]

Eles, P. von - *Guerriero e sacerdote. Autorita e communita nell eta del ferro a Verucchio*
Class R - v54 - i1 - May 2004 - p251(1) [501+]

Eley, Geoff - *Forging Democracy: The History of the Left in Europe, 1850-2000*
CEH - v37 - i3 - Summer 2004 - p453(5) [501+]
CS - v33 - i2 - March 2004 - p215-217 [501+]
S&S - v68 - i2 - Summer 2004 - p236-239 [501+]

Elferink, Alex G. Oude - *Oceans Management in the 21st Century: Institutional Frameworks and Responses*
R&R Bk N - v19 - i3 - August 2004 - p212(1) [1-50]

Elfers, James E. - *The Tour to End All Tours: The Story of Major League Baseball's 1913-1914 World Tour*
JPC - v38 - i1 - August 2004 - p229(3) [501+]

Ellis, Alice Thomas - *Fish, Flesh and Good Red Herring: A Gallimaufry*
CR - v286 - i1669 - Feb 2005 - p123(1) [51-500]
Spec - v296 - i9191 - Oct 2 2004 - p46(1) [501+]
TLS - i5298 - Oct 15 2004 - p30(1) [51-500]
God Has Not Changed
Spec - v296 - i9187 - Sept 4 2004 - p40(2) [501+]

Ellis, Anita J. - *The Ceramic Career of M. Louise McLaughlin*
Ceram Mo - v52 - i3 - March 2004 - p32(2) [501+]

Ellis, B.G. - *The Moving Appeal: Mr. McClanahan, Mrs. Dill, and the Civil War's Great Newspaper Run*
HNet - Sept 2004 - pNA [501+]
JAH - v91 - i2 - Sept 2004 - p638(2) [501+]
JSH - v70 - i4 - Nov 2004 - p935(2) [501+]

Ellis, Bill - *Lucifer Ascending: The Occult in Folklore and Popular Culture*
JouAmCul - v27 - i4 - Dec 2004 - p450(2) [501+]

Ellis, Chris - *Communicating with the African Patient*
SciTech - v28 - i4 - Dec 2004 - p76(1) [51-500]

Ellis, Clyde - *A Dancing People: Powwow Culture on the Southern Plains*
Choice - v42 - i1 - Sept 2004 - p147(1) [501+]
HNet - July 2004 - pNA [501+]
PHR - v73 - i3 - August 2004 - p508(509) [501+]

Ellis, David - *In the Company of Liars*
LJ - v129 - i20 - Dec 1 2004 - p86(1) [1-50]
PW - v252 - i9 - Feb 28 2005 - p41(1) [51-500]
Jury of One (Read by Burr, Sandra). Audiobook Review
BL - v100 - i21 - July 2004 - p1855(1) [1-50]
LJ - v129 - i15 - Sept 15 2004 - p88(1) [51-500]
Jury of One
BooChiTr - April 4 2004 - p3(1) [501+]

Ellis, Deborah - *The Breadwinner*
y VOYA - v27 - i3 - August 2004 - p180(1) [1-50]
A Company of Fools
Can Lit - i182 - Autumn 2004 - p135(2) [501+]
The Heaven Shop
y BL - v101 - i1 - Sept 1 2004 - p120(1) [1-50]
y CC - v121 - i25 - Dec 14 2004 - p24(1) [51-500]
y CCB-B - v58 - i5 - Jan 2005 - p208(2) [51-500]
y Globe & Mail - Sept 11 2004 - pD11 [501+]
y Kliatt - v38 - i5 - Sept 2004 - p8(2) [501+]
c KR - v72 - i15 - August 1 2004 - p740(1) [51-500]
y PW - v251 - i51 - Dec 20 2004 - p60(1) [501+]
c Res Links - v10 - i1 - Oct 2004 - p28(2) [51-500]
y SLJ - v50 - i10 - Oct 2004 - p161(2) [51-500]
y VOYA - v27 - i5 - Dec 2004 - p380(1) [501+]
Mud City
y Kliatt - v39 - i2 - March 2005 - p18(1) [51-500]
y Sch Lib - v52 - i3 - Autumn 2004 - p156(2) [501+]
c TES - v0 - i4587 - June 11 2004 - pssss18(2) [501+]
Parvana's Journey
y Can CL - i111-112 - Fall-Winter 2003 - p153(6) [501+]
c RT - v57 - Oct 2003 - p177 [1-50]
Three Wishes: Palestinian and Israeli Children Speak
y BL - v101 - i1 - Sept 1 2004 - p122(1) [1-50]
c BL - v101 - i7 - Dec 1 2004 - p647(1) [51-500]
y HB - v81 - i1 - Jan-Feb 2005 - p109(2) [51-500]
y Res Links - v10 - i2 - Dec 2004 - p43(2) [501+]
c SLJ - v50 - i10 - Oct 2004 - p190(1) [51-500]
y VOYA - v27 - i4 - Oct 2004 - p324(1) [51-500]

Ellis, Douglas - *Uncovered*
Bwatch - Dec 2004 - pNA [51-500]

Ellis, Edward Robb - *The Epic of New York City*
LJ - v130 - i2 - Feb 1 2005 - p126(1) [1-50]

Ellis, Harold - *Anatomy for Anaesthetists, 8th Ed.*
E-Streams - Nov 2004 - pNA [501+]

Ellis, Hattie - *Sweetness and Light: The Mysterious History of the Honeybee*
KR - v72 - i24 - Dec 15 2004 - p1179(1) [51-500]
PW - v252 - i3 - Jan 17 2005 - p44(1) [51-500]
Spec - v296 - i9193 - Oct 16 2004 - p69(1) [51-500]

The Ellis Island Collection: Artifacts from the Immigrant Experience
Bwatch - Dec 2004 - pNA [51-500]

Ellis, James - *Sexuality and Citizenship: Metamorphosis in Elizabethan Erotic Verse*
Ren Q - v57 - i4 - Winter 2004 - p1508(3) [501+]

Ellis, James E. - *Buying and Owning Your Own Airplane, 3rd Ed.*
SciTech - v28 - i3 - Sept 2004 - p164(1) [51-500]

Ellis, Joseph J. - *His Excellency: George Washington*
Ent W - i790 - Oct 29 2004 - p71 [501+]
y BL - v101 - i2 - Sept 15 2004 - p178(1) [51-500]
BL - v101 - i9-10 - Jan 1 2005 - p766(1) [51-500]
Bus W - i3906 - Nov 1 2004 - p30 [501+]
BW - v34 - i44 - Oct 31 2004 - p2(1) [501+]
KR - v72 - i16 - August 15 2004 - p786(1) [501+]
LJ - v129 - i13 - August 2004 - p90(1) [501+]
NYTBR - Nov 7 2004 - p18 [501+]
PW - v251 - i31 - August 2 2004 - p58(1) [501+]
Time - v164 - i17 - Oct 25 2004 - p97 [501+]

Ellis, Judith A. - *Selected Essays in Electronic Recordkeeping in Australia*
Archiv - i56 - Fall 2003 - p411(3) [501+]

Ellis, Julie (b. 1933 -) - *Small-Town Dreams*
BL - v101 - i5 - Nov 1 2004 - p470(1) [51-500]

Ellis, Julie (b. 1961 -) - *What's Your Angle, Pythagoras?: A Math Adventure (Illus. by Hornung, Phyllis)*
c PW - v251 - i31 - August 2 2004 - p73(1) [51-500]
c SB - v40 - i6 - Nov-Dec 2004 - p265(1) [51-500]
c SLJ - v50 - i10 - Oct 2004 - p140(1) [51-500]

Ellis, Linda - *Travel, Communication, and Geography in Late Antiquity: Sacred and Profane*
R&R Bk N - v19 - i4 - Nov 2004 - p25(1) [501+]

Ellis, Markman - *The Coffee House: A Cultural History*
NS - v133 - i4713 - Nov 8 2004 - p51(2) [501+]
Spec - v296 - i9197 - Nov 13 2004 - p65(1) [501+]
TLS - i5304 - Nov 26 2004 - p11(1) [501+]

Ellis, Mary Relindes - *The Turtle Warrior. Audiobook Review*
c Kliatt - v38 - i4 - July 2004 - p57(1) [51-500]
The Turtle Warrior
y BooChiTr - Jan 18 2004 - p1(2) [501+]
y SLJ - v50 - i8 - August 2004 - p146(1) [51-500]

Ellis, Peter Berresford - *Eyewitness to Irish History*
R&R Bk N - v19 - i3 - August 2004 - p40(1) [51-500]

Ellis, Richard (b. 1938 -) - *Aquagenesis: The Origin and Evolution of Life in the Sea*
Am Bio T - v66 - i8 - Oct 2004 - p579(2) [501+]
The Empty Ocean: Plundering the World's Marine Life
TLS - i5262 - Feb 6 2004 - p5(2) [501+]
No Turning Back: The Life and Death of Animal Species
BL - v100 - i21 - July 2004 - p1807(1) [1-50]
LJ - v129 - i12 - July 2004 - p113(1) [51-500]
PW - v251 - i31 - August 2 2004 - p65(1) [51-500]
SciTech - v28 - i4 - Dec 2004 - p66(1) [51-500]

Ellis, Richard J. - *To the Flag: The Unlikely History of the Pledge of Allegiance*
LJ - v130 - i3 - Feb 15 2005 - p148(1) [51-500]

Ellis, Robert Richmond - *They Dream Not of Angels but of Men: Homoeroticism, Gender, and Race in Latin American Autobiography*
Biomag - v27 - i3 - Summer 2004 - p640(4) [501+]

Ellis, Roger - *The Complete Audition Book for Young Actors: A Comprehensive Guide to Winning by Enhancing Acting Skills*
y SLJ - v50 - i7 - July 2004 - p120(1) [51-500]

Ellis, Sarah - *Pick-Up Sticks*
y Can Lit - i182 - Autumn 2004 - p124(2) [501+]
Several Lives of Orphan Jack (Illus. by St-Aubin, Bruno)
c CBRA - Annual 2003 - p481(2) [51-500]
c LibMed - v22 - i6 - March 2004 - p60(1) [501+]

Ellis, Simon P. - *Roman Housing*
Class R - v54 - i2 - Nov 2004 - p498-499 [501+]

Ellis, Stephen - *Worlds of Power: Religious Thought and Political Practice in Africa*
Choice - v42 - i5 - Jan 2005 - p870(1) [1-50]

Ellis, Sylvia - *Britain, America, and the Vietnam War*
Choice - v42 - i3 - Nov 2004 - p538(1) [1-50]
R&R Bk N - v19 - i3 - August 2004 - p55(1) [51-500]

Ellis, Thomas Sayers - *The Maverick Room*
Black Iss - v7 - i2 - March-April 2005 - p32(1) [51-500]
PW - v252 - i4 - Jan 24 2005 - p237(1) [501+]

Ellis, Warren - *Global Frequency: Planet Ablaze*
LJ - v129 - i12 - July 2004 - p61(1) [51-500]
Orbiter
LibMed - v22 - i4 - Jan 2004 - p69(1) [501+]

Ellison, David - *Ethics and Aesthetics in European Modernist Literature: From the Sublime to the Uncanny*
MP - v102 - i1 - August 2004 - p144(5) [501+]
Neuropathology: A Reference Text of CNS Pathology, 2nd Ed.
SciTech - v28 - i3 - Sept 2004 - p93(1) [51-500]

Ellison, Harlan - *Children of the Streets*
LJ - v129 - i19 - Nov 15 2004 - p103(1) [501+]

Ellison, James - *George Sandys: Travel, Colonialism and Tolerance in the Seventeenth Century*
Albion - v36 - i1 - Spring 2004 - p118(3) [501+]
Six Ct J - v34 - i4 - Winter 2003 - p1136-1137 [501+]

Ellison, Katherine (b. 1957 -) - *The Mommy Brain: How Motherhood Makes Us Smarter.*
KR - v73 - i1 - Jan 1 2005 - p32(1) [501+]
LJ - v130 - i4 - March 1 2005 - p99(2) [51-500]
PW - v252 - i8 - Feb 21 2005 - p167(1) [51-500]

Ellison, Katherine W. - *Stress and the Police Officer, 2nd Ed.*
R&R Bk N - v19 - i3 - August 2004 - p168(1) [501+]

Ellison, Nancy - *Vineyard Days, Vineyard Nights*
R&R Bk N - v19 - i3 - August 2004 - p72(1) [51-500]

Ellison, R.A. - *Geology of London*
New Sci - v185 - i2481 - Jan 8 2005 - p51(1) [51-500]

Elllis, Janice Rider - *Nursing in Today's World: Trends, Issues, and Management, 8th Ed.*
SciTech - v28 - i4 - Dec 2004 - p121 [51-500]

Ellmann, Maud - *Elizabeth Bowen: The Shadow Across the Page*
Choice - v42 - i3 - Nov 2004 - p482(1) [1-50]
TSWL - v23 - i2 - Fall 2004 - p382(3) [501+]

Ellner, Steve - *Venezuelan Politics in the Chavez Era: Class, Polarization and Conflict*
S&S - v68 - i4 - Winter 2004 - p496-3 [501+]

Ellroy, James - *Destination: Morgue! L.A. Tales*
BL - v100 - i22 - August 2004 - p1868(1) [51-500]
Ent W - i786 - Oct 1 2004 - p77 [51-500]
Globe & Mail - Nov 20 2004 - pD24 [501+]
LJ - v129 - i18 - Nov 1 2004 - p83(1) [501+]
PW - v251 - i33 - August 16 2004 - p41(2) [51-500]
TLS - i5304 - Nov 26 2004 - p23(1) [501+]

Ellsberg, Robert - *The Saints' Guide to Happiness*
Comw - v131 - i21 - Dec 3 2004 - p29(2) [501+]

Ellstrand, Norman Carl - *Dangerous Liaisons?: When Cultivated Plants Mate with Their Wild Relatives*
SciTech - v28 - i3 - Sept 2004 - p128(1) [51-500]

Ellsworth, Allan J. - *Mosby's 2005 Medical Drug Reference*
SciTech - v28 - i4 - Dec 2004 - p118(1) [1-50]

Ellsworth, Edward - *The Selected Works of Edward E. Jones*
R&R Bk N - v19 - i2 - May 2004 - p129(1) [501+]

Ellwood, Robert - *Cycles of Faith: The Development of the World's Religions*
R&R Bk N - v19 - i1 - Feb 2004 - p11(1) [51-500]

Elman, Benjamin A. - *Rethinking Confucianism: Past and Present in China, Japan, Korea, and Vietnam*
Ch Rev Int - v10 - i2 - Fall 2003 - p337(14) [501+]

Elman, Colin - *Progress in International Relations Theory: Appraising the Field*
JEL - v42 - i1 - March 2004 - p344(1) [501+]

Elmer Bernstein's Film Music Notebook: A Complete Collection of the Quarterly Journal, 1974-1978
Notes - v61 - i3 - March 2005 - p749(4) [501+]

Elmer, Peter - *The Healing Arts: Health, Disease and Society in Europe 1500-1800, 1st Ed.*
TimHES - v0 - i1680 - Feb 25 2005 - pXV(1) [501+]
Health, Disease and Society in Europe 1500-1800: A Source Book, 1st Ed.
TimHES - v0 - i1680 - Feb 25 2005 - pXV(1) [501+]

Elpel, Thomas J. - *Botany in a Day*
Bwatch - Dec 2004 - pNA [51-500]
Primitive Living, Self-Sufficiency, and Survival Skills: A Field Guide to Primitive Living Skills
y Kliatt - v38 - i5 - Sept 2004 - p48(2) [51-500]

Elphinstone, Margaret - *Voyageurs*
BL - v100 - i22 - August 2004 - p1897(2) [51-500]
LJ - v129 - i13 - August 2004 - p66(1) [51-500]
PW - v251 - i33 - August 16 2004 - p45(1) [51-500]

Elrod, P.N. - *Stepping through the Stargate*
ChrSFF&H - v26 - i10 - Oct 2004 - p28(1) [51-500]

Elsadda, Hoda - *Madkhal ila qadaya al-mar'a fi sutur wa suwar*
HNet - June 2004 - pNA [501+]

Encarnacion, Omar G. - *The Myth of Civil Society: Social Capital and Democratic Consolidation in Spain and Brazil*
> Choice - v42 - i2 - Oct 2004 - p364(1) [51-500]
> PSQ - v119 - i4 - Winter 2004 - p717(3) [501+]
> R&R Bk N - v19 - i1 - Feb 2004 - p148(1) [51-500]

Encyclopaedia Britannica Almanac, 2005
> Choice - v42 - i7 - March 2005 - p1191(1) [51-500]
> R&R Bk N - v20 - i1 - Feb 2005 - p1(1) [51-500]

Encyclopedia Americana, International Ed., Vols. 1-30
> BL - v101 - i2 - Sept 15 2004 - p264(1) [501+]

Encyclopedia Americana Online
> BL - v101 - i2 - Sept 15 2004 - p270(1) [501+]

Encyclopedia Americana
> BL - v101 - i2 - Sept 15 2004 - p270(1) [51-500]

Encyclopedia Britainnica, Inc. - *Annals of America 2003, Vol. 22*
> R&R Bk N - v19 - i3 - August 2004 - p64 [51-500]

Annals of America 2003, Vols. 1-22
> R&R Bk N - v19 - i4 - Nov 2004 - p56(1) [51-500]

The Annals of America, Vols. 1-22
> BL - v101 - i6 - Nov 15 2004 - p613(1) [501+]

Encyclopedia Britannica Online
> BL - v101 - i2 - Sept 15 2004 - p268(2) [501+]

Encyclopedia Britannica Online School Edition
> BL - v101 - i2 - Sept 15 2004 - p268(2) [501+]

Encyclopedia Britannica Original Sources
> Choice - v42 - i2 - Oct 2004 - p274(1) [501+]

The Encyclopedia of Animals: A Complete Visual Guide
> Am Sci - v93 - i1 - Jan-Feb 2005 - p73(1) [501+]
> NH - v113 - i10 - Dec 2004 - p55(1) [501+]

Encyclopedia of British Writers: 19th and 20th Centuries
> LibMed - v22 - i6 - March 2004 - p81(1) [501+]

Encyclopedia of Chicago
> ON - v69 - i2 - August 2004 - p6(1) [51-500]

Encyclopedia of the Aquatic World, Vols. 1-11
> LibMed - v23 - i1 - August-Sept 2004 - p79(1) [51-500]
> y SLJ - v50 - i8 - August 2004 - p56(2) [51-500]

Encyclopedia of the Harlem Renaissance
> LibMed - v22 - i7 - April-May 2004 - p73(1) [501+]
> LJ - v129 - i18 - Nov 1 2004 - p122(2) [51-500]

Encyclopedia of the Lewis and Clark Expedition
> LibMed - v22 - i7 - April-May 2004 - p73(1) [501+]

Encyclopedia of the Presidents, 2nd Ser.
> LibMed - v22 - i7 - April-May 2004 - p66(1) [501+]

The Encyclopedia of the Summer Olympics
> LibMed - v22 - i6 - March 2004 - p88(1) [501+]

Encyclopedia of the World's Minorities
> LJ - v129 - i17 - Oct 15 2004 - p89(1) [51-500]

Encyclopedia of Women in the American West
> LibMed - v22 - i5 - Feb 2004 - p92(1) [501+]

Encyclopedia of World Pop Music, 1980-2001
> LibMed - v22 - i6 - March 2004 - p82(1) [501+]

End the Silence: Stop the Bullying
> SLJ - v50 - i12 - Dec 2004 - p66(1) [501+]

Endangered and Threatened Fishes in the Klamath River Basin: Causes of Decline and Strategies for Recovery
> Choice - v42 - i4 - Dec 2004 - p691(1) [1-50]

Endelman, Todd M. - *The Jews of Britain, 1656 to 2000*
> NYRB - v51 - i20 - Dec 16 2004 - p76(2) [501+]

Enderle, Judith Ross - *Hide-and-Seek Turkeys (Illus. by Murfin, Teresa)*
> KR - v72 - i18 - Sept 15 2004 - p913(1) [501+]
> c SLJ - v50 - i11 - Nov 2004 - p103(1) [501+]

Enderlin, Charles - *Shattered Dreams: The Failure of the Peace Process in the Middle East*
> JPR - v41 - i6 - Nov 2004 - p757-757 [501+]

Enders, Eric - *100 Years of the World Series*
> BL - v101 - i1 - Sept 1 2004 - p46(1) [51-500]

Enders, Jody - *Death by Drama and Other Medieval Urban Legends*
> Theat J - v56 - i1 - March 2004 - p133(2) [501+]

Endich, Roberta Solomon - *Media Literacy: Activities For Understanding the Scripted world*
> LibMed - v22 - i7 - April-May 2004 - p86(1) [501+]

Endicott, Shirley Jane - *China Diary: The Life of Mary Austin Endicott*
> CBRA - Annual 2003 - p43(2) [501+]

Endicott, Stephen Lyon - *Bienfait: The Saskatchewan Miners' Struggle of '31*
> R&R Bk N - v19 - i1 - Feb 2004 - p99(1) [1-50]
> WHQ - v35 - i3 - Autumn 2004 - p404(2) [501+]

Endlich, Lisa - *Optical Illusions: Lucent and the Crash of Telecom*
> BL - v101 - i2 - Sept 15 2004 - p185(1) [51-500]
> LJ - v129 - i15 - Sept 15 2004 - p67(1) [51-500]
> PW - v251 - i34 - August 23 2004 - p46(2) [51-500]

Endo, Shusaku - *The Samurai*
> Globe & Mail - July 10 2004 - pD13 [501+]

Endsley, Mica R. - *Designing for Situation Awareness: An Approach to User-Centered Design*
> SciTech - v28 - i1 - March 2004 - p177(1) [51-500]

Endy, Christopher - *Cold War Holidays: American Tourism in France*
> Choice - v42 - i4 - Dec 2004 - p700(1) [1-50]

Enenkel, Karl A.E. - *Mundus Emblematicus: Studies in Neo-Latin Emblem Books*
> Ren Q - v57 - i4 - Winter 2004 - p1443(2) [501+]

Ener, Mine - *Managing Egypt's Poor and the Politics of Benevolence, 1800-1952*
> AHR - v109 - i3 - June 2004 - p1015(2) [501+]

Energy Balances of Non-OECD Countries 2000-2001
> JEL - v42 - i1 - March 2004 - p333(1) [501+]
> SciTech - v28 - i3 - Sept 2004 - p7(1) [501+]

Energy Balances of OECD Countries 2000-2001
> JEL - v42 - i1 - March 2004 - p333(1) [501+]

Energy Policies of IEA Countries: 2003 Review
> SciTech - v28 - i3 - Sept 2004 - p7(1) [501+]

Energy Policies of IEA Countries: Austria: 2002 Review
> JEL - v42 - i1 - March 2004 - p333(1) [501+]

Energy Policies of IEA Countries: Hungary: 2003 Review
> JEL - v42 - i1 - March 2004 - p333(1) [501+]

Energy Policies of IEA Countries: Switzerland: 2003 Review
> JEL - v42 - i1 - March 2004 - p333(2) [501+]
> SciTech - v28 - i3 - Sept 2004 - p7(1) [501+]

Energy Statistics of Non-OECD Countries: 2000-2001
> JEL - v42 - i1 - March 2004 - p334(1) [501+]

Energy Statistics of Non-OECD Countries 2000-2001
> SciTech - v28 - i3 - Sept 2004 - p8(1) [501+]

Energy Statistics of OECD Countries/Statistiques de L'Energie des Pays de L'OCDE, 2000-2001
> JEL - v42 - i1 - March 2004 - p334(1) [501+]

Energy Statistics Yearbook 2001
> SciTech - v28 - i4 - Dec 2004 - p8(1) [1-50]

Enfield, Edward - *Greece on My Wheels (Read by Enfield, Edward). Audiobook Review*
> Kliatt - v38 - i6 - Nov 2004 - p56(1) [51-500]

Eng, Lai Ah - *Beyond Rituals and Riots: Ethnic Pluralism and Social Cohesion in Singapore*
> R&R Bk N - v19 - i3 - August 2004 - p55(1) [51-500]

Eng, Svein - *Seeking Civility: Common Courtesy and the Common Law*
> R&R Bk N - v19 - i1 - Feb 2004 - pNA [51-500]

Engaging Schools for Fostering High School Students' Motivation to Learn
> Choice - v42 - i2 - Oct 2004 - p344(1) [51-500]

Engammare, Max - *L'Etude de la Renaissance nunc et cras*
> Ren Q - v57 - i4 - Winter 2004 - p1346(4) [501+]

Engberg, Siri - *Robert Motherwell: The Complete Prints 1940/1991*
> NYTBR - July 11 2004 - p20 [51-500]

Engel, Andrew G. - *Myology: Basic and Clinical, 3rd Ed., Vols. 1-2*
> SciTech - v28 - i3 - Sept 2004 - p108(1) [51-500]

Engel, Barbara Alpern - *Women in Russia, 1700-2000.*
> Slav R - v63 - i4 - Winter 2004 - p879(2) [501+]

Engel, David M. - *Rights of Inclusion: Law and Identity in the Life Stories of Americans with Disabilities*
> AJS - v110 - i2 - Sept 2004 - p509(3) [501+]
> CS - v33 - i4 - July 2004 - p491(2) [501+]

Engel, Howard - *Memory Book*
> Globe & Mail - Feb 26 2005 - pD5 [501+]

Engel, Leonard - *Sam Peckinpah's West: New Perspectives*
> Choice - v41 - i7 - March 2004 - p1303(1) [501+]
> R&R Bk N - v19 - i1 - Feb 2004 - p226(1) [51-500]
> WHQ - v35 - i4 - Winter 2004 - p532-532 [501+]

Engel, Marian - *Marian Engel: Life in Letters*
> R&R Bk N - v19 - i4 - Nov 2004 - p244(1) [51-500]

Engel, William E. - *Death and Drama in Renaissance England: Shades of Memory*
> Clio - v33 - i4 - Summer 2004 - p473(5) [501+]
> Ren Q - v57 - i3 - Fall 2004 - p1166(3) [501+]
> RES - v55 - i220 - June 2004 - p457-458 [501+]

Engel, Wolfgang - *Shader X3: Advanced Rendering with DirectX and Open GL*
> Bwatch - Jan 2005 - pNA [51-500]

Engelbert, Thomas - *Ethnic Minorities and Politics in Southeast Asia*
> R&R Bk N - v19 - i3 - August 2004 - p54(1) [51-500]

Engelbreit, Mary - *Queen of Hearts*
> c KR - v72 - i24 - Dec 15 2004 - p1201(1) [501+]
> c PW - v251 - i49 - Dec 6 2004 - p61(2) [501+]
> c SLJ - v50 - i12 - Dec 2004 - p106(1) [501+]

Queen of the Class (Illus. by Engelbreit, Mary)
> c SLJ - v50 - i7 - July 2004 - p69(1) [51-500]

Engelhard, Michael - *Hell's Half Mile: River Runners' Tales of Hilarity and Adventure*
> BL - v101 - i2 - Sept 15 2004 - p192(1) [51-500]

Engelhardt, Elizabeth S.D. - *The Tangled Roots of Feminism, Environmentalism, and Appalachian Literature*
> Choice - v42 - i1 - Sept 2004 - p100(1) [501+]

Engelking, Larry R. - *Textbook of Veterinary Physiological Chemistry*
> SciTech - v28 - i4 - Dec 2004 - p126 [51-500]

Engels, Johannes M.M. - *Managing Plant Genetic Diversity*
> QRB - v79 - i4 - Dec 2004 - p429(2) [501+]

Engerman, David C. - *Staging Growth: Modernization, Development, and the Global Cold War*
> AHR - v109 - i4 - Oct 2004 - p1205-1205 [501+]
> JAH - v91 - i2 - Sept 2004 - p692(2) [501+]
> JAS - v63 - i2 - May 2004 - p475(3) [501+]

Engerman, Stanley L. - *The Cambridge Economic History of the United States, Vol. 3*
> JEL - v41 - i4 - Dec 2003 - p1316(3) [501+]

Finance, Intermediaries, and Economic Development
> BHR - v78 - i2 - Summer 2004 - p331(3) [501+]

Enghag, Per - *Encyclopedia of the Elements: Technical Data, History, Processing, Applications*
> Choice - v42 - i6 - Feb 2005 - p996(1) [51-500]

Engineering Is Elementary: Engineering and Technology Lessons for Children
> Tec Teach - v64 - i4 - Dec 2004 - p3(1) [501+]

Engineering Systems Design and Analysis, Vol. 1
> SciTech - v28 - i4 - Dec 2004 - p133 [51-500]

Engineering Systems Design and Analysis, Vol. 2
> SciTech - v28 - i4 - Dec 2004 - p133 [51-500]

Engineering Systems Design and Analysis, Vol. 3
> SciTech - v28 - i4 - Dec 2004 - p133 [51-500]

Englar, Mary - *Chief Joseph, 1840-1904*
> c SLJ - v50 - i7 - July 2004 - p92(1) [51-500]

Engler, Mira - *Designing America's Waste Landscapes*
> Choice - v42 - i6 - Feb 2005 - p1053(1) [51-500]

English, Daylanne K. - *Unnatural Selections; Eugenics in American Modernism and the Harlem Renaissance*
> Choice - v42 - i1 - Sept 2004 - p100(1) [501+]

English, Elizabeth - *Vajrayogini: Her Visualizations, Rituals, and Forms*
> JR - v84 - i3 - July 2004 - p498(2) [501+]

English, John - *The Hidden Pierre Elliott Trudeau: The Faith Behind the Politics*
> Globe & Mail - Jan 1 2005 - pD8 [501+]

English, Karen - *Hot Day on Abbott Avenue (Illus. by Steptoe, Javaka)*
> c BL - v100 - i21 - July 2004 - p1847(1) [51-500]
> c HB - v80 - i4 - July-August 2004 - p437(1) [51-500]
> c SLJ - v50 - i7 - July 2004 - p75(1) [51-500]

Speak to Me: And I Will Listen between the Lines (Illus. by Bates, Amy June)
> c BL - v100 - i22 - August 2004 - p1933(1) [51-500]
> c KR - v72 - i13 - July 1 2004 - p628(1) [51-500]
> c SLJ - v50 - i8 - August 2004 - p86(1) [51-500]

English, Richard - *Armed Struggle: A History of the IRA*
> Choice - v41 - i7 - March 2004 - p1360(1) [501+]

English, Sharon - *Uncomfortably Numb*
> CBRA - Annual 2003 - p198(2) [51-500]

English, T.J. - *Paddy Whacked: the Untold Story of the Irish American Gangster*
> PW - v252 - i5 - Jan 31 2005 - p60(2) [501+]

Englund, George - *The Way It's Never Been Done Before: My Friendship with Marlon Brando*
> BL - v101 - i5 - Nov 1 2004 - p443(1) [51-500]
> PW - v251 - i43 - Oct 25 2004 - p40(2) [51-500]

Englund, Steven - *Napoleon: A Political Life*
> Choice - v42 - i2 - Oct 2004 - p361(1) [51-500]
> Parameters - v34 - i4 - Winter 2004 - p154(2) [501+]
> TLS - i5264 - Feb 20 2004 - p8-9 [501+]

Engs, Ruth Clifford - *The Progressive Era's Health Reform Movement: A Historical Dictionary*
> Soc Ser R - v78 - i4 - Dec 2004 - p697(1) [51-500]

Engstrand, Iris - *John Sutter: Sutter's Fort and the California Gold Rush*
> c SLJ - v50 - i7 - July 2004 - p115(1) [1-50]

Engstrom, Eric J. - *Clinical Psychiatry in Imperial Germany: A History of Psychiatric Practice*
Choice - v42 - i1 - Sept 2004 - p137(2) [501+]
SciTech - v28 - i3 - Sept 2004 - p96(1) [51-500]

Enguland, Hari - *Rights and the Politics of Recognition in Africa*
Choice - v42 - i6 - Feb 2005 - p1093(1) [501+]

Ennis, Garth - *War Stories, Vol. 1*
BL - v101 - i1 - Sept 1 2004 - p77(1) [501+]

Enns, Carolyn Zerbe - *Feminist Theories and Feminist Psychotherapies: Origins, Themes, and Diversity, 2nd Ed.*
SciTech - v28 - i4 - Dec 2004 - p98(1) [51-500]

Enns, James T. - *The Thinking Eye, the Seeing Brain: Explorations in Visual Cognition*
SciTech - v28 - i4 - Dec 2004 - p2(1) [1-50]

Enoch, Suzanne - *Flirting with Danger*
PW - v252 - i3 - Jan 17 2005 - p39(2) [501+]

Enquist, Per Olov - *Lewi's Journey*
KR - v73 - i3 - Feb 1 2005 - p135(1) [501+]

Enright, Anne - *Making Babies: Stumbling into Motherhood*
NS - v133 - i4702 - August 23 2004 - p34(2) [501+]
TLS - i5301 - Nov 5 2004 - p36(1) [501+]

Enright, Leo - *The Beginner's Observing Guide, 5th Ed.*
Astron - v33 - i2 - Feb 2005 - p98 [51-500]

Ensign, Tod - *America's Military Today: The Challenge of Militarism*
PW - v251 - i47 - Nov 22 2004 - p54(1) [51-500]

Ensler, Eve - *The Good Body (Read by Ensler, Eve). Audiobook Review*
Globe & Mail - Dec 4 2004 - pD38 [1-50]
The Good Body
Globe & Mail - Nov 27 2004 - pD45 [501+]
NS - v133 - i4710 - Oct 18 2004 - p51(2) [501+]

Enstice, Wayne - *Jazzwomen*
Wom R Bks - v21 - i10-11 - July 2004 - p27(1) [51-500]

Enthoven, Alain C. - *Toward a 21st Century Health System: The Contributions and Promise of Prepaid Group Practice*
E-Streams - Oct 2004 - pNA [501+]

Entman, Robert M. - *Projections of Power: Framing News, Public Opinion, and U.S. Foreign Policy*
AJS - v110 - i3 - Nov 2004 - p833(2) [501+]
CS - v33 - i5 - Sept 2004 - p622-622 [501+]
J Broadcst - v48 - i4 - Dec 2004 - p700(5) [501+]

Entzinger, Han - *Migration between States and Markets*
R&R Bk N - v19 - i4 - Nov 2004 - p158(1) [501+]

The Environment
y SLJ - v50 - i8 - August 2004 - p136(1) [501+]

Environmental and Water Resources Institute (U.S.) - *American Society of Civil Engineers Standard Practice for the Design and Operation of Precipitation Enhancement Projects*
SciTech - v28 - i3 - Sept 2004 - p49(1) [1-50]

Environmental Archaeology: The Journal of Human Palaeoecology
R&R Bk N - v19 - i4 - Nov 2004 - p30(1) [501+]
SciTech - v28 - i4 - Dec 2004 - p4(1) [1-50]

Environmental Law Institute - *Legal Tools and Incentives for Private Lands Conservation in Latin America: Building Models for Success: Environmental Law Institute*
NRJ - v44 - i2 - Spring 2004 - p621-651 [501+]

The Environmental Performance of Public Procurement: Issues of Policy Coherence
JEL - v42 - i1 - March 2004 - p273(1) [501+]

The Environmental Resource Handbook 2003
R&R Bk N - v19 - i3 - August 2004 - p80(1) [51-500]

Environmental Spill Reporting and Contingency Planning
SciTech - v28 - i3 - Sept 2004 - p12(1) [501+]

Environmentally Harmful Subsidies: Policy Issues and Challenges
JEL - v42 - i1 - March 2004 - p337(1) [501+]
SciTech - v28 - i3 - Sept 2004 - p7(1) [501+]

Enzensberger, Hans Magnus - *The Number Devil (Illus. by Berner, Rotraut Susanne)*
c SLJ - v50 - i9 - Sept 2004 - p59(1) [501+]

Eom, Sean B. - *Author Co-Citation Analysis Using Custom Bibiographic Databases: An Introduction to the SAS Approach*
R&R Bk N - v19 - i1 - Feb 2004 - p258(1) [51-500]
Inter-Organizational Information Systems in the Internet Age
R&R Bk N - v19 - i4 - Nov 2004 - p107(1) [51-500]

Ephron, Amy - *One Sunday Morning*
KR - v73 - i3 - Feb 1 2005 - p135(1) [501+]
PW - v252 - i11 - March 14 2005 - p44(1) [51-500]

Ephron, G.H. - *Guilt*
KR - v73 - i3 - Feb 1 2005 - p151(1) [51-500]
PW - v252 - i9 - Feb 28 2005 - p46(1) [51-500]

Epicetus - *On Medieval Philosophy*
R&R Bk N - v19 - i3 - August 2004 - p3(1) [1-50]

Epkenhans, Michael - *Das Militar und der Aufbruch in die Moderne 1860-1890*
J Mil H - v68 - i4 - Oct 2004 - p1269-1271 [501+]

Epner, Paul - *There's a Dachshund in My Bed*
c CH Bwatch - v14 - i11 - Nov 2004 - pNA [51-500]

Epp, Marlene - *Sisters or Strangers?: Immigrant, Ethnic, and Racialized Women in Canadian History*
R&R Bk N - v19 - i4 - Nov 2004 - p134(1) [51-500]

Epperson, Michael - *Quantum Mechanics and the Philosophy of Alfred North Whitehead*
SciTech - v28 - i4 - Dec 2004 - p48(1) [51-500]

Epprecht, Marc - *'This Matter of Women Is Getting Very Bad' Gender, Development, and Politics in Colonial Lesotho*
JWH - v16 - i3 - Autumn 2004 - p213(8) [501+]

Eprile, Tony - *The Persistence of Memory*
NYTBR - August 8 2004 - p19 [501+]
NYTBR - August 22 2004 - p18 [501+]
TLS - i5295 - Sept 24 2004 - p21(1) [501+]

Epstein, Catherine - *The Last Revolutionaries: German Communists and Their Century*
AHR - v109 - i3 - June 2004 - p991(2) [501+]
CEH - v37 - i3 - Summer 2004 - p458(2) [501+]

Epstein, Charles L. - *Introduction to the Mathematics of Medical Imaging*
SIAM Rev - v46 - i2 - June 2004 - p362-364 [501+]

Epstein, Cynthia Fuchs - *Fighting for Time: Shifting Boundaries of Work and Social Life*
Choice - v42 - i7 - March 2005 - p1278(1) [51-500]

Epstein, Daniel Mark - *What Lips My Lips Have Kissed: The Loves and Love Poems of Edna St. Vincent Millay*
Sew R - v111 - i3 - Summer 2003 - p463-470 [501+]

Epstein, Edward Jay - *The Big Picture: The New Logic of Money and Power in Hollywood*
BL - v101 - i9-10 - Jan 1 2005 - p792(1) [51-500]
Econ - v374 - i8415 - Feb 26 2005 - p84US [501+]
KR - v72 - i24 - Dec 15 2004 - p1179(1) [501+]
LJ - v130 - i1 - Jan 1 2005 - p114(1) [51-500]
PW - v251 - i50 - Dec 13 2004 - p56(1) [51-500]

Epstein, Emanuel - *Mineral Nutrition of Plants: Principles and Perspectives, 2nd Ed.*
SciTech - v28 - i4 - Dec 2004 - p65(1) [51-500]

Epstein, James - *In Practice: Studies in the Language and Culture of Popular Politics in Modern Britain*
Albion - v36 - i1 - Spring 2004 - p174(3) [501+]
JIH - v35 - i1 - Summer 2004 - p127-129 [501+]
VS - v46 - i4 - Summer 2004 - p675(2) [501+]

Epstein, Joseph - *Envy*
HM - v310 - i1856 - Jan 2005 - p96(6) [501+]
Sew R - v112 - i3 - Summer 2004 - pLXXVI-LXXIX [501+]
Fabulous Small Jews
VQR - v80 - i1 - Wntr 2004 - p271-272 [501+]
Snobbery: The American Version
Sew R - v111 - i4 - Fall 2003 - pcxxiv-cxxvi [501+]

Epstein, Joshua M. - *Toward a Containment Strategy for Smallpox Bioterror: An Individual-Based Computational Approach*
SciTech - v28 - i4 - Dec 2004 - p84(1) [501+]

Epstein, Lawrence J. - *Mixed Nuts: America's Love Affair with Comedy Teams from Burns and Allen to Belushi and Aykroyd*
Bwatch - Feb 2005 - pNA [51-500]
KR - v72 - i15 - August 1 2004 - p722(1) [501+]
PW - v251 - i27 - July 5 2004 - p43(1) [501+]

Epstein, Lee - *Constitutional Law for a Changing America: Institutional Powers and Constraints, 5th Ed.*
R&R Bk N - v19 - i3 - August 2004 - p202(1) [501+]

Epstein, Leslie - *San Remo Drive: A Novel from Memory*
y NYTBR - August 1 2004 - p16 [501+]

Epstein, Mark - *Open to Desire: Embracing a Lust for Life*
PW - v251 - i50 - Dec 13 2004 - p64(1) [51-500]

Epstein, Nicky - *Knitting on the Edge: Ribs, Ruffles, Lace, Fringes, Flora, Points & Picots: The Essential Collection of 350 Decorative Borders*
BL - v100 - i22 - August 2004 - p1890(1) [51-500]
LJ - v129 - i13 - August 2004 - p78(1) [51-500]

Epstein, Richard Allen - *Cases and Materials on Torts, 8th Ed.*
R&R Bk N - v19 - i4 - Nov 2004 - p167(1) [501+]
Competition Laws in Conflict: Antitrust Jurisdiction in the Global Economy
Choice - v42 - i4 - Dec 2004 - p707(1) [1-50]
Skepticism and Freedom: A Modern Case of Classical Liberalism
VQR - v80 - i1 - Wntr 2004 - p275-275 [501+]

Equiano, Olaudah - *The Interesting Narrative and Other Writings*
R&R Bk N - v19 - i4 - Nov 2004 - p137(1) [1-50]

Eraly, Abraham - *The Mughal Throne: The Saga of India's Great Emperors*
KR - v72 - i23 - Dec 1 2004 - p1129(2) [501+]

Erber, Joan T. - *Aging and Older Adulthood*
R&R Bk N - v19 - i4 - Nov 2004 - p11(1) [51-500]

Erbisti, Paulo C.F. - *Design of Hydraulic Gates*
E-Streams - June 2004 - pNA [501+]
SciTech - v28 - i1 - March 2004 - p146(1) [51-500]

Erbsen, Wayne - *Clawhammer Banjo for the Complete Ignoramus!*
Bwatch - v26 - i8 - August 2004 - p3(1) [51-500]
Rural Roots of Bluegrass: Songs, Stories, and History
Teach Mus - v12 - i1 - August 2004 - p61(2) [501+]

Erdal, Jennie - *Ghosting: A Double Life*
KR - v73 - i1 - Jan 1 2005 - p32(2) [501+]
LJ - v129 - i20 - Dec 1 2004 - p92(1) [1-50]
Lon R Bks - v26 - i21 - Nov 4 2004 - p33(2) [501+]
PW - v252 - i7 - Feb 14 2005 - p63(1) [51-500]
Ghosting: A Memoir
NS - v133 - i4712 - Nov 1 2004 - p52(1) [501+]
Spec - v296 - i9194 - Oct 23 2004 - p57(1) [501+]
TLS - i5301 - Nov 5 2004 - p40(1) [501+]

Erdal, Marcel - *A Grammar of Old Turkic*
R&R Bk N - v19 - i4 - Nov 2004 - p219(1) [501+]

Erdcamp, P. - *The Roman Army and the Economy*
Class R - v54 - i1 - May 2004 - p198(3) [501+]

Erdelyi, R. - *Turbulence, Waves and Instabilities in the Solar Plasma*
SciTech - v28 - i1 - March 2004 - p44(1) [51-500]

Erder, Sema - *Irregular Migration and Trafficking in Women: The Case of Turkey*
R&R Bk N - v19 - i2 - May 2004 - p133 [51-500]

Erdly, Jeffrey L. - *Building Facade Maintenance, Repair, and Inspection*
SciTech - v28 - i3 - Sept 2004 - p148(1) [51-500]

Erdman, Andrew L. - *Blue Vaudeville: Sex, Morals and the Mass Marketing of Amusement, 1895-1915*
R&R Bk N - v19 - i3 - August 2004 - p260(1) [51-500]

Erdman, Sarah - *Nine Hills to Nambonkaha*
NYTBR - Sept 19 2004 - p24 [501+]

Erdrich, Liselotte - *Sacagawea (Illus. by Buffalohead, Julie)*
c Five Owls - v18 - i1 - Fall 2004 - p20(2) [51-500]
LibMed - v22 - i5 - Feb 2004 - p76(1) [501+]
RT - v58 - i3 - Nov 2004 - p289(1) [1-50]

Erdrich, Louise - *Four Souls*
Am Ind CRJ - v28 - i1 - Winter 2004 - p97-101 [501+]
Atl - v294 - i1 - July-August 2004 - p164(1) [51-500]
BL - v101 - i9-10 - Jan 1 2005 - p769(1) [51-500]
BW - v34 - i29 - July 18 2004 - p12(1) [501+]
CC - v122 - i2 - Jan 25 2005 - p39(2) [501+]
Globe & Mail - Sept 4 2004 - pD5 [501+]
NYTBR - July 4 2004 - p15 [501+]
NYTBR - July 11 2004 - p22 [501+]
NYTBR - July 18 2004 - p18 [501+]
People - v62 - i3 - July 19 2004 - p45 [51-500]
VQR - v80 - i3 - Summer 2004 - p272(1) [1-50]

Eren, Halit - *Electronic Portable Instruments: Design and Applications*
SciTech - v28 - i1 - March 2004 - p164(1) [51-500]

Erian, Alicia - *Towelhead*
KR - v73 - i2 - Jan 15 2005 - p69(1) [501+]
LJ - v129 - i20 - Dec 1 2004 - p86(1) [51-500]
LJ - v130 - i3 - Feb 15 2005 - p114(1) [51-500]
PW - v252 - i9 - Feb 28 2005 - p41(1) [51-500]

Eslick, Tom - *Mountain Peril: A White Mountains Mystery*
KR - v73 - i4 - Feb 15 2005 - p200(1) [51-500]
LJ - v130 - i4 - March 1 2005 - p71(1) [51-500]
PW - v252 - i10 - March 7 2005 - p53(2) [51-500]

Esolen, Anthony - *Paradise*
LJ - v129 - i20 - Dec 1 2004 - p116(1) [51-500]

Espelage, Dorothy L. - *Bullying in American Schools: A Social-Ecological Perspective on Prevention and Intervention*
Choice - v42 - i1 - Sept 2004 - p157(1) [501+]

Espey, David - *Writing the Journey: Essays, Stories, and Poems on Travel*
R&R Bk N - v19 - i4 - Nov 2004 - p229(1) [501+]

Espinet, Ramabai - *Swinging Bridge*
CBRA - Annual 2003 - p163(1) [51-500]

Espinosa, Felipe Arturo Avila - *Los Origenes del Zapatismo*
HAHR - v84 - i3 - August 2004 - p548(2R) [501+]

Espinosa, Rod - *Neotopia, Vol. 1*
y   BL - v101 - i7 - Dec 1 2004 - p646(2) [51-500]
Neotopia, Vol. 2
LJ - v129 - i18 - Nov 1 2004 - p66(1) [501+]
Neotopia, Vols. 1-2
PW - v251 - i40 - Oct 4 2004 - p72(1) [51-500]

Espiritu, Precy - *Intermediate Ilokano: An Integrated Language and Culture Reading Text*
R&R Bk N - v19 - i4 - Nov 2004 - p220(1) [501+]

Espiritu, Yen Le - *Home Bound: Filipino American Lives Across Cultures, Communities, and Countries*
WHQ - v35 - i2 - Summer 2004 - p232-233 [501+]

Esposito, Dino - *Introducing ASP.NET 2.0*
SciTech - v28 - i4 - Dec 2004 - p152(1) [51-500]
Programming Microsoft ASP.NET
SciTech - v28 - i1 - March 2004 - p158(1) [51-500]

Esposito, John L. - *The Islamic World: Past and Present*
BL - v101 - i6 - Nov 15 2004 - p610(1) [1-50]
Choice - v42 - i3 - Nov 2004 - p466(1) [51-500]
LJ - v129 - i17 - Oct 15 2004 - p86(2) [51-500]
R&USQ - v44 - i2 - Winter 2004 - p174(1) [501+]
y   SLJ - v50 - i10 - Oct 2004 - p92(1) [51-500]
BL - v101 - i6 - Nov 15 2004 - p614(1) [501+]

Esposito, Phil - *Thunder and Lightning: A No-B.S. Hockey Memoir*
CBRA - Annual 2003 - p44(2) [501+]

Espy, Willard R. - *The Game of Words: The Remarkable Exuberance of the English Language*
South CR - v36 - i2 - Spring 2004 - p173-174 [501+]

Esquer, Raul Figueroa - *Espana frente al Mexico amenazado, 1845-1848*
HAHR - v84 - i4 - Nov 2004 - p770(2) [501+]

Esquith, Rafe - *There Are No Shortcuts*
Kliatt - v38 - i6 - Nov 2004 - p32(1) [51-500]
NYRB - v51 - i19 - Dec 2 2004 - p29(4) [501+]

Ess, Charles M. - *Critical Thinking and the Bible in the Age of New Media*
R&R Bk N - v20 - i1 - Feb 2005 - p10(1) [51-500]

Esselborn, Hans - *Utopie, Antiutopie und Science Fiction im Deutschsprachigen Roman des 20*
GSR - v27 - i1 - Feb 2004 - p223-224 [501+]

Esselman, Mary D. - *You Drive Me Crazy: Love Poems for Real Life*
BL - v101 - i9-10 - Jan 1 2005 - p804(1) [51-500]
People - v63 - i6 - Feb 14 2005 - p62 [1-50]

Essentials of Music
SLJ - v50 - i12 - Dec 2004 - p63(1) [501+]

Essex, Christopher - *Taken by Storm: The Troubled Science, Policy and Politics of Global Warming*
CBRA - Annual 2003 - p409(1) [51-500]

Essex, Nathan L. - *School Law and the Public Schools: A Practical Guide for Educational Leaders, 3rd Ed.*
R&R Bk N - v19 - i3 - August 2004 - p201(1) [1-50]

Essien, Effiong - *Sausage Manufacture: Principles and Practice*
E-Streams - Sept 2004 - pNA [501+]

Essig, Mark - *Edison and the Electric Chair: A Story of Light and Death*
Choice - v41 - i7 - March 2004 - p1317(1) [501+]

Essinger, James - *Jacquard's Web: How a Hand-Loom Led to the Birth of the Information Age*
BL - v101 - i4 - Oct 15 2004 - p371(1) [51-500]
Ent W - i795 - Dec 3 2004 - p94 [51-500]
KR - v72 - i17 - Sept 1 2004 - p847(1) [501+]
New Sci - v184 - i2470 - Oct 23 2004 - p54(2) [501+]
TimHES - v0 - i1677 - Feb 4 2005 - p33(1) [501+]

Essington, Michael E. - *Soil and Water Chemistry: An Integrative Approach*
SciTech - v28 - i1 - March 2004 - p128(1) [51-500]

Esteller, Manel - *DNA Methylation: Approaches, Methods, and Applications*
SciTech - v28 - i4 - Dec 2004 - p73(1) [51-500]

Esten, John - *Hamptons Gardens: A 350-Year Legacy*
Choice - v42 - i5 - Jan 2005 - p840(2) [1-50]

Estenne, Robert - *Traicte de Grammaire Francoise*
SLJ - v51 - i3 - July 2004 - p402-402 [51-500]

Estep, Donald - *Accuracy and Stability of Numerical Algorithms*
SIAM Rev - v46 - i1 - March 2004 - p163-166 [501+]

Estep, Maggie - *Gargantuan: A Ruby Murphy Mystery*
LJ - v129 - i12 - July 2004 - p64(1) [51-500]
NYTBR - August 8 2004 - p15 [501+]

Esterhazy, Peter - *Celestial Harmonies*
Globe & Mail - Nov 27 2004 - pD3 [51-500]
RCF - v24 - i3 - Fall 2004 - p132(2) [501+]

Estermann, Monika - *Verzeichnis der gedruckten Briefe deutscher Autoren des 17.Jahrhunderts*
Six Ct J - v34 - i4 - Winter 2003 - p1194-1195 [501+]

Esterson, Samuel H. - *Starting and Managing Your Own Physical Therapy Practice: A Practical Guide for the Rookie Entrepreneur*
SciTech - v28 - i4 - Dec 2004 - p118(1) [1-50]

Estes, Linda S. - *Essentials of Child Care and Early Education*
R&R Bk N - v19 - i1 - Feb 2004 - p130(1) [51-500]

Esteves, Maria Lufsa Oliveira - *Portugaliae Monumenta Africana, Vol. V*
IJAHS - v37 - i1 - Wntr 2004 - p161-162 [501+]

Estey Centre for Law and Economics in International Trade - *Estey Centre Journal of International Law and Trade Policy*
JEL - v41 - i4 - Dec 2003 - p1446(1) [501+]

Estigarribia, Diana - *Cheetahs*
c   SLJ - v51 - i2 - Feb 2005 - p118(1) [51-500]

Estleman, Loren D. - *Little Black Dress*
KR - v73 - i5 - March 1 2005 - p261(1) [51-500]
Retro (Read by Foster, Mel). Audiobook Review
BL - v101 - i1 - Sept 1 2004 - p144(1) [1-50]
LJ - v130 - i4 - Feb 15 2005 - p168(1) [51-500]

Estrada, C. Zesati - *Demostenes: Sobre la corona. Introduction, traduccion y notas*
Class R - v54 - i1 - May 2004 - p242(1) [501+]

Estrin, Marc - *The Education of Arnold Hitler*
KR - v73 - i3 - Feb 1 2005 - p135(2) [501+]
LJ - v130 - i2 - Feb 1 2005 - p67(2) [501+]

Estrin, Mark W. - *Orson Welles*
FQ - v57 - i4 - Summer 2004 - p65(2) [501+]

Esty, Jed - *A Shrinking Island: Modernism and National Culture in England*
ELT - v47 - i3 - Summer 2004 - p367(1) [51-500]

Etcheson, Nicole - *Bleeding Kansas: Contested Liberty in the Civil War Era*
Choice - v42 - i1 - Sept 2004 - p173(1) [501+]
HNet - Oct 2004 - pNA [501+]

Etemad, Hamid - *Globalization and Entrepreneurship: Policy and Strategy Perspectives*
JEL - v41 - i4 - Dec 2003 - p1356(2) [501+]

Ethier, Stephen J. - *AutoCAD in 3 Dimensions Using AutoCAD 2004*
SciTech - v28 - i3 - Sept 2004 - p136(1) [51-500]

Ethridge, Don E. - *Research Methodology in Applied Economics: Organizing, Planning, and Conducting Economic Research, 2nd Ed.*
R&R Bk N - v19 - i3 - August 2004 - p92(1) [51-500]

Ethridge, Robbie - *Creek Country: The Creek Indians and Their World*
RAH - v32 - i3 - Sept 2004 - p374-379 [501+]

Etkind, Aleksandr - *Tolkovanie puteshestvii: Rossiia i Amerika v travelogakh i intertehstakh*
AHR - v109 - i3 - June 2004 - p870(2) [501+]

Etlin, Richard A. - *Art, Culture, and Media under the Third Reich*
Clio - v33 - i4 - Summer 2004 - p487(7) [501+]

Etling, Kathy - *Cougar Attacks: Encounters of the Worst Kind*
Kliatt - v38 - i6 - Nov 2004 - p39(1) [51-500]

Eto, Hiroyuki - *Gadjet, Vol. 1*
PW - v252 - i2 - Jan 10 2005 - p41(1) [51-500]

Ette, Ottmar - *Literature on the Move*
R&R Bk N - v19 - i1 - Feb 2004 - p221(1) [51-500]

Etting, Vivian - *Queen Margrete I, 1353-1412, and the Founding of the Nordic Union*
Choice - v42 - i1 - Sept 2004 - p180(1) [501+]
R&R Bk N - v19 - i3 - August 2004 - p46(1) [51-500]

Ettinger, Alan B. - *Essential Patient Handbook: Getting the Health Care You Need--From Doctors Who Know*
SciTech - v28 - i4 - Dec 2004 - p77(1) [51-500]

Ettinger, Blanche - *Medical Transcription, 2nd Rev. Ed.*
SciTech - v28 - i3 - Sept 2004 - p78(1) [51-500]

Ettus, Samantha - *The Experts' Guide to 100 Things Everyone Should Know How to Do*
BL - v101 - i1 - Sept 1 2004 - p33(1) [51-500]
NW - Oct 18 2004 - p78 [51-500]

Etuk, Emma S. - *Recipe for Success: The 21 Indispensable Things That Can Help You Succeed in Life*
Black Iss - v6 - i5 - Sept-Oct 2004 - p48(1) [51-500]

Etulain, Richard W. - *The American West in 2000: Essays in Honor of Gerald D. Nash*
PHR - v73 - i3 - August 2004 - p495(496) [501+]
WHQ - v35 - i4 - Winter 2004 - p502-502 [501+]
Western Lives: A Biographical History of the American West
Roundup M - v12 - i3 - Feb 2005 - p17(1) [51-500]
Roundup M - v12 - i3 - Feb 2005 - p17(1) [51-500]

Etzel, Barbara - *Webster's New World Finance and Investment Dictionary*
R&R Bk N - v19 - i3 - August 2004 - p133(1) [51-500]

Etzioni, Amitai - *The Communitarian Reader: Beyond the Essentials*
Pers PS - v34 - i1 - Wntr 2005 - p60(1) [501+]
R&R Bk N - v19 - i4 - Nov 2004 - p122(1) [51-500]
From Empire to Community: A New Approach to International Relations
Choice - v42 - i5 - Jan 2005 - p930(1) [51-500]
For Aff - v83 - i5 - Sept-Oct 2004 - p164 [51-500]
Fut - v38 - i6 - Nov-Dec 2004 - p60(1) [51-500]
Globe & Mail - July 24 2004 - pD9 [501+]
PSQ - v119 - i3 - Fall 2004 - p539(2) [501+]
How Patriotic Is the Patriot Act? Freedom versus Security in the Age of Terrorism
y   BL - v101 - i6 - Nov 15 2004 - p536(1) [51-500]
My Brother's Keeper: A Memoir and a Message
CS - v33 - i6 - Nov 2004 - p702(2) [501+]
TLS - i5293 - Sept 10 2004 - p23(1) [501+]
The Wars Within: Peoples and States in Conflict
CS - v33 - i4 - July 2004 - p477(2) [501+]

Eu, Geoffrey - *East African Wildlife, 3rd Ed.*
SciTech - v28 - i1 - March 2004 - p68(1) [51-500]

Eubank, Damon - *The Response of Kentucky to the Mexican War, 1846-1848*
R&R Bk N - v19 - i3 - August 2004 - p67(1) [51-500]

Eubank, Mark - *The Weather Detectives*
c   SLJ - v51 - i2 - Feb 2005 - p118(1) [51-500]

Eubanks, Bob - *It's in the Book, Bob!*
PW - v251 - i29 - July 19 2004 - p152(1) [51-500]

Eudell, Dementrius L. - *The Political Languages of Emancipation in the British Caribbean and the U. S. South*
JIH - v34 - i4 - Spring 2004 - p636-638 [501+]

Eugene, Arnold L. - *Contemporary Diagnosis and Management of Attention Deficit/Hyperactivity Disorder, 3rd Ed.*
SciTech - v28 - i3 - Sept 2004 - p119(1) [51-500]

Eugenides, Jeffrey - *Middlesex*
South R - v39 - Winter 2003 - p209 [501+]

Eun-Ah, Park - *Sweet and Sensitive, Vol. 1*
y   VOYA - v27 - i4 - Oct 2004 - p295(2) [51-500]

Eurell, Jo Ann Coers - *Veterinary Histology*
SciTech - v28 - i3 - Sept 2004 - p132(1) [51-500]

Euripides - *Cretesi*
Class R - v53 - i2 - Nov 2003 - p287-288 [501+]
Euripides: Medea
Class R - v54 - i1 - May 2004 - p34(3) [501+]
Hippolytus
Class R - v53 - i2 - Nov 2003 - p285-286 [501+]

Euromicro Conference on Real-Time Systems -
Euromicro Conference on Real-Time Systems (ECRTS 2004): Proceedings
SciTech - v28 - i3 - Sept 2004 - p19(1) [501+]

Europa World Plus
LJ - v130 - i4 - March 1 2005 - p110(2) [51-500]

European Conference of Ministers of Transport -
Implementing Sustainable Urban Travel Policies: National Review
R&R Bk N - v19 - i1 - Feb 2004 - p68(1) [501+]

European Test Symposium (ETS 2004): Proceedings
SciTech - v28 - i4 - Dec 2004 - p158(1) [51-500]

European Yearbook of Minority Issues, 2002/3, Vol. 2
R&R Bk N - v19 - i4 - Nov 2004 - p174(1) [501+]

Eusepi, Giuseppe - *Changing Institutions in the European Union: A Public Choice Perspective*
   R&R Bk N - v19 - i3 - August 2004 - p134(1) [51-500]

Evanick, Marcia - *A Berry Merry Christmas*
   LJ - v129 - i19 - Nov 15 2004 - p47(1) [51-500]

Evanier, David - *Roman Candle: The Life of Bobby Darin*
   Atl - v295 - i1 - Jan-Feb 2005 - p179(4) [501+]
   Globe & Mail - Dec 11 2004 - pD3 [501+]
   PW - v251 - i42 - Oct 18 2004 - p58(1) [51-500]

Evano, Brigitte - *Cuentos y leyendas de los juegos de Olimpia/Tales and Legends from the Games at Olympia*
   c BL - v100 - i22 - August 2004 - p1950(1) [501+]

Evanovich, Janet - *Full Blast (Read by King, Lorelei). Audiobook Review*
   LJ - v130 - i2 - Feb 1 2005 - p122(1) [51-500]
Full Bloom (Read by King, Lorelei). Audiobook Review
   LJ - v130 - i1 - Jan 1 2005 - p168(1) [501+]
Full Bloom
   PW - v252 - i11 - March 14 2005 - p51(1) [51-500]
Metro Girl
   BL - v101 - i5 - Nov 1 2004 - p443(1) [51-500]
   Bwatch - Feb 2005 - pNA [51-500]
   Ent W - i791 - Nov 5 2004 - p85 [51-500]
   Globe & Mail - Nov 13 2004 - pD18 [51-500]
   LJ - v129 - i20 - Dec 1 2004 - p95(1) [51-500]
   PW - v251 - i45 - Nov 8 2004 - p36(1) [501+]
Rocky Road to Romance
   BW - v34 - i43 - Oct 24 2004 - p13(1) [501+]
Ten Big Ones (Read by Evanovich, Janet). Audiobook Review
   BL - v101 - i4 - Oct 15 2004 - p432(1) [51-500]
Ten Big Ones (Read by Critt, C.J.). Audiobook Review
   y Kliatt - v39 - i1 - Jan 2005 - p50(2) [51-500]
Ten Big Ones (Read by King, Lorelei). Audiobook Review
   LJ - v130 - i1 - Jan 1 2005 - p167(1) [51-500]
To the Nines (Read by King, Lorelei). Audiobook Review
   LJ - v129 - i16 - Oct 1 2004 - p119(1) [51-500]

Evans, A.K.B. - *The Impact of the Railway on Society in Britain: Essays in Honor of Jack Simmons*
   J Hist G - v30 - i3 - July 2004 - p584(2) [501+]

Evans, Al - *Chee Chee: A Study of Aboriginal Suicide*
   R&R Bk N - v19 - i3 - August 2004 - p62(1) [51-500]

Evans, Alfred B. - *The Politics of Local Government in Russia*
   R&R Bk N - v19 - i3 - August 2004 - p184(1) [501+]

Evans, Arthur V. - *Introduction to California Beetles*
   Choice - v42 - i4 - Dec 2004 - p690(1) [1-50]
   QRB - v79 - i4 - Dec 2004 - p434(1) [501+]

Evans, C. Wyatt - *The Legend of John Wilkes Booth: Myth, Memory, and a Mummy*
   LJ - v129 - i17 - Oct 15 2004 - p72(1) [51-500]

Evans, Charles - *Vomeronasal Chemoreception in Vertebrates: A Study of the Second Nose*
   QRB - v79 - i3 - Sept 2004 - p332(2) [501+]

Evans, Christopher H. - *The Faith of Fifty Million: Baseball, Religion and American Culture*
   TT - v61 - i1 - April 2004 - p104-108 [501+]
The Kingdom Is Always but Coming: A Life of Walter Rauschenbusch
   Choice - v42 - i5 - Jan 2005 - p870(1) [1-50]

Evans, Clayton - *Rescue at Sea: An International History of Lifesaving, Coastal Rescue Craft and Organisations*
   R&R Bk N - v19 - i4 - Nov 2004 - p253(1) [501+]

Evans, Colin - *Murder Two: The Second Casebook of Forensic Detection*
   Choice - v42 - i6 - Feb 2005 - p1041(2) [51-500]
   SB - v41 - i1 - Jan-Feb 2005 - p17(2) [51+]

Evans, Craig A. - *From Prophecy to Testament: The Function of the Old Testament in the New*
   Intpr - v59 - i1 - Jan 2005 - p110(2) [51-500]

Evans, Curtis J. - *The Conquest of Labor: Daniel Pratt and Southern Industrialization*
   T&C - v45 - i1 - Jan 2004 - p190(2) [501+]

Evans, D.E. - *Nuclear Envelope*
   SciTech - v28 - i4 - Dec 2004 - p64(1) [51-500]
Plant Cell Culture
   E-Streams - Oct 2004 - pNA [501+]

Evans, David G. - *Healed Without Scars*
   Black Iss - v7 - i2 - March-April 2005 - p61(1) [51-500]

Evans, Douglas - *Math Rashes: And Other Classroom Tales (Illus. by Di Fiori, Larry)*
   c SLJ - v50 - i7 - July 2004 - p43(1) [51-500]
MVP (Illus. by Shelley, John)
   c BL - v101 - i7 - Dec 1 2004 - p651(1) [51-500]
   c KR - v72 - i19 - Oct 1 2004 - p960(1) [51-500]
   y SLJ - v51 - i1 - Jan 2005 - p128(1) [51-500]

Evans, Eric J. - *Thatcher and Thatcherism, 2nd Ed.*
   R&R Bk N - v19 - i4 - Nov 2004 - p36(1) [51-500]

Evans, G. Edward - *Beyond the Basics: The Management Guide for Library and Information Professionals*
   ALJ - v53 - i4 - Nov 2004 - p412(1) [501+]
   R&R Bk N - v19 - i1 - Feb 2004 - p259(1) [51-500]
Introduction to Technical Services
   LRTS - v49 - i1 - Jan 2005 - p67(2) [501+]
Performance Management and Appraisal: A How-To-Do-It Manual for Librarians
   R&USQ - v44 - i2 - Winter 2004 - p178(1) [501+]

Evans, G.R. - *The First Christian Theologians: An Introduction to Theology in the Early Church*
   R&R Bk N - v19 - i3 - August 2004 - p25(1) [1-50]

Evans, Gary - *Handbook of Bioanalysis and Drug Metabolism*
   SciTech - v28 - i3 - Sept 2004 - p124(1) [51-500]

Evans, Geraldine - *Bad Blood*
   BL - v101 - i9-10 - Jan 1 2005 - p825(2) [1-50]
Dying for You
   BL - v100 - i22 - August 2004 - p1904(2) [501+]
   KR - v72 - i16 - August 15 2004 - p780(1) [51-500]

Evans, Gloria - *Implementing e-Government: An Executive Report for Civil Servants and Their Advisors*
   R&R Bk N - v19 - i1 - Feb 2004 - pNA [501+]

Evans, Gregory R.D. - *Reconstructive Surgery of the Chest, Abdomen, and Pelvis*
   E-Streams - Dec 2004 - pNA [501+]
   SciTech - v28 - i3 - Sept 2004 - p111(1) [51-500]

Evans, H.B. - *Aqueduct Hunting in the Seventeenth Century: Raffaello Fabretti's De aquis et aquaeductibus veteris Romae*
   Class R - v53 - i2 - Nov 2003 - p476-478 [501+]

Evans, Harold - *Five Thousand Days: Press Photography in a Changing World Members of The British Press Association*
   PW - v251 - i45 - Nov 8 2004 - p50(1) [501+]
They Made America: From the Steam Engine to the Search Engine: Two Centuries of Innovators
   y BL - v101 - i3 - Oct 1 2004 - p290(1) [51-500]
   LJ - v129 - i17 - Oct 15 2004 - p72(1) [51-500]
   NW - Oct 18 2004 - p69 [51-500]
   NY - v80 - i32 - Oct 25 2004 - p91(1) [51-500]
   NYTBR - Jan 23 2005 - p14 [501+]
   People - v62 - i25 - Dec 20 2004 - p60 [51-500]
   PW - v251 - i37 - Sept 13 2004 - p68(1) [51-500]
   Time - v164 - i16 - Oct 18 2004 - p88 [501+]

Evans, Helen C. - *Byzantium: Faith and Power (1261-1557).*
   Bks & Cult - v10 - i5 - Sept-Oct 2004 - p29(2) [501+]
   CC - v121 - i25 - Dec 14 2004 - p23(1) [51-500]
   Choice - v42 - i2 - Oct 2004 - p280(1) [501+]
   HRNB - v33 - i1 - Fall 2004 - p33(1) [501+]
   LJ - v129 - i16 - Oct 1 2004 - p76(1) [51-500]
Saint Catherine's Monastery, Sinai, Egypt: A Photographic Essay
   R&R Bk N - v19 - i3 - August 2004 - p27(1) [1-50]

Evans, Hilary - *Seeing Ghosts: Experiences of the Paranormal*
   Folkl - v115 - i3 - Dec 2004 - p373(2) [501+]

Evans, Isabel - *Achieving Software Quality through Teamwork*
   SciTech - v28 - i3 - Sept 2004 - p24(1) [51-500]

Evans, J.A.S. - *The Empress Theodora: Partner of Justinian*
   Class R - v54 - i1 - May 2004 - p196(3) [501+]

Evans, J. Bryant - *The Floyd Site: A Terminal Archaic Habitation in the Northern American Bottom*
   Am Ant - v70 - i1 - Jan 2005 - p196(2) [501+]
The Ringering Site and the Archaic-Woodland Transition in the American Bottom
   Am Ant - v70 - i1 - Jan 2005 - p196(2) [501+]

Evans, James R. - *The Management and Control of Quality, 6th Ed.*
   R&R Bk N - v19 - i4 - Nov 2004 - p249(1) [501+]

Evans, Jocelyn - *The French Party System*
   Choice - v41 - i7 - March 2004 - p1365(1) [501+]

Evans, Jodie - *Twilight of Empire: Responses to Occupation*
   Tikkun - v19 - i5 - Sept-Oct 2004 - p74(2) [501+]

Evans, Joel M. - *The Whole Pregnancy Handbook: An Obstetrician's Guide to Integrating Conventional and Alternative Medicine Before, During and After Pregnancy*
   PW - v252 - i11 - March 14 2005 - p62(1) [51-500]

Evans, Joyce J. - *Dreamweaver MX 2004: Complete Course*
   SciTech - v28 - i4 - Dec 2004 - p151(1) [51-500]

Evans, Lawrence Lee, Jr. - *Why the Bubble Burst: US Stock Market Performance Since 1982*
   JEH - v64 - i1 - March 2004 - p279(2) [501+]
   JEL - v41 - i4 - Dec 2003 - p1363(2) [501+]

Evans, Liz - *Sick as a Parrot*
   Globe & Mail - Oct 30 2004 - pD26 [51-500]
   KR - v72 - i16 - August 15 2004 - p780(1) [51-500]
   LJ - v129 - i16 - Oct 1 2004 - p65(1) [51-500]

Evans, Lois K. - *Academic Nursing Practice*
   SciTech - v28 - i3 - Sept 2004 - p126(1) [51-500]

Evans, Mark - *Constitution-Making and the Labour Party*
   CR - v285 - i1662 - July 2004 - p63(1) [51-500]
Ethical Theory in the Study of International Politics
   R&R Bk N - v19 - i3 - August 2004 - p11(1) [1-50]

Evans, Martha M. - *Claude Raguet Hirst: Transforming the American Still Life*
   Mag Antiq - v167 - i1 - Jan 2005 - p129(1) [51-500]
   Mag Antiq - v167 - i2 - Feb 2005 - p55(1) [51-500]
   Mag Antiq - v167 - i3 - March 2005 - p59(1) [501+]

Evans, Mary - *Real Bodies: A Sociological Introduction*
   CS - v33 - i1 - Jan 2004 - p62-63 [501+]

Evans, Michael D. - *The American Prophecies*
   BL - v100 - i21 - July 2004 - p1802(1) [51-500]

Evans, Paul - *The Global Challenge: Frameworks for International Human Resource Management*
   HR Mag - v49 - i7 - July 2004 - pS11(1) [51-500]

Evans, Polly - *It's Not about the Tapas: Around Spain on Two Wheels*
   BL - v101 - i9-10 - Jan 1 2005 - p804(1) [51-500]
   KR - v72 - i20 - Oct 15 2004 - p993(1) [51-500]
   LJ - v129 - i20 - Dec 1 2004 - p146(1) [51-500]

Evans, Poppy - *Exploring the Elements of Design*
   R&R Bk N - v19 - i1 - Feb 2004 - p205(1) [51-500]

Evans, R.J. - *Questioning Reputations: Essays on Nine Roman Republican Politicians*
   Class R - v54 - i2 - Nov 2004 - p490(2) [501+]

Evans, Richard J. - *The Coming of the Third Reich*
   Choice - v42 - i2 - Oct 2004 - p361(1) [51-500]
   For Aff - v83 - i5 - Sept-Oct 2004 - p164 [501+]

Evans, Robert - *Family Matters: How Schools Can Cope with the Crisis in Childrearing*
   Choice - v42 - i3 - Nov 2004 - p536(1) [1-50]
   R&R Bk N - v19 - i2 - May 2004 - p186(1) [51-500]

Evans, Robert G. - *The 16th Mississippi Infantry: Civil War Letters and Reminiscences*
   JSH - v70 - i3 - August 2004 - p691(3) [501+]

Evans, Roger - *The Writer in the Garden*
   TLS - i5303 - Nov 19 2004 - p20-21 [501+]

Evans, Ronald W. - *The Social Studies Wars: What Should We Teach the Children?*
   Choice - v42 - i2 - Oct 2004 - p343(1) [51-500]
   SS - v95 - i5 - Sept-Oct 2004 - p217(3) [501+]

Evans, S.M. - *The Bar U and Canadian Ranching History*
   BIC - v33 - i9 - Dec 2004 - p27(2) [501+]
   R&R Bk N - v19 - i4 - Nov 2004 - p70(1) [51-500]

Evans, Sandra - *Talking over the Years: A Handbook of Dynamic Psychotherapy with Older Adults*
   SciTech - v28 - i4 - Dec 2004 - p97(1) [51-500]

Evans, Sara M. - *Journeys That Opened Up the World: Women, Student Christian Movements, and Social Justice, 1955-1975*
   R&R Bk N - v19 - i1 - Feb 2004 - p22(1) [51-500]
   Soc Ser R - v79 - i1 - March 2005 - p208(1) [51-500]
Tidal Wave: How Women Changed America at Century's End
   JAH - v91 - i1 - June 2004 - p332-333 [501+]

Evans, Sheila - *The Widow's Husband*
   KR - v72 - i23 - Dec 1 2004 - p1104(1) [501+]
   PW - v252 - i1 - Jan 3 2005 - p36(1) [51-500]

Evans, Stewart P. - *Executioner: The Chronicles of James Berry Victorian Hangman*
   CR - v286 - i1669 - Feb 2005 - p126(1) [51-500]

Evans, Susan Toby - *Ancient Mexico and Central America: Archaeology and Culture History*
   Choice - v42 - i5 - Jan 2005 - p895(1) [1-50]
   R&R Bk N - v19 - i3 - August 2004 - p76(1) [51-500]
   TimHES - v0 - i1681 - March 4 2005 - p26(2) [501+]

Evans, Suzanne E. - *Forgotten Crimes: The Holocaust and People with Disabilities*
Bwatch - Dec 2004 - pNA [51-500]
R&R Bk N - v19 - i3 - August 2004 - p34(1) [51-500]

Evans, Walker - *Many Are Called*
LJ - v129 - i16 - Oct 1 2004 - p121(1) [51-500]
NYTBR - Oct 31 2004 - p6 [501+]
Ent W - i789 - Oct 22 2004 - p101 [51-500]

Evanson, Robert E. - *Consumer Acceptance of Genetically Modified Foods*
SciTech - v28 - i4 - Dec 2004 - p164(1) [51-500]

Evaristo, Bernadine - *The Emperor's Babe*
Callaloo - v27 - i2 - Spring 2004 - p565(569) [501+]

Evaristo, Riande - *Electrical Properties of Polymers*
SciTech - v28 - i3 - Sept 2004 - p52(1) [1-50]

Evasdottir, Erika E.S. - *Obedient Autonomy: Chinese Intellectuals and the Achievement of Orderly Life*
Choice - v42 - i3 - Nov 2004 - p527(2) [1-50]
R&R Bk N - v19 - i2 - May 2004 - p129 [51-500]

Evdokimov, Michel - *Light from the East: Icons in Liturgy and Prayer*
CC - v121 - i25 - Dec 14 2004 - p23(1) [51-500]

Evdokimova, Svetlana - *Alexander Pushkin's Little Tragedies: The Poetics of Brevity*
Choice - v42 - i2 - Oct 2004 - p299(1) [51-500]

Evelegh, Tessa - *House Beautiful Decorating School*
LJ - v130 - i1 - Jan 1 2005 - p106(1) [51-500]
House Beautiful Window Workshop
LJ - v129 - i15 - Sept 15 2004 - p56(1) [51-500]

Eveline, Joan - *Ivory Basement Leadership: Power and Invisibility in the Changing University*
R&R Bk N - v19 - i4 - Nov 2004 - p177(1) [501+]

Even Kids Get the Blues
c BL - v100 - i21 - July 2004 - p1857(1) [1-50]

Evenden, Matthew - *Fish Versus Power: An Environmental History of the Fraser River*
Choice - v42 - i6 - Feb 2005 - p1046(1) [51-500]

Evenhuis, Neal L. - *Natural History of Nihoa and Necker Islands*
SciTech - v28 - i4 - Dec 2004 - p59(1) [51-500]

Evensen, Bruce J. - *God's Man for the Gilded Age: D.L. Moody and the Rise of Modern Mass Evangelism*
AHR - v109 - i4 - Oct 2004 - p1267-1268 [501+]
JAH - v91 - i3 - Dec 2004 - p1034(2) [501+]
JR - v84 - i4 - Oct 2004 - p628(2) [501+]

Evenson, Brian - *Wavering Knife*
ABR - v26 - i1 - Nov-Dec 2004 - p23(2) [501+]

Evenson, Debra - *Law and Society in Contemporary Cuba, 2nd Ed.*
R&R Bk N - v19 - i1 - Feb 2004 - pNA [501+]

Everard, J.A. - *Jersey 1204: The Forging of an Island Community*
CR - v285 - i1666 - Nov 2004 - p315(1) [501+]

Everest, Larry - *Oil, Power and Empire: Iraq and the US Global Agenda*
MEJ - v58 - i4 - Autumn 2004 - p708(1) [501+]

Everett-Heath, Tom - *Central Asia: Aspects of Transition*
JAS - v63 - i2 - May 2004 - p504(3) [501+]

Everett, Nicholas - *Literacy in Lombard Italy, c. 568-774*
AHR - v109 - i4 - Oct 2004 - p1290-1291 [501+]

Everett, Percival L. - *American Desert*
BooChiTr - June 6 2004 - p1(2) [501+]
Damned If I Do
BL - v101 - i4 - Oct 15 2004 - p389(1) [51-500]
BW - v34 - i46 - Nov 14 2004 - p6(1) [501+]
LJ - v129 - i19 - Nov 15 2004 - p53(1) [501+]
PW - v251 - i43 - Oct 25 2004 - p27(1) [51-500]
A History of the African-American People [proposed] by Strom Thurmond: A Novel
BooChiTr - June 6 2004 - p4(1) [501+]

Everett, R.E. - *Financial and Managerial Accounting for School Administrators, Superintendents, School Business Administrators, and Principals*
R&R Bk N - v19 - i1 - Feb 2004 - p187(1) [51-500]

Everett, Walter - *The Beatles as Musicians: The Quarry Men through Rubber Soul*
PMS - v27 - i3 - Oct 2004 - p373(2) [501+]

Everett, Wendy - *Cultures of Exile: Images of Displacement*
R&R Bk N - v19 - i4 - Nov 2004 - p123(1) [51-500]
R&R Bk N - v19 - i4 - Nov 2004 - p123(1) [51-500]

Everett, Yayoi Uno - *Locating East Asia in Western Art Music*
Choice - v41 - i11-12 - July-August 2004 - p2054(1) [501+]
Notes - v61 - i2 - Dec 2004 - p454(3) [501+]

Evergates, Theodore - *Littere Baronum: The Earliest Cartulary of the Counts of Champagne*
Med R - August 2004 - pNA [501+]
R&R Bk N - v19 - i1 - Feb 2004 - p36(1) [1-50]
Specu - v79 - i4 - Oct 2004 - p1069(2) [501+]

Everhart, Nancy - *Controversial Issues in School Librarianship: Divergent Perspectives*
LibMed - v22 - i4 - Jan 2004 - p84(1) [501+]
R&R Bk N - v19 - i1 - Feb 2004 - p258(1) [51-500]

Everingham, Christine - *Social Justice and the Politics of Community*
R&R Bk N - v19 - i2 - May 2004 - p127 [51-500]

Evers, Adalbert - *The Third Sector in Europe*
R&R Bk N - v19 - i3 - August 2004 - p114(1) [51-500]

Evers, Alex S. - *Anesthetic Pharmacology: Physiologic Principles and Clinical Practice, A Companion to Miller's Anesthesia*
SciTech - v28 - i1 - March 2004 - p110(1) [51-500]

Evers, Williamson M. - *Testing Student Learning, Evaluating Teaching Effectiveness*
Choice - v42 - i5 - Jan 2005 - p906(1) [1-50]
R&R Bk N - v19 - i3 - August 2004 - p226(1) [1-50]
TCR - v107 - i2 - Feb 2005 - p247(4) [501+]

Everson, S. - *Ethics*
Class R - v54 - i2 - Nov 2004 - p430(3) [501+]

Eversz, Robert - *Digging James Dean: A Nina Zero Novel*
KR - v72 - i24 - Dec 15 2004 - p1167(1) [501+]
PW - v251 - i47 - Nov 22 2004 - p41(1) [51-500]

Everwine, Peter - *From the Meadow: Selected and New Poems*
LJ - v129 - i12 - July 2004 - p87(1) [51-500]

Every Manager's Desk Reference
HR Mag - v50 - i2 - Feb 2005 - pS2(1) [501+]

Eves, Howard W. - *Mathematical Circles Adieu and Return to Mathematical Circles*
Math T - v97 - i3 - March 2004 - p222-222 [501+]

Evetts-Secker, Josephine - *Little Red Riding Hood (Illus. by Ceccoli, Nicoletta)*
c LibMed - v23 - i1 - August-Sept 2004 - p69(1) [51-500]
c SLJ - v50 - i8 - August 2004 - p107(1) [51-500]

Evey, Stuart - *ESPN: The No-Holds-Barred Story of Power, Ego, Money, and Vision That Transformed a Culture*
BL - v101 - i1 - Sept 1 2004 - p47(1) [501+]
LJ - v129 - i15 - Sept 15 2004 - p64(1) [51-500]
PW - v251 - i34 - August 23 2004 - p49(2) [51-500]

Evjen, Bill - *ASP.net 2.0 Beta Preview*
SciTech - v28 - i3 - Sept 2004 - p155(1) [1-50]
Professional VB.NET 2003, 3rd Ed.
SciTech - v28 - i3 - Sept 2004 - p23(1) [51-500]

Evolution of CITES: A Reference to the Convention on International Trade in Endangered Species of Wild Fauna and Flora, 7th Ed.
SciTech - v28 - i3 - Sept 2004 - p10(1) [501+]

Evrigenis, Ioannis D. - *Johann Gottfried Herder: Another Philosophy of History and Selected Political Writings*
For Aff - v83 - i5 - Sept-Oct 2004 - p164 [501+]
R&R Bk N - v19 - i3 - August 2004 - p5(1) [1-50]

Ewart, Claire - *Fossil*
y LibMed - v23 - i1 - August-Sept 2004 - p79(2)

Ewazen, Eric - *Sonata for Horn and Piano*
Notes - v61 - i3 - March 2005 - p874(4) [501+]
Sonata for Trombone and Piano
Notes - v61 - i3 - March 2005 - p874(4) [501+]
Sonata for Trumpet and Piano
Notes - v61 - i3 - March 2005 - p874(4) [501+]

Ewing, E. Thomas - *The Teachers of Stalinism: Policy, Practice, and Power in Soviet Schools of the 1930s*
AHR - v109 - i3 - June 2004 - p1010(2) [501+]
Russ Rev - v63 - i3 - July 2004 - pNA [501+]
Slav R - v63 - i2 - Summer 2004 - p413(2) [501+]

Ewing, Lynne - *Barbarian*
y KR - v72 - i14 - July 15 2004 - p684(1) [51-500]
y SLJ - v50 - i10 - Oct 2004 - p163(1) [51-500]
Escape
y SLJ - v51 - i1 - Jan 2005 - p128(1) [51-500]

Ewing, William A. - *Rico Puhlmann: A Fashion Legacy: Photographs and Illustrations 1955-1996*
PetPho - v33 - i11 - March 2005 - p22(1) [501+]

Exley, Jo Ella Powell - *Frontier Blood: The Saga of the Parker Family*
Am Ind CRJ - v27 - i2 - Spring 2003 - p118-121 [501+]

Exner, Richard - *Ufer: Gedichte 1996-2003*
WLT - v78 - i3-4 - Sept-Dec 2004 - p127(1) [501+]

Explorescience.com
LibMed - v22 - i5 - Feb 2004 - p56(1) [51-500]

Exploring Ancient Civilizations
y Ref Rev - May 2004 - pNA [501+]
R&R Bk N - v19 - i1 - Feb 2004 - p26(1) [51-500]

Exploring Dinosaurs
LibMed - v23 - i3 - Nov-Dec 2004 - p62(1) [51-500]

Exploring the Ocean
LibMed - v22 - i5 - Feb 2004 - p55(1) [501+]

External Corrosion: Introduction to Chemistry and Control, 2nd Ed.
SciTech - v28 - i3 - Sept 2004 - p146(1) [51-500]

External Debt Statistics, 1998-2002, 2003 Ed.
R&R Bk N - v19 - i3 - August 2004 - p140(1) [51-500]

External Debt Statistics: Guide for Compilers and Users
JEL - v42 - i1 - March 2004 - p264(2) [501+]

Extreme Sports
LibMed - v22 - i7 - April-May 2004 - p85(1) [501+]

Exum, Andrew - *This Man's Army: A Soldier's Story from the Front Lines of the War on Terrorism*
Bus W - i3894 - August 2 2004 - p20 [501+]
Bus W - i3895 - August 9 2004 - p10 [501+]
KR - v72 - i24 - Dec 15 2004 - pS9(2) [501+]

Exum, J. Cheryl - *Reading from Right to Left: Essays on the Hebrew Bible in Honour of David J.A. Clines*
R&R Bk N - v19 - i3 - August 2004 - p23(1) [1-50]

Eyal, Gil - *The Origins of Postcommunist Elites: From Prague Spring to the Breakup of Czechoslovakia*
Slav R - v63 - i4 - Winter 2004 - p861(2) [501+]

Eyden, Ton van der - *Public Management of Society: Rediscovering French Institutional Engineering in the European Context*
R&R Bk N - v19 - i3 - August 2004 - p182(1) [501+]

Eye, Alexander von - *Analyzing Rater Agreement: Manifest Variable Methods*
SciTech - v28 - i4 - Dec 2004 - p37(1) [51-500]

Eye View
LibMed - v22 - i7 - April-May 2004 - p78(1) [501+]

Eyerdam, Pamela J. - *Using Internet Primary Sources to Teach Critical Thinking Skills in the Visual Arts*
LibMed - v22 - i4 - Jan 2004 - p84(1) [501+]

Eyewitness Buddhism
LibMed - v22 - i7 - April-May 2004 - p84(1) [501+]

Eyewitness History
LibMed - v22 - i6 - March 2004 - p79(1) [501+]

Eymann, Marcia - *What's Going On?: California and the Vietnam Era*
NYTBR - Dec 19 2004 - p10 [501+]

Eysenck, Michael W. - *Psychology: An International Perspective*
R&R Bk N - v19 - i4 - Nov 2004 - p9(1) [51-500]
TimHES - v0 - i1668 - Nov 26 2004 - pXVIII(2) [501+]

Eyzaguirre, Pablo B. - *Home Gardens and Agrobiodiversity*
SciTech - v28 - i3 - Sept 2004 - p128(1) [51-500]

Ezekiel, Judith - *Feminism in the Heartland*
HNet - Sept 2004 - pNA [501+]
Wom HR - v13 - i2 - Summer 2004 - p303-310 [501+]

Ezra, Elizabeth - *European Cinema*
Choice - v42 - i1 - Sept 2004 - p108(1) [501+]
TimHES - v0 - i1647 - July 2 2004 - p28(1) [501+]

Ezumezu, Nwokedi Francis - *Freedom as Responsibility: The Social Market Economy in the Light of Catholic Social Teaching for the Nigerian Society*
Theol St - v66 - i1 - March 2005 - p231(2) [501+]

Ezzelarab, Abdelazziz - *European Control and Egypt's Traditional Elites: A Case Study in Elite Economic Nationalism*
IJMES - v36 - i3 - August 2004 - p488-490 [501+]

Ezzy, Douglas - *Qualitative Analysis: Practice and Innovation*
CS - v33 - i1 - Jan 2004 - p123-124 [501+]

F

Farber, Paul Lawrence - *Finding Order in Nature: The Naturalist Tradition from Linnaeus to E.O. Wilson*
  Isis - v95 - i3 - Sept 2004 - p504(2) [501+]

Farber, Robert - *American Mood*
  LJ - v130 - i4 - March 1 2005 - p82(1) [51-500]

Farber, Vreneli - *The Prose of Aleksandr Vampilov*
  R&R Bk N - v19 - i1 - Feb 2004 - p218(1) [51-500]
  Slav R - v63 - i4 - Winter 2004 - p913(2) [501+]

Farbman, Suzy - *Back from Betrayal: Saving a Marriage, a Family, a Life*
  BW - v34 - i30 - July 25 2004 - p13(1) [501+]
  Bwatch - v26 - i8 - August 2004 - p5(1) [51-500]

Fardner, Robert - *Forces and Motion Science Fair Projects: Using Water Balloons, Pulleys and Other Stuff*
  y SB - v40 - i4 - July-August 2004 - p164(1) [51-500]

Fare, Rolf - *New Directions: Efficiency and Productivity*
  R&R Bk N - v19 - i1 - Feb 2004 - p90(1) [1-50]

Farhat, Hassan A. - *Digital Design and Computer Organization*
  Choice - v41 - i11-12 - July-August 2004 - p2080(1) [501+]

Fariborz, Amir H. - *High Energy Physics MRST 2003: Proceedings*
  SciTech - v28 - i1 - March 2004 - p52(1) [51-500]
  Scalar Mesons: An Interesting Puzzle for QCD: Proceedings
  SciTech - v28 - i1 - March 2004 - p52(1) [51-500]

Faricy, Katherine - *Artistic Pedal Technique: Lessons for Intermediate and Advanced Pianists*
  Am MT - v54 - i1 - August-Sept 2004 - p103(1) [501+]

Farimah, Daftary - *Radical Ethnic Movements in Contemporary Europe*
  JPR - v41 - i5 - Sept 2004 - p640-640 [501+]

Faris, James C. - *Navajo and Photography: A Critical History of the Representation of an American People*
  R&R Bk N - v19 - i1 - Feb 2004 - p53(1) [51-500]

Faris, Wendy B. - *Ordinary Enchantments: Magical Realism and the Remystification of Narrative*
  R&R Bk N - v19 - i3 - August 2004 - p257(1) [51-500]

Farjani, Nadir - *The Arab Human Development Report 2003: Building a Knowledge Society*
  JPR - v41 - i5 - Sept 2004 - p648-649 [501+]

Farjeon, Eleanor - *The Little Bookroom (Illus. by Ardizzone, Edward)*
  c Sch Lib - v52 - i4 - Winter 2004 - p201(1) [51-500]

Farkas, Cassia - *The Pattern Companion: Decorative Painting*
  LJ - v129 - i17 - Oct 15 2004 - p63(1) [51-500]

Farkas, Daniel H. - *DNA from A to Z, 3rd Ed.*
  Choice - v42 - i5 - Jan 2005 - p830(2) [1-50]
  SciTech - v28 - i4 - Dec 2004 - p73(1) [51-500]

Farkas, Jozsef - *Economic Design of Metal Structures*
  SciTech - v28 - i1 - March 2004 - p137(1) [51-500]

Farley, Marc - *Storage Networking Fundamentals: An Introduction to Storage Devices, Subsystems, Applications, Management, and File Systems*
  Bwatch - March 2005 - pNA [51-500]

Farley, Margaret A. - *Compassionate Respect: A Feminist Approach to Medical Ethics and Other Questions*
  Theol St - v65 - i3 - Sept 2004 - p683(1) [501+]

Farm Babies
  c PW - v251 - i38 - Sept 20 2004 - p64(1) [51-500]

Farmer, Brian R. - *American Domestic Policy: Substance and Process*
  Choice - v41 - i11-12 - July-August 2004 - p2125(1) [501+]

Farmer, Jacqueline - *Pumpkins (Illus. by Tildes, Phyllis Limbacher)*
  c BL - v100 - i22 - August 2004 - p1938(1) [51-500]
  c SLJ - v50 - i7 - July 2004 - p93(1) [51-500]

Farmer, Jerrilyn - *The Flaming Luau of Death: A Madeline Bean Novel*
  KR - v73 - i3 - Feb 1 2005 - p151(1) [51-500]
  LJ - v130 - i4 - March 1 2005 - p70(1) [51-500]
  PW - v252 - i4 - Feb 21 2005 - p161(1) [51-500]

Farmer, John Stephen - *The Correspondence of John Stephen Farmer and W.E. Henley on Their Slang Dictionary, 1890-1904*
  R&R Bk N - v19 - i1 - Feb 2004 - p216(1) [51-500]

Farmer, Lesley S.J. - *How to Conduct Action Research: A Guide for Library Media Specialists*
  Teach Lib - v32 - i2 - Dec 2004 - p37(1) [501+]
  Student Success and Library Media Programs: A Systems Approach to Research and Best Practice
  Kliatt - v39 - i1 - Jan 2005 - p31(2) [501+]
  LibMed - v23 - i1 - August-Sept 2004 - p84(1) [51-500]
  R&R Bk N - v19 - i1 - Feb 2004 - p259(1) [51-500]
  Teach Lib - v32 - i3 - Feb 2005 - p39(1) [51-500]

Farmer, Nancy - *The House of the Scorpion*
  y Kliatt - v38 - i4 - July 2004 - p28(1) [501+]
  y Magpies - v19 - i5 - Nov 2004 - p40(1) [501+]
  The Sea of Trolls
  y BL - v101 - i5 - Nov 1 2004 - p475(1) [51-500]
  c CCB-B - v58 - i3 - Nov 2004 - p119(1) [501+]
  c CH Bwatch - Feb 2005 - pNA [51-500]
  c HB - v80 - i6 - Nov-Dec 2004 - p706(2) [51-500]
  c HB - v81 - i1 - Jan-Feb 2005 - p15(1) [51-500]
  y JAAL - v48 - i1 - Sept 2004 - p73(1) [501+]
  y Kliatt - v38 - i5 - Sept 2004 - p8(2) [501+]
  c KR - v72 - i18 - Sept 15 2004 - p913(1) [501+]
  c PW - v251 - i29 - July 19 2004 - p162(1) [51-500]
  y Sch Lib - v52 - i4 - Winter 2004 - p215(1) [51-500]
  y SLJ - v50 - i10 - Oct 2004 - p163(1) [51-500]
  y VOYA - v27 - i4 - Oct 2004 - p313(1) [51-500]

Farmer, Paul - *Pathologies of Power: Health, Human Rights and the New War on the Poor*
  Comw - v132 - i3 - Feb 11 2005 - p28(2) [501+]
  Globe & Mail - Jan 1 2005 - pD14 [1-50]
  MAQ - v18 - i1 - March 2004 - p108(5) [501+]
  Soc Ser R - v78 - i3 - Sept 2004 - p524(2) [501+]
  The Uses of Haiti
  Comw - v132 - i3 - Feb 11 2005 - p28(2) [501+]

Farmer, Rick - *The Test of Time: Coping with Legislative Term Limits*
  Choice - v41 - i7 - March 2004 - p1373(1) [501+]

Farndon, John - *Dictionary of the Earth*
  SB - v40 - i5 - Sept-Oct 2004 - p195(1) [51-500]
  Human Body
  c SB - v40 - i4 - July-August 2004 - p148(1) [51-500]

Farnsworth, Kevin - *Corporate Power and Social Policy in a Global Economy: British Welfare Under the Influence*
  R&R Bk N - v19 - i3 - August 2004 - p86(1) [51-500]

Farnsworth, Stephen J. - *Political Support in a Frustrated America*
  Choice - v42 - i2 - Oct 2004 - p371(2) [501+]
  R&R Bk N - v19 - i1 - Feb 2004 - pNA [51-500]

Farnsworth, Ward - *Torts: Cases and Questions*
  R&R Bk N - v19 - i3 - August 2004 - p198(1) [1-50]

Faro, Sebastian - *Vaginitis: Differential Diagnosis and Management*
  SciTech - v28 - i1 - March 2004 - p115(1) [51-500]

Farquhar, Judith - *Appetites: Food and Sex in Post-Socialist China*
  MAQ - v18 - i1 - March 2004 - p112(2) [501+]

Farr, David - *John Lambert, Parliamentary Soldier and Cromwellian Major-General, 1619-1684*
  HER - v119 - i483 - Sept 2004 - p1057(1) [501+]
  HER - v119 - i483 - Sept 2004 - p1057(1) [501+]
  HNet - Sept 2004 - pNA [501+]

Farr, Judith - *The Gardens of Emily Dickinson*
  Choice - v42 - i2 - Oct 2004 - p293(1) [501+]
  G&L Rev W - v12 - i2 - March-April 2005 - p35(2) [501+]
  TimHES - v0 - i1649 - July 16 2004 - p27(1) [501+]

Farr, Ken - *The Forests of Canada*
  CG - v124 - i2 - March-April 2004 - p93(1) [501+]

Farr, Michael - *The Very Quick Job Search: Get a Better Job in Half the Time!, 3rd Ed.*
  R&R Bk N - v19 - i4 - Nov 2004 - p109(1) [51-500]

Farr, Moira - *Word Carving: The Craft of Literary Journalism*
  CBRA - Annual 2003 - p271(1) [51-500]

Farrant, Tim - *Balzac's Shorter Fictions: Genesis and Genre*
  NCFS - v32 - i3-4 - Spring-Summer 2004 - p394(3) [501+]

Farrar, Jennifer Gonnerman - *Life on the Outside: The Prison Odyssey of Elaine Bartlett*
  AM - v191 - i15 - Nov 15 2004 - p24 [501+]

Farrell-Beck, Jane - *Uplift: The Bra in America*
  JWH - v16 - i4 - Winter 2004 - p191(16) [501+]

Farrell, Brian P. - *Leadership and Responsibility in the Second World War: Essays in the Honour of Robert Vogel*
  R&R Bk N - v19 - i4 - Nov 2004 - p32(1) [51-500]

Farrell, Chris - *Deflation: What Happens When Prices Fall*
  Bwatch - v26 - i8 - August 2004 - p8(1) [51-500]

Farrell, J.G. - *The Siege of Krishnapur*
  Globe & Mail - Sept 11 2004 - pD21 [1-50]

Farrell, Joseph P. - *Reich of the Black Sun*
  c Bwatch - March 2005 - pNA [51-500]

Farrell, Mary Cronk - *Fire in the Hole!*
  c BL - v101 - i5 - Nov 1 2004 - p484(1) [51-500]
  y CCB-B - v58 - i5 - Jan 2005 - p209(1) [51-500]
  y KR - v72 - i19 - Oct 1 2004 - p960(1) [51-500]
  y SLJ - v51 - i1 - Jan 2005 - p128(1) [51-500]

Farrell, Michael - *Special Educational Needs: A Resource for Practitioners*
  R&R Bk N - v19 - i3 - August 2004 - p226(1) [1-50]

Farrell, Michael P. - *Collaborative Circles: Friendship Dynamics and Creative Work*
  SF - v83 - i1 - Sept 2004 - p433(4) [501+]

Farrell, Nicholas - *Mussolini: A New Life*
  CR - v285 - i1664 - Sept 2004 - p183(2) [501+]

Farrell, S.L. - *Heir of Stone*
  BL - v101 - i9-10 - Jan 1 2005 - p833(1) [1-50]
  PW - v251 - i51 - Dec 20 2004 - p41(1) [51-500]

Farrell, Warren - *Why Men Earn More*
  NW - March 21 2005 - p36 [501+]

Farren, Mick - *Gene Vincent*
  Bwatch - Jan 2005 - pNA [51-500]
  Kindling
  y BL - v100 - i22 - August 2004 - p1912(1) [51-500]
  ChrSFF&H - v26 - i9 - Sept 2004 - p30(1) [51-500]
  LJ - v129 - i13 - August 2004 - p73(1) [51-500]
  PW - v251 - i28 - July 12 2004 - p49(1) [501+]

Farrer, Anne - *Chinese Printmaking Today: Woodblock Printing in China 1980-2000*
  A Aff - v35 - i2 - July 2004 - p252-253 [501+]
  R&R Bk N - v19 - i4 - Nov 2004 - p208(1) [501+]

Farrier, Jasmine - *Passing the Buck: Congress, the Budget, and Deficits*
  Pers PS - v34 - i1 - Wntr 2005 - p48(2) [501+]

Farrington, Debra K. - *The Seasons of a Restless Heart: A Spiritual Companion for Living in Transition*
  PW - v252 - i7 - Feb 14 2005 - p70(2) [51-500]

Farrington, Karen - *Historical Atlas of the Holy Land*
  VOYA - v27 - i5 - Dec 2004 - p419(1) [51-500]

Farrington, Lisa E. - *Creating Their Own Image: The History of African-American Women Artists*
  Black Iss - v7 - i2 - March-April 2005 - p20(1) [501+]
  PW - v251 - i50 - Dec 13 2004 - p60(1) [51-500]
  Faith Ringgold
  Black Iss - v6 - i4 - July-August 2004 - p33(1) [51-500]
  LJ - v129 - i14 - Sept 1 2004 - p146(1) [51-500]

Farris, Catherine - *Women in the New Taiwan: Gender Roles and Gender Consciousness in a Changing Society*
  R&R Bk N - v19 - i4 - Nov 2004 - p135(1) [51-500]

Farris, Christine King - *My Brother Martin: A Sister Remembers Growing up with the Rev. Dr. Martin Luther King Jr. (Illus. by Soentpiet, Chris)*
  c RT - v58 - i3 - Nov 2004 - p287(1) [51-500]

Farris, Jacqueline W. - *Shehu Musa Yar'Adua: A Life of Service*
  R&R Bk N - v19 - i3 - August 2004 - p59(1) [51-500]

Farris, John - *Phantom Nights*
  Ent W - i808 - Feb 25 2005 - p106 [51-500]
  KR - v73 - i1 - Jan 1 2005 - p7(1) [51-500]
  PW - v252 - i2 - Jan 10 2005 - p44(1) [51-500]

Farshtey, Gregory - *The 1920s*
  y CH Bwatch - v14 - i7 - July 2004 - p5(1) [51-500]

Faryon, Cynthia - *Unsung Heroes of the Royal Canadian Air Force*
  y Res Links - v10 - i3 - Feb 2005 - p46(1) [501+]

Fasce, Ferdinando - *An American Family: The Great War and Corporate Culture in America*
  AHR - v109 - i2 - April 2004 - p546(1) [501+]

Feeney, Mark - *Nixon at the Movies: A Book about Belief*
LJ - v129 - i17 - Oct 15 2004 - p76(1) [51-500]
Lon R Bks - v27 - i4 - Feb 17 2005 - p25(2)
[501+]
NYTBR - Dec 12 2004 - p20 [501+]
Spec - v296 - i9198 - Nov 20 2004 - p52(2)
[501+]

Feeney, Michael J. - *The Bora Boys and the Last Big Door*
c CH Bwatch - v14 - i8 - August 2004 - p7(1) [51-500]

Feenie, Rob - *Lumiere Light: Recipes from the Tasting Bar*
BIC - v33 - i8 - Nov 2004 - p26(2) [501+]

Feferman, Anita Burdman - *Alfred Tarski: Life and Logic*
TimHES - v0 - i1680 - Feb 25 2005 - p26(2) [501+]

Feffer, John - *North Korea, South Korea: US Policy at a Time of Crisis*
A Aff - v35 - i2 - July 2004 - p256-257 [501+]

Fegan, Melissa - *Literature and the Irish Famine, 1845-1919*
Nine-C Lit - v59 - i2 - Sept 2004 - p267(5) [501+]

Feghelm, Dagmar - *I, Goya*
LJ - v130 - i4 - March 1 2005 - p82(2) [51-500]

Fehr, Scott Simon - *Introduction to Group Therapy: A Practical Guide, 2nd Ed.*
E-Streams - Nov 2004 - pNA [501+]

Fehrenbach, Frank - *Leonardo da Vinci: Natur im Ubergang*
Ren Q - v57 - i3 - Fall 2004 - p991(3) [501+]

Feiertag, Joe - *Writer's Market Companion*
Bwatch - Feb 2005 - pNA [51-500]

Feig, Barry - *Low-Cost Web Site Promotion*
Bwatch - v26 - i8 - August 2004 - p8(1) [51-500]

Feigenbaum, Gail - *Jefferson's America and Napolean's France: An Exhibition for the Louisiana Purchase Bicentennial*
RAH - v32 - i2 - June 2004 - p166-10 [501+]

Feigon, Lee - *Mao: A Reinterpretation*
A Aff - v35 - i2 - July 2004 - p249-251 [501+]
SPA - v60 - i4 - July-August 2004 - p67(3) [501+]

Feil, Wolfgang - *Ultrasonic Energy for Cutting, Coagulation, and Dissecting*
SciTech - v28 - i4 - Dec 2004 - p107(1) [51-500]

Feilchenfeldt, Rahel·E. - *Paul Cassirer Verlag Berlin 1898-1933. Eine Kommentierte Bibliograhie*
GSR - v27 - i3 - Oct 2004 - p636(2) [501+]

Feiler, Bruce S. - *Walking the Bible: An Illustrated Journey for Kids through the Greatest Stories Ever Told (Illus. by Meret, Sasha)*
c BL - v101 - i3 - Oct 1 2004 - p341(1) [51-500]
c PW - v251 - i43 - Oct 25 2004 - p46(1) [501+]
y SLJ - v50 - i11 - Nov 2004 - p162(1) [51-500]

Feiler, Gil - *Economic Relations between Egypt and the Gulf Oil States, 1967-2000: Petro-Wealth and Patterns of Influence*
Choice - v42 - i1 - Sept 2004 - p153(1) [501+]

Feiler, Karin - *Sustainability Creates New Prosperity: Basis for a New World Order, New Economics, and Environmental Protection*
R&R Bk N - v19 - i4 - Nov 2004 - p88(1) [51-500]

Feinberg, Barbara - *Welcome to Lizard Motel: Children, Stories, and the Mystery of Making Things Up: A Memoir*
HB - v81 - i2 - March-April 2005 - p219(2) [51-500]
Welcome to Lizard Motel: Children, Stories and the Mystery of Making Things Up: A Memoir
People - Sept 20 2004 - p62 [51-500]
Welcome to Lizard Motel: Children, Stories, and the Mystery of Making Things Up: A Memoir
R&R Bk N - v19 - i4 - Nov 2004 - p258(1) [501+]
SLJ - v50 - i12 - Dec 2004 - p178(1) [51-500]

Feinberg, Joel - *Doing Philosophy: A Guide to the Writing of Philosophy Papers, 3rd Ed.*
R&R Bk N - v19 - i3 - August 2004 - p2(1) [1-50]

Feiner, Michael - *Feiner Points of Leadership: The Fifty Basic Laws That Will Make People Want to Perform Better for You*
HR Mag - v49 - i10 - Oct 2004 - p141(1) [501+]
HR Mag - v50 - i2 - Feb 2005 - pS2(1) [501+]

Feiner, Shmuel - *The Jewish Enlightenment*
Choice - v42 - i1 - Sept 2004 - p180(1) [501+]

Feingold, Mordechai - *Jesuit Science and the Republic of Letters*
Six Ct J - v35 - i3 - Fall 2004 - p902-903 [501+]
Theol St - v65 - i4 - Dec 2004 - p899(2) [501+]
The Newtonian Moment: Isaac Newton and the Making of Modern Culture
NYRB - v51 - i19 - Dec 2 2004 - p38(3) [501+]

Feinman, Jay M. - *Un-Making Law: The Conservative Campaign to Roll Back the Common Law*
BL - v101 - i2 - Sept 15 2004 - p182(1) [51-500]
KR - v72 - i15 - August 1 2004 - p722(2) [501+]
Law&PolBR - Oct 2004 - pNA [501+]
R&R Bk N - v19 - i4 - Nov 2004 - p166(1) [501+]

Feinstein, Adam - *Pablo Neruda: A Passion for Life*
BW - v34 - i43 - Oct 24 2004 - p5(1) [501+]
LJ - v129 - i17 - Oct 15 2004 - p63(1) [51-500]
NS - v133 - i4700 - August 9 2004 - p38(2) [501+]
NS - v133 - i4716 - Nov 29 2004 - p44(2) [51-500]
PW - v251 - i31 - August 2 2004 - p64(2) [51-500]
Spec - v295 - i9184 - August 14 2004 - p33(2) [501+]
TLS - i5301 - Nov 5 2004 - p8-9 [501+]

Feinstein, Edward - *Tough Questions Jews Ask: A Young Adult's Guide to Building a Jewish Life*
c BL - v101 - i3 - Oct 1 2004 - p345(1) [51-500]

Feinstein, John - *Last Shot: A Final Four Mystery (Read by Feinstein, John). Audiobook Review*
c PW - v252 - i11 - March 14 2005 - p26(1) [501+]
Last Shot: A Final Four Mystery
c KR - v73 - i1 - Jan 1 2005 - p51(1) [51-500]
y PW - v252 - i4 - Jan 24 2005 - p244(2) [51-500]
y SLJ - v51 - i1 - Jan 2005 - p128(2) [51-500]
Open: Inside the Ropes at Bethpage Black
Kliatt - v38 - i4 - July 2004 - p45(1) [51-500]
The Punch: One Night, Two Lives, and the Fight That Changed Basketball Forever
BL - v101 - i1 - Sept 1 2004 - p52(1) [501+]

Feinstein, Stephen - *Read about Abraham Lincoln*
c SLJ - v50 - i9 - Sept 2004 - p186(1) [51-500]
Read about Cesar Chavez
c SLJ - v50 - i9 - Sept 2004 - p186(1) [51-500]
Read about Martin Luther King
c SLJ - v50 - i9 - Sept 2004 - p186(1) [51-500]
Read about Sacagawea
c SLJ - v50 - i9 - Sept 2004 - p186(1) [51-500]

Feinstein, Wiley - *The Civilization of the Holocaust in Italy: Poets, Artists, Saints, Anti-Semites*
Choice - v41 - i11-12 - July-August 2004 - p2114(1) [501+]

Feireisl, Eduard - *Dynamics of Viscous Compressible Fluids*
SciTech - v28 - i4 - Dec 2004 - p44(1) [501+]

Feischtinger, Johannes - *Das Gewebe der Kultur. Kulturwissenschafliche Analysen zur Geschichte und Identitat Osterreichs in der Moderne*
GSR - v27 - i1 - Feb 2004 - p162-163 [501+]

Feist, Raymond E. - *Exile's Return*
BL - v101 - i7 - Dec 1 2004 - p643(1) [51-500]
KR - v73 - i3 - Feb 1 2005 - p155(1) [51-500]
LJ - v129 - i20 - Dec 1 2004 - p86(1) [1-50]
PW - v252 - i10 - March 7 2005 - p55(1) [51-500]

Feist, Richard - *Husserl and Stein*
R&R Bk N - v19 - i1 - Feb 2004 - p4(1) [51-500]

Feistauer, M. - *Mathematical and Computational Methods for Compressible Flow*
Choice - v41 - i7 - March 2004 - p1325(1) [501+]

Feitell, Merrill - *Here Beneath Low-Flying Planes*
BL - v101 - i2 - Sept 15 2004 - p207(1) [501+]
KR - v72 - i16 - August 15 2004 - p762(1) [501+]
PW - v251 - i34 - August 23 2004 - p36(1) [501+]

Fejfer, Jane - *The Rediscovery of Antiquity: The Role of the Artist*
R&R Bk N - v19 - i2 - May 2004 - p194(1) [51-500]

Fekete, David - *A Rhapsody of Love and Spirituality*
Choice - v41 - i11-12 - July-August 2004 - p2057(1) [501+]

Felber, Lynette - *Literary Liaisons: Auto/biographical Appropriations in Modernist Women's Fiction*
Biomag - v27 - i4 - Fall 2004 - p874(8) [501+]
MFSF - v50 - i3 - Fall 2004 - p786-788 [501+]

Felber, Ron - *Il Dottore: The Double Life of a Mafia Doctor*
BL - v101 - i3 - Oct 1 2004 - p286(1) [51-500]
LJ - v129 - i15 - Sept 15 2004 - p70(1) [51-500]
NYTBR - Oct 31 2004 - p20 [501+]
PW - v251 - i36 - Sept 6 2004 - p58(2) [51-500]
SciTech - v28 - i4 - Dec 2004 - p102(1) [51-500]

Felbinger, Claire L. - *Outstanding Women in Public Administration: Leaders, Mentors, and Pioneers*
R&R Bk N - v19 - i3 - August 2004 - p154(1) [501+]

Feld, Andrew - *Citizen*
Poet - v185 - i6 - March 2005 - p463(13) [501+]
Prog - v69 - i2 - Feb 2005 - p46(3) [501+]

Feldberg, Georgina - *Women, Health, and Nation: Canada and the United States Since 1945*
CBRA - Annual 2003 - p389(2) [501+]

Feldbrugge, F.J.M. - *The Law's Beginnings*
R&R Bk N - v19 - i3 - August 2004 - p189(1) [501+]

Feldbuk, Ole - *The Battle of Copenhagen: Nelson and the Danes*
R&R Bk N - v19 - i1 - Feb 2004 - p39(1) [1-50]

Felder, Deborah G. - *A Bookshelf of Our Own: Works That Changed Women's Lives*
LJ - v130 - i1 - Jan 1 2005 - p111(1) [51-500]

Feldhamer, George A. - *Wild Mammals of North America: Biology, Management, and Conservation*
SciTech - v28 - i3 - Sept 2004 - p66(1) [51-500]

Feldman, Bruce - *Cane Mutiny: How the Miami Hurricanes Overturned the Football Establishment*
PW - v251 - i33 - August 16 2004 - p56(1) [51-500]

Feldman, David - *Do Elephants Jump? (Illus. by Schwan, Kassie)*
y BL - v101 - i5 - Nov 1 2004 - p445(1) [51-500]
y NW - Dec 13 2004 - p10 [501+]
English Public Law
Law Q Rev - v121 - Jan 2005 - p171-174 [501+]

Feldman, Edward C. - *Canine and Feline Endocrinology and Reproduction, 3rd Ed.*
SciTech - v28 - i1 - March 2004 - p132(1) [51-500]

Feldman, Ellen - *The Boy Who Loved Anne Frank*
KR - v73 - i2 - Jan 15 2005 - p69(1) [501+]
LJ - v129 - i20 - Dec 1 2004 - p86(1) [1-50]
LJ - v130 - i4 - March 1 2005 - p78(1) [51-500]
PW - v252 - i10 - March 7 2005 - p51(1) [51-500]

Feldman, Eric A. - *Unfiltered: Conflicts over Tobacco Policy Health*
Choice - v42 - i7 - March 2005 - p1261(1) [51-500]

Feldman, Glenn - *The Disfranchisement Myth: Poor Whites and Suffrage Restriction in Alabama*
Choice - v42 - i5 - Jan 2005 - p934(1) [51-500]

Feldman, Heather - *Copperheads*
c SB - v40 - i6 - Nov-Dec 2004 - p270(1) [51-500]
Coral Snakes
c SB - v40 - i6 - Nov-Dec 2004 - p270(1) [51-500]
Cottonmouths
c SB - v40 - i6 - Nov-Dec 2004 - p270(1) [51-500]
c SLJ - v51 - i2 - Feb 2005 - p118(1) [501+]
Diamondbacks
c SB - v40 - i6 - Nov-Dec 2004 - p270(1) [51-500]
c SLJ - v51 - i2 - Feb 2005 - p118(1) [501+]
King Snakes
c SB - v40 - i6 - Nov-Dec 2004 - p270(1) [51-500]
Milk Snakes
c SB - v40 - i6 - Nov-Dec 2004 - p270(1) [51-500]
c SLJ - v51 - i2 - Feb 2005 - p118(1) [501+]

Feldman, Irving - *Collected Poems, 1954-2004*
BL - v101 - i4 - Oct 15 2004 - p381(1) [51-500]

Feldman, Jay - *When the Mississippi Ran Backwards: Empire, Intrigue, Murder and the New Madrid Earthquakes*
LJ - v130 - i4 - March 1 2005 - p97(2) [51-500]
PW - v252 - i5 - Jan 31 2005 - p60(1) [501+]

Feldman, Leonard C. - *Citizens Without Shelter: Homelessness, Democracy, and Political Exclusion*
Pers PS - v33 - i4 - Fall 2004 - p247(2) [501+]

Feldman, Maryann P. - *Institutions and Systems in the Geography of Innovation*
PG - v23 - i8 - Nov 2004 - p1060-1063 [501+]

Feldman, Noah - *After Jihad: America and the Struggle for Islamic Democracy*
HNet - Sept 2004 - pNA [501+]
What We Owe Iraq: War and the Ethics of Nation Building
BW - v34 - i47 - Nov 21 2004 - p3(2) [501+]
NYTBR - Nov 14 2004 - p12(L) [501+]
PW - v251 - i32 - August 9 2004 - p237(1) [51-500]

Feldman, Roberta M. - *The Dignity of Resistance: Women Residents' Activism in Chicago Public Housing*
Choice - v42 - i6 - Feb 2005 - p1104(1) [51-500]

Feldman, Ruth Tenzer - *World War I*
c SLJ - v50 - i10 - Oct 2004 - p189(1) [51-500]

Feldman, Shai - *After the War in Iraq: Defining the New Strategic Balance*
R&R Bk N - v19 - i1 - Feb 2004 - p41(1) [51-500]

Feldstein, Martin S. - *The Distributional Aspects of Social Security and Social Security Reform*
    JEL - v42 - i1 - March 2004 - p191(1) [501+]
Economic and Financial Crises in Emerging Market Economies
    JEL - v42 - i3 - Sept 2004 - p822(16) [501+]
Social Security Pension Reform in Europe
    JEL - v42 - i1 - March 2004 - p191(3) [501+]

Felfe, Jorg - *Organizational Development and Leadership*
    R&R Bk N - v19 - i1 - Feb 2004 - p91(1) [1-50]

Fell, A. London - *Origins of Legislative Sovereignty and the Legislative State, Vol. 6, Bk. 1*
    R&R Bk N - v19 - i4 - Nov 2004 - p161(1) [501+]

Fell, Derek - *Cezanne's Garden*
    y A Art - v68 - i744 - July 2004 - p74(1) [501+]
    c SLJ - v50 - i9 - Sept 2004 - p236(1) [51-500]
Van Gogh's Women: His Love Affairs and Journey into Madness
    BL - v101 - i9-10 - Jan 1 2005 - p798(1) [51-500]
    KR - v72 - i21 - Nov 1 2004 - p1036(1) [501+]
    PW - v251 - i46 - Nov 15 2004 - p49(1) [51-500]

Fellner, Fritz - *Geschichtssschreibung und nationale Identitat: Probleme und Leistungen der osterreichischen Geschichtswissenschaft*
    JMH - v77 - i1 - March 2005 - p244(3) [501+]

Fellow, Anthony R. - *American Media History*
    R&R Bk N - v19 - i4 - Nov 2004 - p212(1) [501+]

Fellowes, Julian - *Snobs*
    Spec - v296 - i9199 - Nov 27 2004 - p49(1) [501+]
    BL - v101 - i9-10 - Jan 1 2005 - p814(1) [1-50]
    Ent W - i806 - Feb 11 2005 - p66 [501+]
    KR - v72 - i24 - Dec 15 2004 - p1156(1) [501+]
    LJ - v130 - i1 - Jan 1 2005 - p95(1) [51-500]
    People - v63 - i6 - Feb 14 2005 - p59 [501+]
    PW - v252 - i3 - Jan 17 2005 - p34(2) [51-500]
    NYTBR - March 13 2005 - p8 [501+]

Fellows, Alex - *Canvas*
    y BL - v101 - i2 - Sept 15 2004 - p217(1) [51-500]

Fellows, Will - *A Passion to Preserve: Gay Men as Keepers of Culture*
    Advocate - July 6 2004 - p36(1) [501+]
    G&L Rev W - v12 - i2 - March-April 2005 - p37(2) [501+]
    Lam Bk Rpt - v13 - i1-2 - August-Sept 2004 - p17(2) [501+]
    R&R Bk N - v19 - i3 - August 2004 - p148(1) [51-500]

Fells, Robert M. - *George Arliss: The Man Who Played God*
    Choice - v42 - i7 - March 2005 - p1234(1) [51-500]

Fels, Anna - *Necessary Dreams: Ambition in Women's Changing Lives*
    BW - v34 - i30 - July 25 2004 - p5(1) [501+]
    Choice - v42 - i2 - Oct 2004 - p374(1) [51-500]

Felski, Rita - *Literature After Feminism*
    MFSF - v50 - i3 - Fall 2004 - p785-786 [501+]
    VQR - v80 - i1 - Wntr 2004 - p270-270 [501+]
    VQR - v80 - i1 - Wntr 2004 - p270-271 [501+]

Femmes, mystique et missionnaire
    Can Lit - i181 - Summer 2004 - p94-94 [501+]

Fenby, Jonathan - *Generalissimo: Chiang Kai-shek and the China He Lost*
    A Aff - v35 - i2 - July 2004 - p249-251 [501+]
    Choice - v42 - i2 - Oct 2004 - p349(1) [51-500]
    Lon R Bks - v26 - i6 - March 18 2004 - pNA [501+]
    TimHES - v0 - i1669 - Dec 3 2004 - p25(1) [501+]

Fender, J.E. - *On the Spur of Speed*
    KR - v73 - i5 - March 1 2005 - p247(1) [501+]

Feng, Jianfeng - *Computational Neuroscience: A Comprehensive Approach*
    SciTech - v28 - i1 - March 2004 - p73(1) [51-500]

Feng, Jin - *The New Woman in Early Twentieth-Century Chinese Fiction*
    R&R Bk N - v19 - i4 - Nov 2004 - p219(1) [501+]

Feng, Yi - *Democracy, Governance, and Economic Performance: Theory and Evidence*
    AJS - v110 - i3 - Nov 2004 - p805(2) [501+]
    JEL - v42 - i1 - March 2004 - p249(2) [501+]
    JEL - v42 - i4 - Dec 2004 - p1120(2) [501+]

Feng, Zhe Chuan - *Silicon Carbide: Materials, Processing, and Devices*
    E-Streams - Dec 2004 - pNA [501+]
    SciTech - v28 - i1 - March 2004 - p173(1) [51-500]

Fenimore, E.E. - *Gamma-Ray Bursts: 30 Years of Discovery: Proceedings*
    SciTech - v28 - i4 - Dec 2004 - p53(1) [501+]

Fennario, David - *Death of Rene Levesque*
    CBRA - Annual 2003 - p239(2) [501+]

Fennell, Francis L. - *Samuel Johnson's Dictionary: Selections from the 1755 Work That Defined the English Language*
    R&R Bk N - v19 - i1 - Feb 2004 - p216(1) [1-50]

Fennell, Hope-Arlene - *Role of the Principal in Canada*
    CBRA - Annual 2003 - p393(1) [51-500]

Fennell, Patricia A. - *Managing Chronic Illness Using the Four-Phase Treatment Approach: A Mental Health Professional's Guide to Helping Chronically Ill People*
    SciTech - v28 - i1 - March 2004 - p85(1) [51-500]

Fennelly, Beth Ann - *Tender Hooks: Poems*
    Ga R - v58 - i3 - Fall 2004 - p713-714 [501+]

Fenner, Audrey - *Selected Materials for Library Collections*
    R&R Bk N - v19 - i4 - Nov 2004 - p256(1) [501+]

Fenner, Carol - *Snowed in with Grandmother Silk (Illus. by Harvey, Amanda)*
    c SLJ - v50 - i10 - Oct 2004 - pS30(1) [1-50]

Fenner, David E.W. - *Introducing Aesthetics*
    R&R Bk N - v19 - i1 - Feb 2004 - p9(1) [51-500]

Fenner, Pamela J. - *Books for the Journey: A Guide to the World of Reading*
    y Kliatt - v38 - i4 - July 2004 - p35(1) [501+]
    y LibMed - v23 - i1 - August-Sept 2004 - p85(1) [51-500]
    c SLJ - v50 - i8 - August 2004 - p150(1) [501+]
    y VOYA - v27 - i3 - August 2004 - p248(1) [1-50]

Fensham, Peter J. - *Defining an Identity: The Evolution of Science Education as a Field of Research*
    SciTech - v28 - i3 - Sept 2004 - p14(1) [501+]

Fenson, Bill - *Implementing and Managing Telework: A Guide for Those Who Make It Happen*
    Per Psy - v57 - i4 - Winter 2004 - p1091(4) [501+]

Fenster, Thelma - *Fama: The Politics of Talk and Reputation in Medieval Europe*
    AHR - v109 - i3 - June 2004 - p964(1) [501+]

Fenton, Kate - *Vanity and Vexation: A Novel of Pride and Prejudice*
    BL - v100 - i21 - July 2004 - p1817(1) [51-500]
    BW - v34 - i28 - July 11 2004 - p13(1) [501+]

Fenton, Neil - *Understanding the UN Security Council: Coercion or Consent?*
    R&R Bk N - v19 - i3 - August 2004 - p188(1) [501+]

Fenton, Peter - *Eyeing the Flash: The Education of a Carnival Con Artist*
    LJ - v129 - i20 - Dec 1 2004 - p130(1) [501+]
    KR - v72 - i20 - Oct 15 2004 - p993(2) [501+]
    People - v63 - i2 - Jan 17 2005 - p57 [51-500]
    PW - v251 - i45 - Nov 8 2004 - p43(1) [501+]

Fenton, Steve - *Ethnicity*
    AJPS - v39 - i3 - Nov 2004 - p677(2) [501+]

Fenton, Tom - *Bad News: The Decline of Reporting, the Business of News, and the Danger to Us All*
    PW - v252 - i8 - Feb 21 2005 - p172(1) [51-500]

Fenwick, Tara J. - *Learning through Experience: Troubling Orthodoxies and Intersecting Questions*
    R&R Bk N - v19 - i1 - Feb 2004 - p193(1) [51-500]

Feraudi-Gruenais, Francisca - *Ubi diutius nobis habitandum est: Die Innendekoration der kaiserzeitlichen Graber Roms*
    Class R - v53 - i2 - Nov 2003 - p462-463 [501+]

Ferber, Abby L. - *Home-Grown Hate: Gender and Organized Racism*
    Wom R Bks - v22 - i3 - Dec 2004 - p6(2) [501+]

Ferber, Marianne A. - *Feminist Economics Today: Beyond Economic Man*
    Choice - v41 - i11-12 - July-August 2004 - p2091(2) [501+]

Ferdico, John N. - *Criminal Procedure for the Criminal Justice Professional, 9th ed.*
    R&R Bk N - v19 - i4 - Nov 2004 - p173(1) [501+]

Ferenczy, Ilene H. - *2003 Employee Benefits in Mergers and Acquisitions*
    R&R Bk N - v19 - i1 - Feb 2004 - pNA [51-500]

Fergus, Jim - *Wild Girl: The Notebooks of Ned Giles (Read by Baskous, Chris). Audiobook Review*
    LJ - v130 - i1 - Jan 1 2005 - p168(1) [51-500]

Ferguson, Beth - *Digestion*
    c CH Bwatch - v14 - i7 - July 2004 - p5(1) [51-500]
Ears
    c CH Bwatch - v14 - i7 - July 2004 - p5(1) [51-500]
Eyes
    c CH Bwatch - v14 - i7 - July 2004 - p5(1) [51-500]
Teeth
    c CH Bwatch - v14 - i7 - July 2004 - p5(1) [51-500]

Ferguson, Carroy U. - *Transitions in Consciousness from an African American Perspective: Original Essays in Psycho-Historical Context*
    R&R Bk N - v19 - i3 - August 2004 - p66(1) [51-500]

Ferguson, Charles D. - *The Four Faces of Nuclear Terrorism*
    BW - v34 - i38 - Sept 19 2004 - p4(1) [501+]
    SPA - v61 - i2 - March-April 2005 - p67(2) [501+]

Ferguson, Charles H. - *The Broadband Problem: Anatomy of Market Failure and a Policy Dilemma*
    R&R Bk N - v19 - i3 - August 2004 - p122(1) [51-500]

Ferguson, Gary - *Great Divide: The Rocky Mountains in the American Mind*
    R&R Bk N - v19 - i4 - Nov 2004 - p67(1) [1-50]

Ferguson, Ian - *Village of the Small Houses*
    Globe & Mail - August 28 2004 - pD13 [51-500]

Ferguson, Jo Ann - *The Perfect Bride*
    BL - v101 - i2 - Sept 15 2004 - p218(2) [51-500]

Ferguson, Kitty - *Tycho and Kepler: The Unlikely Partnership That Forever Changed Our Understanding of the Heavens*
    y Kliatt - v38 - i5 - Sept 2004 - p48(3) [501+]

Ferguson, Margaret W. - *Dido's Daughters: Literacy, Gender, and Empire in Early Modern England and France*
    Ren Q - v57 - i4 - Winter 2004 - p1457(3) [501+]

Ferguson, Michael - *The Rise of Management Consulting in Britain*
    BHR - v77 - i4 - Winter 2003 - p795(798) [501+]

Ferguson, Neil - *Grandparenting in Divorced Families*
    R&R Bk N - v19 - i3 - August 2004 - p150(1) [51-500]

Ferguson, Niall - *The Cash Nexus: Money and Power in the Modern World, 1700-2000*
    JMH - v76 - i3 - Sept 2004 - p654(3) [501+]
Colossus: The Price of America's Empire
    AM - v191 - i5 - August 30 2004 - p23 [501+]
    Bwatch - Oct 2004 - pNA [51-500]
    Choice - v42 - i3 - Nov 2004 - p560(1) [1-50]
    Globe & Mail - July 31 2004 - pD12 [1-50]
    HM - v309 - i1855 - Dec 2004 - p89(5) [501+]
    NYTBR - July 25 2004 - p11 [501+]
    Reason - v36 - i8 - Jan 2005 - p50(6) [501+]
    TLS - i5285 - July 16 2004 - p11(1) [501+]
Colossus: The Rise and Fall of the American Empire
    CR - v286 - i1668 - Jan 2005 - p47(2) [501+]
    TimHES - v0 - i1651 - July 30 2004 - p26(2) [501+]
Empire: The Rise and Demise of the British World Order and the Lessons for Global Power (Read by Barrett, Sean). Audiobook Review
    y Kliatt - v39 - i2 - March 2005 - p59(1) [501+]
Empire: The Rise and Demise of the British World Order and the Lessons for Global Power
    Dal R - v83 - i3 - Autumn 2003 - p369-390 [501+]
    HM - v309 - i1855 - Dec 2004 - p89(5) [501+]
    NS - v133 - i4702 - August 23 2004 - p39(1) [501+]

Ferguson, Priscilla Parkhurst - *Accounting for Taste: The Triumph of French Cuisine*
    Choice - v42 - i6 - Feb 2005 - p1043(1) [51-500]
    Econ - v372 - i8388 - August 14 2004 - p75US [501+]
    HT - v54 - i8 - August 2004 - p56(1) [501+]

Ferguson, Rob - *Devil and the Disappearing Sea: A True Story About the Aral Sea Catastrophe*
    CBRA - Annual 2003 - p287(1) [51-500]
The Devil and the Disappearing Sea: Or, How I Tried to Stop the World's Worst Ecological Catastrophe
    KR - v73 - i5 - March 1 2005 - p272(2) [501+]
    PW - v252 - i9 - Feb 28 2005 - p50(1) [51-500]

Ferguson, Roderick A. - *Aberrations in Black: Toward a Queer of Color Critique*
    Lam Bk Rpt - v13 - i1-2 - August-Sept 2004 - p36(2) [501+]

Ferguson, Ruby - *Lady Rose and Mrs. Memmary*
    Spec - v296 - i9198 - Nov 20 2004 - p56(1) [501+]

Ferguson, Suzanne - *Jarrell, Bishop, Lowell & Co.: Middle Generation Poets in Context*
    VQR - v80 - i1 - Wntr 2004 - p268-269 [501+]

Ferguson, Will - *Beauty Tips from Moose Jaw: Travels in Search of Canada*
    Globe & Mail - Oct 23 2004 - pD4 [501+]

Fergusson, Adam - *Scone: A Likely Tale*
    Spec - v296 - i9193 - Oct 16 2004 - p73(1) [501+]

Fergusson, James - *Kandahar Cockney: A Tale of Two Worlds*
    TLS - i5290 - August 20 2004 - p32(1) [501+]

188 • FERLATTE
Book Review Index 2005 Cumulation

Ferlatte, Diane - *Knick-Knack Paddy Whack 2: Mother Goose Still on the Loose and a Few Animal Tales Too (Read by Ferlatte, Diane). Audiobook Review*
c SLJ - v50 - i9 - Sept 2004 - p80(1) [51-500]
Ferling, John - *Adams vs. Jefferson: The Tumultuous Election of 1800*
BW - v34 - i44 - Oct 31 2004 - p3(1) [501+]
KR - v72 - i14 - July 15 2004 - p670(2) [501+]
LJ - v129 - i17 - Oct 15 2004 - p72(2) [51-500]
PW - v251 - i31 - August 2 2004 - p61(1) [501+]
A Leap in the Dark: The Struggle to Create the American Republic
AHR - v109 - i2 - April 2004 - p516(2) [501+]
JAH - v91 - i1 - June 2004 - p221-222 [501+]
JSH - v71 - i1 - Feb 2005 - p140(3) [501+]
RAH - v32 - i1 - March 2004 - p14(6) [501+]
W&M Q - v61 - i3 - July 2004 - p573-577 [501+]
Ferlinghetti, Lawrence - *Americus: Book I*
LJ - v129 - i12 - July 2004 - p87(1) [1-50]
Fermi, Enrico - *Fermi Remembered*
Choice - v42 - i6 - Feb 2005 - p1043(2) [51-500]
Fermi, Laura - *Galileo and the Scientific Revolution*
SciTech - v28 - i1 - March 2004 - p43(1) [51-500]
Fernald, Anya - *A World of Presidia*
PW - v252 - i4 - Jan 24 2005 - p229(1) [501+]
Fernald, Daniel Horace - *Spirit's Philosophical Bildung: Image and Rhetoric in Hegel's 'Phenomenology of Spirit' and 'Science of Logic'*
R&R Bk N - v20 - i1 - Feb 2005 - p4(1) [51-500]
Fernandes, Eugenie - *Busy Little Mouse (Illus. by Fernandes, Kim)*
c RT - v57 - Oct 2003 - p164 [1-50]
Fernandez-Armesto, Felipe - *Humankind: A Brief History*
Choice - v42 - i7 - March 2005 - p1267(1) [51-500]
So You Think You're Human? A Brief History of Humankind
Nature - v429 - i6987 - May 6 2004 - p17(2) [501+]
World of Myths, Vol. 2
CR - v285 - i1665 - Oct 2004 - p252(1) [501+]
Fernandez De Lizardi, Jose Joaquin - *The Mangy Parrot: The Life and Times of Periquillo Sarniento, Written by Himself for His Children*
Choice - v42 - i2 - Oct 2004 - p298(1) [501+]
Fernandez Olmos, Margarite - *Creole Religions of the Caribbean: An Introduction from Vodou and Santeria to Obeah and Espiritismo*
JR - v84 - i4 - Oct 2004 - p670(3) [501+]
Fernandez, Susan J. - *Encumbered Cuba: Capital Markets and Revolt, 1878-1895*
HAHR - v84 - i3 - August 2004 - p540(2) [501+]
Fernie, Kate - *Creating and Using Virtual Reality: A Guide for the Arts and Humanities*
R&R Bk N - v19 - i2 - May 2004 - p193(1) [51-500]
Feroci, Marco - *Third Rome Workshop on Gamma-Ray Bursts in the Afterglow Era Proceedings*
SciTech - v28 - i3 - Sept 2004 - p43(1) [1-50]
Ferragamo, Amanda - *Seven Years in Tuscany*
R&R Bk N - v19 - i3 - August 2004 - p242(1) [51-500]
Ferraiolo, James A. - *A Systematic Classification of Minerals*
RocksMiner - v79 - i6 - Nov-Dec 2004 - p423(1) [501+]
Ferrara, Alex - *Collateral Man*
LJ - v129 - i17 - Oct 15 2004 - p53(1) [51-500]
PW - v251 - i33 - August 16 2004 - p43(2) [51-500]
Ferrarese, Carlo - *Excitotoxicity in Neurological Diseases: New Therapeutic Challenge*
SciTech - v28 - i1 - March 2004 - p92(1) [51-500]
Ferrari, Armando R. - *From the Eclipse of the Body, the Dawn of Thought*
SciTech - v28 - i3 - Sept 2004 - p99(1) [51-500]
Ferrari, Gloria - *Figures of Speech: Men and Maidens in Ancient Greece*
AJP - v125 - i3 - Fall 2004 - p453-455 [501+]
Class R - v54 - i2 - Nov 2004 - p435(3) [501+]
Ferrari, Michelle - *Reporting America at War: An Oral History*
R&R Bk N - v19 - i1 - Feb 2004 - p229(1) [1-50]
Reporting America at War (Read by Driscoll, Moira). Audiobook Review
y Kliatt - v38 - i5 - Sept 2004 - p68(3) [51-500]
Ferraris, Giovanni - *Crystallography of Modular Materials*
SciTech - v28 - i3 - Sept 2004 - p54(1) [1-50]
Ferraro, Gary P. - *The Cultural Dimension of International Business*
HR Mag - v49 - i7 - July 2004 - pS10(1) [51-500]
Ferrary, Jeannette - *Out of the Kitchen: Adventures of a Food Writer*
KR - v72 - i15 - August 1 2004 - p723(1) [51-500]
LJ - v129 - i17 - Oct 15 2004 - p81(1) [51-500]
Ferrazzi, Keith - *Never Eat Alone: And Other Secrets to Success, One Relationship at a Time*
PW - v252 - i4 - Jan 24 2005 - p234(1) [501+]
Ferree, Myra Marx - *Shaping Abortion Discourse: Democracy and the Public Sphere in Germany and the United States*
AJS - v110 - i3 - Nov 2004 - p818(3) [501+]
Ferreira, Cesar - *Culture and Customs of Peru*
JRAI - v10 - i4 - Dec 2004 - p917(2) [501+]
Ferreira, J.J.P. - *E-Manufacturing: Business Paradigms and Supporting Technologies*
R&R Bk N - v19 - i1 - Feb 2004 - p103(1) [51-500]
Ferreira, Mario Jorge - *Accessibility and Quality of Health Services: Proceedings*
SciTech - v28 - i3 - Sept 2004 - p81(1) [501+]
Ferreira-Pinto, Cristina - *Gender, Discource, and Desire in Twentieth-Century Brazilian Women's Literature*
Choice - v42 - i6 - Feb 2005 - p1025(2) [51-500]
Ferrell, O.C. - *Marketing Strategy*
R&R Bk N - v19 - i3 - August 2004 - p127(1) [51-500]
Ferrell, Robert H. - *Collapse at Meuse-Argonne: The Failure of the Missouri-Kansas Division*
R&R Bk N - v19 - i4 - Nov 2004 - p31(1) [51-500]
Harry S. Truman
R&R Bk N - v19 - i1 - Feb 2004 - p61(1) [501+]
A Soldier in World War I: The Diary of Elmer W. Sherwood
HNet - Oct 2004 - pNA [501+]
Ferrer, Elizabeth - *Julie Speed: Paintings, Constructions, and Works on Paper (Illus. by Speed, Julie)*
LJ - v129 - i16 - Oct 1 2004 - p79(1) [51-500]
Ferrera, Maurizio - *Rescued by Europe?: Social and Labour Market Reforms in Italy from Maastricht to Berlusoni*
Choice - v42 - i7 - March 2005 - p1276(1) [51-500]
Ferreras, Pipin - *The Dive: A Story of Love and Obsession*
y BL - v101 - i1 - Sept 1 2004 - p47(1) [51-500]
LJ - v129 - i19 - Nov 15 2004 - p67(1) [501+]
PW - v251 - i31 - August 2 2004 - p64(1) [51-500]
Ferretti, Vittorio - *Dictionary of Electronics, Computing, Telecommunications and Media, 3rd Rev. Ed., Pt. 2*
E-Streams - Nov 2004 - pNA [501+]
Ferrey, Steven - *Environmental Law: Examples and Explanations, 3rd Ed.*
R&R Bk N - v19 - i3 - August 2004 - p200(1) [1-50]
Ferri, Fred F. - *Ferri's Best Test: A Practical Guide to Clinical Laboratory Medicine and Diagnostic Imaging*
SciTech - v28 - i4 - Dec 2004 - p87(1) [51-500]
Ferri's Clinical Advisor: Instant Diagnosis and Treatment. 2005 Ed.
SciTech - v28 - i3 - Sept 2004 - p90(1) [51-500]
Practical Guide to the Care of the Medical Patient, 6th Ed.
SciTech - v28 - i4 - Dec 2004 - p89(1) [51-500]
Ferri, Linda - *Enchantments*
KR - v72 - i23 - Dec 1 2004 - p1105(1) [501+]
PW - v252 - i2 - Jan 10 2005 - p37(1) [51-500]
Ferri, Rolando - *Octavia: A Play Attributed to Seneca*
Choice - v42 - i3 - Nov 2004 - p479(1) [1-50]
Ferrigno, Robert - *The Wake-Up*
BL - v100 - i22 - August 2004 - p1905(1) [501+]
KR - v72 - i13 - July 1 2004 - p593(1) [51-500]
LJ - v129 - i12 - July 2004 - p69(1) [51-500]
PW - v251 - i28 - July 12 2004 - p43(2) [51-500]
Ferrington, Esther - *Infinite Variety: Exploring the Folger Shakespeare Library*
Lib & Cul - v39 - i3 - Summer 2004 - p330(3) [501+]
Ferris, David S. - *The Cambridge Companion to Walter Benjamin*
Choice - v42 - i2 - Oct 2004 - p297(1) [501+]
Ferris, Jean - *Once upon a Marigold*
c Kliatt - v38 - i4 - July 2004 - p28(2) [51-500]
Ferris, Monica - *Crewel Yule*
BL - v101 - i4 - Oct 15 2004 - p393(1) [51-500]
PW - v251 - i39 - Sept 27 2004 - p41(1) [501+]
Ferriter, Diarmaid - *The Transformation of Ireland, 1900-2000*
HT - v55 - i2 - Feb 2005 - p58(2) [501+]
NS - v133 - i4717 - Dec 6 2004 - p53(2) [501+]
Spec - v296 - i9195 - Oct 30 2004 - p53(2) [501+]
Ferro, Jeffrey - *Juvenile Crime*
y VOYA - v27 - i3 - August 2004 - p246(1) [1-50]
Ferry, Georgina - *A Computer Called Leo*
New Sci - v183 - i2463 - Sept 4 2004 - p47(1) [51-500]
Fertel, Mort - *Marriage Fitness: 4 Steps to Building & Maintaining Phenomenal Love*
LJ - v129 - i15 - Sept 15 2004 - p72(1) [51-500]
Feschuk, Scott - *Searching for Michael Jackson's Nose: And Other Preoccupations of Our Celebrity-Mad Culture*
CBRA - Annual 2003 - p375(1) [51-500]
Fesmire, Julia A. - *Beth Henley: A Casebook*
Theat J - v56 - i4 - Dec 2004 - p729-730 [501+]
Fesperman, Dan - *The Warlord's Son*
Econ - v373 - i8395 - Oct 2 2004 - p84US [501+]
BL - v101 - i1 - Sept 1 2004 - p60(1) [51-500]
Ent W - i784 - Sept 17 2004 - p86 [51-500]
Globe & Mail - Jan 8 2005 - pD11 [51-500]
KR - v72 - i14 - July 15 2004 - p647(1) [51-500]
LJ - v129 - i14 - Sept 1 2004 - p139(1) [51-500]
NYTBR - Dec 19 2004 - p23 [501+]
PW - v251 - i33 - August 16 2004 - p43(1) [51-500]
Fessler, Henry E. - *Lung Volume Reduction Surgery for Emphysema*
SciTech - v28 - i1 - March 2004 - p111(1) [51-500]
Fest, Joachim - *Inside Hitler's Bunker: The Last Days of the Third Reich*
Choice - v42 - i4 - Dec 2004 - p728(1) [1-50]
CR - v285 - i1666 - Nov 2004 - p318(1) [501+]
Festa-Bianchet, Marco - *Animal Behavior and Wildlife Conservation*
SB - v40 - i3 - May-June 2004 - p117(1) [501+]
Feste, Karen A. - *Intervention: Shaping the Global Order*
R&R Bk N - v19 - i1 - Feb 2004 - p62(1) [501+]
Fetherling, George - *Gold Diggers of 1929: Canada and the Great Stock Market Crash*
Globe & Mail - Sept 11 2004 - pD21 [1-50]
Jericho
Globe & Mail - Feb 5 2005 - pD4 [501+]
Fett, Sharla M. - *Slave to the Body: Black Bodies, White No-Bodies, and the Regulative Dualism of Body-Politics in the Old South*
JAH - v91 - i1 - June 2004 - p233-234 [501+]
Working Cures: Healing, Health, and Power on Southern Slave Plantations
JAH - v91 - i1 - June 2004 - p232-233 [501+]
Fetter, Henry D. - *Taking on the Yankees: Winning and Losing in the Business of Baseball, 1903-2003*
BHR - v78 - i2 - Summer 2004 - p298(3) [501+]
R&R Bk N - v19 - i1 - Feb 2004 - p74(1) [1-50]
Feudtner, Chris - *Bittersweet: Diabetes, Insulin, and the Transformation of Illness*
JIH - v35 - i2 - Autumn 2004 - p319(2) [501+]
Feuer, Alan - *Over There: From the Bronx to Baghdad: Two Months in the Life of a Reluctant Reporter*
KR - v73 - i5 - March 1 2005 - p273(1) [501+]
Feuerhake, Herbert G. - *Basic Civil Litigation, 2nd Ed.*
R&R Bk N - v19 - i4 - Nov 2004 - p173(1) [501+]
Fevre, Ralph - *The New Sociology of Economic Behaviour*
R&R Bk N - v19 - i2 - May 2004 - p126 [51-500]
Few, Martha - *Women Who Live Evil Lives: Gender, Religion, and the Politics of Power in Colonial Guatemala*
Six Ct J - v35 - i1 - Spring 2004 - p311(2) [501+]
Fey, David L. - *Catspaw*
PW - v251 - i27 - July 5 2004 - p39(2) [501+]
Fey, Marshall - *Emigrant Shadows: A History and Guide to the California Trail*
R&R Bk N - v19 - i4 - Nov 2004 - p67(1) [51-500]
Feyder, Vera - *La belle voyageuse endormie dans la brousse*
WLT - v78 - i3-4 - Sept-Dec 2004 - p117(1) [501+]
Feynman, Michelle - *Perfectly Reasonable Deviations from the Beaten Track: The Letters of Richard P. Feynman*
KR - v73 - i4 - Feb 15 2005 - p210(1) [501+]
PW - v252 - i11 - March 14 2005 - p57(1) [51-500]
Fforde, Jasper - *Something Rotten (Read by Gray, Emily). Audiobook Review*
y Kliatt - v39 - i2 - March 2005 - p57(1) [51-500]
Something Rotten (Illus. by Roberts, Stewart)
y BL - v100 - i21 - July 2004 - p1797(1) [51-500]
y BW - v34 - i33 - August 15 2004 - p7(1) [501+]
y Ent W - i777 - August 6 2004 - p85 [51-500]
y Globe & Mail - Oct 2 2004 - pD21 [501+]
y SLJ - v50 - i11 - Nov 2004 - p176(1) [51-500]
y Time - v164 - i5 - August 2 2004 - p80 [51-500]
The Well of Lost Plots (Read by Sastre, Elizabeth). Audiobook Review
y Kliatt - v38 - i4 - July 2004 - p58(1) [51-500]
The Well of Lost Plots
BW - v34 - i12 - March 21 2004 - p15(1) [501+]
Kliatt - v38 - i6 - Nov 2004 - p22(1) [51-500]

Finckenauer, James O. - *The Prediction and Control of Organized Crime: The Experience of Post-Soviet Ukraine*
E-A St - v56 - i8 - Dec 2004 - p1258(2) [501+]

Finckenstein, Maria von - *Nuvisavik: The Place Where We Weave*
Am Ind CRJ - v27 - i2 - Spring 2003 - p136-138 [501+]
Can Hist R - v85 - i3 - Sept 2004 - p583(2) [501+]

Finder, Joseph - *Company Man (Read by Brick, Scott).*
Audiobook Review
KR - v73 - i3 - Feb 1 2005 - p136(1) [501+]
LJ - v129 - i20 - Dec 1 2004 - p86(2) [1-50]
Company Man
PW - v252 - i9 - Feb 28 2005 - p41(1) [51-500]
Paranoia (Read by Brick, Scott). Audiobook Review
y Kliatt - v38 - i5 - Sept 2004 - p63(2) [51-500]
Kliatt - v38 - i6 - Nov 2004 - p49(1) [51-500]

Findlay, Christopher - *Rural Financial Markets in China*
JEL - v41 - i4 - Dec 2003 - p1430(1) [501+]
R&R Bk N - v19 - i1 - Feb 2004 - p114(1) [51-500]

Findlay, Diane (b. 1952 -) - *Lend a Hand: Exploring Service-Learning through Children's Literature*
c LibMed - v22 - i4 - Jan 2004 - p84(1) [501+]

Findlay, Jamieson - *The Blue Roan Child*
y CCB-B - v58 - i1 - Sept 2004 - p15(1) [51-500]
c PW - v251 - i31 - August 2 2004 - p71(1) [51-500]
c Sch Lib - v52 - i4 - Winter 2004 - p201(1) [51-500]
c SLJ - v50 - i7 - July 2004 - p105(1) [51-500]
y VOYA - v27 - i4 - Oct 2004 - p313(1) [51-500]

Findlay, John M. - *Parallel Destinies: Canadian-American Relations West of the Rockies*
JAH - v91 - i1 - June 2004 - p266-267 [501+]
WHQ - v35 - i1 - Spring 2004 - p74-74 [501+]

Findlen, Paula - *Beyond Florence: The Contours of Medieval and Early Modern Italy*
Six Ct J - v35 - i3 - Fall 2004 - p927-928 [501+]

Findley, Roger W. - *Cases and Materials on Environmental Law, 6th Ed.*
R&R Bk N - v19 - i3 - August 2004 - p200(1) [1-50]

Findley, Timothy - *Journeyman: Travels of a Writer*
Globe & Mail - Nov 13 2004 - pD21 [51-500]
The Wars
Mac - v117 - i45 - Nov 8 2004 - p50(1) [1-50]

Findling, John E. - *Encyclopedia of the Modern Olympic Movement*
BL - v100 - i22 - August 2004 - p1974(1) [501+]
Choice - v42 - i2 - Oct 2004 - p262(1) [51-500]
LibMed - v23 - i3 - Nov-Dec 2004 - p89(1) [51-500]
Ref Rev - July 2004 - pNA [501+]
R&R Bk N - v19 - i3 - August 2004 - p88(1) [51-500]

Fine, Anne - *Frozen Billy (Illus. by McBain, Georgina)*
c Sch Lib - v52 - i4 - Winter 2004 - p201(1) [51-500]

Fine, Ben - *Development Policy in the Twenty-First Century: Beyond the Post-Washington Consensus*
JEL - v41 - i4 - Dec 2003 - p1408(2) [501+]

Fine-Dare, Kathleen S. - *Grave Injustice: The American Indian Repatriation Movement and NAGPRA*
Am Ind CRJ - v27 - i2 - Spring 2003 - p124-126 [501+]
WHQ - v35 - i1 - Spring 2004 - p87-88 [501+]

Fine, Doug - *Not Really an Alaskan Mountain Man*
LJ - v129 - i17 - Oct 15 2004 - p78(1) [51-500]

Fine, Edith Hope - *Cryptomania!: Teleporting into Greek and Latin with the CryptoKids (Illus. by Doner, Kim)*
c SLJ - v50 - i11 - Nov 2004 - p143(1) [51-500]

Fine, Gary Alan - *Everyday Genius: Self-Taught Art and the Culture of Authenticity*
Choice - v42 - i7 - March 2005 - p1214(1) [51-500]

Fine, Jil - *Art*
y SLJ - v51 - i1 - Jan 2005 - p139(2) [51-500]

Fine, Lawrence - *Judaism in Practice: From the Middle Ages through the Early Modern Period*
Six Ct J - v35 - i1 - Spring 2004 - p279(2) [501+]
Physician of the Soul, Healer of the Cosmos: Isaac Luria and His Kabbalistic Fellowship
AHR - v109 - i3 - June 2004 - p1014(2) [501+]

Fine, Ruth - *The Art of Romare Bearden*
A Art - v68 - i746 - Sept 2004 - p74(2) [501+]

Fine Woodworking - *Designing & Building Cabinets*
R&R Bk N - v19 - i4 - Nov 2004 - p250(1) [501+]

Fineberg, Jill - *People I Sleep With*
PW - v251 - i45 - Nov 8 2004 - p49(1) [501+]

Fineberg, Jonathan - *Christo and Jeanne-Claude: On the Way to the Gates, Central Park, New York City (Illus. by Volz, Wolfgang)*
Choice - v42 - i3 - Nov 2004 - p471(1) [1-50]
LJ - v129 - i12 - July 2004 - p78(1) [51-500]
Discovering Child Art
JAAC - v61 - Winter 2003 - p93 [501+]

Finegan, Wesley C. - *Trust Me I'm a Cancer Patient*
SciTech - v28 - i3 - Sept 2004 - p92(1) [51-500]

Finello, Dominick - *Cervantes: Essays on Social and Literary Polemics*
Hisp R - v72 - i3 - Summer 2004 - p442-446 [501+]

Fineman, Martha Albertson - *The Autonomy Myth: A Theory of Dependency*
Choice - v42 - i6 - Feb 2005 - p1104(1) [51-500]
R&R Bk N - v19 - i4 - Nov 2004 - p124(1) [51-500]

Fineman, Stephen - *Understanding Emotion at Work*
Per Psy - v57 - i3 - Autumn 2004 - p811(3) [501+]

Finer, Catherine Jones - *Social Policy Reform in China: Views from Home and Abroad*
CS - v33 - i6 - Nov 2004 - p743(1) [1-50]

Finestein, Israel - *Scenes and Personalities in Anglo-Jewry, 1800-2000*
Albion - v36 - i1 - Spring 2004 - p166(2) [501+]

Finestone, Jeanne - *A Girl's Guide to Yoga*
y BL - v101 - i9-10 - Jan 1 2005 - p840(1) [51-500]

Fingarette, Herbert - *Mapping Responsibility: Explorations in Mind, Law, Myth, and Culture*
R&R Bk N - v19 - i4 - Nov 2004 - p13(1) [501+]

Finger, Alan - *Yoga Zone Yoga for Life: An Intermediate Guide to Health, Fitness, and Relaxation*
LJ - v129 - i13 - August 2004 - p107(1) [51-500]

Fingeroth, Danny - *Superman on the Couch: What Superheroes Really Tell Us about Ourselves and Our Society*
Choice - v42 - i1 - Sept 2004 - p84(1) [501+]
y SLJ - v50 - i8 - August 2004 - p147(1) [51-500]

Fingleton, B. - *European Regional Growth*
JEL - v41 - i4 - Dec 2003 - p1437(2) [501+]
Regional Economic Growth, SMEs, and the Wider Europe
JEL - v41 - i4 - March 2004 - p340(1) [501+]

The Finis Jhung Ballet Technique
Dance - v78 - i12 - Dec 2004 - p72(2) [501+]
Dance - v78 - i12 - Dec 2004 - p72(2) [501+]

Fink, A.M. - *Weighted Inequalities of Hardy Type*
SIAM Rev - v46 - i1 - March 2004 - p166-167 [501+]

Fink, Arlene - *Evaluation Fundamentals: Insights into the Outcomes, Effectiveness, and Quality of Health Programs, 2nd Ed.*
SciTech - v28 - i3 - Sept 2004 - p81(1) [501+]

Fink, Joseph L. - *Pharmacy Law Digest, 39th Ed., 2005*
SciTech - v28 - i3 - Sept 2004 - p11(1) [501+]

Fink, L. Dee - *Creating Significant Learning Experiences: An Integrated Approach to Designing Courses*
TCR - v106 - i2 - Feb 2004 - p283-286 [501+]

Fink, Leon - *The Maya of Morganton: Work and Community in the Nuevo New South*
HAHR - v84 - i4 - Nov 2004 - p743(2) [501+]
JAH - v91 - i1 - June 2004 - p339-340 [501+]
JSH - v70 - i4 - Nov 2004 - p975(2) [501+]

Finkam, Susan - *Athletic Training in Occupational Settings*
SciTech - v28 - i3 - Sept 2004 - p109(1) [51-500]

Finkbeiner, Walter E. - *Autopsy Pathology: A Manual and Atlas*
SciTech - v28 - i1 - March 2004 - p85(1) [51-500]

Finke, James H. - *Cancer Immunotherapy at the Crossroads: How Tumors Evade Immunity and What Can Be Done*
SciTech - v28 - i1 - March 2004 - p90(1) [51-500]

Finkeinbine, Roy E. - *Sources of the African American Past: Primary Sources in American History, 2nd Ed.*
R&R Bk N - v19 - i3 - August 2004 - p66(1) [51-500]

Finkel, Michael - *True Story*
PW - v252 - i11 - March 14 2005 - p52(1) [501+]

Finkelstein, Ellen - *AutoCAD 2005 and AutoCAD LT 2005 Bible*
SciTech - v28 - i4 - Dec 2004 - p130 [51-500]

Finkelstein, Marni - *With No Direction Home: Homeless Youth On the Road and In the Streets*
R&R Bk N - v19 - i3 - August 2004 - p161(1) [1-50]

Finkenzeller, Klaus - *RFID Handbook: Fundamentals and Applications in Contactless Smart Cards and Identification, 2nd Ed.*
SciTech - v28 - i1 - March 2004 - p177(1) [51-500]

Finkie, Laurie A. - *King Arthur and the Myth of History*
Choice - v42 - i4 - Dec 2004 - p656(1) [1-50]

Finkielkraut, Alain - *In the Name of the Other: Reflections on the Coming Anti-Semitism*
Wil Q - v29 - i1 - Wntr 2005 - p96(2) [501+]

Finkler, Steven A. - *Finance and Accounting for Nonfinancial Managers, 3rd Ed.*
R&R Bk N - v19 - i1 - Feb 2004 - p112(1) [51-500]

Finlay, Hugh - *Africa on a Shoestring*
Bwatch - Feb 2005 - pNA [51-500]

Finlay, Karen A. - *The Force of Culture: Vincent Massey and Canadian Sovereignty*
Choice - v42 - i6 - Feb 2005 - p1081(1) [51-500]

Finlay, Richard - *Modern Scotland, 1914-2000*
CR - v285 - i1667 - Dec 2004 - p369(2) [501+]
TLS - i5268 - March 19 2004 - p24-24 [501+]

Finlay, Teresa - *Intravenous Therapy*
E-Streams - Oct 2004 - pNA [501+]

Finlay, Triny - *Splitting Off*
Globe & Mail - July 17 2004 - pD12 [501+]
BIC - v33 - i8 - Nov 2004 - p31(3) [501+]

Finlay, Victoria - *Colour: A Natural History of the Palette*
Globe & Mail - Oct 9 2004 - pD31 [501+]

Finlay, William - *Headhunters: Matchmaking in the Labor Market*
CS - v33 - i2 - March 2004 - p185-186 [501+]
JEL - v42 - i1 - March 2004 - p208(2) [501+]

Finlayson, Clive - *Neanderthals and Modern Humans: An Ecological and Evolutionary Perspective*
Sci - v305 - i5680 - July 2 2004 - p45(1) [501+]

Finlayson, George D. - *John J. Robinette: Peerless Mentor: An Appreciation*
CBRA - Annual 2003 - p45(1) [51-500]

Finlayson, Iain - *Browning: A Private Life*
CR - v285 - i1664 - Sept 2004 - p181(1) [501+]

Finlayson, Marcia - *Occupational Therapy Practice and Research with Persons with Multiple Sclerosis*
SciTech - v28 - i3 - Sept 2004 - p94(1) [51-500]
SciTech - v28 - i3 - Sept 2004 - p94(1) [51-500]

Finlayson, Reggie - *We Shall Overcome: The History of the American Civil Rights Movement*
SLJ - v50 - i10 - Oct 2004 - p67(1) [51-500]

Finley, James - *Christian Meditation: Experiencing the Presence of God*
LJ - v129 - i12 - July 2004 - p89(1) [51-500]

Finley, Kathleen - *The Liturgy of Motherhood: Moments of Grace*
PW - v251 - i43 - Oct 25 2004 - p44(1) [51-500]

Finmann, Victor - *Planning for Retirement Distributions: Tax, Financials, and Personal Aspects, 2004 Ed.*
R&R Bk N - v19 - i1 - Feb 2004 - p114(1) [51-500]

Finn, Christine A. - *Artifacts: An Archaeologist's Year in Silicon Valley*
Isis - v95 - i2 - June 2004 - p333(1) [501+]
J Urban H - v31 - i2 - Jan 2005 - p258-268 [501+]

Finn, Margot C. - *The Character of Credit: Personal Debt in English Culture, 1740-1914*
AHR - v109 - i4 - Oct 2004 - p1312-1312 [501+]
BHR - v78 - i2 - Summer 2004 - p338(3) [501+]
Choice - v42 - i1 - Sept 2004 - p178(1) [501+]
HER - v119 - i483 - Sept 2004 - p1000(3) [501+]
HER - v119 - i483 - Sept 2004 - p1000(1002) [501+]
HNet - Sept 2004 - pNA [501+]
VS - v46 - i4 - Summer 2004 - p676(4) [501+]

Finn, Michael R. - *Rachilde-Maurice Barres: Correspondance inedite, 1885-1914*
NCFS - v32 - i3-4 - Spring-Summer 2004 - p410(3) [501+]

Finn, Warren E. - *Handbook of Neuroprosthetic Methods*
E-Streams - June 2004 - pNA [501+]

Finnan, Joseph P. - *John Redmond and Irish Unity, 1912-1918*
R&R Bk N - v19 - i3 - August 2004 - p40(1) [51-500]

Finnegan, Cara A. - *Picturing Poverty: Print Culture and FSA Photographs*
JAH - v91 - i2 - Sept 2004 - p675(2) [501+]

Finney, Ben - *Sailing in the Wake of the Ancestors: Reviving Polynesian Voyaging*
Cont Pac - v17 - i1 - Spring 2005 - p232(4) [501+]

Finney, Kenneth C. - *3D Programming All in One*
SciTech - v28 - i4 - Dec 2004 - p23(1) [51-500]

Finney, Michael - *Michael Finney's Consumer Confidential: The Money-Saving Secrets They Don't Want You to Know*
BL - v101 - i4 - Oct 15 2004 - p385(2) [51-500]
Bwatch - March 2005 - pNA [51-500]

Fisher, Ellie Slott - *Mom, There's a Man in the Kitchen and He's Wearing Your Robe: The Single Mother's Guide to Dating and Parenting*
LJ - v130 - i2 - Feb 1 2005 - p109(2) [51-500]
PW - v251 - i51 - Dec 20 2004 - p53(2) [501+]

Fisher, Erik A. - *The Art of Managing Everyday Conflict: Understanding Emotions and Power Struggles*
Choice - v42 - i3 - Nov 2004 - p567(1) [51-500]
R&R Bk N - v19 - i3 - August 2004 - p144(1) [51-500]

Fisher, George - *Plea Bargaining's Triumph: A History of Plea Bargaining in America*
AHR - v109 - i4 - Oct 2004 - p1245(2) [501+]
JAH - v91 - i2 - Sept 2004 - p660(2) [501+]

Fisher, Helen - *Why We Love: The Nature and Chemistry of Romantic Love*
Globe & Mail - Feb 12 2005 - pD13 [1-50]

Fisher, J.D.C. - *Christian Initiation: Baptism in the Medieval West: A Study in the Disintegration of the Primitive Rite of Initiation*
Theol St - v66 - i1 - March 2005 - p238(1) [501+]

Fisher, James L. - *The Entrepreneurial College President*
R&R Bk N - v19 - i4 - Nov 2004 - p184(1) [501+]

Fisher, Jennifer - *Nutcracker Nation: How an Old World Ballet Became a Christmas Tradition in the New World*
Dance RJ - v35 - i2 - Winter 2003 - p197-200 [501+]

Fisher, John - *Bourbon Peru: 1750-1824*
AHR - v109 - i3 - June 2004 - p952(2) [501+]
R&R Bk N - v19 - i1 - Feb 2004 - p68(1) [501+]

Fisher, John C. - *Catfish, Fiddles, Mules, and More: Missouri's State Symbols*
Pub Hist - v26 - i3 - Summer 2004 - p77(78) [501+]

Fisher, Jude - *The Rose of the World: Book Three of Fool's Gold*
PW - v252 - i3 - Jan 17 2005 - p39(1) [51-500]

Fisher, Len - *How to Dunk A Doughnut*
Bwatch - Nov 2004 - pNA [51-500]
New Sci - v184 - i2469 - Oct 16 2004 - p53(1) [51-500]
Weighing the Soul: Scientific Discovery from the Brilliant to the Bizarre
KR - v72 - i18 - Sept 15 2004 - p900(1) [501+]
PW - v251 - i40 - Oct 4 2004 - p80(1) [51-500]

Fisher, Lester E. - *Dr. Fisher's Life on the Ark: Green Alligators, Bushman, and Other ""Hare-Raising"" Tales from America's Most Popular Zoo and around the World*
y BL - v101 - i1 - Sept 1 2004 - p32(1) [51-500]
Dr. Fisher's Life on the Ark: Green Alligators, Bushman, and Other "Hare-Raising" Tales from America's Most Popular Zoo and around the World
Bwatch - March 2005 - pNA [51-500]

Fisher, Louis - *Nazi Saboteurs on Trial: A Military Tribunal and American Law*
AHR - v109 - i2 - April 2004 - p555(2) [501+]
JAH - v91 - i1 - June 2004 - p295-295 [501+]
The Politics of Executive Privilege
PSQ - v119 - i4 - Winter 2004 - p687(2) [501+]
R&R Bk N - v19 - i3 - August 2004 - p178(1) [501+]
Presidential War Power, 2nd Ed.
Law&PolBR - August 2004 - p639(4) [501+]

Fisher, M.F.K. - *The Art of Eating*
LJ - v129 - i12 - July 2004 - p127(1) [1-50]

Fisher, Mark - *Britain's Best Museums and Galleries*
New Sci - v185 - i2481 - Jan 8 2005 - p51(1) [51-500]
Spec - v296 - i9201 - Dec 11 2004 - p45(1) [501+]

Fisher, Mercedes - *Designing Courses and Teaching on the Web: A "How to" Guide to Proven, Innovative Strategies*
Choice - v42 - i1 - Sept 2004 - p158(1) [501+]
R&R Bk N - v19 - i1 - Feb 2004 - p182(1) [51-500]

Fisher, Philip - *The Vehement Passions*
Ga R - v58 - i2 - Summer 2004 - p471-483 [501+]

Fisher, Rob - *Experiential Psychotherapy with Couples: A Guide for the Creative Pragmatist*
SciTech - v28 - i3 - Sept 2004 - p98(1) [1-50]

Fisher, Robert - *Teaching Thinking: Philosophical Enquiry in the Classroom, 2nd Ed.*
R&R Bk N - v19 - i1 - Feb 2004 - p184(1) [51-500]
R&R Bk N - v19 - i3 - August 2004 - p219(1) [1-50]

Fisher, Steven - *Archival Information: How to Find It, How to Use It*
Choice - v42 - i2 - Oct 2004 - p261(1) [51-500]
R&R Bk N - v19 - i3 - August 2004 - p29(1) [1-50]

Fisher, Vivian C. - *Esteban Jose Martinez: His Voyage in 1779 to Supply Alta California*
HAHR - v84 - i3 - August 2004 - p521(2) [501+]

Fisher, William F. - *Another World Is Possible: Popular Alternatives to Globalization at the World Social Forum*
JEL - v42 - i1 - March 2004 - p259(1) [501+]
PG - v23 - i5 - June 2004 - p625-636 [501+]

Fisher, William W. - *Promises to Keep: Technology, Law, and the Future of Entertainment*
Choice - v42 - i7 - March 2005 - p1276(1) [51-500]
HLR - v118 - i4 - Feb 2005 - p1395-1396 [501+]

Fishlock, Trevor - *Conquerors of Time: Exploration and Invention in the Age of Daring*
CR - v285 - i1663 - August 2004 - p125(1) [501+]
TLS - i5288 - August 6 2004 - p25(1) [501+]

Fishman, Katharine Davis - *Attitude! Eight Young Dancers Come of Age at the Ailey School*
y BL - v101 - i3 - Oct 1 2004 - p293(1) [51-500]
BL - v101 - i5 - Nov 1 2004 - p458(1) [51-500]
Dance - v78 - i12 - Dec 2004 - p72(2) [501+]
KR - v72 - i15 - August 1 2004 - p723(1) [501+]
LJ - v129 - i15 - Sept 15 2004 - p59(1) [51-500]
PW - v251 - i34 - August 23 2004 - p45(1) [51-500]

Fishman, Stephen - *The Copyright Handbook: How to Protect and Use Written Works, 7th Ed.*
R&R Bk N - v19 - i1 - Feb 2004 - pNA [51-500]
Deduct It!: Lower Your Small Business Taxes
R&R Bk N - v19 - i3 - August 2004 - p205(1) [501+]

Fishman, Sylvia Barack - *Double or Nothing?: Jewish Families and Mixed Marriage*
Choice - v42 - i3 - Nov 2004 - p572(1) [1-50]

Fishman, Ted C. - *China, Inc.: How the Rise of the Next Industrial Superpower Challenges America and the World*
KR - v72 - i24 - Dec 15 2004 - p1180(1) [501+]
PW - v252 - i3 - Jan 17 2005 - p47(1) [51-500]
Why China Will Win
Esq - v143 - i3 - March 2005 - p60(1) [1-50]

Fishwick, Duncan - *The Imperial Cult in the Latin West: Studies in the Ruler Cult of the Western Provinces of the Roman Empire, Vol. 3, Pt. 3*
R&R Bk N - v19 - i3 - August 2004 - p14(1) [1-50]

Fishwick, Marshall - *Probing Popular Culture: On and Off the Internet*
JouAmCul - v27 - i4 - Dec 2004 - p456(2) [501+]
R&R Bk N - v19 - i4 - Nov 2004 - p56(1) [51-500]

Fishwick, Sarah - *The Body in the Work of Simone de Beauvoir*
FS - v58 - i2 - April 2004 - p285(2) [501+]

Fisk, Arthur D. - *Designing for Older Adults: Principles and Creative Human Factors*
E-Streams - Dec 2004 - pNA [501+]

Fisk, Pauline - *Midnight Blue*
LibMed - v22 - i7 - April-May 2004 - p60(60) [501+]

Fiske, Edward B. - *Elusive Equity: Education Reform in Post-Apartheid South Africa*
R&R Bk N - v19 - i4 - Nov 2004 - p190(1) [501+]
Fiske Guide to Colleges, 2005
Choice - v42 - i4 - Dec 2004 - p638(1) [1-50]
R&R Bk N - v19 - i4 - Nov 2004 - p185(1) [501+]
Fiske New SAT Insider's Guide
R&R Bk N - v19 - i4 - Nov 2004 - p185(1) [501+]

Fitch, John G. - *Annaeana Tragica: Notes on the Text of Seneca's Tragedies*
R&R Bk N - v19 - i4 - Nov 2004 - p215(1) [501+]
Seneca, Vol. 1
Class R - v53 - i2 - Nov 2003 - p369-370 [501+]

Fitch, Sheree - *Pocket Rocks*
c Res Links - v10 - i1 - Oct 2004 - p4(1) [51-500]

Fitting, Peter - *Subterranean Worlds*
ChrSFF&H - v26 - i10 - Oct 2004 - p28(1) [51-500]

Fittipaldi, Lisa - *A Brush with Darkness*
S Liv - v39 - i12 - Dec 2004 - p54(1) [501+]

Fitz, Brewster E. - *Silko: Writer, Storyteller and Medicine Woman*
Choice - v42 - i2 - Oct 2004 - p293(1) [501+]

Fitz-enz, Jac - *How to Measure Human Resources Management, 3rd Ed.*
HR Mag - v49 - i7 - July 2004 - pS32(1) [501+]
HR Mag - v50 - i2 - Feb 2005 - pS14(1) [501+]

Fitz-Gibbon, Sally - *Lizzie's Storm (Illus. by Wood, Muriel)*
c BL - v101 - i1 - Sept 1 2004 - p120(1) [1-50]
c SLJ - v50 - i10 - Oct 2004 - p112(2) [51-500]
Pig in the Middle (Illus. by Wakelin, Kristi Anne)
c Res Links - v10 - i2 - Dec 2004 - p3(1) [51-500]
Two Shoes, Blue Shoes, New Shoes! (Illus. by Zaman, Farida)
c Can Lit - i182 - Autumn 2004 - p125(3) [501+]

Fitzduff, Mari - *NGO's at the Table: Strategies for Influencing Policies in Areas of Conflict*
R&R Bk N - v19 - i3 - August 2004 - p189(1) [501+]

Fitzgerald, Caroline - *Letters from the Bay of Islands: The Story of Marianne Williams*
CR - v286 - i1668 - Jan 2005 - p59(1) [51-500]

Fitzgerald, Dawn - *Getting in the Game*
y Kliatt - v39 - i2 - March 2005 - p10(1) [51-500]
c KR - v73 - i5 - March 1 2005 - p286(1) [51-500]

Fitzgerald, Deborah - *Every Farm a Factory: The Industrial Ideal in American Agriculture*
J Hist G - v30 - i1 - Jan 2004 - p207(2) [501+]
JAH - v91 - i1 - June 2004 - p284-285 [501+]

Fitzgerald, E. Keith - *Ontario People: 1796-1803*
EFHM - v58 - i2 - March-April 2004 - p88(1) [51-500]

FitzGerald, Edmund V.K. - *Global Markets and the Developing Economy*
JEL - v42 - i1 - March 2004 - pNA [501+]

FitzGerald, Garret - *Reflections on the Irish State*
ILS - v24 - i1 - Fall 2004 - p7(1) [501+]

Fitzgerald, Jack - *Day at the Races: The St. John's Regatta Story*
CBRA - Annual 2003 - p340(1) [501+]

Fitzgerald, James L. - *The Mahabharata*
Choice - v42 - i3 - Nov 2004 - p500(1) [51-500]

Fitzgerald, Joanne - *This Is Me and Where I Am (Illus. by Fitzgerald, Joanne)*
c BL - v101 - i3 - Oct 1 2004 - p334(1) [51-500]
c Globe & Mail - Sept 11 2004 - pD13 [51-500]
c PW - v251 - i50 - Dec 13 2004 - p66(1) [51-500]
c Res Links - v10 - i2 - Dec 2004 - p2(2) [51-500]
c SLJ - v50 - i11 - Nov 2004 - p103(1) [51-500]

Fitzgerald, Mary Ann - *Educational Media and Technology Yearbook 2004, Vol. 29*
R&R Bk N - v19 - i3 - August 2004 - p215(1) [1-50]

Fitzgerald, Michael - *XML Hacks*
Bwatch - Feb 2005 - pNA [501+]
SciTech - v28 - i4 - Dec 2004 - p29(1) [51-500]

Fitzgerald, Michael W. - *Urban Emancipation: Popular Politics in Reconstruction Mobile, 1860-1890*
AHR - v109 - i2 - April 2004 - p531(2) [501+]
JAH - v91 - i1 - June 2004 - p255-254 [501+]
JIH - v35 - i1 - Summer 2004 - p158-159 [501+]

Fitzgerald, Penelope - *The Afterlife: Essays and Criticism*
BIC - v33 - i9 - Dec 2004 - p17(2) [501+]
Comw - v131 - i13 - July 16 2004 - p34(2) [501+]

Fitzgerald, Robert - *The Development of Corporate Governance in Japan and Britain*
R&R Bk N - v19 - i3 - August 2004 - p113(1) [51-500]

Fitzgerald, Ross - *The Pope's Battalions: Santamaria, Catholicism and the Labor Split*
R&R Bk N - v19 - i1 - Feb 2004 - p51(1) [51-500]

FitzGerald, Thomas E. - *The Ecumenical Movement: An Introductory History*
R&R Bk N - v19 - i3 - August 2004 - p27(1) [1-50]

Fitzherbert, Claudia - *Emily Davison*
c TES - v0 - i4587 - June 11 2004 - pssss29(1) [501+]

Fitzhugh, Bill - *Highway 61 Resurfaced*
LJ - v129 - i20 - Dec 1 2004 - p96(1) [51-500]

Fitzhugh, Karla - *Body Image*
Sch Lib - v52 - i3 - Autumn 2004 - p150(1) [501+]

Fitzmaurice, Andrew - *Humanism and America: An Intellectual History of English Colonisation, 1500-1625*
HNet - Sept 2004 - pNA [501+]
JAH - v91 - i3 - Dec 2004 - p989(2) [501+]
Ren Q - v57 - i3 - Fall 2004 - p1127(2) [501+]

Fitzmaurice, Garrett M. - *Applied Longitudinal Analysis*
Choice - v42 - i4 - Dec 2004 - p697(1) [1-50]
SciTech - v28 - i3 - Sept 2004 - p81(1) [501+]

Fitzpatrick, Anne - *Amazon River*
c CH Bwatch - v14 - i11 - Nov 2004 - pNA [501+]
y SLJ - v51 - i1 - Jan 2005 - p146(1) [51-500]
Muscles
c SB - v40 - i4 - July-August 2004 - p148(2) [51-500]

Foley, Robert T. - *Alfred von Schlieffen's Military Writings*
JMH - v77 - i1 - March 2005 - p220(5) [501+]

Foley, Thomas W. - *Father Francis M. Craft: Missionary to the Sioux*
Am Ind CRJ - v27 - i2 - Spring 2003 - p114-117 [501+]

Foley, William E. - *Wilderness Journey: The Life of William Clark*
Bwatch - Oct 2004 - pNA [51-500]
Choice - v42 - i5 - Jan 2005 - p916(1) [1-50]

Folger, Tim - *Best American Science and Nature Writing 2004*
Bwatch - Nov 2004 - pNA [51-500]

Foljanty-Jost, Gesine - *Juvenile Delinquency in Japan: Reconsidering the "Crisis"*
R&R Bk N - v19 - i1 - Feb 2004 - p145(1) [51-500]

Folkart, Jessica - *Angles on Otherness in Post-Franco Spain: The Fiction of Cristina Fernandez Cubas*
Hisp R - v72 - i2 - Spring 2004 - p327-329 [501+]

Folkerts, Menso - *Essays on Early Medieval Mathematics: The Latin Tradition*
Isis - v95 - i2 - June 2004 - p344(2) [51-500]

Follesdal, Dagfinn - *Referential Opacity and Modal Logic*
R&R Bk N - v19 - i4 - Nov 2004 - p7(1) [51-500]

Follett, Ken - *Whiteout (Read by Rosenblat, Barbara). Audiobook Review*
PW - v252 - i1 - Jan 3 2005 - p22(2) [51-500]
Whiteout
BL - v101 - i5 - Nov 1 2004 - p444(1) [51-500]
Ent W - i794 - Nov 26 2004 - p128 [51-500]
Globe & Mail - Dec 18 2004 - pD23 [51-500]
KR - v72 - i19 - Oct 1 2004 - p930(1) [51-500]
LJ - v129 - i18 - Nov 1 2004 - p74(1) [51-500]
People - v62 - i25 - Dec 20 2004 - p57 [51-500]
PW - v251 - i46 - Nov 15 2004 - p42(1) [51-500]

Follett, Kenneth A., Jr. - *Neurosurgical Pain Management*
SciTech - v28 - i3 - Sept 2004 - p113(1) [51-500]

Follows, Mick - *The Ocean Carbon Cycle and Climate*
Choice - v42 - i7 - March 2005 - p1256(1) [51-500]

Folmer, Henk - *The International Yearbook of Environmental and Resource Economics 2003/2004: A Survey of Current Issues*
JEL - v41 - i4 - Dec 2003 - p1432(2) [501+]
The International Yearbook of Environmental and Resource Economics, 2004/2005: A Survey of Current Issues
R&R Bk N - v19 - i3 - August 2004 - p110(1) [51-500]

Folsach, Kjeld von - *From Handaxe to Khan: Essays Presented to Peder Mortensen on the Occasion of His 70th Birthday*
R&R Bk N - v19 - i4 - Nov 2004 - p43(1) [51-500]

Folsom, Allan - *The Exile*
BL - v100 - i22 - August 2004 - p1868(2) [51-500]
KR - v72 - i15 - August 1 2004 - p703(1) [501+]
LJ - v129 - i13 - August 2004 - p66(1) [51-500]
PW - v251 - i29 - July 19 2004 - p145(2) [51-500]

Folsom, W. Davis - *Encyclopedia of American Business*
BL - v100 - i21 - July 2004 - p1862(1) [501+]
Choice - v42 - i1 - Sept 2004 - p77(2) [501+]
y LibMed - v23 - i3 - Nov-Dec 2004 - p89(1) [51-500]
R&R Bk N - v19 - i2 - May 2004 - p110(1) [1-50]

Folson, Allan - *The Exile (Read by Singer, Erik). Audiobook Review*
y Kliatt - v39 - i1 - Jan 2005 - p42(1) [51-500]

Folz, Diane C. - *Microwave and Radio Frequency Applications: Proceedings*
SciTech - v28 - i4 - Dec 2004 - p158(1) [51-500]

Foner, Eric - *Give Me Liberty: An American History*
R&R Bk N - v19 - i4 - Nov 2004 - p57(1) [51-500]

Foner, Nancy - *Not Just Black and White: Historical and Contemporary Perspectives on Immigration, Race, and Ethnicity in the United States*
Choice - v42 - i7 - March 2005 - p1268(1) [51-500]
Fut - v39 - i1 - Jan-Feb 2005 - p49(1) [51-500]

Fong, Grace S. - *Beyond Tradition and Modernity: Gender, Genre, and Cosmopolitanism in Late Qing China*
R&R Bk N - v19 - i3 - August 2004 - p155(1) [51-500]

Fong, Mary - *Communicating Ethnic and Cultural Identity*
R&R Bk N - v19 - i2 - May 2004 - p127 [51-500]

Fong, Rowena - *Culturally Competent Practice with Immigrant and Refugee Children and Families*
R&R Bk N - v19 - i3 - August 2004 - p160(1) [51-500]

Fong, Vanessa L. - *Only Hope: Coming of Age under China's One-Child Policy*
Choice - v42 - i3 - Nov 2004 - p572(1) [1-50]
R&R Bk N - v19 - i2 - May 2004 - p135 [51-500]

Fong, Yem S. - *The Changing Landscape for Electronic Resources: Content, Access, Delivery, and Legal Issues*
R&R Bk N - v19 - i4 - Nov 2004 - p259(1) [501+]

Fonseca, Isabel - *Bury Me Standing: The Gypsies and Their Journey*
LJ - v129 - i20 - Dec 1 2004 - p186(1) [501+]

Font, Mauricio A. - *Reforming Brazil*
R&R Bk N - v19 - i3 - August 2004 - p98(1) [51-500]

Fontova, Humberto - *The Hellpig Hunt*
Bwatch - v26 - i9 - Sept 2004 - p6(1) [51-500]

Food and Nutrition
y SLJ - v50 - i8 - August 2004 - p136(1) [501+]

Foon, Dennis - *The Dirt Eaters*
y CBRA - Annual 2003 - p482(2) [501+]
y SLJ - v50 - i10 - Oct 2004 - pS53(1) [51-500]
Freewalker
Res Links - v10 - i2 - Dec 2004 - p36(1) [51-500]
Skud
y CBRA - Annual 2003 - p483(1) [51-500]

Foos, Laurie - *Before Elvis There Was Nothing*
KR - v73 - i5 - March 1 2005 - p247(1) [501+]
PW - v252 - i10 - March 7 2005 - p48(1) [51-500]

Foot, John - *Modern Italy*
R&R Bk N - v19 - i1 - Feb 2004 - p37(1) [1-50]

Foot, Mirjam M. - *The Decorated Bindings in Marsh's Library*
ILS - v24 - i1 - Fall 2004 - p19(1) [501+]
Eloquent Witnesses: Bookbindings and Their History: A Volume of Essays Dedicated to the Memory of Dr. Phiroze Randeria
R&R Bk N - v19 - i4 - Nov 2004 - p254(1) [501+]

Foot, Paul - *The Vote: How it Was Won and How it Was Undermined*
Spec - v297 - i9211 - Feb 19 2005 - p34(2) [501+]

Foot, Philippa - *Moral Dilemmas and Other Topics in Moral Philosophy*
Ethics - v115 - i1 - Oct 2004 - p142(4) [501+]

Foote, Horton - *Genesis of an American Playwright*
Choice - v42 - i4 - Dec 2004 - p659(1) [1-50]

Foote, William E. - *Evaluating Sexual Harassment: Psychological, Social, and Legal Considerations in Forensic Examinations*
Choice - v42 - i4 - Dec 2004 - p738(1) [1-50]
SciTech - v28 - i3 - Sept 2004 - p87(1) [51-500]

Fooye, Lorien - *Seeking the One Great Remedy: Francis George Shaw and Nineteenth-Century Reform*
Choice - v41 - i11-12 - July-August 2004 - p2106(1) [501+]

Fopp, Michael A. - *The Lancaster Manual: The Official Air Publication for the Lancaster Mk I and III, 1942-1945*
APJ - v18 - i3 - Fall 2004 - p125(1) [51-500]

Foran, Jill - *Caring for Your Guinea Pig*
c SLJ - v50 - i10 - Oct 2004 - p140(1) [51-500]
Caring for Your Hamster
c SLJ - v50 - i10 - Oct 2004 - p140(1) [51-500]
Caring for Your Rabbit
c SLJ - v50 - i10 - Oct 2004 - p140(1) [51-500]
Christmas
c CBRA - Annual 2003 - p549(1) [51-500]
Dinosaurs
c SB - v40 - i3 - May-June 2004 - p131(2) [51-500]
Dr. Seuss
c SLJ - v50 - i10 - Oct 2004 - p139(2) [51-500]
Easter
c CBRA - Annual 2003 - p549(1) [51-500]
Independence Day
c SLJ - v50 - i8 - August 2004 - p106(1) [51-500]
Martin Luther King Jr. Day
c SLJ - v50 - i11 - Nov 2004 - p124(1) [51-500]
Remembrance Day
c CBRA - Annual 2003 - p549(1) [51-500]
The Search for the Northwest Passage
c BL - v101 - i5 - Nov 1 2004 - p477(2) [51-500]
Thanksgiving
c CBRA - Annual 2003 - p549(1) [51-500]
Victoria Day
c CBRA - Annual 2003 - p549(1) [51-500]

Foran, John - *The Future of Revolutions: Rethinking Radical Change in the Age of Globalization*
CS - v33 - i5 - Sept 2004 - p574-576 [501+]

Foran, Max - *Trails and Trials: Markets and Land Use in Alberta Beef Cattle Industry, 1881-1948*
CBRA - Annual 2003 - p417(2) [501+]

Forbeck, Matt - *Secret of the Spiritkeeper*
c BL - v100 - i22 - August 2004 - p1933(1) [51-500]
y VOYA - v27 - i5 - Dec 2004 - p403(1) [51-500]

Forbes, Bruce David - *Rapture, Revelation, and the End Times: Exploring the Left Behind Series*
LJ - v129 - i12 - July 2004 - p88(1) [51-500]

Forbes, David - *Boyz 2 Buddhas: Counseling Urban High School Male Athletes in the Zone*
R&R Bk N - v19 - i4 - Nov 2004 - p80(1) [51-500]

Forbes, Deborah - *Sincerity's Shadow: Self-Consciousness in British Romantic and Mid-Twentieth Century American Poetry*
Choice - v42 - i2 - Oct 2004 - p293(1) [501+]

Forbes, Dennis L. - *Collecting Limited Edition Prints: Contemporary African American Printmakers*
Black Iss - v6 - i5 - Sept-Oct 2004 - p32(1) [501+]

Forbes, Nancy - *Imitation of Life: How Biology Is Inspiring Computing*
Choice - v42 - i4 - Dec 2004 - p686(1) [1-50]
Fut - v39 - i1 - Jan-Feb 2005 - p48(2) [51-500]
Nature - v431 - i7011 - Oct 21 2004 - p908(2) [501+]
SB - v40 - i6 - Nov-Dec 2004 - p252(1) [51-500]

Forbes, Peter - *All the Poems You Need to Say I Do*
Lon R Bks - v26 - i21 - Nov 4 2004 - p44(2) [501+]
We Have Come Through: 100 Poems Celebrating Courage and Overcoming Depression and Trauma
MHR - v30 - i2 - Dec 2004 - p106(2) [501+]

Ford, Aisha - *Flippin' the Script*
LJ - v129 - i14 - Sept 1 2004 - p130(1) [51-500]

Ford, Andrew Laughlin - *The Origins of Criticism: Literary Culture and Poetic Theory in Classical Greece*
CJ - v100 - i1 - Oct-Nov 2004 - p96-98 [501+]
Class R - v54 - i1 - May 2004 - p64(3) [501+]
CML - v24 - i1 - Spring 2004 - p127-131 [501+]

Ford, Bernette - *Don't Hit Me! (Illus. by Grier, Gary)*
c SLJ - v51 - i1 - Jan 2005 - p85(1) [51-500]
Hurry, Up! (Illus. by Kindert, Jennifer)
c SLJ - v51 - i1 - Jan 2005 - p85(1) [51-500]

Ford, Brent A. - *Project Earth Science: Geology*
y SB - v40 - i5 - Sept-Oct 2004 - p194(1) [51-500]

Ford, Carin T. - *African-American Soldiers in the Civil War: Fighting for Freedom*
c LibMed - v23 - i3 - Nov-Dec 2004 - p81(1) [51-500]
c SLJ - v50 - i10 - Oct 2004 - p190(1) [51-500]
The Battle of Gettysburg and Lincoln's Gettysburg Address
y SLJ - v51 - i1 - Jan 2005 - p146(2) [51-500]
Daring Women of the Civil War
c BL - v100 - i21 - July 2004 - p1839(2) [1-50]
c SLJ - v50 - i8 - August 2004 - p136(1) [51-500]
Sacagawea: Meet an American Legend
LibMed - v22 - i5 - Feb 2004 - p76(1) [501+]
Slavery and the Underground Railroad: Bound for Freedom
c BL - v100 - i21 - July 2004 - p1839(1) [1-50]
c SLJ - v50 - i8 - August 2004 - p136(1) [51-500]
Walt Disney: Meet the Cartoonist
LibMed - v22 - i4 - Jan 2004 - p72(1) [501+]

Ford, Colin - *Julia Margaret Cameron: A Critical Biography*
Albion - v36 - i2 - Summer 2004 - p328(4) [501+]

Ford, D.G. - *Laser Metrology and Machine Performance VI*
SciTech - v28 - i3 - Sept 2004 - p151(1) [51-500]

Ford, David F. - *Reading Texts, Seeking Wisdom: Scripture and Theology*
Intpr - v58 - i4 - Oct 2004 - p440(1) [501+]

Ford, Davis L. - *The Last Cowboy: The Personal Story of a Vanishing Cowboy*
SHQ - v107 - i4 - April 2004 - p623(2) [501+]

Ford, Deborah - *Puttin' on the Grits: A Guide to Southern Entertaining*
PW - v252 - i11 - March 14 2005 - p62(1) [51-500]

Ford, Dick - *Cast Iron Toy Cook Stoves and Ranges*
Ant&CM - v108 - i11 - Jan 2004 - p16(1) [501+]

Ford, Donna A. - *Scanning: For Kids of All Ages*
LibMed - v22 - i7 - April-May 2004 - p86(1) [501+]

Ford, Elizabeth A. - *The Makeover in Movies: Before and After in Hollywood Films, 1941-2002*
R&R Bk N - v19 - i3 - August 2004 - p262(1) [51-500]

Ford-Grabowsky, Mary - *Stations of the Light: Rediscovering an Ancient Christian Practice as a Spiritual Tool for Today*
LJ - v130 - i4 - March 1 2005 - p92(1) [51-500]

Ford, James - *Theseus and the Minotaur (Illus. by Andrews, Gary)*
  c   SLJ - v51 - i2 - Feb 2005 - p118(2) [51-500]
The Twelve Labors of Hercules (Illus. by Rutherford, Peter)
  c   SLJ - v51 - i2 - Feb 2005 - p118(2) [51-500]
Ford, Juwanda G. - *Shop Talk (Illus. by Hoston, Jim)*
  c   SLJ - v51 - i1 - Jan 2005 - p92(1) [51-500]
Sunday Best (Illus. by Bootman, Colin)
  c   SLJ - v51 - i1 - Jan 2005 - p92(1) [51-500]
Ford, Kenneth W. - *The Quantum World: Quantum Physics for Everyone*
      Choice - v42 - i1 - Sept 2004 - p142(1) [501+]
      New Sci - v183 - i2465 - Sept 18 2004 - p47(1) [51-500]
      TimHES - v0 - i1658 - Sept 17 2004 - p27(1) [501+]
Ford, Larry R. - *America's New Downtowns: Revitalization or Reinvention?*
      JEL - v41 - i4 - Dec 2003 - p1438(1) [501+]
Ford, Michael (b. 1956 -) - *Disclosures: Conversations Gay and Spiritual*
      TLS - i5292 - Sept 3 2004 - p26(1) [501+]
Ford, Michael Curtis - *The Sword of Attila: A Novel of the Last Years of Rome*
      KR - v73 - i2 - Jan 15 2005 - p70(1) [501+]
Ford, Michael Thomas - *Looking for It*
      BL - v100 - i22 - August 2004 - p1908(2) [51-500]
      PW - v252 - i29 - July 19 2004 - p145(1) [51-500]
Ultimate Gay Sex
      G&L Rev W - v11 - i6 - Nov-Dec 2004 - p42(1) [501+]
Ford, Nick - *Jerusalem under Muslim Rule in the Eleventh Century: Christian Pilgrims under Islamic Government*
  c   SLJ - v50 - i8 - August 2004 - p136(1) [501+]
Ford, Richard - *Independence Day*
      Globe & Mail - Nov 20 2004 - pD31 [501+]
Ford, Richard T. - *Racial Culture: A Critique*
      PW - v251 - i44 - Nov 1 2004 - p52(2) [501+]
Forde, Catherine - *Fat Boy Swim (Read by Lewis, Gary). Audiobook Review*
  c   SLJ - v51 - i2 - Feb 2005 - p76(2) [501+]
Fat Boy Swim
  y   BL - v101 - i1 - Sept 1 2004 - p110(1) [1-50]
  c   CH Bwatch - Feb 2005 - pNA [51-500]
  y   KR - v72 - i17 - Sept 1 2004 - p864(1) [51-500]
  y   SLJ - v50 - i9 - Sept 2004 - p204(2) [51-500]
Forde, Jasper - *Something Rotten*
      PW - v251 - i33 - August 16 2004 - p44(1) [51-500]
Fordham, John - *James Hanley: Modernism and the Working Class*
      RES - v55 - i221 - Sept 2004 - p635(3) [501+]
Fordyce, Deborah - *Welcome to Afghanistan*
  c   SLJ - v50 - i7 - July 2004 - p93(1) [51-500]
Fore, Stephanie - *Proceedings of the 18th North American Prairie Conference: Promoting Prairie*
      SciTech - v28 - i3 - Sept 2004 - p57(1) [1-50]
Foreman, George - *George Foreman's Indoor Grilling Made Easy: More than 100 Simple, Healthy Ways to Feed Family and Friends*
      LJ - v129 - i19 - Nov 15 2004 - p83(1) [51-500]
Foreman, Laura - *Alexander the Conqueror: The Epic Story of the Warrior King*
      New Sci - v184 - i2478 - Dec 18 2004 - p50(1) [501+]
      TLS - i5297 - Oct 8 2004 - p4-5 [501+]
Foreman, Michael - *Cat on the Hill (Illus. by Foreman, Michael)*
  c   KR - v72 - i13 - July 1 2004 - p629(1) [51-500]
Forensic Crime Solvers
  y   LibMed - v23 - i3 - Nov-Dec 2004 - p87(1) [51-500]
Forest, Cary B. - *Radio Frequency Power in Plasmas: Proceedings*
      SciTech - v28 - i1 - March 2004 - p51(1) [51-500]
Forest, Jacques - *The Crustacea: Revised and Updated from the Traite de Zoologie*
      Choice - v42 - i7 - March 2005 - p1253(1) [51-500]
      SciTech - v28 - i3 - Sept 2004 - p64(1) [51-500]
Forest, Jim - *The Wormwood File: E-Mail from Hell*
      BL - v101 - i3 - Oct 1 2004 - p299(1) [51-500]
Foresta, Merry - *At First Sight: Photography and the Smithsonian*
      VQR - v80 - i3 - Summer 2004 - p270(1) [1-50]
Forester, Jeff - *The Forest for the Trees: How Humans Shaped the North Woods*
      Choice - v42 - i5 - Jan 2005 - p879(2) [1-50]
      NH - v113 - i8 - Oct 2004 - p70(2) [501+]

Forgang, William G. - *Strategy-Specific Decision Making: A Guide for Executing Competitive Strategy*
      Choice - v42 - i2 - Oct 2004 - p336(1) [51-500]
      R&R Bk N - v19 - i3 - August 2004 - p102(1) [501+]
Forgette, Richard G. - *Congress, Parties, and Puzzles: Politics as a Team Sport*
      R&R Bk N - v19 - i1 - Feb 2004 - pNA [51-500]
Forhan, Chris - *The Actual Moon, the Actual Stars*
      South CR - v37 - i1 - Fall 2004 - p198-201 [501+]
Forhan, Kate Langdon - *The Political Theory of Christine De Pizan*
      Six Ct J - v34 - i4 - Winter 2003 - p1124-1125 [501+]
Forkey, Neil S. - *Shaping the Upper Canadian Frontier: Environment, Society, and Culture in the Trent Vale*
      Can Hist R - v85 - i3 - Sept 2004 - p591(2) [501+]
Shaping the Upper Canadian Frontier: Environment, Society, and Culture in the Trent Valley
      CBRA - Annual 2003 - p340(2) [501+]
Forlati, Laura Picchio - *Economic Sanctions in International Law*
      R&R Bk N - v19 - i4 - Nov 2004 - p108(1) [51-500]
Forman, Gayle - *You Can't Get There from Here: A Year on the Fringes of a Shrinking World*
      KR - v73 - i2 - Jan 15 2005 - p99(1) [501+]
      LJ - v130 - i2 - Feb 1 2005 - p106(1) [51-500]
      PW - v252 - i6 - Feb 7 2005 - p50(2) [51-500]
Forman, Murray - *That's the Joint!: The Hip-Hop Studies Reader*
      R&R Bk N - v19 - i4 - Nov 2004 - p197(1) [501+]
Forment, Carlos A. - *Democracy in Latin America, 1760-1900*
      AHR - v109 - i4 - Oct 2004 - p1272-1273 [501+]
      CS - v33 - i6 - Nov 2004 - p743(1) [1-50]
Formichella, Joe - *The Wreck of the Twilight Limited*
      KR - v72 - i14 - July 15 2004 - p647(1) [51-500]
Formicola, Jo Renee - *Faith-Based Initiatives and the Bush Administration: The Good, the Bad, and the Ugly*
      Ch Today - v48 - i7 - July 2004 - p65(2) [501+]
      Choice - v41 - i7 - March 2004 - p1372(1) [501+]
Fornahl, Dirk - *Cooperation, Networks and Institutions in Regional Innovation Systems*
      JEL - v41 - i4 - Dec 2003 - p1418(1) [501+]
Fornero, Elsa - *Developing an Annuity Market in Europe*
      R&R Bk N - v19 - i3 - August 2004 - p139(1) [51-500]
Fornerod, Nicolas - *Registres de la Compagnie des Pasteurs de Geneve, Vol. 13*
      Six Ct J - v35 - i1 - Spring 2004 - p229(3) [501+]
Forney, Todd A. - *The Midshipman Culture and Educational Reform: The U.S. Naval Academy 1946-76*
      R&R Bk N - v19 - i4 - Nov 2004 - p253(1) [501+]
Fornieri, Joseph R. - *Abraham Lincoln's Political Faith*
      AHR - v109 - i3 - June 2004 - p911(2) [501+]
      JAH - v91 - i2 - Sept 2004 - p634(2) [501+]
Forrer, Matthi - *Hokusai: Mountains and Water, Flowers and Birds*
      Choice - v42 - i4 - Dec 2004 - p649(1) [1-50]
Forrest, Alan - *Napoleon's Men: The Soldiers of the Revolution and Empire*
      JMH - v76 - i3 - Sept 2004 - p663(3) [501+]
Paris, the Provinces and the French Revolution
      Choice - v42 - i5 - Jan 2005 - p922(1) [1-50]
Forrest, Emma - *Cherries in the Snow*
      PW - v252 - i4 - Jan 24 2005 - p221(2) [501+]
Forrest, Joshua B. - *Lineages of State Fragility: Rural Civil Society in Guinea Bissau*
      HNet - August 2004 - pNA [501+]
Subnationalism in Africa: Ethnicity, Alliances, and Politics
      R&R Bk N - v19 - i1 - Feb 2004 - pNA [501+]
Forrest, Ray - *Housing and Social Change: East-West Perspective*
      R&R Bk N - v19 - i1 - Feb 2004 - p101(1) [51-500]
Forrest, Richard - *Death in the Secret Garden*
      BL - v101 - i7 - Dec 1 2004 - p639(1) [51-500]
      KR - v73 - i2 - Jan 15 2005 - p85(1) [51-500]
Forrester, Andrew - *The Man Who Saw the Future*
      R&R Bk N - v19 - i3 - August 2004 - p77(1) [51-500]
Forrester, Tina - *Birthday Book (Illus. by Langlois, Suzane)*
  c   CBRA - Annual 2003 - p551(2) [51-500]
Forsberg, Clyde R., Jr. - *Equal Rites: Mormonism, Masonry, Gender, and American Culture*
      Choice - v42 - i4 - Dec 2004 - p677(1) [1-50]
Forsmark, Chris E. - *Pancreatitis and Its Complications*
      SciTech - v28 - i4 - Dec 2004 - p105(1) [51-500]

Forssbaeck, Jens - *Money Markets and Politics: A Study of European Financial Integration and Monetary Policy Options*
      R&R Bk N - v19 - i3 - August 2004 - p134(1) [51-500]
Forsten, Char - *Differentiating Textbooks: Strategies to Improve Student Comprehension and Motivation*
      Sci Teach - v71 - i6 - July 2004 - p63-64 [501+]
Forster, E.M. - *A Room with a View (Read by David, Joanna). Audiobook Review*
  y   Kliatt - v38 - i5 - Sept 2004 - p64(2) [51-500]
Forster, Eckart - *Kant's Final Synthesis: An Essay on the Opus Postumum*
      Eight-C St - v37 - i3 - Spring 2004 - p491-497 [501+]
Forster, Gwynne - *After the Loving*
      BL - v101 - i9-10 - Jan 1 2005 - p830(1) [1-50]
If You Walked in My Shoes
  y   BL - v101 - i6 - Nov 15 2004 - p561(1) [51-500]
Forster, Margaret - *Diary of an Ordinary Woman (Read by Jameson, Susan). Audiobook Review*
  y   Kliatt - v39 - i2 - March 2005 - p51(2) [51-500]
Is There Anything You Want?
      Spec - v297 - i9206 - Jan 15 2005 - p44(2) [501+]
Forster, Michael N. - *Philosophical Writings*
      GSR - v27 - i2 - May 2004 - p378-379 [501+]
Wittgenstein on the Arbitrariness of Grammar
      Choice - v42 - i6 - Feb 2005 - p1034(2) [51-500]
Forster, Richard - *Amos Burn: A Chess Biography*
      R&R Bk N - v19 - i4 - Nov 2004 - p82(1) [51-500]
Forster, Roy - *Woodland Garden: Planting in Harmony with Nature*
      E-Streams - August 2004 - pNA [501+]
Forsyth, Christine - *Adrenaline High*
  y   Kliatt - v38 - i6 - Nov 2004 - p16(1) [51-500]
  y   SLJ - v50 - i11 - Nov 2004 - p144(1) [51-500]
  y   VOYA - v27 - i4 - Oct 2004 - p296(1) [51-500]
Forsyth, Peter - *The Economic Regulation of Airports: Recent Developments in Australasia, North America and Europe*
      R&R Bk N - v19 - i4 - Nov 2004 - p107(1) [51-500]
Forsythe, David P. - *Human Rights and Diversity: Area Studies Revisited*
      Choice - v42 - i1 - Sept 2004 - p185(1) [501+]
Fort, Adrian - *Prof: The Life of Frederick Lindemann*
      CR - v285 - i1663 - August 2004 - p116(2) [501+]
      Lon R Bks - v26 - i6 - March 18 2004 - pNA [501+]
      TLS - i5283 - July 2 2004 - p25(1) [501+]
Fort, Meredith - *Sickness and Wealth: The Corporate Assault on Global Health*
      SciTech - v28 - i4 - Dec 2004 - p83(1) [51-500]
Fort, Rodney D. - *International Sports Economics Comparisons*
      Choice - v42 - i2 - Oct 2004 - p339(1) [51-500]
      R&R Bk N - v19 - i3 - August 2004 - p87(1) [51-500]
Sports Economics
      JEL - v41 - i4 - Dec 2003 - p1393(1) [501+]
Forte, Bruno - *The Essence of Christianity*
      TT - v61 - i2 - July 2004 - p240(1) [501+]
Fortea, Jose I. - *Furor et Rabies: Violencia, Conflicto y marginacion en la Edad Moderna*
      JIH - v35 - i1 - Summer 2004 - p120-122 [501+]
Fortelius, Mikael - *Geology and Paleontology of the Miocene Sinap Formation, Turkey*
      Choice - v42 - i1 - Sept 2004 - p134(1) [501+]
      SciTech - v28 - i3 - March 2004 - p59(1) [51-500]
Fortey, Richard - *Earth: An Intimate History*
  y   BL - v101 - i4 - Oct 15 2004 - p370(1) [51-500]
      BL - v101 - i7 - Dec 1 2004 - p632(1) [51-500]
      BL - v101 - i9-10 - Jan 1 2005 - p768(1) [51-500]
      KR - v72 - i19 - Oct 1 2004 - p947(1) [51-500]
      LJ - v129 - i19 - Nov 15 2004 - p84(1) [51-500]
      NYT - Nov 16 2004 - pE8 [501+]
      NYTBR - Dec 12 2004 - p34 [501+]
      PW - v251 - i45 - Nov 8 2004 - p45(1) [501+]
      SciTech - v28 - i4 - Dec 2004 - p57(1) [51-500]
Forth, Christopher E. - *The Dreyfus Affair and the Crisis of French Manhood*
      Choice - v42 - i3 - Nov 2004 - p555(1) [1-50]
      HRNB - v33 - i1 - Fall 2004 - p27(2) [501+]
Fortier, Andrew C. - *The Dash Reeves Site: A Middle Woodland Village and Lithic Production Center in the American Bottom*
      Am Ant - v70 - i1 - Jan 2005 - p196(2) [501+]
Fortier, Minnie - *I Love...*
      PW - v252 - i5 - Jan 31 2005 - p66(1) [501+]

Fortin, Francois - *Major Systems of the Body*
  c SB - v40 - i4 - July-August 2004 - p149(1) [51-500]
  Structure of the Body
  c SB - v40 - i4 - July-August 2004 - p149(1) [51-500]

Fortin, Jeffrey B. - *Chemical Vapor Deposition Polymerization: The Growth and Properties of Parylene Thin Films*
  SciTech - v28 - i1 - March 2004 - p178(1) [51-500]

Fortin, Noonie - *Women at Risk*
  HNet - Sept 2004 - pNA [501+]

Fortin, Sarah - *Forging the Canadian Social Union: SUFA and Beyond*
  R&R Bk N - v19 - i3 - August 2004 - p180(1) [501+]

Fortinash, Katherine M. - *Psychiatric Mental Health Nursing, 3rd Ed.*
  SciTech - v28 - i1 - March 2004 - p95(1) [51-500]

Fortna, Virginia Page - *Peace Time: Cease-Fire Agreements and the Durability of Peace*
  Choice - v42 - i4 - Dec 2004 - p732(1) [1-50]

Fortune, Marie M. - *Sexual Abuse in the Catholic Church: Trusting the Clergy?*
  R&R Bk N - v19 - i4 - Nov 2004 - p27(1) [501+]

Fortwengel, Gerhard - *Guide for Clinical Trial Staff: Implementing Good Clinical Practice*
  SciTech - v28 - i3 - Sept 2004 - p79(1) [51-500]

Forward, Toby - *The First Day at School*
  c Sch Lib - v52 - i4 - Winter 2004 - p187(1) [51-500]
  What Did You Do Today? The First Day of School (Illus. by Thompson, Carol)
  c BL - v100 - i22 - August 2004 - p1947(1) [51-500]
  c KR - v72 - i14 - July 15 2004 - p684(1) [51-500]
  c SLJ - v50 - i10 - Oct 2004 - p113(1) [51-500]

Foshay, Ella M. - *John James Audubon*
  BL - v100 - i22 - August 2004 - p1886(1) [51-500]

Foskett, Ken - *Judging Thomas: The Life and Times of Clarence Thomas*
  BL - v100 - i22 - August 2004 - p1880(1) [51-500]
  Black Iss - v7 - i1 - Jan-Feb 2005 - p68(2) [501+]
  BW - v34 - i34 - August 22 2004 - p10(1) [501+]
  NYTBR - Sept 5 2004 - p10 [501+]
  PW - v251 - i28 - July 12 2004 - p58(1) [51-500]

Foskett, Mary F. - *A Virgin Conceived: Mary and Classical Representations of Virginity*
  CH - v73 - i4 - Dec 2004 - p837(2) [51-500]
  Theol St - v65 - i3 - Sept 2004 - p672(2) [501+]

Fosl, Catherine - *Subversive Southerner: Anne Braden and the Struggle for Racial Justice in the Cold War South*
  JAH - v91 - i2 - Sept 2004 - p706(2) [501+]

Foss, Jason - *Blood and Sandals*
  KR - v72 - i18 - Sept 15 2004 - p893(1) [51-500]

Foss, Karen A. - *Readings in Feminist Rhetorical Theory*
  Choice - v41 - i11-12 - July-August 2004 - p2038(1) [501+]
  R&R Bk N - v19 - i2 - May 2004 - p136 [51-500]

Fossheim, K. - *Superconductivity: Physics and Applications*
  SciTech - v28 - i3 - Sept 2004 - p48(1) [1-50]

Fossum, Karin - *He Who Fears the Wolf*
  Globe & Mail - July 10 2004 - pD12 [501+]
  Globe & Mail - Nov 27 2004 - pD18 [1-50]
  When the Devil Holds the Candle
  Globe & Mail - Oct 30 2004 - pD26 [51-500]
  Globe & Mail - Nov 27 2004 - pD18 [1-50]

Foster, A. Kristen - *Moral Visions and Material Ambitions: Philadelphia Struggles to Define the Republic, 1776-1836*
  Choice - v42 - i3 - Nov 2004 - p546(1) [1-50]
  W&M Q - v62 - i1 - Jan 2005 - p120-3 [501+]

Foster, Alan Dean - *Flinx's Folly*
  Analog - v124 - i1-2 - Jan-Feb 2004 - p233(2) [501+]
  Sliding Scales: A Pip and Flinx Novel
  BL - v101 - i2 - Sept 15 2004 - p215(1) [51-500]
  LJ - v129 - i17 - Oct 15 2004 - p58(1) [51-500]
  PW - v251 - i34 - August 23 2004 - p41(1) [51-500]

Foster, Cecil - *Dry Bone Memories*
  Can Lit - i182 - Autumn 2004 - p127(2) [501+]
  Where Race Does Not Matter: The New Spirit of Modernity
  Globe & Mail - Feb 5 2005 - pD12 [501+]

Foster, Charles - *Feel Better Fast: Overcoming the Emotional Fallout of Your Illness or Injury*
  LJ - v129 - i13 - August 2004 - p107(2) [51-500]
  Once Upon a Time in Paradise: Canadians in the Golden Age of Hollywood
  Beav - v84 - i6 - Dec 2004 - p49(1) [51-500]
  CBRA - Annual 2003 - p105(1) [51-500]

Foster, David (b. 1953 -) - *Accept No Mediocre Life: Living Beyond Labels, Libels and Limitations*
  PW - v251 - i50 - Dec 13 2004 - p62(1) [51-500]

Foster, David R. - *Forests in Time: The Environmental Consequences of 1,000 Years of Change in New England*
  Choice - v42 - i2 - Oct 2004 - p316(2) [51-500]
  Sci - v306 - i5701 - Nov 26 2004 - p1479(2) [501+]
  SciTech - v28 - i3 - Sept 2004 - p57(1) [1-50]

Foster, David Ruel - *The Two Wings of Catholic Thought: Essays on Fides et Ratio*
  Theol St - v65 - i3 - Sept 2004 - p678(1) [501+]

Foster, David William - *Queer Issues in Contemporary Latin American Cinema*
  Film Cr - v28 - i3 - Spring 2004 - p59(6) [501+]

Foster, Gaines M. - *Moral Reconstruction: Christian Lobbyists and the Federal Legislation of Morality, 1865-1920*
  CH - v73 - i3 - Sept 2004 - p699(3) [501+]
  RAH - v32 - i1 - March 2004 - p49(9) [501+]

Foster, Gary D. - *Managing Obesity: A Clinical Guide*
  SciTech - v28 - i1 - March 2004 - p103(1) [51-500]

Foster, Gerald - *American Houses: A Field Guide to the Architecture of the Home*
  Choice - v42 - i3 - Nov 2004 - p475(1) [1-50]

Foster, Graham - *Language Arts Idea Bank: Instructional Strategies for Supporting Student Learning*
  CBRA - Annual 2003 - p394(1) [51-500]

Foster, Gwendolyn Audrey - *Performing Whiteness: Postmodern Re/Constructions in the Cinema*
  FQ - v58 - i1 - Fall 2004 - p73(2) [501+]

Foster, Hal - *Prosthetic Gods*
  Afterimage - v32 - i4 - Jan-Feb 2005 - p15(1) [1-50]

Foster, Harold - *Vikings on the Isle of Man (Illus. by Murphy, John Cullen)*
  LJ - v129 - i14 - Sept 1 2004 - p128(1) [51-500]

Foster, Ian - *Arthur Schnitzler: Zeitgenossenschaften/Contemporaneities*
  GSR - v27 - i3 - Oct 2004 - p616(1) [501+]
  Neighbours and Strangers: Literary and Cultural Relations in Germany, Austria and Central Europe Since 1989
  R&R Bk N - v19 - i4 - Nov 2004 - p244(1) [501+]

Foster, John - *Drift upon a Dream: Poems for Sleepy Babies (Illus. by Williamson, Melanie)*
  c BL - v101 - i1 - Sept 1 2004 - p127(1) [1-50]
  c SLJ - v50 - i12 - Dec 2004 - p130(1) [501+]
  Our Teacher's Gone Bananas
  c Sch Lib - v52 - i4 - Winter 2004 - p210(1) [51-500]
  The Trying Flapeze and Other Puzzle Poems (Illus. by Ross, Tony)
  c Sch Lib - v52 - i3 - Autumn 2004 - p154(1) [1-50]

Foster, John L. - *Ancient Egyptian Literature: An Anthology*
  JNES - v63 - i4 - Oct 2004 - p316(2) [501+]

Foster, John Wilson - *Recoveries: Neglected Episodes in Irish Cultural History, 1860-1912*
  VS - v46 - i3 - Spring 2004 - p507(2) [501+]

Foster, Kit - *The Stanley Steamer: America's Legendary Steam Car*
  SciTech - v28 - i4 - Dec 2004 - p160(1) [51-500]

Foster, Lori - *Just a Hint, Clint*
  BL - v101 - i3 - Oct 1 2004 - p316(1) [51-500]

Foster, Lynn V. - *A Brief History of Mexico, Rev. Ed.*
  R&R Bk N - v19 - i3 - August 2004 - p76(1) [51-500]

Foster, Mary F. - *2004 Miller Not-for-Profit Reporting: GAAP Plus Tax, Financial, and Regulatory Requirements*
  R&R Bk N - v19 - i2 - May 2004 - p120 [51-500]

Foster, Merna - *100 Canadian Heroines: Famous and Forgotten Faces*
  Globe & Mail - Dec 24 2004 - pD13 [1-50]

Foster, Michael - *Plotting Gigantic Worx: The Story of Elgar's Apostles Trilogy*
  MT - v145 - i1887 - Summer 2004 - p105(3) [501+]

Foster, Patricia - *Just Beneath My Skin: Autobiography and Self-Discovery*
  BL - v101 - i1 - Sept 1 2004 - p41(1) [51-500]
  KR - v72 - i15 - August 1 2004 - p723(2) [51-500]
  LJ - v129 - i16 - Oct 1 2004 - p80(1) [51-500]

Foster, R.F. - *W.B. Yeats: A Life, Vol. 2*
  HR - v57 - i1 - Spring 2004 - p141-149 [501+]
  W.B. Yeats: A Life. Vol. 2
  WLT - v78 - i3-4 - Sept-Dec 2004 - p104(1) [501+]

Foster, Russell G. - *Rhythms of Life: The Biological Clocks That Control the Daily Lives of Every Living Thing*
  NW - Oct 11 2004 - p46 [501+]
  PW - v251 - i33 - August 16 2004 - p54(1) [51-500]
  SB - v41 - i1 - Jan-Feb 2005 - p20(1) [501+]
  TimHES - v0 - i1653 - August 13 2004 - p28(1) [501+]

Foster, Verna A. - *The Name and Nature of Tragicomedy*
  R&R Bk N - v19 - i3 - August 2004 - p260(1) [51-500]

Foster, William Henry - *The Captors' Narrative: Catholic Women and Their Puritan Men on the Early American Frontier*
  JAH - v91 - i1 - June 2004 - p215-216 [501+]

Fothergill, Augusta B. - *Wills of Westmoreland County, Virginia, 1654-1800*
  EFHM - v58 - i3 - May-June 2004 - p61(1) [51-500]

Foti, Jeffrey L. - *Blueprints Q&A Step 2: Pediatrics, 2nd Ed.*
  SciTech - v28 - i4 - Dec 2004 - p111(1) [1-50]
  Blueprints Q&A Step 3: Pediatrics, 2nd Ed.
  SciTech - v28 - i4 - Dec 2004 - p111(1) [1-50]

Fotos, Sandra - *New Perspectives on CALL for Second Language Classrooms*
  R&R Bk N - v19 - i4 - Nov 2004 - p211(1) [501+]

Fouarge, Didier - *Poverty and Subsidiarity in Europe: Minimum Protection from an Economic Perspective*
  R&R Bk N - v19 - i4 - Nov 2004 - p89(1) [51-500]

Foucault, Didier - *Un philosophe libertin dans l'Europe baroque: Giulio Cesare Vanini, 1585-1619*
  Ren Q - v57 - i3 - Fall 2004 - p981(2) [501+]

Foucault, Michel - *Abnormal: Lectures at the College de France, 1974-1975*
  TLS - i5289 - August 13 2004 - p27(1) [501+]
  Death and the Labyrinth: The World of Raymond Roussel
  R&R Bk N - v19 - i3 - August 2004 - p5(1) [1-50]
  TLS - i5289 - August 13 2004 - p27(1) [501+]
  Essential Foucault: Selections from Essential Works of Foucault, 1954-1984, Rev. Ed.
  R&R Bk N - v19 - i1 - Feb 2004 - p4(1) [51-500]
  The Hermeneutics of the Subject: Lectures at the College de France, 1981-82
  LJ - v130 - i4 - March 1 2005 - p89(1) [51-500]
  Society Must Be Defended: Lectures at the College de France, 1975-76
  Choice - v41 - i7 - March 2004 - p1309(1) [501+]

Fouche, Rayvon - *Black Inventors in the Age of Segregation: Granville T. Woods, Lewis H. Latimer, and Shelby J. Davidson*
  JEL - v42 - i1 - March 2004 - p279(1) [501+]
  SciTech - v28 - i1 - March 2004 - p133(1) [51-500]
  T&C - v45 - i4 - Oct 2004 - p848(2) [501+]

Fought, Leigh - *Southern Womanhood and Slavery: A Biography of Louisa S. McCord, 1810-1879*
  AHR - v109 - i3 - June 2004 - p915(2) [501+]
  JAH - v91 - i2 - Sept 2004 - p619(2) [501+]

Foukal, Peter V. - *Solar Astrophysics, 2nd Rev. Ed.*
  SciTech - v28 - i3 - Sept 2004 - p44(1) [1-50]

Foulds, Nancy - *Pumpkin Carving: 22 Designs and Step-by-Step Instructions*
  c CBRA - Annual 2003 - p555(1) [51-500]

Foulke, Robert - *The Sea Voyage Narrative*
  Can Lit - i182 - Autumn 2004 - p94(2) [501+]

Foulkes, Julia L. - *Modern Bodies: Dance and American Modernism from Martha Graham to Alvin Ailey*
  Dance RJ - v35 - i2 - Winter 2003 - p193-196 [501+]
  JAH - v91 - i1 - June 2004 - p278-279 [501+]

Foulkes, Richard - *Performing Shakespeare in the Age of Empire*
  RES - v55 - i219 - April 2004 - p292-294 [501+]
  VS - v46 - i3 - Spring 2004 - p544(4) [501+]

Foulston, Lynn - *At the Feet of the Goddess: The Divine Feminine in Local Hindu Religion*
  JR - v85 - i1 - Jan 2005 - p162(2) [501+]

Fourcans, Andree - *Currency Crises: A Theoretical and Empirical Perspective*
  R&R Bk N - v19 - i2 - May 2004 - p122 [51-500]

Fourkas, John T. - *Dynamics in Small Confining Systems: Proceedings*
  SciTech - v28 - i3 - Sept 2004 - p53(1) [1-50]

Fourment, Tiffany - *My Water Comes from the Mountains (Illus. by Emerling, Dorothy)*
  c CH Bwatch - Feb 2005 - pNA [51-500]

Fournel, Paul - *Poils de cairote*
  WLT - v78 - i3-4 - Sept-Dec 2004 - p122(1) [501+]

Fournier, Peter J. - *The Handbook of Mascots and Nicknames: A Guide to the Nicknames of All Senior, Junior and Community Colleges Throughout the United States and Canada*
  R&R Bk N - v19 - i3 - August 2004 - p226(1) [1-50]

Foust, James C. - *Online Journalism: Principles and Practices of News for the Web*
  R&R Bk N - v19 - i4 - Nov 2004 - p228(1) [501+]

Fouz-Hernandez, Santiago - *Madonna's Drowned Worlds: New Approaches to Her Subcultural Transformations, 1983-2003*
  R&R Bk N - v19 - i4 - Nov 2004 - p196(1) [501+]

Fowle, Frances - *Soil and Stone: Impressionism, Urbanism, Environment*
  R&R Bk N - v19 - i1 - Feb 2004 - p209(1) [51-500]

Fowler, Alan - *Lancashire Cotton Operatives and Work, 1900-1950*
  Albion - v36 - i2 - Summer 2004 - p350(3) [501+]

Fowler, Alastair - *Renaissance Realism: Narrative Images in Literature and Art*
  Ren Q - v57 - i3 - Fall 2004 - p1154(2) [501+]
  RES - v55 - i221 - Sept 2004 - p615(3) [501+]

Fowler, Christopher - *Breathe*
  ChrSFF&H - v26 - i10 - Oct 2004 - p26(1) [51-500]
  Full Dark House
  y SLJ - v50 - i10 - Oct 2004 - p198(1) [51-500]

Fowler, Connie May - *The Problem with Murmur Lee*
  BL - v101 - i9-10 - Jan 1 2005 - p814(1) [1-50]
  KR - v72 - i21 - Nov 1 2004 - p1023(1) [501+]
  LJ - v129 - i20 - Dec 1 2004 - p99(1) [51-500]
  PW - v251 - i47 - Nov 22 2004 - p38(1) [51-500]

Fowler, David C. - *E-Serials Collection Management: Transitions, Trends, and Technicalities*
  LRTS - v48 - i4 - Oct 2004 - p306(2) [501+]

Fowler, Elizabeth - *Literary Character: The Human Figure in Early English Writing*
  Med R - July 2004 - pNA [501+]
  Ren Q - v57 - i4 - Winter 2004 - p1511(3) [501+]
  Literary Character: The Human Figure in Early English Writing
  Choice - v41 - i7 - March 2004 - p1295(2) [501+]

Fowler, Karen Joy - *The James Tiptree Award Anthology 1*
  BL - v101 - i9-10 - Jan 1 2005 - p834(1) [1-50]
  Bwatch - Dec 2004 - pNA [51-500]
  The Jane Austen Book Club (Read by Schraf, Kimberly). Audiobook Review
  BL - v100 - i22 - August 2004 - p1953(1) [51-500]
  LJ - v129 - i17 - Oct 15 2004 - p95(1) [51-500]
  The Jane Austen Book Club
  Econ - v372 - i8384 - July 17 2004 - p82US [501+]
  NS - v133 - i4713 - Nov 8 2004 - p55(1) [501+]
  Spec - v296 - i9191 - Oct 2 2004 - p43(1) [501+]
  TLS - i5300 - Oct 29 2004 - p22(1) [501+]
  The Sweetheart Season
  BL - v101 - i1 - Sept 1 2004 - p53(1) [51-500]

Fowler, Kristine K. - *Using the Mathematics Literature*
  E-Streams - Nov 2004 - pNA [501+]
  SciTech - v28 - i3 - Sept 2004 - p16(1) [501+]

Fowler, Loretta - *The Columbia Guide to American Indians of the Great Plains*
  WHQ - v35 - i4 - Winter 2004 - p518-519 [501+]
  Trival Sovereignty and the Historical Imagination: Cheyenne-Arapaho Politics
  HNet - July 2004 - pNA [501+]

Fowler, Peter - *Farming in the First Millennium AD: British Agriculture between Julius Caesar and William the Conqueror*
  Albion - v36 - i2 - Summer 2004 - p280(2) [501+]
  Landscapes for the World: Conserving a Global Heritage
  R&R Bk N - v20 - i1 - Feb 2005 - p83(1) [501+]

Fowler, William - *Barbarossa: The First Seven Days*
  R&R Bk N - v19 - i3 - August 2004 - p33(1) [51-500]
  Empires at War: The French and Indian War and the Struggle for North America, 1754-1763
  BL - v101 - i8 - Dec 15 2004 - p701(1) [51-500]
  KR - v72 - i22 - Nov 15 2004 - p1077(2) [501+]
  LJ - v130 - i1 - Jan 1 2005 - p127(2) [51-500]

Fox, Aaron A. - *Real Country: Music and Language in Working-Class Culture*
  Choice - v42 - i7 - March 2005 - p1030(1) [51-500]

Fox, Andrew - *Bride of the Fat White Vampire*
  y BL - v100 - i22 - August 2004 - p1912(1) [51-500]
  KR - v72 - i13 - July 1 2004 - p594(1) [501+]
  LJ - v129 - i12 - July 2004 - p69(1) [51-500]
  PW - v251 - i28 - July 12 2004 - p49(1) [501+]

Fox, Annie - *Too Stressed to Think? A Teen Guide to Staying Sane When Life Makes You Crazy*
  y Cur R - v44 - i5 - Jan 2005 - p13(1) [51-500]

Fox, Christyan - *Raton, que te pilla el gato!*
  c BL - v100 - i22 - August 2004 - p1950(1) [501+]

Fox, Dan - *A Treasury of Children's Songs: Forty Favorites to Sing and Play*
  c SLJ - v50 - i10 - Oct 2004 - pS26(1) [1-50]

Fox, Dana L. - *Stories Matter: The Complexity of Cultural Authenticity in Children's Literature*
  Bkbird - v42 - i3 - July 2004 - p50(1) [501+]
  SLJ - v50 - i10 - Oct 2004 - pS72(1) [51-500]

Fox, Daniel J. - *Arrowheads of the Central Great Plains: Identification and Value Guide*
  R&R Bk N - v19 - i4 - Nov 2004 - p53(1) [51-500]

Fox, Don M. - *Patton's Vanguard: The United States Army Fourth Armored Division*
  R&R Bk N - v19 - i1 - Feb 2004 - p29(1) [51-500]

Fox, Edward A. - *Electronic Theses and Dissertations: A Sourcebook for Educators, Students, and Librarians*
  A Lib - v35 - i7 - August 2004 - p87(1) [501+]
  R&R Bk N - v19 - i3 - August 2004 - p222(1) [1-50]

Fox, Greg - *Kyle's Bed and Breakfast*
  PW - v251 - i28 - July 12 2004 - p46(1) [51-500]

Fox, Helen - *Eager*
  c CH Bwatch - v14 - i7 - July 2004 - p7(2) [501+]
  c HB - v80 - i4 - July-August 2004 - p451(2) [51-500]
  c SLJ - v50 - i8 - August 2004 - p121(2) [51-500]

Fox, James Alan - *Elementary Statistics in Criminal Justice Research: The Essentials*
  R&R Bk N - v19 - i3 - August 2004 - p91(1) [51-500]
  The Will to Kill: Making Sense of Senseless Murder, 2nd Ed.
  R&R Bk N - v19 - i4 - Nov 2004 - p145(1) [501+]

Fox, Jonathan - *Bringing Religion into International Relations*
  Choice - v42 - i5 - Jan 2005 - p870(1) [1-50]
  Religion, Civilization, and Civil War: 1945 through the New Millennium
  Choice - v42 - i3 - Nov 2004 - p560(1) [1-50]
  R&R Bk N - v19 - i3 - August 2004 - p13(1) [1-50]

Fox, Karen C. - *Einstein: A to Z*
  SB - v41 - i1 - Jan-Feb 2005 - p19(2) [501+]
  Choice - v42 - i5 - Jan 2005 - p874(2) [1-50]

Fox, Laurie - *The Lost Girls*
  MFSF - v107 - i2 - August 2004 - p33(2) [501+]

Fox, Lawrence J. - *Traversing the Ethical Minefield: Problems, Law, and Professional Responsibility*
  R&R Bk N - v19 - i3 - August 2004 - p196(1) [1-50]

Fox, Loren - *Enron: The Rise and Fall*
  En Jnl - v25 - i4 - Oct 2004 - p115(20) [501+]

Fox, Mem - *Hunwick's Egg (Illus. by Lofts, Pamela)*
  c KR - v73 - i2 - Jan 15 2005 - p119(1) [51-500]
  c PW - v252 - i4 - Jan 24 2005 - p242(1) [51-500]
  The Magic Hat (Illus. by Tusa, Tricia)
  c RT - v57 - Oct 2003 - p167 [1-50]
  Where Is the Green Sheep? (Illus. by Horacek, Judy)
  c HB - v81 - i1 - Jan-Feb 2005 - p12(1) [51-500]

Fox, Nik Farrell - *The New Sartre: Explorations in Postmodernism*
  FS - v58 - i3 - July 2004 - p435-436 [501+]

Fox, Richard Wightman - *Jesus in America: Personal Savior, Cultural Hero, National Obsession*
  CC - v121 - i14 - July 13 2004 - p30(2) [501+]
  Choice - v41 - i11-12 - July-August 2004 - p2106(2) [501+]

Fox, Robin Lane - *The Long March: Xenophon and the Ten Thousand*
  Lon R Bks - v26 - i21 - Nov 4 2004 - p12(1) [1-50]

Fox, Seymour - *Visions of Jewish Education*
  Choice - v42 - i2 - Oct 2004 - p312(1) [51-500]
  TCR - v106 - i5 - May 2004 - p916(6) [501+]

Fox, Susan - *Dial with Style*
  c PW - v252 - i4 - Jan 24 2005 - p246(1) [501+]

Foxall, James D. - *Sams Teach Yourself Microsoft Visual C# .NET 2003 in 24 Hours. 2nd Ed.*
  SciTech - v28 - i3 - Sept 2004 - p23(1) [1-50]

Foxman, Abraham H. - *Never Again?: The Threat of the New Anti-Semitism*
  MEJ - v58 - i4 - Autumn 2004 - p667(8) [501+]

Foye, K'wan - *Street Dreams*
  Ent W - i786 - Oct 1 2004 - p77 [51-500]

Foyle, Andrew - *Pevsner Architectural Guides: Bristol*
  Choice - v42 - i6 - Feb 2005 - p1015(1) [51-500]
  CR - v286 - i1669 - Feb 2005 - p127(1) [51-500]

Fradeani, Mauro - *Esthetic Rehabilitation in Fixed Prosthodontics*
  SciTech - v28 - i4 - Dec 2004 - p115(1) [1-50]

Fraden, Rena - *Imagining Media: Rhodessa Jones and Theater for Incarcerated Women*
  Theat J - v56 - i4 - Dec 2004 - p725-726 [501+]

Fradin, Dennis B. - *Who Was Thomas Jefferson?*
  LibMed - v22 - i6 - March 2004 - p76(1) [501+]
  Who Was Thomas Jefferson? (Illus. by O'Brien, John)
  c LibMed - v22 - i6 - March 2004 - p76(1) [501+]

Fradin, Dennis Brindell - *Fight On! Mary Church Terrell's Battle for Integration*
  y RT - v58 - i3 - Nov 2004 - p290(1) [1-50]
  The Signers: The 56 Stories Behind the Declaration of Independence (Illus. by McCurdy, Michael)
  c RT - v57 - Nov 2003 - p278 [51-500]

Fradin, Judith Bloom - *The Power of One: Daisy Bates and the Little Rock Nine*
  y CCB-B - v58 - i6 - Feb 2005 - p251(2) [51-500]
  y HB - v81 - i2 - March-April 2005 - p214(2) [51-500]
  KR - v73 - i1 - Jan 1 2005 - p51(1) [51-500]

Fradkin, Barbara - *Fifth Son*
  Globe & Mail - Oct 2 2004 - pD18 [51-500]

Fragaszy, Dorothy M. - *The Complete Capuchini: The Biology of the Genus Cebus*
  Choice - v42 - i7 - March 2005 - p1253(2) [51-500]

Fragos, Emily - *Little Savage*
  ABR - v25 - i6 - Sept-Oct 2004 - p20(2) [501+]

Fragoulis, Tess - *Musings: An Anthology of Greek-Canadian Literature*
  Globe & Mail - August 28 2004 - pD10 [501+]

Fraiman, Susan - *Cool Men and the Second Sex*
  R&R Bk N - v19 - i1 - Feb 2004 - p131(1) [51-500]
  Wom R Bks - v22 - i3 - Dec 2004 - p23(2) [501+]

Fraina, Blake - *King of Cats: A Life in Five Novellas*
  Lam Bk Rpt - v13 - i4-5 - Nov-Dec 2004 - p41(1) [501+]

Fraisse, Luc - *Les Fondements de l'histoire litteraire: de Saint-Rene Taillandier a Lanson*
  FS - v58 - i2 - April 2004 - p297(2) [501+]

Fraley, R. Chris - *How to Conduct Behavioral Research over the Internet: A Beginner's Guide to HTML and CGI/PERL*
  R&R Bk N - v19 - i4 - Nov 2004 - p9(1) [1-50]

Fram, Mark - *Well-Preserved: The Ontario Heritage Foundation's Manual of Principles and Practice for Architectural Conservation, 3rd Ed.*
  E-Streams - June 2004 - pNA [501+]

Frame, J. Davidson - *Managing Projects in Organizations: How to Make the Best Use of Time, Techniques, and People, 3rd Ed.*
  R&R Bk N - v19 - i1 - Feb 2004 - p94(1) [51-500]

Frame, Melissa J. - *Blind Spots: The Communicative Performance of Visual Impairment in Relationships and Social Interaction*
  R&R Bk N - v19 - i3 - August 2004 - p161(1) [501+]

Frame, Ronald - *Time in Carnbeg*
  Spec - v295 - i9181 - July 24 2004 - p37(1) [501+]
  TLS - i5301 - Nov 5 2004 - p24(1) [501+]

Frampton, David - *At Jerusalem's Gate: Poems of Easter*
  c PW - v252 - i7 - Feb 14 2005 - p79(2) [501+]

Francaviglia, Riccardo - *My Great-Great-Great-Great-Grandfather....Was a Warrior! (Illus. by Sgarlata, Margherita)*
  c SLJ - v50 - i10 - Oct 2004 - p113(1) [51-500]

Francaviglia, Richard V. - *Dueling Eagles: Reinterpreting the U.S.-Mexican War, 1846-1848*
  HAHR - v84 - i3 - August 2004 - p564(3) [501+]

France, David - *Our Fathers: The Secret Life of the Catholic Church in an Age of Scandal*
  G&L Rev W - v11 - i5 - Sept-Oct 2004 - p44(2) [501+]
  Lam Bk Rpt - v13 - i1-2 - August-Sept 2004 - p31(2) [501+]

France-Lanord, Hadrien - *Paul Celan et Martin Heidegger: Le sens d'un dialogue*
  TLS - i5296 - Oct 1 2004 - p4-6 [501+]

France, Peter - *Mapping Lives: The Uses of Biography*
  Biomag - v27 - i3 - Summer 2004 - p597(3) [501+]

Frances, Henry - *Whiteout*
  Can Lit - i182 - Autumn 2004 - p138(2) [501+]

Francia, Peter L. - *The Financiers of Congressional Elections: Investors, Ideologues, and Intimates*
  PSQ - v119 - i4 - Winter 2004 - p693(2) [501+]
  R&R Bk N - v19 - i1 - Feb 2004 - pNA [51-500]

Franciosi, Robert J. - *The Rise and Fall of American Public Schools: The Political Economy of Public Education in the Twentieth Century*
R&R Bk N - v19 - i3 - August 2004 - p213(1) [1-50]

Francis, Brian - *Fruit*
y   BL - v100 - i22 - August 2004 - p1898(1) [51-500]
Ent W - i779 - August 20 2004 - p132 [1-50]
Globe & Mail - July 3 2004 - pD14 [501+]
KR - v72 - i13 - July 1 2004 - p594(1) [51-500]
LJ - v129 - i16 - Oct 1 2004 - p68(2) [51-500]
PW - v251 - i28 - July 12 2004 - p45(1) [51-500]

Francis, Diana Pharaoh - *Path of Honor*
y   BL - v101 - i6 - Nov 15 2004 - p571(1) [51-500]

Francis, Dick - *Bonecrack. Audiobook Review*
y   Kliatt - v39 - i2 - March 2005 - p48(2) [51-500]

Francis, Dorothy - *Pier Pressure*
BL - v101 - i9-10 - Jan 1 2005 - p826(1) [1-50]

Francis, H.E. - *I'll Never Leave You: Stories*
KR - v72 - i18 - Sept 15 2004 - p882(2) [51-500]

Francis, Mark - *Urban Open Space: Designing for User Needs*
R&R Bk N - v19 - i1 - Feb 2004 - p249(1) [1-50]
Village Homes: A Community by Design
R&R Bk N - v19 - i1 - Feb 2004 - p249(1) [51-500]

Francis, Matthew - *W.S. Graham: New Collected Poems*
Poet - v185 - i4 - Jan 2005 - p309(11) [501+]

Francis, Richard C. - *Why Men Won't Ask for Directions: The Seductions of Sociobiology*
Choice - v41 - i11-12 - July-August 2004 - p2126(2) [501+]
NH - v113 - i6 - July-August 2004 - p52(4) [501+]
QRB - v79 - i3 - Sept 2004 - p335(2) [501+]
SB - v40 - i5 - Sept-Oct 2004 - p199(1) [51-500]

Francis, Samuel - *James Burnham*
Quad - v48 - i10 - Oct 2004 - p84(3) [501+]

Francis, Tim - *Professional IBM Websphere 5.0 Application Server*
SciTech - v28 - i3 - Sept 2004 - p158(1) [51-500]

Francisco, Ruth - *Good Morning, Darkness*
KR - v72 - i14 - July 15 2004 - p662(1) [51-500]
PW - v251 - i35 - August 30 2004 - p36(1) [501+]

Franck, Cesar - *Sonata No. 1 in A Major for Violin and Piano Op. 13 (1875-6).*
Notes - v61 - i2 - Dec 2004 - p556(6) [501+]

Franck, Hans Goran - *The Barbaric Punishment: Abolishing the Death Penalty*
R&R Bk N - v19 - i4 - Nov 2004 - p148(1) [501+]

Franco, Betsy - *Counting Our Way to the 100th Day! (Illus. by Salerno, Steven)*
c   BL - v100 - i22 - August 2004 - p1947(1) [51-500]
c   CCB-B - v58 - i1 - Sept 2004 - p16(1) [51-500]
c   SLJ - v50 - i7 - July 2004 - p45(1) [51-500]
c   SLJ - v50 - i7 - July 2004 - p93(1) [51-500]
Mathematickles (Illus. by Salerno, Steven)
c   TC Math - v11 - i4 - Nov 2004 - p238(1) [501+]

Franco, Jean - *The Decline and Fall of the Lettered City: Latin America in the Cold War*
Ams - v61 - i2 - Oct 2004 - p325(3) [501+]
Col Lit - v32 - i1 - Wntr 2005 - p196(4) [501+]

Francoeur, Robert T. - *The Continuum Complete International Encyclopedia of Sexuality*
Choice - v42 - i2 - Oct 2004 - p272(1) [501+]

Francois, Charles - *International Encyclopedia of Systems and Cybernetics, 2nd Ed., Vols. 1-2*
SciTech - v28 - i4 - Dec 2004 - p41(1) [51-500]

Francome, Colin - *Abortion in the U.S.A. and the U.K.*
R&R Bk N - v19 - i3 - August 2004 - p150(1) [51-500]

Francome, John - *Inside Track*
BL - v101 - i3 - Oct 1 2004 - p313(1) [51-500]
KR - v72 - i17 - Sept 1 2004 - p838(1) [51-500]
LJ - v129 - i20 - Dec 1 2004 - p95(2) [51-500]
PW - v251 - i39 - Sept 27 2004 - p41(1) [51-500]

Francouer, Robert T. - *The Continuum Complete International Encyclopedia of Sexuality*
R&R Bk N - v19 - i1 - Feb 2004 - p128(1) [51-500]

Franek, Frantisek - *Memory as a Programming Concept in C and C++*
Choice - v41 - i11-12 - July-August 2004 - p2080(1) [501+]

Frangopol, Dan M. - *Life-Cycle Performance of Deteriorating Structures: Assessment, Design, and Management*
SciTech - v28 - i1 - March 2004 - p142(1) [51-500]

Frangoulidis, S. - *Roles and Performances in Apuleius' Metamorphoses*
Class R - v54 - i2 - Nov 2004 - p412(2) [501+]

Franits, Wayne - *Dutch 17th-Century Genre Painting: Its Stylistic and Thematic Evolution*
Lon R Bks - v27 - i2 - Jan 20 2005 - p23(3) [501+]

Frank, Anne - *Anne Frank: The Diary of a Young Girl*
c   RT - v57 - Sept 2003 - p100 [51-500]

Frank, Arthur W. - *The Renewal of Generosity: Illness, Medicine and How to Live*
Globe & Mail - August 14 2004 - pD4 [501+]

Frank, Daniel - *Search Scripture Well: Karaite Exegetes and the Origins of the Jewish Bible Commentary in the Islamic East*
R&R Bk N - v19 - i4 - Nov 2004 - p22(1) [51-500]

Frank, Daniel H. - *The Cambridge Companion to Medieval Jewish Philosophy*
Med R - Sept 2004 - pNA [501+]

Frank, Dorothea Benton - *Shem Creek: A Lowcountry Tale*
PW - v251 - i31 - August 2 2004 - p53(1) [501+]

Frank, E.R. - *Friction*
y   Kliatt - v39 - i1 - Jan 2005 - p12(2) [51-500]
c   PW - v251 - i47 - Nov 22 2004 - p62(1) [501+]

Frank, Elizabeth - *Cheat and Charmer*
BL - v101 - i1 - Sept 1 2004 - p5(1) [51-500]
KR - v72 - i16 - August 15 2004 - p762(1) [501+]
LJ - v129 - i14 - Sept 1 2004 - p40(1) [501+]
LJ - v129 - i14 - Sept 1 2004 - p139(1) [51-500]
NW - Oct 18 2004 - p67 [501+]
NY - v80 - i32 - Oct 25 2004 - p91(1) [51-500]
NYTBR - Nov 14 2004 - p52 [501+]
PW - v251 - i33 - August 16 2004 - p40(2) [51-500]

Frank, Ellen - *The Raw Deal: How Myths and Misinformation about Deficits, Inflation, and Wealth Impoverish America*
Choice - v42 - i3 - Nov 2004 - p523(1) [1-50]
R&R Bk N - v19 - i4 - Nov 2004 - p116(1) [51-500]

Frank, Hillary - *Better than Running at Night*
y   BL - v101 - i5 - Nov 1 2004 - p496(1) [51-500]
I Can't Tell You (Illus. by Frank, Hillary)
y   BL - v101 - i2 - Sept 15 2004 - p232(1) [51-500]
y   CCB-B - v58 - i4 - Dec 2004 - p166(2) [51-500]
HB - v80 - i6 - Nov-Dec 2004 - p707(1) [51-500]
y   Kliatt - v38 - i5 - Sept 2004 - p10(2) [51-500]
KR - v72 - i17 - Sept 1 2004 - p864(1) [51-500]
SLJ - v50 - i12 - Dec 2004 - p145(2) [501+]
PW - v251 - i41 - Oct 11 2004 - p81(2) [51-500]

Frank, Jeffrey - *Bad Publicity*
BW - v34 - i3 - Jan 18 2004 - p3(2) [501+]

Frank, John - *A Chill in the Air: Nature Poems for Fall and Winter*
c   LibMed - v22 - i6 - March 2004 - p70(1) [501+]
The Toughest Cowboy: Or, How the Wild West Was Tamed (Illus. by Pullen, Zachary)
c   BL - v100 - i22 - August 2004 - p1942(1) [51-500]
c   CCB-B - v58 - i2 - Oct 2004 - p72(1) [51-500]
c   KR - v72 - i13 - July 1 2004 - p629(1) [51-500]
c   PW - v251 - i38 - Sept 20 2004 - p62(1) [51-500]
c   SLJ - v50 - i8 - August 2004 - p86(1) [51-500]

Frank, Joseph - *Dostoevsky: The Mantle of the Prophet, 1871-1881*
Sew R - v112 - i2 - Spring 2004 - p304-307 [501+]

Frank, Justin A. - *Bush on the Couch: Inside the Mind of the President*
Globe & Mail - July 10 2004 - pD16 [501+]

Frank, Katherine - *G-Strings and Sympathy: Strip Club Regulars and Male Desire*
JPC - v38 - i3 - Feb 2005 - p593(2) [501+]

Frank, Lawrence - *Victorian Detective Fiction and the Nature of Evidence: The Scientific Investigations of Poe, Dickens, and Doyle*
Isis - v95 - i3 - Sept 2004 - p510(2) [501+]
JouAmCul - v27 - i3 - Sept 2004 - p362(2) [501+]

Frank, Marcie - *Gender, Theatre, and the Origins of Criticism, from Dryden to Manley*
Ren Q - v57 - i3 - Fall 2004 - p1147(3) [501+]

Frank, Peter - *Luc Leestemaker (Illus. by Leestemaker, Luc)*
LJ - v129 - i16 - Oct 1 2004 - p76(2) [51-500]

Frank, Robert G. - *Primary Care Psychology*
Choice - v41 - i7 - March 2004 - p1375(1) [501+]

Frank, Robert H. - *What Price the Moral High Ground? Ethical Dilemmas in Competitive Environments*
Choice - v41 - i11-12 - July-August 2004 - p2088(2) [501+]
TLS - i5305 - Dec 3 2004 - p32(1) [501+]

Frank, Steven - *The Pen Commandments: A Guide for the Beginning Writer*
y   Kliatt - v39 - i1 - Jan 2005 - p27(1) [51-500]

Frank-Stromborg, Marilyn - *Instruments for Clinical Health-Care Research, 3rd Ed.*
E-Streams - August 2004 - pNA [501+]

Frank, Thomas - *What's the Matter with America?: The Resistible Rise of the American Right*
Lon R Bks - v26 - i21 - Nov 4 2004 - p20(1) [501+]
Lon R Bks - v26 - i23 - Dec 2 2004 - p7(3) [501+]
NS - v133 - i4707 - Sept 27 2004 - p70(3) [501+]
NS - v133 - i4716 - Nov 29 2004 - p46(1) [51-500]
What's the Matter with Kansas?: How Conservatives Won the Heart of America
Atl - v295 - i3 - April 2005 - p99(7) [501+]
BW - v34 - i29 - July 18 2004 - p5(1) [501+]
CC - v122 - i5 - March 8 2005 - p42(2) [501+]
Comw - v131 - i18 - Oct 22 2004 - p7(2) [501+]
Dis - v51 - i4 - Fall 2004 - p104(3) [501+]
G&L Rev W - v12 - i2 - March-April 2005 - p40(1) [501+]
NYRB - v51 - i15 - Oct 7 2004 - p8(2) [501+]
Prog - v68 - i11 - Nov 2004 - p44(5) [501+]

Frank, Zephyr L. - *Dutra's World: Wealth and Family in Nineteenth-Century Rio de Janeiro*
Choice - v42 - i6 - Feb 2005 - p1069(1) [51-500]
R&R Bk N - v19 - i4 - Nov 2004 - p89(1) [51-500]

Frankel, Arthur J. - *Case Management: An Introduction to Concepts and Skills, 2nd Ed.*
R&R Bk N - v19 - i1 - Feb 2004 - p136(1) [51-500]

Frankel, Boris - *Caliban's Shore: The Wreck of the Grosvenor and the Strange Fate of Her Survivors*
R&R Bk N - v19 - i4 - Nov 2004 - p52(1) [51-500]

Frankel, Francine R. - *The India-China Relationship: What the United States Needs to Know*
Choice - v42 - i6 - Feb 2005 - p1094(2) [51-500]
R&R Bk N - v19 - i3 - August 2004 - p54(1) [51-500]

Frankel, Gerald S. - *Corrosion Science: A Retrospective and Current Status in Honor of Robert P. Frankenthal*
SciTech - v28 - i3 - Sept 2004 - p139(1) [51-500]

Frankel, Jeffrey A. - *American Economic Policy in the 1990's*
JEL - v42 - i1 - March 2004 - p178(2) [501+]

Frankel, Lois P. - *Nice Girls Don't Get the Corner Office: 101 Unconscious Mistakes Women Make That Sabotage Their Careers*
HR Mag - v49 - i7 - July 2004 - p137(1) [501+]
HR Mag - v50 - i2 - Feb 2005 - pS4(1) [501+]

Frankel, Max - *High Noon in the Cold War: Kennedy, Khrushchev, and the Cuban Missile Crisis*
BW - v34 - i42 - Oct 17 2004 - p5(1) [501+]
KR - v72 - i15 - August 1 2004 - p724(1) [501+]
LJ - v129 - i16 - Oct 1 2004 - p93(2) [51-500]
NL - v87 - i5 - Sept-Oct 2004 - p20(3) [501+]
NYTBR - Nov 28 2004 - p9 [501+]
PW - v251 - i31 - August 2 2004 - p59(1) [501+]

Frankel, Steven A. - *Intricate Engagements: The Collaborative Basis of Therapeutic Change*
SciTech - v28 - i3 - Sept 2004 - p97(1) [1-50]

Frankel, Valerie - *The Girlfriend Curse*
Ent W - i809 - March 4 2005 - p77 [501+]

Frankenberg, Ruth - *Living Spirit, Living Practice: Poetics, Politics, Epistemology*
J Ch St - v46 - i4 - Autumn 2004 - p909(2) [501+]
Wom R Bks - v22 - i2 - Nov 2004 - p22(1) [501+]

Frankenberry, Nancy K. - *Radical Interpretation in Religion*
JAAR - v72 - i3 - Sept 2004 - p780-783 [501+]

Frankenhuyzen, Robbyn Smith Van - *Saving Samantha: A True Story (Illus. by Frankenhuyzen, Gijsbert Van)*
y   BL - v100 - i21 - July 2004 - p1846(1) [1-50]
c   SLJ - v50 - i9 - Sept 2004 - p194(1) [51-500]

Frankenthal, Hans - *The Unwelcome One: Returning Home from Auschwitz*
HNet - Oct 2004 - pNA [501+]

Franklin, Allan - *Are There Really Neutrinos?: An Evidential History*
SciTech - v28 - i1 - March 2004 - p51(1) [51-500]

Franklin, Arden - *Sewing with Fabulous Vintage Fabrics*
LJ - v129 - i20 - Dec 1 2004 - p110(1) [51-500]

Franklin, Benjamin - *The Political Thought of Benjamin Franklin*
R&R Bk N - v19 - i1 - Feb 2004 - p58(1) [51-500]

Franklin, Caroline - *Mary Wollstonecraft: A Literary Life*
TLS - i5297 - Oct 8 2004 - p31(1) [51-500]

Book Review Index 2005 Cumulation FREED • 201

Franklin, David G. - *The Art of Parmigianino*
A Art - v68 - i745 - August 2004 - p74(1) [501+]
Choice - v41 - i11-12 - July-August 2004 - p2034(1) [501+]
Ren Q - v57 - i4 - Winter 2004 - p1389(3) [501+]
Franklin, Eric - *Conditioning for Dance*
R&R Bk N - v19 - i1 - Feb 2004 - p75(1) [1-50]
Franklin, James (b. 1953 -) - *The Science of Conjecture: Evidence and Probability before Pascal*
Isis - v95 - i3 - Sept 2004 - p460(5) [501+]
Franklin, James L. - *Pompeis difficile est: Studies in the Political Life of Imperial Pompeii*
Class R - v53 - i2 - Nov 2003 - p419-421 [501+]
Franklin, John Hope - *From Slavery to Freedom: A History of African Americans*
Black Iss - v7 - i1 - Jan-Feb 2005 - p28(2) [501+]
Franklin, Kristine L. - *Grape Thief*
LibMed - v22 - i5 - Feb 2004 - p69(1) [501+]
Franklin, Mark N. - *Voter Turnout and the Dynamics of Electoral Competition in Established Democracies since 1945*
CR - v286 - i1668 - Jan 2005 - p58(1) [51-500]
Franklin, Paul M. - *Our Washington, D.C.*
R&R Bk N - v19 - i4 - Nov 2004 - p65(1) [1-50]
Franklin, Sarah - *Remaking Life and Death: Toward an Anthropology of the Biosciences*
SciTech - v28 - i4 - Dec 2004 - p68(1) [51-500]
Franklin, Steven E. - *Remote Sensing for Sustainable Forest Management*
GJ - v170 - i3 - Sept 2004 - p281(1) [501+]
Franklin's Christmas: A Sticker Activity Book
c CBRA - Annual 2003 - p552(1) [51-500]
Franks, Norman - *Dog-Fight: Aerial Tactics of the Aces of World War I*
APJ - v18 - i3 - Fall 2004 - p124(1) [501+]
Franks, Tommy - *American Soldier*
BW - v34 - i33 - August 15 2004 - p1(3) [501+]
Globe & Mail - Oct 9 2004 - pD20 [501+]
NYTBR - Sept 26 2004 - p15 [501+]
Franses, Philip Hans - *A Concise Introduction to Econometrics: An Intuitive Guide*
JEL - v42 - i1 - March 2004 - p234(1) [501+]
Franson, David - *Dark Side of Game Texturing*
SciTech - v28 - i3 - Sept 2004 - p136(1) [51-500]
Frantis, Wayne - *Dutch Seventeenth-Century Genre Paintings: Its Stylistic and Thematic Evolution*
Choice - v42 - i6 - Feb 2005 - p1013(1) [51-500]
Frantz, Susanne K. - *The Other Side of the Looking Glass: The Glass Body and Its Metaphors*
Am Craft - v64 - i2 - April-May 2004 - p30(1) [501+]
Frantzen, Allen J. - *Bloody Good: Chivalry, Sacrifice, and the Great War*
J Mil H - v68 - i3 - July 2004 - p977-978 [501+]
Med R - June 2004 - pNA [501+]
Frantzich, Stephen E. - *Citizen Democracy: Political Activists in a Cynical Age, 2nd Ed.*
R&R Bk N - v19 - i3 - August 2004 - p179(1) [501+]
Franz, Stephen J. - *401(k) Answer Book, 2004 Ed.*
R&R Bk N - v19 - i1 - Feb 2004 - pNA [51-500]
Franz, Steven J. - *401(k) Answer Book*
HR Mag - v49 - i7 - July 2004 - pS6(1) [51-500]
Franzen, Jonathan - *How To Be Alone: Essays*
Dal R - v84 - i1 - Spring 2004 - p182-183 [501+]
Fraschetti, Augusto - *Roman Women*
Wom HR - v13 - i2 - Summer 2004 - p317-319 [501+]
Frasconi, Paolo - *Artificial Intelligence and Heuristic Methods in Bioinformatics: Proceedings*
SciTech - v28 - i4 - Dec 2004 - p62(1) [51-500]
Fraser, Antonia - *The Gunpowder Plot: Terror and Faith in 1605 (Read by Gallimore, Patricia). Audiobook Review*
LJ - v129 - i12 - July 2004 - p125(1) [51-500]
Fraser, Claire M. - *Microbial Genomes*
SciTech - v28 - i3 - Sept 2004 - p59(1) [1-50]
Fraser, Elisabeth A. - *Delacroix, Art, and Patrimony in Post-Revolutionary France*
Choice - v42 - i4 - Dec 2004 - p649(2) [1-50]
Fraser, Flora - *Princesses: The Six Daughters of George III*
Globe & Mail - Dec 24 2004 - pD13 [1-50]
Globe & Mail - Jan 15 2005 - pD14 [1-50]
KR - v73 - i4 - Feb 15 2005 - p210(2) [51-500]
Spec - v296 - i9190 - Sept 25 2004 - p60(1) [501+]
TLS - i5305 - Dec 3 2004 - p26(1) [501+]
Fraser, Hilary - *Gender and the Victorian Periodical*
TLS - i5284 - July 9 2004 - p28(1) [501+]
Fraser, Jennifer Margaret - *Rite of Passage in the Narratives of Dante and Joyce*
ELT - v47 - i3 - Summer 2004 - p360(4) [501+]
Fraser, John - *Close Up: An Actor Telling Tales*
CR - v286 - i1668 - Jan 2005 - p64(1) [51-500]
Spec - v296 - i9197 - Nov 13 2004 - p46(1) [501+]
Fraser, Lyndon - *Shifting Centres: Women and Migration in New Zealand History*
AHS - v35 - i123 - April 2004 - p173-174 [501+]
Fraser, Mark W. - *Risk and Resilience in Childhood: An Ecological Perspective, 2nd Ed.*
R&R Bk N - v19 - i3 - August 2004 - p160(1) [51-500]
Fraser, Matthew - *Weapons of Mass Distraction: Soft Power and American Empire*
CBRA - Annual 2003 - p375(2) [501+]
KR - v72 - i24 - Dec 15 2004 - p1180(1) [501+]
LJ - v130 - i2 - Feb 1 2005 - p101(2) [51-500]
Fraser, Nancy - *Redistribution or Recognition? A Political-Philosophical Exchange*
Arena - i73 - Oct-Nov 2004 - p53(2) [501+]
CS - v33 - i5 - Sept 2004 - p623-623 [501+]
Ethics - v115 - i2 - Jan 2005 - p397(6) [501+]
Fraser, P.M. - *A Lexicon of Greek Personal Names, Volume IIIB*
Class R - v54 - i2 - Nov 2004 - p475(2) [501+]
Fraser, Rebecca - *The Story of Britain: From the Romans to the Present: A Narrative History*
BL - v101 - i9-10 - Jan 1 2005 - p808(1) [51-500]
KR - v72 - i23 - Dec 1 2004 - p1130(1) [501+]
LJ - v130 - i1 - Jan 1 2005 - p128(1) [51-500]
PW - v252 - i1 - Jan 3 2005 - p46(1) [51-500]
Fraser, Russell - *Singing Masters: Poets in English, 1500 to the Present*
Sew R - v111 - i3 - Summer 2003 - pLXIV-LXVI [501+]
Fraser, Sandy - *Doing Research with Children and Young People*
R&R Bk N - v19 - i2 - May 2004 - p134 [51-500]
Fraser, Sarah E. - *Performing the Visual: The Practice of Buddhist Wall Painting in China and Central Asia, 618-960*
Choice - v42 - i1 - Sept 2004 - p89(1) [501+]
Fraser, Simon - *Bill Brandt: A Life*
CHE - v50 - i29 - March 26 2004 - pA18-A18 [501+]
Fraser, Steve - *Every Man a Speculator: A History of Wall Street in American Life*
BL - v101 - i8 - Dec 15 2004 - p696(1) [51-500]
KR - v72 - i23 - Dec 1 2004 - p1130(1) [501+]
LJ - v130 - i4 - March 1 2005 - p96(1) [51-500]
NYTBR - March 13 2005 - p14 [501+]
PW - v252 - i1 - Jan 3 2005 - p46(1) [51-500]
Fraser, Tom - *Designer's Color Manual*
Bwatch - Oct 2004 - pNA [51-500]
Frasier, Debra - *The Incredible Water Show*
c PW - v251 - i38 - Sept 20 2004 - p64(2) [51-500]
c KR - v72 - i15 - August 1 2004 - p741(1) [51-500]
c SLJ - v50 - i12 - Dec 2004 - p106(2) [501+]
Frater, Alexander - *Tales from the Torrid Zone: Travels in the Deep Tropics*
TLS - i5285 - July 16 2004 - p6(1) [501+]
Fratianni, Michele - *Sustainable Global Growth and Development: G7 and IMF Governance*
R&R Bk N - v19 - i1 - Feb 2004 - p116(1) [51-500]
Fratzke, Jenifer Lee - *Alaska's Women Pilots: Contemporary Portraits*
R&R Bk N - v19 - i4 - Nov 2004 - p248(1) [501+]
Fraue, Elizabeth - *Writing the Wrongs: Eva Valesh and the Rise of Labor Journalism*
WHQ - v35 - i1 - Spring 2004 - p100-101 [501+]
Fraught, C. Brad - *The Oxford Movement: A Thematic History of the Tractarians and Their Times*
VS - v46 - i3 - Spring 2004 - p526(4) [501+]
Fraustino, Lisa Rowe - *I Walk In Dread: The Diary of Deliverance Trembley, Witness to the Salem Witch Trials*
y CH Bwatch - Feb 2005 - pNA [51-500]
Frawley, Maria H. - *Invalidism and Identity in Nineteenth-Century Britain*
TLS - i5300 - Oct 29 2004 - p27(1) [501+]
Frawley, Patsie - *Living Safer Sexual Lives--A Training & Resource Pack for People with Learning Disabilities & Those Who Support Them*
TES - v0 - i4586 - June 4 2004 - pss6(1) [501+]
Frayn, Michael - *The Copenhagen Papers: An Intrigue*
Physics T - v42 - i4 - April 2004 - p256-256 [501+]
Frayne, Douglas R. - *Ur III Period*
JNES - v63 - i3 - July 2004 - p207(4) [501+]
Frazer, Margaret - *The Widow's Tale*
KR - v72 - i24 - Dec 15 2004 - p1167(1) [501+]
PW - v251 - i51 - Dec 20 2004 - p40(1) [51-500]
Frazier, Craig - *Stanley Goes for a Drive (Illus. by Frazier, Craig)*
c KR - v72 - i13 - July 1 2004 - p629(1) [51-500]
c PW - v251 - i37 - Sept 13 2004 - p77(1) [501+]
c SLJ - v50 - i9 - Sept 2004 - p160(1) [51-500]
Frazier, Gregory W. - *Riding the World: The Biker's Road Map for a Seven-Continent Adventure*
LJ - v130 - i4 - March 1 2005 - p102(1) [51-500]
Frazier, James Bruce - *What I Learned on the Ranch and Other Stories from a West Texas Childhood*
Bwatch - v26 - i7 - July 2004 - p9(1) [51-500]
Frazier, John W. - *Race and Place: Equity Issues in Urban America*
CS - v33 - i4 - July 2004 - p427(3) [501+]
Freadman, Anne - *The Machinery of Talk: Charles Peirce and the Sign Hypothesis*
R&R Bk N - v19 - i3 - August 2004 - p5(1) [1-50]
Freake, Ross - *Out of the Ashes*
CG - v124 - i2 - March-April 2004 - p97(1) [501+]
Stories from the Firestorm
Globe & Mail - Dec 24 2004 - pD13 [1-50]
Fredd, Carla - *A Valentine's Kiss*
LJ - v130 - i1 - Jan 1 2005 - p91(1) [51-500]
Frederick, Heather Vogel - *The Education of Patience Goodspeed*
y KR - v72 - i15 - August 1 2004 - p741(1) [51-500]
c SLJ - v50 - i10 - Oct 2004 - p163(1) [51-500]
Frederick, Marla F. - *Between Sundays: Black Women and Everyday Struggles of Faith*
Choice - v42 - i1 - Sept 2004 - p119(2) [501+]
Fredericks, Anthony D. - *Around One Cactus: Owls, Bats, and Leaping Rats (Illus. by DiRubbio, Jennifer)*
c LibMed - v22 - i6 - March 2004 - p83(1) [501+]
c RT - v58 - i3 - Nov 2004 - p286(1) [51-500]
Exploring the Oceans: Science Activities for Kids (Illus. by Shea, Shawn)
c SB - v40 - i5 - Sept-Oct 2004 - p193(1) [51-500]
Fredericks, Mariah - *Head Games*
y BL - v101 - i2 - Sept 15 2004 - p232(1) [51-500]
y CCB-B - v58 - i3 - Nov 2004 - p119(2) [501+]
y HB - v80 - i5 - Sept-Oct 2004 - p581(1) [51-500]
y KR - v72 - i15 - August 1 2004 - p741(1) [51-500]
y PW - v251 - i38 - Sept 20 2004 - p63(1) [51-500]
y SLJ - v50 - i10 - Oct 2004 - p164(1) [51-500]
The Smart Girl's Guide to Tarot
LJ - v129 - i16 - Oct 1 2004 - p98(1) [51-500]
The True Meaning of Cleavage
Kliatt - v38 - i4 - July 2004 - p17(1) [501+]
Frederiks, Martha - *Towards an Intercultural Theology: Essays in Honour of Jan A.B. Jongeneel*
y IBMR - v28 - i3 - July 2004 - p142(1) [501+]
Frederiks, Martha T. - *We Have Toiled All Night: Christianity in the Gambia, 1456-2000*
IBMR - v29 - i1 - Jan 2005 - p44(1) [501+]
Frederiksen, Paula - *Jesus, Judaism and Christian Anti-Judaism: Reading the New Testament After the Holocaust*
TT - v61 - i1 - April 2004 - p110-114 [501+]
Fredman, Myer - *The Drama of Opera: Exotic and Irrational Entertainment*
R&R Bk N - v19 - i2 - May 2004 - p192(1) [51-500]
Choice - v41 - i11-12 - July-August 2004 - p2054(1) [501+]
Fredrick, David - *The Roman Gaze: Vision, Power, and the Body*
AHR - v109 - i4 - Oct 2004 - p1288-1289 [501+]
AJP - v125 - i3 - Fall 2004 - p463-465 [501+]
Clio - v33 - i4 - Summer 2004 - p457(6) [501+]
Fredrickson, George M. - *Racism: A Short History*
y CH Bwatch - v14 - i7 - July 2004 - p5(1) [51-500]
Fredrickson, Rebecca - *Secret Envy of the Unsaved*
CBRA - Annual 2003 - p216(1) [51-500]
Fredriksen, John C. - *Biographical Dictionary of Modern World Leaders: 1992 to the Present*
y LibMed - v22 - i6 - March 2004 - p75(1) [501+]
Biographical Dictionary of Modern World Leaders
VOYA - v27 - i5 - Dec 2004 - p422(1) [51-500]
Fredrikson, Eric - *How to Avoid Falling: A Guide for Active Aging and Independence*
LJ - v129 - i16 - Oct 1 2004 - p103(2) [51-500]
Freeborn, Richard - *Dostoevsky*
Bwatch - v26 - i9 - Sept 2004 - p1(1) [51-500]
LJ - v129 - i12 - July 2004 - p82(1) [51-500]
Freed, Les - *PC Magazine Guide to Home Networking*
LJ - v129 - i12 - July 2004 - p112(1) [51-500]
Freed, Lynn - *The Curse of the Appropriate Man*
BL - v100 - i22 - August 2004 - p1898(1) [51-500]
KR - v72 - i15 - August 1 2004 - p704(1) [501+]
NYTBR - Oct 3 2004 - p38 [501+]
PW - v251 - i32 - August 9 2004 - p228(2) [51-500]

Freedberg, David - *The Eye of the Lynx: Galileo, His Friends, and the Beginnings of Modern Natural History*
Ren Q - v57 - i3 - Fall 2004 - p1104(4) [501+]
T&C - v45 - i1 - Jan 2004 - p171(3) [501+]

Freedman, Benedict - *Kathy Little Bird*
BL - v101 - i8 - Dec 15 2004 - p708(1) [51-500]

Freedman, Claire - *Goose on the Loose*
c Sch Lib - v52 - i4 - Winter 2004 - p186(1) [51-500]
Oops-a-Daisy!
c Sch Lib - v52 - i3 - Autumn 2004 - p131(1) [501+]

Freedman, Estelle B. - *No Turning Back: The History of Feminism and the Future of Women*
NWSA Jnl - v16 - i3 - Fall 2004 - p226(4) [501+]
Wom HR - v13 - i2 - Summer 2004 - p303-310 [501+]

Freedman, Jeri - *Sid Fleischman*
y SLJ - v50 - i9 - Sept 2004 - p226(1) [51-500]

Freedman, Lawrence - *Deterrence*
For Aff - v83 - i5 - Sept-Oct 2004 - p164 [501+]
Pers PS - v34 - i1 - Wntr 2005 - p62(2) [501+]

Freedman, Luba - *The Revival of the Olympian Gods in Renaissance Art*
Ren Q - v57 - i4 - Winter 2004 - p1385(3) [501+]

Freedman, Russell - *In Defense of Liberty: The Story of America's Bill of Rights*
RT - v58 - i3 - Nov 2004 - p291(1) [501+]
Martha Graham: A Dancer's Life
y SLJ - v50 - i11 - Nov 2004 - p67(1) [51-500]
The Voice That Challenged a Nation: Marian Anderson and the Struggle for Equal Rights
c CCB-B - v57 - i11 - July-August 2004 - p464(1) [501+]
HB - v81 - i1 - Jan-Feb 2005 - p17(1) [51-500]
c SLJ - v50 - i7 - July 2004 - p120(1) [51-500]
y SLJ - v50 - i10 - Oct 2004 - p67(1) [51-500]
y SLJ - v50 - i12 - Dec 2004 - p60(1) [501+]
y VOYA - v27 - i3 - August 2004 - p237(1) [1-50]

Freedman, Samuel G. - *Who She Was: My Search for My Mother's Life*
KR - v73 - i2 - Jan 15 2005 - p99(1) [501+]
LJ - v129 - i20 - Dec 1 2004 - p92(1) [51-500]
PW - v252 - i10 - March 7 2005 - p60(1) [51-500]

Freeland, James J. - *Fundamentals of Federal Income Taxation: Cases and Materials, 13th Ed.*
R&R Bk N - v19 - i4 - Nov 2004 - p171(1) [501+]

Freeley, Austin J. - *Argumentation and Debate: Critical Thinking for Reasoned Decision Making, 11th Ed.*
R&R Bk N - v19 - i4 - Nov 2004 - p227(1) [501+]

Freely, John - *Byzantine Monuments of Istanbul*
Choice - v42 - i2 - Oct 2004 - p280(2) [501+]
Jem Sultan: The Adventures of a Captive Turkish Prince in Renaissance Europe
TLS - i5293 - Sept 10 2004 - p6(1) [501+]
Strolling through Athens: Fourteen Unforgettable Walks through Europe's Oldest City
TLS - i5284 - July 9 2004 - p7(1) [501+]

Freely, Maureen - *Snow*
NY - v80 - i24 - August 30 2004 - p098 [501+]

Freeman, Adam - *Programming .NET Security*
SciTech - v28 - i4 - Dec 2004 - p153(1) [51-500]

Freeman, Alan - *The New Value Controversy and the Foundations of Economics*
R&R Bk N - v19 - i3 - August 2004 - p94(1) [51-500]

Freeman, Arthur - *Clinical Applications of Cognitive Therapy, 2nd Ed.*
SciTech - v28 - i4 - Dec 2004 - p97(1) [51-500]
Cognition and Psychotherapy, 2nd Ed.
SciTech - v28 - i4 - Dec 2004 - p97(1) [51-500]
John Payne Collier: Scholarship and Forgery in the Nineteenth Century
Choice - v42 - i6 - Feb 2005 - p1022(1) [51-500]
Lon R Bks - v26 - i24 - Dec 16 2004 - p17(2) [501+]
William Shakespeare: Comedies, Histories and Tragedies, First Folio, London, 1623, Folger Shakespeare Library
Lib & Cul - v39 - i3 - Summer 2004 - p328(2) [501+]

Freeman, Brian - *Ultimate Guide to Choosing a Medical Specialty*
SciTech - v28 - i1 - March 2004 - p77(1) [51-500]

Freeman, Charles - *The Closing of the Western Mind: The Rise of Faith and the Fall of Reason*
World&I - v19 - i2 - Feb 2004 - p220 [501+]
The Horses of St. Mark's: A Story of Triumph in Byzantium, Paris and Venice
CR - v285 - i1667 - Dec 2004 - p373(2) [501+]

Freeman, Dena - *Initiating Change in Highland Ethiopia: Causes and Consequences of Cultural Transformation*
IJAHS - v37 - i2 - Spring 2004 - p376-378 [501+]

Freeman, James M. - *Voices from the Camps: Vietnamese Children Seeking Asylum*
CS - v33 - i5 - Sept 2004 - p623-623 [501+]
PHR - v73 - i3 - August 2004 - p521(522) [501+]

Freeman, Jo - *At Berkeley in the Sixties: The Education of an Activist, 1961-1965*
Choice - v41 - i11-12 - July-August 2004 - p2107(1) [501+]
HNet - Sept 2004 - pNA [501+]
JAH - v91 - i3 - Dec 2004 - p1089(2) [501+]
A Room at a Time: How Women Entered Party Politics
Signs - v30 - i2 - Wntr 2005 - p1677(6) [501+]

Freeman, John - *Tracing the Footprints: Documenting the Process of Performance*
R&R Bk N - v19 - i1 - Feb 2004 - p223(1) [51-500]

Freeman, Lisa A. - *Character's Theatre: Genre and Identity on the Eighteenth-Century English Stage*
Critm - v46 - i2 - Spring 2004 - p305(5) [501+]

Freeman, Lorna - *Covenants*
y Kliatt - v38 - i5 - Sept 2004 - p28(2) [51-500]

Freeman, Michael - *Cambodia*
TimHES - v0 - i1648 - July 9 2004 - p30(1) [501+]
Space: Japanese Design Solutions for Compact Living
R&R Bk N - v19 - i4 - Nov 2004 - p203(1) [501+]
Victorians and the Prehistoric: Tracks to a Lost World
Choice - v42 - i6 - Feb 2005 - p1044(1) [51-500]
Lon R Bks - v26 - i21 - Nov 4 2004 - p12(1) [1-50]
New Sci - v184 - i2472 - Nov 6 2004 - p53(1) [51-500]

Freeman, Michael (b. 1945 -) - *Digital Photography Expert: Nature and Landscape Photography*
PetPho - v33 - i10 - Feb 2005 - p18(1) [51-500]

Freeman, Michael (b. 1973 -) - *Freedom and Security and the Consequences for Democracies Using Emergency Powers to Fight Terror*
Choice - v42 - i3 - Nov 2004 - p557(1) [1-50]

Freeman, Michael D.A. - *Children's Rights*
R&R Bk N - v19 - i3 - August 2004 - p190(1) [501+]

Freeman, Paul - *Bondi Classic*
Advocate - August 17 2004 - p82(4) [51-500]

Freeman, Philip - *St. Patrick of Ireland: A Biography*
CHR - v90 - i4 - Oct 2004 - p741(2) [501+]

Freeman, R. Edward - *Business, Science and Ethics*
R&R Bk N - v19 - i3 - August 2004 - p126(1) [51-500]

Freeman, Roger L. - *Telecommunication System Engineering, 4th Ed.*
SciTech - v28 - i3 - Sept 2004 - p154(1) [51-500]

Freeman, Stephen J. - *Grief and Loss: Understanding the Journey*
R&R Bk N - v19 - i3 - August 2004 - p9(1) [1-50]

Freeman, Tor - *Hooray, I'm Five Today! (Illus. by Freeman, Tor)*
c KR - v72 - i14 - July 15 2004 - p684(1) [51-500]
c PW - v251 - i29 - July 19 2004 - p159(1) [51-500]
c SLJ - v50 - i10 - Oct 2004 - p113(1) [51-500]

Freeman, Victoria - *Distant Relations: How My Ancestors Colonized North America*
AHR - v109 - i4 - Oct 2004 - p1216-1216 [501+]

Freemantle, Brian - *Dead End*
BL - v101 - i8 - Dec 15 2004 - p711(1) [51-500]
KR - v73 - i3 - Feb 1 2005 - p136(1) [501+]

Freer, Echo - *Blaggers*
y Sch Lib - v52 - i3 - Autumn 2004 - p158(1) [51-500]

Frees, Edward W. - *Longitudinal and Panel Data: Analysis and Applications in the Social Sciences*
R&R Bk N - v19 - i4 - Nov 2004 - p83(1) [51-500]

Freese, Barbara - *Coal: A Human History (Read by Frasier, Shelly). Audiobook Review*
y Kliatt - v38 - i5 - Sept 2004 - p67(2) [51-500]
Coal: A Human History
Lon R Bks - v27 - i1 - Jan 6 2005 - p12(1) [501+]
SciTech - v28 - i1 - March 2004 - p171(1) [51-500]

Freese, Peter - *The Holodeck in the Garden: Science and Technology in Contemporary American Fiction*
R&R Bk N - v19 - i4 - Nov 2004 - p240(1) [501+]

Freethy, Barbara - *All She Ever Wanted*
PW - v251 - i46 - Nov 15 2004 - p46(1) [51-500]

Fregoso, Rosa Linda - *Mexicana Encounters: The Making of Social Identities on the Borderlands*
Choice - v41 - i11-12 - July-August 2004 - p2128(2) [501+]

Frei, Pierre - *Onkel Toms Hutte, Berlin*
WLT - v79 - i1 - Jan-April 2005 - p99(2) [501+]

Frei, Terry - *Horns, Hogs, and Nixon Coming: Texas Vs. Arkansas in Dixie's Last Stand*
SHQ - v108 - i1 - July 2004 - p127-128 [501+]

Freiberg, H. Jerome - *Universal Teaching Strategies, 4th ed.*
R&R Bk N - v19 - i4 - Nov 2004 - p178(1) [501+]

Freiberg, Jackie - *Guts!*
HR Mag - v49 - i7 - July 2004 - p137(2) [501+]

Freire, Mila - *Enhancing Urban Management in East Asia*
R&R Bk N - v19 - i4 - Nov 2004 - p158(1) [501+]

Freise, Dorothea - *Geistliche Spiele in der Stadt des ausgehenden Mittelalters: Frankfurt, Friedberg, Alsfeld*
HNet - Oct 2004 - pNA [501+]

Freise, Matthias - *Aleksander Wot und "Sein" Jahrhundert*
Slav R - v63 - i3 - Fall 2004 - p630-631 [501+]

Freitag, Ulrike - *Indian Ocean Migrants and State Formation in Hadhramaut: Reforming the Homeland*
R&R Bk N - v19 - i1 - Feb 2004 - pNA [501+]

Freitas, Donna - *Becoming a Goddess of Inner Poise: Spirituality for the Bridget Jones in All of Us*
PW - v251 - i37 - Sept 13 2004 - p75(1) [501+]

Freitas, Gary - *War Movies: The Bell and Blade Guide to Classic War Videos*
R&R Bk N - v19 - i1 - Feb 2004 - p209(1) [51-500]

Freivalds, Andris - *Biomechanics of the Upper Limbs: Mechanics, Modeling and Musculoskeletal Injuries*
SciTech - v28 - i4 - Dec 2004 - p108(1) [51-500]

Fremon, David K. - *The Jim Crow Laws and Racism in American History*
y SLJ - v50 - i10 - Oct 2004 - p67(1) [51-500]

Fremont-Barnes, Gregory - *The Boer War, 1899-1902*
HNet - Sept 2004 - pNA [501+]

French, David - *The British General Staff: Reform and Innovation, c. 1890-1929*
Albion - v36 - i2 - Summer 2004 - p338(2) [501+]

French, Fiona - *Bethlehem*
c CI - v12 - i11 - Dec 2004 - p23(1) [501+]
Easter (Illus. by French, Fiona)
c TES - v0 - i4576 - March 26 2004 - pssss18(2) [501+]
Paradise (Illus. by French, Fiona)
c TES - v0 - i4576 - March 26 2004 - pssss18(2) [501+]

French, Howard W. - *A Continent for the Taking: The Tragedy and Hope of Africa*
BooChiTr - May 16 2004 - p1(2) [501+]
Bwatch - v26 - i8 - August 2004 - p11(1) [51-500]
NYRB - v51 - i16 - Oct 21 2004 - p37(3) [501+]

French, Jackie - *Pete the Sheep (Illus. by Whatley, Bruce)*
c Magpies - v19 - i5 - Nov 2004 - p28(1) [501+]

French, Laurence Armand - *Native American Justice*
Choice - v41 - i7 - March 2004 - p1372(1) [501+]
R&R Bk N - v19 - i1 - Feb 2004 - pNA [51-500]

French, Marilyn - *From Eve to Dawn: A History of Women, Vol. 1*
TimHES - v0 - i1679 - Feb 18 2005 - p28(1) [501+]
From Eve to Dawn: A History of Women, Vol. 2
TimHES - v0 - i1679 - Feb 18 2005 - p28(1) [501+]
From Eve to Dawn: A History of Women, Vol. 3
TimHES - v0 - i1679 - Feb 18 2005 - p28(1) [501+]

French, Nicci - *Secret Smile (Read by Flosnik, Anne). Audiobook Review*
y Kliatt - v39 - i2 - March 2005 - p56(1) [51-500]
Secret Smile
BIC - v33 - i8 - Nov 2004 - p16(3) [501+]
NYTBR - July 11 2004 - p17 [501+]

French, Peter A. - *Ethics and College Sports: Ethics, Sports, and the University*
Choice - v42 - i7 - March 2005 - p1265(1) [51-500]
R&R Bk N - v19 - i4 - Nov 2004 - p80(1) [51-500]

French, Roger - *Medicine Before Science: The Rational and Learned Doctor from the Middle Ages to the Enlightenment*
Med R - Dec 2004 - pNA [501+]
Medicine Before Science: The Rational and Learned Doctors from the Middle Ages to the Enlightenment
AHR - v109 - i2 - April 2004 - p594(2) [501+]

French, Scot - *The Rebellious Slave: Nat Turner in American Memory*
Choice - v42 - i2 - Oct 2004 - p354(1) [51-500]
VQR - v80 - i3 - Summer 2004 - p254(2) [501+]

French, Simon - *Where in the World (Read by Olsen, Dennis). Audiobook Review*
y Magpies - v19 - i5 - Nov 2004 - p43(1) [501+]

French, Vivian - *I Love You, Grandpa (Illus. by Kubick, Dana)*
  c BL - v101 - i5 - Nov 1 2004 - p488(2) [51-500]
      KR - v72 - i17 - Sept 1 2004 - p864(1) [51-500]
  c SLJ - v50 - i10 - Oct 2004 - p113(1) [51-500]
Mrs. Hippo's Pizza Parlor (Illus. by Scruton, Clive)
  c BL - v101 - i8 - Dec 15 2004 - p746(1) [1-50]
T. Rex (Illus. by Bartlett, Alison)
  c BL - v101 - i7 - Dec 1 2004 - p672(1) [51-500]
  c CCB-B - v58 - i4 - Dec 2004 - p167(1) [51-500]
  c HB - v80 - i6 - Nov-Dec 2004 - p726(1) [501+]
  c KR - v72 - i20 - Oct 15 2004 - p1005(1) [51-500]
  c PW - v251 - i48 - Nov 29 2004 - p39(2) [51-500]
  c SLJ - v50 - i12 - Dec 2004 - p108(1) [501+]
French, Wendy - *Going Coastal*
    BL - v101 - i9-10 - Jan 1 2005 - p814(1) [1-50]
Frenette, Christiane - *Whole Night Through*
    BIC - v33 - i7 - Oct 2004 - p6(1) [501+]
Frenkel, Edward - *Vertex Algebras and Algebraic Curves, 2nd Ed.*
    SciTech - v28 - i4 - Dec 2004 - p39(1) [51-500]
Fresan, Rodrigo - *Jardines de Kensington*
    TLS - i5292 - Sept 3 2004 - p31(1) [501+]
Fresch, Mary Jo - *The Spelling List and Word Study Resource Book: Organized Spelling Lists, Greek and Latin Roots, Word Histories, and Other Resources for Dynamic Spelling and Vocabulary Instruction*
    SLJ - v50 - i10 - Oct 2004 - pS72(1) [51-500]
Freschet, Gina - *Up and at 'Em with Winnie and Ernst (Illus. by Freschet, Gina)*
  c KR - v73 - i5 - March 1 2005 - p286(1) [51-500]
Frese, Pamela R. - *Anthropology and the United States Military: Coming of Age in the Twenty-First Century*
    R&R Bk N - v19 - i1 - Feb 2004 - p255(1) [51-500]
Fresnais, Jocelyne - *La protection du patrimoine en Republique populaire de Chine, 1949-1999*
    Ch Rev Int - v10 - i2 - Fall 2003 - p385(5) [501+]
Fresonke, Kris - *Lewis and Clark: Legacies, Memories, and New Perspectives*
    Choice - v42 - i2 - Oct 2004 - p357(1) [51-500]
West of Emerson: The Design of Manifest Destiny
    J Am St - v38 - i1 - April 2004 - p142-143 [501+]
    WHQ - v35 - i2 - Summer 2004 - p227-228 [501+]
Fretes-Cibils, Vicente - *Ecuador: An Economic and Social Agenda in the New Millennium*
    JEL - v41 - i4 - Dec 2003 - p1423(2) [501+]
Fretwell, Sheila S. - *Abstracts of the Cumberland County Virginia, Court Order Books from 26 July, 1762 to 24 July 1764*
    EFHM - v58 - i2 - March-April 2004 - p91(1) [51-500]
Freud, S.A. - *Caged*
  y Magpies - v19 - i5 - Nov 2004 - p34(1) [501+]
Freud, Sigmund - *Studies in Hysteria*
    SciTech - v28 - i4 - Dec 2004 - p99(1) [51-500]
Freudenberger, Herman - *Lost Momentum: Austrian Economic Development, 1750s-1830s*
    BHR - v78 - i2 - Summer 2004 - p354(3) [501+]
Freudenberger, Nell - *Lucky Girls: Stories*
    NYTBR - Sept 26 2004 - p28 [501+]
Freudenburg, K. - *Satires of Rome: Threatening Poses from Lucilius to Juvenal*
    Class R - v54 - i1 - May 2004 - p106(2) [501+]
Freudenheim, Ellen - *Looking Forward: An Optimist's Guide to Retirement*
    BL - v101 - i8 - Dec 15 2004 - p695(2) [51-500]
    LJ - v130 - i1 - Jan 1 2005 - p134(1) [51-500]
Freudenthal, Gideon - *Salomon Maimon: Rational Dogmatist, Empirical Skeptic: Critical Assessments*
    R&R Bk N - v19 - i1 - Feb 2004 - p4(1) [51-500]
Freund, L.B. - *Thin Film Materials*
    TimHES - v0 - i1681 - March 4 2005 - p30(1) [501+]
Freund, Wolfgang - *Looking into HAMAS and other Constituents of the Palestinian-Israeli Confrontation*
    R&R Bk N - v19 - i1 - Feb 2004 - p43(1) [51-500]
Freundel, Barry - *Contemporary Orthodox Judaism's Response to Modernity*
    R&R Bk N - v19 - i3 - August 2004 - p16(1) [1-50]
Freundlieb, Dieter - *Critical Theory after Habermas*
    R&R Bk N - v19 - i3 - August 2004 - pS141(1) [51-500]
Frew, Andrew J. - *Information and Communication Technologies in Tourism 2003: Proceedings of the International Conference in Helsinki, Finland 2003*
    JEL - v42 - i1 - March 2004 - p291(1) [501+]
Frew, Katherine - *Plumber*
  c SLJ - v50 - i7 - July 2004 - p120(2) [51-500]

Frey, Bruno S. - *Inspiring Economics: Human Motivation in Political Economy*
    S&S - v68 - i1 - Spring 2004 - p113-115 [501+]
Frey, Cecelia - *Prisoner of Cage Farm*
    CBRA - Annual 2003 - p163(2) [51-500]
Frey, Hugo - *Louis Malle*
    TLS - i5296 - Oct 1 2004 - p31(1) [51-500]
Frey, James - *A Million Little Pieces*
    NYTBR - Feb 27 2005 - p22 [501+]
Frey, Marc - *The Transformation of Southeast Asia: International Perspectives on Decolonization*
    Pac A - v77 - i3 - Fall 2004 - p606(2) [501+]
Frey, Robert S. - *The Genocidal Temptation: Auschwitz, Hiroshima, Rwanda, and Beyond*
    R&R Bk N - v19 - i3 - August 2004 - p164(1) [501+]
Frey, Stephen - *The Chairman (Read by Singer, Eric). Audiobook Review*
    KR - v73 - i5 - March 1 2005 - p247(2) [501+]
The Chairman
    LJ - v129 - i20 - Dec 1 2004 - p88(1) [51-500]
    PW - v252 - i11 - March 14 2005 - p47(1) [51-500]
Frey, William H. - *The New Great Migration: Black Americans' Return to the South, 1965-2000*
    Atl - v294 - i2 - Sept 2004 - p48(1) [51-500]
Freyhofer, Horst H. - *The Nuremberg Medical Trial: The Holocaust and the Origin of the Nuremberg Medical Code*
    R&R Bk N - v19 - i3 - August 2004 - p210(1) [1-50]
Freymann, Saxton - *Food for Thought: The Complete Book of Concepts for Growing Minds*
    BL - v101 - i9-10 - Jan 1 2005 - p852(1) [1-50]
    KR - v72 - i24 - Dec 15 2004 - p1201(1) [51-500]
Freymann-Weyr, Garret - *My Heartbeat*
  y TES - v0 - i4577 - April 2 2004 - p35(1) [501+]
Freyssenet, Michel - *Globalization or Regionalization of the American and Asian Car Industry?*
    JEL - v42 - i1 - March 2004 - p289(1) [501+]
    JEL - v42 - i1 - March 2004 - p289(2) [501+]
Freystatter, Hanna - *Price Setting Behavior in an Open Economy and the Determination of Finnish Foreign Trade Prices*
    JEL - v41 - i4 - Dec 2003 - p1353(1) [501+]
Freytag, Chris - *Move To Lose: Look and Feel Better in Just Minutes a Day*
    LJ - v130 - i1 - Jan 1 2005 - p144(3) [501+]
Friar, Stephen - *The Local History Companion*
    CR - v286 - i1668 - Jan 2005 - p61(1) [501+]
Friberg, Stig E. - *Food Emulsions. 4th Ed., Rev. and Expanded*
    E-Streams - June 2004 - pNA [501+]
Food Emulsions, 4th Ed., Rev. and Expanded
    SciTech - v28 - i1 - March 2004 - p172(1) [51-500]
Friborg, Flemming - *Ancient Art to Post-Impressionism: Masterpieces from the Ny Carlsberg Glyptotek, Copenhagen*
    LJ - v129 - i20 - Dec 1 2004 - p113(1) [51-500]
Ancient to Post-Impressionism: Masterpieces from the Ny Carlsberg Glyptotek, Copenhagen
    Choice - v42 - i6 - Feb 2005 - p1012(1) [51-500]
Frick, Carole Collier - *Dressing Renaissance Florence: Families, Fortune, and Fine Clothing*
    HNet - August 2004 - pNA [501+]
Dressing Rennaissance Florence: Families, Fortunes, and the Fine Clothing
    AHR - v109 - i2 - April 2004 - p638(2) [501+]
Frick, Don M. - *Robert K. Greenleaf: A Life of Servant-Leadership*
    Choice - v42 - i4 - Dec 2004 - p704(1) [1-50]
    R&R Bk N - v19 - i4 - Nov 2004 - p88(1) [51-500]
Frick, John W. - *Theatre, Culture, and Temperance Reform in Nineteenth-Century America*
    AHR - v109 - i4 - Oct 2004 - p1237(2) [501+]
    JAH - v91 - i2 - Sept 2004 - p625(1) [501+]
Fricke, Eberhard - *Die westfaelische Veme im Bild: Geschichte, Verbreitung und Einfluss der westfaelischen Vemegerichtbarkeit*
    HNet - July 2004 - pNA [501+]
Frickel, Scott - *Chemical Consequences: Environmental Mutagens, Scientist Activism, and the Rise of Genetic Toxicology*
    Choice - v42 - i6 - Feb 2005 - p1055(1) [51-500]
    SciTech - v28 - i4 - Dec 2004 - p87(1) [51-500]
Fricker, Jon D. - *Fundamentals of Transportation Engineering: A Multimodal Approach*
    SciTech - v28 - i3 - Sept 2004 - p142(1) [51-500]

Friday, Chris - *Lelooska: The Life of a Northwest Coast Artist*
    Am Ind CRJ - v28 - i2 - Spring 2004 - p159(5) [501+]
    WHQ - v35 - i4 - Winter 2004 - p523-524 [501+]
Fridell, Ron - *Privacy vs. Security: Your Rights in Conflict*
  y SLJ - v50 - i9 - Sept 2004 - p226(1) [51-500]
Fridman, Alexander - *Plasma Physics and Engineering*
    SciTech - v28 - i3 - Sept 2004 - p48(1) [1-50]
Fridman, Alexei M. - *Observational Manifestation of Chaos in Astrophysical Objects: Invited Talks for a Workshop Held in Moscow: Sternberg Astronomical Institute, 28-29 August 2000*
    SciTech - v28 - i1 - March 2004 - p44(1) [51-500]
Frie, R. - *The Secret in the Attic*
  c CH Bwatch - Jan 2005 - pNA [51-500]
Frie, Roger - *Understanding Experience: Psychotherapy and Postmodernism*
    R&R Bk N - v19 - i1 - Feb 2004 - p1(1) [1-50]
Fried, Charles - *Saying What the Law Is: The Constitution in the Supreme Court*
    Choice - v42 - i2 - Oct 2004 - p372(1) [51-500]
    Law&PolBR - July 2004 - p517(3) [501+]
Fried, Michael - *Menzel's Realism: Art and Embodiment in Nineteenth-Century Berlin*
    HNet - Oct 2004 - pNA [501+]
Menzel's Realism: Art and Embodiment in Nineteeth-Century Berlin
    VQR - v79 - i1 - Winter 2003 - p33 [51-500]
Frieda, Leonie - *Catherine de Medici: Renaissance Queen of France*
    BL - v101 - i8 - Dec 15 2004 - p702(1) [51-500]
    Globe & Mail - March 19 2005 - pD17 [1-50]
    HT - v54 - i10 - Oct 2004 - p61(1) [501+]
    KR - v72 - i23 - Dec 1 2004 - p1130(2) [501+]
    PW - v251 - i50 - Dec 13 2004 - p58(2) [51-500]
    TLS - i5267 - March 12 2004 - p8-9 [501+]
Friedberg, Errol C. - *The Writing Life of James D. Watson*
    New Sci - v185 - i2484 - Jan 29 2005 - p51(1) [501+]
    SciTech - v28 - i4 - Dec 2004 - p63(1) [51-500]
    TimHES - v0 - i1684 - March 25 2005 - p24(2) [501+]
Friedeburg, Robert von - *Self Defence and Religious Strife in Early Modern Europe: England and Germany, 1530-1680*
    Albion - v36 - i1 - Spring 2004 - p116(3) [501+]
    Six Ct J - v34 - i4 - Winter 2003 - p1130-1131 [501+]
Friedemann, Joe - *Victor Hugo, un temps pour rire*
    NCFS - v33 - i1-2 - Fall-Winter 2004 - p206(2) [501+]
Frieden, B. Roy - *Science from Fisher Information: A Unification, 2nd Ed.*
    SciTech - v28 - i4 - Dec 2004 - p47(1) [51-500]
Frieden, Ken - *Classic Yiddish Stories of S.Y. Abramovitsh, Sholem Aleichem, and I.L. Peretz*
    R&R Bk N - v19 - i3 - August 2004 - p255(1) [51-500]
Friedenberg, Zachary B. - *Medicine under Sail*
    J Mil H - v68 - i3 - July 2004 - p959-960 [501+]
Friedes, Peter E. - *2R Manager: When to Relate, When to Require, and How to Do Both Effectively*
    HR Mag - v50 - i2 - Feb 2005 - pS2(1) [501+]
Friedlan, John H. - *Reforming the Law and Structure of the International Financial System*
    R&R Bk N - v19 - i3 - August 2004 - p193(1) [501+]
Friedland, Martin - *The University of Toronto: A History*
    Can Lit - i182 - Autumn 2004 - p129(2) [501+]
Friedman, Avi - *Peeking through the Keyhole: The Evoltuion of North American Homes*
    CBRA - Annual 2003 - p114(1) [51-500]
Friedman, Barbara G. - *Web Search Savvy: Strategies and Shortcuts for Online Research*
    R&R Bk N - v19 - i4 - Nov 2004 - p260(1) [501+]
Friedman, C.S. - *The Wilding*
    ChrSFF&H - v26 - i9 - Sept 2004 - p32(1) [51-500]
Friedman, Daniel - *To Kill and Take Possession: Law, Morality, and Society in Biblical Stories*
    Intpr - v59 - i1 - Jan 2005 - p104(1) [501+]
Friedman, Daniel J. - *Progress in Compound Semiconductor Materials III -- Electronic and Optoelectronic Applications*
    SciTech - v28 - i3 - Sept 2004 - p161(1) [51-500]
Friedman, David M. - *A Mind of Its Own: A Cultural History of the Penis*
    TLS - i5294 - Sept 17 2004 - p4-6 [501+]
Friedman, Debra - *Picture This: Fun Photography and Crafts*
  c CBRA - Annual 2003 - p552(1) [51-500]

Friedman, Ed - *Photonics Rules of Thumb: Optics, Electro-Optics, Fiber Optics, and Lasers, 2nd Ed.*
E-Streams - August 2004 - pNA [501+]
SciTech - v28 - i1 - March 2004 - p145(1) [51-500]

Friedman, Eli A. - *Diabetic Renal-Retinal Syndrome: Pathogenesis and Management Update 2002*
SciTech - v28 - i1 - March 2004 - p104(1) [51-500]

Friedman, Elisabeth J. - *Unfinished Transitions: Women and the Gendered Development of Democracy in Venezuela, 1936-1996*
Signs - v30 - i2 - Wntr 2005 - p1689(6) [501+]

Friedman, Elyse - *Waking Beauty*
Globe & Mail - August 7 2004 - pD7 [501+]

Friedman, George - *America's Secret War: Inside the Hidden Worldwide Struggle between America and Its Enemies*
BL - v101 - i3 - Oct 1 2004 - p286(1) [51-500]
Spec - v296 - i9199 - Nov 27 2004 - p48(2) [501+]

Friedman, Ian C. - *Education Reform*
R&R Bk N - v19 - i1 - Feb 2004 - pNA [51-500]

Friedman, Jack P. - *Dictionary of Real Estate Terms*
R&R Bk N - v19 - i3 - August 2004 - p111(1) [51-500]

Friedman, James - *Reality Squared: Televisual Discourse on the Real*
JPC - v38 - i3 - Feb 2005 - p581(3) [501+]

Friedman, Jonathan - *Globalization, the State, and Violence*
JEL - v41 - i4 - Dec 2003 - p1349(1) [501+]

Friedman, Jonathan C. - *The Literary, Cultural, and Historical Significance of the 1937 Biblical Stage Play The Eternal Road*
R&R Bk N - v19 - i4 - Nov 2004 - p245(1) [501+]

Friedman, Jonathan R. - *Exploring the Quantum/Classical Frontier: Recent Advances in Macroscopic Quantum Phenomena*
SciTech - v28 - i1 - March 2004 - p48(1) [51-500]

Friedman, Josh Alan - *When Sex Was Dirty*
PW - v252 - i4 - Jan 24 2005 - p235(2) [501+]

Friedman, Kinky - *The Great Psychedelic Armadillo Picnic: A "Walk" in Austin*
LJ - v129 - i17 - Oct 15 2004 - p78(1) [51-500]
Kill Two Birds and Get Stoned
y NYTBR - August 1 2004 - p16 [501+]
Ten Little New Yorkers
KR - v73 - i5 - March 1 2005 - p262(1) [51-500]
PW - v252 - i3 - Jan 17 2005 - p37(1) [51-500]

Friedman, Laurie - *Back to School, Mallory (Illus. by Schmitz, Tamara)*
c CCB-B - v58 - i1 - Sept 2004 - p16(1) [51-500]
c SLJ - v50 - i8 - August 2004 - p86(1) [51-500]
Mallory on the Move (Illus. by Schmitz, Tamara)
c CH Bwatch - v14 - i8 - August 2004 - p3(1) [51-500]
Mallory vs. Max (Illus. by Schmitz, Tamara)
c KR - v73 - i4 - Feb 15 2005 - p228(1) [51-500]

Friedman, Lawrence J. - *Charity, Philanthropy, and Civility in American History*
CS - v33 - i1 - Jan 2004 - p126-126 [501+]
JAH - v91 - i1 - June 2004 - p207-208 [501+]
JEH - v64 - i1 - March 2004 - p273(2) [501+]

Friedman, Lester D. - *Cultural Suturers: Medicine and Media*
Choice - v42 - i5 - Jan 2005 - p885(1) [1-50]

Friedman, Lita - *Mary Robinson: Fighter for Human Rights*
c SLJ - v50 - i10 - Oct 2004 - p190(1) [51-500]

Friedman, Marilyn F. - *Selling Good Design: Promoting the Early Modern Interior*
R&R Bk N - v19 - i1 - Feb 2004 - p207(1) [51-500]

Friedman, Mark - *Government: How Local, State, and Federal Government Works*
c BL - v101 - i4 - Oct 15 2004 - p415(2) [51-500]

Friedman, Mary Lusky - *The Self in the Narratives of Jose Donoso: Chile, 1924-1996*
Choice - v42 - i5 - Jan 2005 - p858(1) [1-50]
R&R Bk N - v19 - i4 - Nov 2004 - p232(1) [501+]

Friedman, Max Paul - *Nazis and Good Neighbors: The United States Campaign Against the Germans of Latin America in World War II*
Ams - v61 - i2 - Oct 2004 - p322(2) [501+]
GSR - v27 - i3 - Oct 2004 - p653(3) [501+]
HNet - June 2004 - pNA [501+]
JAH - v91 - i2 - Sept 2004 - p680(2) [501+]
JSH - v70 - i4 - Nov 2004 - p962(3) [501+]
PHR - v73 - i4 - Nov 2004 - p692(3) [501+]
RAH - v32 - i3 - Sept 2004 - p413-421 [501+]

Friedman, Michael D. - *"The World Must Be Peopled": Shakespeare's Comedies of Forgiveness*
Shakes Q - v55 - i1 - Spring 2004 - p85-86 [501+]

Friedman, Michael Jan - *Stargazer Enigma*
y Kliatt - v39 - i2 - March 2005 - p26(1) [51-500]

Friedman, Myles I. - *No School Left Behind: How to Increase Student Achievement*
BL - v101 - i9-10 - Jan 1 2005 - p789(2) [1-50]
LJ - v130 - i2 - Feb 1 2005 - p95(1) [51-500]

Friedman, Norman - *Terrorism, Afghanistan, and America's New Way of War*
Mar Crp G - v88 - i2 - Feb 2004 - p54(2) [501+]
Parameters - v34 - i3 - Autumn 2004 - p172(2) [501+]
U.S. Destroyers: An Illustrated Design History
NWCR - v57 - Autumn 2004 - p173(1) [501+]

Friedman, Stanley - *Dickens Studies Annual: Essays on Victorian Fiction, Vol. 33*
R&R Bk N - v19 - i1 - Feb 2004 - p238(1) [51-500]
Dickens's Fictions: Tapestries of Conscience
R&R Bk N - v19 - i1 - Feb 2004 - p238(1) [51-500]

Friedman, Susan Stanford - *Analyzing Freud: Letters of H.D., Bryher, and Their Circle*
TSWL - v22 - i2 - Fall 2003 - p409-411 [501+]

Friedman, Terry - *The Georgian Parish Church: "Monuments to Posterity"*
Apo - v160 - i512 - Oct 2004 - p87(2) [501+]
TLS - i5292 - Sept 3 2004 - p30(1) [51-500]
Hand to Earth: Andy Goldsworthy Sculpture 1976-1990
R&R Bk N - v19 - i4 - Nov 2004 - p200(1) [501+]

Friedman, Thomas L. - *The World Is Flat: A Brief History of the Twenty-First Century (Read by Wyman, Oliver). Audiobook Review*
LJ - v129 - i20 - Dec 1 2004 - p92(1) [51-500]
The World Is Flat: A Brief History of the Twenty-First Century
Har Bus R - v83 - i2 - Feb 2005 - p57(1) [1-50]

Friedman, Walter A. - *Birth of a Salesman: The Transformation of Selling in America*
BHR - v78 - i3 - Autumn 2004 - p562(3) [501+]
TLS - i5284 - July 9 2004 - p10(1) [501+]

Friedman, Yali - *Building Biotechnology: Starting, Managing, and Understanding Biotechnology Companies*
SciTech - v28 - i3 - Sept 2004 - p167(1) [51-500]

Friedman, Yvonne - *Encounter Between Enemies: Captivity and Ransom in the Latin Kingdom of Jerusalem*
Med R - Sept 2004 - pNA [501+]

Friedman, Daniel - *To Kill and Take Possession: Law, Morality, and Society in Biblical Stories*
Law Q Rev - v120 - Oct 2004 - p707-711 [501+]

Friedrich, Jorg - *Brandstatten: Der Anblick des Bombenkriegs*
HNet - Dec 2004 - pNA [501+]
NYRB - v51 - i16 - Oct 21 2004 - p8(4) [501+]
Der Brand: Deutschland im Bombenkrieg, 1940-1945
GSR - v27 - i1 - Feb 2004 - p184-185 [501+]
NYRB - v51 - i16 - Oct 21 2004 - p8(4) [501+]

Friedrich, Molly - *You're Not My Real Mother! (Illus. by Hale, Christy)*
c BL - v101 - i6 - Nov 15 2004 - p589(2) [51-500]
c PW - v252 - i2 - Jan 10 2005 - p55(1) [51-500]
c SLJ - v51 - i2 - Feb 2005 - p97(1) [51-500]

Friedrich, Wolfgang-Uwe - *Germany and America*
GSR - v27 - i1 - Feb 2004 - p207-208 [501+]

Friedrichsen, Christina - *Intimate Weddings: Planning a Small Wedding That Fits Your Budget and Style*
LJ - v129 - i15 - Sept 15 2004 - p78(2) [51-500]

Friel, Howard - *The Record of the Paper: How the New York Times Misreports U.S. Foreign Policy*
BL - v101 - i6 - Nov 15 2004 - p533(1) [51-500]
LJ - v129 - i19 - Nov 15 2004 - p68(1) [501+]
PW - v251 - i43 - Oct 25 2004 - p37(1) [51-500]
TimHES - v0 - i1683 - March 18 2005 - p28(1) [501+]

Friel, Maeve - *Charlie's Story*
y Kliatt - v38 - i5 - Sept 2004 - p28(2) [51-500]

Frielinghaus, Helmut - *The Gunter Grass Reader*
LJ - v130 - i1 - Jan 1 2005 - p111(2) [51-500]

Frieman, Barry B. - *The Divorcing Father's Manual: 8 Steps to Help You and Your Children Survive and Thrive*
LJ - v130 - i1 - Jan 1 2005 - p134(1) [51-500]

Friend, Catherine - *Eddie the Raccoon*
BL - v100 - i21 - July 2004 - p1850(1) [1-50]
Eddie the Raccoon (Illus. by Yee, Wong Herbert)
c SLJ - v51 - i1 - Jan 2005 - p92(1) [51-500]

Friend, Craig Thompson - *Southern Manhood: Perspectives on Masculinity in the Old South*
JouAmCul - v27 - i4 - Dec 2004 - p462(1) [501+]

Friend, Natasha - *Perfect*
BL - v101 - i9-10 - Jan 1 2005 - p844(1) [501+]
c CCB-B - v58 - i3 - Nov 2004 - p120(1) [51-500]
y Kliatt - v38 - i6 - Nov 2004 - p8(1) [51-500]
y KR - v72 - i20 - Oct 15 2004 - p1006(1) [51-500]
y PW - v251 - i45 - Nov 8 2004 - p57(1) [51-500]
SLJ - v50 - i12 - Dec 2004 - p146(1) [501+]

Friend, Robert - *Dancing with a Tiger: Poems, 1941-1998*
WLT - v78 - i3-4 - Sept-Dec 2004 - p98(2) [501+]

Friend, Robert G.M. - *Growing Orchids in Your Garden*
SciTech - v28 - i4 - Dec 2004 - p124 [51-500]

Friend, Sandra - *Orlando, Central and North Florida: An Explorer's Guide: Includes St. Augustine, Pensacola, and Jacksonville*
Bwatch - Feb 2005 - pNA [51-500]

Friend, Theodore - *Indonesian Destinies*
JAS - v63 - i2 - May 2004 - p549(3) [501+]
Pac A - v77 - i2 - Summer 2004 - p376(2) [501+]

Friend, Tim - *Animal Talk: Breaking the Codes of Animal Language*
y SLJ - v50 - i7 - July 2004 - p133(1) [51-500]

Friere, Maria Raquel - *Conflict and Security in the Former Soviet Union: The Role of the OSCE*
AJPS - v39 - i2 - July 2004 - p448(449) [501+]

Fries, Adelaide L. - *The Moravians in Georgia, 1735-1740*
EFHM - v58 - i2 - March-April 2004 - p89(1) [51-500]

Friesen, John W. - *Aboriginal Education in Canada: A Plea for Integration*
CBRA - Annual 2003 - p363(1) [501+]
The Palgrave Companion to North American Uptopias
Choice - v42 - i4 - Dec 2004 - p741(1) [1-50]

Friesen, Patrick - *The Breath You Take from the Lord*
CBRA - Annual 2003 - p216(2) [51-500]

Friesner, Esther - *Turn the Other Chick*
BL - v101 - i5 - Nov 1 2004 - p472(1) [51-500]

Frifalconi, Ann - *The Village That Vanished (Illus. by Nelson, Kadir)*
c PW - v251 - i49 - Dec 6 2004 - p62(1) [51-500]

Friggieri, Joe - *Tales for Our Times*
TLS - i5299 - Oct 22 2004 - p21(1) [501+]

Frings, Manfred S. - *Lifetime: Max Scheler's Philosophy of Time: A First Inquiry and Presentation*
R&R Bk N - v19 - i1 - Feb 2004 - p5(1) [501+]

Frisby, Mister Mann - *Blinking Red Light*
Black Iss - v6 - i4 - July-August 2004 - p44(2) [501+]

Frisch, Aaron - *The Story of Nike*
c SLJ - v50 - i7 - July 2004 - p122(1) [51-500]

Frisch, Walter - *Brahms: The Four Symphonies*
Notes - v61 - i2 - Dec 2004 - p439(3) [501+]

Frishman, Rick - *Networking Magic*
LJ - v129 - i18 - Nov 1 2004 - p99(1) [51-500]
PW - v251 - i34 - August 23 2004 - p52(1) [51-500]

Frishman, William H. - *Cardiovascular Pharmacotherapeutics Manual, 2nd Ed.*
SciTech - v28 - i1 - March 2004 - p122(1) [51-500]

Frison, George C. - *Survival by Hunting: Prehistoric Human Predators and Animal Prey (Illus. by Frison, George C.)*
Am Sci - v93 - i1 - Jan-Feb 2005 - p71(2) [501+]
Survival by Hunting: Prehistoric Predators and Animal Prey (Illus. by Frison, George C.)
Arch - v57 - i6 - Nov-Dec 2004 - p55-55 [501+]

Fristad, Mary A. - *Raising a Moody Child: How to Cope with Depression and Bipolar Disorder*
SciTech - v28 - i4 - Dec 2004 - p114(1) [1-50]

Frith, Margaret - *Frida Kahlo: The Artist Who Painted Herself (Illus. by De Pada, Tomie)*
c LibMed - v22 - i6 - March 2004 - p74(1) [501+]
Hooray for Ballet! (Illus. by Haley, Amanda)
c LibMed - v22 - i4 - Jan 2004 - p80(1) [501+]

Frith, Simon - *Music and Copyright, 2nd Ed.*
Teach Mus - v12 - i4 - Feb 2005 - p82(1) [51-500]

Frith, Uta - *Autism: Mind and Brain*
Choice - v42 - i1 - Sept 2004 - p136(1) [501+]

Fritsch, Al - *Ecotourism in Appalachia: Marketing the Mountains*
Choice - v42 - i1 - Sept 2004 - p146(1) [501+]

Fritts, Ron - *Ella Fitzgerald: The Chick Webb Years and Beyond*
R&R Bk N - v19 - i1 - Feb 2004 - p197(1) [51-500]

Fritz, Ben - *All the President's Spin: George W. Bush, the Media, and the Truth*
BIC - v17 - i7 - Oct 2004 - p15(2) [501+]

Fritz, Brewster E. - *Silko: Writing Storyteller and Medicine Woman*
Roundup M - v12 - i1 - Oct 2004 - p22(1) [51-500]

Fritz, Deborah A. - *Cataloging with AACR2 and MARC21: For Books, Electronic Resources, Sound Recordings, Videorecordings, and Serials*
   A Lib - v35 - i8 - Sept 2004 - p78(1) [51-500]
   LJ - v129 - i20 - Dec 1 2004 - p174(1) [51-500]

Fritz, Jean - *Leonardo's Horse*
   c Teach Lib - v32 - i1 - Oct 2004 - p16(1) [51-500]
The Lost Colony of Roanoke (Illus. by Talbott, Hudson)
   c NYTBR - August 8 2004 - p16 [501+]
   c SLJ - v50 - i10 - Oct 2004 - pS31(1) [51-500]

Fritz, Sandy - *Mosby's Fundamentals of Therapeutic Massage, 3rd Ed.*
   SciTech - v28 - i1 - March 2004 - p122(1) [51-500]
Robotics and Artificial Intelligence
   y SB - v40 - i3 - May-June 2004 - p129(1) [501+]

Fritze, Ronald H. - *New Worlds: The Voyages of Discovery 1400-1600*
   Six Ct J - v35 - i3 - Fall 2004 - p922-923 [501+]
Reference Sources in History: An Introductory Guide
   BL - v101 - i1 - Sept 1 2004 - p175(1) [1-50]
   Choice - v42 - i1 - Sept 2004 - p78(1) [501+]

Fritzsche, Peter - *Stranded in the Present: Modern Time and the Melancholy of History*
   Choice - v42 - i5 - Jan 2005 - p922(2) [1-50]
   HRNB - v33 - i1 - Fall 2004 - p38(1) [501+]

Fritzsche, Wolfgang - *DNA-Based Molecular Electronics: Proceedings*
   SciTech - v28 - i4 - Dec 2004 - p73(1) [51-500]

Froese Fischer, Charlotte - *Douglas Rayner Hartree: His Life in Science and Computing*
   Choice - v41 - i11-12 - July-August 2004 - p2065(1) [501+]

Froetschel, Susan - *Interruptions*
   KR - v72 - i20 - Oct 15 2004 - p985(2) [51-500]
   LJ - v129 - i18 - Nov 1 2004 - p58(1) [51-500]

Frohlich, Michael - *Die Weimarer Republik: Portrait einer Epoche in Biographien*
   GSR - v27 - i2 - May 2004 - p397-397 [501+]

Frohlich, Stefan - *The Difficulties of EU Governance: What Way Forward for the EU Institutions?*
   R&R Bk N - v19 - i3 - August 2004 - p181(1) [501+]

Frohock, Richard - *Heros of Empire: The British Imperial Protagonist in America, 1596-1764*
   Choice - v42 - i7 - March 2005 - p1227(1) [51-500]

Frojmovic, Eva - *Imagining the Self, Imagining the Other: Visual Representations and Jewish-Christian Dynamics in the Middle Ages and Early Modern Period*
   Six Ct J - v35 - i3 - Fall 2004 - p848-850 [501+]

Frolick, Larry - *Ten Thousand Scorpions: The Search for the Queen of Sheba's Gold*
   CBRA - Annual 2003 - p45(1) [51-500]

Froma Walsh - *Living Beyond Loss*
   Bwatch - March 2005 - pNA [51-500]

Fromkin, David - *Europe's Last Summer: Who Started the Great War in 1914?*
   BW - v34 - i37 - Sept 12 2004 - p5(1) [501+]
   Choice - v42 - i4 - Dec 2004 - p728(1) [1-50]
Europe's Last Summer: Why the World Went to War in 1914
   CR - v286 - i1669 - Feb 2005 - p126(1) [51-500]
   TLS - i5306 - Dec 10 2004 - p36(1) [501+]

Fromm, Peter - *As Cool as I Am*
   BW - v34 - i1 - Jan 4 2004 - p12(1) [501+]

Frommer, Harvey - *New York City Baseball: The Last Golden Age: 1947-1957*
   R&R Bk N - v19 - i3 - August 2004 - p88(1) [51-500]

Fromstein, Joe - *Loveplay: A Conversation in Rhyme*
   Globe & Mail - Feb 12 2005 - pD13 [1-50]

Frosh, Paul - *The Image Factory: Consumer Culture, Photography and the Visual Content Industry*
   Choice - v42 - i4 - Dec 2004 - p644(1) [1-50]

Froslev, Christensen Jens - *The Industrial Dynamics of the New Digital Economy*
   R&R Bk N - v19 - i2 - May 2004 - p116(1) [51-500]

Frost, Brian J. - *The Essential Guide to Werewolf Literature*
   Choice - v42 - i1 - Sept 2004 - p95(1) [501+]
   JouAmCul - v27 - i4 - Dec 2004 - p443(3) [501+]

Frost, Bryan-Paul - *History of American Political Thought*
   Choice - v41 - i7 - March 2004 - p1370(1) [501+]

Frost, Helen - *Boa Constrictors*
   c Am Bio T - v66 - i4 - April 2004 - p309(1) [501+]
Fog
   c SB - v40 - i4 - July-August 2004 - p174(1) [51-500]
Ice
   c SB - v40 - i4 - July-August 2004 - p174(1) [51-500]
Keesha's House. Audiobook Review
   y BL - v101 - i8 - Dec 15 2004 - p754(1) [1-50]
   c BL - v101 - i9-10 - Jan 1 2005 - p778(1) [1-50]
   y Kliatt - v39 - i1 - Jan 2005 - p45(1) [51-500]
   y SLJ - v50 - i12 - Dec 2004 - p78(1) [501+]
   y VOYA - v27 - i5 - Dec 2004 - p371(1) [501+]
Leaf-Cutting Ants
   c Am Bio T - v66 - i4 - April 2004 - p309(1) [501+]
A Look at Kenya
   c HNet - Sept 2004 - pNA [501+]
Snow
   c SB - v40 - i4 - July-August 2004 - p174(1) [51-500]
Spinning through the Universe: A Novel in Poems from Room 214
   c LibMed - v23 - i3 - Nov-Dec 2004 - p70(1) [51-500]
   y VOYA - v27 - i4 - Oct 2004 - p296(1) [51-500]
Tarantulas
   c Am Bio T - v66 - i4 - April 2004 - p309(1) [501+]
Tree Frogs
   c Am Bio T - v66 - i4 - April 2004 - p309(1) [501+]
Wind
   c SB - v40 - i4 - July-August 2004 - p174(1) [51-500]

Frost, J. Williams - *A History of Christian, Jewish, Muslim, Hindu, and Buddhist Perspectives on War and Peace, Vol. 1*
   Choice - v42 - i3 - Nov 2004 - p499(1) [51-500]
A History of Christian, Jewish, Muslim, Hindu, and Buddhist Perspectives on War and Peace, Vol. 2
   Choice - v42 - i3 - Nov 2004 - p499(1) [51-500]

Frost, James D. - *Merchant Princes: Halifax's First Family of Finance, Ships, and Steel*
   Can Hist R - v85 - i4 - Dec 2004 - p818(3) [501+]
   CBRA - Annual 2003 - p45(2) [51-500]

Frost, Jennifer - *"An Interracial Movement of the Poor": Community Organizing and the New Left*
   J Soc H - v38 - i1 - Fall 2004 - p255(3) [501+]

Frost, Joy - *Samantha and Starlight (Read by Frost, Joy). Audiobook Review*
   c SLJ - v50 - i9 - Sept 2004 - p78(1) [51-500]
The Successful Journey (Read by Frost, Joy). Audiobook Review
   c SLJ - v50 - i10 - Oct 2004 - p86(1) [51-500]
Under the Lily Pad
   c SLJ - v50 - i8 - August 2004 - p76(2) [51-500]

Frost, Mark - *The Grand Slam: Bobby Jones, America, and the Story of Golf*
   BL - v101 - i6 - Nov 15 2004 - p545(1) [51-500]
   LJ - v129 - i19 - Nov 15 2004 - p67(1) [501+]
   NYTBR - Feb 13 2005 - p6 [501+]
   PW - v251 - i40 - Oct 4 2004 - p81(2) [51-500]
   Spec - v296 - Dec 18 2004 - p86(2) [501+]

Frost, Orcutt - *Bering: The Russian Discovery of America*
   BIC - v33 - i2 - March 2004 - p18(4) [501+]
   Choice - v42 - i1 - Sept 2004 - p162(1) [501+]

Frost, Robert - *Elected Friends: Robert Frost and Edward Thomas to One Another*
   New R - Dec 20 2004 - p37 [501+]

Frost, Scott - *Run the Risk*
   BL - v101 - i9-10 - Jan 1 2005 - p783(1) [1-50]
   KR - v73 - i1 - Jan 1 2005 - p8(1) [51-500]
   LJ - v130 - i3 - Feb 15 2005 - p114(2) [51-500]
   PW - v252 - i2 - Jan 10 2005 - p40(1) [51-500]

Frowen, Stephen F. - *Economists in Discussion: The Correspondence between G.L.S. Shackle and Stephen F. Frowen, 1951-1992*
   TLS - i5295 - Sept 24 2004 - p28(1) [501+]

Fruehauf, Norbert - *Flexible Electronics-- Materials and Device Technology*
   SciTech - v28 - i1 - March 2004 - p160(1) [51-500]
Flexible Electronics -- Materials and Device Technology: Proceedings
   SciTech - v28 - i4 - Dec 2004 - p155(1) [51-500]

Fruhling, Hugo - *Crime and Violence in Latin America: Citizen Security, Democracy, and the State*
   R&R Bk N - v19 - i1 - Feb 2004 - p143(1) [51-500]

Fruhstuck, Sabine - *Colonizing Sex: Sexology and Social Control in Modern Japan*
   AHR - v109 - i4 - Oct 2004 - p1210-1211 [501+]

Frum, David - *An End to Evil: How to Win the War on Terror*
   BW - v34 - i1 - Jan 4 2004 - p3(1) [501+]
   Parameters - v34 - i4 - Winter 2004 - p140(2) [501+]
   Reason - v36 - i8 - Jan 2005 - p50(6) [501+]
Right Man: An Inside Account of the Bush White House
   CBRA - Annual 2003 - p306(2) [501+]

Frumkin, Howard - *Urban Sprawl and Public Health: Designing, Planning, and Building for Healthy Communities*
   Choice - v42 - i5 - Jan 2005 - p885(1) [1-50]
   R&R Bk N - v19 - i4 - Nov 2004 - p137(1) [1-50]

Frumkin, Norman - *Tracking America's Economy, 4th Ed.*
   R&R Bk N - v19 - i3 - August 2004 - p98(1) [51-500]

Frumkin, Peter - *On Being Nonprofit: A Conceptual and Policy Primer*
   CS - v33 - i2 - March 2004 - p187-188 [501+]

Fry, C. George - *Berthold von Schenk (1895-1974): Pioneer of Lutheran Liturgical Renewal*
   R&R Bk N - v19 - i1 - Feb 2004 - p25(1) [51-500]

Fry, Christopher - *Djomi Dream Child*
   c CH Bwatch - v14 - i11 - Nov 2004 - pNA [51-500]

Fry, Edward B. - *The Vocabulary Teacher's Book of Lists*
   SLJ - v50 - i10 - Oct 2004 - pS72(1) [51-500]

Fry, Katherine - *Constructing the Heartland: Television News and Natural Disaster*
   R&R Bk N - v19 - i1 - Feb 2004 - p230(1) [51-500]

Fry, Lionel - *Atlas of Atopic Exzema*
   E-Streams - Sept 2004 - pNA [501+]

Fry, Michael - *How the Scots Made America*
   BL - v101 - i8 - Dec 15 2004 - p702(1) [51-500]
   KR - v72 - i21 - Nov 1 2004 - p1036(2) [501+]
   LJ - v129 - i19 - Nov 15 2004 - p70(1) [501+]
   PW - v251 - i46 - Nov 15 2004 - p47(1) [51-500]

Fry, Stephen - *Bright Young Things*
   New York - v37 - i29 - August 23 2004 - p138(1) [501+]
Stephen Fry's Incomplete and Utter History of Classical Music
   Spec - v296 - i9196 - Nov 6 2004 - p62(1) [501+]

Frydenberg, Erica - *Thriving, Surviving, or Going Under: Coping with Everyday Lives*
   R&R Bk N - v20 - i1 - Feb 2005 - p8(1) [51-500]

Frye, Northrop - *Biblical and Classical Myths: The Mythological Framework of Western Culture*
   Globe & Mail - Nov 13 2004 - pD21 [51-500]
Northrop Frye on Modern Culture
   CBRA - Annual 2003 - p288(1) [501+]
   R&R Bk N - v19 - i4 - Nov 2004 - p221(1) [501+]
Northrop Frye's Notebooks and Lectures on the Bible and Other Religious Tracts
   CBRA - Annual 2003 - p90(2) [501+]

Fryer, David Ross - *The Intervention of the Other: Ethical Subjectivity in Levinas and Lacan*
   R&R Bk N - v19 - i4 - Nov 2004 - p5(1) [51-500]

Fryer, Mary Beacock - *Bold, Brave and Born to Lead*
   y Res Links - v10 - i3 - Feb 2005 - p46(1) [501+]

Fryer, Paul - *Lina Cavalieri: The Life of Opera's Greatest Beauty, 1874-1944*
   R&R Bk N - v19 - i1 - Feb 2004 - p197(1) [51-500]

Frykenberg, Robert Eric - *Christians and Missionaries in India: Cross-Cultural Communication Since 1500*
   AHR - v109 - i2 - April 2004 - p502(1) [501+]
   IBMR - v29 - i1 - Jan 2005 - p45(1) [501+]

Frykholm, Amy Johnson - *Rapture Culture: Left Behind in Evangelical America*
   Choice - v42 - i4 - Dec 2004 - p677(2) [1-50]
   LJ - v129 - i12 - July 2004 - p88(2) [51-500]

Frymer-Kensky, Tikva - *Reading The Women Of The Bible: A New Interpretation Of Their Stories*
   Bwatch - Feb 2005 - pNA [51-500]

Frymier, Jack - *Changing the School Learning Environment: Where Do We Stand after Decades of Reform?*
   R&R Bk N - v19 - i3 - August 2004 - p214(1) [1-50]
Cultures of the States: A Handbook on the Effectiveness of State Governments
   R&R Bk N - v19 - i1 - Feb 2004 - pNA [501+]

Frynas, Jedrzej George - *Transnational Corporations and Human Rights*
   R&R Bk N - v19 - i1 - Feb 2004 - p97(1) [1-50]

Fryxell, David A. - *Write Faster, Write Better*
   R&R Bk N - v19 - i3 - August 2004 - p258(1) [51-500]

Fu, Poshek - *Between Shanghai and Hong Kong: The Politics of Chinese Cinemas*
R&R Bk N - v19 - i1 - Feb 2004 - p224(1) [51-500]

Fuchs, Bernie - *Ride Like the Wind: A Tale of the Pony Express (Illus. by Fuchs, Bernie)*
c CH Bwatch - v14 - i7 - July 2004 - p4(2) [51-500]
c Five Owls - v18 - i1 - Fall 2004 - p20(1) [51-500]
c LibMed - v22 - i7 - April-May 2004 - p56(1) [501+]

Fuchs, Elinor - *Making an Exit: A Mother-Daughter Drama with Alzheimer's, Machine Tools, and Laughter*
KR - v73 - i2 - Jan 15 2005 - p99(2) [501+]
LJ - v130 - i1 - Jan 1 2005 - p139(1) [51-500]
PW - v252 - i2 - Jan 10 2005 - p46(1) [51-500]

Fuchs, Lucy - *Humanities in the Elementary School: A Handbook for Teachers, 2nd Ed.*
R&R Bk N - v19 - i1 - Feb 2004 - p183(1) [51-500]

Fuchs, Martina - *Karl V. Eine Populare Figur? Zur Rezeption des Kaisers in deutschsprachiger Belletristik*
Six Ct J - v34 - i4 - Winter 2003 - p1115-1117 [501+]

Fuchs, Sabine - *... weil die Kinder nicht ernst genommen werden: zum Werk von Christine Nostlinger*
c Bkbird - v42 - i3 - July 2004 - p46(1) [501+]

Fudge, Erica - *Renaissance Beasts: Of Animals, Humans, and Other Wonderful Creatures*
Choice - v42 - i1 - Sept 2004 - p147(1) [501+]
TLS - i5286 - July 23 2004 - p33(1) [501+]

Fuentes, Carlos - *Inez*
HR - v55 - i4 - Winter 2003 - p685 [501+]
This I Believe: An A to Z of a Life
BL - v101 - i8 - Dec 15 2004 - p690(1) [501+]
BW - v35 - i4 - Jan 30 2005 - p15(1) [51-500]
KR - v72 - i24 - Dec 15 2004 - p1180(2) [501+]
LJ - v130 - i4 - March 1 2005 - p84(1) [51-500]
PW - v252 - i2 - Jan 10 2005 - p46(1) [51-500]
TLS - i5303 - Nov 19 2004 - p37(1) [51-500]

Fuerst, James S. - *When Public Housing Was Paradise: Building Community in Chicago*
BooChiTr - Jan 11 2004 - p4(2) [501+]

Fuess, Harald - *Divorce in Japan: Family, Gender, and the State, 1600-2000*
Law&PolBR - Oct 2004 - pNA [501+]
R&R Bk N - v19 - i2 - May 2004 - p135 [51-500]

Fugerson, Robert A. - *Reading the Early Republic*
Choice - v42 - i5 - Jan 2005 - p915(1) [1-50]

Fuguet, Alberto - *The Movies of My Life*
WLT - v79 - i1 - Jan-April 2005 - p108(1) [501+]

Fuh, Jerry Ying Hsi - *Computer-Aided Injection Mold Design and Manufacture*
SciTech - v28 - i4 - Dec 2004 - p166(1) [51-500]

Fujikawa, Kazuo - *Path Integrals and Quantum Anomalies*
SciTech - v28 - i4 - Dec 2004 - p48(1) [51-500]

Fujimoto, Takashi - *Plasma Spectroscopy*
SciTech - v28 - i4 - Dec 2004 - p51(1) [51-500]

Fujisawa, Yukiho - *Introduction to the H8 Microcontroller*
SciTech - v28 - i3 - Sept 2004 - p163(1) [51-500]

Fujishima, Kosuke - *Oh My Goddess! Traveler*
y VOYA - v27 - i3 - August 2004 - p228(1) [1-50]
Oh My Goddess! Wrong Number
y SLJ - v50 - i10 - Oct 2004 - p29(1) [51-500]

Fujita, Rod - *Heal the Ocean: Solutions for Saving Our Seas*
Choice - v42 - i2 - Oct 2004 - p317(1) [51-500]

Fujita-Rony, Dorothy B. - *American Workers, Colonial Power: Philippine Seattle and the Transpacific West, 1919-1941*
WHQ - v35 - i3 - Autumn 2004 - p373(2) [501+]

Fujita, S. - *Similarity in Diversity*
SciTech - v28 - i1 - March 2004 - p47(1) [51-500]

Fujita, Satoshi - *Seismic Engineering--2004, Vols. 1-2*
SciTech - v28 - i4 - Dec 2004 - p146(1) [501+]

Fukamachi Hideo - *Jindai Guangdong de zhengdang shehui guojia--Zhongguo Guomindang jiqi dangguotizhi de xingchengguocheng*
Ch Rev Int - v11 - i1 - Spring 2004 - p82(2) [501+]

Fukuyama, Francis - *State-Building: Governance and World Order in the 21st Century*
AJES - v63 - i4 - Oct 2004 - p951(4) [501+]
For Aff - v83 - i5 - Sept-Oct 2004 - p164 [501+]
Globe & Mail - August 21 2004 - pD10 [501+]
NS - v133 - i4695 - July 5 2004 - p48(2) [501+]
Pers PS - v33 - i4 - Fall 2004 - p244(1) [501+]
TimHES - v0 - i1658 - Sept 17 2004 - p26(1) [501+]

Fulbright Scholar Program: Grants for U.S. Faculty and Professionals, 2004-2005
JEL - v41 - i4 - Dec 2003 - p1444(2) [501+]

Fulbrook, Mary - *A Concise History of Germany*
CR - v285 - i1663 - August 2004 - p128(1) [501+]
Twentieth-Century Germany: Politics Culture and Society 1918-1990
HNet - Nov 2004 - pNA [501+]

Fulcher, Jane - *Debussy and His World*
NCFS - v32 - i3-4 - Spring-Summer 2004 - p370(3) [501+]

Fulford, Francis - *Bearing Up: The Long View*
Spec - v297 - i9207 - Jan 22 2005 - p34(2) [501+]

Fulford, Tim - *Literature, Science and Exploration in the Romantic Era: Bodies of Knowledge*
Choice - v42 - i7 - March 2005 - p1227(2) [51-500]

Fulkerson, John P. - *Disorders of the Patellofemoral Joint, 4th Ed.*
SciTech - v28 - i3 - Sept 2004 - p112(1) [51-500]

Fullam, Scott - *Hardware Hacking Projects for Geeks*
LJ - v129 - i16 - Oct 1 2004 - p104(1) [51-500]

Fullbrook, Edward - *Intersubjectivity in Economics: Agents and Structures*
JEL - v42 - i3 - Sept 2004 - p844(2) [501+]

Fuller, Alexandra - *Scribbling the Cat: Travels with an African Soldier (Read by Lecat, Lisette). Audiobook Review*
y Kliatt - v39 - i2 - March 2005 - p60(1) [51-500]
LJ - v130 - i4 - March 1 2005 - p125(1) [51-500]
Scribbling the Cat: Travels with an African Soldier
BL - v101 - i9-10 - Jan 1 2005 - p767(1) [51-500]
BooChiTr - May 16 2004 - p1(2) [501+]
NS - v133 - i4703 - August 30 2004 - p39(2) [501+]
NS - v133 - i4716 - Nov 29 2004 - p42(1) [51-500]
Spec - v296 - i9187 - Sept 4 2004 - p40(1) [501+]
TLS - i5304 - Nov 26 2004 - p29(1) [501+]

Fuller, Barry J. - *Life in the Frozen State*
SciTech - v28 - i3 - Sept 2004 - p58(1) [1-50]

Fuller, C.J. - *The Everyday State and Society in Modern India*
JAS - v63 - i2 - May 2004 - p527(1) [501+]

Fuller, Doris - *Promise You Won't Freak Out: A Teenager Tells Her Mother the Truth about Boys, Booze, Body Piercing, and Other Touchy Topics*
y VOYA - v27 - i4 - Oct 2004 - p324(1) [51-500]

Fuller, Graham E. - *The Future of Political Islam*
Prog - v68 - i8 - August 2004 - p45(4) [501+]
Turkey's Strategic Model: Myths and Realities
Wil Q - v28 - i4 - Autumn 2004 - p107(2) [501+]

Fuller, John - *Ghosts*
NS - v133 - i4716 - Nov 29 2004 - p42(1) [51-500]

Fuller, Robert C. - *Spiritual but Not Religious: Understanding Unchurched America*
JR - v84 - i4 - Oct 2004 - p676(3) [501+]

Fuller, Roy Broadbent - *Gut Flora, Nutrition, Immunity, and Health*
SciTech - v28 - i1 - March 2004 - p76(1) [51-500]

Fuller, Samuel - *Scorsese Up Close: A Study of the Films*
R&R Bk N - v19 - i3 - August 2004 - p264(1) [1-50]

Fuller, Sandy Ferguson. Moon Loon
SLJ - v50 - i12 - Dec 2004 - p108(1) [501+]

Fuller, Steve - *Kuhn vs. Popper: The Struggle for the Soul of Science*
KR - v72 - i22 - Nov 15 2004 - p1078(1) [501+]

Fuller, Thomas E. - *Missing*
c SLJ - v50 - i10 - Oct 2004 - p178(1) [51-500]

Fuller, Todd K. - *Wolves of the World*
Bwatch - Dec 2004 - pNA [51-500]
Choice - v42 - i4 - Dec 2004 - p690(1) [1-50]
SB - v40 - i6 - Nov-Dec 2004 - p245(1) [51-500]
y SB - v40 - i6 - Nov-Dec 2004 - p261(1) [51-500]
SciTech - v28 - i3 - Sept 2004 - p66(1) [51-500]

Fuller, Wayne E. - *Morality and the Mail in Nineteenth-Century America*
BHR - v77 - i4 - Winter 2003 - p755(757) [501+]
JAH - v91 - i2 - Sept 2004 - p626(2) [501+]
JSH - v70 - i3 - August 2004 - p664(2) [501+]
WHQ - v35 - i3 - Autumn 2004 - p402(2) [501+]

Fullerton, Alexander - *Storm Force to Narvik*
LJ - v130 - i2 - Feb 1 2005 - p126(1) [1-50]

Fullick, Leisha - *Adult Learners in a Brave New World: Lifelong Learning Policy & Structural Changes Since 1997*
TES - v0 - i4586 - June 4 2004 - pss6(1) [501+]

Fullilove, Mindy Thompson - *Root Shock: How Tearing Up City Neighborhoods Hurts America, and What We Can Do About It*
Black Iss - v7 - i2 - March-April 2005 - p40(2) [501+]
Choice - v42 - i6 - Feb 2005 - p1104(1) [501+]

Fullinwider, Robert K. - *Leveling the Playing Field: Justice, Politics and College Admissions*
R&R Bk N - v19 - i3 - August 2004 - p222(1) [1-50]

Fullinwider, S.P. - *Patterns in Twentieth-Century European Thought*
R&R Bk N - v19 - i3 - August 2004 - p4(1) [1-50]

Fulmer, David - *Jass*
BL - v101 - i9-10 - Jan 1 2005 - p826(1) [1-50]
KR - v72 - i21 - Nov 1 2004 - p1030(1) [51-500]
LJ - v129 - i20 - Dec 1 2004 - p94(1) [51-500]
PW - v251 - i48 - Nov 29 2004 - p26(1) [51-500]

Fulton, Alice - *Cascade Experiment: Selected Poems*
Poet - v184 - i5 - Sept 2004 - p381(4) [501+]

Fulton, Rachel - *From Judgment to Passion: Devotion to Christ and the Virgin Mary, 800-1200*
Med R - June 2004 - pNA [501+]
Specu - v79 - i4 - Oct 2004 - p1071(2) [501+]
Theol St - v65 - i4 - Dec 2004 - p861(4) [501+]

Fumaroli, Marc - *Chateaubriand: Poesie et terreur*
TLS - i5268 - March 19 2004 - p5-6 [501+]
The Poet and the King: Jean de La Fontaine and His Century
JMH - v76 - i3 - Sept 2004 - p689(2) [501+]

Fumento, Michael - *Bioevolution: How Biotechnology Is Changing Our World*
QRB - v79 - i3 - Sept 2004 - p294(2) [501+]

Fumizuki, Kou - *Ai Yori Aoshi, Vol. 1*
y Kliatt - v38 - i5 - Sept 2004 - p34(3) [51-500]
Ai Yori Aoshi, Vol. 2
LJ - v129 - i12 - July 2004 - p61(1) [51-500]

Fumoleau, Rene - *As Long as This Land Shall Last: A History of Treaty 8 and Treaty II, 1870-1939*
R&R Bk N - v19 - i3 - August 2004 - p205(1) [501+]

Fun-to-Make Crafts for Easter
c PW - v252 - i7 - Feb 14 2005 - p79(2) [501+]

Funabashi, Yoichi - *Reconciliation in the Asia-Pacific*
NWCR - v57 - Autumn 2004 - p167(3) [501+]
Pers PS - v33 - i4 - Fall 2004 - p242(1) [501+]

Funaki, Tadahisa - *Stochastic Analysis on Large Scale Interacting Systems*
SciTech - v28 - i3 - Sept 2004 - p37(1) [51-500]

Funck, Bernard - *European Integration, Regional Policy, and Growth*
JEL - v41 - i4 - Dec 2003 - p1353(1) [501+]

Funck, Marcus - *Endangered Cities: Military Power and Urban Societies in the Era of the World Wars*
R&R Bk N - v19 - i3 - August 2004 - p32(1) [51-500]

Funder, Anna - *Stasiland: Stories from Behind the Berlin Wall*
BIC - v33 - i7 - Oct 2004 - p24(1) [501+]
HNet - Sept 2004 - pNA [501+]

Funding Sources for K-12 Education, 2004, 6th Ed.
R&R Bk N - v19 - i3 - August 2004 - p228(1) [1-50]

Fundraising: Handbuch fur Grundlagen, Strategien und Instrumente
HNet - Oct 2004 - pNA [501+]

Fung, Archon - *Deepening Democracy: Institutional Innovations in Empowered Participatory Governance*
CS - v33 - i1 - Jan 2004 - p126-127 [501+]
Empowered Participation: Reinventing Urban Democracy
Choice - v42 - i4 - Dec 2004 - p736(1) [1-50]
Ethics - v115 - i2 - Jan 2005 - p402(5) [501+]

Fung, Jojo M. - *Ripples on the Water: Believers in the Orang Asli's Struggle for a Homeland of Equal Citizens*
Theol St - v66 - i1 - March 2005 - p234(2) [501+]

Funge, John David - *Artificial Intelligence for Computer Games: An Introduction*
SciTech - v28 - i4 - Dec 2004 - p24(1) [51-500]

Funk, Jeffrey L. - *Mobile Disruption: The Technologies and Applications Driving the Mobile Internet*
E-Streams - June 2004 - pNA [501+]
SciTech - v28 - i1 - March 2004 - p154(1) [51-500]

Funk, Robert E. - *Three Sixteenth-Century Mohawk Iroquois Village Sites*
Am Ant - v70 - i1 - Jan 2005 - p197(2) [501+]

Funke, Cornelia - *Dragon Rider (Read by Fraser, Brendan). Audiobook Review*
c PW - v251 - i50 - Dec 13 2004 - p24(1) [51-500]
Dragon Rider (Illus. by Funke, Cornelia)
c BL - v100 - i22 - August 2004 - p1924(1) [51-500]
c CCB-B - v58 - i2 - Oct 2004 - p72(2) [501+]
c HB - v80 - i5 - Sept-Oct 2004 - p583(1) [51-500]
c Inst - v114 - i5 - Jan-Feb 2005 - p73(2) [501+]
c KR - v72 - i14 - July 15 2004 - p685(1) [51-500]
c LibMed - v23 - i3 - Nov-Dec 2004 - p70(1) [51-500]
c PW - v251 - i29 - July 19 2004 - p162(1) [51-500]

c SLJ - v50 - i10 - Oct 2004 - p164(1) [51-500]
y VOYA - v27 - i4 - Oct 2004 - p314(1) [51-500]
Inkheart (Read by Redgrave, Lynn). Audiobook Review
y BL - v101 - i9-10 - Jan 1 2005 - p778(1) [1-50]
Inkheart
c BooChiTr - Jan 4 2004 - p5(1) [501+]
The Princess Knight (Illus. by Meyer, Kerstin)
BL - v101 - i9-10 - Jan 1 2005 - p775(1) [1-50]
c LibMed - v23 - i1 - August-Sept 2004 - p64(1) [51-500]
Thief Lord (Read by Maloney, Michael). Audiobook Review
y Magpies - v19 - i5 - Nov 2004 - p43(1) [501+]
Funke, Cornelia Caroline - *Dragon Rider (Read by Fraser, Brendan). Audiobook Review*
c SLJ - v50 - i12 - Dec 2004 - p73(1) [501+]
Funnell, Barbara E. - *Plasmid Biology*
QRB - v79 - i4 - Dec 2004 - p427(1) [501+]
Funny Honey Valentine (Illus. by Salerno, Steven)
c PW - v251 - i49 - Dec 6 2004 - p61(2) [501+]
Funston, Sylvia - *Magic (Illus. by Weissmann, Joe)*
c CBRA - Annual 2003 - p551(1) [51-500]
Fuqua, Jonathon Scott - *The Willoughby Spit Wonder*
LibMed - v22 - i7 - April-May 2004 - p60(1) [501+]
Furbee, Mary R. - *Outrageous Women of Civil War Times*
LibMed - v22 - i4 - Jan 2004 - p71(1) [501+]
Furdell, Elizabeth Lane - *Publishing and Medicine in Early Modern England*
Albion - v36 - i1 - Spring 2004 - p127(2) [501+]
Six Ct J - v34 - i4 - Winter 2003 - p1252-1253 [501+]
Furedi, Frank - *Where Have All the Intellectuals Gone?: Confronting 21st Century Philistinism*
NS - v133 - i4705 - Sept 13 2004 - p48(2) [501+]
Spec - v296 - i9191 - Oct 2 2004 - p47(2) [501+]
TimHES - v0 - i1670 - Dec 10 2004 - p30(1) [501+]
TLS - i5296 - Oct 1 2004 - p25(1) [501+]
Furey, Leo - *The Long Run*
Globe & Mail - Nov 27 2004 - pD3 [51-500]
Furgurson, Ernest B. - *Freedom Rising: Washington in the Civil War*
BL - v101 - i6 - Nov 15 2004 - p548(2) [51-500]
BW - v34 - i44 - Oct 31 2004 - p4(2) [501+]
KR - v72 - i18 - Sept 15 2004 - p900(2) [501+]
LJ - v129 - i17 - Oct 15 2004 - p73(1) [51-500]
NYRB - v51 - i20 - Dec 16 2004 - p70(2) [501+]
PW - v251 - i39 - Sept 27 2004 - p44(1) [51-500]
Furht, Borko - *Handbook of Video Databases: Design and Applications*
SciTech - v28 - i1 - March 2004 - p145(1) [51-500]
Furie, Karen L. - *Handbook of Stroke Prevention in Clinical Practice*
SciTech - v28 - i3 - Sept 2004 - p95(1) [51-500]
Furlan, Francesco - *Studia Albertiana: Lectures et lecteurs de L.B. Alberti*
Ren Q - v57 - i4 - Winter 2004 - p1357(2) [501+]
Furlong, Dennis J. - *Medicare Myths: 50 Myths We've Endured about the Canadian Health Care System*
Globe & Mail - July 24 2004 - pD14 [51-500]
Furlong, Michael J. - *Issues in School Violence Research*
Cur R - v44 - i5 - Jan 2005 - p12(1) [51-500]
Furman, Laura - *The O. Henry Prize Stories 2005*
BL - v101 - i6 - Nov 15 2004 - p562(1) [51-500]
PW - v252 - i2 - Jan 10 2005 - p39(1) [51-500]

Furman, Leah - *Single Jewish Female: A Modern Guide to Sex and Dating*
PW - v251 - i35 - August 30 2004 - p52(1) [51-500]
Furnham, Adrian - *The Dark Side of Behavior at Work: Understanding and Avoiding Employees Leaving, Thieving, and Deceiving*
Choice - v42 - i5 - Jan 2005 - p898(2) [1-50]
Furnish, Michael D. - *Shock Compression of Condensed Matter - 2004: Proceedings: vol. 2.*
SciTech - v28 - i4 - Dec 2004 - p134 [51-500]
Furno, Martine - *Une "Fantaisie" sur l'Antique: Le gout pour l'epigraphie funeraire dans l'Hypnerotomachia Poliphili de Francesco Colonna*
Ren Q - v57 - i4 - Winter 2004 - p1366(2) [501+]
Furrows, Dwight - *Moral Surroundings: Readings on the Crisis of Values in Contemporary Life*
R&R Bk N - v19 - i3 - August 2004 - p11(1) [1-50]
Furst, Alan - *The Book of Spies: An Anthology of Literary Espionage*
Bks & Cult - v10 - i6 - Nov-Dec 2004 - p27(3) [501+]
Dark Voyage
BL - v100 - i21 - July 2004 - p1798(1) [51-500]
Ent W - i777 - August 6 2004 - p84 [501+]
Globe & Mail - Sept 11 2004 - pD19 [501+]
KR - v72 - i13 - July 1 2004 - p594(2) [51-500]
LJ - v129 - i12 - July 2004 - p69(1) [51-500]
NYTBR - August 15 2004 - p7 [501+]
People - v62 - i11 - Sept 13 2004 - p56 [501+]
PW - v251 - i29 - July 19 2004 - p143(1) [51-500]
TLS - i5291 - August 27 2004 - p21(1) [501+]
Furst, Peter T. - *Visions of a Huichol Shaman*
Lat Ant - v15 - i4 - Dec 2004 - p460(2) [501+]
Furstinger, Nancy - *The Everglades: The Largest Marsh in the United States*
c SLJ - v50 - i8 - August 2004 - p107(1) [501+]
Say It with Music: The Story of Irving Berlin
LibMed - v22 - i5 - Feb 2004 - p76(1) [501+]
Furtig, Henner - *Iran's Rivalry with Saudi Arabia between the Gulf Wars*
IJMES - v36 - i3 - August 2004 - p522-523 [501+]
Furtman, Michael - *Why Birds Do That: 40 Distinctive Bird Behaviors Explained and Photographed*
Bwatch - March 2005 - pNA [51-500]
Furtney, Charles S. - *Tyrconnel*
c CH Bwatch - v14 - i9 - Sept 2004 - p3(2) [51-500]
Furukawa, Hisao - *Ecological Destruction, Health, and Development: Advancing Asian Paradigms*
SciTech - v28 - i4 - Dec 2004 - p4(1) [1-50]
Furuya, Yasubumi - *Materials and Devices for Smart Systems*
SciTech - v28 - i3 - Sept 2004 - p144(1) [51-500]
Fusarelli, Lance D. - *The Political Dynamics of School Choice: Negotiating Contested Terrain*
R&R Bk N - v19 - i1 - Feb 2004 - pNA [51-500]
Fusaro, B.A. - *Environmental Mathematics in the Classroom*
Math T - v97 - i3 - March 2004 - p221-221 [501+]
Fusaro, Peter C. - *What Went Wrong at Enron: Everyone's Guide to the Largest Bankruptcy in U.S. History*
En Jnl - v25 - i4 - Oct 2004 - p115(20) [501+]
Fusco, Coco - *Only Skin Deep: Changing Visions of the American Self*
Choice - v42 - i2 - Oct 2004 - p287(1) [501+]

Fusco, Kimberly Newton - *Tending to Grace*
y BL - v100 - i22 - August 2004 - p1924(1) [51-500]
c BL - v101 - i6 - Nov 15 2004 - p599(1) [501+]
Fusco, Kimberly Newton - *Tending to Grace*
c CH Bwatch - Feb 2005 - pNA [51-500]
Fusco, Kimberly Newton - *Tending to Grace*
c LibMed - v23 - i3 - Nov-Dec 2004 - p70(1) [51-500]
y PW - v251 - i27 - July 5 2004 - p56(2) [51-500]
y SLJ - v50 - i10 - Oct 2004 - pS53(2) [51-500]
Fusilli, Jim - *Hard, Hard City*
BL - v101 - i3 - Oct 1 2004 - p313(1) [51-500]
DroRevMy - v24 - i4 - July-August 2004 - p12(1) [51-500]
KR - v72 - i16 - August 15 2004 - p780(1) [51-500]
NYTBR - Oct 24 2004 - p27 [501+]
PW - v251 - i39 - Sept 27 2004 - p36(2) [51-500]
Fusillo, Archimede - *Bruises*
y Magpies - v19 - i5 - Nov 2004 - p40(1) [501+]
The Dons (Read by Marnika, Dino). Audiobook Review
Kliatt - v38 - i6 - Nov 2004 - p46(1) [51-500]
y VOYA - v27 - i5 - Dec 2004 - p373(1) [501+]
Fuss, Diana - *The Sense of an Interior: Four Writers and the Rooms That Shaped Them*
NYTBR - Oct 24 2004 - p35 [501+]
R&R Bk N - v19 - i3 - August 2004 - p258(1) [51-500]
Fussell, Betty - *The Story of Corn*
y Kliatt - v39 - i2 - March 2005 - p43(1) [51-500]
Fussell, Paul - *The Boys' Crusade: American G.I.s in Europe: Chaos and Fear in World War Two*
CR - v286 - i1669 - Feb 2005 - p122(1) [51-500]
Spec - v296 - i9199 - Nov 27 2004 - p43(2) [501+]
TLS - i5304 - Nov 26 2004 - p12(1) [501+]
The Boys' Crusade: The American Infantry in Northwestern Europe, 1944-1945
NS - v133 - i4702 - August 23 2004 - p35(2) [501+]
Parameters - v34 - i3 - Autumn 2004 - p150(2) [501+]
Fuster, Valentin - *Hurst's the Heart, 11th Ed., Vols. 1-2*
SciTech - v28 - i3 - Sept 2004 - p105(1) [1-50]
Fustukian, Suzanne - *Health Policy in a Globalising World*
CS - v33 - i4 - July 2004 - p490(2) [51-500]
Futai, Masamitsu - *Handbook of ATPases: Biochemistry, Cell Biology, Pathophysiology*
SciTech - v28 - i4 - Dec 2004 - p73(1) [51-500]
Futterer, Kurt - *Emile (Illus. by Futterer, Ralf)*
c BL - v101 - i9-10 - Jan 1 2005 - p869(1) [501+]
Futuyma, Douglas J. - *Annual Review of Ecology, Evolution, and Systematics: Vol. 34, 2003*
QRB - v79 - i3 - Sept 2004 - p331(1) [501+]
SciTech - v28 - i1 - March 2004 - p69(1) [51-500]
Fyfe, Aileen - *Science and Salavations: Evangelical Popular Science Publishing in Victorian Britain*
Choice - v42 - i5 - Jan 2005 - p870(2) [1-50]
Fyleman, Rose - *Mary Middling and Other Silly Folk: Nursery Rhymes and Nonsense Poems (Illus. by Bandlow, Katja)*
c BL - v101 - i6 - Nov 15 2004 - p588(1) [51-500]
c HB - v80 - i5 - Sept-Oct 2004 - p603(2) [51-500]
c KR - v72 - i17 - Sept 1 2004 - p864(1) [51-500]
c PW - v251 - i37 - Sept 13 2004 - p80(2) [51-500]
c SLJ - v50 - i9 - Sept 2004 - p186(1) [51-500]
Fyock, Catherine D. - *Hiring Source Book: A Collection of Practical Samples*
HR Mag - v50 - i2 - Feb 2005 - pNA [501+]
HR Mag - v50 - i2 - Feb 2005 - pS10(1) [501+]

G

Gaarder, Jostein - *The Orange Girl*
  y Kliatt - v38 - i5 - Sept 2004 - p10(2) [51-500]
  y SLJ - v51 - i1 - Jan 2005 - p130(1) [51-500]
Gabaccia, Donna - *Women, Gender, and Transnational Lives: Italian Workers of the World*
  CWS - v23 - i3-4 - Spring-Summer 2004 - p214(1) [501+]
Gabaldon, Diana - *Lord John and the Private Matter*
  Globe & Mail - Nov 20 2004 - pD29 [1-50]
Gabbard, David A. - *Defending Public Schools, Vols. 1-4*
  LJ - v130 - i2 - Feb 1 2005 - p113(1) [51-500]
Gabbin, Joanne V. - *Furious Flower: African American Poetry from the Black Arts Movement to the Present*
  Black Iss - v7 - i2 - March-April 2005 - p31(2) [51-500]
Gabel, Medard - *Global Inc.: An Atlas of Multinational Corporations*
  Fut - v38 - i5 - Sept-Oct 2004 - p62(2) [51-500]
Gable, Craig - *Ebony Rising: Short Fiction of the Greater Harlem Renaissance Era*
  Bl S - v34 - i3 - Fall 2004 - p71-71 [501+]
  Kliatt - v38 - i6 - Nov 2004 - p28(1) [51-500]
  LJ - v129 - i13 - August 2004 - p71(1) [51-500]
Ebony Rising: Short Fiction of the Greater Harlem Renaissance Era
  Choice - v42 - i3 - Nov 2004 - p482(1) [1-50]
Gabler, James M. - *Wine into Words: A History and Bibliography of Wine Books in the English Language*
  ALJ - v53 - i4 - Nov 2004 - p414(1) [501+]
Gabori, Susan - *Good Enough Life: The Dying Speak*
  CBRA - Annual 2003 - p391(1) [51-500]
Gabriel, Barbara - *Post-modernism and the Ethical Subject*
  R&R Bk N - v20 - i1 - Feb 2005 - p9(1) [51-500]
Gabriel, Philip - *Kafka on the Shore*
  NY - v80 - i44 - Jan 24 2005 - p091 [501+]
Gabriel, Richard A. - *Military History of Ancient Israel*
  R&R Bk N - v19 - i1 - Feb 2004 - p19(1) [1-50]
Subotai the Valiant: Genghis Khan's Greatest General
  R&R Bk N - v19 - i4 - Nov 2004 - p43(1) [51-500]
Gabriel, Richard F. - *What Engineers and Managers Need to Know about Human Factors*
  SciTech - v28 - i1 - March 2004 - p136(1) [51-500]
Gaca, Kathy L. - *The Making of Fornication: Eros, Ethics, and Political Reform in Greek Philosophy and Early Christianity*
  TLS - i5301 - Nov 5 2004 - p14(1) [501+]
Gad, Shayne C. - *Selection and Use of Contract Research Organizations: A Guide for the Pharmaceutical and Medical Device Industries*
  SciTech - v28 - i1 - March 2004 - p121(1) [51-500]
  SciTech - v28 - i1 - March 2004 - p122(1) [51-500]
Gadalla, Moustafa - *Egyptian Romany*
  Bwatch - Oct 2004 - pNA [51-500]
Gadamer, Hans-Georg - *Century of Philosophy*
  R&R Bk N - v19 - i1 - Feb 2004 - p4(1) [51-500]
Les Chemins de Heidegger
  Dialogue - v43 - i1 - Wntr 2004 - p200-202 [501+]
Gaddie, Ronald Keith - *Born to Run: Origins of the Political Career*
  Choice - v42 - i3 - Nov 2004 - p564(2) [1-50]
Gaddis, John Lewis - *The Landscape of History: How Historians Map the Past*
  AHR - v109 - i2 - April 2004 - p475(2) [501+]
Surprise, Security, and the American Experience
  APJ - v18 - i4 - Winter 2004 - p113(2) [501+]
  Choice - v42 - i2 - Oct 2004 - p368(1) [51-500]
  J Mil H - v68 - i4 - Oct 2004 - p1327-1328 [501+]
  NYRB - v51 - i15 - Oct 7 2004 - p15(4) [501+]
  Parameters - v34 - i4 - Winter 2004 - p131(3) [501+]
  PSQ - v119 - i4 - Winter 2004 - p681(3) [501+]
  TLS - i5301 - Nov 5 2004 - p4-6 [501+]

Gaddis, William - *Carpenter's Gothic*
  TLS - i5264 - Feb 20 2004 - p21-22 [501+]
J R
  TLS - i5264 - Feb 20 2004 - p21-22 [501+]
The Recognitions
  TLS - i5264 - Feb 20 2004 - p21-22 [501+]
Gade, Anna M. - *Perfection Makes Practice: Learning, Emotion, and the Recited Qur'an in Indonesia*
  R&R Bk N - v19 - i3 - August 2004 - p17(1) [1-50]
Gadrey, Jean - *Productivity Innovation and Knowledge in Services: New Economic and Socio-Economic Approaches*
  JEL - v42 - i3 - Sept 2004 - p865(3) [501+]
Gaebel, R.E. - *Cavalry Operations in the Ancient Greek World*
  Class R - v53 - i2 - Nov 2003 - p403-405 [501+]
Gaetano, Arianne M. - *On the Move: Women and Rural-to-Urban Migration in Contemporary China*
  Ch Rev Int - v11 - i1 - Spring 2004 - p84(4) [501+]
Gaetz, Dayle Campbell - *Barkerville Gold*
  c Res Links - v10 - i1 - Oct 2004 - p12(2) [51-500]
No Problem
  c CBRA - Annual 2003 - p483(2) [51-500]
Gafar, John - *Gunaya: From State Control to Free Markets*
  JEL - v41 - i4 - Dec 2003 - p1424(1) [501+]
Gaff, Alan D. - *Bayonets in the Wilderness: Anthony Wayne's Legion in the Old Northwest*
  J Mil H - v68 - i4 - Oct 2004 - p1254-1255 [501+]
Gaffey, Sheila - *Signifying Place: The Semiotic Realisation of Place in Irish Product Marketing*
  R&R Bk N - v19 - i4 - Nov 2004 - p111(1) [51-500]
Gaffney, Terence - *Real and Complex Singularities: Proceedings*
  SciTech - v28 - i4 - Dec 2004 - p43(1) [51-500]
Gaffield, Chad - *Canadian Distinctiveness into the XX1st Century*
  CBRA - Annual 2003 - p273(1) [501+]
Gaffney, Elizabeth - *Metropolis*
  BL - v101 - i9-10 - Jan 1 2005 - p814(1) [1-50]
  Ent W - i810 - March 11 2005 - p108 [501+]
  KR - v73 - i2 - Jan 15 2005 - p70(1) [501+]
  LJ - v130 - i1 - Jan 1 2005 - p95(1) [51-500]
  NW - March 7 2005 - p55 [51-500]
  NYTBR - March 13 2005 - p12 [501+]
  People - v63 - i12 - March 28 2005 - p48 [51-500]
  PW - v251 - i51 - Dec 20 2004 - p34(1) [51-500]
  Time - v165 - i13 - March 28 2005 - p64 [501+]
Gaffney, John - *The French Presidential and Legislative Elections of 2002*
  R&R Bk N - v19 - i4 - Nov 2004 - p156(1) [501+]
Gaffney, Timothy R. - *Wee and the Wright Brothers (Illus. by Pons, Bernadette)*
  c BL - v101 - i1 - Sept 1 2004 - p131(1) [1-50]
  c KR - v72 - i16 - August 15 2004 - p805(1) [51-500]
  c SLJ - v50 - i12 - Dec 2004 - p108(1) [501+]
Gagan, David - *For Patients of Moderate Means: A Social History of the Voluntary Public General Hospital in Canada, 1890-1950*
  Can Hist R - v85 - i3 - Sept 2004 - p632(2) [501+]
Gagarin, Michael - *Antiphon the Athenian: Oratory, Law and Justice in the Age of the Sophists*
  Class R - v54 - i2 - Nov 2004 - p310-312 [501+]
Gage, Eleni - *North of Ithaka: A Journey Home Through a Family's Extraordinary Past*
  TLS - i5291 - August 27 2004 - p27(1) [501+]
Gage, Eleni N. - *North of Ithaka: A Journey Home Through a Family's Extraordinary Past*
  KR - v73 - i5 - March 1 2005 - p273(1) [501+]

Gage, John - *Color and Meaning: Art, Science, and Symbolism*
  Isis - v95 - i3 - Sept 2004 - p473(2) [501+]
Gagne, Denise - *Alphabet Action Songs*
  c Teach Mus - v12 - i2 - Oct 2004 - p71(1) [51-500]
Gagne, Eric - *Eric Gagne: Break Barriers*
  c BL - v101 - i1 - Sept 1 2004 - p110(1) [1-50]
Gagne, Marcel - *Moving to the Linux Business Desktop*
  LJ - v130 - i1 - Jan 1 2005 - p148(1) [501+]
Gagne, Robert M. - *Principles of Instructional Design, 5th Ed.*
  R&R Bk N - v19 - i3 - August 2004 - p216(1) [1-50]
Gagnon, Alain-G. - *The Conditions of Diversity in Multinational Democracies*
  R&R Bk N - v19 - i3 - August 2004 - p174(1) [501+]
Gagnon, John H. - *Interpretation of Desire: Essays in the Study of Sexuality*
  E-Streams - July 2004 - pNA [501+]
Gahlinger, Paul M. - *Illegal Drugs: A Complete Guide to Their History, Chemistry, Use and Abuse*
  Ref Rev - Dec 2004 - pNA [501+]
  SciTech - v28 - i3 - Sept 2004 - p103(1) [51-500]
Gaidar, Yegor - *The Economics of Russian Transition*
  E-A St - v56 - i3 - May 2004 - p470(2) [501+]
  JEL - v41 - i4 - Dec 2003 - p1427(1) [501+]
  JEL - v42 - i4 - Dec 2004 - p1162(3) [501+]
  Slav R - v63 - i3 - Fall 2004 - p673-673 [501+]
State and Evolution: Russia's Search for a Free Market
  JEL - v41 - i4 - Dec 2003 - p1427(1) [501+]
Gaiduk, Ilya V. - *Confronting Vietnam: Soviet Policy toward the Indochina Conflict, 1954-1963*
  HNet - Nov 2004 - pNA [501+]
  Slav R - v63 - i2 - Summer 2004 - p417(2) [501+]
The Great Confrontation: Europe and Islam Through the Centuries
  Choice - v42 - i1 - Sept 2004 - p162(2) [501+]
  R&R Bk N - v19 - i1 - Feb 2004 - p27(1) [51-500]
Gaige, Amity - *O My Darling*
  KR - v73 - i2 - Jan 15 2005 - p70(1) [501+]
  PW - v252 - i9 - Feb 28 2005 - p40(1) [51-500]
Gaile, Gary L. - *Geography in America at the Dawn of the 21st Century*
  Choice - v42 - i3 - Nov 2004 - p546(2) [1-50]
Gailey, Elizabeth Atwood - *Write to Death: News Framing of the Right-to-Die Conflict From Quinlan's Coma to Kervorkian's Conviction*
  R&R Bk N - v19 - i1 - Feb 2004 - p248(1) [51-500]
Gailey, Jeannine Hall - *Understanding Web Services Specifications and the WSE*
  SciTech - v28 - i1 - March 2004 - p158(1) [51-500]
Gaillard, Frye - *Cradle of Freedom: Alabama and the Movement That Changed America*
  Choice - v42 - i2 - Oct 2004 - p354(2) [51-500]
Gaillemin, Jean-Louis - *Dali: Master of Fantasies*
  R&R Bk N - v19 - i4 - Nov 2004 - p207(1) [501+]
Gaiman, Neil - *1602 (Illus. by Kubert, Andy)*
  PW - v251 - i43 - Oct 25 2004 - p30(1) [51-500]
Coraline (Illus. by McKean, Dave)
  c RT - v57 - Oct 2003 - p176 [1-50]
  c Kliatt - v38 - i4 - July 2004 - p30(1) [51-500]
Creatures of the Night
  BL - v101 - i7 - Dec 1 2004 - p643(1) [51-500]
The Day I Swapped My Dad for Two Goldfish (Illus. by McKean, Dave)
  c BIC - v33 - i8 - Nov 2004 - p35(2) [501+]
  c BW - v34 - i41 - Oct 10 2004 - p12(1) [501+]
  c Globe & Mail - Oct 23 2004 - pD22 [51-500]
  c Sch Lib - v52 - i4 - Winter 2004 - p201(1) [51-500]

Melinda
     PW - v252 - i11 - March 14 2005 - p47(1) [51-500]

The Neil Gaiman Audio Collection (Read by Gaiman, Neil)
     Globe & Mail - Jan 1 2005 - pD14 [1-50]

The Wolves in the Walls
   c LibMed - v22 - i6 - March 2004 - p60(1) [501+]

The Wolves in the Walls (Illus. by McKean, Dave)
     LibMed - v22 - i6 - March 2004 - p60(1) [501+]

Gaimster, David - *The Archaeology of Reformation 1480-1580*
     Ren Q - v57 - i4 - Winter 2004 - p1492(2) [501+]

Gainax - *FLCL, Vol 1. Art (Illus. by Ueda, Hajime)*
   y Kliatt - v38 - i5 - Sept 2004 - p35(2) [501+]

Gaines, Clarence E. - *They Call Me Big House*
     LJ - v129 - i19 - Nov 15 2004 - p67(1) [501+]
     PW - v251 - i34 - August 23 2004 - p49(1) [51-500]

Gaines, James R. - *Evening in the Palace of Reason: Bach Meets Frederick the Great in the Age of Enlightenment*
     Ent W - i811 - March 18 2005 - p74 [51-500]
     KR - v73 - i1 - Jan 1 2005 - p33(1) [501+]
     LJ - v130 - i2 - Feb 1 2005 - p80(2) [51-500]
     People - v63 - i12 - March 28 2005 - p50 [51-500]
     PW - v252 - i6 - Feb 7 2005 - p53(2) [51-500]
     Spec - v297 - i9205 - Jan 8 2005 - p32(2) [501+]
     Time - v165 - i11 - March 14 2005 - p62 [501+]

Gaines, Janet Howe - *Forgiveness in a Wounded World: Jonah's Dilemma*
     R&R Bk N - v19 - i1 - Feb 2004 - p20(1) [1-50]

Gaines, Larry K. - *Drugs, Crime, & Justice: Contemporary Perspectives, 2nd Ed.*
     R&R Bk N - v19 - i1 - Feb 2004 - p140(1) [51-500]

Gaines, Steven - *The Sky's the Limit: Passion and Property in Manhattan*
     PW - v252 - i11 - March 14 2005 - p52(2) [51-500]

Gainor, J. Ellen - *Susan Glaspell in Context: American Theater, Culture, and Politics 1915-48*
     TDR - v48 - i2 - Summer 2004 - p174(5) [501+]

Gaita, Raimond - *The Philosopher's Dog: Friendship with Animals*
     BL - v100 - i21 - July 2004 - p1808(1) [1-50]

Gaiter, Dorothy J. - *Wine for Every Day and Every Occasion: Red, White, and Bubbly to Celebrate the Joy of Living.*
     LJ - v129 - i13 - August 2004 - p109(1) [51-500]
     PW - v251 - i29 - July 19 2004 - p157(1) [51-500]

Gaiter, Leonce - *Bourbon Street*
     KR - v73 - i1 - Jan 1 2005 - p22(2) [51-500]
     LJ - v130 - i3 - Feb 15 2005 - p124(1) [51-500]

Gaither, Carl C. - *Astronomically Speaking: A Dictionary of Quotations on Astronomy and Physics*
     E-Streams - Sept 2004 - pNA [501+]
     S&T - v108 - i3 - Sept 2004 - p112(2) [501+]

Gajano, Sofia Boesch - *Europa Sacra: Raccolte agiografiche e identita politiche in Europa fra Medioevo ed Eta moderna*
     CHR - v90 - i3 - July 2004 - p539(3) [501+]

Galaktionov, Kirill V. - *The Biology and Evolution of Trematodes: An Essay on the Biology, Morphology, Life Cycles, Transmission, and Evolution of Digenetic Trematodes*
     QRB - v79 - i4 - Dec 2004 - p434(2) [501+]
     SciTech - v28 - i1 - March 2004 - p68(1) [51-500]

Galambos, Janos - *Products of Random Variables: Applications to Problems of Physics and to Arithmetical Functions*
     SciTech - v28 - i4 - Dec 2004 - p36(1) [51-500]

Galambos, Louis - *Anytime, Anywhere: Entrepreneurship and the Creation of a Wireless World*
     T&C - v45 - i1 - Jan 2004 - p213(2) [501+]

Galanaki, Rhea - *Eleni, or Nobody*
     TLS - i5284 - July 9 2004 - p6(1) [501+]
     WLT - v78 - i3-4 - Sept-Dec 2004 - p150(1) [501+]

O Aionas Ton Lavyrinthon
     TLS - i5284 - July 9 2004 - p6(1) [501+]

Galand-Hallyn, Perrine - *Poetiques de la Renaissance: Le modele italien, le monde franco-bourguignon et leur heritage en France au XVIe siecle*
     Six Ct J - v35 - i3 - Fall 2004 - p872-874 [501+]

Galanis, Clifford - *Breastfeeding Facts for Fathers*
     E-Streams - Sept 2004 - pNA [501+]

Galante, Pierre - *Operation Valkyrie: The German Generals' Plot Against Hitler*
     HNet - Sept 2004 - pNA [501+]

Galat, Joan Marie - *Dot to Dot in the Sky: Stories of the Moon*
     Res Links - v10 - i3 - Feb 2005 - p17(1) [51-500]

Galbally, Ann - *Charles Conder: The Last Bohemian*
     Quad - v49 - i1-2 - Jan-Feb 2005 - p117(2) [501+]

Galbraith, James K. - *Inequality and Industrial Change: A Global View*
     Econ J - v114 - i499 - Nov 2004 - pF549-F550 [501+]

Galbraith, John Kenneth - *The Economics of Innocent Fraud: Truth for our Time*
     Choice - v42 - i5 - Jan 2005 - p901(2) [1-50]
     R&R Bk N - v19 - i4 - Nov 2004 - p146(1) [501+]
     TimHES - v0 - i1675 - Jan 21 2005 - p28(1) [501+]

Gale, M. - *Virgil on the Nature of Things: The Georgics, Lucretius and the Didactic Tradition*
     Class R - v54 - i2 - Nov 2004 - p371(4) [501+]

Gale, Robert L. - *A Henry Wadsworth Longfellow Companion*
     Choice - v41 - i11-12 - July-August 2004 - p2016(1) [501+]

Gale, Trevor - *Engaging Teachers: Towards a Radical Democratic Agenda for Schooling*
     R&R Bk N - v19 - i1 - Feb 2004 - p190(1) [51-500]
     TCR - v106 - i5 - May 2004 - p1018(3) [501+]

Gale, W.F. - *Smithells Metals Reference Book*
     Choice - v42 - i3 - Nov 2004 - p515(2) [1-50]

Gales, Nick - *Marine Mammals, Fisheries, Tourism and Management Issues*
     SciTech - v28 - i3 - Sept 2004 - p66(1) [51-500]

Galetti, Paola - *I Mulini nell'Europa medievale: Atti del Convegno di San Quirico d'Orcia, 21-23 settembre 2000*
     HER - v119 - i483 - Sept 2004 - p1042(2) [501+]
     HER - v119 - i483 - Sept 2004 - p1042(2) [501+]

Galford, Ellen - *The Trail West: Exploring History through Art*
   c BL - v101 - i5 - Nov 1 2004 - p495(2) [51-500]
   c SLJ - v51 - i2 - Feb 2005 - p146(1) [51-500]

Galford, Robert - *The Leadership Legacy*
     Har Bus R - v83 - i2 - Feb 2005 - p57(1) [1-50]

Galgut, Damon - *The Good Doctor*
   y Kliatt - v39 - i1 - Jan 2005 - p13(1) [51-500]
     BW - v34 - i46 - Nov 14 2004 - p12(1) [1-50]

The Quarry
     BL - v101 - i6 - Nov 15 2004 - p561(1) [51-500]
     Econ - v373 - i8397 - Oct 16 2004 - p82US [501+]
     Globe & Mail - March 5 2005 - pD5 [501+]
     LJ - v130 - i2 - Feb 1 2005 - p68(1) [51-500]
     PW - v251 - i48 - Nov 29 2004 - p21(1) [51-500]
     Spec - v296 - i9189 - Sept 18 2004 - p48(1) [501+]
     TLS - i5293 - Sept 10 2004 - p21(1) [501+]

Galician, Mary-Lou - *Handbook of Product Placement in the Mass Media: New Strategies in Marketing Theory, Practice, Trends, and Ethics*
     R&R Bk N - v19 - i4 - Nov 2004 - p115(1) [51-500]

Sex, Love & Romance in the Mass Media: Analysis & Criticism of Unrealistic Portrayals & Their Influence
     JPC - v38 - i2 - Nov 2004 - p424(2) [501+]
     R&R Bk N - v19 - i1 - Feb 2004 - p130(1) [51-500]

Galilei, Vincenzo - *Dialogue on Ancient and Modern Music*
     Choice - v41 - i11-12 - July-August 2004 - p2054(1) [501+]
     Ren Q - v57 - i4 - Winter 2004 - p1400(2) [501+]

Galileo - *Le mecaniche*
     Isis - v95 - i3 - Sept 2004 - p490(3) [501+]

Galimberti Jarman, Beatriz - *Oxford Spanish Dictionary, 3rd Ed.*
   y SLJ - v50 - i10 - Oct 2004 - pS67(1) [51-500]

Galindo, Alberto Flores - *Los Rostros de la Plebe*
     HAHR - v84 - i2 - May 2004 - p342(2) [501+]

Galindo, Fernando - *Database and Expert Systems Applications: 15th International Conference, DEXA 2004, Zaragoza, Spain, August 30-September 3, 2004: Proceedings*
     SciTech - v28 - i4 - Dec 2004 - p24(1) [51-500]

Galindo-Leal, Carlos - *The Atlantic Forest of South America: Biodiversity Status, Threats, and Outlook*
     Choice - v41 - i7 - March 2004 - p1321(1) [501+]
     QRB - v79 - i3 - Sept 2004 - p324(2) [501+]

Galinou, Mireille - *City Merchants and the Arts 1670-1720*
     Apo - v160 - i511 - Sept 2004 - p101(2) [501+]

Galis, Alex - *Programmable Networks for IP Service Deployment*
     SciTech - v28 - i3 - Sept 2004 - p158(1) [51-500]

Galison, Peter - *Einstein's Clocks, Poincare's Maps: Empires of Time*
     Choice - v41 - i7 - March 2004 - p1317(1) [501+]
     NYTBR - Oct 24 2004 - p30 [501+]
     Phys Today - v57 - i9 - Sept 2004 - p57-57 [501+]
   y SB - v40 - i4 - July-August 2004 - p164(1) [51-500]
     VQR - v80 - i1 - Wntr 2004 - p275-276 [501+]

Gall, Joyce P. - *Applying Educational Research: A Practical Guide, 5th Ed.*
     R&R Bk N - v19 - i3 - August 2004 - p215(1) [1-50]

Gall, Lothar - *Krupp im 20 Jahrhundert: Die Geschichte des Unternehmens vom Ersten Weltkrieg bis zur Grundung der Stiftung*
     HNet - Dec 2004 - pNA [501+]

Wissenschaftskommunikation im 19. Jahrhundert: Nassauer Gespracheder Freiherr-vom-Stein-Gesellschaft
     HNet - Oct 2004 - pNA [501+]

Gall, Timothy L. - *Junior Worldmark Encyclopedia of the Canadian Provinces, 4th Ed.E-book Review*
     BL - v101 - i8 - Dec 15 2004 - p758(2) [501+]

Junior Worldmark Encyclopedia of the Mexican States
   c SLJ - v51 - i2 - Feb 2005 - p84(1) [51-500]

Junior Worldmark Encyclopedia of the Mexican States. E-book Review
     BL - v101 - i8 - Dec 15 2004 - p758(2) [501+]

Gallagher, B.J. - *Who Are "They" Anyway? A Tale of Achieving Success at Work through Personal Accountability*
     BL - v101 - i1 - Sept 1 2004 - p32(1) [51-500]

Gallagher, Clarence - *Church Law and Church Order in Rome and Byzantium: A Comparative Study*
     Specu - v79 - i4 - Oct 2004 - p1072(2) [501+]

Gallagher, Eugene V. - *The New Religious Movements Experience in America*
     LJ - v130 - i2 - Feb 1 2005 - p116(1) [51-500]

Gallagher, Fred - *Megatokyo, Vol. 2*
     NYTBR - July 18 2004 - p14 [501+]
   y SLJ - v50 - i8 - August 2004 - p148(1) [501+]
   y VOYA - v27 - i3 - August 2004 - p228(1) [51-500]

Gallagher, Gary W. - *The Shenandoah Valley Campaign of 1862*
     J Mil H - v68 - i3 - April 2004 - p606-607 [501+]
     JAH - v91 - i2 - Sept 2004 - p636(2) [501+]
     JSH - v70 - i3 - August 2004 - p685(2) [501+]
     SHQ - v107 - i3 - Jan 2004 - p486(2) [501+]

Gallagher, John - *Geisha: A Unique World of Tradition, Elegance, and Art*
   y Choice - v42 - i4 - Dec 2004 - p702(1) [1-50]

J. Roger's School for Pirates. Audiobook Review
   c SLJ - v50 - i9 - Sept 2004 - p80(2) [51-500]

Gallagher, Lisa A. - *Thesaurus of Psychological Index Terms, 10th Ed.*
     R&R Bk N - v19 - i4 - Nov 2004 - p257(1) [501+]

Gallagher, Lynn M. - *Clean Water Handbook, 3rd Ed.*
     SciTech - v28 - i1 - March 2004 - p147(1) [51-500]

Gallagher, Mary - *Soundings in French Caribbean Writing Since 1950: The Shock of Space and Time*
     FS - v58 - i1 - Jan 2004 - p142(2) [501+]

Gallagher, Michael - *Israel and Palestine*
   y Sch Lib - v52 - i4 - Winter 2004 - p218(1) [51-500]

Gallagher-Mundy, Chrissie - *Cesarean Recovery*
     E-Streams - August 2004 - pNA [501+]

Gallagher, Sean - *Western Plainchant in the First Millennium: Studies in the Medieval Liturgy and Its Music*
     R&R Bk N - v19 - i2 - May 2004 - p192(1) [51-500]

Gallagher, Tom - *The Balkans After the Cold War: From Tyranny to Tragedy*
     JPR - v41 - i5 - Sept 2004 - p641-641 [501+]
     Slav R - v63 - i4 - Winter 2004 - p870(2) [501+]

Galland, Nicole - *The Fool's Tale: A Novel*
     KR - v72 - i22 - Nov 15 2004 - p1061(1) [51-500]
     LJ - v129 - i20 - Dec 1 2004 - p100(1) [51-500]
     PW - v251 - i50 - Dec 13 2004 - p45(1) [51-500]

Gallander, Benjamin - *Canadian Small Business Survival Guide*
     CBRA - Annual 2003 - p326(1) [51-500]

Gallant, John - *Bannock, Beans and Black Tea*
     Beav - v84 - i5 - Oct-Nov 2004 - p46(1) [501+]

Gallant, Thomas W. - *Experiencing Dominion: Culture, Identity, and Power in the British Mediterranean*
     JIH - v34 - i3 - Wntr 2004 - p455-2 [501+]
     JMH - v76 - i3 - Sept 2004 - p681(3) [501+]

Gallard, Rolf C. - *The ACTH Axis: Pathogenesis, Diagnosis, and Treatment*
     SciTech - v28 - i1 - March 2004 - p103(1) [51-500]

Gallati, Barbara Dayer - *Children of the Gilded Era: Portraits by Sargent, Renoir, Cassatt, and Their Contemporaries*
    A Art - v69 - i751 - Feb 2005 - p75(2) [501+]
Great Expectations: John Singer Sargent Painting Children
    A Art - v68 - i748 - Nov 2004 - p74(1) [501+]

Gallaway, Jayson - *Diary of a Viagra Fiend*
    NYT - August 8 2004 - pST9 [501+]
    NYTBR - Jan 2 2005 - p19 [501+]

Gallegher, Kathleen - *How Theatre Educates: Convergences and Counterpoints with Artists, Scholars, and Advocates*
    TDR - v48 - i4 - Winter 2004 - p192(11) [501+]

Gallegos, Frederick - *Information Technology Control and Audit, 2nd Ed.*
    SciTech - v28 - i3 - Sept 2004 - p134(1) [51-500]

Galley, Harry A. - *MacArthur's Victory: The War in New Guinea, 1943-1944*
    LJ - v130 - i2 - Feb 1 2005 - p97(1) [51-500]

Gallico, Paul - *Small Miracle (Illus. by Croll, Carolyn)*
    c CBRA - Annual 2003 - p450(2) [51-500]

Gallien, Louis B., Jr. - *Instructing and Mentoring the African American College Student: Strategies for Success in Higher Education*
    Choice - v42 - i2 - Oct 2004 - p343(2) [51-500]
    R&R Bk N - v19 - i3 - August 2004 - p229(1) [1-50]

Gallina, Jill - *Christmas Pins Past and Present, 2nd Ed.*
    Ant&CM - v108 - i10 - Dec 2003 - p16(1) [501+]

Gallo, Donald R. - *First Crossing: Stories about Teen Immigrants*
    y BL - v101 - i6 - Nov 15 2004 - p574(1) [51-500]
    y JAAL - v48 - i2 - Oct 2004 - p174(2) [501+]
    y KR - v72 - i19 - Oct 1 2004 - p960(1) [51-500]
    y SLJ - v50 - i10 - Oct 2004 - p164(2) [51-500]
    y VOYA - v27 - i4 - Oct 2004 - p296(1) [51-500]

Gallo, Melina L. - *Reading the World of Work: A Learner-Centered Approach to Workplace Literacy and ESL*
    R&R Bk N - v19 - i4 - Nov 2004 - p189(1) [501+]

Gallo, Ruben - *The Mexico City Reader*
    LJ - v129 - i17 - Oct 15 2004 - p79(1) [51-500]

Galloway, Gregory - *As Simple as Snow*
    BL - v101 - i9-10 - Jan 1 2005 - p814(1) [1-50]
    KR - v73 - i2 - Jan 15 2005 - p71(1) [501+]
    LJ - v130 - i3 - Feb 15 2005 - p116(1) [51-500]
    PW - v252 - i6 - Feb 7 2005 - p42(1) [501+]

Galloway, Priscilla - *Archers, Alchemists, and 98 Other Medieval Jobs You Might Have Loved or Loathed (Illus. by Newbigging, Martha)*
    c CBRA - Annual 2003 - p535(1) [51-500]
    y SLJ - v50 - i10 - Oct 2004 - pS32(1) [51-500]
Courtesan's Daughter
    y CBRA - Annual 2003 - p484(1) [51-500]
The Courtesan's Daughter
    c CH Bwatch - v14 - i8 - August 2004 - p3(1) [51-500]
    c PW - v251 - i37 - Sept 13 2004 - p81(1) [51-500]
Lisa, Boon One: Overland to Cariboo. Our Canadian Girl
    y Can CL - i111-112 - Fall-Winter 2003 - p128(7) [501+]

Galloway, T.H. - *Dear Old Roswell: Civil War Letters of the King Family of Roswell, Georgia*
    R&R Bk N - v19 - i1 - Feb 2004 - p60(1) [1-50]

Gallp, Rick - *Living the G.I. Diet: Delicious Recipes and Real Life Strategies to Lose Weight and Keep it Off*
    CBRA - Annual 2003 - p129(2) [51-500]

Gallucci, Margaret A. - *Benvenuto Cellini: Sexuality, Masculinity, and Artistic Identity in Renaissance Italy*
    Ren Q - v57 - i4 - Winter 2004 - p1391(3) [501+]

Galluccio, Steve - *Mambo Italiano*
    BIC - v33 - i9 - Dec 2004 - p24(3) [501+]

Gallup, George H., Sr. - *Gallup Poll: Public Opinion 2003*
    R&R Bk N - v19 - i4 - Nov 2004 - p120(1) [51-500]

Gallup, John Luke - *Is Geography Destiny?: Lessons from Latin America*
    Choice - v41 - i7 - March 2004 - p1341(1) [501+]
    JEL - v42 - i1 - March 2004 - p1 [501+]
    R&R Bk N - v19 - i1 - Feb 2004 - p82(1) [1-50]

Galperin, Hernan - *New Television, Old Politics: The Transition to Digital TV in the United States and Britain*
    TimHES - v0 - i1683 - March 18 2005 - p29(1) [501+]

Galperin, William H. - *The Historical Austen*
    Albion - v36 - i1 - Spring 2004 - p149(2) [501+]
    Clio - v33 - i3 - Spring 2004 - p305(10) [501+]
    HR - v57 - i2 - Summer 2004 - p303-310 [501+]

Galster, George C. - *Why Not in My Backyard? Neighborhood Impacts of Deconcentrating Assisted Housing*
    R&R Bk N - v19 - i1 - Feb 2004 - p102(1) [51-500]

Galston, William - *Liberal Pluralism*
    Phil R - v113 - i1 - Jan 2004 - p127(3) [501+]

Galvan, Nelida - *La Revolucion para ninos/The Revolution for children (Illus. by Garcia, Modesto)*
    c BL - v100 - i22 - August 2004 - p1950(1) [501+]

Gambaccini, Piero - *Mountebanks and Medicasters: A History of Italian Charlatans from the Middle Ages to the Present*
    SciTech - v28 - i1 - March 2004 - p79(1) [51-500]

Gambescia, Stephen F. - *Managing a Public Speaker Bureau: A Manual for Health and Human Services Organizations*
    SciTech - v28 - i4 - Dec 2004 - p86(1) [51-500]

Gambito, Sarah - *Matadora*
    LJ - v129 - i13 - August 2004 - p85(1) [501+]

Gamble, Adam - *A Public Betrayed: Japan's Corrupt New Industry and Media Atrocities*
    LJ - v129 - i16 - Oct 1 2004 - p91(1) [51-500]

Gamble, Andrew - *Between Europe and America: The Future of British Politics*
    TimHES - v0 - i1668 - Nov 26 2004 - pV(1) [501+]

Gamble, Richard M. - *The War for Righteousness: Progressive Christianity, The Great War, and the Rise of the Messianic Nation*
    Choice - v41 - i11-12 - July-August 2004 - p2107(1) [501+]

The Game. Audiobook Review
    Globe & Mail - Feb 19 2005 - pD17 [501+]

Gamm, Kate - *Teaching World Cinema*
    TES - v0 - i4587 - June 11 2004 - psssss19(1) [501+]

Gammel, Irene - *Making Avonlea: L.M. Montgomery and Popular Culture*
    Can Hist R - v85 - i3 - Sept 2004 - p634(2) [501+]
    Dal R - v84 - i1 - Spring 2004 - p179-180 [501+]
    R&R Bk N - v19 - i1 - Feb 2004 - p240(1) [51-500]

Gammon, Jim - *Aviation Fuel Quality Control Procedures, 3rd Ed.*
    SciTech - v28 - i4 - Dec 2004 - p161(1) [51-500]

Gamson, Joshua - *The Fabulous Sylvester: The Legend, the Music, the Seventies in San Francisco*
    Ent W - i809 - March 4 2005 - p77 [51-500]
    KR - v73 - i1 - Jan 1 2005 - p33(1) [501+]
    PW - v252 - i2 - Jan 10 2005 - p47(1) [51-500]

Gan, Jay J. - *Pesticide Decontamination and Detoxification: Proceedings*
    SciTech - v28 - i1 - March 2004 - p147(1) [51-500]

Ganci, Chris - *Chief: The Life of Peter J. Ganci, a New York City Firefighter*
    c CE - v80 - i5 - Mid-Summer 2004 - p275(2) [51-500]

Gand, Gale - *Tru: A Cookbook from the Legendary Chicago Restaurant*
    PW - v251 - i39 - Sept 27 2004 - p51(1) [51-500]

Gandara, Patricia - *School Connections: U.S. Mexican Youth, Peers and School Achievement*
    CE - v81 - i2 - Winter 2004 - p112(1) [51-500]

Gander, Eric M. - *On Our Minds: How Evolutionary Psychology Is Reshaping the Nature-Versus-Nurture Debate*
    Choice - v42 - i1 - Sept 2004 - p191(1) [501+]
    QRB - v79 - i4 - Dec 2004 - p410(1) [501+]

Gandhi, Jeeti - *Indian Flavor*
    Bwatch - v26 - i8 - August 2004 - p2(1) [51-500]

Gandolfi, Arthur - *Economics as Evolutiobary Science: From Utility to Fitness*
    S&S - v68 - i4 - Winter 2004 - p523-3 [501+]

Gandolfi, Silvana - *Aldabra: Or the Tortise Who Loved Shakespeare*
    c LibMed - v23 - i1 - August-Sept 2004 - p67(1) [51-500]
Aldabra: Or the Tortoise Who Loved Shakespeare
    c CCB-B - v57 - i11 - July-August 2004 - p464(2) [501+]
    c SLJ - v50 - i8 - August 2004 - p122(1) [501+]
    y VOYA - v27 - i3 - August 2004 - p229(1) [1-50]

Gandy, Matthew - *Concrete and Clay: Reworking Nature in New York City*
    PG - v23 - i2 - Feb 2004 - p222-223 [501+]
    Pub Hist - v26 - i2 - Spring 2004 - p109(111) [501+]

The Return of the White Plague: Global Poverty and the 'New' Tuberculosis
    TimHES - v0 - i1653 - August 13 2004 - p26(2) [501+]

Gane, Nicholas - *The Future of Social Theory*
    Choice - v42 - i6 - Feb 2005 - p1104(1) [51-500]
    R&R Bk N - v19 - i4 - Nov 2004 - p121(1) [51-500]

Ganeri, Anita - *DK First Atlas*
    c SLJ - v51 - i2 - Feb 2005 - p81(1) [51-500]
Food Chains
    c SB - v40 - i6 - Nov-Dec 2004 - p268(2) [51-500]
Martin Luther King, Jr.: From Minister to Civil Rights Leader
    c SLJ - v50 - i10 - Oct 2004 - p67(1) [51-500]
Muslim Festivals throughout the Year
    c SLJ - v51 - i1 - Jan 2005 - p56(1) [51-500]
The Qur'an and Islam (Illus. by Fennell, Tracy)
    c SLJ - v51 - i1 - Jan 2005 - p57(1) [51-500]
Wild Islands (Illus. by Philips, Mike)
    c Sch Lib - v52 - i4 - Winter 2004 - p207(1) [51-500]
The Young Person's Guide to the Opera
    c SLJ - v50 - i12 - Dec 2004 - p60(1) [501+]
The Young Person's Guide to the Orchestra
    c SLJ - v50 - i12 - Dec 2004 - p60(1) [501+]

Gang Lin - *China After Jiang*
    Pac A - v77 - i3 - Fall 2004 - p552(2) [501+]

Gangi, Jane M. - *Encountering Children's Literature: An Arts Approach*
    Choice - v42 - i1 - Sept 2004 - p158(1) [501+]
    R&R Bk N - v19 - i1 - Feb 2004 - p243(1) [51-500]

Ganguly, Gautam - *Amorphous and Nanocrystalline Silicon Science and Technology -- 2004: Proceedings*
    SciTech - v28 - i4 - Dec 2004 - p156(1) [51-500]

Ganguly, Sumit - *The Kashmir Question: Retrospect and Prospect*
    A Aff - v35 - i2 - July 2004 - p240-240 [51-500]
    R&R Bk N - v19 - i1 - Feb 2004 - p47(1) [51-500]

Ganis, John - *Consuming the American Landscape*
    Aftermage - v32 - i2 - Sept-Oct 2004 - p12(1) [501+]

Gann, Kirby - *Our Napoleon in Rags*
    KR - v73 - i4 - Feb 15 2005 - p190(1) [501+]

Gannett, Robert T., Jr. - *L'impense de la democratie: Tocqueville, la citoyennete et la religion*
    TLS - i5283 - July 2 2004 - p3-4 [501+]

Gannon, Michael B. - *Blood, Bedlam, Bullets, and Badguys: A Reader's Guide to Adventure/Suspense Fiction*
    VOYA - v27 - i5 - Dec 2004 - p427(1) [51-500]

Gannon, Todd - *Steven Holl/Simmons Hall: MIT Undergraduate Residence*
    R&R Bk N - v19 - i4 - Nov 2004 - p247(1) [501+]

Ganong, Lawrence H. - *Stepfamily Relationships: Development, Dynamics, and Interventions*
    R&R Bk N - v19 - i2 - May 2004 - p134 [51-500]

Gansberg, Alan L. - *Little Caesar: A Biography of Edward G. Robinson*
    R&R Bk N - v19 - i4 - Nov 2004 - p226(1) [501+]

Gansler, Jacques - *Transforming Government Supply Chain Management*
    R&R Bk N - v19 - i1 - Feb 2004 - p92(1) [1-50]

Gansner, Emden R. - *Standard ML Basis Manual*
    SciTech - v28 - i4 - Dec 2004 - p22(1) [51-500]

Ganson, Barbara - *The Guarani under Spanish Rule in the Rio de la Plata*
    AHR - v109 - i3 - June 2004 - p951(2) [501+]
    HAHR - v84 - i3 - August 2004 - p535(2) [501+]
    J Soc H - v38 - i2 - Winter 2004 - p537(3) [501+]
    JIH - v35 - i2 - Autumn 2004 - p326(2) [501+]

Gansworth, Eric - *Mending Skins*
    PW - v252 - i8 - Feb 21 2005 - p158(2) [51-500]

Ganti, Tibor - *Chemoton Theory*
    SciTech - v28 - i1 - March 2004 - p61(1) [51-500]
The Principles of Life
    QRB - v79 - i4 - Dec 2004 - p408(2) [501+]
    SciTech - v28 - i1 - March 2004 - p62(1) [51-500]

Gantos, Jack - *Desire Lines*
    y TES - v0 - i4577 - April 2 2004 - p35(1) [501+]
Hole in My Life
    Kliatt - v38 - i6 - Nov 2004 - p32(2) [51-500]
    y SLJ - v50 - i11 - Nov 2004 - p67(1) [51-500]
    y Teach Lib - v32 - i1 - Oct 2004 - p51(1) [51-500]
Jack Adrift: Fourth Grade Without a Clue
    c BooChiTr - Jan 4 2004 - p5(1) [501+]
    c LibMed - v22 - i6 - March 2004 - p62(1) [501+]
Jack's New Power: Stories from a Caribbean Year
    c SLJ - v50 - i11 - Nov 2004 - p65(1) [51-500]
Rotten Ralph Feels Rotten (Illus. by Rubel, Nicole)
    c BL - v100 - i21 - July 2004 - p1850(1) [1-50]
    c HB - v80 - i5 - Sept-Oct 2004 - p583(1) [51-500]
    c SLJ - v50 - i9 - Sept 2004 - p160(1) [51-500]
What Would Joey Do?
    y Kliatt - v38 - i4 - July 2004 - p17(1) [51-500]

Ganz, Cheryl R. - *Pots of Promise: Mexicans and Pottery at Hull-House,1920-40*
   Choice - v42 - i3 - Nov 2004 - p472(1) [1-50]
Ganz, Nicholas - *Graffiti World: Street Art from Five Continents*
   BL - v101 - i9-10 - Jan 1 2005 - p798(2) [51-500]
Gao, James Zheng - *The Communist Takeover of Hangzhou: The Transformation of City and Cadre, 1949-1954*
   R&R Bk N - v19 - i3 - August 2004 - p183(1) [501+]
Gao, Xingjian - *Buying a Fishing Rod for My Grandfather*
   RCF - v24 - i3 - Fall 2004 - p131(2) [501+]
Gaquin, Deirdre A. - *The Almanac of American Education 2004*
   R&R Bk N - v19 - i1 - Feb 2004 - p189(1) [51-500]
Garagna, Silvia - *Mouse Genetics After the Mouse Genome*
   SciTech - v28 - i4 - Dec 2004 - p62(1) [51-500]
Garate, Donald T. - *Juan Bautista de Anza: Basque Explorer in the New World*
   Choice - v41 - i7 - March 2004 - p1346(1) [501+]
   JAH - v91 - i2 - Sept 2004 - p603(2) [501+]
Garb, Louis - *International Succession*
   R&R Bk N - v19 - i3 - August 2004 - p194(1) [501+]
Garbade, Kenneth D. - *Pricing Corporate Securities as Contingent Claims*
   JEL - v41 - i4 - Dec 2003 - p1297(2) [501+]
Garber, James F. - *The Ancient Maya of the Belize Valley: Half a Century of Archaeological Research*
   Choice - v42 - i4 - Dec 2004 - p702(1) [1-50]
Garber, Joseph R. - *Whirlwind*
   KR - v72 - i14 - July 15 2004 - p647(1) [51-500]
   LJ - v129 - i16 - Oct 1 2004 - p69(1) [51-500]
   NYTBR - Oct 31 2004 - p15 [51-500]
   PW - v251 - i37 - Sept 13 2004 - p58(1) [51-500]
Garber, Marjorie B. - *A Manifesto for Literary Studies*
   ELT - v48 - i2 - Spring 2005 - p91(4) [501+]
   Shakespeare After All
   KR - v72 - i20 - Oct 15 2004 - pNA [501+]
   NW - Dec 6 2004 - p90 [501+]
   LJ - v129 - i20 - Dec 1 2004 - p116(2) [51-500]
Garber, Peter - *101 Stupid Things Supervisors Do to Sabotage Success*
   HR Mag - v50 - i2 - Feb 2005 - pS8(1) [501+]
Garber, Stephen J. - *Looking Backward, Looking Forward: Forty Years of U.S. Human Spaceflight Symposium*
   Pub Hist - v26 - i2 - Spring 2004 - p104(106) [501+]
Garber, Zev - *Double Takes: Thinking and Rethinking Issues of Modern Judaism in Ancient Contexts*
   Choice - v42 - i6 - Feb 2005 - p1037(1) [51-500]
   R&R Bk N - v19 - i4 - Nov 2004 - p17(1) [51-500]
Garcia, Alma M. - *Narratives of Mexican American Women: Emergent Identities of the Second Generation*
   R&R Bk N - v19 - i1 - Feb 2004 - p56(1) [51-500]
Garcia-Ballester, Luis - *Galen and Galenism: Theory and Medical Practice from Antiquity to the European Renaissance*
   Six Ct J - v34 - i4 - Winter 2003 - p1127-1128 [501+]
Garcia, Eric - *Cassandra French's Finishing School for Boys*
   LJ - v129 - i13 - August 2004 - p67(1) [51-500]
   People - v62 - i1 - July 5 2004 - p46 [51-500]
   Hot and Sweaty Rex (Read by Marosz, Jonathan). Audiobook Review
   y Kliatt - v38 - i5 - Sept 2004 - p61(2) [51-500]
   LJ - v130 - i1 - Jan 1 2005 - p167(1) [51-500]
Garcia, Frank J. - *Trade, Inequality, and Justice: Towards a Liberal Theory of Just Trade*
   R&R Bk N - v19 - i2 - May 2004 - p111(1) [51-500]
Garcia, Guy - *The New Mainstream: How the Multicultural Consumer Is Transforming American Business*
   NYT - Sept 5 2004 - pBU8 [501+]
   PW - v251 - i35 - August 30 2004 - p46(1) [51-500]
Garcia, Jorge J.E. - *Mel Gibson's Passion and Philosophy: The Challenge of Christ's Trial, Conviction, and Crucifixion.*
   LJ - v130 - i2 - Feb 1 2005 - p85(1) [51-500]
Garcia, Jose A. - *Progressive Image Transmission: The Role of Rationality, Cooperation, and Justice*
   SciTech - v28 - i3 - Sept 2004 - p158(1) [51-500]
Garcia, Keith S. - *Washington Manual Psychiatry Survival Guide*
   SciTech - v28 - i3 - Sept 2004 - p96(1) [51-500]

Garcia, Lynne S. - *Clinical Laboratory Management*
   E-Streams - Nov 2004 - pNA [501+]
   SciTech - v28 - i3 - Sept 2004 - p80(1) [51-500]
Garcia Marquez, Gabriel - *Living to Tell the Tale*
   Globe & Mail - Nov 27 2004 - pD3 [501+]
   Living to Tell the Tale. Audiobook Review
   Globe & Mail - Dec 4 2004 - pD38 [1-50]
   Living to Tell the Tale
   Globe & Mail - Jan 1 2005 - pD14 [1-50]
   y Kliatt - v39 - i2 - March 2005 - p34(1) [51-500]
   TimHES - v0 - i1650 - July 23 2004 - p29(1) [501+]
   A Memoir of My Sad Whores
   Econ - v373 - i8404 - Dec 4 2004 - p85US [501+]
   Memoria de Mis Putas Tristes
   TLS - i5306 - Dec 10 2004 - p23(1) [501+]
Garcia, Paulo J.V. - *Very Large Telescope Interferometer: Challenges for the Future: Proceedings*
   SciTech - v28 - i1 - March 2004 - p43(1) [51-500]
Garcia, Ricardo L. - *Brother Bill's Bait Bites Back and Other Tales from the Raton*
   Roundup M - v11 - i6 - August 2004 - p27(1) [501+]
Garcia-Rivera, Alex - *A Wounded Innocence: Sketches for a Theology of Art*
   TT - v61 - i2 - July 2004 - p284(1) [501+]
Garcia-Roza, Luiz Alfredo - *Southwesterly Wind*
   TLS - i5303 - Nov 19 2004 - p25(1) [501+]
   A Window in Copacabana
   BL - v101 - i5 - Nov 1 2004 - p468(1) [51-500]
   BW - v35 - i4 - Jan 30 2005 - p13(1) [51-500]
   KR - v72 - i21 - Nov 1 2004 - p1030(1) [51-500]
   LJ - v129 - i20 - Dec 1 2004 - p95(1) [51-500]
   NYTBR - Jan 9 2005 - p17 [501+]
   PW - v251 - i48 - Nov 29 2004 - p26(1) [51-500]
Garcia, Tomas B. - *Arrhythmia Recognition: The Art of Interpretation*
   SciTech - v28 - i1 - March 2004 - p104(1) [51-500]
Garcia y Robertson, R. - *White Rose*
   y BL - v101 - i3 - Oct 1 2004 - p318(1) [51-500]
   KR - v72 - i16 - August 15 2004 - p762(1) [51-500]
Garcia-Zamor, Jean-Claude - *Bureaucratic, Societal, and Ethical Transformation of the Former East Germany*
   R&R Bk N - v19 - i3 - August 2004 - p42(1) [51-500]
Gardam, Jane - *Old Filth*
   NS - v134 - i4726 - Feb 7 2005 - p54(2) [501+]
   Spec - v296 - i9196 - Nov 6 2004 - p66(2) [501+]
   TLS - i5302 - Nov 12 2004 - p21-22 [501+]
Gardella, Lorrie Greenhouse - *A Dream and a Plan: A Woman's Path to Leadership in Human Services*
   R&R Bk N - v19 - i3 - August 2004 - p158(1) [51-500]
Garden, Nancy - *Molly's Family (Illus. by Wooding, Sharon)*
   c Advocate - July 20 2004 - p51(1) [51-500]
   HB - v80 - i4 - July-August 2004 - p434(2) [51-500]
Garden of Dreams
   PetPho - v33 - i11 - March 2005 - p17(1) [501+]
Gardenfors, Peter - *How Homo Became Sapiens: On the Evolution of Thinking*
   QRB - v79 - i4 - Dec 2004 - p419(1) [501+]
   TLS - i5300 - Oct 29 2004 - p32(1) [501+]
Gardenswartz, Lee - *Diverse Teams at Work: Capitalizing on the Power of Diversity*
   HR Mag - v49 - i7 - July 2004 - pS10(1) [51-500]
   HR Mag - v50 - i2 - Feb 2005 - pS6(1) [501+]
   The Diversity Tool Kit
   HR Mag - v49 - i7 - July 2004 - pS11(1) [51-500]
   The Global Diversity Desk Reference: Managing an International Workforce
   HR Mag - v49 - i7 - July 2004 - pS11(1) [51-500]
   Global Diversity Desk Reference: Managing an International Workforce
   HR Mag - v50 - i2 - Feb 2005 - pS6(1) [501+]
Gardey, Delphine - *La dactylographe et l'expeditionnaire: Histoire des employes de bureau, 1890-1930*
   JMH - v76 - i3 - Sept 2004 - p704(3) [501+]
Gardiner, Harry W. - *Lives Across Cultures: Cross-Cultural Human Development, 3rd Ed.*
   R&R Bk N - v19 - i3 - August 2004 - p83(1) [51-500]
Gardiner, John Rolfe - *The Magellan House: Stories*
   BL - v100 - i22 - August 2004 - p1898(1) [51-500]
   BW - v34 - i34 - August 22 2004 - p5(1) [501+]
   KR - v72 - i13 - July 1 2004 - p595(1) [51-500]
Gardiner, Juliet - *Wartime: Britain 1939-1945*
   Spec - v296 - i9193 - Oct 16 2004 - p76(1) [501+]

Gardiner, Lindsey - *The Loopy Life of Lola*
   c Sch Lib - v52 - i3 - Autumn 2004 - p131(1) [1-50]
Gardiner, Meg - *Jericho Point*
   Globe & Mail - Oct 30 2004 - pD26 [51-500]
Gardner, Bruce L. - *American Agriculture in the Twentieth Century: How It Flourished and What It Cost*
   T&C - v45 - i3 - July 2004 - p655-656 [501+]
Gardner, Catherine Villanueva - *Women Philosophers: Genre and the Boundaries of Philosophy*
   R&R Bk N - v19 - i3 - August 2004 - p2(1) [1-50]
Gardner, Charlie - *The Beatles: Yellow Submarine (Illus. by Edelmann, Heinz)*
   c HB - v80 - i5 - Sept-Oct 2004 - p564(1) [51-500]
   c KR - v72 - i13 - July 1 2004 - p638(1) [51-500]
   c PW - v251 - i33 - August 16 2004 - p62(1) [51-500]
   c SLJ - v50 - i10 - Oct 2004 - p109(1) [51-500]
Gardner, Daniel K. - *Zhu Xi's Reading of the Analects: Canon, Commentary, and the Classical Tradition*
   Ch Rev Int - v11 - i1 - Spring 2004 - p87(5) [501+]
   JAS - v63 - i2 - May 2004 - p494(2) [501+]
Gardner, Daniel L. - *Supply Chain Vector: Methods for Linking the Execution of Global Business Models with Financial Performance*
   R&R Bk N - v19 - i3 - August 2004 - p103(1) [1-50]
Gardner, David K - *A Laboratory Guide To The Mammalian Embryo*
   QRB - v79 - i4 - Dec 2004 - p426(1) [501+]
Gardner, Debbie - *Raising Kids Who Can Protect Themselves*
   Globe & Mail - Sept 4 2004 - pF6 [1-50]
Gardner, Garth - *Gardner's Guide to Colleges for Multimedia and Animation, 4th Ed.*
   SciTech - v28 - i3 - Sept 2004 - p136(1) [51-500]
   Gardner's Guide to Multimedia and Animation Studios: The Industry Directory. 2d Ed.
   SciTech - v28 - i3 - Sept 2004 - p20(1) [51-500]
Gardner, Graham - *Inventing Elliot (Read by Taylor, Dominic). Audiobook Review*
   y Kliatt - v38 - i5 - Sept 2004 - p62(2) [51-500]
Gardner, Hall - *NATO and the European Union: New World, New Europe, New Threats*
   R&R Bk N - v19 - i3 - August 2004 - p187(1) [501+]
Gardner, Howard - *Changing Minds: The Art and Science of Changing Our Own and Other People's Minds*
   Bwatch - v26 - i8 - August 2004 - p1(1) [51-500]
   Choice - v42 - i3 - Nov 2004 - p567(1) [51-500]
   SciTech - v28 - i3 - Sept 2004 - p3(1) [501+]
Gardner, James Alan - *Gravity Wells: Speculative Fiction Stories*
   PW - v252 - i11 - March 14 2005 - p49(2) [51-500]
   Radiant
   BL - v100 - i22 - August 2004 - p1913(1) [51-500]
Gardner, James B. - *The AAM Guide to Collections Planning*
   R&R Bk N - v19 - i3 - August 2004 - p1(1) [1-50]
Gardner, Jenny - *French Thru Art*
   TES - v0 - i4587 - June 11 2004 - psssss18(1) [501+]
   French Thru Verbs
   TES - v0 - i4587 - June 11 2004 - psssss18(2) [501+]
Gardner, John - *Unknown Fears*
   KR - v73 - i1 - Jan 1 2005 - p23(1) [51-500]
   PW - v252 - i4 - Jan 24 2005 - p225(2) [501+]
Gardner, Judith - *Somalia-The Untold Story: The War through the Eyes of Small Somali Women*
   Choice - v42 - i3 - Nov 2004 - p540(1) [1-50]
Gardner, Lisa - *Alone*
   BL - v101 - i7 - Dec 1 2004 - p639(1) [51-500]
   Globe & Mail - Feb 5 2005 - pD15 [51-500]
   KR - v72 - i21 - Nov 1 2004 - p1030(1) [51-500]
   LJ - v129 - i20 - Dec 1 2004 - p100(1) [51-500]
   People - v63 - i4 - Jan 31 2005 - p53 [51-500]
   PW - v251 - i49 - Dec 6 2004 - p45(1) [51-500]
Gardner, Martin - *Are Universes Thicker than Blackberries?*
   Bwatch - Feb 2005 - pNA [51-500]
   VQR - v80 - i1 - Wntr 2004 - p276-276 [501+]
   Smart Science Tricks
   KR - v72 - i24 - Dec 15 2004 - p1201(1) [51-500]

Gardner, Robert - *Bicycle Science Projects: Physics on Wheels*
  y BL - v101 - i8 - Dec 15 2004 - p733(1) [51-500]
  y SLJ - v51 - i2 - Feb 2005 - p146(2) [51-500]
Chemistry Science Fair Projects Using Acids, Bases, Metals, Salts, and Inorganic Stuff
  y SLJ - v51 - i2 - Feb 2005 - p147(1) [51-500]
Light, Sound, and Waves Science Fair Projects: Using Sunglasses, Guitars, CDs, and Other Stuff
  y SB - v40 - i5 - Sept-Oct 2004 - p208(1) [51-500]
Science Fair Projects about the Properties of Matter: Using Marbles, Water, Balloons, and More
  y SB - v40 - i5 - Sept-Oct 2004 - p208(2) [51-500]
Science Project Ideas about Rain
  y SB - v40 - i5 - Sept-Oct 2004 - p194(1) [51-500]
Gardner, Sarah E. - *Blood and Irony: Southern White Women's Narratives of the Civil War, 1861-1937*
  Choice - v42 - i2 - Oct 2004 - p355(1) [51-500]
Gardner, Thomas - *Regions of Unlikeness: Explaining Contemporary Poetry*
  RES - v55 - i219 - April 2004 - p304-306 [501+]
Gardner, Thomas J. - *Criminal Evidence: Principles and Cases, 5th Ed.*
  R&R Bk N - v19 - i1 - Feb 2004 - pNA [51-500]
Gardner, Tim Alan - *The Naked Soul: God's Amazing, Everyday Solution to Loneliness*
  PW - v251 - i35 - August 30 2004 - p50(1) [51-500]
Gardyne, John - *Producing Musicals: A Practical Guide*
  Choice - v42 - i3 - Nov 2004 - p492(1) [51-500]
Gare, Deborah - *The Fuss That Never Ended: The Life and Work of Geoffrey Blainey*
  AHS - v35 - i124 - Oct 2004 - p400(2) [501+]
Gareth Stevens Atlas of the World
  c LibMed - v23 - i3 - Nov-Dec 2004 - p80(1) [51-500]
Garff, Joakim - *Soren Kierkegaard*
  BL - v101 - i5 - Nov 1 2004 - p447(1) [51-500]
  HM - v310 - i1857 - Feb 2005 - p83(2) [51-500]
Garfield, Brian - *Hopscotch*
  LJ - v129 - i14 - Sept 1 2004 - p204(1) [51-500]
The Thousand Mile War: World War Two in Alaska and the Aleutians
  TLS - i5302 - Nov 12 2004 - p30(1) [51-500]
Garfield, Henry - *The Lost Voyage of John Cabot*
  PW - v251 - i32 - August 9 2004 - p251(2) [51-500]
  y SLJ - v50 - i9 - Sept 2004 - p205(1) [51-500]
  VOYA - v27 - i5 - Dec 2004 - p381(1) [501+]
Garfield, Patricia - *Dream Catcher: A Young Person's Journal for Exploring Dreams*
  y CBRA - Annual 2003 - p562(1) [51-500]
Garfield, Simon - *Our Hidden Lives: The Everyday Diaries of a Forgotten Britain 1945-1948*
  CR - v286 - i1669 - Feb 2005 - p122(1) [51-500]
Our Hidden Lives: The Everyday Diaries of a Forgotten Britain, 1945-1948
  HT - v54 - i12 - Dec 2004 - p58(1) [501+]
  Spec - i9201 - Dec 11 2004 - p43(1) [501+]
Garfunkel, Trudy - *Kosher for Everybody: The Complete Guide to Understanding, Shopping, Cooking, and Eating the Kosher Way*
  LJ - v129 - i15 - Sept 15 2004 - p79(2) [51-500]
  PW - v251 - i28 - July 12 2004 - p60(1) [51-500]
Garg, Vijay K. - *Concurrent and Distributed Computing in Java*
  Choice - v42 - i1 - Sept 2004 - p140(1) [501+]
Garibaldi, Luciano - *Mussolini: The Secrets of His Death*
  LJ - v129 - i18 - Nov 1 2004 - p101(2) [51-500]
Garibaldo, Francesco - *Globalisation, Company Strategies and the Quality of Working Life in Europe*
  R&R Bk N - v19 - i3 - August 2004 - p116(1) [51-500]
Gariepy, Henry - *Daily Meditations on Golden Texts of the Bible*
  LJ - v129 - i12 - July 2004 - p89(1) [51-500]
Garlake, Margaret - *The Drawings of Peter Lanyon*
  TLS - i5305 - Dec 3 2004 - p19(1) [501+]
Garland, Alex - *The Coma*
  Globe & Mail - July 24 2004 - pD4 [501+]
  NS - v133 - i4695 - July 5 2004 - p55(1) [501+]
  NYTBR - July 4 2004 - p19 [501+]
  TLS - i5283 - July 2 2004 - p19(1) [501+]
Garland, Glenda - *Her Other Thief*
  BL - v101 - i7 - Dec 1 2004 - p641(1) [51-500]
Garland, Michael - *The Great Easter Egg Hunt*
  c KR - v72 - i24 - Dec 15 2004 - p1201(1) [51-500]
  c SLJ - v51 - i2 - Feb 2005 - p97(1) [51-500]
Joan of Arc: Heroine of France
  LibMed - v22 - i4 - Jan 2004 - p72(1) [501+]
Look Again Book
  c PW - v252 - i7 - Feb 14 2005 - p79(2) [501+]
Miss Smith's Incredible Storybook
  c LibMed - v22 - i6 - March 2004 - p56(1) [501+]

Garland, Nicole - *The Fool's Tale*
  y BL - v101 - i6 - Nov 15 2004 - p553(1) [51-500]
Garland, Sarah - *Billy and Belle*
  c Sch Lib - v52 - i4 - Winter 2004 - p191(1) [51-500]
Eddie's Garden: And How to Make Things Grow (Illus. by Garland, Sarah)
  c SLJ - v50 - i7 - July 2004 - p75(1) [51-500]
Garlick, Mark A. - *Astronomy: A Visual Guide*
  Astron - v32 - i11 - Nov 2004 - p98 [51-500]
  y BL - v101 - i4 - Oct 15 2004 - p370(1) [51-500]
  Choice - v42 - i6 - Feb 2005 - p1044(2) [51-500]
  Globe & Mail - Dec 4 2004 - pD4 [501+]
  y SB - v40 - i6 - Nov-Dec 2004 - p256(1) [51-500]
  SciTech - v28 - i4 - Dec 2004 - p45(1) [51-500]
  S&T - v108 - i6 - Dec 2004 - p119(3) [501+]
Garmendia, Joseba Irazu - *Soinujolearen Semea*
  TLS - i5289 - August 13 2004 - p28(1) [501+]
Garnaut, Ross - *China: New Engine of World Growth*
  R&R Bk N - v19 - i1 - Feb 2004 - p106(1) [51-500]
Garner, Abigail - *Families Like Mine: Children of Gay Parents Tell It Like It Is*
  Advocate - July 20 2004 - p51(1) [51-500]
  y VOYA - v27 - i4 - Oct 2004 - p324(2) [51-500]
Garner, Bryan A. - *Garner's Modern American Usage*
  R&R Bk N - v19 - i1 - Feb 2004 - p217(1) [51-500]
Garner, Carolyn - *Teaching Library Media Skills in Grades K-6: A How-to-Do-It Manual for Librarians (Illus. by Crabtree, Jaime)*
  c SLJ - v50 - i9 - Sept 2004 - p238(1) [51-500]
Garner, Karen - *Precious Fire: Maud Russell and the Chinese Revolution*
  AHR - v109 - i3 - June 2004 - p884(1) [501+]
  Choice - v41 - i7 - March 2004 - p1350(1) [501+]
  JAH - v91 - i2 - Sept 2004 - p691(2) [501+]
  Pac A - v77 - i2 - Summer 2004 - p328(3) [501+]
Garner, Mary - *The Hidden Souls of Words: Keys to Transformation through the Power of Words*
  LJ - v129 - i16 - Oct 1 2004 - p87(1) [51-500]
Garner, Ruth-Miriam - *Laelia*
  Black Iss - v6 - i4 - July-August 2004 - p44(2) [501+]
Garner, Steve - *Racism in the Irish Experience*
  Choice - v42 - i1 - Sept 2004 - p180(1) [501+]
Garnett, Eve - *The Family from One End Street (Read by Sands, Julia). Audiobook Review*
  y Kliatt - v38 - i5 - Sept 2004 - p58(2) [51-500]
Garnett, Gale Zoe - *Transient Dancing*
  Globe & Mail - Nov 6 2004 - pD25 [51-500]
Garnett, Henrietta - *Anny: A Life of Anne Thackeray Ritchie*
  Lon R Bks - v26 - i23 - Dec 2 2004 - p31(1) [501+]
Garnett, Mark - *The Snake That Swallowed Its Tail: Some Contradictions in Modern Liberalism*
  NS - v133 - i4714 - Nov 15 2004 - p50(1) [501+]
Garnham, A. M. - *Hans Keller and the BBC: The Musical Conscience of British Broadcasting, 1959-79*
  Albion - v36 - i2 - Summer 2004 - p369(3) [501+]
Garnier, Katja von - *Iron Jawed Angels*
  JAH - v91 - i3 - Dec 2004 - p1131(2) [501+]
Garnier, Philippe - *Social Funds: Lessons for a New Future*
  ILR - v143 - i3 - Autumn 2004 - p293(1) [51-500]
Garon, Lise - *Dangerous Alliances: Civil Society, the Media and Democratic Transition in North Africa*
  R&R Bk N - v19 - i1 - Feb 2004 - pNA [501+]
Garoogian, David - *America's Top Rated Cities: A Statistical Handbook, 2004, 11th Ed., Vols. 1-4*
  R&R Bk N - v19 - i3 - August 2004 - p155(1) [51-500]
America's Top-Rated Cities: A Statistical Handbook: Central Region, 11th Ed., Vol. 3
  Choice - v42 - i5 - Jan 2005 - p834-1 [1-50]
America's Top-Rated Cities: A Statistical Handbook: Eastern Region, 11th Ed., Vol. 4th
  Choice - v42 - i5 - Jan 2005 - p834-1 [1-50]
America's Top-Rated Cities: A Statistical Handbook: Southern Region, 11th Ed., Vol. 1
  Choice - v42 - i5 - Jan 2005 - p834-1 [1-50]
America's Top-Rated Cities: A Statistical Handbook: Western Region, 11th Ed., Vol. 2
  Choice - v42 - i5 - Jan 2005 - p834-1 [1-50]
America's Top-Rated Smaller Cities: A Statistical Profile, 2004/05, 5th Ed.
  R&R Bk N - v19 - i4 - Nov 2004 - p136(1) [51-500]

The Asian Databook: Detailed Statistics and Rankings on the Asian and Pacific Islander Population, Including 23 Ethnic Backgrounds from Bangladeshi to Vietnamese, for 1,883 U.S. Countries and Cities
  Choice - v42 - i7 - March 2005 - p1203(1) [51-500]
The Hispanic Databook: Detailed Statistics and Rankings on the Hispanic Population, 2nd Ed.
  R&R Bk N - v19 - i3 - August 2004 - p65(1) [51-500]
The Hispanic Databook: Detailed Statistics and Rankings on the Hispanic Population, Including 23 Ethnic Backgrounds from Argentinian to Venezuelan, for 1,266 U.S. Counties and Cities
  Choice - v42 - i1 - Sept 2004 - p78(1) [501+]
Garrard, Graeme - *Rousseau's Counter-Enlightenment: A Republican Critique of the Philosophes*
  FS - v58 - i1 - Jan 2004 - p112(2) [501+]
Garratt, James - *Palestrina and the German Romantic Imagination: Interpreting Histoticism in Nineteenth-Century Music*
  GSR - v27 - i1 - Feb 2004 - p156-157 [501+]
Garreton, Manuel Antonio - *Incomplete Democracy: Political Democratization in Chile and Latin America*
  PSQ - v119 - i2 - Summer 2004 - p365(2) [501+]
Latin America in the 21st Century: Towards a New Sociopolitical Matrix
  Ams - v61 - i2 - Oct 2004 - p335(2) [501+]
Garrett, Aaron - *Meaning in Spinoza's Method*
  RM - v58 - i2 - Dec 2004 - p434(3) [501+]
Garrett, Eilidh - *Changing Family Size in England and Wales: Place, Class and Demography, 1891-1911*
  JIH - v34 - i3 - Wntr 2004 - p458(2) [501+]
Garrett, Garet - *Ex America: The 50th Anniversary of The People's Pottage*
  R&R Bk N - v19 - i4 - Nov 2004 - p63(1) [51-500]
Garrett, George - *Going to See the Elephant: Pieces of a Writing Life*
  South CR - v37 - i1 - Fall 2004 - p194-198 [501+]
Garrett, Howard - *Texas Gardening the Natural Way: The Complete Handbook (Illus. by Celusniak, Chris)*
  E-Streams - Sept 2004 - pNA [501+]
Garrett, Klink - *Ten Turtles to Tucumcari: A Personal History of the Railway Express Agency*
  R&R Bk N - v19 - i1 - Feb 2004 - p104(1) [1-50]
Garrett, Leah - *Journeys Beyond the Pale: Yiddish Travel Writing in the Modern World*
  Slav R - v63 - i2 - Summer 2004 - p392(2) [501+]
Garrett, Leslie - *Helen Keller: A Photographic Story of a Life*
  y Kliatt - v39 - i1 - Jan 2005 - p29(2) [51-500]
Garrett, Martin - *Cambridge: A Cultural and Literary History*
  HT - v54 - i11 - Nov 2004 - p86(4) [501+]
  R&R Bk N - v19 - i4 - Nov 2004 - p37(1) [51-500]
  TLS - i5306 - Dec 10 2004 - p32(1) [51-500]
Garrett, Peter K. - *Gothic Reflections: Narrative Force in Nineteenth-Century Fiction*
  Nine-C Lit - v59 - i1 - June 2004 - p115(119) [501+]
Garrett, Sheryl - *Just Give Me the Answer: Expert Advisors Address Your Most Pressing Financial Questions*
  R&R Bk N - v19 - i4 - Nov 2004 - p116(1) [51-500]
Garriel, Barbara S. - *I Know a Shy Fellow Who Swallowed a Cello (Illus. by O'Brien, John)*
  c BL - v100 - i22 - August 2004 - p1942(1) [51-500]
  c CE - v80 - i5 - Mid-Summer 2004 - p273(1) [1-50]
Garrigan, Siobhan - *Beyond Ritual: Sacramental Theology After Habermas*
  R&R Bk N - v19 - i4 - Nov 2004 - p19(1) [51-500]
Garrioch, David - *The Making of Revolutionary Paris*
  JIH - v34 - i4 - Spring 2004 - p640-642 [501+]
  JMH - v76 - i3 - Sept 2004 - p693(2) [501+]
  Lib & Cul - v39 - i4 - Fall 2004 - p470(2) [501+]
Garriott, James C. - *Medical-Legal Aspects of Alcohol, 4th Ed.*
  SciTech - v28 - i1 - March 2004 - p85(1) [51-500]
Garrison, D.R. - *E-Learning in the 21st Century: A Framework for Research and Practice*
  TCR - v106 - i8 - August 2004 - p1661(2) [501+]
Garrison, Dee - *Apostles of Culture: The Public Librarian and American Society, 1876-1920, 2nd Ed.*
  Lib & Cul - v39 - i3 - Summer 2004 - p332(2) [501+]
Garrison, Gary - *Perfect 10: Writing and Producing the 10-Minute Play*
  Theat J - v56 - i1 - March 2004 - p145(3) [501+]

Garrison, Gene - *Unless Victory Comes: Combat with a Machine Gunner in Patton's Third Army*
    R&R Bk N - v19 - i4 - Nov 2004 - p33(1) [51-500]

Garrison, Jim - *America as Empire: Global Leader or Rogue Power?*
    Choice - v41 - i11-12 - July-August 2004 - p2120(1) [501+]

Garrison, Odessa S. - *Descendants of Joseph Stanford Garrison of Somerset Maryland 1694-1999*
    EFHM - v58 - i3 - May-June 2004 - p57(1) [1-50]

Garrity, Jane - *Step-Daughters of England: British Women Modernists and the National Imaginary*
    ELT - v48 - i2 - Spring 2005 - p114(5) [501+]
    J Hist G - v30 - i3 - July 2004 - p585(2) [501+]
    JGS - v13 - i2 - July 2004 - p183-184 [501+]
    R&R Bk N - v19 - i1 - Feb 2004 - p234(1) [51-500]
    TSWL - v23 - i2 - Fall 2004 - p377(3) [501+]

Garrod, Andrew C. - *Adolescent Portraits: Identity, Relationships, and Challenges, 5th ed.*
    R&R Bk N - v19 - i4 - Nov 2004 - p131(1) [1-50]

Garroutte, Eva Marie - *Real Indians: Identity and the Survival of Native America*
    AJS - v110 - i3 - Nov 2004 - p852(2) [501+]
    Am Ind CRJ - v28 - i2 - Spring 2004 - p176(4) [501+]
    CS - v33 - i2 - March 2004 - p192-194 [501+]
    JRAI - v10 - i3 - Sept 2004 - p720(2) [501+]

Garry-Boussel, Claire - *Statut et fonction du personnage masculin chez Madame de Stael*
    FS - v58 - i2 - April 2004 - p266(2) [501+]

Garson, Derek - *Mere Observations*
    y CBRA - Annual 2003 - p525(2) [51-500]

Garsten, Christina - *New Technologies at Work: People, Screens and Social Virtuality*
    JRAI - v10 - i4 - Dec 2004 - p944(2) [501+]

Garten, Ina - *Barefoot in Paris: Easy French Food You Can Make at Home*
    Globe & Mail - Nov 27 2004 - pD26 [51-500]
    LJ - v129 - i17 - Oct 15 2004 - p82(1) [51-500]
    PW - v251 - i41 - Oct 11 2004 - p70(1) [51-500]

Garth, John - *Tokien and the Great War: The Threshold of Middle-earth*
    TLS - i5264 - Feb 20 2004 - p25-25 [501+]
Tolkien and the Great War: The Threshold of Middle-earth
    R&R Bk N - v19 - i1 - Feb 2004 - p240(1) [51-500]
    WLT - v79 - i1 - Jan-April 2005 - p93(1) [501+]

Garthwait, Cynthia L. - *The Social Work Practicum: A Guide and Workbook for Students, 3rd Ed.*
    R&R Bk N - v19 - i4 - Nov 2004 - p137(1) [1-50]

Gartner, H. - *Diogenes Laertius: Vitae Philosophorum. Vol III. Indices*
    Class R - v54 - i2 - Nov 2004 - p568-569 [501+]

Gartner, John D. - *The Hypomanic Edge: The Bipolar Disorder that Made America the Most Successful Nation in the World*
    KR - v73 - i1 - Jan 1 2005 - p33(2) [501+]

Garton, Alison F. - *Exploring Cognitive Development: The Child as Problem Solver*
    Choice - v42 - i2 - Oct 2004 - p374(2) [51-500]

Garton Ash, Timothy - *Free World: America, Europe, and the Surprising Future of the West*
    BL - v101 - i6 - Nov 15 2004 - p547(2) [51-500]
    KR - v72 - i18 - Sept 15 2004 - p897(2) [501+]
    LJ - v129 - i19 - Nov 15 2004 - p75(1) [501+]
    PW - v251 - i40 - Oct 4 2004 - p76(2) [51-500]
Free World: Why a Crisis of the West Reveals the Opportunity of Our Time
    Econ - v372 - i8385 - July 24 2004 - p77US [501+]
    Globe & Mail - Oct 23 2004 - pD6 [501+]
    TLS - i5295 - Sept 24 2004 - p8(1) [501+]

Garver, Eugene - *For the Sake of Argument: Practical Reasoning, Character, and the Ethics of Belief*
    Choice - v42 - i3 - Nov 2004 - p497(2) [51-500]

Garvin, Charles D. - *Handbook of Social Work with Groups*
    Fam in Soc - v85 - i3 - July-Sept 2004 - p432(3) [501+]
    R&R Bk N - v19 - i3 - August 2004 - p159(1) [501+]

Garvin, Peggy - *The United States Government Internet Manual, 2003-2004*
    Choice - v42 - i1 - Sept 2004 - p83(1) [501+]
    R&USQ - v44 - i3 - Fall 2004 - p95(2) [501+]

Gary, Morecambe - *Cary Grant in Name Only*
    LJ - v129 - i15 - Sept 15 2004 - p59(2) [51-500]

Gary, Romain - *White Dog*
    Globe & Mail - Nov 13 2004 - pD21 [51-500]

Garza, Ale - *Ninja Boy: Faded Dreams*
    LibMed - v22 - i6 - March 2004 - p70(1) [501+]

Garza, Encarnacion - *Resiliency and Success: Migrant Children in the United States*
    R&R Bk N - v19 - i3 - August 2004 - p230 [1-50]

Garza, Phyllis de la - *Death for Dinner: The Benders of (Old) Kansas*
    Roundup M - v12 - i1 - Oct 2004 - p23(1) [51-500]
Silk and Sagebrush: Women of the old West
    Roundup M - v12 - i3 - Feb 2005 - p27(1) [51-500]

Garza, Rodolfo O. de la - *Muted Voices: Latinos and the 2000 Elections*
    Choice - v42 - i6 - Feb 2005 - p1099(1) [51-500]

Garzo, Vicente - *Kinetic Theory of Gases in Shear Flows: Nonlinear Transport*
    SciTech - v28 - i1 - March 2004 - p48(1) [51-500]

Gascoigne, Bamber - *How to Identify Prints: A Complete Guide to Manual and Mechanical Processes from Woodcut to Inkjet, 2nd Ed.*
    R&R Bk N - v19 - i3 - August 2004 - p244(1) [51-500]

Gascoine, Russell - *Rebels*
    c Sch Lib - v52 - i4 - Winter 2004 - p201(1) [51-500]

Gash, John - *Caravaggio*
    LJ - v130 - i2 - Feb 1 2005 - p76(1) [51-500]

Gasinski, Leszek - *Nonsmooth Critical Point Theory and Nonlinear Boundary Value Problems*
    SciTech - v28 - i4 - Dec 2004 - p43(1) [51-500]

Gasiorowski, Mark J. - *Mohammad Mosaddeq and the 1953 Coup in Iran*
    Choice - v42 - i5 - Jan 2005 - p913(1) [1-50]
    R&R Bk N - v19 - i3 - August 2004 - p53(1) [51-500]

Gask, Linda - *A Short Introduction to Psychiatry*
    SciTech - v28 - i4 - Dec 2004 - p95(1) [51-500]

Gaskin, James E. - *Broadband Bible, Desktop Ed.*
    SciTech - v28 - i3 - Sept 2004 - p153(1) [51-500]

Gaskins, Pearl - *I Believe in ... : Christian, Jewish, and Muslim Young People Speak about Their Faith*
    y BL - v101 - i3 - Oct 1 2004 - p340(1) [51-500]
    y CCB-B - v58 - i1 - Sept 2004 - p17(1) [51-500]
    y HB - v80 - i4 - July-August 2004 - p467(1) [51-500]
    c SLJ - v50 - i8 - August 2004 - p136(1) [501+]

Gaspar de Alba, Alicia - *Desert Blood: The Juarez Murders*
    LJ - v130 - i4 - March 1 2005 - p70(1) [51-500]

Gaspar, Frank X. - *Night of a Thousand Blossoms*
    LJ - v129 - i12 - July 2004 - p87(1) [51-500]

Gasparino, Charles - *Blood on the Street: The Sensational Inside Story of How Wall Street Analysts Duped a Generation of Investors*
    Bus W - Jan 31 2005 - p18 [501+]

Gasper, Giles E.M. - *Anselm of Canterbury and His Theological Inheritance*
    R&R Bk N - v19 - i4 - Nov 2004 - p20(1) [51-500]

Gasper, Larry - *Princes in Waiting*
    Globe & Mail - August 7 2004 - pD10 [501+]
    y Kliatt - v39 - i1 - Jan 2005 - p26(1) [51-500]

Gass, Thomas Edward - *Nobody's Home: Candid Reflections of a Nursing Home Aide*
    Choice - v42 - i2 - Oct 2004 - p325(1) [51-500]
    SciTech - v28 - i3 - Sept 2004 - p85(1) [501+]

Gaston, Anthony J. - *Seabirds: A Natural History*
    Choice - v42 - i5 - Jan 2005 - p881(1) [1-50]
    SB - v41 - i1 - Jan-Feb 2005 - p21(1) [501+]

Gaston, Bill - *The Cameraman*
    Can Lit - i182 - Autumn 2004 - p153(2) [501+]
Mount Appetite
    Can Lit - i181 - Summer 2004 - p129-130 [501+]
    KR - v73 - i5 - March 1 2005 - p248(1) [501+]
    PW - v252 - i6 - Feb 7 2005 - p39(1) [51-500]
Sointula
    BIC - v33 - i8 - Nov 2004 - p8(2) [501+]
    Globe & Mail - Sept 18 2004 - pD16 [501+]
    Globe & Mail - Dec 24 2004 - pD3 [1-50]

Gatchalian, C.E. - *Motifs & Repetitions & Other Plays*
    Lam Bk Rpt - v13 - i4-5 - Nov-Dec 2004 - p22(3) [501+]

Gatchel, Robert J. - *Clinical Essentials of Pain Management*
    SciTech - v28 - i4 - Dec 2004 - p88(1) [51-500]

Gatenholm, Paul - *Hemicelluloses: Science and Technology: Proceedings*
    SciTech - v28 - i1 - March 2004 - p55(1) [51-500]

Gates, Gary J. - *The Gay and Lesbian Atlas*
    Choice - v42 - i2 - Oct 2004 - p274(2) [501+]
    R&R Bk N - v19 - i3 - August 2004 - p149(1) [1-50]

Gates, Henry Louis, Jr. - *African American Lives*
    y BL - v100 - i21 - July 2004 - p1860(1) [501+]
    y BL - v101 - i9-10 - Jan 1 2005 - p779(1) [1-50]
    y Choice - v42 - i3 - Nov 2004 - p445(1) [1-50]
    y Ref Rev - Sept 2004 - pNA [501+]
    y SLJ - v50 - i8 - August 2004 - p57(1) [501+]
America Behind the Color Line: Dialogues with African Americans
    BooChiTr - March 7 2004 - p1(2) [501+]
Critical Essays on the Bondwoman's Narrative
    BL - v101 - i9-10 - Jan 1 2005 - p766(1) [51-500]

Gates, Susan - *Sugar Bug Baby*
    c Sch Lib - v52 - i4 - Winter 2004 - p203(1) [51-500]
When I Had Wings (Illus. by Frankland, David)
    c Sch Lib - v52 - i3 - Autumn 2004 - p145(1) [501+]

Gathercole, Simon J. - *Where Is Boasting? Early Jewish Soteriology and Paul's Response in Romans 1-5*
    Intpr - v58 - i3 - July 2004 - p315(2) [501+]
    JR - v84 - i3 - July 2004 - p455(2) [501+]

Gathorne-Hardy, Jonathan - *Half An Arch*
    Spec - v296 - i9201 - Dec 11 2004 - p42(2) [501+]

Gatiss, Mark - *The Vesuvius Club*
    TLS - i5303 - Nov 19 2004 - p24(1) [501+]

Gatti, Hilary - *Giordano Bruno: Philosopher of the Renaissance*
    Six Ct J - v35 - i3 - Fall 2004 - p824-826 [501+]

Gatzweiler, Franz W. - *Sustainable Agriculture in Central and Eastern European Countries*
    JEL - v41 - i4 - Dec 2003 - p1430(1) [501+]

Gauci, Perry - *The Politics of Trade: The Overseas Merchant in State and Society, 1660-1720*
    JIH - v34 - i4 - Spring 2004 - p632-633 [501+]
    JMH - v76 - i3 - Sept 2004 - p653(2) [501+]

Gaude, Laurent - *Death of an Ancient King*
    TLS - i5290 - August 20 2004 - p20(1) [501+]

Gauderman, Kimberly - *Women's Lives in Colonial Quito: Gender, Law and Economy in Spanish America*
    AHR - v109 - i4 - Oct 2004 - p1280-1281 [501+]

Gauer, James - *The New American Dream: Living Well in Small Homes*
    LJ - v130 - i1 - Jan 1 2005 - p106(1) [51-500]

Gauger, Soren A. - *Hymns to Millionaires*
    Globe & Mail - Oct 30 2004 - pD23 [501+]

Gaughen, Shasta - *The Arab-Israeli Conflict*
    y SLJ - v51 - i1 - Jan 2005 - p148(1) [51-500]

Gauglitz, G. - *Handbook of Spectroscopy*
    E-Streams - June 2004 - pNA [501+]

Gauguin, Paul - *Letters to His Wife*
    R&R Bk N - v19 - i1 - Feb 2004 - p206(1) [51-500]

Gault, Fred - *Understanding Innovation in Canadian Industry*
    R&R Bk N - v19 - i3 - August 2004 - p97(1) [51-500]

Gaunt, Peter - *Oliver Cromwell*
    y BL - v101 - i4 - Oct 15 2004 - p383(1) [51-500]
    LJ - v129 - i18 - Nov 1 2004 - p95(1) [51-500]

Gaunt, Richard A. - *Unhappy Reactionary: The Diaries of the Fourth Duke of Newcastle-under-Lyne, 1822-50*
    CR - v286 - i1668 - Jan 2005 - p57(1) [51-500]
    HER - v119 - i483 - Sept 2004 - p1072(2) [501+]

Gausche-Hill, Marianne - *Pediatric Airway Management for the Prehospital Professional*
    SciTech - v28 - i4 - Dec 2004 - p112(1) [1-50]

Gaustad, Edwin S. - *Benjamin Franklin: Inventing America*
    c SLJ - v51 - i2 - Feb 2005 - p145(2) [501+]
Documentary History of Religion in America: Since 1877, 3d ed.
    R&R Bk N - v19 - i1 - Feb 2004 - p13(1) [1-50]

Gautam, Madhur - *Debt Relief for the Poorest: An OED Review of the HIPC Initiative*
    JEL - v41 - i4 - Dec 2003 - p1360(1) [501+]

Gauthier, Gail - *Saving the Planet & Stuff*
    y LibMed - v22 - i4 - Jan 2004 - p65(1) [501+]

Gauthier, Gilles - *Dear Old Dumpling (Illus. by Derome, Pierre-Andre)*
    y Can CL - i111-112 - Fall-Winter 2003 - p134(6) [501+]

Gauthier, Michel - *Olivier Mosset: Works, 1966-2003*
    R&R Bk N - v19 - i1 - Feb 2004 - p205(1) [51-500]

Gautier, Theophile - *Lettres a la Presidente & Poesies erotiques*
    NCFS - v33 - i1-2 - Fall-Winter 2004 - p202(2) [501+]

Gautreaux, Tim - *The Clearing*
WLT - v78 - i3-4 - Sept-Dec 2004 - p93(1) [501+]
NYTBR - August 29 2004 - p20 [501+]
Gauvin, Pierre - *Educating our Children: The Guide to Reading, Writing, Speaking and Listening Activities*
Res Links - v10 - i2 - Dec 2004 - p52(1) [51-500]
Gavalda, Anna - *I Wish Someone Were Waiting for Me Somewhere*
WLT - v78 - i3-4 - Sept-Dec 2004 - p115(2) [501+]
Someone I Loved
KR - v73 - i3 - Feb 1 2005 - p136(2) [51-500]
PW - v252 - i11 - March 14 2005 - p45(1) [51-500]
Gavanas, Anna - *Fatherhood Politics in the United States: Masculinity, Sexuality, Race and Marriage*
Choice - v42 - i3 - Nov 2004 - p572(1) [1-50]
Gavenda, Victor - *GarageBand for Mac OS X: Visual QuickStart Guide*
LJ - v129 - i14 - Sept 1 2004 - p182(1) [501+]
Gaventa, Beverly Roberts - *Blessed One: Protestant Perspectives on Mary*
Comw - v131 - i16 - Sept 24 2004 - p35(3) [501+]
Gavin, Adrienne E. - *Dark Horse: A Life of Anna Sewell*
CR - v285 - i1664 - Sept 2004 - p188(1) [51-500]
Gavin, Philip - *The Fall of Vietnam*
SLJ - v50 - i10 - Oct 2004 - pS58(1) [51-500]
Gavin, Robin Farwell - *Ceramica y Cultra: The Story of Spanish and Mexican Mayolica*
Ceram Mo - v52 - i1 - Jan 2004 - p28(1) [501+]
Ceramica y Cultura: The Story of Spanish and Mexican Mayolica
Ams - v61 - i2 - Oct 2004 - p263(1) [501+]
Gavrilovici, Ovidiu - *European Perspectives on Chronically Ill People*
SciTech - v28 - i3 - Sept 2004 - p87(1) [51-500]
Gavron, Daniel - *The Other Side of Despair: Jews and Arabs in the Promised Land*
Choice - v41 - i11-12 - July-August 2004 - p2104(1) [501+]
Gawalt, Gerard W. - *First Daughters: Letters between U.S. Presidents and Their Daughters*
y SLJ - v51 - i1 - Jan 2005 - p160(1) [51-500]
Gay, Jane de - *Languages of Theatre Shaped by Women*
TDR - v48 - i4 - Winter 2004 - p192(11) [501+]
Gay, Kathlyn - *Cultural Diversity: Conflicts and Challenges, the Ultimate Teen Guide*
R&R Bk N - v19 - i2 - May 2004 - p129 [51-500]
Gay, Marie-Louise - *Good Night Sam*
c CBRA - Annual 2003 - p451(1) [51-500]
Stella, Princess of the Sky (Illus. by Gay, Marie-Louise)
c BL - v101 - i5 - Nov 1 2004 - p489(1) [51-500]
c CCB-B - v58 - i2 - Oct 2004 - p73(1) [51-500]
c Globe & Mail - Nov 6 2004 - pD22 [1-50]
c SLJ - v50 - i10 - Oct 2004 - p113(2) [51-500]
Stella, Princess of the Sky
c Res Links - v10 - i3 - Feb 2005 - p4(1) [51-500]
Gay, Oonagh - *Conduct Unbecoming: The Regulation of Parliamentary Behaviour*
R&R Bk N - v19 - i3 - August 2004 - p182(1) [501+]
Gay, Penny - *Jane Austin and the Theater*
Theat J - v56 - i4 - Dec 2004 - p716-718 [501+]
Gay, Ruth - *Safe among the Germans: Liberated Jews after World War II*
GSR - v27 - i1 - Feb 2004 - p192-193 [501+]
HNet - Oct 2004 - pNA [501+]
Gayheart, Willard - *Willard Gayheart, Appalachian Artist*
R&R Bk N - v19 - i1 - Feb 2004 - p205(1) [51-500]
Gayle, Curtis Anderson - *Marxist History and Postwar Japanese Nationalism*
Pac A - v77 - i2 - Summer 2004 - p340(2) [501+]
Gayle, Mike - *Dinner for Two: Real Life Doesn't Come in Single Servings*
Kliatt - v38 - i6 - Nov 2004 - p16(2) [51-500]
Gaylin, Alison - *Hide Your Eyes*
PW - v252 - i6 - Feb 7 2005 - p47(1) [51-500]
Gaylin, Ann - *Eavesdropping in the Novel from Austen to Proust*
FS - v58 - i2 - April 2004 - p270(2) [501+]
NCFS - v33 - i1-2 - Fall-Winter 2004 - p178(2) [501+]
Gazeau, J.P. - *Group 24; Physical and Mathematical Aspects of Symmetries*
SciTech - v28 - i3 - Sept 2004 - p46(1) [1-50]
Gazendam, Henk W.M. - *Dynamics and Change in Organizations*
R&R Bk N - v19 - i1 - Feb 2004 - p91A(1) [51-500]

Gazit, Shlomo - *Trapped Fools: Thirty Years of Israeli Policy in the Territories*
R&R Bk N - v19 - i1 - Feb 2004 - p43(1) [51-500]
Gaztambide-Fernandez, Ruben A. - *Cultural Studies and Education: Perspectives on Theory, Methodology, and Practice*
SLJ - v50 - i10 - Oct 2004 - pS72(1) [51-500]
TCR - v106 - i8 - August 2004 - p1650(4) [501+]
Gazur, Wayne M. - *Case Studies in Estate Planning: with Abridged Student Forms*
R&R Bk N - v19 - i3 - August 2004 - p197(1) [1-50]
Gazzara, Ben - *In the Moment: My Life as an Actor*
KR - v72 - i18 - Sept 15 2004 - p901(1) [501+]
PW - v251 - i38 - Sept 20 2004 - p52(1) [51-500]
Gazzini Isabelle Fellrath - *Cultural Property Disputes: The Role of Arbitration in Resolving Non-Contractual Disputes*
R&R Bk N - v19 - i3 - August 2004 - p192(1) [501+]
Geagley, Brad - *Year of the Hyenas*
BL - v101 - i9-10 - Jan 1 2005 - p826(1) [1-50]
KR - v72 - i24 - Dec 15 2004 - p1167(1) [501+]
LJ - v130 - i1 - Jan 1 2005 - p83(1) [51-500]
Gear, Alan D. - *The Complete Guide to Stamping: Over 70 Techniques with 20 Original Projects and 300 Motifs*
LJ - v129 - i17 - Oct 15 2004 - p62(1) [51-500]
Gear, Kathleen O'Neal - *It Sleeps in Me (Read by Patel, Lina). Audiobook Review*
LJ - v130 - i3 - Feb 15 2005 - p171(1) [1-50]
Geary, Brent B. - *Handbook of Ericksonian Psychotherapy*
SciTech - v28 - i3 - Sept 2004 - p97(1) [51-500]
Geary, David - *Core JavaServer Faces*
SciTech - v28 - i4 - Dec 2004 - p150(1) [51-500]
Geary, Rick - *The Beast of Chicago: An Account of the Life and Crimes of Herman W. Mudgett, Known to the World as H.H. Holmes*
y Teach Lib - v32 - i1 - Oct 2004 - p17(2) [501+]
Gebara, Ivone - *Out of the Depths: Women's Experience of Evil and Salvation*
TT - v61 - i3 - Oct 2004 - p374(2) [501+]
Gebesmair, Andreas - *Global Repertoires: Popular Music Within and Beyond the Transnational Music Industry*
PMS - v27 - i4 - Dec 2004 - p542(4) [501+]
Gebhard, David - *An Architectural Guidebook to Los Angeles*
R&R Bk N - v19 - i1 - Feb 2004 - p202(1) [51-500]
Gebhard, Wilfried - *What Eddie Can Do (Illus. by Gebhard, Wilfried)*
c SLJ - v50 - i7 - July 2004 - p75(1) [51-500]
Gebhardt, A. - *Imperiale Politik und Provinziale Entwicklung Untersuchungen Zum Verhaltnis von Kaiser, Heer und Stadten im Syrein der Vorseverischen Zeit*
Class R - v54 - i2 - Nov 2004 - p504-506 [501+]
Gebissa, Ezekiel - *Leaf of Allah: Khat and Agricultural Transformations in Harerge, Ethiopia, 1875-1991*
SciTech - v28 - i4 - Dec 2004 - p65(1) [51-500]
Gecan, Michael - *Going Public: An Organizer's Guide to Citizen Action*
y Kliatt - v38 - i5 - Sept 2004 - p44(2) [51-500]
Gedacht, Daniel C. - *Land and Resources of Ancient Rome*
c SLJ - v50 - i12 - Dec 2004 - p130(1) [51-500]
Gedatus, Gus - *Exercise for Weight Management*
y SB - v40 - i4 - July-August 2004 - p149(1) [51-500]
Geddes, Andrew - *The European Union and British Politics*
TimHES - v0 - i1668 - Nov 26 2004 - pIV(1) [501+]
Geddes, Anne - *Miracle: A Celebration of New Life*
LJ - v130 - i2 - Feb 1 2005 - p76(1) [51-500]
PW - v251 - i41 - Oct 11 2004 - p74(1) [51-500]
Small Miracles
People - v62 - i17 - Oct 25 2004 - p53 [501+]
Geddes, Barbara - *Paradigms and Sand Castles: Theory Building and Research Design in Comparative Politics*
Choice - v41 - i11-12 - July-August 2004 - p2116(1) [501+]
Geddes, Gary - *Kingdom of Ten Thousand Things: An Impossible Journey from Kabul to Chiapas*
Globe & Mail - Feb 26 2005 - pD4 [501+]
Geddes, R. Richard - *Competing with the Government: Anticompetitive Behavior and Public Enterprise*
Choice - v42 - i4 - Dec 2004 - p707(1) [1-50]
Gedge, Karin E. - *Without Benefit of Clergy: Women and the Pastoral Relationship in Nineteenth-Century American Culture*
Choice - v42 - i1 - Sept 2004 - p120(1) [501+]
JR - v85 - i1 - Jan 2005 - p138(2) [501+]

Gedney, Mona - *The Affair at Greengage Manor*
LJ - v129 - i13 - August 2004 - p55(1) [501+]
On the Twelfth Day of Christmas
LJ - v129 - i19 - Nov 15 2004 - p47(2) [501+]
Gedutis, Susan - *See You at the Hall: Boston's Golden Era of Irish Music and Dance*
Bwatch - v26 - i8 - August 2004 - p4(1) [51-500]
Choice - v42 - i4 - Dec 2004 - p671(2) [1-50]
Gee, Austin - *The British Volunteer Movement: 1794-1814*
AHR - v109 - i4 - Oct 2004 - p1312-1312 [501+]
Gee, Henry - *Jacob's Ladder: The History of the Human Genome*
Am Sci - v92 - i5 - Sept-Oct 2004 - p465(1) [501+]
BL - v100 - i21 - July 2004 - p1807(1) [1-50]
CR - v285 - i1664 - Sept 2004 - p191(1) [51-500]
LJ - v129 - i12 - July 2004 - p113(1) [51-500]
Lon R Bks - v27 - i1 - Jan 6 2005 - p33(2) [501+]
NYTBR - August 29 2004 - p22 [501+]
SB - v40 - i4 - July-August 2004 - p159(1) [51-500]
SciTech - v28 - i3 - Sept 2004 - p59(1) [1-50]
TimHES - v0 - i1668 - Nov 26 2004 - p26(1) [501+]
Gee, Lisa - *Friends: Why Men and Women Are from the Same Planet*
PW - v251 - i34 - August 23 2004 - p51(1) [51-500]
Gee, Maggie - *The Flood*
TLS - i5265 - Feb 27 2004 - p23-23 [501+]
Gee, Sue - *The Mysteries of Glass*
TLS - i5284 - July 9 2004 - p20(1) [501+]
Geelhoed, E. Bruce - *Eisenhower, Macmillan, and Allied Unity, 1957-1961*
Albion - v36 - i2 - Summer 2004 - p366(2) [501+]
JAH - v91 - i2 - Sept 2004 - p694(1) [501+]
Geen, Rob - *Kinship Care: Making the Most of a Valuable Resource*
R&R Bk N - v19 - i1 - Feb 2004 - p137(1) [51-500]
Geer, Charlie - *Outbound: The Curious Secession of Latter-Day Charleston*
KR - v73 - i5 - March 1 2005 - p248(1) [501+]
Geer, John G. - *Public Opinion and Polling around the World: A Historical Encyclopedia, Vols. 1-2*
BL - v101 - i9-10 - Jan 1 2005 - p908(1) [501+]
Choice - v42 - i6 - Feb 2005 - p1005(1) [51-500]
Geerlings, W. - *Der Kommentar in Antike und Mittelalte. Beittrage zu seiner Erforschung*
Class R - v53 - i2 - Nov 2003 - p472-474 [501+]
Geertz, Hildred - *The Life of a Balinese Temple: Artistry, Imagination, and History in a Peasant Village*
Choice - v42 - i7 - March 2005 - p1269(1) [51-500]
R&R Bk N - v19 - i4 - Nov 2004 - p49(1) [51-500]
Geeslin, Campbell - *Elena's Serenade (Illus. by Juan, Ana)*
c SLJ - v50 - i10 - Oct 2004 - pS26(1) [1-50]
Geeson, Eileen - *Ultimate Dog Grooming*
E-Streams - Oct 2004 - pNA [501+]
Geest, Gerrit de - *Comparative Law and Economics*
R&R Bk N - v19 - i3 - August 2004 - p189(1) [501+]
Geever, Jane C. - *The Foundation Center's Guide to Proposal Writing, 4th Ed.*
R&R Bk N - v19 - i3 - August 2004 - p133(1) [51-500]
Gehlbach, Stephen H. - *American Plagues: Lessons from Our Battles with Disease*
SciTech - v28 - i4 - Dec 2004 - p84(1) [51-500]
Gehring, Verna V. - *The Internet in Public Life*
R&R Bk N - v19 - i4 - Nov 2004 - p122(1) [51-500]
War after September 11
Ethics - v114 - i4 - July 2004 - p860(1) [501+]
WP - v56 - i2 - Jan 2004 - p303-325 [501+]
Gehring, Wes D. - *Irene Dunne: First Lady of Hollywood*
R&R Bk N - v19 - i1 - Feb 2004 - p227(1) [51-500]
Gehrman, Jody - *Summer in the Land of Skin*
y BL - v100 - i22 - August 2004 - p1909(1) [51-500]
PW - v251 - i31 - August 2 2004 - p54(1) [51-500]
Gehrmann, Christian - *Bluetooth Security*
SciTech - v28 - i3 - Sept 2004 - p153(1) [51-500]
Geiger, John - *Chapel of Extreme Experience: A Short History of Stroboscopic Light and the Dream Machine*
BIC - v33 - i6 - Sept 2004 - p13(2) [501+]
Geiger, Till - *Ireland, Europe and the Marshall Plan*
R&R Bk N - v19 - i4 - Nov 2004 - p89(1) [51-500]

Geirnaert, Eric - *L'Ambre, Miel de Fortune et Memoire de Vie.*
RocksMiner - v79 - i4 - July-August 2004 - p275(2) [501+]

Geisel, Theodore Seuss - *The Cat in the Hat*
c   RT - v57 - Sept 2003 - p98 [1-50]

Geiser, Kenneth - *Materials Matter: Toward a Sustainable Materials Policy*
JEL - v42 - i1 - March 2004 - p228(2) [501+]

Geisert, Arthur - *Pigaroons (Illus. by Geisert, Arthur)*
c   BL - v101 - i2 - Sept 15 2004 - p249(1) [51-500]
c   CCB-B - v58 - i3 - Nov 2004 - p120(2) [501+]
Pigaroons
c   KR - v72 - i17 - Sept 1 2004 - p865(1) [51-500]
c   SLJ - v50 - i12 - Dec 2004 - p108(2) [501+]
Roman Numerals I to MM (Illus. by Geisert, Arthur)
c   SLJ - v50 - i9 - Sept 2004 - p58(1) [51-500]

Geisert, Bonnie - *Lessons*
y   HB - v81 - i2 - March-April 2005 - p201(1) [51-500]

Geisler, Barbara Reichmuth - *Graven Images*
LJ - v130 - i4 - March 1 2005 - p70(1) [51-500]

Geisler, Cheryl - *Analyzing Streams of Language: Twelve Steps to the Systematic Coding of Text, Talk, and Other Verbal Data*
R&R Bk N - v19 - i1 - Feb 2004 - p213 [51-500]

Geisst, Charles R. - *Undue Influence: How the Wall Street Elite Put the Financial System at Risk*
LJ - v130 - i2 - Feb 1 2005 - p94(1) [51-500]
PW - v251 - i46 - Nov 15 2004 - p52(1) [51-500]

Geist, Anthony L. - *Modernism and Its Margins: Reinscribing Cultural Modernity from Spain and Latin America*
Hisp R - v72 - i3 - Summer 2004 - p450-452 [501+]

Geisthoevel, Alexa - *Eigentuemlichkeit und Macht: Deutscher Nationalismus 1830-1851*
HNet - Sept 2004 - pNA [501+]

Gelardi, Julia P. - *Born to Rule: Five Reigning Granddaughters of Queen Victoria.*
KR - v72 - i24 - Dec 15 2004 - p1181(1) [501+]
LJ - v129 - i20 - Dec 1 2004 - p135(2) [51-500]

Gelb, Arthur - *City Room*
NYTBR - Nov 14 2004 - p58 [501+]

Gelb, Michael J. - *Da Vinci Decoded: Discovering the Spiritual Secrets of Da Vinci's Seven Principles*
LJ - v129 - i16 - Oct 1 2004 - p87(1) [51-500]
How To Think Like Leonardo Da Vinci
Bwatch - Nov 2004 - pNA [51-500]

Gelber, Harry G. - *Opium, Soldiers and Evangelicals: England's 1840-42 War with China and Its Aftermath*
TLS - i5283 - July 2 2004 - p29(1) [501+]

Gelber, Hester Goodenough - *It Could Have Been Otherwise: Contingency and Necessity in Dominican Theology at Oxford, 1300-1350*
R&R Bk N - v19 - i4 - Nov 2004 - p23(1) [51-500]

Gelber, Yoav - *Israeli-Jordanian Dialogue, 1948-1953: Cooperation, Conspiracy, or Collusion?*
R&R Bk N - v19 - i4 - Nov 2004 - p45(1) [51-500]

Gelbmann, Gerhard - *Wittgenstein Archived: Bergenser Essays*
R&R Bk N - v19 - i3 - August 2004 - p6(1) [1-50]

Gelbspan, Ross - *Boiling Point: How Politicians, Big Oil and Coal, Journalists, and Activists are Fueling the Climate Crisis--and What We Can Do to Avert Disaster*
Am Sci - v93 - i2 - March-April 2005 - p174(1) [51-500]
BL - v100 - i22 - August 2004 - p1880(1) [51-500]
Choice - v42 - i7 - March 2005 - p1264(1) [51-500]
Hum - v64 - i6 - Nov-Dec 2004 - p39(2) [501+]
NYTBR - August 15 2004 - p5 [501+]
NYTBR - August 22 2004 - p18 [501+]

Geldart, Lloyd P. - *Problems in Exploration Seismology and Their Solutions*
SciTech - v28 - i4 - Dec 2004 - p162(1) [51-500]

Gelderblom, Arie-Jan - *The Low Countries as a Crossroads of Religious Beliefs*
R&R Bk N - v19 - i4 - Nov 2004 - p20(1) [501+]

Gelderen, C.J. van - *Encyclopedia of Hydrangeas*
Choice - v42 - i6 - Feb 2005 - p996(1) [51-500]

Gelfand, Donald E. - *Aging and Ethnicity: Knowledge and Services, 2nd Ed.*
R&R Bk N - v19 - i1 - Feb 2004 - p130(1) [51-500]

Gelfand, Michele J. - *The Handbook of Negotiation and Culture*
Choice - v42 - i6 - Feb 2005 - p1101(1) [51-500]
R&R Bk N - v19 - i4 - Nov 2004 - p10(1) [51-500]

Gelinas, Ulric J. - *Accounting Information Systems, 6th Ed.*
R&R Bk N - v19 - i4 - Nov 2004 - p114(1) [51-500]

Gell-Mann, Murray - *Nonextensive Entropy--Interdisciplinary Applications*
SciTech - v28 - i3 - Sept 2004 - p46(1) [1-50]

Gellately, Robert - *The Nuremberg Interviews*
NW - Oct 18 2004 - p68 [501+]
The Specter of Genocide: Mass Murder in Historical Perspective
GSR - v27 - i3 - Oct 2004 - p647(2) [501+]
JPR - v41 - i6 - Nov 2004 - p757-758 [501+]

Geller, Ewa - *Warschauer Jiddisch*
JEGP - v103 - i4 - Oct 2004 - p547-550 [501+]

Gelletly, LeeAnne - *Bolivia*
LibMed - v22 - i4 - Jan 2004 - p74(1) [501+]
Mexican Immigration
LibMed - v23 - i1 - August-Sept 2004 - p82(1) [51-500]

Gellner, David N. - *The Anthropology of Buddhism and Hinduism: Weberian Themes*
JRAI - v10 - i3 - Sept 2004 - p732(2) [501+]
Inside Organizations: Anthropologists at Work
JRAI - v10 - i4 - Dec 2004 - p945(2) [501+]

Gellner, Winardi - *The Berlin Republic: German Unification and a Decade of Changes*
HNet - June 2004 - pNA [501+]

Gelman, Andrew - *Teaching Statistics: A Bag of Tricks*
Math T - v98 - i1 - August 2004 - p63-63 [501+]

Gelman, Rita Golden - *Doodler Doodling (Illus. by Zelinsky, Paul O.)*
c   BL - v100 - i21 - July 2004 - p1842(1) [1-50]
    HB - v80 - i6 - Nov-Dec 2004 - p696(1) [51-500]
c   KR - v72 - i13 - July 1 2004 - p629(1) [51-500]
c   NYTBR - March 13 2005 - p21 [501+]
c   PW - v251 - i29 - July 19 2004 - p161(1) [51-500]
c   SLJ - v50 - i8 - August 2004 - p86(2) [501+]

Gel'man, Vladimir - *Avtonomiia ili kontrol'? Reforma mestnoi vlasti v gorodakh Rossii 1991-2001*
Slav R - v63 - i2 - Summer 2004 - p424(2) [501+]
Making and Breaking Democratic Transitions: The Comparative Politics of Russia's Regions
Russ Rev - v63 - i2 - April 2004 - pNA [501+]
Slav R - v63 - i3 - Fall 2004 - p670-671 [501+]

Gemelli, B. - *Isaac Becham, atomista e lettore critico di Lucrezio*
Class R - v54 - i2 - Nov 2004 - p549(2) [501+]

Gemignani, Michael C. - *Basic Concepts of Mathematics and Logic*
SciTech - v28 - i3 - Sept 2004 - p17(1) [501+]

Gemmeke, Mascha - *Frances Burney and the Female Bildungsroman: An Interpretation of The Wanderer, or Female Difficulties*
R&R Bk N - v19 - i4 - Nov 2004 - p236(1) [501+]

Gemmel, David - *The Swords of Night and Day*
y   VOYA - v27 - i5 - Dec 2004 - p404(1) [51-500]

Genazzani, A.R. - *Hormone Replacement Therapy and the Brain: The Current Status of Research and Practice*
SciTech - v28 - i1 - March 2004 - p99(1) [51-500]

Gendron, Michael P. - *Integrating Newly Merged Organizations*
R&R Bk N - v19 - i3 - August 2004 - p105(1) [1-50]

Genechten, Guido van - *The Cuddle Book (Illus. by Genechten, Guido van)*
c   BL - v101 - i7 - Dec 1 2004 - p663(1) [51-500]
c   CCB-B - v58 - i5 - Jan 2005 - p231(1) [51-500]
c   KR - v72 - i22 - Nov 15 2004 - p1094(1) [51-500]
c   SLJ - v50 - i12 - Dec 2004 - p123(1) [51-500]

General Index to the Collected Courses of the Hague Academy of International Law, Vols. 201-250 (1987-1994)/ Index General du Recueil des Cours ...
R&R Bk N - v19 - i3 - August 2004 - p185(1) [501+]

Generation X: Americans Born 1965 to 1976
Choice - v42 - i6 - Feb 2005 - p1005(1) [51-500]

Genet, Jean - *The Declared Enemy*
Choice - v41 - i11-12 - July-August 2004 - p2049(2) [501+]

A Genetic Puzzle: The Search for a Solution, Sects. 1-5, Student Book & Teacher Guide
Sci Teach - v71 - i7 - Sept 2004 - p85-85 [501+]

Geneva International Centre for Humanitarian Demining - *A Guide to Mine Action*
JPR - v41 - i6 - Nov 2004 - p758-758 [501+]

Genevois, Daniele Bussy - *Les Espagnoles dans l'histoire: une sociabilite democratique*
AHR - v109 - i4 - Oct 2004 - p1317(2) [501+]

Geng, Hwaiyu - *Manufacturing Engineering Handbook*
Choice - v42 - i5 - Jan 2005 - p884(1) [1-50]

Genge, N.E. - *The Forensic Casebook*
TLS - i5292 - Sept 3 2004 - p28(1) [501+]

Genna, Giuseppe - *In the Name of Ishmael*
TLS - i5288 - August 6 2004 - p20(1) [501+]

Gennes, Pierre-Gilles de - *Capillarity and Wetting Phenomena: Drops, Bubbles, Pearls, Waves*
Phys Today - v57 - i12 - Dec 2004 - p66-67 [501+]

Gennett, Andrew - *Sound Wormy*
VQR - v79 - i1 - Winter 2003 - p18 [501+]

Genoa, Chris - *Poof!*
LJ - v130 - i3 - Feb 15 2005 - p122(1) [51-500]

Genosko, Gary - *Party Without Bosses: Lessons on Anti-Capitalism from Felix Guattari and Luis Inacio 'Lula' da Silva*
CBRA - Annual 2003 - p288(2) [501+]

Genovese, Michael A. - *Encyclopedia of the American Presidency*
c   SLJ - v50 - i8 - August 2004 - p49(1) [51-500]
y   SLJ - v50 - i10 - Oct 2004 - p92(2) [501+]
c   BL - v101 - i3 - Oct 1 2004 - p359(1) [501+]

Genovese, Robert - *Disaster Prepardness Manual (1988), 2003 Rev. Ed.*
R&R Bk N - v19 - i1 - Feb 2004 - p261(1) [51-500]

Genoways, Hugh H. - *Museum Administration: An Introduction*
R&R Bk N - v19 - i1 - Feb 2004 - p1(1) [51-500]

Genoways, Ted - *Walt Whitman: The Correspondence, Vol. VII*
BW - v34 - i32 - August 8 2004 - p13(1) [501+]

Gentile, Douglas A. - *Media Violence and Children: A Complete Guide for Parents and Professionals*
Choice - v42 - i1 - Sept 2004 - p192(1) [501+]
R&R Bk N - v19 - i1 - Feb 2004 - p130(1) [51-500]

Gentile, Emilio - *The Struggle for Modernity: Nationalism, Futurism, and Fascism*
Choice - v42 - i2 - Oct 2004 - p361(1) [501+]
R&R Bk N - v19 - i1 - Feb 2004 - p37(1) [1-50]

Gentile, Lance M. - *The Oral Language Acquisition Inventory: Linking Research and Theory to Assessment and Instruction*
CE - v81 - i2 - Winter 2004 - p117(1) [51-500]

Gentili, B. - *Poetae elegiaci. Testimonia et fragmenta. Pars altera. Editio altera novis Simonidis fragmentis aucta*
Class R - v54 - i2 - Nov 2004 - p299-300 [501+]

Gentle, James E. - *Random Number Generation and Monte Carlo Methods*
JEL - v41 - i4 - Dec 2003 - p1338(2) [501+]

Genton, Marc G. - *Skew-Elliptical Distributions and Their Applications: A Journey Beyond Normality*
SciTech - v28 - i4 - Dec 2004 - p36(1) [51-500]

Gentry, Christine - *Carnosaur Crimes*
KR - v73 - i5 - March 1 2005 - p262(1) [51-500]

Gentry, Howard Scott - *Agaves of Continental North America*
E-Streams - Dec 2004 - pNA [501+]

Gentzler, JYL - *The Attractions and Delights of Goodness*
RM - v58 - i1 - Sept 2004 - p225(3) [501+]

Genz, Marcella D. - *A History of the Eragny*
TLS - i5304 - Nov 26 2004 - p30(1) [501+]

Geoff, Johns - *The Flash: Crossfire*
LibMed - v23 - i3 - Nov-Dec 2004 - p74(1) [51-500]

Geoghegan, Luke - *ICT for Social Welfare: A Toolkit for Managers*
R&R Bk N - v19 - i4 - Nov 2004 - p124(1) [1-50]

Geoghegan, Patrick M. - *Robert Emmet: A Life*
Albion - v36 - i2 - Summer 2004 - p385(2) [501+]

Geography on File, Rev. Ed.
c   LibMed - v22 - i5 - Feb 2004 - p85(1) [501+]

George, Alan - *Syria: Neither Bread nor Freedom*
Choice - v41 - i7 - March 2004 - p1365(1) [501+]

George, Alice L. - *Awaiting Armageddon: How Americans Faced the Cuban Missile Crisis*
HNet - Sept 2004 - pNA [501+]
JAH - v91 - i2 - Sept 2004 - p697(2) [501+]
T&C - v45 - i3 - July 2004 - p635-636 [501+]

George, Arthur L. - *St. Petersburg: Russia's Window to the Future, the First Three Centuries*
Choice - v41 - i7 - March 2004 - p1351(1) [501+]

George, Charles - *Buddhist*
　y　SLJ - v50 - i11 - Nov 2004 - p162(1) [51-500]
The Comanche
　c　SLJ - v50 - i7 - July 2004 - p117(1) [51-500]
What Makes Me a Buddhist?
　c　BL - v101 - i4 - Oct 15 2004 - p417(1) [51-500]
What Makes Me a Hindu?
　c　BL - v101 - i4 - Oct 15 2004 - p417(1) [51-500]

George, David - *Flash And Crash Days: Brazilian Theatre in the Post-Dictatorship*
　Theat J - v56 - i3 - Oct 2004 - p525-526 [501+]

George, David B. - *The Boethian Commentaries of Claembald of Arras*
　RM - v58 - i1 - Sept 2004 - p173(2) [501+]

George, Diana - *Reading Culture: Contexts for Critical Reading and Writing, 5th Ed.*
　R&R Bk N - v19 - i1 - Feb 2004 - p216(1) [51-500]

George, Earl Maquinna - *Living on the Edge: Nuu-Chah-Nulth History from an Ahousaht Chief's Perspective*
　Can Hist R - v85 - i4 - Dec 2004 - p825(2) [501+]
　CBRA - Annual 2003 - p364(1) [501+]

George, Elizabeth - *A Moment on the Edge: 100 Years of Crime Stories by Women*
　Globe & Mail - July 24 2004 - pD11 [51-500]
　LJ - v129 - i13 - August 2004 - p61(1) [501+]
　PW - v251 - i27 - July 5 2004 - p39(2) [501+]
With No One As Witness
　Ent W - i811 - March 18 2005 - p74 [51-500]
　Globe & Mail - March 5 2005 - pD15 [51-500]
　KR - v73 - i3 - Feb 1 2005 - p151(1) [51-500]
　PW - v252 - i8 - Feb 21 2005 - p161(1) [51-500]

George, Gerald - *Starting Right: A Basic Guide to Museum Planning, 2nd Ed.*
　R&R Bk N - v19 - i4 - Nov 2004 - p1(1) [51-500]

George, Jean Craighead - *Charlie's Raven*
　c　BL - v100 - i22 - August 2004 - p1933(1) [51-500]
　c　KR - v72 - i17 - Sept 1 2004 - p865(1) [51-500]
　c　PW - v251 - i40 - Oct 4 2004 - p88(1) [51-500]
　y　SLJ - v50 - i9 - Sept 2004 - p205(2) [51-500]
　y　VOYA - v27 - i5 - Dec 2004 - p381(1) [501+]
On the Far Side of the Mountain
　c　Teach Lib - v32 - i1 - Oct 2004 - p14(1) [51-500]
Snowboard Twist (Illus. by Minor, Wendell)
　c　BL - v101 - i4 - Oct 15 2004 - p410(1) [51-500]
　c　SLJ - v50 - i11 - Nov 2004 - p103(2) [51-500]
Tree Castle Island
　c　Teach Lib - v32 - i1 - Oct 2004 - p14(1) [51-500]

George, Judith St. - *Take the Lead, George Washington (Illus. by Powers, George)*
　c　PW - v252 - i5 - Jan 31 2005 - p70(1) [501+]

George, Kristine O'Connell - *Fold Me a Poem (Illus. by Stringer, Lauren)*
　c　KR - v73 - i5 - March 1 2005 - p286(1) [51-500]
Hummingbird Nest: A Journal of Poems (Illus. by Moser, Barry)
　c　NYTBR - Oct 17 2004 - p21 [501+]
　c　SLJ - v50 - i10 - Oct 2004 - pS52(1) [51-500]
One Mitten (Illus. by Smith, Maggie)
　c　BL - v101 - i6 - Nov 15 2004 - p590(1) [51-500]
　c　SLJ - v50 - i12 - Dec 2004 - p109(1) [501+]
Swimming Upstream (Illus. by Tilley, Debbie)
　c　RT - v57 - Oct 2003 - p178 [1-50]

George, Lindsay Barrett - *Inside Mouse, Outside Mouse (Illus. by George, Lindsay Barrett)*
　c　BL - v100 - i22 - August 2004 - p1942(1) [51-500]
　c　NYTBR - July 11 2004 - p18 [501+]
The Secret
　KR - v73 - i2 - Jan 15 2005 - p120(1) [51-500]

George, Melanie - *Naughty or Nice*
　BL - v101 - i7 - Dec 1 2004 - p641(2) [51-500]

George, Nelson - *The Accidental Hunter: A D. Hunter Mystery*
　Black Iss - v7 - i1 - Jan-Feb 2005 - p64(1) [51-500]
　KR - v72 - i21 - Nov 1 2004 - p1030(1) [51-500]
　LJ - v129 - i20 - Dec 1 2004 - p94(1) [51-500]
　PW - v251 - i50 - Dec 13 2004 - p48(1) [51-500]
Post-Soul Nation: The Explosive, Contradictory, Triumphant, and Tragic 1980's as Experienced by African Americans
　Black Iss - v6 - i4 - July-August 2004 - p55(1) [51-500]

George, Robert P. - *The Clash of Orthodoxies: Law, Religion and Morality in Crisis*
　Soc - v41 - i3 - March-April 2004 - p75(5) [501+]

George, Robley E. - *Socioeconomic Democracy: An Advanced Socioeconomic System*
　S&S - v68 - i4 - Winter 2004 - p510-4 [501+]

George, Rose - *A Life Removed: Hunting for Refuge in the Modern World*
　TLS - i5298 - Oct 15 2004 - p26(1) [501+]

George, Susan - *Another World Is Possible If...*
　R&R Bk N - v19 - i4 - Nov 2004 - p124(1) [51-500]

George, Susan Ella - *Visual Perception of Music Notation: On-Line and Off-Line Recognition*
　R&R Bk N - v19 - i4 - Nov 2004 - p194(1) [501+]

George, Terry - *Hotel Rwanda: Bringing the True Story of an African Hero to Film*
　LJ - v130 - i3 - Feb 15 2005 - p132(1) [51-500]
　c　PW - v252 - i6 - Feb 7 2005 - p57(1) [51-500]

George, Twig C. - *Seahorses*
　c　CH Bwatch - March 2005 - pNA [51-500]

George-Warren, Holly - *Shake, Rattle & Roll: The Founders of Rock & Roll (Illus. by Levine, Laura)*
　c　SLJ - v50 - i12 - Dec 2004 - p60(1) [501+]

George Washington
　c　SLJ - v50 - i7 - July 2004 - p55(1) [51-500]

Georges, Gregory - *50 Fast Photoshop CS Techniques*
　SciTech - v28 - i4 - Dec 2004 - p166(1) [51-500]

Georgiades, George - *2004 Miller GAAS Practice Manual: Current SASs, SSAEs, and SSARSs in Practice*
　R&R Bk N - v19 - i1 - Feb 2004 - p112(1) [51-500]

Georgiadou, Maria - *Constantin Caratheodory: Mathematics and Politics in Turbulent Times*
　Choice - v42 - i1 - Sept 2004 - p141(1) [501+]

Gephart, Roy E. - *Hanford: A Conversation about Nuclear Waste and Cleanup*
　HNet - June 2004 - pNA [501+]

Geraci, Victor W. - *Salud! The Rise of Santa Barbara's Wine Country*
　Pub Hist - v26 - i4 - Fall 2004 - p125(3) [501+]

Geraghty, Paul - *Dinosaur in Danger (Illus. by Geraghty, Paul)*
　c　SLJ - v50 - i11 - Nov 2004 - p124(1) [51-500]

Gerald, Debra E. - *Federal Forecasters Conference--2000: Papers and Proceedings*
　JEL - v42 - i1 - March 2004 - p246(1) [501+]

Gerald, Paul - *60 Hikes within 60 Miles*
　Bwatch - v26 - i7 - July 2004 - p1(1) [51-500]

Gerard, Anthony - *Tsubasa, Vol. 1 (Illus. by Dana, Hayward)*
　LJ - v129 - i14 - Sept 1 2004 - p128(1) [51-500]
　PW - v251 - i28 - July 12 2004 - p46(2) [51-500]

Gerardi, Michael H. - *Wastewater Pathogens*
　SciTech - v28 - i4 - Dec 2004 - p83(1) [51-500]

Geras, Adele - *Lizzie's Wish*
　c　Sch Lib - v52 - i4 - Winter 2004 - p203(1) [1-50]
Other Echoes
　y　Kliatt - v39 - i2 - March 2005 - p10(1) [51-500]
　c　Sch Lib - v52 - i3 - Autumn 2004 - p145(1) [501+]
Rebecca's Passover (Illus. by Moxley, Sheila)
　c　TES - v0 - i4576 - March 26 2004 - pssss18(2) [501+]
Sleeping Beauty (Illus. by Birmingham, Christian)
　c　SLJ - v50 - i8 - August 2004 - p107(1) [51-500]
Time for Ballet (Illus. by McNicholas, Shelagh)
　c　SLJ - v50 - i10 - Oct 2004 - pS26(2) [1-50]

Gerber, Carole - *Leaf Jumpers (Illus. by Evans, Leslie)*
　c　BL - v101 - i1 - Sept 1 2004 - p127(1) [1-50]
　c　SLJ - v50 - i8 - August 2004 - p107(2) [51-500]
Leaf Jumpers
　c　SB - v40 - i6 - Nov-Dec 2004 - p269(1) [51-500]

Gerber, D.E. - *A Commentary on Pindar Olympian Nine*
　Class R - v54 - i1 - May 2004 - p22(2) [501+]

Gerber, Merrill Joan - *This Is a Voice from Your Past: New and Selected Stories*
　KR - v73 - i2 - Jan 15 2005 - p71(1) [51-500]

Gerber, Richard - *Programming with Hyper-Threading Technology*
　SciTech - v28 - i3 - Sept 2004 - p20(1) [501+]

Gerber, Rudolph Joseph - *Legalizing Marijuana: Drug Policy Reform and Prohibition Politics*
　Choice - v42 - i6 - Feb 2005 - p1098(1) [51-500]
　R&R Bk N - v19 - i3 - August 2004 - p163(1) [501+]

Gerber, Steve - *Hard Time: 50 to Life (Illus. by Hurtt, Brian)*
　y　BL - v101 - i8 - Dec 15 2004 - p716(1) [51-500]
Hard Time: 50 to Life
　PW - v251 - i46 - Nov 15 2004 - p42(1) [51-500]

Gerber, Theodore P. - *Research in Social Stratification and Mobility, Vol. 19*
　CS - v33 - i5 - Sept 2004 - p539-540 [501+]

Gerdes, Louise I. - *Endangered Oceans: Opposing Viewpoints*
　y　SB - v41 - i1 - Jan-Feb 2005 - p23(2) [501+]
Espionage and Intelligence Gathering
　y　SLJ - v50 - i11 - Nov 2004 - p162(1) [51-500]
Media Violence
　SLJ - v50 - i10 - Oct 2004 - pS59(1) [51-500]

Gerdts, William H. - *American Art at the Flint Institute of Arts*
　R&R Bk N - v19 - i2 - May 2004 - p195(1) [51-500]

Gere, Charlie - *Digital Culture*
　Afterimage - v32 - i1 - July-August 2004 - p16(1) [501+]

Gere, David - *How to Make Dances in an Epidemic: Tracking Choreography in the Age of AIDS*
　R&R Bk N - v19 - i4 - Nov 2004 - p82(1) [51-500]

Gere, James M. - *Mechanics of Materials, 6th Ed.*
　SciTech - v28 - i1 - March 2004 - p139(1) [1-50]

Gergen, Mary - *Social Construction: A Reader*
　R&R Bk N - v19 - i3 - August 2004 - p144(1) [51-500]

Gerhardt, Uta - *Talcott Parsons: An Intellectual Biography*
　CS - v33 - i1 - Jan 2004 - p117-119 [501+]

Gerhards, Albert - *Identitat durch Gebet: Zur gemeinschaftsbildenden Funktion institutionalisierten Betens in Judentum und Christentum*
　Theol St - v66 - i1 - March 2005 - p217(2) [501+]

Gerhardt, Christoph - *Das Munchner Gedicht von den funfzehn zeichen vor dem jungsten gericht: Nach der handschrift der bayerischen Staatsbibliothek*
　Specu - v79 - i3 - July 2004 - p756-758 [501+]

Gerhardt, Uta - *Talcott Parsons: An Intellectual Biography*
　JAH - v91 - i3 - Dec 2004 - p1086(2) [501+]

Gerhart, Ann - *The Perfect Wife: The Life and Choices of Laura Bush*
　BW - v34 - i5 - Feb 1 2004 - p9(1) [501+]

Gerhart, Mary - *New Maps for Old: Explorations in Science and Religion*
　JR - v85 - i1 - Jan 2005 - p141(2) [501+]

Gerieco, Allen - *The Italian Renaissance in the Twentieth Century: Acts of an International Conference Florence, Villa I Tatti, June 9-11, 1999*
　Six Ct J - v35 - i1 - Spring 2004 - p307(3) [501+]

Geringer, Laura - *So B. It*
　c　NYTBR - Oct 17 2004 - p21 [501+]

Gerits, Anton - *Books, Friends, and Bibliophilia: Reminiscences of an Antiquarian Bookseller*
　R&R Bk N - v19 - i4 - Nov 2004 - p255(1) [501+]

Gerlach, Allen - *Indians, Oil, and Politics: A Recent History of Ecuador*
　HAHR - v84 - i3 - August 2004 - p555(3) [501+]

Gerlach, Arch C. - *National Atlas of the United States of America*
　LibMed - v22 - i7 - April-May 2004 - p91(1) [501+]

Gerlach, Larry R. - *The Winter Olympics: From Chamonix to Salt Lake City*
　Choice - v42 - i2 - Oct 2004 - p332(1) [51-500]
　R&R Bk N - v19 - i3 - August 2004 - p88(1) [51-500]

Gerlach, U. Henry - *Einwande und Einsichten. Revidierte Deutungen deutschsprachiger Literatur des 19. und 20. Jahrhunderts*
　Ger Q - v77 - i1 - Wntr 2004 - p103(2) [501+]

Gerler, Edwin R. - *Handbook of School Violence*
　R&R Bk N - v19 - i4 - Nov 2004 - p188(1) [501+]

Gerloff, Roswith - *Mission Is Crossing Frontiers: Essays in Honour of Bongai A. Mazibuko*
　IBMR - v28 - i4 - Oct 2004 - p181(1) [501+]

Germain, Georges-Hebert - *Adventures in the New World: The Saga of the Coureurs des Bois*
　CBRA - Annual 2003 - p275(2) [501+]

Germain, Sheryl St. - *Swamp Songs: The Making of an Unruly Woman*
　NWSA Jnl - v16 - i3 - Fall 2004 - p220(2) [501+]

German, Christopher R. - *Mid-Ocean Ridges: Hydrothermal Interactions Between the Lithosphere and Oceans*
　R&R Bk N - v20 - i1 - Feb 2005 - p82(1) [51-500]

German, Tracey C. - *Russia's Chechen War*
　Choice - v41 - i7 - March 2004 - p1368(1) [501+]
　HNet - Sept 2004 - pNA [501+]

Germond, Jack W. - *Fat Man Fed Up: How American Politics Went Bad*
　BL - v100 - i21 - July 2004 - p1802(1) [1-50]
　Wil Q - v28 - i4 - Autumn 2004 - p123(2) [501+]

Gernard, Bradley E. - *Quantico: Semper Progredi-Always Forward*
　Mar Crp G - v88 - i12 - Dec 2004 - p46(1) [501+]

Gerolymatos, Andre - *The Balkan Wars: Conquest, Revolution, and Retribution from the Ottoman Era to the Twentieth Century and Beyond*
R&R Bk N - v19 - i1 - Feb 2004 - p40(1) [1-50]
Red Acropolis, Black Terror: The Greek Civil War and the Origins of the Soviet-American Rivalry, 1943-1949
LJ - v129 - i13 - August 2004 - p93(1) [501+]

Geronimo Stilton!
c LibMed - v23 - i3 - Nov-Dec 2004 - p69(1) [51-500]

Gerovitch, Slava - *From Newspeak to Cyberspeak: A History of Soviet Cybernetics*
JEL - v42 - i1 - March 2004 - p214(2) [501+]
T&C - v45 - i1 - Jan 2004 - p208(2) [501+]

Gerritsen, Resi - *K9 Complete Care: A Manual for Physically and Mentally Healthy Working Dogs*
CBRA - Annual 2003 - p14(1) [51-500]

Gerritsen, Tess - *Body Double (Read by Mazur, Kathe). Audiobook Review*
BL - v101 - i8 - Dec 15 2004 - p751(2) [1-50]
Body Double
BL - v100 - i21 - July 2004 - p1797(1) [51-500]
Ent W - i779 - August 20 2004 - p131 [51-500]

Gers, Juan M. - *Protection of Electricity Distribution Networks, 2nd Ed.*
SciTech - v28 - i4 - Dec 2004 - p148(1) [501+]

Gersao, Teolinda - *O mensageiro e outras historias com anjos*
WLT - v78 - i3-4 - Sept-Dec 2004 - p151(2) [501+]

Gersemann, Olaf - *Cowboy Capitalism: European Myths, American Reality*
Choice - v42 - i6 - Feb 2005 - p1069(1) [51-500]
R&R Bk N - v19 - i4 - Nov 2004 - p88(1) [51-500]

Gersh, Stephen - *Medieval and Renaissance Humanism: Rhetoric, Representation, and Reform*
Ren Q - v57 - i4 - Winter 2004 - p1451(2) [501+]
R&R Bk N - v19 - i1 - Feb 2004 - p222(1) [51-500]

Gershator, Phillis - *The Babysitter Sings (Illus. by Potter, Melisande)*
c SLJ - v50 - i7 - July 2004 - p75(1) [51-500]
Wise ... and Not So Wise: Ten Tales from the Rabbis (Illus. by Ginsburg, Alexa)
c BL - v101 - i3 - Oct 1 2004 - p341(2) [51-500]
c SLJ - v51 - i1 - Jan 2005 - p109(1) [51-500]

Gershenfeld, Neil - *FAB: The Coming Revolution on Your Desktop--From Personal Computers to Personal Fabrication*
KR - v73 - i5 - March 1 2005 - p273(2) [501+]

Gershenhorn, Jerry - *Melville J. Herskovits and the Racial Politics of Knowledge*
Choice - v42 - i5 - Jan 2005 - p895(1) [1-50]
New R - Feb 14 2005 - p32 [501+]

Gershon, Anne A. - *Krugman's Infectious Diseases of Children, 11th Ed.*
E-Streams - June 2004 - pNA [501+]

Gershoni, Israel - *Whose Pharaohs? Archaeology, Museums and Egyptian National Identity from Napolean to World War I*
IJMES - v36 - i1 - Feb 2004 - p125-127 [501+]

Gershwin, M. Eric - *Handbook of Nutrition and Immunity*
SciTech - v28 - i3 - Sept 2004 - p75(1) [51-500]

Gerson, Carole - *E. Pauline Johnson, Tekahionwake: Collected Poems and Selected Prose*
Can Hist R - v85 - i3 - Sept 2004 - p618(2) [501+]

Gerson, Fabian - *Electron Spin Resonance Spectroscopy of Organic Radicals*
SciTech - v28 - i1 - March 2004 - p54(1) [51-500]

Gerson, Joel - *Milady's Standard Fundamentals for Estheticians, 9th Ed.*
R&R Bk N - v19 - i1 - Feb 2004 - p252(1) [51-500]

Gerson, Lloyd P. - *Aristotle and Other Platonists*
LJ - v129 - i20 - Dec 1 2004 - p121(1) [51-500]

Gerson, Stephane - *The Pride of Place: Local Memories and Political Culture in Nineteenth-Century France*
AHR - v109 - i3 - June 2004 - p987(2) [501+]

Gerstein, Emma - *Moscow Memoirs: Memories of Anna Akhmatova, Osip Mandelstam, and Literary Russia under Stalin*
BW - v34 - i42 - Oct 17 2004 - p15(1) [501+]
Choice - v42 - i5 - Jan 2005 - p858(1) [1-50]
KR - v72 - i15 - August 1 2004 - p724(1) [501+]
LJ - v129 - i15 - Sept 15 2004 - p57(1) [501+]
R&R Bk N - v19 - i4 - Nov 2004 - p217(1) [501+]

Gerstein, Mordicai - *The Man Who Walked between the Towers*
HB - v81 - i1 - Jan-Feb 2005 - p19(4) [501+]
What Charlie Heard (Read by Gerstein, Mordicai). Audiobook Review
c BL - v101 - i5 - Nov 1 2004 - p508(1) [51-500]
c SLJ - v50 - i9 - Sept 2004 - p82(1) [51-500]
What Charlie Heard
c SLJ - v50 - i12 - Dec 2004 - p61(1) [501+]

Gerstein, Ralph M. - *Education Law: An Essential Guide for Attorneys, Teachers, Parents and Student Advocates*
R&R Bk N - v19 - i4 - Nov 2004 - p171(1) [501+]

Gerstenberger, Erhard S. - *Theologies in the Old Testament*
TT - v61 - i2 - July 2004 - p244(3) [501+]

Gerstenfeld, Phyllis B. - *Crimes of Hate: Selected Readings*
R&R Bk N - v19 - i1 - Feb 2004 - p142(1) [51-500]

Gerster, Robin - *On the Warpath: An Anthology of Australian Military Travel*
Quad - v49 - i1-2 - Jan-Feb 2005 - p120(3) [501+]

Gerstmann, Evan - *Same-Sex Marriage and the Constitution*
PSQ - v119 - i4 - Winter 2004 - p696(2) [501+]

Gerstner, David A. - *Authorship and Film*
J Film & Vid - v56 - i1 - Spring 2004 - p51-52 [501+]

Gerston, Larry N. - *Public Policy Making: Process and Principles, 2nd Ed.*
R&R Bk N - v19 - i3 - August 2004 - p178(1) [501+]
Public Policymaking in a Democractic Society: A Guide to Civic Engagement
R&R Bk N - v19 - i1 - Feb 2004 - p76(1) [501+]
Recall!: California's Political Earthquake
Choice - v42 - i4 - Dec 2004 - p736(1) [1-50]
R&R Bk N - v19 - i3 - August 2004 - p180(1) [501+]

Gerth, Karl - *China Made: Consumer Culture and the Creation of the Nation*
BHR - v78 - i2 - Summer 2004 - p373(3) [501+]
Pac A - v77 - i3 - Fall 2004 - p560(2) [501+]

Gertler, Eric - *Prying Eyes: Protect Your Privacy from People Who Sell to You, Snoop on You, and Steal from You*
SEP - v277 - i1 - Jan-Feb 2005 - p46(1) [501+]

Gertler, Mark - *NBER Macroeconomics Annual 2002, Vol. 17*
JEL - v41 - i4 - Dec 2003 - p1344(1) [501+]

Gertler, Stephanie - *To Love, Honor, and BETRAY: The Secret Life of Suburban Wives*
Globe & Mail - Feb 12 2005 - pD13 [1-50]
The Windmill
BL - v101 - i3 - Oct 1 2004 - p310(1) [51-500]
PW - v251 - i41 - Oct 11 2004 - p55(1) [51-500]

Gertsler, Amy - *Ghost Girl*
LJ - v129 - i12 - July 2004 - p87(1) [51-500]

Gertz, Bill - *Breakdown: The Failure of American Intelligence to Defeat Global Terror, rev. ed.*
R&R Bk N - v19 - i4 - Nov 2004 - p252(1) [501+]

Gertz, Jan Christian - *Abschied vom Jahwisten: Die Komposition des Hexateuch in der jungsten Diskussion*
Theol St - v66 - i1 - March 2005 - p178(2) [501+]

Gertz, S.K. - *Echoes and Reflections: Memory and Memorials in Ovid and Marie de France*
FS - v58 - i2 - April 2004 - p235(2) [501+]

Gertzog, Alice - *Administration of the Public Library*
R&R Bk N - v19 - i1 - Feb 2004 - p259(1) [51-500]

Gertzog, Irwin N. - *Women and Power on Capitol Hill: Reconstructing the Congressional Women's Caucus*
Choice - v42 - i4 - Dec 2004 - p736(1) [1-50]
Pers PS - v33 - i4 - Fall 2004 - p231(1) [501+]
PSQ - v119 - i2 - Summer 2004 - p383(2) [501+]

Gervais, Ricky - *Flanimals*
PW - v252 - i5 - Jan 31 2005 - p66(1) [501+]
The Office: The Complete Second Series. Audiobook Review
LJ - v129 - i19 - Nov 15 2004 - p96(1) [501+]

Gervase, William Clarence-Smith - *The Global Coffee Economy in Africa, Asia and Latin America, 1500-1989*
JIH - v35 - i2 - Autumn 2004 - p325(2) [501+]

Gerwehr, Scott - *Unweaving the Web: Deception and Adaption in Future Urban Operations*
R&R Bk N - v19 - i1 - Feb 2004 - p254(1) [51-500]

Gery, Robin - *Melville and Milton: An Edition and Analysis of Melville's Annotations on Milton*
Choice - v42 - i3 - Nov 2004 - p485(1) [1-50]

Gerzina, Gretchen Holbrook - *Frances Hodgson Burnett: The Unexpected Life of the Author of The Secret Garden*
Bwatch - v26 - i9 - Sept 2004 - p4(1) [51-500]
Frances Hodgson Burnett: The Unexpected Life of the Author of 'The Secret Garden'
Ent W - i785 - Sept 24 2004 - p114 [51-500]
Frances Hodgson Burnett: The Unexpected Life of the Author of The Secret Garden
NYT - July 28 2004 - pE9 [501+]

Geschwind, Carl-Henry - *California Earthquakes: Science, Risk, and the Politics of Hazard Mitigation*
Isis - v95 - i3 - Sept 2004 - p529(2) [501+]

Geshe Kelsang Gyatso - *How to Solve Our Human Problems: The Four Noble Truths*
BL - v101 - i3 - Oct 1 2004 - p304(1) [51-500]

Gessen, Masha - *Ester and Ruzya: How My Grandmothers Survived Hitler's War and Stalin's Peace*
BL - v101 - i4 - Oct 15 2004 - p383(1) [51-500]
KR - v72 - i18 - Sept 15 2004 - p901(1) [501+]
NYTBR - March 6 2005 - p18 [501+]
PW - v251 - i45 - Nov 8 2004 - p45(1) [501+]

Gessner, David - *Sick of Nature*
LJ - v129 - i12 - July 2004 - p113(2) [501+]

Getes, William Preston - *Lake George Boats and Steamboats*
R&R Bk N - v19 - i3 - August 2004 - p88(1) [51-500]

Getty, Adam - *Reconciliation*
BIC - v33 - i5 - August 2004 - p33(2) [501+]

Getty, Michael - *The Metre of Beowulf: A Constraint-Based Approach*
JEGP - v103 - i4 - Oct 2004 - p535-538 [501+]

Getz, Ken - *Access Cookbook, 2nd Ed.*
SciTech - v28 - i3 - Sept 2004 - p29(1) [51-500]

Getz, Trevor R. - *Slavery and Reform in West Africa: Toward Emancipation in Nineteenth-Century Senegal and the Gold Coast*
Choice - v42 - i2 - Oct 2004 - p347(1) [51-500]
R&R Bk N - v19 - i3 - August 2004 - p157(1) [51-500]

Getzinger, Donna - *Antonio Vivaldi and the Baroque Tradition*
y VOYA - v27 - i4 - Oct 2004 - p333(1) [51-500]
George Frideric Handel and Music for Voices
y SLJ - v50 - i11 - Nov 2004 - p162(1) [51-500]
Johann Sebastian Bach and the Art of Baroque Music
c SLJ - v50 - i8 - August 2004 - p136(2) [51-500]
y VOYA - v27 - i4 - Oct 2004 - p333(1) [51-500]
Richard Wagner and German Opera
y SLJ - v50 - i11 - Nov 2004 - p162(2) [51-500]

Geurts, Kathryn Linn - *Culture and the Senses: Bodily Ways of Knowing in an African Community*
IJAHS - v37 - i2 - Spring 2004 - p380-382 [501+]

Geus, C.H.J. de - *Towns in Ancient Israel and in the Southern Levant*
R&R Bk N - v19 - i3 - August 2004 - p155(1) [51-500]

Geus, Eelco de - *Sometimes I Just Stutter*
SLJ - v50 - i12 - Dec 2004 - p67(1) [501+]

Geus, K. - *Eratosthenes von Kyrene. Studien zur hellenistischen Kultur und Wissenschaftgeschichte*
Class R - v54 - i1 - May 2004 - p47(2) [501+]

Gevitz, Norman - *The DOs: Osteopathic Medicine in America, 2nd Ed.*
E-Streams - Nov 2004 - pNA [501+]
SciTech - v28 - i4 - Dec 2004 - p122 [51-500]

Gewanter, David - *The Sleep of Reason*
Poet - v185 - i5 - Feb 2005 - p401(2) [501+]

Geybels, Hans - *Vulgariter Beghinae: Eight Centuries of Beguine History in the Low Countries*
R&R Bk N - v19 - i4 - Nov 2004 - p26(1) [501+]

Geyer, Georgie Anne - *Tunisia: A Journey through a Country That Works*
BL - v101 - i2 - Sept 15 2004 - p200(1) [501+]
R&R Bk N - v19 - i4 - Nov 2004 - p51(1) [51-500]

Geyer, John B. - *Mythology and Lament: Studies in the Oracles About the Nations*
R&R Bk N - v19 - i4 - Nov 2004 - p22(1) [51-500]

Geyer, Michael - *Shattered Past: Reconstructing German Histories*
CEH - v37 - i3 - Summer 2004 - p461(5) [501+]

Geyman, John P. - *Corporate Transformation of Health Care: Can the Public Interest Still be Served?*
SciTech - v28 - i4 - Dec 2004 - p78(1) [51-500]

Gezelius, Stig S. - *Regulation and Compliance in the Atlantic Fisheries: State/Society Relations in the Management of Natural Resources*
SciTech - v28 - i1 - March 2004 - p132(1) [51-500]

Gibson, R.K. - *The Classical Commentary: Histories, Practices, Theory*
Class R - v54 - i1 - May 2004 - p5(8) [501+]

Gibson, R.N. - *Oceanography and Marine Biology: An Annual Review, Vol. 42*
SciTech - v28 - i4 - Dec 2004 - p6(1) [1-50]

Gibson, Rachel - *The Trouble With Valentine's Day*
PW - v251 - i49 - Dec 6 2004 - p48(1) [501+]
BL - v101 - i9-10 - Jan 1 2005 - p830(1) [1-50]

Gibson, Roger F., Jr. - *The Cambridge Companion to Quine*
Choice - v42 - i4 - Dec 2004 - p674(1) [1-50]

Gibson, Scott - *The Workshop: Celebrating the Place Where Craftsmanship Begins*
Am Craft - v64 - i1 - Feb-March 2004 - p24(1) [501+]
SciTech - v28 - i1 - March 2004 - p178(1) [51-500]

Gibson, Shimon - *The Cave of John the Baptist: The First Archaeological Evidence of the Historical Reality of the Gospel Story*
TLS - i5302 - Nov 12 2004 - p31(1) [51-500]
The Cave of John the Baptist: The Stunning Archaeological Discovery That has Redefined Christian History
Arch - v57 - i6 - Nov-Dec 2004 - p52-52 [501+]
BL - v101 - i2 - Sept 15 2004 - p179(1) [51-500]
Choice - v42 - i7 - March 2005 - p1242(1) [51-500]
LJ - v129 - i18 - Nov 1 2004 - p92(1) [51-500]

Gibson, Timothy A. - *Securing the Spectacular City: The Politics of Revitalization and Homelessness in Downtown Seattle*
R&R Bk N - v19 - i1 - Feb 2004 - p134(1) [51-500]

Gibson, William - *Neuromancer*
MFSF - v108 - i4 - April 2005 - p28(3) [501+]

Giddens, Anthony - *The Progressive Manifesto: New Ideas for the Centre-Left*
AJPS - v39 - i3 - Nov 2004 - p678(2) [501+]

Giddings, Geoffrey Jahwara - *Contemporary Afrocentric Scholarship: Toward a Functional Cultural Philosophy*
R&R Bk N - v19 - i1 - Feb 2004 - p56(1) [51-500]

Giddings, Philip - *Britain in the European Union: Law, Policy and Parliament*
CR - v285 - i1665 - Oct 2004 - p256(1) [501+]

Giddins, Gary - *Weather Bird: Jazz at the Dawn of Its Second Century*
Globe & Mail - Dec 24 2004 - pD13 [1-50]
LJ - v129 - i17 - Oct 15 2004 - p65(1) [51-500]

Giddy, Patrick - *Protest and Engagement: Philosophy After Apartheid at an Historically Black South African University*
HNet - Sept 2004 - pNA [501+]

Gidengil, Elisabeth - *Citizens*
R&R Bk N - v19 - i3 - August 2004 - p180(1) [501+]

Gidl, Anneliese - *In Einer Weiblichen Gesellschaft? Eine Analyse der Osterreichischen Printmedien 1945-1995*
GSR - v27 - i2 - May 2004 - p436-437 [501+]

Gidley, Mick - *Edward S. Curtis and the North American Indian Project in the Field*
SHQ - v107 - i4 - April 2004 - p620(2) [501+]

Giele, Janet Zollinger - *Women and Equality in the Workplace: A Reference Handbook*
Choice - v42 - i5 - Jan 2005 - p899(1) [1-50]

Gielen, Uwe P. - *Handbook of Culture, Therapy, and Healing*
Choice - v42 - i3 - Nov 2004 - p568(1) [51-500]
SciTech - v28 - i3 - Sept 2004 - p96(1) [51-500]

Gienapp, William E. - *This Fiery Trial: The Speeches and Writings of Abraham Lincoln*
HNet - June 2004 - pNA [501+]

Gierach, John - *Still Life with Brook Trout*
LJ - v130 - i3 - Feb 15 2005 - p137(1) [51-500]
PW - v252 - i8 - Feb 21 2005 - p166(1) [51-500]

Giesbrecht, Francis G. - *Planning, Construction, and Statistical Analysis of Comparative Experiments*
Choice - v42 - i2 - Oct 2004 - p329(1) [51-500]

Giese, Xenia - *Cisco Networking Academy Program: Fundamentals of Web Design Companion Guide*
SciTech - v28 - i3 - Sept 2004 - p156(1) [51-500]

Giff, Patricia Reilly - *Don't Tell the Girls: A Family Memoir*
PW - v252 - i10 - March 7 2005 - p69(2) [51-500]
A House of Tailors (Read by Brown, Blair). Audiobook Review
c HB - v81 - i2 - March-April 2005 - p220(2) [51-500]
A House of Tailors
c BL - v101 - i2 - Sept 15 2004 - p244(1) [51-500]
c CCB-B - v58 - i3 - Nov 2004 - p121(1) [501+]
c HB - v80 - i6 - Nov-Dec 2004 - p707(2) [51-500]
c KR - v72 - i19 - Oct 1 2004 - p960(1) [51-500]
c SLJ - v50 - i10 - Oct 2004 - p165(1) [51-500]
Maggie's Door (Read by Flanagan, Fionnula). Audiobook Review
c SLJ - v50 - i10 - Oct 2004 - pS54(1) [51-500]
Maggie's Door
LibMed - v22 - i6 - March 2004 - p63(1) [501+]
Pictures of Hollis Woods
c CH Bwatch - v14 - i7 - July 2004 - p7(2) [501+]
y Kliatt - v38 - i5 - Sept 2004 - p20(2) [51-500]
c RT - v57 - Nov 2003 - p275 [51-500]

Giffin, Emily - *Something Borrowed*
BW - v34 - i28 - July 11 2004 - p13(1) [501+]

Gifford, Clive - *The Arms Trade*
y BL - v101 - i9-10 - Jan 1 2005 - p840(1) [51-500]
The Kingfisher Geography Encyclopedia
LibMed - v22 - i6 - March 2004 - p77(1) [501+]
Soccer: The Ultimate Guide to the Beautiful Game
y LibMed - v23 - i3 - Nov-Dec 2004 - p90(1) [51-500]
c RT - v57 - Oct 2003 - p177 [1-50]
Summer Olympics: The Definitive Guide to the World's Greatest Sports Celebration
c SLJ - v50 - i8 - August 2004 - p137(1) [51-500]

Gifford, Courtney D. - *Directory of U.S. Labor Organizations, 2003 Ed.*
R&R Bk N - v19 - i1 - Feb 2004 - p100(1) [51-500]

Gifford, Darcy - *PeaceJam: How Young People Can Make Peace in their Schools and Communities*
R&R Bk N - v19 - i3 - August 2004 - p151(1) [51-500]

Gifford, Rebecca - *Cancer Happens*
CH Bwatch - Feb 2005 - pNA [51-500]

Gifford, Scott - *Piece = Part = Portion: Fractions = Decimals = Percents*
c TC Math - v11 - i2 - Sept 2004 - p109(1) [51-500]

Giger, Joyce Newman - *Transcultural Nursing: Assessment and Intervention, 4th Ed.*
SciTech - v28 - i1 - March 2004 - p126(1) [51-500]

Giggle Poetry
c SLJ - v50 - i10 - Oct 2004 - pS28(1) [1-50]

Gigliotti, Jim - *The Atlantic Division*
BL - v101 - i1 - Sept 1 2004 - p111(1) [1-50]

Gijsberts, Merove - *Nationalism and Exclusion of Migrants: Cross-National Comparisons*
R&R Bk N - v19 - i4 - Nov 2004 - p150(1) [501+]

Gikow, Louise A. - *The Big Game (Illus. by Garner, Phil)*
c SLJ - v50 - i12 - Dec 2004 - p109(1) [51-500]
A Day with Daddy (Illus. by Mazali, Gustavo)
c SLJ - v50 - i7 - July 2004 - p75(2) [51-500]

Gil, Moshe - *Jews in Islamic Countries in the Middle Ages*
Choice - v42 - i4 - Dec 2004 - p718(1) [1-50]
R&R Bk N - v19 - i3 - August 2004 - p52(1) [51-500]

Gilb, Dagoberto - *Gritos: Essays*
NYTBR - July 25 2004 - p20 [501+]

Gilbert, Brad - *I've Got Your Back: Coaching Top Performers from Center Court to the Corner Office*
PW - v251 - i28 - July 12 2004 - p55(1) [51-500]

Gilbert, David - *Geographies of British Modernity: Space and Society Twentieth Century*
J Hist G - v30 - i3 - July 2004 - p587(2) [51-500]
The Normals
BL - v101 - i2 - Sept 15 2004 - p207(1) [501+]
KR - v72 - i14 - July 15 2004 - p648(1) [501+]
NY - v80 - i33 - Nov 1 2004 - p105(1) [1-50]
NYTBR - Oct 17 2004 - p25 [501+]
PW - v251 - i34 - August 23 2004 - p35(2) [501+]

Gilbert, Erik - *Dhows and the Colonial Economy of Zanzibar, 1860-1970*
R&R Bk N - v19 - i4 - Nov 2004 - p52(1) [51-500]

Gilbert, Geoffrey - *World Poverty: A Reference Handbook*
Choice - v42 - i6 - Feb 2005 - p1069(1) [51-500]

Gilbert, Jack - *Refusing Heaven*
LJ - v130 - i2 - Feb 1 2005 - p83(1) [51-500]

Gilbert, Jimmie - *Elements of Modern Algebra, 6th Ed.*
SciTech - v28 - i4 - Dec 2004 - p34(1) [51-500]

Gilbert, Joanne R. - *Performing Marginality: Humor, Gender, and Cultural Critique*
Choice - v42 - i2 - Oct 2004 - p287(1) [501+]

Gilbert, Martin - *Churchill at War: His "Finest Hour" in Photographs, 1940-1945*
VQR - v80 - i3 - Summer 2004 - p254(1) [501+]
Dearest Auntie Fori,: The Story of the Jewish People
Globe & Mail - Jan 22 2005 - pD5 [501+]
The Second World War
LJ - v129 - i12 - July 2004 - p127(1) [51-500]

Gilbert, Michael B. - *Communicating Effectively: Tools for Educational Leaders*
R&R Bk N - v19 - i3 - August 2004 - p217(1) [1-50]

Gilbert, Neil - *Transformation of the Welfare State: The Silent Surrender of Public Responsibility*
CS - v33 - i1 - Jan 2004 - p81-82 [501+]

Gilbert, Oliver - *The Lichen Hunters*
New Sci - v185 - i2483 - Jan 22 2005 - p50(1) [501+]

Gilbert, Oscar E. - *Marine Corps Tank Battles in Korea*
HNet - Dec 2004 - pNA [501+]

Gilbert, Pat - *Passion Is a Fashion: The Real Story of the Clash*
NS - v133 - i4713 - Nov 8 2004 - p53(2) [501+]

Gilbert, Paul - *Evolutionary Theory and Cognitive Therapy*
SciTech - v28 - i4 - Dec 2004 - p98(1) [51-500]

Gilbert, Robert P. - *Maple Projects for Differential Equations*
SciTech - v28 - i3 - Sept 2004 - p39(1) [51-500]

Gilbert, Roger - *Epoch*
Poet - v184 - i5 - Sept 2004 - p394(1) [51-500]

Gilbert, Sandra M. - *Belongings: Poems*
LJ - v129 - i16 - Oct 1 2004 - p85(1) [51-500]

Gilbert, Sheri L. - *The Legacy of Gloria Russell*
c CH Bwatch - v14 - i7 - July 2004 - p7(2) [501+]
c LibMed - v22 - i7 - April-May 2004 - p61(1) [501+]

Gilbert, Sky - *An English Gentleman*
Globe & Mail - July 17 2004 - pD6 [501+]
Temptations for a Juvenile Delinquent
CBRA - Annual 2003 - p217(1) [501+]

Gilbert, Steven G. - *A Small Dose of Toxicology: The Health Effects of Common Chemicals*
Choice - v42 - i2 - Oct 2004 - p325(1) [51-500]
SciTech - v28 - i3 - Sept 2004 - p87(1) [51-500]

Gilbert, Steven W. - *Understanding Models in Earth and Space Science*
SB - v40 - i3 - May-June 2004 - p113(1) [501+]

Gilbert, Thomas R. - *Chemistry: The Science in Context, 1st Ed.*
TimHES - v0 - i1680 - Feb 25 2005 - pXIII(1) [501+]

Gilbert, Val - *The Daily Telegraph: 80 Years of Cryptic Crosswords*
Spec - v296 - i9198 - Nov 20 2004 - p48(1) [501+]

Gilbert, W. S. - *H.M.S. Pinafore in Full Score*
Notes - v61 - i2 - Dec 2004 - p532(5) [501+]
H.M.S. Pinafore: Or, the Lass That Loved a Sailor
Notes - v61 - i2 - Dec 2004 - p532(5) [501+]
H.M.S. Pinafore: Vocal score
Notes - v61 - i2 - Dec 2004 - p532(5) [501+]
The Mikado in Full Score
Notes - v61 - i2 - Dec 2004 - p532(5) [501+]
The Mikado: Vocal score
Notes - v61 - i2 - Dec 2004 - p532(5) [501+]
The Pirates of Penzance in Full Score
Notes - v61 - i2 - Dec 2004 - p532(5) [501+]
The Pirates of Penzance: Vocal score
Notes - v61 - i2 - Dec 2004 - p532(5) [501+]

Gilbertson, Michael - *God and History in the Book of Revelation: New Testament Studies in Dialogue with Pannenberg and Moltmann*
TT - v61 - i3 - Oct 2004 - p377(2) [501+]

Gilbey, Ryan - *"Groundhog Day"*
TLS - i5291 - August 27 2004 - p29(1) [51-500]

Gilbrt, Lara - *I Might be Nothing: Journal Writing*
Globe & Mail - Oct 9 2004 - pD24 [501+]

Gilchrist, Alan - *Information Architecture: Designing Information Environments for Purpose*
SciTech - v28 - i3 - Sept 2004 - p134(1) [51-500]

Gilchrist, Alison - *The Well-Connected Community: A Networking Approach to Community Development*
R&R Bk N - v19 - i2 - May 2004 - p131 [51-500]

Gilchrist, Ellen - *The Writing Life*
PW - v252 - i8 - Feb 21 2005 - p170(1) [51-500]

Gildart, Keith - *North Wales Miners: A Fragile Unity, 1945-1996*
CS - v33 - i4 - July 2004 - p442(2) [501+]
JEL - v42 - i1 - March 2004 - p300(1) [501+]

Gillmor, Stewart C. - *Fed Terman at Stanford: Building a Discipline, a University, and Silicon Valley*
Choice - v42 - i7 - March 2005 - p1247(1) [51-500]

Gillock, William - *More New Orleans Jazz Styles*
Am MT - v54 - i2 - Oct-Nov 2004 - p84(2) [501+]
New Orleans Jazz Styles
Am MT - v54 - i2 - Oct-Nov 2004 - p84(2) [501+]
Still More New Orleans Jazz Styles with Interactive Instrumental Accompaniments
Am MT - v54 - i2 - Oct-Nov 2004 - p84(2) [501+]

Gillon, Gail T. - *Phonological Awareness: From Research to Practice*
R&R Bk N - v19 - i4 - Nov 2004 - p181(1) [501+]

Gillon, Steven M. - *Boomer Nation: The Largest and Richest Generation Ever, and How it Changed America*
R&R Bk N - v19 - i3 - August 2004 - p145(1) [51-500]

Gillot de Beaucour, Louise-Genevieve de Gomes de Vasconcellos - *A Critical Edition of Penelope Aubin's Translation of Mme Gillot de Beaucour's The Adventures of the Prince of Clermont and Madam de Ravezan 1722*
R&R Bk N - v19 - i1 - Feb 2004 - p231(1) [51-500]

Gillow, John - *World Textiles: A Visual Guide to Traditional Techniques*
y Kliatt - v39 - i2 - March 2005 - p43(1) [51-500]

Gilman, Caroline - *Distance Learning and University Effectiveness: Changing Educational Paradigms for Online Learning*
R&R Bk N - v19 - i1 - Feb 2004 - p193(1) [51-500]

Gilman, Charlotte Perkins - *His Religion and Hers: A Study of the Faith of Our Fathers and the Work of Our Mothers*
R&R Bk N - v19 - i1 - Feb 2004 - p11(1) [51-500]
Social Ethics: Sociology and the Future of Society
R&R Bk N - v19 - i4 - Nov 2004 - p121(1) [51-500]

Gilman, James - *Fidelity of Heart: An Ethic of Christian Virtue*
J Ch St - v46 - i4 - Autumn 2004 - p911(2) [501+]

Gilman, John - *Electronic Basis of the Strength of Materials*
Phys Today - v57 - i8 - August 2004 - p56-57 [501+]

Gilman, Laura Anne - *Staying Dead*
ChrSFF&H - v26 - i9 - Sept 2004 - p33(1) [51-500]

Gilman, Nils - *Mandarins of the Future: Modernization Theory in Cold War America*
Choice - v42 - i2 - Oct 2004 - p368(1) [51-500]

Gilman, Phoebe - *The Balloon Tree*
c Res Links - v10 - i3 - Feb 2005 - p4(1) [501+]

Gilman, Rhoda R. - *Henry Hastings Sibley: Divided Heart*
Choice - v42 - i5 - Jan 2005 - p916(1) [1-50]

Gilman, Sander L. - *Fat Boys: A Slim Book*
Choice - v42 - i2 - Oct 2004 - p325(2) [51-500]
New Sci - v183 - i2461 - August 21 2004 - p51(1) [501+]
NYTBR - July 11 2004 - p20 [51-500]
Tikkun - v19 - i6 - Nov-Dec 2004 - p76(1) [501+]
TLS - i5293 - Sept 10 2004 - p10(1) [501+]
Franz Kafka: The Jewish Patient
NYRB - v52 - i2 - Feb 10 2005 - p4(4) [501+]
Jurek Becker: A Life in Five Worlds
Choice - v42 - i1 - Sept 2004 - p105(1) [51-500]
TLS - i5265 - Feb 27 2004 - p26-26 [501+]
Smoke: A Global History of Smoking
Spec - v296 - i9199 - Nov 27 2004 - p44(1) [501+]
TimHES - v0 - i1683 - March 18 2005 - p29(1) [501+]

Gilman, Susan Jane - *Hypocrite in a Pouffy White Dress: Tales of Growing up Groovy and Clueless*
PW - v251 - i44 - Nov 1 2004 - p51(2) [501+]
y BL - v101 - i1 - Sept 1 2004 - p41(1) [51-500]
Globe & Mail - Feb 12 2005 - pD9 [501+]
KR - v72 - i19 - Oct 1 2004 - p947(2) [501+]
People - v63 - i1 - Jan 10 2005 - p45 [51-500]

Gilmore, David - *Monsters: Evil Beings, Mythical Beasts, and All Manners of Imaginary Terrors*
Col Lit - v32 - i1 - Wntr 2005 - p199(3) [501+]

Gilmore, Gary D. - *Needs and Capacity Assessment Strategies for Health Promotion and Health Education, 3rd Ed.*
SciTech - v28 - i4 - Dec 2004 - p82(1) [51-500]

Gilmore, Michael T. - *Surface and Depth: The Quest for Legibility in American Culture*
RES - v55 - i219 - April 2004 - p299-301 [501+]

Gilmore, Rachna - *Ellen's Terrible TV Troubles*
y Can CL - i111-112 - Fall-Winter 2003 - p134(6) [501+]

Gilmore, Robert - *Elementary Quantum Mechanics in One Dimension*
Choice - v42 - i7 - March 2005 - p1264(1) [51-500]
SciTech - v28 - i4 - Dec 2004 - p48(1) [51-500]
Once Upon A Universe: Not-so-Grimm Tales of Cosmology
Phys Today - v57 - i12 - Dec 2004 - p64-66 [501+]

Gilmour, David - *Curzon: Imperial Statesman*
VQR - v80 - i1 - Wntr 2004 - p264-264 [501+]

Gilmour, Iain - *An Introduction to Astrobiology*
Choice - v42 - i5 - Jan 2005 - p878(1) [1-50]
S&T - v109 - i1 - Jan 2005 - p120(2) [501+]

Gilmour, Michael J. - *Tangled up in the Bible: Bob Dylan and Scripture*
Ch Today - v48 - i11 - Nov 2004 - p86(1) [501+]

Gilpin, Patrick J. - *Charles S. Johnson: Leadership beyond the Veil in the Age of Jim Crow*
JAH - v91 - i3 - Dec 2004 - p1084(2) [501+]

Gilroy, Amanda - *Green and Pleasant Land: English Culture and the Romantic Countryside*
R&R Bk N - v19 - i4 - Nov 2004 - p36(1) [51-500]

Gilson, Etienne - *Thomism: The Philosophy of Thomas Aquinas*
RM - v58 - i1 - Sept 2004 - p178(2) [501+]

Gilster, Paul - *Centauri Dreams: Imagining and Planning Interstellar Exploration*
Choice - v42 - i7 - March 2005 - p1248(1) [51-500]
PW - v252 - i2 - Jan 10 2005 - p51(2) [51-500]

Giltrow, Janet Lesley - *Academic Reading: Reading and Writing in the Disciplines, 2nd Ed.*
R&R Bk N - v19 - i1 - Feb 2004 - p216(1) [51-500]
Academic Writing: Writing and Reading in the Disciplines, 3rd Ed.
R&R Bk N - v19 - i1 - Feb 2004 - p216(1) [51-500]

Gimbel, Howard V. - *Lasik Complications: Trends and Techniques, 3rd Ed.*
SciTech - v28 - i3 - Sept 2004 - p114(1) [51-500]

Gimenez, Carmen - *Constantin Brancusi: The Essence of Things*
R&R Bk N - v19 - i4 - Nov 2004 - p205(1) [501+]

Giminez, Carmen - *Calder: Gravity and Grace*
Choice - v42 - i4 - Dec 2004 - p648(1) [1-50]

Gimlette, John - *At the Tomb of the Inflatable Pig: Travels through Paraguay*
Bwatch - Feb 2005 - pNA [51-500]
Comw - v131 - i20 - Nov 19 2004 - p29(2) [501+]
Theatre of Fish
Spec - v297 - i9212 - Feb 26 2005 - p40(1) [501+]

Gimpel, James G. - *Cultivating Democracy: Civic Environments and Political Socialization in America*
CS - v33 - i5 - Sept 2004 - p623-623 [501+]
R&R Bk N - v19 - i1 - Feb 2004 - p130(1) [51-500]
Patchwork Nation: Sectionalism and Political Change in American Politics
Pers PS - v34 - i1 - Wntr 2005 - p51(1) [501+]

Gina, Lloyd Maepeza - *Journeys in a Small Canoe: The Life and Times of a Solomon Islander*
Pac A - v77 - i3 - Fall 2004 - p615(2) [501+]

Gindroz, Ray - *The Architectural Pattern Book*
R&R Bk N - v19 - i3 - August 2004 - p242(1) [51-500]

Ginevan, Michael E. - *Statistical Tools for Environmental Quality Measurement*
R&R Bk N - v19 - i1 - Feb 2004 - p70(1) [501+]

Gingerich, Owen - *Annotated Census of Copernicus; "De Revolutionibus"*
BSA-P - v98 - i3 - Sept 2004 - p374-379 [501+]
The Book Nobody Read: Chasing the Revolutions of Nicolaus Copernicus
BL - v101 - i7 - Dec 1 2004 - p632(1) [51-500]
Bwatch - Nov 2004 - pNA [51-500]
Choice - v41 - i11-12 - July-August 2004 - p2065(1) [501+]
E-Streams - Sept 2004 - pNA [501+]
NS - v133 - i4701 - August 16 2004 - p37(2) [501+]
NYTBR - July 18 2004 - p13 [501+]
SB - v40 - i3 - May-June 2004 - p113(1) [501+]
SB - v40 - i6 - Nov-Dec 2004 - p240(1) [501+]
TimHES - v0 - i1666 - Nov 12 2004 - p22(1) [501+]

Gingher, Marianne - *Bobby Rex's Greatest Hit*
BL - v101 - i6 - Nov 15 2004 - p557(1) [501+]

Gingold, Alfred - *Dog World: And the Humans Who Live There*
LJ - v130 - i3 - Feb 15 2005 - p150(1) [51-500]
PW - v252 - i3 - Jan 17 2005 - p52(1) [51-500]

Gingras, Francis - *Erotisme et merveilles dans le recitt Francis des XII*
Specu - v79 - i3 - July 2004 - p760-763 [501+]

Gingrich, Newt - *Gettysburg: A Novel of the Civil War*
New R - Sept 6 2004 - p32 [501+]
Grant Comes East: A Novel of the Civil War
New R - Sept 6 2004 - p32 [501+]
Winning the Future: A 21st Century Contract with America
NYTBR - Feb 6 2005 - p14 [501+]

Gini, Al - *The Importance of Being Lazy: In Praise of Play, Leisure, and Vacations*
JEL - v41 - i4 - Dec 2003 - p1340(1) [501+]

Ginkas, Kama - *Provoking Theater: Kama Ginkas Directs*
R&R Bk N - v19 - i1 - Feb 2004 - p227(1) [51-500]

Ginsberg, Allen - *The Allen Ginsberg Audio Collection. Audiobook Review*
Globe & Mail - Dec 4 2004 - pD38 [1-50]

Ginsberg, Margery B. - *Motivating Matters: A Workbook for School Change*
R&R Bk N - v19 - i1 - Feb 2004 - p111(1) [51-500]

Ginsberg, Martin D. - *Mergers, Acquisitions, and Buyouts: A Transactional Analysis of the Governing Tax, Legal, and Accounting Considerations, Vols. 1-4*
R&R Bk N - v19 - i1 - Feb 2004 - p117(1) [51-500]
R&R Bk N - v19 - i4 - Nov 2004 - p117(1) [51-500]
Mergers, Acquisitions, and Buyouts on CD-ROM. E-book Review
R&R Bk N - v19 - i1 - Feb 2004 - p117(1) [1-50]
Mergers, Acquisitions, and Buyouts (Through December 2003) 4v.
R&R Bk N - v19 - i2 - May 2004 - p123 [51-500]

Ginsberg, Robert - *The Aesthetics of Ruins*
R&R Bk N - v19 - i4 - Nov 2004 - p8(1) [51-500]

Ginsborg, Paul - *Italy and Its Discontents: Family, Civil Society State 1980-2001*
AHR - v109 - i4 - Oct 2004 - p1335-1336 [501+]
Silvio Berlusconi: Television, Power and Patrimony
CJR - v43 - i2 - July-August 2004 - p56(1) [51-500]
Globe & Mail - July 10 2004 - pD11 [501+]
Lon R Bks - v27 - i1 - Jan 6 2005 - p31(2) [501+]
TLS - i5307 - Dec 17 2004 - p30(1) [1-50]

Ginsburg, Daniel E. - *The Fix Is In: A History of Baseball Gambling and Game Fixing Scandals*
R&R Bk N - v19 - i3 - August 2004 - p88(1) [51-500]

Ginsburg, Michal Peled - *Shattered Vessels: Memory, Identity, and Creation in the Work of David Shahar*
Choice - v42 - i2 - Oct 2004 - p289(1) [501+]

Ginsburg, Tom - *Legal Reform in Korea*
Law&PolBR - Oct 2004 - pNA [501+]

Ginter, C.R. - *Realm of the Golden Feather*
c CBRA - Annual 2003 - p484(2) [51-500]

Ginway, Elizabeth M. - *Brazilian Science Fiction: Cultural Myths and Nationhood in the Land of the Future*
Choice - v42 - i2 - Oct 2004 - p298(1) [501+]

Ginwright, Shawn A. - *Black in School: Afrocentric Reform, Urban Youth, and the Promise of Hip-Hop Culture*
TCR - v106 - i12 - Dec 2004 - p2286(5) [501+]

Ginzburg, Lev R. - *Ecological Orbits: How Planets Move and Populations Grow*
SciTech - v28 - i3 - Sept 2004 - p58(1) [1-50]
Ecological Orbits: How Plants Move and Populations Grow
Choice - v42 - i6 - Feb 2005 - p1046(1) [51-500]

Ginzburg, Natalia - *It's Hard to Talk about Yourself*
TLS - i5264 - Feb 20 2004 - p24-24 [501+]

Giocoli, Nicola - *Modeling Rational Agents: From Interwar Economics to Early Modern Game Theory*
Econ J - v114 - i499 - Nov 2004 - pF544-F545 [501+]
JEL - v42 - i1 - March 2004 - p239(2) [501+]

Gioia, Dana - *Disappearing Ink: Poetry at the End of Print Culture*
BL - v101 - i4 - Oct 15 2004 - p377(1) [51-500]
LJ - v129 - i20 - Dec 1 2004 - p117(1) [51-500]
NYTBR - Nov 21 2004 - p16 [501+]
Nosferatu: An Opera Libretto
Sew R - v111 - i3 - Summer 2003 - pLXXXVIII-LC [501+]

Twentieth-Century American Poetics
Poet - v184 - i4 - August 2004 - p317(7) [501+]
Gioia, Ted - *The History of Jazz*
Globe & Mail - July 3 2004 - pD15 [501+]
Giono, Jean - *The Serpent of Stars*
LJ - v129 - i14 - Sept 1 2004 - p139(1) [51-500]
Giordan, Daniel - *Art of Photoshop*
SciTech - v28 - i1 - March 2004 - p135(1) [51-500]
Giordano, Antonio - *Cell Cycle Control and Dysregulation Protocols: Cyclins, Cyclin-Dependent Kinases, and Other Factors*
SciTech - v28 - i4 - Dec 2004 - p64(1) [51-500]
Giordano, F. - *L'idea di Roma nella cultura antica*
Class R - v54 - i1 - May 2004 - p167(3) [501+]
Giordano, Gerard - *Wartime Schools: How World War II Changed American Education*
R&R Bk N - v19 - i1 - Feb 2004 - pNA [51-500]
Giordano, Marie - *I Love You Like a Tomato*
Kliatt - v38 - i4 - July 2004 - p17(2) [51-500]
Giordano, Ralph G. - *Fun and Games in Twentieth-Century America: A Historical Guide to Leisure*
LibMed - v22 - i7 - April-May 2004 - p71(1) [501+]
R&R Bk N - v19 - i1 - Feb 2004 - p73(1) [1-50]
Giovanni, Janine di - *Madness Visible: A Memoir of the War*
TLS - i5264 - Feb 20 2004 - p24-24 [501+]
Giovanni, Nikki - *The Girls in the Circle (Illus. by Johnson, Cathy Ann)*
c SLJ - v51 - i2 - Feb 2005 - p97(1) [51-500]
Giovannini, A. - *La revolution romaine apres Ronald Syme. Bilans et perspectives*
Class R - v54 - i1 - May 2004 - p173(2) [501+]
Giovannini, Joseph - *Subway Style: 100 Years of Architecture & Design in the New York City Subway (Illus. by Garn, Andrew)*
PW - v251 - i39 - Sept 27 2004 - p53(1) [51-500]
Giovino, Andrea - *Divorced from the Mob: My Journey from Organized Crime to Independent Woman. Audiobook Review*
BL - v101 - i5 - Nov 1 2004 - p504(1) [51-500]
Divorced from the Mob: My Journey from Organized Crime to Independent Woman (Read by Rosenblat, Barbara). Audiobook Review
y Kliatt - v39 - i1 - Jan 2005 - p52(1) [51-500]
PW - v251 - i27 - July 5 2004 - p18(1) [51-500]
Divorced from the Mob: My Journey from Organized Crime to Independent Woman
NYTBR - Oct 31 2004 - p20 [501+]
Gipe, Paul - *Wind Power: Renewable Energy for Home, Farm, and Business*
Bwatch - v26 - i9 - Sept 2004 - p11(1) [51-500]
Choice - v42 - i3 - Nov 2004 - p514(1) [1-50]
Giraffes
c SLJ - v50 - i9 - Sept 2004 - p187(2) [51-500]
Girard, James E. - *Principles of Environmental Chemistry*
Bwatch - Jan 2005 - pNA [51-500]
SciTech - v28 - i4 - Dec 2004 - p54(1) [51-500]
Girard, Rodolphe - *Marie Calumet*
Essays CW - Winter 2003 - p110 [501+]
Girardet, Edward - *Jonathan Walter, Charles Norchi and Miswais Masood*
A Aff - v35 - i2 - July 2004 - p233-234 [501+]
Girardot, Norman J. - *The Victorian Translation of China: James Legge's Oriental Pilgrimage*
BCS - v24 - Annual 2004 - p276(3) [501+]
Ch Rev Int - v11 - i1 - Spring 2004 - p8(7) [501+]
IBMR - v28 - i4 - Oct 2004 - p185(1) [501+]
Girdner, Eddie J. - *Killing Me Softly: Toxic Waste, Corporate Profit, and the Struggle for Environmental Justice*
CS - v33 - i1 - Jan 2004 - p67-67 [501+]
Giri, Ananta Kumar - *Creative Social Research: Rethinking Theories and Methods*
R&R Bk N - v19 - i4 - Nov 2004 - p82(1) [51-500]
Girling, Paul - *Family Life: The Project Management Game*
R&R Bk N - v19 - i1 - Feb 2004 - p93(1) [51-500]
Girot, Jean-Eudes - *Pindare avant Ronsard: de l'emergence du grec a la publication des 'Quatre premiers livres des Odes' de Ronsard*
Six Ct J - v34 - i4 - Winter 2003 - p1182-1183 [501+]
FS - v58 - i1 - Jan 2004 - p88(2) [501+]
Giroud, Axele - *Transnational Corporations, Technology and Economic Development: Backward Linkages and Knowledge Transfer in South-East Asia*
JEL - v41 - i4 - Dec 2003 - p1357(1) [501+]

Giroux, Henry A. - *The Abandoned Generation: Democracy Beyond the Culture Fear*
TCR - v106 - i2 - Feb 2004 - p383-386 [501+]
Beyond the Corporate University: Culture and Pedagogy in the New Millennium
Col Lit - v31 - i4 - Fall 2004 - p172(9) [501+]
Breaking in to the Movies
Afterimage - v30 - Winter 2003 - p17 [501+]
Proto-Fascism in America: Neoliberalism and the Demise of Democracy
TCR - v106 - i12 - Dec 2004 - p2324(4) [501+]
Public Spaces, Private Lives: Democracy Beyond 9/11
CS - v33 - i5 - Sept 2004 - p623-623 [501+]
Take Back Higher Education: Race, Youth, and the Crisis of Democracy in the Post-Civil Rights Era
Choice - v42 - i5 - Jan 2005 - p893(2) [1-50]
Take Back Higher Education: Race, Youth, and the Crisis of Democracy in the Post-Civil War Era
Black Iss - v6 - i5 - Sept-Oct 2004 - p41(1) [501+]
Girzone, Joseph F. - *Joshua in a Troubled World: A Story for Our Time*
BL - v101 - i6 - Nov 15 2004 - p531(1) [51-500]
LJ - v130 - i2 - Feb 1 2005 - p60(1) [51-500]
PW - v251 - i48 - Nov 29 2004 - p21(2) [51-500]
Gischler, Victor - *Suicide Squeeze*
LJ - v129 - i20 - Dec 1 2004 - p96(1) [1-50]
PW - v252 - i11 - March 14 2005 - p48(1) [51-500]
Gish Jen - *The Love Wife*
Globe & Mail - Oct 23 2004 - pD15 [501+]
Gisonni, Debbie - *The Goddess of Happiness: A Down-to-Earth Guide for Heavenly Balance and Bliss*
PW - v252 - i9 - Feb 28 2005 - p61(1) [51-500]
Gispen, Kees - *Poems in Steel: National Socialism and the Politics of Inventing from Weimar to Bonn*
GSR - v27 - i1 - Feb 2004 - p188-190 [501+]
HNet - Nov 2004 - pNA [501+]
JMH - v76 - i3 - Sept 2004 - p724(3) [501+]
Gispert, Carlos - *Diccionario de literatura universal*
y BL - v101 - i6 - Nov 15 2004 - p612(1) [501+]
Gispert, Helene - *"Par la science, pour la patrie": L'association francaise pour l'avancement des sciences*
T&C - v45 - i4 - Oct 2004 - p878(2) [501+]
Gitchel, Sam - *Let's Talk About S-E-X: A Guide for Kids 9 to 12 and Their Parents*
y PW - v252 - i4 - Jan 24 2005 - p246(1) [51-500]
Gitelman, Claudia - *Liebe Hanya: Mary Wigman's Letters to Hanya Holm*
Dance - v78 - i8 - August 2004 - p52(2) [501+]
Gitelman, Lisa - *New Media, 1740-1915*
JAH - v91 - i2 - Sept 2004 - p620(2) [501+]
T&C - v45 - i1 - Jan 2004 - p259(3) [501+]
Gitelman, Zvi - *The Emergence of Modern Jewish Politics: Bundism and Zionism in Eastern Europe*
Slav R - v63 - i2 - Summer 2004 - p381(3) [501+]
Jewish Life after USSR
Slav R - v63 - i2 - Summer 2004 - p428(3) [501+]
New Jewish Identities: Contemporary Europe and Beyond
R&R Bk N - v19 - i1 - Feb 2004 - p44(1) [501+]
Gitelson, I.I. - *Manmade Closed Ecological Systems*
E-Streams - July 2004 - pNA [501+]
SciTech - v28 - i1 - March 2004 - p65(1) [51-500]
Gitler, Carlos - *Cellular Implications of Redox Signaling*
SciTech - v28 - i4 - Dec 2004 - p70(1) [51-500]
Gitlin, Laura N. - *Successful Grant Writing: Strategies for Health and Human Service Professionals. 2nd Ed.*
SciTech - v28 - i3 - Sept 2004 - p10(1) [501+]
Gitlin, Todd - *Letters to a Young Activist*
HER - v74 - i3 - Fall 2004 - p352(3) [501+]
Media Unlimited: How the Torrent of Images and Sounds Overwhelms Our Lives
JPC - v38 - i1 - August 2004 - p217(3) [501+]
Gitman, Lawrence J. - *Personal Financial Planning, 10th Ed.*
R&R Bk N - v19 - i3 - August 2004 - p134(1) [51-500]
Gitomer, Jeffrey H. - *The Patterson Principles of Selling*
R&R Bk N - v19 - i3 - August 2004 - p128(1) [51-500]
Gittins, Chrissie - *Armature*
y Sch Lib - v52 - i3 - Autumn 2004 - p166(1) [501+]
Gittleman, Art - *C# .Net illuminated*
SciTech - v28 - i4 - Dec 2004 - p19(1) [1-50]
Giugni, Marco - *Social Protest and Policy Change: Ecology, Antinuclear, and Peace Movements in Comparative Perspective*
R&R Bk N - v19 - i3 - August 2004 - p144(1) [51-500]
Giuliani, Massimo - *A Centaur in Auschwitz: Reflections on Primo Levi's Thinking*
Choice - v41 - i7 - March 2004 - p1301(2) [501+]

Giuliani, Rudolph W. - *Leadership*
Fed Prob - v68 - i1 - June 2004 - p72-73 [501+]
Giulietti, Alexandre - *Turbo Codes: Desirable and Designable*
SciTech - v28 - i1 - March 2004 - p153(1) [51-500]
Giunta, Anna - *Restructuring Industry and Territory: The Experience of Europe's Regions*
JEL - v41 - i4 - Dec 2003 - p1438(1) [501+]
Giustino, Cathleen M. - *Tearing Down Prague's Jewish Town: Ghetto Clearance and the Legacy of Middle-Class Ethnic Politics Around 1900*
HNet - Sept 2004 - pNA [501+]
Given, Michael - *The Sydney Cyprus Survey Project: Social Approaches to Regional Archaeological Survey*
Am Ant - v70 - i1 - Jan 2005 - p205(2) [501+]
Given-Wilson, Chris - *Fourteenth Century England II*
Albion - v36 - i1 - Spring 2004 - p98(2) [501+]
Givens, David - *Love Signals: A Practical Guide to the Body Language of Courtship*
LJ - v130 - i1 - Jan 1 2005 - p134(1) [51-500]
Givens, R. - *The Eight Ball Bible: A Guide to Bar Table Play*
BL - v100 - i22 - August 2004 - p1890(1) [51-500]
Givens, Terry L. - *By the Hand of Mormon: The American Scripture That Launched a New World Religion*
Bks & Cult - v10 - i6 - Nov-Dec 2004 - p38(3) [501+]
Givner, Joan - *Ellen Fremedon*
c BL - v101 - i6 - Nov 15 2004 - p582(1) [51-500]
c Globe & Mail - Nov 20 2004 - pD26 [51-500]
c Res Links - v10 - i3 - Feb 2005 - p17(2) [501+]
Gizzi, Peter - *Some Values of Landscape and Weather*
Poet - v185 - i5 - Feb 2005 - p392(2) [501+]
TLS - i5265 - Feb 27 2004 - p30-30 [501+]
Glachant, Jean-Michel - *Competition in European Electricity Markets: A Cross-Country Comparison*
JEL - v41 - i4 - Dec 2003 - p1396(1) [501+]
Gladding, Samuel T. - *Counseling as an Art: The Creative Arts in Counseling, 3rd Ed.*
SciTech - v28 - i3 - Sept 2004 - p3(1) [501+]
Gladman, T. - *Grain Size Control*
SciTech - v28 - i4 - Dec 2004 - p162(1) [51-500]
Gladney, Dru C. - *Dislocating China: Reflections on Muslims, Minorities, and Other Subaltern Subjects*
Choice - v42 - i5 - Jan 2005 - p910(1) [1-50]
Choice - v42 - i5 - Jan 2005 - p910(1) [1-50]
Gladstone, Alan - *International Labour Law Reports, Vol. 22*
R&R Bk N - v19 - i3 - August 2004 - p191(1) [501+]
Gladwell, Malcolm - *Blink: The Power of Thinking Without Thinking. Audiobook Review*
Globe & Mail - Jan 22 2005 - pD13 [51-500]
Blink: The Power of Thinking Without Thinking
BL - v101 - i1 - Sept 1 2004 - p2(1) [51-500]
Black Iss - v6 - i6 - Nov-Dec 2004 - p64(2) [501+]
Bus W - i3914 - Dec 27 2004 - p26 [501+]
Ent W - i801 - Jan 14 2005 - p92 [51-500]
Globe & Mail - Jan 8 2005 - pD4 [501+]
KR - v72 - i19 - Oct 1 2004 - p948(1) [501+]
LJ - v129 - i19 - Nov 15 2004 - p75(2) [501+]
New R - Jan 24 2005 - p27 [501+]
New Sci - v185 - i2486 - Feb 12 2005 - p48(1) [501+]
NS - v134 - i4727 - Feb 14 2005 - p51(2) [501+]
NYTBR - Jan 16 2005 - p1 [501+]
PW - v251 - i44 - Nov 1 2004 - p52(1) [501+]
Time - v165 - i2 - Jan 10 2005 - p57 [501+]
Glaeser, Andreas - *Divided in Unity: Identity, Germany, and the Berlin Police*
JRAI - v10 - i4 - Dec 2004 - p946(2) [501+]
Glaeser, Edward L. - *The Governance of Not-for-Profit Organizations*
JEL - v41 - i4 - Dec 2003 - p1368(1) [501+]
JEL - v42 - i3 - Sept 2004 - p854(3) [501+]
Soc Ser R - v78 - i4 - Dec 2004 - p698(1) [51-500]
Glaessner, Thomas C. - *Electronic Safety and Soundness: Securing Finance in a New Age*
R&R Bk N - v19 - i3 - August 2004 - p135(1) [51-500]
Glain, Stephen - *Mullahs, Merchants and Militants: The Economic Collapse of the Arab World*
MEJ - v59 - i1 - Wntr 2005 - p155(2) [501+]
Glaister, L. - *As Far as You Can Go*
MHR - v30 - i2 - Dec 2004 - p106(2) [51-500]
Glaisyer, Natasha - *Didactic Literature in England 1500-1800*
Ren Q - v57 - i3 - Fall 2004 - p1132(3) [501+]

Glancy, Diane - *American Gypsy: Six Native American Plays*
　　Am Ind CRJ - v28 - i1 - Winter 2004 - p83-85 [501+]
The Shadow's Horse
　　Am Ind CRJ - v27 - i4 - Fall 2003 - p175-176 [501+]
　　Prog - v69 - i2 - Feb 2005 - p46(3) [501+]
Stone Heart: A Novel of Sacajawea
　　South HR - v38 - i2 - Spring 2004 - p207(3) [501+]

Glantz, David M. - *Battle for the Ukraine: The Red Army's Korsun'-Shevchenkovkii Operation, 1944*
　　R&R Bk N - v19 - i1 - Feb 2004 - p29(1) [51-500]
Soviet Operational and Tactical Combat in Manchuria, 1945: August Storm
　　APJ - v18 - i3 - Fall 2004 - p115(2) [501+]
　　J Mil H - v68 - i4 - Oct 2004 - p1299-1301 [501+]
The Soviet Strategic Offensive in Manchuria, 1945: August Storm
　　APJ - v18 - i3 - Fall 2004 - p115(2) [501+]
　　J Mil H - v68 - i4 - Oct 2004 - p1299-1301 [501+]

Glanz, James - *City in the Sky: The Rise and Fall of the World Trade Center*
　　NYTBR - August 8 2004 - p20 [501+]

Glanz, Jeffrey - *Finding Your Leadership Style: A Guide for Educators*
　　TCR - v106 - i2 - Feb 2004 - p221-224 [501+]

Glasbeek, Harry - *Wealth by Stealth: Corporate crime, Corporate Law, and the Perversion of Democracy*
　　CBRA - Annual 2003 - p326(2) [501+]

Glasby, Jon - *The Health and Social Care Divide: The Experiences of Older People, 2nd Ed.*
　　SciTech - v28 - i3 - Sept 2004 - p80(1) [51-500]

Glasco, Laurence A. - *The WPA History of the Negro in Pittsburgh*
　　Bl S - v34 - i3 - Fall 2004 - p71-71 [501+]

Glasell, Pamela - *Collector's Guide to Vintage Tablecloths*
　　Ant&CM - v108 - i12 - Feb 2004 - p16(1) [501+]

Glaser, Bruno - *Amazonian Dark Earths: Explorations in Space and Time*
　　Choice - v42 - i5 - Jan 2005 - p876(2) [1-50]

Glaser, Byron - *Bonz Inside-Out! A Rhythm, Rhyme, and Reason Bonz-anza! (Illus. by Glaser, Byron)*
　　c SB - v40 - i4 - July-August 2004 - p149(1) [51-500]

Glaser, Linda - *Brilliant Bees*
　　c LibMed - v22 - i7 - April-May 2004 - p78(1) [501+]
Mrs. Greenberg's Messy Hanukkah (Illus. by Cote, Nancy)
　　c BL - v101 - i2 - Sept 15 2004 - p249(2) [51-500]
　　c CCB-B - v58 - i4 - Dec 2004 - p167(2) [51-500]
　　c HB - v80 - i6 - Nov-Dec 2004 - p659(1) [51-500]
　　c KR - v72 - i21 - Nov 1 2004 - p1049(1) [51-500]

Glaser, Matt - *Berklee Practice Method: Violin: Get Your Band Together*
　　Teach Mus - v12 - i1 - August 2004 - p60(1) [501+]

Glasgow, Neil A. - *What Successful Teachers Do: 91 Research-Based Classroom Strategies for New and Veteran Teachers*
　　Adoles - v39 - i156 - Winter 2004 - p831(1) [51-500]

Glasgow, Nina - *Critical Issues in Rural Health*
　　SciTech - v28 - i4 - Dec 2004 - p84(1) [51-500]

Glasmeier, Amy K. - *Manufacturing Time: Global Competition in the Watch Industry, 1795-2000*
　　Isis - v95 - i2 - June 2004 - p320(2) [501+]

Glasner, Peter - *Reconfiguring Nature: Issues and Debates in the New Genetics*
　　SciTech - v28 - i3 - Sept 2004 - p59(1) [1-50]
Splicing Life?: The New Genetics and Society
　　SciTech - v28 - i4 - Dec 2004 - p88(1) [51-500]

Glasrud, Bruce A. - *Bibliophiling Tejano Scholarship: Secondary Sources on Hispanic Texans*
　　Choice - v41 - i11-12 - July-August 2004 - p2026(1) [501+]
　　JSH - v70 - i4 - Nov 2004 - p992(1) [501+]

Glass, Isabel - *Daughter of Exile*
　　y VOYA - v27 - i4 - Oct 2004 - p314(1) [51-500]

Glass, Leslie - *For Love and Money: A Novel of Stocks and Robbers*
　　KR - v72 - i20 - Oct 15 2004 - p986(1) [51-500]
　　PW - v251 - i47 - Nov 22 2004 - p39(1) [501+]

Glass, Loren - *Authors Inc: Literary Celebrity in the Modern United States, 1880-1980*
　　Choice - v42 - i5 - Jan 2005 - p852(1) [1-50]

Glass, Thomas E. - *The History of Educational Administration Viewed through Its Textbooks*
　　TCR - v106 - i8 - August 2004 - p1519(2) [501+]

The Glasse Cafe
　　LibMed - v22 - i5 - Feb 2004 - p70(1) [501+]

Glassgold, Judith M. - *Lesbians, Feminism, and Psychoanalysis: The Second Wave*
　　SciTech - v28 - i4 - Dec 2004 - p100(1) [51-500]

Glassman, Audrey - *Bark & Tim: A True Story of Friendship Based on the Paintings of Tim Brown*
　　LibMed - v22 - i7 - April-May 2004 - p58(1) [501+]

Glassner, Andrew - *Morphs, Mallards & Montages: Computer-Aided Imagination*
　　SciTech - v28 - i4 - Dec 2004 - p131 [51-500]

Glassner, Barry - *Our Studies, Ourselves: Sociologists' Lives and Work*
　　Choice - v42 - i1 - Sept 2004 - p195(1) [501+]

Glassner, Jean-Jacques - *The Invention of Cuneiform: Writing in Sumer*
　　Choice - v41 - i11-12 - July-August 2004 - p2100(1) [501+]
　　TimHES - v0 - i1661 - Oct 8 2004 - p29(1) [501+]

Glaudes, Pierre - *Leon Bloy: Les Funerailles du naturalisme*
　　FS - v58 - i1 - Jan 2004 - p126(2) [501+]
L'Essai: metamorphoses d'un genre
　　FS - v58 - i1 - Jan 2004 - p148(2) [501+]

Glausiusz, Josie - *Buzz: The Intimate Bond Between Humans and Insects (Illus. by Steger, Volker)*
　　NH - v113 - i10 - Dec 2004 - p54(2) [51-500]

Glausner, Friedrich - *Thumbprint*
　　PW - v251 - i39 - Sept 27 2004 - p41(1) [501+]

Glayman, Claude - *Henri Duttileux: Music, Mystery and Memory*
　　M Ed J - v91 - i2 - Nov 2004 - p60(1) [501+]

Glaze, Dave - *Waiting for Pelly*
　　c CBRA - Annual 2003 - p485(1) [51-500]

Glazer, Neil T. - *Averting the Homework Crisis*
　　CE - v81 - i1 - Fall 2004 - p56(2) [51-500]

Glazier, Ira A. - *Germans to America, vol. 6*
　　HNet - Oct 2004 - pNA [501+]

Glazier, Teresa Ferster - *The Least You Should Know About Vocabulary Building: Word Roots, 5th ed.*
　　R&R Bk N - v19 - i4 - Nov 2004 - p216(1) [501+]

Gleadle, Kathryn - *Radical Writing on Women, 1800-1850: An Anthology*
　　JGS - v13 - i2 - July 2004 - p178-180 [501+]

Gleason, Gregory - *Markets and Politics in Central Asia: Structural Reform and Political Change*
　　JEL - v41 - i4 - Dec 2003 - p1409(1) [501+]

Gledhill, Christine - *Reframing British Cinema 1918-1928: Between Restraint and Passion*
　　TimHES - v0 - i1647 - July 2 2004 - p26(1) [501+]

Gleeson, James - *Bloody Sunday: How Michael Collins' Agents Assassinated Britain's Secret Service in Dublin on November 21, 1920*
　　R&R Bk N - v19 - i3 - August 2004 - p40(1) [51-500]

Gleeson, Janet - *The Grenadillo Box*
　　BooChiTr - Jan 11 2004 - p3(1) [501+]
The Serpent in the Garden
　　BL - v101 - i9-10 - Jan 1 2005 - p827(1) [1-50]
　　KR - v72 - i23 - Dec 1 2004 - p1106(1) [501+]
　　LJ - v130 - i1 - Jan 1 2005 - p85(1) [1-50]
　　PW - v252 - i4 - Jan 24 2005 - p225(1) [501+]

Gleeson, Libby - *Cuddle Time (Illus. by Vivas, Julie)*
　　c BL - v101 - i5 - Nov 1 2004 - p489(1) [51-500]
　　c HB - v80 - i6 - Nov-Dec 2004 - p697(1) [51-500]
　　c KR - v72 - i22 - Nov 15 2004 - p1089(1) [51-500]
　　c SLJ - v50 - i12 - Dec 2004 - p109(1) [501+]

Gleick, James - *Isaac Newton*
　　Kliatt - v38 - i6 - Nov 2004 - p33(1) [51-500]

Gleijeses, Piero - *Conflicting Missions: Havana, Washington, and Africa, 1959-1976*
　　RAH - v32 - i1 - March 2004 - p114(8) [501+]

Gleissner, Ruth-Maria - *Der Unpolitische Komponist als Politikum: Die Rezeption von Jean Sibilius im NS-Staat*
　　GSR - v27 - i3 - Oct 2004 - p640(3) [501+]

Gleitman, Henry - *Psychology. 6th Ed.*
　　TimHES - v0 - i1668 - Nov 26 2004 - pXVIII(8) [501+]

Gleitzman, Morris - *Girl Underground (Read by Fahey, Mary-Anne). Audiobook Review*
　　c SLJ - v50 - i12 - Dec 2004 - p74(1) [501+]
Toad Heaven
　　c KR - v72 - i24 - Dec 15 2004 - p1202(1) [51-500]
　　c PW - v252 - i1 - Jan 3 2005 - p57(2) [501+]
　　c SLJ - v51 - i1 - Jan 2005 - p130(1) [51-500]

Glen, Heather - *Charlotte Bronte: The Imagination in History*
　　Nine-C Lit - v59 - i2 - Sept 2004 - p264(4) [501+]

Glendenning, Norman - *After the Beginning: A Cosmic Journey through Space and Time*
　　PW - v251 - i47 - Nov 22 2004 - p53(1) [51-500]

Glenmullen, Joseph - *The Antidepressant Solution*
　　Bwatch - March 2005 - pNA [51-500]

Glenn, Cheryl - *Rhetorical Education in America*
　　Choice - v42 - i7 - March 2005 - p1224(1) [51-500]

Glenn, Jerome C. - *2004 State of the Future*
　　Choice - v42 - i7 - March 2005 - p1207(1) [51-500]
　　Fut - v38 - i6 - Nov-Dec 2004 - p59(1) [501+]
　　Fut - v38 - i6 - Nov-Dec 2004 - p61(1) [51-500]

Glenn, John - *Neorealism Versus Strategic Culture*
　　R&R Bk N - v19 - i3 - August 2004 - p172(1) [501+]

Glenn, Phillip - *Studies in Language and Social Interaction: In Honor of Robert Hopper*
　　Lang Soc - v33 - i3 - June 2004 - p446-450 [501+]

Glenn, Walter - *MCDST self-paced training kit (exam 70-270); supporting users and troubleshooting a Microsoft Windows XP operating system*
　　SciTech - v28 - i4 - Dec 2004 - p18(1) [1-50]
MCDST Self-Paced Training Kit (Exam 70-272): Supporting Users and Troubleshooting Desktop Applications on a Microsoft Windows XP Operating System
　　SciTech - v28 - i3 - Sept 2004 - p19(1) [501+]

Glenn, Wendy J. - *Portrait of a Profession: Teaching and Teachers in the 21st Century*
　　Cur R - v44 - i6 - Feb 2005 - p13(1) [501+]

Glennan, Kathryn P. - *Music Cataloging Bulletin: Index/Supplement to Volumes 21-30, 1990-1999*
　　R&R Bk N - v19 - i1 - Feb 2004 - p194(1) [51-500]

Glennon, John C. - *Piercing the veil of secrecy; litigation against U.S. intelligence*
　　R&R Bk N - v19 - i3 - August 2004 - p199(1) [1-50]
Roadway Safety and Tort Liability, 2nd Ed
　　R&R Bk N - v19 - i3 - August 2004 - p199(1) [1-50]

Glennon, Sean - *This Past Year: A Trek through a Season as a Football Fan*
　　LJ - v129 - i12 - July 2004 - p91(1) [501+]

Gleria, M. - *Applicative Aspects of Cyclophosphazenes*
　　SciTech - v28 - i3 - Sept 2004 - p52(1) [1-50]

Gleria, Mario - *Synthesis and Characterizations of Poly*
　　SciTech - v28 - i3 - Sept 2004 - p52(1) [1-50]

Glick, Andrew S. - *A comprehensive dictionary of gods, goddesses, demigods, and other subjects in Greek and Roman mythology*
　　R&R Bk N - v19 - i3 - August 2004 - p14(1) [1-50]

Glick, Daniel - *Monkey Dancing: A Father, Two Kids, and a Journey to the Ends of the Earth*
　　y Kliatt - v38 - i5 - Sept 2004 - p48(2) [51-500]
Monkey Dancing
　　Bwatch - v26 - i8 - August 2004 - p1(1) [51-500]

Glick, Lyz - *Your Father's Voice: Letters for Emmy about Life with Jeremy--and Without Him After 9/11*
　　KR - v72 - i13 - July 1 2004 - p616(1) [501+]

Glick, Reuven - *Financial Crises in Emerging Markets*
　　JEL - v42 - i1 - March 2004 - p215(2) [501+]

Glickman, Carl D. - *Holding Sacred Ground: Essays on Leadership, Courage, and Endurance*
　　TCR - v106 - i8 - August 2004 - p1516(3) [501+]
Letters to the Next President: What We Can Do about the Real Crisis in Public Education
　　TCR - v106 - i12 - Dec 2004 - p2322(2) [501+]

Glickman, Susan - *Running in Prospect Cemetery: New and Selected Poems*
　　Globe & Mail - July 17 2004 - pD12 [501+]

Glickman, Sylvia - *From Convent to Concert Hall: A Guide to Women Composers*
　　R&R Bk N - v19 - i1 - Feb 2004 - p194(1) [51-500]

Glickstein, Jonathan A. - *American Exceptionalism, American Anxiety: Wages, Competition, and Degraded Labor in the Antebellum United States*
　　JAH - v91 - i3 - Dec 2004 - p1012(2) [501+]

Glimcher, Paul W. - *Decisions, Uncertainty, and the Brain: the Science of Neuroeconomics*
　　QRB - v79 - i4 - Dec 2004 - p454(2) [501+]

Glimp, David - *Arts of Calculation: Quantifying Thought in Early Modern Europe*
　　Choice - v42 - i4 - Dec 2004 - p682(2) [1-50]
Increase and Multiply: Governing Cultural Reproduction in Early Modern England
　　Critm - v46 - i2 - Spring 2004 - p281(18) [501+]
　　Ren Q - v57 - i3 - Fall 2004 - p1149(2) [501+]

Goff, Philip - *Themes in Religion and American Culture*
Choice - v42 - i7 - March 2005 - p1245(1) [51-500]

Goff, Robert C.A. - *Counterspell: Guardian of the Ruins*
LJ - v130 - i3 - Feb 15 2005 - p122(1) [51-500]

Goffart, Walter A. - *Historical Atlases: The First Three Hundred Years, 1570-1870*
AHR - v109 - i2 - April 2004 - p598(2) [501+]
J Hist G - v30 - i3 - July 2004 - p564(5) [501+]
JIH - v35 - i2 - Autumn 2004 - p289(2) [501+]

Goffman, Ken - *Counterculture through the Ages: From Abraham to Acid House*
BL - v101 - i3 - Oct 1 2004 - p286(1) [51-500]
KR - v72 - i16 - August 15 2004 - p786(1) [51+]
LJ - v129 - i15 - Sept 15 2004 - p71(1) [51-500]

Gogerly, Liz - *Autumn*
c BL - v101 - i6 - Nov 15 2004 - p575(1) [51-500]
Pablo Picasso: Master of Modern Art
c SLJ - v51 - i1 - Jan 2005 - p110(1) [51-500]
Sigmund Freud
c LibMed - v22 - i4 - Jan 2004 - p73(1) [501+]

Gogotsi, Yury - *High-Pressure Surface Science and Engineering*
E-Streams - July 2004 - pNA [501+]

Goh, Beng-Lan - *Modern Dreams: An Inquiry into Power, Cultural Production, and the Cityscape in Contemporary Urban Penang Malaysia*
JAS - v63 - i3 - August 2004 - p846-847 [501+]

Goh, David S. - *Assessment Accommodations for Diverse Learners*
R&R Bk N - v19 - i1 - Feb 2004 - p188(1) [51-500]

Goh, Swee Chiew - *Studies in Educational Learning Environments: An International Perspective*
R&R Bk N - v19 - i1 - Feb 2004 - p190(1) [51-500]

Gohberg, Seymour Goldberg - *Basic Classes of Linear Operators*
SIAM Rev - v46 - i4 - Dec 2004 - p758-759 [501+]

Goichi, Yamada - *Manshukoku no ahensenbai: "Waga ManMo no tokushu ken'eki" no kenkyu/The opium Monopoly in Manchukuo: Research into the "Special Rights of Prewar Japanese Manchuria-Mongolia"*
Ch Rev Int - v10 - i2 - Fall 2003 - p477(9) [501+]

Going, K.L. - *Fat Kid Rules the World*
y LibMed - v22 - i5 - Feb 2004 - p71(1) [501+]

Goins, Wayne E. - *The Jazz Band Director's Handbook: A Guide for Success*
Choice - v41 - i7 - March 2004 - p1306(1) [501+]

Gokhale, Jagadeesh - *Fiscal and Generational Imbalances: New Budget Measures for New Budget Priorities*
JEL - v42 - i1 - March 2004 - p273(2) [501+]

Goksen, Fatos - *Integrating and Articulating Environments: A Challenge for Northern and Southern Europe*
E-Streams - June 2004 - pNA [501+]
R&R Bk N - v19 - i1 - Feb 2004 - p70(1) [51-500]

Golahny, Amy - *Points of Contact: Crossing Cultural Boundaries*
R&R Bk N - v19 - i3 - August 2004 - p141(1) [51-500]

Golan, David E. - *Principles of Pharmacology: The Pathophysiologic Basis of Drug Therapy*
SciTech - v28 - i3 - Sept 2004 - p122(1) [51-500]

Golan, Jonathan S. - *The Linear Algebra a Beginning Graduate Student Ought to Know*
Choice - v41 - i11-12 - July-August 2004 - p2081(1) [501+]

Golan, Tal - *Laws of Men and Laws of Nature: The History of Scientific Expert Testimony in England and America*
Am Sci - v92 - i6 - Nov-Dec 2004 - p556(3) [501+]
Choice - v42 - i6 - Feb 2005 - p1042(1) [51-500]
New Sci - v183 - i2462 - August 28 2004 - p51(1) [501+]
Laws of Men and Laws of Nature The History of Scientific Expert Testimony in England and America
Sci - v306 - i5695 - Oct 15 2004 - p412(2) [501+]
Laws of Men and Laws of Nature: The History of Scientific Expert Testimony in England and America
TimHES - v0 - i1678 - Feb 11 2005 - p29(1) [501+]

Golas, Peter J. - *Science and Civilisation in China, Vol. 5, Pt. 13*
Isis - v95 - i3 - Sept 2004 - p474(2) [501+]

Golash, Deirdre - *The Case Against Punishment: Retribution, Crime Prevention, and the Law*
LJ - v130 - i2 - Feb 1 2005 - p100(1) [51-500]

Golay, Michael - *The Tide of Empire: America's March to the Pacific*
JAH - v91 - i3 - Dec 2004 - p1019(2) [501+]

Golberg, Michael A. - *Introduction to Regression Analysis*
Choice - v42 - i6 - Feb 2005 - p1058(1) [51-500]
SciTech - v28 - i4 - Dec 2004 - p38(1) [51-500]

Gold, Alison Leslie - *Fiet's Vase: And Other Stories of Survival, Europe 1939-1945*
TLS - i5283 - July 2 2004 - p29(1) [501+]

Gold, August - *Does God Hear My Prayer? (Illus. by Waller, Diane Hardy)*
c PW - v252 - i7 - Feb 14 2005 - p81(1) [501+]

Gold, Aviva - *Painting from the Source: Awakening the Artist's Soul in Everyone*
LibMed - v22 - i4 - Jan 2004 - p91(1) [501+]

Gold, Bernice - *Strange School, Secret Wish*
y Can CL - i111-112 - Fall-Winter 2003 - p128(7) [501+]

Gold, Dore - *Hatred's Kingdom: How Saudi Arabia Supports the New Global Terrorism*
NYRB - v51 - i16 - Oct 21 2004 - p22(4) [501+]

Gold, Elizabeth - *Brief Intervals of Horrible Sanity: One Season in a Progressive School*
BooChiTr - Jan 25 2004 - p5(1) [501+]

Gold, Glen David - *Carter Beats the Devil (Read by Harding, Jeff). Audiobook Review*
Spec - v296 - i9187 - Sept 4 2004 - p43(1) [501+]

Gold, Hal - *Neutral War*
Ant R - v63 - i1 - Wntr 2005 - p190(2) [51-500]

Gold, Jack - *Kilter: 55 Fictions*
CBRA - Annual 2003 - p199(1) [51-500]

Gold, John C. - *Circulatory and Lymphatic Systems*
y SB - v40 - i4 - July-August 2004 - p168(2) [51-500]

Gold, Joseph - *Story Species: Our Life-Literature Connection*
CBRA - Annual 2003 - p269(2) [501+]

Gold, Liza H. - *Sexual harassment; psychiatric assessment in employment litigation*
SciTech - v28 - i4 - Dec 2004 - p11(1) [1-50]

Gold, Lois Swirsky - *Misconceptions About the Causes of Cancer*
CBRA - Annual 2003 - p430(1) [501+]

Gold, Lorna - *The Sharing Economy: Solidarity Networks Transforming Globalization*
R&R Bk N - v19 - i4 - Nov 2004 - p107(1) [51-500]

Gold, Malcolm - *Hybridization of an Assembly of God Church: Proselytism, Retention, and Re-Affiliation*
R&R Bk N - v19 - i1 - Feb 2004 - p25(1) [51-500]

Gold, Martha V. - *Nervous System*
y SB - v40 - i6 - Nov-Dec 2004 - p262(2) [51-500]

Gold, Michael - *New Frontiers of Democratic Participation at Work*
ILR - v143 - i3 - Autumn 2004 - p279(4) [501+]
R&R Bk N - v19 - i1 - Feb 2004 - p99(1) [51-500]

Gold, Penny Schine - *Making the Bible Modern: Children's Bibles and Jewish Education in Twentieth-Century America*
Choice - v42 - i3 - Nov 2004 - p499(2) [51-500]

Gold, Philip - *Take Back the Right: How the Neocons and the Religious Right Have Betrayed the Conservative Movement*
BW - v34 - i38 - Sept 19 2004 - p11(1) [51-500]
LJ - v129 - i16 - Oct 1 2004 - p98(2) [51-500]

Gold, Sharlya - *The Answered Prayer*
c CH Bwatch - v14 - i9 - Sept 2004 - p3(1) [51-500]

Gold, Steven H. - *High Energy Density and High Power RF: Proceedings*
SciTech - v28 - i1 - March 2004 - p164(1) [51-500]

Gold, Steven J. - *The Israeli Diaspora*
AJS - v110 - i2 - Sept 2004 - p525(3) [501+]
CS - v33 - i1 - Jan 2004 - p70-71 [501+]

Gold, Susan Dudley - *Brown v. Board of Education: Separate but Equal?*
y SLJ - v51 - i1 - Jan 2005 - p148(1) [51-500]
The Pentagon Papers: National Security or the Right to Know
y SLJ - v51 - i1 - Jan 2005 - p148(1) [51-500]
Roe v. Wade: A Woman's Choice?
y SLJ - v51 - i1 - Jan 2005 - p148(1) [51-500]

Gold, Thomas W. - *The Lega Nord and Contemporary Politics in Italy*
Choice - v41 - i7 - March 2004 - p1365(1) [501+]

Gold, Victor - *Liberwocky: What Liberals Say and What they Really Mean*
Am Spect - v37 - i9 - Nov 2004 - p58(2) [501+]

Gold, Victoria - *Ohio Employer's Guide, 12th ed.*
R&R Bk N - v19 - i4 - Nov 2004 - p169(1) [501+]

Gold-Vukson, Marji E. - *Grandpa and Me on Tu B'Shevat (Illus. by Evans, Leslie)*
c BL - v101 - i3 - Oct 1 2004 - p346(1) [51-500]
c SLJ - v50 - i11 - Nov 2004 - p104(1) [51-500]

Goldbarth, Albert - *Budget Travel through Space and Time*
LJ - v130 - i3 - Feb 15 2005 - p134(2) [51-500]
PW - v252 - i10 - March 7 2005 - p66(1) [51-500]

Goldberg, Arnold - *Misunderstanding Freud*
Choice - v42 - i3 - Nov 2004 - p567(1) [51-500]
SciTech - v28 - i4 - Dec 2004 - p2(1) [1-50]

Goldberg, Bernard - *Arrogance: Rescuing America from the Media Elite*
Am Spect - v37 - i1 - Feb 2004 - p58(3) [501+]
R&R Bk N - v19 - i1 - Feb 2004 - p229(1) [51-500]

Goldberg, Carl - *Seeking the Compassionate Life: The Moral Crisis for Psychotherapy and Society*
Choice - v42 - i5 - Jan 2005 - p937(1) [51-500]
SciTech - v28 - i3 - Sept 2004 - p98(1) [51-500]

Goldberg, Danny - *Dispatches from the Culture Wars: How the Left Lost Teen Spirit*
Lon R Bks - v26 - i20 - Oct 21 2004 - p22(1) [501+]

Goldberg, David J. - *Photodamaged Skin*
SciTech - v28 - i3 - Sept 2004 - p120(1) [51-500]

Goldberg, Esther - *Holocaust Memoir Digest: Survivors' Published Memoirs with Study Guide and Maps, vol. 1*
R&R Bk N - v19 - i3 - August 2004 - p34(1) [51-500]

Goldberg, Giora - *Ben-Gurion against the Knesset*
R&R Bk N - v19 - i1 - Feb 2004 - pNA [501+]

Goldberg, Halina - *The Age of Chopin: Interdisciplinary Inquiries*
Choice - v42 - i4 - Dec 2004 - p670(1) [1-50]

Goldberg, Jan - *The Louisiana Purchase: A Primary Source History of Jefferson's Landmark Purchase from Napoleon*
y SLJ - v50 - i10 - Oct 2004 - p188(1) [51-500]

Goldberg, Karen I. - *Activation and Functionalization of C-H Bonds*
SciTech - v28 - i3 - Sept 2004 - p51(1) [1-50]

Goldberg, Merryl - *Teaching English Language Learners through the Arts: A SUAVE Experience*
R&R Bk N - v19 - i1 - Feb 2004 - p192(1) [51-500]

Goldberg, Myla - *Time's Magpie: A Walk in Prague*
BL - v101 - i2 - Sept 15 2004 - p201(1) [501+]
LJ - v129 - i18 - Nov 1 2004 - p110(1) [51-500]

Goldberg, Natalie - *The Great Failure: A Bartender, a Monk, and My Unlikely Path to Truth*
BL - v100 - i22 - August 2004 - p1891(1) [51-500]
LJ - v129 - i15 - Sept 15 2004 - p63(1) [51-500]

Goldberg, P.J.P. - *Youth in the Middle Ages*
Med R - July 2004 - pNA [501+]

Goldberg, Stan - *Ready To Learn: How To Help Your Preschooler Succeed*
LJ - v130 - i4 - March 1 2005 - p104(2) [51-500]
PW - v252 - i3 - Jan 17 2005 - p49(1) [51-500]

Goldberger, Nancy - *Art and the River: Views and Visions of the Housatonic*
Choice - v42 - i4 - Dec 2004 - p648(1) [1-50]

Goldberger, Paul - *Up from Zero: Politics, Architecture, and the Rebuilding of New York*
Art N - v104 - i2 - Feb 2005 - p106(1) [501+]
BL - v101 - i1 - Sept 1 2004 - p37(1) [51-500]
Bus W - i3900 - Sept 20 2004 - p24 [501+]
BW - v34 - i42 - Oct 17 2004 - p8(1) [501+]
KR - v72 - i15 - August 1 2004 - p724(2) [501+]
LJ - v129 - i20 - Dec 1 2004 - p114(1) [51-500]
Up from Zero: Politics, Architecture and the Rebuilding of New York
Nation - v280 - i4 - Jan 31 2005 - p25 [501+]
Up from Zero: Politics, Architecture, and the Rebuilding of New York
NYTBR - Sept 12 2004 - p12 [501+]
NYTBR - Sept 19 2004 - p22 [501+]
PW - v251 - i32 - August 9 2004 - p241(1) [51-500]

Golden Books - *Animal Tales*
c PW - v251 - i37 - Sept 13 2004 - p80(2) [51-500]

Golden, Catherine J. - *Images of the Woman Reader in Victorian British and American Fiction*
ELT - v48 - i2 - Spring 2005 - p79(4) [501+]

Golden, Christopher - *Last Breath*
y Kliatt - v39 - i1 - Jan 2005 - p13(2) [51-500]
The Nimble Man
y BL - v101 - i4 - Oct 15 2004 - p395(1) [51-500]
Outcast
KR - v72 - i14 - July 15 2004 - p685(1) [51-500]
The Un-Magician
c SLJ - v50 - i10 - Oct 2004 - p165(1) [51-500]
Wildwood Road
y KR - v73 - i3 - Feb 1 2005 - p137(1) [51-500]
c PW - v252 - i8 - Feb 21 2005 - p162(1) [51-500]

Golden, Janet - *Children and Youth in Sickness and in Health: A Historical Handbook and Guide*
    E-Streams - Nov 2004 - pNA [501+]
    SciTech - v28 - i3 - Sept 2004 - p117(1) [51-500]
    VOYA - v27 - i5 - Dec 2004 - p421(1) [51-500]
Message in a Bottle: The Making of Fetal Alcohol Syndrome
    LJ - v129 - i18 - Nov 1 2004 - p112(1) [51-500]

Golden, M. - *Sport in the Ancient World from A to Z*
    Class R - v54 - i2 - Nov 2004 - p531(4) [501+]

Golden, Marita - *Don't Play in the Sun: One Woman's Journey Through the Color Complex*
    Bl S - v34 - i3 - Fall 2004 - p72-72 [501+]

Golden, Mark - *Sex and Differences in Ancient Greece and Rome*
    Choice - v42 - i5 - Jan 2005 - p909(1) [1-50]

Golden, Peter B. - *Nomads and Their Neighbors in the Russian Steppe: Turks, Khazars, and Qipchaqs*
    Russ Rev - v63 - i2 - April 2004 - pNA [501+]

Goldenberg, David M. - *The Curse of Ham: Race and Slavery in Early Judaism, Christianity, and Islam*
    CC - v121 - i18 - Sept 7 2004 - p55(2) [501+]
    JR - v84 - i3 - July 2004 - p511(2) [501+]

Goldenflame, Jake - *Overcoming Sexual Terrorism: 40 Ways to Protect Your Children from Sexual Predators*
    LJ - v129 - i17 - Oct 15 2004 - p81(1) [51-500]

Goldensohn, Leon - *The Nuremberg Interviews: An American Psychiatrist's Conversations with the Defendants and Witnesses*
    BL - v100 - i22 - August 2004 - p1879(1) [51-500]
    KR - v72 - i14 - July 15 2004 - p671(1) [501+]
    LJ - v129 - i12 - July 2004 - p97(1) [51-500]
    PW - v251 - i28 - July 12 2004 - p52(1) [51-500]
    Wil Q - v28 - i4 - Autumn 2004 - p120(1) [501+]

Goldfarb, Larry - *Daddy I Wanna Be a Lawyer*
    c CH Bwatch - v14 - i12 - Dec 2004 - pNA [51-500]

Goldfarb, Warren - *Deductive Logic*
    R&R Bk N - v19 - i1 - Feb 2004 - p5(1) [501+]

Goldfield, David R. - *Southern Histories: Public, Personal, and Sacred*
    HNet - Dec 2004 - pNA [501+]
    R&R Bk N - v19 - i3 - August 2004 - p73(1) [51-500]

Goldfinger, Eliot - *Animal Anatomy for Artists: The Elements of Form*
    A Art - v69 - i751 - Feb 2005 - p77(1) [51-500]
    R&R Bk N - v19 - i4 - Nov 2004 - p205(1) [501+]

Goldgar, Anne - *Institutional Culture in Early Modern Society*
    R&R Bk N - v19 - i3 - August 2004 - p143(1) [51-500]

Goldgeier, James M. - *Power and Purpose: U.S. Policy Toward Russia After the Cold War*
    E-A St - v56 - i8 - Dec 2004 - p1249(4) [501+]
    JPR - v41 - i6 - Nov 2004 - p758-759 [501+]
    Slav R - v63 - i4 - Winter 2004 - p895(3) [501+]

Goldhaber, A. - *Symmetry and Modern Physics: Proceedings*
    SciTech - v28 - i1 - March 2004 - p46(1) [51-500]

Goldhawk, Dale - *Getting What You Deserve: The Adventures of Goldhawk Fights Back*
    CBRA - Annual 2003 - p78(2) [51-500]

Goldhill, S. - *Being Greek under Rome: Cultural Identity, the Second Sophistic and the Development of Empire*
    Class R - v53 - i2 - Nov 2003 - p329-331 [501+]

Goldhill, Simon - *Love, Sex and Tragedy: How the Ancient World Shapes our Lives*
    HT - v54 - i12 - Dec 2004 - p57(1) [501+]
    TimHES - v0 - i1659 - Sept 24 2004 - p26(1) [501+]
The Temple of Jerusalem
    TimHES - v0 - i1680 - Feb 25 2005 - p33(1) [501+]
    TLS - i5303 - Nov 19 2004 - p32(1) [501+]

Goldie, Peter - *On Personality*
    TLS - i5288 - August 6 2004 - p29(1) [501+]

Goldie, Terry - *Pink Snow: Homotextual Possibilities in Canadian Fiction*
    CBRA - Annual 2003 - p255(2) [501+]

Goldin, Barbara - *Ten Holiday Jewish Children's Stories*
    c CH Bwatch - v14 - i12 - Dec 2004 - pNA [51-500]

Goldin-Meadow, Susan - *Hearing Gesture: How Our Hands Help Us Think*
    Nature - v429 - i6992 - June 10 2004 - p606(2) [501+]
    TimHES - v0 - i1660 - Oct 1 2004 - p24(2) [501+]

Goldin, Nan - *The Devil's Playground*
    Art N - v103 - i1 - Jan 2004 - p98(1) [501+]

Goldin, Paul Rakita - *The Culture of Sex in Ancient China*
    JAAR - v72 - i4 - Dec 2004 - p1031(4) [501+]

Golding, Joshua L. - *Rationality and Religious Theism*
    Rel St - v40 - i4 - Dec 2004 - p508(3) [501+]
    R&R Bk N - v19 - i1 - Feb 2004 - p14(1) [1-50]

Golding, Paul - *Senseless*
    TLS - i5299 - Oct 22 2004 - p23(1) [501+]

Golding, Theresa Martin - *Memorial Day Surprise (Illus. by Artigas, Alexandra)*
    c CE - v80 - i5 - Mid-Summer 2004 - p273(2) [1-50]
The Truth about Twelve
    c CCB-B - v58 - i2 - Oct 2004 - p74(1) [51-500]
    c KR - v72 - i18 - Sept 15 2004 - p914(1) [501+]
    y SLJ - v50 - i11 - Nov 2004 - p144(2) [51-500]

Golding, William - *Lord of the Flies*
    Globe & Mail - Oct 30 2004 - pD31 [501+]

Goldingay, John - *Old Testament Theology Vol. 1*
    TT - v61 - i3 - Oct 2004 - p380(2) [501+]

Goldish, Matt - *The Sabbatean Prophets*
    Choice - v42 - i4 - Dec 2004 - p678(1) [1-50]

Goldman, Emily O. - *The Diffusion of Military Technology and Ideas*
    Choice - v41 - i7 - March 2004 - p1362(1) [501+]
The Diffusion of Military Technology and Ideas
    R&R Bk N - v19 - i1 - Feb 2004 - p254(1) [51-500]

Goldman, Emma - *An Exceedingly Dangerous Woman*
    AHR - v109 - i4 - Oct 2004 - p1248(2) [501+]

Goldman, Francisco - *The Divine Husband*
    BL - v100 - i22 - August 2004 - p1899(1) [51-500]
    BW - v34 - i37 - Sept 12 2004 - p15(1) [501+]
    Globe & Mail - Oct 30 2004 - pD22 [501+]
    Globe & Mail - Nov 27 2004 - pD3 [501+]
    LJ - v129 - i12 - July 2004 - p70(1) [51-500]
    Lon R Bks - v27 - i4 - Feb 17 2005 - p35(3) [501+]
    NY - v80 - i26 - Sept 13 2004 - p89(1) [1-50]
    NYTBR - Sept 26 2004 - p29 [501+]

Goldman, Howard - *Choose What Works*
    NACEJou - v64 - i4 - Summer 2004 - p12-12 [501+]

Goldman, Irving - *Cubeo Hehenewa Religious Thought: Metaphysics of a Northwestern Amazonian People*
    Choice - v42 - i7 - March 2005 - p1269(1) [51-500]
    R&R Bk N - v19 - i3 - August 2004 - p16(1) [1-50]

Goldman, Judy - *Early Leaving*
    BL - v101 - i1 - Sept 1 2004 - p60(1) [51-500]
    KR - v72 - i13 - July 1 2004 - p595(1) [501+]
    LJ - v129 - i13 - August 2004 - p67(1) [51-500]

Goldman, Larry S. - *Psychiatry for Primary Care Physicians. 2nd Ed.*
    E-Streams - July 2004 - pNA [501+]
    SciTech - v28 - i1 - March 2004 - p96(1) [51-500]

Goldman, Lawrence - *Science, Reform, and Politics in Victorian Britain: The Social Science Association, 1857-1886.*
    JMH - v77 - i1 - March 2005 - p178(2) [501+]

Goldman, Lee - *Cecil Textbook of Medicine. 22nd Ed.*
    SciTech - v28 - i1 - March 2004 - p88(1) [51-500]

Goldman, Merle - *Changing Meanings of Citizenship in Modern China*
    Ch Rev Int - v11 - i1 - Spring 2004 - p95(8) [501+]

Goldman, Robert D. - *Live Cell Imaging: A Laboratory Manual*
    SciTech - v28 - i4 - Dec 2004 - p63(1) [51-500]

Goldman, Ron - *Topics in Algebraic Geometry and Geometric Modeling: Proceedings*
    SciTech - v28 - i1 - March 2004 - p41(1) [51-500]

Goldman, Shalom - *God's Sacred Tongue: Hebrew and the American Imagination*
    Choice - v42 - i3 - Nov 2004 - p500(1) [51-500]

Goldman, Stephen Robert - *Handbook of Computer and Computerized System Validation for the Pharmaceutical Industry*
    SciTech - v28 - i3 - Sept 2004 - p124(1) [51-500]

Goldman, Wendy Z. - *Women at the Gates: Gender and Industry in Stalin's Russia*
    JMH - v77 - i1 - March 2005 - p260(3) [501+]

Goldmark, Kathi Kamen - *And My Shoes Keep Walking Back to You: A Novel*
    BL - v101 - i6 - Nov 15 2004 - p557(1) [501+]

Goldratt, Eli - *The Goal: A Process of Ongoing Improvement, 3rd ed.*
    TimHES - v0 - i1680 - Feb 25 2005 - pVIII(1) [501+]

Goldreich, Gloria - *Walking Home*
    BL - v101 - i9-10 - Jan 1 2005 - p814(2) [1-50]

Goldscheider, Calvin - *Studying the Jewish Future*
    R&R Bk N - v19 - i4 - Nov 2004 - p46(1) [51-500]

Goldschmidt, Arthur - *Historical Dictionary of Egypt, 3rd. Ed.*
    R&R Bk N - v19 - i1 - Feb 2004 - p50(1) [51-500]
Modern Egypt: The Formation of a Nation State
    MEJ - v59 - i1 - Wntr 2005 - p167(1) [51-500]

Goldschmidt, Simon - *Strategic Affiliate Marketing*
    JEL - v42 - i1 - March 2004 - p297(1) [501+]
    R&R Bk N - v19 - i1 - Feb 2004 - p108(1) [51-500]

Goldsmith, Alan - *Waldo Chicken Wakes the Dead: A Murder Mystery of Uncommon Proportions (Illus. by King, David)*
    LJ - v129 - i16 - Oct 1 2004 - p62(1) [51-500]

Goldsmith, Annabel - *Annabel: An Unconventional Life: The Memoirs of Lady Annabel Goldsmith*
    KR - v73 - i3 - Feb 1 2005 - p163(2) [501+]

Goldsmith, Barbara - *Obsessive Genius: The Inner World of Marie Curie*
    y BL - v101 - i7 - Dec 1 2004 - p630(1) [51-500]
    KR - v72 - i20 - Oct 15 2004 - p994(1) [501+]
    LJ - v129 - i18 - Nov 1 2004 - p116(2) [51-500]
    New Sci - v185 - i2488 - Feb 26 2005 - p55(1) [51-500]
    NYTBR - Nov 28 2004 - p8 [501+]
    PW - v251 - i44 - Nov 1 2004 - p56(1) [501+]
    Wil Q - v29 - i1 - Wntr 2005 - p120(2) [501+]

Goldsmith, David A. - *The Documentary Makers: Interviews with 15 of the Best in the Business*
    TimHES - v0 - i1647 - July 2 2004 - p26(1) [501+]

Goldsmith, Elizabeth B. - *Resource Management for Individuals and Families, 3rd ed.*
    R&R Bk N - v19 - i4 - Nov 2004 - p135(1) [51-500]

Goldsmith, James Lowth - *Lordship in France: 500-1500*
    R&R Bk N - v19 - i1 - Feb 2004 - p95(1) [51-500]

Goldsmith, Kenneth - *I'll Be Your Mirror: The Selected Andy Warhol Interviews, 1962-1987*
    BL - v100 - i22 - August 2004 - p1888(1) [51-500]
    LJ - v129 - i13 - August 2004 - p76(1) [501+]
    NYTBR - Sept 12 2004 - p16 [501+]

Goldsmith, Marshall - *Leading Organizational Learning*
    HR Mag - v49 - i7 - July 2004 - p138(2) [501+]

Goldsmith, Olivia - *Dumping Billy (Read by Quigley, Bernadette). Audiobook Review*
    BL - v101 - i3 - Oct 1 2004 - p350(1) [51-500]
    LJ - v130 - i3 - Feb 15 2005 - p168(1) [51-500]

Goldsmith, Thomas - *The Bluegrass Reader*
    LJ - v129 - i12 - July 2004 - p84(1) [51-500]

Goldstein, Diane E. - *Once Upon a Virus: AIDS Legends and Vernacular Risk Perception*
    SciTech - v28 - i4 - Dec 2004 - p84(1) [1-50]

Goldstein, Donna M. - *Laughter out of Place: Race, Class, Violence, and Sexuality in a Rio Shantytown*
    Choice - v41 - i11-12 - July-August 2004 - p2102(2) [501+]
    JRAI - v10 - i4 - Dec 2004 - p947(2) [501+]

Goldstein, E. Bruce - *Cognitive Psychology: Connecting Mind, Research, and Everyday Experience*
    SciTech - v28 - i3 - Sept 2004 - p2(1) [501+]

Goldstein, Eda G. - *Object Relations Theory and Self Psychology in Social Work Practice*
    Adoles - v39 - i156 - Winter 2004 - p831(2) [51-500]

Goldstein, Erik - *Power and stability; British foreign policy, 1865-1965*
    R&R Bk N - v19 - i1 - Feb 2004 - p33(1) [1-50]

Goldstein, Jan - *All That Matters*
    BL - v101 - i1 - Sept 1 2004 - p60(1) [51-500]
    KR - v72 - i16 - August 15 2004 - p763(1) [51-500]
    PW - v251 - i32 - August 9 2004 - p229(2) [51-500]

Goldstein, Jeffrey - *Toys, Games, and Media*
    R&R Bk N - v19 - i4 - Nov 2004 - p179(1) [501+]

Goldstein, Jonathan - *Schmelvis: In Search of Elvis Presley's Jewish Roots*
    CBRA - Annual 2003 - p84(1) [501+]

Goldstein, Joshua S. - *International Relations Brief, 2nd Ed.*
    R&R Bk N - v19 - i1 - Feb 2004 - pNA [501+]
The Real Price of War: How You Pay for the War on Terror
    KR - v72 - i13 - July 1 2004 - p616(1) [501+]
    LJ - v129 - i15 - Sept 15 2004 - p70(1) [51-500]
    PW - v251 - i39 - Sept 27 2004 - p50(1) [51-500]

Goldstein, Joyce - *Italian Slow and Savory: A Cookbook*
    PW - v251 - i39 - Sept 27 2004 - p51(1) [51-500]

Goldstein, Leonard - *The Origin of Medieval Drama*
    Choice - v42 - i6 - Feb 2005 - p1019(2) [51-500]
    R&R Bk N - v19 - i4 - Nov 2004 - p215(1) [501+]

Goldstein, Margaret J. - *Irish in America*
  c BL - v101 - i6 - Nov 15 2004 - p575(1) [51-500]
World War II: Europe
  c SLJ - v50 - i10 - Oct 2004 - p189(1) [51-500]
Goldstein, Melvyn C. - *A Tibetan Revolutionary: The Political Life and Times of Bapa Phuntso Wangye*
  Choice - v42 - i5 - Jan 2005 - p910(1) [1-50]
  NYRB - v51 - i19 - Dec 2 2004 - p45(3) [501+]
Goldstein, Morris - *Controlling Currency Mismatches in Emerging Economies*
  R&R Bk N - v19 - i3 - August 2004 - p136(1) [51-500]
Goldstein, Natalie - *Earth Almanac. 2nd Ed.*
  SB - v40 - i5 - Sept-Oct 2004 - p195(1) [51-500]
Goldstein, Rebecca - *Incompleteness: the Proof and Paradox of Kurt Godel*
  PW - v251 - i51 - Dec 20 2004 - p46(1) [501+]
Goldstein, Sid - *The Wine Lover Cooks with Wine: Great Recipes for the Essential Ingredient*
  PW - v251 - i37 - Sept 13 2004 - p72(1) [501+]
Goldstein, Stephen L. - *30 Days to Successful Fundraising*
  R&R Bk N - v19 - i3 - August 2004 - p133(1) [1-50]
Goldstein, T. - *Teaching and Learning in a Multilingual School: Choices, Risks, and Dilemmas*
  CE - v80 - i5 - Mid-Summer 2004 - p278(1) [501+]
Goldstein, Warren - *William Sloane Coffin, Jr: A Holy Impatience*
  Choice - v42 - i4 - Dec 2004 - p721(1) [1-50]
William Sloane Coffin, Jr.: A Holy Impatience
  Nation - v279 - i2 - July 12 2004 - p34 [501+]
Goldstein, William N. - *Using the Transference in Psychotherapy*
  SciTech - v28 - i4 - Dec 2004 - p98(1) [51-500]
Goldstone, Lawrence - *The Friar and the Cipher: Roger Bacon and the Unsolved Mystery of the Most Unusual Manuscript in the World*
  BL - v101 - i9-10 - Jan 1 2005 - p786(1) [1-50]
  KR - v72 - i23 - Dec 1 2004 - p1131(1) [501+]
  LJ - v130 - i2 - Feb 1 2005 - p78(2) [51-500]
  PW - v251 - i50 - Dec 13 2004 - p54(2) [51-500]
Goldsworthy, Andy - *Passage*
  BL - v101 - i9-10 - Jan 1 2005 - p799(1) [51-500]
  LJ - v129 - i19 - Nov 15 2004 - p57(1) [51-500]
  PW - v251 - i45 - Nov 8 2004 - p49(1) [501+]
  R&R Bk N - v19 - i4 - Nov 2004 - p204(1) [501+]
Goldwasser, Orly - *Prophets, Lovers and Giraffes: Wor(l)d Classification in Ancient Egypt*
  R&R Bk N - v19 - i4 - Nov 2004 - p218(1) [501+]
Gole, Henry G. - *The Road to Rainbow: Army Planning for Global War, 1934-1940*
  APJ - v18 - i4 - Winter 2004 - p120(2) [501+]
Golembe, Carla - *The Story Of Hula*
  c CH Bwatch - v14 - i12 - Dec 2004 - pNA [51-500]
Golenbock, Peter - *Bums: An Oral History of the Brooklyn Dodgers (Read by Todd, Raymond). Audiobook Review*
  Kliatt - v38 - i6 - Nov 2004 - p55(1) [51-500]
Hank Aaron: Brave in Every Way (Illus. by Lee, Paul)
  c PW - v252 - i6 - Feb 7 2005 - p62(1) [51-500]
Goletz, DeBorah - *Ceramic Art Title for the Home*
  Ant&CM - v108 - i6 - August 2003 - p16(1) [501+]
Golia, Maria - *Cairo City of Sand*
  LJ - v129 - i13 - August 2004 - p105(2) [51-500]
Golightley, Malcolm - *Social Work and Mental Health, 1st ed.*
  TimHES - v0 - i1680 - Feb 25 2005 - pIV(1) [501+]
Gollehon, John - *How to Buy Antiques at Bargain Prices!*
  Ant&CM - v108 - i6 - July 2003 - p16(1) [501+]
Gollin, Rita K. - *Annie Adams Fields: Woman of Letters*
  Legacy - v21 - i2 - June 2004 - p256(3) [501+]
Golomb, Jacob - *Nietzsche and Zion*
  Choice - v42 - i3 - Nov 2004 - p497(1) [51-500]
Nietzsche, Godfather of Fascism? On the Uses and Abuses of a Philosophy
  Dialogue - v43 - i1 - Wntr 2004 - p181-184 [501+]
  HNet - Nov 2004 - pNA [501+]
Golonna, G. - *Il santuario di Portonaccio a Veio. I.Gli scavi di Massimo Pallottino nella zona dell'altare*
  Class R - v54 - i1 - May 2004 - p250(1) [501+]
Golosov, Grigorii - *Political Parties in the Regions of Russia: Democracy Unclaimed*
  R&R Bk N - v19 - i1 - Feb 2004 - pNA [501+]
  Slav R - v63 - i4 - Winter 2004 - p898(2) [501+]
Golshiri, Houshang - *Black Parrot, Green Crow: A Collection of Short Fiction*
  WLT - v78 - i3-4 - Sept-Dec 2004 - p151(1) [501+]

Goluboff, Sacha L. - *Russian Trade Unions and Industrial Relations in Transition*
  Slav R - v63 - i3 - Fall 2004 - p675-676 [501+]
Goluboff, Sascha L. - *Jewish Russians: Upheavals in a Moscow Synagogue*
  Slav R - v63 - i3 - Fall 2004 - p676-677 [501+]
Golumbic, Martin Charles - *Tolerance Graphs*
  Choice - v42 - i5 - Jan 2005 - p888(1) [501+]
Golway, Terry - *So Others Might Live: A History of New York's Bravest; the FDNY From 1700 to the Present*
  R&R Bk N - v19 - i1 - Feb 2004 - p250(1) [51-500]
Washington's General: Nathanael Greene and the Triumph of the American Revolution
  BL - v101 - i8 - Dec 15 2004 - p702(1) [51-500]
  KR - v72 - i22 - Nov 15 2004 - p1078(1) [501+]
  LJ - v130 - i2 - Feb 1 2005 - p97(1) [51-500]
  PW - v252 - i2 - Jan 10 2005 - p50(1) [51-500]
Gomaa, Hassan - *Designing Software Product Lines with UML: From Use Cases to Pattern-Based Software Architectures*
  SciTech - v28 - i4 - Dec 2004 - p23(1) [51-500]
Gombrowicz, Witold - *Bacacay*
  Globe & Mail - Dec 11 2004 - pD6 [501+]
  KR - v72 - i20 - Oct 15 2004 - p984(1) [51-500]
  Nation - v280 - i3 - Jan 24 2005 - p32 [501+]
  LJ - v129 - i20 - Dec 1 2004 - p106(1) [51-500]
A Guide to Philosophy in Six Hours and Fifteen Minutes
  BW - v34 - i51 - Dec 19 2004 - p5(1) [501+]
  Globe & Mail - Dec 11 2004 - pD6 [501+]
  Nation - v280 - i3 - Jan 24 2005 - p32 [501+]
Polish Memories
  BW - v34 - i51 - Dec 19 2004 - p5(1) [501+]
  Globe & Mail - Dec 11 2004 - pD6 [501+]
  Nation - v280 - i3 - Jan 24 2005 - p32 [501+]
Gomel, Elana - *Bloodscripts: Writing the Violent Subject*
  SFS - v31 - i2 - July 2004 - p306-311 [501+]
Gomella, Leonard G. - *Clinician's Pocket Reference 10th Ed.*
  SciTech - v28 - i1 - March 2004 - p123(1) [1-50]
Gomes, Leonard - *The Economics and Ideology of Free Trade: A Historical Review*
  Choice - v42 - i1 - Sept 2004 - p153(2) [501+]
  JEL - v41 - i4 - Dec 2003 - p1336(1) [501+]
Gomes, Merico P. - *The Indians and Brazil*
  JRAI - v10 - i4 - Dec 2004 - p918(2) [501+]
Gomes, Rita Costa - *The Making of a Court Society: Kings and Nobles in Late Medieval Portugal*
  Ren Q - v57 - i4 - Winter 2004 - p1413(2) [501+]
Gomez Gallego, Mar - *Organic Reaction Mechanism: 40 Solved Cases*
  Choice - v41 - i11-12 - July-August 2004 - p2073(2) [501+]
Organic Reaction Mechanisms: 40 Solved Cases
  TimHES - v0 - i1680 - Feb 25 2005 - pXIII(1) [501+]
Gomez-Ibanez, Jose A. - *Regulating Infrastructure: Monopoly, Contracts, and Discretion*
  BHR - v78 - i1 - Spring 2004 - p156(4) [501+]
  JEL - v41 - i4 - Dec 2003 - p1392(1) [501+]
Gomez-Jefferson, Annetta L. - *The Sage of Tawawa: Reverdy Cassius Ransom, 1861-1959*
  JSH - v70 - i4 - Nov 2004 - p942(2) [501+]
Gomez, Juan Carlos - *Apes, Monkeys, Children, and the Growth of Mind*
  Choice - v42 - i3 - Nov 2004 - p568(1) [51-500]
Gomez-Pompa, Arturo - *The Lowland Maya Area: Three Millennia at the Human-Wildland Interface*
  QRB - v79 - i3 - Sept 2004 - p340(2) [501+]
  R&R Bk N - v19 - i1 - Feb 2004 - p67(1) [501+]
Gomez, Ricardo - *Negotiating the Euro-Mediterranean Partnership: Strategic Action in EU Foreign Policy?*
  R&R Bk N - v19 - i1 - Feb 2004 - pNA [51-500]
Gomi, Taro - *Bus Stops*
  People - v62 - i25 - Dec 20 2004 - p58 [51-500]
Gomm, Roger - *Social Research Methodology: A Critical Introduction, 1st ed.*
  TimHES - v0 - i1680 - Feb 25 2005 - pVI(1) [501+]
Gommans, Jos - *Circumambulations in South Asian History: Essays in Honour of Dirk H.A. Kolff*
  R&R Bk N - v19 - i1 - Feb 2004 - p46(1) [51-500]
Mughal Warfare: Indian Frontiers and High Roads to Empire, 1500-1700
  AHR - v109 - i2 - April 2004 - p501(2) [501+]
Gomme, Robert - *George Herbert Perris, 1866-1920: the Life and Times of a Radical*
  R&R Bk N - v19 - i1 - Feb 2004 - p32(1) [1-50]
Gomory, Ralph E. - *Global Trade and Conflicting National Interests*
  JEL - v41 - i4 - Dec 2003 - p1290(2) [501+]

Gomulka, Gene Thomas - *The Survival Guide for Marriage in the Military*
  Mar Crp G - v88 - i11 - Nov 2004 - p89(1) [501+]
Gonen, Jay Y. - *The Roots of Nazi Psychology: Hitler's Utopian Barbarism*
  HNet - June 2004 - pNA [501+]
Gonen, Rivka - *Contested Holiness: Jewish, Muslim, and Christian Perspective on the Temple Mount in Jerusalem*
  R&R Bk N - v19 - i1 - Feb 2004 - p42(1) [51-500]
Gonget, Hans - *Brentidae (Coleoptera) of Northern Europe*
  SciTech - v28 - i4 - Dec 2004 - p66(1) [51-500]
Gonick, Cy - *A Very Red Life: the Story of Bill Walsh*
  Can Hist R - v85 - i4 - Dec 2004 - p862(3) [501+]
Gonnerman, Jennifer - *Life on the Outside: The Prison Odyssey of Elaine Bartlett*
  BooChiTr - March 28 2004 - p1(2) [501+]
Gonsalves, Rob - *Imagine a Day (Illus. by Thomson, Sarah)*
  c PW - v252 - i5 - Jan 31 2005 - p70(1) [501+]
Gonzales Bertrand, Diane - *Upside Down and Backwards/De cabeza y al reves*
  c SLJ - v51 - i1 - Jan 2005 - p120(1) [51-500]
Gonzales, Doreen - *The Arctic Ocean*
  y SB - v40 - i4 - July-August 2004 - p165(1) [51-500]
The Indian Ocean
  y SB - v40 - i6 - Nov-Dec 2004 - p260(1) [51-500]
The Pacific Ocean
  y SB - v40 - i4 - July-August 2004 - p165(1) [51-500]
Gonzales, Linda Dawson - *Sustaining Teacher Leadership: Beyond the Boundaries of an Enabling School Culture*
  R&R Bk N - v19 - i4 - Nov 2004 - p183(1) [501+]
Gonzales, Susan - *Cecilia's Year*
  y Kliatt - v39 - i2 - March 2005 - p10(1) [51-500]
Gonzalez, Alberto - *Our Voices: Essays in Culture, Ethnicity, and Communication, 4th ed*
  R&R Bk N - v19 - i3 - August 2004 - p82(1) [51-500]
Gonzalez, Anita - *Jarocho's Soul: Cultural Identity and Afro-Mexican Dance*
  R&R Bk N - v19 - i3 - August 2004 - p89(1) [51-500]
Gonzalez-Crussi, F. - *On Being Born*
  NYTBR - July 11 2004 - p20 [51-500]
Gonzalez, Edward - *Cuba After Castro: Legacies, Challenges, and Impediments, Appendices*
  R&R Bk N - v19 - i4 - Nov 2004 - p70(1) [51-500]
Gonzalez, Evelyn Diaz - *The Bronx*
  Choice - v42 - i5 - Jan 2005 - p916(1) [1-50]
  R&R Bk N - v19 - i3 - August 2004 - p72(1) [51-500]
Gonzalez, Gilbert G. - *A Century of Chicano History: Empire, Nations, and Migration*
  HAHR - v84 - i4 - Nov 2004 - p745(2) [501+]
  JAH - v91 - i3 - Dec 2004 - p1112(1) [501+]
  PHR - v73 - i4 - Nov 2004 - p679(2) [501+]
Labor versus Empire: Race, Gender, and Migration
  R&R Bk N - v19 - i4 - Nov 2004 - p151(1) [501+]
Gonzalez, Guillermo - *The Privileged Planet: How Our Planet in the Cosmos is Designed for Discovery*
  Astron - v32 - i12 - Dec 2004 - p104 [501+]
  Nature - v429 - i6994 - June 24 2004 - p808(1) [501+]
Gonzalez, J.F. - *Survivor*
  NYTBR - Oct 31 2004 - p18 [501+]
Gonzalez, Jose Antonio - *Latin American Macroeconomic Reforms: The Second Stage*
  JEL - v41 - i4 - Dec 2003 - p1409(1) [501+]
Gonzalez, Joseph - *Complete Idiot's Guide to Geography, 2nd Ed.*
  SB - v40 - i6 - Nov-Dec 2004 - p253(1) [51-500]
Gonzalez, Julie - *Wings*
  y Kliatt - v39 - i2 - March 2005 - p10(2) [51-500]
  KR - v73 - i5 - March 1 2005 - p286(1) [51-500]
Gonzalez, Justo L. - *The Changing Shape of Church History*
  Theol St - v66 - i1 - March 2005 - p225(1) [501+]
Gonzalez, Lisa Sanchez - *Boricua Literature: A Literary History of the Puerto Rican Diaspora*
  AL - v76 - i2 - June 2004 - p407(3) [501+]
Gonzalez, Ray - *Human Crying Daisies*
  ABR - v26 - i1 - Nov-Dec 2004 - p22(1) [501+]
Gonzalez, Roberto J. - *Zapotec science: farming and food in the northern Sierra of Oaxaca*
  JRAI - v10 - i4 - Dec 2004 - p948(2) [501+]
Gonzalez, Victoria - *Radical Women in Latin America: Left and Right*
  AHR - v109 - i2 - April 2004 - p571(2) [501+]

Gonzalez-Wippler, Migene - *Keys to the Kingdom: Jesus & the Mystic Kabbalah*
  LJ - v129 - i20 - Dec 1 2004 - p124(1) [51-500]
  PW - v251 - i41 - Oct 11 2004 - p76(1) [51-500]
Gonzenbach, Laura - *The Brothers Grimm: From Enchanted Forest to the Modern World, 2nd Ed.*
  HNet - Oct 2004 - pNA [501+]
  The Robber with A Witch's Head: More Stories from the Great Treasury of Sicilian Folk and Fairy Tales,
  Bwatch - Feb 2005 - pNA [51-500]
  The Robber with a Witch's Head: More Stories from the Great Treasury of Sicilian Folk and Fairy Tales
  Globe & Mail - Sept 11 2004 - pD22 [1-50]
  R&R Bk N - v19 - i4 - Nov 2004 - p77(1) [51-500]
Goobie, Beth - *Flux*
  c CCB-B - v57 - i11 - July-August 2004 - p465(1) [501+]
  c Kliatt - v38 - i4 - July 2004 - p7(2) [51-500]
  c LibMed - v23 - i3 - Nov-Dec 2004 - p70(1) [51-500]
  y SLJ - v50 - i9 - Sept 2004 - p206(1) [51-500]
  y VOYA - v27 - i4 - Oct 2004 - p314(1) [51-500]
  Lottery
  y Can CL - i111-112 - Fall-Winter 2003 - p153(6) [501+]
  Who Owns Kelly Paddik?
  c CBRA - Annual 2003 - p485(2) [51-500]
Good, Anthony - *Worship and the Ceremonial Economy of a Royal South Indian Temple*
  R&R Bk N - v19 - i4 - Nov 2004 - p15(1) [51-500]
Good, Charles M. - *The Steamer Parish: The Rise and Fall of Missionary Medicine on an African Frontier*
  IBMR - v28 - i4 - Oct 2004 - p188(1) [501+]
Good, Diane L. - *Brown v. Board of Education*
  c SLJ - v50 - i7 - July 2004 - p122(1) [51-500]
Good Jobs Wanted: Labor Markets in Latin America
  R&R Bk N - v19 - i3 - August 2004 - p115(1) [51-500]
Good, Michael - *The Search for Major Plagge: The Nazi Who Saved Jews*
  KR - v73 - i3 - Feb 1 2005 - p164(1) [501+]
Good, Phillip I. - *Common Errors in Statistics, and How to Avoid Them*
  E-Streams - Sept 2004 - pNA [501+]
Good, Stephanie R. - *Law school 101; survival techniques from pre-law to being an attorney*
  R&R Bk N - v19 - i3 - August 2004 - p196(1) [1-50]
Good, Steven L. - *Churches, Jails, and Gold Mines: Mega-Deals From a Real Estate Maverick*
  R&R Bk N - v19 - i1 - Feb 2004 - p95(1) [51-500]
Goodale, Melvyn A. - *Sight Unseen: An Exploration of Conscious and Unconscious Vision*
  Choice - v41 - i11-12 - July-August 2004 - p2069(1) [501+]
  Nature - v429 - i6993 - June 17 2004 - p703(1) [501+]
  TLS - i5286 - July 23 2004 - p27(1) [501+]
Goodall, Hollis - *The Raymond and Frances Bushnell Collection of Netsuke: A Legend at the Los Angeles County Museum of Art*
  R&R Bk N - v19 - i1 - Feb 2004 - p208(1) [51-500]
Goodall, Jane - *Rickie & Henri (Illus. by Marks, Alan)*
  c BL - v101 - i4 - Oct 15 2004 - p404(1) [51-500]
  c PW - v251 - i37 - Sept 13 2004 - p81(1) [51-500]
  c SLJ - v50 - i12 - Dec 2004 - p130(1) [501+]
Goodall, Lian - *Singing Towards the Future: The Story of Portia White (Illus. by Milkau, Liz)*
  c CH Bwatch - v14 - i12 - Dec 2004 - pNA [51-500]
  c Globe & Mail - August 28 2004 - pD12 [501+]
  y Res Links - v10 - i2 - Dec 2004 - p44(1) [501+]
Goodan, Kevin - *In the Ghost-House Acquainted*
  LJ - v129 - i13 - August 2004 - p85(1) [501+]
Gooday, Graeme J.N. - *The Morals of Measurement Accuracy, Irony, and Trust in Late Victorian Electrical Practice*
  Sci - v305 - i5690 - Sept 10 2004 - p1569(2) [501+]
Goodchild, Peter - *Edward Teller: The Real Dr. Strangelove*
  BL - v101 - i4 - Oct 15 2004 - p371(1) [51-500]
  BL - v101 - i7 - Dec 1 2004 - p632(1) [51-500]
  Choice - v42 - i7 - March 2005 - p1247(1) [51-500]
  Globe & Mail - Jan 15 2005 - pD10 [501+]
  LJ - v129 - i15 - Sept 15 2004 - p80(1) [51-500]
  Nation - v279 - i14 - Nov 1 2004 - p31 [501+]
  Nature - v430 - i6997 - July 15 2004 - p293(2) [501+]
  PW - v251 - i36 - Sept 6 2004 - p56(1) [51-500]
  Queens Q - v111 - i4 - Winter 2004 - p562(10) [501+]
  SPA - v61 - i2 - March-April 2005 - p69(1) [501+]
  TimHES - v0 - i1668 - Nov 26 2004 - p22(2) [501+]

Goode, Caroline - *Cupidity*
  y BL - v101 - i8 - Dec 15 2004 - p736(1) [51-500]
  y Kliatt - v39 - i2 - March 2005 - p26(2) [51-500]
  y PW - v252 - i3 - Jan 17 2005 - p57(1) [51-500]
  y SLJ - v51 - i2 - Feb 2005 - p136(1) [51-500]
Goode, Diane - *Thanksgiving is Here!*
  LibMed - v22 - i6 - March 2004 - p57(1) [51-500]
Goodell, Jill Jeffers - *Learning HTML for Kids*
  y LibMed - v22 - i7 - April-May 2004 - p91(1) [501+]
Gooden, Philip - *An Honorable Murderer*
  KR - v73 - i4 - Feb 15 2005 - p201(1) [51-500]
  PW - v252 - i11 - March 14 2005 - p48(1) [51-500]
Goodger, John - *The Druperman Tapes*
  BL - v101 - i4 - Oct 15 2004 - p392(1) [51-500]
  KR - v72 - i18 - Sept 15 2004 - p893(2) [51-500]
  PW - v251 - i42 - Oct 18 2004 - p51(1) [51-500]
Goodhart, Charles - *Essays in Honour of Charles Goodhart, Vol. 1*
  JEL - v41 - i4 - Dec 2003 - p1347(2) [501+]
  Essays in Honour of Charles Goodhart, Vol. 2
  JEL - v41 - i4 - Dec 2003 - p1360(1) [501+]
  Intervention to Save Hong Kong: The Authorities' Counter-Speculation in Financial Markets
  JEL - v42 - i1 - March 2004 - p267(2) [501+]
Goodheart, Lawrence B. - *Mad Yankees: The Hartford Retreat for the Insane and Nineteenth-Century Psychiatry*
  JAH - v91 - i3 - Dec 2004 - p1015(2) [501+]
  NEQ - v77 - i2 - June 2004 - p315-319 [501+]
Goodin, Robert E. - *Reflective Democracy*
  AJPS - v39 - i2 - July 2004 - p465(466) [501+]
  Pub Op Q - v68 - i4 - Winter 2004 - p641(4) [501+]
Goodlad, John I. - *Education for Everyone: Agenda for Education in a Democracy*
  Choice - v42 - i3 - Nov 2004 - p536(1) [1-50]
  TCR - v106 - i12 - Dec 2004 - p2259(2) [501+]
  The Teaching Career
  Choice - v42 - i1 - Sept 2004 - p160(1) [501+]
  TCR - v106 - i12 - Dec 2004 - p2372(4) [501+]
Goodman, Alan H. - *Genetic Nature/Culture: Anthropology and Science Beyond the Two-Culture Divide*
  QRB - v79 - i4 - Dec 2004 - p459(2) [501+]
Goodman, Alison - *Singing the Dogstar Blues*
  y Teach Lib - v32 - i1 - Oct 2004 - p18(1) [51-500]
Goodman, Amy - *The Exception to the Rulers: Exposing Oily Politicians, War Profiteers, and the Media That Love Them*
  Wom R Bks - v21 - i12 - Sept 2004 - p19(2) [501+]
Goodman, Barbara Scott - *The Beach House Cookbook*
  PW - v252 - i5 - Jan 31 2005 - p64(1) [501+]
Goodman, Bryan - *American Cars in Prewar England: A Pictorial Survey*
  SciTech - v28 - i1 - March 2004 - p166(1) [51-500]
Goodman, Calvin J. - *Art Marketing Handbook: Art Marketing in the 21st Century*
  A Art - v68 - i747 - Oct 2004 - p76(1) [501+]
Goodman, Carl F. - *The Rule of Law in Japan: A Comparative Analysis*
  HNet - Dec 2004 - pNA [501+]
Goodman, Carol - *The Drowning Tree (Read by Marshall, Christine). Audiobook Review*
  BL - v101 - i7 - Dec 1 2004 - p677(1) [51-500]
  The Drowning Tree. Audiobook Review
  Globe & Mail - Jan 15 2005 - pD13 [1-50]
  The Drowning Tree
  LJ - v129 - i12 - July 2004 - p70(1) [51-500]
Goodman, Danny - *JavaScript and DHTML Cookbook*
  CBRA - Annual 2003 - p21(1) [50-500]
  SciTech - v28 - i4 - Dec 2004 - p21(1) [51-500]
Goodman-Davies, Mara - *When Harry Hit the Hamptons*
  KR - v73 - i5 - March 1 2005 - p248(2) [501+]
  PW - v252 - i11 - March 14 2005 - p44(1) [51-500]
Goodman, Eric - *Child of My Right Hand*
  BL - v101 - i1 - Sept 1 2004 - p61(1) [51-500]
  KR - v72 - i15 - August 1 2004 - p704(1) [501+]
  PW - v251 - i39 - Sept 27 2004 - p37(1) [51-500]
Goodman, Geoffrey - *From Bevan to Blair: Fifty Years' Reporting from the Political Frontline*
  R&R Bk N - v19 - i1 - Feb 2004 - p230(1) [51-500]
Goodman, Greg S. - *Ubiquitous Assessment: Evaluation Techniques for the New Millennium*
  R&R Bk N - v19 - i4 - Nov 2004 - p188(1) [501+]
Goodman, Hannah R. - *My Sister's Wedding*
  y Kliatt - v39 - i1 - Jan 2005 - p14(1) [501+]

Goodman, Hirsh - *Let Me Create a Paradise, God Said to Himself: A Childhood Spent in South Africa and a Life in Israel*
  PW - v252 - i8 - Feb 21 2005 - p171(1) [51-500]
Goodman, Jacob E. - *Handbook of Discrete and Computational Geometry. 2nd Ed.*
  SciTech - v28 - i3 - Sept 2004 - p35(1) [51-500]
Goodman, James - *Blackout*
  RAH - v32 - i2 - June 2004 - p267-273 [501+]
Goodman, Jeremy - *The Washington Manual Surgery Survival Guide*
  SciTech - v28 - i3 - Sept 2004 - p110(1) [51-500]
Goodman, Jo - *Beyond a Wicked Kiss*
  BL - v100 - i22 - August 2004 - p1909(1) [51-500]
Goodman, Joan Elizabeth - *Bernard Wants a Baby (Illus. by Catalano, Dominic)*
  c SLJ - v50 - i7 - July 2004 - p76(1) [51-500]
Goodman, Jordan - *The Rattlesnake: A Voyage of Discovery to the Coral Sea*
  Econ - v374 - i8418 - March 19 2005 - p89US [501+]
  Tobacco in History and Culture: An Encyclopedia, 2 Vols.
  Ref Rev - Dec 2004 - pNA [501+]
  Tobacco in History and Culture: An Encyclopedia Vols. 1-2
  LJ - v130 - i1 - Jan 1 2005 - p156(2) [51-500]
  Useful Bodies: Humans in the Service of Medical Science in the Twentieth Century
  AHR - v109 - i4 - Oct 2004 - p1200-1200 [501+]
  Choice - v41 - i11-12 - July-August 2004 - p2079(1) [501+]
  SciTech - v28 - i1 - March 2004 - p80(1) [51-500]
Goodman, Joyce - *Gender, Colonialism and Education: The Politics of Experience*
  Wom HR - v13 - i2 - Summer 2004 - p330-332 [501+]
Goodman, Kevis - *Georgic Modernity and British Romanticism: Poetry and the Mediation History*
  Choice - v42 - i6 - Feb 2005 - p1022(2) [51-500]
Goodman, Laura J. - *Eating Disorders: the Journey to Recovery Workbook*
  Adoles - v39 - i156 - Winter 2004 - p832(1) [51-500]
Goodman, Lenn E. - *Islamic Humanism*
  JAAR - v72 - i4 - Dec 2004 - p1035(3) [501+]
  JR - v84 - i4 - Oct 2004 - p663(3) [501+]
Goodman, Linda J. - *Singing the Songs of My Ancestors: The Life and Music of Helma Swan, Makah Elder*
  Am Ind CRJ - v28 - i1 - Winter 2004 - p105-107 [501+]
  WHQ - v35 - i2 - Summer 2004 - p248-249 [501+]
Goodman, Loren - *Famous Americans*
  BooChiTr - April 11 2004 - p1(2) [501+]
  WLT - v78 - i3-4 - Sept-Dec 2004 - p99(1) [501+]
Goodman, Matthew - *Jewish Food: The World at Table*
  LJ - v130 - i3 - Feb 15 2005 - p152(1) [51-500]
  PW - v252 - i3 - Jan 17 2005 - p48(2) [51-500]
Goodman, Philomena - *Women, Sexuality and War*
  Signs - v30 - i2 - Wntr 2005 - p1695(5) [501+]
Goodman, Randall L. - *Ophtho Notes: The Essential Guide*
  SciTech - v28 - i1 - March 2004 - p113(1) [51-500]
Goodman, Richard - *The Oxford American Writer's Thesaurus*
  LJ - v129 - i20 - Dec 1 2004 - p170(1) [51-500]
Goodman, Robert M. - *Encyclopedia of Plant and Crop Science*
  Choice - v42 - i2 - Oct 2004 - p271(1) [501+]
  E-Streams - Sept 2004 - pNA [501+]
  R&USQ - v44 - i2 - Winter 2004 - p171(1) [501+]
  SB - v40 - i5 - Sept-Oct 2004 - p206(2) [51-500]
Goodman, Robin Truth - *World, Class, Women: Global Literature, Education, and Feminism*
  TCR - v106 - i12 - Dec 2004 - p2290(4) [501+]
Goodman, Roger - *Children of the Japanese State: The Changing Role of Child Protection Institutions in Contemporary Japan*
  AJS - v110 - i2 - Sept 2004 - p518(3) [501+]
Goodman, Stephen A. - *Collaborative Assessment: Working With Students Who Are Blind or Visually Impaired, Including Those With Additional Disabilities*
  R&R Bk N - v19 - i3 - August 2004 - p161(1) [501+]
Goodman, Steve - *The Train They Call the City of New Orleans (Read by Chapin, Tom). Audiobook Review*
  c BL - v101 - i5 - Nov 1 2004 - p508(1) [51-500]
  c SLJ - v50 - i11 - Nov 2004 - p82(1) [51-500]
  The Train They Call the City of New Orleans
  c CE - v80 - i5 - Mid-Summer 2004 - p274(1) [1-50]

Gordon, Joanne - *Be Happy at Work: 100 Women Who Love Their Jobs, and Why*
LJ - v130 - i2 - Feb 1 2005 - p94(1) [51-500]

Gordon, John (b. 1945 -) - *Joyce and Reality: The Empirical Strike Back*
Choice - v42 - i3 - Nov 2004 - p483(1) [1-50]

Gordon, John Steele - *An Empire of Wealth: The Epic History of American Economic Power*
Barron's - v84 - i44 - Nov 1 2004 - p41(1) [501+]
BL - v101 - i4 - Oct 15 2004 - p386(1) [51-500]
BW - v34 - i51 - Dec 19 2004 - p6(2) [501+]
Choice - v42 - i7 - March 2005 - p1276(2) [51-500]
KR - v72 - i15 - August 1 2004 - p725(1) [501+]
LJ - v129 - i17 - Oct 15 2004 - p73(1) [51-500]
NW - Nov 29 2004 - p45 [501+]
NYTBR - Nov 28 2004 - p29 [501+]
PW - v251 - i31 - August 2 2004 - p59(2) [501+]
Thread Across the Ocean: The Heroic Story of the Transatlantic Cable
SciTech - v28 - i1 - March 2004 - p158(1) [51-500]

Gordon, Jon W. - *The Science and Ethics of Engineering the Human Germ Line: Mendel's Maze*
E-Streams - July 2004 - pNA [501+]
QRB - v79 - i4 - Dec 2004 - p408(1) [501+]

Gordon, Karen Ferguson - *Black Politics in New Deal Atlanta*
JIH - v34 - i3 - Wntr 2004 - p488(2) [501+]

Gordon, Linda - *The Moral Property of Women: A History of Birth Control Politics in America*
JouAmCul - v27 - i3 - Sept 2004 - p360(3) [501+]
S&S - v68 - i1 - Spring 2004 - p120-123 [501+]

Gordon, Lyndall - *Mary Wollstonecraft: A New Genus*
Econ - v374 - i8415 - Feb 26 2005 - p85US [501+]
Spec - v297 - i9208 - Jan 29 2005 - p34(1) [501+]

Gordon, Malcolm S. - *Experimental Approaches to Conservation Biology*
SciTech - v28 - i4 - Dec 2004 - p58(1) [51-500]

Gordon, Mary - *Pearl*
BL - v101 - i3 - Oct 1 2004 - p282(1) [51-500]
BW - v35 - i4 - Jan 30 2005 - p6(1) [501+]
Globe & Mail - Feb 19 2005 - pD9 [501+]
LJ - v129 - i17 - Oct 15 2004 - p53(2) [51-500]
Ms - v14 - i4 - Winter 2004 - p91(2) [501+]
NL - v87 - i6 - Nov-Dec 2004 - p33(3) [501+]
NYTBR - Feb 20 2005 - p28 [501+]
PW - v251 - i42 - Oct 18 2004 - p45(1) [501+]

Gordon, Matthew S. - *The Breaking of a Thousand Swords: A History of the Turkish Military of Samarra*
Specu - v79 - i3 - July 2004 - p763-764 [501+]

Gordon, Michael D. - *A Well-Ordered Thing*
Bwatch - Nov 2004 - pNA [51-500]

Gordon, Nancy D. - *Stream Hydrology: An Introduction for Ecologists. 2nd Ed.*
SciTech - v28 - i3 - Sept 2004 - p5(1) [501+]

Gordon, Neil - *The Company You Keep*
NYTBR - July 11 2004 - p24 [501+]

Gordon, Phil - *Poker: The Real Deal*
PW - v251 - i41 - Oct 11 2004 - p70(1) [51-500]

Gordon, Phillip H. - *Allies at War: America, Europe, and the Crisis over Iraq*
Choice - v42 - i4 - Dec 2004 - p732(1) [1-50]

Gordon, R. Michael - *The American Murders of Jack the Ripper*
R&R Bk N - v19 - i1 - Feb 2004 - p142(1) [51-500]

Gordon, Rachel Singer - *The Librarian's Guide to Writing for Publication*
BL - v101 - i1 - Sept 1 2004 - p164(1) [1-50]
R&R Bk N - v19 - i4 - Nov 2004 - p255(1) [501+]

Gordon, Richard L. - *Antitrust Abuse in the New Economy: The Microsoft Case*
JEL - v42 - i1 - March 2004 - p204(2) [501+]

Gordon, Robert S.C. - *Primo Levi: Le virtu dell'uomo normale*
TLS - i5290 - August 20 2004 - p22(1) [501+]

Gordon, Sarah Barringer - *The Mormon Question, Polygamy and Constitutional Conflict in Nineteenth-Century America*
JIH - v34 - i3 - Wntr 2004 - p477(2) [501+]
The Mormon Question: Polygamy and Constitutional Conflict in Nineteenth-Century America
PHR - v73 - i4 - Nov 2004 - p671(3) [501+]

Gordon, Stephen P. - *Professional Development for School Improvement: Empowering Learning Communities*
R&R Bk N - v19 - i1 - Feb 2004 - p184(1) [51-500]

Gordon, Steven R. - *Information Technology and E-business in the Financial Services: A Global Anthology of Case Studies and Analytical Research*
R&R Bk N - v19 - i4 - Nov 2004 - p116(1) [51-500]

Gordon, Wendy J. - *The Economics of Copyright: Developments in Research and Analysis*
JEL - v42 - i1 - March 2004 - p318(1) [501+]
R&R Bk N - v19 - i1 - Feb 2004 - pNA [51-500]

Gordon, Wendy M. - *Mill Girls and Strangers: Single Women's Independent Migration in England, Scotland, and the United States, 1850-1881*
VS - v46 - i3 - Spring 2004 - p512(2) [501+]

Gore, Amanda - *You Can Be Happy: The Essential Guide to a Healthy Body, Mind and Soul. (Read by Macauley, Rebecca). Audiobook Review*
LJ - v129 - i18 - Nov 1 2004 - p132(1) [51-500]

Gore, Chris - *The Ultimate Film Festival Survival Guide, 3rd Ed.*
Bwatch - Nov 2004 - pNA [51-500]
R&R Bk N - v19 - i4 - Nov 2004 - p223(1) [51-500]

Gore, Kristin - *Sammy's Hill*
y BL - v100 - i22 - August 2004 - p1871(1) [51-500]
BW - v34 - i37 - Sept 12 2004 - p11(1) [1-50]
KR - v72 - i13 - July 1 2004 - p595(2) [501+]
LJ - v129 - i13 - August 2004 - p67(1) [51-500]
NYTBR - Sept 12 2004 - p23(L) [501+]
PW - v251 - i28 - July 12 2004 - p42(1) [51-500]

Gorenburg, Dmitry P - *Minority Ethnic Mobilization in the Russian Federation*
AJS - v110 - i3 - Nov 2004 - p856(2) [501+]

Gorenburg, Dmitry P. - *Minority Ethnic Mobilization in the Russian Federation*
E-A St - v56 - i7 - Nov 2004 - p1092(1094) [501+]
Slav R - v63 - i4 - Winter 2004 - p903(2) [501+]

Gorey, Edward - *The Gashlycrumb Tinies*
People - v62 - i25 - Dec 20 2004 - p58 [51-500]

Gorga, Carmine - *The Economic Process: An Instantaneous Non-Newtonian Picture*
JEL - v41 - i4 - Dec 2003 - p1284(2) [501+]

G'Orge-Walker, Pat - *Mother Eternal Ann Everlastin's Dead*
Black Iss - v6 - i6 - Nov-Dec 2004 - p74(1) [51-500]

Gorham, Michael S. - *Speaking in Soviet Tongues: Language, Culture, and the Politics of Voice in Revolutionary Russia*
AHR - v109 - i3 - June 2004 - p1007(1) [501+]
Slav R - v63 - i3 - Fall 2004 - p683-684 [501+]

Gorild, Heggelund - *Environment and Resettlement Politics in China: The Three Gorges Project*
R&R Bk N - v19 - i3 - August 2004 - p100(1) [51-500]

Goring, Jeremy - *Burn Holy Fire! Religion in Lewes since the Reformation*
HER - v119 - i483 - Sept 2004 - p1082(2) [501+]
Burn, Holy Fire! Religion in Lewis Since the Reformation
HER - v119 - i483 - Sept 2004 - p1082(2) [501+]

Gorini, Catherine A. - *The Facts on File Geometry Handbook*
LibMed - v22 - i4 - Jan 2004 - p78(1) [501+]
Math T - v97 - i5 - May 2004 - p381-382 [501+]

Goris, Richard C. - *Guide to the Amphibians and Reptiles of Japan*
SciTech - v28 - i4 - Dec 2004 - p67(1) [51-500]

Goris, Wouter - *The Scattered Field: History of Metaphysics in the Postmetaphysical Era, Inaugural Address at the Free University of Amsterdam on January 16, 2004*
R&R Bk N - v20 - i1 - Feb 2005 - p6(1) [51-500]

Gorke, Martin - *Death of Our Planet's Species: A Challenge to Ecology and Ethics*
SciTech - v28 - i1 - March 2004 - p64(1) [1-50]

Gorlee, Dinda L. - *On Translating Signs: Exploring Text and Semio-Translation*
R&R Bk N - v19 - i4 - Nov 2004 - p212(1) [501+]

Gorlizki, Yoram - *Cold Peace: Stalin and the Soviet Ruling Circle, 1945-1953*
Choice - v42 - i2 - Oct 2004 - p350(1) [51-500]
CR - v285 - i1667 - Dec 2004 - p367(2) [501+]
HNet - Dec 2004 - pNA [501+]

Gorman, Carma - *Industrial Design Reader*
SciTech - v28 - i1 - March 2004 - p177(1) [51-500]

Gorman, Dave - *Dave Gorman's Googlewhack! Adventure*
BL - v101 - i2 - Sept 15 2004 - p201(1) [51-500]
LJ - v129 - i14 - Sept 2004 - p175(1) [501+]
PW - v251 - i30 - July 26 2004 - p47(1) [501+]

Gorman, Ed - *Breaking up Is Hard to Do*
DroRevMy - v24 - i3 - May-June 2004 - p7(2) [501+]

The Long Ride Back
Roundup M - v11 - i6 - August 2004 - p27(2) [501+]
Roundup M - v12 - i1 - Oct 2004 - p30(1) [51-500]
Texas Rangers
Roundup M - v12 - i3 - Feb 2005 - p27(1) [51-500]
The World's Finest Mystery and Crime Stories: Fifth Annual Collection
PW - v251 - i38 - Sept 20 2004 - p49(1) [51-500]

Gorman, G.E. - *International Yearbook of Library and Information Management 2003-2004: Metadata Applications and Management*
ALJ - v53 - i4 - Nov 2004 - p413(1) [501+]

Gorman, Jack M. - *Fear and Anxiety: The Benefits of Translational Research*
SciTech - v28 - i3 - Sept 2004 - p100(1) [1-50]

Gorman, Michael (b. 1941 -) - *The Enduring Library: Technology, Tradition, and the Quest for Balance*
Lib & Cul - v39 - i4 - Fall 2004 - p452(9) [501+]
LRTS - v48 - i4 - Oct 2004 - p308(2) [501+]

Gorman, Michael E. - *Scientific and Technological Thinking*
SciTech - v28 - i4 - Dec 2004 - p128 [51-500]

Gorman, Michael J. - *Apostle of the Crucified Lord: a Theological Introduction to Paul and His Letters*
CC - v121 - i24 - Nov 30 2004 - p44(2) [501+]
Intpr - v58 - i3 - July 2004 - p325(1) [501+]
Theol St - v65 - i4 - Dec 2004 - p894(2) [501+]

Gorman, Michele - *Getting Graphic! Using Graphic Novels to Promote Literacy with Preteens and Teens*
y Kliatt - v38 - i4 - July 2004 - p40(1) [51-500]
Getting Graphic!: Using Graphic Novels to Promote Literacy with Preteens and Teens
LibMed - v23 - i1 - August-Sept 2004 - p85(1) [51-500]
Getting Graphic! Using Graphic Novels to Promote Literacy with Preteens and Teens
VOYA - v27 - i4 - Oct 2004 - p266(1) [51-500]

Gorman, Tom - *The Complete Idiot's Guide to Economics*
JEL - v42 - i1 - March 2004 - p234(1) [501+]

Gorman, V.B. - *Oikistes: Studies in Constitutions, Colonies, and Military Power in the Ancient World Offered in Honor of A.J. Graham*
Class R - v54 - i1 - May 2004 - p148(2) [501+]

Gormley, Beatrice - *Maria Mitchell: The Soul of an Astronomer*
y Kliatt - v39 - i2 - March 2005 - p34(1) [51-500]

Gormley, Greg - *Cat Trap!*
c Sch Lib - v52 - i4 - Winter 2004 - p187(1) [51-500]

Gormley, William T. - *Bureaucracy and Democracy: Accountability and Performance*
R&R Bk N - v19 - i1 - Feb 2004 - pNA [51-500]

Gorn, Michael H. - *Expanding the Envelope: Flight Research at NACA and NASA*
Isis - v95 - i3 - Sept 2004 - p530(2) [501+]

Gornick, Janet C. - *Families that Work: Policies for Reconciling Parenthood and Employment*
Choice - v41 - i7 - March 2004 - p1338(1) [501+]
JEL - v42 - i1 - March 2004 - p279(1) [501+]
M Lab R - v127 - i9 - Sept 2004 - p57(2) [501+]

Gorny, Yosef - *Between Auschwitz and Jerusalem*
R&R Bk N - v19 - i1 - Feb 2004 - p30(1) [51-500]

Gorodetsky, Gabriel - *Russia between East and West: Russian Foreign Policy on the Threshold of the Twenty-First Century*
Slav R - v63 - i3 - Fall 2004 - p680-681 [501+]

Gorog, Veronika - *La fille difficile: un conte-type africain*
WestFolk - v62 - i3 - Summer 2003 - p215-219 [501+]

Gorra, Michael - *The Bells in Their Silence: Travels through Germany*
CHE - v51 - i19 - Jan 14 2005 - pB13-B14 [501+]
Globe & Mail - August 7 2004 - pT12 [501+]
Sew R - v112 - i1 - Wntr 2004 - pXXXI-XXXIII [501+]
TLS - i5285 - July 16 2004 - p7(1) [501+]

Gorrara, Claire - *The Roman Noir in Post-War French Culture*
MLN - v119 - i4 - Sept 2004 - p897-900 [501+]

Gorringe, T.J. - *Furthering Humanity: A Theology of Culture*
R&R Bk N - v19 - i4 - Nov 2004 - p19(1) [51-500]

Gorski, Philip S. - *The Disciplinary Revolution: Calvinism and the Rise of the State in Early Modern Europe*
AHR - v109 - i3 - June 2004 - p966(2) [501+]
Choice - v41 - i11-12 - July-August 2004 - p2114(1) [501+]
HNet - Sept 2004 - pNA [501+]

Gorsuch, Joseph W. - *Silver: Environmental Transport, Fate, Effects, and Models, Papers from Environmental Toxicology and Chemistry, 1983 to 2002*
SciTech - v28 - i1 - March 2004 - p147(1) [51-500]

Goschler, Constantin - *Rudolf Virchow: Mediziner-Anthropologe-Politiker*
CEH - v37 - i2 - Spring 2004 - p302(3) [501+]

Gosden, Caroline - *Really Useful Handbook of Reptile Husbandry*
E-Streams - Sept 2004 - pNA [501+]

Goshgarian, Gary - *Exploring Language, 10th ed.*
R&R Bk N - v19 - i1 - Feb 2004 - p212 [51-500]

Gosling, David L. - *Religion and Ecology in India and SouthEast Asia*
ER - v56 - i3 - July 2004 - p376(2) [501+]

Gosling, Ray - *Sum Total*
NS - v133 - i4702 - August 23 2004 - p37(2) [501+]

Gospodinov, Georgi - *Natural Novel*
KR - v72 - i23 - Dec 1 2004 - p1106(1) [51-500]
LJ - v130 - i2 - Feb 1 2005 - p68(1) [51-500]
PW - v252 - i5 - Jan 31 2005 - p50(2) [51-500]

Goss, Mini - *When Mum Was Little (Illus. by Goss, Mini)*
c   KR - v72 - i16 - August 15 2004 - p806(1) [51-500]

Goss, Thomas J. - *The War Within the Union High Command: Politics and Generalship During the Civil War*
HNet - Sept 2004 - pNA [501+]
JAH - v91 - i2 - Sept 2004 - p636(2) [501+]

Gosse, Van - *The World the Sixties Made: Politics and Culture in Recent America*
CS - v33 - i5 - Sept 2004 - p624-624 [501+]

Gossen, Gary H. - *Four Creations: An Epic Story of the Chiapas Mayas*
Ams - v61 - i2 - Oct 2004 - p345(2) [501+]

Gosseries, Axel - *Denser la Justice Entre les Generations: De l'affaire Perruche a la Reforme de Retraites*
Ethics - v115 - i2 - Jan 2005 - p412(4) [501+]

Gostin, Lawrence O. - *The AIDS Pandemic: Complacency, Injustice, and Unfulfilled Expectations*
Choice - v42 - i3 - Nov 2004 - p517(1) [1-50]
Nation - v279 - i7 - Sept 13 2004 - p56 [501+]

Got, Olivier - *Les Jardins de Zola: Psyanalyse et paysage myique dans 'Les Rougon-Macquart'*
FS - v58 - i1 - Jan 2004 - p125(2) [501+]
Les Jardins de Zola, psychanalyse et paysage mythique dans les Rougon-Macquart
NCFS - v33 - i1-2 - Fall-Winter 2004 - p224(3) [501+]

Gotelli, Nicholas J. - *A Primer of Ecological Statistics*
SciTech - v28 - i3 - Sept 2004 - p61(1) [51-500]

Gotham, Kevin Fox - *Race, Real Estate, and Uneven Development: The Kansas City Experience, 1900-2000*
CS - v33 - i2 - March 2004 - p165-166 [501+]
HNet - Nov 2004 - pNA [501+]

Goto, Ken'ichi - *Tensions of Empire: Japan and Southeast Asia in the Colonial and Postcolonial World*
R&R Bk N - v19 - i3 - August 2004 - p55(1) [51-500]

Gotschmann, Dirk - *Bayerischer Parlamentarismus im Vormarz: Die Standeversammlung des Konigreichs Bayern, 1819-1848*
HNet - Oct 2004 - pNA [501+]
JMH - v76 - i4 - Dec 2004 - p988(3) [501+]

Gott, Jonatha - *RNA Interference, Editing, and Modification: Methods and Protocols*
SciTech - v28 - i3 - Sept 2004 - p60(1) [1-50]

Gott, Kendall D. - *Where the South Lost the War: An Analysis of the Fort Henry-Fort Donelson Campaign, February 1862.*
JSH - v71 - i1 - Feb 2005 - p165(2) [501+]

Gott, Richard - *Cuba: A New History*
LJ - v129 - i17 - Oct 15 2004 - p73(1) [51-500]
Nation - v279 - i13 - Oct 25 2004 - p36 [501+]
NS - v133 - i4715 - Nov 22 2004 - p48(2) [501+]
TLS - i5303 - Nov 19 2004 - p7(1) [501+]

Gottesman, Evan - *Cambodia After the Khmer Rouge: Inside the Politics of Nation Building*
Pac A - v77 - i2 - Summer 2004 - p367(2) [501+]

Gottfried, Heidi - *Equity in the Workplace: Gendering Workplace Policy Analysis*
CWS - v23 - i3-4 - Spring-Summer 2004 - p210(2) [501+]
Equity in Workplace: Gendering Workplace Policy Analysis
Choice - v42 - i2 - Oct 2004 - p336(1) [51-500]

Gottfried, Kurt - *Quantum Mechanics: Fundamentals*
Phys Today - v57 - i8 - August 2004 - p55-55 [501+]

Gottfried, Martin - *Arthur Miller: A Life*
CR - v285 - i1664 - Sept 2004 - p177(2) [51-500]
Lon R Bks - v26 - i6 - March 18 2004 - pNA [501+]
TimHES - v0 - i1672 - Dec 24 2004 - p26(2) [501+]
Arthur Miller: His Life and Work
Choice - v42 - i1 - Sept 2004 - p100(1) [501+]
Queens Q - v111 - i3 - Fall 2004 - p405(12) [501+]

Gottfried, Maya - *Good Dog*
KR - v73 - i1 - Jan 1 2005 - p51(1) [51-500]

Gottfried, Ted - *Homeland Security Versus Constitutional Rights*
LibMed - v22 - i7 - April-May 2004 - p82(1) [501+]

Gottfried, Theodore Mark - *Homeland Security Versus Constitutional Rights*
SLJ - v50 - i10 - Oct 2004 - pS59(1) [51-500]

Gottheil, Fred M. - *Principles of Macroeconomics, 4th ed.*
R&R Bk N - v19 - i4 - Nov 2004 - p85(1) [1-50]

Gottheimer, Josh - *Ripples of Hope: Great American Civil Rights Speeches*
Kliatt - v38 - i6 - Nov 2004 - p31(1) [51-500]

Gottinger, Hans-Werner - *Economies of Networks Industries*
JEL - v41 - i4 - Dec 2003 - p1390(2) [501+]

Gottlieb, Alma - *The Afterlife Is Where We Come from: The Culture of Infancy in West Africa*
MAQ - v18 - i3 - Sept 2004 - p399-402 [501+]

Gottlieb, Daphne - *Final Girl*
Lam Bk Rpt - v13 - i4-5 - Nov-Dec 2004 - p16(2) [501+]

Gottlieb, Erika - *Dystopian Fiction East and West: Universe of Terror and Trial*
MFSF - v50 - i2 - Summer 2004 - p534-536 [501+]

Gottlieb, Jack - *Funny, It Doesn't Sound Jewish: How Yiddish Songs and Synagogue Melodies Influenced Tin Pan Alley, Broadway, and Hollywood*
Choice - v42 - i4 - Dec 2004 - p671(1) [1-50]

Gottlieb, Julie V. - *The Culture of Fascism: Visions of the Far Right in Britian*
Choice - v42 - i2 - Oct 2004 - p359(2) [51-500]
Feminine Fascism: Women in Britain's Fascist Movement, 1923-1945
Albion - v36 - i2 - Summer 2004 - p359(2) [501+]
Signs - v30 - i2 - Wntr 2005 - p1695(5) [501+]

Gottlieb, Nanette - *Japanese Cybercultures*
CS - v33 - i6 - Nov 2004 - p743(1) [1-50]

Gottlieb, Richard - *2004 Sports Market Place Directory*
Ref Rev - August 2004 - pNA [501+]
The Directory of Business Information Resources 2005, 12th ed.
R&R Bk N - v19 - i4 - Nov 2004 - p107(1) [51-500]
The Directory of Mail Order Catalogs: A Comprehensive Guide to Consumer Mail Order Catalog Companies. 18th Ed.
R&R Bk N - v19 - i2 - May 2004 - p115(1) [51-500]
Sports Market Place Directory, 2004 Ed.
BL - v101 - i2 - Sept 15 2004 - p278(1) [501+]
R&R Bk N - v19 - i3 - August 2004 - p121(1) [51-500]

Gottlieb, Robert - *George Balanchine: The Ballet Maker*
y   BL - v101 - i5 - Nov 1 2004 - p459(1) [501+]
BW - v34 - i48 - Nov 28 2004 - p7(1) [501+]
Dance - v79 - i1 - Jan 2005 - p106(5) [501+]
Ent W - i790 - Oct 29 2004 - p71 [501+]
KR - v72 - i21 - Nov 1 2004 - p1037(1) [501+]
LJ - v129 - i18 - Nov 1 2004 - p87(1) [501+]
NYTBR - Nov 28 2004 - p16 [501+]
PW - v251 - i41 - Oct 11 2004 - p72(1) [501+]

Gottlieb, Roger S. - *Liberating Faith: Religious Voices for Justice, Peace, and Ecological Wisdom*
R&R Bk N - v19 - i1 - Feb 2004 - p11(1) [1-50]

Gottlieb, Sussannah Young-ah - *Regions of Sorrow - Anxiety and Messianism in Hannah and W.H. Auden*
MLN - v118 - i5 - Dec 2003 - p1317-1323 [501+]

Gottlieb, Vera - *Anton Chekhov at the Moscow Art Theatre: Illustrations of the Original Productions*
TimHES - v0 - i1677 - Feb 4 2005 - p26(2) [501+]

Gottman, John M. - *The Mathematics of Marriage Dynamic Nonlinear Models*
CS - v33 - i2 - March 2004 - p179-181 [501+]

Gottschalk, Louis A. - *World War II: Neuropsychiatric Casualties, Out of Sight, Out of Mind*
SciTech - v28 - i3 - Sept 2004 - p101(1) [51-500]

Gottschall, Terrell D. - *By Order of the Kaiser: Otto von Diederichs and the Rise of the Imperial German Navy, 1865-1902*
J Mil H - v68 - i3 - April 2004 - p615-616 [501+]
R&R Bk N - v19 - i1 - Feb 2004 - p256(1) [51-500]

Gottschild, Brenda Dixon - *The Black Dancing Body: A Geography from Coon to Cool*
Choice - v42 - i2 - Oct 2004 - p304(2) [51-500]
Dance - v78 - i9 - Sept 2004 - p58(2) [51-500]

Gottstein, Gunter - *Physical Foundations of Materials Science*
Choice - v42 - i5 - Jan 2005 - p884(1) [1-50]

Gotz, Norbert - *Civil Society in the Baltic Sea Region*
R&R Bk N - v19 - i1 - Feb 2004 - pNA [501+]

Gotz, Schroth - *Agroforestry and Biodiversity Conservation in Tropical Landscape*
SciTech - v28 - i4 - Dec 2004 - p122 [51-500]

Gotzkowsky, Bodo - *Die Buchholzschnitte Hans Brosamers zu den Frankfurter "Volksbuch": Ausgaben und ihre Wiederverwendungen*
Six Ct J - v35 - i3 - Fall 2004 - p895-896 [501+]

Gotzmann, Andreas - *Juden, Burger, Deutsche: Zur Geschichte von Vielfalt und Differenz 1800-1933*
HNet - Oct 2004 - pNA [501+]

Goudail, Francois - *Statistical Image Processing for Noisy Images: An Application-Oriented Approach*
SciTech - v28 - i1 - March 2004 - p145(1) [51-500]

Goudge, Paulette - *The Power of Whiteness: Racism in Third World Development and Aid*
JEL - v42 - i1 - March 2004 - p265(2) [501+]

Goudie, A.S. - *Encyclopedia of Geomorphology*
Choice - v42 - i1 - Sept 2004 - p68(1) [501+]
SciTech - v28 - i3 - Sept 2004 - p5(1) [501+]

Goudsmit, Jaap - *Viral Fitness: The Next SARS and West Nile in the Making*
Choice - v42 - i5 - Jan 2005 - p885(2) [1-50]
SciTech - v28 - i4 - Dec 2004 - p75(1) [51-500]

Goudsouzian, Aram - *Sidney Poitier: Man, Actor, Icon*
Black Iss - v6 - i5 - Sept-Oct 2004 - p45(2) [501+]
Choice - v42 - i1 - Sept 2004 - p107(2) [501+]

Gouge, Earnest - *New Fire: Creek Folktales*
Choice - v42 - i7 - March 2005 - p1270(1) [51-500]

Gough, Alex - *Breed Predispositions to Disease in Dogs and Cats*
SciTech - v28 - i3 - Sept 2004 - p133(1) [51-500]

Gough, Laurence - *Cloud of Suspects*
CBRA - Annual 2003 - p165(2) [51-500]

Gouinlock, James S. - *Eros and the Good: Wisdom According to Nature*
Choice - v42 - i4 - Dec 2004 - p675(1) [1-50]
Eros and the good; wisdom according to nature
R&R Bk N - v19 - i3 - August 2004 - p11(1) [1-50]

Gouk, Penelope - *Music, Science, and Natural Magic in Seventeenth-Century England*
Isis - v95 - i3 - June 2004 - p293(1) [501+]

Goukowsky, P. - *Appien: Histoire romaine. Tome iv, livre viii. La guerre de MithridateAppien: Histoire romaine. Tome iv, livre viii. La guerre de Mithridate*
Class R - v53 - i2 - Nov 2003 - p319-321 [501+]

Goulart, Ron - *Comic Book Encyclopedia*
MFSF - v108 - i4 - April 2005 - p31(2) [501+]

Gould, Allan - *Anne of Green Gables vs. G.I. Joe: Friendly Fire Between Canada and the U.S.*
CBRA - Annual 2003 - p84(2) [501+]

Gould, Carol Grant - *The Remarkable Life of William Beebe: Explorer and Naturalist*
BL - v101 - i7 - Dec 1 2004 - p630(1) [51-500]

Gould, Eric - *The University in a Corporate Culture*
J Hi E - v75 - i6 - Nov-Dec 2004 - p707(3) [501+]

Gould, Joan - *Spinning Straw into Gold: What Fairy Tales Reveal about the Transformations in a Woman's Life.*
KR - v72 - i24 - Dec 15 2004 - p1181(1) [51-500]
LJ - v130 - i2 - Feb 1 2005 - p105(1) [51-500]
PW - v251 - i51 - Dec 20 2004 - p47(1) [501+]

Gould, Judith - *The Parisian Affair*
BL - v101 - i1 - Sept 1 2004 - p5(1) [51-500]
KR - v72 - i16 - August 15 2004 - p763(1) [501+]
PW - v251 - i36 - Sept 6 2004 - p46(1) [51-500]

Gould, Lewis L. - *Grand Old Party: A History of the Republicans*
Choice - v41 - i11-12 - July-August 2004 - p2107(1) [501+]
The Modern American Presidency
JAH - v91 - i1 - June 2004 - p321-321 [501+]

Gould, Mike - *Page to Stage*
c   Sch Lib - v52 - i4 - Winter 2004 - p210(1) [51-500]

Gould, Nick - *Social Work, Critical Reflection, and the Learning Organisation*
R&R Bk N - v19 - i4 - Nov 2004 - p137(1) [51-500]

Gould, Peter - *Geographical Voices: Fourteen Autobiographical Essays*
Biomag - v27 - i3 - Summer 2004 - p628(4) [501+]

Gould, Roger V. - *Collision of Wills: How Ambiguity about Social Rank Breeds Conflict*
AJS - v110 - i1 - July 2004 - p231(2) [501+]

Gould, Stephen Jay - *Triumph And Tragedy In Mudville*
TLS - i5262 - Feb 6 2004 - p10(1) [501+]

Gould, Steven - *Reflex*
y BL - v101 - i8 - Dec 15 2004 - p715(1) [51-500]
KR - v72 - i20 - Oct 15 2004 - p990(1) [51-500]
MFSF - v108 - i3 - March 2005 - p26(2) [501+]
PW - v251 - i44 - Nov 1 2004 - p47(2) [501+]
LJ - v129 - i20 - Dec 1 2004 - p105(1) [51-500]

Gould, Terry - *Paper Fan: The Hunt for Triad Gangster Steven Wong*
LJ - v129 - i17 - Oct 15 2004 - p75(1) [51-500]
PW - v251 - i38 - Sept 20 2004 - p54(1) [51-500]

Gould, Tony - *Don't Fence Me In: Leprosy in Modern Times*
NS - v134 - i4726 - Feb 7 2005 - p48(2) [501+]
Spec - v297 - i9206 - Jan 15 2005 - p44(1) [501+]

Gould, Veronica Franklin - *G.F. Watts: The Last Great Victorian*
LJ - v130 - i4 - March 1 2005 - p83(1) [51-500]
The Vision of G.F. Watts
Spec - v295 - i9186 - August 28 2004 - p40(2) [501+]

Gould, Virginia Meacham - *No Cross, No Crown: Black Nuns in Nineteenth-Century New Orleans*
JWH - v16 - i3 - Autumn 2004 - p187(10) [501+]

Gould, William - *Maximum Likelihood Estimation with Stata*
JEL - v42 - i1 - March 2004 - p246(2) [501+]

Goulden, Ian P. - *Combinatorial Enumeration*
SciTech - v28 - i4 - Dec 2004 - p35(1) [51-500]

Goulder, Michael - *Isaiah as Liturgy*
R&R Bk N - v19 - i4 - Nov 2004 - p22(1) [51-500]

Goulding, Gill - *Creative Perseverance: Sustaining Life-Giving Ministry in Today's Church*
CBRA - Annual 2003 - p91(1) [501+]

Goulding, Marrack - *Peacemonger*
R&R Bk N - v19 - i1 - Feb 2004 - pNA [51-500]

Goulet, d'Alain - *Le litteraire, qu'est-ce que c'est?*
FS - v58 - i1 - Jan 2004 - p149(2) [501+]

Goulson, Dave - *Bumblebees: Their Behaviour and Ecology*
QRB - v79 - i3 - Sept 2004 - p315(1) [501+]

Gouraud, Jean-Louis - *Horses (Read by Arthus-Bertrand, Yann)*
LJ - v129 - i18 - Nov 1 2004 - p80(1) [501+]

Gourlay, Alexander S. - *Prophetic Character: Essays on William Blake in Honor of John E. Grant*
Albion - v36 - i1 - Spring 2004 - p147(2) [501+]

Gourlay, Jharna - *Florence Nightingale and the Health of the Raj*
SciTech - v28 - i1 - March 2004 - p125(1) [51-500]

Gourley, Catherine - *Society's Sisters: Stories of Women Who Fought for Social Justice in America*
LibMed - v22 - i7 - April-May 2004 - p71(1) [501+]

Gourley, Miriam - *Dollmaking for the First Time*
LJ - v130 - i3 - Feb 15 2005 - p126(1) [51-500]

Gourluck, Russ - *A Store Like No Other: Eaton's of Winnipeg*
Globe & Mail - Dec 18 2004 - pD14 [1-50]

Gourmet Magazine - *The Gourmet Cookbook*
USNews & Wrld Rpt - v137 - i11 - Oct 4 2004 - p61 [501+]

Gournay, Marie de - *Les Advis: ou, les presens de la Demoiselle de Gournay*
FS - v58 - i3 - July 2004 - p404-404 [501+]
OEuvres completes
FS - v58 - i2 - April 2004 - p248(2) [501+]

Gousseff, Catherine - *The Perfect Knight (Illus. by Negrin, Fabian)*
c SLJ - v50 - i9 - Sept 2004 - p160(1) [51-500]

Govan, Michael - *Dan Flavin: A Retrospective*
BL - v101 - i6 - Nov 15 2004 - p541(1) [51-500]
LJ - v129 - i20 - Dec 1 2004 - p114(1) [51-500]
Dan Flavin: The Complete Lights 1961-1996
LJ - v129 - i20 - Dec 1 2004 - p114(1) [51-500]

Goverde, Henri - *Power and Gender in European Rural Development*
R&R Bk N - v19 - i3 - August 2004 - p147(1) [51-500]

Govier, Katherine - *Creation*
BL - v100 - i22 - August 2004 - p1886(1) [51-500]
CBRA - Annual 2003 - p166(1) [51-500]

Govier, Trudy - *A Practical Study of Argument, 6th ed.*
R&R Bk N - v19 - i4 - Nov 2004 - p7(1) [51-500]

Govinden, Niven - *We Are the New Romantics*
KR - v72 - i19 - Oct 1 2004 - p930(2) [501+]

Gow, James - *The Serbian Project and its Adversaries: A Strategy of War Crimes*
Slav R - v63 - i4 - Winter 2004 - p866(2) [501+]

Gowan, Donald E. - *The Westminster Theological Wordbook of the Bible*
TT - v61 - i2 - July 2004 - p284(3) [501+]

Gowdy, Barbara - *The Romantic*
CBRA - Annual 2003 - p166(1) [501+]

Gowen, L. Kris - *Making Sexual Decisions: The Ultimate Teen Guide*
SLJ - v50 - i10 - Oct 2004 - pS64(1) [51-500]

Gower, Catherine - *Long-Long's New Year: A Story About the Chinese Spring Festival (Illus. by He Zhihong)*
c PW - v252 - i5 - Jan 31 2005 - p67(2) [51-500]

Gowing, Laura - *Common Bodies: Women, Touch, and Power in Seventeenth-Century England*
Critm - v46 - i2 - Spring 2004 - p281(18) [501+]
Common Bodies: Women, Touch and Power in Seventeenth-Century England
HNet - Sept 2004 - pNA [501+]
Common Bodies: Women, Touch and Power in Seventeenth Century England
HRNB - v33 - i1 - Fall 2004 - p22(1) [501+]

Gownley, Jimmy - *Amelia Rules! What Makes You Happy*
c VOYA - v27 - i5 - Dec 2004 - p375(1) [501+]

Goy-Blanquet, Dominique - *Joan of Arc, a saint for all reasons; studies in myth and politics*
R&R Bk N - v19 - i1 - Feb 2004 - p35(1) [1-50]
Shakespeare's Early History Plays: From Chronicle to Stage
Ren Q - v57 - i4 - Winter 2004 - p1518(3) [501+]
TLS - i5289 - August 13 2004 - p9-10 [501+]

Goyal, Amit - *Processing of High Temperature Superconductors: Proceedings*
SciTech - v28 - i4 - Dec 2004 - p157(1) [51-500]

Goyer, Tricia - *Night Song*
BL - v101 - i1 - Sept 1 2004 - p55(1) [501+]

Goyette, Linda - *Edmonton in Our Own Words*
CG - v125 - i1 - Jan-Feb 2005 - p99(1) [501+]
Kidmonton: True stories of River City Kids
CG - v125 - i1 - Jan-Feb 2005 - p99(1) [501+]

Goyette, Sue - *Lures*
CBRA - Annual 2003 - p166(2) [501+]
Undone
Globe & Mail - July 3 2004 - pD6 [501+]

Goytisolo, Juan - *Forbidden Territory and Realms of Strife: The Memoirs of Juan Goytisolo*
R&R Bk N - v19 - i1 - Feb 2004 - p233(1) [51-500]

Graafland, Johan J. - *Economic Assessment of Election Programmes: Does it Make Sense?*
JEL - v42 - i1 - March 2004 - p250(1) [501+]

Grab, Alexander - *Napoleon and the Transformation of Europe*
HNet - June 2004 - pNA [501+]
R&R Bk N - v19 - i1 - Feb 2004 - p35(1) [1-50]

Graber, Jetan - *Resistance*
KR - v73 - i5 - March 1 2005 - p286(1) [51-500]

Graber, Thomas M. - *Risk Management in Orthodontics: Experts' Guide to Malpractice*
SciTech - v28 - i3 - Sept 2004 - p120(1) [51-500]

Grabien, Deborah - *The Famous Flower of Serving Men*
BL - v101 - i6 - Nov 15 2004 - p565(1) [51-500]
KR - v72 - i17 - Sept 1 2004 - p838(2) [51-500]
LJ - v129 - i18 - Nov 1 2004 - p60(1) [51-500]
PW - v251 - i41 - Oct 11 2004 - p59(2) [51-500]

Grabowski, Ralph - *The Illustrated AutoCAD 2005 Quick Reference*
LJ - v129 - i18 - Nov 1 2004 - p114(1) [51-500]
Using AutoCAD 2005: Advanced
LJ - v129 - i18 - Nov 1 2004 - p114(1) [51-500]
Using AutoCAD 2005: Basics
LJ - v129 - i18 - Nov 1 2004 - p114(1) [51-500]

Grace, Catherine O'Neill - *Forces of Nature: The Awesome Power of Volcanoes, Earthquakes, and Tornadoes*
c BL - v101 - i1 - Sept 1 2004 - p116(1) [501+]
c SB - v40 - i5 - Sept-Oct 2004 - p210(2) [501+]
y SLJ - v50 - i11 - Nov 2004 - p164(1) [51-500]
The White House: An Illustrated History
c LibMed - v22 - i6 - March 2004 - p79(1) [501+]

Grace, Christopher - *Medical Management of Infectious Disease*
E-Streams - July 2004 - pNA [501+]

Grace, Louis - *The British Political Elite and the Soviet Union, 1937-1939*
HER - v119 - i483 - Sept 2004 - p1012(3) [501+]

Grace, Nancy M. - *Breaking the Rule of Cool: Interviewing and Reading Women Beat Writers*
Choice - v42 - i3 - Nov 2004 - p483(1) [1-50]

Grace, Sherill - *Canada and the Idea of North*
Can Lit - i181 - Summer 2004 - p132-134 [501+]

Grace, Sherrill - *Performing National Identities: International Perspectives on Contemporary Canadian Theatre*
CBRA - Annual 2003 - p107(2) [51-500]

Grace, Will - *Caterpillar Dance (Illus. by McBee, Scott)*
c SLJ - v50 - i9 - Sept 2004 - p160(1) [51-500]

Gracia-Arenal, Mercedes - *A Man of Three Words: Samuel Pallache, a moroccan Jew in Catholic and Protestant Europe*
AHR - v109 - i2 - April 2004 - p596(2) [501+]

Gracia, Jorge J.E. - *A Companion to Philosophy in the Middle Ages*
RM - v58 - i2 - Dec 2004 - p436(3) [501+]

Gradel, I. - *Emperor Worship and Roman Religion*
Class R - v53 - i2 - Nov 2003 - p426-428 [501+]

Gradon, Leon - *Optimization of Aerosol Drug Delivery*
SciTech - v28 - i1 - March 2004 - p124(1) [51-500]

Graduate Programs in the Humanities, Arts and Social Sciences, 2003, 37th Ed.
R&R Bk N - v19 - i1 - Feb 2004 - pNA [51-500]

Graduate Study in Psychology, 2005 25th Ed.
R&R Bk N - v19 - i4 - Nov 2004 - p9(1) [51-500]

Grady, Alan - *When Good Men Do Nothing: The Assassination of Albert Patterson*
JSH - v70 - i4 - Nov 2004 - p967(2) [501+]

Grady, Hugh - *Shakespeare, Machiavelli, and Montaigne: Power and Subjectivity from Richard II to Hamlet*
RES - v55 - i220 - June 2004 - p455-457 [501+]
Six Ct J - v35 - i3 - Fall 2004 - p909-911 [501+]

Graeme-Evans, Posie - *The Innocent*
y Kliatt - v38 - i4 - July 2004 - p18(1) [51-500]

Graen, George B. - *Dealing with Diversity*
R&R Bk N - v19 - i3 - August 2004 - p129(1) [51-500]

Graf, Mike - *The Amazon River*
c SLJ - v50 - i10 - Oct 2004 - p140(1) [51-500]
The Nile River
c SLJ - v50 - i10 - Oct 2004 - p140(1) [51-500]

Graf, William L. - *Dam Removal Research: Status and Prospects*
Env - v46 - i6 - July-August 2004 - p43(1) [51-500]

Graff, David A. - *A Diplomatic Revolution: Algeria's Fight for Independence and the Origins of the Post-Cold War Era*
JIH - v34 - i3 - Wntr 2004 - p497(2) [501+]

Graff, E.J. - *What is Marriage For?*
R&R Bk N - v19 - i4 - Nov 2004 - p129(1) [1-50]

Graff, Joakim - *Soren Kierkegaard: a Biography*
PW - v251 - i51 - Dec 20 2004 - p55(1) [51-500]

Graff, Nancy Price - *Looking Back at Vermont: Farm Security Administration Photographs, 1936-1942*
NEQ - v77 - i2 - June 2004 - p330-332 [501+]

Graffi, Giorgio - *Two Hundred Years of Syntax: a Critical Survey*
Isis - v95 - i3 - Sept 2004 - p475(2) [501+]

Grafton, Anthony - *Bring Out Your Dead: The Past as Revelation*
HNet - Sept 2004 - pNA [501+]

Grafton, Carol Belanger - *Great Woodcuts of Albrecht Durer*
A Art - v68 - i748 - Nov 2004 - p75(1) [51-500]

Grafton, R. Quentin - *The Economics of the Environment and Natural Resources*
TimHES - v0 - i1675 - Jan 21 2005 - p27(1) [501+]

Grafton, Sue - *R Is for Ricochet (Read by Kaye, Judy). Audiobook Review*
BL - v101 - i4 - Oct 15 2004 - p432(1) [51-500]
y Kliatt - v39 - i1 - Jan 2005 - p49(1) [51-500]
R Is for Ricochet
BL - v100 - i22 - August 2004 - p1870(1) [51-500]
BW - v34 - i31 - August 1 2004 - p8(1) [501+]
Ent W - i774 - July 16 2004 - p80 [501+]
Globe & Mail - August 7 2004 - pD12 [501-500]
LJ - v129 - i12 - July 2004 - p64(1) [51-500]
NYTBR - August 8 2004 - p15 [501+]
People - v62 - i6 - August 9 2004 - p45 [51-500]
SLJ - v50 - i12 - Dec 2004 - p174(1) [51-500]

Gragg, Larry - *Englishmen Transplanted: The English Colonization of Barbados, 1627-1660*
  HNet - Oct 2004 - pNA [501+]
  W&M Q - v61 - i4 - Oct 2004 - p753-756 [501+]

Gragoudas, Evangelos S. - *Photodynamic Therapy of Ocular Diseases*
  SciTech - v28 - i1 - March 2004 - p114(1) [51-500]

Graham, Amy - *Discovering Antarctica's Land, People, and Wildlife*
  c   SLJ - v50 - i8 - August 2004 - p137(1) [51-500]

Graham-Barber, Lynda - *Spy Hops and Belly Flops: Curious Behaviors of Woodland Animals (Illus. by Lies, Brian)*
  c   LibMed - v23 - i3 - Nov-Dec 2004 - p76(1) [51-500]
  c   SLJ - v51 - i1 - Jan 2005 - p110(1) [51-500]

Graham, Bob (b. 1936 -) - *Intelligence Matters: The CIA, the FBI, Saudi Arabia, and the Failure of America's War on Terror*
  BW - v34 - i38 - Sept 19 2004 - p12(1) [501+]

Graham, Bob (b. 1942 -) - *Tales from the Waterhole (Illus. by Graham, Bob)*
  c   Sch Lib - v52 - i3 - Autumn 2004 - p131(1) [501+]
  c   SLJ - v50 - i7 - July 2004 - p76(1) [51-500]
  c   SLJ - v50 - i10 - Oct 2004 - pS29(1) [1-50]

Graham, Brandon - *Escalator*
  PW - v251 - i30 - July 26 2004 - p40(2) [501+]

Graham, Caroline - *A Ghost in the Machine: A Chief Inspector Barnaby Mystery*
  BL - v100 - i22 - August 2004 - p1905(1) [501+]
  LJ - v129 - i13 - August 2004 - p60(1) [501+]
  PW - v251 - i28 - July 12 2004 - p47(1) [51-500]

Graham, Clare - *Ordering Law: The Architectural and Social History of the English Law Court to 1914*
  R&R Bk N - v19 - i1 - Feb 2004 - p203(1) [51-500]

Graham, David - *An Interregnum of the Sign: The Emblematic Age in France*
  Six Ct J - v35 - i1 - Spring 2004 - p238(2) [501+]

Graham, Don - *Kings of Texas: The 150-Year Saga of an American Ranching Empire*
  AHR - v109 - i3 - June 2004 - p931(2) [501+]
  SHQ - v107 - i4 - April 2004 - p624(2) [501+]
  Lone Star Literature
  VQR - v80 - i2 - Spring 2004 - p257-258 [501+]

Graham, Duncan - *People Next Door: Understanding Indonesia*
  R&R Bk N - v19 - i4 - Nov 2004 - p49(1) [1-50]

Graham, Edward M. - *Reforming Korea's Industrial Conglomerates*
  JEL - v42 - i1 - March 2004 - p216(3) [501+]

Graham, Elaine L. - *Representations of the Post/Human: Monsters, Aliens and Others in Popular Culture*
  SFS - v31 - i1 - March 2004 - p132-137 [501+]

Graham, Ellen - *The Bad and the Beautiful*
  LJ - v130 - i3 - Feb 15 2005 - p125(1) [51-500]

Graham, Georgia - *A Team Like No Other*
  c   Globe & Mail - Jan 1 2005 - pD11 [51-500]

Graham, Heather - *Killing Kelly*
  PW - v252 - i8 - Feb 21 2005 - p158(1) [51-500]
  The Presence
  BL - v101 - i1 - Sept 1 2004 - p72(1) [51-500]
  PW - v251 - i31 - August 2 2004 - p57(1) [501+]

Graham, Helen - *The Spanish Republic at War, 1936-1939*
  AHR - v109 - i2 - April 2004 - p622(2) [501+]
  J Mil H - v68 - i3 - July 2004 - p985-986 [501+]

Graham, Herman, III - *The Brothers' Vietnam War: Black Power, Manhood, and the Military Experience*
  Afr Am R - v38 - i2 - Summer 2004 - p345(4) [501+]
  CS - v33 - i5 - Sept 2004 - p586-587 [501+]
  J Mil H - v68 - i2 - April 2004 - p653(2) [501+]
  JAH - v91 - i2 - Sept 2004 - p713(2) [501+]
  JSH - v70 - i4 - Nov 2004 - p972(1) [501+]

Graham, Ian - *Alfred Maudslay and the Maya*
  HAHR - v84 - i2 - May 2004 - p365(2) [501+]

Graham, Jorie - *Overlord*
  LJ - v130 - i2 - Feb 1 2005 - p83(1) [51-500]
  PW - v252 - i4 - Jan 24 2005 - p236(1) [501+]

Graham, Judith - *Writing Under Control*
  TCR - v106 - i8 - August 2004 - p1541(3) [501+]

Graham, Judith S. - *Puritan Family Life: The Diary of Samuel Sewall*
  R&R Bk N - v19 - i1 - Feb 2004 - p63(1) [501+]

Graham, Keith - *Practical Reasoning in a Social World: How We Act Together*
  Phil R - v113 - i1 - Jan 2004 - p130(3) [501+]

Graham, L.B. - *Beyond the Summerland*
  VOYA - v27 - i5 - Dec 2004 - p404(1) [51-500]

Graham, Margaret Baker - *Victorian America: A Family Record from the Heartland*
  NWSA Jnl - v16 - i3 - Fall 2004 - p215(2) [501+]

Graham, Mark - *Josef Fuchs on Natural Law Mid-init=E .*
  TT - v60 - i4 - Jan 2004 - p570-571 [501+]

Graham, Nancy - *Afraid of the Day: A Daughter's Journey*
  CBRA - Annual 2003 - p46(1) [51-500]

Graham, Paul - *Hackers and Painters: Big Ideas from the Computer Age*
  Choice - v42 - i3 - Nov 2004 - p519(1) [1-50]
  SciTech - v28 - i3 - Sept 2004 - p31(1) [51-500]

Graham, Rosemary - *My Not-So-Terrible Time at the Hippie Hotel*
  LibMed - v22 - i5 - Feb 2004 - p69(1) [501+]

Graham, Sandra Lauderdale - *Caetana Says No: Women's Stories from a Brazilian Slave Society*
  AHR - v109 - i2 - April 2004 - p581(1) [501+]
  CS - v33 - i1 - Jan 2004 - p127-127 [501+]

Graham, Stedman - *Move without the Ball: Put Your Skills and Your Magic to Work for You*
  Black Iss - v6 - i5 - Sept-Oct 2004 - p28(2) [501+]
  y   SLJ - v50 - i11 - Nov 2004 - p164(1) [1-50]

Graham, Stephen - *Cybercities Reader*
  SciTech - v28 - i3 - Sept 2004 - p133(1) [51-500]
  Splintering Urbanism: Networked Infrastructures, Technological Mobilities and the Urban Condition
  J Urban H - v30 - i4 - May 2004 - p627-635 [501+]

Graham, Toni - *Waiting For Elvis: Stories*
  KR - v73 - i1 - Jan 1 2005 - p8(1) [501+]

Graham, William H. - *Newton County, Mississippi Marriage Records, 1872-1952*
  EFHM - v58 - i3 - May-June 2004 - p59(1) [51-500]

Grahame, Kenneth - *The Reluctant Dragon (Illus. by Moore, Inga)*
  c   BL - v100 - i22 - August 2004 - p1942(1) [51-500]
  c   CH Bwatch - v14 - i7 - July 2004 - p1(1) [51-500]
  y   Magpies - v19 - i5 - Nov 2004 - p20(4) [501+]
  c   NYTBR - Oct 17 2004 - p21 [501+]
  c   SLJ - v50 - i11 - Nov 2004 - p104(1) [51-500]
  The Wind in the Willows
  c   RT - v57 - Sept 2003 - p98 [1-50]

Grahn, Geoffrey - *What's Going on in There? (Illus. by Grahn, Geoffrey)*
  c   KR - v73 - i3 - Feb 1 2005 - p176(1) [51-500]
  c   PW - v252 - i11 - March 14 2005 - p70(1) [501+]

Grainge, Paul - *Memory and Popular Film*
  J Am St - v38 - i1 - April 2004 - p145-146 [501+]
  JouAmCul - v27 - i3 - Sept 2004 - p346(2) [501+]
  Monochrome Memories: Nostalgia and Style in Retro America
  J Am St - v38 - i2 - August 2004 - p359(1) [501+]
  J Am St - v38 - i2 - August 2004 - p359-359 [501+]

Grainger, Guy - *The Anglo-Saxon Cemetery at Worthy Park, Kingsworthy near Winchester, Hampshire*
  Med R - Nov 2004 - pNA [501+]

Grainger, James - *The Long Slide: Stories*
  Globe & Mail - Nov 27 2004 - pD44 [501+]

Grainger, John D. - *Maritime Blockade of Germany in the Great War: The Northern Patrol, 1914-1928*
  R&R Bk N - v19 - i1 - Feb 2004 - p28(1) [51-500]

Graizbord, David L. - *Souls in Dispute: Converso Identities in Iberia and the Jewish Diaspora, 1580-1700*
  JR - v85 - i1 - Jan 2005 - p152(3) [501+]

Grajetzki, Wolfram - *Burial Customs in Ancient Egypt: Life and Death for Rich and Poor*
  R&R Bk N - v19 - i1 - Feb 2004 - p50(1) [51-500]

Gralla, Preston - *Windows XP Power Hound: Teach Yourself New Tricks*
  LJ - v130 - i2 - Feb 1 2005 - p110(1) [501+]

Gralley, Jean - *The Moon Came Down on Milk Street (Illus. by Gralley, Jean)*
  c   BW - v34 - i45 - Nov 7 2004 - p12(1) [501+]
  c   HB - v81 - i1 - Jan-Feb 2005 - p76(2) [51-500]
  c   KR - v72 - i20 - Oct 15 2004 - p1006(1) [51-500]
  c   SLJ - v50 - i11 - Nov 2004 - p104(1) [51-500]

Gram, Malene - *Grounds to Play: Culture-specific Ideals in the Upbringing of Children in France, Germany, and the Netherlands*
  R&R Bk N - v19 - i2 - May 2004 - p135 [51-500]

Grambling, Lois G. - *Shoo! Scat! (Illus. by Newman, Barbara Johansen)*
  c   SLJ - v50 - i11 - Nov 2004 - p104(1) [51-500]
  The Witch Who Wanted to Be a Princess (Illus. by Love, Judy)
  c   RT - v57 - Oct 2003 - p172 [1-50]

Grambo, Rebecca L. - *Digging Canadian Dinosaurs*
  c   Res Links - v10 - i1 - Oct 2004 - p23(1) [51-500]
  Lupe: A Wolf Pup's First Year (Illus. by Cox, Daniel J.)
  c   Globe & Mail - Dec 11 2004 - pD43 [51-500]

Grambs, Alison - *Hilarious Halloween Jokes (Illus. by Harpster, Steve)*
  c   SLJ - v50 - i10 - Oct 2004 - p140(1) [51-500]

Gramm, Kent - *Somebody's Darling: Essays on the Civil War*
  Sew R - v112 - i1 - Wntr 2004 - p138-147 [501+]

Grammer, Elizabeth Elkin - *Some Wild Visions: Autobiographies by Female Itinerant Evangelists in 19th-Century America*
  JR - v85 - i1 - Jan 2005 - p124(2) [501+]

Gramsch, Robert - *Erfurter Juristen im Spatmittelalter: Die Karrieremuster und Tatigkeitsfelder einer gelehrten Elite des 14. und 15. Jahrhunderts*
  Ren Q - v57 - i3 - Fall 2004 - p1045(3) [501+]
  CHR - v90 - i3 - July 2004 - p535(2) [501+]

Granado, Alberto - *Traveling with Che Guevara: The Making of a Revolutionary*
  y   Kliatt - v39 - i2 - March 2005 - p41(2) [51-500]
  KR - v72 - i15 - August 1 2004 - p725(1) [501+]
  LJ - v129 - i14 - Sept 1 2004 - p162(1) [51-500]
  PW - v251 - i35 - August 30 2004 - p42(1) [51-500]

Granas, Andrzej - *Fixed Point Theory*
  JEL - v41 - i4 - Dec 2003 - p1339(1) [501+]

Granatstein, J.L. - *Battle Lines: Eyewitness Accounts from Canada's Military History*
  Beav - v85 - i1 - Feb-March 2005 - p49(1) [51-500]
  Globe & Mail - Nov 6 2004 - pD15 [501+]
  Canada and the Two World Wars
  CBRA - Annual 2003 - p289(1) [51-500]
  Canada's Army: Waging War and Keeping the Peace
  HNet - Sept 2004 - pNA [501+]
  R&R Bk N - v19 - i4 - Nov 2004 - p252(1) [501+]
  Hell's Corner: An Illustrated History of Canada's Great War, 1914-1918
  Globe & Mail - August 28 2004 - pD8 [501+]
  Who Killed the Canadian Military?
  HNet - Oct 2004 - pNA [501+]

Granby, Alan - *A Yachtsman's Eye: The Glen S. Foster Collection of Marine Paintings*
  Mag Antiq - v167 - i1 - Jan 2005 - p128(1) [51-500]
  Mag Antiq - v167 - i2 - Feb 2005 - p54(1) [51-500]
  Mag Antiq - v167 - i3 - March 2005 - p58(1) [501+]

Grand, Joe - *Hardware Hacking: Have Fun While Voiding Your Warranty*
  LJ - v129 - i16 - Oct 1 2004 - p104(1) [51-500]

Grand, Steve - *Growing up with Lucy: How to Build an Android in Twenty Easy Steps*
  TimHES - v0 - i1661 - Oct 8 2004 - p31(1) [501+]

Grande, Natalie - *Madeleine De Scudery: Mathilde*
  FS - v58 - i1 - Jan 2004 - p99(2) [501+]

Grande, Sandy - *Red Pedagogy: Native American Social and Political Thought*
  R&R Bk N - v19 - i4 - Nov 2004 - p54(1) [51-500]

Grandi, Guido - *Genomics, Proteomics and Vaccines*
  E-Streams - Oct 2004 - pNA [501+]

Grandin, Greg - *The Last Colonial Massacre: Latin America in the Cold War*
  Lon R Bks - v26 - i22 - Nov 18 2004 - p3(3) [501+]

Grandin, Temple - *Animals in Translation: Using the Mysteries of Autism to Decode Animal Behavior*
  BL - v101 - i6 - Nov 15 2004 - p539(1) [501+]
  Ent W - i798 - Dec 24 2004 - p73 [501+]
  Globe & Mail - Jan 29 2005 - pD3 [501+]
  LJ - v129 - i20 - Dec 1 2004 - p154(2) [51-500]
  NYTBR - Dec 26 2004 - p16 [501+]
  People - v63 - i4 - Jan 31 2005 - p47 [51-500]
  PW - v251 - i42 - Oct 18 2004 - p55(1) [51-500]

Grandits, Hannes - *Familie und sozialer Wandel im landlichen Kroatien 18.-20. Jahrhundert*
  HNet - June 2004 - pNA [501+]

Grandits, John - *Technically, It's Not My Fault: Concrete Poems (Illus. by Grandits, John)*
  c   BL - v101 - i8 - Dec 15 2004 - p739(1) [51-500]
  c   CCB-B - v58 - i5 - Jan 2005 - p210(1) [51-500]
  c   KR - v72 - i20 - Oct 15 2004 - p1006(1) [51-500]
  c   PW - v251 - i49 - Dec 6 2004 - p61(1) [51-500]
  c   SLJ - v50 - i12 - Dec 2004 - p161(1) [51-500]

Granfield, Linda - *America Votes: How Our President Is Elected (Illus. by Bjorkman, Steve)*
  c   BL - v101 - i3 - Oct 1 2004 - p327(1) [51-500]
  c   LibMed - v22 - i6 - March 2004 - p86(1) [501+]
  c   SLJ - v50 - i8 - August 2004 - p49(1) [51-500]

Grange, Jean-Christophe - *The Empire of the Wolves*
  BL - v101 - i8 - Dec 15 2004 - p711(1) [51-500]
  Globe & Mail - March 19 2005 - pD15 [51-500]
  KR - v72 - i22 - Nov 15 2004 - p1061(1) [51-500]
  NYTBR - Jan 9 2005 - p17 [501+]
  PW - v251 - i48 - Nov 29 2004 - p22(1) [51-500]
Granger, Ann - *Flowers for His Funeral (Read by Boyd, Judith). Audiobook Review*
  y Kliatt - v39 - i1 - Jan 2005 - p42(1) [51-500]
  That Way Murder Lies: A Mitchell and Markby Mystery
  BL - v101 - i9-10 - Jan 1 2005 - p826(2) [1-50]
  KR - v72 - i24 - Dec 15 2004 - p1167(2) [501+]
  LJ - v130 - i2 - Feb 1 2005 - p57(1) [1-50]
  PW - v252 - i4 - Jan 24 2005 - p226(1) [51-500]
Granger, John - *Looking for God in Harry Potter*
  Ch Today - v48 - i10 - Oct 2004 - p111(2) [501+]
Granger, Pip - *Trouble in Paradise*
  BL - v101 - i8 - Dec 15 2004 - p711(1) [51-500]
  KR - v72 - i23 - Dec 1 2004 - p1120(1) [51-500]
  PW - v251 - i51 - Dec 20 2004 - p40(2) [51-500]
Granieri, Ronald J. - *The Ambivalent Alliance: Konrad Adenauer, the CDU/CSU, and the West, 1949-1966*
  AHR - v109 - i3 - June 2004 - p992(2) [501+]
  GSR - v27 - i1 - Feb 2004 - p197-199 [501+]
Grant, Barry Keith - *John Ford's Stagecoach*
  FQ - v58 - i1 - Fall 2004 - p70(2) [501+]
Grant Gould, Carol - *The Remarkable Life of William Beebe, Explorer and Naturalist*
  New Sci - v184 - i2473 - Nov 13 2004 - p56(2) [51-500]
Grant, Ian Lyall - *Burma: The Turning Point, The Seven Battles on the Tiddim Road Which Turned the Tide of the Burma War*
  R&R Bk N - v19 - i3 - August 2004 - p55(1) [51-500]
Grant, James - *John Adams: Party of One*
  BL - v101 - i9-10 - Jan 1 2005 - p808(2) [51-500]
  KR - v72 - i23 - Dec 1 2004 - p1131(2) [501+]
  LJ - v130 - i1 - Jan 1 2005 - p123(1) [51-500]
  PW - v252 - i11 - March 14 2005 - p56(2) [51-500]
Grant, Jessica - *Making Light of Tragedy*
  Globe & Mail - Sept 25 2004 - pD24 [501+]
Grant, Jon E. - *Munchausen by Proxy: Identification, Intervention, and Case Management*
  SciTech - v28 - i4 - Dec 2004 - p101(1) [51-500]
Grant, K.M. - *Blood Red Horse Bk. 1*
  c KR - v73 - i5 - March 1 2005 - p287(1) [51-500]
Grant, Mark N. - *The Rise and Fall of the Broadway Musical*
  BL - v101 - i5 - Nov 1 2004 - p457(1) [51-500]
  LJ - v129 - i18 - Nov 1 2004 - p86(2) [51-500]
Grant, Michael - *Cleopatra*
  LJ - v129 - i15 - Sept 15 2004 - p91(1) [51-500]
Grant, Michael Johnston - *Down and Out on the Family Farm: Rural Rehabilitation in the Great Plains, 1929-1945*
  JAH - v91 - i1 - June 2004 - p285-286 [501+]
  WHQ - v35 - i1 - Spring 2004 - p98-99 [501+]
Grant, Nathan - *Masculinist Impulses: Toomer, Horston, Black Writing, and Modernity*
  Choice - v42 - i3 - Nov 2004 - p483(1) [1-50]
Grant, Nicola - *Don't Be so Nosy, Posy!*
  c Sch Lib - v52 - i4 - Winter 2004 - p187(1) [51-500]
Grant, Paul - *Stanley Park Companion*
  CBRA - Annual 2003 - p341(1) [51-500]
Grant, Paul D. - *Baptism by Ice: How Hockey Taught an American to Love Canada*
  Globe & Mail - Oct 30 2004 - pD18 [501+]
Grant, Peter (b. 1948 -) - *Wish You Were Here: Life on Vancouver Island in Historical Postcards*
  CBRA - Annual 2003 - p114(1) [501+]
Grant, Peter S. - *Blockbusters and Trade Wars: Popular Culture in a Globalized World*
  R&R Bk N - v19 - i4 - Nov 2004 - p121(1) [51-500]
Grant, Phil - *The Law of Escalating Marginal Sacrifice: Explaining a Plethora of Heretofore Unresolved Motivation Phenomena*
  R&R Bk N - v19 - i3 - August 2004 - p127(1) [51-500]
Grant, R.G. - *The African-American Slave Trade*
  LibMed - v22 - i4 - Jan 2004 - p76(1) [501+]
  Protesting Capitalism
  y SLJ - v50 - i7 - July 2004 - p122(1) [51-500]
Grant, Richard P. - *Computational Genomics: Theory and Application*
  SciTech - v28 - i4 - Dec 2004 - p62(1) [51-500]
Grant, Rickford - *Linux for Non-Geeks: A Hands-on, Project-Based, Take-It-Slow Guidebook*
  SciTech - v28 - i3 - Sept 2004 - p26(1) [51-500]

Grant, Robert (b. 1945 -) - *Imagining the Real: Essays on Politics, Ideology, and Literature*
  R&R Bk N - v19 - i1 - Feb 2004 - p147(1) [51-500]
Grant, Robert M. - *Paul in the Roman World: the Conflict at Corinth*
  JR - v84 - i4 - Oct 2004 - p604(2) [501+]
Grant, Roger - *Getting Around: Exploring Transportation History*
  Pub Hist - v26 - i2 - Spring 2004 - p106(107) [501+]
Grant, Susan - *The Scarlet Empress*
  BL - v101 - i6 - Nov 15 2004 - p568(1) [51-500]
  PW - v251 - i47 - Nov 22 2004 - p44(1) [51-500]
Grant, Susan-Mary - *Legacy of Disunion: The Enduring Significance of the American Civil War*
  AHR - v109 - i3 - June 2004 - p913(2) [501+]
  JSH - v70 - i3 - August 2004 - p696(2) [501+]
Grant, Ted - *Women in Medicine: A Celebration of Their Work*
  Globe & Mail - August 14 2004 - pD12 [1-50]
  SciTech - v28 - i4 - Dec 2004 - p76(1) [51-500]
Grant, Vicki - *Halifax Citadel (Illus. by Pilsworth, Graham)*
  c CBRA - Annual 2003 - p535(2) [51-500]
  The Puppet Wrangler
  c CCB-B - v57 - i11 - July-August 2004 - p466(1) [501+]
  y Kliatt - v38 - i5 - Sept 2004 - p20(2) [51-500]
  c SLJ - v50 - i8 - August 2004 - p122(1) [51-500]
  c VOYA - v27 - i5 - Dec 2004 - p404(1) [51-500]
Grantley, Darryll - *English Dramatic Interludes, 1300-1580: A Reference Guide*
  Choice - v42 - i2 - Oct 2004 - p266(1) [51-500]
The Grants Register 2005, 23rd Ed.
  Choice - v42 - i4 - Dec 2004 - p625(1) [1-50]
Granville, Brigitte - *The Economics of Essential Medicines*
  JEL - v42 - i1 - March 2004 - p195(3) [501+]
Granville, Johanna C. - *The First Domino: International Decision Making During the Hungarian Crisis of 1956*
  Choice - v42 - i1 - Sept 2004 - p168(1) [501+]
  J Mil H - v68 - i4 - Oct 2004 - p1310-1311 [501+]
Granz, Nicholas - *Graffiti World: Street Art from the Five Continents*
  PW - v251 - i41 - Oct 11 2004 - p73(1) [51-500]
Grapham, Otis L. - *Unguarded Gates*
  Bwatch - v26 - i9 - Sept 2004 - p12(1) [501+]
Graphic, David B. - *Epileptic*
  Ent W - i801 - Jan 14 2005 - p95 [51-500]
Grare, Frederic - *Beyond the Rhetoric: The Economics of India's Look East Policy*
  JAS - v63 - i2 - May 2004 - p532(2) [501+]
Grassian, Daniel - *Hybrid Fictions: American Literature and Generation X*
  Choice - v41 - i7 - March 2004 - p1296(1) [501+]
Grasso, June M. - *Modernization and Revolution in China: From the Opium Wars to World Power, 3rd Ed.*
  R&R Bk N - v19 - i4 - Nov 2004 - p49(1) [51-500]
Grasso, Patrick G. - *World Bank Operations Evaluation Department: The First Thirty Years*
  JEL - v41 - i4 - Dec 2003 - p1360(1) [501+]
Graton Ash, Timothy - *Free World: Why a Crisis of the West Reveals the Opportunity of Our Time*
  NS - v133 - i4698 - July 26 2004 - p48(2) [501+]
  Spec - v295 - i9184 - August 14 2004 - p32(2) [501+]
Grau, Oliver - *Virtual Art: From Illusion to Immersion*
  Afterimage - v32 - i4 - Jan-Feb 2005 - p15(1) [51-500]
  T&C - v45 - i3 - July 2004 - p670-671 [501+]
Grau, Shirley Ann - *The Keepers of the House*
  LJ - v129 - i17 - Oct 15 2004 - p99(1) [51-500]
Graubard, Stephen - *Command of Office: How War, Secrecy, and Deception Transformed the Presidency, from Theodore Roosevelt to George W. Bush*
  KR - v72 - i18 - Sept 15 2004 - p901(2) [501+]
  LJ - v129 - i17 - Oct 15 2004 - p76(1) [51-500]
  Command of Office: How War, Secrecy and Deception Transformed the Presidency From Theodore Roosevelt to George W. Bush
  NYTBR - Feb 27 2005 - p21 [501+]
  Command of Office: How War, Secrecy, and Deception Transformed the Presidency, from Theodore Roosevelt to George W. Bush
  PW - v251 - i43 - Oct 25 2004 - p38(1) [51-500]
  The Presidents: The Transformation of the American Presidency from Theodore Roosevelt to George W. Bush
  Spec - v297 - i9209 - Feb 5 2005 - p45(2) [501+]
Graulich, Melody - *Reading The Virginian in the New West*
  WHQ - v35 - i2 - Summer 2004 - p227-227 [501+]

Graumann, L.A. - *Die Krankengeschichten der Epidemienbucher des Corpus Hippocraticum. Medizinhistorische Bedeutung und Moglichkeiten der retrospektiven Diagnose*
  Class R - v54 - i2 - Nov 2004 - p294-295 [501+]
Gravelle, Karen - *The Driving Book: Everything New Drivers Need to Know But Don't Know to Ask (Illus. by Flook, Helen)*
  c PW - v252 - i11 - March 14 2005 - p70(1) [501+]
Graves, Alun - *Tiles and Tilework*
  Ceram Mo - v52 - i2 - Feb 2004 - p30(2) [501+]
Graves, Donald E. - *In Peril on the Sea: The Royal Canadian Navy and the Battle of the Atlantic*
  CBRA - Annual 2003 - p289(1) [501+]
Graves, Donald H. - *Writing: Teachers and Children at Work, 20th ed.*
  R&R Bk N - v19 - i1 - Feb 2004 - p184(1) [51-500]
Graves, Jane - *Light My Fire*
  PW - v251 - i42 - Oct 18 2004 - p53(1) [51-500]
Graves, Joseph L., Jr. - *The Race Myth: Why We Pretend Race Exists in America*
  Choice - v42 - i6 - Feb 2005 - p1104(1) [51-500]
  R&R Bk N - v19 - i4 - Nov 2004 - p59(1) [51-500]
Graves, Joseph L., Jr. - *The Race Myth: Why We Pretend Race Exists in America*
  Bwatch - Jan 2005 - pNA [51-500]
Graves, Keith - *Three Nasty Gnarlies*
  LibMed - v22 - i4 - Jan 2004 - p58(1) [501+]
Graves, Michael A.R. - *Henry VIII: A Study in Kingship*
  CR - v285 - i1662 - July 2004 - p62(2) [51-500]
Graves Myers, Beverle - *Interrupted Aria: A Baroque Mystery*
  DroRevMy - v24 - i3 - May-June 2004 - p3(1) [501+]
Graves, Sarah - *Mallets Aforethought (Read by Ellison, Lindsay). Audiobook Review*
  y Kliatt - v38 - i5 - Sept 2004 - p62(3) [51-500]
  Tool & Die
  KR - v72 - i23 - Dec 1 2004 - p1120(1) [51-500]
  LJ - v129 - i20 - Dec 1 2004 - p95(1) [51-500]
  PW - v251 - i44 - Nov 1 2004 - p46(2) [501+]
Graves, Theodore D. - *Behavioral Anthropology: Toward an Integrated Science of Human Behavior*
  R&R Bk N - v19 - i3 - August 2004 - p83(1) [51-500]
  Studies in Behavioral Anthropology (reprint, 2002).
  R&R Bk N - v19 - i3 - August 2004 - p83(1) [51-500]
Gravett, Paul - *Manga: Sixty Years of Japanese Comics*
  LJ - v130 - i1 - Jan 1 2005 - p89(1) [51-500]
Grawe, Klaus - *Psychological Therapy*
  SciTech - v28 - i4 - Dec 2004 - p96(1) [51-500]
Gray, Alex - *A Small Weeping*
  LJ - v130 - i2 - Feb 1 2005 - p57(1) [51-500]
Gray, Anne - *The Edwardians: Secrets and Desires*
  Choice - v42 - i5 - Jan 2005 - p843(2) [51-500]
  LJ - v129 - i20 - Dec 1 2004 - p110(2) [51-500]
Gray, Breda - *Women and the Irish Diaspora*
  Choice - v42 - i4 - Dec 2004 - p741(2) [1-50]
Gray, Charlotte - *Canada: A Portrait in Letters, 1800-2000*
  CBRA - Annual 2003 - p276(1) [501+]
  Canada: A Portrait in Letters. Audiobook Review
  Globe & Mail - Dec 4 2004 - pD38 [1-50]
  Flint and Feather: The Life and Times of E. Pauline Johnson, Tekahionwake
  Can Lit - i182 - Autumn 2004 - p132(2) [501+]
  The Museum Called Canada: 25 Rooms of Wonder
  Beav - v84 - i6 - Dec 2004 - p49(1) [51-500]
  Globe & Mail - Nov 6 2004 - pD4 [501+]
  Globe & Mail - Nov 13 2004 - pF2 [501+]
Gray, Colin S. - *The Sheriff: America's Defense of the New World Order*
  Choice - v42 - i6 - Feb 2005 - p1094(1) [51-500]
  NWCR - v57 - Autumn 2004 - p153(3) [501+]
Gray, David - *Dead Is Forever*
  PW - v252 - i1 - Jan 3 2005 - p39(1) [51-500]
Gray, Douglas - *The Oxford Companion to Chaucer*
  Choice - v42 - i1 - Sept 2004 - p66(1) [501+]
Gray, Ed - *40 Days to a Life of G.O.L.D.*
  Black Iss - v6 - i6 - Nov-Dec 2004 - p18(1) [51-500]
Gray, Farrah - *Reallionaire: Nine Steps to Becoming Rich from the Inside Out*
  BL - v101 - i7 - Dec 1 2004 - p623(1) [51-500]
  PW - v251 - i47 - Nov 22 2004 - p46(1) [51-500]

Gray, Frances Clayton - *Born to Win: The Authorized Biography of Althea Gibson*
  BL - v101 - i1 - Sept 1 2004 - p47(1) [51-500]
  PW - v251 - i32 - August 9 2004 - p242(1) [51-500]

Gray, Francine du Plessix - *Them: A Memoir of Parents*
  KR - v73 - i4 - Feb 15 2005 - p209(2) [501+]
  PW - v252 - i10 - March 7 2005 - p58(1) [51-500]

Gray, Gregory E. - *Concise Guide to Evidence-Based Psychiatry*
  E-Streams - August 2004 - pNA [501+]
  SciTech - v28 - i1 - March 2004 - p96(1) [51-500]

Gray, H. Peter - *Extending the Eclectic Paradigm in International Business: Essays in Honor of John Dunning*
  JEL - v41 - i4 - Dec 2003 - p1356(1) [501+]

Gray, J.S. - *Lyme Borreliosis: Biology, Epidemiology and Control*
  QRB - v79 - i3 - Sept 2004 - p343(2) [501+]

Gray, Janet - *Race and Time: American Women's Poetics from Antislavery to Racial Modernity*
  Choice - v42 - i1 - Sept 2004 - p100(2) [501+]

Gray, Jeremy J. - *Janos Bolyai, Non-Euclidean Geometry, and the Nature of Space*
  Sci - v306 - i5703 - Dec 10 2004 - p1893(2) [501+]

Gray, John (b. 1934 -) - *Paul Martin in the Balance. Audiobook Review*
  Globe & Mail - Dec 18 2004 - pD25 [1-50]

Gray, John (b. 1937 -) - *Paul Martin: The Power of Ambition*
  BIC - v33 - i2 - March 2004 - p32(2) [501+]
  CBRA - Annual 2003 - p46(2) [51-500]

Gray, John (b. 1938 -) - *Long Live Latin: A Latin Miscellany*
  Spec - v297 - i9209 - Feb 5 2005 - p43(2) [501+]

Gray, John (b. 1948 -) - *Al Qaeda and What It Means to Be Modern*
  Soc - v41 - i6 - Sept-Oct 2004 - p86(3) [501+]
  Heresies
  NS - v133 - i4716 - Nov 29 2004 - p42(1) [51-500]

Gray, John (b. 1965 -) - *Programmed Cell Death in Plants*
  QRB - v79 - i3 - Sept 2004 - p310(2) [501+]

Gray, John MacLachlan - *Fiend in Human*
  CBRA - Annual 2003 - p167(1) [51-500]

Gray, Keith - *Creepers*
  y Sch Lib - v52 - i4 - Winter 2004 - p211(1) [51-500]

Gray, Kes - *Baby on Board (Illus. by Nayler, Sarah)*
  c SLJ - v50 - i7 - July 2004 - p76(1) [51-500]
  Bebe a bordo/Baby on Board (Illus. by Nayler, Sarah)
  c BL - v100 - i22 - August 2004 - p1950(1) [501+]
  Our Twitchy
  c Sch Lib - v52 - i4 - Winter 2004 - p186(1) [51-500]

Gray, Leon - *Iodine*
  c BL - v101 - i7 - Dec 1 2004 - p665(1) [51-500]

Gray, Madeleine - *Protestant Reformation: Belief, Practice, and Tradition*
  R&R Bk N - v19 - i1 - Feb 2004 - p16(1) [51-500]

Gray, Margaret - *The Lovesick Salesman (Illus. by Cecil, Randy)*
  c BL - v101 - i9-10 - Jan 1 2005 - p858(1) [1-50]
  c CCB-B - v58 - i3 - Nov 2004 - p122(1) [501+]
  c KR - v72 - i20 - Oct 15 2004 - p1006(1) [51-500]
  SLJ - v50 - i12 - Dec 2004 - p146(1) [501+]

Gray, Martin - *Blues for Bird*
  Can Lit - i181 - Summer 2004 - p96-97 [501+]

Gray, Mike - *Warning; Accident at Three Mile Island*
  SciTech - v28 - i3 - Sept 2004 - p151(1) [51-500]

Gray, Patrick - *Godly fear; the Epistle to the Hebrews and Greco-Roman critiques of superstition*
  R&R Bk N - v19 - i3 - August 2004 - p25(1) [1-50]

Gray, Peter - *Victoria's Ireland?: Irishness and Britishness, 1837-1901*
  R&R Bk N - v19 - i4 - Nov 2004 - p38(1) [51-500]

Gray, Ralph D. - *IUPUI: The Making of an Urban University*
  HNet - August 2004 - pNA [501+]

Gray, Rich - *Click or Treat: The Best of Halloween and Horror on the Internet*
  R&R Bk N - v19 - i4 - Nov 2004 - p79(1) [51-500]

Gray, Richard - *A Companion to the Literature and Culture of the American South*
  Choice - v42 - i4 - Dec 2004 - p628(1) [1-50]
  A History of American Literature
  Choice - v41 - i11-12 - July-August 2004 - p2043(2) [501+]
  TimHES - v0 - i1656 - Sept 3 2004 - p26(1) [501+]

Gray, Rita - *Nonna's Porch (Illus. by Widener, Terry)*
  c KR - v72 - i20 - Oct 15 2004 - p1007(1) [51-500]
  c PW - v251 - i48 - Nov 29 2004 - p39(1) [51-500]
  c SLJ - v50 - i11 - Nov 2004 - p104(1) [51-500]

Gray, Ross - *Standing Ovation: Performing Social Science Research about Cancer*
  CS - v33 - i1 - Jan 2004 - p121-122 [501+]

Gray, Simon - *The Smoking Diaries*
  Globe & Mail - August 28 2004 - pD13 [501+]
  NS - v133 - i4716 - Nov 29 2004 - p43(1) [51-500]
  TLS - i5284 - July 9 2004 - p18(1) [51-500]

Gray, Susan H. - *Apatosaurus*
  c SLJ - v50 - i9 - Sept 2004 - p188(1) [51-500]
  Circulatory System
  c SB - v40 - i4 - July-August 2004 - p149(1) [51-500]
  Coelophysis
  c SLJ - v50 - i9 - Sept 2004 - p188(1) [51-500]
  Digestive System
  c SB - v40 - i4 - July-August 2004 - p149(1) [51-500]
  Iguanodon
  c SLJ - v50 - i9 - Sept 2004 - p188(1) [51-500]
  Megalosaurus
  c SLJ - v51 - i2 - Feb 2005 - p120(1) [51-500]
  Muscular System
  c SB - v40 - i4 - July-August 2004 - p149(1) [51-500]
  Nervous System
  c SB - v40 - i4 - July-August 2004 - p149(1) [51-500]
  Oviraptor
  c SLJ - v50 - i9 - Sept 2004 - p188(1) [51-500]
  Psittacosaurus
  c SLJ - v51 - i2 - Feb 2005 - p120(1) [51-500]
  Respiratory System
  c SB - v40 - i4 - July-August 2004 - p149(1) [51-500]
  Skeletal System
  c SB - v40 - i4 - July-August 2004 - p149(1) [51-500]

Gray, T.M. - *Ghosts of Eden*
  LJ - v130 - i1 - Jan 1 2005 - p103(1) [51-500]

Gray, William - *Robert Louis Stevenson: A Literary Life*
  Choice - v42 - i3 - Nov 2004 - p483(1) [1-50]
  CR - v285 - i1665 - Oct 2004 - p252(2) [501+]

Graydon, Shari - *The Culture of Beauty*
  y BL - v101 - i8 - Dec 15 2004 - p738(1) [51-500]
  Made You Look: How Advertising Works and Why You Should Know (Illus. by Clark, Warren)
  c CBRA - Annual 2003 - p550(1) [501+]
  c Mac - Jan 26 2004 - p47(1) [51-500]
  SLJ - v50 - i10 - Oct 2004 - pS47(1) [51-500]
  y Teach Lib - v32 - i3 - Feb 2005 - p15(1) [51-500]

Grayling, A.C. - *The Mystery of Things*
  Globe & Mail - Dec 24 2004 - pD14 [51-500]
  Mac - May 17 2004 - p55(1) [51-500]
  What Is Good? The Search for the Best Way to Live
  CR - v285 - i1662 - July 2004 - p57(2) [501+]

Grazia, Victoria De - *Irresistible Empire: America's Advance Through 20th-Century Europe*
  PW - v252 - i7 - Feb 14 2005 - p64(2) [501+]

Graziani, Augusto - *The Monetary Theory of Production*
  JEL - v42 - i1 - March 2004 - p257(1) [501+]

Graziani, Robert - *Robert Smithson and the American Landscape*
  TLS - i5300 - Oct 29 2004 - p12(1) [501+]

Graziano, Frank - *Wounds of Love: The Mystical Marriage of Saint Rose of Lima*
  Choice - v42 - i1 - Sept 2004 - p84(1) [501+]

Graziosi, Barbara - *Inventing Homer: The Early Reception of Epic*
  CJ - v99 - i3 - Feb-March 2004 - p343-345 [501+]
  Class R - v54 - i1 - May 2004 - p20(3) [501+]

Gready, Paul - *Fighting for Human Rights*
  CR - v285 - i1667 - Dec 2004 - p384(1) [51-500]

Greaney, Michael - *Conrad, Language, and Narrative*
  ELT - v47 - i4 - Fall 2004 - p470(5) [501+]

Greaser, Galen D. - *Catalogue of the Spanish Collection of the General Land Office, Part I*
  SHQ - v108 - i1 - July 2004 - p114-114 [501+]
  Catalogue of the Spanish Collection of the General Land Office, Part II
  SHQ - v108 - i1 - July 2004 - p114-115 [501+]

Great Battles through the Ages
  LibMed - v23 - i1 - August-Sept 2004 - p75(1) [51-500]

Great Cities of the World
  y Ref Rev - June 2004 - pNA [501+]

The Great Depression
  LibMed - v22 - i4 - Jan 2004 - p76(1) [501+]

Great Events from History: The Ancient World, Prehistory-476 C.E., Vols. 1-2
  Choice - v42 - i4 - Dec 2004 - p638(2) [1-50]

Great Events from History: The Ancient World, Prehistory--476 C.E., Vols. 1-2
  y SLJ - v50 - i10 - Oct 2004 - p91(1) [51-500]

Great Life Stories- Inventors And Scientists
  LibMed - v22 - i7 - April-May 2004 - p66(1) [501+]

Great Life Stories- Political Figures
  LibMed - v22 - i7 - April-May 2004 - p66(1) [501+]

Great Life Stories- Writers and Poets
  LibMed - v22 - i7 - April-May 2004 - p66(1) [501+]

Great Lives from History: The Ancient World, Prehistory--476 C.E., Vols. 1-2
  y SLJ - v50 - i10 - Oct 2004 - p91(1) [51-500]

Great Military Leaders of the 20th Century
  LibMed - v22 - i7 - April-May 2004 - p66(1) [501+]

Great Moments in Baseball
  c LibMed - v22 - i4 - Jan 2004 - p82(1) [501+]

Great Moments in Hockey
  c LibMed - v22 - i4 - Jan 2004 - p82(1) [501+]

Great Scientists
  LibMed - v22 - i4 - Jan 2004 - p72(1) [501+]

Greatrex, Geoffrey - *The Roman Eastern Frontier and the Persian Wars, Part II: AD 363-630*
  Class R - v54 - i1 - May 2004 - p186(2) [501+]

Greatshell, Walter - *Xombies*
  ChrSFF&H - v26 - i10 - Oct 2004 - p27(1) [51-500]

Greaves, David - *The Healing Tradition: Reviving the Soul of Western Medicine*
  SciTech - v28 - i4 - Dec 2004 - p81(1) [51-500]

Greaves, J. David - *Clinical Teaching: A Guide to Teaching Practical Anaesthesia*
  E-Streams - July 2004 - pNA [501+]

Greaves, Malcolm W. - *Urticaria and Angioedema*
  SciTech - v28 - i3 - Sept 2004 - p120(1) [51-500]

Greaves, Richard L. - *Glimpses of Glory: John Bunyan and English Dissent*
  AHR - v109 - i3 - June 2004 - p971(2) [501+]
  Lon R Bks - v26 - i24 - Dec 16 2004 - p11(4) [501+]
  CHR - v90 - i3 - July 2004 - p556(2) [501+]

Greban, Tanguy - *Sarah So Small (Illus. by Greban, Quentin)*
  c BL - v101 - i9-10 - Jan 1 2005 - p869(1) [51-500]
  c SLJ - v50 - i10 - Oct 2004 - p114(1) [51-500]

Grebenikov, E.A. - *Asymptotic Methods in Resonance Analytical Dynamics*
  SciTech - v28 - i3 - Sept 2004 - p39(1) [51-500]

Grebennikov, Andrei - *RF and Microwave Power Amplifier Design*
  SciTech - v28 - i4 - Dec 2004 - p157(1) [51-500]
  SciTech - v28 - i4 - Dec 2004 - p157(1) [51-500]

Grebler, Eric - *Adobe Audition Ignite!*
  R&R Bk N - v19 - i4 - Nov 2004 - p197(1) [501+]

Grebler, Ron - *Adobe Photoshop CS Image Effects*
  SciTech - v28 - i4 - Dec 2004 - p130 [51-500]

Greco, Francesca - *Cyril the Mandrill*
  KR - v73 - i1 - Jan 1 2005 - p52(1) [51-500]

Greco, Kathleen - *Yummy Yarns: Learn To Knit in 20+ Easy Projects Featuring Fun Novelty Yarns*
  LJ - v129 - i20 - Dec 1 2004 - p110(1) [51-500]

Greece
  R&R Bk N - v19 - i4 - Nov 2004 - p40(1) [51-500]

Greeley, Andrew M. - *The Catholic Revolution. New Wine, Old Wineskins, and the Second Vatican Council*
  AM - v191 - i5 - August 30 2004 - p22 [501+]
  The Catholic Revolution: New Wine, Old Wineskins, and the Second Vatican Council
  Choice - v41 - i11-12 - July-August 2004 - p2061(1) [501+]
  Theol St - v66 - i1 - March 2005 - p237(2) [501+]
  TLS - i5306 - Dec 10 2004 - p26(1) [501+]

Golden Years: the Sixth Chronicle of the O'Malley Family in the Twentieth Century
 KR - v72 - i16 - August 15 2004 - p778(1) [51-500]

Irish Cream: A Nuala Anne McGrail Novel
 KR - v73 - i1 - Jan 1 2005 - p23(1) [51-500]

Greeley, Andrew M - *Irish Cream: A Nuala Anne McGrail Novel*
 PW - v252 - i3 - Jan 17 2005 - p38(1) [51-500]

Greeley, Andrew M. - *The Priestly Sins (Read by Marosz, Jonathan). Audiobook Review*
 LJ - v130 - i2 - Feb 1 2005 - p122(1) [51-500]

Priests: A Calling in Crisis
 CI - v12 - i9 - Oct 2004 - p46(2) [501+]
 Theol St - v66 - i1 - March 2005 - p237(2) [501+]
 TLS - i5292 - Sept 3 2004 - p31(1) [501+]

Green, Andrew - *Writing the Great War: Sir James Edmonds and the Official Histories, 1915-1948*
 J Mil H - v68 - i3 - April 2004 - p624-625 [501+]

Green, Anna L. - *Journey to the Ph.D.: How to Navigate the Process as African Americans*
 R&R Bk N - v19 - i1 - Feb 2004 - p192(1) [51-500]

Green, Archie - *Torching the Fink Books and Other Essays on Vernacular Culture*
 WestFolk - v62 - i4 - Fall 2003 - p299(3) [501+]

Green, Arthur - *A Guide to the Zohar*
 Choice - v41 - i11-12 - July-August 2004 - p2061(1) [501+]
 Parabola - v29 - i2 - Summer 2004 - p92-98 [501+]

Green, Candida Lycett - *The Dangerous Edge of Things*
 Spec - v297 - i9211 - Feb 19 2005 - p39(1) [501+]

Green, Carl R. - *Apollo 11 Rockets to First Moon Landing*
 c BL - v101 - i1 - Oct 1 2004 - p325(1) [51-500]
 y SLJ - v51 - i1 - Jan 2005 - p148(1) [51-500]

Gemini 4 Spacewalk Mission
 c SB - v40 - i6 - Nov-Dec 2004 - p274(1) [51-500]

Green, Cheryl - *World Wide Search: The Savvy Christian's Guide to Online Dating*
 LJ - v129 - i12 - July 2004 - p106(1) [51-500]

Green, Christine - *Deadly Night*
 BL - v101 - i9-10 - Jan 1 2005 - p827(1) [1-50]

Green, Christopher D. - *Early Psychological Thought: Ancient Accounts of Mind and Soul*
 Choice - v41 - i7 - March 2004 - p1334(1) [501+]

Green, D.H. - *The Beginnings of Medieval Romance: Fact and Fiction, 1150-1220*
 RES - v55 - i221 - Sept 2004 - p613(2) [501+]

The Continental Saxons from the Migration Period to the Tenth Century: An Ethnographic Perspective
 Med R - June 2004 - pNA [501+]

Green, David - *Bleeding Disorders*
 SciTech - v28 - i4 - Dec 2004 - p102(1) [51-500]

Green, Dominic - *The Double Life of Doctor Lopez*
 BIC - v33 - i2 - March 2004 - p22(1) [501+]

Green, Donald P. - *Get Out the Vote: How to Increase Voter Turnout*
 R&R Bk N - v19 - i3 - August 2004 - p180(1) [501+]

Green, Duncan - *Silent Revolution: The Rise and Crisis of Market Economics in Latin America, 2nd Ed.*
 R&R Bk N - v19 - i1 - Feb 2004 - p82(1) [51-500]

Green, Edmund P. - *World Atlas of Seagrasses*
 E-Streams - August 2004 - pNA [501+]

Green, Edward C. - *Rethinking AIDS Prevention: Learning from Successes in Developing Countries*
 Choice - v42 - i1 - Sept 2004 - p138(1) [501+]
 SciTech - v28 - i1 - March 2004 - p83(1) [51-500]

Green, Edwin - *Crisis and Renewal in Twentieth Century Banking: Exploring History and Archives of Banking at Times of Political and Social Stress*
 R&R Bk N - v19 - i4 - Nov 2004 - p116(1) [51-500]

Green, Elna C. - *The New Deal and Beyond: Social Welfare in the South Since 1930*
 RAH - v32 - i2 - June 2004 - p231-8 [501+]

This Business of Relief: Confronting Poverty in a Southern City, 1740-1940
 HRNB - v33 - i1 - Fall 2004 - p13(1) [501+]
 JAH - v91 - i3 - Dec 2004 - p1043(2) [501+]
 R&R Bk N - v19 - i3 - August 2004 - p160(1) [51-500]

Green, Garo - *Dreamweaver MX: H.O.T, Hands-On Training*
 SciTech - v28 - i1 - March 2004 - p156(1) [51-500]

Green, Gene L. - *The Letters to the Thessalonians*
 Intpr - v59 - i1 - Jan 2005 - p94(1) [501+]

Green, George W. - *Special Use Vehicles*
 Ant&CM - v108 - i5 - July 2003 - p16(1) [501+]

Green, Gillian - *Traditional Textiles of Cambodia: Cultural Threads and Material Heritage*
 TimHES - v0 - i1673 - Jan 7 2005 - p25(1) [501+]

Green, Hardy - *The Age of Napoleon*
 Bus W - i3894 - August 2 2004 - p21 [501+]

Green, Heidi - *Rattlesnake Plantain*
 CBRA - Annual 2003 - p218(1) [51-500]

Green, Helen - *East Texas Daughter*
 SHQ - v108 - i1 - July 2004 - p133-134 [501+]

Green, Ian - *Print and Protestantism in Early Modern England*
 HNet - Sept 2004 - pNA [501+]

Green, J. Ronald - *With a Crooked Stick--The Films of Oscar Micheaux*
 Bl S - v34 - i3 - Fall 2004 - p72-72 [501+]

Green, Jamison - *Becoming a Visible Man*
 Advocate - Nov 23 2004 - p96(1) [51-500]
 R&R Bk N - v19 - i4 - Nov 2004 - p128(1) [1-50]

Green, Jane - *The Other Woman*
 Ent W - i809 - March 4 2005 - p77 [501+]
 KR - v73 - i2 - Jan 15 2005 - p71(1) [501+]

Green, John - *Looking for Alaska*
 y CCB-B - v58 - i6 - Feb 2005 - p252(1) [51-500]
 y HB - v81 - i2 - March-April 2005 - p201(2) [51-500]
 y Kliatt - v39 - i2 - March 2005 - p12(1) [51-500]
 KR - v73 - i5 - March 1 2005 - p287(1) [51-500]
 y PW - v252 - i6 - Feb 7 2005 - p61(1) [51-500]
 y SLJ - v51 - i2 - Feb 2005 - p136(1) [501+]

Green, John (b. 1945 -) - *Excel 2000 VBA Programmer's Reference*
 R&R Bk N - v19 - i4 - Nov 2004 - p112(1) [1-50]

Green, John C. - *The Christian Right in American Politics: Marching to the Millennium*
 J Ch St - v46 - i3 - Summer 2004 - p669(2) [501+]

Green, John F. - *Alice and the Birthday Giant (Illus. by Kovalski, Maryann)*
 y Can CL - i111-112 - Fall-Winter 2003 - p134(6) [501+]

Green, Joseph Michael - *Your Past and the Press: Controversial Presidential Appointments, a Study Focusing on the Impact of Interest Groups and Media Activity on the Appointment Process*
 R&R Bk N - v19 - i3 - August 2004 - p178(1) [501+]

Green, Mark - *What We Stand For: A Program for Progressive Patriotism*
 R&R Bk N - v19 - i3 - August 2004 - p179(1) [501+]

Green, Mark M. - *Organic Chemistry Principles and Industrial Practice*
 J Chem Ed - v81 - i8 - August 2004 - p1125-1126 [501+]

Green, Michael S. - *Freedom, Union, and Power: Lincoln and his Party During the Civil War*
 R&R Bk N - v19 - i3 - August 2004 - p67(1) [51-500]

Green, Michael Steven - *Nietsche and the Transcendental Tradition*
 GSR - v27 - i2 - May 2004 - p403-406 [501+]

Green MiniAtlas
 LJ - v129 - i16 - Oct 1 2004 - p109(2) [51-500]

Green, Peter - *Alexander of Macedon, 356-323 B.C.: A Historical Biography*
 New R - Nov 15 2004 - p28 [501+]

Green, Rhonda Gowler - *This Is the Teacher (Illus. by Lester, Mike)*
 c BL - v100 - i22 - August 2004 - p1948(1) [51-500]

Green, Richard K. - *A Primer on U.S. Housing Markets and Housing Policy*
 Choice - v41 - i7 - March 2004 - p1341(1) [501+]
 R&R Bk N - v19 - i1 - Feb 2004 - p101(1) [51-500]

Green, Risa - *Notes from the Underbelly*
 KR - v73 - i1 - Jan 1 2005 - p9(1) [51-500]
 PW - v252 - i4 - Jan 24 2005 - p118(1) [501+]

Green, Roger - *Hydra and the Bananas of Leonard Cohen: A Search for Serenity in the Sun*
 BIC - v33 - i8 - Nov 2004 - p18(1) [501+]

Green, Ronald J. - *With a Crooked Stick- The Films of Oscar Micheaux*
 Choice - v42 - i2 - Oct 2004 - p300(1) [51-500]

Green, Sidney - *Rise and Fall of a Political Animal: A Memoir*
 CBRA - Annual 2003 - p47(1) [51-500]

Green, Simon F. - *An Introduction to the Sun and Stars*
 S&T - v109 - i1 - Jan 2005 - p120(2) [501+]

Green, Simon R. - *Deathstalker Coda*
 BL - v101 - i7 - Dec 1 2004 - p643(1) [51-500]
 Bwatch - March 2005 - pNA [51-500]
 PW - v252 - i1 - Jan 3 2005 - p41(1) [51-500]

Green, Thomas - *Pediatrics: Just the facts*
 SciTech - v28 - i4 - Dec 2004 - p111(1) [1-50]

Green, Thomas Arthur - *Martial Arts in the Modern World*
 Choice - v42 - i1 - Sept 2004 - p143(2) [501+]

Green, Thomas J. - *Building Dynamic Web Sites with Macromedia Studio MX 2004*
 SciTech - v28 - i1 - March 2004 - p156(1) [51-500]

Green, Tom - *Hollywood Causes Cancer: The Tom Green Story*
 Ent W - i786 - Oct 1 2004 - p77 [51-500]
 PW - v251 - i38 - Sept 20 2004 - p55(1) [51-500]

Green, W. John - *Gaitanismo, Left Liberalism, and Popular Mobilization in Colombia*
 AHR - v109 - i2 - April 2004 - p577(1) [501+]

Gaitanismo, Left Liberalism, and Popular Mobilization in Columbia
 HAHR - v84 - i4 - Nov 2004 - p758(3) [501+]

Greenan, Nathalie - *Productivity, Inequality, and the Digital Economy: A Transatlantic Perspective*
 JEL - v42 - i1 - March 2004 - p218(2) [501+]

Greenawalt, Kent - *Does God Belong in Public Schools?*
 LJ - v129 - i20 - Dec 1 2004 - p133(2) [51-500]
 PW - v251 - i40 - Oct 4 2004 - p76(1) [51-500]

Greenaway, John - *Drink and British Politics Since 1830: A Study in Policy-Making*
 R&R Bk N - v19 - i1 - Feb 2004 - p140(1) [51-500]

Greenberg, David - *Nixon's Shadow: The History of an Image*
 BW - v34 - i42 - Oct 17 2004 - p12(1) [501+]
 Choice - v41 - i11-12 - July-August 2004 - p2107(1) [501+]
 HNet - Sept 2004 - pNA [501+]
 HNet - Oct 2004 - pNA [501+]
 JAH - v91 - i3 - Dec 2004 - p1095(2) [501+]
 Lon R Bks - v26 - i21 - Nov 4 2004 - p15(4) [501+]
 NYTBR - Oct 31 2004 - p26 [501+]
 RAH - v32 - i1 - March 2004 - p122(6) [501+]

Greenberg, David (b. 1968 -) - *Nixon's Shadow: The History of an Image*
 R&R Bk N - v19 - i1 - Feb 2004 - p62(1) [501+]

Greenberg, David H. - *The Digest of Social Experiments, 3rd Ed.*
 Choice - v42 - i7 - March 2005 - p1206(2) [51-500]
 R&R Bk N - v19 - i4 - Nov 2004 - p124(1) [51-500]

Social Experimentation and Public Policymaking
 Choice - v41 - i7 - March 2004 - p1334(2) [501+]

Greenberg, Ellen - *The House and Senate Explained: The People's Guide to Congress*
 c SLJ - v50 - i8 - August 2004 - p49(1) [51-500]

Greenberg, Irving - *For the Sake of Heaven and Earth: The New Encounter Between Judaism and Christianity*
 PW - v251 - i37 - Sept 13 2004 - p73(1) [51-500]

For the Sake of Heaven and Earth: The New Encounter beween Judaism and Christianity
 Comw - v131 - i19 - Nov 5 2004 - p49(5) [501+]

Greenberg, Jan - *Andy Warhol: Prince of Pop*
 y BL - v101 - i9-10 - Jan 1 2005 - p772(1) [51-500]
 y CCB-B - v58 - i4 - Dec 2004 - p168(1) [51-500]
 y HB - v81 - i1 - Jan-Feb 2005 - p111(2) [51-500]
 y KR - v72 - i19 - Oct 1 2004 - p960(1) [51-500]
 y PW - v251 - i43 - Oct 25 2004 - p49(1) [51-500]
 y SLJ - v50 - i11 - Nov 2004 - p164(1) [51-500]
 y VOYA - v27 - i4 - Oct 2004 - p326(1) [51-500]

Chuck Close, Up Close
 c SLJ - v50 - i11 - Nov 2004 - p66(1) [51-500]

Heart to Heart: New Poems Inspired by Twentieth-Century American Art
 c SLJ - v50 - i11 - Nov 2004 - p66(1) [51-500]

Romare Bearden: Collage of Memories
 BooChiTr - Jan 4 2004 - p5(1) [501+]
 LibMed - v22 - i5 - Feb 2004 - p76(1) [501+]
 y Teach Lib - v32 - i1 - Oct 2004 - p30(1) [501+]

Greenberg, Judith - *Trauma at Home: After 9/11*
 Biomag - v27 - i3 - Summer 2004 - p663(3) [501+]

Greenberg, Karen J. - *The Torture Papers: The Road to Abu Ghraib*
 Globe & Mail - March 12 2005 - pD10 [501+]
 Lon R Bks - v27 - i4 - Feb 17 2005 - p21(4) [501+]
 Nation - v280 - i5 - Feb 7 2005 - p23 [501+]

Greenberg, Kenneth S. - *Nat Turner: A Slave Rebellion in History and Memory*
 HNet - June 2004 - pNA [501+]

Greenberg, Martin H. - *Faerie Tales*
  y Kliatt - v38 - i4 - July 2004 - p30(1) [51-500]
  Little Red Riding Hood in the Big Bad City
  y Kliatt - v39 - i2 - March 2005 - p28(1) [51-500]
Greenberg, Mitchell - *Baroque Bodies: Psychoanalysis and the Culture of French Absolutism*
  Comp L - v56 - i2 - Spring 2004 - p198-200 [501+]
Greenberg, Paul - *CRM at the Speed of Light: Essential Customer Strategies for the 21st Century, 3rd Ed.*
  R&R Bk N - v19 - i4 - Nov 2004 - p110(1) [51-500]
Greenberg, Raymond S. - *Medical Epidemiology, 4th ed.*
  SciTech - v28 - i4 - Dec 2004 - p84(1) [51-500]
Greenberg, Robert - *Kant's Theory of a Prior Knowledge*
  Dialogue - v43 - i1 - Wntr 2004 - p165-167 [501+]
Greenberg, Robert D. - *Language and Identity in the Balkans: Serbo-Croatian and its Disintegration*
  Choice - v42 - i5 - Jan 2005 - p858(2) [1-50]
Greenberg, Steve - *I Remember Woody: Recollections of the Man They Called Coach Hayes*
  BL - v101 - i1 - Sept 1 2004 - p47(2) [51-500]
Greenberg, Steven - *Wrestling with God and Men: Homosexuality in the Jewish Tradition*
  Choice - v42 - i3 - Nov 2004 - p500(1) [51-500]
  Lam Bk Rpt - v13 - i4-5 - Nov-Dec 2004 - p32(2) [501+]
  R&R Bk N - v19 - i4 - Nov 2004 - p17(1) [51-500]
Greenberg, Suzanne - *Speed-Walk and Other Stories*
  Ga R - v58 - i3 - Fall 2004 - p685-696 [501+]
Greenblatt, Stephen - *Will in the World: How Shakespeare Became Shakespeare*
  Atl - v294 - i5 - Dec 2004 - p129(5) [501+]
  BL - v101 - i1 - Sept 1 2004 - p39(2) [51-500]
  BW - v34 - i45 - Nov 7 2004 - p6(1) [501+]
  Forbes - v174 - i6 - Oct 4 2004 - p148 [501+]
  Globe & Mail - Oct 16 2004 - pD11 [501+]
  HM - v309 - i1852 - Sept 2004 - p85(2) [501+]
  KR - v72 - i13 - July 1 2004 - p616(2) [501+]
  LJ - v129 - i13 - August 2004 - p76(1) [51-500]
  Lon R Bks - v27 - i2 - Jan 20 2005 - p9(3) [501+]
  New R - Nov 22 2004 - p21 [501+]
  NS - v133 - i4714 - Nov 15 2004 - p48(2) [501+]
  NS - v133 - i4716 - Nov 29 2004 - p43(1) [51-500]
  NYRB - v51 - i20 - Dec 16 2004 - p34(4) [501+]
  NYTBR - Oct 3 2004 - p22 [501+]
  NYTBR - Jan 23 2005 - p31 [501+]
  PW - v251 - i29 - July 19 2004 - p152(2) [51-500]
  SLJ - v50 - i12 - Dec 2004 - p54(4) [501+]
  Spec - v296 - i9192 - Oct 9 2004 - p54(1) [501+]
  TimHES - v0 - i1672 - Dec 24 2004 - p24(2) [501+]
Greene, Alexis - *Lucille Lortel: The Queen of Off Broadway*
  Am Theat - v21 - i7 - Sept 2004 - p80(2) [501+]
  Women Who Write Plays: Interviews with American Dramatists
  Theat J - v56 - i1 - March 2004 - p151(3) [501+]
Greene, Bob - *Fraternity: A Journey in Search of Five Presidents*
  BL - v100 - i21 - July 2004 - p1795(1) [51-500]
  Esq - v142 - i5 - Nov 2004 - p48(1) [51-500]
  KR - v72 - i13 - July 1 2004 - p617(1) [501+]
  LJ - v129 - i12 - July 2004 - p97(1) [51-500]
  PW - v251 - i28 - July 12 2004 - p54(2) [51-500]
Greene, Bob W. - *Bob Greene's Total Body Makeover: An Accelerated Program of Exercise and Nutrition for Maximum Results in Minimum Time*
  LJ - v130 - i1 - Jan 1 2005 - p144(3) [501+]
Greene, Brian - *The Elegant Universe: Superstrings, Hidden Dimensions, and the Quest for the Ultimate Theory*
  Isis - v95 - i2 - June 2004 - p327(1) [501+]
  The Fabric of the Cosmos: Space, Time, and the Texture of Reality (Read by Prichard, Michael). Audiobook Review
  Kliatt - v38 - i6 - Nov 2004 - p55(1) [501+]
  LJ - v129 - i12 - July 2004 - p125(1) [51-500]
  The Fabric of the Cosmos: Space, Time, and the Texture of Reality
  Am Sci - v92 - i4 - July-August 2004 - p371(3) [501+]
  BL - v101 - i7 - Dec 1 2004 - p632(1) [51-500]
  Choice - v41 - i11-12 - July-August 2004 - p2067(1) [501+]

The Fabric of the Cosmos: Space, Time and the Texture of Reality
  NYTBR - March 13 2005 - p32 [501+]
The Fabric of the Cosmos: Space, Time, and the Texture of Reality
  Time - v165 - i11 - March 14 2005 - p68 [501+]
  TimHES - v0 - i1653 - August 13 2004 - p24(2) [501+]
Greene, Carol - *The Story of Halloween (Illus. by Bronson, Linda)*
  c BL - v101 - i1 - Sept 1 2004 - p116(2) [501+]
  c CCB-B - v58 - i1 - Sept 2004 - p18(1) [51-500]
  c KR - v72 - i14 - July 15 2004 - p685(1) [51-500]
  c SLJ - v50 - i8 - August 2004 - p108(1) [51-500]
Greene, Diana - *Reinventing Romantic Poetry: Russian Women Poets of the Mid-Nineteenth Century*
  Choice - v42 - i1 - Sept 2004 - p107(1) [501+]
Greene, Graham - *The Comedians*
  LJ - v130 - i4 - March 1 2005 - p126(1) [1-50]
  The Heart of the Matter (Read by Kitchen, Michael). Audiobook Review
  y Kliatt - v39 - i2 - March 2005 - p53(1) [51-500]
Greene, Jack - *The Black Prince and the Sea Devils*
  Bwatch - v26 - i9 - Sept 2004 - p6(1) [51-500]
Greene, Jeffrey D. - *Public Administration in the New Century: A Concise Introduction*
  R&R Bk N - v19 - i4 - Nov 2004 - p153(1) [501+]
Greene, Jerome A. - *Morning Star Dawn: The Powder River Expedition and the Northern Cheyennes, 1876*
  HNet - Sept 2004 - pNA [501+]
  Washita: The U.S. Army and the Southern Cheyennes, 1867-1869
  Roundup M - v12 - i1 - Oct 2004 - p22(1) [51-500]
Greene, John N. - *Infections in Cancer Patients*
  SciTech - v28 - i3 - Sept 2004 - p91(1) [51-500]
Greene, John Robert - *Betty Ford: Candor and Courage in the White House*
  PW - v251 - i51 - Dec 20 2004 - p51(1) [501+]
Greene, Lawrence J. - *The Resistant Learner: Helping Your Child Knock Down the Barriers to School Success*
  LJ - v130 - i1 - Jan 1 2005 - p126(1) [51-500]
Greene, Meg - *The Eiffel Tower*
  c SLJ - v50 - i7 - July 2004 - p123(1) [1-50]
  Louis Sachar
  y SLJ - v50 - i9 - Sept 2004 - p226(1) [51-500]
  c SLJ - v50 - i11 - Nov 2004 - p66(1) [51-500]
  y VOYA - v27 - i5 - Dec 2004 - p419(1) [51-500]
  Pope John Paul II: A Biography
  R&R Bk N - v19 - i1 - Feb 2004 - p24(1) [51-500]
Greene, Molly - *A Shared World: Christians and Muslims in the Early Modern Mediterranean*
  IJMES - v36 - i3 - August 2004 - p476-477 [501+]
Greene, Rachel - *Internet Art*
  Choice - v42 - i3 - Nov 2004 - p471(1) [1-50]
  TimHES - v0 - i1667 - Nov 19 2004 - p27(1) [501+]
Greene, Rhonda Gowler - *Santa's Stuck (Illus. by Cole, Henry)*
  c CCB-B - v58 - i4 - Dec 2004 - p168(2) [51-500]
  c PW - v251 - i39 - Sept 27 2004 - p61(1) [51-500]
  This Is the Teacher (Illus. by Lester, Mike)
  c SLJ - v50 - i8 - August 2004 - p87(1) [51-500]
Greene, Richard - *The Sopranos and Philosophy: I Kill Therefore I Am*
  Bwatch - v26 - i7 - July 2004 - p1(1) [51-500]
  Globe & Mail - July 10 2004 - pD16 [51-500]
  JPC - v38 - i3 - Feb 2005 - p586(3) [501+]
Greene, Sandra E. - *Sacred Sites and the Colonial Encounter: A History of Meaning and Memory in Ghana*
  HNet - August 2004 - pNA [501+]
  JAAR - v72 - i4 - Dec 2004 - p1037(4) [501+]
Greene, Stephanie - *Owen Foote, Mighty Scientist (Illus. by Smith, Cat Bowman)*
  c BL - v100 - i22 - August 2004 - p1933(1) [51-500]
  c CCB-B - v58 - i2 - Oct 2004 - p74(2) [51-500]
  c CH Bwatch - v14 - i1 - Nov 2004 - pNA [51-500]
  HB - v80 - i5 - Scpt-Oct 2004 - p583(2) [51-500]
  c SLJ - v50 - i10 - Oct 2004 - p114(1) [51-500]
Greene, Stuart - *Making Race Visible: Literacy Research for Cultural Understanding*
  Choice - v42 - i1 - Sept 2004 - p158(2) [501+]
Greene, Thomas C. - *Computer Security for the Home and Small Office*
  Bwatch - v26 - i7 - July 2004 - p7(2) [51-500]
  SciTech - v28 - i3 - Sept 2004 - p30(1) [51-500]
Greene, Victor - *A Singing Ambivalence: American Immigrants Between Old World and New, 1830-1930*
  Choice - v42 - i6 - Feb 2005 - p1062(1) [51-500]
Greenebaum, Ken - *Audio Anecdotes II: Tools, Tips, And Techniques For Digital Audio*
  Bwatch - Jan 2005 - pNA [51-500]

Greenewalt, Crawford H., Jr. - *The City of Sardis: Approaches in Graphic Recording*
  R&R Bk N - v19 - i1 - Feb 2004 - p45(1) [51-500]
Greenfeld, Liah - *The Spirit of Nationalism: Nationalism and Economic Growth*
  AJS - v110 - i2 - Sept 2004 - p492(3) [501+]
Greenfield, Amy Butler - *A Perfect Red: Empire, Espionage, and the Quest for the Color of Desire*
  KR - v73 - i4 - Feb 15 2005 - p211(1) [501+]
  PW - v252 - i11 - March 14 2005 - p55(1) [51-500]
  Virginia Bound
  LibMed - v22 - i6 - March 2004 - p63(1) [501+]
  LibMed - v22 - i6 - March 2004 - p63(1) [501+]
Greenfield, Eloise - *In the Land of Words: New and Selected Poems (Illus. by Gilchrist, Jan Spivey)*
  c LibMed - v23 - i1 - August-Sept 2004 - p70(1) [51-500]
  Me and Neesie (Illus. by Gilchrist, Jan Spivey)
  c SLJ - v51 - i1 - Jan 2005 - p92(1) [51-500]
Greenfield, Nathan M. - *The Battle of the St. Lawrence: The Second World War in Canada*
  Globe & Mail - Nov 6 2004 - pD14 [501+]
  TLS - i5299 - Oct 22 2004 - p31(1) [51-500]
Greenfield, Patricia Marks - *Weaving Generations Together: Evolving Creativity among the Mayas of Chiapas*
  Choice - v42 - i7 - March 2005 - p1214(1) [51-500]
Greenfieldt, John - *Play Index 1998-2002: An Index to 4,114 Plays*
  y Ref Rev - June 2004 - pNA [501+]
Greenhut, M.L. - *Our Teleological Economic World: Correlative Underpinnings of the Economic and Physical Sciences*
  JEL - v41 - i4 - Dec 2003 - p1437(1) [501+]
Greenhut, Steven - *Abuse of Power: How the Government Misuses Eminent Domain*
  Am Spect - v37 - i9 - Nov 2004 - p56(3) [501+]
Greenland, Seth - *The Bones*
  KR - v73 - i2 - Jan 15 2005 - p72(1) [501+]
  LJ - v130 - i3 - Feb 15 2005 - p116(1) [51-500]
  PW - v252 - i5 - Jan 31 2005 - p49(1) [51-500]
  Ent W - i809 - March 4 2005 - p78 [501+]
Greenlaw, Linda - *All Fishermen Are Liars (Read by Greenlaw, Linda). Audiobook Review*
  Kliatt - v38 - i6 - Nov 2004 - p53(2) [51-500]
  All Fishermen Are Liars: True Tales from the Dry Dock Bar (Read by Greenlaw, Linda). Audiobook Review
  LJ - v130 - i2 - Feb 1 2005 - p124(1) [51-500]
  All Fishermen Are Liars: True Tales from the Dry Dock Bar
  LJ - v129 - i13 - August 2004 - p89(1) [501+]
Greenman, Philip E. - *Principles of Manual Medicine. 3rd Ed.*
  SciTech - v28 - i1 - March 2004 - p123(1) [51-500]
Greenough, Paul - *Nature in the Global South: Environmental Projects in South and Southeast Asia*
  CS - v33 - i5 - Sept 2004 - p623-624 [501+]
  TimHES - v0 - i1672 - Dec 24 2004 - p27(1) [501+]
Greenslade, Macmillan - *Press Gang: How Newspapers Make Profits from Propaganda*
  CR - v285 - i1662 - July 2004 - p52(2) [501+]
Greenslade, William - *Thomas Hardy's Facts Notebook*
  Spec - v296 - i9198 - Nov 20 2004 - p51(1) [501+]
Greenspan, Frederick E. - *An Introduction to Aramaic, 2nd Ed.*
  R&R Bk N - v19 - i1 - Feb 2004 - p218(1) [51-500]
Greenspan, Amy L. - *U.S. employer's guide, 11th ed*
  R&R Bk N - v19 - i3 - August 2004 - p200(1) [1-50]
Greenspan, Anders - *Creating Colonial Williamburg*
  JAH - v91 - i1 - June 2004 - p283-284 [501+]
Greenspan, Erza - *Studies in Classic American Literature*
  ELT - v47 - i4 - Fall 2004 - p484(5) [501+]
Greenspan, Nancy Thorndike - *End of the Certain World: the Life and Science of Max Born, the Nobel Physicist Who Ignited the Quantum Revolution*
  PW - v252 - i6 - Feb 7 2005 - p54(1) [51-500]
Greenspan, Ralph J. - *Fly Pushing: The Theory and Practice of Drosophila Genetics. 2nd Ed.*
  SciTech - v28 - i3 - Sept 2004 - p60(1) [1-50]

Greenspan, Stanley I. - *The First Idea: How Symbols, Language, and Intelligence Evolved from Our Primate Ancestors to Modern Humans*
  BL - v101 - i2 - Sept 15 2004 - p181(1) [51-500]
  Choice - v42 - i5 - Jan 2005 - p937(1) [51-500]
  Globe & Mail - Dec 24 2004 - pD13 [1-50]
  KR - v72 - i14 - July 15 2004 - p671(2) [501+]
  Nature - v431 - i7005 - Sept 9 2004 - p127(2) [501+]
  PW - v251 - i30 - July 26 2004 - p46(1) [501+]
The First Idea: How Symbols, Language, and Intelligence Evolved in Early Primates and Humans
  LJ - v129 - i18 - Nov 1 2004 - p118(1) [51-500]
Greenstein, Elaine - *Ice-Cream Cones for Sale!*
  c CH Bwatch - v14 - i7 - July 2004 - p4(2) [51-500]
  LibMed - v22 - i6 - March 2004 - p80(1) [501+]
One Little Lamb (Illus. by Greenstein, Elaine)
  c BL - v100 - i21 - July 2004 - p1842(1) [1-50]
  c BL - v101 - i7 - Dec 1 2004 - p670(1) [51-500]
  c BL - v101 - i9-10 - Jan 1 2005 - p775(1) [1-50]
  c SLJ - v50 - i9 - Sept 2004 - p160(1) [51-500]
One Little Seed (Illus. by Greenstein, Elaine)
  c BL - v100 - i21 - July 2004 - p1842(1) [1-50]
  c BL - v101 - i7 - Dec 1 2004 - p670(1) [51-500]
  c BL - v101 - i9-10 - Jan 1 2005 - p775(1) [1-50]
  c SLJ - v50 - i9 - Sept 2004 - p160(1) [51-500]
Greenstein, Fred I. - *The George W. Bush Presidency: An Early Assessment*
  R&R Bk N - v19 - i1 - Feb 2004 - p63(1) [501+]
The Presidential Difference: Leadership Style from FDR to George W. Bush
  Globe & Mail - Jan 15 2005 - pD15 [501+]
Greenstein, Michael - *Contemporary Jewish Writing in Canada*
  BIC - v33 - i6 - Sept 2004 - p2(1) [501+]
Greenwald, Bruce - *Competition Demystified: A Radically Simplified Approach to Business Strategy*
  Har Bus R - v83 - i2 - Feb 2005 - p57(1) [1-50]
Greenwald, Marilyn S. - *The Secret of the Hardy Boys: Leslie McFarlane and the Stratemeyer Syndicate*
  Globe & Mail - Oct 2 2004 - pD7 [51-500]
  JouAmCul - v27 - i4 - Dec 2004 - p461(2) [501+]
  R&R Bk N - v19 - i4 - Nov 2004 - p239(1) [501+]
Greenwald, Michelle - *The Magical Melting Pot: The All-Family Cookbook That Celebrates America's Diversity*
  SLJ - v50 - i10 - Oct 2004 - pS62(1) [51-500]
Greenwald, Rick - *Oracle Application Server 10g Essentials*
  SciTech - v28 - i4 - Dec 2004 - p32(1) [51-500]
Greenwood - *Discovering world cultures: The Middle East*
  y VOYA - v27 - i5 - Dec 2004 - p422(1) [51-500]
Greenwood, Barbara - *Hidden Treasure: Amazing Stories of Discovery*
  c CBRA - Annual 2003 - p536(1) [51-500]
Greenwood Daily Life Online. E-book Review
  BL - v101 - i9-10 - Jan 1 2005 - p780(1) [51-500]
  SLJ - v50 - i12 - Dec 2004 - p91(2) [501+]
Greenwood, Daniel R. - *Action! in the Classroom: A Guide to Student Produced Digital Video in K-12 Education*
  LibMed - v22 - i5 - Feb 2004 - p83(1) [501+]
Greenwood, Ed. - *The Silent House: A Chronicle of Aglirta*
  LJ - v129 - i12 - July 2004 - p75(1) [51-500]
Greenwood, Justin - *Interest Representation in the European Union*
  PSQ - v119 - i4 - Winter 2004 - p702(2) [501+]
Greenwood, Kerry - *Away with the Fairies (Read by Daniel, Stephanie). Audiobook Review*
  LJ - v129 - i17 - Oct 15 2004 - p96(1) [51-500]
Away with the Fairies
  BL - v101 - i8 - Dec 15 2004 - p711(1) [51-500]
  KR - v72 - i23 - Dec 1 2004 - p1120(1) [51-500]
The Castlemaine Murders: A Phryne Fisher Mystery
  BL - v101 - i2 - Sept 15 2004 - p212(1) [51-500]
  DroRevMy - v24 - i4 - July-August 2004 - p4(2) [501+]
  PW - v251 - i34 - August 23 2004 - p40(1) [51-500]
Greenwood Press - *Life and Times in 20th-Century America, Vols. 1-5*
  R&R Bk N - v19 - i1 - Feb 2004 - p60(1) [51-500]
  y VOYA - v27 - i3 - August 2004 - p246(1) [1-50]
Greer, Alan - *Colonial Saints: Discovering the Holy in the Americas, 1500-1800*
  AHR - v109 - i4 - Oct 2004 - p1194-1195 [501+]
Greer, Andrew Sean - *The Confessions of Max Tivoli*
  NS - v133 - i4698 - July 26 2004 - p55(1) [501+]
  NYTBR - Feb 20 2005 - p26(L) [501+]
  TLS - i5287 - July 30 2004 - p20(1) [501+]
Greer, Darren - *Still Life with June. Audiobook Review*
  Globe & Mail - August 14 2004 - pD13 [1-50]

Greer, Germaine - *The Beautiful Boy*
  Art N - v103 - i1 - Jan 2004 - p100(2) [501+]
Whitefella Jump Up: the Shortest Way to Nationhood
  KR - v72 - i21 - Nov 1 2004 - p1037(1) [501+]
  NS - v133 - i4699 - August 2 2004 - p36(2) [501+]
  Spec - v295 - i9178 - July 3 2004 - p35(2) [501+]
Greger, Debora - *Western Art*
  Poet - v185 - i5 - Feb 2005 - p403(2) [501+]
Greger, Michael - *Carbophobia: The Scary Truth about America's Low-Carb Craze*
  PW - v252 - i7 - Feb 14 2005 - p69(1) [51-500]
Gregg, Samuel - *On Ordered Liberty: A Treatise on the Free Society*
  R&R Bk N - v19 - i1 - Feb 2004 - p149(1) [51-500]
Grego, Peter - *Moon Observer's Guide*
  E-Streams - August 2004 - pNA [501+]
  y VOYA - v27 - i4 - Oct 2004 - p326(1) [51-500]
Gregoire, Elizabeth - *Whose House Is This? A Look at Animal Homes--Webs, Nests, and Shells (Illus. by Alderman, Derrick)*
  c BL - v101 - i5 - Nov 1 2004 - p486(1) [51-500]
Gregor, Arthur - *Hand Upon His Head: Selected Poems 1947-2003*
  ABR - v26 - i1 - Nov-Dec 2004 - p25(2) [501+]
Gregorian, Vartan - *Islam: A Mosaic, Not a Monolith*
  J Ch St - v46 - i3 - Summer 2004 - p647(2) [501+]
  MEQ - v12 - i1 - Wntr 2005 - p93(2) [501+]
The Road to Home: My Life and Times
  LQ - v74 - i3 - July 2004 - p386(4) [501+]
Gregoriou, Greg N. - *Hedge Funds: Strategies, Risk Assessment, and Returns*
  R&R Bk N - v19 - i3 - August 2004 - p137(1) [51-500]
Performance Evaluation of Hedge Funds
  R&R Bk N - v19 - i3 - August 2004 - p137(1) [51-500]
Gregorkiewicz, Tom - *Optoelectronics of Group-IV Based Materials: Proceedings*
  SciTech - v28 - i1 - March 2004 - p146(1) [51-500]
Gregory, Alan P.R. - *Coleridge and the Conservative Imagination*
  R&R Bk N - v19 - i1 - Feb 2004 - p238(1) [51-500]
Gregory, Danny - *Lessons From the Golden Age of Classroom Filmstrips: Change Your Underwear Twice a Week*
  Choice - v42 - i6 - Feb 2005 - p1073(1) [51-500]
Gregory, Elizabeth - *Critical Response to Marianne Moore*
  R&R Bk N - v19 - i1 - Feb 2004 - p245(1) [51-500]
Gregory, Ian N. - *A Place in History: A Guide to Using GIS in Historical Research*
  JIH - v35 - i2 - Autumn 2004 - p283(1) [501+]
Gregory, Jeremy - *The National Church in Local Perspective: The Church of England and the Regions, 1660-1800.*
  Albion - v36 - i1 - Spring 2004 - p136(2) [501+]
Gregory, John S. - *The West and China Since 1500*
  E-A St - v56 - i3 - May 2004 - p483(2) [501+]
Gregory, Patrick - *The Daguerreotype*
  PW - v251 - i27 - July 5 2004 - p39(2) [501+]
Gregory, Paul R. - *The Economics of Forced Labor: The Soviet Gulag*
  R&R Bk N - v19 - i1 - Feb 2004 - p145(1) [51-500]
The Political Economy of Stalinism: Evidence from the Soviet Secret Archives
  Choice - v42 - i2 - Oct 2004 - p339(1) [51-500]
Gregory, Philippa - *The Virgin's Lover*
  Globe & Mail - Feb 12 2005 - pD13 [1-50]
  BL - v101 - i5 - Nov 1 2004 - p464(1) [51-500]
  Ent W - i794 - Nov 26 2004 - p123 [51-500]
  LJ - v129 - i15 - Sept 15 2004 - p48(1) [51-500]
  PW - v251 - i38 - Sept 20 2004 - p43(2) [501+]
Gregory, Raymond F. - *Unwelcome and Unlawful: Sexual Harassment in the American Workplace*
  Choice - v42 - i4 - Dec 2004 - p704(1) [1-50]
  Law&PolBR - Oct 2004 - pNA [501+]
  LJ - v129 - i12 - July 2004 - p101(1) [51-500]
Gregory, Richard L. - *The Oxford Companion to the Mind, 2nd Ed.*
  R&R Bk N - v20 - i1 - Feb 2005 - p6(1) [501+]
Gregory, Stan V. - *Ecology and Management of Wood in World Rivers*
  SciTech - v28 - i1 - March 2004 - p64(1) [51-500]
Gregory, Susanna - *The Hand of Justice: the Tenth Chronicle of Matthew Bartholomew*
  KR - v72 - i17 - Sept 1 2004 - p839(1) [51-500]

Gregory, William H. - *Inside the Ironworks: How Grumman's Glory Days Faded*
  SciTech - v28 - i4 - Dec 2004 - p161(1) [51-500]
Gregson, Ian - *Irresistible Force*
  Globe & Mail - August 14 2004 - pD15 [501+]
Gregson, J.M. - *Just Desserts*
  BL - v101 - i3 - Oct 1 2004 - p313(1) [51-500]
  KR - v72 - i20 - Oct 15 2004 - p986(1) [51-500]
Greider, William - *The Soul of Capitalism: Opening Paths to a Moral Economy*
  Comw - v131 - i13 - July 16 2004 - p32(2) [501+]
  OS - v40 - i4 - July-August 2004 - p39(2) [501+]
Greiff, Susanne - *Das Grab des Bin Wang: Wandmalereien der Ostlichen Han Zeit in China*
  Ch Rev Int - v10 - i2 - Fall 2003 - p389(5) [501+]
Greig, Denise - *Ornamental Foliage Plants*
  BL - v101 - i6 - Nov 15 2004 - p539(1) [501+]
Grein, Eberhard - *Ways Into a New Social Market Economy: Analytical Approaches for the Democratically Legitimized States in Central and Eastern Europe with Special References to the Work of Oswald von Nell-Breuning*
  R&R Bk N - v19 - i4 - Nov 2004 - p90(1) [51-500]
Greiner, Joy M. - *Exemplary Public Libraries: Lessons in Leadership, Management, and Service*
  BL - v101 - i9-10 - Jan 1 2005 - p909(1) [501+]
Greiner, Larry - *Goal Directed Project Management: Effective Techniques and Strategies*
  R&R Bk N - v19 - i3 - August 2004 - p109(1) [501+]
Greivenkamp, John E. - *Field Guide to Geometrical Optics*
  Choice - v42 - i2 - Oct 2004 - p330(1) [51-500]
Grekul, Lisa - *Kalyna's Song*
  Can Lit - i181 - Summer 2004 - p134-135 [501+]
  Globe & Mail - July 24 2004 - pD7 [501+]
Gremillion, Helen - *Feeding Anorexia: Gender and Power at a Treatment Center*
  AJS - v110 - i2 - Sept 2004 - p514(3) [501+]
  JRAI - v10 - i3 - Sept 2004 - p743(2) [501+]
  MAQ - v18 - i4 - Dec 2004 - p516(4) [501+]
Grencouillet, Corinne - *Lectures et lectures des 'Communistes' d'Aragon*
  FS - v58 - i1 - Jan 2004 - p139(2) [501+]
Grendler, Paul F. - *The Universities of the Italian Renaissance*
  JMH - v76 - i4 - Dec 2004 - p972(3) [501+]
  Specu - v79 - i4 - Oct 2004 - p1078(3) [501+]
  TLS - i5289 - August 13 2004 - p22(1) [501+]
Grenfell, Diana - *The Color Encyclopedia of Hostas*
  Choice - v42 - i1 - Sept 2004 - p68(1) [51-500]
  E-Streams - Nov 2004 - pNA [501+]
  SciTech - v28 - i3 - Sept 2004 - p129(1) [51-500]
Grenfell, Michael - *Pierre Bourdieu: Language, Culture, and Education, Theory into Practice*
  R&R Bk N - v19 - i2 - May 2004 - p127 [51-500]
Grenfell, Wilfred T. - *Adrift on an Icepan (Read by Brookes, Chris)*
  Globe & Mail - Dec 24 2004 - pD14 [51-500]
Grennan, Eamon - *The Quick of It*
  LJ - v130 - i3 - Feb 15 2005 - p135(1) [51-500]
Grenoble, Lenore A. - *Language Policy in the Soviet Union*
  R&R Bk N - v19 - i1 - Feb 2004 - p212 [51-500]
Grenouillet, Corinne - *Recherches croises Aragon/Elsa Triolet, no. 8*
  FS - v58 - i2 - April 2004 - p283(2) [501+]
Grensing-Pophal, Lin - *Human Resource Essentials*
  HR Mag - v50 - i2 - Feb 2005 - pNA [501+]
Grescoe, Audrey - *The Book of War Letters*
  Beav - v84 - i5 - Oct-Nov 2004 - p44(2) [501+]
Grescoe, Paul - *The Book of Love Letters: Canadian Kinship, Friendship, and Romance*
  Globe & Mail - Feb 12 2005 - pD3 [501+]
Grescoe, Taras - *End of Elsewhere: Travels Among the Tourists*
  CBRA - Annual 2003 - p23(2) [501+]
Gresh, Alain - *The New A-Z of the Middle East*
  Choice - v42 - i5 - Jan 2005 - p837(1) [1-50]
Gresh, Lois - *The Science of Supervillians*
  USNews & Wrld Rpt - v137 - i20 - Dec 6 2004 - p82 [51-500]
Gresson, Aaron David - *America's Atonement: Racial Pain, Recovery Rhetoric, and the Pedagogy of Healing*
  R&R Bk N - v19 - i3 - August 2004 - p66(1) [51-500]
Grethe, Harald - *Effects of Including Agricultural Products in the Customs Union Between Turkey and the EU: A Partial Equilibrium Analysis for Turkey*
  R&R Bk N - v19 - i4 - Nov 2004 - p104(1) [51-500]

Grimes, Martha - *Foul Matter (Read by Hoye, Stephen).*
Audiobook Review
    LJ - v129 - i13 - August 2004 - p128(1) [51-500]
Foul Matter
    Globe & Mail - Sept 18 2004 - pD26 [1-50]
The Winds of Change: A Richard Jury Mystery (Read by Lee, John). Audiobook Review
    BL - v101 - i7 - Dec 1 2004 - p677(1) [1-50]
The Winds of Change: A Richard Jury Mystery
    BL - v100 - i22 - August 2004 - p1870(1) [51-500]
    PW - v251 - i30 - July 26 2004 - p41(2) [501+]

Grimes, Nikki - *At Jerusalem's Gate (Illus. by Frampton, David)*
    y KR - v73 - i1 - Jan 1 2005 - p52(1) [51-500]
Bronx Masquerade
    y SLJ - v50 - i11 - Nov 2004 - p67(1) [51-500]
A Day with Daddy (Illus. by Tadgell, Nicole)
    c BL - v101 - i4 - Oct 15 2004 - p409(2) [51-500]
    c SLJ - v51 - i2 - Feb 2005 - p97(1) [51-500]
Tai Chi Morning: Snapshots of China (Illus. by Young, Ed)
    c SLJ - v50 - i11 - Nov 2004 - p66(1) [51-500]
What is Goodbye? (Illus. by Colon, Raul)
    c Black Iss - v6 - i5 - Sept-Oct 2004 - p59(1) [51-500]

Grimes, William - *Eating Your Words*
    Globe & Mail - Feb 12 2005 - pD14 [51-500]
    NYTBR - Dec 19 2004 - p32 [501+]

Grimley, Daniel M. - *The Cambridge Companion to Sibelius*
    Choice - v42 - i3 - Nov 2004 - p491(1) [51-500]

Grimm, Cherry Barbara - *The Wanderer*
    y VOYA - v27 - i3 - August 2004 - p234(1) [1-50]

Grimm, Jacob - *The Annotated Brothers Grimm*
    LJ - v129 - i14 - Sept 1 2004 - p149(1) [51-500]
    NYTBR - Dec 5 2004 - p64 [501+]
    R&R Bk N - v19 - i4 - Nov 2004 - p245(1) [501+]
The Elves and the Shoemaker (Illus. by LaMarche, Jim)
    c RT - v58 - i3 - Nov 2004 - p286(1) [51-500]

Grimmett, Richard - *Birds of Northern India (Illus. by Byers, Clive)*
    E-Streams - August 2004 - pNA [501+]

Grimshaw, Nicholas - *The Architecture of Eden*
    Choice - v42 - i1 - Sept 2004 - p91(1) [501+]

Grimsley, Jim - *The Ordinary*
    Analog - v124 - i11 - Nov 2004 - p134(6) [501+]

Grimsley, Mark - *Soldiers as Citizens: Former Wehrmacht Officers in the Federal Republic of Germany, 1945-1955*
    JMH - v76 - i4 - Dec 2004 - p997(2) [501+]

Grimwood, Jon Courtenay - *Pashazade: The First Arabesk*
    KR - v73 - i1 - Jan 1 2005 - p25(1) [51-500]
    LJ - v130 - i3 - Feb 15 2005 - p122(1) [51-500]
    PW - v252 - i5 - Jan 31 2005 - p53(1) [51-500]
    Ent W - i810 - March 11 2005 - p108 [51-500]

Grindle, Merilee S. - *Proclaiming Revolution: Bolivia in Comparative Perspective*
    JEL - v42 - i1 - March 2004 - p302(1) [501+]
    Pers PS - v33 - i4 - Fall 2004 - p236(1) [501+]

Grindley, Sally - *A Little Bit of Trouble (Illus. by Taylor, Eleanor)*
    c KR - v72 - i16 - August 15 2004 - p806(1) [51-500]
    c Sch Lib - v52 - i3 - Autumn 2004 - p131(1) [501+]
    c SLJ - v50 - i12 - Dec 2004 - p110(1) [501+]
Polar Skater (Illus. by Hieta, Heli)
    c Globe & Mail - Feb 26 2005 - pD11 [501+]
    c SLJ - v51 - i1 - Jan 2005 - p92(1) [51-500]
Spilled Water
    c BL - v101 - i2 - Sept 15 2004 - p244(2) [51-500]
    c CCB-B - v58 - i2 - Oct 2004 - p75(1) [51-500]
    y KR - v72 - i15 - August 1 2004 - p741(1) [51-500]
    c PW - v251 - i46 - Nov 15 2004 - p60(1) [501+]
    c SLJ - v50 - i9 - Sept 2004 - p206(1) [51-500]

Grindstaff, Laura - *The Money Shot: Trash, Class, and the Making of TV Talk Shows*
    CS - v33 - i2 - March 2004 - p199-200 [501+]
    JC - v54 - i3 - Sept 2004 - p574(3) [501+]

Gring-Pemble, Lisa M. - *Grim Fairy Tales: The Rhetorical Construction of American Welfare Policy*
    Choice - v41 - i11-12 - July-August 2004 - p2037(1) [501+]

Gringore, Pierre - *OEuvres polemiques redigees sous le regne de Louis XII*
    Ren Q - v57 - i4 - Winter 2004 - p1431(3) [501+]

Grinley, David S. - *Critical Interfacial Issues in Thin-Film Optoelectronic and Energy Conversion Devices: Proceedings*
    SciTech - v28 - i3 - Sept 2004 - p161(1) [51-500]

Grippando, James - *Hear No Evil (Read by Sullivan, Nick). Audiobook Review*
    BL - v101 - i7 - Dec 1 2004 - p678(1) [51-500]
Hear No Evil
    KR - v72 - i14 - July 15 2004 - p648(1) [51-500]
    PW - v251 - i31 - August 2 2004 - p52(1) [501+]

Grisham, John - *The Broker*
    Globe & Mail - Jan 29 2005 - pD13 [1-50]
    Globe & Mail - Jan 22 2005 - pD12 [51-500]
    NYTBR - Jan 9 2005 - p18 [501+]
    People - v63 - i2 - Jan 17 2005 - p55 [51-500]
    PW - v252 - i2 - Jan 10 2005 - p39(2) [501+]
    Ent W - i801 - Jan 14 2005 - p91 [501+]
The Last Juror (Read by Beck, Michael). Audiobook Review
    LJ - v129 - i13 - August 2004 - p128(1) [51-500]

Grisolia, R. - *Oikovouia: Structure e tecnica drammatica negli scoli antichi ai testi drammatici*
    Class R - v54 - i1 - May 2004 - p241(1) [501+]

Grisso, Thomas - *Double Jeopardy: Adolescent Offenders with Mental Disorders*
    Choice - v42 - i4 - Dec 2004 - p694(1) [1-50]

Gristwood, Sarah - *Perdita: Royal Mistress, Writer, Romantic*
    Spec - v297 - i9207 - Jan 22 2005 - p37(1) [501+]

Griswold, Wendy - *Cultures and Societies in Changing World, 2nd ed.*
    R&R Bk N - v19 - i2 - May 2004 - p127 [501+]

Gritsch, Eric W. - *A History of Lutheranism*
    Intpr - v59 - i1 - Jan 2005 - p98(1) [501+]

Grmek, Mirko D. - *Western Medical Thought from Antiquity to the Middle Ages*
    Isis - v95 - i2 - June 2004 - p282(2) [501+]

Grob-Fitzgibbon, Benjamin - *Irish Experience During the Second World War: An Oral History*
    R&R Bk N - v20 - i1 - Feb 2005 - p32(1) [51-500]

Grob, Gerald N. - *The Deadly Truth: A History of Disease in America*
    Isis - v95 - i3 - Sept 2004 - p492(1) [501+]
    J Soc H - v38 - i1 - Fall 2004 - p267(3) [501+]
    RAH - v32 - i1 - March 2004 - p128(9) [501+]

Grob, Robert L. - *Modern Practice of Gas Chromatography, 4th Ed.*
    Choice - v42 - i5 - Jan 2005 - p882(1) [1-50]
    E-Streams - Dec 2004 - pNA [501+]
    SciTech - v28 - i3 - Sept 2004 - p51(1) [1-50]

Grobel, Lawrence - *The Art of the Interview: Lessons from a Master of the Craft*
    y BL - v100 - i22 - August 2004 - p1876(1) [51-500]
    LJ - v129 - i17 - Oct 15 2004 - p69(1) [51-500]

Grobler, Hanka - *Person-Centered Communication: Theory and Practice, 2nd Ed.*
    R&R Bk N - v19 - i1 - Feb 2004 - p210(1) [51-500]

Grobman, Alex - *Battling for Souls: The Vaad Hatzala Rescue Committee in Post-Holocaust Europe*
    Bwatch - Nov 2004 - pNA [51-500]
    Choice - v42 - i6 - Feb 2005 - p1075(1) [51-500]

Grobman, Gary M. - *An Introduction to the Nonprofit Sector: A Practical Approach for the 21st Century*
    R&R Bk N - v19 - i3 - August 2004 - p108(1) [51-500]

Grodin, Elissa - *D Is for Democracy: A Citizen's Alphabet (Illus. by Juhasz, Victor)*
    c BL - v101 - i9-10 - Jan 1 2005 - p848(1) [1-50]
    c CH Bwatch - Oct 2004 - pNA [51-500]
    c SLJ - v50 - i10 - Oct 2004 - p140(2) [51-500]
D Is for Democracy: A Citizen's Alphabet
    c PW - v251 - i34 - August 23 2004 - p56(2) [501+]

Grodzins, Dean - *American Heretic: Theodore Parker and Transcendentalism*
    AHR - v109 - i3 - June 2004 - p906(2) [501+]
    HNet - Sept 2004 - pNA [501+]

Grodzinsky, Yosef - *In the Shadow of the Holocaust: The Struggle Between Jews and Zionists in the Aftermath of World War II*
    Nation - v280 - i2 - Jan 10 2005 - p29 [501+]

Groebner, Valentin - *Liquid Assets, Dangerous Gifts: Presents and Politics at the End of the Middle Ages*
    Six Ct J - v34 - i4 - Winter 2003 - p1250-1252 [501+]
    Specu - v79 - i3 - July 2004 - p764-765 [501+]

Groenhout, Ruth E. - *Connected Lives: Human Nature and an Ethics of Care*
    R&R Bk N - v19 - i3 - August 2004 - p12(1) [1-50]

Groff, James L. - *Advanced Nutrition and Human Metabolism, 4th Ed.*
    SciTech - v28 - i3 - Sept 2004 - p68(1) [51-500]

Grogan, Tamara - *Boys And Girls Together: Improving Gender Relationships in K-6 Classrooms*
    CE - v81 - i2 - Winter 2004 - p116(1) [51-500]

Grohol, John M. - *Insider's Guide to Mental Health Resources Online, Rev. Ed.*
    SciTech - v28 - i3 - Sept 2004 - p95(1) [51-500]

Grolier Multimedia Encyclopedia
    BL - v101 - i2 - Sept 15 2004 - p270(2) [51-500]
    BL - v101 - i2 - Sept 15 2004 - p270(1) [51-500]

Grolier Online
    BL - v101 - i2 - Sept 15 2004 - p270(1) [51-500]

Grolier Student Encyclopedia
    c LibMed - v23 - i3 - Nov-Dec 2004 - p62(2) [51-500]

Grollman, Stephen A. - *Heinrich Mann: Narratives of Wilhelmine Germany*
    GSR - v27 - i1 - Feb 2004 - p166-167 [501+]

Grondahl, Jens Christian - *An Altered Light*
    KR - v73 - i2 - Jan 15 2005 - p72(1) [51-500]
    PW - v252 - i5 - Jan 31 2005 - p46(1) [51-500]

Grondin, Jean - *Hans-Georg Gadamer: A Biography*
    TimHES - v0 - i1672 - Dec 24 2004 - p26(2) [501+]

Groner, Paul - *Ryogen and Mount Hiei: Japanese Tendai in the Tenth Century*
    HJAS - v64 - i2 - Dec 2004 - p516-529 [501+]
    HJAS - v64 - i2 - Dec 2004 - p516-529 [501+]

Gronfeldt, Svafa - *The Nature, Impact and Development of Customer Oriented Behaviour*
    R&R Bk N - v19 - i2 - May 2004 - p114(1) [51-500]

Gronowski, Ann M. - *Handbook of Clinical Laboratory Testing During Pregnancy*
    SciTech - v28 - i3 - Sept 2004 - p116(1) [51-500]

Groody, Daniel G. - *Border of Death, Valley of Life: An Immigrant Journey of Heart and Spirit*
    JR - v85 - i1 - Jan 2005 - p139(3) [501+]
    WHQ - v35 - i3 - Autumn 2004 - p394(2) [501+]

Groom, Simon - *A Secret History of Clay*
    TLS - i5286 - July 23 2004 - p19(1) [501+]

Groom, Winston - *1942: The Year that Tried Men's Souls*
    KR - v73 - i4 - Feb 15 2005 - p211(2) [501+]
    PW - v252 - i10 - March 7 2005 - p59(1) [51-500]

Grooms, Duffy - *Ten Little Elvi (Illus. by Gorissen, Dean)*
    c PW - v251 - i48 - Nov 29 2004 - p39(1) [51-500]

Groopman, Jerome E. - *The Anatomy of Hope: How People Prevail in the Face of Illness (Read by Michael, Paul). Audiobook Review*
    c Kliatt - v38 - i4 - July 2004 - p59(1) [51-500]
The Anatomy of Hope: How People Prevail in the Face of Illness
    y Kliatt - v39 - i2 - March 2005 - p36(1) [51-500]
    SciTech - v28 - i3 - Sept 2004 - p77(1) [1-50]
    SEP - v277 - i1 - Jan-Feb 2005 - p50(2) [51-500]

Groos, Arthur - *Perceval/Parzival: A Casebook*
    Specu - v79 - i3 - July 2004 - p766-767 [501+]

Groos, Jonathan L. - *Handbook of Graph Theory*
    Choice - v42 - i5 - Jan 2005 - p888(1) [501+]

Groot, Tracy - *Stones of My Accusers*
    BL - v101 - i3 - Oct 1 2004 - p303(1) [51-500]

Groover, Kristina K. - *Things of the Spirit: Women Writers Constructing Spirituality*
    LJ - v129 - i13 - August 2004 - p88(1) [501+]

Gropp, William - *Beowulf Cluster Computing with Linux, 2nd Ed.*
    E-Streams - August 2004 - pNA [501+]

Groppa, Carlos G. - *The Tango in the United States: A History*
    Choice - v42 - i2 - Oct 2004 - p305(1) [51-500]

Gros, Jean-Germain - *Cameroon: Politics and Society in Critical Perspectives*
    Choice - v42 - i1 - Sept 2004 - p182(1) [501+]

Grosbard, Ofer - *Israel on the Conch: The Psychology of the Peace Process*
    MEQ - v11 - i3 - Summer 2004 - p87(2) [501+]

Grosby, Steven - *Biblical Ideas of Nationality: Ancient and Modern*
    Hist Geo - v32 - Annual 2004 - p193(2) [501+]

Grose, Francis - *The Vulgar Tongue: British Slang and Pickpocket Eloquence*
    TLS - i5294 - Sept 17 2004 - p24(1) [501+]

Grosfoguel, Ramon - *The Modern/Colonial/Capitalist World-System in the Twentieth Century: Global Processes, Antisystemic Movements, and the Geopolitics of Knowledge*
    CS - v33 - i2 - March 2004 - p221-222 [501+]

Grosholz, Emily R. - *The Legacy of Simone de Beauvoir*
    TimHES - v0 - i1656 - Sept 3 2004 - p28(1) [501+]

Grosjean, Alexis - *An Unofficial Alliance: Scotland and Sweden, 1569-1654*
    J Mil H - v68 - i4 - Oct 2004 - p1248-1250 [501+]

Gross, Abraham - *Struggling with Tradition: Reservations About Active Martyrdom in the Middle Ages*
R&R Bk N - v19 - i4 - Nov 2004 - p16(1) [51-500]

Gross, Alan G. - *Communicating Science: The Scientific Article from the Seventeenth Century to the Present*
Isis - v95 - i2 - June 2004 - p341(2) [501+]

Gross, Chuck - *Rattler One-Seven: A Vietnam Helicopter Pilot's War Story*
PW - v251 - i31 - August 2 2004 - p64(1) [51-500]

Gross, Claudia - *Scholarium*
DroRevMy - v24 - i3 - May-June 2004 - p12(1) [1-50]

Gross, Gloria Sybil - *In a Fast Coach with a Pretty Woman: Jane Austen and Samuel Johnson*
RES - v55 - i218 - Feb 2004 - p142-143 [501+]

Gross, James A. - *Workers' Rights as Human Rights*
JEL - v41 - i4 - Dec 2003 - p1390(1) [501+]

Gross, John - *A Double Thread: Growing Up English and Jewish in London*
NYRB - v51 - i20 - Dec 16 2004 - p76(2) [501+]

Gross, Jurgen H. - *Mass Spectrometry: A Textbook*
Choice - v42 - i2 - Oct 2004 - p321(1) [51-500]

Gross, Michael Joseph - *Starstruck: When a Fan Gets Close to Fame*
KR - v73 - i3 - Feb 1 2005 - p164(1) [501+]
PW - v252 - i8 - Feb 21 2005 - p167(1) [51-500]

Gross, Miraca U.M. - *Exceptionally Gifted Children*
TCR - v107 - i2 - Feb 2005 - p261(5) [501+]

Gross, Norman - *America's Lawyer-Presidents: From Law Office to Oval Office*
BL - v100 - i22 - August 2004 - p1878(2) [51-500]
Choice - v42 - i6 - Feb 2005 - p1000(1) [51-500]
LJ - v129 - i15 - Sept 15 2004 - p70(1) [51-500]

Gross, Terry - *All I Did Was Ask*
y BL - v100 - i22 - August 2004 - p1867(1) [51-500]
KR - v72 - i13 - July 1 2004 - p617(1) [51-500]
LJ - v129 - i15 - Sept 15 2004 - p65(2) [51-500]
PW - v251 - i29 - July 19 2004 - p155(1) [51-500]
R&R Bk N - v19 - i4 - Nov 2004 - p106(1) [51-500]

Gross, Thomas - *Legal Scholarship in International and Comparative Law*
R&R Bk N - v19 - i1 - Feb 2004 - pNA [51-500]

Grossbard-Shechtman, Shoshana A. - *Marriage and the Economy: Theory and Evidence from Advanced Industrial Societies*
JEL - v41 - i4 - Dec 2003 - p1383(1) [501+]

Grosse, Robert E. - *The Future of Global Financial Services*
R&R Bk N - v19 - i4 - Nov 2004 - p117(1) [51-500]

Grosskurth, Phyllis - *Byron: The Flawed Angel*
Globe & Mail - Feb 12 2005 - pD15 [501+]

Grossman, Andrea - *Designer Scrapbooks with Mrs. Grossman*
BL - v101 - i8 - Dec 15 2004 - p706(1) [501+]
Bwatch - Feb 2005 - pNA [51-500]

Grossman, Bill - *My Little Sister Hugged an Ape (Illus. by Hawkes, Kevin)*
c HB - v80 - i6 - Nov-Dec 2004 - p697(1) [51-500]
c KR - v72 - i17 - Sept 1 2004 - p865(1) [51-500]
c PW - v251 - i41 - Oct 11 2004 - p79(1) [51-500]
c SLJ - v50 - i11 - Nov 2004 - p104(1) [51-500]

Grossman, David - *Death as a Way of Life: Dispatches from Jerusalem*
Lon R Bks - v26 - i6 - March 18 2004 - pNA [501+]
Duel
c BL - v101 - i1 - Sept 1 2004 - p121(1) [1-50]
y BL - v101 - i5 - Nov 1 2004 - p496(1) [51-500]
c KR - v72 - i14 - July 15 2004 - p685(1) [51-500]
c NYTBR - July 11 2004 - p18 [501+]
c SLJ - v50 - i8 - August 2004 - p122(1) [51-500]
Someone to Run With
Lon R Bks - v26 - i6 - March 18 2004 - pNA [501+]

Grossman, Edith - *Don Quixote*
Globe & Mail - Nov 27 2004 - pD3 [51-500]

Grossman, Gary - *Executive Actions: A Presidential Thriller*
PW - v251 - i29 - July 19 2004 - p145(1) [51-500]

Grossman, Herbert - *Classroom Behavior Management for Diverse and Inclusive Schools, 3rd Ed.*
R&R Bk N - v19 - i1 - Feb 2004 - p188(1) [51-500]
TCR - v106 - i12 - Dec 2004 - p2381(4) [501+]

Grossman, James R. - *The Encyclopedia of Chicago*
Atl - v294 - i5 - Dec 2004 - p121(4) [501+]
BL - v101 - i9-10 - Jan 1 2005 - p779(1) [1-50]
LJ - v129 - i20 - Dec 1 2004 - p162(1) [51-500]
BL - v101 - i7 - Dec 1 2004 - p685(1) [501+]

Grossman, Janet Burnett - *Looking at Greek and Roman Sculpture in Stone: A Guide to Terms, Styles, and Techniques*
Choice - v42 - i4 - Dec 2004 - p650(1) [1-50]

Grossman, Jay - *Reconstituting the American Renaissance: Emerson, Whitman, and the Politics of Representation*
JAH - v91 - i2 - Sept 2004 - p631(2) [501+]
NEQ - v77 - i4 - Dec 2004 - p662-664 [501+]

Grossman, Joan Delaney - *Williams James in Russian Culture*
Slav R - v63 - i2 - Summer 2004 - p434(3) [501+]

Grossman, Lev - *Codex*
ABR - v26 - i2 - Jan-Feb 2005 - p19(1) [501+]

Grossman, Mark - *Political Corruption in America: An Encyclopedia of Scandals, Power, and Greed*
Ref Rev - August 2004 - pNA [501+]
R&R Bk N - v19 - i1 - Feb 2004 - pNA [501+]
Technology Law: What Every Business (and Business-Minded Person) Needs to Know
SciTech - v28 - i3 - Sept 2004 - p11(1) [501+]

Grossman, Peter Z. - *The End of a Natural Monopoly: Deregulation and Competition in the Electric Power Industry*
En Jnl - v25 - i4 - Oct 2004 - p135(4) [501+]
How Cartels Endure and How They Fail: Studies of Industrial Collusion
Choice - v42 - i4 - Dec 2004 - p707(1) [1-50]
R&R Bk N - v19 - i3 - August 2004 - p113(1) [51-500]

Grossman, Robert I. - *Neuroradiology: The Requisites, 2nd Ed.*
SciTech - v28 - i1 - March 2004 - p93(1) [51-500]

Grosz, Elizabeth - *Architecture from the Outside*
JAAC - v61 - Winter 2003 - p81 [501+]

Grotberg, Edith Henderson - *Resilience for Today: Gaining Strength from Adversity*
R&R Bk N - v19 - i1 - Feb 2004 - p8(1) [51-500]

Groten, Martin - *Clincal Investigations of Medical Devices in Dentistry: Specification, Interpretation, and Practical Guidance*
SciTech - v28 - i3 - Sept 2004 - p119(1) [51-500]

Grotenhuis, Elizabeth Ten - *Along the Silk Road*
Six Ct J - v34 - i4 - Winter 2003 - p1256-1256 [501+]

Groth, Alexander J. - *Holocaust Voices: An Attitudinal Survey of Survivors*
R&R Bk N - v19 - i1 - Feb 2004 - p30(1) [51-500]

Groth, Gary - *The Comics Journal Special Edition: Conversations among Four Generations of Cartoonists*
BL - v100 - i21 - July 2004 - p1809(1) [1-50]
Drawing the Line: The Comics Journal Library
BL - v101 - i9-10 - Jan 1 2005 - p799(1) [51-500]

Groth, Helen - *Victorian Photography and Literary Nostalgia*
Choice - v41 - i11-12 - July-August 2004 - p2044(1) [501+]
VS - v46 - i4 - Summer 2004 - p714(2) [501+]

Groth, Miles - *Translating Heidegger*
R&R Bk N - v19 - i1 - Feb 2004 - p5(1) [51-500]

Grothaus, L.H. - *Manlines and its Discontents: The Black Middle Class and the Transformation of Masculinity, 1900-1930*
Choice - v42 - i4 - Dec 2004 - p725(1) [1-50]

Grotius, Hugo - *The Free Sea*
R&R Bk N - v19 - i3 - August 2004 - p212(1) [1-50]

Grotschel, Martin - *The Sharpest Cut: The Impact of Manfred Padberg and His Work*
SciTech - v28 - i3 - Sept 2004 - p41(1) [1-50]

Grounds, Richard A. - *Native Voices: American Indian Identity and Resistance*
JAH - v91 - i2 - Sept 2004 - p716(2) [501+]

Grounds, Roger - *Gardening with Ornamental Grasses*
LJ - v129 - i18 - Nov 1 2004 - p111(2) [51-500]

Groupe d'etudes balzaciennes - *L'Annee balzacienne 2002*
NCFS - v33 - i1-2 - Fall-Winter 2004 - p191(3) [501+]

Groupe interdisciplinaire de recherche en archivistique - *Les archives electroniques: une memoire orpheline ou en mutation? Actes du 4ieme symposium du GIRA, Archives nationales du Quebec (Montreal), le 22 mars 2002*
Archiv - i56 - Fall 2003 - p413(5) [501+]

Grove, Fred - *Soldier Returns*
Roundup M - v12 - i1 - Oct 2004 - p30(1) [51-500]

Grover, Lorie Ann - *Hold me Tight*
y Kliatt - v39 - i2 - March 2005 - p12(1) [51-500]
On Pointe
c BL - v100 - i21 - July 2004 - p1844(1) [1-50]
c CH Bwatch - v14 - i7 - July 2004 - p7(1) [51-500]
c PW - v251 - i28 - July 12 2004 - p64(1) [51-500]

Grover, Velma I. - *Climate Change: Five Years After Kyoto*
Choice - v42 - i5 - Jan 2005 - p890(1) [1-50]
SciTech - v28 - i4 - Dec 2004 - p53(1) [51-500]

Grover, Warren - *Nazis in Newark*
Choice - v41 - i7 - March 2004 - p1355(2) [501+]

Groves, Leslie Christine - *Inclusive Aid: Changing Power and Relationships in International Development*
R&R Bk N - v19 - i4 - Nov 2004 - p87(1) [51-500]

Grubb, Lisa - *Happy Dog!*
c LibMed - v22 - i6 - March 2004 - p57(1) [501+]

Grubb, W. Norton - *The Education Gospel: The Economic Power of Schooling*
LJ - v129 - i17 - Oct 15 2004 - p71(1) [51-500]

Grubbs, Bruce - *Backpacking Arizona: From Deep Canyons to Sky Islands*
R&R Bk N - v19 - i1 - Feb 2004 - p65(1) [51-500]

Grubbs, J. Evans - *Women and Law in the Roman Empire: A Sourcebook on Marriage, Divorce and Widowhood*
Class R - v53 - i2 - Nov 2003 - p421-423 [501+]

Grubbs, Robert H. - *Handbook of Metathesis*
E-Streams - July 2004 - pNA [501+]

Grube, Ernst J. - *Carolinda Tolstoy: Ceramics*
Ceram Mo - v52 - i5 - May 2004 - p36(1) [501+]

Gruber, Mayer I. - *Rashi's commentary on Psalms*
R&R Bk N - v19 - i3 - August 2004 - p23(1) [1-50]

Gruber, Michael - *Valley of Bones*
BL - v101 - i7 - Dec 1 2004 - p639(1) [51-500]
Ent W - i802 - Jan 21 2005 - p93 [51-500]
KR - v72 - i19 - Oct 1 2004 - p931(1) [51-500]
LJ - v130 - i1 - Jan 1 2005 - p85(1) [51-500]
PW - v251 - i45 - Nov 8 2004 - p33(1) [501+]

Gruber, Samuel D. - *American Synagogues: A Century of Architecture and Jewish Community*
R&R Bk N - v19 - i1 - Feb 2004 - p203(1) [51-500]

Grubgeld, Elizabeth - *Anglo-Irish Autobiography: Class, Gender, and the Forms of Narrative*
Choice - v42 - i2 - Oct 2004 - p293(1) [501+]

Grubov, V.I. - *Plants of Central Asia: Plant Collections from China and Mongolia, Vol. 8b*
SciTech - v28 - i1 - March 2004 - p67(1) [51-500]

Gruchy, John W. De - *Reconciliation: Restoring Justice*
TT - v61 - i1 - April 2004 - p100-102 [501+]

Grudens, Richard - *Chattanooga Choo Choo: The Life and Times of the World Famous Glenn Miller Orchestra*
Bwatch - v26 - i7 - July 2004 - p11(1) [51-500]

Gruen, Erich S. - *Diaspora: Jews Amidst Greeks and Romans*
Class R - v54 - i2 - Nov 2004 - p508-511 [501+]
JIH - v34 - i4 - Spring 2004 - p620-622 [501+]

Gruenbaum, Thelma - *Nesarim: Child Survivors of Terezin*
R&R Bk N - v19 - i3 - August 2004 - p52(1) [51-500]

Gruending, Dennis - *Great Canadian Speeches*
Beav - v85 - i1 - Feb-March 2005 - p47(2) [501+]
Globe & Mail - Jan 1 2005 - pD13 [501+]

Gruenwald, Kim M. - *River of Enterprise: The Commercial Origins of Regional Identity in the Ohio Valley, 1790-1850*
JEH - v64 - i1 - March 2004 - p262(2) [501+]
WHQ - v35 - i1 - Spring 2004 - p79-80 [501+]

Grummitt, David - *The English Experience in France 1450-1558: War, Diplomacy and Cultural Exchange*
Six Ct J - v34 - i4 - Winter 2003 - p1122-1124 [501+]

Grunbein, D. - *Seneca: Thyestes Mit Materialien Zur Ubersetzung und Zu Leben und Werk Senecas*
Class R - v54 - i2 - Nov 2004 - p570-571 [501+]

Grundman, Adolph H. - *The Golden Age of Amateur Basketball: The AAU Tournament, 1921-1968*
Choice - v42 - i7 - March 2005 - p1265(1) [51-500]

Gruntman, Mike - *Blazing the Trail: The Early History of Spacecraft and Rocketry*
Choice - v42 - i5 - Jan 2005 - p875(1) [1-50]
SciTech - v28 - i3 - Sept 2004 - p164(1) [51-500]

Grushkin, Paul - *Art of Modern Rock: The Poster Explosion*
LJ - v129 - i14 - Sept 1 2004 - p42(1) [501+]
NW - Dec 6 2004 - p10 [501+]
NYTBR - Dec 5 2004 - p53 [501+]

Gupta, Arjun K. - *Handbook of Beta Distribution and Its Applications*
Choice - v42 - i6 - Feb 2005 - p1058(1) [51-500]
SciTech - v28 - i4 - Dec 2004 - p37(1) [51-500]

Gupta, Jatinder N.D. - *Intelligent Enterprises of the 21st Century*
R&R Bk N - v19 - i1 - Feb 2004 - p89(1) [1-50]

Gupta, Piyush - *Advances in Network Information Theory: Proceedings*
SciTech - v28 - i4 - Dec 2004 - p150(1) [51-500]

Gupta, Rahila - *From Homebreakers to Jailbreakers: Southall Black Sisters*
TimHES - v0 - i1656 - Sept 3 2004 - p29(1) [501+]

Gupta, Ram S. - *Introduction to Environmental Engineering and Science, 2nd Ed.*
SciTech - v28 - i3 - Sept 2004 - p5(1) [501+]

Gupta, Uma Das - *Rabindranath Tagore: A Biography*
CR - v286 - i1669 - Feb 2005 - p118(2) [501+]

Gur, Batya - *Bethlehem Road Murder*
BL - v101 - i9-10 - Jan 1 2005 - p827(1) [1-50]
LJ - v129 - i18 - Nov 1 2004 - p62(2) [51-500]
PW - v251 - i45 - Nov 8 2004 - p39(1) [501+]
NYTBR - Dec 12 2004 - p26 [501+]

Gura, Philip F. - *C.F. Martin and His Guitars, 1796-1873*
BHR - v78 - i2 - Summer 2004 - p292(3) [501+]
Choice - v41 - i7 - March 2004 - p1306(1) [501+]
Notes - v61 - i1 - Sept 2004 - p147(4) [501+]
Jonathan Edwards: America's Evangelical
KR - v72 - i24 - Dec 15 2004 - p1182(1) [501+]
LJ - v130 - i4 - March 1 2005 - p90(1) [51-500]
PW - v252 - i4 - Jan 24 2005 - p237(1) [501+]

Guralnick, Peter - *Martin Scorsese Presents The Blues: A Musical Journey*
Notes - v61 - i1 - Sept 2004 - p104(3) [501+]

Gurewitsch, Edna P. - *Kindred Souls: The Friendship of Eleanor Roosevelt and David Gurewitsch. Audiobook Review*
LJ - v129 - i13 - August 2004 - p129(1) [51-500]

Gurib-Fakim, Ameenah - *Medicinal and Aromatic Plants in the Indian Ocean Islands*
SciTech - v28 - i3 - Sept 2004 - p123(1) [51-500]
Medicinal and Aromatic Plants of Indian Ocean Islands: Madagascar, Comoros, Seychelles and Mascarenes
Choice - v42 - i4 - Dec 2004 - p689(1) [1-50]

Gurman, Alan S. - *Essential Psychotherapies: Theory and Practice, 2nd Ed.*
SciTech - v28 - i1 - March 2004 - p98(1) [51-500]

Gurney, Alan - *Compass: A Story of Exploration and Innovation*
Am Sci - v92 - i5 - Sept-Oct 2004 - p467(1) [501+]
R&R Bk N - v19 - i4 - Nov 2004 - p253(1) [501+]
TimHES - v0 - i1674 - Jan 14 2005 - p25(1) [501+]

Guroian, Vigen - *Ancestral Shadows: An Anthology of Ghostly Tales*
BW - v34 - i44 - Oct 31 2004 - p15(1) [501+]

Gurr, Andrew - *Playgoing in Shakespeare's London, 3rd Ed.*
Choice - v42 - i7 - March 2005 - p1238(1) [51-500]
The Shakespare Company, 1594-1642
Choice - v42 - i5 - Jan 2005 - p863(2) [1-50]
Shakespeare & Co.
Wil Q - v29 - i1 - Wntr 2005 - p109(3) [501+]

Gurstelle, William - *The Art of the Catapult: Build Greek Ballistae, Roman Onagers, English Trebuchets, and More Ancient Artillery*
y SLJ - v50 - i11 - Nov 2004 - p164(1) [501+]
NH - v113 - i10 - Dec 2004 - p51 [501+]

Gushee, David P. - *Getting Marriage Right: Realistic Counsel for Saving & Strengthening Relationships*
Ch Today - v48 - i7 - July 2004 - p66(1) [501+]
Righteous Gentiles of the Holocaust: Genocide and Moral Obligation, 2nd Ed.
R&R Bk N - v19 - i1 - Feb 2004 - p21(1) [501+]

Gustafson, Chris - *Acting Cool! Using Reader's Theatre to Teach Language Arts & Social Studies in Your Classroom*
LibMed - v22 - i5 - Feb 2004 - p83(1) [501+]

Gustafson, James M. - *An Examined Faith: The Grace of Self-Doubt*
JR - v85 - i1 - Jan 2005 - p151(2) [501+]

Gustafson, Jan - *Object-Oriented Real-Time Distributed Computing: Proceedings*
SciTech - v28 - i3 - Sept 2004 - p32(1) [51-500]

Gustafson, Lowell S. - *Economic Performance under Democratic Regimes in Latin America in the Twenty-First Century*
R&R Bk N - v19 - i1 - Feb 2004 - pNA [501+]

Gustafson, Scott - *Classic Fairy Tales*
c CH Bwatch - v14 - i9 - Sept 2004 - p3(1) [51-500]

Gustanski, Julie Ann - *Protecting the Land: Conservation Easements Past, Present, and Future*
NRJ - v44 - i2 - Spring 2004 - p621-651 [501+]

Gusterson, Hugh - *People of the Bomb: Portraits of America's Nuclear Complex*
Bwatch - Oct 2004 - pNA [51-500]
SciTech - v28 - i4 - Dec 2004 - p171(1) [51-500]

Gutcheon, Beth - *Leeway Cottage Book)*
KR - v73 - i3 - Feb 1 2005 - p137(2) [501+]
Leeway Cottage
PW - v252 - i9 - Feb 28 2005 - p40(1) [51-500]

Gutek, Gerald Lee - *The Montessori Method: The Origins of an Educational Innovation, Including an Abridged and Annotated Edition of Maria Montessori's "The Montessori Method"*
R&R Bk N - v19 - i3 - August 2004 - p215(1) [1-50]
Philosophical and Ideological Voices in Education
R&R Bk N - v19 - i1 - Feb 2004 - pNA [51-500]

Gutenschwager, Gerald A. - *Planning and Social Science: A Humanistic Approach*
R&R Bk N - v19 - i3 - August 2004 - p155(1) [51-500]

Guter, Bob - *Queer Crips: Disabled Gay Men and Their Stories*
R&R Bk N - v19 - i1 - Feb 2004 - p128(1) [51-500]

Guterson, David - *East of the Mountains (Read by Herrmann, Edward). Audiobook Review*
Globe & Mail - Jan 8 2005 - pD13 [1-50]
Our Lady of the Forest
Globe & Mail - August 21 2004 - pD13 [1-50]
y NYTBR - August 1 2004 - p16 [501+]

Guterson, Mary - *We Are All Fine Here*
KR - v72 - i21 - Nov 1 2004 - p1024(1) [51-500]
LJ - v129 - i20 - Dec 1 2004 - p100(1) [51-500]
PW - v251 - i47 - Nov 22 2004 - p37(1) [51-500]

Gutfield, Arnon - *American Exceptionalism: The Effects of Plenty on the American Experience*
Am St - v45 - i1 - Spring 2004 - p137-138 [501+]

Guthman, Julie - *Agrarian Dreams: The Paradox of Organic Farming in California*
Choice - v42 - i5 - Jan 2005 - p877(1) [1-50]

Guthrie, Allan - *Kiss Her Goodbye*
PW - v252 - i6 - Feb 7 2005 - p47(1) [51-500]

Guthrie, Arlo - *Sing Along with Putumayo*
Teach Mus - v12 - i1 - August 2004 - p61(2) [501+]

Guthrie, John T. - *Motivating Reading Comprehension: Concept-Oriented Reading Instruction*
R&R Bk N - v19 - i3 - August 2004 - p218(1) [1-50]

Guthrie, William P. - *The Later Thirty Years War: From the Battle of Wittstock to the Treaty of Westphalia*
GSR - v27 - i2 - May 2004 - p370-371 [501+]
J Mil H - v68 - i2 - April 2004 - p586(2) [501+]

Guthrie, Woody - *New Baby Train (Illus. by Frazee, Marla)*
c BL - v101 - i4 - Oct 15 2004 - p407(1) [51-500]
c HB - v80 - i5 - Sept-Oct 2004 - p566(2) [51-500]
c KR - v72 - i17 - Sept 1 2004 - p865(1) [51-500]
c PW - v251 - i31 - August 2 2004 - p69(1) [51-500]
c SLJ - v50 - i10 - Oct 2004 - p74(1) [51-500]
This Land Is Your Land (Illus. by Jakobsen, Kathy)
c SLJ - v50 - i12 - Dec 2004 - p59(1) [501+]

Gutierrez, Martha - *Macro-Economics: Making Gender Matter: Concepts, Policies and Institutional Change in Developing Countries*
JEL - v42 - i1 - March 2004 - p253(1) [501+]

Gutierrez, Nancy A. - *"Shall She Famish Then?": Female Food Refusal in Early Modern England*
R&R Bk N - v19 - i1 - Feb 2004 - p234(1) [51-500]

Gutierrez, Pedro Juan - *The Insatiable Spiderman*
NS - v134 - i4728 - Feb 21 2005 - p55(1) [501+]
Tropical Animal
BL - v101 - i9-10 - Jan 1 2005 - p816(2) [1-50]
KR - v72 - i22 - Nov 15 2004 - p1061(2) [501+]
LJ - v130 - i1 - Jan 1 2005 - p97(1) [51-500]
PW - v252 - i1 - Jan 3 2005 - p35(1) [51-500]

Gutierrez, Ricky S. - *Social Equity and the Funding of Community Policing*
R&R Bk N - v19 - i1 - Feb 2004 - p144(1) [51-500]

Gutkind, Lee - *Forever Fat: Essays by the Godfather*
Sew R - v112 - i3 - Summer 2004 - p427-438 [501+]
In Fact: The Best of Creative Nonfiction
y BL - v101 - i6 - Nov 15 2004 - p546(1) [51-500]
y Kliatt - v39 - i2 - March 2005 - p32(1) [51-500]
LJ - v129 - i20 - Dec 1 2004 - p117(2) [51-500]

Gutman, Anne - *Gaspard and Lisa's Ready for School Words (Illus. by Hallensleben, Georg)*
c BL - v100 - i22 - August 2004 - p1948(1) [51-500]
c SLJ - v50 - i10 - Oct 2004 - p114(1) [51-500]
Penelope at School (Illus. by Hallensleben, Georg)
c PW - v251 - i41 - Oct 11 2004 - p82(1) [501+]

Gutman, Dan - *Abner and Me*
y BL - v101 - i9-10 - Jan 1 2005 - p858(1) [1-50]
The Get Rich Quick Club (Read by Goethals, Angela). Audiobook Review
c PW - v251 - i50 - Dec 13 2004 - p24(1) [51-500]
The Get Rich Quick Club (Illus. by Gutman, Dan)
c BL - v100 - i22 - August 2004 - p1934(1) [51-500]
c KR - v72 - i13 - July 1 2004 - p629(1) [51-500]
c PW - v251 - i36 - Sept 6 2004 - p63(1) [51-500]
c SLJ - v50 - i8 - August 2004 - p87(1) [51-500]
Jackie and Me: A Baseball Card Adventure (Read by Heller, Johnny). Audiobook Review
y Kliatt - v39 - i1 - Jan 2005 - p44(2) [51-500]
c SLJ - v50 - i10 - Oct 2004 - p74(1) [501+]
The Kid Who Ran for President
c BL - v101 - i3 - Oct 1 2004 - p327(1) [51-500]
The Million Dollar Strike
c BL - v101 - i1 - Sept 1 2004 - p111(1) [1-50]
c SLJ - v50 - i12 - Dec 2004 - p146(1) [501+]
Miss Daisy Is Crazy! (Illus. by Paillot, Jim)
c BL - v101 - i1 - Sept 1 2004 - p121(1) [1-50]
Mr. Klutz Is Nuts! (Illus. by Paillot, Jim)
c SLJ - v50 - i11 - Nov 2004 - p104(2) [501+]

Gutmann, Amy - *Identity in Democracy*
Ethics - v114 - i4 - July 2004 - p820(4) [501+]

Gutmann, Ethan - *Losing the New China: A Story of American Commerce, Desire and Betrayal*
R&R Bk N - v19 - i3 - August 2004 - p125(1) [51-500]

Gutmann, Matthew C. - *Changing Men and Masculinities in Latin America*
CS - v33 - i2 - March 2004 - p176-177 [501+]

Gutner, Tamar L. - *Banking on the Environmental: Multilateral Development Banks and Their Environmental Performance in Central and Eastern Europe*
Slav R - v63 - i3 - Fall 2004 - p623-624 [501+]

Gutschow, Kim - *Being a Buddhist Nun: The Struggle for Enlightenment in the Himalayas*
Choice - v42 - i4 - Dec 2004 - p678(1) [1-50]
Wom R Bks - v21 - i10-11 - July 2004 - p27(1) [51-500]

Gutschow, Niels - *Sacred Landscape of the Himalaya: Proceedings*
R&R Bk N - v19 - i4 - Nov 2004 - p47(1) [51-500]

Gutteddge, Rene - *The Splitting Storm*
BL - v101 - i3 - Oct 1 2004 - p300(1) [501+]

Gutteridge, Alex - *Oven Chips for Tea*
c Sch Lib - v52 - i3 - Autumn 2004 - p145(1) [501+]

Gutteridge, Don - *Turncoat: A Marc Edwards Mystery*
CBRA - Annual 2003 - p168(1) [501+]

Guttmann, Allen - *Sports: The First Five Millennia*
LJ - v130 - i3 - Feb 15 2005 - p137(1) [51-500]

Guttridge, Peter - *No Laughing Matter*
DroRevMy - v24 - i4 - July-August 2004 - p12(1) [501+]
LJ - v129 - i16 - Oct 1 2004 - p62(1) [51-500]

Guttteridge, Rene - *Boo Who*
PW - v251 - i30 - July 26 2004 - p38(1) [501+]

Guy-Bray, Stephen - *Homoerotic Space: The Poetics of Loss in Renaissance Literature*
Six Ct J - v34 - i4 - Winter 2003 - p1255-1256 [501+]

Guy, Geoffrey W. - *Medicinal Uses of Cannabis and Cannabinoids*
E-Streams - Dec 2004 - pNA [501+]

Guy, J.A. - *Queen of Scots: The True Life of Mary Stuart*
Choice - v42 - i5 - Jan 2005 - p920(1) [1-50]
R&R Bk N - v19 - i3 - August 2004 - p40(1) [51-500]

Guy, Jasmine - *Afeni Shakur: Evolution of a Revolutionary*
Black Iss - v6 - i4 - July-August 2004 - p53(2) [51-500]

Guy, John - *My Heart Is My Own: The Life of Mary Queen of Scots*
Lon R Bks - v26 - i20 - Oct 21 2004 - p1(3) [501+]
TLS - i5267 - March 12 2004 - p8-9 [501+]
Queen of Scots: The True Life of Mary Stuart
BW - v34 - i28 - July 11 2004 - p6(1) [501+]
HRNB - v33 - i1 - Fall 2004 - p23(1) [501+]

Guy, Kolleen M. - *When Champagne Became French: Wine and the Making of a National Identity*
J Hist G - v30 - i1 - Jan 2004 - p202(2) [501+]
J Soc H - v38 - i1 - Fall 2004 - p219(3) [501+]
T&C - v45 - i2 - April 2004 - p423-423 [501+]

H

Haa-Wilson, Deborah - *Managed Care and Monopoly Power: The Antitrust Challenge*
JEL - v41 - i4 - Dec 2003 - p1374(1) [501+]

Haab, Sherri - *The Art of Metal Clay: Techniques for Creating Jewelry and Decorative Objects*
Ceram Mo - v52 - i6 - June-August 2004 - p36(1) [501+]

The Hip Handbag Book: 25 Easy-to-Make Totes, Purses, and Bags
y Kliatt - v39 - i2 - March 2005 - p44(1) [51-500]

Haack, Susan - *Defending Science--Within Reason: Between Scientism and Cynicism*
Choice - v41 - i7 - March 2004 - p1315-1 [501+]
Sci - v305 - i5680 - July 2 2004 - p44(2) [501+]

Haacker, Klaus - *The Theology of Paul's Letter to the Romans*
Intpr - v58 - i3 - July 2004 - p313(1) [501+]

Haag, Michael - *Alexandria: City of Memory*
CR - v286 - i1669 - Feb 2005 - p121(1) [51-500]
G&L Rev W - v12 - i1 - Jan-Feb 2005 - p45(2) [501+]

Haager, Diane - *Differentiating Instruction in Inclusive Classrooms: The Special Educator's Guide*
R&R Bk N - v19 - i4 - Nov 2004 - p192(1) [501+]

Haak, Martine - *Approaches to Arabic Dialects: Collection of Articles Presented to Manfred Woidich on the Occasion of His Sixtieth Birthday*
R&R Bk N - v19 - i1 - Feb 2004 - p218(1) [51-500]

Haan, Ellen de - *Boomer Shock: Preparing Communities for the Retirement Generation*
R&R Bk N - v19 - i2 - May 2004 - p136 [51-500]

Haan, Linda de - *King and King and Family (Illus. by Haan, Linda de)*
HB - v80 - i4 - July-August 2004 - p434(2) [51-500]

King & King & Family (Illus. by Haan, Linda de)
c Advocate - July 20 2004 - p51(1) [51-500]
c CCB-B - v57 - i11 - July-August 2004 - p459(1) [501+]
c SLJ - v50 - i9 - Sept 2004 - p158(1) [51-500]

Haanappel, P.P.C. - *The Law and Policy of Air Space and Outer Space: A Comparative Approach*
R&R Bk N - v19 - i1 - Feb 2004 - pNA [501+]

Haar, B. J. ter - *Ritual and Mythology of the Chinese Triads: Creating an Identity*
Ch Rev Int - v11 - i1 - Spring 2004 - p180(2) [501+]

Haar, Jaap ter - *The Ice Road*
c Sch Lib - v52 - i4 - Winter 2004 - p192(1) [51-500]

Haardt, Anton - *Mose T, A to Z: The Folk Art of Mose Tolliver*
Black Iss - v7 - i1 - Jan-Feb 2005 - p44(1) [51-500]

Haas, Andrew W. - *Poetics of Critique: The Interdisciplinarity of Textuality*
R&R Bk N - v19 - i1 - Feb 2004 - p16(1) [1-50]

Haas, Birgit - *Modern German Political Drama 1980-2000*
Ger Q - v77 - i4 - Fall 2004 - p502-503 [501+]

Haas, Jack - *Roots and Wings: Adventures of a Spirit on Earth*
CBRA - Annual 2003 - p47(1) [51-500]

Haas, Jessie - *Birthday Pony (Illus. by Apple, Margot)*
c BL - v100 - i22 - August 2004 - p1934(1) [51-500]
c HB - v80 - i5 - Sept-Oct 2004 - p584(2) [51-500]
c KR - v72 - i13 - July 1 2004 - p630(1) [51-500]
c SLJ - v50 - i10 - Oct 2004 - p114(1) [51-500]

Scamper and the Horse Show (Illus. by Apple, Margot)
c SLJ - v50 - i7 - July 2004 - p77(1) [51-500]

Haasen, Adolf - *New Corporate Cultures That Motivate*
R&R Bk N - v19 - i1 - Feb 2004 - p91(1) [1-50]

Habeck, Mary R. - *Storm of Steel: The Development of Armor Doctrine in Germany and the Soviet Union, 1919-1939*
Slav R - v63 - i3 - Fall 2004 - p662-663 [501+]

Habel, Dorothy Metzger - *The Urban Development of Rome in the Age of Alexander VII*
Six Ct J - v34 - i4 - Winter 2003 - p1161-1162 [501+]

Haber, Karen - *Science Fiction: The Best of 2003*
ChrSFF&H - v26 - i10 - Oct 2004 - p49(2) [501+]

Haber, Melissa - *The Heroic Adventures of Hercules Amsterdam*
LibMed - v22 - i5 - Feb 2004 - p67(1) [501+]

Haber, Stephen - *The Politics of Property Rights: Political Instability, Credible Commitments, and Economic Growth in Mexico, 1876-1929*
JEL - v41 - i4 - Dec 2003 - p1409(1) [501+]
PSQ - v119 - i3 - Fall 2004 - p556(3) [501+]

Haberman, Rex S. - *Middle Ear and Mastoid Surgery*
SciTech - v28 - i1 - March 2004 - p115(1) [51-500]

Habermas, Gary R. - *Risen Jesus and Future Hope*
R&R Bk N - v19 - i4 - Nov 2004 - p22(1) [1-50]

Habermas, Jurgen - *The Future of Human Nature*
QRB - v79 - i4 - Dec 2004 - p460(2) [501+]

Religion and Rationality: Essays on Reason, God, and Modernity
Theol St - v65 - i4 - Dec 2004 - p907(2) [501+]

Truth and Justification
CS - v33 - i5 - Sept 2004 - p624-624 [501+]
Ethics - v115 - i1 - Oct 2004 - p187(2) [501+]
HER - v74 - i2 - Summer 2004 - p209-218 [501+]
RM - v58 - i2 - Dec 2004 - p438(3) [501+]

Habib, Jasmin - *Israel, Diaspora, and the Routes of National Belonging*
Globe & Mail - Nov 20 2004 - pD17 [501+]

Habib, S. Irfan - *Situating the History of Science: Dialogues with Joseph Needham*
T&C - v45 - i1 - Jan 2004 - p173(3) [501+]

Hachey, Michael - *A Matter of Motive*
BL - v101 - i7 - Dec 1 2004 - p639(1) [51-500]
PW - v251 - i47 - Nov 22 2004 - p42(1) [51-500]

Hachler, Bruno - *Blue-Footed Booby Dance (Illus. by Ratto, Cinzia)*
c PW - v251 - i47 - Nov 22 2004 - p60(1) [51-500]
c SLJ - v50 - i11 - Nov 2004 - p106(1) [51-500]

What Does My Teddy Bear Do All Day? (Illus. by Mailer, Binte)
c SLJ - v51 - i1 - Jan 2005 - p92(2) [51-500]

What Does My Teddy Bear Do All Day? (Illus. by Muller, Birte)
c KR - v72 - i20 - Oct 15 2004 - p1007(1) [51-500]

Hachmeister, Gretchen L. - *Italy in German Literary Imagination: Goethe's "Italian Journey" and Its Reception by Eichendorff, Platen, and Heine*
GSR - v27 - i3 - Oct 2004 - p615(2) [501+]

Hachmeister, Lutz - *Die Herren Journalisten: Die Elite der deutschen Presse nach 1945*
HNet - Oct 2004 - pNA [501+]

Hack, Richard - *Clash of Titans: How the Unbridled Ambition of Ted Turner and Rupert Murdoch Has Created Global Empires That Control What We Read and Watch Each Day*
TV Q - v34 - i2 - Wntr 2004 - p82-83 [501+]

Puppetmaster: The Secret Life of J. Edgar Hoover (Read by Cashman, Dan). Audiobook Review
y Kliatt - v39 - i1 - Jan 2005 - p53(1) [51-500]
LJ - v130 - i1 - Jan 1 2005 - p170(1) [51-500]

Hacker, Jacob S. - *The Divided Welfare State: The Battle over Public and Private Social Benefits in the United States*
JIH - v34 - i3 - Wntr 2004 - p487(2) [501+]

The Dividend Welfare State: The Battle over Public and Private Social Benefits in the United States
JAH - v91 - i1 - June 2004 - p332-333 [501+]

Hacker, Marilyn - *Desesperanto: Poems, 1999-2002*
PSQ - v78 - i3 - Fall 2004 - p169(6) [501+]
WLT - v78 - i3-4 - Sept-Dec 2004 - p99(2) [501+]
Wom R Bks - v21 - i10-11 - July 2004 - p6(2) [501+]

Hacker, Neville F. - *Essential Obstetrics and Gynecology, 4th Ed.*
SciTech - v28 - i4 - Dec 2004 - p110(1) [51-500]

Hacker, Stephen - *Transformational Leadership: Creating Organizations of Meaning*
R&R Bk N - v19 - i1 - Feb 2004 - p90(1) [1-50]

Hackett, Robin - *Sapphic Primitivism: Production of Race, Class, and Sexuality in Key Works of Modern Fiction*
Choice - v42 - i4 - Dec 2004 - p659(1) [1-50]

Hacking, Norm - *When Cats Go Wrong (Illus. by Nugent, Cynthia)*
c Res Links - v10 - i3 - Feb 2005 - p4(2) [51-500]

Hackman, Gene - *Justice for None (Read by Peakes, John). Audiobook Review*
y Kliatt - v39 - i2 - March 2005 - p54(1) [51-500]

Haddad, Michael - *The Screenwriter's Sourcebook: A Comprehensive Marketing Guide for Screen and Television Writers*
BL - v101 - i9-10 - Jan 1 2005 - p802(1) [51-500]
LJ - v130 - i3 - Feb 15 2005 - p131(1) [51-500]

Haddad, Yvonne Yazbeck - *Islamic Law and the Challenges of Modernity*
R&R Bk N - v19 - i3 - August 2004 - p194(1) [501+]

Religion and Immigration: Christian, Jewish, and Muslim Experiences in the United States
AHR - v109 - i2 - April 2004 - p563(2) [501+]

Haddam, Jane - *The Headmaster's Wife*
KR - v73 - i5 - March 1 2005 - p262(1) [51-500]
LJ - v130 - i4 - March 1 2005 - p71(1) [51-500]
PW - v252 - i9 - Feb 28 2005 - p45(1) [51-500]

Haddix, Margaret Peterson - *Among the Betrayed*
c RT - v57 - Oct 2003 - p175 [1-50]

Among the Brave
y BIC - v33 - i6 - Sept 2004 - p39(2) [501+]
y VOYA - v27 - i3 - August 2004 - p230(1) [1-50]

Among the Hidden (Read by Davis, Jonathan). Audiobook Review
c Kliatt - v38 - i4 - July 2004 - p46(1) [51-500]

Among the Hidden
y Storyworks - v12 - i5 - Feb-March 2005 - p7(1) [51-500]

Escape from Memory
y LibMed - v22 - i6 - March 2004 - p64(1) [501+]

The House on the Gulf
c BL - v101 - i1 - Sept 1 2004 - p124(1) [1-50]
c CCB-B - v58 - i2 - Oct 2004 - p75(1) [51-500]
c CH Bwatch - Feb 2005 - pNA [51-500]
c KR - v72 - i15 - August 1 2004 - p741(1) [51-500]
c SLJ - v50 - i10 - Oct 2004 - p165(2) [51-500]

Leaving Fishers
y Kliatt - v38 - i5 - Sept 2004 - p20(2) [51-500]

Turnabout
c Teach Lib - v32 - i3 - Feb 2005 - p54(1) [1-50]

Haddon, Mark - *The Curious Incident of the Dog in the Night-Time (Read by Woodman, Jeff). Audiobook Review*
BL - v101 - i6 - Nov 15 2004 - p607(1) [501+]
VOYA - v27 - i5 - Dec 2004 - p372(1) [501+]

The Curious Incident of the Dog in the Night-Time
    Globe & Mail - July 3 2004 - pD13 [1-50]
    y Kliatt - v38 - i4 - July 2004 - p18(1) [51-500]

Hadfield, Andrew - *Amazons, Savages, and Machiavels: Travel and Colonial Writing in English, 1550-1630*
    Six Ct J - v35 - i3 - Fall 2004 - p918(1) [501+]

Hadley, Leila - *A Garden by the Sea: A Practical Guide and Journal*
    PW - v252 - i9 - Feb 28 2005 - p56(2) [51-500]

Hadot, Pierre - *What is Ancient Philosophy?*
    Class R - v54 - i1 - May 2004 - p69(2) [501+]
    South HR - v38 - i3 - Summer 2004 - p292-296 [501+]

Hadow, Pen - *The North Pole: Alone and Unsupported*
    Spec - v296 - i9197 - Nov 13 2004 - p61(2) [501+]

Haduch, Bill - *Go Fly a Bike!: The Ultimate Book about Bicycle Fun, Freedom & Science (Illus. by Murphy, Chris)*
    c SLJ - v50 - i10 - Oct 2004 - pS48(1) [51-500]

Haduck, Bill - *Food Rules! The Stuff You Munch, Its Crunch, and Why You Sometimes Lose Your Lunch*
    c SB - v40 - i4 - July-August 2004 - p149(2) [51-500]

Hadziic, Admir - *Peripheral Nerve Blocks*
    SciTech - v28 - i1 - March 2004 - p110(1) [51-500]

Haeckel, Ernest - *Art Forms in Nature*
    Bwatch - Oct 2004 - pNA [51-500]

Haedrich, Ken - *Pie: 300 Tried-and-True Recipes for Delicious Homemade Pie*
    BL - v101 - i2 - Sept 15 2004 - p189(1) [51-500]
    LJ - v129 - i15 - Sept 15 2004 - p78(1) [51-500]
    PW - v251 - i33 - August 16 2004 - p57(1) [51-500]

Haefeli, Evan - *Captors and Captives: The 1704 French and Indian Raid on Deerfield*
    Choice - v42 - i11-12 - July-August 2004 - p2107(2) [501+]
    JAH - v91 - i3 - Dec 2004 - p991(2) [501+]
    NEQ - v77 - i4 - Dec 2004 - p653-655 [501+]

Haefner, H. - *IRAOs: Interview for the Retrospective Assessment of the Onset and Course of Schizophrenia and Other Psychosis*
    SciTech - v28 - i3 - Sept 2004 - p100(1) [51-500]

Haeg, Lawrence Peter - *In Gatsby's Shadow: The Story of Charles Macomb Flandrau*
    Choice - v42 - i6 - Feb 2005 - p1023(1) [51-500]
    R&R Bk N - v19 - i4 - Nov 2004 - p243(1) [501+]

Haeger, John Winthrop - *North American Pinot Noir*
    LJ - v129 - i14 - Sept 1 2004 - p181(1) [51-500]

Haelewyck, Jean-Claude - *Hester. Fascicule 1. Introduction*
    Theol St - v66 - i1 - March 2005 - p224(1) [501+]

Haeri, Shahla - *No Shame for the Sun: Lives of Professional Pakistani Women*
    IJMES - v36 - i3 - August 2004 - p498-499 [501+]

Haerle, Dan - *Jazz Improvisation: A Pocket Guide*
    Teach Mus - v12 - i4 - Feb 2005 - p78(1) [51-500]

Hafen, Leroy R. - *To the Pike's Peak Gold Fields*
    Roundup M - v12 - i1 - Oct 2004 - p22(1) [51-500]

Hafez, E.S.E. - *Atlas of Reproductive Physiology in Men*
    E-Streams - Sept 2004 - pNA [501+]
    SciTech - v28 - i1 - March 2004 - p72(1) [51-500]

Haffner, Sebastian - *Isherwood: A Life*
    Quad - v48 - i11 - Nov 2004 - p83(3) [501+]

Haffner, Stephen - *Seventy-Five: The Diamond Anniversary of a Science Fiction Pioneer (Illus. by Hauptmann, Richard A.)*
    LJ - v129 - i20 - Dec 1 2004 - p184(1) [501+]

Hafiz, Ed - *Hafiz of Shiraz: Thirty Poems, an Introduction to the Sufi Master*
    R&R Bk N - v19 - i1 - Feb 2004 - p218(1) [51-500]

Hafner, Ralph - *Gotter im Exil: Fruhneuzeitliches Dichtungsverstandnis im Spannungsfeld christlicher Apologetik und philologischer Kritik*
    Ren Q - v57 - i4 - Winter 2004 - p1454(2) [501+]

Hagan, Charles C., Jr. - *Not Guilty Every Time: Keys to Courtroom Victory*
    R&R Bk N - v19 - i4 - Nov 2004 - p173(1) [501+]

Hagan, Frank E. - *Essentials of Research Methods in Criminal Justice and Criminology*
    R&R Bk N - v19 - i3 - August 2004 - p163(1) [501+]

Hagan, John - *Justice in the Balkans: Prosecuting War Crimes in the Hague Tribunal*
    TimHES - v0 - i1665 - Nov 5 2004 - p26(1) [501+]

Hagan, William T. - *Taking Indian Lands: The Cherokee (Jerome) Commission, 1889-1893*
    SHQ - v107 - i4 - April 2004 - p618(2) [501+]
    WHQ - v35 - i2 - Summer 2004 - p243-244 [501+]
    JAH - v91 - i2 - Sept 2004 - p652(2) [501+]

Hagberg, Karen A. - *Stage Presence from Head to Toe: A Manual for Musicians*
    M Ed J - v91 - i1 - Sept 2004 - p63(1) [501+]
    R&R Bk N - v19 - i1 - Feb 2004 - p198(1) [51-500]

Hage, Christine Lind - *Public Library Start-Up Guide*
    R&R Bk N - v19 - i1 - Feb 2004 - p259(1) [51-500]

Hagedorn, Ann - *Beyond the River: The Untold Story of the Heroes of the Underground Railroad*
    JAH - v91 - i1 - June 2004 - p235-236 [501+]

Hagedorn, Suzanne C. - *Abandoned Women: Rewriting the Classics in Dante, Boccaccio, & Chaucer*
    Choice - v41 - i11-12 - July-August 2004 - p2038 [501+]
    Med R - June 2004 - pNA [501+]

Hagelia, Hallvard - *Coram Deo: Spirituality in the Book of Isaiah, with Particular Attention to Faith in Yahweh*
    JNES - v63 - i4 - Oct 2004 - p304(2) [501+]

Hagelin, Ove - *Old and Rare Books on Materia Medica in the Library of the Swedish Pharmaceutical Society [Apotekarsocieteten]*
    SciTech - v28 - i1 - March 2004 - p124(1) [51-500]

Hageman, Louis A. - *Applied Iterative Methods*
    SciTech - v28 - i4 - Dec 2004 - p38(1) [51-500]

Hagemann, Harald - *The Economics of Structural Change*
    JEL - v41 - i4 - Dec 2003 - p1420(2) [501+]

Hagen, Anja - *Gedachtnisort Romantik*
    Ger Q - v77 - i2 - Spring 2004 - p244-246 [501+]

Hagen, George - *The Laments (Read by Matthews, Richard). Audiobook Review*
    y Kliatt - v39 - i1 - Jan 2005 - p46(1) [51-500]
The Laments
    KR - v72 - i24 - Dec 15 2004 - pS10(1) [501+]
    NYTBR - August 22 2004 - p8 [501+]
    People - v62 - i1 - July 5 2004 - p47 [51-500]
    y SLJ - v50 - i10 - Oct 2004 - p198(1) [51-500]

Hagen, Susan - *Women at Ground Zero: Stories of Courage and Compassion*
    HNet - Sept 2004 - pNA [501+]

Hagen, William W. - *Ordinary Prussians: Brandenburg Junkers and Villagers, 1500-1840*
    CEH - v37 - i2 - Spring 2004 - p291(3) [501+]
    JIH - v35 - i1 - Summer 2004 - p135-136 [501+]
    JMH - v77 - i1 - March 2005 - p216(2) [501+]

Hager, Alan - *The Age of Milton: An Encyclopedia of Major 17th-Century British and American Authors*
    BL - v100 - i22 - August 2004 - p1972(1) [501+]
    LJ - v129 - i14 - Sept 1 2004 - p186(1) [51-500]
    TLS - i5289 - August 13 2004 - p29(1) [501+]

Hagg, Thomas - *The Virgin and Her Lover: Fragments of an Ancient Greek Novel and a Persian Epic Poem*
    R&R Bk N - v19 - i1 - Feb 2004 - p218(1) [51-500]

Haggard, Howard Wilcox - *From Medicine Man to Doctor: The Story of the Science of Healing*
    SciTech - v28 - i4 - Dec 2004 - p76(1) [51-500]

Haggard, Stephan - *Economic Crisis and Corporate Restructuring in Korea: Reforming the Chaebol*
    JAS - v63 - i2 - May 2004 - p520(1) [501+]
    JEL - v42 - i4 - Dec 2004 - p1138(2) [501+]

Haggart, Ron - *Rumours of War*
    Globe & Mail - March 12 2005 - pD19 [501+]

Haggh, Barbara - *Essays on Music and Culture in Honor of Herbert Kellman*
    Six Ct J - v35 - i3 - Fall 2004 - p900-902 [501+]

Hagiioannu, Andrew - *The Man Who Would Be Kipling: The Colonial Fiction and the Frontiers of Exile*
    ELT - v48 - i2 - Spring 2005 - p88(4) [501+]

Hagman, Harvey - *Majesty from Assateague*
    CH Bwatch - v14 - i9 - Sept 2004 - p6(1) [51-500]

Hagstrom, David - *From Outrageous to Inspired: How to Build a Community of Leaders in Our Schools*
    R&R Bk N - v19 - i3 - August 2004 - p224(1) [1-50]

Hagstrom, Robert G. - *The Detective and the Investor: Uncovering Investment Techniques from Legendary Sleuths*
    R&R Bk N - v19 - i3 - August 2004 - p137(1) [51-500]

Hague, Paul - *Market Research in Practice: A Guide to the Basics*
    R&R Bk N - v19 - i3 - August 2004 - p127(1) [51-500]

Hague, William - *William Pitt the Younger*
    CR - v286 - i1669 - Feb 2005 - p124(1) [51-500]
    NS - v133 - i4716 - Nov 29 2004 - p48(2) [51-500]
    Spec - v296 - i9191 - Oct 2 2004 - p48(2) [51-500]
    TLS - i5297 - Oct 8 2004 - p36(1) [501+]

Hahn, Daniel - *The Tower Menagerie: The Amazing 600-Year History of the Royal Collection of Wild and Ferocious Beasts Kept at the Tower of London*
    SciTech - v28 - i3 - Sept 2004 - p63(1) [51-500]

Hahn, Johannes - *Zerstorungen des Jerusalemer Tempels: Geschehen--Wahrnehmung--Bewaltigung*
    Theol St - v65 - i4 - Dec 2004 - p850(2) [501+]

Hahn, Mary Downing - *Following My Own Footsteps*
    c Storyworks - v12 - i1 - Sept 2004 - p9(1) [51-500]
Hear the Wind Blow
    LibMed - v22 - i5 - Feb 2004 - p69(1) [501+]
The Old Willis Place: A Ghost Story
    c BL - v101 - i1 - Sept 1 2004 - p124(1) [1-50]
    c CCB-B - v58 - i3 - Nov 2004 - p122(2) [501+]
    c KR - v72 - i17 - Sept 1 2004 - p866(1) [51-500]
    c SLJ - v50 - i12 - Dec 2004 - p146(1) [501+]

Hahn, Peter L. - *Caught in the Middle East: U.S. Policy toward the Arab-Israeli Conflict, 1945-1961*
    Choice - v42 - i3 - Nov 2004 - p560(2) [1-50]
    MEJ - v58 - i4 - Autumn 2004 - p679(2) [501+]
    Nation - v279 - i6 - August 30 2004 - p38 [501+]

Hahn, Regina U. - *The Democratic Dream: Stefan Heym in America*
    GSR - v27 - i3 - Oct 2004 - p674(2) [501+]

Hahn, Robert W. - *High-Stakes Antitrust: The Last Hurrah?*
    R&R Bk N - v19 - i1 - Feb 2004 - pNA [51-500]

Hahn, Scott - *Catholic for a Reason 111: Scripture & the Mystery of the Mass*
    CI - v12 - i9 - Oct 2004 - p44(1) [501+]

Hahn, Steven - *A Nation under Our Feet: Black Political Struggles in the Rural South from Slavery to the Great Migration*
    HNet - Sept 2004 - pNA [501+]
    JAH - v91 - i3 - Dec 2004 - p981(2) [501+]
Nation under Our Feet: Black Political Struggles in the Rural South from Slavery to the Great Migration
    New R - August 2 2004 - p33 [501+]

Hahn, Thich Nhat - *True Love: A Practice for Awakening the Heart*
    PW - v251 - i35 - August 30 2004 - p52(1) [51-500]

Hahn, Thomas - *Robin Hood and Popular Culture: Violence, Transgression, and Justice*
    JEGP - v103 - i2 - April 2004 - p271-272 [501+]

Haid, Regis W. - *Advances in Spinal Stabilization*
    SciTech - v28 - i1 - March 2004 - p111(1) [51-500]
Lumbar Interbody Fusion Techniques: Cages, Dowels and Grafts
    SciTech - v28 - i3 - Sept 2004 - p114(1) [51-500]

Haidu, Peter - *The Subject Medieval/Modern: Text and Governance in the Middle Ages*
    Med R - July 2004 - pNA [501+]

Haig, Brian - *The President's Assassin*
    Ent W - i808 - Feb 25 2005 - p106 [51-500]
    KR - v73 - i1 - Jan 1 2005 - p9(1) [501+]
    PW - v252 - i2 - Jan 10 2005 - p37(1) [51-500]

Haig-Brown, Roderick Langmere - *Starbuck Valley Winter*
    y Can CL - i111-112 - Fall-Winter 2003 - p153(6) [501+]
Whale People
    y CBRA - Annual 2003 - p486(1) [51-500]

Haig, Scott V. - *Orthopedic Emergencies: A Radiographic Atlas*
    SciTech - v28 - i4 - Dec 2004 - p109(1) [51-500]

Haigh, Gideon - *The Uncyclopedia*
    Globe & Mail - Feb 5 2005 - pD17 [501+]
    R&R Bk N - v20 - i1 - Feb 2005 - p1(1) [51-500]

Haigh, Jennifer - *Baker Towers*
    People - v63 - i3 - Jan 24 2005 - p49 [51-500]
    y BL - v101 - i5 - Nov 1 2004 - p464(1) [51-500]
    KR - v72 - i18 - Sept 15 2004 - p883(1) [501+]
    LJ - v129 - i20 - Dec 1 2004 - p100(1) [51-500]
    PW - v251 - i47 - Nov 22 2004 - p38(2) [51-500]
    Ent W - i801 - Jan 14 2005 - p94 [51-500]

Haight, David F. - *The Scandal of Reason: Or Shadow of God*
    R&R Bk N - v19 - i3 - August 2004 - p26(1) [1-50]

Haight, Roger - *Christian Community in History, Vol. 1*
AM - v192 - i4 - Feb 7 2005 - p35 [501+]
Comw - v132 - i2 - Jan 28 2005 - p34(3) [501+]

Hailey, Elizabeth Forsythe - *Woman of Independent Means*
LJ - v130 - i1 - Jan 1 2005 - p174(1) [501+]

Hails, Rosie S. - *Genes in the Environment*
QRB - v79 - i3 - Sept 2004 - p307(2) [501+]

Hailwood, Simon - *How to Be a Green Liberal: Nature, Value and Liberal Philosophy*
R&R Bk N - v19 - i3 - August 2004 - p172(1) [501+]

Haim, Alexander - *24 Hour MBA*
Bwatch - v26 - i8 - August 2004 - p8(1) [51-500]

Haiman, Franklyn S. - *Religious Expression and the American Constitution*
JouAmCul - v27 - i3 - Sept 2004 - p350(4) [501+]
R&R Bk N - v19 - i3 - August 2004 - p203(1) [1-50]

Haine, Malou - *L'Apollonide de Leconte de Lisle et Franz Servais*
Notes - v61 - i3 - March 2005 - p758(3) [501+]

Haines, John Dickinson - *Eight Centuries of Troubadours and Trouveres: The Changing Identity of Medieval Music*
Choice - v42 - i5 - Jan 2005 - p861(1) [1-50]
Music and Medieval Manuscripts: Paleography and Performance: Essays Dedicated to Andrew Hughes
R&R Bk N - v19 - i4 - Nov 2004 - p195(1) [501+]

Haines, Robin - *Charles Trevelyan and the Great Irish Famine*
R&R Bk N - v19 - i4 - Nov 2004 - p37(1) [51-500]
Life and Death in the Age of Sail
AHS - v35 - i124 - 2004 - p392(2) [501+]

Hainsfurther, Stephanie - *Covering the Business Beat: Strategies for Publishing What You Write*
R&R Bk N - v19 - i4 - Nov 2004 - p228(1) [501+]

Haitovsky, Yoel - *Foundations of Statistical Inference: Proceedings of the Shoresh Conference 2000*
JEL - v42 - i1 - March 2004 - p244(1) [501+]

Hajdu, I. - *Kommentar zur 4. Philippischen Rede des Demosthenes*
Class R - v53 - i2 - Nov 2003 - pNA [501+]

Hajek, Alan - *Waging War on Pascal's Wager*
RM - v58 - i1 - Sept 2004 - p228(1) [501+]

Hajek, Ann E. - *Natural Enemies: An Introduction to Biological Control*
QRB - v79 - i4 - Dec 2004 - p451(1) [501+]

Haji, Ishtiyaque - *Dialectical Delicacies in the Debate about Freedom and Alternative Possibilities*
RM - v58 - i1 - Sept 2004 - p220(1) [501+]

Hajiyev, Chingis - *Fault Diagnosis and Reconfiguration in Flight Control Systems*
SciTech - v28 - i1 - March 2004 - p169(1) [51-500]

Hajjar, Lisa - *The Palestine People: A History*
CS - v33 - i5 - Sept 2004 - p583-585 [501+]

Hakakian, Roya - *Journey from the Land of No: A Girlhood Caught in Revolutionary Iran*
BL - v100 - i21 - July 2004 - p1812(1) [1-50]
BW - v34 - i36 - Sept 5 2004 - p4(1) [501+]
Ent W - i778 - August 13 2004 - p92 [51-500]
Globe & Mail - Sept 18 2004 - pD21 [501+]
SLJ - v50 - i12 - Dec 2004 - p176(1) [51-500]

Haken, Hermann - *Molecular Physics and Elements of Quantum Chemistry: Introduction to Experiments and Theory*
Choice - v42 - i4 - Dec 2004 - p698(1) [1-50]

Hakes, Trinka - *The Scarlet Stockings Spy (Illus. by Papp, Robert)*
c Inst - v114 - i5 - Jan-Feb 2005 - p73(2) [501+]

Hakim, Catherine - *Key Issues in Women's Work: Female Diversity and the Polarisation of Women's Employment*
TimHES - v0 - i1679 - Feb 18 2005 - p26(1) [501+]
Models of the Family in Modern Societies: Ideals and Realities
R&R Bk N - v19 - i1 - Feb 2004 - p129(1) [51-500]

Hakim, Joy - *The Story of Science: Aristotle Leads the Way*
c BL - v101 - i4 - Oct 15 2004 - p417(2) [51-500]
y NH - v113 - i10 - Dec 2004 - p52(1) [1-50]
c NYT - Nov 7 2004 - p11 [501+]
y SLJ - v50 - i12 - Dec 2004 - p161(1) [501+]

Halaas, David Fridtjof - *Halfbreed: The Remarkable True Story of George Bent-Caught Between the Worlds of the Indian and the White Man*
Choice - v42 - i2 - Oct 2004 - p355(1) [51-500]

Halabi, Rabah - *Israeli and Palestinian Identities in Dialogue: The School for Peace Approach*
MEJ - v58 - i4 - Autumn 2004 - p684(2) [501+]

Haladyna, Thomas M. - *Developing and Validating Multiple-Choice Test Items, 3rd Ed.*
R&R Bk N - v19 - i4 - Nov 2004 - p188(1) [501+]

Halam, Ann - *Taylor Five*
c CH Bwatch - v14 - i7 - July 2004 - p7(2) [501+]

Halasa, Malu - *Transit Beirut*
TLS - i5296 - Oct 1 2004 - p30-31 [51-500]

Halberstam, David - *The Teammates: A Portrait of a Friendship*
Kliatt - v38 - i4 - July 2004 - p45(1) [51-500]

Halbert, Terry - *CyberEthics, 2nd Ed.*
SciTech - v28 - i3 - Sept 2004 - p30(1) [51-500]

Halcoussis, Dennis - *Understanding Econometrics*
R&R Bk N - v19 - i4 - Nov 2004 - p85(1) [51-500]

Halda, Josef J. - *The Genus Paeonia*
Choice - v42 - i2 - Oct 2004 - p319(1) [51-500]

Haldane, J.B.S. - *My Friend Mr Leakey (Illus. by Blake, Quentin)*
c Sch Lib - v52 - i4 - Winter 2004 - p201(1) [51-500]

Haldeman, Joe W. - *Camouflage*
BL - v100 - i22 - August 2004 - p1913(1) [51-500]
BW - v34 - i40 - Oct 3 2004 - p17(1) [501+]
LJ - v129 - i13 - August 2004 - p72(1) [501+]
NYTBR - July 18 2004 - p19 [501+]
Preventing Earth Defects
Ent W - Sept 10 2004 - p167 [501+]

Haldeman, Scott - *Principles and Practice of Chiropractic, 3rd Ed.*
SciTech - v28 - i4 - Dec 2004 - p122 [51-500]

Haldi, Stacy Bergstrom - *Why Wars Widen: A Theory of Predation and Balancing*
Choice - v41 - i7 - March 2004 - p1346(1) [501+]

Hale, Bruce - *The Hamster of the Baskervilles (Illus. by Hale, Bruce)*
c RT - v57 - Oct 2003 - p173 [1-50]
Murder, My Tweet: From the Tattered Casebook of Chet Gecko, Private Eye (Illus. by Hale, Bruce)
c SLJ - v50 - i10 - Oct 2004 - p114(1) [51-500]

Hale, Charles D. - *The Assessment Center Handbook for Police and Fire Personnel, 2nd Ed.*
R&R Bk N - v19 - i4 - Nov 2004 - p113(1) [51-500]

Hale, Deborah - *Highland Rogue*
BL - v101 - i3 - Oct 1 2004 - p316(1) [51-500]

Hale, Frank W., Jr. - *What Makes Racial Diversity Work in Higher Education: Academic Leaders Present Successful Policies and Strategies*
R&R Bk N - v19 - i1 - Feb 2004 - p192(1) [51-500]

Hale, Geoffrey - *Politics of Taxation in Canada*
CBRA - Annual 2003 - p307(1) [501+]

Hale, James B. - *School Neuropsychology: A Practitioner's Handbook*
SciTech - v28 - i3 - Sept 2004 - p117(1) [51-500]

Hale, Judith - *Performance-Based Management: What Every Manager Should Do to Get Results*
R&R Bk N - v19 - i1 - Feb 2004 - p87(1) [1-50]

Hale, Lucretia - *The Peterkins' Christmas (Illus. by Anderson, Wendy)*
c KR - v72 - i21 - Nov 1 2004 - p1049(1) [501+]

Hale, Marian - *The Truth about Sparrows*
c BL - v101 - i3 - Oct 1 2004 - p326(1) [51-500]
c BL - v101 - i6 - Nov 15 2004 - p599(1) [501+]
c CCB-B - v58 - i4 - Dec 2004 - p169(2) [51-500]
c HB - v80 - i5 - Sept-Oct 2004 - p585(1) [51-500]
c KR - v72 - i14 - July 15 2004 - p685(1) [51-500]
c SLJ - v50 - i10 - Oct 2004 - p166(1) [51-500]
y BL - v101 - i9-10 - Jan 1 2005 - p773(1) [1-50]

Hale, Shannon - *Enna Burning*
y BL - v101 - i2 - Sept 15 2004 - p232(1) [51-500]
y CCB-B - v58 - i3 - Nov 2004 - p123(1) [501+]
y Kliatt - v38 - i6 - Nov 2004 - p8(1) [51-500]
y KR - v72 - i17 - Sept 1 2004 - p866(1) [51-500]
MFSF - v108 - i1 - Jan 2005 - p31(5) [501+]
y SLJ - v50 - i9 - Sept 2004 - p206(1) [51-500]
y VOYA - v27 - i5 - Dec 2004 - p404(1) [51-500]
The Goose Girl
y SLJ - v50 - i12 - Dec 2004 - p40(2) [501+]

Hale, Tudor - *Exercise Physiology: A Thematic Approach*
SciTech - v28 - i3 - Sept 2004 - p69(1) [51-500]

Haleem, M.A.S. Abdel - *The Qur'an*
TLS - i5301 - Nov 5 2004 - p15(1) [501+]

Haleman, Steven L. - *But Is it Garbage?: On Rock and Trash*
Choice - v42 - i2 - Oct 2004 - p302(1) [51-500]

Hales, Dianne - *Invitation to Health, 11th Ed.*
SciTech - v28 - i3 - Sept 2004 - p85(1) [51-500]

Hales, Douglas - *A Southern Family in White and Black: The Cuneys of Texas*
SHQ - v108 - i1 - July 2004 - p123-124 [501+]
WHQ - v35 - i1 - Spring 2004 - p97-98 [501+]

Hales, Robert E. - *Essentials of Clinical Psychiatry, 2nd Ed.*
SciTech - v28 - i1 - March 2004 - p95(1) [51-500]

Halevi, Gideon - *Process and Operation Planning*
SciTech - v28 - i1 - March 2004 - p178(1) [51-500]

Halevi-Wise, Yael - *Interactive Fictions: Scenes of Storytelling in the Novel*
R&R Bk N - v19 - i1 - Feb 2004 - p228(1) [51-500]

Haley, James (b. 1968 -) - *Foreign Oil Dependence*
y SLJ - v50 - i11 - Nov 2004 - p164(1) [51-500]
Pollution
Sci Teach - v71 - i8 - Oct 2004 - p76-78 [501+]
Women in the Military
y SLJ - v51 - i1 - Jan 2005 - p148(1) [51-500]

Haley, James L. - *Sam Houston*
HNet - Sept 2004 - pNA [501+]

Halfin, Igal - *Languages and Revolution: Making Modern Politics Identities*
Slav R - v63 - i4 - Winter 2004 - p884(2) [501+]
Terror in My Soul: Communist Autobiographies on Trial
AHR - v109 - i3 - June 2004 - p1008(1) [501+]
Russ Rev - v63 - i2 - April 2004 - pNA [501+]
Slav R - v63 - i3 - Fall 2004 - p660-661 [501+]

Halford, Nigel G. - *Genetically Modified Crops*
Choice - v41 - i7 - March 2004 - p1321(1) [501+]

Haliczer, Stephen - *Between Exaltation and Infamy: Female Mystics in the Golden Age of Spain*
CHR - v90 - i4 - Oct 2004 - p797(2) [501+]
Six Ct J - v34 - i4 - Winter 2003 - p1212-1213 [501+]

Hall, Alex M. - *Discovering Eden: A Lifetime of Paddling Arctic Rivers*
CBRA - Annual 2003 - p142(1) [51-500]
CG - v124 - i1 - Jan-Feb 2004 - p87(1) [501+]

Hall, Anthony J. - *The American Empire and the Fourth World*
BIC - v33 - i6 - Sept 2004 - p26(2) [501+]
CBRA - Annual 2003 - p290(2) [501+]
Globe & Mail - July 31 2004 - pD4 [501+]

Hall, Barry G. - *Phylogenetic Trees Made Easy: A How-to Manual, 2nd Ed.*
SciTech - v28 - i3 - Sept 2004 - p59(1) [1-50]

Hall, Bradford J. - *Among Cultures: The Challenge of Communication, 2nd Ed.*
R&R Bk N - v19 - i4 - Nov 2004 - p76(1) [51-500]

Hall, Brian - *Religion and the Formation of Taiwanese Identities*
CS - v33 - i5 - Sept 2004 - p555-557 [501+]

Hall, Bruce Edward - *Henry and the Kite Dragon (Illus. by Low, William)*
c CCB-B - v57 - i11 - July-August 2004 - p466(2) [501+]
c SLJ - v50 - i8 - August 2004 - p87(1) [51-500]

Hall, C. Michael - *Tourism, Mobility, and Second Homes: Between Elite Landscape and Common Ground*
R&R Bk N - v19 - i4 - Nov 2004 - p104(1) [51-500]

Hall, Catherine - *Civilising Subjects: Colony and Metropole in the English Imagination, 1830-1867*
AHR - v109 - i2 - April 2004 - p611(2) [501+]
Civilising Subjects: Metropole and Colony in the English Imagination, 1830-1867
Albion - v36 - i1 - Spring 2004 - p195(2) [501+]

Hall, Christopher T. - *Aggregate Analysis in Chipped Stone*
R&R Bk N - v19 - i4 - Nov 2004 - p77(1) [51-500]

Hall, D. Geoffrey - *Weaving a Lexicon*
QRB - v79 - i4 - Dec 2004 - p462(1) [501+]

Hall, David D. - *Puritans in the New World: A Critical Anthology*
Choice - v42 - i5 - Jan 2005 - p918(1) [1-50]

Hall, Donald (b. 1928 -) - *The Best Day the Worst Day: Life with Jane Kenyon*
PW - v252 - i10 - March 7 2005 - p57(1) [51-500]
Breakfast Served Any Time All Day: Essays on Poetry New and Selected
TLS - i5305 - Dec 3 2004 - p30(1) [501+]

Hall, Donald E. - *Subjectivity*
TLS - i5297 - Oct 8 2004 - p31(1) [51-500]

Hall, Douglas John - *The Cross in Our Context; Jesus and the Suffering World*
CC - v121 - i14 - July 13 2004 - p36(3) [501+]

Hall, Edith - *Dionysus Since 69: Greek Tragedy at the Dawn of the Third Millennium*
Choice - v42 - i1 - Sept 2004 - p113(1) [501+]
TLS - i5298 - Oct 15 2004 - p11(1) [501+]

Hall, Ellen - *High Schools in Crisis: What Every Parent Should Know*
Choice - v42 - i3 - Nov 2004 - p536(1) [1-50]
R&R Bk N - v19 - i3 - August 2004 - p226(1) [1-50]
VOYA - v27 - i5 - Dec 2004 - p427(1) [51-500]

Hall-Ellis, Sylvia D. - *Grants for School Libraries*
LibMed - v22 - i7 - April-May 2004 - p87(1) [501+]
R&R Bk N - v19 - i1 - Feb 2004 - p260(1) [51-500]
SLJ - v50 - i8 - August 2004 - p150(1) [501+]
y   Teach Lib - v32 - i1 - Oct 2004 - p38(2) [501+]

Hall, Greg - *Harvest Wobblies: The Industrial Workers of the World and Agricultural Laborers in the American West, 1905-1930*
Hist Geo - v32 - Annual 2004 - p202(3) [501+]

Hall, Halbert W. - *Louis L'Amour: An Annotated Bibliography and Guide*
R&R Bk N - v19 - i1 - Feb 2004 - p245(1) [51-500]

Hall, James A. - *Information Technology Auditing and Assurance, 2nd Ed.*
R&R Bk N - v19 - i4 - Nov 2004 - p114(1) [51-500]

Hall, James (b. 1963 -) - *Michelangelo and the Reinvention of the Human Body*
PW - v252 - i10 - March 7 2005 - p59(1) [51-500]

Hall, James Baker - *Tobacco Harvest: An Elegy*
BL - v101 - i5 - Nov 1 2004 - p451(2) [51-500]

Hall, James W. - *Forests of the Night (Read by Merlington, Laural). Audiobook Review*
PW - v252 - i10 - March 7 2005 - p27(1) [51-500]
Forests of the Night
BL - v101 - i6 - Nov 15 2004 - p531(1) [51-500]
Globe & Mail - Feb 5 2005 - pD15 [51-500]
KR - v72 - i20 - Oct 15 2004 - p977(2) [501+]
LJ - v129 - i18 - Nov 1 2004 - p63(1) [51-500]
PW - v251 - i43 - Oct 25 2004 - p25(1) [51-500]

Hall, Jason - *The Crush*
PW - v251 - i41 - Oct 11 2004 - p59(1) [51-500]
Trigger (Illus. by Watkiss, John)
Ent W - i808 - Feb 25 2005 - p105 [501+]

Hall, Jessica - *Heat of the Moment*
BL - v101 - i3 - Oct 1 2004 - p316(1) [51-500]

Hall, Joan Wylie - *Conversations with Audre Lorde*
Black Iss - v6 - i5 - Sept-Oct 2004 - p55(1) [501+]
Choice - v42 - i6 - Feb 2005 - p1021(2) [51-500]

Hall, John A. - *The Disciplinary Revolution: Calvinism and the Rise of the State in Early Modern Europe*
CS - v33 - i5 - Sept 2004 - p573-574 [501+]

Hall, Katy - *Piggy Riddles (Illus. by Andriani, Renee)*
c   SLJ - v50 - i7 - July 2004 - p93(1) [51-500]

Hall, Kirsten - *Kids in Sports: A Chapter Book*
c   SLJ - v51 - i1 - Jan 2005 - p148(1) [51-500]

Hall, Loretta - *Underground Buildings: More than Meets the Eye*
Bwatch - Oct 2004 - pNA [51-500]

Hall, M.C. - *John Deere*
c   BL - v100 - i21 - July 2004 - p1840(1) [1-50]
c   SLJ - v50 - i9 - Sept 2004 - p187(1) [51-500]
Samuel Morse
c   SLJ - v50 - i9 - Sept 2004 - p187(1) [51-500]

Hall, Margaret - *Beavers*
c   SB - v40 - i4 - July-August 2004 - p177(1) [51-500]
Herons
c   SB - v40 - i4 - July-August 2004 - p177(1) [51-500]
Mallards
c   SB - v40 - i4 - July-August 2004 - p177(1) [51-500]
Muskrats
c   SB - v40 - i4 - July-August 2004 - p177(1) [51-500]

Hall, Marie Boas - *Henry Oldenburg: Shaping the Royal Society*
Isis - v95 - i2 - June 2004 - p289(2) [501+]

Hall, Michael C. - *Safety and Security in Tourism: Relationships, Management, and Marketing*
R&R Bk N - v19 - i3 - August 2004 - p79(1) [51-500]

Hall, Michael N. - *Cell Growth: Control of Cell Size*
Nature - v431 - i7005 - Sept 9 2004 - p128(2) [501+]
SciTech - v28 - i3 - Sept 2004 - p61(1) [51-500]

Hall, N. John - *Max Beerbohm: A Kind of a Life*
ELT - v47 - i4 - Fall 2004 - p449(4) [501+]
VS - v46 - i3 - Spring 2004 - p535(2) [501+]

Hall, Oakley - *Ambrose Bierce and the Ace of Shoots*
KR - v73 - i4 - Feb 15 2005 - p201(1) [51-500]
PW - v252 - i10 - March 7 2005 - p53(1) [51-500]

Hall, Parnell - *And a Puzzle to Die On: A Puzzle Lady Mystery*
BL - v101 - i5 - Nov 1 2004 - p466(1) [51-500]
PW - v251 - i43 - Oct 25 2004 - p32(1) [51-500]

Hall, Patricia - *Dead Reckoning*
KR - v73 - i5 - March 1 2005 - p262(1) [51-500]

Hall, Peter A. - *The First-Year Principal*
R&R Bk N - v19 - i4 - Nov 2004 - p187(1) [501+]

Hall, Peter, Sir (b. 1930 -) - *Shakespeare's Advice to the Players*
TLS - i5289 - August 13 2004 - p10-11 [501+]

Hall, Philip S. - *Educating Oppositional and Defiant Children*
Choice - v41 - i7 - March 2004 - p1344(1) [501+]

Hall, Randolph W. - *Handbook of Transportation Science, 2nd Ed.*
JEL - v41 - i4 - Dec 2003 - p1440(1) [501+]

Hall, Ronald E. - *Scientific Fallacy and Political Misuse of the Concept of Race*
R&R Bk N - v19 - i4 - Nov 2004 - p59(1) [51-500]
Skin Color as a Post-Colonial Issue Among Asian-Americans
R&R Bk N - v19 - i1 - Feb 2004 - p57(1) [51-500]

Hall, Thomas E. - *The Rotten Fruits of Economic Controls and the Rise from the Ashes, 1965-1989*
R&R Bk N - v19 - i1 - Feb 2004 - p78(1) [1-50]

Hall, Timothy L. - *The U.S. Legal System, Vols. 1-2*
BL - v101 - i2 - Sept 15 2004 - p279(1) [501+]
Choice - v42 - i2 - Oct 2004 - p277(1) [501+]
y   Ref Rev - August 2004 - pNA [501+]
R&R Bk N - v19 - i3 - August 2004 - p196(1) [1-50]
R&USQ - v44 - i2 - Winter 2004 - p175(2) [501+]
y   SLJ - v50 - i10 - Oct 2004 - p93(1) [51-500]

Hall-Wallace, Michelle K. - *Exploring the Ocean Environment: GIS Investigations for the Earth Sciences*
SciTech - v28 - i4 - Dec 2004 - p6(1) [1-50]

Hall, William C. - *The Superior Colliculus: New Approaches for Studying Sensorimotor Integration*
QRB - v79 - i4 - Dec 2004 - p457(1) [501+]
SciTech - v28 - i1 - March 2004 - p73(1) [51-500]

Hallahan, William H. - *The Day the Revolution Ended-19 October 1781*
J Mil H - v68 - i2 - April 2004 - p594(2) [501+]

Hallahan, Daniel P. - *Learning Disabilities: Foundations, Characteristics and Effective Teaching, 3rd Ed.*
R&R Bk N - v19 - i3 - August 2004 - p230(1) [1-50]

Hallam, Tony - *Catastrophes and Lesser Calamities: The Causes of Mass Extinctions*
New Sci - v183 - i2460 - August 14 2004 - p46(1) [51-500]
SciTech - v28 - i4 - Dec 2004 - p56(1) [51-500]

Halle, David - *New York and Los Angeles: Politics, Society, and Culture: A Comparative View*
JEL - v41 - i4 - Dec 2003 - p1438(1) [501+]
PHR - v73 - i4 - Nov 2004 - p688(2) [501+]
Soc Ser R - v78 - i3 - Sept 2004 - p507(2) [501+]

Halleck, Elaine - *Living in Nazi Germany*
y   BL - v100 - i22 - August 2004 - p1918(1) [51-500]
y   CH Bwatch - v14 - i7 - July 2004 - p5(1) [51-500]
y   CH Bwatch - v14 - i7 - July 2004 - p5(1) [51-500]

Hallenberg, Mats - *Kungen, fogdarna och riket: Lokalforvaltning och statsbyggande under tidig Vasatid*
Scan St - v76 - i3 - Fall 2004 - p385(34) [501+]

Hallett, John W. - *Comprehensive Vascular and Endovascular Surgery*
SciTech - v28 - i3 - Sept 2004 - p113(1) [51-500]

Halley, Patrice - *Far North*
CG - v124 - i3 - May-June 2004 - p134(1) [501+]

Halliday, Candy - *Dream Guy*
PW - v251 - i50 - Dec 13 2004 - p51(1) [51-500]

Halliday, M.A.K. - *The Language of Science*
SciTech - v28 - i4 - Dec 2004 - p12(1) [1-50]
Lexicology and Corpus Linguistics: An Introduction
R&R Bk N - v19 - i4 - Nov 2004 - p214(1) [501+]
On Language and Linguistics
R&R Bk N - v19 - i1 - Feb 2004 - p212 [51-500]

Halliday, Simon - *Judicial Review and Compliance with Administrative Law*
Law&PolBR - Nov 2004 - p878(4) [501+]

Hallifax, Michael - *Let Me Set the Scene: Twenty Years at the Heart of British Theatre, 1956 to 1976*
Choice - v42 - i3 - Nov 2004 - p495(1) [51-500]

Halligan, John - *Civil Service Systems in Anglo-American Countries*
R&R Bk N - v19 - i3 - August 2004 - p177(1) [501+]

Hallin, Daniel C. - *Comparing Media Systems: Three Models of Media and Politics*
Choice - v42 - i3 - Nov 2004 - p477(1) [1-50]

Hallion, Richard P. - *Taking Flight: Inventing the Aerial Age from Antiquity through the First World War*
Isis - v95 - i3 - Sept 2004 - p477(1) [501+]
T&C - v45 - i3 - July 2004 - p626-627 [501+]

Halliwell, Leslie - *Halliwell's Film Guide 2004*
Globe & Mail - Dec 10 2004 - pR21 [1-50]
Halliwell's Film, Video & DVD Guide 2005
LJ - v130 - i4 - March 1 2005 - p114(1) [51-500]

Halliwell, Martin - *Images of Idiocy: The Idiot Figure in Modern Fiction and Film*
TLS - i5296 - Oct 1 2004 - p30(1) [51-500]

Halliwell, Stephen - *The Aesthetics of Mimesis: Ancient Texts and Modern Problems*
CJ - v100 - i1 - Oct-Nov 2004 - p102-104 [501+]
Class R - v54 - i1 - May 2004 - p67(3) [501+]
Dialogue - v43 - i1 - Wntr 2004 - p194-196 [501+]

Hallman, Diana R. - *Opera, Liberalism, and Antisemitism in Nineteenth-Century France: The Politics of Halevy's La Juive*
FS - v58 - i1 - Jan 2004 - p122(2) [501+]
NCFS - v33 - i1-2 - Fall-Winter 2004 - p179(3) [501+]

Hallman, J.C. - *The Chess Artist: Genius, Obsession, and the World's Oldest Game*
BIC - v33 - i7 - Oct 2004 - p20(2) [501+]
BL - v101 - i1 - Sept 1 2004 - p46(1) [51-500]
World&I - v19 - i12 - Dec 2004 - pNA [501+]

Hallock, Marylin R. - *Central Glass Company: The First Thirty Years, 1863-1893*
Ant&CM - v108 - i8 - Oct 2003 - p16(1) [501+]

Hallock, Thomas - *From the Fallen Tree: Frontier Narratives, Environmental Politics, and the Roots of a National Pastoral, 1749-1826*
JAH - v91 - i3 - Dec 2004 - p1008(2) [501+]
W&M Q - v62 - i1 - Jan 2005 - p126-3 [501+]

Hallof, K. - *Inscriptiones Graecae consilio et auctoritate Academiae Scientiarum Berolinensis et Brandenburgensis editae. Voluminis IX Partis I Editio altera. Fasciculus IV. Inscriptiones insularum Maris Ionii*
Class R - v54 - i1 - May 2004 - p215(4) [501+]
Inscriptiones Graecae consilio et auctoritate Academiae Scientiarum Berolinensis et Brandenburgensis editae. Voluminis XII Fasciculus VI. Inscriptiones Chii et Sami cum Corassiis Icariaque
Class R - v54 - i1 - May 2004 - p219(4) [501+]

Hallowell, Edward M. - *Delivered from Distraction: Getting the Most Out of Life with Attention Deficit Disorder*
LJ - v129 - i19 - Nov 15 2004 - p77(1) [501+]
PW - v251 - i47 - Nov 22 2004 - p56(1) [51-500]
A Walk In The Rain With A Brain (Illus. by Mayer, Bill)
c   PW - v251 - i46 - Nov 15 2004 - p59(1) [501+]
c   SLJ - v51 - i1 - Jan 2005 - p94(1) [51-500]

Hallowell, Gerald - *The Oxford Companion to Canadian History*
Globe & Mail - August 28 2004 - pD9 [501+]
TLS - i5297 - Oct 8 2004 - p31(1) [51-500]
BL - v101 - i9-10 - Jan 1 2005 - p906(2) [501+]

Hallowell, Janis - *The Annunciation of Francesca Dunn (Read by Bunch, Tyler). Audiobook Review*
y   Kliatt - v38 - i5 - Sept 2004 - p52(2) [501+]
y   LJ - v129 - i15 - Sept 15 2004 - p88(1) [51-500]
y   VOYA - v27 - i5 - Dec 2004 - p372(1) [501+]
The Annunciation of Francesca Dunn. Audiobook Review
y   BL - v101 - i1 - Sept 1 2004 - p146(1) [1-50]
The Annunciation of Francesca Dunn
BL - v101 - i9-10 - Jan 1 2005 - p771(1) [51-500]
y   VOYA - v27 - i4 - Oct 2004 - p296(2) [51-500]

Hallowell, Nina - *Reflections on Research: The Realities of Doing Research in the Social Sciences, 1st Ed.*
TimHES - v0 - i1680 - Feb 25 2005 - pVI(1) [501+]

Halls, Kelly Milner - *Albino Animals*
c   SLJ - v50 - i8 - August 2004 - p137(1) [51-500]
Dinosaur Mummies: Beyond Bare-Bone Fossils (Illus. by Spears, Rick)
c   LibMed - v22 - i5 - Feb 2004 - p57(1) [501+]
y   SLJ - v50 - i10 - Oct 2004 - pS40(1) [51-500]

Halls, Monty - *Dive: The Ultimate Guide to 60 of the World's Top Dive Locations*
LJ - v130 - i1 - Jan 1 2005 - p122(1) [51-500]

Halls, Nigel - *Microbiological Contamination Control in Pharmaceutical Clean Rooms*
SciTech - v28 - i4 - Dec 2004 - p119(1) [1-50]

250 • HALLSMITH *Book Review Index 2005 Cumulation*

Hallsmith, Gwendolyn - *The Key to Sustainable Cities: Meeting Human Needs and Transforming Community Systems*
Fut - v39 - i1 - Jan-Feb 2005 - p49(1) [51-500]
Hallstrom, Kristina Tamm - *Organizing International Standardization: ISO and the LASC in Quest of Authority*
R&R Bk N - v19 - i3 - August 2004 - p108(1) [51-500]
Hallstron, Jonas - *Constructing a Pipe-Bound City: A History of Water Supply, Sewerage and Excreta Removal in Norrkoping and Linkoping Sweden, 1860-1910*
T&C - v45 - i2 - April 2004 - pNA [501+]
Hallward, Peter - *Think Again: Alain Badiou and the Future of Philosophy*
R&R Bk N - v19 - i4 - Nov 2004 - p5(1) [51-500]
Hally, Mike - *Electronic Brains*
New Sci - v185 - i2490 - March 12 2005 - p51(1) [501+]
Halonen, Timo - *GSM, GPRS and EDGE Performance: Evolution Towards 3G/UMTS, 2nd Ed.*
E-Streams - July 2004 - pNA [501+]
Halper, Stefan - *America Alone: The Neo-Conservatives and the Global Order*
BW - v34 - i33 - August 15 2004 - p1(2) [501+]
Globe & Mail - Jan 15 2005 - pD6 [501+]
TLS - i5301 - Nov 5 2004 - p4-6 [501+]
Halperin, David M. - *How to Do the History of Homosexuality*
AHR - v109 - i2 - April 2004 - p476(2) [501+]
Halperin-Kaddari, Ruth - *Women in Israel: A State of Their Own*
Choice - v42 - i1 - Sept 2004 - p194(1) [501+]
Halperin, Morton - *The Democracy Advantage: How Democracies Promote Prosperity and Peace*
Har Bus R - v82 - i12 - Dec 2004 - p28(1) [1-50]
Halpern, Brian - *The Knee Crisis Handbook: Understanding Pain, Preventing Trauma, Recovering from Injury, and Building Healthy Knees for Life*
NYT - July 27 2004 - pF7 [501+]
Halpern, Greg - *Harvard Works Because We Do*
NEQ - v77 - i3 - Sept 2004 - p511-512 [501+]
Halpern, Joseph Y. - *Reasoning About Uncertainty*
JEL - v42 - i1 - March 2004 - p234(1) [501+]
Halpern, Julie - *Toby and the Snowflakes (Illus. by Cordell, Matthew)*
c CCB-B - v58 - i4 - Dec 2004 - p157(2) [501+]
c KR - v72 - i13 - July 1 2004 - p630(1) [51-500]
c PW - v251 - i44 - Nov 1 2004 - p61(1) [501+]
c SLJ - v50 - i10 - Oct 2004 - p114(1) [51-500]
Halpern, Martin - *Unions, Radicals, and Democratic Presidents: Seeking Social Change in the Twentieth Century*
Choice - v42 - i1 - Sept 2004 - p173(1) [501+]
R&R Bk N - v19 - i1 - Feb 2004 - p100(1) [51-500]
Halpern, Monda - *And on That Farm He Had a Wife: Ontario Farm Women and Feminism, 1900-1970.*
Can Hist R - v85 - i3 - Sept 2004 - p608(3) [501+]
Halpern, Monica - *Railroad Fever: Building the Transcontinental Railroad 1830-1870*
c BL - v100 - i22 - August 2004 - p1926(1) [51-500]
c SLJ - v50 - i7 - July 2004 - p123(1) [51-500]
Halpern, Nick - *Everyday and Prophetic: The Poetry of Lowell, Ammons, Merrill, and Rich*
Choice - v41 - i7 - March 2004 - p1296(1) [501+]
Halpern, Paul - *Faraway Worlds: Planets Beyond Our Solar System (Illus. by Cook, Lynette R.)*
c Astron - v33 - i1 - Jan 2005 - p92 [51-500]
c BL - v100 - i22 - August 2004 - p1926(1) [51-500]
c SB - v40 - i6 - Nov-Dec 2004 - p266(1) [51-500]
The Great Beyond: Higher Dimensions, Parallel Universes, and the Extraordinary Search for a Theory of Everything
Choice - v42 - i5 - Jan 2005 - p891(1) [1-50]
LJ - v129 - i12 - July 2004 - p114(1) [51-500]
y SB - v40 - i6 - Nov-Dec 2004 - p256(2) [51-500]
Halpern, Paul G. - *The Battle of the Otranto Straits: Controlling the Gateway to the Adriatic in World War I*
R&R Bk N - v19 - i4 - Nov 2004 - p32(1) [51-500]
Halpern, Richard - *Shakespeare's Perfume: Sodomy and Sublimity in the Sonnets, Wilde, Freud, and Lacan*
Six Ct J - v35 - i1 - Spring 2004 - p306(2) [501+]
Halpern, Robert - *Making Play Work: The Promise of After-School Programs for Low-Income Children*
Choice - v41 - i7 - March 2004 - p1376(1) [501+]
Halpern, Sydney A. - *Lesser Harms: The Morality of Risk in Medical Research*
New Sci - v185 - i2483 - Jan 22 2005 - p51(1) [1-50]
Halpin, Anne - *Homescaping: Designing Your Landscape to Match Your Home*
PW - v252 - i9 - Feb 28 2005 - p60(2) [51-500]
Halpin, Brendan - *Donorboy: A Novel*
y BL - v100 - i21 - July 2004 - p1817(1) [51-500]
BL - v101 - i9-10 - Jan 1 2005 - p771(1) [51-500]
KR - v72 - i13 - July 1 2004 - p596(1) [51-500]
PW - v251 - i32 - August 9 2004 - p233(1) [51-500]
Losing My Faculties: A Teacher's Story
HER - v74 - i4 - Winter 2004 - p456-458 [501+]
Halpin, Mikki - *It's Your World--If You Don't Like It, Change It: Activism for Teenagers*
y BL - v101 - i8 - Dec 15 2004 - p733(1) [51-500]
y PW - v251 - i42 - Oct 18 2004 - p66(1) [51-500]
y SLJ - v50 - i12 - Dec 2004 - p161(2) [51-500]
y Teach Lib - v32 - i3 - Feb 2005 - p15(1) [51-500]
y VOYA - v27 - i5 - Dec 2004 - p414(1) [51-500]
Halppin, David M.G. - *COPD: Your Questions Answered*
SciTech - v28 - i1 - March 2004 - p106(1) [1-50]
Halsall, Guy - *Humour, History and Politics in Late Antiquity and the Early Middle Ages*
Class R - v54 - i2 - Nov 2004 - p449(2) [501+]
Warfare and Society in the Barbarian West, 450-900
AHR - v109 - i3 - June 2004 - p959(1) [501+]
Halsey, A.H. - *A History of Sociology in Britain: Science, Literature, and Society*
TimHES - v0 - i1665 - Nov 5 2004 - p25(1) [501+]
Halstead, Ted - *The Real State of the Union: From the Best Minds in America, Bold Solutions to the Problems Politicians Dare Not to Address*
R&R Bk N - v19 - i3 - August 2004 - p145(1) [51-500]
Halteman, J. - *The Boundaries of Technique: Ordering Positive and Normative Concerns in Economic Research*
Choice - v42 - i3 - Nov 2004 - pNA [1-50]
Halter, Marek - *Sarah: A Novel (Read by Dunne, Bernadette). Audiobook Review*
Kliatt - v38 - i6 - Nov 2004 - p50(1) [51-500]
Sarah: A Novel
y SLJ - v50 - i10 - Oct 2004 - p198(1) [51-500]
Haltof, Marek - *The Cinema of Krzysztof Kieslowski: Variations on Destiny and Chance*
Choice - v42 - i5 - Jan 2005 - p860(1) [501+]
Haltom, William - *Distorting the Law: Politics, Media, and the Litigation Crisis*
Law&PolBR - Sept 2004 - pNA [501+]
Halvering, Sandi Patti - *Broken on the Back Row: A Journey through Grace and Forgiveness*
PW - v252 - i3 - Jan 17 2005 - p52(1) [51-500]
Halverson, James L. - *Peter Aureol on Predestination: A Challenge to Late Medieval Thought*
Specu - v79 - i4 - Oct 2004 - p1080(3) [501+]
Halvorson, Marilyn - *Bull Rider*
c CBRA - Annual 2003 - p486(2) [51-500]
Let It Go
y Kliatt - v39 - i1 - Jan 2005 - p14(1) [51-500]
Halweil, Brian - *Eat Here: Reclaiming Homegrown Pleasures in a Global Supermarket*
Fut - v39 - i2 - March-April 2005 - p60(1) [51-500]
State of the World 2004: A Worldwatch Institute Report on Progress Toward a Sustainable Society
R&R Bk N - v19 - i2 - May 2004 - p115(1) [1-50]
SLJ - v50 - i10 - Oct 2004 - pS59(1) [51-500]
State of the World 2004
VQR - v80 - i3 - Summer 2004 - p258(2) [501+]
Ham, Eldon - *Larceny and Old Leather: The Mischievous Legacy of Major League Baseball*
PW - v252 - i11 - March 14 2005 - p60(1) [51-500]
Hamad, Taj I. - *Culture of Responsibility and the Role of NGOs*
Choice - v41 - i11-12 - July-August 2004 - p2120(1) [501+]
R&R Bk N - v19 - i1 - Feb 2004 - p125(1) [51-500]
Hamadeh, Hisham K. - *Toxicogenomics: Principles and Applications*
SciTech - v28 - i4 - Dec 2004 - p87(1) [51-500]
Hamadeh, Samer - *Vault Guide to Top Internships*
Choice - v42 - i7 - March 2005 - p1191(1) [51-500]
Hamalainen, Timo J. - *National Competitiveness and Economic Growth: The Changing Determination of Economic Performance in the World Economy*
JEL - v41 - i4 - Dec 2003 - p1418(2) [501+]
Hamann, Donald L. - *Strategies for Teaching Strings: Building a Successful String and Orchestra Program*
M Ed J - v91 - i1 - Sept 2004 - p60(1) [501+]
Hamann, Edmund T. - *The Educational Welcome of Latinos in the New South*
R&R Bk N - v19 - i1 - Feb 2004 - p191(1) [51-500]
Hamann, Jack - *On American Soil: Murder, the Military, and How Justice Became a Casualty of World War II*
KR - v73 - i4 - Feb 15 2005 - p212(1) [501+]
PW - v252 - i6 - Feb 7 2005 - p50(1) [51-500]
Hamblet, Wendy C. - *The Sacred Monstrous: A Reflection on Violence in Human Communities*
Choice - v41 - i11-12 - July-August 2004 - p2057(1) [501+]
Hambleton, Laura - *Welcome to Lizard Lounge*
c CH Bwatch - Oct 2004 - pNA [51-500]
c Sch Lib - v52 - i3 - Autumn 2004 - p131(1) [501+]
c SLJ - v50 - i12 - Dec 2004 - p110(1) [501+]
Hamblin, V.L. - *Le Mistere du Siege d'Orleans*
FS - v58 - i1 - Jan 2004 - p81(2) [501+]
Hambling, David - *Weapons Grade: How Modern Warfare Gave Birth to Our High-Tech World*
KR - v73 - i3 - Feb 1 2005 - p164(2) [501+]
PW - v252 - i11 - March 14 2005 - p60(1) [51-500]
Hambly, Barbara - *Dead Water*
BL - v100 - i21 - July 2004 - p1798(1) [51-500]
PW - v251 - i27 - July 5 2004 - p41(1) [51-500]
The Emancipator's Wife: A Novel of Mary Todd Lincoln
BL - v101 - i7 - Dec 1 2004 - p618(1) [51-500]
KR - v72 - i24 - Dec 15 2004 - p1156(1) [501+]
LJ - v130 - i1 - Jan 1 2005 - p97(1) [51-500]
PW - v252 - i2 - Jan 10 2005 - p38(2) [51-500]
Hambourg, Maria Morris - *Guest (Illus. by Bucklow, Christopher)*
LJ - v130 - i2 - Feb 1 2005 - p76(1) [51-500]
Walker Evans
NYTBR - August 8 2004 - p20 [501+]
Hambric, Julia - *Charreada: Mexican Rodeo in Texas*
SHQ - v107 - i3 - Jan 2004 - p476(3) [501+]
Hamburg, David A. - *No More Killing Fields: Preventing Deadly Conflict*
R&R Bk N - v19 - i1 - Feb 2004 - p30(1) [51-500]
Hamburger, Aaron - *The View from Stalin's Head*
Advocate - August 17 2004 - pS30(1) [51-500]
Lam Bk Rpt - v13 - i1-2 - August-Sept 2004 - p26(1) [501+]
Hamburger, Jeffrey F. - *St. John the Divine: The Deified Evangelist in Medieval Art and Theology*
Six Ct J - v34 - i4 - Winter 2003 - p1241-1242 [501+]
Specu - v79 - i3 - July 2004 - p767-769 [501+]
Hamburger, Kenneth E. - *Leadership in the Crucible: The Korean War Battles of Twin Tunnels and Chipyong-Ni*
J Mil H - v68 - i2 - April 2004 - p647(2) [501+]
Hamburger, Michael - *Wild and Wounded*
TLS - i5289 - August 13 2004 - p28(1) [501+]
Hamburger, Philip - *Separation of Church and State*
CH - v73 - i4 - Dec 2004 - p885(3) [501+]
J Am St - v38 - i1 - April 2004 - p144-145 [501+]
J Ch St - v46 - i4 - Autumn 2004 - p904(2) [501+]
Hamby, Alonzo - *For the Survival of Democracy: Franklin Roosevelt and the World Crisis of the 1930s*
Bks & Cult - v10 - i6 - Nov-Dec 2004 - p24(3) [501+]
Hamby, Barbara - *Babel*
BL - v101 - i6 - Nov 15 2004 - p547(1) [51-500]
LJ - v129 - i20 - Dec 1 2004 - p122(1) [51-500]
Hameka, Hendrik F. - *Quantum Mechanics: A Conceptual Approach*
Choice - v42 - i2 - Oct 2004 - p330(1) [51-500]
Hamel, D. - *Trying Neaira: The True Story of a Courtesan's Scandalous Life in Ancient Greece*
Class R - v54 - i2 - Nov 2004 - p312-314 [501+]
Hamel, Therese - *De la terre a l'ecole. Histoire de l' enseignement agricole au Quebec, 1926-1969*
Can Hist R - v85 - i3 - Sept 2004 - p606(3) [501+]
Hamelman, Steven L. - *But Is It Garbage?*
JouAmCul - v27 - i4 - Dec 2004 - p436(2) [501+]
Hamer, Dean - *The God Gene: How Faith Is Hardwired into Our Genes*
y BL - v101 - i1 - Sept 1 2004 - p22(2) [51-500]
BW - v34 - i36 - Sept 5 2004 - p5(1) [501+]
Globe & Mail - Jan 1 2005 - pD2 [501+]
KR - v72 - i15 - August 1 2004 - p725(2) [501+]
PW - v251 - i28 - July 12 2004 - p55(2) [51-500]
Hamermesh, Daniel S. - *Stressed out on Four Continents: Time Crunch or Yuppie Kvetch?*
M Lab R - v127 - i10 - Oct 2004 - p48(1) [501+]
Hamerow, Helena - *Early Medieval Settlements: The Archeology of Rural Communities in Northwest Europe 400-900*
JIH - v35 - i1 - Summer 2004 - p119-120 [501+]

Hamerow, Theodore - *Remembering a Vanished World: A Jewish Childhood in Interwar Poland*
  GSR - v27 - i1 - Feb 2004 - p177-178 [501+]
Hames-Garcia, Michael - *Fugitive Thought: Prison Movements, Race, and the Meaning of Justice*
  R&R Bk N - v19 - i4 - Nov 2004 - p126(1) [51-500]
Hames, Harvey J. - *Jews, Muslims and Christians in and around the Crown of Aragon: Essays in Honour of Professor Elena Lourie*
  R&R Bk N - v19 - i1 - Feb 2004 - p39(1) [1-50]
Hamilakis, Y. - *Labyrinth Revisited: Rethinking Minoan Archaeology*
  Class R - v53 - i2 - Nov 2003 - p446-448 [501+]
Hamill, Pete - *Downtown: My Manhattan (Read by Hamill, Pete)*
  PW - v252 - i1 - Jan 3 2005 - p23(1) [51-500]
  Downtown: My Manhattan
  Ent W - i798 - Dec 24 2004 - p74 [501+]
  BL - v101 - i6 - Nov 15 2004 - p549(1) [51-500]
  Globe & Mail - Jan 1 2005 - pD3 [501+]
  KR - v72 - i20 - Oct 15 2004 - p994(1) [501+]
  LJ - v129 - i20 - Dec 1 2004 - p136(1) [51-500]
  PW - v251 - i46 - Nov 15 2004 - p53(1) [501+]
Hamill, Sam - *Almost Paradise: New and Selected Poems and Translations*
  PW - v252 - i10 - March 7 2005 - p66(1) [51-500]
  The Poetry of Zen
  BL - v100 - i21 - July 2004 - p1812(1) [1-50]
  War and Poets
  Ga R - v57 - i4 - Winter 2003 - p839-848 [501+]
Hamill, Thomas - *Escape in Iraq: The Thomas Hamill Story*
  LJ - v129 - i20 - Dec 1 2004 - p130(1) [51-500]
  PW - v251 - i41 - Oct 11 2004 - p68(1) [51-500]
Hamilton, Alastair - *Andre du Ryer and Oriental Studies in Seventeenth-Century France*
  TLS - i5299 - Oct 22 2004 - p5(1) [501+]
Hamilton, Bernard - *The Christian World of the Middle Ages*
  Six Ct J - v35 - i3 - Fall 2004 - p928-930 [501+]
Hamilton, Bethany - *Soul Surfer: A True Story of Faith, Family, and Fighting to Get Back on the Board*
  y BL - v101 - i9-10 - Jan 1 2005 - p840(1) [51-500]
  PW - v251 - i45 - Nov 8 2004 - p57(1) [51-500]
  Time - v164 - i14 - Oct 4 2004 - p95 [1-50]
Hamilton, Bill - *ADO.NET in a Nutshell*
  SciTech - v28 - i3 - Sept 2004 - p24(1) [51-500]
Hamilton, Charles - *Beyond Racism: Race and Inequality in Brazil, South Africa, and United States*
  CS - v33 - i2 - March 2004 - p162-163 [501+]
Hamilton, Denise - *Last Lullaby*
  Globe & Mail - July 10 2004 - pD12 [501+]
  Savage Garden
  KR - v73 - i5 - March 1 2005 - p263(1) [51-500]
  LJ - v130 - i4 - March 1 2005 - p72(1) [51-500]
  PW - v252 - i9 - Feb 28 2005 - p39(1) [51-500]
Hamilton, Garry - *Frog Rescue: Changing the Future for Endangered Wildlife*
  c Globe & Mail - Jan 29 2005 - pD10 [51-500]
  c Res Links - v10 - i3 - Feb 2005 - p24(1) [501+]
Hamilton, Hamish - *Father Joe: The Man Who Saved My Soul*
  NS - v134 - i4725 - Jan 31 2005 - p53(1) [501+]
Hamilton, James - *A Life of Discovery: Michael Faraday, Giant of the Scientific Revolution*
  BL - v101 - i7 - Dec 1 2004 - p631(1) [51-500]
  LJ - v130 - i1 - Jan 1 2005 - p142(2) [51-500]
  NYTBR - March 13 2005 - p16 [501+]
  PW - v251 - i48 - Nov 29 2004 - p33(1) [51-500]
Hamilton, Jane - *A Short History of a Prince*
  BL - v101 - i5 - Nov 1 2004 - p458(1) [51-500]
Hamilton, Janet - *Solving the Mystery of DNA*
  SB - v40 - i5 - Sept-Oct 2004 - p211(1) [51-500]
Hamilton, Janice - *Nigeria in Pictures*
  y HNet - June 2004 - pNA [51-500]
Hamilton, Jill - *God, Guns and Israel: Britain, the First World War and the Jews in the Holy Land*
  CR - v285 - i1664 - Sept 2004 - p175(2) [501+]
Hamilton, John T. - *Soliciting Darkness: Pindar, Obscurity and the Classical Tradition*
  Lon R Bks - v27 - i4 - Feb 17 2005 - p33(2) [501+]
Hamilton, Laura S. - *Making Sense of Test-Based Accountability in Education*
  R&R Bk N - v19 - i1 - Feb 2004 - p189(1) [51-500]
Hamilton, Laurell K. - *Bite*
  LJ - v130 - i1 - Jan 1 2005 - p104(1) [51-500]
  PW - v252 - i1 - Jan 3 2005 - p42(1) [51-500]

Cravings
  BL - v100 - i21 - July 2004 - p1828(1) [1-50]
Incubus Dreams
  BL - v101 - i4 - Oct 15 2004 - p395(1) [51-500]
  KR - v72 - i17 - Sept 1 2004 - p825(1) [51-500]
  LJ - v129 - i16 - Oct 1 2004 - p69(1) [51-500]
  PW - v251 - i37 - Sept 13 2004 - p63(1) [51-500]
Hamilton, Lawrence A. - *The Political Philosophy of Needs*
  Choice - v41 - i7 - March 2004 - p1369(2) [501+]
Hamilton, Lyn - *The Moai Murders*
  KR - v73 - i5 - March 1 2005 - p263(1) [51-500]
  PW - v252 - i11 - March 14 2005 - p48(1) [51-500]
Hamilton, Lynn - *Labor Day*
  c SLJ - v50 - i8 - August 2004 - p106(1) [51-500]
  Memorial Day
  c SLJ - v50 - i11 - Nov 2004 - p124(1) [51-500]
  Presidents' Day
  c SLJ - v50 - i11 - Nov 2004 - p124(1) [51-500]
Hamilton, Masha - *The Distance Between Us*
  BL - v101 - i3 - Oct 1 2004 - p310(1) [51-500]
  KR - v72 - i21 - Nov 1 2004 - p1024(1) [501+]
  LJ - v129 - i18 - Nov 1 2004 - p74(1) [501+]
  PW - v251 - i43 - Oct 25 2004 - p26(2) [51-500]
Hamilton-Meritt, Jane - *Tragic Mountains: The Hmong, the Americans, and the Secret Wars for Laos, 1942-1992*
  JTWS - v21 - i1 - Spring 2004 - p273(5) [501+]
Hamilton-Paterson, James - *Cooking with Fernet Branca*
  TLS - i5283 - July 2 2004 - p20(1) [501+]
Hamilton, Paul - *Metaromanticism, Aesthetics, Literature, Theory*
  Nine-C Lit - v59 - i2 - Sept 2004 - p249(6) [501+]
Hamilton, Phillip - *The Making and Unmaking of a Revolutionary Family: The Tuckers of Virginia, 1752-1830*
  AHR - v109 - i3 - June 2004 - p896(2) [501+]
  JAH - v91 - i2 - Sept 2004 - p612(2) [501+]
  JSH - v70 - i4 - Nov 2004 - p899(2) [501+]
  W&M Q - v61 - i3 - July 2004 - p571-573 [501+]
Hamilton, Richard - *Educational Interventions for Refugee Children: Theoretical Perspectives and Implementing Best Practice*
  TCR - v107 - i2 - Feb 2005 - p319(4) [501+]
Hamilton, Richard F. - *The Empire of the Raj: India, Eastern Africa and the Middle East, 1858-1947*
  AHR - v109 - i2 - April 2004 - p485(2) [501+]
  The Origins of World War I
  GSR - v27 - i3 - Oct 2004 - p629(2) [501+]
  y TimHES - v0 - i1652 - August 6 2004 - p24(2) [501+]
Hamilton, Roy W. - *The Art of Rice: Spirit and Sustenance in Asia*
  Choice - v42 - i5 - Jan 2005 - p895(2) [1-50]
Hamilton, Scott - *An Analog Electronics Companion: Basic Circuit Design for Engineers and Scientists*
  Phys Today - v57 - i10 - Oct 2004 - p80-80 [501+]
Hamilton, Stanley - *Machine Gun Kelly's Last Stand*
  SHQ - v108 - i1 - July 2004 - p121-122 [501+]
Hamilton, Stephen F. - *The Youth Development Handbook: Coming of Age in American Communities*
  R&R Bk N - v19 - i1 - Feb 2004 - p138(1) [51-500]
Hamilton, Steve - *Ice Run (Read by Bond, Jim). Audiobook Review*
  LJ - v129 - i20 - Dec 1 2004 - p180(1) [51-500]
Hamilton, Virginia - *Bruh Rabbit and the Tar Baby Girl (Illus. by Ransome, James E.)*
  c Five Owls - v18 - i1 - Fall 2004 - p18(1) [51-500]
  The People Could Fly: The Picture Book (Illus. by Dillon, Leo)
  c BL - v101 - i2 - Sept 15 2004 - p240(1) [51-500]
  y KR - v72 - i21 - Nov 1 2004 - p1044(1) [51-500]
  c PW - v251 - i47 - Nov 22 2004 - p58(1) [51-500]
  c SLJ - v50 - i12 - Dec 2004 - p130(2) [51-500]
  y BL - v101 - i9-10 - Jan 1 2005 - p773(1) [1-50]
  Time Pieces (Read by Pitts, Lisa Renee). Audiobook Review
  c PW - v252 - i11 - March 14 2005 - p26(1) [501+]
  Wee Winnie Witch's Skinny: An Original African American Scare Tale (Illus. by Moser, Barry)
  c CCB-B - v58 - i1 - Sept 2004 - p18(2) [501+]
  c HB - v80 - i5 - Sept-Oct 2004 - p567(2) [51-500]
  c KR - v72 - i14 - July 15 2004 - p686(1) [51-500]
  c LibMed - v23 - i3 - Nov-Dec 2004 - p66(1) [51-500]
  c PW - v251 - i32 - August 9 2004 - p248(2) [51-500]
  c SLJ - v50 - i8 - August 2004 - p88(1) [51-500]
Hamin, Elisabeth M. - *Mojave Lands: Interpretive Planning and the National Preserve*
  JEL - v42 - i1 - March 2004 - p331(1) [501+]

Hamington, Maurice - *Embodied Care: Jane Addams, Maurice Merleau-Ponty, and Feminist Ethics*
  Choice - v42 - i6 - Feb 2005 - p1035(1) [51-500]
Hamley, Dennis - *The Second World War*
  c Sch Lib - v52 - i4 - Winter 2004 - p207(1) [51-500]
Hamley, Ian W. - *Developments in Block Copolymer Science and Technology*
  SciTech - v28 - i3 - Sept 2004 - p52(1) [1-50]
Hamlin, Charles Hughes - *Virginia Ancestors and Adventurers, Vols. 1-3*
  EFHM - v58 - i2 - March-April 2004 - p91(1) [51-500]
Hamlin, Roger E. - *Financing Small Business in America: Debt Capital in a Global Economy*
  R&R Bk N - v19 - i1 - Feb 2004 - p116(1) [51-500]
Hamm, Berndt - *The Reformation of Faith in the Context of Late Medieval Theology and Piety: Essays by Berndt Hamm*
  Med R - Nov 2004 - pNA [501+]
Hamm, Keith David - *Scarred For Life: Eleven Stories About Skateboarders*
  PW - v251 - i45 - Nov 8 2004 - p48(1) [501+]
Hamm, Mia - *Winners Never Quit! (Illus. by Thompson, Carol)*
  c BL - v101 - i1 - Sept 1 2004 - p114(1) [501+]
  c PW - v251 - i40 - Oct 4 2004 - p87(1) [51-500]
  c SLJ - v50 - i9 - Sept 2004 - p161(1) [51-500]
Hamm, Richard F. - *Murder, Honor, and Law: 4 Virginia Homicides from Reconstruction to the Great Depression*
  AHR - v109 - i3 - June 2004 - p920(2) [501+]
  JAH - v91 - i3 - Dec 2004 - p1036(1) [501+]
Hamm, Thomas D. - *The Quakers in America*
  JAH - v91 - i3 - Dec 2004 - p1098(2) [501+]
  JR - v84 - i4 - Oct 2004 - p615(3) [501+]
Hammack, Floyd M. - *The Comprehensive High School Today*
  Choice - v42 - i6 - Feb 2005 - p1072(1) [51-500]
Hammer, Dean - *The Iliad as Politics: The Performance of Political Thought*
  CJ - v99 - i3 - Feb-March 2004 - p345-349 [501+]
  Class R - v53 - i2 - Nov 2003 - p275-276 [501+]
Hammer, Friederike - *Industry in North-West Roman Southwark: Excavations 1984-8*
  R&R Bk N - v19 - i3 - August 2004 - p39(1) [51-500]
Hammer, Jill - *Sisters at Sinai*
  Bwatch - Nov 2004 - pNA [51-500]
Hammer, Olav - *Claiming Knowledge: Strategies of Epistemology from Theosophy to the New Age*
  R&R Bk N - v19 - i3 - August 2004 - p12(1) [1-50]
Hammer, Torild - *Youth Unemployment and Social Exclusion in Europe: A Comparative Study*
  R&R Bk N - v19 - i1 - Feb 2004 - p99(1) [1-50]
Hammermeister, Kai - *The German Aesthetic Tradition*
  GSR - v27 - i3 - Oct 2004 - p600(2) [501+]
  JAAC - v62 - i3 - Summer 2004 - p302-304 [501+]
Hammerschmidt, Peter - *Finanzierung und Management von Wohlfahrtsanstalten 1920 bis 1936*
  HNet - Dec 2004 - pNA [501+]
Hammersley, Ben - *Content Syndication with RSS*
  SciTech - v28 - i4 - Dec 2004 - p24(1) [51-500]
Hammerslough, Jane - *Owl Puke*
  Am Sci - v92 - i4 - July-August 2004 - p376(1) [501+]
  CH Bwatch - Oct 2004 - pNA [51-500]
Hammerson, Geoffrey A. - *Connecticut Wildlife: Biodiversity, Natural History, and Conservation*
  Choice - v42 - i5 - Jan 2005 - p877(2) [1-50]
Hammerstaedt, J. - *Apuleius: de Magia. Eingeleitet, ubersetzt und mit interpretierenden Essays versehen*
  Class R - v54 - i1 - May 2004 - p115(2) [501+]
Hammerstein, Peter - *Genetic and Cultural Evolution of Cooperation*
  QRB - v79 - i4 - Dec 2004 - p458(2) [501+]
Hammes, Thomas - *The Sling and the Stone: On War in the 21st Century*
  BL - v101 - i1 - Sept 1 2004 - p27(1) [51-500]
  LJ - v129 - i18 - Nov 1 2004 - p109(1) [51-500]
  Mar Crp G - v88 - i11 - Nov 2004 - p91(1) [501+]
Hammett, Brian - *A Concise History of Mexico*
  y VOYA - v27 - i3 - August 2004 - p181(1) [1-50]
Hammett, Dashiell - *The Maltese Falcon (Read by Dufris, William). Audiobook Review*
  Globe & Mail - Feb 5 2005 - pD17 [1-50]
  The Maltese Falcon
  LJ - v130 - i3 - Feb 15 2005 - p172(1) [51-500]
  Red Harvest
  LJ - v130 - i3 - Feb 15 2005 - p172(1) [51-500]
  The Thin Man
  LJ - v130 - i3 - Feb 15 2005 - p172(1) [51-500]

Hanson, Stephanie L. - *Health Care Ethics for Psychologists: A Casebook*
SciTech - v28 - i4 - Dec 2004 - p77(1) [51-500]

Hanson, Susan - *Icons of Loss and Grace: Moments from the Natural World*
Ch Today - v49 - i1 - Jan 2005 - p70(1) [51-500]
Roundup M - v11 - i6 - August 2004 - p24(1) [501+]

Hansson, Joacim - *Libraries in Times of Utopian Thoughts and Social Protests--The Libraries of the Late 1960s and Early 1970s*
Lib & Cul - v39 - i3 - Summer 2004 - p320(3) [501+]

Hansten, Philip D. - *Managing Clinically Important Drug Interactions*
SciTech - v28 - i3 - Sept 2004 - p122(1) [51-500]

Hantrais, Linda - *Family Policy Matters: Responding to Family Change in Europe*
R&R Bk N - v19 - i3 - August 2004 - p149(1) [51-500]

Hantula, Richard - *Isaac Asimov's 21st Century Library of the Universe: The Solar System*
S&T - v108 - i1 - July 2004 - p118(1) [501+]

Hanushek, Eric A. - *The Economics of Schooling and School Quality*
JEL - v41 - i4 - Dec 2003 - p1377(2) [501+]

Hanzo, L. - *OFDM and MC-CDMA for Broadband Multi-User Communications, WLANS, and Broadcasting*
E-Streams - June 2004 - pNA [501+]
SciTech - v28 - i1 - March 2004 - p154(1) [51-500]

Single and Multi-Carrier DS-CDMA: Multi-User Detection, Space-Time Spreading, Synchronisation, Networking, and Standards
E-Streams - June 2004 - pNA [501+]
SciTech - v28 - i1 - March 2004 - p154(1) [51-500]

Hapka, Catherine - *Always Dreamin'*
c SLJ - v50 - i8 - August 2004 - p123(1) [51-500]
Supernova
c SLJ - v50 - i8 - August 2004 - p123(1) [51-500]

Happian-Smith, Julian - *Introduction to Modern Vehicle Design*
SciTech - v28 - i1 - March 2004 - p167(1) [51-500]

Haptie, Charlotte - *Otto and the Bird Charmers*
y Magpies - v19 - i5 - Nov 2004 - p38(1) [501+]
c Sch Lib - v52 - i4 - Winter 2004 - p203(1) [51-500]

Harada, Violet H. - *Inquiry Learning through Librarian-Teacher Partnerships*
SLJ - v50 - i9 - Sept 2004 - p238(1) [51-500]

Haran, Alexandre Y. - *Le lys et le globe: Messianisme dynastique et reve imperial en France a l'aube des temps modernes*
JMH - v77 - i1 - March 2005 - p185(3) [501+]

Harasymiw, Bohdan - *Post-Communist Ukraine*
E-A St - v56 - i6 - Sept 2004 - p921(922) [501+]
Slav R - v63 - i2 - Summer 2004 - p396(2) [501+]

Harayda, Janice - *Manhattan, on the Rocks*
BL - v101 - i4 - Oct 15 2004 - p389(1) [51-500]
KR - v72 - i16 - August 15 2004 - p764(1) [51-500]

Harbeke, Dan - *Get In!: How to Market Yourself and Become Successful at a Young Age*
y R&R Bk N - v19 - i2 - May 2004 - p113(1) [1-50]
y VOYA - v27 - i3 - August 2004 - p237(1) [1-50]

Harber, Erika - *The Myth of the Non-Russian: Iskander and Aitmatov's Magical Universe*
Slav R - v63 - i3 - Fall 2004 - p642-643 [501+]

Harbison, Peter - *Ireland's Treasures: 5,000 Years of Artistic Expression*
Choice - v42 - i2 - Oct 2004 - p281(1) [501+]

Harbour, Jonathan S. - *Game Programming All in One, 2nd Ed.*
SciTech - v28 - i4 - Dec 2004 - p24(1) [51-500]

Harbury, Katherine E. - *Colonial Virginia's Cooking Dynasty*
Choice - v42 - i2 - Oct 2004 - p355(1) [51-500]
VQR - v80 - i3 - Summer 2004 - p266(1) [501+]

Harbus, Antonina - *The Life of the Mind in Old English Poetry*
Specu - v79 - i4 - Oct 2004 - p1082(3) [501+]

Harcave, Sidney - *Count Sergei Witte and the Twilight of Imperial Russia: A Biography*
Choice - v42 - i3 - Nov 2004 - p542(1) [1-50]
R&R Bk N - v19 - i3 - August 2004 - p45(1) [51-500]

Harchar, Gloria - *Enchanted by Magic*
BL - v101 - i3 - Oct 1 2004 - p316(1) [51-500]

Harcourt, Mike - *Plan B: One Man's Journey from Tragedy to Triumph*
Globe & Mail - Dec 18 2004 - pD9 [501+]

Hard, Robin - *The Routledge Handbook of Greek Mythology*
TimHES - v0 - i1664 - Oct 29 2004 - p24(1) [501+]

Hardaker, J. Brian - *Coping with Risk in Agriculture, 2nd Ed.*
SciTech - v28 - i4 - Dec 2004 - p123 [51-500]

Hardaway, Robert M. - *No Price Too High: Victimless Crimes and the Ninth Amendment*
Choice - v42 - i2 - Oct 2004 - p372(1) [51-500]
R&R Bk N - v19 - i1 - Feb 2004 - pNA [51-500]

Hardbound, Michael Pratt - *Mid-Century Modern Dinnerware: A Pictorial Guide Redwing to Winfield*
Ant&CM - v108 - i11 - Jan 2004 - p16(1) [501+]

Hardcastle, David A. - *Community Practice: Theories and Skills for Social Workers, 2nd Ed.*
R&R Bk N - v19 - i3 - August 2004 - p158(1) [51-500]

Harder, A. - *'Noch einmal zu...' Kleine Schriften von Stefan Radt zu seinem 75. Geburtstag*
Class R - v54 - i2 - Nov 2004 - p303-305 [501+]

Harder, Jens - *Leviathan*
BL - v100 - i21 - July 2004 - p1830(1) [501+]
y VOYA - v27 - i5 - Dec 2004 - p404(1) [51-500]

Hardesty, Von - *Air Force One: The Aircraft That Shaped the Modern Presidency*
SLJ - v50 - i10 - Oct 2004 - pS57(1) [51-500]

Hardgrave, Robert L., Jr. - *A Portrait of the Hindus: Balthazar Solvyns and the European Image of India, 1760-1824*
Choice - v42 - i3 - Nov 2004 - p471(1) [1-50]
A Portrait of the Hindus: Balthazar Solvyns and the European Image of India 1760-1824
TimHES - v0 - i1662 - Oct 15 2004 - p24(2) [501+]

Hardie, P. - *Ovid's Poetics of Illusion*
Class R - v54 - i2 - Nov 2004 - p384(5) [501+]

Hardiman, David - *Gandhi in His Time and Ours: The Global Legacy of His Ideas*
Choice - v42 - i3 - Nov 2004 - p538(1) [1-50]
HRNB - v33 - i1 - Fall 2004 - p34(1) [501+]
R&R Bk N - v19 - i3 - August 2004 - p54(1) [51-500]
TimHES - v0 - i1650 - July 23 2004 - p28(1) [501+]

Hardin, Joe - *Teaching, Research, and Service in the Twenty-First Century English Department: A Delicate Balance*
R&R Bk N - v19 - i4 - Nov 2004 - p215(1) [501+]

Hardin, Russell - *Indeterminacy and Society*
JEL - v42 - i1 - March 2004 - p250(1) [501+]

Hardin, Stephen - *Alamo 1836: Santa Anna's Texas Campaign*
R&R Bk N - v19 - i4 - Nov 2004 - p62(1) [51-500]

Harding, Alan - *Medieval Law and the Foundation of the State*
Specu - v79 - i4 - Oct 2004 - p1084(2) [501+]

Harding, David - *Mastering the Merger: Four Critical Decisions That Make or Break the Deal*
Time - v164 - i17 - Oct 25 2004 - pA3 [51-500]

Harding, James M. - *Contours of the Theatrical Avantgarde: Performance and Textuality*
Theat J - v56 - i2 - May 2004 - p336(3) [501+]

Harding, Rebecca - *The Future of the German Economy: An End to the Miracle?*
GSR - v27 - i2 - May 2004 - p430-432 [501+]

Harding, Robyn - *The Journal of Mortifying Moments*
Ent W - i794 - Nov 26 2004 - p123 [51-500]
LJ - v129 - i14 - Sept 1 2004 - p139(1) [51-500]
PW - v251 - i40 - Oct 4 2004 - p70(1) [51-500]

Harding, Vanessa - *The Dead and the Living in Paris and London, 1500-1670*
CH - v73 - i3 - Sept 2004 - p693(2) [501+]
JIH - v34 - i3 - Wntr 2004 - p447-3 [501+]
Six Ct J - v34 - i4 - Winter 2003 - p1164-1165 [501+]

Hardman, Malcolm - *Classic Soil: Community, Aspiration, and Debate in the Bolton Region of Lancashire, 1819-1845*
R&R Bk N - v19 - i1 - Feb 2004 - p33(1) [1-50]

Hardman, Phillipa - *The Matter of Identity in Medieval Romance*
JEGP - v103 - i3 - July 2004 - p390-392 [501+]

Hardorff, Richard - *Indian Views of the Custer Fight: A Source Book*
R&R Bk N - v19 - i3 - August 2004 - p61(1) [51-500]

Hardt, John P. - *Russia's Uncertain Economic Future*
E-A St - v56 - i8 - Dec 2004 - p1252(5) [501+]

Hardt, Michael - *Multitude: War and Democracy in the Age of Empire*
BL - v100 - i21 - July 2004 - p1804(1) [51-500]
Choice - v42 - i5 - Jan 2005 - p930(1) [51-500]
NYRB - v51 - i17 - Nov 4 2004 - p38(4) [501+]
NYT - August 7 2004 - pB11 [501+]
NYTBR - July 25 2004 - p12 [501+]
PW - v251 - i28 - July 12 2004 - p57(2) [51-500]
Tikkun - v20 - i1 - Jan-Feb 2005 - p68(4) [501+]
Time - v164 - i6 - August 9 2004 - p94 [501+]

Hardten, David R. - *Phakic Intraocular Lenses: Principles and Practice*
SciTech - v28 - i1 - March 2004 - p114(1) [51-500]

Hardwick, Gary - *The Executioner's Game*
KR - v72 - i24 - Dec 15 2004 - p1156(2) [501+]
PW - v251 - i49 - Dec 6 2004 - p43(2) [51-500]

Hardwick, M. Jeffrey - *Mall Maker: Victor Gruen, Architect of an American Dream*
BHR - v78 - i1 - Spring 2004 - p142(3) [501+]
HRNB - v33 - i1 - Fall 2004 - p9(1) [501+]

Hardwick, Susan Wiley - *Mystic Galveston: Reinventing America's Third Coast*
SHQ - v107 - i4 - April 2004 - p632(2) [501+]
Mythic Galveston: Reinventing America's Third Coast
AHR - v109 - i2 - April 2004 - p533(2) [501+]
JAH - v91 - i1 - June 2004 - p274-275 [501+]

Hardwick, William H. - *Down South: One Tour in Vietnam*
y Kliatt - v39 - i1 - Jan 2005 - p30(1) [501+]

Hardy, Anne - *Where to Eat in Canada, 02-03*
CBRA - Annual 2003 - p30(2) [51-500]
Where to Eat in Canada, 03-04
CBRA - Annual 2003 - p30(1) [51-500]

Hardy, Clarence E., III - *James Baldwin's God: Sex, Hope, and Crisis in Black Holiness Culture*
Choice - v41 - i11-12 - July-August 2004 - p2044(1) [501+]
R&R Bk N - v19 - i1 - Feb 2004 - p246(1) [51-500]

Hardy, David A. - *Futures: 50 Years in Space: The Challenge of the Stars*
Astron - v33 - i1 - Jan 2005 - p92 [51-500]
SciTech - v28 - i4 - Dec 2004 - p46(1) [51-500]
S&T - v109 - i2 - Feb 2005 - p109(2) [501+]

Hardy, David T. - *Michael Moore Is a Big Fat Stupid White Man*
Econ - v372 - i8383 - July 10 2004 - p75US [501+]
Globe & Mail - August 14 2004 - pD12 [1-50]

Hardy, George - *Americans in Paris, 1850-1910: The Academy, the Salon, the Studio, and the Artists' Colony*
Choice - v41 - i11-12 - July-August 2004 - p2033(1) [501+]

Hardy, Henry - *Isaiah Berlin: Letters 1928-1946*
Globe & Mail - Nov 27 2004 - pD3 [51-500]

Hardy, Melissa - *Handbook of Data Analysis*
SciTech - v28 - i3 - Sept 2004 - p37(1) [51-500]

Hardy, Thomas - *Thomas Hardy's "Facts" Notebook, Critical Ed.*
Choice - v42 - i5 - Jan 2005 - p852(1) [1-50]
R&R Bk N - v19 - i4 - Nov 2004 - p237(1) [501+]

Hare, Rom - *The Self and Others: Positioning Individuals and Groups in Personal, Political, and Cultural Contexts*
R&R Bk N - v19 - i1 - Feb 2004 - p124(1) [51-500]

Hare, William - *L.A. Noir: Nine Dark Visions of the City of Angels*
R&R Bk N - v19 - i3 - August 2004 - p262(1) [51-500]

Hareven, Tamara K. - *The Silk Weavers of Kyoto: Family and Work in a Changing Traditional Industry*
CS - v33 - i2 - March 2004 - p181-182 [501+]
T&C - v45 - i1 - Jan 2004 - p177(2) [501+]

Hargadon, Andrew - *How Breakthroughs Happen: The Surprising Truth about How Companies Innovate*
T&C - v45 - i2 - April 2004 - p464-465 [501+]

Hargittai, Istvan - *Candid Science III: More Conversations with Famous Chemists*
SciTech - v28 - i4 - Dec 2004 - p54(1) [51-500]
Candid Science IV: Conversations with Famous Physicists
SB - v40 - i4 - July-August 2004 - p158(1) [51-500]
Candid Science IV; Conversations with Famous Physicists
SciTech - v28 - i3 - Sept 2004 - p50(1) [1-50]
Our Lives: Encounters of a Scientist
Nature - v432 - i7014 - Nov 11 2004 - p150(2) [501+]

Hargrave, Terry D. - *The New Contextual Therapy: Guiding the Power of Give and Take*
Adoles - v39 - i154 - Summer 2004 - p399(2) [51-500]

Hargraves, John A. - *Music in the Works of Broch, Mann, and Kafka*
Ger Q - v77 - i2 - Spring 2004 - p243-244 [501+]
GSR - v27 - i1 - Feb 2004 - p163-165 [501+]

Hargreaves, David H. - *Learning for Life: The Foundations for Lifelong Learning*
R&R Bk N - v19 - i4 - Nov 2004 - p193(1) [501+]

Hargreaves, Ian - *Journalism: Truth or Dare*
TV Q - v34 - i2 - Wntr 2004 - p77-79 [501+]

Hargrove, Erwin C. - *Leadership in Context*
R&R Bk N - v19 - i2 - May 2004 - p125 [51-500]

Harhvell, David - *Christmas Stars*
PW - v251 - i42 - Oct 18 2004 - p52(2) [501+]

Harik, Judith Palmer - *Hezbollah: The Changing Face of Terrorism*
MEQ - v11 - i4 - Fall 2004 - p78(2) [501+]

Harington, Donald - *The Cockroaches of Staymore*
LJ - v129 - i12 - July 2004 - p127(1) [1-50]

Harink, Douglas - *Paul among the Postliberals: Pauline Theology beyond Christendom and Modernity*
Intpr - v58 - i4 - Oct 2004 - p399(3) [501+]

Harir, Salim - *Tools and Environments for Parallel and Distributed Computing*
E-Streams - August 2004 - pNA [501+]

Haritonow, Alexander - *Ideologie als Institution und soziale Praxis: Die Adaption des hoheren sowjetischen Parteischulensystems in der SBZ/DDR*
HNet - June 2004 - pNA [501+]

Harkam, Sammy - *Kramer's Ergot 5*
PW - v251 - i48 - Nov 29 2004 - p26(1) [51-500]

Harkin, Michael E. - *Reassessing Revitalization Movements: Perspectives from North America and the Pacific Islands*
Choice - v42 - i4 - Dec 2004 - p703(1) [1-50]

Harkins, Anthony - *Hillbilly: A Cultural History of an American Icon*
Choice - v41 - i11-12 - July-August 2004 - p2108(1) [501+]
JouAmCul - v27 - i4 - Dec 2004 - p446(2) [501+]

Harkins, Paul H. - *How to Become a Highly Paid Corporate Programme*
SciTech - v28 - i3 - Sept 2004 - p20(1) [501+]

Harkness, Peter - *Rose: An Illustrated History*
E-Streams - July 2004 - pNA [501+]
SciTech - v28 - i1 - March 2004 - p130(1) [51-500]

Harkness, Philip - *Reliable Roses*
E-Streams - August 2004 - pNA [501+]

Harkness, Richard - *Mosby's Handbook of Drug-Herb and Drug-Supplement Interactions*
SciTech - v28 - i1 - March 2004 - p122(1) [51-500]

Harlan, Elizabeth - *George Sand*
PW - v251 - i48 - Nov 29 2004 - p31(1) [51-500]

Harlan, James - *Atlas of Lewis and Clark in Missouri*
BL - v100 - i21 - July 2004 - p1858(1) [1-50]
Choice - v41 - i11-12 - July-August 2004 - p2108(1) [501+]

Harlan, Lindsey - *The Goddesses' Henchmen: Gender in Indian Hero Worship*
JAAR - v72 - i4 - Dec 2004 - p1040(3) [501+]
JAS - v63 - i3 - August 2004 - p825-827 [501+]

Harland, David M. - *The Story of the Space Shuttle*
Choice - v42 - i4 - Dec 2004 - p693(1) [1-50]

Harland, Philip A. - *Associations, Synagogues, and Congregations: Claiming a Place in Ancient Mediterranean Society*
CH - v73 - i4 - Dec 2004 - p836(2) [501+]

Harlem Boys Choir - *O Holy Night: Christmas with the Boys Choir of Harlem (Illus. by Ringgold, Faith)*
c KR - v72 - i21 - Nov 1 2004 - p1053(1) [501+]

Harlen, Jonathan - *The Cockroach War*
c BL - v100 - i22 - August 2004 - p1934(1) [51-500]
y Kliatt - v38 - i5 - Sept 2004 - p28(3) [501+]
c Sch Lib - v52 - i4 - Winter 2004 - p202(1) [51-500]

Harless, Hal - *How Firm a Foundation: The Dispensations in the Light of the Divine Covenants*
R&R Bk N - v19 - i3 - August 2004 - p22(1) [1-50]

Harley, J.B. - *The New Nature of Maps: Essays in the History of Cartography*
Hist Geo - v32 - Annual 2004 - p189(3) [501+]

Harlick, R.J. - *Death's Golden Whisper*
Globe & Mail - Dec 4 2004 - pD35 [51-500]

Harlow, Barbara - *Archives of Empire, Vols. 1-2*
ELT - v47 - i3 - Summer 2004 - p366(1) [51-500]

Harlow, Francis Harvey - *The Pottery of Zia Pueblo*
Ceram Mo - v52 - i3 - March 2004 - p36(1) [501+]
Pottery of Zia Pueblo
R&R Bk N - v19 - i4 - Nov 2004 - p55(1) [51-500]

Harlow, James H. - *Electric Power Transformer Engineering*
Choice - v41 - i7 - March 2004 - p1325(1) [501+]

Harlow, Joan Hiatt - *Shadows on the Sea*
y Kliatt - v39 - i2 - March 2005 - p18(2) [51-500]
y LibMed - v22 - i6 - March 2004 - p64(1) [501+]
y LibMed - v22 - i6 - March 2004 - p64(1) [501+]
c SLJ - v50 - i8 - August 2004 - p76(1) [51-500]
Thunder from the Sea
c BL - v100 - i22 - August 2004 - p1934(1) [51-500]
c Globe & Mail - July 31 2004 - pD11 [51-500]
c HB - v80 - i4 - July-August 2004 - p452(2) [51-500]
c SLJ - v50 - i9 - Sept 2004 - p207(1) [51-500]

Harlow, Katherine - *The London Bible: A Guide to Living and Working in the Capital*
R&R Bk N - v19 - i3 - August 2004 - p39(1) [51-500]

Harman, Claire - *Robert Louis Stevenson: A Biography*
Econ - v374 - i8411 - Jan 29 2005 - p79US [501+]
Lon R Bks - v27 - i4 - Feb 17 2005 - p10(3) [501+]
Spec - v297 - i9208 - Jan 29 2005 - p32(1) [501+]

Harman, Eleanor - *The Thesis and the Book: A Guide for First-Time Academic Authors, 2nd Ed.*
CBRA - Annual 2003 - p19(1) [51-500]
JEL - v41 - i4 - Dec 2003 - p1445(1) [501+]

Harman, Graham - *Tool-Being: Heidegger and the Metaphysics of Objects*
T&C - v45 - i1 - Jan 2004 - p232(3) [501+]

Harman, Hollis Page - *Money Sense for Kids!*
y SLJ - v50 - i11 - Nov 2004 - p165(1) [51-500]

Harman, Oren Solomon - *The Man Who Invented the Chromosome: The Life of Cyril Darlington*
Am Sci - v92 - i6 - Nov-Dec 2004 - p570(3) [501+]
Choice - v42 - i4 - Dec 2004 - p687(1) [1-50]
Nature - v431 - i7008 - Sept 30 2004 - p512(1) [501+]
New Sci - v184 - i2468 - Oct 9 2004 - p49(1) [501+]

Harmel, Anne Peters - *Davidson's Diabetes Mellitus: Diagnosis and Treatment, 5th Ed.*
SciTech - v28 - i1 - March 2004 - p103(1) [51-500]

Harmes, Adam - *The Return of the State: Protesters, Power-Brokers and the New Global Compromise*
Globe & Mail - Oct 30 2004 - pD20 [501+]

Harmon, William - *Classic Writings on Poetry*
Poet - v184 - i4 - August 2004 - p317(7) [501+]

Harmsen, Dorothy - *Sweet on the West: How Candy Built a Colorado Treasure*
JouAmCul - v27 - i3 - Sept 2004 - p358(1) [501+]

Harmsen, Robert - *Euroscepticism: Party Politics, National Identity and European Integration*
R&R Bk N - v19 - i3 - August 2004 - p99(1) [51-500]

Harness, Cheryl - *Franklin and Eleanor*
c BL - v101 - i5 - Nov 1 2004 - p478(1) [501+]
c KR - v72 - i24 - Dec 15 2004 - p1202(1) [51-500]
c PW - v252 - i3 - Jan 17 2005 - p55(2) [51-500]
c SLJ - v50 - i12 - Dec 2004 - p132(1) [501+]
Ghosts of the Nile (Illus. by Harness, Cheryl)
c KR - v72 - i15 - August 1 2004 - p742(1) [51-500]
c SLJ - v50 - i10 - Oct 2004 - p142(1) [51-500]
Rabble Rousers: 20 Women Who Made a Difference
LibMed - v22 - i4 - Jan 2004 - p72(1) [501+]
Thomas Jefferson
LibMed - v22 - i7 - April-May 2004 - p66(1) [501+]
SLJ - v50 - i10 - Oct 2004 - pS31(1) [51-500]

Harnett, Gerald - *Calculus 1*
Math T - v97 - i3 - March 2004 - p223-223 [501+]

Harold, Elliotte Rusty - *Effective XML: 50 Specific Ways to Improve Your XML*
Bwatch - March 2005 - pNA [51-500]
XML In a Nutshell, 3rd Ed.
SciTech - v28 - i4 - Dec 2004 - p29(1) [51-500]

Harold, James A. - *An Introduction to the Love of Wisdom: An Essential and Existential Approach to Philosophy*
R&R Bk N - v20 - i1 - Feb 2005 - p6(1) [501+]

Harold, Stanley - *The Rise of Aggressive Abolitionism: Addresses to the Slaves*
Choice - v42 - i3 - Nov 2004 - p547(1) [1-50]

Harp, Gillis J. - *Brahmin Prophet: Phillips Brooks and the Path of Liberal Protestantism*
AHR - v109 - i4 - Oct 2004 - p1266-1267 [501+]
J Ch St - v46 - i4 - Autumn 2004 - p898(3) [501+]
JAH - v91 - i3 - Dec 2004 - p1035(2) [501+]
R&R Bk N - v19 - i1 - Feb 2004 - p25(1) [1-50]

Harp, Jerry - *Creature*
ABR - v25 - i5 - July-August 2004 - p27(2) [501+]

Harper, Charise Mericle - *The Monster Show: Everything You Never Knew about Monsters (Illus. by Harper, Charise Mericle)*
c KR - v72 - i14 - July 15 2004 - p686(1) [51-500]
c PW - v251 - i32 - August 9 2004 - p250(1) [51-500]
c SLJ - v50 - i9 - Sept 2004 - p161(1) [51-500]
Yes, No, Maybe So (Illus. by Harper, Charise Mericle)
c SLJ - v50 - i7 - July 2004 - p77(1) [51-500]

Harper, Charles A. - *Electronic Packaging and Interconnection Handbook, 4th Ed.*
SciTech - v28 - i4 - Dec 2004 - p155(1) [51-500]

Harper, David A. - *Foundations of Entrepreneurship and Economic Development*
JEL - v41 - i4 - Dec 2003 - p1398(2) [501+]

Harper, David G. - *Investing in Biotech: How to Profit from the Biopharmaceutical Revolution*
CBRA - Annual 2003 - p327(2) [501+]

Harper, Doug A. - *The Cultural Study of Work*
R&R Bk N - v19 - i1 - Feb 2004 - p101(1) [1-50]

Harper, Douglas A. - *The Cultural Study of Work*
Choice - v41 - i11-12 - July-August 2004 - p2128(1) [501+]
TLS - i5299 - Oct 22 2004 - p28(1) [501+]

Harper, Jamie - *Me Too!*
c KR - v73 - i2 - Jan 15 2005 - p120(1) [51-500]
c SLJ - v51 - i2 - Feb 2005 - p97(1) [51-500]

Harper, Jessica - *Four Boys Named Jordan (Illus. by King, Tara Calahan)*
c PW - v251 - i30 - July 26 2004 - p54(1) [51-500]
c SLJ - v50 - i9 - Sept 2004 - p161(1) [51-500]
Hey, Picasso
c BL - v101 - i8 - Dec 15 2004 - p754(1) [1-50]
I Like Where I Am (Illus. by Karas, G. Brian)
c BooChiTr - March 28 2004 - p2(1) [501+]
Lizzy's Ups and Downs: Not an Ordinary School Day
c BL - v101 - i1 - Sept 1 2004 - p131(2) [1-50]

Harper, John Lamberton - *American Machiavelli: Alexander Hamilton and the Origins of U.S. Foreign Policy*
Choice - v42 - i5 - Jan 2005 - p914(1) [501+]
HNet - August 2004 - pNA [501+]

Harper, Judith E. - *Women During the Civil War: An Encyclopedia*
J Mil H - v68 - i3 - July 2004 - p966-967 [501+]
LibMed - v23 - i1 - August-Sept 2004 - p75(2) [51-500]
R&R Bk N - v19 - i1 - Feb 2004 - p60(1) [51-500]

Harper, Karen - *The Fyre Mirror: An Elizabeth I Mystery*
KR - v73 - i2 - Jan 15 2005 - p86(1) [51-500]
LJ - v130 - i2 - Feb 1 2005 - p56(1) [51-500]
PW - v252 - i5 - Jan 31 2005 - p52(1) [51-500]

Harper, Lea - *Shadowcrossing*
Can Lit - i182 - Autumn 2004 - p116(3) [501+]

Harper, M.A. - *The Year of Past Things: A New Orleans Ghost Story*
BL - v101 - i4 - Oct 15 2004 - p389(1) [51-500]
KR - v72 - i20 - Oct 15 2004 - p978(1) [501+]
PW - v251 - i50 - Dec 13 2004 - p50(1) [51-500]

Harper, Pat - *Change One for Diabetes: The Natural Solution Program for Lowering Your Blood Sugar, Losing Weight, and Living a Healthier Life*
PW - v251 - i51 - Dec 20 2004 - p53(1) [501+]

Harper, Piers - *Little Owl*
c PW - v251 - i41 - Oct 11 2004 - p82(1) [501+]

Harper, Russell David - *Bald: A Novel*
PW - v251 - i39 - Sept 27 2004 - p37(1) [501+]

Harper, Sarah Billington - *In the Shadow of the Mahatma: Bishop V.S. Azariah and the Travails of Christianity in British India*
CH - v73 - i4 - Dec 2004 - p901(3) [501+]

Harper, Steven - *Offspring*
BL - v101 - i3 - Oct 1 2004 - p318(1) [51-500]

Harper, Sue - *British Cinema of the 1950s: The Decline of Deference*
Choice - v42 - i2 - Oct 2004 - p300(1) [51-500]
CR - v285 - i1663 - August 2004 - p119(2) [501+]

Harper, William T. - *Eleven Days in Hell: The 1974 Carrasco Prison Siege in Huntsville, Texas*
Roundup M - v12 - i3 - Feb 2005 - p17(1) [51-500]
R&R Bk N - v19 - i4 - Nov 2004 - p149(1) [501+]

Harrison, Stephan - *Patterned Ground: Entanglements of Nature and Culture*
> Choice - v42 - i3 - Nov 2004 - p472(1) [1-50]

Harrison, Troon - *Eye of the Wolf*
> c   CBRA - Annual 2003 - p487(1) [501+]

Harriss-White, Barbara - *India Working: Essays on Society and Economy*
> Pac A - v77 - i2 - Summer 2004 - p355(3) [501+]

Harrod, Tanya - *Carol McNicoll*
> Ceram Mo - v52 - i4 - April 2004 - p30(1) [501+]

Harroff, Stephen Bowers - *The Amish Schools of Indiana: Faith in Education*
> Choice - v42 - i5 - Jan 2005 - p905(1) [1-50]
> R&R Bk N - v19 - i3 - August 2004 - p228(1) [1-50]

Harrold, Stanley - *The Rise of Aggressive Abolitionism: Addresses to the Slaves*
> HNet - Oct 2004 - pNA [501+]
>
> *Subversives: Antislavery Community in Washington, D.C., 1828-1865*
> AHR - v109 - i2 - April 2004 - p526(1) [501+]
>
> *Subversives: Antislavery Community in Washington D.C, 1828-1865*
> JIH - v35 - i1 - Summer 2004 - p154-155 [501+]

Harrop, Jane - *Finishing Touches: Step-by-Step Instructions for Over 70 Projects*
> LJ - v129 - i14 - Sept 1 2004 - p178(1) [51-500]

Harrow, Sharon - *Adventures in Domesticity: Gender and Colonial Adulteration in Eighteenth-Century British Literature*
> Choice - v42 - i7 - March 2005 - p1228(1) [51-500]

Harrow, Susan - *The Material, The Real, and the Fractured Self: Subjectivity and Representation from Rimbaud to Reda*
> R&R Bk N - v19 - i4 - Nov 2004 - p230(1) [501+]

Harry, Karen - *Economic Organization and Settlement Hierarchies: Ceramic Production and Exchange Among the Hohokam*
> R&R Bk N - v19 - i1 - Feb 2004 - p53(1) [51-500]

Harry, Rebecca - *Ruby in Her Own Time*
> LibMed - v22 - i7 - April-May 2004 - p56(1) [501+]

Harryhausen, Ray - *Ray Harryhausen: An Animated Life*
> Bwatch - v26 - i7 - July 2004 - p9(1) [51-500]

Harshav, Benjamin - *Marc Chagall and His Times: A Documentary Narrative*
> R&R Bk N - v19 - i1 - Feb 2004 - p200(1) [51-500]

Harsin, Jill - *Barricades: The War of the Streets in Revolutionary Paris, 1830-1848*
> HNet - August 2004 - pNA [501+]
> JMH - v76 - i3 - Sept 2004 - p698(3) [501+]

Hart, Carolyn - *Death of the Party: A Death on Demand Mystery*
> KR - v73 - i3 - Feb 1 2005 - p151(1) [51-500]
> LJ - v129 - i20 - Dec 1 2004 - p96(1) [51-500]
> c   PW - v252 - i10 - March 7 2005 - p54(1) [51-500]
>
> *Design for Murder*
> LJ - v129 - i13 - August 2004 - p131(1) [51-500]
>
> *Letter from Home (Read by Reading, Kate). Audiobook Review*
> c   Kliatt - v38 - i4 - July 2004 - p52(2) [51-500]
> LJ - v129 - i15 - Sept 15 2004 - p88(1) [51-500]
>
> *Murder Walks the Plank (Read by Reading, Kate). Audiobook Review*
> LJ - v129 - i18 - Nov 1 2004 - p129(1) [51-500]

Hart, Christine - *Ancient Greece*
> c   Teach Lib - v32 - i3 - Feb 2005 - p42(1) [51-500]

Hart, Christopher - *Drawing Cutting Edge Anatomy: The Ultimate Reference for Comic Book Artists*
> Bwatch - Feb 2005 - pNA [51-500]

Hart, Christopher - *Kids Draw Animals*
> c   LibMed - v22 - i6 - March 2004 - p73(1) [501+]
> c   SLJ - v50 - i10 - Oct 2004 - pS49(1) [51-500]
>
> *Kids Draw Manga (Illus. by Hart, Christopher)*
> c   SLJ - v50 - i9 - Sept 2004 - p227(1) [51-500]
>
> *Manga Mania Shoujo: How to Draw the Charming and Romantic Characters of Japanese Comics*
> Bwatch - Oct 2004 - pNA [51-500]
>
> *Manhwa Mania: How to Draw Korean Comics*
> Bwatch - Feb 2005 - pNA [51-500]

Hart, Clive - *James Joyce's Dublin: A Topographical Guide to the Dublin of Ulysses*
> CR - v285 - i1666 - Nov 2004 - p313(1) [501+]

Hart, D.G. - *Deconstructing Evangelicalism: Conservative Protestantism in the Age of Billy Graham*
> CH - v73 - i4 - Dec 2004 - p888(2) [501+]
> JR - v85 - i1 - Jan 2005 - p120(2) [501+]
>
> *The Lost Soul of American Protestantism*
> TT - v61 - i2 - July 2004 - p246(5) [501+]
>
> *Reforming Mother Kirk: The Case for Liturgy in the Reformed Tradition*
> TT - v61 - i3 - Oct 2004 - p382(2) [501+]
>
> *That Old-Time Religion in Modern America: Evangelical Protestantism in the Twentieth Century*
> JAH - v91 - i2 - Sept 2004 - p720(2) [501+]

Hart Davalos, Armando - *Aldabonazo: Inside the Cuban Revolutionary Underground, 1952-58: A Paticipant's Account*
> Choice - v42 - i3 - Nov 2004 - p544(1) [1-50]

Hart, David Bentley - *The Beauty of the Infinite: The Aesthetics of Christian Truth*
> CC - v121 - i18 - Sept 7 2004 - p42(4) [501+]
> CC - v121 - i25 - Dec 14 2004 - p21(1) [501+]
> JR - v85 - i1 - Jan 2005 - p183(2) [501+]

Hart-Davis, Duff - *Audubon's Elephant: America's Greatest Naturalist and the Making of The Birds of America*
> Aud - v106 - i5 - Nov-Dec 2004 - p94(4) [501+]
> BL - v100 - i22 - August 2004 - p1886(1) [51-500]
> BooChiTr - May 30 2004 - p1(2) [501+]
> LJ - v129 - i13 - August 2004 - p112(1) [51-500]

Hart-Davis, Guy - *How To Do Everything with Your iPod & iPod Mini, 2nd Ed.*
> LJ - v129 - i13 - August 2004 - p114(1) [501+]

Hart Dyke, Tom - *Cloud Garden: The True Story of Adventure, Survival and Extreme Horticulture*
> R&R Bk N - v19 - i4 - Nov 2004 - p70(1) [51-500]

Hart, Ellen - *An Intimate Ghost*
> Lam Bk Rpt - v13 - i3 - Oct 2004 - p34(2) [501+]

Hart, Erin - *Lake of Sorrows*
> BL - v101 - i4 - Oct 15 2004 - p363(1) [51-500]
> KR - v72 - i15 - August 1 2004 - p716(1) [51-500]
> LJ - v129 - i14 - Sept 1 2004 - p125(2) [51-500]
> PW - v251 - i33 - August 16 2004 - p41(1) [51-500]

Hart, Gary - *The Fourth Power: A Grand Strategy for the United States in the Twenty-First Century*
> BL - v100 - i21 - July 2004 - p1805(1) [51-500]
> BW - v34 - i29 - July 18 2004 - p3(1) [1-50]
> NYTBR - July 18 2004 - p8 [501+]

Hart, George - *Literature and the Environment*
> R&R Bk N - v19 - i4 - Nov 2004 - p240(1) [501+]

Hart, Henk't - *Sedums of Europe: Stonecrops and Wallpeppers*
> SciTech - v28 - i1 - March 2004 - p130(1) [51-500]

Hart, James S., Jr. - *The Rule of Law, 1603-1660: Crowns, Courts and Judges*
> Choice - v42 - i1 - Sept 2004 - p178(1) [501+]

Hart, John P. - *Custer and His Times, Bk. 4*
> WHQ - v34 - i4 - Winter 2003 - p514 [501+]

Hart, Jonathan - *Comparing Empires: European Colonialism from Portuguese Expansion to the Spanish-American War*
> AHR - v109 - i4 - Oct 2004 - p1301-1302 [501+]
> Ren Q - v57 - i4 - Winter 2004 - p1467(2) [501+]
> R&R Bk N - v19 - i1 - Feb 2004 - pNA [501+]

Hart, Kevin - *The Power of Contestation: Perspectives on Maurice Blanchot*
> Choice - v42 - i7 - March 2005 - p1212(1) [51-500]

Hart, Lenore - *Ordinary Springs*
> BL - v101 - i9-10 - Jan 1 2005 - p817(1) [1-50]
> KR - v72 - i22 - Nov 15 2004 - p1062(1) [501+]
> PW - v252 - i1 - Jan 3 2005 - p36(1) [51-500]

Hart, Matthew - *The Irish Game: A True Story of Crime and Art*
> Apo - v159 - i510 - August 2004 - p80(1) [501+]
> R&R Bk N - v19 - i1 - Feb 2004 - p201(1) [501+]

Hart, Mickey - *Da Capo Best Music Writing, 2004: The Year's Finest Writing on Rock, Hip-Hop, Jazz, Pop, Country, and More*
> BL - v101 - i4 - Oct 15 2004 - p373(1) [51-500]
>
> *A Trading Nation: Canadian Trade Policy from Colonialism to Globalization*
> Can Hist R - v85 - i3 - Sept 2004 - p564(3) [501+]

Hart, Peter - *The IRA at War*
> HER - v119 - i483 - Sept 2004 - p1093(1) [501+]

Hart, Roderick P. - *The Political Pulpit Revisited*
> Choice - v42 - i7 - March 2005 - p1244(1) [51-500]

Hart, Susan - *Learning Without Limits*
> TES - v0 - i4586 - June 4 2004 - psss18(2) [501+]

Hart, Tom - *Hutch Owen: Unmarketable*
> PW - v252 - i4 - Jan 24 2005 - p223(2) [501+]

Hart, William - *Evil: A Primer: A History of a Bad Idea from Beelzebub to Bin Laden*
> BL - v100 - i22 - August 2004 - p1876(1) [51-500]
> KR - v72 - i14 - July 15 2004 - p672(1) [501+]

Hartas, Leo - *How to Draw and Sell Digital Cartoons*
> y   VOYA - v27 - i4 - Oct 2004 - p326(1) [51-500]

Harte, Amanda - *Laughing at the Thunder*
> BL - v101 - i6 - Nov 15 2004 - p567(1) [51-500]

Harte, May - *Halloween/Halloween*
> c   SLJ - v50 - i9 - Sept 2004 - p196(1) [1-50]
>
> *Thanksgiving/Dia de Accion de Gracias*
> c   SLJ - v50 - i9 - Sept 2004 - p196(1) [1-50]

Harte, Verity - *Plato on Parts and Wholes: The Metaphysics of Structure*
> J Phil - v101 - i9 - Sept 2004 - p492-496 [501+]

Hartemink, Alfred E. - *Soil Fertility Decline in the Tropics: With Case Studies on Plantations*
> QRB - v79 - i3 - Sept 2004 - p313(2) [501+]
> SciTech - v28 - i1 - March 2004 - p128(1) [51-500]

Harter, Hugh A. - *Dairy of a Newlywed Poet: A Bilingual Edition of Diario de un Poeta Reciencasado*
> Choice - v42 - i2 - Oct 2004 - p298(1) [51-500]

Hartfield, Ronne - *Another Way Home: The Tangled Roots of Race in One Chicago Family*
> BL - v101 - i3 - Oct 1 2004 - p297(1) [51-500]

Harthorn, Barbara Herr - *Risk, Culture, and Health Inequality: Shifting Perceptions of Danger and Blame*
> CS - v33 - i6 - Nov 2004 - p728(2) [501+]

Hartin, Patrick J. - *James*
> Intpr - v58 - i4 - Oct 2004 - p415(3) [501+]

Hartinger, Brent - *The Last Chance Texaco*
> c   BooChiTr - March 7 2004 - p2(1) [501+]
> y   CE - v81 - i2 - Winter 2004 - p107(1) [51-500]
> c   LibMed - v23 - i1 - August-Sept 2004 - p68(1) [51-500]
>
> *The Order of the Poison Oak*
> y   BL - v101 - i9-10 - Jan 1 2005 - p845(1) [1-50]
> KR - v73 - i2 - Jan 15 2005 - p120(1) [51-500]

Hartjen, Clayton A. - *Delinquency and Juvenile Justice: An International Bibliography*
> Choice - v42 - i5 - Jan 2005 - p838(1) [1-50]
> R&R Bk N - v19 - i3 - August 2004 - p170(1) [501+]

Hartl, Daniel L. - *Genetics: Analysis of Genes and Genomes, 6th Ed.*
> SciTech - v28 - i4 - Dec 2004 - p61(1) [51-500]

Hartland, Jessie - *The Perfect Puppy for Me!*
> c   LibMed - v22 - i5 - Feb 2004 - p65(1) [501+]

Hartle, Ann - *Michel de Montaigne: Accidental Philosopher*
> Choice - v41 - i7 - March 2004 - p1309(2) [501+]
> FS - v58 - i1 - Jan 2004 - p90(2) [501+]

Hartley, Aidan - *The Zanzibar Chest: A Memoir of Love and War*
> A Aff - v35 - i2 - July 2004 - p226-228 [501+]
>
> *The Zanzibar Chest: A Story of Life, Love, and Death in Foreign Lands*
> BIC - v33 - i6 - Sept 2004 - p4(2) [501+]
> Kliatt - v38 - i6 - Nov 2004 - p33(1) [51-500]
> NYTBR - Jan 30 2005 - p24 [501+]

Hartley, George - *The Abyss of Representation: Marxism and the Postmodern Sublime*
> Choice - v41 - i7 - March 2004 - p1310(1) [501+]

Hartley, John - *A Short History of Cultural Studies*
> R&R Bk N - v19 - i2 - May 2004 - p127 [51-500]

Hartley, Michael - *Christy Mathewson: A Biography*
> R&R Bk N - v19 - i3 - August 2004 - p88(1) [51-500]

Hartling, Neil - *Alaska to Nunavut: The Great Rivers*
> CBRA - Annual 2003 - p24(1) [51-500]
> R&R Bk N - v19 - i1 - Feb 2004 - p52(1) [51-500]

Hartman, Bob - *The Lion Storyteller Book of Animal Tales (Illus. by Poole, Susie)*
> c   SLJ - v50 - i8 - August 2004 - p108(1) [51-500]
>
> *The Wolf Who Cried Boy (Illus. by Raglin, Tim)*
> c   RT - v57 - Oct 2003 - p168 [1-50]

Hartman, Chester - *Between Eminence and Notoriety: Four Decades of Radical Urban Planning*
> S&S - v68 - i2 - Summer 2004 - p242-243 [501+]

Hartman, Gary R. - *Landmark Supreme Court Cases: The Most Influential Decisions of the Supreme Court of the United States*
> BL - v101 - i4 - Oct 15 2004 - p438(1) [501+]
> Choice - v42 - i3 - Nov 2004 - p462(2) [1-50]
> SLJ - v50 - i12 - Dec 2004 - p84(1) [501+]

Hartman, Geoffrey - *Scars of the Spirit: The Struggle Against Authenticity*
> Tikkun - v19 - i6 - Nov-Dec 2004 - p72(2) [501+]

Hartman, George E. - *Pencil Points Reader: A Journal for the Drafting Room, 1920-1943*
> Choice - v42 - i2 - Oct 2004 - p286(1) [501+]

Hartman, Laura P. - *Rising Above Sweatshops: Innovative Approaches to Global Labor Challenges*
Choice - v42 - i2 - Oct 2004 - p337(1) [51-500]
R&R Bk N - v19 - i2 - May 2004 - p117 [51-500]

Hartman, Mary S. - *The Household and the Making of History: A Subversive View of the Western Past*
Choice - v42 - i5 - Jan 2005 - p923(1) [1-50]
TLS - i5290 - August 20 2004 - p24(1) [501+]

Hartman, Michelle - *Jesus, and Job: Reading Rescripting of Religious Figures in Lebanese Womens Fiction, Literaturen im Kontext, Band 12*
IJMES - v36 - i1 - Feb 2004 - p142-143 [501+]

Hartman, Rodney - *Ali: The Life of Ali Bacher*
Econ - v372 - i8385 - July 24 2004 - p78US [501+]

Hartmann, Alexander K. - *New Optimization Algorithms in Physics*
SciTech - v28 - i4 - Dec 2004 - p47(1) [51-500]

Hartmann, Arthur - *Claude Debussy As I Knew Him and Other Writings*
MT - v145 - i1889 - Winter 2004 - p101-103 [501+]

Hartmann, Lynn C. - *Mayo Clinic Guide to Women's Cancers*
Bwatch - Nov 2004 - pNA [51-500]

Hartmann, Pierre - *Le Contrat et la Seduction*
Eight-C St - v36 - i2 - Winter 2003 - p270 [501+]

Hartmann, U. - *Das palmyrenische Teilreich*
Class R - v53 - i2 - Nov 2003 - p433-435 [501+]

Hartmann, William K. - *Moons and Planets, 5th Ed.*
SciTech - v28 - i3 - Sept 2004 - p44(1) [1-50]
A Traveler's Guide to Mars
S&T - v107 - i1 - Jan 2004 - p72(2) [501+]

Hartnett, Sonya - *Silver Donkey (Illus. by Spudvilas, Anne)*
y Magpies - v19 - i5 - Nov 2004 - p33(1) [501+]
Stripes of the Sidestep Wolf
y KR - v73 - i1 - Jan 1 2005 - p52(1) [51-500]
y PW - v252 - i2 - Jan 10 2005 - p57(1) [51-500]

Hartnup, Karen - *'On the Beliefs of the Greeks': Leo Allatios and Popular Orthodoxy*
R&R Bk N - v19 - i3 - August 2004 - p27(1) [1-50]

Hartocollis, Anemona - *Seven Days of Possibilities: One Teacher, 24 Kids, and the Music That Changed Their Lives Forever*
LJ - v129 - i12 - July 2004 - p95(2) [51-500]

Hartog, Hendrik - *Man and Wife in America: A History*
AHR - v109 - i3 - June 2004 - p892(2) [501+]
Signs - v30 - i2 - Wntr 2005 - p1659(12) [501+]

Hartog, Kristen den - *Water Wings*
Can Lit - i181 - Summer 2004 - p138-140 [501+]

Hartquist, T.W. - *Blowing Bubbles in the Cosmos: Astronomical Winds, Jets, and Explosions*
Astron - v32 - i10 - Oct 2004 - p90 [51-500]
Choice - v42 - i1 - Sept 2004 - p127(1) [501+]

Hartsfield, Carla - *Your Last Day on Earth*
CBRA - Annual 2003 - p218(1) [51-500]

Hartsfield, Nora - *Pearls in Graph Theory: A Comprehensive Introduction*
SciTech - v28 - i3 - Sept 2004 - p34(1) [51-500]

Hartwell, David G. - *Christmas Stars*
LJ - v129 - i17 - Oct 15 2004 - p58(1) [51-500]
Year's Best Fantasy 4
ChrSFF&H - v26 - i10 - Oct 2004 - p49(2) [501+]
Year's Best Science Fiction 9
ChrSFF&H - v26 - i10 - Oct 2004 - p49(2) [501+]

Harty, Kevin J. - *Strategies for Business and Technical Writing, 5th Ed.*
R&R Bk N - v19 - i4 - Nov 2004 - p115(1) [51-500]

Hartz, Jill - *Siting Jefferson: Contemporary Artists Interpret Thomas Jefferson's Legacy*
R&R Bk N - v19 - i1 - Feb 2004 - p208(1) [51-500]
VQR - v80 - i2 - Spring 2004 - p255-255 [501+]

Haruf, Kent - *Eventide (Read by Hearn, George).*
Audiobook Review
BL - v101 - i3 - Oct 1 2004 - p350(2) [51-500]
Kliatt - v38 - i6 - Nov 2004 - p46(1) [51-500]
LJ - v129 - i18 - Nov 1 2004 - p129(1) [51-500]
PW - v251 - i27 - July 5 2004 - p17(2) [51-500]
Eventide
BooChiTr - May 16 2004 - p1(1) [501+]
Globe & Mail - July 31 2004 - pD10 [501+]
y SLJ - v50 - i10 - Oct 2004 - p198(1) [51-500]
y VOYA - v27 - i4 - Oct 2004 - p297(1) [51-500]

Harvard Business Essentials: Business Communication
R&R Bk N - v19 - i1 - Feb 2004 - p113(1) [51-500]

Harvard Business Essentials: Managing Creativity and Innovation
R&R Bk N - v19 - i1 - Feb 2004 - p89(1) [51-500]

Harvard Business Essentials: Negotiation
R&R Bk N - v19 - i3 - August 2004 - p105(1) [51-500]

Harvard Business Review on Building Personal and Organizational Resilience
R&R Bk N - v19 - i1 - Feb 2004 - p89(1) [51-500]

Harvard Business Review on Corporate Responsibility
R&R Bk N - v19 - i1 - Feb 2004 - p92(1) [1-50]

Harvard Business Review on Leadership at the Top
R&R Bk N - v19 - i1 - Feb 2004 - p90(1) [1-50]

Harvard Business Review on Motivating People
R&R Bk N - v19 - i1 - Feb 2004 - p111(1) [51-500]

Harvard Business Review on Negotiation and Conflict Resolution
HR Mag - v49 - i7 - July 2004 - pS3(1) [51-500]

Harvard Business School Press - *The Results-Driven Manager: Managing Yourself for the Career You Want*
R&R Bk N - v19 - i3 - August 2004 - p103(1) [1-50]
The Results-Driven Manager: Presentations That Persuade and Motivate
R&R Bk N - v19 - i3 - August 2004 - p132(1) [1-50]
When Good People Behave Badly
R&R Bk N - v19 - i4 - Nov 2004 - p113(1) [51-500]
When Marketing Becomes a Minefield
R&R Bk N - v19 - i4 - Nov 2004 - p110(1) [51-500]

Harvard, Joe - *The Velvet Underground and Nico*
Bwatch - v26 - i8 - August 2004 - p3(2) [51-500]
TimHES - v0 - i1669 - Dec 3 2004 - p22(2) [501+]

Harvell, Tony A. - *Latin American Dramatists Since 1945: A Bio-Bibliographical Guide*
R&R Bk N - v19 - i1 - Feb 2004 - p233(1) [51-500]

Harvey, Adrian - *The Beginnings of a Commercial Sporting Culture in Britain, 1793-1850*
R&R Bk N - v19 - i3 - August 2004 - p87(1) [51-500]

Harvey, Barbara - *The Twelfth and Thirteenth Centuries, 1066-1280*
Specu - v79 - i3 - July 2004 - p769-770 [501+]

Harvey, Bill - *Texas Cemeteries*
SHQ - v107 - i3 - Jan 2004 - p496(2) [501+]

Harvey, Brian - *China's Space Program: From Conception to Manned Spaceflight*
Astron - v33 - i2 - Feb 2005 - p98 [501+]
TimHES - v0 - i1681 - March 4 2005 - p28(1) [501+]
Choice - v42 - i5 - Jan 2005 - p876(1) [1-50]

Harvey, Brian W. - *Edward Heron-Allen's Journal of the Great War: From Sussex Shore to Flanders Fields*
ELT - v47 - i4 - Fall 2004 - p452(4) [501+]

Harvey, David - *The New Imperialism*
NYRB - v51 - i17 - Nov 4 2004 - p38(4) [501+]

Harvey, Elizabeth - *Women and the Nazi East: Agents and Witnesses of Germanization*
AHR - v109 - i4 - Oct 2004 - p1329(2) [501+]
HNet - Sept 2004 - pNA [501+]

Harvey, Greg - *Roxio Easy Media Creator for Dummies*
LJ - v129 - i18 - Nov 1 2004 - p114(1) [51-500]

Harvey, John - *Flesh and Blood (Read by Griffin, Gordon).*
Audiobook Review
LJ - v130 - i2 - Feb 1 2005 - p122(1) [51-500]
Flesh and Blood
BW - v34 - i31 - August 1 2004 - p8(2) [501+]
DroRevMy - v24 - i3 - May-June 2004 - p6(1) [501+]
LJ - v129 - i12 - July 2004 - p64(2) [51-500]
NYTBR - July 25 2004 - p19 [501+]
Men from Boys
LJ - v129 - i20 - Dec 1 2004 - p96(1) [51-500]

Harvey, John H. - *The Handbook of Sexuality in Close Relationships*
Choice - v42 - i2 - Oct 2004 - p332(2) [51-500]
R&R Bk N - v19 - i3 - August 2004 - p148(1) [51-500]

Harvey, Kenneth J. - *Shack: The Cutland Junction Stories*
Globe & Mail - Dec 4 2004 - pD10 [501+]

Harvey, Mark - *Exploring the Tomato: Transformations of Nature, Society, and Economy*
T&C - v45 - i1 - Jan 2004 - p222(3) [501+]

Harvey, Matthea - *Sad Little Breathing Machine*
BooChiTr - April 11 2004 - p1(2) [501+]

Harvey, Paul - *Themes in Religion & American Culture*
PW - v251 - i45 - Nov 8 2004 - p53(1) [51-500]

Harvey, Robert - *A Short History of Communism: The Rise and Fall of World Communism*
BL - v101 - i6 - Nov 15 2004 - p537(1) [51-500]
KR - v72 - i18 - Sept 15 2004 - p902(1) [501+]
PW - v251 - i41 - Oct 11 2004 - p65(1) [51-500]

Harvey, Roland - *At the Beach*
c Magpies - v19 - i5 - Nov 2004 - p28(1) [501+]

Harvey, Ross - *Organising Knowledge in a Global Society: Principles and Practice in Libraries and Information Centres*
LRTS - v49 - i1 - Jan 2005 - p62(4) [501+]

Harvey, Sheila Dansby - *Illegal Affairs*
BL - v101 - i6 - Nov 15 2004 - p561(1) [51-500]

Harvey, Stephanie - *Strategic Thinking: Reading and Responding, Grades 4-8*
SLJ - v50 - i10 - Oct 2004 - pS72(1) [51-500]
Think Nonfiction! Modeling Reading and Research
SLJ - v50 - i10 - Oct 2004 - pS72(1) [51-500]

Harvill, Jose Saramago - *The Double*
Spec - v295 - i9185 - August 21 2004 - p33(1) [501+]

Harvor, Elisabeth - *All Times Have Been Modern*
BIC - v33 - i9 - Dec 2004 - p9(1) [501+]
Globe & Mail - Sept 18 2004 - pD17 [501+]

Harwood, Herbert H. - *Invisible Giants: The Empires of Cleveland's Van Sweringen Brothers*
T&C - v45 - i2 - April 2004 - p444-446 [501+]

Harwood, John - *The Ghost Writer*
BW - v34 - i31 - August 1 2004 - p6(1) [501+]
LJ - v129 - i12 - July 2004 - p70(1) [51-500]

Harwood, Lee - *Collected Poems, 1964-2004*
TLS - i5304 - Nov 26 2004 - p8(1) [501+]

Harzig, Christiane - *The Social Construction of Diversity: Recasting the Master Narrative of Industrial Nations*
R&R Bk N - v19 - i2 - May 2004 - p130 [51-500]

Hasak-Lowy, Todd - *The Task of This Translator*
KR - v73 - i3 - Feb 1 2005 - p138(1) [501+]

Hasan, Asma Gull - *American Muslims: The New Generation, 2nd Ed.*
R&R Bk N - v19 - i1 - Feb 2004 - p14(1) [51-500]
Why I Am a Muslim: An American Odyssey
y VOYA - v27 - i4 - Oct 2004 - p326(1) [51-500]

Hasan, Heather - *American Women of the Gulf War*
y BL - v101 - i4 - Oct 15 2004 - p412(1) [51-500]
y SLJ - v50 - i12 - Dec 2004 - p162(1) [51-500]

Hasan, Iftekhar - *Credit Risk, Capital Structure, and the Pricing of Equity Options*
JEL - v41 - i4 - Dec 2003 - p1364(1) [501+]

Hasan, Mushirul - *India's Colonial Encounter: Essays in Memory of Eric Stokes, 2nd Rev. Ed.*
R&R Bk N - v19 - i4 - Nov 2004 - p47(1) [51-500]

Hasan, Rana - *The Impact of Trade on Labor: Issues, Perspectives, and Experiences from Developing Asia*
JEL - v41 - i4 - Dec 2003 - p1353(1) [501+]

Hasan, S.S. - *Christians Versus Muslims in Modern Egypt: The Century-Long Struggle for Coptic Equality*
Choice - v42 - i2 - Oct 2004 - p310(1) [51-500]
IBMR - v28 - i3 - July 2004 - p134(2) [501+]

Hasan, Samiul - *The Failure of the United Nations Development Mangement: Examples and Lessons*
R&R Bk N - v19 - i3 - August 2004 - p99(1) [51-500]

Hasburgh, Patrick - *Aspen Pulp*
KR - v72 - i18 - Sept 15 2004 - p894(1) [51-500]
LJ - v129 - i16 - Oct 1 2004 - p64(1) [51-500]
PW - v251 - i39 - Sept 27 2004 - p40(1) [51-500]

Hascher-Burger, Ulrike - *Gesungene Innigkeit: Studien zu einer Musikhandschrift der Devotio Moderna (Utrecht, Universitätsbibliotheek, MS. 16 H 34, Olim B 113), Mit einer Edition der Gesange.*
Theol St - v65 - i4 - Dec 2004 - p864(2) [501+]

Hasday, Judy L. - *Agnes de Mille*
y VOYA - v27 - i5 - Dec 2004 - p421(1) [51-500]
Albert Einstein: The Giant of 20th Century Science
y SB - v40 - i6 - Nov-Dec 2004 - p257(1) [51-500]

Hasegawa, Koichi - *Constructing Civil Society in Japan: Voices of Environmental Movements*
R&R Bk N - v19 - i4 - Nov 2004 - p157(1) [501+]

Haseley, Dennis - *Photographer Mole (Illus. by Kangas, Juli)*
c PW - v251 - i27 - July 5 2004 - p55(1) [51-500]
c SLJ - v50 - i7 - July 2004 - p77(1) [51-500]
Trick of the Eye
y BL - v100 - i22 - August 2004 - p1919(1) [51-500]
y BL - v101 - i5 - Nov 1 2004 - p496(1) [51-500]
y CCB-B - v57 - i11 - July-August 2004 - p467(1) [501+]
c LibMed - v23 - i3 - Nov-Dec 2004 - p72(1) [1-50]

Haycock, Ken - *Neal-Schuman Authoritative Guide to Kids' Search Engines, Subject Directories, and Portals*
LibMed - v22 - i4 - Jan 2004 - p84(1) [501+]
y VOYA - v27 - i3 - August 2004 - p249(1) [1-50]

Haycox, Stephen - *Frigid Embrace: Politics, Economics and Environment in Alaska*
Pub Hist - v26 - i1 - Wntr 2004 - p169(2) [501+]

Hayden, Brian - *Shamans, Sorcerers, and Saints: A Prehistory of Religion*
Choice - v42 - i6 - Feb 2005 - p1064(2) [51-500]

Hayden, Dolores - *Building Suburbia: Green Fields and Urban Growth, 1820-2000*
Am Q - v56 - i4 - Dec 2004 - p1067(12) [501+]
R&R Bk N - v19 - i1 - Feb 2004 - p134(1) [51-500]
A Field Guide to Sprawl (Illus. by Wark, Jim)
Am Sci - v93 - i2 - March-April 2005 - p170(1) [51-500]
JPC - v38 - i3 - Feb 2005 - p596(3) [501+]
R&R Bk N - v19 - i4 - Nov 2004 - p136(1) [51-500]

Hayden, Patrick - *America's War on Terror*
AJPS - v39 - i2 - July 2004 - p449(450) [501+]

Hayden, Patrick Nielsen - *New Magics: An Anthology of Today's Fantasy*
y VOYA - v27 - i3 - August 2004 - p232(1) [1-50]
New skies: An Anthology of Today's Science Fiction
y Kliatt - v39 - i2 - March 2005 - p28(1) [51-500]

Hayden, Tom - *Street Wars: Gangs and the Future of Violence*
LJ - v129 - i13 - August 2004 - p104(1) [51-500]
NYTBR - Jan 9 2005 - p14 [501+]

Hayden, Torey L. - *Twilight Children: Three Voices No One Heard Until a Therapist Listened*
PW - v252 - i6 - Feb 7 2005 - p52(1) [51-500]
The Very Worst Thing
LibMed - v22 - i4 - Jan 2004 - p62(1) [501+]

Hayder, Mo - *The Devil of Nanking*
KR - v73 - i4 - Feb 15 2005 - p191(1) [501+]
PW - v252 - i5 - Jan 31 2005 - p48(1) [51-500]
Tokyo
Globe & Mail - Dec 24 2004 - pD3 [1-50]

Haydon, Elizabeth - *Elegy for a Lost Star*
y BL - v100 - i22 - August 2004 - p1913(1) [51-500]
y PW - v251 - i28 - July 12 2004 - p48(1) [51-500]

Haydon, Julie - *Astronomers*
c BL - v101 - i4 - Oct 15 2004 - p420(1) [51-500]

Hayes, Alan - *Women's Studies Review, Vol. 7*
Wom HR - v13 - i2 - Summer 2004 - p313-315 [501+]

Hayes, Ann - *Meet the Orchestra (Illus. by Thomson, Karmen)*
c SLJ - v50 - i12 - Dec 2004 - p59(1) [501+]

Hayes, Bill - *Five Quarts: A Personal and Natural History of Blood*
BW - v35 - i4 - Jan 30 2005 - p8(2) [501+]
Ent W - Feb 4 2005 - p139 [51-500]
KR - v72 - i22 - Nov 15 2004 - p1079(1) [501+]
PW - v251 - i47 - Nov 22 2004 - p51(1) [51-500]

Hayes, Dade - *Open Wide: How Hollywood Box Office Became a National Obsession*
Bwatch - Nov 2004 - pNA [51-500]
Globe & Mail - Nov 15 2004 - pR3 [501+]
LJ - v129 - i14 - Sept 1 2004 - p152(2) [51-500]
NYTBR - Dec 5 2004 - p79 [501+]
PW - v251 - i34 - August 23 2004 - p50(1) [51-500]

Hayes, Daniel - *Tearjerker*
BL - v101 - i2 - Sept 15 2004 - p207(1) [501+]
KR - v72 - i16 - August 15 2004 - p764(1) [501+]
LJ - v129 - i16 - Oct 1 2004 - p69(2) [51-500]
PW - v251 - i41 - Oct 11 2004 - p58(1) [51-500]

Hayes, David F. - *Mathematical Adventures for Students and Amateurs*
y SB - v40 - i6 - Nov-Dec 2004 - p255(2) [51-500]
SciTech - v28 - i3 - Sept 2004 - p18(1) [501+]

Hayes, David L. - *Resynchronization and Defibrillation for Heart Failures: A Practical Approach*
SciTech - v28 - i3 - Sept 2004 - p106(1) [51-500]

Hayes, Dawn Marie - *Body and Sacred Place in Medieval Europe, 1100-1389*
AHR - v109 - i2 - April 2004 - p589(2) [501+]

Hayes, Derek - *America Discovered: A Historical Atlas of North American Exploration*
LJ - v130 - i1 - Jan 1 2005 - p154(1) [51-500]
Canada: An Illustrated History
Beav - v85 - i1 - Feb-March 2005 - p49(1) [51-500]
Historical Atlas of Canada: Canada's History Illustrated with Original Maps
Can Hist R - v85 - i3 - Sept 2004 - p549(4) [501+]
Can Lit - i181 - Summer 2004 - p140-141 [501+]

Historical Atlas of the Arctic
Can Hist R - v85 - i3 - Sept 2004 - p597(3) [501+]
CBRA - Annual 2003 - p24(2) [51-500]

Hayes, J.M. - *Plains Crazy: A Mad Dog and Englishman Mystery*
BL - v101 - i2 - Sept 15 2004 - p211(1) [51-500]
Bwatch - Dec 2004 - pNA [501+]
DroRevMy - v24 - i4 - July-August 2004 - p12(1) [51-500]
PW - v251 - i38 - Sept 20 2004 - p49(2) [51-500]

Hayes, Joe - *Ghost Fever: Mal de Fantasma*
c SLJ - v51 - i1 - Jan 2005 - p120(1) [51-500]
La Llorona: The Weeping Woman (Illus. by Hill, Vicki Trego)
y CCB-B - v58 - i5 - Jan 2005 - p211(1) [51-500]
c CH Bwatch - Feb 2005 - pNA [51-500]
y KR - v72 - i22 - Nov 15 2004 - p1090(1) [51-500]
c SLJ - v51 - i1 - Jan 2005 - p120(1) [51-500]

Hayes, Kathleen - *The Winter King: Frederick V of the Palatinate and the Coming of the Thirty Years' War*
HNet - Oct 2004 - pNA [501+]

Hayes, Kevin J. - *Charlie Chaplin: Interviews*
Globe & Mail - Feb 26 2005 - pD13 [51-500]
PW - v252 - i1 - Jan 3 2005 - p47(1) [51-500]

Hayes, Peter - *From Cooperation to Complexity: Degussa in the Third Reich*
Choice - v42 - i7 - March 2005 - p1270(1) [51-500]

Hayes, Rosemary - *Bright Horizons*
y Sch Lib - v52 - i4 - Winter 2004 - p215(1) [51-500]

Hayes, Stephen F. - *The Connection: How Al Qaeda's Collaboration with Saddam Hussein Has Endangered America*
NYTBR - Sept 19 2004 - p19 [501+]

Hayford, Harrison - *Melville's Prisoner*
R&R Bk N - v19 - i1 - Feb 2004 - p244(1) [51-500]

Hayford, Marc - *The Global Economy: Financial, Monetary, Trade and Knowledge Asymmetries*
JEL - v42 - i1 - March 2004 - p321(1) [501+]

Haygood, Wil - *In Black and White: The Life of Sammy Davis, Jr (Read by Free, Kevin R.). Audiobook Review*
BL - v101 - i5 - Nov 1 2004 - p504(1) [51-500]
In Black and White: The Life of Sammy Davis, Jr.
TLS - i5303 - Nov 19 2004 - p27(1) [501+]

Hayhoe, Ruth - *Full Circle: A Life with Hong Kong and China*
Pac A - v77 - i3 - Fall 2004 - p567(2) [501+]

Hayhurst, Chris - *Coli*
c SLJ - v50 - i8 - August 2004 - p137(1) [51-500]
Israel's War of Independence
y BL - v101 - i5 - Nov 1 2004 - p474(1) [51-500]
y SLJ - v51 - i1 - Jan 2005 - p142(1) [51-500]

Hayhurst, Jim, Sr. - *Where Have I Gone Right?: The Right Mountain Guide to Getting the Job and Life You Want*
NACEJou - v64 - i4 - Summer 2004 - p11-11 [501+]

Hayle, Tamara - *Dying in the Dark: A Tamara Hayle Mystery*
PW - v251 - i37 - Sept 13 2004 - p62(1) [51-500]

Hayles, Marsha - *Pajamas Anytime (Illus. by Nakata, Hiroe)*
c KR - v73 - i2 - Jan 15 2005 - p121(1) [51-500]
c PW - v252 - i10 - March 7 2005 - p67(1) [51-500]

Hayles, N. Katherine - *Nanoculture: Implications of the New Technoscience*
R&R Bk N - v19 - i4 - Nov 2004 - p227(1) [501+]
Choice - v42 - i5 - Jan 2005 - p873(1) [1-50]
Writing Machines
MFSF - v50 - i2 - Summer 2004 - p528-529 [501+]

Hayman, Richard - *Trees, Woodlands and Western Civilisation*
TLS - i5267 - March 12 2004 - p29-29 [501+]

Hayman, Sally - *Thomas T. Wilson: Paintings*
Choice - v42 - i6 - Feb 2005 - p1013(1) [51-500]
R&R Bk N - v19 - i4 - Nov 2004 - p206(1) [501+]
LJ - v129 - i20 - Dec 1 2004 - p112(1) [51-500]

Haynes, Alan - *Irish Women's History*
Choice - v42 - i2 - Oct 2004 - p362(1) [51-500]
Walsingham: Elizabethan Spymaster & Statesman
CR - v286 - i1669 - Feb 2005 - p122(2) [51-500]

Haynes, David - *The Full Matilda*
Black Iss - v6 - i4 - July-August 2004 - p44(2) [501+]
BW - v34 - i28 - July 11 2004 - p7(1) [501+]

Haynes, Douglas M. - *Imperial Medicine: Patrick Manson and the Conquest of Tropical Disease*
JMH - v76 - i3 - Sept 2004 - p683(3) [501+]

Haynes, Gary - *The Early Settlement of North America: The Clovis Era*
Am Ant - v70 - i1 - Jan 2005 - p202(3) [501+]

Haynes, Holly - *The History of Make-Believe: Tacitus on Imperial Rome*
TLS - i5285 - July 16 2004 - p24(1) [501+]

Haynes, John - *New Soviet Man: Gender and Masculinity in Stalinist Soviet Cinema*
R&R Bk N - v19 - i1 - Feb 2004 - p224(1) [51-500]
Slav R - v63 - i4 - Winter 2004 - p908(2) [501+]

Haynes, John Earl - *In Denial: Historians, Communism, and Espionage*
JAH - v91 - i3 - Dec 2004 - p1102(2) [501+]
R&R Bk N - v19 - i1 - Feb 2004 - pNA [501+]

Haynes, Kenneth - *English Literature and Ancient Languages*
Choice - v41 - i11-12 - July-August 2004 - p2039(1) [501+]

Haynes, Michael - *A Century of State Murder?: Death and Policy in Twentieth-Century Russia*
R&R Bk N - v19 - i1 - Feb 2004 - p79(1) [51-500]

Haynes, Stephen R. - *The Bonhoeffer Phenomenon: Portraits of a Protestant Saint*
CC - v121 - i19 - Sept 21 2004 - p42(3) [501+]

Haynes, Sterling - *Bloody Practice: Doctoring in the Cariboo and Around the World*
CBRA - Annual 2003 - p49(1) [51-500]

Hayot, Eric - *Chinese Dreams: Pound, Brecht, Tel Quel*
Choice - v41 - i11-12 - July-August 2004 - p2040(1) [501+]

Hays, Constance - *Pop: Truth and Power at the Coca-Cola Company*
TLS - i5284 - July 9 2004 - p10(1) [501+]

Hays, Edward - *The Passionate Troubadour*
BL - v101 - i2 - Sept 15 2004 - p207(1) [501+]

Hays-Gilpin, Kelley A. - *Ambiguous Images: Gender and Rock Art*
R&R Bk N - v19 - i1 - Feb 2004 - p72(1) [51-500]

Hays, Kate F. - *You're On: Consulting for Peak Performance*
R&R Bk N - v19 - i1 - Feb 2004 - p8(1) [1-50]

Hays, Mary - *The Correspondence of Mary Hays (1779-1843), British Novelist*
R&R Bk N - v19 - i4 - Nov 2004 - p237(1) [501+]

Hays, Michael L. - *Shakespearean Tragedy as Chivalric Romance: Rethinking Macbeth, Hamlet, Othello, and King Lear*
Ren Q - v57 - i4 - Winter 2004 - p1520(2) [501+]

Hays, Otis - *Alaska's Hidden Wars: Secret Campaigns on the North Pacific Rim*
J Mil H - v68 - i4 - Oct 2004 - p1288-1289 [501+]
R&R Bk N - v19 - i3 - August 2004 - p33(1) [51-500]

Hays, Tommy - *The Pleasure Was Mine*
KR - v73 - i1 - Jan 1 2005 - p9(1) [501+]

Hayse, Michael R. - *Recasting West German Elites: Higher Civil Servants, Business Leaders, and Physicians in Hesse Between Nazism and Democracy, 1945-1955*
HNet - Dec 2004 - pNA [501+]
R&R Bk N - v19 - i2 - May 2004 - p132 [51-500]

Hayter, Sparkle - *Bandit Queen Boogie*
LJ - v129 - i12 - July 2004 - p70(1) [51-500]

Haythornthwaite, Caroline - *Learning, Culture, and Community in Online Education: Research and Practice*
R&R Bk N - v19 - i4 - Nov 2004 - p193(1) [501+]

Hayton, D.W. - *Ruling Ireland, 1685-1742: Politics, Politicians and Parties*
HNet - Dec 2004 - pNA [501+]

Hayward, Anthony - *Which Side Are You On? Ken Loach and His Films*
TimHES - v0 - i1681 - March 4 2005 - p24(1) [501+]

Hayward, Gordon - *The Intimate Garden: Twenty Years and Four Seasons*
PW - v252 - i3 - Jan 17 2005 - p50(1) [51-500]
The Intimate Garden: Twenty Years and Four Seasons in Our Garden
BL - v101 - i9-10 - Jan 1 2005 - p796(2) [51-500]

Hayward, Jane - *English and French Medieval Stained Glass in the Collection of the Metropolitan Museum of Art, Vols. 1-2*
R&R Bk N - v19 - i1 - Feb 2004 - p208(1) [51-500]

Hayward, Mary Ellen - *The Architecture of Baltimore: An Illustrated History*
Choice - v42 - i5 - Jan 2005 - p845(1) [1-50]
R&R Bk N - v19 - i4 - Nov 2004 - p202(1) [501+]

Hayward, Steven - *The Secret Mitzvah of Lucio Burke*
Globe & Mail - Feb 26 2005 - pD10 [501+]

Hayward, Steven F. - *The Real Jimmy Carter: How our Worst Ex-President Undermines American Foreign Policy, Coddles Dictators, and Created the Party of Clinton and Kerry*
Am Spect - v37 - i6 - July-August 2004 - p70(2) [501+]
R&R Bk N - v19 - i3 - August 2004 - p70(1) [51-500]

Hayward, Susan - *Simone Signoret: The Star as Cultural Sign*
Choice - v42 - i6 - Feb 2005 - p1028(1) [51-500]

Haywood, Chanta M. - *Prophesying Daughters: Black Women Preachers and the Word, 1823-1913*
JSH - v70 - i3 - August 2004 - p665(2) [501+]

Haywood, Eric G. - *Dante Metamorphoses: Episodes in a Literary Afterlife*
Choice - v41 - i7 - March 2004 - p1301(1) [501+]
Ren Q - v57 - i4 - Winter 2004 - p1350(3) [501+]
R&R Bk N - v19 - i1 - Feb 2004 - p232(1) [51-500]
TLS - i5294 - Sept 17 2004 - p3-4 [501+]

Haywood, John - *The Celts: From Bronze Age to New Age*
R&R Bk N - v19 - i4 - Nov 2004 - p31(1) [51-500]

Hazan, Marcella - *Marcella Says ...: Italian Cooking Wisdom from the Legendary Teacher's Master Classes, with 120 of Her Irresistible New Recipes*
BL - v101 - i1 - Sept 1 2004 - p35(1) [51-500]
Marcella Says...Italian Cooking Wisdom from the Legendary Teacher's Master Classes, with 120 of Her Irresistible New Recipes
Globe & Mail - Nov 27 2004 - pD26 [51-500]
Marcella Says ...: Italian Cooking Wisdom from the Legendary Teacher's Master Classes, with 120 of Her Irresistible New Recipes
LJ - v129 - i13 - August 2004 - p112(1) [51-500]

Hazan, Pierre - *Justice in a Time of War*
LJ - v129 - i16 - Oct 1 2004 - p99(1) [51-500]

Hazard, Mark - *The Literal Sense and the Gospel of John in Late-Medieval Commentary and Literature*
JR - v85 - i1 - Jan 2005 - p114(2) [501+]

Hazareesingh, Sudhir - *The Legend Of Napoleon*
Spec - v296 - Dec 18 2004 - p83(3) [501+]
TLS - i5297 - Oct 8 2004 - p6(1) [501+]
The Saint-Napoleon: Celebrations of Sovereignty in Nineteenth-Century France
Choice - v42 - i5 - Jan 2005 - p923(1) [1-50]
TLS - i5284 - July 9 2004 - p22(1) [501+]

Hazen, Craig James - *The Village Enlightenment in America: Popular Religion and Science in the Nineteenth Century*
Isis - v95 - i2 - June 2004 - p303(2) [501+]

Hazen, Lynn E. - *Mermaid Mary Margaret. (Illus. by Hazen, Lynn E.)*
c SLJ - v50 - i9 - Sept 2004 - p161(1) [51-500]

Hazlegrove, Cary - *Nantucket: The Quiet Season*
LJ - v130 - i4 - March 1 2005 - p102(1) [51-500]

Hazleton, Lesley - *Mary: A Flesh-and-Blood Biography of the Virgin Mother*
BIC - v33 - i5 - August 2004 - p18(2) [501+]
BL - v101 - i3 - Oct 1 2004 - p302(1) [51-500]

Hazlewood, Nick - *The Queen's Slave Trader: John Hawkyns, Elizabeth I, and the Trafficking in Human Souls*
BL - v101 - i6 - Nov 15 2004 - p537(1) [51-500]
KR - v72 - i19 - Oct 1 2004 - p948(2) [501+]
LJ - v129 - i20 - Dec 1 2004 - p136(1) [51-500]
Nation - v280 - i6 - Feb 14 2005 - p23 [501+]
PW - v251 - i43 - Oct 25 2004 - p38(2) [51-500]

Hazlitt, William - *Liber Amoris: Or, The New Pygmalion*
Atl - v294 - i2 - Sept 2004 - p139(1) [501+]

Hazzard, R.A. - *Imagination of a Monarchy. Studies in Polemaic Propaganda*
Class R - v54 - i2 - Nov 2004 - p472(2) [501+]

Hazzard, Shirley - *The Great Fire (Read by Leishman, Virginia). Audiobook Review*
BW - v34 - i32 - August 8 2004 - p12(1) [501+]
LJ - v129 - i17 - Oct 15 2004 - p95(1) [51-500]
The Great Fire
BW - v34 - i32 - August 8 2004 - p11(1) [501+]
YR - v92 - i3 - July 2004 - p160-169 [501+]
People in Glass Houses
LJ - v129 - i18 - Nov 1 2004 - p134(1) [1-50]

Heaberlin, Scott W. - *Case for Nuclear-Generated Electricity*
SciTech - v28 - i1 - March 2004 - p166(1) [51-500]

Heacox, Kim - *The Only Kayak*
KR - v73 - i3 - Feb 1 2005 - p165(1) [51-500]
PW - v252 - i11 - March 14 2005 - p55(2) [51-500]

Head, John - *Standing in the Shadows: Understanding and Overcoming Depression in Black Men*
BL - v101 - i1 - Sept 1 2004 - p34(1) [51-500]
Black Iss - v7 - i1 - Jan-Feb 2005 - p41(1) [501+]
LJ - v129 - i13 - August 2004 - p102(1) [51-500]

Head, Tom - *Bill of Rights*
y CH Bwatch - v14 - i7 - July 2004 - p5(1) [51-500]

Headley, Jason - *Small Town Odds*
BL - v101 - i2 - Sept 15 2004 - p207(1) [501+]
KR - v72 - i16 - August 15 2004 - p764(1) [51-500]
LJ - v129 - i14 - Sept 1 2004 - p140(1) [51-500]
PW - v251 - i33 - August 16 2004 - p41(1) [51-500]

Headley, Stephen C. - *From Cosmogony to Exorcism in a Javanese Genesis: The Spilt Seed*
JAS - v63 - i3 - August 2004 - p847-849 [501+]

Headliner - *The Face of Appalachia: Portraits from the Mountain Farm*
R&R Bk N - v19 - i1 - Feb 2004 - p63(1) [501+]
VQR - v80 - i3 - Summer 2004 - p269(2) [1-50]

Headlines From History: The Civil War
LibMed - v23 - i3 - Nov-Dec 2004 - p63(1) [51-500]

Headquarters USA: A Directory of Contact Information for Headquarters and Other Central Offices of Major Business and Organizations in the US and in Canada, 2004, vols. 1-2, 26th ed.
R&R Bk N - v19 - i1 - Feb 2004 - p113(1) [51-500]

Heal, Felicity - *Reformation in Britain and Ireland*
TLS - i5264 - Feb 20 2004 - p32-32 [501+]

Heal, S.C. - *Ugly Ducklings: Japan's WWII Liberty Type Standard Ships*
R&R Bk N - v19 - i1 - Feb 2004 - p29(1) [51-500]

Heale, Elizabeth - *Autobiography and Authorship in Renaissance Verse: Chronicles of the Self*
Ren Q - v57 - i3 - Fall 2004 - p1152(2) [501+]

Heale, M.J. - *Twentieth Century America: Politics and Power in the United States, 1900-2000, 1st Ed.*
Choice - v42 - i4 - Dec 2004 - p721(1) [1-50]
TimHES - v0 - i1680 - Feb 25 2005 - pX(1) [501+]

Healey, Joseph F. - *Statistics: A Tool for Social Research, 7th Ed.*
R&R Bk N - v19 - i4 - Nov 2004 - p83(1) [51-500]

Healey, Kimberley J. - *The Modernist Traveler: French Detours, 1900-1930*
Choice - v41 - i11-12 - July-August 2004 - p2050(1) [501+]

Healey, Mark Alan - *Clerical Ideology in a Revolutionary Age: The Guadalajara Church and the Idea of the Mexican Nation*
HAHR - v84 - i4 - Nov 2004 - p748(2) [501+]

Healthcare Engineering - Latest Developments and Applications: Proceedings
SciTech - v28 - i1 - March 2004 - p84(1) [51-500]

Healy, David - *Let Them Eat Prozac: The Unhealthy Relationship Between the Pharmaceutical Industry and Depression*
Choice - v42 - i2 - Oct 2004 - p326(1) [51-500]
Dis - v51 - i3 - Summer 2004 - p95(8) [501+]
Globe & Mail - Dec 24 2004 - pD3 [1-50]
Nature - v430 - i7001 - August 12 2004 - p727(2) [501+]

Heaney, Seamus - *Beowolf*
NYTBR - Nov 21 2004 - p34(L) [501+]
The Burial at Thebes: A Version of Sophocles' Antigone
Am Theat - v21 - i8 - Oct 2004 - p139(4) [51-500]
BL - v101 - i3 - Oct 1 2004 - p294(1) [51-500]
NYTBR - Dec 5 2004 - p43 [501+]
Wintering Out
Globe & Mail - Jan 22 2005 - pD15 [501+]

Heap, Shaun Hargreaves - *Game Theory: A Critical Text, 2nd Ed.*
R&R Bk N - v19 - i4 - Nov 2004 - p82(1) [1-50]

Heap, Sue - *Four Friends in the Garden (Illus. by Heap, Sue)*
c Sch Lib - v52 - i4 - Winter 2004 - p187(1) [51-500]
c SLJ - v50 - i9 - Sept 2004 - p161(2) [51-500]
Red Rockets & Rainbow Jelly (Illus. by Heap, Sue)
c TES - v0 - i4577 - April 2 2004 - p35(1) [501+]

Heard, Kieron - *Investigating the Maritime History of Rotherhithe: Excavations at Pacific Wharf, 165 Rotherhithe Street, Southwark*
R&R Bk N - v19 - i3 - August 2004 - p39(1) [51-500]

Hearden, Patrick J. - *Architects of Globalism: Building a New World Order During World War II*
JAH - v91 - i1 - June 2004 - p294-295 [501+]
Tragedy of Vietnam, 2nd Ed.
R&R Bk N - v19 - i4 - Nov 2004 - p48(1) [51-500]

Hearfield, Colin - *Adorno and the Modern Ethos of Freedom*
R&R Bk N - v20 - i1 - Feb 2005 - p5(1) [51-500]

Hearn, Chester G. - *Circuits in the Sea: The Men, the Ships, and the Atlantic Cable*
BL - v101 - i5 - Nov 1 2004 - p448(1) [51-500]
Choice - v42 - i7 - March 2005 - p1247(1) [51-500]
Sorties into Hell: The Hidden War on Chichi Jima
J Mil H - v68 - i2 - April 2004 - p641(2) [501+]
Mar Crp G - v88 - i5 - May 2004 - p85(2) [501+]
R&R Bk N - v19 - i3 - August 2004 - p34(1) [51-500]

Hearn, Lafcadio - *In Ghostly Japan*
ChrSFF&H - v26 - i10 - Oct 2004 - p26(1) [51-500]

Hearn, Lian - *The Brilliance of the Moon*
NYTBR - July 18 2004 - p19 [501+]

Hearn, Maxwell K. - *Cultivated Landscapes: Chinese Paintings from the Collection of Marie-Helene and Guy Weill*
JAS - v63 - i2 - May 2004 - p496(3) [501+]

Hearn, Michael Patrick - *The Porcelain Cat (Illus. by Dillon, Leo)*
c BL - v101 - i3 - Oct 1 2004 - p334(1) [51-500]

Hearn, Mona - *Thomas Edmondson and the Dublin Laundry*
ILS - v24 - i1 - Fall 2004 - p6(2) [501+]

Heart So Hungry: The Extraordinary Expedition of Mina Hubbard into the Labrador Wilderness
Globe & Mail - Nov 27 2004 - pD3 [51-500]

Heartfield, John - *How To Make Your Small Business Website Work: Easy Answers to Content, Navigation and Design*
Bwatch - Oct 2004 - pNA [51-500]

Heartney, Eleanor - *Postmodern Heretics: The Catholic Imagination in Contemporary Art*
ABR - v26 - i1 - Nov-Dec 2004 - p29(1) [501+]

Heartz, Daniel - *Music in European Capitals: The Galant Style, 1720-1780*
MT - v145 - i1886 - Spring 2004 - p112-116 [501+]

Heath, Christopher - *Industrial Property in the Bio-Medical Age: Challenges for Asia*
R&R Bk N - v19 - i1 - Feb 2004 - pNA [51-500]
Parallel Imports in Asia
R&R Bk N - v19 - i3 - August 2004 - p209(1) [51-500]

Heath, David - *The Presidency of the United States*
c SLJ - v50 - i8 - August 2004 - p48(1) [51-500]

Heath, Fred - *Introduction to Southern California Butterflies (Illus. by Clarke, Herbert)*
E-Streams - Nov 2004 - pNA [501+]

Heath, Joseph - *Nation of Rebels: Why Counterculture Became Consumer Culture*
Atl - v295 - i3 - April 2005 - p99(7) [501+]
BL - v101 - i7 - Dec 1 2004 - p622(1) [51-500]
Bus W - i3919 - Feb 7 2005 - p20 [501+]
KR - v72 - i21 - Nov 1 2004 - p1038(1) [51-500]
LJ - v129 - i19 - Nov 15 2004 - p77(1) [501+]
PW - v251 - i46 - Nov 15 2004 - p51(1) [51-500]
The Rebel Sell: Why the Culture Can't Be Jammed
Globe & Mail - Sept 25 2004 - pD10 [501+]

Heath, Kingston William - *Patina of Place: The Cultural Weathering of a New England Industrial Landscape*
Hist Geo - v32 - Annual 2004 - p213(2) [501+]

Heath, Sue - *Young, Free, and Single?: Twenty-Somethings and Household Change*
Choice - v42 - i1 - Sept 2004 - p146(1) [51-500]

Heathcote, Joelene - *What's between Us Can't Be Heard*
CBRA - Annual 2003 - p218(2) [51-500]

Heaton, Hannah - *World of Hannah Heaton: The Diary of an Eighteenth-Century New England Farm Woman*
R&R Bk N - v19 - i1 - Feb 2004 - p17(1) [51-500]

Heaton, Janet - *Reworking Qualitative Data*
R&R Bk N - v19 - i3 - August 2004 - p90(1) [51-500]

Heavilin, Barbara A. - *Steinbeck Yearbook, Vol. 3*
R&R Bk N - v19 - i1 - Feb 2004 - p245(1) [51-500]

Hebert, Earl - *Zydeco Shoes*
Bwatch - Jan 2005 - pNA [51-500]

Hebert, Pierre - *Censure et litterature au Quebec, Vol. 1*
Can Lit - i181 - Summer 2004 - p141-142 [501+]

Hebert, Raymond M. - *Manitoba's French-Language Crisis: A Cautionary Tale*
R&R Bk N - v19 - i3 - August 2004 - p78(1) [51-500]

Hebert, Yvonne M. - *Citizenship in Transformation in Canada*
R&R Bk N - v19 - i1 - Feb 2004 - pNA [501+]

Hebra, Alex - *Measure for Measure: The Story of Imperial, Metric, and Other Units*
T&C - v45 - i2 - April 2004 - p438-439 [501+]

Hechel, Waldermar - *Alexander the Great: Historical Texts in Translation*
Choice - v42 - i2 - Oct 2004 - p348(1) [51-500]

Hecht, Anthony - *Melodies Unheard: Essays on the Mysteries of Poetry*
Sew R - v111 - i3 - Summer 2003 - p455-462 [501+]

Hecht, Cornelia - *Deutsche Juden und Antisemitismus in der Weimarer Republik*
HNet - June 2004 - pNA [501+]

Hecht, Daniel - *Land of Echoes (Read by Fields, Anna). Audiobook Review*
Kliatt - v38 - i6 - Nov 2004 - p48(1) [51-500]
LJ - v129 - i20 - Dec 1 2004 - p180(1) [501+]

Hecht, Herbert - *Systems Reliability and Failure Prevention*
SciTech - v28 - i1 - March 2004 - p136(1) [51-500]

Hecht, Jeff - *City of Light: The Story of Fiber Optics, Rev. Ed.*
SciTech - v28 - i3 - Sept 2004 - p144(1) [51-500]

Hecht, Jennifer Michael - *Doubt: A History*
BW - v34 - i5 - Feb 1 2004 - p4(1) [501+]
Hum - v65 - i2 - March-April 2005 - p43(2) [501+]
The End of Soul: Scientific Modernity, Atheism, and Anthropology in France
AHR - v109 - i4 - Oct 2004 - p1322(2) [501+]

Hecht, Tobias - *Minor Omissions: Children in Latin American History and Society*
HAHR - v84 - i2 - May 2004 - p333(3) [501+]
J Soc H - v38 - i1 - Fall 2004 - p246(3) [501+]

Heck, Andre - *Astronomy Communication*
Choice - v42 - i1 - Sept 2004 - p126(1) [501+]
StarBriefs Plus: A Dictionary of Abbreviations, Acronyms, and Symbols in Astronomy and Related Space Sciences
Choice - v42 - i6 - Feb 2005 - p996(1) [51-500]
StarGuides Plus: A World-Wide Directory of Organizations in Astronomy and Related Space Sciences
Choice - v42 - i7 - March 2005 - p1202(1) [51-500]

Hecker, Lorna L. - *An Introduction to Marriage and Family Therapy*
Fam in Soc - v85 - i3 - July-Sept 2004 - p434(2) [501+]

Heckett, Elizabeth Wincott - *Viking Age Headcoverings from Dublin*
R&R Bk N - v19 - i4 - Nov 2004 - p37(1) [51-500]

Heckman, Charles W. - *Encyclopedia of South American Aquatic Insects: Plecoptera, Illustrated Keys to Known Families, Genera, and Species in South America*
SciTech - v28 - i1 - March 2004 - p69(1) [51-500]

Heckman, James J. - *Handbook of Econometrics, Vol. 5*
JEL - v42 - i3 - Sept 2004 - p842(3) [501+]
Inequality in America: What Role for Human Capital Policies?
Choice - v41 - i11-12 - July-August 2004 - p2092(1) [501+]
CS - v33 - i5 - Sept 2004 - p624-624 [501+]
Law and Employment: Lessons from Latin America and the Caribbean
Law&PolBR - Dec 2004 - p950(3) [501+]

Heckscher, Charles - *Agents of Change: Crossing the Post-Industrial Divide*
JEL - v41 - i4 - Dec 2003 - p1387(1) [501+]

Heckstall-Smith, Dick - *Blowing The Blues*
Bwatch - v26 - i9 - Sept 2004 - p10(1) [51-500]

Hedayat, Sadegh - *The Blind Owl*
Globe & Mail - July 24 2004 - pD15 [501+]

Hedelin, Francois - *Abbe d'Aubignac: Des Satyres brutes, monstres et demons*
FS - v58 - i3 - July 2004 - p405-406 [501+]

Hedetoft, Ulf - *The Global Turn: National Encounters with the World*
R&R Bk N - v19 - i1 - Feb 2004 - p123(1) [51-500]

Hedge, Juliet - *Horse Conformation: Structure, Soundness, and Performance*
SciTech - v28 - i4 - Dec 2004 - p126 [51-500]

Hedges, Chris - *War Is a Force That Gives Us Meaning*
Mar Crp G - v87 - i8 - August 2004 - p53(2) [501+]
NYT - Sept 7 2004 - pA23 [501+]

Hedin, Benjamin - *Studio A: The Bob Dylan Reader*
BL - v101 - i4 - Oct 15 2004 - p374(1) [51-500]
Globe & Mail - Oct 23 2004 - pD3 [501+]
LJ - v129 - i16 - Oct 1 2004 - p82(1) [51-500]
NYTBR - Oct 24 2004 - p15 [501+]
TLS - i5302 - Nov 12 2004 - p8-9 [501+]

Hedin, Robert - *Old Glory: American War Poems from the Revolutionary War to the War on Terror*
Kliatt - v38 - i6 - Nov 2004 - p30(1) [501+]
LJ - v129 - i13 - August 2004 - p86(1) [501+]

Hedley, Jo - *Francois Boucher: Seductive Visions*
TLS - i5301 - Nov 5 2004 - p20-21 [501+]

Hedley, R. Alan - *Running Out of Control: Dilemmas of Globalization*
R&R Bk N - v19 - i1 - Feb 2004 - pNA [501+]

Hedreen, G. - *Capturing Troy: The Narrative Functions of Landscape in Archaic and Early Classical Greek Art*
Class R - v53 - i2 - Nov 2003 - p452-454 [501+]

Hedrick, C.W., Jr. - *History and Silence: Purge and the Rehabilitation of Memory in Late Antiquity*
Class R - v54 - i2 - Nov 2004 - p523-524 [501+]

Heede, Dag - *Herman Bang: Morkvordige losninger. Toogfirs tableauer*
Scan Stud - v76 - i3 - Fall 2004 - p431(4) [501+]

Heelan, Judith Stephenson - *Cases in Human Parasitology*
SciTech - v28 - i4 - Dec 2004 - p91(1) [51-500]

Heelas, Paul - *The Spiritual Revolution: Why Religion Is Giving Way to Spirituality*
LJ - v130 - i2 - Feb 1 2005 - p84(2) [51-500]

Heeney, Gwen - *Brickworks*
Ceram Mo - v52 - i6 - June-August 2004 - p38(1) [501+]
Choice - v42 - i1 - Sept 2004 - p85(1) [501+]

Heer, Hannes - *Vom Verschwinden der Taeter*
HNet - June 2004 - pNA [501+]
Wie Geschichte gemacht wird: Zur Konstruktion von Erinnerungen an Wehrmacht und Zweiten Weltkrieg
HNet - June 2004 - pNA [501+]

Heer, Jeet - *Arguing Comics: Literary Masters on a Popular Medium*
BL - v101 - i6 - Nov 15 2004 - p540(1) [51-500]

Heers, Jacques - *The Barbary Corsairs: Warfare in the Mediterranean, 1480-1580*
J Mil H - v68 - i2 - April 2004 - p585(1) [501+]

Heesen, Anke te - *The World in a Box: The Story of an Eighteenth-Century Picture Encyclopedia*
Isis - v95 - i2 - June 2004 - p297(2) [501+]
JMH - v76 - i3 - Sept 2004 - p660(2) [501+]

Heffernan, Rob - *Lily's Garden Of India*
LibMag - v22 - i4 - Jan 2004 - p79(1) [501+]

Heffernan, Kevin - *Ghouls, Gimmicks, and Gold: Horror Films and the American Movie Business, 1953-1968*
Choice - v42 - i2 - Oct 2004 - p282(1) [51-500]

Heffernan, Margaret - *The Naked Truth: A Modern Woman's Manifesto on Business and What Really Matters*
BL - v101 - i4 - Oct 15 2004 - p386(1) [51-500]
PW - v251 - i38 - Sept 20 2004 - p58(1) [51-500]

Heflin, Wilson L. - *Herman Melville's Whaling Years*
R&R Bk N - v19 - i4 - Nov 2004 - p242(1) [501+]

Heftmann, E. - *Chromatography: Fundamentals and Applications of Chromatography and Related Differential Migration Methods: Part A: Fundamentals and Techniques*
Choice - v42 - i5 - Jan 2005 - p882(1) [1-50]

Hefzallah, Ibrahim Michail - *The New Educational Technologies and Learning: Empowering Teachers to Teach and Students to Learn in the Information Age, 2nd Ed.*
R&R Bk N - v19 - i4 - Nov 2004 - p179(1) [501+]

Hegarty, Paul - *Jean Baudrillard: Live Theory*
Choice - v42 - i5 - Jan 2005 - p866(1) [1-50]
R&R Bk N - v19 - i4 - Nov 2004 - p5(1) [51-500]

Hegel, Claudette - *Randolph Caldecott: An Illustrated Life*
c BL - v101 - i3 - Oct 1 2004 - p321(1) [51-500]
y SLJ - v50 - i11 - Nov 2004 - p166(1) [51-500]

Heger, Joel W. - *Cardiology, 5th Ed.*
SciTech - v28 - i1 - March 2004 - p104(1) [51-500]

Heggstad, Glen - *Two Wheels Through Terror: Diary of a South American Motorcycle Odyssey*
R&R Bk N - v19 - i4 - Nov 2004 - p69(1) [1-50]

Heggy, Tarek - *Culture, Civilization and Humanity*
MEQ - v12 - i1 - Wntr 2005 - p71(8) [501+]

Hegi, Ursula - *Sacred Time (Read by Ruehl, Mercedes). Audiobook Review*
Kliatt - v38 - i6 - Nov 2004 - p49(2) [51-500]
Sacred Time
NYTBR - Nov 7 2004 - p30 [501+]

Heginbotham, Eleanor Elson - *Reading the Fascicles of Emily Dickinson: Dwelling in Possibilities*
Legacy - v21 - i2 - June 2004 - p251(2) [501+]

Hehn, Paul N. - *A Low Dishonest Decade: The Great Powers, Eastern Europe, and the Economic Origins of World War II, 1930-1941*
GSR - v27 - i2 - May 2004 - p400-401 [501+]
IndRev - v9 - i2 - Fall 2004 - p293(4) [501+]

Heiberger, Michael H. - *Emergency Care in the Optometric Setting*
SciTech - v28 - i1 - March 2004 - p114(1) [51-500]

Heid, Matt - *Camping and Backpacking the San Francisco Bay Area*
R&R Bk N - v19 - i1 - Feb 2004 - p65(1) [501+]

Heidbreder, Robert - *Drumheller Dinosaur Dance (Illus. by Slavin, Bill)*
c Globe & Mail - Sept 11 2004 - pD13 [51-500]
Drumheller Dinosaur Dance (Illus. by Slavin, Bill)
c PW - v251 - i41 - Oct 11 2004 - p78(1) [51-500]
c Res Links - v10 - i2 - Dec 2004 - p3(1) [51-500]
c SLJ - v50 - i12 - Dec 2004 - p110(1) [51-500]

Heidegger, Martin - *Four Seminars*
Choice - v41 - i11-12 - July-August 2004 - p2057(2) [501+]
RM - v58 - i1 - Sept 2004 - p181(3) [501+]
On the Essence of Language: The Metaphysics of Language and the Essencing of the World: Concerning Herder's Treatise On the Origin of Language
Choice - v42 - i5 - Jan 2005 - p848(1) [1-50]
The Phenomenology of Religious Life
Choice - v42 - i1 - Sept 2004 - p115(1) [51-500]
RM - v58 - i2 - Dec 2004 - p442(4) [501+]

Heidelberger-Leonard, Irene - *Jean Amery: Revolte in der Resignation*
TLS - i5296 - Oct 1 2004 - p10(1) [501+]

Heidemann, Stefan - *Islamic History and Civilization, Studies and Texts, Vol. 40*
IJMES - v36 - i4 - Nov 2004 - p675(2) [501+]

Heider, Don - *Class and News*
Choice - v42 - i5 - Jan 2005 - p846(1) [1-50]
R&R Bk N - v19 - i3 - August 2004 - p146(1) [51-500]

Heidrich, Wolfgang - *Graphics Interface Proceedings*
SciTech - v28 - i4 - Dec 2004 - p130 [51-500]

Heighton, Steven - *The Address Book*
BIC - v33 - i8 - Nov 2004 - p26(3) [501+]

Heijboer, J. - *Westerschelde Tunnel: Approaching Limits*
E-Streams - Oct 2004 - pNA [501+]

Heijkoop, Henk - *Muwassah, Zajal, Kharja: Bibliography of Strophic Poetry and Music from al-Andalus and Their Influence on East and West*
Choice - v42 - i5 - Jan 2005 - p828(1) [1-50]
R&R Bk N - v19 - i3 - August 2004 - p255(1) [51-500]

Heilbron, J.L. - *The Oxford Companion to the History of Modern Science*
Isis - v95 - i3 - Sept 2004 - p477(2) [501+]

Heiligman, Deborah - *High Hopes: A Photobiography of John F. Kennedy*
c SLJ - v50 - i10 - Oct 2004 - pS31(1) [51-500]

Heiman, Gary W. - *Essential Statistics for the Behavioral Sciences*
SciTech - v28 - i4 - Dec 2004 - p37(1) [51-500]

Heimberg, Richard G. - *Generalized Anxiety Disorder: Advances in Research and Practice*
Choice - v42 - i6 - Feb 2005 - p1101(1) [51-500]
E-Streams - Oct 2004 - pNA [501+]
SciTech - v28 - i3 - Sept 2004 - p101(1) [51-500]

Hein, Carola - *Rebuilding Urban Japan After 1945*
Choice - v42 - i1 - Sept 2004 - p167(1) [501+]
Pac A - v77 - i3 - Fall 2004 - p583(2) [501+]

Hein, Christoph - *Landnahme*
TLS - i5296 - Oct 1 2004 - p23(1) [501+]
WLT - v78 - i3-4 - Sept-Dec 2004 - p124(2) [501+]

Hein, David - *The Episcopalians*
Choice - v42 - i1 - Sept 2004 - p120(1) [501+]
JR - v85 - i1 - Jan 2005 - p123(2) [501+]

Hein, Laura - *Islands of Discontent: Okinawan Responses to Japanese and American Power*
JAS - v63 - i2 - May 2004 - p508(3) [501+]

Heinaman, Robert - *Plato and Aristotle's Ethics*
R&R Bk N - v19 - i1 - Feb 2004 - p1(1) [1-50]

Heinberg, Richard - *Powerdown: Options and Actions for a Post-Carbon World*
    Fut - v39 - i2 - March-April 2005 - p61(1) [51-500]
Powerdown: Options for Actions for a Post-Carbon World
    Choice - v42 - i6 - Feb 2005 - p1094(1) [51-500]
Heine, Steven - *Buddhism in the Modern World: Adaption of an Ancient Tradition*
    JAS - v63 - i3 - August 2004 - p760-761 [501+]
The Koan: Texts and Contexts in Zen Buddhism
    BCS - v24 - Annual 2004 - p284(5) [501+]
Opening a Mountain: Koans of the Zen Masters
    BCS - v24 - Annual 2004 - p284(5) [501+]
    HNet - Oct 2004 - pNA [501+]
Heine, Theresa - *Elephant Dance: Memories of India*
    c KR - v72 - i19 - Oct 1 2004 - p961(1) [51-500]
Heine, Theresa. Elephant Dance: Memories of India. (Illus. by Moxley, Sheila)
    c SLJ - v50 - i12 - Dec 2004 - p110(1) [501+]
Heinecken, Dawn - *The Warrior Women of Television: A Feminist Cultural Analysis of the New Female Body in Popular Media*
    JPC - v38 - i3 - Feb 2005 - p576(2) [501+]
Heineman, Elisabeth D. - *What Difference Does a Husband Make? Women and Marital Status in Nazi and Post-War Germany*
    HNet - Oct 2004 - pNA [501+]
Heineman, Kenneth J. - *A Catholic New Deal: Religion and Reform in Depression Pittsburgh*
    J Urban H - v31 - i2 - Jan 2005 - p249-257 [501+]
Heinemann, Larry - *Black Virgin Mountain: A Return to Vietnam*
    BL - v101 - i8 - Dec 15 2004 - p691(1) [51-500]
    BL - v101 - i9-10 - Jan 1 2005 - p782(1) [1-50]
    KR - v73 - i2 - Jan 15 2005 - p101(1) [501+]
    LJ - v129 - i20 - Dec 1 2004 - p92(1) [1-50]
    LJ - v130 - i3 - Feb 15 2005 - p138(1) [51-500]
    PW - v252 - i4 - Jan 24 2005 - p229(1) [501+]
Heinemann State Studies
    y LibMed - v23 - i1 - August-Sept 2004 - p73(2) [51-500]
Heinfeld, Gary - *GASB Statement No. 34, Implementation Recommendations for School Districts, 2nd Ed.*
    R&R Bk N - v19 - i1 - Feb 2004 - p187(1) [51-500]
Heininen, Simo - *Kirchengeschichte Finnlands*
    Six Ct J - v34 - i4 - Winter 2003 - p1262-1263 [501+]
    Six Ct J - v35 - i1 - Spring 2004 - p316(2) [501+]
Heinlein, Robert A. - *Citizen of the Galaxy (Read by James, Lloyd). Audiobook Review*
    Globe & Mail - Feb 5 2005 - pD17 [1-50]
Farmer in the Sky (Read by Brick, Scott). Audiobook Review
    y Kliatt - v38 - i5 - Sept 2004 - p58(2) [51-500]
Heinrich, Bernd - *Bumblebee Economics. Audiobook Review*
    Globe & Mail - Dec 18 2004 - pD25 [1-50]
The Geese of Beaver Bog
    Globe & Mail - August 21 2004 - pD11 [51-500]
    NH - v113 - i9 - Nov 2004 - p53(1) [501+]
    SciTech - v28 - i4 - Dec 2004 - p67(1) [51-500]
Winter World: The Ingenuity of Animal Survival
    QRB - v79 - i4 - Dec 2004 - p433(1) [501+]
Heinrich, Michael - *Fundamentals of Pharmacognosy and Phytotherapy*
    SciTech - v28 - i1 - March 2004 - p124(1) [1-50]
Heinrichs, Ann - *Adjectives*
    c SLJ - v50 - i10 - Oct 2004 - p142(1) [51-500]
Bats
    c SB - v40 - i3 - May-June 2004 - p132(1) [501+]
Fireflies
    c SB - v40 - i3 - May-June 2004 - p132(1) [501+]
Pakistan
    c SLJ - v50 - i11 - Nov 2004 - p124(1) [51-500]
Prepositions
    c SLJ - v50 - i10 - Oct 2004 - p142(1) [51-500]
Pronouns
    c SLJ - v50 - i10 - Oct 2004 - p142(1) [51-500]
Verbs
    c SLJ - v50 - i10 - Oct 2004 - p142(1) [51-500]
Heinricks, Geoff - *A Fool and His Forty Acres: Conjuring a Vineyard Three Thousand Miles from Burgundy*
    Globe & Mail - August 28 2004 - pD4 [501+]
Heintz, James A. - *College Accounting: Chapters 1-16, 18th Ed.*
    R&R Bk N - v19 - i2 - May 2004 - p119 [51-500]
College Accounting: Chapters 1-29, 18th Ed.
    R&R Bk N - v19 - i3 - August 2004 - p131(1) [51-500]

Heintzelman, Donald S. - *Guide to Hawk Watching in North America, 2nd Ed.*
    SciTech - v28 - i3 - Sept 2004 - p65(1) [51-500]
Hawks and Owls of Eastern North America
    QRB - v79 - i3 - Sept 2004 - p318(2) [501+]
Heintzman, Andrew - *Beyond the Oil Patch*
    CG - v124 - i2 - March-April 2004 - p99(1) [501+]
Feeding the Future: From Fat to Famine: How to Solve the World's Food Crises
    Globe & Mail - Jan 8 2005 - pD6 [501+]
Fueling the Future: How the Battle over Energy is Changing Everything
    CG - v124 - i3 - May-June 2004 - p127(1) [501+]
Heinz, W.C. - *The Professional*
    BL - v101 - i1 - Sept 1 2004 - p52(1) [501+]
Heinze, Andrew R. - *Jews and the American Soul: How Jewish Thinkers Changed American Ideas of Human Nature in the 20th Century*
    LJ - v129 - i17 - Oct 15 2004 - p73(1) [51-500]
    New R - Feb 21 2005 - p31 [501+]
    PW - v251 - i34 - August 23 2004 - p46(1) [501+]
Heinzelman, Kurt - *Make it New: The Rise of Modernism*
    VQR - v80 - i3 - Summer 2004 - p261(1) [1-50]
Heinzen, James W. - *Inventing a Soviet Countryside: Soviet State Power and the Transformation of Rural Russia, 1917-1929*
    Choice - v42 - i2 - Oct 2004 - p350(2) [51-500]
Heinzig, Dieter - *The Soviet Union and Communist China, 1945-1950: The Arduous Road to the Alliance*
    Pac A - v77 - i3 - Fall 2004 - p564(2) [501+]
    R&R Bk N - v19 - i1 - Feb 2004 - p38(1) [1-50]
Heiser, Charles B. - *Weeds in My Garden: Observation on Some Misunderstood Weeds*
    Am Bio T - v66 - i3 - March 2004 - p226(2) [501+]
Heiser, William C. - *Gene Delivery to Mammalian Cells, Vol. 1*
    SciTech - v28 - i1 - March 2004 - p63(1) [51-500]
Heisey, M.J. - *Peace and Persistence: Tracing the Brethren in Christ Peace Witness through Three Generations*
    Choice - v41 - i11-12 - July-August 2004 - p2061(1) [501+]
Heisig, James W. - *Philosophers of Nothingness: An Essay on the Kyoto School*
    BCS - v24 - Annual 2004 - p271(6) [501+]
Heisler, Heinz - *Advanced Vehicle Technology, 2nd Ed.*
    SciTech - v28 - i1 - March 2004 - p139(1) [51-500]
Heith, Diane J. - *Polling to Govern: Public Opinion and Presidential Leadership*
    Choice - v42 - i2 - Oct 2004 - p372(1) [51-500]
    Pres St Q - v34 - i4 - Dec 2004 - p896(3) [501+]
    Pub Op Q - v68 - i3 - Fall 2004 - p426(5) [501+]
    R&R Bk N - v19 - i1 - Feb 2004 - pNA [51-500]
Heitman, Jane - *Rhymes and Reasons: Librarians and Teachers Using Poetry to Foster Literacy, Grades K-6*
    LibMed - v22 - i5 - Feb 2004 - p83(1) [501+]
    c SLJ - v50 - i7 - July 2004 - p135(1) [501+]
Heitmeyer, Wilhelm - *The International Handbook on Violence Research*
    Choice - v42 - i1 - Sept 2004 - p78(2) [501+]
    R&R Bk N - v19 - i2 - May 2004 - p128 [51-500]
Heitzman, James - *Networks City: Planning the Information Society in Banglore*
    Choice - v42 - i5 - Jan 2005 - p894(1) [1-50]
The World in the Year 1000
    R&R Bk N - v19 - i3 - August 2004 - p29(1) [1-50]
Heitzmann, Kristen - *A Rush of Wings (Read by Bresnahan, Alyssa). Audiobook Review*
    LJ - v129 - i17 - Oct 15 2004 - p95(1) [51-500]
Secrets
    LJ - v129 - i14 - Sept 1 2004 - p134(1) [51-500]
Hejiboer, J. - *Westerschelde Tunnel: Approaching Limits*
    SciTech - v28 - i1 - March 2004 - p144(1) [51-500]
Hejinian, Lyn - *The Best American Poetry 2004*
    LJ - v129 - i16 - Oct 1 2004 - p84(2) [51-500]
    NYTBR - Nov 21 2004 - p24 [501+]
Hek, Gill - *Making Sense of Research: An Introduction for Health and Social Care Practitioners, 2nd Ed.*
    SciTech - v28 - i4 - Dec 2004 - p82(1) [51-500]
Hekster, O. - *Commodus: An Emperor at the Crossroads*
    Class R - v54 - i1 - May 2004 - p184(2) [501+]
Helbig, Alethea K. - *Dictionary of American Young Adult Fiction, 1997-2001: Books of Recognized Merit*
    BL - v101 - i1 - Sept 1 2004 - p162(2) [501+]
    Choice - v42 - i3 - Nov 2004 - p448(1) [1-50]
    LJ - v129 - i13 - August 2004 - p118(1) [51-500]
    y VOYA - v27 - i4 - Oct 2004 - p336(1) [51-500]
The Oxford Dictionary of Proverbs
    Choice - v42 - i3 - Nov 2004 - p450(2) [1-50]

Helco, Hugh - *Religion Returns to the Public Square, Faith and Policy in America*
    Soc - v41 - i3 - March-April 2004 - p82(4) [501+]
Held, Elissa - *A Squishy Exterior, Velcro Buckles and a Convenient Handle Make My Sleepover Bag (Illus. by Smith, Tammy)*
    c PW - v251 - i48 - Nov 29 2004 - p41(2) [501+]
Held, Gilbert - *Enhancing LAN Performance, 4th Ed.*
    SciTech - v28 - i3 - Sept 2004 - p156(1) [51-500]
Practical Networking Design Techniques: A Complete Guide for WANs and LANs, 2nd Ed.
    SciTech - v28 - i4 - Dec 2004 - p152(1) [51-500]
Helden, Anne C. Van - *Science in the Provinces: A Descriptive Catalogue of the 'Deventer' Collection*
    Isis - v95 - i3 - Sept 2004 - p465(1) [501+]
Heldman, Dennis R. - *Encyclopedia of Agricultural, Food, and Biological Engineering*
    E-Streams - July 2004 - pNA [501+]
Heldrich, Philip - *Out Here in the Out There: Essays in a Region of Superlatives*
    KR - v72 - i21 - Nov 1 2004 - p1038(1) [501+]
Heley, Veronica - *Murder in the Garden*
    KR - v73 - i2 - Jan 15 2005 - p86(1) [51-500]
Helfand, Gloria E. - *The Theory and Practice of Command and Control in Environmental Policy*
    R&R Bk N - v19 - i1 - Feb 2004 - p81(1) [1-50]
Helfat, Constance E. - *The SMS Blackwell Handbook of Organizational Capabilities: Emergence, Development, and Change*
    JEL - v42 - i1 - March 2004 - p247(2) [501+]
Helferich, Gerard - *Humboldt's Cosmos: Alexander von Humboldt and the Latin American Journey That Changed the Way We See the World*
    Choice - v42 - i2 - Oct 2004 - p314(1) [51-500]
Helferich, Gereard - *Humboldt's Cosmos: Alexander von Humboldt and the Latin American Journey That Changed the Way We See the World*
    y SB - v40 - i6 - Nov-Dec 2004 - p255(1) [501+]
Helferty, Seamus - *Directory of Irish Archives*
    Choice - v42 - i1 - Sept 2004 - p59(1) [501+]
Helgason, Gail - *Swimming into Darkness*
    Can Lit - i182 - Autumn 2004 - p136(3) [501+]
Helgeby, Stein - *Action as History: The Historical Thought of R.G. Collingwood*
    R&R Bk N - v20 - i1 - Feb 2005 - p4(1) [51-500]
Helgensen, Sally - *Wildcatters: A Story of Texans, Oil and Money*
    R&R Bk N - v19 - i3 - August 2004 - p199(1) [51-500]
Helgerson, Richard - *Adulterous Alliances: Home, State, and History in Early Modern European Drama and Painting*
    Ren Q - v57 - i3 - Fall 2004 - p1082(2) [501+]
Helgeson, James - *Harmonie Divine et Subjectivite Poetique chez Maurice Sceve*
    Six Ct J - v35 - i3 - Fall 2004 - p877-878 [501+]
Heling, Antje - *Zu Haus bei Martin Luther: Ein alltagsgeschichtlicher Rundgang*
    Six Ct J - v35 - i3 - Fall 2004 - p795-809 [501+]
Hellberg-Hirn, Elena - *Imperial Imprints: Post-Soviet St. Petersburg*
    Slav R - v63 - i4 - Winter 2004 - p914(2) [501+]
Hellden, Jan - *Inclinate Aurem: Oral Perspectives on Early European Verbal Culture*
    Specu - v79 - i4 - Oct 2004 - p1090(3) [501+]
Helldorfer, Mary-Claire - *Got to Dance (Illus. by Nakata, Hiroe)*
    c CCB-B - v57 - i11 - July-August 2004 - p468(2) [501+]
    c SLJ - v50 - i8 - August 2004 - p88(1) [51-500]
Helle, Knut - *The Cambridge History of Scandinavia, Vol. 1*
    Scan St - v76 - i3 - Fall 2004 - p434(3) [501+]
Hellebust, Rolf - *Flesh to Metal: Soviet Literature and the Alchemy of Revolution*
    AHR - v109 - i4 - Oct 2004 - p1340(1) [501+]
    Choice - v41 - i7 - March 2004 - p1302(1) [501+]
    R&R Bk N - v19 - i1 - Feb 2004 - p217(1) [51-500]
    Slav R - v63 - i4 - Winter 2004 - p906(2) [501+]
Hellegers, Dale M. - *We, the Japanese People: World War II and the Origins of the Japanese Constitution*
    HNet - June 2004 - pNA [501+]
Helleiner, Eric - *The Making of National Money: Territorial Currencies in Historical Perspective*
    BHR - v78 - i1 - Spring 2004 - p101(4) [501+]
    JEL - v42 - i3 - Sept 2004 - p847(2) [501+]
    JIH - v34 - i4 - Spring 2004 - p616-617 [501+]
Heller, Agnes - *The Time Is Out of Joint: Shakespeare as Philosopher of History*
    Shakes Q - v55 - i2 - Summer 2004 - p228-232 [501+]

Hendershot, Heather - *Nickelodeon Nation: The History, Politics, and Economics of America's Only TV Channel for Kids*
 Choice - v41 - i11-12 - July-August 2004 - p2037(1) [501+]
Shaking the World for Jesus: Media and Conservative Evangelical Culture
 Choice - v42 - i2 - Oct 2004 - p310(1) [51-500]
 TV Q - v35 - i1 - Fall 2004 - p68(3) [501+]
Hendershott, Anne - *The Politics of Deviance*
 CS - v33 - i1 - Jan 2004 - p94-95 [501+]
Henderson, Aileen Kilgore - *Hard Times for Jake Smith*
 c CCB-B - v57 - i11 - July-August 2004 - p469(1) [501+]
 c CH Bwatch - v14 - i8 - August 2004 - p2(1) [51-500]
 y Kliatt - v38 - i4 - July 2004 - p18(1) [51-500]
 c SLJ - v50 - i9 - Sept 2004 - p207(2) [51-500]
 y VOYA - v27 - i4 - Oct 2004 - p303(1) [51-500]
Henderson, Allan J. - *The E-Learning Question and Answer Book: A Survival Guide for Trainers and Business Managers*
 Per Psy - v57 - i3 - Autumn 2004 - p818(3) [501+]
Henderson, Bill - *The Pushcart Prize XXIX, 2005*
 PW - v252 - i1 - Jan 3 2005 - p36(1) [51-500]
Henderson, Bruce - *True North: Peary, Cook, and the Race to the Pole*
 BL - v101 - i9-10 - Jan 1 2005 - p804(1) [51-500]
 KR - v72 - i23 - Dec 1 2004 - p1132(1) [501+]
 LJ - v130 - i1 - Jan 1 2005 - p128(1) [51-500]
 PW - v252 - i3 - Jan 17 2005 - p48(1) [51-500]
Henderson, Daryl S. - *Drosophila Cytogenetics Protocols*
 SciTech - v28 - i1 - March 2004 - p69(1) [51-500]
Henderson, Dee - *God's Gift*
 LJ - v130 - i2 - Feb 1 2005 - p64(1) [51-500]
Henderson, Eric - *When I Was a Child: Stories for Grown-Ups and Children*
 y CBRA - Annual 2003 - p527(1) [51-500]
Henderson, Fergus - *Nose to Tail Eating: A Kind of British Cooking*
 NS - v133 - i4707 - Sept 27 2004 - p84(1) [501+]
 NS - v133 - i4716 - Nov 29 2004 - p49(1) [51-500]
 TLS - i5297 - Oct 8 2004 - p30(1) [51-500]
Henderson, Genie Chipps - *A Woman of the World*
 PW - v251 - i44 - Nov 1 2004 - p49(1) [501+]
Henderson, George (b. 1931 -) - *The Art of the Picts: Sculpture and Metalwork in Early Medieval Scotland*
 TLS - i5290 - August 20 2004 - p3-4 [501+]
Henderson, George (b. 1932 -) - *Psychosocial Aspects of Disability, 3rd Ed.*
 SciTech - v28 - i4 - Dec 2004 - p109(1) [51-500]
Henderson, Gordon D. - *Tax Planning for Troubled Corporations: Bankruptcy and Nonbankruptcy Restructurings, 2004 Ed.*
 R&R Bk N - v19 - i1 - Feb 2004 - pNA [51-500]
Henderson, Harry - *Career Opportunities in Computers and Cyberspace*
 SLJ - v50 - i7 - July 2004 - p118(1) [51-500]
Global Terrorism
 R&R Bk N - v19 - i3 - August 2004 - p164(1) [501+]
 y SLJ - v50 - i10 - Oct 2004 - p93(1) [51-500]
Library in a Book: Power of the News Media
 Choice - v42 - i6 - Feb 2005 - p1004(1) [51-500]
 R&R Bk N - v19 - i4 - Nov 2004 - p229(1) [501+]
Terrorist Challenge to America
 LibMed - v22 - i5 - Feb 2004 - p88(1) [501+]
Henderson, Hazel - *Planetary Citizenship: Your Values, Beliefs and Actions Can Shape a Sustainable World*
 Fut - v38 - i5 - Sept-Oct 2004 - p63(1) [51-500]
Henderson, Jason - *Sword of Dracula (Illus. by Scott, Greg)*
 PW - v252 - i11 - March 14 2005 - p47(2) [51-500]
 Ent W - i808 - Feb 25 2005 - p105 [501+]
Henderson, John - *Pliny's Statue: The Letters, Self-Portraiture and Classical Art*
 Class R - v54 - i1 - May 2004 - p109(3) [501+]
Henderson, John M. - *The Interface of Language, Vision, and Action: Eye Movements and the Visual World*
 SciTech - v28 - i4 - Dec 2004 - p3(1) [51-500]
Henderson, Joseph L. - *Transformation of the Psyche: The Symbolic Alchemy of the 'Splendor Solis'*
 R&R Bk N - v19 - i4 - Nov 2004 - p9(1) [51-500]
Henderson, Kathy - *And the Good Brown Earth*
 c LibMed - v22 - i7 - April-May 2004 - p57(1) [501+]
Dog Story (Illus. by Granstrom, Brita)
 c KR - v73 - i5 - March 1 2005 - p287(1) [51-500]
Pets, Pets, Pets!
 c Sch Lib - v52 - i4 - Winter 2004 - p210(1) [51-500]

Henderson, Lauren - *Don't Even Think about It*
 BL - v101 - i6 - Nov 15 2004 - p567(1) [51-500]
 Ent W - i794 - Nov 26 2004 - p123 [51-500]
Girls' Night In
 BL - v101 - i2 - Sept 15 2004 - p220(1) [51-500]
 PW - v251 - i34 - August 23 2004 - p37(1) [501+]
Jane Austen's Guide to Dating
 LJ - v130 - i1 - Jan 1 2005 - p134(2) [501+]
 NYTBR - March 13 2005 - p23 [501+]
Henderson, Mary C. - *The City and the Theatre: The History of New York Playhouses: A 250 Year Journey from Bowling Green to Times Square*
 Choice - v42 - i6 - Feb 2005 - p1033(1) [51-500]
 R&R Bk N - v19 - i4 - Nov 2004 - p226(1) [501+]
Henderson, Meryl - *Whales!: Strange and Wonderful*
 CE - v81 - i1 - Fall 2004 - p48(1) [51-500]
 LibMed - v22 - i5 - Feb 2004 - p60(1) [501+]
Henderson, Richard I. - *Compensation Management in a Knowledge-Based World*
 HR Mag - v49 - i7 - July 2004 - pS6(1) [51-500]
Henderson, Roy - *Laser Safety*
 E-Streams - June 2004 - pNA [501+]
Henderson, Sarah L. - *Building Democracy in Contemporary Russia: Western Support for Grassroots Organizations*
 Choice - v41 - i11-12 - July-August 2004 - p2116(1) [501+]
 HNet - Sept 2004 - pNA [501+]
 PSQ - v119 - i3 - Fall 2004 - p562(2) [501+]
Henderson, Saras - *Consuming Health: The Commodification of Health Care*
 CS - v33 - i2 - March 2004 - p245-246 [501+]
Henderson, Simon - *The New Pillar: Conservative Arab Gulf States and U.S. Strategy*
 R&R Bk N - v19 - i1 - Feb 2004 - p45(1) [51-500]
Henderson, Stewart - *All Things Weird and Wonderful*
 c Sch Lib - v52 - i4 - Winter 2004 - p210(1) [51-500]
Hendin, Josephine G. - *A Concise Companion to Postwar American Literature and Culture*
 Choice - v42 - i7 - March 2005 - p1227(1) [51-500]
Heartbreakers: Women and Violence in Contemporary Culture and Literature
 R&R Bk N - v19 - i3 - August 2004 - p153(1) [51-500]
Hendra, Tony - *Father Joe: The Man Who Saved My Soul (Read by Hendra, Tony). Audiobook Review*
 y Kliatt - v39 - i2 - March 2005 - p59(1) [51-500]
Father Joe: The Man Who Saved My Soul
 Comw - v131 - i16 - Sept 24 2004 - p27(2) [501+]
 People - v62 - i1 - July 5 2004 - p45 [51-500]
 y SLJ - v50 - i11 - Nov 2004 - p178(1) [51-500]
 Spec - v297 - i9206 - Jan 15 2005 - p43(1) [501+]
Hendrick, George - *Fleeing for Freedom: Stories of the Underground Railroad*
 Black Iss - v7 - i1 - Jan-Feb 2005 - p25(2) [51-500]
 HNet - Sept 2004 - pNA [501+]
 VQR - v80 - i3 - Summer 2004 - p255(1) [501+]
Why Not Every Man?: African Americans and Civil Disobedience in the Quest for the Dream
 KR - v73 - i3 - Feb 1 2005 - p165(1) [501+]
Hendricks, Judith Ryan - *The Baker's Apprentice*
 BL - v101 - i6 - Nov 15 2004 - p561(1) [51-500]
 KR - v72 - i23 - Dec 1 2004 - p1107(1) [501+]
 LJ - v130 - i2 - Feb 1 2005 - p68(1) [51-500]
Hendricks, Vincent F. - *Trends in Logic: 50 Years of Studia Logica*
 R&R Bk N - v19 - i1 - Feb 2004 - p5(1) [51-500]
Hendrickson, David C. - *Peace Pact: The Lost World of the American Founding*
 AHR - v109 - i3 - June 2004 - p897(2) [501+]
 JAH - v91 - i1 - June 2004 - p220-221 [501+]
Hendrickson, Edward L. - *Treating Co-Occurring Disorders: A Handbook for Mental Health and Substance Abuse Professionals*
 E-Streams - Oct 2004 - pNA [501+]
 Fam in Soc - v85 - i3 - July-Sept 2004 - p430(2) [501+]
 SciTech - v28 - i3 - Sept 2004 - p103(1) [51-500]
Hendrickson, Kenneth E., Jr. - *The Spanish-American War*
 J Mil H - v68 - i3 - July 2004 - p969-970 [501+]
Hendrickson, Paul - *Sons of Mississippi: A Story of Race and Its Legacy*
 CC - v121 - i23 - Nov 16 2004 - p43(2) [501+]

Hendrickson, Robert - *The Facts on File Encyclopedia of Word and Phrase Origins, 3rd Ed.*
 Choice - v42 - i1 - Sept 2004 - p59(1) [501+]
 LibMed - v23 - i1 - August-Sept 2004 - p78(1) [51-500]
 R&R Bk N - v19 - i1 - Feb 2004 - p217(1) [51-500]
Hendrickson, Sep - *Trolling Truths: For Trout, Kokanee, and Landlocked King Salmon*
 Bwatch - v26 - i8 - August 2004 - p4(1) [51-500]
Hendrix, Harville - *Receiving Love: Transform Your Relationship by Letting Yourself Be Loved*
 PW - v251 - i37 - Sept 13 2004 - p70(1) [51-500]
Hendrix, John - *Platonic Architectonics: Platonic Philosophies and the Visual Arts*
 R&R Bk N - v19 - i3 - August 2004 - p3(1) [1-50]
Hendrix, Paul - *Sir Henri Deterding and Royal Dutch-Shell: Changing Control of World Oil, 1900-1940*
 BHR - v77 - i4 - Winter 2003 - p803(805) [501+]
Hendry, Andrew P. - *Evolution Illuminated: Salmon and Their Relatives*
 SciTech - v28 - i1 - March 2004 - p69(1) [51-500]
Hendry, John - *Between Enterprise and Ethics: Business and Management in a Bimoral Society*
 Choice - v42 - i7 - March 2005 - p1274(1) [51-500]
Heneghan, James - *Flood*
 y Can CL - i111-112 - Fall-Winter 2003 - p139(8) [501+]
Hit Squad
 y CBRA - Annual 2003 - p488(1) [51-500]
Torn Away
 y CBRA - Annual 2003 - p488(2) [51-500]
Heneman, Robert L. - *Strategic Reward Management: Design, Implementation, and Evaluation*
 HR Mag - v49 - i7 - July 2004 - pS9(1) [51-500]
Heng, Geraldine - *Empire of Magic: Medieval Romance and the Politics of Cultural Fantasy*
 Med R - July 2004 - pNA [501+]
 Specu - v79 - i4 - Oct 2004 - p1092(3) [501+]
Henig, Jeffrey R. - *Mayors in the Middle: Politics, Race, and Mayoral Control of Urban Schools*
 Choice - v42 - i1 - Sept 2004 - p189(1) [501+]
Henig, Martin - *Alban and St. Albans: Roman and Medieval Architecture, Art and Archaeology*
 Albion - v36 - i1 - Spring 2004 - p84(2) [501+]
Henig, Robin Marantz - *Pandora's Baby: How the First Test Tube Babies Sparked the Reproductive Revolution*
 Choice - v41 - i11-12 - July-August 2004 - p2077(1) [501+]
Henighan, Stephen - *The Streets of Winter*
 BIC - v33 - i5 - August 2004 - p07(2) [501+]
Henighan, Tom - *Coming of Age in Arabia: A Memoir of Aden Before the Terror*
 Globe & Mail - March 12 2005 - pD11 [501+]
Mercury Man
 Res Links - v10 - i2 - Dec 2004 - p36(2) [51-500]
Henke, James - *Lennon Legend: An Illustrated Life of John Lennon*
 BIC - v33 - i6 - Sept 2004 - p38(2) [501+]
 SLJ - v50 - i10 - Oct 2004 - pS66(1) [501+]
Henke, Robert - *Performance and Literature in the Commedia dell'Arte*
 Theat J - v56 - i3 - Oct 2004 - p539-540 [501+]
Henkes, Kevin - *Kitten's First Full Moon*
 c BL - v101 - i9-10 - Jan 1 2005 - p775(1) [1-50]
 c Inst - v114 - i6 - March 2005 - p65(3) [501+]
Olive's Ocean
 c Five Owls - v18 - i1 - Fall 2004 - p24(2) [51-500]
 c JAAL - v48 - i1 - Sept 2004 - p73(2) [501+]
 c LibMed - v22 - i6 - March 2004 - p64(1) [51-500]
 c LibMed - v22 - i6 - March 2004 - p64(1) [51-500]
So Happy! (Illus. by Lobel, Anita)
 c HB - v81 - i2 - March-April 2005 - p188(2) [51-500]
 c KR - v73 - i4 - Feb 15 2005 - p228(1) [51-500]
 c PW - v252 - i8 - Feb 21 2005 - p173(1) [51-500]
Wemberly Worried (Illus. by Henkes, Kevin)
 c SLJ - v50 - i7 - July 2004 - p43(1) [51-500]
Henley, Darren - *The Story of Classical Music (Read by Alsop, Marin). Audiobook Review*
 y Kliatt - v39 - i1 - Jan 2005 - p54(1) [501+]
 c PW - v252 - i2 - Jan 10 2005 - p24(1) [51-500]
Henley, Irene M.A. - *Aviation Education and Training: Adult Learning Principles and Teaching Strategies*
 SciTech - v28 - i1 - March 2004 - p169(1) [51-500]
Henley, Patricia - *In the River Sweet*
 y Kliatt - v38 - i5 - Sept 2004 - p21(2) [51-500]
 LJ - v129 - i18 - Nov 1 2004 - p135(1) [501+]

Henley, Virginia - *Insatiable*
　BL - v101 - i4 - Oct 15 2004 - p394(1) [51-500]
　PW - v251 - i42 - Oct 18 2004 - p53(1) [51-500]
Henn, David - *Old Spain and New Spain: The Travel Narratives of Camilo Jose Cela*
　Choice - v42 - i6 - Feb 2005 - p1026(1) [51-500]
　R&R Bk N - v19 - i4 - Nov 2004 - p231(1) [51-500]
Hennen, Insa Christiane - *Das Lutherhaus Wittenberg: Ein Bauhistorischer Rundgang*
　Six Ct J - v35 - i3 - Fall 2004 - p795-809 [501+]
Hennen, Thomas J. - *Hennen's Public Library Planner: A Manual and Interactive CD-ROM*
　A Lib - v35 - i8 - Sept 2004 - p78(1) [51-500]
　R&R Bk N - v19 - i4 - Nov 2004 - p255(1) [501+]
Hennessy, B.G. - *The Attic Christmas (Illus. by Andreasen, Dan)*
　c KR - v72 - i21 - Nov 1 2004 - p1050(1) [51-500]
　c PW - v251 - i39 - Sept 27 2004 - p62(1) [51-500]
The Once Upon a Time Map Book (Illus. by Joyce, Peter)
　c BL - v101 - i3 - Oct 1 2004 - p329(1) [51-500]
　c PW - v251 - i36 - Sept 6 2004 - p64(2) [51-500]
Hennessy, Michael A. - *War in the Twentieth Century: Reflections at Century's End*
　R&R Bk N - v19 - i1 - Feb 2004 - p254(1) [51-500]
Hennigan, Peter C. - *The Birth of a Legal Institution: The Formation of the Waqf in the Third-Century A.H. Hanafi Legal Discourse*
　R&R Bk N - v19 - i1 - Feb 2004 - pNA [51-500]
Henninger, Maureen - *The Hidden Web: Finding Quality Information on the Net*
　Choice - v42 - i1 - Sept 2004 - p140(1) [501+]
Henninger-Voss, Mary J. - *Animals in Human Histories: The Mirror of Nature and Culture*
　TLS - i5287 - July 30 2004 - p23(1) [501+]
Henningfeld, Jochem - *Friedrich Wilhelm Joseph Schellings "Philosophische Untersuchungen uber das Wesen der menschlichen Freiheit und die damit zusammenhangenden Gegenstande"*
　GSR - v27 - i2 - May 2004 - p381-381 [501+]
Henrich, William L. - *Principles and Practice of Dialysis, 3rd Ed.*
　SciTech - v28 - i1 - March 2004 - p106(1) [51-500]
Henricksen, Noel - *Island and Otherland: Christopher Koch and His Books*
　Quad - v48 - i3 - March 2004 - p91(2) [501+]
Henriques, Adrian - *The Triple Bottom Line: Does It All Add Up? Assessing the Sustainability of Business and CSR*
　R&R Bk N - v19 - i3 - August 2004 - p107(1) [1-50]
Henry, Beth - *Mending Wounded Minds: Seeking Help for a Mentally Ill Child*
　SciTech - v28 - i3 - Sept 2004 - p118(1) [51-500]
Henry, Carla - *Microfinance Poverty Assessment Tool*
　JEL - v42 - i1 - March 2004 - p308(1) [501+]
Henry, Clement M. - *Globalization and the Politics of Development in the Middle East*
　World&I - v19 - i10 - Oct 2004 - pNA [501+]
The Politics of Islamic Finance
　Choice - v42 - i2 - Oct 2004 - p340(1) [51-500]
　MEJ - v59 - i1 - Wntr 2005 - p152(2) [501+]
Henry, Colette - *Entrepreneurship Education and Training: The Issue of Effectiveness*
　R&R Bk N - v19 - i1 - Feb 2004 - p92(1) [51-500]
Henry, Douglas V. - *Faithful Learning and the Christian Scholarly Vocation*
　TT - v61 - i3 - Oct 2004 - p383(2) [501+]
Henry, Frances - *Reclaiming African Religions in Trinidad: The Socio-Political Legitimation of the Orisha and Spiritual Baptist Faiths*
　JR - v85 - i1 - Jan 2005 - p166(2) [501+]
Henry, Holly - *Virginia Woolf and the Discourse of Science: The Aesthetics of Astronomy*
　Albion - v36 - i2 - Summer 2004 - p349(2) [501+]
　MFSF - v50 - i1 - Spring 2004 - p224-240 [501+]
　RES - v55 - i219 - April 2004 - p297-299 [501+]
Henry, Jacques M. - *Blue Collar Bayou: Louisiana Cajuns in the New Economy of Ethnicity*
　CS - v33 - i4 - July 2004 - p419(3) [501+]
Henry, James S. - *The Blood Bankers: Tales from the Global Underground Economy*
　R&R Bk N - v19 - i1 - Feb 2004 - p141(1) [51-500]
Henry, Michel - *I Am the Truth: Toward a Philosophy of Christianity*
　Theol St - v65 - i4 - Dec 2004 - p890(2) [501+]
Henry, Paget - *Caliban's Reason: Introducing Afro-Caribbean Philosophy*
　Phil R - v112 - i3 - July 2003 - p413(4) [501+]

Henry, Sue - *Murder at Five Finger Light*
　KR - v73 - i4 - Feb 15 2005 - p201(1) [51-500]
The Serpents Trail (Read by Adams, Lee). Audiobook Review
　Kliatt - v38 - i5 - Sept 2004 - p64(2) [51-500]
Henry the Minstrel - *The Wallace*
　TLS - i5290 - August 20 2004 - p6(1) [501+]
Henry's 100 Days of Kindergarten
　c PW - v252 - i6 - Feb 7 2005 - p61(2) [501+]
Henschke, Claudia I. - *Lung Cancer Myths, Facts, Choices--and Hope*
　Am Bio T - v66 - i7 - Sept 2004 - p514(514) [501+]
Hensel, Jana - *After the Wall: Confessions from an East German Childhood and the Life That Came Next*
　y BL - v101 - i6 - Nov 15 2004 - p549(1) [51-500]
　PW - v251 - i43 - Oct 25 2004 - p38(1) [51-500]
Henshen, Beverly - *Bible Records, Vol. 2*
　EFHM - v58 - i2 - March-April 2004 - p90(1) [51-500]
Hensher, Philip - *The Fit*
　NS - v133 - i4696 - July 12 2004 - p55(1) [501+]
　Spec - v295 - i9179 - July 10 2004 - p33(2) [501+]
　TLS - i5286 - July 23 2004 - p23(1) [501+]
Henshon, Suzanna E. - *Mildew on the Wall*
　c CH Bwatch - v14 - i11 - Nov 2004 - pNA [51-500]
Henslin, James M. - *Life in Society: Readings to Accompany Sociology, a Down-to-Earth Approach, 7th Ed.*
　R&R Bk N - v19 - i3 - August 2004 - p142(1) [51-500]
Henslowe, Philip - *Public Relations: A Practical Guide to the Basics, 2nd Ed.*
　R&R Bk N - v19 - i1 - Feb 2004 - p91(1) [1-50]
Henson, Kenneth T. - *Constructivist Methods for Teaching in Diverse Middle-Level Classrooms*
　R&R Bk N - v19 - i1 - Feb 2004 - p184(1) [51-500]
Henson, Laura J. - *Ten Little Elvi (Illus. by Gorissen, Dean)*
　c SLJ - v51 - i2 - Feb 2005 - p97(1) [51-500]
Hensperger, Beth - *Not Your Mother's Slow Cooker Cookbook*
　LJ - v129 - i20 - Dec 1 2004 - p151(1) [51-500]
　PW - v252 - i1 - Jan 3 2005 - p51(2) [51-500]
Hentoff, Nat - *American Music Is*
　Bwatch - v26 - i8 - August 2004 - p4(1) [51-500]
The War on the Bill of Rights and the Gathering Resistance
　R&R Bk N - v19 - i1 - Feb 2004 - p150(1) [51-500]
Henton, Douglas - *Civic Revolutionaries: Igniting the Passion for Change in America's Communities*
　R&R Bk N - v19 - i1 - Feb 2004 - p126(1) [51-500]
Hentschel, Uwe - *Mythos Schweiz. Zum Deutschen Literarischen Philhelvetismus Zwischen 1700 und 1850*
　Eight-C St - v37 - i4 - Summer 2004 - p692-694 [501+]
Hentz, James J. - *New and Critical Security and Regionalism: Beyond the Nation State*
　AJPS - v39 - i2 - July 2004 - p450(451) [501+]
　R&R Bk N - v19 - i1 - Feb 2004 - p255(1) [51-500]
Henwood, Doug - *After the New Economy*
　Choice - v42 - i1 - Sept 2004 - p154(1) [501+]
　Comw - v131 - i13 - July 16 2004 - p32(2) [501+]
　R&R Bk N - v19 - i3 - August 2004 - p97(1) [51-500]
Hepburn, A.C. - *Contested Cities in the Modern West*
　Choice - v42 - i5 - Jan 2005 - p939(1) [51-500]
Hepburn, James - *A Book of Scattered Leaves: Poetry of Poverty in Broadside Ballads of Nineteenth-Century England*
　Sew R - v111 - i3 - Summer 2003 - p450-455 [501+]
Hepp, John Henry - *The Middle-Class City: Transforming Space and Time in Philadelphia, 1876-1926*
　JAH - v91 - i3 - Dec 2004 - p1052(2) [501+]
　T&C - v45 - i4 - Oct 2004 - p842(3) [501+]
The Middle-Class City: Transforming Space and Time in Philadelphia, 1876-1926
　Choice - v41 - i7 - March 2004 - p1356(1) [501+]
Heppner, Darrell - *Great Children's Illustrators, 1880-1930*
　R&R Bk N - v19 - i4 - Nov 2004 - p205(1) [501+]
Herald, Diana Tixier - *Teen Genreflecting: A Guide to Reading Interests, 2nd Ed.*
　R&R Bk N - v19 - i1 - Feb 2004 - p243(1) [51-500]
　VOYA - v27 - i4 - Oct 2004 - p266(1) [51-500]

Heras, Theo - *What Will We Do With the Baby-O? (Illus. by Herbert, Jennifer)*
　c Globe & Mail - Jan 15 2005 - pD16 [51-500]
　c KR - v72 - i21 - Nov 1 2004 - p1044(1) [51-500]
　c PW - v251 - i51 - Dec 20 2004 - p57(1) [51-500]
　c Res Links - v10 - i1 - Oct 2004 - p4(1) [51-500]
　c SLJ - v51 - i1 - Jan 2005 - p110(1) [51-500]
Herb, Michael - *All in the Family: Absolutism, Revolution, and Democracy in the Middle Eastern Monarchies*
　IJMES - v36 - i1 - Feb 2004 - p103-119 [501+]
Herbert, Alan - *Official Price Guide to Mint Errors, 6th Ed.*
　Ant&CM - v109 - i1 - March 2004 - p16(1) [501+]
Herbert, Bob - *Promises Betrayed: Waking Up from the American Dream*
　PW - v252 - i8 - Feb 21 2005 - p163(1) [51-500]
Herbert, Brian - *The Battle of Corrin*
　y BL - v100 - i22 - August 2004 - p1871(1) [51-500]
Dune: The Battle of Corrin (Read by Brick, Scott). Audiobook Review
　BL - v101 - i8 - Dec 15 2004 - p751(1) [1-50]
Dune: The Machine Crusade. Audiobook Review
　LJ - v129 - i15 - Sept 15 2004 - p88(2) [51-500]
The Heroic Story of the United States Merchant Marine
　HRNB - v33 - i1 - Fall 2004 - p11(2) [501+]
Herbert-Brown, Geraldine - *Ovid's Fasti: Historical Readings at Its Bimillennium*
　Class R - v54 - i1 - May 2004 - p99(3) [501+]
Herbert, David - *Simply Perfect Every Time: 130 Classic, Foolproof Recipes*
　LJ - v129 - i20 - Dec 1 2004 - p151(1) [51-500]
Herbert, Edward D. - *The Bible as Book: The Hebrew Bible and the Judean Desert Discoveries*
　BSA-P - v98 - i2 - June 2004 - p233-235 [501+]
Herbert, Hans - *Das System: Die Machenschaften der Macht*
　GSR - v27 - i1 - Feb 2004 - p201-203 [501+]
Herbert, Maire - *Retrospect and Prospect in Celtic Studies: Proceedings of the 11th International Congress of Celtic Studies Held in University College, Cork, 25-31 July 1999*
　Med R - Dec 2004 - pNA [501+]
Herbert, Thomas F. - *The Linux TCP/IP Stack: Networking for Embedded Systems (Illus. by Herbert, Thomas F.)*
　SciTech - v28 - i3 - Sept 2004 - p22(1) [1-50]
Herbin, R. - *Finite Volumes for Complex Applications III: Proceedings*
　SciTech - v28 - i1 - March 2004 - p42(1) [51-500]
Herbold, Robert - *The Fiefdom Syndrome: The Turf Battles That Undermine Careers and Companies--and How to Overcome Them*
　BL - v101 - i1 - Sept 1 2004 - p31(2) [501+]
　LJ - v129 - i14 - Sept 1 2004 - p164(2) [51-500]
　PW - v251 - i32 - August 9 2004 - p245(2) [51-500]
Herbrechter, Stefan - *Cultural Studies: Interdisciplinarity and Translation*
　R&R Bk N - v19 - i1 - Feb 2004 - p220(1) [51-500]
Discipline and Practice: The (Ir)resistiblity of Theory
　R&R Bk N - v19 - i3 - August 2004 - p257(1) [51-500]
Herbst, Anri - *Musical Arts in Africa: Theory, Practice and Education*
　Notes - v61 - i1 - Sept 2004 - p111(3) [501+]
Herbst, Judith - *Hoaxes*
　c SLJ - v51 - i2 - Feb 2005 - p120(1) [51-500]
Monsters
　c SLJ - v51 - i2 - Feb 2005 - p120(1) [51-500]
Herbst, Willy - *Industrial Organic Pigments: Production, Properties, Applications, 3rd Ed.*
　E-Streams - Dec 2004 - pNA [501+]
　SciTech - v28 - i3 - Sept 2004 - p168(1) [51-500]
Herbstein, Manu - *Ama: A Story of the Atlantic Slave Trade*
　IJAHS - v37 - i1 - Wntr 2004 - p165-165 [501+]
Herd, Graeme P. - *Russian Regions and Regionalism: Strength through Weakness*
　E-A St - v56 - i6 - Sept 2004 - p926(927) [501+]
　Slav R - v63 - i4 - Winter 2004 - p899(2) [501+]
Herder, Johann Gottfried - *Another Philosophy of History and Selected Political Writings*
　HNet - Sept 2004 - pNA [501+]
Herdewijn, Piet - *Oligonucleotide Synthesis: Methods and Applications*
　SciTech - v28 - i4 - Dec 2004 - p73(1) [51-500]

Herschel, Caroline - *Caroline Herschel's Autobiographies*
Isis - v95 - i3 - Sept 2004 - p505(1) [501+]

Herscher, Elaine - *Generation Extra Large: Rescuing Our Children from Obesity*
PW - v251 - i48 - Nov 29 2004 - p30(1) [51-500]

Herschkowitz, Norbert - *A Good Start in Life: Understanding Your Child's Brain and Behavior from Birth to Age 6*
Globe & Mail - Nov 6 2004 - pF8 [51-500]

Hersen, Michael - *Comprehensive Handbook of Psychological Assessment*
Choice - v42 - i2 - Oct 2004 - p374(1) [51-500]

Hersey, John - *A Bell for Adano*
Mar Crp G - v88 - i3 - March 2004 - p63(1) [501+]

Hersey, Mary Jane - *This Teaching I Present: Fraktur from the Skippack and Salford Mennonite Meetinghouse Schools, 1747-1836*
Choice - v41 - i11-12 - July-August 2004 - p2032(1) [501+]

Hersh, Seymour - *Chain of Command: the Road From 9/11 to Abu Ghraib*
NYTBR - Oct 17 2004 - p13 [501+]

Hersh, Seymour M. - *Chain of Command: The Road From 9/11 to Abu Ghraib*
BW - v34 - i40 - Oct 3 2004 - p4(1) [501+]
Econ - v373 - i8398 - Oct 23 2004 - p83US [501+]
Globe & Mail - Oct 2 2004 - pD6 [501+]
MEP - v11 - i4 - Winter 2004 - p129(5) [501+]
Nation - v280 - i5 - Feb 7 2005 - p23 [501+]
Spec - i9195 - Oct 30 2004 - p50(3) [501+]
TLS - i5299 - Oct 22 2004 - p12-13 [501+]

Hershkowita, Howard - *101 Canadian Jokes*
Res Links - v10 - i3 - Feb 15 2005 - p24(1) [501+]

Hershock, Marin J. - *The Paradox of Progress: Economic Change, Individual Enterprise, and Political Culture in Michigan, 1837-1878*
Choice - v42 - i1 - Sept 2004 - p174(1) [501+]

Hershock, Peter D. - *Technology and Cultural Values: On the Edge of the Third Millennium*
SciTech - v28 - i1 - March 2004 - p133(1) [51-500]

Herskowitz, Mickey - *Lawyer: My Trials and Jubilations*
SHQ - v108 - i1 - July 2004 - p131-132 [501+]

Herspring, Dale R. - *Putin's Russia: Past Imperfect, Future Uncertain*
Russ Rev - v63 - i2 - April 2004 - pNA [501+]

Hertz, Neil - *George Eliot's Pulse*
VS - v46 - i3 - Spring 2004 - p536(3) [501+]

Hertz, Noreena - *The Debt Threat: How Debt Is Destroying the Developing World*
Globe & Mail - March 5 2005 - pD9 [501+]
PW - v252 - i1 - Jan 3 2005 - p50(1) [51-500]
Time - v165 - i11 - March 14 2005 - pA6 [501+]
IOU: The Debt Threat And Why We Must Defuse It
NS - v133 - i4713 - Nov 8 2004 - p52(2) [501+]

Hertzberg, Hendrik - *Politics: Observations and Arguments, 1966-2004*
AM - v192 - i6 - Feb 21 2005 - p26 [501+]
BW - v34 - i29 - July 18 2004 - p4(1) [1-50]
Econ - v373 - i8396 - Oct 9 2004 - p80US [501+]
Globe & Mail - August 21 2004 - pD1(1) [501+]
LJ - v129 - i12 - July 2004 - p103(1) [51-500]
Nation - v279 - i11 - Oct 11 2004 - p36 [501+]
NYTBR - July 4 2004 - p7 [501+]
NYTBR - July 11 2004 - p22 [501+]
NYTBR - July 18 2004 - p18 [501+]
NYTBR - July 25 2004 - p18 [501+]
R&R Bk N - v19 - i4 - Nov 2004 - p63(1) [51-500]

Hertzke, Allen D. - *Freeing God's Children: The Unlikely Alliance for Global Human Rights*
Ch Today - v48 - i10 - Oct 2004 - p106(2) [501+]
R&R Bk N - v19 - i4 - Nov 2004 - p25(1) [501+]

Herumin, Wendy - *Censorship on the Internet: From Filters to Freedom of Speech*
y VOYA - v27 - i4 - Oct 2004 - p333(1) [51-500]

Hervadstveit, Daniel - *Oil in the Gulf: Obstacles to Democracy and Development*
R&R Bk N - v19 - i3 - August 2004 - p52(1) [51-500]

Hervey, Tamara K. - *Economic and Social Rights under the EU Charter of Fundamental Rights: A Legal Perspective*
R&R Bk N - v19 - i1 - Feb 2004 - p83(1) [1-50]

Herwald, Heiko - *Concepts in Bacterial Virulence*
SciTech - v28 - i4 - Dec 2004 - p75(1) [51-500]

Herz, Norman - *Operation Alacrity: The Azores and the War in the Atlantic*
Choice - v42 - i2 - Oct 2004 - p361(2) [51-500]

Herzfeld, Andy - *Revolution in the Valley*
NW - Feb 21 2005 - p32 [51-500]

Herzfeld, Michael - *The Body Impolitic: Artisans and Artifice in the Global Hierarchy of Value*
Choice - v41 - i11-12 - July-August 2004 - p2087(1) [501+]
TLS - i5284 - July 9 2004 - p26(1) [501+]

Herzig, Arno - *Judentum und Aufklaerung*
HNet - June 2004 - pNA [501+]

Herzlinger, Regina E. - *Consumer-Driven Health Care: Implications for Providers, Payers, and Policymakers*
E-Streams - Sept 2004 - pNA [501+]

Herzog, Brad - *H Is for Home Run: A Baseball Alphabet (Illus. by Rose, Melanie)*
c SLJ - v50 - i8 - August 2004 - p108(1) [51-500]
T Is for Touchdown: A Football Alphabet (Illus. by Braught, Mark)
c SLJ - v51 - i2 - Feb 2005 - p120(1) [51-500]

Herzog, Chaim - *The War of Atonement: The Inside Story of the Yom Kippur War*
HNet - August 2004 - pNA [501+]

Herzog, Tamar - *Upholding Justice: Society, State, and the Penal System in Quito*
Choice - v42 - i4 - Dec 2004 - p718(1) [1-50]

Heschel, Abraham Joshua - *Heavenly Torah: As Refracted through the Generations*
BL - v101 - i6 - Nov 15 2004 - p534(1) [51-500]
LJ - v130 - i3 - Feb 15 2005 - p135(2) [51-500]

Hesk, J. - *Deception and Democracy in Classical Athens*
Class R - v54 - i1 - May 2004 - p144(3) [501+]

Heskett, James L. - *The Value Profit Chain: Treat Employees Like Customers and Customers Like Employees*
HR Mag - v49 - i7 - July 2004 - pS52(1) [51-500]

Heslam, Peter - *Globalization and the Good*
TLS - i5307 - Dec 17 2004 - p30(1) [1-50]

Hesli, Vicki L. - *The 1999-2000 Elections in Russia: Their Impact and Legacy*
Slav R - v63 - i4 - Winter 2004 - p897(2) [501+]

Hess, Alan - *The Ranch House (Illus. by Sheldon, Noah)*
LJ - v130 - i1 - Jan 1 2005 - p107(1) [51-500]

Hess, Cathy Thomas - *Wound Care, 5th Ed.*
SciTech - v28 - i4 - Dec 2004 - p108(1) [51-500]

Hess, Debra - *The American Flag: Symbols of America*
y Teach Lib - v32 - i1 - Oct 2004 - p20(1) [51-500]

Hess, Frederick M. - *Common Sense School Reform*
Choice - v42 - i4 - Dec 2004 - p710(1) [1-50]
R&R Bk N - v19 - i3 - August 2004 - p223(1) [1-50]
A Qualified Teacher in Every Classroom?: Appraising Old Answers and New Ideas
Choice - v42 - i4 - Dec 2004 - p711(1) [1-50]
SLJ - v50 - i10 - Oct 2004 - pS73(1) [51-500]
TCR - v107 - i2 - Feb 2005 - p323(5) [501+]

Hess, Gary R. - *Presidential Decisions for War: Korea, Vietnam and the Persian Gulf*
AJPS - v39 - i2 - July 2004 - p451(452) [501+]

Hess, Joan - *The Goodbye Body*
KR - v73 - i3 - Feb 1 2005 - p152(1) [51-500]
PW - v252 - i10 - March 7 2005 - p53(1) [51-500]

Hess, Jonathan M. - *Germans, Jews and the Claims of Modernity*
GSR - v27 - i2 - May 2004 - p374-375 [501+]

Hess, Richard S. - *Family in the Bible: Exploring Customs, Culture, and Context*
Intpr - v59 - i1 - Jan 2005 - p109(1) [51-500]

Hesse, Carla - *The Other Enlightenment: How French Women Became Modern*
JWH - v16 - i4 - Winter 2004 - p226(8) [501+]
Lib & Cul - v39 - i3 - Summer 2004 - p325(2) [501+]

Hesse, Hans - *Persecution and Resistance of Jehovah's Witnesses During the Nazi-Regime 1933-1945*
GSR - v27 - i1 - Feb 2004 - p178-181 [501+]

Hesse, Karen - *Aleutian Sparrow*
c BooChiTr - Jan 11 2004 - p5(1) [501+]
c CE - v80 - i5 - Mid-Summer 2004 - p274(1) [51-500]
The Cats in Krasinski Square (Illus. by Watson, Wendy)
c BL - v101 - i4 - Oct 15 2004 - p404(1) [51-500]
c CCB-B - v58 - i2 - Oct 2004 - p76(1) [51-500]
c HB - v80 - i5 - Sept-Oct 2004 - p569(1) [51-500]
c Inst - v114 - i5 - Jan-Feb 2005 - p73(2) [501+]
c KR - v72 - i15 - August 1 2004 - p742(1) [51-500]
c PW - v251 - i34 - August 23 2004 - p54(1) [501+]
c SLJ - v50 - i10 - Oct 2004 - p106(1) [51-500]
The Music of Dolphins
y Sch Lib - v52 - i4 - Winter 2004 - p215(1) [51-500]
The Stone Lamp: Eight Stories of Hanukkah through History (Illus. by Pinkney, Brian)
c BL - v101 - i3 - Oct 1 2004 - p345(1) [51-500]
c LibMed - v22 - i5 - Feb 2004 - p86(1) [51-500]

Hesse, Rolf - *Syntax of the Modern Greek Verbal System: The Use of the Forms, Particularly in Combination with Ea and Va, 2nd Rev. Ed.*
R&R Bk N - v19 - i1 - Feb 2004 - p213 [51-500]

Hessel, Dieter T. - *Christianity and Ecology: Seeking the Well-Being of Earth and Humans*
Parabola - v29 - i3 - Fall 2004 - p107(3) [501+]

Hessel, Karen M. - *Case Studies in School Leadership: Keys to a Successful Principalship*
R&R Bk N - v19 - i3 - August 2004 - p224(1) [1-50]

Hessel, Rudi - *Modelling Soil Erosion in a Small Catchment on the Chinese Loess Plateau: Applying LISEM to Extreme Conditions*
GJ - v170 - i3 - Sept 2004 - p285(2) [501+]

Hessel, Volker - *Chemical Micro Process Engineering*
Choice - v42 - i1 - Sept 2004 - p136(1) [501+]

Hesselson, Aaron B. - *Simplified Interpretation of Pacemaker ECGs*
E-Streams - July 2004 - pNA [501+]

Hessler, Julie - *A Social History of Soviet Trade: Trade Policy, Retail Practices, and Consumption, 1917-1953.*
BHR - v78 - i3 - Autumn 2004 - p589(3) [501+]
Choice - v42 - i2 - Oct 2004 - p351(1) [501+]

Hesson, James L. - *Weight Training for Life, 7th Ed.*
R&R Bk N - v19 - i3 - August 2004 - p87(1) [51-500]

Hesson, Julie Chapin - *Mason County, West Virginia Marriages, 1806-1915*
EFHM - v58 - i3 - May-June 2004 - p61(1) [51-500]

Hest, Amy - *Mr. George Baker (Illus. by Muth, Jon J.) (Read by Bottino, Pat)*
c SLJ - v50 - i9 - Sept 2004 - p162(1) [51-500]
Mr. George Baker (Illus. by Muth, Jon J.)
c BL - v101 - i1 - Sept 1 2004 - p132(1) [1-50]
c CCB-B - v58 - i1 - Sept 2004 - p20(1) [51-500]
c KR - v72 - i14 - July 15 2004 - p686(1) [51-500]
c PW - v251 - i36 - Sept 6 2004 - p62(2) [51-500]

Hester, Charley - *True Life Wild West Memoir of a Bush-Popping Cow Waddy*
y BL - v101 - i1 - Sept 1 2004 - p41(2) [51-500]

Hester, Denia Lewis - *Grandma Lena's Big Ol' Turnip (Illus. by Urbanovic, Jackie)*
c KR - v73 - i4 - Feb 15 2005 - p229(1) [51-500]

Hester, Joseph P. - *Ethical Leadership for School Administrators and Teachers*
LibMed - v22 - i7 - April-May 2004 - p87(1) [501+]

Hester, Nolan - *Creating a Web Page in Dreamweaver: Visual QuickProject Guide*
LJ - v130 - i1 - Jan 1 2005 - p148(1) [501+]
Microsoft Frontpage For Windows 2002
Bwatch - v26 - i9 - Sept 2004 - p5(2) [501+]

Hester, Phil - *Firebreather, Vol. 1*
y Teach Lib - v32 - i3 - Feb 2005 - p58(1) [1-50]

Heti, Sheila - *Ticknor*
Globe & Mail - March 19 2005 - pD8 [501+]

Hetley, James A. - *The Winter Oak*
y BL - v101 - i6 - Nov 15 2004 - p571(1) [51-500]
Bwatch - Dec 2004 - pNA [501+]
y Kliatt - v39 - i2 - March 2005 - p28(1) [51-500]
y LJ - v129 - i17 - Oct 15 2004 - p57(2) [51-500]
MFSF - v108 - i4 - April 2005 - p30(2) [501+]
y PW - v251 - i41 - Oct 11 2004 - p61(1) [51-500]

Hetnarski, Richard B. - *Mathematical Theory of Elasticity*
Choice - v42 - i2 - Oct 2004 - p323(1) [51-500]
TimHES - v0 - i1668 - Nov 26 2004 - pXIII(1) [501+]

Hett, Benjamin Carter - *Death in the Tiergarten: Murder and Criminal Justice in the Kaiser's Berlin*
Choice - v42 - i6 - Feb 2005 - p1088(1) [51-500]

Hettich, Paul I. - *Connect College to Career: A Student's Guide to Work and Life Transitions*
R&R Bk N - v19 - i3 - August 2004 - p221(1) [1-50]

Heudier, Jean-Louis - *Night Sky: Month-by-Month: January-December 2004*
SciTech - v28 - i1 - March 2004 - p43(1) [51-500]

Heuer, Karsten - *Walking the Big Wild: From Yellowstone to the Yukon on the Grizzly Bears' Trail*
LJ - v130 - i1 - Jan 1 2005 - p147(1) [51-500]
PW - v251 - i46 - Nov 15 2004 - p49(1) [51-500]

Heugel, Ines - *Classic Garden Style: Planters, Furniture, Accessories and Ornaments (Illus. by Sarramon, Christian)*
LJ - v129 - i15 - Sept 15 2004 - p56(1) [51-500]

Heumann, Milton - *Good Cop, Bad Cop: Racial Profiling and Competing Views of Justice*
Law&PolBR - Sept 2004 - pNA [501+]

Heuser, Richard R. - *Textbook of Peripheral Vascular Interventions*
  E-Streams - August 2004 - pNA [501+]

Heuser, Sabine - *Virtual Geographies: Cyberpunk at the Intersection of the Postmodern and Science Fiction*
  Ext - v45 - i2 - Summer 2004 - p209(2) [501+]
  Ext - v45 - i2 - Summer 2004 - p210(5) [501+]

Heuston, Kimberley Burton - *Dante's Daughter*
  c LibMed - v22 - i6 - March 2004 - p67(1) [501+]

Hevia, James L. - *English Lessons: The Pedagogy of Imperialism in Nineteenth-Century China*
  Choice - v42 - i1 - Sept 2004 - p166(1) [501+]

Hew, C.S. - *The Physiology of Tropical Orchids in Relation to the Industry, 2nd Ed.*
  SciTech - v28 - i4 - Dec 2004 - p124 [51-500]

Hewes, Lauren B. - *Portraits in the Collection of the American Antiquarian Society*
  Choice - v42 - i3 - Nov 2004 - p474(1) [1-50]

Hewett, Ivan - *Music: Healing the Rift*
  MT - v145 - i1888 - Autumn 2004 - p106-108 [501+]

Hewett, Joan - *A Monkey Baby Grows Up (Illus. by Hewett, Richard)*
  c SB - v40 - i3 - May-June 2004 - p133(1) [501+]
  c SLJ - v50 - i10 - Oct 2004 - p142(1) [51-500]

Hewison, Alistair - *Management for Nurses and Health Professionals: Theory into Practice*
  SciTech - v28 - i4 - Dec 2004 - p122 [51-500]

Hewitt, C.N. - *Handbook of Atmospheric Science*
  Choice - v41 - i7 - March 2004 - p1331(1) [501+]

Hewitt, David - *A Bit of Grit on Haystacks: A Celebration of Wainwright*
  Spec - v296 - Dec 18 2004 - p94(1) [501+]

Hewitt, Eben - *Java Garage*
  CBRA - Annual 2003 - p21(1) [51-500]
  SciTech - v28 - i4 - Dec 2004 - p21(1) [51-500]

Hewitt, Hugh - *Blog: Understanding the Information Reformation That's Changing Your World*
  Am Spect - v38 - i1 - Feb 2005 - p60(3) [501+]

Hewitt, Jema - *Complete Beading: Jewelry and Accessories*
  LJ - v130 - i3 - Feb 15 2005 - p126(1) [51-500]

Hewitt, Lawrence - *Lousianians in the Civil War*
  VQR - v79 - i1 - Winter 2003 - p8 [51-500]

Hewitt, Maria - *Childhood Cancer Survivorship: Improving Care and Quality of Life*
  SciTech - v28 - i1 - March 2004 - p92(1) [51-500]

Hewitt, Steve - *Spying 101: The RCMP's Secret Activities at Canadian Universities, 1917-1997*
  CBRA - Annual 2003 - p314(2) [501+]
  R&R Bk N - v19 - i1 - Feb 2004 - p145(1) [51-500]

Hewson, David - *Lucifer's Shadow*
  Globe & Mail - August 7 2004 - pD12 [51-500]
  KR - v72 - i13 - July 1 2004 - p596(1) [501+]
  The Villa of Mysteries
  BL - v101 - i8 - Dec 15 2004 - p711(1) [51-500]
  Globe & Mail - July 24 2004 - pD11 [51-500]
  Globe & Mail - March 12 2005 - pD17 [1-50]
  KR - v72 - i23 - Dec 1 2004 - p1121(1) [51-500]
  LJ - v129 - i16 - Oct 1 2004 - p64(1) [501+]
  PW - v251 - i51 - Dec 20 2004 - p37(1) [51-500]

Hewson, Stephen Fletcher - *A Mathematical Bridge: An Intuitive Journey in Higher Mathematics, 1st Ed.*
  TimHES - v0 - i1668 - Nov 26 2004 - pXIV(1) [501+]

Hexham, Irving - *Encountering New Religious Movements: A Holistic Evangelical Approach*
  Ch Today - v48 - i7 - July 2004 - p67(1) [501+]

Heyde, K. - *Basic Ideas and Concepts in Nuclear Physics: An Introductory Approach, 3rd Ed.*
  SciTech - v28 - i4 - Dec 2004 - p51(1) [51-500]

Heydemann, Steven - *Networks of Privilege in the Middle East: The Politics of Economic Reform Revisited*
  Choice - v42 - i6 - Feb 2005 - p1070(1) [51-500]

Heyer, Friedrich - *Kirchengeschichte der Ukraine im 20. Jahrhundert: Von der Epochenwende des ersten Weltkrieges bis zu den Anfängen in einem unabhängigen ukrainischen Staat*
  CHR - v90 - i3 - July 2004 - p562(2) [501+]

Heyking, John von - *Augustine and Politics as Longing in the World*
  Theol St - v65 - i4 - Dec 2004 - p860(2) [501+]

Heylin, Clinton - *Despite the System: Orson Welles Versus the Hollywood Studios*
  LJ - v130 - i2 - Feb 1 2005 - p81(1) [51-500]

Heym, Georg - *Poems*
  TLS - i5293 - Sept 10 2004 - p28(1) [501+]

Heyman, Anita - *Gretchen: The Bicycle Dog*
  c LibMed - v22 - i4 - Jan 2004 - p71(1) [51-500]

Heyman, Kathryn - *The Accomplice (Read by Halligan, Gerri). Audiobook Review*
  y Kliatt - v38 - i5 - Sept 2004 - p52(2) [51-500]

Heymann, C. David - *The Georgetown Ladies' Social Club: Power, Passion, and Politics in the Nation's Capital*
  R&R Bk N - v19 - i4 - Nov 2004 - p133(1) [1-50]

Heyneman, Stephen P. - *The Challenges of Education in Central Asia*
  R&R Bk N - v19 - i3 - August 2004 - p214(1) [1-50]
  Islam and Social Policy
  R&R Bk N - v19 - i4 - Nov 2004 - p18(1) [51-500]

Hiaasen, Carl - *Hoot*
  y Kliatt - v38 - i4 - July 2004 - p18(2) [51-500]
  c RT - v57 - Nov 2003 - p277 [51-500]
  Skinny Dip (Read by Hoye, Stephen). Audiobook Review
  BL - v101 - i5 - Nov 1 2004 - p505(1) [51-500]
  BW - v34 - i32 - August 8 2004 - p12(1) [501+]
  Skinny Dip
  BW - v34 - i30 - July 25 2004 - p15(1) [501+]
  Econ - v372 - i8384 - July 17 2004 - p82US [51-500]
  Ent W - i774 - July 16 2004 - p80 [501+]
  Globe & Mail - July 24 2004 - pD11 [51-500]
  New R - Nov 15 2004 - p33 [501+]
  NW - July 19 2004 - p58 [51-500]
  NYT - July 12 2004 - pE1 [501+]
  NYTBR - July 11 2004 - p17 [501+]

Hib, Nora - *Fair-Weather Friend*
  LibMed - v22 - i4 - Jan 2004 - p62(1) [501+]

Hibbert, Adam - *Why Do People Bully?*
  y TES - v0 - i4586 - June 4 2004 - psss19(1) [501+]

Hibbert, Christopher - *Disraeli: A Personal History*
  Spec - v296 - i9195 - Oct 30 2004 - p52(1) [501+]
  TLS - i5298 - Oct 15 2004 - p30(1) [51-500]

Hibbert, Clare - *The Life of a Chicken*
  c SLJ - v50 - i9 - Sept 2004 - p188(1) [51-500]
  The Life of a Dog
  c SLJ - v50 - i9 - Sept 2004 - p188(1) [51-500]
  The Life of a Guinea Pig
  c SLJ - v50 - i9 - Sept 2004 - p188(1) [51-500]
  The Life of an Apple
  c Sch Lib - v52 - i3 - Autumn 2004 - p131(1) [1-50]
  Looking After Your Pet Rabbit
  c Sch Lib - v52 - i4 - Winter 2004 - p207(1) [51-500]

Hickam, Homer - *The Ambassador's Son*
  BL - v101 - i9-10 - Jan 1 2005 - p783(1) [1-50]
  PW - v252 - i6 - Feb 7 2005 - p41(2) [501+]

Hickey, Elizabeth - *The Painted Kiss*
  KR - v73 - i5 - March 1 2005 - p249(1) [501+]

Hickey, Eric W. - *Encyclopedia of Murder and Violent Crime*
  LibMed - v22 - i7 - April-May 2004 - p80(1) [501+]

Hickey, Georgina - *Hope and Danger in the New South City: Working-Class Women and Urban Development in Atlanta, 1890-1940*
  HNet - August 2004 - pNA [501+]

Hickham, Homer - *Rocket Boys*
  BL - v101 - i7 - Dec 1 2004 - p633(1) [51-500]

Hickling-Hudson, Anne - *Disrupting Preconceptions: Postcolonialism and Education*
  TCR - v106 - i12 - Dec 2004 - p2304(8) [501+]

Hickman Brynie, Faith - *101 Questions about Blood and Circulation: Your Answers Straight from the Heart*
  y SB - v40 - i4 - July-August 2004 - p150(1) [51-500]

Hickman, David - *Lincoln Wills*
  Six Ct J - v34 - i4 - Winter 2003 - p1137-1138 [501+]

Hickman, Pamela - *Animals and Their Mates: How Animals Attract, Fight and Protect Each Other (Illus. by Stephens, Pat)*
  c BL - v101 - i4 - Oct 15 2004 - p401(1) [501+]
  c KR - v72 - i17 - Sept 1 2004 - p866(1) [501+]
  c Res Links - v10 - i2 - Dec 2004 - p26(2) [501+]
  Animals and Their Young: How Animals Produce and Care for Their Babies (Illus. by Stephens, Pat)
  c CBRA - Annual 2003 - p564(2) [51-500]

Hickman, Tom - *The Call-Up: A History of National Service*
  TLS - i5304 - Nov 26 2004 - p12(1) [501+]

Hickman, Tracy - *Mystic Warrior (Read by James, Lloyd). Audiobook Review*
  Kliatt - v38 - i6 - Nov 2004 - p48(1) [51-500]
  LJ - v130 - i2 - Feb 1 2005 - p122(1) [51-500]

Hicks, Barbara Jean - *Jitterbug Jam (Illus. by Deacon, Alexis)*
  c KR - v73 - i3 - Feb 1 2005 - p177(1) [51-500]
  c PW - v252 - i11 - March 14 2005 - p66(1) [51-500]

Hicks, Betty - *Busted!*
  c BL - v101 - i4 - Oct 15 2004 - p406(1) [51-500]
  c CCB-B - v58 - i2 - Oct 2004 - p77(1) [51-500]
  y KR - v72 - i16 - August 15 2004 - p807(1) [51-500]
  c PW - v251 - i42 - Oct 18 2004 - p64(1) [51-500]
  c SLJ - v50 - i10 - Oct 2004 - p166(1) [51-500]

Hicks, Brian - *Ghost Ship: The Mysterious Trite Story of the Mary Celeste and Her Missing Crew*
  c SLJ - v50 - i9 - Sept 2004 - p236(1) [51-500]

Hicks, Douglas A. - *Religion and the Workplace: Pluralism, Spirituality, Leadership*
  Choice - v41 - i11-12 - July-August 2004 - p2061(2) [501+]
  Har Bus R - v82 - i5 - May 2004 - p30(1) [501+]

Hicks, Greg - *Leadershock--and How to Triumph over It: Eight Revolutionary Rules for Becoming a Powerful and Exhilarated Leader*
  HR Mag - v50 - i2 - Feb 2005 - pS16(1) [501+]

Hicks, Michael - *English Political Culture in the Fifteenth Century*
  Albion - v36 - i1 - Spring 2004 - p102(2) [501+]
  Six Ct J - v35 - i1 - Spring 2004 - p282(2) [501+]

Hicks, Michael - *Optimizing Applications on Cisco Networks*
  Bwatch - Feb 2005 - pNA [501+]

Hicks, Tyler G. - *Standard Handbook of Engineering Calculations, 4th Ed.*
  Choice - v42 - i6 - Feb 2005 - p1054(1) [51-500]
  SciTech - v28 - i4 - Dec 2004 - p132 [51-500]

Hicks, Wynford - *Quite Literally: Problem Words and How to Use Them*
  R&R Bk N - v19 - i4 - Nov 2004 - p216(1) [501+]

Hicyilmaz, Gaye - *Girl in Red (Read by Aspel, Richard). Audiobook Review*
  y Kliatt - v38 - i5 - Sept 2004 - p60(2) [51-500]

Hidy, Ralph W. - *The Great Northern Railway: A History*
  R&R Bk N - v19 - i3 - August 2004 - p122(1) [51-500]

Hientzelman, Donald S. - *Hawks and Owls of Eastern North America*
  Choice - v42 - i2 - Oct 2004 - p320(1) [51-500]

Hietala, Marjatta - *The Landscape of Food: The Food Relationship of Town and Country in Modern Times*
  J Hist G - v30 - i1 - Jan 2004 - p203(3) [501+]

Higashi/Glaser Design, Inc. - *Hello Kitty's Graduation Day (Illus. by Hirashima, Jean)*
  c CH Bwatch - v14 - i12 - Dec 2004 - pNA [501+]

Higbie, Frank Tobias - *Indispensable Outcasts: Hobo Workers and Community in the American Midwest, 1880-1930*
  JEL - v42 - i1 - March 2004 - p300(2) [501+]
  JAH - v91 - i2 - Sept 2004 - p649(2) [501+]

Higdon, Jane - *Evidence-Based Approach to Vitamins and Minerals: Health Implications and Intake Recommendations*
  E-Streams - Nov 2004 - pNA [501+]

Higgens-Evenson, R. Rudy - *The Price of Progress: Public Services, Taxation, and the American Corporate State, 1877 to 1929*
  BHR - v78 - i2 - Summer 2004 - p305(3) [501+]
  JAH - v91 - i3 - Dec 2004 - p1055(2) [501+]
  JEH - v64 - i1 - March 2004 - p266(2) [501+]
  JEL - v41 - i4 - Dec 2003 - p1404(1) [501+]

Higginbotham, Don - *George Washington: Uniting a Nation*
  JSH - v70 - i3 - August 2004 - p651(2) [501+]

Higginbotham, Eve Juliet - *Clinical Guide to Glaucoma Management*
  SciTech - v28 - i1 - March 2004 - p114(1) [51-500]

Higgins, Aidan - *A Bestiary*
  BL - v100 - i21 - July 2004 - p1811(1) [1-50]
  LJ - v129 - i13 - August 2004 - p76(1) [51-500]
  NYRB - v51 - i19 - Dec 2 2004 - p55(3) [501+]
  Flotsam & Jetsam
  NYRB - v51 - i19 - Dec 2 2004 - p55(3) [501+]
  Langrishe, Go Down
  NYRB - v51 - i19 - Dec 2 2004 - p55(3) [501+]

Higgins, Billy D. - *A Stranger and a Sojourner: Peter Caulder, Free Black Frontiersman in Antebellum Arkansas*
  BL - v101 - i5 - Nov 1 2004 - p456(1) [51-500]

Higgins, Chester, Jr. - *Echo of the Spirit: A Photographer's Journey (Illus. by Higgins, Chester, Jr.)*
Black Iss - v6 - i6 - Nov-Dec 2004 - p45(1) [501+]
PW - v251 - i31 - August 2 2004 - p66(1) [51-500]

Higgins, Dick - *Life Flowers*
PAJ - v26 - i3 - Sept 2004 - p128-135 [501+]
Octette
PAJ - v26 - i3 - Sept 2004 - p128-135 [501+]

Higgins, George V. - *The Easiest Thing in the World: The Uncollected Fiction of George V. Higgins*
BL - v101 - i7 - Dec 1 2004 - p639(1) [51-500]
KR - v72 - i20 - Oct 15 2004 - p986(1) [51-500]

Higgins, Hannah - *Fluxus Experience*
PAJ - v26 - i3 - Sept 2004 - p128-135 [501+]
TDR - v48 - i3 - Fall 2004 - p190(3) [501+]

Higgins, J. Brian - *Home Schooling: Educating with Head, Heart, and Hand*
LJ - v129 - i20 - Dec 1 2004 - p134(1) [51-500]

Higgins, Jack - *Dark Justice (Read by Page, Michael). Audiobook Review*
BL - v101 - i7 - Dec 1 2004 - p678(1) [1-50]
Dark Justice
BL - v101 - i1 - Sept 1 2004 - p68(1) [51-500]
PW - v251 - i30 - July 26 2004 - p40(1) [501+]
The Keys of Hell (Read by Rodska, Christian). Audiobook Review
LJ - v129 - i15 - Sept 15 2004 - p89(1) [51-500]

Higgins, James - *Lima: A Cultural History*
y BL - v101 - i6 - Nov 15 2004 - p548(1) [51-500]

Higgins, John - *Music of Our World: Multicultural Festivals, Songs, and Activities*
Teach Mus - v12 - i4 - Feb 2005 - p82(1) [51-500]

Higgins, Lesley - *Walter Pater: Transparencies of Desire*
ELT - v48 - i2 - Spring 2005 - p94(4) [501+]

Higgins, Mark - *Concepts in Federal Taxation, 2005 Ed.*
R&R Bk N - v19 - i3 - August 2004 - p204(M) [1-50]

Higgins, Michael W. - *Power and Peril: The Catholic Church at the Crossroads*
CBRA - Annual 2003 - p92(1) [501+]

Higgins, Monica C. - *Career Imprints: Creating Leaders Across an Industry*
Har Bus R - v83 - i2 - Feb 2005 - p56(1) [1-50]

Higgins, P.J. - *Handbook of Australian, New Zealand and Antarctic Birds, Vol. 6 (Illus. by Marsack, P.)*
E-Streams - Nov 2004 - pNA [501+]

Higgins, Pamela L. - *Libraries and Electronic Resources: New Partnerships, New Practicies, New Perspectives*
ALJ - v53 - i4 - Nov 2004 - p422(2) [501+]

Higgs, Edward - *The Information State in England: The Central Collection of Information on Citizens Since 1500*
Choice - v41 - i11-12 - July-August 2004 - p2112(1) [501+]

Higgs, Robert - *Against Leviathan: Government Power and a Free Society*
Choice - v42 - i7 - March 2005 - p1277(1) [51-500]
R&R Bk N - v19 - i4 - Nov 2004 - p89(1) [51-500]
What Have I Ever Done to You?
y TES - v0 - i4586 - June 4 2004 - psssss19(1) [501+]

High, Linda Oatman - *City of Snow: The Great Blizzard of 1888 (Illus. by Filippucci, Laura)*
c BL - v101 - i5 - Nov 1 2004 - p489(2) [51-500]
c KR - v72 - i18 - Sept 15 2004 - p914(1) [501+]
c SLJ - v50 - i11 - Nov 2004 - p106(2) [51-500]
Sister Slam and the Poetic Motormouth Road Trip
y VOYA - v27 - i3 - August 2004 - p216(1) [1-50]

High School Environmental Center
LibMed - v22 - i7 - April-May 2004 - p90(1) [501+]

High, Steven - *Industrial Sunset: The Making of North America's Rust Belt, 1969-1984*
Am St - v45 - i1 - Spring 2004 - p172-173 [501+]
JAH - v91 - i2 - Sept 2004 - p727(2) [501+]
JEL - v41 - i4 - Dec 2003 - p1405(1) [501+]

Higham, C.L. - *One West, Two Myths: A Comparative Reader*
R&R Bk N - v19 - i4 - Nov 2004 - p57(1) [51-500]

Higham, Charles - *Murder in Hollywood: Solving a Silent Screen Mystery*
KR - v72 - i18 - Sept 15 2004 - p902(1) [501+]
PW - v251 - i40 - Oct 4 2004 - p79(1) [51-500]
Murdering Mr. Lincoln: A New Detection of the 19th Century's Most Famous Crime (Read by Cashman, Dan). Audiobook Review
y Kliatt - v38 - i5 - Sept 2004 - p68(2) [51-500]

Higham, Charles F.W. - *Encyclopedia of Ancient Asian Civilizations*
BL - v101 - i1 - Sept 1 2004 - p166(2) [501+]
y Choice - v42 - i2 - Oct 2004 - p276(1) [501+]
R&R Bk N - v19 - i3 - August 2004 - p48(1) [51-500]
y SLJ - v50 - i10 - Oct 2004 - p93(2) [51-500]

Higham, N.J. - *King Arthur: Myth-Making and History*
HER - v119 - i483 - Sept 2004 - p976(3) [501+]
HER - v119 - i483 - Sept 2004 - p976(978) [501+]

Higham, Robin - *100 Years of Airpower and Aviation*
APH - v51 - i3 - Fall 2004 - p50(1) [501+]
J Mil H - v68 - i4 - Oct 2004 - p1319-1320 [501+]
The Military History of the Soviet Union
Russ Rev - v63 - i3 - July 2004 - pNA [501+]
The Military History of Tsarist Russia
Russ Rev - v63 - i3 - July 2004 - pNA [501+]
Researching World War I: A Handbook
Choice - v42 - i1 - Sept 2004 - p82(1) [501+]
J Mil H - v68 - i4 - Oct 2004 - p1274-1275 [501+]
Ref Rev - June 2004 - pNA [501+]

Highmore, Julie - *Play It Again?*
BL - v101 - i7 - Dec 1 2004 - p642(1) [51-500]

Highsmith, Patricia - *Library Lingo!*
c SLJ - v50 - i8 - August 2004 - p79(1) [51-500]
Small g: A Summer Idyll
BW - v34 - i28 - July 11 2004 - p15(1) [501+]
Globe & Mail - August 21 2004 - pD12 [51-500]
Lam Bk Rpt - v13 - i1-2 - August-Sept 2004 - p28(2) [501+]

Hight, Eleanor - *Colonialist Photography: Imag(in)ing Race and Place*
HNet - June 2004 - pNA [501+]

Hightman, Jason - *The Saint of Dragons*
y BL - v100 - i22 - August 2004 - p1920(1) [51-500]
c CCB-B - v58 - i2 - Oct 2004 - p77(1) [51-500]
y Kliatt - v38 - i4 - July 2004 - p8(1) [51-500]
y KR - v72 - i17 - Sept 1 2004 - p866(1) [51-500]
y PW - v251 - i49 - Dec 6 2004 - p60(1) [51-500]
y Sch Lib - v52 - i4 - Winter 2004 - p214(2) [51-500]
y SLJ - v50 - i9 - Sept 2004 - p208(1) [51-500]
y VOYA - v27 - i5 - Dec 2004 - p406(1) [51-500]

Hightower, Jim - *Let's Stop Beating around the Bush: More Politicial Subversion from Jim Hightower*
R&R Bk N - v19 - i4 - Nov 2004 - p124(1) [1-50]
Thieves in High Places: They've Stolen Our Country and It's Time to Take it Back
R&R Bk N - v19 - i3 - August 2004 - p180(1) [501+]

Highway Innovative Technology Evaluation Center - *Evaluation of Anchor Wall Systems' Landmark Reinforced Soil Wall System: With TC Mirafi's Miragrid and Miratex Geogrid Reinforcements, Final Report*
SciTech - v28 - i1 - March 2004 - p144(1) [51-500]

Highway, Tomson - *Caribou Song/Atihko Nikamon (Illus. by Deines, Brian)*
Can Lit - i181 - Summer 2004 - p143-145 [501+]
Fox on the Ice (Illus. by Deines, Brian)
c CBRA - Annual 2003 - p452(1) [51-500]
Rose
CBRA - Annual 2003 - p240(1) [51-500]

Hignutt, Diana - *Empress of Clouds*
PW - v251 - i45 - Nov 8 2004 - p40(2) [51-500]

Higonnet, Patrice - *Paris: Capital of the World*
JMH - v77 - i1 - March 2005 - p201(3) [501+]

Higson, Charlie - *SilverFin*
c PW - v252 - i10 - March 7 2005 - p68(1) [51-500]

Higson, Seamus P.J. - *Analytical Chemistry, 1st Ed.*
TimHES - v0 - i1680 - Feb 25 2005 - pXIII(1) [501+]

Higton, Mike - *Difficult Gospel: The Theology of Rowan Williams*
TLS - i5304 - Nov 26 2004 - p27(1) [501+]

Higuchi, Daisuke - *Whistle! Vol. 1*
PW - v251 - i47 - Nov 22 2004 - p41(1) [51-500]

Higurashi, Yoshinobu - *Tokyo Saiban no Kokusai Kankei: Kokusai Seiji ni Okeru Kenryoku to Kihan*
JAH - v91 - i2 - Sept 2004 - p688(2) [501+]

Hijazi, Ziyad - *Essential Pediatric Cardiology*
SciTech - v28 - i4 - Dec 2004 - p112(1) [1-50]

Hikawa, Kyoko - *From Far Away*
y Kliatt - v39 - i2 - March 2005 - p30(1) [51-500]

Hil, Richard - *Hard Lessons: Reflections on Governance and Crime Control in Late Modernity*
Law&PolBR - Oct 2004 - pNA [501+]

Hilaire, Michel - *French Paintings from the Musee Fabre, Montpellier*
Choice - v42 - i4 - Dec 2004 - p650(1) [1-50]

Hildebrand, Adam - *One Person at a Time*
Bwatch - v26 - i7 - July 2004 - p1(1) [51-500]

Hildebrand, David - *Basic Statistical Ideas for Managers, 2nd Ed.*
R&R Bk N - v19 - i4 - Nov 2004 - p92(1) [51-500]

Hildermeier, Manfred - *Geschichte der Sowjetunion 1917-1991*
HNet - June 2004 - pNA [501+]

Hildinger, Erik - *Swords Against the Senate: The Rise of the Roman Army and the Fall of the Republic*
HNet - June 2004 - pNA [501+]

Hildreth, Denise - *Savannah from Savannah*
S Liv - v39 - i8 - August 2004 - p205(1) [501+]

Hildreth, Paul M. - *Going Virtual: Distributed Communities in Practice*
R&R Bk N - v19 - i1 - Feb 2004 - p87(1) [1-50]
Knowledge Networks: Innovation through Communities of Practice
R&R Bk N - v19 - i3 - August 2004 - p102(1) [501+]

Hilfiker, David - *Urban Injustice: How Ghettos Happen*
Black Iss - v7 - i2 - March-April 2005 - p40(2) [501+]

Hilgartner, Peter - *HighPocket's War Stories: And Other Tall Tales*
Mar Crp G - v89 - i1 - Jan 2005 - p69(1) [501+]

Hilger, Andreas - *Sowjetische Militartribunale*
HNet - July 2004 - pNA [501+]

Hilhorst, A. - *The Apostolic Age in Patristic Thought*
R&R Bk N - v19 - i3 - August 2004 - p26(1) [1-50]

Hilhorst, Dorothea - *The Real World of NGO's: Discourses, Diversity, and Development*
JEL - v41 - i4 - Dec 2003 - p1409(2) [501+]
R&R Bk N - v19 - i1 - Feb 2004 - p132(1) [51-500]

Hill, Beth - *Remarkable World of Frances Barkley, 1769-1845*
CBRA - Annual 2003 - p49(1) [51-500]

Hill, Catharine B. - *Promoting and Sustaining Economic Reform in Zambia*
Choice - v42 - i2 - Oct 2004 - p340(1) [51-500]

Hill, Charles E. - *The Glory of the Atonement: Biblical, Historical & Practical Perspectives: Essays in Honor of Roger R. Nicole*
Bks & Cult - v11 - i1 - Jan-Feb 2005 - p20(3) [501+]

Hill, Christopher - *The Changing Politics of Foreign Policy*
AJPS - v39 - i3 - Nov 2004 - p671(2) [501+]

Hill, Clara E. - *Helping Skills: Facilitating Exploration, Insight, and Action, 2nd Ed.*
SciTech - v28 - i3 - Sept 2004 - p3(1) [501+]

Hill Collins, Patricia - *Black Sexual Politics: African Americans, Gender and the New Racism*
Black Iss - v6 - i5 - Sept-Oct 2004 - p44(1) [501+]

Hill, Dave - *Marxism Against Postmodernism in Educational Theory*
TCR - v106 - i2 - Feb 2004 - p389-392 [501+]

Hill, David (b. 1942 -) - *Coming Back*
y Magpies - v19 - i5 - Nov 2004 - p8S(1) [501+]

Hill, David (b. 1943 -) - *Literature of the Sturm und Drang*
Ger Q - v77 - i4 - Fall 2004 - p496-497 [501+]

Hill, Donna - *Big Girls Don't Cry*
LJ - v130 - i1 - Jan 1 2005 - p91(1) [51-500]
Dare to Dream
BL - v101 - i2 - Sept 15 2004 - p220(1) [51-500]
Divas, Inc.
BL - v100 - i21 - July 2004 - p1817(1) [51-500]

Hill, Douglas - *The Dragon Charmer*
c Sch Lib - v52 - i4 - Winter 2004 - p192(1) [51-500]

Hill, Elizabeth Starr - *Wildfire! (Illus. by Shepperson, Rob)*
c BL - v101 - i2 - Sept 15 2004 - p245(1) [51-500]
c CCB-B - v58 - i3 - Nov 2004 - p125(1) [51-500]
c HB - v80 - i6 - Nov-Dec 2004 - p710(1) [51-500]
c KR - v72 - i19 - Oct 1 2004 - p961(1) [51-500]
c SLJ - v50 - i12 - Dec 2004 - p110(1) [501+]

Hill, Errol G. - *A History of African American Theatre*
Afr Am R - v38 - i2 - Summer 2004 - p335(3) [501+]

Hill, Fiona - *The Siberian Curse: How Communist Planners Left Russia Out in the Cold*
JPR - v41 - i4 - July 2004 - p519-519 [501+]
Lon R Bks - v26 - i13 - July 8 2004 - p3(2) [501+]
NYRB - v51 - i15 - Oct 7 2004 - p39(3) [501+]
R&R Bk N - v19 - i1 - Feb 2004 - p84(1) [1-50]

Hill, Geoffrey - *Scenes from Comus*
Spec - v297 - i9209 - Feb 5 2005 - p44(1) [501+]
Style and Faith
JR - v84 - i3 - July 2004 - p510(2) [501+]

Hill, Gregg - *On the Run: A Mafia Childhood*
    BL - v101 - i1 - Sept 1 2004 - p27(2) [51-500]
    KR - v72 - i15 - August 1 2004 - p726(1) [501+]
    LJ - v129 - i13 - August 2004 - p98(1) [501+]
    NYTBR - Oct 31 2004 - p20 [501+]
    PW - v251 - i33 - August 16 2004 - p54(2) [51-500]

Hill, Hal - *East Timor: Development Challenges to the World's Newest Nation*
    JTWS - v21 - i1 - Spring 2004 - p267(2) [501+]

Hill, Harvey - *The Politics of Modernism: Alfred Loisy and the Scientific Study of Religion*
    CH - v73 - i4 - Dec 2004 - p873(2) [501+]

Hill, Henry - *Gangsters and Goodfellas: The Mob, Witness Protection, and Life on the Run*
    NYTBR - Oct 31 2004 - p20 [501+]

Hill, Ingrid - *Ursula, Under*
    BW - v34 - i34 - August 22 2004 - p5(1) [501+]
    CC - v121 - i25 - Dec 14 2004 - p22(1) [51-500]

Hill, Janet - *Stages and Playgoers: From Guild Plays to Shakespeare*
    Shakes Q - v55 - i1 - Spring 2004 - p80-83 [501+]

Hill, Janet Muirhead - *Starlight Shines for Miranda*
    c CH Bwatch - v14 - i7 - July 2004 - p6(1) [51-500]

Hill, Jeffrey - *Sport, Leisure and Culture in Twentieth-Century Britain*
    Wom HR - v13 - i1 - Spring 2004 - p154(3) [501+]

Hill, John M. - *The Rhetorical Poetics of the Middle Ages: Reconstructive Polyphony: Essays in Honor of Robert O. Payne*
    JEGP - v103 - i1 - Jan 2004 - p125-127 [501+]

Hill, John S. - *World Business: Globalization, Analysis, and Strategy*
    R&R Bk N - v19 - i3 - August 2004 - p132(1) [51-500]

Hill, Jonathan - *The History of Christian Thought: The Fascinating Story of the Great Christian Thinkers and How They Helped Shape the World as We Know It Today*
    Choice - v42 - i2 - Oct 2004 - p310(1) [51-500]

Hill, Justin - *Ciao Asmara: A Classic Account of Contemporary Africa*
    KR - v73 - i1 - Jan 1 2005 - p34(1) [501+]
    LJ - v130 - i2 - Feb 1 2005 - p106(1) [51-500]
    Passing under Heaven
    TLS - i5288 - August 6 2004 - p21(1) [501+]

Hill, Karen - *A Special Thanks (Illus. by Gevry, Claudine)*
    c PW - v252 - i7 - Feb 14 2005 - p81(1) [501+]

Hill, Kathleen Thompson - *Encyclopedia of Federal Agencies and Commissions*
    BL - v101 - i4 - Oct 15 2004 - p436(2) [501+]
    Choice - v42 - i3 - Nov 2004 - p463(1) [1-50]
    R&R Bk N - v19 - i4 - Nov 2004 - p154(1) [501+]
    R&USQ - v44 - i2 - Winter 2004 - p168(2) [501+]

Hill, Kevin R. - *Nietzsche's Critiques: The Kantian Foundation of His Thought*
    Choice - v41 - i11-12 - July-August 2004 - p2058(1) [501+]

Hill, Kirkpatrick - *The Year of Miss Agnes*
    c SLJ - v50 - i7 - July 2004 - p43(1) [51-500]

Hill, Laban Carrick - *Harlem Stomp!: A Cultural History of the Harlem Renaissance*
    SLJ - v50 - i10 - Oct 2004 - pS66(1) [501+]

Hill, Lance - *The Deacons for Defense: Armed Resistance and the Civil Rights Movement*
    Bl S - v34 - i3 - Fall 2004 - p72-72 [501+]
    Choice - v42 - i4 - Dec 2004 - p721(1) [1-50]
    Nation - v279 - i1 - July 5 2004 - p54 [501+]

Hill, Laura E. - *The Socioeconomic Well-Being of California's Immigrant Youth*
    R&R Bk N - v19 - i4 - Nov 2004 - p131(1) [51-500]

Hill, Linda A. - *Becoming a Manager: How New Managers Master the Challenge of Leadership, 2nd Ed.*
    R&R Bk N - v19 - i2 - May 2004 - p113(1) [1-50]

Hill, Marcia - *Diary of a Country Therapist*
    SciTech - v28 - i4 - Dec 2004 - p94(1) [51-500]

Hill, Mary - *Let's Go to a Baseball Game*
    c SLJ - v50 - i12 - Dec 2004 - p132(1) [501+]

Hill, Michael Ortiz - *Dreaming the End of the World: Apocalypse as a Rite of Passage, 2nd Ed.*
    SciTech - v28 - i4 - Dec 2004 - p4(1) [1-50]

Hill, Mike - *After Whiteness: Unmaking an American Majority*
    Choice - v41 - i11-12 - July-August 2004 - p2129(1) [501+]

Hill-Miller, Katherine - *From the Light House to the Monk's House: A Guide to Virginia Woolf's Literary Landscapes*
    Choice - v42 - i2 - Oct 2004 - p293(2) [501+]

Hill, Nemo R. - *The Strange Music of Erich Zann*
    PW - v251 - i51 - Dec 20 2004 - p41(2) [501+]

Hill, Nigel - *How to Measure Customer Satisfaction, 2nd Ed.*
    R&R Bk N - v19 - i2 - May 2004 - p114(1) [1-50]

Hill, Patti - *Like a Watered Garden*
    LJ - v130 - i2 - Feb 1 2005 - p62(1) [51-500]
    PW - v251 - i46 - Nov 15 2004 - p40(1) [51-500]

Hill, Peter B.E. - *The Japanese Mafia: Yakuza, Law, and the State*
    Choice - v42 - i1 - Sept 2004 - p166(1) [501+]

Hill, Reginald - *Good Morning, Midnight*
    BL - v101 - i1 - Sept 1 2004 - p68(2) [51-500]
    Globe & Mail - Sept 18 2004 - pD22 [51-500]
    Globe & Mail - Nov 27 2004 - pD18 [1-50]
    KR - v72 - i16 - August 15 2004 - p780(2) [51-500]
    LJ - v129 - i14 - Sept 1 2004 - p125(1) [51-500]
    PW - v251 - i33 - August 16 2004 - p45(2) [51-500]
    NYTBR - Oct 24 2004 - p27 [501+]

Hill, Richard L. - *Volcanoes of the Cascades: Their Ruse and Their Risks*
    SciTech - v28 - i4 - Dec 2004 - p57(1) [51-500]

Hill, Richard W. - *Animal Physiology*
    QRB - v79 - i4 - Dec 2004 - p432(1) [501+]
    SciTech - v28 - i3 - Sept 2004 - p67(1) [51-500]

Hill, Sam - *Buzz Riff*
    BL - v100 - i22 - August 2004 - p1905(1) [501+]
    KR - v72 - i16 - August 15 2004 - p781(1) [51-500]
    LJ - v129 - i14 - Sept 1 2004 - p121(1) [51-500]
    PW - v251 - i38 - Sept 20 2004 - p49(1) [51-500]

Hill, Sandra - *The Cajun Cowboy*
    y BL - v101 - i2 - Sept 15 2004 - p222(1) [51-500]
    Wet and Wild
    BL - v101 - i6 - Nov 15 2004 - p567(1) [51-500]
    PW - v251 - i40 - Oct 4 2004 - p75(1) [51-500]

Hill, Thomas E. - *The Philosophy of the Good Life*
    R&R Bk N - v19 - i4 - Nov 2004 - p8(1) [51-500]

Hill, Tony - *The Contemporary Encyclopedia of Herbs and Spices: Seasonings for the Global Kitchen*
    LJ - v130 - i1 - Jan 1 2005 - p154(1) [51-500]

Hill, Tracey - *Anthony Munday and Civic Culture: Theatre, History and Power in Early Modern London, 1580-1633*
    TLS - i5286 - July 23 2004 - p33(1) [501+]

Hill, William E. - *Lewis and Clark Trail Yesterday and Today*
    R&R Bk N - v19 - i4 - Nov 2004 - p67(1) [1-50]

Hillar, Marian - *Michael Servetus: Intellectual Giant, Humanist, and Martyr*
    Ren Q - v57 - i3 - Fall 2004 - p1053(3) [501+]
    Six Ct J - v35 - i3 - Fall 2004 - p949-951 [501+]

Hillard, Randy - *Emergency Psychiatry*
    SciTech - v28 - i1 - March 2004 - p98(1) [51-500]

Hillard, Shirley - *Who's Not Asleep?*
    c CH Bwatch - v14 - i12 - Dec 2004 - pNA [51-500]

Hilldorfer, Joseph - *The Cyanide Canary*
    y BL - v100 - i22 - August 2004 - p1880(1) [51-500]
    KR - v72 - i13 - July 1 2004 - p618(1) [501+]

Hillenbrand, Will - *Asleep in the Stable (Illus. by Hillenbrand, Will)*
    c CCB-B - v58 - i3 - Nov 2004 - p125(2) [501+]
    HB - v80 - i6 - Nov-Dec 2004 - p659(2) [51-500]
    c KR - v72 - i21 - Nov 1 2004 - p1050(1) [51-500]
    c PW - v251 - i39 - Sept 27 2004 - p61(1) [51-500]

Hillerbrand, Hans Joachim - *The Encyclopedia of Protestantism*
    Choice - v41 - i11-12 - July-August 2004 - p2016(1) [501+]
    R&USQ - v44 - i1 - Fall 2004 - p85(2) [501+]
    Theol St - v66 - i1 - March 2005 - p192(3) [501+]

Hillerman, Tony - *Skeleton Man*
    BL - v101 - i2 - Sept 15 2004 - p179(1) [51-500]
    Ent W - i794 - Nov 26 2004 - p123 [51-500]
    Globe & Mail - Dec 4 2004 - pD35 [51-500]
    KR - v72 - i18 - Sept 15 2004 - p894(1) [51-500]
    LJ - v129 - i18 - Nov 1 2004 - p63(1) [51-500]
    NYTBR - Nov 28 2004 - p17 [501+]
    People - v62 - i23 - Dec 6 2004 - p55 [51-500]
    PW - v251 - i42 - Oct 18 2004 - p50(2) [51-500]
    Roundup M - v12 - i3 - Feb 2005 - p27(1) [51-500]
    SLJ - v51 - i2 - Feb 2005 - p156(1) [501+]

Hilley, Joseph H. - *Sober Justice*
    BL - v101 - i3 - Oct 1 2004 - p300(1) [51-500]

Hillhouse, Raelynn - *Rift Zone*
    BL - v101 - i10 - July 2004 - p1798(1) [51-500]
    DroRevMy - v24 - i4 - July-August 2004 - p12(1) [51-500]
    KR - v72 - i13 - July 1 2004 - p596(2) [501+]
    LJ - v129 - i12 - July 2004 - p70(2) [51-500]

Hilliam, Paul - *Islamic Weapons, Warfare, and Armies: Muslim Military Operations Against the Crusaders*
    c SLJ - v50 - i8 - August 2004 - p136(1) [501+]

Hilliard, Bryan - *The U.S. Supreme Court and Medical Ethics: From Contraception to Managed Health Care*
    Choice - v42 - i4 - Dec 2004 - p736(2) [1-50]
    R&R Bk N - v19 - i3 - August 2004 - p201(1) [1-50]

Hilliard, Bukkfalvi - *Living Fully with Shyness and Social Anxiety: A Comprehensive Guide to Gaining Social Confidence*
    PW - v252 - i11 - March 14 2005 - p55(1) [51-500]

Hilliard, John E. - *Stereology and Stochastic Geometry*
    SciTech - v28 - i1 - March 2004 - p145(1) [51-500]

Hillier, Bevis - *Betjeman: The Bonus Of Laughter*
    Spec - v296 - i9197 - Nov 13 2004 - p52(3) [501+]
    TLS - i5305 - Dec 3 2004 - p36(1) [501+]

Hilliker, Amy Warren - *Little One, God Loves You (Illus. by Thompson, Carol)*
    c BL - v101 - i3 - Oct 1 2004 - p346(1) [51-500]
    c PW - v251 - i43 - Oct 25 2004 - p46(1) [501+]
    Little One, God Made You (Illus. by Thompson, Carol)
    c BL - v101 - i3 - Oct 1 2004 - p346(1) [51-500]
    c PW - v251 - i43 - Oct 25 2004 - p46(1) [501+]

Hillis, Craig D. - *Texas Trilogy: Life in a Small Texas Town*
    SHQ - v107 - i3 - Jan 2004 - p494(2) [501+]

Hillix, William A. - *Animal Bodies, Human Minds: Ape, Dolphin, and Parrot Language Skills*
    SciTech - v28 - i1 - March 2004 - p70(1) [51-500]

Hillman, Arye L. - *Public Finance and Public Policy: Responsibilities and Limitations of Government*
    JEL - v42 - i1 - March 2004 - p235(1) [501+]

Hillman, James - *A Terrible Love of War*
    BIC - v33 - i8 - Nov 2004 - p21(2) [501+]
    CC - v122 - i4 - Feb 22 2005 - p56(7) [501+]
    Choice - v42 - i2 - Oct 2004 - p375(1) [51-500]
    Sew R - v112 - i1 - Wntr 2004 - pXXIV-XXVII [501+]

Hillman, Mayer - *How We Can Save the Planet*
    New Sci - v183 - i2457 - July 24 2004 - p55(1) [501+]

Hillman, Richard - *Shakespeare, Marlowe and the Politics of France*
    Shakes Q - v55 - i1 - Spring 2004 - p93-94 [501+]

Hillmann, Diane I. - *Metadata in Practice*
    BL - v101 - i1 - Sept 1 2004 - p164(2) [1-50]

Hills, Larry - *The Bicycle*
    c SLJ - v51 - i1 - Jan 2005 - p110(1) [51-500]
    The Camera
    c SLJ - v51 - i1 - Jan 2005 - p110(1) [51-500]

Hillsbery, Thorn Kief - *What We Do Is Secret*
    KR - v73 - i4 - Feb 15 2005 - p191(1) [501+]

Hillsman, Bill - *Run the Other Way: Fixing the Broken Two-Party System, One Campaign at a Time*
    R&R Bk N - v19 - i3 - August 2004 - p179(1) [501+]

Hillson, David - *Effective Opportunity Management for Projects: Exploiting Positive Risk*
    R&R Bk N - v19 - i1 - Feb 2004 - p93(1) [51-500]

Hillstrom, Kevin - *Latin America and the Caribbean: A Continental Overview of Environmental Issues*
    Choice - v42 - i2 - Oct 2004 - p317(1) [51-500]
    Watergate
    R&R Bk N - v19 - i4 - Nov 2004 - p64(1) [51-500]

Hillyard, Susan - *Before the Oil: A Personal Memoir of Abu Dhabi 1954-1958*
    A Aff - v35 - i2 - July 2004 - p220-222 [501+]

Hilmes, Michele - *Radio Reader: Essays in the Cultural History of Radio*
    JC - v54 - i3 - Sept 2004 - p576(3) [501+]

Hiltner, Ken - *Milton and Ecology*
    Ren Q - v57 - i4 - Winter 2004 - p1534(2) [501+]

Hilton, Matthew - *Consumerism in Twentieth-Century Britain*
    CR - v285 - i1665 - Oct 2004 - p241(3) [501+]

Hilton, Paris - *Confessions of an Heiress: A Tongue-in-Chic Peek Behind the Pose*
    Ent W - i786 - Oct 1 2004 - p77 [51-500]
    Globe & Mail - Oct 16 2004 - pD22 [501+]

Hilton, Richard P. - *Dinosaurs and Other Mesozoic Reptiles of California (Illus. by Kirkland, Ken)*
    QRB - v79 - i4 - Dec 2004 - p412(1) [501+]

Hilton, Tim - *One More Kilometre and We're in the Showers: Memoirs of a Cyclist*
    TLS - i5287 - July 30 2004 - p32(1) [501+]

Hirschmann, Werner - *Another Place, Another Time: A U-Boat Officer's Wartime Album*
R&R Bk N - v19 - i4 - Nov 2004 - p33(1) [51-500]

Hirsh, David - *Law Against Genocide: Cosmopolitan Trials*
CS - v33 - i6 - Nov 2004 - p744(1) [1-50]

Hirsh, Dwight C. - *Veterinary Microbiology, 2nd Ed.*
SciTech - v28 - i3 - Sept 2004 - p133(1) [51-500]

Hirsh, John C. - *Medieval Lyric: Middle English Lyrics, Ballads, and Carols*
Choice - v42 - i7 - March 2005 - p1230(1) [51-500]

Hirsh, Michael - *None Braver: U.S. Air Force Pararescuemen in the War on Terrorism*
R&R Bk N - v19 - i4 - Nov 2004 - p47(1) [51-500]

Hirsh, Rae Ann - *Early Childhood Curriculum: Incorporating Multiple Intelligences, Developmentally Appropriate Practice, and Play*
R&R Bk N - v19 - i1 - Feb 2004 - p183(1) [51-500]

Hirshberg, Charles - *ESPN 25: 25 Mind-Bending, Eye-Popping, Culture-Morphing Years of Highlights*
BL - v101 - i1 - Sept 1 2004 - p47(1) [501+]
ESPN25: 25 Mind-Bending, Eye-Popping, Culture-Morphing Years of Highlights
Ent W - Sept 10 2004 - p171 [51-500]

Hirst, Anthony - *Alexandria, Real and Imagined*
R&R Bk N - v19 - i3 - August 2004 - p58(1) [51-500]

Hirstein, James - *Beatus Rhenanus (1485-1547), lecteur et editeur des textes anciens: Actes du Colloque International tenu a Strasbourg a Selestat du 13 au 15 novembre 1998*
Ren Q - v57 - i4 - Winter 2004 - p1477(2) [501+]

Hirt, Hans C. - *The Enforcement of Directors' Duties in Britain and Germany: A Comparative Study with Particular Reference to Large Companies*
R&R Bk N - v19 - i4 - Nov 2004 - p110(1) [51-500]

Hirt, Robert P. - *Organelles, Genomes, and Eukaryote Phylogeny: An Evolutionary Synthesis in the Age of Genomics*
SciTech - v28 - i4 - Dec 2004 - p60(1) [51-500]

Hirth, Kenneth G. - *Mexoamerican Lithic Technology: Experimentation and Interpretation: Proceedings*
R&R Bk N - v19 - i1 - Feb 2004 - p66(1) [501+]

Hirtler, Julia Kristeva - *Mourning Revolution*
Col Lit - v31 - i4 - Fall 2004 - p188(15) [501+]

Hischak, Thomas S. - *Through the Screen Door: What Happened to the Broadway Musical When It Went to Hollywood*
Choice - v42 - i5 - Jan 2005 - p861(2) [1-50]
R&R Bk N - v19 - i4 - Nov 2004 - p197(1) [501+]

Hiscock, Nigel - *The White Mantle of the Churches: Architecture, Liturgy, and Art around the Millennium*
CH - v73 - i3 - Sept 2004 - p686(3) [501+]
Med R - Sept 2004 - pNA [501+]

Hispalensis, Isidorus - *Isidori Hispalensis Chronica*
Specu - v79 - i4 - Oct 2004 - p1101(2) [501+]

Historical Atlas of the Ancient Greece
LibMed - v22 - i5 - Feb 2004 - p79(1) [501+]

Historical Atlas of the Holy Lands
LibMed - v22 - i5 - Feb 2004 - p79(1) [501+]

Historical Documents Index 1972-2002
R&R Bk N - v19 - i1 - Feb 2004 - p61(1) [501+]

Historical Review of Developments Relating to Aggression
R&R Bk N - v19 - i1 - Feb 2004 - p253(1) [51-500]

History of American Literature
LibMed - v22 - i4 - Jan 2004 - p92(1) [501+]

History of Fashion
LibMed - v22 - i7 - April-May 2004 - p90(1) [501+]

History of Sports
LibMed - v22 - i7 - April-May 2004 - p85(1) [501+]

A History of the Third Reich
LibMed - v22 - i4 - Jan 2004 - p75(1) [501+]

The History of Tibet, Vol. II
TimHES - v0 - i1678 - Feb 11 2005 - p22(2) [501+]

The History of Tibet, Vol. III
TimHES - v0 - i1678 - Feb 11 2005 - p22(2) [501+]

History of World War II
y Ref Rev - Nov 2004 - pNA [501+]

History of World War II, Vols. 1-3
Ref Rev - Nov 2004 - pNA [501+]
R&R Bk N - v19 - i4 - Nov 2004 - p32(1) [51-500]

Hitchcock, Barbara - *The Polaroid Book*
Ent W - i808 - Feb 25 2005 - p106 [51-500]

Hitchcock, James - *The Supreme Court and Religion in American Life, Vol. 1*
Choice - v42 - i6 - Feb 2005 - p1098(1) [51-500]
The Supreme Court and Religion in American Life, Vol. 2
Choice - v42 - i6 - Feb 2005 - p1098(1) [51-500]

Hitchcock, Peter - *Imaginary States: Studies in Cultural Transnationalism*
WestFolk - v62 - i4 - Fall 2003 - p314(3) [501+]

Hitchcock, Susan Tyler - *Geography of Religion: Where God Lives, Where Pilgrims Walk*
CC - v121 - i25 - Dec 14 2004 - p23(1) [51-500]
LJ - v130 - i4 - March 1 2005 - p90(2) [51-500]
PW - v251 - i45 - Nov 8 2004 - p53(1) [51-500]
Mad Mary Lamb: Lunacy and Murder in Literary London
BL - v101 - i6 - Nov 15 2004 - p546(1) [51-500]
KR - v72 - i19 - Oct 1 2004 - p949(1) [501+]
LJ - v130 - i2 - Feb 1 2005 - p79(1) [51-500]
PW - v252 - i2 - Jan 10 2005 - p53(1) [51-500]
Mad Mary Lamb: Lunancy and Murder in Literary London
Globe & Mail - Jan 29 2005 - pD8 [501+]

Hitchens, Christopher - *Love, Poverty, and War: Journeys and Essays*
BL - v101 - i9-10 - Jan 1 2005 - p802(1) [51-500]
Globe & Mail - Dec 24 2004 - pD13 [501+]
KR - v72 - i22 - Nov 15 2004 - p1079(2) [501+]
LJ - v130 - i1 - Jan 1 2005 - p124(1) [51-500]
NYTBR - Feb 6 2005 - p16 [501+]
PW - v251 - i46 - Nov 15 2004 - p51(1) [51-500]

Hite, Katherine - *Authoritarian Legacies and Democracy in Latin America and Southern Europe*
Choice - v42 - i2 - Oct 2004 - p364(1) [51-500]

Hite, Shere - *The Hite Report: A National Study of Female Sexuality*
LJ - v130 - i1 - Jan 1 2005 - p172(1) [1-50]

Hite, Sid - *The King of Slippery Falls*
c CCB-B - v57 - i11 - July-August 2004 - p469(2) [501+]
y VOYA - v27 - i3 - August 2004 - p216(1) [1-50]

Hitler, Adolf - *Hitler's Second Book: The Unpublished Sequel to Mein Kampf*
Am Spect - v37 - i3 - April 2004 - p62(2) [501+]

Hitz, Frederick P. - *The Great Game: The Myth and Reality of Espionage*
Bks & Cult - v10 - i6 - Nov-Dec 2004 - p27(3) [501+]
MEJ - v58 - i4 - Autumn 2004 - p707(1) [501+]

Hitze, Guido - *rl Ulitzka (1873-1953) oder Ohersehlesien zwischen den Weltkriegen*
JMH - v76 - i3 - Sept 2004 - p716(4) [501+]

Hjartarson, Paul - *Politics of Cultural Mediation: Baroness Elsa von Freytag-Loringhoven and Felix Paul Greve*
CBRA - Annual 2003 - p261(1) [501+]

Hlawitschka, Eduard - *Konradiner-Genealogie, unstatthafte Verwandtenehen und spatottonisch-fruhsalische Thronbesetzungspraxis*
Med R - June 2004 - pNA [501+]

HMO/PPO Directory, 2004: Detailed Profiles of U.S. Managed Healthcare Organizations and Key Decision Makers, 16th ed.
SciTech - v28 - i1 - March 2004 - p82(1) [51-500]

Ho, Alfred K. - *China's Reforms and Reformers*
Choice - v42 - i5 - Jan 2005 - p927(1) [51-500]
R&R Bk N - v19 - i3 - August 2004 - p56(1) [51-500]

Ho, Chuimei - *Splendors of China's Forbidden City: The Glorious Reign of Emperor Qianlong*
Choice - v42 - i2 - Oct 2004 - p281(1) [501+]

Ho-Kim, Q. - *Invitation to Contemporary Physics, 2nd Ed.*
SB - v40 - i6 - Nov-Dec 2004 - p249(2) [51-500]
SciTech - v28 - i1 - March 2004 - p46(1) [51-500]

Ho, Man Keung - *Family Therapy with Ethnic Minorities, 2nd Ed.*
SciTech - v28 - i1 - March 2004 - p95(1) [51-500]

Ho, Minfong - *Peek!: A Thai Hide-and-Seek (Illus. by Meade, Holly)*
c BL - v101 - i3 - Oct 1 2004 - p334(2) [51-500]
c CCB-B - v58 - i4 - Dec 2004 - p170(2) [51-500]
c HB - v80 - i6 - Nov-Dec 2004 - p697(2) [51-500]
c KR - v72 - i17 - Sept 1 2004 - p867(1) [51-500]
c SLJ - v50 - i10 - Oct 2004 - p115(1) [51-500]

Ho, Tse-Lok - *Flesers' Reagents for Organic Synthesis: Vol. 22*
SciTech - v28 - i4 - Dec 2004 - p55(1) [51-500]

Ho, Wah Kam - *English Language Teaching in East Asia Today: Changing Policies and Practices, 2nd Ed.*
R&R Bk N - v19 - i4 - Nov 2004 - p215(1) [51-500]
Language Policies and Language Education: The Impact of East Asian Countries in the Next Decade, 2nd Ed.
R&R Bk N - v19 - i4 - Nov 2004 - p48(1) [51-500]

Hoag, Tami - *Kill the Messenger (Read by Brick, Scott). Audiobook Review*
BL - v101 - i5 - Nov 1 2004 - p504(1) [51-500]
y Kliatt - v39 - i1 - Jan 2005 - p45(1) [51-500]
Kill the Messenger
BL - v100 - i21 - July 2004 - p1799(1) [51-500]
Globe & Mail - August 7 2004 - pD12 [51-500]

Hoagland, Alison K. - *Constructing Image, Identity, and Place*
Pub Hist - v26 - i3 - Summer 2004 - p80(82) [501+]
R&R Bk N - v19 - i1 - Feb 2004 - p201(1) [51-500]

Hoagland, Tony - *What Narcissism Means to Me*
BW - v34 - i36 - Sept 5 2004 - p12(1) [501+]

Hoban, Russell - *Come Dance with Me*
Spec - v297 - i9209 - Feb 5 2005 - p46(1) [501+]
Her Name Was Lola
BW - v34 - i31 - August 1 2004 - p15(1) [501+]
LJ - v129 - i12 - July 2004 - p70(1) [51-500]
NYTBR - August 8 2004 - p14 [51-500]
RCF - v24 - i3 - Fall 2004 - p134(2) [501+]

Hobart, Alice Tisdale - *Oil for the Lamps of China*
Pac A - v77 - i3 - Fall 2004 - p568(3) [501+]

Hobbes, Nicholas - *Essential Militaria*
Globe & Mail - July 31 2004 - pD13 [51-500]

Hobbie, Holly - *Toot and Puddle: The New Friend (Illus. by Hobbie, Holly)*
c KR - v72 - i14 - July 15 2004 - p687(1) [51-500]
c SLJ - v50 - i10 - Oct 2004 - p115(2) [51-500]

Hobbie, Nathaniel - *Priscilla and the Pink Planet (Illus. by Hobbie, Jocelyn)*
c KR - v72 - i20 - Oct 15 2004 - p1007(1) [51-500]
c PW - v251 - i43 - Oct 25 2004 - p47(1) [51-500]
c SLJ - v50 - i12 - Dec 2004 - p110(1) [501+]

Hobbs, Leigh - *Fiona the Pig*
c PW - v251 - i29 - July 19 2004 - p160(1) [51-500]
Old Tom's Holiday (Illus. by Hobbs, Leigh)
c KR - v72 - i16 - August 15 2004 - p807(1) [51-500]
c SLJ - v50 - i11 - Nov 2004 - p107(1) [51-500]

Hobbs, Richard - *Treasure: Finding Our Past*
R&R Bk N - v19 - i3 - August 2004 - p85(1) [51-500]

Hobbs, Thomas - *The Jewel Box Garden*
SciTech - v28 - i4 - Dec 2004 - p125 [51-500]

Hobbs, Valerie - *Letting Go of Bobby James, or, How I Found Myself of Steam*
y BL - v100 - i21 - July 2004 - p1834(1) [1-50]
y CCB-B - v58 - i2 - Oct 2004 - p78(1) [51-500]
y HB - v80 - i5 - Sept-Oct 2004 - p586(1) [51-500]
y Kliatt - v38 - i4 - July 2004 - p8(1) [51-500]
y KR - v72 - i14 - July 15 2004 - p687(1) [51-500]
PW - v251 - i29 - July 19 2004 - p163(1) [51-500]
y SLJ - v50 - i9 - Sept 2004 - p208(1) [51-500]
y VOYA - v27 - i5 - Dec 2004 - p382(1) [51-500]

Hobbs, Will - *Far North*
y Kliatt - v38 - i4 - July 2004 - p19(1) [51-500]
Jackie's Wild Seattle (Read by Nielsen, Stina). Audiobook Review
c BL - v100 - i21 - July 2004 - p1857(1) [1-50]
c Kliatt - v38 - i4 - July 2004 - p52(1) [51-500]
Jackie's Wild Seattle
Sci Teach - v71 - i4 - April 2004 - p78-78 [501+]
Leaving Protection
y VOYA - v27 - i4 - Oct 2004 - p303(1) [51-500]

Hobday, Peter - *The Girl in Rose: Haydn's Last Love*
CR - v285 - i1667 - Dec 2004 - p381(1) [51-500]
KR - v73 - i5 - March 1 2005 - p274(1) [501+]

Hobelt, Lothar - *Defiant Populist: Jorg Haider and the Politics of Austria*
GSR - v27 - i2 - May 2004 - p435-436 [501+]

Hoberg, George - *Capacity for Choice: Canada in a New North America*
R&R Bk N - v19 - i1 - Feb 2004 - p82(1) [1-50]

Hoberman, J. - *The Dream Life: Movies, Media, and the Mythology of the Sixties*
JPC - v38 - i3 - Feb 2005 - p591(3) [501+]

Hoberman, Mary Ann - *I Know an Old Lady Who Swallowed a Fly*
  c CH Bwatch - v14 - i7 - July 2004 - p4(1) [51-500]
Whose Garden Is It? (Illus. by Dyer, Jane)
  c CE - v81 - i2 - Winter 2004 - p107(1) [51-500]
Yankee Doodle
  c CH Bwatch - v14 - i7 - July 2004 - p4(1) [51-500]
You Read to Me, I'll Read to You: Very Short Fairy Tales to Read Together
    BL - v100 - i21 - July 2004 - p1840(1) [1-50]

Hobhouse, Henry - *Seeds of Wealth: Four Plants That Made Men Rich*
    BL - v101 - i6 - Nov 15 2004 - p539(1) [501+]
    Bwatch - March 2005 - pNA [51-500]
    CR - v285 - i1662 - July 2004 - p57(2) [501+]

Hobson, Anthony - *Renaissance Book Collecting: Jean Grolier and Diego Hurtado de Mendoza, Their Books and Bindings*
    BSA-P - v98 - i2 - June 2004 - p235-237 [501+]

Hobson, Charles F. - *The Papers of John Marshall, Vol. 11*
    JSH - v70 - i3 - August 2004 - p669(2) [501+]

Hobson, J. Allan - *13 Dreams Freud Never Had: The New Mind Science*
    LJ - v129 - i17 - Oct 15 2004 - p77(1) [51-500]
    PW - v251 - i46 - Nov 15 2004 - p55(1) [501+]

Hobson, John M. - *The Eastern Origins Of Western Civilisation*
    NS - v133 - i4713 - Nov 8 2004 - p48(3) [501+]

Hobson, R. Peter - *The Cradle of Thought: Exploring the Origins of Thinking*
    Choice - v42 - i5 - Jan 2005 - p937(2) [51-500]
    R&R Bk N - v19 - i3 - August 2004 - p10(1) [1-50]

Hobson, Robert W., II - *Vascular Surgery: Principles and Practice, 3rd Ed.*
    E-Streams - July 2004 - pNA [501+]

Hobson, Theo - *Against Establishment: An Anglican Polemic*
    TLS - i5265 - Feb 27 2004 - p30-30 [501+]

Hoccleve, Thomas - *A Facsimile of the Autograph Verse Manuscripts*
    RES - v55 - i220 - June 2004 - p452-453 [501+]

Hoce, Charley - *Beyond Old MacDonald: Funny Poems from Down on the Farm (Illus. by Fernandes, Eugenie)*
  c KR - v73 - i5 - March 1 2005 - p287(1) [51-500]

Hoch, James - *A Parade of Hands*
    Ant R - v63 - i1 - Wntr 2005 - p192(2) [501+]

Hochain, Serge - *Building Liberty: A Statue Is Born (Illus. by Hochain, Serge)*
  c CCB-B - v57 - i11 - July-August 2004 - p470(1) [501+]
  c LibMed - v23 - i3 - Nov-Dec 2004 - p82(1) [51-500]
  c SLJ - v50 - i8 - August 2004 - p108(2) [501+]

Hochedlinger, Michael - *Austria's Wars of Emergence: War, State, and Society in the Habsburg Monarchy, 1683-1797*
    J Mil H - v68 - i4 - Oct 2004 - p1240-1241 [501+]
    J Mil H - v68 - i4 - Oct 2004 - p1241-1242 [501+]

Hochhauser, Jennifer - *Misery Is a Spider in the Bathtub (Illus. by Rapp, Jennifer)*
  c SLJ - v51 - i2 - Feb 2005 - p97(2) [51-500]

Hochschild, Adam - *Bury the Chains: Prophets and Rebels in the Fight to Free an Empire's Slaves*
    Econ - v374 - i8412 - Feb 5 2005 - p76US [501+]
    Ent W - i801 - Jan 14 2005 - p94 [51-500]
    Globe & Mail - Jan 29 2005 - pD4 [501+]
    KR - v72 - i21 - Nov 1 2004 - p1038(2) [501+]
    Nation - v280 - i6 - Feb 14 2005 - p23 [501+]
    PW - v252 - i1 - Jan 3 2005 - p48(1) [501+]
    Spec - v297 - i9209 - Feb 5 2005 - p40(2) [501+]
Bury the Chains: Prophets, Slaves, and Rebels in the First Human Rights Crusade
    BL - v101 - i1 - Sept 1 2004 - p2(1) [51-500]
    LJ - v129 - i19 - Nov 2004 - p70(2) [501+]

Hochschild, Arlie Russell - *The Commercialization of Intimate Life: Notes from Home and Work*
    SF - v83 - i2 - Dec 2004 - p867(3) [501+]
Global Woman: Nannies, Maids and Sex Workers in the New Economy
    Dis - v51 - i2 - Spring 2004 - p90(8) [501+]

Hochschild, Jennifer L. - *The American Dream and the Public Schools*
    CS - v33 - i2 - March 2004 - p242-244 [501+]

Hochstrasser, T.J. - *Early Modern Natural Law Theories: Contexts and Strategies in the Early Enlightenment*
    R&R Bk N - v19 - i1 - Feb 2004 - pNA [51-500]

Hockenberry, Dee - *Collecting Golliwoggs: Teddy Bear's Best Friends*
    Ant&CM - v108 - i6 - August 2003 - p16(1) [501+]

Hockenbury, Don H. - *Psychology, 3rd Ed. (Illus. by Hockenbury, Sandra E.)*
    R&R Bk N - v19 - i3 - August 2004 - p8(1) [1-50]

Hocking, Jenny - *It's Time Again: Whitlam and Modern Labor*
    AJPS - v39 - i2 - July 2004 - p441(442) [501+]

Hockney, David - *Hockney's Pictures*
    Spec - v296 - Dec 18 2004 - p87(1) [501+]

Hockx, Michel - *The Literary Field of Twentieth-Century China*
    Ch Rev Int - v10 - i2 - Fall 2003 - p403(6) [501+]

Hocstrasser, T. J. - *Natural Law Theories in the Early Enlightenment*
    GSR - v27 - i1 - Feb 2004 - p140-141 [501+]

Hodaway, Simon - *Record in Stone: The Study of Australia's Flaked Stone Artefacts*
    R&R Bk N - v19 - i4 - Nov 2004 - p77(1) [51-500]

Hodder, Ian - *Archaeology Beyond Dialogue*
    Choice - v42 - i4 - Dec 2004 - p702(2) [1-50]
    R&R Bk N - v19 - i3 - August 2004 - p29(1) [1-50]

Hodder, Rupert - *Between Two Worlds: Society, Politics, and Business in the Philippines*
    JAS - v63 - i2 - May 2004 - p553(2) [501+]

Hodel, Steve - *Black Dahlia Avenger: A Genius for Murder*
    Globe & Mail - July 10 2004 - pD13 [501+]

Hodess, Robin - *Global Corruption Report, 2004*
    Choice - v42 - i4 - Dec 2004 - p730(2) [1-50]

Hodge, Bonnie MacLean - *Explorations in College Algebra and Trigonometry Using the TI 83/83 Plus/84 Plus/86, 3rd Ed.*
    SciTech - v28 - i4 - Dec 2004 - p34(1) [51-500]

Hodge, Deborah - *Emma's Story (Illus. by Zhang, Song Nan)*
  c CBRA - Annual 2003 - p452(2) [51-500]

Hodge, Jacqueline C. - *Musculoskeletal Procedures: Diagnostic and Therapeutic*
    E-Streams - Sept 2004 - pNA [501+]

Hodge, Jonathan - *The Cambridge Companion to Darwin*
    QRB - v79 - i4 - Dec 2004 - p407(2) [501+]

Hodge, Sheida - *Global Smarts: The Art of Communicating and Deal Making Anywhere in the World.*
    HR Mag - v49 - i7 - July 2004 - pS12(1) [51-500]

Hodges, Anthony - *Drawing*
  c BL - v101 - i5 - Nov 1 2004 - p496(1) [51-500]
Painting
  c BL - v101 - i5 - Nov 1 2004 - p496(1) [51-500]

Hodges, Ben - *Forbidden Acts: Pioneering Gay and Lesbian Plays of the Twentieth Century*
    R&R Bk N - v19 - i1 - Feb 2004 - p230(1) [1-50]

Hodges, Bonni C. - *Assessment and Planning in Health Programs*
    SciTech - v28 - i4 - Dec 2004 - p82(1) [501+]

Hodges, Donald - *Mexico under Siege: Popular Resistance to Presidential Despotism*
    Ams - v61 - i2 - Oct 2004 - p336(2) [501+]

Hodges, Graham Russell Gao - *Anna May Wong: From Laundryman's Daughter to Hollywood Legend*
    NYRB - v52 - i1 - Jan 13 2005 - p40(2) [501+]

Hodges, Lynn - *Dear God, It's Me! (Illus. by Bendall-Brunello, John)*
  c PW - v251 - i7 - Feb 14 2005 - p81(1) [501+]

Hodges, Margaret - *Merlin and the Making of the King (Illus. by Hyman, Trina Schart)*
  c BL - v101 - i2 - Sept 15 2004 - p241(1) [51-500]
  c KR - v72 - i15 - August 1 2004 - p742(1) [51-500]
  c PW - v251 - i32 - August 9 2004 - p251(1) [51-500]
  c SLJ - v50 - i9 - Sept 2004 - p188(1) [51-500]
  c BL - v101 - i9-10 - Jan 1 2005 - p773(1) [1-50]

Hodges, Rick - *What Muslims Think and How They Live*
  y SLJ - v50 - i10 - Oct 2004 - p188(1) [51-500]

Hodges, Tony - *Angola: Anatomy of an Oil State*
    IJAHS - v37 - i1 - 2004 - p158-160 [501+]

Hodgetts, Richard M. - *Modern Human Relations at Work*
    R&R Bk N - v19 - i3 - August 2004 - p130(1) [51-500]

Hodgins, Bruce W. - *Blockades and Resistance: Studies in Actions of Peace and the Temagami Blockades of 1988-89*
    Can Hist R - v85 - i3 - Sept 2004 - p537(4) [501+]
    CBRA - Annual 2003 - p361(2) [501+]

Hodgins, Jack - *Broken Ground*
    Mac - v117 - i45 - Nov 8 2004 - p50(1) [1-50]
Damage Done by the Storm
    BIC - v33 - i9 - Dec 2004 - p8(2) [501+]
    Globe & Mail - Oct 2 2004 - pD10 [501+]

Hodgkinson, Peter - *Capital Punishment: Strategies for Abolition*
    Law&PolBR - August 2004 - p603(3) [501+]

Hodgkinson, Tom - *How to Be Idle*
    Econ - v373 - i8397 - Oct 16 2004 - p82US [501+]
    Spec - v296 - i9188 - Sept 11 2004 - p48(1) [501+]

Hodgson, Barbara B. - *Saunders Nursing Drug Handbook 2004*
    E-Streams - June 2004 - pNA [501+]

Hodgson, Damian E. - *Management Knowledge and the New Employee*
    R&R Bk N - v19 - i3 - August 2004 - p130(1) [51-500]

Hodgson, Dorothy L. - *Once Intrepid Warriors: Gender, Ethnicity, and the Cultural Politics of Maasai Development*
    JWH - v16 - i3 - Autumn 2004 - p213(8) [501+]
'Wicked' Women and the Reconfiguration of Gender in Africa
    JGS - v13 - i2 - July 2004 - p170-171 [501+]

Hodgson, Geoffrey M. - *Evolution of Institutional Economics: Agency, Structure and Darwinism in American Institutionalism*
    R&R Bk N - v19 - i4 - Nov 2004 - p84(1) [51-500]
Recent Developments in Institutional Economics
    R&R Bk N - v19 - i1 - Feb 2004 - p78(1) [1-50]

Hodgson, Godfrey - *More Equal than Others: America from Nixon to the New Century*
    NYTBR - August 15 2004 - p13 [51-500]

Hodgson, Heather - *The Great Gift of Tears*
    Can Lit - i182 - Autumn 2004 - p183(3) [501+]

Hodgson, Katherine - *Voicing the Soviet Experience: The Poetry of O'Ga Berggol'ts*
    Choice - v41 - i11-12 - July-August 2004 - p2051(1) [501+]

Hodgson, Ken - *God's Pocket*
    BL - v100 - i22 - August 2004 - p1899(1) [51-500]
    Roundup M - v11 - i6 - August 2004 - p28(1) [501+]

Hodgson, Mona - *Bedtime in the Southwest*
  c CH Bwatch - v14 - i12 - Dec 2004 - pNA [51-500]

Hodgson, Richard G. - *La Femme au XVII siecle: actes du colloque de Vancouver, University of British*
    FS - v58 - i1 - Jan 2004 - p94(2) [501+]

Hodkinson, Ron - *Lightweight Electric/Hybrid Vehicle Design*
    SciTech - v28 - i1 - March 2004 - p167(1) [51-500]

Hodkinson, S. - *Property and Wealth in Classical Sparta*
    Class R - v53 - i2 - Nov 2003 - p397-400 [501+]

Hoe, Ban Seng - *Enduring Hardship: The Chinese Laundry in Canada*
    CBRA - Annual 2003 - p356(1) [501+]

Hoeckner, Berthold - *Programming the Absolute: Nineteenth-Century German Music and the Hermeneutics of the Moment*
    GSR - v27 - i2 - May 2004 - p383-384 [501+]
    MT - v145 - i1886 - Spring 2004 - p109-111 [501+]

Hoehner, Harold - *Ephesians: An Exegetical Commentary*
    Intpr - v59 - i1 - Jan 2005 - p94(2) [51-500]

Hoekstra, Valerie J. - *Public Reaction to Supreme Court Decisions*
    Pers PS - v33 - i4 - Fall 2004 - p234(1) [501+]

Hoel, Michael - *Recent Developments in Environmental Economics, Vols. 1-2*
    R&R Bk N - v19 - i4 - Nov 2004 - p88(1) [51-500]

Hoena, B.A. - *The Farm*
  c SLJ - v50 - i10 - Oct 2004 - p142(1) [51-500]
The Fire Station
  c SLJ - v50 - i10 - Oct 2004 - p142(1) [51-500]
The Library
  c SLJ - v50 - i10 - Oct 2004 - p142(1) [51-500]

Hoenselaars, Ton - *Shakespeare's History Plays: Performance, Translation and Adaptation in Britian and Abroad*
    Choice - v42 - i7 - March 2005 - p1232(1) [51-500]

Hoerder, Dirk - *Cultures in Contact: World Migrations in the Second Millennium*
    J Soc H - v38 - i1 - Fall 2004 - p215(3) [501+]
The Historical Practice of Diversity: Transcultural Interaction from the Early Modern Mediterranean to the Postcolonial World
    R&R Bk N - v19 - i2 - May 2004 - p130 [51-500]

Hoerig, Karl - *Under the Palace Portal: Native Amercan Artists in Sante Fe*
    Am Ind CRJ - v28 - i2 - Spring 2004 - p186(3) [501+]

Hoeveler, Diane Long - *Approaches to Teaching Gothic Fiction: The British and American Traditions*
    Choice - v41 - i11-12 - July-August 2004 - p2041(1) [501+]

Hoeveler, J. David - *Creating the American Mind: Intellect and Politics in the Colonial Colleges*
    JAH - v91 - i1 - June 2004 - p218-219 [501+]
    JSH - v70 - i3 - August 2004 - p645(2) [501+]

Hoeven, Rolph van der - *Perspectives on Growth and Poverty*
    JEL - v42 - i1 - March 2004 - p276(2) [501+]

Hoeye, Michael - *No Time Like Show Time: A Hermux Tantamoq Adventure (Read by Scott, Campbell).* Audiobook Review
    c SLJ - v51 - i2 - Feb 2005 - p75(1) [501+]
No Time Like Show Time: A Hermux Tantamoq Adventure
    c KR - v72 - i15 - August 1 2004 - p742(1) [51-500]
    y SLJ - v50 - i11 - Nov 2004 - p145(1) [51-500]
    c VOYA - v27 - i5 - Dec 2004 - p406(1) [51-500]
Time Stops for No Mouse
    c Storyworks - v12 - i2 - Oct 2004 - p7(1) [501+]

Hofbauer, Karl G. - *Pharmacotherapy of Obesity: Options and Alternatives*
    SciTech - v28 - i4 - Dec 2004 - p102(1) [51-500]

Hofer, Matthias - *Teaching Manual of Color Duplex Sonography: A Workbook on Color Duplex Ultrasound and Echocardiography*
    SciTech - v28 - i4 - Dec 2004 - p103(1) [51-500]

Hoff, Joan - *The Cooper's Wife is Missing: The Trials of Bridget Cleary*
    JWH - v16 - i3 - Autumn 2004 - p206(7) [501+]

Hoff, Mary - *Mimicry and Camouflage*
    c RT - v57 - Nov 2003 - p275 [51-500]

Hoff, R. von den - *Konstruktionen von Wirklichkeit. Bilder im Griechenland des 5. und 4. Jahrhunderts v. Chr*
    Class R - v54 - i1 - May 2004 - p228(2) [501+]

Hoffelt, Jane E. - *We Share One World (Illus. by Husted, Marty)*
    c SLJ - v50 - i9 - Sept 2004 - p162(1) [51-500]

Hoffenberg, Peter H. - *An Empire on Display*
    VS - v45 - i2 - Winter 2003 - p343 [501+]

Hoffer, Peter Charles - *The Great New York Conspiracy of 1741: Slavery, Crime, and Colonial Law*
    AHR - v109 - i3 - June 2004 - p894(2) [501+]
    JAH - v91 - i1 - June 2004 - p219-219 [501+]
Past Imperfect: Facts, Fictions, and Fraud in the writing of American History
    BW - v34 - i46 - Nov 14 2004 - p4(1) [501+]
    KR - v72 - i16 - August 15 2004 - p788(2) [501+]
    LJ - v129 - i17 - Oct 15 2004 - p73(1) [51-500]
    PW - v251 - i37 - Sept 13 2004 - p70(1) [501+]
    Wil Q - v29 - i1 - Wntr 2005 - p112(3) [501+]
Sensory Worlds in Early America
    AHR - v109 - i4 - Oct 2004 - p1223(1) [501+]
    JAH - v91 - i3 - Dec 2004 - p992(2) [501+]
    R&R Bk N - v19 - i1 - Feb 2004 - p58(1) [51-500]

Hoffman, Alice - *Blackbird House*
    Ent W - i775 - July 23 2004 - p81 [51-500]
    LJ - v129 - i12 - July 2004 - p76(1) [51-500]
    MFSF - v108 - i1 - Jan 2005 - p31(5) [501+]
    People - v62 - i4 - July 26 2004 - p47 [51-500]
    SLJ - v51 - i2 - Feb 2005 - p156(1) [51-500]
    TLS - i5289 - August 13 2004 - p20(1) [501+]
Green Angel
    y Kliatt - v38 - i5 - Sept 2004 - p30(2) [51-500]
The Ice Queen (Read by Travis, Nancy). Audiobook Review
    KR - v73 - i5 - March 1 2005 - p249(1) [501+]
    LJ - v129 - i20 - Dec 1 2004 - p88(1) [1-50]
Moondog (Illus. by Heo, Yumi)
    c KR - v72 - i13 - July 1 2004 - p631(1) [51-500]
    c PW - v251 - i32 - August 9 2004 - p248(1) [51-500]
    c SLJ - v50 - i10 - Oct 2004 - p118(1) [51-500]
The Probable Future
    y Kliatt - v38 - i4 - July 2004 - p19(1) [51-500]
    NYTBR - July 18 2004 - p20 [501+]
Property Of
    BL - v101 - i6 - Nov 15 2004 - p557(1) [501+]

Hoffman, Cheryl M. - *Comprehensive Reference Manual for Signers and Interpreters, 5th Ed.*
    R&R Bk N - v19 - i1 - Feb 2004 - p139(1) [51-500]

Hoffman, Daniel - *Darkening Water*
    HR - v55 - Winter 2003 - p671 [501+]

Hoffman, Don - *A Counting Book with Billy and Abigail (Illus. by Dakins, Todd)*
    c SLJ - v50 - i7 - July 2004 - p77(1) [51-500]
Good Morning, Good Night: Billy and Abigail (Illus. by Dakins, Todd)
    c SLJ - v50 - i7 - July 2004 - p77(1) [51-500]

Hoffman, Eva - *After Such Knowledge: Memory, History, and the Legacy of the Holocaust*
    Biomag - v27 - i4 - Fall 2004 - p845(3) [501+]
    BW - v34 - i5 - Feb 1 2004 - p12(1) [501+]
    TLS - i5286 - July 23 2004 - p23(1) [501+]
    Wom R Bks - v21 - i12 - Sept 2004 - p24(2) [501+]

Hoffman, Frank J. - *Breaking Barriers: Essays in Asian and Comparative Philosophy*
    Choice - v42 - i2 - Oct 2004 - p305(1) [51-500]

Hoffman, Frank W. - *Encyclopedia of Recorded Sound, 2nd Ed.*
    Choice - v42 - i7 - March 2005 - p1200(1) [51-500]

Hoffman, James V. - *The Texts in Elementary Classrooms*
    R&R Bk N - v19 - i4 - Nov 2004 - p181(1) [51-500]

Hoffman, Jilliane - *Retribution (Read by Mazur, Kathe).* Audiobook Review
    LJ - v129 - i13 - August 2004 - p128(2) [51-500]
Retribution
    BooChiTr - Jan 25 2004 - p2(1) [501+]

Hoffman, Joan Serra - *Youth Violence, Resilience and Rehabilitation*
    R&R Bk N - v19 - i3 - August 2004 - p170(1) [501+]

Hoffman, Joel M. - *In the Beginning: A Short History of the Hebrew Language*
    TLS - i5302 - Nov 12 2004 - p30(1) [51-500]

Hoffman, Joseph F. - *Annual Review of Physiology 2004*
    QRB - v79 - i4 - Dec 2004 - p409(1) [501+]

Hoffman, Joshua - *The Divine Attributes*
    Theol St - v65 - i3 - Sept 2004 - p688(1) [501+]

Hoffman, K. Douglas - *Marketing Principles and Best Practices, 3rd Ed.*
    R&R Bk N - v19 - i2 - May 2004 - p114(1) [1-50]

Hoffman, Kurt - *System Integration: From Transistor Design to Large Scale Integrated Circuits*
    SciTech - v28 - i3 - Sept 2004 - p161(1) [51-500]

Hoffman, Lance H. - *First Exposure to Emergency Medicine*
    SciTech - v28 - i3 - Sept 2004 - p90(1) [1-50]

Hoffman, Lawrence A. - *What You Will See Inside a Synagogue (Illus. by Aron, Bill)*
    c BL - v101 - i9-10 - Jan 1 2005 - p849(1) [1-50]
    KR - v72 - i24 - Dec 15 2004 - p1202(1) [51-500]
    c SLJ - v51 - i2 - Feb 2005 - p120(1) [51-500]

Hoffman, Lily M. - *Cities and Visitors: Regulating People, Markets, and City Space*
    R&R Bk N - v19 - i1 - Feb 2004 - p68(1) [501+]

Hoffman, Mary - *The Color of Home (Illus. by Littlewood, Karin)*
    c RT - v57 - Nov 2003 - p272 [51-500]
    c RT - v57 - Dec 2003 - p395 [51-500]
How to Be a Cat (Illus. by Martins, Pam)
    c SLJ - v51 - i1 - Jan 2005 - p94(1) [51-500]
Lines in the Sand: New Writing on War and Peace
    y VOYA - v27 - i4 - Oct 2004 - p327(2) [501+]
Seven Wonders of the Ancient World (Illus. by Robertson, M. P.)
    c SLJ - v50 - i8 - August 2004 - p110(1) [51-500]
Stravaganza: City of Masks
    y Kliatt - v39 - i1 - Jan 2005 - p20(1) [51-500]
    y PW - v251 - i40 - Oct 4 2004 - p90(1) [1-50]

Hoffman, Nick - *Tropic of Murder*
    BW - v34 - i39 - Sept 26 2004 - p10(1) [501+]

Hoffman, Paul - *Wings of Madness: Alberto Santos-Dumont and the Invention of Flight*
    y Kliatt - v38 - i5 - Sept 2004 - p41(2) [501+]
    y NYTBR - August 1 2004 - p16 [501+]

Hoffman, Robert V. - *Organic Chemistry: An Intermediate Text, 2nd Ed.*
    SciTech - v28 - i4 - Dec 2004 - p55(1) [51-500]

Hoffman, Roy - *Chicken Dreaming Corn*
    Ent W - i786 - Oct 1 2004 - p79 [51-500]
    KR - v72 - i15 - August 1 2004 - p705(1) [51-500]

Hoffman, Steven J. - *Race, Class and Power in the Building of Richmond, 1870-1920*
    Bl S - v34 - i3 - Fall 2004 - p73-73 [501+]
    R&R Bk N - v19 - i4 - Nov 2004 - p62(1) [51-500]

Hoffman, Susanna - *The Olive and the Caper: Adventures in Greek Cooking*
    PW - v251 - i27 - July 5 2004 - p52(2) [501+]

Hoffman, Susanna M. - *Catastrophe and Culture: The Anthropology of Disaster*
    JRAI - v10 - i4 - Dec 2004 - p920(2) [501+]

Hoffman, William H. - *West Federal Taxation: Corporations, Partnerships, Estates, and Trusts, 2005 Ed.*
    R&R Bk N - v19 - i3 - August 2004 - p204(1) [1-50]

West Federal Taxation: Individual Income Taxes, 2005 Ed.
    R&R Bk N - v19 - i3 - August 2004 - p204(1) [1-50]

Hoffmann, Banesh - *Albert Einstein: Creator and Rebel*
    Astron - v33 - i2 - Feb 2005 - p100 [501+]

Hoffmann, Charlotte - *Trilingualism in Family, School, and Community*
    R&R Bk N - v19 - i1 - Feb 2004 - p212 [51-500]

Hoffmann, David L. - *Stalinist Values: The Cultural Norms of Soviet Modernity, 1917-1941*
    AHR - v109 - i3 - June 2004 - p1009(2) [501+]
    Choice - v41 - i7 - March 2004 - p1351(1) [501+]
    Slav R - v63 - i3 - Fall 2004 - p659-660 [501+]

Hoffmann, Dierk - *Aufbau und Krise der Planwirtschaft: Die Arbeitskraftelenkung in der SBZ/DDR 1945 bis 1963*
    Slav R - v63 - i4 - Winter 2004 - p855(3) [501+]
Die DDR unter Ulbricht: Gewaltsame Neuordnung und gescheiterte Modernisierung
    HNet - June 2004 - pNA [501+]

Hoffmann, E.T.A. - *Nutcracker (Illus. by Zwerger, Lisbeth)*
    c BL - v101 - i3 - Oct 1 2004 - p328(1) [51-500]
    c HB - v80 - i6 - Nov-Dec 2004 - p660(2) [51-500]

Hoffmann-Eifert, Susanne - *Ferroelectric Thin Films XII: Proceedings*
    SciTech - v28 - i3 - Sept 2004 - p139(1) [51-500]

Hoffmann, Elizabeth A. - *In Litigation: Do the "Haves" Still Come out Ahead?*
    CS - v33 - i5 - Sept 2004 - p592-593 [501+]

Hoffmann, Frank W. - *Encyclopedia of Recorded Sound, 2nd Ed., Vols. 1-2*
    LJ - v129 - i19 - Nov 15 2004 - p85(1) [51-500]

Hoffmann, Karl - *Erwin Rommel*
    Bwatch - Oct 2004 - pNA [51-500]

Hoffmann, Nancy E. - *America's Curious Botanist: A Tercentennial Reappraisal of John Bartram, 1699-1777*
    Choice - v42 - i7 - March 2005 - p1251(2) [51-500]
    SciTech - v28 - i4 - Dec 2004 - p12(1) [1-50]

Hoffmann, Peter - *Stauffenberg: A Family History, 1905-1944, 2nd Ed.*
    CBRA - Annual 2003 - p49(2) [51-500]
    R&R Bk N - v19 - i3 - August 2004 - p43(1) [51-500]

Hoffmeyer-Zlotnik, Jurgen H.P. - *Advances in Cross-National Comparison: A European Working Book for Demographic and Socio-Economic Variables*
    CS - v33 - i5 - Sept 2004 - p624-624 [501+]

Hofmann, Gert - *Lichtenberg and the Little Flower Girl*
    NYRB - v51 - i13 - August 12 2004 - p43(2) [501+]
    TLS - i5286 - July 23 2004 - p22(1) [501+]
Schweigende Tropen: Studien zu einer Asthetik der Ohnmacht
    Ger Q - v77 - i4 - Fall 2004 - p515-516 [501+]

Hofmann, Jerry - *Jerry Hofmann on Final Cut Pro*
    SciTech - v28 - i1 - March 2004 - p176(1) [51-500]

Hofmann, Paul - *Vatican's Women: Female Influence in the Holy See*
    R&R Bk N - v19 - i1 - Feb 2004 - p24(1) [1-50]

Hofmann-Randall, Christina - *Die Einblattdrucke der Universitatsbibliothek Erlangen-Nurnberg*
    GSR - v27 - i3 - Oct 2004 - p603(3) [501+]

Hofmann, Thomas - *Challenges in Taste Chemistry and Biology*
    SciTech - v28 - i1 - March 2004 - p174(1) [51-500]

Hofmeester, Karin - *Jewish Workers and the Labour Movement: A Comparative Study of Amsterdam, London and Paris, 1870-1914*
    R&R Bk N - v19 - i3 - August 2004 - p116(1) [51-500]

Hofmeyr, Diane - *The Star-Bearer: A Creation Myth from Ancient Egypt*
    c Teach Lib - v32 - i1 - Oct 2004 - p22(1) [51-500]

Hofmeyr, Isabel - *The Portable Bunyan: A Transnational History of 'The Pilgrim's Progress'*
    Lon R Bks - v26 - i24 - Dec 16 2004 - p11(4) [501+]

Hofrichter, Richard - *Health and Social Justice: Politics, Ideology, and Inequity in the Distribution of Disease, a Public Health Reader*
    SciTech - v28 - i1 - March 2004 - p82(1) [51-500]

Hofschroer, Peter - *Wellington's Smallest Victory: The Duke, the Model Maker and the Secret of Waterloo*
    Lon R Bks - v27 - i1 - Jan 6 2005 - p29(2) [501+]
    Spec - v295 - i9181 - July 24 2004 - p37(1) [501+]

Hofstra, Warren R. - *The Planting of New Virginia: Settlement and Landscape in the Shenandoah Valley*
Choice - v42 - i5 - Jan 2005 - p916(1) [1-50]
R&R Bk N - v19 - i3 - August 2004 - p73(1) [51-500]
W&M Q - v61 - i4 - Oct 2004 - p759-761 [501+]

Hogan, Chuck - *Prince of Thieves*
BW - v34 - i36 - Sept 5 2004 - p12(1) [501+]
KR - v72 - i13 - July 1 2004 - p597(1) [501+]

Hogan, James F. - *Groundwater Recharge in a Desert Environment: The Southwestern United States*
SciTech - v28 - i4 - Dec 2004 - p5(1) [1-50]

Hogan, John P. - *Credible Signs of Christ Alive: Case Studies from the Catholic Campaign for Human Development*
HNet - Sept 2004 - pNA [501+]
R&R Bk N - v19 - i1 - Feb 2004 - p126(1) [51-500]
Theol St - v66 - i1 - March 2005 - p235(2) [501+]

Hogan, Linda - *Face to Face: Women Writers on Faith, Mysticism, and Awakening*
Parabola - v29 - i4 - Winter 2004 - p100-106 [501+]
PW - v251 - i30 - July 26 2004 - p50(1) [501+]

Hogan, Mary - *The Serious Kiss*
y KR - v72 - i24 - Dec 15 2004 - p1202(1) [51-500]
y PW - v252 - i3 - Jan 17 2005 - p57(1) [51-500]
y SLJ - v51 - i1 - Jan 2005 - p130(1) [51-500]

Hogan, Patrick Colm - *Empire and Poetic Voice: Cognitive and Culture Studies of Literacy Tradition and Colonialism*
Choice - v41 - i11-12 - July-August 2004 - p2044(1) [501+]

Hogan, Richard - *The Failure of Planning: Permitting Sprawl in San Diego Suburbs, 1970-1999*
AJS - v110 - i3 - Nov 2004 - p795(3) [501+]

Hogeland, Lisa Maria - *The Aunt Lute Anthology of U.S. Women Writers, Vol. 1*
LJ - v130 - i2 - Feb 1 2005 - p78(1) [51-500]

Hogg, Michael - *The Sage Handbook of Social Psychology*
R&R Bk N - v19 - i1 - Feb 2004 - p121(1) [51-500]

Hogg, Tracy - *The Baby Whisperer Solves All Your Problems (By Teaching You How to Ask the Right Questions): Sleeping, Feeding, and Behavior--Beyond the Basics from Infancy through Toddlerhood*
LJ - v130 - i2 - Feb 1 2005 - p111(1) [51-500]
The Baby Whisperer Solves All Your Problems: Sleeping, Feeding, and Behavior--Beyond the Basics from Infancy through Toddlerhood
PW - v252 - i3 - Jan 17 2005 - p49(2) [51-500]

Hoggart, Richard - *Everyday Language and Everyday Life*
TimHES - v0 - i1650 - July 23 2004 - p28(1) [501+]
Mass Media in a Mass Society: Myth and Reality
Choice - v42 - i4 - Dec 2004 - p654(1) [1-50]
TLS - i5296 - Oct 1 2004 - p24-25 [501+]

Hoghughi, Masud - *Handbook of Parenting: Theory and Research for Practice*
R&R Bk N - v19 - i3 - August 2004 - p150(1) [51-500]

Hohendahl, Peter Uwe - *Patriotism, Cosmpolitanism, and National Culture: Public Culture in Hamburg, 1700-1933*
R&R Bk N - v19 - i1 - Feb 2004 - p247(1) [51-500]

Hohmuth, Jurgen - *Labyrinths and Mazes*
SciTech - v28 - i3 - Sept 2004 - p130(1) [51-500]

Hohn, Maria - *GIs and Frauleins: The German-American Encounter in 1950s West Germany*
CEH - v37 - i3 - Summer 2004 - p487(3) [501+]
JMH - v76 - i3 - Sept 2004 - p730(3) [501+]

Hohpe, Gregor - *Enterprise Integration Patterns: Designing, Building, and Deploying Messaging Solutions*
SciTech - v28 - i1 - March 2004 - p153(1) [51-500]

Hoig, Stan - *Western Odyssey of John Simpson Smith: Frontiersman and Indian Interpreter*
Roundup M - v12 - i1 - Oct 2004 - p23(2) [51-500]

Hojrup, Thomas - *State, Culture and Life-Modes: The Foundations of Life-Mode Analysis*
CS - v33 - i5 - Sept 2004 - p624-624 [501+]

Hojte, J.M. - *Images of Ancestors*
Class R - v54 - i2 - Nov 2004 - p482(2) [501+]

Hoke, Ahmed - *@Large*
y Kliatt - v38 - i5 - Sept 2004 - p35(2) [501+]

Hol, Eugenie M.J.H. - *Empirical Studies on Volatility in International Stock Markets*
R&R Bk N - v19 - i1 - Feb 2004 - p119(1) [51-500]

Holbeche, Linda - *Aligning Human Resources and Business Strategy*
HR Mag - v50 - i2 - Feb 2005 - pNA [501+]

Holbrook, Gretchen - *Black Victorians, Black Victoriana*
VS - v46 - i4 - Summer 2004 - p696(3) [501+]

Holcomb, Brent H. - *Marriages of Granville County, North Carolina, 1753-1868*
EFHM - v58 - i2 - March-April 2004 - p90(1) [51-500]
York County, South Carolina, Will Abstracts, 1787-1862
EFHM - v58 - i2 - March-April 2004 - p91(1) [51-500]

Holcomb, Julie - *Southern Sons, Northern Soldiers: The Civil War Letters of the Remley Brothers, 22nd Iowa Infantry*
J Mil H - v68 - i4 - Oct 2004 - p1261-1262 [501+]

Holdcroft, Tina - *Hidden Depths: Amazing Underwater Discoveries*
Res Links - v10 - i2 - Dec 2004 - p27(1) [51-500]
Hidden Treasure: Amazing Stories of Discovery
c CBRA - Annual 2003 - p536(1) [51-500]

Holden, A.J. - *History of William Marshal*
FS - v58 - i3 - July 2004 - p396-397 [501+]

Holden, Anthony - *The Wit in the Dungeon: A Life of Leigh Hunt*
Econ - v374 - i8411 - Jan 29 2005 - p81US [501+]
Spec - v297 - i9211 - Feb 19 2005 - p35(2) [501+]

Holden, Charles J. - *In the Great Maelstrom: Conservatives in Post-Civil War South Carolina*
AHR - v109 - i4 - Oct 2004 - p1235(2) [501+]

Holden, Clive - *Trains of Winnipeg*
CBRA - Annual 2003 - p219(2) [51-500]

Holden, Colin - *Church in a Landscape: A History of the Diocese of Wangaratta*
AHS - v35 - i123 - April 2004 - p197-197 [501+]

Holden, Craig - *The Narcissist's Daughter*
BL - v101 - i7 - Dec 1 2004 - p634(2) [51-500]
KR - v72 - i23 - Dec 1 2004 - p1107(1) [501+]
LJ - v130 - i3 - Feb 15 2005 - p116(1) [51-500]
PW - v252 - i3 - Jan 17 2005 - p35(1) [51-500]

Holden, Geoffrey - *Thermoplastic Elastomers, 3rd Ed.*
SciTech - v28 - i4 - Dec 2004 - p170(1) [51-500]

Holden, Greg - *eBay PowerUser's Bible*
LJ - v129 - i14 - Sept 1 2004 - p182(1) [501+]
How To Do Everything with eBay
LJ - v129 - i14 - Sept 1 2004 - p182(1) [501+]
R&R Bk N - v19 - i4 - Nov 2004 - p111(1) [51-500]

Holden, Henry M. - *Living and Working Aboard the International Space Station*
c BL - v101 - i3 - Oct 1 2004 - p325(1) [51-500]
c SLJ - v51 - i2 - Feb 2005 - p147(2) [51-500]
The Tragedy of the Space Shuttle Challenger
c SLJ - v51 - i2 - Feb 2005 - p147(2) [51-500]

Holden, Len - *Vauxhall Motors and the Luton Economy, 1900-2002*
BHR - v78 - i2 - Summer 2004 - p346(3) [501+]

Holden, Mark - *The Use and Abuse of Office Politics: How To Survive and Thrive in the Corporate Jungle*
LJ - v129 - i12 - July 2004 - p95(1) [51-500]

Holden, Philip - *Imperial Desire: Dissident Sexualities and Colonial Literature*
ELT - v47 - i3 - Summer 2004 - p339(4) [501+]

Holden, Robert H. - *Armies Without Nations: Public Violence and State Formation in Central America, 1821-1960*
Choice - v42 - i4 - Dec 2004 - p718(1) [1-50]

Holden, Wendy - *The Wives of Bath*
Spec - v297 - i9207 - Jan 22 2005 - p38(1) [501+]

Holder, Julian - *The Architecture of British Transport in the 20th Century*
NS - v133 - i4712 - Nov 1 2004 - p54(2) [501+]

Holder, Nancy - *Spirited*
Kliatt - v38 - i6 - Nov 2004 - p22(1) [51-500]
y KR - v72 - i22 - Nov 15 2004 - p1090(1) [51-500]

Holder, R.W. - *The Dictionary Men: Their Lives and Times*
Spec - v296 - i9198 - Nov 20 2004 - p47(2) [501+]

Holderlin, Johann Christian Friedrich - *Poems and Fragments*
Lon R Bks - v26 - i18 - Sept 23 2004 - p21(2) [501+]

Holding, Elisabeth Sanxay - *Death Wish: Net of Cobwebs*
DroRevMy - v24 - i4 - July-August 2004 - p1(2) [501+]

Holdstock, Pauline - *Beyond Measure*
Globe & Mail - Nov 27 2004 - pD3 [51-500]
Mortal Distractions
Globe & Mail - Nov 20 2004 - pD30 [51-500]
A Rare and Curious Gift
BL - v101 - i9-10 - Jan 1 2005 - p817(2) [1-50]
KR - v72 - i23 - Dec 1 2004 - p1107(2) [501+]
NYTBR - March 6 2005 - p17 [501+]
PW - v251 - i45 - Nov 8 2004 - p32(1) [501+]

Holdstock, Robert - *Celtika*
y Kliatt - v38 - i5 - Sept 2004 - p30(2) [51-500]

Holeman, Linda - *The Linnet Bird*
Globe & Mail - Oct 9 2004 - pD23 [501+]
Search of the Moon King's Daughter
y Can CL - i111-112 - Fall-Winter 2003 - p128(7) [501+]
Toxic Love
y CBRA - Annual 2003 - p489(1) [51-500]

Holguin, Sandie - *Creating Spaniards: Culture and National Identity in Republican Spain*
HNet - Nov 2004 - pNA [501+]
JMH - v77 - i1 - March 2005 - p208(3) [501+]

Holick, Michael G. - *Nutrition and Bone Health*
SciTech - v28 - i3 - Sept 2004 - p68(1) [51-500]

Holiday, Billie - *God Bless the Child (Illus. by Pinkney, Jerry)*
c SLJ - v50 - i10 - Oct 2004 - p21(1) [51-500]

Holidays around the World
SLJ - v50 - i12 - Dec 2004 - p62(2) [501+]

Holidays on the Net
SLJ - v50 - i12 - Dec 2004 - p63(1) [501+]

Holifield, E. Brooks - *Theology in America: Christian Thought from the Age of the Puritans to the Civil war*
AHR - v109 - i4 - Oct 2004 - p1265-1266 [501+]
CH - v73 - i3 - Sept 2004 - p666(16) [501+]
Intpr - v59 - i1 - Jan 2005 - p78(3) [501+]
JAH - v91 - i2 - Sept 2004 - p607(2) [501+]
RAH - v32 - i1 - March 2004 - p1(6) [501+]
TLS - i5263 - Feb 13 2004 - p24-24 [501+]
TT - v61 - i2 - July 2004 - p250(5) [501+]

Holl, Augustin - *The Land of Houlouf: Genesis of a Chadic Polity, 1900 B.C.-A.D. 1800*
Am Ant - v70 - i1 - Jan 2005 - p194(2) [501+]
Saharan Rock Art: Archaeology of Tassilian Pastoralist Iconography
R&R Bk N - v19 - i3 - August 2004 - p85(1) [51-500]

Holladay, Hilary - *Wild Blessings: The Poetry of Lucille Clifton*
Choice - v42 - i6 - Feb 2005 - p1023(1) [51-500]

Holland, Barbara - *When All the World Was Young: A Memoir*
KR - v73 - i2 - Jan 15 2005 - p101(1) [501+]
NYTBR - March 6 2005 - p25 [501+]
PW - v252 - i5 - Jan 31 2005 - p57(1) [51-500]

Holland, Cecilia - *The Soul Thief*
y Kliatt - v38 - i4 - July 2004 - p30(1) [51-500]

Holland-Crossley, Kevin - *How Many Miles to Bethlehem? (Illus. by Malone, Peter)*
c R Today - v22 - i3 - Dec 2004 - p28(1) [501+]

Holland, Eric C. - *Mouse Models of Cancer*
SciTech - v28 - i4 - Dec 2004 - p92(1) [51-500]

Holland, Gini - *I Live in a Town/Vivo en un pueblo*
c SLJ - v50 - i9 - Sept 2004 - p196(1) [1-50]
I Live in the Country/Vivo en el campo
c SLJ - v50 - i9 - Sept 2004 - p196(1) [1-50]
I Live in the Desert/Vivo en el desierto
c SLJ - v50 - i9 - Sept 2004 - p196(1) [1-50]

Holland, H.D. - *Treatise on Geochemistry*
Choice - v42 - i1 - Sept 2004 - p135(1) [501+]

Holland, Joe - *Modern Catholic Social Teaching: The Popes Confront the Industrial Age, 1740-1958*
CHR - v90 - i3 - July 2004 - p520(2) [501+]

Holland, John - *Designing Mobile Autonomous Robots*
Choice - v42 - i3 - Nov 2004 - p514(1) [1-50]

Holland, Martin - *Common Foreign and Security Policy: The First Ten Years, 2nd Ed.*
R&R Bk N - v19 - i4 - Nov 2004 - p174(1) [501+]

Holland, Max - *The Kennedy Assassination Tapes: The White House Conversations of Lyndon B. Johnson Regarding the Assassination, the Warren Commission, and the Aftermath*
BL - v101 - i1 - Sept 1 2004 - p28(1) [51-500]
KR - v72 - i15 - August 1 2004 - p726(1) [501+]
NYTBR - Oct 31 2004 - p14 [501+]
PW - v251 - i28 - July 12 2004 - p56(1) [51-500]
RAH - v32 - i4 - Dec 2004 - p580-590 [501+]

The Kennedy Assassination Tapes:The White House Conversations of Lyndon B. Johnson Regarding the Assassinan Tapes
   BW - v34 - i38 - Sept 19 2004 - p5(1) [501+]
The Presidential Recordings: Lyndon B. Johnson: The Kennedy Assassination and the Transfer of Power, November 1963-January 1964
   LJ - v129 - i20 - Dec 1 2004 - p92(1) [51-500]
Holland, Merlin - *The Real Trial of Oscar Wilde: With an Introduction and Commentary*
   ELT - v47 - i3 - Summer 2004 - p352(4) [501+]
Holland, Patricia - *Picturing Childhood: The Myth of the Child in Popular Imagery*
   TES - v0 - i4576 - March 26 2004 - psss18(2) [501+]
Holland, Penny - *We Don't Play with Guns Here: War, Weapon, and Superhero Play in the Early Years*
   R&R Bk N - v19 - i1 - Feb 2004 - p130(1) [51-500]
Holland, Richard - *Augustus: Godfather of Europe*
   CR - v286 - i1668 - Jan 2005 - p60(1) [51-500]
Holland, Robert Gray - *To Build a Better Teacher: The Emergence of a Competitive Education Industry*
   R&R Bk N - v19 - i3 - August 2004 - p219(1) [1-50]
Holland, Sally - *Child and Family Assessment in Social Work Practice*
   R&R Bk N - v19 - i3 - August 2004 - p160(1) [51-500]
Holland, Tom - *Rubicon: The Last Years of the Roman Republic*
   Choice - v42 - i2 - Oct 2004 - p348(1) [51-500]
Hollander, Anthony P. - *Biopolymer Methods in Tissue Engineering*
   SciTech - v28 - i1 - March 2004 - p80(1) [51-500]
Hollander, John - *American Poetry (Illus. by Comport, Sally Wern)*
  c BW - v34 - i31 - August 1 2004 - p11(1) [51-500]
  c SLJ - v50 - i8 - August 2004 - p137(2) [51-500]
Poetry for Young People: Animal Poems (Illus. by Mulazzani, Simona)
  c KR - v72 - i24 - Dec 15 2004 - p1202(1) [51-500]
  c PW - v252 - i5 - Jan 31 2005 - p70(1) [51-500]
Hollander, Malika - *Brazil, the Culture*
  c CBRA - Annual 2003 - p547(2) [51-500]
Brazil, the Land
  c CBRA - Annual 2003 - p547(2) [501+]
Brazil, the People
  c CBRA - Annual 2003 - p547(2) [501+]
Hollander, Paul - *Understanding Anti-Americanism: Its Origins and Impact at Home and Abroad*
   Choice - v42 - i6 - Feb 2005 - p1075(1) [51-500]
   R&R Bk N - v19 - i3 - August 2004 - p70(1) [51-500]
Hollas, J. Michael - *Modern Spectroscopy*
   Choice - v42 - i1 - Sept 2004 - p134(1) [501+]
Hollein, Max - *Julian Schnabel: Malerei/Paintings 1978-2003*
   LJ - v129 - i17 - Oct 15 2004 - p60(1) [51-500]
Holleman, Marybeth - *The Heart of the Sound*
   E Mag - v15 - i4 - July-August 2004 - p61(1) [501+]
Hollen, Cecilia Van - *Birth on the Threshold: Childbirth and Modernity in South India*
   MAQ - v18 - i3 - Sept 2004 - p399-402 [501+]
Hollen, Kathryn H. - *The Reproductive System*
   SciTech - v28 - i4 - Dec 2004 - p110(1) [51-500]
Hollenbach, David - *Global Face of Public Faith: Politics, Human Rights, and Christian Ethics*
   R&R Bk N - v19 - i1 - Feb 2004 - p10(1) [51-500]
Hollenbeck, Josette - *Apercu Culturel de Films Francophones*
   R&R Bk N - v19 - i3 - August 2004 - p260(1) [51-500]
Hollender, Jeffrey - *What Matters Most: How a Small Group of Pioneers is Teaching Social Responsibility to Big Business, and Why Big Business is Listening*
   Choice - v42 - i1 - Sept 2004 - p150(1) [501+]
   Per Psy - v57 - i4 - Winter 2004 - p1065(4) [501+]
Hollensen, Svend - *Global Marketing: A Decision-Oriented Approach, 3rd Ed.*
   TimHES - v0 - i1680 - Feb 25 2005 - pIX(1) [501+]
Holley, William H. - *The Labor Relations Process, 8th Ed.*
   R&R Bk N - v19 - i4 - Nov 2004 - p104(1) [51-500]
Holliday, Alesia - *American Idle*
   BL - v100 - i22 - August 2004 - p1909(1) [51-500]
   LJ - v129 - i13 - August 2004 - p55(1) [51-500]
   PW - v251 - i30 - July 26 2004 - p38(2) [501+]
Holliday, Barbara - *To Be A Cowboy*
   Bwatch - v26 - i9 - Sept 2004 - p2(1) [51-500]

Holliday, Vance T. - *Soils in Archaeological Research*
   R&R Bk N - v19 - i4 - Nov 2004 - p30(1) [51-500]
Hollihan, Tony - *Crazy Horse: Spirit of the Sioux*
   CBRA - Annual 2003 - p365(1) [51-500]
Great Chiefs
   CBRA - Annual 2003 - p365(1) [51-500]
   SHQ - v107 - i4 - April 2004 - p619(2) [501+]
Mountain Men: Frontier Adventurers Alone Against the Wilderness
   R&R Bk N - v19 - i3 - August 2004 - p75(1) [51-500]
Hollin, Clive R. - *Essential Handbook of Offender Assessment and Treatment*
   E-Streams - Sept 2004 - pNA [501+]
Holling, Holling Clancy - *Paddle-to-the-Sea (Read by Bregy, Terry). Audiobook Review*
  c BL - v100 - i22 - August 2004 - p1954(1) [51-500]
  c SLJ - v50 - i10 - Oct 2004 - pS54(1) [51-500]
Hollinghurst, Alan - *The Line of Beauty*
   BL - v101 - i4 - Oct 15 2004 - p389(1) [51-500]
   BW - v34 - i39 - Sept 26 2004 - p15(1) [501+]
   G&L Rev W - v11 - i6 - Nov-Dec 2004 - p35(2) [501+]
   Globe & Mail - Oct 9 2004 - pD14 [501+]
   KR - v72 - i16 - August 15 2004 - p765(1) [501+]
   Lam Bk Rpt - v13 - i4-5 - Nov-Dec 2004 - p34(2) [501+]
   Mac - v117 - i46 - Nov 15 2004 - p129(3) [501+]
   New R - Dec 13 2004 - p47 [501+]
   NS - v133 - i4716 - Nov 29 2004 - p43(1) [51-500]
   NS - v133 - i4716 - Nov 29 2004 - p43(2) [51-500]
   NY - v80 - i33 - Nov 1 2004 - p105(1) [51-500]
   NYRB - v52 - i1 - Jan 13 2005 - p6(3) [501+]
   NYTBR - Oct 31 2004 - p19 [501+]
   PW - v251 - i38 - Sept 20 2004 - p46(1) [501+]
   Advocate - Dec 7 2004 - p73(1) [501+]
   Ent W - i789 - Oct 22 2004 - p98 [501+]
Hollingshead, Greg - *Bedlam*
   Globe & Mail - August 28 2004 - pD6 [501+]
   Globe & Mail - Nov 27 2004 - pD3 [51-500]
Hollingsworth, A.B. - *University Boulevard*
   KR - v72 - i17 - Sept 1 2004 - p825(1) [501+]
   PW - v251 - i39 - Sept 27 2004 - p38(1) [51-500]
Hollingsworth, Amy - *The Simple Faith of Mister Rogers: Spiritual Insights*
   PW - v252 - i7 - Feb 14 2005 - p73(1) [51-500]
Hollingsworth, J. Rogers - *Advancing Socio-Economics: An Institutionalist Perspective*
   CS - v33 - i2 - March 2004 - p188-189 [501+]
Hollingsworth, Margaret - *Be Quiet*
  y BIC - v33 - i5 - August 2004 - p30(2) [501+]
Hollingsworth, Mary - *Art in World History*
   BL - v100 - i21 - July 2004 - p1860(2) [501+]
   LibMed - v23 - i3 - Nov-Dec 2004 - p77(1) [51-500]
   R&R Bk N - v19 - i2 - May 2004 - p194(1) [51-500]
The Cardinal's Hat: Money, Ambition and Housekeeping in a Renaissance Court
   TLS - i5290 - August 20 2004 - p25(1) [501+]
Hollis, Matthew - *Ground Water*
   TLS - i5287 - July 30 2004 - p28(1) [51-500]
Hollis, Selwyn L. - *A Mathematical Companion for Differential Equations*
   SciTech - v28 - i3 - Sept 2004 - p39(1) [51-500]
Holloran, Peter C. - *Historical Dictionary of New England*
   Choice - v41 - i11-12 - July-August 2004 - p2026(1) [501+]
   JouAmCul - v27 - i3 - Sept 2004 - p340(2) [501+]
Hollos, Marida - *Scandal in a Small Town: Understanding Modern Hungary through the Stories of Three Families*
   E-A St - v56 - i3 - May 2004 - p473(4) [501+]
Holloway, Brenda Walters - *Nurse's Fast Facts: Your Quick Source for Core Clinical Content, 3rd Ed.*
   SciTech - v28 - i3 - Sept 2004 - p126(1) [51-500]
Holloway, Brian - *Interpreting the Legacy: John Neihardt and Black Elk Speaks*
   Am Ind CRJ - v27 - i4 - Fall 2003 - p159-161 [501+]
Holloway, Brian R. - *Technical Writing Basics: A Guide to Style and Form, 3rd Ed.*
   SciTech - v28 - i3 - Sept 2004 - p13(1) [51-500]
Holloway, Joel Ellis - *Dictionary of Birds of the United States*
   Am Bio T - v66 - i8 - Oct 2004 - p579(1) [501+]
   BIC - v33 - i5 - August 2004 - p28(3) [501+]
Holloway, John - *Change the World Without Taking Power: The Meaning of Revolution Today*
   Ams - v61 - i2 - Oct 2004 - p333(2) [501+]

Holloway, Karla F.C. - *Passed On: African American Mourning Stories*
   TLS - i5265 - Feb 27 2004 - p32-32 [501+]
Holloway, Nancy M. - *Medical-Surgical Care Planning, 4th Ed.*
   SciTech - v28 - i1 - March 2004 - p125(1) [1-50]
Holloway, Paul A. - *Consolation in Philippians: Philosophical Sources and Rhetorical Strategy*
   Intpr - v58 - i3 - July 2004 - p324(2) [501+]
Holloway, R. Ross - *Constantine and Rome*
   Choice - v42 - i3 - Nov 2004 - p475(2) [1-50]
Holloway, Ralph L. - *The Human Fossil Record, Vol. 3*
   Choice - v42 - i4 - Dec 2004 - p703(1) [1-50]
   SciTech - v28 - i3 - Sept 2004 - p6(1) [501+]
Holloway, Richard - *Looking into the Distance: The Human Search for Meaning*
   Globe & Mail - Feb 19 2005 - pD11 [501+]
Holloway, Robin - *Robin Holloway on Music: Essays and Diversions: 1963-2003*
   MT - v145 - i1886 - Spring 2004 - p97-101 [501+]
Holloway, Sarah I. - *Cyberkids: Children in the Information Age*
   CS - v33 - i6 - Nov 2004 - p744(1) [1-50]
Holloway, Stephen - *Straight and Level: Practical Airline Economics*
   JEL - v41 - i4 - Dec 2003 - p1396(2) [501+]
Holly, Emma - *The Demon's Daughter*
   BL - v101 - i5 - Nov 1 2004 - p470(1) [51-500]
Hollyer, Beatrice - *Let's Eat!: What Children Eat around the World*
  c BL - v101 - i6 - Nov 15 2004 - p576(1) [51-500]
  c CH Bwatch - Feb 2005 - pNA [51-500]
  c SLJ - v51 - i2 - Feb 2005 - p122(1) [51-500]
Hollywood Creative Directory - *Hollywood Music Industry Directory*
   Choice - v42 - i1 - Sept 2004 - p62(1) [501+]
Hollywood Representation Directory, 27th Ed.
   R&R Bk N - v19 - i3 - August 2004 - p264(1) [51-500]
Hollywood Creative Directory: Contact Information for Studies and Networks, Film and TV Executives, Production Companies, Independent Producers, TV Shows and Staff
   Choice - v41 - i11-12 - July-August 2004 - p2017(1) [501+]
Holm, Anne - *I Am David*
   SLJ - v50 - i10 - Oct 2004 - pS10(1) [51-500]
Holm & Hamel - *To Scratch a Thief (Illus. by Weinman, Brad)*
  c SLJ - v51 - i2 - Feb 2005 - p103(1) [51-500]
Holm, Ian - *Acting My Life: The Autobiography*
   Spec - v296 - i9189 - Sept 18 2004 - p54(1) [501+]
Holm, Jennifer L. - *Boston Jane: Wilderness Days*
  y Kliatt - v38 - i4 - July 2004 - p19(1) [51-500]
The Creek: A Novel of Suspense
  y Kliatt - v38 - i6 - Nov 2004 - p18(1) [51-500]
Holman, J. Alan - *Fossil Frogs and Toads of North America*
   E-Streams - August 2004 - pNA [501+]
   SciTech - v28 - i1 - March 2004 - p59(1) [51-500]
Holman, Katherine - *Historical Dictionary of the Vikings*
   Choice - v41 - i11-12 - July-August 2004 - p2028(1) [501+]
Holman, Sheri - *The Mammoth Cheese*
  y Kliatt - v38 - i5 - Sept 2004 - p21(2) [51-500]
   NYTBR - July 25 2004 - p20 [501+]
Holmberg, Diane - *Thrice-Told Tales: Married Couples Tell Their Stories*
   R&R Bk N - v19 - i1 - Feb 2004 - p129(1) [51-500]
Holmberg, James J. - *Exploring with Lewis and Clark*
   Bwatch - March 2005 - pNA [51-500]
Holmes, Anna - *Hell Hath No Fury: Women's Letters from the End of the Affair*
   Spec - v296 - i9191 - Oct 2 2004 - p43(2) [501+]
Holmes, Diana - *Rachilde: Decadence, Gender and the Woman Writer*
   NCFS - v32 - i3-4 - Spring-Summer 2004 - p418(2) [501+]
Holmes, Frederic Lawrence - *Instruments and Experimentation in the History of Chemistry*
   Isis - v95 - i3 - Sept 2004 - p506(2) [501+]
Investigative Pathways: Patterns and Stages in the Careers of Experimental Scientists
   Am Sci - v93 - i1 - Jan-Feb 2005 - p86(2) [501+]
   Choice - v41 - i11-12 - July-August 2004 - p2064(1) [501+]
   Nature - v430 - i7002 - August 19 2004 - p834(1) [501+]
   QRB - v79 - i4 - Dec 2004 - p404(2) [501+]
   TimHES - v0 - i1683 - March 18 2005 - p24(1) [501+]

Reworking the Bench: Research Notebooks in the History of Science
CS - v33 - i1 - Jan 2004 - p127-127 [501+]
Holmes, Frederick - *The Sickly Stuarts: The Medical Downfall of a Dynasty*
TLS - i5266 - March 5 2004 - p31-31 [501+]
Holmes, Gillian - *Who's Who in Canadian Business*
CBRA - Annual 2003 - p77(1) [51-500]
Holmes, Hannah - *Suburban Safari: A Year on the Lawn*
BL - v101 - i9-10 - Jan 1 2005 - p794(1) [51-500]
Ent W - i808 - Feb 25 2005 - p106 [51-500]
KR - v72 - i24 - Dec 15 2004 - p1182(1) [501+]
PW - v252 - i1 - Jan 3 2005 - p43(1) [51-500]
Holmes, James - *Struts: The Complete Reference*
SciTech - v28 - i3 - Sept 2004 - p28(1) [51-500]
Holmes, Madelyn - *American Women Conservationists: Twelve Profiles*
y BL - v101 - i1 - Sept 1 2004 - p28(1) [51-500]
y SciTech - v28 - i3 - Sept 2004 - p55(1) [1-50]
Holmes, Marjorie - *A Practical Guide to National Competition Rules Across Europe*
R&R Bk N - v19 - i4 - Nov 2004 - p174(1) [501+]
Holmes, Martha - *Nile*
BL - v101 - i5 - Nov 1 2004 - p456(1) [51-500]
Holmes, Perry - *Mountains Against the Sun*
Roundup M - v12 - i3 - Feb 2005 - p28(1) [51-500]
Holmes, Richard - *Britain at War: Famous British Battles from Hastings to Normandy, 1066-1944*
R&R Bk N - v19 - i3 - August 2004 - p37(1) [51-500]
Southey on Nelson
NS - v133 - i4716 - Nov 29 2004 - p44(1) [51-500]
Tommy: The British Soldier on the Western Front, 1914-1918
CR - v285 - i1666 - Nov 2004 - p320(1) [501+]
TLS - i5291 - August 27 2004 - p22(1) [501+]
Holmes, Rupert - *Swing*
KR - v73 - i2 - Jan 15 2005 - p73(1) [51-500]
PW - v252 - i5 - Jan 31 2005 - p49(2) [51-500]
Holmes, Thom - *Great Dinosaur Expeditions and Discoveries: Adventures with the Fossil Hunters*
c Sci Teach - v71 - i3 - March 2004 - p57-64 [501+]
Holmes, Victoria - *Rider in the Dark: An Epic Horse Story.*
c BL - v101 - i3 - Oct 1 2004 - p322(1) [51-500]
y CCB-B - v58 - i5 - Jan 2005 - p211(1) [51-500]
y Kliatt - v38 - i5 - Sept 2004 - p10(3) [51-500]
c KR - v72 - i15 - August 1 2004 - p743(1) [51-500]
c SLJ - v50 - i10 - Oct 2004 - p166(1) [51-500]
Holmesly, Sterlin - *Hemisfair '68 and the Transformation of San Antonio*
SHQ - v108 - i1 - July 2004 - p128-129 [501+]
Holmgren, Beth - *The Russian Memoir: History and Literature*
Biomag - v27 - i4 - Fall 2004 - p847(5) [501+]
Choice - v42 - i1 - Sept 2004 - p107(1) [501+]
Holmlund, Mona - *Inspiring Women: A Celebration of Herstory*
CBRA - Annual 2003 - p383(1) [501+]
Holmsten, Richard B. - *Ready to Fire: Memoir of an American Artilleryman in the Korean War*
R&R Bk N - v19 - i1 - Feb 2004 - p49(1) [51-500]
Holoka, James P. - *Simine Weil's The Iliad: Or, The Poem of Force: A Critical Edition*
FS - v58 - i3 - July 2004 - p437-438 [501+]
Holoman, D. Kern - *The Societe des Concerts du Conservatoire, 1828-1967*
Notes - v61 - i2 - Dec 2004 - p417(3) [501+]
Holowchak, Andrew - *Lucretius on the Gates of Horn and Ivory: A Psychophysical Challenge to Prophecy by Dreams*
RM - v58 - i1 - Sept 2004 - p217(2) [501+]
Holowchak, M. Andrew - *Critical Reasoning and Philosophy: A Concise Guide to Reading, Evaluating, and Writing Philosophical Works*
Choice - v42 - i2 - Oct 2004 - p307(1) [51-500]
R&R Bk N - v19 - i3 - August 2004 - p6(1) [1-50]
Holowchak, Mark Andrew - *Happiness and Greek Ethical Thought*
R&R Bk N - v20 - i1 - Feb 2005 - p9(1) [51-500]
Holquist, Peter - *Making War, Forging Revolution: Russia's Continuum of Crisis, 1914-1921*
Slav R - v63 - i2 - Summer 2004 - p408(2) [501+]
Holroyd, Michael - *Mosaic: Portraits in Fragments*
BL - v100 - i22 - August 2004 - p1893(1) [51-500]
LJ - v129 - i13 - August 2004 - p78(2) [501+]
TLS - i5268 - March 19 2004 - p11-11 [501+]
Holst, Gerald C. - *Holst's Practical Guide to Electro-Optical Systems*
SciTech - v28 - i1 - March 2004 - p146(1) [1-50]
Holsti, K.J. - *Taming the Sovereigns: Institutional Change in International Politics*
Choice - v42 - i1 - Sept 2004 - p184(2) [501+]
For Aff - v83 - i5 - Sept-Oct 2004 - p164 [501+]
Pers PS - v34 - i1 - Wntr 2005 - p58(2) [501+]
Holt, Charles A. - *Experiments Investigating Market Power*
JEL - v42 - i4 - Dec 2004 - p1153(2) [501+]
Holt, Cheryl - *More Than Seduction*
BL - v101 - i1 - Sept 1 2004 - p72(1) [51-500]
Holt, D. Eric - *Optimality Theory and Language Change*
R&R Bk N - v19 - i1 - Feb 2004 - p213 [51-500]
Holt, Daniel J. - *Hydrogen and Its Future as a Transportation Fuel*
SciTech - v28 - i1 - March 2004 - p167(1) [51-500]
Holt, David - *The Exploding Toilet: Modern Urban Legends (Illus. by Pope, Kevin)*
y Kliatt - v38 - i5 - Sept 2004 - p40(2) [51-500]
c SLJ - v50 - i8 - August 2004 - p138(1) [51-500]
Holt, Frank L. - *Alexander the Great and the Mystery of the Elephant Medallions*
J Mil H - v68 - i2 - April 2004 - p579-581 [501+]
TLS - i5264 - Feb 20 2004 - p28-28 [501+]
Holt, John - *Artic Aurora: Canada's Yukon and Northwest Territories*
BL - v101 - i8 - Dec 15 2004 - p702(1) [51-500]
Holt, John Clifford - *Constituting Communities: Theravada Buddhism and the Religious Cultures of South and Southeast Asia*
JAS - v63 - i2 - May 2004 - p477(2) [501+]
Pac A - v77 - i3 - Fall 2004 - p597(2) [501+]
Holt, Marilyn Irvin - *Children of the Western Plains: The Nineteenth-Century Experience*
J Soc H - v38 - i1 - Fall 2004 - p248(3) [501+]
Holt, Stephen S. - *The Search for Other Worlds: Proceedings*
SciTech - v28 - i3 - Sept 2004 - p43(1) [1-50]
Holt, Thaddeus - *The Deceivers: Allied Military Deception in the Second World War*
Sew R - v112 - i1 - Wntr 2004 - pVI-XI [501+]
Spec - v296 - i9200 - Dec 4 2004 - p39(1) [501+]
TLS - i5286 - July 23 2004 - p12(1) [501+]
Holt, Tim A. - *Complexity for Clinicians*
SciTech - v28 - i4 - Dec 2004 - p80(1) [51-500]
Holt, Tom - *In Your Dreams*
BL - v101 - i9-10 - Jan 1 2005 - p833(2) [1-50]
Holt-Watson, Jo Anna - *A Taste of the Sweet Apple: A Memoir*
BL - v101 - i3 - Oct 1 2004 - p296(1) [51-500]
PW - v251 - i36 - Sept 6 2004 - p52(1) [51-500]
Holt, Ysanne - *British Artists and the Modernist Landscape*
R&R Bk N - v19 - i1 - Feb 2004 - p206(1) [51-500]
Holter, Knut - *Deuteronomy 4 and the Second Commandment*
R&R Bk N - v19 - i1 - Feb 2004 - p20(1) [1-50]
Old Testament Research for Africa: A Critical Analysis and Annotated Bibliography of African Old Testament Dissertations, 1967-2000
IBMR - v28 - i3 - July 2004 - p138(1) [501+]
Holtfrerich, Michael - *College Algebra: Preliminary Ed.*
SciTech - v28 - i4 - Dec 2004 - p34(1) [51-500]
Holtje, Hans-Dieter - *Molecular Modeling: Basic Principles and Applications, 2nd Ed.*
SciTech - v28 - i1 - March 2004 - p56(1) [51-500]
Holton, Karina - *Irish Villages: Studies in Local History*
R&R Bk N - v19 - i1 - Feb 2004 - p34(1) [1-50]
Holtz, Eddie - *Full Court Press*
BL - v101 - i1 - Sept 1 2004 - p53(1) [51-500]
Holtzman, Debra Smiley - *The Safe Baby: A Do-It-Yourself Guide to Home Safety*
LJ - v130 - i1 - Jan 1 2005 - p140(1) [51-500]
Holub, Allen - *Holub on Patterns: Learning Design Patterns by Looking at Code*
SciTech - v28 - i4 - Dec 2004 - p25(1) [51-500]
Holub, Joan - *Geogra-Fleas!: Riddles All over the Map (Illus. by Dunnick, Regan)*
c SLJ - v50 - i11 - Nov 2004 - p124(2) [51-500]
The Halloween Queen (Illus. by Smythe, Theresa)
c SLJ - v50 - i10 - Oct 2004 - p118(1) [51-500]
Happy Easter Eggs
c PW - v252 - i7 - Feb 14 2005 - p79(2) [501+]
Riddle-Iculous Math
c SLJ - v50 - i9 - Sept 2004 - p58(1) [51-500]
c TC Math - v11 - i1 - August 2004 - p43(1) [51-500]
Why Do Birds Sing? (Illus. by DiVito, Anna)
c BL - v101 - i5 - Nov 1 2004 - p487(1) [51-500]
c SLJ - v50 - i11 - Nov 2004 - p126(1) [51-500]
Why do Horses Neigh?
c LibMed - v22 - i4 - Jan 2004 - p70(1) [501+]
Why Do Rabbits Hop?: And Other Questions about Rabbits, Guinea Pigs, Hamsters, and Gerbils
c LibMed - v22 - i4 - Jan 2004 - p70(1) [501+]
Why Do Snakes Hiss?: And Other Questions about Snakes, Lizards, and Turtles (Illus. by DiVito, Anna)
c BL - v101 - i5 - Nov 1 2004 - p487(1) [51-500]
c KR - v72 - i17 - Sept 1 2004 - p867(1) [51-500]
c SLJ - v50 - i11 - Nov 2004 - p126(1) [51-500]
Holubitsky, Katherine - *The Hippie House*
y Kliatt - v38 - i4 - July 2004 - p8(1) [51-500]
y Res Links - v10 - i1 - Oct 2004 - p29(2) [51-500]
y VOYA - v27 - i4 - Oct 2004 - p303(1) [51-500]
Holweg, Matthias - *The Second Century: Reconnecting Customer and Value Chain through Build-to-Order*
Har Bus R - v82 - i10 - Oct 2004 - p32(1) [501+]
Holz, Carsten A. - *China's Industrial State-Owned Enterprises: Between Profitability and Bankruptcy*
JEL - v42 - i1 - March 2004 - p326(1) [501+]
Holz, Klaus - *Nationaler Antisemitismus*
HNet - Nov 2004 - pNA [501+]
Holzapfel, Kathleen G. - *Pure Dynamite*
BL - v101 - i1 - Sept 1 2004 - p71(1) [51-500]
Holzer, Harold - *Lincoln at Cooper Union: The Speech That Made Abraham Lincoln President*
NYRB - v51 - i13 - August 12 2004 - p20(3) [501+]
The President Is Shot: The Assassination of Abraham Lincoln
c LibMed - v23 - i3 - Nov-Dec 2004 - p82(1) [51-500]
The President Is Shot! The Assassination of Abraham Lincoln
y VOYA - v27 - i3 - August 2004 - p237(1) [1-50]
Holzer, Harry J. - *The Economics of Affirmative Action*
R&R Bk N - v19 - i4 - Nov 2004 - p113(1) [51-500]
Holzhey, Magdalena - *Frida Kahlo: The Artist in the Blue House*
c SLJ - v50 - i11 - Nov 2004 - p66(1) [51-500]
Holzman, Morey - *Deceptions and Doublecross: How the NHL Conquered Hockey*
CBRA - Annual 2003 - p142(2) [51-500]
Holzmann, Robert - *Pension Reform in Europe: Process and Progress*
JEL - v41 - i4 - Dec 2003 - p1371(1) [501+]
Holzmann, Verena - *"Ich beswer dich wurm und wyrmin...." Formen und Typen altdeutscher Zaubersspruche und Segen*
Folkl - v115 - i3 - Dec 2004 - p375(2) [501+]
"Ich beswer dich wurm und wyrmin...":formen und Typen altdeutscher Zaubersspruche und Segen
Specu - v79 - i3 - July 2004 - p771-772 [501+]
Holzner, Steve - *Eclipse Cookbook*
LJ - v129 - i16 - Oct 1 2004 - p104(1) [51-500]
SciTech - v28 - i3 - Sept 2004 - p22(1) [1-50]
SciTech - v28 - i3 - Sept 2004 - p22(1) [1-50]
Holzschlag, Molly E. - *250 HTML and Web Design Secrets*
SciTech - v28 - i4 - Dec 2004 - p150(1) [51-500]
Hom, Ken - *Ken Hom's Top 100 Stir-Fry Recipes: Quick and Easy Dishes for Every Occasion*
LJ - v130 - i3 - Feb 15 2005 - p152(1) [51-500]
Homan, Elizabeth A. - *Acting Across the Disciplines: Performance Technique for Everyday Life*
R&R Bk N - v19 - i1 - Feb 2004 - p226(1) [51-500]
Homan, Lynn M. - *Women Who Fly (Illus. by Shepherd, Rosalie M.)*
BL - v100 - i21 - July 2004 - p1840(1) [1-50]
y SLJ - v50 - i9 - Sept 2004 - p227(1) [51-500]
Homan, Sidney - *Directing Shakespeare: A Scholar Onstage*
Choice - v42 - i2 - Oct 2004 - p278(1) [501+]
Staging Modern Playwrights: From Director's Concept to Performance
R&R Bk N - v19 - i1 - Feb 2004 - p226(1) [51-500]
Homberger, Eric - *Mrs. Astor's New York: Money and Social Power in a Gilded Age*
JAH - v91 - i2 - Sept 2004 - p644(1) [501+]
Home, Alistair - *Friend or Foe: An Anglosaxon History of France*
Spec - v296 - i9199 - Nov 27 2004 - p42(2) [501+]
Home, Stewart - *Down & Out in Shoreditch and Horton*
KR - v72 - i16 - August 15 2004 - p765(1) [501+]
Homem, Rui Carvalho - *Translating Shakespeare for the Twenty-First Century*
R&R Bk N - v19 - i4 - Nov 2004 - p235(1) [501+]
Homemeyer, Jane - *Techniques of Crime Scene Investigation: An Interactive Training CD-ROM*
R&R Bk N - v19 - i4 - Nov 2004 - p147(1) [501+]
Homer - *The Homeric Hymns*
TLS - i5290 - August 20 2004 - p23(1) [501+]
Homeric Hymns, Homeric Apocrypha, Lives of Homer
TLS - i5290 - August 20 2004 - p23(1) [501+]
Iliad, Bk. 1
Class R - v54 - i2 - Nov 2004 - p275-276 [501+]
Odyssey
LJ - v129 - i12 - July 2004 - p82(1) [51-500]

Homer, Alex - *ASP.NET v. 2.0: The Beta Version*
SciTech - v28 - i4 - Dec 2004 - p150(1) [51-500]
First Look at ASP.NET v.2.0
SciTech - v28 - i1 - March 2004 - p156(1) [51-500]

Homer, Avril - *European Gothic: A Spirited Exchange 1760-1960*
Clio - v33 - i2 - Wntr 2004 - p215(6) [501+]

Homer, Sidney - *Inside the Yield Book: The Classic That Created the Science of Bond Analysis*
R&R Bk N - v19 - i3 - August 2004 - p138(1) [51-500]

Hommes, O. - *Early Indicators, Early Treatment, Neuroprotection in Multiple Sclerosis*
SciTech - v28 - i3 - Sept 2004 - p94(1) [51-500]
SciTech - v28 - i3 - Sept 2004 - p94(1) [51-500]

Homo Promo
Advocate - Dec 21 2004 - p51(1) [51-500]

Hon, Bernard - *Design and Manufacture for Sustainable Development 2003: Proceedings*
SciTech - v28 - i1 - March 2004 - p177(1) [51-500]

Hond, Paul - *Mothers and Sons*
KR - v73 - i2 - Jan 15 2005 - p74(1) [501+]
PW - v252 - i8 - Feb 21 2005 - p156(1) [51-500]

Honderich, Ted - *After the Terror, Rev. Ed.*
R&R Bk N - v19 - i3 - August 2004 - p142(1) [51-500]
On Consciousness
Bwatch - Nov 2004 - pNA [51-500]
Choice - v42 - i7 - March 2005 - p1240(1) [51-500]

Honey, Elizabeth - *Honey Sandwich*
c LibMed - v22 - i7 - April-May 2004 - p64(1) [501+]
Remote Man
y Kliatt - v38 - i4 - July 2004 - p19(1) [51-500]

The Honeynet Project - *Know Your Enemy: Learning About Security Threats, 2d ed*
SciTech - v28 - i3 - Sept 2004 - p32(1) [51-500]

Hong, Fan - *Soccer, Women, Sexual Liberation: Kicking off a New Era*
Choice - v42 - i1 - Sept 2004 - p144(1) [501+]

Hong, Seungbum - *Nanoscale PHenomena in Ferroelectric Thin Films*
SciTech - v28 - i1 - March 2004 - p141(1) [51-500]

Hong, Ying - *Peacock Cries*
KR - v72 - i14 - July 15 2004 - p648(2) [501+]
LJ - v129 - i20 - Dec 1 2004 - p100(1) [51-500]

Honigsbaum, Mark - *Valverde's Gold: In Search of the Last Great Inca Treasure*
BL - v100 - i22 - August 2004 - p1892(1) [51-500]
BW - v34 - i36 - Sept 5 2004 - p7(1) [501+]
LJ - v129 - i12 - July 2004 - p97(2) [51-500]
New Sci - v183 - i2460 - August 14 2004 - p46(1) [51-500]

Honna, Jun - *Military Politics and Democratization in Indonesia*
JAS - v63 - i2 - May 2004 - p554(3) [501+]

Honnay, O. - *Forest Biodiversity: Lessons from History for Conservation*
SciTech - v28 - i3 - Sept 2004 - p131(1) [51-500]

Honneland, Geir - *Health as International Politics: Combating Communicable Diseases in the Baltic Sea Region*
SciTech - v28 - i4 - Dec 2004 - p83(1) [51-500]
Russia and the West: Environmental Co-operation and Conflict
E-A St - v56 - i5 - July 2004 - p774(2) [501+]
Russian Fisheries Management: The Precautionary Approach in Theory and Practice
SciTech - v28 - i3 - Sept 2004 - p133(1) [51-500]

Honnold, RoseMary - *Serving Seniors: A How-to-Do-It Manual for Librarians*
BL - v100 - i21 - July 2004 - p1859(1) [501+]

Honohan, Patrick - *Taxation of Financial International: Theory and Practice for Emerging Economics*
JEL - v41 - i4 - Dec 2003 - p1369(2) [501+]

Honore, Carl - *In Praise of Slow: How a Worldwide Movement Is Challenging the Cult of Speed. Audiobook Review*
Globe & Mail - Jan 8 2005 - pD13 [1-50]
In Praise of Slowness: How a Worldwide Movement Is Challenging the Cult of Speed
Fut - v39 - i2 - March-April 2005 - p12(2) [501+]
Fut - v39 - i2 - March-April 2005 - p60(2) [51-500]
Prog - v69 - i3 - March 2005 - p46(3) [501+]

Honos-Webb, Lara - *The Gift of ADHD: How to Transform Your Child's Problems into Strengths*
PW - v252 - i7 - Feb 14 2005 - p70(1) [51-500]

Honsberger, Ross - *Mathematical Delights*
SciTech - v28 - i4 - Dec 2004 - p33(1) [51-500]

Hoobler, Dorothy - *The 1960s: Rebels*
c SLJ - v50 - i10 - Oct 2004 - p66(1) [51-500]
We are Americans: Voices of the Immigrant Experience
c LibMed - v22 - i6 - March 2004 - p87(1) [51-500]
c SLJ - v50 - i10 - Oct 2004 - p836(2) [501+]

Hoock, Holger - *The King's Artists, the Royal Academy of Arts and the Politics of British Culture, 1760-1840*
Apo - v160 - i512 - Oct 2004 - p89(1) [501+]

Hood, Adrienne D. - *The Weaver's Craft: Cloth, Commerce, and Industry in Early Pennsylvania*
AHR - v109 - i3 - June 2004 - p895(2) [501+]
JAH - v91 - i2 - Sept 2004 - p613(1) [501+]
T&C - v45 - i4 - Oct 2004 - p836(2) [501+]

Hood, Ann - *An Ornithologist's Guide to Life*
BL - v100 - i21 - July 2004 - p1817(2) [501+]
Somewhere Off the Coast of Maine
BL - v101 - i6 - Nov 15 2004 - p557(1) [501+]

Hood, Hugh - *After All!: The Collected Stories V*
CBRA - Annual 2003 - p199(1) [51-500]

Hood, Steven J. - *Political Development and Democratic Theory: Rethinking Comparative Politics*
R&R Bk N - v19 - i3 - August 2004 - p174(1) [501+]

Hood, Susan - *Pup and Hound*
c Res Links - v10 - i2 - Dec 2004 - p6(1) [51-500]
Pup and Hound Move In
c Res Links - v10 - i2 - Dec 2004 - p6(1) [51-500]

Hooft, Stan van - *Life, Death, and Subjectivity: Moral Sources in Bioethics*
SciTech - v28 - i4 - Dec 2004 - p77(1) [51-500]

Hook, Glenn D. - *Japan's Contested Constitution: Documents and Analysis*
HNet - June 2004 - pNA [501+]

Hook, Jason - *Roald Dahl: the Storyteller*
c CCB-B - v57 - i11 - July-August 2004 - p459(1) [501+]

Hooker, Forrestine C. - *Child of the Fighting Tenth: On the Frontier with the Buffalo Soldiers*
LibMed - v22 - i7 - April-May 2004 - p67(1) [501+]

Hooker, John - *Working Across Cultures*
Choice - v41 - i7 - March 2004 - p1338(1) [501+]
JEL - v42 - i1 - March 2004 - p343(1) [51-500]

Hooker, Morna D. - *Paul: A Short Introduction*
TLS - i5264 - Feb 20 2004 - p32-32 [501+]

Hooker, Virginia Matheson - *A Short History of Malaysia: Linking East and West*
R&R Bk N - v19 - i1 - Feb 2004 - p47(1) [51-500]

Hooks, Bell - *Skin Again (Illus. by Raschka, Chris)*
c BL - v101 - i2 - Sept 15 2004 - p250(1) [51-500]
c CCB-B - v58 - i4 - Dec 2004 - p171(1) [51-500]
c HB - v80 - i6 - Nov-Dec 2004 - p698(1) [51-500]
c KR - v72 - i16 - August 15 2004 - p807(1) [51-500]
c PW - v251 - i42 - Oct 18 2004 - p62(2) [501+]
c SLJ - v50 - i9 - Sept 2004 - p162(1) [51-500]

Hooks, Ed - *Acting for Animators: A Complete Guide to Performance Animation, Rev. Ed.*
R&R Bk N - v19 - i1 - Feb 2004 - p252(1) [51-500]
The Actor's Field Guide: Acting Notes on the Run
R&R Bk N - v19 - i3 - August 2004 - p264(1) [1-50]

Hooks, Gwendolyn - *The Mystery of the Missing Dog (Illus. by Devard, Nancy)*
c SLJ - v51 - i1 - Jan 2005 - p86(1) [51-500]
Three's a Crowd (Illus. by Walker, Sylvia)
c SLJ - v51 - i1 - Jan 2005 - p86(1) [51-500]

Hooper, Barbara - *Time To Stand And Stare*
Spec - v295 - i9185 - August 21 2004 - p35(1) [501+]

Hooper, Brian - *Voices in the Heart: Postcolonialism and Identity in Hong Kong Literature*
R&R Bk N - v19 - i1 - Feb 2004 - p241(1) [501+]

Hooper, David C. - *Quinolone Antimicrobial Agents, 3rd ed.*
E-Streams - July 2004 - pNA [501+]

Hooper, Glenn - *Perspectives on Travel Writing*
R&R Bk N - v19 - i3 - August 2004 - p78(1) [501+]

Hooper-Greenhill, Eilean - *Museums and the Interpretation of Visual Culture*
JAAC - v62 - i3 - Summer 2004 - p306-307 [501+]

Hooper, Kay - *The Delaney Christmas Carol*
Globe & Mail - Dec 18 2004 - pD23 [51-500]
Hunting Fear (Read by Hill, Dick). Audiobook Review
y Kliatt - v39 - i1 - Jan 2005 - p44(1) [51-500]
Hunting Fear
PW - v251 - i31 - August 2 2004 - p54(1) [501+]
The Real Thing.
LJ - v129 - i19 - Nov 15 2004 - p48(1) [501+]

Hooper, Mary - *At the Sign of the Sugared Plum*
c LibMed - v22 - i7 - April-May 2004 - p61(1) [501+]
Megan (Read by Walton, Gillian). Audiobook Review
SLJ - v50 - i12 - Dec 2004 - p78(1) [501+]
Petals in the Ashes
c BL - v100 - i22 - August 2004 - p1934(1) [51-500]
c CCB-B - v58 - i1 - Sept 2004 - p20(2) [51-500]
c PW - v251 - i28 - July 12 2004 - p65(2) [501+]
y Sch Lib - v52 - i3 - Autumn 2004 - p158(1) [51-500]
c SLJ - v50 - i8 - August 2004 - p123(2) [51-500]
y VOYA - v27 - i3 - August 2004 - p218(1) [1-50]

Hooper, Meredith - *The Island That Moved: How Shifting Forces Shape Our Earth (Illus. by De Leiris, Lucia)*
c BL - v100 - i22 - August 2004 - p1926(1) [51-500]
c Sch Lib - v52 - i4 - Winter 2004 - p207(1) [51-500]
c SLJ - v50 - i12 - Dec 2004 - p162(1) [51-500]
Race to the Pole (Read by Mantle, Clive). Audiobook Review
y Kliatt - v39 - i2 - March 2005 - p60(1) [51-500]
Stephen Biesty's Castles (Illus. by Biesty, Stephen)
y KR - v72 - i21 - Nov 1 2004 - p1045(1) [51-500]
y Magpies - v19 - i5 - Nov 2004 - p44(2) [501+]
c SLJ - v51 - i2 - Feb 2005 - p122(1) [51-500]

Hoopes, James - *False Prophets: The Gurus Who Created Modern Management and Why Their Ideas Are Bad for Business Today*
R&R Bk N - v19 - i1 - Feb 2004 - p94(1) [1-50]

Hoopmann, Kathy - *Tremada*
y Magpies - v19 - i5 - Nov 2004 - p35(1) [501+]

Hoose, Phillip - *The Race to Save the Lord God Bird*
c BL - v101 - i7 - Dec 1 2004 - p670(1) [51-500]
y BW - v34 - i37 - Sept 12 2004 - p12(1) [51-500]
y Bwatch - Nov 2004 - pNA [501+]
c CCB-B - v58 - i3 - Nov 2004 - p126(1) [501+]
c Globe & Mail - Feb 12 2005 - pD11 [51-500]
c HB - v80 - i5 - Sept-Oct 2004 - p605(2) [51-500]
c KR - v72 - i13 - July 1 2004 - p631(1) [51-500]
y NH - v113 - i10 - Dec 2004 - p51 [501+]
c NYTBR - August 8 2004 - p17 [51-500]
c PW - v251 - i34 - August 23 2004 - p56(1) [501+]
c SLJ - v50 - i9 - Sept 2004 - p227(2) [51-500]
y VOYA - v27 - i4 - Oct 2004 - p326(2) [51-500]

Hoover, John - *How to Work for an Idiot: Survive and Thrive*
HR Mag - v49 - i7 - July 2004 - pS3(1) [51-500]

Hoover, Judith D. - *Effective Small 2nd Group and Team Communication, Ed.*
R&R Bk N - v19 - i3 - August 2004 - p143(1) [51-500]

Hoover, Kenneth R. - *Economics as Ideology: Keynes, Laski, Hayek, and the Creation of Contemporary Politics*
R&R Bk N - v19 - i1 - Feb 2004 - p77(1) [51-500]
The Future of Identity: Centennial Reflections on the Legacy of Erik Erikson
Choice - v42 - i5 - Jan 2005 - p937(1) [51-500]
R&R Bk N - v20 - i1 - Feb 2005 - p8(1) [51-500]

Hoover, Stewart M. - *Practicing Religion in the Age of the Media: Explorations in Media, Religion, and Culture*
JAAR - v72 - i4 - Dec 2004 - p1043(3) [501+]

Hope, Geoffroy - *Le violier des histoires rommaines*
Six Ct J - v35 - i3 - Fall 2004 - p876-877 [501+]

Hope, Judith Richards - *Pinstripes and Pearls: The Women of the Harvard Law Class of '64 who Forged an Old-girl Network and Paved the Way for Future Generations*
HER - v74 - i3 - Fall 2004 - p351(2) [501+]

Hope, Nicholas C. - *How Far Across the River? Chinese Policy Reform at the Millennium*
JEL - v41 - i4 - Dec 2003 - p1427(2) [501+]
JEL - v42 - i3 - Sept 2004 - p884(2) [501+]

Hope, V.M. - *Death and Disease in the Ancient City*
Class R - v54 - i1 - May 2004 - p162(3) [501+]

Hopkin, David M. - *Soldier and Peasant in French Popular Culture 1766-1870*
Folkl - v115 - i3 - Dec 2004 - p367(3) [501+]

Hopkins, Andrea - *Damsels Not in Distress: The True Story of Women in Medieval Times*
y VOYA - v27 - i4 - Oct 2004 - p334(1) [51-500]

Hopkins, Cathy - *Mates, Dates, and Mad Mistakes*
  c SLJ - v50 - i10 - Oct 2004 - p166(1) [51-500]
Mates, Dates, and Sequin Smiles
  y Kliatt - v39 - i1 - Jan 2005 - p14(1) [51-500]
  y SLJ - v50 - i9 - Sept 2004 - p208(1) [51-500]
The Princess of Pop
  y Kliatt - v38 - i4 - July 2004 - p19(2) [501+]
  c SLJ - v50 - i7 - July 2004 - p106(1) [51-500]
Teens, Queens and Has-Beens
  c PW - v251 - i50 - Dec 13 2004 - p70(1) [501+]
Truth or Dare Series
  y Kliatt - v38 - i4 - July 2004 - p19(2) [501+]
White Lies and Barefaced Truths. Bk. #1
  c SLJ - v50 - i7 - July 2004 - p106(1) [51-500]
Hopkins, Dwight, N. - *Heart and Head: Black Theology - Past, Present, and Future*
  JAAR - v72 - i3 - Sept 2004 - p783-785 [501+]
Hopkins, Ellen - *Crank*
  y BL - v101 - i6 - Nov 15 2004 - p595(1) [51-500]
  y Kliatt - v38 - i5 - Sept 2004 - p21(2) [51-500]
  y KR - v72 - i19 - Oct 1 2004 - p961(1) [51-500]
  y SLJ - v50 - i11 - Nov 2004 - p145(1) [51-500]
  PW - v251 - i44 - Nov 1 2004 - p63(2) [501+]
Hopkins, Evans D. - *Life After Life: A Story of Rage and Redemption*
  KR - v73 - i5 - March 1 2005 - p274(1) [501+]
Hopkins, Gerard Manley - *The Mystic Poets*
  AM - v191 - i11 - Oct 18 2004 - p25 [501+]
Hopkins, James K. - *Into the Heart of the Fire: The British in the Spanish Civil War*
  S&S - v68 - i3 - Fall 2004 - p369-376 [501+]
Hopkins, Janet - *Assistive Technology: An Introductory Guide for K-12 Library Media Specialists*
  LibMed - v23 - i3 - Nov-Dec 2004 - p63(1) [51-500]
  c SLJ - v50 - i9 - Sept 2004 - p238(1) [51-500]
  Teach Lib - v32 - i2 - Dec 2004 - p38(1) [501+]
Hopkins, Jasper - *Hugh of Balma on Mystical Theology: A Translation and an Overview of his De Theologia Mystica*
  Med R - July 2004 - pNA [501+]
Hopkins, Johns - *The Roots of American Industrialization*
  JAH - v91 - i3 - Dec 2004 - p1013(2) [501+]
Hopkins, Karen M. - *Supervision as Collaboration in the Human Services: Building a Learning Culture*
  R&R Bk N - v19 - i3 - August 2004 - p158(1) [51-500]
Hopkins, Lee Bennett - *Christmas Presents: Holiday Poetry (Illus. by Hall, Melanie)*
  c BL - v100 - i22 - August 2004 - p1938(1) [51-500]
  c HB - v80 - i6 - Nov-Dec 2004 - p661(1) [51-500]
  c KR - v72 - i21 - Nov 1 2004 - p1050(1) [51-500]
  c PW - v251 - i39 - Sept 27 2004 - p60(1) [51-500]
Days to Celebrate: A Full Year of Poetry, People, Holidays, History, Fascinating Facts, and More (Illus. by Alcorn, Stephen)
  KR - v72 - i24 - Dec 15 2004 - p1203(1) [51-500]
  c PW - v251 - i51 - Dec 20 2004 - p61(1) [501+]
  c SLJ - v51 - i1 - Jan 2005 - p110(2) [51-500]
Hanukkah Lights: Holiday Poetry (Illus. by Hall, Melanie)
  c HB - v80 - i6 - Nov-Dec 2004 - p661(1) [51-500]
  c KR - v72 - i21 - Nov 1 2004 - p1050(1) [51-500]
  c PW - v251 - i39 - Sept 27 2004 - p60(1) [51-500]
Oh No! Where Are My Pants? and Other Disasters: Poems (Illus. by Erlbruch, Wolf)
  c CCB-B - v58 - i6 - Feb 2005 - p252(2) [51-500]
  c KR - v73 - i2 - Jan 15 2005 - p121(1) [51-500]
Oh, No! Where Are My Pants? and Other Disasters: Poems (Illus. by Erlbruch, Wolf)
  c SLJ - v51 - i2 - Feb 2005 - p122(1) [51-500]
School Supplies: A Book of Poems (Illus. by Flower, Renee)
  c SLJ - v50 - i7 - July 2004 - p45(1) [51-500]
Valentine Hearts: Holiday Poetry (Illus. by Adinolfi, JoAnn)
  c BL - v101 - i9-10 - Jan 1 2005 - p867(1) [51-500]
  c PW - v251 - i49 - Dec 6 2004 - p61(2) [501+]
  c SLJ - v51 - i1 - Jan 2005 - p112(1) [51-500]
Wonderful Words: Poems about Reading, Writing, Speaking, and Listening (Illus. by Barbour, Karen)
  c LibMed - v23 - i3 - Nov-Dec 2004 - p75(1) [51-500]
Hopkins, Lisa - *Giants of the Past: Popular Fictions and the Idea of Evolution*
  Choice - v42 - i4 - Dec 2004 - p660(1) [1-50]
Hopkins, Roz - *The Travel Book: A Journey through Every Country in the World*
  BL - v101 - i7 - Dec 1 2004 - p627(1) [51-500]
  LJ - v129 - i18 - Nov 1 2004 - p110(1) [51-500]

Hopkinson, Deborah - *Apples to Oregon: Being the (Slightly) True Narrative of How a Brave Pioneer Father Brought Apples, Peaches, Pears, Plums, Grapes, and Cherries (and Children) across the Plains (Illus. by Carpenter, Nancy)*
  c BL - v101 - i1 - Sept 1 2004 - p132(1) [1-50]
  c CCB-B - v58 - i2 - Oct 2004 - p78(2) [51-500]
  c KR - v72 - i16 - August 15 2004 - p807(1) [51-500]
  c PW - v251 - i35 - August 30 2004 - p53(1) [51-500]
  c SLJ - v50 - i9 - Sept 2004 - p162(2) [51-500]
Billy and the Rebel
  c KR - v73 - i2 - Jan 15 2005 - p121(1) [51-500]
Fannie in the Kitchen: The Whole Story from Soup to Nuts of How Fannie Farmer Invented Recipes with Precise Measurements
  c SLJ - v51 - i2 - Feb 2005 - p57(1) [51-500]
Hear My Sorrow: The Diary of Angela Denoto, a Shirtwaist Worker
  y CH Bwatch - Feb 2005 - pNA [51-500]
The Long Trail (Illus. by Farnsworth, Bill)
  c SLJ - v50 - i10 - Oct 2004 - p107(1) [51-500]
Sailing for Gold (Illus. by Farnsworth, Bill)
  c SLJ - v50 - i7 - July 2004 - p77(1) [51-500]
Shutting out the Sky: Life in the Tenements of New York, 1880-1924
  c LibMed - v22 - i5 - Feb 2004 - p80(1) [501+]
  c RT - v58 - i3 - Nov 2004 - p291(2) [501+]
  c SLJ - v50 - i10 - Oct 2004 - pS31(1) [51-500]
Under the Quilt of Night (Illus. by Ransome, James E.)
  c PW - v252 - i1 - Jan 3 2005 - p58(1) [51-500]
  c RT - v57 - Oct 2003 - p175 [1-50]
Hopkinson, Michael - *The Irish War of Independence*
  Albion - v36 - i1 - Spring 2004 - p192(2) [501+]
Hopkinson, Nalo - *So Long Been Dreaming: Postcolonial Science Fiction & Fantasy*
  y BL - v101 - i1 - Sept 1 2004 - p76(1) [51-500]
Hopp, Glenn - *Billy Wilder: The Complete Films*
  TimHES - v0 - i1647 - July 2 2004 - p26(1) [501+]
Hoppe, Kirk Arden - *Lords of the Fly: Sleeping Sickness Control in British East Africa, 1900-1960*
  SciTech - v28 - i3 - Sept 2004 - p85(1) [501+]
Hoppenfeld, Stanley - *Surgical Exposures in Orthopaedics: The Anatomic Approach, 3d ed. (Illus. by Thomas, Hugh A.)*
  SciTech - v28 - i1 - March 2004 - p113(1) [51-500]
Hopper, Helen M. - *Fukuzawa Yukichi: From Samurai to Capitalist*
  R&R Bk N - v19 - i4 - Nov 2004 - p50(1) [51-500]
Hopper, Kim - *Reckoning with Homelessness*
  CS - v33 - i4 - July 2004 - p484(3) [501+]
Hoppit, Julian - *Parliaments, Nations and Identities in Britain and Ireland, 1650-1850*
  HNet - Dec 2004 - pNA [501+]
Hopt, Klaus J. - *Capital Markets and Company Law*
  Law Q Rev - v120 - Jan 2004 - p183-185 [501+]
Hoque, Serajul - *Global Trade Liberalization: Impact on the Readymade Garments Industry in Bangladesh*
  R&R Bk N - v19 - i4 - Nov 2004 - p105(1) [51-500]
Horace - *Horace, the Odes*
  Class R - v53 - i2 - Nov 2003 - p360-361 [501+]
Horacek, Petr - *A New House for Mouse (Illus. by Horacek, Petr)*
  c BL - v101 - i7 - Dec 1 2004 - p659(1) [51-500]
  c HB - v81 - i1 - Jan-Feb 2005 - p77(1) [51-500]
  c KR - v72 - i22 - Nov 15 2004 - p1090(1) [51-500]
  c PW - v252 - i2 - Jan 10 2005 - p54(1) [51-500]
Hordeski, Michael F. - *Dictionary of Energy Efficiency Technologies*
  SciTech - v28 - i4 - Dec 2004 - p145(1) [501+]
Horgan, John - *Rational Mysticism: Dispatches from the Border between Science and Spirituality*
  Parabola - v29 - i3 - Fall 2003 - p113(3) [501+]
Rational Mysticism: Spirituality Meets Science in the Search for Enlightenment
  y Kliatt - v38 - i4 - July 2004 - p40(1) [51-500]
Horn, Ariel - *Help Wanted, Desperately*
  BL - v101 - i1 - Sept 1 2004 - p61(1) [51-500]
  PW - v251 - i39 - Sept 27 2004 - p37(1) [51-500]
Horn, Art - *Face It: Recognizing and Conquering the Hidden Fear That Drives All Conflict at Work*
  LJ - v129 - i12 - July 2004 - p95(1) [51-500]
Horn, Barbara Lee - *Edward Albee: A Research and Production Source-Book*
  Choice - v42 - i2 - Oct 2004 - p267(1) [51-500]

Horn, Bernd - *Paras Versus the Reich: Canada's Paratroopers at War, 1942-45*
  Can Hist R - v85 - i4 - Dec 2004 - p802(4) [501+]
  CBRA - Annual 2003 - p292(2) [501+]
Horn, Evelyn - *Following the Sandhill Cranes in Colorado*
  Bwatch - Dec 2004 - pNA [51-500]
Horn, Geoffrey M. - *The Bill of Rights and Other Amendments*
  c SLJ - v50 - i9 - Sept 2004 - p228(1) [51-500]
Margaret Mead
  c SLJ - v50 - i7 - July 2004 - p118(1) [51-500]
Political Parties, Interest Groups, and the Media
  c SLJ - v50 - i9 - Sept 2004 - p228(1) [51-500]
Horn, Gerd-Ranier - *Transnational Moments of Change in Europe: 1945, 1968, 1989*
  R&R Bk N - v19 - i3 - August 2004 - p36(1) [51-500]
Horn, James - *The Revolution of 1800: Democracy, Race, and the New Republic*
  AHR - v109 - i2 - April 2004 - p518(2) [501+]
  JAH - v91 - i1 - June 2004 - p222-223 [501+]
Horn, Laurence R. - *The Handbook of Pragmatics*
  Choice - v41 - i11-12 - July-August 2004 - p2039(1) [501+]
Horn, Pamela - *Flunkeys and Scullions: Life Below Stairs in Georgian England*
  CR - v285 - i1666 - Nov 2004 - p319(1) [501+]
Horn, Raymond A. - *Standards Primer*
  R&R Bk N - v19 - i3 - August 2004 - p226(1) [1-50]
Horn, Tammy - *Bees in America: How the Honey Bee Shaped a Nation*
  PW - v252 - i3 - Jan 17 2005 - p44(1) [51-500]
Hornbacher, Marya - *The Center of Winter*
  BL - v101 - i9-10 - Jan 1 2005 - p819(1) [501+]
  KR - v72 - i24 - Dec 15 2004 - p1157(1) [501+]
  LJ - v130 - i1 - Jan 1 2005 - p97(1) [51-500]
  People - v63 - i11 - March 21 2005 - p60 [51-500]
  PW - v252 - i3 - Jan 17 2005 - p36(1) [51-500]
Hornby, Nick - *A Long Way Down*
  KR - v73 - i5 - March 1 2005 - p249(2) [501+]
The Polysyllabic Spree
  Globe & Mail - March 5 2005 - pD17 [501+]
Hornby, Simonetta Agnello - *The Almond Picker*
  BL - v101 - i9-10 - Jan 1 2005 - p819(1) [501+]
  KR - v73 - i1 - Jan 1 2005 - p10(1) [501+]
  LJ - v130 - i1 - Jan 1 2005 - p97(2) [51-500]
  PW - v252 - i8 - Feb 21 2005 - p158(1) [51-500]
Horne, Alistair - *The Age of Napoleon*
  Bus W - i3895 - August 9 2004 - p11 [501+]
  Spec - v295 - i9180 - July 17 2004 - p35(2) [501+]
  TLS - i5297 - Oct 8 2004 - p6(1) [501+]
Friend or Foe: An Anglo-Saxon History of France
  NS - v133 - i4716 - Nov 29 2004 - p46(1) [51-500]
  NS - v133 - i4717 - Dec 6 2004 - p48(2) [501+]
Horne, Arthur M. - *Bully Busters; A Teacher's Manual for Helping Bullies, Victims, and Bystanders, Grades K-5*
  R&R Bk N - v19 - i1 - Feb 2004 - p188(1) [51-500]
Horne, Fiona - *Pop! Goes the Witch: The Disinformation Guide to 21st Century Witchcraft*
  Bwatch - v26 - i8 - August 2004 - p12(1) [51-500]
Horne, Jed - *Desire Street: A True Story of Death and Deliverance in New Orleans*
  KR - v72 - i24 - Dec 15 2004 - p1183(1) [501+]
  LJ - v130 - i1 - Jan 1 2005 - p130(1) [51-500]
Horne, John - *The German Atrocities of 1914: A History of Denial*
  HNet - Oct 2004 - pNA [501+]
Horne, Marilyn - *Marilyn Horne: The Song Continues*
  ON - v69 - i1 - July 2004 - p68(2) [51-500]
Horner, Jeremy - *Island Dreams: Mediterranean*
  LJ - v129 - i20 - Dec 1 2004 - p146(1) [51-500]
Horner, Nigel - *What Is Social Work? Context and Perspectives, 1st Ed.*
  TimHES - v0 - i1680 - Feb 25 2005 - pIV(1) [501+]
Hornfischer, James D. - *The Last Stand of the Tin Can Sailors: The Extraordinary World War II Story of the U.S. Navy's Finest Hour (Read by Whitener, Barrett). Audiobook Review*
  BL - v100 - i21 - July 2004 - p1855(1) [1-50]
The Last Stand of the Tin Can Sailors: The Extraordinary World War II Story of the U.S. Navy's Finest Hour (Read by Gardner, Grover). Audiobook Review
  Kliatt - v38 - i4 - July 2004 - p60(1) [51-500]
The Last Stand of the Tin Can Sailors: The Extraordinary World War II Story of the U.S. Navy's Finest Hour (Read by Whitener, Barrett). Audiobook Review
  LJ - v129 - i17 - Oct 15 2004 - p96(2) [51-500]

Hotchkiss, Julie L. - *The Labor Market Experience Of Workers With Disabilities: The ADA And Beyond*
Soc Ser R - v78 - i3 - Sept 2004 - p523(1) [51-500]

Hotchkiss, Melissa - *Storm Damage*
PSQ - v78 - i4 - Winter 2004 - p197(6) [501+]

Hothem, Lar - *Indian Trade Relics: Identification and Values*
R&R Bk N - v19 - i1 - Feb 2004 - p52(1) [51-500]

Hotten, Jon - *Muscle*
NS - v133 - i4715 - Nov 22 2004 - p49(2) [501+]

Hou, Xianguang - *The Cambrian Fossils of Chengjiang, China: The Flowering of Early Animal Life*
Choice - v41 - i11-12 - July-August 2004 - p2074(1) [501+]
E-Streams - Sept 2004 - pNA [501+]

Hou Xianguang - *The Cambrian Fossils of Chengjiang, China: The Flowering of Early Animal Life*
Nature - v430 - i6998 - July 22 2004 - p405(1) [501+]

Hou, Xianguang - *The Cambrian Fossils of Chengjiang, China: The Flowering of Early Animal Life*
TimHES - v0 - i1682 - March 11 2005 - p30(1) [501+]

Houck, Davis W. - *FDR and Fear Itself: The First Inaugural Address*
Pres St Q - v34 - i3 - Sept 2004 - p696(3) [501+]
FDR's Body Politics: The Rhetoric of Disability
AHR - v109 - i2 - April 2004 - p554(2) [501+]
JAH - v91 - i2 - Sept 2004 - p680(1) [51-500]

Houde, Olivier - *Dictionary of Cognitive Science: Neuroscience, Psychology, Artificial Intelligence, Linguistics, and Philosophy*
R&USQ - v44 - i2 - Winter 2004 - p166(1) [501+]

Hough, Harold - *Satellite Imagery for the Masses*
Bwatch - v26 - i7 - July 2004 - p1(1) [51-500]

Hough, Richard Lee - *The Nation-States: Concert or Chaos*
R&R Bk N - v19 - i1 - Feb 2004 - p148(1) [51-500]

Hough, Robert - *The Final Confession of Mabel Stark (Read by Bobbitt, Betty). Audiobook Review*
LJ - v130 - i1 - Jan 1 2005 - p167(2) [51-500]
The Stowaway
BL - v101 - i1 - Sept 1 2004 - p61(1) [51-500]
Globe & Mail - Nov 27 2004 - pD3 [51-500]
KR - v72 - i13 - July 1 2004 - p597(1) [51-500]
LJ - v129 - i15 - Sept 15 2004 - p48(1) [51-500]
PW - v251 - i39 - Sept 27 2004 - p38(2) [51-500]

Hough, Susan Elizabeth - *Earthshaking Science*
Bwatch - Nov 2004 - pNA [51-500]
Finding Fault in California: An Earthquake Touist's Guide
Bwatch - Nov 2004 - pNA [51-500]
Finding Fault in California: An Earthquake Tourist's Guide
y SB - v41 - i1 - Jan-Feb 2005 - p26(2) [501+]
SciTech - v28 - i3 - Sept 2004 - p55(1) [1-50]

Houghton, Elise - *Breath of Fresh Air: Celebrating Nature and School Gardens*
CBRA - Annual 2003 - p419(2) [51-500]

Houghton, Gillian - *Easter/Pascua*
c SLJ - v50 - i9 - Sept 2004 - p196(1) [1-50]

Houghton, Margaret - *Hamiltonians: 100 Fascinating Lives*
CBRA - Annual 2003 - p341(1) [501+]

Houghton Mifflin - *100 Words Almost Everybody Confuses and Misuses*
NW - Oct 4 2004 - p68 [51-500]
The American Heritage College Thesaurus
Choice - v42 - i4 - Dec 2004 - p626(2) [1-50]
The American Heritage Science Dictionary
LJ - v130 - i4 - March 1 2004 - p110(1) [51-500]
The American Heritage Stedman's Medical Dictionary
LJ - v130 - i1 - Jan 1 2005 - p150(1) [51-500]
The American Heritage Stedman's Medical Dictionary, 2nd Ed.
Choice - v42 - i7 - March 2005 - p1198(1) [51-500]
The American Heritage Student Dictionary
y LibMed - v22 - i4 - Jan 2004 - p80(1) [501+]
The Riverside Dictionary of Biography
LJ - v130 - i4 - March 1 2005 - p112(1) [51-500]

Houghton Mifflin Company - *The Houghton Mifflin Dictionary of Biography*
JSH - v70 - i4 - Nov 2004 - p992(1) [501+]
The Houghton Mifflin Dictionary of Biography: The most Comprehensive Coverage, From Ancient time to the Present Day.
LibMed - v22 - i6 - March 2004 - p75(1) [501+]

Houghton, Sarah - *Bloodsuckers: Bats, Bugs, and Other Bloodthirsty Creatures*
y SLJ - v50 - i7 - July 2004 - p94(1) [51-500]

Hougton, John - *Global Warming: The Complete Briefing, 3rd Ed.*
Choice - v42 - i7 - March 2005 - p1264(2) [51-500]

Houkes, John M. - *An Annotated Bibliography on the History of Usury and Interest from the Earliest Times through the Eighteenth Century*
Choice - v42 - i3 - Nov 2004 - p463(2) [1-50]

Houlden, Leslie - *Jesus in History, Thought and Culture: An Encyclopedia*
TLS - i5294 - Sept 17 2004 - p25-26 [501+]

Houlihan, Barrie - *Sport and Society: A Student Introduction*
TimHES - v0 - i1665 - Nov 5 2004 - p26(1) [501+]

Hountondji, Paulin J. - *The Struggle for Meaning: Reflections on Philosophy, Culture, and democracy in Africa*
IJAHS - v37 - i1 - Wntr 2004 - p147-153 [501+]

Houppermans, Sjef - *Samuel Beckett Compagnie*
FS - v58 - i3 - July 2004 - p442-443 [501+]

Houppert, Karen - *Home Fires Burning: Married to the Military, for Better or Worse*
LJ - v130 - i4 - March 1 2005 - p100(1) [51-500]
PW - v252 - i8 - Feb 21 2005 - p172(1) [51-500]

Houran, James - *From Shaman to Scientist: Essays on Humanity's Search for Spirits*
Choice - v42 - i6 - Feb 2005 - p1101(1) [51-500]
R&R Bk N - v19 - i4 - Nov 2004 - p11(1) [51-500]

Hourcade, A. - *Antiphon d' Athenes. Une pensee de l'individu*
Class R - v54 - i2 - Nov 2004 - p310-312 [501+]

Housden, Roger - *How Rembrandt Reveals Your Beautiful, Imperfect Self: Life Lessons from the Master*
PW - v252 - i11 - March 14 2005 - p57(1) [51-500]
Ten Poems to Last a Lifetime
BL - v101 - i3 - Oct 1 2004 - p294(1) [51-500]

House, James E. - *Descriptive Inorganic Chemistry*
J Chem Ed - v81 - i5 - May 2004 - p647-648 [501+]

House, James S. - *A Telescope on Society: Survey Research and Social Science at the University of Michigan and Beyond*
Choice - v42 - i4 - Dec 2004 - p701(1) [1-50]

House, John (b. 1945 -) - *Impressionism: Paint and Politics*
CR - v286 - i1669 - Feb 2005 - p121(1) [51-500]

House, John H. - *Gifts of the Great River: Arkansas Effigy Pottery from the Edwin Curtiss Collection*
R&R Bk N - v19 - i3 - August 2004 - p61(1) [51-500]

House, Kirk W. - *Hell-Rider to King of the Air: Glenn Curtiss's Life of Innovation*
SciTech - v28 - i1 - March 2004 - p168(1) [51-500]

House, Laurel - *The Guru's Guide to Serenity: A Me-Time Menu of Celebrity Stress Reducers*
LJ - v129 - i19 - Nov 15 2004 - p76(1) [51-500]
PW - v251 - i43 - Oct 25 2004 - p42(1) [51-500]

House, Raelynn Hill - *Rift Zone*
PW - v251 - i32 - August 9 2004 - p233(1) [51-500]

House, Robert J. - *Culture, Leadership, and Organizations: The GLOBE Study of 62 Societies*
Choice - v42 - i7 - March 2005 - p1273(1) [51-500]
R&R Bk N - v19 - i3 - August 2004 - p104(1) [1-50]

House, Silas - *The Coal Tattoo*
BL - v100 - i21 - July 2004 - p1818(1) [51-500]
KR - v72 - i15 - August 1 2004 - p705(1) [51-500]
PW - v251 - i31 - August 2 2004 - p52(1) [51-500]

House, Tom - *The Beginning of Calamities*
BooChiTr - Jan 4 2004 - p3(1) [501+]

Housely, Norman - *The Experience of Crusading I: Western Approaches*
HRNB - v33 - i1 - Fall 2004 - p33(1) [501+]

Houseman, Gerald L. - *Researching Indonesia: A Guide to Political Analysis*
R&R Bk N - v19 - i3 - August 2004 - p182(1) [501+]

Houseman, Susan - *Nonstandard Work in Developed Economies: Causes and Consequences*
M Lab R - v127 - i7 - July 2004 - p63(2) [501+]

Houser, Rick A. - *Gaining Power and Control through Diversity and Group Affiliation*
R&R Bk N - v19 - i3 - August 2004 - p142(1) [51-500]

Housley, Norman - *Religious Warfare in Europe, 1400-1536*
Specu - v79 - i4 - Oct 2004 - p1096(3) [501+]

Houssa, Michel - *High-k Gate Dielectrics*
E-Streams - August 2004 - pNA [501+]

Houston, Alan - *A Nation Transformed: England after the Restoration*
Six Ct J - v35 - i1 - Spring 2004 - p211(2) [501+]

Houston, C. Stuart - *Birds of Yorkton-Duck Mountain*
BIC - v33 - i5 - August 2004 - p28(3) [501+]

Houston, M. Sue - *IGF and Nutrition in Health and Disease*
SciTech - v28 - i4 - Dec 2004 - p72(1) [51-500]

Houston, Pam - *Sight Hound*
y BL - v101 - i6 - Nov 15 2004 - p553(1) [51-500]
KR - v72 - i21 - Nov 1 2004 - p1024(1) [51-500]
LJ - v130 - i1 - Jan 1 2005 - p98(1) [51-500]
NYTBR - Feb 27 2005 - p12 [501+]
People - v63 - i5 - Feb 7 2005 - p52 [501+]
PW - v251 - i46 - Nov 15 2004 - p39(2) [501+]

Houston, Stuart - *Eighteenth-Century Naturalists of Hudson Bay*
Beav - v84 - i4 - August-Sept 2004 - p48(1) [51-500]
Choice - v42 - i1 - Sept 2004 - p129(1) [501+]

Houswitschka, Christoph - *Freedom-Treason-Revolution: Uncollected Sources of the Political and Legal Culture of the London Treason Trials*
R&R Bk N - v19 - i4 - Nov 2004 - p164(1) [501+]

Houtepen, Anton - *God: An Open Question*
TT - v60 - i4 - Jan 2004 - p574-576 [501+]

Houtman, Ronald - *Variegated Trees and Shrubs: The Illustrated Encyclopedia*
BL - v101 - i2 - Sept 15 2004 - p189(1) [51-500]
Bwatch - Nov 2004 - pNA [51-500]
Ref Rev - Nov 2004 - pNA [501+]
SciTech - v28 - i4 - Dec 2004 - p125 [51-500]

Houtzager, Peter P. - *Changing Paths: International Development and the New Politics of Inclusion*
Soc Ser R - v79 - i1 - March 2005 - p210(1) [51-500]

Houzel, Christian - *La geometrie algebrique: Recherches historiques*
Isis - v95 - i2 - June 2004 - p279(1) [51-500]

Hovannisian, Richard G. - *Armenian People from Ancient to Modern Times*
CR - v285 - i1664 - Sept 2004 - p183(2) [501+]

Hovath, Imre - *Tools and Methods of Competitive Engineering: Proceedings, 2 vols.*
SciTech - v28 - i3 - Sept 2004 - p170(1) [51-500]

Hove, Chenjerai - *Blind Moon*
WLT - v79 - i1 - Jan-April 2005 - p85(1) [501+]

Hoverson, Joelle - *Last-Minute Knitted Gifts (Illus. by Williams, Anna)*
y BL - v101 - i8 - Dec 15 2004 - p705(2) [51-500]
LJ - v129 - i20 - Dec 1 2004 - p110(1) [51-500]

Hovey, Kate - *Voices of the Trojan War (Illus. by Gore, Leonid)*
y CCB-B - v58 - i2 - Oct 2004 - p80(1) [51-500]
c KR - v72 - i13 - July 1 2004 - p631(1) [51-500]
y SLJ - v50 - i9 - Sept 2004 - p228(1) [51-500]

Hoveyda, Fereydoun - *The Broken Crescent: The "Threat" of Militant Islamic Fundamentalism, National Committee on American Foreign Policy Study*
IJMES - v36 - i1 - Feb 2004 - p151-152 [501+]

How, Alan - *Critical Theory*
Choice - v41 - i11-12 - July-August 2004 - p2129(1) [501+]
CS - v33 - i6 - Nov 2004 - p732(3) [501+]

How to Reverse Diabetes
SEP - v277 - i1 - Jan-Feb 2005 - p89(1) [501+]

Howard, Andy J. - *Alluvial Archaeology in Europe; Proceedings*
R&R Bk N - v19 - i1 - Feb 2004 - p31(1) [1-50]

Howard, Bradley Reed - *Indigenous Peoples and the State: The Struggle for Native Rights*
R&R Bk N - v19 - i1 - Feb 2004 - p71(1) [1-50]

Howard, David John (b. 1947 -) - *Coloring the Nation: Race and Ethnicity in the Dominican Republic*
JTWS - v21 - i1 - Spring 2004 - p318(3) [501+]
How to Build a Great Screenplay
LJ - v129 - i14 - Sept 1 2004 - p164(2) [501+]

Howard, Elizabeth Fitzgerald - *Flower Girl Butterflies (Illus. by Kromer, Christiane)*
c Black Iss - v6 - i4 - July-August 2004 - p61(1) [51-500]

Virgie Goes to School with Us Boys (Read by Lewis,
E.B.)
  c PW - v252 - i1 - Jan 3 2005 - p58(1) [51-500]
Howard-Hassmann, Rhoda E. - *Compassionate*
Canadians: Civic Leaders Discuss Human Rights
  CBRA - Annual 2003 - p307(1) [51-500]
  R&R Bk N - v19 - i1 - Feb 2004 - p149(1) [51-
  500]
Howard, Heather H. - *Chore Whore: Adventures of a*
Celebrity Personal Assistant
  KR - v73 - i1 - Jan 1 2005 - p10(1) [501+]
  PW - v252 - i6 - Feb 7 2005 - p40(1) [501+]
  PW - v252 - i4 - Jan 24 2005 - p114(1) [501+]
Howard, Hugh - *Natchez: The Houses and History of the*
Jewel of the Mississippi
  Choice - v41 - i11-12 - July-August 2004 -
  p2036(1) [501+]
Howard, Ian - *Swein Forkbeard's Invasions and the*
Danish Conquest of England, 991-1017
  Med R - Dec 2004 - pNA [501+]
Howard, Linda - *Kiss Me While I Sleep (Read by Bean,*
Joyce). Audiobook Review
  y Kliatt - v39 - i1 - Jan 2005 - p46(1) [51-500]
  PW - v251 - i36 - Sept 6 2004 - p25(1) [51-500]
To Die For
  PW - v251 - i49 - Dec 6 2004 - p48(1) [51-500]
Howard, Madeline - *The Hidden Stars*
  LJ - v129 - i19 - Nov 15 2004 - p54(1) [501+]
  PW - v251 - i40 - Oct 4 2004 - p74(2) [501+]
Howard, Marc Morje - *The Weakness of Civil Society in*
Post-Communist Europe
  Slav R - v63 - i3 - Fall 2004 - p621-622 [501+]
Howard, Margaret - *Archeological Survey and History of*
Pedernales Falls State Park, Blanco County, Texas
  SHQ - v108 - i1 - July 2004 - p107-108 [501+]
Howard, Margo - *A Life in Letters: Ann Landers' Letters*
to Her Only Child
  Wom R Bks - v21 - i10-11 - July 2004 - p8(2)
  [501+]
Howard, Maureen - *Big as Life: Three Tales for Spring*
  BL - v100 - i22 - August 2004 - p1886(1) [51-500]
The Silver Screen
  NL - v87 - i4 - July-August 2004 - p29(3) [501+]
  NYRB - v51 - i20 - Dec 16 2004 - p78(2) [501+]
  NYTBR - August 29 2004 - p17 [501+]
  NYTBR - Sept 5 2004 - p18 [501+]
Howard, Patricia L. - *Women and Plants: Gender*
Relations in Biodiversity Management and Conservation
  SciTech - v28 - i1 - March 2004 - p66(1) [51-500]
Howard, Philip N. - *Society Online: The Internet in*
Context
  R&R Bk N - v19 - i1 - Feb 2004 - p124(1) [51-
  500]
Howard, Richard - *Inner Voices: Selected Poems,*
1963-2003
  BL - v101 - i4 - Oct 15 2004 - p380(1) [501+]
  PW - v251 - i38 - Sept 20 2004 - p58(2) [501+]
  NYTBR - Nov 21 2004 - p18 [501+]
Paper Trail: Selected Prose, 1965-2003
  BL - v101 - i4 - Oct 15 2004 - p380(1) [501+]
  KR - v72 - i15 - August 1 2004 - p727(1) [501+]
  LJ - v129 - i16 - Oct 1 2004 - p80(1) [501+]
  NYTBR - Nov 21 2004 - p18 [501+]
Howard, Robert E. - *The Bloody Crown of Conan (Illus.*
by Gianni, Gary)
  LJ - v129 - i13 - August 2004 - p131(1) [51-500]
  PW - v251 - i42 - Oct 18 2004 - p52(2) [501+]
Howard, Robert Ervin - *The Savage Tales of Solomon*
Kane
  ChrSFF&H - v26 - i10 - Oct 2004 - p26(1) [51-
  500]
  Globe & Mail - July 31 2004 - pD14 [1-50]
Howard, Rosalyn - *Black Seminoles in the Bahamas*
  HNet - June 2004 - pNA [501+]
Howard-Snyder, Daniel - *Divine Hiddenness: New Essays*
  TT - v61 - i1 - April 2004 - p118-120 [501+]
Howard, Tracie - *Never Kiss and Tell*
  BL - v101 - i4 - Oct 15 2004 - p389(1) [51-500]
Howarth, David - *The European Central Bank: The New*
European Leviathan?
  JEL - v42 - i1 - March 2004 - p257(1) [501+]
Howarth, Lesley - *Colossus*
  y Sch Lib - v52 - i3 - Autumn 2004 - p158(1) [51-500]
Howatt, Betty - *Tales from Willowshade Farm: An Island*
Woman's Notebook
  CBRA - Annual 2003 - p403(1) [51-500]
Howe, Brian - *Spirit of Australia II: Religion in*
Citizenship and National Life
  AJPS - v39 - i2 - July 2004 - p442(443) [501+]
Howe, Christopher - *China's Economic Reform: A Study*
with Documents
  JEL - v41 - i4 - Dec 2003 - p1428(1) [51-500]

Howe, Deborah - *Bunnicula: A Rabbit-Tale of Mystery,*
25th Anniversary Ed. (Illus. by Daniel, Alan)
  c CH Bwatch - Feb 2005 - pNA [51-500]
Bunnicula: A Rabbit-Tale of Mystery, 25th Anniversary
Edition
  c PW - v251 - i37 - Sept 13 2004 - p80(1) [51-500]
Howe, Elizabeth - *Roman and Medieval Cripplegate, City*
of London: Archaeological Excavations 1992-8
  R&R Bk N - v19 - i4 - Nov 2004 - p36(1) [51-
  500]
Howe, Fanny - *On the Ground*
  Poet - v185 - i5 - Feb 2005 - p397(2) [501+]
Howe, Fisher - *The Nonprofit Leadership Team: Building*
the Board-Executive Director Partnership
  R&R Bk N - v19 - i1 - Feb 2004 - p92(1) [1-50]
Howe, James - *Kaddish for Grandpa in Jesus' Name Amen*
(Illus. by Stock, Catherine)
  c BL - v101 - i3 - Oct 1 2004 - p345(1) [51-500]
  c BL - v101 - i9-10 - Jan 1 2005 - p775(1) [1-50]
  c SLJ - v50 - i7 - July 2004 - p78(1) [51-500]
Howe, John R. - *Language and Political Meaning in*
Revolutionary America
  RAH - v32 - i4 - Dec 2004 - p486-492 [501+]
  R&R Bk N - v19 - i4 - Nov 2004 - p217(1) [501+]
Howe, K.R. - *The Quest for Origins: Who First Discovered*
and Settled New Zealand and the Pacific Islands?
  AHS - v35 - i124 - Oct 2004 - p402(3) [501+]
Howe, Karen - *The Golf Widow Travels Scotland*
  Bwatch - Dec 2004 - pNA [51-500]
Howe, Mary Byle - *A Baptist among the Jews*
  Bks & Cult - v10 - i6 - Nov-Dec 2004 - p14(2)
  [501+]
Howe, Nicholas - *Visions of Community in the Pre-Modern*
World
  Six Ct J - v34 - i4 - Winter 2003 - p1247-1249
  [501+]
Howe, Rufus S. - *Disease Manager's Handbook*
  SciTech - v28 - i4 - Dec 2004 - p80(1) [51-500]
Howe, Sean - *Give Our Regards to the Atomsmashers:*
Writers on Comics
  Globe & Mail - August 21 2004 - pD13 [501+]
Howell, David - *MacDonald's Party: Labour Identities and*
Crisis, 1922-1931
  Albion - v36 - i2 - Summer 2004 - p357(3) [501+]
Howell, Dusti - *Digital Storytelling: Creating an Estory*
  LibMed - v22 - i4 - Jan 2004 - p84(1) [501+]
Howell, Hannah - *The Eternal Highlander*
  BL - v101 - i1 - Sept 1 2004 - p72(1) [51-500]
  LJ - v129 - i13 - August 2004 - p55(1) [51-500]
Howell, Jude - *Governance in China*
  Choice - v42 - i1 - Sept 2004 - p182(1) [501+]
  R&R Bk N - v19 - i1 - Feb 2004 - pNA [501+]
Howells, Edward - *John of the Cross and Teresa of Avila:*
Mystical Knowing and Self-hood
  Theol St - v65 - i4 - Dec 2004 - p898(1) [501+]
Howells, Robin - *Playing Simplicity: Polemical Stupidity in*
the Writing of the French Enlightenment
  FS - v58 - i2 - April 2004 - p255(2) [501+]
Howells, William Dean - *Indian Summer*
  Globe & Mail - Jan 1 2005 - pD14 [1-50]
Hower, Edward - *The Storms of May*
  KR - v73 - i2 - Jan 15 2005 - p74(1) [501+]
  LJ - v130 - i3 - Feb 15 2005 - p116(1) [501+]
Howett, Jerry - *Contemporary's Number Power: Real*
World Math Skills
  Bwatch - Nov 2004 - pNA [501+]
Howgego, Raymond John - *Encyclopedia of Exploration*
1800-1850
  Spec - v297 - i9206 - Jan 15 2005 - p45(2) [501+]
Encyclopedia of Exploration to 1800
  Spec - v297 - i9206 - Jan 15 2005 - p45(2) [501+]
Howitt, Arnold M. - *Countering Terrorism: Dimensions of*
Preparedness
  Choice - v42 - i1 - Sept 2004 - p188(1) [501+]
Howitt, Mary - *The Spider and the Fly (Illus. by*
DiTerlizzi, Tony)
  c RT - v57 - Oct 2003 - p174 [1-50]
Howland, Douglas - *Asia-Pacific Constitutional Systems*
  JAS - v63 - i3 - August 2004 - p758-760 [501+]
Howse, Christopher - *Comfort*
  TLS - i5292 - Sept 3 2004 - p26(1) [501+]
One Hundred and Fifty Years of The Daily Telegraph
  Spec - v296 - i9194 - Oct 23 2004 - p51(1) [501+]
Hox, Joop - *Multilevel Analysis: Techniques and*
Applications
  Per Psy - v57 - i4 - Winter 2004 - p1113(4) [501+]
Hoxby, Blair - *Mammon's Music: Literature and*
Economics in the Age of Milton
  HNet - July 2004 - pNA [501+]

Hoxby, Caroline M. - *The Economics of School Choice*
  JEL - v42 - i3 - Sept 2004 - p861(2) [501+]
A Straightforward Comparison of Charter Schools and
Regular Public Schools in the United States
  Wil Q - v29 - i1 - Wntr 2005 - p93(2) [501+]
Hoy, Claire - *Canadians in the Civil War*
  TLS - i5307 - Dec 17 2004 - p31(1) [1-50]
Hoy, Ronald - *Metaphysics: Classic and Contemporary*
Readings, 2nd Ed.
  R&R Bk N - v19 - i4 - Nov 2004 - p8(1) [51-500]
Hoy, Wayne R. - *Educational Administration, Policy and*
Reform: Research and Measurement
  R&R Bk N - v19 - i3 - August 2004 - p222(1)
  [1-50]
Hoyer, Patricia B. - *Ovarian Toxicology*
  SciTech - v28 - i3 - Sept 2004 - p69(1) [51-500]
Hoyt, Beth Caldwell - *The Ultimate Girls' Guide to*
Science: from Backyard Experiments to Winning the
Nobel Prize!
  c SLJ - v50 - i8 - August 2004 - p138(1) [51-500]
Hoyt-Goldsmith, Diane - *Celebrating Ramadan*
  c SLJ - v51 - i1 - Jan 2005 - p56(1) [51-500]
Three Kings Day: A Celebration at Christmastime (Illus.
by Migdale, Lawrence)
  c BL - v101 - i2 - Sept 15 2004 - p238(2) [51-500]
  HB - v80 - i6 - Nov-Dec 2004 - p661(1) [51-500]
Three Kings Day: A Celebration of Christmastime (Illus.
by Migdale, Lawrence)
  c KR - v72 - i21 - Nov 1 2004 - p1050(1) [51-500]
Hoyt, Linda - *Make It Real*
  RT - v57 - Nov 2003 - p296 [501+]
Hoyt-O'Connor, Paul - *Bernard Lonergan's*
Macroeconomic Dynamics
  R&R Bk N - v19 - i4 - Nov 2004 - p83(1) [51-
  500]
Hoyt, Richard - *Pony Girls*
  Roundup M - v11 - i6 - August 2004 - p28(1)
  [501+]
HR Department Benchmarks and Analysis 2004
  HR Mag - v50 - i2 - Feb 2005 - pNA [51-500]
HR Flipcards: HR Complicance Reference Set
  HR Mag - v49 - i7 - July 2004 - pS33(1) [501+]
Hrdlitschka, Shelley - *Kat's Fall*
  y Kliatt - v38 - i4 - July 2004 - p20(1) [51-500]
  c SLJ - v50 - i8 - August 2004 - p124(1) [51-500]
  y VOYA - v27 - i5 - Dec 2004 - p382(1) [51-500]
Hrechuk, Irene - *Grandma's Kitchen: Comfort Cooking*
from Canadian Grandmas
  CBRA - Annual 2003 - p131(1) [51-500]
Hricak, Hedvig - *Gynecology: Top 100 Diagnoses*
  SciTech - v28 - i3 - Sept 2004 - p115(1) [51-500]
Hrushevsky, Mykhailo - *History of Ukraine-Rus'*
  Six Ct J - v35 - i3 - Fall 2004 - p868-869 [501+]
Hsi, Stephen D. - *Closing the Chart: A Dying Physician*
Examines Family, Faith and Medicine
  SciTech - v28 - i3 - Sept 2004 - p78(1) [51-500]
Hsia, C.T. - *C.T. Hsia on Chinese Literature*
  Choice - v42 - i1 - Sept 2004 - p97(1) [501+]
Hsia, R. Po-Chia - *Calvinism and Religious Toleration in*
the Dutch Golden Age
  JMH - v77 - i1 - March 2005 - p212(3) [501+]
A Companion to the Reformation World
  Choice - v41 - i11-12 - July-August 2004 -
  p2098(1) [501+]
Hsieh, Chiao-min - *Changing China: A Geographical*
Appraisal
  R&R Bk N - v19 - i1 - Feb 2004 - p84(1) [1-50]
Hsieh, Fang-Lan - *An Annotated Bibliography of Church*
Music
  R&R Bk N - v19 - i1 - Feb 2004 - p195(1) [51-
  500]
Hsiung, Ping-Chun - *Chinese Women Organizing: Cadres,*
Feminists, Muslims, Queers
  Ch Rev Int - v10 - i2 - Fall 2003 - p409(3) [501+]
Hsu, Bertrand D. - *Practical Diesel-Engine Combustion*
Analysis
  SciTech - v28 - i1 - March 2004 - p151(1) [51-
  500]
Hsu, D. Frank - *Parallel Architectures, Algorithms, and*
Networks (I-SPAN 2004): Proceedings
  SciTech - v28 - i3 - Sept 2004 - p18(1) [501+]
Hsu, Elizabeth - *Innovation in Chinese Medicine*
  JIH - v35 - i1 - Summer 2004 - p177-179 [501+]
Hsu, Kenneth J. - *Physics of Sedimentology: Textbook and*
Reference
  Choice - v42 - i3 - Nov 2004 - p512(1) [1-50]
Hsueh, Willa A. - *Contemporary Diagnosis and*
Management of Type 2 Diabetes
  SciTech - v28 - i3 - Sept 2004 - p105(1) [51-500]

Htun, Mala - *Sex and the State: Abortion, Divorce, and the Family under Latin American Dictatorships and Democracies*
   CS - v33 - i1 - Jan 2004 - p127-127 [501+]
   PSQ - v119 - i3 - Fall 2004 - p555(2) [501+]
Hu, Evelyn - *Annual Review of Materials Research, Vol. 34*
   SciTech - v28 - i4 - Dec 2004 - p134 [51-500]
Huang, Jianrong - *The Dynamics of China's Rejuvenation*
   Choice - v42 - i6 - Feb 2005 - p1092(1) [51-500]
Huang, Martin W. - *Desire and Fictional Narrative in Late Imperial China*
   HJAS - v64 - i1 - June 2004 - p152-158 [501+]
Huang, Philip C.C. - *Code, Custom, and Legal Practice in China: The Qing and the Republic Compared*
   Ch Rev Int - v10 - i2 - Fall 2003 - p411(4) [501+]
Huang, Xiang - *A Bilingual Edition of Poetry out of Communist China*
   R&R Bk N - v19 - i3 - August 2004 - p257(1) [51-500]
Huang, Yasheng - *Selling China: Foreign Direct Investment During the Reform Era*
   JEL - v41 - i4 - Dec 2003 - p1430(1) [501+]
Huaolelo, Komike - *Mamaka Kaiao: A Modern Hawaiian Vocabulary, a Compilation of Hawaiian Words That Have Been Created, Collected, and Approved by the Hawaiian Lexicon Committee from 1987 through 2000*
   R&R Bk N - v19 - i1 - Feb 2004 - p220(1) [51-500]
Huband, Mark - *The Skull Beneath the Skin: Africa after the Cold War*
   HNet - June 2004 - pNA [501+]
Hubbard, Charles M. - *Lincoln Reshapes the Presidency*
   JSH - v70 - i4 - Nov 2004 - p923(2) [501+]
Hubbard, Edward E. - *The Diversity Scorecard: Evaluating the Impact of Diversity on Organizational Performance*
   HR Mag - v49 - i7 - July 2004 - pS11(1) [51-500]
   Diversity Scorecard: Evaluating the Impact of Diversity on Organizational Performance
   HR Mag - v50 - i2 - Feb 2005 - pS6(1) [501+]
Hubbard, Kirsten A. - *Physics Toolbox: A Survival Guide for Introductory Physics*
   SciTech - v28 - i1 - March 2004 - p46(1) [51-500]
Hubbard, L. Ron - *L. Ron Hubbard Presents Writers of the Future, Vol. XX*
   PW - v251 - i39 - Sept 27 2004 - p43(1) [51-500]
   To the Stars
   Ent W - i790 - Oct 29 2004 - p71 [501+]
   LJ - v129 - i18 - Nov 1 2004 - p134(1) [1-50]
   PW - v251 - i35 - August 30 2004 - p37(1) [501+]
Hubbard, Mina Benson - *A Woman's Way through Unknown Labrador*
   R&R Bk N - v19 - i3 - August 2004 - p77(1) [51-500]
   TLS - i5295 - Sept 24 2004 - p26(1) [51-500]
Hubbard, Phil - *Key Thinkers on Space and Place*
   Choice - v42 - i5 - Jan 2005 - p838(1) [1-50]
   R&R Bk N - v19 - i3 - August 2004 - p81(1) [51-500]
   Thinking Geographically: Space, Theory and Contemporary Human Geography
   PG - v23 - i6 - August 2004 - p804-806 [501+]
Hubbard, T.K - *Homosexuality in Greece and Rome. A Sourcebook of Basic Documents*
   Class R - v54 - i2 - Nov 2004 - p439(3) [501+]
Hubbartt, William S. - *HIPAA Privacy Source Book: A Collection of Practical Samples*
   HR Mag - v50 - i2 - Feb 2005 - pS12(1) [501+]
Hubble, Christopher - *Lord Given Lovers: The Holy Union of David and Jonathan*
   Lam Bk Rpt - v13 - i4-5 - Nov-Dec 2004 - p27(2) [501+]
Hubbs, G. Ward - *Guarding Greensboro: A Confederate Company in the Making of a Southern Community*
   J Mil H - v68 - i3 - July 2004 - p964-965 [501+]
   JSH - v71 - i1 - Feb 2005 - p159(2) [501+]
   Voices from Company D: Diaries by the Greensboro Guards, Fifth Alabama Infantry Regiment, Army of Northern Virginia
   J Mil H - v68 - i3 - July 2004 - p964-965 [501+]
Hubbs, Nadine - *The Queer Composition of America's Sound: Gay Modernists, American Music, and National Identity*
   Choice - y42 - i6 - Feb 2005 - p1030(1) [51-500]
Hubbuch, Susan M. - *Writing Research Papers Across the Curriculum, 5th Ed.*
   R&R Bk N - v19 - i4 - Nov 2004 - p185(1) [501+]
Hubeny, Ivan - *Stellar Atmosphere Modeling: Proceedings*
   SciTech - v28 - i1 - March 2004 - p45(1) [51-500]
Huber, Christopher - *Der "Tristan" Gottfried von Strafburg*
   GSR - v27 - i1 - Feb 2004 - p137-138 [501+]

Huber, Joseph - *New Technologies and Environmental Innovation*
   R&R Bk N - v19 - i3 - August 2004 - p96(1) [51-500]
Huber, Peter - *Hard Green: Saving the Environment*
   Forbes - v174 - i5 - Sept 20 2004 - p146 [501+]
Huber, Peter W. - *The Bottomless Well: The Twilight of Fuel, the Virtue of Waste, and Why We Will Never Run out of Energy*
   BL - v101 - i8 - Dec 15 2004 - p693(1) [51-500]
   BL - v101 - i8 - Dec 15 2004 - p693(1) [51-500]
   BL - v101 - i8 - Dec 15 2004 - p693(1) [51-500]
   BL - v101 - i8 - Dec 15 2004 - p693(1) [51-500]
   BL - v101 - i8 - Dec 15 2004 - p693(1) [51-500]
   Har Bus R - v83 - i3 - March 2005 - p28(1) [51-500]
   The Bottomless Well: the Twilight of Fuel, the Virtue of Waste and Why We Will Never Run out of Energy
   PW - v251 - i50 - Dec 13 2004 - p57(2) [51-500]
   The Twilight of Fuel, the Virtue of Waste, and Why We Will Never Run out of Energy
   Bus W - i3924 - March 14 2005 - p23 [501+]
Huber, Stephan Gerhard - *Preparing School Leaders for the 21st century: an International Comparison of Development Programs in 15 Countries*
   R&R Bk N - v19 - i3 - August 2004 - p220(1) [1-50]
Hubert, Jennifer - *Reading Rants!*
   LibMed - v22 - i4 - Jan 2004 - p88(1) [501+]
Hubler, Marsha - *The Trouble with Skye*
   y SLJ - v51 - i1 - Jan 2005 - p130(2) [51-500]
Huchel, Peter - *The Garden of Theophrastus*
   TLS - i5304 - Nov 26 2004 - p31(1) [501+]
Huchthausen, Peter A. - *America's Splendid Little Wars: A Short History of U.S. Military Engagements: 1975-2000*
   Choice - v41 - i7 - March 2004 - p1368(1) [501+]
   Mar Crp G - v88 - i1 - Jan 2004 - p62(1) [501+]
   Shadow Voyage: The Extraordinary Wartime Escape of the Legendary Liner S.S. Bremen
   KR - v73 - i3 - Feb 1 2005 - p165(2) [501+]
Huckman, Robert - *Human Wildlife: The Life That Lives on Us*
   CBRA - Annual 2003 - p424(1) [51-500]
Hudak, Paul F. - *Principles of Hydrogeology, 3rd Ed.*
   SciTech - v28 - i4 - Dec 2004 - p5(1) [1-50]
Hudgens, Dallas - *Drive Like Hell*
   BL - v101 - i6 - Nov 15 2004 - p553(2) [51-500]
   KR - v72 - i23 - Dec 1 2004 - p1108(1) [51-500]
   LJ - v129 - i20 - Dec 1 2004 - p100(2) [51-500]
   PW - v251 - i44 - Nov 1 2004 - p40(2) [501+]
Hudis, Peter - *The Rosa Luxemburg Reader*
   Choice - v42 - i5 - Jan 2005 - p925(1) [1-50]
Hudson, Aida - *Windows and Words: A Look at Canadian Children's Literature in English*
   Can CL - i113/114 - Spring-Summer 2004 - p129(3) [501+]
   CBRA - Annual 2003 - p265(1) [501+]
Hudson, Charles M. - *Conversation with the High Priest of Coosa*
   Am Ind CRJ - v27 - i4 - Fall 2003 - p148-150 [501+]
Hudson, Cheryl Willis - *What Do You Know? Snow! (Illus. by Walker, Sylvia)*
   c SLJ - v51 - i2 - Feb 2005 - p97(1) [51-500]
Hudson, David L., Jr. - *Rights of Students*
   y VOYA - v27 - i4 - Oct 2004 - p334(1) [51-500]
Hudson, Elizabeth - *Snow Bodies: One Woman's Life on the Streets*
   Wom R Bks - v21 - i12 - Sept 2004 - p27(1) [501+]
Hudson, Judith - *Undelivered Letters to Hudson's Bay Company Men on the Northwest Coast of America, 1830-57*
   CBRA - Annual 2003 - p75(1) [501+]
Hudson, Kate - *Breaking the South Slav Dream: The Rise and Fall of Yugoslavia*
   Choice - v41 - i7 - March 2004 - p1351(1) [501+]
   Slav R - v63 - i4 - Winter 2004 - p864(2) [501+]
Hudson, Lynn H. - *The Making of "Mammy Pleasant": A Black Entrepreneur in Nineteenth-Century San Francisco*
   WHQ - v35 - i3 - Autumn 2004 - p383(2) [501+]
Hudson, Marc - *The Disappearing Poet Blues*
   Sew R - v111 - i3 - Summer 2003 - pXC-XCII [501+]
Hudson, Miles - *Intervention in Russia 1918-1920: A Cautionary Tale*
   R&R Bk N - v19 - i3 - August 2004 - p45(1) [51-500]
   Intervention in Russia, 1918-1920: A Cautionary Tale
   Spec - v295 - i9181 - July 24 2004 - p36(1) [501+]

Hudson, Nicholas - *Samuel Johnson and the Making of Modern England*
   HNet - Sept 2004 - pNA [501+]
   TimHES - v0 - i1676 - Jan 28 2005 - p24(2) [501+]
Hudson, Valerie M. - *Bare Branches: The Security Implications of Asia's Surplus Male Population*
   Choice - v42 - i5 - Jan 2005 - p931(1) [51-500]
   Fut - v39 - i1 - Jan-Feb 2005 - p48(1) [51-500]
Hudson, Wade - *Powerful Words: Excerpts from Famous Speeches and Writings by African Americans (Illus. by Qualls, Sean)*
   c LibMed - v23 - i1 - August-Sept 2004 - p76(1) [51-500]
   Powerful Words: More Than 200 Years of Extraordinary Writing by African Americans
   c SLJ - v50 - i10 - Oct 2004 - pS31(1) [51-500]
   y Teach Lib - v32 - i1 - Oct 2004 - p51(1) [51-500]
   The Two Tyrones (Illus. by Page, Mark)
   c SLJ - v51 - i1 - Jan 2005 - p92(1) [51-500]
Hudson, William E. - *American Democracy in Peril: Eight Challenges to America's Future, 4th Ed.*
   R&R Bk N - v19 - i3 - August 2004 - p177(1) [501+]
Huebert, Ronald - *The Performance of Pleasure in English Renaissance Drama*
   Choice - v41 - i11-12 - July-August 2004 - p2044(1) [501+]
   R&R Bk N - v19 - i1 - Feb 2004 - p235(1) [51-500]
Huebner, Mark - *Sports Bloopers: All-Star Blubs and Fumbles*
   CBRA - Annual 2003 - p143(1) [501+]
Huebner, Timothy S. - *The Taney Court: Justices, Rulings, and Legacy*
   R&R Bk N - v19 - i1 - Feb 2004 - pNA [51-500]
Huebscher, Roxana - *Natural, Alternative, and Complementary Health Care Practices*
   E-Streams - June 2004 - pNA [501+]
Huegel, Kelly - *GLBTQ: The Survival Guide for Queer and Questioning Teens*
   y SLJ - v50 - i10 - Oct 2004 - pS65(1) [501+]
Huel, Raymond J.A. - *Archbishop A.-A. Tache of St. Boniface: The "Good Fight" and the Illusive Vision*
   CBRA - Annual 2003 - p50(1) [51-500]
Huelfer, Evan Andrew - *The Casualty Issue" in American Military Practice: The Impact of World War I*
   R&R Bk N - v19 - i1 - Feb 2004 - p255(1) [51-500]
Huener, Jonathan - *Auschwitz, Poland, and the Politics of Commemoration, 1945-1979*
   Choice - v42 - i1 - Sept 2004 - p168(1) [501+]
Huesca-Dorantes, Patricia - *The Emergence of Multiparty Competition in Mexican Politics*
   R&R Bk N - v19 - i1 - Feb 2004 - pNA [501+]
Hueston, Marie Proeller - *Country Living Collection Style: Arranging and Displaying Your Treasures*
   LJ - v130 - i1 - Jan 1 2005 - p107(1) [51-500]
Huet, Pierre-Daniel - *Against Cartesian Philosophy*
   R&R Bk N - v19 - i1 - Feb 2004 - p3(1) [51-500]
Huet, Sylvie - *Statistical Tools for Nonlinear Regression: A Practical Guide with S-PLUS and R Examples*
   JEL - v42 - i1 - March 2004 - p245(1) [501+]
Huettel, Scott A. - *Functional Magnetic Resonance Imaging*
   Choice - v42 - i4 - Dec 2004 - p695(1) [1-50]
   SciTech - v28 - i3 - Sept 2004 - p95(1) [51-500]
Huey, Michael - *Viennese Silver- Modern Design 1780-1918*
   Ant&CM - v108 - i8 - Oct 2003 - p16(1) [501+]
Huff, Tanya - *Smoke and Shadows*
   MFSF - v107 - i3 - Sept 2004 - p34(5) [501+]
Huffaker, Bob - *When the News Went Live: Dallas 1963*
   LJ - v129 - i13 - August 2004 - p91(1) [501+]
Huffington, Arianna - *Pigs at the Trough: How Corporate Greed and Political Corruption Are Undermining America*
   R&R Bk N - v19 - i3 - August 2004 - p146(1) [51-500]
Huffman, Alan - *Mississippi in Africa: The Saga of the Slaves of Prospect Hill Plantation and their Legacy in Liberia Today*
   BW - v34 - i5 - Feb 1 2004 - p2(1) [501+]
Huffman, Fred - *Practical IP and Telecom for Broadcast Engineering and Operations*
   E-Streams - Nov 2004 - pNA [501+]
Huffman, James L. - *A Yankee in Meiji Japan: The Crusading Journalist Edward H. House*
   JAS - v63 - i3 - August 2004 - p798-799 [501+]
   Pac A - v77 - i2 - Summer 2004 - p342(2) [501+]

Huffman, Jane Bumpers - *Reculturing Schools as Professional Learning Communities*
 R&R Bk N - v19 - i1 - Feb 2004 - p187(1) [51-500]

Huggan, Isabel - *Belonging: Home Away from Home*
 CBRA - Annual 2003 - p50(1) [51-500]

Huggens, Karin - *Ferris Wheel Fun*
 c CH Bwatch - v14 - i12 - Dec 2004 - pNA [51-500]

Huggett, Richard J. - *Fundamentals of Biogeography, 2nd Ed.*
 SciTech - v28 - i4 - Dec 2004 - p59(1) [51-500]

Huggins, Barry - *Creative Photoshop Lighting Techniques*
 SciTech - v28 - i3 - Sept 2004 - p169(1) [51-500]

Huggins, James Byron - *Nightbringer*
 LJ - v129 - i14 - Sept 1 2004 - p132(1) [51-500]

Huggins, Martha K. - *Violence Workers: Police Torturers and Murderers Reconstruct Brazilian Atrocities*
 CS - v33 - i1 - Jan 2004 - p60-62 [501+]

Hugh-Jones, Stephen - *The essential Edmund Leach, vol. 1*
 JRAI - v10 - i4 - Dec 2004 - p949(2) [501+]

Hughes, Aaron W. - *The Texture of the Divine: Imagination in Medieval Islamic and Jewish Thought*
 Choice - v42 - i2 - Oct 2004 - p310(1) [51-500]

Hughes, Alan - *Signs and Circumstances: A Study of Allegory in Chaucer's Canterbury Tales*
 Med R - Dec 2004 - pNA [501+]

Hughes, Cheryl - *Web Wizard's Guide to XHTML*
 SciTech - v28 - i4 - Dec 2004 - p28(1) [51-500]

Hughes, Christopher - *Kripke: Names, Necessity and Identity*
 Lon R Bks - v26 - i20 - Oct 21 2004 - p17(3) [501+]

Hughes, Christopher W. - *Japan's Security Agenda: Military, Economic and Environmental Dimensions*
 Choice - v42 - i2 - Oct 2004 - p368(1) [51-500]
 Pac A - v77 - i3 - Fall 2004 - p577(2) [501+]

Hughes, David A. - *Diet and Human Immune Function*
 SciTech - v28 - i1 - March 2004 - p76(1) [51-500]

Hughes, Dean - *Take Me Home: Hearts of the Children, vol. 4*
 PW - v251 - i34 - August 23 2004 - pS16(1) [51-500]

Hughes, Dennie - *Dateworthy*
 LJ - v129 - i17 - Oct 15 2004 - p77(1) [51-500]

Hughes, Dorothy B. - *In a Lonely Place*
 NYTBR - August 8 2004 - p15 [501+]

Hughes, Frieda - *Waxworks*
 South HR - v38 - i1 - Wntr 2004 - p88-91 [501+]

Hughes, Gerard - *Reforming Pensions in Europe: Evolution of Pension Financing and Sources of Retirement Income*
 R&R Bk N - v19 - i3 - August 2004 - p117(1) [51-500]

Hughes, Graham - *Worship as Meaning: A Liturgical Theology for Late Modernity*
 Intpr - v59 - i1 - Jan 2005 - p106(1) [501+]
 TT - v61 - i2 - July 2004 - p254(3) [501+]

Hughes-Hallett, Lucy - *Heroes: Saviours, Traitors And Supermen*
 Spec - v296 - i9192 - Oct 9 2004 - p44(1) [501+]
 TLS - i5305 - Dec 3 2004 - p27(1) [501+]

Hughes-Hallett, Penelope - *The Immortal Dinner*
 Sew R - v112 - i3 - Summer 2004 - p467-475 [501+]

Hughes, Howard - *Once Upon a Time in the Italian West: A Filmgoer's Guide to Spaghetti Westerns*
 LJ - v130 - i1 - Jan 1 2005 - p115(1) [51-500]

Hughes, James E. - *Family Wealth: Keeping It in the Family: How Family Members and Their Advisers Preserve Human, Intellectual, and Financial Assets for Generations, Rev. and Expanded Ed.*
 R&R Bk N - v19 - i3 - August 2004 - p197(1) [1-50]

Hughes, James H. - *Citizen Cyborg: Why Democratic Societies Must Respond to the Redesigned Human of the Future*
 Fut - v39 - i1 - Jan-Feb 2005 - p48(1) [501+]
 SciTech - v28 - i4 - Dec 2004 - p81(1) [51-500]

Hughes, Jason - *Learning to Smoke: Tobacco Use in the West*
 CS - v33 - i2 - March 2004 - p247-248 [501+]

Hughes, Jeff - *The Manhattan Project: Big Science and the Atom Bomb*
 Choice - v41 - i7 - March 2004 - p1332(1) [501+]
 SciTech - v28 - i1 - March 2004 - p51(1) [51-500]

Hughes, John A. - *Understanding Classical Sociology: Marx, Weber, Durkheim, 2nd Ed.*
 R&R Bk N - v19 - i2 - May 2004 - p126 [51-500]

Hughes, Karen - *Ten Minutes from Normal (Read by Hughes, Karen). Audiobook Review*
 BL - v101 - i1 - Sept 1 2004 - p146(1) [1-50]
 LJ - v129 - i17 - Oct 15 2004 - p98(1) [51-500]

Hughes, Kathleen - *Dear Mrs. Lindbergh*
 y Kliatt - v39 - i2 - March 2005 - p20(1) [51-500]

Hughes, Langston - *Autobiography: I Wonder as I Wander, Vol. 14*
 Afr Am R - v38 - i3 - Fall 2004 - p529(2) [501+]

Hughes, Lee - *Biggest Boat I Could Afford*
 Bwatch - v26 - i8 - August 2004 - p12(1) [51-500]

Hughes, Lindsey - *Peter the Great: A Biography*
 JMH - v76 - i3 - Sept 2004 - p732(3) [501+]

Hughes, Lorna M. - *Digitizing Collections: Strategic Issues for the Information Manager*
 LRTS - v49 - i1 - Jan 2005 - p65(2) [501+]

Hughes, Matthew - *Black Brillion: A Novel of the Archonate*
 BL - v101 - i5 - Nov 1 2004 - p472(1) [51-500]
 PW - v251 - i44 - Nov 1 2004 - p48(1) [51-500]

Hughes, Meredith Sayles - *Plants We Eat*
 c CH Bwatch - Feb 2005 - pNA [51-500]

Hughes, Monica - *Water Cycle*
 c SB - v40 - i6 - Nov-Dec 2004 - p949(2) [51-500]
Weather Patterns
 c SB - v40 - i6 - Nov-Dec 2004 - p268(1) [51-500]

Hughes, Pat - *The Breaker Boys*
 c BL - v101 - i2 - Sept 15 2004 - p233(1) [51-500]
 c BW - v34 - i43 - Oct 24 2004 - p11(1) [51-500]
Breaker Boys
 y CCB-B - v58 - i2 - Oct 2004 - p80(2) [51-500]
The Breaker Boys
 y KR - v72 - i15 - August 1 2004 - p743(1) [51-500]
 y SLJ - v50 - i11 - Nov 2004 - p145(2) [51-500]
Guerrilla Season
 c LibMed - v22 - i6 - March 2004 - p67(1) [501+]

Hughes, Richard - *Capricorn: David Stirling's Second African Campaign*
 IJAHS - v37 - i2 - Spring 2004 - p361-363 [501+]

Hughes, Richard (b. 1941 -) - *Lament, Death, and Destiny*
 R&R Bk N - v19 - i4 - Nov 2004 - p24(1) [51-500]
Myths America Lives By
 JR - v85 - i1 - Jan 2005 - p175(2) [501+]

Hughes, Robert - *Goya*
 Lon R Bks - v26 - i18 - Sept 23 2004 - p17(2) [501+]
 R&R Bk N - v19 - i1 - Feb 2004 - p200(1) [51-500]
 World&I - v19 - i2 - Feb 2004 - p210 [501+]

Hughes, Shirley - *Alfie Wins a Prize*
 c Magpies - v19 - i5 - Nov 2004 - p28(1) [501+]
 c Sch Lib - v52 - i4 - Winter 2004 - p187(1) [51-500]
Ella's Big Chance: A Jazz-Age Cinderella (Illus. by Hughes, Shirley)
 c BL - v101 - i5 - Nov 1 2004 - p490(1) [51-500]
 c CCB-B - v58 - i3 - Nov 2004 - p126(2) [501+]
 c KR - v72 - i19 - Oct 1 2004 - p961(1) [51-500]
 c PW - v251 - i46 - Nov 15 2004 - p59(1) [501+]
Ella's Big Chance: A Jazz-Age Cinderella. (Illus. by Hughes, Shirley)
 c SLJ - v50 - i12 - Dec 2004 - p132(1) [501+]

Hughes, Susan - *Beluga en danger*
 c Res Links - v10 - i2 - Dec 2004 - p54(2) [501+]
Bobcat Rescue
 c CBRA - Annual 2003 - p490(1) [51-500]
Cubs All Alone
 c Res Links - v10 - i3 - Feb 2005 - p18(1) [501+]
Lonely Wolf Pup
 c CBRA - Annual 2003 - p490(1) [51-500]
Not-Quite World Famous Scientist (Illus. by Taylor, Stephen)
 y Can CL - i111-112 - Fall-Winter 2003 - p134(6) [501+]
Sauvons Les Bebes Lievres!
 y Res Links - v10 - i1 - Oct 2004 - p52(2) [501+]

Hughes, Ted - *Collected Poems*
 BooChiTr - Jan 11 2004 - p2(1) [501+]
 Globe & Mail - Nov 27 2004 - pD3 [51-500]
 Quad - v48 - i9 - Sept 2004 - p88(2) [501+]

Hughes, Thomas P. - *American Genesis: A Century of Invention and Technological Enthusiasm*
 y SB - v40 - i6 - Nov-Dec 2004 - p262(1) [51-500]
Human-Built World: How to Think about Technology and Culture
 Am Sci - v92 - i6 - Nov-Dec 2004 - p576(2) [501+]
 HT - v54 - i11 - Nov 2004 - p85(2) [501+]
 Nature - v429 - i6990 - May 27 2004 - p348(1) [501+]
 Sci - v305 - i5690 - Sept 10 2004 - p1568(2) [501+]
 TimHES - v0 - i1681 - March 4 2005 - p29(1) [501+]
 TLS - i5288 - August 6 2004 - p27(1) [501+]

Hughes, William C. - *James Agee, Omnibus, and Mr. Lincoln: The Culture of Liberalism and the Challenge of Television, 1952-1953*
 R&R Bk N - v19 - i4 - Nov 2004 - p222(1) [51-500]
James Agee, Omnibus, and Mr. Lincoln: The Culture of Liberalism and the Challenge of Televison, 1952-1953
 Choice - v42 - i7 - March 2005 - p1222(1) [51-500]

Hughes-Wilson, John - *The Puppet Masters: Spies, Traitors and the Real Forces Behind World Events*
 Spec - v295 - i9181 - July 24 2004 - p33(1) [501+]

Hugo, Leon - *Bernard Shaw's The Black Girl in Search of God: The Story Behind the Story*
 ELT - v47 - i3 - Summer 2004 - p363(3) [501+]

Hugo, Richard - *The Real West Marginal Way: A Poet's Autobiography*
 A Lib - v35 - i7 - August 2004 - p88(1) [501+]

Hugo, Victor - *Bug-Jargal*
 TLS - i5294 - Sept 17 2004 - p31(1) [501+]
The Distance, The Shadows
 TLS - i5268 - March 19 2004 - p8-8 [501+]
Selected Poems
 TLS - i5268 - March 19 2004 - p8-8 [501+]
Selected Poems of Victor Hugo
 TLS - i5268 - March 19 2004 - p8-8 [501+]

Huhn, Rick - *The Sizzler: George Sisler, Baseball's Forgotten Great*
 Choice - v42 - i7 - March 2005 - p1266(1) [51-500]
 PW - v251 - i41 - Oct 11 2004 - p67(2) [51-500]

Hui, Y.H. - *Handbook of Food and Beverage Fermentation Technology*
 E-Streams - Oct 2004 - pNA [501+]
Handbook of Frozen Foods
 E-Streams - Oct 2004 - pNA [501+]
Handbook of Vegetable Preservation and Processing
 E-Streams - Sept 2004 - pNA [501+]

Huie, William Bradford - *The Execution of Private Slovik*
 LJ - v129 - i18 - Nov 1 2004 - p134(1) [51-500]

Huisman, Frank - *Locating Medical History: The Stories and Their Meanings*
 Sci - v307 - i5708 - Jan 21 2005 - p356(1) [501+]
 SciTech - v28 - i4 - Dec 2004 - p76(1) [51-500]

Huizenga, Edward I. - *Innovation Management in the ICT Sector: How Frontrunners Stay Ahead*
 R&R Bk N - v19 - i3 - August 2004 - p101(1) [501+]

Huler, Scott - *Defining the Wind: The Beaufort Scale, and How a Nineteenth-Century Admiral Turned Science into Poetry*
 BL - v100 - i21 - July 2004 - p1807(1) [1-50]
 LJ - v129 - i12 - July 2004 - p114(2) [51-500]
 NH - v113 - i9 - Nov 2004 - p51(2) [501+]
Defining The Wind: The Beaufort Scale, and How the Nineteenth-Century Admiral Turned Science into Poetry
 Ent W - i778 - August 13 2004 - p91 [51-500]
 NY - v80 - i26 - Sept 13 2004 - p89(1) [1-50]
 SLJ - v50 - i12 - Dec 2004 - p54(4) [501+]

Huliska-Beth, Laura - *Favourite Things*
 c LibMed - v22 - i4 - Jan 2004 - p56(1) [501+]

Hulit, Lloyd M. - *Straight Talk on Stuttering: Information, Encouragement, and Counsel for Stutterers, Caregivers, and Speech-Language Clinicians, 2nd Ed.*
 SciTech - v28 - i4 - Dec 2004 - p94(1) [51-500]

Hull, Derek - *Celtic and Anglo-Saxon Art Geometric Aspects*
 Choice - v42 - i1 - Sept 2004 - p85(1) [501+]

Hull, Maureen - *Rainy Days with Bear (Illus. by Franson, Leanne)*
 c Globe & Mail - August 28 2004 - pD12 [501+]
 c Res Links - v10 - i2 - Dec 2004 - p4(1) [501+]

Hull, N.E.H. - *The Abortion Rights Controversy in America: A Legal Reader*
 Pers PS - v34 - i1 - Wntr 2005 - p49(1) [501+]

Hull, Tanya - *Smoke and Shadows*
 y VOYA - v27 - i4 - Oct 2004 - p315(1) [51-500]

Hullen, Werner - *A History of Roget's Thesaurus: Origins, Development and Design*
 TimHES - v0 - i1661 - Oct 8 2004 - p26(1) [501+]
 TLS - i5263 - Feb 13 2004 - p7-7 [501+]

Hulliung, Mark - *Citizens and Citoyens: Republicans and Liberals in America and France*
 JMH - v76 - i3 - Sept 2004 - p662(2) [501+]

Hulme, Joy N. - *Climbing the Rainbow*
 c LibMed - v23 - i1 - August-Sept 2004 - p67(1) [51-500]

Hulme, Karen - *War Torn Environment: Interpreting the Legal Threshold*
 R&R Bk N - v19 - i4 - Nov 2004 - p163(1) [501+]

Hyland, William G. - *George Gershwin: A New Biography*
Choice - v41 - i7 - March 2004 - p1306(1) [501+]
Notes - v61 - i1 - Sept 2004 - p116(4) [501+]
Hylton, Keith N. - *Antitrust Law: Economic Theory and Common Law Evolution*
JEL - v41 - i4 - Dec 2003 - p1390(1) [501+]
JEL - v42 - i4 - Dec 2004 - p1146(2) [501+]
Hylton, Stuart - *A History of Manchester*
R&R Bk N - v19 - i1 - Feb 2004 - p33(1) [1-50]
Hyman, Bruce M. - *Obsessive-Compulsive Disorder*
SLJ - v50 - i10 - Oct 2004 - pS64(1) [501+]
Hyman, David N. - *Public Finance: A Contemporary Application of Theory to Policy, 8th Ed.*
R&R Bk N - v19 - i2 - May 2004 - p124 [51-500]
Hyman, Michael H. - *The Power of Global Capital: New International Rules--New Global Risks*
R&R Bk N - v19 - i2 - May 2004 - p123(1) [501+]
Hyman, Peter - *1 out of 10: From Downing Street Vision to Classroom Reality*
Econ - v374 - i8415 - Feb 26 2005 - p85US [501+]

The Reluctant Metrosexual: Dispatches from an Almost Hip Life (Read by Hyman, Peter). Audiobook Review
BL - v101 - i9-10 - Jan 1 2005 - p884(2) [51-500]
The Reluctant Metrosexual: Dispatches from an Almost Hip Life
LJ - v129 - i12 - July 2004 - p82(2) [51-500]
NYT - August 8 2004 - pST9 [501+]
Hyman, Steven E. - *Annual Review of Neuroscience: Vol. 26, 2003*
SciTech - v28 - i1 - March 2004 - p73(1) [51-500]
Hympendahl, Klaus - *Pirates Aboard! Forty Cases of Piracy Today and What Bluewater Cruisers Can Do About It*
R&R Bk N - v19 - i1 - Feb 2004 - p69(1) [501+]
Pirates Aboard! Forty Cases of Piracy Today and Whate Bluewater Cruisers Can Do About It
Bwatch - v26 - i8 - August 2004 - p12(1) [51-500]
Hyndman, Chris - *Designerguys: Finding Your Personal Style*
CBRA - Annual 2003 - p115(1) [51-500]
Hynes, James - *Kings of Infinite Space*
ABR - v26 - i2 - Jan-Feb 2005 - p17(2) [501+]

Hynes, Joel - *Down to the Dirt*
CBRA - Annual 2003 - p169(1) [51-500]
Hynes, Steven J. - *Planetary Nebulae and Practical Guide Handbook for Amateur Astronomers*
Astron - v33 - i2 - Feb 2005 - p100 [501+]
Hyser, Raymond M. - *Voices of the American Past: Documents in U.S. History, 3rd Ed., Vol.1*
R&R Bk N - v19 - i4 - Nov 2004 - p57(1) [1-50]
Voices of the American Past: Documents in U.S. History, 3rd Ed., Vol. 2
R&R Bk N - v19 - i4 - Nov 2004 - p57(1) [1-50]
Hyslop, Stephen G. - *Bound for Santa Fe: The Road to New Mexico and the American Conquest, 1806-1848*
HAHR - v84 - i3 - August 2004 - p538(2) [501+]
Hyson, Marilou - *The Emotional Development of Young Children: Building an Emotion-Centred Curriculum*
TCR - v106 - i5 - May 2004 - p931(4) [501+]
Hyun, Gang-Suk - *Sky Blade: Sword of the Heavens*
y VOYA - v27 - i5 - Dec 2004 - p407(1) [51-500]
Hyun, Theresa - *Writing Women in Korea: Translation and Feminism in the Colonial Period*
R&R Bk N - v19 - i1 - Feb 2004 - p213 [51-500]

I

Ikenberry, G. John - *American Foreign Policy: Theoretical Essays, 5th Ed.*
> R&R Bk N - v19 - i3 - August 2004 - p160(1) [501+]
>
> *Reinventing the Alliance: U.S.-Japan Security Partnership in an Era of Change*
> Choice - v42 - i1 - Sept 2004 - p186(1) [501+]

Ikenson, Ben - *Patents: Ingenious Inventions: How They Work and How They Came to Be*
> Choice - v42 - i3 - Nov 2004 - p514(2) [1-50]
> SciTech - v28 - i3 - Sept 2004 - p134(1) [51-500]
> y SLJ - v50 - i8 - August 2004 - p147(1) [501+]

Ikeuchi, Satoru - *Asian-Pacific Regional Meeting, Vol. 1*
> SciTech - v28 - i3 - Sept 2004 - p42(1) [1-50]

Ikumi, Mia - *Tokyo Mew Mew, Volume 1*
> c Teach Lib - v32 - i3 - Feb 2005 - p24(1) [51-500]

Ilari, Virgilio - *Bella Italia Militar: Eserciti e Marine nell'Italia pre-napoleonica*
> J Mil H - v68 - i2 - April 2004 - p595(4) [501+]
>
> *Storia Militare dell'Italia Giacobina (1796-1802), Tomo 1, La Guerra Continentale*
> J Mil H - v68 - i2 - April 2004 - p595(4) [501+]
>
> *Storia Militare dell'Italia Giacobina (1796-1802), Tomo 2, La Guerra Peninsulare*
> J Mil H - v68 - i2 - April 2004 - p595(4) [501+]

Iles, Chrissie - *Whitney Biennial 2004: Whitney Museum of American Art*
> Art N - v103 - i5 - May 2004 - p145(1) [501+]

Iles, Greg - *Blood Memory*
> BL - v101 - i7 - Dec 1 2004 - p618(1) [51-500]
> KR - v73 - i3 - Feb 1 2005 - p139(1) [501+]
> LJ - v130 - i3 - Feb 15 2005 - p119(1) [51-500]
> PW - v252 - i1 - Jan 3 2005 - p33(1) [51-500]

Illetschko, Georgia - *I, Michelangelo*
> Choice - v42 - i2 - Oct 2004 - p284(1) [501+]
> Lam Bk Rpt - v13 - i4-5 - Nov-Dec 2004 - p46(2) [501+]
>
> *Masterworks*
> LJ - v129 - i15 - Sept 15 2004 - p54(1) [51-500]

Illies, Christian - *The Grounds of Ethical Judgement: New Transcendental Arguments in Moral Philosophy*
> Ethics - v114 - i4 - July 2004 - p823(5) [501+]

Illner, Reinhard - *Mathematical Foundation of Classical Statistical Mechanics: Continous Systesms. Second Edition*
> SIAM Rev - v46 - i1 - March 2004 - p168-169 [501+]

Illouz, Eva - *Oprah Winfrey and the Glamour of Misery: An Essay on Popular Culture*
> Afr Am R - v38 - i3 - Fall 2004 - p539(3) [501+]
> AJS - v110 - i3 - Nov 2004 - p839(2) [501+]
> JouAmCul - v27 - i4 - Dec 2004 - p453(2) [501+]
> R&R Bk N - v19 - i1 - Feb 2004 - p223(1) [51-500]

Illustrated World Atlas
> LJ - v129 - i16 - Oct 1 2004 - p112(1) [501+]
> y BL - v101 - i8 - Dec 15 2004 - p758(1) [501+]

Ilyas, Mohammad - *Handbook of Sensor Networks: Compact Wireless and Wired Sensing Systems*
> Choice - v42 - i6 - Feb 2005 - p1053(1) [51-500]
>
> *Silicon Carbide 2004 -- Materials, Processing and Devices: Proceedings*
> SciTech - v28 - i4 - Dec 2004 - p157(1) [51-500]

I'm Learning My Phonics. Audiobook Review
> SLJ - v50 - i12 - Dec 2004 - p74(1) [501+]

Imagawa, Yasuhiro - *Seven of Seven: Volume 3 (Illus. by Imagawa, Yasuhiro)*
> c SLJ - v50 - i8 - August 2004 - p148(2) [501+]

Image Comics Presents: Flight, vol. 1
> LJ - v130 - i1 - Jan 1 2005 - p88(1) [51-500]

Images from Science, An Exhibition of Scientific Photography
> Am Bio T - v66 - i7 - Sept 2004 - p514(515) [501+]

Imagine a House: A Journey to Fascinating houses around the World
> LibMed - v22 - i4 - Jan 2004 - p79(1) [501+]

Imamoghu, Y. - *Novel Metathesis Chemistry: Well-Defined Initiator Systems for Specialty Chemical Synthesis, Tailored Polymers, and Advanced Material Applications*
> SciTech - v28 - i1 - March 2004 - p57(1) [51-500]

Imber, Colin - *The Ottoman Empire, 1300-1650: The Structure of Power*
> HNet - Oct 2004 - pNA [501+]
> Six Ct J - v35 - i1 - Spring 2004 - p268(2) [501+]

Imber, Michael - *Education Law, 3rd Ed.*
> R&R Bk N - v19 - i4 - Nov 2004 - p170(1) [501+]

Imboden, John B. - *Current Rheumatology Diagnosis and Treatment*
> SciTech - v28 - i3 - Sept 2004 - p108(1) [51-500]

Imbriaco, Alison - *Vietnam*
> c SLJ - v50 - i9 - Sept 2004 - p228(1) [51-500]

Imlay, Talbot C. - *Facing the Second World War: Strategy, Politics, and Economics in Britain and France, 1938-1940*
> J Mil H - v68 - i3 - July 2004 - p990-991 [501+]

Immer, Andrea - *Everyday Dining with Wine: 125 Wonderful Recipes To Match and Enjoy with Wine*
> LJ - v129 - i19 - Nov 15 2004 - p80(1) [51-500]

Immergluck, Daniel - *Credit to the Community: Community Reinvestment and Fair Lending Policy in the United States*
> Choice - v42 - i4 - Dec 2004 - p707(1) [1-50]
> R&R Bk N - v19 - i3 - August 2004 - p135(1) [501+]

Immigration and Migration: Primary Sources, Vols. 1-2
> y R&USQ - v44 - i2 - Winter 2004 - p176(1) [501+]

The Impact of Trade Agreements: Effect of the Tokyo Round, U.S.-Israel FTA, U.S.-Canada FTA, NAFTA, and the Uruguay Round on the U.S. Economy
> JEL - v42 - i1 - March 2004 - p261(2) [501+]

Impacts of a Warming Arctic: Arctic Climate Impact Assessment
> Lon R Bks - v27 - i1 - Jan 6 2005 - p9(3) [501+]

Imparato, Ivo - *Slum Upgrading and Participation: Lessons from Latin America*
> JEL - v41 - i4 - Dec 2003 - p1441(1) [501+]

Impe, W.F. van - *Deep Foundations on Bored and Auger Piles: Proceedings*
> SciTech - v28 - i1 - March 2004 - p144(1) [51-500]

Impelluso, Lucia - *Nature and Its Symbols*
> PW - v251 - i48 - Nov 29 2004 - p35(1) [51-500]

Imperato, Teresa - *Morning in the Jungle (Illus. by McDonald, Mercedes)*
> c PW - v251 - i36 - Sept 6 2004 - p64(2) [51-500]

Imperial Hubris: Why the West is Losing the War on Terror
> PW - v251 - i32 - August 9 2004 - p245(1) [501+]
> TLS - i5301 - Nov 5 2004 - p4-6 [501+]

Impey, Rose - *The Ankle Grabber (Illus. by Kemp, Moira)*
> c SLJ - v51 - i1 - Jan 2005 - p94(1) [51-500]
>
> *The Flying Vampire*
> c Sch Lib - v52 - i4 - Winter 2004 - p187(1) [51-500]
>
> *Jumble Joan (Illus. by Kemp, Moira)*
> c SLJ - v51 - i1 - Jan 2005 - p94(1) [51-500]
>
> *The Midnight Ship*
> c Sch Lib - v52 - i4 - Winter 2004 - p187(1) [51-500]
>
> *Scare Yourself to Sleep (Illus. by Kemp, Moira)*
> c SLJ - v51 - i1 - Jan 2005 - p94(1) [51-500]
>
> *Titchy Witch and the Bully Boggarts*
> c Sch Lib - v52 - i3 - Autumn 2004 - p131(1) [501+]

Important People, Vol. 2
> y SB - v40 - i6 - Nov-Dec 2004 - p259(1) [51-500]

Imran, Ali - *Chiral Pollutants: Distribution, Toxicity and Analysis by Chromatography and Capillary Electophoresis*
> SciTech - v28 - i3 - Sept 2004 - p88(1) [51-500]

Imsen, Steinar - *Ecclesia Nidrosiensis 1153-1537*
> HNet - June 2004 - pNA [501+]

In Defense of Liberty: The Story America's Bill of Rights
> LibMed - v22 - i6 - March 2004 - p79(1) [501+]

In Focus
> PW - v251 - i40 - Oct 4 2004 - p21(1) [501+]

In Focus: National Geographic Greatest Portraits
> CC - v121 - i25 - Dec 14 2004 - p23(1) [51-500]
> LJ - v129 - i14 - Sept 1 2004 - p41(1) [51-500]

Inaba, Kay - *Guidelines for Developing Instructions*
> SciTech - v28 - i3 - Sept 2004 - p133(1) [51-500]

Inati, Shams C. - *Iraq: Its History, People, and Politics*
> HNet - Sept 2004 - pNA [501+]

Inayatullah, Naeem - *International Relations and the Problem of Difference*
> CR - v285 - i1664 - Sept 2004 - p187(1) [501+]

Inbar, Efraim - *Democracies and Small Wars*
> J Mil H - v68 - i2 - April 2004 - p663(4) [501+]

Inca, Don Justo Apu Sahuaraura - *Recuerdos de la Monarquia Peruana: O Bosquejo de la Historia de Los Incas Compendio Breve, 2 Vols*
> HAHR - v84 - i2 - May 2004 - p344(2) [501+]

The Incredible Submersible Alvin Discovers a Strange Deep-Sea World
> c LibMed - v22 - i5 - Feb 2004 - p57(1) [501+]

Inda, Jonathan Xavier - *The Anthropology of Globalization: A Reader*
> JRAI - v10 - i3 - Sept 2004 - p722(2) [501+]

Indelible Acts: Stories
> Globe & Mail - Sept 4 2004 - pD18 [1-50]

Indergaard, Michael - *Silicon Alley: The Rise and Fall of a New Media District*
> R&R Bk N - v19 - i2 - May 2004 - p107(1) [51-500]

Inderjit - *Weed Biology and Management*
> Choice - v42 - i5 - Jan 2005 - p879(1) [1-50]

Index to Proceedings of the Security Council: Fifty-Seventh Year, 2002
> R&R Bk N - v19 - i1 - Feb 2004 - pNA [501+]

Indian Development Review
> JEL - v41 - i4 - Dec 2003 - p1446(1) [501+]

Indiana, Gary - *Do Everything in the Dark*
> G&L Rev W - v11 - i5 - Sept-Oct 2004 - p42(1) [51-500]

Indicators of Educations Systems (Project) - *Education at a Glance: OECD Indicators 2003*
> JEL - v42 - i1 - March 2004 - p276(1) [501+]

Indick, William - *Psychology for Screenwriters: Building Conflict in Your Script*
> R&R Bk N - v19 - i4 - Nov 2004 - p224(1) [501+]

Indigenous Peoples
> LibMed - v23 - i1 - August-Sept 2004 - p82(1) [51-500]

Indridason, Arnaldur - *Jar City*
> TLS - i5303 - Nov 19 2004 - p25(1) [501+]

Industrial Revolution Reference Library
> LibMed - v22 - i6 - March 2004 - p80(1) [501+]

Infante, Dominic A. - *Building Communication Theory, 4th Ed.*
> R&R Bk N - v19 - i1 - Feb 2004 - p210(1) [51-500]

Infinite Life: Seven Virtues for Living Well
> Atl - v294 - i5 - Dec 2004 - p137(1) [501+]

Information Handling Skills. E-book Review
> Sch Lib - v52 - i4 - Winter 2004 - p198(1) [501+]

Information Today - *American Book Trade Directory, 2004-2005, 50th Ed.*
> R&R Bk N - v19 - i4 - Nov 2004 - p255(1) [501+]

Information Today, Inc. - *Literary Market Place 2004, 64th Ed. Vols. 1-2.*
> R&R Bk N - v19 - i3 - August 2004 - p258(1) [51-500]

Ingalls, Robert P. - *Tampa Cigar Workers: A Pictorial History*
> HNet - Oct 2004 - pNA [501+]

Ingarden, Roman - *Husserl, La Controverse Idealisme-realisme*
> Dialogue - v43 - i1 - Wntr 2004 - p196-199 [501+]

Ingco, Merlinda D. - *Agriculture and the WTO: Creating a Trading System for Development*
> R&R Bk N - v19 - i1 - Feb 2004 - p107(1) [51-500]
>
> *Agriculture, Trade, and the WTO in South Asia*
> JEL - v42 - i1 - March 2004 - p283(1) [501+]

Ingebretsen, Edward J. - *At Stake: Monsters and the Rhetoric of Fear in Public Culture*
> JouAmCul - v27 - i3 - Sept 2004 - p336(1) [501+]

Ingebretsen, Mark - *Why Companies Fail: The 10 Big Reasons Businesses Crumble, and to Keep Yours Strong and Solid*
> Choice - v41 - i7 - March 2004 - p1338(2) [501+]

Ingermanson, Randall - *Double Vision*
> BL - v101 - i9-10 - Jan 1 2005 - p818(1) [1-50]

Ingermanson, Randall Scott - *Retribution*
> LJ - v129 - i14 - Sept 1 2004 - p134(1) [51-500]

Ingersoll, Julie - *Baptist and Methodist Faiths in America*
> SLJ - v50 - i10 - Oct 2004 - pS62(1) [51-500]
>
> *Evangelical Christian Women: War Stories in the Gender Battles*
> Choice - v41 - i11-12 - July-August 2004 - p2062(1) [501+]
> Wom R Bks - v22 - i3 - Dec 2004 - p6(2) [501+]

Ingham, Geoffrey - *The Nature of Money*
> Choice - v42 - i5 - Jan 2005 - p902(1) [1-50]

Ingham, Mary Beth - *The Philosophical Vision of John Duns Scotus: An Introduction*
> Choice - v42 - i5 - Jan 2005 - p866(1) [1-50]

Ingham, Mike Anthony - *The Prose Fiction Stage Adaptation as Social Allegory in Contemporary British Drama: Staging Fictions*
> R&R Bk N - v19 - i4 - Nov 2004 - p234(1) [501+]

Ingle, James N. - *Advances in Endocrine Therapy of Breast Cancer: Proceedings*
> SciTech - v28 - i4 - Dec 2004 - p92(1) [51-500]

Ingles, Ernie B. - *Peel's Bibliography of the Canadian Prairies to 1953, 3rd Ed.*
> CBRA - Annual 2003 - p10(1) [51-500]

Inglis, John - *On Medieval Philosophy*
> R&R Bk N - v19 - i3 - August 2004 - p3(1) [1-50]

Inglis, John R. - *Inspiring Science: Jim Watson and the Age of DNA*
> QRB - v79 - i3 - Sept 2004 - p293(1) [501+]

Inglis, Mike - *Astronomy of the Milky Way:[pt. 1]: The Observer's Guide to the Northern Milkyway;[pt. 2]: The Observer's Guide to the Southern Milky Way*
Choice - v41 - i11-12 - July-August 2004 - p2067(2) [501+]

Ingold, Tim - *The Perception of the Environment: Essays in Livelihood, Dwelling and Skill*
JRAI - v10 - i3 - Sept 2004 - p723(2) [501+]

Ingoldsby, Bron B. - *Exploring Family Theories*
R&R Bk N - v19 - i3 - August 2004 - p149(1) [51-500]

Ingraham, Patricia W. - *Government Performance: Why Management Matters*
Choice - v42 - i2 - Oct 2004 - p372(1) [51-500]
R&R Bk N - v19 - i1 - Feb 2004 - pNA [51-500]

Ingram, Catherine - *In the Footsteps of Gandhi: Conversations with Spiritual Social Activists, Rev. Ed.*
R&R Bk N - v19 - i3 - August 2004 - p145(1) [51-500]

Ingram, Chip - *God: as He Longs for You to See Him*
PW - v251 - i28 - July 12 2004 - p61(1) [51-500]

Ingram, David - *Rights, Democracy, and Fulfillment in the Era of Identity Politics: Principled Compromises in a Compromised World*
Law&PolBR - Oct 2004 - pNA [501+]
R&R Bk N - v19 - i3 - August 2004 - p175(1) [501+]

Ingram, Heather E. - *Risking It All: My Student, My Lover, My Story*
BIC - v33 - i2 - March 2004 - p28(2) [501+]
CBRA - Annual 2003 - p51(1) [51-500]

Ingram, Jay - *The Velocity of Honey and More Science of Everyday Life*
CBRA - Annual 2003 - p424(2) [51-500]
New Sci - v185 - i2482 - Jan 15 2005 - p51(1) [51-500]

Ingram, Robert W. - *Accounting: Information for Decisions, 3rd Ed.*
R&R Bk N - v19 - i2 - May 2004 - p119 [51-500]

Ingram, Scott - *Frank Lloyd Wright*
c LibMed - v22 - i4 - Jan 2004 - p72(1) [501+]
Indian Americans
y CH Bwatch - v14 - i7 - July 2004 - p5(1) [51-500]
Kim Il Sung
BL - v100 - i21 - July 2004 - p1832(1) [1-50]
y CH Bwatch - v14 - i7 - July 2004 - p5(1) [51-500]
The Panama Canal
c LibMed - v22 - i7 - April-May 2004 - p70(1) [501+]
The Song Dynasty
c SLJ - v50 - i8 - August 2004 - p138(1) [501+]

Ingram-Smith, Cheryl - *Biochemistry and Genetics: PreTest Self-Assessment and Review, 2nd Ed.*
SciTech - v28 - i4 - Dec 2004 - p71(1) [51-500]

Ingram, Susan - *Ports of Call: Central European and North American Culture/s in Motion*
R&R Bk N - v19 - i3 - August 2004 - p41(1) [51-500]
Zarathustra's Sisters: Women's Autobiography and the Shaping of Cultural History
Biomag - v27 - i3 - Summer 2004 - p638(3) [501+]
TSWL - v23 - i2 - Fall 2004 - p393(2) [501+]

Ingstad, Helge - *The Apache Indians: In Search of the Missing Tribe*
LJ - v130 - i3 - Feb 15 2005 - p144(2) [51-500]

Inikori, Joseph E - *Africans and the Industrial Revolution in England: A Study in International Trade and Economic Development*
Albion - v36 - i1 - Spring 2004 - p159(2) [501+]

Initiatives for E-Commerce Capacity-Building of Small and Medium Enterprises
R&R Bk N - v19 - i1 - Feb 2004 - p110(1) [51-500]

Injury Chartbook: A Graphical Overview of the Global Burden of Injuries
SciTech - v28 - i1 - March 2004 - p110(1) [51-500]

Inkheart
LibMed - v22 - i4 - Jan 2004 - p64(1) [501+]

Inman, James A. - *Computers and Writing: The Cyborg Era*
Choice - v42 - i1 - Sept 2004 - p95(1) [501+]

Innerst, Stacy - *M Is for Music (Illus. by Innerst, Stacy)*
c SLJ - v50 - i12 - Dec 2004 - p58(1) [501+]

Innes, Jay - *Secrets in High Places*
CBRA - Annual 2003 - p328(1) [501+]

Innes, Robert B. - *Reconstructing Undergraduate Education: Using Learning Science to Design Effective Courses*
R&R Bk N - v19 - i4 - Nov 2004 - p183(1) [501+]

Inness, Sherrie A. - *Action Chicks: New Images of Tough Women in Popular Culture*
JPC - v38 - i3 - Feb 2005 - p585(2) [501+]
Disco Divas: Women and Popular Culture in the 1970
J Am St - v38 - i1 - April 2004 - p146-147 [501+]

Innocent III, Pope - *Between God and Man: Six Sermons on the Priestly Office*
CH - v73 - i4 - Dec 2004 - p841(2) [51-500]
CHR - v90 - i3 - July 2004 - p530(3) [501+]

Inns, Christopher - *Help!*
HB - v80 - i6 - Nov-Dec 2004 - p698(2) [51-500]
c Sch Lib - v52 - i3 - Autumn 2004 - p131(1) [501+]

Inoarcerea huliganului
WLT - v78 - i3-4 - Sept-Dec 2004 - p153(2) [501+]

Inoue, Katsuro - *Principles of Software Evolution: Proceedings*
SciTech - v28 - i4 - Dec 2004 - p17(1) [1-50]

Inoue, M. - *People and Forest: Policy and Local Reality in Southeast Asia, the Russian Far East, and Japan*
SciTech - v28 - i1 - March 2004 - p131(1) [51-500]

Inoue, Santa - *Tokyo Tribes*
PW - v251 - i39 - Sept 27 2004 - p39(1) [51-500]

Inoue, Yoshihisa - *Chiral Photochemistry*
SciTech - v28 - i4 - Dec 2004 - p56(1) [51-500]

Insects and Other Invertebrates, Vols. 1-10
BL - v101 - i7 - Dec 1 2004 - p687(1) [501+]

Inside Grandad
LibMed - v22 - i7 - April-May 2004 - p58(1) [501+]

Inside Out
LibMed - v22 - i5 - Feb 2004 - p73(1) [501+]

Inside Special Operations, 6 vol.
y VOYA - v27 - i4 - Oct 2004 - p333(1) [51-500]

Insoll, Timothy - *The Archaeology of Islam in Sub-Saharan Africa*
HNet - Sept 2004 - pNA [501+]
The Archeology of Islam in Sub-Saharan Africa
IJAHS - v37 - i1 - Wntr 2004 - p131-133 [501+]

Inspection Panel - *Accountability at the World Bank: The Inspection Panel Ten Years On*
JEL - v42 - i1 - March 2004 - p266(1) [501+]

InstallAnywhere Tutorial and Reference Guide
SciTech - v28 - i4 - Dec 2004 - p25(1) [51-500]

Institute for Laboratory Animal Research - *Guidelines for the Care and Use of Mammals in Neuroscience and Behavioral Research*
SciTech - v28 - i1 - March 2004 - p92(1) [51-500]

Institute for Research on Public Policy - *At the Global Crossroads: The Sylvia Ostry Foundation Lectures*
BIC - v33 - i7 - Oct 2004 - p26(1) [501+]

Institute of Electrical and Electronics Engineers - *Bioinformatics and bioengineering (BIBE 2004): proceedings*
SciTech - v28 - i3 - Sept 2004 - p72(1) [51-500]

Institute of Medicine - *Advancing Prion Science: Guidance for the National Prion Research Program*
SciTech - v28 - i3 - Sept 2004 - p85(1) [51-500]
Financing Vaccines in the 21st Century: Assuring Access and Availability
SciTech - v28 - i3 - Sept 2004 - p84(1) [501+]
Hidden Costs, Value Lost: Uninsurance in America
SciTech - v28 - i3 - Sept 2004 - p82(1) [501+]
Testosterone and Aging: Clinical Research Directions
SciTech - v28 - i3 - Sept 2004 - p86(1) [501+]

Institute of Medicine. Committee on Assessing Integrity in Research Environments - *Integrity in Scientific Research: Creating an Environment That Promotes Responsible Conduct*
SciTech - v28 - i3 - Sept 2004 - p14(1) [501+]

Institute of Medicine (U.S.) - *Dietary Reference Intakes: Applications in Dietary Planning*
SciTech - v28 - i1 - March 2004 - p72(1) [51-500]
Safety of Genetically Engineered Foods: Approaches to Assessing Unintended Health Effects
Choice - v42 - i6 - Feb 2005 - p1056(1) [51-500]

Institute of Medicine (U.S.). Committee on Assuring the Health of the Public in the 21st Century - *The Future of the Public's Health in the 21st Century*
SciTech - v28 - i1 - March 2004 - p83(1) [51-500]

Institute of Medicine (U.S.). Committee on Damp Indoor Spaces and Health - *Damp Indoor Spaces and Health*
Choice - v42 - i7 - March 2005 - p1260(1) [51-500]

Institute of Medicine (U.S.). Committee on the Ryan White CARE Act - *Measuring What Matters: Allocation, Planning, and Quality Assessment for the Ryan White Care Act*
SciTech - v28 - i3 - Sept 2004 - p84(1) [501+]

Insurance and Expanding Systemic Risks
JEL - v42 - i1 - March 2004 - p269(1) [501+]

Insurance Fundamentals
R&R Bk N - v19 - i2 - May 2004 - p124 [51-500]

Insurance Statistics Yearbook/Annuaire des Statisques D'Assurance: 1994-2001
JEL - v42 - i1 - March 2004 - p269(1) [501+]

Insuring America's Health: Principles and Recommendations
SciTech - v28 - i3 - Sept 2004 - p9(1) [501+]

Inter-American Development Bank - *Beyond Borders: The New Regionalism in Latin America*
JEL - v42 - i1 - March 2004 - p308(1) [501+]

International Astronautical Federation - *Highlights in Space 2003; Progress in Space Science, Technology and Applications, International Cooperation and Space Law*
SciTech - v28 - i3 - Sept 2004 - p43(1) [1-50]

International Bank for Reconstruction and Development - *World Bank Atlas, 36th ed.*
R&R Bk N - v20 - i1 - Feb 2005 - p82(1) [51-500]

International Campaign for Tibet - *When the Sky Fell to Earth: The New Crackdown on Buddhism in Tibet*
NYRB - v51 - i19 - Dec 2 2004 - p45(3) [501+]

International Ceramics Studio: Kecskemet, Hungary
Ceram Mo - v52 - i6 - June-August 2004 - p38(1) [501+]

International Children's Digital Library
LibMed - v22 - i4 - Jan 2004 - p88(1) [501+]

International Commission on Intervention and State Sovereignty - *The Responsibility to Protect: Report of the International Commission on Intervention and State Sovereignty*
AJPS - v39 - i2 - July 2004 - p430(430) [501+]

International Conference of the International Plutarch Society (6th: 2002: Nijemgen/Castle Hernen, Netherlands) - *The Statesman in Plutarch's Works: Proceedings; vol. 1*
R&R Bk N - v19 - i4 - Nov 2004 - p214(1) [501+]

International Conference on Autonomic Computing Proceedings: New York, New York, May 17-18, 2004
SciTech - v28 - i3 - Sept 2004 - p29(1) [51-500]

International Conference on Dependable Systems and Networks - *Dependable Systems and Networks: Proceedings*
SciTech - v28 - i3 - Sept 2004 - p21(1) [51-500]

International Conference on Difference Equations and Aplications - *Difference and Differential Equations: Proceedings*
SciTech - v28 - i4 - Dec 2004 - p42(1) [51-500]

International Conference on Enterprise Distributed Object Computing - *Enterprise Distributed Object Computing: Proceedings*
SciTech - v28 - i4 - Dec 2004 - p30(1) [51-500]

International Conference on Mobile and Ubiquitous Systems - *Mobiquitous 2004: Mobile and Ubiquitous Systems, Networking and Services, Proceedings*
SciTech - v28 - i4 - Dec 2004 - p32(1) [51-500]

International Conference on Quality Software - *Quality Software (QSIC 2004): Proceedings*
SciTech - v28 - i4 - Dec 2004 - p27(1) [51-500]

International Conference on Software Engineering and Formal Methods - *Software Engineering and Formal Methods: Proceedings*
SciTech - v28 - i4 - Dec 2004 - p28(1) [51-500]

International Conference on Sustainable Planning and Development - *Sustainable Planning and Development: Proceedings*
R&R Bk N - v19 - i3 - August 2004 - p100(1) [51-500]

International Congress of Celtic Studies - *Retrospect and Prospect in Celtic Studies: Proceedings*
R&R Bk N - v19 - i1 - Feb 2004 - p34(1) [1-50]

International Crisis Group - *Sudan: Now or Never in Darfur*
For Aff - v83 - i5 - Sept-Oct 2004 - p164 [501+]

International Electronic Countermeasures Handbook, 2004 ed.
SciTech - v28 - i3 - Sept 2004 - p172(1) [51-500]

International Encyclopedia of Dance: A Project of Dance Perspectives Foundation, Inc., Vols. 1-6
LJ - v130 - i4 - March 1 2005 - p114(1) [51-500]

International Encyclopedia of Information and Library Science Second Edition
LibMed - v22 - i6 - March 2004 - p88(1) [501+]

International Energy Agency - *Oil Information 2003: With 2002 Data*
SciTech - v28 - i3 - Sept 2004 - p8(1) [501+]
Oil Information/Donnees Sur le Petrole: 2003
JEL - v42 - i1 - March 2004 - p334(2) [501+]

International Geneva Yearbook 2003-2004: Organization and Activities of International Institutions in Geneva, vol. 17
R&R Bk N - v19 - i1 - Feb 2004 - pNA [501+]

J

Jackson, Phil - *The Last Season: A Team in Search of Its Soul*
NYTBR - Nov 7 2004 - p28 [501+]

Jackson, Richard, (b. 1966 -) - *(Re)constructing Cultures of Violence and Peace*
R&R Bk N - v19 - i3 - August 2004 - p144(1) [51-500]

Jackson, Robert H. - *That Man: An Insider's Portrait of Franklin D. Roosevelt*
JSH - v70 - i4 - Nov 2004 - p961(2) [501+]

Jackson, Ronald L., II - *African American Communication and Identities: Essential Readings*
R&R Bk N - v19 - i1 - Feb 2004 - p211 [51-500]

Jackson, Shannon - *Professing Performance: Theatre in the Academy from Philology to Performativity*
Choice - v42 - i4 - Dec 2004 - p667(1) [1-50]

Jackson, Sherri L. - *Statistics: Plain and Simple*
SciTech - v28 - i3 - Sept 2004 - p37(1) [51-500]

Jackson, Stephen - *Australian Mammals: Biology and Captive Management*
Choice - v41 - i11-12 - July-August 2004 - p2073(1) [501+]
SciTech - v28 - i3 - Sept 2004 - p66(1) [51-500]

Jackson, Tom - *Fluorine*
y   SB - v40 - i4 - July-August 2004 - p164(1) [51-500]

Jacob, Gregory - *Criminal*
New York - v37 - i31 - Sept 13 2004 - p126(3) [501+]

Jacob, Karen - *Quick Reference Dictionary for Occupational Therapy, 4th Ed.*
E-Streams - June 2004 - pNA [501+]

Jacob, Madeleine K. - *The Mommy Fund*
BL - v101 - i9-10 - Jan 1 2005 - p819(1) [501+]
LJ - v130 - i2 - Feb 1 2005 - p68(1) [51-500]

Jacob, Pierre - *Ways of Seeing: The Scope and Limits of Visual Cognition*
SciTech - v28 - i1 - March 2004 - p73(1) [51-500]

Jacob, Suzanne - *Rouge, mere et fils*
Can Lit - i182 - Autumn 2004 - p169(3) [501+]

Jacobi, Derek - *Kings and Queens of England: The Story of 1000 Years of English Monarchy. (Read by Jacobi, Derek)*
y   Sch Lib - v52 - i4 - Winter 2004 - p218(1) [51-500]

Jacobs, A.J. - *I Am Not a Jackass*
NYTBR - Feb 13 2005 - p4 [501+]
The Know-It-All: One Man's Humble Quest to Become the Smartest Person in the World
NW - Sept 27 2004 - p12 [51-500]
y   BL - v101 - i1 - Sept 1 2004 - p22(1) [51-500]
Ent W - i785 - Sept 24 2004 - p111 [501+]
KR - v72 - i15 - August 1 2004 - p727(1) [501+]
LJ - v129 - i16 - Oct 1 2004 - p80(1) [51-500]
NYTBR - Oct 3 2004 - p13 [501+]
PW - v251 - i28 - July 12 2004 - p52(1) [51-500]
SLJ - v51 - i2 - Feb 2005 - p158(1) [51-500]
Time - v164 - i14 - Oct 4 2004 - p78 [501+]

Jacobs, Alan - *Shaming the Devil: Essays in Truthtelling*
BL - v101 - i1 - Sept 1 2004 - p22(1) [51-500]
LJ - v129 - i19 - Nov 15 2004 - p65(1) [501+]
PW - v251 - i33 - August 16 2004 - p61(1) [51-500]

Jacobs, Andrew S. - *Remains of the Jews: The Holy Land and Christian Empire in Late Antiquity*
CH - v73 - i4 - Dec 2004 - p845(3) [501+]

Jacobs, Anna - *Marrying Miss Martha*
BL - v100 - i22 - August 2004 - p1909(1) [51-500]

Jacobs, Brian - *Essays on Kant's Anthropology*
Eight-C St - v37 - i3 - Spring 2004 - p491-497 [501+]

Jacobs, Bruce A. - *Race Manners: Navigating the Minefield Between Black and White Americans*
HR Mag - v50 - i2 - Feb 2005 - pS7(1) [501+]

Jacobs, Carol - *Acts of Narrative*
MLN - v118 - i5 - Dec 2003 - p1323-1327 [501+]

Jacobs, Dale - *A Way to Move: Rhetorics of Emotion and Composition Studies*
R&R Bk N - v19 - i1 - Feb 2004 - p215(1) [51-500]

Jacobs, David G. - *The Foundation Directory 2004*
R&R Bk N - v19 - i4 - Nov 2004 - p2(1) [51-500]
R&R Bk N - v19 - i4 - Nov 2004 - p2(1) [51-500]
Guide to U.S. Foundations, Their Trustees, Officers, and Donors
Choice - v42 - i4 - Dec 2004 - p626(1) [1-50]

Jacobs, Don - *Interpersonal Psychology: Communicating Effective People Skills, 2nd Ed.*
R&R Bk N - v19 - i1 - Feb 2004 - p113(1) [51-500]

Jacobs, Elizabeth Derr - *The Nehalem Tillamook: An Ethnography*
Choice - v42 - i2 - Oct 2004 - p334(1) [51-500]

Jacobs, Eva E. - *Handbook of U.S. Labor Statistics: Employment, Earnings, Prices, Productivity, and Other Labor Data*
Choice - v42 - i1 - Sept 2004 - p78(1) [51-500]

Jacobs, Francine - *Lonesome George, the Giant Tortoise (Illus. by Cassels, Jean)*
LibMed - v22 - i4 - Jan 2004 - p71(1) [501+]
c   SLJ - v50 - i10 - Oct 2004 - pS23(1) [51-500]

Jacobs, Harvey M. - *The Character Factor: How We Judge America's Presidents*
Choice - v42 - i3 - Nov 2004 - p566(1) [1-50]

Jacobs, James A. - *Engineering Materials Technology: Structures, Processing, Properties and Selection. 5th Ed.*
SciTech - v28 - i3 - Sept 2004 - p138(1) [51-500]

Jacobs, Jane - *Dark Age Ahead*
Bus W - i3890 - July 5 2004 - p26 [501+]
Globe & Mail - Nov 27 2004 - pD3 [51-500]

Jacobs, Jay S. - *Wild Years: The Music and Myth of Tom Waits*
CBRA - Annual 2003 - p105(1) [51-500]

Jacobs, Jerry A. - *The Time Divide: Work, Family and Gender Inequality*
TLS - i5299 - Oct 22 2004 - p28(1) [501+]
Wom R Bks - v22 - i3 - Dec 2004 - p7(2) [501+]

Jacobs, Jo Ellen - *The Voice of Harriet Taylor Mill*
Albion - v36 - i1 - Spring 2004 - p156(2) [501+]
VS - v46 - i3 - Spring 2004 - p515(4) [501+]

Jacobs, Jonathan A. - *Aristotle's Virtues: Nature, Knowledge, and Human Good*
R&R Bk N - v19 - i4 - Nov 2004 - p3(1) [51-500]

Jacobs, Karen - *Quick Reference Dictionary for Occupational Therapy, 4th Ed.*
SciTech - v28 - i1 - March 2004 - p123(1) [51-500]

Jacobs, Louis - *We Have Reason to Believe: Some Aspects of Jewish Theology Examined in the Light of Modern Thought, 5th Ed.*
R&R Bk N - v19 - i3 - August 2004 - p16(1) [1-50]

Jacobs, Martin S. - *Before They Were Champions: The San Francisco 49er's 1958 Season*
SSJ - v21 - i2 - June 2004 - p230-237 [501+]

Jacobs, Meg - *The Democratic Experiment: New Directions in American Political History*
BHR - v78 - i2 - Summer 2004 - p289(4) [501+]
Choice - v41 - i11-12 - July-August 2004 - p2106(1) [501+]

Jacobs, Michael - *Cards That Pop-Up, Flip and Slide*
LJ - v130 - i3 - Feb 15 2005 - p126(1) [51-500]

Jacobs, Miriam - *Silent Invaders: Pesticides, Livelihoods, and Women's Health*
CS - v33 - i6 - Nov 2004 - p745(1) [1-50]

Jacobs, Paul Dubois - *My Subway Ride (Illus. by Alko, Selina)*
c   KR - v72 - i16 - August 15 2004 - p808(1) [51-500]
c   PW - v251 - i29 - July 19 2004 - p92(1) [51-500]
c   PW - v251 - i37 - Sept 13 2004 - p77(2) [501+]
c   SLJ - v50 - i9 - Sept 2004 - p169(1) [51-500]

Jacobs, Sean - *Thabo Mbeki's World: The Politics and Ideology of the South African President*
Choice - v42 - i1 - Sept 2004 - p184(1) [501+]

Jacobs, Steven Leonard - *Dismantling the Big Lie: The Protocols of the Elders of Zion*
R&R Bk N - v19 - i1 - Feb 2004 - p44(1) [51-500]

Jacobs, Thomas A. - *They Broke the Law, You Be the Judge: True Cases of Teen Crime*
y   VOYA - v27 - i3 - August 2004 - p238(1) [1-50]

Jacobsen, Douglas - *Scholarship and Christian Faith: Enlarging the Conversation*
CC - v121 - i23 - Nov 16 2004 - p45(3) [501+]
Thinking in the Spirit: Theologies of the Early Pentecostal Movement
Choice - v41 - i11-12 - July-August 2004 - p2062(1) [501+]

Jacobsen, Gene Samuel - *We Refused to Die: My Time as a Prisoner of War in Bataan and Japan, 1942-1945*
R&R Bk N - v19 - i4 - Nov 2004 - p34(1) [51-500]

Jacobsen, Knut A. - *South Asians in the Diaspora: Histories and Religious Traditions*
Choice - v42 - i1 - Sept 2004 - p312(1) [51-500]

Jacobsen, Kurt - *Hooked On Growth*
Bwatch - v26 - i9 - Sept 2004 - p12(1) [501+]
Maverick Voices: Conversations with the Political and Cultural Rebels
R&R Bk N - v19 - i4 - Nov 2004 - p30(1) [501+]

Jacobsen, Werner - *Die Maler von Florenz: zu Beginn der Renaissance*
Ren Q - v57 - i3 - Fall 2004 - p987(3) [501+]

Jacobsohn, Gary - *The Wheel of Law: India's Secularism in Comparative Constitutional Context*
JR - v85 - i1 - Jan 2005 - p160(3) [501+]

Jacobson, Arthur J. - *Weimar: A Jurisprudence of Crisis*
GSR - v27 - i2 - May 2004 - p397-398 [501+]

Jacobson, Bonnie - *The Shy Single: A Bold Guide to Dating for the Less-than-Bold Dater*
LJ - v129 - i12 - July 2004 - p106(1) [51-500]

Jacobson, D.M. - *Rapid Design, Prototyping, and Manufacturing Proceedings*
SciTech - v28 - i4 - Dec 2004 - p168(1) [51-500]

Jacobson, Dan - *All For Love*
Spec - v297 - i9209 - Feb 5 2005 - p42(1) [501+]

Jacobson, David - *Place and Belonging in America*
CS - v33 - i1 - Jan 2004 - p59-60 [501+]

Jacobson, Howard - *The Making of Henry*
BL - v100 - i22 - August 2004 - p1899(1) [51-500]
KR - v72 - i14 - July 15 2004 - p649(1) [501+]
y   NYTBR - Sept 26 2004 - p24 [501+]

Jacobson, Jennifer Richard - *Stained*
y   CCB-B - v58 - i6 - Feb 2005 - p253(1) [51-500]
y   HB - v81 - i2 - March-April 2005 - p202(2) [51-500]
y   Kliatt - v39 - i1 - Jan 2005 - p8(1) [51-500]
y   KR - v73 - i5 - March 1 2005 - p288(1) [51-500]
y   PW - v252 - i8 - Feb 21 2005 - p176(1) [51-500]
Truly Winnie (Illus. by Gels, Alissa Imre)
c   SLJ - v50 - i10 - Oct 2004 - pS30(1) [1-50]

Jacobson, Judy - *A Field Guide for Genealogists, 2nd Ed.*
EFHM - v58 - i3 - May-June 2004 - p57(1) [51-500]
R&R Bk N - v19 - i1 - Feb 2004 - p27(1) [51-500]

Jacobson, Mark - *12,000 Miles in the Nick of Time*
y   Kliatt - v38 - i5 - Sept 2004 - p48(2) [51-500]

Jacobson, Michael - *Downsizing Prisons: How to Reduce Crime and End Mass Incarceration*
LJ - v130 - i2 - Feb 1 2005 - p101(1) [51-500]

Jacobson, Nora - *In Recovery: The Making of Mental Health Policy*
Choice - v42 - i6 - Feb 2005 - p1055(2) [51-500]
SciTech - v28 - i4 - Dec 2004 - p85(1) [51-500]

Jacobson, Rick - *Picasso: Soul on Fire (Illus. by Fernandez, Laura)*
c   BL - v101 - i5 - Nov 1 2004 - p496(2) [51-500]
c   Globe & Mail - Sept 11 2004 - pD13 [51-500]
c   Res Links - v10 - i1 - Oct 2004 - p23(2) [501+]
c   SLJ - v50 - i12 - Dec 2004 - p132(1) [501+]

Jacobson, Trudi E. - *Motivating Students in Information Literacy Classes*
R&USQ - v44 - i2 - Winter 2004 - p177(1) [501+]

Jacoby, Rebecca - *Between Stress and Hope: From a Disease-Centered to a Health-Centered Perspective*
SciTech - v28 - i1 - March 2004 - p78(1) [51-500]

Jacoby, Sanford M. - *The Embedded Corporation: Corporate Governance and Employment Relations in Japan and the United States*
Har Bus R - v83 - i3 - March 2005 - p28(1) [51-500]
Employing Bureaucracy: Managers, Unions, and the Transformation of Work in the 20th Century
Choice - v42 - i1 - Sept 2004 - p150(1) [501+]

Jacoby, Susan - *Freethinkers: A History of American Secularism*
BL - v101 - i3 - Oct 1 2004 - p302(1) [51-500]
HM - v309 - i1854 - Nov 2004 - p91(6) [501+]

Jacoby, Tamar - *Reinventing the Melting Pot: The New Immigrants and What It Means to Be American*
Choice - v42 - i4 - Dec 2004 - p743(1) [1-50]

Jacoby, Wade - *Imitation and Politics, Redesigning Modern Germany*
GSR - v27 - i1 - Feb 2004 - p203-205 [501+]

Jacques, Brian - *Loamhedge (Read by Jacques, Brian). Audiobook Review*
y   Kliatt - v38 - i5 - Sept 2004 - p62(2) [501+]
Mariel of Redwall (Read by Jacques, Brian). Audiobook Review
y   Kliatt - v39 - i1 - Jan 2005 - p47(1) [51-500]
c   SLJ - v51 - i2 - Feb 2005 - p75(1) [501+]
Marlfox: A Tale from Redwall
c   PW - v252 - i2 - Jan 10 2005 - p58(1) [1-50]
Mattimeo
c   SLJ - v50 - i8 - August 2004 - p76(1) [51-500]
Rakkety Tam (Illus. by Elliot, David)
c   BL - v101 - i2 - Sept 15 2004 - p245(1) [51-500]
y   SLJ - v50 - i9 - Sept 2004 - p208(2) [51-500]
The Ribbajack & Other Curious Yarns
c   BL - v100 - i22 - August 2004 - p1935(1) [51-500]
c   CH Bwatch - v14 - i7 - July 2004 - p6(1) [51-500]
y   VOYA - v27 - i3 - August 2004 - p230(1) [1-50]

300 • JACQUES
Book Review Index 2005 Cumulation

Jacques, Daniel - *La Revolution technique. Essai sur le devoir d'humanite*
Dialogue - v43 - i3 - Summer 2004 - p612-615 [501+]
Jacques, Roland - *Des nations a evangeliser: Genese de la mission catholique pour l'Exteme-Orient*
CHR - v90 - i4 - Oct 2004 - p766(2) [501+]
Jae-Suk Lee, Edward - *The Good Man*
KR - v72 - i22 - Nov 15 2004 - p1062(1) [51-500]
Jae-Won, Lim - *The Boss, Vol. 1*
VOYA - v27 - i5 - Dec 2004 - p384(1) [51-500]
Jaeger, Barrie - *Making Work Work for the Highly Sensitive Person*
Bwatch - v26 - i8 - August 2004 - p8(1) [51-500]
Jaegwon, Kim - *Nous*
TLS - i5267 - March 12 2004 - p23-23 [501+]
Jaffe, Adam B. - *Innovation and Its Discontents*
New Sci - v185 - i2483 - Jan 22 2005 - p51(1) [501+]
Innovation Policy and the Economy, Vol. 3
JEL - v41 - i4 - Dec 2003 - p1419(1) [501+]
Patents, Citations, and Innovations: A Window on the Knowledge Economy
JEL - v42 - i4 - Dec 2004 - p1158(3) [501+]
Jaffe, Harold - *15 Serial Killers*
ABR - v25 - i5 - July-August 2004 - p25(2) [501+]
Jaffe, Irma B. - *Shining Eyes, Cruel Fortune: The Lives and Loves of Italian Renaissance Women Poets*
HNet - Sept 2004 - pNA [501+]
Jaffe, James A. - *Striking a Bargain: Work and Industrial Relations in England, 1815-65*
JIH - v34 - i3 - Wntr 2004 - p453-3 [501+]
Jaffe, John - *Shenandoah Summer*
KR - v72 - i13 - July 1 2004 - p597(2) [51-500]
PW - v251 - i33 - August 16 2004 - p44(1) [51-500]
Jaffe, Michael Grant - *Whirlwind: A Novel*
BL - v101 - i1 - Sept 1 2004 - p61(1) [51-500]
KR - v72 - i16 - August 15 2004 - p766(1) [51-500]
LJ - v129 - i14 - Sept 1 2004 - p140(1) [51-500]
People - Nov 29 2004 - p57 [501+]
PW - v251 - i40 - Oct 4 2004 - p69(1) [51-500]
Jaffe, Peter G. - *Protecting Children from Domestic Violence: Strategies for Community Intervention*
R&R Bk N - v19 - i4 - Nov 2004 - p146(1) [501+]
Jaffe, Richard A. - *Anesthesiologist's Manual of Surgical Procedures, 3rd Ed.*
SciTech - v28 - i1 - March 2004 - p109(1) [51-500]
Jaffee, Lee - *The Technique and Practice of Psychoanalysis, Vol. 3*
SciTech - v28 - i4 - Dec 2004 - p98(1) [51-500]
Jagdev, Harinder Singh - *Strategic, Decision Making in Modern Manufacturing*
R&R Bk N - v19 - i1 - Feb 2004 - p103(1) [51-500]
Jagels, Martin G. - *Hospitality Management Accounting, 8th Ed.*
R&R Bk N - v19 - i2 - May 2004 - p120 [51-500]
Jager, Eric - *The Last Duel: A True Story of Crime, Scandal, and Trial by Combat in Medieval France*
BL - v101 - i1 - Sept 1 2004 - p24(1) [51-500]
KR - v72 - i14 - July 15 2004 - p672(2) [501+]
LJ - v129 - i15 - Sept 15 2004 - p68(1) [51-500]
PW - v251 - i30 - July 26 2004 - p47(1) [501+]
Spec - v297 - i9204 - Jan 1 2005 - p26(2) [501+]
Jager, Lorenz - *Adorno: A Political Biography*
Choice - v42 - i7 - March 2005 - p1240(1) [51-500]
Nation - v280 - i5 - Feb 7 2005 - p30 [501+]
Jager, Ronald - *The Fate of Family Farming*
VQR - v80 - i3 - Summer 2004 - p265(1) [1-50]
Jager, Sheila Miyoshi - *Narratives of Nation Building in Korea: A Genealogy of Patriotism*
Pac A - v77 - i2 - Summer 2004 - p352(3) [501+]
Jagodzinski, Jan - *Youth Fantasies: The Perverse Landscape of the Media*
Choice - v42 - i5 - Jan 2005 - p846(1) [1-50]
Jagtenberg, Yvonne - *Jack's Kite (Illus. by Jagtenberg, Yvonne)*
c HB - v81 - i1 - Jan-Feb 2005 - p77(1) [51-500]
c SLJ - v51 - i2 - Feb 2005 - p103(2) [51-500]
Jahanbegloo, Ramin - *Iran between Tradition and Modernity*
Choice - v42 - i5 - Jan 2005 - p913(1) [1-50]
R&R Bk N - v19 - i3 - August 2004 - p53(1) [51-500]
Jahn-Clough, Lisa - *Country Girl, City Girl*
y BL - v101 - i6 - Nov 15 2004 - p574(1) [51-500]
c KR - v72 - i20 - Oct 15 2004 - p1007(1) [51-500]
c PW - v251 - i49 - Dec 6 2004 - p60(1) [51-500]
y SLJ - v50 - i11 - Nov 2004 - p146(1) [51-500]
y VOYA - v27 - i4 - Oct 2004 - p303(1) [51-500]
Jahne, Bernd - *Practical Handbook on Image Processing for Scientific and Technical Applications, 2nd Ed.*
Choice - v42 - i2 - Oct 2004 - p327(1) [51-500]
E-Streams - Dec 2004 - pNA [501+]
SciTech - v28 - i3 - Sept 2004 - p143(1) [51-500]
Jahnert, Tina - *A Gift for the Christ Child (Illus. by Roberti, Alessandra)*
c KR - v72 - i21 - Nov 1 2004 - p1051(1) [51-500]
Jahnke, Klaus - *Middle Ear Surgery: Recent Advances and Future Directions*
SciTech - v28 - i1 - March 2004 - p115(1) [51-500]
Jailall, Peter - *When September Comes and Other Poems*
CBRA - Annual 2003 - p220(1) [51-500]
Jain, Harish C. - *Employment Equity and Affirmative Action: An International Comparison*
JEL - v41 - i4 - Dec 2003 - p1388(1) [501+]
Per Psy - v57 - i3 - Autumn 2004 - p789(3) [501+]
Jain, K.K. - *Textbook of Hyperbaric Medicine, 4th Ed.*
SciTech - v28 - i4 - Dec 2004 - p117(1) [1-50]
Jain, S. Mohan - *Banana Improvement: Cellular, Molecular Biology, and Induced Mutations*
SciTech - v28 - i3 - Sept 2004 - p129(1) [51-500]
Jain, Subhash C. - *Handbook of Research in International Marketing: Proceedings*
R&R Bk N - v19 - i1 - Feb 2004 - p106(1) [51-500]
Toward a Global Confederation: A Blueprint for Globalization
R&R Bk N - v19 - i1 - Feb 2004 - p106(1) [51-500]
Jakelic, Slavica - *The Future of the Study of Religion: Proceedings of Congress 2000*
R&R Bk N - v19 - i4 - Nov 2004 - p13(1) [51-500]
Jakeman, Jane - *Let There Be Blood*
KR - v72 - i14 - July 15 2004 - p662(1) [51-500]
LJ - v129 - i14 - Sept 1 2004 - p122(1) [51-500]
PW - v251 - i33 - August 16 2004 - p46(1) [51-500]
Jakes, John - *Savannah, or, A Gift for Mr. Lincoln*
c BL - v100 - i21 - July 2004 - p1799(1) [51-500]
c LJ - v129 - i15 - Sept 15 2004 - p49(1) [51-500]
Savannah, or, A Gift for Mr. Lincoln
c PW - v251 - i33 - August 16 2004 - p40(1) [51-500]
Jakes, Susan Scherffius - *Understanding Ecological Programming: Merging Theory, Research and Practice*
SciTech - v28 - i4 - Dec 2004 - p83(1) [51-500]
Jakes, T.D. - *He-Motions: Even Strong Men Struggle*
BL - v101 - i1 - Sept 1 2004 - p24(1) [51-500]
PW - v251 - i27 - July 5 2004 - p51(1) [51-500]
The Ten Commandments of Working in a Hostile Environment
BL - v101 - i9-10 - Jan 1 2005 - p789(1) [1-50]
Jakle, John A. - *Lots of Parking: Land Use in a Car Culture*
Choice - v42 - i5 - Jan 2005 - p884(1) [1-50]
SciTech - v28 - i3 - Sept 2004 - p163(1) [51-500]
Signs in America's Auto Age: Signature of Landscape and Place
Choice - v42 - i4 - Dec 2004 - p700(1) [1-50]
Signs in America's Auto Age: Signatures of Landscape and Place
JouAmCul - v27 - i3 - Sept 2004 - p356(1) [501+]
Jaklic, Andreja - *Enhanced Transition through Outward Internationalization: Outward FDI by Slovenian Firms*
JEL - v41 - i4 - Dec 2003 - p1357(1) [501+]
Jakobsen, Janet R. - *Love the Sin: Sexual Regulation and the Limits of Religious Tolerance*
R&R Bk N - v19 - i3 - August 2004 - p19(1) [1-50]
Jakobsh, Doris R. - *Relocating Gender in Sikh History: Transformation, Meaning, and Identity*
AHR - v109 - i3 - June 2004 - p889(2) [501+]
JAS - v63 - i2 - May 2004 - p533(3) [501+]
Jakobsson, Armann - *Stadur i nyjum Heimi: Konungasagan Morkinskinna*
JEGP - v103 - i4 - Oct 2004 - p505-528 [501+]
Jakubowski, Maxim - *The Best British Mysteries 2005*
LJ - v129 - i20 - Dec 1 2004 - p96(1) [51-500]
Confessions of a Romantic Pornographer
BL - v101 - i5 - Nov 1 2004 - p468(1) [51-500]
PW - v251 - i42 - Oct 18 2004 - p50(1) [51-500]
Jalbert, Brad - *Roses for British Columbia*
CBRA - Annual 2003 - p420(1) [51-500]
Jalongo, Mary Renck - *The World's Children and Their Companion Animals: Developmental and Educational Significance of the Child/Pet Bond*
R&R Bk N - v19 - i3 - August 2004 - p10(1) [1-50]
Jaman, Julia - *Kangaroo's Cancan Cafe*
c Sch Lib - v52 - i3 - Autumn 2004 - p131(2) [501+]
James, Annabelle - *Abigail's Ballet Class (Illus. by Beckes, Shirley)*
c PW - v251 - i38 - Sept 20 2004 - p65(1) [51-500]
James, B.J. - *Supertwins and the Sneaky, Slimy Book Worms (Illus. by Demarest, Chris L.)*
c BL - v100 - i21 - July 2004 - p1850(1) [1-50]
James, Betsy - *My Chair (Illus. by DePalma, Mary Newell)*
c BL - v101 - i2 - Sept 15 2004 - p250(2) [51-500]
c CCB-B - v58 - i1 - Sept 2004 - p23(2) [51-500]
c SLJ - v50 - i7 - July 2004 - p78(1) [51-500]
James, Bill - *The Neyer/James Guide to Pitchers: An Historical Compendium of Pitching Pitchers, and Pitches*
Globe & Mail - Oct 23 2004 - pD25 [51-500]
James, Clive - *As of this Writing: The Essential Essay, 1968-2002*
VQR - v80 - i1 - Wntr 2004 - p270-270 [501+]
VQR - v80 - i1 - Wntr 2004 - p270-270 [501+]
James, Darryl Dean - *Baked to Death: A Simon Kirby-Jones Mystery*
LJ - v130 - i1 - Jan 1 2005 - p83(1) [51-500]
James, David - *Buying Information Systems: Selecting, Implementing and Assessing Off-the-Shelf Systems*
SciTech - v28 - i3 - Sept 2004 - p134(1) [51-500]
James, Dean - *Baked to Death: a Simon Kirby-Jones Mystery*
PW - v252 - i5 - Jan 31 2005 - p52(1) [51-500]
James, Delores C.S. - *Nutrition and Well-Being A to Z*
Choice - v42 - i4 - Dec 2004 - p634(1) [1-50]
LJ - v129 - i15 - Sept 15 2004 - p82(1) [51-500]
y Ref Rev - Nov 2004 - pNA [501+]
SciTech - v28 - i3 - Sept 2004 - p86(1) [501+]
y SLJ - v50 - i10 - Oct 2004 - p94(2) [51-500]
BL - v101 - i7 - Dec 1 2004 - p686(2) [501+]
James, Elizabeth - *Charles Dickens*
y SLJ - v51 - i1 - Jan 2005 - p149(1) [51-500]
Macmillan: A Publishing Tradition from 1843
BSA-P - v98 - i3 - Sept 2004 - p388-390 [501+]
James, Eloisa - *Much Ado about You*
BL - v101 - i7 - Dec 1 2004 - p640(1) [51-500]
PW - v251 - i51 - Dec 20 2004 - p42(1) [51-500]
James-Enger, Kelly - *White Bikini Panties*
BL - v101 - i5 - Nov 1 2004 - p470(2) [51-500]
PW - v251 - i41 - Oct 11 2004 - p56(1) [51-500]
James, Glyn - *Advanced Modern Engineering Mathematics, 3rd Ed.*
TimHES - v0 - i1668 - Nov 26 2004 - pXVI(1) [501+]
James, Harold - *End of Globalization: Lessons from the Great Depression*
JMH - v76 - i4 - Dec 2004 - p945(3) [501+]
Enterprise in the Period of Facism in Europe
JEH - v64 - i1 - March 2004 - p252(2) [501+]
The Interwar Depression in an International Context
BHR - v78 - i2 - Summer 2004 - p329(3) [501+]
James, Henry - *The Beast in the Jungle*
Sew R - v111 - i1 - Winter 2003 - p116 [501+]
Beloved Boy: Letters to Hendrik C. Andersen, 1899-1915
Choice - v42 - i3 - Nov 2004 - p483(2) [1-50]
Lam Bk Rpt - v13 - i4-5 - Nov-Dec 2004 - p35(1) [501+]
TLS - i5305 - Dec 3 2004 - p24(1) [501+]
The Uncollected Henry James: Newly Discovered Stories
Choice - v42 - i1 - Sept 2004 - p101(1) [501+]
Lon R Bks - v26 - i18 - Sept 23 2004 - p20(1) [501+]
James, I.M. - *Remarkable Physicists: From Galileo to Yukawa*
Choice - v42 - i1 - Sept 2004 - p124(1) [501+]
James, Jeffrey - *Bridging the Global Digital Divide*
JEL - v41 - i4 - Dec 2003 - p1394(1) [501+]
James, Nick - *Heat*
FQ - v57 - i2 - Winter 2003 - p55(2) [501+]
James, P.D. - *The Murder Room (Read by Jayston, Michael). Audiobook Review*
Spec - v296 - i9187 - Sept 4 2004 - p43(1) [501+]
The Murder Room
NYTBR - Oct 31 2004 - p26 [501+]
James, Patrick - *The Myth of the Sacred: The Charter, the Courts, and the Politics of the Constitution in Canada*
Law&PolBR - August 2004 - p655(4) [501+]
James, Peet - *Verification Plans: The Five-Day Verification Strategy for Modern Hardware Verification Languages*
SciTech - v28 - i1 - March 2004 - p165(1) [51-500]

James, Richard K. - *Crisis Intervention Strategies, 5th Ed.*
SciTech - v28 - i4 - Dec 2004 - p96(1) [51-500]

James, S.L. - *Learned Girls and Male Persuasion: Gender and Reading in Roman Love Elegy*
Class R - v54 - i1 - May 2004 - p96(3) [501+]

James, Sara N. - *Signorelli and Fra Angelico at Orvieto: Liturgy, Poetry and a Vision of the End Time*
Ren Q - v57 - i4 - Winter 2004 - p1393(2) [501+]

James, Simon (b. 1957 -) - *The Arms and Armour and Other Military Equipment*
R&R Bk N - v19 - i4 - Nov 2004 - p44(1) [51-500]

James, Simon (b. 1961 -) - *Baby Brains (Illus. by James, Simon)*
c BL - v101 - i6 - Nov 15 2004 - p584(1) [51-500]
c CCB-B - v58 - i5 - Jan 2005 - p212(2) [51-500]
c HB - v80 - i6 - Nov-Dec 2004 - p699(2) [51-500]
   HB - v81 - i1 - Jan-Feb 2005 - p13(1) [51-500]
c KR - v72 - i19 - Oct 1 2004 - p962(1) [51-500]
c Magpies - v19 - i5 - Nov 2004 - p28(1) [501+]
c PW - v251 - i41 - Oct 11 2004 - p79(1) [51-500]
c SLJ - v50 - i11 - Nov 2004 - p107(2) [51-500]

James, Simon J. - *Unsettled Accounts: Money and Narrative in the Novels of George Gissing*
ELT - v48 - i2 - Spring 2005 - p97(4) [501+]
VS - v46 - i4 - Summer 2004 - p690(3) [501+]

James, Simon P. - *Zen Buddhism and Environmental Ethics*
R&R Bk N - v19 - i4 - Nov 2004 - p19(1) [51-500]

James, Tom Beaumont - *Edward V: The Prince in the Tower*
Choice - v42 - i6 - Feb 2005 - p1086(1) [51-500]

James, W. Martin - *Historical Dictionary of Angola*
Choice - v42 - i3 - Nov 2004 - p466(1) [1-50]

James, Wendy - *The Ceremonial Animal: A New Portrait of Anthropology*
Choice - v42 - i2 - Oct 2004 - p334(1) [51-500]
TimHES - v0 - i1669 - Dec 3 2004 - p29(1) [501+]

Marcel Mauss: A Centenary Tribute
JRAI - v10 - i3 - Sept 2004 - p727(2) [501+]

James, Will - *Horses I've Known*
Roundup M - v12 - i1 - Oct 2004 - p31(1) [51-500]

Jameson, E.W., Jr. - *Mammals of California (Illus. by Jameson, E.W., Jr.)*
QRB - v79 - i4 - Dec 2004 - p440(2) [501+]

Jameson, Fredric - *A Singular Modernity: Essay on the Ontology of the Present*
CS - v33 - i2 - March 2004 - p201-202 [501+]
South HR - v38 - i1 - Wntr 2004 - p79-88 [501+]

Jameson, Jenna - *How To Make Love Like A Porn Star: A Cautionary Tale*
Ent W - i778 - August 13 2004 - p93 [501+]
Globe & Mail - Oct 16 2004 - pD22 [501+]
NYTBR - Sept 5 2004 - p14 [501+]
PW - v251 - i32 - August 9 2004 - p246(1) [501+]

Jameson, W.C. - *Billy the Kid: Beyond the Grave*
BL - v101 - i9-10 - Jan 1 2005 - p790(1) [1-50]

Jamie, Kathleen - *Mr. and Mrs. Scotland Are Dead, Poems 1980-1994*
BIC - v33 - i2 - March 2004 - p38(2) [501+]

The Tree House
TLS - i5303 - Nov 19 2004 - p34(1) [501+]

Jamieson, Alan G. - *Ebb Tide in the British Maritime Industries: Change and Adaptation, 1918-1990*
R&R Bk N - v19 - i1 - Feb 2004 - p31(1) [1-50]

Jamieson, Barrie G.M. - *Reproductive Biology and Phylogeny of Anura*
QRB - v79 - i4 - Dec 2004 - p438(1) [501+]

Jamieson, Patsy - *The Essential Eating Well Cookbook: Good Carbs, Good Fats, Great Flavors*
PW - v251 - i31 - August 2 2004 - p67(2) [51-500]

Jamieson, Perry D. - *Winfield Scott Hancock: Gettysburg Hero*
J Mil H - v68 - i4 - Oct 2004 - p1264-1266 [501+]
R&R Bk N - v19 - i3 - August 2004 - p68(1) [501+]

Jamison, Kay Redfield - *Exuberance: The Passion for Life*
BL - v101 - i1 - Sept 1 2004 - p2(1) [51-500]
BW - v34 - i41 - Oct 10 2004 - p3(1) [501+]
Globe & Mail - Nov 6 2004 - pD16 [501+]
KR - v72 - i16 - August 15 2004 - p789(1) [501+]
LJ - v129 - i16 - Oct 1 2004 - p100(1) [51-500]
NYTBR - Dec 5 2004 - p56 [501+]
PW - v251 - i39 - Sept 27 2004 - p48(1) [51-500]
R&R Bk N - v19 - i4 - Nov 2004 - p9(1) [51-500]
SEP - v276 - i6 - Nov-Dec 2004 - p52(2) [501+]

Touched with Fire
Globe & Mail - August 21 2004 - pD15 [501+]

Jampoler, Andrew C.A. - *Adak: The Rescue of Alfa Foxtrot 586*
APJ - v18 - i3 - Fall 2004 - p121(1) [501+]

Jana, B.B. - *Sustainable Aquaculture: Global Perspectives*
QRB - v79 - i4 - Dec 2004 - p443(2) [501+]

Janacek, Leoes - *The Janacek Opera Libretti, Vol. 2*
R&R Bk N - v19 - i4 - Nov 2004 - p194(1) [51-500]

Jance, Judith A. - *After the Fire*
DroRevMy - v24 - i4 - July-August 2004 - p8(1) [501+]

Day of the Dead (Read by Jerome, Tim). Audiobook Review
BL - v101 - i5 - Nov 1 2004 - p502(1) [1-50]

Day of the Dead
KR - v72 - i13 - July 1 2004 - p606(1) [51-500]
NYTBR - July 25 2004 - p19 [501+]

Jancovich, Marc - *Quality Popular Television*
JouAmCul - v27 - i3 - Sept 2004 - p349(2) [501+]

Janeczko, Paul B. - *Blushing: Expressions of Love in Poems and Letters*
LibMed - v23 - i1 - August-Sept 2004 - p70(1) [51-500]
y SLJ - v50 - i10 - Oct 2004 - pS67(2) [51-500]
y Teach Lib - v32 - i1 - Oct 2004 - p10(1) [51-500]
   JAAL - v48 - i4 - Dec 2004 - p349(4) [501+]

A Kick in the Head: An Everyday Guide to Poetic Forms (Illus. by Raschka, Chris)
c KR - v73 - i5 - March 1 2005 - p288(1) [51-500]
c PW - v252 - i11 - March 14 2005 - p67(1) [51-500]

Opening a Door
RT - v57 - Nov 2003 - p296 [501+]

Top Secret: A Handbook of Codes, Ciphers, and Secret Writing (Illus. by LaReau, Jenna)
y Magpies - v19 - i5 - Nov 2004 - p44(1) [501+]
y SLJ - v50 - i10 - Oct 2004 - pS48(2) [51-500]
y VOYA - v27 - i3 - August 2004 - p238(1) [1-50]
c BL - v101 - i9-10 - Jan 1 2005 - p774(1) [1-50]

Worlds Afire
LibMed - v23 - i1 - August-Sept 2004 - p70(1) [51-500]
SLJ - v50 - i10 - Oct 2004 - pS68(1) [51-500]

Writing Winning Reports and Essays
LibMed - v22 - i6 - March 2004 - p84(1) [501+]
SLJ - v50 - i10 - Oct 2004 - pS50(1) [51-500]

Janelidze, George - *Galois Theory, Hopf Algebras, and Semiabelian Categories*
SciTech - v28 - i4 - Dec 2004 - p35(1) [51-500]

Janes, Joseph - *Introduction to Reference Work in the Digital Age*
LQ - v74 - i3 - July 2004 - p389(3) [501+]

Janeway, Charles A., Jr. - *Immunobiology: The Immune System in Health and Disease, 6th Ed.*
SciTech - v28 - i3 - Sept 2004 - p75(1) [51-500]

Janeway, Eliot - *The House of Janeway*
BooChiTr - April 18 2004 - p1(2) [501+]

Janeway, Michael - *The Fall of the House of Roosevelt: Brokers of Ideas and Power from FDR to LBJ*
BooChiTr - April 18 2004 - p1(2) [501+]
Choice - v42 - i3 - Nov 2004 - p547(1) [1-50]

Jango-Cohen, Judith - *The Bald Eagle*
c LibMed - v22 - i4 - Jan 2004 - p82(1) [501+]

Camels
c SLJ - v51 - i2 - Feb 2005 - p118(1) [51-500]

Chinese New Year
c BL - v101 - i9-10 - Jan 1 2005 - p866(1) [51-500]

Rhinoceroses
c SLJ - v51 - i2 - Feb 2005 - p118(1) [51-500]

Janich, Michael D. - *Speak Like a Native*
Bwatch - Nov 2004 - pNA [51-500]

Janik, Vicki K. - *The Merchant of Venice: A Guide to the Play*
R&R Bk N - v19 - i1 - Feb 2004 - p237(1) [51-500]

Janin, Hunt - *Medieval Justice: Cases and Laws in France, England, and Germany, 500-1500*
R&R Bk N - v19 - i3 - August 2004 - p207(1) [1-50]

Janis, Irving L. - *Victims of Groupthink: A Psychological Study of Foreign-Policy Decisions and Fiascoes*
Globe & Mail - Jan 15 2005 - pD15 [501+]

Janis, Mark W. - *Religion and International Law*
R&R Bk N - v19 - i4 - Nov 2004 - p176(1) [501+]

Janiskee, Brian P. - *The California Republic: Institutions, Statesmanship, and Policies*
Choice - v42 - i6 - Feb 2005 - p1097(1) [51-500]
R&R Bk N - v19 - i3 - August 2004 - p180(1) [501+]

Democracy in California: Politics and Government in the Golden State, Post-Recall Edition
Choice - v42 - i6 - Feb 2005 - p1098(2) [51-500]
R&R Bk N - v19 - i3 - August 2004 - p180(1) [501+]

Janka, M. - *Platon als Mythologe. Neue Interpretationen zu den Mythen in Platons Dialogen*
Class R - v54 - i2 - Nov 2004 - p320-322 [501+]

Jankelevitch, Vladimir - *Music and the Ineffable*
Choice - v41 - i7 - March 2004 - p1306(1) [51-500]

Janken, Kenneth Robert - *White: The Biography of Walter White, Mr. NAACP*
Bl S - v34 - i3 - Fall 2004 - p66-66 [501+]
Choice - v41 - i7 - March 2004 - p1356(1) [501+]

Jankiraman, Mohinder - *Space-Time Codes and MIMO Systems*
SciTech - v28 - i4 - Dec 2004 - p149(1) [51-500]

Jankowiak, William - *Drugs, Labor, and Colonial Expansion*
J Soc H - v38 - i1 - Fall 2004 - p250(2) [501+]

Janku, Andrea - *Nur leere Reden: Politischer Diskurs und die Shanghaier Presse im China des spaten 19*
Ch Rev Int - v10 - i2 - Fall 2003 - p414(5) [501+]

Jankulak, Karen - *The Medieval Cult of St. Petroc*
Specu - v79 - i4 - Oct 2004 - p1102(2) [501+]

Janney, Rachel - *Modifying Schoolwork, 2nd Ed.*
R&R Bk N - v19 - i4 - Nov 2004 - p191(1) [501+]

Janove, Jathan - *Managing to Stay Out of Court: How to Avoid the 8 Deadly Sins of Mismanagement*
HR Mag - v50 - i2 - Feb 2005 - p131(2) [501+]
HR Mag - v50 - i2 - Feb 2005 - pS12(1) [501+]
LJ - v130 - i1 - Jan 1 2005 - p126(1) [51-500]

Janowitz, Tama - *Area Code 212*
People - v62 - i25 - Dec 20 2004 - p58 [51-500]

Area Code 212: New York Days, New York Nights
Globe & Mail - Jan 1 2005 - pD3 [501+]

Area Code 212 with 718, 649, 917, 516, and a Brief Foray to 518: New York Days, New York Nights
BL - v101 - i5 - Nov 1 2004 - p443(1) [51-500]
KR - v72 - i20 - Oct 15 2004 - p994(2) [51-500]
LJ - v72 - i20 - Dec 1 2004 - p146(1) [51-500]
NYTBR - Jan 30 2005 - p23 [501+]
PW - v251 - i44 - Nov 1 2004 - p54(1) [501+]

Janowski, Maciej - *Polish Liberal Thought before 1918*
Choice - v42 - i5 - Jan 2005 - p911(1) [1-50]
R&R Bk N - v19 - i3 - August 2004 - p175(1) [501+]

Janowski, Monica - *The Forest, Source of Life: The Kelabit of Sarawak*
R&R Bk N - v19 - i3 - August 2004 - p55(1) [51-500]

Jan's Illustrated Computer Literary 101
LibMed - v22 - i7 - April-May 2004 - p90(1) [501+]

Jansen, Dirk - *Electronic Design Automation Handbook*
SciTech - v28 - i1 - March 2004 - p159(1) [51-500]

Jansen, Katherine Ludwig - *The Making of the Magdalen: Preaching and Popular Devotion in the Later Middle Ages*
Specu - v79 - i3 - July 2004 - p775-776 [501+]

Jansen, Marc - *Stalin's Loyal Executioner: People's Commissar Nikolai Ezhov, 1895-1940*
JMH - v76 - i3 - Sept 2004 - p738(2) [501+]

Janssens, David - *Tussen Athene en Jeruzalem: Filosofie, profetie en politiek in het werk van Leo Strauss*
NYRB - v51 - i16 - Oct 21 2004 - p58(3) [501+]

Janssens, Jules - *Avicenna and His Heritage: Proceedings*
R&R Bk N - v19 - i1 - Feb 2004 - p2(1) [51-500]

Jansson, Bruce S. - *The Reluctant Welfare State, American Welfare Policies: Past, Present, and Future, 5th Ed.*
R&R Bk N - v19 - i4 - Nov 2004 - p124(1) [1-50]

Jansson, M. - *Principles of Lake Sedimentology*
SciTech - v28 - i4 - Dec 2004 - p58(1) [51-500]

January, Brendan - *Globalize It!: The Stories of the IMF, the World Bank, the WTO--and Those Who Protest*
SLJ - v50 - i10 - Oct 2004 - pS59(1) [51-500]

Little Bighorn, June 25, 1876
c BL - v101 - i5 - Nov 1 2004 - p476(2) [51-500]

Janusonis, Stepas - *Self-Formation Theory and Applications: Proceedings*
SciTech - v28 - i3 - Sept 2004 - p15(1) [51-500]

Janz, Denis R. - *A Reformation Reader*
Six Ct J - v34 - i4 - Winter 2003 - p1131-1132 [501+]

Janz, Paul D. - *God, the Mind's Desire: Reference, Reason and Christian Thinking*
TLS - i5307 - Dec 17 2004 - p4-6 [501+]

Japan, 3rd Rev. Ed
R&R Bk N - v19 - i1 - Feb 2004 - p147(1) [51-500]

Japrisot, Sebastien - *A Very Long Engagement*
  Ent W - i801 - Jan 14 2005 - p92 [501+]
Jaramillo, Alvaro - *Birds of Chile (Illus. by Burke, Peter)*
  E-Streams - Oct 2004 - pNA [501+]
Jarausch, Konrad H. - *Die historische Meisterezahlung: Deutungslinien der deutschen Nationalgeschichte nach 1945*
  CEH - v37 - i3 - Summer 2004 - p461(5) [501+]
  Shattered Past: Reconstructing German Histories
  GSR - v27 - i3 - Oct 2004 - p669(2) [501+]
Jardine, Lisa - *The Curious Life of Robert Hooke: The Man Who Measured London*
  BW - v34 - i12 - March 21 2004 - p4(2) [501+]
  SciTech - v28 - i3 - Sept 2004 - p13(1) [501+]
Jardine, Quintin - *Alarm Call*
  KR - v73 - i4 - Feb 15 2005 - p201(2) [51-500]
  LJ - v130 - i4 - March 1 2005 - p71(1) [51-500]
  Stay of Execution
  Globe & Mail - Oct 2 2004 - pD18 [51-500]
  KR - v72 - i19 - Oct 1 2004 - p941(1) [501+]
Jardins, Julie Des - *Women and the Historical Enterprise in America: Gender, Race, and the Politics of Memory, 1880-1945*
  AHR - v109 - i4 - Oct 2004 - p1250(2) [501+]
  JAH - v91 - i3 - Dec 2004 - p1064(2) [501+]
  JouAmCul - v27 - i3 - Sept 2004 - p365(2) [501+]
  JSH - v70 - i4 - Nov 2004 - p946(2) [501+]
  Pub Hist - v26 - i3 - Summer 2004 - p63(65) [501+]
Jarecke, George W. - *Seeking Civility: Common Courtesy and the Common Law*
  R&R Bk N - v19 - i1 - Feb 2004 - pNA [51-500]
Jarl, Ann-Cathrin - *In Justice: Women and Global Economics*
  Choice - v41 - i11-12 - July-August 2004 - p2058(1) [501+]
Jarlby, Janne - *H.C. Branner: Splittelse og kontinuitet*
  Scan St - v76 - i4 - Winter 2004 - p557(4) [501+]
Jarmai, Karoly - *Metal Structures: Design, Fabrication, Economy: Proceedings*
  SciTech - v28 - i1 - March 2004 - p137(1) [51-500]
Jarman, Derek - *Chroma: A Book of Colour*
  Globe & Mail - Oct 9 2004 - pD31 [501+]
Jarman, Julia - *Big Red Tub (Illus. by Reynolds, Adrian)*
  c BL - v101 - i9-10 - Jan 1 2005 - p869(2) [51-500]
  c PW - v252 - i3 - Jan 17 2005 - p54(1) [51-500]
  The Magic Backpack (Illus. by Gon, Adriano)
  c SLJ - v50 - i8 - August 2004 - p85(1) [501+]
  Peace Weavers
  c TES - v0 - i4587 - June 11 2004 - pssss18(2) [501+]
Jarman, Mark - *To the Green Man*
  BL - v100 - i21 - July 2004 - p1811(2) [1-50]
Jarman, Mark Anthony - *Coming Attractions 03*
  CBRA - Annual 2003 - p243(2) [501+]
Jarman, Robert L. - *Sabah Al-Salim Al-Sabah, Amir of Kuwait, 1965-77: A Political Biography*
  A Aff - v35 - i2 - July 2004 - p214-215 [501+]
  IJMES - v36 - i3 - August 2004 - p492-493 [501+]
Jaros, Patrik - *Fish and Seafood*
  PW - v251 - i33 - August 16 2004 - p57(1) [51-500]
Jarrard, Alice - *Architecture as Performance in Seventeenth-Century Europe: Court Ritual in Modena, Rome, and Paris*
  Ren Q - v57 - i4 - Winter 2004 - p1398(2) [501+]
Jarrard, Kyle - *Cognac: The Seductive Saga of the World's Most Coveted Spirit*
  LJ - v130 - i2 - Feb 1 2005 - p111(1) [51-500]
  PW - v252 - i2 - Jan 10 2005 - p46(1) [51-500]
Jarrell, Donna - *Scoot over, Skinny: The FAT Nonfiction Anthology*
  BW - v35 - i4 - Jan 30 2005 - p10(1) [501+]
  What Are You Looking At? An Anthology of Fat Fiction
  NS - v133 - i4713 - Nov 8 2004 - p54(2) [501+]
  What Are You Looking At? The First Fat Fiction Anthology
  JPC - v38 - i2 - Nov 2004 - p445(2) [501+]
Jarrell, Wallace E. - *The Randolph Hornets in the Civil War: A History and Roster of Company M, 22nd North Carolina Regiment*
  R&R Bk N - v19 - i3 - August 2004 - p69(1) [51-500]
Jarrett, Clare - *The Best Picnic Ever (Illus. by Jarrett, Clare)*
  c BL - v100 - i22 - August 2004 - p1942(1) [51-500]
  c SLJ - v50 - i7 - July 2004 - p78(1) [51-500]
Jarrett, Sandra - *Edvard Grieg and His Songs*
  M Ed J - v91 - i1 - Sept 2004 - p64(1) [501+]
Jarrow, Gail - *Chiggers*
  c SB - v40 - i5 - Sept-Oct 2004 - p224(1) [501+]

Jarry, Isabelle - *J'ai nom sans bruit*
  WLT - v79 - i1 - Jan-April 2005 - p98(1) [501+]
Jarviluoma, Helmi - *Gender and Qualitative Methods*
  R&R Bk N - v19 - i1 - Feb 2004 - p122(1) [51-500]
Jarvis, Brian - *Cruel and Unusual: Punishment and US Culture*
  Choice - v42 - i1 - Sept 2004 - p84(1) [501+]
Jarvis, Christina S. - *The Male Body at War: American Masculinity During World War II*
  HNet - August 2004 - pNA [501+]
  R&R Bk N - v19 - i2 - May 2004 - p136 [51-500]
Jarvis, Robert M. - *Theater Law: Cases and Materials*
  R&R Bk N - v19 - i3 - August 2004 - p202(1) [1-50]
Jarvis, Robin - *The Alchemist's Cat*
  c BL - v101 - i5 - Nov 1 2004 - p484(2) [51-500]
  c KR - v72 - i18 - Sept 15 2004 - p915(1) [51-500]
  y SLJ - v50 - i12 - Dec 2004 - p148(1) [51-500]
  Thorn Ogres of Hagwood
  y Kliatt - v38 - i4 - July 2004 - p30(1) [51-500]
  c PW - v251 - i28 - July 12 2004 - p66(1) [51-500]
Jasanoff, Jay - *Hittite and the Indo-European Verb*
  TLS - i5266 - March 5 2004 - p29-29 [501+]
Jaskunas, Paul - *Hidden*
  BW - v34 - i32 - August 8 2004 - p6(1) [501+]
  PW - v251 - i28 - July 12 2004 - p45(2) [501+]
Jason, Leonard - *Havens: Stories of True Community Healing*
  SciTech - v28 - i3 - Sept 2004 - p86(1) [501+]
  Participatory Community Research: Theories and Methods in Action, Proceedings
  R&R Bk N - v19 - i2 - May 2004 - p130 [51-500]
Jason, Philip K. - *Don't Wave Goodbye: The Children's Flight from Nazi Persecution to American Freedom*
  LJ - v129 - i12 - July 2004 - p96(1) [51-500]
Jasper, Kenji - *Seeking Salamanca Mitchel*
  PW - v251 - i27 - July 5 2004 - p39(2) [501+]
Jasper, Margaret C. - *Law for the Small Business Owner, 2nd Revised Ed.*
  R&R Bk N - v19 - i1 - Feb 2004 - pNA [1-50]
  Privacy and the Internet: Your Expectations and Rights Under the Law
  R&R Bk N - v19 - i4 - Nov 2004 - p167(1) [501+]
Javeline, Debra - *Protest and the Politics of Blame: The Russian Response to Unpaid Wages*
  AJS - v110 - i1 - July 2004 - p243(3) [501+]
  JEL - v41 - i4 - Dec 2003 - p1428(1) [501+]
  Social Capital and Social Cohesion in Post-Soviet Russia
  Slav R - v63 - i4 - Winter 2004 - p900(3) [501+]
Jawad, Maan H. - *Design of Plate and Shell Structures*
  SciTech - v28 - i1 - March 2004 - p143(1) [51-500]
Jawara, Fatoumata - *Behind the Scenes at the WTO: The Real World of International Trade Negotiations*
  Choice - v41 - i7 - March 2004 - p1342(1) [501+]
Jay, Edward - *The Big Picture*
  Ent W - i807 - Feb 18 2005 - p81 [51-500]
Jay, Kathryn - *More Than Just a Game: Sports in American Life Since 1945*
  R&R Bk N - v19 - i3 - August 2004 - p87(1) [51-500]
Jay, M. Ellen - *Teaching with Computers: Strategies that Work in Grades K-6*
  LibMed - v22 - i5 - Feb 2004 - p83(1) [501+]
Jayaram, N. - *The Indian Diaspora: Dynamics of Migration*
  R&R Bk N - v19 - i3 - August 2004 - p54(1) [51-500]
Jayasuriya, Ruwan - *Efficiency in Reaching the Millennium Development Goals*
  JEL - v42 - i1 - March 2004 - p308(1) [501+]
  R&R Bk N - v19 - i1 - Feb 2004 - p125(1) [51-500]
Jayawardena, Kumari - *The White Woman's Other Burden*
  Globe & Mail - Jan 29 2005 - pD15 [501+]
Jayaweera, Swarna - *Women in Post-Independence Sri Lanka*
  JAS - v63 - i2 - May 2004 - p535(2) [501+]
Jaynes, E.T. - *Probability Theory: The Logic of Science*
  Phys Today - v57 - i10 - Oct 2004 - p76-77 [501+]
Jaynes, Ela - *Planet Yumthing: Do-It-Yourself (Illus. by Greenblatt, Darren)*
  c SLJ - v50 - i8 - August 2004 - p138(1) [51-500]
Jaynes, Gerald David - *Encyclopedia of African American Society, 2 Vols.*
  LJ - v129 - i20 - Dec 1 2004 - p166(1) [501+]
Je peux lire! Series
  Res Links - v10 - i2 - Dec 2004 - p56(1) [501+]

Jeanloz, Raymond - *Annual Review of Earth and Planetary Sciences: Vol. 31, 2003*
  SciTech - v28 - i1 - March 2004 - p44(1) [51-500]
  Annual Review of Earth and Planetary Sciences. Vol. 32, 2004
  SciTech - v28 - i3 - Sept 2004 - p44(1) [1-50]
Jeanneret, Michel - *Eros Rebelle: Litterature et Dissidence a Lage Classique*
  FS - v58 - i2 - April 2004 - p249(2) [501+]
  MLN - v119 - i4 - Sept 2004 - p887-892 [501+]
Jeans, Peter D. - *Ship to Shore: A Dictionary of Everyday Words and Phrases Derived from the Sea*
  Choice - v42 - i6 - Feb 2005 - p990(1) [51-500]
Jeapes, Ben - *The New World Order*
  y BL - v101 - i9-10 - Jan 1 2005 - p845(1) [1-50]
  y CCB-B - v58 - i6 - Feb 2005 - p253(2) [51-500]
  y Kliatt - v39 - i2 - March 2005 - p13(1) [51-500]
  y KR - v73 - i2 - Jan 15 2005 - p122(1) [51-500]
Jebb, Cindy R. - *Bridging the Gap: Ethnicity, Legitimacy, and State Alignment in the International Scene*
  R&R Bk N - v19 - i3 - August 2004 - p160(1) [501+]
Jecks, Michael - *The Tolls of Death*
  PW - v251 - i39 - Sept 27 2004 - p41(1) [501+]
Jedicke Peter - *Cosmology: Exploring the Universe*
  y SB - v40 - i4 - July-August 2004 - p163(1) [51-500]
Jeeves, Malcolm - *Science, Life and Christian Belief: A Survey of Contemporary Issues*
  Zygon - v39 - i4 - Dec 2004 - pNA [501+]
The Jeff Corwin Experience Series
  c LibMed - v23 - i1 - August-Sept 2004 - p72(1) [501+]
Jeff Gordon
  y LibMed - v22 - i5 - Feb 2004 - p76(1) [501+]
Jeffares, A. Norman - *The Poems and Plays of Oliver St. John Gogarty*
  ELT - v48 - i1 - Wntr 2005 - p217(4) [501+]
Jefferies, William McK. - *Safe Uses of Cortisol, 3rd Ed.*
  SciTech - v28 - i4 - Dec 2004 - p116(1) [1-50]
Jeffers, Jennifer - *The Irish Novel at the End of the Twentieth Century*
  MFSF - v50 - i2 - Summer 2004 - p505-506 [501+]
Jeffers, Oliver - *How to Catch a Star (Illus. by Jeffers, Oliver)*
  c BL - v100 - i22 - August 2004 - p1942(2) [51-500]
  c PW - v251 - i29 - July 19 2004 - p159(2) [51-500]
  c Sch Lib - v52 - i4 - Winter 2004 - p202(1) [51-500]
  c SLJ - v50 - i9 - Sept 2004 - p169(1) [51-500]
Jeffers, Raymond - *Global Business Workforce Restructuring: Labour and Employment Law and Benefits*
  R&R Bk N - v19 - i2 - May 2004 - p117 [51-500]
Jeffers, Susan - *Cinderella (Illus. by Jeffers, Susan)*
  c BW - v34 - i39 - Sept 26 2004 - p11(1) [501+]
Jefferson, Ann - *Stendhal: ' La Chartreuse de Parme'*
  FS - v58 - i2 - April 2004 - p272(2) [501+]
Jefferson, Lisa - *Wardens' Accounts and Court Minute Books of the Goldsmiths' Mistery of London, 1334-1446*
  HER - v119 - i483 - Sept 2004 - p1038(2) [501+]
  Med R - Dec 2004 - pNA [501+]
Jeffery, David L. - *Houses of the Interpreter: Reading Scripture, Reading Culture*
  Choice - v42 - i2 - Oct 2004 - p310(2) [51-500]
Jeffery, Gary - *Abraham Lincoln: The Life of America's Sixteenth President (Illus. by Lacey, Mike)*
  PW - v252 - i8 - Feb 21 2005 - p160(1) [51-500]
Jeffey, Sean - *Franklin's Big Life-and-Learn Book*
  c CBRA - Annual 2003 - p453(1) [51-500]
Jeffrey, Alan - *Essentials of Engineering Mathematics: Worked Examples and Problems, 2nd Ed.*
  SciTech - v28 - i4 - Dec 2004 - p132 [51-500]
  Handbook of Mathematical Formulas and Integrals, 3rd Ed.
  Choice - v42 - i7 - March 2005 - p1263(1) [51-500]
  E-Streams - Oct 2004 - pNA [501+]
  Mathematics for Engineers and Scientists, 6th Ed.
  SciTech - v28 - i4 - Dec 2004 - p16(1) [1-50]
Jeffrey, David Lyle - *House of Interpretation; Reading Scripture, Reading Culture*
  TT - v61 - i3 - Oct 2004 - p386(3) [501+]
Jeffrey, Laura S. - *All about Braille: Reading by Touch*
  c SLJ - v50 - i12 - Dec 2004 - p132(1) [51-500]
  Cats: How to Choose and Care for a Cat
  c SLJ - v51 - i2 - Feb 2005 - p122(2) [51-500]
  c BL - v101 - i4 - Oct 15 2004 - p420(2) [51-500]
  Dogs: How to Choose and Care for a Dog
  c SLJ - v51 - i2 - Feb 2005 - p122(2) [51-500]
  Horses: How to Choose and Care for a Horse
  c SLJ - v51 - i2 - Feb 2005 - p122(2) [51-500]
  c BL - v101 - i4 - Oct 15 2004 - p420(2) [51-500]

304 • JENNINGS Book Review Index 2005 Cumulation

Jennings, Paul - *Quirky Tails (Read by Pacey, Steven). Audiobook Review*
y Magpies - v19 - i5 - Nov 2004 - p43(1) [501+]
Rascal the Dragon (Read by Macauley, Rebecca). Audiobook Review
c CH Bwatch - Feb 2005 - pNA [51-500]
c SLJ - v51 - i1 - Jan 2005 - p77(1) [51-500]
The Reading Bug
c Sch Lib - v52 - i3 - Autumn 2004 - p167(1) [501+]
Jennings, Phillip - *Nam-A-Rama*
KR - v72 - i24 - Dec 15 2004 - p1157(1) [501+]
PW - v252 - i8 - Feb 21 2005 - p159(1) [51-500]
Jennings, Richard W. - *Scribble: A Dog Story, a Ghost Story, a Love Story*
c BL - v101 - i5 - Nov 1 2004 - p475(1) [51-500]
y KR - v72 - i19 - Oct 1 2004 - p962(1) [51-500]
y SLJ - v50 - i11 - Nov 2004 - p146(1) [51-500]
y HB - v81 - i1 - Jan-Feb 2005 - p93(2) [51-500]
Jennings, Roger - *Introducing Microsoft Office InfoPath 2003*
R&R Bk N - v19 - i3 - August 2004 - p125(1) [51-500]
Jennings, Sharon - *Bats in the Garbage*
c CBRA - Annual 2003 - p491(2) [51-500]
Bearcub and Mama (Illus. by Watt, Melanie)
c KR - v73 - i4 - Feb 15 2005 - p230(1) [51-500]
Benjamin Pardonne
c Res Links - v10 - i3 - Feb 2005 - p59(1) [51-500]
Franklin and the New Teacher
c Res Links - v10 - i2 - Dec 2004 - p4(2) [51-500]
Franklin Annual
c CBRA - Annual 2003 - p453(1) [51-500]
Franklin Stays Up (Illus. by Jeffrey, Sean)
c CBRA - Annual 2003 - p453(2) [51-500]
Franklin the Detective
c Res Links - v10 - i2 - Dec 2004 - p6(1) [51-500]
Franklin's Nickname (Illus. by Lei, John)
c Res Links - v10 - i2 - Dec 2004 - p5(2) [51-500]
Franklin's Pumpkin
c Res Links - v10 - i2 - Dec 2004 - p6(1) [51-500]
Franklin's Reading Club (Illus. by Koren, Mark)
c CBRA - Annual 2003 - p454(1) [51-500]
Franklin's Surprise (Illus. by Jeffrey, Sean)
c CBRA - Annual 2003 - p454(1) [51-500]
Franklin's Trading Cards (Illus. by Jeffrey, Sean)
c CBRA - Annual 2003 - p453(2) [51-500]
No Monsters Here (Illus. by Ohi, Ruth)
c BL - v101 - i1 - Sept 1 2004 - p133(1) [51-500]
c Res Links - v10 - i2 - Dec 2004 - p6(1) [501+]
c SLJ - v50 - i10 - Oct 2004 - p119(1) [51-500]
Jennings, Theodore W., Jr. - *The Man Jesus Loved*
Lam Bk Rpt - v13 - i4-5 - Nov-Dec 2004 - p28(3) [501+]
Jensen, Alexander S. - *John's Gospel as Witness: The Development of the Early Christian Language of Faith*
R&R Bk N - v19 - i3 - August 2004 - p25(1) [1-50]
Jensen, Bill - *Work 2.0: Building the Future, One Employee at a Time*
R&R Bk N - v19 - i1 - Feb 2004 - p91(1) [1-50]
Jensen, Candi - *Knit Scarves!: 16 Cool Patterns To Keep You Warm*
LJ - v129 - i13 - August 2004 - p78(1) [501+]
Jensen, David G. - *Selling with Science and Soul*
R&R Bk N - v19 - i1 - Feb 2004 - p109(1) [51-500]
Jensen, Derrick - *Listening to the Land: Conversations about Nature, Culture, and Eros*
R&R Bk N - v19 - i3 - August 2004 - p82(1) [51-500]
Walking on Water: Reading, Writing, and Revolution
y VOYA - v27 - i4 - Oct 2004 - p338(1) [51-500]
Welcome to the Machine: Science, Surveillance, and the Culture of Control
Bwatch - Jan 2005 - pNA [51-500]
LJ - v129 - i17 - Oct 15 2004 - p85(1) [51-500]
Jensen, George H. - *Identities across Texts*
Col Lit - v32 - i1 - Wntr 2005 - p177(10) [501+]
Jensen, Hans Jorgen - *The Ivan Galamian Scale System for Violoncello, Vol. 2*
Am MT - v54 - i3 - Dec 2004 - p84(1) [501+]
Jensen, Hans Siggaard - *The Evolution of Scientific Knowledge*
JEL - v42 - i1 - March 2004 - p251(2) [501+]
Jensen, Jan Lars - *Nervous System: Or, Losing My Mind in Literature*
KR - v73 - i3 - Feb 1 2005 - p166(1) [501+]
Jensen, Jane Richardson - *She Who Prays: A Woman's Interfaith Prayer Book*
LJ - v130 - i4 - March 1 2005 - p92(1) [51-500]
Jensen, Jeppe Sinding - *The Study of Religion in a New Key: Theoretical and Philosophical Soundings in the Comparative and General Study of Religion*
R&R Bk N - v20 - i1 - Feb 2005 - p10(1) [51-500]
Jensen, Jonathan E. - *Globetrotter's Pocket Doc*
Bwatch - Nov 2004 - pNA [51-500]
Jensen, Julio Hans Casado - *The Object of Study in the Humanities: Proceedings*
R&R Bk N - v19 - i2 - May 2004 - p127 [51-500]
Jensen, Laura - *Patriots, Settlers, and the Origins of American Social Policy*
JAH - v91 - i3 - Dec 2004 - p1002(1) [501+]
JIH - v35 - i2 - Autumn 2004 - p306(2) [501+]
Jensen, Liz - *The Ninth Life of Louis Drax*
y BL - v101 - i6 - Nov 15 2004 - p561(1) [51-500]
PW - v251 - i45 - Nov 8 2004 - p34(2) [501+]
Ent W - i801 - Jan 14 2005 - p95 [51-500]
KR - v72 - i21 - Nov 1 2004 - p1025(1) [501+]
People - v63 - i4 - Jan 31 2005 - p47 [51-500]
Jensen, Michael - *Firelands*
Advocate - Nov 23 2004 - p97(1) [501+]
Jensen, Peter S. - *Making the System Work for Your Child with ADHD: How To Cut through Red Tape and Get What You Need from Doctors, Teachers, School, and Healthcare Plans*
LJ - v129 - i13 - August 2004 - p109(2) [51-500]
Jensen, Richard D. - *Tristeza*
Roundup M - v11 - i6 - August 2004 - p28 [501+]
Jensen, Richard J. - *Trans-Pacific Relations: America, Europe and Asia in the Twentieth Century*
JAH - v91 - i1 - June 2004 - p296-297 [501+]
Jensen, Robert - *Citizens of the Empire: The Struggle to Claim our Humanity*
R&R Bk N - v19 - i3 - August 2004 - p71(1) [51-500]
Jensen, Trish - *Phi Beta Bimbo*
BL - v101 - i9-10 - Jan 1 2005 - p830(1) [1-50]
Jenson, Deborah - *Trauma and Its Representations: The Social Life Of Mimesis in Post-Revolutionary France*
FS - v58 - i2 - April 2004 - p269(2) [501+]
Jenson, Robert W. - *On Thinking the Human: Resolutions of Difficult Notions*
TT - v61 - i3 - Oct 2004 - p424(1) [501+]
Jentleson, Bruce W. - *American Foreign Policy: The Dynamics of Choice in the 21st Century, 2nd ed.*
TimHES - v0 - i1668 - Nov 26 2004 - pV(1) [501+]
Jentsch, Birgit - *Young People in Rural Areas of Europe*
R&R Bk N - v19 - i3 - August 2004 - p152(1) [51-500]
Jephson, Patrick - *Portraits of a Princess: Travels with Diana (Illus. by Gavin, Kent)*
Globe & Mail - Dec 18 2004 - pD14 [1-50]
Jergen, Robert - *The Little Monster: Growing Up with ADHD*
R&R Bk N - v19 - i3 - August 2004 - p230(1) [1-50]
Jergovic, Miljenko - *Dvori od oraha*
WLT - v78 - i3-4 - Sept-Dec 2004 - p135(1) [501+]
Jermyn, Deborah - *The Cinema of Kathryn Bigelow: Hollywood Transgressor*
FQ - v58 - i1 - Fall 2004 - p61(3) [501+]
Jerome, Roy - *Conceptions of Postwar German Masculiity*
GSR - v27 - i1 - Feb 2004 - p221-222 [501+]
Jerrum, Mark - *Counting, Sampling and Integrating: Algorithms and Complexity*
SIAM Rev - v46 - i1 - March 2004 - p147-149 [501+]
Jesch, Judith - *The Scandinavians, from the Vendel Period to the Tenth Century: An Ethnographic Perspective*
HER - v119 - i483 - Sept 2004 - p978(979) [501+]
Jesenko, Joze - *Management in Tourism*
R&R Bk N - v19 - i4 - Nov 2004 - p72(1) [51-500]
Jesness, Jerry - *Teaching English Language Learners K-12: A Quick Guide for the New Teacher*
Choice - v42 - i6 - Feb 2005 - p1073(1) [51-500]
Jespersen, Knud J.V. - *A History of Denmark*
Choice - v42 - i5 - Jan 2005 - p924(1) [1-50]
Jesperson, Leon - *A Revolution from Above?: The Power State of 16th and 17th Century Scandinavia*
Scan St - v76 - i3 - Fall 2004 - p385(34) [501+]
Jessee, W. Scott - *Robert the Burgundian and the Counts of Anjou*
Specu - v79 - i3 - July 2004 - p776-777 [501+]
Jessop, Violet - *Titanic Survivor: The Newly Discovered Memoirs of Violet Jessop Who Survived Both the Titanic and Britannic Disasters*
R&R Bk N - v19 - i4 - Nov 2004 - p73(1) [51-500]
Jessup, Harsley - *Flower Girl*
LibMed - v22 - i4 - Jan 2004 - p57(1) [501+]
Jessup, Mariell - *Heart Failure: Providing Optimal Care*
E-Streams - Sept 2004 - pNA [501+]
SciTech - v28 - i1 - March 2004 - p105(1) [51-500]
Jeswald, Mary J. - *The Crazy Adventure of Nicholas Mouse (Illus. by Trimble, Anne M.)*
c CH Bwatch - March 2005 - pNA [51-500]
Jeswald, Peter - *How To Build Paths, Steps & Footbridges: The Fundamentals of Planning, Designing, and Constructing Creative Walkways in Your Home Landscape*
LJ - v130 - i4 - March 1 2005 - p108(1) [51-500]
Jett, Terri - *Agenda-Setting and Decision-Making of African American County Officials: The Case of Wilcox County, Alabama*
R&R Bk N - v19 - i4 - Nov 2004 - p62(1) [51-500]
Jeudy-Ballini, Monique - *People and Things: Social Mediations in Oceania*
Cont Pac - v16 - i2 - Fall 2004 - p452(3) [501+]
Jeune, Veronique le - *Feeling Freakish*
y TES - v0 - i4586 - June 4 2004 - pssss18(2) [501+]
Jewell, K. Sue - *Survival of the African American Family: The Institutional Impact of U.S. Social Policy*
Choice - v41 - i11-12 - July-August 2004 - p2129(1) [501+]
R&R Bk N - v19 - i1 - Feb 2004 - p58(1) [51-500]
Jewell, Keala - *The Art of Enigma: The De Chirico Brothers & the Politics of Modernism*
Choice - v42 - i1 - Sept 2004 - p89(2) [501+]
Jewett, Clayton E. - *Slavery in the South: A State-by-State History*
Choice - v42 - i2 - Oct 2004 - p356(1) [51-500]
y SLJ - v50 - i8 - August 2004 - p57(2) [501+]
Jewett, Robert - *Captain America and the Crusade against Evil: The Dilemma of Zealous Nationalism*
Ext - v45 - i3 - Fall 2004 - p320(3) [501+]
TT - v60 - i4 - Jan 2004 - p576-580 [501+]
Jewison, Norman - *This Terrible Business Has Been Good to Me: An Autobiography*
Globe & Mail - Nov 27 2004 - pD20 [501+]
Jewkes, Yvonne - *Media and Crime*
R&R Bk N - v19 - i4 - Nov 2004 - p212(1) [501+]
Jewler, A. Jerome - *Creative Strategy in Advertising, 8th Ed.*
R&R Bk N - v19 - i4 - Nov 2004 - p115(1) [51-500]
Jeyaveeran, Ruth - *The Road to Mumbai (Illus. by Jeyaveeran, Ruth)*
c BL - v101 - i1 - Sept 1 2004 - p133(1) [51-500]
c BW - v34 - i35 - August 2004 - p12(1) [51-500]
c CCB-B - v58 - i2 - Oct 2004 - p81(2) [51-500]
c KR - v72 - i14 - July 15 2004 - p687(1) [51-500]
c SLJ - v50 - i9 - Sept 2004 - p169(1) [51-500]
Jeyifo, Biodun - *Wole Soyinka: Politics, Poetics, Postcolonialism*
Choice - v42 - i1 - Sept 2004 - p96(2) [501+]
Jeynes, William - *Religion, Education, and Academic Success*
R&R Bk N - v19 - i1 - Feb 2004 - p190(1) [51-500]
Jha, Praveen K. - *Land Reforms in India, Vol. 7*
Pac A - v77 - i2 - Summer 2004 - p359(3) [501+]
Land Reforms in India, Vol. 8
Pac A - v77 - i2 - Summer 2004 - p359(3) [501+]
Jha, Prem Shankar - *The Perilous Road to Market: The Political Economy of Reform in Russia, India and China*
Russ Rev - v63 - i3 - July 2004 - pNA [501+]
Jha, Raj Kamal - *If You Are Afraid of Heights*
BL - v100 - i22 - August 2004 - p1899(1) [51-500]
KR - v72 - i14 - July 15 2004 - p649(2) [51-500]
LJ - v129 - i15 - Sept 15 2004 - p49(1) [51-500]
Lon R Bks - v26 - i24 - Dec 16 2004 - p29(2) [501+]
Jhabvala, Renana - *Informal Economy Centrestage: New Structures of Employment*
JEL - v42 - i1 - March 2004 - p309(1) [501+]
R&R Bk N - v19 - i1 - Feb 2004 - p97(1) [51-500]
Jhabvala, Ruth Prawer - *My Nine Lives: Chapters of a Possible Past (Illus. by Jhabvala, C.S.H.)*
BW - v34 - i31 - August 1 2004 - p7(1) [501+]
Econ - v371 - i8380 - June 19 2004 - p83US [501+]
Globe & Mail - August 7 2004 - pD5 [501+]
NYTBR - July 18 2004 - p12 [501+]
NYTBR - July 25 2004 - p18 [501+]
TLS - i5285 - July 16 2004 - p22(1) [501+]

Jhorth, Daniel - *Narrative and Discursive Approaches in Entrepreneurship: A Second Movements in Entrepreneurship Book*
    R&R Bk N - v19 - i4 - Nov 2004 - p85(1) [51-500]

Ji, Fengyuan - *Linguistic Engineering: Language and Politics in Mao's China*
    R&R Bk N - v19 - i1 - Feb 2004 - p212 [51-500]

Ji, Xiao-bin - *Facts About China*
    LJ - v129 - i13 - August 2004 - p118(1) [51-500]

Ji, Zhaojin - *A History of Modern Shanghai Banking: The Rise and Decline of China's Finance Capitalism*
    AHR - v109 - i3 - June 2004 - p879(2) [501+]

Jia, Wenshan - *Chinese Communication Theory and Research: Reflections, New Frontiers, and New Directions*
    Ch Rev Int - v10 - i2 - Fall 2003 - p418(4) [501+]

Jian, Ma - *The Noodle Maker*
    BL - v101 - i9-10 - Jan 1 2005 - p819(1) [501+]
    PW - v251 - i47 - Nov 22 2004 - p37(1) [51-500]

Jiang, Ji-Li - *The Magical Monkey King*
    c CH Bwatch - v14 - i8 - August 2004 - p4(1) [51-500]

Jiang, Tao - *Intimacy or Integrity: Philosophy and Cultural Difference*
    JAAR - v72 - i3 - Sept 2004 - p786-789 [501+]

Jiirgs, Michael - *Bürger Grass: Biografie eines deutschen Dichters*
    GSR - v27 - i1 - Feb 2004 - p212-214 [501+]

Jiles, Paulette - *Celestial Navigation*
    BIC - v33 - i7 - Oct 2004 - p29(2) [501+]
    North Spirit: Travels among the Cree and Ojibway Nations and Their Star Maps
    Can Lit - i182 - Autumn 2004 - p139(2) [501+]
    Sitting in the Club Car Drinking Rum and Karma-Kola: A Manual of Etiquette for Ladies Crossing Canada by Train
    CBRA - Annual 2003 - p170(1) [51-500]

Jillette, Penn - *Sock*
    Ent W - i775 - July 23 2004 - p82 [51-500]
    Globe & Mail - July 17 2004 - pD13 [1-50]
    LJ - v129 - i12 - July 2004 - p71(1) [51-500]
    NYTBR - August 1 2004 - p19 [501+]

Jillson, Carl - *Pursuing the American Dream: Opportunity & Exclusion over Four Centuries*
    LJ - v129 - i14 - Sept 1 2004 - p168(1) [51-500]

Jimenez, Ivan Molina - *Costarricense por dicha: Identidad nacional y cambio cultural en costa rica durantr los siglos XIX y XX*
    AHR - v109 - i4 - Oct 2004 - p1284-1285 [501+]

Jimenez, Marc - *Qu'est-Ce Que L'Esthetique?*
    JAAC - v61 - Winter 2003 - p91 [501+]

Jimenez, Phil - *The DC Comics Encyclopedia: The Definitive Guide to the Characters of the DC Universe*
    c SLJ - v51 - i2 - Feb 2005 - p84(1) [51-500]

Jimoh, A. Yemisi - *Spiritual, Blues and Jazz People in African American Fiction: Living in Paradox*
    MFSF - v50 - i2 - Summer 2004 - p483-484 [501+]

Jin, Cheng - *Building Scalable Network Services: Theory and Practice*
    SciTech - v28 - i1 - March 2004 - p156(1) [51-500]

Jin, Ha - *War Trash*
    BL - v100 - i22 - August 2004 - p1872(1) [51-500]
    BL - v101 - i9-10 - Jan 1 2005 - p769(1) [1-50]
    BW - v34 - i40 - Oct 3 2004 - p8(1) [501+]
    CC - v121 - i25 - Dec 14 2004 - p22(1) [51-500]
    Ent W - i787 - Oct 8 2004 - p120 [501+]
    Globe & Mail - Oct 23 2004 - pD14 [501+]
    Globe & Mail - Dec 24 2004 - pD3 [1-50]
    KR - v72 - i16 - August 15 2004 - p763(1) [51-500]
    LJ - v129 - i13 - August 2004 - p67(2) [51-500]
    Mac - v117 - i46 - Nov 15 2004 - p129(3) [501+]
    NYTBR - Oct 10 2004 - p1 [501+]
    PW - v251 - i31 - August 2 2004 - p49(1) [51-500]

Jinkins, Jim - *Pinky Dinky Doo: Polka Dot Pox*
    c BL - v100 - i21 - July 2004 - p1850(2) [1-50]
    Pinky Dinky Doo: Where Are My Shoes? (Illus. by Jinkins, Jim)
    c BL - v100 - i21 - July 2004 - p1850(2) [1-50]
    c SLJ - v50 - i7 - July 2004 - p78(1) [51-500]

Jinks, Catherine - *Pagan in Exile*
    y PW - v252 - i6 - Feb 7 2005 - p62(1) [51-500]
    Pagan's Crusade
    y Kliatt - v38 - i6 - Nov 2004 - p18(1) [51-500]
    y PW - v251 - i36 - Sept 6 2004 - p65(1) [51-500]
    Pagan's Scribe
    y HB - v81 - i2 - March-April 2005 - p203(1) [51-500]
    y Kliatt - v39 - i2 - March 2005 - p13(1) [51-500]
    y KR - v73 - i5 - March 1 2005 - p288(1) [51-500]
    Pagan's Vows
    y BL - v101 - i3 - Oct 1 2004 - p322(1) [51-500]
    y CCB-B - v58 - i3 - Nov 2004 - p127(2) [501+]
    y HB - v80 - i5 - Sept-Oct 2004 - p587(1) [51-500]
    y KR - v72 - i15 - August 1 2004 - p743(1) [51-500]
    y PW - v251 - i34 - August 23 2004 - p56(1) [501+]
    y SLJ - v50 - i9 - Sept 2004 - p209(1) [51-500]
    y VOYA - v27 - i4 - Oct 2004 - p303(1) [51-500]

Jirankova-Limbrick, Martina - *The Artful Alphabet*
    LibMed - v23 - i1 - August-Sept 2004 - p65(1) [51-500]

Jirsaek, Jan E. - *An Atlas of Human Prenatal Developmental Mechanics: Anatomy and Staging*
    SciTech - v28 - i3 - Sept 2004 - p67(1) [51-500]

Jjemba, Patrick K. - *Environmental Microbiology: Principles and Applications*
    Choice - v42 - i7 - March 2005 - p1251(1) [51-500]
    SciTech - v28 - i4 - Dec 2004 - p74(1) [51-500]

Joachim, Martin D. - *Historical Aspects of Cataloging and Classification*
    LRTS - v49 - i1 - Jan 2005 - p60(2) [501+]

Jobe, Ron - *Info-Kids: How to Use Nonfiction to Turn Reluctant Readers into Enthusiastic Learners*
    RT - v57 - Nov 2003 - p296 [501+]

Jobling, Mark A. - *Human Evolutionary Genetics: Origins, Peoples and Disease*
    Choice - v42 - i4 - Dec 2004 - p687(1) [1-50]
    E-Streams - July 2004 - pNA [501+]

Joby, John - *Fundamentals of Customer Focused Management: Competing through Service*
    R&R Bk N - v19 - i3 - August 2004 - p126(1) [51-500]

Jocelyn, Marthe - *Earthly Astonishments*
    y Can CL - i111-112 - Fall-Winter 2003 - p153(6) [501+]
    Mabel Riley: A Reliable Record Of Humdrum, Peril and Romance
    LibMed - v22 - i7 - April-May 2004 - p61(1) [501+]
    Mayfly (Illus. by Jocelyn, Marthe)
    c BL - v100 - i22 - August 2004 - p1943(1) [51-500]
    Over Under (Illus. by Slaughter, Tom)
    c KR - v73 - i5 - March 1 2005 - p288(1) [51-500]
    c PW - v252 - i5 - Jan 31 2005 - p70(1) [501+]

Jochelson, Waldemar - *Archaeological Investigations in the Aleutian Islands*
    Am Ant - v69 - i4 - Oct 2004 - p789(3) [501+]

Jochems, Wim - *Integrated E-Learning: Implications for Pedagogy, Technology, and Organization*
    R&R Bk N - v19 - i3 - August 2004 - p217(1) [1-50]
    TCR - v107 - i2 - Feb 2005 - p336(4) [501+]

Jochimsen, Maren A. - *A Careful Economics: Integrating Caring Activities and Economic Science*
    JEL - v42 - i1 - March 2004 - p232(2) [501+]

Jode, Martin de - *Programming Java 2 Micro Edition for Symbian OS: A Developer's Guide to MIDP 2.0*
    SciTech - v28 - i3 - Sept 2004 - p23(1) [51-500]

Jodorowsky, Alexandro - *The Metabarons: Oton and Honorata. Book 1*
    Kliatt - v38 - i6 - Nov 2004 - p27(1) [501+]

Jodral, Manuel Miro - *Illicium, Pimpinella, and Foeniculum*
    SciTech - v28 - i4 - Dec 2004 - p117(1) [1-50]

Joe, Donna - *Ch'askin: A Legend of the Sechelt People (Illus. by Jeffries, Jamie)*
    c CBRA - Annual 2003 - p528(2) [51-500]

Joel, Billy - *Goodnight, My Angel: A Lullabye (Illus. by Gilbert, Yvonne)*
    c KR - v72 - i20 - Oct 15 2004 - p1008(1) [51-500]
    c PW - v251 - i41 - Oct 11 2004 - p78(1) [51-500]
    c SLJ - v51 - i2 - Feb 2005 - p104(1) [51-500]

Joel, Lucille A. - *Advanced Practice Nursing: Essentials for Role Development*
    SciTech - v28 - i1 - March 2004 - p126(1) [51-500]

Joellenbeck, Lois M. - *Giving Full Measure to Countermeasures: Addressing Problems in the DoD Program to Develop Medical Countermeasures Against Biological Warfare Agents*
    SciTech - v28 - i4 - Dec 2004 - p172(1) [51-500]

Joens, Michael - *Blood Reins*
    KR - v72 - i22 - Nov 15 2004 - p1071(1) [51-500]
    PW - v252 - i1 - Jan 3 2005 - p39(1) [51-500]

Joerges, Christian - *Darker Legacies of Law in Europe: The Shadow of National Socialism and Fascism Over Europe and Its Legal Traditions*
    TLS - i5289 - August 13 2004 - p26(1) [501+]

Joestel, Volkmar - *Luthers Bild und Lutherbilder: Ein Rundgang durch die Wirkungsgeschichte*
    Six Ct J - v35 - i3 - Fall 2004 - p795-809 [501+]

Jogdand, P.G. - *Dalit Women in India: Issues and Perspectives*
    CS - v33 - i6 - Nov 2004 - p654(4) [501+]

Joglekar, Anand M. - *Statistical Methods for Six Sigma in R&D and Manufacturing*
    SciTech - v28 - i1 - March 2004 - p177(1) [51-500]

Johanek, Michael C. - *A Faithful Mirror: Reflections on the College Board and Education in America*
    TCR - v106 - i2 - Feb 2004 - p228-234 [501+]

Johansen, Bruce E. - *Enduring Legacies: Native American Treaties and Contemporary Controversies*
    Choice - v42 - i5 - Jan 2005 - p915(1) [1-50]
    LJ - v129 - i14 - Sept 1 2004 - p168(1) [51-500]
    R&R Bk N - v19 - i3 - August 2004 - p205(1) [501+]

Johansen, Heidi Leigh - *What I Look Like When I Am Angry*
    y SLJ - v50 - i7 - July 2004 - p94(1) [51-500]
    What I Look Like When I Am Happy
    c SLJ - v50 - i8 - August 2004 - p110(1) [51-500]

Johansen, Iris - *Blind Alley*
    y BL - v100 - i22 - August 2004 - p1871(1) [51-500]
    Ent W - i784 - Sept 17 2004 - p84 [501+]
    KR - v72 - i16 - August 15 2004 - p766(1) [501+]
    PW - v251 - i34 - August 23 2004 - p37(1) [501+]
    Countdown
    LJ - v129 - i20 - Dec 1 2004 - p88(1) [51-500]
    The Delaney Christmas Carol
    LJ - v129 - i19 - Nov 15 2004 - p48(1) [51-500]
    Firestorm (Read by Dunne, Bernadette). Audiobook Review
    Kliatt - v38 - i6 - Nov 2004 - p46(1) [51-500]

Johansen, Jergen Dines - *Literary Discourse: A Semiotic-Pragmatic Approach to Literature*
    Can Lit - i181 - Summer 2004 - p97-99 [501+]

Johansen, Linda - *Fast, Fun & Easy Fabric Boxes*
    LJ - v129 - i20 - Dec 1 2004 - p110(1) [51-500]

Johansen, Michael - *Confession in Moscow*
    CBRA - Annual 2003 - p170(2) [51-500]

Johanson, Sue - *Sex, Sex, and More Sex*
    Globe & Mail - July 10 2004 - pD8 [501+]
    NYTBR - Sept 26 2004 - p31 [501+]

Johansson, Frans - *The Medici Effect: Breakthrough Insights at the Intersection of Ideas, Concepts, and Cultures*
    Fut - v39 - i2 - March-April 2005 - p61(1) [51-500]
    PW - v251 - i32 - August 9 2004 - p244(2) [51-500]

Johansson, Philip - *The Forested Taiga: A Web of Life*
    c SB - v40 - i4 - July-August 2004 - p176(1) [51-500]
    c SLJ - v50 - i8 - August 2004 - p110(1) [51-500]
    Frozen Tundra: A Web of Life
    c SB - v40 - i4 - July-August 2004 - p176(1) [51-500]
    The Temperate Forest: A Web of Life
    c SB - v40 - i4 - July-August 2004 - p176(1) [51-500]
    c SLJ - v50 - i8 - August 2004 - p110(1) [51-500]
    The Tropical Rain Forest: A Web of Life
    c SB - v40 - i4 - July-August 2004 - p176(1) [51-500]
    c SLJ - v50 - i8 - August 2004 - p110(1) [51-500]

John, Barnard - *The Cambridge History of the Book in Britain, Vol 4*
    BSA-P - v98 - i1 - March 2004 - p97-104 [501+]

John, Catherine A. - *Clear Word and Third Sight: Folk Groundings and Diasporic Consciousness in African Caribbean Writing*
    Choice - v41 - i11-12 - July-August 2004 - p2044(2) [501+]

John, Fritz - *Plane Waves and Spherical Means Applied to Partial Differential Equations*
    SciTech - v28 - i4 - Dec 2004 - p40(1) [51-500]

John, Joby - *Fundamentals of Customer-Focused Management: Competing through Service*
    Choice - v42 - i1 - Sept 2004 - p150(1) [501+]

John, Paul - *Qulirat Qanemcit-Ilu Kinguvarcimalriit = Stories for Future Generations: The Oratory of Yup'ik Elder Paul John*
R&R Bk N - v19 - i1 - Feb 2004 - p53(1) [51-500]

John Paul II, Pope - *Body and Gift: Reflections on Creation*
Bks & Cult - v10 - i5 - Sept-Oct 2004 - p28(1) [501+]
Purity of Heart: Reflections on Love and Lust
Bks & Cult - v10 - i5 - Sept-Oct 2004 - p28(1) [501+]
Rise, Let Us Be on Our Way
AM - v192 - i7 - Feb 28 2005 - p16 [501+]
LJ - v130 - i2 - Feb 1 2005 - p85(1) [51-500]
NS - v133 - i4710 - Oct 18 2004 - p54(2) [501+]

John, Raymond - *Encyclopedia of Exploration, 1800 to 1850*
Quad - v48 - i12 - Dec 2004 - p85(1) [501+]

Johns, Andreas - *Baba Yaga: The Ambiguous Mother and Witch of the Russian Folktale*
R&R Bk N - v19 - i3 - August 2004 - p85(1) [51-500]

Johns, Geoff - *Hawkman: Allies and Enemies*
c LibMed - v23 - i3 - Nov-Dec 2004 - p74(2) [51-500]
Teen Titans: A Kid's Game
y Kliatt - v38 - i4 - July 2004 - p33(2) [51-500]
Teen Titans: Family Lost
PW - v251 - i47 - Nov 22 2004 - p40(2) [51-500]

Johns, Jeremy - *Arabic Administration in Norman Sicily: The Royal Diwan*
AHR - v109 - i4 - Oct 2004 - p1296-1297 [501+]

Johns, Mark D. - *Online Social Research: Methods, Issues & Ethics*
R&R Bk N - v19 - i1 - Feb 2004 - p122(1) [51-500]

Johns, Richard - *Theory of Physical Probability*
CBRA - Annual 2003 - p92(2) [501+]

Johns, Robert - *Using the Law in Social Work, 1st ed.*
TimHES - v0 - i1680 - Feb 25 2005 - pIV(1) [501+]

Johns, Susan M. - *Noblewomen, Aristocracy and Power in the Twelfth-Century Anglo-Norman Realm*
HER - v119 - i483 - Sept 2004 - p984(2) [501+]
HER - v119 - i483 - Sept 2004 - p984(2) [501+]

Johnsen, William A. - *Violence and Modernism: Ibsen, Joyce, and Woolf*
Choice - v41 - i7 - March 2004 - p1296(1) [501+]
ELT - v48 - i2 - Spring 2005 - p111(4) [501+]

Johnsgard, Keith W. - *Conquering Depression and Anxiety through Exercise*
SciTech - v28 - i3 - Sept 2004 - p101(1) [1-50]

Johnson, A.J.B. - *Louisbourg: An 18th Century Town*
c Res Links - v10 - i1 - Oct 2004 - p38(1) [51-500]

Johnson, A.W. - *Dream No Little Dreams: A Biography of the Douglas Government of Saskatchewan, 1944-1961*
R&R Bk N - v19 - i3 - August 2004 - p79(1) [51-500]

Johnson, Allan G. - *The Gender Knot*
OOB - v34 - i9-10 - Sept-Oct 2004 - p51(2) [501+]

Johnson, Amy J. - *Reconstructing Rural Egypt: Ahmed Hussein and the History of Egyptian Development*
Choice - v42 - i1 - Sept 2004 - p170(1) [501+]
MEJ - v59 - i1 - Wntr 2005 - p142(3) [501+]

Johnson, Andrew P. - *A Short Guide to Action Research, 2nd Ed.*
R&R Bk N - v19 - i4 - Nov 2004 - p179(1) [501+]

Johnson, Angela - *Bird*
y BL - v101 - i1 - Sept 1 2004 - p108(1) [1-50]
c CCB-B - v58 - i4 - Dec 2004 - p172(2) [51-500]
c HB - v80 - i5 - Sept-Oct 2004 - p587(2) [51-500]
y Kliatt - v38 - i5 - Sept 2004 - p12(2) [51-500]
c KR - v72 - i14 - July 15 2004 - p688(1) [51-500]
c PW - v251 - i42 - Oct 18 2004 - p65(1) [51-500]
c SLJ - v50 - i9 - Sept 2004 - p209(1) [51-500]
A Cool Moonlight
LibMed - v22 - i7 - April-May 2004 - p61(1) [501+]
*The First Part Last (Read by Oldjohn, Khalipa).
Audiobook Review*
y HB - v81 - i2 - March-April 2005 - p221(1) [51-500]
c SLJ - v51 - i2 - Feb 2005 - p77(1) [501+]
The First Part Last
y Kliatt - v39 - i1 - Jan 2005 - p14(2) [51-500]
y PW - v252 - i1 - Jan 3 2005 - p58(1) [51-500]
I Dream of Trains (Illus. by Long, Lauren)
c LibMed - v22 - i4 - Jan 2004 - p58(1) [501+]
Just Like Josh Gibson (Illus. by Peck, Beth)
c BooChiTr - Feb 1 2004 - p5(1) [501+]
c CE - v81 - i2 - Winter 2004 - p107(2) [51-500]
A Sweet Smell of Roses (Illus. by Velasquez, Eric)
c CCB-B - v58 - i6 - Feb 2005 - p254(1) [51-500]
c HB - v81 - i1 - Jan-Feb 2005 - p79(1) [51-500]
c KR - v73 - i1 - Jan 1 2005 - p53(1) [51-500]
c PW - v252 - i1 - Jan 3 2005 - p55(1) [51-500]

Johnson, B.S. - *Albert Angelo*
Lon R Bks - v26 - i15 - August 5 2004 - p11(3) [501+]
House Mother Normal
Lon R Bks - v26 - i15 - August 5 2004 - p11(3) [501+]
Trawl
Lon R Bks - v26 - i15 - August 5 2004 - p11(3) [501+]

Johnson, Bankole A. - *Handbook of Clinical Alcoholism Treatment*
SciTech - v28 - i1 - March 2004 - p102(1) [51-500]

Johnson, Ben Campbell - *The God Who Speaks: Learning the Language of God*
Ch Today - v48 - i8 - August 2004 - p58(1) [51-500]
Hearing God's Call: Ways of Discernment for Laity and Clergy
Intpr - v59 - i1 - Jan 2005 - p103(1) [501+]

Johnson, Benjamin (b. 1972 -) - *Steal This University*
J Hi E - v75 - i5 - Sept-Oct 2004 - p594(3) [501+]

Johnson, Benjamin Heber - *Revolution in Texas: How a Forgotten Rebellion and Its Bloody Suppression Turned Mexicans into Americans*
HNet - Sept 2004 - pNA [501+]
HNet - Sept 2004 - pNA [501+]
JSH - v71 - i1 - Feb 2005 - p195(2) [501+]
SHQ - v108 - i1 - July 2004 - p116-117 [501+]

Johnson-Bennett, Pam - *Cat vs. Cat: Keeping Peace When You Have More Than One Cat*
LJ - v129 - i12 - July 2004 - p109(1) [51-500]
SciTech - v28 - i4 - Dec 2004 - p126 [51-500]

Johnson, Bethany L. - *"Origins of the New South" Fifty Years Later: The Continuing Influence of a Historical Classic*
BHR - v78 - i3 - Autumn 2004 - p524(3) [501+]

Johnson, Boris - *Seventy-Two Virgins: A Comedy of Errors*
NS - v133 - i4710 - Oct 18 2004 - p55(1) [501+]
Spec - v296 - i9189 - Sept 18 2004 - p53(2) [501+]

Johnson, Brooks - *Photography Speaks: 150 Photographers on Their Art*
Afterimage - v32 - i4 - Jan-Feb 2005 - p14(1) [501+]
LJ - v130 - i4 - March 1 2005 - p83(1) [51-500]

Johnson, Burke - *Educational Research: Quantitative, Qualitative, and Mixed Approaches, 2nd Ed.*
R&R Bk N - v19 - i1 - Feb 2004 - pNA [51-500]

Johnson, C.D. - *Recent Advances in Surgery: Vol. 27*
SciTech - v28 - i3 - Sept 2004 - p110(1) [51-500]

Johnson, C. Richard - *Telecommunication Breakdown: Concepts of Communication Transmitted Via Software-Defined Radio*
SciTech - v28 - i1 - March 2004 - p154(1) [51-500]

Johnson, Carolyn - *Using Internet Primary Sources to Teach Critical Thinking Skills in the Sciences*
SLJ - v50 - i10 - Oct 2004 - pS73(1) [51-500]

Johnson-Cartee, Karen S. - *Strategic Political Communication: Rethinking Social Influence, Persuasion, and Propaganda*
R&R Bk N - v19 - i1 - Feb 2004 - p124(1) [51-500]

Johnson, Chalmers - *Blowback: The Costs and Consequences of American Empire*
A Aff - v35 - i2 - July 2004 - p206-209 [501+]
The Sorrows of Empire: Militarism, Secrecy, and the End of the Republic
A Aff - v35 - i2 - July 2004 - p206-209 [501+]
J Mil H - v68 - i4 - Oct 2004 - p1324-1326 [501+]
NYTBR - Jan 23 2005 - p28 [501+]

Johnson, Charles - *Dr. King's Refrigerator and Other Bedtime Stories*
BL - v101 - i6 - Nov 15 2004 - p561(2) [51-500]
Black Iss - v7 - i1 - Jan-Feb 2005 - p63(1) [501+]
KR - v72 - i20 - Oct 15 2004 - p978(2) [501+]
LJ - v129 - i19 - Nov 15 2004 - p53(2) [501+]
NYTBR - March 6 2005 - p7 [501+]
PW - v251 - i44 - Nov 1 2004 - p40(1) [501+]

Johnson, Chris - *Afghanistan: The Mirage of Peace*
NS - v134 - i4726 - Feb 7 2005 - p52(2) [501+]

Johnson, Christopher - *Claude Levi-Strauss: The Formative Years*
FS - v58 - i1 - Jan 2004 - p138(2) [501+]

Johnson, Claudia Durst - *Youth Gangs in Literature*
R&R Bk N - v19 - i4 - Nov 2004 - p240(1) [501+]

Johnson, Clifford V. - *D-Branes*
Phys Today - v57 - i7 - July 2004 - p62-63 [501+]

Johnson, Craig - *The Cold Dish*
BW - v35 - i4 - Jan 30 2005 - p13(1) [501+]
KR - v72 - i23 - Dec 1 2004 - p1108(1) [501+]
PW - v251 - i50 - Dec 13 2004 - p48(1) [51-500]

Johnson, D.A. - *Metals and Chemical Change*
J Chem Ed - v81 - i3 - March 2004 - p337-342 [501+]

Johnson, D.B. - *Henry Works (Illus. by Johnson, D.B.)*
c BL - v101 - i1 - Sept 1 2004 - p133(1) [51-500]
c PW - v251 - i29 - July 19 2004 - p161(1) [51-500]
c SLJ - v50 - i9 - Sept 2004 - p169(1) [51-500]

Johnson, D.B. (American illustrator) - *Henry Works (Illus. by Johnson, D.B.)*
c CCB-B - v58 - i3 - Nov 2004 - p128(1) [501+]
HB - v80 - i5 - Sept-Oct 2004 - p569(2) [51-500]
c KR - v72 - i14 - July 15 2004 - p688(1) [51-500]

Johnson, D. LaMont - *Technology in Education: A Twenty-Year Retrospective*
R&R Bk N - v19 - i1 - Feb 2004 - p181(1) [51-500]

Johnson, D.P. - *English Episcopal Acta. London: 1189-1228*
CHR - v90 - i4 - Oct 2004 - p762(2) [501+]

Johnson, David A. - *On Sand Island*
c LibMed - v22 - i6 - March 2004 - p58(1) [501+]

Johnson, David (b. 1957 -) - *Thinking Government: Public-Sector Management in Canada*
CBRA - Annual 2003 - p307(2) [501+]

Johnson, David D. - *Douglas Southall Freeman*
South CR - v37 - i1 - Fall 2004 - p203-207 [501+]

Johnson, David K. - *The Lavender Scare: The Cold War Persecution of Gays and Lesbians in the Federal Government*
AJS - v110 - i3 - Nov 2004 - p848(3) [501+]
Choice - v42 - i2 - Oct 2004 - p356(1) [501+]
G&L Rev W - v11 - i5 - Sept-Oct 2004 - p46(2) [501+]
HNet - June 2004 - pNA [501+]
Lam Bk Rpt - v13 - i1-2 - August-Sept 2004 - p16(2) [501+]

Johnson, David Martel - *How History Made the Mind: The Cultural Origins of Objective Thinking*
Choice - v42 - i1 - Sept 2004 - p115(2) [501+]

Johnson, Denis - *Seek: Reports from the Edges of America and Beyond*
BIC - v33 - i2 - March 2004 - p11(1) [501+]

Johnson, Dennis W. - *Congress Online: Bridging the Gap Between Citizens and their Representatives*
Choice - v42 - i4 - Dec 2004 - p737(1) [1-50]

Johnson, Diane - *L'Affaire*
TLS - i5297 - Oct 8 2004 - p23(1) [501+]
Spec - v296 - i9194 - Oct 23 2004 - p46(1) [501+]

Johnson, Diane Chalmers - *American Symbolist Art: Nineteenth-Century "Poets in Paint" Washington Allston, John La Farge, William Rimmer, George Inness, and Albert Pinkham Ryder*
R&R Bk N - v19 - i4 - Nov 2004 - p200(1) [501+]

Johnson, Dolores - *Taking the Wrap: A Mandy Dyer Mystery*
BL - v101 - i1 - Sept 1 2004 - p69(1) [51-500]
LJ - v129 - i18 - Nov 1 2004 - p60(2) [51-500]

Johnson, Dominic D.P. - *Overconfidence and War: The Havoc and Glory of Positive Illusions*
LJ - v129 - i18 - Nov 1 2004 - p109(1) [51-500]
PW - v251 - i28 - July 12 2004 - p52(1) [51-500]
TimHES - v0 - i1676 - Jan 28 2005 - p30(2) [501+]

Johnson, Doug (b. 1952-) - *Learning Right from Wrong in the Digital Age: An Ethnics Guide for Parents, Teachers, Librarians, and Others Who Care about Computer-using Young People*
LibMed - v22 - i5 - Feb 2004 - p83(2) [501+]

Johnson, Douglas H. - *The Root Causes of Sudan's Civil Wars*
PSQ - v119 - i2 - Summer 2004 - p363(3) [501+]
TLS - i5288 - August 6 2004 - p6(1) [501+]

Johnson, Drew Heath - *Capturing Light: Masterpieces of California Photography, 1850-2000*
R&R Bk N - v19 - i4 - Nov 2004 - p248(1) [501+]

Johnson, Elaine B. - *The Dismantling of Public Education and How to Stop It*
R&R Bk N - v19 - i1 - Feb 2004 - pNA [51-500]

Johnson, Elizabeth A. - *Truly Our Sister: A Theology of Mary in the Communion of Saints*
Choice - v42 - i2 - Oct 2004 - p311(1) [51-500]

Johnson, Emily Pauline - *The Lost Island (Illus. by Matsoureff, Atanas)*
c BL - v101 - i9-10 - Jan 1 2005 - p849(1) [1-50]

Johnson, Eric - *What We Knew: Terror, Mass Murder, and Everyday Life in Nazi Germany: An Oral History*
PW - v252 - i5 - Jan 31 2005 - p60(1) [501+]

Johnson, Steve - *Show Me! Microsoft Windows XP*
  LJ - v130 - i2 - Feb 1 2005 - p110(1) [501+]
Johnson, Steven - *Mind Wide Open: Your Brain and the Neuroscience of Everyday Life*
  Choice - v41 - i11-12 - July-August 2004 - p2127(1) [501+]
  TES - v0 - i4586 - June 4 2004 - psss19(1) [501+]
Johnson, Susan M. - *Attachment Processes in Couple and Family Therapy*
  SciTech - v28 - i1 - March 2004 - p96(1) [51-500]
  The Practice of Emotionally Focused Couple Therapy: Creating Connection, 2nd Ed.
  SciTech - v28 - i4 - Dec 2004 - p97(1) [51-500]
Johnson, Susan Moore - *Finders and Keepers: Helping New Teachers Survive and Thrive in Our Schools*
  Choice - v42 - i3 - Nov 2004 - p536(1) [1-50]
  R&R Bk N - v19 - i3 - August 2004 - p224(1) [1-50]
Johnson, Sylvia - *Crows*
  c BL - v101 - i7 - Dec 1 2004 - p665(2) [51-500]
Johnson, Timothy A. - *Baseball and the Music of Charles Ives: A Proving Ground*
  R&R Bk N - v19 - i4 - Nov 2004 - p195(1) [501+]
Johnson, Tom - *The Christopher Lee Filmography*
  LJ - v129 - i13 - August 2004 - p83(1) [501+]
Johnson, Tora - *Entanglements: The Intertwined Fates of Whales and Fishermen*
  BL - v101 - i9-10 - Jan 1 2005 - p790(1) [1-50]
Johnson, Valen E. - *Grade Inflation: A Crisis in College Education*
  AJE - v110 - i4 - August 2004 - p404(3) [501+]
  Choice - v41 - i11-12 - July-August 2004 - p2096(1) [501+]
Johnson, Wayne - *The Devil You Know*
  BL - v101 - i9-10 - Jan 1 2005 - p769(1) [1-50]
  BooChiTr - May 9 2004 - p3(1) [501+]
  y SLJ - v50 - i8 - August 2004 - p146(1) [501+]
Johnson, William C. - *Superior Customer Value in the New Economy: Concepts and Cases, 2nd Ed.*
  R&R Bk N - v19 - i4 - Nov 2004 - p111(1) [51-500]
Johnson, Winslow - *Powerhouse Marketing Plans: 14 Outstanding Real-Life Plans and What You Can Learn from Them to Supercharge Your Own Campaigns*
  Bwatch - Feb 2005 - pNA [501+]
  Choice - v42 - i6 - Feb 2005 - p1066(2) [51-500]
  R&R Bk N - v19 - i4 - Nov 2004 - p110(1) [51-500]
Johnston, Alan B. - *SIP: Understanding the Session Initiation Protocol. 2nd Ed.*
  SciTech - v28 - i1 - March 2004 - p158(1) [51-500]
Johnston, Andrew James - *Clerks and Courtiers: Chaucer, Late Medieval Literature and the State Formation Process*
  JEGP - v103 - i1 - Jan 2004 - p134-138 [501+]
Johnston, Andrew K. - *Earth from Space: Smithsonian National Air and Space Museum*
  y BL - v101 - i7 - Dec 1 2004 - p629(2) [51-500]
  LJ - v130 - i1 - Jan 1 2005 - p147(1) [51-500]
Johnston, Anna - *Missionary Writing and Empire, 1800-1860*
  Nine-C Lit - v59 - i1 - June 2004 - p119(122) [501+]
Johnston, Basil - *Honour Earth Mother*
  y Kliatt - v39 - i2 - March 2005 - p36(1) [501+]
Johnston, Carolyn Ross - *Cherokee Women in Crisis: Trail of Tears, Civil War, and Allotment, 1838-1907*
  Choice - v41 - i11-12 - July-August 2004 - p2108(1) [501+]
Johnston, David Cay - *Perfectly Legal: The Covert Campaign to Rig Our Tax System to Benefit the Super Rich--and Cheat Everybody Else*
  Har Bus R - v82 - i1 - Feb 2004 - p39(1) [501+]
Johnston, David W. - *The History of Ornithology in Virginia*
  SciTech - v28 - i3 - Sept 2004 - p65(1) [51-500]
Johnston, Dorothy - *The Trojan Dog*
  KR - v73 - i2 - Jan 15 2005 - p86(1) [51-500]
  PW - v252 - i9 - Feb 28 2005 - p46(1) [51-500]
Johnston, Harold - *A Bridge Not Attacked: Chemical Warfare Civilian Research during World War II*
  Choice - v41 - i11-12 - July-August 2004 - p2065(1) [501+]
Johnston, Jennifer - *This Is Not a Novel (Read by Lowe, Emma). Audiobook Review*
  Kliatt - v38 - i6 - Nov 2004 - p52(1) [51-500]
Johnston, Joan - *The Rivals*
  PW - v251 - i35 - August 30 2004 - p38(1) [501+]
  Sweetwater Seduction
  LJ - v129 - i19 - Nov 15 2004 - p48(1) [51-500]

Johnston, Julie - *Susanna's Quill*
  c Globe & Mail - Dec 11 2004 - pD20 [501+]
  y Res Links - v10 - i3 - Feb 2005 - p35(2) [501+]
  y SLJ - v51 - i2 - Feb 2005 - p138(1) [51-500]
Johnston, Lynn - *Suddenly Silver: Celebrating 25 Years Of For Better Or For Worse*
  Bwatch - Feb 2005 - pNA [51-500]
Johnston, Mark - *Alamein: The Australian Story*
  AHS - v35 - i123 - April 2004 - p190-192 [501+]
Johnston, Peter H. - *Choice Words, How Our Language Affects Children's Learning*
  Inst - v114 - i5 - Jan-Feb 2005 - pS4(1) [501+]
Johnston, Peter R. - *Fluid Sterilization by Filtration. 3rd Ed.*
  SciTech - v28 - i1 - March 2004 - p124(1) [51-500]
Johnston, Richard - *The 2000 Presidential Election and the Foundations of Party Politics*
  Choice - v42 - i6 - Feb 2005 - p1099(1) [51-500]
Johnston, Robert D. - *The Radical Middle Class: Populist Democracy and the Question of Capitalism in Progressive Era Portland, Oregon*
  AHR - v109 - i4 - Oct 2004 - p1247(2) [501+]
  BHR - v78 - i1 - Spring 2004 - p131(4) [501+]
  RAH - v32 - i1 - March 2004 - p58(10) [501+]
  WHQ - v35 - i4 - Winter 2004 - p502-503 [501+]
  JAH - v91 - i2 - Sept 2004 - p659(1) [501+]
Johnston, Robert E., Jr. - *The Power of Strategy Innovation: A New Way of Linking Creativity and Strategic Planning to Discover Great Business Opportunities*
  R&R Bk N - v19 - i1 - Feb 2004 - p87(1) [1-50]
Johnston, Robert K. - *Useless Beauty: Ecclesiastes through the Lens of Contemporary Film*
  PW - v251 - i41 - Oct 11 2004 - p75(1) [51-500]
Johnston, Ron - *A Century of British Geography*
  Choice - v41 - i11-12 - July-August 2004 - p2111(2) [501+]
  J Hist G - v30 - i3 - July 2004 - p588(3) [501+]
Johnston, Sarah Iles - *Religions of the Ancient World: A Guide*
  LJ - v130 - i1 - Jan 1 2005 - p156(1) [51-500]
Johnston, Sean - *Day Does Not Go By*
  CBRA - Annual 2003 - p200(1) [501+]
Johnston, Tony - *Chicken in the Kitchen (Illus. by Taylor, Eleanor)*
  c BL - v101 - i9-10 - Jan 1 2005 - p870(1) [51-500]
  c KR - v73 - i1 - Jan 1 2005 - p53(1) [51-500]
  c PW - v252 - i9 - Feb 28 2005 - p66(1) [51-500]
  The Harmonica (Illus. by Mazellan, Ron)
  c Inst - v114 - i5 - Jan-Feb 2005 - p73(2) [501+]
  The Mummy's Mother
  c LibMed - v22 - i4 - Jan 2004 - p63(1) [501+]
  Uncle Rain Cloud
  c RT - v57 - Dec 2003 - p398 [51-500]
  The Worm Family (Illus. by Innerst, Stacy)
  c CCB-B - v58 - i1 - Sept 2004 - p23(1) [51-500]
  c KR - v72 - i19 - Oct 1 2004 - p963(1) [51-500]
  c PW - v251 - i49 - Dec 6 2004 - p58(2) [51-500]
  c SLJ - v51 - i2 - Feb 2005 - p104(1) [51-500]
Johnston, Wayne - *Human Amusements*
  NYTBR - August 8 2004 - p14 [51-500]
Johnston, Whit - *'80*
  KR - v72 - i14 - July 15 2004 - p650(1) [51-500]
  PW - v251 - i34 - August 23 2004 - p37(1) [501+]
Johnston, William - *Geisha, Harlot, Strangler, Star: A Woman, Sex, and Morality in Modern Japan*
  BL - v101 - i6 - Nov 15 2004 - p537(1) [51-500]
  LJ - v129 - i17 - Oct 15 2004 - p74(1) [51-500]
  A War of Patrols: Canadian Army Operations in Korea
  Can Hist R - v85 - i4 - Dec 2004 - p805(3) [501+]
  J Mil H - v68 - i2 - April 2004 - p648(3) [501+]
Johnstone, Craig - *New Horizons in British Urban Policy: Perspectives on New Labour's Urban Renaissance*
  R&R Bk N - v19 - i4 - Nov 2004 - p135(1) [51-500]
Johnstone, James - *Quickies 3: Short Short Fiction on Gay Male Desire*
  CBRA - Annual 2003 - p248(2) [51-500]
Johnstone, Jyll - *Throwing Curves: Eva Zeisel*
  Am Craft - v64 - i1 - Feb-March 2004 - p20(1) [501+]
  Am Craft - v64 - i1 - Feb-March 2004 - p20(1) [501+]
Johnstone, Nick - *The Environmental Performance of Public Procurement: Issues of Policy Coherence*
  R&R Bk N - v19 - i4 - Nov 2004 - p82(1) [1-50]
Johnstone, William W. - *First Mountain Man: Preacher's Justice*
  Roundup M - v12 - i1 - Oct 2004 - p31(1) [51-500]

The Last Gunfighter: No Man's Land
  Roundup M - v11 - i6 - August 2004 - p28(2) [501+]
Joint FAO/WHO Expert Committee on Food Additives - *Evaluation of Certain Food Additives and Contaminants: Proceedings*
  SciTech - v28 - i4 - Dec 2004 - p80(1) [51-500]
Jolas, Maria - *Maria Jolas, Woman of Action: A Memoir and Other Writings*
  Choice - v42 - i7 - March 2005 - p1228(1) [51-500]
Joldersma, Hermina - *Elisabeth's Manly Courage: Testimonials and Songs of Martyred Anabaptist Women in the Low Countries*
  Six Ct J - v34 - i4 - Winter 2003 - p1203-1204 [501+]
Jolivet, Jean-Christophe - *Allusion et epistolaire dans les Heroides Recherches sur l'intertextualite ovidienne*
  Class R - v54 - i1 - May 2004 - p98(2) [501+]
Joll, Evelyn - *The Oxford Companion to J.M.W. Turner*
  VS - v45 - i2 - Winter 2003 - p358 [501+]
Jolles, Carol Zane - *Faith, Food, and Family in a Yupik Whaling Community*
  WHQ - v35 - i3 - Autumn 2004 - p391(1) [501+]
Jolley, Dan - *ISA: The Liberty Files*
  LJ - v129 - i12 - July 2004 - p61(2) [51-500]
Jolly, Alison - *Lords and Lemurs: Mad Scientists, Kings and Spears, with the Survival of Diversity in Madagascar*
  Bwatch - v26 - i8 - August 2004 - p1(1) [51-500]
  Lords and Lemurs: Mad Scientists, Kings with Spears, and the Survival of Diversity in Madagascar
  Am Sci - v92 - i4 - July-August 2004 - p383(2) [501+]
Jolly, Penny Howell - *Hair: Untangling a Social History*
  R&R Bk N - v19 - i3 - August 2004 - p85(1) [51-500]
Jolly, Richard - *UN Contributions to Development Thinking and Practice*
  Choice - v42 - i5 - Jan 2005 - p904(1) [1-50]
Joly, Daniele - *International Migration in the New Millennium: Global Movement and Settlement*
  R&R Bk N - v19 - i3 - August 2004 - p185(1) [501+]
Joly, Herve - *Des barrages, des usiness, et des hommes: L'industrialisation des Alpes du Nord entre ressources locales et apports exterieurs*
  T&C - v45 - i4 - Oct 2004 - p879(2) [501+]
Jomo, K.S. - *Manufacturing Competitiveness in Asia: How Internationally Competitive National Firms and Industries Developed in East Asia*
  JEL - v41 - i4 - Dec 2003 - p1410(1) [501+]
  Southeast Asian Paper Tigers? From Miracle to Debacle and Beyond
  JAS - v63 - i2 - May 2004 - p556(3) [501+]
Jomphe, Claudine - *Les Theories de la dispositio et le grand oeuvre de Ronsard*
  Six Ct J - v34 - i4 - Winter 2003 - p1173-1175 [501+]
Jonakait, Randolph N. - *The American Jury System*
  Law&PolBR - June 2004 - p389(4) [501+]
Jonas, Hans - *Erinnerungen*
  TLS - i5283 - July 2 2004 - p22(1) [501+]
Jonas, Klaus W. - *Golo Mann: Leben und Werk, Chronik und Bibliographie (1929-2003).*
  WLT - v79 - i1 - Jan-April 2005 - p100(1) [501+]
Jonas, Peter M. - *Secrets of Connecting Leadership and Learning with Humor*
  R&R Bk N - v19 - i4 - Nov 2004 - p183(1) [501+]
Jonas, Raymond - *France and the Cult of the Sacred Heart*
  JIH - v33 - i3 - Winter 2003 - p472 [501+]
Jonassen, David H. - *Handbook of Research on Educational Communications and Technology: A Project of the Association for Educational Communications and Technology, 2nd Ed.*
  R&R Bk N - v19 - i1 - Feb 2004 - pNA [51-500]
Joneja, Janice M. Vickerstaff - *Digestion, Diet, and Disease: Irritable Bowel Syndrome and Gastrointestinal Function*
  Choice - v42 - i7 - March 2005 - p1260(1) [51-500]
Jones, Adam - *Beyond the Barricades: Nicaragua and the Struggle for the Sandinista Press*
  HAHR - v84 - i2 - May 2004 - p375(3) [501+]
  Gendercide and Genocide
  R&R Bk N - v19 - i3 - August 2004 - p164(1) [501+]
  Genocide, War Crimes and the West: History and Complicity
  Choice - v42 - i5 - Jan 2005 - p930(1) [51-500]

Jones, Alan - *Reimagining Christianity: Reconnect Your Spirit without Disconnecting Your Mind*
    BL - v101 - i4 - Oct 15 2004 - p365(1) [51-500]
    LJ - v130 - i1 - Jan 1 2005 - p120(1) [51-500]
    PW - v251 - i37 - Sept 13 2004 - p76(1) [501+]

Jones, Alice - *Gorgeous Mourning*
    Poet - v185 - i2 - Nov 2004 - p131(2) [501+]

Jones, Allen - *Royal Academy Illustrated 2004: A Selection from the 236th Summer Exhibition*
    R&R Bk N - v19 - i4 - Nov 2004 - p200(1) [501+]

Jones, Ann Rosalind - *Renaissance Clothes and the Materials of Memory*
    MP - v102 - i1 - August 2004 - p101(5) [501+]

Jones, Arthur - *Pierre Toussaint*
    CHR - v90 - i4 - Oct 2004 - p819(2) [501+]
    Comw - v131 - i16 - Sept 24 2004 - p35(3) [501+]

Jones, Barrie W. - *Life in the Solar System and Beyond*
    Choice - v42 - i2 - Oct 2004 - p315(1) [51-500]

Jones, Ben - *The Rope Eater*
    BL - v101 - i6 - Nov 15 2004 - p558(1) [51-500]

Jones, Bill - *British Politics Today, 7th Ed.*
    CR - v285 - i1666 - Nov 2004 - p316(1) [501+]
    TimHES - v0 - i1668 - Nov 26 2004 - pIII(1) [501+]
Politics UK, 5th Ed.
    TimHES - v0 - i1668 - Nov 26 2004 - pIII(1) [501+]

Jones, Brian W. - *Suetonius: The Flavian Emperors. A Historical Commentary*
    Class R - v53 - i2 - Nov 2003 - p378-379 [501+]

Jones, Colin - *Paris: Biography of a City*
    KR - v73 - i3 - Feb 1 2005 - p166(2) [501+]
    PW - v252 - i10 - March 7 2005 - p60(1) [51-500]
    Spec - v296 - i9197 - Nov 13 2004 - p57(1) [501+]

Jones, Daniel B. - *Laparoscopic Surgery: Principles and Procedures. 2nd Ed.*
    SciTech - v28 - i3 - Sept 2004 - p110(1) [51-500]

Jones, Daniel (b. 1962 -) - *The Bastard on the Couch: 27 Men Try Really Hard to Explain Their Feelings About Love, Loss, Fatherhood, and Freedom*
    Atl - v294 - i3 - Oct 2004 - p165(10) [501+]

Jones, Darryl - *Jane Austen*
    Choice - v42 - i5 - Jan 2005 - p853(1) [1-50]
    CR - v285 - i1665 - Oct 2004 - p245(3) [501+]

Jones, Daryl - *Agriculture, Trade and the Environment: The Pig Sector*
    SciTech - v28 - i3 - Sept 2004 - p132(1) [51-500]

Jones, David (b. 1945) - *U.S. Subs Down Under: Brisbane, 1942-1945*
    R&R Bk N - v20 - i1 - Feb 2005 - p33(1) [51-500]

Jones, David C. - *Empire of Dust: Settling and Abandoning the Prairie Dry Belt*
    WHQ - v35 - i1 - Spring 2004 - p99-100 [501+]

Jones, David E. - *Combat, Ritual, and Performance: Anthropology of the Martial Arts*
    JRAI - v10 - i3 - Sept 2004 - p745(1) [501+]
Native North American Armor, Shields, and Fortifications
    J Mil H - v68 - i4 - Oct 2004 - p1253-1254 [501+]
    Roundup M - v12 - i1 - Oct 2004 - p22(2) [51-500]

Jones, David Laurence - *See This World before the Next: Cruising with CPR Ships in the Twenties and Thirties*
    Globe & Mail - Sept 4 2004 - pT6 [501+]

Jones, David Martin - *Globalization and the New Terror: The Asia Pacific Dimension*
    R&R Bk N - v19 - i3 - August 2004 - p164(1) [501+]

Jones, David W. - *Reforming the Morality of Usury: A Study of the Differences that Separated the Protestant Reformers*
    R&R Bk N - v19 - i3 - August 2004 - p20(1) [1-50]

Jones-Davis, M.-T. - *Memoire et oubli au temps de la renaissance*
    FS - v58 - i2 - April 2004 - p245(1) [501+]

Jones, Diana Wynne - *Changeover*
    ChrSFF&H - v26 - i9 - Sept 2004 - p37(1) [51-500]
Charmed Life (Read by Doyle, Gerard). Audiobook Review
    y   HB - v80 - i4 - July-August 2004 - p474(1) [51-500]
    y   Kliatt - v38 - i5 - Sept 2004 - p54(3) [51-500]
    y   SLJ - v50 - i10 - Oct 2004 - p84(1) [51-500]
The Lives of Christopher Chant (Read by Doyle, Gerard). Audiobook Review
    Kliatt - v38 - i6 - Nov 2004 - p48(1) [51-500]
    y   SLJ - v50 - i9 - Sept 2004 - p78(1) [51-500]
The Magicians of Caprona (Read by Doyle, Gerard). Audiobook Review
    y   SLJ - v51 - i1 - Jan 2005 - p76(2) [51-500]
Unexpected Magic: Collected Stories
    c   SLJ - v50 - i9 - Sept 2004 - p209(1) [51-500]

Jones, Dorothy V. - *Toward a Just World: The Critical Years in the Search for International Justice*
    JAH - v91 - i1 - June 2004 - p298-299 [501+]

Jones, E. Michael - *The Slaughter of Cities: Urban Renewal as Ethnic Cleansing*
    Choice - v42 - i2 - Oct 2004 - p376(2) [51-500]

Jones, Edward D. - *HIPAA Transactions: A Nontechnical Business Guide for Health Care*
    SciTech - v28 - i1 - March 2004 - p81(1) [51-500]

Jones, Edward P. - *The Known World*
    Ant R - v63 - i1 - Wntr 2005 - p190(1) [51-500]
    BooChiTr - Jan 18 2004 - p1(2) [501+]
    NYRB - v51 - i16 - Oct 21 2004 - p14(4) [501+]
    VQR - v80 - i1 - Wntr 2004 - p271-271 [501+]

Jones, Edward Powis - *Faith, Hope and Love*
    LJ - v129 - i20 - Dec 1 2004 - p112(1) [51-500]

Jones, Edward R. - *Known World (Read by Free, Kevin R.). Audiobook Review*
    BW - v34 - i32 - August 8 2004 - p12(1) [501+]

Jones, Edward Trostle - *All or Nothing: The Cinema of Mike Leigh*
    R&R Bk N - v19 - i4 - Nov 2004 - p224(1) [501+]

Jones, Eli - *Selling ASAP: Art, Science, Agility, Performance*
    R&R Bk N - v19 - i2 - May 2004 - p115(1) [1-50]

Jones, Frankie J. - *Survival of Love*
    Lam Bk Rpt - v13 - i4-5 - Nov-Dec 2004 - p42(2) [501+]

Jones, Gail - *Sixty Lights*
    NS - v133 - i4716 - Nov 29 2004 - p44(1) [51-500]
    TLS - i5303 - Nov 19 2004 - p25(1) [501+]

Jones, Gareth E. - *People and Environment: A Global Approach*
    TimHES - v0 - i1677 - Feb 4 2005 - p32(1) [501+]

Jones, Gareth Stedman - *An End to Poverty? A Historical Debate*
    CR - v285 - i1667 - Dec 2004 - p382(1) [51-500]

Jones, Gerard - *Men of Tomorrow: Geeks, Gangsters, and the Birth of the Comic Book*
    BL - v101 - i2 - Sept 15 2004 - p190(1) [51-500]
    Bus W - i3911 - Dec 6 2004 - p24 [501+]
    KR - v72 - i17 - Sept 1 2004 - p848(1) [51-500]
    LJ - v129 - i14 - Sept 1 2004 - p41(1) [501+]
    LJ - v130 - i1 - Jan 1 2005 - p89(1) [51-500]

Jones, Greta - *Herbert Spencer*
    New Sci - v183 - i2466 - Sept 25 2004 - p49(1) [51-500]

Jones, Gwyneth A. - *Life*
    LJ - v129 - i15 - Sept 15 2004 - p52(1) [51-500]
    NYTBR - Nov 14 2004 - p51 [501+]
Taylor Five
    LibMed - v22 - i6 - March 2004 - p67(1) [501+]
    y   VOYA - v27 - i4 - Oct 2004 - p314(1) [501+]

Jones, Hettie - *All Told*
    WLT - v78 - i3-4 - Sept-Dec 2004 - p100(1) [501+]

Jones, Howard - *Samnium: Settlement and Cultural Change, Proceedings*
    R&R Bk N - v19 - i4 - Nov 2004 - p40(1) [51-500]

Jones, Howard (b. 1940 -) - *Death of a Generation: How the Assassinations of Diem and JFK Prolonged the Vietnam War*
    AHR - v109 - i4 - Oct 2004 - p1259(2) [501+]

Jones, Ian - *Morning Glory: A History of British Breakfast Television*
    TLS - i5292 - Sept 3 2004 - p31(1) [501+]

Jones, J. Stephen - *Overcoming Impotence: A Leading Urologist Tells You Everything You Need to Know*
    SciTech - v28 - i1 - March 2004 - p106(1) [1-50]

Jones, Jac - *In Chatter Wood*
    c   Sch Lib - v52 - i3 - Autumn 2004 - p146(1) [501+]

Jones, Jacqueline - *Early Literacy Assessment Systems*
    CE - v81 - i2 - Winter 2004 - p117(1) [51-500]

Jones, James H. - *Alfred Kinsey: A Life*
    Globe & Mail - Dec 24 2004 - pD14 [51-500]

Jones, Jami Biles - *Helping Teens Cope: Resources for School Library Media Specialists and Other Youth Workers*
    LibMed - v22 - i4 - Jan 2004 - p85(1) [501+]
Helping Teens Cope: Resources for School Library Media Specialists
    R&R Bk N - v19 - i1 - Feb 2004 - p261(1) [51-500]

Jones, Jane - *Classic Still Life Painting: A Contemporary Master Shows How to Achieve Old Master Effects Using Today's Art Materials*
    LJ - v129 - i19 - Nov 15 2004 - p58(2) [501+]

Jones, Janna - *The Southern Movie Palace: Rise, Fall, and Resurrection.*
    BHR - v78 - i1 - Spring 2004 - p144(3) [501+]
    Pub Hist - v26 - i2 - Spring 2004 - p92(94) [501+]

Jones, Jennifer B. - *The (Short) Story of My Life*
    c   BL - v100 - i21 - July 2004 - p1844(1) [1-50]
    c   SLJ - v50 - i8 - August 2004 - p124(1) [51-500]

Jones, Jennifer (b. 1961 -) - *Medea's Daughters: Forming and Performing the Woman Who Kills*
    Theat J - v56 - i4 - Dec 2004 - p726-727 [501+]

Jones, Jennifer Vaughan - *Anna Wickham: A Poet's Daring Life*
    Lam Bk Rpt - v13 - i4-5 - Nov-Dec 2004 - p25(1) [501+]
    TLS - i5263 - Feb 13 2004 - p12-12 [501+]

Jones, John E. - *New Supervisor Training*
    HR Mag - v50 - i2 - Feb 2005 - pS16(1) [501+]

Jones, John Philip - *Fables, Fashions and Facts about Advertising: A Study of 28 Enduring Myths*
    R&R Bk N - v19 - i1 - Feb 2004 - p114(1) [51-500]

Jones, John R.W.D. - *International Criminal Practice*
    R&R Bk N - v19 - i1 - Feb 2004 - pNA [51-500]

Jones, Karen M. - *The Difference a Day Makes: 365 Ways to Change Your World in Just 24 Hours*
    LJ - v130 - i1 - Jan 1 2005 - p135(1) [51-500]

Jones, Karen R. - *Wolf Mountains: A History of Wolves along the Great Divide*
    HNet - June 2004 - pNA [501+]

Jones, Kent - *Who's Afraid of the WTO?*
    Choice - v41 - i11-12 - July-August 2004 - p2092(2) [501+]

Jones, Landon Y. - *William Clark and the Shaping of the West*
    BW - v34 - i37 - Sept 12 2004 - p5(1) [501+]
    Choice - v42 - i5 - Jan 2005 - p916(1) [1-50]
    RAH - v32 - i3 - Sept 2004 - p365-373 [501+]

Jones, Larry - *Black Box*
    PW - v251 - i39 - Sept 27 2004 - p39(1) [51-500]

Jones, Laura - *Managing Fish: Ten Case Studies from Canada's Pacific Coast*
    CBRA - Annual 2003 - p413(2) [501+]
    CBRA - Annual 2003 - p413(2) [501+]

Jones, Linda Winstead - *The Sun Witch*
    BL - v101 - i7 - Dec 1 2004 - p641(1) [51-500]

Jones, Lyle V. - *The Nation's Report Card: Evolution and Prespectives*
    Choice - v42 - i2 - Oct 2004 - p344(2) [51-500]
    TCR - v106 - i8 - August 2004 - p1618(2) [501+]

Jones, Lynne - *Then They Started Shooting: Growing Up in Wartime Bosnia*
    BL - v101 - i3 - Oct 1 2004 - p286(1) [51-500]
    Globe & Mail - March 5 2005 - pD6 [501+]
    LJ - v130 - i2 - Feb 1 2005 - p105(1) [51-500]
    PW - v251 - i35 - August 30 2004 - p39(1) [501+]

Jones, Marion - *Marion Jones: Life in the Fast Lane, An Illustrated Autobiography*
    Black Iss - v6 - i6 - Nov-Dec 2004 - p51(1) [501+]

Jones, Mark H. - *An Introduction to Galaxies and Cosmology*
    S&T - v109 - i1 - Jan 2005 - p120(2) [501+]

Jones, Mark W. - *Theory and Practice of Computer Graphics: Proceedings*
    SciTech - v28 - i3 - Sept 2004 - p137(1) [51-500]

Jones, Max - *The Last Great Quest: Captain Scott's Antarctic Sacrifice*
    J Hist G - v30 - i1 - Jan 2004 - p198(3) [501+]
    TimHES - v0 - i1647 - July 2 2004 - p30(1) [501+]

Jones, Melissa M. - *Whisper Writing: Teenage Girls Talk about Ableism and Sexism in School*
    R&R Bk N - v19 - i4 - Nov 2004 - p193(1) [501+]

Jones, Michael C.E. - *Between France and England: Politics, Power, and Society in Late Medieval Brittany*
    R&R Bk N - v19 - i1 - Feb 2004 - p36(1) [1-50]

Jones, Miranda - *Little Genie: Castle Magic*
    c   CH Bwatch - v14 - i11 - Nov 2004 - pNA [501+]
Make a Wish! (Illus. by Calver, David)
    c   BL - v101 - i2 - Sept 15 2004 - p233(1) [501+]

Jones, Nicholas F. - *Rural Athens under the Democracy*
    Choice - v42 - i3 - Nov 2004 - p540(1) [1-50]

Jones, Norman - *Structures Under Shock and Impact VIII: Proceedings*
    SciTech - v28 - i3 - Sept 2004 - p141(1) [51-500]

Jones, P.C. - *Fraud and Corruption in Public Services: A Guide to Risk and Prevention*
    R&R Bk N - v19 - i4 - Nov 2004 - p153(1) [501+]

Jones, Pamela M. - *From Rome to Eternity: Catholicism and the Arts in Italy, ca. 1550-1650*
    CHR - v90 - i4 - Oct 2004 - p793(3) [501+]

Jones, Patricia - *The Color of Family*
 BL - v101 - i2 - Sept 15 2004 - p207(2) [501+]
 Black Iss - v6 - i6 - Nov-Dec 2004 - p71(1) [51-500]

Jones, Patrick - *Connecting Young Adults and Libraries: A How-to-Do-It Manual for Librarians, 3rd Ed.*
 y CCB-B - v58 - i4 - Dec 2004 - p189(1) [1-50]
 R&R Bk N - v19 - i4 - Nov 2004 - p257(1) [501+]
 y SLJ - v50 - i12 - Dec 2004 - p178(2) [51-500]
 A Core Collections for Young Adults
 LibMed - v22 - i4 - Jan 2004 - p87(1) [501+]

Jones, Paul - *Raymond Williams's Sociology of Culture: A Critical Reconstruction*
 Choice - v42 - i4 - Dec 2004 - p742(1) [1-50]

Jones, Peder - *College Writing Skills, 5th Ed.*
 R&R Bk N - v19 - i1 - Feb 2004 - p216(1) [51-500]

Jones, Peter (b. 1949 -) - *Liberty and Locality in Revolutionary France: Six Villages Compared, 1760-1820*
 AHR - v109 - i4 - Oct 2004 - p1319(2) [501+]

Jones, Pip - *Introducing Social Theory*
 AJPS - v39 - i3 - Nov 2004 - p677(2) [501+]
 CS - v33 - i6 - Nov 2004 - p745(1) [1-50]
 JEL - v42 - i1 - March 2004 - p344(1) [501+]

Jones, Ray - *USA to Z: A Celebration of American Popular Culture*
 R&R Bk N - v19 - i4 - Nov 2004 - p56(1) [1-50]

Jones, Richard A.L. - *Soft Machines: Nanotechnology and Life*
 Am Sci - v93 - i2 - March-April 2005 - p183(2) [501+]
 SciTech - v28 - i4 - Dec 2004 - p130 [51-500]

Jones, Roger - *Thailand: A Quick Guide to Culture and Etiquette*
 R&R Bk N - v19 - i1 - Feb 2004 - p47(1) [1-50]

Jones, Shirley R. - *Law and the Midwife, 2nd Ed.*
 E-Streams - Oct 2004 - pNA [501+]

Jones, Solomon - *Ride or Die*
 KR - v72 - i13 - July 1 2004 - p598(1) [51-500]
 PW - v251 - i34 - August 23 2004 - p38(1) [51-500]

Jones, Stephen - *Captivity Narrative 109*
 South CR - v36 - i2 - Spring 2004 - p19-23 [501+]

Jones, Stephen Graham - *The Bird Is Gone: A Manifesto*
 Am Ind CRJ - v28 - i2 - Spring 2004 - p142(3) [501+]

Jones, Stephen R. - *The North American Prairie*
 Atl - v294 - i1 - July-August 2004 - p144(1) [501+]

Jones, Steven E. - *Satire and Romanticism*
 JEGP - v103 - i2 - April 2004 - p273-274 [501+]

Jones, Steven H. - *Coping with Schizophrenia: A Guide for Patients, Families, and Caregivers*
 LJ - v130 - i1 - Jan 1 2005 - p132(1) [501+]

Jones, Stuart - *The Decline of the South African Economy*
 JEH - v64 - i1 - March 2004 - p258(2) [501+]

Jones, Susan D. - *Valuing Animals: Veterinarians and Their Patients in Modern America*
 AHR - v109 - i2 - April 2004 - p566(2) [501+]
 JAH - v91 - i1 - June 2004 - p336-337 [501+]

Jones, Suzanne W. - *Race Mixing: Southern Fiction since the Sixties*
 Choice - v42 - i1 - Sept 2004 - p101(1) [501+]

Jones, Tayari - *The Untelling*
 KR - v73 - i2 - Jan 15 2005 - p75(1) [51-500]
 PW - v252 - i9 - Feb 28 2005 - p40(1) [51-500]
 Black Iss - v7 - i2 - March-April 2005 - p51(1) [51-500]

Jones, Ted - *Fredericton Flashbacks: Stories and Photography from the Past*
 CBRA - Annual 2003 - p342(1) [501+]

Jones, Terri - *Culinary Calculations: Simplified Math for Culinary Professionals*
 R&R Bk N - v19 - i1 - Feb 2004 - p253(1) [51-500]

Jones, Terry - *Who Murdered Chaucer?: A Medieval Mystery*
 Ent W - Feb 4 2005 - p141 [51-500]
 LJ - v130 - i2 - Feb 1 2005 - p79(1) [51-500]

Jones, Thai - *A Radical Line: From the Labor Movement to the Weather Underground, One Family's Century of Conscience*
 BW - v34 - i47 - Nov 21 2004 - p13(1) [501+]
 A Radical Line: One Family's Century of Conscience: The Story of the Radical Movement in America
 y BL - v101 - i4 - Oct 15 2004 - p368(1) [51-500]
 KR - v72 - i15 - August 1 2004 - p727(1) [501+]
 LJ - v129 - i14 - Sept 1 2004 - p168(1) [51-500]
 PW - v251 - i32 - August 9 2004 - p239(1) [51-500]

Jones, Tod E. - *The Broad Church: A Biography of a Movement*
 CH - v73 - i3 - Sept 2004 - p695(3) [501+]

Jones, Tracy - *The Smart-Carb Guide to Eating Out: Fast Food and Family Restaurants*
 LJ - v130 - i1 - Jan 1 2005 - p144(3) [501+]

Jones, Ursula - *The Witches Children and the Queen*
 c Sch Lib - v52 - i4 - Winter 2004 - p186(1) [51-500]

Jones, V.M. - *Prince of the Wind*
 y Magpies - v19 - i5 - Nov 2004 - p38(1) [501+]

Jones, Vivien - *Women and Literature in Britain 1700-1800*
 Eight-C St - v36 - i2 - Winter 2003 - p289 [501+]

Jones, Weyman - *Broken Glass*
 LJ - v129 - i14 - Sept 1 2004 - p122(1) [51-500]

Jones, Wilmer L. - *Generals in Blue and Gray*
 BL - v101 - i8 - Dec 15 2004 - p702(1) [51-500]

Jong, Erica - *Sappho's Leap*
 Lon R Bks - v26 - i1 - Jan 8 2004 - pNA [501+]
 TLS - i5295 - Sept 24 2004 - p20(1) [501+]

Jong-Fast, Molly - *The Sex Doctors in the Basement: True Stories from a Semi-Celebrity Childhood*
 KR - v73 - i1 - Jan 1 2005 - p35(1) [501+]
 PW - v251 - i51 - Dec 20 2004 - p43(1) [51-500]

Jong, Irene J.F. De - *A Narratological Commentary on the Odyssey*
 Class R - v54 - i1 - May 2004 - p17(2) [501+]

Jongen, Hubertus Th. - *Optimization Theory*
 Choice - v42 - i4 - Dec 2004 - p697(1) [1-50]

Jongsma, Arthur E., Jr. - *Adult Psychotherapy Homework Planner*
 SciTech - v28 - i1 - March 2004 - p97(1) [51-500]
 Adult Psychotherapy Progress Notes Planner. 2nd Ed.
 SciTech - v28 - i1 - March 2004 - p97(1) [51-500]

Jonsdottir, Sigurlini - *Children's Recorder Method, Vol. 1. Audiobook Review*
 c Teach Mus - v12 - i2 - Oct 2004 - p72(1) [51-500]

Joosse, Barbara M. - *Bad Dog School (Illus. by Plecas, Jennifer)*
 c CCB-B - v58 - i2 - Oct 2004 - p82(1) [51-500]
 c KR - v72 - i14 - July 15 2004 - p688(1) [51-500]
 c SLJ - v50 - i9 - Sept 2004 - p169(2) [51-500]
 Hot City (Illus. by Christie, Gregory)
 c BL - v100 - i21 - July 2004 - p1847(2) [51-500]
 c NYTBR - July 11 2004 - p18 [501+]
 c PW - v251 - i28 - July 12 2004 - p63(1) [51-500]
 c SLJ - v50 - i7 - July 2004 - p78(1) [51-500]
 Nikolai, the Only Bear (Illus. by Liwska, Renata)
 c CCB-B - v58 - i5 - Jan 2005 - p213(1) [51-500]
 c HB - v81 - i1 - Jan-Feb 2005 - p79(2) [51-500]
 c KR - v73 - i5 - March 1 2005 - p288(1) [51-500]

Joosse, Nanne Peter - *A Syriac Encyclopedia of Aristolelian Philosophy: Barhebraeus (13th c.), 'Butyrum Sapientiae', Books of Ethics, Economy, and Politics*
 R&R Bk N - v19 - i4 - Nov 2004 - p12(1) [51-500]

Jordan, A. Van - *M-A-C-N-O-L-I-A: Poems*
 Black Iss - v6 - i5 - Sept-Oct 2004 - p54(1) [501+]
 BW - v34 - i43 - Oct 24 2004 - p12(1) [501+]

Jordan, Andrew - *Environmental Policy in the European Union: Actors, Institutions and Processes*
 JEL - v42 - i1 - March 2004 - p336(1) [501+]

Jordan, Bill - *Irregular Migration-The Dilemmas of Transnational Mobility*
 PG - v23 - i4 - May 2004 - p495-497 [501+]
 Migration: The Boundaries of Equality and Justice
 AJPS - v39 - i3 - Nov 2004 - p679(2) [501+]
 JEL - v41 - i4 - Dec 2003 - p1383(2) [501+]

Jordan, Brian Matthew - *Triumphant Mourner*
 Bwatch - v26 - i8 - August 2004 - p5(1) [51-500]
 Bwatch - v26 - i9 - Sept 2004 - p4(1) [51-500]

Jordan-Bychkov, Terry G. - *The Upland South: The Making of an American Folk Region and Landscape*
 JSH - v70 - i3 - August 2004 - p647(2) [501+]

Jordan, Carol E. - *Intimate Partner Violence: A Clinical Training Guide for Mental Health Professionals*
 SciTech - v28 - i4 - Dec 2004 - p101(1) [51-500]

Jordan, David K. - *The Minor Arts of Daily Life: Popular Culture in Taiwan*
 R&R Bk N - v19 - i3 - August 2004 - p147(1) [51-500]

Jordan, David M. - *Pete Rose: A Biography*
 Bwatch - March 2005 - pNA [51-500]

Jordan, Deloris - *Did I Tell You I Love You Today? (Illus. by Evans, Shane)*
 c SLJ - v50 - i12 - Dec 2004 - p112(1) [501+]
 Did I Tell You I Love You?
 KR - v72 - i24 - Dec 15 2004 - p1203(1) [51-500]

Jordan, Frank - *Thiamine: Catalytic Mechanisms in Normal and Disease States*
 SciTech - v28 - i1 - March 2004 - p72(1) [51-500]

Jordan, Harry - *Meat Harry*
 CBRA - Annual 2003 - p132(1) [51-500]

Jordan, Jennifer - *Savage Summit: The True Stories of the First Five Women Who Climbed K2, the World's Most Feared Mountain*
 BL - v101 - i9-10 - Jan 1 2005 - p801(1) [51-500]
 LJ - v129 - i20 - Dec 1 2004 - p126(1) [51-500]
 NYTBR - Feb 6 2005 - p9 [501+]
 PW - v251 - i48 - Nov 29 2004 - p31(1) [51-500]

Jordan, June - *Soulscript: A Collection of African American Poetry*
 LJ - v129 - i16 - Oct 1 2004 - p121(1) [51-500]

Jordan, Karin - *Handbook of Couple and Family Assessment*
 SciTech - v28 - i1 - March 2004 - p99(1) [51-500]

Jordan, Louis - *John Hull, the Mint and the Economics of Massachusetts Coinage*
 JEH - v64 - i1 - March 2004 - p263(2) [501+]

Jordan, Margaret I. - *African American Servitude and Historical Imaginings: Retrospective Fiction and Representation*
 Choice - v42 - i5 - Jan 2005 - p896(1) [1-50]
 Choice - v42 - i7 - March 2005 - p1226(1) [51-500]

Jordan, Mark D. - *Telling Truths in Church: Scandal, Flesh and Christian Speech*
 Lam Bk Rpt - v13 - i1-2 - August-Sept 2004 - p34(3) [501+]

Jordan, Mary - *The Prison Angel: Mother Antonia's Journey from Beverly Hills to a Life of Service in a Mexican Jail*
 KR - v73 - i5 - March 1 2005 - p275(1) [501+]

Jordan, Michael - *Dictionary of Gods and Goddesses, 2nd Ed.*
 Choice - v42 - i6 - Feb 2005 - p992(1) [501+]
 LJ - v130 - i2 - Feb 1 2005 - p114(1) [51-500]
 R&R Bk N - v19 - i4 - Nov 2004 - p14(1) [51-500]
 y SLJ - v51 - i2 - Feb 2005 - p84(1) [51-500]

Jordan, Neil - *Shade (Read by Donnelly, Terry). Audiobook Review*
 KR - v72 - i15 - August 1 2004 - p706(1) [501+]
 Shade
 BL - v101 - i1 - Sept 1 2004 - p61(2) [501+]
 Ent W - i788 - Oct 15 2004 - p78 [51-500]
 Globe & Mail - July 17 2004 - pD3 [501+]
 LJ - v129 - i15 - Sept 15 2004 - p49(1) [51-500]
 NYTBR - Oct 24 2004 - p20 [501+]
 People - v62 - i20 - Nov 15 2004 - p47 [51-500]
 PW - v251 - i35 - August 30 2004 - p30(2) [501+]

Jordan, Nicole - *Lord of Seduction*
 PW - v251 - i46 - Nov 15 2004 - p46(1) [51-500]

Jordan, Peter - *Material Culture and Sacred Landscape:The Anthropology of the Siberian Khanty*
 JRAI - v10 - i4 - Dec 2004 - p921(2) [501+]

Jordan, Robert - *New Spring, the Novel (Read by Reading, Kate). Audiobook Review*
 Kliatt - v38 - i4 - July 2004 - p53(1) [51-500]

Jordan, Ronald R. - *Planned Giving: Management, Marketing, and Law, 3rd Ed.*
 R&R Bk N - v19 - i1 - Feb 2004 - p136(1) [51-500]

Jordan, Rosa - *Lost Goat Lane*
 c CCB-B - v58 - i6 - Feb 2005 - p254(2) [51-500]
 c KR - v72 - i19 - Oct 1 2004 - p963(1) [51-500]
 c SLJ - v50 - i12 - Dec 2004 - p148(1) [51-500]

Jordan, Sandra - *Frog Hunt*
 c CH Bwatch - March 2005 - pNA [51-500]

Jordan, Sarah - *The Anxieties of Idleness in Eighteenth-Century British Literature and Culture*
 RES - v55 - i221 - Sept 2004 - p622(3) [501+]

Jordan, Sarah Clark - *The BossQueen, Little BigBark, and the Sentinel Pup*
 c SLJ - v50 - i12 - Dec 2004 - p148(2) [51-500]

Jordan, Sherryl - *The Raging Quiet*
 y Kliatt - v38 - i4 - July 2004 - p20(2) [51-500]

Jordan, William Chester - *Dictionary of Middle Ages: Supplement I*
 Choice - v42 - i1 - Sept 2004 - p77(1) [501+]

Jordon, Deloris - *Did I Tell You I Love You Today? (Illus. by Evans, Shane)*
 c PW - v251 - i49 - Dec 6 2004 - p58(1) [51-500]

Jordy, William H. - *Buildings of Rhode Island*
 Choice - v42 - i2 - Oct 2004 - p285(1) [51-500]

Jorgensen, Christer - *Hitler's Espionage Machine: The True Story Behind One of the World's Most Ruthless Spy Networks*
 R&R Bk N - v19 - i4 - Nov 2004 - p34(1) [51-500]

Jorgensen, James H. - *Clinician's Dictionary of Pathogenic Microorganisms*
 E-Streams - August 2004 - pNA [501+]

Jorgensen, Karen - *Pay for Results: A Practical Guide to Effective Employee Compensation.*
HR Mag - v49 - i7 - July 2004 - pS7(1) [51-500]

Jorgensen, Norman - *The Call of the Osprey (Illus. by Harrison-Lever, Brian)*
c SLJ - v51 - i2 - Feb 2005 - p104(1) [51-500]

Jorisch, Stephane - *Suki's Kimono*
LibMed - v22 - i6 - March 2004 - p60(1) [501+]

Jory, Jon - *Tips II: More Ideas for Actors*
Choice - v42 - i6 - Feb 2005 - p1028(1) [51-500]

Joselit, Jenna Weissman - *A Perfect Fit: Clothes, Character, and the Promise of America*
JWH - v16 - i4 - Winter 2004 - p191(16) [501+]

Joseph, Anne - *From the Edge of the World: The Jewish Refugee Experience through Letters and Stories*
R&R Bk N - v19 - i1 - Feb 2004 - p30(1) [51-500]

Joseph, Betty - *Reading the East India Company, 1720-1840: Colonial Currencies of Gender*
TLS - i5266 - March 5 2004 - p30-30 [501+]

Joseph, Frank - *The Atlantis Encyclopedia*
LJ - v129 - i20 - Dec 1 2004 - p166(1) [501+]

Joseph, Giles Foden Michael - *Mimi and Toutou Go Forth: The Bizzare Battle of Lake Tanganyika*
Spec - v296 - i9193 - Oct 16 2004 - p68(2) [501+]

Joseph, J.W. - *Another's Country: Archaeological and Historical Perspectives on Cultural Interactions in the Southern Colonies*
JouAmCul - v27 - i3 - Sept 2004 - p335(2) [501+]
JSH - v70 - i4 - Nov 2004 - p889(3) [501+]

Joseph, James - *110 Car and Driving Emergencies--and How to Survive Them*
SciTech - v28 - i4 - Dec 2004 - p160(1) [51-500]

Joseph, Jeffrey T. - *Functional Neuroanatomy: An Interactive Text and Manual*
SciTech - v28 - i1 - March 2004 - p71(1) [51-500]

Joseph, John E. - *Language and Identity: National, Ethnic, and Religious*
Choice - v42 - i5 - Jan 2005 - p848(1) [1-50]

Joseph, Jonathan - *Hegemony: A Realist Analysis*
CS - v33 - i2 - March 2004 - p256-257 [501+]

Joseph, Miranda - *Against the Romance of Community*
Col Lit - v31 - i4 - Fall 2004 - p181(7) [501+]

Joseph, Richard J. - *The Origins of the American Income Tax: The Revenue Act of 1894 and Its Aftermath*
Choice - v42 - i3 - Nov 2004 - p533(1) [1-50]
R&R Bk N - v19 - i3 - August 2004 - p204(1) [1-50]

Joseph, Robert - *Bordeaux and Its Wines*
E-Streams - July 2004 - pNA [501+]

Joseph, Suad - *Encyclopedia of Women and Islamic Cultures, vol. 1*
HNet - Nov 2004 - pNA [501+]
R&R Bk N - v19 - i2 - May 2004 - p136 [51-500]

Josephson, Allan M. - *Handbook of Spirituality and Worldview in Clinical Practice*
SciTech - v28 - i4 - Dec 2004 - p98(1) [1-50]

Josephus, Flavius - *Great Roman-Jewish War*
R&R Bk N - v19 - i4 - Nov 2004 - p45(1) [51-500]

Joshel, S.R. - *Imperial Projections. Ancient Rome in Modern Popular Culture*
Class R - v54 - i1 - May 2004 - p234(3) [501+]

Joshi, P.B. - *Materials for Electrical and Electronic Contacts: Processing, Properties, and Applications*
SciTech - v28 - i4 - Dec 2004 - p148(1) [501+]

Joshi, P.C. - *Marxism and Social Revolution in India and Other Essays*
JEL - v41 - i4 - Dec 2003 - p1410(1) [501+]

Joshi, Priya - *In Another Country: Colonialism, Culture, and the English Novel in India*
MFSF - v50 - i2 - Summer 2004 - p506-508 [501+]

Joshi, S.T. - *The Collected Jorkens, Vols 1-2*
BW - v34 - i44 - Oct 31 2004 - p15(1) [501+]
The Evolution of the Weird Tale
MFSF - v108 - i3 - March 2005 - p30(5) [501+]
Mencken's America
Choice - v42 - i2 - Oct 2004 - p295(1) [501+]
Out of the Immortal Night: Selected Works of Samuel Loveman
PW - v251 - i51 - Dec 20 2004 - p41(2) [501+]

Joshi, Vandana - *Gender and Power in the Third Reich: Female Denouncers and the Gestapo, 1933-45*
HNet - Sept 2004 - pNA [501+]

Josipovici, Gabriel - *Goldberg: Variations*
BIC - v33 - i6 - Sept 2004 - p13(1) [501+]

Joslin, Katherine - *Jane Addams: A Writer's Life*
Choice - v42 - i7 - March 2005 - p1228(2) [51-500]

Josling, Timothy Edward - *Food Regulation and Trade: Toward a Safe and Open Global Food System*
Choice - v42 - i1 - Sept 2004 - p154(1) [501+]
R&R Bk N - v19 - i2 - May 2004 - p106(1) [51-500]

Joss, Morag - *Funeral Music*
PW - v252 - i11 - March 14 2005 - p51(1) [51-500]

Jossey-Bass Inc. - *The Jossey-Bass Reader on Teaching*
TCR - v106 - i2 - Feb 2004 - p406-408 [501+]

Jost, Hermand - *Beethoven: Werk und Wirkung*
Ger Q - v77 - i4 - Fall 2004 - p494-496 [501+]

Jost, Kenneth - *The Supreme Court A to Z, 3rd Ed.*
R&R Bk N - v19 - i1 - Feb 2004 - pNA [51-500]

Jost, Walter - *A Companion to Rhetoric and Rhetorical Criticism*
Choice - v42 - i3 - Nov 2004 - p478(1) [1-50]
Rhetorical Investigations: Studies in Ordinary Language Criticism
R&R Bk N - v19 - i3 - August 2004 - p259(1) [501+]

Jotisalikorn, Chami - *Contemporary Asian Bathrooms*
R&R Bk N - v19 - i4 - Nov 2004 - p247(1) [501+]

Jotischky, Andrew - *The Carmelites and Antiquity: Mencicants and their Pasts in the Middle Ages*
AHR - v109 - i2 - April 2004 - p593(2) [501+]
Crusading and the Crusader States
R&R Bk N - v20 - i1 - Feb 2005 - p31(1) [51-500]

Jouanna, Jacques - *Hippocrates*
Isis - v95 - i2 - June 2004 - p285(2) [501+]

Jouet, Jacques - *Mountain R*
ABR - v25 - i6 - Sept-Oct 2004 - p1(3) [501+]

Joughin, Sheena - *Things to Do Indoors*
KR - v73 - i3 - Feb 1 2005 - p140(1) [501+]

Jouhaud, Christian - *De la publication: Entre Renaissance et Lumieres*
JMH - v76 - i4 - Dec 2004 - p938(3) [501+]

Jour, Belle de - *The Intimate Adventures of a London Call Girl*
NS - v134 - i4722 - Jan 17 2005 - p50(2) [501+]
Spec - v297 - i9206 - Jan 15 2005 - p41(2) [501+]

Jourda, Pierre - *Le Theatre a Montpellier: 1755-1851*
FS - v58 - i2 - April 2004 - p263(2) [501+]

Jourdane, Maurice - *The Struggle for the Health and Legal Protection of Farm Workers: El Cortito*
R&R Bk N - v19 - i4 - Nov 2004 - p174(1) [501+]

Journal of Behavioral Finance
JEL - v42 - i1 - March 2004 - p345(1) [501+]

Journal of Human Development
JEL - v41 - i4 - Dec 2003 - p1447(1) [501+]

The Journal of Human Rights
TLS - i5267 - March 12 2004 - p25-26 [501+]

Journel, Andre G. - *Evaluation of Mineral Reserves: A Simulation Approach (Illus. by Aedon, C. Kyriakidis)*
SciTech - v28 - i3 - Sept 2004 - p165(1) [501+]

Journey to Freedom: The African American Library
LibMed - v22 - i6 - March 2004 - p75(1) [501+]

Jovanovic, Rob - *In Perfect Sound Forever: The Story of Pavement*
NYTBR - Dec 5 2004 - p52 [501+]

Jovanovich, William - *The Temper of the West*
PSQ - v78 - i3 - Fall 2004 - p167(3) [501+]

Jowett, John - *Timon of Athens*
TLS - i5298 - Oct 15 2004 - p30-31 [501+]

Jowett, Peter - *Nahanni River Guide, 3rd Ed.*
CBRA - Annual 2003 - p143(2) [51-500]

Jowitt, Claire - *Voyage Drama and Gender Politics, 1589-1642: Real and Imagined Worlds*
R&R Bk N - v19 - i1 - Feb 2004 - p235(1) [51-500]

Jowitt, Deborah - *Jerome Robbins: His Life, His Theater, His Dance*
Advocate - August 31 2004 - p62(2) [501+]
AM - v192 - i1 - Jan 3 2005 - p26 [501+]
BL - v100 - i22 - August 2004 - p1888(1) [51-500]
BW - v34 - i33 - August 15 2004 - p9(1) [501+]
Choice - v42 - i6 - Feb 2005 - p1033(1) [51-500]
Dance - v78 - i11 - Nov 2004 - p60(2) [501+]
Ent W - i778 - August 13 2004 - p92 [51-500]
Lam Bk Rpt - v13 - i3 - Oct 2004 - p23(3) [501+]
LJ - v129 - i13 - August 2004 - p83(1) [501+]
NYTBR - August 1 2004 - p8 [501+]
NYTBR - August 8 2004 - p18 [501+]
NYTBR - August 22 2004 - p18 [501+]

Joy, Angela - *My Dog (Illus. by Slater, Nicola)*
c PW - v252 - i4 - Jan 24 2005 - p246(1) [51-500]

Joy, Flora - *Treasures from Europe: Stories and Classroom Activities*
LibMed - v22 - i4 - Jan 2004 - p85(1) [501+]

Joy-Matthews, Jennifer - *Human Resource Development, 3rd Ed.*
R&R Bk N - v19 - i4 - Nov 2004 - p113(1) [51-500]

Joyal, Serge - *Protecting Canadian Democracy: The Senate You Never Knew*
PSQ - v119 - i3 - Fall 2004 - p553(3) [501+]

Joyce, Barry Alan - *The Shaping of American Ethnography: The Wilkes Exploring Expedition, 1838-1842.*
Isis - v95 - i2 - June 2004 - p306(2) [501+]

Joyce, Bruce - *Models of Teaching, 7th ed.*
R&R Bk N - v19 - i1 - Feb 2004 - pNA [51-500]

Joyce, Davis D. - *Howard Zinn: A Radical American Vision*
R&R Bk N - v19 - i1 - Feb 2004 - p55(1) [51-500]

Joyce, Graham - *The Limits Of Enchantment*
Ent W - i808 - Feb 25 2005 - p106 [51-500]
KR - v72 - i24 - Dec 15 2004 - p1157(2) [501+]
PW - v252 - i4 - Jan 24 2005 - p226(1) [501+]

Joyce, James - *James Joyce: The Complete Recordings*
ABR - v26 - i2 - Jan-Feb 2005 - p20(2) [501+]
Joyce's Dublin, A Topographical Guide to the Dublin of Ulysses
ILS - v24 - i1 - Fall 2004 - p32(1) [51-500]

Joyce, Jerry - *Microsoft Windows XP Plain and Simple, 2nd Ed.*
SciTech - v28 - i4 - Dec 2004 - p26(1) [51-500]

Joyce, Nancy - *Building Stata: The Design and Construction of Frank O. Gehry's Stata Center at MIT*
Choice - v42 - i2 - Oct 2004 - p285(1) [501+]

Joyce, Patrick - *The Rule of Freedom: The City and Modern Liberalism*
J Hist G - v30 - i1 - Jan 2004 - p192(2) [501+]
J Soc H - v38 - i1 - Fall 2004 - p242(2) [501+]

Joyce, Patrick D. - *No Fire Next Time: Black Korean Conflicts and the Future of America's Cities*
AJS - v110 - i2 - Sept 2004 - p522(2) [501+]
No Fire Next Time: Black-Korean Conflicts and the Future of America's Cities
Black Iss - v7 - i2 - March-April 2005 - p40(2) [501+]
CS - v33 - i5 - Sept 2004 - p532-533 [501+]

Joyce, Simon - *Capital Offenses: Geographies of Class and Crime in Victorian London*
ELT - v47 - i4 - Fall 2004 - p466(5) [501+]
J Soc H - v38 - i1 - Fall 2004 - p261(3) [501+]

Joynt, Amanda - *Fish of Alberta*
CBRA - Annual 2003 - p403(1) [51-500]

Juan, Ana - *The Night Eater (Illus. by Juan, Ana)*
c BL - v101 - i8 - Dec 15 2004 - p738(1) [51-500]
c CCB-B - v58 - i4 - Dec 2004 - p173(2) [51-500]
c KR - v72 - i20 - Oct 15 2004 - p1008(1) [51-500]
c PW - v251 - i47 - Nov 22 2004 - p60(1) [51-500]
c SLJ - v51 - i1 - Jan 2005 - p94(1) [51-500]

Juan, Luis de - *Postmodernist Strategies in Alasdair Gray's 'Lanark, a Life in 4 Books'*
R&R Bk N - v19 - i1 - Feb 2004 - p240(1) [51-500]

Juarez, Jose Roberto - *Reclaiming Church Wealth: The Recovery of Church Property after Expropriation in the Archdiocese of Guadalajara, 1860-1911*
CHR - v90 - i4 - Oct 2004 - p833(2) [501+]

Juarez, Juan Antonio - *Brotherhood of Corruption: A Cop Breaks the Silence on Police Abuse, Brutality, and Racial Profiling*
BL - v101 - i2 - Sept 15 2004 - p182(2) [51-500]

Jubb, Kendhal Jan - *Colorful Captivating Coral Reefs (Illus. by Jubb, Kendhal Jan)*
LibMed - v22 - i5 - Feb 2004 - p60(1) [501+]

Juby, Susan - *Alice I think*
y LibMed - v22 - i5 - Feb 2004 - p72(1) [501+]
Miss Smithers
y CCB-B - v57 - i11 - July-August 2004 - p471(2) [501+]
y HB - v80 - i4 - July-August 2004 - p454(1) [51-500]
y SLJ - v50 - i10 - Oct 2004 - p168(2) [51-500]
y VOYA - v27 - i4 - Oct 2004 - p304(1) [51-500]

Judah, Eleanor Hannon - *Criminal Justice: Retribution vs. Restoration*
R&R Bk N - v19 - i4 - Nov 2004 - p149(1) [51-500]

Judd, Cameron - *Beggar's Gulch*
Roundup M - v11 - i6 - August 2004 - p29(1) [501+]
War at Fire Creek
Roundup M - v12 - i3 - Feb 2005 - p28(1) [51-500]

Judd, Denis - *The Boer War*
AHR - v109 - i3 - June 2004 - p868(2) [501+]
Albion - v36 - i2 - Summer 2004 - p341(1) [501+]
VS - v46 - i3 - Spring 2004 - p549(3) [501+]

The Lion and the Tiger: The Rise and Fall of the British Raj, 1600-1947
  A Aff - v35 - i2 - July 2004 - p236-237 [501+]
  CR - v285 - i1663 - August 2004 - p128(1) [501+]
  TLS - i5289 - August 13 2004 - p23(1) [501+]
Judd, Dennis R. - *City Politics: Private Power and Public Policy, 4th Ed.*
  R&R Bk N - v19 - i1 - Feb 2004 - pNA [501+]
Judd, Ellen R. - *The Chinese Women's Movement: Between State and Marker*
  CS - v33 - i6 - Nov 2004 - p745(1) [1-50]
Judd, Garrit Parmele - *Anatomia: 1838*
  SciTech - v28 - i3 - Sept 2004 - p67(1) [51-500]
Judd, Richard W. - *Natural States: The Environmental Imagination in Maine, Oregon, and the Nation.*
  Env - v46 - i7 - Sept 2004 - p39(1) [501+]
  JAH - v91 - i3 - Dec 2004 - p1107(2) [501+]
  R&R Bk N - v19 - i1 - Feb 2004 - p70(1) [501+]
  T&C - v45 - i4 - Oct 2004 - p862(3) [501+]
Judd, Sandra - *Breast Cancer Sourcebook*
  Bwatch - March 2005 - pNA [51-500]
Judet de la Combe, Pierre - *L'Agamemnon d'Eschyle: Commentaire des dialogues*
  Class R - v54 - i1 - May 2004 - p25(3) [501+]
Judge, David - *The European Parliament*
  PSQ - v119 - i4 - Winter 2004 - p703(2) [501+]
Judge for Yourself
  c LibMed - v23 - i3 - Nov-Dec 2004 - p79(1) [51-500]
  c Ref Rev - June 2004 - pNA [501+]
Judis, John B. - *The Folly of Empire: What George W. Bush Could Learn from Theodore Roosevelt and Woodrow Wilson*
  BW - v34 - i32 - August 8 2004 - p5(1) [501+]
  Comw - v131 - i21 - Dec 3 2004 - p28(1) [501+]
  NYTBR - Sept 12 2004 - p20(L) [501+]
  PW - v251 - i30 - July 26 2004 - p48(2) [501+]
Judson, Bruce - *Go It Alone: The Secret to Building a Successful Business on Your Own*
  BL - v101 - i5 - Nov 1 2004 - p450(1) [51-500]
Judson, Horace Freeland - *The Great Betrayal: Fraud in Science*
  Am Sci - v93 - i1 - Jan-Feb 2005 - p72(3) [501+]
  BL - v101 - i3 - Oct 1 2004 - p286(2) [51-500]
  BW - v35 - i4 - Jan 30 2005 - p8(2) [501+]
  NYRB - v51 - i18 - Nov 18 2004 - p38(3) [501+]
  PW - v251 - i37 - Sept 13 2004 - p67(1) [51-500]
Judson, Karen - *Chemical and Biological Warfare*
  y SLJ - v50 - i7 - July 2004 - p123(2) [51-500]
Judson, Olivia - *Dr. Tatiana's Sex Advice to All Creation*
  Am Bio T - v66 - i4 - April 2004 - p309(2) [501+]
Judson, Theodore - *Fitzpatrick's War*
  LJ - v129 - i13 - August 2004 - p72(1) [51-500]
  PW - v251 - i29 - July 19 2004 - p149(1) [51-500]
Juenger, Ernst - *Storm of Steel*
  BW - v34 - i29 - July 18 2004 - p15(1) [501+]
  Sew R - v112 - i1 - Wntr 2004 - pXXI-XXIII [501+]
Juergensmeyer, Mark - *Global Religions: An Introduction*
  CS - v33 - i4 - July 2004 - p449(2) [501+]
  Terror in the Mind of God, the Global Rise of Religious Violence
  JTWS - v21 - i1 - Spring 2004 - p328(2) [501+]
Juettner, Bonnie - *Light*
  c SB - v40 - i5 - Sept-Oct 2004 - p218(2) [51-500]
  Weather
  y SB - v40 - i5 - Sept-Oct 2004 - p196(1) [51-500]
  c SB - v40 - i5 - Sept-Oct 2004 - p219(1) [51-500]
Juhany, Uwaidah M. Al - *Najd before the Salafi Reform Movement: Social, Political and Religious Conditions during the Three Centuries Preceeding the Rise of the Saudi State*
  IJMES - v36 - i1 - Feb 2004 - p124-125 [501+]
Juhasz, A.L. - *Waste Management*
  SciTech - v28 - i3 - Sept 2004 - p147(1) [51-500]
Juhasz, Suzanne - *A Desire for Women: Relational Psychoanalysis, Writing, and Relationships between Women*
  TSWL - v23 - i2 - Fall 2004 - p388(6) [501+]
Jukes, Mavis - *Be Healthy! It's a Girl Thing: Food, Fitness, and Feeling Great (Illus. by Ziss, Debra)*
  c SLJ - v50 - i10 - Oct 2004 - pS46(1) [51-500]
  You're a Bear (Illus. by Johnson, Steve)
  c Five Owls - v18 - i1 - Fall 2004 - p17(2) [51-500]
Jukna, Stasys - *Extremal Combinatorics: With Applications in Computer Science*
  SIAM Rev - v46 - i1 - March 2004 - p169-170 [501+]

Julavits, Heidi - *The Effect of Living Backwards*
  NYTBR - Oct 17 2004 - p26 [501+]
Julian, Russell - *Busy Dog*
  c PW - v252 - i4 - Jan 24 2005 - p245(2) [51-500]
  Happy Cockerel
  c PW - v252 - i4 - Jan 24 2005 - p245(2) [51-500]
  Hungry Pig
  c PW - v252 - i4 - Jan 24 2005 - p245(2) [51-500]
  Lost Calf
  c PW - v252 - i4 - Jan 24 2005 - p245(2) [51-500]
Julien, Robert M. - *A Primer of Drug Action: A Comprehensive Guide to the Actions, Uses, and Side Effects of Psychoactive Drugs, 10th Ed.*
  SciTech - v28 - i4 - Dec 2004 - p117(1) [1-50]
  A Primer of Drug Action: A Concise, Nontechnical Guide to the Actions, Uses, and Side Effects of Psychoactive Drugs, 9th Ed.
  SciTech - v28 - i4 - Dec 2004 - p116(1) [1-50]
Julius, Bryant - *Anthony Caro: A Life in Sculpture*
  Choice - v42 - i5 - Jan 2005 - p843(1) [1-50]
Jullien, Francois - *In Praise of Blandness: Proceeding from Chinese Thought and Aesthetic*
  TimHES - v0 - i1664 - Oct 29 2004 - p28(1) [501+]
  A Treatise on Efficacy: Between Western and Chinese Thinking
  R&R Bk N - v19 - i3 - August 2004 - p2(1) [1-50]
Juluri, Vamsee - *Becoming a Global Audience: Longing and Belonging in Indian Music Television*
  R&R Bk N - v19 - i1 - Feb 2004 - p223(1) [1-50]
Jump, Shirley - *The Bird Wore Chocolate*
  BL - v101 - i1 - Sept 1 2004 - p72(1) [51-500]
Jung - *Kwaidan (Illus. by Jung)*
  LJ - v129 - i12 - July 2004 - p62(1) [51-500]
Jung, Carl Gustav - *The Plight of the Individual in Modern Society*
  Spec - v297 - i9205 - Jan 8 2005 - p45(1) [501+]
Jung-Huttl, Angelika - *Earthsong (Illus. by Edmaier, Bernhard)*
  NH - v113 - i10 - Dec 2004 - p55(1) [51-500]
Jung, Reinhardt - *Bambert's Book of Missing Stories (Illus. by Allen, Peter)*
  y KR - v72 - i19 - Oct 1 2004 - p963(1) [51-500]
  y PW - v252 - i1 - Jan 3 2005 - p56(1) [51-500]
  y SLJ - v50 - i11 - Nov 2004 - p146(1) [51-500]
Jung, Thomas - *Alles Nur Pop? Anmerkungen zur Popularen und Pop-Literatur seit 1990*
  GSR - v27 - i3 - Oct 2004 - p677(2) [501+]
Junge, Traudl - *Until the Final Hour: Hitler's Last Secretary*
  TLS - i5266 - March 5 2004 - p30-30 [501+]
Junger-Tas, Josine - *Delinquency in an International Perspective: The International Self-Reported Delinquency Study*
  Adoles - v39 - i156 - Winter 2004 - p833(1) [51-500]
Junghans, Helmar - *Martin Luther: Exploring His Life and Times, 1483-1546*
  Six Ct J - v35 - i3 - Fall 2004 - p795-809 [501+]
Jungk, Peter Stephan - *Tigor*
  BL - v101 - i2 - Sept 15 2004 - p208(1) [501+]
  KR - v72 - i15 - August 1 2004 - p706(1) [501+]
  LJ - v129 - i13 - August 2004 - p68(1) [51-500]
Jungman, Ann - *Lucy and the Big Bad Wolf*
  c Sch Lib - v52 - i4 - Winter 2004 - p192(1) [51-500]
  The Most Magnificent Mosque (Illus. by Fowles, Shelley)
  c SLJ - v50 - i9 - Sept 2004 - p170(1) [51-500]
  c TES - v0 - i4576 - March 26 2004 - pssss18(2) [501+]
Junior Worldmark Encyclopedia of the Nations, 4th Ed., Vols. 1-10. E-book Review
  BL - v101 - i8 - Dec 15 2004 - p759(1) [501+]
Juniper, Andrew - *Wabi Sabi: The Japanese Art of Impermanence*
  R&R Bk N - v19 - i1 - Feb 2004 - p200(1) [51-500]
Juniper, Andy - *Sunforth Chronicles*
  CBRA - Annual 2003 - p171(1) [51-500]
Junker, Thomas - *Die Entdeckung der Evolution: Eine revolutionare Theorie und ihre Geschichte*
  Isis - v95 - i2 - June 2004 - p314(2) [501+]
Junkin, Tim - *Bloodsworth: The True Story of the First Death Row Inmate Exonerated by DNA*
  BW - v34 - i43 - Oct 24 2004 - p6(2) [501+]
  KR - v72 - i13 - July 1 2004 - p618(2) [501+]
  PW - v251 - i35 - August 30 2004 - p44(1) [51-500]

Jupp, James - *The Australian People: An Encyclopedia of the Nation, Its People and Their Origins*
  AHS - v35 - i123 - April 2004 - p177-179 [501+]
  The English in Australia
  Quad - v48 - i10 - Oct 2004 - p89(2) [501+]
  TLS - i5293 - Sept 10 2004 - p27(1) [501+]
  From White Australia to Woomera: The Story of Australian Immigration
  AHS - v35 - i123 - April 2004 - p176-177 [501+]
Jurca, Catherine - *White Diaspora: The Suburb and the Twentieth-Century American Novels*
  Am Q - v56 - i4 - Dec 2004 - p1067(12) [501+]
Jurd, Richard D. - *Instant Notes Animal Biology, 2nd Ed.*
  E-Streams - Nov 2004 - pNA [501+]
  SciTech - v28 - i3 - Sept 2004 - p63(1) [51-500]
Jurgs, Michael - *Bürger Grass: Biografie eines deutschen Ditchters*
  GSR - v27 - i1 - Feb 2004 - p212-214 [501+]
Jurinski, James John - *Religion on Trail: A Handbook with Cases, Laws, and Documents*
  Choice - v41 - i11-12 - July-August 2004 - p2062(1) [501+]
Jurmain, Robert - *Introduction to Physical Anthropology, 10th Ed.*
  R&R Bk N - v19 - i4 - Nov 2004 - p76(1) [51-500]
Jury, David - *Letterpress: The Allure of the Handmade*
  TimHES - v0 - i1673 - Jan 7 2005 - p24(2) [501+]
Juska, Elise - *The Hazards of Sleeping Alone*
  BL - v101 - i2 - Sept 15 2004 - p208(1) [51-500]
  KR - v72 - i16 - August 15 2004 - p766(2) [501+]
Juska, Jane - *A Round Heeled Woman: My Late-Life Adventures in Sex and Romance*
  BIC - v33 - i2 - March 2004 - p28(2) [501+]
Jussawalla, Feroza - *Chiffon Saris*
  WLT - v79 - i1 - Jan-April 2005 - p89(1) [501+]
Just the Facts: Fluids and Electrolytes
  SciTech - v28 - i3 - Sept 2004 - p104(1) [1-50]
Just the Facts: I.V. Therapy
  SciTech - v28 - i3 - Sept 2004 - p121(1) [51-500]
Just, Ward - *An Unfinished Season*
  Econ - v372 - i8384 - July 17 2004 - p82US [501+]
  Ent W - i774 - July 16 2004 - p82 [501+]
  Globe & Mail - July 17 2004 - pD6 [501+]
  NYTBR - July 25 2004 - p7 [501+]
  NYTBR - August 1 2004 - p14 [501+]
  NYTBR - August 8 2004 - p18 [501+]
  The Weather in Berlin (Read by Dean, Robertson). Audiobook Review
  Kliatt - v38 - i6 - Nov 2004 - p53(1) [51-500]
Juster, Norton - *The Hello, Goodbye Window (Illus. by Raschka, Chris)*
  c KR - v73 - i5 - March 1 2005 - p289(1) [51-500]
  c PW - v252 - i8 - Feb 21 2005 - p173(2) [51-500]
Juster, Susan - *Doomsayers: Anglo-American Prophecy in the Age of Revolution*
  AHR - v109 - i4 - Oct 2004 - p1197-1198 [501+]
  HNet - Oct 2004 - pNA [501+]
  J Am St - v38 - i1 - April 2004 - p147-148 [501+]
  JAH - v91 - i2 - Sept 2004 - p607(1) [501+]
Justice, Donald Rodney - *Collected Poems*
  BL - v100 - i22 - August 2004 - p1891(2) [51-500]
  BW - v34 - i33 - August 15 2004 - p15(1) [501+]
  LJ - v129 - i16 - Oct 1 2004 - p85(1) [51-500]
  Poet - v185 - i2 - Nov 2004 - p122(9) [501+]
  NYTBR - August 29 2004 - p16 [501+]
Justice, George L. - *Women's Writing and the Circulation of Ideas: Manuscript Publication in England, 1550-1800*
  Ren Q - v57 - i4 - Winter 2004 - p1507(2) [501+]
  RES - v55 - i218 - Feb 2004 - p135-137 [501+]
Justice, Glenn - *Little Known History of the Texas Big Bend: Documented Chronicles from Cabeza de Vaca to the Era of the Pancho Villa*
  SHQ - v107 - i3 - Jan 2004 - p480(2) [501+]
Justice, Jennifer - *The Kingfisher Children's Encyclopedia*
  y PW - v251 - i44 - Nov 1 2004 - p64(2) [501+]
Justin, Anne - *The Ultimate Sourcebook for Curtains, Blinds, Fabrics and Hardware*
  BL - v101 - i9-10 - Jan 1 2005 - p800(1) [51-500]
Juteau, Danielle - *Social Differentiation: Patterns and Processes*
  R&R Bk N - v19 - i1 - Feb 2004 - p123(1) [51-500]
Jweid, Rosann - *Building Character through Multicultural Literature: A Guide for Middle School Readers*
  y R&R Bk N - v19 - i4 - Nov 2004 - p258(1) [501+]
Jwing-Ming, Yang - *Back Pain Relief*
  Bwatch - Jan 2005 - pNA [51-500]
Jyh-Cheng Chen - *IP-Based Next-Generation Wireless Networks: Systems, Architectures, and Protocols*
  E-Streams - August 2004 - pNA [501+]

K

Kaaberbol, Lene - *The Shamer's Daughter*
  c CH Bwatch - v14 - i8 - August 2004 - p3(1) [51-500]
  c LibMed - v23 - i3 - Nov-Dec 2004 - p70(1) [51-500]

Kaartinen, Marjo - *Religious Life and English Culture in the Reformation*
  Six Ct J - v35 - i1 - Spring 2004 - p263(2) [501+]

Kabat-Zinn, Jon - *Coming to Our Senses: Healing Ourselves and the World Through Mindfulness*
  PW - v251 - i51 - Dec 20 2004 - p50(1) [501+]

Kabatek, Wolfgang - *Imagerie des Anderen im Weimarer Kino*
  HNet - Sept 2004 - pNA [501+]

Kabbani, Nizar - *Republic of Love: Selected Poems in English and Arabic*
  WLT - v79 - i1 - Jan-April 2005 - p110(1) [501+]

Kabili, Jan - *How To WOW: Photoshop For The Web*
  Bwatch - March 2005 - pNA [501+]
  Photoshop Elements 2: Complete Course
  SciTech - v28 - i3 - Sept 2004 - p168(1) [51-500]

Kabir, Abulfazal M. Fasle - *Acquisition in Different and Special Subject Areas*
  SciTech - v28 - i1 - March 2004 - p180(1) [51-500]

Kacer, Kathy - *Margit: Home Free (Illus. by Wilson, Janet)*
  y Can CL - i111-112 - Fall-Winter 2003 - p128(7) [501+]
  c CBRA - Annual 2003 - p492(1) [51-500]
  Night Spies
  y CBRA - Annual 2003 - p492(2) [51-500]
  The Underground Reporters
  c KR - v73 - i2 - Jan 15 2005 - p122(1) [51-500]

Kachanov, L.M. - *Fundamentals of Theory of Plasticity*
  SciTech - v28 - i4 - Dec 2004 - p44(1) [51-500]

Kachroo, Pushkin - *Mobile Robotic Car Design*
  SciTech - v28 - i4 - Dec 2004 - p160(1) [51-500]

Kachun, Mitch - *Festivals of Freedom: Memory and Meaning in African American Emancipation Celebrations, 1808-1915*
  Afr Am R - v38 - i3 - Fall 2004 - p535(3) [501+]
  JAH - v91 - i3 - Dec 2004 - p1026(2) [501+]
  JSH - v70 - i4 - Nov 2004 - p909(3) [501+]

Kachur, B.A. - *Etherege and Wycherley*
  Choice - v42 - i5 - Jan 2005 - p853(1) [1-50]

Kachurek, Sandra J. - *George W. Bush*
  c BL - v101 - i2 - Sept 15 2004 - p239(1) [51-500]

Kaczynski, Tomasz - *Computational Homology*
  Choice - v42 - i4 - Dec 2004 - p698(1) [1-50]

Kadar, Gabor - *Self-Financing Genocide: The Gold Train, the Becher Case and the Wealth of Hungarian Jews*
  R&R Bk N - v19 - i4 - Nov 2004 - p46(1) [51-500]

Kadare, Ismail - *Le Successeur*
  WLT - v78 - i3-4 - Sept-Dec 2004 - p149(1) [501+]
  Pasardhesi
  WLT - v78 - i3-4 - Sept-Dec 2004 - p149(1) [501+]

Kadhim, Hussein - *The Poetics of Anti-Colonialism in the Arabic Qasidah*
  R&R Bk N - v19 - i3 - August 2004 - p255(1) [51-500]

Kadison, Richard - *College of the Overwhelmed: The Campus Mental Health Crisis and What to Do about It*
  LJ - v129 - i18 - Nov 1 2004 - p99(1) [51-500]
  NW - Oct 11 2004 - p13 [1-50]
  PW - v251 - i35 - August 30 2004 - p41(2) [51-500]
  SciTech - v28 - i4 - Dec 2004 - p95(1) [51-500]

Kadlec, David - *Mosaic Modernism: Anarchism, Pragmatism, Culture*
  MP - v102 - i1 - August 2004 - p148(4) [501+]

Kadlec, Dusan - *Inspired Halifax: The Art of Dusan Kadlec*
  CBRA - Annual 2003 - p116(1) [501+]

Kadohata, Cynthia - *Kira-Kira*
  y BL - v101 - i9-10 - Jan 1 2005 - p772(1) [51-500]
  c BooChiTr - March 7 2004 - p2(1) [501+]
  c CC - v121 - i25 - Dec 14 2004 - p24(1) [51-500]
  y VOYA - v27 - i3 - August 2004 - p218(1) [1-50]

Kadushin, Raphael - *Wonderlands: Good Gay Travel Writing*
  R&R Bk N - v19 - i3 - August 2004 - p148(1) [1-50]

Kaegi, Walter E. - *Heraclius: Emperor of Byzantium*
  AHR - v109 - i2 - April 2004 - p584(2) [501+]
  J Mil H - v68 - i3 - July 2004 - p949-950 [501+]

Kael, Pauline - *For Keeps: 30 Years at the Movies*
  Globe & Mail - Sept 4 2004 - pD19 [501+]

Kaelble, Hartmut - *The European Way: European Societies During the Nineteenth and Twentieth Centuries*
  R&R Bk N - v19 - i3 - August 2004 - p147(1) [51-500]
  Choice - v42 - i5 - Jan 2005 - p922(1) [1-50]

Kaelin, Carolyn M. - *Living through Breast Cancer: What a Harvard Doctor Wants You to Know about Getting the Best Care while Preserving Your Self-Image*
  LJ - v130 - i3 - Feb 15 2005 - p150(1) [51-500]
  PW - v252 - i9 - Feb 28 2005 - p60(1) [51-500]

Kaeo, Merike - *Designing Network Security, 2d ed.*
  SciTech - v28 - i4 - Dec 2004 - p151(1) [51-500]

Kaese, Harold - *The Boston Braves, 1871-1953*
  Choice - v42 - i3 - Nov 2004 - p524(1) [1-50]
  R&R Bk N - v19 - i3 - August 2004 - p88(1) [51-500]

Kaese, Jim - *The Athletic-Minded Traveler*
  Bwatch - Jan 2005 - pNA [51-500]
  NW - Dec 20 2004 - p38 [501+]

Kaewert, Julie - *Unsolicited: A Booklover's Mystery*
  LJ - v129 - i14 - Sept 1 2004 - p207(1) [51-500]

Kafai, Yasmin B. - *Embracing Diversity in the Learning Sciences: Proceedings*
  SciTech - v28 - i3 - Sept 2004 - p12(1) [501+]

Kafer, Peter - *Charles Brockden Brown's Revolution and the Birth of American Gothic*
  Choice - v42 - i3 - Nov 2004 - p484(1) [1-50]
  HRNB - v33 - i1 - Fall 2004 - p16(2) [501+]

Kafka, Phillipa - *On the Outside Looking In(dian): Indian Women Writers at Home and Abroad*
  Choice - v42 - i1 - Sept 2004 - p97(2) [501+]
  R&R Bk N - v19 - i1 - Feb 2004 - p241(1) [501+]

Kagami, Mitsuhiro - *Information Technology Policy and the Digital Divide: Lessons for Developing Countries*
  R&R Bk N - v19 - i3 - August 2004 - p96(1) [51-500]

Kagan, Donald - *The Peloponnesian War*
  BIC - v33 - i6 - Sept 2004 - p20(2) [501+]
  HNet - Nov 2004 - pNA [501+]
  Sew R - v112 - i1 - Wntr 2004 - pII-VI [501+]
  TLS - i5262 - Feb 6 2004 - p28(1) [501+]

Kagan, Richard - *Rebuilding Attachments with Traumatized Children: Healing from Losses, Violence, Abuse, and Neglect*
  SciTech - v28 - i3 - Sept 2004 - p119(1) [51-500]

Kagan, Richard L. - *Inquisitorial Inquiries: Brief Lives of Secret Jews and Other Heretics*
  R&R Bk N - v19 - i4 - Nov 2004 - p46(1) [51-500]
  Spain in America: The Origins of Hispanism in the United States
  AHR - v109 - i2 - April 2004 - p511(2) [501+]

Kagis, Indra - *Vitruvius: Writing the Body of Architecture*
  RM - v58 - i2 - Dec 2004 - p458(3) [501+]

Kahan, Alan S. - *Liberalism in Nineteenth-Century Europe: The Political Culture of Limited Suffrage*
  Choice - v42 - i2 - Oct 2004 - p362(1) [51-500]

Kahan, Scott - *In a Page, Signs and Symptoms*
  SciTech - v28 - i3 - Sept 2004 - p90(1) [51-500]
  In a Page Surgery
  E-Streams - August 2004 - pNA [501+]
  SciTech - v28 - i1 - March 2004 - p109(1) [51-500]

Kahane, Adam - *Solving Tough Problems: An Open Way of Talking, Listening, and Creating New Realities*
  R&R Bk N - v19 - i4 - Nov 2004 - p123(1) [1-50]

Kahera, Akel Ismail - *Deconstructing the American Mosque: Space, Gender, and Aesthetics*
  HNet - July 2004 - pNA [501+]
  IJMES - v36 - i1 - Feb 2004 - p142-145 [501+]
  JR - v84 - i3 - July 2004 - p505(2) [501+]

Kahl, Gunter - *The Dictionary of Gene Technology: Genomics, Transcriptomics, Proteomics, 3rd Ed., Vols. 1-2*
  Choice - v42 - i7 - March 2005 - p1202(1) [51-500]
  SciTech - v28 - i4 - Dec 2004 - p63(1) [51-500]

Kahle, Lynn R. - *Euromarketing and the Future*
  R&R Bk N - v19 - i2 - May 2004 - p113(1) [1-50]
  Sports Marketing and the Psychology of Marketing Communication
  Choice - v42 - i1 - Sept 2004 - p144(1) [51-500]
  R&R Bk N - v19 - i3 - August 2004 - p88(1) [51-500]

Kahn, Ada P. - *Encyclopedia of Work-Related Illnesses, Injuries, and Health Issues*
  E-Streams - August 2004 - pNA [501+]
  SciTech - v28 - i1 - March 2004 - p108(1) [51-500]

Kahn, Alfred E. - *Lessons from Deregulation: Telecommunications and Airlines After the Crunch*
  R&R Bk N - v19 - i3 - August 2004 - p123(1) [51-500]

Kahn, Ashley - *Kind of Blue: The Making of the Miles Davis Masterpiece*
  Am M - v22 - i2 - Summer 2004 - p319-321 [501+]

Kahn, Ava F. - *California Jews*
  HNet - August 2004 - pNA [501+]
  PHR - v73 - i4 - Nov 2004 - p683(4) [501+]
  Jewish Life in the American West: Perspectives on Migration, Settlement, and Community
  WestFolk - v62 - i4 - Fall 2003 - p313(2) [501+]

Kahn, Cedric - *Red Lights*
  New York - v37 - i31 - Sept 13 2004 - p126(3) [501+]

Kahn, Charles H. - *Pythagoras and the Pythagoreans: A Brief History*
  CJ - v99 - i3 - Feb-March 2004 - p353-358 [501+]

Kahn, Charlotte - *Resurgence of Jewish Life in Germany*
  R&R Bk N - v19 - i4 - Nov 2004 - p46(1) [51-500]

Kahn, David - *The Reader of Gentlemen's Mail: Herbert O. Yardley and the Birth of American Codebreaking*
  Am Sci - v92 - i4 - July-August 2004 - p387(1) [501+]
  TimHES - v0 - i1674 - Jan 14 2005 - p26(1) [501+]

Kahn, Gerard - *Beaumarchais: Le Marriage de Figaro*
  FS - v58 - i3 - July 2004 - p416-417 [501+]

Kahn, James R. - *Economic Approach to Environmental and Natural Resources, 3d ed.*
  R&R Bk N - v19 - i4 - Nov 2004 - p87(1) [51-500]

Kalodner, Cynthia R. - *Too Fat or Too Thin: A Reference Guide to Eating Disorders*
Choice - v41 - i11-12 - July-August 2004 - p2078(1) [501+]
LibMed - v22 - i6 - March 2004 - p77(1) [501+]
LibMed - v22 - i6 - March 2004 - p77(1) [501+]

Kalogjera-Sackellares, Dalma - *Psychodynamics and Psychotherapy of Pseudoseizures*
SciTech - v28 - i4 - Dec 2004 - p100(1) [51-500]

Kalotay, Daphne - *Calamity and Other Stories*
BL - v101 - i5 - Nov 1 2004 - p464(1) [51-500]
Ent W - i810 - March 11 2005 - p109 [51-500]
KR - v72 - i22 - Nov 15 2004 - p1062(2) [501+]
PW - v251 - i46 - Nov 15 2004 - p39(1) [51-500]

Kalpakian, Jack - *Identity, Conflict and Cooperation in International River Systems*
TimHES - v0 - i1656 - Sept 3 2004 - p30(1) [501+]

Kalpan, Amy - *The Anarchy of Empire in the Making of U.S. Culture*
AHR - v109 - i2 - April 2004 - p552(2) [501+]

Kalpan, E. Ann - *Trauma and Cinema: Cross-Cultural Explorations*
Choice - v42 - i3 - Nov 2004 - p468(2) [1-50]

Kalpan, Lawrence - *Between Ocean and City: The Transformation of Rockaway, New York*
JAH - v91 - i2 - Sept 2004 - p703(2) [501+]

Kalpan, Leslie - *Primary Sources of Ancient Civilizations: Egypt*
c LibMed - v23 - i3 - Nov-Dec 2004 - p82(2) [51-500]

Kalu, Athonia C. - *Broken Lives and Other Stories*
IJAHS - v37 - i1 - Wntr 2004 - p175-176 [501+]

Kalu, Kelechi A. - *Agenda Setting and Public Policy in Africa*
R&R Bk N - v19 - i4 - Nov 2004 - p91(1) [501+]

Kalumuck, Karen E. - *Human Body Explorations: Hands-On Investigations of What Makes Us Tick*
c SB - v40 - i4 - July-August 2004 - p150(1) [51-500]

Kalunta-Crumpton, Anita - *Pan-African Issues in Crime and Justice*
R&R Bk N - v19 - i3 - August 2004 - p169(1) [501+]

Kaluta, John - *The Perfect Stage Crew: The Compleat Technical Guide for High School, College, and Community Theater*
Choice - v42 - i3 - Nov 2004 - p495(1) [51-500]

Kaluzniacky, Eugene - *Managing Psychological Factors in Information Systems Work: An Orientation to Emotional Intelligence*
SciTech - v28 - i3 - Sept 2004 - p2(1) [501+]

Kalyanaraman, S. - *Sarasvati. Vol.1: Civilization*
Choice - v42 - i1 - Sept 2004 - p166(1) [501+]
Sarasvati. Vol. 2: Rigveda
Choice - v42 - i1 - Sept 2004 - p166(1) [501+]
Sarasvati. Vol. 3: River
Choice - v42 - i1 - Sept 2004 - p166(1) [501+]
Sarasvati. Vol. 4: Bharati
Choice - v42 - i1 - Sept 2004 - p166(1) [501+]
Sarasvati. Vol. 5: Technology
Choice - v42 - i1 - Sept 2004 - p166(1) [501+]
Sarasvati. Vol. 6: Language
Choice - v42 - i1 - Sept 2004 - p166(1) [501+]
Sarasvati. Vol. 7: Epigraphs
Choice - v42 - i1 - Sept 2004 - p166(2) [501+]

Kalyn, Wayne - *Design Ideas For Basements (Illus. by Ennis, Phillip H.)*
Bwatch - v26 - i9 - Sept 2004 - p3(1) [51-500]
LJ - v129 - i15 - Sept 15 2004 - p56(1) [51-500]

Kalz, Jill - *Mount Everest*
c CH Bwatch - v14 - i11 - Nov 2004 - pNA [51-500]
y SLJ - v51 - i1 - Jan 2005 - p146(1) [51-500]

Kamakura, Yasuhiko - *Best Practices in Work-Flexibility Schemes and Their Impact on the Quality of Working Life in the Chemical Industries*
ILR - v143 - i3 - Autumn 2004 - p287(2) [51-500]

Kamal, Raj - *If You Are Afraid of Heights*
PW - v251 - i31 - August 2 2004 - p50(1) [501+]

Kamaliour, Yahya R. - *War, Media, and Propaganda: A Global Perspective*
Choice - v42 - i7 - March 2005 - p1223(1) [51-500]

Kamat, Prashant V. - *Fullerenes and Nanotubes: The Building Blocks of Next Generation Nanodevices. Vol. 23: Proceedings*
SciTech - v28 - i1 - March 2004 - p54(1) [51-500]

Kambayashi, Yahiko - *Creating, Connecting and Collaborating through Computing: Proceedings*
SciTech - v28 - i3 - Sept 2004 - p18(1) [501+]

Kamen, Henry - *The Duke of Alba*
TLS - i5304 - Nov 26 2004 - p11(1) [501+]

Kamen, Paula - *All in My Head: An Epic Quest to Cure an Unrelenting, Totally Unreasonable, and Only Slightly Enlightening Headache*
KR - v73 - i1 - Jan 1 2005 - p35(1) [501+]
LJ - v130 - i3 - Feb 15 2005 - p150(1) [51-500]
PW - v252 - i3 - Jan 17 2005 - p44(2) [51-500]

Kamensky, John M. - *Collaboration: Using Networks and Partnerships*
R&R Bk N - v19 - i3 - August 2004 - p177(1) [501+]

Kamerick, Kathleen - *Popular Piety and Art in the Late Middle Ages: Image Worship and Idolatry in England 1350-1500*
AHR - v109 - i4 - Oct 2004 - p1298-1299 [501+]

Kamerman, Gary W. - *Laser Radar Technology and Applications VII: Proceedings*
SciTech - v28 - i3 - Sept 2004 - p160(1) [51-500]

Kamholz, Edward J. - *The Oregon-American Lumber Company: Ain't No More*
Pub Hist - v26 - i1 - Wntr 2004 - p182(3) [501+]

Kamii, Constance - *Young Children Continue to Reinvent Arithmetic--2nd Grade: Implications of Piaget's Theory*
TCR - v106 - i5 - May 2004 - p928(4) [501+]

Kaminski, John P. - *The Documentary History of the Ratification of the Constitution, Vol. 20*
R&R Bk N - v19 - i3 - August 2004 - p202(1) [1-50]

Kaminski, Robert J. - *The Murder of Police Officers*
R&R Bk N - v19 - i3 - August 2004 - p168(1) [501+]

Kaminsky, Ilya - *Dancing in Odessa*
LJ - v129 - i15 - Sept 15 2004 - p61(1) [51-500]

Kaminsky, Jessica - *I Hate the Gym*
People - v63 - i1 - Jan 10 2005 - p49 [51-500]

Kaminsky, Peter - *Pig Perfect: Encounters with Remarkable Swine and the Best Ways to Cook Them*
PW - v252 - i11 - March 14 2005 - p55(1) [51-500]

Kaminsky, Stuart M. - *The Last Dark Place: An Abe Lieberman Mystery*
BL - v101 - i5 - Nov 1 2004 - p468(1) [51-500]
Globe & Mail - Jan 22 2005 - pD12 [51-500]
KR - v72 - i19 - Oct 1 2004 - p942(1) [501+]
PW - v251 - i41 - Oct 11 2004 - p59(1) [51-500]
Midnight Pass (Read by Brick, Scott). Audiobook Review
LJ - v129 - i13 - August 2004 - p129(1) [51-500]
Now You See It: A Toby Peters Mystery
y BL - v101 - i3 - Oct 1 2004 - p313(1) [51-500]
KR - v72 - i20 - Oct 15 2004 - p987(1) [51-500]
PW - v251 - i37 - Sept 13 2004 - p61(1) [501+]
Show Business Is Murder
PW - v251 - i29 - July 19 2004 - p148(2) [501+]

Kamio, Yoko - *Boys Over Flowers*
y Kliatt - v38 - i5 - Sept 2004 - p35(2) [51-500]

Kammen, Carol - *On Doing Local History. 2nd Ed.*
Pub Hist - v26 - i2 - Spring 2004 - p81(82) [501+]

Kammen, Michael - *A Time To Every Purpose: The Four Seasons in American Culture*
Bks & Cult - v10 - i6 - Nov-Dec 2004 - p34(2) [501+]
Choice - v42 - i3 - Nov 2004 - p547(2) [1-50]
HNet - August 2004 - pNA [501+]

Kammerer, Paul - *Environmental Vitalism: The Inheritance of Acquired Characteristics*
SciTech - v28 - i4 - Dec 2004 - p61(1) [51-500]

Kamp, Albert H. - *Inner Worlds: A Cognitive-Linguistic Approach to the Book of Jonah*
R&R Bk N - v19 - i4 - Nov 2004 - p23(1) [51-500]

Kamp, J.W. van der - *Dietary Fibre: Bio-active Carbohydrates for Food and Feed*
SciTech - v28 - i3 - Sept 2004 - p69(1) [51-500]

Kampen, Bettina von - *Blue Becomes You*
BIC - v33 - i2 - March 2004 - p43(1) [51-500]

Kamra, Sukeshi - *Bearing Witness: Partition Independence, End of the Raj*
CBRA - Annual 2003 - p293(1) [501+]

Kamran, Etemad - *CDMA2000 Evolution: System Concepts and Design Principals*
SciTech - v28 - i4 - Dec 2004 - p149(1) [51-500]

Kamrin, Janice - *Ancient Egyptian Hieroglyphs: A Practical Guide*
R&R Bk N - v19 - i4 - Nov 2004 - p218(1) [501+]

Kamstra, Ryan - *Late Capitalist Sublime*
CBRA - Annual 2003 - p220(1) [51-500]

Kanaaneh, Rhoda Ann - *Birthing the Nation: Strategies of Palestinian Women in Israel*
CS - v33 - i1 - Jan 2004 - p85-87 [501+]

Kanari, Yozaburo - *The Kindaichi Case Files: The Legend of Lake Hiren*
y Teach Lib - v32 - i1 - Oct 2004 - p17(2) [501+]

Kanas, Nick - *Space Psychology and Psychiatry*
SciTech - v28 - i1 - March 2004 - p109(1) [51-500]

Kanawati, Naguib - *The Tomb and Beyond: Burial Customs of Egyptian Officials*
JNES - v63 - i4 - Oct 2004 - p315(2) [501+]
The Unis Cemetery at Saqqara, Vol. 2
R&R Bk N - v19 - i4 - Nov 2004 - p51(1) [51-500]
R&R Bk N - v19 - i4 - Nov 2004 - p51(1) [51-500]

Kandasamy, W.B. Vasantha - *Analysis of Social Aspects of Migrant Labourers Living with HIV/AIDS Using Fuzzy Theory and Neutrosophic Cognitive Maps*
SciTech - v28 - i3 - Sept 2004 - p104(1) [51-500]
Fuzzy Relational Equations and Neutrosophic Relational Equations
SciTech - v28 - i4 - Dec 2004 - p36(1) [51-500]
Linear Algebra and Smarandache Linear Algebra
SciTech - v28 - i3 - Sept 2004 - p35(1) [51-500]
Smarandache Fuzzy Algebra
SciTech - v28 - i3 - Sept 2004 - p36(1) [51-500]

Kandel, Denise B. - *Stages and Pathways of Drug Involvement. Examining the Gateway Hypothesis*
Adoles - v39 - i156 - Winter 2004 - p833(1) [51-500]

Kandel, Susan - *I Dreamed I Married Perry Mason*
DroRevMy - v24 - i3 - May-June 2004 - p12(1) [1-50]
SLJ - v50 - i12 - Dec 2004 - p175(1) [51-500]

Kander, John - *Colored Lights: Forty Years of Words and Music, Show Biz, Collaboration, and All That Jazz*
Lam Bk Rpt - v13 - i3 - Oct 2004 - p27(2) [501+]

Kandlikar, Satish G. - *Microchannels and Minichannels: Proceedings*
SciTech - v28 - i3 - Sept 2004 - p157(1) [51-500]

Kane, Adam I. - *The Western River Steamboat*
Choice - v42 - i4 - Dec 2004 - p722(1) [1-50]

Kane, Andrea - *I'll Be Watching You*
BL - v101 - i5 - Nov 1 2004 - p468(1) [51-500]
PW - v251 - i49 - Dec 6 2004 - p45(1) [51-500]

Kane, Daniel - *All Poets Welcome: The Lower East Side Poetry Scene in the 1960s*
AL - v76 - i2 - June 2004 - p402(3) [501+]
ANQ:QJ - v17 - i4 - Fall 2004 - p54(4) [501+]

Kane, Joseph Nathan - *Facts about the Presidents*
BL - v101 - i3 - Oct 1 2004 - p358(1) [501+]

Kane, Lawrence A. - *Martial Arts Instruction: Applying Educational Theory and Communication Techniques in the Dojois*
Bwatch - Feb 2005 - pNA [51-500]

Kane, Leslie - *The Art of Crime: The Plays and Films of Harold Pinter and David Mamet*
R&R Bk N - v19 - i4 - Nov 2004 - p224(1) [501+]

Kane, Nancy M. - *Managing Health: An International Perspective*
SciTech - v28 - i1 - March 2004 - p85(1) [51-500]

Kane, Ousmane - *Muslim Modernity in Postcolonial Nigeria: A Study of the Society for the Removal of Innovation and Reinstatement of Tradition*
JR - v85 - i1 - Jan 2005 - p178(2) [501+]

Kane, Stephanie - *Seeds of Doubt*
BL - v101 - i2 - Sept 15 2004 - p212(1) [51-500]
KR - v72 - i18 - Sept 15 2004 - p883(2) [51-500]
PW - v251 - i39 - Sept 27 2004 - p36(1) [51-500]

Kanellos, Nicolas - *Hispanic Literature of the United States: A Comprehensive Reference*
Choice - v42 - i1 - Sept 2004 - p62(1) [501+]
LibMed - v23 - i1 - August-Sept 2004 - p77(2) [51-500]

Kaner, Etta - *Animal Groups: How Animals Live Together (Illus. by Stephens, Pat)*
c SB - v40 - i4 - July-August 2004 - p179(1) [51-500]

Kanerva, Lasse - *Condensed Handbook of Occupational Dermatology*
E-Streams - Nov 2004 - pNA [501+]

Kanes, Levie - *Outrage 2000*
R&R Bk N - v19 - i4 - Nov 2004 - p46(1) [51-500]

Kanevski, Mikhail - *Analysis and Modelling of Spatial Environmental Data*
SciTech - v28 - i4 - Dec 2004 - p6(1) [1-50]

Kanfer, Stefan - *Ball of Fire: The Tumultuous Life and Comic Art of Lucille Ball*
Choice - v41 - i7 - March 2004 - p1302(1) [501+]
TV Q - v34 - i2 - Wntr 2004 - p80-81 [501+]

Kang, David C. - *Nuclear North Korea: A Debate on Engagement Strategies*
JAS - v63 - i3 - August 2004 - p808-810 [501+]

Kang, S.G. - *Designing, Processing and Properties of Advanced Engineering Materials: Proceedings*
SciTech - v28 - i3 - Sept 2004 - p138(1) [51-500]

Kangas, Juli - *The Surprise Visitor*
c   KR - v73 - i2 - Jan 15 2005 - p122(1) [51-500]
c   PW - v252 - i10 - March 7 2005 - p67(1) [51-500]

Kangas, Kalle - *Business Strategies for Information Technology Management*
JEL - v41 - i4 - Dec 2003 - p1399(1) [501+]

Kanie, Norichika - *Emerging Forces in Environmental Governance*
R&R Bk N - v19 - i4 - Nov 2004 - p74(1) [51-500]

Kaniut, Larry - *Tales from the Edge: True Adventures in Alaska*
LJ - v130 - i2 - Feb 1 2005 - p107(1) [51-500]

Kannaday, Wayne Campbell - *Apologetic Discourse and the Scribal Tradition: Evidence of the Influence of Apologetic Interests on the Text of the Canonical Gospels*
R&R Bk N - v19 - i4 - Nov 2004 - p21(1) [51-500]

Kannaiyan, S. (b. 1944 -) - *Biotechnology of Biofertilizers*
SciTech - v28 - i1 - March 2004 - p128(1) [51-500]

Kanner, Bernice - *Pocketbook Power: How to Reach the Hearts and Minds of Today's Most Coveted Consumers-Women*
Choice - v42 - i2 - Oct 2004 - p336(1) [51-500]
The Superbowl of Advertising: How the Commercials Won the Game
TV Q - v34 - i2 - Wntr 2004 - p64-66 [501+]

Kanner, Ellie - *How Not to Audition: Avoiding the Common Mistakes Most Actors Make*
Choice - v41 - i7 - March 2004 - p1302(1) [501+]
R&R Bk N - v19 - i1 - Feb 2004 - p226(1) [51-500]

Kanon, Joseph - *Alibi*
KR - v73 - i5 - March 1 2005 - p250(1) [51-500]
PW - v252 - i11 - March 14 2005 - p46(1) [51-500]

Kant, Immanuel - *Critique of Practical Reason*
Eight-C St - v37 - i3 - Spring 2004 - p491-497 [501+]
R&R Bk N - v19 - i3 - August 2004 - p5(1) [1-50]

Kant, John H. - *Birth of Anthropology*
RM - v58 - i1 - Sept 2004 - p205(2) [501+]

Kante, Jodi - *Modern Drama: Defining the Field*
Theat J - v56 - i3 - Oct 2004 - p534-535 [501+]

Kanter, Rosabeth Moss - *Confidence: How Winning Streaks and Losing Streaks Begin and End*
BL - v101 - i2 - Sept 15 2004 - p185(2) [51-500]
BW - v34 - i46 - Nov 14 2004 - p5(1) [1-50]
LJ - v129 - i15 - Sept 15 2004 - p67(1) [51-500]
NYT - August 8 2004 - pBU8 [501+]
PW - v251 - i29 - July 19 2004 - p155(1) [51-500]
Time - v164 - i15 - Oct 11 2004 - pA16 [51-500]

Kantner, Seth - *Ordinary Wolves*
BL - v101 - i6 - Nov 15 2004 - p558(1) [51-500]
Globe & Mail - July 3 2004 - pD5 [501+]
NYTBR - August 1 2004 - p14 [501+]
NYTBR - August 8 2004 - p18 [501+]
NYTBR - August 15 2004 - p14 [501+]
y   SLJ - v51 - i2 - Feb 2005 - p156(1) [51-500]
y   VOYA - v27 - i4 - Oct 2004 - p304(1) [51-500]

Kantor, Martin - *Distancing: Avoidant Personality Disorder. Rev. Ed.*
SciTech - v28 - i1 - March 2004 - p102(1) [51-500]
Understanding Paranoia: A Guide for Professionals, Families, and Sufferers
Choice - v42 - i4 - Dec 2004 - p739(1) [1-50]
LJ - v129 - i14 - Sept 1 2004 - p172(1) [51-500]

Kantor, Melissa - *Confessions of a Not It Girl*
y   BL - v101 - i2 - Sept 15 2004 - p236(1) [51-500]
y   HB - v80 - i4 - July-August 2004 - p454(2) [51-500]
c   NYTBR - August 8 2004 - p16 [501+]

Kantor, Michael - *Broadway: The American Musical*
Am Theat - v22 - i1 - Jan 2005 - p92(3) [501+]
Bwatch - Jan 2005 - pNA [51-500]

Kantor, Susan - *An Illustrated Treasury of African American Read-Aloud Stories (Illus. by Clayton, Christian)*
Cur R - v44 - i6 - Feb 2005 - p12(1) [501+]

Kantowitz, Barry H. - *Experimental Psychology: Understanding Psychological Research, 8th Ed.*
SciTech - v28 - i4 - Dec 2004 - p1(1) [51-500]

Kanzaka, Hajime - *Slayers Return (Illus. by Yoshinaka, Shoko)*
y   SLJ - v50 - i8 - August 2004 - p149(1) [51-500]
Slayers Special (Illus. by Ohtsuka, Tommy)
c   SLJ - v50 - i7 - July 2004 - p134(1) [51-500]

Kao, Deborah Martin - *Gary Schneider: Portraits*
Choice - v42 - i1 - Sept 2004 - p92(2) [501+]

Kao, Mary Liu - *Cataloging and Classification for Library Technicians*
LRTS - v49 - i1 - Jan 2005 - p67(2) [501+]

Kaouk, Aida - *The Lands Within Me: Expressions by Canadian Artists of Arab Origins*
CBRA - Annual 2003 - p117(1) [501+]
Choice - v41 - i11-12 - July-August 2004 - p2032(1) [501+]

Kapanadze, David - *Crack Theory and Edge Singularities*
SciTech - v28 - i1 - March 2004 - p41(1) [51-500]

Kapell, Matthew - *Jacking into the Matrix Franchise: Cultural Reception and Interpretation*
Choice - v42 - i5 - Jan 2005 - p860(1) [1-50]

Kapelonis, Steve - *The Pump Energy Food: A Revolutionary Cookbook and Eating Plan to Create the Body of Your Dreams*
LJ - v130 - i1 - Jan 1 2005 - p144(3) [501+]
PW - v251 - i51 - Dec 20 2004 - p53(1) [501+]

Kaplan, Amy - *The Anarchy of Empire in the Making of U.S. Culture*
Am Q - v56 - i2 - June 2004 - p429(9) [501+]

Kaplan, Carla - *Zora Neale Hurston: A Life in Letters*
Afr Am R - v38 - i3 - Fall 2004 - p532(3) [501+]

Kaplan, Edgar - *Bridge Master: The Best of Edgar Kaplan: A Tribute to One of the Game's Leading Personalities and Inventors*
NYT - August 28 2004 - pB12 [501+]

Kaplan, Esther - *With God on Their Side*
Globe & Mail - Nov 13 2004 - pD23 [501+]

Kaplan, Fred - *The Singular Mark Twain: A Biography*
BW - v34 - i5 - Feb 1 2004 - p5(2) [501+]
Nine-C Lit - v58 - i4 - March 2004 - p559(562) [501+]
R&R Bk N - v19 - i1 - Feb 2004 - p244(1) [51-500]

Kaplan, H. Roy - *Failing Grades: How Schools Breed Frustration, Anger and Violence, and How to Prevent It*
R&R Bk N - v19 - i3 - August 2004 - p225(1) [1-50]

Kaplan, Howard - *John F. Kennedy: A Photographic Story of a Life*
y   Kliatt - v39 - i1 - Jan 2005 - p29(2) [51-500]

Kaplan, Jane - *Interfaith Families: Personal Stories of Jewish-Christian Intermarriage*
R&R Bk N - v19 - i3 - August 2004 - p152(1) [1-50]

Kaplan, Janice - *The Botox Diaries*
BW - v34 - i31 - August 1 2004 - p10(1) [51-500]
LJ - v129 - i13 - August 2004 - p68(1) [51-500]

Kaplan, Joel A. - *Vascular Anesthesia. 2nd Ed.*
SciTech - v28 - i3 - Sept 2004 - p113(1) [51-500]

Kaplan, John (b. 1929 - 1989) - *Criminal Law: Cases and Materials, 5th Ed.*
R&R Bk N - v19 - i3 - August 2004 - p206(1) [501+]

Kaplan, John (b. 1959 -) - *Photo Portfolio Success*
R&R Bk N - v19 - i1 - Feb 2004 - p251(1) [51-500]

Kaplan, Kalman - *Biblical Stories for Psychotherapy: A Sourcebook*
R&R Bk N - v19 - i4 - Nov 2004 - p9(1) [51-500]

Kaplan, Laurie - *Help Your Dog Fight Cancer: An Overview of Home Care Options*
LJ - v129 - i15 - Sept 15 2004 - p74(1) [51-500]

Kaplan, Lawrence S. - *NATO Divided, NATO United: The Evolution of an Alliance*
Pers PS - v33 - i4 - Fall 2004 - p242(2) [501+]
R&R Bk N - v19 - i3 - August 2004 - p189(1) [501+]

Kaplan, Leslie C. - *Chinese New Year*
c   SLJ - v50 - i8 - August 2004 - p110(1) [51-500]
Cinco de Mayo
c   SLJ - v50 - i8 - August 2004 - p110(1) [51-500]
Flag Day
c   SLJ - v50 - i8 - August 2004 - p110(1) [51-500]
Home Life in Ancient Egypt
c   Teach Lib - v32 - i3 - Feb 2005 - p42(1) [51-500]

Kaplan, Marion - *Geschichte des judischen Alltags in Deutschland vom 17 Jahrhundert bis 1945*
HNet - Nov 2004 - pNA [501+]

Kaplan, Michael - *The Best Time to Do Everything: Expert Advice on How to Live Cooler, Smarter, Faster, Better*
LJ - v130 - i1 - Jan 1 2005 - p135(1) [51-500]

Kaplan, Philip - *Battleship*
R&R Bk N - v19 - i4 - Nov 2004 - p253(1) [501+]

Kaplan, Richard L. - *Politics and the American Press: The Rise of Objectivity, 1865-1920*
BHR - v77 - i4 - Winter 2003 - p757(760) [501+]
JC - v54 - i3 - Sept 2004 - p578(3) [501+]

Kaplan, Robert (b. 1933 -) - *Art of the Infinite: The Pleasures of Mathematics*
SciTech - v28 - i4 - Dec 2004 - p38(1) [51-500]

Kaplan, Robert M. - *Psychological Testing: Principles, Applications, and Issues. 6th Ed.*
SciTech - v28 - i3 - Sept 2004 - p1(1) [51-500]

Kaplan, Robert S. - *The Strategy-Focused Organization: How Balanced Scorecard Companies Thrive in the New Business Environment*
HR Mag - v49 - i7 - July 2004 - pS52(1) [51-500]

Kaplan, Steven L. - *Cherchez lebon pain: Guide des Meilleurs Boulangeries de Paris*
TLS - i5283 - July 2 2004 - p28(1) [501+]

Kaplan, Steven M. - *Wiley Electrical and Electronics Engineering Dictionary*
Choice - v41 - i11-12 - July-August 2004 - p2022(1) [501+]
E-Streams - July 2004 - pNA [501+]
SciTech - v28 - i1 - March 2004 - p152(1) [51-500]

Kaplan, Temma - *Taking Back the Streets: Women, Youth, and Direct Democracy*
Choice - v41 - i11-12 - July-August 2004 - p2103(1) [501+]

Kaplan, Vivian Jeanette - *Ten Green Bottles: The True Story of One Family's Journey from War-Torn Austria to the Ghettos of Shanghai*
y   BL - v101 - i3 - Oct 1 2004 - p297(2) [51-500]
KR - v72 - i17 - Sept 1 2004 - p848(2) [501+]
LJ - v129 - i18 - Nov 1 2004 - p95(1) [51-500]
PW - v251 - i36 - Sept 6 2004 - p52(1) [51-500]

Kaplan, William - *A Secret Trial: Brian Mulroney, Stevie Cameron and the Public Trust*
Mac - Oct 25 2004 - p80(1) [501+]
A Secret Trust: Brian Mulroney, Stevie Cameron, and the Public Trust
Globe & Mail - Oct 2 2004 - pD3 [501+]

Kaplinski, Jaan - *Evening Brings Everything Back*
Ant R - v63 - i1 - Wntr 2005 - p194(1) [501+]
Ood valged ja Mustad: Kirjavahetus Aastast 2001
WLT - v78 - i3-4 - Sept-Dec 2004 - p113(1) [501+]

Kaplow, Robert - *Me and Orson Welles*
World&I - v19 - i2 - Feb 2004 - p230 [501+]

Kapp, Marshall B. - *Assuring Safety in Long-Term Care*
R&R Bk N - v19 - i1 - Feb 2004 - pNA [501+]
The Law and Older Persons: Is Geriatric Jurisprudence Therapeutic?
Choice - v41 - i11-12 - July-August 2004 - p2115(2) [501+]

Kappeler, Andreas - *Culture, Nation, and Identity: The Ukrainian-Russian Encounter, 1600-1945*
CBRA - Annual 2003 - p285(1) [501+]
Russ Rev - v63 - i2 - April 2004 - pNA [501+]
Slav R - v63 - i4 - Winter 2004 - p872(2) [501+]

Kappeler, Peter M. - *Primate Life Histories and Socioecology*
QRB - v79 - i4 - Dec 2004 - p441(2) [501+]

Kappeler, Thomas - *KdV & KAM*
Choice - v41 - i7 - March 2004 - p1330(1) [501+]

Kapsch, Robert J. - *Canals*
SciTech - v28 - i4 - Dec 2004 - p8(1) [1-50]

Kaptein, Ethan B. - *Income and Influence: Social Policy in Emerging Market Economics*
JEL - v41 - i4 - Dec 2003 - p1380(2) [501+]

Kaptein, Hendrik - *Crime, Victims and Justice: Essays on Principles and Practice*
R&R Bk N - v19 - i3 - August 2004 - p169(1) [501+]

Kapustka, L. - *Landscape Ecology and Wildlife Habitat Evaluation: Critical Information for Ecological Risk Assessment, Land-Use Management Activities, and Biodiversity Enhancement, Proceedings*
SciTech - v28 - i4 - Dec 2004 - p63(1) [51-500]

Kar, Law - *Hong Kong Cinema: A Cross-Cultural View*
Bwatch - Nov 2004 - pNA [51-500]
Choice - v42 - i7 - March 2005 - p1234(2) [51-500]

Kara, Yade - *Selam Berlin*
WLT - v78 - i3-4 - Sept-Dec 2004 - p125(1) [501+]

Karabell, Zachary - *Chester Alan Arthur*
BW - v34 - i37 - Sept 12 2004 - p5(1) [501+]
Parting the Desert: The Creation of the Suez Canal
T&C - v45 - i4 - Oct 2004 - p871(2) [501+]

Karady, Viktor - *Jews of Europe in the Modern Era: A Socio-Historical Outline*
R&R Bk N - v19 - i4 - Nov 2004 - p46(1) [51-500]

Kaufman, Matthew H. - *The Regius Chair of Military Surgery in the University of Edinburgh, 1806-55*
HNet - Nov 2004 - pNA [501+]
SciTech - v28 - i1 - March 2004 - p111(1) [51-500]

Kaufman, Peter Iver - *Thinking of the Laity in Late Tudor England*
Choice - v42 - i7 - March 2005 - p1242(2) [51-500]

Kaufman, Scott - *The Pig War: The United States, Britain, and the Balance of Power in the Pacific Northwest, 1846-72*
Choice - v42 - i3 - Nov 2004 - p548(1) [1-50]
J Mil H - v68 - i4 - Oct 2004 - p1258-1259 [501+]

Kaufman, Sharon R. - *...And a Time to Die: How American Hospitals Shape the End of Life*
KR - v73 - i1 - Jan 1 2005 - p36(1) [501+]
LJ - v130 - i4 - March 1 2005 - p104(1) [51-500]
PW - v252 - i7 - Feb 14 2005 - p65(1) [51-500]

Kaufman, Wallace - *Coming out of the Woods: The Solitary Life of a Maverick Naturalist*
NRJ - v44 - i2 - Spring 2004 - p621-651 [501+]

Kaufmann, Bruno - *Direct Democracy in Europe: A Comprehensive Reference Guide to the Initiative and Referendum Process in Europe*
Choice - v42 - i3 - Nov 2004 - p462(1) [1-50]

Kaufmann, Dorothy - *Edith Thomas: A Passion for Resistance*
BL - v101 - i1 - Sept 1 2004 - p39(1) [51-500]
Choice - v42 - i6 - Feb 2005 - p1026(1) [51-500]

Kaufmann, Eric P. - *The Rise and Fall of Anglo-America*
Choice - v42 - i6 - Feb 2005 - p1082(1) [51-500]
RM - v58 - i1 - Sept 2004 - p184(2) [501+]

Kaufmann, Karen M. - *The Partisan Paradox: Religious Commitment and the Gender Gap in Party Identification*
Wil Q - v29 - i1 - Wntr 2005 - p87(1) [501+]

Kaufmann-Kohler, Gabrielle - *International Arbitration in Switzerland: A Handbook for Practitioners*
R&R Bk N - v19 - i4 - Nov 2004 - p175(1) [501+]

Kaufmann, Stefan H.E. - *The Innate Immune Response to Infection*
SciTech - v28 - i3 - Sept 2004 - p75(1) [51-500]
Novel Vaccination Strategies
E-Streams - Oct 2004 - pNA [501+]

Kaufmann, Thomas - *Evangelische Kirchenhistoriker im "Dritten Reich"*
HNet - Nov 2004 - pNA [501+]

Kaufmann, Thomas DaCosta - *Toward a Geography of Art*
Art Bull - v86 - i4 - Dec 2004 - p783(5) [501+]

Kaul, Chandrika - *Reporting the Raj: The British Press and India, 1880-1922*
Choice - v41 - i11-12 - July-August 2004 - p2101(1) [501+]

Kaul, Inge - *Providing Global Public Goods: Managing Globalization*
JEL - v41 - i4 - Dec 2003 - p1370(1) [501+]
JEL - v42 - i1 - March 2004 - p194(2) [501+]

Kaul, Sunil C. - *Aging of Cells in and Outside the Body*
SciTech - v28 - i1 - March 2004 - p66(1) [51-500]

Kaul, Suvir - *The Partitions of Memory: The Afterlife of the Division of India*
AHR - v109 - i2 - April 2004 - p503(2) [501+]

Kault, David - *Statistics with Common Sense*
LibMed - v22 - i4 - Jan 2004 - p78(1) [501+]
Math T - v97 - i4 - April 2004 - p302-302 [501+]

Kaup, Monika - *Mixing Race, Mixing Culture: Inter-American Literary Dialogues*
J Am St - v38 - i1 - April 2004 - p148-149 [501+]
Rewriting North American Borders in Chicano and Chicana Narrative
MFSF - v50 - i2 - Summer 2004 - p469-476 [501+]

Kaupp, Martin - *Calculation of NMR and EPR Parameters: Theory and Applications*
SciTech - v28 - i4 - Dec 2004 - p55(1) [51-500]

Kaur, Sat Dharam - *The Complete Natural Medicine Guide to Breast Cancer: A Practical Manual for Understanding, Prevention and Care*
E-Streams - August 2004 - pNA [501+]
LJ - v129 - i14 - Sept 1 2004 - p184(2) [501+]
SciTech - v28 - i1 - March 2004 - p91(1) [1-50]

Kautsky, John H. - *Social Democracy and the Aristocracy*
S&S - v68 - i4 - Winter 2004 - p505-3 [501+]

Kava, Alex - *One False Move (Read by Reed, Maggi-Meg). Audiobook Review*
y Kliatt - v39 - i1 - Jan 2005 - p48(1) [51-500]
One False Move
PW - v251 - i29 - July 19 2004 - p146(1) [51-500]

Kavale, Kenneth A. - *The Positive Side of Special Education: Minimizing Its Fads, Fancies, and Follies*
R&R Bk N - v19 - i4 - Nov 2004 - p192(1) [501+]

Kavanagh, James - *In God's Kitchen (Illus. by Belisle, John)*
c Globe & Mail - August 14 2004 - pD16 [51-500]

Kavanagh, Kathryn Hopkins - *Many Voices: Toward Caring Culture in Healthcare and Healing*
Choice - v42 - i6 - Feb 2005 - p1056(1) [51-500]
SciTech - v28 - i4 - Dec 2004 - p122 [51-500]

Kavanagh, Patrick Joseph (b. 1931 -) - *Something About*
Spec - v296 - i9189 - Sept 18 2004 - p52(2) [501+]

Kawabata, Yasunari - *The Lake*
Bwatch - Dec 2004 - pNA [51-500]

Kawaguchi, Kazuko Hirose - *A Social Theory of International Law: International Relations as a Complex System*
R&R Bk N - v19 - i3 - August 2004 - p210(1) [1-50]

Kawakatsu, Toshihiro - *Statistical Physics of Polymers: An Introduction*
Choice - v42 - i5 - Jan 2005 - p891(1) [1-50]

Kawamoto, Kevin - *Digital Journalism: Emerging Media and the Changing Horizons of Journalism*
R&R Bk N - v19 - i1 - Feb 2004 - p229(1) [51-500]

Kawano, Satoyuki - *Computational Technologies for Fluid/Thermal/Structural/Chemical Systems with Industrial Applications: Proceedings, Vols. 1-2.*
SciTech - v28 - i4 - Dec 2004 - p164(1) [51-500]

Kawasaki, Guy - *The Art of the Start: The Time-Tested, Battle-Hardened Guide for Anyone Starting Anything*
Bus W - i3906 - Nov 1 2004 - p92 [501+]
Forbes - v174 - i5 - Sept 20 2004 - p45 [501+]
LJ - v129 - i18 - Nov 1 2004 - p99(1) [51-500]
NW - Oct 4 2004 - p38 [501+]
PW - v251 - i30 - July 26 2004 - p47(1) [501+]

Kawashima, Yutaka - *Japanese Foreign Policy at the Crossroads: Challenges and Options for the Twenty-First Century*
R&R Bk N - v19 - i1 - Feb 2004 - p49(1) [51-500]

Kay, Alan N. - *No Girls Allowed*
c SLJ - v50 - i10 - Oct 2004 - p169(2) [51-500]

Kay, Carolyn - *Art and the German Bourgeoisie: Alfred Lichtwark and Modern Painting in Hamburg, 1886-1914*
AHR - v109 - i4 - Oct 2004 - p1327(2) [51-500]
CEH - v37 - i3 - Summer 2004 - p446(3) [501+]
JMH - v77 - i1 - March 2005 - p218(3) [501+]

Kay, Charles E. - *Wilderness and Political Ecology: Aboriginal Influences and the Original State of Nature*
WHQ - v35 - i1 - Spring 2004 - p81-82 [501+]

Kay, Devra - *Seyder Tkhines: The Forgotten Book of Common Prayer for Jewish Women*
LJ - v129 - i16 - Oct 1 2004 - p87(1) [51-500]

Kay, Elizabeth - *Back to the Divide (Illus. by Dewan, Ted)*
c PW - v251 - i28 - July 12 2004 - p65(2) [501+]
c Sch Lib - v52 - i4 - Winter 2004 - p202(1) [51-500]
y SLJ - v50 - i9 - Sept 2004 - p209(1) [51-500]

Kay, Ellie - *Heroes at Home: Help & Hope for America's Military Families (Read by Kay, Ellie). Audiobook Review*
LJ - v129 - i15 - Sept 15 2004 - p90(1) [51-500]

Kay, Guy Gavriel - *The Last Light of the Sun*
BIC - v33 - i7 - Oct 2004 - p19(2) [501+]
BW - v34 - i12 - March 21 2004 - p13(1) [501+]

Kay, J.A. - *Culture and Prosperity: The Truth about Markets: Why Some Nations Are Rich but Most Remain Poor*
Choice - v42 - i3 - Nov 2004 - p533(1) [1-50]
The Economics of Business Strategy
R&R Bk N - v19 - i1 - Feb 2004 - p86(1) [51-500]

Kay, Janet - *Protecting Children: A Practical Guide, 2nd Ed.*
R&R Bk N - v19 - i3 - August 2004 - p166(1) [501+]

Kay, John - *Culture and Prosperity: The Truth about Markets--Why Some Nations Are Rich but Most Remain Poor*
BW - v34 - i41 - Oct 10 2004 - p6(1) [501+]
Bwatch - v26 - i8 - August 2004 - p8(1) [51-500]
Har Bus R - v82 - i6 - June 2004 - p28(1) [501+]
The Economics of Business Strategy
JEL - v42 - i1 - March 2004 - p297(1) [501+]

Kay, Michael - *XSLT 2.0 Programmer's Reference, 3rd Ed.*
SciTech - v28 - i4 - Dec 2004 - p19(1) [1-50]
XSLT: Programmer's Reference. 2nd Ed.
SciTech - v28 - i3 - Sept 2004 - p21(1) [51-500]

Kay, N.M. - *Ausonius: Epigrams*
Class R - v53 - i2 - Nov 2003 - p384-385 [501+]

Kay, Richard - *The Council of Bourges, 1225: A Documentary History*
Specu - v79 - i4 - Oct 2004 - p1105(3) [501+]

Kay, Sarah - *A Short History of French Literature*
FS - v58 - i3 - July 2004 - p391-391 [501+]
TLS - i5285 - July 16 2004 - p20(1) [501+]

Kay, Verla - *Orphan Train (Illus. by Stark, Ken)*
c CE - v80 - i5 - Mid-Summer 2004 - p274(1) [51-500]

Kaya, Ibrahim - *Equitable Utilization: The Law of Non-Navigational Uses of International Watercourses*
R&R Bk N - v19 - i1 - Feb 2004 - pNA [51-500]
Social Theory and Later Modernities: The Turkish Experience
R&R Bk N - v19 - i3 - August 2004 - p47(1) [51-500]

Kaye, Andrew M. - *The Pussycat of Prizefighting: Tiger Flowers and the Politics of Black Celebrity*
Choice - v42 - i3 - Nov 2004 - p524(1) [1-50]
TLS - i5295 - Sept 24 2004 - p27(1) [501+]

Kaye, Beverly L. - *Love 'em or Lose 'em: Getting Good People to Stay. 2nd Ed.*
HR Mag - v49 - i7 - July 2004 - pS20(1) [51-500]

Kaye, Cathryn Berger - *The Complete Guide to Service Learning: Proven, Practical Ways to Engage Students in Civic Responsibility, Academic Curriculum, and Social Action*
LibMed - v23 - i1 - August-Sept 2004 - p85(2) [51-500]
VOYA - v27 - i4 - Oct 2004 - p266(1) [51-500]
y VOYA - v27 - i4 - Oct 2004 - p338(1) [51-500]

Kaye, Dalia Dassa - *Beyond the Handshake: Multilateral Cooperation in the Arab-Israeli Peace Process, 1991-1996*
IJMES - v36 - i3 - August 2004 - p524-525 [501+]

Kaye, David L. - *Child and Adolescent Mental Health*
Adoles - v39 - i156 - Winter 2004 - p833(2) [51-500]

Kaye, Frances W. - *Hiding the Audience: Viewing Arts and Arts Institutions on the Prairies*
CBRA - Annual 2003 - p116(2) [501+]
HNet - July 2004 - pNA [501+]

Kaye, Lenny - *You Call It Madness: The Sensuous Song of the Croon*
BW - v34 - i39 - Sept 26 2004 - p13(1) [501+]
Choice - v42 - i6 - Feb 2005 - p1031(1) [51-500]
Ent W - i777 - August 6 2004 - p85 [51-500]
NY - v80 - i27 - Sept 20 2004 - p102(1) [1-50]
NYTBR - August 15 2004 - p13 [501+]

Kaye, Marvin - *The Dragon Quintent*
y VOYA - v27 - i3 - August 2004 - p228(1) [1-50]

Kaynak, Erdener - *Strategic Global Marketing: Issues and Trends*
JEL - v41 - i4 - Dec 2003 - p1400(1) [501+]

Kayser, Oliver - *Pharmaceutical Biotechnology: Drug Discovery and Clinical Applications*
E-Streams - Oct 2004 - pNA [501+]

Kaywell, Joan F. - *Using Literature to Help Troubled Teenagers Cope with Abuse Issues*
SLJ - v51 - i1 - Jan 2005 - p162(1) [51-500]

Kaza, Stephanie - *Hooked!: Buddhist Writings on Greed, Desire, and the Urge to Consume*
LJ - v130 - i4 - March 1 2005 - p93(1) [51-500]
PW - v252 - i4 - Jan 24 2005 - p240(1) [501+]

Kazack, Sherene H. - *Dark Threats and White Knights: The Somalia Affair, Peacekeeping, and the New Imperialism*
R&R Bk N - v19 - i3 - August 2004 - p59(1) [51-500]

Kazadi wa Mukuna - *An Interdisciplinary Study of The Ox and the Slave (Bumba-Meu-Boi): A Satirical Music Drama in Brazil*
Choice - v41 - i7 - March 2004 - p1306(1) [501+]

Kazal, Russell A. - *Becoming Old Stock: The Paradox of German-American Identity*
Choice - v42 - i5 - Jan 2005 - p939(1) [51-500]

Kazanjian, David - *The Colonizing Trick: National Culture and Imperial Citizenship in Early America*
Am Q - v56 - i4 - Dec 2004 - p1107(7) [501+]

Kazanjian, Howard - *The Cowboy and the Senorita: A Biography of Roy Rogers and Dale Evans*
Bwatch - v26 - i7 - July 2004 - p10(1) [51-500]
HRNB - v33 - i1 - Fall 2004 - p9(2) [51-500]

Kazanjian, Kirk - *Making Dough: The 12 Secret Ingredients of Krispy Kreem's Sweet Success*
R&R Bk N - v19 - i1 - Feb 2004 - p102(2) [51-500]

Kazemzadeh, Masoud - *Islamic Fundamentalism, Feminism and Gender Inequality in Iran under Khomeini*
IJMES - v36 - i1 - Feb 2004 - p137-138 [501+]

Kazimee, Bashir A. - *Place, Meaning, and Form in the Architecture and Urban Structure of Eastern Islamic Cities*
R&R Bk N - v19 - i1 - Feb 2004 - p203(1) [51-500]

Kazis, Richard - *Double the Numbers: Increasing Postsecondary Credentials for Underrepresented Youth*
TCR - v107 - i2 - Feb 2005 - p303(4) [501+]

Kazumi, Yuana - *Flower of the Deep Sleep, Vol. 1*
PW - v252 - i8 - Feb 21 2005 - p160(1) [51-500]

Keagy, Blair A. - *Essentials of Physician Practice Management*
SciTech - v28 - i4 - Dec 2004 - p78(1) [51-500]

Keahey, Deborah - *Madwoman in the Academy: 43 Women Boldly Take on the Ivory Tower*
CBRA - Annual 2003 - p385(1) [501+]

Kean, Thomas H. - *The 9/11 Commission Report: Final Report of the National Commission on Terrorist Attacks Upon the United States*
Globe & Mail - August 7 2004 - pD8 [501+]

Keane, Angela - *Women Writers and English Nation in the 1790's*
RES - v55 - i219 - April 2004 - p284-285 [501+]

Keane, John - *Global Civil Society?*
AJS - v110 - i1 - July 2004 - p234(2) [501+]
Choice - v41 - i7 - March 2004 - p1369(1) [501+]
Musician's Guide to Pro Tools
SciTech - v28 - i3 - Sept 2004 - p162(1) [51-500]

Keane, Kahlee - *The Standing People: Field Guide of the Medicinal Plants for the Prairie Provinces*
SciTech - v28 - i3 - Sept 2004 - p62(1) [51-500]

Kearney, Chris - *The Monkey's Mask: Identity, Memory, Narrative and Voice*
Choice - v42 - i1 - Sept 2004 - p158(1) [501+]

Kearney-Cooke, Ann - *Change Your Mind, Change Your Body: Feeling Good about Your Body and Self after 40*
LJ - v129 - i12 - July 2004 - p106(1) [51-500]

Kearney, Michael - *Changing Fields in Anthropology: From Local to Global*
R&R Bk N - v19 - i3 - August 2004 - p82(1) [51-500]

Kearney, Milo - *Indian Ocean in World History*
R&R Bk N - v19 - i4 - Nov 2004 - p47(1) [51-500]

Kearney, Richard - *The God Who May Be: A Hermeneutics of Religion*
JR - v84 - i4 - Oct 2004 - p632(3) [501+]
On Paul Ricoeur: The Owl of Minerva
Choice - v42 - i7 - March 2005 - p1240(2) [51-500]
R&R Bk N - v20 - i1 - Feb 2005 - p4(1) [501+]
On Stories
ILS - v24 - i1 - Fall 2004 - p27(1) [501+]

Keating, Frank - *Will Rogers: An American Legend (Illus. by Wimmer, Mike)*
c RT - v57 - Oct 2003 - p175 [1-50]

Keating, H.R.F. - *The Dreaming Detective*
KR - v72 - i22 - Nov 15 2004 - p1071(1) [51-500]
PW - v251 - i49 - Dec 6 2004 - p46(1) [51-500]

Keating, Peter (b. 1953 -) - *Biomedical Platforms: Realigning the Normal and the Pathological in Late-Twentieth-Century Medicine*
CS - v33 - i3 - Sept 2004 - p624-625 [501+]
QRB - v79 - i3 - Sept 2004 - p343(1) [501+]

Keating, Richard C. - *Anatomy of the Monocotyledons, IW: Acoraceae and Araceae*
E-Streams - Dec 2004 - pNA [501+]

Keating, Tom - *Building Sustainable Peace*
R&R Bk N - v19 - i3 - August 2004 - p188(1) [501+]

Keay, Julia - *Alexander the Corrector: The Tormented Genius Who Unwrote the Bible*
TLS - i5307 - Dec 17 2004 - p3-4 [501+]

Kebede, Messay - *Africa's Quest for a Philosophy of Decolonization*
Choice - v42 - i5 - Jan 2005 - p866(1) [1-50]
R&R Bk N - v19 - i3 - August 2004 - p36(1) [51-500]

Kechnie, Margaret C. - *Organizing Rural Women: The Federating Women's Institutes of Ontario, 1897-1919*
CBRA - Annual 2003 - p383(2) [501+]

Keddie, Nikki R. - *Modern Iran: Roots and Results of Revolution*
MEQ - v11 - i3 - Summer 2004 - p88(2) [501+]

Keding, Dan - *Stories of Hope And Spirit: Folktales from Eastern Europe*
KR - v72 - i20 - Oct 15 2004 - p1008(1) [51-500]

Kedourie, Elie - *The Chatham House Version and Other Middle-Eastern Studies*
R&R Bk N - v19 - i3 - August 2004 - p48(1) [51-500]

Kedro, M. James - *Aligning Resources for Student Outcomes: School-Based Steps to Success*
R&R Bk N - v19 - i4 - Nov 2004 - p186(1) [501+]

Keefe, Alice A. - *Woman's Body and the Social Body in Hosea*
R&R Bk N - v19 - i4 - Nov 2004 - p23(1) [51-500]

Keefe, Patrick Radden - *Chatter: Dispatches from the Secret World of Global Eavesdropping*
KR - v72 - i24 - Dec 15 2004 - p1183(1) [51-500]
LJ - v130 - i2 - Feb 1 2005 - p101(1) [51-500]

Keefe, Simon P. - *The Cambridge Companion to Mozart*
Choice - v41 - i7 - March 2004 - p1305(1) [501+]
Notes - v61 - i1 - Sept 2004 - p122(3) [501+]

Keefer, Janice Kulyk - *Thieves*
Globe & Mail - Nov 27 2004 - pD3 [51-500]
Globe & Mail - March 12 2005 - pD17 [1-50]

Keegan, Abigail F. - *Byron's Othered Self and Voice: Contextualizing the Homographic Signature*
R&R Bk N - v19 - i1 - Feb 2004 - p238(1) [51-500]

Keegan, Jeff - *Hacking TiVo: The Expansion, Enhancement, and Development Starter Kit*
SciTech - v28 - i1 - March 2004 - p159(1) [51-500]

Keegan, John - *The Face of Battle*
Globe & Mail - Nov 6 2004 - pD27 [501+]
Intelligence in War: Knowledge of the Enemy from Napoleon to Al-Qaeda
BIC - v33 - i6 - Sept 2004 - p19(2) [501+]
NWCR - v57 - Autumn 2004 - p162(3) [501+]
T&C - v45 - i4 - Oct 2004 - p881(3) [501+]
World&I - v19 - i4 - April 2004 - p214 [501+]
Intelligence in War: The Value and Limitations of What the Military Can Learn about the Enemy
NYTBR - Dec 19 2004 - p30 [501+]
The Iraq War
Bwatch - Oct 2004 - pNA [51-500]
Choice - v42 - i4 - Dec 2004 - p733(1) [1-50]
CR - v285 - i1666 - Nov 2004 - p303(2) [501+]
For Aff - v83 - i5 - Sept-Oct 2004 - p164 [501+]
Parameters - v34 - i3 - Autumn 2004 - p148(3) [501+]

Keegan, William - *The Prudence of Mr. Gordon Brown*
Lon R Bks - v26 - i7 - April 1 2004 - p17(2) [501+]
TLS - i5267 - March 12 2004 - p10-10 [501+]

Keehn, Sally M. - *Gnat Stokes and the Foggy Bottom Swamp Queen*
c KR - v73 - i5 - March 1 2005 - p289(1) [51-500]

Keel, William D. - *German Language Varieties Worldwide: Internal and External Perspectives*
R&R Bk N - v19 - i1 - Feb 2004 - p217(1) [51-500]

Keelan, Brian - *Free at Last! Stop Smoking: How I Did It, How You Can Too*
Globe & Mail - Sept 4 2004 - pF6 [1-50]

Keelan, Claudia - *The Devotion Field*
PW - v251 - i47 - Nov 22 2004 - p56(2) [51-500]

Keeley, James F. - *Commercial Satellite Imagery and United Nations Peacekeeping: A View from Above*
SciTech - v28 - i4 - Dec 2004 - p172(1) [51-500]

Keeling, Clinton - *Where the Camel Strode*
Spec - v296 - i9193 - Oct 16 2004 - p72(1) [501+]

Keeling, Jim - *Flowerpots*
Bwatch - v26 - i7 - July 2004 - p4(2) [51-500]

Keen, Ian - *Aboriginal Economy and Society: Australia at the Threshold of Colonisation*
Choice - v42 - i5 - Jan 2005 - p896(1) [1-50]

Keen, Paul - *The Popular Radical Press in Britain, 1817-1821, Vols. 1-6*
R&R Bk N - v19 - i3 - August 2004 - p38(1) [51-500]

Keen, Richard A. - *Skywatch West: The Complete Weather Guide, Rev. Ed.*
Bwatch - Jan 2005 - pNA [51-500]
y SB - v41 - i1 - Jan-Feb 2005 - p27(1) [51-500]

Keen, Suzanne - *Romances of the Archive in Contemporary British Fiction*
MFSF - v50 - i2 - Summer 2004 - p501-503 [501+]
TLS - i5286 - July 23 2004 - p31(1) [501+]

Keenan, Celia - *Studies in Children's Literature, 1500-2000*
Choice - v42 - i7 - March 2005 - p1224(1) [501+]

Keenan, Edward L. - *Josef Dobrovsky and the Origins of the Igor Tale*
TimHES - v0 - i1678 - Feb 11 2005 - p24(2) [501+]

Keenan, James, S.J. - *Moral Wisdom: Lessons and Texts from the Catholic Tradition*
LJ - v129 - i16 - Oct 1 2004 - p87(2) [51-500]

Keenan, Sheila - *O, Say Can You See? America's Symbols, Landmarks, and Inspiring Words (Illus. by Boyajian, Ann)*
c BL - v101 - i4 - Oct 15 2004 - p402(1) [51-500]
c KR - v72 - i15 - August 1 2004 - p743(1) [51-500]
y PW - v251 - i44 - Nov 1 2004 - p64(2) [501+]
O, Say Can You See? America's Symbols, Landmarks, and Inspiring Words (Illus. by Boyanian, Ann)
c SLJ - v50 - i12 - Dec 2004 - p132(2) [501+]
Scholastic Book of Outstanding Americans
c LibMed - v22 - i6 - March 2004 - p75(1) [501+]
c LibMed - v22 - i6 - March 2004 - p75(1) [501+]

Keene, Brian - *The Rising*
NYTBR - Oct 31 2004 - p18 [501+]

Keene, Derek - *St. Paul's: The Cathedral Church of London, 604-2004*
Bks & Cult - v11 - i1 - Jan-Feb 2005 - p18(2) [501+]
Choice - v42 - i7 - March 2005 - p1221(1) [51-500]
CR - v285 - i1666 - Nov 2004 - p315(1) [501+]
HT - v54 - i9 - Sept 2004 - p58(1) [501+]
St Paul's: The Cathedral Church of London, 604-2004
TimHES - v0 - i1671 - Dec 17 2004 - p21(2) [501+]

Keene, Donald - *Yoshimasa and the Silver Pavilion: The Creation of the Soul of Japan*
Choice - v41 - i11-12 - July-August 2004 - p2101(1) [501+]
JAS - v63 - i3 - August 2004 - p799-800 [501+]
R&R Bk N - v19 - i1 - Feb 2004 - p49(1) [51-500]

Keene, Judith - *Fighting for Franco: International Volunteers in Nationalist Spain during the Spanish Civil War, 1936-39*
S&S - v68 - i3 - Fall 2004 - p381-385 [501+]

Keener, Craig S. - *The Gospel of John: A Commentary, Vols. 1-2*
R&R Bk N - v19 - i1 - Feb 2004 - p21(1) [51-500]
Theol St - v65 - i3 - Sept 2004 - p631(3) [501+]

Keener, James - *Mathematical Physiology*
SIAM Rev - v46 - i3 - Sept 2004 - p587(4) [501+]

Keens-Douglas, Ricardo - *Tales from the Isle of Spice*
Res Links - v10 - i2 - Dec 2004 - p20(1) [51-500]

Keep, Richard - *Clatter Bash!: A Day of the Dead Celebration*
c KR - v72 - i17 - Sept 1 2004 - p867(1) [51-500]
c SLJ - v51 - i2 - Feb 2005 - p104(1) [51-500]

Keeping Unusual Pets
c LibMed - v23 - i3 - Nov-Dec 2004 - p76(1) [51-500]

Keeran, Roger - *Socialism Betrayed: Behind the Collapse of the Soviet Union*
R&R Bk N - v19 - i3 - August 2004 - p46(1) [51-500]

Kees, Weldon - *Collected Poems*
TLS - i5286 - July 23 2004 - p9-10 [501+]

Keesling, Catherine M. - *The Votive Statues of the Athenian Acropolis*
TLS - i5294 - Sept 17 2004 - p29(1) [501+]

Keetley, Dawn - *Public Women, Public Words: A Documentary History of American Feminism, Vols. 2-3*
HNet - Sept 2004 - pNA [501+]

Keever, John M. - *The Cornell Manual for Lifeboatmen, Able Seamen, and Qualified Members of Engine Department, 2nd Ed.*
SciTech - v28 - i4 - Dec 2004 - p172(1) [501+]

Keeves, John P. - *International Handbook of Educational Research in the Asia-Pacific Region, Vols. 1-2*
R&R Bk N - v19 - i1 - Feb 2004 - p181(1) [51-500]

Kefalas, Maria - *Working-Class Heroes: Protecting Home, Community, and Nation in a Chicago Neighborhood*
CS - v33 - i2 - March 2004 - p196-198 [501+]

Kehal, Harbhajan - *Digital Economy: Impacts, Influences, and Challenges*
R&R Bk N - v19 - i3 - August 2004 - p96(1) [51-500]

Kehily, Mary Jane - *Children's Cultural Worlds*
Adoles - v39 - i155 - Fall 2004 - p624(1) [51-500]

Kehm, Michelle - *No Place Like Home: Staying In, Kicking Back, and Living It Up*
LJ - v130 - i2 - Feb 1 2005 - p111(1) [51-500]

Kehoe, Elisabeth - *Fortune's Daughters: The Extravagant Lives of the Jerome Sisters: Jennie Churchill, Clara Frewen, and Leonie Leslie*
Spec - v296 - i9197 - Nov 13 2004 - p59(1) [501+]

Kehoe, Elisabeth - *Fortune's Daughters: The Extravagant Lives of the Jerome Sisters: Jennie Churchill, Clara Frewen, and Leonie Leslie*
TimHES - v0 - i1679 - Feb 18 2005 - p24(1) [501+]
TLS - i5297 - Oct 8 2004 - p26(1) [501+]

The Titled Americans: Three American Sisters and the English Aristocratic World into Which They Married
- BL - v101 - i5 - Nov 1 2004 - p456(1) [51-500]
- KR - v72 - i17 - Sept 1 2004 - p849(1) [501+]
- LJ - v129 - i20 - Dec 1 2004 - p136(1) [51-500]
- PW - v251 - i37 - Sept 13 2004 - p65(1) [51-500]

Kehr, J. Alan - *Fusion-bonded Epoxy (FBE): A Foundation for Pipeline Corrosion Protection*
- SciTech - v28 - i3 - Sept 2004 - p150(1) [51-500]

Kehres, Jean-Marc - *Sade et la Rhetorique de l'exemplarite*
- FS - v58 - i2 - April 2004 - p264(2) [501+]

Kehret, Peg - *Abduction!*
- c BL - v101 - i5 - Nov 1 2004 - p485(1) [51-500]
- c Kliatt - v38 - i6 - Nov 2004 - p8(1) [51-500]
- y KR - v72 - i22 - Nov 15 2004 - p1090(1) [51-500]
- c SLJ - v50 - i12 - Dec 2004 - p149(1) [51-500]

Keider, Erik M. - *Nanostructured Materials in Alternative Energy Devices: Proceedings*
- SciTech - v28 - i4 - Dec 2004 - p158(1) [51-500]

Keil, Charles - *Bright Balkan Morning: Romani Lives and the Power of Music in Greek Macedonia*
- Notes - v61 - i1 - Sept 2004 - p142(4) [501+]

Keil, Charlie - *American Cinema's Transitional Era: Audiences, Institutions, Practices*
- Choice - v42 - i6 - Feb 2005 - p1028(1) [51-500]

Keillor, Garrison - *Daddy's Girl (Illus. by Glasser, Robin Preiss)*
- c PW - v252 - i8 - Feb 21 2005 - p173(1) [51-500]

Homegrown Democrat: A Few Plain Thoughts from the Heart of America
- BL - v100 - i21 - July 2004 - p1795(2) [51-500]
- BW - v34 - i29 - July 18 2004 - p3(1) [1-50]
- LJ - v129 - i13 - August 2004 - p100(1) [501+]

Homegrown Democrat: A Few Plain Thoughts from the Heart of America (Read by Keillor, Garrison). Audiobook Review
- PW - v251 - i40 - Oct 4 2004 - p32(1) [51-500]

Homegrown Democrat: A Few Plain Thoughts from the Heart of America
- R&R Bk N - v19 - i4 - Nov 2004 - p154(1) [501+]

Keillor, Steven J. - *Grand Excursion: Antebellum America Discovers the Upper Mississippi*
- Choice - v42 - i6 - Feb 2005 - p1081(2) [51-500]

Keinan, Ehud - *Life Sciences for the 21st Century*
- E-Streams - August 2004 - pNA [501+]
- QRB - v79 - i3 - Sept 2004 - p298(1) [501+]

Keister, Douglas - *Stories In Stone: A Field Guide to Cemetery Symbolism and Iconography*
- Bwatch - v26 - i9 - Sept 2004 - p2(1) [51-500]
- R&R Bk N - v19 - i3 - August 2004 - p242(1) [51-500]

Keiter, Robert B. - *Keeping Faith with Nature: Ecosystems, Democracy, & America's Public Lands*
- Choice - v41 - i7 - March 2004 - p1320(1) [501+]
- Env - v46 - i6 - July-August 2004 - p44(2) [501+]
- JEL - v42 - i1 - March 2004 - p337(1) [501+]
- QRB - v79 - i4 - Dec 2004 - p452(2) [501+]

Keith, Pat M. - *Doing Good for the Aged: Volunteers in an Ombudsman Program*
- CS - v33 - i2 - March 2004 - p175-176 [501+]

Keithley, Joey - *I, Shithead: A Life in Punk*
- CBRA - Annual 2003 - p106(1) [51-500]

Keizer, Garret - *Help: The Original Human Dilemma*
- BW - v34 - i46 - Nov 14 2004 - p5(1) [1-50]
- CC - v121 - i23 - Nov 16 2004 - p40(2) [501+]
- LJ - v129 - i16 - Oct 1 2004 - p84(1) [51-500]
- PW - v251 - i31 - August 2 2004 - p63(1) [51-500]

Keizer, Gregg - *The Longest Night*
- PW - v251 - i31 - August 2 2004 - p54(1) [501+]

Kekelidz, T. - *Creatine Kinase and Brain Energy Metabolism: Function and Disease, Proceedings*
- SciTech - v28 - i4 - Dec 2004 - p73(1) [51-500]

Kekes, John - *The Illusions of Egalitarianism*
- Choice - v41 - i11-12 - July-August 2004 - p2124(1) [501+]

Kekki, Lasse - *From Gay to Queer: Gay Male Identity in Selected Fiction by David Leavitt and in Tony Kushner's Play Angels in America I-II*
- R&R Bk N - v19 - i1 - Feb 2004 - p246(1) [51-500]

Keklik, Mumtaz - *Schumpeter, Innovation and Growth: Long-Cycle Dynamics in the Post-WWII American Manufacturing Industries*
- JEL - v41 - i4 - Dec 2003 - p1345(2) [501+]

Kelby, Scott - *Classic Photoshop Effects*
- Bwatch - v26 - i9 - Sept 2004 - p5(2) [501+]

Kelemen, R. Daniel - *The Rules of Federalism: Institutions and Regulatory Politics in the EU and Beyond*
- Choice - v42 - i3 - Nov 2004 - p557(2) [1-50]

Kelin, Daniel A. - *Marshall Islands Legends and Stories*
- Cont Pac - v17 - i1 - Spring 2005 - p252(3) [501+]

Kell, Peter - *Adult Education @ 21st Century*
- R&R Bk N - v19 - i1 - Feb 2004 - p193(1) [51-500]

Kellar, Clare - *Scotland, England, and the Reformation, 1534-1561*
- CR - v285 - i1664 - Sept 2004 - p180(2) [501+]
- HNet - Nov 2004 - pNA [501+]

Kellaway, Roy - *Feeding Concentrates: Supplements for Dairy Cows. Rev. Ed.*
- SciTech - v28 - i3 - Sept 2004 - p131(1) [51-500]

Kellehear, Allan - *Eternity and Me: The Everlasting Things in Life and Death*
- R&R Bk N - v20 - i1 - Feb 2005 - p6(1) [51-500]

Kelleher, Anne - *Silver's Edge*
- ChrSFF&H - v26 - i9 - Sept 2004 - p33(1) [51-500]

Kelleher, William F., Jr. - *The Troubles in Ballybogoin: Memory and Identity in Northern Ireland*
- Choice - v41 - i7 - March 2004 - p1360(1) [501+]
- Pub Hist - v26 - i3 - Summer 2004 - p71(73) [501+]

Keller, Benno - *Competition and Regulation in Telecommunications: Theory and Application to Switzerland*
- R&R Bk N - v19 - i2 - May 2004 - p109(1) [1-50]

Keller, Berndt - *Industrial Relations and European Integration: Trans- and Supranational Developments and Prospects*
- JEL - v42 - i1 - March 2004 - p283(1) [501+]

Keller, Catherine - *Face of the Deep: A Theology of Becoming*
- Intpr - v59 - i1 - Jan 2005 - p82(2) [501+]
- JR - v84 - i4 - Oct 2004 - p639(2) [501+]
- TT - v61 - i3 - Oct 2004 - p389(2) [501+]

Keller-Dall, Barbara - *Heilsplan und Gedachtnis: Zur Mnemologis des 16. Jahrhunderts in Italien*
- Six Ct J - v34 - i4 - Winter 2003 - p1265-1266 [501+]

Keller, Edwige - *Poetique de la Mort dans la Nouvelles Classique: 1660-1680*
- FS - v58 - i2 - April 2004 - p253(2) [501+]

Keller, Erik - *Technology Paradise Lost: Why Companies Will Spend Less to Get More from Information Technology*
- Choice - v42 - i3 - Nov 2004 - p530(1) [1-50]

Keller, Harald - *Dictionary of Engineering Materials*
- Choice - v42 - i1 - Sept 2004 - p72(1) [501+]
- E-Streams - Oct 2004 - pNA [501+]

Keller, Helen - *The World I Live In*
- YR - v92 - i4 - Oct 2004 - p140-149 [501+]

Keller, Holly - *Pearl's New Skates (Illus. by Keller, Holly)*
- c BL - v101 - i9-10 - Jan 1 2005 - p870(1) [51-500]
- c CCB-B - v58 - i5 - Jan 2005 - p213(2) [51-500]
- c KR - v72 - i24 - Dec 15 2004 - p1203(1) [51-500]
- c PW - v251 - i51 - Dec 20 2004 - p58(1) [51-500]
- c SLJ - v51 - i2 - Feb 2005 - p104(1) [51-500]

What a Hat!
- c LibMed - v22 - i6 - March 2004 - p57(1) [501+]

Keller, James R. - *Almost Shakespeare: Reinventing His Works for Cinema and Television*
- Choice - v42 - i6 - Feb 2005 - p1008(1) [51-500]

Keller, Jean A. - *Empty Beds: Indian Student Health at Sherman Institute, 1902-1922*
- WHQ - v35 - i2 - Summer 2004 - p245-246 [501+]

Keller, John Robert - *Samuel Beckett and the Primacy of Love*
- RES - v55 - i219 - April 2004 - p301-303 [501+]

Keller, Keith - *Wildlife Wars: Frontline Stories of BC's Worst Forest Fires*
- CBRA - Annual 2003 - p414(1) [51-500]

Keller, Kristin Thoennes - *From Maple Trees to Maple Syrup*
- c SLJ - v51 - i2 - Feb 2005 - p123(1) [51-500]

From Oranges to Orange Juice
- c SLJ - v51 - i2 - Feb 2005 - p123(1) [51-500]

From Peanuts to Peanut Butter
- c SLJ - v51 - i2 - Feb 2005 - p123(1) [51-500]

Keller, Mary - *The Hammer and the Flute: Women, Power and Spirit Possession*
- JR - v84 - i4 - Oct 2004 - p592(12) [501+]

Keller, Robert P. - *Three Wars...One Marine*
- Mar Crp G - v88 - i5 - May 2004 - p88(2) [501+]

Keller, Suzanne - *Community: Pursuing the Dream, Living the Reality*
- AJS - v110 - i1 - July 2004 - p249(2) [501+]

Keller, Sven - *Gunzburg und der Fall Josef Mengele: Die Heimatstadt und die Jagd nach dem NS-Verbrecher*
- HNet - Oct 2004 - pNA [501+]

Keller, Teresa - *Television News: A Handbook for Writing, Reporting, Shooting and Editing, 2nd Ed.*
- R&R Bk N - v19 - i4 - Nov 2004 - p228(1) [51-500]

Keller, Thomas - *Bouchon*
- BL - v101 - i9-10 - Jan 1 2005 - p798(1) [51-500]
- Globe & Mail - Nov 27 2004 - pD26 [51-500]
- LJ - v129 - i20 - Dec 1 2004 - p153(2) [51-500]
- NW - Dec 6 2004 - p88 [501+]
- PW - v251 - i43 - Oct 25 2004 - p41(1) [51-500]

Keller, William L. - *International Labor and Employment Laws, 2nd Ed., Vol. 1*
- R&R Bk N - v19 - i4 - Nov 2004 - p163(1) [501+]

International Labor and Employment Laws, 2nd Ed., Vol. 2
- R&R Bk N - v19 - i4 - Nov 2004 - p162(1) [501+]

Keller, William W. - *Crisis and Innovation in Asian Technology*
- T&C - v45 - i2 - April 2004 - p465-467 [501+]

Keller, Wolfgang - *Wavelets in Geodesy and Geodynamics*
- SciTech - v28 - i3 - Sept 2004 - p54(1) [1-50]

Kellerhals-Stewart, Heather - *Skookun Sal, Birling Gal (Illus. by Blaine, Janice)*
- c CBRA - Annual 2003 - p454(1) [51-500]

Kellerman, Barbara - *Bad Leadership: What It Is, How It Happens, Why It Matters*
- BL - v101 - i2 - Sept 15 2004 - p186(1) [51-500]
- PW - v251 - i35 - August 30 2004 - p46(1) [51-500]

Kellerman, Faye - *Double Homicide: Boston Double Homicide: Santa Fe*
- BL - v101 - i1 - Sept 1 2004 - p5(2) [51-500]
- Ent W - i787 - Oct 8 2004 - p120 [51-500]
- LJ - v129 - i14 - Sept 1 2004 - p125(1) [51-500]

Kellerman, Jonathan - *The Conspiracy Club (Read by Rahn, Rob). Audiobook Review*
- LJ - v129 - i12 - July 2004 - p124(1) [51-500]

Double Homicide: Boston Double Homicide: Santa Fe
- KR - v72 - i16 - August 15 2004 - p781(1) [51-500]
- PW - v251 - i36 - Sept 6 2004 - p49(1) [51-500]

Therapy (Read by Rubinstein, John). Audiobook Review
- Globe & Mail - July 24 2004 - pD13 [51-500]
- LJ - v129 - i19 - Nov 15 2004 - p97(1) [51-500]
- PW - v251 - i31 - August 2 2004 - p20(1) [501+]

Twisted: A Novel
- BL - v101 - i3 - Oct 1 2004 - p283(1) [51-500]
- Ent W - i794 - Nov 26 2004 - p123 [51-500]
- Globe & Mail - Nov 27 2004 - pD16 [51-500]
- LJ - v129 - i18 - Nov 1 2004 - p75(1) [501+]
- PW - v251 - i50 - Dec 13 2004 - p47(1) [51-500]

Twisted (Read by Crouse, Lindsay). Audiobook Review
- Globe & Mail - Jan 15 2005 - pD13 [1-50]

Kelley, Beverly Merrill - *Reelpolitik II: Political Ideologies in '50s and '60s Films*
- Choice - v42 - i1 - Sept 2004 - p109(1) [501+]
- R&R Bk N - v19 - i3 - August 2004 - p262(1) [51-500]

Kelley, C.T. - *Solving Nonlinear Equations with Newton's Method*
- SIAM Rev - v46 - i4 - Dec 2004 - p770-771 [501+]

Kelley, Charles T. - *High-Technology Manufacturing and U.S. Competitiveness*
- SciTech - v28 - i4 - Dec 2004 - p7(1) [1-50]

Kelley, Kitty - *The Family: The Real Story of the Bush Dynasty*
- BL - v101 - i4 - Oct 15 2004 - p362(1) [51-500]
- BW - v34 - i39 - Sept 26 2004 - p3(1) [501+]
- Econ - v372 - i8394 - Sept 25 2004 - p97US [501+]
- Globe & Mail - Sept 25 2004 - pD8 [501+]
- NYTBR - Oct 10 2004 - p28 [501+]
- Spec - v296 - i9191 - Oct 2 2004 - p55(1) [501+]

Kelley, Mark R. - *Milton and the Grounds of Contention*
- Ren Q - v57 - i3 - Fall 2004 - p1171(3) [501+]
- R&R Bk N - v19 - i1 - Feb 2004 - p238(1) [51-500]

Kelley, Norman - *The Head Negro in Charge Syndrome: The Dead End of Black Politics*
- LJ - v129 - i12 - July 2004 - p103(1) [51-500]

Kelley, Paul B. - *Stories for Nothing: Samuel Beckett's Narrative Poetics*
- FS - v58 - i2 - April 2004 - p288(2) [501+]

Kellman, Peter - *Divided We Fall: The Story of the Paperworkers' Union and the Future of Labor*
- Bwatch - v26 - i7 - July 2004 - p10(1) [51-500]

Kellner, Douglas - *The New Left and the 1960s: Collected Papers of Herbert Marcuse, Vol. 3*
- Nation - v280 - i5 - Feb 7 2005 - p30 [501+]

Kelloff, Gary J. - *Cancer Chemoprevention, Vol. 1*
- SciTech - v28 - i3 - Sept 2004 - p91(1) [51-500]

Kellogg, Steven - *Give the Dog a Bone*
  c PW - v251 - i36 - Sept 6 2004 - p65(1) [51-500]
Millions to Measure
  c TC Math - v11 - i4 - Nov 2004 - p238(1) [501+]
The Three Sillies
  c PW - v251 - i36 - Sept 6 2004 - p65(1) [51-500]
Kellow, Brian - *The Bennetts: An Acting Family*
     Globe & Mail - Dec 18 2004 - pD25 [51-500]
     PW - v251 - i43 - Oct 25 2004 - p35(1) [51-500]
Kelly, A.V. - *The Curriculum: Theory and Practice, 5th Ed.*
     R&R Bk N - v19 - i4 - Nov 2004 - p186(1) [501+]
Kelly, Anthony J. - *Experiencing God in the Gospel of John*
     TT - v61 - i3 - Oct 2004 - p424(2) [501+]
Kelly, Barbara L. - *Tradition and Style in the Works of Darius Milhaud 1912-1939*
     Choice - v41 - i7 - March 2004 - p1306(2) [501+]
     M Ed J - v91 - i4 - March 2005 - p66(1) [501+]
Kelly, Brent P. - *The San Francisco Seals, 1946-1957: Interviews with 25 Former Baseballers*
     SSJ - v21 - i2 - June 2004 - p230-237 [501+]
Kelly, Brian - *Race, Class, and Power in the Alabama Coalfields, 1908-21*
     JAH - v91 - i3 - Dec 2004 - p1066(1) [501+]
Kelly, Brigit Pegeen - *The Orchard*
     NYTBR - August 15 2004 - p19 [501+]
     Ant R - v62 - i4 - Fall 2004 - p775(1) [501+]
Kelly, Cathy - *Best of Friends*
     PW - v251 - i51 - Dec 20 2004 - p36(1) [51-500]
Kelly, Christopher - *Rousseau as Author: Consecrating One's Life to the Truth*
     FS - v58 - i3 - July 2004 - p414-415 [501+]
Kelly, Daniel - *James Burnham and the Struggle for the World: A Life*
     Quad - v48 - i10 - Oct 2004 - p84(3) [501+]
Kelly, Donna Darling - *Uncovering the History of Children's Drawing and Art*
     R&R Bk N - v19 - i2 - May 2004 - p194(1) [51-500]
Kelly, Douglas - *Chretien de Troyes: An Analytical Bibliography*
     Specu - v79 - i3 - July 2004 - p777-778 [501+]
Kelly, Eugene - *The Basics of Western Philosophy*
     LJ - v129 - i13 - August 2004 - p84(1) [501+]
     R&R Bk N - v19 - i3 - August 2004 - p2(1) [1-50]
Kelly, Evelyn B. - *Skeletal System*
     SciTech - v28 - i4 - Dec 2004 - p68(1) [51-500]
Kelly, Franklin - *American Masters from Bingham to Eakins: The John Wilmerding*
     Choice - v42 - i2 - Oct 2004 - p283(1) [501+]
Kelly, Ian - *Cooking for Kings*
     NY - v80 - i25 - Sept 6 2004 - p163(1) [1-50]
Kelly, Irene - *Bloodlines*
     PW - v251 - i51 - Dec 20 2004 - p40(1) [51-500]
Kelly, Jack - *Gunpowder: Alchemy, Bombards, and Pyrotechnics: The History of the Explosive that Changed the World*
     Bwatch - v26 - i9 - Sept 2004 - p1(1) [51-500]
     Choice - v42 - i1 - Sept 2004 - p126(1) [501+]
     HRNB - v33 - i1 - Fall 2004 - p40(1) [501+]
Kelly, James - *Sir Edward Newenham, MP, 1734-1814: Defender of the Protestant Constitution*
     HER - v119 - i483 - Sept 2004 - p1067(2) [501+]
Kelly, Jennifer - *Borrowed Identities*
     Bl S - v34 - i3 - Fall 2004 - p73-73 [501+]
     R&R Bk N - v19 - i1 - Feb 2004 - p123(1) [51-500]
Kelly, Jim - *The Fire Baby*
     BL - v101 - i8 - Dec 15 2004 - p713(1) [51-500]
     KR - v72 - i20 - Oct 15 2004 - p987(1) [51-500]
     LJ - v129 - i20 - Dec 1 2004 - p95(1) [51-500]
     PW - v251 - i43 - Oct 25 2004 - p30(1) [51-500]
Kelly, John (b. 1945 -) - *The Great Mortality: An Intimate History of the Black Death, the Most Devastating Plague of All Time*
     KR - v73 - i1 - Jan 1 2005 - p36(1) [501+]
     LJ - v130 - i3 - Feb 15 2005 - p151(1) [51-500]
     PW - v252 - i3 - Jan 17 2005 - p47(2) [501+]
Kelly, John (b. 1964 -) - *The Mystery of Eatum Hall (Illus. by Kelly, John)*
     c CCB-B - v58 - i2 - Oct 2004 - p82(2) [51-500]
     c HB - v81 - i1 - Jan-Feb 2005 - p80(1) [51-500]
     c KR - v72 - i17 - Sept 1 2004 - p868(1) [51-500]
     c PW - v251 - i38 - Sept 20 2004 - p62(1) [51-500]
The Mystery of Eatum Hall (Illus. by Kelly, John (b. 1964 -))
     c SLJ - v50 - i12 - Dec 2004 - p112(1) [501+]
Kelly, John P. - *A Business & Tax Guide for Antiques & Collectibles*
     R&R Bk N - v19 - i4 - Nov 2004 - p209(1) [501+]
Kelly, John S. - *A W.B. Yeats Chronology*
     Choice - v42 - i2 - Oct 2004 - p267(1) [51-500]

Kelly, Joseph F. - *The Origins of Christmas*
  y LJ - v129 - i18 - Nov 1 2004 - p92(1) [51-500]
Kelly, Katy - *Lucy Rose: Here's the Thing about Me (Illus. by Rex, Adam)*
     c BL - v101 - i5 - Nov 1 2004 - p485(1) [51-500]
     c CCB-B - v58 - i2 - Oct 2004 - p83(1) [51-500]
     c CH Bwatch - v14 - i11 - Nov 2004 - pNA [51-500]
     c KR - v72 - i17 - Sept 1 2004 - p868(1) [51-500]
     c PW - v251 - i38 - Sept 20 2004 - p63(1) [51-500]
     c SLJ - v50 - i9 - Sept 2004 - p170(1) [51-500]
     c USNews & Wrld Rpt - v137 - i12 - Oct 11 2004 - p68 [501+]
Kelly, Kristin A. - *Domestic Violence and The Politics Of Privacy*
     Soc Ser R - v78 - i3 - Sept 2004 - p524(1) [51-500]
Kelly, Larson - *Irish Wit and Wisdom*
     BooChiTr - March 14 2004 - p1(2) [501+]
Kelly, Laurie J. - *Essentials of Human Physiology for Pharmacy*
     SciTech - v28 - i3 - Sept 2004 - p67(1) [51-500]
Kelly, Leisha - *Katie's Dream*
     BL - v101 - i9-10 - Jan 1 2005 - p818(1) [1-50]
Kelly, Linda - *Susanna, the Captain and the Castrato: Scenes from the Burney Salon, 1779-1980*
     TLS - i5296 - Oct 1 2004 - p30(1) [51-500]
Kelly, Linda Armstrong - *No Mountain High Enough: Raising Lance, Raising Me*
     KR - v73 - i2 - Jan 15 2005 - p102(1) [501+]
     LJ - v129 - i20 - Dec 1 2004 - p90(1) [1-50]
     PW - v252 - i7 - Feb 14 2005 - p62(2) [51-500]
Kelly, Louise - *Dictionary of Strategy: Strategic Management A-Z*
     Choice - v42 - i3 - Nov 2004 - p466(1) [1-50]
     R&R Bk N - v19 - i3 - August 2004 - p101(1) [501+]
Kelly, Marjorie - *The Divine Right of Capital: Dethroning the Economic Aristocracy*
     Comw - v131 - i13 - July 16 2004 - p32(2) [501+]
Kelly, Mary - *The Media in Europe*
     Choice - v42 - i2 - Oct 2004 - p266(1) [51-500]
Kelly, Matthew - *The Rhythm of Life: Living Every Day with Passion and Purpose*
     PW - v251 - i41 - Oct 11 2004 - p66(1) [51-500]
Kelly, Michael - *Things Worth Fighting For: Collected Writings*
     Am Spect - v37 - i6 - July-August 2004 - p68(3) [501+]
     Nation - v279 - i11 - Oct 11 2004 - p36 [501+]
Kelly, Patrick (Fashion designer) - *Current Biography International Yearbook, 2003*
  y Ref Rev - July 2004 - pNA [501+]
     R&R Bk N - v19 - i3 - August 2004 - p30(1) [1-50]
Kelly, Richard J. - *The Blickling Homilies*
     CH - v73 - i4 - Dec 2004 - p847(3) [501+]
Kelly, Richard T. - *Sean Penn: His Life and Times*
     KR - v72 - i22 - Nov 15 2004 - p1080(1) [501+]
     NYTBR - Jan 23 2005 - p7 [501+]
     PW - v251 - i40 - Oct 4 2004 - p80(2) [51-500]
Kelly, Robert L. - *Prehistory of the Carson Desert and Stillwater Mountains: Environment, Mobility, and Subsistence in a Great Basin Wetland*
     Am Ant - v69 - i3 - July 2004 - p590(2) [501+]
Kelly, Samantha - *The New Solomon: Robert of Naples (1309-1343) and Fourteenth-Century Kingship*
     Med R - Nov 2004 - pNA [501+]
     Ren Q - v57 - i3 - Fall 2004 - p984(2) [501+]
Kelly, Sarah - *The Complete Mosaic Handbook: Projects, Techniques, Designs*
     BL - v101 - i8 - Dec 15 2004 - p706(1) [51-500]
Kelly, Thomas - *Empire Rising*
     BL - v101 - i8 - Dec 15 2004 - p708(1) [51-500]
     Globe & Mail - Feb 19 2005 - pD15 [501+]
     KR - v72 - i22 - Nov 15 2004 - p1063(1) [501+]
     LJ - v130 - i1 - Jan 1 2005 - p98(1) [51-500]
     NYTBR - Feb 13 2005 - p12 [501+]
     PW - v252 - i3 - Jan 17 2005 - p34(1) [51-500]
     Time - v165 - i13 - March 28 2005 - p64 [501+]
Kelly, Thomas Forrest - *First Nights at the Opera*
     Choice - v42 - i6 - Feb 2005 - p1031(1) [51-500]
     LJ - v129 - i18 - Nov 1 2004 - p87(2) [51-500]
     ON - v69 - i7 - Jan 2005 - p75(1) [501+]
Kelman, Ari - *A River and Its City: The Nature of Landscape in New Orleans*
     Hist Geo - v32 - Annual 2004 - p204(5) [501+]
     JIH - v35 - i1 - Summer 2004 - p151-152 [501+]
     Pub Hist - v26 - i1 - Wntr 2004 - p159(3) [501+]
     T&C - v45 - i2 - April 2004 - p433-434 [501+]

Kelman, James - *You Have to be Careful in the Land of the Free*
     BW - v34 - i28 - July 11 2004 - p15(1) [501+]
     Lon R Bks - v26 - i14 - July 22 2004 - p15(2) [501+]
Kelman, Nic - *Girls: A Paean*
     ABR - v25 - i5 - July-August 2004 - p29(1) [501+]
Kelsey, Elin - *Canadian Dinosaurs*
     c CBRA - Annual 2003 - p567(2) [51-500]
     y SB - v40 - i4 - July-August 2004 - p166(1) [51-500]
     c SLJ - v50 - i7 - July 2004 - p124(1) [51-500]
Kelsey, Harry - *Sir John Hawkins: Queen Elizabeth's Slave Trader*
     Albion - v36 - i2 - Summer 2004 - p292(3) [501+]
     BIC - v33 - i2 - March 2004 - p18(4) [501+]
Kelsey, Paul - *Outreach Services in Academic and Special Libraries*
     LJ - v129 - i16 - Oct 1 2004 - p114(1) [51-500]
Kelsey, Todd - *Sams Teach Yourself iMovie and iDVD in 24 Hours*
     SciTech - v28 - i1 - March 2004 - p176(1) [51-500]
Kelso, Megan - *Scheherazade: Stories of Love, Treachery, Mothers and Monsters*
     PW - v251 - i39 - Sept 27 2004 - p39(1) [51-500]
Kelton, Elmer - *Jericho's Road*
     BL - v101 - i4 - Oct 15 2004 - p390(1) [51-500]
     KR - v72 - i16 - August 15 2004 - p767(1) [501+]
     LJ - v129 - i17 - Oct 15 2004 - p54(1) [51-500]
     PW - v251 - i44 - Nov 1 2004 - p43(1) [501+]
My Kind of Heroes
     Roundup M - v12 - i3 - Feb 2005 - p19(1) [51-500]
Kely, L.A. - *Tahn*
     PW - v252 - i1 - Jan 3 2005 - p37(1) [51-500]
Kemme, Thomas J. - *Patterns of Power in American Political Fiction*
     R&R Bk N - v19 - i1 - Feb 2004 - p243(1) [51-500]
Kemp, Adriana - *Israelis in Conflict: Hegemonies, Identities and Challenges*
     R&R Bk N - v19 - i4 - Nov 2004 - p45(1) [51-500]
Kemp, Daren - *New Age: A Guide: Alternative Spiritualities from Aquarian Conspiracy to Next Age*
     Choice - v42 - i4 - Dec 2004 - p678(1) [1-50]
Kemp, David D. - *Exploring Environmental Issues: An Integrated Approach*
     R&R Bk N - v19 - i3 - August 2004 - p80(1) [51-500]
Kemp, Gene - *Seriously Weird (Read by Coleman, Lisa). Audiobook Review*
     y Kliatt - v39 - i2 - March 2005 - p56(1) [51-500]
Kemp, James W. - *The Gospel According to Dr. Seuss*
     Bks & Cult - v11 - i1 - Jan-Feb 2005 - p16(2) [501+]
Kemp, John R. - *Vanishing Paradise: Duck Hunting in the Louisiana Marsh*
     R&R Bk N - v19 - i4 - Nov 2004 - p246(1) [501+]
Kemp, Kathryn W. - *God's Capitalist: Asa Candler of Coca-Cola*
     BHR - v78 - i2 - Summer 2004 - p295(3) [501+]
Kemp, Kristen - *The Dating Diaries*
     y Kliatt - v38 - i5 - Sept 2004 - p22(2) [51-500]
Kemp, Mark - *Dixie Lullaby: A Story of Music, Race, and New Beginnings in a New South*
     LJ - v129 - i13 - August 2004 - p83(2) [501+]
     BL - v101 - i1 - Sept 1 2004 - p37(1) [501+]
     KR - v72 - i13 - July 1 2004 - p619(1) [501+]
     PW - v251 - i27 - July 5 2004 - p47(1) [51-500]
Kemp, Martin - *Leonardo*
     Art N - v103 - i11 - Dec 2004 - p106(2) [501+]
     BW - v34 - i48 - Nov 28 2004 - p10(1) [501+]
     CR - v286 - i1669 - Feb 2005 - p127(1) [51-500]
     Econ - v373 - i8405 - Dec 11 2004 - p81US [501+]
     Globe & Mail - Jan 8 2005 - pD8 [501+]
     KR - v72 - i18 - Sept 15 2004 - p903(1) [501+]
     LJ - v129 - i17 - Oct 15 2004 - p60(1) [51-500]
     Nature - v432 - i7014 - Nov 11 2004 - p151(1) [501+]
     NS - v133 - i4708 - Oct 4 2004 - p50(2) [501+]
     Spec - v296 - i9200 - Dec 4 2004 - p38(1) [501+]
     TimHES - v0 - i1667 - Nov 19 2004 - p26(2) [501+]
     TLS - i5300 - Oct 29 2004 - p4-6 [501+]
Visualizations: The Nature Book of Art and Science
     Isis - v95 - i2 - June 2004 - p277(3) [501+]
Kemp, Paul - *Goodbye Canada?*
     CBRA - Annual 2003 - p329(1) [501+]

Kemp, Sid - *Business Statistics Demystified*
Bwatch - Nov 2004 - pNA [501+]
Kemple, Kristen Mary - *Let's Be Friends: Peer Competence and Social Inclusion in Early Childhood Programs*
Choice - v42 - i2 - Oct 2004 - p344(1) [51-500]
TCR - v106 - i5 - May 2004 - p922(4) [501+]
Kempler, Daniel - *Neurocognitive Disorders in Aging*
SciTech - v28 - i4 - Dec 2004 - p100(1) [51-500]
Kendall, Diana - *Sociology in Our Times, 4th Ed.*
R&R Bk N - v19 - i2 - May 2004 - p126 [51-500]
Kendall, Lauren - *Under Construction: The Gendering of Modernity, Class, and Consumption in the Republic of Korea*
JWH - v16 - i3 - Autumn 2004 - p197(9) [501+]
Kendall, Lisa See - *Dragon Bones (Read by Ross, Liza).* Audiobook Review
y Kliatt - v39 - i2 - March 2005 - p52(1) [51-500]
Kendall, Lori - *Hanging Out in the Virtual Pub: Masculinities and Relationships Online*
CS - v33 - i1 - Jan 2004 - p31-32 [501+]
Kendall, Roy - *Christopher Marlowe and Richard Baines: Journeys through the Elizabethan Underground*
Lon R Bks - v26 - i16 - August 19 2004 - p11(4) [501+]
Kendall-Tackett, Kathleen A. - *Health Consequences of Abuse in the Family: A Clinical Guide for Evidence-Based Practice*
SciTech - v28 - i1 - March 2004 - p119(1) [51-500]
Kendrick, J. Richard - *Social Statistics: An Introduction Using SPSS for Windows, 2nd Ed.*
R&R Bk N - v19 - i3 - August 2004 - p91(1) [51-500]
Kendrick, John - *Alejandro Malaspina: Portrait of a Visionary*
R&R Bk N - v19 - i1 - Feb 2004 - p40(1) [1-50]
Kendrick, Maureen - *Converging Worlds: Play, Literacy, and Culture in Early Childhood*
R&R Bk N - v19 - i1 - Feb 2004 - p183(1) [51-500]
Kendrick, Stephen - *Sarah's Long Walk: The Free Blacks of Boston and How Their Struggle for Equality Changed America*
BL - v101 - i8 - Dec 15 2004 - p694(1) [51-500]
KR - v72 - i23 - Dec 1 2004 - p1134(1) [501+]
PW - v251 - i46 - Nov 15 2004 - p47(1) [51-500]
Kendrick, T.D. - *A History of the Vikings*
R&R Bk N - v19 - i3 - August 2004 - p46(1) [51-500]
Keneally, Thomas - *The Tyrant's Novel*
BW - v34 - i27 - July 4 2004 - p5(1) [501+]
LJ - v129 - i13 - August 2004 - p68(1) [51-500]
NL - v87 - i4 - July-August 2004 - p31(2) [501+]
NYTBR - July 18 2004 - p11 [501+]
NYTBR - July 25 2004 - p18 [501+]
NYTBR - August 1 2004 - p14 [501+]
Kenelly, Brendan - *Positive Strangers: New and Selected Poems 1960-2004*
y Sch Lib - v52 - i3 - Autumn 2004 - p166(1) [501+]
Kengor, Paul - *God and Ronald Reagan: A Spiritual Life*
J Ch St - v46 - i3 - Summer 2004 - p670(2) [501+]
Kenkyukai, Ayumi - *Zusetsu kodomo no hon honyaku no ayumi jiten*
c Bkbird - v42 - i3 - July 2004 - p48(1) [501+]
Kenmotsu, Katsuei - *Surfaces with Constant Mean Curvature*
SciTech - v28 - i1 - March 2004 - p42(1) [51-500]
Kennard, Mark - *Freshwater Fishes of North-Eastern Australia*
Choice - v42 - i7 - March 2005 - p1254(1) [51-500]
Kenneally, James J. - *A Compassionate Conservative: A Political Biography of Joseph W. Martin, Jr., Speaker of the U.S. House of Representatives*
R&R Bk N - v19 - i1 - Feb 2004 - p61(1) [501+]
Kennedy, A.L. - *Indelible Acts: Stories*
NYTBR - August 22 2004 - p20 [501+]
Paradise
BL - v101 - i8 - Dec 15 2004 - p690(2) [51-500]
Globe & Mail - Oct 23 2004 - pD10 [501+]
Globe & Mail - Dec 24 2004 - pD3 [1-50]
KR - v73 - i1 - Jan 1 2005 - p11(1) [501+]
LJ - v130 - i2 - Feb 1 2005 - p68(1) [51-500]
Lon R Bks - v26 - i19 - Oct 7 2004 - p26(1) [501+]
NS - v133 - i4705 - Sept 13 2004 - p55(1) [501+]
PW - v252 - i8 - Feb 21 2005 - p157(1) [51-500]
Spec - v296 - i9188 - Sept 11 2004 - p46(1) [501+]
TLS - i5291 - August 27 2004 - p19(1) [501+]
Ent W - i811 - March 18 2005 - p75 [51-500]

Kennedy, Cecilia - *The Robbie Burns Revival*
Globe & Mail - July 24 2004 - pD4 [501+]
Kennedy, Craig H. - *Including Students with Severe Disabilities*
R&R Bk N - v19 - i1 - Feb 2004 - p192(1) [51-500]
Kennedy, David (1954-) - *The Dark Sides of Virtue: Reassessing International Humanitarianism*
Choice - v42 - i4 - Dec 2004 - p733(1) [1-50]
HLR - v118 - i3 - Jan 2005 - p1031-1038 [501+]
Law&PolBR - Oct 2004 - pNA [501+]
Pers PS - v33 - i4 - Fall 2004 - p243(1) [501+]
TimHES - v0 - i1671 - Dec 17 2004 - p22(2) [501+]
Freedom from Fear: The American People In Depression and War, 1929-1945
Bks & Cult - v10 - i6 - Nov-Dec 2004 - p24(3) [501+]
Kennedy, David M. - *Over Here: The First World War and American Society*
LJ - v129 - i20 - Dec 1 2004 - p184(1) [51-500]
Kennedy-Day, Kiki - *Books of Definition in Islamic Philosophy: The Limits of Works*
IJMES - v36 - i4 - Nov 2004 - p686(2) [501+]
Kennedy, Dennis - *The Oxford Encyclopedia of Theatre and Performance*
TDR - v48 - i3 - Fall 2004 - p194(3) [501+]
Kennedy, Dorothy M. - *I Thought I'd Take My Rat to School: Poems for September to June (Illus. by Carter, Abby)*
c SLJ - v50 - i7 - July 2004 - p45(1) [51-500]
Kennedy, Duncan - *Legal Education and the Reproduction of Hierarchy: A Polemic Against the System*
HLR - v118 - i3 - Jan 2005 - p1096-1097 [1-50]
Law&PolBR - August 2004 - p667(6) [501+]
Kennedy, Duncan F. - *Rethinking Reality: Lucretius and the Textualization of Nature*
Class R - v53 - i2 - Nov 2003 - p352-354 [501+]
Kennedy, Erica - *Bling*
LJ - v129 - i12 - July 2004 - p71(1) [51-500]
NYTBR - July 11 2004 - p26 [501+]
Kennedy, Frances - *The Pickle Patch Bathtub (Illus. by Aldridge, Sheila)*
c SLJ - v50 - i10 - Oct 2004 - p120(1) [51-500]
Kennedy, Gerry - *The Voynich Manuscript*
Apo - v159 - i510 - August 2004 - p80(1) [501+]
TimHES - v0 - i1658 - Sept 17 2004 - p25(1) [501+]
TLS - i5303 - Nov 19 2004 - p31(1) [501+]
Kennedy, Graeme D. - *Structure and Meaning in English: A Guide for Teachers*
TimHES - v0 - i1668 - Nov 26 2004 - pX(2) [501+]
Kennedy, Hugh - *The Court of the Caliphs: The Rise and Fall of Islam's Greatest Dynasty*
TLS - i5306 - Dec 10 2004 - p24(1) [501+]
Kennedy, Mary M. - *Inside Teaching: How Classroom Life Undermines Reform*
LJ - v130 - i4 - March 1 2005 - p97(1) [51-500]
Kennedy, Matthew - *Edmund Goulding's Dark Victory: Hollywood's Genius Bad Boy*
R&R Bk N - v19 - i3 - August 2004 - p263(1) [51-500]
Kennedy, Michael - *A Brief History of Disease, Science and Medicine: From the Ice Age to the Genome Project*
Choice - v42 - i1 - Sept 2004 - p138(1) [501+]
Kennedy, Michael (b. 1926 -) - *The Life of Elgar*
MT - v145 - i1887 - Summer 2004 - p105(3) [501+]
Kennedy, Michael (b. 1938 -) - *A Brief History of Disease, Science and Medicine: From the Ice Age to the Genome Project*
SciTech - v28 - i1 - March 2004 - p77(1) [51-500]
Kennedy, Michael D. - *Cultural Formations of Postcommunism: Emancipation, Transition, Nation, and War*
CS - v33 - i2 - March 2004 - p219-220 [501+]
Kennedy, Michael P.J. - *Words on Ice: A Collection of Hockey Prose*
CBRA - Annual 2003 - p251(1) [501+]
Kennedy, Michelle - *Without a Net: Middle Class and Homeless (with Kids) in America: My Story*
BL - v101 - i9-10 - Jan 1 2005 - p790(1) [1-50]
Ent W - i808 - Feb 25 2005 - p107 [51-500]
KR - v72 - i24 - Dec 15 2004 - p1183(1) [501+]
NYTBR - Feb 27 2005 - p19 [501+]
PW - v251 - i42 - Oct 18 2004 - p54(1) [51-500]
Kennedy, Paul D. - *Doing Business with Kuwait, 2nd Ed.*
R&R Bk N - v19 - i4 - Nov 2004 - p109(1) [51-500]
Kennedy, Peter - *A Guide to Econometrics*
JEL - v41 - i4 - Dec 2003 - p1334(1) [501+]

Kennedy, Robert Francis - *Saint Francis of Assisi: A Life of Joy (Illus. by Nolan, Dennis)*
c KR - v73 - i4 - Feb 15 2005 - p230(1) [51-500]
c PW - v252 - i9 - Feb 28 2005 - p69(1) [51-500]
Kennedy, Roger G. - *Mr. Jefferson's Lost Cause: Land, Farmers, Slavery, and the Louisiana Purchase*
W&M Q - v61 - i3 - July 2004 - p588-592 [501+]
Kennedy, Terry - *Fix It Before It Breaks: Seasonal Checklist Guide to Home Maintenance*
LJ - v129 - i14 - Sept 1 2004 - p178(1) [51-500]
Kennedy, William J. - *The Site of Petrarchism: Early Modern National Sentiment in Italy, France, and England*
Ren Q - v57 - i4 - Winter 2004 - p1352(2) [501+]
R&R Bk N - v19 - i1 - Feb 2004 - p232(1) [51-500]
Kennedy, X.J. - *Handbook of Literary Terms: Literature, Language, Theory*
R&R Bk N - v19 - i4 - Nov 2004 - p220(1) [51-500]
The Longman Dictionary of Literary Terms
LJ - v130 - i2 - Feb 1 2005 - p116(2) [51-500]
The Kennedy Years
c SLJ - v51 - i2 - Feb 2005 - p86(1) [51-500]
Kennell, S.A.H. (b. 1950 -) - *Magnus Felix Ennodius: A Gentleman of the Church*
Class R - v53 - i2 - Nov 2003 - p391-394 [501+]
Kennett, David - *A New View of Comparative Economic Systems, 2nd Ed.*
R&R Bk N - v19 - i1 - Feb 2004 - p78(1) [1-50]
Kenney, Charles D. - *Fujimori's Coup and the Breakdown of Democracy in Latin America*
Choice - v42 - i2 - Oct 2004 - p365(1) [51-500]
Kenney, Martin - *Locating Global Advantage: Industry Dynamics in the International Economy*
R&R Bk N - v19 - i2 - May 2004 - p112(1) [51-500]
Kenney, Matthew T. - *A Theoretical Examination of Political Values and Attitudes in New and Old Democracies*
R&R Bk N - v19 - i1 - Feb 2004 - p147(1) [51-500]
Kennington, Richard - *On Modern Origins: Essays in Early Modern Philosophy*
R&R Bk N - v19 - i4 - Nov 2004 - p3(1) [51-500]
Kennish, Michael J. - *Estuarine Research, Monitoring, and Resource Protection*
SciTech - v28 - i1 - March 2004 - p60(1) [51-500]
Kennon, Donald R. - *American Pantheon: Sculptural and Artistic Decoration of the United States Capitol*
R&R Bk N - v19 - i4 - Nov 2004 - p204(1) [501+]
Kenny, Anthony - *The Unknown God: Agnostic Essays*
TLS - i5284 - July 9 2004 - p24(1) [501+]
Kenny, Anthony John Patrick - *Aquinas on Being*
JR - v84 - i4 - Oct 2004 - p634(3) [501+]
New History of Western Philosophy, Vol. 1
Lon R Bks - v27 - i4 - Feb 17 2005 - p31(2) [501+]
A New History of Western Philosophy, Vol. I
CR - v286 - i1668 - Jan 2005 - p58(1) [51-500]
Kenny, Mary - *Germany Calling: A Personal Biography of William Joyce, Lord Haw-Haw*
Lon R Bks - v26 - i13 - July 8 2004 - p22(3) [501+]
TLS - i5285 - July 16 2004 - p10(1) [501+]
Kenrick, Paul - *Fossil Plants*
New Sci - v185 - i2484 - Jan 29 2005 - p51(1) [501+]
Kenry, Chris - *Confessions of Casanova*
BL - v101 - i2 - Sept 15 2004 - p220(1) [51-500]
Kensett, Robert C. - *Walk in the Valley*
CBRA - Annual 2003 - p52(1) [51-500]
Kent, Alison - *The Bane Affair*
BL - v101 - i1 - Sept 1 2004 - p72(1) [51-500]
The McKenzie Artifact
BL - v101 - i9-10 - Jan 1 2005 - p830(1) [1-50]
The Shaughnessey Accord
BL - v101 - i3 - Oct 1 2004 - p316(1) [51-500]
Kent, Carol - *When I Lay My Isaac Down: Unshakable Faith in Unthinkable Circumstances*
Ch Today - v48 - i8 - August 2004 - p57(3) [501+]
Ch Today - v48 - i8 - August 2004 - p58(1) [51-500]
Kent, Deborah - *American Sign Language*
c CH Bwatch - Oct 2004 - pNA [51-500]
Dorothy Day: Friend to the Forgotten
c Kliatt - v38 - i6 - Nov 2004 - p33(1) [51-500]
The Freedom Riders
c SLJ - v50 - i10 - Oct 2004 - p66(1) [51-500]
Mario Molina: Chemist and Nobel Prize Winner
c SLJ - v50 - i10 - Oct 2004 - p144(1) [51-500]
Snake Pits, Talking Cures, and Magic Bullets: A History of Mental Illness
c Sci Teach - v71 - i4 - April 2004 - p72-73 [501+]

Kent, Eliza F. - *Converting Women: Gender and Protestant Christianity in Colonial South India*
Choice - v42 - i4 - Dec 2004 - p678(1) [1-50]

Kent, Gordon - *Force Protection*
BL - v101 - i1 - Sept 1 2004 - p62(1) [501+]
KR - v72 - i15 - August 1 2004 - p706(1) [51-500]

Kent, Jacqueline C. - *Business Builders in Cosmetics*
y SLJ - v50 - i9 - Sept 2004 - p228(1) [51-500]

Kent, Kathryn R. - *Making Girls into Women: American Women's Writing and the Rise of Lesbian Identity*
Am Q - v56 - i4 - Dec 2004 - p1099(7) [501+]

Kent, Margaret - *How to Marry the Man of Your Choice*
LJ - v130 - i1 - Jan 1 2005 - p134(2) [501+]

Kent, Martha - *Eine Porzellanscherbe im Graben: Eine deutsche Fluechtlingskindheit*
HNet - Oct 2004 - pNA [501+]

Kent, Neil - *Helsinki: A Cultural and Literary History*
LJ - v129 - i19 - Nov 15 2004 - p78(1) [501+]
R&R Bk N - v19 - i4 - Nov 2004 - p42(1) [51-500]

Kent, Raymond D. - *MIT Encyclopedia of Communication Disorders*
E-Streams - Sept 2004 - pNA [501+]

Kent, Richard - *Air Bag Development and Performance: New Perspectives from Industry, Government and Academia*
SciTech - v28 - i1 - March 2004 - p167(1) [51-500]

Kent, Thomas De - *Le Roman d'Alexandre: ou, Le Roman de Toute Chevalerie*
FS - v58 - i3 - July 2004 - p394-394 [501+]

Kent, Timothy J. - *Ft. Pontchartrain at Detroit: A Guide to the Daily Lives of Fur Trade and Military Personnel, Settlers, and Missionaries at French Posts*
Can Hist R - v85 - i4 - Dec 2004 - p813(2) [501+]

Kent, Zachary - *James Madison: Creating a Nation*
c LibMed - v23 - i3 - Nov-Dec 2004 - p78(1) [51-500]

Kenway, Jane - *Innovation and Tradition: The Arts, Humanities, and the Knowledge Economy*
R&R Bk N - v19 - i3 - August 2004 - p2(1) [1-50]

Kenyon, Sherrilyn - *Night Play*
BL - v100 - i22 - August 2004 - p1909(1) [51-500]
PW - v251 - i29 - July 19 2004 - p150(1) [51-500]
Seize the Night
PW - v251 - i51 - Dec 20 2004 - p42(1) [51-500]
BL - v101 - i9-10 - Jan 1 2005 - p831(1) [1-50]

Keogh, Barbara K. - *Temperament in the Classroom: Understanding Individual Differences*
HER - v74 - i2 - Summer 2004 - p224-225 [501+]

Keogh, Pamela Clarke - *Elvis Presley the Man, The Life, the Legend*
People - v62 - i2 - July 12 2004 - p45 [51-500]

Kepcher, Carolyn - *Carolyn 101: Business Lessons from The Apprentice's Straight Shooter*
PW - v251 - i42 - Oct 18 2004 - p60(1) [51-500]

Kepel, Gilles - *Bad Moon Rising: A Chronicle of Middle East Today*
A Aff - v35 - i2 - July 2004 - p209-210 [501+]
Jihad: The Trail of Political Islam
Dis - v50 - i1 - Winter 2003 - p89 [501+]
IJMES - v36 - i3 - August 2004 - p512-514 [501+]
The War for Muslim Minds: Islam and the West
Econ - v373 - i8397 - Oct 16 2004 - p80US [501+]
For Aff - v84 - i1 - Jan-Feb 2005 - p148 [501+]
Globe & Mail - Nov 20 2004 - pD16 [501+]
NYTBR - Feb 6 2005 - p28 [501+]
TimHES - v0 - i1684 - March 25 2005 - p24(2) [501+]

Kephart, Beth - *Ghosts in the Garden: Reflections on Endings, Beginnings, and the Unearthing of Self*
PW - v252 - i3 - Jan 17 2005 - p43(1) [51-500]
Seeing Past Z: Nurturing the Imagination in a Fast-Forward World
R&R Bk N - v19 - i4 - Nov 2004 - p180(1) [501+]

Kepler, Johannes - *Optics: Paralipomena to Witelo and Optical Part of Astronomy*
Isis - v95 - i2 - June 2004 - p296(2) [501+]

Kepnes, Caroline - *Stephen Crane*
y SLJ - v51 - i1 - Jan 2005 - p140(1) [51-500]

Keptron, Wayne - *Cystic Fibrosis: Everything You Need to Know*
E-Streams - August 2004 - pNA [501+]

Ker, I.T. - *The Catholic Revival in English Literature, 1845-1961*
Quad - v48 - i9 - Sept 2004 - p90(1) [501+]
The Catholic Revival in English Literature, 1845-1961: Newman, Hopkins, Belloc, Chesterton, Greene, Waugh
Sew R - v112 - i2 - Spring 2004 - pLIX-LXII [501+]
TLS - i5268 - March 19 2004 - p22-22 [501+]

Kerber, Linda K. - *No Constitutional Right to Be Ladies: Women and the Obligations of Citizenship*
Signs - v30 - i2 - Wntr 2005 - p1659(12) [501+]

Keren, Michael - *The Citizen's Voice: Twentieth-Century Politics and Literature*
Choice - v41 - i11-12 - July-August 2004 - p2039(1) [501+]
International Intervention: Sovereignty Versus Responsibility
AJPS - v39 - i2 - July 2004 - p430(430) [501+]

Keret, Etgar - *Dad Runs Away with the Circus (Illus. by Modan, Rutu)*
c CCB-B - v58 - i3 - Nov 2004 - p129(1) [501+]
SLJ - v50 - i12 - Dec 2004 - p112(1) [501+]
Gaza Blues: Different Stories
TLS - i5285 - July 16 2004 - p22(1) [501+]

Kerievsky, Joshua - *Refactoring to Patterns*
SciTech - v28 - i4 - Dec 2004 - p27(1) [51-500]

Kerisel, Francoise - *Diogenes' Lantern (Illus. by Mansot, Frederick)*
c SLJ - v50 - i9 - Sept 2004 - p160(1) [51-500]

Kerkering, John D. - *The Poetics of National and Racial Identity in Nineteenth-Century American Literature*
Choice - v42 - i1 - Sept 2004 - p101(1) [501+]

Kerkvliet, Melinda Tria - *Unbending Cane: Pablo Manlapit, a Filipino Labor Leader in Hawai'i*
Pac A - v77 - i3 - Fall 2004 - p612(2) [501+]

Kerley, Barbara - *Walt Whitman: Words for America (Illus. by Selznick, Brian)*
c BL - v101 - i6 - Nov 15 2004 - p575(1) [51-500]
c CCB-B - v58 - i6 - Feb 2005 - p255(1) [51-500]
c HB - v80 - i6 - Nov-Dec 2004 - p729(2) [501+]
KR - v72 - i18 - Sept 15 2004 - p915(1) [501+]
c NYTBR - Nov 14 2004 - p36(L) [501+]
c PW - v251 - i42 - Oct 18 2004 - p64(1) [51-500]
y SLJ - v50 - i11 - Nov 2004 - p166(1) [51-500]

Kerley, Jack - *The Hundredth Man (Read by Hill, Dick). Audiobook Review*
y Kliatt - v39 - i1 - Jan 2005 - p44(1) [51-500]
LJ - v130 - i1 - Jan 1 2005 - p168(1) [51-500]

Kerlogue, Fiona - *Arts of Southeast Asia*
Choice - v42 - i7 - March 2005 - p1215(1) [51-500]
Batik: Design, Style and History
Bwatch - Jan 2005 - pNA [51-500]

Kerman, Phillip - *Macromedia Flash MX 2004 for Rich Internet Applications*
SciTech - v28 - i1 - March 2004 - p175(1) [51-500]

Kermani, Navid - *Offenbarung als Kommunikation: Das konzept wahy in Nasr Hamid Abu Zayds Mafhum an-nass*
IJMES - v36 - i4 - Nov 2004 - p684(2) [501+]

Kermel-Torres, Doryane - *Atlas of Thailand: Spatial Structures and Development*
Choice - v42 - i5 - Jan 2005 - p834(1) [1-50]
LJ - v129 - i16 - Oct 1 2004 - p112(1) [51-500]

Kermode, Frank - *The Age of Shakespeare*
y BooChiTr - Feb 1 2004 - p4(1) [501+]
CR - v286 - i1668 - Jan 2005 - p49(2) [501+]
y NS - v133 - i4695 - July 5 2004 - p53(1) [501+]
y SLJ - v50 - i10 - Oct 2004 - pS67(1) [51-500]
y TimHES - v0 - i1666 - Nov 12 2004 - p32(1) [501+]
Pieces of My Mind: Essays and Criticisms, 1958-2002
ELT - v47 - i3 - Summer 2004 - p355(3) [501+]
NYTBR - Oct 10 2004 - p26 [501+]

Kern, Gary - *A Death in Washington: Walter G. Krivitsky and the Stalin Terror*
Choice - v41 - i7 - March 2004 - p1346(1) [501+]

Kern, Morton J. - *Interventional Cardiac Catheterization Handbook. 2nd Ed.*
SciTech - v28 - i1 - March 2004 - p104(1) [51-500]

Kern, Stephen - *A Cultural History of Causality: Science, Murder Novels, and Systems of Thought*
Choice - v42 - i6 - Feb 2005 - p1018(1) [51-500]
Globe & Mail - Nov 13 2004 - pD16 [501+]
New Sci - v184 - i2476 - Dec 4 2004 - p57(1) [501+]
Sci - v306 - i5705 - Dec 24 2004 - p2193(2) [501+]

Kern, Tom - *The Tennis Book: A Young Player's Guide to Tennis*
c Globe & Mail - July 3 2004 - pD11 [501+]
c Res Links - v10 - i1 - Oct 2004 - p38(1) [51-500]

Kernaghan, Eileen - *The Alchemist's Daughter*
y Res Links - v10 - i3 - Feb 2005 - p36(1) [501+]

Kernberg, Otto F. - *Aggressivity, Narcissism, and Self-Destructiveness in the Psychotherapeutic Relationship: New Developments in the Psychopathology and Psychotherapy of Severe Personality Disorders*
Adoles - v39 - i156 - Winter 2004 - p834(1) [51-500]

Kernell, Samuel - *James Madison: The Theory and Practice of Republican Government*
Choice - v41 - i7 - March 2004 - p1370(1) [501+]

Kerner, Elizabeth - *Redeeming the Lost*
BL - v100 - i21 - July 2004 - p1828(1) [1-50]

Kerner, Ian - *Be Honest: You're Not That into Him Either*
People - v63 - i6 - Feb 14 2005 - p62 [1-50]

Kernick, David - *Complexity and Healthcare Organization: A View from the Street*
SciTech - v28 - i3 - Sept 2004 - p86(1) [501+]
SciTech - v28 - i3 - Sept 2004 - p86(1) [51-500]

Kernodle, Tammy L. - *Soul on Soul: The Life and Music of Mary Lou Williams*
Black Iss - v6 - i4 - July-August 2004 - p35(1) [501+]
Bwatch - v26 - i9 - Sept 2004 - p9(1) [51-500]
Choice - v42 - i2 - Oct 2004 - p302(1) [51-500]

Kerns, David V. - *Essentials of Electrical and Computer Engineering*
SciTech - v28 - i3 - Sept 2004 - p151(1) [51-500]

Kerns, Virginia - *Scenes from the High Desert: Julian Steward's Life and Theory*
Choice - v41 - i7 - March 2004 - p1336(2) [501+]
JRAI - v10 - i3 - Sept 2004 - p728(1) [501+]
WHQ - v35 - i4 - Winter 2004 - p924-925 [501+]

Kerouac, Jack - *Departed Angels: The Lost Paintings*
LJ - v130 - i1 - Jan 1 2005 - p108(1) [51-500]
Windblown World: The Journals of Jack Kerouac, 1947-1954
y BL - v101 - i4 - Oct 15 2004 - p378(1) [51-500]
Choice - v42 - i7 - March 2005 - p1229(1) [51-500]
y KR - v72 - i16 - August 15 2004 - p790(1) [501+]
NYTBR - Oct 10 2004 - p6 [501+]
PW - v251 - i33 - August 16 2004 - p52(2) [51-500]
Time - v164 - i16 - Oct 18 2004 - p88 [501+]

Kerr, Anne - *Genetics and Society: A Sociology of Disease*
SciTech - v28 - i4 - Dec 2004 - p88(1) [51-500]

Kerr, Fergus - *After Aquinas: Versions of Thomism*
JR - v84 - i3 - July 2004 - p481(2) [501+]

Kerr, Ian J. - *Railways in Modern India*
T&C - v45 - i1 - Jan 2004 - p180(2) [501+]

Kerr, M.E. - *Snakes Don't Miss Their Mothers*
c BooChiTr - Jan 11 2004 - p5(1) [501+]

Kerr, P.B. - *The Akhenaten Adventure*
c BL - v101 - i2 - Sept 15 2004 - p233(1) [51-500]
c CCB-B - v58 - i5 - Jan 2005 - p214(1) [51-500]
c Globe & Mail - Dec 11 2004 - pD39 [501+]
c HB - v81 - i1 - Jan-Feb 2005 - p95(1) [51-500]
c KR - v72 - i19 - Oct 1 2004 - p963(1) [51-500]
c SLJ - v50 - i12 - Dec 2004 - p149(1) [51-500]
The Akhenaten
c PW - v251 - i40 - Oct 4 2004 - p88(1) [51-500]

Kerr, Peter - *Viva Mallorca!: One Mallorcan Autumn*
KR - v73 - i4 - Feb 15 2005 - p213(1) [51-500]

Kerret, Etgar - *Dad Runs Away with the Circus (Illus. by Modan, Rutu)*
c KR - v72 - i17 - Sept 1 2004 - p868(1) [51-500]
c PW - v251 - i43 - Oct 25 2004 - p47(1) [51-500]

Kerridge, Roy - *From Blues to Rap*
Spec - v296 - i9196 - Nov 6 2004 - p62(2) [501+]

Kerrin, Jessica Scott - *Martin Bridge: Ready for Takeoff! (Illus. by Kelly, Joseph)*
c KR - v73 - i4 - Feb 15 2005 - p230(1) [51-500]

Kerrod, Robin - *Hubble: The Mirror on the Universe*
CBRA - Annual 2003 - p425(1) [51-500]
SB - v40 - i6 - Nov-Dec 2004 - p245(1) [51-500]
The Way the Universe Works
c RT - v57 - Oct 2003 - p178 [1-50]

Kerry, Richard J. - *Star-Spangled Mirror: A Father's Legacy Shapes John Kerry's Worldview*
R&R Bk N - v19 - i4 - Nov 2004 - p63(1) [51-500]

Kersey, Harry A., Jr. - *The Stranahans of Fort Lauderdale: A Pioneer Family of New River*
JSH - v71 - i1 - Feb 2005 - p190(2) [501+]

Kersh, Rogan - *Dreams of a More Perfect Union*
W&M Q - v61 - i3 - July 2004 - p582-588 [501+]

Killam, Edward W. - *The Detection of Human Remains, 2nd Ed.*
SciTech - v28 - i4 - Dec 2004 - p7(1) [1-50]

Killebrew, Tom - *The Royal Air Force in Texas: Training British Pilots in Terrell During World War II*
APH - v51 - i3 - Fall 2004 - p52(1) [501+]
R&R Bk N - v19 - i1 - Feb 2004 - p256(1) [51-500]
SHQ - v108 - i1 - July 2004 - p124-125 [501+]

Killeen, Anthony A. - *Principles of Molecular Pathology*
SciTech - v28 - i1 - March 2004 - p86(1) [51-500]

Killen, Patricia O'Connell - *Religion and Public Life in the Pacific Northwest: The None Zone*
R&R Bk N - v19 - i3 - August 2004 - p15(1) [1-50]

Killham, Nina - *Mounting Desire*
KR - v73 - i5 - March 1 2005 - p250(2) [501+]

Killius, Rosemarie - *Frauen fur die Front: Gesprdche mit Wehrmachtshelferinnen*
HNet - July 2004 - pNA [501+]

Killy, Walther - *Dictionary of German Biography, Vols. 1-5*
GSR - v27 - i3 - Oct 2004 - p599(2) [501+]

Kilpatrick, Jacquelyn - *Louis Owens: Literary Reflections on His Life and Work*
JouAmCul - v27 - i4 - Dec 2004 - p450(1) [51-500]

Kilpatrick, Nancy - *The Goth Bible: A Compendium for the Darkly Inclined*
y BL - v101 - i4 - Oct 15 2004 - p368(1) [51-500]

Kilpatrick, Scott E. - *Diagnostic Musculoskeletal Surgical Pathology: Clinicradiologic and Cytologic Correlations*
SciTech - v28 - i1 - March 2004 - p107(1) [51-500]

Kilroy, David P. - *For Race and Country: The Life and Career of Colonel Charles Young*
R&R Bk N - v19 - i1 - Feb 2004 - p254(1) [51-500]

Kilworth, Garry - *The Winter Soldiers (Read by Wale, Terry). Audiobook Review*
y Kliatt - v39 - i1 - Jan 2005 - p51(1) [51-500]

Kim, Cherng-ju - *Advanced Pharmaceutics: Physiochemical Principles*
SciTech - v28 - i3 - Sept 2004 - p125(1) [51-500]

Kim, Chongho - *Korean Shamanism: The Cultural Paradox*
J Ch St - v46 - i4 - Autumn 2004 - p891(3) [501+]
R&R Bk N - v19 - i1 - Feb 2004 - p13(1) [51-500]

Kim, Dong-One - *Employment Relations and the HRM in South Korea*
R&R Bk N - v19 - i3 - August 2004 - p118(1) [51-500]

Kim, Elizabeth - *Ten Thousand Sorrows: The Extraordinary Journey of a Korean War Orphan*
Can Lit - i181 - Summer 2004 - p147-148 [501+]

Kim, Ho-dong - *Holy War in China: The Muslim Rebellion and State in Chinese Central Asia, 1864-1877*
TLS - i5306 - Dec 10 2004 - p30-31 [501+]

Kim, Ho Sik - *My Sassy Girl: Vol. 4*
PW - v251 - i32 - August 9 2004 - p234(1) [51-500]

Kim, Hodong - *Holy War in China: The Muslim Rebellion and State in Chinese Central Asia, 1864-1877*
Choice - v42 - i3 - Nov 2004 - p541(1) [1-50]
R&R Bk N - v19 - i3 - August 2004 - p57(1) [51-500]

Kim, Hyun Chul Paul - *Ambiguity, Tension, and Multiplicity in Deutero-Isaiah*
R&R Bk N - v19 - i1 - Feb 2004 - p20(1) [51-500]

Kim, Karen E. - *Acute Gastrointestinal Bleeding: Diagnosis and Treatment*
E-Streams - Sept 2004 - pNA [501+]

Kim, Kyung Hyun - *The Remasculinization of Korean Cinema*
Choice - v42 - i2 - Oct 2004 - p301(1) [51-500]

Kim, Mi Gyung - *Affinity, That Elusive Dream: A Genealogy of the Chemical Revolution*
Choice - v41 - i7 - March 2004 - p1317(2) [501+]
T&C - v45 - i3 - July 2004 - p645-647 [501+]

Kim-Renaud, Young-Key - *Creative Women of Korea: The Fifteenth through the Twentieth Centuries*
JAS - v63 - i3 - August 2004 - p814-817 [501+]
Creative Women of Korea: The Fifteenth through the Twentieth Century
R&R Bk N - v19 - i1 - Feb 2004 - p219(1) [51-500]

Kim, Samuel S. - *The International Relations of Northeast Asia*
R&R Bk N - v19 - i1 - Feb 2004 - p47(1) [51-500]

Kim, Soonsik - *Colonial and Postcolonial Discourse in the Novels of Yom Sang-Sop, Chinua Achebe, and Salman Rushdie*
R&R Bk N - v19 - i4 - Nov 2004 - p222(1) [501+]

Kim, Sue Kwock - *Notes from a Divided Country*
Ga R - v58 - i1 - Spring 2004 - p198-199 [501+]

Kim, Sun Pyo - *Maritime Delimitation and Interim Arrangements in North East Asia*
R&R Bk N - v19 - i3 - August 2004 - p212(1) [1-50]

Kim, Sung Ho - *Max Weber's Politics of Civil Society*
Pers PS - v34 - i1 - Wntr 2005 - p60(2) [501+]

Kim, Young-Won - *Gamma Titanium Aluminides 2003: Proceedings*
SciTech - v28 - i3 - Sept 2004 - p52(1) [1-50]

Kim, Yung-Hee - *Readings in Modern Korean Literature*
R&R Bk N - v19 - i3 - August 2004 - p256(1) [1-50]

Kim, Yuonkyoo - *The Resource Curse in a Post-Communist Regime: Russia in Comparative Prespective*
JEL - v41 - i4 - Dec 2003 - p1428(1) [501+]

Kimball, Anne S. - *Lettres de Marcel Jouhandeau a Max Jacob*
FS - v58 - i1 - Jan 2004 - p135(2) [501+]

Kimball, Bob - *Selling in the New World of Business*
Choice - v42 - i5 - Jan 2005 - p899(2) [1-50]
R&R Bk N - v19 - i3 - August 2004 - p128(1) [501-500]

Kimball, Chad T. - *Healthy Children Sourcebook: Basic Consumer Health Information about the Physical and Mental Development of Children Between the Ages of 3 and 2 ...*
E-Streams - June 2004 - pNA [501+]
SciTech - v28 - i1 - March 2004 - p117(1) [51-500]

Kimball, Cheryl - *Horse Showing for Kids*
c SLJ - v51 - i2 - Feb 2005 - p148(1) [51-500]

Kimball, Christopher - *The New Best Recipe: From the Editors of Cook's Illustrated*
People - v62 - i21 - Nov 22 2004 - p56 [51-500]

Kimball, D. Scott - *Top Gun Prospecting for Financial Professionals*
R&R Bk N - v19 - i1 - Feb 2004 - p118(1) [51-500]

Kimball, Jean - *Joyce and the Early Freudians: A Synchronic Dialogue of Texts*
ELT - v47 - i4 - Fall 2004 - p474(2) [501+]

Kimball, Jeffrey P. - *The Vietnam War Files: Uncovering the Secret History of Nixon-Era Strategy*
Choice - v42 - i1 - Sept 2004 - p174(1) [501+]
PSQ - v119 - i2 - Summer 2004 - p353(3) [501+]

Kimball, Marie Goebel - *The Martha Washington Cook Book*
SEP - v276 - i6 - Nov-Dec 2004 - p70(1) [501+]

Kimball, Richard Ian - *Sports in Zion: Mormon Recreation, 1890-1940*
JAH - v91 - i3 - Dec 2004 - p1039(2) [501+]

Kimball, Roger - *Art's Prospect (Read by Lane, Christopher). Audiobook Review*
c Kliatt - v38 - i4 - July 2004 - p59(1) [51-500]
Lengthened Shadows: America and Its Institutions in the Twenty-first Century
BL - v101 - i6 - Nov 15 2004 - p537(2) [501+]
The Rape of the Masters: How Political Correctness Sabotages Art
Choice - v42 - i5 - Jan 2005 - p841(1) [1-50]
Quad - v48 - i11 - Nov 2004 - p93(2) [501+]
R&R Bk N - v19 - i4 - Nov 2004 - p199(1) [501+]

Kimbel, William H. - *The Skull of Australopithecus Afarensis*
Choice - v42 - i2 - Oct 2004 - p334(2) [51-500]
QRB - v79 - i4 - Dec 2004 - p413(1) [501+]
R&R Bk N - v19 - i3 - August 2004 - p82(1) [51-500]

Kimber, Stephen - *Sailors, Slackers and Blind Pigs: Halifax at War*
CBRA - Annual 2003 - p342(1) [51-500]

Kimble, John M. - *Cryosols: Permafrost-Affected Soils*
Choice - v42 - i5 - Jan 2005 - p877(1) [1-50]

Kimenyi, Mwangi S. - *Devolution and Development: Governance Prospects in Decentralizing States*
R&R Bk N - v19 - i4 - Nov 2004 - p157(1) [501+]
Restarting and Sustaining Economic Growth and Development in Africa: The Case of Kenya
JEL - v41 - i4 - Dec 2003 - p1424(1) [501+]

Kimes, Joanne - *Pregnancy Sucks for Men: What to Do When Your Miracle Makes You Both Miserable*
LJ - v129 - i17 - Oct 15 2004 - p77(1) [51-500]

Kimmel, Allan J. - *Rumors and Rumor Controls: A Manager's Guide to Understanding and Combatting Rumors*
R&R Bk N - v19 - i1 - Feb 2004 - p88(1) [1-50]

Kimmel, Daniel M. - *The Fourth Network: How Fox Broke the Rules and Reinvented Television*
Atl - v295 - i1 - Jan-Feb 2005 - p163(4) [501+]
Bwatch - Nov 2004 - pNA [51-500]
Choice - v42 - i4 - Dec 2004 - p654(1) [1-50]
R&R Bk N - v19 - i4 - Nov 2004 - p222(1) [501+]
TV Q - v35 - i1 - Fall 2004 - p77(3) [501+]

Kimmel, Elizabeth Cody - *Lily B. on the Brink of Cool (Read by Vernoff, Kaili). Audiobook Review*
c Kliatt - v38 - i4 - July 2004 - p53(1) [51-500]
Lily B. on the Brink of Cool
y Sch Lib - v52 - i3 - Autumn 2004 - p156(1) [501+]
The Look-It-Up-Book of Explorers
y SLJ - v51 - i1 - Jan 2005 - p149(2) [51-500]
My Penguin Osbert (Illus. by Lewis, H.B.)
c BL - v101 - i7 - Dec 1 2004 - p659(1) [51-500]
c HB - v80 - i6 - Nov-Dec 2004 - p662(1) [51-500]
c KR - v72 - i21 - Nov 1 2004 - p1051(1) [51-500]
c PW - v251 - i47 - Nov 22 2004 - p60(1) [51-500]

Kimmel, Eric A. - *Cactus Soup (Illus. by Huling, Paul)*
y CCB-B - v58 - i3 - Nov 2004 - p129(2) [501+]
c HB - v81 - i1 - Jan-Feb 2005 - p103(1) [51-500]
Cactus Soup (Illus. by Huling, Phil)
c BL - v101 - i2 - Sept 15 2004 - p241(1) [51-500]
c KR - v72 - i17 - Sept 1 2004 - p868(1) [51-500]
c PW - v251 - i45 - Nov 8 2004 - p54(1) [51-500]
c SLJ - v50 - i10 - Oct 2004 - p144(1) [51-500]
The Castle of the Cats (Illus. by Krenina, Katya)
c BL - v101 - i4 - Oct 15 2004 - p410(1) [51-500]
c KR - v72 - i20 - Oct 15 2004 - p1008(1) [51-500]
c SLJ - v50 - i11 - Nov 2004 - p126(1) [51-500]
Don Quixote and the Windmills (Illus. by Fisher, Leonard Everett)
c CCB-B - v57 - i11 - July-August 2004 - p472(1) [501+]
c SLJ - v50 - i10 - Oct 2004 - pS50(1) [51-500]
Wonders and Miracles: A Passover Companion
c BL - v101 - i3 - Oct 1 2004 - p345(1) [51-500]
c LibMed - v23 - i3 - Nov-Dec 2004 - p86(1) [51-500]
c SLJ - v50 - i10 - Oct 2004 - pS37(1) [51-500]

Kimmel, Michael S. - *Handbook of Studies on Men and Masculinities*
R&R Bk N - v19 - i4 - Nov 2004 - p132(1) [51-500]
Men and Masculinities: A Social, Cultural, and Historical Encyclopedia
Ref Rev - June 2004 - pNA [501+]
R&R Bk N - v19 - i2 - May 2004 - p136 [51-500]
R&USQ - v44 - i1 - Fall 2004 - p80(2) [501+]
Privilege: A Reader
CS - v33 - i1 - Jan 2004 - p126-126 [501+]

Kimmel, Stacey - *Virtual Reference Services: Issues and Trends*
R&R Bk N - v19 - i1 - Feb 2004 - p261(1) [51-500]

Kimmelman, Burt - *The Facts on File Companion to 20th-Century American Poetry*
LJ - v130 - i4 - March 1 2005 - p114(1) [51-500]

Kimmerle, Constance - *Edward W. Redfield: Just Values and Fine Seeing*
Choice - v42 - i7 - March 2005 - p1217(1) [51-500]

Kimmerling, Baruch - *The Palestinian People: A History*
JTWS - v21 - i1 - Spring 2004 - p329(1) [501+]
MEP - v11 - i4 - Winter 2004 - p141(4) [501+]
MEQ - v11 - i3 - Summer 2004 - p89(3) [501+]
Politicide: Ariel Sharon's War against the Palestinians
CS - v33 - i4 - July 2004 - p410(4) [501+]
MEQ - v11 - i3 - Summer 2004 - p91(2) [501+]
PSQ - v119 - i2 - Summer 2004 - p361(3) [501+]
R&R Bk N - v19 - i1 - Feb 2004 - p43(1) [51-500]

Kimpton, Diana - *Edison's Fantastic Phonograph (Illus. by Robertson, M.P.)*
c SLJ - v50 - i8 - August 2004 - p89(1) [51-500]

Kimura, Stephanie - *Bags with Style*
LJ - v129 - i17 - Oct 15 2004 - p62(2) [51-500]

Kimura, T. - *Electroceramics in Japan VI: Proceedings*
SciTech - v28 - i1 - March 2004 - p142(1) [51-500]

Kincaid, Jamaica - *Among Flowers: A Walk in the Himalaya*
LJ - v130 - i1 - Jan 1 2005 - p137(1) [51-500]
PW - v251 - i51 - Dec 20 2004 - p47(1) [501+]
Mr. Potter
HR - v55 - Winter 2003 - p685 [501+]

Kincaid, Nanci - *As Hot as It Was You Ought to Thank Me*
 y BL - v101 - i8 - Dec 15 2004 - p707(1) [51-500]
  KR - v72 - i24 - Dec 15 2004 - p1158(1) [501+]
  LJ - v130 - i3 - Feb 15 2005 - p119(1) [51-500]
  PW - v252 - i4 - Jan 24 2005 - p222(2) [501+]
Balls
  BL - v101 - i1 - Sept 1 2004 - p53(1) [51-500]

Kincheloe, Joe L. - *Critical Pedagogy Primer*
  R&R Bk N - v19 - i3 - August 2004 - p227(1)
  [1-50]
Critical Thinking and Learning: An Encyclopedia for Parents and Teachers
  Choice - v42 - i2 - Oct 2004 - p273(2) [501+]
  LJ - v129 - i12 - July 2004 - p115(2) [51-500]
  R&R Bk N - v19 - i3 - August 2004 - p219(1)
  [1-50]
The Miseducation of the West: How Schools and the Media Distort Our Understanding of the Islamic World
  R&R Bk N - v19 - i4 - Nov 2004 - p191(1) [501+]
Multiple Intelligences Reconsidered
  R&R Bk N - v19 - i3 - August 2004 - p8(1) [1-50]
The Sign of the Burger: McDonald's and the Culture of Power
  HER - v74 - i3 - Fall 2004 - p349(3) [501+]

Kind, John - *Financial Games for Training*
  R&R Bk N - v19 - i3 - August 2004 - p131(1)
  [51-500]

Kinder, Chuck - *Last Mountain Dancer: Hard-Earned Lessons in Love, Loss, and Honky-Tonk Outlaw Life*
  BL - v101 - i3 - Oct 1 2004 - p298(1) [51-500]
  KR - v72 - i15 - August 1 2004 - p728(1) [501+]
  LJ - v129 - i19 - Nov 15 2004 - p68(1) [51-500]
  PW - v251 - i33 - August 16 2004 - p51(1) [51-500]

Kindl, Patrice - *Owl in Love: Schoolgirl by Day, Owl by Night*
 y Kliatt - v38 - i4 - July 2004 - p30(2) [51-500]

Kindsvatter, Peter S. - *American Soldiers: Ground Combat in the World Wars, Korea, and Vietnam*
  AHR - v109 - i4 - Oct 2004 - p1251(2) [501+]
  APH - v51 - i4 - Winter 2004 - p59(1) [501+]

Kindt, Matt - *2 Sisters: A Super-Spy Graphic Novel*
  BL - v101 - i5 - Nov 1 2004 - p473(1) [51-500]
  PW - v251 - i28 - July 12 2004 - p46(1) [51-500]

Kinealy, Christine - *A New History of Ireland*
  CR - v285 - i1665 - Oct 2004 - p253(1) [501+]

Kiner, Ralph - *Baseball Forever: Reflections on 60 Years in the Game*
  NYTBR - July 18 2004 - p16 [501+]

King, A.C. - *Differential Equations: Linear, Nonlinear, Ordinary, Partial*
  SIAM Rev - v46 - i3 - Sept 2004 - p587(1) [501+]

King, Alan - *Matzo Balls for Breakfast: And Other Memories of Growing Up Jewish*
  BL - v101 - i5 - Nov 1 2004 - p443(1) [51-500]
  LJ - v130 - i2 - Feb 1 2005 - p79(2) [51-500]
  PW - v251 - i43 - Oct 25 2004 - p39(1) [51-500]

King, Alan C. - *Double Cohort Study Phase 3 Report*
  BIC - v33 - i7 - Oct 2004 - p37(2) [501+]

King, Amy M. - *Bloom: The Botanical Vernacular in the English Novel*
  Nine-C Lit - v59 - i2 - Sept 2004 - p260(5) [501+]
  VS - v46 - i3 - Spring 2004 - p510(3) [501+]

King, Andrew - *Building/Art*
  CBRA - Annual 2003 - p111(2) [51-500]
  R&R Bk N - v19 - i4 - Nov 2004 - p136(1) [1-50]

King, Anthony - *The European Ritual: Football in the New Europe*
  Choice - v41 - i11-12 - July-August 2004 - p2083(1) [501+]

King, Averil - *Isaak Levitan: Lyrical Landscape*
  HT - v54 - i11 - Nov 2004 - p71(2) [501+]

King, Barbara J. - *The Dynamic Dance: Nonvocal Communication in African Great Apes*
  BL - v101 - i5 - Nov 1 2004 - p451(1) [51-500]
  Nature - v432 - i7019 - Dec 16 2004 - p804(2) [501+]

King, Bart - *The Big Book of Boy Stuff*
 c PW - v251 - i28 - July 12 2004 - p66(1) [501+]
 y SLJ - v50 - i11 - Nov 2004 - p166(1) [51-500]

King, Bente Starcke - *Beautiful Botanicals: Painting and Drawing Flowers and Plants*
  LJ - v129 - i17 - Oct 15 2004 - p63(1) [51-500]

King, Brian A. - *Performance Assurance for IT Systems*
  SciTech - v28 - i4 - Dec 2004 - p129 [51-500]

King, Bruce - *The Internationalization of English Literature, Vol. 13*
  LJ - v129 - i13 - August 2004 - p79(2) [501+]

King, C. Richard - *Native Americans in Sports*
  Choice - v41 - i11-12 - July-August 2004 - p2013(1) [501+]
  R&USQ - v44 - i1 - Fall 2004 - p92(2) [501+]

King, Cassandra - *Making Waves (Read by Delany, Colleen). Audiobook Review*
  BL - v101 - i9 - Nov 1 2004 - p504(1) [51-500]
 y Kliatt - v39 - i1 - Jan 2005 - p47(1) [51-500]
The Same Sweet Girls
  BL - v101 - i1 - Sept 1 2004 - p6(1) [51-500]
  LJ - v130 - i3 - Feb 15 2005 - p119(1) [51-500]
  PW - v251 - i47 - Nov 22 2004 - p38(1) [51-500]
  S Liv - v40 - i2 - Feb 2005 - p151(1) [51-500]

King, Charles - *The Black Sea: A History*
  Choice - v42 - i5 - Jan 2005 - p907(1) [1-50]
  CR - v285 - i1664 - Sept 2004 - p192(1) [51-500]
  HT - v55 - i2 - Feb 2005 - p59(1) [501+]

King, Dave - *The Ha-Ha (Read by Kinney, Terry). Audiobook Review*
  PW - v252 - i10 - March 7 2005 - p26(1) [51-500]
The Ha-Ha
  BL - v101 - i7 - Dec 1 2004 - p637(1) [501+]
  KR - v72 - i17 - Sept 1 2004 - p825(1) [501+]
  LJ - v129 - i18 - Nov 1 2004 - p75(1) [501+]
  NYTBR - Jan 23 2005 - p25 [501+]
  People - v63 - i5 - Feb 7 2005 - p50 [501+]
  PW - v251 - i46 - Nov 15 2004 - p37(2) [501+]
  Time - v165 - i5 - Jan 31 2005 - p70 [501+]

King, David A. - *The Ciphers of the Monks: A Forgotten Number-Notation of the Middle Ages*
  TimHES - v0 - i1664 - Oct 29 2004 - p22(1) [501+]

King, David C. - *The Right to Speak Out*
 c SLJ - v50 - i8 - August 2004 - p49(1) [51-500]

King, Dean - *Skeletons on the Zahara (Read by Prichard, Michael). Audiobook Review*
  Kliatt - v38 - i6 - Nov 2004 - p57(1) [51-500]

King, Dexter - *Growing up King: An Intimate Memoir*
 y Kliatt - v38 - i4 - July 2004 - p37(1) [51-500]

King, Dwight Y. - *Half-Hearted Reform: Electoral Institutions and the Struggle for Democracy in Indonesia*
  JAS - v63 - i2 - May 2004 - p558(2) [501+]

King, Geoff - *New Hollywood Cinema: An Introduction*
  FQ - v57 - i2 - Winter 2003 - p59(2) [501+]

King, Gilbert - *Woman, Child for Sale: The New Slave Trade in the 21st Century*
  PW - v251 - i33 - August 16 2004 - p55(1) [51-500]

King, Glenn E. - *Traditional Cultures: A Survey of Nonwestern Experience and Achievement*
  R&R Bk N - v19 - i1 - Feb 2004 - p71(1) [1-50]

King, Greg - *The Fate of the Romanovs*
  R&R Bk N - v19 - i1 - Feb 2004 - p38(1) [1-50]

King, Helen - *The Disease of Virgins: Green Sickness, Chlorosis and the Problems of Puberty*
  Lon R Bks - v26 - i5 - March 4 2004 - p14(5) [501+]
  TLS - i5265 - Feb 27 2004 - p30-31 [501+]

King, Hueston C. - *Allergy in ENT Practice: The Basic Guide, 2nd Ed.*
  SciTech - v28 - i4 - Dec 2004 - p101(1) [51-500]

King, J.E. - *The Elgar Companion to Post Keynesian Economics*
  R&R Bk N - v19 - i1 - Feb 2004 - p78(1) [1-50]

King, J.L. - *On the Down Low: A Journey into the Lives of "Straight" Black Men Who Sleep with Men*
  Black Iss - v6 - i5 - Sept-Oct 2004 - p46(1) [501+]
  G&L Rev W - v11 - i4 - July-August 2004 - p40(1) [51-500]

King, Jan B. - *Business Plans to Game Plans: A Practical System for Turning Strategies Into Action, Rev. Ed.*
  R&R Bk N - v19 - i2 - May 2004 - p117 [51-500]

King, Jean A. - *Roots of Mental Illness in Children*
  SciTech - v28 - i3 - Sept 2004 - p118(1) [51-500]

King, Jeremy - *Budweisers into Czechs and Germans: A Local History of Bohemian Politics, 1848-1948*
  GSR - v27 - i2 - May 2004 - p432-433 [501+]
  HNet - June 2004 - pNA [501+]

King, John - *The Cambridge Companion to Modern Latin American Culture*
  Choice - v42 - i2 - Oct 2004 - p278(1) [501+]
  TimHES - v0 - i1683 - March 18 2005 - p28(1) [501+]

King, Jonathon - *A Killing Night*
  BL - v101 - i9-10 - Jan 1 2005 - p827(1) [1-50]
  LJ - v130 - i4 - March 1 2005 - p72(1) [51-500]
  PW - v252 - i6 - Feb 7 2005 - p46(1) [51-500]
Shadow Men (Read by Colacci, David). Audiobook Review
  LJ - v129 - i20 - Dec 1 2004 - p180(1) [51-500]

King, Joseph F. - *The Development of Modern Police History in the United Kingdom and the United States*
  R&R Bk N - v19 - i4 - Nov 2004 - p148(1) [501+]

King, Julia - *The Library of Leonard and Virginia Woolf: A Short-Title Catalog*
  Choice - v42 - i2 - Oct 2004 - p267(1) [501+]

King, Karen L. - *The Wedding Runaway*
  BL - v101 - i9-10 - Jan 1 2005 - p830(2) [1-50]
What Is Gnosticism?
  Theol St - v65 - i3 - Sept 2004 - p639(3) [501+]

King, Kenneth - *Knowledge for Development?: Comparing British, Japanese, Swedish and World Bank Aid*
  Choice - v42 - i6 - Feb 2005 - p1069(2) [51-500]

King, Larry - *Taking on Heart Disease*
  Bwatch - Dec 2004 - pNA [51-500]
Why I Love Baseball (Read by King, Larry). Audiobook Review
  Kliatt - v38 - i6 - Nov 2004 - p57(1) [51-500]
  LJ - v129 - i13 - August 2004 - p130(1) [51-500]

King, Laurie R. - *The Game (Read by Sterlin, Jenny). Audiobook Review*
  BL - v101 - i1 - Sept 1 2004 - p142(1) [51-500]

King, Lawrence Peter - *Theories of the New Class: Intellectuals and Power*
  Choice - v42 - i6 - Feb 2005 - p1105(1) [51-500]

King, Lovalerie - *A Student's Guide to the Study of African American Literature, 1760 to the Present*
  R&R Bk N - v19 - i1 - Feb 2004 - p241(1) [501+]

King, Lyn - *Walking into the Night Sky*
  CBRA - Annual 2003 - p220(2) [51-500]

King, Michael R. - *Who Killed King Tut? Using Modern Forensics to Solve a 3,300-Year-Old Mystery*
  Bwatch - Oct 2004 - pNA [51-500]
Who Killed King Tut?: Using Modern Forensics to Solve a 3,300-Year-Old Mystery
  R&R Bk N - v19 - i3 - August 2004 - p58(1) [51-500]

King, Peter - *Crime, Justice, and Discretion in England 1740-1820*
  J Soc H - v38 - i1 - Fall 2004 - p259(3) [501+]
A Social Philosophy of Housing
  CS - v33 - i6 - Nov 2004 - p745(1) [1-50]
  Soc Ser R - v78 - i4 - Dec 2004 - p699(1) [51-500]

King, Philip - *International Economics and International Economic Policy: A Reader*
  R&R Bk N - v19 - i3 - August 2004 - p124(1) [51-500]

King, R.A.H. - *Aristotle on Life and Death*
  Class R - v54 - i2 - Nov 2004 - p329-331 [501+]

King, Richard - *That Sleep of Death*
  CBRA - Annual 2003 - p172(1) [501+]

King, Richard C. - *Beyond the Cheers: Race as Spectacle in College Sport*
  SSJ - v21 - i2 - June 2004 - p221-223 [501+]

King, Richard H. - *Race, Culture, and the Intellectuals, 1940-1970*
  R&R Bk N - v19 - i4 - Nov 2004 - p60(1) [51-500]

King, Robert H. - *Autumn Years: Taking the Contemplative Path*
  PW - v251 - i28 - July 12 2004 - p59(1) [51-500]

King, Roger - *The State, Democracy and Globalization*
  TimHES - v0 - i1668 - Nov 26 2004 - pVIII(1) [501+]

King, Rosamond S. - *Voices of the City*
 y Kliatt - v38 - i4 - July 2004 - p36(1) [51-500]

King, Ross - *Michelangelo & the Pope's Ceiling*
  R&R Bk N - v19 - i3 - August 2004 - p243(1) [51-500]

King-Shaver, Barbara - *Differentiated Instruction in the English Classroom: Content, Process, Product, and Assessment*
  JAAL - v48 - i4 - Dec 2004 - p358(2) [501+]
  R&R Bk N - v19 - i1 - Feb 2004 - p184(1) [51-500]

King-Smith, Dick - *The Adventurous Snail*
 c Sch Lib - v52 - i4 - Winter 2004 - p203(1) [51-500]
The Golden Goose (Illus. by Kronheimer, Ann)
 c HB - v81 - i1 - Jan-Feb 2005 - p95(2) [501+]
 c KR - v73 - i3 - Feb 1 2005 - p177(1) [51-500]
 y PW - v252 - i7 - Feb 14 2005 - p77(1) [51-500]
Just Binnie (Illus. by Frankland, David)
 c Sch Lib - v52 - i3 - Autumn 2004 - p146(1) [501+]

King, Stephen - *The Dark Tower (Illus. by Whelan, Michael)*
  BL - v101 - i1 - Sept 1 2004 - p6(1) [51-500]
  BW - v34 - i38 - Sept 19 2004 - p7(1) [501+]
  KR - v72 - i17 - Sept 1 2004 - pNA [501+]
  LJ - v129 - i15 - Sept 15 2004 - p49(1) [51-500]
  NYTBR - Oct 17 2004 - p14 [501+]
  People - v62 - i13 - Sept 27 2004 - p53 [501+]
  PW - v251 - i35 - August 30 2004 - p30(1) [501+]
Faithful: Two Diehard Boston Red Sox Fans Chronicle the Historic 2004 Season
  People - v62 - i24 - Dec 13 2004 - p53 [51-500]
  PW - v251 - i48 - Nov 29 2004 - p32(1) [501+]

The Girl Who Loved Tom Gordon: A Pop-up Book (Illus. by Dingman, Alan)
c BIC - v33 - i8 - Nov 2004 - p35(2) [501+]
c PW - v251 - i38 - Sept 20 2004 - p62(1) [51-500]
c SLJ - v50 - i11 - Nov 2004 - p148(1) [51-500]
The Girl Who Loved Tom Gordon
c BW - v34 - i50 - Dec 12 2004 - p13(1) [501+]
Salem's Lot (Read by McLarty, Ron). Audiobook Review
   LJ - v129 - i13 - August 2004 - p129(1) [51-500]
The Stephen King Collection (Read by Glover, John). Audiobook Review
   LJ - v129 - i17 - Oct 15 2004 - p96(1) [51-500]
Wolves of the Calla (Read by Guidall, George). Audiobook Review
c Kliatt - v38 - i4 - July 2004 - p58(1) [51-500]
Wolves of the Calla (Illus. by Wrightson, Bernie)
   NYTBR - Jan 23 2005 - p28 [501+]
King, Stephen J. - *Liberlization against Democracy: The Local Politics of Economic Reform in Tunisia*
   Choice - v42 - i2 - Oct 2004 - p365(1) [51-500]
King, Stephen Michael - *Mutt Dog!*
c Magpies - v19 - i5 - Nov 2004 - p29(2) [501+]
King, Thomas - *Coyote's New Suit (Illus. by Wales, Johnny)*
c Globe & Mail - Dec 11 2004 - pD18 [501+]
King, Thomas F. - *Cultural Resource Laws and Practice: An Introductory Guide, 2nd Ed.*
   R&R Bk N - v19 - i3 - August 2004 - p202(1) [1-50]
Places That Count: Traditional Cultural Properties in Cultural Resources Management
   R&R Bk N - v19 - i1 - Feb 2004 - p54(1) [51-500]
King, Trish - *Parenting Your Dog*
   Bwatch - Nov 2004 - pNA [51-500]
King, Ursula - *Gender, Religion, and Diversity; Cross-Cultural Perspectives*
   R&R Bk N - v19 - i3 - August 2004 - p13(1) [1-50]
King, Valerie - *An Adventurous Lady*
y BL - v101 - i4 - Oct 15 2004 - p394(1) [51-500]
King, Venita - *The Voice of My Boundaries: Life-Changing Exercises Your Other Coaches Didn't Tell You About!*
   Black Iss - v7 - i2 - March-April 2005 - p61(1) [51-500]
King, Woodie, Jr. - *The Impact of Race: Theatre and Culture*
   Afr Am R - v38 - i3 - Fall 2004 - p544(2) [501+]
King, Yolanda - *Open My Eyes, Open My Soul: Celebrating Our Common Humanity*
   Black Iss - v6 - i4 - July-August 2004 - p31(1) [51-500]
Kingdon, John W. - *Reaganism and the Death of Representative Democracy*
   R&R Bk N - v19 - i1 - Feb 2004 - pNA [51-500]
Kingdon, Jonathan - *The Kingdon Pocket Guide to African Mammals*
   New Sci - v185 - i2489 - March 5 2005 - p57(1) [51-500]
Lowly Origin: Where, When and Why Our Ancestors First Stood Up
   Am Bio T - v66 - i5 - May 2004 - p390(1) [501+]
   Lon R Bks - v26 - i19 - Oct 7 2004 - p28(1) [501+]
Kingfisher - *The Kingfisher History Encyclopedia*
y PW - v251 - i44 - Nov 1 2004 - p64(2) [501+]
Kingfisher, Catherine - *Western Welfare in Decline: Globalization and Women's Poverty*
   Soc Ser R - v78 - i4 - Dec 2004 - p699(2) [51-500]
Kingfisher Young Knowledge
   LibMed - v22 - i6 - March 2004 - p85(1) [501+]
Kingsbury, Celia Malone - *The Peculiar Sanity of War: Hysteria in the Literature of World War I*
   MFSF - v50 - i2 - Summer 2004 - p511-513 [501+]
Kingsbury, Karen - *Beyond Tuesday Morning*
   LJ - v130 - i2 - Feb 1 2005 - p60(1) [51-500]
   Time - v165 - i11 - March 14 2005 - p65 [501+]
   Ent W - i812 - March 25 2005 - p76 [501+]
Born to Write
   PW - v251 - i34 - August 23 2004 - pS17(3) [501+]
A Thousand Tomorrows
   PW - v252 - i10 - March 7 2005 - p51(2) [501+]
Kingsley-Hughes, Adrian W. - *The PC Doctor's Fix-It-Yourself Guide*
   SciTech - v28 - i4 - Dec 2004 - p159(1) [51-500]
Kingsley, Karen - *Buildings of Louisiana*
   JSH - v70 - i4 - Nov 2004 - p981(2) [501+]

Kingsley, Peter - *Reality*
   Choice - v41 - i11-12 - July-August 2004 - p2058(1) [501+]
   Parabola - v29 - i2 - Summer 2004 - p106-111 [501+]
Kingsley, S. - *Economy and Exchange in the East Mediterranean During Late Antiquity: Proceedings*
   Class R - v53 - i2 - Nov 2003 - p442-444 [501+]
Kingston, Anne - *The Meaning of Wife*
   Globe & Mail - Nov 27 2004 - pD3 [51-500]
   KR - v72 - i24 - Dec 15 2004 - p1184(1) [501+]
   LJ - v129 - i20 - Dec 1 2004 - p145(1) [51-500]
   PW - v252 - i3 - Jan 17 2005 - p45(2) [501+]
Kingston, Madeline - *Something in the Head: The Life and Work of John Broderick*
   TLS - i5307 - Dec 17 2004 - p21-22 [501+]
Kingston, Maxine Hong - *The Fifth Book Of Peace*
   NYTBR - Dec 19 2004 - p30 [501+]
Kingston, Paul - *States-Within-States: Incipient Political Entities in the Post-Cold War Era*
   Choice - v42 - i5 - Jan 2005 - p932(1) [51-500]
Kingston, Simon - *Ulster and the Isles in the Fifteenth Century: The Lordship of the Clann Domhnaill of Antrim*
   R&R Bk N - v19 - i3 - August 2004 - p40(1) [51-500]
Kingwell, Mark - *Catch And Release: Trout Fishing and the Meaning of Life*
   Wil Q - v28 - i4 - Autumn 2004 - p126(2) [501+]
Practical Judgments: Essays in Culture, Politics, and Interpretation
   R&R Bk N - v19 - i4 - Nov 2004 - p150(1) [501+]
Kinkade, Thomas - *A Christmas Promise*
   PW - v251 - i40 - Oct 4 2004 - p71(1) [501+]
Kinkead, Jonathan - *Build Your Own Acoustic Guitar: Complete Instructions and Full-Size Plans*
   LJ - v129 - i14 - Sept 1 2004 - p178(1) [51-500]
Kinkoph, Sherry Willard - *Teach Yourself Visually: Macromedia Flash MX 2004*
   LJ - v129 - i20 - Dec 1 2004 - p152(1) [51-500]
Kinley, Harold - *Radioman's Manual of RF Devices, Principles, and Practices*
   SciTech - v28 - i1 - March 2004 - p159(1) [51-500]
Kinnamon, Michael - *The Vision of the Ecumenical Movement and How It Has Been Impoverished by Its Friends*
   Intpr - v58 - i4 - Oct 2004 - p434(2) [501+]
Kinnear, Mary - *Woman of the World: Mary McGeachy and International Cooperation*
   R&R Bk N - v19 - i3 - August 2004 - p77(1) [51-500]
Kinnear, Paul R. - *SPSS 12 made simple*
   SciTech - v28 - i4 - Dec 2004 - p7(1) [1-50]
Kinney, Anne Behnke - *Representations of Childhood and Youth in Early China*
   Choice - v42 - i2 - Oct 2004 - p349(1) [51-500]
   R&R Bk N - v19 - i2 - May 2004 - p135 [51-500]
Kinney, Arthur F. - *Hamlet: New Critical Essays*
   Shakes Q - v55 - i1 - Spring 2004 - p88-91 [501+]
Kinney, Thomas A. - *The Carriage Trade*
   Bwatch - Dec 2004 - pNA [51-500]
Kinni, Theodore - *No Substitute for Victory: Lessons in Strategy and Leadership from General Douglas MacArthur*
   LJ - v130 - i3 - Feb 15 2005 - p141(1) [51-500]
   PW - v252 - i2 - Jan 10 2005 - p49(2) [51-500]
Kinoshita, Sakura - *The Mythical Detective Loki Ragnarok, Vol. 1*
   PW - v251 - i42 - Oct 18 2004 - p50(1) [51-500]
Kinro, Gerald Y. - *A Cup of Aloha*
   Pac A - v77 - i2 - Summer 2004 - p383(1) [501+]
Kinsella, Sophie - *Can You Keep a Secret? (Read by Reading, Kate). Audiobook Review*
y Kliatt - v38 - i5 - Sept 2004 - p54(2) [51-500]
Shopaholic and Sister (Read by Kellgren, Katherine). Audiobook Review
   PW - v251 - i44 - Nov 1 2004 - p27(1) [501+]
Shopaholic and Sister
   BL - v101 - i1 - Sept 15 2004 - p208(1) [501+]
   Ent W - i787 - Oct 8 2004 - p119 [501+]
   KR - v72 - i15 - August 1 2004 - p707(1) [501+]
   LJ - v129 - i15 - Sept 15 2004 - p49(1) [51-500]
   People - v62 - i15 - Oct 11 2004 - p56 [501+]
   PW - v251 - i35 - August 30 2004 - p32(1) [501+]
Kinservik, Matthew J. - *Disciplining Satire: The Censorship of Satiric Comedy on the Eighteenth-Century London Stage*
   Theat J - v56 - i1 - March 2004 - p136(3) [501+]
Kinsey, Leland - *In the Rain Shadow*
   BL - v101 - i2 - Sept 15 2004 - p195(2) [501+]

Kinsey-Warnock, Natalie - *A Christmas Like Helen's (Illus. by Azarian, Mary)*
c BL - v101 - i4 - Oct 15 2004 - p405(1) [51-500]
c KR - v72 - i21 - Nov 1 2004 - p1051(1) [51-500]
c PW - v251 - i39 - Sept 27 2004 - p61(2) [51-500]
Kinsler, Gwen Glakely - *Crocheting (Illus. by Melo, Esperanza)*
c CBRA - Annual 2003 - p553(1) [51-500]
Kinsley, Peter - *The Shy Pornographer*
   Spec - v296 - i9200 - Dec 4 2004 - p48(1) [501+]
Kinsman, Anna - *The Politics of Knowledge: Public Schools in the Nation's Capital*
   R&R Bk N - v19 - i1 - Feb 2004 - pNA [51-500]
Kintzig, Claude - *Communicating with Smart Objects*
   SciTech - v28 - i1 - March 2004 - p164(1) [51-500]
Kinzer, Stephen - *All the Shah's Men: An American Coup and the Roots of Middle East Terror*
   MEP - v11 - i4 - Winter 2004 - p122(8) [501+]
   MEQ - v11 - i3 - Summer 2004 - p81(2) [501+]
Kipling, Rudyard - *A Collection of Rudyard Kipling's Just So Stories*
c BL - v101 - i7 - Dec 1 2004 - p651(2) [51-500]
c PW - v251 - i50 - Dec 13 2004 - p69(2) [501+]
c SLJ - v50 - i12 - Dec 2004 - p112(1) [501+]
The Jungle Book
c RT - v57 - Sept 2003 - p98 [1-50]
Kim
c HR - v55 - i4 - Winter 2003 - p537 [501+]
Kipnis, Laura - *Against Love: A Polemic*
   BIC - v33 - i5 - August 2004 - p24(1) [501+]
   Bks & Cult - v10 - i5 - Sept-Oct 2004 - p18(2) [501+]
   NYTBR - Oct 10 2004 - p26 [501+]
Kipp, Charles D. - *Because We Are Canadians: A Battlefield Memoir*
   Can Hist R - v85 - i3 - Sept 2004 - p624(3) [501+]
Kipp, Woody - *Viet Cong at Wounded Knee: The Trail of a Blackfeet Activist*
   BL - v101 - i1 - Sept 1 2004 - p42(1) [51-500]
Kipper, Rainer - *Der Germanenmythos im Deutschen Kaiserreich: Formen und Funktionen historischer Selbstthematisierung*
   HNet - June 2004 - pNA [501+]
Kirby, David - *Mercury in Vaccines and the Autism Epidemic: A Medical Controversy*
   KR - v73 - i4 - Feb 15 2005 - p213(1) [501+]
Kirby, F.E. - *Wagner's Themes: A Study in Musical Expression*
   Choice - v42 - i6 - Feb 2005 - p1031(1) [51-500]
   R&R Bk N - v19 - i4 - Nov 2004 - p198(1) [501+]
Kirby, Huguette - *Halloween Crafts: Step-by-Step Projects for Spooky Fun!*
c CBRA - Annual 2003 - p553(2) [51-500]
Kirby, Jack - *Challengers of the Unknown Archives*
   BL - v101 - i1 - Sept 1 2004 - p77(1) [501+]
Jimmy Olsen: Adventures by Jack Kirby, Vol. 2 (Illus. by Kirby, Jack)
y BL - v101 - i8 - Dec 15 2004 - p716(1) [51-500]
   LibMed - v22 - i6 - March 2004 - p69(1) [501+]
y PW - v251 - i49 - Dec 6 2004 - p45(1) [501+]
Kirby, Linda D. - *The Executor's Guide: How to Administer an Estate under a Will*
   R&R Bk N - v19 - i3 - August 2004 - p198(1) [1-50]
Kirby, Maurice W - *Operational Research in War and Peace: The British Experience from the 1930s to 1970*
   BHR - v78 - i2 - Summer 2004 - p343(3) [501+]
Kirby, Peter - *Child Labour in Britain, 1750-1870*
   HER - v119 - i482 - June 2004 - p811(3) [501+]
   R&R Bk N - v19 - i1 - Feb 2004 - p100(1) [1-50]
Kirby, Roger S. - *Atlas of Erectile Dysfunction, 2nd Ed.*
   E-Streams - v8 - i3 - Sept 2004 - pNA [501+]
An Illustrated Pocketbook of Prostatic Diseases
   SciTech - v28 - i4 - Dec 2004 - p105(1) [51-500]
Prostate Cancer, 4th ed.
   SciTech - v28 - i3 - Sept 2004 - p92(1) [51-500]
Kirby, William C. - *Realms of Freedom in Modern China*
   R&R Bk N - v19 - i1 - Feb 2004 - p150(1) [51-500]
Kiribati: Monetization in an Atoll Society: Managing Economic and Social Change
   JEL - v41 - i4 - Dec 2003 - p1422(2) [501+]
Kirienko, Alexander - *Ilizarov Technique for Complex Foot and Ankle Deformities*
   SciTech - v28 - i1 - March 2004 - p113(1) [51-500]
Kirino, Natsuo - *Out*
   Time - v165 - i11 - March 14 2005 - p68 [501+]

Kirjuchina, Ljubow - *Sowjetdeutsche Lyrik (1941-1989) Zu den Themen "Mutter-Sprache" und "Heimat" als Narrativer Identitatsakt*
  GSR - v27 - i3 - Oct 2004 - p668(2) [501+]
Kirk, Andrew - *Civil Disobedience*
  y Kliatt - v39 - i2 - March 2005 - p36(2) [51-500]
Kirk, Connie Ann - *Emily Dickinson: A Biography*
  R&R Bk N - v19 - i4 - Nov 2004 - p241(1) [501+]
  Mark Twain: A Biography
  R&R Bk N - v19 - i4 - Nov 2004 - p241(1) [501+]
  Sky Dancers (Illus. by Hale, Christy)
  c BL - v101 - i6 - Nov 15 2004 - p590(1) [51-500]
     KR - v72 - i20 - Oct 15 2004 - p1009(1) [51-500]
  c SLJ - v51 - i1 - Jan 2005 - p94(1) [51-500]
Kirk, Daniel - *Jack and Jill*
  LibMed - v22 - i5 - Feb 2004 - p64(1) [501+]
  Lunchroom Lizard
  c SLJ - v50 - i8 - August 2004 - p89(1) [51-500]
  Rex Tabby: Cat Detective
  c BL - v100 - i22 - August 2004 - p1935(1) [51-500]
  c PW - v251 - i30 - July 26 2004 - p54(2) [51-500]
  c SLJ - v50 - i8 - August 2004 - p89(1) [51-500]
  Snow Dude (Illus. by Kirk, Daniel)
  c BL - v101 - i6 - Nov 15 2004 - p590(1) [51-500]
  c PW - v251 - i51 - Dec 20 2004 - p58(1) [51-500]
  c SLJ - v51 - i1 - Jan 2005 - p95(1) [51-500]
Kirk, David - *Miss Spider's Sunny Patch Kids*
  c SLJ - v50 - i8 - August 2004 - p89(1) [51-500]
Kirk-Duggan, Cheryl A. - *Pregnant Passion: Gender, Sex, and Violence in the Bible*
  Intpr - v58 - i3 - July 2004 - p334(2) [51-500]
Kirk, Dylan - *Canada at War*
  c CBRA - Annual 2003 - p532(1) [51-500]
Kirk, Gordon - *The Chartered Teacher*
  R&R Bk N - v19 - i3 - August 2004 - p226(1) [1-50]
Kirk, H. Ray - *EPA Compliance Guide for Hazardous Waste, 10th Ed.*
  SciTech - v28 - i3 - Sept 2004 - p12(1) [501+]
  OSHA Training Guide, 6th Ed.
  R&R Bk N - v19 - i4 - Nov 2004 - p170(1) [501+]
Kirk, Heather - *A Drop Of Rain*
  c CH Bwatch - Oct 2004 - pNA [51-500]
     Res Links - v10 - i2 - Dec 2004 - p37(1) [501+]
Kirk, Kevin L. - *Cystic Fibrosis Transmembrane Conductance Regulator*
  SciTech - v28 - i1 - March 2004 - p106(1) [51-500]
Kirk, Mark T. - *Predictive Material Modeling: Combining Fundamental Physics Understanding, Computational Methods and Empirically Observed Behavior: Proceedings*
  SciTech - v28 - i3 - Sept 2004 - p166(1) [51-500]
Kirk, Neville - *Comrades and Cousins: Globalization, Workers, and Labour Movements in Britain, the USA, and Australia from the 1880s to 1914*
  JAH - v91 - i3 - Dec 2004 - p1058(2) [501+]
Kirk, Paul G. - *Paul Kirk's Championship Barbecue: BBQ Your Way to Greatness with 575 Lip-Smackin' Recipes from the Baron of Barbecue*
  Bwatch - v26 - i8 - August 2004 - p3(1) [1-50]
  Paul Kirk's Championship Barbeque Sauces: 175 Make-Your-Own Sauces, Marinades, Dry Rubs, Wet Rubs, Mops, and Salsas
  Bwatch - v26 - i8 - August 2004 - p3(1) [1-50]
Kirk, Robin - *More Terrible than Death: Massacres, Drugs, and America's War in Colombia*
  Nation - v279 - i5 - August 16 2004 - p31 [501+]
Kirk, Russell - *Ancestral Shadows: An Anthology of Ghostly Tales*
  BL - v101 - i2 - Sept 15 2004 - p216(1) [51-500]
  PW - v251 - i34 - August 23 2004 - p42(1) [51-500]
  The Roots of American Order, 4th Ed.
  R&R Bk N - v19 - i3 - August 2004 - p173(1) [501+]
Kirkbright, Suzanne - *Karl Jaspers: A Biography: Navigations in Truth*
  LJ - v129 - i20 - Dec 1 2004 - p121(1) [51-500]
Kirkendale, Warren - *Emilio de' Cavalieri "Gentiluomo Romano." His Life and Letters, His Role as Superintendent of All the Arts at the Medici Court, and His Musical Compositions*
  Notes - v61 - i2 - Dec 2004 - p428(3) [501+]
Kirkham, Victoria - *Fabulous Vernacular: Boccaccio's "Filocolo" and the Art of Medieval Fiction*
  Specu - v79 - i4 - Oct 2004 - p1107(2) [501+]
Kirkland, Jane - *Take a Walk with Butterflies and Dragonflies*
  c CH Bwatch - v14 - i11 - Nov 2004 - pNA [51-500]
     Sci Teach - v71 - i8 - Oct 2004 - p78-80 [51-500]

Kirkley, Harriet - *A Biographer at Work: Samuel Johnson's Notes for the 'Life of Pope'*
  Biomag - v27 - i3 - Summer 2004 - p611(3) [501+]
Kirkman, Rick - *Two Plus One Is Enough*
  Bwatch - Feb 2005 - pNA [51-500]
Kirkman, Robert - *Family Matters*
  y Teach Lib - v32 - i3 - Feb 2005 - p58(1) [1-50]
Kirkos, Linda A. - *Women's Studies: A Recommended Bibliography*
  Choice - v42 - i7 - March 2005 - p1208(1) [51-500]
Kirkpatrick, Jane - *Hold Tight the Thread*
  Roundup M - v11 - i6 - August 2004 - p29(1) [501+]
Kirkpatrick, Katherine - *Escape across the Wide Sea (Illus. by Gao, Long)*
  c BL - v101 - i9-10 - Jan 1 2005 - p858(2) [1-50]
     KR - v72 - i18 - Sept 15 2004 - p915(1) [501+]
  y SLJ - v50 - i11 - Nov 2004 - p148(1) [51-500]
Kirkpatrick, Lee A. - *A Simple Guide to SPSS for Windows: For Versions 12.0*
  SciTech - v28 - i3 - Sept 2004 - p6(1) [501+]
Kirkwood, Gwen - *Children of the Glens*
  BL - v101 - i5 - Nov 1 2004 - p464(1) [51-500]
Kirmse, Andrew - *Game Programming Gems 4*
  Bwatch - v26 - i7 - July 2004 - p8(1) [51-500]
  SciTech - v28 - i3 - Sept 2004 - p25(1) [51-500]
Kirp, David L. - *Shakespeare, Einstein, and the Bottom Line: The Marketing of Higher Education*
  JEL - v42 - i1 - March 2004 - p275(2) [501+]
  JEL - v42 - i4 - Dec 2004 - p1141(2) [501+]
Kirsch, Adam - *The Wounded Surgeon: Confession and Transformation in Six American Poets: Robert Lowell, Elizabeth Bishop, John Berryman, Randall Jarrell, Delmore Schwartz, Sylvia Plath*
  KR - v73 - i2 - Jan 15 2005 - p102(1) [501+]
  PW - v252 - i9 - Feb 28 2005 - p56(1) [51-500]
Kirsch, David - *The Ultimate New York Body Plan*
  LJ - v129 - i16 - Oct 1 2004 - p106(1) [51-500]
  PW - v251 - i35 - August 30 2004 - p47(1) [51-500]
Kirsch, George B. - *Baseball in Blue and Gray: The National Pastime during the Civil War*
  AHR - v109 - i3 - June 2004 - p921(2) [501+]
  JAH - v91 - i1 - June 2004 - p248-248 [501+]
  JSH - v70 - i3 - August 2004 - p684(2) [501+]
Kirschenbaum, Alan - *Chaos Organization and Disaster Management*
  R&R Bk N - v19 - i1 - Feb 2004 - p121(1) [51-500]
Kirschmann, Anne Taylor - *A Vital Force: Women in American Homeopathy*
  QRB - v79 - i3 - Sept 2004 - p290(2) [501+]
  SciTech - v28 - i1 - March 2004 - p127(1) [51-500]
Kirshenbaum, Sandra - *Complete Index to Fine Print, 1975-1990*
  R&R Bk N - v19 - i1 - Feb 2004 - p258(1) [51-500]
Kirstein, Klaus-Peter - *Die lateinischen Patriarchen von Jerusalem: Von der Eroberung der Heiligen Stadt durch die Kreuzfahrer 1099 bis zum Ende der Kreuzfahrerstaaten 1291*
  CHR - v90 - i4 - Oct 2004 - p756(3) [501+]
Kirstein, Lincoln Edward - *The Classic Ballet: Basic Technique & Terminology*
  LJ - v129 - i18 - Nov 1 2004 - p134(1) [1-50]
Kirstein, Rosemary - *The Language of Power*
  BL - v100 - i22 - August 2004 - p1913(1) [51-500]
  LJ - v129 - i13 - August 2004 - p73(1) [51-500]
  PW - v251 - i30 - July 26 2004 - p42(1) [501+]
Kirtsoglou, Elisabeth - *For the Love of Women*
  TLS - i5284 - July 9 2004 - p4(1) [501+]
Kirwan, Anna - *Lady of Palenque: Flower of Bacal*
  c SLJ - v50 - i7 - July 2004 - p106(1) [51-500]
Kirwan, James - *The Aesthetic in Kant, a Critique*
  R&R Bk N - v19 - i4 - Nov 2004 - p6(1) [51-500]
Kirwan, Larry - *Green Suede Shoes: An Irish-American Odyssey*
  KR - v73 - i2 - Jan 15 2005 - p102(2) [501+]
Kirwan, Laurence - *Studies on the History of Late Antique and Christian Nubia*
  Class R - v54 - i1 - May 2004 - p226(3) [501+]
Kis, Janos - *Constitutional Democracy*
  Slav R - v63 - i4 - Winter 2004 - p863(1) [501+]
Kishimoto, Kikuo - *Advances in Fracture and Failure Prevention: Proceedings*
  SciTech - v28 - i3 - Sept 2004 - p139(1) [51-500]
Kishinevsky, Mike - *Application of Concurrency to System Design: Proceedings*
  SciTech - v28 - i3 - Sept 2004 - p19(1) [501+]

Kisilevsky, Hershy - *Number Theory: Proceedings*
  SciTech - v28 - i3 - Sept 2004 - p35(1) [51-500]
Kiskaddon, Bruce - *Shorty's Yarns: Western Stories and Poems of Bruce Kiskaddon*
  Roundup M - v11 - i6 - August 2004 - p32(1) [501+]
Kislenko, Arne - *Culture and Customs of Thailand*
  y Ref Rev - Nov 2004 - pNA [501+]
  R&R Bk N - v19 - i4 - Nov 2004 - p48(1) [51-500]
Kissam, Philip C. - *The Discipline of Law Schools: The Making of Modern Lawyers*
  CS - v33 - i6 - Nov 2004 - p726(2) [501+]
Kissinger, Henry A. - *Crisis: The Anatomy of Two Major Foreign Policy Crises*
  MEQ - v11 - i4 - Fall 2004 - p75(2) [501+]
Kissock, Heather - *Canada Day*
  c CBRA - Annual 2003 - p549(1) [51-500]
Kistler, John M. - *Animals Are the Issue: Library Resources on Animal Issues*
  Choice - v42 - i7 - March 2005 - p1198(1) [51-500]
Kistler, Max - *Causalite et lois de la nature*
  Dialogue - v43 - i1 - Wntr 2004 - p192-194 [501+]
Kitamura, Satoshi - *Me and My Cat?*
  c PW - v252 - i6 - Feb 7 2005 - p62(1) [51-500]
Kitch, Carolyn - *The Girl on the Magazine Cover: The Origins of Visual Stereotypes in American Mass Media*
  JIH - v34 - i3 - Wntr 2004 - p480(3) [501+]
  JWH - v16 - i4 - Winter 2004 - p191(16) [501+]
Kitch, Sally L. - *Higher Ground: From Utopianism to Realism in American Feminist Thought and Theory*
  Wom HR - v13 - i2 - Summer 2004 - p303-310 [501+]
Kitchell, Catherine A. - *BNA's Directory of State and Federal Courts, Judges, and Clerks: A State-by-State and General Listing, 2004 Ed.*
  R&R Bk N - v19 - i3 - August 2004 - p205(1) [501+]
Kitchen, K.A. - *On the Reliability of the Old Testament*
  Choice - v41 - i11-12 - July-August 2004 - p2062(2) [501+]
  R&R Bk N - v19 - i1 - Feb 2004 - p19(1) [51-500]
Kitcher, Philip - *Finding an Ending: Reflections on Wagner's Ring*
  Lon R Bks - v26 - i15 - August 5 2004 - p8(3) [501+]
  ON - v69 - i1 - July 2004 - p67(2) [501+]
  TLS - i5304 - Nov 26 2004 - p20(1) [501+]
Kitchin, C.R. - *Astrophysical Techniques, 4th Ed.*
  SciTech - v28 - i4 - Dec 2004 - p45(1) [51-500]
Kitching, Carolyn J., - *Britain and the Geneva Disarmament Conference: A Study in International History*
  JPR - v41 - i5 - Sept 2004 - p641-641 [501+]
Kitching, Gavin - *Wittgenstein and Society: Essays in Conceptual Puzzlement*
  R&R Bk N - v19 - i1 - Feb 2004 - p5(1) [51-500]
Kitroeff, Alexander - *Wrestling with the Ancients: Modern Greek Identity and the Olympics*
  NY - v80 - i24 - August 30 2004 - p97(1) [1-50]
  NYRB - v51 - i16 - Oct 21 2004 - p19(3) [501+]
Kitsch, Jonathan - *God against the Gods: The History of the War between Monotheism and Polytheism*
  BL - v101 - i3 - Oct 1 2004 - p302(1) [51-500]
Kitson, Frank - *Old Ironsides: The Military Biography of Oliver Cromwell*
  CR - v285 - i1666 - Nov 2004 - p314(1) [501+]
Kitson, Peter J. - *Nineteenth-Century Travels, Explorations and Empires: Writings from the Era of Imperial Consolidation 1835-1910, Vols. 1-4*
  R&R Bk N - v19 - i4 - Nov 2004 - p73(1) [51-500]
Kitt, Sandra - *Southern Comfort*
  y BL - v100 - i21 - July 2004 - p1827(1) [51-500]
Kittler, Josef - *Pattern Recognition: Proceedings*
  SciTech - v28 - i3 - Sept 2004 - p143(1) [51-500]
Kittredge, William - *The Best of Montana's Short Fiction*
  BL - v101 - i4 - Oct 15 2004 - p388(1) [51-500]
  Owning It All
  A Lib - v35 - i7 - August 2004 - p88(1) [501+]
Kittrie, Nicholas N. - *The Future of Peace in the Twenty-First Century: To Mitigate Domestic Discontents and Harmonize Global Diversity*
  R&R Bk N - v19 - i1 - Feb 2004 - pNA [51-500]
Kivelson, Valerie A. - *Orthodox Russia: Belief and Practice under the Tsars*
  AHR - v109 - i3 - June 2004 - p1003(2) [501+]
  Choice - v41 - i7 - March 2004 - p1352(1) [501+]
  Choice - v41 - i7 - March 2004 - p1352(1) [501+]
  Slav R - v63 - i3 - Fall 2004 - p649-650 [501+]

Kivimaki, Timo - *Development Cooperation as an Instrument in the Prevention of Terrorism*
JPR - v41 - i6 - Nov 2004 - p759-760 [501+]
U.S. Indonesian Hegemonic Bargaining: Strength of Weakness
R&R Bk N - v19 - i1 - Feb 2004 - p56(1) [51-500]
Kivisto, Peter - *Key Ideas in Sociology, 2nd Ed.*
R&R Bk N - v19 - i2 - May 2004 - p126 [51-500]
Kivy, Peter - *The Blackwell Guide to Aesthetics*
Choice - v42 - i2 - Oct 2004 - p305(1) [51-500]
Introduction to a Philosophy of Music
JAAC - v62 - i3 - Summer 2004 - p299-300 [501+]
The Possessor and the Possessed
JAAC - v61 - Winter 2003 - p73 [501+]
The Seventh Sense: Francis Hutcheson and Eighteenth-Century British Aesthetics
RM - v58 - i2 - Dec 2004 - p445(3) [501+]
Kiyosaki, Robert T. - *Rich Dad, Poor Dad for Teens: The Secrets about Money--That You Don't Learn in School!*
y PW - v251 - i31 - August 2 2004 - p73(1) [51-500]
Rich Dad's Success Stories (Read by Butiu, Melody). Audiobook Review
LJ - v129 - i13 - August 2004 - p130(1) [51-500]
Kiyota, Minoru - *The Case of Japanese Americans During World War II: Suppression of Civil Liberty*
R&R Bk N - v19 - i3 - August 2004 - p33(1) [51-500]
Kizenko, Nadieszda - *A Prodigal Saint: Father John of Kronstadt and the Russian People*
CHR - v90 - i3 - July 2004 - p560(3) [501+]
Kizlik, Sandy - *Algebraic Equations*
Math T - v97 - i3 - March 2004 - p223-223 [501+]
QuickStudy Laminated Reference Guides, Algebra 1
Math T - v97 - i3 - March 2004 - p223-223 [501+]
Kizny, Tomasz - *Gulag: Life and Death Inside the Soviet Concentration Camps*
BIC - v33 - i9 - Dec 2004 - p13(2) [501+]
BL - v101 - i7 - Dec 1 2004 - p623(1) [51-500]
LJ - v129 - i20 - Dec 1 2004 - p137(1) [51-500]
Kjelle, Marylou Morano - *Katherine Patterson*
y BL - v101 - i9-10 - Jan 1 2005 - p849(1) [1-50]
Klabunde, Richard E. - *Cardiovascular Physiology Concepts*
SciTech - v28 - i3 - Sept 2004 - p68(1) [51-500]
Klagge, James C. - *Wittgenstein: Biography and Philosophy*
GSR - v27 - i1 - Feb 2004 - p215-217 [501+]
Klandermans, Bert - *Methods of Social Movements Research*
CS - v33 - i1 - Jan 2004 - p120-121 [501+]
Klapdor-Kleingrothaus, Hans Voker - *Beyond the Desert 2002; Accelerator, Non-accelerator, and Space Approaches into the Next Millennium; Proceedings*
SciTech - v28 - i3 - Sept 2004 - p49(1) [1-50]
Klapper, Melissa R. - *Jewish Girls Coming of Age in America, 1860-1920*
PW - v251 - i43 - Oct 25 2004 - p43(1) [51-500]
Klare, Michael T. - *Blood and Oil: The Dangers and Consequences of America's Growing Petroleum Dependency*
BL - v101 - i1 - Sept 1 2004 - p28(1) [51-500]
KR - v72 - i13 - July 1 2004 - p619(1) [501+]
PW - v251 - i29 - July 19 2004 - p155(1) [51-500]
Klarman, Michael J. - *From Jim Crow to Civil Rights: The Supreme Court and the Struggle for Racial Equality*
Choice - v42 - i3 - Nov 2004 - p525(1) [1-50]
HLR - v118 - i3 - Jan 2005 - p973-1029 [501+]
Law&PolBR - July 2004 - p507(6) [501+]
New R - July 5 2004 - p29 [501+]
RAH - v32 - i4 - Dec 2004 - p602-609 [501+]
Klarsfeld, Andre - *The Biology of Death: Origins of Mortality*
Choice - v41 - i11-12 - July-August 2004 - p2069(2) [501+]
QRB - v79 - i3 - Sept 2004 - p338(1) [501+]
SB - v40 - i3 - May-June 2004 - p115(1) [501+]
SciTech - v28 - i1 - March 2004 - p64(1) [51-500]
Klasky, Mindy L. - *The Glasswright's Master*
ChrSFF&H - v26 - i9 - Sept 2004 - p36(1) [51-500]
Klass, David - *You Don't Know Me (Read by Landrum, Nick). Audiobook Review*
Kliatt - v38 - i6 - Nov 2004 - p53(1) [51-500]
You Don't Know Me
c SLJ - v50 - i8 - August 2004 - p78(1) [51-500]
Klass, Perri - *The Mystery of Breathing*
Ms - v14 - i1 - Spring 2004 - p87(1) [501+]
Quirky Kids: Understanding and Helping Your Child Who Doesn't Fit In: When to Worry and When Not to Worry
Globe & Mail - Oct 9 2004 - pF6 [501+]
Klassen, Henry C. - *Eye on the Future: Business People in Calgary and the Bow Valley, 1870-1900*
BHR - v78 - i1 - Spring 2004 - p151(3) [501+]
WHQ - v35 - i4 - Winter 2004 - p534-535 [501+]
Klassen, Pamela E. - *Blessed Events: Religion and Home Birth in America*
JR - v84 - i4 - Oct 2004 - p669(2) [501+]
Klauck, Hans-Josef - *Apocryphal Gospels: An Introduction*
R&R Bk N - v19 - i3 - August 2004 - p23(1) [1-50]
Klausen, Soren Harnow - *Reality Lost and Found: An Essay on the Realism-Antirealism Controversy*
Choice - v42 - i6 - Feb 2005 - p1035(1) [51-500]
R&R Bk N - v19 - i4 - Nov 2004 - p4(1) [51-500]
Klavan, Andrew - *Shotgun Alley*
BL - v101 - i4 - Oct 15 2004 - p393(1) [51-500]
PW - v251 - i39 - Sept 27 2004 - p37(1) [51-500]
Klavan, Laurence - *The Shooting Script (Read by Sullivan, Nick). Audiobook Review*
LJ - v129 - i20 - Dec 1 2004 - p182(1) [501+]
The Shooting Script
BL - v101 - i7 - Dec 1 2004 - p639(2) [51-500]
KR - v72 - i24 - Dec 15 2004 - p1168(1) [501+]
PW - v252 - i7 - Feb 14 2005 - p54(1) [51-500]
Klawitter, George - *The Agony of Words*
Lam Bk Rpt - v13 - i4-5 - Nov-Dec 2004 - p18(3) [501+]
Kleber, John E. - *Thomas D. Clark of Kentucky: An Uncommon Life in the Commonwealth*
JSH - v70 - i4 - Nov 2004 - p982(2) [501+]
Klee, Wanda G. - *Leibhaftige Dekadenz: Studien zur Korperlichkeit in ausgewahlten Werken von Joris-Karl Huysmans und Oscar Wilde*
NCFS - v33 - i1-2 - Fall-Winter 2004 - p181(3) [501+]
Kleeman, Faye Yuan - *Under an Imperial Sun: Japanese Colonial Literature of Taiwan and the South*
R&R Bk N - v19 - i1 - Feb 2004 - p219(1) [1-50]
Kleiber, Christian - *Statistical Size Distributions in Economics and Actuarial Sciences*
JEL - v42 - i1 - March 2004 - p244(1) [501+]
Klein, Abby - *Tooth Trouble (Illus. by McKinley, John K.)*
c KR - v72 - i13 - July 1 2004 - p631(1) [51-500]
c PW - v251 - i35 - August 30 2004 - p55(1) [51-500]
Klein, Barry - *Mail Order Business Directory, 19th ed.*
R&R Bk N - v19 - i1 - Feb 2004 - p109(1) [51-500]
Klein, Christina - *Cold War Orientalism: Asia in the Middlebrow Imagination, 1945-1961*
Am Q - v56 - i2 - June 2004 - p461(9) [501+]
J Am St - v38 - i1 - April 2004 - p149-150 [501+]
Klein, Daniel - *Such Vicious Minds: A Murder Mystery Featuring Elvis Presley*
PW - v251 - i27 - July 5 2004 - p41(2) [51-500]
Klein, David R. - *Organic Chemistry as a Second Language: Translating the Basic Concepts*
J Chem Ed - v81 - i12 - Dec 2004 - p1717-1718 [501+]
Klein, Donna - *The PDQ (Pretty Darn Quick!) Vegetarian Cookbook: 240 Healthy and Easy No-Prep Recipes for Busy Cooks*
LJ - v129 - i20 - Dec 1 2004 - p150(2) [51-500]
Klein, Eric A. - *Management of Prostate Cancer, 2nd Ed.*
SciTech - v28 - i3 - Sept 2004 - p92(1) [51-500]
Klein, Felix - *Elementary Mathematics from an Advanced Standpoint: Arithmetic, Algebra, Analysis*
SciTech - v28 - i4 - Dec 2004 - p16(1) [1-50]
Elementary Mathematics from an Advanced Standpoint: Geometry
SciTech - v28 - i4 - Dec 2004 - p42(1) [51-500]
Klein, Herbert S. - *A Population History of the United States*
Choice - v42 - i3 - Nov 2004 - p548(1) [1-50]
SF - v83 - i1 - Sept 2004 - p451(3) [501+]
Klein, Jacky - *The Bone Beneath the Pulp: Drawings by Wyndham Lewis (Illus. by Lewis, Wyndham)*
Apo - v161 - i516 - Feb 2005 - p16(1) [501+]
Klein, Jake - *Then and Now: Santa Monica*
R&R Bk N - v19 - i1 - Feb 2004 - p65(1) [501+]
Klein, Jennifer - *For All These Rights: Business, Labor, and the Shaping of America's Public-Private Welfare State*
CS - v33 - i6 - Nov 2004 - p729(3) [501+]
JAH - v91 - i3 - Dec 2004 - p1056(2) [501+]
RAH - v32 - i2 - June 2004 - p214-9 [501+]
Klein, Kathleen Gregory - *The Deadly Garden Tour*
BL - v101 - i4 - Oct 15 2004 - p393(1) [51-500]
Klein, Kim - *Fundraising in Times of Crisis*
R&R Bk N - v19 - i3 - August 2004 - p159(1) [51-500]
Klein, Lawrence A. - *Sensor and Data Fusion: A Tool for Information Assessment and Decision Making*
SciTech - v28 - i3 - Sept 2004 - p153(1) [51-500]
Klein, Leigh - *My Favorite Moves: Making the Big Plays*
SLJ - v50 - i10 - Oct 2004 - pS66(1) [501+]
Klein, Malcom W. - *Gang Cop: The Words and Ways of Officer Paco Domingo*
Choice - v42 - i3 - Nov 2004 - p572(1) [1-50]
Klein, Mason - *Modigliani: Beyond the Myth*
Choice - v42 - i4 - Dec 2004 - p650(2) [1-50]
LJ - v129 - i13 - August 2004 - p74(1) [51-500]
Klein, Michael U. - *The Private Sector in Development: Enterpreneurship, Regulation, and Competitive Discipline*
JEL - v41 - i4 - Dec 2003 - p1381(1) [501+]
Klein, Norman M. - *The Vatican to Vegas: The History of Special Effects*
R&R Bk N - v19 - i4 - Nov 2004 - p249(1) [501+]
Klein, Robert M. - *Anatomy, Histology and Cell Biology: PreTest Self-Assessment and Review, 2nd Ed.*
SciTech - v28 - i4 - Dec 2004 - p68(1) [51-500]
Klein, Robin - *Came Back to Show You I Could Fly (Read by Marnika, Dino). Audiobook Review*
Kliatt - v38 - i6 - Nov 2004 - p44(1) [51-500]
y SLJ - v50 - i9 - Sept 2004 - p77(1) [51-500]
Klein, Saul D. - *Real Estate Technology Guide*
R&R Bk N - v19 - i3 - August 2004 - p111(1) [51-500]
Klein, Susan - *Through a Ruby Window: A Martha's Vineyard Childhood*
y Kliatt - v39 - i1 - Jan 2005 - p30(1) [51-500]
Klein, Terrance W. - *How Things Are in the World: Metaphysics and Theology in Wittgenstein and Rahner*
R&R Bk N - v19 - i1 - Feb 2004 - p5(1) [51-500]
Klein, Ursula - *Experiments, Models, Paper Tools: Cultures of Organic Chemistry in the Nineteenth Century*
JIH - v35 - i2 - Autumn 2004 - p279(2) [501+]
Kleinberg, Tamara - *Bootcamp 360: A Complete Fitness Programs for Brides: The Few, the Proud, the Fit*
LJ - v130 - i1 - Jan 1 2005 - p144(3) [501+]
Kleine, Karynne L.M. - *Becoming a Mentor Leader in a Professional Community*
R&R Bk N - v19 - i2 - May 2004 - p117 [51-500]
Kleiner, Fred - *Gardner's Art through the Ages, 12th Ed.*
R&R Bk N - v19 - i2 - May 2004 - p194(1) [51-500]
Kleiner, Lynn - *Kids Can Listen, Kids Can Move!*
c Teach Mus - v12 - i2 - Oct 2004 - p72(1) [51-500]
Kleinhenz, Christopher - *Medieval Italy: An Encyclopedia*
Ref Rev - May 2004 - pNA [501+]
Kleinknecht, Alfred - *Innovation and Firm Performance: Econometric Explorations of Survey Data*
JEL - v41 - i4 - Dec 2003 - p1322(3) [501+]
Kleinman, Daniel Lee - *Impure Cultures: University Biology and the World of Commerce*
Isis - v95 - i3 - Sept 2004 - p532(1) [501+]
SciTech - v28 - i3 - Sept 2004 - p57(1) [1-50]
Kleinschmidt, Harald - *People on the Move: Attitudes Toward and Perceptions of Migration in Medieval and Modern Europe*
Choice - v42 - i2 - Oct 2004 - p362(1) [51-500]
Kleinwort, Malte - *KafkasVerfahren: Literatur, Individuum und Gesellschaft im Umkreis von Kafkas Briefen an Milena*
MLN - v119 - i3 - April 2004 - p627-629 [501+]
Kleinzahler, August - *Cutty, One Rock: Low Characters and Strange Places, Gently Explained*
BL - v101 - i5 - Nov 1 2004 - p454(1) [51-500]
Ent W - i790 - Oct 29 2004 - p75 [51-500]
Esq - v142 - i5 - Nov 2004 - p48(1) [51-500]
Globe & Mail - Dec 11 2004 - pD50 [501+]
KR - v72 - i17 - Sept 1 2004 - p849(2) [501+]
PW - v251 - i38 - Sept 20 2004 - p52(2) [51-500]
Klemp, Klaus - *Nackt fur Stalin: Korperbilder in der russischen Fotografie der 20er und 30er Jahre*
HNet - July 2004 - pNA [501+]
Klemperer, Victor - *The Lesser Evil: The Diaries of Victor Klemperer, 1945-1959*
Atl - v294 - i5 - Dec 2004 - p140(6) [501+]
Choice - v42 - i2 - Oct 2004 - p362(1) [51-500]
The Lesser Evil: The Diaries of Victor Klemperer 1945-1959
LJ - v129 - i16 - Oct 1 2004 - p91(1) [51-500]
PW - v251 - i28 - July 12 2004 - p56(1) [51-500]
Klempner, Daniel - *Handbook of Polymeric Foams and Foam Technology, 2nd Ed.*
Choice - v42 - i3 - Nov 2004 - p511(1) [1-50]
SciTech - v28 - i3 - Sept 2004 - p168(1) [51-500]
Klempner, Geoff - *Operation and Maintenance of Large Turbo Generators*
SciTech - v28 - i4 - Dec 2004 - p148(1) [501+]
Klempt, Eberhard - *Hadron Spectroscopy: Proceedings*
SciTech - v28 - i4 - Dec 2004 - p52(1) [51-500]

Klenk, Hans-Dieter - *Ebola and Marburg Viruses: Molecular and Cellular Biology*
E-Streams - Dec 2004 - pNA [501+]
SciTech - v28 - i1 - March 2004 - p77(1) [51-500]

Klensch, Elsa - *Live at 10:00, Dead at 10:15*
BL - v101 - i2 - Sept 15 2004 - p214(2) [51-500]
DroRevMy - v24 - i3 - May-June 2004 - p12(1) [1-50]
Ent W - Sept 10 2004 - p170 [51-500]
KR - v72 - i14 - July 15 2004 - p662(1) [51-500]
LJ - v129 - i18 - Nov 1 2004 - p63(1) [51-500]

Klep, P.M.M. - *The Statistical Mind in a Pre-Statistical Era: The Netherlands, 1750-1850*
Isis - v95 - i3 - Sept 2004 - p508(2) [501+]

Klerks, Cat - *Emily Carr: The Incredible Life and Adventures of a West Coast Artist*
CBRA - Annual 2003 - p52(1) [51-500]

Klerkx, Greg - *Lost in Space: The Fall of NASA and the Dream of a New Space Age*
TLS - i5284 - July 9 2004 - p11(1) [501+]

Klett, Mark - *Third Views, Second Sights: A Rephotographic Survey of the American West*
Afterimage - v32 - i3 - Nov-Dec 2004 - p14(1) [501+]

Kleveman, Lutz - *The New Great Game: Blood and Oil in Central Asia*
A Aff - v35 - i2 - July 2004 - p230-232 [501+]
HT - v54 - i11 - Nov 2004 - p86(4) [501+]
JPR - v41 - i5 - Sept 2004 - p641-642 [501+]
y Kliatt - v39 - i2 - March 2005 - p37(1) [51-500]

Kleypas, Lisa - *Secrets of a Summer Night*
PW - v251 - i41 - Oct 11 2004 - p61(1) [51-500]

Klieforth, Alexander Leslie - *The Scottish Invention of America, Democracy and Human Rights: A History of Liberty and Freedom from the Ancient Celts to the New Millennium*
R&R Bk N - v19 - i3 - August 2004 - p12(1) [1-50]

Kliegman, Robert M. - *Practical Strategies in Pediatric Diagnosis and Therapy, 2nd Ed.*
SciTech - v28 - i4 - Dec 2004 - p111(1) [1-50]

Klieman, Kairn A. - *The Pygmies Were Our Compass: Bantu and Batwa in the History of West Central Africa, Early Times to c.1900 C.E.*
Choice - v42 - i2 - Oct 2004 - p348(1) [51-500]
IJAHS - v37 - i1 - Wntr 2004 - p183-185 [501+]

Kliger, Benjamin - *Integrative Medicine: Principles for Practice*
SciTech - v28 - i3 - Sept 2004 - p78(1) [51-500]

Klilmov, Victor I. - *Semiconductor and Metal Nanocrystals: Synthesis and Electronic and Optical Properties*
SciTech - v28 - i1 - March 2004 - p166(1) [51-500]

Klimi, Julia - *At Home in Greece*
LJ - v130 - i1 - Jan 1 2005 - p106(1) [51-500]

Klimo, Arpad von - *Nation, Konfession, Geschichte: Zur nationalen Geschichtskultur Ungarns im europdischen Kontext*
HNet - June 2004 - pNA [501+]

Klinck, Anne L. - *Medieval Woman's Song: Cross-Cultural Approaches*
JEGP - v103 - i3 - July 2004 - p392-394 [501+]

Kline, Frank M. - *The Educator's Guide to Mental Health Issues in the Classroom*
R&R Bk N - v19 - i4 - Nov 2004 - p189(1) [501+]

Kline, Kevin E. - *SQL in a Nutshell, 2nd Ed.*
SciTech - v28 - i4 - Dec 2004 - p22(1) [51-500]

Kline, Lanning B. - *Neuro-Ophthalmology Review Manual, 5th ed.*
SciTech - v28 - i1 - March 2004 - p114(1) [51-500]

Kline, Rex B. - *Beyond Significance Testing: Reforming Data Analysis Methods in Behavioral Research*
SciTech - v28 - i3 - Sept 2004 - p1(1) [501+]

Kline, Stephen - *Digital Play: The Interaction of Technology, Culture, and Marketing*
CBRA - Annual 2003 - p444(1) [501+]

Kline, Suzy - *Horrible Harry and the Locked Closet (Illus. by Remkiewicz, Frank)*
c CH Bwatch - v14 - i11 - Nov 2004 - pNA [51-500]
c SLJ - v50 - i11 - Nov 2004 - p108(1) [51-500]

Kline, Wendy - *Building a Better Race: Gender, Sexuality, and Eugenics From the Turn of the Century to the Baby Boom*
JWH - v16 - i4 - Winter 2004 - p215(11) [501+]

Kling, Christine - *Cross Current*
BL - v101 - i1 - Sept 1 2004 - p69(1) [51-500]
PW - v251 - i40 - Oct 4 2004 - p71(1) [51-500]

Kling, David W. - *The Bible in History: How the Texts Have Shaped the Times*
CC - v122 - i1 - Jan 11 2005 - p37(1) [501+]
LJ - v129 - i14 - Sept 1 2004 - p157(1) [51-500]
PW - v251 - i28 - July 12 2004 - p60(2) [51-500]

Jonathan Edwards at Home and Abroad: Historical Memories, Cultural Movements, Global Horizons
Choice - v41 - i11-12 - July-August 2004 - p2062 [501+]

Klinge, Matti - *Den politiske Runeberg*
Scan St - v76 - i4 - Winter 2004 - p571(3) [501+]

Klinger, Cornelia - *Continental Philosophy in Feminist Perspective: Re-reading the Canon in German*
Signs - v30 - i2 - Wntr 2005 - p1706(6) [501+]

Klinger, Leslie S. - *The New Annotated Sherlock Holmes*
KR - v72 - i18 - Sept 15 2004 - pNA [501+]
Spec - v296 - i9200 - Dec 4 2004 - p36(2) [501+]

Klinghoffer, David - *Why the Jews Rejected Jesus: The Turning Point in Western History*
KR - v72 - i24 - Dec 15 2004 - p1184(1) [501+]
LJ - v130 - i1 - Jan 1 2005 - p118(1) [51-500]
PW - v252 - i4 - Jan 24 2005 - p238(1) [501+]

Klinken, Gerry Van - *Minorities, Modernity, and the Emerging Nation: Christians in Indonesia: A Biographical Approach*
IBMR - v28 - i4 - Oct 2004 - p186(2) [501+]

Klinkenberg, Jeff - *Seasons of Real Florida*
HNet - July 2004 - pNA [501+]

Klinkenborg, Verlyn - *The Last Fine Time*
Bwatch - v26 - i9 - Sept 2004 - p7(1) [51-500]

Klinkowitz, Jerome - *The Vonnegut Effect*
R&R Bk N - v19 - i4 - Nov 2004 - p244(1) [501+]
TLS - i5289 - August 13 2004 - p29(1) [501+]

Klionsky, Daniel J. - *Autophagy*
SciTech - v28 - i1 - March 2004 - p66(1) [51-500]

Klise, Kate - *Deliver Us from Normal*
y CCB-B - v58 - i6 - Feb 2005 - p256(1) [501+]
y Kliatt - v39 - i2 - March 2005 - p31(1) [51-500]
y KR - v73 - i4 - Feb 15 2005 - p231(1) [51-500]
People - v63 - i11 - March 21 2005 - p60 [51-500]

Regarding the Sink: Where, Oh Where, Did Waters Go? (Illus. by Klise, M. Sarah)
c BL - v101 - i1 - Sept 1 2004 - p124(2) [1-50]
c HB - v80 - i5 - Sept-Oct 2004 - p588(2) [51-500]
c KR - v72 - i14 - July 15 2004 - p688(1) [51-500]
c SLJ - v50 - i10 - Oct 2004 - p170(1) [51-500]

Shall I Knit You a Hat? A Christmas Yarn (Illus. by Klise, M. Sarah)
c BL - v101 - i7 - Dec 1 2004 - p659(2) [51-500]
c KR - v72 - i21 - Nov 1 2004 - p1051(1) [51-500]
c PW - v251 - i39 - Sept 27 2004 - p61(1) [51-500]

Klitzman, Robert - *Mortal Secrets: Truth and Lies in the Age of AIDS*
SciTech - v28 - i3 - Sept 2004 - p84(1) [501+]

Klock, Geoff - *How to Read Superhero Comics and Why*
Col Lit - v32 - i1 - Wntr 2005 - p166(11) [501+]

Klockars, Carl - *The Contours of Police Integrity*
R&R Bk N - v19 - i1 - Feb 2004 - p143(1) [51-500]

Klodt, C. - *Bescheidene Grobe: Die Herrschergestalt, der Kaiserpalast und die Stadt Rom: Literarische Reflexuinen monarchischer Selbstdarstellung*
Class R - v54 - i2 - Nov 2004 - p380(2) [501+]

Klohr, Cynthia - *Nature from Within: Gustav Theodor Fechner and His Psychophysical Worldview*
Choice - v42 - i2 - Oct 2004 - p307(1) [51-500]

Klopper, Susan M. - *Introduction to Online Accounting and Financial Research: Search Strategies, Research Case Study, Research Problems, and Data Source Evaluations and Reviews*
R&R Bk N - v19 - i3 - August 2004 - p131(1) [501+]

Klose, Andreas R. - *Dogmas of Democratic Historical Thought: The Writing of Monumental National History in the USA*
JAH - v91 - i3 - Dec 2004 - p1065(1) [501+]

Klose, Liz - *Roses for Ontario*
CBRA - Annual 2003 - p420(1) [51-500]

Klosek, Jacqueline - *The Legal Guide to e-Business*
R&R Bk N - v19 - i1 - Feb 2004 - pNA [51-500]

Klosko, George - *The Principle of Fairness and Political Obligation, New Ed.*
Ethics - v115 - i2 - Jan 2005 - p418(5) [501+]
R&R Bk N - v19 - i3 - August 2004 - p174(1) [501+]

Klotter, James C. - *The Human Tradition in the Old South*
JSH - v70 - i3 - August 2004 - p679(2) [501+]

Kentucky Justice, Southern Honor, and American Manhood: Understanding the Life and Death of Richard Reid
JSH - v71 - i1 - Feb 2005 - p188(2) [501+]
JAH - v91 - i2 - Sept 2004 - p648(2) [501+]

Klotter, John C. - *Criminal Law, 7th Ed.*
R&R Bk N - v19 - i1 - Feb 2004 - pNA [51-500]

Klotz, Robert J. - *The Politics of Internet Communication*
PSQ - v119 - i2 - Summer 2004 - p395(2) [501+]
R&R Bk N - v19 - i2 - May 2004 - p128 [51-500]

Klucas, Gillian - *Leadville: The Struggle to Revive an American Town*
BL - v101 - i5 - Nov 1 2004 - p448(1) [51-500]
KR - v72 - i18 - Sept 15 2004 - p903(2) [501+]
PW - v251 - i38 - Sept 20 2004 - p54(1) [51-500]

Klug, Beverly J. - *Widening the Circle: Culturally Relevant Pedagogy for American Indian Children*
TCR - v106 - i5 - May 2004 - p911(6) [501+]

Kluge, Alexander - *The Devil's Blind Spot: Tales from the New Century*
KR - v72 - i18 - Sept 15 2004 - p884(1) [501+]

Kluger, Jeffrey - *Splendid Solution: Jonas Salk and the Conquest of Polio*
Bus W - i3923 - March 7 2005 - p22 [501+]
Ent W - i810 - March 11 2005 - p109 [51-500]
Globe & Mail - March 19 2005 - pD10 [501+]
KR - v72 - i24 - Dec 15 2004 - p1184(2) [501+]
LJ - v130 - i1 - Jan 1 2005 - p139(1) [51-500]
PW - v252 - i2 - Jan 10 2005 - p47(1) [51-500]

Kluger, Richard - *Simple Justice: The History of Brown v. Board of Education and Black America's Struggle for Equality*
HNet - Sept 2004 - pNA [501+]
LJ - v129 - i12 - July 2004 - p127(1) [51-500]
New R - July 5 2004 - p29 [501+]
NYRB - v51 - i14 - Sept 23 2004 - p47(4) [501+]

Kluger, Steve - *Last Days of Summer*
LJ - v130 - i1 - Jan 1 2005 - p174(1) [501+]

Kluwer Academic Publishers - *International Journal of Health Care Finance and Economics*
JEL - v41 - i4 - Dec 2003 - p1447(1) [501+]

Knack, Martha C. - *Boundaries Between: The Southern Paiutes, 1775-1995*
WHQ - v35 - i1 - Spring 2004 - p82-83 [501+]

Knack, Stephen - *Democracy, Governance, and Growth*
JEL - v42 - i3 - Sept 2004 - p858(3) [501+]

Knapen, Hans - *Forests of Fortune: The Environmental History of Southeast Borneo, 1600-1880*
Pac A - v77 - i3 - Fall 2004 - p605(2) [501+]

Knapp, Brian - *Earth and Moon, Vols. 1-8*
c SB - v40 - i5 - Sept-Oct 2004 - p209(1) [501+]
Earth's Resources
y SB - v40 - i5 - Sept-Oct 2004 - p195(2) [51-500]
Space Science
c SLJ - v50 - i10 - Oct 2004 - p95(1) [51-500]

Knapp, Caroline - *Appetites: Why Women Want*
Kliatt - v38 - i6 - Nov 2004 - p36(1) [51-500]
Drinking: A Love Story
BL - v101 - i2 - Sept 15 2004 - p225(1) [51-500]
Globe & Mail - Jan 8 2005 - pD15 [51-500]

Knapp, Connie L. - *Making Community Connections: The Orton Family Foundation Community Mapping Program*
SE - v68 - i7 - Nov-Dec 2004 - p490(1) [501+]

Knapp, Eva - *Emblematics in Hungary: A Study of the History of Symbolic Representation in Renaissance and Baroque Literature*
Ren Q - v57 - i4 - Winter 2004 - p1441(3) [501+]

Knapp, Jeffrey - *Shakespeare's Tribe: Church, Nation, and Theater in Renaissance England*
Clio - v33 - i3 - Spring 2004 - p330(7) [501+]
Shakes Q - v55 - i2 - Summer 2004 - p221-223 [501+]

Knapp, Raymond - *Symphonic Metamorphoses: Subjectivity and Alienation in Mahler's Re-Cycled Songs*
Notes - v61 - i1 - Sept 2004 - p126(3) [501+]

Knapp, Sandra - *Plant Discoveries: A Botanist's Voyage through Plant Exploration*
SciTech - v28 - i1 - March 2004 - p66(1) [51-500]

Knapp, Sarah Edison - *The School Counseling and School Social Work Treatment Planner*
R&R Bk N - v19 - i1 - Feb 2004 - pNA [51-500]

Knappert, Jan - *A Survey of Swahili Songs with English Translations*
R&R Bk N - v19 - i3 - August 2004 - p257(1) [51-500]

Knasas, John F.X. - *Being and Some Twentieth-Century Thomists*
RM - v58 - i2 - Dec 2004 - p447(3) [501+]

Kneale, Matthew - *Small Crimes in an Age of Abundance*
KR - v73 - i3 - Feb 1 2005 - p140(2) [501+]
LJ - v130 - i2 - Feb 2005 - p73(1) [51-500]
PW - v252 - i2 - Jan 10 2005 - p36(1) [51-500]

Kneebone, Susan - *The Refugees Convention 50 Years On: Globalisation and International Law*
R&R Bk N - v19 - i1 - Feb 2004 - pNA [51-500]

Kneib, Martha - *Women Soldiers, Spies, and Patriots of the American Revolution*
 y   SLJ - v50 - i12 - Dec 2004 - p162(1) [51-500]

Knell, Simon J. - *The Culture of English Geology 1815-1851*
   VS - v45 - i2 - Winter 2003 - p344 [501+]
Museums and the Future of Collecting, 2nd Ed.
   R&R Bk N - v19 - i3 - August 2004 - p1(1) [1-50]

Knerr, Douglas - *Suburban Steel: The Magnificent Failure of the Lustron Corporation, 1945-1951*
   Choice - v42 - i3 - Nov 2004 - p504(1) [1-50]

Knetsch, Joe - *Florida's Seminole Wars, 1817-1858*
   HNet - Sept 2004 - pNA [501+]

Knezevic, Boban - *Black Blossom*
   PW - v252 - i4 - Jan 24 2005 - p227(1) [501+]

Knife - *Dinosaur Adventure*
   Sch Lib - v52 - i3 - Autumn 2004 - p151(1) [501+]

Knight, Alan E. - *Les Mysteres de la Procession de Lille*
   FS - v58 - i3 - July 2004 - p397-398 [501+]

Knight, Anthony P. - *Guide to Plant Poisoning of Animals in North America*
   SciTech - v28 - i3 - Sept 2004 - p130(1) [51-500]

Knight, Bernard - *Fear in the Forest (Read by Matthews, Paul). Audiobook Review*
 c   Kliatt - v38 - i4 - July 2004 - p51(1) [51-500]

Knight, Carlo - *La "Memorie delle Piture" di Angelica Kauffman*
   Eight-C St - v37 - i3 - Spring 2004 - p478-482 [501+]

Knight, Charles A. - *The Literature of Satire*
   Choice - v42 - i2 - Oct 2004 - p288(1) [501+]

Knight, Christopher J. - *Uncommon Readers: Denis Donoghue, Frank Kermode, George Steiner, and the Tradition of the Common Reader*
   BIC - v33 - i5 - August 2004 - p20(1) [501+]
   Choice - v42 - i1 - Sept 2004 - p95(2) [501+]

Knight, Erika - *Simple Knits with a Twist: Unique Projects for Creative Knitters*
   LJ - v129 - i13 - August 2004 - p78(1) [501+]

Knight, Hilary - *A Firefly in a Fir Tree: A Carol for Mice*
 c   BL - v101 - i2 - Sept 15 2004 - p251(1) [51-500]

Knight, James R. - *Bonnie and Clyde: A Twenty-First-Century Update*
   SHQ - v108 - i1 - July 2004 - p122-123 [501+]

Knight, John - *Waiting for the Wolves in Japan: An Anthropological Study of People-Wildlife Relations*
   JAS - v63 - i3 - August 2004 - p800-802 [501+]
Wildlife in Asia: Cultural Perspectives
   JRAI - v10 - i4 - Dec 2004 - p922(2) [501+]

Knight, Joseph A. - *A Crisis Call for New Preventive Medicine: Emerging Effects of Lifestyle on Morbidity and Mortality*
   SciTech - v28 - i4 - Dec 2004 - p82(1) [51-500]

Knight, Peter - *Conspiracy Theories in American History: An Encyclopedia*
   Choice - v41 - i11-12 - July-August 2004 - p2024(2) [501+]
   Ref Rev - July 2004 - pNA [501+]
   R&R Bk N - v19 - i3 - August 2004 - p64(1) [51-500]

Knight, Randall D. - *Physics for Scientists and Engineers: A Strategic Approach with Modern Physics*
   SciTech - v28 - i3 - Sept 2004 - p45(1) [1-50]
   TimHES - v0 - i1668 - Nov 26 2004 - pXIV(2) [501+]

Knight, Richard L. - *Ranching West of the 100th Meridian: Culture, Ecology, and Economics*
   WHQ - v35 - i3 - Autumn 2004 - p378(2) [501+]

Knight, Rory - *Timothy The Tortoise: The Remarkable Story of the Nation's Oldest Pet*
   Spec - v296 - i9200 - Dec 4 2004 - p48(1) [501+]

Knight, Sian - *Muscles, Bones, and Skin, 2nd Ed.*
   SciTech - v28 - i1 - March 2004 - p107(1) [1-50]

Knight, Stephen - *Robin Hood: A Mythic Biography*
   Lon R Bks - v26 - i14 - July 22 2004 - p22(3) [501+]
Sardines and Other Poems
 c   Sch Lib - v52 - i3 - Autumn 2004 - p154(1) [501+]

Knight, W. Nicolas - *Autobiography in Shakespeare's Plays*
   Six Ct J - v34 - i4 - Winter 2003 - p1226-1226 [501+]

Knight, Wendy - *Far from Home: Father-Daughter Travel Adventures*
   LJ - v129 - i12 - July 2004 - p108(1) [51-500]

Knighton, C.S. - *Pepys's Later Diaries*
   CR - v286 - i1668 - Jan 2005 - p62(2) [501+]
Westminster Abbey Reformed, 1540-1640
   R&R Bk N - v19 - i1 - Feb 2004 - p33(1) [1-50]

Knighton, Monica - *Tarot of the Dead*
   Bwatch - Dec 2004 - pNA [501+]

Knijn, Trudie - *Solidarity between the Sexes and the Generations: Transformations in Europe*
   R&R Bk N - v19 - i3 - August 2004 - p147(1) [51-500]

Knippschild, S. - *'Drum Bietet zum Bunde die Hande'. Rechtssymbolische Akte in zwischenstaatlichen Beziehungen im oreintalischen und griechisch-romischen Altertum*
   Class R - v54 - i2 - Nov 2004 - p476(3) [501+]

Knishinsky, Ran - *Prickly Pear Cactus Medicine: Treatments For Diabetes, Cholesterol, And The Immune System*
   Bwatch - March 2005 - pNA [51-500]

Kniskern, Nancy V. - *Moving and Relocation Directory 2004, 4th Ed.*
   R&R Bk N - v19 - i1 - Feb 2004 - p134(1) [51-500]

Knobler, Stacey L. - *Learning from SARS: Preparing for the Next Disease Outbreak: Workshop Summary*
   SciTech - v28 - i3 - Sept 2004 - p85(1) [501+]
Resistance Phenomenon in Microbes and Infectious Disease Vectors: Implications for Human Health and Strategies for Containment: Workshop Summary: Proceedings
   SciTech - v28 - i1 - March 2004 - p76(1) [51-500]

Knobloch, Manfred - *Web Design with XML*
   SciTech - v28 - i3 - Sept 2004 - p29(1) [51-500]

Knoepfler, D. - *Eretria fouilles et recherches XI. Decrets eretriens de proxenie et de citoyennete*
   Class R - v53 - i2 - Nov 2003 - p454-458 [501+]

Knohl, Israel - *The Divine Symphony: The Bible's Many Voices*
   Intpr - v58 - i3 - July 2004 - p304(3) [501+]

Knoll, Andrew - *Life on a Young Planet*
   New Sci - v184 - i2472 - Nov 6 2004 - p53(1) [51-500]

Knollenberg, Bernhard - *Growth of the American Revolution: 1766-1775*
   R&R Bk N - v19 - i1 - Feb 2004 - p58(1) [51-500]

Knoop, Todd A. - *Recessions and Depressions: Understanding Business Cycles*
   Choice - v42 - i7 - March 2005 - p1277(1) [51-500]
   R&R Bk N - v19 - i4 - Nov 2004 - p86(1) [51-500]

Knopf, David Thomson - *The Whole Equation: A History of Hollywood*
   NL - v87 - i6 - Nov-Dec 2004 - p43(2) [501+]

Knopf-Newman, Marcy Jane - *Beyond Slash, Burn, and Poison: Transforming Breast Cancer Stories into Action*
   LJ - v129 - i14 - Sept 1 2004 - p184(2) [501+]

Knoppers, Bartha Maria - *Populations and Genetics; Legal and Socio-ethical Perspectives*
   R&R Bk N - v19 - i3 - August 2004 - p201(1) [1-50]

Knoppers, Laura Lunger - *Puritanism and Its Discontents*
   AHR - v109 - i4 - Oct 2004 - p1196-1197 [501+]
   Ren Q - v57 - i3 - Fall 2004 - p1125(3) [501+]

Knott, Bill - *The Unsubscriber*
   BL - v101 - i4 - Oct 15 2004 - p382(1) [51-500]
   LJ - v129 - i17 - Oct 15 2004 - p66(1) [51-500]
   Poet - v185 - i5 - Feb 2005 - p387(5) [501+]
   PW - v251 - i47 - Nov 22 2004 - p57(1) [51-500]

Knouff, Gregory T. - *The Soldiers' Revolution: Pennsylvanians in Arms and the Forging of Early American Identity*
   Choice - v42 - i2 - Oct 2004 - p356(1) [51-500]
The Soliders' Revolution: Pennsylvanians in Arms and the Forging of Early American Identity
   W&M Q - v61 - i4 - Oct 2004 - p773-776 [501+]

Know it: Communicating
   LibMed - v22 - i5 - Feb 2004 - p86(1) [501+]

Know Your Enemy, 2d Ed.
   Bwatch - v26 - i8 - August 2004 - p7(1) [51-500]

Knowles, Alison - *Spoken Text*
   PAJ - v26 - i3 - Sept 2004 - p128-135 [501+]

Knowles, Elizabeth - *The Oxford Dictionary of Quotations, 6th Ed.*
   LJ - v129 - i14 - Sept 1 2004 - p188(1) [51-500]
Talk about Books! A Guide for Book Clubs, Literature Circles, and Discussion Groups
   LibMed - v22 - i4 - March 2004 - p88(1) [51-500]

Knowles, M. - *Micro Energy Systems*
   SciTech - v28 - i4 - Dec 2004 - p145(1) [501+]

Knowles, Richard Paul - *Shakespeare and Canada: Essays on Production, Translation, and Adaptation*
   R&R Bk N - v19 - i4 - Nov 2004 - p236(1) [501+]

Knowles, Valerie - *Come Blow Your Horne*
   Beav - v84 - i5 - Oct-Nov 2004 - p42(1) [501+]

Knox, Barbara - *Afghanistan*
 c   SLJ - v50 - i8 - August 2004 - p110(1) [51-500]

Knox, Caroline - *He Paves the Road with Iron Bars*
   Ant R - v63 - i1 - Wntr 2005 - p191(2) [51-500]

Knox, David - *Choices in Relationships: An Introduction to Marriage and the Family, 8th Ed.*
   R&R Bk N - v19 - i4 - Nov 2004 - p127(1) [1-50]

Knox, Lorna Ann - *Scary News*
 c   CH Bwatch - Feb 2005 - pNA [51-500]

Knox, Melanie N. - *Pension Distribution Answer Book, 2004 Ed.*
   R&R Bk N - v19 - i1 - Feb 2004 - pNA [51-500]

Knox, Susan - *Financial Basics: A Money-Management Guide for Students*
 y   VOYA - v27 - i4 - Oct 2004 - p327(1) [51-500]

Knuckle, Essie - *Other People's Rotten Kids*
   Bwatch - Oct 2004 - pNA [51-500]

Knudsen, Michelle - *A Slimy Story (Illus. by Billin-Frye, Paige)*
 c   SLJ - v51 - i1 - Jan 2005 - p95(1) [51-500]

Knudsen, Shannon - *Police Officers*
 c   BL - v101 - i4 - Oct 15 2004 - p426(1) [51-500]

Knudsen, Steen - *Guide to Analysis of DNA Microarray Data, 2nd Ed.*
   E-Streams - Nov 2004 - pNA [501+]

Knutson, Barbara - *Love and Roast Chicken: A Trickster Tale from the Andes Mountains (Illus. by Knutson, Barbara)*
 c   BL - v101 - i2 - Sept 15 2004 - p247(1) [51-500]
 c   CCB-B - v58 - i2 - Oct 2004 - p83(1) [51-500]
   HB - v80 - i6 - Nov-Dec 2004 - p720(2) [501+]
 c   KR - v72 - i15 - August 1 2004 - p743(1) [51-500]
 c   SLJ - v50 - i11 - Nov 2004 - p126(2) [51-500]

Koakowski, Leszek - *The Two Eyes of Spinoza and Other Essays on Philosophers*
   R&R Bk N - v20 - i1 - Feb 2005 - p5(1) [51-500]

Kobak, Annette - *Joe's War: My Father Decoded*
   BooChiTr - March 14 2004 - p2(1) [501+]
   CR - v285 - i1664 - Sept 2004 - p185(1) [501+]
   TLS - i5284 - July 9 2004 - p27(1) [501+]

Kobayashi, Makoto - *What's Michael? The Ideal Cat*
 c   BL - v100 - i22 - August 2004 - p1935(1) [51-500]

Kobayashi, Motofumi - *Apocalypse Meow*
   Ent W - i808 - Feb 25 2005 - p105 [501+]
   VOYA - v27 - i5 - Dec 2004 - p407(1) [51-500]
Apocalypse Meow: Vol. 1
   PW - v251 - i30 - July 26 2004 - p41(1) [501+]

Kobeisy, Ahmed Nezar - *Counseling American Muslims: Understanding the Faith and Helping the People*
   Choice - v42 - i3 - Nov 2004 - p568(1) [51-500]

Koblinsky, Marjorie - *Reducing Material Mortality: Learning from Bolivia, China, Egypt, Honduras, Indonesia, Jamaica, and Zimbabwe*
   JEL - v41 - i4 - Dec 2003 - p1374(1) [501+]

Kobrak, Christopher - *National Cultures and International Competition. The Experience of Schering Ag, 1851-1950*
   GSR - v27 - i1 - Feb 2004 - p190-191 [501+]

Koch, Christof - *The Quest for Consciousness: A Neurobiological Approach*
   Choice - v42 - i3 - Nov 2004 - p508(1) [1-50]
   NYRB - v52 - i1 - Jan 13 2005 - p36(4) [501+]
   TimHES - v0 - i1657 - Sept 10 2004 - p28(2) [501+]

Koch, Edward I. - *Eddie: Harold's Little Brother (Illus. by Warhola, James)*
 c   BL - v101 - i1 - Sept 1 2004 - p114(1) [501+]
 c   KR - v72 - i14 - July 15 2004 - p688(1) [51-500]
 c   PW - v251 - i33 - August 16 2004 - p63(1) [51-500]
 c   SLJ - v50 - i11 - Nov 2004 - p108(1) [51-500]

Koch, Eric - *Arabian Nights 1914: A Novel About Kaiser Wilhelm II*
   CBRA - Annual 2003 - p172(2) [51-500]

Koch, John T. - *The Celtic Heroic Age; Literary Sources for Ancient Celtic Europe and Early Ireland and Wales, 4th Ed.*
   R&R Bk N - v19 - i1 - Feb 2004 - p32(1) [1-50]

Koch, Jonathan - *Pitching Hollywood: How to Sell Your TV and Movie Ideas*
   Bwatch - Nov 2004 - pNA [51-500]
   R&R Bk N - v19 - i3 - August 2004 - p260(1) [51-500]

Koch, Stefan - *Free/Open Source Software Development*
   SciTech - v28 - i3 - Sept 2004 - p25(1) [51-500]

Koch, Stephen - *The Breaking Point: Hemingway, Dos Passos, and the Murder of Jose Robles*
   KR - v73 - i2 - Jan 15 2005 - p103(1) [501+]
   PW - v252 - i7 - Feb 14 2005 - p65(1) [51-500]

Koch, Tom - *The Wreck of the William Brown: A True Tale of Overcrowded Lifeboats and Murder at Sea*
   Beav - v84 - i4 - August-Sept 2004 - p48(1) [51-500]
   CBRA - Annual 2003 - p440(2) [51-500]

Koch-Westenholz, Ulla - *Babylonian Liver Omens: The Chapters Manzazu, Padanu and Pan Takalti of the Babylonian Extispicy Series Mainly from Assurbanipal's Library*
    JNES - v63 - i4 - Oct 2004 - p310(2) [501+]

Kochalka, James - *American Elf: James Kochalka's Sketchbook Diaries*
    BL - v100 - i21 - July 2004 - p1831(1) [1-50]

Kochan, Frances K. - *Global Perspectives on Mentoring: Transforming Contexts, Communities, and Cultures*
    R&R Bk N - v19 - i3 - August 2004 - p9(1) [1-50]

Kochan, Thomas A. - *Management: Inventing and Delivering Its Future*
    JEL - v41 - i4 - Dec 2003 - p1399(1) [501+]

Kochendorfer-Lucius, Gudrun - *Service Provision for the Poor: Public and Private Sector Cooperation, Proceedings*
    R&R Bk N - v19 - i3 - August 2004 - p159(1) [51-500]

Kociejowski, Marius - *So Dance the Lords of Language*
    CBRA - Annual 2003 - p221(1) [501+]

Kocienski, Philip J. - *Protecting Groups, 3d Ed.*
    SciTech - v28 - i3 - Sept 2004 - p51(1) [1-50]

Koda-Kimble, Mary Anne - *Applied Therapeutics: The Clinical Use of Drugs, 8th Ed.*
    SciTech - v28 - i3 - Sept 2004 - p121(1) [51-500]

Kodaka, Kazuma - *Kimera, Vol. 1*
    PW - v251 - i47 - Nov 22 2004 - p41(1) [51-500]

Kodis, Michelle - *Blueprint Affordable: How to Build a Beautiful House Without Breaking the Bank*
    LJ - v129 - i20 - Dec 1 2004 - p156(1) [51-500]
    PW - v251 - i37 - Sept 13 2004 - p73(1) [501+]

Kodrzcki, Yolanda - *Education in the Twenty-First Century: Meeting the Challenges of a Changing World*
    JEL - v41 - i4 - Dec 2003 - p1378(1) [501+]

Koechlin, Carol - *Build Your Own Information Literate School*
    LibMed - v23 - i1 - August-Sept 2004 - p86(1)

Koehler, Jan - *Potentials of Disorders*
    E-A St - v56 - i3 - May 2004 - p478(2) [501+]

Koehler-Pentacoff, Elizabeth - *The ABC's of Writing for Children: 114 Children's Authors and Illustrators Talk About the Art, Business, the Craft, and the Life of Writing Children's Literature*
    R&R Bk N - v19 - i1 - Feb 2004 - p221(1) [51-500]

Koehn, Daryl - *The Nature of Evil*
    PW - v252 - i10 - March 7 2005 - p64(1) [51-500]

Koeneke, Rodney - *Empires of the Mind: I.A. Richards and Basic English in China, 1929-1979*
    AHR - v109 - i4 - Oct 2004 - p1209-1210 [501+]

Koenig, Bernie - *Natural Law, Science, and the Social Construction of Reality*
    SciTech - v28 - i4 - Dec 2004 - p10(1) [1-50]

Koenig, Harold G. - *Faith in the Future: Religion, Aging, and Healthcare*
    AM - v191 - i15 - Nov 15 2004 - p23 [501+]
    Ch Today - v49 - i1 - Jan 2005 - p69(2) [501+]
Faith in the Future: Religion, Aging, and the Role of Religion
    Choice - v42 - i2 - Oct 2004 - p326(1) [51-500]

Koenig, Michael E.D. - *Knowledge Management Lessons Learned: What Works and What Doesn't*
    Choice - v42 - i1 - Sept 2004 - p140(1) [501+]

Koenig, Walter D. - *Ecology and Evolution of Cooperative Breeding in Birds*
    Choice - v42 - i5 - Jan 2005 - p881(1) [1-50]

Koenigsberger, H.G. - *Monarchies, States Generals and Parliaments: The Netherlands in the Fifteenth and Sixteenth Centuries*
    AHR - v109 - i3 - June 2004 - p989(2) [501+]
    JMH - v77 - i1 - March 2005 - p214(3) [501+]
    Six Ct J - v35 - i3 - Fall 2004 - p859-860 [501+]

Koenraad, P.M. - *Scanning Tunneling Microscopy/Spectroscopy and Related Techniques: Proceedings*
    SciTech - v28 - i1 - March 2004 - p61(1) [51-500]

Koepnick, Lutz - *The Dark Mirror: German Cinema between Hitler and Hollywood*
    GSR - v27 - i2 - May 2004 - p413-415 [501+]

Koeppel, Dan - *To See Every Bird on Earth: A Father, a Son, and a Lifelong Obsession*
    PW - v252 - i11 - March 14 2005 - p53(1) [51-500]

Koerner, Joseph Leo - *The Reformation of the Image*
    Apo - v159 - i509 - July 2004 - p66(2) [501+]
    Lon R Bks - v26 - i16 - August 19 2004 - p15(2) [501+]
    TLS - i5300 - Oct 29 2004 - p3-4 [501+]

Koertge, Ron - *The Brimstone Journals*
    y Kliatt - v38 - i5 - Sept 2004 - p22(2) [51-500]
Margaux with an X
    y BL - v101 - i2 - Sept 15 2004 - p233(2) [51-500]
    y CCB-B - v58 - i2 - Oct 2004 - p83(2) [51-500]
    y HB - v80 - i6 - Nov-Dec 2004 - p711(1) [501+]
    y Kliatt - v38 - i5 - Sept 2004 - p12(3) [51-500]
    y KR - v72 - i15 - August 1 2004 - p744(1) [51-500]
    y LibMed - v23 - i3 - Nov-Dec 2004 - p72(1) [51-500]
    y PW - v251 - i38 - Sept 20 2004 - p64(1) [51-500]
    y SLJ - v50 - i9 - Sept 2004 - p209(1) [51-500]
    y VOYA - v27 - i5 - Dec 2004 - p384(1) [51-500]
Shakespeare Bats Cleanup
    y Teach Lib - v32 - i1 - Oct 2004 - p10(1) [51-500]

Koestenbaum, Wayne - *Model Homes*
    PW - v251 - i47 - Nov 22 2004 - p57(1) [51-500]
Moira Orfei in Aigues-Mortes
    KR - v72 - i15 - August 1 2004 - p707(1) [501+]
    Lam Bk Rpt - v13 - i4-5 - Nov-Dec 2004 - p39(2) [501+]

Koester, Craig R. - *Revelation and the End of All Things*
    Intpr - v59 - i1 - Jan 2005 - p96(2) [501+]

Koestler-Grack, Rachel A. - *Mary Baker Eddy*
    y SLJ - v50 - i10 - Oct 2004 - p190(1) [51-500]
The Story of Clara Barton
    c SLJ - v50 - i9 - Sept 2004 - p188(2) [51-500]

Koestler, Kathleen - *Theophile Gautier's Espana*
    FS - v58 - i2 - April 2004 - p275(1) [501+]

Koetke, Walter - *Number Wonder: Book 1 of the Series Real Mathematics*
    Math T - v98 - i1 - August 2004 - p63-63 [501+]

Koetzle, Hans-Michael - *Rene Burri, Photographs (Illus. by Burri, Reni)*
    Afterimage - v32 - i1 - July-August 2004 - p18(1) [501+]

Kofas, Jon V. - *Under the Eagle's Claw: Exceptionalism in Postwar U.S.-Greek Relations*
    Choice - v42 - i2 - Oct 2004 - p369(1) [501+]
    R&R Bk N - v19 - i1 - Feb 2004 - p56(1) [51-500]

Koff, Clea - *The Bone Woman: A Forensic Anthropologist's Search for Truth in the Mass Graves of Rwanda, Bosnia, Croatia, and Kosovo*
    BIC - v33 - i6 - Sept 2004 - p6(1) [501+]
    Globe & Mail - Feb 26 2005 - pD13 [1-50]
    TimHES - v0 - i1680 - Feb 25 2005 - p26(1) [501+]

Kofoed, Karl - *Galactic Geographic Annual 3003*
    Analog - v124 - i3 - March 2004 - p137(1) [501+]

Kogan, Rick - *America's More: The Life, Lessons, and Legacy of Ann Landers*
    Wom R Bks - v21 - i10-11 - July 2004 - p8(2) [501+]

Kogawa, Joy - *Garden of Anchors: Selected Poems*
    CBRA - Annual 2003 - p221(2) [501+]

Kogels, Han A. - *Consumption Taxation and Financial Services*
    R&R Bk N - v19 - i1 - Feb 2004 - p121(1) [51-500]

Koggel, Christine M. - *Confidential Relationships: Psychoanalytic, Ethical, and Legal Contexts*
    SciTech - v28 - i1 - March 2004 - p98(1) [51-500]

Kogler, Jennifer Anne - *Ruby Tuesday*
    y Kliatt - v39 - i2 - March 2005 - p13(1) [51-500]
    y KR - v73 - i5 - March 1 2005 - p289(1) [51-500]

Koglmeier, Georg - *Die Zentralen Rategremien in Bayern 1918/19: Legitimation-Organisation-Funktion*
    JMH - v77 - i1 - March 2005 - p226(3) [501+]

Kogman-Appel, Katrin - *Jewish Book Art between Islam and Christianity: The Decoration of Hebrew Bibles in Medieval Spain*
    R&R Bk N - v19 - i4 - Nov 2004 - p207(1) [501+]

Kogut, Bruce - *The Global Internet Economy*
    CS - v33 - i4 - July 2004 - p446(2) [501+]
    JEL - v42 - i2 - June 2004 - p205(2) [501+]

Koh, Tommy - *The New Global Threat: Severe Acute Respiratory Syndrome and Its Impacts*
    Choice - v41 - i11-12 - July-August 2004 - p2078(1) [501+]

Kohanski, Tamarah - *The Book of John Mandeville: An Edition of the Pynson Text with commentary on the Defective Version*
    JEGP - v103 - i2 - April 2004 - p267-269 [501+]
The Book of John Mandeville: An Edition of the Pyson Text with Commentary on the Defective Version
    RES - v55 - i218 - Feb 2004 - p117-119 [501+]

Kohl, Christiane - *The Maiden and the Jew: The Story of a Fatal Friendship in Nazi Germany*
    KR - v72 - i13 - July 1 2004 - p619(1) [501+]
    LJ - v129 - i13 - August 2004 - p94(1) [501+]
    TLS - i5301 - Nov 5 2004 - p12(1) [501+]

Kohl, Helmut - *Erinnerungen 1930-1982*
    HNet - June 2004 - pNA [501+]

Kohl, Herbert - *Stupidity and Tears: Teaching and Learning in Troubled Times*
    BooChiTr - Jan 25 2004 - p5(1) [501+]

Kohl, Karl-Heinz - *Die Macht der Dinge: Geschichte und Theorie sakraler Objekte*
    HNet - Oct 2004 - pNA [501+]

Kohlberg, Etan - *Shi'ism*
    R&R Bk N - v19 - i1 - Feb 2004 - p15(1) [51-500]

Kohler, Joachim - *Richard Wagner: The Last of the Titans*
    LJ - v129 - i20 - Dec 1 2004 - p120(1) [51-500]
    BL - v101 - i6 - Nov 15 2004 - p541(1) [51-500]
    CR - v286 - i1669 - Feb 2005 - p128(1) [51-500]
    Nation - v279 - i20 - Dec 13 2004 - p44 [501+]

Kohler, Michael - *Nanotechnology: An Introduction to Nanostructuring Techniques*
    SciTech - v28 - i3 - Sept 2004 - p135(1) [51-500]

Kohler, Robert E. - *Landscapes and Labscapes: Exploring the Lab-Field Border in Biology*
    Isis - v95 - i3 - Sept 2004 - p509(2) [501+]

Kohler, Sheila - *Crossways*
    BL - v101 - i2 - Sept 15 2004 - p208(1) [501+]
    KR - v72 - i16 - August 15 2004 - p767(2) [51-500]
    LJ - v129 - i16 - Oct 1 2004 - p70(1) [51-500]
    PW - v251 - i41 - Oct 11 2004 - p57(2) [51-500]

Kohler, Timothy A. - *Archaeology of Bandelier National Monument: Village Formation on the Pajarito Plateau, New Mexico*
    Choice - v42 - i2 - Oct 2004 - p334(1) [51-500]
    Roundup M - v12 - i1 - Oct 2004 - p24(1) [51-500]

Kohler, Werner - *Elementary Differential Equations with Boundary Value Problems*
    SciTech - v28 - i3 - Sept 2004 - p39(1) [51-500]

Kohlhoff, Dean W. - *Amchitka and the Bomb*
    WHQ - v34 - i4 - Winter 2003 - p517 [501+]

Kohlmann, Evan F. - *Al-Qaida's Jihad in Europe: The Afghan-Bosnian Network*
    Spec - v296 - i9200 - Dec 4 2004 - p46(2) [501+]

Kohm, Amelia - *Strategic Restructuring for Nonprofit Organizations: Mergers, Integrations, and Alliances*
    R&R Bk N - v19 - i1 - Feb 2004 - p93(1) [51-500]

Kohn, Abigail A. - *Shooters: Myths and Realities of America's Gun Cultures*
    Choice - v42 - i6 - Feb 2005 - p1105(1) [51-500]
    Globe & Mail - Dec 4 2004 - pD39 [51-500]
    Reason - v36 - i9 - Feb 2005 - p56(3) [501+]

Kohn, Alfie - *Harvard Business Review on Compensation*
    HR Mag - v49 - i7 - July 2004 - pS7(1) [51-500]
Unconditional Parenting: Moving from Rewards and Punishments to Love and Reason
    PW - v252 - i7 - Feb 14 2005 - p70(1) [51-500]
What Does It Mean to be Well Educated? And More Essays on Standards, Grading, and Other Follies
    BIC - v33 - i7 - Oct 2004 - p37(2) [501+]
    R&R Bk N - v19 - i4 - Nov 2004 - p177(1) [501+]

Kohn, Daniel B. - *Sex, Drugs, and Violence in the Jewish Tradition, Moral Perspectives*
    R&R Bk N - v19 - i4 - Nov 2004 - p16(1) [51-500]

Kohn, Joan - *It's Your Bed and Bath: Hundreds of Beautiful Design Ideas*
    PW - v251 - i35 - August 30 2004 - p48(1) [51-500]

Kohn, Linda T. - *Academic Health Centers: Leading Change in the 21st Century*
    SciTech - v28 - i3 - Sept 2004 - p86(1) [501+]

Kohn, Livia - *Cosmos and Community: The Ethical Dimensions of Daoism*
    Choice - v42 - i7 - March 2005 - p1243(1) [51-500]
The Daoist Monastic Manual: A Translation of the Fengdao Kejie
    Choice - v42 - i7 - March 2005 - p1241(2) [51-500]
Monastic Life in Medieval Daoism: A Cross-Cultural Perspective
    Choice - v41 - i7 - March 2004 - p1313(2) [501+]

Kohn, Marek - *A Reason for Everything: Natural Selection and the English Imagination*
    Nature - v431 - i7004 - Sept 2 2004 - p21(2) [501+]
    New Sci - v183 - i2463 - Sept 4 2004 - p46(1) [501+]
    TimHES - v0 - i1666 - Nov 12 2004 - p22(2) [501+]
    TLS - i5305 - Dec 3 2004 - p12(1) [501+]

Kohn, Margaret - *Brave New Neighborhood: The Privatization of Public Space*
  Choice - v42 - i3 - Nov 2004 - p565(1) [1-50]
  R&R Bk N - v19 - i3 - August 2004 - p155(1) [1-50]

Kohn, Meir - *Financial Institutions and Markets*
  JEL - v42 - i1 - March 2004 - p235(1) [501+]

Kohnle, Armin - *Reichstag und Reformation: Kaiserliche und standische Religionspolitik von den Anfangen der Causa Lutheri bis zum Nurnberger Religionsfrieden*
  Six Ct J - v35 - i1 - Spring 2004 - p246(3) [501+]

Kohr, M. - *Viscous Incompressible Flow for Low Reynolds Numbers*
  SciTech - v28 - i4 - Dec 2004 - p44(1) [51-500]

Kohring, Rolf - *Tilly Edinger, Leben und Werk einer judischen Wissenschaftlerin*
  HNet - Nov 2004 - pNA [501+]

Kohso, Sabu - *Transcritique on Kant and Marx*
  Choice - v42 - i2 - Oct 2004 - p370(1) [51-500]

Kohut, David R. - *Historical Dictionary of the "Dirty Wars".*
  R&R Bk N - v19 - i1 - Feb 2004 - p67(1) [501+]

Kohwi, Yoshimori - *Trinucleotide Repeat Protocols*
  SciTech - v28 - i3 - Sept 2004 - p72(1) [51-500]

Koike, Kazuo - *When the Demon Knife Weeps*
  BL - v101 - i5 - Nov 1 2004 - p473(1) [51-500]

Koistinen, Olli - *Spinoza: Metaphysical Themes*
  Phil R - v113 - i1 - Jan 2004 - p139(5) [501+]

Koja, Kathe - *The Blue Mirror (Read by Kellgren, Katherine). Audiobook Review*
  y Kliatt - v39 - i1 - Jan 2005 - p38(1) [51-500]
  The Blue Mirror
  c LibMed - v23 - i3 - Nov-Dec 2004 - p72(1) [51-500]
  Buddha Boy (Read by Murphy, Spencer). Audiobook Review
  y SLJ - v50 - i9 - Sept 2004 - p79(1) [51-500]
  Buddha Boy
  y Kliatt - v38 - i6 - Nov 2004 - p18(2) [51-500]
  c PW - v251 - i45 - Nov 8 2004 - p58(1) [51-500]
  Talk
  y HB - v81 - i2 - March-April 2005 - p203(2) [51-500]
  y KR - v73 - i4 - Feb 15 2005 - p231(1) [51-500]
  y PW - v252 - i7 - Feb 14 2005 - p77(1) [51-500]

Koje, Kathe - *The Blue Mirror (Read by Kellgren, Katherine). Audiobook Review*
  SLJ - v50 - i12 - Dec 2004 - p76(1) [501+]

Kokis, Sergio - *Art of Deception*
  CBRA - Annual 2003 - p173(1) [501+]
  Les amants de l'Alfama
  WLT - v78 - i3-4 - Sept-Dec 2004 - p117(1) [501+]

Kokkotas, K.D. - *Recent Developments in Gravity: Proceedings*
  SciTech - v28 - i4 - Dec 2004 - p45(1) [51-500]

Kola, Paulin - *The Myth of Greater Albania*
  Slav R - v63 - i3 - Fall 2004 - p636-638 [501+]

Kolago, Lech - *Studia Niemcoznawcze/Studien zur Deutschkunde*
  GSR - v27 - i1 - Feb 2004 - p224-226 [501+]

Kolakowski, Leszek - *The Two Eyes of Spinoza and Other Essays on Philosophy*
  Choice - v42 - i3 - Nov 2004 - p497(1) [1-50]

Kolanowski, Bernard F. - *Guide to Microturbines*
  SciTech - v28 - i4 - Dec 2004 - p147(1) [501+]

Kolb, A. - *Transport und Nachrichtentransfer im Romischen Reich*
  Class R - v54 - i2 - Nov 2004 - p493-494 [501+]

Kolb, Bryan - *Fundamentals of Human Neuropsychology, 5th Ed.*
  SciTech - v28 - i3 - Sept 2004 - p70(1) [51-500]

Kolb, Deborah M. - *Her Place at the Table: A Woman's Guide to Negotiating Five Key Challenges to Leadership Success*
  HR Mag - v50 - i2 - Feb 2005 - pS6(1) [501+]

Kolb, F. - *Herrscherideologie in der Spatantike*
  Class R - v54 - i1 - May 2004 - p189(3) [501+]

Kolb, Katherine - *Proust in Perspective: Visions and Revisions*
  FS - v58 - i1 - Jan 2004 - p134(2) [501+]

Kolb, Larry J. - *Overworld: The Life and Times of a Reluctant Spy*
  BL - v101 - i4 - Oct 15 2004 - p368(1) [51-500]
  BW - v34 - i44 - Oct 31 2004 - p13(1) [501+]
  LJ - v129 - i18 - Nov 1 2004 - p96(1) [51-500]
  PW - v251 - i38 - Sept 20 2004 - p56(2) [51-500]

Kolb, Patricia J. - *Caring for Our Elders: Multicultural Experiences with Nursing Home Placement*
  SciTech - v28 - i1 - March 2004 - p108(1) [51-500]
  Soc Ser R - v79 - i1 - March 2005 - p209(1) [51-500]

Kolbell, Erik - *Were You There?: Finding Ourselves at the Foot of the Cross*
  LJ - v130 - i4 - March 1 2005 - p94(1) [51-500]

Kolber, Leo - *Leo, a Life*
  CBRA - Annual 2003 - p52(2) [501+]

Kolbert, Elizabeth - *The Prophet of Love: and Other Tales of Power and Deceit*
  KR - v72 - i24 - Dec 15 2004 - pS7(2) [501+]

Kolbesen, Bernd O. - *Analytical and Diagnostic Techniques for Semiconductor Materials, Devices, and Processes: Proceedings*
  SciTech - v28 - i1 - March 2004 - p161(1) [51-500]

Kolchin, Peter - *American Slavery*
  Black Iss - v7 - i1 - Jan-Feb 2005 - p28(2) [501+]
  A Sphinx on the American Land: The Nineteenth-Century South in Comparative Perspective
  AHR - v109 - i3 - June 2004 - p864(2) [501+]
  HNet - Sept 2004 - pNA [501+]
  JAH - v91 - i1 - June 2004 - p228-229 [501+]
  JIH - v35 - i2 - Autumn 2004 - p311(2) [501+]
  JSH - v70 - i3 - August 2004 - p660(3) [501+]
  SHQ - v107 - i4 - April 2004 - p628(2) [501+]

Kolin, Andrew - *One Family: Before and During the Holocaust, 2nd Ed.*
  R&R Bk N - v19 - i1 - Feb 2004 - p44(1) [51-500]

Kolin, Philip C. - *Othello: New Critical Essays*
  ANQ:QJ - v18 - i1 - Wntr 2005 - p69(4) [501+]
  The Tennessee Williams Encyclopedia
  BL - v100 - i22 - August 2004 - p1982(1) [51-500]
  Choice - v42 - i2 - Oct 2004 - p268(1) [501+]
  The Undiscovered Country: The Later Plays of Tennessee Williams
  ANQ:QJ - v18 - i1 - Wntr 2005 - p65(5) [501+]
  Theat J - v56 - i3 - Oct 2004 - p530-531 [501+]

Kolinsky, Eva - *Reinventing Gender: Women in Eastern Germany Since Unification*
  HNet - June 2004 - pNA [501+]

Kolko, Gabriel - *Another Century of War?*
  IndRev - v9 - i2 - Fall 2004 - p286(4) [501+]

Koll, Elisabeth - *From Cotton Mill to Business Empire: The Emergence of Regional Enterprises in Modern China*
  Choice - v41 - i11-12 - July-August 2004 - p2093(1) [501+]
  From Cotton Mill to Business Enterprise: The Emergence of Regional Enterprises in Modern China
  BHR - v78 - i3 - Autumn 2004 - p591(3) [501+]

Koll-Schretzenmayr, Martina - *The Real and Virtual Worlds of Spatial Planning*
  JEL - v42 - i1 - March 2004 - p342(2) [501+]

Koller, Jackie French - *Horace the Horrible: A Knight Meets His Match (Illus. by Urbanovie, Jackie)*
  LibMed - v22 - i4 - Jan 2004 - p59(1) [501+]

Kollins, Michael J. - *Pioneers of the Automobile Industry*
  SciTech - v28 - i1 - March 2004 - p166(1) [51-500]

Kollman, Ken - *Computational Models in Political Economy*
  JEL - v42 - i1 - March 2004 - p250(1) [501+]

Kollner, Thomas - *Land Use in Product Life Cycles and Ecosystem Quality*
  SciTech - v28 - i3 - Sept 2004 - p7(1) [51-500]

Kolman, Bernard - *Elementary Linear Algebra, 8th Ed.*
  SciTech - v28 - i3 - Sept 2004 - p35(1) [51-500]

Kolodko, Grzegorz W. - *Emerging Market Economies: Globalization and Development*
  R&R Bk N - v19 - i1 - Feb 2004 - p106(1) [51-500]

Kolodziej, Edward A. - *A Force Profonde: The Power, Politics, and Promise of Human Rights*
  Choice - v41 - i7 - March 2004 - p1368(1) [501+]

Kolomay, Richard - *Firefighter Rescue and Survival*
  R&R Bk N - v19 - i1 - Feb 2004 - p250(1) [51-500]

Kolonitskii, B.V. - *Simvoly vlasti i bor'ba za vlast': Kizucheniiu politicheskoi kul'tury rossiskoi revoliutsii 1917 goda*
  AHR - v109 - i3 - June 2004 - p1006(2) [501+]

Kolsto, Pal - *National Integration and Violent Conflict in Post-Soviet Societies: The Cases of Estonia and Moldova*
  Russ Rev - v63 - i4 - Oct 2004 - p728(1) [501+]
  Slav R - v63 - i2 - Summer 2004 - p393(2) [501+]

Kolving, Ulla - *Cahiers Voltaire, I: revue annuelle de la Societe Voltaire*
  FS - v58 - i3 - July 2004 - p413-414 [501+]

Komar, Brian - *Firewalls for Dummies, 2d ed.*
  SciTech - v28 - i1 - March 2004 - p156(1) [51-500]
  Microsoft Windows Server 2003 PKI and Certificate Security
  SciTech - v28 - i3 - Sept 2004 - p27(1) [51-500]

Komar, Kathleen L. - *Reclaiming Klytemnestra: Revenge or Reconciliation*
  AJP - v125 - i2 - Summer 2004 - p283-287 [501+]
  Ger Q - v77 - i1 - Wntr 2004 - p116(3) [501+]
  MFSF - v50 - i3 - Fall 2004 - p783-784 [501+]

Komarovsky, Mirra - *Dilemmas of Masculinity: A Study of College Youth*
  R&R Bk N - v19 - i4 - Nov 2004 - p128(1) [1-50]
  Women in the Modern World: Their Education and Their Dilemmas
  R&R Bk N - v19 - i4 - Nov 2004 - p191(1) [501+]

Komblatt, Judith Deutsch - *Doubly Chosen: Jewish Identity, the Soviet Intelligentsia, and the Russian Orthodox Church*
  Choice - v42 - i3 - Nov 2004 - p542(1) [1-50]

Komlosy, Andrea - *Grenze und ungleiche regionale Entwicklung: Binnenmarkt und Migration in der Habsburgermonarchie*
  HNet - June 2004 - pNA [501+]

Kommers, Donald P. - *American Constitutional Law: Essays, Cases, and Comparative Notes, 2nd Ed.*
  R&R Bk N - v19 - i3 - August 2004 - p202(1) [1-50]

Komunyakaa, Yusef - *Taboo*
  BL - v101 - i2 - Sept 15 2004 - p196(1) [501+]
  Black Iss - v7 - i2 - March-April 2005 - p33(1) [501+]
  LJ - v129 - i17 - Oct 15 2004 - p66(1) [51-500]
  Poet - v185 - i5 - Feb 2005 - p394(1) [51-500]
  c PW - v251 - i38 - Sept 20 2004 - p60(1) [51-500]

Kona, Prakash - *Streets That Smell of Dying Roses*
  WLT - v78 - i3-4 - Sept-Dec 2004 - p87(2) [501+]

Konakov, N.D. - *Komi Mythology*
  R&R Bk N - v19 - i1 - Feb 2004 - p12(1) [501+]

Koncel, Mary A. - *You Can Tell the Horse Anything*
  ABR - v26 - i2 - Jan-Feb 2005 - p1(2) [501+]

Kondos, Yannis - *Absurd Athlete*
  TLS - i5284 - July 9 2004 - p28(1) [501+]

Kondratyev, Kirill Ya. - *Stability of Life on Earth: Principal Subject of Scientific Research in the 21st Century*
  Choice - v42 - i3 - Nov 2004 - p509(1) [1-50]

Kongoli, Florian - *Modeling, Control and Optimization in Ferrous and Nonferrous Industry*
  SciTech - v28 - i1 - March 2004 - p138(1) [51-500]

Konieczny, Vladimir - *Struggling for Perfection: The Story of Glenn Gould (Illus. by Wysotski, Chrissie)*
  BL - v100 - i21 - July 2004 - p1840(2) [1-50]
  c SLJ - v50 - i9 - Sept 2004 - p228(1) [51-500]

Konig, Christoph - *Hofmannsthal: Ein Moderner Dichter unter den Philologen*
  Ger Q - v77 - i1 - Wntr 2004 - p105(5) [501+]

Konig, Rita - *Rita's Culinary Trickery: How to Get Dinner On the Table Even If You Can't Cook*
  NS - v133 - i4715 - Nov 22 2004 - p56(1) [501+]

Konigsburg, E.L. - *The Outcasts of 19 Schuyler Place (Read by Ringwald, Molly). Audiobook Review*
  c BL - v100 - i21 - July 2004 - p1857(1) [1-50]
  c Kliatt - v38 - i4 - July 2004 - p54(1) [51-500]
  The Outcasts of 19 Schuyler Place
  y BIC - v33 - i7 - Oct 2004 - p40(1) [501+]
  y BL - v101 - i5 - Nov 1 2004 - p496(1) [51-500]
  CC - v121 - i25 - Dec 14 2004 - p24(1) [501+]
  y SLJ - v50 - i10 - Oct 2004 - pS54(1) [51-500]
  y Teach Lib - v32 - i1 - Oct 2004 - p18(1) [51-500]

Konik, Michael - *Ella in Europe: An American Dog's International Adventures*
  KR - v72 - i23 - Dec 1 2004 - p1134(1) [501+]
  LJ - v129 - i20 - Dec 1 2004 - p146(2) [51-500]

Konkle, Maureen - *Writing Indian Nations: Native Intellectuals and the Politics of Historiography, 1827-1863*
  Choice - v41 - i11-12 - July-August 2004 - p2108(1) [501+]

Konomi, Takeshi - *The Prince of Tennis*
  y Kliatt - v38 - i5 - Sept 2004 - p35(3) [51-500]
  The Prince of Tennis: Volume 2
  PW - v251 - i36 - Sept 6 2004 - p48(1) [51-500]

Konopka, Andrzej K. - *Compact Handbook of Computational Biology*
  SciTech - v28 - i4 - Dec 2004 - p60(1) [51-500]

Konrad, Michaela - *Der spatromische Limes in Syrien: Archaologische Untersuchungen an den Grenzkastellen von Sura, Tetrapyrgium, Cholle und in Resafa*
  JNES - v64 - i1 - Jan 2005 - p70(2) [501+]

Konrad, Ulrich - *Wolfgang Amadeus Mozart. Fragmente Notes* - v61 - i1 - Sept 2004 - p231(7) [501+]

Konrath, J.A. - *Whiskey Sour (Read by Breck, Susan). Audiobook Review*
LJ - v129 - i19 - Nov 15 2004 - p97(1) [51-500]

Konstadakopulos, Dimitrios - *Learning for Innovation in the Global Knowledge Economy: A European and South-East Asian Perspective*
R&R Bk N - v19 - i3 - August 2004 - p106(1) [1-50]

Konstam, Angus - *Fair Oaks 1862: McClellan's Peninsula Campaign*
R&R Bk N - v19 - i4 - Nov 2004 - p61(1) [51-500]
Guilford Courthouse, 1781: Lord Cornwallis's Ruinous Victory
R&R Bk N - v19 - i4 - Nov 2004 - p60(1) [51-500]
Hampton Roads 1862: First Clash of the Ironclads
R&R Bk N - v19 - i4 - Nov 2004 - p61(1) [51-500]
Historical Atlas of the Napoleonic Era
R&R Bk N - v19 - i1 - Feb 2004 - p36(1) [1-50]
Seven Days Battles: Lee's Defence of Richmond
R&R Bk N - v19 - i4 - Nov 2004 - p61(1) [51-500]

Konstantinos - *Speak with the Dead: Seven Methods for Spirit Communication*
Bwatch - Feb 2005 - pNA [51-500]

Kontje, Todd - *A Companion to German Realism, 1848-1900*
Ger Q - v77 - i2 - Spring 2004 - p236-237 [501+]
GSR - v27 - i1 - Feb 2004 - p154-155 [501+]

Kontogeorgos, Goerge - *Molecular Pathology of the Pituitary*
SciTech - v28 - i3 - Sept 2004 - p92(1) [51-500]

Konzett, Delia Caparoso - *Ethnic Modernisms: Anziz Yezierska, Zora Neale Hurston, Jean Rhys and the Aesthetics of Dislocation*
MFSF - v50 - i2 - Summer 2004 - p517-519 [501+]

Koon, Larry - *Roycroft Furniture and Collectibles*
Ant&CM - v109 - i1 - March 2004 - p16(1) [501+]

Koonce, Jefferson M. - *Human Factors in the Training of Pilots*
SciTech - v28 - i3 - Sept 2004 - p164(1) [51-500]

Koonooka, Christopher - *Ungipaghaghlanga = Let Me Tell a Story: Quutmiit Yupigita Ungipaghaatangit = Legends of the Siberian Eskimos*
R&R Bk N - v19 - i1 - Feb 2004 - p54(1) [51-500]

Koons, Jon - *A Confused Hanukkah: An Original Story of Chelm (Illus. by Schindler, S.D.)*
c CCB-B - v58 - i3 - Nov 2004 - p130(1) [501+]
c CH Bwatch - v14 - i11 - Nov 2004 - pNA [51-500]
c KR - v72 - i21 - Nov 1 2004 - p1051(1) [51-500]
c PW - v251 - i39 - Sept 27 2004 - p60(1) [51-500]

Koontz, Dean - *Dean Koontz's Frankenstein: Book One, Prodigal Son*
BL - v101 - i9-10 - Jan 1 2005 - p784(1) [1-50]
LJ - v130 - i2 - Feb 1 2005 - p68(2) [51-500]
PW - v252 - i3 - Jan 17 2005 - p40(1) [51-500]
Every Day's A Holiday (Illus. by Parks, Phil)
y CE - v81 - i2 - Winter 2004 - p108(1) [51-500]
Life Expectancy
BL - v101 - i5 - Nov 1 2004 - p444(1) [51-500]
Globe & Mail - Dec 18 2004 - pD23 [501+]
KR - v72 - i22 - Nov 15 2004 - p1063(1) [501+]
LJ - v129 - i20 - Dec 1 2004 - p101(1) [51-500]
NYT - Dec 6 2004 - pE8 [501+]
PW - v251 - i46 - Nov 15 2004 - p41(2) [501+]
Lightning (Read by Marinker, Peter). Audiobook Review
Globe & Mail - July 24 2004 - pD13 [501+]
Midnight (Read by Charles, J.). Audiobook Review
LJ - v129 - i15 - Sept 15 2004 - p89(1) [51-500]
Odd Thomas (Read by Baker, David Aaron). Audiobook Review
c Kliatt - v38 - i4 - July 2004 - p53(2) [51-500]
LJ - v129 - i14 - Sept 1 2004 - p200(2) [51-500]
The Taking (Read by Meyers, Ariadne). Audiobook Review
BL - v101 - i3 - Oct 1 2004 - p351(1) [51-500]
Kliatt - v38 - i6 - Nov 2004 - p51(2) [51-500]
LJ - v129 - i18 - Nov 1 2004 - p129(2) [51-500]
The Taking
Globe & Mail - July 10 2004 - pD12 [501+]

Koonz, Claudia - *The Nazi Conscience*
GSR - v27 - i3 - Oct 2004 - p643(2) [501+]

Koopmann, Helmut - *Goethe und Frau von Stein: Geschite einer Liebe*
Ger Q - v77 - i2 - Spring 2004 - p231-232 [501+]

Koopmans, Tim - *Courts and Political Institutions: A Comparative View*
Choice - v42 - i1 - Sept 2004 - p183(1) [501+]
HNet - Oct 2004 - pNA [501+]

Kooser, Ted - *Delights and Shadows*
Poet - v185 - i5 - Feb 2005 - p396(1) [51-500]

Koot, Willem - *Organizational Relationships in the Networking Age: The Dynamics of Identity Formation and Bonding*
JEL - v42 - i1 - March 2004 - p248(1) [501+]
R&R Bk N - v19 - i1 - Feb 2004 - p101(1) [51-500]

Kooyman, Brian - *Archaeology on the Edge: New Perspectives from the Northern Plains*
Bwatch - Feb 2005 - pNA [501+]

Kopas, Cliff - *Bella Coola: "...a Romantic History..."*
CBRA - Annual 2003 - p365(2) [501+]

Kopelke, Lisa - *Tissue, Please! (Illus. by Kopelke, Lisa)*
c KR - v72 - i19 - Oct 1 2004 - p964(1) [51-500]
c SLJ - v50 - i11 - Nov 2004 - p108(2) [51-500]

Kopelow, Gerry - *How to Photograph Buildings and Interiors, 3rd Ed.*
R&R Bk N - v19 - i1 - Feb 2004 - p251(1) [51-500]

Koper, Carsten - *Real-Financial Interaction in Contemporary Models of AS-AD Growth*
R&R Bk N - v19 - i1 - Feb 2004 - p117(1) [51-500]

Kopley, Richard - *Threads of The Scarlet Letter: A Study of Hawthorne's Transformative Art*
R&R Bk N - v19 - i1 - Feb 2004 - p244(1) [51-500]

Koplow, David - *Smallpox: The Fight to Eradicate a Global Scourge*
Isis - v95 - i2 - June 2004 - p331(1) [501+]

Koponen, Libby - *Blow Out the Moon*
c CCB-B - v58 - i1 - Sept 2004 - p24(2) [51-500]
c CH Bwatch - v14 - i9 - Sept 2004 - p3(1) [51-500]
c SLJ - v50 - i11 - Nov 2004 - p148(2) [51-500]

Kopp, Jaine - *Algebraic Reasoning*
TC Math - v11 - i1 - August 2004 - p45(1) [51-500]
Early Adventures in Algebra: Featuring Zero the Hero
c SB - v40 - i5 - Sept-Oct 2004 - p217(1) [51-500]

Koppel, Tom - *Lost World: Rewriting Prehistory--How New Science Is Tracing America's Ice Age Mariners*
Am Ant - v70 - i1 - Jan 2005 - p202(3) [501+]
BIC - v33 - i5 - August 2004 - p09(2) [501+]
Lost World: Rewriting Prehistory-- How New Science Is Tracing America's Ice Age Mariners
CG - v124 - i1 - Jan-Feb 2004 - p86(1) [501+]

Koppelman, Charles - *Behind the Seen: How Walter Murch Edited Cold Mountain Using Apple's Final Cut Pro and What This Means for Cinema*
LJ - v130 - i1 - Jan 1 2005 - p148(1) [51-500]

Koppelman, Kent L. - *Understanding Human Differences: Multicultural Education for a Diverse American*
R&R Bk N - v19 - i3 - August 2004 - p228(1) [1-50]

Koppelman, Susan - *The Strange History of Suzanne LaFleshe and Other Stories of Women and Fatness*
OOB - v34 - Nov-Dec 2004 - p66(2) [501+]
Wom R Bks - v22 - i3 - Dec 2004 - p22(2) [501+]

Koppes, Steven N. - *Killer Rocks from Outer Space: Asteroids, Comets, and Meteorites*
y LibMed - v22 - i7 - April-May 2004 - p78(1) [501+]

Koppl, Roger - *Austrian Economics and Entrepreneurial Studies*
JEL - v42 - i1 - March 2004 - p243(1) [501+]

Kops, Deborah - *Women's Suffrage*
y SLJ - v50 - i9 - Sept 2004 - p228(2) [51-500]

Koralek, Jenny - *The Coat of Many Colors (Illus. by Baynes, Pauline)*
c BL - v101 - i4 - Oct 15 2004 - p410(1) [51-500]
c KR - v72 - i16 - August 15 2004 - p808(1) [51-500]
c PW - v251 - i43 - Oct 25 2004 - p46(1) [51-500]
c SLJ - v50 - i11 - Nov 2004 - p127(1) [51-500]

Korb, Lawrence J. - *A New National Security Strategy in an Age of Terrorists, Tyrants, and Weapons of Mass Destruction: Three Options Presented as Presidential Speeches*
NWCR - v57 - Autumn 2004 - p155(2) [501+]

Korbonski, Stefan - *Fighting Warsaw: The Story of the Polish Underground State, 1939-1945*
R&R Bk N - v19 - i3 - August 2004 - p34(1) [51-500]

Korczak, Janusz - *King Matt the First*
LJ - v129 - i14 - Sept 1 2004 - p140(1) [51-500]

Kord, Susanne - *Hollywood Divas, Indie Queens, and TV Heroines: Contemporary Screen Images of Women*
PW - v51 - i51 - Dec 20 2004 - p45(1) [51-500]
Women Peasant Poets in Eighteenth-Century England, Scotland, and Germany: Milkmaids on Parnassus
Ger Q - v77 - i1 - Wntr 2004 - p100(2) [501+]

Korda, Michael - *Crystal Lite*
NYTBR - March 13 2005 - p30 [501+]
Ulysses S. Grant: The Unlikely Hero
NYTBR - Nov 14 2004 - p13 [501+]
BL - v101 - i2 - Sept 15 2004 - p197(1) [501+]
BW - v34 - i38 - Sept 19 2004 - p2(1) [501+]
KR - v72 - i15 - August 1 2004 - p728(1) [501+]
LJ - v129 - i14 - Sept 1 2004 - p162(1) [51-500]
PW - v251 - i30 - July 26 2004 - p44(1) [501+]

Korda, Natasha - *Shakespeare's Domestic Economies: Gender and Property in Early Modern England*
RES - v55 - i218 - Feb 2004 - p129-131 [501+]

Kordan, Bohdan S. - *A Bare and Impolitic Right: Internment and Ukrainian-Canadian Redress*
R&R Bk N - v19 - i3 - August 2004 - p95(1) [51-500]

Korelitz, Jean Hanff - *The White Rose*
BL - v101 - i3 - Oct 1 2004 - p310(1) [51-500]
Ent W - i802 - Jan 21 2005 - p94 [51-500]
KR - v72 - i18 - Sept 15 2004 - p884(1) [501+]
NYTBR - Feb 27 2005 - p12 [501+]
PW - v251 - i46 - Nov 15 2004 - p39(1) [51-500]
LJ - v129 - i18 - Nov 1 2004 - p75(1) [501+]

Koremenos, Barbara - *The Rational Design of International Institutions*
Choice - v42 - i1 - Sept 2004 - p186(1) [501+]

Koren, Edward - *Very Hairy Harry*
c LibMed - v22 - i6 - March 2004 - p57(1) [501+]

Koren, Gideon - *The Complete Guide to Everyday Risks in Pregnancy & Breastfeeding: Answers to Your Questions about Morning Sickness, Medications, Herbs, Diseases, Chemical Exposures and More*
LJ - v130 - i1 - Jan 1 2005 - p139(1) [51-500]

Koren, Herman - *Illustrated Dictionary and Resource Directory of Environmental and Occupational Health, 2nd Ed.*
Choice - v42 - i4 - Dec 2004 - p634(1) [1-50]
SciTech - v28 - i4 - Dec 2004 - p83(1) [51-500]

Koretchuk, Patricia - *Chasing the Cornet: A Scottish-Canadian Life*
Can Hist R - v85 - i3 - Sept 2004 - p619(3) [501+]

Koreto, Richard - *Run It Like a Business: Top Financial Planners Weigh in on Practice Management*
R&R Bk N - v19 - i3 - August 2004 - p134(1) [51-500]

Koretsky, J. Lea - *Domino*
LJ - v129 - i18 - Nov 1 2004 - p60(1) [51-500]

Korman, Gordon - *Son of the Mob: Hollywood Hustle*
y PW - v251 - i34 - August 23 2004 - p56(1) [501+]

Korman, Gordon Richard - *Go Jump in the Pool!*
y CBRA - Annual 2003 - p493(1) [501+]
I Want to Go Home
c Res Links - v10 - i1 - Oct 2004 - p13(2) [51-500]
Jake, Reinvented (Read by Colby, Jim). Audiobook Review
c BL - v101 - i1 - Sept 1 2004 - p148(1) [51-500]
Jake, Reinvented
c CBRA - Annual 2003 - p493(2) [51-500]
The Joke's on Us
Res Links - v10 - i3 - Feb 2005 - p18(2) [501+]
Maxx Comedy
c CBRA - Annual 2003 - p494(1) [51-500]
Mefiez Vous du Poisson
Res Links - v10 - i1 - Oct 2004 - p53(1) [51-500]
Son of the Mob: Hollywood Hustle
y BL - v101 - i3 - Oct 1 2004 - p323(1) [51-500]
Kliatt - v38 - i6 - Nov 2004 - p8(2) [51-500]
Kliatt - v38 - i6 - Nov 2004 - p19(1) [51-500]
KR - v72 - i17 - Sept 1 2004 - p868(1) [51-500]
y Res Links - v10 - i3 - Feb 2005 - p36(2) [51-500]
y SLJ - v50 - i9 - Sept 2004 - p209(2) [51-500]
VOYA - v27 - i5 - Dec 2004 - p384(1) [51-500]
This Can't Be Happening!
y CBRA - Annual 2003 - p493(1) [501+]

Korn, Peter - *Woodworking Basics: Mastering the Essentials of Craftsmanship*
SciTech - v28 - i1 - March 2004 - p178(1) [51-500]

Kornak, Adam - *Enterprise Guide to Gaining Business Value from Mobile Technologies*
R&R Bk N - v19 - i4 - Nov 2004 - p112(1) [51-500]

Kornblatt, Judith Deutsch - *Doubly Chosen: Jewish Identity, the Soviet Intelligentsia, and the Russian Orthodox Church*
R&R Bk N - v19 - i4 - Nov 2004 - p19(1) [51-500]

Kornbluh, Peter - *The Pinochet File: A Declassified Dossier on Atrocity and Accountability*
CC - v122 - i1 - Jan 11 2005 - p28(7) [501+]
Globe & Mail - Sept 11 2004 - pD21 [1-50]
R&R Bk N - v19 - i1 - Feb 2004 - p67(1) [501+]

Korneev, V. - *Modern Microprocessors, 3rd Ed.*
SciTech - v28 - i4 - Dec 2004 - p159(1) [51-500]

Kornfeld, Marcel - *Islands on the Plains: Ecological, Social, and Ritual Use of Landscapes*
R&R Bk N - v19 - i1 - Feb 2004 - p52(1) [51-500]

Korosi, Zsuzsanna - *Carrying a Secret in My Heart... Children of the Victims of the Reprisals after the Hungarian Revolution in 1956: An Oral History*
TimHES - v0 - i1650 - July 23 2004 - p30(2) [501+]

Korotaev, Andrey V. - *World Religions and Social Evolution of the Old World Oikumene Civilizations, a Cross-Cultural Perspective*
R&R Bk N - v19 - i4 - Nov 2004 - p14(1) [51-500]

Korr, Charles P. - *The End of Baseball as We Knew It: The Players Union, 1960-1981*
Am St - v45 - i1 - Spring 2004 - p160-162 [501+]

Korros, Alexandra - *A Reluctant Parliament: Stolypin, Nationalism, and the Politics of the Russian Imperial State Council, 1906-1911*
Slav R - v63 - i2 - Summer 2004 - p407(2) [501+]

Korsch, Karl - *Briefe 1908-1939, 1940-1958*
GSR - v27 - i1 - Feb 2004 - p170-171 [501+]

Korstad, Robert Rodgers - *Civil Rights Unionism: Tobacco Workers and the Struggle for Democracy in the Mid-Twentieth Century South*
JEL - v41 - i4 - Dec 2003 - p1387(1) [501+]
Civil Rights Unionism: Tobacco Workers and the Struggle for Democracy in the Mid-Twentieth-Century South
RAH - v32 - i4 - Dec 2004 - p558-564 [501+]

Kort, Michael - *Central Asian Republics*
SLJ - v50 - i10 - Oct 2004 - pS58(1) [51-500]

Kort, Wesley A. - *Place and Space in Modern Fiction*
Choice - v42 - i4 - Dec 2004 - p660(1) [51-500]

Korte, Anne-Marie - *Women and Miracle Stories: A Multidisciplinary Exploration*
R&R Bk N - v19 - i3 - August 2004 - p13(1) [1-50]

Kortekaas, G.A.A. - *The Story of Appolonius, King of Tyre: A Study of Its Greek Origin and an Edition of the Two Oldest Latin Recensions*
Choice - v42 - i4 - Dec 2004 - p657(1) [1-50]
R&R Bk N - v19 - i4 - Nov 2004 - p215(1) [501+]

Korutcheva, Elka - *Advances in Condensed Matter and Statistical Physics*
SciTech - v28 - i3 - Sept 2004 - p45(1) [1-50]

Koryta, Michael - *Tonight I Said Goodbye*
Globe & Mail - Oct 2 2004 - pD18 [51-500]
KR - v72 - i16 - August 15 2004 - p781(1) [51-500]
LJ - v129 - i14 - Sept 1 2004 - p125(1) [51-500]
PW - v251 - i35 - August 30 2004 - p32(2) [501+]

Korzeniowska, Victoria B. - *Giraudoux: La Guerre de Troie n'aura pas lieu*
FS - v58 - i3 - July 2004 - p432-433 [501+]

Kos, David - *A Measure of Undoing*
BIC - v33 - i2 - March 2004 - p43(1) [501+]

Kosaka, Fumi - *If You'll Be My Valentine*
PW - v251 - i49 - Dec 6 2004 - p59(1) [501+]

Kosch, Harald - *Distributed Multimedia Database Technologies Supported by MPEG-7 and MPEG-21*
SciTech - v28 - i3 - Sept 2004 - p160(1) [51-500]

Koschorke, Albrecht - *The Holy Family and Its Legacy: Religious Imagination from the Gospels to Star Wars*
Choice - v42 - i1 - Sept 2004 - p84(1) [501+]
R&R Bk N - v19 - i1 - Feb 2004 - p22(1) [51-500]

Koscielniak, Bruce - *About Time: A First Look at Time and Clocks (Illus. by Koscielniak, Bruce)*
c BL - v101 - i7 - Dec 1 2004 - p666(1) [51-500]
c KR - v72 - i20 - Oct 15 2004 - p1009(1) [51-500]
c SLJ - v50 - i11 - Nov 2004 - p127(1) [51-500]
The Story of the Incredible Orchestra
c SLJ - v50 - i12 - Dec 2004 - p59(1) [501+]

Koselleck, Reinhart - *Futures Past: On the Semantics of Historical Time*
R&R Bk N - v19 - i3 - August 2004 - p30(1) [1-50]
The Practice of Conceptual History: Timing History, Spacing Concepts
J Soc H - v38 - i1 - Fall 2004 - p211(3) [501+]

Koser, Khalid - *New African Diasporas*
AJS - v110 - i2 - Sept 2004 - p527(3) [501+]
JPR - v41 - i5 - Sept 2004 - p642-642 [501+]

Koshar, Rudy - *Germany's Transient Pasts: Preservation and National Memory in the Twentieth Century*
J Urban H - v30 - i4 - May 2004 - p583-593 [501+]

Kositsky, Lynne - *Rachel, Book Four: An Elephant Tree Christmas*
c Res Links - v10 - i1 - Oct 2004 - p14(1) [501+]
Rachel, Book Two: The Maybe House: Our Canadian Girl
y Can CL - i111-112 - Fall-Winter 2003 - p128(7) [501+]
Rachel: Certificate of Freedom
c Can CL - i113/114 - Spring-Summer 2004 - p136(3) [501+]
c CBRA - Annual 2003 - p494(2) [51-500]
The Thought of High Windows
c Can CL - i113/114 - Spring-Summer 2004 - p136(3) [501+]
JAAL - v48 - i3 - Nov 2004 - p272(2) [501+]
c LibMed - v23 - i1 - August-Sept 2004 - p68(1) [51-500]
y VOYA - v27 - i3 - August 2004 - p219(1) [1-50]

Koskenniemi, Martti - *Finnish Yearbook of International Law, Vol. 12*
R&R Bk N - v19 - i3 - August 2004 - p210(1) [1-50]

Koslova, Natalia - *Ur III-Texte der St. Petersburger Eremitage*
JNES - v63 - i4 - Oct 2004 - p311(2) [501+]

Koslowski, Peter - *Philosophy Bridging the World Religions*
R&R Bk N - v19 - i1 - Feb 2004 - p11(1) [51-500]

Kosmoski, Georgia J. - *Managing Difficult, Frustrating, and Hostile Conversations: Strategies for Savvy Administrators, 2nd Ed.*
Cur R - v44 - i6 - Feb 2005 - p12(1) [501+]

Kosofsky, Scott-Martin - *The Book of Customs: A Complete Handbook for the Jewish Year*
BL - v101 - i3 - Oct 1 2004 - p304(2) [51-500]
LJ - v129 - i17 - Oct 15 2004 - p68(1) [51-500]

Koss, Amy G. - *Gossip Times Three*
LibMed - v22 - i6 - March 2004 - p64(1) [501+]

Kosta, Barbara - *Writing Against Boundaries: Nationality, Ethnicity and Gender in the German-Speaking Context*
GSR - v27 - i3 - Oct 2004 - p673(2) [501+]

Koster, Maren - *Musik-Zeit-Geschehen. Zu den Musikverhaltnissen in der SBZ/DDR 1945 bis 1952*
GSR - v27 - i3 - Oct 2004 - p664(2) [501+]

Koster, Ralph - *Theory of Fun for Game Design*
Bwatch - Feb 2005 - pNA [51-500]

Kostova, Elizabeth - *The Historian*
PW - v252 - i4 - Jan 24 2005 - p26(1) [501+]

Kot, Dave - *Wilco: Learning How to Die*
y SLJ - v50 - i10 - Oct 2004 - p200(1) [51-500]

Kota, Sastri L. - *Broadband Satellite Communications for Internet Access*
SciTech - v28 - i1 - March 2004 - p153(1) [51-500]

Kotani, Motoko - *Discrete Geometric Analysis: Proceedings*
SciTech - v28 - i3 - Sept 2004 - p42(1) [1-50]

Koterbay, Scott - *The Potential Role of Art in Kierkegaard's Description of the Individual*
R&R Bk N - v19 - i4 - Nov 2004 - p7(1) [51-500]

Koth, Karl B. - *Waking the Dictator: Veracruz, the Struggle for Federalism, and the Mexican Revolution, 1870-1927*
HAHR - v84 - i4 - Nov 2004 - p750(2) [501+]

Kothari, Brij - *Reading Beyond the Alphabet: Innovations in Lifelong Literacy*
R&R Bk N - v19 - i1 - Feb 2004 - p189(1) [51-500]

Kotin, Joel - *Getting Started: An Introduction to Dynamic Psychotherapy*
SciTech - v28 - i3 - Sept 2004 - p99(1) [501+]

Kotjabopoulou, Eleni - *Zooarchaeology in Greece: Recent Advances, Abstracts*
R&R Bk N - v19 - i1 - Feb 2004 - p26(1) [51-500]

Kotkin, Joel - *The City: A Global History*
KR - v73 - i3 - Feb 1 2005 - p167(1) [501+]
LJ - v130 - i4 - March 1 2005 - p102(1) [51-500]

Kotler, Philip - *Lateral Marketing: New Techniques for Finding Breakthrough Ideas*
R&R Bk N - v19 - i3 - August 2004 - p127(1) [51-500]

Kotlikoff, Laurence J. - *The Coming Generational Storm: What You Need to Know about America's Economic Future*
Bus W - i3897 - August 30 2004 - p28 [501+]
Choice - v42 - i1 - Sept 2004 - p154(1) [501+]
Fut - v38 - i6 - Nov-Dec 2004 - p60(1) [51-500]
Har Bus R - v82 - i6 - June 2004 - p28(1) [501+]

Kotlowitz, Alex - *Never a City So Real: A Walk in Chicago (Read by Brick, Scott). Audiobook Review*
y Kliatt - v39 - i1 - Jan 2005 - p54(1) [51-500]
Never a City So Real: A Walk in Chicago
BL - v100 - i21 - July 2004 - p1812(1) [1-50]
BW - v34 - i32 - August 8 2004 - p4(2) [501+]
Globe & Mail - July 31 2004 - pD12 [1-50]

Kotschevar, Lendal H. - *Managing Beverage Service*
R&R Bk N - v19 - i4 - Nov 2004 - p251(1) [501+]

Kotsonouris, Mary - *The Winding-Up of the Dail Courts, 1922-1925: An Obvious Duty*
R&R Bk N - v19 - i4 - Nov 2004 - p164(1) [501+]

Kottick, Edward L. - *A History of the Harpsichord*
TLS - i5263 - Feb 13 2004 - p10-10 [501+]

Kotz, Mary Lynn - *Rauschenberg: Art and Life*
Art N - v104 - i1 - Jan 2005 - p94(1) [501+]
LJ - v130 - i2 - Feb 1 2005 - p76(1) [51-500]

Kotz, Nick - *Judgment Days: Lyndon Baines Johnson, Martin Luther King, Jr., and the Laws That Changed America*
BL - v101 - i8 - Dec 15 2004 - p694(1) [51-500]
Black Iss - v7 - i2 - March-April 2005 - p54(1) [51-500]
KR - v72 - i22 - Nov 15 2004 - p1080(1) [501+]
LJ - v129 - i19 - Nov 15 2004 - p71(1) [51-500]
NYTBR - Feb 6 2005 - p21 [501+]
PW - v251 - i48 - Nov 29 2004 - p29(2) [51-500]

Kotze, Annemare - *Augustine's 'Confessions': Communicative Purpose and Audience*
R&R Bk N - v19 - i4 - Nov 2004 - p19(1) [51-500]

Kotzwinkle, William - *Rough Weather for Walter the Farting Dog (Illus. by Colman, Audrey)*
c PW - v252 - i11 - March 14 2005 - p69(1) [501+]

Kouchoukos, Nicholas T. - *Kirklin/Barratt-Boyes Cardiac Surgery: Morphology, Diagnostic Criteria, Natural History, Techniques, Results and Indications, 3rd Ed.*
SciTech - v28 - i1 - March 2004 - p112 [51-500]

Koul, Opender - *Transgenic Crop Protection: Concepts and Strategies*
Choice - v42 - i6 - Feb 2005 - p1047(2) [51-500]
SciTech - v28 - i3 - Sept 2004 - p128(1) [51-500]

Kouloglou, Stelios - *Min Pas Pote Monos Sto Tachydromio*
TLS - i5284 - July 9 2004 - p7(1) [51-500]

Koundouri, Phoebe - *The Countries of Water Management in Developing Countries: Problems, Principles, and Policies, Proceedings*
R&R Bk N - v19 - i1 - Feb 2004 - p96(1) [51-500]
The Economics of Water Management in Developing Countries: Problems, Principles and Policies
JEL - v42 - i1 - March 2004 - p309(1) [501+]

Kourou, N. - *Limestone Statuettes of Cypriot Type Found in the Aegean: Provenance Studies*
Class R - v54 - i2 - Nov 2004 - p542(3) [501+]

Kourouma, Ahmadou - *Quand on refuse on dit non*
Econ - v372 - i8390 - August 28 2004 - p76US [501+]

Koustrup, Birthe - *Handbook of Decorative Motifs*
R&R Bk N - v19 - i4 - Nov 2004 - p209(1) [501+]

Koutsky, Jan Dale - *My Grandma, My Pen Pal (Illus. by Koutsky, Jan Dale)*
c RT - v57 - Nov 2003 - p272 [51-500]

Kouvaros, George - *Where Does It Happen?: John Cassavetes and Cinema at the Breaking Point*
R&R Bk N - v19 - i3 - August 2004 - p264(1) [51-500]

Kouzminov, Alexander - *Biological Espionage: Special Operations of the Soviet and Russian Foreign Intelligence Services in the West*
LJ - v129 - i20 - Dec 1 2004 - p137(1) [51-500]
PW - v251 - i47 - Nov 22 2004 - p45(2) [51-500]

Kovach, Robert - *Firefly Guide to Global Hazards*
CG - v124 - i3 - May-June 2004 - p134(1) [501+]

Kovach, Robert L. - *Early Earthquakes of the Americas*
Am Ant - v70 - i1 - Jan 2005 - p200(2) [501+]
Choice - v42 - i4 - Dec 2004 - p692(1) [1-50]
Firefly Guide to Global Hazards
c Kliatt - v38 - i4 - July 2004 - p44(1) [51-500]
Sci Teach - v72 - i3 - March 2005 - p81(2) [51-500]

Kovacs, D. - *Euripidea Tertia*
Class R - v54 - i2 - Nov 2004 - p306-307 [501+]
Euripides VI: Bacchae, Iphigenia at Aulis Rhesus
Class R - v54 - i2 - Nov 2004 - p305-306 [501+]

Kovacs, Diane K. - *The Kovacs Guide to Electronic Library Collection Development: Essential Core Subject Collections, Selection Criteria, and Guidelines*
    BL - v100 - i21 - July 2004 - p1859(1) [501+]

Kovacs, Judith - *Revelation*
    TLS - i5289 - August 13 2004 - p24(1) [501+]

Kovalev, Vladimir A. - *Elastic Lidar: Theory, Practice, and Analysis Methods*
    E-Streams - Nov 2004 - pNA [501+]
    SciTech - v28 - i3 - Sept 2004 - p160(1) [51-500]

Kovalevsky, Jean - *Fundamentals of Astrometry*
    Choice - v42 - i6 - Feb 2005 - p1045(1) [51-500]

Kovalski, Maryann - *Take Me Out to the Ball Game (Illus. by Kovalski, Maryann)*
  c BL - v100 - i22 - August 2004 - p1943(1) [51-500]
  c Globe & Mail - July 17 2004 - pD11 [1-50]
    Res Links - v10 - i2 - Dec 2004 - p9(1) [51-500]
  c SLJ - v50 - i10 - Oct 2004 - p120(1) [51-500]

Koven, Seth (b. 1958 -) - *Slumming: Sexual and Social Politics in Victorian London*
    CHE - v51 - i9 - Oct 22 2004 - pA23-A23 [501+]
    HM - v309 - i1853 - Oct 2004 - p91(2) [501+]
    LJ - v129 - i16 - Oct 1 2004 - p94(1) [51-500]
    TimHES - v0 - i1679 - Feb 18 2005 - p26(2) [501+]

Koves, W.J. - *Elevated Temperature Design and Analysis, Nonlinear Analysis, and Plastic Components: Proceedings*
    SciTech - v28 - i4 - Dec 2004 - p163(1) [51-500]

Kowalczuk, Ilko-Sascha - *Freiheit und Offentlichkeit: Politischer Samisdat in der DDR 1985-1989, Eine Dokumentation*
    HNet - Nov 2004 - pNA [501+]

Kowaleski, Maryanne - *The Havener's Accounts of the Earldom and Duchy of Cornwall, 1287-1356.*
    Albion - v36 - i1 - Spring 2004 - p97(2) [501+]

Kowalick, Thomas M. - *Fatal Exit: The Automotive Black Box Debate*
    SciTech - v28 - i4 - Dec 2004 - p8(1) [1-50]

Kowalski, Kathiann M. - *Poverty in America: Causes and Issues*
  c SLJ - v50 - i10 - Oct 2004 - pS36(1) [51-500]

Kowalski, Theodore J. - *Case Studies on Educational Administration, 4th Ed.*
    R&R Bk N - v19 - i4 - Nov 2004 - p186(1) [501+]

Kowalski, William - *The Good Neighbor*
    BL - v101 - i3 - Oct 1 2004 - p310(2) [51-500]
    KR - v72 - i17 - Sept 1 2004 - p826(1) [501+]
    LJ - v129 - i16 - Oct 1 2004 - p70(1) [51-500]
    PW - v251 - i43 - Oct 25 2004 - p25(2) [51-500]

Kowalsky, Richard J. - *Radiopharmaceuticals in Nuclear Pharmacy and Nuclear Medicine, 2nd Ed.*
    SciTech - v28 - i4 - Dec 2004 - p90(1) [51-500]

Kozaczuk, Wadysaw - *Enigma: How the Poles Broke the Nazi Code*
    R&R Bk N - v19 - i3 - August 2004 - p35(1) [51-500]

Kozak, Harley Jane - *Dating is Murder*
    PW - v252 - i6 - Feb 7 2005 - p45(1) [51-500]

Kozak, Metin - *Destination Benchmarking: Concepts, Practices, and Operations*
    R&R Bk N - v19 - i3 - August 2004 - p79(1) [51-500]

Kozak, Susan Jane - *Dating Is Murder*
    BL - v101 - i5 - Nov 1 2004 - p468(1) [51-500]
    KR - v72 - i23 - Dec 1 2004 - p1121(1) [51-500]
    LJ - v129 - i18 - Nov 1 2004 - p63(1) [51-500]
    Ent W - i811 - March 18 2005 - p75 [51-500]

Kozak, Warren - *The Rabbi of 84th Street: The Extraordinary Life of Haskel Besser*
    BL - v100 - i21 - July 2004 - p1802(1) [51-500]
    LJ - v129 - i12 - July 2004 - p90(1) [51-500]

Kozinn, Allan - *Classical Music: A Critic's Guide to the 100 Most Important Recordings*
  y BL - v100 - i22 - August 2004 - p1888(1) [51-500]

Kozma, P. - *Floral Biology, Pollination and Fertilisation in Temperate Zone Fruit Species and Grape*
    SciTech - v28 - i1 - March 2004 - p129(1) [51-500]

Krabbendam, Hans - *Religion in America: European and American Perspectives*
    CH - v73 - i4 - Dec 2004 - p890(2) [501+]

Kracauer, Siegfried - *From Caligari to Hitler: A Psychological History of the German Film*
    Globe & Mail - July 3 2004 - pD13 [1-50]
  Jacques Offenbach and the Paris of His Time
    South HR - v38 - i2 - Spring 2004 - p199(3) [501+]

Krach, Aaron - *Half-Life*
    Lam Bk Rpt - v13 - i1-2 - August-Sept 2004 - p40(1) [501+]

Krader, Lawrence - *Labor and Value*
    R&R Bk N - v19 - i1 - Feb 2004 - p99(1) [51-500]

Kraemer, Ross - *Religions of Star Trek*
    R&R Bk N - v19 - i4 - Feb 2004 - p244(1) [1-50]

Kraft, Betsy Harvey - *Theodore Roosevelt: Champion of the American Spirit*
  c SLJ - v50 - i10 - Oct 2004 - pS32(1) [51-500]

Kraft, Chris - *Flight: My Life in Mission Control*
    BL - v101 - i7 - Dec 1 2004 - p633(1) [51-500]

Kraft, Eric - *Passionate Spectator*
    BL - v100 - i21 - July 2004 - p1818(1) [51-500]
    PW - v251 - i28 - July 12 2004 - p45(1) [51-500]

Kraft, Erik - *Lenny and Mel: After-School Confidential (Illus. by Kraft, Erik)*
  c SLJ - v50 - i9 - Sept 2004 - p170(1) [51-500]
  Lenny and Mel: After-School Confidential
  c PW - v251 - i28 - July 12 2004 - p65(2) [501+]

Krahenbuhl, Gary S. - *Building the Academic Deanship: Strategies for Success*
    R&R Bk N - v19 - i3 - August 2004 - p221(1) [1-50]

Krahn, Betina - *The Marriage Test*
  y BL - v101 - i2 - Sept 15 2004 - p222(1) [51-500]

Krajewski, Bruce - *Gadamer's Repercussions: Reconsidering Philosophical Hermeneutics*
    Choice - v42 - i2 - Oct 2004 - p306(1) [51-500]

Krakauer, Jon - *Under the Banner of Heaven: A Story of Violent Faith (Read by Brick, Scott). Audiobook Review*
    LJ - v129 - i2 - Feb 1 2004 - p144(1) [51-500]

Krall, Jennifer L. - *Simply Shakespeare: Readers Theatre for Young People*
    LibMed - v22 - i6 - March 2004 - p82(1) [501+]

Kralovec, Etta - *The End of Homework: How Homework Disrupts Families, Overburdens Children, and Limits Learning*
    CE - v81 - i1 - Fall 2004 - p56(1) [51-500]

KramarzBein, Susanne - *Die pidreks saga im Kontext der altnorwegischen Literatur*
    JEGP - v103 - i4 - Oct 2004 - p505-528 [501+]

Kramer, Daniel C. - *The Price of Rights: The Courts, Government Largesse, and Fundamental Liberties*
    Law&PolBR - June 2004 - p453(5) [501+]

Kramer, Eric Mark - *The Emerging Monoculture: Assimilation and the "Model Minority"*
    CS - v33 - i4 - July 2004 - p422(3) [501+]

Kramer, Greg - *Wally*
    Globe & Mail - August 21 2004 - pD14 [501+]

Kramer, John E. - *The American College Novel: An Annotated Bibliography*
    Choice - v41 - i11-12 - July-August 2004 - p2018(1) [501+]

Kramer, Larry D. - *The People Themselves: Popular Constitutionalism and Judicial Review*
    Choice - v42 - i6 - Feb 2005 - p1099(1) [51-500]
    Law&PolBR - Nov 2004 - p916(11) [501+]
    New R - July 19 2004 - p32 [51-500]
    NYTBR - Oct 24 2004 - p32 [501+]

Kramer, Laura - *The Sociology of Gender: A Brief Introduction, 2nd Ed.*
    R&R Bk N - v19 - i4 - Nov 2004 - p132(1) [1-50]

Kramer, Lawerence - *Opera and Modern Culture: Wagner and Strauss*
    Choice - v42 - i7 - March 2005 - p1270(1) [51-500]

Kramer, Matthew H. - *The Quality of Freedom*
    Law&PolBR - June 2004 - p410(6) [501+]

Kramer, Pat - *Alaska's Totem Poles*
    R&R Bk N - v19 - i4 - Nov 2004 - p53(1) [51-500]

Kramer, Peter - *American Film: An A-Z Guide*
    LibMed - v23 - i1 - August-Sept 2004 - p78(1) [51-500]

Kramer, Peter D. - *Against Depression*
    KR - v73 - i5 - March 1 2005 - p275(1) [501+]

Krane, Julia - *What's Mother Got to Do with It? Protecting Children from Sexual Abuse*
    CBRA - Annual 2003 - p384(1) [501+]

Kranish, Michael - *Daniel Patrick Moynihan: The Intellectual in Public Life, 2nd Ed.*
    R&R Bk N - v19 - i4 - Nov 2004 - p63(1) [51-500]
  John F. Kerry: The Complete Biography by the Boston Globe Reporters Who Know Him Best
    NYTBR - August 15 2004 - p11 [501+]
    TimHES - v0 - i1650 - July 23 2004 - p25(1) [501+]

Krannich, Caryl Rae - *101 Secrets of Highly Effective Speakers: Controlling Fear, Commanding Attention*
    Bwatch - Feb 2005 - pNA [51-500]
  Nail the Job Interview!: 101 Dynamite Answers to Interview Questions (Read by Rohan, Richard). Audiobook Review
    LJ - v130 - i3 - Feb 15 2005 - p169(2) [51-500]
  Nail the Job Interview!: 101 Dynamite Answers to Interview Questions
    NACEJou - v64 - i2 - Wntr 2004 - p14(1) [501+]

Krannich, Ronald L. - *America's Top 100 Jobs for People Without a Four-Year Degree: Great Jobs with a Promising Future*
    Bwatch - Feb 2005 - pNA [51-500]
    Choice - v42 - i6 - Feb 2005 - p1004(1) [51-500]
    R&R Bk N - v19 - i4 - Nov 2004 - p109(1) [51-500]
  The Treasures and Pleasures of Thailand and Myanmar
    Bwatch - Nov 2004 - pNA [51-500]

Krantz, Les - *Not Till the Fat Lady Sings: The Most Dramatic Finishes of All Time*
    BL - v101 - i1 - Sept 1 2004 - p46(1) [51-500]

Krantz, Steven G. - *Differential Equations Demystified*
    Choice - v42 - i6 - Feb 2005 - p1058(1) [51-500]
    SciTech - v28 - i4 - Dec 2004 - p40(1) [51-500]

Kranz, Gene - *Failure Is Not an Option: Mission Control from Mercury to Apollo 13 and Beyond*
    BL - v101 - i7 - Dec 1 2004 - p633(1) [51-500]

Kranz, Linda - *My Nature Book: A Journal and Activity Book for Kids (Illus. by Kranz, Linda)*
  c PW - v251 - i37 - Sept 13 2004 - p81(1) [501+]

Kranz, Rachel - *African-American Business Leaders and Entrepreneurs*
    Choice - v42 - i2 - Oct 2004 - p276(1) [501+]

Kranzler, Henry R. - *Dual Diagnosis and Psychiatric Treatment: Substance Abuse and Comorbid Disorders, 2nd Ed.*
    E-Streams - Dec 2004 - pNA [501+]
  Dual Diagnosis and Psychiatric Treatment: Substance Abuse and Comorbid Disorders, 2nd Ed.
    SciTech - v28 - i3 - Sept 2004 - p103(1) [51-500]

Krapp, Peter - *Deja Vu: Aberrations on Cultural Memory*
    Afterimage - v32 - i3 - Nov-Dec 2004 - p13(1) [501+]

Krashen, Stephen D. - *The Power of Reading: Insights from the Research, 2nd Ed.*
    R&R Bk N - v19 - i4 - Nov 2004 - p258(1) [51-500]

Kraska, Peter B. - *Theorizing Criminal Justice: Eight Essential Orientations*
    R&R Bk N - v19 - i4 - Nov 2004 - p147(1) [501+]

Krasno, Jean E. - *Leveraging for Success in United Nations Peace Operations*
    R&R Bk N - v19 - i1 - Feb 2004 - pNA [51-500]
  The United Nations: Confronting the Challenges of a Global Society
    R&R Bk N - v19 - i3 - August 2004 - p188(1) [501+]

Krass, Peter - *Blood and Whiskey: The Life and Times of Jack Daniel*
    Choice - v42 - i3 - Nov 2004 - p504(2) [1-50]
  Carnegie
    BHR - v78 - i3 - Autumn 2004 - p501(6) [501+]

Krastev, Ivan - *Shifting Obsessions: Three Essays on the Politics of Anticorruption*
    R&R Bk N - v19 - i4 - Nov 2004 - p153(1) [501+]

Kratter, Paul - *Living Rain Forest: An Animal Alphabet*
  c SB - v40 - i4 - July-August 2004 - p179(1) [51-500]

Krau, Edgar - *A Meta-Psychological Perspective on the Individual Course of Life*
    R&R Bk N - v19 - i3 - August 2004 - p11(1) [1-50]

Kraus, Caroline - *Borderlines: A Memoir*
    BW - v34 - i30 - July 25 2004 - p13(1) [501+]
  y SLJ - v50 - i7 - July 2004 - p133(1) [51-500]

Kraus, Hans-Christof - *Konservative Zeitschriften zwischen Kaiserreich und Diktatur: Funf Fallstudien*
    HNet - Nov 2004 - pNA [501+]

Krause, Peter - *Combating Poverty in Europe: The German Welfare Regime in Practice*
    R&R Bk N - v19 - i1 - Feb 2004 - p139(1) [51-500]

Krause, Virginia - *Idle Pursuits: Literature and Oisivete in the French Renaissance*
    Ren Q - v57 - i4 - Winter 2004 - p1425(2) [501+]
    R&R Bk N - v19 - i1 - Feb 2004 - p231(1) [51-500]

Kraushaar, Wolfgang - *Fischer in Frankfurt. Karriere eines aubenseiters*
    GSR - v27 - i1 - Feb 2004 - p206-207 [501+]

Krauss, Ellis S. - *Beyond Bilateralism: U.S.-Japan Relations in the New Asia-Pacific*
Choice - v42 - i2 - Oct 2004 - p367(1) [51-500]
HNet - Sept 2004 - pNA [501+]

Krauss, Hartmut - *Zoonoses: Infectious Diseases Transmissible from Animals to Humans*
QRB - v79 - i3 - Sept 2004 - p344(2) [501+]

Krauss, Marita - *Frauen und Migration*
GSR - v27 - i1 - Feb 2004 - p132-133 [501+]

Krauss, Nicole - *The History of Love*
KR - v73 - i4 - Feb 15 2005 - p191(1) [501+]
PW - v252 - i8 - Feb 21 2005 - p154(1) [51-500]

Krauss, Rosalind - *October*
TLS - i5267 - March 12 2004 - p23-23 [501+]

Krauss, Ruth - *Goodnight Goodnight Sleepyhead (Illus. by Krauss, Ruth)*
c SLJ - v50 - i7 - July 2004 - p78(2) [51-500]

Kraut, Alan M. - *Goldberger's War: The Life and Work of a Public Health Crusader*
JSH - v70 - i4 - Nov 2004 - p950(2) [501+]
SciTech - v28 - i1 - March 2004 - p77(1) [51-500]
JAH - v91 - i2 - Sept 2004 - p662(2) [501+]

Krauth, Leland - *Mark Twain & Company: Six Literary Relations*
Choice - v41 - i7 - March 2004 - p1296(2) [501+]

Krautwurst, Terry - *Night Science for Kids: Exploring the World after Dark*
c BL - v101 - i7 - Dec 1 2004 - p670(1) [51-500]
Sci Teach - v71 - i8 - Oct 2004 - p74-74 [501+]
c SLJ - v50 - i10 - Oct 2004 - pS40(1) [51-500]

Kravchenko, Alexander - *Sign, Meaning, Knowledge: An Essay in the Cognitive Philosophy of Language*
R&R Bk N - v19 - i1 - Feb 2004 - p212 [51-500]

Kravchuk, Robert S. - *Ukrainian Political Economy: The First Ten Years*
Slav R - v63 - i2 - Summer 2004 - p397(2) [501+]

Kravetz, Dennis J. - *Measuring Human Capital: Converting Workplace Behavior into Dollars*
HR Mag - v49 - i11 - Nov 2004 - p147(1) [51-500]
HR Mag - v50 - i2 - Feb 2005 - pS15(1) [501+]

Kravetz, Stacy - *The Dating Race: An Undercover Report from the Front Lines of Modern-Day Romance*
LJ - v130 - i2 - Feb 1 2005 - p105(1) [51-500]

Kravitz, Noah - *Teaching and Learning with Technology: Learning Where to Look*
R&R Bk N - v19 - i4 - Nov 2004 - p179(1) [501+]

Kraybill, Donald R. - *Amish Enterprise: From Plows to Profits, 2nd Ed.*
R&R Bk N - v19 - i3 - August 2004 - p28(1) [1-50]

Kraye, Jill - *Classical Traditions in Renaissance Philosophy*
Six Ct J - v35 - i3 - Fall 2004 - p828-829 [501+]

Krebs, Laurie - *A Day in the Life of a Colonial Doctor*
c BL - v101 - i1 - Sept 1 2004 - p127(1) [1-50]
SLJ - v50 - i12 - Dec 2004 - p133(1) [501+]
A Day in the Life of a Colonial Sailmaker
c BL - v101 - i1 - Sept 1 2004 - p127(1) [1-50]
We All Went on Safari: A Counting Journey Through Tanzania (Illus. by Cairns, Julia)
RT - v58 - i3 - Nov 2004 - p287(2) [1-50]

Krebs, Robert E. - *Basics of Earth Science*
E-Streams - June 2004 - pNA [501+]
Groundbreaking Scientific Experiments, Inventions, and Discoveries of the Ancient World
SB - v40 - i4 - July-August 2004 - p156(1) [51-500]
Groundbreaking Scientific Experiments, Inventions, and Discoveries of the Middle Ages and the Renaissance
Choice - v42 - i3 - Nov 2004 - p505(1) [1-50]
E-Streams - Dec 2004 - pNA [501+]
SB - v40 - i6 - Nov-Dec 2004 - p247(1) [501+]
TES - v0 - i4587 - June 11 2004 - psss28(1) [501+]

Krech, Shepard - *Encyclopedia of World Environmental History*
LibMed - v23 - i1 - August-Sept 2004 - p82(1) [51-500]
Ref Rev - Sept 2004 - pNA [501+]

Krehbiel, Joyce L. - *Lanier: The Descendants of John Lanier and Nancy C. Morris*
EFHM - v58 - i2 - March-April 2004 - p88(1) [51-500]

Kreider, Glenn R. - *Jonathan Edwards's Interpretation of Revelation 4:1-8:1*
R&R Bk N - v19 - i4 - Nov 2004 - p28(1) [501+]

Kreijen, Gerard - *State Failure, Sovereignty and Effectiveness: Legal Lessons from the Decolonization of Sub-Saharan Africa*
R&R Bk N - v19 - i3 - August 2004 - p184(1) [501+]

Kreinath, Jens - *Dynamics of Changing Rituals: The Transformation of Religious Rituals Within Their Social and Cultural Context*
R&R Bk N - v19 - i1 - Feb 2004 - p12(1) [51-500]

Kreisel, Henry - *The Almost Meeting: And Other Stories*
Globe & Mail - Nov 20 2004 - pD29 [1-50]

Kreitler, Shulamith - *Psychosocial Aspects of Pediatric Oncology*
E-Streams - Dec 2004 - pNA [501+]
SciTech - v28 - i3 - Sept 2004 - p92(1) [51-500]

Kreitman, Esther Singer - *Deborah*
y BL - v100 - i22 - August 2004 - p1899(1) [51-500]
Choice - v42 - i6 - Feb 2005 - p1019(1) [51-500]
LJ - v129 - i13 - August 2004 - p68(1) [51-500]

Kreizenbeck, Alan - *Zoe Akins: Broadway Playwright*
Choice - v42 - i7 - March 2005 - p1229(2) [51-500]
R&R Bk N - v19 - i4 - Nov 2004 - p242(1) [501+]

Krelle, Wilhelm E. - *Economics and Ethics*
JEL - v42 - i1 - March 2004 - p233(1) [501+]

Kremer, Mark - *Plato's Cleitophon: On Socrates and the Modern Mind*
RM - v58 - i2 - Dec 2004 - p449(3) [501+]
R&R Bk N - v19 - i3 - August 2004 - p3(1) [1-50]

Kremer, Michael - *Strong Medicine: Creating Incentives for Pharmaceutical Research on Neglected Diseases*
Nature - v431 - i7009 - Oct 7 2004 - p629(2) [501+]

Kremer, S. Lillian - *Holocaust Literature: An Encyclopedia of Writers and Their Work*
GSR - v27 - i2 - May 2004 - p439-440 [501+]

Kremer, Thomas - *The Missing Heart of Europe*
Spec - v297 - i9207 - Jan 22 2005 - p36(1) [501+]

Kren, Jan - *Die Konfliktgemeinschaft: Tschechen und Deutsche, 1780-1918*
Slav R - v63 - i2 - Summer 2004 - p381(3) [501+]

Kren, Thomas - *Illuminating the Renaissance: The Triumph of Flemish Manuscript Painting in Europe*
Ren Q - v57 - i3 - Fall 2004 - p1032(2) [501+]

Krensky, Stephen - *Dangerous Crossing: The Revolutionary Voyage of John Quincy Adams (Illus. by Harlin, Greg)*
c KR - v73 - i1 - Jan 1 2005 - p53(1) [51-500]
c SLJ - v51 - i2 - Feb 2005 - p104(2) [51-500]
Davy Crockett: A Life on the Frontier (Illus. by Dacey, Bob)
c BL - v101 - i7 - Dec 1 2004 - p656(1) [51-500]
There Once Was a Very Odd School: And Other Lunch-Box Limericks (Illus. by Petrosino, Tamara)
c BL - v101 - i1 - Sept 1 2004 - p117(1) [501+]
c SLJ - v50 - i8 - August 2004 - p110(1) [51-500]

Krentz, Jayne Ann - *Falling Awake*
y BL - v101 - i3 - Oct 1 2004 - p283(1) [51-500]
KR - v72 - i18 - Sept 15 2004 - p884(2) [501+]
LJ - v129 - i17 - Oct 15 2004 - p54(1) [51-500]
PW - v251 - i41 - Oct 11 2004 - p55(2) [51-500]
Truth or Dare (Read by Bean, Joyce). Audiobook Review
LJ - v129 - i12 - July 2004 - p124(1) [51-500]

Krenz, Kim - *Deep Waters: The Ottawa River and Canada's Nuclear Adventure*
SciTech - v28 - i3 - Sept 2004 - p151(1) [51-500]

Krepon, Michael - *Cooperative Threat Reduction, Missile Defense and the Nuclear Future*
JPR - v41 - i5 - Sept 2004 - p642-642 [501+]

Kress, Nancy - *Crucible*
Analog - v125 - i1-2 - Jan-Feb 2005 - p230(6) [501+]
BL - v100 - i22 - August 2004 - p1913(1) [51-500]
LJ - v129 - i13 - August 2004 - p72(1) [51-500]
y VOYA - v27 - i4 - Oct 2004 - p315(1) [51-500]

Kressel, Gideon M. - *Let Shepherding Endure: Applied Anthropology and the Preservation of a Cultural Tradition in Israel and the Middle East*
JRAI - v10 - i3 - Sept 2004 - p724(2) [501+]

Kressley, Carson - *Off the Cuff: The Essential Style Guide for Men and the Women Who Love Them (Illus. by O'Malley, Jason)*
PW - v251 - i33 - August 16 2004 - p58(1) [51-500]
Time - v164 - i12 - Sept 20 2004 - p80 [51-500]

Krethlow-Benziger, Donata Maria - *Glanz und Elend der Diplomatie*
GSR - v27 - i2 - May 2004 - p388-389 [501+]

Kreuer, Klaus-Dieter - *Annual Review of Materials Research: Vol. 33, 2003*
SciTech - v28 - i1 - March 2004 - p139(1) [51-500]

Kreuger, Gary - *Enterprise Restructuring and the Role of Managers in Russia: Case Studies of Firms in Transition*
R&R Bk N - v19 - i3 - August 2004 - p110(1) [501+]

Krich, Rochelle - *Grave Endings*
BL - v100 - i22 - August 2004 - p1905(1) [51-500]
KR - v72 - i17 - Sept 1 2004 - p839(1) [51-500]
LJ - v129 - i17 - Oct 15 2004 - p54(1) [51-500]
PW - v251 - i32 - August 9 2004 - p230(2) [51-500]

Krick-Aigner, Kirsten - *Ingeborg Bachmann's Telling Stories: Fairy Tale Beginnings & Holocaust Endings*
Ger Q - v77 - i1 - Wntr 2004 - p109(2) [501+]

Krick, Robert E.L. - *Staff Officers in Gray: A Biographical Register of the Staff Officers in the Army of Northern Virginia*
HNet - Oct 2004 - pNA [501+]
VQR - v80 - i1 - Wntr 2004 - p264-265 [501+]

Kricka, Larry J. - *Optical Methods: A Guide to the "-Escences"*
Choice - v42 - i1 - Sept 2004 - p72(1) [501+]

Kricorian, Nancy - *Dreams of Bread and Fire*
Kliatt - v38 - i5 - Sept 2004 - p22(2) [501+]

Krieg, Robert Anthony - *Catholic Theologians in Nazi Germany*
AM - v191 - i19 - Dec 13 2004 - p14 [501+]
J Ch St - v46 - i4 - Autumn 2004 - p893(2) [501+]
R&R Bk N - v19 - i4 - Nov 2004 - p27(1) [501+]
CHR - v90 - i3 - July 2004 - p565(2) [501+]

Kriegel, Mark - *Namath: A Biography (Read by Brick, Scott). Audiobook Review*
LJ - v130 - i4 - March 1 2005 - p125(1) [51-500]
Namath: A Biography
BL - v100 - i21 - July 2004 - p1810(1) [1-50]
BW - v34 - i34 - August 22 2004 - p2(1) [501+]
Ent W - i781 - Sept 3 2004 - p78 [51-500]
Nation - v280 - i8 - Feb 28 2005 - p30 [501+]
People - v62 - i10 - Sept 6 2004 - p58 [51-500]
PW - v251 - i27 - July 5 2004 - p49(2) [51-500]

Krieger, Alex D. - *We Came Naked and Barefoot: The Journey of Cabeza de Vaca across North America*
Ams - v61 - i2 - Oct 2004 - p273(2) [501+]
SHQ - v107 - i4 - April 2004 - p616(3) [501+]

Krieger, Ellie - *Small Changes, Big Results: A 12-Week Action Plan for Eating Well, Staying Fit, and Feeling Good*
LJ - v130 - i1 - Jan 1 2005 - p144(3) [501+]

Krieger, Melanie Jacobs - *How to Excel in Science Competitions*
SB - v40 - i5 - Sept-Oct 2004 - p191(1) [51-500]

Kriek, Eric - *Gutsman Comics, Vol. 1*
Kliatt - v38 - i6 - Nov 2004 - p27(1) [51-500]

Krienert, Jessie L. - *Crime and Employment: Critical Issues in Crime Reduction for Corrections*
R&R Bk N - v19 - i1 - Feb 2004 - p145(1) [51-500]

Krier, Theresa - *Spenser Studies: A Renaissance Poetry Annual, Vol. 18*
R&R Bk N - v19 - i1 - Feb 2004 - p237(1) [51-500]

Kriger, Norma - *Guerrilla Veterans in Post-War Zimbabwe: Symbolic and Violent Politics, 1980-1987*
IJAHS - v37 - i1 - Wntr 2004 - p156-158 [501+]
J Mil H - v68 - i4 - Oct 2004 - p1314-1315 [501+]

Krigstein, Bernard - *B. Krigstein: Comics*
BL - v101 - i5 - Nov 1 2004 - p473(1) [51-500]
PW - v251 - i38 - Sept 20 2004 - p48(1) [51-500]

Krijff, J.Th.J. - *Een Aengenaeme Vrientschap: An Amicable Friendship: A Collection of Historical Events Between the Netherlands and Canada from 1862 to 1914*
CBRA - Annual 2003 - p356(2) [501+]

Krikos, Linda A. - *Women's Studies: A Recommended Bibliography, 3rd Ed.*
R&R Bk N - v19 - i4 - Nov 2004 - p133(1) [51-500]

Krimsky, Sheldon - *Science in the Private Interest: Has the Lure of Profits Corrupted Biomedical Research?*
Hast Cen R - v34 - i5 - Sept-Oct 2004 - p44(2) [501+]
QRB - v79 - i3 - Sept 2004 - p341(3) [501+]
SciTech - v28 - i4 - Dec 2004 - p79(1) [51-500]
TimHES - v0 - i1655 - August 27 2004 - p25(1) [501+]

Kring, Sandka - *Carry Me Home*
PW - v251 - i45 - Nov 8 2004 - p35(1) [501+]

Krinsky, Natalie - *Chloe Does Yale*
Ent W - i809 - March 4 2005 - p77 [501+]
KR - v73 - i1 - Jan 1 2005 - p12(1) [51-500]
People - v63 - i11 - March 21 2005 - p62 [51-500]
PW - v252 - i6 - Feb 7 2005 - p43(1) [51-500]

Krippendorff, Kaihan - *The Art of the Advantage: 36 Strategies to Seize the Competitive Edge*
Har Bus R - v82 - i3 - March 2004 - pNA [501+]
R&R Bk N - v19 - i1 - Feb 2004 - p105(1) [51-500]

Krippendorff, Klaus - *Content Analysis: An Introduction to Its Methodology, 2nd Ed.*
Per Psy - v57 - i4 - Winter 2004 - p1110(4) [501+]

Krippner, Stanley - *Becoming Psychic: Spiritual Lessons for Focusing Your Hidden Abilities*
Bwatch - Feb 2005 - pNA [501+]

Krisak, Len - *Even as We Speak*
Sew R - v111 - i3 - Summer 2003 - pXCIII-XCIV [501+]

Krishna, S. - *Digital Challenge: Information Technology in the Development Context*
SciTech - v28 - i1 - March 2004 - p133(1) [51-500]

Krishnaswami, Uma - *Naming Maya*
HB - v80 - i4 - July-August 2004 - p455(1) [51-500]

Krishnaswamy, Venkataraman - *Private Sector Participation in the Power Sector in Europe and Central Asia: Lessons from the Last Decade*
JEL - v42 - i1 - March 2004 - p292(1) [501+]

Krisnky, Norman I. - *Carotenoids in Health and Disease*
SciTech - v28 - i4 - Dec 2004 - p74(1) [51-500]

Kristeva, Julia - *Colette*
Wom R Bks - v22 - i2 - Nov 2004 - p23(1) [501+]
The Sense and Non-Sense of Revolt: The Powers and Limits of Psychoanalysis
Col Lit - v31 - i4 - Fall 2004 - p188(15) [501+]

Kristiansen, Sonbo - *Evidence Based Medicine: In Whose Interests?*
SciTech - v28 - i4 - Dec 2004 - p77(1) [51-500]

Kristjansson, Kristjan - *Justifying Emotions: Pride and Jealousy*
Dialogue - v43 - i2 - Spring 2004 - p404(3) [501+]

Kristmanson, Mark - *Plateaus of Freedom: Nationality, Culture, and State Security in Canada, 1940-1960.*
Can Hist R - v85 - i4 - Dec 2004 - p871(3) [501+]

Kristo, Janice V. - *Nonfiction in Focus: A Comprehensive Framework for Helping Students Become Independent Readers and Writers of Nonfiction, K-6*
SLJ - v50 - i10 - Oct 2004 - pS73(1) [51-500]

Kristrom, Bengt - *Economic Theory for the Environment: Essays in Honor of Karl-Goran Maler*
JEL - v42 - i3 - Sept 2004 - p888(2) [501+]

Krisztal, Ruben - *Nursing Home Litigation: Pretrial Practices and Trial, 2nd Ed.*
R&R Bk N - v19 - i1 - Feb 2004 - pNA [51-500]

Kritzer, Herbert M. - *In Litigation: Do the "Haves" Still Come out Ahead?*
Choice - v41 - i7 - March 2004 - p1372(1) [501+]
Risks, Reputations, and Rewards: Contingency Fee Legal Practice in the United States
CHE - v51 - i2 - Sept 3 2004 - pA20(1) [501+]
HLR - v118 - i3 - Jan 2005 - p1097-1098 [1-50]

Krivopissko, Guy - *La Vie A En Mourir*
TLS - i5262 - Feb 6 2004 - p23(1) [501+]

Krizan, A.C. - *Business Communication, 6th Ed.*
R&R Bk N - v19 - i2 - May 2004 - p120 [51-500]

Krizmanic, Judy - *The Teen's Vegetarian Cookbook (Illus. by Wawiorka, Matthew)*
y SLJ - v51 - i2 - Feb 2005 - p59(1) [51-500]

Krizsan, Andrea - *Reshaping Globalization: Multilateral Dialogues and New Policy Initiatives*
JEL - v41 - i4 - Dec 2003 - p1350(1) [501+]

Krobb, Florian - *Poetry Project, Irish Germanists Interpret German Verse*
GSR - v27 - i2 - May 2004 - p445-446 [501+]

Kroeber, Karl - *Ishi in Three Centuries*
Am Ind CRJ - v28 - i2 - Spring 2004 - p158(2) [501+]
NYRB - v51 - i15 - Oct 7 2004 - p4(3) [501+]
PHR - v73 - i4 - Nov 2004 - p676(3) [501+]
Native American Storytelling: A Reader of Myths and Legends
Choice - v42 - i5 - Jan 2005 - p840(1) [1-50]

Kroener, Bernhard R. - *Organization and Mobilization of the German Sphere of Power, Pt. 2*
HNet - Oct 2004 - pNA [501+]

Kroeper, Karla - *Minshat Abu Omar II: Ein vor- und fruhgeschichtlicher Friedhof im Nildelta, Graber 115-204. Vol. 2/1.*
JNES - v63 - i3 - July 2004 - p218(2) [501+]

Kroetsch, Robert - *The Snowbird Poems*
Globe & Mail - Nov 20 2004 - pD8 [501+]

Krogh, Steffen - *Das Ostjiddisch im Sprachkontakt. Deutsch im Spannungsfeld zwischen Semitism und Slavisch*
JEGP - v103 - i4 - Oct 2004 - p545-547 [501+]

Krogius, Henrik - *New York You're A Wonderful Town!: Fifty-Plus Years of Chronicling Gotham*
Bwatch - Oct 2004 - pNA [51-500]
New York, You're a Wonderful Town: Fifty-Plus Years of Chronicling Gotham
R&R Bk N - v19 - i3 - August 2004 - p73(1) [51-500]

Krogstie, John - *Information Modeling Methods and Methodologies*
SciTech - v28 - i4 - Dec 2004 - p31(1) [51-500]

Krohn, Leena - *Tainaron: Mail from Another City*
PW - v251 - i46 - Nov 15 2004 - p45(1) [51-500]

Kroker, Arthur - *The Will to Technology and the Culture of Nihilism: Heidegger, Nietzsche, and Marx*
R&R Bk N - v19 - i4 - Nov 2004 - p8(1) [51-500]

Kroll, Steven - *A Tale of Two Dogs (Illus. by Reed, Mike)*
c SLJ - v50 - i7 - July 2004 - p80(1) [51-500]

Kroller, Eva-Marie - *Cambridge Companion to Canadian Literature*
BIC - v33 - i7 - Oct 2004 - p28(1) [501+]

Kronenfeld, Jennie J. - *Reorganizing Health Care Delivery Systems: Problems of Managed Care and Other Models of Health Care Delivery*
CS - v33 - i5 - Sept 2004 - p610-611 [501+]

Kronenfeld, Jennie Jacobs - *Healthcare Reform in America: A Reference Handbook*
Choice - v42 - i6 - Feb 2005 - p998(1) [51-500]
y Ref Rev - Oct 2004 - pNA [501+]
SciTech - v28 - i4 - Dec 2004 - p80(1) [51-500]
Research in the Sociology of Health Care, Vol. 20: Social Inequalities, Health Care Delivery
CS - v33 - i1 - Jan 2004 - p127-127 [501+]

Kronenwetter, Michael - *America in the 1960s*
y SLJ - v50 - i10 - Oct 2004 - p67(1) [51-500]
Terrorism: A Guide to Events and Documents
BL - v101 - i6 - Nov 15 2004 - p615(1) [501+]
Choice - v42 - i4 - Dec 2004 - p640(1) [1-50]

Kronick, David A. - *"Devant le Deluge": And Other Essays on Early Modern Scientific Communication*
R&R Bk N - v19 - i4 - Nov 2004 - p228(1) [501+]

Kronk, Gary W. - *Cometography: A Catalog of Comets, Vol. 2*
S&T - v107 - i4 - April 2004 - p74(1) [501+]

Kronman, Anthony T. - *A History of the Yale Law School: The Tercentennial Lectures*
LJ - v129 - i12 - July 2004 - p96(1) [51-500]

Kroodsma, Donald E. - *The Singing Life of Birds: The Art and Science of Listening to Birdsong*
PW - v252 - i8 - Feb 21 2005 - p167(1) [51-500]

Krooth, Richard - *A Century Passing: Carnegie, Steel and the Fate of Homestead*
R&R Bk N - v19 - i3 - August 2004 - p73(1) [51-500]

Kropf, Latifa Berry - *It's Hanukkah Time! (Illus. by Cohen, Tod)*
c BL - v101 - i4 - Oct 15 2004 - p411(1) [51-500]
c PW - v251 - i39 - Sept 27 2004 - p60(1) [51-500]
It's Purim Time! (Illus. by Cohen, Tod)
c PW - v252 - i7 - Feb 14 2005 - p81(1) [51-500]
It's Seder Time! (Illus. by Cohen, Tod)
c SLJ - v50 - i12 - Dec 2004 - p133(2) [501+]

Kropp, Paul - *Countess and Me*
y Can CL - i111-112 - Fall-Winter 2003 - p153(6) [501+]

Krosoczka, Jarrett - *Max for President*
c BL - v100 - i21 - July 2004 - p1848(1) [1-50]
c PW - v251 - i31 - August 2 2004 - p69(1) [51-500]
c SLJ - v50 - i7 - July 2004 - p80(1) [51-500]

Kross, Jaan - *Omaeluloolisus ja alltekst*
WLT - v78 - i3-4 - Sept-Dec 2004 - p109(1) [501+]

Krossing, Karen - *Take the Stairs*
y CBRA - Annual 2003 - p495(1) [51-500]
y Kliatt - v39 - i1 - Jan 2005 - p26(1) [51-500]

Krotzl, Christian - *The Roman Curia, the Apostolic Penitentiary and the Partes in the Later Middle Ages*
CHR - v90 - i3 - July 2004 - p532(2) [501+]

Krouwer, Jan S. - *Managing Risk in Hospitals Using Integrated Fault Trees and Failure Mode Effects and Criticality Analysis*
SciTech - v28 - i4 - Dec 2004 - p86(1) [51-500]

Kruckeberg, Arthur - *Geology and Plant Life: The Effects of Landforms and Rock Types on Plants*
SciTech - v28 - i3 - Sept 2004 - p61(1) [51-500]

Krude, Torsten - *DNA: Changing Science and Society*
E-Streams - Nov 2004 - pNA [501+]
TimHES - v0 - i1661 - Oct 8 2004 - p24(2) [501+]

Krudwig, Vickie Leigh - *Searching for Chipeta: The Story of a Ute and Her People*
c BL - v101 - i1 - Sept 1 2004 - p117(1) [1-50]
y Kliatt - v38 - i4 - July 2004 - p37(2) [51-500]
VOYA - v27 - i5 - Dec 2004 - p414(1) [51-500]

Krueger, Anne O. - *Reforming India's External, Financial, and Fiscal Policies*
JEL - v41 - i4 - Dec 2003 - p1416(1) [501+]

Krueger, Ronald R. - *Wavefront Customized Visual Correction: The Quest for Super Vision II*
E-Streams - Oct 2004 - pNA [501+]

Krug, Rebecca - *Reading Families: Women's Literate Practice in Late Medieval England*
Specu - v79 - i3 - July 2004 - p780-782 [501+]

Kruggeler, Thomas - *Muchas Hispanoamericas. Antropologia, Historia y Enfoques Culturales en los Estudios Latinoamericanistas*
Ams - v61 - i2 - Oct 2004 - p271(2) [501+]

Kruglanski, Arie W. - *Psychology of Closed Mindedness*
SciTech - v28 - i3 - Sept 2004 - p2(1) [501+]

Krugman, Paul - *The Great Unravelling: Losing Our Way in the New Century*
VQR - v80 - i1 - Wntr 2004 - p266-267 [501+]

Kruk, Laurie - *Voice Is the Story: Conversations with Canadian Writers of Short Fiction*
CBRA - Annual 2003 - p256(2) [501+]

Krukowski, Artur - *DSP System Design: Complexity Reduced IIR Filter Implementation for Practical Applications*
SciTech - v28 - i1 - March 2004 - p153(1) [51-500]

Kruks, Sonia - *Retrieving Experience: Subjectivity and Recognition in Feminist Politics*
Signs - v30 - i2 - Wntr 2005 - p1706(6) [501+]

Krulic, Brigitte - *Nietzsche penseur de la hierarchie. Pour une lecture tocquevillienne de Nietsche*
Dialogue - v43 - i1 - Wntr 2004 - p186-189 [501+]

Krulik, Nancy - *Love and SK8*
c SLJ - v50 - i10 - Oct 2004 - p170(1) [51-500]
y VOYA - v27 - i5 - Dec 2004 - p384(1) [51-500]
Love & SK8
y Kliatt - v38 - i4 - July 2004 - p21(1) [51-500]
Newly Wed
y PW - v252 - i5 - Jan 31 2005 - p69(1) [51-500]
Ripped at the Seams
c PW - v251 - i28 - July 12 2004 - p65(2) [501+]
y SLJ - v50 - i7 - July 2004 - p106(1) [51-500]
She's Got the Beat
y Kliatt - v39 - i2 - March 2005 - p21(1) [51-500]

Krull, Kathleen - *The Book of Rock Stars: 24 Musical Icons that Shine through History*
LibMed - v22 - i5 - Feb 2004 - p76(1) [501+]
SLJ - v50 - i10 - Oct 2004 - pS49(2) [51-500]
y VOYA - v27 - i3 - August 2004 - p238(1) [1-50]
The Boy on Fairfield Street: How Ted Geisel Grew Up to Become Dr. Seuss (Illus. by Johnson, Steve)
c SLJ - v50 - i10 - Oct 2004 - pS27(1) [51-500]
Gonna Sing My Head Off!: American Folk Songs for Children (Illus. by Allen, Garns)
SLJ - v50 - i12 - Dec 2004 - p59(2) [501+]
Harvesting Hope: the Story of Cesar Chavez (Illus. by Morales, Yuyi)
c RT - v58 - i3 - Nov 2004 - p288(1) [1-50]
Houdini: World's Greatest Mystery Man and Escape King (Illus. by Velasquez, Eric)
c KR - v73 - i5 - March 1 2005 - p289(1) [51-500]
How to Trick or Treat in Outer Space (Illus. by Brewer, Paul)
PW - v251 - i32 - August 9 2004 - p248(1) [51-500]
c SLJ - v50 - i11 - Nov 2004 - p110(1) [51-500]
Ireland and the British Empire
CR - v285 - i1667 - Dec 2004 - p383(2) [501+]
Lives of the Musicians: Good Times, Bad Times, and What the Neighbors Thought (Illus. by Hewitt, Kathryn)
c SLJ - v50 - i12 - Dec 2004 - p60(2) [501+]
What Really Happened in Roswell? Just the Facts (Plus the Rumors) about UFOs and Aliens
LibMed - v22 - i5 - Feb 2004 - p87(2) [501+]
A Woman for President: The Story of Victoria Woodhull (Illus. by Dyer, Jane)
c BL - v101 - i3 - Oct 1 2004 - p327(1) [51-500]
c CCB-B - v58 - i2 - Oct 2004 - p84(1) [51-500]
c KR - v72 - i15 - August 1 2004 - p744(1) [51-500]
c NYTBR - Oct 17 2004 - p20 [501+]
c PW - v251 - i31 - August 2 2004 - p70(1) [51-500]
c SLJ - v50 - i8 - August 2004 - p48(1) [51-500]
c SLJ - v50 - i9 - Sept 2004 - p189(1) [51-500]
c SLJ - v50 - i10 - Oct 2004 - pS21(1) [51-500]

Krumeich, R. - *Das griechische Satyrspiel*
Class R - v53 - i2 - Nov 2003 - p288-290 [501+]

Krupat, Arnold - *Red Matters: Native American Studies*
MFSF - v50 - i2 - Summer 2004 - p492-494 [501+]

Krupinski, Loretta - *The Royal Mice: The Sword and the Horn (Illus. by Krupinski, Loretta)*
c   BL - v101 - i2 - Sept 15 2004 - p251(1) [51-500]
KR - v72 - i17 - Sept 1 2004 - p869(1) [51-500]
c   SLJ - v50 - i10 - Oct 2004 - p120(1) [51-500]

Krupp, Lauren B. - *Fatigue in Multiple Sclerosis: A Guide to Diagnosis and Management*
SciTech - v28 - i3 - Sept 2004 - p89(1) [51-500]

Kruttschnitt, Candace - *Advancing the Federal Research Agenda on Violence Against Women*
R&R Bk N - v19 - i4 - Nov 2004 - p143(1) [501+]

Kruuk, Hans - *Niko's Nature*
New Sci - v184 - i2476 - Dec 4 2004 - p55(1) [501+]
Niko's Nature: The Life of Niko Tinbergen and His Science of Animal Behaviour
New Sci - v183 - i2457 - July 24 2004 - p54(1) [501+]
SB - v40 - i5 - Sept-Oct 2004 - p203(2) [51-500]
TLS - i5265 - Feb 27 2004 - p27-27 [501+]

Krygier, Leora - *When She Sleeps*
y   BL - v101 - i3 - Oct 1 2004 - p311(1) [51-500]
KR - v72 - i18 - Sept 15 2004 - p885(1) [51-500]
LJ - v129 - i18 - Nov 1 2004 - p75(1) [501+]

Kryk, John - *Natural Enemies: Major College Football's Oldest, Fiercest Rivalry--Michigan vs. Notre Dame*
BL - v101 - i2 - Sept 15 2004 - p192(2) [501+]
PW - v251 - i32 - August 9 2004 - p242(1) [51-500]

Krysinska, Marie - *Rythmes pittoresques*
NCFS - v33 - i1-2 - Fall-Winter 2004 - p211(3) [501+]

Ku, Hok Bun - *Moral Politics in a South Chinese Village: Responsibility, Reciprocity, and Resistance*
R&R Bk N - v19 - i1 - Feb 2004 - p49(1) [51-500]

Kuang, Yang - *Dynamical Systems and Their Applications in Biology*
SIAM Rev - v46 - i1 - March 2004 - p174-175 [501+]

Kubale, Marek - *Graph Colorings*
SciTech - v28 - i3 - Sept 2004 - p34(1) [51-500]

Kubert, Joe - *Tor: Volume 3*
LibMed - v23 - i1 - August-Sept 2004 - p70(1) [51-500]
Yossel: April 19, 1943: A Story of the Warsaw Ghetto Uprising (Illus. by Kubert, Joe)
y   SLJ - v50 - i7 - July 2004 - p134(1) [51-500]
y   VOYA - v27 - i3 - August 2004 - p210(1) [1-50]

Kubey, Robert - *Creating Television: Conversations with the People Behind 50 Years of American TV*
TV Q - v34 - i3-4 - Spring-Summer 2004 - p65-68 [501+]

Kubiak, Anthony - *Agitated States: Performance in the American Theater of Cruelty*
Theat J - v56 - i1 - March 2004 - p130(2) [501+]

Kubo, Tite - *Bleach*
y   Kliatt - v39 - i1 - Jan 2005 - p25(1) [51-500]

Kucera, David - *Gender, Growth and Trade: The Miracle Economies of the Postwar Years*
ILR - v143 - i3 - Autumn 2004 - p275(3) [501+]

Kuch, Peter - *Irelands in the Asia-Pacific*
ILS - v24 - i1 - Fall 2004 - p32(1) [51-500]

Kuchana, Partha - *Software Architecture Design Patterns in Java*
Choice - v42 - i6 - Feb 2005 - p1057(1) [51-500]
SciTech - v28 - i3 - Sept 2004 - p23(1) [51-500]

Kuchler, Bonnie Louise - *One Heart: Universal Wisdom from the World's Scriptures*
LJ - v129 - i18 - Nov 1 2004 - p92(2) [51-500]

Kuchment, Peter - *Waves in Periodic and Random Media: Proceedings*
SciTech - v28 - i1 - March 2004 - p42(1) [51-500]

Kuchta, David - *The Three-Piece Suit and Modern Masculinity: England, 1550-1850*
JIH - v34 - i3 - Wntr 2004 - p450-3 [501+]
JMH - v76 - i4 - Dec 2004 - p947(2) [501+]

Kuczma, Marcin E. - *International Mathematical Olympiads, 1986-1999*
Choice - v41 - i7 - March 2004 - p1330(1) [501+]
Math T - v97 - i4 - April 2004 - p300-301 [501+]

Kudler, David - *Sake & Satori: Asian Journals, Japan*
Parabola - v28 - i3 - Fall 2003 - p117(3) [501+]

Kudlinski, Kathleen - *The Spirit Catchers: An Encounter With Georgia O'Keeffe*
y   Kliatt - v38 - i4 - July 2004 - p21(1) [51-500]
y   KR - v72 - i17 - Sept 1 2004 - p869(1) [51-500]
c   SLJ - v50 - i10 - Oct 2004 - p170(1) [51-500]

Kudrova, Irma - *The Death of a Poet: The Last Days of Marina Tsvetaeva*
Choice - v42 - i1 - Sept 2004 - p107(1) [501+]
New R - Oct 25 2004 - p34 [501+]
TLS - i5301 - Nov 5 2004 - p9(1) [501+]

Kuechel, Marie Czenko - *Aesthetic Medicine: Practicing for Success*
SciTech - v28 - i3 - Sept 2004 - p111(1) [51-500]

Kuehnast, Kathleen - *Post-Soviet Women Encountering Transition: Nation Building, Economic Survival*
Choice - v42 - i3 - Nov 2004 - p543(1) [1-50]

Kuehr, Rudiger - *Computers and the Environment: Understanding and Managing Their Impacts*
SciTech - v28 - i1 - March 2004 - p165(1) [51-500]

Kuersten, Ashlyn K. - *Women and the Laws, Leaders, Cases, and Documents*
y   VOYA - v27 - i4 - Oct 2004 - p336(1) [51-500]

Kuftinec, Sonja - *Staging America: Cornerstone and Community-Based Theater*
Theat J - v56 - i2 - May 2004 - p328(3) [501+]

Kugel, James L. - *The God of Old: Inside the Lost World of the Bible*
Intpr - v59 - i1 - Jan 2005 - p64(3) [501+]

Kugiya, Hugo - *58 Degrees North: The Mysterious Sinking of the Arctic Rose*
KR - v73 - i2 - Jan 15 2005 - p103(1) [501+]
LJ - v130 - i4 - March 1 2005 - p98(1) [51-500]
PW - v252 - i7 - Feb 14 2005 - p63(1) [51-500]

Kuhlthau, Carol Collier - *Seeking Meaning: A Process Approach to Library and Information Services, 2nd Ed.*
ALJ - v53 - i4 - Nov 2004 - p415(1) [501+]
Teach Lib - v32 - i3 - Feb 2005 - p38(1) [501+]

Kuhn, Annette - *Dreaming of Fred and Ginger: Cinema and Cultural Memory*
FQ - v57 - i4 - Summer 2004 - p51(3) [501+]

Kuhn, Cynthia - *Buzzed: The Straight Facts about the Most Used and Abused Drugs from Alcohol to Ecstasy*
E-Streams - July 2004 - pNA [501+]

Kuhn, Jerald P. - *Caffey's Pediatric Diagnostic Imaging. 10th Ed.*
SciTech - v28 - i1 - March 2004 - p117(1) [51-500]

Kuhn, Jim - *Ronald Reagan in Private: A Memoir of My Years in the White House*
PW - v251 - i31 - August 2 2004 - p65(2) [51-500]

Kuhn, Philip A. - *Origins of the Modern Chinese State*
JIH - v34 - i3 - Wntr 2004 - p498(3) [501+]

Kuhn, Robert Lawrence - *The Man Who Changed China: The Life and Legacy of Jiang Zemin*
BL - v101 - i8 - Dec 15 2004 - p703(1) [51-500]
PW - v251 - i50 - Dec 13 2004 - p59(1) [51-500]

Kuhns, Elizabeth - *Habit: A History of the Clothing of Catholic Nuns*
R&R Bk N - v19 - i1 - Feb 2004 - p25(1) [1-50]

Kuhnst, Peter - *Physique: Classic Photographs of Naked Athletes*
LJ - v129 - i12 - July 2004 - p78(1) [51-500]

Kuhthau, Carol Collier - *Seeking Meaning: A Process Approach to Library and Information Services, 2nd Ed.*
R&R Bk N - v19 - i1 - Feb 2004 - p261(1) [51-500]

Kuitenbrouwer, Peter - *Our Song: The Story of O Canada, the Canadian National Anthem*
c   Res Links - v10 - i1 - Oct 2004 - p24(1) [501+]

Kujiradou, Misaho - *Princess Ai: Vol. 1: Destitution (Illus. by Kujiradou, Misaho)*
BW - v34 - i37 - Sept 12 2004 - p13(1) [501+]
LJ - v129 - i18 - Nov 1 2004 - p66(1) [501+]
PW - v251 - i35 - August 30 2004 - p35(1) [501+]

Kukathas, Chandran - *The Liberal Archipelago: A Theory of Diversity and Freedom*
AJPS - v39 - i2 - July 2004 - p466(467) [501+]
Ethics - v115 - i2 - Jan 2005 - p422(6) [501+]

Kuki, Shuzo - *Kuki Shuzo: A Philosopher's Poetry and Poetics*
R&R Bk N - v19 - i3 - August 2004 - p256(1) [51-500]

Kukis, Mark - *"My Heart Became Attached": The Strange Journey of John Walker Lindh*
R&R Bk N - v19 - i1 - Feb 2004 - p141(1) [51-500]

Kukla, Andre - *Social Constructivism and the Philosophy of Science*
Isis - v95 - i3 - Sept 2004 - p538(2) [501+]

Kukla, Jon - *A Wilderness So Immense: The Louisiana Purchase and the Destiny of America*
AHR - v109 - i2 - April 2004 - p509(2) [501+]
JAH - v91 - i1 - June 2004 - p223-225 [501+]
RAH - v32 - i2 - June 2004 - p166-10 [501+]
TLS - i5264 - Feb 20 2004 - p9-10 [501+]

Kuklin, Susan - *All Aboard! A True Train Story*
LibMed - v22 - i5 - Feb 2004 - p87(2) [501+]

Kukowski, Martin - *Die Chemnitzer Auto Union AG und die "Demokratizierung" der Wirtschaft in der Sowjetischen Besatzungszone von 1945 bis 1948*
HNet - Oct 2004 - pNA [501+]

Kulaev, I.S. - *The Biochemistry of Inorganic Polyphosphates, 2nd Ed.*
SciTech - v28 - i3 - Sept 2004 - p71(1) [51-500]

Kularatna, Nihal - *Essentials of Modern Telecommunications Systems*
Choice - v42 - i2 - Oct 2004 - p323(1) [51-500]
SciTech - v28 - i3 - Sept 2004 - p152(1) [51-500]

Kulavig, Erik - *Dissent in the Years of Khrushchev: Nine Stories about Disobedient Russians*
Russ Rev - v63 - i2 - April 2004 - pNA [501+]
Slav R - v63 - i2 - Summer 2004 - p419(2) [501+]

Kulick, Don - *Fat: The Anthropology of an Obsession*
PW - v251 - i47 - Nov 22 2004 - p47(1) [51-500]
Language and Sexuality
JGS - v13 - i1 - March 2004 - p92-93 [501+]

Kulik, Carol T. - *Human Resources for the Non-HR Manager*
Choice - v42 - i3 - Nov 2004 - p530(1) [1-50]

Kulikowski, Michael - *Rex Germanorum, Populos Sclavorum: An Inquiry into the Origin and Early History of the Serbs/Slavs of Sarmatia, Germania and Illyria*
Specu - v79 - i4 - Oct 2004 - p1173(3) [501+]

Kulisch, Ulrich W. - *Advanced Arithmetic for the Digital Computer: Design of Arithmetic Units*
SIAM Rev - v46 - i4 - Dec 2004 - p755-756 [501+]

Kulkarni, S.V. - *Transformer Engineering: Design and Practice*
E-Streams - Dec 2004 - pNA [501+]
SciTech - v28 - i3 - Sept 2004 - p152(1) [51-500]

Kulling, Monica - *Eat My Dust! Henry Ford's First Race (Illus. by Walz, Richard)*
c   BL - v100 - i22 - August 2004 - p1943(1) [51-500]

Kumar, Amitava - *Passport Photos*
Can Lit - i182 - Autumn 2004 - p112(3) [501+]

Kumar, Krishan - *1989: Revolutionary Ideas and Ideals*
Slav R - v63 - i4 - Winter 2004 - p851(2) [501+]
The Making of English National Identity
CS - v33 - i6 - Nov 2004 - p685(3) [501+]
JIH - v35 - i2 - Autumn 2004 - p294(2) [501+]

Kumar, Krishna Dev - *Introductory Operations Research: Theory and Applications*
Choice - v42 - i6 - Feb 2005 - p1057(1) [51-500]

Kumar, Nirmalya - *Marketing as Strategy: The CEO's Agenda for Driving Growth and Innovation*
R&R Bk N - v19 - i3 - August 2004 - p127(1) [51-500]

Kumar, Radha - *The History of Doing: An Illustrated Account of Movements for Women's Rights and Feminism in India, 1800 to 1900*
CS - v33 - i6 - Nov 2004 - p640(3) [501+]

Kumar, Sandeep - *Molecular Genetics and Breeding of Forest Trees*
E-Streams - Nov 2004 - pNA [501+]

Kumar, Vinay - *Robbins and Cotran Pathologic Basis of Disease, 7th Ed.*
SciTech - v28 - i4 - Dec 2004 - p88(1) [51-500]

Kumashiro, Kevin K. - *Restored Selves: Autobiographies of Queer Asian/Pacific American Activists*
R&R Bk N - v19 - i2 - May 2004 - p133 [51-500]
Troubling Education: Queer Activism and Anti-Oppressive Pedagogy
HER - v74 - i4 - Winter 2004 - p460-463 [501+]

Kumin, Maxine - *Jack and Other New Poems*
BL - v101 - i9-10 - Jan 1 2005 - p804(1) [51-500]
PW - v251 - i51 - Dec 20 2004 - p52(1) [501+]
LJ - v129 - i19 - Nov 15 2004 - p63(1) [501+]

Kummer, Patricia K. - *Currency*
c   SLJ - v51 - i2 - Feb 2005 - p148(1) [51-500]

Kun, Miklos - *Stalin: An Unknown Portrait*
TimHES - v0 - i1657 - Sept 10 2004 - p30(1) [501+]

Kunast, Hans-Jorg - *Die Bibliothek Konard Peutingers. Edition der historischen Kataloge und Rekonstrucktion der Bestande. Band I: Die autographen Kataloge Peutings. Der nicht-juristische Bibliotheksteil*
BSA-P - v98 - i1 - March 2004 - p121-124 [501+]

Kune, Jan B. - *On Global Aging: Old-Age Income Systems in the EU and Other Major Parts of the World*
JEL - v42 - i1 - March 2004 - p279(1) [501+]

Kunhardt, Dorothy - *Pat the Bunny*
c   PW - v252 - i6 - Feb 7 2005 - p61(2) [501+]

Kunhardt, Edith - *Daddy's Scratchy Face (Illus. by Kunhardt, Edith)*
c   SLJ - v51 - i1 - Jan 2005 - p95(2) [51-500]

Kunhardt, Philip B. - *Dreaming Game: A Portrait of a Passionate Life*
BL - v101 - i4 - Oct 15 2004 - p378(1) [51-500]
The Dreaming Game: A Portrait of a Passionate Life
Ent W - i785 - Sept 24 2004 - p114 [51-500]
Kunin, Seth D. - *Religion: The Modern Theories*
R&R Bk N - v19 - i1 - Feb 2004 - p10(1) [51-500]
Kunita, Hiroshi - *Stochastic Analysis and Related Topics in Kyoto: In Honour of Kiyosi Ito*
SciTech - v28 - i4 - Dec 2004 - p36(1) [51-500]
Kunitzsch, Paul - *Stars and Numbers: Astronomy and Mathematics in the Medieval Arab and Western Worlds*
SciTech - v28 - i4 - Dec 2004 - p45(1) [51-500]
Kunkel, Mike - *Herobear and the Kid: The Inheritance*
c Teach Lib - v32 - i3 - Feb 2005 - p24(1) [51-500]
The Land of Sokmunster
c VOYA - v27 - i5 - Dec 2004 - p375(1) [501+]
Kuns, J. Irvin - *While You Were Out*
c BL - v101 - i6 - Nov 15 2004 - p602(1) [51-500]
c CCB-B - v58 - i3 - Nov 2004 - p130(2) [501+]
c CH Bwatch - Feb 2005 - pNA [51-500]
y KR - v72 - i22 - Nov 15 2004 - p1091(1) [51-500]
c PW - v251 - i50 - Dec 13 2004 - p68(2) [51-500]
c SLJ - v50 - i12 - Dec 2004 - p149(1) [51-500]
Kunstler, Barton - *The Hothouse Effect*
Fut - v38 - i4 - July-August 2004 - p52(2) [501+]
Kunstler, William M. - *The Emerging Police State*
Bl S - v34 - i3 - Fall 2004 - p73-73 [501+]
Kuntz, Marion Leathers - *The Anointment of Dionisio: Prophecy and Politics in Renaissance Italy*
JMH - v76 - i3 - Sept 2004 - p709(2) [501+]
Six Ct J - v34 - i4 - Winter 2003 - p1224-1225 [501+]
Kunz, Christina L. - *The Process of Legal Research, 6th Ed.*
R&R Bk N - v19 - i4 - Nov 2004 - p165(1) [501+]
Kunz, Dieter - *Deadly Medicine: Creating the Master Race*
LJ - v129 - i19 - Nov 15 2004 - p81(2) [51-500]
Kunz, Georg - *Verotete Geschichte. Regionales Geschintsbewubtsein in den deutschen Historischen Vereinen des 19*
GSR - v27 - i1 - Feb 2004 - p161-162 [501+]
Kunzig, Robert - *The Restless Sea: Exploring the World beneath the Waves*
LibMed - v22 - i7 - April-May 2004 - p79(1) [501+]
Kunzle, David - *From Criminal to Courtier: The Soldier in Netherlandish Art 1550-1672*
Six Ct J - v35 - i3 - Fall 2004 - p847-848 [501+]
Kunzru, Hari - *Transmission*
NYTBR - March 13 2005 - p32 [501+]
y SLJ - v50 - i10 - Oct 2004 - p199(1) [51-500]
Kuo, Peter - *Novell's Guide to Troubleshooting eDirectory*
Bwatch - v26 - i8 - August 2004 - p6(1) [51-500]
Kuortti, Joel - *Tense Past, Tense Present: Women Writing in English*
WLT - v78 - i3-4 - Sept-Dec 2004 - p157(1) [501+]
Kupecek, Linda - *Rebel Women: Achievements Beyond the Ordinary*
CBRA - Annual 2003 - p53(1) [51-500]
y Res Links - v10 - i1 - Oct 2004 - p36(2) [501+]
Kupel, Douglas E. - *Fuel for Growth: Water and Arizona's Urban Environment*
JAH - v91 - i1 - June 2004 - p337-338 [501+]
WHQ - v35 - i3 - Autumn 2004 - p379(2) [501+]
Kuper, Daniela - *Hunger and Thirst*
BL - v101 - i1 - Sept 1 2004 - p62(1) [501+]
KR - v72 - i16 - August 15 2004 - p768(1) [51-500]
Kuper, Jack - *After the Smoke Cleared*
y Can CL - i111-112 - Fall-Winter 2003 - p146(6) [501+]
Kuper, Peter - *The Jungle*
BL - v101 - i6 - Nov 15 2004 - p572(1) [51-500]
Sticks and Stones: An Epic in Pictures
PW - v251 - i34 - August 23 2004 - p39(1) [51-500]
Sticks and Stones (Illus. by Kuper, Peter)
y SLJ - v51 - i2 - Feb 2005 - p25(1) [51-500]
Kupersmidt, Janis B. - *Children's Peer Relations: From Development to Intervention*
SciTech - v28 - i3 - Sept 2004 - p3(1) [501+]
Kupfer, Marcia - *The Art of Healing: Painting for the Sick and the Sinner in a Medieval Town*
AHR - v109 - i3 - June 2004 - p960-2 [501+]
Kuppens, Thea - *Banking Supervision at the Crossroads*
R&R Bk N - v19 - i2 - May 2004 - p122 [51-500]
Kupper, Patrick - *Atomenergie und Gespaltene Gesellschaft: Die Geschichte des Gescheiterten Projektes Kernkraftwerk Kaiseraugst*
HNet - Sept 2004 - pNA [501+]
Kupperman, Joel J. - *Learning from Asian Philosophy*
Ethics - v115 - i2 - Jan 2005 - p438(1) [501+]
Kuppevelt, Jan van - *Current and New Directions in Discourse and Dialogue*
R&R Bk N - v19 - i1 - Feb 2004 - p213 [51-500]
Kuppner, Frank - *A God's Breakfast*
TLS - i5304 - Nov 26 2004 - p7(1) [501+]
Kuran, Timur - *Islam and Mammon: The Economic Predicaments of Islamism*
Choice - v42 - i5 - Jan 2005 - p902(1) [1-50]
Kureishi, Hanif - *Buddha of Suburbia (Read by Simpson, Christopher). Audiobook Review*
c Kliatt - v38 - i4 - July 2004 - p49(1) [51-500]
My Ear at His Heart
Lon R Bks - v27 - i1 - Jan 6 2005 - p26(2) [501+]
NS - v133 - i4716 - Nov 29 2004 - p46(1) [51-500]
Kurian, George Thomas - *Datapedia of the United States: American History in Numbers, 3rd Ed.*
Choice - v42 - i3 - Nov 2004 - p462(1) [1-50]
R&R Bk N - v19 - i3 - August 2004 - p92(1) [51-500]
The Encyclopedia of the Republican Party; The Encyclopedia of the Democratic Party
BL - v101 - i3 - Oct 1 2004 - p358(1) [501+]
The Nobel Scientists: A Biographical Encyclopedia
Am Bio T - v66 - i2 - Feb 2004 - p153(153) [501+]
Physics T - v42 - i8 - Nov 2004 - p511(1) [501+]
Kurihashi, Shinsuke - *Maniac Road, Vol. 1*
LJ - v130 - i1 - Jan 1 2005 - p88(1) [51-500]
Kuriyama, Constance Brown - *Christopher Marlowe: A Renaissance Life*
Six Ct J - v35 - i1 - Spring 2004 - p222(3) [501+]
Kurke, Lance B. - *The Wisdom of Alexander the Great: Enduring Leadership Lessons from the Man Who Created an Empire*
Bwatch - Dec 2004 - pNA [51-500]
R&R Bk N - v19 - i4 - Nov 2004 - p39(1) [51-500]
Kurkela, Robert W. - *Lilies on the Moon (Illus. by Kurkela, Cassidy S.)*
c CH Bwatch - March 2005 - pNA [51-500]
Kurland, Michael - *Sherlock Holmes: The Hidden Years*
PW - v251 - i41 - Oct 11 2004 - p59(1) [51-500]
Kurlansky, Mark - *1968: The Year That Rocked the World (Read by Cazenove, Christopher). Audiobook Review*
y Kliatt - v39 - i1 - Jan 2005 - p53(1) [51-500]
LJ - v129 - i13 - August 2004 - p130(1) [51-500]
1968: The Year That Rocked the World
BooChiTr - Jan 25 2004 - p1(2) [501+]
Choice - v42 - i1 - Sept 2004 - p163(1) [501+]
HNet - Nov 2004 - pNA [501+]
Boogaloo on 2nd Avenue: A Novel of Pastry, Guilt, and Music
BL - v101 - i8 - Dec 15 2004 - p691(1) [51-500]
KR - v73 - i2 - Jan 15 2005 - p75(1) [501+]
LJ - v129 - i20 - Dec 1 2004 - p88(1) [51-500]
LJ - v130 - i2 - Feb 1 2005 - p69(1) [51-500]
Kurniawan, Budi - *JavaServer Faces Programming*
SciTech - v28 - i1 - March 2004 - p157(1) [51-500]
Kuronen, Darcy - *Musical Instruments*
R&R Bk N - v19 - i4 - Nov 2004 - p196(1) [501+]
Kurose, James F. - *Computer Networking: A Top-Down Approach Featuring the Internet, 3rd Ed.*
SciTech - v28 - i4 - Dec 2004 - p150(1) [51-500]
Kurrer, Karl-Eugen - *Geschichte der Baustatik*
T&C - v45 - i3 - July 2004 - p664-666 [501+]
T&C - v45 - i3 - July 2004 - p664-666 [501+]
Kurson, Robert - *Shadow Divers: The True Adventure of Two Americans Who Discovered Hitler's Lost Sub (Read by Prichard, Michael). Audiobook Review*
BL - v101 - i5 - Nov 1 2004 - p505(1) [51-500]
Shadow Divers: The True Adventure of Two Americans Who Discovered Hitler's Lost Sub
Ent W - i773 - July 9 2004 - p93 [501+]
Shadow Divers: The True Adventure of Two Americans Who Risked Everything to Solve One of the Last Mysteries of World War II (Read by Prichard, Michael). Audiobook Review
y Kliatt - v39 - i1 - Jan 2005 - p53(2) [51-500]
Shadow Divers: The True Adventure of Two Americans Who Risked Everything to Solve One of the Last Mysteries of World War II (Read by Campbell, Scott). Audiobook Review
PW - v251 - i31 - August 2 2004 - p21(1) [501+]
Shadow Divers: The True Adventure of Two Americans Who Risked Everything to Solve One of the Last Mysteries of World War II
SLJ - v51 - i2 - Feb 2005 - p158(1) [51-500]
Shadow Drivers: The True Adventure of Two Americans Who Risked Everything to Solve One of the Last Mysteries of World War II
NYTBR - July 18 2004 - p7 [501+]
Kurth, Peter - *Isadora: A Sensational Life*
BL - v101 - i5 - Nov 1 2004 - p458(1) [51-500]
Theat J - v56 - i4 - Dec 2004 - p721-722 [501+]
Kurtis, Bill - *The Death Penalty on Trial: Crisis in American Justice*
y BL - v101 - i2 - Sept 15 2004 - p179(1) [51-500]
KR - v72 - i16 - August 15 2004 - p790(1) [501+]
PW - v251 - i39 - Sept 27 2004 - p46(1) [51-500]
Kurtz, Donald W. - *Variable Stars in the Local Group: Proceedings*
SciTech - v28 - i3 - Sept 2004 - p44(1) [1-50]
Kurtz, Jane - *Do Kangaroos Wear Seat Belts? (Illus. by Manning, Jane K.)*
c KR - v73 - i1 - Jan 1 2005 - p53(1) [51-500]
c PW - v252 - i9 - Feb 28 2005 - p65(1) [51-500]
In the Small, Small Night (Illus. by Isadora, Rachel)
c KR - v73 - i1 - Jan 1 2005 - p54(1) [51-500]
c PW - v252 - i4 - Jan 24 2005 - p243(1) [51-500]
c SLJ - v51 - i2 - Feb 2005 - p106(1) [51-500]
Johnny Appleseed (Illus. by Haverfield, Mary)
c KR - v72 - i16 - August 15 2004 - p808(1) [51-500]
c SLJ - v50 - i12 - Dec 2004 - p134(1) [501+]
Memories of Sun: Stories of Africa and America
c CE - v81 - i1 - Fall 2004 - p46(1) [51-500]
c LibMed - v23 - i1 - August-Sept 2004 - p68(1) [51-500]
Saba: Under the Hyena's Foot
c HNet - Oct 2004 - pNA [501+]
Kurtz, Jean-Paul - *Dictionary of Civil Engineering: English-French*
Choice - v42 - i7 - March 2005 - p1202(1) [51-500]
Kurtz, Marcus J. - *Free Market Democracy and the Chilean and Mexican Countryside*
Choice - v42 - i3 - Nov 2004 - p558(1) [1-50]
Kurtz, Paul - *Affirmations: Joyful and Creative Exuberance*
Hum - v64 - i6 - Nov-Dec 2004 - p41(1) [51-500]
Kurtz, Sharon - *Workplace Justice: Organizing Multi-Identity Movements*
CS - v33 - i1 - Jan 2004 - p35-37 [501+]
Kurtzman, Joel - *MBA in a Box: The Practical Guide to the Big Ideas of Business*
BL - v101 - i4 - Oct 15 2004 - p387(1) [51-500]
Kurz, Heinz D. - *The Legacy of Piero Sraffa*
JEL - v42 - i1 - March 2004 - p241(1) [501+]
Kurzman, Charles - *The Unthinkable Revolution in Iran*
Choice - v42 - i4 - Dec 2004 - p719(1) [1-50]
TimHES - v0 - i1665 - Nov 5 2004 - p27(1) [501+]
Kurzman, Dan - *No Greater Glory: The Four Immortal Chaplains and the Sinking of the Dorchester in World War II (Read by Dufris, William). Audiobook Review*
BL - v101 - i4 - Oct 15 2004 - p432(1) [51-500]
Kliatt - v38 - i6 - Nov 2004 - p56(1) [51-500]
Kurzon, Dennis - *Where East Looks West: Success in English in Goa and on the Konkan Coast*
R&R Bk N - v19 - i1 - Feb 2004 - p215(1) [51-500]
Kusek, David - *The Future of Music*
PW - v252 - i4 - Jan 24 2005 - p232(1) [501+]
Kusek, Jody Zall - *Ten Steps to a Results-Based Monitoring and Evaluation System: A Handbook for Development Practitioners*
R&R Bk N - v19 - i4 - Nov 2004 - p154(1) [501+]
Kusenbach, Margarethe - *Newcomers to Old Towns: Suburbanization of the Heartland*
CS - v33 - i5 - Sept 2004 - p570-571 [501+]
Kusher, Harold - *The Lord is My Shepherd: Healing Wisdom of the Twenty-third Psalm*
CI - v12 - i8 - Sept 2004 - p43(1) [501+]
Kushner, Donn - *Peter's Pixie (Illus. by Daigneault, Sylvie)*
c CBRA - Annual 2003 - p454(2) [51-500]
Kushner, Eva - *The Living Prism: Itineraries in Comparative Literature*
Can Lit - i182 - Autumn 2004 - p141(3) [501+]
Kushner, Tony - *The Art of Maurice Sendak: 1980 to the Present*
Lam Bk Rpt - v13 - i3 - Oct 2004 - p18(1) [501+]
Brundibar (Illus. by Sendak, Maurice)
c TES - v0 - i4586 - June 4 2004 - p21(1) [501+]
Wrestling with Zion: Progressive Jewish-American Responses to the Israeli-Palestinian Conflict
ABR - v26 - i1 - Nov-Dec 2004 - p17(2) [501+]
Kusimba, Sibel Barut - *African Foragers: Environment, Technology, Interactions*
T&C - v45 - i3 - July 2004 - p641-643 [501+]

Kuska, Bob - *Hot Potato: How Washington and New York Gave Birth to Black Basketball and Changed America's Game Forever*
R&R Bk N - v19 - i3 - August 2004 - p88(1) [51-500]

Kuskin, Karla - *The Philharmonic Gets Dressed (Illus. by Simont, Marc)*
c   SLJ - v50 - i12 - Dec 2004 - p58(1) [501+]
Under My Hood I Have a Hat (Illus. by Kosaka, Fumi)
c   BL - v101 - i5 - Nov 1 2004 - p490(1) [51-500]
c   HB - v81 - i1 - Jan-Feb 2005 - p80(2) [51-500]
c   KR - v72 - i19 - Oct 1 2004 - p964(1) [51-500]
c   PW - v251 - i50 - Dec 13 2004 - p66(1) [51-500]
c   SLJ - v50 - i11 - Nov 2004 - p110(1) [51-500]

Kusky, Timothy M. - *Geological Hazards: A Sourcebook*
LibMed - v22 - i5 - Feb 2004 - p57(2) [501+]

Kusnetz, Marc - *Operation Iraqi Freedom*
R&R Bk N - v19 - i1 - Feb 2004 - p42(1) [51-500]

Kuspit, Donald B. - *Anthony Quinn's Eye: A Lifetime of Creating and Collecting Art*
R&R Bk N - v19 - i4 - Nov 2004 - p200(1) [501+]
The End of Art
Choice - v42 - i2 - Oct 2004 - p281(1) [501+]
Steve Tobin's Natural History
R&R Bk N - v19 - i1 - Feb 2004 - p204(1) [51-500]

Kustow, Michael - *Peter Brook: A Biography*
Econ - v374 - i8418 - March 19 2005 - p89US [501+]

Kuther, Tara L. - *Gimme Your Lunch Money! The Complete Guide to Bullies and Bullying*
LibMed - v22 - i4 - Jan 2004 - p85(1) [501+]

Kutner, Marc L. - *Astronomy: A Physical Perspective*
Choice - v41 - i7 - March 2004 - p1319(1) [501+]

Kuttner, Robert - *Family Re-Union: Reconnecting Parents and Children in Adulthood*
Adoles - v39 - i154 - Summer 2004 - p400(1) [501+]

Kutz, Christopher - *Complicity: Ethics and Law for a Collective Age*
Ethics - v114 - i4 - July 2004 - p827(4) [501+]
Law&PolBR - June 2004 - p420(4) [501+]

Kutz, Myer - *Handbook of Transportation Engineering*
Choice - v42 - i3 - Nov 2004 - p514(1) [1-50]

Kuwahara, Ryuichi - *In Front of the Ant: Walking with Beetles and Other Insects (Illus. by Kuribayashi, Satoshi)*
c   SLJ - v50 - i7 - July 2004 - p80(1) [51-500]

Kuwayama, Takami - *Native Anthropology: The Japanese Challenge to Western Academic Hegemony*
Choice - v42 - i4 - Dec 2004 - p703(1) [1-50]
R&R Bk N - v19 - i3 - August 2004 - p82(1) [51-500]

Kuyk, Betty M. - *African Voices in the African American Heritage*
JSH - v70 - i4 - Nov 2004 - p905(2) [501+]

Kuzmany, Hans - *Electronic Properties of Synthetic Nanostructures: Proceedings*
SciTech - v28 - i4 - Dec 2004 - p49(1) [51-500]
Molecular Nanostructures: Proceedings
SciTech - v28 - i1 - March 2004 - p48(1) [51-500]

Kwan Chi Kao - *Dielectric Phenomena in Solids: With Emphasis on Physical Concepts of Electronic Processes*
E-Streams - Oct 2004 - pNA [501+]

Kwen-Jen Chang - *Delta Receptor*
E-Streams - June 2004 - pNA [501+]

Kwiatkowska, Barbara - *International organizations and the law of the sea; documentary yearbook; v.17, 2001*
R&R Bk N - v19 - i3 - August 2004 - p213(1) [1-50]

Kwiek, Marek - *The University, Globalization, Central Europe*
R&R Bk N - v19 - i1 - Feb 2004 - pNA [51-500]

Kwok, Sun - *Cosmic Butterflies*
Astron - v33 - i2 - Feb 2005 - p100 [501+]
Planetary Nebulae: Their Evolution and Role in the Universe: Proceedings
SciTech - v28 - i1 - March 2004 - p45(1) [51-500]

Kwoka, John E., Jr. - *The Antitrust Revolution: Economics, Competition, and Policy*
JEL - v42 - i1 - March 2004 - p286(1) [501+]

Kwon, Okyun - *Buddhist and Protestant Korean Immigrants: Religious Beliefs and Socioeconomic Aspects of Life*
R&R Bk N - v19 - i1 - Feb 2004 - p13(1) [51-500]

Kyi, Tanya Lloyd - *Fires!: Ten Stories That Chronicle Some of the Most Destructive Fires in Human History*
y   BL - v101 - i9-10 - Jan 1 2005 - p840(1) [501+]
c   Res Links - v10 - i2 - Dec 2004 - p27(2) [501+]
My Time as Caz Hazard
y   Res Links - v10 - i3 - Feb 2005 - p37(1) [51-500]
Truth
c   CBRA - Annual 2003 - p495(1) [51-500]

Kyker, Keith - *Educator's Survival Guide for Television Production and Activities, 2nd Ed.*
LibMed - v22 - i4 - Jan 2004 - p85(1) [501+]

Kyle, Chris R. - *Parliament at Work: Parliamentary Committees, Political Power and Public Access in Early Modern England*
Albion - v36 - i1 - Spring 2004 - p115(2) [501+]

Kyle, Keith - *Suez: Britain's End of Empire in the Middle East*
Albion - v36 - i1 - Spring 2004 - p197(2) [501+]

Kymlicka, Will - *Language Rights and Political Theory*
Law&PolBR - August 2004 - p630(4) [501+]

Kynell-Hunt, Teresa - *Power and Legitimacy in Technical Communication, Vol. II*
SciTech - v28 - i3 - Sept 2004 - pNA [51-500]

Kyoko, Ariyoshi - *Swan, Vol. 1*
Dance - v79 - i3 - March 2005 - p72(2) [501+]

Kyriacou, Andreas P. - *A Viable Solution to the Cyprus Problem: Lessons from Political Economy*
JEL - v41 - i4 - Dec 2003 - p1343(1) [501+]

Kyriakoudes, Louis M. - *The Social Origins of the Urban South: Race, Gender and Migration in Nashville and Middle Tennessee, 1890-1930*
AJS - v110 - i2 - Sept 2004 - p523(3) [501+]
The Social Origins of the Urban South: Race, Gender, and Migration in Nashville and Middle Tennessee, 1890-1930
JAH - v91 - i3 - Dec 2004 - p1042(2) [501+]
JSH - v71 - i1 - Feb 2005 - p186(3) [501+]

Kyriazakis, I. - *Organic Meat and Milk from Ruminants: Proceedings*
SciTech - v28 - i1 - March 2004 - p178(1) [51-500]

Kyuchukov, Hristo - *My Name Was Hussein (Illus. by Eitzen, Allan)*
c   SLJ - v50 - i10 - Oct 2004 - pS21(1) [1-50]
c   SLJ - v51 - i1 - Jan 2005 - p55(1) [51-500]

Kyuma, Kazutake - *Paddy Soil Science*
SciTech - v28 - i3 - Sept 2004 - p128(1) [51-500]

Kyvig, David E. - *Daily Life in the United States, 1920-1940: How Americans Lived through the "Roaring Twenties" and the Great Depression*
Atl - v294 - i3 - Oct 2004 - p164(1) [51-500]
LJ - v129 - i12 - July 2004 - p98(1) [51-500]
R&R Bk N - v19 - i4 - Nov 2004 - p56(1) [51-500]

L

La Corte, Daniel Marcel - *Regular Life: Monastic, Canonical, and Mendicant Rules, 2nd Ed.*
R&R Bk N - v19 - i3 - August 2004 - p28(1) [1-50]

La Faye, Deirdre - *Jane Austen's "Outlandish Cousin": The Life and Letters of Eliza de Feuillide*
R&R Bk N - v19 - i1 - Feb 2004 - p238(1) [51-500]

La Fevers, Robin L. - *Forging of the Blade*
c CCB-B - v58 - i3 - Nov 2004 - p131(1) [501+]
The Forging of the Blade
SLJ - v50 - i12 - Dec 2004 - p112(1) [501+]

La Grange, Henry-Louis de - *Gustav Mahler: Letters to His Wife*
TLS - i5302 - Nov 12 2004 - p6-7 [501+]

La Morte, Michael W. - *School Law: Cases and Concepts, 8th Ed.*
R&R Bk N - v19 - i3 - August 2004 - p201(1) [1-50]

La Plante, Lynda - *Royal Heist*
Globe & Mail - August 7 2004 - pD12 [51-500]
KR - v72 - i13 - July 1 2004 - p599(1) [51-500]
LJ - v129 - i12 - July 2004 - p72(1) [51-500]

La Rochefoucauld - *Maxims*
Sew R - v112 - i3 - Summer 2004 - pLXXIV-LXXVI [501+]
Moral Maxims
Sew R - v112 - i3 - Summer 2004 - p467-475 [501+]

La sociabilite litteraire - *Voix et images*
Can Lit - i181 - Summer 2004 - p182-183 [501+]

La Van, David A. - *Micro--and Nanosystems: Proceedings*
SciTech - v28 - i3 - Sept 2004 - p47(1) [1-50]

La Vere, David - *The Texas Indians*
Choice - v42 - i2 - Oct 2004 - p356(1) [51-500]

Laato, Antti - *Theodicy in the World of the Bible*
R&R Bk N - v19 - i1 - Feb 2004 - p22(1) [51-500]

Lab, Steven P. - *Explaining Criminal Justice*
R&R Bk N - v19 - i3 - August 2004 - p171(1) [501+]

Laba, Mark - *Dummy Spit*
CBRA - Annual 2003 - p222(1) [501+]

L'Abate, Luciano - *Family Psychology III: Theory Building, Theory Testing, and Psychological Interventions*
Adoles - v39 - i154 - Summer 2004 - p400(2) [51-500]
Guide to Self-Help Workbooks for Mental Health Clinicians and Researchers
E-Streams - Nov 2004 - pNA [501+]
Using Workbooks in Mental Health: Resources in Prevention, Psychotherapy, and Rehabilitation for Clinicians and Researchers
SciTech - v28 - i4 - Dec 2004 - p85(1) [51-500]

Labaton, Vivien - *The Fire This Time: Young Activists and the New Feminism*
Lam Bk Rpt - v13 - i3 - Oct 2004 - p16(2) [501+]
Wom R Bks - v22 - i1 - Oct 2004 - p18(2) [501+]

Labatt, Mary - *Friend for Sam (Illus. by Sarrazin, Marisol)*
c CBRA - Annual 2003 - p455(1) [51-500]
Pizza for Sam (Illus. by Sarrazin, Marisol)
c CBRA - Annual 2003 - p455(1) [51-500]
Sam Finds a Monster (Illus. by Sarrazin, Marisol)
c CBRA - Annual 2003 - p455(1) [51-500]
Sam Gets Lost
c BL - v100 - i21 - July 2004 - p1851(1) [1-50]
Sam Goes to School
c BL - v100 - i21 - July 2004 - p1851(1) [1-50]
Sam's First Halloween (Illus. by Sarrazin, marisol)
c CBRA - Annual 2003 - p455(1) [51-500]

Labbe, Ronald M. - *The Slaughterhouse Cases: Regulation, Reconstruction, and the Fourteenth Amendment*
Choice - v42 - i2 - Oct 2004 - p372(2) [51-500]
HNet - June 2004 - pNA [501+]
JAH - v91 - i3 - Dec 2004 - p1030(1) [501+]

LaBelle, Charlene G. - *A Guide to Backpacking with Your Dog*
Bwatch - Oct 2004 - pNA [51-500]

Labio, Catherine - *Belgian Memories*
FS - v58 - i2 - April 2004 - p293(2) [501+]

Labouret-Grare, Mireille - *Balzac, la Duchesse et l'idole. Poetique du Corps Aristocratique*
NCFS - v33 - i1-2 - Fall-Winter 2004 - p193(2) [501+]

Labrianidis, Lois - *The Future of Europe's Rural Peripheries*
R&R Bk N - v19 - i4 - Nov 2004 - p126(1) [51-500]

Labrie, Fernand - *Prostate Cancer: Understanding the Pathophysiology and Re-designing a Therapeutic Approach*
SciTech - v28 - i4 - Dec 2004 - p93(1) [51-500]

Labus, Diane - *Heart Sounds Made Incredibly Easy*
SciTech - v28 - i4 - Dec 2004 - p103(1) [51-500]

LaBute, Neil - *Seconds of Pleasure*
Ent W - i788 - Oct 15 2004 - p78 [51-500]
Seconds of Pleasure: Stories
BL - v100 - i22 - August 2004 - p1899(2) [51-500]
KR - v72 - i15 - August 1 2004 - p707(2) [501+]
LJ - v129 - i14 - Sept 1 2004 - p145(1) [501+]
NYTBR - Nov 28 2004 - p24 [501+]
Spec - v296 - i9195 - Oct 30 2004 - p54(2) [501+]
TLS - i5300 - Oct 29 2004 - p22(1) [501+]

Lacaita, Carlo G. - *La Biblioteca Di Carlo Cattaneo*
TLS - i5291 - August 27 2004 - p4-6 [501+]

Lacave, Jose Luis - *Medieval Ketubot from Sefarad*
Specu - v79 - i4 - Oct 2004 - p1108(3) [501+]

Lace, William W. - *The Vatican*
y BL - v101 - i3 - Oct 1 2004 - p340(1) [51-500]

Lacey, Andrew - *The Cult of King Charles the Martyr*
Albion - v36 - i2 - Summer 2004 - p303(2) [501+]

Lacey, Greg - *Germany 1918-1945*
y TES - v0 - i4586 - June 4 2004 - psssss14(2) [501+]

Lacey, Nicola - *A Life of H.L.A. Hart: The Nightmare and the Noble Dream*
Lon R Bks - v27 - i3 - Feb 3 2005 - p12(1) [501+]
Spec - v296 - i9200 - Dec 4 2004 - p44(1) [501+]
TimHES - v0 - i1670 - Dec 10 2004 - p25(2) [501+]

Lacey, Robert - *Great Tales from English History: Joan of Arc, the Princes in the Tower, Bloody Mary, Oliver Cromwell, Sir Isaac Newton, and More*
PW - v252 - i11 - March 14 2005 - p52(1) [51-500]
Great Tales from English History, Vol. 1 (Read by Lacey, Robert). Audiobook Review
y Kliatt - v39 - i2 - March 2005 - p59(1) [51-500]

Lachenmeyer, Nathaniel - *13: the Story of the World's Most Popular Superstition*
KR - v72 - i16 - August 15 2004 - p790(2) [51-500]

Lachev, Teo - *Microsoft Reporting Services in Action*
SciTech - v28 - i4 - Dec 2004 - p32(1) [51-500]

Lachman, Gary - *A Dark Muse: The History of the Occult*
LJ - v130 - i4 - March 1 2005 - p93(1) [51-500]

Lachtman, Ofelia Dumas - *Looking for La Unica*
y BL - v101 - i9-10 - Jan 1 2005 - p845(2) [1-50]

Lack, H. Walter - *Jardin de la Malmaison: Empress Josephine's Garden*
Choice - v42 - i7 - March 2005 - p1252(1) [51-500]

Lackey, Mercedes - *Alta*
y VOYA - v27 - i4 - Oct 2004 - p315(1) [51-500]
The Fairy Godmother
y BL - v101 - i2 - Sept 15 2004 - p222(1) [51-500]
Phoenix and Ashes
Bwatch - Dec 2004 - pNA [51-500]
This Rough Magic
y VOYA - v27 - i3 - August 2004 - p230(1) [1-50]
To Light a Candle: The Obsidian Trilogy, Book Two
LJ - v129 - i17 - Oct 15 2004 - p57(1) [51-500]
PW - v251 - i42 - Oct 18 2004 - p52(2) [501+]
The Wizard of Karres
y BL - v100 - i22 - August 2004 - p1913(2) [51-500]
y SLJ - v50 - i11 - Nov 2004 - p176(1) [51-500]

Lackner, Michael - *Mapping Meanings: The Field of New Learning in Late Qing China*
R&R Bk N - v19 - i3 - August 2004 - p56(1) [51-500]

Lacobbo, Karen - *Vegetarian America--A History*
Veg J - v23 - i4 - July-August 2004 - p32(1) [501+]

Lacombe, Herve - *The Keys to French Opera in the Nineteenth Century*
NCFS - v32 - i3-4 - Spring-Summer 2004 - p372(3) [501+]

Lacoste, Jean-Yves - *Encyclopedia of Christian Theology*
LJ - v130 - i1 - Jan 1 2005 - p152(2) [501+]

Lacroux, Jean - *Discover the Moon*
Astron - v32 - i10 - Oct 2004 - p90 [51-500]

Ladd, Grace F. - *Quite a Curiosity: The Sea Letters of Grace F. Ladd*
CBRA - Annual 2003 - p53(2) [51-500]

Ladegaard, Peter - *From Red Tape to Smart Tape: Administrative Simplification in OECD Countries*
JEL - v42 - i1 - March 2004 - p288(1) [501+]

Lader, Malcolm - *Psychiatry Highlights, 2003-04*
SciTech - v28 - i3 - Sept 2004 - p96(1) [51-500]

Laderman, David - *Driving Visions: Exploring the Road Movie*
FQ - v57 - i2 - Winter 2003 - p53(2) [501+]

Laderman, Gary - *Rest in Peace: A Cultural History of Death and the Funeral Home in Twentieth-Century America*
J Soc H - v38 - i2 - Winter 2004 - p541(3) [501+]

Ladeur, Karl-Heinz - *Public Governance in the Age of Globalization*
R&R Bk N - v19 - i4 - Nov 2004 - p153(1) [501+]

Ladson-Billings, Gloria - *Critical Race Theory Perspectives on the Social Studies: The Profession, Policies, and Curriculum*
R&R Bk N - v19 - i1 - Feb 2004 - p76(1) [51-500]

LaDuke, Dee - *Making Great Television: Four Essential Ingredients*
R&R Bk N - v19 - i3 - August 2004 - p260(1) [51-500]

Ladutke, Lawrence Michael - *Freedom of Expression in El Salvador: The Struggle for Human Rights and Democracy*
Choice - v42 - i5 - Jan 2005 - p927(1) [51-500]

Ladwig, Tim - *Especially Heroes*
LibMed - v22 - i4 - Jan 2004 - p59(1) [501+]

Laechele, Rainer - *Wuerttembergs Protestantismus in der Weimarer Republik*
HNet - Dec 2004 - pNA [501+]

Laer, Lutz von - *Pediatric Fractures and Dislocations*
SciTech - v28 - i3 - Sept 2004 - p113(1) [51-500]

Laeri, Franco - *Host-Guest Systems Based on Nanoporous Crystals*
SciTech - v28 - i1 - March 2004 - p140(1) [51-500]

Lal, Brij V. - *Pacific Lives, Pacific Places: Bursting Boundaries in Pacific History*
   Cont Pac - v16 - i2 - Fall 2004 - p462(4) [501+]
Pacific Places, Pacific Histories: Essays in Honor of Robert C. Kiste
   Choice - v42 - i5 - Jan 2005 - p910(1) [1-50]
   R&R Bk N - v19 - i3 - August 2004 - p60(1) [51-500]

Lal, Deepak - *Trade, Development and Political Economy: Essays in Honour of Anne O. Krueger*
   JEL - v41 - i4 - Dec 2003 - p1324(2) [501+]

Lal, Rattan - *Principles of Soil Physics*
   SciTech - v28 - i3 - Sept 2004 - p127(1) [51-500]
Soil Degradation in the United States: Extent, Severity, and Trends
   Choice - v41 - i11-12 - July-August 2004 - p2071(1) [501+]
   SciTech - v28 - i1 - March 2004 - p128(1) [51-500]
Sustainable Agriculture and the International Rice-Wheat System
   SciTech - v28 - i3 - Sept 2004 - p127(1) [51-500]

Lalander, Philip - *Hooked and Heroin : Drugs and Drifters in a Globalized World*
   CS - v33 - i5 - Sept 2004 - p593-594 [501+]

Lalicki, Tom - *Grierson's Raid: A Daring Cavalry Strike through the Heart of the Confederacy*
  y BL - v100 - i22 - August 2004 - p1917(2) [51-500]
  y HB - v80 - i4 - July-August 2004 - p468(1) [51-500]
  y VOYA - v27 - i3 - August 2004 - p238(1) [1-50]

Lall, Sanjaya - *Competitiveness, FDI and Technological Activity in East Asia*
   R&R Bk N - v19 - i1 - Feb 2004 - p85(1) [51-500]

Lallemand, Marie-Gabrielle - *Madeleine De Scudery: La Promenade de Versailles*
   FS - v58 - i1 - Jan 2004 - p99(2) [501+]

Lallukka, Seppo - *From Fugitive Peasants to Diaspora: The Eastern Mari in Tsarist and Federal Russia*
   Slav R - v63 - i4 - Winter 2004 - p904(2) [501+]

Lalor, Brian - *The Encyclopedia of Ireland*
   ILS - v24 - i1 - Fall 2004 - p5(1) [501+]
   TLS - i5294 - Sept 17 2004 - p27(1) [501+]

Lalou, Frank - *The Gospel of Thomas*
   Parabola - v29 - i2 - Summer 2004 - p100-106 [501+]

Lalouette, Jacqueline - *Les congregations hors la loi?: Autour de la loi du [1.sup.er] juillet 1901*
   CHR - v90 - i4 - Oct 2004 - p809(4) [501+]

Lalumiere, Claude - *Open Space: New Candian Fantastic Fiction*
   CBRA - Annual 2003 - p247(2) [51-500]

Lam, Fiona Tinwei - *Intimate Distances*
   CBRA - Annual 2003 - p222(2) [501+]

Lam, Kai S. - *Topics in Contemporary Mathematical Physics*
   SciTech - v28 - i4 - Dec 2004 - p47(1) [51-500]

Lam, Kevin - *Assessing Network Security*
   SciTech - v28 - i3 - Sept 2004 - p155(1) [51-500]

Lam, Poh-Sang - *Fracture Methodologies and Manufacturing Processes: Proceedings*
   SciTech - v28 - i4 - Dec 2004 - p163(1) [51-500]

Lam, Wai-man - *Understanding the Political Culture of Hong Kong: The Paradox of Activism and Depoliticization*
   R&R Bk N - v19 - i3 - August 2004 - p183(1) [501+]

Lamadrid, Enrique R. - *Hermanitos Comanchitos*
   Roundup M - v12 - i1 - Oct 2004 - p24(1) [51-500]
Hermanitos Comanchitos: Indo-Hispano Rituals of Captivity and Redemption
   Choice - v42 - i1 - Sept 2004 - p146(1) [501+]
   SHQ - v108 - i1 - July 2004 - p111-112 [501+]

Lamarre, Jean (b. 1958-) - *The French Canadians of Michigan: Their Contribution to the Development of the Saginaw Valley and the Keweenaw Peninsula, 1840-1914*
   Can Hist R - v85 - i3 - Sept 2004 - p603(2) [501+]
   JAH - v91 - i2 - Sept 2004 - p650(1) [501+]
Les Canadiens Francais du Michigan: Leur Contribution dans le Developpement de la Vallee de la Saginaw et de la Peninsule de Keweenaw, 1840-1914
   Can Hist R - v85 - i3 - Sept 2004 - p603(2) [501+]

LaMarre, Thomas - *Uncovering Heian Japan: An Archaeology of Sensation and Inscription*
   HJAS - v64 - i1 - June 2004 - p184-200 [501+]

Lamb, Brian - *Booknotes: On American Character*
   Bwatch - v26 - i7 - July 2004 - p1(1) [51-500]

Lamb, Charles - *The Essays of Elia*
   NYRB - v51 - i16 - Oct 21 2004 - p54(4) [501+]

Lamb, Charles W. - *Essentials of Marketing, 4th Ed.*
   R&R Bk N - v19 - i2 - May 2004 - p113(1) [1-50]

Lamb, Chris - *Blackout: The Untold Story of Jackie Robinson's First Spring Training*
   BL - v101 - i1 - Sept 1 2004 - p48(1) [51-500]
   Choice - v42 - i7 - March 2005 - p1266(1) [51-500]
   LJ - v129 - i14 - Sept 1 2004 - p161(1) [51-500]
Drawn to Extremes: The Use and Abuse of Editorial Cartoons
   CJR - v43 - i6 - March-April 2005 - p63(1) [51-500]

Lamb, Christina - *The Africa House: The True Story of an English Gentleman and His African Dream*
   BL - v101 - i7 - Dec 1 2004 - p628(1) [51-500]
   KR - v72 - i22 - Nov 15 2004 - p1080(2) [501+]
   LJ - v130 - i2 - Feb 1 2005 - p98(1) [51-500]
   PW - v251 - i49 - Dec 6 2004 - p54(1) [51-500]

Lamb, Jane - *The Grand Masters of Maine Gardening: And Some of Their Disciples*
   Bwatch - v26 - i7 - July 2004 - p5(1) [51-500]

Lamb, John - *IBM WebSphere and Lotus: And Implementing Collaborative Solutions*
   SciTech - v28 - i4 - Dec 2004 - p151(1) [51-500]

Lamb, Jonathan - *Exploration & Exchange: A South Seas Anthology, 1680-1900*
   Cont Pac - v16 - i2 - Fall 2004 - p465(5) [501+]
Preserving the Self in the South Seas, 1680-1840
   Cont Pac - v16 - i2 - Fall 2004 - p465(5) [501+]

Lamb, Joyce - *Found Wanting*
   BL - v101 - i2 - Sept 15 2004 - p220(1) [51-500]

Lamb, Simon - *Devil in the Mountain: A Search for the Origin of the Andes*
   Am Sci - v93 - i1 - Jan-Feb 2005 - p81(2) [501+]
   Bwatch - v26 - i8 - August 2004 - p11(1) [51-500]
   Nature - v429 - i6987 - May 6 2004 - p21(2) [501+]
   NYTBR - July 25 2004 - p21 [501+]
   NYTBR - August 1 2004 - p14 [501+]
   SB - v40 - i6 - Nov-Dec 2004 - p251(1) [501+]
   TLS - i5295 - Sept 24 2004 - p23(1) [501+]

Lamb, Sydney M. - *Language and Reality*
   R&R Bk N - v19 - i4 - Nov 2004 - p212(1) [501+]

Lambdin, Dewey - *The Captain's Vengeance*
   KR - v72 - i17 - Sept 1 2004 - p826(1) [51-500]
   PW - v251 - i36 - Sept 6 2004 - p43(2) [51-500]

Lambert, Andrew - *Nelson: Britannia's God of War*
   TimHES - v0 - i1673 - Jan 7 2005 - p20(2) [501+]

Lambert, Frank - *Britain and the American South: From Colonialism to Rock and Roll*
   Choice - v41 - i11-12 - July-August 2004 - p2098(1) [501+]
The Founding Fathers and the Place of Religion in America
   Am St - v45 - i1 - Spring 2004 - p144-145 [501+]

Lambert, Gavin - *The Ivan Moffat File: Life Among the Beautiful and Damned in London, Paris, New York and Hollywood*
   KR - v72 - i16 - August 15 2004 - p791(1) [501+]
   PW - v251 - i34 - August 23 2004 - p44(2) [51-500]
Natalie Wood: a Life (Read by Blumenfeld, Robert). Audiobook Review
   LJ - v129 - i12 - July 2004 - p126(1) [51-500]
Natalie Wood
   TLS - i5283 - July 2 2004 - p16-17 [501+]

Lambert, Jonamay - *Trainer's Diversity Source Book: 50 Ready-to-Use Activities from Icebreakers through Wrap-Ups*
   HR Mag - v49 - i12 - Dec 2004 - p121(1) [501+]
   HR Mag - v50 - i2 - Feb 2005 - pS7(1) [501+]

Lambert, Katherine - *The Longest Winter: The Incredible Survival of Captain Scott's Lost Party*
   BL - v101 - i3 - Oct 1 2004 - p295(1) [51-500]
   LJ - v129 - i16 - Oct 1 2004 - p94(2) [51-500]
   PW - v251 - i33 - August 16 2004 - p51(1) [51-500]
   R&R Bk N - v20 - i1 - Feb 2005 - p81(1) [51-500]

Lambert, Ladina Bezzola - *Shifting the Scene: Shakespeare in European Culture*
   R&R Bk N - v19 - i4 - Nov 2004 - p235(1) [51-500]

Lambert, Linda - *Leadership Capacity for Lasting School Improvement*
   TCR - v106 - i8 - August 2004 - p1513(3) [501+]

Lambert, Thomas A. - *Registres du Consistoire de Geneve au temps de Calvin, Tome II*
   CHR - v90 - i3 - July 2004 - p550(2) [501+]
Registres du Consistoire de Geneve au temps de Calvin, Tome III
   CHR - v90 - i4 - Oct 2004 - p791(2) [501+]

Lamberth, Minnie - *Life with Strings Attached*
   LJ - v130 - i2 - Feb 1 2005 - p60(2) [51-500]

Lamberton, Ken - *Beyond Desert Walls: Essays from Prison*
   E Mag - v16 - i2 - March-April 2005 - p62(2) [501+]

Lambeth, Benjamin S. - *Mastering the Ultimate High Ground: Next Steps in the Military Uses of Space*
   APH - v51 - i3 - Fall 2004 - p53(1) [501+]
   APJ - v18 - i3 - Fall 2004 - p122(2) [501+]

Lambin, G. - *Anacreon. Fragments et imitations*
   Class R - v54 - i2 - Nov 2004 - p297-299 [501+]

Lamblin, Bianca - *A Disgraceful Affair: Simone de Beauvoir, Jean-Paul Sartre, and Bianca Lamblin*
   Atl - v294 - i2 - Sept 2004 - p139(1) [501+]

Lambrecht, Bill - *Big Muddy Blues: True Tales and Twisted Politics Along Lewis and Clark's Missouri River*
   KR - v73 - i4 - Feb 15 2005 - p214(1) [501+]
   PW - v252 - i8 - Feb 21 2005 - p170(1) [51-500]

Lambright, Slim - *The Sweethearts of Soul*
   Black Iss - v7 - i1 - Jan-Feb 2005 - p64(1) [51-500]
   KR - v72 - i19 - Oct 1 2004 - p932(1) [501+]
   PW - v251 - i47 - Nov 22 2004 - p39(2) [51-500]

Lambton, Gunda - *Sun in Winter: A Toronto Wartime Journal, 1942-1945.*
   Can Hist R - v85 - i4 - Dec 2004 - p843(3) [501+]
   CBRA - Annual 2003 - p54(1) [501+]
   Beav - v84 - i5 - Oct-Nov 2004 - p44(2) [501+]

Lamedman, Debbie - *55 Short Scenes*
  c SLJ - v50 - i8 - August 2004 - p140(1) [51-500]

Lamensdorf, Len - *The Raging Dragon (Illus. by Swingle, Bob)*
  c RT - v57 - Oct 2003 - p177 [1-50]

Lamia, Stephen - *Decorations for the Holy Dead: Visual Embellishment on Tombs and Shrines of Saints*
   Med R - June 2004 - pNA [501+]

Laminack, Lester L. - *Saturdays and Teacakes (Illus. by Soentpiet, Chris K.)*
  c LibMed - v23 - i1 - August-Sept 2004 - p65(1) [51-500]

Laming, Donald - *Understanding Human Motivation: What Makes People Tick?*
   Choice - v41 - i7 - March 2004 - p1374(2) [501+]

Lamm, Drew - *Bittersweet*
  y LibMed - v22 - i6 - March 2004 - p67(1) [501+]

Lamm, Richard D. - *The Brave New World of Health Care*
   Bwatch - v26 - i7 - July 2004 - p3(1) [51-500]
   Bwatch - Dec 2004 - pNA [51-500]
   Fut - v38 - i6 - Nov-Dec 2004 - p60(1) [51-500]

Lammers, William J. - *Fundamentals of Behavioral Research*
   SciTech - v28 - i4 - Dec 2004 - p1(1) [1-50]

Lammertse, Friso - *Peter Paul Rubens: The Life of Achilles*
   LJ - v129 - i12 - July 2004 - p78(2) [51-500]

Lamonde, Yvan - *Histoire sociale des idees au Quebec*
   Can Hist R - v85 - i4 - Dec 2004 - p845(5) [501+]
Le rouge et le bleu: Une anthologie de la pensee politique au Quebec de la Conquete a la Revolution tranquile
   Can Lit - i182 - Autumn 2004 - p143(2) [501+]

Lamont-Brown, Raymond - *Humphry Davy: Life Beyond the Lamp*
   CR - v285 - i1667 - Dec 2004 - p378(1) [51-500]

Lamont, Peter - *The Rise of the Indian Rope Trick: How a Spectacular Hoax Became History*
   NYTBR - Feb 13 2005 - p24 [501+]

LaMonte, Bob - *Winning the N.F.L. Way: Leadership Lessons from Football's Top Head Coaches*
   NYT - July 11 2004 - pBU8 [501+]

Lamoreaux, John C. - *The Early Muslim Tradition of Dream Interpretation*
   Specu - v79 - i3 - July 2004 - p782-783 [501+]

Lamothe, Lee - *The Last Thief*
   BIC - v33 - i5 - August 2004 - p15(1) [501+]

Lamott, Anne - *Bird by Bird*
  c SLJ - v50 - i11 - Nov 2004 - p67(1) [51-500]
Plan B: Further Thoughts on Faith
   BL - v101 - i9-10 - Jan 1 2005 - p782(1) [1-50]
   KR - v73 - i1 - Jan 1 2005 - p36(1) [501+]
   LJ - v130 - i4 - March 1 2005 - p84(2) [51-500]
   People - v63 - i10 - March 14 2005 - p49 [51-500]
   PW - v252 - i6 - Feb 7 2005 - p55(1) [51-500]
Twist of Faith
   Ent W - i809 - March 4 2005 - p76 [501+]

L'Amour, Louis - *The Collected Short Stories of Louis L'Amour: The Frontier Stories, Vol. 2*
  c BL - v101 - i5 - Nov 1 2004 - p464(1) [51-500]
  c KR - v72 - i20 - Oct 15 2004 - p984(1) [51-500]
  c LJ - v129 - i18 - Nov 1 2004 - p79(1) [501+]
The Collected Short Stories of Luis L'Amour, Vol 1. (Read by Lloyd, John Bedford). Audiobook Review
  c Kliatt - v38 - i4 - July 2004 - p50(1) [51-500]
Son of a Wanted Man. Audiobook Review
   PW - v252 - i10 - March 7 2005 - p27(1) [51-500]

Lang, Karen C. - *Four Illusions: Candrakirti's Advice to Travelers on the Bodhisattva Path*
JAS - v63 - i3 - August 2004 - p827-828 [501+]

Lang, Kenneth R. - *The Cambridge Guide to the Solar System*
TimHES - v0 - i1649 - July 16 2004 - p26(1) [501+]

Lang, Richard S. - *Clinical Preventive Medicine, 2nd Ed.*
SciTech - v28 - i3 - Sept 2004 - p82(1) [501+]

Lang, Robert J. - *Origami Design Secrets: Mathematical Methods for an Ancient Art*
Choice - v41 - i11-12 - July-August 2004 - p2032(1) [501+]
Math T - v98 - i2 - Sept 2004 - p143-143 [501+]

Lang, Tim - *Food Wars: The Global Battle for Mouths, Minds and Markets*
Choice - v42 - i6 - Feb 2005 - p1042(1) [51-500]
New Sci - v184 - i2468 - Oct 9 2004 - p44(4) [501+]
SciTech - v28 - i4 - Dec 2004 - p170(1) [51-500]

Lang, W. Patrick - *Intelligence: the Human Factor*
c SLJ - v50 - i7 - July 2004 - p124(1) [51-500]

Langa, Helen - *Radical Art: Printmaking and the Left in 1930's New York*
Choice - v42 - i1 - Sept 2004 - p90(1) [501+]

Langbehn, Volker - *Arno Schmidt's Zettels Traum: An Analysis*
Ger Q - v77 - i4 - Fall 2004 - p504-505 [501+]

Langbein, Hermann - *People in Auschwitz*
Choice - v42 - i4 - Dec 2004 - p729(1) [1-50]

Langbein, John H. - *The Origins of Adversary Criminal Trial*
Law Q Rev - v120 - Jan 2004 - p185-188 [501+]

Langdell, Cheri Colby - *Adrienne Rich: The Moment of Change*
Choice - v42 - i5 - Jan 2005 - p853(1) [1-50]

Langdon, Simon P. - *Cancer Cell Culture: Methods and Protocols*
SciTech - v28 - i1 - March 2004 - p90(1) [51-500]

Langdridge, Darren - *Introduction to Research Methods and Data Analysis in Psychology*
TimHES - v0 - i1668 - Nov 26 2004 - pXVIII(2) [501+]

Lange, Armin - *Die Damonen: Die Damonologie der Israelitisch-Judischen und Fruhchristlichen Literatur im Kontext ihrer Umwelt = Demons: The Demonology of Israelite-Jewish and Early Christian Literature in Context of Their Environment*
Theol St - v65 - i3 - Sept 2004 - p630(2) [501+]

Lange, Barbara Rose - *Holy Brotherhood: Romani Music in a Hungarian Pentecostal Church*
Slav R - v63 - i2 - Summer 2004 - p385(2) [501+]

Lange, Glenn-Marie - *Environmental Accounting in Action: Case Studies from Southern Africa*
JEL - v41 - i4 - Dec 2003 - p1410(2) [501+]

Lange, Lis - *White, Poor, and Angry: White Working Class Families in Johannesburg*
CS - v33 - i4 - July 2004 - p453(2) [501+]

Lange, Marc - *A Note on Scientific Essentialism, Laws of Nature, and Counterfactual Conditionals*
RM - v58 - i1 - Sept 2004 - p213(3) [501+]

Lange, Vladimir - *Be a Survivor: Your Guide to Breast Cancer Treatment. 2nd Ed.*
LJ - v129 - i14 - Sept 1 2004 - p184(2) [501+]
Fatal Memories
PW - v252 - i7 - Feb 14 2005 - p55(1) [51-500]

Langellier, John P. - *Second Manassas 1862: Robert E. Lee's Greatest Victory*
R&R Bk N - v19 - i4 - Nov 2004 - p61(1) [51-500]

Langemack, Chapple - *The Booktalker's Bible: How to Talk about the Books You Love to Any Audience*
VOYA - v27 - i4 - Oct 2004 - p296(1) [51-500]

Langenfeld, Friedrich Spee von - *Cautio Criminalis, or A Book on Witch Trials*
Theol St - v65 - i3 - Sept 2004 - p674(2) [501+]

Langer, Adam - *Crossing California*
BL - v101 - i6 - Nov 15 2004 - p558(1) [51-500]
BW - v34 - i30 - July 25 2004 - p6(1) [501+]
y SLJ - v50 - i10 - Oct 2004 - p199(1) [501+]

Langer, Ellen J. - *On Becoming an Artist: Reinventing Yourself through Mindful Creativity*
LJ - v130 - i4 - March 1 2005 - p100(1) [51-500]
PW - v252 - i2 - Jan 10 2005 - p45(1) [501+]

Langer, G.M. - *Collaborative Analysis of Student Work: Improving Teaching and Learning*
TCR - v106 - i5 - May 2004 - p1026(4) [501+]

Langer, Judith A. - *Getting to Excellent: How to Create Better Schools*
TCR - v107 - i2 - Feb 2005 - p300(4) [501+]

Langer, Maria - *Creating Resumes, Letters, Business Cards, and Flyers in Word: Visual QuickProject Guide*
LJ - v130 - i1 - Jan 1 2005 - p148(1) [501+]
Microsoft Office Word 2003 for Windows
SciTech - v28 - i4 - Dec 2004 - p172(1) [51-500]
Quicken 2005: The Official Guide
SciTech - v28 - i4 - Dec 2004 - p9(1) [1-50]

Langer, Nieli - *Aging Education: Teaching and Practice Strategies*
R&R Bk N - v19 - i3 - August 2004 - p152(1) [51-500]

Langerbein, Helmut - *Hitlers's Death Squads: The Logic of Mass Murder*
Slav R - v63 - i4 - Winter 2004 - p854(2) [501+]

Langewiesche, William - *The Outlaw Sea: A World of Freedom, Chaos, and Crime (Read by Langewiesche, William). Audiobook Review*
y Kliatt - v38 - i5 - Sept 2004 - p68(2) [51-500]
The Outlaw Sea: A World of Freedom, Chaos, and Crime
Globe & Mail - July 17 2004 - pD13 [501+]
NYRB - v51 - i13 - August 12 2004 - p23(3) [501+]

Langewiesche, Wolfgang - *America from the Air: An Aviator's Story*
y Kliatt - v38 - i5 - Sept 2004 - p42(2) [501+]
R&R Bk N - v19 - i4 - Nov 2004 - p56(1) [51-500]

Langford, Ian H. - *Environmental Decision Making and Risk Management: Selected Essays*
R&R Bk N - v19 - i4 - Nov 2004 - p87(1) [51-500]

Langford, Jean M. - *Fluent Bodies: Ayurvedic Remedies for Postcolonial Imbalance*
AHR - v109 - i4 - Oct 2004 - p1213-1214 [501+]

Langford, Martha - *Suspended Conversations: The Afterlife of Memory in Photographic Albums*
WestFolk - v62 - i4 - Fall 2003 - p303(3) [501+]

Langford, R. Everett - *Introduction to Weapons of Mass Destruction: Radiological, Chemical, and Biological*
Choice - v42 - i2 - Oct 2004 - p369(1) [51-500]
E-Streams - August 2004 - pNA [501+]

Langham, Tony - *Creepy Crawly Calypso (Illus. by Hatter, Debbie)*
c PW - v251 - i41 - Oct 11 2004 - p82(1) [501+]

Langholm, Odd - *The Merchant in the Confessional: Trade and Price in the Pre-Reformation Penitential Handbooks*
Ren Q - v57 - i3 - Fall 2004 - p1047(2) [501+]

Langholm, Siri - *The Sweeter Side of Pain: A Critical Look at Some Modern Feminist Classics*
R&R Bk N - v19 - i1 - Feb 2004 - p132(1) [51-500]

Langholtz, Harvey J. - *The Psychology of Diplomacy*
Choice - v42 - i4 - Dec 2004 - p734(1) [1-50]
R&R Bk N - v19 - i3 - August 2004 - p186(1) [501+]

Langhorne, Mary Jo - *Developing an Information Literacy Program K-12: A How-to-Do-It Manual and CD-ROM Package*
LJ - v130 - i3 - Feb 15 2005 - p164(1) [501+]

Langley, Andrew - *Michaelangelo*
LibMed - v22 - i4 - Jan 2004 - p72(1) [501+]
Pablo Picasso
LibMed - v22 - i4 - Jan 2004 - p72(1) [501+]

Langley, Helen - *Benjamin Disraeli: Scenes from an Extraordinary Life*
Globe & Mail - Dec 18 2004 - pD27 [51-500]

Langley, Lester D. - *The Americas in the Modern Age*
JAH - v91 - i3 - Dec 2004 - p1115(2) [501+]

Langley, Ricky L. - *Sex and Gender Differences in Health and Disease*
SciTech - v28 - i3 - Sept 2004 - p89(1) [51-500]

Langmead, Donald - *Frank Lloyd Wright: A Bio-Bibliography*
R&R Bk N - v19 - i1 - Feb 2004 - p262(1) [51-500]

Langmead, Ross - *The Word Made Flesh: Towards an Incarnational Missiology*
R&R Bk N - v19 - i4 - Nov 2004 - p25(1) [501+]

Langness, L.L. - *Study of Culture, 3rd Ed.*
R&R Bk N - v19 - i4 - Nov 2004 - p76(1) [51-500]

Langran, Robert - *The Supreme Court: A Concise History*
R&R Bk N - v19 - i1 - Feb 2004 - pNA [51-500]

Langridge, Roger - *Fred the Clown*
y BL - v101 - i5 - Nov 1 2004 - p473(1) [51-500]
y Kliatt - v39 - i2 - March 2005 - p30(1) [51-500]

Langrish, Katherine - *Troll Fell*
c CCB-B - v58 - i1 - Sept 2004 - p25(2) [51-500]
y Magpies - v19 - i5 - Nov 2004 - p40(1) [501+]
c MFSF - v107 - i2 - August 2004 - p35(6) [501+]
c SLJ - v50 - i7 - July 2004 - p106(1) [51-500]

Langston, Douglas C. - *Conscience and Other Virtues: From Bonaventure to MacIntyre*
Dialogue - v43 - i1 - Wntr 2004 - p202-204 [501+]

Langston, Laura - *Lesia's Dream*
c Can CL - i113/114 - Spring-Summer 2004 - p136(3) [501+]
Mile-High Apple Pie (Illus. by Gardiner, Lindsey)
c Globe & Mail - Feb 26 2005 - pD11 [501+]
Taste of Perfection
y Can CL - i111-112 - Fall-Winter 2003 - p139(8) [501+]

Langston, Nancy - *Where Land & Water Meet: A Western Landscape Transformed*
HNet - August 2004 - pNA [501+]
WHQ - v35 - i1 - Spring 2004 - p75-76 [501+]
Where Land & Water Meet: A Western Landscape Trasformed
JAH - v91 - i3 - Dec 2004 - p1108(2) [501+]

Langston, Thomas S. - *Uneasy Balance: Civil-Military Relations in Peacetime America since 1783*
Choice - v41 - i11-12 - July-August 2004 - p2125(2) [501+]
J Mil H - v68 - i3 - July 2004 - p1021-1022 [501+]
NWCR - v57 - Autumn 2004 - p169(2) [501+]

Langston, William - *Research Methods Laboratory Manual for Psychology, 2nd Ed.*
SciTech - v28 - i4 - Dec 2004 - p1(1) [1-50]

Langstrom, Tarja - *Transformation in Russia and International Law*
R&R Bk N - v19 - i3 - August 2004 - p207(1) [1-50]

Langstroth, L.L. - *Langstroth's Hive and the Honey-Bee*
Bwatch - v26 - i9 - Sept 2004 - p2(1) [51-500]

Langton, Christian M. - *Physical Measurement of Bone*
E-Streams - August 2004 - pNA [501+]

Langton, Christopher - *The Military Balance, 2003-2004*
Choice - v41 - i11-12 - July-August 2004 - p2028(1) [501+]

Langton, Marcia - *Honor Among Nations?: Treaties and Agreements with Indigenous People*
Choice - v42 - i6 - Feb 2005 - p1090(1) [51-500]

Lanham, Richard Lee Hough - *The Nation-States: Concert or Chaos*
IndRev - v9 - i3 - Wntr 2005 - p459(3) [501+]

Lanier, Doris - *Absinthe: The Cocaine of the Nineteenth Century: A History of the Hallucinogenic Drug and Its Effect on Artists and Writers in Europe and the United States*
R&R Bk N - v19 - i3 - August 2004 - p86(1) [501+]

Lanik, Monika - *Freie Ruerger und Freimaurerinnen: Lokalpolitik am Ende des 20. Jahrhunderts*
HNet - June 2004 - pNA [501+]

Lankford, George E. - *Native American Legends*
LibMed - v22 - i7 - April-May 2004 - p67(1) [501+]

Lankford, Nelson - *Richmond Burning: The Last Days of the Confederate Capital*
Sew R - v112 - i1 - Wntr 2004 - p138-147 [501+]

Lankford, Terill Lee - *Earthquake Weather*
BooChiTr - May 2 2004 - p3(1) [501+]

Lankina, Tomila - *Governing the Locals: Local Self-Government and Ethnic Mobilization in Russia*
Choice - v42 - i5 - Jan 2005 - p927(1) [51-500]
R&R Bk N - v19 - i3 - August 2004 - p184(1) [501+]

Lankov, Andrei - *From Stalin to Kim II Sung: The Formation of North Korea 1945-1960*
E-A St - v56 - i5 - July 2004 - p777(2) [501+]

Lanning, Scott - *Essential Reference Services for Today's School Media Specialists*
Teach Lib - v32 - i2 - Dec 2004 - p38(1) [501+]

L'Annunziata, Michael F. - *Handbook of Radioactivity Analysis*
Choice - v41 - i7 - March 2004 - p1331(1) [501+]

Lansdale, Joe R. - *Bumper Crop*
MFSF - v107 - i3 - Sept 2004 - p30(2) [501+]
Sunset and Sawdust (Read by Marlowe, Deborah). Audiobook Review
c Kliatt - v38 - i4 - July 2004 - p57(1) [51-500]

Lansdown, A.R. - *Lubrication and Lubricant Selection: A Practical Guide, 3rd Ed.*
SciTech - v28 - i1 - March 2004 - p151(1) [51-500]

Lansford, Tom - *A Bitter Harvest: US Foreign Policy and Afghanistan*
Choice - v42 - i1 - Sept 2004 - p185(1) [501+]
R&R Bk N - v19 - i1 - Feb 2004 - p55(1) [51-500]

Debating the War on Terrorism
  R&R Bk N - v19 - i3 - August 2004 - p165(1)
  [501+]
George W. Bush
  c CH Bwatch - March 2005 - pNA [51-500]
Lanski, Charles - *Concepts in Abstract Algebra*
  SciTech - v28 - i4 - Dec 2004 - p34(1) [51-500]
Lansky, Aaron - *Outwitting History: The Amazing Adventures of a Man Who Rescued a Million Yiddish Books*
  y BL - v101 - i4 - Oct 15 2004 - p369(1) [501+]
  KR - v72 - i14 - July 15 2004 - p673(2) [501+]
  LJ - v129 - i18 - Nov 1 2004 - p83(2) [501+]
  PW - v251 - i27 - July 5 2004 - p43(1) [51-500]
Lansky, Bruce - *Rolling in the Aisles: A Collection of Laugh-Out-Loud Poems (Illus. by Carpenter, Stephen)*
  c SLJ - v51 - i1 - Jan 2005 - p150(1) [51-500]
Lantz, Hays B. - *Rubrics for Assessing Student Achievement in Science, Grades K-12*
  R&R Bk N - v19 - i3 - August 2004 - p219(1)
  [1-50]
Lantz, Kenneth - *The Dostoevsky Encyclopedia*
  LJ - v129 - i18 - Nov 1 2004 - p124(1) [51-500]
  R&R Bk N - v19 - i4 - Nov 2004 - p218(1) [501+]
  BL - v101 - i6 - Nov 15 2004 - p613(1) [501+]
Lanyon, Anna - *The New World of Martin Cortes: A True Story of Poignant Loss and Resilient Courage*
  BL - v100 - i21 - July 2004 - p1812(1) [1-50]
  LJ - v129 - i12 - July 2004 - p98(1) [51-500]
New World of Martin Cortes
  R&R Bk N - v19 - i4 - Nov 2004 - p69(1) [51-500]
Lanza, Joseph - *Elevator Music: A Surreal History of Muzak, Easy-Listening, and Other Moodsong*
  Choice - v42 - i6 - Feb 2005 - p1031(1) [51-500]
Lanzetta, Beverly J. - *The Other Side of Nothingness: Toward a Theology of Radical Openness*
  BCS - v24 - Annual 2004 - p306(4) [501+]
Laos and Cambodia, rev. ed
  R&R Bk N - v19 - i1 - Feb 2004 - p47(1) [51-500]
Lapadat, Judith - *Mixed Messages*
  CBRA - Annual 2003 - p223(1) [501+]
Lapan, Richard T. - *Career Development Across the K-16 Years: Bridging the Present to Satisying and Successful Futures*
  R&R Bk N - v19 - i3 - August 2004 - p125(1)
  [501+]
Lapatin, Kenneth D.S. - *Mysteries of the Snake Goddess: Art, Desire, and the Forging of History*
  ABR - v26 - i1 - Nov-Dec 2004 - p23(2) [501+]
Mysteries of the Snake Goddess. Art, Desire, and the Forging of History
  Class R - v53 - i2 - Nov 2003 - p481-482 [501+]
Lapavitsas, Costas - *Social Foundations of Markets, Money and Credit*
  JEL - v42 - i1 - March 2004 - p323(1) [501+]
Lapcharoensap, Rattawut - *Sightseeing: Stories*
  BL - v101 - i8 - Dec 15 2004 - p708(1) [51-500]
  y BL - v101 - i8 - Dec 15 2004 - p708(1) [51-500]
  BL - v101 - i8 - Dec 15 2004 - p708(2) [51-500]
  Ent W - i803 - Jan 28 2005 - p86 [501+]
  KR - v72 - i20 - Oct 15 2004 - p979(1) [501+]
  LJ - v129 - i17 - Oct 15 2004 - p58(1) [51-500]
  NYTBR - Jan 9 2005 - p26 [501+]
  People - v63 - i5 - Feb 7 2005 - p49 [501+]
  PW - v251 - i46 - Nov 15 2004 - p37(1) [51-500]
  Globe & Mail - Feb 19 2005 - pD4 [501+]
Lape, Susan - *Reproducing Athens: Menader's Comedy, Democratic Culture, and the Hellenistic City*
  Choice - v42 - i2 - Oct 2004 - p290(1) [501+]
Lapham, Alexander - *Deathwatch*
  ChrSFF&H - v26 - i10 - Oct 2004 - p28(1) [51-500]
Lapham, F. - *An Introduction to the New Testament Apocrypha*
  JR - v85 - i1 - Jan 2005 - p111(2) [501+]
Lapham, Lewis H. - *Gag Rule: On the Suppression of Dissent and the Stifling of Democracy*
  Globe & Mail - July 24 2004 - pD8 [501+]
  LJ - v129 - i12 - July 2004 - p103(2) [51-500]
  Nation - v279 - i11 - Oct 11 2004 - p36 [501+]
  NYT - August 9 2004 - pE6 [501+]
  R&R Bk N - v19 - i4 - Nov 2004 - p152(1) [501+]
Lapidus, Rina - *Between Snow and Desert Heat: Russian Influences on Hebrew Literature, 1870-1970*
  Choice - v41 - i7 - March 2004 - p1302(1) [501+]
LaPierre, Janet - *Death Duties*
  KR - v72 - i14 - July 15 2004 - p662(2) [51-500]
LaPlante, Eve - *American Jezebel: The Uncommon Life of Anne Hutchinson, the Woman Who Defied the Puritans*
  ABR - v26 - i2 - Jan-Feb 2005 - p29(1) [501+]
  Choice - v42 - i6 - Feb 2005 - p1082(1) [51-500]

Lapomarda, Vincent A. - *The Jesuits in the United States: The Italian Heritage*
  CHR - v90 - i3 - July 2004 - p573(2) [501+]
LaPorte, Joseph - *Natural Kinds and Conceptual Change*
  Choice - v42 - i1 - Sept 2004 - p116(1) [501+]
Laporte, Leo - *Leo Laporte's Guide To TiVo*
  Bwatch - Dec 2004 - pNA [51-500]
LaPorte, Norman - *The German Communist Party in Saxony, 1924-1933*
  GSR - v27 - i3 - Oct 2004 - p634(1) [501+]
Lapp, Diane - *Teaching All the Children*
  SLJ - v50 - i10 - Oct 2004 - pS73(1) [501+]
Lapp, Nancy D. - *Landing Votes: Representation and Land Reform in Latin America*
  Choice - v42 - i5 - Jan 2005 - p928(1) [501+]
Lappe, Anthony - *True Lies*
  PW - v251 - i38 - Sept 20 2004 - p56(1) [51-500]
  R&R Bk N - v19 - i4 - Nov 2004 - p229(1) [501+]
Lappi, Megan - *Birds*
  c SB - v40 - i3 - May-June 2004 - p131(2) [501+]
Lappin, Anthony - *The Medieval Cult of Saint Dominic of Silos*
  JR - v84 - i3 - July 2004 - p464(3) [501+]
  CHR - v90 - i3 - July 2004 - p524(3) [501+]
Lapsley, Daniel K. - *Moral Development, Self, and Identity*
  Adoles - v39 - i155 - Fall 2004 - p624(2) [51-500]
  Choice - v42 - i3 - Nov 2004 - p569(1) [51-500]
  R&R Bk N - v19 - i3 - August 2004 - p10(1)
  [1-50]
Laqueur, Thomas W. - *Solitary Sex: A Cultural History of Masturbation*
  Afterimage - v32 - i4 - Jan-Feb 2005 - p15(1) [51-500]
  AHR - v109 - i2 - April 2004 - p478(2) [501+]
  J Soc H - v38 - i1 - Fall 2004 - p205(6) [501+]
  J Soc H - v38 - i1 - Fall 2004 - p278(1) [501+]
  JIH - v35 - i1 - Summer 2004 - p116-117 [501+]
Laqueur, Walter - *No End to War: Terrorism in the Twenty-First Century*
  TLS - i5301 - Nov 5 2004 - p4-6 [501+]
Voices of Terror: Manifestos, Writings and Manuals of Al Qaeda, Hamas, and Other Terrorists from around the World and Throughout the Ages
  Parameters - v34 - i4 - Winter 2004 - p129(2)
  [501+]
Larbalestier, Justine - *Magic or Madness*
  KR - v73 - i3 - Feb 1 2005 - p178(1) [51-500]
Larcent, Manu - *Astronauts of the Future*
  Bwatch - Feb 2005 - pNA [51-500]
Larch, Maureen - *Serving Homeschooled Teens and Their Parents*
  Teach Lib - v32 - i2 - Dec 2004 - p39(1) [501+]
Lardellier, Pascal - *Les Miroirs du paon: Rites et Rhetoriques Politiques dans la France de l'Ancien Regime*
  Ren Q - v57 - i3 - Fall 2004 - p1022(2) [501+]
Lardinois, Andre - *Making Silence Speak: Women's Voices in Greek Literature and Society*
  Signs - v30 - i2 - Wntr 2005 - p1715(5) [501+]
  Wom HR - v13 - i2 - Summer 2004 - p317-319
  [501+]
Lardo, Vincent - *McNally's Bluff*
  PW - v251 - i32 - August 9 2004 - p233(1) [51-500]
Lare, Gary A. - *Acquiring and Organizing Curriculum Materials: A Guide and Directory of Resources, 2nd Ed.*
  R&R Bk N - v19 - i3 - August 2004 - p225(1)
  [1-50]
Lareau, Annette - *Unequal Childhoods: Class, Race, and Family Life*
  HER - v74 - i4 - Winter 2004 - p431-439 [501+]
  NYRB - v51 - i19 - Dec 2 2004 - p29(4) [501+]
Lareau, Kara - *Rocko and Spanky Go to a Party (Illus. by LaReau, Jenna)*
  c SLJ - v50 - i10 - Oct 2004 - p120(1) [51-500]
LaReau, Renee M. - *Getting a Life: How to Find Your True Vocation*
  CI - v13 - i1 - Jan 2005 - p44(2) [501+]
Large, David Clay - *And the World Closed Its Doors: The Story of One Family Abandoned to the Holocaust*
  HNet - July 2004 - pNA [501+]
Large, Mark F. - *Tree Ferns*
  Choice - v42 - i4 - Dec 2004 - p689(1) [1-50]
  E-Streams - Dec 2004 - pNA [501+]
  SciTech - v28 - i3 - Sept 2004 - p62(1) [51-500]
Lark, Michael - *Batman in Nine Lives*
  LibMed - v22 - i6 - March 2004 - p70(1) [501+]

Larkin, Emma - *Secret Histories: Finding George Orwell in a Burmese Teashop*
  Globe & Mail - Nov 3 2004 - pT1 [501+]
  TimHES - v0 - i1658 - Sept 17 2004 - p26(1)
  [501+]
  TLS - i5294 - Sept 17 2004 - p30(1) [501+]
Larkin, Philip - *Collected Poems*
  ABR - v26 - i2 - Jan-Feb 2005 - p18(1) [501+]
  LJ - v129 - i12 - July 2004 - p88(1) [1-50]
  NY - v80 - i20 - July 26 2004 - p084 [501+]
  YR - v92 - i3 - July 2004 - p170-178 [501+]
Larkin, Tanya - *Jacques Marquette and Louis Jolliet: Explorers of the Mississippi*
  VOYA - v27 - i5 - Dec 2004 - p419(1) [51-500]
Larkum, Anthony W.D. - *Photosynthesis in Algae*
  SciTech - v28 - i1 - March 2004 - p67(1) [51-500]
LaRochelle, David - *The Best Pet of All (Illus. by Wakiyama, Hanako)*
  c PW - v251 - i28 - July 12 2004 - p63(2) [51-500]
  c SLJ - v50 - i7 - July 2004 - p80(2) [51-500]
LaRosa, Michael - *The United States Discovers Panama: The Writings of Soldiers, Scholars, Scientists, and Scoundrels, 1850-1905*
  R&R Bk N - v19 - i1 - Feb 2004 - p67(1) [501+]
Larose, Lawrence - *Cottage for Sale, Must Be Moved: A Woman Moves a House to Make a Home*
  LJ - v129 - i12 - July 2004 - p106(2) [501+]
Gutted: Down to the Studs in My House, My Marriage, My Entire Life
  LJ - v129 - i12 - July 2004 - p106(2) [501+]
Larousse de Poche, 2005 Ed.
  R&R Bk N - v20 - i1 - Feb 2005 - p1(1) [51-500]
Laroussi, Farid - *French and Francophone: The Challenge of Expanding Horizons*
  FS - v58 - i3 - July 2004 - p441-442 [501+]
Larrabee, Eric - *Commander in Chief: Franklin Delano Roosevelt, His Lieutenants and Their War*
  R&R Bk N - v19 - i3 - August 2004 - p69(1) [51-500]
Larrabee, Wayne F. - *Surgical Anatomy of the Face, 2nd Ed.*
  SciTech - v28 - i3 - Sept 2004 - p67(1) [51-500]
Larrick, Geary - *Theory and Composition of Percussion Music*
  Choice - v42 - i7 - March 2005 - p1236(1) [51-500]
  R&R Bk N - v19 - i4 - Nov 2004 - p196(1) [501+]
Larsen, Jack Lenor - *Jack Lenor Larsen: Creator and Collector*
  Choice - v42 - i4 - Dec 2004 - p646(1) [1-50]
Larsen, Timothy - *Christabel Pankhurst: Fundamentalism and Feminism in Coalition*
  AHR - v109 - i2 - April 2004 - p616(2) [501+]
  Albion - v36 - i1 - Spring 2004 - p177(2) [501+]
  JR - v84 - i4 - Oct 2004 - p622(3) [501+]
Larsen, Wayne - *A.Y. Jackson: A Love for the Land*
  y CBRA - Annual 2003 - p537(1) [501+]
  Globe & Mail - July 17 2004 - pD14 [1-50]
  y Res Links - v10 - i3 - Feb 2005 - p46(2) [501+]
Larson, Bruce A. - *Property Rights and Environmental Problems*
  JEL - v41 - i4 - Dec 2003 - p1433(1) [501+]
Larson, Catherine - *Games and Play in the Theater of Spanish American Women*
  Choice - v42 - i4 - Dec 2004 - p666(1) [1-50]
Larson, Douglas - *The Urban Cliff Revolution: New Findings on the Origins and Evolution of Human Habitats*
  Choice - v42 - i6 - Feb 2005 - p1048(1) [51-500]
  Nature - v431 - i7006 - Sept 16 2004 - p248(1)
  [501+]
Larson, Edward J. - *Evolution: The Remarkable History of a Scientific Theory (Read by McDonough, John). Audiobook Review*
  y Kliatt - v39 - i2 - March 2005 - p59(1) [51-500]
Evolution: The Remarkable History of a Scientific Theory
  Choice - v42 - i3 - Nov 2004 - p508(1) [1-50]
  HRNB - v33 - i1 - Fall 2004 - p39(1) [501+]
  y SB - v40 - i4 - July-August 2004 - p167(1) [51-500]
  SB - v40 - i6 - Nov-Dec 2004 - p242(1) [51-500]
Larson, Erik - *The Devil in the White City: Murder, Magic, and Madness at the Fair That Changed America*
  HNet - Nov 2004 - pNA [501+]
  Lon R Bks - v26 - i7 - April 1 2004 - p27(1)
  [501+]
  World&I - v19 - i3 - March 2004 - p221 [501+]
Larson, Gerald James - *Religion and Personal Law in Secular India: A Call to Judgement*
  JAS - v63 - i2 - May 2004 - p527(4) [501+]

Larson, Jeanette - *Bringing Mysteries Alive for Children and Young Adults*
   y LibMed - v22 - i5 - Feb 2004 - p84(1) [501+]
   c SLJ - v50 - i8 - August 2004 - p150(1) [501+]
   y VOYA - v27 - i3 - August 2004 - p250(1) [1-50]

Larson, Jennifer - *Greek Nymphs: Myth, Cult, Lore*
   Class R - v54 - i2 - Nov 2004 - p433(3) [501+]
   Signs - v30 - i2 - Wntr 2005 - p1715(5) [501+]

Larson, Kate Clifford - *Bound for the Promised Land: Harriet Tubman, Portrait of an American Hero*
   y Choice - v42 - i2 - Oct 2004 - p355(2) [501+]
   y RAH - v32 - i4 - Dec 2004 - p512-517 [501+]
   y SLJ - v50 - i9 - Sept 2004 - p236(1) [51-500]

Larson, Olaf F. - *Sociology in Government: The Galpin-Taylor Years in the U.S. Department of Agriculture, 1919 to 1953*
   CS - v33 - i4 - July 2004 - p462(2) [501+]

Larson, Paul B. - *Stationary Tower: Notes on a Course by W. Hugh Woodin*
   SciTech - v28 - i3 - Sept 2004 - p16(1) [501+]

Larson, Paul Clifford - *Mississippi Escapade: Reliving the Grand Excursion of 1854.*
   c SLJ - v50 - i9 - Sept 2004 - p230(1) [51-500]

Larson, Peter - *Bones Rock!: Everything You Need to Know to Be a Paleontologist*
   y SLJ - v50 - i11 - Nov 2004 - p166(2) [51-500]

Larsson, Patrik - *Yr-rune: Use and Phonetic Value in Scandinavian Runic Inscriptions*
   JEGP - v103 - i4 - Oct 2004 - p529-530 [501+]

Larsson, Stig - *Partial Differential Equations with Numerical Methods*
   Choice - v41 - i7 - March 2004 - p1330(1) [501+]

L'art gothique dans l'Oise et ses environs
   Specu - v79 - i3 - July 2004 - p733-735 [501+]

Lartey, Emmanuel Y. - *In Living Color: An Intercultural Approach to Pastoral Care and Counseling, 2nd Ed.*
   R&R Bk N - v19 - i1 - Feb 2004 - p23(1) [1-50]

Larzelere, Alex R. - *The Coast Guard in World War I: An Untold Story*
   Choice - v41 - i7 - March 2004 - p1356(1) [501+]

LaSalle, Mick - *Dangerous Men: Pre-Code Hollywood and the Birth of the Modern Man*
   JPC - v38 - i2 - Nov 2004 - p440(2) [501+]

Laschever, Barnett - *Connecticut: An Explorer's Guide*
   Bwatch - v26 - i8 - August 2004 - p2(1) [51-500]

Laschquinn, Elisabeth - *Race Experts: How Racial Etiquette, Sensitivity Training and New Age Therapy Hijacked the Civil Rights Revolution*
   CS - v33 - i1 - Jan 2004 - p23-24 [501+]

Lasenby, Jack - *Aunt Effie and the Island that Sank*
   c Magpies - v19 - i5 - Nov 2004 - p7S(1) [501+]

Laser, G. - *Quintus Tullius Cicero: Commentariolum petitionis, Herausgegeben ubersetzt und kommentiert*
   Class R - v54 - i2 - Nov 2004 - p362(2) [501+]

Lasher, Louisa J. - *Munchausen by Proxy: Identification, Intervention, and Case Management*
   SciTech - v28 - i4 - Dec 2004 - p101(1) [51-500]

Lashner, William - *Past Due*
   DroRevMy - v24 - i3 - May-June 2004 - p12(1) [1-50]

Lasine, Stuart - *Knowing Kings: Knowledge, Power, and Narcissism in the Hebrew Bible*
   JNES - v63 - i4 - Oct 2004 - p303(2) [501+]

Laskaris, George - *Color Atlas of Oral Diseases, 3rd Ed.*
   E-Streams - Nov 2004 - pNA [501+]

Laskaris, J. - *The Art is Long: On the Sacred Disease and the Scientific Tradition*
   Class R - v54 - i2 - Nov 2004 - p295-297 [501+]

Laskey, Elizabeth - *Gross and Gory*
   y Teach Lib - v32 - i1 - Oct 2004 - p44(1) [501+]

Laskey, Heather - *Night Voices: Heard in the Shadow of Hitler and Stalin*
   R&R Bk N - v19 - i1 - Feb 2004 - p39(1) [1-50]

Laski, Marghanita - *The Village*
   Spec - v296 - i9194 - Oct 23 2004 - p49(2) [501+]
   TLS - i5298 - Oct 15 2004 - p22(1) [501+]

Laskier, Michael M. - *Israel and the Maghreb: From Statehood to Oslo*
   Choice - v42 - i6 - Feb 2005 - p1078(2) [51-500]
   MEJ - v58 - i4 - Autumn 2004 - p690(2) [51-500]

Laskin, David - *The Children's Blizzard*
   y BL - v101 - i4 - Oct 15 2004 - p384(1) [51-500]
   Ent W - i793 - Nov 19 2004 - p87 [51-500]
   KR - v72 - i18 - Sept 15 2004 - p904(1) [51-500]
   PW - v251 - i43 - Oct 25 2004 - p37(1) [51-500]

Lasky, Kathryn - *Blood Secret*
   y BL - v101 - i3 - Oct 1 2004 - p340(1) [51-500]
   y CCB-B - v58 - i2 - Oct 2004 - p85(2) [501+]
   y Kliatt - v38 - i4 - July 2004 - p8(2) [51-500]
   y KR - v72 - i14 - July 15 2004 - p689(1) [51-500]
   y SLJ - v50 - i8 - August 2004 - p124(1) [51-500]
   y VOYA - v27 - i4 - Oct 2004 - p316(1) [51-500]
Broken Song
   y BL - v101 - i9-10 - Jan 1 2005 - p859(1) [1-50]
   y HB - v81 - i2 - March-April 2005 - p204(1) [51-500]
   y KR - v73 - i3 - Feb 1 2005 - p178(1) [51-500]
The Capture (Illus. by Cowdrey, Richard)
   c CE - v80 - i5 - Mid-Summer 2004 - p274(1) [51-500]
The Capture
   c LibMed - v22 - i4 - Jan 2004 - p65(1) [501+]
First Painter
   c Teach Lib - v32 - i1 - Oct 2004 - p16(1) [501+]
Humphrey, Albert, and the Flying Machine (Illus. by Manders, John)
   c BL - v101 - i3 - Oct 1 2004 - p335(1) [51-500]
   c PW - v251 - i44 - Nov 1 2004 - p64(1) [501+]
   c SLJ - v50 - i10 - Oct 2004 - p120(1) [51-500]
Kazunomiya Prisoner of Heaven
   y CH Bwatch - Feb 2005 - pNA [51-500]
Lucille Camps In (Illus. by Hafner, Marilyn)
   c LibMed - v22 - i5 - Feb 2004 - p64(1) [501+]
The Man Who Made Time Travel
   c TC Math - v11 - i4 - Nov 2004 - p237(1) [501+]
A Voice of Her Own: The Story of Phillis Wheatley, Slave Poet (Illus. by Lee, Paul)
   c RT - v58 - i3 - Nov 2004 - p289(1) [1-50]

Lasser, William - *Benjamin V. Cohen: Architect of the New Deal*
   J Am St - v38 - i2 - August 2004 - p361(2) [501+]

Lassieur, Allison - *The Ancient Greeks*
   c SLJ - v51 - i2 - Feb 2005 - p148(1) [51-500]
The Ancient Romans
   y BL - v101 - i4 - Oct 15 2004 - p412(1) [51-500]
   y SLJ - v51 - i1 - Jan 2005 - p150(1) [51-500]

Lassister, Luke E. - *The Other Side of Middletown: Exploring Muncie's African American Community*
   Bl S - v34 - i3 - Fall 2004 - p73-73 [501+]

Lassiter, Linda Elizabeth - *An Etymological Vocabulary and Study of La Estoria de Los Godos, 1243*
   R&R Bk N - v19 - i4 - Nov 2004 - p215(1) [501+]

Lassiter, Luke E. - *The Other Side of Middletown: Exploring Muncie's African American Community*
   Black Iss - v7 - i2 - March-April 2005 - p40(2) [501+]
   Choice - v42 - i6 - Feb 2005 - p1083(1) [51-500]
   R&R Bk N - v19 - i3 - August 2004 - p74(1) [51-500]

Lassiter, Luke Eric - *Invitation to Anthropology*
   JRAI - v10 - i3 - Sept 2004 - p729(1) [501+]

Lasswitz, Kurd - *Auf Zwei Planeten*
   Comp L - v55 - i1 - Winter 2003 - p24 [501+]

Last Chance to Eat: The Fate of Taste in a Fast: Food World
   BIC - v33 - i8 - Nov 2004 - p26(2) [501+]

Laszlo, Chris - *The Sustainable Company: How to Create Lasting Value through Social and Environmental Performance*
   Choice - v41 - i7 - March 2004 - p1339(1) [501+]
   R&R Bk N - v19 - i1 - Feb 2004 - p88(1) [1-50]

Latham, Alison - *Sing, Ariel: Essays and Thoughts for Alexander Goehr's Seventieth Birthday*
   MT - v145 - i1886 - Spring 2004 - p97-101 [501+]
   R&R Bk N - v19 - i1 - Feb 2004 - p194(1) [501+]

Latham, David - *Haunted Texts: Studies in Pre-Raphaelitisim*
   CBRA - Annual 2003 - p114(2) [51-500]

Lathers, Marie - *Bodies of Art: French Literary Realism and the Artist's Model*
   NCFS - v32 - i3-4 - Spring-Summer 2004 - p374(3) [501+]

Lathrop, Charles E. - *The Literary Spy: The Ultimate Source for Quotations on Espionage and Intelligence*
   Choice - v42 - i6 - Feb 2005 - p1004(2) [51-500]
   LJ - v129 - i19 - Nov 15 2004 - p88(2) [51-500]

Lathrop, Douglas A. - *The Campaign Continues: How Political Consultants and Campaign Tactics Affect Public Policy*
   Choice - v41 - i7 - March 2004 - p1372(2) [501+]
   PSQ - v119 - i2 - Summer 2004 - p373(2) [501+]

Lathrop, Gordon W. - *Christian Assembly: Marks of the Church in a Pluralistic Age*
   Intpr - v59 - i1 - Jan 2005 - p107(1) [501+]
Holy Ground: A Liturgical Cosmology
   Intpr - v58 - i3 - July 2004 - p309(3) [501+]

Lathrop, Tad - *This Business of Music Marketing & Promotion*
   Choice - v41 - i7 - March 2004 - p1307(1) [501+]

Latifi, Afschineh - *Even After All This Time: A Story of Love, Revolution, and Leaving Iran*
   KR - v73 - i2 - Jan 15 2005 - p103(2) [501+]
   LJ - v130 - i4 - March 1 2005 - p96(1) [51-500]
   PW - v252 - i3 - Jan 17 2005 - p42(1) [51-500]

Latifi, Rifat - *Biology and Practice of Current Nutritional Support, 2nd Ed.*
   E-Streams - Nov 2004 - pNA [501+]

Latimer, Jon - *Burma: The Forgotten War*
   CR - v286 - i1669 - Feb 2005 - p127(1) [51-500]

The Latin Feminist Group - *Telling to Live: Latina Feminist Testimonios*
   Can Lit - i181 - Summer 2004 - p150-152 [501+]

Latini, Brunetto - *Li lives doug tresor*
   R&R Bk N - v19 - i3 - August 2004 - p1(1) [1-50]

Latini, G. - *Earthquake Resistant Engineering Structures IV*
   SciTech - v28 - i3 - Sept 2004 - p141(1) [51-500]

Latour, Bruno - *Politics of Nature: How to Bring the Sciences into Democracy*
   Am Sci - v93 - i1 - Jan-Feb 2005 - p89(2) [501+]
   QRB - v79 - i4 - Dec 2004 - p405(2) [501+]
   R&R Bk N - v19 - i3 - August 2004 - p172(1) [501+]
   Sci - v305 - i5688 - August 27 2004 - p1241(2) [501+]

LaTrenta, Gregory S. - *Atlas of Aesthetic Face and Neck Surgery*
   SciTech - v28 - i1 - March 2004 - p110(1) [51-500]

Lattimer, Heather - *Thinking through Genre: Units of Study in Reading and Writing Workshops 4-12*
   JAAL - v48 - i1 - Sept 2004 - p87(1) [501+]

Lau, Jenny Kwok Wah - *Multiple Modernities: Cinemas and Popular Media in Transcultural East Asia*
   FQ - v57 - i4 - Summer 2004 - p61(4) [501+]

Lau, Linda K. - *Managing Business with SAP: Planning, Implementation and Evaluation*
   R&R Bk N - v19 - i4 - Nov 2004 - p112(1) [51-500]

Lau, Matthias - *Pressepolitik als Chance: Staatliche Oeffentlichkeitsarbeit in den Laendern der Weimarer Republik*
   HNet - August 2004 - pNA [501+]

Lau, Richard R. - *Negative Campaigning: An Analysis of U.S. Senate Elections*
   R&R Bk N - v19 - i4 - Nov 2004 - p155(1) [501+]

Laub, John H. - *Shared Beginnings, Divergent Lives: Delinquent Boys to Age 70*
   Choice - v41 - i11-12 - July-August 2004 - p?129(1) [501+]
   TLS - i5304 - Nov 26 2004 - p9-10 [501+]

Laubach, Christyna M. - *Raptor!*
   c CH Bwatch - March 2005 - pNA [51-500]

Laube, Adolf - *Flugschriften Gegen die Reformation*
   Six Ct J - v35 - i1 - Spring 2004 - p186(2) [501+]

Laube, David R. - *Business-driven Information Technology: Answers to 100 Critical Questions for Every Manager*
   R&R Bk N - v19 - i1 - Feb 2004 - p86(1) [51-500]

Lauber, David - *Barth on the Descent into Hell: God, Antonement, and the Christian Life*
   R&R Bk N - v19 - i4 - Nov 2004 - p24(1) [51-500]

Lauber, Leah - *Soccer Dreams*
   c CH Bwatch - v14 - i9 - Sept 2004 - p2(1) [51-500]

Lauber, Lynn - *Listen to Me: Writing Life into Meaning*
   R&R Bk N - v19 - i1 - Feb 2004 - p221(1) [1-50]

Lauer, Betty - *Hiding in Plain Sight: The Incredible True Story of a German-Jewish Teenager's Struggle to Survive in Nazi-Occupied Poland*
   LJ - v129 - i15 - Sept 15 2004 - p65(1) [51-500]
   PW - v251 - i27 - July 5 2004 - p44(2) [51-500]

Lauer, Brett Fletcher - *Isn't it Romantic: 100 Love Poems by Younger American Poets*
   y Kliatt - v39 - i2 - March 2005 - p32(1) [51-500]

Laufer, Stefan - *Inflammation and Rheumatic Diseases: The Molecular Basis of Novel Therapies*
   SciTech - v28 - i1 - March 2004 - p108(1) [51-500]

Laufgraben, Jodi Levine - *Sustaining and Improving Learning Communities*
   R&R Bk N - v19 - i4 - Nov 2004 - p184(1) [501+]

Laughing Matters
   c LibMed - v23 - i3 - Nov-Dec 2004 - p84(1) [51-500]

Laughlin, Charles A. - *Chinese Reportage: The Aesthetics of Historical Experience*
   HJAS - v64 - i1 - June 2004 - p234-242 [501+]

Laughlin, Robert B. - *A Different Universe: Reinventing Physics from the Bottom Down*
New Sci - v185 - i2488 - Feb 26 2005 - p54(2) [51-500]
PW - v252 - i6 - Feb 7 2005 - p54(1) [51-500]

Laughlin, Sarah - *The Library's Continuous Improvement Fieldbook: 29 Ready-To-Use Tools*
ALJ - v53 - i4 - Nov 2004 - p411(1) [501+]

Laughton, Bruce - *William Coldstream*
Apo - v161 - i515 - Jan 2005 - p67(2) [501+]
Lon R Bks - v26 - i23 - Dec 2 2004 - p23(2) [501+]
Spec - v295 - i9184 - August 14 2004 - p36(1) [501+]

Lauglo, Jon - *Education, Training, and Contexts: Studies and Essays*
R&R Bk N - v19 - i1 - Feb 2004 - p190(1) [51-500]

Laumann, Edward O. - *The Sexual Organization of the City*
Choice - v42 - i4 - Dec 2004 - p743(1) [1-50]
G&L Rev W - v11 - i6 - Nov-Dec 2004 - p41(2) [501+]
The Social Organization of Sexuality: Sexual Practices in the United States
Globe & Mail - March 5 2005 - pD19 [501+]

Launchlan, Iain - *Russian Hide-and-Seek: The Tsarist Secret in St. Petersburg, 1906-1914*
Slav R - v63 - i2 - Summer 2004 - p405(2) [501+]

Launius, Roger D. - *Frontiers of Space Exploration, 2nd Ed.*
SB - v41 - i1 - Jan-Feb 2005 - p19(1) [501+]
Frontiers of Space Exploration
BL - v101 - i1 - Sept 1 2004 - p172(1) [1-50]
Choice - v42 - i1 - Sept 2004 - p127(1) [501+]
Reconsidering a Century of Flight
J Mil H - v68 - i3 - July 2004 - p1025-1026 [501+]

Laurel, Blossom - *Wednesday: New and Selected Poems*
ABR - v26 - i1 - Nov-Dec 2004 - p17(2) [501+]

Lauren, Emily - *Maryland*
c SLJ - v51 - i2 - Feb 2005 - p114(2) [51-500]

Laurence, Iain - *B for Buster*
c LibMed - v23 - i3 - Nov-Dec 2004 - p72(1) [51-500]

Laurence, Margaret - *Heart of a Stranger*
CBRA - Annual 2003 - p55(1) [51-500]

Laurence, Patricia - *Lily Briscoe's Chinese Eyes: Bloomsbury, Modernism, and China*
RCF - v24 - i3 - Fall 2004 - p136(2) [501+]
R&R Bk N - v19 - i1 - Feb 2004 - p234(1) [51-500]

Laurence, Ray - *The Roads of Roman Italy: Mobility and Cultural Change*
Class R - v53 - i2 - Nov 2003 - p412-414 [501+]

Laurenceson, James - *Financial Reform and Economic Development in China*
JEL - v41 - i4 - Dec 2003 - p1430(2) [501+]

Laurencin, Cato T. - *Bone Graft Substitutes*
SciTech - v28 - i1 - March 2004 - p113(1) [51-500]

Laurens, Stephanie - *The Truth about Love*
PW - v252 - i9 - Feb 28 2005 - p42(1) [51-500]

Laurent, Natacha - *L'Oeil du Kemlin: Cinema et censure en URSS sous Staline*
Slav R - v63 - i2 - Summer 2004 - p414(2) [501+]

Laurent, Patricia - *Santiago's Way*
BL - v101 - i7 - Dec 1 2004 - p637(1) [51-500]

Laurenti, Jean-Noel - *Valeurs Morales et Religieuses sur la Scene de l'Academie Royale de Musique: 1669-1737*
FS - v58 - i1 - Jan 2004 - p103(2) [501+]

Laurey, Rosemary - *Kiss Me Forever/ Love Me Forever*
ChrSFF&H - v26 - i10 - Oct 2004 - p27(1) [51-500]

Lauria, Frank - *Pitch Black*
ChrSFF&H - v26 - i9 - Sept 2004 - p36(2) [51-500]

Lauria-Santiago, Aldo - *Landscapes of Struggle: Politics, Society, and Community in El Salvador*
Choice - v42 - i5 - Jan 2005 - p912(1) [1-50]
HRNB - v33 - i1 - Fall 2004 - p19(1) [501+]

Lauristin, Marju - *The Challenge of the Russian Minority: Emerging Multicultural Democracy in Estonia*
E-A St - v56 - i4 - June 2004 - p624(625) [501+]

Laursen, Finn - *Comparative Regional Integration: Theoretical Perspectives*
R&R Bk N - v19 - i2 - May 2004 - p111(1) [51-500]

Lautenbach, Ebbing - *Practical Handbook for Healthcare Epidemiologists, 2nd Ed.*
SciTech - v28 - i4 - Dec 2004 - p85(1) [51-500]

Lauw, Darlene - *Air*
y CBRA - Annual 2003 - p572(3) [501+]
Earth and the Solar System
y CBRA - Annual 2003 - p572(3) [501+]
Electricity
y CBRA - Annual 2003 - p572(3) [501+]
Heat
y CBRA - Annual 2003 - p572(3) [501+]
Human Body
y CBRA - Annual 2003 - p572(3) [501+]
Light
y CBRA - Annual 2003 - p572(3) [501+]
Magnets
y CBRA - Annual 2003 - p573(2) [501+]
Materials
y CBRA - Annual 2003 - p573(2) [501+]
Motion
y CBRA - Annual 2003 - p573(2) [501+]
Sound
y CBRA - Annual 2003 - p573(2) [501+]
Water
y CBRA - Annual 2003 - p573(2) [501+]
Weather
y CBRA - Annual 2003 - p573(2) [501+]

Laven, David - *Venice and Veneita under the Habsburgs 1815-1835*
AHR - v109 - i2 - April 2004 - p640(2) [501+]

Lavender, Bee - *Mamaphonic: Balancing Motherhood and Other Creative Acts*
LJ - v129 - i18 - Nov 1 2004 - p110(1) [51-500]

Lavender, Peter - *Testing, Testing--Assessment in Adult Literacy, Language & Numeracy*
TES - v0 - i4586 - June 4 2004 - pss6(1) [501+]

Laverack, Glenn - *Health Promotion Practice: Power and Empowerment*
SciTech - v28 - i3 - Sept 2004 - p83(1) [501+]

Lavery, Brian - *Jack Aubrey Commands: An Historical Companion to the Naval World of Patrick O'Brian*
R&R Bk N - v19 - i1 - Feb 2004 - p239(1) [51-500]

Lavery, Jason - *Germany's Northern Challenge: The Holy Roman Empire and the Scandinavian Struggle for Baltic, 1563-1576*
AHR - v109 - i2 - April 2004 - p598(1) [501+]

Lavie, Peretz - *Restless Nights: Understanding Snoring and Sleep Apnea*
Choice - v42 - i1 - Sept 2004 - p138(1) [501+]

Laville, Helen - *Cold War Women: The International Activities of American Women's Organisations*
JAH - v91 - i1 - June 2004 - p301-302 [501+]

Lavin, Maud - *The Business of Holidays*
NYTBR - Dec 26 2004 - p23 [501+]

Lavinthal, Andrea - *The Hookup Handbook: A Single Girl's Guide to Living It Up*
LJ - v130 - i3 - Feb 15 2005 - p142(1) [51-500]

Lavrent'ev, M.M. - *Inverse Problems of Mathematical Physics*
SciTech - v28 - i1 - March 2004 - p46(1) [51-500]

Law Commission of Canada - *Personal Relationships of Dependence and Interdependence in Law*
CBRA - Annual 2003 - p318(1) [51-500]
What Is a Crime? Defining Criminal Conduct in Contemporary Society
Choice - v42 - i6 - Feb 2005 - p1107(1) [51-500]
Law&PolBR - Oct 2004 - pNA [501+]
R&R Bk N - v19 - i3 - August 2004 - p163(1) [501+]

Law, John - *Aircraft Stories: Decentering the Object in Technoscience*
CS - v33 - i1 - Jan 2004 - p116-117 [501+]
T&C - v45 - i2 - April 2004 - p406-412 [501+]

Law, Karina - *The Truth about Hansel and Gretel (Illus. by Counsell, Elke)*
c SLJ - v50 - i11 - Nov 2004 - p94(1) [51-500]

The Law School Survival Guide
NACEJou - v64 - i2 - Wntr 2004 - p12(1) [501+]

Law, Stephen - *The Xmas Files: The Philosophy of Christmas*
New Sci - v184 - i2476 - Dec 4 2004 - p55(1) [501+]

Lawerence, D.H. - *Late Essays and Articles*
Choice - v42 - i3 - Nov 2004 - p484(1) [1-50]

Lawler, Edward E. - *Human Resources Business Process Outsourcing: Transforming How HR Gets Its Work Done*
HR Mag - v50 - i2 - Feb 2005 - pS15(1) [501+]
R&R Bk N - v19 - i4 - Nov 2004 - p113(1) [51-500]

Lawler, Jennifer - *Dojo Wisdom for Writers: 100 Simple Ways to Become a More Inspired, Successful, and Fearless Writer*
LJ - v129 - i14 - Sept 1 2004 - p164(2) [501+]
Encyclopedia of the Byzantine Empire
BL - v101 - i9-10 - Jan 1 2005 - p902(1) [501+]
Choice - v42 - i5 - Jan 2005 - p838(1) [1-50]
Encyclopedia of Women in the Middle Ages
Wom HR - v13 - i1 - Spring 2004 - p142(3) [501+]
Punch: Why Women Participate in Violent Sports
SSJ - v21 - i1 - March 2004 - p110-112 [501+]

Lawler, Peter Augustine - *Democracy and Its Friendly Critics: Tocqueville and Political Life Today*
R&R Bk N - v19 - i4 - Nov 2004 - p150(1) [501+]

Lawler, Suzanne - *Cotton, Cornbread, and Conversations: 50 Adventures in Central Georgia*
R&R Bk N - v19 - i3 - August 2004 - p73(1) [51-500]

Lawlor, Edward F. - *Redesigning the Medicare Contract: Politics, Markets, and Agency*
JEL - v42 - i1 - March 2004 - p275(1) [501+]

Lawlor, Leonard - *Thinking through French Philosophy: The Being of the Question*
RM - v58 - i2 - Dec 2004 - p452(2) [501+]

Lawrence, Barry F. - *ERP in Distribution*
R&R Bk N - v19 - i2 - May 2004 - p116(1) [51-500]

Lawrence, Bruce B. - *New Faiths, Old Fears: Muslims and Other Asian Immigrants in American Religious Life*
TLS - i5288 - August 6 2004 - p3-4 [501+]

Lawrence, Candida - *Fear Itself*
y BL - v101 - i4 - Oct 15 2004 - p368(1) [51-500]

Lawrence, Caroline - *Assassins of Rome*
y VOYA - v27 - i3 - August 2004 - p181(1) [1-50]
The Gladiators from Capua
c Sch Lib - v52 - i3 - Autumn 2004 - p146(1) [501+]
The Thieves of Ostia: The Roman Mysteries (Read by Hicks, Kim). Audiobook Review
c Kliatt - v38 - i4 - July 2004 - p57(1) [51-500]
c SLJ - v50 - i7 - July 2004 - p60(1) [51-500]
The Twelve Tasks of Flavia Gemina
y SLJ - v51 - i2 - Feb 2005 - p138(1) [51-500]

Lawrence, Carolyn McKenzie - *Literacy for All Children: A Formula for Leaving No Child Behind*
R&R Bk N - v19 - i3 - August 2004 - p224(1) [1-50]

Lawrence, Colton - *Big Fat Paycheck: A Young Person's Guide to Writing for the Movies*
c BL - v101 - i1 - Sept 1 2004 - p79(1) [1-50]
y Ref Rev - Sept 2004 - pNA [501+]

Lawrence, D.H. - *Studies in Classic American Literature*
TLS - i5267 - March 12 2004 - p5-6 [501+]

Lawrence, David - *The Dead Sit Round in a Ring*
BooChiTr - June 6 2004 - p4(1) [501+]

Lawrence, Felicity - *Not on the Label: What Really Goes into the Food on Your Plate*
Lon R Bks - v26 - i22 - Nov 18 2004 - p28(2) [501+]

Lawrence, Iain - *B for Buster*
y BW - v34 - i29 - July 18 2004 - p11(1) [1-50]
y CCB-B - v58 - i1 - Sept 2004 - p26(1) [51-500]
y NYTBR - Sept 19 2004 - p16 [501+]
y PW - v251 - i27 - July 5 2004 - p57(1) [51-500]
c SLJ - v50 - i7 - July 2004 - p106(2) [51-500]
y VOYA - v27 - i3 - August 2004 - p219(1) [1-50]
Buccaneers
y CBRA - Annual 2003 - p496(1) [51-500]
The Convicts
y HB - v81 - i2 - March-April 2005 - p204(2) [51-500]
The Lightkeeper's Daughter
y Kliatt - v38 - i6 - Nov 2004 - p19(1) [51-500]
Lord of the Nutcracker Men
y CBRA - Annual 2003 - p496(1) [51-500]
The Smugglers
y BL - v101 - i1 - Sept 1 2004 - p121(1) [501+]

Lawrence, Jack - *They All Sang My Songs: The Times of My Life*
LJ - v129 - i16 - Oct 1 2004 - p82(2) [51-500]

Lawrence, James T. - *Human Rights in Asia and the Pacific*
Choice - v42 - i4 - Dec 2004 - p640(1) [1-50]

Lawrence, John C. - *Voyage to a Thousand Cares: Master's Mate Lawrence with the African Squadron, 1844-1846*
Choice - v42 - i2 - Oct 2004 - p356(1) [51-500]
J Mil H - v68 - i3 - July 2004 - p961 [501+]

Lawrence, Katherine - *Life in the Desert*
VOYA - v27 - i5 - Dec 2004 - p420(1) [51-500]

Le Blanc, Marcel - *The History of Siam, 1688*
  Choice - v42 - i3 - Nov 2004 - p541(1) [1-50]
Le Blanc, Paul - *Black Liberation and the American Dream: The Struggle for Racial and Economic Justice: Analysis, Strategy, Readings*
  R&R Bk N - v19 - i1 - Feb 2004 - p57(1) [51-500]
Le Bon, Gustave - *The Psychology of Revolution*
  R&R Bk N - v19 - i3 - August 2004 - p144(1) [1-50]
Le Calvez, Eric - *La Production du Descriptif: Exogenese et Endogenese de L'Education Sentimentale*
  NCFS - v33 - i1-2 - Fall-Winter 2004 - p199(3) [501+]
Le Carre, John - *Absolute Friends (Read by Le Carre, John). Audiobook Review*
  LJ - v129 - i14 - Sept 1 2004 - p202(1) [51-500]
  Absolute Friends
  BooChiTr - Jan 18 2004 - p3(1) [501+]
  Absolute Friends. Audiobook Review
  Globe & Mail - Jan 22 2005 - pD13 [51-500]
  Absolute Friends
  NYRB - v51 - i13 - August 12 2004 - p12(4) [501+]
  Atl - v295 - i3 - April 2005 - p111(6) [501+]
  Call for the Dead
  LJ - v129 - i14 - Sept 1 2004 - p204(1) [51-500]
  The Little Drummer Girl
  NYRB - v51 - i13 - August 12 2004 - p12(4) [501+]
  A Murder of Quality
  LJ - v129 - i14 - Sept 1 2004 - p204(1) [51-500]
Le Clezio, J.M.G. - *Wandering Star*
  BL - v101 - i2 - Sept 15 2004 - p208(2) [501+]
Le Doeuff, Michele - *The Sex of Knowing*
  Wom R Bks - v22 - i2 - Nov 2004 - p14(2) [501+]
Le Fanu, Joseph Sheridan - *Uncle Silas*
  BW - v34 - i5 - Feb 1 2004 - p15(1) [501+]
Le Grand, Julian - *Motivation Agency and Public Policy: Of Knights and Knaves, Pawns and Queens*
  AJPS - v39 - i3 - Nov 2004 - p680(2) [501+]
Le Guin, Ursula K. - *Changing Planes*
  NYTBR - August 8 2004 - p20 [501+]
  TLS - i5265 - Feb 27 2004 - p22-22 [501+]
  Gifts
  y BL - v100 - i22 - August 2004 - p1924(1) [51-500]
  y BL - v101 - i9-10 - Jan 1 2005 - p772(1) [51-500]
  y BW - v34 - i45 - Nov 7 2004 - p11(1) [501+]
  y CCB-B - v58 - i2 - Oct 2004 - p86(1) [51-500]
     HB - v80 - i5 - Sept-Oct 2004 - p589(1) [51-500]
  c Inst - v114 - i5 - Jan-Feb 2005 - p73(2) [501+]
  y Kliatt - v38 - i5 - Sept 2004 - p13(2) [51-500]
  c KR - v72 - i15 - August 1 2004 - p744(1) [51-500]
  c PW - v251 - i29 - July 19 2004 - p163(1) [501+]
  y SLJ - v50 - i9 - Sept 2004 - p210(1) [51-500]
     TLS - i5306 - Dec 10 2004 - p22(1) [501+]
  y VOYA - v27 - i5 - Dec 2004 - p408(1) [51-500]
  The Wave in the Mind: Talks and Essays on the Writer, the Reader, and the Imagination
  Wom R Bks - v21 - i10-11 - July 2004 - p25(2) [501+]
Le Guyader, Herve - *Etienne Geoffroy Saint-Hilaire, 1772-1844: A Visionary Naturalist.*
  QRB - v79 - i4 - Dec 2004 - p407(1) [501+]
  Etienne Geoffroy Saint-Hilaire, 1772-1884: A Visionary Naturalist
  Nature - v429 - i6987 - May 6 2004 - p18(2) [501+]
Le Hardy de Beaulieu, Antoine - *An Illustrated Guide to Maples*
  Choice - v41 - i7 - March 2004 - p1321(1) [501+]
  E-Streams - June 2004 - pNA [501+]
  SB - v40 - i3 - May-June 2004 - p116(1) [501+]
Le Jeune, Francoise - *Legacy and Contribution to Canada of European Female Immigrants*
  R&R Bk N - v19 - i1 - Feb 2004 - pNA [501+]
Le Jeune, Veronique - *Feeling Freakish? How to be Comfortable in Your Own Skin (Illus. by Princess H.)*
  y Sch Lib - v52 - i3 - Autumn 2004 - p164(1) [501+]
  y VOYA - v27 - i4 - Oct 2004 - p335(1) [501+]
Le Naour, Jean-Yves - *The Living Unknown Soldier: A Story of Grief and the Great War*
  BL - v101 - i1 - Sept 1 2004 - p42(1) [51-500]
  KR - v72 - i13 - July 1 2004 - p620(1) [501+]
  LJ - v129 - i13 - August 2004 - p94(1) [51-500]
Le Person, Xavier - *"Practiques" et "Practiqueurs": La vie Politique a la fin du Regne de Henri III*
  AHR - v109 - i3 - June 2004 - p984(2) [501+]
Le Quellec, Jean-Loic - *Impressions of the Sahara (Illus. by Baldizzone, Tiziana)*
  LJ - v129 - i16 - Oct 1 2004 - p78(1) [51-500]
  R&R Bk N - v19 - i3 - August 2004 - p58(1) [51-500]

Le Roux, Peter D. - *Management of Cerebral Aneurysms*
  SciTech - v28 - i1 - March 2004 - p105(1) [51-500]
Le Roy, Julien-David - *The Ruins of the Most Beautiful Monuments of Greece*
  Choice - v42 - i3 - Nov 2004 - p476(1) [1-50]
  TLS - i5302 - Nov 12 2004 - p12-13 [501+]
Le Roy, Michael K. - *Comparative Politics Using MicroCase ExplorIt, 3rd Ed.*
  R&R Bk N - v19 - i3 - August 2004 - p176(1) [501+]
Le Sueur, Andrew - *Building the UK's New Supreme Court: National and Comparative Perspectives*
  Law&PolBR - Dec 2004 - p953(3) [501+]
Le, Tao - *First Aid for the USMLE Step 2 CS*
  SciTech - v28 - i3 - Sept 2004 - p90(1) [51-500]
Le, Thi Diem Thuy - *The Gangster We Are All Looking For*
  Kliatt - v38 - i5 - Sept 2004 - p23(2) [501+]
  Sew R - v112 - i3 - Summer 2004 - p456-463 [501+]
Le Toquin, Alain - *The Most Beautiful Gardens in the World*
  BL - v101 - i7 - Dec 1 2004 - p625(2) [501+]
Le Tord, Biou - *A Story about Henri Matisse*
  c Teach Lib - v32 - i1 - Oct 2004 - p16(1) [51-500]
Le Vine, Victor T. - *Politics in Francophone Africa*
  R&R Bk N - v19 - i4 - Nov 2004 - p157(1) [501+]
Lea, Brent - *Mountain Odyssey: One Man's Summer in the Canadian Rockies*
  CBRA - Annual 2003 - p25(1) [51-500]
Lea, Virginia - *Identifying Race and Transforming Whiteness in the Classroom*
  R&R Bk N - v19 - i4 - Nov 2004 - p190(1) [501+]
Leach, Eleanor Winsor - *The Social Life of Painting in Ancient Rome and on the Bay of the Naples*
  Choice - v42 - i7 - March 2005 - p1215(2) [51-500]
Leach, Jim - *Candid Eyes: Essays on Canadian Documentaries*
  CBRA - Annual 2003 - p103(2) [501+]
  R&R Bk N - v19 - i1 - Feb 2004 - p225(1) [51-500]
Leachteneauer, Jon C. - *Electronic Image Display: Equipment Selection and Operation*
  SciTech - v28 - i1 - March 2004 - p164(1) [51-500]
Leacock, J.C. - *Our Colorado*
  R&R Bk N - v19 - i1 - Feb 2004 - p65(1) [51-500]
Leacock, Stephen - *Charles Dickens: His Life and Work*
  Globe & Mail - August 7 2004 - pD14 [1-50]
League of Women Voters (U.S.) - *Choosing the President 2004: A Citizen's Guide to the Electoral Process*
  c SLJ - v50 - i8 - August 2004 - p49(2) [51-500]
Leahy, Christopher W. - *The Birdwatcher's Companion to North American Birdlife*
  Am Sci - v92 - i5 - Sept-Oct 2004 - p469(1) [501+]
  Choice - v42 - i3 - Nov 2004 - p458(1) [1-50]
Leahy, J.F. - *Ask the Chief: Backbone of the Navy*
  R&R Bk N - v19 - i4 - Nov 2004 - p253(1) [501+]
Leahy, Michael - *When Nothing Else Matters: Michael Jordan's Last Comeback*
  BL - v101 - i5 - Nov 1 2004 - p453(2) [501+]
  KR - v72 - i17 - Sept 1 2004 - p850(1) [51-500]
  LJ - v129 - i16 - Oct 1 2004 - p89(2) [51-500]
  PW - v251 - i38 - Sept 20 2004 - p53(1) [51-500]
Leahy, Robert L. - *Cognitive Therapy Techniques: A Practioner's Guide*
  SciTech - v28 - i1 - March 2004 - p100(1) [51-500]
  Cognitive Therapy Techniques: A Practitioner's Guide
  E-Streams - Oct 2004 - pNA [501+]
Leak, Graeme - *Performance Making: A Manual for Music Workshops*
  R&R Bk N - v19 - i4 - Nov 2004 - p198(1) [501+]
Leake, Elizabeth - *The Reinvention of Ignazio Silone*
  R&R Bk N - v19 - i1 - Feb 2004 - p232(1) [51-500]
Leal, Robert Barry - *Wilderness in the Bible*
  R&R Bk N - v19 - i4 - Nov 2004 - p22(1) [51-500]
Leander, Kevin M. - *Spatializing Literacy Research and Practice*
  R&R Bk N - v19 - i4 - Nov 2004 - p189(1) [501+]
Leap, William L. - *Speaking in Queer Tongues: Globalization and Gay Language*
  Choice - v42 - i1 - Sept 2004 - p147(1) [501+]
Leapman, Michael - *Inigo: The Troubled Life of Inigo Jones, Architect of the English Renaissance*
  Choice - v42 - i6 - Feb 2005 - p1086(1) [51-500]
  LJ - v129 - i12 - July 2004 - p79(1) [51-500]

Lear, Edward - *The Book of Nonsense*
  c RT - v57 - Sept 2003 - p97 [51-500]
  Nonsense! (Illus. by Fisher, Valorie)
  c KR - v72 - i16 - August 15 2004 - p808(1) [51-500]
  c PW - v251 - i44 - Nov 1 2004 - p61(1) [501+]
  c SLJ - v50 - i11 - Nov 2004 - p127(2) [51-500]
  The Quangle Wangle's Hat (Illus. by Voce, Louise)
  c KR - v72 - i24 - Dec 15 2004 - p1204(1) [51-500]
  c PW - v252 - i4 - Jan 24 2005 - p242(1) [51-500]
  c SLJ - v51 - i1 - Jan 2005 - p112(1) [51-500]
Lears, Jackson - *Something for Nothing: Luck in America*
  AHR - v109 - i2 - April 2004 - p510(2) [501+]
  NEQ - v77 - i3 - Sept 2004 - p517-520 [501+]
  RAH - v32 - i4 - Dec 2004 - p532-538 [501+]
Leary, Ann - *An Innocent, A Broad*
  NYT - Nov 7 2004 - pST13 [501+]
Leatherbarrow, David - *Uncommon Ground*
  JAAC - v61 - Winter 2003 - p81 [501+]
Leatherdale, Mary Beth - *My Class and Me: 1st Grade (Illus. by Ritchie, Scot)*
  c CBRA - Annual 2003 - p554(1) [51-500]
  My Class and Me: 2nd Grade (Illus. by Ritchie, Scot)
  c CBRA - Annual 2003 - p554(1) [51-500]
  My Class and Me: 3rd Grade (Illus. by Ritchie, Scot)
  c CBRA - Annual 2003 - p554(1) [51-500]
  My Class and Me: Kindergarten (Illus. by Ritchie, Scot)
  c CBRA - Annual 2003 - p554(1) [51-500]
Leatherman, Janie - *From Cold War to Democratic Peace: Third Parties, Peaceful Change, and the OSCE*
  Choice - v41 - i11-12 - July-August 2004 - p2121(1) [501+]
  From Cold War to democratic peace; third parties, peaceful change, and the OSCE
  R&R Bk N - v19 - i1 - Feb 2004 - p38(1) [1-50]
Leavell, Chuck - *Forever Green: The History and Hope of the American Forest, 2nd Ed.*
  E-Streams - Nov 2004 - pNA [501+]
Leaver, Peter K. - *The History of Moorfields Eye Hospital, Vol. 3*
  SciTech - v28 - i4 - Dec 2004 - p110(1) [51-500]
Leavey, Peggy Dymond - *Deep End Gang*
  c CBRA - Annual 2003 - p497(2) [51-500]
Leavitt, Caroline - *Girls in Trouble*
  BW - v34 - i3 - Jan 18 2004 - p5(1) [51-500]
Leavitt, David - *The Body of Jonah Boyd*
  BW - v34 - i27 - July 4 2004 - p13(1) [501+]
  NS - v133 - i4716 - Nov 29 2004 - p48(1) [51-500]
  TLS - i5302 - Nov 12 2004 - p23(1) [501+]
Leavitt, Harold J. - *Top Down: Why Hierarchies Are Here to Stay and How to Manage Them More Effectively*
  Time - v165 - i5 - Jan 31 2005 - pA4 [501+]
Leavitt, Martine - *Heck Superhero*
  c BIC - v33 - i7 - Oct 2004 - p39(1) [501+]
  y BL - v101 - i3 - Oct 1 2004 - p323(1) [51-500]
  c CCB-B - v58 - i2 - Oct 2004 - p85(2) [501+]
  y HB - v81 - i1 - Jan-Feb 2005 - p96(1) [51-500]
  c Inst - v114 - i5 - Jan-Feb 2005 - p73(2) [501+]
  c KR - v72 - i17 - Sept 1 2004 - p869(1) [51-500]
  c SLJ - v50 - i10 - Oct 2004 - p171(1) [51-500]
  c Res Links - v10 - i2 - Dec 2004 - p20(2) [51-500]
  Tom Finder
  y CBRA - Annual 2003 - p498(1) [51-500]
Leavitt, Sarah Abigail - *From Catharine Beecher to Martha Stewart: A Cultural History of Domestic Advice*
  JIH - v35 - i2 - Autumn 2004 - p316(2) [501+]
  NWSA Jnl - v16 - i3 - Fall 2004 - p217(3) [501+]
Leazes, Francis J. - *Providence, the Renaissance City*
  Choice - v42 - i6 - Feb 2005 - p1063(1) [51-500]
  R&R Bk N - v19 - i4 - Nov 2004 - p136(1) [51-500]
Lebans, Gertrude - *In All Things Goodness: A Christian Vision for the 21st Century*
  CBRA - Annual 2003 - p93(1) [51-500]
LeBaron, Michelle - *Bridging Cultural Conflict: A New Approach for a Changing World*
  R&R Bk N - v19 - i4 - Nov 2004 - p11(1) [51-500]
Lebbon, Tim - *Dead Man's Hands*
  MFSF - v108 - i1 - Jan 2005 - p31(5) [501+]
  Fears Unnamed
  NYTBR - Oct 31 2004 - p18 [501+]
LeBeau, Bryan F. - *The Atheist: Madalyn Murray O'Hair*
  AHR - v109 - i3 - June 2004 - p942(1) [501+]
Lebedev, Leonid P. - *Approximating Perfection: A Mathematician's Journey into the World of Mechanics*
  Choice - v42 - i3 - Nov 2004 - p521(1) [1-50]
Lebedoff, David - *The Uncivil War: How a New Elite Is Destroying Our Democracy*
  NYTBR - Nov 28 2004 - p21 [501+]

Leben, Ulrich - *Object Design in the Age of Enlightenment: The History of the Royal Free Drawing School in Paris*
   Mag Antiq - v167 - i1 - Jan 2005 - p128(1) [51-500]
   Mag Antiq - v167 - i2 - Feb 2005 - p54(1) [51-500]
   Mag Antiq - v167 - i3 - March 2005 - p58(1) [501+]

LeBesco, Kathleen - *Revolting Bodies?: The Struggle to Redefine Fat Identity*
   SciTech - v28 - i3 - Sept 2004 - p104(1) [51-500]

LeBey, Barbara - *Remarried with Children: Ten Secrets for Successfully Blending and Extending Your Family*
   Globe & Mail - Oct 9 2004 - pF6 [501+]
Remarried with Children: Ten Secrets for Successfully Blending and Extending Your Family
   LJ - v129 - i17 - Oct 15 2004 - p77(1) [51-500]

LeBlanc, Barbara - *Postcards from Acadie: Grand Pre, Evangeline and the Acadian Identity*
   CBRA - Annual 2003 - p343(1) [501+]

LeBlanc, David C. - *Statistics: Concepts and Applications for Science*
   QRB - v79 - i4 - Dec 2004 - p409(1) [501+]
Workbook to Accompany Statistics: Concepts and Applications for Science
   QRB - v79 - i4 - Dec 2004 - p409(1) [501+]

LeBlanc, Dee-Ann - *Linux for Dummies, 5th Ed.*
   SciTech - v28 - i3 - Sept 2004 - p26(1) [51-500]

Leblanc, Louise - *Maddie's Millionaire Dreams (Illus. by Gay, Marie-Louise)*
   y Can CL - i111-112 - Fall-Winter 2003 - p134(6) [501+]

LeBlanc, Maurice - *Hollow Needle*
   ChrSFF&H - v26 - i10 - Oct 2004 - p28(1) [51-500]

Leblanc, Suzanne - *Cassiar, a Jewel in the Wilderness*
   CBRA - Annual 2003 - p343(1) [51-500]

LeBlond, Richard F. - *DeGowin's Diagnostic Examination, 8th Ed.*
   SciTech - v28 - i3 - Sept 2004 - p90(1) [51-500]

LeBor, Adam - *Milosevic: A Biography*
   Choice - v42 - i5 - Jan 2005 - p928(1) [51-500]
   HRNB - v33 - i1 - Fall 2004 - p24(2) [501+]

Leboutillier, Nate - *Day in the Life of a Zookeeper*
   c SLJ - v51 - i1 - Jan 2005 - p109(1) [51-500]

Lebovics, Herman - *Bringing the Empire Back Home: France in the Global Age*
   BW - v34 - i41 - Oct 10 2004 - p6(1) [501+]
   Choice - v42 - i6 - Feb 2005 - p1092(1) [51-500]

Lebow, Richard Ned - *The Tragic Vision of Politics: Ethics, Interests and Orders*
   Choice - v42 - i2 - Oct 2004 - p370(1) [51-500]

Lebowitz, Michael A. - *Beyond Capital: Marx's Political Economy of the Working Class*
   JEL - v42 - i1 - March 2004 - p241(1) [501+]

Lebsock, Suzanne - *A Murder in Virginia: Southern Justice on Trial*
   HNet - Oct 2004 - pNA [501+]
   JAH - v91 - i1 - June 2004 - p254-255 [501+]
   JSH - v70 - i3 - August 2004 - p704(2) [501+]
   NYRB - v51 - i12 - July 15 2004 - p50(2) [501+]

Lebwohl, Mark G. - *Skin and Systemic Disease: A Color Atlas and Text, 2nd Ed.*
   SciTech - v28 - i1 - March 2004 - p119(1) [51-500]

Lecca, Pedro J. - *Allied Health: Practice Issues and Trends in the New Millennium*
   E-Streams - June 2004 - pNA [501+]
   SciTech - v28 - i1 - March 2004 - p78(1) [51-500]

Leckie, Scott - *Returning Home: Housing and Property Restitution Rights of Refugees and Displaced Persons*
   R&R Bk N - v19 - i1 - Feb 2004 - pNA [51-500]

LeClaire, Anne D. - *The Law of Bound Hearts*
   BL - v100 - i22 - August 2004 - p1900(1) [51-500]
   KR - v72 - i13 - July 1 2004 - p599(1) [501+]
   LJ - v129 - i12 - July 2004 - p72(1) [51-500]

Leclercq, Dom Jean - *Camaldolese Extraordinary: The Life, Doctrine, and Rule of Blessed Paul Giustiniani*
   CHR - v90 - i3 - July 2004 - p543(2) [501+]

LeClercq, Terri - *Guide to Legal Writing Style, 3rd Ed.*
   R&R Bk N - v19 - i4 - Nov 2004 - p165(1) [501+]

Lecompte, Luc - *Rouge malsain*
   Can Lit - i182 - Autumn 2004 - p144(2) [501+]

LeCompte, Tom - *The Last Sure Thing*
   Bwatch - v26 - i9 - Sept 2004 - p4(1) [51-500]

Ledbetter, Grace M. (b. 1965-) - *Poetics before Plato: Interpretation and Authority in Early Greek Theories of Poetry*
   Class R - v54 - i1 - May 2004 - p66(2) [501+]

Leder, Michelle - *Financial Fine Print: Uncovering a Company's True Value*
   R&R Bk N - v19 - i2 - May 2004 - p123 [51-500]

Lederer, Richard - *The Revenge of Anguished English*
   SEP - v277 - i2 - March-April 2005 - p30(1) [501+]

Lederer, Susan E. - *Frankenstein: Penetrating the Secrets of Nature*
   SFS - v31 - i1 - March 2004 - p147-149 [501+]

Lederman, Leon Max - *Portraits of Great American Scientists*
   Isis - v95 - i3 - Sept 2004 - p532(2) [501+]
Symmetry and the Beautiful Universe
   Choice - v42 - i7 - March 2005 - p1265(1) [51-500]
   PW - v251 - i35 - August 30 2004 - p43(1) [51-500]
   Sci Teach - v72 - i3 - March 2005 - p82-4 [501+]
   SciTech - v28 - i4 - Dec 2004 - p13(1) [1-50]

Ledford, Janice K. - *Certified Ophthalmic Technician Exam Review Manual, 2nd Ed.*
   SciTech - v28 - i3 - Sept 2004 - p114(1) [51-500]

Ledgin, Stephanie P. - *Homegrown Music: Discovering Bluegrass*
   LJ - v129 - i16 - Oct 1 2004 - p83(1) [51-500]

LeDonne, John P. - *The Grand Strategy of the Russian Empire, 1650-1831*
   Choice - v42 - i1 - Sept 2004 - p168(2) [501+]
   J Mil H - v68 - i4 - Oct 2004 - p1250-1251 [501+]

LeDoux, Joseph - *Self: From Soul to Brain.*
   SciTech - v28 - i3 - Sept 2004 - p3(1) [501+]

LeDuc, Lawrence - *The Politics of Direct Democracy: Referendums in Global Perspective*
   R&R Bk N - v19 - i3 - August 2004 - p176(1) [501+]

Lee, Anthony W. - *Yun Gee: Poetry, Writings, Art, Memories*
   R&R Bk N - v19 - i1 - Feb 2004 - p209(1) [51-500]

Lee, Bill - *Have Glove, Will Travel: Adventures of a Baseball Vagabond*
   BL - v101 - i9-10 - Jan 1 2005 - p801(1) [51-500]
   KR - v72 - i24 - Dec 15 2004 - p1185(1) [501+]
Have glove will travel: Adventures of a Baseball Vagabond
   PW - v251 - i51 - Dec 20 2004 - p43(1) [51-500]

Lee, Bradford A. - *The Dream of Civilized Warfare: World War I Flying Aces and the American Imagination*
   J Mil H - v68 - i3 - July 2004 - p983-985 [501+]
Strategic Logic and Political Rationality: Essays in Honor of Michael I. Handel
   R&R Bk N - v19 - i1 - Feb 2004 - p254(1) [51-500]

Lee, Cecilia Hae-Jin - *Eating Korean: From Barbecue to Kimchi, Recipes from My Home*
   LJ - v130 - i3 - Feb 15 2005 - p153(1) [51-500]

Lee, Chang-Rae - *Aloft (Read by Leslie, Don). Audiobook Review*
   BL - v100 - i22 - August 2004 - p1952(1) [51-500]
Aloft
   ABR - v26 - i2 - Jan-Feb 2005 - p16(2) [501+]
   BW - v34 - i12 - March 21 2004 - p7(1) [501+]
   New York - v37 - i8 - March 8 2004 - p66(2) [501+]
   NYTBR - March 13 2005 - p32 [501+]
   Time - v165 - i11 - March 14 2005 - p68 [501+]

Lee, Cheng-Few - *Advances in Financial Planning and Forecasting*
   JEL - v41 - i4 - Dec 2003 - p1368(2) [501+]

Lee, Cheng-Sheng - *Biosecurity in Aquaculture Production Systems: Exclusion of Pathogens and Other Undesirables*
   SciTech - v28 - i3 - Sept 2004 - p133(1) [51-500]

Lee, Chinlun - *Good Dog, Paw!*
   c Sch Lib - v52 - i3 - Autumn 2004 - p132(1) [501+]
   c SLJ - v50 - i8 - August 2004 - p89(1) [51-500]

Lee, Christopher - *Meadows*
   Bwatch - v26 - i9 - Sept 2004 - p2(2) [51-500]
This Sceptred Isle, 1901-1919 (Read by Massey, Anna). Audiobook Review
   y Kliatt - v39 - i2 - March 2005 - p57(1) [501+]

Lee, Claudia M. - *Messengers of Rain and Other Poems from Latin America (Illus. by Yockteng, Rafael)*
   c Can Lit - i182 - Autumn 2004 - p125(3) [501+]

Lee, Cyndi - *Yoga Body, Buddha Mind*
   BL - v101 - i2 - Sept 15 2004 - p188(2) [51-500]
   LJ - v129 - i14 - Sept 1 2004 - p176(1) [51-500]

Lee David W. - *2004 Handbook of Section 1983 Litigation*
   R&R Bk N - v19 - i4 - Nov 2004 - p167(1) [501+]

Lee, Debbie - *Slavery and the Romantic Imagination*
   Critm - v46 - i2 - Spring 2004 - p299(5) [501+]

Lee, Dennis - *So Cool*
   y Globe & Mail - Dec 11 2004 - pD17 [501+]
   y Res Links - v10 - i3 - Feb 2005 - p37(2) [501+]

Lee, Der-Horng - *Urban and Regional Transportation Modeling: Essays in Honor of David Boyce*
   R&R Bk N - v19 - i3 - August 2004 - p121(1) [51-500]

Lee, Don - *Country of Origin*
   Ent W - i774 - July 16 2004 - p82 [501+]
   Globe & Mail - August 21 2004 - pD12 [51-500]
   Globe & Mail - Nov 27 2004 - pD18 [1-50]
   NYTBR - July 11 2004 - p8 [501+]

Lee, Edward (b. 1957-) - *Messenger*
   ChrSFF&H - v26 - i10 - Oct 2004 - p28(1) [51-500]

Lee, Edward Jae-Suk - *The Good Man*
   BL - v101 - i6 - Nov 15 2004 - p556(1) [51-500]
   LJ - v129 - i20 - Dec 1 2004 - p101(1) [51-500]

Lee, Ellie - *Abortion, Motherhood, and Mental Health: Medicalizing Reproduction in the United States and Great Britain*
   CS - v33 - i6 - Nov 2004 - p727(2) [501+]

Lee, Erika - *At America's Gates: Chinese Immigration during the Exclusion Era, 1882-1943*
   JEL - v41 - i4 - Dec 2003 - p1404(1) [501+]
   RAH - v32 - i4 - Dec 2004 - p539-544 [501+]
   JAH - v91 - i2 - Sept 2004 - p666(2) [501+]

Lee, Eun-Joo - *Integrated Korean: Advanced 1*
   R&R Bk N - v19 - i4 - Nov 2004 - p219(1) [501+]
Integrated Korean: Advanced 2
   R&R Bk N - v19 - i4 - Nov 2004 - p219(1) [501+]

Lee, Gregory D. - *Global Drug Enforcement: Practical Investigative Techniques*
   R&R Bk N - v19 - i1 - Feb 2004 - p144(1) [51-500]

Lee, Helen Morton - *Tongans Overseas: Between Two Shores*
   Cont Pac - v16 - i2 - Fall 2004 - p455(5) [501+]

Lee, Henry C. - *Cracking More Cases: The Forensic Science of Solving Crimes*
   PW - v251 - i31 - August 2 2004 - p65(1) [51-500]
   R&R Bk N - v19 - i4 - Nov 2004 - p148(1) [501+]
   SB - v41 - i1 - Jan-Feb 2005 - p18(1) [501+]
   Choice - v42 - i5 - Jan 2005 - p873(1) [1-50]

Lee, Hermione - *Body Parts: Essays on Life-Writing*
   Spec - v297 - i9211 - Feb 19 2005 - p38(2) [501+]
Virginia Woolf's Nose: Essays on Biography
   HM - v310 - i1858 - March 2005 - p89(2) [501+]
   PW - v252 - i6 - Feb 7 2005 - p51(1) [51-500]

Lee, Ida J. - *Lancaster County, Virginia, Marriage Bonds, 1652-1850*
   EFHM - v58 - i2 - March-April 2004 - p91(1) [51-500]

Lee, J. Ardian - *Sword of the White Rose*
   y Kliatt - v38 - i5 - Sept 2004 - p30(2) [51-500]

Lee, James Kyung-Jin - *Urban Triage: Race and Fictions of Multiculturalism*
   R&R Bk N - v19 - i3 - August 2004 - p66(1) [51-500]

Lee, James Ward - *Adventures with a Texas Humanist*
   Roundup M - v12 - i3 - Feb 2005 - p19(1) [51-500]

Lee, Janie - *Arshile Gorky: A Retrospective of Drawings*
   Lon R Bks - v26 - i7 - April 1 2004 - p7(2) [501+]

Lee, Jeffrey - *True Blue: A Novel*
   LibMed - v22 - i6 - March 2004 - p67(1) [51-500]

Lee, Jennifer - *Civility in the City: Blacks, Jews, and Koreans in Urban America*
   CS - v33 - i2 - March 2004 - p163-164 [501+]

Lee, John B. - *In the Terrible Weather of Guns*
   CBRA - Annual 2003 - p55(2) [51-500]

Lee, Jon - *A First Course in Combinatorial Optimization*
   Choice - v42 - i3 - Nov 2004 - p521(1) [501+]

Lee, Josephine - *Recollecting Early Asian America: Essays in Cultural History*
   JAH - v91 - i1 - June 2004 - p257-257 [501+]

Lee, Kathy H. (b. 1968-) - *Solutions for Early Childhood Directors: Real Answers to Everyday Challenges*
   CE - v80 - i5 - Mid-Summer 2004 - p278(1) [51-500]

Lee, Katie - *Sandstone Seduction: Rivers and Lovers, Canyons and Friends*
   R&R Bk N - v19 - i4 - Nov 2004 - p68(1) [51-500]

Lee, Kelley - *Globalization and Health: An Introduction*
   Choice - v42 - i1 - Sept 2004 - p138(1) [51-500]

Lee, Lanniko L. - *Shaping Survival: Essays by four American Indian Tribal Women.*
   Am Ind CRJ - v27 - i2 - Spring 2003 - p141-144 [501+]

Lehey, Greg - *The Complete FreeBSD: Documentation from the Source. 4th Ed.*
SciTech - v28 - i3 - Sept 2004 - p25(1) [51-500]
Lehman, Barbara - *The Red Book*
c HB - v80 - i5 - Sept-Oct 2004 - p570(2) [51-500]
The Red Book (Illus. by Lehman, Barbara)
c BL - v101 - i3 - Oct 1 2004 - p335(1) [51-500]
HB - v81 - i1 - Jan-Feb 2005 - p13(1) [51-500]
KR - v72 - i17 - Sept 1 2004 - p869(1) [51-500]
c PW - v251 - i37 - Sept 13 2004 - p78(1) [51-500]
c SLJ - v50 - i11 - Nov 2004 - p110(1) [51-500]
Lehman, Carol M. - *Business Communication, 14th Ed.*
R&R Bk N - v19 - i2 - May 2004 - p120 [51-500]
Lehman, David - *When a Woman Loves a Man*
LJ - v130 - i3 - Feb 15 2005 - p135(1) [51-500]
Lehman, Jeffrey - *West's Encyclopedia of American Law*
LJ - v130 - i1 - Jan 1 2005 - p158(1) [51-500]
Lehman, Peter - *Roy Orbison: The Invention of an Alternative Rock Masculinity*
Am St - v45 - i1 - Spring 2004 - p169-170 [501+]
Lehman-Wilzig, Tami - *Keeping the Promise: A Torah's Journey (Illus. by Orback, Craig)*
c SLJ - v50 - i8 - August 2004 - p111(1) [51-500]
Lehmann, Courtney - *Shakespeare Remains: Theatre to Film, Early Modern to Postmodern*
Six Ct J - v34 - i4 - Winter 2003 - p1177-1178 [501+]
Lehmann, Detlef - *Mathematical Methods of Many-Body Quantum Field Theory*
SciTech - v28 - i4 - Dec 2004 - p48(1) [51-500]
Lehmann, Jennifer - *Current Perspectives in Social Theory. Vol. 21*
CS - v33 - i1 - Jan 2004 - p112-113 [501+]
Lehmann, Kay Johnson - *How to Be a Great Online Teacher*
R&R Bk N - v19 - i3 - August 2004 - p215(1) [1-50]
Surviving Inclusion
Choice - v42 - i4 - Dec 2004 - p710(1) [1-50]
R&R Bk N - v19 - i4 - Nov 2004 - p192(1) [501+]
Lehmann, Ulrich - *Tigersprung: Fashion in Modernity*
JMH - v76 - i4 - Dec 2004 - p943(3) [501+]
Lehmkuhl, Ursula - *Deutschland, Grossbritannien, Amerika: Politik, Gesellschaft und Internationale Geschichte im 20. Jahrhundert*
HNet - Oct 2004 - pNA [501+]
Lehner, Ernst - *Folklore and Symbolism of Flowers, Plants, and Trees: With Over 200 Rare and Unusual Floral Designs and Illustrations*
R&R Bk N - v19 - i3 - August 2004 - p85(1) [51-500]
Lehnert, Hendrik - *Pheochromocytoma: Pathophysiology and Clinical Management*
SciTech - v28 - i1 - March 2004 - p92(1) [51-500]
Lehnert, Herbert - *A Companion to the Works of Thomas Mann*
Choice - v42 - i5 - Jan 2005 - p857(1) [1-50]
Lehning, James R. - *To Be a Citizen: the Political Culture of the Early French Third Republic*
JMH - v76 - i4 - Dec 2004 - p968(3) [501+]
Lehoucq, Fabrice E. - *Stuffing the Ballot Box: Fraud, Electoral Reform, and Democratization in Costa Rica*
Ams - v61 - i2 - Oct 2004 - p341(2) [501+]
CS - v33 - i6 - Nov 2004 - p746(1) [1-50]
Lehr, Jay H. - *Wiley's Remediation Technologies Handbook: Major Contaminant Chemicals and Chemical Groups*
SciTech - v28 - i3 - Sept 2004 - p148(1) [51-500]
Lehr, Jennifer - *Ill-Equipped for a Life of Sex: A Memoir*
BL - v101 - i1 - Sept 1 2004 - p2(1) [51-500]
Ent W - i790 - Oct 29 2004 - p70 [501+]
PW - v251 - i31 - August 2 2004 - p62(1) [501+]
Lehrak, Otto J. - *First Battle: Operation Starlite and the Beginning of the Blood Debt in Vietnam*
R&R Bk N - v19 - i4 - Nov 2004 - p48(1) [51-500]
Lehrer, Jim - *The Franklin Affair*
KR - v73 - i3 - Feb 1 2005 - p141(1) [501+]
LJ - v130 - i4 - March 1 2005 - p78(2) [51-500]
PW - v252 - i9 - Feb 28 2005 - p39(1) [51-500]
Lehrhaupt, Linda Myoki - *T'ai Chi As a Path of Wisdom*
Parabola - v29 - i1 - Spring 2004 - p116(4) [501+]
Lehrich, Christopher I. - *Language of Demons and Angels: Cornelius Agrippa's Occult Philosophy*
R&R Bk N - v19 - i1 - Feb 2004 - p2(1) [51-500]
Lehring, Gary L. - *Officially Gay: The Political Construction of Sexuality by the U.S. Military*
CS - v33 - i6 - Nov 2004 - p710(3) [501+]
Lam Bk Rpt - v13 - i1-2 - August-Sept 2004 - p16(2) [501+]
PSQ - v119 - i2 - Summer 2004 - p389(2) [501+]

Lehtinen, Ari Aukusti - *Politics of Forests: Northern Forest-Industrial Regimes in the Age of Globalization*
R&R Bk N - v19 - i4 - Nov 2004 - p246(1) [501+]
Lehtonen, Risto - *Practical Methods for Design and Analysis of Complex Surveys, 2nd Ed.*
SciTech - v28 - i3 - Sept 2004 - p37(1) [51-500]
Leib, Ethan J. - *Deliberative Democracy in America: A Proposal for a Popular Branch of Government*
Choice - v42 - i3 - Nov 2004 - p565(1) [1-50]
PSQ - v119 - i3 - Fall 2004 - p544(2) [501+]
Leiber, Fritz (b. 1910-) - *Gonna Roll the Bones (Illus. by Wiesner, David)*
c BIC - v33 - i8 - Nov 2004 - p35(2) [501+]
c BW - v34 - i43 - Oct 24 2004 - p11(1) [51-500]
c CCB-B - v58 - i3 - Nov 2004 - p132(2) [501+]
c PW - v251 - i41 - Oct 11 2004 - p80(1) [51-500]
c SLJ - v50 - i12 - Dec 2004 - p210(2) [51-500]
Leiberg, Carolyn - *West with Hopeless*
y BL - v100 - i22 - August 2004 - p1920(1) [51-500]
Leibovitz, Annie - *American Music*
New Cr - v39 - i6 - March 2005 - p18(2) [501+]
NYTBR - Dec 19 2004 - p30 [501+]
Leibs, Andrew - *Sports and the Games of Renassiance*
Choice - v42 - i7 - March 2005 - p1266(1) [51-500]
Leibson-Hawkins, Beth - *I'm Too Young to Have Breast Cancer!: Regain Control of Your Life, Career, Family, Sexuality, and Faith*
LJ - v129 - i14 - Sept 1 2004 - p184(2) [501+]
Leicester, Mal - *Lifelong Learning: Education Across the Lifespan*
TCR - v106 - i12 - Dec 2004 - p2315(4) [501+]
Leichsenring, Jana - *Frauen und Widerstand.*
HNet - July 2004 - pNA [501+]
Leider, Emily - *Dark Lover: The Life and Death of Rudolph Valentino*
Lon R Bks - v26 - i24 - Dec 16 2004 - p31(2) [501+]
Leiding, Darlene - *Managers Make the Difference: Managing vs. Leading in Our Schools*
R&R Bk N - v19 - i3 - August 2004 - p222(1) [1-50]
Leifer, Gloria - *Growth and Development across the Lifespan: A Health Promotion Focus*
SciTech - v28 - i1 - March 2004 - p82(1) [51-500]
Leifer, Michael - *Singapore's Foreign Policy: Coping with Vulnerability*
JAS - v63 - i3 - August 2004 - p849-850 [501+]
Leifs, Igo - *Weimarer Republik 1918-1933*
Ger Q - v77 - i2 - Spring 2004 - p238-240 [501+]
Leigh, Andrew - *Dramatic Success: Theatre Techniques to Transform and Inspire Your Working Life*
R&R Bk N - v19 - i3 - August 2004 - p126(1) [51-500]
Leigh, David S. - *Ichiro Suzuki*
c SLJ - v50 - i11 - Nov 2004 - p168(1) [51-500]
Leigh, G.J. - *The World's Greatest Fix: A History of Nitrogen and Agriculture*
Choice - v42 - i6 - Feb 2005 - p1046(1) [51-500]
Nature - v431 - i7011 - Oct 21 2004 - p909(2) [501+]
SciTech - v28 - i4 - Dec 2004 - p123 [51-500]
Leigh, John - *Football Lexicon: A Dictionary of Usage in Football Journalism and Commentary*
TLS - i5305 - Dec 3 2004 - p30-31 [51-500]
Leigh, Tera - *Faux Mosaics: Make 20 Paper Projects in Three Simple Steps*
BL - v100 - i21 - July 2004 - p1809(2) [1-50]
Leighton, Myriam - *HeartSmart Nutrition: Shopping on the Run*
CBRA - Annual 2003 - p132(1) [51-500]
Leilberg, Carolyn - *West with Hopeless*
y VOYA - v27 - i3 - August 2004 - p220(1) [1-50]
Leimberg, Stephan R. - *The Tools & Techniques of Employee Benefit and Retirement Planning, 8th Ed.*
HR Mag - v49 - i7 - July 2004 - pS9(1) [51-500]
Leimgruber, Walter - *Between Global and Local: Marginality and Marginal Regions in the Context of Globalization and Deregulation*
R&R Bk N - v19 - i3 - August 2004 - p157(1) [51-500]
Policies and Strategies in Marginal Regions: Summary and Valuations
R&R Bk N - v19 - i1 - Feb 2004 - p135(1) [51-500]
Leinbach, S.J. - *The Lost Island: Alone Among the Fruitful and Multiplying*
BW - v34 - i40 - Oct 3 2004 - p14(1) [501+]
Leinhardt, Gaea - *Listening in on Museum Conversations*
R&R Bk N - v19 - i3 - August 2004 - p1(1) [1-50]

Leinwand, Gerald - *Mackerels in the Moonlight: Four Corrupt American Mayors*
LJ - v130 - i2 - Feb 1 2005 - p98(1) [51-500]
Leiris, Michel - *La Regle Du Jeu*
TLS - i5268 - March 19 2004 - p10-10 [501+]
Leis, Jeffrey M. - *The Larvae of Indo-Pacific Coastal Fishes: An Identification Guide to Marine Fish Larvae, 2nd Ed.*
SciTech - v28 - i3 - Sept 2004 - p64(1) [51-500]
Leitch, Thomas - *Crime Films*
FQ - v57 - i4 - Summer 2004 - p49(3) [501+]
Leitch, Vincent B. - *The Norton Anthology of Theory and Criticism*
Sew R - v111 - i3 - Summer 2003 - pLXXXI-LXXXIV [501+]
Leite, Adam - *Is Fallibility an Epistemological Shortcoming*
RM - v58 - i1 - Sept 2004 - p224(2) [501+]
Leite, Joao Alexandre - *Evolving Knowledge Bases: Specification and Semantics*
SciTech - v28 - i4 - Dec 2004 - p10(1) [1-50]
Leiter, Samuel L. - *Frozen Moments: Writings on Kabuki, 1966-2001*
Theat J - v56 - i3 - Oct 2004 - p540-541 [501+]
Leith, Denise - *The Politics of Power: Freeport in Suharto's Indonesia*
Pac A - v77 - i2 - Summer 2004 - p379(3) [501+]
Leith, Prue - *A Lovesome Thing*
BL - v100 - i22 - August 2004 - p1900(1) [501+]
Leithe-Jasper, Manfred - *European Bronzes from the Quentin Collection*
Choice - v42 - i6 - Feb 2005 - p1013(2) [51-500]
LJ - v130 - i2 - Feb 1 2005 - p76(1) [51-500]
Leitner, Michael J. - *Leisure in Later Life, 3rd Ed.*
R&R Bk N - v19 - i4 - Nov 2004 - p80(1) [1-50]
Leitz, Robert C. - *Imagining the Sciences: Expressions of New Knowledge in the Long Eighteenth Century*
SciTech - v28 - i4 - Dec 2004 - p12(1) [1-50]
Lejeune, Philippe - *Un Journal a soi: Histoire d'une pratique*
Biomag - v27 - i3 - Summer 2004 - p645(5) [501+]
LeJeune, Veronique - *How to Be Comfortable in Your Own Skin (Illus. by H., Princess)*
y SLJ - v50 - i9 - Sept 2004 - p224(1) [51-500]
Lekan, Thomas M. - *Imagining the Nation in Nature: Landscape Preservation and German Identity, 1885-1945*
HRNB - v33 - i1 - Fall 2004 - p26(1) [501+]
Lekkas, E.L. - *Earthquake Geodynamics: Seismic Case Studies*
SciTech - v28 - i3 - Sept 2004 - p55(1) [51-500]
Lekuton, Joseph - *Facing the Lion: Growing Up Maasai on the African Savanna*
y LibMed - v22 - i4 - Jan 2004 - p79(1) [501+]
Leland, John - *Hip: The History*
y BL - v101 - i3 - Oct 1 2004 - p287(1) [51-500]
BW - v34 - i43 - Oct 24 2004 - p7(1) [501+]
KR - v72 - i16 - August 15 2004 - p791(1) [501+]
LJ - v129 - i14 - Sept 1 2004 - p173(2) [51-500]
NYTBR - Oct 24 2004 - p9 [501+]
PW - v251 - i33 - August 16 2004 - p51(1) [51-500]
Time - v164 - i16 - Oct 18 2004 - p88 [501+]
Lelchuk, Alan - *Ziff: A Life?*
NYTBR - Oct 10 2004 - p26 [501+]
Lelieur, Isabelle - *Law and Policy of Substantial Ownership and Effective Control of Airlines: Prospects for Change*
R&R Bk N - v19 - i1 - Feb 2004 - pNA [51-500]
Lelieveld, H.L.M. - *Hygiene in Food Processing*
E-Streams - Sept 2004 - pNA [501+]
Lelis, Arnold - *The Age of Marriage in Ancient Rome*
R&R Bk N - v19 - i1 - Feb 2004 - p129(1) [51-500]
Leloup, Jean-Yves - *The Gospel of Philip: Jesus, Mary Magdalene, and the Gnosis of Sacred Union*
BL - v101 - i3 - Oct 1 2004 - p305(1) [51-500]
LJ - v129 - i20 - Dec 1 2004 - p125(1) [51-500]
The Gospel of Thomas: The Gnostic Wisdom of Jesus
PW - v252 - i11 - March 14 2005 - p64(1) [51-500]
Lelyveld, Joseph - *Omaha Blues: A Memory Loop*
Econ - v374 - i8410 - Jan 22 2005 - p80US [501+]
KR - v73 - i2 - Jan 15 2005 - p104(1) [501+]
LJ - v129 - i20 - Dec 1 2004 - p92(1) [51-500]
PW - v252 - i9 - Feb 28 2005 - p51(1) [51-500]
Lemaire, Andre - *Prophetes et Rois: Bible et Proche-Orient.*
JNES - v63 - i4 - Oct 2004 - p298(2) [501+]
Lemaire de Belges, Jean - *Des Anciennes Pompes Funeralles*
FS - v58 - i2 - April 2004 - p242(2) [501+]

LeMarquand, Grant - *An Issue of Relevance: A Comparative Study of the Story of the Bleeding Woman (Mk 5: 25-34; Mt 9:20-22; LK 8:43-48) in North Atlantic and African Contexts*
R&R Bk N - v19 - i4 - Nov 2004 - p24(1) [51-500]

Lembke, Janet - *Skinny Dipping and Other Immersions in Water, Myth, and Being Human*
SciTech - v28 - i4 - Dec 2004 - p59(1) [51-500]

Lemche, Niels Peter - *Historical Dictionary of Ancient Israel*
Choice - v42 - i1 - Sept 2004 - p80(1) [501+]

Leme-Hebuterne, Kristiane - *Autour des Stalles de Picardie et Normandie: Tradition Iconographique au Moyen-age*
Specu - v79 - i3 - July 2004 - p787-789 [501+]

Lement, Wendy - *Keri Tarr: Cat Detective (Illus. by Burrows, Jeffrey Scott)*
c BL - v101 - i6 - Nov 15 2004 - p583(1) [51-500]

Lemercier, Claire - *Un si discret pouvoir: Aux origines de la chambre de commerce de Paris 1803-1853*
AHR - v109 - i2 - April 2004 - p631(2) [501+]

Lemke, Judy - *Microsoft Office Visio 2003 Step by Step*
SciTech - v28 - i4 - Dec 2004 - p131 [51-500]

Lemmon, Alfred E. - *Charting Louisiana: Five Hundred Years of Maps*
Choice - v42 - i1 - Sept 2004 - p172(1) [501+]

Lemoine, Serge - *Paintings in the Musee d'Orsay*
LJ - v130 - i2 - Feb 1 2005 - p78(1) [51-500]
PW - v251 - i45 - Nov 8 2004 - p48(1) [501+]
TimHES - v0 - i1681 - March 4 2005 - p24(2) [501+]

Lemonick, Michael D. - *Echo of the Big Bang*
Physics T - v43 - i3 - March 2005 - p192(1) [501+]

Lemons, John - *Conserving Biodiversity in Arid Regions: Best Practices in Developing Nations*
SciTech - v28 - i1 - March 2004 - p64(1) [51-500]

Lemos, Irene S. - *The Protogeometric Aegean: The Archaeology of the Late Eleventh and Tenth Centuries BC*
Class R - v54 - i1 - May 2004 - p210(3) [501+]

LeMoult, Dolph - *Running Horsemen*
c CH Bwatch - v14 - i7 - July 2004 - p7(1) [51-500]

Lempert, Robert J. - *Shaping the Next One Hundred Years: New Methods for Quantitative Long-term Policy Analysis*
R&R Bk N - v19 - i1 - Feb 2004 - p77(1) [1-50]

Lempicka, Tamara de - *Tamara de Lempicka: Art Deco Icon*
Choice - v42 - i6 - Feb 2005 - p1014(1) [51-500]

LeMura, Linda M. - *Clinical Exercise Physiology: Application and Physiological Principles*
SciTech - v28 - i1 - March 2004 - p123(1) [51-500]

Lenard-Cook, Lisa - *Coyote Morning: A Novel*
LJ - v129 - i16 - Oct 1 2004 - p70(1) [51-500]

Lence, Matthew - *Closer to the Masses: Stalinist Culture, Social Revolution, and Soviet Newspaper*
Choice - v42 - i6 - Feb 2005 - p1078(1) [51-500]

Lencioni, Patrick - *Death by Meeting: A Leadership Fable about Solving the Most Painful Problem in Business*
Har Bus R - v82 - i5 - May 2004 - p30(1) [501+]

Lenclos, Jean-Philippe - *Colors of the World: The Geography of Color*
R&R Bk N - v19 - i3 - August 2004 - p241(1) [51-500]

Lende, Heather - *If You Lived Here, I'd Know Your Name: News from Small-Town Alaska*
KR - v73 - i5 - March 1 2005 - p275(1) [501+]

Lendeckel, Uwe - *Proteases in Tissue Remodeling of Lung and Heart*
SciTech - v28 - i1 - March 2004 - p87(1) [51-500]

Lendvai, Paul - *The Hungarians*
Bwatch - Dec 2004 - pNA [51-500]

Lenehan, Pat - *Anabolic Steroids and Other Performance-Enhancing Drugs*
E-Streams - June 2004 - pNA [501+]

Leng, Rainer - *Ars Belli: Deutsche Taktische und Kriegstechnische Bilderhandschriften und Traktate im 15. und 16. Jahrhundert.*
T&C - v45 - i1 - Jan 2004 - p168(3) [501+]

Lengel, Edward G. - *World War I Memories: An Annotated Bibliography of Personal Accounts Published in English Since 1919*
Choice - v42 - i4 - Dec 2004 - p640(1) [1-50]
R&R Bk N - v19 - i4 - Nov 2004 - p32(1) [51-500]

Lengel, James G. - *Web Wizard's Guide to Dreamweaver*
SciTech - v28 - i3 - Sept 2004 - p159(1) [51-500]

Lengen, R. - *Form und Funktion der aristotelischen Pragmatie. Die Kommunikation mit dem Rezipienten*
Class R - v54 - i2 - Nov 2004 - p326-327 [501+]

Lenger, Friedrich - *Towards an Urban Nation: Germany since 1780*
HNet - July 2004 - pNA [501+]

L'Engle, Madeleine - *A Wrinkle in Time*
c RT - v57 - Sept 2003 - p100 [51-500]

Lenihan, Padraig - *1690: Battle of the Boyne*
HRNB - v33 - i1 - Fall 2004 - p22(1) [501+]
Conquest and Resistance: War in Seventeenth-Century Ireland
HNet - Sept 2004 - pNA [501+]
Six Ct J - v34 - i4 - Winter 2003 - p1142-1143 [501+]

Lening, Arthur - *The Immortal Count: The Life and Films of Bela Lugosi*
VQR - v80 - i1 - Wntr 2004 - p274-275 [501+]

Lenius, Brian J. - *Genealogical Gazetter of Galicia: Expanded Data Edition*
EFHM - v58 - i2 - March-April 2004 - p88(1) [51-500]

Lenke, Lawrence G. - *Modern Anterior Scoliosis Surgery*
SciTech - v28 - i3 - Sept 2004 - p114(1) [51-500]

Lennard-Brown, Sarah - *Cannabis*
y Sch Lib - v52 - i4 - Winter 2004 - p218(1) [51-500]
Sports Injuries
y Sch Lib - v52 - i4 - Winter 2004 - p218(1) [51-500]

Lennard, Erica - *American Writers at Home*
NYTBR - Oct 24 2004 - p35 [501+]

Lenner, Andrew C. - *The Federal Principle in American Politics, 1790-1833*
W&M Q - v61 - i3 - July 2004 - p582-588 [501+]

Lennon, Alexander T. J. - *The Battle for Hearts and Minds: Using Soft Power to Undermine Terrorist Networks*
JPR - v41 - i4 - July 2004 - p520-521 [501+]
Reshaping Rogue States: Preemption, Regime Change, and U.S. Policy toward Iran, Iraq, and North Korea
Pers PS - v34 - i1 - Wntr 2005 - p53(1) [501+]

Lennon, J. Robert - *Mailman*
Ga R - v58 - i1 - Spring 2004 - p197-198 [501+]

Lennon, Joseph - *Irish Orientalism: A Literary and Intellectual History*
Choice - v42 - i3 - Nov 2004 - p484(1) [1-50]

Lennon, M.T. - *Making It Up as I Go Along*
LJ - v130 - i4 - March 1 2005 - p79(1) [51-500]

Lennon, Thomas M. - *Cartesian Views: Papers Presented to Richard A. Watson*
Ren Q - v57 - i4 - Winter 2004 - p1476(2) [501+]
R&R Bk N - v19 - i1 - Feb 2004 - p3(1) [51-500]
Reading Bayle
Eight-C St - v37 - i3 - Spring 2004 - p510-520 [501+]

Lennox, Doug - *Now You Know: The Book of Answers*
CBRA - Annual 2003 - p14(2) [51-500]
Now You Know: The Book of Answers. Vol. 2
Globe & Mail - Nov 6 2004 - pF8 [51-500]

Lennox, John C. - *Theory of Infinite Soluble Groups*
SciTech - v28 - i4 - Dec 2004 - p35(1) [51-500]

Leno, Jay - *If Roast Beef Could Fly*
c CH Bwatch - v14 - i8 - August 2004 - p6(1) [51-500]

Lenoble, Jacques - *Toward a Theory of Governance: The Action of Norms*
R&R Bk N - v19 - i1 - Feb 2004 - p147(1) [51-500]

Lenski, Noel - *Failure of Empire: Valens and the Roman State in the Fourth Century A.D.*
AHR - v109 - i4 - Oct 2004 - p1289-1290 [501+]
Class R - v54 - i1 - May 2004 - p192(4) [501+]

Lenski, Susan Davis - *Transforming Teacher Education through Partnerships*
R&R Bk N - v19 - i3 - August 2004 - p219(1) [1-50]

Lent, John A. - *Comic Art of Africa, Asia, Australia, and Latin America through 2000: An International Bibliography*
Choice - v42 - i7 - March 2005 - p1196(1) [51-500]

Lent, ReLeah Cossett - *Silent No More: Voices of Courage in American Schools*
TCR - v106 - i5 - May 2004 - p1020(4) [501+]

Lentin, Ronit - *Re-presenting the Shoah for the Twenty-First Century*
R&R Bk N - v19 - i3 - August 2004 - p34(1) [51-500]

Lentz, Harris M., III - *Biographical Dictionary of Professional Wrestling, 2nd Ed.*
R&R Bk N - v19 - i1 - Feb 2004 - p75(1) [51-500]

Lenz, Evan - *Office 2003 XML*
SciTech - v28 - i3 - Sept 2004 - p27(1) [51-500]

Lenz, Mary Jane - *Small Spirits: Native American Dolls from the National Museum of the American Indian*
Choice - v42 - i5 - Jan 2005 - p841(2) [1-50]
LJ - v129 - i17 - Oct 15 2004 - p60(1) [51-500]
R&R Bk N - v19 - i3 - August 2004 - p60(1) [51-500]

Leo, Jennifer L. - *Whose Panties are These? More Misadventures from Funny Women on the Road*
Globe & Mail - Feb 5 2005 - pT14 [501+]

Leok, Goh Chee - *The Asian Skin: A Reference Atlas of Dermatology*
SciTech - v28 - i4 - Dec 2004 - p115(1) [1-50]

Leon, Arnoldo De - *Racial Frontiers: Africans, Chinese and Mexicans in Western America, 1848-1890*
JAH - v91 - i1 - June 2004 - p256-257 [501+]

Leon, Bonnie - *The Heart of Thornton Creek*
LJ - v130 - i2 - Feb 1 2005 - p62(1) [51-500]

Leon, Dan - *Who's Left in Israel?: Radical Political Alternatives for the Future of Israel*
R&R Bk N - v19 - i3 - August 2004 - p51(1) [51-500]

Leon, David De - *Artefactual Intelligence: The Development and Use of Cognitively Congenial Artefacts*
T&C - v45 - i3 - July 2004 - p668-669 [501+]

Leon, Donna - *Acqua Alta*
PW - v251 - i33 - August 16 2004 - p48(1) [501+]
Doctored Evidence (Read by Colacci, David). Audiobook Review
BL - v101 - i3 - Oct 1 2004 - p350(1) [51-500]

Leon, Donna - *Doctored Evidence (Read by Colacci, David). Audiobook Review*
Globe & Mail - Jan 22 2005 - pD13 [51-500]

Leon, Donna - *Doctored Evidence (Read by Colacci, David). Audiobook Review*
Kliatt - v38 - i6 - Nov 2004 - p44(1) [51-500]

Leon-Dufour, Xavier - *Un bibliste Cherche Dieu*
Theol St - v65 - i4 - Dec 2004 - p895(1) [501+]

Leon, Luis D. - *La Llorona's Children: Religion, Life, and Death in the U.S. Mexican Borderlands*
Choice - v42 - i5 - Jan 2005 - p871(1) [1-50]

Leon Portilla, Miguel - *Aztec Poets*
y VOYA - v27 - i3 - August 2004 - p182(1) [1-50]

Leonard, David P. - *Evidence; a Structured Approach*
R&R Bk N - v19 - i3 - August 2004 - p206(1) [501+]

Leonard, Elizabeth D. - *Lincoln's Avengers: Justice, Revenge, and Reunion after the Civil War*
BooChiTr - April 11 2004 - p2(1) [501+]
Choice - v42 - i3 - Nov 2004 - p548(1) [1-50]
CR - v285 - i1667 - Dec 2004 - p382(1) [51-500]
NYRB - v51 - i13 - August 12 2004 - p20(3) [501+]
R&R Bk N - v19 - i4 - Nov 2004 - p60(1) [51-500]

Leonard, Elmore - *Be Cool. Audiobook Review*
Globe & Mail - Feb 19 2005 - pD17 [501+]
Be Cool (Read by Scott, Campbell). Audiobook Review
PW - v252 - i10 - March 7 2005 - p26(1) [51-500]
A Coyote's in the House (Read by Harris, Neil Patrick). Audiobook Review
y BL - v101 - i4 - Oct 15 2004 - p433(1) [51-500]
A Coyote's in the House (Illus. by Child, Lauren)
c HB - v80 - i5 - Sept-Oct 2004 - p589(2) [51-500]
c Sch Lib - v52 - i4 - Winter 2004 - p202(1) [51-500]
c SLJ - v50 - i10 - Oct 2004 - p171(1) [51-500]
A Coyote's in the House
c NYTBR - July 11 2004 - p18 [501+]
The Hot Kid
KR - v73 - i4 - Feb 15 2005 - p192(1) [501+]
Mr. Paradise (Read by Forster, Robert). Audiobook Review
LJ - v129 - i13 - August 2004 - p129(1) [51-500]
Mr. Paradise
BooChiTr - Jan 11 2004 - p3(1) [501+]
BW - v34 - i3 - Jan 18 2004 - p15(1) [501+]
TLS - i5283 - July 2 2004 - p21(1) [501+]

Leonard, Hal - *The Art of the Piano: Its Performers, Literature, and Recordings*
LJ - v130 - i2 - Feb 1 2005 - p113(2) [51-500]
Jazz Saxophone: An In-Depth Look at the Styles of the Tenor Masters
Teach Mus - v12 - i4 - Feb 2005 - p78(1) [51-500]

Leonard, Hugh - *Fillums*
TLS - i5288 - August 6 2004 - p21(1) [501+]

Leonard, Karen Isaksen - *Muslims in the United States: The State of Research*
  Choice - v42 - i1 - Sept 2004 - p194(1) [501+]
  CS - v33 - i5 - Sept 2004 - p625-625 [501+]
  SF - v83 - i1 - Sept 2004 - p444(2) [501+]

Leonard, Kurt J. - *Fusarium Head Blight of Wheat and Barley*
  SciTech - v28 - i3 - Sept 2004 - p130(1) [51-500]

Leonard, Mark - *Why Europe Will Run the 21st Century*
  Econ - v374 - i8415 - Feb 26 2005 - p83US [501+]

Leonard, Michael - *Achieving Safe and Reliable Healthcare: Strategies and Solutions*
  SciTech - v28 - i4 - Dec 2004 - p78(1) [51-500]

Leonard, Penny - *Promoting Welfare?: Government Information Policy and Social Citizenship*
  R&R Bk N - v19 - i1 - Feb 2004 - p136(1) [51-500]
  Soc Ser R - v79 - i1 - March 2005 - p209(1) [51-500]

Leonard, R.L. - *American Art Deco: An Illustrated Survey*
  Bwatch - v26 - i8 - August 2004 - p1(1) [51-500]
  R&R Bk N - v19 - i4 - Nov 2004 - p209(1) [501+]

Leonard, Robin - *Money Troubles: Legal Strategies to Cope with Your Debts, 9th Ed.*
  R&R Bk N - v19 - i1 - Feb 2004 - pNA [51-500]

Leonard, Stephen J. - *Lynching in Colorado, 1859-1919*
  JAH - v91 - i1 - June 2004 - p258-259 [501+]
  WHQ - v35 - i2 - Summer 2004 - p231-232 [501+]

Leonard, Thomas M. - *Encyclopedia of Cuban-United States Relations*
  BL - v101 - i1 - Sept 1 2004 - p168(1) [501+]
  R&R Bk N - v19 - i3 - August 2004 - p64(1) [51-500]
  Fidel Castro: A Biography
  R&R Bk N - v19 - i3 - August 2004 - p77(1) [51-500]

Leonardo, Zeus - *Ideology, Discourse, and School Reform*
  Choice - v41 - i11-12 - July-August 2004 - p2096(1) [501+]
  R&R Bk N - v19 - i1 - Feb 2004 - p190(1) [51-500]
  TCR - v106 - i12 - Dec 2004 - p2330(3) [501+]

Leoncini, Riccardo - *Technological Systems and Intersectoral Innovation Flows*
  SciTech - v28 - i1 - March 2004 - p134(1) [51-500]

Leondes, Cornelius T. - *Computer Aided and Integrated Manufacturing Systems, Vol. 1*
  SciTech - v28 - i4 - Dec 2004 - p167(1) [51-500]

Leone, Stephen R. - *Annual Review of Physical Chemistry: Vol. 54, 2003*
  SciTech - v28 - i1 - March 2004 - p55(1) [51-500]
  Annual Review of Physical Chemistry: Vol. 55, 2004
  SciTech - v28 - i3 - Sept 2004 - p52(1) [1-50]

Leonetti, Mike - *The Maple Leafs Trivia Book, 1927-2003*
  CBRA - Annual 2003 - p144(1) [51-500]
  Number Four, Bobby Orr! (Illus. by Letain, Shayne)
  c CBRA - Annual 2003 - p456(1) [51-500]

Leong, Ho Khai - *Shared Responsibilities, Unshared Power: The Politics of Policy-Making in Singapore, Rev. Ed.*
  R&R Bk N - v19 - i1 - Feb 2004 - pNA [51-500]

Leonhardt, Alice - *Samuel's Horses*
  y Kliatt - v39 - i2 - March 2005 - p20(1) [51-500]

Leonori, Ann - *Francesco D'Adamo: Iqbal (Read by Moore, Christina). Audiobook Review*
  HB - v80 - i6 - Nov-Dec 2004 - p733(2) [501+]

Leoshko, Janice - *Sacred Traces: British Explorations of Buddhism in South Asia*
  TimHES - v0 - i1647 - July 2 2004 - p24(2) [501+]

Lepa, Jack H. - *The Shenandoah Valley Campaign of 1864*
  R&R Bk N - v19 - i1 - Feb 2004 - p59(1) [51-500]

Lepard, Brian D. - *Rethinking Humanitarian Intervention: A Fresh Legal Approach Based on Fundamental Ethical Principles in International Law and World Religions.*
  AJPS - v39 - i2 - July 2004 - p430(430) [501+]

Lepenies, Wolf - *Sainte-Beuve: Au Seuil de la Modernite*
  FS - v58 - i2 - April 2004 - p273(1) [501+]

Lepidus, D.L. - *The Best Men's Stage Monologues of 2004*
  LJ - v129 - i20 - Dec 1 2004 - p116(1) [501+]
  The Best Women's Stage Monologues of 2004
  LJ - v129 - i20 - Dec 1 2004 - p116(1) [501+]

Lepik, Andres - *Skyscrapers*
  Bwatch - March 2005 - pNA [51-500]
  LJ - v129 - i20 - Dec 1 2004 - p113(1) [501+]

Leppert, Phyllis, C. - *Primary Care for Women, 2nd Ed.*
  SciTech - v28 - i3 - Sept 2004 - p89(1) [51-500]

Leppin, Volker - *Wilhelm von Ockham: Gelehrter, Streiter, Bettelmonch*
  Theol St - v66 - i1 - March 2005 - p191(2) [501+]

Lerch, Maureen T. - *Serving Homeschooled Teens and Their Parents*
  BL - v101 - i9-10 - Jan 1 2005 - p911(1) [501+]
  SLJ - v50 - i12 - Dec 2004 - p179(1) [51-500]

Lerda, Valeria Gennaro - *Canadian and American Women: Moving from Private to Public Experiences in the Atlantic World*
  JAH - v91 - i1 - June 2004 - p266-267 [501+]

Lerman, James - *Essential Websites for Educational Leaders in the 21st Century*
  Choice - v42 - i5 - Jan 2005 - p905(1) [1-50]
  R&R Bk N - v19 - i4 - Nov 2004 - p180(1) [501+]
  Tec Teach - v64 - i4 - Dec 2004 - p4(1) [501+]

Lerman, Nina E. - *Gender and Technology: A Reader*
  T&C - v45 - i4 - Oct 2004 - p908(3) [501+]

Lerner, Ben - *The Lichtenberg Figures*
  LJ - v129 - i17 - Oct 15 2004 - p66(2) [501+]

Lerner, Claire - *Bringing Up Baby: Three Steps to Making Good Decisions in Your Child's First Years*
  BL - v101 - i7 - Dec 1 2004 - p625(1) [501+]

Lerner, David N. - *Urban Groundwater Pollution*
  E-Streams - June 2004 - pNA [501+]
  SciTech - v28 - i1 - March 2004 - p148(1) [51-500]

Lerner, K. Lee - *Encyclopedia of Espionage, Intelligence, and Security*
  R&R Bk N - v19 - i1 - Feb 2004 - p150(1) [51-500]

Lerner, Mark D. - *A Practical Guide for Crisis Response in Our Schools, 5th Ed.*
  Tec Teach - v64 - i4 - Dec 2004 - p4(1) [501+]
  A Practical Guide for University Crisis Response
  Tec Teach - v64 - i4 - Dec 2004 - p4(1) [501+]

Lerner, Paul - *Hysterical Men: War, Psychiatry, and the Politics of Trauma in Germany, 1890-1930*
  AHR - v109 - i2 - April 2004 - p635(2) [501+]
  Hysterical Men: War, Psychiatry, and the Politics of Trauma in Germany 1890-1930
  GSR - v27 - i2 - May 2004 - p391-393 [501+]

Lerner, Richard M. - *Liberty: Thriving and Civic Engagement among America's Youth*
  R&R Bk N - v19 - i3 - August 2004 - p151(1) [51-500]

Lerner, Robert E. - *The Feast of Saint Abraham: Medieval Millenarians and the Jews*
  Specu - v79 - i3 - July 2004 - p789-792 [501+]

Lerner, Steve - *Diamond: A Struggle for Environmental Justice in Louisiana's Chemical Corridor*
  PW - v251 - i39 - Sept 27 2004 - p45(1) [51-500]

Leroi, Armand Marie - *Mutants: On Genetic Variety and the Human Body*
  New Sci - v185 - i2486 - Feb 12 2005 - p49(1) [501+]
  Mutants: On the Form, Varieties and Errors of the Human Body
  Lon R Bks - v27 - i1 - Jan 6 2005 - p33(2) [501+]
  TimHES - v0 - i1668 - Nov 26 2004 - p26(1) [501+]

Leroux, Bob - *Murder in the Glen*
  CBRA - Annual 2003 - p174(1) [51-500]

Leroux, Neil R. - *Luther's Rhetoric: Strategies and Style from the Invocavit Sermons*
  Six Ct J - v34 - i4 - Winter 2003 - p1178-1179 [501+]

Leroy, Catherine - *Under Fire: Great Photographers and Writers in Vietnam*
  PW - v252 - i9 - Feb 28 2005 - p57(1) [51-500]

LeRoy, J.T. - *Harold's End (Illus. by Hood, Cherry)*
  BW - v35 - i4 - Jan 30 2005 - p7(1) [501+]
  G&L Rev W - v12 - i2 - March-April 2005 - p45(1) [501+]
  NYTBR - Feb 27 2005 - p17 [501+]
  Advocate - Dec 21 2004 - p65(1) [501+]

Lersten, Nels R. - *Flowering Plant Embryology: With Emphasis on Economic Species*
  Choice - v42 - i4 - Dec 2004 - p689(2) [1-50]
  QRB - v79 - i4 - Dec 2004 - p428(1) [501+]

Lesage, Julia - *Making a Difference: University Students of Color Speak Out*
  J Hi E - v75 - i4 - July-August 2004 - p483(3) [501+]

Lescroart, John - *The Motive (Read by Colacci, David). Audiobook Review*
  PW - v252 - i6 - Feb 7 2005 - p34(1) [501+]
  The Motive
  BL - v101 - i6 - Nov 15 2004 - p532(1) [51-500]
  PW - v251 - i48 - Nov 29 2004 - p22(1) [51-500]
  Ent W - i798 - Dec 24 2004 - p73 [501+]

Lesesne, Teri S. - *Making the Match: The Right Book for the Right Reader at the Right Time, Grades 4-12*
  JAAL - v48 - i1 - Sept 2004 - p81(2) [501+]
  LibMed - v23 - i1 - August-Sept 2004 - p86(1) [51-500]
  TCR - v106 - i8 - August 2004 - p1544(3) [501+]
  VOYA - v27 - i4 - Oct 2004 - p266(2) [501+]

Lesh, Phil - *Searching for the Sound: My Life in the Grateful Dead*
  LJ - v129 - i20 - Dec 1 2004 - p92(1) [1-50]

LeShan, Lawrence - *The World of the Paranormal: The Next Frontier*
  Bwatch - Feb 2005 - pNA [51-500]

Lesk, Arthur M. - *Introduction to Protein Science: Architecture, Function, and Genomics, 1st Ed.*
  TimHES - v0 - i1680 - Feb 25 2005 - pIII(1) [501+]

Lesko, Wendy Schaetzel - *Knock-Your-Socks-Off: Training Teens to be Successful Activists!*
  VOYA - v27 - i5 - Dec 2004 - p427(1) [51-500]

Leslie, John - *Infinite Minds: A Philosophical Cosmology*
  Dialogue - v43 - i2 - Spring 2004 - p409(4) [501+]
  Infinite Minds
  Rel St - v40 - i4 - Dec 2004 - p499(4) [501+]

Leslie, Roger - *Isak Dinesen: Gothic Storyteller*
  y CH Bwatch - v14 - i11 - Nov 2004 - pNA [51-500]

Lesniczak, Peter - *Alte Landschaftskuechen im Sog der Modernisierung: Studien zu einer Ernaehrungsgeographie Deutschlands zwischen 1860 und 1930*
  HNet - Nov 2004 - pNA [501+]

Lessac, Frane - *Island Counting 1 2 3*
  c PW - v252 - i6 - Feb 7 2005 - p61(2) [501+]

Lesseig, Corey T. - *Automobility: Social Changes in the American South, 1909-1939*
  JSH - v70 - i3 - August 2004 - p713(3) [501+]

Lessem, Don - *Armored Dinosaurs (Illus. by Bindon, John)*
  c SLJ - v51 - i2 - Feb 2005 - p123(1) [51-500]
  Dinosaur Atlas (Illus. by Bindon, John)
  c CBRA - Annual 2003 - p568(1) [51-500]
  Giant Meat-Eating Dinosaurs (Illus. by Bindon, John)
  c SLJ - v51 - i2 - Feb 2005 - p123(1) [51-500]
  Horned Dinosaurs (Illus. by Bindon, John)
  c SLJ - v51 - i2 - Feb 2005 - p123(1) [51-500]
  Scholastic Dinosaurs A to Z: The Ultimate Dinosaur Encyclopedia (Illus. by Sovak, Jan)
  c SLJ - v50 - i10 - Oct 2004 - p40(1) [51-500]

Lesser, Gary S. - *SIMPLE, SEP, and SARSEP Answer Book, 9th Ed.*
  R&R Bk N - v19 - i1 - Feb 2004 - pNA [51-500]

Lesser, Jeffery - *Searching for Home Abroad: Japanese Brazilians and Transnationalism*
  Pac A - v77 - i3 - Fall 2004 - p585(3) [501+]

Lesser, W. Hunter - *Rebels at the Gate: Lee and McClellan on the Front Line of a Nation Divided*
  R&R Bk N - v19 - i4 - Nov 2004 - p61(1) [51-500]

Lesser, Wendy - *The Genius of Language: Fifteen Writers Reflect on Their Mother Tongues*
  BL - v100 - i21 - July 2004 - p1810(2) [1-50]
  BW - v34 - i32 - August 8 2004 - p15(1) [501+]
  Globe & Mail - August 21 2004 - pD4 [501+]
  SLJ - v51 - i2 - Feb 2005 - p158(2) [501+]

Lessig, Lawrence - *Free Culture: How Big Media Uses Technology and the Law to Lock Down Culture and Control Creativity*
  Choice - v42 - i3 - Nov 2004 - p525(1) [1-50]
  Har Bus R - v82 - i3 - March 2004 - pNA [501+]

Lessing, Doris - *The Grandmothers*
  BooChiTr - Jan 11 2004 - p2(1) [501+]
  BW - v34 - i5 - Feb 1 2004 - p6(1) [501+]
  Time Bites: Views and Reviews
  Spec - v296 - i9194 - Oct 23 2004 - p55(2) [501+]
  TLS - i5302 - Nov 12 2004 - p27(1) [501+]

Lester, Alison - *Are We There Yet?: A Journey around Australia*
  c KR - v73 - i2 - Jan 15 2005 - p123(1) [51-500]
  c Magpies - v19 - i5 - Nov 2004 - p29(1) [51-500]

Lester, Andrew W. - *The Angry Christian: A Theology for Care and Counseling*
  Intpr - v59 - i1 - Jan 2005 - p100(2) [501+]

Lester, Barry M. - *NICU Network Neurobehavioral Scale*
  SciTech - v28 - i4 - Dec 2004 - p112(1) [1-50]
  Why Is My Baby Crying?: The Parent's Survival Guide for Coping with Crying Problems and Colic
  LJ - v130 - i1 - Jan 1 2005 - p140(1) [51-500]

Lester, Frank K. - *Proceedings of the NCTM Research Catalyst Conference*
  SciTech - v28 - i4 - Dec 2004 - p16(1) [1-50]
  Teaching Mathematics through Problem Solving: Prekindergarten-Grade 6
  TC Math - v11 - i1 - August 2004 - p44(1) [501+]

Lester, Helen - *Hooway for Wodney Wat (Illus. by Munsinger, Lynn). Audiobook Review*
  c SLJ - v50 - i10 - Oct 2004 - pS29(1) [51-500]
Hurty Feelings (Illus. by Munsinger, Lynn)
  c BL - v101 - i2 - Sept 15 2004 - p251(2) [51-500]
  c CCB-B - v58 - i3 - Nov 2004 - p133(1) [501+]
  c KR - v72 - i13 - July 1 2004 - p632(1) [51-500]
  c SLJ - v50 - i10 - Oct 2004 - p120(1) [51-500]
Something Might Happen
  BooChiTr - Jan 18 2004 - p5(1) [501+]
Lester, Julius - *The Autobiography of God: A Novel*
  BL - v101 - i6 - Nov 15 2004 - p562(1) [51-500]
  LJ - v129 - i18 - Nov 1 2004 - p76(1) [501+]
  PW - v251 - i43 - Oct 25 2004 - p28(1) [51-500]
The Blues Singers: Ten Who Rocked the World (Illus. by Cohen, Lisa)
  SLJ - v50 - i12 - Dec 2004 - p61(1) [501+]
Day of Tears: a Novel in Dialogue
  y KR - v73 - i5 - March 1 2005 - p289(1) [51-500]
Let's Talk About Race (Illus. by Barbour, Karen)
  c KR - v72 - i24 - Dec 15 2004 - p1204(1) [51-500]
  c PW - v252 - i4 - Jan 24 2005 - p244(1) [51-500]
  c SLJ - v51 - i1 - Jan 2005 - p112(1) [51-500]
On Writing for Children and Other People.
  y BL - v101 - i3 - Oct 1 2004 - p321(1) [51-500]
  c CCB-B - v58 - i2 - Oct 2004 - p105(1) [51-500]
  KR - v72 - i20 - Oct 15 2004 - p1009(1) [51-500]
  c SLJ - v50 - i10 - Oct 2004 - p202(1) [51-500]
  c SLJ - v50 - i11 - Nov 2004 - p67(1) [51-500]
  y VOYA - v27 - i5 - Dec 2004 - p416(1) [51-500]
Shining
  HNet - June 2004 - pNA [501+]
What a Truly Cool World
  c Teach Lib - v32 - i1 - Oct 2004 - p22(1) [51-500]
Lester, Katherine Morris - *Accessories of Dress: An Illustrated Encyclopedia*
  R&R Bk N - v19 - i4 - Nov 2004 - p79(1) [51-500]
Lester, Meera - *Blooming Rooms*
  Bwatch - v26 - i9 - Sept 2004 - p1(1) [51-500]
Lester, Paul Martin - *Images That Injure: Pictorial Stereotypes in the Media, 2nd Ed.*
  R&R Bk N - v19 - i1 - Feb 2004 - p211 [51-500]
Lester, Richard K. - *Innovation: The Missing Dimension*
  Choice - v42 - i7 - March 2005 - p1274(1) [51-500]
  Har Bus R - v82 - i11 - Nov 2004 - p31(1) [501+]
Lester, Valerie Browne - *Phiz: The Man Who Drew Dickens*
  TLS - i5306 - Dec 10 2004 - p10(1) [501+]
Lesynski, Loris - *Cabbagehead*
  y CBRA - Annual 2003 - p526(1) [51-500]
Zigzag: Zoems for Zindergarten (Illus. by Lesynski, Loris)
  c BL - v101 - i7 - Dec 1 2004 - p656(2) [51-500]
  c Globe & Mail - Sept 11 2004 - pD13 [51-500]
  c Res Links - v10 - i3 - Feb 2005 - p6(1) [51-500]
  c SLJ - v51 - i1 - Jan 2005 - p112(1) [51-500]
L'Etang, Jacquie - *Public Relations in Britain: A History of Professional Practice in the 20th Century*
  R&R Bk N - v19 - i4 - Nov 2004 - p124(1) [51-500]
LeTendre, Gerald K. - *Learning to be Adolescent: Growing up in U.S. and Japanese Middle Schools*
  CS - v33 - i1 - Jan 2004 - p98-99 [501+]
Letexier, Gerard - *Madame de Villedieu: une Chroniqueuse qux Origines de 'La Princesse de Cleves*
  FS - v58 - i2 - April 2004 - p252(2) [501+]
Lethbridge, Lucy - *Annie Oakley: Sharpshooter of the West*
  c Sch Lib - v52 - i4 - Winter 2004 - p207(1) [51-500]
Lethem, Jonathan - *The Disappointment Artist and Other Essays*
  KR - v72 - i24 - Dec 15 2004 - p1185(1) [501+]
  PW - v251 - i50 - Dec 13 2004 - p53(1) [51-500]
  Ent W - i811 - March 18 2005 - p74 [51-500]
The Fortress of Solitude
  BIC - v33 - i2 - March 2004 - p3(1) [501+]
  BW - v34 - i40 - Oct 3 2004 - p15(1) [501+]
  NYTBR - Sept 19 2004 - p24 [501+]
Men and Cartoons (Read by Lenthem, Jonathan). Audiobook Review
  PW - v251 - i44 - Nov 1 2004 - p26(1) [501+]
Men and Cartoons
  BL - v101 - i1 - Sept 1 2004 - p62(1) [501+]
  Ent W - i791 - Nov 5 2004 - p89 [51-500]
  Globe & Mail - Nov 13 2004 - pD4 [501+]
  KR - v72 - i15 - August 1 2004 - p708(1) [501+]
  LJ - v129 - i15 - Sept 15 2004 - p52(1) [51-500]
  NS - v134 - i4722 - Jan 17 2005 - p55(1) [501+]
  People - v62 - i25 - Dec 20 2004 - p60 [501+]
  PW - v251 - i43 - Oct 25 2004 - p28(1) [51-500]

Men and Cartoons: Stories
  NYTBR - Nov 7 2004 - p14 [501+]
Letourneau, Jocelyn - *History for the Future: Rewriting Memory and Identity in Quebec*
  R&R Bk N - v19 - i4 - Nov 2004 - p70(1) [51-500]
Let's Draw with Shapes
  c LibMed - v23 - i1 - August-Sept 2004 - p71(1) [51-500]
Let's Look at Feelings
  LibMed - v23 - i1 - August-Sept 2004 - p73(1) [51-500]
Let's See Library-Economics
  c LibMed - v22 - i7 - April-May 2004 - p83(1) [501+]
Lette, Kathy - *Dead Sexy, Shelly*
  PW - v251 - i27 - July 5 2004 - p39(2) [501+]
Letters from Battlefront
  LibMed - v23 - i1 - August-Sept 2004 - p76(1) [51-500]
Lettow, Paul - *Ronald Reagan and His Quest to Abolish Nuclear Weapons*
  BL - v101 - i9-10 - Jan 1 2005 - p790(1) [1-50]
  KR - v72 - i24 - Dec 15 2004 - p1185(2) [501+]
  NYTBR - Feb 13 2005 - p7 [501+]
  PW - v252 - i2 - Jan 10 2005 - p48(2) [51-500]
Letts, Billie - *Shoot the Moon (Read by Mazur, Kathe). Audiobook Review*
  c BL - v101 - i6 - Nov 15 2004 - p606(1) [501+]
  c Kliatt - v38 - i6 - Nov 2004 - p50(1) [51-500]
Shoot the Moon
  c Ent W - i774 - July 16 2004 - p82 [501+]
Leuci, Robert - *All the Centurions*
  Ent W - i774 - July 16 2004 - p82 [501+]
Leuck, Laura - *My Creature Teacher (Illus. by Nash, Scott)*
  c SLJ - v50 - i7 - July 2004 - p81(1) [51-500]
One Witch
  c LibMed - v22 - i4 - Jan 2004 - p59(1) [501+]
Leung, Hok-Lin - *Land Use Planning Made Plain, 2nd Ed.*
  R&R Bk N - v19 - i1 - Feb 2004 - p95(1) [1-50]
Leung, Jacqueline M. - *Cardiac and Vascular Anesthesia: The Requisites in Anesthesiology*
  SciTech - v28 - i3 - Sept 2004 - p111(1) [51-500]
Leung, Joseph Y-T. - *Handbook of Scheduling: Algorithms, Models and Performance Analysis*
  SciTech - v28 - i3 - Sept 2004 - p31(1) [51-500]
Leupin, Alexandre - *Fiction and Incarnation: Rhetoric, Theology, and Literature in the Middle Ages*
  Comp L - v56 - i3 - Summer 2004 - p262-266 [501+]
Leupp, Gary P. - *Interracial Intimacy in Japan: Western Men and Japanese Women, 1543-1900*
  R&R Bk N - v19 - i1 - Feb 2004 - p130(1) [51-500]
Leutwiler, Anita - *Excuse Me, Is This India?*
  SLJ - v50 - i12 - Dec 2004 - p118(1) [501+]
Lev, Arlene Istar - *Transgender Emergence: Therapeutic Guidelines for Working with Gender-variant People and Their Families*
  SciTech - v28 - i3 - Sept 2004 - p102(1) [51-500]
Levander, Caroline F. - *The American Child: A Cultural Studies Reader*
  Adoles - v39 - i154 - Summer 2004 - p401(1) [51-500]
  HB - v80 - i4 - July-August 2004 - p472(2) [51-500]
Levanon, Nadav - *Radar Signals*
  SciTech - v28 - i3 - Sept 2004 - p160(1) [51-500]
Levantrosser, William - *Noble Calling: Character and the George H.W. Bush Presidency*
  R&R Bk N - v19 - i4 - Nov 2004 - p64(1) [51-500]
Levchev, Lyubomir - *And Here I Am*
  WLT - v78 - i3-4 - Sept-Dec 2004 - p134(2) [501+]
Levchin, Rafael - *Ludus Danielis*
  WLT - v78 - i3-4 - Sept-Dec 2004 - p137(1) [501+]
Leveen, Steve - *The Little Guide to Your Well-Read Life: How to Get More Books in Your Life and More Life from Your Books*
  PW - v252 - i9 - Feb 28 2005 - p54(1) [501+]
Leveille, J.R. - *The Setting Lake Sun*
  Can Lit - i182 - Autumn 2004 - p183(3) [501+]
Leveille, Kathy-Diane - *Roads Unravelling*
  CBRA - Annual 2003 - p200(1) [51-500]
Levenda, Peter - *Unholy Alliance: A History of Nazi Involvement with the Occult*
  J Ch St - v46 - i3 - Summer 2004 - p659(2) [501+]

Levene, D.S. - *Clio and the Poets. Augustan Poetry and the Ancient Traditions of Ancient Historiography*
  Class R - v53 - i2 - Nov 2003 - p357-358 [501+]
Levene, Donna B. - *American Musicians Making History*
  LibMed - v23 - i1 - August-Sept 2004 - p86(1) [51-500]
Levenson, George - *Bread Comes to Life: A Garden of Wheat and a Loaf to Eat. (Illus. by Thaler, Shmuel)*
  c BL - v101 - i3 - Oct 1 2004 - p331(2) [51-500]
Bread Comes to Life: A Garden of Wheat and a Loaf to Eat (Illus. by Thaler, Shmuel)
  c SLJ - v50 - i12 - Dec 2004 - p134(1) [51-500]
Levenson, Jacob - *The Secret Epidemic: The Story of Aids and Black America*
  Nation - v279 - i7 - Sept 13 2004 - p56 [501+]
Levenson, Thomas - *Einstein in Berlin*
  Physics T - v43 - i1 - Jan 2005 - p58-59 [501+]
Levenstein, Harvey A. - *We'll Always Have Paris: American Tourists in France Since 1930*
  CHE - v51 - i19 - Jan 14 2005 - pB13-B14 [501+]
  LJ - v129 - i20 - Dec 1 2004 - p145(1) [51-500]
Leveque, Christian - *Biodiversity*
  Choice - v42 - i1 - Sept 2004 - p129(1) [51-500]
  E-Streams - August 2004 - pNA [501+]
Ecology From Ecosystem to Biosphere
  SciTech - v28 - i1 - March 2004 - p65(1) [51-500]
Leveque, Laure - *Le Roman de l'Histoire*
  NCFS - v32 - i3-4 - Spring-Summer 2004 - p382(5) [501+]
Levere, Trevor - *Discussing Chemistry and Steam: The Minutes of a Coffee House Philosophical Society, 1780-1787*
  T&C - v45 - i3 - July 2004 - p647-648 [501+]
Leverenz, David - *Paternalism Incorporated: Fables of American Fatherhood, 1865-1940*
  Choice - v42 - i1 - Sept 2004 - p101(1) [501+]
  JAH - v91 - i3 - Dec 2004 - p1033(2) [501+]
  JEL - v42 - i1 - March 2004 - p301(1) [501+]
Leverington, David - *Babylon to Voyager and Beyond: A History of Planetary Astronomy*
  Choice - v41 - i7 - March 2004 - p1319(1) [501+]
Levert, Mireille - *Lucy's Secret*
  c Res Links - v10 - i1 - Oct 2004 - p6(1) [51-500]
LeVert, Suzanne - *The Congress*
  c SLJ - v50 - i8 - August 2004 - p48(1) [51-500]
Levesque, Roger J.R. - *Sexuality education: What Adolescents Rights Require*
  R&R Bk N - v19 - i2 - May 2004 - p132 [51-500]
Levey, Michael - *The Burlington Magazine: A Centenary Anthology*
  Sew R - v112 - i2 - Spring 2004 - pLXII-LXV [501+]
Levi, Anthony - *Louis XIV*
  CR - v285 - i1664 - Sept 2004 - p185(2) [51-500]
Levi, Carlo - *Fleeting Rome: In Search of "La Dolce Vita"*
  TLS - i5303 - Nov 19 2004 - p32(1) [501+]
Levi, Charles Morden - *Comings and Goings: University Students in Canadian Society, 1834-1973*
  CBRA - Annual 2003 - p394(2) [501+]
Levi, Vicki Gold - *Times Square Style: Graphics from the Great White Way*
  AH - v55 - i5 - Oct 2004 - p20(1) [51-500]
Leviant, Curt - *King Artus: A Hebrew Arthurian Romance of 1279*
  R&R Bk N - v19 - i1 - Feb 2004 - p218(1) [51-500]
Levick, Stephen E. - *Clone Being: Exploring the Psychological and Social Dimensions*
  Choice - v42 - i3 - Nov 2004 - p508(1) [1-50]
  SciTech - v28 - i1 - March 2004 - p63(1) [51-500]
Levin, Bridget - *Rules of the Wild: An Unruly Book of Manners (Illus. by Shepherd, Amanda)*
  c KR - v72 - i16 - August 15 2004 - p809(1) [51-500]
Rules of the Wild;: An Unruly Book of Manners (Illus. by Shepherd, Amanda)
  c PW - v251 - i46 - Nov 15 2004 - p58(1) [501+]
Rules of the Wild: An Unruly Book of Manners (Illus. by Shepherd, Amanda)
  c SLJ - v50 - i10 - Oct 2004 - p120(2) [51-500]
Levin, Carole - *Elizabeth I: Always Her Own Free Woman*
  HNet - August 2004 - pNA [501+]
  R&R Bk N - v19 - i1 - Feb 2004 - p32(1) [1-50]
Levin, David H. - *Bridge Puzzles For Children*
  c CH Bwatch - v14 - i8 - August 2004 - p4(1) [51-500]
Levin, Donald A. - *The Role of Chromosomal Change in Plant Evolution*
  QRB - v79 - i3 - Sept 2004 - p311(2) [501+]

Levin, Henry M. - *Privatizing Education: Can the Marketplace Deliver Choice, Efficiency, Equity, and Social Cohesion?*
JEL - v41 - i4 - Dec 2003 - p1305(2) [501+]

Levin, Itamar - *His Majesty's Enemies: Great Britain's War against Holocaust Victims and Survivors*
GSR - v27 - i2 - May 2004 - p417-418 [501+]
Walls Around: The Plunder of Warsaw Jewry during World War II and Its Aftermath
Choice - v42 - i5 - Jan 2005 - p911(1) [1-50]
R&R Bk N - v19 - i3 - August 2004 - p35(1) [51-500]

Levin, Jack - *Elementary Statistics in Social Research: The Essentials*
R&R Bk N - v19 - i1 - Feb 2004 - p77(1) [51-500]
Sociological Snapshots 4: Seeing Social Structure and Change in Everyday Life
R&R Bk N - v19 - i2 - May 2004 - p127 [51-500]
Why We Hate
R&R Bk N - v19 - i4 - Nov 2004 - p146(1) [501+]

Levin, Jack S. - *Structuring Venture Capital, Private Equity, and Entrepreneurial Transactions, 2004 Ed.*
R&R Bk N - v19 - i3 - August 2004 - p199(1) [1-50]

Levin, James - *Principles of Classroom Management: A Professional Decision-Making Model, 4th ed.*
R&R Bk N - v19 - i1 - Feb 2004 - p188(1) [51-500]

Levin, Judy - *Life at a High Altitude*
y SLJ - v51 - i1 - Jan 2005 - p150(1) [51-500]
VOYA - v27 - i5 - Dec 2004 - p420(1) [51-500]

Levin, Richard A. - *Shakespeare's Secret Schemers: The Study of an Early Modern Dramatic Device*
Shakes Q - v55 - i2 - Summer 2004 - p236-238 [501+]

Levinas, Emmanuel - *Unforeseen History*
Choice - v41 - i11-12 - July-August 2004 - p2058(1) [501+]

Levine, Abby - *This Is the Matzah*
c PW - v252 - i7 - Feb 14 2005 - p81(1) [51-500]

Levine, Alan - *Sensual Philosophy: Toleration, Skepticism, and Montaigne's Politics of the Self*
Ren Q - v57 - i4 - Winter 2004 - p1427(2) [501+]
RM - v58 - i2 - Dec 2004 - p454(2) [501+]

Levine, Alan J. - *From the Normandy Beaches to the Baltic Sea: The Northwest Europe Campaign, 1944-1945*
GSR - v27 - i3 - Oct 2004 - p652(2) [501+]

Levine, Amy-Jill - *Feminist Companion to the New Testament and Early Christian Writings*
OS - v40 - i4 - July-August 2004 - p39(1) [501+]

Levine, Andrew - *A Future for Marxism? Althusser, the Analytical Turn, and the Revival of Socialist Theory*
S&S - v68 - i1 - Spring 2004 - p93-101 [501+]

Levine, Anna - *Running on Eggs*
c BL - v101 - i7 - Dec 1 2004 - p647(1) [51-500]

Levine, Carol - *Cultures of Caregiving: Conflict and Common Ground Among Families, Health Professionals, and Policy Makers*
E-Streams - Nov 2004 - pNA [501+]

Levine, Caroline - *The Serious Pleasures of Suspense: Victorian Realism and Narrative Doubt*
R&R Bk N - v19 - i1 - Feb 2004 - p235(1) [51-500]

Levine-Clark, Marjorie - *Beyond the Reproductive Body: The Politics of Women's Health and Work in Early Victorian England*
Choice - v42 - i3 - Nov 2004 - p554(1) [1-50]

Levine, Ed - *Pizza: A Slice of Heaven*
PW - v252 - i7 - Feb 14 2005 - p68(2) [51-500]

Levine, Ellen - *Freedom's Children: Young Civil Rights Activists Tell Their Own Stories*
y SLJ - v50 - i10 - Oct 2004 - p67(2) [51-500]

Levine, Gail Carson - *Betsy Who Cried Wolf (Illus. by Nash, Scott)*
c RT - v57 - Oct 2003 - p168 [1-50]

Levine, John R. - *UNIX for Dummies. 5th Ed.*
SciTech - v28 - i3 - Sept 2004 - p28(1) [51-500]

Levine, Joseph M. - *Re-Enacting the Past: Essays on the Evolution of Modern English Historiography*
R&R Bk N - v19 - i4 - Nov 2004 - p35(1) [51-500]

Levine, Judith - *Do You Remember Me?: A Father, a Daughter, and a Search for the Self*
R&R Bk N - v19 - i3 - August 2004 - p150(1) [51-500]

Levine, Karen - *Hana's Suitcase*
CE - v81 - i1 - Fall 2004 - p48(1) [51-500]
RT - v58 - i3 - Nov 2004 - p290(2) [51-500]

Levine, Marsha - *Prehistoric Steppe Adaptation and the Horse*
Choice - v42 - i3 - Nov 2004 - p528(1) [1-50]

Levine, Melvin D. - *Ready or Not, Here Life Comes*
LJ - v130 - i4 - March 1 2005 - p105(1) [51-500]
PW - v252 - i1 - Jan 3 2005 - p52(1) [51-500]

Levine, Michael - *Charming Your Way to the Top: Hollywood's Premier P.R. Executive Shows You How to Get Ahead*
BL - v101 - i5 - Nov 1 2004 - p450(1) [51-500]
PW - v251 - i45 - Nov 8 2004 - p45(2) [501+]

Levine, Michael (b. 1954-) - *The Broken Windows, Broken Business*
Har Bus R - v83 - i2 - Feb 2005 - p57(1) [1-50]

Levine, Michael P. - *Racism in Mind*
Bl S - v34 - i3 - Fall 2004 - p73-73 [501+]

Levine, Michelle - *Rosa Parks*
c SLJ - v51 - i1 - Jan 2005 - p112(1) [51-500]

Levine, Myron M. - *New Generation Vaccines, 3rd Rev. Ed.*
E-Streams - Sept 2004 - pNA [501+]

Levine, Norman (b. 1923-) - *The Ability to Forget: Short Stories*
Can Lit - i182 - Autumn 2004 - p145(3) [501+]
CBRA - Annual 2003 - p200(2) [51-500]

Levine, Norman (b. 1945-) - *Dermatology Therapy: A-Z Essentials*
E-Streams - Nov 2004 - pNA [501+]

Levine, Patt - *Eating Well after Weight Loss Surgery*
LJ - v129 - i14 - Sept 1 2004 - p176(1) [51-500]

Levine, Paul - *Arms Trade, Security and Conflict*
JEL - v41 - i4 - Dec 2003 - p1354(1) [501+]

Levine, Philip - *Breath*
c BL - v100 - i22 - August 2004 - p1892(1) [51-500]
c LJ - v129 - i13 - August 2004 - p86(1) [501+]
c NL - v87 - i4 - July-August 2004 - p33(3) [501+]
c NYTBR - Nov 21 2004 - p19 [501+]
c PW - v251 - i38 - Sept 20 2004 - p60(1) [51-500]

Levine, Philippa - *Prostitution, Race, and Politics: Policing Venereal Disease in the British Empire*
AHR - v109 - i2 - April 2004 - p483(2) [501+]
Albion - v36 - i2 - Summer 2004 - p386(2) [501+]

Levine, Phillip B. - *Sex and Consequences: Abortion, Public Policy, and the Economics of Fertility*
Choice - v42 - i5 - Jan 2005 - p894(1) [1-50]
Pub Int - i158 - Wntr 2005 - p131(4) [501+]

Levine, Robert - *Aging with Attitude: Growing Older with Dignity and Vitality*
Choice - v42 - i4 - Dec 2004 - p739(1) [1-50]
R&R Bk N - v19 - i3 - August 2004 - p152(1) [51-500]

LeVine, Robert A. - *Childhood Socialization: Comparative Studies of Parenting, Learning and Educational Change*
TCR - v106 - i2 - Feb 2004 - p305-307 [501+]

Levine, Robert M. - *Secret Missions to Cuba: Fidel Castro, Benardo Benes, and Cuban Miami*
HAHR - v84 - i3 - August 2004 - p570(3) [501+]

Levine, Robert S. - *Martin R. Delany: A Documentary Reader*
JSH - v70 - i3 - August 2004 - p697(3) [501+]

Levine, Shar - *First Science Experiments: Mighty Machines (Illus. by Harpster, Steve)*
c SLJ - v50 - i9 - Sept 2004 - p189(1) [51-500]
Play Marbles!
c PW - v251 - i43 - Oct 25 2004 - p50(1) [51-500]
Wonderful Weather
c SB - v40 - i5 - Sept-Oct 2004 - p195(1) [51-500]

Levine, Stephen - *Unattended Sorrow: Recovering from Loss and Reviving the Heart*
PW - v251 - i51 - Dec 20 2004 - p44(1) [51-500]

LeVine, Steven M. - *Redox-Active Metals in Neurological Disorders*
SciTech - v28 - i4 - Dec 2004 - p93(1) [51-500]

Levine, Stuart - *J.R.R. Tolkien*
y CH Bwatch - v14 - i7 - July 2004 - p5(1) [51-500]
Life in a Rain Forest
c SB - v40 - i6 - Nov-Dec 2004 - p269(2) [51-500]

Levine, Suzanne Braun - *Inventing the Rest of Our Lives: Women in Second Adulthood*
KR - v72 - i19 - Oct 1 2004 - p949(1) [501+]
PW - v251 - i42 - Oct 18 2004 - p55(1) [51-500]

Levinson, Bradley A.U. - *Ethnography and Education Policy Across the Americas*
CS - v33 - i6 - Nov 2004 - p746(1) [1-50]

Levinson, Brett - *The Ends of Literature: The Latin American "Boom" in the Neoliberal Marketplace*
MFSF - v50 - i2 - Summer 2004 - p496-498 [501+]

Levinson, Conrad - *Guerrilla Marketing in 30 Days*
PW - v252 - i1 - Jan 3 2005 - p47(1) [51-500]

Levinson, David - *Encyclopedia of Homelessness*
BL - v101 - i4 - Oct 15 2004 - p437(1) [501+]
Encyclopedia of Homelessness, Vols. 1-2
BL - v101 - i9-10 - Jan 1 2005 - p779(1) [1-50]
Choice - v42 - i5 - Jan 2005 - p836(1) [1-50]
LJ - v129 - i15 - Sept 15 2004 - p81(1) [51-500]
Ref Rev - Oct 2004 - pNA [501+]
The Wilson Chronology of Human Rights
R&R Bk N - v19 - i1 - Feb 2004 - p149(1) [51-500]

Levinson, Edward M. - *Transition from School to Post-School Life for Individuals with Disabilities: Assessment from an Educational and School Psychological Perspective*
R&R Bk N - v19 - i4 - Nov 2004 - p193(1) [501+]

Levinson, Elizabeth - *Edible Journey: Exploring the Islands' Fine Food, Farms and Vineyards*
CBRA - Annual 2003 - p133(1) [51-500]

Levinson, Nancy - *Cars (Illus. by Rogers, Jacqueline)*
c BL - v101 - i6 - Nov 15 2004 - p588(2) [51-500]
KR - v72 - i17 - Sept 1 2004 - p870(1) [51-500]
c SLJ - v50 - i12 - Dec 2004 - p134(1) [501+]

Levinson, Paul - *Cellphone: The Story of the World's Most Mobile Medium and How it Has Transformed Everything!*
SciTech - v28 - i3 - Sept 2004 - p159(1) [51-500]
The Pixel Eye
Analog - v124 - i1-2 - Jan-Feb 2004 - p231(2) [501+]
Realspace
Analog - v124 - i3 - March 2004 - p135(2) [501+]

Levinson, Robert S. - *Ask a Dead Man*
BL - v101 - i6 - Nov 15 2004 - p565(1) [51-500]
KR - v72 - i20 - Oct 15 2004 - p987(1) [51-500]
PW - v251 - i51 - Dec 20 2004 - p38(1) [51-500]

Levinson, Sanford - *Torture: A Collection*
Nation - v280 - i5 - Feb 7 2005 - p23 [501+]
NYTBR - Jan 23 2005 - p11 [501+]
PW - v251 - i40 - Oct 4 2004 - p85(1) [51-500]
LJ - v129 - i20 - Dec 1 2004 - p141(1) [51-500]

Levinson, Warren - *Medical Microbiology and Immunology: Examination and Board Review*
SciTech - v28 - i3 - Sept 2004 - p73(1) [51-500]

Levinson, William - *Lean Enterprise*
Bwatch - v26 - i7 - July 2004 - p3(2) [51-500]

Levitan, Sar A. - *Programs in Aid of the Poor*
JEL - v42 - i1 - March 2004 - p277(1) [501+]

Levith, Murray J. - *Shakespeare in China*
R&R Bk N - v19 - i4 - Nov 2004 - p236(1) [501+]

Levithan, David - *Boy Meets Boy*
LibMed - v22 - i6 - March 2004 - p68(1) [501+]
The Realm of Possibility
y BL - v101 - i1 - Sept 1 2004 - p108(1) [1-50]
y KR - v72 - i14 - July 15 2004 - p689(1) [51-500]
c LibMed - v23 - i3 - Nov-Dec 2004 - p72(1) [51-500]
y PW - v251 - i36 - Sept 6 2004 - p63(1) [51-500]
y SLJ - v50 - i9 - Sept 2004 - p211(1) [51-500]
y VOYA - v27 - i3 - August 2004 - p220(1) [1-50]

Levitin, Jacqueline - *Women Filmmakers Refocusing*
CBRA - Annual 2003 - p110(1) [501+]
J Film & Vid - v56 - i1 - Spring 2004 - p55-56 [501+]

Levitin, Sonia - *Room in the Heart*
LibMed - v22 - i7 - April-May 2004 - p63(1) [501+]

Levitt, Joel - *Managing Maintenance Shutdowns and Outages*
SciTech - v28 - i3 - Sept 2004 - p171(1) [51-500]

Levitt, Kari - *Silent Surrender: The Multinational Corporation in Canada*
CBRA - Annual 2003 - p329(1) [51-500]

Levitt, Leonard - *Conviction: Solving the Moxley Murder: A Reporter and a Detective's 20-Year Search for Justice*
PW - v251 - i35 - August 30 2004 - p43(1) [51-500]

Levitt, Steven D. - *Freakonomics: A Rogue Economist Explores the Hidden Side of Everything*
PW - v252 - i11 - March 14 2005 - p53(2) [51-500]

LeVitus, Bob - *Mac OS X Panther for Dummies*
SciTech - v28 - i3 - Sept 2004 - p26(1) [51-500]

Levrini, Aurelio - *Masters of Functional Orthodontics*
SciTech - v28 - i1 - March 2004 - p120(1) [51-500]

Levy, Allison - *Widowhood and Visual Culture in Early Modern Europe*
Choice - v41 - i7 - March 2004 - p1362(1) [501+]
Ren Q - v57 - i3 - Fall 2004 - p1080(3) [501+]

Levy, Andrea - *Small Island*
  Globe & Mail - Nov 27 2004 - pD3 [51-500]
  Globe & Mail - Dec 24 2004 - pD3 [1-50]
  KR - v73 - i4 - Feb 15 2005 - p192(1) [501+]
  PW - v252 - i10 - March 7 2005 - p50(1) [51-500]
  Ent W - i810 - March 11 2005 - p107 [51-500]
Levy, Bernard Henri - *Sartre: The Philosopher of the Twentieth Century*
  Choice - v41 - i7 - March 2004 - p1310(1) [501+]
War, Evil and the End of History
  NS - v133 - i4712 - Nov 1 2004 - p48(2) [501+]
Levy, Constance - *The Story of Red Rubber Ball (Illus. by Nakata, Hiroe)*
  c CE - v81 - i1 - Fall 2004 - p46(2) [51-500]
  c SLJ - v50 - i7 - July 2004 - p81(1) [51-500]
Levy, Daniel - *Challenging Ethnic Citizenships. German and Israeli Perspectives on Immigration*
  Ger Q - v77 - i1 - Wntr 2004 - p123(2) [501+]
A Change of Heart: How the Framingham Heart Study Helped Unravel the Mysteries of Cardiovascular Disease
  LJ - v130 - i2 - Feb 1 2005 - p108(2) [51-500]
Levy, David H. - *David Levy's Guide to Observing and Discovering Comets*
  S&T - v107 - i4 - April 2004 - p72(2) [501+]
Levy, David M. - *Scrolling Forward*
  Bwatch - Oct 2004 - pNA [51-500]
Levy, Donald R. - *Quick Reference to IRAs, 2003 Ed.*
  R&R Bk N - v19 - i1 - Feb 2004 - pNA [51-500]
Levy, Evonne - *Propaganda and the Jesuit Baroque*
  TLS - i5287 - July 30 2004 - p28(1) [501+]
Levy, F.J. - *Tudor Historical Thought*
  HRNB - v33 - i1 - Fall 2004 - p40(2) [501+]
Levy, Frank - *The New Division of Labor: How Computers are Creating the Next Job Market*
  Choice - v42 - i4 - Dec 2004 - p704(2) [1-50]
Levy, Frederick - *Short Films 101: How to Make a Short Film and Launch Your Filmmaking Career*
  R&R Bk N - v19 - i3 - August 2004 - p263(1) [51-500]
Levy, Ian Christopher - *John Wyclif: Scriptural Logic, Real Presence, and the Parameters of Orthodoxy*
  R&R Bk N - v19 - i3 - August 2004 - p27(1) [1-50]
Levy, Jo Ann - *Unsettling the West: Eliza Farnham and Georgiana Bruce Kirby in Frontier California*
  Choice - v42 - i5 - Jan 2005 - p916(2) [1-50]
Unsettling the West: Eliza Farnham and Georgiana Bruce Kirby in Frontier California
  R&R Bk N - v19 - i3 - August 2004 - p75(1) [51-500]
Levy, Leonard W. - *Emergence of a Free Press*
  R&R Bk N - v19 - i3 - August 2004 - p203(1) [1-50]
Levy, Peter B. - *Civil War on Race Street: The Civil Rights Movement in Cambridge, Maryland*
  HNet - Sept 2004 - pNA [501+]
  JAH - v91 - i3 - Dec 2004 - p1085(2) [501+]
  JSH - v71 - i1 - Feb 2005 - p212(1) [501+]
Levy, Robert - *Analysis of Geometrically Nonlinear Structures, 2nd Ed.*
  SciTech - v28 - i1 - March 2004 - p143(1) [51-500]
Levy, Silvano - *The Scandalous Eye: The Surrealism of Conroy Maddox*
  Choice - v42 - i2 - Oct 2004 - p285(1) [501+]
Levy, Sophie - *A Transalantic Avant-Garde: American Artists in Paris*
  Choice - v41 - i11-12 - July-August 2004 - p2033(1) [501+]
Levy-Yamamori, Ran - *Garden Plants of Japan*
  BL - v101 - i4 - Oct 15 2004 - p372(1) [51-500]
Lew, Alan A. - *A Companion to Tourism*
  Choice - v42 - i2 - Oct 2004 - p346(1) [51-500]
  R&R Bk N - v19 - i3 - August 2004 - p79(1) [51-500]
Lew, Douglas - *Painting from Life: Explorations in Watercolor*
  LJ - v129 - i19 - Nov 15 2004 - p59(1) [501+]
Lewan, Todd - *The Last Run*
  Ent W - i773 - July 9 2004 - p93 [501+]
Lewandrowski, Kai-Uwe - *Advances in Spinal Fusion: Molecular Science, Biomechanics, and Clinical Management*
  SciTech - v28 - i1 - March 2004 - p113(1) [51-500]
Lewars, Errol - *Computational Chemistry: Introduction to the Theory and Applications of Molecular and Quantum Mechanics*
  Choice - v41 - i7 - March 2004 - p1324(1) [501+]
Lewellen, Ted C. - *Political Anthropology: An Introduction, 3rd Ed.*
  R&R Bk N - v19 - i1 - Feb 2004 - p71(1) [1-50]

Lewin, Alison Williams - *Negotiating Survival: Florence and the Great Schism, 1378-1417*
  AHR - v109 - i4 - Oct 2004 - p1299-1300 [501+]
Lewin, Betsy - *Animal Snackers (Illus. by Lewin, Betsy)*
  c KR - v72 - i16 - August 15 2004 - p809(1) [51-500]
  c SLJ - v50 - i10 - Oct 2004 - p144(1) [51-500]
Lewin, David - *Advances in Industrial and Labor Relations*
  JEL - v41 - i4 - Dec 2003 - p1387(2) [501+]
Lewin, Jackie - *Fear of Dying*
  BL - v100 - i22 - August 2004 - p1905(1) [51-500]
  LJ - v129 - i13 - August 2004 - p60(1) [501+]
Lewin, Linda (b. 1941-) - *Surprise Heirs, Vol. 1*
  AHR - v109 - i3 - June 2004 - p953(1) [501+]
Surprise Heirs, Vol. 2
  AHR - v109 - i3 - June 2004 - p953(2) [501+]
Surprise Heirs, Vol. II
  HAHR - v84 - i3 - August 2004 - p530(4) [501+]
Lewin, Michael Z. - *Eye Opener*
  BL - v101 - i8 - Dec 15 2004 - p711(1) [51-500]
Lewin, Roger - *Principles of Human Evolution*
  QRB - v79 - i3 - Sept 2004 - p339(1) [501+]
Lewin, Ted - *Big Jimmy's Kum Kau Chinese Take Out (Illus. by Lewin, Ted)*
  c SLJ - v51 - i2 - Feb 2005 - p57(2) [51-500]
Girl on the High-Diving Horse: An Adventure in the Atlantic City
  c LibMed - v22 - i5 - Feb 2004 - p67(1) [501+]
Losing Is not an Option
  y LibMed - v22 - i6 - March 2004 - p68(1) [501+]
Lost City: The Discovery of Machu Picchu
  c LibMed - v22 - i4 - Jan 2004 - p76(1) [501+]
Top to Bottom Down Under (Illus. by Lewin, Ted)
  c PW - v252 - i5 - Jan 31 2005 - p70(1) [501+]
  c BL - v101 - i9-10 - Jan 1 2005 - p866(1) [51-500]
Top to Bottom Down Under. (Illus. by Lewin, Ted)
  c KR - v73 - i4 - Feb 15 2005 - p231(1) [51-500]
Lewington, Anna - *Plants for People*
  LJ - v129 - i13 - August 2004 - p113(1) [51-500]
Lewinski, John Scott - *Alone in a Room: The Secrets of Professional Screenwriters*
  LJ - v129 - i14 - Sept 1 2004 - p164(2) [501+]
Lewis, Adrian - *Roger Hilton*
  R&R Bk N - v19 - i1 - Feb 2004 - p199(1) [51-500]
Lewis, Amanda - *Jumbo Book of Paper Crafts (Illus. by Kurisu, Jane)*
  c CBRA - Annual 2003 - p554(2) [51-500]
Lewis, Amanda E. - *Race in the Schoolyard: Negotiating the Color Line in Classrooms and Communities*
  CS - v33 - i2 - March 2004 - p244-245 [501+]
The Lewis and Clark Expedition
  R&R Bk N - v19 - i3 - August 2004 - p74(1) [51-500]
Lewis-Beck, Michael S. - *The Sage Encyclopedia of Social Science Research Methods*
  Choice - v42 - i1 - Sept 2004 - p82(1) [501+]
  R&USQ - v44 - i1 - Fall 2004 - p94(2) [501+]
Lewis, Bernard - *The Crisis of Islam: Holy War and Unholy Terror*
  J Ch St - v46 - i3 - Summer 2004 - p648(3) [501+]
From Babel to Dragomans: Interpreting the Middle East
  Nation - v279 - i7 - Sept 13 2004 - p49 [501+]
  NYRB - v51 - i17 - Nov 4 2004 - p31(4) [501+]
Land of Enchanters: Egyptian Short Stories from the Earliest Times to the Present Day
  JNES - v63 - i4 - Oct 2004 - p317(1) [501+]
Lewis, Bonnie Sue - *Creating Christian Indians: Native Clergy in the Presbyterian Church*
  CH - v73 - i4 - Dec 2004 - p887(2) [501+]
  HNet - Sept 2004 - pNA [501+]
  IBMR - v28 - i3 - July 2004 - p135(1) [501+]
  JAH - v91 - i1 - June 2004 - p261-261 [501+]
  JR - v84 - i4 - Oct 2004 - p631(2) [501+]
  WHQ - v35 - i4 - Winter 2004 - p518-518 [501+]
  CHR - v90 - i3 - July 2004 - p579(2) [501+]
Lewis, C.S. - *The Chronicles of Narnia. Audiobook Review*
  c Globe & Mail - Dec 11 2004 - pD53 [1-50]
The Collected Letters of C.S. Lewis, Vol. I
  Bks & Cult - v10 - i5 - Sept-Oct 2004 - p8(2) [501+]
The Collected Letters of C.S. Lewis, Vol. II
  Bks & Cult - v10 - i5 - Sept-Oct 2004 - p8(2) [501+]
The Last Battle (Read by Stewart, Patrick). Audiobook Review
  c BL - v101 - i7 - Dec 1 2004 - p678(1) [1-50]
The Lion, the Witch, and the Wardrobe
  c RT - v57 - Sept 2003 - p98 [1-50]
The Magician's Nephew
  c Storyworks - v12 - i3 - Nov-Dec 2004 - p7(1) [51-500]

The Silver Chair (Read by Northam, Jeremy). Audiobook Review
  c HB - v80 - i6 - Nov-Dec 2004 - p734(1) [501+]
Lewis, Charles - *The Buying of the President 2004: Who's Really Bankrolling Bush and His Democratic Challengers--And What They Expect in Return*
  PSQ - v119 - i3 - Fall 2004 - p529(2) [501+]
Lewis, Colin M. - *Argentina: A Short History*
  HAHR - v84 - i3 - August 2004 - p561(2) [501+]
Lewis, Darrell R. - *The Public Research University: Serving the Public Good in New Times*
  JEL - v41 - i4 - Dec 2003 - p1378(1) [501+]
Lewis, David E. - *Presidents and the Politics of Agency Design: Political Insulation in the United States Government Bureaucracy, 1946-1997*
  Choice - v41 - i7 - March 2004 - p1373(1) [501+]
Lewis, David T. - *The Family Limited Partnership Deskbook: Forming and Funding FLPs and Other Closely Held Business Entities*
  R&R Bk N - v19 - i4 - Nov 2004 - p167(1) [501+]
Lewis, Donald M. - *Christianity Reborn: the Global Expansion of Evangelicalism in the Twentieth Century*
  R&R Bk N - v19 - i3 - August 2004 - p21(1) [1-50]
Lewis, E.B. - *Aston, Dianna Hutts. When You Were Born*
  SLJ - v50 - i12 - Dec 2004 - p96(1) [501+]
This Little Light of Mine
  KR - v72 - i24 - Dec 15 2004 - p1204(1) [51-500]
Lewis, E.E. - *Masterworks of Technology: The Story of Creative Engineering, Architecture, and Design*
  Choice - v42 - i6 - Feb 2005 - p1042(1) [51-500]
  New Sci - v183 - i2463 - Sept 4 2004 - p46(2) [501+]
  SciTech - v28 - i4 - Dec 2004 - p128 [51-500]
Lewis, Frank L. - *Robot Manipulator Control: Theory and Practice, 2nd Ed.*
  SciTech - v28 - i1 - March 2004 - p150(1) [51-500]
Lewis, Gail - *Citizenship: Personal Lives and Social Policy*
  R&R Bk N - v19 - i4 - Nov 2004 - p153(1) [501+]
Lewis, Gwyneth - *Keeping Mum*
  MHR - v30 - i2 - Dec 2004 - p106(2) [501+]
Sunbathing in the Rain
  MHR - v30 - i2 - Dec 2004 - p106(2) [501+]
Lewis, Gwynne - *France, 1715-1804: Power and the People*
  R&R Bk N - v19 - i4 - Nov 2004 - p38(1) [51-500]
Lewis, H.J. - *Big Split*
  y CBRA - Annual 2003 - p498(1) [51-500]
Lewis, Hal M. - *Models and Meanings in the History of Jewish Leadership*
  R&R Bk N - v19 - i4 - Nov 2004 - p17(1) [51-500]
Lewis, Heather - *Notice*
  Advocate - Oct 12 2004 - p96(1) [501+]
  Lam Bk Rpt - v13 - i3 - Oct 2004 - p36(2) [501+]
  PW - v251 - i29 - July 19 2004 - p144(1) [51-500]
Lewis, Henry William - *I Got Somebody in Staunton*
  PW - v252 - i9 - Feb 28 2005 - p40(1) [51-500]
Lewis, J. Patrick - *Heroes and She-roes: Poems of Amazing and Everyday Heroes (Illus. by Cooke, Jim)*
  y BL - v101 - i9-10 - Jan 1 2005 - p849(1) [1-50]
  c KR - v73 - i4 - Feb 15 2005 - p231(1) [51-500]
Please Bury Me in the Library (Illus. by Stone, Kyle M.)
  c PW - v252 - i11 - March 14 2005 - p67(1) [51-500]
The Stolen Smile (Illus. by Kelley, Gary)
  c SLJ - v51 - i1 - Jan 2005 - p132(1) [51-500]
A World of Wonders (Illus. by Jay, Alison)
  c RT - v57 - Nov 2003 - p276 [1-50]
Lewis, James F. - *The Oxford Handbook of New Religious Movements*
  Choice - v42 - i3 - Nov 2004 - p501(1) [51-500]
Lewis, James R. - *The Astrology Book: The Encyclopedia Of Heavenly Influences*
  Bwatch - Feb 2005 - pNA [51-500]
  Choice - v41 - i11-12 - July-August 2004 - p2018(1) [501+]
The Encyclopedia Sourcebook of New Age Religious
  Choice - v42 - i6 - Feb 2005 - p992(1) [51-500]
Encyclopedic Sourcebook of UFO Religions
  Bwatch - v26 - i8 - August 2004 - p12(1) [51-500]
  R&USQ - v44 - i1 - Fall 2004 - p88(1) [501+]
Legitimating New Religions
  R&R Bk N - v19 - i1 - Feb 2004 - p15(1) [1-50]
Lewis, Jeffrey - *Meritocracy: A Love Story*
  PW - v251 - i29 - July 19 2004 - p141(2) [51-500]

Lewis, Jill - *Educators on the Frontline: Advocacy Strategies for Your Classroom, Your School, and Your Profession*
R Today - v22 - i2 - Oct-Nov 2004 - p34(1) [501+]

Lewis, Jim - *The King is Dead*
NYTBR - Nov 21 2004 - p36 [501+]

Lewis, Joanna - *Empire State-Building: War and Welfare in Kenya, 1925-52*
AHR - v109 - i3 - June 2004 - p1023(2) [501+]

Lewis, John - *Atlanta: An Illustrated History*
JSH - v70 - i4 - Nov 2004 - p990(2) [501+]

Lewis, Jon - *The End of Cinema as We Know It: American Film in the Nineties*
J Broadcst - v48 - i3 - Sept 2004 - p525(3) [501+]

Lewis, Kevin - *The Runaway Pumpkin*
c LibMed - v22 - i5 - Feb 2004 - p65(1) [501+]

Lewis, Kim - *Good Night Harry*
c LibMed - v22 - i7 - April-May 2004 - p57(1) [501+]

Lewis, Laura A. - *Hall of Mirrors: Power, Witchcraft, and Caste in Colonial Mexico*
AHR - v109 - i3 - June 2004 - p946(2) [501+]

Lewis, Linda M. - *Germaine de Stael, George Sand, and the Victorian Woman Artist*
NCFS - v33 - i1-2 - Fall-Winter 2004 - p219(3) [501+]

Lewis, Linden - *The Culture of Gender and Sexuality in the Caribbean*
CS - v33 - i6 - Nov 2004 - p689(2) [501+]

Lewis, Lucy M. - *American Indian Potter*
Ceram Mo - v52 - i6 - June-August 2004 - p34(1) [501+]

Lewis, Marla - *We All Laugh In The Same Language*
c CH Bwatch - Jan 2005 - pNA [51-500]

Lewis, Michael - *Moneyball: The Art of Winning an Unfair Game (Read by Brick, Scott). Audiobook Review*
Kliatt - v38 - i4 - July 2004 - p61(1) [51-500]
Moneyball: The Art of Winning an Unfair Game
TLS - i5262 - Feb 6 2004 - p8(1) [501+]
Spec - v296 - i9189 - Sept 18 2004 - p50(1) [501+]

Lewis, Michael L. - *Inventing Global Ecology: Tracking the Biodiversity Idea in India, 1947-1997*
Choice - v42 - i5 - Jan 2005 - p878(1) [1-50]
Inventing Global Ecology; Tracking the Biodiversity Ideal in India, 1947-1997
SciTech - v28 - i3 - Sept 2004 - p56(1) [1-50]

Lewis, Miles Marshall - *Scars of the Soul Are Why Kids Wear Bandages When They Don't Have Bruises*
Black Iss - v6 - i6 - Nov-Dec 2004 - p65(2) [501+]

Lewis, Naomi - *East o' the Sun and West o' the Moon, the Norwegian fairy tale*
c PW - v252 - i8 - Feb 21 2005 - p177(1) [51-500]

Lewis, Nathaniel - *Unsettling the Literary West: Aunthenticity and Authorship*
Am St - v45 - i1 - Spring 2004 - p141-142 [501+]

Lewis, Norah L. - *Freedom to Play: We Made Our Own Fun*
Can Hist R - v85 - i3 - Sept 2004 - p635(3) [501+]

Lewis, Norman - *The Tomb in Seville*
BL - v101 - i9-10 - Jan 1 2005 - p804(1) [51-500]
KR - v73 - i1 - Jan 1 2005 - p37(1) [501+]
PW - v252 - i1 - Jan 3 2005 - p43(2) [51-500]

Lewis, Paddy Greenwall - *Helping Children Cope with the Death of a Parent: A Guide for the First Year*
Choice - v42 - i1 - Sept 2004 - p192(1) [501+]

Lewis, Paeony - *No More Cookies! (Illus. by Granstrom, Brita)*
c KR - v73 - i5 - March 1 2005 - p290(1) [501+]

Lewis, Pam - *Speak Softly, She Can Hear*
BL - v101 - i9-10 - Jan 1 2005 - p819(1) [501+]
KR - v73 - i2 - Jan 15 2005 - p76(1) [501+]
PW - v252 - i4 - Jan 24 2005 - p219(1) [501+]

Lewis, Pamela - *Talking Funny for Money: An Introduction to the Cartoon/Character/Looping Area of Voice-Overs*
R&R Bk N - v19 - i1 - Feb 2004 - p225(1) [51-500]

Lewis, Patrick J. - *The Stolen Smile (Illus. by Kelley, Gary)*
c NYTBR - March 13 2005 - p21 [501+]

Lewis, Paul S. - *Superconductivity Research at the Leading Edge*
SciTech - v28 - i3 - Sept 2004 - p48(1) [1-50]

Lewis, Peirce F. - *New Orleans: The Making of an Urban Landscape*
Hist Geo - v32 - Annual 2004 - p209(2) [501+]

Lewis, Peter B. - *Wittgenstein, Aesthetics, and Philosophy*
R&R Bk N - v19 - i4 - Nov 2004 - p6(1) [51-500]

Lewis, Peter Rhys - *Forensic Materials Engineering: Case Studies*
SciTech - v28 - i1 - March 2004 - p137(1) [51-500]

Lewis, Philip - *Islamic Britain: Religion, Politics and Identity among British Muslims*
IJMES - v36 - i1 - Feb 2004 - p152-154 [501+]

Lewis, Rachael - *Scarlet Pony: Adventures in the Great Canadian North Country (Illus. by Verheyen, Stephanie)*
c CBRA - Annual 2003 - p456(2) [51-500]

Lewis, Richard - *The Flame Tree*
y CCB-B - v58 - i3 - Nov 2004 - p133(2) [501+]
y KR - v72 - i14 - July 15 2004 - p689(1) [51-500]
y PW - v251 - i36 - Sept 6 2004 - p63(2) [51-500]
y Sch Lib - v52 - i4 - Winter 2004 - p215(2) [51-500]
y SLJ - v50 - i10 - Oct 2004 - p171(1) [51-500]
y VOYA - v27 - i4 - Oct 2004 - p304(1) [51-500]

Lewis, Richard J., Sr. - *Sax's Dangerous Properties of Industrial Materials*
Choice - v42 - i7 - March 2005 - p1255(1) [51-500]

Lewis, Robert M. - *From Traveling Show to Vaudeville: Theatrical Spectacle in America, 1830-1910*
JouAmCul - v27 - i3 - Sept 2004 - p339(1) [501+]
R&R Bk N - v19 - i1 - Feb 2004 - p227(1) [51-500]

Lewis, Roger - *Anthony Burgess*
Choice - v41 - i11-12 - July-August 2004 - p2045(1) [501+]

Lewis, Roland W. - *Fundamentals of the Finite Element Method for Heat and Fluid Flow. 1st Ed.*
TimHES - v0 - i1668 - Nov 26 2004 - pXIII(1) [501+]

Lewis, Sian - *The Athenian Woman: An Iconographic Handbook*
Class R - v53 - i2 - Nov 2003 - p450-452 [501+]

Lewis, Simon - *White Women Writers and Their African Invention*
Choice - v41 - i7 - March 2004 - p1297(1) [501+]

Lewis, Sinclair - *Work of Art*
New ER - v25 - i3 - Summer 2004 - p161-171 [501+]

Lewis, Timothy - *In the Long Run We're All Dead: The Canadian Turn to Fiscal Restraint*
R&R Bk N - v19 - i3 - August 2004 - p140(1) [51-500]

Lewis, Valerie V. - *Valerie and Walter's Best Books for Children: A Lively, Opinionated Guide, 2nd Ed.*
SLJ - v51 - i2 - Feb 2005 - p160(1) [501+]

Lewis, Vicky - *The Reality of Research With Children and Young People*
R&R Bk N - v19 - i2 - May 2004 - p134 [51-500]

Lewis, Wayne - *Ph.D.'s CCNP 4: Network Troubleshooting Companion Guide*
Bwatch - Feb 2005 - pNA [501+]

Lewis, Wendy A. - *In Abby's Hands (Illus. by Mets, Marilyn)*
c CBRA - Annual 2003 - p457(1) [501+]

Lewis, William Henry - *I Got Somebody in Staunton: Stories*
KR - v73 - i1 - Jan 1 2005 - p12(1) [501+]

Lewis, William W. (b. 1942 -) - *The Power of Productivity: Wealth, Poverty, and the Threat to Global Stability*
Har Bus R - v82 - i6 - June 2004 - p28(1) [501+]
TimHES - v0 - i1666 - Nov 12 2004 - p26(2) [501+]

Lewis-Williams, J. David - *San Spirituality: Roots, Expression, and Social Consequences*
Choice - v42 - i7 - March 2005 - p1270(1) [501+]
R&R Bk N - v19 - i4 - Nov 2004 - p52(1) [1-50]

Lewise, Mark - *Troubleshooting Virtual Private Networks*
Bwatch - Oct 2004 - pNA [501+]

Lewison, Kim - *The Interpretation of Contracts, 3rd Ed.*
Law Q Rev - v121 - Jan 2005 - p158-161 [501+]

Lewycka, Marina - *At the Villa of Reduced Circumstances*
KR - v72 - i23 - Dec 1 2004 - p1108(2) [501+]
A Short History of Tractors in Ukrainian
BL - v101 - i9-10 - Jan 1 2005 - p820(1) [501+]
PW - v252 - i3 - Jan 17 2005 - p33(2) [51-500]
Ent W - i809 - March 4 2005 - p78 [51-500]

Leys, Colin - *Socialist Register 2004: The New Imperial Challenge*
Dis - v51 - i2 - Spring 2004 - p104(5) [501+]

Lhabitant, Francois-Serge - *Hedge Funds: Quantitative Insights*
R&R Bk N - v19 - i4 - Nov 2004 - p118(1) [51-500]

Lhamon, W.T., Jr. - *Jump Jim Crow: Lost Plays, Lyrics, and Street Prose of the First Atlantic Popular Culture*
Afr Am R - v38 - i2 - Summer 2004 - p337(3) [501+]
JAH - v91 - i2 - Sept 2004 - p624(2) [501+]
JouAmCul - v27 - i3 - Sept 2004 - p343(1) [501+]
JPC - v38 - i2 - Nov 2004 - p446(3) [501+]

L'Hoeste, Hector Fernandez - *Rockin' Las Americas: The Global Politics of Rock in Latin/o America*
Choice - v42 - i3 - Nov 2004 - p493(1) [51-500]

Li, Andres de - *Critical Edition of Andres de Li's Summa de Paciencia, 1505*
R&R Bk N - v19 - i1 - Feb 2004 - p23(1) [51-500]

Li, Cunxin - *Mao's Last Dancer (Read by English, Paul). Audiobook Review*
Kliatt - v38 - i6 - Nov 2004 - p56(1) [51-500]
LJ - v129 - i16 - Oct 1 2004 - p119(2) [51-500]

Li, Eldon Y. - *Advances in Electronic Business, Vol. 1*
R&R Bk N - v19 - i4 - Nov 2004 - p112(1) [51-500]

Li, Gui - *A Journey to the East: Li Gui's A New Account of a Trip Around the Globe*
Choice - v42 - i4 - Dec 2004 - p713(1) [1-50]

Li, He - *From Revolution to Reform: A Comparative Study of China And Mexico*
R&R Bk N - v19 - i3 - August 2004 - p56(1) [51-500]

Li-Hua, Richard - *Technology and Knowledge Transfer in China*
SciTech - v28 - i3 - Sept 2004 - p135(1) [51-500]

Li, Jie Jack - *Contemporary Drug Synthesis*
Choice - v42 - i4 - Dec 2004 - p691(1) [1-50]
SciTech - v28 - i3 - Sept 2004 - p125(1) [51-500]
Name Reactions: A Collection of Detailed Reaction Mechanisms
Choice - v41 - i7 - March 2004 - p1324(1) [501+]
Name Reactions in Heterocyclic Chemistry
SciTech - v28 - i4 - Dec 2004 - p56(1) [51-500]

Li, Jinquan - *Chinese Media, Global Contexts*
Ch Rev Int - v11 - i1 - Spring 2004 - p133(5) [501+]

Li, Leslie - *Daughter of Heaven: a Memoir with Earthly Recipes*
KR - v73 - i5 - March 1 2005 - p276(1) [501+]

Li, Peter S. - *Destination Canada: Immigration Debates and Issues*
Can Lit - i182 - Autumn 2004 - p90(3) [501+]
CBRA - Annual 2003 - p308(1) [51-500]

Li, Tiger - *Reviving Traditions in Research on International Market Entry*
JEL - v42 - i1 - March 2004 - p297(1) [501+]

Li, X.D. (b. 1969 -) - *High Energy Processes and Phenomena in Astrophysics: Proceedings*
SciTech - v28 - i1 - March 2004 - p44(1) [51-500]

Li, Yong-ping - *Retribution: The Jiling Chronicles*
WLT - v78 - i3-4 - Sept-Dec 2004 - p85(2) [501+]

Lial, Margaret L. - *Beginning and Intermediate Algebra. 3rd Ed.*
SciTech - v28 - i3 - Sept 2004 - p34(1) [51-500]
Essentials of Geometry for College Students. 2nd Ed.
SciTech - v28 - i3 - Sept 2004 - p41(1) [1-50]

Liang, G.H. - *Genetically Modified Crops: Their Development, Uses, and Risks*
Choice - v42 - i7 - March 2005 - p1252(1) [51-500]
SciTech - v28 - i4 - Dec 2004 - p123 [51-500]

Liang, Shunlin - *Quantitative Remote Sensing of Land Surfaces*
E-Streams - August 2004 - pNA [501+]

Liao, Ming - *Levy Processes in Lie Groups*
SciTech - v28 - i4 - Dec 2004 - p36(1) [51-500]

Liao, Shijun - *Beyond Perturbation: Introduction to Homotopy Analysis Method*
SciTech - v28 - i1 - March 2004 - p41(1) [51-500]

Libal, Autumn - *Runaway Train: Youth with Emotional Disturbance*
y SLJ - v50 - i12 - Dec 2004 - p162(2) [51-500]

Libal, Joyce - *A House between Homes: Youth in the Foster Care System*
c SLJ - v50 - i7 - July 2004 - p120(1) [51-500]

Libaridian, Gerard J. - *Modern Armenia: People, Nation, State*
Choice - v41 - i11-12 - July-August 2004 - p2104(1) [501+]
Nation - v279 - i8 - Sept 20 2004 - p39 [501+]

Libbrecht, Kenneth - *The Snowflake: Winter's Secret Beauty*
SB - v40 - i6 - Nov-Dec 2004 - p245(1) [51-500]
Sci Teach - v71 - i3 - March 2004 - p90-92 [501+]
SciTech - v28 - i1 - March 2004 - p53(1) [51-500]

Libby, David J. - *Slavery and Frontier Mississippi, 1720-1835*
Choice - v42 - i3 - Nov 2004 - p548(1) [1-50]

Libel, Joyce - *Finding My Voice: Youth with Speech Impairments*
y VOYA - v27 - i4 - Oct 2004 - p335(2) [51-500]

Liber, George O. - *Alexander Dovzhenko: A Life in Soviet Film*
JMH - v76 - i4 - Dec 2004 - p1008(2) [501+]
Russ Rev - v63 - i2 - April 2004 - pNA [501+]

Libera, Anne - *The Second City Almanac of Improvisation*
Choice - v42 - i4 - Dec 2004 - p673(1) [1-50]
R&R Bk N - v19 - i3 - August 2004 - p264(1) [51-500]

Liberman, Sherri - *Historical Atlas of Azerbaijan*
c BL - v101 - i7 - Dec 1 2004 - p649(1) [51-500]
A Historical Atlas of Azerbaijan
y SLJ - v50 - i11 - Nov 2004 - p166(1) [51-500]

Liberto, Lorenzo - *Matt the Rat and His Magic Cloud/A Day at School/Raton Mateo y su nube Magica/Un dia de escuela (Illus. by Torres, Irving)*
c SLJ - v50 - i9 - Sept 2004 - p197(1) [51-500]
Matt The Rat And His Magic Cloud
c CH Bwatch - v14 - i12 - Dec 2004 - pNA [51-500]
Matt the Rat and His Sister Maggie/When I Grow Up/Raton Mateo y su Hermana Maggie/Cuando yo Crezca (Illus. by Torres, Irving)
c SLJ - v50 - i9 - Sept 2004 - p197(1) [51-500]

Liberto, Nicholas - *User's Guide to Power Coating, 4th Ed.*
SciTech - v28 - i4 - Dec 2004 - p166(1) [51-500]

Liberty, Jesse - *Programming ASP.NET, 2nd Ed.*
SciTech - v28 - i4 - Dec 2004 - p153(1) [51-500]
Programming Visual Basic .NET, 2nd Ed.
SciTech - v28 - i4 - Dec 2004 - p22(1) [51-500]

Libeskind, Daniel - *Breaking Ground: Adventures in Life and Architecture*
Globe & Mail - Dec 24 2004 - pD11 [501+]
New R - Feb 7 2005 - p28 [501+]
Spec - v297 - i9205 - Jan 8 2005 - p34(2) [501+]
TLS - i5300 - Oct 29 2004 - p10-11 [501+]
Daniel Libeskind: The Space of Encounter
TLS - i5300 - Oct 29 2004 - p10-11 [501+]

Libet, Benjamin - *Mind Time: The Temporal Factor in Consciousness*
Choice - v42 - i2 - Oct 2004 - p317(2) [51-500]
Nature - v429 - i6989 - May 20 2004 - p243(2) [501+]
TimHES - v0 - i1660 - Oct 1 2004 - p26(1) [501+]

Librarie Larousse - *Le Petit Larousse Illustre en Couleurs, 100th (2005) Ed.*
R&R Bk N - v20 - i1 - Feb 2005 - p1(1) [51-500]

Library Media Connection - *Above the Rim: The NBA Library*
y LibMed - v23 - i3 - Nov-Dec 2004 - p89(1) [51-500]

Library of the Civil Rights Movement
LibMed - v23 - i1 - August-Sept 2004 - p76(1) [51-500]

Library Skills For Children
LibMed - v22 - i4 - Jan 2004 - p92(1) [501+]

Licari, James J. - *Coating Materials for Electronic Applications: Polymers, Processes, Reliability, Testing*
E-Streams - Oct 2004 - pNA [501+]
SciTech - v28 - i1 - March 2004 - p140(1) [51-500]

Lichstein, Kenneth L. - *Epidemiology of Sleep: Age, Gender, and Ethnicity*
SciTech - v28 - i3 - Sept 2004 - p101(1) [51-500]

Lichtenberg, Ronna - *Pitch Like a Girl: How a Woman Can Be Herself and Still Succeed*
BL - v101 - i8 - Dec 15 2004 - p696(1) [501+]
LJ - v129 - i20 - Dec 1 2004 - p132(1) [51-500]
PW - v251 - i51 - Dec 20 2004 - p50(1) [501+]

Lichtenheld, Tom - *Everything I Know about Cars*
c BL - v101 - i9-10 - Jan 1 2005 - p849(1) [1-50]
c KR - v73 - i2 - Jan 15 2005 - p123(1) [51-500]
c PW - v252 - i6 - Feb 7 2005 - p61(2) [501+]

Lichtenthal, J. David - *Fundamentals of Business Marketing Education: A Guide for Univeristy-level Faculty and Policymakers*
R&R Bk N - v19 - i2 - May 2004 - p114(1) [51-500]

Lichtman, Robert M. - *Deadly Farce: Harvey Matusow and the Informer System in the McCarthy Era*
Bwatch - v26 - i7 - July 2004 - p9(1) [51-500]
Choice - v42 - i4 - Dec 2004 - p722(1) [1-50]

Lichtman, Susan A. - *Conversations with Male Inmates at Indiana State Prison Concerning Education and its Rehabilitation Effects*
R&R Bk N - v19 - i3 - August 2004 - p170(1) [501+]

Lickona, Matthew - *Swimming with Scapulars: True Confessions of a Young Catholic*
PW - v252 - i9 - Feb 28 2005 - p61(1) [51-500]

Liddiard, Robert - *Anglo-Norman Castles*
Albion - v36 - i1 - Spring 2004 - p88(3) [501+]

Liddick, Don R. - *The Global Underworld: Transnational Crime and the United States*
R&R Bk N - v19 - i4 - Nov 2004 - p143(1) [501+]

Liddle, Rod - *Too Beautiful for You: Tales of Improper Behavior*
KR - v72 - i18 - Sept 15 2004 - p885(1) [501+]
PW - v251 - i44 - Nov 1 2004 - p42(1) [501+]

Lide, David R. - *CRC Handbook of Chemistry and Physics: A Ready-Reference Book of Chemical and Physical Data, 85th Ed, 2004-2005*
SciTech - v28 - i4 - Dec 2004 - p54(1) [51-500]

Lidegaard, Bo - *Defiant Diplomacy: Henrik Kauffmann, Denmark, and the United States in World War II and Cold War, 1939-1958*
R&R Bk N - v19 - i1 - Feb 2004 - p39(1) [1-50]

Lidstone, John - *Presentation Planning and Media Relations for the Pharmaceutical Industry*
SciTech - v28 - i1 - March 2004 - p124(1) [51-500]

Lie, John - *Modern Peoplehood*
CC - v122 - i2 - Jan 25 2005 - p36(3) [501+]

Lie-Nielsen, Thomas - *Taunton's Complete Illustrated Guide to Sharpening*
SciTech - v28 - i4 - Dec 2004 - p170(1) [51-500]

Liebeherr, Jorg - *Mastering Networks: An Internet Lab Manual*
SciTech - v28 - i3 - Sept 2004 - p157(1) [51-500]

Lieberg, Carolyn - *West with Hopeless*
c CCB-B - v58 - i1 - Sept 2004 - p26(2) [51-500]
c SLJ - v50 - i7 - July 2004 - p108(1) [51-500]

Lieberman, Alicia F. - *Losing a Parent to Death in the Early Years: Guidelines for Treating Traumatic Bereavement in Infancy and Early Childhood*
SciTech - v28 - i1 - March 2004 - p96(1) [51-500]

Lieberman, Ann - *Inside the National Writing Project: Connecting Network Learning and Classroom Teaching*
JNE - v73 - i1 - Wntr 2004 - p99-100 [501+]

Lieberman-Cline, Nancy - *Admissions*
KR - v72 - i14 - July 15 2004 - p650(2) [501+]
NYTBR - Nov 7 2004 - p15 [501+]
PW - v251 - i27 - July 5 2004 - p35(1) [501+]

Lieberman, David J. - *How To Change Anybody: Proven Techniques To Reshape Anyone's Attitude, Behavior, Feelings, or Beliefs*
LJ - v130 - i3 - Feb 15 2005 - p142(2) [51-500]

Lieberman, Evan S. - *Race and Regionalism in the Politics of Taxation in Brazil and South Africa*
Ams - v61 - i2 - Oct 2004 - p297(2) [501+]
JEL - v42 - i1 - March 2004 - p271(1) [501+]

Lieberman, Howard B. - *Cell Cycle Checkpoint Control Protocols*
SciTech - v28 - i1 - March 2004 - p66(1) [51-500]

Lieberman, Julie Lyonn - *Alternative Strings: The New Curriculum*
Am MT - v54 - i2 - Oct-Nov 2004 - p82(2) [501+]
Bwatch - Feb 2005 - pNA [51-500]
Alternative Strings: The New Curriculum. Audiobook Review
Teach Mus - v12 - i2 - Oct 2004 - p70(1) [51-500]

Lieberman, Marc - *Introduction to Economics, 2nd Ed.*
R&R Bk N - v19 - i3 - August 2004 - p93(1) [51-500]

Liebermann, Robbie - *Prairie Power: Voices of 1960s Midwestern Student Protest*
R&R Bk N - v19 - i3 - August 2004 - p226(1) [1-50]

Liebig, Phoebe S. - *An Aging India: Perspectives, Prospects, and Policies*
R&R Bk N - v19 - i2 - May 2004 - p136 [51-500]

Liebler, Naomi Conn - *The Female Tragic Hero in English Renaissance Drama*
NWSA Jnl - v16 - i3 - Fall 2004 - p231(3) [501+]
Shakes Q - v55 - i2 - Summer 2004 - p238-239 [501+]
Theat J - v56 - i4 - Dec 2004 - p712-714 [501+]
The Female Tragic Hero in English Renaissance Tragedy
Theat J - v56 - i4 - Dec 2004 - p712-714 [501+]

Lieblich, Amia - *Healing Plots: The Narrative Basis of Psychotherapy*
Choice - v42 - i5 - Jan 2005 - p937(1) [51-500]
SciTech - v28 - i3 - Sept 2004 - p100(1) [51-500]

Liebling, A.J. - *Between Meals: An Appetite for Paris*
NYRB - v51 - i18 - Nov 18 2004 - p12(3) [501+]
Just Enough Liebling: Classic Work by the Legendary New Yorker Writer
BL - v101 - i4 - Oct 15 2004 - p378(1) [51-500]
BW - v34 - i37 - Sept 12 2004 - p15(1) [501+]
Globe & Mail - Oct 30 2004 - pD8 [501+]
HM - v309 - i1855 - Dec 2004 - p93(5) [501+]
LJ - v129 - i15 - Sept 15 2004 - p68(1) [51-500]
Nation - v279 - i20 - Dec 13 2004 - p19 [501+]
NYRB - v51 - i18 - Nov 18 2004 - p12(3) [501+]
NYTBR - Sept 26 2004 - p7 [501+]
PW - v251 - i30 - July 26 2004 - p47(1) [501+]
Mollie and Other War Pieces
Nation - v279 - i20 - Dec 13 2004 - p19 [501+]
The Sweet Science
NYRB - v51 - i18 - Nov 18 2004 - p12(3) [501+]
The Telephone Booth Indian
NYRB - v51 - i18 - Nov 18 2004 - p12(3) [501+]

Liebman, Daniel - *Librarian*
c LibMed - v22 - i5 - Feb 2004 - p77(1) [501+]

Liebmann, George W. - *Neighborhood Futures: Citizen Rights and Local Control*
Fut - v39 - i1 - Jan-Feb 2005 - p11(1) [501+]
Fut - v39 - i1 - Jan-Feb 2005 - p49(1) [51-500]

Liebovich, Louis W. - *Richard Nixon, Watergate, and the Press: A Historical Retrospective*
JAH - v91 - i2 - Sept 2004 - p723(2) [501+]

Liebregts, P.Th.M.G. - *Ezra Pound and Neoplatonism*
Choice - v42 - i5 - Jan 2005 - p853(1) [1-50]
R&R Bk N - v19 - i4 - Nov 2004 - p243(1) [501+]

Liebreich, Karen - *Fallen Order: Intrigue, Heresy, and Scandal in the Rome of Galileo and Caravaggio*
LJ - v129 - i15 - Sept 15 2004 - p63(1) [51-500]
PW - v251 - i28 - July 12 2004 - p59(1) [51-500]

Lief, Michael S. - *And the Walls Came Tumbling Down: Closing Arguments That Changed the Way We Live, from Protecting Free Speech to Winning Women's Suffrage to Defending the Right to Die*
LJ - v129 - i16 - Oct 1 2004 - p98(1) [51-500]
PW - v251 - i34 - August 23 2004 - p47(1) [51-500]

Liehr, Reinhard - *Ein Institut und sein General: Wilhelm Faupel und das Ibero-Amerikanische Institut in der Zeit des Nationalsozialismus*
HAHR - v84 - i4 - Nov 2004 - p774(1) [501+]

Liehu, Rakel - *Helene*
WLT - v78 - i3-4 - Sept-Dec 2004 - p111(2) [501+]

Lien, Pei-te - *The Politics of Asian Americans: Diversity and Community*
R&R Bk N - v19 - i3 - August 2004 - p66(1) [51-500]

Lienert, Elisabeth - *Deutsche Antikenromane des Mittelaters*
Specu - v79 - i3 - July 2004 - p792-794 [501+]

Lienert, T.J. - *Joining of Advanced and Specialty Materials: Proceedings*
SciTech - v28 - i3 - Sept 2004 - p140(1) [51-500]

Lienhard, John H. - *Engines of Our Ingenuity: An Engineer Looks at Technology and Culture*
SciTech - v28 - i1 - March 2004 - p133(1) [51-500]

Liepe-Levinson, Katherine - *Strip Show: Performances of Gender and Desire*
Theat J - v56 - i1 - March 2004 - p143(3) [501+]

Lieshout, Elle van - *The Nothing King (Illus. by Gerritsen, Paula)*
c BL - v101 - i8 - Dec 15 2004 - p747(1) [1-50]
c CH Bwatch - Feb 2005 - pNA [51-500]
c KR - v72 - i22 - Nov 15 2004 - p1094(1) [51-500]
c PW - v252 - i2 - Jan 10 2005 - p54(2) [501+]

Lieuallen, Gwendolyn Griffith - *Basic Federal Income Tax*
R&R Bk N - v19 - i3 - August 2004 - p204(1) [1-50]

Lieurance, Suzanne - *The Philippines*
c SLJ - v50 - i9 - Sept 2004 - p228(1) [51-500]

Lieven, Anatol - *America Right or Wrong: An Anatomy of American Nationalism*
Lon R Bks - v26 - i21 - Nov 4 2004 - p15(4) [501+]
NS - v133 - i4716 - Nov 29 2004 - p48(1) [51-500]
PW - v251 - i42 - Oct 18 2004 - p60(1) [51-500]

Lievesley, Geraldine - *The Cuban Revolution: Past, Present and Future Perspectives*
Choice - v42 - i6 - Feb 2005 - p1078(1) [51-500]

Liew, Ten Chin - *Was Mill a Liberal?*
R&R Bk N - v20 - i1 - Feb 2005 - p4(1) [51-500]

Life Balance. Vols. 1-8
c LibMed - v22 - i6 - March 2004 - p77(1) [501+]

Littauer, Marita - *Your Spiritual Personality: Using the Strengths of Your Personality to Deepen Your Relationship with God*
　　PW - v251 - i43 - Oct 25 2004 - p45(1) [51-500]
Littell, David A. - *Financial Decision Making at Retirement, 7th Ed.*
　　R&R Bk N - v19 - i4 - Nov 2004 - p116(1) [51-500]
Littell, Robert - *The Debriefing*
　　LJ - v129 - i13 - August 2004 - p131(1) [51-500]
　　The Sisters (Read by Brick, Scott). Audiobook Review
　c　Kliatt - v38 - i4 - July 2004 - p56(1) [51-500]
Litten, Troy M. - *Wanderlust*
　　Bwatch - v26 - i8 - August 2004 - p2(1) [51-500]
Litterman, Bob - *Modern Investment Management: An Equilibrium Approach*
　　R&R Bk N - v19 - i1 - Feb 2004 - p117(1) [51-500]
Little, Benilde - *Who Does She Think She Is?*
　　KR - v73 - i4 - Feb 15 2005 - p193(1) [501+]
Little, Bentley - *The Resort*
　　PW - v251 - i33 - August 16 2004 - p48(1) [51-500]
Little, Bruce A. - *A Creation-Order Theodicy: God and Gratuitous Evil*
　　R&R Bk N - v20 - i1 - Feb 2005 - p10(1) [51-500]
The Little Data Book 2003
　　JEL - v41 - i4 - Dec 2003 - p1345(1) [501+]
Little, Doug - *Losing Mariposa: The Memoir of a Compulsive Gambler*
　　CBRA - Annual 2003 - p56(2) [51-500]
Little, Douglas - *American Orientalism: The United States and the Middle East since 1945*
　　AHR - v109 - i2 - April 2004 - p569(2) [501+]
　　Nation - v279 - i6 - August 30 2004 - p38 [501+]
Little, George - *A Garden Gallery: The Plants, Art, and Hardscape of Little and Lewis*
　　BL - v101 - i9-10 - Jan 1 2005 - p798(1) [51-500]
Little, Ian Malcolm David - *Ethics, Economics and Politics: Principles of Public Policy*
　　Choice - v41 - i11-12 - July-August 2004 - p2093(1) [501+]
　　JEL - v41 - i4 - Dec 2003 - p1333(1) [501+]
Little, Jean - *The Birthday Girl (Illus. by Lawrason, June)*
　c　BL - v101 - i8 - Dec 15 2004 - p742(1) [51-500]
　　Brothers Far From Home: The World War I Diary of Eliza Bates
　y　CBRA - Annual 2003 - p499(1) [51-500]
　　I Gave My Mom a Castle (Illus. by Denton, Kady MacDonald)
　c　Five Owls - v18 - i1 - Fall 2004 - p23(1) [51-500]
　　Pippin the Christmas Pig (Illus. by Zimmerman, H. Werner)
　c　BL - v101 - i2 - Sept 15 2004 - p253(1) [51-500]
　c　KR - v72 - i21 - Nov 1 2004 - p1052(1) [51-500]
　c　PW - v251 - i39 - Sept 27 2004 - p61(1) [51-500]
　c　R Today - v22 - i3 - Dec 2004 - p28(1) [501+]
　　Rescue Pup
　　Res Links - v10 - i3 - Feb 2005 - p19(2) [501+]
Little, Jeffrey B. - *Understanding Wall Street*
　　Choice - v41 - i11-12 - July-August 2004 - p2093(2) [501+]
Little, Kimberley Griffiths - *The Last Snake Runner*
　y　Kliatt - v39 - i2 - March 2005 - p28(1) [51-500]
Little, Mark - *JAVA Transaction Processing: Design and Implementation*
　　CBRA - Annual 2003 - p21(1) [51-500]
　　SciTech - v28 - i4 - Dec 2004 - p21(1) [51-500]
Little, Ruth - *The Young Vic Book: Theatre Work & Play*
　　TES - v0 - i4577 - April 2 2004 - p26(2) [501+]
Little, Stephen - *...Isms: Understanding Art*
　　Choice - v42 - i7 - March 2005 - p1216(1) [51-500]
Littlejohn, Randy - *Life in Outer Space*
　y　SLJ - v51 - i1 - Jan 2005 - p150(1) [51-500]
　　VOYA - v27 - i5 - Dec 2004 - p420(1) [51-500]
Littlejohn, Stephen W. - *Theories of Human Communication, 8th Ed.*
　　R&R Bk N - v19 - i4 - Nov 2004 - p212(1) [501+]
Littlesugar, Amy - *Freedom School, Yes*
　c　RT - v57 - Dec 2003 - p394 [51-500]
Littman, Sarah Darer - *Confessions of a Closet Catholic*
　c　CCB-B - v58 - i6 - Feb 2005 - p257(1) [51-500]
　c　KR - v73 - i1 - Jan 1 2005 - p54(1) [51-500]
　c　PW - v251 - i9 - Feb 28 2005 - p68(1) [51-500]
　　SLJ - v51 - i1 - Jan 2005 - p132(1) [51-500]
Littman, Sol - *Pure Soldiers or Sinister Legion: The Ukrainian 14th Waffen-SS Division*
　　CBRA - Annual 2003 - p293(2) [51-500]

Litton, Josie - *Believe in Me (Read by Bailey, Josephine). Audiobook Review*
　　Kliatt - v38 - i5 - Sept 2004 - p58(2) [51-500]
　　Come Back to Me (Read by Bailey, Josephine). Audiobook Review
　　Kliatt - v38 - i5 - Sept 2004 - p58(2) [51-500]
　　Dream of Me (Read by Bailey, Josephine). Audiobook Review
　　Kliatt - v38 - i5 - Sept 2004 - p58(2) [51-500]
Litvin, Alter A. - *Writing History in Twentieth-Century Russia: A View from Within*
　　Russ Rev - v63 - i2 - April 2004 - pNA [501+]
Litwak, Mark - *Risky Business: Financing and Distributing Independent Films*
　　R&R Bk N - v19 - i3 - August 2004 - p261(1) [51-500]
Litwin, Val - *Cool to Be Kind: Random Acts and How to Commit Them*
　　Globe & Mail - July 31 2004 - pD12 [1-50]
Litz, Brett T. - *Early Intervention for Trauma and Traumatic Loss*
　　Choice - v42 - i2 - Oct 2004 - p374(1) [51-500]
　　E-Streams - Oct 2004 - pNA [501+]
　　SciTech - v28 - i3 - Oct 2004 - p101(1) [51-500]
Litz, Courtney - *Live from New York, It's Lena Sharpe*
　　BL - v101 - i4 - Oct 15 2004 - p394(1) [51-500]
Litz, Joyce - *The Montana Frontier: One Woman's West*
　　Roundup M - v11 - i6 - August 2004 - p25(1) [501+]
Litzenburg, Thomas V., Jr. - *Chinese Export Porcelain in the Reeves Center Collection at Washington and Lee University*
　　Ceram Mo - v52 - i6 - June-August 2004 - p34(1) [501+]
Litzgus, Hazel - *Where the Meadowlark Sang: Cherished Scenes from an Artist's Childhood*
　c　CBRA - Annual 2003 - p538(1) [501+]
Liu, Chongyun - *Chinese Herbal Medicine: Modern Applications of Traditional Formulas*
　　SciTech - v28 - i4 - Dec 2004 - p117(1) [1-50]
Liu, Eric - *Guiding Lights: The People Who Lead Us toward Our Purpose in Life*
　　BL - v101 - i7 - Dec 1 2004 - p620(1) [51-500]
　　PW - v251 - i42 - Oct 18 2004 - p56(2) [51-500]
Liu, Fangtong - *China's Contemporary Philosophical Journey: Western Philosophy and Marxism Chinese Philosophical Studies*
　　R&R Bk N - v19 - i4 - Nov 2004 - p7(1) [1-50]
Liu, Hong - *Singapore Chinese Society in Transition: Business, Politics, and Socio-Economic Change, 1945-1965*
　　R&R Bk N - v19 - i3 - August 2004 - p55(1) [51-500]
Liu, Jianmei - *Revolution Plus Love: Literary History, Women's Bodies, and Thematic Repetition in Twentieth-Century Chinese Fiction*
　　R&R Bk N - v19 - i1 - Feb 2004 - p219(1) [51-500]
Liu, Kwang-Ching - *Heterodoxy in Late Imperial China*
　　Choice - v42 - i1 - Sept 2004 - p165(2) [501+]
Liu, Leo - *Taiwanese Polity in the Twenty-First Century: Politics and Culture in a Global Context*
　　R&R Bk N - v19 - i4 - Nov 2004 - p50(1) [51-500]
Liu, Li - *State Formation in Early China*
　　R&R Bk N - v19 - i1 - Feb 2004 - p48(1) [51-500]
Liu, Marjorie M. - *Tiger Eye*
　　PW - v252 - i4 - Jan 24 2005 - p227(1) [501+]
Liu, Xiaoyuan - *Frontier Passages: Ethnopolitics and the Rise of Chinese Communism, 1921-1945*
　　Choice - v41 - i11-12 - July-August 2004 - p2101(1) [501+]
　　Pac A - v77 - i3 - Fall 2004 - p565(2) [501+]
Liu, Xin - *The Otherness of Self: A Genealogy of the Self in Contemporary China*
　　CS - v33 - i2 - March 2004 - p183-185 [501+]
Livak, Leonid - *How It Was Done in Paris: Russian Empire Literature and French Modernism*
　　Slav R - v63 - i3 - Fall 2004 - p685-686 [501+]
Lively, Penelope - *Goldilocks and the Three Bears (Illus. by Gliori, Debi)*
　c　SLJ - v51 - i1 - Jan 2005 - p107(2) [51-500]
　　The House in Norham Gardens
　c　Sch Lib - v52 - i4 - Winter 2004 - p201(1) [51-500]
Liverman, Matthew - *Animator's Motion Capture Guide: Organizing, Managing, and Editing*
　　SciTech - v28 - i3 - Sept 2004 - p169(1) [1-50]
Lives of the Artists
　y　Ref Rev - June 2004 - pNA [501+]

Livesey, Graham - *Passages: Explorations Of The Contemporary City*
　　Bwatch - Feb 2005 - pNA [501+]
Livesey, Margot - *Banishing Verona*
　　BL - v101 - i1 - Sept 1 2004 - p6(1) [51-500]
　　Globe & Mail - Nov 27 2004 - pD24 [501+]
　　KR - v72 - i18 - Sept 15 2004 - p885(2) [501+]
　　LJ - v129 - i16 - Oct 1 2004 - p71(1) [51-500]
　　NYTBR - Dec 5 2004 - p80 [501+]
　　People - v62 - i25 - Dec 20 2004 - p57 [51-500]
　　PW - v251 - i35 - August 30 2004 - p29(1) [501+]
　　Ent W - i791 - Nov 5 2004 - p84 [501+]
Livet, George - *Histoire des Routes et des Transports en Europe: Des Chemins de Saint-Jacques a l'age d'or des Diligences*
　　JIH - v35 - i2 - Autumn 2004 - p288(2) [501+]
Living Habitats
　y　LibMed - v23 - i1 - August-Sept 2004 - p78(1) [51-500]
Livingston, Carolyn - *Charles Faulkner Bryan: His Life and Music*
　　JSH - v70 - i3 - August 2004 - p716(2) [501+]
　　M Ed J - v91 - i3 - Jan 2005 - p62(1) [501+]
Livingston, David J. - *Healing Violent Men: A Model for Christian Communities*
　　Intpr - v58 - i4 - Oct 2004 - p418(1) [501+]
Livingston, Ivor L. - *Praeger Handbook of Black American Health: Policies and Issues behind Disparities in Health, 2nd Ed., Vols. 1-2*
　　Choice - v42 - i5 - Jan 2005 - p887(1) [1-50]
Livingston, Ivor Lensworth - *Praeger Handbook of Black American Health: Policies and Issues behind Disparities in Health, 2nd Ed., Vols. 1-2*
　　LJ - v129 - i14 - Sept 1 2004 - p190(1) [51-500]
　　SciTech - v28 - i3 - Sept 2004 - p83 [501+]
Livingston, Tobie Gene - *Soul on Bikes: The East Bay Dragons MC and the Black Biker Set*
　　Black Iss - v6 - i4 - July-August 2004 - p55(1) [51-500]
Livingston, Todd - *The Black Forest*
　　KR - v72 - i19 - Oct 1 2004 - pNA [501+]
Livingstone, David N. - *Putting Science in Its Place: Geographies of Scientific Knowledge*
　　Choice - v42 - i2 - Oct 2004 - p313(1) [51-500]
　　E-Streams - June 2004 - pNA [501+]
Livingstone, Grace - *Inside Colombia: Drugs, Democracy and War*
　　Nation - v279 - i5 - August 16 2004 - p31 [501+]
Livingstone, Tess - *George Pell: Defender of the Faith Down Under*
　c　CI - v12 - i11 - Dec 2004 - p23(1) [501+]
Livo, Norma J. - *Bringing out Their Best: Values, Education and Character Development through Traditional Tales*
　　LibMed - v22 - i5 - Feb 2004 - p84(2) [501+]
Livoti, Carol - *Vaginas: An Owner's Manual*
　　LJ - v129 - i14 - Sept 1 2004 - p176(2) [51-500]
　　PW - v251 - i33 - August 16 2004 - p58(1) [51-500]
Ljubisic, Davorka - *A Politics of Sorrow: The Disintegration of Yugoslavia*
　　Choice - v41 - i11-12 - July-August 2004 - p2117(1) [501+]
Llamazares, Julio - *The Yellow Rain*
　　VQR - v80 - i3 - Summer 2004 - p263(1) [1-50]
Llamosas, V. Munoz - *La Intervencion Divina en el Hombre a Traves de la Literatura Griega de Epoca Arcaica y Clasica*
　　Class R - v54 - i1 - May 2004 - p62(3) [501+]
Llewellyn, Bryn - *The Rat and the Serpent*
　　PW - v252 - i1 - Jan 3 2005 - p41(1) [51-500]
Llewellyn, Claire - *Crocodile (Illus. by Mendez, Simon)*
　c　SLJ - v50 - i11 - Nov 2004 - p128(1) [51-500]
　　Duck (Illus. by Mendez, Simon)
　c　SLJ - v50 - i11 - Nov 2004 - p128(1) [51-500]
　　Eating
　c　BL - v101 - i5 - Nov 1 2004 - p487(1) [51-500]
　c　CH Bwatch - Feb 2005 - pNA [51-500]
　　Electricity
　c　Sch Lib - v52 - i4 - Winter 2004 - p187(2) [51-500]
　　Great Discoveries and Amazing Adventures: The Stories of Hidden Marvels and Lost Treasures
　y　SLJ - v51 - i1 - Jan 2005 - p150(1) [51-500]
　　Ladybug (Illus. by Mendez, Simon)
　c　SLJ - v50 - i11 - Nov 2004 - p128(1) [51-500]
　　Saints and Angels
　c　BL - v101 - i3 - Oct 1 2004 - p345(1) [51-500]
　　Tree (Illus. by Mendez, Simon)
　c　SLJ - v50 - i11 - Nov 2004 - p128(1) [51-500]

Llewellyn-Jones, Lloyd - *Aphrodite's Tortoise: The Veiled Woman of Ancient Greece*
Choice - v42 - i1 - Sept 2004 - p164(2) [501+]
R&R Bk N - v19 - i2 - May 2004 - p136 [51-500]
TLS - i5303 - Nov 19 2004 - p36(1) [51-500]

Llewellyn, Sam - *Admiral Nelson*
c TES - v0 - i4587 - June 11 2004 - pssss29(1) [501+]

Lliteras, D.S. - *The Silence of John*
BL - v101 - i9-10 - Jan 1 2005 - p818(1) [1-50]
LJ - v130 - i2 - Feb 1 2005 - p62(1) [51-500]

Llobera, Josep R. - *An Invitation to Anthropology: The Structure, Evolution and Cultural Identity of Human Societies*
JRAI - v10 - i4 - Dec 2004 - p923(2) [501+]

Lloyd, Annette D'Agostino - *The Harold Lloyd Encyclopedia*
BIC - v33 - i5 - August 2004 - p21(2) [501+]
R&R Bk N - v19 - i1 - Feb 2004 - p227(1) [51-500]

Lloyd, Cathie - *Rethinking Anti-Racisms: From Theory to Practice*
CS - v33 - i2 - March 2004 - p229-230 [501+]

Lloyd, Cristopher - *Meadows*
SciTech - v28 - j4 - Dec 2004 - p125 [51-500]

Lloyd, Dan - *Radiant Cool: A Novel Theory of Consciousness*
Lon R Bks - v26 - i5 - March 4 2004 - p30(2) [501+]

Lloyd, Elisabeth A. - *The Case of the Female Orgasm: Bias in the Science of Evolution*
PW - v252 - i10 - March 7 2005 - p59(1) [51-500]

Lloyd, G.E.R. - *The Ambitions of Curiosity: Understanding the World in Ancient Greece and China*
CJ - v99 - i4 - April-May 2004 - p467-469 [501+]
Ancient Worlds, Modern Reflections: Philosophical Perspectives on Greek and Chinese Science and Culture
Quad - v48 - i12 - Dec 2004 - p92(2) [501+]
TLS - i5304 - Nov 26 2004 - p28(1) [501+]
In the Grip of Disease: Studies in the Greek Imagination
TLS - i5264 - Feb 20 2004 - p28-28 [501+]

Lloyd, Geoffrey - *The Way and the Word: Science and Medicine in Early China and Greece*
Ch Rev Int - v10 - i2 - Fall 2003 - p422(4) [501+]

Lloyd, John - *What the Media Are Doing to Our Politics*
NS - v133 - i4696 - July 12 2004 - p53(1) [501+]

Lloyd-Jones, Stewart - *The Last Empire: Thirty Years of Portuguese Decolonization*
R&R Bk N - v19 - i3 - August 2004 - p36(1) [51-500]

Lloyd, Peter - *Models of the 'Chinese Economy'*
JEL - v42 - i3 - Sept 2004 - p875(3) [501+]

Lloyd, Peter J. - *Global Trade Policy 2002*
JEL - v41 - i4 - Dec 2003 - p1354(1) [501+]
Intra-Industry Trade
JEL - v41 - i4 - Dec 2003 - p1354(1) [501+]

Lloyd, Roseann - *Because of the Light*
Wom R Bks - v22 - i3 - Dec 2004 - p26(2) [501+]

Lloyd, Rosemary - *Baudelaire's World*
NCFS - v33 - i1-2 - Fall-Winter 2004 - p196(3) [501+]

Lloyd, Sam - *Yummy Yummy! Food for My Tummy! (Illus. by Tickle, Jack)*
c SLJ - v50 - i7 - July 2004 - p81(1) [501+]

Lloyd-Smith, Allan - *American Gothic Fiction: An Introduction*
Choice - v42 - i7 - March 2005 - p1230(1) [51-500]

Lloyd, Sue - *The Man Who Was Cyrano: A Life of Edmond Rostand, Creator of "Cyrano de Bergerac"*
NCFS - v33 - i1-2 - Fall-Winter 2004 - p218(2) [501+]

Lloyd, Thomas - *Pembrokeshire*
Choice - v42 - i2 - Oct 2004 - p286(1) [501+]

Lloyd Webber, Andrew - *The Phantom of the Opera Companion*
LJ - v130 - i3 - Feb 15 2005 - p133(1) [51-500]

Llwyd, Humphrey - *Cronica Walliae*
HER - v119 - i483 - Sept 2004 - p1049(2) [501+]

Llywelyn, Morgan - *1949: A Novel of the Irish Free State*
Kliatt - v38 - i5 - Sept 2004 - p23(2) [501+]
1972: A Novel of Ireland's Unfinished Revolution
KR - v73 - i3 - Feb 1 2005 - p149(1) [51-500]

Lo, Alison - *Job 28 as Rhetoric: An Analysis of Job 28 in the Context of Job 22-31*
R&R Bk N - v19 - i1 - Feb 2004 - p18(1) [51-500]

Lo, Benny K.C. - *Antibody Engineering: Methods and Protocols*
SciTech - v28 - i1 - March 2004 - p172(1) [51-500]

Lo, Bobo - *Russian Foreign Policy in the Post-Soviet Era: Realty, Illusion and Mythmaking*
Slav R - v63 - i3 - Fall 2004 - p679-680 [501+]
Vladimir Putin and the Evolution of Russian Foreign Policy
E-A St - v56 - i4 - June 2004 - p627(628) [501+]

Lo, Ginnie - *Mahjong All Day Long (Illus. by Lo, Beth)*
c KR - v73 - i5 - March 1 2005 - p290(1) [51-500]

Lo, Ming-Cheng Miriam - *Doctors Within Borders: Profession, Ethnicity, and Modernity in Colonial Taiwan*
CS - v33 - i2 - March 2004 - p233-234 [501+]
MAQ - v18 - i1 - March 2004 - p116(2) [501+]

Loader, Ian - *Policing and the Condition of England: Memory, Politics and Culture*
AJS - v110 - i1 - July 2004 - p261(3) [501+]

Loader, William - *Sexuality and the Jesus Tradition*
PW - v252 - i3 - Jan 17 2005 - p52(2) [51-500]

Loades, David - *Elizabeth I: The Golden Reign of Gloriana*
AHR - v109 - i2 - April 2004 - p605(2) [501+]
Six Ct J - v35 - i3 - Fall 2004 - p905-906 [501+]
John Foxe at Home and Abroad
R&R Bk N - v19 - i4 - Nov 2004 - p28(1) [501+]
Reader's Guide to British History, Vols. 1-2
Albion - v36 - i2 - Summer 2004 - p279(2) [501+]
Ref Rev - June 2004 - pNA [501+]
Reader's Guide to British History; Vols. 1-2
R&R Bk N - v19 - i1 - Feb 2004 - p31(1) [1-50]

Loayza, Norman - *Economic Growth: Sources, Trends, and Cycles*
JEL - v42 - i1 - March 2004 - p320(1) [501+]
Inflation Targeting: Design, Performance, Challenges
JEL - v41 - i4 - Dec 2003 - p1285(2) [501+]
Monetary Policy: Rules and Transmission Mechanisms
JEL - v42 - i4 - Dec 2004 - p1129(2) [501+]

Lobato, Arcadio - *The Secret of the North Pole (Illus. by Lobato, Arcadio)*
c RT - v57 - Oct 2003 - p170 [1-50]

Lobban, Richard A., Jr. - *Historical Dictionary of Ancient and Medieval Nubia*
Choice - v41 - i11-12 - July-August 2004 - p2028(1) [501+]
R&USQ - v44 - i1 - Fall 2004 - p89(2) [501+]

Lobdell, Jared - *The Scientification Novels of C.S. Lewis: Space and Time in the Ransom Stories*
Choice - v42 - i4 - Dec 2004 - p660(1) [1-50]
The World of the Rings: Language, Religion, and Adventure in Tolkien
Globe & Mail - Sept 25 2004 - pD30 [1-50]
R&R Bk N - v19 - i4 - Nov 2004 - p238(1) [501+]

Lobel, Jules - *Success Without Victory: Lost Legal Battles and the Long Road to Justice in America*
Law&PolBR - Oct 2004 - pNA [501+]

Lobenthal, Joel - *Tallulah!: The Life and Times of a Leading Lady*
BL - v101 - i5 - Nov 1 2004 - p459(1) [51-500]
BW - v34 - i45 - Nov 7 2004 - p8(1) [501+]
Globe & Mail - Feb 5 2005 - pD9 [501+]
PW - v251 - i42 - Oct 18 2004 - p57(1) [51-500]

Loberg, Kristin - *Identity Theft: How to Protect Your Name, Your Credit and Your Vital Information, and What to Do When Someone Hijacks Any of These*
Bwatch - Feb 2005 - pNA [51-500]

Lobo, Hubert - *Handbook of Plastics Analysis*
E-Streams - July 2004 - pNA [501+]

Locher, James R., III - *Victory on the Potomac: The Goldwater-Nichols Act Unifies the Pentagon*
APH - v51 - i4 - Winter 2004 - p59(3) [501+]

Lochhead, Douglas - *Midgic*
BIC - v33 - i2 - March 2004 - p41(1) [501+]
CBRA - Annual 2003 - p224(1) [51-500]
Weathers: Poems New and Selected
CBRA - Annual 2003 - p224(1) [51-500]

Lock, Dennis - *Project Management in Construction*
SciTech - v28 - i4 - Dec 2004 - p8(1) [1-50]

Lock, James - *Help Your Teenager Beat an Eating Disorder*
PW - v252 - i5 - Jan 31 2005 - p65(1) [51-500]

Lock, Joan - *Dead End*
BL - v100 - i22 - August 2004 - p1906(1) [51-500]
KR - v72 - i19 - Oct 1 2004 - p942(1) [501+]

Lock, Margaret - *Bookbinding Materials and Techniques, 1700-1920*
BSA-P - v98 - i3 - Sept 2004 - p390-392 [501+]

Lock, Norman - *Tango in Amsterdam*
New ER - v24 - i4 - Fall 2003 - p152-157 [501+]

Lockard, James - *Computers for Twenty-First Century Educators, 6th Ed.*
R&R Bk N - v19 - i1 - Feb 2004 - pNA [501+]

Locke, Edwin A. - *Postmodernism and Management: Pros, Cons, and the Alternative*
Per Psy - v57 - i3 - Autumn 2004 - p783(4) [501+]

Locke, John - *Open Source Solutions for Small Business Problems*
Bwatch - Oct 2004 - pNA [51-500]
SciTech - v28 - i3 - Sept 2004 - p9(1) [501+]

Locke, Lawrence F. - *Reading and Understanding Research. 2nd Ed.*
SciTech - v28 - i3 - Sept 2004 - p14(1) [501+]

Locker, Thomas - *John Muir: America's Naturalist*
c Five Owls - v18 - i1 - Fall 2004 - p24(1) [51-500]
Rachel Carson: Preserving a Sense of Nature
c SB - v40 - i6 - Nov-Dec 2004 - p264(1) [51-500]

Lockhart, Andrew - *Network Security Hacks*
SciTech - v28 - i3 - Sept 2004 - p32(1) [51-500]

Lockhart, Darrell B. - *Latin American Mystery Writers: An A-to-Z Guide*
BL - v101 - i1 - Sept 1 2004 - p172(1) [501+]
Choice - v42 - i2 - Oct 2004 - p267(1) [51-500]
JouAmCul - v27 - i4 - Dec 2004 - p449(2) [501+]
Latin American Science Fiction Writers: An A-to-Z Guide
BL - v101 - i1 - Sept 1 2004 - p172(1) [501+]
Choice - v42 - i3 - Nov 2004 - p450(1) [1-50]

Lockhart, E. - *The Boyfriend List*
y KR - v73 - i4 - Feb 15 2005 - p232(1) [51-500]
y PW - v252 - i9 - Feb 28 2005 - p68(1) [51-500]

Lockhart Fleming, Patricia - *History of the Book in Canada: Vol. 1 -- Beginnings to 1840*
Globe & Mail - Oct 23 2004 - pD17 [501+]

Lockhart, Paul Douglas - *Frederik II and the Protestant Cause: Denmark's Role in the Wars of Religion, 1559-1596*
Choice - v42 - i5 - Jan 2005 - p924(1) [1-50]
R&R Bk N - v19 - i3 - August 2004 - p46(1) [51-500]
Sweden in the Seventeenth Century
Choice - v42 - i5 - Jan 2005 - p924(1) [1-50]

Lockman, Zachary - *Contending Visions of the Middle East: the History and Politics of Orientalism*
Choice - v42 - i6 - Feb 2005 - p1079(1) [51-500]

Lockshin, Richard A. - *When Cells Die II: A Comprehensive Evaluation of Apoptosis and Programmed Cell Death*
SciTech - v28 - i4 - Dec 2004 - p64(1) [51-500]

Locksley, Rebecca - *The Three Sisters*
ChrSFF&H - v26 - i9 - Sept 2004 - p36(1) [51-500]

Lockwood, Anne Turnbaugh - *The Charter Schools Decade*
R&R Bk N - v19 - i4 - Nov 2004 - p186(1) [501+]

Lockwood, Charles - *Bricks and Brownstones: The New York Row House 1783-1929, 2nd Ed.*
R&R Bk N - v19 - i1 - Feb 2004 - p201(1) [51-500]

Lockwood, Diane - *Eve's Red Dress*
PSQ - v78 - i4 - Winter 2004 - p197(6) [501+]

Lockwood, Jeffrey A. - *Locust: The Devastating Rise and Mysterious Disappearance of the Insect that Shaped the American Frontier*
Choice - v42 - i6 - Feb 2005 - p1050(1) [51-500]
NH - v113 - i6 - July-August 2004 - p56(1) [501+]
SciTech - v28 - i3 - Sept 2004 - p130(1) [51-500]

Lockwood, Lewis - *The Beethoven Violin Sonatas: History, Criticism, Performance*
Choice - v42 - i5 - Jan 2005 - p861(1) [1-50]

Lockwood, Mark W. - *The TOS Handbook of Texas Birds*
Choice - v42 - i3 - Nov 2004 - p511(1) [1-50]
E-Streams - Oct 2004 - pNA [51-500]

Lockwood, Robert P. - *A Faith for Grownups: A Midlife Conversation about What Really Matters*
CI - v12 - i9 - Oct 2004 - p44(1) [501+]

Lockyer, Andrew - *Education for Democratic Citizenship: Issues of Theory and Practice*
R&R Bk N - v19 - i3 - August 2004 - p228(1) [1-50]

Lockyer, Herbert Jr. - *All the Music of the Bible: An Exploration of Musical Expression in Scripture and Church Hymnody*
Ch Today - v48 - i12 - Dec 2004 - p71(1) [51-500]

Lococo, Donald - *Towards a Theology of Science*
CBRA - Annual 2003 - p93(2) [51-500]

Locricchio, Matthew - *Brazil (Illus. by McConnell, Jack)*
c CH Bwatch - Feb 2005 - pNA [51-500]
The Cooking of India
c SLJ - v51 - i2 - Feb 2005 - p148(2) [51-500]
The Cooking of Thailand
c SLJ - v51 - i2 - Feb 2005 - p148(2) [51-500]
Greece (Illus. by McConnell, Jack)
c CH Bwatch - Feb 2005 - pNA [51-500]
India (Illus. by McConnell, Jack)
c CH Bwatch - Feb 2005 - pNA [51-500]
The International Cookbook For Kids
c CH Bwatch - Jan 2005 - pNA [51-500]
c PW - v252 - i2 - Jan 10 2005 - p58(1) [51-500]
y SLJ - v51 - i1 - Jan 2005 - p150(2) [51-500]
y SLJ - v51 - i2 - Feb 2005 - p59(1) [51-500]
Thailand (Illus. by McConnell, Jack)
c CH Bwatch - Feb 2005 - pNA [51-500]

Loden, Marilyn - *Implementing Diversity.*
  HR Mag - v49 - i7 - July 2004 - pS12(1) [51-500]
Loder, Elizabeth W. - *Headache: A Guide for the Primary Care Physician*
  SciTech - v28 - i4 - Dec 2004 - p94(1) [51-500]
Lodge, Annette - *Bird*
  y Magpies - v19 - i5 - Nov 2004 - p32(1) [501+]
Lodge, David - *Author, Author*
  BL - v101 - i2 - Sept 15 2004 - p179(1) [51-500]
  BW - v34 - i45 - Nov 7 2004 - p6(2) [501+]
  Ent W - i788 - Oct 15 2004 - p81 [51-500]
  Globe & Mail - Nov 20 2004 - pD8 [501+]
  KR - v72 - i14 - July 15 2004 - p651(1) [501+]
  Lon R Bks - v26 - i18 - Sept 23 2004 - p23(2) [501+]
  Nation - v279 - i14 - Nov 1 2004 - p34 [501+]
  New R - Oct 18 2004 - p28 [501+]
  NS - v133 - i4704 - Sept 6 2004 - p48(3) [501+]
  NS - v133 - i4716 - Nov 29 2004 - p43(2) [51-500]
  NS - v133 - i4716 - Nov 29 2004 - p44(1) [51-500]
  NS - v133 - i4716 - Nov 29 2004 - p49(1) [51-500]
  NYRB - v51 - i18 - Nov 18 2004 - p41(2) [501+]
  NYTBR - Oct 10 2004 - p30 [501+]
  People - v62 - i17 - Oct 25 2004 - p51 [501+]
  Spec - v296 - i9188 - Sept 11 2004 - p45(1) [501+]
  TLS - i5292 - Sept 3 2004 - p12(1) [501+]
  NL - v87 - i5 - Sept-Oct 2004 - p31(3) [501+]
Therapy
  BL - v101 - i9-10 - Jan 1 2005 - p816(1) [501+]
Lodge, David (b. 1969 -) - *Author, Author*
  PW - v251 - i35 - August 30 2004 - p29(1) [501+]
Lodge, Stephen - *Charley Sunday's Texas Outfit!*
  Roundup M - v12 - i3 - Feb 2005 - p28(1) [51-500]
Lodge, Thomas E. - *The Everglades Handbook: Understanding the Ecosystem, 2nd Ed.*
  Choice - v42 - i7 - March 2005 - p1251(1) [51-500]
  SciTech - v28 - i4 - Dec 2004 - p59(1) [51-500]
Loe, Meika - *The Rise of Viagra: How the Little Blue Pill Changed Sex in America*
  BL - v101 - i2 - Sept 15 2004 - p188(1) [51-500]
  BW - v34 - i41 - Oct 10 2004 - p4(1) [501+]
  Choice - v42 - i6 - Feb 2005 - p1056(1) [51-500]
  LJ - v129 - i13 - August 2004 - p103(1) [51-500]
Loeb, Carol - *Lucia Joyce: To Dance in the Wake*
  VQR - v80 - i3 - Summer 2004 - p269(1) [1-50]
Loeb, Carolyn S. - *Entrepreneurial Vernacular: Developers' Subdivisions in the 1920s*
  BHR - v78 - i2 - Summer 2004 - p300(3) [501+]
  Hist Geo - v32 - Annual 2004 - p211(2) [501+]
Loeb, Jeph - *Batman: The Long Halloween*
  y Teach Lib - v32 - i1 - Oct 2004 - p17(2) [501+]
Batman. Vol. 1: Hush
  LibMed - v22 - i4 - Jan 2004 - p69(1) [501+]
Challengers of the Unknown Must Die!
  y BL - v101 - i7 - Dec 1 2004 - p643(2) [51-500]
Hulk: Gray
  PW - v251 - i32 - August 9 2004 - p234(1) [51-500]
Public Enemies
  BL - v101 - i1 - Sept 1 2004 - p77(1) [501+]
Spider-Man: Blue
  y SLJ - v50 - i7 - July 2004 - p21(1) [501+]
Loeb, Paul Rogat - *The Impossible Will Take a Little While*
  E Mag - v16 - i1 - Jan-Feb 2005 - p60(1) [51-500]
Loebel-Fried, Caren - *Hawaiian Legends of the Guardian Spirits*
  Parabola - v29 - i2 - Summer 2004 - p112-114 [501+]
Loertscher, David V. - *We Boost Achievement: Evidence-Based Practice for School Library Media Specialists*
  LibMed - v23 - i1 - August-Sept 2004 - p86(1) [51-500]
Loeschnig, Louis V. - *Simple Earth Science Experiments with Everyday Materials*
  c SB - v40 - i5 - Sept-Oct 2004 - p194(1) [51-500]
Loesser, Frank - *I Love You! A Bushel and a Peck (Illus. by Wells, Rosemary)*
  c BL - v101 - i6 - Nov 15 2004 - p589(1) [51-500]
  c Globe & Mail - Feb 12 2005 - pD11 [51-500]
  c KR - v72 - i24 - Dec 15 2004 - p1204(1) [51-500]
  c PW - v251 - i49 - Dec 6 2004 - p61(2) [501+]
  c SLJ - v51 - i2 - Feb 2005 - p123(1) [51-500]

Loetz, Francisca - *Mit Gott Handeln: Von den Zurcher Gotteslasterern der Fruhen Neuzeit zu einer Kulturageschichte des Religiosen*
  HNet - August 2004 - pNA [501+]
Loewe, Michael - *The Men Who Governed Han China: Companion to a Biographical Dictionary of the Qin, Former Han and Xin Periods*
  R&R Bk N - v19 - i3 - August 2004 - p56(1) [51-500]
Loewen, G.V. - *Hermeneutic Apprenticeships: Essays, Epigrams, Verse*
  R&R Bk N - v19 - i1 - Feb 2004 - p4(1) [51-500]
Loewenstein, David - *The Cambridge History of Early Modern Literature of Early Modern English Literature*
  RES - v55 - i219 - April 2004 - p266-268 [501+]
Loewenstein, George - *Time and Decision: Economic and Psychological Perspectives on Intertemporal Choice*
  CS - v33 - i1 - Jan 2004 - p127-128 [501+]
  JEL - v41 - i4 - Dec 2003 - p1344(1) [501+]
Loewenstein, Joseph (b. 1951-) - *The Author's Due: Printing and the Prehistory of Copyright*
  Comp L - v56 - i2 - Spring 2004 - p192-197 [501+]
  RES - v55 - i221 - Sept 2004 - p619(2) [501+]
Ben Jonson and Possessive Authorship
  RES - v55 - i218 - Feb 2004 - p134-135 [501+]
  Six Ct J - v34 - i4 - Winter 2003 - p1152-1153 [501+]
  TLS - i5264 - Feb 20 2004 - p26-26 [501+]
Loewenthal, Del - *Post-Modernism for Psychotherapists*
  TLS - i5286 - July 23 2004 - p32(1) [501+]
Lofaro, Michael A. - *Daniel Boone: An American Life*
  JSH - v71 - i1 - Feb 2005 - p144(2) [501+]
Lofficier, Jean-Marc - *Robonocchio*
  ChrSFF&H - v26 - i10 - Oct 2004 - p26(1) [51-500]
Loffler, Bernhard - *Soziale Marktwirtschaft und Administrative Praxis: Das Bundeswirt-schaftsministerium unter Ludwig Erhard*
  BHR - v78 - i1 - Spring 2004 - p168(3) [501+]
Loffler, Elke - *Improving the Quality of East and West European Public Services*
  R&R Bk N - v19 - i3 - August 2004 - p184(1) [501+]
Lofstedt, B. - *Virgilius Maro grammaticus: Opera omnia*
  Class R - v54 - i2 - Nov 2004 - p419(2) [501+]
Loft, Abram - *How to Succeed in an Ensemble: Reflections on a Life in Chamber Music*
  R&R Bk N - v19 - i1 - Feb 2004 - p198(1) [51-500]
Loft, Leonore - *Passion, Politics and Philosophie: Rediscovering*
  FS - v58 - i2 - April 2004 - p265(2) [501+]
Loftus, Ronald P. - *Telling Lives: Women's Self-Writing in Modern Japan*
  HNet - Nov 2004 - pNA [501+]
  R&R Bk N - v19 - i4 - Nov 2004 - p30(1) [51-500]
Logan, Bari M. - *McMinn's Color Atlas of Head and Neck Anatomy*
  E-Streams - Dec 2004 - pNA [501+]
Logan, Michael F. - *The Lessening Stream: An Environmental History of the Santa Cruz River*
  J Urban H - v31 - i2 - Jan 2005 - p258-268 [501+]
Logan, Tom - *How to Act and Eat at the Same Time: The Sequel, the Do's and Dont's of Landing a Professional Acting Job*
  R&R Bk N - v19 - i3 - August 2004 - p264(1) [51-500]
Logan, William - *Desperate Measures*
  Sew R - v111 - i3 - Summer 2003 - pLXVI-LXX [501+]
Logevall, Fredrik - *Choosing War: The Lost Chance for Peace and the Escalation of War in Vietnam*
  APH - v51 - i3 - Fall 2004 - p53(1) [501+]
Logne, Calvin M. - *Representative American Speeches 2002-2003*
  y Ref Rev - June 2004 - pNA [501+]
Logowski, J.J. - *Chemistry: Foundations and Applications. Vol. 1-4*
  y BL - v101 - i1 - Sept 1 2004 - p162(1) [501+]
Logsdon, Gene - *All Flesh Is Grass: The Pleasures and Promises of Pasture Farming*
  BL - v101 - i6 - Nov 15 2004 - p539(1) [501+]
  BL - v101 - i7 - Dec 1 2004 - p632(1) [51-500]
  LJ - v129 - i16 - Oct 1 2004 - p103(1) [51-500]
Wyeth People
  R&R Bk N - v19 - i1 - Feb 2004 - p206(1) [51-500]
Logue, A.W. - *The Psychology of Eating and Drinking, 3rd Ed.*
  SciTech - v28 - i4 - Dec 2004 - p170(1) [51-500]

Logue, Christopher - *All Day Permanent Red: The First Battle Scenes of Homer's Iliad Rewritten*
  BooChiTr - Jan 4 2004 - p1(2) [501+]
  WLT - v78 - i3-4 - Sept-Dec 2004 - p100(2) [501+]
Loh, Eric - *Nationalizing the Russian Empire: The Campaign Against Enemy Aliens During World War I*
  AHR - v109 - i2 - April 2004 - p648(2) [501+]
Lohfink, Norbert - *Qoheleth: A Continental Commentary*
  Intpr - v59 - i1 - Jan 2005 - p88(1) [51-500]
  Theol St - v65 - i3 - Sept 2004 - p670(2) [501+]
Lohlein, Daniela - *An Economic Analysis of Public Good Provision in Rural Russia: The Case of Education and Health Care*
  R&R Bk N - v19 - i1 - Feb 2004 - p127(1) [51-500]
Lohmann, Roger Ivar - *Dream Travelers: Sleep Experiences and Culture in the Western Pacific*
  R&R Bk N - v19 - i1 - Feb 2004 - p72(1) [51-500]
Lohn, Jason - *Evolvable Hardware: Proceedings*
  SciTech - v28 - i3 - Sept 2004 - p163(1) [51-500]
Lohr, Eric - *Military and Society in Russia, 1450-1917*
  JMH - v76 - i4 - Dec 2004 - p1002(3) [501+]
  Russ Rev - v63 - i2 - April 2004 - pNA [501+]
  Nationalizing the Russian Empire: The Campaign against Enemy Aliens during World War I
  HNet - July 2004 - pNA [501+]
Loibl, Gerhard - *Austrian Review of International and European Law, Vol. 6*
  R&R Bk N - v19 - i3 - August 2004 - p186(1) [501+]
Lois, Jennifer - *Heroic Efforts: The Emotional Culture of Search and Rescue Volunteers*
  SF - v83 - i1 - Sept 2004 - p449(3) [501+]
Loiselle, Andre - *Stage-Bound: Feature Film Adaptions of Canadian and Quebecois Drama*
  CBRA - Annual 2003 - p106(2) [501+]
Loiselle, Carmen G. - *Canadian Essentials of Nursing Research*
  SciTech - v28 - i4 - Dec 2004 - p121 [51-500]
Loizeaux, Elizabeth Bergman - *Yeats and the Visual Arts Syracuse*
  ILS - v24 - i1 - Fall 2004 - p22(2) [501+]
Loker, William M. - *Changing Places: Environment, Development, and Social Change in Rural Honduras*
  R&R Bk N - v19 - i4 - Nov 2004 - p126(1) [51-500]
Lomakin, S.M. - *Modern Polymer Flame Retardancy*
  SciTech - v28 - i1 - March 2004 - p55(1) [51-500]
Lomas, Kathryn - *Bread and Circuses: Euergetism and Municipal Patronage in Roman Italy*
  AJP - v125 - i2 - Summer 2004 - p293-296 [501+]
  Greek Identity in the Western Mediterranean: Papers in Honour of Brian Shefton
  R&R Bk N - v19 - i3 - August 2004 - p43(1) [51-500]
Lomax, Paul - *VBScript in a Nutshell, 2nd Ed.*
  SciTech - v28 - i4 - Dec 2004 - p28(1) [51-500]
Lombard, Anne S. - *Making Manhood: Growing Up Male in Colonial New England*
  AHR - v109 - i2 - April 2004 - p514(2) [501+]
Lombard, Joseph E.B. - *Islam, Fundamentalism, and the Betrayal of Tradition: Essays by Western Muslim Scholars*
  LJ - v129 - i13 - August 2004 - p88(1) [501+]
Lombard, Maurice - *The Golden Age of Islam*
  R&R Bk N - v19 - i3 - August 2004 - p48(1) [51-500]
Lombardi, Daniela - *Matrimoni di antico regime*
  CHR - v90 - i4 - Oct 2004 - p795(2) [501+]
  JMH - v77 - i1 - March 2005 - p203(2) [501+]
Lombardo, Daniel - *All about Techniques in Acrylics*
  LJ - v129 - i19 - Nov 15 2004 - p59(1) [501+]
  Painter's Quick Reference: Painting Trees & Foliage
  LJ - v129 - i19 - Nov 15 2004 - p59(1) [51-500]
Lombardo, Mary A. - *Rhymes Writing and Role-Play: Quick and Easy Lessons for Beginning Readers*
  LibMed - v22 - i7 - April-May 2004 - p87(1) [501+]
Lomberg, Michelle - *The Grand Canyon: The Largest Canyon in the United States*
  c SLJ - v50 - i8 - August 2004 - p107(1) [501+]
  Planets
  c SLJ - v50 - i8 - August 2004 - p105(1) [51-500]
Lomborg, Bjorn - *Global Crises, Global Solutions*
  Bwatch - Feb 2005 - pNA [51-500]
Lombroso, Cesare - *The Criminal Anthropological Writings of Cesare Lombroso Published in English Language Periodical Literature during the Late 19th and Early 20th Centuries: With Bibliographic Appendices of Books*
  R&R Bk N - v19 - i4 - Nov 2004 - p143(1) [501+]

Lomer, Kathryn - *Spare Room*
  y Magpies - v19 - i5 - Nov 2004 - p40(2) [501+]

Lomicka, Lara - *The Heinle Professional Series in Language Instruction, Vol. 1*
    R&R Bk N - v19 - i1 - Feb 2004 - p210(1) [51-500]

Lomolino, Mark V. - *Foundations of Biogeography: Classic Papers with Commentaries*
    Nature - v431 - i7007 - Sept 23 2004 - p401(1) [501+]

LoMonaco, Martha Schmoyer - *Summer Stock!: An American Theatrical Phenomenon*
    CHE - v50 - i49 - August 13 2004 - pA16(1) [501+]
    Choice - v42 - i4 - Dec 2004 - p673(1) [1-50]
    LJ - v129 - i13 - August 2004 - p84(1) [501+]
    Wom R Bks - v21 - i12 - Sept 2004 - p27(1) [501+]

Lomonaco, Michael - *Nightly Specials: 125 Recipes for Spontaneous, Creative Cooking at Home*
    BL - v101 - i4 - Oct 15 2004 - p372(1) [501+]

Londero, Elio H. - *Shadow Prices for Project Appraisal: Theory and Practice*
    R&R Bk N - v19 - i1 - Feb 2004 - p78(1) [51-500]

London, Joan - *Gilgamesh*
  y Kliatt - v38 - i5 - Sept 2004 - p23(2) [51-500]
    NYTBR - July 11 2004 - p24 [501+]

London, Jonathan - *Do Your ABC's, Little Brown Bear (Illus. by Moore, Margie)*
  c HB - v81 - i2 - March-April 2005 - p191(2) [51-500]
    Froggy Goes to the Doctor (Illus. by Remkiewicz, Frank)
  c RT - v57 - Oct 2003 - p165 [1-50]
    Froggy Plays in the Band (Illus. by Remkiewicz, Frank)
  c RT - v57 - Oct 2003 - p165 [1-50]
    Froggy's Sleepover (Illus. by Remkiewicz, Frank)
    KR - v73 - i1 - Jan 1 2005 - p54(1) [51-500]
  c PW - v252 - i6 - Feb 7 2005 - p61(2) [501+]

London, Julia - *Highlander in Disguise*
    PW - v251 - i50 - Dec 13 2004 - p51(1) [51-500]
    Miss Fortune
    BL - v101 - i5 - Nov 1 2004 - p471(1) [51-500]
    LJ - v129 - i19 - Nov 15 2004 - p46(1) [501+]

London, Lorna H. - *Community Interventions to Create Change in Children*
    CE - v81 - i1 - Fall 2004 - p50(1) [501+]

Londono-Vega, Patricia - *Religion, Culture, and Society in Colombia: Medellin and Antioquia, 1850-1930*
    HAHR - v84 - i2 - May 2004 - p368(2) [501+]

Lonergan, Bernard J.F. - *Collected Works of Bernard Lonergan, Vol. 17*
    R&R Bk N - v19 - i4 - Nov 2004 - p26(1) [501+]

Long, A.R. - *Physics of Semiconductors 2002: Proceedings*
    SciTech - v28 - i3 - Sept 2004 - p48(1) [1-50]

Long, Alecia P. - *The Great Southern Babylon: Sex, Race, and Respectability in New Orleans, 1865-1920*
    Choice - v42 - i3 - Nov 2004 - p549(1) [1-50]

Long, Alex - *Refutation and Relativism in Theaetetus 161-171*
    RM - v58 - i1 - Sept 2004 - p238(2) [501+]

Long, Bob - *Guide to Storage Tanks and Equipment*
    SciTech - v28 - i3 - Sept 2004 - p141(1) [51-500]

Long, Douglas - *Ecoterrorism*
    Choice - v42 - i7 - March 2005 - p1202(1) [51-500]
    R&R Bk N - v19 - i4 - Nov 2004 - p75(1) [51-500]
    Global Warming
    SciTech - v28 - i1 - March 2004 - p53(1) [51-500]
    International Logistics: Global Supply Chain Management
    R&R Bk N - v19 - i1 - Feb 2004 - p88(1) [1-50]

Long, J.C. - *Roy D. Chapin: The Man Behind the Hudson Motor Car Company*
    Choice - v42 - i7 - March 2005 - p1247(1) [51-500]

Long, J.J. - *W.G. Sebald: A Critical Companion*
    Choice - v42 - i5 - Jan 2005 - p857(1) [1-50]
    R&R Bk N - v19 - i4 - Nov 2004 - p245(1) [501+]

Long, J. Scott - *Regression Models for Categorical Dependent Variables Using Stata*
    JEL - v42 - i1 - March 2004 - p247(1) [501+]

Long, Jeff - *The Reckoning*
    BL - v100 - i21 - July 2004 - p1818(1) [51-500]
    LJ - v129 - i12 - July 2004 - p72(1) [51-500]

Long, Jerry M. - *Saddam's War of Words: Politics, Religion, and the Iraqi Invasion of Kuwait*
    Pers PS - v34 - i1 - Wntr 2005 - p55(2) [501+]

Long, John L. - *Introduced Mammals of the World: Their History, Distribution, and Influence*
    Choice - v42 - i1 - Sept 2004 - p131(1) [501+]
    Introduced Mammals of the World: Their History, Distribution and Influence
    QRB - v79 - i4 - Dec 2004 - p440(2) [501+]
    Introduced Mammals of the World: Their History, Distribution, and Influence
    SciTech - v28 - i1 - March 2004 - p70(1) [51-500]
    SciTech - v28 - i3 - Sept 2004 - p65(1) [51-500]

Long, Kate - *The Bad Mother's Handbook*
    KR - v73 - i1 - Jan 1 2005 - p13(1) [501+]

Long, Kathleen - *Get Bunny Love*
    BL - v101 - i9-10 - Jan 1 2005 - p831(1) [1-50]

Long, Kathleen P. - *High Anxiety: Masculinity in Crisis in Early Modern France*
    Six Ct J - v34 - i4 - Winter 2003 - p1236-1237 [501+]

Long, Larry - *Personal Computing Demystified*
    SciTech - v28 - i4 - Dec 2004 - p18(1) [1-50]

Long, Laurel - *The Lady and the Lion: A Brothers Grimm Tale (Illus. by Long, Laurel)*
  c SLJ - v50 - i10 - Oct 2004 - pS27(1) [1-50]

Long, Lisa A. - *Rehabilitating Bodies: Health, History, and the American Civil War*
    Choice - v42 - i1 - Sept 2004 - p175(1) [501+]

Long, Lucy M. - *Culinary Tourism*
    HNet - Sept 2004 - pNA [501+]
    JouAmCul - v27 - i4 - Dec 2004 - p439(2) [501+]
    VQR - v80 - i3 - Summer 2004 - p268(1) [1-50]

Long, Lynellyn D. - *Coming Home?: Refugees, Migrants, and Those Who Stayed Behind*
    Choice - v42 - i3 - Nov 2004 - p526(2) [1-50]

Long, Lynette - *Great Graphs and Sensational Statistics: Games and Activities That Make Math Easy and Fun (Illus. by Cash-Walsh, Tina)*
  c SLJ - v50 - i9 - Sept 2004 - p168(1) [51-500]

Long, Pamela O. - *Openness, Secrecy, Authorship: Technical Arts and the Culture of Knowledge from Antiquity to the Renaissance*
    Isis - v95 - i3 - Sept 2004 - p479(2) [501+]
    Six Ct J - v34 - i4 - Winter 2003 - p1198-1200 [501+]
    T&C - v45 - i2 - April 2004 - p415-416 [501+]

Long, Robert Emmet - *James Ivory in Conversation: How Merchant Ivory Makes Its Movies*
    LJ - v130 - i3 - Feb 15 2005 - p131(1) [51-500]

Long, Thomas G. - *Testimony: Talking Ourselves into Being Christian*
    CC - v122 - i5 - March 8 2005 - p43(3) [501+]

Longacre, Edward G. - *Lee's Cavalrymen: A History of the Mounted Forces of the Army of Northern Virginia*
    HNet - Sept 2004 - pNA [501+]

Longacre, Glenn V. - *To Battle for God and the Right: The Civil War Letterbooks of Emerson Opdycke*
    JSH - v70 - i3 - August 2004 - p690(2) [501+]

Longair, Malcolm S. - *Theoretical Concepts in Physics: An Alternative View of Theoretical in Physics*
    Choice - v41 - i11-12 - July-August 2004 - p2082(1) [501+]
    Theoretical Concepts in Physics: An Alternative View of Theoretical Reasoning in Physics
    TimHES - v0 - i1682 - March 11 2005 - p26(1) [501+]

Longenbach, James - *The Resistance to Poetry*
    Choice - v42 - i3 - Nov 2004 - p484(1) [1-50]
    Poet - v185 - i5 - Feb 2005 - p405(2) [501+]

Longenecker, Bruce W. - *Narrative Dynamics in Paul: A Critical Assessment*
    Intpr - v58 - i3 - July 2004 - p316(1) [501+]

Longenecker, Dwight - *Mary: A Catholic-Evangelical Debate*
    Comw - v131 - i16 - Sept 24 2004 - p35(3) [501+]

Longest, Beaufort B. - *Managing Health Programs and Projects*
    SciTech - v28 - i3 - Sept 2004 - p83(1) [501+]

Longfield, Kevin - *From Fire to Flood: A History of Theatre in Manitoba*
    Can Lit - i181 - Summer 2004 - p155-157 [501+]

Longino, Helen E. - *The Fate of Knowledge*
    Isis - v95 - i3 - Sept 2004 - p539(2) [501+]

Longley, Michael - *Snow Water*
    TLS - i5294 - Sept 17 2004 - p28(1) [501+]
    The Weather in Japan
    Sew R - v111 - i3 - Summer 2003 - p486-492 [501+]

Longman, Jere - *The Girls of Summer*
    BL - v101 - i1 - Sept 1 2004 - p53(1) [51-500]

Longman, Phillip - *The Empty Cradle: How Falling Birthrates Threaten World Prosperity and What to Do about It*
    Choice - v42 - i2 - Oct 2004 - p339(1) [51-500]
    Har Bus R - v82 - i5 - May 2004 - p30(1) [501+]
    The Empty Cradles: How Falling Birthrates Threaten World Prosperity and What To Do about It
    R&R Bk N - v19 - i4 - Nov 2004 - p86(1) [51-500]

Longman, Stanley Vincent - *Page and Stage: An Approach to Script Analysis*
    R&R Bk N - v19 - i1 - Feb 2004 - p223(1) [51-500]

Longmore, Paul - *Why I Burned My Book and Other Essays on Disability*
    RAH - v32 - i2 - June 2004 - p282-292 [501+]

Longnecker, Brent M. - *Rethinking Strategic Compensation*
    HR Mag - v50 - i2 - Feb 2005 - pS5(1) [501+]

Longo, Lawrence D. - *"Our Lords, the Sick": McGovern Lectures in the History of Medicine and Medical Humanism*
    SciTech - v28 - i3 - Sept 2004 - p77(1) [51-500]

Longrigg, Clare - *No Questions Asked: The Secret Life of Women in the Mob*
    BL - v100 - i21 - July 2004 - p1805(1) [1-50]
    NYTBR - Oct 31 2004 - p20 [501+]

Longstaffe-Gowan, Todd - *The Gardens and Parks at Hampton Court Palace*
    Apo - v161 - i516 - Feb 2005 - p72(3) [501+]

Longuski, Jim - *Advice to Rocket Scientists: A Career Survival Guide for Scientists and Engineers*
    SciTech - v28 - i1 - March 2004 - p170(1) [51-500]

Longworth, Gay - *The Unquiet Dead*
    KR - v72 - i20 - Oct 15 2004 - p987(1) [51-500]
    PW - v251 - i45 - Nov 8 2004 - p39(1) [501+]

Lonie, Bridie - *Marilynn Webb: Prints and Pastels*
    Choice - v42 - i1 - Sept 2004 - p90(1) [501+]

Lonien, Claude - *The Japanese Economic and Social System: From a Rocky Past to an Uncertain Future*
    R&R Bk N - v19 - i4 - Nov 2004 - p91(1) [501+]

Lonnrot, Elias - *Vandraren: Reseberattelser fran Karelen 1828-1842*
    Scan St - v76 - i3 - Fall 2004 - p419(3) [501+]

Lonsdale, David - *Alexander the Great, Killer of Men: History's Greatest Conqueror and the Macedonian Way of War*
    PW - v251 - i47 - Nov 22 2004 - p53(1) [51-500]

Look after Yourself
  c LibMed - v22 - i7 - April-May 2004 - p69(1) [501+]

Look at the Sky and Tell the Weather
    Bwatch - v26 - i9 - Sept 2004 - p2(1) [51-500]

Look, Lenore - *Ruby Lu, Brave and True (Illus. by Wilsdoff, Anne)*
  c LibMed - v23 - i3 - Nov-Dec 2004 - p69(1) [51-500]
  c SLJ - v50 - i10 - Oct 2004 - pS30(1) [51-500]

Lookadoo, Justin - *The Dirt on Sex: A Dateable Book*
  y SLJ - v50 - i11 - Nov 2004 - p168(1) [51-500]

Looking at Paintings: An Introduction to Fine Art for Young People
  c CH Bwatch - Feb 2005 - pNA [51-500]

Lookofsky, Joseph - *Understanding the CISG in the USA: A Compact Guide to the 1980 United Nations Convention on Contracts for the International Sale of Goods, 2nd Ed.*
    R&R Bk N - v19 - i3 - August 2004 - p190(1) [501+]
    R&R Bk N - v19 - i4 - Nov 2004 - p161(1) [501+]

Loomba, Ania - *Shakespeare, Race, and Colonialism*
    Six Ct J - v35 - i1 - Spring 2004 - p258(3) [501+]

Loomis, Burdett A. - *The Contemporary Congress, 4th Ed.*
    R&R Bk N - v19 - i1 - Feb 2004 - pNA [51-500]

Loon, Joost van - *Risk and Technological Culture: Towards a Sociology of Virulence*
    CS - v33 - i1 - Jan 2004 - p115-116 [501+]

Loos, Adolf - *On Architecture*
    South HR - v38 - i1 - Wntr 2004 - p91-94 [501+]

Looseley, David L. - *Popular Music in Contemporary France: Authenticity, Politics Debate*
    FS - v58 - i3 - July 2004 - p443-444 [501+]

Loosemore, Martin - *Human Resource Management in Construction Projects: Strategic and Operational Approaches*
    R&R Bk N - v19 - i1 - Feb 2004 - p103(1) [51-500]

Lopata, Helena Z. - *Social Problems Across the Life Course*
    R&R Bk N - v19 - i1 - Feb 2004 - p123(1) [51-500]

Loughran, Donna - *How Long Is It?*
c BL - v101 - i4 - Oct 15 2004 - p426(1) [51-500]

Lougy, Robert E. - *Inaugural Wounds: The Shaping of Desire in Five Nineteenth-Century English Narratives*
Choice - v42 - i6 - Feb 2005 - p1023(1) [51-500]

Louis, Dupre - *The Enlightenment and the Intellectual Foundations of Modern Culture*
LJ - v129 - i14 - Sept 1 2004 - p166(2) [501+]

Louis, Shirley - *Q'sapi: A History of Okanagan People as Told by Okanagan Families*
Can Hist R - v85 - i4 - Dec 2004 - p822(4) [501+]

Lourenco-Lindell, Ilda - *Walking the Tight Rope: Informal Livelihoods and Social Networks in a West African City*
R&R Bk N - v19 - i1 - Feb 2004 - p86(1) [51-500]

Lourie, Peter - *The Lost World of the Anasazi: Exploring the Mysteries of Chaco Canyon*
c LibMed - v22 - i6 - March 2004 - p72(1) [501+]
c LibMed - v22 - i6 - March 2004 - p72(1) [501+]

Loury, Glenn C. - *The Anatomy of Racial Inequality*
J Am St - v38 - i1 - April 2004 - p150-151 [501+]

Louth, Andrew - *St. John Damascene: Tradition and Originality in Byzantine Theology*
CH - v73 - i3 - Sept 2004 - p685(1) [51-500]
JR - v84 - i4 - Oct 2004 - p618(2) [501+]

Louv, Richard - *Last Child in the Woods: Saving Our Children from Nature Deficit Disorder*
PW - v252 - i11 - March 14 2005 - p56(1) [51-500]

Louvish, Simon - *Keystone: The Life and Clowns of Mack Sennett*
BIC - v33 - i7 - Oct 2004 - p21(3) [501+]

Lovallo, William R. - *Stress and Health: Biological and Psychological Interactions, 2nd Ed.*
SciTech - v28 - i4 - Dec 2004 - p69(1) [51-500]

Lovano, Michael - *The Age of Cinna: Crucible of Late Republican Rome*
Class R - v53 - i2 - Nov 2003 - p414-415 [501+]

Love, Ann - *The Kids Book of the Night Sky (Illus. by Collins, Heather)*
c Globe & Mail - July 3 2004 - pD11 [501+]
c Res Links - v10 - i1 - Oct 2004 - p25(1) [501+]
y SB - v40 - i4 - July-August 2004 - p163(2) [51-500]
c SLJ - v50 - i7 - July 2004 - p124(2) [51-500]
c S&T - v108 - i1 - July 2004 - p118(1) [501+]

Love Bites
y TES - v0 - i4586 - June 4 2004 - psssss18(2) [501+]

Love, D. Anne - *The Secret Prince*
c BL - v101 - i9-10 - Jan 1 2005 - p859(1) [1-50]
c CCB-B - v58 - i6 - Feb 2005 - p257(1) [51-500]
y Kliatt - v39 - i2 - March 2005 - p13(2) [51-500]

Love, Kathy - *Wanting What You Get*
y BL - v101 - i5 - Nov 1 2004 - p471(1) [51-500]

Love, Michael - *Incidents of Archaeology in Central America and Yucatan: Essays in Honor of Edwin M. Shook*
Lat Ant - v15 - i4 - Dec 2004 - p464(3) [501+]

Love, Pamela - *A Cub Explores (Illus. by Sycks, Shannon)*
c CH Bwatch - v14 - i12 - Dec 2004 - pNA [51-500]
c SLJ - v51 - i1 - Jan 2005 - p96(1) [51-500]

Love, Patrick G. - *Rethinking Student Affairs Practice*
R&R Bk N - v19 - i3 - August 2004 - p221(1) [1-50]

Lovecraft, H.P. - *Tales*
KR - v72 - i23 - Dec 1 2004 - p1109(1) [501+]
PW - v252 - i1 - Jan 3 2005 - p40(2) [51-500]

Lovejoy, Paul E. - *Slavery on the Frontiers of Islam*
Choice - v42 - i3 - Nov 2004 - p540(1) [1-50]
R&R Bk N - v19 - i3 - August 2004 - p157(1) [51-500]

Lovelace, Merline - *Untamed*
BL - v101 - i2 - Sept 15 2004 - p224(1) [51-500]

Loveland, Anne C. - *From Meetinghouse to Megachurch: A Material and Cultural History*
Choice - v42 - i1 - Sept 2004 - p120(1) [501+]
JAH - v91 - i3 - Dec 2004 - p1097(2) [501+]
JR - v84 - i4 - Oct 2004 - p611(2) [501+]

Loveland, Scott - *Software Testing Techniques: Finding the Defects That Matter*
Bwatch - Feb 2005 - pNA [51-500]

Lovell, George I. - *Legislative Deferrals: Statutory Ambiguity, Judicial Power, and American Democracy*
AHR - v109 - i3 - June 2004 - p934(2) [501+]
JAH - v91 - i3 - Dec 2004 - p1057(2) [501+]

Lovell, Glenville - *Love and Death in Brooklyn*
BL - v100 - i21 - July 2004 - p1824(1) [1-50]
KR - v72 - i13 - July 1 2004 - p607(1) [51-500]
PW - v251 - i30 - July 26 2004 - p40(1) [501+]

Lovell, Margaretta M. - *Art in a Season of Revolution: Painters, Artisans, and Patrons in Early America*
Mag Antiq - v167 - i1 - Jan 2005 - p128(1) [51-500]
Mag Antiq - v167 - i2 - Feb 2005 - p54(1) [51-500]
Mag Antiq - v167 - i3 - March 2005 - p58(1) [501+]

Lovell, Mark R. - *Traumatic Brain Injury in Sports: An International Neuropsychological Perspective*
E-Streams - July 2004 - pNA [501+]

Lovell, Patty - *Stand Tall, Molly Lou Melon (Illus. by Catrow, David)*
c SLJ - v50 - i7 - July 2004 - p43(1) [51-500]

Lovell, Stephen - *Summerfolk: A History of the Dacha, 1710-2000*
AHR - v109 - i2 - April 2004 - p645(2) [501+]
J Soc H - v38 - i2 - Winter 2004 - p526(3) [501+]
JMH - v77 - i1 - March 2005 - p251(3) [501+]
Russ Rev - v63 - i2 - April 2004 - pNA [501+]
Slav R - v63 - i3 - Fall 2004 - p647-648 [501+]

Lovelock, Robin - *Reflecting on Social Work: Discipline and Profession*
R&R Bk N - v19 - i3 - August 2004 - p160(1) [51-500]

Lovenheim, Peter - *Becoming a Mediator: Your Guide to Career Opportunities*
R&R Bk N - v19 - i4 - Nov 2004 - p123(1) [51-500]
Mediate, Don't Litigate
R&R Bk N - v19 - i3 - August 2004 - p206(1) [501+]

Loverance, Rowena - *Byzantium*
y Kliatt - v38 - i5 - Sept 2004 - p46(3) [51-500]

Lovett, Marsha - *Cognitive Modeling: Proceedings*
SciTech - v28 - i4 - Dec 2004 - p2(1) [1-50]

Lovett, William A. - *U.S. Trade Policy: History, Theory, and the WTO*
Choice - v42 - i1 - Sept 2004 - p155(1) [501+]
U.S. Trade Policy: History, Theory and the WTO
R&R Bk N - v19 - i3 - August 2004 - p125(1) [51-500]

Loving, George G. - *Woodbine Red Leader: A P-51 Mustang Ace in the Mediterranean Theater*
APJ - v18 - i3 - Fall 2004 - p117(2) [501+]

Loving, Jerome - *The Last Titan: A Life of Theodore Dreiser*
KR - v72 - i24 - Dec 15 2004 - p1186(1) [501+]
LJ - v130 - i2 - Feb 1 2005 - p80(1) [51-500]
PW - v252 - i8 - Feb 21 2005 - p171(1) [501+]

Lovinger, Jay - *The Gospel According to ESPN: Saints, Saviors, and Sinners*
Bks & Cult - v11 - i1 - Jan-Feb 2005 - p16(2) [501+]

Lovink, Geert - *Uncanny Networks: Dialogues with the Virtual Intelligentsia*
CS - v33 - i1 - Jan 2004 - p128-128 [501+]

Lovric, Michelle - *The Floating Book*
BW - v34 - i3 - Jan 18 2004 - p5(1) [501+]
The World's Greatest Letters: From Ancient Greece to the Twentieth Century
LJ - v129 - i14 - Sept 1 2004 - p151(1) [51-500]

Low, Andrea - *Deutsche-Juden-Polen: Geschichte einer wechselvollen Beziehung im 20 Jahrhundert*
HNet - June 2004 - pNA [501+]

Low, Anthony - *Aspects of Subjectivity: Society and Individuality from the Middle Ages to Shakespeare and Milton*
Ren Q - v57 - i3 - Fall 2004 - p1150(3) [501+]

Low, Setha M. - *Behind the Gates: Life, Security and the Pursuit of Happiness in Fortress America*
Am Q - v56 - i4 - Dec 2004 - p1067(12) [501+]
Behind the Gates: Life, Security, and the Pursuit of Happiness in Fortress America
JEL - v41 - i4 - Dec 2003 - p1445(1) [501+]

Low, Shari - *Why Not?*
BL - v101 - i3 - Oct 1 2004 - p316(1) [51-500]
PW - v251 - i34 - August 23 2004 - p35(1) [501+]

Lowance, Mason I., Jr. - *A House Divided: The Antebellum Slavery Debates in America, 1776-1865*
JSH - v70 - i3 - August 2004 - p648(2) [501+]

Lowden, Stephanie Golightly - *Time of the Eagle*
c CH Bwatch - March 2005 - pNA [51-500]

Lowder, Ellie - *Section 403(b) Compliance Guide for Public Education Employers*
R&R Bk N - v19 - i3 - August 2004 - p204(1) [1-50]

Lowe, Andrew - *Ecological Genetics: Design, Analysis, and Application*
Choice - v42 - i4 - Dec 2004 - p687(1) [1-50]

Lowe, Barbara J. - *Decorated Medieval Floor Tiles of Somerset*
R&R Bk N - v19 - i4 - Nov 2004 - p208(1) [501+]

Lowe, David Garrard - *Art Deco New York*
Bwatch - March 2005 - pNA [51-500]
Choice - v42 - i7 - March 2005 - p1216(1) [51-500]

Lowe, Denise Nola-Faye - *An Encyclopedic Dictionary of Women in Early American Films; 1895-1930.*
LJ - v129 - i16 - Oct 1 2004 - p110(1) [51-500]
An Encyclopedic Dictionary Of Women In Early American Films
Bwatch - Feb 2005 - pNA [51-500]

Lowe, E.Jonathan - *Subjects of Experience*
Phil R - v112 - i3 - July 2003 - p416(4) [501+]

Lowe, J. Andreas - *Richard Smyth and the Language of Orthodoxy: Re-Imagining Tudor Catholic Polemicism*
Ren Q - v57 - i3 - Fall 2004 - p1114(3) [501+]

Lowe, Kate - *Nuns' Chronicles and Convent Culture in Renaissance and Counter-Reformation Italy*
Ren Q - v57 - i4 - Winter 2004 - p1371(2) [501+]

Lowe, Keith - *New Free Chocolate Sex*
KR - v72 - i24 - Dec 15 2004 - p1158(2) [51-500]

Lowe, Margaret A. - *Looking Good: College Women and Body Image, 1875-1930*
Am Q - v56 - i4 - Dec 2004 - p1115(10) [501+]
Am St - v45 - i1 - Spring 2004 - p153-154 [501+]
J Soc H - v38 - i1 - Fall 2004 - p231(2) [501+]
JAH - v91 - i2 - Sept 2004 - p656(2) [501+]

Lowe, Pat - *Hunters and Trackers of The Australian Desert*
Bwatch - Oct 2004 - pNA [51-500]

Lowe, Roger - *Family Therapy: A Constructive Framework*
SciTech - v28 - i4 - Dec 2004 - p97(1) [51-500]

Lowe, Sarah M. - *Tina Modotti and Edward Weston: The Mexico Years*
Choice - v42 - i2 - Oct 2004 - p286(1) [501+]

Lowell, Christopher - *Christopher Lowell, the Hassle-Free Host: Super-Simple Tablescapes and Recipes for Stunning Parties*
BL - v101 - i1 - Sept 1 2004 - p35(1) [51-500]
LJ - v129 - i13 - August 2004 - p110(1) [51-500]
PW - v251 - i27 - July 5 2004 - p52(1) [51-500]

Lowell, David W. - *Asia-Pacific Security: Policy Challenges*
R&R Bk N - v19 - i1 - Feb 2004 - p256(1) [51-500]

Lowell, Heather - *No Escape*
PW - v251 - i29 - July 19 2004 - p150(1) [51-500]

Lowell, Robert - *Collected Poems*
Ga R - v58 - i1 - Spring 2004 - p185-195 [501+]
J Am St - v38 - i1 - April 2004 - p151-152 [501+]
Ken R - v27 - i1 - Wntr 2005 - p134(36) [501+]
NEQ - v77 - i2 - June 2004 - p291-299 [501+]
WLT - v78 - i3-4 - Sept-Dec 2004 - p103(1) [501+]

Lowenstein, Felicia - *All about Sign Language: Talking with Your Hands*
c SLJ - v50 - i12 - Dec 2004 - p163(1) [51-500]

Lowenstein, Roger - *Origin of the Crash: The Great Bubble and Its Undoing*
NYTBR - Jan 30 2005 - p24 [501+]

Lowery, Charles D. - *The Greenwood Encyclopedia of African American Civil Rights: From Emancipation to the Twenty-First Century*
Choice - v41 - i11-12 - July-August 2004 - p2026(1) [501+]
y SLJ - v50 - i10 - Oct 2004 - p95(1) [51-500]

Lowery, Joseph W. - *Dreamweaver MX 2004 Bible*
LJ - v129 - i12 - July 2004 - p112(1) [501+]
SciTech - v28 - i3 - Sept 2004 - p156(1) [51-500]

Lowery, Ron - *Chasing Lewis and Clark Across America*
S Liv - v40 - i2 - Feb 2005 - p151(1) [51-500]

Lowi, Theodore J. - *American Government: Power and Purpose, core 8th Core Ed.*
R&R Bk N - v19 - i3 - August 2004 - p177(1) [501+]

Lowie, Robert H. - *The Crow Indians*
Atl - v294 - i1 - July-August 2004 - p144(1) [501+]
LJ - v129 - i17 - Oct 15 2004 - p99(1) [51-500]

Lowitt, Richard - *Fred Harris: His Journey from Liberalism to Populism*
SHQ - v107 - i3 - Jan 2004 - p492(2) [501+]
WHQ - v35 - i2 - Summer 2004 - p251-252 [501+]

Lowndes, Marie Bellock - *The Lodger (Read by Raver, Lorna). Audiobook Review*
BL - v100 - i21 - July 2004 - p1855(2) [1-50]

Lowney, Chris - *Heroic Leadership: Best Practices from a 450-Year-Old Company That Changed the World*
   CC - v121 - i21 - Oct 19 2004 - p62(3) [501+]
A Vanished World: Medieval Spain's Golden Age of Enlightenment
   KR - v73 - i3 - Feb 1 2005 - p167(1) [501+]
   PW - v252 - i9 - Feb 28 2005 - p56(1) [51-500]
Lowrie, Charlotte K. - *Teach Yourself Visually Digital Photography. 2nd Ed.*
   SciTech - v28 - i3 - Sept 2004 - p169(1) [51-500]
Lowry, Brigid - *Follow the Blue*
   y   HB - v80 - i4 - July-August 2004 - p456(1) [51-500]
       VOYA - v27 - i5 - Dec 2004 - p384(1) [51-500]
Lowry, Lois - *Anastasia Vive Aqui/Anastasia at This Address (Illus. by Alonso, Juan Ramon)*
   c   BL - v100 - i22 - August 2004 - p1950(1) [501+]
Messenger (Read by Morse, David). Audiobook Review
   y   Kliatt - v38 - i5 - Sept 2004 - p63(2) [51-500]
   c   SLJ - v50 - i9 - Sept 2004 - p78(1) [51-500]
Messenger
   c   BooChiTr - May 9 2004 - p2(1) [501+]
   c   CH Bwatch - v14 - i7 - July 2004 - p7(1) [51-500]
   y   JAAL - v48 - i1 - Sept 2004 - p80(1) [501+]
   c   LibMed - v23 - i3 - Nov-Dec 2004 - p70(2) [51-500]
   y   Teach Lib - v32 - i1 - Oct 2004 - p18(1) [51-500]
Number the Stars (Read by Brown, Blair). Audiobook Review
   c   BL - v100 - i21 - July 2004 - p1857(1) [1-50]
       Kliatt - v38 - i3 - May 2004 - p54(1) [51-500]
   c   SLJ - v50 - i7 - July 2004 - p60(1) [51-500]
Number the Stars
   c   RT - v57 - Sept 2003 - p98 [1-50]
The Silent Boy
       JAAL - v48 - i1 - Sept 2004 - p75(2) [501+]
   y   PW - v252 - i4 - Jan 24 2005 - p246(1) [51-500]
Lowry, William R. - *Dam Politics: Restoring America's Rivers*
   R&R Bk N - v19 - i1 - Feb 2004 - p250(1) [51-500]
Lowy, Alex - *The Power of the 2x2 Matrix; Using 2x2 Thinking to Solve Business Problems and Make Better Decisions*
   R&R Bk N - v19 - i3 - August 2004 - p102(1) [501+]
Lowy, Joan A. - *Pat Schroeder: A Woman of the House*
   R&R Bk N - v19 - i1 - Feb 2004 - p61(1) [501+]
Lowy, Jonathan - *The Temple of Music*
   KR - v72 - i19 - Oct 1 2004 - p932(1) [501+]
   PW - v251 - i48 - Nov 29 2004 - p24(1) [51-500]
Lowy, Juval - *Programming .NET Components*
   SciTech - v28 - i4 - Dec 2004 - p27(1) [51-500]
Lowy, Michael - *Romanticism Against the Tide of Modernity*
   CS - v33 - i2 - March 2004 - p254-256 [501+]
Loxley, Simon - *Type: The Secret History of Letters*
   LJ - v129 - i14 - Sept 1 2004 - p146(1) [51-500]
   TimHES - v0 - i1673 - Jan 7 2005 - p24(2) [501+]
   TLS - i5292 - Sept 3 2004 - p33(1) [501+]
Loy, David L. - *The Dharma of Dragons and Daemons: Buddhist Themes in Modern Fantasy*
   PW - v251 - i43 - Oct 25 2004 - p45(1) [51-500]
Loya, Joe (b. 1961 -) - *The Man Who Outgrew His Prison Cell: Confessions of a Bank Robber*
   BL - v100 - i22 - August 2004 - p1881(1) [51-500]
   KR - v72 - i14 - July 15 2004 - p674(1) [51-500]
   NY - v80 - i33 - Nov 1 2004 - pNA [1-50]
   PW - v251 - i28 - July 12 2004 - p54(1) [51-500]
Loyd, Gary E. - *Practical Health Care Simulations*
   SciTech - v28 - i4 - Dec 2004 - p81(1) [51-500]
Lozada, Eriberto P. - *God Aboveground: Catholic Church, Postsocialist State, and Transnational Processes in a Chinese Village*
   JR - v84 - i3 - July 2004 - p472(3) [501+]
Lozowick, Yaacov - *Right to Exist: A Moral Defense of Israel's Wars*
   MEQ - v11 - i4 - Fall 2004 - p83(2) [501+]
Lu, Chun-Shien - *Multimedia Security: Steganography and Digital Watermarking Techniques for Protection of Intellectual Property*
   Choice - v42 - i4 - Dec 2004 - p696(1) [1-50]
   SciTech - v28 - i3 - Sept 2004 - p32(1) [51-500]
Lu, Ding - *China's Economic Globalization through the WTO*
   JEL - v42 - i1 - March 2004 - p326(1) [501+]
China's Telecommunications Market: Entering a New Competitive Age
   R&R Bk N - v19 - i2 - May 2004 - p109(1) [51-500]

Lu, Mi - *Arithmetic and Logic in Computer Systems*
   Choice - v41 - i11-12 - July-August 2004 - p2080(1) [501+]
Lu, Ming - *Development and Application of Discontinous Modelling for Rock Engineering*
   SciTech - v28 - i1 - March 2004 - p144(1) [51-500]
Lu, Xing - *Chinese Communication Studies: Contexts and Comparisons*
   Ch Rev Int - v10 - i2 - Fall 2003 - p418(4) [501+]
Rhetoric of the Chinese Cultural Revolution: The Impact on Chinese Thought, Culture, and Communication
   R&R Bk N - v19 - i4 - Nov 2004 - p227(1) [501+]
Lu, Yan - *Re-Understanding Japan: Chinese Perspectives, 1895-1945*
   R&R Bk N - v19 - i3 - August 2004 - p56(1) [51-500]
Lu, Yichen - *AIDS in Asia*
   Choice - v42 - i5 - Jan 2005 - p885(1) [1-50]
Lu, Yunfeng - *Self-Assembled Nanostructured Materials: Proceedings*
   SciTech - v28 - i1 - March 2004 - p141(1) [51-500]
Lubar, David - *Dunk*
   y   Kliatt - v38 - i4 - July 2004 - p21(1) [51-500]
Flip
   y   Kliatt - v38 - i4 - July 2004 - p31(1) [51-500]
   y   LibMed - v22 - i5 - Feb 2004 - p69(1) [501+]
Wizards of the Game
   y   LibMed - v22 - i4 - Jan 2004 - p65(1) [501+]
Lubaroff, Scott - *An Examination of the Neo-Classical Wind Works of Igor Stravinsky: The Octet for Winds and Concerto for Piano and Winds*
   R&R Bk N - v19 - i4 - Nov 2004 - p198(1) [501+]
Lubell, Pamela - *The Chinese Communist Party and the Cultural Revolution: The Case of the Sixty-One Renegades*
   JAS - v63 - i3 - August 2004 - p772-773 [501+]
Lubelski, Nava - *The Starving Artist's Way: Easy Projects for Low-Budget Living*
   Globe & Mail - Jan 22 2005 - pL4 [501+]
Lubertozzi, Alex - *The War of the Worlds: Mars' Invasion of Earth, Inciting Panic and Inspiring Terror from H.G. Wells to Orson Welles and Beyond*
   R&R Bk N - v19 - i1 - Feb 2004 - p239(1) [51-500]
Lubet, Steven - *Murder in Tombstone: The Forgotten Trial of Wyatt Earp*
   LJ - v129 - i17 - Oct 15 2004 - p74(1) [51-500]
   PW - v251 - i35 - August 30 2004 - p41(1) [51-500]
Lubimiv, Greg - *My Sister is an Angeline*
   c   CBRA - Annual 2003 - p457(1) [51-500]
Lubin, David M. - *Shooting Kennedy: JFK and the Culture of Images*
   JAH - v91 - i3 - Dec 2004 - p1087(2) [501+]
Lubka, S. Ruth - *Pupniks: The Story of Two Space Dogs*
   LibMed - v22 - i5 - Feb 2004 - p58(1) [501+]
Lublin, David - *The Republican South: Democratization and Partisan Change*
   Choice - v42 - i4 - Dec 2004 - p737(1) [1-50]
   HRNB - v33 - i1 - Fall 2004 - p8(2) [501+]
Lucado, Max - *Come Thirsty: No Heart Too Dry for His Touch*
   PW - v251 - i35 - August 30 2004 - p50(1) [51-500]
Lucarelli, Carlo - *Day After Day*
   TLS - i5300 - Oct 29 2004 - p24(1) [501+]
Lucarotti, Rolli - *Recipes from Corsica*
   TLS - i5289 - August 13 2004 - p28(1) [501+]
Lucas, Alexander R. - *Demystifying Anorexia Nervosa: An Optimistic Guide to Understanding and Healing*
   SciTech - v28 - i4 - Dec 2004 - p99(1) [51-500]
Lucas, Ceil - *Language and the Law in Deaf Communities*
   R&R Bk N - v19 - i1 - Feb 2004 - pNA [51-500]
What's Your Sign for Pizza? An Introduction to Variation in American Sign Language
   R&R Bk N - v19 - i1 - Feb 2004 - p139(1) [51-500]
Lucas, David - *Halibut Jackson*
   c   BooChiTr - March 28 2004 - p2(1) [501+]
       LibMed - v22 - i7 - April-May 2004 - p57(1) [501+]
Lucas, Geralyn - *Why I Wore Lipstick*
   LJ - v129 - i14 - Sept 1 2004 - p184(2) [501+]
   PW - v251 - i33 - August 16 2004 - p51(2) [51-500]
Lucas, John - *A World Perhaps: New and Selected Poems*
   TLS - i5291 - August 27 2004 - p28(1) [501+]

Lucas, John Meredyth - *Eighty Odd Years in Hollywood: Memoir of a Career in Film and Television*
   R&R Bk N - v19 - i3 - August 2004 - p260(1) [51-500]
Lucas, John Scott - *Astrology and Numerology in Medieval and Early Modern Catalonia: 'The Tractat de Prenostication de la Vida Natural dels Homens'*
   R&R Bk N - v19 - i1 - Feb 2004 - p9(1) [51-500]
Lucas, Karen - *Running on Empty: Transport, Social Exclusion and Environmental Justice*
   R&R Bk N - v19 - i4 - Nov 2004 - p106(1) [51-500]
Lucas, Michele Claire - *A High and Hidden Place*
   KR - v73 - i2 - Jan 15 2005 - p77(1) [501+]
   LJ - v130 - i2 - Feb 1 2005 - p62(1) [51-500]
Lucas, Peter W. - *Dental Functional Morphology: How Teeth Work*
   Nature - v431 - i7007 - Sept 23 2004 - p400(2) [501+]
   Sci - v306 - i5704 - Dec 17 2004 - p2045(1) [501+]
Lucas, Philip Charles - *New Religious Movements in the 21st Century: Legal, Political, and Social Challenges in Global Perspective*
   J Ch St - v46 - i3 - Summer 2004 - p663(1) [501+]
Lucas, Robert E. - *Lectures on Economic Growth*
   JEL - v42 - i3 - Sept 2004 - p877(2) [501+]
Lucas, Scott - *The Betrayal of Dissent: Beyond Orwell, Hitchens and the New American Century*
   Nation - v279 - i19 - Dec 6 2004 - p40 [501+]
Luceigh, Betty A. - *Organic Chemistry and Biochemistry: Strucutre Visualization Workbook*
   SciTech - v28 - i4 - Dec 2004 - p55(1) [51-500]
Luceno, James - *Star Wars: Labyrinth of Evil*
   BL - v101 - i9-10 - Jan 1 2005 - p834(1) [1-50]
   PW - v251 - i51 - Dec 20 2004 - p41(2) [501+]
   LJ - v129 - i20 - Dec 1 2004 - p104(1) [51-500]
Worlds of Star Wars Trilogy: The Ultimate Guide to the Incredible Locations of Episodes (Illus. by Chasemore, Richard)
   y   PW - v251 - i36 - Sept 6 2004 - p65(1) [51-500]
Luchetti, Cathy - *Men of the West: Life on the American Frontier*
   R&R Bk N - v19 - i3 - August 2004 - p75(1) [51-500]
Luciani, Brigitte - *Those Messy Hempels (Illus. by Hie, Vanessa)*
   c   CCB-B - v57 - i11 - July-August 2004 - p473(1) [501+]
   c   LibMed - v23 - i3 - Nov-Dec 2004 - p66(1) [51-500]
   c   SLJ - v50 - i9 - Sept 2004 - p170(2) [51-500]
Lucie-Smith, Edward - *Erotica: The Fine Art of Sex*
   Art N - v103 - i1 - Jan 2004 - p100(1) [501+]
Lucifora, Rose Marie - *Voci Politiche in Properzio 'Erotico'. Ideologia e Progetto Elegiaco in II, 16 e III, 11*
   Class R - v53 - i2 - Nov 2003 - p363-365 [501+]
Luckhurst, Roger - *The Invention of Telepathy, 1870-1901*
   VS - v46 - i3 - Spring 2004 - p503(3) [501+]
Lucking, David - *Ancestors and Gods: Margaret Laurence and the Dialectics of Identity*
   Can Lit - i181 - Summer 2004 - p157-159 [501+]
Luckins, Tanja - *The Gates of Memory: Australian People's Experiences and Memories of Loss and the Great War*
   HNet - Sept 2004 - pNA [501+]
Luconi, Stefano - *Italian-American Vote in Providence, Rhode Island, 1916-1948*
   R&R Bk N - v19 - i4 - Nov 2004 - p65(1) [51-500]
Lucs, Scott C. - *Constructive Critics, Hadith Literature, and the Articulation of Sunni Culture: The Legacy of the Generation of Ibn Sa'd, Ibn Ma'in, and Ibn Hanbal*
   R&R Bk N - v19 - i3 - August 2004 - p18(1) [1-50]
Lucy, Niall - *A Derrida Dictionary*
   Choice - v42 - i1 - Sept 2004 - p62(1) [501+]
   TLS - i5284 - July 9 2004 - p25(1) [501+]
Luczanits, Christian - *Buddhist Sculpture in Clay: Early Western Himalayan Art, Late 10th to Early 13th Centuries*
   R&R Bk N - v19 - i4 - Nov 2004 - p205(1) [501+]
Luddy, Maria - *Crimean Journals of the Sisters of Mercy, 1854-56*
   R&R Bk N - v19 - i4 - Nov 2004 - p41(1) [51-500]
Ludemann, Gerd - *The Resurrection of Christ: A Historical Inquiry*
   BL - v101 - i3 - Oct 1 2004 - p305(1) [51-500]
Ludington, Jake - *Easy Digital Home Movies*
   Bwatch - v26 - i7 - July 2004 - p8(1) [51-500]

Lynch, Peter - *Wiring Prometheus: Globalisation, History and Technology*
   R&R Bk N - v19 - i4 - Nov 2004 - p88(1) [51-500]
Lynch, Sarah-Kate - *By Bread Alone*
   BL - v101 - i2 - Sept 15 2004 - p209(1) [501+]
   LJ - v129 - i15 - Sept 15 2004 - p49(1) [51-500]
   PW - v251 - i38 - Sept 20 2004 - p47(1) [51-500]
Lynch, Stephen - *Dynamical Systems with Applications Using Maple*
   SIAM Rev - v46 - i3 - Sept 2004 - p575(3) [501+]
Lynch, Stephen J. - *As You Like It: A Guide to the Play*
   R&R Bk N - v19 - i1 - Feb 2004 - p237(1) [51-500]
Lynch, Wayne - *Baby Lion*
   c Can Lit - i182 - Autumn 2004 - p122(3) [501+]
Lynd, Staughton - *Lucasville: the Untold Story of a Prison Uprising*
   LJ - v129 - i13 - August 2004 - p98(1) [501+]
Lynda, Sandoval - *Who's Your Daddy?*
   SLJ - v51 - i1 - Jan 2005 - p136(1) [51-500]
Lynds, Gayle - *The Coil*
   BooChiTr - April 18 2004 - p6(1) [501+]
Lyndsay, Dave - *Dave's Quick 'n' Easy Web Pages 2: A Guide to Creating Multi-Page Web Sites*
   LJ - v129 - i20 - Dec 1 2004 - p152(1) [501+]
Lyne, Alison Davis - *Vidrine, Beverly Barras. Halloween Alphabet*
   SLJ - v50 - i12 - Dec 2004 - p138(1) [501+]
Lynes, Barbara Buhler - *Georgia O'Keeffe and New Mexico: A Sense of Place*
   A Art - v68 - i745 - August 2004 - p75(1) [501+]
   Georgia O'Keeffe and New Mexico: A Sense of Place
   TLS - i5289 - August 13 2004 - p28-29 [501+]
   Maria Chabot--Georgia O'Keeffe: Correspondence 1941-1949
   R&R Bk N - v19 - i1 - Feb 2004 - p206(1) [51-500]
Lyness, Anne M. Prouty - *Feminist Perspectives in Medical Family Therapy*
   SciTech - v28 - i3 - Sept 2004 - p98(1) [51-500]
Lyng, Stephen - *Edgework: The Sociology of Risk-Taking*
   CHE - v51 - i16 - Dec 10 2004 - pA17-A17 [501+]
Lynn, Allison - *Now You See It*
   People - v62 - i6 - August 9 2004 - p48 [51-500]
Lynn, Bill - *Actors and Writers: A Guidebook for Improv Lessons in Comedy*
   Bwatch - Feb 2005 - pNA [51-500]
Lynn, Cari - *Leg the Spread: A Woman's Adventures inside the Trillion-Dollar Boys' Club of Commodities Trading*
   BL - v101 - i2 - Sept 15 2004 - p186(1) [51-500]
   KR - v72 - i14 - July 15 2004 - p674(1) [501+]
   LJ - v129 - i13 - August 2004 - p91(1) [501+]
   NW - Nov 1 2004 - p34 [501+]
   PW - v251 - i28 - July 12 2004 - p52(1) [51-500]

Lynn, Dennis - *What Is My Song? (Illus. by Miranda, Francisco)*
   c BL - v101 - i7 - Dec 1 2004 - p657(1) [51-500]
Lynn, Elizabeth A. - *Dragon's Treasure*
   y BL - v101 - i1 - Sept 1 2004 - p75(1) [51-500]
   PW - v251 - i33 - August 16 2004 - p47(1) [51-500]
Lynn, John A. (b. 1943 -) - *Battle: A History of Combat and Culture*
   J Mil H - v68 - i3 - July 2004 - p943-945 [501+]
   Battle: A History of Combat and Culture from Ancient Greece to Modern America
   AHR - v109 - i3 - June 2004 - p862(1) [501+]
   APJ - v18 - i3 - Fall 2004 - p112(3) [501+]
Lynn, Loretta - *You're Cookin' It Country: My Favorite Recipes and Memories*
   LJ - v129 - i14 - Sept 1 2004 - p181(2) [51-500]
   PW - v251 - i29 - July 19 2004 - p157(1) [51-500]
Lynn, Martha Drexler - *American Studio Glass, 1960-1990*
   R&R Bk N - v19 - i4 - Nov 2004 - p209(1) [501+]
Lynn, Richard - *IQ and the Wealth of Nations*
   JEL - v42 - i1 - March 2004 - p220(2) [501+]
Lynton, Norbert - *William Scott*
   Spec - v296 - i9194 - Oct 23 2004 - p53(1) [501+]
Lyon, Annabel - *The Best Thing for You*
   Globe & Mail - Jan 6 2005 - pR1 [501+]
Lyon, David - *Surveillance after September 11*
   AJPS - v39 - i2 - July 2004 - p467(468) [501+]
Lyon, George Ella - *Sonny's House of Spies*
   y CCB-B - v58 - i1 - Sept 2004 - p27(1) [51-500]
   y HB - v80 - i5 - Sept-Oct 2004 - p590(1) [51-500]
   y PW - v251 - i27 - July 5 2004 - p56(1) [51-500]
   c SLJ - v50 - i8 - August 2004 - p126(1) [501+]
   y VOYA - v27 - i3 - August 2004 - p221(1) [1-50]
Lyon, James - *South America on a Shoestring*
   Bwatch - Feb 2005 - pNA [51-500]
Lyons, Andrew O. - *Irregular Connections: A History of Anthropology and Sexuality*
   Choice - v42 - i7 - March 2005 - p1270(2) [51-500]
Lyons, Carol A. - *Teaching Struggling Readers: How to Use Brain-based Research to Maximize Learning*
   SLJ - v50 - i10 - Oct 2004 - pS73(1) [51-500]
Lyons, Greg - *Literature of the American West: A Cultural Approach*
   ANQ:QJ - v17 - i4 - Fall 2004 - p52(3) [501+]
Lyons, James - *Selling Seattle: Representing Contemporary Urban America.*
   LJ - v129 - i13 - August 2004 - p104(1) [51-500]

Lyons, John S. - *Redressing the Emperor: Improving Our Children's Public Mental Health System*
   Choice - v42 - i6 - Feb 2005 - p1102(1) [51-500]
   LJ - v129 - i18 - Nov 1 2004 - p110(1) [51-500]
   SciTech - v28 - i4 - Dec 2004 - p112(1) [1-50]
Lyons, Kelly Starling - *Eddie's Ordeal*
   y CH Bwatch - Jan 2005 - pNA [51-500]
Lyons, Lenore - *A State of Ambivalence: The Feminist Movement in Singapore*
   R&R Bk N - v19 - i4 - Nov 2004 - p135(1) [1-50]
Lyons, Mary E. - *Roy Makes a Car (Illus. by Widener, Terry)*
   c Black Iss - v7 - i2 - March-April 2005 - p66(2) [501+]
Lyons, Mary Evelyn - *Roy Makes a Car (Illus. by Widener, Terry)*
   c CCB-B - v58 - i6 - Feb 2005 - p258(1) [51-500]
   c HB - v81 - i2 - March-April 2005 - p211(2) [51-500]
   c KR - v72 - i24 - Dec 15 2004 - p1204(1) [51-500]
   c PW - v252 - i4 - Jan 24 2005 - p243(1) [51-500]
Lyons, Paul - *Button Man*
   BL - v100 - i21 - July 2004 - p1818(1) [51-500]
   The People of Generation: The Rise and Fall of the New Left in Philadelphia
   JAH - v91 - i2 - Sept 2004 - p717(2) [501+]
Lyons, Richard E. - *Success Strategies for Adjunct Faculty*
   R&R Bk N - v19 - i1 - Feb 2004 - p185(1) [51-500]
Lyons, Stephen J. - *A View from the Inland Northwest*
   PW - v251 - i34 - August 23 2004 - p51(1) [51-500]
Lyons, Steve - *The Gift Moves*
   c LibMed - v23 - i3 - Nov-Dec 2004 - p73(1) [51-500]
Lyons, Tanya - *Guns and Guerilla Girls: Women in the Zimbabwean Liberation Struggle*
   HNet - Nov 2004 - pNA [501+]
Lyons, Thomas P. - *China Maritime Customs and China's Trade Statistics, 1859-1948*
   JEL - v41 - i4 - Dec 2003 - p1405(2) [501+]
Lyons, Tryna - *The Artists of Nathadwara: The Practice of Painting in Rajasthan*
   Choice - v42 - i2 - Oct 2004 - p281(1) [501+]
Lystra, Karen - *Dangerous Intimacy: The Untold Story of Mark Twain's Final Years*
   Choice - v42 - i3 - Nov 2004 - p484(2) [1-50]
   JouAmCul - v27 - i4 - Dec 2004 - p459(2) [501+]
Lytle, Richard M. - *Soldiers of America's First Army, 1791*
   R&R Bk N - v19 - i4 - Nov 2004 - p53(1) [51-500]
Lytwyn, Victor P. - *Muskekowuck Athinuwick: Original People of the Great Swampy Land*
   Can Hist R - v85 - i3 - Sept 2004 - p574(3) [501+]

M

Ma, Jian - *The Noodle Maker*
  KR - v72 - i19 - Oct 1 2004 - p932(2) [501+]
  Lon R Bks - v26 - i13 - July 8 2004 - p12(2)
  [501+]
Ma, Jun - *China's Water Crisis*
  R&R Bk N - v19 - i3 - August 2004 - p112(1)
  [51-500]
Ma, Jyoti - *Sparkling Together: Starbright and His
  Earthling Friends (Illus. by Devi, Chandra)*
  c SLJ - v50 - i10 - Oct 2004 - p123(1) [51-500]
Ma, Mingda - *Shuo jian cong gao*
  Ch Rev Int - v11 - i1 - Spring 2004 - p141(5)
  [501+]
Ma, O. John - *Emergency Medicine: Just the Facts, 2nd
  Ed.*
  SciTech - v28 - i3 - Sept 2004 - p113(1) [51-500]
  Emergency Medicine Manual, 6th Ed.
  SciTech - v28 - i1 - March 2004 - p89(1) [51-500]
Ma, Zhong-Qi - *Problems and Solutions in Group Theory
  for Physicists*
  SciTech - v28 - i4 - Dec 2004 - p47(1) [51-500]
Maag, Karin - *Worship in Medieval and Early Modern
  Europe: Change and Continuity in Religious Practice*
  Med R - Nov 2004 - pNA [501+]
Maalouf, Amin - *In the Name of Identity: Violence and the
  Need to Belong*
  Globe & Mail - Sept 11 2004 - pD23 [501+]
Maar, Michael - *Bluebeard's Chamber: Guilt and
  Confession in Thomas Mann*
  CHE - v50 - i23 - Feb 13 2004 - pA15-A15 [501+]
  Choice - v41 - i7 - March 2004 - p1301(1) [501+]
Maart, Rozena - *Rosa's District 6*
  Globe & Mail - March 5 2005 - pD7 [501+]
Maas, A.J.P. - *Atomisme en individualisme: De
  Amsterdamse Natuurkunde tussen 1877 en 1940*
  Isis - v95 - i2 - June 2004 - p307(2) [501+]
Mabanckou, Alain - *African Psycho*
  WLT - v78 - i3-4 - Sept-Dec 2004 - p82(1) [501+]
Mabey, Richard - *Nature Cure*
  Spec - v297 - i9212 - Feb 26 2005 - p36(2) [501+]
Mabillon, Dom Jean - *Treatise on Monastic Studies: 1691*
  R&R Bk N - v19 - i4 - Nov 2004 - p19(1) [51-
  500]
Mabrouk, Ann Patricia - *The Ethical Chemist:
  Professionalism and Ethics in Science*
  J Chem Ed - v81 - i6 - June 2004 - p806-807
  [501+]
Mabry, Celia Hales - *Cooperative Reference: Social
  Interaction in the Workplace*
  LJ - v129 - i19 - Nov 15 2004 - p92(1) [51-500]
Mac, Carrie - *The Beckoners*
  y BL - v101 - i6 - Nov 15 2004 - p595(2) [51-500]
  y Kliatt - v38 - i5 - Sept 2004 - p13(3) [51-500]
  c Res Links - v10 - i1 - Oct 2004 - p34(1) [501+]
  y SLJ - v50 - i12 - Dec 2004 - p150(1) [51-500]
  Charmed
  y Res Links - v10 - i3 - Feb 2005 - p38(1) [501+]
Macaire, Jennifer - *The Secret of Shabaz*
  VOYA - v27 - i5 - Dec 2004 - p408(1) [51-500]
MacAlister, Katie - *Hard Day's Knight*
  BL - v101 - i9-10 - Jan 1 2005 - p831(1) [1-50]
  You Slay Me
  BL - v101 - i1 - Sept 1 2004 - p73(1) [51-500]
MacAndrew, Craig - *Drunken Comportment: A Social
  Explanation*
  R&R Bk N - v19 - i1 - Feb 2004 - p139(1) [51-
  500]
Macaulay, Adam - *Don't Tell Me, Show Me: Directors
  Talk about Acting*
  R&R Bk N - v19 - i3 - August 2004 - p261(1)
  [501+]

Macaulay, David - *Mosque (Illus. by Macaulay, David)*
  c BL - v101 - i3 - Oct 1 2004 - p345(1) [51-500]
Macauley, David - *Mosque*
  LibMed - v22 - i6 - March 2004 - p80(1) [501+]
  y SLJ - v51 - i1 - Jan 2005 - p57(1) [51-500]
MacAvoy, Paul W. - *The Recurrent Crisis in Corporate
  Governance*
  Choice - v41 - i11-12 - July-August 2004 -
  p2089(1) [501+]
Macbain, Jennifer - *Chien-Shiung Wu: Pioneering
  Physicist and Atomic Researcher*
  c SLJ - v50 - i9 - Sept 2004 - p220(2) [51-500]
MacCabe, Colin - *Godard: A Portrait of the Artist at
  Seventy*
  Bks & Cult - v10 - i5 - Sept-Oct 2004 - p36(2)
  [501+]
  Lon R Bks - v26 - i7 - April 1 2004 - pNA [501+]
MacCambridge, Michael - *America's Game: The Epic
  Story of How Pro Football Captured a Nation*
  BL - v101 - i6 - Nov 15 2004 - p545(1) [51-500]
  BW - v34 - i45 - Nov 7 2004 - p2(1) [501+]
  Choice - v42 - i7 - March 2005 - p1266(1) [51-
  500]
  LJ - v129 - i16 - Oct 1 2004 - p90(1) [51-500]
  Nation - v280 - i8 - Feb 28 2005 - p30 [501+]
  NYTBR - Nov 7 2004 - p20 [501+]
  PW - v251 - i37 - Sept 13 2004 - p68(1) [51-500]
Maccarone, Grace - *Bless Me (Illus. by Williams, San)*
  c PW - v251 - i43 - Oct 25 2004 - p46(1) [501+]
MacCarthy, Robert - *Preached at St. Patrick's: Sermons
  from Different Ages*
  R&R Bk N - v19 - i4 - Nov 2004 - p20(1) [51-
  500]
Maccioni, Sirio - *Sirio: The Story of My Life and Le
  Cirque*
  LJ - v129 - i12 - July 2004 - p110(1) [51-500]
  NYTBR - July 11 2004 - p16 [501+]
  NYTBR - July 18 2004 - p18 [501+]
  NYTBR - July 25 2004 - p18 [501+]
MacCotter, Paul - *Colman of Cloyne: A Study*
  R&R Bk N - v19 - i4 - Nov 2004 - p37(1) [51-
  500]
MacCulloch, Diarmaid - *The Reformation: A History*
  AM - v191 - i11 - Oct 18 2004 - p24 [501+]
  Atl - v294 - i5 - Dec 2004 - p123(1) [501+]
  Bks & Cult - v10 - i5 - Sept-Oct 2004 - p31(1)
  [501+]
  CC - v122 - i3 - Feb 8 2005 - p41(2) [501+]
  Choice - v42 - i4 - Dec 2004 - p678(2) [1-50]
  Reformation: Europe's House Divided 1490-1700
  Lon R Bks - v26 - i14 - July 22 2004 - p22(2)
  [501+]
MacCullough, Carolyn - *Falling through Darkness*
  y LibMed - v22 - i5 - Feb 2004 - p72(1) [501+]
  Stealing Henry
  y KR - v73 - i5 - March 1 2005 - p290(1) [51-500]
MacDiarmid, Hugh - *The Revolutionary Art of the Future:
  Rediscovered Poems*
  TLS - i5295 - Sept 24 2004 - p24(1) [501+]
MacDonagh, Oliver - *The Union and its Aftermath*
  ILS - v24 - i1 - Fall 2004 - p4(1) [501+]
MacDonald, Alasdair A. - *Scholarly Environments:
  Centres of Learning and Institutional Contexts,
  1560-1960*
  R&R Bk N - v19 - i3 - August 2004 - p213(1)
  [1-50]
  *Schooling and Society: The Ordering and Reordering of
  Knowledge in the Western Middle Ages*
  R&R Bk N - v19 - i3 - August 2004 - p213(1)
  [1-50]

MacDonald, Amy - *No More Nasty (Read by Heller,
  Johnny). Audiobook Review*
  c SLJ - v50 - i7 - July 2004 - p59(1) [51-500]
MacDonald, Ann-Marie - *Fall on Your Knees*
  Essays CW - Winter 2003 - p86 [501+]
  The Way the Crow Flies
  CBRA - Annual 2003 - p174(1) [501+]
  Globe & Mail - August 21 2004 - pD13 [1-50]
MacDonald, Cheryl - *Niagara Daredevils: Thrills and
  Spills over Niagara Falls*
  y Res Links - v10 - i1 - Oct 2004 - p36(2) [501+]
Macdonald, Copthorne - *Matters of Consequence*
  Fut - v38 - i5 - Sept-Oct 2004 - p63(1) [51-500]
Macdonald, Cynthia - *Alms*
  Globe & Mail - July 31 2004 - pD14 [1-50]
MacDonald, D.R. - *All the Men are Sleeping*
  CBRA - Annual 2003 - p201(1) [51-500]
Macdonald, F. - *Molecular Biology of Cancer, 2nd Ed.*
  SciTech - v28 - i4 - Dec 2004 - p92(1) [51-500]
MacDonald, Fiona - *The First "Test-Tube Baby."*
  c SLJ - v50 - i7 - July 2004 - p116(1) [51-500]
MacDonald, Gayle - *Massage for the Hospital Patient and
  Medically Frail Client*
  SciTech - v28 - i4 - Dec 2004 - p118(1) [1-50]
MacDonald, Gordon - *A Resilient Life: You Can Move
  Ahead No Matter What*
  PW - v251 - i51 - Dec 20 2004 - p56(1) [51-500]
MacDonald, Graeme - *Tales from the Bully Pulpit: Vol. 1*
  PW - v251 - i45 - Nov 8 2004 - p37(1) [501+]
MacDonald, Ian - *Born to Die: A Cop Killer's Final
  Message*
  CBRA - Annual 2003 - p315(1) [51-500]
MacDonald, Jake - *Houseboat Chronicles: Notes from a
  Life in Shield Country*
  BIC - v33 - i2 - March 2004 - p12(1) [501+]
  BL - v101 - i4 - Oct 15 2004 - p379(1) [51-500]
  Globe & Mail - July 17 2004 - pD15 [501+]
  PW - v251 - i36 - Sept 6 2004 - p56(1) [51-500]
MacDonald, Joyce Green - *Women and Race in Early
  Modern Texts*
  Clio - v33 - i4 - Summer 2004 - p439(11) [501+]
  JWH - v16 - i4 - Winter 2004 - p207(8) [501+]
Macdonald, M.C.A. - *Seminar for Arabian Studies, Vol. 33*
  R&R Bk N - v19 - i1 - Feb 2004 - p72(1) [51-500]
Macdonald, Malcolm - *Varese: Astronomer in Sound*
  MT - v145 - i1888 - Autumn 2004 - p109-111
  [501+]
MacDonald, Margaret F. - *Palaces in the Night: Whistler
  in Venice*
  VS - v46 - i3 - Spring 2004 - p524(3) [501+]
  Whistler, Women and Fashion
  J Am St - v38 - i1 - April 2004 - p152-153 [501+]
MacDonald, Margaret Read - *Three Minute Tales: Stories
  from around the World to Tell or Read When Time Is
  Short*
  y BL - v101 - i2 - Sept 15 2004 - p183(1) [51-500]
  y Kliatt - v39 - i1 - Jan 2005 - p28(1) [51-500]
  KR - v72 - i17 - Sept 1 2004 - p870(1) [51-500]
  SLJ - v50 - i10 - Oct 2004 - p202(1) [51-500]
MacDonald, Marianne - *Death's Autograph: An
  Atiquarian Book Mystery*
  LJ - v129 - i14 - Sept 1 2004 - p207(1) [501+]
MacDonald, Mark - *Flat*
  Can Lit - i181 - Summer 2004 - p176-178 [501+]
MacDonald, Matthew - *Microsoft .NET Distributed
  Applications: Integrating XML Web Services and .NET
  Remoting*
  SciTech - v28 - i3 - Sept 2004 - p27(1) [51-500]
Macdonald, Neil W. - *The League That Lasted: 1876 and
  the Founding of the National League of Professional
  Base Ball Clubs*
  Choice - v42 - i4 - Dec 2004 - p699(1) [1-50]

Mack, Tracy - *Drawing Lessons*
y BL - v101 - i5 - Nov 1 2004 - p496(1) [51-500]
Mackall, Dandi Daley - *Are We There Yet? (Illus. by McNeill, Shannon)*
c LibMed - v22 - i4 - Jan 2004 - p59(1) [501+]
Problem Solving, 2nd Ed.
y SLJ - v51 - i1 - Jan 2005 - p144(1) [51-500]
MacKay, Anne - *Sailing the Edge*
Lam Bk Rpt - v13 - i1-2 - August-Sept 2004 - p42(2) [501+]
MacKay, David J.C. - *Information Theory, Inference, and Learning Algorithms*
Am Sci - v92 - i6 - Nov-Dec 2004 - p578(2) [501+]
Mackay, Harvey - *We Got Fired! ... And It's the Best Thing That Ever Happened to Us*
BL - v101 - i2 - Sept 15 2004 - p186(1) [51-500]
LJ - v129 - i15 - Sept 15 2004 - p67(1) [51-500]
MacKay, K.M. - *Introduction to Modern Inorganic Chemistry, 6th Ed.*
J Chem Ed - v81 - i5 - May 2004 - p648-649 [501+]
MacKay, Robert - *Half the Battle: Civilian Morale in Britain During the Second World War*
AHR - v109 - i2 - April 2004 - p619(2) [501+]
Mackay, Steve - *Practical Industrial Data Networks: Design, Installation and Troubleshooting*
E-Streams - Nov 2004 - pNA [501+]
Mackel, Kathryn - *The Departed*
PW - v252 - i8 - Feb 21 2005 - p159(1) [51-500]
Mackel, Kathy - *Alien in a Bottle*
c BL - v101 - i2 - Sept 15 2004 - p233(1) [51-500]
MadCat
c KR - v73 - i5 - March 1 2005 - p290(1) [51-500]
Mackell, Jan - *Brothels, Bordellos & Bad Girls: Prostitution in Colorado 1860-1930*
Roundup M - v12 - i3 - Feb 2005 - p20(1) [51-500]
MacKellar, Landis - *Economic Impacts of Population Ageing in Japan*
R&R Bk N - v19 - i4 - Nov 2004 - p86(1) [51-500]
Macken, JoAnn Early - *Bears/Los osos*
c SLJ - v50 - i9 - Sept 2004 - p197(1) [1-50]
Elephants/Los elefantes
c SLJ - v50 - i9 - Sept 2004 - p197(1) [1-50]
Penguins/Los pinguinos
c SLJ - v50 - i9 - Sept 2004 - p197(1) [1-50]
Sing-Along Song (Illus. by Pham, LeUyen)
y BL - v100 - i21 - July 2004 - p1848(2) [1-50]
y NYTBR - Sept 19 2004 - p16 [501+]
Macken, Walter - *Island of the Great Yellow Ox. Audiobook Review*
c SLJ - v50 - i7 - July 2004 - p58(1) [51-500]
Mackendrick, Alexander - *On Film-Making: An Introduction to the Craft of the Director*
Si & So - v14 - i8 - August 2004 - p38(1) [501+]
TimHES - v0 - i1647 - July 2 2004 - p27(1) [501+]
MacKenna, Wolf - *The Hellraisers*
Roundup M - v11 - i6 - August 2004 - p29(1) [501+]
Mackenney, Richard - *Renaissances: The Cultures of Italy, 1300-1600, 1st Ed.*
TimHES - v0 - i1680 - Feb 25 2005 - pXI(1) [501+]
MacKenzie, Donald - *Mechanizing Proof: Computing, Risk, and Trust*
T&C - v45 - i4 - Oct 2004 - p893(2) [501+]
Mackenzie, Iain - *The Idea of Pure Critique*
R&R Bk N - v19 - i4 - Nov 2004 - p6(1) [51-500]
MacKenzie, John - *Shaken by Physics*
Can Lit - i182 - Autumn 2004 - p149(3) [501+]
Mackenzie, Nancy - *Illuminated Life*
CBRA - Annual 2003 - p224(2) [501+]
Mackenzie, S.P. - *The Colditz Myth: British and Commonwealth Prisoners of War in Nazi Germany*
CR - v286 - i1668 - Jan 2005 - p61(1) [51-500]
Lon R Bks - v27 - i1 - Jan 6 2005 - p20(1) [501+]
MacKenzie, Sally - *The Naked Duke*
BL - v101 - i9-10 - Jan 1 2005 - p831(1) [1-50]
MacKenzie, Scott - *Screening Quebec: Quebecois Moving Images, National Identity, and the Public Sphere*
Choice - v42 - i4 - Dec 2004 - p668(2) [1-50]
Mackerras, Colin - *Ethnicity in Asia*
JAS - v63 - i2 - May 2004 - p481(2) [501+]
JEL - v42 - i1 - March 2004 - p279(2) [501+]
R&R Bk N - v19 - i3 - August 2004 - p54(1) [51-500]

Mackey, Chris - *The Interrogators: Inside the Secret War against Al Qaeda*
Globe & Mail - July 24 2004 - pD14 [51-500]
Nation - v280 - i5 - Feb 7 2005 - p23 [501+]
NYTBR - Jan 23 2005 - p11 [501+]
PW - v251 - i29 - July 19 2004 - p156(1) [51-500]
Mackey, Frank - *Black Then: Blacks and Montreal, 1780s-1880s*
R&R Bk N - v19 - i4 - Nov 2004 - p70(1) [51-500]
Mackey, George Whitelaw - *Mathematical Foundation of Quantum Mechanics*
SciTech - v28 - i3 - Sept 2004 - p46(1) [1-50]
Mackey, Louis - *An Ancient Quarrel Continued: The Troubled Marriage of Philosophy and Literature*
JAAC - v62 - i3 - Summer 2004 - p311-312 [501+]
Mackey, Michael C. - *Time's Arrow: The Origins of Thermodynamic Behavior*
SciTech - v28 - i1 - March 2004 - p48(1) [51-500]
SciTech - v28 - i1 - March 2004 - p48(1) [51-500]
Mackie, Evelyn A. - *Editing Robert Grosseteste: Papers Given at the Thirty-Sixth Annual Conference on Editorial Problems, University of Toronto, 3-4 November 2000*
Med R - Dec 2004 - pNA [501+]
Mackie, Gerry - *Democracy Defended*
Choice - v42 - i1 - Sept 2004 - p187(1) [501+]
Pers PS - v33 - i4 - Fall 2004 - p228(2) [501+]
Mackie, Gillian - *Early Christian Chapels in the West: Decoration, Function, and Patronage*
CBRA - Annual 2003 - p118(1) [51-500]
R&R Bk N - v19 - i1 - Feb 2004 - p203(1) [51-500]
Mackie, Hilary Susan - *Graceful Errors: Pindar and the Performance of Praise*
Class R - v54 - i2 - Nov 2004 - p300-301 [501+]
Mackinlay, John - *Regional Peacekeepers: The Paradox of Russian Peacekeeping*
JPR - v41 - i6 - Nov 2004 - p761-761 [501+]
MacKinnon, Aran S. - *The Making of South Africa: Culture and Politics*
y HNet - Sept 2004 - pNA [501+]
MacKinnon, Catharine A. - *Directions in Sexual Harassment Law*
Choice - v42 - i1 - Sept 2004 - p186(2) [501+]
Law&PolBR - July 2004 - p558(5) [501+]
Women's Lives, Men's Laws
LJ - v129 - i19 - Nov 15 2004 - p74(1) [501+]
MacKinnon, Fiona J.D. - *Rentz's Student Affairs Practice in Higher Education, 3rd Ed.*
R&R Bk N - v19 - i3 - August 2004 - p221(1) [1-50]
MacKinnon, Janice - *Minding the Public Purse: The Fiscal Crisis, Political Trade-offs, and Canada's Future*
Can Hist R - v85 - i3 - Sept 2004 - p641(3) [501+]
CWS - v23 - i3-4 - Spring-Summer 2004 - p208(2) [501+]
MacKinnon, M.R. - *Excavations of San Giovanni di Ruoti, Vol. 3*
CBRA - Annual 2003 - p294(1) [501+]
Macklem, Timothy - *Beyond Comparison: Sex and Discrimination*
PSQ - v119 - i4 - Winter 2004 - p697(3) [501+]
Mackler, Aaron L. - *Introduction to Jewish and Catholic Bioethics: A Comparative Analysis*
SciTech - v28 - i1 - March 2004 - p78(1) [51-500]
Theol St - v66 - i1 - March 2005 - p212(3) [501+]
Mackler, Carolyn - *The Earth, My Butt, and Other Big Round Things (Read by Parker, Johanna). Audiobook Review*
y Kliatt - v39 - i1 - Jan 2005 - p40(2) [51-500]
y SLJ - v50 - i12 - Dec 2004 - p76(2) [501+]
y VOYA - v27 - i5 - Dec 2004 - p371(1) [501+]
y BL - v101 - i7 - Dec 1 2004 - p678(1) [1-50]
The Earth, My Butt, and Other Big Round Things
y LibMed - v22 - i5 - Feb 2004 - p72(1) [501+]
Vegan Virgin Valentine
y CCB-B - v58 - i2 - Oct 2004 - p88(1) [51-500]
y JAAL - v48 - i2 - Oct 2004 - p173(2) [501+]
y Kliatt - v38 - i4 - July 2004 - p10(1) [51-500]
y KR - v72 - i13 - July 1 2004 - p632(1) [51-500]
y LibMed - v23 - i1 - August-Sept 2004 - p69(1) [51-500]
c SLJ - v50 - i8 - August 2004 - p126(1) [51-500]
y Teach Lib - v32 - i3 - Feb 2005 - p18(1) [51-500]
y VOYA - v27 - i4 - Oct 2004 - p304(1) [51-500]
Macklin, Ruth - *Double Standards in Medical Research in Developing Countries*
Choice - v42 - i5 - Jan 2005 - p886(2) [1-50]

Macksey, Kenneth - *Searchers: How Radio Interception Changed the Course of Both World Wars*
R&R Bk N - v19 - i1 - Feb 2004 - p256(1) [51-500]
Maclachlan, Ian - *Jacques Derrida: Critical Thought*
CR - v285 - i1667 - Dec 2004 - p377(2) [51-500]
R&R Bk N - v20 - i1 - Feb 2005 - p4(1) [51-500]
MacLachlan, Patricia - *Bittle (Illus. by Yaccarino, Dan)*
c CCB-B - v58 - i1 - Sept 2004 - p27(2) [51-500]
c PW - v251 - i27 - July 5 2004 - p55(1) [51-500]
The Facts and Fictions of Minna Pratt
c SLJ - v50 - i12 - Dec 2004 - p61(2) [501+]
More Perfect than the Moon (Read by Close, Glenn). Audiobook Review
c BL - v101 - i8 - Dec 15 2004 - p754(1) [1-50]
More Perfect than the Moon
c CCB-B - v58 - i3 - Nov 2004 - p134(1) [501+]
c HB - v80 - i5 - Sept-Oct 2004 - p590(2) [51-500]
c KR - v72 - i14 - July 15 2004 - p690(1) [51-500]
c SLJ - v50 - i8 - August 2004 - p90(1) [51-500]
Sarah, Plain and Tall
c RT - v57 - Sept 2003 - p98 [1-50]
Maclaren-Ross, J. - *Collected Memoirs*
Spec - v296 - Dec 18 2004 - p91(2) [501+]
TLS - i5306 - Dec 10 2004 - p22(1) [501+]
Selected Stories
Spec - v296 - Dec 18 2004 - p91(2) [501+]
TLS - i5306 - Dec 10 2004 - p22(1) [501+]
MacLaren, Roy - *Canadians Behind Enemy Lines, 1939-1945*
BIC - v33 - i5 - August 2004 - p26(2) [501+]
Canadians Behind Enemy Lines, 1939-1945
R&R Bk N - v19 - i3 - August 2004 - p35(1) [51-500]
MacLean, Christine Kole - *Mary Margaret and the Perfect Pet Plan*
c CH Bwatch - v14 - i7 - July 2004 - p7(2) [501+]
c SLJ - v50 - i7 - July 2004 - p109(1) [51-500]
MacLean, D.J.H. - *Evaluating Feedback in Amplifiers and Oscillators: Theory, Design and Analogue Applications*
SciTech - v28 - i4 - Dec 2004 - p156(1) [51-500]
MacLean, Gerald - *The Rise of Oriental Travel: English Visitors to the Ottoman Empire 1580-1720*
TLS - i5285 - July 16 2004 - p6(1) [501+]
MacLean, Kerry Lee - *Peaceful Piggy Meditation (Illus. by MacLean, Kerry Lee)*
c BL - v101 - i4 - Oct 15 2004 - p411(1) [51-500]
c PW - v251 - i45 - Nov 8 2004 - p55(1) [51-500]
c SLJ - v50 - i11 - Nov 2004 - p112(1) [51-500]
MacLean Rogers, Guy - *Alexander: The Ambiguity of Greatness*
Globe & Mail - Nov 20 2004 - pD5 [501+]
Maclellan, Nic - *Louise Michel*
Kliatt - v38 - i6 - Nov 2004 - p34(1) [51-500]
MacLennan, Christopher - *Toward the Charter: Canadians and the Demand for a National Bill of Rights, 1929-1960*
R&R Bk N - v19 - i3 - August 2004 - p176(1) [501+]
MacLennan, David - *Santa's Stormy Christmas Eve*
c CBRA - Annual 2003 - p458(1) [51-500]
MacLennan, Hugh - *Barometer Rising*
Mac - v117 - i45 - Nov 8 2004 - p50(1) [1-50]
Macleod, Beth Abelson - *Women Performing Music: The Emergence of American Women as Instrumentalists and Conductors*
Am M - v22 - i2 - Summer 2004 - p321-323 [501+]
MacLeod, Dag - *Downsizing the State: Pivatization and the Limits of Neoliberal Reform in Mexico*
Choice - v42 - i2 - Oct 2004 - p339(1) [51-500]
Macleod, Donald V.L. - *Tourism, Globalisation and Cultural Change: An Island Community Perspective*
R&R Bk N - v19 - i3 - August 2004 - p79(1) [51-500]
MacLeod, Donnie M. - *Participation and Entitlement in Educational Development: Accounts of Participatory Practitioner Research in Botswana*
R&R Bk N - v19 - i1 - Feb 2004 - p187(1) [51-500]
MacLeod, Doug - *Spiky, Spunky, My Pet Monkey (Illus. by Smith, Craig)*
y Magpies - v19 - i5 - Nov 2004 - p35(2) [501+]
MacLeod, Elizabeth - *Albert Einstein: A Life of Genius*
c CBRA - Annual 2003 - p538(2) [51-500]
c LibMed - v22 - i5 - Feb 2004 - p58(2) [501+]
Bake and Make Amazing Cookies (Illus. by Bradford, June)
Res Links - v10 - i1 - Oct 2004 - p25(2) [51-500]
c SLJ - v51 - i2 - Feb 2005 - p150(1) [51-500]
Helen Keller: A Determined Life
c LibMed - v23 - i3 - Nov-Dec 2004 - p79(1) [51-500]
Marie Curie: A Brilliant Life
c KR - v72 - i15 - August 1 2004 - p744(1) [51-500]
c Res Links - v10 - i2 - Dec 2004 - p28(1) [501+]
y SB - v40 - i6 - Nov-Dec 2004 - p258(1) [51-500]
c SLJ - v50 - i11 - Nov 2004 - p169(1) [51-500]

MacLeod, Ian R. - *Breathmoss and Other Exhalations*
Bwatch - v26 - i7 - July 2004 - p6(1) [51-500]
The Light Ages
y Kliatt - v38 - i4 - July 2004 - p31(1) [51-500]

Macleod, Iseabail - *The Illustrated Encyclopedia of Scotland*
LJ - v129 - i17 - Oct 15 2004 - p86(1) [51-500]
R&R Bk N - v19 - i4 - Nov 2004 - p37(1) [51-500]

Macleod, Jenny - *Uncovered Fields: Perspectives in First World War Studies*
J Mil H - v68 - i3 - July 2004 - p976-977 [501+]

MacLeod, Ken - *Newton's Wake*
Analog - v124 - i11 - Nov 2004 - p134(6) [501+]
New Sci - v183 - i2458 - July 31 2004 - p53(1) [51-500]
NYTBR - July 18 2004 - p19 [501+]

MacLeod, Malcolm - *Connection Newfoundland's Pre-Confederation Links with Canada and the World*
CBRA - Annual 2003 - p344(2) [501+]

MacLeod, Roderick - *Meeting of the People: School Boards and Protestant Communities in Quebec, 1801-1998*
R&R Bk N - v19 - i4 - Nov 2004 - p68(1) [1-50]

MacInnis, Joseph - *Breathing Underwater: The Quest to Live in the Sea*
CG - v125 - i1 - Jan-Feb 2005 - p99(1) [501+]

MacLure, Maggie - *Discourse in Educational and Social Research*
R&R Bk N - v19 - i1 - Feb 2004 - pNA [51-500]

Macmillan, Donovan Webster - *The Burma Road: The Epic Story of One of World War II's Most Remarkable Endeavours*
CR - v285 - i1663 - August 2004 - p127(1) [501+]

Macmillan, John Hemming - *Die If You Must: Brazilian Indians in the Twentieth Century*
CR - v285 - i1663 - August 2004 - p113(2) [501+]

MacMillan, Margaret - *Canada's House: Rideau Hall and the Invention of a Canadian Home*
Globe & Mail - Dec 4 2004 - pD3 [501+]
Parties Long Estranged: Canada and Australia in the Twentieth Century
Pac A - v77 - i3 - Fall 2004 - p609(2) [501+]

Macmillan, Neil A. - *Detection Theory: A User's Guide, 2nd Ed.*
SciTech - v28 - i4 - Dec 2004 - p2(1) [1-50]

MacMillian, Dianne M. - *Humpback Whales*
y SB - v40 - i3 - May-June 2004 - p125(1) [501+]

MacMullen, Ramsay - *Feelings in History, Ancient and Modern*
Choice - v41 - i11-12 - July-August 2004 - p2098(1) [501+]

Macnair, Patricia - *Life Cycle*
c BL - v101 - i4 - Oct 15 2004 - p424(1) [51-500]
Movers and Shapers
c BL - v101 - i4 - Oct 15 2004 - p424(1) [51-500]

MacNair, Rachel M. - *The Psychology of Peace: An Introduction*
HNet - June 2004 - pNA [501+]

MacNamara, Matthew - *La Textualisation de Madame Bovary*
NCFS - v33 - i1-2 - Fall-Winter 2004 - p201(2) [501+]

Macnee, Carol L. - *Understanding Nursing Research: Reading and Using Research in Practice*
SciTech - v28 - i4 - Dec 2004 - p121 [51-500]

MacNee, William - *Chronic Obstructive Pulmonary Disease*
SciTech - v28 - i3 - Sept 2004 - p107(1) [51-500]

MacNeil, Anne - *Music and Women of the Commedia dell'Arte in the Late Sixteenth Century*
Ren Q - v57 - i3 - Fall 2004 - p1091(2) [501+]

MacNeil, Rita - *Christmas at Home with Rita MacNeil*
CBRA - Annual 2003 - p57(1) [51-500]

MacNeil, Robert - *Do You Speak American?*
BL - v101 - i7 - Dec 1 2004 - p623(2) [51-500]
Globe & Mail - Feb 12 2005 - pD14 [51-500]
Looking for My Country: Finding Myself in America
CBRA - Annual 2003 - p57(1) [51-500]
R&R Bk N - v19 - i4 - Nov 2004 - p228(1) [501+]

Macomber, Debbie - *44 Cranberry Point*
BL - v101 - i1 - Sept 1 2004 - p73(1) [51-500]
PW - v251 - i36 - Sept 6 2004 - p51(1) [51-500]
When Christmas Comes
BL - v101 - i4 - Oct 15 2004 - p394(1) [51-500]
PW - v251 - i44 - Nov 1 2004 - p45(1) [501+]

MacPhail, Catherine - *Catch Us If You Can*
y Sch Lib - v52 - i3 - Autumn 2004 - p158(1) [501+]
Underworld
y Sch Lib - v52 - i3 - Autumn 2004 - p159(1) [501+]

Macphail, Euan - *Do Animals Think?*
Sci - v305 - i5682 - July 16 2004 - p344(1) [501+]

MacPherson, Andrea - *When She Was Electric*
KR - v73 - i5 - March 1 2005 - p251(1) [501+]

Macpherson, Gordon - *Black's Medical Dictionary, 40th Ed.*
Choice - v42 - i2 - Oct 2004 - p270(1) [501+]
SciTech - v28 - i3 - Sept 2004 - p76(1) [51-500]

MacPherson, Margaret - *Nellie McClung: Voice for the Voiceless*
y CBRA - Annual 2003 - p539(1) [51-500]

MacPherson, Nelson - *American Intelligence in War-Time London: The Story of the OSS*
Choice - v41 - i11-12 - July-August 2004 - p2108(2) [501+]
R&R Bk N - v19 - i1 - Feb 2004 - p30(1) [51-500]

MacPherson, Rett - *Thicker Than Water*
KR - v73 - i3 - Feb 1 2005 - p153(1) [51-500]
PW - v252 - i8 - Feb 21 2005 - p161(2) [501+]

MacPherson, Suzanne - *She Woke Up Married*
PW - v252 - i7 - Feb 14 2005 - p59(1) [51-500]

MacPhillips, Kathleen - *Local Heroes: Australian Crusades from the Environmental Frontine*
AJPS - v39 - i3 - Nov 2004 - p665(2) [501+]

MacQuarrie, Charles W. - *The Biography of the Irish God of the Sea from 'The Voyage of Bran' (700 A.D.) to 'Finnegans Wake' (1939): The Waves of Manannan*
R&R Bk N - v19 - i4 - Nov 2004 - p15(1) [51-500]

Macqueen, Adam - *The King of Sunlight: How William Lever Cleaned Up the World*
Econ - v372 - i8385 - July 24 2004 - p76US [501+]

Macromedia Inc. - *Macromedia Flash MX 2004 ActionScript 2.0 Dictionary*
SciTech - v28 - i1 - March 2004 - p175(1) [1-50]

MacShamhrain, Ailbhe - *The Island of St. Patrick: Church and Ruling Dynasties in Fingal and Meath, 400-1148*
R&R Bk N - v19 - i3 - August 2004 - p20(1) [1-50]

MacSkimming, Roy - *The Perilous Trade: Publishing Canada's Writers*
BIC - v33 - i2 - March 2004 - p26(1) [501+]
CBRA - Annual 2003 - p79(1) [51-500]

Macunovich, Diane J. - *Birth Quake: The Baby Boom and Its Aftershocks*
JEL - v42 - i1 - March 2004 - p198(3) [501+]

Macy, Sue - *Swifter, Higher, Stronger: A Photographic History of the Summer Olympics*
c BL - v100 - i21 - July 2004 - p1843(1) [1-50]
Swifter, Higher, Stronger: A Photographic History of the Summer Olympics
c CCB-B - v57 - i11 - July-August 2004 - p473(2) [501+]

Madancy, Joyce A. - *The Troublesome Legacy of Commissioner Lin: The Opium Trade and Opium Suppression in Fujian Province, 1820s to 1920s*
Choice - v42 - i4 - Dec 2004 - p715(1) [1-50]

Madden, Bill - *The Zen of Zim: Baseballs, Beanballs, and Bosses*
NYTBR - July 18 2004 - p16 [501+]

Madden, Gary - *The International Handbook of Telecommunications Economics, Vol 1*
JEL - v41 - i4 - Dec 2003 - p1397(1) [501+]

Madden, Kerry - *Gentle's Holler*
y KR - v73 - i4 - Feb 15 2005 - p232(1) [51-500]

Madden, Robert G. - *Essential Law for Social Workers*
R&R Bk N - v19 - i1 - Feb 2004 - pNA [51-500]

Madden, Thomas F. - *Crusades: The Illustrated History*
LJ - v129 - i18 - Nov 1 2004 - p101(1) [51-500]
Enrico Dandolo & the Rise of Venice
AHR - v109 - i4 - Oct 2004 - p1294-1295 [501+]
Med R - August 2004 - pNA [501+]
R&R Bk N - v19 - i1 - Feb 2004 - p37(1) [1-50]

Maddern, Eric - *Death in a Nut (Illus. by Hess, Paul)*
c KR - v72 - i24 - Dec 15 2004 - p1205(1) [51-500]
c PW - v252 - i7 - Feb 14 2005 - p76(1) [51-500]

Maddison, Angus - *The World Economy: Historical Statistics*
JEL - v42 - i1 - March 2004 - p299(1) [501+]

Maddock, Shane J. - *The Struggle Against the Bomb, Vol. 2*
HNet - June 2004 - pNA [501+]

Maddox, Donald - *The Medieval French Alexander*
Specu - v79 - i3 - July 2004 - p794-795 [501+]

Maddox, Tony - *Fergus the Sea Dog*
c Sch Lib - v52 - i3 - Autumn 2004 - p132(1) [501+]

Maddux, James E. - *Psychopathology: Foundations for a Contemporary Understanding*
SciTech - v28 - i4 - Dec 2004 - p95(1) [51-500]

Maddy, Penelope - *Naturalism in Mathematics*
Phil R - v112 - i3 - July 2003 - p425(3) [501+]

Mader, Charles L. - *Numerical Modeling of Water Waves, 2nd Ed.*
SciTech - v28 - i4 - Dec 2004 - p44(1) [51-500]

Madhubuti, Haki R. - *Run Toward Fear: New Poems and a Poet's Handbook*
Black Iss - v6 - i5 - Sept-Oct 2004 - p54(1) [501+]
ABR - v25 - i6 - Sept-Oct 2004 - p8(2) [501+]

Madigan, Charles - *Global Chicago*
Bwatch - Nov 2004 - pNA [51-500]

Madigan, Mary Jean Smith - *Steuben Design: A Legacy of Light and Form*
Ant&CM - v109 - i6 - August 2004 - p16(1) [501+]
Choice - v42 - i4 - Dec 2004 - p646(1) [1-50]
LJ - v129 - i16 - Oct 1 2004 - p78(1) [51-500]
R&R Bk N - v19 - i4 - Nov 2004 - p209(1) [501+]

Madison, Daniel Lee Kleinman. - *Impure Cultures: University Biology and the World of Commerce*
AJS - v110 - i3 - Nov 2004 - p815(2) [501+]

Madison, Deborah - *Vegetarian Suppers from Deborah Madison's Kitchen*
PW - v252 - i1 - Jan 3 2005 - p51(1) [51-500]

Madison, Lynda - *The Feelings Book*
c PW - v252 - i8 - Feb 21 2005 - p177(1) [501+]

Madoff, Steven Henry - *Christopher Wilmarth: Light and Gravity*
Art N - v104 - i1 - Jan 2005 - p96(1) [501+]

Madonna - *The Adventures of Abdi (Illus. by Dugina, Olga)*
c PW - v251 - i47 - Nov 22 2004 - p59(2) [51-500]
Yakov and the Seven Thieves (Illus. by Spirin, Gennadii)
c Econ - v371 - i8381 - June 26 2004 - p85US [501+]
c PW - v251 - i27 - July 5 2004 - p55(1) [51-500]

Madrick, Jeffrey - *Taking America: How We Got from the First Hostile Takeover to Megamergers, Corporate Raiding, and Scandal*
R&R Bk N - v19 - i2 - May 2004 - p123 [51-500]

Madrid, Raul L. - *The Limits of Stabilization: Infrastructure, Public Deficits, and Growth in Latin America*
JEL - v42 - i1 - March 2004 - p272(2) [501+]
Retiring the State: The Politics of Pension Privatization in Latin America and Beyond
CS - v33 - i5 - Sept 2004 - p579-580 [501+]

Madsen, D.B. - *Entering America: Northeast Asia and Beringa Before the Last Glacial Maximum*
R&R Bk N - v19 - i4 - Nov 2004 - p53(1) [51-500]

Madsen, Daniel - *Ressurection: Salvaging the Battle Fleet at Pearl Harbor*
J Mil H - v68 - i3 - April 2004 - p631-632 [501+]

Madsen, Deborah L. - *Beyond the Borders: American Literature and Post-Colonial Theory*
Choice - v41 - i7 - March 2004 - p1294(1) [501+]
R&R Bk N - v19 - i1 - Feb 2004 - p241(1) [501+]

Madsen, Gunnar - *Old Mr. Mackle Hackle (Illus. by Shepherd, Irana)*
c KR - v73 - i5 - March 1 2005 - p290(1) [51-500]

Maekawa, K. - *Nonlinear Mechanics of Reinforced Concrete*
E-Streams - June 2004 - pNA [501+]

Maeland, Bard - *Rewarding Encounters: Islam and the Comparative Theologies of Kenneth Cragg and Wilfred Cantwell Smith*
IBMR - v29 - i1 - Jan 2005 - p44(2) [501+]

Maeroff, Gene I. - *A Classroom of One: How Online Learning Is Changing Our Schools and Colleges*
Choice - v41 - i7 - March 2004 - p1344(1) [501+]
TCR - v106 - i2 - Feb 2004 - p413-416 [501+]

Maestripieri, Dario - *Primate Psychology*
Am Sci - v92 - i5 - Sept-Oct 2004 - p483(2) [501+]

Maestro, Betsy - *The Voice of the People: American Democracy in Action*
c SLJ - v50 - i8 - August 2004 - p48(1) [51-500]

Maeurer, Juergen - *Imaging Strategies for the Shoulder*
SciTech - v28 - i3 - Sept 2004 - p108(1) [51-500]

Maffei, Massimo - *Dietary Supplements of Plant Origin: A Nutrition and Health Approach*
SciTech - v28 - i1 - March 2004 - p121(1) [51-500]

Maffini, Mary Jane - *Little Boy Blues: A Camilla MacPhee Mystery*
CBRA - Annual 2003 - p175(1) [501+]

Mafundikwa, Saki - *Afrikan Alphabets: The Story of Writing in Afrika*
Black Iss - v6 - i6 - Nov-Dec 2004 - p44(1) [501+]
R&R Bk N - v19 - i4 - Nov 2004 - p220(1) [501+]

Maga, Timothy P. - *America Attacks Japan*
VQR - v79 - i1 - Winter 2003 - p26 [51-500]

Mahoney, Sylvia Gann - *College Rodeo: From Show to Sport*
Choice - v42 - i3 - Nov 2004 - p524(1) [1-50]

Mahovlich, Ted - *Triple Crown: The Marcel Dionne Story*
Globe & Mail - Oct 30 2004 - pD25 [51-500]

Mahy, Margaret - *Al borde del acantilado*
y   VOYA - v27 - i3 - August 2004 - p180(1) [1-50]
Alchemy
y   Kliatt - v38 - i5 - Sept 2004 - p30(2) [51-500]
Watch Me!
c   Sch Lib - v52 - i4 - Winter 2004 - p203(1) [51-500]

Maidstone, Richard - *Concordia: The Reconciliation of Richard II with London*
R&R Bk N - v19 - i1 - Feb 2004 - p214 [51-500]

Maienschein, Jane - *Whose View of Life?: Embryos, Cloning, and Stem Cells*
QRB - v79 - i4 - Dec 2004 - p404(1) [501+]
TLS - i5267 - March 12 2004 - p11-11 [501+]

Maier, Bernhard - *The Celts: A History from Earliest Times to the Present*
Albion - v36 - i2 - Summer 2004 - p372(2) [501+]

Maier, Carolina M. - *Hypothermia and Cerebral Ischemia: Mechanisms and Clinical Applications*
SciTech - v28 - i1 - March 2004 - p94(1) [51-500]

Maier, Eugene A. - *Gene's Corner and Other Nooks and Crannies: Perspectives on Math*
Math T - v98 - i2 - Sept 2004 - p143-143 [501+]

Maier, Frith - *Vagabond Life: The Caucasus Journals of George Kennan*
TLS - i5265 - Feb 27 2004 - p30-30 [501+]

Maier, Hans-Joachim - *Zwischen Bestimmung und Autonomie*
GSR - v27 - i1 - Feb 2004 - p144-146 [501+]

Maier, Joe - *Welcome to the Bangkok Slaughterhouse: The Battle for Human Dignity in Bangkok's Bleakest Slums*
PW - v252 - i8 - Feb 21 2005 - p172(1) [51-500]

Maier, Linda S. - *Woman as Witness: Essays on Testimonial Literature by Latin American Women*
Biomag - v27 - i4 - Fall 2004 - p855(5) [501+]

Maier, Martin - *Metropolitan Area WDM Networks: An AWG Based Approach*
SciTech - v28 - i1 - March 2004 - p157(1) [51-500]

Maier, Pauline - *A History of the United State: Inventing America*
BHR - v77 - i4 - Winter 2003 - p731(737) [501+]

Maile, Stella - *Stakeholding and the New International Order*
JEL - v42 - i1 - March 2004 - p259(1) [501+]

Mailer, Norman - *Miami and the Siege of Chicago*
BW - v34 - i39 - Sept 26 2004 - p4(1) [501+]
The Spooky Art: Some Thoughts on Writing
Choice - v41 - i11-12 - July-August 2004 - p2039(1) [501+]

Mailis-Gagnon, Angela - *Let Them Eat Prozac*
CBRA - Annual 2003 - p430(2) [51-500]

Maillard, Keith - *The Clarinet Polka*
Can Lit - i182 - Autumn 2004 - p153(2) [501+]

Maillet, Antonine - *The Tale of Don l'Orignal. Audiobook Review*
c   Globe & Mail - Dec 11 2004 - pD53 [1-50]

Maillet, Arnaud - *The Claude Glass: Use and Meaning of the Black Mirror in Western Art*
Afterimage - v32 - i4 - Jan-Feb 2005 - p15(1) [51-500]

Maimonides, Moses - *Maimonides Medical Aphorisms. Treatises 105=Kitab al-Fusul fi al-Tibbi: A Parallel Arabic-English Text*
SciTech - v28 - i4 - Dec 2004 - p76(1) [51-500]

Main, Elizabeth C. - *Murder of the Month*
KR - v73 - i3 - Feb 1 2005 - p153(1) [51-500]

Maine, David - *The Flood*
TLS - i5301 - Nov 5 2004 - p25(1) [51-500]
The Preservationist (Read by Bunch, Tyler). Audiobook Review
BL - v101 - i5 - Nov 1 2004 - p505(1) [51-500]
BL - v101 - i6 - Nov 15 2004 - p607(1) [501+]
The Preservationist (Read by Tyler, Bunch). Audiobook Review
y   Kliatt - v39 - i1 - Jan 2005 - p49(1) [51-500]
The Preservationist
Globe & Mail - July 17 2004 - pD13 [501+]
LJ - v129 - i12 - July 2004 - p72(1) [51-500]
Time - July 5 2004 - p88 [501+]

Maine, Jeffrey A. - *Intellectual Property Taxation: Transaction and Litigation Issues*
R&R Bk N - v19 - i4 - Nov 2004 - p172(1) [501+]

Maiorino, Giancarlo - *At the Margins of the Renaissance: Lazarillo de Tormes and the Picaresque Art of Survival*
Ren Q - v57 - i3 - Fall 2004 - p1007(2) [501+]

Mair, Christian - *The Politics of English as a World Language: New Horizons in Postcolonial Cultural Studies*
R&R Bk N - v19 - i1 - Feb 2004 - p215(1) [51-500]

Mair, George - *A Life with Purpose: The Story of the Man Behind the Purpose-Driven Life*
PW - v252 - i9 - Feb 28 2005 - p64(1) [51-500]

Mair, Victor H. - *An Alphabetical Index to the Hanyu Da Cidian*
R&R Bk N - v19 - i2 - May 2004 - p218(1) [501+]

Maisel, Eric - *The Art of the Book Proposal: From Focused Idea to Finished Proposal*
LJ - v129 - i14 - Sept 1 2004 - p164(2) [501+]
R&R Bk N - v19 - i3 - August 2004 - p258(1) [1-50]
Coaching the Artist Within: Advice from Writers, Actors, Visual Artists & Musicians from America's Foremost Creativity Coach
BL - v101 - i9-10 - Jan 1 2005 - p789(1) [1-50]

Maisel, L. Sandy - *Jews in American Politics: Essays*
R&R Bk N - v19 - i1 - Feb 2004 - p56(1) [51-500]
Parties and Elections in America: The Electoral Process, 4th Ed.
R&R Bk N - v19 - i4 - Nov 2004 - p155(1) [501+]
Running on Empty?: Political Discourse in Congressional Elections
Choice - v42 - i4 - Dec 2004 - p738(1) [1-50]
R&R Bk N - v19 - i3 - August 2004 - p173(1) [501+]

Maisel, Richard - *Biting the Hand That Starves You: Inspiring Resistance to Anorexia/Bulimia*
SciTech - v28 - i4 - Dec 2004 - p99(1) [51-500]

Maisner, Heather - *Time to See the Doctor*
c   BL - v101 - i9-10 - Jan 1 2005 - p870(2) [51-500]
We're Moving (Illus. by Stephenson, Kristina)
c   BL - v101 - i7 - Dec 1 2004 - p661(1) [51-500]

Maistre, Xavier de - *A Journey around My Room*
TLS - i5301 - Nov 5 2004 - p35(1) [51-500]

Maitland, Alexander - *Wilfred Thesiger: A Life in Pictures (Illus. by Thesiger, Wilfred)*
TimHES - v0 - i1675 - Jan 21 2005 - p22(2) [501+]

Majd, Mohammad Gholi - *Persia in World War I and Its Conquest by Great Britain*
R&R Bk N - v19 - i3 - August 2004 - p53(1) [51-500]

Majer, Diemut - *'Non Germans' under the Third Reich: The Nazi Judicial and Administrative System in Germany and Occupied Eastern Europe, and Special Regard to Occupied Poland 1939-1945*
HER - v119 - i483 - Sept 2004 - p1008(3) [501+]

Majewski, Henry F. - *Transposing Art into Texts in French Romantic Literature*
NCFS - v33 - i1-2 - Fall-Winter 2004 - p183(4) [501+]

Majewski, Karen - *Traitors and True Poles: Narrating a Polish-American Identity, 1880-1939*
JAH - v91 - i1 - June 2004 - p276-277 [501+]
Slav R - v63 - i4 - Winter 2004 - p858(2) [501+]

Majid, Anouar - *Freedom and Orthodoxy: Islam and Difference in the Post-Andalusian Age*
MEJ - v59 - i1 - Wntr 2005 - p158(4) [501+]
NS - v133 - i4716 - Nov 29 2004 - p46(1) [51-500]

Major, Kevin - *Ann and Seamus (Illus. by Blackwood, David)*
c   CBRA - Annual 2003 - p526(1) [501+]
Ann and Seamus
CE - v81 - i1 - Fall 2004 - p47(1) [501+]
Far from Shore
y   Res Links - v10 - i3 - Feb 2005 - p38(2) [51-500]

Major, Marcus - *A Family Affair. Audiobook Review*
LJ - v129 - i17 - Oct 15 2004 - p95(2) [51-500]

Major, Patrick - *The Workers' and Peasants' State: Communism and Society in East Germany under Ulbricht, 1945-71*
JMH - v77 - i1 - March 2005 - p237(4) [501+]
The Workers' and Peasants' State: Communism and Society in East Germany Under Ulbricht, 1945-1971
GSR - v27 - i1 - Feb 2004 - p210-211 [501+]

Majors, Inman - *Wonderdog*
BL - v101 - i4 - Oct 15 2004 - p390(1) [51-500]
KR - v72 - i17 - Sept 1 2004 - p827(1) [51-500]
PW - v251 - i41 - Oct 11 2004 - p55(1) [51-500]

Majumdar, Margaret - *Francophone Studies: The Essential Glossary*
FS - v58 - i2 - April 2004 - p294(2) [501+]

Majure, Janet - *Elections*
c   SLJ - v50 - i8 - August 2004 - p49(1) [51-500]

Majzels, Robert - *Apikoros Sleuth*
Globe & Mail - Feb 19 2005 - pD8 [501+]

Majzer, Jean-Pierre - *Un parcours de l'oeuvre poetique de Jean-Claude Renard*
FS - v58 - i1 - Jan 2004 - p141(2) [501+]

Mak, James - *Tourism and the Economy: Understanding the Economics of Tourism*
HNet - Sept 2004 - pNA [501+]

Makdisi, Samir - *The Lessons of Lebanon: The Economics of War and Development*
Choice - v42 - i5 - Jan 2005 - p902(1) [1-50]

Makdisi, Saree - *William Blake and the Impossible History of the 1790s*
Albion - v36 - i2 - Summer 2004 - p313(2) [501+]
Clio - v33 - i4 - Summer 2004 - p483(4) [501+]

Make Your Own Itty-Bitty Angels
c   PW - v252 - i4 - Jan 24 2005 - p246(1) [501+]

Make Your Own Itty-Bitty Ballerinas
c   PW - v252 - i4 - Jan 24 2005 - p246(1) [501+]

Make Your Own Itty Bitty Princesses
c   PW - v252 - i4 - Jan 24 2005 - p246(1) [501+]

Maki, John M. - *A Yankee in Hokkaido: The Life of William Smith Clark*
HNet - Sept 2004 - pNA [501+]

Maki, Peggy - *Assessing for Learning: Building a Sustainable Commitment Across the Institution*
R&R Bk N - v19 - i4 - Nov 2004 - p185(1) [501+]

Maki, Uskali - *Fact and Fiction in Economics: Models, Realism, and Social Construction*
JEL - v41 - i4 - Dec 2003 - p1338(1) [501+]

Makine, Andrei - *The Earth and Sky of Jacques Dorme*
KR - v72 - i24 - Dec 15 2004 - p1159(1) [501+]
LJ - v130 - i2 - Feb 1 2005 - p69(1) [51-500]
NYTBR - March 6 2005 - p17 [501+]
PW - v251 - i51 - Dec 20 2004 - p34(2) [51-500]

Makinson, Randell L. - *Greene and Greene: Creating a Style*
LJ - v130 - i1 - Jan 1 2005 - p107(1) [51-500]

Makitra, R.G. - *Correlation Analysis in Chemistry of Solutions*
SciTech - v28 - i4 - Dec 2004 - p55(1) [51-500]

Makiya, Kanan - *The Monument: Art and Vulgarity in Saddam Hussein's Iraq*
MEQ - v11 - i4 - Fall 2004 - p82(2) [501+]

Makkai, Adam - *In Quest of the Miracle Stag: The Poetry of Hungary, Vol. 1 (Illus. by Buday, George)*
WLT - v79 - i1 - Jan-April 2005 - p94(2) [501+]
In Quest of the Miracle Stag: The Poetry of Hungary, Vol. 2 (Illus. by Szasz, Endre)
WLT - v79 - i1 - Jan-April 2005 - p94(2) [501+]

Makkar, Harinder P.S. - *Quantification of Tannins in Tree and Shrub Foliage: A Laboratory Manual*
SciTech - v28 - i1 - March 2004 - p68(1) [51-500]

Makover, Richard B. - *Treatment Planning for Psychotherapists: A Practical Guide to Better Outcomes, 2nd Ed.*
SciTech - v28 - i1 - March 2004 - p98(1) [51-500]

MAKS - *Breaking News!: Trilogy*
y   CBRA - Annual 2003 - p501(1) [51-500]

Maksakovsky, Pavel V. - *Pavel V. Maksakovsky: The Capitalist Cycle, an Essay on the Marxist Theory of the Cycle*
R&R Bk N - v19 - i3 - August 2004 - p95(1) [51-500]

Mal-Maeder, D.K. Van - *Apuleius Madaurensis: Metamorphoses, Livre II*
Class R - v53 - i2 - Nov 2003 - p379-381 [501+]

Malachi, Tim - *Gnosis of the Cosmic Christ: A Gnostic Christian Kabbalah*
LJ - v130 - i2 - Feb 1 2005 - p85(1) [51-500]

Malacrida, Claudia - *Cold Comfort: Mothers, Professionals, and Attention Deficit Disorder*
CBRA - Annual 2003 - p385(2) [501+]
SciTech - v28 - i1 - March 2004 - p119(1) [51-500]
Soc Ser R - v78 - i3 - Sept 2004 - p524(1) [51-500]

Malam, John - *Ancient Egypt*
c   SLJ - v50 - i11 - Nov 2004 - p123(1) [51-500]
Ancient Greece
c   BL - v101 - i4 - Oct 15 2004 - p415(1) [51-500]
c   SLJ - v50 - i11 - Nov 2004 - p123(1) [51-500]
Jason and the Argonauts (Illus. by Antram, David)
c   SLJ - v51 - i2 - Feb 2005 - p118(2) [51-500]

Malan, Roy - *Efrem Zimbalist: A Life*
Bwatch - v26 - i9 - Sept 2004 - p9(1) [51-500]
Choice - v42 - i5 - Jan 2005 - p862(1) [1-50]
R&R Bk N - v19 - i4 - Nov 2004 - p196(1) [501+]

Malanga, Steven - *The New New Left: How American Politics Works Today*
KR - v73 - i5 - March 1 2005 - p277(1) [501+]

Malarcher, Jay - *The Classically American Comedy of Larry Gelbart*
R&R Bk N - v19 - i1 - Feb 2004 - p223(1) [1-50]

Malarek, Victor - *The Natashas: Inside the New Global Sex Trade*
Globe & Mail - Oct 30 2004 - pD29 [51-500]
KR - v72 - i14 - July 15 2004 - p674(1) [51-500]
PW - v251 - i33 - August 16 2004 - p55(1) [51-500]
Natashas: The New Global Sex Trade
CBRA - Annual 2003 - p315(2) [51-500]

Malaspina, E. - *L. Annaei Senecae De clementia libri duo*
Class R - v53 - i2 - Nov 2003 - p367-369 [501+]

Malaspina, Margaret A. - *Cracking Your Retirement Nest Egg (Read by Lawson, Celeste). Audiobook Review*
LJ - v129 - i14 - Sept 1 2004 - p203(1) [51-500]

Malaurie, Jean - *Ultima Thule: Explorers and Natives in the Polar North*
R&R Bk N - v19 - i1 - Feb 2004 - p69(1) [501+]

Malavet, Pedro A. - *America's Colony: The Political and Cultural Conflict between the United States and Puerto Rico*
Choice - v42 - i6 - Feb 2005 - p1092(2) [51-500]
HLR - v118 - i4 - Feb 2005 - p1398(1) [501+]

Malbin, Michael J. - *Life after Reform: When the Bipartisan Campaign Reform Act Meets Politics*
R&R Bk N - v19 - i1 - Feb 2004 - pNA [51-500]

Malcolm, Jahnna N. - *Mixed Messages*
y SLJ - v51 - i1 - Jan 2005 - p132(2) [51-500]

Malcolmson, Cristina - *Debating Gender in Early Modern England, 1500-1700*
Six Ct J - v34 - i4 - Winter 2003 - p1222-1223 [501+]
George Herbert: A Literary Life
TLS - i5287 - July 30 2004 - p29(1) [501+]

Malcom, David - *Understanding Graham Swift*
Choice - v41 - i11-12 - July-August 2004 - p2045(1) [501+]

Malcomson, Robert - *A Very Brilliant Affair: The Battle of Queenston Heights, 1812*
Can Hist R - v85 - i4 - Dec 2004 - p828(3) [501+]
CBRA - Annual 2003 - p277(1) [501+]
R&R Bk N - v19 - i4 - Nov 2004 - p60(1) [51-500]

Malek, Roman - *The Chinese Face of Jesus Christ*
Theol St - v65 - i3 - Sept 2004 - p660(3) [501+]

Malenfant, Marie-Claude - *Argumentaires de l'une et l'autre espece de femme: Le statut de l'exemplum dans les discours litteraires sur la femme*
Ren Q - v57 - i4 - Winter 2004 - p1421(2) [501+]

Maler, Karl-Goran - *Economic Theory for the Environment: Essays in Honour of Karl Goran Maler*
Econ J - v114 - i499 - Nov 2004 - pF539-F540 [501+]
Handbook of Environmental Economics
JEL - v41 - i4 - Dec 2003 - p1436(1) [501+]

Maler, Thomas - *Dr. Spock: An American Life*
SciTech - v28 - i1 - March 2004 - p117(1) [51-500]

Malesevic, Sinisa - *The Sociology of Ethnicity*
CS - v33 - i6 - Nov 2004 - p746(1) [1-50]

Maley, William - *The Afghanistan Wars*
E-A St - v56 - i7 - Nov 2004 - p1099(1100) [501+]
From Civil Strife to Civil Society: Civil and Military Responsibilities in Disrupted States
R&R Bk N - v19 - i1 - Feb 2004 - p148 [51-500]

Maley, Willy - *British Identities and English Renaissance Literature*
Ren Q - v57 - i4 - Winter 2004 - p1538(3) [501+]

Malgorzata, Bartula - *On Improvisation: Nine Conversations with Roberto Ciulli*
R&R Bk N - v19 - i1 - Feb 2004 - p227(1) [501+]

Malhotra, Anshu - *Gender, Caste, and Religious Identities: Restructing Class In Colonial Punjab*
JIH - v34 - i3 - Wntr 2004 - p506(2) [501+]

Malhotra, Sonali - *Welcome to Iraq*
c SLJ - v50 - i7 - July 2004 - p93(1) [51-500]

Mali, Joseph - *Isaiah Berlin's Counter-Enlightenment*
R&R Bk N - v19 - i4 - Nov 2004 - p5(1) [51-500]
Mythistory: The Making of a Modern Historiography
AHR - v109 - i3 - June 2004 - p859(2) [501+]

Malick Sidibe: Photographs Hasselblad Center/Steidl March 2004 (Illus. by Sidibe, Malick)
Black Iss - v6 - i5 - Sept-Oct 2004 - p33(1) [501+]

Malik, Iftikhar H. - *Islam and Modernity: Muslims in Europe and the United States*
Choice - v41 - i11-12 - July-August 2004 - p2098(1) [501+]

Malik, Marek - *Dynamic Electrocardiography*
SciTech - v28 - i3 - Sept 2004 - p105(1) [51-500]

Malik, Saadat - *Network Security Principles and Practices*
SciTech - v28 - i3 - Sept 2004 - p157(1) [51-500]

Malin, Jo - *Herspace: Women, Writing, and Solitude*
TSWL - v23 - i2 - Fall 2004 - p388(6) [501+]

Malin, Shimon - *Nature Loves to Hide: Quantum Physics and the Nature of Reality: A Western Perspective*
Isis - v95 - i2 - June 2004 - p335(2) [501+]

Malinowski, Stephan - *Vom Konig zum Fuhrer: Sozialer Niedergang und politische Radikalisierung im deutschen Adel zwischen Kaiserreich und NS-Staat*
AHR - v109 - i4 - Oct 2004 - p1328(2) [501+]

Malkia, Matti - *eTransformation in Governance: New Directions in Government and Politics*
R&R Bk N - v19 - i1 - Feb 2004 - p150(1) [51-500]

Malkin, I - *Ancient Perceptions of Greek Ethnicity*
Class R - v53 - i2 - Nov 2003 - p405-407 [501+]

Malkin, Lawrence - *What Ifs? of American History*
NYTBR - Sept 5 2004 - p23 [501+]

Malkoo, Lauri - *Illegal Annexation and State Continuity: The Case of the Incorporation of the Baltic States by the USSR, a Study of the Tension between Normativity...*
R&R Bk N - v19 - i3 - August 2004 - p207(1) [1-50]

Mallaby, Sebastian - *The World's Banker: A Story of Failed States, Financial Crises, and the Wealth and Poverty of Nations*
BL - v101 - i4 - Oct 15 2004 - p386(1) [51-500]
Bus W - i3905 - Oct 25 2004 - p30 [501+]
BW - v34 - i40 - Oct 3 2004 - p5(1) [501+]
KR - v72 - i16 - August 15 2004 - p792(1) [501+]
NS - v134 - i4722 - Jan 17 2005 - p52(2) [501+]
NYTBR - Dec 5 2004 - p77 [501+]
PW - v251 - i42 - Oct 18 2004 - p60(1) [51-500]

Malladi, Amulya - *Serving Crazy with Curry*
BL - v101 - i1 - Sept 1 2004 - p62(1) [501+]
KR - v72 - i19 - Oct 1 2004 - p933(1) [501+]
PW - v251 - i16 - Oct 1 2004 - p71(1) [51-500]

Mallarme, Stephane - *For Anatole's Tomb*
TLS - i5268 - March 19 2004 - p9-9 [501+]

Mallary, Michael - *Our Implorable Universe: A Physicist Considers How We Got There*
Choice - v42 - i5 - Jan 2005 - p876(1) [1-50]

Mallen, Enrique - *The Visual Grammar of Pablo Picasso*
R&R Bk N - v19 - i1 - Feb 2004 - p200(1) [51-500]

Mallery, Susan - *Falling for Gracie*
PW - v252 - i7 - Feb 14 2005 - p59(1) [51-500]

Mallet, Gina - *Last Chance to Eat: The Fate of Taste in a Fast Food World*
BL - v100 - i22 - August 2004 - p1887(1) [51-500]
Globe & Mail - Sept 18 2004 - pD20 [501+]
LJ - v129 - i12 - July 2004 - p110(2) [51-500]
NY - v80 - i25 - Sept 6 2004 - p163(1) [1-50]

Mallet, Shelley - *Conceiving Cultures: Reproducing People and Places on Nuakata, Papua New Guinea*
JRAI - v10 - i3 - Sept 2004 - p745(2) [501+]

Mallett, Ashley - *The Black Lords of Summer: The Story of the 1868 Aboriginal Tour of England and Beyond*
SSJ - v21 - i1 - March 2004 - p97-99 [501+]

Mallett, Phillip - *Palgrave Advances in Thomas Hardy Studies*
Choice - v42 - i4 - Dec 2004 - p661(1) [1-50]
Rudyard Kipling: A Literary Life
ELT - v48 - i1 - Wntr 2005 - p252(2) [501+]
R&R Bk N - v19 - i1 - Feb 2004 - p238(1) [51-500]
Thomas Hardy: Texts and Contexts
VS - v46 - i3 - Spring 2004 - p538(4) [501+]

Mallett, Robert - *Mussolini and the Origins of the Second World War, 1933-1940*
J Mil H - v68 - i1 - April 2004 - p627-628 [501+]
R&R Bk N - v19 - i1 - Feb 2004 - p29(1) [51-500]

Mallette, Gloria - *Distant Lover*
BL - v101 - i1 - Sept 1 2004 - p62(1) [501+]
Black Iss - v7 - i1 - Jan-Feb 2005 - p65(1) [501+]
PW - v251 - i41 - Oct 11 2004 - p56(1) [501+]

Malley, Brian - *How the Bible Works: An Anthropological Study of Evangelical Biblicism*
R&R Bk N - v19 - i3 - August 2004 - p21(1) [1-50]

Malley-Morrison, Kathleen - *Family Violence in a Cultural Perspective: Defining, Understanding, and Combating Abuse*
R&R Bk N - v19 - i1 - Feb 2004 - p142(1) [51-500]
International Perspectives on Family Violence and Abuse: A Cognitive Ecological Approach
Adoles - v39 - i155 - Fall 2004 - p625(1) [51-500]
Choice - v42 - i6 - Feb 2005 - p1104(1) [51-500]

Mallick, Heather - *Pearls in Vinegar: The Pillow Book of Heather Mallick*
Globe & Mail - Sept 11 2004 - pD7 [501+]

Mallinson, Allan - *A Call to Arms (Read by Graham, Errick). Audiobook Review*
y Kliatt - v38 - i5 - Sept 2004 - p54(2) [51-500]

Mallinson, Jeffrey - *Faith, Reason, and Revelation in Theodore Beza*
CH - v73 - i4 - Dec 2004 - p857(2) [501+]

Mallon, Gerald P. - *Gay Men Choosing Parenthood*
Advocate - July 20 2004 - p51(1) [51-500]

Mallon, Sean - *Samoan Art & Artists: O Measina a Samoa*
Cont Pac - v17 - i1 - Spring 2005 - p255(3) [501+]
Pac A - v77 - i2 - Summer 2004 - p384(2) [501+]

Mallon, Thomas - *Bandbox*
BooChiTr - Jan 18 2004 - p1(2) [501+]
NYTBR - Jan 30 2005 - p24 [501+]

Malloy, John - *Amnesia*
y VOYA - v27 - i5 - Dec 2004 - p408(1) [51-500]

Malloy, Jonathan - *Between Colliding Worlds: The Ambiguous Existence of Government Agencies for Aboriginal and Women's Policy*
CBRA - Annual 2003 - p308(2) [501+]
Choice - v42 - i2 - Oct 2004 - p366(1) [51-500]
R&R Bk N - v19 - i1 - Feb 2004 - pNA [501+]

Malloy, Judy - *Women, Art, and Technology*
ABR - v25 - i5 - July-August 2004 - p15(1) [501+]

Malmfors, Birgitta - *Writing and Presenting Scientific Papers*
Choice - v42 - i4 - Dec 2004 - p634(1) [1-50]

Malnar, Joy Monice - *Sensory Design*
R&R Bk N - v19 - i4 - Nov 2004 - p209(1) [501+]

Malo, Paul - *Fool's Paradise: Remembering the Thousand Islands*
R&R Bk N - v19 - i3 - August 2004 - p72(1) [51-500]

Malone, Bill C. - *Don't Get Above Your Raisin': Country Music and the Southern Working Class*
WestFolk - v62 - i4 - Fall 2003 - p297(3) [501+]

Malone, Carolyn Marino - *Facade as Spectacle: Ritual and Ideology at Wells Cathedral*
R&R Bk N - v19 - i4 - Nov 2004 - p204(1) [501+]

Malone, Geoffrey - *Cadoc*
c Sch Lib - v52 - i3 - Autumn 2004 - p146(1) [501+]

Malone, Linda A. - *Defending the Environment: Civil Society Strategies to Enforce International Environmental Law*
R&R Bk N - v19 - i4 - Nov 2004 - p75(1) [51-500]

Malone, Paul M. - *Franz Kafka's The Trial: Four Stage Adaptations*
R&R Bk N - v19 - i1 - Feb 2004 - p248(1) [51-500]

Malone, Robert - *Ultimate Robot*
y BL - v101 - i7 - Dec 1 2004 - p630(1) [51-500]

Malone, Thomas W. - *The Future of Work: How the New Order of Business Will Shape Your Organization, Your Management Style, and Your Life*
Choice - v41 - i11-12 - July-August 2004 - p2089(1) [501+]
Organizing Business Knowledge: The MIT Process Handbook
Per Psy - v57 - i3 - Autumn 2004 - p835(3) [501+]

Maloney, Paul - *Scotland and the Music Hall 1850-1914*
TLS - i5265 - Feb 27 2004 - p19-19 [501+]

Maloney, Peter - *Bronto Eats Meat*
LibMed - v22 - i4 - Jan 2004 - p59(1) [501+]

Malory, Thomas - *Le Morte Darthur, or, the Hoole Book of Kyng Arthur and of His Noble Knyghtes of the Rounde Table: Authoritative Text, Sources and Backgrounds, Criticism*
R&R Bk N - v19 - i1 - Feb 2004 - p236(1) [1-50]

Malotki, Ekkehart - *Hopi Tales of Destruction*
Am Ind CRJ - v27 - i2 - Spring 2003 - p126-128 [501+]

Malsberger, Brian M. - *Trade Secrets: A State-by-State Survey, 2nd Ed.*
R&R Bk N - v19 - i3 - August 2004 - p200(1) [1-50]

Malt, Johanna - *Obscure Objects of Desire: Surrealism, Fetishism and Politics*
TLS - i5302 - Nov 12 2004 - p31(1) [51-500]

Maltbie, P.I. - *Picasso and Minou (Illus. by Estrada, Pau)*
c PW - v252 - i2 - Jan 10 2005 - p56(1) [51-500]

Maltby, John Wingate - *A Brief History of Science*
y Sch Lib - v52 - i3 - Autumn 2004 - p166(1) [501+]

Maltby, Paul - *The Visionary Moment: A Postmodern Critique*
MFSF - v50 - i2 - Summer 2004 - p490-492 [501+]

Maltby, R. - *Tibullus: Elegies, Text, Introduction and Commentary*
   Class R - v54 - i2 - Nov 2004 - p382(3) [501+]
Maltby, Tony - *Ageing and the Transition to Retirement: A Comparative Analysis of European Welfare States*
   R&R Bk N - v19 - i3 - August 2004 - p160(1) [51-500]
Maltby, William S. - *The Reign of Charles V*
   Six Ct J - v35 - i1 - Spring 2004 - p264(3) [501+]
Maltin, Leonard - *Leonard Maltin's 2005 Movie Guide*
   Globe & Mail - Dec 10 2004 - pR21 [1-50]
Maltori, H. Mel - *One Large Coffin to Go*
   CBRA - Annual 2003 - p175(2) [501+]
Maluf, Nadim - *Introduction to Microelectromechanical Systems Engineering, 2nd Ed.*
   SciTech - v28 - i3 - Sept 2004 - p162(1) [51-500]
Maluszynski, M. - *Doubled Haploid Production in Crop Plants: A Manual*
   SciTech - v28 - i1 - March 2004 - p129(1) [51-500]
Malvern, Sue - *Modern Art, Britain and the Great War: Witnessing, Testimony and Remembrance*
   Choice - v42 - i7 - March 2005 - p1217(1) [51-500]
   TLS - i5300 - Oct 29 2004 - p7(1) [501+]
Malyon, Carol - *Colville's People*
   Can Lit - i182 - Autumn 2004 - p131(2) [501+]
The Migration of Butterflies
   Globe & Mail - Jan 22 2005 - pD12 [501+]
Malyschev, L.I. - *Flora of Siberia, Vol. 7*
   SciTech - v28 - i4 - Dec 2004 - p65(1) [51-500]
Flora of Siberia, Vol. 8
   SciTech - v28 - i3 - Sept 2004 - p62(1) [51-500]
Mamdani, Mahmood - *Good Muslim, Bad Muslim: America, the Cold War and the Roots of Terror*
   Choice - v42 - i3 - Nov 2004 - p561(1) [1-50]
When Victims Become Killers: Colonialism, Nativism, and the Genocide in Rwanda
   HNet - June 2004 - pNA [501+]
Mammoli, A.A. - *Computation Methods in Multiphase Flow 2: Proceedings*
   SciTech - v28 - i3 - Sept 2004 - p138(1) [51-500]
Computational Methods in Materials Characterisation: Proceedings
   SciTech - v28 - i3 - Sept 2004 - p138(1) [51-500]
Moving Boundaries VII: Computational Modelling of Free and Moving Boundary Problems
   SciTech - v28 - i3 - Sept 2004 - p45(1) [1-50]
Man-Cheong, Iona D. - *The Class of 1761: Examinations, State, and Elites in Eighteenth-Century China*
   R&R Bk N - v19 - i4 - Nov 2004 - p156(1) [501+]
Man, John - *Genghis Khan: Life, Death and Resurrection*
   BL - v101 - i9-10 - Jan 1 2005 - p809(1) [1-50]
   LJ - v130 - i2 - Feb 1 2005 - p93(1) [51-500]
Man-Made Disasters Series
   LibMed - v23 - i1 - August-Sept 2004 - p83(1) [51-500]
Mana, Ka - *Christians and Churches of Africa: Salvation in Christ and Building a New African Society*
   IBMR - v29 - i1 - Jan 2005 - p48(2) [501+]
Manalansan, Martin F. - *Global Divas: Filipino Gay Men in the Diaspora*
   CS - v33 - i5 - Sept 2004 - p625-625 [501+]
   JRAI - v10 - i4 - Dec 2004 - p952(2) [501+]
Manas, Todd M. - *Creating a Total Rewards Strategy: A Toolkit for Designing Business-Based Plans*
   HR Mag - v50 - i2 - Feb 2005 - pS5(1) [501+]
   HR Mag - v49 - i7 - July 2004 - pS6(1) [51-500]
Manassiev, Nikolai - *Female Reproductive Health*
   SciTech - v28 - i1 - March 2004 - p115(1) [51-500]
Manby, Chris - *Getting Personal*
   BW - v34 - i28 - July 11 2004 - p13(1) [501+]
Manchee, William - *Deadly Distractions: A Stan Turner Mystery*
   LJ - v129 - i14 - Sept 1 2004 - p122(1) [51-500]
Mancilla, Michael - *Love in the Time of HIV: The Gay Man's Guide to Sex, Dating and Relationships*
   R&R Bk N - v19 - i2 - May 2004 - p133 [51-500]
Mancing, Howard - *The Cervantes Encyclopedia*
   Choice - v42 - i1 - Sept 2004 - p62(1) [51-500]
   Ref Rev - July 2004 - pNA [501+]
Mancini, Julie R. - *Guide to Backyard Birds*
   Bwatch - March 2005 - pNA [51-500]
   PW - v251 - i45 - Nov 8 2004 - p47(1) [501+]
Mancoske, Ronald J. - *Practice Issues in HIV/AIDS Services: Empowerment-Based Models and Program Applications*
   SciTech - v28 - i4 - Dec 2004 - p84(1) [51-500]

Mandaville, Peter G. - *Transnational Muslim Politics: Reimagining the Umma*
   R&R Bk N - v19 - i3 - August 2004 - p173(1) [501+]
Mandel, Maud S. - *In the Aftermath of Genocide: Armenians and Jews in Twentieth-Century France*
   AHR - v109 - i2 - April 2004 - p487(2) [501+]
Mandel, Michael J. - *Rational Exuberance: Silencing the Enemies of Growth and Why the Future Is Better than You Think*
   LJ - v129 - i13 - August 2004 - p91(2) [501+]
Mandel, Peter - *Boats on the River (Illus. by Miller, Edward)*
   c SLJ - v50 - i9 - Sept 2004 - p173(1) [1-50]
Planes at the Airport (Illus. by Miller, Edward)
   c SLJ - v50 - i9 - Sept 2004 - p173(1) [1-50]
Mandel, Robert - *Security, Strategy, and the Quest for Bloodless War*
   R&R Bk N - v19 - i4 - Nov 2004 - p251(1) [501+]
Mandel, Scott - *The New-Teacher Toolbox: Proven Tips and Strategies for a Great First Year*
   JAAL - v48 - i1 - Sept 2004 - p87(1) [501+]
   SLJ - v50 - i10 - Oct 2004 - pS73(1) [51-500]
Mandela, Nelson - *Long Walk to Freedom (Read by Glover, Danny). Audiobook Review*
   Globe & Mail - Jan 8 2005 - pD13 [1-50]
Nelson Mandela in His Own Words
   PW - v251 - i48 - Nov 29 2004 - p32(1) [51-500]
Mandelbaum, Michael - *The Meaning of Sports: Why Americans Watch Baseball, Football, and Basketball and What They See When They Do*
   Choice - v42 - i3 - Nov 2004 - p524(1) [1-50]
   R&R Bk N - v19 - i3 - August 2004 - p87(1) [51-500]
Mandelbaum, Paul - *Garrett in Wedlock: A Novel-in-Stories*
   KR - v72 - i19 - Oct 1 2004 - p933(1) [501+]
Mandelbrot, Benoit B. - *Fractals and Chaos: The Mandelbrot Set and Beyond*
   E-Streams - Oct 2004 - pNA [501+]
   Nature - v430 - i6995 - July 1 2004 - p18(3) [501+]
The (Mis)behavior of Markets: A Fractal View of Risk, Ruin, and Reward
   Choice - v42 - i6 - Feb 2005 - p1070(1) [51-500]
Mandelbrote, Scott - *Footprints of the Lion: Isaac Newton at Work*
   Isis - v95 - i2 - June 2004 - p294(3) [501+]
Mandell, Deena - *Deadbeat Dads: Subjectivity and Social Construction*
   CBRA - Annual 2003 - p386(1) [501+]
Mandelman, Avner - *Cuckoo*
   BIC - v33 - i6 - Sept 2004 - p5(1) [501+]
   Globe & Mail - July 10 2004 - pD7 [501+]
Manderson, Lenore - *Teaching Gender, Teaching Women's Health: Case Studies in Medical and Health Science Education*
   SciTech - v28 - i1 - March 2004 - p78(1) [51-500]
Violence Against Women in Asian Societies: Gender Inequality and Technologies of Violence
   Pac A - v77 - i2 - Summer 2004 - p308(3) [501+]
Mandle, Jay R. - *Globalization and the Poor*
   JEL - v42 - i3 - Sept 2004 - p853(2) [501+]
Mandler, Martin - *Market Expections and Option Prices: Techniques and Applications*
   JEL - v41 - i4 - Dec 2003 - p1364(2) [501+]
Mandrioli, Paolo - *Cultural Heritage and Aerobiology: Methods and Measurement Techniques for Biodeterioration Monitoring*
   SciTech - v28 - i1 - March 2004 - p76(1) [51-500]
Mandrosov, Valery I. - *Coherent Fields and Images in Remote Sensing*
   SciTech - v28 - i3 - Sept 2004 - p4(1) [501+]
Mandry, Christof - *Ethische Identitat und christlicher Glaube. Theologische Ethik im Spannungsfeld von Theologie und Philosophie*
   Theol St - v65 - i3 - Sept 2004 - p664(2) [501+]
Mandvi, Aasif - *Magic Seeds*
   PW - v252 - i6 - Feb 7 2005 - p34(2) [51-500]
Mandy, Ross - *Victorian Toys*
   Sch Lib - v52 - i3 - Autumn 2004 - p151(1) [501+]
Mandy, Stanley - *Lettice The Flying Rabbit*
   c CE - v81 - i1 - Fall 2004 - p47(1) [51-500]
Manea, Norman - *The Hooligan's Return: A Memoir*
   TLS - i5266 - March 5 2004 - p6-7 [501+]
   WLT - v78 - i3-4 - Sept-Dec 2004 - p153(2) [501+]
Manekin, Charles H. - *On Maimonides*
   R&R Bk N - v19 - i4 - Nov 2004 - p16(1) [51-500]

Manelis, G.B. - *Thermal Decomposition and Combustion of Explosives and Propellants*
   E-Streams - June 2004 - pNA [501+]
   SciTech - v28 - i1 - March 2004 - p171(1) [51-500]
Maness, Terry S. - *Short-Term Financial Management, 3rd Ed.*
   R&R Bk N - v19 - i4 - Nov 2004 - p117(1) [51-500]
Manetta, Alberto - *Cancer Prevention and Early Diagnosis in Women*
   SciTech - v28 - i1 - March 2004 - p92(1) [51-500]
Manetti, Giannozzo - *Biographical Writings*
   Ren Q - v57 - i4 - Winter 2004 - p1354(4) [501+]
Maney, Mabel - *The Girl with the Golden Bouffant: An Original Jane Bond Parody*
   Advocate - August 17 2004 - pS30(1) [51-500]
Manfredi, Christopher P. - *Feminist Activism in the Supreme Court: Legal Mobilization and the Women's Legal Education and Action Fund*
   Law&PolBR - Nov 2004 - p861(6) [501+]
   R&R Bk N - v19 - i3 - August 2004 - p153(1) [51-500]
Mangal, Melina - *Anne Hutchinson: Religious Reformer*
   c LibMed - v23 - i3 - Nov-Dec 2004 - p78(2) [51-500]
Mangan, James Clarence - *Selected Writings*
   ILS - v24 - i1 - Fall 2004 - p32(1) [51-500]
   LJ - v129 - i16 - Oct 1 2004 - p80(1) [51-500]
Mangan, Richard - *Gielgud's Letters*
   Lon R Bks - v26 - i15 - August 5 2004 - p14(2) [501+]
Sir John Gielgud: A Life in Letters
   Choice - v42 - i2 - Oct 2004 - p299(1) [51-500]
   G&L Rev W - v11 - i6 - Nov-Dec 2004 - p43(1) [501+]
Mangan, Timothy - *Paul Bowles on Music*
   M Ed J - v91 - i4 - March 2005 - p65(1) [501+]
Manganelli, Giorgio - *Centuria: One Hundred Ouroboric Novels*
   LJ - v130 - i2 - Feb 1 2005 - p73(1) [51-500]
Mangels, Reed - *The Dietician's Guide to Vegetarian Diets: Issues and Applications, 2nd Ed.*
   SciTech - v28 - i3 - Sept 2004 - p121(1) [51-500]
Mangiapane, John - *It's All in the Cards: Tarot Reading Made Easy*
   LJ - v129 - i13 - August 2004 - p99(1) [501+]
Mango, Andrew - *The Turks Today*
   BL - v101 - i8 - Dec 15 2004 - p703(1) [51-500]
   CR - v286 - i1668 - Jan 2005 - p62(1) [51-500]
   KR - v72 - i23 - Dec 1 2004 - p1135(1) [501+]
   LJ - v129 - i20 - Dec 1 2004 - p142(1) [51-500]
   PW - v251 - i47 - Nov 22 2004 - p47(1) [51-500]
   Spec - v295 - i9185 - August 21 2004 - p30(1) [501+]
Manguel, Alberto - *A Reading Diary: A Passionate Reader's Reflections on a Year of Books*
   BL - v101 - i2 - Sept 15 2004 - p194(1) [501+]
   BW - v34 - i49 - Dec 5 2004 - p12(1) [501+]
   KR - v72 - i14 - July 15 2004 - p675(1) [501+]
   LJ - v129 - i14 - Sept 1 2004 - p149(2) [501+]
A Reading Diary: A Year of Favourite Books
   Globe & Mail - Oct 9 2004 - pD12 [501+]
   Globe & Mail - Dec 24 2004 - pD3 [1-50]
Stevenson under the Palm Trees
   BIC - v33 - i2 - March 2004 - p5(2) [501+]
   BL - v101 - i2 - Sept 15 2004 - p214(1) [51-500]
   BW - v34 - i49 - Dec 5 2004 - p12(1) [501+]
   KR - v72 - i17 - Sept 1 2004 - p827(1) [501+]
   LJ - v129 - i17 - Oct 15 2004 - p55(1) [51-500]
   PW - v251 - i34 - August 23 2004 - p40(1) [51-500]
With Borges
   Globe & Mail - July 31 2004 - pD5 [501+]
Manheim, Jarol B. - *Biz-War and the Out-of-Power Elite: The Progressive-Left Attack on the Corporation*
   R&R Bk N - v19 - i3 - August 2004 - p114(1) [51-500]
Manheimer, Ann S. - *Martin Luther King Jr: Dreaming of Equality*
   c SLJ - v51 - i2 - Feb 2005 - p150(1) [51-500]
Mani, Sunil - *Innovation, Learning, and Technological Dynamism of Developing Countries*
   SciTech - v28 - i4 - Dec 2004 - p129 [51-500]
Manicom, David - *The Burning Eaves*
   BIC - v33 - i8 - Nov 2004 - p26(3) [501+]
Manji, Irshad - *The Trouble with Islam: A Muslim's Call for Reform in Her Faith*
   CBRA - Annual 2003 - p94(2) [51-500]
   Ga R - v58 - i3 - Fall 2004 - p705-707 [501+]

Mankell, Henning - *Before the Frost*
  BL - v101 - i9-10 - Jan 1 2005 - p828(1) [1-50]
  Econ - v373 - i8395 - Oct 2 2004 - p84US [501+]
  KR - v72 - i24 - Dec 15 2004 - p1168(1) [501+]
  LJ - v130 - i3 - Feb 15 2005 - p124(1) [51-500]
  NS - v133 - i4704 - Sept 6 2004 - p54(2) [501+]
  NYTBR - Jan 23 2005 - p21 [501+]
  PW - v252 - i5 - Jan 31 2005 - p52(1) [51-500]
  TLS - i5300 - Oct 29 2004 - p24(1) [501+]
  Firewall
  Globe & Mail - Dec 24 2004 - pD3 [1-50]
  Secrets in the Fire
  y SLJ - v50 - i10 - Oct 2004 - pS36(1) [51-500]
Mankiller, Wilma - *Every Day Is a Good Day: Reflections by Contemporary Indigenous Women*
  BL - v101 - i3 - Oct 1 2004 - p287(1) [51-500]
Mankin, Don - *Business Without Boundaries: An Action Framework for Collaborating Across Time, Distance, Organization, and Culture*
  Bwatch - March 2005 - pNA [51-500]
Mankoff, Robert - *The Complete Cartoons of the New Yorker*
  BL - v101 - i2 - Sept 15 2004 - p190(1) [51-500]
  LJ - v129 - i19 - Nov 15 2004 - p56(2) [51-500]
  NYTBR - Dec 26 2004 - p1 [501+]
  PW - v251 - i38 - Sept 20 2004 - p58(1) [51-500]
Mankowitz, Zeev W. - *Life between Memory and Hope: The Survivors of the Holocaust in Occupied Germany*
  GSR - v27 - i2 - May 2004 - p422-423 [501+]
  JMH - v77 - i1 - March 2005 - p235(3) [501+]
Manley, Bill - *Seventy Great Mysteries of Ancient Egypt*
  R&R Bk N - v19 - i1 - Feb 2004 - p26(1) [1-50]
Manlow, James - *Attraction*
  BIC - v33 - i8 - Nov 2004 - p16(3) [501+]
  KR - v72 - i16 - August 15 2004 - p769(1) [51-500]
Manly, Bryan F.J. - *Multivariate Statistical Methods: A Primer, 3rd Ed.*
  SciTech - v28 - i4 - Dec 2004 - p38(1) [51-500]
Mann, Barbara Alice - *Native Americans, Archaelogists, and the Mounds*
  Am Ind CRJ - v27 - i4 - Fall 2003 - p167-168 [501+]
Mann, Bruce H. - *Republic of Debtors: Bankruptcy in the Age of American Independence*
  AHR - v109 - i3 - June 2004 - p898(2) [501+]
  BHR - v78 - i2 - Summer 2004 - p285(3) [501+]
  HNet - Sept 2004 - pNA [501+]
  NEQ - v77 - i4 - Dec 2004 - p655-659 [501+]
Mann, Douglas - *Philosophy: A New Introduction*
  R&R Bk N - v19 - i3 - August 2004 - p6(1) [1-50]
Mann, Elizabeth - *Empire State Building: When New York Reached for the Skies (Illus. by Witschonke, Alan)*
  c SLJ - v50 - i10 - Oct 2004 - p540(1) [51-500]
Mann, Emily - *Political Stages: Plays That Shaped a Century*
  TDR - v48 - i2 - Summer 2004 - p180(2) [501+]
Mann, Ingrid - *The Danube Testament*
  Spec - v295 - i9185 - August 21 2004 - p32(1) [501+]
Mann, James - *Peace Signs: The Anti-War Movement in Pictures*
  Choice - v42 - i1 - Sept 2004 - p86(1) [501+]
  Rise of the Vulcans: The History of Bush's War Cabinet
  For Aff - v83 - i5 - Sept-Oct 2004 - p164 [501+]
  Globe & Mail - Dec 24 2004 - pD3 [1-50]
  Lon R Bks - v26 - i21 - Nov 4 2004 - p15(4) [501+]
  NYRB - v51 - i14 - Sept 23 2004 - p40(4) [501+]
  Parameters - v34 - i3 - Autumn 2004 - p146(3) [501+]
  YR - v92 - i4 - Oct 2004 - p128-139 [501+]
Mann, Jeffrey K. - *Shall We Sin?: Responding to the Antinomian Question in Lutheran Theology*
  Choice - v42 - i4 - Dec 2004 - p679(1) [1-50]
Mann, John W.W. - *Sacajawea's People: The Lemhi Shoshones and the Salmon River Country*
  BL - v101 - i4 - Oct 15 2004 - p384(1) [51-500]
Mann, Michael - *The Dark Side of Democracy: Explaining Ethnic Cleansing*
  PW - v251 - i34 - August 23 2004 - p43(2) [51-500]
  Fascists
  For Aff - v83 - i5 - Sept-Oct 2004 - p164 [501+]
  HRNB - v33 - i1 - Fall 2004 - p38(2) [501+]
Mann, Michael - *Fascists*
  HT - v54 - i11 - Nov 2004 - p78(1) [501+]
Mann, Randall - *Complaint in the Garden*
  G&L Rev W - v11 - i5 - Sept-Oct 2004 - p42(1) [501+]
  Poet - v185 - i5 - Feb 2005 - p395(2) [501+]

Mann, Richard A. - *Business Law and the Regulation of Business, 8th Ed.*
  R&R Bk N - v19 - i3 - August 2004 - p198(1) [1-50]
Mann, Thomas - *Buddenbrooks*
  NS - v133 - i4716 - Nov 29 2004 - p44(1) [51-500]
  Thomas Mann's Addresses Delivered at the Library of Congress
  R&R Bk N - v19 - i1 - Feb 2004 - p248(1) [51-500]
Mann, William E. - *The Blackwell Guide to the Philosophy of Religion*
  Choice - v42 - i6 - Feb 2005 - p1036(1) [51-500]
Mann, William J. - *Edge of Midnight: The Life of John Schlesinger*
  Spec - v295 - i9183 - August 7 2004 - p30(2) [501+]
  TimHES - v0 - i1674 - Jan 14 2005 - p27(1) [501+]
  TLS - i5293 - Sept 10 2004 - p18(1) [501+]
Manne, Robert - *The Howard Years*
  AJPS - v39 - i2 - July 2004 - p443(444) [501+]
Mannes, Aaron - *Profiles in Terror*
  Bwatch - Jan 2005 - pNA [501+]
Mannheim, Karl - *Selected Correspondence (1911-1946) of Karl Mannheim, Scientist, Philosopher, and Sociologist*
  CS - v33 - i5 - Sept 2004 - p566-567 [501+]
  Isis - v95 - i3 - Sept 2004 - p512(2) [501+]
Manning, Christel - *Sex and Religion*
  R&R Bk N - v19 - i4 - Nov 2004 - p21(1) [51-500]
Manning, Frederick J. - *NIH Extramural Center Programs: Criteria for Initiation and Evaluation*
  SciTech - v28 - i3 - Sept 2004 - p79(1) [51-500]
Manning, Howard - *The Cervantes Encyclopedia*
  BL - v100 - i21 - July 2004 - p1861(1) [501+]
Manning, Jason - *War Lovers*
  Roundup M - v12 - i1 - Oct 2004 - p31(1) [51-500]
Manning, Joe - *Disappearing into North Adams*
  Pub Hist - v26 - i2 - Spring 2004 - p83(84) [501+]
Manning, John - *The Emblem*
  Six Ct J - v34 - i4 - Winter 2003 - p1227-1228 [501+]
Manning, Kathleen - *San Francisco's Ocean Beach*
  Bwatch - v26 - i7 - July 2004 - p2(1) [51-500]
Manning, Martin J. - *Historical Dictionary of American Propaganda*
  LJ - v129 - i20 - Dec 1 2004 - p166(1) [51-500]
Manning, Maurice - *A Companion for Owls: Being the Commonplace Book of D. Boone, Long Hunter, Back Woodsman*
  BL - v101 - i1 - Sept 1 2004 - p40(1) [51-500]
Manning, Nick - *Poverty and Social Exclusion in the New Russia*
  R&R Bk N - v19 - i4 - Nov 2004 - p90(1) [51-500]
Manning, Peter (b. 1948 -) - *Electronic and Computer Music, Rev. and Expanded Ed.*
  Notes - v61 - i3 - March 2005 - p746(4) [501+]
Manning, Peter K. - *Policing Contingencies*
  AJS - v110 - i1 - July 2004 - p259(3) [501+]
Manning, Preston - *Think Big: Adventures in Life and Democracy*
  BIC - v33 - i2 - March 2004 - p34(3) [501+]
Manning, Richard - *Against the Grain: How Agriculture Has Hijacked Civilization*
  BooChiTr - May 2 2004 - p3(1) [501+]
  Choice - v42 - i1 - Sept 2004 - p129(1) [501+]
  SB - v40 - i5 - Sept-Oct 2004 - p207(1) [51-500]
Manning, Roger B. - *Swordsmen: The Martial Ethos in the Three Kingdoms*
  Choice - v42 - i3 - Nov 2004 - p554(1) [1-50]
  HNet - Oct 2004 - pNA [501+]
Manning, Russ - *Russ Manning's Magnus, Robot Fighter*
  y BL - v101 - i7 - Dec 1 2004 - p644(1) [51-500]
Manning, Tara Jon - *The Gift Knitter: Knitting Chunky for Babies with Four Legs and Two*
  BL - v101 - i2 - Sept 15 2004 - p192(1) [51-500]
Mannings, Mick - *Roman Fort*
  c Sch Lib - v52 - i4 - Winter 2004 - p209(1) [51-500]
Mannino, Stephanie - *Cool Careers Without College for People Who Love Crafts*
  y SLJ - v50 - i10 - Oct 2004 - p186(1) [51-500]
Mannion, Gerard - *Schopenhauer, Religion and Morality: The Humble Path to Ethics*
  R&R Bk N - v19 - i1 - Feb 2004 - p4(1) [51-500]
Mannion, Lawrence P. - *Employee Assistance Programs: What Works and What Doesn't*
  R&R Bk N - v19 - i2 - May 2004 - p117 [51-500]

Mannis, Celeste Davidson - *The Queen's Progress: An Elizabethan Alphabet (Illus. by Ibatoulline, Bagram)*
  c LibMed - v22 - i4 - Jan 2004 - p60(1) [501+]
Mannlein-Robert, I. - *Longin: Philologe und Philosoph. Eine Interpretation der erhaltenen Zeugnisse*
  Class R - v53 - i2 - Nov 2003 - p323-326 [501+]
Manolis, Tim - *Dragonflies and Damselflies of California*
  QRB - v79 - i4 - Dec 2004 - p435(2) [501+]
Manoni, Laurent - *Eyes, Lies and Illusions*
  TLS - i5301 - Nov 5 2004 - p22(1) [501+]
Mansal, Bibhat K. - *Lecture Notes on Infectious Diseases, 6th Ed.*
  E-Streams - Oct 2004 - pNA [501+]
Mansbach, Adam - *Angry Black White Boy*
  NYTBR - March 6 2005 - p21 [501+]
Mansel, Philip - *Prince of Europe: The Life of Charles-Joseph de Ligne, 1735-1814*
  R&R Bk N - v19 - i1 - Feb 2004 - p28(1) [51-500]
Mansell, Wade - *A Critical Introduction to Law, 3rd Ed.*
  Law&PolBR - Dec 2004 - p956(5) [501+]
Manser, Martin H. - *The Facts on File Dictionary of Classical and Biblical Allusions*
  LibMed - v22 - i7 - April-May 2004 - p73(1) [501+]
  R&R Bk N - v19 - i1 - Feb 2004 - p220(1) [51-500]
  Getting to Grips with Grammar
  LibMed - v22 - i6 - March 2004 - p83(1) [501+]
Mansfield, Bruce - *Erasmus in the 20th Century: Interpretations c. 1920-2000*
  R&R Bk N - v19 - i1 - Feb 2004 - p214 [51-500]
Mansfield, Edward D. - *Economic Interdependence and International Conflict: New Perspectives on an Enduring Debate*
  JEL - v41 - i4 - Dec 2003 - p1343(1) [501+]
  The Evolution of Political Knowledge: Theory and Inquiry in American Politics
  Choice - v42 - i4 - Dec 2004 - p729(1) [1-50]
Mansfield, Howard - *The Bones of the Earth*
  BL - v101 - i3 - Oct 1 2004 - p298(1) [51-500]
  PW - v251 - i41 - Oct 11 2004 - p66(1) [51-500]
Mansfield, Stephen - *The Faith of George W. Bush (Read by Charles, J.). Audiobook Review*
  BL - v101 - i1 - Sept 1 2004 - p146(1) [1-50]
Mansini, Guy - *Ethics and Theological Disclosures: The Thought of Robert Sokolowski*
  RM - v58 - i1 - Sept 2004 - p185(3) [501+]
  TT - v61 - i3 - Oct 2004 - p426(1) [501+]
Manson, Ainslie - *Alexander Mackenzie: From Canada by Land*
  c CBRA - Annual 2003 - p540(1) [51-500]
  Leaving the Log House
  c CBRA - Annual 2003 - p501(1) [51-500]
Manson, Neil A. - *God and Design: The Teleological Argument and Modern Science*
  Rel St - v40 - i3 - Sept 2004 - p386(3) [501+]
  TT - v60 - i4 - Jan 2004 - p584-586 [501+]
Manson, Sarah - *A History of the Golden Cockerel Press, 1920-1960*
  BSA-P - v98 - i3 - Sept 2004 - p367-369 [501+]
Mantel, Hilary - *Beyond Black*
  KR - v73 - i5 - March 1 2005 - p251(1) [501+]
  Giving Up the Ghost: A Memoir
  Globe & Mail - Nov 27 2004 - pD3 [51-500]
  NYTBR - Oct 24 2004 - p30 [501+]
Mantell, Paul - *Stealing Home*
  c SLJ - v50 - i11 - Nov 2004 - p150(1) [51-500]
Manu, Peter - *Psychopathology of Functional Somatic Syndromes: Neurobiology and Illness Behavior in Chronic Fatigue Syndrome, Fibromyalgia, Gulf War Illness, Irritable Bowel, and Premenstrual Dysphoria*
  E-Streams - Dec 2004 - pNA [501+]
Manuel, Frances - *Desert Indian Woman: Stories and Dreams*
  WestFolk - v62 - i3 - Summer 2003 - p230-232 [501+]
Manuel, Frank E. - *James Bowdoin and the Patriot Philosophers*
  Bwatch - Dec 2004 - pNA [51-500]
Manuel, Lynn - *Camels Always Do (Illus. by Charko, Kasia)*
  c SLJ - v50 - i11 - Nov 2004 - p112(2) [51-500]
Manuel, Tara - *Filling the Belly*
  CBRA - Annual 2003 - p176(1) [51-500]
Manushkin, Fran - *The Little Sleepyhead (Illus. by Gore, Leonid)*
  c SLJ - v50 - i9 - Sept 2004 - p173(1) [51-500]
Manusov, Valerie - *The Sourcebook of Nonverbal Measures: Going Beyond Words*
  Choice - v42 - i7 - March 2005 - p1223(1) [51-500]

Manuwald, G. - *Der Satiriker Lucilius und seine Zeit*
　　Class R - v54 - i1 - May 2004 - p88(2) [501+]
　Fabulae Pratextae. Spuren Einer Literarischen Gattung der Romer
　　Class R - v54 - i1 - May 2004 - p86(3) [501+]
Manwaring, Randle - *Songs of the Spirit in Poetry and Hymnody*
　　R&R Bk N - v19 - i4 - Nov 2004 - p216(1) [501+]
Manz, Beatriz - *Paradise in Ashes: A Guatemalan Journey of Courage, Terror, and Hope*
　　Choice - v42 - i3 - Nov 2004 - p544(1) [1-50]
Manzano, Sonia - *No Dogs Allowed! (Illus. by Muth, Jon J.)*
　　c   SLJ - v50 - i7 - July 2004 - p82(1) [51-500]
Manzer, Ronald A. - *Educational Regimes and Anglo-American Democracy*
　　R&R Bk N - v19 - i1 - Feb 2004 - p189(1) [51-500]
Manzini, Francesco - *Stendhal's Parallel Lives*
　　R&R Bk N - v19 - i4 - Nov 2004 - p230(1) [501+]
Manzo, Anthony V. - *Reading Assessment for Diagnostic-Prescriptive Teaching, 2nd Ed.*
　　R&R Bk N - v19 - i1 - Feb 2004 - p183(1) [51-500]
Manzoni, G. - *Pugnae Maioris Imago. Intertestualita e Rovesciamento Nella Seconda esade Dell Eneide*
　　Class R - v54 - i2 - Nov 2004 - p569-570 [501+]
Mao, Dun - *The Shop of the Lin Family and Spring Silkworms*
　　Choice - v42 - i4 - Dec 2004 - p657(1) [1-50]
Maogoto, Jackson Nyamuya - *State Sovereignty and International Criminal Law: Versailles to Rome*
　　R&R Bk N - v19 - i1 - Feb 2004 - pNA [51-500]
Maor, Eli - *The Facts of File Calculus Handbook*
　　Math T - v97 - i4 - April 2004 - p300-300 [501+]
Maoz, Zeev - *Multiple Paths to Knowledge in International Relations: Methodology in the Study of Conflict Management and Conflict Resolution*
　　R&R Bk N - v19 - i3 - August 2004 - p159(1) [501+]
Mapp, Alf J., Jr. - *The Faiths of Our Fathers: What America's Founders Really Believed*
　　R&R Bk N - v19 - i1 - Feb 2004 - p58(1) [51-500]
Mapp, Edward - *African Americans and the Oscar: Seven Decades of Struggle and Achievement*
　　R&R Bk N - v19 - i1 - Feb 2004 - p225(1) [51-500]
Mapquest.com, Inc. - *Gareth Stevens Atlas of the World*
　　c   CH Bwatch - v14 - i11 - Nov 2004 - pNA [51-500]
Maps on File, 2004 Ed., Vols. 1-2
　　R&R Bk N - v19 - i1 - Feb 2004 - p70(1) [51-500]
Maqueira, Enzo - *Cortazar: About "Cronopios" and Commitments*
　　y   VOYA - v27 - i3 - August 2004 - p181(1) [1-50]
Mar, David Peterson Del - *Beaten Down: A History of Interpersonal Violence in the West*
　　JAH - v91 - i1 - June 2004 - p257-259 [501+]
Mara, Duncan - *Handbook of Water and Wastewater Microbiology*
　　Choice - v41 - i7 - March 2004 - p1320(1) [501+]
Mara, Wil - *Franklin D. Roosevelt*
　　c   SLJ - v50 - i8 - August 2004 - p105(2) [51-500]
　Thomas Alva Edison
　　c   SLJ - v50 - i8 - August 2004 - p105(2) [51-500]
Maracin, Paul R. - *The Night of the Long Knives: Forty-Eight Hours That Changed the History of the World*
　　LJ - v129 - i12 - July 2004 - p99(1) [51-500]
Maracle, Lee - *Daughters are Forever*
　　Can Lit - i182 - Autumn 2004 - p154(3) [501+]
Marai, Sandor - *Casanova in Bolzano*
　　BL - v101 - i5 - Nov 1 2004 - p464(2) [51-500]
　　BW - v34 - i45 - Nov 7 2004 - p7(1) [501+]
　　KR - v72 - i18 - Sept 15 2004 - p886(1) [501+]
　　NYTBR - Dec 5 2004 - p74 [501+]
　　PW - v251 - i40 - Oct 4 2004 - p67(1) [501+]
　Conversations in Bolzano
　　Lon R Bks - v26 - i20 - Oct 21 2004 - p35(2) [501+]
　　Spec - v296 - i9196 - Nov 6 2004 - p61(1) [501+]
　　TLS - i5303 - Nov 19 2004 - p24(1) [501+]
Maral, Alexandre - *La Chapelle royale de Versailles sous Louis XIV: Ceremonial, Liturgie et musique*
　　FS - v58 - i2 - April 2004 - p251(2) [501+]
　　JMH - v77 - i1 - March 2005 - p187(3) [501+]
Marangos, John - *Alternative Economic Models of Transition*
　　R&R Bk N - v19 - i3 - August 2004 - p92(1) [51-500]
Maraniss, David - *They Marched into Sunlight: War and Peace, Vietnam and America, October 1967*
　　Mar Crp G - v88 - i12 - Dec 2004 - p47(1) [501+]

Marano, Jeff - *Eros*
　　Bwatch - March 2005 - pNA [51-500]
Marano, Richard Michael - *Vote Your Conscience: The Last Campaign of George McGovern*
　　PSQ - v119 - i3 - Fall 2004 - p530(3) [501+]
　　R&R Bk N - v19 - i1 - Feb 2004 - p61(1) [501+]
Marans, Steven - *Listening to Fear: Helping Kids Cope, from Nightmares to the Nightly News*
　　LJ - v129 - i20 - Dec 1 2004 - p154(1) [51-500]
Marazzi, Martino - *Voices of Italian America: A History of Early Italian American Literature with a Critical Anthology*
　　Choice - v42 - i5 - Jan 2005 - p858(1) [1-50]
　　R&R Bk N - v19 - i4 - Nov 2004 - p231(1) [501+]
Marbas, Laurie L. - *Blueprints Clinical Procedures*
　　SciTech - v28 - i3 - Sept 2004 - p89(1) [51-500]
　Visual Mnemonics for Behavioral Sciences
　　SciTech - v28 - i4 - March 2004 - p97(1) [51-500]
Marberry, Craig - *Cuttin' Up: Wit and Wisdom from Black Barber Shops*
　　PW - v252 - i11 - March 14 2005 - p56(1) [51-500]
Marcatto, Dario - *"Questo Passo dell'Heresia": Pietrantonio di Capua tra Valdesiani, 'Spirituali' e Inquisizione*
　　CHR - v90 - i4 - Oct 2004 - p792(2) [501+]
Marceau, T.E. - *Hanford Site Historic District: History of the Plutonium Production Facilities, 1943-1990*
　　HNet - July 2004 - pNA [501+]
Marcel, Gabriel - *Awakenings: A Translation of Gabriel Marcel's Autobiography*
　　Theol St - v65 - i4 - Dec 2004 - p908(2) [501+]
Marcello, Patricia Cronin - *Gloria Steinem: A Biography*
　　R&R Bk N - v19 - i3 - August 2004 - p154(1) [51-500]
March, Ivan - *The Penguin Guide to Compact Discs and DVDs, 2003/4 Ed.*
　　R&R Bk N - v19 - i4 - Nov 2004 - p195(1) [501+]
March, W. Eugene - *The Wide, Wide Circle of Divine Love: A Biblical Case for Religious Diversity*
　　LJ - v130 - i1 - Jan 1 2005 - p121(1) [51-500]
　　PW - v251 - i48 - Nov 29 2004 - p38(1) [51-500]
Marchand, Amanda - *Without Cease the Earth Faintly Trembles*
　　CBRA - Annual 2003 - p241(1) [51-500]
Marchand-Martella, Nancy E. - *Introduction to Direct Instruction*
　　R&R Bk N - v19 - i1 - Feb 2004 - pNA [51-500]
Marchand, Trevor H.J. - *Minaret Building and Apprenticeship in Yemen*
　　IJMES - v36 - i4 - Nov 2004 - p676(3) [501+]
Marchant, Kerena - *Muhammad and Islam*
　　c   SLJ - v51 - i1 - Jan 2005 - p56(1) [51-500]
Marchant, Steve - *The Cartoonist's Workshop*
　　LJ - v129 - i19 - Nov 15 2004 - p59(1) [51-500]
Marche, Stephen - *Raymond and Hannah*
　　Globe & Mail - Jan 15 2005 - pD11 [501+]
　　KR - v73 - i3 - Feb 1 2005 - p141(1) [501+]
　　BL - v101 - i9-10 - Jan 1 2005 - p820(1) [501+]
Marchesani, Robert B. - *Saints and Rogues: Conflicts and Covergence in Psychotherapy*
　　SciTech - v28 - i4 - Dec 2004 - p97(1) [51-500]
Marchetta, Melina - *Saving Francesca (Read by Macauley, Rebecca). Audiobook Review*
　　y   Kliatt - v38 - i6 - Nov 2004 - p50(1) [51-500]
　　c   SLJ - v50 - i7 - July 2004 - p61(1) [51-500]
　　y   VOYA - v27 - i5 - Dec 2004 - p371(1) [501+]
　Saving Francesca
　　y   BL - v101 - i3 - Oct 1 2004 - p323(2) [51-500]
　　y   CCB-B - v58 - i2 - Oct 2004 - p88(2) [51-500]
　　y   HB - v80 - i5 - Sept-Oct 2004 - p591(1) [51-500]
　　y   Kliatt - v38 - i5 - Sept 2004 - p14(2) [501+]
　　y   KR - v72 - i17 - Sept 1 2004 - p870(1) [51-500]
　　y   PW - v251 - i36 - Sept 6 2004 - p64(1) [51-500]
　　y   SLJ - v50 - i9 - Sept 2004 - p212(1) [51-500]
　　y   VOYA - v27 - i4 - Oct 2004 - p304(2) [51-500]
Marchetti, Ciro - *The Gilded Tarot*
　　Bwatch - Dec 2004 - pNA [51-500]
Marchettini, N. - *The Sustainable City 3: Urban Regeneration and Sustainability, Proceedings*
　　R&R Bk N - v19 - i4 - Nov 2004 - p136(1) [51-500]
Marchica, John - *The Accountable Organization: Reclaiming Integrity, Restoring Trust*
　　HR Mag - v50 - i2 - Feb 2005 - p131(1) [501+]
　　R&R Bk N - v19 - i3 - August 2004 - p107(1) [1-50]
Marchus, Linda - *Shy Sherman*
　　c   CH Bwatch - v14 - i8 - August 2004 - p6(1) [51-500]

Marciano, Alain - *From Economic to Legal Competition: New Perspectives on Law and Institutions in Europe*
　　R&R Bk N - v19 - i1 - Feb 2004 - pNA [51-500]
Marcinko, David E. - *Business of Medical Practice: Advanced Profit Maximization Techniques for Savvy Doctors, 2nd Ed.*
　　SciTech - v28 - i3 - Sept 2004 - p78(1) [51-500]
　Financial Planning Handbook for Physicians and Advisors: An Integrated Approach
　　SciTech - v28 - i4 - Dec 2004 - p78(1) [51-500]
　Insurance and Risk Management Strategies for Physicians and Advisors: A Strategic Approach
　　SciTech - v28 - i4 - Dec 2004 - p9(1) [1-50]
Marco, David - *Universal Meta Data Models*
　　SciTech - v28 - i4 - Dec 2004 - p33(1) [51-500]
Marcombe, David - *Leper Knights: The Order of St. Lazarus of Jerusalem in England, c. 1150-1544*
　　Albion - v36 - i2 - Summer 2004 - p282(2) [501+]
Marcone, A. - *Costantino il Grande*
　　Class R - v54 - i1 - May 2004 - p191(2) [501+]
Marconi, Joe - *Public Relations: The Complete Guide*
　　Choice - v42 - i4 - Dec 2004 - p705(1) [1-50]
Marcum, Deanna B. - *Development of Digital Libraries: An American Perspective*
　　LRTS - v49 - i1 - Jan 2005 - p66(2) [501+]
Marcus Aurelius, Emperor of Rome - *Meditations*
　　VQR - v79 - i1 - Winter 2003 - p15 [51-500]
Marcus, Ben - *The Anchor Book of New American Short Stories*
　　y   BL - v100 - i22 - August 2004 - p1895(1) [51-500]
　　y   Kliatt - v39 - i1 - Jan 2005 - p26(1) [51-500]
Marcus, Daniel - *Happy Days and Wonder Years: The Fifties and the Sixties in Contemporary Cultural Politics*
　　Choice - v42 - i5 - Jan 2005 - p917(1) [1-50]
Marcus, David L. - *What It Takes to Pull Me Through: Why Teenagers Get in Trouble--and How Four of Them Got Out*
　　y   BL - v101 - i7 - Dec 1 2004 - p622(1) [51-500]
　　LJ - v130 - i1 - Jan 1 2005 - p132(1) [51-500]
　　PW - v251 - i49 - Dec 6 2004 - p53(1) [501+]
Marcus, Eric R. - *Psychosis and Near Psychosis: Ego Function, Symbol Structure, Treatment, 2nd Rev. Ed.*
　　SciTech - v28 - i1 - March 2004 - p100(1) [51-500]
Marcus, Evan - *Blueprints for High Availability, 2nd Ed.*
　　SciTech - v28 - i3 - Sept 2004 - p30(1) [51-500]
Marcus, Gary - *The Birth of the Mind: How a Tiny Number of Genes Creates the Complexity of Human Thought*
　　Globe & Mail - Nov 27 2004 - pD34 [501+]
　　NYTBR - August 15 2004 - p13 [51-500]
Marcus, Greil - *Like a Rolling Stone: Bob Dylan at the Crossroads*
　　KR - v73 - i5 - March 1 2005 - p277(1) [501+]
　　PW - v252 - i8 - Feb 21 2005 - p169(1) [51-500]
Marcus, James - *Amazonia: Five Years at the Epicenter of the Dot.com Juggernaut*
　　BL - v101 - i4 - Oct 15 2004 - p387(1) [51-500]
　　BW - v34 - i27 - July 4 2004 - p2(1) [501+]
Marcus, Jane - *Hearts of Darkness: White Women Write Race*
　　Choice - v42 - i1 - Sept 2004 - p101(2) [501+]
Marcus, Julie - *The Indomitable Miss Pink: A Life in Anthropology*
　　Isis - v95 - i2 - June 2004 - p328(2) [501+]
Marcus, Maeva - *The Documentary History of the Supreme Court of the United States, 1789-1800, Vol. 7*
　　R&R Bk N - v19 - i4 - Nov 2004 - p172(1) [501+]
Marcus, Yizhak - *Ion Exchange and Solvent Extraction: A Series of Advances, Vol. 17*
　　SciTech - v28 - i4 - Dec 2004 - p56(1) [51-500]
Marcuse, Irene - *Under the Manhattan Bridge: An Anita Servi Mystery*
　　LJ - v129 - i12 - July 2004 - p64(1) [51-500]
Marcuse, Peter - *Of States and Cities: The Partitioning of Urban Space*
　　CS - v33 - i6 - Nov 2004 - p747(1) [1-50]
Marder, Brenda L. - *Stewards of the Land: The American Farm School and Greece in the Twentieth Century*
　　SciTech - v28 - i1 - March 2004 - p127(1) [51-500]
Marechal, Brigitte - *Muslims in the Enlarged Europe: Religion and Society*
　　Choice - v41 - i11-12 - July-August 2004 - p2114(1) [501+]
Maredia, K.M. - *Integrated Pest Management in the Global Arena*
　　QRB - v79 - i3 - Sept 2004 - p327(2) [501+]
　　SciTech - v28 - i1 - March 2004 - p130(1) [51-500]
Marek, Elizabeth - *Beyond the Waves*
　　BL - v101 - i6 - Nov 15 2004 - p556(2) [51-500]

Marenbon, John - *Boethuis*
  Choice - v41 - i7 - March 2004 - p1310(1) [501+]
Mares, Isabela - *The Politics of Social Risk: Business and Welfare State Development*
  AJS - v110 - i3 - Nov 2004 - p808(3) [501+]
  BHR - v78 - i3 - Autumn 2004 - p583(3) [501+]
  Choice - v41 - i7 - March 2004 - p1339(1) [501+]
  JEL - v42 - i1 - March 2004 - p277(1) [501+]
Mares, Radu - *Business and Human Rights: A Compilation of Documents*
  R&R Bk N - v19 - i3 - August 2004 - p190(1) [501+]
Marg, Susan - *Las Vegas Weddings: A Brief History, Celebrity Gossip, Everything Elvis and the Complete Chapel Guide*
  PW - v251 - i40 - Oct 4 2004 - p83(1) [51-500]
Margadant, Jo Burr - *The New Biography: Performing Femininity in Nineteenth-Century France*
  HER - v119 - i482 - June 2004 - p815(2) [501+]
Margaritondo, Giorgio - *Elements of Synchrotron Light for Biology, Chemistry, and Medical Research*
  Phys Today - v57 - i3 - March 2004 - p83-83 [501+]
Margereson, Carl - *Cardiothoracic Surgical Nursing*
  E-Streams - July 2004 - pNA [501+]
  SciTech - v28 - i1 - March 2004 - p111(1) [51-500]
Margolf, Diane C. - *Religion and Royal Justice in Early Modern France: The Paris Chambre de l'Edit, 1598-1665*
  Choice - v42 - i1 - Sept 2004 - p180(2) [501+]
Margolies, Luisa - *My Mother's Hip: Lessons from the World of Eldercare*
  Choice - v42 - i4 - Dec 2004 - p695(1) [1-50]
Margolin, Jean-Claude - *Lettres et poemes de Charles de Bovelles*
  FS - v58 - i1 - Jan 2004 - p87(2) [501+]
Margolin, Phillip - *Lost Lake (Read by Hazlett, Deborah). Audiobook Review*
  KR - v73 - i4 - Feb 15 2005 - p193(1) [501+]
  Lost Lake
  PW - v252 - i8 - Feb 21 2005 - p158(1) [51-500]
  Sleeping Beauty (Read by Houston, Suzanne). Audiobook Review
  LJ - v130 - i3 - Feb 15 2004 - p169(1) [51-500]
Margolis, Jonathan - *O: The Intimate History of the Orgasm*
  BL - v101 - i4 - Oct 15 2004 - p369(1) [51-500]
  KR - v72 - i16 - August 15 2004 - p792(1) [501+]
  LJ - v129 - i16 - Oct 1 2004 - p100(2) [51-500]
  PW - v251 - i34 - August 23 2004 - p43(1) [51-500]
Margolis, Joseph - *Moral Philosophy After 9/11*
  Choice - v42 - i6 - Feb 2005 - p1035(1) [51-500]
Margolis, Sue - *Original Cyn*
  KR - v73 - i5 - March 1 2005 - p251(2) [501+]
Margoshes, Dave - *Drowning Man*
  BIC - v33 - i2 - March 2004 - p12(1) [501+]
Marguerat, Daniel - *The First Christian Historian: Writing the Acts of the Apostles*
  Intpr - v58 - i4 - Oct 2004 - p428(1) [501+]
Marguerat, Philippe - *Banques et entreprises en Europe de l'ouest, XIXe-XXe siecles: Aspects nationaux et regionaux*
  JEH - v64 - i1 - March 2004 - p248(2) [501+]
Margulies, Donald - *Brooklyn Boy*
  Ent W - i806 - Feb 11 2005 - p71 [51-500]
  Sight Unseen (Read by Gunn, Anna). Audiobook Review
  LJ - v130 - i1 - Jan 2005 - p168(1) [501+]
Margulies, Paul - *What Julianna Could See (Illus. by Zonneveld, Famke)*
  c CH Bwatch - March 2005 - pNA [51-500]
Margulies, Phillip - *Creutzfeldt-Jakob Disease*
  c SLJ - v50 - i8 - August 2004 - p137(1) [51-500]
  West Nile Virus
  c SLJ - v50 - i8 - August 2004 - p137(1) [51-500]
Margulies, Sam - *A Man's Guide to a Civilized Divorce: How To Divorce with Grace, a Little Class, and a Lot of Common Sense*
  LJ - v129 - i12 - July 2004 - p101(1) [51-500]
  NYTBR - August 22 2004 - p17 [501+]
Mari, Jean-Luc - *Well Seismic Surveying*
  SciTech - v28 - i1 - March 2004 - p171(1) [51-500]
Marias, Javier - *Dark Back of Time*
  LJ - v129 - i13 - August 2004 - p68(2) [51-500]
Mariaux, Pierre Alain - *Warmond d'Ivree et ses images: politique et creation iconographique autour de l'an mil*
  Specu - v79 - i3 - July 2004 - p795-798 [501+]
Marie, Jean - *My First Five Years: Baby Record Book (Illus. by Marie, Jean)*
  PetPho - v33 - i6 - Oct 2004 - p57(1) [51-500]

Marie, Queen of Romania - *Last Chapters of My Life: The Lost Memoir of Queen Marie of Romania*
  Spec - v295 - i9181 - July 24 2004 - p32(1) [501+]
Marien, Mary Warner - *Fleming's Arts & Ideas, 10th Ed., Vol. 1*
  R&R Bk N - v19 - i4 - Nov 2004 - p210(1) [501+]
  Fleming's Arts & Ideas, 10th Ed., Vol. 2
  R&R Bk N - v19 - i4 - Nov 2004 - p210(1) [501+]
Marillier, Juliet - *Foxmask*
  BL - v100 - i21 - July 2004 - p1829(1) [501+]
  BL - v101 - i9-10 - Jan 1 2005 - p771(1) [501+]
  LJ - v129 - i13 - August 2004 - p73(1) [51-500]
  PW - v251 - i28 - July 12 2004 - p48(1) [51-500]
  y VOYA - v27 - i3 - August 2004 - p230(1) [1-50]
  Wolfskin
  y Kliatt - v39 - i1 - Jan 2005 - p20(1) [501+]
Marin, Pamela - *Motherland: A Memoir*
  KR - v73 - i2 - Jan 15 2005 - p105(1) [501+]
  PW - v252 - i8 - Feb 21 2005 - p167(2) [51-500]
Marin, Reva - *Oscar: The Life and Music of Oscar Peterson*
  y CBRA - Annual 2003 - p540(1) [51-500]
  c Res Links - v10 - i1 - Oct 2004 - p39(1) [501+]
Marinescu, Ioan D. - *Tribology of Abrasive Machining Processes*
  SciTech - v28 - i3 - Sept 2004 - p151(1) [51-500]
Marini, Stephen A. - *Sacred Song in America: Religion, Music, and Public Culture*
  JSH - v70 - i4 - Nov 2004 - p977(2) [501+]
Marinick, Richard - *Boyos*
  KR - v72 - i15 - August 1 2004 - p716(1) [51-500]
  LJ - v129 - i14 - Sept 1 2004 - p126(1) [51-500]
  PW - v251 - i35 - August 30 2004 - p36(2) [501+]
Marino, Bradley S. - *Blueprints Pediatrics, 3rd Ed.*
  SciTech - v28 - i1 - March 2004 - p117(1) [51-500]
Marino, Jay - *Quality Across The Curriculum: Integrating Quality Tools and PDSA with Standards, K-5*
  Bwatch - Oct 2004 - pNA [51-500]
  R&R Bk N - v19 - i3 - August 2004 - p218(1) [1-50]
Marino, John A. - *Early Modern History and the Social Sciences: Testing the Limits of Braudel's Mediterranean*
  Six Ct J - v34 - i4 - Winter 2003 - p1235-1236 [501+]
Marinova, Svetla Trifonova - *Foreign Direct Investment in Central and Eastern Europe*
  JEL - v42 - i1 - March 2004 - p326(1) [501+]
Mario, Mouzinho - *Higher Education in Mozambique: A Case Study*
  TimHES - v0 - i1676 - Jan 28 2005 - p26(1) [501+]
Marion, Forrest L. - *Fixing Intelligence: For a More Secure America*
  APJ - v18 - i4 - Winter 2004 - p123(2) [501+]
Marion, Jim - *The Death of the Mythic God: The Rise of Evolutionary Spirituality*
  LJ - v129 - i12 - July 2004 - p89(1) [51-500]
Mariotte, Jeff - *Fall*
  y SLJ - v51 - i2 - Feb 2005 - p138(2) [51-500]
  Winter
  y Kliatt - v39 - i1 - Jan 2005 - p20(1) [51-500]
  Witch Season: Fall
  Kliatt - v38 - i6 - Nov 2004 - p22(1) [51-500]
  Witch Season: Summer
  y Kliatt - v38 - i4 - July 2004 - p31(1) [51-500]
  PW - v251 - i32 - August 9 2004 - p252(1) [51-500]
Mariposas Bonaerenses
  QRB - v79 - i3 - Sept 2004 - p315(2) [501+]
Mariposas de Misiones
  QRB - v79 - i3 - Sept 2004 - p315(2) [501+]
Mariss, R. - *Alkidamas: Uber Diejenigen, die schriftliche Reden sichern, oder Uber die Sophisten. Eine Sophistenrede aus dem 4. Jahrhundert v. Chr. eingeleitet und kommentiert*
  Class R - v54 - i2 - Nov 2004 - p331-333 [501+]
Maristed, Kai - *Broken Ground (Read by Ward, Johanna). Audiobook Review*
  c Kliatt - v38 - i4 - July 2004 - p49(1) [51-500]
Marix Evans, Martin - *Invasion!: Operation Sealion, 1940*
  R&R Bk N - v20 - i1 - Feb 2005 - p33(1) [51-500]
Marjit, Sugata - *International Trade, Wage Inequality and the Developing Economy: A General Equilibrium Approach*
  JEL - v42 - i1 - March 2004 - p309(2) [501+]
Mark, Colin B.D. - *The Gaelic-English Dictionary*
  TLS - i5263 - Feb 13 2004 - p28-28 [501+]

Mark, Jan - *A Jetblack Sunrise: Poems about War and Conflict*
  c Globe & Mail - Nov 20 2004 - pD26 [51-500]
  Useful Idiots
  y BL - v101 - i1 - Sept 1 2004 - p107(1) [501+]
  y BW - v34 - i43 - Oct 24 2004 - p11(1) [51-500]
  y CCB-B - v58 - i2 - Oct 2004 - p89(1) [51-500]
  y KR - v72 - i14 - July 15 2004 - p690(1) [51-500]
  y PW - v251 - i38 - Sept 20 2004 - p64(1) [51-500]
  y Sch Lib - v52 - i3 - Autumn 2004 - p165(1) [501+]
  y SLJ - v50 - i11 - Nov 2004 - p150(1) [51-500]
  y VOYA - v27 - i5 - Dec 2004 - p408(1) [51-500]
Mark, Peter - *"Portuguese" Style and Luso-African Identity: Precolonial Senegambia, Sixteenth-Nineteenth Centuries*
  AHR - v109 - i3 - June 2004 - p1019(2) [501+]
  JIH - v35 - i1 - Summer 2004 - p173-174 [501+]
Mark, Powell, J. - *The Curse of Cain*
  KR - v73 - i3 - Feb 1 2005 - p145(1) [501+]
Markale, Jean - *Cathedral of the Black Madonna: The Druids and the Mysteries of Chartres*
  Bwatch - Feb 2005 - pNA [51-500]
  PW - v251 - i48 - Nov 29 2004 - p38(1) [51-500]
  The Church of Mary Magdalene: The Sacred Feminine and the Treasure of Rennes-le-Chateau
  LJ - v129 - i16 - Oct 1 2004 - p88(1) [51-500]
Markandaya, Kamala - *A Handful of Rice*
  Globe & Mail - Dec 24 2004 - pD15 [51-500]
  Nectar in a Sieve
  Globe & Mail - Dec 24 2004 - pD15 [51-500]
Markantonatos, A. - *Tragic Narrative: A Narratological Study of Sophocles' Oedipus at Colonus*
  Class R - v54 - i1 - May 2004 - p32(3) [501+]
Markaris, Petros - *Deadline in Athens*
  BL - v100 - i22 - August 2004 - p1906(1) [51-500]
  BW - v34 - i36 - Sept 5 2004 - p10(1) [501+]
  DroRevMy - v24 - i4 - July-August 2004 - p5(2) [501+]
  KR - v72 - i14 - July 15 2004 - p663(1) [51-500]
  LJ - v129 - i14 - Sept 1 2004 - p121(1) [51-500]
Markel, Howard - *When Germs Travel: Six Major Epidemics That Have Invaded America Since 1900 and the Fears They Have Unleashed*
  Wil Q - v28 - i4 - Autumn 2004 - p116(1) [501+]
Markel, Scott - *Sequence Analysis in a Nutshell: A Guide to Tools and Databases*
  SciTech - v28 - i1 - March 2004 - p63(1) [51-500]
Markell, David L. - *Greening NAFTA: The North American Commission for Environmental Cooperation*
  HNet - June 2004 - pNA [501+]
Markell, Denis - *The Great Stroller Adventure (Illus. by Iwai, Melissa)*
  c PW - v251 - i41 - Oct 11 2004 - p82(1) [501+]
  c SLJ - v50 - i10 - Oct 2004 - p123(1) [51-500]
Markels, Julian - *The Marxian Imagination: Representing Class in Literature*
  R&R Bk N - v19 - i1 - Feb 2004 - p235(1) [51-500]
Markert, James - *Glioblastomas Multiforme*
  SciTech - v28 - i4 - Dec 2004 - p93(1) [51-500]
Markes, Julie - *Shhhhh! Everybody's Sleeping (Illus. by Parkins, David)*
  c BL - v101 - i8 - Dec 15 2004 - p738(1) [51-500]
  c KR - v72 - i24 - Dec 15 2004 - p1205(1) [51-500]
  c PW - v252 - i5 - Jan 31 2005 - p66(1) [50-51]
  Thanks for Thanksgiving (Illus. by Barrette, Doris)
  c KR - v72 - i15 - August 1 2004 - p745(1) [51-500]
  c PW - v251 - i39 - Sept 27 2004 - p59(1) [51-500]
Markesinis, Basil - *Comparative Law in the Courtroom and Classroom: The Story of the Last Thirty-Five Years*
  Law Q Rev - v120 - Jan 2004 - p175-179 [501+]
Market and Business Development Ltd. - *The UK Kitchen Furniture Market Development*
  R&R Bk N - v19 - i3 - August 2004 - p120(1) [51-500]
  The UK Residential Window and Door Market Development
  R&R Bk N - v19 - i3 - August 2004 - p120(1) [51-500]
Market and Business Development, Ltd. - *UK Timber and Joinery Market*
  R&R Bk N - v19 - i3 - August 2004 - p120(1) [51-500]
Market & Business Development Ltd. - *UK Timber Distribution*
  R&R Bk N - v19 - i2 - May 2004 - p108(1) [51-500]
Markey, Judy - *Just Trust Me*
  BL - v100 - i22 - August 2004 - p1900(1) [501+]
  PW - v251 - i35 - August 30 2004 - p33(1) [501+]
Markham, Wendy - *Mike, Mike, and Me*
  BL - v101 - i6 - Nov 15 2004 - p567(2) [51-500]

Markle, Donald E. - *Spies and Spymasters of the Civil War, Rev. Ed.*
R&R Bk N - v19 - i3 - August 2004 - p69(1) [51-500]

Markle, Sandra - *Animal Predators*
c CH Bwatch - v14 - i11 - Nov 2004 - pNA [51-500]
Crocodiles
c BL - v101 - i2 - Sept 15 2004 - p239(1) [51-500]
c SB - v40 - i6 - Nov-Dec 2004 - p271(1) [51-500]
c SLJ - v50 - i10 - Oct 2004 - p192(1) [51-500]
Great White Sharks
c SB - v40 - i6 - Nov-Dec 2004 - p271(1) [51-500]
c SLJ - v50 - i12 - Dec 2004 - p163(2) [51-500]
Killer Whales
c BL - v101 - i7 - Dec 1 2004 - p666(1) [51-500]
c SLJ - v51 - i1 - Jan 2005 - p152(1) [51-500]
Lions
c BL - v101 - i2 - Sept 15 2004 - p239(1) [51-500]
c SLJ - v50 - i10 - Oct 2004 - p192(1) [51-500]
Math Mini-Mysteries
c SLJ - v50 - i9 - Sept 2004 - p59(1) [51-500]
Outside and Inside: Giant Squid
LibMed - v22 - i5 - Feb 2004 - p59(1) [501+]
Outside and Inside Killer Bees
c BL - v101 - i7 - Dec 1 2004 - p668(1) [51-500]
y HB - v81 - i1 - Jan-Feb 2005 - p112(1) [51-500]
KR - v72 - i20 - Oct 15 2004 - p1009(1) [51-500]
c SLJ - v51 - i1 - Jan 2005 - p152(1) [51-500]
Owls
c SLJ - v50 - i12 - Dec 2004 - p163(2) [51-500]
Polar Bears
c SLJ - v51 - i1 - Jan 2005 - p152(1) [51-500]
Snakes (Illus. by McDonald, Joe)
c KR - v73 - i5 - March 1 2005 - p291(1) [51-500]
Spiders: Biggest! Littlest! (Illus. by Pollard, Simon)
c SLJ - v50 - i12 - Dec 2004 - p134(1) [501+]
Spiders
c KR - v72 - i20 - Oct 15 2004 - p1009(1) [51-500]
Wolves
c SB - v40 - i6 - Nov-Dec 2004 - p271(1) [51-500]
c SLJ - v50 - i10 - Oct 2004 - p192(1) [51-500]

Markley, Nelson G. - *Principles of Differential Equations*
SciTech - v28 - i3 - Sept 2004 - p39(1) [51-500]

Markoe, Glenn - *Petra Rediscovered: Lost City of the Nabateans*
R&R Bk N - v19 - i1 - Feb 2004 - p45(1) [51-500]

Markoe, Merrill - *The Psycho Ex Game*
BL - v100 - i21 - July 2004 - p1818(1) [1-50]
People - v62 - i2 - July 12 2004 - p48 [51-500]

Markoff, John - *What the Dormouse Said...How the 60s Counterculture Shaped the Personal Computer Industry*
KR - v73 - i5 - March 1 2005 - p277(1) [501+]

Markopoulos, Athanasios - *History and Literature of Byzantium in the 9th-10th Centuries*
R&R Bk N - v19 - i4 - Nov 2004 - p40(1) [51-500]

Markova, Ivana - *Dialogicality and Social Representations: The Dynamics of Mind*
Choice - v42 - i1 - Sept 2004 - p192(1) [501+]

Markovits, Benjamin - *The Syme Papers*
TLS - i5264 - Feb 20 2004 - p22-22 [501+]

Markovitz, Jonathan - *Legacies of Lynching: Racial Violence and Memory*
HNet - Oct 2004 - pNA [501+]
R&R Bk N - v19 - i4 - Nov 2004 - p145(1) [501+]

Markowitz, Gerald - *Deceit and Denial: The Deadly Politics of Industrial Pollution*
AHR - v109 - i2 - April 2004 - p567(2) [501+]
Pub Hist - v26 - i2 - Spring 2004 - p113(115) [501+]
T&C - v45 - i1 - Jan 2004 - p219(3) [501+]

Marks, David - *Research Methods for Clinical and Health Psychology*
SciTech - v28 - i1 - March 2004 - p97(1) [51-500]
TimHES - v0 - i1668 - Nov 26 2004 - pXVIII(2) [501+]

Marks, Diona - *Glues, Brews and Goos: Recipes and Formulas for Almost Any Classroom Project*
y LibMed - v22 - i4 - Jan 2004 - p85(1) [501+]

Marks, Gary - *European Integration and Political Conflict*
Choice - v42 - i5 - Jan 2005 - p927(1) [1-50]
CR - v285 - i1663 - August 2004 - p125(1) [501+]

Marks, Graham - *How It Works: Everyone Gets the Angel They Deserve*
y BL - v101 - i3 - Oct 1 2004 - p340(1) [51-500]
y SLJ - v50 - i12 - Dec 2004 - p150(2) [51-500]
Radio Radio
y BL - v101 - i9-10 - Jan 1 2005 - p846(1) [1-50]
SLJ - v51 - i1 - Jan 2005 - p133(1) [51-500]

Marks, Laurie J. - *Earth Logic*
MFSF - v107 - i4-5 - Oct-Nov 2004 - p31(4) [501+]

Fire Logic
MFSF - v107 - i4-5 - Oct-Nov 2004 - p31(4) [501+]

Marks, Michael P. - *The Prison as Metaphor: Re-Imagining International Relations*
R&R Bk N - v19 - i1 - Feb 2004 - pNA [501+]

Marks, Richard - *Gothic: Art for England, 1400-1547*
Med R - Dec 2004 - pNA [501+]

Marks, Richard - *Image and Devotion in Late Medieval England*
HT - v54 - i7 - July 2004 - p57(2) [501+]

Marks, Robert B. - *The Origins of the Modern World: A Global and Ecological Narrative*
Pac A - v77 - i2 - Summer 2004 - p306(3) [501+]

Marks, Steven G. - *How Russia Shaped the Modern World: From Art to Anti-Semitism, Ballet to Bolshevism*
Slav R - v63 - i2 - Summer 2004 - p400(2) [501+]
South CR - v36 - i2 - Spring 2004 - p182-184 [501+]

Marks, Susan - *Finding Betty Crocker: The Secret Life of America's First Lady of Food*
KR - v73 - i2 - Jan 15 2005 - p105(1) [501+]
LJ - v130 - i2 - Feb 1 2005 - p111(1) [51-500]
PW - v252 - i7 - Feb 14 2005 - p60(2) [51-500]

Markson, David - *The Vanishing Point*
ABR - v26 - i1 - Nov-Dec 2004 - p25(2) [501+]
BW - v34 - i12 - March 21 2004 - p6(1) [501+]

Markusen, Bruce - *Ted Williams, a Biography*
R&R Bk N - v19 - i4 - Nov 2004 - p81(1) [51-500]

Markusen, James R. - *Multinational Firms and the Theory of International Trade*
JEL - v42 - i1 - March 2004 - p181(2) [501+]

Marland, Ken - *High Frequency Words: Strategies That Build Skills in Spelling, Vocabulary, and Word Play*
CBRA - Annual 2003 - p395(1) [51-500]
CBRA - Annual 2003 - p395(1) [51-500]

Marlatt, Daphne - *Salvage*
Can Lit - i182 - Autumn 2004 - p107(2) [501+]

Marler, Regina - *Queer Beats: How the Beats Turned America on to Sex*
G&L Rev W - v12 - i1 - Jan-Feb 2005 - p43(1) [501+]
R&R Bk N - v19 - i4 - Nov 2004 - p241(1) [501+]

Marley, James A. - *Family Involvement in Treating Schizophrenia; Models, Essential Skills, and Process*
SciTech - v28 - i1 - March 2004 - p100(1) [51-500]

Marley, Louise - *The Child Goddess*
y VOYA - v27 - i4 - Oct 2004 - p316(1) [51-500]

Marley, Rita - *No Woman No Cry*
Bwatch - v26 - i8 - August 2004 - p3(1) [51-500]

Marlin-Bennett, Renee - *Knowledge Power: Intellectual Property, Information, and Privacy*
Choice - v42 - i6 - Feb 2005 - p1090(1) [51-500]
Law&PolBR - Nov 2004 - p874(4) [501+]

Marlin, John - *Mickey Mantle*
c BL - v101 - i1 - Sept 1 2004 - p111(1) [501+]
c SLJ - v50 - i11 - Nov 2004 - p168(1) [51-500]

Marlow, Christine - *Research Methods for Generalist Social Work, 4th Ed.*
R&R Bk N - v19 - i3 - August 2004 - p158(1) [51-500]

Marlowe, Cecile - *Sunsets Romantico and Other Scenery*
Bwatch - v26 - i8 - August 2004 - p11(1) [51-500]

Marlowe, Gertrude Woodruff - *A Right Worthy Grand Mission: Maggie Lena Walker and the Quest for Black Economic Empowerment*
Black Iss - v6 - i4 - July-August 2004 - p51(1) [501+]
R&R Bk N - v19 - i1 - Feb 2004 - p63(1) [501+]

Marlowe, Joelyn D. - *Evidence for Paralegals, 3rd Ed.*
R&R Bk N - v19 - i1 - Feb 2004 - pNA [51-500]

Marmarelis, Vasilis Z. - *Nonlinear Dynamic Modeling of Physiological Systems*
SciTech - v28 - i4 - Dec 2004 - p79(1) [51-500]

Marmot, Michael - *The Status Syndrome: How Social Standing Affects Our Health and Longevity*
BW - v34 - i31 - August 1 2004 - p3(1) [501+]
LJ - v129 - i12 - July 2004 - p109(1) [51-500]
NYTBR - August 22 2004 - p16 [501+]
Status Syndrome: How Your Social Standing Directly Affects Your Health and Life Expectancy
TimHES - v0 - i1684 - March 25 2005 - p26(2) [501+]

Maron, Margaret - *High Country Fall*
DroRevMy - v24 - i4 - July-August 2004 - p6(2) [501+]
LJ - v129 - i12 - July 2004 - p64(1) [51-500]
NYTBR - August 22 2004 - p15 [501+]

Maron, Monika - *Geburtsort Berlin*
WLT - v79 - i1 - Jan-April 2005 - p99(1) [501+]

Maronites, D.N. - *Homeric Megathemes: War-Homilia-Homecoming*
R&R Bk N - v19 - i4 - Nov 2004 - p214(1) [501+]

Maroukis, Thomas Constantine - *Peyote and the Yankton Sioux: The Life and Times of Sam Necklace*
Roundup M - v12 - i3 - Feb 2005 - p19(1) [51-500]

Marowitz, Charles - *The Other Chekhov*
Am Theat - v21 - i8 - Oct 2004 - p139(4) [51-500]

Marozzi, Justin - *Tamerlane: Sword of Islam, Conqueror of the World*
CR - v286 - i1668 - Jan 2005 - p61(1) [51-500]
Econ - v372 - i8390 - August 28 2004 - p75US [501+]
Spec - v295 - i9185 - August 21 2004 - p29(2) [501+]

Marple, Basil R. - *Thermal Spray 2003: Advancing the Science and Applying the Technology: Proceedings, Vols. 1-2*
SciTech - v28 - i4 - Dec 2004 - p169(1) [51-500]

Marple, Jorea M. - *An Insider's Guide to Making School Systems Work*
TCR - v106 - i5 - May 2004 - p876(4) [501+]

Marples, David R. - *The Collapse of the Soviet Union: 1985-1991*
CR - v285 - i1666 - Nov 2004 - p318(2) [501+]
R&R Bk N - v19 - i3 - August 2004 - p45(1) [51-500]

Marquand, David - *Decline of the Public: The Hollowing Out of Citizenship*
TimHES - v0 - i1659 - Sept 24 2004 - p31(1) [501+]

Marquardt, Karl Heinz - *The Global Schooner: Origins, Development, Design and Construction, 1695-1845*
SciTech - v28 - i1 - March 2004 - p180(1) [51-500]

Marquez, Benjamin - *Constructing Identities in Mexican American Political Organizations*
CS - v33 - i6 - Nov 2004 - p710(2) [501+]

The Marquis de Sade: A Life
Eight-C St - v37 - i3 - Spring 2004 - p469-474 [501+]

Marquis, Fernand D.S. - *Powder Materials: Current Research and Industrial Practices III, Proceedings*
SciTech - v28 - i1 - March 2004 - p170(1) [51-500]

Marquit, Amanda - *Shut the Door*
KR - v72 - i19 - Oct 1 2004 - p933(2) [501+]
PW - v251 - i51 - Dec 20 2004 - p37(1) [51-500]

Marqusee, Mark - *Chimes of Freedom: The Politics of Bob Dylan's Art*
RAH - v32 - i2 - June 2004 - p274-281 [501+]

Marr, Andrew - *My Trade: A Short History of British Journalism*
NS - v133 - i4707 - Sept 27 2004 - p77(2) [501+]
Spec - v296 - i9189 - Sept 18 2004 - p47(2) [501+]

Marr, Phebe - *The Modern History of Iraq, 2nd Ed.*
R&R Bk N - v19 - i1 - Feb 2004 - p42(1) [51-500]

Marra, Kim - *Staging Desire: Queer Readings of American Theater History*
Lam Bk Rpt - v13 - i3 - Oct 2004 - p17(3) [501+]
TDR - v48 - i4 - Winter 2004 - p192(11) [501+]

Marrese, Michelle Lamarche - *A Woman's Kingdom: Noblewomen and the Control of Property in Russia, 1700-1861*
J Soc H - v38 - i2 - Winter 2004 - p553(3) [501+]

Marrett, George J. - *Howard Hughes: Aviator*
BL - v101 - i4 - Oct 15 2004 - p371(1) [51-500]
Choice - v42 - i7 - March 2005 - p1247(2) [51-500]

Marrin, Albert - *Old Hickory: Andrew Jackson and the American People*
y BL - v101 - i7 - Dec 1 2004 - p645(1) [51-500]
y CCB-B - v58 - i5 - Jan 2005 - p214(2) [51-500]
y HB - v80 - i6 - Nov-Dec 2004 - p730(1) [501+]
y KR - v72 - i22 - Nov 15 2004 - p1091(1) [51-500]
y SLJ - v50 - i12 - Dec 2004 - p164(1) [51-500]

Marritt, A. - *The Moon Pool*
Choice - v42 - i4 - Dec 2004 - p661(1) [1-50]

Marrouchi, Mustapha - *Edward Said at the Limits*
Choice - v42 - i1 - Sept 2004 - p96(1) [501+]

Marry, Martin - *Martin Luther (Read by Michael, Paul). Audiobook Review*
y Kliatt - v39 - i1 - Jan 2005 - p53(1) [51-500]

Mars-Proietti, Laura - *The Complete Directory for Pediatric Disorders 2005, 3rd Ed*
SciTech - v28 - i4 - Dec 2004 - p113(1) [1-50]
The Complete Mental Health Directory: Comprehensive Source Book for Individuals and Professionals. 4th Ed.
LJ - v129 - i17 - Oct 15 2004 - p86(1) [51-500]
Directory of Health Care Group Purchasing Organizations 2004
SciTech - v28 - i4 - Dec 2004 - p86(1) [51-500]

Marsalis, Wynton - *To Young Jazz Musician: Letters from the Road*
PW - v251 - i41 - Oct 11 2004 - p69(2) [51-500]

Marscher, Bill - *The Great Sea Island Storm of 1893*
R&R Bk N - v19 - i4 - Nov 2004 - p245(1) [501+]

Marschler, Thomas - *Auferstehung und Himmelfahrt Christi in der Scholastichen Theologie bis zu Thomas von Aquin*
Theol St - v66 - i1 - March 2005 - p189(3) [501+]

Marsden, Ben - *Watt's Perfect Engine: Steam and the Age of Invention*
Choice - v41 - i11-12 - July-August 2004 - p2065(2) [501+]

Marsden, Carolyn - *Moon Runner*
c KR - v73 - i5 - March 1 2005 - p291(1) [51-500]
Silk Umbrellas
c BooChiTr - April 18 2004 - p3(1) [501+]
c SLJ - v50 - i10 - Oct 2004 - pS37(1) [1-50]

Marsden, George M. - *Jonathan Edwards: A Life*
NYTBR - Nov 7 2004 - p30 [501+]
TT - v60 - i4 - Jan 2004 - p588-590 [501+]

Marsden, John - *Roomful of Magic (Illus. by Jackson, Mark)*
y Magpies - v19 - i5 - Nov 2004 - p36(1) [501+]
So Much to Tell You
y Sch Lib - v52 - i4 - Winter 2004 - p211(1) [51-500]
Tomorrow, When the War Began
c SLJ - v50 - i8 - August 2004 - p78(1) [51-500]
Winter (Read by Hosking, Kate). Audiobook Review
y Kliatt - v38 - i5 - Sept 2004 - p66(2) [51-500]

Marsden, Richard - *The Cambridge Old English Reader*
Choice - v42 - i4 - Dec 2004 - p661(1) [1-50]
Med R - Dec 2004 - pNA [51-500]

Marsh, Charles - *The Beloved Community: How Faith Shapes Social Justice, from the Civil Rights Movement to Today*
BL - v101 - i8 - Dec 15 2004 - p694(1) [51-500]
BW - v35 - i4 - Jan 30 2005 - p4(1) [501+]
KR - v72 - i23 - Dec 1 2004 - p1135(2) [501+]
NL - v87 - i6 - Nov-Dec 2004 - p23(3) [501+]
PW - v251 - i50 - Dec 13 2004 - p63(2) [51-500]

Marsh, Christopher - *U.S.-China Relations in the Twenty-First Century: Policies, Prospects, and Possibilities*
R&R Bk N - v19 - i1 - Feb 2004 - p56(1) [51-500]

Marsh, Helen - *Land Deed Genealogy of Bedford County, Tennessee, 1807-1852, Vol. 1*
EFHM - v58 - i3 - May-June 2004 - p61(1) [1-50]

Marshak, Stephen - *Essentials of Geology*
SciTech - v28 - i1 - March 2004 - p58(1) [51-500]

Marshall, Alan - *Oliver Cromwell: Soldier: The Military Life of a Revolutionary at War*
HT - v55 - i1 - Jan 2005 - p57(1) [501+]

Marshall, Carmen Rose - *Black Professional Women in Recent American Fiction*
R&R Bk N - v19 - i1 - Feb 2004 - p242(1) [501+]

Marshall Cavendish Corporation - *Explorers and Exploration, Vols. 1-11*
c SLJ - v51 - i2 - Feb 2005 - p82(2) [51-500]

Marshall Cavendish Wildlife Reference Center
LibMed - v22 - i7 - April-May 2004 - p92(1) [501+]

Marshall, David - *Wild About Flying!: Dreamers, Doers, and Dare-Devils*
SciTech - v28 - i1 - March 2004 - p168(1) [51-500]

Marshall, Diana - *Aboriginal Australians*
c SLJ - v50 - i7 - July 2004 - p94(1) [51-500]

Marshall, Evan - *Crushing Crystal: A Jane Stuart and Winky Mystery*
PW - v251 - i43 - Oct 25 2004 - p32(1) [51-500]

Marshall, Gerald F. - *Handbook of Optical and Laser Scanning*
SciTech - v28 - i4 - Dec 2004 - p159(1) [51-500]

Marshall, Hazel - *Troublesome Angels and Flying Machines*
c Sch Lib - v52 - i4 - Winter 2004 - p203(1) [51-500]

Marshall, I. Howard - *Beyond the Bible*
Intpr - v58 - i3 - July 2004 - p276(1) [51-500]

Marshall, James - *Let's Not Let a Little Thing Like the End of the World Come Between Us*
Globe & Mail - Dec 18 2004 - pD20 [501+]

Marshall, Jim - *Proof*
Bwatch - March 2005 - pNA [51-500]

Marshall, John Douglas - *Place of Learning, Place of Dreams: A History of the Seattle Public Library*
LJ - v129 - i14 - Sept 1 2004 - p195(1) [51-500]

Marshall, Joseph M. - *The Journey of Crazy Horse: A Lakota History*
BL - v101 - i4 - Oct 15 2004 - p384(1) [51-500]
KR - v72 - i16 - August 15 2004 - p793(1) [501+]
PW - v251 - i37 - Sept 13 2004 - p68(1) [51-500]

Marshall, Katherine - *Mind, Heart, and Soul in the Fight Against Poverty*
R&R Bk N - v19 - i4 - Nov 2004 - p124(1) [51-500]

Marshall, Kerry James - *One True Thing: Meditations on Black Aesthetics*
Black Iss - v6 - i5 - Sept-Oct 2004 - p33(1) [501+]

Marshall, Leslie - *A Girl Could Stand Up*
Kliatt - v38 - i5 - Sept 2004 - p23(2) [501+]

Marshall, Megan - *The Peabody Sisters: Three Women Who Ignited American Romanticism*
KR - v73 - i4 - Feb 15 2005 - p214(1) [501+]
LJ - v129 - i20 - Dec 1 2004 - p92(1) [51-500]
PW - v252 - i9 - Feb 28 2005 - p55(1) [51-500]

Marshall, Oliver - *Brazil in British and Irish Archives*
HAHR - v84 - i2 - May 2004 - p329(2) [501+]

Marshall, Pam - *From Idea to Book (Illus. by Strand, Todd)*
c SLJ - v50 - i9 - Sept 2004 - p190(1) [51-500]

Marshall, Paul Victor - *One, Catholic, and Apostolic: Samuel Seabury and the Early Episcopal Church.*
Choice - v42 - i7 - March 2005 - p1243(1) [51-500]

Marshall, Perry S. - *Industrial Ethernet: How to Plan, Install, and Maintain TCP/IP Ethernet Networks: The Basic Reference Guide for Automation and Process Control Engineers, 2nd Ed.*
SciTech - v28 - i3 - Sept 2004 - p157(1) [51-500]
Industrial Ethernet: How to Plan, Install, and Maintain TCP/IP Ethernet Networks: The Basic Reference Guide for Automation and Process Control Engineers, 2nd. Ed.
SciTech - v28 - i4 - Dec 2004 - p152(1) [51-500]

Marshall, Peter - *Beliefs and the Dead in Reformation England*
CH - v73 - i4 - Dec 2004 - p859(3) [501+]
Six Ct J - v34 - i4 - Winter 2003 - p1215-1217 [501+]
Reformation England, 1480-1642
Choice - v42 - i1 - Sept 2004 - p179(1) [501+]

Marshall, Rita - *The Illustrated Treasury of Fairy Tales*
c CH Bwatch - v14 - i7 - July 2004 - p1(1) [51-500]
The Illustrated Treasury of Fairy Tales (Illus. by Marshall, Rita)
c CH Bwatch - v14 - i7 - July 2004 - p1(1) [51-500]

Marshall, Shane A. - *On Call: Principles and Protocols, 4th Ed.*
SciTech - v28 - i4 - Dec 2004 - p90(1) [51-500]

Marshall-Slack, Doris L. - *Perseverance Lane: A Teacher's Story*
Bwatch - Oct 2004 - pNA [51-500]

Marshall, Steward - *Using Community Informatics to Transform Regions*
R&R Bk N - v19 - i1 - Feb 2004 - p126(1) [51-500]

Marshall, Suzanne - *"Lord, We're Just Trying to Save Your Water": Environmental Activism and Dissent in the Appalachian South*
JAH - v91 - i1 - June 2004 - p340-342 [501+]
JSH - v70 - i3 - August 2004 - p726(3) [501+]

Marshall, Wendy L. - *William Beaudine: From Silences to Televison*
Choice - v42 - i7 - March 2005 - p1235(1) [51-500]

Marsiglio, William - *Stepdads: Stories of Love, Hope, and Repair*
Choice - v42 - i4 - Dec 2004 - p742(1) [1-50]
R&R Bk N - v19 - i3 - August 2004 - p150(1) [51-500]

Marson, Bonnie - *Sleeping with Schubert (Read by Snell, Staci). Audiobook Review*
y Kliatt - v39 - i1 - Jan 2005 - p50(1) [51-500]
Sleeping with Schubert
BW - v34 - i27 - July 4 2004 - p8(1) [501+]
ON - v69 - i4 - Oct 2004 - p84(1) [501+]

Marston, Daniel P. - *Phoenix from the Ashes: The Indian Army in the Burma Campaign*
J Mil H - v68 - i3 - April 2004 - p632-633 [501+]
R&R Bk N - v19 - i1 - Feb 2004 - p29(1) [51-500]

Marston, Edward - *The Counterfeit Crank*
BL - v100 - i21 - July 2004 - p1824(2) [1-50]
DroRevMy - v24 - i3 - May-June 2004 - p5(2) [501+]
LJ - v129 - i13 - August 2004 - p60(1) [501+]
PW - v251 - i29 - July 19 2004 - p148(1) [51-500]

Marston, Elsa - *Figs and Fate: Stories about Growing Up in the Arab World Today*
KR - v73 - i1 - Jan 1 2005 - p13(1) [51-500]
LJ - v130 - i3 - Feb 15 2005 - p123(2) [51-500]
Muhammad of Mecca: Prophet of Islam
y SLJ - v51 - i1 - Jan 2005 - p57(1) [51-500]

Marston, Gwen - *Mary Schafer, American Quilt Maker*
Choice - v42 - i5 - Jan 2005 - p842(1) [1-50]
LJ - v129 - i12 - July 2004 - p79(1) [51-500]

Marston, John - *History, Buddhism, and New Religious Movements in Cambodia*
R&R Bk N - v19 - i4 - Nov 2004 - p18(1) [51-500]

Marszalek, John F. - *Commander of All Lincoln's Armies: A Life of General Henry W. Halleck*
LJ - v129 - i16 - Oct 1 2004 - p91(1) [51-500]

Martchenko, Michael - *Ma I'm a Farmer*
c CBRA - Annual 2003 - p458(1) [51-500]

Martel, Gordon - *The Origins of the First World War*
CR - v285 - i1662 - July 2004 - p61(1) [51-500]

Martel, Yann - *The Facts Behind the Helsinki Roccamatios*
BL - v101 - i5 - Nov 1 2004 - p465(1) [51-500]
BL - v101 - i9-10 - Jan 1 2005 - p769(2) [1-50]
BW - v34 - i50 - Dec 12 2004 - p5(1) [501+]
Ent W - i795 - Dec 3 2004 - p92 [51-500]
Globe & Mail - Nov 20 2004 - pD29 [1-50]
KR - v72 - i20 - Oct 15 2004 - p979(1) [51-500]
LJ - v129 - i14 - Sept 1 2004 - p44(1) [51-500]
LJ - v129 - i18 - Nov 1 2004 - p79(1) [51-500]
NYTBR - Dec 5 2004 - p63 [501+]
People - v62 - i25 - Dec 20 2004 - p58 [51-500]
PW - v251 - i44 - Nov 1 2004 - p41(2) [501+]
Spec - v296 - i9192 - Oct 9 2004 - p48(2) [501+]
TLS - i5301 - Nov 5 2004 - p25(1) [501+]
Life of Pi
Globe & Mail - Dec 24 2004 - pD3 [1-50]

Martell, Christopher R. - *Cognitive-Behavioral Therapies with Lesbian, Gay, and Bisexual Clients*
Choice - v41 - i11-12 - July-August 2004 - p2127(1) [51-500]

Marten, James Alan - *Children for the Union: The War Spirit on the Northern Home Front*
BooChiTr - May 16 2004 - p3(1) [501+]
Bwatch - Dec 2004 - pNA [51-500]
Choice - v42 - i3 - Nov 2004 - p549(1) [1-50]
R&R Bk N - v19 - i3 - August 2004 - p68(1) [51-500]

Martens, Bertin - *The Institutional Economics of Foreign Aid*
IndRev - v9 - i2 - Fall 2004 - p299(4) [501+]

Martens, Claus-Peter - *German Environmental Law for Practitioners, 2nd Ed.*
R&R Bk N - v19 - i4 - Nov 2004 - p175(1) [501+]

Martens, Helen - *Hutterite Songs*
Notes - v61 - i2 - Dec 2004 - p462(3) [501+]

Martens, Koen - *Aquatic Biodiversity: A Celebratory Volume in Honour of Henri J. Dumont*
SciTech - v28 - i1 - March 2004 - p60(1) [51-500]

Martens, Oscar - *Girl with the Full Figure Is Your Daughter*
CBRA - Annual 2003 - p202(1) [501+]

Marthouret, Alin - *Art Fraud: Memoirs of a Master Forger*
KR - v72 - i13 - July 1 2004 - p620(1) [501+]

Marti, Susan - *Malen, Schreiben und Beten: Die spatmittelalterliche Handschriftenproduktion im Doppelkloster Engelberg*
Med R - Oct 2004 - pNA [501+]

Martignacco, Carole - *The Everything Seed*
c CH Bwatch - v14 - i12 - Dec 2004 - pNA [51-500]

Martin, Alex - *Knights and Castles: Exploring History through Art*
c BL - v101 - i5 - Nov 1 2004 - p495(2) [51-500]
c SLJ - v51 - i2 - Feb 2005 - p146(1) [51-500]

Martin, Andrew - *The Blackpool Highflyer*
Globe & Mail - August 21 2004 - pD12 [501+]
NS - v133 - i4704 - Sept 6 2004 - p55(1) [501+]
NS - v133 - i4716 - Nov 29 2004 - p42(1) [51-500]
Vampires Don't Believe in Flanagans
y VOYA - v27 - i3 - August 2004 - p180(1) [1-50]

Martin, Ann M. - *Here Today (Read by Kaye, Judy). Audiobook Review*
y Kliatt - v39 - i1 - Jan 2005 - p44(1) [51-500]
c SLJ - v51 - i2 - Feb 2005 - p74(1) [501+]
Here Today
c BIC - v33 - i7 - Oct 2004 - p39(2) [501+]
c BL - v100 - i22 - August 2004 - p1924(2) [501+]
c CCB-B - v58 - i5 - Jan 2005 - p215(1) [51-500]
c CH Bwatch - Oct 2004 - pNA [51-500]
c HB - v80 - i6 - Nov-Dec 2004 - p712(1) [501+]
c KR - v72 - i20 - Oct 15 2004 - p1010(1) [51-500]
c PW - v251 - i40 - Oct 4 2004 - p88(1) [51-500]
c SLJ - v50 - i10 - Oct 2004 - p172(1) [51-500]
y BL - v101 - i9-10 - Jan 1 2005 - p774(1) [1-50]
y VOYA - v27 - i5 - Dec 2004 - p385(1) [51-500]

Martin, Bill, Jr. - *Chicka Chicka 1, 2, 3 (Illus. by Ehlert, Lois)*
  c BIC - v33 - i7 - Oct 2004 - p40(1) [501+]
  c HB - v80 - i5 - Sept-Oct 2004 - p571(1) [51-500]
  c KR - v72 - i13 - July 1 2004 - p632(1) [51-500]
  c PW - v251 - i29 - July 19 2004 - p159(1) [51-500]
  c SLJ - v50 - i8 - August 2004 - p90(1) [51-500]

Martin, Bradley K. - *Under the Loving Care of the Fatherly Leader: North Korea and the Kim Dynasty*
  BL - v101 - i2 - Sept 15 2004 - p183(1) [51-500]
  KR - v72 - i14 - July 15 2004 - p675(1) [501+]
  LJ - v129 - i15 - Sept 15 2004 - p70(1) [51-500]
  NYRB - v52 - i2 - Feb 10 2005 - p25(3) [501+]

Martin, Bruce - *Wayside Attractions: The Negotiation of Aspirations and Careers among African-American Adolescent Males in an Urban Alternative School*
  R&R Bk N - v19 - i1 - Feb 2004 - p191(1) [51-500]

Martin, C.L.G. - *Uff Da! (Illus. by Clark, Richard)*
  c LibMed - v23 - i3 - Nov-Dec 2004 - p66(1) [51-500]
  c SLJ - v50 - i7 - July 2004 - p82(1) [51-500]

Martin, Carol - *Catharine Parr Traill: Backwoods Pioneer*
  c Globe & Mail - Dec 11 2004 - pD20 [501+]

Martin, Catherine - *An Australian Girl*
  AHS - v35 - i123 - April 2004 - p196-196 [501+]

Martin, Charles - *Healing America: The Life of Senate Majority Leader William H. Frist, M.D., and the Issues That Shape Our Time*
  BL - v100 - i22 - August 2004 - p1881(1) [51-500]
  Metamorphoses
  HR - v57 - i2 - Summer 2004 - p345-351 [501+]
  Wrapped in Rain
  LJ - v130 - i2 - Feb 1 2005 - p64(1) [51-500]
  PW - v252 - i6 - Feb 7 2005 - p44(1) [51-500]

Martin, Charles Trice - *The Record Interpreter: A Collection of Abbreviations, Latin Words and Names Used in English Historical Manuscripts and Records, 2nd Ed.*
  EFHM - v58 - i3 - May-June 2004 - p57(1) [51-500]

Martin, Christopher R. - *Framed! Labor and the Corporate Media*
  Har Bus R - v82 - i4 - April 2004 - p28(1) [501+]

Martin, Dale - *Inventing Superstition: From the Hippocratics to the Christians*
  LJ - v129 - i14 - Sept 1 2004 - p157(1) [51-500]

Martin, Daniel - *Rabelais: mode d'emploi*
  FS - v58 - i2 - April 2004 - p244(2) [501+]

Martin, David - *Three Little Bears (Illus. by Gutierrez, Akemi)*
  c SLJ - v51 - i1 - Jan 2005 - p92(1) [51-500]
  We've All Got Bellybuttons! (Illus. by Cecil, Randy)
  c CCB-B - v58 - i6 - Feb 2005 - p258(1) [51-500]
  c KR - v73 - i1 - Jan 1 2005 - p54(1) [51-500]
  c SLJ - v51 - i2 - Feb 2005 - p107(1) [51-500]

Martin, Deana - *Memories Are Made of This: Dean Martin through His Daughter's Eyes*
  BL - v101 - i1 - Sept 1 2004 - p37(1) [51-500]
  BW - v34 - i45 - Nov 7 2004 - p8(1) [501+]
  KR - v72 - i17 - Sept 1 2004 - p851(1) [501+]
  LJ - v129 - i14 - Sept 1 2004 - p153(1) [51-500]
  PW - v251 - i36 - Sept 6 2004 - p57(1) [51-500]

Martin, Dick - *Tough Calls: AT&T and the Hard Lessons Learned from the Telecom Wars*
  BL - v101 - i6 - Nov 15 2004 - p538(1) [51-500]
  Bwatch - Feb 2005 - pNA [501+]
  Fortune - v150 - i10 - Nov 15 2004 - p54 [501+]
  PW - v251 - i43 - Oct 25 2004 - p38(1) [51-500]

Martin, Doug - *A Study of Walt Whitman's Mimetic Prosody: Free-Bound and Full Circle*
  R&R Bk N - v19 - i4 - Nov 2004 - p242(1) [501+]

Martin, Eric B. - *Winners*
  KR - v72 - i23 - Dec 1 2004 - p82(1) [501+]
  LJ - v129 - i20 - Dec 1 2004 - p101(1) [51-500]
  PW - v251 - i45 - Nov 8 2004 - p32(2) [501+]

Martin, Ged - *The Cambridge Union and Ireland 1815-1914*
  VS - v45 - i2 - Winter 2003 - p382 [501+]
  Past Futures: The Impossible Necessity of History, Based on the 1996 Joanne Goodman Lectures
  R&R Bk N - v19 - i3 - August 2004 - p31(1) [51-500]

Martin, George - *CCB: The Life and Century of Charles C. Burlingham, New York's First Citizen, 1858-1959*
  KR - v73 - i4 - Feb 15 2005 - p214(2) [501+]

Martin, George R.R. - *A Clash of Kings (Read by Dotrice, Roy). Audiobook Review*
  c Kliatt - v38 - i4 - July 2004 - p50(1) [51-500]
  The Hedge Knight
  PW - v251 - i31 - August 2 2004 - p55(1) [501+]
  Legends II: "A Song of Ice and Fire: The Sworn Sword" (Read by Malcolm, Graeme). Audiobook Review
  c Kliatt - v38 - i4 - July 2004 - p52(1) [51-500]
  A Storm of Swords (Read by Dotrice, Roy). Audiobook Review
  Kliatt - v38 - i6 - Nov 2004 - p51(1) [51-500]

Martin, Gord - *Tongue Twisters: Sexy Food from Bin 941 and Bin 942*
  CBRA - Annual 2003 - p133(1) [51-500]

Martin, Henry - *Essential Jazz: The First 100 Years*
  R&R Bk N - v19 - i4 - Nov 2004 - p194(1) [501+]

Martin, James W. - *Historical Dictionary of Angola, Rev. Ed.*
  R&R Bk N - v19 - i3 - August 2004 - p59(1) [51-500]

Martin, Jane - *Women and Education, 1800-1980*
  Choice - v42 - i4 - Dec 2004 - p710(2) [1-50]

Martin, Janet M. - *The Presidency and Women: Promise, Performance and Illusion*
  JAH - v91 - i1 - June 2004 - p322-324 [501+]
  PSQ - v119 - i2 - Summer 2004 - p381(3) [501+]

Martin, Jean-Hubert - *Andy Warhol: The Late Work: Paintings and Wallpapers, Vol. 3 (Illus. by Warhol, Andy)*
  LJ - v129 - i14 - Sept 1 2004 - p148(2) [51-500]

Martin, Joanna - *Wives and Daughters: Women and Children in the Georgian Country House*
  HT - v54 - i7 - July 2004 - p56(1) [501+]
  Spec - v295 - i9185 - August 21 2004 - p31(1) [501+]

Martin, John Jeffries - *Myths of Renaissance Individualism*
  R&R Bk N - v20 - i1 - Feb 2005 - p3(1) [51-500]

Martin, John N. - *Themes in Neoplatonic and Aristotelian Logic: Order, Negotiation, and Abstraction*
  R&R Bk N - v20 - i1 - Feb 2005 - p6(1) [51-500]

Martin, Jonathan D. - *Divided Mastery: Slave Hiring in the American South*
  Choice - v42 - i3 - Nov 2004 - p549(1) [1-50]

Martin, Judith - *Miss Manners' Guide to Excruciatingly Correct Behavior*
  LJ - v129 - i20 - Dec 1 2004 - p92(1) [51-500]

Martin, Justin - *Nader: Crusader, Spoiler, Icon*
  R&R Bk N - v19 - i1 - Feb 2004 - p81(1) [1-50]

Martin, Kat - *The Bride's Necklace*
  LJ - v130 - i1 - Jan 1 2005 - p92(1) [51-500]
  PW - v252 - i1 - Jan 3 2005 - p42(1) [51-500]
  BL - v101 - i9-10 - Jan 1 2005 - p831(1) [1-50]
  Deep Blue
  PW - v252 - i7 - Feb 14 2005 - p58(2) [51-500]

Martin, Katherine - *Those Who Dare: Real People, Real Courage*
  LJ - v129 - i19 - Nov 15 2004 - p76(1) [501+]
  y VOYA - v27 - i5 - Dec 2004 - p416(1) [51-500]

Martin, Laura (b. 1961 -) - *Harmony in Discord: German Women Writers in the Eighteenth and Nineteenth Centuries*
  GSR - v27 - i2 - May 2004 - p371-372 [501+]

Martin, Laura C. - *Recycled Crafts Box*
  c CH Bwatch - v14 - i11 - Nov 2004 - pNA [51-500]
  c SLJ - v50 - i7 - July 2004 - p94(1) [51-500]

Martin, Lawrence - *Iron Man: The Defiant Reign of Jean Chretien*
  Globe & Mail - Nov 6 2004 - pD25 [51-500]
  The Presidents and the Prime Ministers--Washington and Ottawa Face to Face: The Myth of Bilateral Bliss 1867-1982
  Globe & Mail - Nov 27 2004 - pD51 [501+]

Martin, Lee - *The Bright Forever*
  KR - v73 - i5 - March 1 2005 - p252(1) [501+]

Martin, Lenore G. - *The Future of Turkish Foreign Policy*
  Choice - v42 - i3 - Nov 2004 - p557(1) [1-50]

Martin, Louis F. - *Obesity Surgery*
  SciTech - v28 - i1 - March 2004 - p111(1) [51-500]

Martin, Marvin - *Extraordinary People in Jazz*
  y SLJ - v51 - i1 - Jan 2005 - p152(1) [51-500]

Martin, Nancy - *Cross Your Heart and Hope to Die: A Blackbird Sisters Mystery*
  BL - v101 - i9-10 - Jan 1 2005 - p827(1) [1-50]
  KR - v73 - i1 - Jan 1 2005 - p24(1) [51-500]
  LJ - v130 - i1 - Jan 1 2005 - p84(1) [51-500]
  PW - v252 - i7 - Feb 14 2005 - p57(1) [51-500]

Martin, Nicholas - *Nietzsche and the German Tradition: Selected Papers*
  R&R Bk N - v19 - i1 - Feb 2004 - p5(1) [51-500]

Martin, Nora - *A Perfect Snow*
  y Kliatt - v38 - i5 - Sept 2004 - p24(2) [51-500]

Martin-Ogunsola, Dellita - *The Eve/Hagar Paradigm in the Fiction of Quince Duncan*
  Choice - v42 - i4 - Dec 2004 - p666(1) [1-50]

Martin, Patricia - *Made Possible By: Succeeding with Sponsorship*
  R&R Bk N - v19 - i1 - Feb 2004 - p91(1) [1-50]

Martin, Paul - *Counting Sheep: The Science and Pleasure of Sleep and Dreams*
  BL - v100 - i21 - July 2004 - p1808(1) [1-50]

Martin, Philip L. - *Promise Unfulfilled: Unions, Immigration and the Farm Workers*
  JEL - v42 - i1 - March 2004 - p283(1) [501+]

Martin, Ralph - *Teaching Science for All Children: Inquiry Methods for Constructing Understanding, 3rd Ed.*
  SciTech - v28 - i4 - Dec 2004 - p14(1) [1-50]

Martin, Ralph E. - *Teaching Science for All Children: Inquiry Lessons for Constructing Understanding, 3rd Ed.*
  SciTech - v28 - i3 - Sept 2004 - p15(1) [501+]

Martin, Randall - *Henry VI*
  TLS - i5289 - August 13 2004 - p9-10 [501+]

Martin, Randy - *Financialization of Daily Life*
  S&S - v68 - i2 - Summer 2004 - p255-257 [501+]

Martin, Raquel - *The Estrogen Alternative: A Guide to Natural HRT*
  PW - v251 - i49 - Dec 6 2004 - p57(1) [51-500]

Martin, Reinhold - *The Oraganizational Complex: Architecture, Media, and Corporate Space*
  T&C - v45 - i2 - April 2004 - p468-470 [501+]
  The Organizational Complex: Architecture, Media, and Corporate Space
  BHR - v78 - i3 - Autumn 2004 - p557(3) [501+]

Martin, Richard C. - *Encyclopedia of Islam and the Muslim World*
  y Ref Rev - May 2004 - pNA [501+]
  R&USQ - v44 - i2 - Winter 2004 - p169(1) [501+]

Martin, Robert Ivan - *Most Dangerous Branch: How the Supreme Court of Canada Has Undermined Our Law and Our Democracy*
  CBRA - Annual 2003 - p316(1) [501+]

Martin, Robert M. - *There Are Two Errors in the Title of This Book: A Sourcebook of Philosophical Puzzles, Problems, and Paradoxes, Rev. Ed.*
  CBRA - Annual 2003 - p95(1) [51-500]

Martin, Rosemary - *It's a Mod, Mod, Mod, Mod Murder: A Murder A-Go-Go Mystery*
  PW - v252 - i10 - March 7 2005 - p55(1) [51-500]

Martin, Sherrill V. - *Henry F. Gilbert: A Bio-Bibliography*
  Choice - v42 - i6 - Feb 2005 - p992(1) [51-500]
  R&R Bk N - v19 - i4 - Nov 2004 - p194(1) [501+]

Martin, Terry - *The Affirmative Action Empire: Nations and Nationalism in the Soviet Union, 1923-1939*
  Russ Rev - v63 - i2 - April 2004 - pNA [501+]

Martin, Valerie - *Italian Fever*
  NS - v133 - i4697 - July 19 2004 - p54(2) [501+]
  Spec - v296 - Dec 18 2004 - p96(1) [501+]
  Property
  Globe & Mail - Dec 24 2004 - pD3 [1-50]

Martin, Waldo E., Jr. - *No Coward Soldiers: Black Cultural Politics and Postwar America*
  LJ - v130 - i4 - March 1 2005 - p98(1) [51-500]

Martin, Wendy - *More Stories We Tell: The Best Contemporary Short Stories by North American Women*
  y Kliatt - v38 - i5 - Sept 2004 - p37(2) [51-500]

Martin, William R. - *Handbook for Teaching Reflectively in Grades K-12*
  R&R Bk N - v19 - i1 - Feb 2004 - pNA [501+]

Martindale, Charles - *Shakespeare and the Classics*
  Choice - v42 - i7 - March 2005 - p1232(1) [51-500]

Martineau, Harriet - *Harriet Martineau's Writing on the British Empire, Vols. 1-5*
  Choice - v42 - i5 - Jan 2005 - p920(1) [501+]
  R&R Bk N - v19 - i3 - August 2004 - p37(1) [51-500]

Martineau, Pierre - *I Was a Killer for the Hells Angels: The Story of Serge Quesnel*
  CBRA - Annual 2003 - p57(2) [51-500]

Martineau, Robert J. - *Clean Air Act Handbook, 2nd Ed.*
  SciTech - v28 - i3 - Sept 2004 - p11(1) [501+]

Martines, Lauro - *April Blood: Florence and the Plot Against the Medici*
  HNet - Oct 2004 - pNA [501+]
  Ren Q - v57 - i4 - Winter 2004 - p1376(3) [501+]
  Strong Words: Winning and Social Strain in the Italian Renaissance
  JIH - v34 - i3 - Wntr 2004 - p462(3) [501+]

Martinez, A. Lee - *Gil's All Fright Diner*
  KR - v73 - i5 - March 1 2005 - p267(1) [51-500]

Martinez, Agnes - *Poe Park*
  c BL - v101 - i6 - Nov 15 2004 - p602(1) [501+]
  c Black Iss - v7 - i1 - Jan-Feb 2005 - p70(2) [501+]
  c CCB-B - v58 - i4 - Dec 2004 - p174(2) [51-500]
  c KR - v72 - i19 - Oct 1 2004 - p964(1) [51-500]
  c SLJ - v50 - i10 - Oct 2004 - p172(1) [51-500]
Martinez Aleman, Ana M. - *Women in Higher Education: An Encyclopedia*
  J Hi E - v75 - i6 - Nov-Dec 2004 - p712(4) [501+]
Martinez, Andrea - *Out of the Ivory Tower: Feminist Research for Social Change*
  CBRA - Annual 2003 - p389(1) [501+]
Martinez, Consuelo Abdres - *Camino al espanol: A Comprehensive Course in Spanish, 1st Ed.*
  TimHES - v0 - i1668 - Nov 26 2004 - pX(2) [501+]
Martinez, D.P. - *Identity and Ritual in a Japanese Diving Village: The Making and Becoming of Person and Place*
  Choice - v42 - i5 - Jan 2005 - p896(1) [1-50]
  R&R Bk N - v19 - i3 - August 2004 - p84(1) [51-500]
Martinez, David - *The Legends and Lands of Native Americans*
  R&R Bk N - v19 - i1 - Feb 2004 - p53(1) [51-500]
Martinez, Fernando - *Wheezing Disorders in the Preschool Child: Pathophysiology and Management*
  E-Streams - June 2004 - pNA [501+]
Martinez, Florentino Garcia - *Jerusalem, Alexandria, Rome: Studies in Ancient Cultural Interaction in Honour of A. Hilhorst*
  R&R Bk N - v19 - i1 - Feb 2004 - p16(1) [51-500]
Martinez, Guillermo - *Los Crimenes De Oxford*
  TLS - i5290 - August 20 2004 - p29(1) [51-500]
The Oxford Murders
  Lon R Bks - v27 - i2 - Jan 20 2005 - p29(1) [501+]
Martinez, J. Michael - *Life and Death in Civil War Prisons: The Parallel Torments of Corporal John Wesley Minnich, C.S.A. and Sergeant Warren Lee Goss, U.S.A.*
  R&R Bk N - v19 - i3 - August 2004 - p69(1) [51-500]
Martinez, Manuel Luis - *Drift*
  WLT - v78 - i3-4 - Sept-Dec 2004 - p95(1) [501+]
Martinez, Mario - *Postsecondary Participation and State Policy: Meeting the Future Demand*
  R&R Bk N - v19 - i4 - Nov 2004 - p189(1) [501+]
Martinez, Michele - *Most Wanted*
  KR - v73 - i1 - Jan 1 2005 - p13(1) [501+]
  LJ - v130 - i3 - Feb 15 2005 - p119(1) [51-500]
  PW - v252 - i4 - Jan 24 2005 - p219(1) [501+]
Martinez, Nina Marie - *Caramba! A Tale Told in Turns of the Card*
  BW - v34 - i27 - July 4 2004 - p8(1) [501+]
  Wom R Bks - v21 - i10-11 - July 2004 - p26(2) [501+]
Martinez, Ramon Carrilero - *La emperatriz Isabel de Portugal, Senora de Albacete y de Alcaraz, 1526-1539: Estudio historico-documental*
  Six Ct J - v35 - i3 - Fall 2004 - p823-824 [501+]
Martinez, Ruben - *The New Americans*
  R&R Bk N - v19 - i3 - August 2004 - p185(1) [501+]
Martinez, Tomas Eloy - *El Cantor De Tango*
  TLS - i5291 - August 27 2004 - p28(1) [51-500]
Martini, Clem - *The Mob*
  c BL - v101 - i3 - Oct 1 2004 - p329(1) [51-500]
  c CCB-B - v58 - i3 - Nov 2004 - p134(2) [501+]
  y KR - v72 - i16 - August 15 2004 - p809(1) [51-500]
  y Res Links - v10 - i2 - Dec 2004 - p38(1) [501+]
  y SLJ - v50 - i12 - Dec 2004 - p151(1) [51-500]
Martino, Alfred C. - *Pinned*
  y KR - v73 - i4 - Feb 15 2005 - p232(1) [51-500]
  y SLJ - v51 - i2 - Feb 2005 - p139(1) [51-500]
Martino, J.A. - *Microelectronics Technology and Devices: Proceedings*
  SciTech - v28 - i1 - March 2004 - p163(1) [51-500]
Silicon Nitride and Silicon Dioxide Thin Insulating Films VII: Proceedings
  SciTech - v28 - i1 - March 2004 - p162(1) [51-500]
Martins, Susanna Wade - *Farmers, Landlords and Landscapes: Rural Britain, 1720 to 1870*
  R&R Bk N - v19 - i4 - Nov 2004 - p246(1) [501+]
Martinsen, Deborah A. - *Surprised by Shame: Dostoevsky's Liars and Narrative Exposure*
  Slav R - v63 - i2 - Summer 2004 - p432(2) [501+]
Martinson, Deborah - *In the Presence of Audience: The Self in Diaries and Fiction*
  Choice - v41 - i7 - March 2004 - p1298(1) [501+]
  ELT - v47 - i3 - Summer 2004 - p349(4) [501+]

Martland, Peter - *Lord Haw-Haw: The English Voice of Nazi Germany*
  Lon R Bks - v26 - i13 - July 8 2004 - p22(3) [501+]
  TLS - i5285 - July 16 2004 - p10(1) [501+]
Martocchio, Joseph J. - *Employee Benefits: A Primer for Human Resource Professionals*
  HR Mag - v49 - i7 - July 2004 - pS6(1) [51-500]
Research in Personnel and Human Resources Management
  JEL - v42 - i1 - March 2004 - p298(1) [501+]
Strategic Compensation: A Human Resource Management Approach, 3rd Ed.
  HR Mag - v49 - i7 - July 2004 - pS9(1) [51-500]
Martone, Cynthia - *Loving through Bars: Children with Parents in Prison*
  LJ - v130 - i4 - March 1 2005 - p101(1) [51-500]
  PW - v252 - i3 - Jan 17 2005 - p46(1) [51-500]
Marty, Martin E. - *Fundamentalisms Comprehended*
  MEJ - v58 - i4 - Autumn 2004 - p709(1) [501+]
Martin Luther (Read by Michael, Paul). Audiobook Review
  LJ - v130 - i1 - Jan 1 2005 - p170(1) [51-500]
Martin Luther
  AM - v191 - i6 - Sept 13 2004 - p27 [501+]
The Protestant Voice in American Pluralism
  R&R Bk N - v19 - i3 - August 2004 - p20(1) [1-50]
  CHR - v90 - i3 - July 2004 - p572(1) [501+]
Martyn, David - *Sublime Failures: The Ethics of Kant and Sade*
  Eight-C St - v37 - i3 - Spring 2004 - p491-497 [501+]
Martyn, J. Louis - *History and Theology in the Fourth Gospel*
  BTB - v34 - i3 - Fall 2004 - p130(1) [501+]
Martyn, John R.C. - *A Translation of Abbot Leontios' 'Life of Saint Gregory, Bishop of Agrigento'*
  R&R Bk N - v19 - i4 - Nov 2004 - p21(1) [51-500]
Martyr, Philippa - *Paradise of Quacks: An Alternative History of Medicine in Australia*
  AHS - v35 - i123 - April 2004 - p189-190 [501+]
Martz, Fraidie - *Open Your Hearts: The Story of the Jewish War Orphans in Canada*
  y Can CL - i111-112 - Fall-Winter 2003 - p146(6) [501+]
Martz, Linda - *A Network of Converso Families in Early Modern Toledo: Assimilating a Minority*
  AHR - v109 - i3 - June 2004 - p983(2) [501+]
  JIH - v35 - i2 - Autumn 2004 - p302(2) [501+]
Maruna, Shadd - *After Crime and Punishment: Pathways to Offender Reintegration*
  R&R Bk N - v19 - i3 - August 2004 - p170(1) [501+]
Maruska, Don - *How Great Decisions Get Made: 10 Easy Steps for Reaching Agreement on Even the Toughest Issues*
  HR Mag - v49 - i7 - July 2004 - pS20(1) [51-500]
  R&R Bk N - v19 - i1 - Feb 2004 - p87(1) [1-50]
Marvel, William - *A Place Called Appomattox*
  Sew R - v112 - i1 - Wntr 2004 - p138-147 [501+]
Marvell, Andrew - *The Poems of Andrew Marvell*
  CR - v285 - i1662 - July 2004 - p64(1) [51-500]
Marven, Nigel - *Chased by Sea Monsters: Prehistoric Predators of the Deep*
  LibMed - v23 - i1 - August-Sept 2004 - p80(1) [51-500]
  y SB - v40 - i4 - July-August 2004 - p166(1) [51-500]
  Sci Teach - v71 - i7 - Sept 2004 - p85-85 [501+]
  y VOYA - v27 - i3 - August 2004 - p238(1) [1-50]
Marvis, Barbara - *The Story of the Peanuts Gang*
  c SLJ - v50 - i12 - Dec 2004 - p125(1) [51-500]
Marwedel, Peter - *Embedded System Design*
  SciTech - v28 - i1 - March 2004 - p165(1) [51-500]
Marwick, Arthur - *British Society Since 1945, 4th Ed.*
  R&R Bk N - v19 - i1 - Feb 2004 - p127(1) [51-500]
A History of Human Beauty
  Spec - v296 - i9198 - Nov 20 2004 - p48(3) [501+]
Marx, Anthony W. - *Faith in Nation: Exclusionary Origins of Nationalism*
  AJS - v110 - i3 - Nov 2004 - p824(2) [501+]
  CH - v73 - i4 - Dec 2004 - p862(3) [501+]

Marx, Christy - *Grace Hopper: The First Woman to Program the First Computer in the United States*
  c SLJ - v50 - i7 - July 2004 - p114(1) [1-50]
The Great Chicago Fire of 1871
  y SLJ - v51 - i1 - Jan 2005 - p140(1) [51-500]
Life in the Ocean Depths
  y SLJ - v51 - i1 - Jan 2005 - p150(1) [51-500]
  c VOYA - v27 - i5 - Dec 2004 - p420(1) [51-500]
Marx, Edward - *The Idea of a Colony: Cross-Culturalism in Modern Poetry*
  R&R Bk N - v19 - i3 - August 2004 - p259(1) [51-500]
Marx, Jeffrey - *Physics Education Research: Proceedings*
  SciTech - v28 - i4 - Dec 2004 - p47(1) [51-500]
Season of Life: A Football Star, a Ballboy, a Journey to Manhood
  BL - v101 - i1 - Sept 1 2004 - p48(1) [51-500]
  CC - v121 - i23 - Nov 16 2004 - p39(1) [501+]
Marx, Robert F. - *Treasure Lost at Sea: Diving to the World's Great Shipwrecks*
  E-Streams - August 2004 - pNA [501+]
Marx, Trish - *Everglades Forever: Restoring America's Great Wetland (Illus. by Karp, Cindy)*
  c SLJ - v51 - i1 - Jan 2005 - p152(2) [51-500]
Marx, William - *Naissance de la critique moderne: la litterature selon Eliot et Valery*
  FS - v58 - i3 - July 2004 - p430-431 [501+]
Marzano, Michela - *G.E. Moore's Ethics: Good as Intrinsic Value*
  R&R Bk N - v20 - i1 - Feb 2005 - p4(1) [51-500]
Marzano, Robert J. - *Building Background Knowledge for Academic Achievement: Research on What Works in Schools*
  Bwatch - Oct 2004 - pNA [51-500]
  R&R Bk N - v19 - i4 - Nov 2004 - p180(1) [51-500]
What Works in Schools: Translating Research into Action
  Sci Teach - v71 - i5 - May 2004 - p70-72 [501+]
Marzilli, Alan - *Affirmative Action*
  y VOYA - v27 - i4 - Oct 2004 - p334(1) [51-500]
Capital Punishment
  c LibMed - v22 - i4 - Jan 2004 - p82(1) [501+]
Marzollo, Jean - *Daniel in the Lion's Den*
  c SLJ - v50 - i8 - August 2004 - p111(1) [51-500]
Jonah and the Whale (and the Worm): A Bible Story (Illus. by Marzollo, Jean)
  c SLJ - v50 - i11 - Nov 2004 - p128(1) [51-500]
Miriam and Her Brother Moses
  c SLJ - v50 - i8 - August 2004 - p111(1) [51-500]
Shanna's Bear Hunt (Illus. by Roos, Maryn)
  c BL - v100 - i22 - August 2004 - p1943(1) [51-500]
  c SLJ - v50 - i10 - Oct 2004 - p123(1) [51-500]
Shanna's Hip, Hop, Hooray! (Illus. by Roos, Maryn)
  c BL - v100 - i22 - August 2004 - p1943(1) [51-500]
  c SLJ - v50 - i10 - Oct 2004 - p123(1) [51-500]
Shanna's Party Surprise (Illus. by Roos, Maryn)
  c SLJ - v50 - i10 - Oct 2004 - p123(1) [51-500]
Marzolph, Ulrich - *The Arabian Nights Encyclopedia*
  Choice - v42 - i5 - Jan 2005 - p828(2) [1-50]
Masala Trois Collective - *Desilicious: Sexy. Subversive. South Asian*
  CBRA - Annual 2003 - p244(1) [51-500]
Masamune, Shirow - *Ghost in the Shell 2: Man-Made Interface*
  PW - v252 - i8 - Feb 21 2005 - p160(1) [51-500]
Ghost in the Shell
  PW - v251 - i49 - Dec 6 2004 - p46(1) [51-500]
Mascagni, Pietro - *Cavalleria Rusticana*
  ON - v69 - i4 - Oct 2004 - p77(2) [501+]
Mascarelli, Gloria - *The Ceramics of China: 5000 B.C. to 1912 A.D.*
  Ceram Mo - v52 - i4 - April 2004 - p28(1) [501+]
Mascarelli, Robert - *The Ceramics of China: 5000 B.C. to 1912 A.D.*
  R&R Bk N - v19 - i1 - Feb 2004 - p207(1) [51-500]
Maschio, Giorgio - *La Figura Di Cristo Nel Commento Al salmo 118 Di Ambrogio di Milano*
  Theol St - v65 - i3 - Sept 2004 - p674(1) [501+]
Masciandaro, Donato - *Global Financial Crime: Terrorism, Money Laundering and Off Shore Centres*
  R&R Bk N - v19 - i3 - August 2004 - p166(1) [501+]
Masekela, Hugh - *Still Grazing: The Musical Journey of Hugh Masekela*
  Black Iss - v6 - i5 - Sept-Oct 2004 - p27(1) [501+]
Maseko, Zola - *The Return of Sara Bartman*
  IJAHS - v37 - i1 - Wntr 2004 - p128-130 [501+]
Mash, Eric J. - *Abnormal Child Psychology, 3rd Ed*
  SciTech - v28 - i4 - Dec 2004 - p113(1) [1-50]

Mastro, Jim - *Antarctic Ice (Illus. by Wu, Norbert)*
c CE - v81 - i1 - Fall 2004 - p48(1) [51-500]
c SLJ - v50 - i10 - Oct 2004 - pS23(1) [1-50]
*Under Antarctic Ice: The Photographs of Norbert Wu
(Illus. by Wu, Norbert)*
Am Sci - v93 - i1 - Jan-Feb 2005 - p77(1) [501+]
NH - v113 - i10 - Dec 2004 - p54(1) [501+]

Mastro, Robin - *Altars of Power and Grace: Create the
Life You Desire*
LJ - v129 - i12 - July 2004 - p89(1) [51-500]

Mastronarde, Donald J. - *Euripides: Medea*
CJ - v100 - i1 - Oct-Nov 2004 - p93-96 [501+]

Masumoto, David Mas - *Letters to the Valley: A Harvest
of Memories*
BL - v101 - i4 - Oct 15 2004 - p371(1) [51-500]

Masur, Harald - *Scales and Scores in Neurology:
Quantification of Neurological Deficits in Research and
Practice*
SciTech - v28 - i1 - March 2004 - p104(1) [51-
500]

Masurel, Claire - *Big Bad Wolf (Illus. by Iwai, Melissa)*
c RT - v57 - Oct 2003 - p164 [1-50]

Matar, Khalil I. - *Lockerbie and Libya: A Study in
International Relations*
Choice - v42 - i1 - Sept 2004 - p185(1) [501+]
R&R Bk N - v19 - i1 - Feb 2004 - p141(1) [51-
50]

Matar, Nabil - *In the Lands of the Christians: Arab Travel
Writing in the Seventeenth Century*
NYRB - v51 - i17 - Nov 4 2004 - p31(4) [501+]
Islam in Britain: 1558-1685
NYRB - v51 - i17 - Nov 4 2004 - p31(4) [501+]
Turks, Moors, and Englishmen in the Age of Discovery
NYRB - v51 - i17 - Nov 4 2004 - p31(4) [501+]

Matas, Carol - *In My Enemy's House*
y Can CL - i111-112 - Fall-Winter 2003 - p146(6)
[501+]
Rosie in New York City: Gotcha!
c Can CL - i113/114 - Spring-Summer 2004 - p136(3)
[501+]
c CBRA - Annual 2003 - p501(2) [51-500]

Matcha, Duane A. - *Health Care Systems of the Developed
World: How the United States' System Remains an
Outlier*
SciTech - v28 - i1 - March 2004 - p83(1) [51-500]

Matera, Frank J. - *II Corinthians: A Commentary*
Intpr - v58 - i3 - July 2004 - p301(3) [501+]
Theol St - v65 - i3 - Sept 2004 - p633(2) [501+]

Materials Science
LibMed - v22 - i5 - Feb 2004 - p59(1) [501+]

Mates, Barbara T. - *5-Star Programming and Services for
Your 55+ Library Customers*
ALJ - v53 - i4 - Nov 2004 - p416(1) [501+]

Math and My World Series
LibMed - v22 - i7 - April-May 2004 - p73(1)
[501+]

Math Forum - *Dr. Math Explains Algebra: Learning
Algebra Is Easy! Just Ask Dr. Math! (Illus. by
Wolk-Stanley, Jessica)*
c Math T - v98 - i2 - Sept 2004 - p142-142 [501+]

Math Matters Series
LibMed - v22 - i6 - March 2004 - p82(1) [501+]

Mathad, G.S. - *Copper Interconnects, New Contact
Metallurgies/Structures and Low-K Interlevel Dielectrics
2: Proceedings*
SciTech - v28 - i1 - March 2004 - p160(1) [51-
500]
Plasma Processing XIV: Proceedings
SciTech - v28 - i1 - March 2004 - p161(1) [51-
500]

Mathai, Kimberly - *The Cancer Lifeline Cookbook, 2nd
Ed.*
LJ - v129 - i14 - Sept 1 2004 - p184(2) [501+]

Matheij, Robert M.M. - *Mathematical Modeling for
Polymer Processing: Polymerization, Crystalization,
Manufacturing*
SIAM Rev - v46 - i1 - March 2004 - p175-176
[501+]

Mather, Richard B. - *The Age of Eternal Brilliance: Three
Lyric Poets of the Yung-ming Era (483-493), Vols. 1-2*
R&R Bk N - v19 - i1 - Feb 2004 - p219(1) [51-
500]

Mathers, Chris - *Crime School: Money Laundering: True
Crime Meets the World of Business and Finance*
BL - v101 - i1 - Sept 1 2004 - p28(1) [51-500]
Bwatch - March 2005 - pNA [51-500]
LJ - v129 - i19 - Nov 15 2004 - p74(1) [501+]
R&R Bk N - v19 - i4 - Nov 2004 - p146(1) [501+]

Mathers, E. Powys - *Black Marigolds and Coloured Stars*
TLS - i5306 - Dec 10 2004 - p33(1) [51-500]

Matheson, Dawn - *Ruby Lee the Bumble Bee (Illus. by
Barcita, Pamela)*
c CH Bwatch - March 2005 - pNA [51-500]

Matheson, Richard - *Somewhere in Time*
BL - v101 - i2 - Sept 15 2004 - p225(1) [501+]

Matheson, Robert E. - *Special Report on Surnames in
Ireland...[and]...Surnames and Christian Names in
Ireland*
R&R Bk N - v19 - i1 - Feb 2004 - p27(1) [51-500]

Matheson, Shirlee Smith - *Fastback Beach*
c CBRA - Annual 2003 - p502(1) [51-500]

Mathews, Gordon - *Consuming Hong Kong*
Can Lit - i181 - Summer 2004 - p159-160 [501+]

Mathews, Jean V. - *The Rise of New Woman: The Women's
Movement in America, 1875-1930*
AHR - v109 - i3 - June 2004 - p925(2) [501+]

Mathez, Edmond A. - *The Earth Machine: The Science of
a Dynamic Planet*
Bwatch - v26 - i9 - Sept 2004 - p8(1) [51-500]
Bwatch - Nov 2004 - pNA [51-500]
Choice - v42 - i4 - Dec 2004 - p692(2) [1-50]
E-Streams - Dec 2004 - pNA [501+]
SB - v40 - i6 - Nov-Dec 2004 - p251(2) [51-500]
SciTech - v28 - i3 - Sept 2004 - p44(1) [1-50]

Mathhews, J.F. - *Laying Down the Law. A Study of the
Theodosian Code*
Class R - v54 - i2 - Nov 2004 - p524-526 [501+]

Mathieu, Paul - *Sex Pots: Eroticism in Ceramics*
Am Craft - v64 - i2 - April-May 2004 - p32(1)
[501+]
Art N - v103 - i1 - Jan 2004 - p102(1) [501+]

Mathijs, Ernest - *The Cinema of the Low Countries*
Choice - v42 - i5 - Jan 2005 - p859(1) [1-50]

Mathis, Robert L. - *Human Resource Management, 11th
Ed.*
HR Mag - v50 - i2 - Feb 2005 - pS14(1) [501+]
*Human Resources Management: Essential Perspectives,
3rd Ed.*
R&R Bk N - v19 - i2 - May 2004 - p118 [51-500]

Mathisen, Ralph W. - *People, Personal Expression and
Social Relations in Late Antiquity, Vol. 1*
Class R - v54 - i2 - Nov 2004 - p521-522 [501+]
*People, Personal Expression and Social Relations in Late
Antiquity, Vol. 2*
Class R - v54 - i2 - Nov 2004 - p521-522 [501+]

Mathison, Sandra - *Encyclopedia of Evaluation*
LJ - v130 - i4 - March 1 2005 - p110(1) [51-500]

Matibag, Eugenio - *Haitian-Dominican Counterpoint:
Nation, State, and Race in Hispaniola*
Choice - v41 - i7 - March 2004 - p1352(1) [501+]

Matic, Gordana - *Topology and Geometry of Manifolds:
Proceedings*
SciTech - v28 - i1 - March 2004 - p41(1) [501+]

Matignon, Karine Lou - *Tiger, Tiger*
BL - v101 - i5 - Nov 1 2004 - p451(1) [51-500]
Bwatch - Dec 2004 - pNA [51-500]

Matlak, Richard E. - *Deep Distress: William Wordsworth,
John Wordsworth, Sir George Beaumont*
Choice - v41 - i11-12 - July-August 2004 -
p2045(1) [501+]

Matlock, Curtiss Ann - *Sweet Dreams at the Goodnight
Motel*
BL - v101 - i2 - Sept 15 2004 - p224(1) [51-500]

Matlock, Jack F. - *Reagan and Gorbachev: How the Cold
War Ended*
BL - v100 - i22 - August 2004 - p1867(1) [51-500]
Bus W - i3895 - August 9 2004 - p16 [501+]
BW - v34 - i30 - July 25 2004 - p3(1) [501+]
For Aff - v83 - i5 - Sept-Oct 2004 - p164 [501+]
LJ - v129 - i16 - Oct 1 2004 - p99(1) [501+]
NL - v87 - i4 - July-August 2004 - p22(3) [501+]
NYRB - v51 - i17 - Nov 4 2004 - p26(4) [501+]
NYTBR - August 1 2004 - p7 [501+]
R&R Bk N - v19 - i4 - Nov 2004 - p57(1) [1-50]

Maton, Kenneth I. - *Investing in Children, Youth, Families
and Communities: Strengths-Based Research and Policy*
R&R Bk N - v19 - i1 - Feb 2004 - p125(1) [51-
500]

Matovina, Timothy - *Horizons of the Sacred: Mexican
Traditions in U.S. Catholicism*
Theol St - v65 - i4 - Dec 2004 - p904(2) [501+]
WHQ - v35 - i3 - Autumn 2004 - p394(1) [501+]

Matravers, Matt - *Scanlon and Contractualism*
R&R Bk N - v19 - i1 - Feb 2004 - p10(1) [51-500]

Matricon, Jean - *The Cold Wars: A History of
Superconductivity*
Phys Today - v57 - i11 - Nov 2004 - p68-70
[501+]

Matsen, Brad - *Descent: The Heroic Discovery of the
Abyss*
KR - v73 - i2 - Jan 15 2005 - p105(2) [501+]
LJ - v130 - i4 - March 1 2005 - p105(2) [51-500]
PW - v252 - i8 - Feb 21 2005 - p170(1) [51-500]
An Extreme Dive under the Antarctic Ice
y SB - v40 - i3 - May-June 2004 - p122(1) [501+]
Go Wild in New York City! (Illus. by Corio, Paul)
c KR - v73 - i4 - Feb 15 2005 - p233(1) [51-500]
*The Incredible Record-Setting Deep-Sea Dive of the
Bathysphere*
c LibMed - v22 - i5 - Feb 2004 - p57(1) [501+]

Matson, Gienna - *Celtic Mythology A to Z*
c SLJ - v50 - i10 - Oct 2004 - p95(2) [51-500]
c BL - v101 - i3 - Oct 1 2004 - p354(1) [51-500]

Matson, Gregory A. - *Elements of STIL: Principles and
Applications of IEEE Std. 1450*
SciTech - v28 - i1 - March 2004 - p162(1) [51-
500]

Matson, Jack V. - *Effective Expert Witnessing: Practices
for the 21st Century, 4th Ed.*
R&R Bk N - v19 - i3 - August 2004 - p206(1)
[501+]

Matson, Pamela A. - *Annual Review of Environment and
Resources: Vol. 28, 2003*
SciTech - v28 - i1 - March 2004 - p147(1) [51-
500]

Matson, R.G. - *Emerging from the Mist: Studies in
Northwest Coast Culture History*
Can Hist R - v85 - i4 - Dec 2004 - p820(3) [501+]
R&R Bk N - v19 - i1 - Feb 2004 - p52(1) [51-500]

Matsumoto, Gary - *Vaccine A: The Covert Government
Experiment That's Killing Our Soldiers and Why GI's
Are Only the First Victims*
BW - v34 - i45 - Nov 7 2004 - p5(1) [501+]

Matsuoka, Takashi - *Autumn Bridge (Read by Dyck,
Jennifer Van). Audiobook Review*
y Kliatt - v39 - i2 - March 2005 - p46(1) [51-500]
Autumn Bridge
BL - v100 - i21 - July 2004 - p1818(2) [1-50]
PW - v251 - i29 - July 19 2004 - p144(1) [51-500]
*Cloud of Sparrows (Read by Gardner, Grover).
Audiobook Review*
BL - v101 - i6 - Nov 15 2004 - p607(1) [501+]

Matt, Daniel Chanan - *The Zohar. Pritzker Edition*
Choice - v41 - i11-12 - July-August 2004 -
p2063(1) [501+]
Parabola - v29 - i2 - Summer 2004 - p92-98
[501+]

Mattar, Philip - *Encyclopedia of the Modern Middle East
and North Africa, 2nd Ed., Vols. 1-4*
Choice - v42 - i4 - Dec 2004 - p638(1) [1-50]
LJ - v129 - i16 - Oct 1 2004 - p109(1) [51-500]
R&R Bk N - v19 - i3 - August 2004 - p48(1) [51-
500]

Mattei, Ugo - *The European Codification Process: Cut and
Paste*
R&R Bk N - v19 - i1 - Feb 2004 - pNA [51-500]

Matteo, Steve - *Let It Be*
y BL - v101 - i2 - Sept 15 2004 - p191(1) [501+]
TimHES - v0 - i1669 - Dec 3 2004 - p22(2)
[501+]

Mattern, Joanne - *The Chunnel*
c SLJ - v50 - i7 - July 2004 - p123(1) [1-50]
Lebron James: Young Basketball Star
c BL - v101 - i6 - Nov 15 2004 - p576(1) [51-500]

Matteson, Robert S. - *A Large Private Park: The
Collection of Archbishop William King, 1650-1729*
TLS - i5297 - Oct 8 2004 - p27(1) [501+]

Matthew, H.C.G. - *Oxford Dictionary of National
Biography: In Association with the British Academy:
From the Earliest Times to the Year 2000*
Atl - v294 - i5 - Dec 2004 - p123(1) [501+]
Choice - v42 - i6 - Feb 2005 - p986(1) [501+]
Lon R Bks - v27 - i2 - Jan 20 2005 - p3(5) [501+]
TLS - i5306 - Dec 10 2004 - p5-7 [501+]
Atl - v294 - i5 - Dec 2004 - p121(4) [501+]
BL - v101 - i9-10 - Jan 1 2005 - p780(1) [501+]
BL - v101 - i9-10 - Jan 1 2005 - p901(1) [501+]
Spec - v296 - i9190 - Sept 25 2004 - p47(3)
[501+]
TLS - i5307 - Dec 17 2004 - p12-13 [501+]

Matthew, Kathryn I. - *Guide to Celebrations and
Holidays around the World: The Best Books, Media, and
Multicultural Learning Activities*
BL - v101 - i1 - Sept 1 2004 - p164(1) [1-50]

Matthew, Richard A. - *Landmines and Human Security:
International Politics and War's Hidden Legacy*
Choice - v42 - i4 - Dec 2004 - p733(1) [1-50]

Matthews, Alice P. - *Marriage Made in Eden: A
Pre-Modern Perspective for a Post-Christian World*
LJ - v129 - i12 - July 2004 - p90(2) [51-500]

Matthews, Andrew - *The Flip Side*
 y   PW - v252 - i4 - Jan 24 2005 - p246(1) [51-500]
The Light Witch, Bks. 1-2
 y   Sch Lib - v52 - i3 - Autumn 2004 - p159(1) [501+]
A Winter Night's Dream
 y   BL - v101 - i1 - Sept 1 2004 - p123(1) [1-50]
 y   Kliatt - v38 - i4 - July 2004 - p10(1) [51-500]
 y   PW - v251 - i31 - August 2 2004 - p72(1) [51-500]
 c   SLJ - v50 - i8 - August 2004 - p126(1) [51-500]
 y   VOYA - v27 - i5 - Dec 2004 - p386(1) [51-500]
Matthews, Beryl - *Wings of the Morning*
     BL - v101 - i6 - Nov 15 2004 - p568(1) [51-500]
Matthews, Bonnie - *Coral Reefs*
     LibMed - v22 - i5 - Feb 2004 - p55(1) [501+]
Matthews, Brenda - *Niagara Flavours: Recipes from Southwest Ontario's Finest Chefs*
     CBRA - Annual 2003 - p133(2) [51-500]
Matthews, Brian S. - *New Wilderness*
     Mac - v117 - i48 - Nov 29 2004 - p77(1) [51-500]
Matthews, Carole - *Let's Meet on Platform 8*
     BL - v101 - i1 - Sept 1 2004 - p73(1) [51-500]
The Scent of Scandal
     KR - v72 - i17 - Sept 1 2004 - p827(1) [501+]
Matthews, Carolyn - *Heroic Rescues at Sea: True Stories of the Canadian Coast Guard*
     CBRA - Annual 2003 - p345(1) [51-500]
Matthews, Christopher - *Eyelevel: Fifty Histories*
     HR - v57 - i2 - Summer 2004 - p325-334 [501+]
Matthews, Clifford - *Handbook of Mechanical In-Service Inspection*
     SciTech - v28 - i1 - March 2004 - p149(1) [51-500]
Pressure Systems Safety Regulations: PSSRs, SI 128
     SciTech - v28 - i1 - March 2004 - p178(1) [51-500]
Matthews, Dawn D. - *Child Abuse Sourcebook*
     Bwatch - Nov 2004 - pNA [51-500]
     Choice - v42 - i7 - March 2005 - p1206(1) [51-500]
     R&R Bk N - v19 - i4 - Nov 2004 - p145(1) [51-500]
Domestic Violence Sourcebook, 2nd Ed.
     Choice - v42 - i5 - Jan 2005 - p836(1) [51-500]
     R&R Bk N - v19 - i4 - Nov 2004 - p146(1) [51-500]
Domestic Violence Sourcebook
     Bwatch - Nov 2004 - pNA [51-500]
Hypertension Sourcebook
     Bwatch - March 2005 - pNA [51-500]
Matthews, Francine - *As You Wish*
 y   BL - v101 - i6 - Nov 15 2004 - p568(1) [51-500]
Matthews, Gerald - *Personality Traits, 2nd Ed.*
     Per Psy - v57 - i4 - Winter 2004 - p1084(4) [501+]
Matthews, Glenna - *Silicon Valley, Women, and the California Dream: Gender, Class and Opportunity in the Twentieth Century.*
     BHR - v78 - i2 - Summer 2004 - p313(3) [501+]
Silicon Valley, Women, and the California Dream: Gender, Class, and Opportunity in the Twentieth Century
     CS - v33 - i4 - July 2004 - p426(2) [501+]
Silicon Valley, Women and the California Dream: Gender, class and Opportunity in the Twentieth Century
     WHQ - v35 - i1 - Spring 2004 - p92-93 [501+]
Silicon Valley, Women, and the California Dream: Gender, Class, and Opportunity in Twentieth Century
     AHR - v109 - i2 - April 2004 - p542(3) [501+]
Matthews-Grieco, Sara F. - *Monaca, Moglie, Serva, Cortigiana: Vita e immagine delle donne tra Rinascimento e Controriforma*
     Six Ct J - v35 - i1 - Spring 2004 - p256(3) [501+]
Matthews, Jean V. - *The Rise of the New Woman: The Women's Movement in America, 1875-1930*
     Am St - v45 - i1 - Spring 2004 - p152-153 [501+]
The Rise of the New Woman: The Women's Movement in America, 1875 to 1930
     CS - v33 - i6 - Nov 2004 - p747(1) [1-50]
Matthews, Jeffrey J. - *Alanson B. Houghton: Ambassador in the New Era*
     R&R Bk N - v19 - i4 - Nov 2004 - p63(1) [51-500]
Matthews, Jenny - *Women and War*
     HNet - Dec 2004 - pNA [501+]
Matthews, John - *King Arthur: Dark Age Warrior and Mythic Hero*
 y   SLJ - v51 - i1 - Jan 2005 - p160(1) [51-500]
Matthews, Joseph R. - *Bottom Line: Determining and Communicating the Value of the Special Library*
     R&R Bk N - v19 - i1 - Feb 2004 - p258(1) [51-500]
Measuring for Results: The Dimensions of Public Library Effectiveness
     A Lib - v35 - i7 - August 2004 - p86(1) [51-500]

Matthews, L.S. - *Fish: A Novel (Read by Lamia, Jenna). Audiobook Review*
     Kliatt - v38 - i6 - Nov 2004 - p46(1) [51-500]
Fish (Read by Lamia, Jenna). Audiobook Review
 c   BL - v101 - i3 - Oct 1 2004 - p352(1) [51-500]
 c   SLJ - v50 - i11 - Nov 2004 - p81(1) [51-500]
Fish
 c   BL - v100 - i21 - July 2004 - p1844(1) [1-50]
 c   CCB-B - v58 - i2 - Oct 2004 - p89(2) [51-500]
 c   Globe & Mail - July 31 2004 - pD11 [51-500]
 c   Inst - v114 - i5 - Jan-Feb 2005 - p73(2) [501+]
 c   NYTBR - July 11 2004 - p18 [501+]
 c   SLJ - v50 - i7 - July 2004 - p109(1) [51-500]
 y   VOYA - v27 - i3 - August 2004 - p221(1) [1-50]
Matthews, Marty D. - *Forgotten Founder: The Life and Times of Charles Pinckney*
     R&R Bk N - v19 - i4 - Nov 2004 - p60(1) [51-500]
Matthews, Roger - *Ancient Perspectives on Egypt*
     R&R Bk N - v19 - i1 - Feb 2004 - p50(1) [51-500]
     TimHES - v0 - i1671 - Dec 17 2004 - p24(1) [501+]
Matthews, Rupert - *Everyday Rituals*
 c   Sch Lib - v52 - i4 - Winter 2004 - p209(1) [51-500]
Matthews, Shelly - *Walk in the Ways of Wisdom: Essays in Honor of Elisabeth Schussler Fiorenza*
     Intpr - v58 - i4 - Oct 2004 - p440(1) [501+]
Matthews, Tom - *Like We Care*
     BL - v100 - i22 - August 2004 - p1900(1) [501+]
 y   SLJ - v50 - i11 - Nov 2004 - p177(1) [51-500]
 y   VOYA - v27 - i5 - Dec 2004 - p386(1) [51-500]
Matthews, Tony - *Memory Trees: Family Trees for the Scrapbooker*
     EFHM - v58 - i2 - March-April 2004 - p88(1) [51-500]
Matthews, William - *Search Party: Collected Poems*
     ABR - v25 - i6 - Sept-Oct 2004 - p14(2) [501+]
Matthewson, Tim - *A Proslavery Foreign Policy: Haitian-American Relations During the Early Republic*
     JAH - v91 - i3 - Dec 2004 - p1000(2) [501+]
     JSH - v71 - i1 - Feb 2005 - p146(2) [501+]
     R&R Bk N - v19 - i1 - Feb 2004 - p55(1) [501+]
Matthias, Driess - *Molecular Clusters of the Main Group Elements*
     SciTech - v28 - i3 - Sept 2004 - p45(1) [1-50]
Matthiessen, Peter - *Under the Mountain Wall: A Chronicle of Two Seasons in the Stone Age*
     Globe & Mail - Dec 24 2004 - pD15 [51-500]
Matthys, Robert James - *Accurate Clock Pendulums*
     SciTech - v28 - i4 - Dec 2004 - p169(1) [51-500]
Mattia, Martha B. - *Conversations with George Bush: Beyond Polls and Partisanship: Real Life in the USA*
     PW - v252 - i5 - Jan 31 2005 - p61(1) [501+]
Mattiace, Shannan L. - *To See with Two Eyes: Peasant Activism and Indian Autonomy in Chiapas, Mexico*
     R&R Bk N - v19 - i1 - Feb 2004 - p66(1) [51-500]
To See with Two Eyes: Peasant Activism and Indian Autonomy in Chipas, Mexico
     Choice - v41 - i11-12 - July-August 2004 - p2103(1) [501+]
Mattingly, Paul H. - *Suburban Landscapes: Culture and Politics in a New York Metropolitan Community*
     BHR - v78 - i1 - Spring 2004 - p128(4) [501+]
Mattis, Daniel C. - *Statistical Mechanics Made Simple: A Guide for Students and Researchers*
     Phys Today - v57 - i7 - July 2004 - p63-64 [501+]
Mattison, Alice - *The Wedding of the Two-Headed Woman*
     BL - v100 - i22 - August 2004 - p1900(1) [501+]
     BW - v34 - i33 - August 15 2004 - p6(1) [501+]
     LJ - v129 - i16 - Oct 1 2004 - p71(1) [51-500]
     NYTBR - August 8 2004 - p14 [51-500]
     PW - v251 - i29 - July 19 2004 - p143(1) [51-500]
Mattison, Steve - *The Complete Potter*
     Ceram Mo - v52 - i6 - June-August 2004 - p32(2) [501+]
Mattoo, Aaditya - *Domestic Regulation and Service Trade Liberalization*
     JEL - v42 - i1 - March 2004 - p260(2) [501+]
     R&R Bk N - v19 - i2 - May 2004 - p108(1) [51-500]
India and the WTO
     JEL - v41 - i4 - Dec 2003 - p1411(1) [501+]
     JEL - v42 - i3 - Sept 2004 - p878(3) [501+]
     R&R Bk N - v19 - i2 - May 2004 - p112(1) [51-500]
Moving People to Deliver Services
     JEL - v42 - i1 - March 2004 - p262(2) [501+]
Mattox, Kenneth L. - *Top Knife: The Art and Craft of Trauma Surgery*
     SciTech - v28 - i4 - Dec 2004 - p108(1) [51-500]

Mattox, Mickey Leland - *Defender of the Most Holy Matriarchs: Martin Luther's Interpretation of the Women of Genesis in the Enarrationes in Genesin, 1535-45*
     Ren Q - v57 - i3 - Fall 2004 - p1049(2) [501+]
     Theol St - v65 - i4 - Dec 2004 - p898(2) [501+]
Mattson, Kevin - *When America Was Great: The Fighting Faith of Postwar Liberalism*
     KR - v72 - i16 - August 15 2004 - p793(1) [501+]
     LJ - v129 - i19 - Nov 15 2004 - p75(1) [501+]
Matturro, Claire - *Skinny-Dipping*
     KR - v72 - i16 - August 15 2004 - p782(1) [51-500]
     PW - v251 - i38 - Sept 20 2004 - p44(2) [501+]
Matuz, Roger - *The Presidents Fact Book*
     Bwatch - Jan 2005 - pNA [51-500]
U.S. Immigration and Migration: Primary Sources, Vols. 1-2
     Choice - v42 - i5 - Jan 2005 - p839(1) [1-50]
Matveev, Sergei - *Algorithmic Topology and Classification of 3-Manifolds*
     Choice - v41 - i7 - March 2004 - p1331(1) [501+]
Matyssek, Angela - *Rudolf Virchow: Das Pathologische Museum: Geschichte einer wissenschaftlichen Sammlung um 1900*
     HNet - Nov 2004 - pNA [501+]
Matz, Judith - *Beyond a Shadow of a Diet: The Therapist's Guide to Treating Compulsive Eating*
     SciTech - v28 - i3 - Sept 2004 - p101(1) [51-500]
Mau, Bruce - *Massive Change: The Future of Global Design*
     PW - v251 - i50 - Dec 13 2004 - p61(1) [51-500]
Mauch, Christof - *Nature in German History*
     R&R Bk N - v20 - i1 - Feb 2005 - p83(1) [51-500]
The Shadow War Against Hitler: The Covert Operations of America's Wartime Secret Intelligence Service
     J Mil H - v68 - i3 - July 2004 - p1001-1002 [501+]
     JAH - v91 - i2 - Sept 2004 - p683(2) [501+]
Mauer, Marc - *Invisible Punishment: The Collateral Consequences of Mass Imprisonment*
     Comw - v132 - i3 - Feb 11 2005 - p24(2) [501+]
Maugham, Somerset - *Collected Stories*
     LJ - v129 - i14 - Sept 1 2004 - p204(1) [51-500]
     TLS - i5298 - Oct 15 2004 - p21(1) [501+]
Maughan, William L. - *The Artist's Complete Guide to Drawing the Head*
     LJ - v129 - i12 - July 2004 - p81(1) [51-500]
     R&R Bk N - v19 - i3 - August 2004 - p242(1) [51-500]
Mauk, Kristen - *Spiritual Care in Nursing Practice*
     SciTech - v28 - i4 - Dec 2004 - p121 [51-500]
Mauldin, Barbara - *Carnaval!*
     LJ - v130 - i4 - March 1 2005 - p82(1) [51-500]
Mauldin, John - *Bull's Eye Investing: Targeting Real Returns in a Smoke and Mirrors Market*
     NYT - July 11 2004 - pBU8 [501+]
     R&R Bk N - v19 - i4 - Nov 2004 - p118(1) [51-500]
Mauldon, Margaret - *Madame Bovary*
     BW - v34 - i35 - August 2004 - p15(1) [501+]
     Atl - v294 - i3 - Oct 2004 - p175(9) [501+]
Maume, David J., Jr. - *Whitewashing Race: The Myth of Color-Blind Society*
     CS - v33 - i5 - Sept 2004 - p537-539 [501+]
Maunder, Andrew - *Varieties of Women's Sensation Fiction: 1855-1890, Vols. 1-6*
     R&R Bk N - v19 - i4 - Nov 2004 - p234(1) [501+]
Maunder, Richard - *The Scoring of Baroque Concertos*
     MT - v145 - i1889 - Winter 2004 - p85-89 [501+]
Maurer, David W. - *Whiz Mob: A Correlation of the Technical Argot of Pickpockets with Their Behavior Pattern*
     R&R Bk N - v19 - i1 - Feb 2004 - pNA [51-500]
Maurer, Gerd - *Thermodynamic Properties of Complex Fluid Mixtures*
     SciTech - v28 - i3 - Sept 2004 - p53(1) [1-50]
Maurer, Helen E. - *Margaret of Anjou: Queenship and Power in Late Medieval England*
     Albion - v36 - i2 - Summer 2004 - p287(2) [501+]
Maurer, John H. - *Churchill and Strategic Dilemmas Before the World Wars: Essays in Honor of Michael I. Handel*
     J Mil H - v68 - i3 - July 2004 - p983-985 [501+]
     R&R Bk N - v19 - i1 - Feb 2004 - p255(1) [51-500]
Maurer, Konrad - *Alzheimer: The Life of a Physician and the Career of a Disease*
     HNet - Sept 2004 - pNA [501+]
Maurer, Noel - *The Power and the Money: The Mexican Financial System*
     JEL - v42 - i3 - Sept 2004 - p870(3) [501+]

McAuliffe, Jane Dammen - *Encyclopaedia of the Qur'an, Vol. 3*
R&R Bk N - v19 - i1 - Feb 2004 - p15(1) [51-500]
With Reverence for the Word: Medieval Scriptural Exegesis in Judaism, Christianity, and Islam
JAAR - v72 - i4 - Dec 2004 - p1053(4) [501+]

McAuslan, I. - *Sophocles: Oedipus Tyrannus. A New Translation and Commentary*
Class R - v54 - i2 - Nov 2004 - p562-563 [501+]

McAvoy, Muriel - *Sugar Baron: Manuel Rionda and the Fortunes of Pre-Castro Cuba*
JEH - v64 - i1 - March 2004 - p254(2) [501+]

McBain, Ed - *Alice in Jeopardy*
BL - v101 - i5 - Nov 1 2004 - p444(1) [51-500]
BW - v35 - i4 - Jan 30 2005 - p13(1) [51-500]
Ent W - i802 - Jan 21 2005 - p95 [51-500]
KR - v72 - i19 - Oct 1 2004 - p942(1) [501+]
LJ - v130 - i1 - Jan 1 2005 - p98(1) [51-500]
People - v63 - i3 - Jan 24 2005 - p52 [51-500]
PW - v251 - i46 - Nov 15 2004 - p40(1) [51-500]
The Frumious Bandersnatch (Read by McLarty, Ron). Audiobook Review
LJ - v130 - i2 - Feb 1 2005 - p123(1) [51-500]
Hark!: A Novel of the 87th Precinct
BW - v34 - i36 - Sept 5 2004 - p10(1) [501+]
LJ - v129 - i13 - August 2004 - p60(2) [51-500]
Hark! An 87th Precinct Novel
Spec - v296 - i9192 - Oct 9 2004 - p47(1) [501+]
Transgressions
KR - v73 - i5 - March 1 2005 - p252(1) [501+]

McBarnet, Doreen J. - *Crime, Compliance and Control*
R&R Bk N - v19 - i4 - Nov 2004 - p147(1) [501+]

McBay, Bruce - *Waiting for Sarah*
y CBRA - Annual 2003 - p502(1) [51-500]
c CH Bwatch - v14 - i8 - August 2004 - p2(1) [51-500]

McBee, Randy D. - *Dance Hall Days: Intimacy and Leisure among Working-Class Immigrants in the United States*
J Soc H - v38 - i1 - Fall 2004 - p244(3) [501+]
JAH - v91 - i1 - June 2004 - p269-269 [501+]

McBratney, Sam - *Little Red Riding Hood (Illus. by Chichester-Clark, Emma)*
c SLJ - v51 - i1 - Jan 2005 - p107(2) [51-500]
You're All My Favorites (Illus. by Jeram, Anita)
c HB - v80 - i5 - Sept-Oct 2004 - p571(2) [51-500]
c KR - v72 - i19 - Oct 1 2004 - p965(1) [51-500]
c PW - v251 - i38 - Sept 20 2004 - p61(1) [51-500]
c SLJ - v50 - i11 - Nov 2004 - p110(2) [51-500]

McBride-Chang, Catherine - *Children's Literacy Development*
TimHES - v0 - i1684 - March 25 2005 - p28(1) [501+]

McBride, Dwight A. - *Why I Hate Abercrombie & Fitch: Essays on Race and Sexuality*
PW - v251 - i51 - Dec 20 2004 - p46(1) [501+]

McBride, Lawrence W. - *Reading Irish Histories: Texts, Contexts, and Memory in Modern Ireland*
AHR - v109 - i2 - April 2004 - p471(2) [501+]
ILS - v24 - i1 - Fall 2004 - p15(1) [501+]

McBride, Mary - *Say It Again, Sam*
BL - v101 - i6 - Nov 15 2004 - p568(1) [51-500]
PW - v251 - i46 - Nov 15 2004 - p46(1) [51-500]

McBride, Neil - *An Introduction to the Solar System*
Astron - v32 - i8 - August 2004 - p98 [501+]
S&T - v109 - i1 - Jan 2005 - p120(2) [501+]

McBride-Smith, Barbara - *The Button Box: Stories about Mama (Read by McBride-Smith, Barbara). Audiobook Review*
c PW - v252 - i7 - Feb 14 2005 - p20(1) [51-500]

McBride, Susan - *The Good Girl's Guide to Murder*
PW - v251 - i4 - Jan 24 2005 - p227(1) [501+]

McBride, William I. - *Idea of Values*
R&R Bk N - v19 - i1 - Feb 2004 - p10(1) [1-50]

McBrien, Judith Paine - *Pocket Guide to Chicago Architecture, 2nd Ed.*
R&R Bk N - v19 - i4 - Nov 2004 - p202(1) [501+]

McCabe, Herbert - *God, Christ and Us*
CC - v122 - i2 - Jan 25 2005 - p20(6) [501+]
TLS - i5286 - July 23 2004 - p26(1) [501+]
God Matters
CC - v122 - i2 - Jan 25 2005 - p20(6) [501+]
God Still Matters
CC - v122 - i2 - Jan 25 2005 - p20(6) [501+]
Law, Love and Language
CC - v122 - i2 - Jan 25 2005 - p20(6) [501+]

McCabe, Joel - *Hanging Out with the Dream King: Conversations with Neil Gaiman & His Collaborators*
SLJ - v51 - i2 - Feb 2005 - p25(1) [501+]

McCabe, Marilyn - *The Paradox of Loss: Toward a Relational Theory of Grief*
Choice - v42 - i2 - Oct 2004 - p375(1) [51-500]
SciTech - v28 - i1 - March 2004 - p96(1) [51-500]

McCabe, Mary Margaret - *Plato and His Predecessors: The Dramatization of Reason*
CJ - v99 - i3 - Feb-March 2004 - p358-362 [501+]

McCabe, Patrick - *The Butcher Boy*
Critq - v44 - Winter 2003 - p196 [501+]

McCabe, Paul T. - *Contemporary Ergonomics, 2003: Proceedings*
SciTech - v28 - i1 - March 2004 - p136(1) [51-500]
Contemporary Ergonomics, 2004: Proceedings
SciTech - v28 - i3 - Sept 2004 - p137(1) [51-500]

McCabe, Richard A. - *Spenser's Monstrous Regiment: Elizabethan Ireland and the Poetics of Difference*
RES - v55 - i218 - Feb 2004 - p124-124 [501+]

McCabe, Richard E. - *Prairie Ghost: Proghorn and Human Interaction in Early America*
Choice - v42 - i6 - Feb 2005 - p1050(1) [51-500]

McCafferty, Megan - *Sixteen: Stories about That Sweet and Bitter Birthday*
y SLJ - v50 - i9 - Sept 2004 - p234(1) [51-500]
VOYA - v27 - i5 - Dec 2004 - p396(1) [51-500]

McCaffrey, Anne - *Acorna's Triumph: The Further Adventures of the Unicorn Girl (Read by Fields, Anna). Audiobook Review*
Kliatt - v38 - i6 - Nov 2004 - p41(1) [51-500]
LJ - v130 - i4 - March 1 2005 - p122(1) [51-500]
Acorna's Triumph: The Further Adventures of the Unicorn Girl
y VOYA - v27 - i4 - Oct 2004 - p316(1) [51-500]
Legends II: "Pern: Beyond Between" (Read by Malcolm, Graeme). Audiobook Review
c Kliatt - v38 - i4 - July 2004 - p52(1) [51-500]

McCaffrey, Laura Williams - *Alia Waking*
c LibMed - v22 - i4 - Jan 2004 - p65(1) [501+]
Planning the Family in Egypt: New Bodies, New Selves
IJMES - v36 - i1 - Feb 2004 - p132-134 [501+]

McCaffrey, Robert - *Practitioner's Guide to Symptom Base Rates in Clinical Neuropsychology*
SciTech - v28 - i1 - March 2004 - p94(1) [51-500]

McCaffrey, Todd J. - *Dragonsblood*
y BL - v101 - i5 - Nov 1 2004 - p444(1) [51-500]
KR - v72 - i22 - Nov 15 2004 - p1072(1) [51-500]
LJ - v129 - i20 - Dec 1 2004 - p104(1) [51-500]
PW - v251 - i45 - Nov 8 2004 - p40(1) [51-500]

McCaig, JoAnn - *Reading in Alice Munro's Archives*
Can Lit - i181 - Summer 2004 - p161-163 [501+]

McCain, John - *Why Courage Matters: The Way to a Braver Life*
y SLJ - v50 - i11 - Nov 2004 - p178(2) [51-500]

McCain, Roger A. - *Game Theory: A Non-Technical Introduction to the Analysis of Strategy*
R&R Bk N - v19 - i1 - Feb 2004 - p78(1) [1-50]

McCall, J.B. - *The Cavalry of the Roman Republic: Cavalry Combat and Elite Reputations in the Middle and Late Republic*
Class R - v54 - i2 - Nov 2004 - p488(3) [501+]

McCall, Junietta Baker - *Bereavement Counseling: Pastoral Care for Complicated Grieving*
R&R Bk N - v19 - i3 - August 2004 - p27(1) [1-50]

McCall, Morgan W. - *Developing Global Executives.*
HR Mag - v49 - i7 - July 2004 - pS10(1) [501+]

McCall, Renee M. - *Purposeful Play: Early Childhood Movement Activities on a Budget*
R&R Bk N - v19 - i4 - Nov 2004 - p80(1) [51-500]

McCall Smith, Alexander - *At the Villa of Reduced Circumstances*
Globe & Mail - Dec 18 2004 - pD4 [51-500]
Death Takes a Holiday
NYTBR - August 29 2004 - p23 [501+]
The Finer Points of Sausage Dogs
Globe & Mail - Dec 18 2004 - pD4 [51-500]
The Full Cupboard of Life (Read by Lecat, Lisette). Audiobook Review
BL - v101 - i4 - Oct 15 2004 - p432(1) [51-500]
The Girl Who Married a Lion and Other Tales from Africa
y BL - v101 - i5 - Nov 1 2004 - p442(1) [51-500]
Ent W - i797 - Dec 17 2004 - p89 [501+]
In the Company of Cheerful Ladies
Spec - v295 - i9185 - August 21 2004 - p33(1) [501+]

The Kalahari Typing School for Men (Read by Lecat, Lisette). Audiobook Review
People - v62 - i4 - July 26 2004 - p48 [51-500]
Portuguese Irregular Verbs
Globe & Mail - Dec 18 2004 - pD4 [51-500]
The Sunday Philosophy Club (Read by Porter, Davina). Audiobook Review
BL - v101 - i9-10 - Jan 1 2005 - p886(1) [51-500]
The Sunday Philosophy Club
BL - v100 - i22 - August 2004 - p1872(1) [51-500]
Globe & Mail - Oct 9 2004 - pD4 [501+]
KR - v72 - i15 - August 1 2004 - p717(1) [51-500]
LJ - v129 - i13 - August 2004 - p62(1) [501+]
NS - v133 - i4704 - Sept 6 2004 - p52(3) [501+]
NYTBR - Oct 3 2004 - p30 [501+]
PW - v251 - i31 - August 2 2004 - p51(1) [501+]
Spec - v296 - i9191 - Oct 2 2004 - p45(1) [501+]
TLS - i5296 - Oct 1 2004 - p22(1) [501+]

McCallum, Lawrence - *Italian Horror Films of the 1960's: A Critical Catalog of 62 Chillers*
R&R Bk N - v19 - i3 - August 2004 - p262(1) [51-500]

McCallus, Joseph P. - *Gentleman Soldier: John Clifford Brown and the Philippine-American War*
J Mil H - v68 - i3 - July 2004 - p970-971 [501+]

McCally, Michael - *Life Support: The Environment and Human Health*
NRJ - v44 - i2 - Spring 2004 - p656-659 [501+]

McCamley, Nick - *Disasters Underground*
R&R Bk N - v19 - i4 - Nov 2004 - p252(1) [501+]

McCane, Byron R. - *Roll Back the Stone: Death and Burial in the World of Jesus*
Theol St - v65 - i4 - Dec 2004 - p893(2) [501+]

McCann, Bryan - *Hello, Hello Brazil: Popular Music in the Making of Modern Brazil*
Choice - v42 - i4 - Dec 2004 - p671(1) [1-50]

McCann, Charles Robert, Jr. - *The Elgar Dictionary of Economic Quotations*
Choice - v42 - i1 - Sept 2004 - p77(1) [501+]

McCann, Colum - *Dancer. Audiobook Review*
LJ - v129 - i15 - Sept 15 2004 - p89(1) [51-500]
Dancer
BL - v101 - i5 - Nov 1 2004 - p458(1) [51-500]

McCann, David R. - *The Columbia Anthology of Modern Korean Poetry*
Choice - v42 - i3 - Nov 2004 - p479(1) [1-50]
R&R Bk N - v19 - i3 - August 2004 - p256(1) [51-500]

McCann, Frank D. - *Soldiers of the Patria: A History of the Brazilian Army, 1889-1937*
Choice - v42 - i2 - Oct 2004 - p352(1) [51-500]

McCann, Graham - *Frankie Howerd*
NS - v133 - i4716 - Nov 29 2004 - p43(1) [51-500]
Spec - v296 - i9197 - Nov 13 2004 - p64(2) [501+]

McCann, Michael - *Health Hazards Manual for Artists, 5th Rev. Ed.*
R&R Bk N - v19 - i4 - Nov 2004 - p245(1) [501+]

McCann, Richard - *Mother of Sorrows*
KR - v73 - i2 - Jan 15 2005 - p77(1) [51-500]
LJ - v129 - i20 - Dec 1 2004 - p88(1) [1-50]
LJ - v130 - i4 - March 1 2005 - p79(1) [51-500]
PW - v252 - i10 - March 7 2005 - p51(1) [51-500]

McCants, Clyde T. - *Opera for Libraries: A Guide to Core Works, Audio and Video Recordings, Books and Serials*
ALJ - v53 - i3 - August 2004 - p328(2) [501+]

McCargo, Duncan - *Media and Politics in Pacific Asia*
Pac A - v77 - i3 - Fall 2004 - p549(2) [501+]

McCarney, Patricia - *Governance on the Ground Innovations and Discontinuties in Cities of Developing World*
CS - v33 - i5 - Sept 2004 - p625-625 [501+]

McCarroll, Stacey - *California Dreamin': Camera Clubs in the Pictorial Photography Tradition*
Choice - v42 - i1 - Sept 2004 - p93(1) [501+]

McCarry, Charles - *Old Boys*
Econ - v373 - i8395 - Oct 2 2004 - p84US [501+]
KR - v72 - i24 - Dec 15 2004 - pS6(1) [501+]
Spec - v296 - i9189 - Sept 18 2004 - p56(1) [501+]
TLS - i5304 - Nov 26 2004 - p23(1) [501+]
The Tears of Autumn
LJ - v130 - i2 - Feb 1 2005 - p126(1) [1-50]

McCarthy, Conor - *Love, Sex and Marriage in the Middle Ages: A Sourcebook*
CH - v73 - i4 - Dec 2004 - p841(1) [51-500]

McCarthy, Dayton - *The Once and Future Army: A History of the Citizen Military Forces 1947-1974*
AHR - v109 - i2 - April 2004 - p505(2) [501+]

McCarthy, Erin - *Houston, We Have a Problem*
BL - v100 - i22 - August 2004 - p1909(1) [51-500]
Mouth to Mouth
BL - v101 - i7 - Dec 1 2004 - p642(1) [51-500]

McCarthy, George E. - *Classical Horizons: The Origins of Sociology in Ancient Greece*
CS - v33 - i6 - Nov 2004 - p736(3) [501+]

McCarthy, Gerry - *The Theatres of Moliere*
Theat J - v56 - i1 - March 2004 - p131(3) [501+]

McCarthy, Jim - *Voices of Latin Rock*
Bwatch - Jan 2005 - pNA [51-500]

McCarthy, John A. - *The Many Faces of Germany: Transformations in the Study of German Culture and History, Festschrift for Frank Trommler*
R&R Bk N - v19 - i3 - August 2004 - p42(1) [51-500]

McCarthy, Julia - *Stormthrower*
CBRA - Annual 2003 - p225(1) [51-500]

McCarthy, Justin - *The Ottoman Peoples and the End of Empire*
HER - v119 - i482 - June 2004 - p824(2) [501+]

McCarthy, Kathleen D. - *American Creed: Philanthropy and the Rise of Civil Society, 1700-1865*
JAH - v91 - i3 - Dec 2004 - p982(3) [501+]
JSH - v70 - i4 - Nov 2004 - p893(2) [501+]
NEQ - v77 - i2 - June 2004 - p323-325 [501+]
RAH - v32 - i4 - Dec 2004 - p506-511 [501+]

McCarthy, Keith - *The Silent Sleep of the Dying*
BL - v100 - i22 - August 2004 - p1906(1) [51-500]
KR - v72 - i14 - July 15 2004 - p663(1) [51-500]
PW - v251 - i32 - August 9 2004 - p234(1) [51-500]

McCarthy, Meghan - *The Adventures of Patty and the Big Red Bus (Illus. by McCarthy, Meghan)*
c KR - v73 - i5 - March 1 2005 - p291(1) [51-500]
George Upside Down
c LibMed - v22 - i4 - Jan 2004 - p60(1) [501+]

McCarthy, Michael (b. 1932 -) - *Journey Home*
y CBRA - Annual 2003 - p502(2) [51-500]

McCarthy, Michael R. - *Carlisle and Cumbria: Roman and Medieval Architecture, Art and Archaeology*
Choice - v42 - i7 - March 2005 - p1219(2) [51-500]
R&R Bk N - v19 - i4 - Nov 2004 - p35(1) [51-500]

McCarthy, Muriel - *The Making of Marsh's Library: Learning, Politics and Religion in Ireland, 1650-1750*
R&R Bk N - v19 - i4 - Nov 2004 - p257(1) [501+]
Marsh's Library, Dublin: All Graduates and Gentlemen
R&R Bk N - v19 - i1 - Feb 2004 - p194(1) [51-500]

McCarthy, Pat - *Canada*
c CH Bwatch - Feb 2005 - pNA [51-500]
Famous Confederate Generals and Leaders of the South
c SLJ - v51 - i2 - Feb 2005 - p150(1) [51-500]
Famous Union Generals and Leaders of the North
c SLJ - v51 - i2 - Feb 2005 - p150(1) [51-500]

McCarthy, Pete - *The Road to McCarthy: Around the World in Search of Ireland*
BL - v101 - i2 - Sept 15 2004 - p201(1) [501+]

McCarthy, Robert L. - *Introduction to Health Care Delivery: A Primer for Pharmacists, 3rd Ed.*
SciTech - v28 - i3 - Sept 2004 - p81(1) [51-500]

McCarthy, Susan - *Becoming a Tiger: How Baby Animals Learn to Live in the Wild*
New Sci - v183 - i2456 - July 17 2004 - p46(1) [501+]
y SLJ - v50 - i11 - Nov 2004 - p179(1) [51-500]

McCartney, Laton - *Across the Great Divide: Robert Stuart and the Discovery of the Oregon Trail*
Choice - v41 - i7 - March 2004 - p1357(1) [501+]
CR - v286 - i1668 - Jan 2005 - p59(1) [51-500]

McCartney, Paul - *Each One Believing: Paul McCartney on Stage, Off Stage, and Backstage*
PW - v251 - i46 - Nov 15 2004 - p56(1) [501+]

McCarty, Betsy Lee - *Knit Socks!: 15 Cool Patterns for Toasty Feet*
LJ - v129 - i13 - August 2004 - p78(1) [51-500]

McCarty, Bill - *Learning Red Hat Enterprise Linux and Fedora, 4th ed.*
SciTech - v28 - i3 - Sept 2004 - p26(1) [51-500]
Learning Red Hat Enterprise Linux and Fedora
LJ - v130 - i1 - Jan 1 2005 - p148(1) [51-500]

McCarty, John - *Bullets over Hollywood: The American Gangster Picture from the Silents to The Sopranos*
Choice - v42 - i5 - Jan 2005 - p860(1) [1-50]
R&R Bk N - v19 - i4 - Nov 2004 - p223(1) [501+]

McCarty, Peter - *T Is for Terrible (Illus. by McCarty, Peter)*
c KR - v72 - i13 - July 1 2004 - p633(1) [51-500]
c PW - v251 - i29 - July 19 2004 - p159(1) [51-500]
c SLJ - v50 - i8 - August 2004 - p89(2) [51-500]

McCaslin, Richard B. - *Last Stronghold: The Campaign for Fort Fisher*
R&R Bk N - v19 - i4 - Nov 2004 - p62(1) [51-500]

McCaughey, Martha - *Reel Knockouts: Violent Women in the Movies*
Signs - v30 - i2 - Wntr 2005 - p1700(4) [501+]

McCaughey, Robert A. - *Stand, Columbia: A History of Columbia University in the City of New York, 1754-2004*
R&R Bk N - v19 - i1 - Feb 2004 - p194(1) [51-500]

McCaughrean, Geraldine - *The Kite Rider (Illus. by Bishop, Cynthia). Audiobook Review*
y SLJ - v50 - i9 - Sept 2004 - p77(2) [51-500]
The Kite Rider (Read by Druke, Galen). Audiobook Review
y BL - v101 - i3 - Oct 1 2004 - p352(1) [51-500]
The Kite Rider (Read by Bishop, Cynthia). Audiobook Review
y Kliatt - v38 - i5 - Sept 2004 - p62(2) [51-500]
The Kite Rider
c WLT - v79 - i1 - Jan-April 2005 - p69(4) [501+]
Odysseus
c BL - v101 - i8 - Dec 15 2004 - p739(2) [51-500]
y KR - v72 - i22 - Nov 15 2004 - p1091(1) [51-500]
y PW - v251 - i50 - Dec 13 2004 - p69(1) [51-500]
c SLJ - v50 - i12 - Dec 2004 - p163(1) [51-500]
The Pirate's Son
y BL - v101 - i1 - Sept 1 2004 - p121(1) [501+]
Smile! (Illus. by McCaughrean, Ian)
c Sch Lib - v52 - i4 - Winter 2004 - p202(1) [51-500]
Stop the Train!
c PW - v252 - i2 - Jan 10 2005 - p58(1) [1-50]

McCauley, Cynthia D. - *The Center for Creative Leadership Handbook of Leadership Development*
Per Psy - v57 - i3 - Autumn 2004 - p798(4) [501+]
R&R Bk N - v19 - i3 - August 2004 - p104(1) [1-50]

McCauley, Dana - *"Homemaker's" Menu of the Month Cookbook*
CBRA - Annual 2003 - p131(1) [51-500]

McCauley, Gary F. - *Soldier Boys*
CBRA - Annual 2003 - p176(2) [51-500]

McCauley, Robert N. - *Bringing Ritual to Mind: Psychological Foundations of Cultural Forms*
JR - v85 - i1 - Jan 2005 - p174(2) [501+]

McCauley, William - *Need: Stories from Africa*
KR - v72 - i18 - Sept 15 2004 - p886(1) [501+]
PW - v251 - i43 - Oct 25 2004 - p26(1) [51-500]

McCay, Frances - *Into the Blue*
c Sch Lib - v52 - i4 - Winter 2004 - p188(1) [51-500]

McCay, Kay - *The Potion Maker*
c Sch Lib - v52 - i4 - Winter 2004 - p202(2) [51-500]

McChesney, Robert W. - *The Problem of the Media: U.S. Communication Politics in the Twenty-First Century*
Choice - v42 - i1 - Sept 2004 - p94(1) [501+]

McClanan, Anne L. - *The Material Culture of Sex, Procreation and Marriage in Premodern Europe*
Six Ct J - v34 - i4 - Winter 2003 - p1217-1218 [501+]

McClane, Patrick W. - *The Architecture of James Gamble Rogers II in Winter Park Florida*
Choice - v42 - i7 - March 2005 - p1220(1) [51-500]

McClaren, Bill - *Encyclopedia of Dahlias*
SciTech - v28 - i4 - Dec 2004 - p125 [51-500]

McClatchy, J.D. - *American Writers at Home*
Globe & Mail - Dec 18 2004 - pD14 [1-50]

McClatchy, Will - *Index Funds: Strategies for Investment Success*
R&R Bk N - v19 - i2 - May 2004 - p123 [51-500]

McClean, Barbara - *Lambsquarters: Scenes from a Handmade Life*
Can Lit - i182 - Autumn 2004 - p178(3) [501+]

McCleary, John Bassett - *Hippie Dictionary*
NW - July 12 2004 - p15 [501+]

McClellan, Lawrence - *The Later Swing Era, 1942 to 1955*
Choice - v42 - i7 - March 2005 - p1236(2) [501+]
R&R Bk N - v19 - i4 - Nov 2004 - p197(1) [501+]

McClellan, Marilyn - *The Big Deal about Alcohol: What Teens Need to Know about Drinking*
c SLJ - v50 - i10 - Oct 2004 - p190(2) [51-500]

McClelland, Charles E. - *Prophets, Paupers, or Professionals?: A Social History of Everyday Visual Artists in Modern Germany, 1850-Present*
R&R Bk N - v19 - i2 - May 2004 - p193(1) [51-500]

McClelland, Deke - *Adobe Photoshop CS: One-on-One*
SciTech - v28 - i3 - Sept 2004 - p136(1) [51-500]

McClelland, Doug - *Eleanor Parker: Woman of a Thousand Faces, a Bio-Bibliography and Filmography*
R&R Bk N - v19 - i1 - Feb 2004 - p227(1) [51-500]

McClelland, Ted - *Horseplayers: Life at the Track*
KR - v73 - i5 - March 1 2005 - p278(1) [501+]

McClenahan, William M., Jr. - *The Market, the State, and the Export-Import Bank of the United States, 1934-2000*
JAH - v91 - i3 - Dec 2004 - p1080(2) [501+]

McClendon, McKee J. - *Statistical Analysis in the Social Sciences*
R&R Bk N - v19 - i1 - Feb 2004 - p77(1) [1-50]

McClendon, Muriel C. - *The Quiet Reformation: Magistrates and the Emergence of Protestantism in Tudor Norwich*
CH - v73 - i4 - Dec 2004 - p861(2) [501+]

McClennen, Sophia A. - *The Dialectics of Exile: Nation, Time, Language, and Space in Hispanic Literatures*
Choice - v42 - i1 - Sept 2004 - p106(1) [501+]

McClernon, John P. - *Sermon in a Sentence*
CI - v13 - i2 - Feb 2005 - p39(1) [501+]

McCleverty, Jon A. - *Comprehensive Coordination Chemistry II: From Biology to Nanatechnology*
Choice - v41 - i11-12 - July-August 2004 - p2073(1) [501+]

McClintock, Norah - *Dead and Gone*
y Res Links - v10 - i3 - Feb 2005 - p38(1) [51-500]
Hit and Run
y CBRA - Annual 2003 - p503(1) [51-500]
Truth and Lies
c Globe & Mail - August 14 2004 - pD16 [51-500]

McCloskey, Robert - *Make Way for Ducklings*
c RT - v57 - Sept 2003 - p98 [1-50]

McCloud, Sean - *Making the American Religious Fringe: Exotics, Subversives, and Journalists, 1955-1993*
Choice - v42 - i2 - Oct 2004 - p311(1) [51-500]

McClowry, Sandee Graham - *Your Child's Unique Temperment: Insights and Strategies for Responsive Parenting*
R&R Bk N - v19 - i4 - Nov 2004 - p130(1) [1-50]

McClung, Nellie - *Nellie McClung: The Complete Autobiography: Clearing in the West and the Stream Runs Fast*
R&R Bk N - v19 - i4 - Nov 2004 - p239(1) [51-500]

McClure, George W. - *The Culture of Profession in Late Renaissance Italy*
R&R Bk N - v19 - i4 - Nov 2004 - p40(1) [51-500]

McClure, Laura K. - *Courtesans at Table: Gender and Greek Literary Culture in Athenaeus*
R&R Bk N - v19 - i4 - Nov 2004 - p214(1) [501+]
Sexuality and Gender in the Classical World: Readings and Sources
HNet - June 2004 - pNA [501+]

McClure, Stuart - *Web Hacking*
Bwatch - v26 - i8 - August 2004 - p7(1) [51-500]

McClure, Wendy - *I'm Not the New Me*
KR - v73 - i4 - Feb 15 2005 - p215(1) [501+]
PW - v252 - i11 - March 14 2005 - p58(2) [51-500]

McClymond, Michael J. - *Familiar Stranger: An Introduction to Jesus of Nazareth*
AM - v191 - i7 - Sept 20 2004 - p26 [501+]
Ch Today - v49 - i2 - Feb 2005 - p89(2) [501+]
Choice - v42 - i4 - Dec 2004 - p679(1) [1-50]

McColl, Michael - *Metaprogramming GPUs with Sh*
SciTech - v28 - i4 - Dec 2004 - p130 [51-500]

McCollum, Jonathan - *Armenian Music: A Comprehensive Bibliography and Discography*
Choice - v42 - i2 - Oct 2004 - p267(2) [51-500]

McCombie, John - *Productivity Growth and Economic Performance: Essays on Verdoorn's Law*
JEL - v42 - i3 - Sept 2004 - p862(3) [501+]

McConachie, Bruce - *American Theater in the Culture of the Cold War: Producing and Contesting Containment, 1947-1962*
Am St - v45 - i1 - Spring 2004 - p166-167 [501+]

McConchie, Lyn - *The Duke's Ballad*
PW - v251 - i51 - Dec 20 2004 - p41(2) [501+]

McConell, Andy - *The Decanter: An Illustrated History of Glass from 1650*
Apo - v161 - i517 - March 2005 - p102(1) [501+]

McConkey, James - *The Telescope in the Parlor: Essays on Life and Literature*
PW - v251 - i46 - Nov 15 2004 - p54(1) [501+]

McConkey, Kenneth - *Memory and Desire: Painting in Britain and Ireland at the Turn of the Twentieth Century*
Albion - v36 - i1 - Spring 2004 - p170(3) [501+]

McConnell, John H. - *Auditing Your Human Resources Department: A Step-by-Step Guide*
HR Mag - v49 - i7 - July 2004 - pS32(1) [501+]
HR Mag - v50 - i2 - Feb 2005 - pS14(1) [501+]
How to Develop Essential HR Policies and Procedures
HR Mag - v50 - i2 - Feb 2005 - pS9(1) [501+]

McConnell, Kevin - *Redware: America's Folk Art Pottery*
Ceram Mo - v52 - i3 - March 2004 - p32(1) [501+]

McConnell, Melissa - *Evidence of Love*
KR - v73 - i3 - Feb 1 2005 - p141(2) [501+]
PW - v252 - i4 - Jan 24 2005 - p118(1) [501+]
PW - v252 - i11 - March 14 2005 - p43(1) [51-500]

McConnell, Steve - *Code Complete, 2nd Ed.*
SciTech - v28 - i3 - Sept 2004 - p25(1) [51-500]

McConville, Sean - *Use of Punishment*
Law&PolBR - August 2004 - p606(3) [501+]

McCoog, Thomas M. - *"Promising Hope": Essays on the Suppression and Restoration of the English Province of the Society of Jesus*
CHR - v90 - i4 - Oct 2004 - p804(2) [501+]

McCook, Kathleen de la Pena - *Introduction to Public Librarianship*
LJ - v129 - i20 - Dec 1 2004 - p174(1) [51-500]
R&R Bk N - v19 - i4 - Nov 2004 - p257(1) [501+]

McCool, Daniel - *Native Waters: Contemporary Indian Water Setlements and the Second Treaty Era*
WHQ - v35 - i1 - Spring 2004 - p80-81 [501+]

McCoole, Sinead - *No Ordinary Women: Irish Female Activists in the Revolutionary Years 1900-1923*
ELT - v48 - i1 - Wntr 2005 - p220(4) [501+]

Mccord, Charline R. - *Christmas in the South*
S Liv - v39 - i12 - Dec 2004 - p54(1) [501+]

McCord, Patricia - *Pictures in the Dark*
y HB - v80 - i4 - July-August 2004 - p457(1) [51-500]
JAAL - v48 - i1 - Sept 2004 - p77(1) [501+]
y VOYA - v27 - i4 - Oct 2004 - p306(1) [51-500]

McCorduck, Pamela - *Machines Who Think: A Personal Inquiry into the History and Prospects of Artificial Intelligence*
Choice - v42 - i2 - Oct 2004 - p314(1) [51-500]

McCorkle, Sandra K. - *Web Pages for Your Classroom: The Easy Way*
LibMed - v22 - i5 - Feb 2004 - p85(1) [501+]
VOYA - v27 - i5 - Dec 2004 - p424(1) [51-500]

McCorkle, Suzanne - *Mediation Theory and Practice*
R&R Bk N - v19 - i3 - August 2004 - p144(1) [1-50]

McCormack, Derek - *Grab Bag*
Lam Bk Rpt - v13 - i3 - Oct 2004 - p38(2) [501+]
The Haunted Hillbilly
Globe & Mail - Nov 27 2004 - pD3 [51-500]
Lam Bk Rpt - v13 - i3 - Oct 2004 - p38(2) [501+]

McCormack, Guy L. - *Occupational Therapy Manager, 4th Ed.*
SciTech - v28 - i3 - Sept 2004 - p123(1) [51-500]

McCormack, Patrick - *The Last Companion: A Novel of Arthurian Britain*
KR - v72 - i24 - Dec 15 2004 - p1160(1) [501+]

McCormack, William J. - *'10-45' Spells Death*
Globe & Mail - Oct 2 2004 - pD7 [51-500]

McCormick, Donald B. - *Annual Review of Nutrition, Vol. 24, 2004*
QRB - v79 - i4 - Dec 2004 - p461(2) [501+]
SciTech - v28 - i3 - Sept 2004 - p171(1) [51-500]

McCormick, John - *Contemproary Britain*
R&R Bk N - v19 - i1 - Feb 2004 - p33(1) [1-50]

McCormick, Neil - *Killing Bono*
PW - v251 - i34 - August 23 2004 - p45(1) [51-500]

McCormick, Richard W. - *German Essays on Film*
R&R Bk N - v19 - i3 - August 2004 - p261(1) [51-500]

McCormick, Rosie - *Life Is a Pueblo*
c CBRA - Annual 2003 - p533(2) [51-500]

McCormmach, Russell - *Speculative Truth: Henry Cavendish, Natural Philosophy, and the Rise of Modern Theoretical Science*
Choice - v42 - i1 - Sept 2004 - p126(1) [501+]

McCorquodale, Robert - *Human Rights*
R&R Bk N - v19 - i1 - Feb 2004 - pNA [501+]

McCouch, Hannah - *Mountain Betty*
y BL - v101 - i8 - Dec 15 2004 - p708(1) [51-500]

McCourt, James - *Queer Street: Rise and Fall of an American Culture, 1947-1985*
Lam Bk Rpt - v13 - i1-2 - August-Sept 2004 - p21(2) [501+]
NYTBR - Jan 30 2005 - p24 [501+]
R&R Bk N - v19 - i1 - Feb 2004 - p128(1) [51-500]

McCourt, Lisa - *The Most Thankful Thing (Illus. by Moore, Cyd)*
KR - v72 - i20 - Oct 15 2004 - p1010(1) [51-500]
c PW - v251 - i49 - Dec 6 2004 - p58(1) [51-500]

McCourt, Malachy - *Malachy McCourt's History of Ireland*
Ent W - i785 - Sept 24 2004 - p114 [501+]
Globe & Mail - Dec 11 2004 - pD4 [501+]
KR - v72 - i17 - Sept 1 2004 - p851(1) [501+]
LJ - v129 - i17 - Oct 15 2004 - p74(1) [51-500]
PW - v251 - i40 - Oct 4 2004 - p83(1) [51-500]

McCourt, Willy - *Global Human Resource Management: Managing People in Developing and Traditional Countries*
R&R Bk N - v19 - i2 - May 2004 - p117 [501+]

McCown, Clint - *The Weatherman*
BL - v100 - i22 - August 2004 - p1906(1) [51-500]
KR - v72 - i14 - July 15 2004 - p651(2) [501+]
LJ - v129 - i14 - Sept 1 2004 - p140(1) [51-500]
Ent W - i789 - Oct 22 2004 - p101 [51-500]
PW - v251 - i37 - Sept 13 2004 - p58(2) [501+]

McCoy, Edain - *Advanced Witchcraft: Go Deeper, Reach Further, Fly Higher*
Bwatch - Feb 2005 - pNA [51-500]

McCoy, Ken - *Mad Carew*
LJ - v130 - i1 - Jan 1 2005 - p84(1) [51-500]

McCoy, Maureen - *Junebug*
NYTBR - August 22 2004 - p23 [501+]

McCoy, Richard - *Alterations of State: Sacred Kingship in the English Reformation*
Six Ct J - v34 - i4 - Winter 2003 - p1175-1176 [501+]

McCoy, Robert Wayne - *The King of Ice Cream*
PW - v251 - i35 - August 30 2004 - p38(1) [501+]

McCracken, Kathleen - *Geography of Souls*
CBRA - Annual 2003 - p225(2) [51-500]

McCracken, Peggy - *The Curse of Eve, the Wound of the Hero: Blood, Gender, and Medieval Literature*
Clio - v33 - i2 - Wntr 2004 - p226(4) [501+]

McCray, W. Patrick - *Giant Telescopes: Astronomical Ambition and the Promise of Technology*
Am Sci - v93 - i1 - Jan-Feb 2005 - p82(3) [501+]
Astron - v32 - i9 - Sept 2004 - p92 [501+]
Choice - v42 - i1 - Sept 2004 - p127(1) [501+]
Nature - v430 - i7002 - August 19 2004 - p833(1) [501+]
TimHES - v0 - i1650 - July 23 2004 - p26(1) [501+]

McCrea, Brian - *Impotent Fathers*
Eight-C St - v36 - i2 - Winter 2003 - p275 [501+]

McCreary, Alf - *Nobody's Fool: The Life of Archbishop Robin Eames*
TLS - i5305 - Dec 3 2004 - p31(1) [501+]

McCreery, Cindy - *The Satirical Gaze: Prints of Women in Late Eighteenth-Century England*
Apo - v159 - i509 - July 2004 - p70(2) [501+]
HRNB - v33 - i1 - Fall 2004 - p20(2) [501+]

McCrorie, Edward - *Odyssey*
Choice - v42 - i3 - Nov 2004 - p479(1) [1-50]

McCrossen, Alexis - *Holy Day, Holiday: The American Sunday*
CHR - v90 - i3 - July 2004 - p572(2) [501+]

McCrudden, Christopher - *Anti-Discrimination Law*
Law&PolBR - Sept 2004 - pNA [501+]

McCrum, Robert - *Wodehouse: A Life*
Am Theat - v21 - i8 - Oct 2004 - p139(4) [501+]
Atl - v294 - i4 - Nov 2004 - p136(7) [501+]
BL - v101 - i2 - Sept 15 2004 - p194(1) [501+]
BW - v34 - i49 - Dec 5 2004 - p8(2) [501+]
Econ - v373 - i8402 - Nov 20 2004 - p87US [501+]
Globe & Mail - Nov 20 2004 - pD6 [501+]
Globe & Mail - Nov 27 2004 - pD3 [51-500]
KR - v72 - i18 - Sept 15 2004 - p904(1) [501+]
LJ - v129 - i15 - Sept 15 2004 - p58(1) [51-500]
NS - v133 - i4706 - Sept 20 2004 - p49(2) [501+]
NS - v133 - i4716 - Nov 29 2004 - p43(1) [51-500]
NYTBR - Dec 5 2004 - p48 [501+]
PW - v251 - i35 - August 30 2004 - p39(1) [501+]
Spec - v295 - i9186 - August 28 2004 - p28(2) [501+]
TLS - i5297 - Oct 8 2004 - p12(1) [501+]
Wil Q - v29 - i1 - Wntr 2005 - p117(2) [501+]

McCrumb, Sharyn - *St. Dale*
BL - v101 - i9-10 - Jan 1 2005 - p827(2) [1-50]
KR - v72 - i23 - Dec 1 2004 - p1109(2) [51-500]
LJ - v129 - i19 - Nov 15 2004 - p50(1) [501+]
PW - v252 - i3 - Jan 17 2005 - p35(2) [51-500]

McCuen, Jo Ray - *From Idea to Essay: A Rhetoric, Reader, and Handbook, 10th Ed.*
R&R Bk N - v19 - i1 - Feb 2004 - p216(1) [51-500]

McCullers, Carson - *The Heart Is a Lonely Hunter. Audiobook Review*
BL - v101 - i5 - Nov 1 2004 - p504(1) [51-500]
The Heart Is a Lonely Hunter
Globe & Mail - August 7 2004 - pD14 [1-50]

McCulloch, Diarmaid - *The Reformation: A History*
BW - v34 - i37 - Sept 12 2004 - p11(1) [1-50]

McCulloch, Fiona - *The Fictional Role of Childhood in Victorian and Early Twentieth Century Children's Literature*
R&R Bk N - v19 - i4 - Nov 2004 - p234(1) [501+]

McCulloch, Gregory - *The Life of the Mind: An Essay on Phenomenological Externalism*
RM - v58 - i2 - Dec 2004 - p457(2) [501+]

McCulloch, Margery Palmer - *Modernism and Nationalism: Literature and Society in Scotland, 1918-1939*
TLS - i5307 - Dec 17 2004 - p31(1) [1-50]

McCulloh, Mark R. - *Understanding W.G. Sebald*
Ger Q - v77 - i4 - Fall 2004 - p505-506 [501+]

McCullors, Tia - *A Heart of Devotion*
BL - v101 - i9-10 - Jan 1 2005 - p818(1) [1-50]

McCullough, David - *1776*
PW - v252 - i8 - Feb 21 2005 - p164(1) [501+]
The Great Bridge: The Epic Story of the Building of the Brooklyn Bridge (Read by Herrmann, Edward). Audiobook Review
PW - v251 - i36 - Sept 6 2004 - p26(1) [51-500]

McCullough, David Willis - *The Unending Mystery: A Journey through Labyrinths and Mazes*
BL - v101 - i3 - Oct 1 2004 - p287(1) [51-500]
KR - v72 - i16 - August 15 2004 - p793(2) [501+]
PW - v251 - i32 - August 9 2004 - p240(1) [51-500]

McCully, Emily Arnold - *Squirrel and John Muir (Illus. by McCully, Emily Arnold)*
c BL - v100 - i21 - July 2004 - p1849(1) [1-50]
c HB - v81 - i1 - Jan-Feb 2005 - p81(1) [51-500]
c KR - v72 - i16 - August 15 2004 - p809(1) [51-500]
c PW - v251 - i34 - August 23 2004 - p54(1) [501+]
c SLJ - v50 - i10 - Oct 2004 - p122(1) [51-500]

McCumber, John - *Assessing and Managing Security Risk in IT Systems: A Structured Methodology*
SciTech - v28 - i4 - Dec 2004 - p29(1) [51-500]

McCunn, Ruthanne Lum - *Sole Survivor (Read by Ward, Johanna). Audiobook Review*
y Kliatt - v38 - i5 - Sept 2004 - p69(2) [51-500]

McCurdy, Michael - *The Train They Call the City of New Orleans*
c LibMed - v22 - i4 - Jan 2004 - p57(1) [501+]

McCusker, Kristine M. - *A Boy Named Sue: Gender and Country Music*
Bwatch - Feb 2005 - pNA [51-500]
Choice - v42 - i7 - March 2005 - p1236(1) [51-500]

McCusker, Paul - *The Mill House*
BL - v101 - i9-10 - Jan 1 2005 - p818(1) [501+]

McCutchan, Philip - *Halfhyde and the Admiral (Read by Scott, Christopher). Audiobook Review*
y Kliatt - v39 - i1 - Jan 2005 - p42(1) [51-500]

McCutchen, H.L. - *LightLand*
Kliatt - v38 - i6 - Nov 2004 - p22(1) [51-500]

McCutcheon, Marc - *Kid Who Named Pluto*
c CH Bwatch - v14 - i7 - July 2004 - p2(1) [51-500]

McCutcheon, Scott - *Facts on File Marine Science Handbook*
c LibMed - v22 - i5 - Feb 2004 - p59(1) [501+]

McDaniel, Carl N. - *Wisdom for a Livable Planet*
PW - v252 - i6 - Feb 7 2005 - p55(2) [501+]

McDaniel, Charlotte - *Organizational Ethics: Research and Ethical Environments*
R&R Bk N - v19 - i4 - Nov 2004 - p110(1) [51-500]

McDaniel, Josh - *Burn Baby, Burn!*
Bwatch - v26 - i9 - Sept 2004 - p5(2) [501+]

McDaniel, June - *Offering Flowers, Feeding Skulls: Popular Goddess Worship in West Bengal*
Choice - v42 - i6 - Feb 2005 - p1039(1) [501+]

McDaniel, Lurlene - *Angels in Pink*
c CH Bwatch - Feb 2005 - pNA [51-500]
Journey of Hope
c CH Bwatch - Feb 2005 - pNA [51-500]

McDaniel, Melissa - *Pushing the Limits: A Chapter Book*
c SLJ - v51 - i1 - Jan 2005 - p148(1) [51-500]

McDaniel, Patricia A. - *Shrinking Violets and Caspar Milquetoasts: Shyness, Power, and Intimacy in the United States, 1950-1995*
JAH - v91 - i3 - Dec 2004 - p1082(2) [501+]
McDaniels, Timothy - *Risk Analysis and Society: An Interdisciplinary Characterization of the Field*
Env - v46 - i9 - Nov 2004 - p40(1) [501+]
McDermid, Val - *The Distant Echo (Read by Kotcher, Tom). Audiobook Review*
BL - v101 - i2 - Sept 15 2004 - p258(1) [51-500]
The Torment of Others
Globe & Mail - Oct 2 2004 - pD18 [51-500]
Globe & Mail - Nov 27 2004 - pD18 [1-50]
McDermott, Alice - *That Night*
BL - v101 - i2 - Sept 15 2004 - p225(1) [501+]
McDermott, Gerald - *Creation*
c   Teach Lib - v32 - i1 - Oct 2004 - p22(1) [51-500]
McDermott, Gerald A. - *Embedded Politics: Industrial Networks and Institutional Change in Postcommunism*
CS - v33 - i2 - March 2004 - p218-219 [501+]
JEL - v42 - i1 - March 2004 - p225(2) [501+]
McDermott, Keith - *Acqua Calda*
KR - v72 - i24 - Dec 15 2004 - p1160(1) [51-500]
LJ - v130 - i4 - March 1 2005 - p79(1) [51-500]
PW - v252 - i5 - Jan 31 2005 - p48(1) [51-500]
McDermott, M.T. - *Electrochemistry of Carbon Materials; Proceedings*
SciTech - v28 - i3 - Sept 2004 - p51(1) [1-50]
McDermott, Michael - *Boogers are Blessings (Illus. by Ross, Bill)*
c   PW - v251 - i43 - Oct 25 2004 - p47(1) [51-500]
McDermott, Terry - *Perfect Soldiers: The Hijackers: Who They Were, Why They Did It*
KR - v73 - i5 - March 1 2005 - p278(1) [501+]
PW - v252 - i7 - Feb 14 2005 - p60(1) [51-500]
McDevitt, Jack - *Polaris*
BL - v101 - i5 - Nov 1 2004 - p472(1) [51-500]
KR - v72 - i18 - Sept 15 2004 - p896(1) [51-500]
LJ - v129 - i19 - Nov 15 2004 - p54(1) [501+]
PW - v251 - i38 - Sept 20 2004 - p50(1) [51-500]
McDevitt, Patrick F. - *May the Best Man Win: Sport, Masculinity, and the Nationalism in Great Britain and the Empire, 1880-1935*
Choice - v42 - i2 - Oct 2004 - p331(1) [51-500]
McDevitt, Theresa - *Women and the American Civil War: An Annotated Bibliography*
J Mil H - v68 - i3 - July 2004 - p965(1) [501+]
JSH - v70 - i4 - Nov 2004 - p987(2) [501+]
R&R Bk N - v19 - i1 - Feb 2004 - p262(1) [51-500]
McDonagh, Josephine - *Child Murder and British Culture: 1720-1900*
TLS - i5296 - Oct 1 2004 - p28(1) [501+]
McDonald, Beth E. - *Vampire as Numinous Experience*
ChrSFF&H - v26 - i10 - Oct 2004 - p30(1) [51-500]
McDonald, Bob - *Quirks and Quarks Question Book: 101 Answers to Listeners' Questions*
CBRA - Annual 2003 - p17(1) [51-500]
McDonald, Deborah - *Clara Collet, 1860-1948: An Educated Working Woman*
Choice - v42 - i2 - Oct 2004 - p360(1) [51-500]
McDonald, Forrest - *Recovering the Past: A Historian's Memoir*
HRNB - v33 - i1 - Fall 2004 - p7(2) [501+]
States' Rights and the Union: Imperium in Imperio, 1776-1876
W&M Q - v61 - i3 - July 2004 - p582-588 [501+]
McDonald, Frederick F. - *Ancestral Portraits: The Colour of My People*
CBRA - Annual 2003 - p366(1) [501+]
McDonald, Furman S. - *Mayo Clinic Images in Internal Medicine: Self-Assessment for Board Exam Review*
SciTech - v28 - i4 - Dec 2004 - p89(1) [501+]
McDonald, Gregory - *The Buck Passes Flynn*
LJ - v129 - i12 - July 2004 - p127(1) [1-50]
Fletch and the Man Who
LJ - v130 - i3 - Feb 15 2005 - p172(1) [51-500]
McDonald, Heather - *Blood, Bones and Spirit: Aboriginal Christianity in an East Kimberley Town*
Quad - v48 - i11 - Nov 2004 - p86(2) [501+]
McDonald, Henry - *UDA: Inside the Heart of Loyalist Terror*
CR - v286 - i1668 - Jan 2005 - p64(1) [51-500]
McDonald, Hugh P. - *John Dewey and Environmental Philosophy*
Choice - v41 - i11-12 - July-August 2004 - p2058(1) [501+]
Radical Axiology: A First Philosophy of Values
R&R Bk N - v19 - i4 - Nov 2004 - p8(1) [501+]

McDonald, Ian - *River of Gods*
ChrSFF&H - v26 - i10 - Oct 2004 - p26(1) [51-500]
New Sci - v183 - i2465 - Sept 18 2004 - p47(1) [51-500]
McDonald, Janet - *Brother Hood*
y   BL - v101 - i1 - Sept 1 2004 - p108(2) [1-50]
y   CCB-B - v58 - i5 - Jan 2005 - p216(2) [51-500]
y   HB - v81 - i1 - Jan-Feb 2005 - p96(1) [51-500]
y   Kliatt - v38 - i5 - Sept 2004 - p14(2) [51-500]
y   KR - v72 - i15 - August 1 2004 - p745(1) [51-500]
y   SLJ - v50 - i11 - Nov 2004 - p149(2) [51-500]
Chill Wind
y   Sch Lib - v52 - i3 - Autumn 2004 - p159(1) [501+]
Twists and Turns
y   LibMed - v22 - i6 - March 2004 - p68(1) [501+]
McDonald, John D. - *Electric Power Substations Engineering*
E-Streams - Sept 2004 - pNA [501+]
McDonald, Joyce - *Devil on My Heels*
y   CCB-B - v58 - i1 - Sept 2004 - p28(2) [51-500]
c   LibMed - v23 - i3 - Nov-Dec 2004 - p73(1) [51-500]
c   SLJ - v50 - i7 - July 2004 - p108(2) [51-500]
y   VOYA - v27 - i3 - August 2004 - p222(1) [1-50]
McDonald, Laughlin - *A Voting Rights Odyssey: Black Enfranchisement in Georgia*
JSH - v71 - i1 - Feb 2005 - p214(2) [501+]
McDonald, Lynn - *Florence Nightingale's European Travels*
Bwatch - Jan 2005 - pNA [51-500]
McDonald, Malcolm - *Marketing: A Complete Guide*
R&R Bk N - v19 - i1 - Feb 2004 - p108(1) [51-500]
McDonald, Marianne - *The Living Art of Greek Tragedy*
Theat J - v56 - i3 - Oct 2004 - p532-533 [501+]
McDonald, Marie A. - *Na Lei Makamae: The Treasured Lei*
R&R Bk N - v19 - i1 - Feb 2004 - p249(1) [51-500]
McDonald, Mark P. - *The Print Collection of Ferdinand Columbus (1488-1539): A Renaissance Collector in Seville, Vol. 1-2*
R&R Bk N - v19 - i4 - Nov 2004 - p208(1) [501+]
The Print Collection of Ferdinand Columbus (1488-1539): A Renaissance Collector in Seville, Vols. 1-2
Apo - v160 - i514 - Dec 2004 - p49(2) [501+]
McDonald, Maurice S. - *Photobiology of Higher Plants*
Choice - v41 - i7 - March 2004 - p1321(2) [501+]
McDonald, Megan - *Ant and Honey Bee: What a Pair! (Illus. by Karas, G. Brian)*
c   CCB-B - v58 - i6 - Feb 2005 - p258(2) [51-500]
c   KR - v73 - i1 - Jan 1 2005 - p55(1) [51-500]
c   PW - v252 - i5 - Jan 31 2005 - p66(1) [51-500]
Beetle McGrady Eats Bugs! (Illus. by Manning, Jane)
c   PW - v252 - i9 - Feb 28 2005 - p66(1) [51-500]
Judy Moody (Illus. by Reynolds, Peter H.)
c   SLJ - v50 - i7 - July 2004 - p43(1) [51-500]
Judy Moody, M.D.: The Doctor Is In! (Illus. by Reynolds, Peter H.)
c   BL - v101 - i4 - Oct 15 2004 - p406(1) [51-500]
c   CH Bwatch - v14 - i11 - Nov 2004 - pNA [51-500]
c   SLJ - v50 - i9 - Sept 2004 - p172(1) [51-500]
Judy Moody Predicts the Future (Illus. by Reynolds, Peter H.)
c   PW - v252 - i5 - Jan 31 2005 - p70(1) [1-50]
c   Storyworks - v12 - i4 - Jan 2005 - p6(1) [501+]
Judy Moody Saves the World (Illus. by Reynolds, Peter H.)
c   RT - v57 - Oct 2003 - p174 [1-50]
Stink: The Incredible Shrinking Kid (Illus. by Reynolds, Peter H.)
c   PW - v252 - i9 - Feb 28 2005 - p67(1) [51-500]
McDonald, Nicola - *Pulp Fictions of Medieval England: Essays in Popular Romance*
Choice - v42 - i6 - Feb 2005 - p1024(1) [51-500]
TLS - i5297 - Oct 8 2004 - p30(1) [51-500]
McDonald, Steven E. - *Waystation*
BL - v100 - i21 - July 2004 - p1829(1) [501+]
McDonald, W. Wesley - *Russell Kirk and the Age of Ideology*
Choice - v42 - i3 - Nov 2004 - p562(1) [1-50]
McDonell, Chris - *The Football Game I'll Never Forget: 100 NFL Stars' Stories*
BL - v101 - i1 - Sept 1 2004 - p47(1) [51-500]
McDonnell, Greg - *Canadian Pacific: Stand Fast, Craigellachie!*
CBRA - Annual 2003 - p441(1) [51-500]
R&R Bk N - v19 - i1 - Feb 2004 - p104(1) [51-500]

McDonnell, Kathleen - *Honey, We Lost the Kids: Re-Thinking Childhood in the Multimedia Age*
y   Teach Lib - v32 - i1 - Oct 2004 - p38(2) [501+]
Not an Easy Choice Re-Examining Abortion
CBRA - Annual 2003 - p386(2) [501+]
Putting on a Show
Bwatch - Dec 2004 - pNA [51-500]
Shining World
y   CBRA - Annual 2003 - p503(1) [51-500]
McDonnell, Kilian - *The Other Hand of God: The Holy Spirit as the Universal Touch and Goal*
TT - v61 - i3 - Oct 2004 - p390(3) [501+]
McDonnough, Kevin - *Education and Citizenship in Liberal-Democratic Societies: Teaching for Cosmopolitan Values and Collective Identities*
Choice - v42 - i1 - Sept 2004 - p157(2) [501+]
McDonough, John - *The Advertising Age Encyclopedia of Advertising*
BHR - v78 - i2 - Summer 2004 - p377(1) [501+]
McDonough, Stefan I. - *Calcium Channel Pharmacology*
SciTech - v28 - i1 - March 2004 - p122(1) [51-500]
McDonough, Yona Zeldis - *In Dahlia's Wake*
KR - v73 - i2 - Jan 15 2005 - p77(1) [501+]
LJ - v130 - i2 - Feb 1 2005 - p69(1) [51-500]
PW - v252 - i10 - March 7 2005 - p51(1) [51-500]
McDougal, Stuart Y. - *Stanley Kubrick's A Clockwork Orange*
Choice - v41 - i7 - March 2004 - p1304(1) [51-500]
McDougall, Bonnie S. - *Fictional Authors, Imaginary Audiences: Modern Chinese Literature in the Twentieth Century*
Ch Rev Int - v10 - i2 - Fall 2003 - p425(6) [501+]
Love-Letters and Privacy in Modern China: The Intimate Lives of Lu Xun and Xu Guangping
HJAS - v64 - i1 - June 2004 - p167-175 [501+]
McDougall, Walter A. - *Let the Sea Make a Noise...: A History of the North Pacific from Magellan to MacArthur*
Globe & Mail - August 21 2004 - pD13 [1-50]
LJ - v129 - i14 - Sept 1 2004 - p204(1) [51-500]
McDowell, Julie - *Lymphatic System*
SciTech - v28 - i4 - Dec 2004 - p69(1) [51-500]
Nervous System and Sense Organs
SciTech - v28 - i4 - Dec 2004 - p70(1) [51-500]
McDowell, Linda - *Redundant Masculinities? Employment Change and White Working Class Youth*
AJS - v110 - i2 - Sept 2004 - p503(2) [51-500]
McDowell, Nicholas - *The English Radical Imagination: Culture, Religion, and Revolution, 1630-1660*
Critm - v46 - i2 - Spring 2004 - p311(5) [501+]
Ren Q - v57 - i4 - Winter 2004 - p1495(2) [501+]
McDowell, Robert - *On Foot, in Flames*
HR - v55 - i4 - Winter 2003 - p671 [501+]
McDuff, Dusa - *J-Holomorphic Curves and Symplectic Topology*
SciTech - v28 - i3 - Sept 2004 - p41(1) [1-50]
McDuffee, Michael B. - *Small-Town Protestantism in Nineteenth-Century Germany: Living Lost Faith*
HNet - June 2004 - pNA [501+]
McElfish, James M., Jr. - *Nature Friendly Ordinances*
NRJ - v44 - i3 - Summer 2004 - p907-916 [501+]
McElheny, Victor K. - *Watson and DNA: Making a Scientistific Revolution*
T&C - v45 - i2 - April 2004 - p457-458 [501+]
McElligott, Matthew - *Absolutely Not*
c   LibMed - v23 - i1 - August-Sept 2004 - p65(1) [51-500]
McElmeel, Sharron L. - *Children's Authors and Illustrators Too Good to Miss: Biographical Sketches and Bibliographies*
R&R Bk N - v19 - i4 - Nov 2004 - p241(1) [501+]
SLJ - v51 - i1 - Jan 2005 - p162(1) [51-500]
McElmurray, Karen Salyer - *Surrendered Child: A Birth Mother's Journey*
KR - v72 - i14 - July 15 2004 - p675(1) [51-500]
McElroy, Nan - *Italy: Instructions for Use*
Bwatch - Dec 2004 - pNA [51-500]
McElvaine, Robert S. - *Encyclopedia of the Great Depression, Vols. 1-2*
BL - v101 - i9-10 - Jan 1 2005 - p779(1) [1-50]
LJ - v129 - i12 - July 2004 - p116(1) [51-500]
Ref Rev - Sept 2004 - pNA [501+]
R&USQ - v44 - i1 - Fall 2004 - p86(2) [501+]
McEnteer, James - *Deep in the Heart: The Texas Tendency in American Politics*
Pers PS - v34 - i1 - Wntr 2005 - p52(1) [501+]
R&R Bk N - v19 - i4 - Nov 2004 - p62(1) [51-500]

McEntegart, Rory - *Henry VIII, the League of Schmalkalden, and the English Reformation*
   Albion - v36 - i1 - Spring 2004 - p107(3) [501+]
   Six Ct J - v34 - i4 - Winter 2003 - p1228-1230 [501+]

McEvilley, T. - *The Shape of Ancient Thought: Comparative Studies in Greek and Indian Philosophies*
   Class R - v54 - i2 - Nov 2004 - p420(4) [501+]

McEvoy, John - *Blind Switch*
   LJ - v129 - i12 - July 2004 - p63(1) [51-500]
   PW - v251 - i28 - July 12 2004 - p47(2) [51-500]

McEvoy, Thomas J. - *Positive Impact Forestry: A Sustainable Approach to Managing Woodlands*
   Choice - v42 - i4 - Dec 2004 - p690(1) [1-50]
   SciTech - v28 - i3 - Sept 2004 - p131(1) [51-500]

McEwan, Ian - *Atonement*
   HR - v55 - i4 - Winter 2003 - p685 [501+]
   Black Dogs
   Globe & Mail - July 10 2004 - pD15 [501+]
   The Child in Time (Read by Prebble, Simon). Audiobook Review
   y Kliatt - v39 - i2 - March 2005 - p50(1) [51-500]
   Saturday
   KR - v73 - i2 - Jan 15 2005 - p78(1) [501+]
   LJ - v129 - i20 - Dec 1 2004 - p88(1) [51-500]
   NS - v134 - i4724 - Jan 24 2005 - p48(2) [501+]
   NW - March 21 2005 - p60 [501+]
   PW - v252 - i5 - Jan 31 2005 - p48(1) [51-500]
   Atl - v295 - i3 - April 2005 - p107(4) [501+]
   Globe & Mail - Feb 19 2005 - pD6 [501+]
   Spec - v297 - i9208 - Jan 29 2005 - p38(1) [501+]

McEwan, Jenny - *The Verdict of the Court: Passing Judgment in Law and Psychology*
   R&R Bk N - v19 - i1 - Feb 2004 - pNA [51-500]

McEwen, Bruce S. - *The End of Stress as We Know It*
   Per Psy - v57 - i3 - Autumn 2004 - p830(3) [501+]
   SciTech - v28 - i4 - Dec 2004 - p68(1) [51-500]

McEwen, I.K. - *Vitruvius: Writing the Body of Architecture*
   Class R - v54 - i1 - Nov 2004 - p393(3) [501+]

McFadden, Anna Hicks - *The Social Construction of Educational Leadership: Southern Appalachian Ceilings*
   R&R Bk N - v19 - i4 - Nov 2004 - p187(1) [501+]

McFadden, David W. - *An Innocent in Newfoundland: Even More Curious Rambles and Singular Ecounters*
   R&R Bk N - v19 - i3 - August 2004 - p76(1) [51-500]
   An Innocent in Newfoundland: Even More Curious Rambles and Singular Encounters
   CBRA - Annual 2003 - p58(2) [51-500]

McFadden, Susan H. - *New Directions in the Study of Late Life Religiousness and Spirituality*
   R&R Bk N - v19 - i1 - Feb 2004 - p12(1) [51-500]

McFall, Liz - *Advertising: A Cultural Economy*
   R&R Bk N - v19 - i3 - August 2004 - p133(1) [51-500]

McFarland, David Sawyer - *Dreamweaver MX 2004: The Missing Manual*
   LJ - v129 - i12 - July 2004 - p112(1) [501+]

McFarland, Dennis - *Prince Edward*
   BW - v34 - i33 - August 15 2004 - p12(1) [501+]
   y SLJ - v50 - i7 - July 2004 - p131(2) [51-500]

McFarland, Lyn Rossiter - *Mouse Went out to Get a Snack (Illus. by McFarland, Jim)*
   c KR - v73 - i4 - Feb 15 2005 - p233(1) [51-500]
   Widget & the Puppy (Illus. by McFarland, Jim)
   c KR - v72 - i14 - July 15 2004 - p690(1) [51-500]
   c SLJ - v50 - i9 - Sept 2004 - p172(1) [51-500]

McFarland, Philip - *Hawthorne in Concord*
   AM - v192 - i5 - Feb 14 2005 - p22 [501+]
   AS - v73 - i4 - Autumn 2004 - p170(3) [501+]
   BL - v100 - i21 - July 2004 - p1811(1) [1-50]
   Bwatch - Oct 2004 - pNA [51-500]

McFarlane, Ann - *Mastabas at Saqqara: Kaiemheset, Kaipunesut, Kaiemsenu, Sehetepu and Others*
   R&R Bk N - v19 - i4 - Nov 2004 - p51(1) [51-500]

McFarlane, J.A. - *Globe and Mail Style Book: A Guide to Language and Usage, 9th Ed.*
   CBRA - Annual 2003 - p15(1) [51-500]

McFarlane, Sheryl - *This Is the Dog*
   c CBRA - Annual 2003 - p458(1) [51-500]
   What's That Sound? In the City (Illus. by LaFave, Kim)
   c Res Links - v10 - i1 - Oct 2004 - p6(2) [51-500]
   c SLJ - v50 - i12 - Dec 2004 - p113(1) [501+]
   What's That Sound? On the Farm
   c Res Links - v10 - i1 - Oct 2004 - p6(2) [51-500]

McFarren, Todd - *Workplace Injury Litigation*
   SciTech - v28 - i3 - Sept 2004 - p11(1) [501+]

McFaul, Michael - *Between Dictatorship and Democracy: Russian Post-Communist Political Reform*
   Choice - v42 - i2 - Oct 2004 - p366(1) [51-500]
   For Aff - v83 - i5 - Sept-Oct 2004 - p164 [501+]

McFedries, Paul - *Formulas and Functions with Microsoft Excel 2003.*
   LJ - v130 - i4 - March 1 2005 - p106(1) [51-500]
   Word Spy: The Word Lover's Guide to Modern Culture
   JPC - v38 - i3 - Feb 2005 - p590(2) [501+]

McFerson, Hazel M. - *Mixed Blessing: The Impact of the American Colonial Experience on Politics and Society in the Philippines*
   JTWS - v21 - i1 - Spring 2004 - p262(4) [501+]

McFetridge, John - *Below the Line*
   CBRA - Annual 2003 - p177(1) [51-500]

McGadden, Bernice L. - *Camilla's Roses (Read by Floyd, Patricia R.). Audiobook Review*
   y Kliatt - v39 - i2 - March 2005 - p50(1) [51-500]

McGahey, Jo - *Return to Warrah*
   y Magpies - v19 - i5 - Nov 2004 - p41(1) [501+]

McGann, Oisin - *The Gods and Their Machines*
   y BL - v101 - i8 - Dec 15 2004 - p736(2) [51-500]
   LJ - v129 - i19 - Nov 15 2004 - p55(1) [501+]

McGarrity, Michael - *Slow Kill*
   BL - v100 - i22 - August 2004 - p1906(1) [51-500]
   PW - v251 - i30 - July 26 2004 - p39(1) [501+]

McGary, Jane - *Rock Garden Design and Construction*
   E-Streams - June 2004 - pNA [501+]
   R&R Bk N - v19 - i1 - Feb 2004 - p249(1) [51-500]

Mcgaughey, Kathyrn - *Below the Rimrocks: A Story of the Early Days in Paradox Valley, Colorado*
   R&R Bk N - v19 - i1 - Feb 2004 - p65(1) [501+]

McGaughey, William - *The Independence Party and the Future of Third-Party Politics: Adventures & Opinions of an IP Senate Candidate*
   PSQ - v119 - i2 - Summer 2004 - p371(3) [501+]

McGaw, Laurie - *Avram's Gift*
   LibMed - v22 - i7 - April-May 2004 - p56(1) [501+]

McGaw, Michael A. - *Thermomechanical Fatigue Behavior of Materials, Vol. 4*
   SciTech - v28 - i1 - March 2004 - p143(1) [51-500]

McGee, Harold - *An Encyclopedia of Kitchen Science, History and Culture*
   TLS - i5303 - Nov 19 2004 - p36(1) [51-500]
   On Food and Cooking: The Science and Lore of the Kitchen
   BL - v101 - i6 - Nov 15 2004 - p540(1) [51-500]
   Globe & Mail - Nov 27 2004 - pD26 [51-500]
   LJ - v130 - i1 - Jan 1 2005 - p140(2) [51-500]
   PW - v251 - i47 - Nov 22 2004 - p53(1) [51-500]

McGee, Kenneth G. - *Heads up: How to Anticipate Business Surprises and Seize Opportunities First*
   Bwatch - v26 - i7 - July 2004 - p4(1) [51-500]
   R&R Bk N - v19 - i4 - Nov 2004 - p92(1) [501+]

McGee, Marni - *The Noisy Farm (Illus. by Shearing, Leonie)*
   c SLJ - v50 - i10 - Oct 2004 - p122(1) [51-500]

McGee, Paula - *Advanced Nursing Practice, 2nd Ed.*
   SciTech - v28 - i1 - March 2004 - p126(1) [51-500]

McGee, September - *Let's Sail Away (Illus. by McGee, September)*
   c CH Bwatch - March 2005 - pNA [51-500]

McGee, Timothy J. - *Improvisation in the Arts of the Middle Ages and Renaissance*
   Ren Q - v57 - i3 - Fall 2004 - p1088(2) [501+]
   Singing Early Music: The Pronunciation of European Languages in the Late Middle Ages and Renaissance
   Choice - v42 - i6 - Feb 2005 - p1032(1) [51-500]

McGee, William L. - *The Divorce Seekers: A Photo Memoir of a Nevada Dude Wrangler*
   R&R Bk N - v19 - i3 - August 2004 - p75(1) [51-500]

McGeorge, Constance W. - *Chestnut (Illus. by Whyte, Mary)*
   c BL - v101 - i7 - Dec 1 2004 - p661(1) [51-500]
   c SLJ - v50 - i9 - Sept 2004 - p172(2) [51-500]

McGeorge, Pamela - *Lilies*
   E-Streams - August 2004 - pNA [501+]

McGeough, Paul - *Manhattan to Baghdad*
   R&R Bk N - v19 - i3 - August 2004 - p164(1) [501+]

McGerr, Michael - *A Fierce Discontent: The Rise and Fall of the Progressive Movement in America, 1870-1920*
   JAH - v91 - i3 - Dec 2004 - p1048(1) [501+]
   RAH - v32 - i2 - June 2004 - p223-8 [501+]

McGhee, Alison - *Countdown to Kindergarten (Read by Lillis, Rachael). Audiobook Review*
   c SLJ - v50 - i11 - Nov 2004 - p81(1) [51-500]
   Countdown to Kindergarten (Illus. by Bliss, Harry)
   c SLJ - v50 - i7 - July 2004 - p43(1) [51-500]
   Mrs. Watson Wants Your Teeth (Illus. by Bliss, Harry)
   c CCB-B - v58 - i1 - Sept 2004 - p29(1) [51-500]
   c KR - v72 - i13 - July 1 2004 - p633(1) [51-500]
   c PW - v251 - i27 - July 5 2004 - p54(1) [51-500]
   c SLJ - v50 - i9 - Sept 2004 - p173(1) [51-500]
   Snap (Read by Moore, Christina). Audiobook Review
   c BL - v101 - i9-10 - Jan 1 2005 - p887(1) [501+]
   y SLJ - v51 - i1 - Jan 2005 - p77(1) [51-500]
   Snap
   c LibMed - v23 - i1 - August-Sept 2004 - p67(1) [51-500]
   y Sch Lib - v52 - i3 - Autumn 2004 - p159(1) [501+]

McGhee, Sally - *Take Back Your Life!: Using Microsoft Outlook to Get Organized and Stay Organized*
   Bwatch - Feb 2005 - pNA [51-500]

McGill, Meredith L. - *American Literature and the Culture of Reprinting, 1834-1853*
   AL - v76 - i2 - June 2004 - p398(3) [501+]
   RAH - v32 - i3 - Sept 2004 - p358-364 [501+]

McGill, Robert - *The Mysteries*
   BIC - v33 - i9 - Dec 2004 - p38(2) [51-500]
   Globe & Mail - Sept 18 2004 - pD9 [501+]
   TLS - i5302 - Nov 12 2004 - p23(1) [501+]

McGill, T.N. - *Most of My Life Has Been about Waiting*
   Bwatch - Jan 2005 - pNA [51-500]

McGilligan, Patrick - *A Life in Darkness and Light*
   FQ - v58 - i1 - Fall 2004 - p56(3) [501+]

McGillis, Roderick - *Children's Literature and the Fin de Siecle*
   R&R Bk N - v19 - i1 - Feb 2004 - p222(1) [51-500]

McGillivray, Fiona - *Privileging Industry: The Comparative Politics of Trade and Industrial Policy*
   Pers PS - v33 - i4 - Fall 2004 - p248(1) [501+]

McGinn, Bernard J. - *Continuum History of Apocalypticism*
   R&R Bk N - v19 - i1 - Feb 2004 - p12(1) [51-500]

McGinn, Colin - *Mindsight: Image, Dream, Meaning*
   LJ - v129 - i15 - Sept 15 2004 - p60(1) [51-500]

McGinn, Ellen - *From Dark Horse Road*
   Can Lit - i182 - Autumn 2004 - p131(2) [501+]

McGinn, Thomas A.J. - *The Economy of Prostitution in the Roman World: A Study of Social History & the Brothel*
   Choice - v42 - i3 - Nov 2004 - pNA [1-50]

McGinnis, Jon - *Interpreting Avicenna: Science and Philosophy in Medieval Islam, Proceedings*
   R&R Bk N - v20 - i1 - Feb 2005 - p3(1) [51-500]

McGinnis, Paul J. - *The British Union: A Criticsl Edition and Translation of David Hume of Godscroff's De Unione Insulae Britannicae*
   Six Ct J - v35 - i1 - Spring 2004 - p189(2) [501+]

McGinnis, Pearl Yeadon - *The Solo Vocal Music of American Composer John La Montaine: Compositions for Voice on Piano*
   R&R Bk N - v19 - i4 - Nov 2004 - p196(1) [501+]

McGinniss, Joe - *The Big Horse*
   BL - v100 - i21 - July 2004 - p1796(1) [51-500]
   BL - v101 - i1 - Sept 1 2004 - p46(1) [51-500]
   BW - v34 - i29 - July 18 2004 - p6(1) [501+]

McGinnity, Frances - *Welfare for the Unemployed in Britain and Germany: Who Benefits?*
   R&R Bk N - v19 - i4 - Nov 2004 - p104(1) [51-500]

McGlen, Nancy E. - *Women, Politics, and American Society, 4th Ed.*
   R&R Bk N - v19 - i4 - Nov 2004 - p134(1) [1-50]

McGlew, James F. - *Citizens on Stage: Comedy and Political Culture in the Athenian Democracy*
   AHR - v109 - i3 - June 2004 - p955(1) [501+]
   Class R - v54 - i1 - May 2004 - p42(3) [501+]

McGlone, Catherine - *Visiting Volcanoes with a Scientist*
   c SLJ - v51 - i2 - Feb 2005 - p124(1) [51-500]
   c SB - v40 - i4 - July-August 2004 - p174(2) [51-500]

McGlothin, Victor - *Every Sistah Wants It*
   BL - v101 - i5 - Nov 1 2004 - p465(1) [51-500]

McGoldrick, Dominic - *From '9-11' to the 'Iraq War 2003': International Law in an Age of Complexity*
   Law&PolBR - Sept 2004 - pNA [501+]
   R&R Bk N - v19 - i3 - August 2004 - p193(1) [501+]
   The Permanent International Criminal Court: Legal and Policy Issues
   Law&PolBR - Oct 2004 - pNA [501+]
   R&R Bk N - v19 - i3 - August 2004 - p212(1) [1-50]

McGonagle, John J. - *The Manager's Guide to Competitive Intelligence*
R&R Bk N - v19 - i1 - Feb 2004 - p89(1) [51-500]
McGoogan, Ken - *Ancient Mariner: The Amazing Adventures of Samuel Hearne, the Sailor Who Walked to the Arctic Ocean*
Globe & Mail - Sept 18 2004 - pD26 [1-50]
Ancient Mariner: The Arctic Adventures of Samuel Hearne, the Sailor Who Inspired Coleridge's Masterpiece
Choice - v42 - i2 - Oct 2004 - p346(2) [51-500]
McGough, Matthew - *Bat Boy: My True Life Adventures Coming of Age with the New York Yankees (Read by Harris, Jason). Audiobook Review*
KR - v73 - i3 - Feb 1 2005 - p168(1) [501+]
Bat Boy: My True Life Adventures Coming of Age with the New York Yankees
PW - v252 - i10 - March 7 2005 - p57(1) [51-500]
McGough, Roger - *Daniel and the Beast of Babylon (Illus. by Newton, Jill)*
c Sch Lib - v52 - i4 - Winter 2004 - p207(1) [51-500]
Dotty Inventions and Some Real Ones Too (Illus. by Swain, Holly)
c BW - v34 - i31 - August 1 2004 - p11(1) [51-500]
c Sch Lib - v52 - i3 - Autumn 2004 - p151(1) [501+]
c SLJ - v50 - i7 - July 2004 - p82(1) [51-500]
Wicked Poems (Illus. by Layton, Neal)
c CH Bwatch - March 2005 - pNA [51-500]
c Sch Lib - v52 - i4 - Winter 2004 - p210(1) [51-500]
y SLJ - v51 - i1 - Jan 2005 - p152(1) [51-500]
McGovern, Ann - *The Lady in the Box (Illus. by Backer, Marni)*
c SLJ - v50 - i10 - Oct 2004 - pS22(1) [51-500]
McGovern, George - *The Essential America: Our Founders and the Liberal Tradition*
BL - v100 - i22 - August 2004 - p1893(1) [51-500]
NYTBR - July 18 2004 - p8 [501+]
PW - v251 - i32 - August 9 2004 - p246(1) [51-500]
McGovern, Patrick E. - *Ancient Wine: The Search for the Origins of Viniculture*
E-Streams - Sept 2004 - pNA [501+]
McGovern, Una - *Dictionary of Literacy Characters*
Choice - v42 - i7 - March 2005 - p1194(1) [51-500]
Dictionary of Literary Characters
LJ - v130 - i2 - Feb 1 2005 - p113(1) [51-500]
McGowan, Christopher - *The Dragon Seekers (Read by Langston, Stuart). Audiobook Review*
BL - v100 - i22 - August 2004 - p1953(1) [51-500]
Kliatt - v38 - i6 - Nov 2004 - p55(1) [51-500]
Rail, Steam, and Speed: The "Rocket" and the Birth of Steam Locomotion
LJ - v129 - i19 - Nov 15 2004 - p71(1) [501+]
The Rainhill Trials: The Greatest Contest of Industrial Britain and the Birth of Commercial Rail
CR - v285 - i1665 - Oct 2004 - p255(1) [501+]
McGowan, Jeffrey - *Major Conflict: One Gay Man's Life in the Don't-Ask-Don't-Tell Military*
KR - v73 - i1 - Jan 1 2005 - p37(1) [501+]
PW - v252 - i6 - Feb 7 2005 - p54(1) [51-500]
McGowan, Maryrose - *Interior Graphic Standards*
E-Streams - Oct 2004 - pNA [501+]
McGowan, Todd - *Lacan and Contemporary Film*
R&R Bk N - v19 - i4 - Nov 2004 - p223(1) [501+]
McGown, Jill - *Unlucky for Some*
Ent W - i803 - Jan 28 2005 - p89 [51-500]
KR - v72 - i23 - Dec 1 2004 - p1122(1) [51-500]
LJ - v130 - i1 - Jan 1 2005 - p85(1) [51-500]
PW - v251 - i50 - Dec 13 2004 - p48(1) [51-500]
McGrade, A.S. - *The Cambridge Companion to Medieval Philosophy*
Med R - Dec 2004 - pNA [501+]
Rel St - v40 - i4 - Dec 2004 - p516(5) [501+]
McGrandle, Piers - *Trevor Huddleston: Turbulent Priest*
TLS - i5292 - Sept 3 2004 - p30-31 [501+]
McGrann, Molly - *360-Flip*
TLS - i5284 - July 9 2004 - p21(1) [501+]
McGrath, Alister E. - *Dawkins' God: Genes, Memes, and the Meaning of Life*
TimHES - v0 - i1670 - Dec 10 2004 - p26(2) [501+]
In the Beginning: The Story of the King James Bible and How It Changed a Nation, a Language, and a Culture
CHR - v90 - i4 - Oct 2004 - p719(5) [501+]
A Scientific Theology, Vol. 1
Zygon - v39 - i4 - Dec 2004 - pNA [501+]
A Scientific Theology, Vol. 2
TT - v61 - i1 - April 2004 - p121-122 [501+]
A Scientific Theology, Vol. 3
Theol St - v66 - i1 - March 2005 - p209(2) [501+]
Theology: The Basics
R&R Bk N - v19 - i3 - August 2004 - p25(1) [1-50]

The Twilight of Atheism: The Rise and Fall of Disbelief in the Modern World
Choice - v42 - i3 - Nov 2004 - p500(1) [51-500]
TLS - i5307 - Dec 17 2004 - p6-7 [501+]
McGrath, Anne - *Ultimate Guide to Law Schools*
Choice - v42 - i4 - Dec 2004 - p640(2) [1-50]
McGrath, Barbara Barbieri - *Soccer Counts!*
TC Math - v11 - i2 - Sept 2004 - p110(1) [51-500]
McGrath, Campbell - *Pax Atomica*
PW - v251 - i51 - Dec 20 2004 - p52(1) [501+]
LJ - v129 - i20 - Dec 1 2004 - p122(1) [51-500]
McGrath, Carmelia - *Boston Box*
c CBRA - Annual 2003 - p458(2) [51-500]
McGrath, Joseph E. - *Temporal Matters in Social Psychology: Examining the Role of Time in the Lives of Groups and Individuals*
R&R Bk N - v19 - i1 - Feb 2004 - p122(1) [51-500]
McGrath, Kevin - *The Sanskrit Hero: Karna in Epic Mahabharata*
R&R Bk N - v19 - i3 - August 2004 - p14(1) [1-50]
McGrath, Lynette - *Subjectivity and Women's Poetry in Early Modern England: 'Why on the Ridge Should She Desire to Go'?*
Wom HR - v13 - i2 - Summer 2004 - p327-329 [501+]
McGrath, Michael J. - *Religious Celebrations in Segovia, 1577-1697*
Six Ct J - v35 - i3 - Fall 2004 - p898-900 [501+]
McGrath, Patrick - *Port Mungo (Read by Van Dyke, Jennifer). Audiobook Review*
y Kliatt - v39 - i1 - Jan 2005 - p49(1) [51-500]
Port Mungo
BW - v34 - i30 - July 25 2004 - p6(1) [501+]
Globe & Mail - July 3 2004 - pD2 [501+]
Lon R Bks - v26 - i16 - August 19 2004 - p22(1) [501+]
McGrath, Renee Vaillancourt - *Excellence in Library Services to Young Adults*
VOYA - v27 - i5 - Dec 2004 - p426(1) [51-500]
McGrath, Wendy - *Recurring Fictions*
CBRA - Annual 2003 - p177(1) [51-500]
McGraw, Erin - *The Good Life*
AM - v191 - i8 - Sept 27 2004 - p27 [501+]
LJ - v129 - i15 - Sept 15 2004 - p52(2) [51-500]
McGraw-Hill Concise Encyclopedia of Chemistry
Choice - v42 - i6 - Feb 2005 - p998(1) [51-500]
McGraw-Hill Dictionary of Electrical and Computer Engineering
Choice - v42 - i5 - Jan 2005 - p832(1) [1-50]
McGraw, J. Kevin - *Interventional Radiology of the Spine: Image-Guided Pain Therapy*
SciTech - v28 - i1 - March 2004 - p109(1) [51-500]
McGraw, Tug - *My Hope-Filled Fight Against Brain Cancer*
NYTBR - July 18 2004 - p16 [501+]
Ya Gotta Believe! My Roller-Coaster Life as a Screwball Pitcher and Part-Time Father
NYTBR - July 18 2004 - p16 [501+]
McGreevy, John T. - *Catholicism and American Freedom: A History*
AHR - v109 - i3 - June 2004 - p905(1) [501+]
JAH - v91 - i1 - June 2004 - p202-204 [501+]
JR - v85 - i1 - Jan 2005 - p136(3) [501+]
Theol St - v65 - i3 - Sept 2004 - p656(2) [501+]
McGregor, Ewan - *Long Way Round: Chasing Shadows Across the World*
PW - v251 - i44 - Nov 1 2004 - p56(2) [501+]
McGregor, Jon - *If Nobody Speaks of Remarkable Things (Read by Bond, Jilly). Audiobook Review*
Kliatt - v38 - i6 - Nov 2004 - p47(2) [501+]
McGregor, Joy - *Collection Management for School Libraries*
ALJ - v53 - i3 - August 2004 - p310(2) [501+]
McGruder, Aaron - *Birth of a Nation: A Comic Novel (Illus. by Baker, Kyle)*
BL - v100 - i21 - July 2004 - p1831(1) [1-50]
BW - v34 - i41 - Oct 10 2004 - p9(2) [501+]
LJ - v129 - i14 - Sept 1 2004 - p128(1) [51-500]
Time - v164 - i5 - August 2 2004 - p83 [51-500]
McGuane, John - *The Essential Pine Book*
LJ - v129 - i20 - Dec 1 2004 - p156(1) [51-500]
McGuckian, Medbh - *The Face of the Earth*
TLS - i5297 - Oct 8 2004 - p28(1) [501+]
Shelmalier
Sew R - v111 - i3 - Summer 2003 - p486-492 [501+]
McGuffin, Gary - *Great Lakes Journey: Exploring the Heritage Coast*
CBRA - Annual 2003 - p25(1) [501+]

McGuinness, Patrick - *The Canals of Mars*
TLS - i5303 - Nov 19 2004 - p34(1) [501+]
McGuire, Robert A. - *To Form a More Perfect Union: A New Economic Interpretation of the United States Constitution*
HNet - June 2004 - pNA [501+]
JEL - v42 - i1 - March 2004 - p285(1) [501+]
JEL - v42 - i4 - Dec 2004 - p1149(2) [501+]
McGuirk, Leslie - *Snail Boy*
LibMed - v22 - i4 - Jan 2004 - p60(1) [501+]
McGuirk, Niall - *Please Feed Me: A Punk Vegan Cookbook*
PW - v252 - i7 - Feb 14 2005 - p68(1) [51-500]
McGurn, Barrett - *Yank, the Army Weekly: Reporting the Greatest Generation*
CJR - v43 - i6 - March-April 2005 - p63(1) [51-500]
R&R Bk N - v20 - i1 - Feb 2005 - p33(1) [51-500]
McHale, Brian - *The Obligation Toward the Difficult Whole: Postmodernist Long Poems*
Choice - v42 - i1 - Sept 2004 - p102(1) [501+]
McHale, John - *The Real Split in the International: Theses on the Situationist International and Its Time, 1972, Enlarged Ed.*
R&R Bk N - v19 - i1 - Feb 2004 - p125(1) [51-500]
McHale, Shawn Frederick - *Print and Power: Confucianism, Communism, and Buddhism in the Making of Modern Vietnam*
R&R Bk N - v19 - i1 - Feb 2004 - p47(1) [51-500]
McHenry, E.B. - *Poodlena (Illus. by McHenry, E.B.)*
c SLJ - v50 - i11 - Nov 2004 - p112(1) [51-500]
McHenry, Elizabeth - *Forgotten Readers: Recovering the Lost History of African American Literary Societies*
AHR - v109 - i2 - April 2004 - p525(2) [501+]
AL - v76 - i2 - June 2004 - p398(3) [501+]
Am St - v45 - i1 - Spring 2004 - p146-147 [501+]
Col Lit - v32 - i1 - Wntr 2005 - p191(3) [501+]
JSH - v70 - i3 - August 2004 - p670(3) [501+]
Lib & Cul - v39 - i4 - Fall 2004 - p469(2) [501+]
NEQ - v77 - i3 - Sept 2004 - p507-511 [501+]
McHugh, Heather - *Eyeshot*
Ga R - v58 - i2 - Summer 2004 - p484-501 [501+]
Poet - v184 - i4 - August 2004 - p305(12) [501+]
McHugh, James T. - *The Essential Concept of Law*
Law&PolBR - June 2004 - p428(7) [501+]
McIlvoy, Kevin - *The Complete History of New Mexico: Stories*
KR - v72 - i22 - Nov 15 2004 - p1064(1) [501+]
LJ - v130 - i2 - Feb 1 2005 - p73(1) [51-500]
PW - v251 - i50 - Dec 13 2004 - p45(1) [51-500]
McIlwraith, T.F. - *At Home with the Bella Coola Indians: T.F. McIlawraith's Field Letters, 1922-4*
CBRA - Annual 2003 - p59(1) [51-500]
McInerney, Maud Burnett - *Eloquent Virgins: From Thecla to Joan of Arc*
JR - v85 - i1 - Jan 2005 - p126(2) [501+]
McInerney, Monica - *The Alphabet Sisters*
KR - v73 - i5 - March 1 2005 - p252(1) [501+]
McInerny, D.Q. - *Being Logical: A Guide to Good Thinking*
y BL - v100 - i22 - August 2004 - p1876(1) [51-500]
McInerny, Ralph - *Green Thumb*
BL - v101 - i6 - Nov 15 2004 - p565(1) [51-500]
Irish Coffee
LJ - v129 - i18 - Nov 1 2004 - p135(1) [51-500]
Requiem for a Realtor
BL - v100 - i22 - August 2004 - p1906(1) [51-500]
The Very Rich Hours of Jacques Maritain: A Spiritual Life
TLS - i5265 - Feb 27 2004 - p28-28 [501+]
CHR - v90 - i3 - July 2004 - p568(2) [501+]
McInnes, Gavin - *Dos and Dont's*
Advocate - Oct 12 2004 - p98(1) [501+]
McInnes, Graham - *One Man's Documentary: A Memoir of the Early Years of the National Film Board*
Globe & Mail - Jan 15 2005 - pD5 [501+]
McInnis-Dittrich, Kathleen - *Social Work with Elders: A Biopsychosocial Approach to Assessment and Intervention, 2nd Ed.*
R&R Bk N - v19 - i3 - August 2004 - p161(1) [501+]
McInnis, Sheri - *Devil May Care*
Globe & Mail - August 7 2004 - pD14 [1-50]
McIntire, C.T. - *Herbert Butterfield: Historian as Dissenter*
CR - v286 - i1668 - Jan 2005 - p60(2) [51-500]
Spec - v296 - i9194 - Oct 23 2004 - p50(1) [501+]
TLS - i5299 - Oct 22 2004 - p7(1) [501+]
McIntosh, Barbara-Jo - *Great Chef's Cook at Barbara-Jo's*
BIC - v33 - i8 - Nov 2004 - p26(2) [501+]

McIntosh, Christopher - *The Swan King: Ludwig II of Bavaria*
 HNet - Sept 2004 - pNA [501+]
McIntosh, Fiona - *Myrren's Gift*
 KR - v73 - i2 - Jan 15 2005 - p90(1) [51-500]
 LJ - v130 - i1 - Jan 1 2005 - p103(1) [51-500]
 PW - v252 - i2 - Jan 10 2005 - p43(1) [51-500]
McIntosh, Keuneth - *Apache*
 SLJ - v50 - i10 - Oct 2004 - pS60(2) [51-500]
 Iroquois
 SLJ - v50 - i10 - Oct 2004 - pS60(2) [51-500]
McIntosh, Malcolm - *Raising a Ladder to the Moon: The Complexities of Corporate Social and Environmental Responsibility*
 R&R Bk N - v19 - i1 - Feb 2004 - p92(1) [1-50]
McIntosh, Pat - *The Harper's Quine*
 KR - v72 - i13 - July 1 2004 - p607(1) [51-500]
 LJ - v129 - i12 - July 2004 - p63(1) [51-500]
 PW - v251 - i28 - July 12 2004 - p47(1) [51-500]
McIntosh, Tom - *Building the Social Union: Perspectives, Directions and Challenges*
 CBRA - Annual 2003 - p303(2) [501+]
McIntyre, Lisa J. - *Need to Know: Social Science Research Methods, 1st Ed.*
 TimHES - v0 - i1680 - Feb 25 2005 - pVI(1) [501+]
McIntyre, Robert J. - *Small and Medium Enterprises in Transitional Economies*
 E-A St - v56 - i8 - Dec 2004 - p1256(2) [501+]
McIntyre, Tom - *The Behavior Survival Guide for Kids: How to Make Good Choices and Stay out of Trouble*
 y SLJ - v50 - i10 - Oct 2004 - pS47(1) [51-500]
 y VOYA - v27 - i4 - Oct 2004 - p328(1) [51-500]
McIntyre, Vestal - *You Are Not the One: Stories*
 KR - v72 - i21 - Nov 1 2004 - p1025(1) [501+]
 PW - v251 - i48 - Nov 29 2004 - p23(2) [51-500]
McIntyre, Vonda N. - *Nebula Awards Showcase 2004*
 ChrSFF&H - v26 - i10 - Oct 2004 - p49(2) [501+]
McIver, Katherine A. - *Art and Music in the Early Modern Period: Essays in Honor of Franca Trinchieri Camiz.*
 Ren Q - v57 - i3 - Fall 2004 - p1090(2) [501+]
McIver, Stuart B. - *Death in the Everglades: The Murder of Guy Bradley, America's First Martyr to Environmentalism*
 HNet - Oct 2004 - pNA [501+]
McIvor, Maura Conlon- - *FBI Girl: How I Learned to Crack My Father's Code*
 Comw - v131 - i18 - Oct 22 2004 - p30(3) [501+]
McKanan, Dan - *Identifying the Image of God: Radical Christians and Nonviolent Power in the Antebellum United States*
 AL - v76 - i2 - June 2004 - p394(3) [501+]
 JAH - v91 - i1 - June 2004 - p243-244 [501+]
McKanna, Clare V., Jr. - *Race and Homicide in Nineteenth-Century California*
 JIH - v34 - i4 - Spring 2004 - p657-658 [501+]
 WHQ - v35 - i1 - Spring 2004 - p92-92 [501+]
 The Trial of "Indian Joe": Race and Justice in the Nineteenth-Century West
 JAH - v91 - i3 - Dec 2004 - p1037(2) [501+]
McKay, Alex - *The History of Tibet, Vol. I*
 TimHES - v0 - i1678 - Feb 11 2005 - p22(2) [501+]
 Tibet and Her Neighbours: A History
 R&R Bk N - v19 - i3 - August 2004 - p56(1) [51-500]
McKay, Andy - *The Definitive Guide to Plone*
 Bwatch - Feb 2005 - pNA [51-500]
McKay, Claude - *Complete Poems*
 VQR - v80 - i3 - Summer 2004 - p272(1) [1-50]
McKay, Don - *Camber: Selected Poems, 1983-2000*
 BIC - v33 - i6 - Sept 2004 - p32(2) [501+]
 Globe & Mail - Nov 27 2004 - pD3 [51-500]
McKay, Floyd J. - *Reporting the Pacific Northwest: An Annotated Bibliography of Journalism History in Oregon and Washington*
 R&R Bk N - v19 - i4 - Nov 2004 - p229(1) [501+]
McKay, George - *The Encyclopedia of Animals: A Complete Visual Guide*
 Bwatch - Nov 2004 - pNA [51-500]
 Bwatch - Jan 2005 - pNA [51-500]
 LJ - v129 - i19 - Nov 15 2004 - p85(1) [51-500]
 New Sci - v184 - i2473 - Nov 13 2004 - p57(1) [51-500]

McKay, Hilary - *Indigo's Star (Read by Lederer, Helen). Audiobook Review*
 c BL - v101 - i9-10 - Jan 1 2005 - p887(1) [51-500]
 y HB - v81 - i1 - Jan-Feb 2005 - p122(1) [51-500]
 c SLJ - v51 - i2 - Feb 2005 - p77(1) [501+]
 Indigo's Star
 c BL - v101 - i2 - Sept 15 2004 - p245(1) [51-500]
 y CCB-B - v58 - i1 - Sept 2004 - p29(2) [51-500]
 c HB - v80 - i5 - Sept-Oct 2004 - p591(2) [51-500]
 c HB - v81 - i1 - Jan-Feb 2005 - p15(1) [51-500]
 c KR - v72 - i15 - August 1 2004 - p745(1) [51-500]
  PW - v251 - i35 - August 30 2004 - p56(1) [51-500]
 y SLJ - v50 - i9 - Sept 2004 - p211(2) [51-500]
 Saffey's Angel
 c CH Bwatch - v14 - i8 - August 2004 - p3(1) [51-500]
McKay, Jane - *Tess and the Star Traveller*
 c CH Bwatch - March 2005 - pNA [51-500]
McKay, Jenn - *Power of Thirteen*
 y CBRA - Annual 2003 - p503(2) [51-500]
McKay, Kathryn L. - *Currents and Undercurrents: An Administrative History of Roosevelt National Recreation Area*
 Pub Hist - v26 - i1 - Wntr 2004 - p176(3) [501+]
McKay, Sharon E. - *Charlie Wilcox''s Great War*
 y CBRA - Annual 2003 - p504(1) [51-500]
 Esther
 c Globe & Mail - Nov 6 2004 - pD22 [1-50]
 c Res Links - v10 - i2 - Dec 2004 - p37(2) [51-500]
 Penelope: An Irish Penny
 c Can CL - i113/114 - Spring-Summer 2004 - p136(3) [501+]
 Penelope: Christmas Reunion
 y Res Links - v10 - i2 - Dec 2004 - p21(1) [51-500]
 Penelope: The Glass Castle
 y Can CL - i111-112 - Fall-Winter 2003 - p128(7) [501+]
McKean, Erin - *More Weird and Wonderful Words*
 R&R Bk N - v19 - i1 - Feb 2004 - p216(1) [1-50]
McKean, John - *Giancarlo de Carlo: Layered Places*
 R&R Bk N - v19 - i4 - Nov 2004 - p203(1) [501+]
McKee, David - *Charlotte's Piggy Bank (Illus. by McKee, David)*
 c KR - v72 - i24 - Dec 15 2004 - p1205(1) [51-500]
 The Conquerors (Illus. by McKee, David)
 c CCB-B - v58 - i5 - Jan 2005 - p217(1) [51-500]
 c HB - v81 - i1 - Jan-Feb 2005 - p82(1) [51-500]
 c KR - v72 - i24 - Dec 15 2004 - p1205(1) [51-500]
 c PW - v252 - i2 - Jan 10 2005 - p55(1) [51-500]
McKee, Lex - *The Accelerated Trainer: Using Accelerated Learning Techniques to Revolutionize Your Training*
 R&R Bk N - v19 - i3 - August 2004 - p216(1) [1-50]
McKee, Neill - *Strategic Communication in the HIV/AIDS Epidemic*
 SciTech - v28 - i4 - Dec 2004 - p84(1) [51-500]
McKeen, Wendy - *Money in Their Own Name: The Feminist Voice in Poverty Debate in Canada, 1970-1995*
 CBRA - Annual 2003 - p387(1) [501+]
 CWS - v23 - i3-4 - Spring-Summer 2004 - p211(2) [501+]
McKeever, Sean - *Marvel Age Fantastic Four: All for One*
 PW - v251 - i40 - Oct 4 2004 - p73(1) [501+]
 Mary Jane: Circle of Friends
 PW - v251 - i49 - Dec 6 2004 - p45(1) [51-500]
McKellar, Shelly - *Surgical Limits: The Life of Gordon Murray*
 Can Hist R - v85 - i4 - Dec 2004 - p860(3) [501+]
McKelvey, Maureen - *The Economic Dynamics of Modern Biotechnology*
 R&R Bk N - v19 - i4 - Nov 2004 - p105(1) [51-500]
McKendrick, Jamie - *The Faber Book of Twentieth-Century Italian Poems*
 TLS - i5306 - Dec 10 2004 - p28(1) [501+]
McKendrick, Scot - *Bible as Book: The Transmission of the Greek Text*
 R&R Bk N - v19 - i1 - Feb 2004 - p17(1) [51-500]
 Flemish Illuminated Manuscripts, 1400-1550
 R&R Bk N - v19 - i1 - Feb 2004 - p206(1) [51-500]
McKendry, Joe - *Beneath the Streets of Boston: Building America's First Subway*
 c PW - v251 - i29 - July 19 2004 - p92(1) [51-500]
McKenna, Bernard - *James Joyce's Ulysses: A Reference Guide*
 ELT - v47 - i4 - Fall 2004 - p491(3) [501+]
McKenna, Erin - *Animal Pragmatism: Rethinking Human-Nonhuman Realtionships*
 Choice - v42 - i7 - March 2005 - p1238(2) [51-500]

McKenna, Mark - *Australian Republicanism: A Reader (Illus. by Hudson, Wayne)*
 AJPS - v39 - i2 - July 2004 - p444(445) [501+]
 Looking for Blackfellas' Paint: An Australian History of Place
 AHS - v35 - i123 - April 2004 - p184-185 [501+]
 This Country: A Reconciled Republic?
 TLS - i5287 - July 30 2004 - p29(1) [501+]
McKenna, Maryn - *Beating Back the Devil: On the Front Lines with the Disease Detectives of the Epidemic Intelligence Service*
 BL - v101 - i1 - Sept 1 2004 - p34(1) [51-500]
 y BW - v34 - i45 - Nov 7 2004 - p5(1) [51-500]
  Choice - v42 - i7 - March 2005 - p1260(2) [51-500]
 LJ - v129 - i13 - August 2004 - p108(1) [51-500]
 New Sci - v183 - i2466 - Sept 25 2004 - p49(1) [51-500]
McKenna, Neil - *The Secret Life of Oscar Wilde*
 KR - v73 - i4 - Feb 15 2005 - p215(1) [501+]
 PW - v252 - i9 - Feb 28 2005 - p48(1) [51-500]
McKenzie, Donald Francis - *Making Meaning: "Printers of the Mind" and Other Essays*
 Lib & Cul - v39 - i3 - Summer 2004 - p346(2) [501+]
McKenzie, Elizabeth - *Stop That Girl: A Novel in Stories*
 KR - v72 - i22 - Nov 15 2004 - p1064(1) [501+]
 LJ - v129 - i19 - Nov 15 2004 - p50(2) [501+]
 PW - v251 - i44 - Nov 1 2004 - p40(1) [51-500]
 NYTBR - March 13 2005 - p26 [501+]
McKenzie, Joy - *Exploring Basic Black and White Photography*
 R&R Bk N - v19 - i1 - Feb 2004 - p251(1) [51-500]
McKenzie, Kirsten - *Scandal in the Colonies: Sydney and Cape Town, 1829-1850*
 Quad - v48 - i10 - Oct 2004 - p90(2) [501+]
McKenzie, Lionel W. - *Classical General Equilibrium Theory*
 JEL - v41 - i4 - Dec 2003 - p1280(2) [501+]
McKenzie, Neil - *Australian Soils and Landscapes: An Illustrated Compendium*
 Choice - v42 - i6 - Feb 2005 - p1045(1) [51-500]
 SciTech - v28 - i4 - Dec 2004 - p123 [51-500]
McKenzie, Stephanie - *The Backyards of Heaven: An Anthology of Contemporary Poetry from Ireland and Newfoundland and Labrador*
 CBRA - Annual 2003 - p241(2) [501+]
 ILS - v24 - i1 - Fall 2004 - p32(1) [51-500]
McKenzie, Tim A. - *Baxter Barret Brown's Bass Fiddle (Illus. by Shaw, Charles)*
 c SLJ - v50 - i12 - Dec 2004 - p113(1) [501+]
McKenzie, Walter - *Standards-Based Lessons for Tech-Savvy Students: A Multiple Intelligence Approach*
 y VOYA - v27 - i4 - Oct 2004 - p338(2) [51-500]
McKeown, Adam - *Romeo and Juliet (Illus. by Fiore, Peter)*
 c BL - v100 - i22 - August 2004 - p1918(1) [51-500]
 c SLJ - v50 - i10 - Oct 2004 - p192(1) [51-500]
McKeown, Adam, Ph.D. - *Chinese Migrant Networks and Cultural Change: Peru, Chicago, Hawaii, 1990-1936*
 J Urban H - v30 - i4 - May 2004 - p604-615 [501+]
McKeown, Julie - *Burleigh: The Story of a Pottery*
 Ceram Mo - v53 - i1 - Jan 2005 - p76(1) [501+]
McKeown, William - *Idaho Falls: The Untold Story of America's First Nuclear Accident*
 SPA - v60 - i5 - Sept-Oct 2004 - p68(2) [501+]
McKernan, Victoria - *Shackleton's Stowaway*
 y CCB-B - v58 - i6 - Feb 2005 - p259(1) [51-500]
 y Kliatt - v39 - i1 - Jan 2005 - p8(2) [51-500]
 y KR - v73 - i1 - Jan 1 2005 - p55(1) [51-500]
 y PW - v252 - i11 - March 14 2005 - p68(2) [51-500]
 y SLJ - v51 - i2 - Feb 2005 - p138(1) [51-500]
McKerrow, Andrew J. - *Materials, Technology and Reliability for Advanced Interconnects and Low-K Dielectrics 2003: Proceedings*
 SciTech - v28 - i1 - March 2004 - p161(1) [51-500]
McKevett, G.A. - *Murder a La Mode: A Savannah Reid Mystery*
 KR - v72 - i21 - Nov 1 2004 - p1031(1) [51-500]
 LJ - v130 - i1 - Jan 1 2005 - p84(1) [51-500]
 PW - v251 - i49 - Dec 6 2004 - p46(2) [51-500]
McKibben, Bill - *Wandering Home: A Long Walk Across America's Most Hopeful Landscape, Vermont's Champlain Valley and New York's Adirondacks*
 KR - v73 - i1 - Jan 1 2005 - p38(1) [501+]
 LJ - v130 - i3 - Feb 15 2005 - p149(1) [51-500]

McLeod, Wilson - *Divided Gaels: Gaelic Cultural Identities in Scotland and Ireland, c.1200-c.1650.*
HRNB - v33 - i1 - Fall 2004 - p23(2) [501+]

McIllwain, Jeffery Scott - *Organizing Crime in Chinatown: Race and Racketeering in New York City, 1890-1910*
Choice - v42 - i3 - Nov 2004 - p549(1) [1-50]

McIlroy, Claire Elizabeth - *The English Prose Treatises of Richard Rolle*
Choice - v42 - i3 - Nov 2004 - p485(1) [1-50]

McIlwraith, Hiro - *Shahnaz: A Novel*
Can Lit - i182 - Autumn 2004 - p156(3) [501+]

McInerny, D.Q. - *Being Logical: A Guide to Good Thinking*
Choice - v42 - i6 - Feb 2005 - p1035(1) [51-500]

M'Closkey, Kathy - *Swept under the Rug: A Hidden History of Navajo Weaving*
WHQ - v35 - i1 - Spring 2004 - p88-89 [501+]

McLoughlin, Tim - *Brooklyn Noir*
BL - v100 - i21 - July 2004 - p1823(1) [1-50]

McLoughlin, Barry - *Stalin's Terror: High Politics and Mass Repression in the Soviet Union*
Russ Rev - v63 - i2 - April 2004 - pNA [501+]
Slav R - v63 - i3 - Fall 2004 - p663-665 [501+]

McLynn, Frank - *1759: The Year Britain Became Master of the World*
CR - v285 - i1664 - Sept 2004 - p188(1) [51-500]
KR - v72 - i24 - Dec 15 2004 - p1186(2) [501+]
PW - v251 - i45 - Nov 8 2004 - p42(1) [501+]

McMahan, Alison - *Alice Guy Blache: Lost Visionary of the Cinema*
TimHES - v0 - i1654 - August 20 2004 - p28(1) [501+]

McMahon, Cliff - *Reframing the Theory of the Sublime: Pillars and Modes*
R&R Bk N - v19 - i4 - Nov 2004 - p12(1) [51-500]

McMahon, Deidre - *Moynihan Brothers in Peace and War, 1909-1918: Their New Ireland*
R&R Bk N - v20 - i1 - Feb 2005 - p32(1) [51-500]

McMahon, George - *Prescription Pot: A Leading Advocate's Heroic Battle to Legalize Medical Marijuana*
SciTech - v28 - i3 - Sept 2004 - p12(1) [501+]

McMahon, Kevin J. - *Minnie Fisher Cunningham: A Suffragist's Life in Politics*
Choice - v42 - i1 - Sept 2004 - p175(1) [501+]
Reconsidering Roosevelt on Race: How the Presidency Paved the Road to Brown
JSH - v71 - i1 - Feb 2005 - p201(2) [501+]
Law&PolBR - Dec 2004 - pNA [501+]
Reason - v36 - i5 - Oct 2004 - p59(5) [501+]
VQR - v80 - i3 - Summer 2004 - p257(1) [501+]

McMahon, Neil - *Revolution No. 9*
BL - v101 - i8 - Dec 15 2004 - p711(2) [51-500]
LJ - v130 - i1 - Jan 1 2005 - p98(2) [51-500]
PW - v251 - i48 - Nov 29 2004 - p24(2) [51-500]

McMahon, P.J. - *The Mystery of the Swimming Gorilla, Vol. 1 (Illus. by Manders, John)*
c SLJ - v50 - i10 - Oct 2004 - p122(2) [51-500]

McMahon, Patricia - *Just Add One Chinese Sister (Illus. by Jerome, Karen A.)*
c KR - v73 - i3 - Feb 1 2005 - p178(1) [51-500]
c SLJ - v51 - i2 - Feb 2005 - p124(1) [51-500]

McMahon, Peter - *Global Control: Information Technology and Globalization since 1845*
T&C - v45 - i1 - Jan 2004 - p214(3) [501+]

McMahon, Robert J. - *Helping the Noncompliant Child: Family-Based Treatment for Oppositional Behavior, 2nd Ed.*
SciTech - v28 - i1 - March 2004 - p99(1) [51-500]

McMahon, Thomas F. - *Ethical Leadership through Transforming Justice*
R&R Bk N - v19 - i3 - August 2004 - p174(1) [51-500]

McManners, Hugh - *Ultimate Special Forces*
y VOYA - v27 - i4 - Oct 2004 - p328(1) [51-500]

McManus, Caroline - *Spenser's Faerie Queene and the Reading of Women*
Six Ct J - v35 - i1 - Spring 2004 - p300(2) [501+]

McManus, James - *Positively 5th Street*
TLS - i5262 - Feb 6 2004 - p8(1) [501+]

McManus, John C. - *Americans at D-Day: The American Experience at the Normandy Invasion*
R&R Bk N - v20 - i1 - Feb 2005 - p32(1) [51-500]
The Americans at Normandy: The Summer of 1944--the American War from the Normandy Beaches to Falaise
BL - v101 - i2 - Sept 15 2004 - p197(1) [501+]
KR - v72 - i15 - August 1 2004 - p728(1) [501+]
R&R Bk N - v20 - i1 - Feb 2005 - p32(1) [51-500]

McManus, Stephen - *The Civil War Research Guide*
J Mil H - v68 - i3 - July 2004 - p967(1) [501+]

McMaster, Gerald - *Native Universe: Voices of Indian America*
y BL - v100 - i22 - August 2004 - p1893(1) [51-500]
LJ - v129 - i16 - Oct 1 2004 - p96(1) [501+]

McMaster, Juliet - *Reading the Body in the Eighteenth-Century Novel*
Choice - v42 - i3 - Nov 2004 - p485(1) [1-50]
TLS - i5285 - July 16 2004 - p28(1) [501+]

McMaster, Robert B. - *A Research Agenda for Geographic Information Science*
SciTech - v28 - i4 - Dec 2004 - p5(1) [1-50]

McMasters, Gretchen - *Aesock's Travels*
c CH Bwatch - Oct 2004 - pNA [501-500]

McMeekin, Sean - *The Red Millionaire: A Political Biography of Willi Muenzenberg, Moscow's Secret Propaganda Tsar in the West*
Quad - v48 - i7-8 - July-August 2004 - p119(3) [501+]

McMillan, Alan D. - *First Peoples in Canada*
Globe & Mail - Sept 11 2004 - pD21 [1-50]

McMillan, Bruce - *Eating Fractions*
c SLJ - v50 - i9 - Sept 2004 - p58(1) [51-500]

McMillan, Dawn - *Coming Home (Illus. by Gunson, Dave)*
c Magpies - v19 - i5 - Nov 2004 - p6S(1) [501+]
Wood for the Winter (Illus. by Durkin, Denise)
c Magpies - v19 - i5 - Nov 2004 - p6S(1) [501+]

McMillan, Dennis - *Monkology*
PW - v251 - i31 - August 2 2004 - p56(1) [501+]

McMillan, Franklin D. - *Unlocking the Animal Mind: How Your Pet's Feelings Hold the Key to His Health and Happiness*
BL - v101 - i4 - Oct 15 2004 - p371(2) [51-500]
PW - v251 - i35 - August 30 2004 - p44(1) [51-500]

McMillan, Gregory K. - *Models Unleashed: Virtual Plant and Model Predictive Control Applications*
SciTech - v28 - i1 - March 2004 - p151(1) [51-500]

McMillan, James H. - *Classroom Assessment: Principles and Practice for Effective Instruction, 3rd Ed.*
R&R Bk N - v19 - i1 - Feb 2004 - p189(1) [51-500]

McMillan, John - *The New Left Revisited*
CS - v33 - i1 - Jan 2004 - p128-128 [501+]

McMillan, Michael - *Object-Oriented Programming with Visual Basic.Net*
Choice - v42 - i3 - Nov 2004 - p520(1) [1-50]

McMillan, Robin - *Us Against Them: An Oral History of the Ryder Cup*
BL - v100 - i22 - August 2004 - p1890(1) [51-500]

McMillen, Sally G. - *Southern Women: Black and White in the Old South, 2nd Ed.*
HNet - Dec 2004 - pNA [501+]

McMillian, Elizabeth Jean - *Deco & Streamline Architecture in L.A.: A Moderne City Survey*
R&R Bk N - v19 - i3 - August 2004 - p241(1) [51-500]

McMillian, John - *The New Left Revisited*
JAH - v91 - i1 - June 2004 - p326-327 [501+]
NEQ - v77 - i4 - Dec 2004 - p668-670 [501+]

McMillin, James A. - *The Final Victims: Foreign Slave Trade to North America, 1783-1810*
R&R Bk N - v19 - i4 - Nov 2004 - p137(1) [1-50]

McMinn, Lisa Graham - *Sexuality and Holy Longing: Embracing Intimacy in a Broken World*
Bks & Cult - v10 - i5 - Sept-Oct 2004 - p20(2) [501+]
CC - v121 - i16 - August 10 2004 - p40(2) [501+]

McMonnies, Alistair - *Object-Oriented Programming in Visual Basic .NET.*
SciTech - v28 - i3 - Sept 2004 - p21(1) [51-500]

McMullan, Kate - *Baby Goose (Illus. by Lemaitre, Pascal)*
c BL - v101 - i6 - Nov 15 2004 - p588(1) [51-500]
c KR - v72 - i20 - Oct 15 2004 - p1010(1) [51-500]
c NYTBR - March 13 2005 - p20 [501+]
c PW - v251 - i44 - Nov 1 2004 - p60(1) [501+]
c SLJ - v50 - i11 - Nov 2004 - p128(1) [51-500]
Fluffy Plants a Jelly Bean (Illus. by Smith, Mavis)
c SLJ - v50 - i8 - August 2004 - p82(1) [51-500]
I Stink! (Illus. by McMullan, Jim)
c RT - v57 - Oct 2003 - p169 [1-50]
My Travels with Capts. Lewis and Clark by George Shannon (Illus. by Yorinks, Adrienne)
y BL - v101 - i4 - Oct 15 2004 - p398(2) [501+]
c CCB-B - v58 - i2 - Oct 2004 - p90(1) [51-500]
c HB - v80 - i6 - Nov-Dec 2004 - p712(2) [501+]
c KR - v72 - i13 - July 1 2004 - p633(1) [51-500]
c NYTBR - August 8 2004 - p16 [501+]
c SLJ - v50 - i9 - Sept 2004 - p212(1) [51-500]
Pearl and Wagner: Three Secrets (Illus. by Alley, R.W.)
c CCB-B - v58 - i1 - Sept 2004 - p30(1) [51-500]
c HB - v80 - i5 - Sept-Oct 2004 - p593(2) [51-500]
c SLJ - v50 - i10 - Oct 2004 - pS30(1) [1-50]

McMullan, Margaret - *How I Found the Strong: A Civil War Story*
c BL - v101 - i6 - Nov 15 2004 - p599(1) [501+]

McMullen, Margaret - *In My Mother's House*
Wom R Bks - v22 - i2 - Nov 2004 - p17(2) [501+]

McMullen, Sean - *Glass Dragons*
y VOYA - v27 - i3 - August 2004 - p232(1) [1-50]

McMullin, Stan - *Anatomy of a Seance: A History of Spirit Communication in Central Canada*
R&R Bk N - v19 - i3 - August 2004 - p11(1) [1-50]

McMurdo, Kathleen - *Structured Writing II: Using Inspiration Software to Teach Essay Development*
LibMed - v23 - i3 - Nov-Dec 2004 - p63(1) [51-500]

McMurray, Jonathan S. - *Distant Ties: Germany, the Ottoman Empire, and the Construction of the Baghdad Railway*
T&C - v45 - i4 - Oct 2004 - p872(3) [501+]

McMurry, Andrew - *Environmental Renaissance: Emerson, Thoreau, and the Systems of Nature*
Choice - v41 - i7 - March 2004 - p1315(1) [501+]
NEQ - v77 - i2 - June 2004 - p300-307 [501+]
R&R Bk N - v19 - i3 - August 2004 - p81(1) [51-500]

McMurtry, Larry - *Folly and Glory (Read by Molina, Alfred). Audiobook Review*
LJ - v130 - i4 - March 1 2005 - p122(1) [51-500]
Horseman, Pass By
BL - v101 - i6 - Nov 15 2004 - p556(1) [501+]
The Last Picture Show
Globe & Mail - Sept 4 2004 - pD19 [501+]
Loop Group
BL - v101 - i4 - Oct 15 2004 - p363(1) [51-500]
KR - v72 - i18 - Sept 15 2004 - p886(2) [501+]
LJ - v129 - i17 - Oct 15 2004 - p54(1) [51-500]
NYTBR - Jan 2 2005 - p5 [501+]
PW - v251 - i45 - Nov 8 2004 - p35(1) [501+]
PW - v252 - i6 - Feb 7 2005 - p34(1) [51-500]
Ent W - i795 - Dec 3 2004 - p94 [51-500]

McNab, Chris - *Network Security Assessment*
LJ - v129 - i12 - July 2004 - p112(1) [501+]

McNab, Claire - *Death by Death*
Lam Bk Rpt - v13 - i3 - Oct 2004 - p30(2) [501+]

McNab, Robert - *Ghost Ships: A Surrealist Love Triangle*
Spec - v296 - i9197 - Nov 13 2004 - p62(1) [501+]

McNabb, David E. - *Research Methods for Political Science: Quantitative and Qualitative Methods*
R&R Bk N - v19 - i4 - Nov 2004 - p150(1) [501+]

McNabb, Linda - *Stonekeeper's Daughter*
y Magpies - v19 - i5 - Nov 2004 - p36(1) [501+]

McNair, Brian - *Striptease Culture: Sex, Media, and the Democratization of Desire*
Theat J - v56 - i1 - March 2004 - p143(3) [501+]

McNall, Bruce - *Fun While It Lasted: My Rise and Fall in the Land of Fame and Fortune*
R&R Bk N - v19 - i1 - Feb 2004 - p142(1) [51-500]

McNally, Dennis - *A Long Strange Trip: The Inside History of the Grateful Dead*
JouAmCul - v27 - i3 - Sept 2004 - p333(2) [501+]

McNally, John - *The Book of Ralph: A Fiction*
ABR - v26 - i2 - Jan-Feb 2005 - p30(1) [501+]
VQR - v80 - i3 - Spring 2004 - p259-259 [501+]
Brains of the Operation
New ER - v24 - i4 - Fall 2003 - p38-96 [501+]

McNally, Richard J. - *Remembering Trauma*
Choice - v41 - i7 - March 2004 - p1375(1) [51-500]

McNally, Robert Aquinas - *Men's Health Concerns Sourcebook, 2nd Ed.*
E-Streams - Sept 2004 - pNA [501+]
Skin Health Information for Teens
LibMed - v22 - i6 - March 2004 - p78(1) [501+]

McNally, T.M. - *Quick*
BL - v101 - i3 - Oct 1 2004 - p311(1) [51-500]

McNamara, Brooks - *The New York Concert Saloon: The Devil's Own Nights*
Theat J - v56 - i2 - May 2004 - p335(2) [501+]

McNamara, Margaret - *Election Day (Illus. by Gordon, Mike)*
c BL - v101 - i1 - Sept 1 2004 - p133(2) [51-500]
c BL - v101 - i3 - Oct 1 2004 - p327(1) [51-500]
c SLJ - v50 - i11 - Nov 2004 - p112(1) [51-500]

McNamara, Martin - *Apocalyptic and Eschatological Heritage: The Middle East and Celtic Realms*
R&R Bk N - v19 - i1 - Feb 2004 - p19(1) [51-500]

McNamara, Timothy J, - *Key Concepts in Mathematics: Strengthening Standard Practice in Grades 6-12*
Math T - v97 - i5 - May 2004 - p382-382 [501+]

McNamee, Roger - *New Normal: Great Opportunities in a Time of Great Risk*
  PW - v251 - i46 - Nov 15 2004 - p55(1) [501+]
McNamee, Stephen J. - *The Meritocracy Myth*
  Choice - v42 - i6 - Feb 2005 - p1105(2) [51-500]
  R&R Bk N - v19 - i3 - August 2004 - p146(1) [1-50]
McNaught, Judith - *Someone to Watch Over Me (Read by Rosenblat, Barbara). Audiobook Review*
  c Kliatt - v38 - i4 - July 2004 - p57(1) [51-500]
McNaughton, Colin - *If Dinosaurs Were Cats and Dogs*
  c Sch Lib - v52 - i4 - Winter 2004 - p210(1) [51-500]
  Once Upon an Ordinary School Day (Illus. by Kitamura, Satoshi)
  c HB - v81 - i2 - March-April 2005 - p192(1) [51-500]
  c KR - v73 - i3 - Feb 1 2005 - p178(1) [51-500]
  c PW - v252 - i11 - March 14 2005 - p66(1) [51-500]
  c Sch Lib - v52 - i3 - Autumn 2004 - p167(1) [501+]
McNaughton, Janet - *An Earthly Knight*
  y CBRA - Annual 2003 - p504(1) [51-500]
  y Kliatt - v39 - i2 - March 2005 - p28(2) [51-500]
  y Teach Lib - v32 - i3 - Feb 2005 - p54(1) [1-50]
  y VOYA - v27 - i4 - Oct 2004 - p317(1) [51-500]
  The Secret under My Skin
  y CCB - v58 - i5 - Jan 2005 - p218(1) [51-500]
  c HB - v81 - i1 - Jan-Feb 2005 - p97(1) [51-500]
  c Kliatt - v39 - i3 - March 2005 - p14(1) [51-500]
  c KR - v73 - i4 - Feb 15 2005 - p233(1) [51-500]
  y SLJ - v51 - i2 - Feb 2005 - p138(1) [51-500]
McNeal, Laura - *Zipped*
  y Kliatt - v39 - i1 - Jan 2005 - p15(2) [501+]
  y PW - v251 - i42 - Oct 18 2004 - p66(1) [51-500]
McNeely, Ian - *The Emancipation of Writing: German Civil Society in the Making, 1790-1820*
  GSR - v27 - i2 - May 2004 - p386-387 [501+]
McNeely, Trevor - *Proteus Unmasked: Sixteenth-Century Rhetoric and the Art of Shakespeare*
  Choice - v42 - i2 - Oct 2004 - p294(1) [501+]
McNeese, Tim - *The Rise and Fall of American Slavery: Freedom Denied, Freedom Gained*
  y BL - v101 - i1 - Sept 1 2004 - p79(1) [501+]
  c CH Bwatch - v14 - i7 - July 2004 - p5(1) [51-500]
  c SLJ - v50 - i8 - August 2004 - p135(1) [501+]
McNeil, Jean - *Private View*
  Can Lit - i182 - Autumn 2004 - p114(3) [501+]
McNeil, Legs - *The Other Hollywood: The Uncensored Oral History of the Porn Film Industry*
  Ent W - Feb 4 2005 - p136 [501+]
  PW - v252 - i2 - Jan 10 2005 - p47(2) [501+]
McNeill, Elisabeth - *The Lady of Cawnpore*
  BL - v101 - i1 - Sept 1 2004 - p62(1) [501+]
McNeill, J.R. William - *The Human Web: A Birds's Eye View of World History*
  J Hist G - v30 - i3 - July 2004 - p578(2) [501+]
McNeill, Laurie S. - *Field Measurement Methods for Arsenic in Drinking Water*
  SciTech - v28 - i3 - Sept 2004 - p145(1) [51-500]
McNeill, William H. - *Berkshire Encyclopedia of World History, Vols. 1-5*
  BL - v101 - i9-10 - Jan 1 2005 - p779(1) [1-50]
  BL - v101 - i9-10 - Jan 1 2005 - p888(1) [501+]
  LJ - v130 - i1 - Jan 1 2005 - p150(2) [51-500]
McNeillie, John - *My Childhood*
  TLS - i5303 - Nov 19 2004 - p36(1) [51-500]
McNicholl, Damian - *A Son Called Gabriel*
  Lam Bk Rpt - v13 - i1-2 - August-Sept 2004 - p27(2) [501+]
McNicoll, Sylvia - *A Different Kind of Beauty*
  y CBRA - Annual 2003 - p505(1) [51-500]
  c SLJ - v50 - i8 - August 2004 - p126(1) [51-500]
  y VOYA - v27 - i3 - August 2004 - p222(1) [1-50]
McNish, Cliff - *The Doomspell Trilogy*
  y Sch Lib - v52 - i4 - Winter 2004 - p212(1) [51-500]
  The Silver Child
  y PW - v252 - i11 - March 14 2005 - p68(1) [51-500]
  y Sch Lib - v52 - i4 - Winter 2004 - p212(1) [51-500]
McNish, Jacquie - *Wrong Way: The Fall of Conrad Black*
  Globe & Mail - Nov 6 2004 - pD10 [501+]
  NYTBR - Jan 2 2005 - p13 [501+]
McNulty, Faith - *If Dogs Ruled the World (Illus. by Durrell, Julie)*
  c RT - v57 - Oct 2003 - p169 [1-50]
McNulty, Thomas - *Errol Flynn: The Life and Career*
  Choice - v42 - i4 - Dec 2004 - p668(2) [1-50]

McPhail, David - *Mole Music (Read by Weiss, Jim). Audiobook Review*
  c SLJ - v50 - i12 - Dec 2004 - p58(1) [51-500]
  Mole Music
  c SLJ - v50 - i12 - Dec 2004 - p58(1) [501+]
  My Little Brother (Illus. by McPhail, David)
  c CE - v81 - i2 - Winter 2004 - p108(1) [51-500]
  A Pot o' Gold: A Treasury of Irish Stories, Poetry, Folkore and (of Course) Blarney
  c LibMed - v22 - i5 - Feb 2004 - p73(1) [501+]
  Wynken, Blynken, and Nod
  c LibMed - v22 - i7 - April-May 2004 - p56(1) [501+]
McPhee, Jenny - *No Ordinary Matter*
  BW - v34 - i31 - August 1 2004 - p10(1) [51-500]
McPhee, Peter - *Out of Time*
  y Kliatt - v38 - i6 - Nov 2004 - p19(1) [51-500]
  y SLJ - v50 - i11 - Nov 2004 - p144(1) [51-500]
  y VOYA - v27 - i4 - Oct 2004 - p306(1) [51-500]
McPherson, Alan - *Yankee No! Anti-Americanism in U.S. Latin American Relations*
  Choice - v41 - i11-12 - July-August 2004 - p2121(1) [501+]
McPherson, Anne - *Ways of the Wilderness: A Personal Journey through Religion and Literature*
  CBRA - Annual 2003 - p257(1) [501+]
McPherson, Edward - *Buster Keaton: Tempest in a Flat Hat*
  TimHES - v0 - i1681 - March 4 2005 - p25(1) [501+]
  TLS - i5300 - Oct 29 2004 - p18-19 [501+]
McPherson, James M. - *Crossroads of Freedom: Antietam*
  J Mil H - v68 - i3 - April 2004 - p607-608 [501+]
  The Illustrated Battle Cry of Freedom: The Civil War Era
  JSH - v70 - i4 - Nov 2004 - p987(1) [501+]
  The Most Fearful Ordeal: Original Coverage of the Civil War by Writers and Reporters of the New York Times
  For Aff - v83 - i5 - Sept-Oct 2004 - p164 [501+]
McPherson, Kathryn - *Gendered Pasts: Historical Essays in Femininity and Masculinity in Canada*
  R&R Bk N - v19 - i4 - Nov 2004 - p132(1) [51-500]
McPherson, Robert - *New Owners in Their Own Land: Minerals and Inuit Land Claims*
  CBRA - Annual 2003 - p366(2) [501+]
  Choice - v42 - i3 - Nov 2004 - p549(2) [1-50]
McPherson, Stephanie Sammartino - *Wilbur and Orville Wright Taking Flight*
  c LibMed - v23 - i1 - August-Sept 2004 - p72(1) [51-500]
McPherson, Tara - *Reconstructing Dixie: Race, Gender, and Nostalgia in the Imagined South*
  AHR - v109 - i3 - June 2004 - p917(2) [501+]
  J Am St - v38 - i2 - August 2004 - p362(2) [501+]
  JAH - v91 - i2 - Sept 2004 - p674(1) [501+]
  JouAmCul - v27 - i4 - Dec 2004 - p457(3) [501+]
  JSH - v70 - i3 - August 2004 - p730(2) [501+]
McPhillips, Robert - *The New Formalism: A Critical Introduction*
  Sew R - v111 - i3 - Summer 2003 - pLXX-LXXIV [501+]
McQuaid, Kim - *A Response to Industrialism: Liberal Businessmen and the Evolving Spectrum of Capitalist Reform, 1886-1960*
  R&R Bk N - v19 - i1 - Feb 2004 - p81(1) [1-50]
McQuaig, Linda - *It's the Crude, Dude: War, Big Oil and the Fight for the Planet*
  Globe & Mail - Sept 25 2004 - pD21 [501+]
McQuail, Lisa - *The Masai of Africa*
  c HNet - Sept 2004 - pNA [501+]
McQuarrie, Donald A. - *Mathematical Methods for Scientists and Engineers*
  J Chem Ed - v81 - i10 - Oct 2004 - p1425(1) [501+]
McQueary, Carl R. - *Dining at the Governor's Mansion*
  SHQ - v107 - i3 - Jan 2004 - p497(2) [501+]
McQueen, E.I. - *Herodotus Book*
  Class R - v53 - i2 - Nov 2003 - pNA [501+]
McQueen, Humphrey - *Essence of Capitalism: The Origins of Our Future*
  CBRA - Annual 2003 - p330(1) [501+]
McQueen, Mike - *Land Conservation Financing*
  NRJ - v44 - i2 - Spring 2004 - p621-651 [501+]
  R&R Bk N - v19 - i1 - Feb 2004 - p95(1) [51-500]
McQueen, Rod - *The Icarus Factor: The Rise and Fall of Edgar Bronfman Jr.*
  Globe & Mail - Oct 16 2004 - pD3 [501+]
McQuerry, Steve - *CCNA Self-Study: Introduction to Cisco Networking Technologies*
  LJ - v129 - i18 - Nov 1 2004 - p114(1) [51-500]

McQuiston, John, II - *Finding Time for the Timeless: Spirituality in the Workweek*
  PW - v251 - i45 - Nov 8 2004 - p52(1) [51-500]
McQuiston, Liz - *Graphic Agitation 2: Social and Political Graphics in the Digital Age*
  LJ - v130 - i1 - Jan 1 2005 - p108(1) [51-500]
McRae, Andrew - *Literature, Satire, and the Early Stuart State*
  Choice - v42 - i2 - Oct 2004 - p294(2) [501+]
  Critm - v46 - i2 - Spring 2004 - p311(5) [501+]
McRae, Bard - *Seven Strategies of Master Negotiators: Featuring Real-Life Insights from Canada's Top Negotiators*
  CBRA - Annual 2003 - p330(1) [51-500]
McRae, John R. - *Seeing through Zen: Encounter, Transformation, and Genealogy in Chinese Chan Buddhism*
  Choice - v42 - i1 - Sept 2004 - p121(1) [501+]
  Parabola - v29 - i4 - Winter 2004 - p112-117 [501+]
McReynolds, Kathy - *Enhancing Our Way to Happiness?: Aristotle Versus Bacon on the Nature of True Happiness*
  R&R Bk N - v20 - i1 - Feb 2005 - p10(1) [51-500]
McReynolds, Louise - *Russia at Play: Leisure Activities at the End of the Tsarist Era*
  AHR - v109 - i3 - June 2004 - p1004(2) [501+]
  HNet - July 2004 - pNA [501+]
McSheffrey, Shannon - *Lollards of Coventry, 1486-1522*
  Med R - July 2004 - pNA [501+]
McSherry, Peter - *Mean Streets: Confessions of a Nighttime Taxi Driver*
  CBRA - Annual 2003 - p59(1) [51-500]
McSween, Harry Y. - *Geochemistry: Pathways and Processes, 2nd Ed.*
  SciTech - v28 - i1 - March 2004 - p58(1) [51-500]
McSweeney, Joyelle - *The Commandrine and Other Poems*
  c PW - v252 - i10 - March 7 2005 - p66(1) [51-500]
McTavish, Jan R. - *Pain and Profits: The History of the Headache and Its Remedies in America*
  CHE - v51 - i12 - Nov 12 2004 - pA28-1 [501+]
  Choice - v42 - i6 - Feb 2005 - p1056(1) [51-500]
  SciTech - v28 - i4 - Dec 2004 - p88(1) [51-500]
  SEP - v277 - i2 - March-April 2005 - p44(2) [501+]
McTavish, Karen - *Knitted Toys: 21 Easy-to-Knit Patterns for Irresistible Soft Toys*
  LJ - v129 - i13 - August 2004 - p78(1) [51-500]
  Whitework Quilting: Creative Techniques for Designing Wholecloth and Adding Trapunto to Your Quilts
  LJ - v129 - i13 - August 2004 - p78(2) [501+]
McTeer, Maureen - *In My Own Name: A Memoir*
  CBRA - Annual 2003 - p60(1) [51-500]
  Globe & Mail - Nov 13 2004 - pD21 [51-500]
McVary, Kevin T. - *Management of Benign Prostatic Hypertrophy*
  SciTech - v28 - i1 - March 2004 - p106(1) [51-500]
McVeagh, John - *Daniel Defoe: A Review of the Affairs of France, 1704-1705, Vols. 1-2*
  R&R Bk N - v19 - i3 - August 2004 - p38(1) [51-500]
McVeigh, Brian J. - *Nationalisms of Japan: Managing and Mystifying Identity*
  Choice - v41 - i11-12 - July-August 2004 - p2101(1) [501+]
  R&R Bk N - v19 - i1 - Feb 2004 - p49(1) [51-500]
McVeigh, Frank J. - *Brief History of Social Problems: A Critical Thinking Approach*
  R&R Bk N - v19 - i4 - Nov 2004 - p121(1) [51-500]
McVicker, Mary - *Secret of Belle Meadow*
  c CH Bwatch - v14 - i8 - August 2004 - p3(1) [51-500]
McVitie, Stephen - *Electron Microscopy and Analysis 2003: Proceedings*
  SciTech - v28 - i3 - Sept 2004 - p57(1) [1-50]
McWatt, Tessa - *This Body*
  Globe & Mail - Sept 25 2004 - pD25 [501+]
  Globe & Mail - Oct 16 2004 - pR1 [501+]
  Globe & Mail - Nov 27 2004 - pD3 [51-500]
McWeeny, R. - *Spins in Chemistry*
  SciTech - v28 - i3 - Sept 2004 - p53(1) [1-50]
McWhinney, Edward - *Chretien and Canadian Federalism: Politics and the Constitution, 1993-2003*
  CBRA - Annual 2003 - p309(1) [501+]
McWhirter, Teresa - *Some Girls Do*
  KR - v72 - i16 - August 15 2004 - p769(1) [51-500]

McWhorter, Diane - *A Dream of Freedom: The Civil Rights Movement from 1954 to 1968*
y BL - v101 - i6 - Nov 15 2004 - p584(1) [51-500]
y BL - v101 - i9-10 - Jan 1 2005 - p772(1) [51-500]
c CCB-B - v58 - i5 - Jan 2005 - p219(1) [51-500]
c HB - v81 - i1 - Jan-Feb 2005 - p17(1) [51-500]
c HB - v81 - i1 - Jan-Feb 2005 - p112(2) [51-500]
y KR - v72 - i19 - Oct 1 2004 - p965(1) [51-500]
y NYTBR - Nov 14 2004 - p43 [501+]
y PW - v251 - i47 - Nov 22 2004 - p61(1) [51-500]
c SLJ - v50 - i12 - Dec 2004 - p163(1) [51-500]
McWhorter, John - *Doing Our Own Thing: The Degradation of Language and Music and Why We Should, Like, Care*
NYTBR - Nov 7 2004 - p30 [501+]
World&I - v19 - i3 - March 2004 - p227 [501+]
McWilliam, Andrew - *Paths of Origin, Gates of Life: A Study of Place and Precedence in Southwest Timor*
JAS - v63 - i3 - August 2004 - p850-854 [501+]
McWilliams, Bill - *On Hallowed Ground: The Last Battle for Pork Chop Hill*
J Mil H - v68 - i4 - Oct 2004 - p1308-1309 [501+]
McWilliams, Brian - *Spam Kings: The Real Story Behind the High-Rolling Hucksters Pushing Porn, Pills, and @*#?Enlargements*
LJ - v129 - i18 - Nov 1 2004 - p112(1) [51-500]
PW - v251 - i43 - Oct 25 2004 - p41(1) [51-500]
McWilliams, Jeff - *Whimsical Accents for Your Home*
LJ - v129 - i20 - Dec 1 2004 - p157(1) [51-500]
McWilliams, Kelly - *Doormat*
y BL - v101 - i7 - Dec 1 2004 - p647(1) [51-500]
y CCB-B - v58 - i5 - Jan 2005 - p219(2) [51-500]
y Kliatt - v38 - i5 - Sept 2004 - p14(2) [51-500]
c KR - v72 - i17 - Sept 1 2004 - p870(1) [51-500]
y PW - v251 - i42 - Oct 18 2004 - p65(1) [51-500]
c SLJ - v50 - i9 - Sept 2004 - p212(1) [51-500]
y Black Iss - v7 - i2 - March-April 2005 - p16(1) [51-500]
y VOYA - v27 - i5 - Dec 2004 - p386(1) [51-500]
McWilliams, Nancy - *Psychoanalytic Psychotherapy: A Practitioner's Guide*
SciTech - v28 - i3 - Sept 2004 - p100(1) [1-50]
McWilliams, Tracy - *Dress to Express*
Bwatch - Nov 2004 - pNA [51-500]
Mda, Zakes - *The Madonna of Excelsior*
AM - v191 - i1 - July 5 2004 - p25 [501+]
IJAHS - v37 - i2 - Spring 2004 - p389-391 [501+]
She Plays with the Darkness
AM - v191 - i1 - July 5 2004 - p25 [501+]
Meacham, Jon - *Franklin and Winston: An Intimate Portrait of an Epic Friendship*
NYTBR - Oct 31 2004 - p26 [501+]
Meacham, Margaret - *A Mid-Semester Night's Dream*
c SLJ - v50 - i8 - August 2004 - p126(2) [51-500]
Meacham, Rebecca - *Let's Do*
PW - v251 - i50 - Dec 13 2004 - p46(2) [51-500]
Mead, Alice - *Madame Squidley and Beanie*
c CCB-B - v58 - i1 - Sept 2004 - p30(2) [51-500]
c CH Bwatch - v14 - i8 - August 2004 - p3(1) [51-500]
Swimming to America
c KR - v73 - i4 - Feb 15 2005 - p234(1) [51-500]
Year of No Rain (Read by Lecat, Lisette). Audiobook Review
c Kliatt - v38 - i4 - July 2004 - p58(2) [51-500]
Mead-Ferro, Muffy - *Confessions of a Slacker Wife*
KR - v73 - i4 - Feb 15 2005 - p215(1) [501+]
PW - v252 - i8 - Feb 21 2005 - p168(1) [51-500]
Mead, George R. - *Ethnobotany of the California Indians*
R&R Bk N - v19 - i4 - Nov 2004 - p53(1) [51-500]
Mead, Lawrence M. - *Government Matters: Welfare Reform in Wisconsin*
Choice - v42 - i3 - Nov 2004 - p565-1 [1-50]
Mead, Rebecca J. - *How the Vote Was Won: Woman Suffrage in the Western United States, 1868-1914*
Choice - v42 - i2 - Oct 2004 - p357(1) [51-500]
PHR - v73 - i4 - Nov 2004 - p673(2) [501+]
Mead, Walter Russell - *Power, Terror, Peace, and War: America's Grand Strategy in a World at Risk*
CC - v121 - i20 - Oct 5 2004 - p42(1) [501+]
Choice - v42 - i5 - Jan 2005 - p935(1) [51-500]
Globe & Mail - Nov 27 2004 - pD3 [51-500]
MEJ - v58 - i4 - Autumn 2004 - p707(2) [501+]
Mead, William R. - *Pehr Kalm: A Finnish Visitor to the Chilterns in 1748*
J Hist G - v30 - i1 - Jan 2004 - p205(2) [501+]
Meade, James G. - *The Human Resources Software Handbook.*
HR Mag - v49 - i7 - July 2004 - pS54(1) [51-500]
Meade, Teresa A. - *A Companion to Gender History*
Choice - v42 - i2 - Oct 2004 - p346(1) [51-500]
Meadow-Orlans, Kathryn P. - *The World of Deaf Infants: A Longitudinal Study*
R&R Bk N - v19 - i3 - August 2004 - p162(1) [501+]
Meadows, Donella - *The Limits to Growth: The 30-Year Update*
Choice - v42 - i3 - Nov 2004 - p503(1) [1-50]
E Mag - v15 - i5 - Sept-Oct 2004 - p63(1) [51-500]
PW - v251 - i29 - July 19 2004 - p156(2) [51-500]
Meadows, Eddie S. - *Bebop to Cool: Context, Ideology, and Musical Identity*
M Ed J - v91 - i2 - Nov 2004 - p60(2) [501+]
Meadows, Sammye J. - *Lewis and Clark for Dummies*
R&R Bk N - v19 - i1 - Feb 2004 - p64(1) [501+]
Meagher, John C. - *Pursuing Shakespeare's Dramaturgy: Some Contexts, Resources, and Strategies in His Playmaking*
R&R Bk N - v19 - i1 - Feb 2004 - p237(1) [51-500]
Meagher, R.P. - *Meagher, Gummow and Lehane's Doctrines and Remedies, 4th Ed.*
Law Q Rev - v120 - April 2004 - p344-348 [501+]
Meaker, Marijane - *Highsmith: A Romance of the 1950's*
MLN - v118 - i5 - Dec 2003 - p1311-1317 [501+]
Mealing, Stuart - *Computers and Art, 2nd Ed.*
R&R Bk N - v19 - i1 - Feb 2004 - p250(1) [51-500]
Meaney, James A. - *How to Buy a Franchise*
Bwatch - Feb 2005 - pNA [51-500]
Meaney, John - *Paradox*
Ent W - i810 - March 11 2005 - p108 [51-500]
KR - v73 - i1 - Jan 1 2005 - p25(2) [51-500]
LJ - v130 - i3 - Feb 15 2005 - p123(1) [51-500]
PW - v252 - i8 - Feb 21 2005 - p162(1) [51-500]
Means, Barbara - *Using Technology Evalution to Enhance Student Learning*
TCR - v106 - i8 - August 2004 - p1666(3) [501+]
Means Coleman, Robin R. - *Say It Loud!: African-American Audiences, Media, and Identity*
JC - v54 - i3 - Sept 2004 - p567(4) [501+]
Means, David - *The Secret Goldfish: Stories*
BL - v101 - i1 - Sept 1 2004 - p62(2) [501+]
BW - v34 - i40 - Oct 3 2004 - p6(1) [501+]
KR - v72 - i14 - July 15 2004 - p652(1) [51-500]
LJ - v129 - i13 - August 2004 - p73(1) [51-500]
NYTBR - Sept 5 2004 - p16 [501+]
PW - v251 - i27 - July 5 2004 - p34(1) [51-500]
Means, Robin - *From Community Care to Market Care?: The Development of Welfare Services for Older People*
R&R Bk N - v19 - i1 - Feb 2004 - p138(1) [51-500]
Means, Thomas L. - *Business Communications*
R&R Bk N - v19 - i3 - August 2004 - p132(1) [1-50]
Mearns, Linda O. - *Issues in the Impacts of Climate Variability and Change on Agriculture: Applications to the Southeastern United States*
SciTech - v28 - i1 - March 2004 - p128(1) [51-500]
Measor, Lynda - *Young People and Community Safety: Inclusion, Risk, Tolerance and Disorder*
Adoles - v39 - i154 - Summer 2004 - p402(1) [51-500]
Mebus, Scott - *Booty Nomad (Read by Feverstein, Michael). Audiobook Review*
LJ - v129 - i12 - July 2004 - p124(1) [51-500]
Mecke, Viola - *Fatal Attachments: The Instigation to Suicide*
Choice - v42 - i4 - Dec 2004 - p739(1) [1-50]
R&R Bk N - v19 - i4 - Nov 2004 - p145(1) [501+]
Meckelnborg, C. - *Odyssea: Responsio Ulixis ad Penelopen*
Class R - v54 - i1 - May 2004 - p233(2) [501+]
Meckna, Michael - *Satchmo: The Louis Armstrong Encyclopedia*
Choice - v42 - i3 - Nov 2004 - p450(1) [1-50]
LJ - v129 - i12 - July 2004 - p118(1) [51-500]
BL - v101 - i5 - Nov 1 2004 - p527(1) [501+]
Medavoy, Mike - *You're Only as Good as Your Next One (Read by Dean, Robertson). Audiobook Review*
BL - v101 - i2 - Sept 15 2004 - p259(1) [51-500]
BL - v101 - i5 - Nov 1 2004 - p506(1) [51-500]
Medawar, Charles - *Medicines out of Control: Antidepressants and the Conspiracy of Goodwill*
Nature - v430 - i7001 - August 12 2004 - p727(2) [501+]
Meddeb, Abdelwahab - *The Malady of Islam*
BIC - v33 - i6 - Sept 2004 - p23(2) [501+]
R&R Bk N - v19 - i1 - Feb 2004 - p15(1) [51-500]
Medearis, Angela Shelf - *Lights Out! (Illus. by Tadgell, Nicole)*
c SLJ - v51 - i1 - Jan 2005 - p85(1) [51-500]
Lucy's Quiet Book (Illus. by Ernst, Lisa Campbell)
c BL - v100 - i21 - July 2004 - p1851(1) [1-50]
c SLJ - v50 - i12 - Dec 2004 - p114(1) [501+]
Singing for Dr. King (Illus. by Van Wright, Cornelius)
c SLJ - v51 - i1 - Jan 2005 - p92(1) [51-500]
Snug in Mama's Arms (Illus. by Sandford, John)
c BL - v100 - i21 - July 2004 - p1849(1) [1-50]
c SLJ - v50 - i7 - July 2004 - p82(1) [51-500]
Medeiros, Teresa - *Yours Until Dawn*
PW - v251 - i28 - July 12 2004 - p49(1) [51-500]
Medhus, Elisa - *Hearing Is Believing: How Words Can Make or Break Our Kids*
Bwatch - v26 - i7 - July 2004 - p6(1) [51-500]
R&R Bk N - v19 - i3 - August 2004 - p149(1) [51-500]
SLJ - v50 - i10 - Oct 2004 - pS74(1) [51-500]
Raising Everyday Heroes
Bwatch - Oct 2004 - pNA [51-500]
Media, Kikim - *Muhammad: Legacy of a Prophet*
LJ - v129 - i14 - Sept 1 2004 - p199(1) [501+]
Media Projects Incorporated - *Life and Times in 20th Century America*
VOYA - v27 - i5 - Dec 2004 - p422(1) [51-500]
Student Almanac of African American History
LibMed - v22 - i6 - March 2004 - p81(1) [501+]
Student Almanac of Asian American History
y VOYA - v27 - i3 - August 2004 - p247(1) [1-50]
Student Almanac of Hispanic American History
y Ref Rev - May 2004 - pNA [501+]
Student Almanac of Native American History
LibMed - v22 - i6 - March 2004 - p81(1) [501+]
Mediavilla, Claude - *Virtue and Happiness: The Manual of Epictetus*
Parabola - v29 - i2 - Summer 2004 - p100-106 [501+]
Medical-Surgical Nursing, 4th ed.
SciTech - v28 - i4 - Dec 2004 - p121 [51-500]
Medical Terminology Made Incredibly Easy, 2nd Ed.
SciTech - v28 - i3 - Sept 2004 - p77(1) [51-500]
Medici, Lorenzino de' - *Apology for a Murder*
Bwatch - v26 - i9 - Sept 2004 - p1(1) [51-500]
TLS - i5293 - Sept 10 2004 - p26-27 [501+]
Medieval World
LibMed - v22 - i7 - April-May 2004 - p71(1) [501+]
Medina, Carmen - *Compliance Handbook for Pharmaceuticals, Medical Devices, and Biologics*
E-Streams - July 2004 - pNA [501+]
SciTech - v28 - i1 - March 2004 - p123(1) [51-500]
Medina, Jane - *Tomas Rivera*
BL - v100 - i21 - July 2004 - p1851(2) [1-50]
Medina, Laurie Kroshus - *Negotiating Economic Development: Identity Formation and Collective Action in Belize*
R&R Bk N - v19 - i4 - Nov 2004 - p105(1) [51-500]
Medina, Loreta - *Bilingual Education*
y SLJ - v50 - i7 - July 2004 - p125(2) [51-500]
Medina, Manuel Ramos - *Historia de la Ciudad de Mexico en los fines de siglo*
HAHR - v84 - i3 - August 2004 - p513(2) [501+]
Medina, Pablo - *The Cigar Roller*
BL - v101 - i9-10 - Jan 1 2005 - p820(1) [501+]
KR - v72 - i24 - Dec 15 2004 - p1160(1) [51-500]
LJ - v130 - i1 - Jan 1 2005 - p99(1) [51-500]
NYTBR - March 13 2005 - p17 [501+]
PW - v252 - i5 - Jan 31 2005 - p48(1) [51-500]
Medlicott, Mary - *Open Secret*
c Sch Lib - v52 - i3 - Autumn 2004 - p146(1) [501+]
Medoff, Mark Howard - *The Dramaturgy of Mark Medoff: Five Plays Dealing with Deafness and Social Issues*
R&R Bk N - v19 - i4 - Nov 2004 - p244(1) [501+]
Medoro, Dana - *The Bleeding of America: Menstruation as Symbolic Economy in Pynchon, Faulkner and Morrison*
TSWL - v22 - i2 - Fall 2003 - p417-419 [501+]
Medrano, Juan Diez - *Framing Europe: Attitudes to European Integration in Germany, Spain, and the United Kingdom*
AJS - v110 - i2 - Sept 2004 - p494(3) [501+]
Medres, Israel - *Between the Wars: Canadian Jews in Transition*
CBRA - Annual 2003 - p357(1) [501+]
Medved, Michael - *Right Turns: Unconventional Lessons from a Controversial Life*
NYTBR - Feb 13 2005 - p26 [501+]
Medvedev, Roy - *Post-Soviet Russia: A Journey through the Yeltsin Era*
HNet - Sept 2004 - pNA [501+]

Medvedev, Sergei - *Russia and the West at the Millennium: Global Imperatives and Domestic Policies*
Parameters - v34 - i4 - Winter 2004 - p149(2) [501+]

Medvedev, Zhores A. - *The Unknown Stalin*
TLS - i5301 - Nov 5 2004 - p10(1) [501+]

Mee, Brad - *Outdoor Spaces: Design Is in the Details*
R&R Bk N - v19 - i4 - Nov 2004 - p204(1) [501+]

Mee, Jon - *Romanticism, Enthusiasm, and Regulation: Poetics and the Policing of Culture in the Romantic Period*
TimHES - v0 - i1676 - Jan 28 2005 - p24(1) [501+]

Mee, Margaret - *Margaret Mee's Amazon: Diaries of an Artist Explorer*
LJ - v130 - i2 - Feb 1 2005 - p112(1) [51-500]

Meek, Anna George - *Acts of Contortion*
Sew R - v111 - i3 - Summer 2003 - pXCV-XCVIII [501+]

Meek, Gary K. - *Developments in Country Studies in International Accounting: Americas and the Far East, 2nd Ed.*
R&R Bk N - v19 - i3 - August 2004 - p131(1) [51-500]

Meek, Jay - *Trains in Winter*
y Kliatt - v38 - i5 - Sept 2004 - p38(2) [51-500]

Meek, M.R.D. - *Kemp's Last Case*
BL - v101 - i3 - Oct 1 2004 - p314(1) [51-500]
LJ - v129 - i20 - Dec 1 2004 - p95(1) [51-500]

Meek, Margaret - *Coming of Age in Children's Literature*
Choice - v42 - i1 - Sept 2004 - p102(1) [501+]
R&R Bk N - v19 - i3 - August 2004 - p259(1) [51-500]

Meeker, Michael E. - *A Nation of Empire: The Ottoman Legacy of Turkish Modernity*
JIH - v34 - i3 - Wntr 2004 - p501(3) [501+]

Meer, Michael N. - *Formation and Reformulation: The Redaction of the Book of Joshua in the Light of the Oldest Textual Witnesses*
R&R Bk N - v19 - i3 - August 2004 - p21(1) [1-50]

Meerman, Marije - *Keten van Liefde: Chain of Love*
JAS - v63 - i2 - May 2004 - p559(2) [501+]

Meernik, James David - *The Political Use of Military Force in US Foreign Policy*
R&R Bk N - v19 - i4 - Nov 2004 - p251(1) [501+]

Meet MINITAB: Student Release 14 for Windows
SciTech - v28 - i3 - Sept 2004 - p37(1) [1-50]

Meezan, William - *Research Methods with Gay, Lesbian, Bisexual, and Transgender Populations*
R&R Bk N - v19 - i1 - Feb 2004 - p138(1) [51-500]

MeGeorge, Constance W. - *Chestnut (Illus. by Whyte, Mary)*
c KR - v72 - i16 - August 15 2004 - p809(1) [51-500]

Meharg, Andrew - *Venomous Earth: How Arsenic Caused the World's Worst Mass Poisoning*
New Sci - v184 - i2477 - Dec 11 2004 - p51(1) [501+]

Meharry, Dot - *Up the Creek (Illus. by Watene, Joshua)*
c Magpies - v19 - i5 - Nov 2004 - p6S(2) [501+]

Mehigan, Tim - *The Critical Response to Robert Musil's The Man Without Qualities*
Ger Q - v77 - i4 - Fall 2004 - p507-508 [501+]
GSR - v27 - i2 - May 2004 - p410-411 [501+]

Mehl, Dieter - *Plotting Early Modern London: New Essays on Jacobean City Comedy*
R&R Bk N - v19 - i4 - Nov 2004 - p234(1) [501+]

Mehmedinovic, Semezdin - *Nine Alexandrias*
ABR - v25 - i5 - July-August 2004 - p10(1) [501+]

Meho, Lokman I. - *The Kurdish Question in U.S. Foriegn Policy: A Documentary Sourcebook*
Choice - v41 - i11-12 - July-August 2004 - p2028(1) [501+]

Mehra, Ajay K. - *Political Parties and Party Systems*
Pac A - v77 - i2 - Summer 2004 - p362(2) [501+]

Mehran, Alfred - *The Terminal Man*
NS - v133 - i4709 - Oct 11 2004 - p52(1) [501+]

Mehrotra, Amit - *Noise Analysis of Radio Frequency Circuits*
SciTech - v28 - i1 - March 2004 - p163(1) [51-500]

Mehta-Jones, Shilpa - *Disaster Alert! Series*
c Res Links - v10 - i1 - Oct 2004 - p22(2) [51-500]

Mehta, Kishor C. - *Guide to the Use of the Wind Load Provisions of ASCE 7-02*
SciTech - v28 - i1 - March 2004 - p149(1) [51-500]

Mehta, Paulette - *Pediatric Stem Cell Transplantation*
SciTech - v28 - i1 - March 2004 - p111(1) [51-500]

Mehta, Suketu - *Maximum City: Bombay Lost and Found*
BL - v101 - i2 - Sept 15 2004 - p197(1) [501+]
Globe & Mail - Oct 23 2004 - pD20 [501+]
HM - v310 - i1857 - Feb 2005 - p90(4) [501+]
KR - v72 - i14 - July 15 2004 - p676(1) [501+]
LJ - v129 - i15 - Sept 15 2004 - p72(2) [51-500]
Nation - v279 - i12 - Oct 18 2004 - p31 [501+]
NYRB - v51 - i18 - Nov 18 2004 - p17(3) [501+]
NYTBR - Nov 21 2004 - p35 [501+]
People - v62 - i18 - Nov 1 2004 - p45 [51-500]
PW - v251 - i29 - July 19 2004 - p153(2) [51-500]
Spec - v297 - i9211 - Feb 19 2005 - p39(2) [501+]
USNews & Wrld Rpt - v137 - i15 - Nov 1 2004 - p76 [51-500]

Mehta, Ved - *Dark Harbor*
Spec - v297 - i9207 - Jan 22 2005 - p31(2) [501+]
The Red Letters: My Father's Enchanted Period
BL - v101 - i3 - Oct 1 2004 - p284(1) [51-500]
KR - v72 - i14 - July 15 2004 - p676(1) [501+]
LJ - v129 - i15 - Sept 15 2004 - p58(1) [51-500]
Spec - v297 - i9207 - Jan 22 2005 - p31(2) [501+]
Remembering Mr. Shawn's New Yorker
Spec - v297 - i9207 - Jan 22 2005 - p31(2) [501+]

Mei, Jianping - *Asset Pricing*
JEL - v41 - i4 - Dec 2003 - p1366(2) [501+]

Meibach, Howard - *Ask the Pros: Screenwriting, 101 Questions Answered by Industry Professionals*
R&R Bk N - v19 - i3 - August 2004 - p263(1) [51-500]

Meier, Andrew - *Black Earth: A Journey through Russia after the Fall*
NYTBR - Feb 20 2005 - p26(L) [501+]
VQR - v80 - i2 - Spring 2004 - p257-257 [501+]
Chechnya: To the Heart of a Conflict
PW - v251 - i48 - Nov 29 2004 - p34(1) [51-500]

Meier, Daniel R. - *The Young Child's Memory for Words: Developing First and Second Language and Literacy*
CE - v81 - i2 - Winter 2004 - p110(2) [501+]

Meier, Deborah - *Keeping School: Letters to Families from Principals of Two Small Schools*
BL - v100 - i22 - August 2004 - p1881(1) [51-500]
LJ - v129 - i12 - July 2004 - p96(1) [51-500]
Many Children Left Behind: How the No Child Left Behind Act Is Damaging Our Children and Our Schools
BL - v101 - i1 - Sept 1 2004 - p28(2) [51-500]
PW - v251 - i34 - August 23 2004 - p52(1) [51-500]
R&R Bk N - v19 - i4 - Nov 2004 - p187(1) [501+]

Meier, Frederick A. - *Instrumentation and Control Systems Documentation*
SciTech - v28 - i3 - Sept 2004 - p170(1) [51-500]

Meier, Heinrich - *Das theologisch-politische Problem: Zum Thema von Leo Strauss*
NYRB - v51 - i16 - Oct 21 2004 - p58(3) [501+]
Die Denkbewegung von Leo Strauss: Die Geschichte der Philosophie und die Intentionen des Philosophen
NYRB - v51 - i16 - Oct 21 2004 - p58(3) [501+]

Meier, John P. - *A Marginal Jew, Vol. 3*
JR - v84 - i4 - Oct 2004 - p609(3) [501+]

Meier, Matt S. - *The Mexican American Experience: An Encyclopedia*
c BL - v100 - i22 - August 2004 - p1982(1) [51-500]
y Choice - v42 - i1 - Sept 2004 - p80(1) [501+]
y VOYA - v27 - i4 - Oct 2004 - p336(1) [51-500]

Meier, Richard - *Architect: 2000-2004*
LJ - v129 - i20 - Dec 1 2004 - p113(1) [51-500]

Meier, Scott T. - *The Elements of Counseling, 5th Ed.*
R&R Bk N - v19 - i4 - Nov 2004 - p10(1) [51-500]

Meilleur, Helen - *A Pour of Rain: Stories from a West Coast Fort*
Can Lit - i181 - Summer 2004 - p165-166 [51-500]

Mein, Andrew - *Ezekiel and the Ethics of Exile*
TT - v61 - i2 - July 2004 - p258(3) [501+]

Meinbach, Anita Meyer - *Memories of the Night: Studies of the Holocaust, 2nd Ed.*
c LibMed - v23 - i3 - Nov-Dec 2004 - p90(2) [51-500]

Meinel, Carolyn - *Uberhacker II: More Ways to Break into a Computer*
R&R Bk N - v19 - i1 - Feb 2004 - p248(1) [51-500]

Meiner, Sue F. - *Care of Gastrointestinal Problems in the Older Adult*
SciTech - v28 - i3 - Sept 2004 - p107(1) [51-500]

Meiners, Cheri J. - *Be Polite and Kind (Illus. by Johnson, Meredith)*
c SLJ - v50 - i8 - August 2004 - p111(1) [51-500]
Join in and Play (Illus. by Johnson, Meredith)
c SLJ - v50 - i8 - August 2004 - p111(1) [51-500]
Listen and Learn
c LibMed - v22 - i5 - Feb 2004 - p78(1) [51-500]

Meinong, Alexius - *Theorie De L'Objet 1904 Et Presentation Personnelle 1921*
Dialogue - v42 - i1 - Winter 2003 - p164 [501+]

Meirav, Ariel - *Wholes, Sums, and Unities*
R&R Bk N - v19 - i1 - Feb 2004 - p6(1) [51-500]

Meisch, Lynn A. - *Andean Entrepreneurs: Otavalo Merchants and the Musicians in the Global Arena*
JEL - v42 - i3 - Sept 2004 - p880(2) [501+]
TLS - i5298 - Oct 15 2004 - p29(1) [501+]

Meisel, Alan - *The Right to Die: The Law of End-of-Life Decisionmaking, 3rd Ed*
R&R Bk N - v19 - i3 - August 2004 - p201(1) [1-50]

Meissner, B. - *Die technologische Fachliteratur der Antike. Struktur, Uberlieferung und Wirkung technischen Wissens in der Antike*
Class R - v53 - i2 - Nov 2003 - p331-334 [501+]

Meissner, Susan - *A Window to the World*
PW - v251 - i46 - Nov 15 2004 - p40(2) [51-500]

Meissner, W.W. - *Psyche and Spirit: Dialectics of Transformation*
R&R Bk N - v19 - i1 - Feb 2004 - p7(1) [51-500]

Meister, Cari - *Luther's Halloween (Illus. by Petrone, Valeria)*
c CCB-B - v58 - i1 - Sept 2004 - p31(1) [51-500]
c KR - v72 - i13 - July 1 2004 - p633(1) [51-500]
c PW - v251 - i32 - August 9 2004 - p248(1) [51-500]
c SLJ - v50 - i9 - Sept 2004 - p174(1) [51-500]

Melamed, Abraham - *The Philosopher-King in Medieval and Renaissance Jewish Thought*
Specu - v79 - i4 - Oct 2004 - p1115(2) [501+]

Melancon, Glenn - *Britain's China Policy and the Opium Crisis: Balancing Drugs, Violence, and National Honour, 1833-1840*
Ch Rev Int - v10 - i2 - Fall 2003 - p307(20) [501+]
VS - v46 - i3 - Spring 2004 - p547(3) [501+]

Melander, Goran - *The Raoul Wallenberg Institute Compilation of Human Rights Instruments, 2nd Ed.*
R&R Bk N - v19 - i3 - August 2004 - p192(1) [501+]

Melantschuk, Gregor - *Kierkegaard's Concept of Existence*
RM - v58 - i2 - Dec 2004 - p460(2) [501+]

Melas, Dimitrios - *Air Pollution Processes in Regional Scale*
SciTech - v28 - i1 - March 2004 - p148(1) [51-500]

Melber, Henning - *Re-Examining Liberation in Namibia: Political Culture Since Independence*
HNet - Sept 2004 - pNA [501+]

Meldrum, Andrew - *Where We Have Hope: A Memoir of Zimbabwe*
CR - v286 - i1669 - Feb 2005 - p111(2) [501+]

Meldrum, D. Jeffrey - *From Biped to Strider: The Emergence of Modern Human Walking, Running, and Resource Transport*
SciTech - v28 - i3 - Sept 2004 - p69(1) [51-500]

Mele, Alfred R. - *Motivation and Agency*
Ethics - v115 - i1 - Oct 2004 - p145(4) [501+]

Melendez, Mariselle - *Mapping Colonial Spanish America: Places and Commonplaces of Identity, Culture and Experience*
Hisp R - v72 - i3 - Summer 2004 - p441-442 [501+]

Meleshkina, E.IU. - *Vtoroi elektoral'nyi tsikl v Rossii 1999-2000*
Slav R - v63 - i2 - Summer 2004 - p425(2) [501+]

Melia, Fulvio - *The Black Hole at the Center of Our Galaxy*
Phys Today - v57 - i7 - July 2004 - p61-62 [501+]
S&T - v107 - i1 - Jan 2004 - p74(2) [501+]
Edge of Infinity: Supermassive Black Holes in the Universe
SciTech - v28 - i1 - March 2004 - p45(1) [51-500]

Melia, Kath - *Health Care Ethics: Lessons from Intensive Care*
Choice - v42 - i5 - Jan 2005 - p887(1) [1-50]
SciTech - v28 - i3 - Sept 2004 - p77(1) [51-500]

Meligrana, John - *Redrawing Local Government Boundaries: An International Study of Politics, Procedures, and Decisions*
R&R Bk N - v19 - i3 - August 2004 - p184(1) [501+]

Melikoff, Irene - *Hadji bektach: Un Mythe et Ses Avatars. Genese et Evolution du Soufisme Populaire en Turquie*
IJMES - v36 - i4 - Nov 2004 - p687(3) [501+]

Melina, Vesanto - *Food Allergy Survival Guide*
Veg J - v24 - i1 - Jan-Feb 2005 - p32(1) [501+]

Menon, Ram K. - *Pediatric Diabetes*
SciTech - v28 - i1 - March 2004 - p118(1) [51-500]

Menon, Ramesh - *The Ramayana: A Modern Retelling of the Great Indian Epic*
Parabola - v29 - i3 - Fall 2004 - p130(4) [501+]

Menon, Visalakshi - *From Movement to Government: The Congress in the United Provinces, 1937-42*
R&R Bk N - v19 - i1 - Feb 2004 - pNA [501+]

Mentzer, John T. - *Fundamentals of Supply Chain Management: Twelve Drivers of Competitive Advantage*
R&R Bk N - v19 - i3 - August 2004 - p103(1) [1-50]

Mentzer, Raymond A. - *Society and Culture in the Huguenot World, 1559-1685*
Six Ct J - v35 - i1 - Spring 2004 - p217(2) [501+]

Menuge, Angus J.L. - *Agents under Fire: Materialism and the Rationality of Science*
R&R Bk N - v19 - i4 - Nov 2004 - p14(1) [51-500]

Menz, Deb - *Colorworks*
Bwatch - v26 - i7 - July 2004 - p6(2) [51-500]

Menz, Robert L. - *Pastoral Counselor's Model for Wellness in the Workplace: Psychergonomics*
R&R Bk N - v19 - i1 - Feb 2004 - p23(1) [1-50]

Menzel, Marcus - *Doomed to Cooperate?: American Foreign Policy in the Caspian Region*
R&R Bk N - v19 - i1 - Feb 2004 - p39(1) [1-50]

Mercader, Julio - *Under the Canopy: The Archaeology of Tropical Rain Forests*
JRAI - v10 - i3 - Sept 2004 - p712(2) [501+]
QRB - v79 - i3 - Sept 2004 - p323(2) [501+]

Mercado, Nancy E. - *Tripping over the Lunch Lady and Other School Stories*
c BL - v100 - i21 - July 2004 - p1845(1) [1-50]
c CCB-B - v58 - i3 - Nov 2004 - p135(1) [501+]
y PW - v251 - i31 - August 2 2004 - p71(1) [51-500]
c SLJ - v50 - i7 - July 2004 - p109(1) [51-500]
y VOYA - v27 - i3 - August 2004 - p225(1) [1-50]

Mercatante, Anthony S. - *The Facts on File Encyclopedia of World Mythology and Legend, 2nd Ed.*
BL - v100 - i21 - July 2004 - p1863(1) [501+]
Choice - v42 - i1 - Sept 2004 - p80(1) [501+]
LibMed - v23 - i3 - Nov-Dec 2004 - p85(1) [51-500]
y SLJ - v50 - i8 - August 2004 - p58(1) [501+]

Mercer, Michelle - *Footprints: The Life and Work of Wayne Shorter*
LJ - v129 - i20 - Dec 1 2004 - p120(1) [51-500]
KR - v72 - i23 - Dec 1 2004 - p1136(1) [501+]
PW - v251 - i50 - Dec 13 2004 - p58(1) [51-500]

Merchant, Carolyn - *The Columbia Guide to American Environmental History*
Isis - v95 - i3 - Sept 2004 - p480(2) [501+]
Green versus Gold: Sources in California's Environmental History
Isis - v95 - i2 - June 2004 - p310(2) [501+]
Reinventing Eden: The Fate of Nature in Western Culture
Choice - v41 - i7 - March 2004 - p1347(1) [501+]
T&C - v45 - i2 - April 2004 - p413-414 [501+]

Mercier, Raymond - *Studies on the Transmission of Medieval Mathematical Astronomy*
SciTech - v28 - i4 - Dec 2004 - p44(1) [51-500]

Mercure, Daniel - *Le travail dans l'histoire de la pensee occidentale*
ILR - v143 - i3 - Autumn 2004 - p277(3) [501+]

Mercuri, Becky - *American Sandwich: Great Eats from All 50 States*
LJ - v129 - i20 - Dec 1 2004 - p150(1) [51-500]

Mercy, David - *Berserk: My Voyage to Antarctica in a Twenty-Seven-Foot Sailboat*
LJ - v129 - i14 - Sept 1 2004 - p175(1) [51-500]
R&R Bk N - v19 - i4 - Nov 2004 - p73(1) [51-500]

Meredith, D.R. - *Murder in Volume*
LJ - v129 - i14 - Sept 1 2004 - p207(1) [501+]

Meredith, Martin - *Elephant Destiny: Biography of an Endangered Species in Africa*
Kliatt - v38 - i6 - Nov 2004 - p39(1) [51-500]

Meredith, Peter A. - *Hypertension and Related Disorders*
SciTech - v28 - i1 - March 2004 - p105(1) [1-50]

Mergel, Thomas - *Parlamentarische Kultur in der Weimarer Republik: Politische Kommunikation, symbolische Politik und Offentlichkeit im Reichstag*
JMH - v76 - i3 - Sept 2004 - p723(2) [501+]

Merges, Robert P. - *Intellectual Property in the New Technological Age: 2004 Case and Statutory Supplement*
R&R Bk N - v19 - i4 - Nov 2004 - p168(1) [501+]

Meri, Josef W. - *The Cult of Saints among Muslims and Jews in Medieval Syria*
HNet - August 2004 - pNA [501+]

Merian, E. - *Elements and Their Compounds in the Environment: Occurrence, Analysis and Biological Relevance, 2nd Rev. Ed.*
E-Streams - Nov 2004 - pNA [501+]

Mericle, Kenneth S. - *Gainsharing and Goalsharing: Aligning Pay and Strategic Goals*
R&R Bk N - v19 - i3 - August 2004 - p115(1) [51-500]

Meriggioli, Matthew N. - *Neuromuscular Junction Disorders: Diagnosis and Treatment*
SciTech - v28 - i1 - March 2004 - p93(1) [51-500]

Meritt, Lucy Shoe - *Etruscan and Republican Roman Mouldings. 2nd Ed.*
Class R - v54 - i1 - May 2004 - p251(2) [501+]

Merki, Christoph - *Die holprige Siegeszug des Automobils, 1895-1930*
T&C - v45 - i1 - Jan 2004 - p195(3) [501+]

Merkl, Peter H. - *Right-Wing Extremism in the Twenty-First Century, 2nd Rev. Ed.*
Choice - v42 - i1 - Sept 2004 - p183(1) [501+]
CR - v285 - i1664 - Sept 2004 - p176(2) [51-500]
R&R Bk N - v19 - i1 - Feb 2004 - p125(1) [51-500]

Merkle, John C. - *Faith Transformed: Christian Encounters with Jews and Judaism*
Comw - v131 - i16 - Sept 24 2004 - p35(3) [501+]

Merkley, Paul Charles - *American Presidents, Religion, and Israel: The Heirs of Cyrus*
R&R Bk N - v19 - i4 - Nov 2004 - p57(1) [1-50]

Merleau-Ponty, Maurice - *The World of Perception*
R&R Bk N - v19 - i4 - Nov 2004 - p4(1) [1-50]

Merletti, Roberto - *Electromyography: Physiology, Engineering, and Noninvasive Applications*
SciTech - v28 - i4 - Dec 2004 - p90(1) [51-500]

Merlevede, Patrick E. - *Mastering Mentoring and Coaching with Emotional Intelligence: Increase Your Job EQ*
R&R Bk N - v19 - i4 - Nov 2004 - p119(1) [51-500]

Merli, Geno J. - *Peripheral Vascular Disorders: Management in Primary Care*
SciTech - v28 - i1 - March 2004 - p105(1) [51-500]

Merlin, Bella - *Konstantin Stanislavsky*
TimHES - v0 - i1655 - August 27 2004 - p26(1) [501+]

Merobaudes, Flavius - *Panegirico in versi*
Class R - v54 - i1 - May 2004 - p130(2) [501+]

Merom, Gil - *How Democracies Lose Small Wars: State, Society, and the Failures of France in Algeria, Israel in Lebanon, and the United States in Vietnam*
AJS - v110 - i2 - Sept 2004 - p535(3) [501+]
J Mil H - v68 - i2 - April 2004 - p663(4) [501+]
Parameters - v34 - i3 - Autumn 2004 - p170(3)

Merrell, Floyd - *Sensing Corporeally: Toward a Posthuman Understanding*
R&R Bk N - v19 - i1 - Feb 2004 - p211 [501+]

Merrell, Frederica - *Seattle's Beacon Hill*
Bwatch - v26 - i7 - July 2004 - p2(1) [51-500]

Merrett, Christopher D. - *Cooperatives and Local Development: Theory and Applications for the 21st Century*
R&R Bk N - v19 - i1 - Feb 2004 - p98(1) [51-500]

Merriam-Webster, Inc. - *Merriam-Webster's Intermediate Dictionary*
y R&R Bk N - v19 - i4 - Nov 2004 - p217(1) [501+]
Merriam-Webster's School Dictionary
CH Bwatch - v14 - i9 - Sept 2004 - p2(1) [51-500]
y R&R Bk N - v19 - i4 - Nov 2004 - p217(1) [501+]
Webster's New Explorer Dictionary of American Writers
Choice - v42 - i6 - Feb 2005 - p994(1) [51-500]
LJ - v129 - i17 - Oct 15 2004 - p89(1) [51-500]
R&R Bk N - v19 - i4 - Nov 2004 - p239(1) [501+]
Webster's New Explorer Dictionary of Word Origins
Bwatch - Nov 2004 - pNA [501+]
Webster's New Explorer Guide to English Usage
Bwatch - Nov 2004 - pNA [51-500]
LJ - v129 - i17 - Oct 15 2004 - p90(1) [51-500]

Merrick, Janna C. - *Reproductive Issues in America: A Reference Handbook*
E-Streams - August 2004 - pNA [501+]

Merrifield, John - *School Choices: True and False*
TCR - v106 - i2 - Feb 2004 - p326-328 [501+]

Merrill, Andrea T. - *The Strategic Stewardship of Cultural Resources: To Preserve and Protect*
LRTS - v48 - i3 - July 2004 - p228(2) [501+]
R&R Bk N - v19 - i1 - Feb 2004 - p260(1) [51-500]

Merrill, Boynton - *Jefferson's Nephews: A Frontier Tragedy*
LJ - v129 - i15 - Sept 15 2004 - p91(1) [1-50]

Merrill, Christopher - *Things of the Hidden God: Journey to the Holy Mountain.*
KR - v72 - i24 - Dec 15 2004 - p1187(1) [501+]
PW - v252 - i3 - Jan 17 2005 - p52(1) [51-500]

Merrill, James - *Collected Prose*
BL - v101 - i6 - Nov 15 2004 - p546(1) [51-500]
KR - v72 - i14 - July 15 2004 - p676(1) [501+]
LJ - v129 - i18 - Nov 1 2004 - p84(2) [51-500]
NYTBR - Nov 21 2004 - p28(L) [501+]

Merrill, Yvonne Y. - *Hands-on Ancient People: Art Activities about Minoans, Mycenaeans, Trojans, Ancient Greeks, Etruscans and Romans, Vol. 2* (Illus. by Simpson, Mary)
c SLJ - v51 - i2 - Feb 2005 - p150(1) [51-500]

Merrillees, Parvine H. - *Ancient Near Eastern Glyptic in the National Gallery of Victoria, Melbourne, Australia*
JNES - v63 - i3 - July 2004 - p216(2) [501+]

Merriner, James L. - *Grafters and Goo Goos: Corruption and Reform in Chicago, 1833-2003*
Choice - v42 - i2 - Oct 2004 - p357(1) [51-500]
LJ - v129 - i13 - August 2004 - p94(1) [501+]

Merritt, A. - *The Moon Pool*
MFSF - v108 - i1 - Jan 2005 - p36(8) [501+]

Merritt, Elizabeth E. - *Data by Dscipline: 2003 Museum Financial Information*
R&R Bk N - v19 - i3 - August 2004 - p1(1) [1-50]

Merritt, Jane T. - *At the Crossroads: Indians and Empires on a Mid-Atlantic Frontier, 1700-1763*
Am St - v45 - i1 - Spring 2004 - p142-143 [501+]
JAH - v91 - i1 - June 2004 - p213-214 [501+]
JIH - v35 - i1 - Summer 2004 - p143-145 [501+]
WHQ - v35 - i4 - Winter 2004 - p521-522 [501+]

Merritt, Juliette - *Beyond Spectacle: Eliza Haywood's Female Spectators*
R&R Bk N - v19 - i4 - Nov 2004 - p236(1) [501+]

Merry, Bruce - *Encyclopedia of Modern Greek Literature*
Choice - v42 - i3 - Nov 2004 - p450(1) [1-50]
Ref Rev - Oct 2004 - pNA [501+]
TLS - i5293 - Sept 10 2004 - p27(1) [501+]

Merry, Sally Engle - *Law and Empire in the Pacific: Fiji and Hawaii*
Choice - v42 - i4 - Dec 2004 - p715(1) [1-50]
R&R Bk N - v19 - i4 - Nov 2004 - p77(1) [51-500]

Mersky, Peter B. - *From the Flight Deck: An Anthology of the Best Writing on Carrier Warfare*
R&R Bk N - v19 - i1 - Feb 2004 - p257(1) [1-50]

Mertens, Donna M. - *Research and Evaluation Methods in Special Education*
Choice - v42 - i1 - Sept 2004 - p159(1) [501+]

Mertig, Angela G. - *Social Movements and Networks: Relational Approaches to Collective Action*
CS - v33 - i5 - Sept 2004 - p578-579 [501+]

Mertler, Craig A. - *Introduction to Educational Research, 5th Ed.*
R&R Bk N - v19 - i3 - August 2004 - p216(1) [1-50]

Merton, Robert K. - *Mass Persuasion: The Social Psychology of a War Bond Drive*
R&R Bk N - v19 - i4 - Nov 2004 - p123(1) [1-50]
The Travels and Adventures of Serendipity: A Study in Sociological Semantics and the Sociology of Science
Am Sci - v92 - i4 - July-August 2004 - p374(3) [501+]
Isis - v95 - i3 - Sept 2004 - p540(1) [501+]
Lon R Bks - v26 - i18 - Sept 23 2004 - p29(2) [501+]

Merton, Thomas - *Peace in the Post-Christian Era*
PW - v251 - i39 - Sept 27 2004 - p58(1) [51-500]
A Year with Thomas Merton: Daily Meditations from His Journals
LJ - v130 - i1 - Jan 1 2005 - p121(1) [51-500]

Mertus, Julie - *Bait and Switch? Human Rights and U.S. Foreign Policy*
R&R Bk N - v19 - i3 - August 2004 - p175(1) [501+]

Mertz, Barbara - *Guardian of the Horizon* (Read by Rosenblat, Barbara)
BL - v100 - i22 - August 2004 - p1953(1) [51-500]
Guardian of the Horizon. Audiobook Review
BL - v101 - i9-10 - Jan 1 2005 - p778(1) [1-50]
The Serpent on the Crown (Read by Rosenblat, Barbara). Audiobook Review
KR - v73 - i4 - Feb 15 2005 - p202(1) [51-500]
LJ - v129 - i20 - Dec 1 2004 - p96(1) [51-500]
The Serpent on the Crown
PW - v252 - i10 - March 7 2005 - p53(1) [51-500]

Mertz, Leslie A. - *Circulatory System*
SciTech - v28 - i4 - Dec 2004 - p69(1) [51-500]

Mertz, Ursula R. - *Composition Dolls 1900-1950, Vol. 2*
Bwatch - v26 - i9 - Sept 2004 - p9(1) [51-500]

Merwin, W.S. - *The Ends of the Earth*
LJ - v129 - i12 - July 2004 - p83(1) [51-500]
Migration: New and Selected Poems
LJ - v130 - i4 - March 1 2005 - p89(2) [51-500]
Sir Gawain and the Green Knight
TLS - i5285 - July 16 2004 - p29(1) [501+]

Merz, Jennifer J. - *That Dancin' Dolly: A Retelling of "Buffalo Gals," a Traditional American Song (Illus. by Merz, Jennifer J.)*
c PW - v251 - i29 - July 19 2004 - p161(1) [51-500]
c SLJ - v50 - i10 - Oct 2004 - p146(1) [51-500]

Merz, Jon F. - *Danger-Close*
KR - v72 - i20 - Oct 15 2004 - p988(1) [51-500]

Merz-Perez, Linda - *Animal Cruelty: Pathway to Violence Against People*
Choice - v41 - i11-12 - July-August 2004 - p2129(2) [501+]
R&R Bk N - v19 - i1 - Feb 2004 - p139(1) [51-500]

Merzoni, Guido S. - *Strategic Delegation in Firms and in the Trade Union*
JEL - v42 - i1 - March 2004 - p283(2) [501+]

Mesce, Bill, Jr. - *Peckinpah's Women: A Reappraisal of the Portrayal of Women in the Period Westerns of Sam Peckinpah*
JGS - v13 - i1 - March 2004 - p80-81 [501+]

Meserve, Adria - *Cleopatra Silverwing*
c Sch Lib - v52 - i3 - Autumn 2004 - p131(1) [1-50]

Meshaka, Walter E. - *The Exotic Amphibians and Reptiles of Florida*
Choice - v42 - i4 - Dec 2004 - p690(1) [1-50]
QRB - v79 - i4 - Dec 2004 - p436(2) [501+]

Mesic, Stipe - *The Demise of Yugoslavia: A Political Memoir*
R&R Bk N - v19 - i3 - August 2004 - p47(1) [51-500]

Mesnier, Roland - *Dessert University: More than 300 Spectacular Recipes and Essential Lessons from White House Pastry Chef Roland Mesnier*
BL - v100 - i22 - August 2004 - p1887(1) [51-500]
LJ - v129 - i13 - August 2004 - p112(1) [51-500]

Mesquita, Bruce Bueno de - *The Logic of Political Survival*
Choice - v42 - i1 - Sept 2004 - p185(1) [501+]
IndRev - v9 - i3 - Wntr 2005 - p456(4) [501+]

Messbarger, Rebecca - *The Century of Women: Representations of Women in Eighteenth-Century Italian Public Discourse*
AHR - v109 - i3 - June 2004 - p994(2) [501+]

Messenger, Charles - *The D-Day Atlas: Anatomy of the Normandy Campaign*
Choice - v42 - i1 - Sept 2004 - p80(2) [501+]
R&R Bk N - v19 - i3 - August 2004 - p32(1) [51-500]

Messer, Sarah - *Red House: Being a Mostly Accurate Account of New England's Oldest Continuously Lived-in House*
Bwatch - Oct 2004 - pNA [51-500]

Messer, Wendel - *Sink: The Last Days of Driving*
CBRA - Annual 2003 - p177(2) [51-500]

Messere, Ken - *Tax Policy: Theory and Practice in OECD Countries*
JEL - v41 - i4 - Dec 2003 - p1370(1) [501+]

Messerlin, Patrick A. - *Measuring the Costs of Protection in Europe: European Commercial Policy in the 2000s*
JEL - v42 - i1 - March 2004 - p182(2) [501+]

Messick, David M. - *The Psychology of Leadership: New Perspectives and Research*
R&R Bk N - v19 - i4 - Nov 2004 - p10(1) [51-500]

Messier, Mireille - *Competition: Deal with It from Start to Finish (Illus. by Murray, Stephen)*
y Res Links - v10 - i2 - Dec 2004 - p25(2) [51-500]

Messina, Lynn - *Mim Warner's Lost Her Cool*
PW - v252 - i9 - Feb 28 2005 - p43(1) [51-500]

Messinger, Robert - *Why Me? Why Did I Have to Get Diabetes?*
c CH Bwatch - Jan 2005 - pNA [51-500]

Messner, Michael - *Taking the Field: Men, Women and Sports*
JPC - v38 - i2 - Nov 2004 - p426(2) [501+]

Mesta, Gabriel - *The Martian War: A Thrilling Eyewitness Account of the Recent Alien Invasion as Reported by Mr. H.G. Wells*
KR - v73 - i3 - Feb 1 2005 - p155(2) [51-500]
PW - v252 - i6 - Feb 7 2005 - p46(1) [51-500]

Mesthrie, Rajend - *Language in South Africa*
Lang Soc - v33 - i4 - Sept 2004 - p632-637 [501+]

Mestre-Reed, Ernesto - *The Second Death of Unica Aveyano*
y Kliatt - v38 - i4 - July 2004 - p21(1) [51-500]
NYTBR - July 4 2004 - p16 [51-500]

Metaphor and Musical Thought
MT - v145 - i1889 - Winter 2004 - p95-98 [501+]

Metaphrog - *Louis: Dreams Never Die*
c PW - v251 - i35 - August 30 2004 - p35(1) [501+]
c SLJ - v50 - i9 - Sept 2004 - p213(1) [51-500]

Metcalf, Allan - *Presidential Voices*
NW - July 26 2004 - p14 [51-500]

Metcalf, John - *Aesthetic Underground: A Literary Memoir*
CBRA - Annual 2003 - p60(2) [501+]
Standing Stones: The Best Stories of John Metcalf
Globe & Mail - July 3 2004 - pD4 [501+]

Metcalf, Linda - *Teaching Towards Solutions: A Solution-Focused Guide to Improving Student Behavior, Grades, Parental Support and Staff Morale, 2nd Ed.*
R&R Bk N - v19 - i1 - Feb 2004 - p188(1) [51-500]

Metcalf, Michael - *Fortran 95/2003 Explained*
Choice - v42 - i7 - March 2005 - p1262(1) [51-500]
SciTech - v28 - i4 - Dec 2004 - p20(1) [1-50]

Metcalf, R. Warren - *Termination's Legacy: The Discarded Indians of Utah*
AHR - v109 - i2 - April 2004 - p559(1) [501+]
WHQ - v35 - i3 - Autumn 2004 - p401(1) [501+]

Metcalfe, Alex - *Muslims and Christians in Norman Italy: Arabic Speakers and the End of Islam*
AHR - v109 - i4 - Oct 2004 - p1296-1297 [501+]

Metcalfe, Gayden - *Being Dead Is No Excuse: The Official Southern Ladies Guide to Hosting the Perfect Funeral*
PW - v252 - i3 - Jan 17 2005 - p49(1) [51-500]

Metcalfe, J.S. - *Change, Transformation and Development*
JEL - v42 - i1 - March 2004 - p318(2) [501+]
Market Relations and the Competitive Process
JEL - v42 - i1 - March 2004 - p287(1) [501+]

Metchnikoff, Ilya Ilyich - *Prolongation of Life: Optimistic Studies*
SciTech - v28 - i1 - March 2004 - p71(1) [501+]

Metra, C. - *On-Line Testing Symposium (IOLTS 2004): Proceedings*
SciTech - v28 - i3 - Sept 2004 - p160(1) [51-500]

Mets, David R. - *Plotting a True Course: Reflections on USAF Strategic Attack Theory and Doctrine, the Post-World War II Experience*
J Mil H - v68 - i2 - April 2004 - p659(2) [501+]

Metsker, Steven John - *Design Patterns in C#*
SciTech - v28 - i3 - Sept 2004 - p21(1) [51-500]

Metter, Dean - *Batman: Nine Lives (Illus. by Lark, Michael)*
LibMed - v22 - i6 - March 2004 - p70(1) [501+]

Mettinger, Tryggve N.D. - *The Riddle of Resurrection: "Dying and Rising Gods" in the Ancient Near East*
JR - v84 - i4 - Oct 2004 - p665(2) [501+]

Metz, Allan - *Blondie, from Punk to the Present: A Pictorial History*
PMS - v28 - i1 - Feb 2005 - p129(2) [501+]

Metz, David C. - *Esophagus and Stomach*
SciTech - v28 - i1 - March 2004 - p111(1) [51-500]

Metz, Matthew - *Bacillus Thuringiensis: A Cornerstone of Modern Agriculture*
QRB - v79 - i3 - Sept 2004 - p309(1) [501+]
SciTech - v28 - i1 - March 2004 - p129(1) [51-500]

Metz, Melinda - *Raven's Point*
y CCB-B - v58 - i2 - Oct 2004 - p90(2) [51-500]
y Kliatt - v39 - i1 - Jan 2005 - pD10(1) [51-500]
y KR - v72 - i13 - July 1 2004 - p633(1) [51-500]
c SLJ - v50 - i10 - Oct 2004 - p172(1) [51-500]
y VOYA - v27 - i5 - Dec 2004 - p408(1) [51-500]

Metz, Walter - *Engaging Film Criticism: Film History and Contemporary American Cinema*
R&R Bk N - v19 - i3 - August 2004 - p261(1) [51-500]

Metzenthen, David - *Time Turns on Spooky Hill (Illus. by Webb, Philip)*
y Magpies - v19 - i5 - Nov 2004 - p36(1) [51-500]

Metzer, David - *Quotation and Cultural Meaning in Twentieth-Century Music*
Choice - v41 - i7 - March 2004 - p1307(1) [501+]

Metzger, Barbara - *The Duel*
BL - v101 - i9-10 - Jan 1 2005 - p831(2) [501+]
LJ - v130 - i1 - Jan 1 2005 - p92(1) [51-500]
A Perfect Gentleman
y BL - v101 - i3 - Oct 1 2004 - p317(1) [51-500]
LJ - v129 - i13 - August 2004 - p56(1) [51-500]
PW - v251 - i37 - Sept 13 2004 - p64(1) [51-500]
Wedded Bliss
y BL - v101 - i2 - Sept 15 2004 - p222(1) [51-500]

Metzger, Robert A. - *CUSP*
BL - v101 - i9-10 - Jan 1 2005 - p834(1) [1-50]
KR - v72 - i22 - Nov 15 2004 - p1072(1) [51-500]
LJ - v130 - i1 - Jan 1 2005 - p102(1) [51-500]
PW - v251 - i50 - Dec 13 2004 - p50(1) [51-500]

Metzl, Jamie - *The Depths of the Sea*
BooChiTr - May 23 2004 - p2(1) [501+]

Metzl, Jonathan Michel - *Prozac on the Couch: Prescribing Gender in the Era of Wonder Drugs*
Isis - v95 - i3 - Sept 2004 - p533(2) [501+]
JAH - v91 - i2 - Sept 2004 - p730(1) [501+]
TLS - i5265 - Feb 27 2004 - p32-32 [501+]

Metzler, David E. - *Biochemistry: The Chemical Reactions of Living Cells, 2nd Ed.*
J Chem Ed - v81 - i5 - May 2004 - p646-647 [501+]

Metzler, Michael W. - *Instructional Models for Physical Education, 2nd Ed.*
R&R Bk N - v19 - i4 - Nov 2004 - p80(1) [51-500]

Meuse-Dallien, Theresa - *Sharing Circle*
c CBRA - Annual 2003 - p459(1) [51-500]

Mews, Constant J. - *Abelard and Heloise*
Bks & Cult - v11 - i1 - Jan-Feb 2005 - p15(1) [501+]
Listen, Daughter: The "Speculum Virginum" and the Formation of Religious Women in the Middle Ages
Med R - Dec 2004 - pNA [501+]
Rhetoric and Renewal in the Latin West 1100-1540: Essays in Honor of John O. Ward
Med R - June 2004 - pNA [501+]

Mewshaw, Michael - *Do I Owe You Something?: A Memoir of the Literary Life*
Sew R - v112 - i2 - Spring 2004 - pLIV-LVII [501+]
Island Tempest
BL - v101 - i4 - Oct 15 2004 - p390(1) [51-500]
KR - v72 - i17 - Sept 1 2004 - p828(1) [501+]
LJ - v129 - i16 - Oct 1 2004 - p71(2) [51-500]
NYTBR - Dec 19 2004 - p23 [501+]
PW - v251 - i40 - Oct 4 2004 - p71(1) [51-500]

Meyer, Ann R. - *Medieval Allegory and the Building of the New Jerusalem*
HER - v119 - i483 - Sept 2004 - p1041(2) [501+]

Meyer, Carolyn - *Doomed Queen Anne*
y Kliatt - v38 - i4 - July 2004 - p22(1) [51-500]
Patience, Princess Catherine
c SLJ - v50 - i7 - July 2004 - p110(1) [51-500]
y VOYA - v27 - i3 - August 2004 - p222(1) [1-50]

Meyer, Carter Jones - *Selling the Indian: Commercializing and Appropriating American Indian Cultures*
Folkl - v115 - i2 - August 2004 - p236(3) [501+]
WestFolk - v62 - i3 - Summer 2003 - p228-230 [501+]

Meyer, Christopher - *It's Alive: The Coming Convergence of Information, Biology, and Business*
Choice - v41 - i11-12 - July-August 2004 - p2090(1) [501+]

Meyer, David R. - *The Roots of American Industrialization*
BHR - v78 - i3 - Autumn 2004 - p509(4) [501+]
JEL - v41 - i4 - Dec 2003 - p1402(1) [501+]
T&C - v45 - i4 - Oct 2004 - p837(2) [501+]

Meyer, Deon - *Heart of the Hunter*
BL - v100 - i21 - July 2004 - p1825(1) [1-50]
PW - v251 - i29 - July 19 2004 - p146(1) [51-500]

Meyer, Eric A. - *Cascading Style Sheets: The Definitive Guide, 2nd Ed.*
SciTech - v28 - i3 - Sept 2004 - p25(1) [51-500]

Meyer, Esther da Costa - *Schoenberg, Kandinsky, and the Blue Rider*
Russ Rev - v63 - i3 - July 2004 - pNA [501+]
TLS - i5267 - March 12 2004 - p16-17 [501+]

Meyer-Fong, Tobie - *Building Culture in Early Qing Yangzhou*
HJAS - v64 - i1 - June 2004 - p201-205 [501+]
JAS - v63 - i2 - May 2004 - p498(2) [501+]

Meyer, Gordon - *Smart Home Hacks*
Bwatch - March 2005 - pNA [51-500]

Meyer, Howard N. - *The World Court in Action: Judging among the Nations*
HNet - June 2004 - pNA [501+]

Meyer, Jimmy Elaine Wilkinson - *Any Friend of the Movement: Networking for Birth Control, 1920-1940*
Choice - v42 - i5 - Jan 2005 - p940(1) [51-500]
SciTech - v28 - i3 - Sept 2004 - p90(1) [501+]

Meyer, John - *Kids Talking: Learning Relationships and Culture with Children*
R&R Bk N - v19 - i1 - Feb 2004 - p8(1) [51-500]
TES - v0 - i4586 - June 4 2004 - psss17(1) [501+]

Meyer, Joyce - *In Pursuit of Peace: 21 Ways to Conquer Anxiety, Fear, and Discontentment*
PW - v251 - i33 - August 16 2004 - p61(1) [51-500]

Meyer, Karl E. - *The Dust of Empire: The Race for Mastery in the Asian Heartland*
NYTBR - July 25 2004 - p20 [501+]
R&R Bk N - v19 - i3 - August 2004 - p53(1) [51-500]

Meyer, L.A. - *Bloody Jack: Being an Account of the Curious Adventures of Mary "Jacky" Faber, Ship's Boy*
y BL - v101 - i1 - Sept 1 2004 - p121(1) [501+]
y Kliatt - v38 - i4 - July 2004 - p22(1) [501+]
Curse of the Blue Tattoo: Being an Account of the Misadventures of Jacky Faber, Midshipman and Fine Lady
y CCB-B - v58 - i1 - Sept 2004 - p31(2) [51-500]
y HB - v80 - i4 - July-August 2004 - p457(2) [51-500]
y SLJ - v50 - i7 - July 2004 - p110(1) [51-500]
y VOYA - v27 - i3 - August 2004 - p222(1) [1-50]

Meyer, Larry L. - *No Paltry Thing: Memoirs of a Geezer Dad*
PW - v252 - i1 - Jan 3 2005 - p47(1) [51-500]

Meyer, Laurence - *A Term at the Fed: An Insider's View*
BL - v100 - i21 - July 2004 - p1806(1) [51-500]
Bus W - i3892 - July 19 2004 - p26 [501+]
Bwatch - Oct 2004 - pNA [51-500]
Choice - v42 - i4 - Dec 2004 - p708(1) [1-50]
Fortune - v150 - i2 - July 26 2004 - p38 [501+]
LJ - v129 - i12 - July 2004 - p95(1) [51-500]

Meyer, Laurine Morrison - *Sacred Home: Creating Shelter for Your Soul*
LJ - v129 - i16 - Oct 1 2004 - p87(1) [51-500]

Meyer, Maisie J. - *From the Rivers of Babylon to the Whangpoo: A Century of Sephardi Jewish Life in Shanghai*
Ch Rev Int - v11 - i1 - Spring 2004 - p146(5) [501+]

Meyer, Marjorie Teetor - *One Man's Vision: The Life of Automotive Pioneer Ralph R. Teetor*
SEP - v276 - i5 - Sept-Oct 2004 - p18(1) [501+]

Meyer, Marshall T. - *You Are My Witness: The Living Words of Rabbi Marshall T. Meyer*
LJ - v129 - i16 - Oct 1 2004 - p87(1) [51-500]

Meyer, P. Mirecki - *Magic and Ritual in the Ancient World*
Class R - v54 - i2 - Nov 2004 - p443(3) [501+]

Meyer, Paul W. - *The Word in This World: Essays in New Testament Exegesis and Theology*
CC - v121 - i21 - Oct 19 2004 - p32(2) [501+]
Intpr - v59 - i1 - Jan 2005 - p90(1) [51-500]

Meyer, Philip - *The Vanishing Newspaper: Saving Journalism in the Information Age*
AJR - v27 - i1 - Feb-March 2005 - p57(1) [501+]
LJ - v130 - i2 - Feb 1 2005 - p94(1) [51-500]

Meyer, R Charles - *Contemporary Financial Management Fundamentals*
R&R Bk N - v19 - i2 - May 2004 - p122 [51-500]

Meyer, Stephanie H. - *Teen Ink: Written in the Dirt*
y VOYA - v27 - i3 - August 2004 - p242(1) [1-50]

Meyer, Thomas - *Media Democracy: How the Media Colonize Politics*
AJPS - v39 - i2 - July 2004 - p468(468) [501+]

Meyerbeer, Giacomo - *The Diaries of Giacomo Meyerbeer, Vol. 4*
Choice - v42 - i3 - Nov 2004 - p492(1) [51-500]

Meyers, Annette - *Hedging: A Smith and Wetzon Mystery*
LJ - v130 - i2 - Feb 1 2005 - p57(1) [51-500]
PW - v252 - i5 - Jan 31 2005 - p52(2) [51-500]

Meyers, Bruce F. - *Swift, Silent, and Deadly: Marine Amphibious Reconnaissance in the Pacific, 1942-1945*
Mar Crp G - v89 - i1 - Jan 2005 - p70(1) [501+]

Meyers, Debra - *Common Whores, Vertuous Women, and Loveing Wives: Free Will Christian Women in Colonial Maryland*
JAH - v91 - i1 - June 2004 - p212-213 [501+]
JSH - v70 - i4 - Nov 2004 - p894(2) [501+]
W&M Q - v61 - i3 - July 2004 - p565-568 [501+]

Meyers, Diana Tietjens - *Being Yourself: Essays on Identity, Action, and Social Life*
R&R Bk N - v19 - i3 - August 2004 - p154(1) [51-500]

Meyers, Jeffrey - *Impressionist Quartet: The Intimate Genius of Manet and Morisot, Degas and Cassatt*
KR - v73 - i4 - Feb 15 2005 - p216(1) [501+]
PW - v252 - i11 - March 14 2005 - p56(1) [51-500]

Somerset Maugham: A Life
Choice - v42 - i6 - Feb 2005 - p1023(1) [51-500]
ELT - v48 - i1 - Wntr 2005 - p236(4) [501+]
G&L Rev W - v11 - i4 - July-August 2004 - p45(1) [501+]
NYRB - v51 - i20 - Dec 16 2004 - p72(4) [501+]
TimHES - v0 - i1660 - Oct 1 2004 - p23(1) [501+]

Meyers, Miriam - *A Bite Off Mama's Plate: Mothers' and Daughters' Connections through Food*
JWH - v16 - i3 - Autumn 2004 - p197(9) [501+]

Meyers, Richard - *Basics of Chemistry*
LibMed - v22 - i5 - Feb 2005 - p54(1) [501+]

Meyerson, Daniel - *The Linguist and the Emperor: Napoleon and Champollion's Quest to Decipher the Rosetta Stone*
Choice - v42 - i1 - Sept 2004 - p97(1) [501+]

Meyerson, Mark D. - *Jews in an Iberian Frontier Kingdom: Society, Economy, and Politics in Morvedre, 1248-1391*
Choice - v42 - i5 - Jan 2005 - p924(1) [1-50]
R&R Bk N - v19 - i3 - August 2004 - p51(1) [501+]

Mezeske, Richard J. - *Finding Our Way: Reforming Teacher Education in the Liberal Arts Setting*
R&R Bk N - v19 - i3 - August 2004 - p219(1) [1-50]

Mezey, Mathy D. - *The Encyclopedia of Elder Care*
Choice - v42 - i6 - Feb 2005 - p1002(1) [51-500]
SciTech - v28 - i4 - Dec 2004 - p106(1) [51-500]
Nurse Practitioners: Evolution of Advanced Practice, 4th Ed.
SciTech - v28 - i1 - March 2004 - p126(1) [51-500]

Mezhiba, Andrey V. - *Power Distribution Networks in High Speed Integrated Circuits*
SciTech - v28 - i1 - March 2004 - p163(1) [51-500]

Mezrich, Ben - *Ugly Americans*
Bwatch - v26 - i8 - August 2004 - p7(1) [51-500]

Mgadla, P.T. - *A History of Education in the Bechuanaland Protectorate to 1965*
HNet - August 2004 - pNA [501+]

Mgbeoji, Ikechi - *Collective Insecurity: The Liberian Crisis, Unilateralism, and Global Order*
Law&PolBR - July 2004 - p567(5) [501+]

Mhlophe, Gcina - *Stories of Africa*
c SLJ - v50 - i10 - Oct 2004 - p146(1) [51-500]

Mi, Jiayan - *Self-Fashioning and Reflexive Modernity in Modern Chinese Poetry, 1919-1949*
R&R Bk N - v19 - i4 - Nov 2004 - p219(1) [501+]

Micale, Mark S. - *Traumatic Pasts: History, Psychiatry and Trauma in the Modern Age, 1870-1930*
JIH - v34 - i4 - Spring 2004 - p619-620 [501+]

Michael Bendis, Brian - *New Avengers #1*
Ent W - i797 - Dec 17 2004 - p88 [501+]

Michael, George - *Confronting Right-Wing Extremism and Terrorism in the USA*
JSH - v71 - i1 - Feb 2005 - p216(2) [501+]

Michael, Judith - *The Real Mother*
y BL - v101 - i6 - Nov 15 2004 - p532(1) [51-500]
KR - v73 - i1 - Jan 1 2005 - p14(1) [501+]
LJ - v130 - i1 - Jan 1 2005 - p69(2) [51-500]
PW - v252 - i2 - Jan 10 2005 - p37(1) [51-500]

Michael, Moser - *Engineering Acoustics: An Introduction to Noise Control*
Choice - v42 - i2 - Oct 2004 - p323(1) [51-500]

Michaels, Anne - *Fugitive Pieces*
Globe & Mail - Jan 22 2005 - pD15 [501+]

Michaels, Axel - *Hinduism: Past and Present*
Choice - v42 - i1 - Sept 2004 - p121(1) [501+]
TimHES - v0 - i1665 - Nov 5 2004 - p27(1) [501+]

Michaels, Fern - *Family Blessings*
BL - v101 - i3 - Oct 1 2004 - p283(1) [51-500]
KR - v72 - i19 - Oct 1 2004 - p939(1) [501+]
LJ - v129 - i19 - Nov 15 2004 - p48(1) [501+]
PW - v251 - i40 - Oct 4 2004 - p70(1) [51-500]
Jingle All the Way
LJ - v129 - i19 - Nov 15 2004 - p48(1) [501+]
Payback
PW - v252 - i2 - Jan 10 2005 - p40(1) [51-500]
Pretty Woman
PW - v252 - i11 - March 14 2005 - p45(2) [51-500]
The Real Deal
BL - v100 - i22 - August 2004 - p1909(2) [51-500]

Michaels, Kasey - *The Butler Did It*
PW - v251 - i34 - August 23 2004 - p42(1) [51-500]
Maggie Without a Clue
BL - v100 - i21 - July 2004 - p1825(1) [1-50]

Michaels, Lynn - *Honeymoon Suite*
LJ - v130 - i1 - Jan 1 2005 - p92(1) [51-500]
PW - v252 - i3 - Jan 17 2005 - p40(1) [51-500]

Michaels, Marcy - *Blow Him Away: How to Give Him Mind Blowing Oral Sex*
LJ - v129 - i20 - Dec 1 2004 - p143(1) [51-500]
The Low Down on Going Down: How to Give Her Mind-Blowing Oral Sex
LJ - v129 - i20 - Dec 1 2004 - p143(1) [51-500]

Michaels, Melisa - *World-Walker*
LJ - v129 - i17 - Oct 15 2004 - p57(1) [51-500]

Michaels, Patrick J. - *Meltdown: The Predictable Distortion of Global Warming by Scientists, Politicians, and the Media*
New Sci - v185 - i2481 - Jan 8 2005 - p51(1) [51-500]
SciTech - v28 - i4 - Dec 2004 - p53(1) [51-500]

Michaels, Paula A. - *Curative Powers: Medicine and Empire in Stalin's Central Asia*
AHR - v109 - i2 - April 2004 - p650(1) [501+]

Michaels, Vaughn - *Dodi's Prince (Illus. by Rogers, Jacqueline)*
c LibMed - v22 - i4 - Jan 2004 - p63(1) [501+]

Michaels, Walter Benn - *The Shape of the Signifer: 1967 to the End of History*
Choice - v42 - i4 - Dec 2004 - p656(1) [1-50]
LJ - v129 - i14 - Sept 1 2004 - p150(1) [51-500]

Michaely, Michael - *Trade Liberalization and Trade Preferences*
R&R Bk N - v19 - i3 - August 2004 - p124(1) [51-500]

Michalczyk, John J. - *Confront!: Resistance in Nazi Germany*
R&R Bk N - v19 - i1 - Feb 2004 - p36(1) [1-50]

Michalos, Alex C. - *Bernard Shaw and the Webbs*
Theat J - v56 - i1 - March 2004 - p138(2) [501+]
Essays on the Quality of Life
R&R Bk N - v19 - i1 - Feb 2004 - p126(1) [51-500]

Michalowski, Sabine - *Medical Confidentiality and Crime*
R&R Bk N - v19 - i1 - Feb 2004 - pNA [51-500]

Michaud, Andre A. - *Le ravissement*
Can Lit - i181 - Summer 2004 - p166-168 [501+]

Michaud, Eric - *The Cult of Art in Nazi Germany*
HRNB - v33 - i1 - Fall 2004 - p25(2) [501+]

Michaud, Mararet A. - *Beautiful Smiles, Gentle Spirits: Fetal Alcohol Spectrum Disorder: A Misunderstood Problem*
CBRA - Annual 2003 - p431(2) [501+]

Michel, Arlette - *Le Reel et la beaute dans le roman balzacien*
FS - v58 - i3 - July 2004 - p419-420 [501+]

Michel, Cecile - *Correspondance des marchands de Kanis au debut du IIe millenaire avant J.-C.*
JNES - v63 - i3 - July 2004 - p210(2) [501+]

Michel, Prince of Greece - *The White Night of St. Petersburg*
Globe & Mail - Jan 8 2005 - pD10 [501+]
LJ - v129 - i16 - Oct 1 2004 - p72(1) [51-500]
PW - v251 - i36 - Sept 6 2004 - p46(1) [51-500]

Michelakis, P. - *Achilles in Greek Tragedy*
Class R - v54 - i1 - May 2004 - p28(3) [501+]

Micheletti, Michele - *Political Virtue and Shopping: Individuals, Consumerism, and Collective Action*
AJS - v110 - i3 - Nov 2004 - p842(3) [501+]
R&R Bk N - v19 - i1 - Feb 2004 - p80(1) [501+]

Michelson, Karin - *Oneida-English/English-Oneida Dictionary*
Can Lit - i182 - Autumn 2004 - p158(2) [501+]

Michie, Helena - *Nineteenth-Century Geographies: The Transformation of Space from the Victorian Age to the American Century*
PG - v23 - i2 - Feb 2004 - p219-221 [501+]

Michie, Jonathan - *The Handbook of Globalisation*
R&R Bk N - v19 - i2 - May 2004 - p110(1) [1-50]

Michman, Ronald D. - *Lifestyle Marketing: Reaching the New American Consumer*
R&R Bk N - v19 - i1 - Feb 2004 - p108(1) [51-500]

Michod, Alec - *The White City*
Globe & Mail - Nov 27 2004 - pD18 [1-50]

Michtl, Max - *Herbal Drugs and Phytopharmaceuticals: A Handbook for Practice on a Scientific Basis, 3rd Ed.*
SciTech - v28 - i3 - Sept 2004 - p123(1) [51-500]

Mickel, John T. - *Ferns for American Gardens*
E-Streams - June 2004 - pNA [501+]
Pteridophytes of Mexico
SciTech - v28 - i4 - Dec 2004 - p64(1) [51-500]

Mickelson, Phil - *One Magical Sunday: But Winning Isn't Everything*
KR - v73 - i4 - Feb 15 2005 - p216(1) [501+]

Micklem, Sarah - *Firethorn*
  BW - v34 - i46 - Nov 14 2004 - p13(1) [1-50]
Micklethwait, John - *The Right Nation: Conservative Power in America*
  BW - v34 - i29 - July 18 2004 - p4(1) [1-50]
  CC - v121 - i25 - Dec 14 2004 - p43(5) [501+]
  For Aff - v83 - i5 - Sept-Oct 2004 - p164 [501+]
  NYRB - v51 - i17 - Nov 4 2004 - p38(4) [501+]
  NYTBR - Nov 28 2004 - p20 [501+]
  Reason - v36 - i6 - Nov 2004 - p62(5) [501+]
  R&R Bk N - v19 - i4 - Nov 2004 - p152(1) [501+]
  The Right Nation: Why America Is Different
  Lon R Bks - v26 - i21 - Nov 4 2004 - p15(4) [501+]
  NS - v133 - i4707 - Sept 27 2004 - p70(3) [501+]
  Spec - v296 - i9189 - Sept 18 2004 - p51(1) [501+]
Micklethwait, Lucy - *Animals: A First Art Book*
  c SLJ - v50 - i7 - July 2004 - p94(2) [51-500]
  I Spy Shapes in Art
  c BL - v100 - i22 - August 2004 - p1938(2) [51-500]
  c KR - v72 - i13 - July 1 2004 - p634(1) [51-500]
  c PW - v251 - i34 - August 23 2004 - p56(2) [501+]
  c SLJ - v50 - i9 - Sept 2004 - p190(1) [51-500]
Mickoleit, Gerhard - *Phylogenetische Systematik der Wirbeltiere*
  QRB - v79 - i3 - Sept 2004 - p320(1) [501+]
Microhabitats, Set 2
  LibMed - v22 - i7 - April-May 2004 - p74(1) [501+]
Microsoft Corporation - *Microsoft Manual of Style for Technical Publications*
  Bwatch - Dec 2004 - pNA [51-500]
Micucci, Charles - *The Life and Times of the Ant*
  c LibMed - v22 - i5 - Feb 2004 - p59(1) [501+]
Midcalf, Brian - *Pharmaceutical Isolators: A Guide to Their Application, Design and Control*
  SciTech - v28 - i3 - Sept 2004 - p124(1) [51-500]
The Middle Ages
  c LibMed - v22 - i5 - Feb 2004 - p79(1) [501+]
Middlebrook, Diane Wood - *Her Husband: Hughes and Plath--A Marriage (Read by Dunne, Bernadette). Audiobook Review*
  y Kliatt - v39 - i1 - Jan 2005 - p53(1) [51-500]
  Her Husband: Hughes and Plath--A Marriage
  CR - v286 - i1669 - Feb 2005 - p117(2) [501+]
  TLS - i5307 - Dec 17 2004 - p11 [501+]
  TSWL - v23 - i2 - Fall 2004 - p386(2) [501+]
  Her Husband: Ted Hughes & Sylvia Plath -- A Marriage
  Globe & Mail - Sept 4 2004 - pD18 [1-50]
  Globe & Mail - Sept 25 2004 - pD30 [1-50]
Middlekauff, Robert - *The Glorious Cause: The American Revolution, 1763-1789, Rev. Ed.*
  Atl - v295 - i2 - March 2005 - p103(2) [501+]
  LJ - v130 - i3 - Feb 15 2005 - p145(1) [51-500]
Middleton, Charlotte - *Enrico Starts School (Illus. by Middleton, Charlotte)*
  c BL - v101 - i1 - Sept 1 2004 - p134(1) [51-500]
  c SLJ - v50 - i7 - July 2004 - p82(1) [51-500]
Middleton, Chris - *Complete Guide to Digital Audio: A Comprehensive Introduction to Digital Sound and Music-Making*
  SciTech - v28 - i1 - March 2004 - p164(1) [51-500]
Middleton, Christopher - *Crypto-Topographia: Stories of Secret Places*
  WLT - v78 - i3-4 - Sept-Dec 2004 - p101(1) [501+]
  Of the Mortal Fire: Poems 1999-2002
  WLT - v79 - i1 - Jan-April 2005 - p89(2) [501+]
Middleton, David - *The Language of the Heart*
  South CR - v36 - i2 - Spring 2004 - p187-190 [501+]
  The Nature of Vermont: A Year-Long Photographic Journal
  SciTech - v28 - i3 - Sept 2004 - p57(1) [1-50]
  The Photographer's Guide to the Oregon Coast
  PetPho - v33 - i10 - Feb 2005 - p18(1) [1-50]
Middleton, Kent R. - *The Law of Public Communication, 6th Ed.*
  R&R Bk N - v19 - i1 - Feb 2004 - pNA [51-500]
Middleton, Neil - *Rio Plus Ten: Politics, Poverty and the Environment*
  PG - v23 - i8 - Nov 2004 - p1055-1057 [501+]
  R&R Bk N - v19 - i1 - Feb 2004 - p95(1) [51-500]
Middleton, Stanley - *Brief Garlands*
  BL - v101 - i4 - Oct 15 2004 - p390(1) [51-500]
  KR - v72 - i18 - Sept 15 2004 - p887(1) [501+]
  TLS - i5286 - July 23 2004 - p23(1) [501+]
Middleton, Stephen - *Black Congressmen During Reconstruction: A Documentary Sourcebook*
  JSH - v70 - i4 - Nov 2004 - p941(2) [501+]

Middleton, Valerie A. - *Explorations in Privilege, Oppression, and Diversity*
  R&R Bk N - v19 - i4 - Nov 2004 - p121(1) [1-50]
Middleton, William D. - *Ultrasound: The Requisites, 2nd Ed.*
  SciTech - v28 - i1 - March 2004 - p89(1) [51-500]
Middleton, William D. (b. 1928 -) - *Metropolitan Railways: Rapid Transit in America*
  T&C - v45 - i2 - April 2004 - p446-447 [501+]
Midgley, David - *Abramovich*
  Spec - v296 - i9200 - Dec 4 2004 - p42(2) [501+]
Midgley, P.A. - *Microscopy of Semiconducting Materials 2003: Proceedings*
  SciTech - v28 - i4 - Dec 2004 - p51(1) [51-500]
Midkiff, Ken - *The Meat You Eat: Corporate Farming and the Decline of the American Diet*
  PW - v251 - i28 - July 12 2004 - p58(1) [51-500]
Miele, Matthew - *Lit Riffs: Writers "Cover" Songs They Love*
  y SLJ - v51 - i1 - Jan 2005 - p160(1) [51-500]
Miers, Suzanne - *Slavery in the Twentieth Century: The Evolution of a Global Problem*
  AHR - v109 - i3 - June 2004 - p869(2) [501+]
  Choice - v41 - i7 - March 2004 - p1347(1) [501+]
Mieville, China - *Iron Council*
  BW - v34 - i34 - August 22 2004 - p15(1) [501+]
  LJ - v129 - i12 - July 2004 - p75(1) [51-500]
  NYTBR - July 18 2004 - p19 [501+]
  PW - v251 - i27 - July 5 2004 - p42(1) [51-500]
  TLS - i5293 - Sept 10 2004 - p20(1) [501+]
Mighton, John - *In the Myth of Ability: Nurturing Mathematical Talent in Every Child*
  Cur R - v44 - i5 - Jan 2005 - p12(2) [51-500]
  LJ - v129 - i13 - August 2004 - p92(1) [501+]
Miglio, Massimo - *Saggi di stampa: Tipografi e cultura a Roma nel Quattrocento*
  Ren Q - v57 - i3 - Fall 2004 - p1002(3) [501+]
Mignola, Dean - *The Single Guy's Survival Guide: 7 Secrets of the Modern Alpha Male*
  LJ - v130 - i3 - Feb 15 2005 - p143(1) [51-500]
Mignola, Mike - *The Dark Horse Book of Witchcraft*
  y VOYA - v27 - i4 - Oct 2004 - p317(1) [51-500]
  The Soul of Venice and Other Stories
  BL - v101 - i1 - Sept 1 2004 - p77(1) [501+]
Miguel, Jose Martinez Carrion - *El Nivel de vida en la Espana rural, siglos XVIII-XX*
  JIH - v35 - i2 - Autumn 2004 - p301(2) [501+]
Mihailovich, Vasa D. - *Jagnje i vuk: Basne za veliku i malu decu*
  WLT - v78 - i3-4 - Sept-Dec 2004 - p140(1) [501+]
  Tango
  WLT - v79 - i1 - Jan-April 2005 - p105(2) [501+]
Mihalkanin, Edward S. - *American Statesman: Secretaries of State from John Jay to Collin Powell*
  Choice - v42 - i7 - March 2005 - p1203(1) [51-500]
Mihesuah, Devon Abbott - *Indigenizing the Academy: Transforming Scholarship and Empowering Communities*
  Choice - v42 - i6 - Feb 2005 - p1063(1) [51-500]
Mihesuah, Henry - *First to Fight*
  Am Ind CRJ - v27 - i2 - Spring 2003 - p117-118 [501+]
  WHQ - v35 - i1 - Spring 2004 - p86-87 [501+]
Miike, Lawrence H. - *Water and the Law in Hawaii*
  Choice - v42 - i2 - Oct 2004 - p363(1) [51-500]
Mijares, John - *Statistics*
  Math T - v97 - i3 - March 2004 - p223-223 [51-500]
Mikaelsen, Ben - *Touching Spirit Bear*
  y Kliatt - v39 - i1 - Jan 2005 - p16(1) [501+]
Mikalson, Jon D. - *Ancient Greek Religion*
  Choice - v42 - i6 - Feb 2005 - p1039(1) [51-500]
  R&R Bk N - v20 - i1 - Feb 2005 - p12(1) [51-500]
  Herodotus and Religion in the Persian Wars
  AHR - v109 - i3 - June 2004 - p955(2) [501+]
  AJP - v125 - i3 - Fall 2004 - p456-459 [501+]
Mike Dyer - *The Essential Guide to Geocaching: Tracking Treasure with Your GPS*
  Bwatch - March 2005 - pNA [51-500]
Mikesell, Margaret - *Culture and Change: Attending to Early Modern Women*
  Ren Q - v57 - i4 - Winter 2004 - p1459(2) [501+]
  R&R Bk N - v19 - i1 - Feb 2004 - p131(1) [51-500]
Mikhail, Mona N. - *Seen and Heard: A Century of Arab Women in Literature and Culture*
  Choice - v41 - i11-12 - July-August 2004 - p2040(1) [501+]
Mikhalev, Vladimir - *Inequality and Social Structure During the Transition*
  E-A St - v56 - i7 - Nov 2004 - p1098(1099) [501+]

Mikhalevsky, Nina - *Dear Daughters: A History of Mount Vernon Seminary and College*
  HNet - Sept 2004 - pNA [501+]
Mikheev, Yu - *The Concept of Micellar-spongy Nanophases in Chemical Physics of Polymers*
  SciTech - v28 - i3 - Sept 2004 - p51(1) [1-50]
Mikhelson, Ilya - *Structural Engineering Formulas*
  Choice - v42 - i3 - Nov 2004 - p515(1) [1-50]
Miki, Roy - *Meanwhile: The Critical Writings of bpNichol*
  Can Lit - i182 - Autumn 2004 - p159(2) [501+]
  Redress: Inside the Japanese Canadian Call for Justice
  Globe & Mail - Nov 27 2004 - pD32 [501+]
Mikkelsen, Glen - *Checkered Courage: Chuckwagon Racing's Glass Family*
  CBRA - Annual 2003 - p144(2) [51-500]
Mikkelsen, Susan R. - *Bioanalytical Chemistry*
  Choice - v42 - i2 - Oct 2004 - p321(1) [51-500]
  J Chem Ed - v81 - i9 - Sept 2004 - p1270-1271 [501+]
Mikkelson, Douglas K. - *The Greatest Story Ever Told: A Silver Screen Gospel*
  R&R Bk N - v19 - i3 - August 2004 - p263(1) [51-500]
Miksic, John - *Earthenware in Southeast Asia*
  Ceram Mo - v52 - i4 - April 2004 - p30(1) [501+]
Mikunda, Christian - *Brand Lands, Hot Spots, and Cool Spaces: Welcome to the Third Place and the Total Marketing Experience*
  Bwatch - Nov 2004 - pNA [51-500]
  R&R Bk N - v19 - i4 - Nov 2004 - p79(1) [51-500]
Milani, Abbas - *Lost Wisdom: Rethinking Modernity in Iran*
  Choice - v42 - i3 - Nov 2004 - p558(1) [1-50]
  MEJ - v58 - i4 - Autumn 2004 - p688(3) [501+]
Milanovic, Petar T. - *Water Resources Engineering in Karst*
  Choice - v42 - i5 - Jan 2005 - p882(2) [1-50]
  SciTech - v28 - i4 - Dec 2004 - p5(1) [1-50]
Milavsky, Adelle - *Take Your RV to Europe: The Low-Cost Route to Long-Term Touring*
  LJ - v130 - i3 - Feb 15 2005 - p149(1) [51-500]
Milbourne, Anna - *On the Moon*
  c Magpies - v19 - i5 - Nov 2004 - p44(1) [501+]
Milburn, Ken - *Digital Photography: Expert Techniques*
  SciTech - v28 - i3 - Sept 2004 - p168(1) [1-50]
Milburn, Sharon Seidman - *iSearch: Human Development*
  R&R Bk N - v19 - i2 - May 2004 - p129 [51-500]
Milde, Jeanette - *Once upon a Wedding*
  c CCB-B - v58 - i2 - Oct 2004 - p91(1) [51-500]
  c Sch Lib - v52 - i3 - Autumn 2004 - p131(1) [1-50]
Mileck, Joseph - *Hermann Hesse: Between the Perils of Politics and the Allure of the Orient*
  R&R Bk N - v19 - i1 - Feb 2004 - p248(1) [51-500]
Milem, Bruce - *The Unspoken Word: Negative Theology in Meister Eckhart's German Sermons*
  Specu - v79 - i4 - Oct 2004 - p1116(2) [501+]
Miles, Barry - *Hippie*
  y BL - v100 - i22 - August 2004 - p1881(1) [51-500]
  BW - v34 - i36 - Sept 5 2004 - p8(1) [501+]
  NYTBR - Dec 19 2004 - p10 [501+]
  Zappa: A Biography
  BL - v101 - i5 - Nov 1 2004 - p460(1) [51-500]
  NYTBR - Nov 14 2004 - p61(L) [501+]
  KR - v72 - i18 - Sept 15 2004 - p904(2) [501+]
  LJ - v129 - i16 - Oct 1 2004 - p83(1) [51-500]
  PW - v251 - i43 - Oct 25 2004 - p36(1) [501+]
Miles, Greg - *Security Assessment: Case Studies for Implementing the NSA IAM*
  LJ - v129 - i12 - July 2004 - p112(1) [501+]
Miles, Hugh - *Al-Jazeera: How Arab TV News Challenged the World*
  NS - v134 - i4722 - Jan 17 2005 - p51(2) [501+]
  Al-Jazeera: The Inside Story of the Arab News Channel That Is Challenging the West
  BL - v101 - i9-10 - Jan 1 2005 - p786(1) [1-50]
  BW - v35 - i4 - Jan 30 2005 - p4(2) [501+]
  KR - v72 - i23 - Dec 1 2004 - p1136(1) [501+]
  NYTBR - March 6 2005 - p8 [501+]
  PW - v251 - i49 - Dec 6 2004 - p50(1) [51-500]
Miles, Murray - *Insight and Inference: Descartes's Founding Principle and Modern Philosophy*
  Dialogue - v43 - i1 - Wntr 2004 - p178-181 [501+]
Miles, Robert P. - *Warren Buffett Wealth: Principles and Practical Methods Used by the World's Greatest Investor*
  R&R Bk N - v19 - i3 - August 2004 - p137(1) [51-500]

Miles, Rosalind - *The Lady of the Sea: The Third of the Tristan and Isolde Novels*
  BL - v101 - i4 - Oct 15 2004 - p390(1) [51-500]
  KR - v72 - i17 - Sept 1 2004 - p829(1) [501+]
  LJ - v129 - i15 - Sept 15 2004 - p49(1) [51-500]
  PW - v251 - i41 - Oct 11 2004 - p53(1) [51-500]
Miles, Steven H. - *The Hippocratic Oath and the Ethics of Medicine*
  Choice - v42 - i2 - Oct 2004 - p326(1) [51-500]
Miles, Timothy S. - *Clinical Oral Physiology*
  SciTech - v28 - i3 - Sept 2004 - p67(1) [51-500]
Miles, Victoria - *Wild Science: Amazing Encounters between Animals and the People Who Study Them (Illus. by Buzzard, Garth)*
  c BL - v101 - i7 - Dec 1 2004 - p666(1) [51-500]
  c CCB-B - v58 - i4 - Dec 2004 - p176(1) [51-500]
  c CG - v124 - i5 - Sept-Oct 2004 - p114(1) [501+]
  c KR - v72 - i19 - Oct 1 2004 - p965(1) [51-500]
  c Res Links - v10 - i1 - Oct 2004 - p39(2) [501+]
  y SLJ - v50 - i12 - Dec 2004 - p164(1) [51-500]
Milford, Nancy - *Savage Beauty: The Life of Edna St. Vincent Millay*
  Sew R - v111 - i3 - Summer 2003 - p463-470 [501+]
Milgate, Michael A. - *Transforming Corporate Performance: Measuring and Managing the Drivers of Business Success*
  R&R Bk N - v19 - i3 - August 2004 - p106(1) [1-50]
Milgram, Avraham - *Entre la Aceptacion y el Rechazo: America Latina y los Refugiados Judios delnazismo*
  Ams - v61 - i2 - Oct 2004 - p277(1) [501+]
Milgram, Goldie - *Make Your Own Bar/Bat Mitzvah: A Personal Approach to Creating a Meaningful Rite of Passage*
  PW - v251 - i28 - July 12 2004 - p60(1) [51-500]
  Reclaiming Judaism as a Spiritual Practice: Holy Days and Shabbat
  PW - v251 - i33 - August 16 2004 - p59(2) [51-500]
Milgrim, David - *See Santa Nap (Illus. by Milgrim, David)*
  c HB - v80 - i6 - Nov-Dec 2004 - p662(1) [51-500]
  c KR - v72 - i21 - Nov 1 2004 - p1052(1) [51-500]
  Swing Otto Swing! (Illus. by Milgrim, David)
  c BL - v100 - i21 - July 2004 - p1852(1) [1-50]
  c BooChiTr - May 9 2004 - p2(1) [501+]
  c HB - v81 - i1 - Jan-Feb 2005 - p14(1) [51-500]
  c SLJ - v50 - i7 - July 2004 - p83(1) [51-500]
Milgrom, Etan C. - *Practical Allergy*
  SciTech - v28 - i1 - March 2004 - p102(1) [51-500]
Milhaupt, Curtis J. - *Global Markets, Domestic Institutions: Corporate Law and Governance in a New Era of Cross-Border Deals*
  R&R Bk N - v19 - i1 - Feb 2004 - pNA [51-500]
Milich, Zoran - *City 123 (Illus. by Milich, Zoran)*
  c KR - v73 - i5 - March 1 2005 - p291(1) [51-500]
  The City ABC Book
  c PW - v252 - i5 - Jan 31 2005 - p70(1) [501+]
Miliora, Maria T. - *The Scorsese Psyche on Screen: Roots of Themes and Characters in the Films*
  R&R Bk N - v19 - i3 - August 2004 - p264(1) [51-500]
Milito, Lynda - *Mafia Wife: My Story of Love, Murder, and Madness*
  TLS - i5283 - July 2 2004 - p6-7 [501+]
Milivojevic, JoAnn - *Bosnia and Herzegovina*
  c BL - v101 - i1 - Sept 1 2004 - p118(1) [1-50]
  c SLJ - v50 - i7 - July 2004 - p126(1) [51-500]
Miljan, Lydia - *Hidden Agendas: How Journalists Influence the News*
  CBRA - Annual 2003 - p80(1) [501+]
  R&R Bk N - v19 - i1 - Feb 2004 - p230(1) [51-500]
Miljan, Toivo - *Historical Dictionary of Estonia*
  Choice - v42 - i3 - Nov 2004 - p467(1) [1-50]
  R&R Bk N - v19 - i3 - August 2004 - p46(1) [51-500]
Millan, Jaime - *Keeping the Lights On: Power Sector Reform in Latin America*
  R&R Bk N - v19 - i2 - May 2004 - p107(1) [51-500]
Millar, A. Lynn - *Action Plan for Arthritis*
  E-Streams - June 2004 - pNA [501+]
Millar, Dan P. - *Responding to Crisis: A Rhetorical Approach to Crisis Communication*
  R&R Bk N - v19 - i1 - Feb 2004 - p89(1) [1-50]
Millar, F. - *The Roman Republic in Political Thought: The Menahem Stern Jerusalem Lectures*
  Class R - v54 - i1 - May 2004 - p169(3) [501+]

Millar, James R. - *Encyclopedia of Russian History*
  Choice - v41 - i11-12 - July-August 2004 - p2025(2) [501+]
  y Ref Rev - May 2004 - pNA [501+]
  Ref Rev - July 2004 - pNA [501+]
  R&R Bk N - v19 - i1 - Feb 2004 - p38(1) [1-50]
  R&USQ - v44 - i1 - Fall 2004 - p86(1) [501+]
Millar, Joseph - *The Gods Hate Kansas*
  MFSF - v107 - i1 - July 2004 - p162(1) [51-500]
Millar, Kenneth - *Meet Me at the Morgue (Read by Gardner, Grover). Audiobook Review*
  y Kliatt - v39 - i1 - Jan 2005 - p47(2) [51-500]
Millar, Margaret - *The Couple Next Door: Collected Short Mysteries*
  Globe & Mail - March 5 2005 - pD15 [51-500]
  KR - v73 - i1 - Jan 1 2005 - p24(1) [51-500]
  PW - v252 - i4 - Jan 24 2005 - p226(1) [51-500]
Millar, Mark - *The Ultimates: Homeland Security, Vol. 2 (Illus. by Hitch, Bryan)*
  LJ - v129 - i14 - Sept 1 2004 - p128(1) [51-500]
  PW - v251 - i27 - July 5 2004 - p41(1) [51-500]
Millar, Roderick - *Directory of International Direct and E-Marketing: A Country-by-Country Sourcebook of Providers, Legislation and Data 7th Ed.*
  R&R Bk N - v19 - i2 - May 2004 - p113(1) [51-500]
Millar, Sandra - *Sage of Our Seniors*
  CBRA - Annual 2003 - p376(1) [51-500]
Millard, Andre - *The Electric Guitar: A History of an American Icon*
  Bwatch - Jan 2005 - pNA [51-500]
  Choice - v42 - i4 - Dec 2004 - p670(1) [1-50]
  R&R Bk N - v19 - i4 - Nov 2004 - p196(1) [501+]
Millard, Anne - *Story of the Nile: A Journey through Time along the World's Longest River (Illus. by Noon, Steve)*
  LibMed - v22 - i6 - March 2004 - p77(1) [501+]
  SLJ - v50 - i10 - Oct 2004 - pS34(1) [51-500]
Millard, Glenda - *Heart of the Tiger (Illus. by Chapman, Gaye)*
  c Magpies - v19 - i5 - Nov 2004 - p30(1) [501+]
Millard, Mike - *Jihad in Paradise: Islam and Politics in Southeast Asia*
  R&R Bk N - v19 - i3 - August 2004 - p165(1) [501+]
Millard, Scott - *Introduction to Serials Work for Library Technicians*
  R&R Bk N - v19 - i4 - Nov 2004 - p256(1) [501+]
Millas, Aristides J. - *Coral Cables Miami Riviera: An Architectural Guide*
  HNet - Sept 2004 - pNA [501+]
Millay, Edna St. Vincent - *Early Poems*
  Sew R - v111 - i3 - Summer 2003 - p463-470 [501+]
Millen, C.M. - *Blue Bowl Down: An Appalachian Rhyme (Illus. by Meade, Holly)*
  c BooChiTr - June 6 2004 - p2(1) [501+]
  c SLJ - v50 - i9 - Sept 2004 - p174(1) [51-500]
  c Teach Lib - v32 - i3 - Feb 2005 - p20(1) [51-500]
Millen, Rochelle L. - *Women, Birth, and Death in Jewish Law and Practice*
  Choice - v42 - i2 - Oct 2004 - p311(1) [51-500]
Millener, Denene - *Angry Black Woman's Guide to Life*
  NW - Sept 27 2004 - p90 [501+]
Miller-Adams, Michelle - *Magic and Modernity: Interfaces of Revolution and Concealment*
  CS - v33 - i1 - Jan 2004 - p128-128 [501+]
Miller, Adrienne - *The Coast of Akron*
  KR - v73 - i5 - March 1 2005 - p253(1) [501+]
  PW - v252 - i10 - March 7 2005 - p47(1) [51-500]
Miller, Albert G. - *Elevating the Race: Theophilus G. Steward, Black Theology, and the Making of an African American Civil Society, 1865-1924*
  Choice - v41 - i7 - March 2004 - p1357(1) [501+]
Miller, Alex - *Journey to the Stone Country*
  Quad - v48 - i11 - Nov 2004 - p89(3) [501+]
Miller, Alexander - *An Introduction to Contemporary Metaethics*
  Choice - v41 - i7 - March 2004 - p1310(2) [501+]
  Ethics - v114 - i4 - July 2004 - p860(3) [501+]
Miller, Alexei - *The Ukrainian Question: The Russian Empire and Nationalism in the Nineteenth Century*
  AHR - v109 - i4 - Oct 2004 - p1338(1) [501+]
  R&R Bk N - v19 - i1 - Feb 2004 - p39(1) [1-50]
Miller, Andrew - *The Optimists*
  BL - v101 - i9-10 - Jan 1 2005 - p820(1) [501+]
  KR - v73 - i1 - Jan 1 2005 - p14(1) [501+]
  LJ - v129 - i20 - Dec 1 2004 - p88(1) [51-500]
  LJ - v130 - i1 - Jan 1 2005 - p99(1) [51-500]
  PW - v252 - i3 - Jan 17 2005 - p33(1) [51-500]

Miller, Anna M. - *Illustrated Guide to Jewelry Appraising, 3rd Ed.*
  Ant&CM - v109 - i6 - August 2004 - p16(1) [501+]
Miller, Anne Meeker - *Baby Sing and Sign: A Play-Filled Language Development Program for Hearing Infants and Toddlers*
  c Teach Mus - v12 - i2 - Oct 2004 - p70(2) [51-500]
Miller, Anthony G. - *Ethno Flora of the Soqotra Archipelago*
  Nature - v432 - i7019 - Dec 16 2004 - p805(2) [501+]
Miller, Arthur - *The Man Who Had All the Luck*
  LJ - v129 - i13 - August 2004 - p131(1) [51-500]
Miller, Arthur G. - *The Social Psychology of Good and Evil*
  Choice - v42 - i3 - Nov 2004 - p570(1) [1-50]
  R&R Bk N - v19 - i4 - Nov 2004 - p123(1) [51-500]
Miller, Arthur I. - *Empire of the Stars: Obsession, Friendship, and Betrayal in the Quest for Black Holes*
  KR - v73 - i4 - Feb 15 2005 - p216(1) [501+]
  LJ - v129 - i20 - Dec 1 2004 - p92(1) [51-500]
  PW - v252 - i11 - March 14 2005 - p57(1) [51-500]
Miller, Berna - *Developing Nations*
  SLJ - v50 - i10 - Oct 2004 - pS59(1) [51-500]
Miller-Bernal, Leslie - *Going Coed: Women's Experiences in Formerly Men's Colleges and Universities, 1950-2000*
  R&R Bk N - v19 - i4 - Nov 2004 - p189(1) [501+]
  Wom R Bks - v21 - i12 - Sept 2004 - p27(1) [501+]
Miller, Beth - *The Women's Book of Resilience: 12 Qualities to Cultivate*
  PW - v252 - i7 - Feb 14 2005 - p68(1) [51-500]
Miller, Brandon Marie - *Good Women of a Well-Blessed Land: Women's Lives in Colonial America*
  y VOYA - v27 - i3 - August 2004 - p240(1) [1-50]
Miller, Brenda Rhodes - *The Church Ladies' Celestial Suppers & Sensible Advice: A Heaping of Comfort Food with a Side of Good Old-Fashioned Values*
  LJ - v129 - i19 - Nov 15 2004 - p83(1) [51-500]
Miller, Calvin - *The Unfinished Soul: Happening upon Jesus in the Happenstance of Life*
  Ch Today - v48 - i10 - Oct 2004 - p112(1) [51-500]
Miller, Carman - *Canada's Little War: Fighting for the British Empire in Southern Africa, 1899-1902*
  Beav - v84 - i4 - August-Sept 2004 - p48(1) [51-500]
  Can Hist R - v85 - i4 - Dec 2004 - p836(2) [501+]
  CBRA - Annual 2003 - p295(1) [501+]
Miller, Catherine - *Jean Cocteau, Guillaume Apollinaire, Paul Claudel et le Groupe des Six: Rencontres poetico-musicales autour des melodies et des chansons*
  Notes - v61 - i2 - Dec 2004 - p421(3) [501+]
  The Sexual Life of Catherine M.
  BIC - v33 - i2 - March 2004 - p28(2) [501+]
Miller, Char - *The Atlas of US and Canadian Environmental History*
  Can Hist R - v85 - i3 - Sept 2004 - p638(2) [501+]
  Fifty Years of the Texas Observer
  CJR - v43 - i4 - Nov-Dec 2004 - p69(1) [501+]
  On the Border: An Environmental History of San Antonio
  HNet - Oct 2004 - pNA [501+]
  Pub Hist - v26 - i1 - Wntr 2004 - p166(4) [501+]
Miller, Charles B. - *Biological Oceanography*
  Choice - v41 - i11-12 - July-August 2004 - p2070(1) [501+]
Miller, Clyde Lee - *Reading Cusanus: Metaphor and Dialectic in a Conjectural Universe*
  Ren Q - v57 - i3 - Fall 2004 - p1038(2) [501+]
Miller, D.A. - *Jane Austen, or, The Secret of Style*
  HR - v57 - i2 - Summer 2004 - p303-310 [501+]
  Lon R Bks - v26 - i21 - Nov 4 2004 - p41(3) [501+]
Miller, David (b. 1935 -) - *Athens to Athens: The Official History of the Olympic Games and the IOC, 1896-2004*
  TLS - i5284 - July 9 2004 - p3-4 [501+]
Miller, David (b. 1946 -) - *Political Philosophy: A Very Short Introduction, 1st Ed.*
  TimHES - v0 - i1668 - Nov 26 2004 - pVII(1) [501+]
Miller, David (b. 1964 -) - *Tell Me Lies: Propaganda and Media Distortion in the Attack on Iraq*
  MEQ - v11 - i4 - Fall 2004 - p85(2) [501+]
Miller, David Philip - *Discovering Water: James Watt, Henry Cavendish, and the Nineteenth Century 'Water Controversy'*
  SciTech - v28 - i3 - Sept 2004 - p51(1) [1-50]

Miller-Day, Michelle A. - *Communication among Grandmothers, Mothers, and Adult Daughters: A Qualitative Study of Maternal Relationships*
R&R Bk N - v19 - i4 - Nov 2004 - p129(1) [51-500]

Miller, Debbie (b. 1948 -) - *Reading with Meaning: Teaching Comprehension in the Primary Grades*
SLJ - v50 - i10 - Oct 2004 - pS74(1) [51-500]

Miller, Debbie S. - *Arctic Lights, Arctic Nights (Illus. by Van Zyle, Jon)*
c LibMed - v22 - i5 - Feb 2004 - p59(1) [501+]
c Sci Teach - v71 - i3 - March 2004 - p57-64 [501+]
Are Trees Alive? (Illus. by Schuett, Stacey)
c RT - v57 - Nov 2003 - p272 [51-500]

Miller, Debra A. - *Iraq*
c SLJ - v50 - i8 - August 2004 - p140(1) [51-500]
North Korea
y SLJ - v50 - i7 - July 2004 - p126(1) [51-500]
The War Against Iraq
LibMed - v23 - i1 - August-Sept 2004 - p77(1) [51-500]

Miller, Dennis - *Designing High-Speed Interconnect Circuits; Advanced Signal Integrity for Engineers*
SciTech - v28 - i4 - Dec 2004 - p148(1) [501+]

Miller, Denny - *Didn't You Used to Be What's His Name?*
Bwatch - v26 - i8 - August 2004 - p5(1) [51-500]

Miller, Dick R. - *Putting XML to Work in the Library: Tools for Improving Access and Management*
ALJ - v53 - i3 - August 2004 - p311(2) [501+]
LibMed - v23 - i1 - August-Sept 2004 - p86(1) [51-500]
R&R Bk N - v19 - i1 - Feb 2004 - p259(1) [51-500]
R&USQ - v44 - i1 - Fall 2004 - p100(1) [501+]

Miller, Donald - *Searching for God Knows What*
Ch Today - v48 - i11 - Nov 2004 - p87(1) [501+]
PW - v251 - i37 - Sept 13 2004 - p75(1) [501+]

Miller, Donald E. - *Armenia: Portraits of Survival and Hope*
Slav R - v63 - i4 - Winter 2004 - p875(2) [501+]

Miller, Donna - *The Standards-Based Integrated Library: A Collaborative Approach for Aligning the Library Program with the Classroom Curriculum*
LibMed - v23 - i1 - August-Sept 2004 - p86(2) [51-500]
y VOYA - v27 - i4 - Oct 2004 - p339(1) [51-500]

Miller, Donna P. - *Day-by-Day: Professional Journaling for Library Media Specialists*
LibMed - v22 - i4 - Jan 2004 - p86(1) [501+]

Miller, Douglas B. - *Symbol and Rhetoric in Ecclesiastes: The Place of Hebel in Qohelet's Work*
JR - v85 - i1 - Jan 2005 - p112(3) [501+]

Miller, E. Ethelbert - *How We Sleep on the Nights We Don't Make Love*
Black Iss - v7 - i2 - March-April 2005 - p34(1) [51-500]
BW - v34 - i43 - Oct 24 2004 - p12(1) [501+]

Miller, Edward - *Elf Elementary*
c PW - v251 - i39 - Sept 27 2004 - p62(1) [51-500]

Miller, Edward D. - *Emergency Broadcasting and 1930s American Radio*
JAH - v91 - i1 - June 2004 - p292-294 [501+]

Miller, Edward L. - *New Orleans and the Texas Revolution*
Roundup M - v12 - i3 - Feb 2005 - p20(1) [51-500]

Miller, Evie Yoder - *Eyes at the Window*
BL - v101 - i3 - Oct 1 2004 - p303(1) [51-500]

Miller, Franklin G. - *The Nature and Prospect of Bioethics: Interdisciplinary Perspectives*
QRB - v79 - i3 - Sept 2004 - p295(2) [501+]

Miller, Frederick H. - *The ABCs of the UCC: Related and Supplementary Consumer Law, 2nd Ed.*
R&R Bk N - v19 - i4 - Nov 2004 - p168(1) [501+]

Miller, G. Ann Stamp - *The Cultural Politics of the German Democratic Republic: The Voices of Wolf Biermann, Christa Wolf, and Heiner Muller*
R&R Bk N - v19 - i4 - Nov 2004 - p39(1) [51-500]

Miller, G. Tyler, Jr. - *Essentials of Ecology, 3rd Ed.*
SciTech - v28 - i4 - Dec 2004 - p63(1) [51-500]
Living in the environment: Principles, Connections, and Solutions, 14th Ed.
SciTech - v28 - i4 - Dec 2004 - p6(1) [1-50]
Sustaining the Earth: An Integrated Approach, 7th Ed.
R&R Bk N - v20 - i1 - Feb 2005 - p82(1) [51-500]

Miller, Gareth - *Frontiers of Family Law*
Law&PolBR - August 2004 - p652(3) [501+]

Miller, Geralyn M. - *Changing the Way America Votes: Election Reform, Incrementalism, and Cutting Deals*
R&R Bk N - v19 - i4 - Nov 2004 - p155(1) [51-500]

Miller, Geri A. - *Learning the Language of Addiction Counseling, 2nd Ed.*
SciTech - v28 - i4 - Dec 2004 - p101(1) [51-500]

Miller, Hamish - *Dowsing: A Journey Beyond Our Five Senses*
R&R Bk N - v19 - i4 - Nov 2004 - p12(1) [51-500]

Miller, Heather - *Cricket*
c SLJ - v50 - i12 - Dec 2004 - p135(1) [51-500]
Wheels, Wings, and Water
c LibMed - v22 - i5 - Feb 2004 - p88(2) [501+]

Miller, Henry - *Tropic of Cancer*
BL - v101 - i2 - Sept 15 2004 - p224(1) [501+]

Miller, Henry I. - *The Frankenfood Myth: How Protest and Politics Threaten the Biotech Revolution*
Choice - v42 - i7 - March 2005 - p1245(2) [51-500]

Miller, Irwin - *John E. Freund's Mathematical Statistics: With Applications, 7th Ed.*
SciTech - v28 - i3 - Sept 2004 - p37(1) [51-500]

Miller, J. Philip - *We All Sing with the Same Voice (Illus. by Meisel, Paul)*
c PW - v252 - i2 - Jan 10 2005 - p58(1) [1-50]

Miller, J.R. - *Reflections on Native-Newcomer Relations: Selected Essays*
R&R Bk N - v19 - i4 - Nov 2004 - p53(1) [51-500]

Miller, Jacueline Y. - *The Butterfly Handbook*
y SB - v40 - i5 - Sept-Oct 2004 - p215(1) [51-500]

Miller, Jake - *Brown Recluse Spiders*
y Teach Lib - v32 - i1 - Oct 2004 - p44(1) [51-500]

Miller, James - *The North Atlantic Front: Orkney, Shetland, Faroe and Iceland at War*
R&R Bk N - v19 - i3 - August 2004 - p34(1) [51-500]

Miller, James David - *South by Southwest: Planter Emigration and Identity in the Slave South*
HNet - Sept 2004 - pNA [501+]
JAH - v91 - i1 - June 2004 - p231-232 [501+]
JSH - v70 - i3 - August 2004 - p674(2) [501+]

Miller, Jane - *Relations*
TLS - i5302 - Nov 12 2004 - p29(1) [501+]

Miller, Jeffrey C. - *The Transcendent Function: Jung's Model of Psychological Growth through Dialogue with the Unconscious*
Choice - v41 - i11-12 - July-August 2004 - p2127(1) [501+]

Miller, John - *Featherbed*
CBRA - Annual 2003 - p178(1) [51-500]

Miller, John C. - *The Handbook of Nanotechnology: Business, Policy, and Intellectual Property Law*
SciTech - v28 - i4 - Dec 2004 - p8(1) [1-50]

Miller, John G. - *QBQ!: The Question Behind the Question: Practicing Personal Accountability at Work and in Life*
LJ - v129 - i15 - Sept 15 2004 - p73(1) [51-500]
PW - v251 - i34 - August 23 2004 - p49(1) [51-500]

Miller, John J. - *Our Oldest Enemy: A History of America's Disastrous Relationship with France*
BL - v101 - i2 - Sept 15 2004 - p183(1) [51-500]
KR - v72 - i15 - August 1 2004 - p729(1) [501+]
LJ - v129 - i15 - Sept 15 2004 - p68(2) [51-500]
NYTBR - Dec 5 2004 - p73 [501+]
PW - v251 - i40 - Oct 4 2004 - p84(1) [51-500]

Miller, Jon - *Missionary Zeal and Institutional Control: Organizational Contradictions in the Basel Mission on the Gold Coast, 1828-1917*
HNet - Nov 2004 - pNA [501+]
IBMR - v28 - i4 - Oct 2004 - p182(1) [501+]

Miller, Judith - *Costume Jewelry*
Ant&CM - v108 - i12 - Feb 2004 - p16(1) [501+]
The Style Sourcebook: The Definitive Illustrated Directory of Fabrics, Wallpapers, Paints, Flooring, Tiles
R&R Bk N - v19 - i1 - Feb 2004 - p207(1) [51-500]

Miller, Karen E. Quinones - *Ida B*
BL - v100 - i22 - August 2004 - p1901(1) [501+]
KR - v72 - i13 - July 1 2004 - p599(2) [501+]
PW - v251 - i35 - August 30 2004 - p33(1) [501+]

Miller, Karl - *The Electric Shepherd: A Likeness of James Hogg*
Lon R Bks - v26 - i22 - Nov 18 2004 - p24(2) [501+]

Miller, Kenneth E. - *The Mental Health of Refugees: Ecological Approaches to Healing and Adaptation*
Choice - v42 - i4 - Dec 2004 - p695(1) [1-50]
SciTech - v28 - i3 - Sept 2004 - p96(1) [51-500]

Miller, Kerby A. - *Irish Immigrants in the Land of Canaan: Letters and Memoirs from Colonial and Revolutionary America*
RAH - v32 - i3 - Sept 2004 - p305-316 [501+]

Miller, Kevin A. - *Surviving Information Overload: The Clear, Practical Guide to Help You Stay on Top of What You Need to Know*
Ch Today - v48 - i9 - Sept 2004 - p91(1) [51-500]

Miller, Kirk - *Policing World Society: Historical Foundations of International Police Cooperation*
CS - v33 - i5 - Sept 2004 - p597-599 [501+]

Miller, Kristie - *Isabella Greenway: An Enterprising Woman*
Roundup M - v12 - i3 - Feb 2005 - p20(1) [51-500]
R&R Bk N - v19 - i4 - Nov 2004 - p63(1) [1-50]

Miller, Leta E. - *Composing a World: Lou Harrison, Musical Wayfarer*
G&L Rev W - v12 - i1 - Jan-Feb 2005 - p41(2) [501+]

Miller, Lila - *Shelter Medicine for Veterinarians and Staff*
E-Streams - Dec 2004 - pNA [501+]

Miller, Linda Lael - *Never Look Back*
BW - v34 - i43 - Oct 24 2004 - p13(1) [501+]
Secondhand Bride
PW - v251 - i48 - Nov 29 2004 - p28(1) [51-500]

Miller, Linda S. - *Community Policing: Partnerships for Problem Solving, 4th Ed.*
R&R Bk N - v19 - i4 - Nov 2004 - p147(1) [501+]

Miller, M. Rex - *The Millennium Matrix: Reclaiming the Past, Reframing the Future of the Church*
Fut - v38 - i6 - Nov-Dec 2004 - p60(1) [51-500]
LJ - v129 - i19 - Nov 15 2004 - p65(2) [501+]

Miller, Madeleine S. - *Harper's Encyclopedia of Bible Life*
LJ - v130 - i2 - Feb 1 2005 - p126(1) [1-50]

Miller, Marcianne - *The Artful Cupcake: Baking and Decorating Delicious Indulgences*
LJ - v129 - i13 - August 2004 - p113(1) [51-500]
Creative Scarecrows
LJ - v129 - i17 - Oct 15 2004 - p63(1) [51-500]

Miller, Margaret J. - *Credit Reporting Systems and the International Economy*
JEL - v41 - i4 - Dec 2003 - p1367(1) [501+]

Miller, Marilyn L. - *Pioneers and Leaders in Library Services to Youth: A Biographical Dictionary*
LibMed - v22 - i7 - April-May 2004 - p87(1) [501+]

Miller, Mark A. - *Internet Technology Handbook: Optimizing the IP Network*
Choice - v42 - i2 - Oct 2004 - p327(1) [51-500]
E-Streams - Oct 2004 - pNA [501+]

Miller, Mark C. - *The Dark Sides of Virtue: Reassessing International Humanitarianism*
Law&PolBR - Oct 2004 - pNA [501+]

Miller, Mark Crispin - *Cruel and Unusual: Bush/Cheney's New World Order*
BL - v100 - i21 - July 2004 - p1812(2) [1-50]
LJ - v129 - i12 - July 2004 - p104(1) [51-500]
R&R Bk N - v19 - i4 - Nov 2004 - p64(1) [51-500]

Miller, Mark D. - *Review of Orthopaedics, 4th Ed.*
SciTech - v28 - i3 - Sept 2004 - p113(1) [51-500]
Textbook of Arthroscopy
SciTech - v28 - i3 - Sept 2004 - p113(1) [51-500]

Miller, Marvin - *A Whole Different Ball Game: The Inside Story of the Baseball Revolution*
Bwatch - March 2005 - pNA [51-500]

Miller, Mary - *Courtly Art of the Ancient Maya*
Choice - v42 - i3 - Nov 2004 - p472(1) [1-50]
R&R Bk N - v19 - i3 - August 2004 - p77(1) [51-500]
TimHES - v0 - i1681 - March 4 2005 - p26(2) [501+]

Miller, Mary-Kay F. - *(Re)productions: Autobiography, Colonialism, and Infanticide*
R&R Bk N - v19 - i1 - Feb 2004 - p230(1) [51-500]

Miller, Michael - *Bargain Hunter's Secrets to Online Shopping*
LJ - v130 - i4 - March 1 2005 - p106(1) [51-500]

Miller, Naomi - *Fort Steele: Gold Rush to Boom Town*
CBRA - Annual 2003 - p345(1) [51-500]

Miller, Naomi J. - *Mapping the City: The Language and Culture of Cartography in the Renaissance*
Ren Q - v57 - i4 - Winter 2004 - p1469(3) [501+]

Miller, Nicholas Andrew - *Modernism, Ireland, and the Erotics of Memory*
Clio - v33 - i2 - Wntr 2004 - p189(22) [501+]

Miller, Page Putnam - *Landmarks of American Women's History*
y Ref Rev - May 2004 - pNA [501+]
y SLJ - v50 - i9 - Sept 2004 - p230(1) [51-500]

Miller, Pat - *Stretchy Library Lessons: Seasons & Celebrations*
c SLJ - v50 - i8 - August 2004 - p150(1) [501+]

Mills, Lauren - *Hans Christian Andersen's Thumbelina (Illus. by Mills, Lauren)*
   c KR - v73 - i5 - March 1 2005 - p291(1) [51-500]

Mills, Mark - *Amagansett*
   BL - v100 - i22 - August 2004 - p1907(1) [51-500]
   BL - v101 - i3 - Oct 1 2004 - p360(1) [501+]
   KR - v72 - i14 - July 15 2004 - p652(1) [51-500]
   LJ - v129 - i12 - July 2004 - p72(1) [51-500]
   NYTBR - August 29 2004 - p12 [501+]
   PW - v251 - i28 - July 12 2004 - p44(2) [51-500]
   y SLJ - v51 - i1 - Jan 2005 - p159(1) [51-500]

Mills, Nicolaus - *50 Years of Dissent*
   CJR - v43 - i4 - Nov-Dec 2004 - p69(1) [501+]
   LJ - v129 - i14 - Sept 1 2004 - p171(1) [51-500]
Their Last Battle: The Fight for the National World War II Memorial
   New R - v231 - August 16 2004 - p30 [501+]

Mills, Pat - *Charley's War: 2 June 1916-1 August 1916*
   PW - v252 - i4 - Jan 24 2005 - p223(1) [501+]

Mills, Sara - *An Anthology of Women's Travel Writing*
   JGS - v13 - i1 - March 2004 - p94-95 [501+]

Mills, Stephen - *Tiger*
   y BL - v101 - i5 - Nov 1 2004 - p451(1) [51-500]
   Globe & Mail - August 21 2004 - pD11 [51-500]
   y Kliatt - v39 - i2 - March 2005 - p43(1) [51-500]
   y Res Links - v10 - i2 - Dec 2004 - p45(1) [51-500]

Mills, Terence C. - *Modelling Trends and Cycles in Economic Time Series*
   JEL - v42 - i1 - March 2004 - p235(1) [501+]

Mills, Watson - *An Index of Periodical Literature for the Study of the New Testament*
   R&R Bk N - v19 - i3 - August 2004 - p21(1) [1-50]

Mills, William James - *Exploring Polar Frontiers: A Historical Encyclopedia*
   Choice - v42 - i1 - Sept 2004 - p81(1) [501+]
   Ref Rev - June 2004 - pNA [501+]

Mills, Wilmer - *Light for the Orphans*
   HR - v55 - i4 - Winter 2003 - p671 [501+]

Millstein, Ira M. - *The Limits of Corporate Power: Existing Constraints on the Exercise of Corporate Discretion*
   R&R Bk N - v19 - i1 - Feb 2004 - p98(1) [51-500]

Milne, A.A. - *Winnie-the-Pooh (Illus. by Shephard, Ernest H.)*
   c RT - v57 - Sept 2003 - p99 [51-500]

Milne, Frank - *Finance Theory and Asset Pricing*
   JEL - v41 - i4 - Dec 2003 - p1334(1) [501+]

Milne, G.W.A. - *Pesticides: An International Guide to 1800 Pest Control Chemicals, 2nd Ed.*
   E-Streams - Nov 2004 - pNA [501+]
   SciTech - v28 - i3 - Sept 2004 - p130(1) [51-500]

Milner, Craig S. - *Ralph Stanley: Tales of a Maine Boatbuilder*
   Bwatch - v26 - i9 - Sept 2004 - p3(1) [51-500]

Milner, George R. - *The Moundbuilders: Ancient Peoples of Eastern North America*
   Choice - v42 - i3 - Nov 2004 - p528(1) [1-50]

Milner, Judith - *Assessment in Counselling: Theory, Process, and Decision-Making*
   SciTech - v28 - i3 - Sept 2004 - p2(1) [501+]

Milner, Lisa - *Fighting Films*
   Arena - i72 - August-Sept 2004 - p52(2) [501+]

Milner, Marc - *Battle of the Atlantic*
   Choice - v42 - i3 - Nov 2004 - p538(1) [1-50]
   TLS - i5266 - March 5 2004 - p30-31 [501+]

Milner, Murray, Jr. - *Freaks, Geeks, and Cool Kids: American Teenagers, Schools, and the Culture of Consumption*
   Atl - v294 - i1 - July-August 2004 - p147(4) [501+]
   Choice - v42 - i3 - Nov 2004 - p525(2) [1-50]
   Choice - v42 - i3 - Nov 2004 - pNA [1-50]

Milnes, Tim - *Knowledge and Indifference in English Romantic Prose*
   RES - v55 - i221 - Sept 2004 - p629(2) [501+]

Milosevic, Mario - *Animal Life*
   MFSF - v108 - i2 - Feb 2005 - p41(3) [51-500]
Fantasy Life
   MFSF - v108 - i2 - Feb 2005 - p41(3) [51-500]

Milosz, Czeslaw - *Second Space: New Poems*
   AM - v191 - i10 - Oct 11 2004 - p35 [501+]
   BL - v101 - i3 - Oct 1 2004 - p299(1) [501+]
   BL - v101 - i9-10 - Jan 1 2005 - p768(1) [51-500]
   BW - v34 - i41 - Oct 10 2004 - p15(1) [501+]
   LJ - v129 - i15 - Sept 15 2004 - p61(1) [51-500]
   NYTBR - Nov 21 2004 - p22 [501+]
   Poet - v185 - i5 - Feb 2005 - p378(9) [501+]
   PW - v251 - i42 - Oct 18 2004 - p60(2) [51-500]
To Begin Where I Am: Selected Essays
   Sew R - v112 - i3 - Summer 2004 - pLXXXV-LXXXVII [501+]

Milrod, Barbara - *Psychodynamic Approaches to the Adolescent with Panic Disorder*
   SciTech - v28 - i4 - Dec 2004 - p113(1) [1-50]

Milsom, David - *Theory and Practice in Late Nineteenth-Century Violin Performance: An Examination of Style in Performance, 1850-1900*
   M Ed J - v91 - i4 - March 2005 - p64(1) [501+]

Milsom, S.F.C. - *A Natural History of the Common Law*
   Law Q Rev - v120 - Oct 2004 - p696-700 [501+]

Milstein, Sarah - *Google: The Missing Manual*
   SciTech - v28 - i3 - Sept 2004 - p156(1) [51-500]

Milton-Edwards, Beverley - *Islam and Politics in the Contemporary World, 1st Ed.*
   Choice - v42 - i6 - Feb 2005 - p1095(1) [51-500]
   TimHES - v0 - i1668 - Nov 26 2004 - pIV(1) [501+]

Milton, Giles - *White Gold: The Extraordinary Story of Thomas Pellow and North Africa's One Million European Slaves*
   Globe & Mail - Dec 24 2004 - pD13 [1-50]
   TLS - i5304 - Nov 26 2004 - p33(1) [51-500]

Milton, Lorraine - *Step by Step to Grace: A Spiritual Walk Through the Bible and the Twelve Steps*
   CBRA - Annual 2003 - p96(1) [51-500]

Milton, Ralph - *Julian's Cell*
   CBRA - Annual 2003 - p178(1) [51-500]

Milton, Robert - *Straight from the Top: The Truth about Air Canada*
   Globe & Mail - Oct 30 2004 - pD10 [501+]

Milton, Steve - *Figure Skating Now: Olympic and World Stars*
   CBRA - Annual 2003 - p145(1) [51-500]

Milward, Bob - *Globalisation? Internalisation and Monopoly Capitalism: Historical Processes and Capital Dynamism*
   R&R Bk N - v19 - i3 - August 2004 - p94(1) [51-500]

Mimouni, Rachid - *Tombeza*
   Col Lit - v30 - i1 - Winter 2003 - p124 [501+]

Min, Anchee - *Empress Orchid*
   Wom R Bks - v21 - i10-11 - July 2004 - p24(1) [501+]

Min, Pyong Gap - *Mass Migration to the United States: Classical and Contemporary Periods*
   CS - v33 - i1 - Jan 2004 - p128-129 [501+]

Mina, Denise - *Deception (Read by Matthews, Richard). Audiobook Review*
   y Kliatt - v39 - i2 - March 2005 - p51(1) [51-500]
Deception
   BL - v100 - i21 - July 2004 - p1825(1) [1-50]
   DroRevMy - v24 - i3 - May-June 2004 - p7(1) [501+]
   Ent W - i779 - August 20 2004 - p133 [501+]
   LJ - v129 - i12 - July 2004 - p72(1) [51-500]
   NYTBR - Sept 5 2004 - p15 [501+]
   People - v62 - i8 - August 23 2004 - p49 [501+]
   PW - v251 - i30 - July 26 2004 - p39(2) [501+]

Minahan, James - *The Former Soviet Union's Diverse Peoples: A Reference Sourcebook*
   Choice - v42 - i4 - Dec 2004 - p642(1) [1-50]

Minchin, Timothy J. - *Forging a Common Bond: Labor and Environmental Activism During the BASF Lockout*
   J Soc H - v38 - i1 - Fall 2004 - p251(3) [501+]
   JAH - v91 - i1 - June 2004 - p340-342 [501+]
   JEH - v64 - i1 - March 2004 - p276(3) [501+]

Mindell, Jodi A. - *Sleeping through the Night: How Infants, Toddlers, and Their Parents Can Get a Good Night's Sleep*
   LJ - v130 - i3 - Feb 15 2005 - p151(4) [501+]

Mindess, Anna - *Reading between the Signs Workbook: A Cultural Guide for Sign Language Students and Interpreters*
   R&R Bk N - v19 - i3 - August 2004 - p162(1) [501+]

Mindich, David T.Z. - *Tuned Out: Why Americans under 40 Don't Follow the News*
   AJR - v26 - i6 - Dec 2004 - p62(1) [1-50]
   BW - v34 - i41 - Oct 10 2004 - p13(1) [501+]
   PW - v251 - i39 - Sept 27 2004 - p47(1) [51-500]

Mindiola, Tatcho - *Black-Brown Relations and Stereotypes*
   Aztlan - v29 - i2 - Fall 2004 - p223-226 [501+]
   CS - v33 - i4 - July 2004 - p416(3) [501+]

Mineau, Andre - *Operation Barbarossa: Ideology and Ethics Against Human Dignity*
   R&R Bk N - v20 - i1 - Feb 2005 - p32(1) [501+]

Mineo, E. Igor - *Nobilta di stato: Famiglie e identita aristocratiche nel tardo medioevo*
   Specu - v79 - i4 - Oct 2004 - p1117(3) [501+]

Miner, Earl - *Paradise Lost, 1668-1968: Three Centuries of Commentary*
   Choice - v42 - i5 - Jan 2005 - p854(2) [1-50]
   R&R Bk N - v19 - i4 - Nov 2004 - p236(1) [501+]

Miner, Jeff - *The Children Are Free: Re-Examining the Biblical Evidence on Same-Sex Relationships*
   Lam Bk Rpt - v13 - i4-5 - Nov-Dec 2004 - p27(2) [501+]

Miner, Jeremy T. - *Directory of Biomedical and Health Care Grants 2004, 18th Ed.*
   SciTech - v28 - i1 - March 2004 - p79(1) [51-500]
Directory of Grants in the Humanites 2004/2005, 18th Ed.
   R&R Bk N - v19 - i4 - Nov 2004 - p2(1) [51-500]
Funding Sources for Children and Youth Programs 2004, 3rd Ed.
   R&R Bk N - v19 - i3 - August 2004 - p96(1) [51-500]
Funding Sources for Community and Economic Development 2003/2004, 9th Ed.
   R&R Bk N - v19 - i1 - Feb 2004 - p80(1) [51-500]

Miner, Robert C. - *Vico, Genealogist of Modernity*
   Six Ct J - v35 - i1 - Spring 2004 - p303(3) [501+]

Miner, Steven Merritt - *Stalin's Holy War: Religion, Nationalism, and Alliance Politics, 1941-1945*
   AHR - v109 - i3 - June 2004 - p1012(2) [501+]
   Russ Rev - v63 - i2 - April 2004 - pNA [501+]
   Slav R - v63 - i2 - Summer 2004 - p415(2) [501+]

Minford, Patrick - *Money Matters: Essays in Honour of Alan Walters*
   R&R Bk N - v19 - i3 - August 2004 - p134(1) [51-500]

Ming, Yao - *Yao: A Life in Two Worlds*
   PW - v251 - i32 - August 9 2004 - p243(1) [51-500]

Mingat, Alain - *Tools for Education Policy Analysis*
   JEL - v41 - i4 - Dec 2003 - p1378(1) [501+]
   R&R Bk N - v19 - i1 - Feb 2004 - p187(1) [51-500]

Minges, Patrick N. - *Slavery in the Cherokee Nation: The Keetowah Society and the Defining of a People, 1855-1867*
   JSH - v71 - i1 - Feb 2005 - p156(2) [501+]

Minghelli, Giuliana - *In the Shadow of the Mammoth: Italo Svevo and the Emergence of Modernism*
   R&R Bk N - v19 - i1 - Feb 2004 - p232(1) [51-500]

Mingins, Rosemary - *The Beacon Controversy and Challenges to British Quaker Tradition in the Early 19th Century: Some Responses to the Evangelical Revival by Friends in Manchester and Kendal*
   R&R Bk N - v19 - i4 - Nov 2004 - p28(1) [501+]

Mingo, Jack - *Inside and Out: From Comic Books to Cult TV and Beyond*
   BL - v101 - i5 - Nov 1 2004 - p452(1) [51-500]

Mingst, Karen A. - *Essentials of International Relations, 3rd Ed.*
   R&R Bk N - v19 - i3 - August 2004 - p159(1) [501+]

Minh, Y.C. - *New Technologies in VLBI: Proceedings*
   SciTech - v28 - i1 - March 2004 - p45(1) [51-500]

Mink, Eric - *This Is Today: A Window on Our Times*
   TV Q - v34 - i3-4 - Spring-Summer 2004 - p71-73 [501+]

Mink, Gwendolyn - *Welfare: A Documentary History of U.S. Policy and Politics*
   Soc Ser R - v78 - i3 - Sept 2004 - p516(4) [501+]

Minkin, Mary Jane - *Manual of Menopause Counseling for the Perimenopausal and Menopausal Patient: A Clinican's Guide*
   SciTech - v28 - i1 - March 2004 - p116(1) [51-500]
A Woman's Guide to Menopause and Perimenopause
   LJ - v130 - i1 - Jan 1 2005 - p139(2) [51-500]

Minkoff, Eli C. - *Biology Today: An Issue Approach, 3rd Ed.*
   E-Streams - Sept 2004 - pNA [501+]

Minkov, Anton - *Conversion to Islam in the Balkans: Kisve Bahasi Petitions and Ottoman Social Life, 1670-1730*
   R&R Bk N - v19 - i3 - August 2004 - p17(1) [1-50]

Minkova, Donka - *Chaucer and the Challenges of Medievalism: Studies in Honour of H.A. Kelly*
   R&R Bk N - v19 - i1 - Feb 2004 - p236(1) [51-500]
Studies in the History of the English Language: A Millennial Perspective
   JEGP - v103 - i3 - July 2004 - p381-382 [501+]

Minne, Brigitte - *The Best Bottom (Illus. by Pottie, Marjolein)*
   c SLJ - v50 - i9 - Sept 2004 - p174(2) [51-500]

Minnerly, Denise B. - *Molly Meets Mona and Friends*
   c CH Bwatch - v14 - i11 - Nov 2004 - pNA [51-500]

Minnick, Lisa Cohen - *Dialect and Dichotomy: Literary Representations of African American Speech*
Choice - v42 - i5 - Jan 2005 - p854(1) [1-50]

Minnis, A.J. - *Middle English Poetry: Texts and Traditions: Essays in Honour of Derek Pearsall*
RES - v55 - i221 - Sept 2004 - p608(3) [501+]

Minnis, Ivan - *You Are in Ancient China*
c BL - v101 - i7 - Dec 1 2004 - p649(1) [51-500]
c SLJ - v51 - i2 - Feb 2005 - p124(1) [51-500]
You Are in Ancient Egypt
c SLJ - v51 - i2 - Feb 2005 - p124(1) [51-500]
You Are in Ancient Greece
c SLJ - v51 - i2 - Feb 2005 - p124(1) [51-500]
You Are in Ancient Rome
c SLJ - v51 - i2 - Feb 2005 - p124(1) [51-500]

Minnis, Paul E. - *People and Plants in Ancient Eastern North America*
JRAI - v10 - i3 - Sept 2004 - p713(2) [501+]
People and Plants in Ancient Western North America
R&R Bk N - v19 - i4 - Nov 2004 - p53(1) [51-500]

Minocha, Anil - *The Encyclopedia of the Digestive System and Digestive Disorders*
BL - v101 - i9-10 - Jan 1 2005 - p903(1) [501+]
Choice - v42 - i6 - Feb 2005 - p998(1) [51-500]
LJ - v129 - i20 - Dec 1 2004 - p166(2) [51-500]
SciTech - v28 - i4 - Dec 2004 - p104(1) [51-500]
The Handbook of Digestive Diseases
SciTech - v28 - i3 - Sept 2004 - p107(1) [51-500]

Minohara, Toshi-hiro - *Hainichi Iminho to Nichibei Kankei: "Hanihara Shokan" No Shinso to Sono "Judainaru Kekka"*
JAH - v91 - i2 - Sept 2004 - p665(2) [501+]

Minois, Georges - *History of Suicide: Voluntary Death in Western Culture*
Eight-C St - v37 - i4 - Summer 2004 - p683-686 [501+]

Minor, William - *Jazz Journeys to Japan: The Heart Within*
Choice - v42 - i4 - Dec 2004 - p671(1) [1-50]

Minow, Mary - *The Library's Legal Answer Book*
ALJ - v53 - i3 - August 2004 - p313(2) [501+]
LQ - v74 - i3 - July 2004 - p391(3) [501+]

Minteer, Ben A. - *Reconstructing Conservation: Finding Common Ground*
SB - v40 - i3 - May-June 2004 - p112(1) [501+]

Minter, J. - *The Insiders*
y VOYA - v27 - i3 - August 2004 - p222(1) [1-50]
Pass It On: An Insiders Novel
y Kliatt - v39 - i1 - Jan 2005 - p16(1) [51-500]
c PW - v251 - i50 - Dec 13 2004 - p70(1) [501+]
y SLJ - v51 - i2 - Feb 2005 - p139(1) [51-500]

Mintrop, Heinrich - *Schools on Probation: How Accountability Works*
TCR - v106 - i8 - August 2004 - p1614(4) [501+]

Mintz, Paul D. - *Transfusion Therapy: Clinical Principles and Practice, 2nd Ed.*
SciTech - v28 - i4 - Dec 2004 - p115(1) [1-50]

Mintz, Steven - *Huck's Raft: A History of American Childhood*
Atl - v294 - i3 - Oct 2004 - p163(2) [501+]
BL - v101 - i5 - Nov 1 2004 - p448(1) [51-500]
BL - v101 - i9-10 - Jan 1 2005 - p768(1) [51-500]
BW - v34 - i50 - Dec 12 2004 - p15(1) [501+]
LJ - v129 - i12 - July 2004 - p99(1) [51-500]
NYTBR - Oct 24 2004 - p26 [501+]
PW - v251 - i36 - Sept 6 2004 - p54(1) [51-500]

Mintzberg, Henry - *Managers, Not MBAs: A Hard Look at the Soft Practice of Managing and Management Development*
BL - v100 - i21 - July 2004 - p1806(2) [1-50]
Choice - v42 - i2 - Oct 2004 - p336(2) [51-500]
HR Mag - v49 - i9 - Sept 2004 - p180(2) [501+]
R&R Bk N - v19 - i3 - August 2004 - p102(1) [501+]

Miozzo, Marcela - *Innovation in Construction: A European Analysis*
R&R Bk N - v19 - i4 - Nov 2004 - p105(1) [51-500]

Miraldi, Robert - *The Pen Is Mightier: The Muckraking Life of Charles Edward Russell*
AHR - v109 - i2 - April 2004 - p545(2) [501+]
JAH - v91 - i2 - Sept 2004 - p654(2) [501+]
R&R Bk N - v19 - i1 - Feb 2004 - p220(1) [1-50]

Miranda, Marie Keta - *Homegirls in the Public Sphere*
Am Q - v56 - i4 - Dec 2004 - p1135(10) [501+]

Miree, Kathryn W. - *Professional Advisors' Guide to Planned Giving, 2004 Ed.*
R&R Bk N - v19 - i1 - Feb 2004 - pNA [51-500]

Miron, Louis F. - *Reinterpreting Urban School Reform: Have Urban Schools Failed, or Has the Reform Movement Failed Urban Schools?*
TCR - v106 - i2 - Feb 2004 - p314-317 [501+]

Miroshnichenko, Leonty I. - *Radiation Hazard in Space*
SciTech - v28 - i1 - March 2004 - p49(1) [51-500]

Mirowski, Philip - *The Effortless Economy of Science?*
Am Sci - v93 - i2 - March-April 2005 - p187(2) [501+]
Science Bought and Sold: Essays in the Economics of Science
Isis - v95 - i2 - June 2004 - p339(3) [501+]

Mirra, Amy J. - *Administrator's Guide: How to Support and Improve Mathematics Education in Your School*
Math T - v97 - i5 - May 2004 - p381-381 [501+]
TC Math - v11 - i1 - August 2004 - p43(2) [51-500]

Mirvis, Stuart E. - *Imaging In Trauma and Critical Care, 2nd Ed.*
SciTech - v28 - i1 - March 2004 - p88(1) [51-500]

Mirvis, Tova - *The Outside World.*
y SLJ - v50 - i8 - August 2004 - p146(1) [501+]

Mirzayan, Raffy - *Shoulder and Elbow Trauma*
SciTech - v28 - i3 - Sept 2004 - p112(1) [51-500]

Misa, Thomas J. - *Leonardo to the Internet: Technology and Culture from the Renaissance to the Present*
Choice - v42 - i4 - Dec 2004 - p683(2) [1-50]
SciTech - v28 - i3 - Sept 2004 - p133(1) [51-500]
Modernity and Technology
T&C - v45 - i2 - April 2004 - p471-473 [501+]

Misak, Cheryl - *The Cambridge Companion to Peirce*
Choice - v42 - i5 - Jan 2005 - p865(1) [1-50]

Miser, Brad - *iPod And iTunes Starter Kit*
Bwatch - Feb 2005 - pNA [501+]

Misfeldt, Trevor - *The Elements of C++ Style*
Bwatch - Dec 2004 - pNA [501+]
Choice - v42 - i2 - Oct 2004 - p327(1) [51-500]
SciTech - v28 - i4 - Dec 2004 - p17(1) [1-50]

Mishel, Lawrence - *The State of Working America 2004-2005.*
LJ - v130 - i2 - Feb 1 2005 - p118(1) [51-500]

Mishkin, Andrew - *Sojourner: An Insider's View of the Mars Pathfinder Mission*
Choice - v41 - i11-12 - July-August 2004 - p2068(1) [501+]

Mishler, Craig - *Han, People of the River: Han Hwech'in: An Ethnography and Ethnohistory*
Choice - v42 - i2 - Oct 2004 - p335(1) [51-500]

Mishler, William - *A Measure of Endurance: The Unlikely Triumph of Steven Sharp*
R&R Bk N - v19 - i1 - Feb 2004 - p138(1) [51-500]

Mishra, Lakshmi Chandra - *Scientific Basis for Ayurvedic Therapies*
SciTech - v28 - i1 - March 2004 - p77(1) [51-500]

Mishra, Pankaj - *An End to Suffering: The Buddha in the World*
BL - v101 - i8 - Dec 15 2004 - p692(1) [51-500]
BW - v34 - i49 - Dec 5 2004 - p15(1) [501+]
Globe & Mail - Feb 19 2005 - pD10 [501+]
KR - v72 - i20 - Oct 15 2004 - p995(1) [51-500]
LJ - v130 - i2 - Feb 1 2005 - p85(2) [51-500]
Nation - v280 - i7 - Feb 21 2005 - p26 [501+]
NS - v133 - i4712 - Nov 1 2004 - p51(2) [501+]
NYTBR - Feb 6 2005 - p18 [501+]
PW - v251 - i45 - Nov 8 2004 - p52(1) [51-500]
Spec - v296 - i9196 - Nov 6 2004 - p65(2) [501+]
TLS - i5306 - Dec 10 2004 - p26(1) [501+]
India in Mind: An Anthology
LJ - v130 - i1 - Jan 1 2005 - p137(1) [51-500]

Mishra, Sanjay - *Interactive Multimedia in Education and Training*
SciTech - v28 - i4 - Dec 2004 - p25(1) [51-500]
Mastering Oracle SQL, 2nd Ed.
Bwatch - Dec 2004 - pNA [501+]
SciTech - v28 - i4 - Dec 2004 - p22(1) [51-500]

Miskolczy, Ambrus - *Hitler's Library*
R&R Bk N - v19 - i1 - Feb 2004 - p36(1) [1-50]

Misner, Stacia - *Microsoft SQL Server 2000 Reporting Services Step by Step*
SciTech - v28 - i4 - Dec 2004 - p32(1) [51-500]

Misra, D. - *Dielectrics in Emerging Technologies: Proceedings of the International Symposium*
SciTech - v28 - i1 - March 2004 - p50(1) [51-500]

Misra, Devendra K. - *Radio-Frequency and Microwave Communication Circuits: Analysis and Design, 2nd Ed.*
SciTech - v28 - i3 - Sept 2004 - p159(1) [51-500]

Misra, Kalpana - *Jewish Feminism in Israel: Some Contemporary Perspectives*
Choice - v41 - i7 - March 2004 - p1377(1) [501+]

Missant, Frank - *Canticle of the Sun: The Spirit of Francis of Assisi*
Parabola - v29 - i2 - Summer 2004 - p100-106 [501+]

Mitchard, Jacquelyn - *Baby Bat's Lullaby (Illus. by Noonan, Julia)*
c BL - v101 - i2 - Sept 15 2004 - p253(1) [51-500]
c KR - v72 - i16 - August 15 2004 - p810(1) [51-500]
c PW - v251 - i43 - Oct 25 2004 - p47(1) [51-500]
c SLJ - v50 - i10 - Oct 2004 - p124(1) [51-500]
The Breakdown Lane (Read by Fields, Anna). Audiobook Review
LJ - v129 - i20 - Dec 1 2004 - p88(1) [51-500]
The Breakdown Lane
KR - v73 - i3 - Feb 1 2005 - p142(1) [501+]
LJ - v130 - i3 - Feb 15 2005 - p119(2) [51-500]
PW - v252 - i5 - Jan 31 2005 - p47(2) [51-500]
Rosalie, My Rosalie: The Tale of a Duckling (Illus. by Bendall-Brunello, John)
c KR - v73 - i5 - March 1 2005 - p292(1) [51-500]
Starring Prima! The Mouse of the Ballet Jolie (Read by Mitchard, Jacquelyn). Audiobook Review
c BL - v101 - i5 - Nov 1 2004 - p508(1) [51-500]
c PW - v251 - i41 - Oct 11 2004 - p27(1) [51-500]
Starring Prima! The Mouse of the Ballet Jolie (Illus. by Tusa, Tricia)
c BL - v100 - i21 - July 2004 - p1844(1) [1-50]
c SLJ - v50 - i9 - Sept 2004 - p175(1) [51-500]

Mitchell, Alanna - *Dancing at the Dead Sea: Tracking the World's Environmental Hotspots*
CG - v124 - i3 - May-June 2004 - p128(1) [501+]

Mitchell, Allan - *The Great Train Race: Railways and the Franco-German Rivalry, 1815-1914*
CEH - v37 - i2 - Spring 2004 - p298(3) [501+]

Mitchell, B. - *An Engagement with Plato's Republic: A Companion to the Republic*
Class R - v54 - i2 - Nov 2004 - p314-315 [501+]

Mitchell, Brian S. - *An Introduction to Materials Engineering and Science for Chemical and Materials Engineers*
SciTech - v28 - i1 - March 2004 - p139(1) [51-500]

Mitchell, C. Ben - *Aging, Death, and the Quest for Immoratality*
Choice - v42 - i6 - Feb 2005 - p1036(1) [501+]

Mitchell, David - *Cloud Atlas*
BW - v34 - i34 - August 22 2004 - p1(2) [501+]
Ent W - i779 - August 20 2004 - p133 [51-500]
Globe & Mail - August 21 2004 - pD6 [501+]
Globe & Mail - Nov 27 2004 - pD3 [501+]
Mac - v117 - i46 - Nov 15 2004 - p129(3) [501+]
MFSF - v108 - i4 - April 2005 - p33(8) [501+]
NS - v133 - i4716 - Nov 29 2004 - p42(1) [51-500]
NYTBR - August 29 2004 - p7 [501+]
People - v62 - i11 - Sept 13 2004 - p58 [51-500]
RCF - v24 - i3 - Fall 2004 - p133(2) [501+]
Time - v164 - i8 - August 23 2004 - p67 [501+]
TLS - i5265 - Feb 27 2004 - p21-22 [501+]

Mitchell, Don - *The Right to the City: Social Justice and the Fight for Public Space*
JAH - v91 - i3 - Dec 2004 - p1110(2) [501+]
S&S - v68 - i4 - Winter 2004 - p515-3 [501+]

Mitchell, Donald - *Letters from a Life: Selected Letters of Benjamin Britten, Volume III, 1946-1951*
Spec - v296 - i9193 - Oct 16 2004 - p70(2) [501+]

Mitchell, Donald G. - *MRI Principles, 2nd Ed.*
SciTech - v28 - i1 - March 2004 - p89(1) [51-500]

Mitchell, Douglas R. - *Ancient Burial Practices in the American Southwest: Archaeology, Physical Anthropology, and Native American Perspectives*
Roundup M - v12 - i1 - Oct 2004 - p24(1) [51-500]

Mitchell, Edward W. - *Self-Made Madness: Rethinking Illness and Criminal Responsibility*
SciTech - v28 - i1 - March 2004 - p86(1) [51-500]

Mitchell, Elizabeth - *Journey to the Bottomless Pit: The Story of Stephen Bishop & Mammoth Cave (Illus. by Alder, Kelynn)*
c BL - v101 - i5 - Nov 1 2004 - p485(2) [51-500]
c CCB-B - v58 - i5 - Jan 2005 - p220(2) [51-500]
c KR - v72 - i19 - Oct 1 2004 - p965(1) [51-500]
c SLJ - v50 - i12 - Dec 2004 - p151(2) [51-500]

Mitchell, Ella Pearson - *Those Preaching Women, Vol. 4*
Black Iss - v6 - i6 - Nov-Dec 2004 - p18(1) [51-500]

Mitchell, Ellen - *Beyond Tears: Living After Losing a Child*
LJ - v130 - i1 - Jan 1 2005 - p135(1) [51-500]

Mitchell, Elyne - *The Silver Brumby (Read by Lee, Caroline).* Audiobook Review
  c SLJ - v50 - i10 - Oct 2004 - p85(1) [51-500]

Mitchell, Gladys - *Sleuth's Alchemy: Cases of Mrs. Bradley and Others*
  KR - v73 - i3 - Feb 1 2005 - p153(1) [51-500]

Mitchell, Ian - *The Geology of Northern Ireland: Our Natural Foundation*
  New Sci - v183 - i2457 - July 24 2004 - p54(2) [501+]

Mitchell, James C. - *Choke Point*
  BL - v101 - i3 - Oct 1 2004 - p314(1) [51-500]
  KR - v72 - i17 - Sept 1 2004 - p840(1) [51-500]
  PW - v251 - i40 - Oct 4 2004 - p74(1) [51-500]

Mitchell, John Hanson - *Looking for Mr. Gilbert: The Reimagined Life of an African American*
  Black Iss - v7 - i2 - March-April 2005 - p54(2) [501+]
  KR - v72 - i24 - Dec 15 2004 - p1187(1) [501+]

Mitchell, Jon P. - *Ambivalent Europeans: Ritual, Memory and the Public Sphere in Malta*
  JRAI - v10 - i4 - Dec 2004 - p938(2) [501+]

Mitchell, Joni - *Chelsea Morning (Illus. by Froud, Brian)*
  c KR - v72 - i18 - Sept 15 2004 - p916(1) [51-500]
  c PW - v251 - i42 - Oct 18 2004 - p63(1) [51-500]

Mitchell, Joseph - *Up in the Old Hotel*
  LJ - v129 - i20 - Dec 1 2004 - p186(1) [501+]

Mitchell, Judith Claire - *The Last Day of the War*
  BooChiTr - June 6 2004 - p3(1) [501+]

Mitchell, Juliet - *Siblings: Sex and Violence*
  JGS - v13 - i2 - July 2004 - p167-168 [501+]

Mitchell, Kathleen - *The World of Gregory of Tours*
  Specu - v79 - i3 - July 2004 - p804-805 [501+]

Mitchell, Kirk - *Dance of the Thunder Dogs*
  LJ - v129 - i18 - Nov 1 2004 - p60(1) [51-500]
  PW - v251 - i43 - Oct 25 2004 - p31(1) [51-500]

Mitchell, Linda E. - *Portraits of Medieval Women: Family, Marriage, and Politics in England, 1225-1350*
  Med R - Oct 2004 - pNA [501+]
  R&R Bk N - v19 - i1 - Feb 2004 - p131(1) [51-500]

  Portraits of Medieval Women: Family, Marriage, and Politics in England, 1255-1350
  AHR - v109 - i2 - April 2004 - p590(2) [501+]

Mitchell, Marianne - *Firebug*
  JAAL - v48 - i2 - Oct 2004 - p172(2) [501+]

Mitchell, Mark G. - *Raising La Belle*
  SHQ - v107 - i3 - Jan 2004 - p500(1) [501+]

Mitchell, Melanie - *Butterflies*
  LibMed - v22 - i4 - Jan 2004 - p70(1) [501+]

Mitchell, Michael - *The Molly Fire: A Memoir*
  Globe & Mail - Feb 26 2005 - pD3 [501+]
  Monsters: Human Freaks in America's Gilded Age: The Photographs of Chas. Eisenmann
  CBRA - Annual 2003 - p118(2) [501+]

Mitchell, Missy - *Ballet: Pointe by Pointe*
  c SLJ - v50 - i12 - Dec 2004 - p162(1) [51-500]

Mitchell, Mykel - *Word: For Everybody Who Thought Christianity Was for Suckas*
  PW - v252 - i4 - Jan 24 2005 - p240(1) [501+]

Mitchell, Nancy - *The Danger of Dreams: German and American Imperialism in Latin America*
  HAHR - v84 - i4 - Nov 2004 - p773(2) [501+]

Mitchell, Neil J. - *Agents of Atrocity: Leaders, Followers, and the Violations of Human Rights in Civil War*
  PW - v251 - i27 - July 5 2004 - p48(2) [501+]

Mitchell, Olivia S. - *Benefits for the Workplace of the Future*
  JEL - v41 - i4 - Dec 2003 - p1401(1) [501+]

Mitchell, Paulette - *The Spirited Vegetarian: Over 100 Recipes Made Lively with Wine and Spirits*
  PW - v252 - i3 - Jan 17 2005 - p48(1) [51-500]

Mitchell, Peter - *Researching Africa's Past: New Contributions from British Archaeologists: Proceedings*
  R&R Bk N - v19 - i3 - August 2004 - p57(1) [51-500]

Mitchell, Robin - *Sunny*
  c CBRA - Annual 2003 - p459(2) [51-500]
  Windy
  c CBRA - Annual 2003 - p459(2) [51-500]

Mitchell, Roger - *Delicate Bait*
  HR - v57 - i2 - Summer 2004 - p325-334 [501+]

Mitchell, Sally - *Frances Power Cobbe: Victorian Feminist, Journalist, Reformer*
  R&R Bk N - v19 - i4 - Nov 2004 - p236(1) [501+]

Mitchell, Sam - *Tourism and Development in Yunnan: Yunnan through Foreign Students' Eyes, Vol. 1*
  JPR - v41 - i4 - July 2004 - p521-521 [501+]

Mitchell, Sandra D. - *Biological Complexity and Integrative Pluralism*
  QRB - v79 - i4 - Dec 2004 - p406(1) [501+]

Mitchell, Scott - *ASP.NET Data Web Controls Kick Start*
  SciTech - v28 - i1 - March 2004 - p155(1) [51-500]

Mitchell, Stacy Ann - *Livin' Large: African American Sisters Confront Obesity*
  LJ - v129 - i18 - Nov 1 2004 - p116(1) [51-500]
  Time - v164 - i14 - Oct 4 2004 - p93 [51-500]

Mitchell, Stephen - *Gilgamesh: A New English Version*
  BL - v101 - i4 - Oct 15 2004 - p381(2) [501+]
  BW - v34 - i46 - Nov 14 2004 - p6(1) [501+]
  G&L Rev W - v12 - i2 - March-April 2005 - p38(2) [501+]
  Globe & Mail - Dec 4 2004 - pD16 [501+]
  LJ - v129 - i12 - July 2004 - p83(1) [51-500]
  NYTBR - Dec 5 2004 - p78 [501+]
  PW - v251 - i33 - August 16 2004 - p41(1) [501+]

Mitchell, Susan - *Fat Is Not Your Fate: Outsmart Your Genes and Lose the Weight Forever*
  LJ - v130 - i1 - Jan 1 2005 - p144(3) [501+]

Mitchell, Terence N. - *NMR--From Spectra to Structures: An Experimental Approach*
  Choice - v41 - i11-12 - July-August 2004 - p2074(1) [501+]

Mitchell, Thomas G. - *Indian Fighters Turned American Politicians: From Military to Public Service*
  R&R Bk N - v19 - i1 - Feb 2004 - p55(1) [51-500]

Mitchenhill, Barbara - *How to Be a Detective*
  c Sch Lib - v52 - i4 - Winter 2004 - p185(1) [51-500]

Mitford, Nancy - *The Bookshop at 10 Curzon Street: Letters between Nancy Mitford and Heywood Hill, 1952-1973*
  Spec - v296 - i9187 - Sept 4 2004 - p34(2) [501+]

Mithcell, Ken - *Heroic Adventures of Donny Coyote*
  CBRA - Annual 2003 - p178(2) [501+]

Mithen, Steven - *After the Ice: A Global Human History, 20,000-5,000 BC*
  Arch - v58 - i1 - Jan-Feb 2005 - p54-55 [501+]
  BL - v101 - i1 - Sept 1 2004 - p42(1) [51-500]
  JRAI - v10 - i3 - Sept 2004 - p714(1) [501+]
  Quad - v49 - i1-2 - Jan-Feb 2005 - p119(2) [501+]

Mithridates, Flavius - *The Great Parchment: Flavius Mithridate's Latin Translation, the Hebrew Text, and an English Version*
  TLS - i5298 - Oct 15 2004 - p28(1) [501+]

Mitnick, Kevin D. - *The Art of Intrusion: The Real Stories Behind the Exploits of Hackers, Intruders and Deceivers*
  LJ - v130 - i1 - Jan 1 2005 - p139(1) [51-500]
  PW - v252 - i7 - Feb 14 2005 - p66(1) [51-500]

Mitoma, Judy - *Envisioning Dance on Film and Video*
  Dance RJ - v35 - i2 - Winter 2003 - p176-181 [501+]

Mitra, Kalita - *Suburban Sahibs: Three Immigrant Families and Their Passage from India to America*
  R&R Bk N - v19 - i1 - Feb 2004 - p63(1) [501+]

Mitroff, Ian I. - *Why Some Companies Emerge Stronger and Better from a Crisis: 7 Essential Lessons for Surviving Disaster*
  Fut - v39 - i2 - March-April 2005 - p6(1) [501+]

Mitroff, Ian L. - *Why Some Companies Emerge Stronger and Better from a Crisis: 7 Essential Lessons for Surviving Disaster*
  Fut - v39 - i2 - March-April 2005 - p61(1) [51-500]

Mitropoulos, Atanasios - *Economic Learning Experiments and the Limits to Information*
  R&R Bk N - v19 - i4 - Nov 2004 - p83(1) [51-500]

Mitrovic, Branko - *Learning from Palladio*
  CR - v285 - i1667 - Dec 2004 - p381(1) [51-500]
  R&R Bk N - v19 - i3 - August 2004 - p241(1) [51-500]

Mitsch, William J. - *Ecological Engineering and Ecosystem Restoration*
  SciTech - v28 - i1 - March 2004 - p64(1) [51-500]

Mitsilegas, Valsamis - *Money Laundering Counter-Measures in the European Union: A New Paradigm of Security Governance Versus Fundamental Legal Principles*
  R&R Bk N - v19 - i1 - Feb 2004 - pNA [51-500]

Mittal, K.L. - *Contact Angle, Wettability and Adhesion, Vol. 3*
  SciTech - v28 - i1 - March 2004 - p57(1) [51-500]
  Particles on Surfaces 8: Detection, Adhesion and Removal
  SciTech - v28 - i1 - March 2004 - p141(1) [51-500]
  Polimer Surface Modification: Relevance to Adhesion, Vol. 3
  SciTech - v28 - i4 - Dec 2004 - p165(1) [51-500]
  Silanes and Other Coupling Agents: Proceedings, Vol. 3
  SciTech - v28 - i4 - Dec 2004 - p49(1) [51-500]

Mittal, Sushil - *Surprising Bedfellows: Hindus and Muslims in Medieval and Early Modern India*
  R&R Bk N - v19 - i1 - Feb 2004 - p46(1) [51-500]

Mittelbach, Margaret - *Carnivorous Nights: On the Trail of the Tasmanian Tiger*
  KR - v73 - i4 - Feb 15 2005 - p217(1) [501+]
  PW - v252 - i11 - March 14 2005 - p60(1) [51-500]

Mittelstaedt, Robert E., Jr. - *Will Your Next Mistake Be Fatal?: Avoiding the Chain of Mistakes That Can Destroy Your Organization*
  LJ - v129 - i17 - Oct 15 2004 - p70(1) [51-500]

Mitter, Matt - *Once Upon a Rhyme: Story Rhymes (Illus. by Banta, Susan)*
  c SLJ - v50 - i8 - August 2004 - p111(1) [51-500]

Mitter, Rana - *Across the Blocks: Cold War Cultural and Social History*
  Choice - v42 - i2 - Oct 2004 - p345(1) [51-500]
  A Bitter Revolution: China's Struggle with the Modern World
  LJ - v129 - i12 - July 2004 - p104(1) [51-500]
  TimHES - v0 - i1676 - Jan 28 2005 - p28(2) [501+]

Mitterauer, Michael - *Warum Europa? Mittelalterliche Grundlagen eines Sonderwegs*
  CEH - v37 - i3 - Summer 2004 - p430(3) [501+]

Mittleman, Alan - *Religion as a Public Good: Jews and Other Americans on Religion in the Public Square*
  Choice - v42 - i1 - Sept 2004 - p122(1) [501+]
  HNet - Sept 2004 - pNA [501+]
  R&R Bk N - v19 - i4 - Nov 2004 - p16(1) [51-500]

Mittler, Barbara - *A Newspaper for China?: Power, Identity, and Change in Shanghai's News Media, 1872-1912*
  Choice - v42 - i4 - Dec 2004 - p654(1) [1-50]

Mitton, Jacqueline - *Once upon a Starry Night: A Book of Constellation Stories*
  c LibMed - v22 - i7 - April-May 2004 - p79(1) [501+]
  c S&T - v108 - i1 - July 2004 - p118(1) [501+]

Mitton, Maureen - *Interior Design Visual Presentation: A Guide to Graphics, Models, and Presentation Techniques, 2nd Ed.*
  R&R Bk N - v19 - i1 - Feb 2004 - p207(1) [51-500]

Mitton, Simon - *Conflict in the Cosmos: Fred Hoyle's Life in Science*
  PW - v252 - i6 - Feb 7 2005 - p54(1) [51-500]

Mitton, Tony - *Amazing Machines Jigsaw Book*
  c PW - v251 - i41 - Oct 11 2004 - p82(1) [501+]
  Down by the Cool of the Pool (Illus. by Parker-Rees, Guy)
  c RT - v57 - Oct 2003 - p165 [1-50]
  Goodnight Me, Goodnight You
  c BooChiTr - June 6 2004 - p5(1) [501+]
  Plum: Poems by Tony Mitton (Illus. by GrandPre, Mary)
  c Teach Lib - v32 - i3 - Feb 2005 - p20(1) [51-500]
  Riddley Piggledy: A Book of Rhymes and Riddles (Illus. by Mounter, Paddy)
  c KR - v72 - i17 - Sept 1 2004 - p871(1) [51-500]
  c PW - v251 - i38 - Sept 20 2004 - p65(1) [51-500]
  c SLJ - v50 - i11 - Nov 2004 - p128(1) [51-500]
  Spooky Hour (Illus. by Parker-Rees, Guy)
  c KR - v72 - i13 - July 1 2004 - p634(1) [51-500]
  c SLJ - v50 - i8 - August 2004 - p90(1) [51-500]
  The Tale of Tales (Illus. by Bailey, Peter)
  c NYTBR - August 8 2004 - p17 [501+]

Mitzman, Arthur - *Prometheus Revisited: The Quest for Global Justice in the Twenty-First Century*
  Choice - v41 - i7 - March 2004 - p1335(2) [501+]

Mixing It Up: Integrated, Interdisciplinary, Intriguing Science in the Elementary Classroom
  CE - v81 - i2 - Winter 2004 - p117(1) [51-500]

Miya, Kimio - *Complex Analysis in Several Variables: Memorial Conference of Kiyoshi Oka's Centennial Birthday: Proceedings*
  SciTech - v28 - i4 - Dec 2004 - p40(1) [51-500]

Miyabe, Miyuki - *Shadow Family*
  BL - v101 - i9-10 - Jan 1 2005 - p828(1) [1-50]
  KR - v72 - i23 - Dec 1 2004 - p1122(1) [51-500]
  LJ - v130 - i3 - Feb 15 2005 - p124(1) [51-500]
  PW - v252 - i3 - Jan 17 2005 - p38(1) [51-500]
  NYTBR - Feb 6 2005 - p25 [501+]

Miyaki, Takahashi - *Musashi #9: Vol. 1*
  PW - v251 - i46 - Nov 15 2004 - p43(1) [51-500]

Miyaoka, Isao - *Legitimacy in International Society: Japan's Reaction to Global Wildlife Preservation*
  SciTech - v28 - i3 - Sept 2004 - p63(1) [51-500]

Miyashita, Akitoshi - *Limits to Power: Asymmetric Dependence and Japanese Foreign Aid Policy*
  Pac A - v77 - i2 - Summer 2004 - p345(2) [501+]

Miyazaki, Hayao - *Castle in the Sky*
  y Kliatt - v38 - i5 - Sept 2004 - p36(2) [51-500]
  Nausicaa of the Valley of the Wind, Vol. 1
    LJ - v129 - i12 - July 2004 - p62(1) [51-500]
Miyoshi, Masao - *Learning Places: The Afterlife of Area Studies*
    Pac A - v77 - i2 - Summer 2004 - p305(2) [501+]
Mize, Ronald L. - *Politics and the Past: On Repairing Historical Injustices*
    CS - v33 - i5 - Sept 2004 - p582-583 [501+]
  Should America Pay? Slavery and the Raging Debate on Reparations
    CS - v33 - i5 - Sept 2004 - p582-583 [501+]
Mizejewski, Linda - *Hardboiled & High Heeled: The Woman Detective in Popular Culture*
    Choice - v42 - i2 - Oct 2004 - p278(2) [501+]
Mizner, David - *Political Animal*
    BL - v100 - i22 - August 2004 - p1901(1) [501+]
    Ent W - Sept 10 2004 - p168 [51-500]
    KR - v72 - i14 - July 15 2004 - p652(1) [501+]
Mizrahi, Eli M. - *Atlas of Neonatal Electroencephalography, 3rd Ed.*
    SciTech - v28 - i1 - March 2004 - p118(1) [51-500]
Mizrahi, Yemile - *From Martyrdom to Power: The Partido Accion Nacional in Mexico*
    Ams - v61 - i2 - Oct 2004 - p338(2) [501+]
    Pers PS - v33 - i4 - Fall 2004 - p236(1) [501+]
Mizuki, Sakura - *The Ring, Vol. 4*
    PW - v252 - i2 - Jan 10 2005 - p41(1) [51-500]
Mizuno, Junko - *Princess Mermaid*
  y Kliatt - v39 - i2 - March 2005 - p30(1) [51-500]
Mizuno, Katsuhiko - *The Hidden Gardens of Kyoto*
    BL - v101 - i4 - Oct 15 2004 - p372(1) [51-500]
    Bwatch - Oct 2004 - pNA [51-500]
Mizuno, Ryou - *Louie the Rune Soldier (Illus. by Sasameyuki, Jun)*
  y SLJ - v50 - i8 - August 2004 - p149(1) [501+]
Mkude, Daniel - *Higher Education in Tanzania: A Case Study*
    TimHES - v0 - i1676 - Jan 28 2005 - p26(1) [501+]
Mller, Jane E. - *The Chicago Guide to Writing about Numbers*
    Econ - v374 - i8408 - Jan 8 2005 - p75US [501+]
Mlynowski, Sarah - *Bras and Broomsticks*
  y BL - v101 - i9-10 - Jan 1 2005 - p846(1) [1-50]
  y CCB-B - v58 - i5 - Jan 2005 - p221(1) [51-500]
  y KR - v73 - i2 - Jan 15 2005 - p123(1) [51-500]
  y PW - v252 - i6 - Feb 7 2005 - p60(2) [51-500]
    SLJ - v51 - i1 - Jan 2005 - p134(1) [51-500]
  Monkey Business
    BL - v101 - i2 - Sept 15 2004 - p224(2) [51-500]
Mnookin, Seth - *Hard News: The Scandals at The New York Times and Their Meaning for American Media*
    BW - v34 - i46 - Nov 14 2004 - p3(2) [501+]
    CJR - v43 - i4 - Nov-Dec 2004 - p63(2) [501+]
    Econ - v374 - i8410 - Jan 22 2005 - p80US [501+]
    Ent W - i792 - Nov 12 2004 - p128 [51-500]
    New York - v37 - i40 - Nov 15 2004 - p116(2) [501+]
    NYTBR - Dec 26 2004 - p13 [501+]
Mo, Phyllis Lai Lan - *Tax Avoidance and Anti-Avoidance Measures in Major Developing Economies*
    R&R Bk N - v19 - i1 - Feb 2004 - p120(1) [51-500]
Mo, Yan - *Big Breasts and Wide Hips*
    BL - v101 - i6 - Nov 15 2004 - p563(1) [51-500]
    BW - v34 - i48 - Nov 28 2004 - p2(1) [501+]
    KR - v72 - i19 - Oct 1 2004 - p934(1) [501+]
    LJ - v129 - i20 - Dec 1 2004 - p101(1) [51-500]
    PW - v251 - i47 - Nov 22 2004 - p40(1) [501+]
Moats, David - *Civil Wars: A Battle for Gay Marriage*
    R&R Bk N - v19 - i2 - May 2004 - p135 [51-500]
Moaveni, Azadeh - *Lipstick Jihad: A Memoir of Growing Up Iranian in America and American in Iran*
    KR - v73 - i2 - Jan 15 2005 - p106(1) [501+]
    LJ - v130 - i3 - Feb 15 2005 - p140(1) [51-500]
    NYTBR - March 13 2005 - p29 [501+]
    PW - v252 - i3 - Jan 17 2005 - p42(1) [51-500]
Mobberley, Martin - *The New Amateur Astronomer*
    Choice - v42 - i7 - March 2005 - p1248(2) [51-500]
Mobius, Siegurd - *LSC 2001, Advances in Liquid Scintillation Spectrometry*
    SciTech - v28 - i1 - March 2004 - p51(1) [51-500]
Mocek, Reinhard - *Biologie und soziale Befreiung: Zur Geschichte des Biologismus und der Rassenhygiene in der Arbeiterbewegung*
    GSR - v27 - i2 - May 2004 - p395-396 [501+]

Moch, Leslie Page - *Moving Europeans: Migration in Western Europe since 1650*
    Choice - v41 - i7 - March 2004 - p1361(2) [501+]
Mock, Douglas W. - *More Than Kin and Less Than Kind: The Evolution of Family Conflict*
    Choice - v42 - i3 - Nov 2004 - p508(2) [1-50]
    Nature - v429 - i6987 - May 6 2004 - p23(2) [501+]
Mockaitis, Thomas R. - *Grand Strategy in the War Against Terrorism*
    Choice - v41 - i11-12 - July-August 2004 - p2120(1) [501+]
  Grand Strategy in the War Against Terrrorism
    R&R Bk N - v19 - i1 - Feb 2004 - p141(1) [51-500]
Mockler, Robert J. - *International Strategic Management: An Integrative Entrepreneurial Context-Specific Process*
    JEL - v41 - i4 - Dec 2003 - p1357(2) [501+]
Modell, Judith S. - *A Sealed and Secret Kinship: The Culture of Policies and Practices in American Adoption*
    JRAI - v10 - i4 - Dec 2004 - p953(2) [501+]
The Modern Social Science.
    CS - v33 - i5 - Sept 2004 - p626-626 [501+]
Modernism/Modernity
    TLS - i5267 - March 12 2004 - p25-25 [501+]
Modesitt, Jeanne - *Mouse's Halloween Party (Illus. by Spowart, Robin)*
  c BL - v100 - i22 - August 2004 - p1943(2) [51-500]
  c SLJ - v50 - i8 - August 2004 - p90(1) [51-500]
Modesitt, L.E. - *The Ethos Effect*
    Analog - v124 - i3 - March 2004 - p134(2) [501+]
  Flash
    Analog - v125 - i1-2 - Jan-Feb 2005 - p230(6) [501+]
  y BL - v101 - i1 - Sept 1 2004 - p75(1) [51-500]
    ChrSFF&H - v26 - i9 - Sept 2004 - p30(1) [51-500]
    KR - v72 - i15 - August 1 2004 - p718(1) [51-500]
    PW - v251 - i34 - August 23 2004 - p41(1) [51-500]
  Ordermaster
    BL - v101 - i9-10 - Jan 1 2005 - p834(1) [1-50]
    LJ - v130 - i1 - Jan 1 2005 - p102(1) [51-500]
  Scepters
    BL - v100 - i21 - July 2004 - p1829(1) [501+]
  y VOYA - v27 - i3 - August 2004 - p232(1) [1-50]
Modeste, Naomi N. - *Dictionary of Public Health Promotion and Education: Terms and Concepts, 2nd Ed.*
    SciTech - v28 - i4 - Dec 2004 - p82(1) [51-500]
Modiano, Patrick - *Accident Nocturne*
    WLT - v78 - i3-4 - Sept-Dec 2004 - p118(1) [501+]
Modiano, Raimonda - *Voice, Text, Hypertext: Emerging Practices in Textual Studies*
    Choice - v42 - i2 - Oct 2004 - p289(1) [501+]
Modoc Press Inc. - *Teacher Education Programs in the United States: A Guide*
    R&R Bk N - v19 - i4 - Nov 2004 - p182(1) [501+]
Moe, Christian H. - *Masterplots II: Drama Series, Rev. Ed., Vols. 1-4*
    R&R Bk N - v19 - i1 - Feb 2004 - p230(1) [51-500]
  c SLJ - v50 - i8 - August 2004 - p58(1) [501+]
Moe, Nelson - *The View from Vesuvius: Italian Culture and the Southern Question*
    JIH - v35 - i1 - Summer 2004 - p134-135 [501+]
    JMH - v77 - i1 - March 2005 - p204(3) [501+]
Moe, Ronald C. - *Administrative Renewal: Reorganization Commissions in the 20th Century*
    Pres St Q - v34 - i3 - Sept 2004 - p704(3) [501+]
Moed, Pnina - *Kass Real Time*
  y HB - v81 - i1 - Jan-Feb 2005 - p94(1) [51-500]
Moeglin, Jean-Marie - *Les bourgeois de Calais: Essai sur un myhte historique*
    Specu - v79 - i4 - Oct 2004 - p1119(3) [501+]
Moehn, Heather - *The U.S. Constitution: A Primary Source Investigation into the Fundamental Law of the United States*
    LibMed - v22 - i4 - Jan 2004 - p75(1) [501+]
Moeller, Bill - *Custer: A Photographic Biography*
    R&R Bk N - v19 - i1 - Feb 2004 - p59(1) [51-500]
Moeller, Hans-Bernhard - *Volker Schlondorff's Cinema: Adaptation, Politics, and the "Movie-Appropriate"*
    Ger Q - v77 - i1 - Wntr 2004 - p113(2) [501+]
    GSR - v27 - i2 - May 2004 - p440-441 [501+]
Moeller, James L. - *Winter Sports Medicine Handbook*
    SciTech - v28 - i3 - Sept 2004 - p110(1) [51-500]
Moen, Christine Boardman - *Read-Alouds and Performance Reading: A Handbook of Activities for the Middle School Classroom*
    LibMed - v23 - i3 - Nov-Dec 2004 - p91 [51-500]
    RT - v58 - i4 - Dec 2004 - p386(1) [501+]

Moffat, Anthony C. - *Clarke's Analysis of Drugs and Poisons in Pharmaceuticals, Body Fluids and Postmortem Material, 3rd Ed.*
    E-Streams - August 2004 - pNA [501+]
Moffat, Ivan - *The Ivan Moffat File: Life among the Beautiful and Damned in London, Paris, New York and Hollywood*
    LJ - v129 - i15 - Sept 15 2004 - p60(1) [51-500]
Moffatt, Gregory K. - *The Parenting Journey: From Conception through the Teen Years*
    Choice - v42 - i3 - Nov 2004 - p569(1) [51-500]
    R&R Bk N - v19 - i3 - August 2004 - p150(1) [51-500]
Moffitt, John F. - *Picturing Extraterrestrials: Alien Images in Modern Mass Culture*
    JPC - v38 - i3 - Feb 2005 - p588(2) [501+]
Mofina, Rick - *Be Mine*
    Globe & Mail - July 24 2004 - pD11 [51-500]
Moggach, Deborah - *These Foolish Things*
    NS - v133 - i4716 - Nov 29 2004 - p43(2) [51-500]
Moggach, Douglas - *The Philosophy and Politics of Bruno Bauer*
    Choice - v42 - i3 - Nov 2004 - p562(1) [1-50]
    HNet - Dec 2004 - pNA [501+]
    TLS - i5295 - Sept 24 2004 - p22(1) [501+]
Mogil, H. Michael - *The Amateur Meteorologist: Explorations and Investigations*
    SB - v40 - i5 - Sept-Oct 2004 - p192(1) [51-500]
Mogil, Jeffrey S. - *Genetics of Pain*
    SciTech - v28 - i4 - Dec 2004 - p88(1) [51-500]
Mogren, Eric W. - *Warm Sands: Uranium Mill Tailings Policy in the Atomic West*
    T&C - v45 - i4 - Oct 2004 - p866(3) [501+]
Mohammad-Djafari, Ali - *Bayesian Inference and Maximum Entropy Methods in Science and Engineering: Proceedings*
    SciTech - v28 - i3 - Sept 2004 - p16(1) [501+]
Mohammad, K. Silem - *A Thousand Devils*
    PW - v251 - i42 - Oct 18 2004 - p61(1) [51-500]
Mohammad, Jamshid - *NDT Methods Applied to Fatigue Reliability Assessment of Structures*
    SciTech - v28 - i3 - Sept 2004 - p139(1) [51-500]
Mohammadi, S. - *Discontinuum Mechanics: Using Finite and Discrete Elements*
    SciTech - v28 - i3 - Sept 2004 - p142(1) [51-500]
Mohammadian, Masoud - *Intelligent Agents for Data Mining and Information Retrieval*
    Choice - v42 - i4 - Dec 2004 - p696(1) [1-50]
Mohammed, Nadeya Sayed Ali - *Population and Development of the Arab Gulf States: The Case of Bahrain, Oman and Kuwait*
    R&R Bk N - v19 - i1 - Feb 2004 - p84(1) [1-50]
Mohan, C. Raja - *Crossing the Rubicon: The Shaping of India's New Foreign Policy*
    For Aff - v83 - i5 - Sept-Oct 2004 - p164 [501+]
Mohanty, Chandra Talpade - *Feminism Without Borders: Decolonizing Theory, Practicing Solidarity*
    R&R Bk N - v19 - i4 - Nov 2004 - p135(1) [1-50]
Mohanty, Manoranjan - *Class, Caste, Gender*
    R&R Bk N - v19 - i4 - Nov 2004 - p127(1) [51-500]
Moholy-Nagy, Hattula - *The Artifacts of Tikal: Utilitarian Artifacts and Unworked Material*
    Lat Ant - v15 - i4 - Dec 2004 - p458(3) [501+]
Mohowski, Robert E. - *The New York, Susquehanna & Western Railroad*
    BHR - v78 - i3 - Autumn 2004 - p531(4) [501+]
    R&R Bk N - v19 - i1 - Feb 2004 - p104(1) [51-500]
Mohr, Angie - *Bookkeepers' Boot Camp: Get a Grip on Accounting Basics*
    CBRA - Annual 2003 - p330(2) [51-500]
  Financial Management 101: Get a Grip on Your Business Numbers
    CBRA - Annual 2003 - p330(2) [51-500]
Mohr, James C. - *Plague and Fire: Battling Black Death and the 1900 Burning of Honolulu's Chinatown.*
    KR - v72 - i17 - Sept 1 2004 - p852(1) [501+]
    PW - v251 - i36 - Sept 6 2004 - p55(1) [501+]
Mohr, Jay - *Gasping for Airtime: Two Years in the Trenches of Saturday Night Live (Read by Mohr, Jay). Audiobook Review*
  y Kliatt - v39 - i1 - Jan 2005 - p52(1) [51-500]
Mohr, Marian M. - *Teacher Research for Better Schools*
    HER - v74 - i3 - Fall 2004 - p356(3) [501+]
Mohr, Richard D. - *Pottery, Politics, Art: George Ohr and the Brothers Kirkpatrick*
    Am Craft - v64 - i2 - April-May 2004 - p32(1) [501+]
    Am Craft - v64 - i2 - April-May 2004 - p32(1) [501+]

Mohrig, Jerry R. - *Modern Projects and Experiments in Organic Chemistry: Miniscale and Williamson Microscale, 2nd Ed.*
J Chem Ed - v81 - i5 - May 2004 - p649-651 [501+]

Moinereau, Dominique - *RPV Integrity and Fracture Mechanics: Proceedings*
SciTech - v28 - i4 - Dec 2004 - p160(1) [51-500]

Moir, John S. - *Christianity in Canada: Historical Essays*
Can Hist R - v85 - i3 - Sept 2004 - p552(3) [501+]
Early Presbyterianism in Canada
Can Hist R - v85 - i3 - Sept 2004 - p599(2) [501+]
CBRA - Annual 2003 - p96(2) [51-500]

Moisala, Pirkko - *Music and Gender*
Signs - v30 - i2 - Wntr 2005 - p1722(5) [501+]

Moisienko, Anatolii - *Spaleni kameni*
WLT - v79 - i1 - Jan-April 2005 - p106(1) [501+]

Moitra, Stefan - *"Wo bleibt der Arbeiterfilm?": Die Auseinandersetzung der IG Bergbau und Energie mit dem Medium Film in den 1950er und 1960er Jahren*
HNet - July 2004 - pNA [501+]

Moitt, Bernard - *Women and Slavery in the French Antilles, 1635-1848*
W&M Q - v61 - i3 - July 2004 - p568-570 [501+]

Moix, Ana Maria - *Julia*
BL - v101 - i1 - Sept 1 2004 - p63(1) [501+]

Mok, Ka-Ho - *Globalization and Educational Restructuring in the Asia Pacific Region*
Pac A - v77 - i3 - Fall 2004 - p546(2) [501+]
Globalization and Marketization in Education: A Comparative Analysis of Hong Kong and Singapore
R&R Bk N - v19 - i4 - Nov 2004 - p189(1) [501+]

Moka - *Just Us Girls: Secrets to Feeling Good about Yourself, Inside and Out (Illus. by Heliot, Eric)*
y SLJ - v50 - i9 - Sept 2004 - p223(1) [51-500]
y TES - v0 - i4586 - June 4 2004 - psssss18(2) [501+]
y VOYA - v27 - i4 - Oct 2004 - p335(1) [501+]

Mokyr, Joel - *The Gifts of Athena: Historical Origins of the Knowledge Economy*
IndRev - v9 - i3 - Wntr 2005 - p439(3) [501+]
JEL - v42 - i3 - Sept 2004 - p805(6) [501+]
Lib & Cul - v39 - i3 - Summer 2004 - p340(3) [501+]
The Oxford Encyclopedia of Economic History, vols. 1-5
BHR - v78 - i2 - Summer 2004 - p377(1) [501+]
JEL - v42 - i1 - March 2004 - p298(2) [501+]
JEL - v42 - i3 - Sept 2004 - p872(3) [501+]
R&USQ - v44 - i2 - Winter 2004 - p131(1) [501+]
TimHES - v0 - i1664 - Oct 29 2004 - p24(2) [501+]

Mol, Annemarie - *The Body Multiple: Ontology in Medical Practice*
MAQ - v18 - i4 - Dec 2004 - p520(2) [501+]

Mol, Arthur P.J. - *Greening Industrialization in Asian Transitional Economies: China and Vietnam*
CS - v33 - i6 - Nov 2004 - p747(1) [1-50]

Molander, Per - *Fiscal Federalism in Unitary States*
R&R Bk N - v19 - i1 - Feb 2004 - pNA [501+]

Molano, Alfred - *Loyal Soldiers in the Cocaine Kingdom: Tales of Drugs, Mules and Gunmen*
Nation - v279 - i5 - August 16 2004 - p31 [501+]

Molasky, Michael S. - *The American Occupation of Japan and Okinawa: Literature and Memory*
HNet - Dec 2004 - pNA [501+]

Molella, Arthur - *Inventing for the Environment*
JEL - v42 - i1 - March 2004 - p337(1) [501+]
QRB - v79 - i4 - Dec 2004 - p453(2) [501+]
Sci - v305 - i5690 - Sept 10 2004 - p1570(1) [501+]

Moler, Cleve B. - *Numerical Computing With MATLAB*
Choice - v42 - i6 - Feb 2005 - p1058(1) [51-500]

Moletin, Giuseppe (b. 1531-1588) - *The Unfinished Mechanics of Giuseppe Moletti: An Edition and English Translation of His Dialogue on Mechanics, 1576*
Isis - v95 - i2 - June 2004 - p288(2) [501+]

Molinari, A. - *From Nuclei and Their Constituents to Stars: Proceedings*
SciTech - v28 - i4 - Dec 2004 - p51(1) [51-500]

Moliterno, James E. - *Ethics of the Lawyer's Work, 2nd Ed.*
R&R Bk N - v19 - i1 - Feb 2004 - pNA [51-500]
Professional Responsibility
R&R Bk N - v19 - i1 - Feb 2004 - pNA [1-50]

Molk, Laurel - *When You Were Just a Heartbeat (Illus. by Molk, Laurel)*
c CCB-B - v57 - i11 - July-August 2004 - p474(2) [501+]
c SLJ - v50 - i7 - July 2004 - p83(1) [51-500]

Moll, Don - *The Ecology, Exploitation, and Conservation of River Turtles*
Choice - v42 - i4 - Dec 2004 - p690(2) [1-50]
QRB - v79 - i4 - Dec 2004 - p446(1) [501+]
SciTech - v28 - i3 - Sept 2004 - p65(1) [51-500]

Moll, Richard J. - *Before Malory: Reading Arthur in Later Medieval England*
Med R - Dec 2004 - pNA [501+]
TLS - i5287 - July 30 2004 - p24(1) [501+]

Mollan, Charles - *Irish Innovators in Science and Technology*
Isis - v95 - i2 - June 2004 - p275(1) [501+]

Molle, Elizabeth A. - *Lippincott Williams and Wilkins' Administrative Medical Assisting*
SciTech - v28 - i1 - March 2004 - p79(1) [51-500]

Moller, Peter Ulf - *Under Vitus Bering's Command: New Perspectives on the Russian Kamchatka Expeditions*
R&R Bk N - v19 - i4 - Nov 2004 - p73(1) [51-500]

Moller, Verner - *The Essence of Sport*
SSJ - v21 - i3 - Sept 2004 - p346-348 [501+]

Molles, Manuel C., Jr. - *Ecology: Concepts and Applications, 3rd Ed.*
TimHES - v0 - i1680 - Feb 25 2005 - pIII(1) [501+]

Mollinga, Peter P. - *The Politics of Irrigation Reform: Contested Policy Formulation and the Implementation in Asia and Africa and Latin America*
R&R Bk N - v19 - i3 - August 2004 - p112(1) [51-500]

Mollod, Phineas - *The Modern Lover: A Playbook for Suitors, Spouses & Ringless Carousers*
LJ - v129 - i19 - Nov 15 2004 - p76(1) [501+]

Molloy, Dorothy - *Hare Soup*
TLS - i5287 - July 30 2004 - p25(1) [501+]

Molloy, Michael - *The House on Falling Star Hill*
c LibMed - v23 - i1 - August-Sept 2004 - p67(2) [51-500]
y VOYA - v27 - i3 - August 2004 - p232(1) [1-50]
The Witch Trade (Read by Wallis, Bill). Audiobook Review
y SLJ - v51 - i1 - Jan 2005 - p78(1) [51-500]

Molnar, George - *Powers: A Study in Metaphysics*
J Phil - v101 - i8 - August 2004 - p438-443 [501+]

Molnar, Paul D. - *Divine Freedom and the Doctrine of the Immanent Trinity: In Dialogue with Karl Barth and Contemporary Theology*
TT - v60 - i4 - Jan 2004 - p590-592 [501+]

Molnar, Ralph E. - *Dragons in the Dust: The Paleobiology of the Giant Monitor Lizard Megalania*
Choice - v42 - i3 - Nov 2004 - p513(1) [1-50]
QRB - v79 - i4 - Dec 2004 - p411(1) [501+]

Moloney, Catriona - *Irish Women Writers Speak Out: Voices from the Field*
ILS - v24 - i1 - Fall 2004 - p22(1) [501+]

Moloney, Francis J. - *Mark: Storyteller, Interpreter, Evangelist*
Intpr - v58 - i3 - July 2004 - p334(1) [51-500]

Moloney, James - *Black Taxi*
y Kliatt - v39 - i2 - March 2005 - p14(1) [51-500]
KR - v73 - i3 - Feb 1 2005 - p179(1) [51-500]

Moloney, Jerome V. - *Nonlinear Optics*
SciTech - v28 - i1 - March 2004 - p49(1) [51-500]

Moloney, Susie - *Dwelling*
CBRA - Annual 2003 - p179(1) [51-500]

Moltmann, Jurgen - *Science and Wisdom*
JR - v84 - i4 - Oct 2004 - p645(2) [501+]
Theol St - v65 - i3 - Sept 2004 - p679(1) [501+]
TT - v61 - i3 - Oct 2004 - p393(2) [501+]
Theology of Hope
CC - v121 - i26 - Dec 28 2004 - p31(1) [501+]

Moltz, Barry J. - *You Need to Be a Little Crazy: The Truth About Starting and Growing Your Business*
R&R Bk N - v19 - i1 - Feb 2004 - p93(1) [1-50]

Molyneux, Robert E. - *The Internet under the Hood: An Introduction to Network Technologies for Information Professionals*
ALJ - v53 - i3 - August 2004 - p316(2) [501+]

Mom, Gijs - *The Electric Vehicle: Technology and Expectations in the Automobile Age*
BHR - v78 - i3 - Autumn 2004 - p548(3) [501+]
Choice - v42 - i2 - Oct 2004 - p323(1) [51-500]
New Sci - v183 - i2455 - July 10 2004 - p48(2) [501+]
SciTech - v28 - i3 - Sept 2004 - p163(1) [51-500]

Mombauer, Annika - *Helmuth von Moltke and the Origins of the First World War*
CEH - v37 - i3 - Summer 2004 - p468(5) [501+]
The Kaiser: New Research on Wilhelm's Role in Imperial Germany
HNet - Nov 2004 - pNA [501+]

Mommaerts, Robb - *Mason Moves Away: Mason Se Muda*
LibMed - v22 - i7 - April-May 2004 - p57(1) [501+]

Mommsen, Wolfgang J. - *Der Erste Weltkrieg: Anfang vom Ende des burgerlichen Zeitalters*
TLS - i5299 - Oct 22 2004 - p11(1) [501+]

Momochi, Reiko - *Confidential Confessions*
Kliatt - v38 - i5 - Sept 2004 - p36(2) [501+]

Monaco, James Martin - *Fee Mining and Rockhunting Adventures in the West, Rev. Ed.*
SciTech - v28 - i4 - Dec 2004 - p57(1) [51-500]

Monagan, David - *Jaywalking with the Irish*
LJ - v129 - i17 - Oct 15 2004 - p79(1) [51-500]
PW - v251 - i37 - Sept 13 2004 - p69(2) [501+]

Monaghan, Frank - *Practical Ways to Support New Arrivals in the Classroom*
Sch Lib - v52 - i4 - Winter 2004 - p222(1) [51-500]

Monaghan, Kelly - *The Other Orlando*
Bwatch - Nov 2004 - pNA [51-500]

Monaghan, Patricia - *The Encyclopedia of Celtic Mythology and Folklore*
y SLJ - v50 - i10 - Oct 2004 - p96(1) [51-500]
The Red-Haired Girl from the Bog
Bwatch - v26 - i9 - Sept 2004 - p3(1) [51-500]

Monahan, Edward J. - *Collective Autonomy: A History of the Council of Ontario Universities, 1962-2000*
R&R Bk N - v19 - i4 - Nov 2004 - p183(1) [501+]

Monahan, Evelyn M. - *And If I Perish: Frontline U.S. Army Nurses in World War II*
Choice - v42 - i1 - Sept 2004 - p175(2) [501+]
y Kliatt - v39 - i2 - March 2005 - p39(1) [51-500]
R&R Bk N - v19 - i1 - Feb 2004 - p30(1) [51-500]

Monaingo, Robert A. - *Introduction to Adaptive Arrays*
SciTech - v28 - i1 - March 2004 - p161(1) [51-500]

Monakov, Yuri B. - *Leading Edge Research on Polymers and Composites*
SciTech - v28 - i3 - Sept 2004 - p139(1) [51-500]

Monbiot, George - *The Age of Consent: A Manifesto for a New World Order*
JPR - v41 - i4 - July 2004 - p521-522 [501+]

Mondini, Mariana - *Colonisation, Migration and Marginal Areas: A Zooarchaeological Approach*
R&R Bk N - v19 - i4 - Nov 2004 - p30(1) [501+]

Monenembo, Tierno - *Peuls*
WLT - v79 - i1 - Jan-April 2005 - p82(1) [501+]

Monetary Policy Report: January 2003
JEL - v41 - i4 - Dec 2003 - p1347(1) [501+]

Monette, Duane R. - *Applied Social Research: Tool for the Human Services, 6th Ed.*
R&R Bk N - v19 - i4 - Nov 2004 - p137(1) [1-50]

Moneymaker, Chris - *Moneymaker: How an Amateur Poker Player Turned $40 into $2.5 Million at the World Series of Poker*
KR - v73 - i1 - Jan 1 2005 - p38(1) [501+]
PW - v252 - i6 - Feb 7 2005 - p55(1) [51-500]

Monfrin, Jacques - *Etudes de philologie romane*
FS - v58 - i1 - Jan 2004 - p152(2) [501+]

Mongello, Louis A. - *The Walt Disney World Trivia Book*
Bwatch - Dec 2004 - pNA [51-500]

Mongillo, John F. - *Teen Guides to Environmental Science, vols. 1-5*
Cur R - v44 - i5 - Jan 2005 - p12(1) [51-500]
SciTech - v28 - i4 - Dec 2004 - p6(1) [1-50]

Monhollon, Rusty L. - *"This Is America?" The Sixties in Lawrence, Kansas*
J Am St - v38 - i2 - August 2004 - p364(1) [501+]

Monin, Lydia - *The Devil's Gardens: A History of Landmines*
JPR - v41 - i4 - July 2004 - p522-522 [501+]

Moning, Karen Marie - *The Immortal Highlander*
BL - v100 - i22 - August 2004 - p1910(1) [51-500]

Moniz, B.J. - *Welding Skills, 3rd Ed.*
SciTech - v28 - i4 - Dec 2004 - p169(1) [51-500]

Monk, Isabell - *Blackberry Stew (Illus. by Porter, Janice Lee)*
c KR - v73 - i2 - Jan 15 2005 - p123(1) [51-500]

Monk, Paul M.S. - *Physical Chemistry; Understanding Our Chemical World*
SciTech - v28 - i3 - Sept 2004 - p52(1) [1-50]

Monks, Lydia - *Aaaarrgghh! Spider!*
c KR - v72 - i13 - July 1 2004 - p634(1) [51-500]
c SLJ - v50 - i9 - Sept 2004 - p181(1) [51-500]

Monks, Robert A.G. - *Corporate Governance, 3rd Ed.*
R&R Bk N - v19 - i1 - Feb 2004 - p97(1) [51-500]

Monks, William - *A History of Southern Missouri and Northern Arkansas: Being an Account of the Early Settlements, the Civil War, the Ku-Klux, and Times of Peace*
Choice - v42 - i1 - Sept 2004 - p176(1) [501+]

Monmonier, Mark - *Rhumb Lines and Map Wars: A Social History of the Mercator Projection*
Lon R Bks - v26 - i21 - Nov 4 2004 - p6(1) [1-50]

Monmonier, Mark S. - *Rhumb Lines and Map Wars: A Social History of the Mercator Projection*
New Sci - v184 - i2472 - Nov 6 2004 - p53(1) [51-500]
TimHES - v0 - i1677 - Feb 4 2005 - p30(1) [501+]

Spying with Maps: Surveillance Technologies and the Future of Privacy
T&C - v45 - i3 - July 2004 - p675-676 [501+]

Monod, Paul Kleber - *The Murder of Mr. Grebell: Madness and Civility in an English Town*
CHE - v50 - i25 - Feb 27 2004 - pA17-A17 [501+]

Monolescu, Dominique - *The Distance Education Evolution: Issues and Case Studies*
Choice - v42 - i1 - Sept 2004 - p159(1) [501+]
R&R Bk N - v19 - i1 - Feb 2004 - p193(1) [51-500]

Monoson, S. Sara - *Plato's Democratic Entanglements: Athenian Politics and the Practice of Philosophy*
Phil R - v112 - i4 - Oct 2003 - p561(6) [501+]

Monpetit, Eric - *Misplaced Distrust: Policy Networks and the Environment in France , the United States, and Canada*
R&R Bk N - v19 - i3 - August 2004 - p91(1) [51-500]

Monroe, Barbara - *Crossing the Digital Divide: Race, Writing, and Technology in the Classroom*
Choice - v42 - i4 - Dec 2004 - p711(1) [1-50]
TCR - v107 - i2 - Feb 2005 - p339(4) [501+]

Monroe, Colleen - *A Is For Ark (Illus. by Monroe, Michael Glenn)*
c CH Bwatch - v14 - i9 - Sept 2004 - p3(1) [51-500]
A Is for Ark: Noah's Journey (Illus. by Monroe, Michael Glenn)
c SLJ - v51 - i1 - Jan 2005 - p96(1) [51-500]

Monroe, Dan - *The Republican Vision of John Tyler*
AHR - v109 - i3 - June 2004 - p904(1) [501+]
JAH - v91 - i1 - June 2004 - p238-239 [501+]
JSH - v70 - i3 - August 2004 - p672(2) [501+]
SHQ - v107 - i3 - Jan 2004 - p482(2) [501+]

Monroe, James S. - *Physical Geology: Exploring the Earth, 5th Ed.*
SciTech - v28 - i3 - Sept 2004 - p54(1) [1-50]

Monroe, Judy - *Chief Red Cloud, 1822-1909*
c SLJ - v50 - i7 - July 2004 - p92(1) [51-500]
A Day in the Life of a Librarian
c SLJ - v51 - i1 - Jan 2005 - p109(1) [51-500]

Monroe, Lucy - *3 Brides for 3 Bad Boys*
BL - v101 - i9-10 - Jan 1 2005 - p832(1) [1-50]
The Real Deal
BL - v101 - i1 - Sept 1 2004 - p73(1) [51-500]

Monroe, Mary - *Red Light Wives*
Black Iss - v7 - i1 - Jan-Feb 2005 - p65(1) [51-500]

Monroy, Manuel - *Daybreak, Nightfall*
LibMed - v22 - i4 - Jan 2004 - p70(1) [501+]

Monseau, Virginia R. - *A Curriculum of Peace: Selected Essays from English Journal*
y VOYA - v27 - i4 - Oct 2004 - p337(1) [51-500]

Monserud, Robert A. - *Compatible Forest Management*
SciTech - v28 - i1 - March 2004 - p131(1) [51-500]

Monsma, Bradley John - *The Sespe Wild: Southern California's Last Free River*
Choice - v42 - i6 - Feb 2005 - p1047(1) [51-500]

Monsma, Stephen V. - *Putting Faith in Partnerships: Welfare-to-Work in Four Cities*
Choice - v42 - i5 - Jan 2005 - p935(2) [51-500]

Monson-Haefel, Richard - *Enterprise JavaBeans, 4th Ed.*
SciTech - v28 - i4 - Dec 2004 - p20(1) [1-50]
Exceptional C++ Style; 40 New Engineering Puzzles, Programming Problems, and Solutions
SciTech - v28 - i4 - Dec 2004 - p20(1) [1-50]
J2EE Web Services
SciTech - v28 - i1 - March 2004 - p156(1) [51-500]

Monson, Ingrid - *The African Diaspora: A Musical Perspective*
Notes - v61 - i1 - Sept 2004 - p109(3) [501+]

Montague, John - *Smashing the Piano*
Sew R - v111 - i3 - Summer 2003 - p486-492 [501+]

Montague, Terrence - *Patients First: Closing the Health Care Gap in Canada*
Globe & Mail - Dec 24 2004 - pD13 [1-50]

Montanari, Eva - *Dino Bikes*
c SLJ - v50 - i9 - Sept 2004 - p175(1) [51-500]
Tiff, Taff, and Lulu
c CCB-B - v58 - i2 - Oct 2004 - p91(2) [51-500]
c HB - v80 - i5 - Sept-Oct 2004 - p573(1) [51-500]
c KR - v72 - i14 - July 15 2004 - p691(1) [51-500]
c PW - v251 - i30 - July 26 2004 - p53(2) [51-500]
c SLJ - v50 - i9 - Sept 2004 - p175(2) [51-500]

Montanari, F. - *Omero tremila anni dopo. Atti del Congresso di Genova 6-8 luglio 2000. Con la collaborazione di P. Ascheri*
Class R - v54 - i2 - Nov 2004 - p278-281 [501+]

Montanari, Julie - *Knit It Now!*
Bwatch - v26 - i9 - Sept 2004 - p10(2) [51-500]

Montanari, Richard - *The Rosary Girls*
BL - v101 - i8 - Dec 15 2004 - p691(1) [51-500]
KR - v72 - i23 - Dec 1 2004 - p1122(1) [501+]
LJ - v130 - i1 - Jan 1 2005 - p99(1) [51-500]
PW - v251 - i50 - Dec 13 2004 - p43(1) [51-500]

Montandon, Alain - *Desirs d'hospitalite: de Homere a Kafka*
FS - v58 - i1 - Jan 2004 - p145(2) [501+]
L'Hospitalite dans les contes
FS - v58 - i2 - April 2004 - p296(2) [501+]
L'Hospitalite: signes et rites
FS - v58 - i1 - Jan 2004 - p146(2) [501+]

Montano, John Patrick - *Courting the Moderates: Ideology, Propaganda, and the Emergence of Party, 1660-1678.*
Albion - v36 - i1 - Spring 2004 - p128(3) [501+]

Montano, Josie - *Snot Fair!*
c Sch Lib - v52 - i3 - Autumn 2004 - p146(2) [501+]

Montefiore, Sebag - *Stalin: The Court of the Red Tsar*
Atl - v294 - i1 - July-August 2004 - p165(4) [501+]
Choice - v42 - i4 - Dec 2004 - p717(1) [1-50]
CR - v285 - i1662 - July 2004 - p50(2) [501+]
NL - v87 - i4 - July-August 2004 - p24(1) [501+]
VQR - v80 - i2 - Spring 2004 - p253-253 [501+]

Monteith, Moira - *ICT for Curriculum Enhancement*
R&R Bk N - v19 - i3 - August 2004 - p216(1) [1-50]

Monteleone, Thomas F. - *Fearful Symmetries*
PW - v251 - i46 - Nov 15 2004 - p45(2) [51-500]

Montero, Alfred - *Decentralization and Democracy in Latin America Notre Dame*
Pers PS - v33 - i4 - Fall 2004 - p235(1) [501+]

Montero, Maritza - *Leadership and Organization for Community Prevention and Intervention in Venezuela*
R&R Bk N - v19 - i4 - Nov 2004 - p126(1) [51-500]

Montford, Angela - *Health, Sickness, Medicine and the Friars in the Thirteenth and Fourteenth Centuries*
SciTech - v28 - i4 - Dec 2004 - p76(1) [51-500]

Montgomery, Arch - *Jake*
y VOYA - v27 - i3 - August 2004 - p222(1) [1-50]

Montgomery, Charles - *The Last Heathen: Encounters with Ghosts and Ancestors in Melanesia*
Globe & Mail - Sept 25 2004 - pD3 [501+]
Globe & Mail - Nov 3 2004 - pT1 [501+]
Globe & Mail - Nov 27 2004 - pD3 [51-500]

Montgomery, John - *Tikal: An Illustrated History of the Ancient Maya Capital*
Lat Ant - v15 - i4 - Dec 2004 - p472(2) [501+]

Montgomery, John D. - *Beyond Reconstruction in Afghanistan: Lessons from Development Experience*
Choice - v42 - i7 - March 2005 - p1275(1) [51-500]

Montgomery, Kathleen - *Creating e-Portfolios using PowerPoint: A Guide for Educators*
R&R Bk N - v19 - i3 - August 2004 - p216(1) [1-50]

Montgomery, L.M. - *Anne of Green Gables. Audiobook Review*
Globe & Mail - Nov 27 2004 - pD49 [1-50]
Anne's House of Dreams (Read by Caruso, Barbara). Audiobook Review
c BL - v101 - i1 - Sept 1 2004 - p148(1) [51-500]
c Kliatt - v38 - i6 - Nov 2004 - p41(1) [51-500]
c SLJ - v50 - i10 - Oct 2004 - p83(2) [51-500]
Rainbow Valley (Read by Caruso, Barbara). Audiobook Review
c SLJ - v51 - i2 - Feb 2005 - p76(1) [501+]
The Selected Journals of L.M. Montgomery: Volume V, 1935-1942
Globe & Mail - Oct 16 2004 - pD6 [501+]
Globe & Mail - Nov 27 2004 - pD3 [51-500]

Montgomery, M.R. - *A Cow's Life: The Surprising History of Cattle and How the Black Angus Came to Be Home on the Range*
y BL - v101 - i4 - Oct 15 2004 - p372(1) [51-500]
LJ - v129 - i7 - Oct 15 2004 - p80(1) [51-500]
PW - v251 - i34 - August 23 2004 - p46(1) [51-500]

Montgomery, Marion - *Eudora Welty and Walker Percy: The Concept of Home in Their Lives and Literature*
R&R Bk N - v19 - i1 - Feb 2004 - p246(1) [51-500]

Montgomery, Michael B. - *Dictionary of Smoky Mountain English*
Choice - v42 - i2 - Oct 2004 - p268(1) [501+]
JSH - v70 - i4 - Nov 2004 - p991(1) [501+]
NYTBR - Nov 21 2004 - p32 [501+]

Montgomery, S. - *The Tarantula Scientist (Illus. by Bishop, Nic)*
SLJ - v50 - i10 - Oct 2004 - pS42(1) [51-500]

Montgomery, Scott L. - *The Chicago Guide to Communicating Science*
Phys Today - v57 - i7 - July 2004 - p59-60 [501+]
QRB - v79 - i4 - Dec 2004 - p395(5) [501+]

Montgomery, Sy - *Search for the Golden Moon Bear: Science and Adventure in Southeast Asia*
c BL - v101 - i7 - Dec 1 2004 - p665(1) [51-500]
Search for the Golden Moon Bear: Science and Adventure in the Asian Tropics
c CCB-B - v58 - i4 - Dec 2004 - p176(2) [51-500]
y KR - v72 - i21 - Nov 1 2004 - p1045(1) [51-500]
y SLJ - v50 - i12 - Dec 2004 - p164(1) [51-500]
The Tarantula Scientist (Illus. by Bishop, Nic)
c Five Owls - v18 - i1 - Fall 2004 - p25(2) [51-500]
y HB - v80 - i4 - July-August 2004 - p469(1) [51-500]

Monthei, Betty - *Looking for Normal*
c KR - v73 - i5 - March 1 2005 - p292(1) [51-500]

Monticello, Valentino - *Opera & Wine/Wine in Opera*
ON - v69 - i8 - Feb 2005 - p80(2) [501+]

Montiel, Peter J. - *Macroeconomics in Emerging Markets*
JEL - v41 - i4 - Dec 2003 - p1334(1) [501+]

Montparker, Carol - *The Blue Piano and Other Stories.*
Am MT - v54 - i1 - August-Sept 2004 - p98(1) [501+]

Montreal Protocol on Substances that Deplete the Ozone Layer: Report of the Technology and Economic Assessment Panel, April 2002, vols. 1-3
SciTech - v28 - i4 - March 2004 - p53(1) [51-500]

Montric, Chad - *To Save the Land and People: A History of Opposition to Surface Coal Mining in Appalachia*
JAH - v91 - i1 - June 2004 - p338-339 [501+]

Montuschi, Eleonora - *The Objects of Social Science*
R&R Bk N - v19 - i3 - August 2004 - p90(1) [501+]

Montville, Leigh - *Ted Williams: The Biography of an American Hero (Read by Brick, Scott). Audiobook Review*
BL - v101 - i1 - Sept 1 2004 - p146(1) [51-500]
BL - v101 - i9-10 - Jan 1 2005 - p778(1) [1-50]
Kliatt - v38 - i6 - Nov 2004 - p57(1) [51-500]
Ted Williams: The Biography of an American Hero
BL - v101 - i1 - Sept 1 2004 - p46(1) [51-500]
BooChiTr - May 9 2004 - p1(2) [501+]
Choice - v42 - i2 - Oct 2004 - p331(1) [51-500]

Monypenny, William - *The Life of Benjamin Disraeli, Earl of Beaconsfield*
Globe & Mail - Dec 18 2004 - pD27 [51-500]

Moock, Colin - *Essential ActionScript 2.0.*
SciTech - v28 - i3 - Sept 2004 - p21(1) [51-500]

Mood, Terry Ann - *American Regional Folklore: A Sourcebook and Research Guide*
LJ - v130 - i1 - Jan 1 2005 - p154(2) [51-500]
American Regional Folkore: A Sourcebook and Research Guide
Bwatch - Nov 2004 - pNA [51-500]
Choice - v42 - i6 - Feb 2005 - p1005(1) [51-500]

Moody, Glyn - *Digital Code of Life: How Bioinformatics Is Revolutionizing Science, Medicine, and Business*
Choice - v42 - i2 - Oct 2004 - p318(1) [51-500]
SB - v40 - i5 - Sept-Oct 2004 - p204(1) [501+]

Moody, Joanna - *The Private Correspondence of Jane Lady Cornwallis Bacon, 1613-1644*
R&R Bk N - v19 - i1 - Feb 2004 - p32(1) [1-50]

Moody, Neville R. - *Hydrogen Effects on Material Behavior and Corrosion Deformation Interactions: Proceedings*
SciTech - v28 - i3 - Sept 2004 - p53(1) [1-50]

Moody, Skye Kathleen - *The Good Diamond*
BL - v100 - i22 - August 2004 - p1906(2) [51-500]
BW - v34 - i36 - Sept 5 2004 - p10(1) [501+]
LJ - v129 - i13 - August 2004 - p60(1) [501+]

Moogk, Peter - *Building a House in New France: An Account of the Perplexities of Client and Craftsmen in Early Canada*
CBRA - Annual 2003 - p119(1) [51-500]

Mooij, Marieke K. de - *Ageless Marketing: Strategies for Reaching Hearts and Minds of the New Customer Majority*
R&R Bk N - v19 - i1 - Feb 2004 - p107(1) [51-500]

Moon, Bruce L. - *Art and Soul: Reflections on an Artistic Psychology, 2nd Ed.*
SciTech - v28 - i4 - Dec 2004 - p97(1) [51-500]

Moon, Dawne - *God, Sex, and Politics: Homosexuality and Everyday Theologies*
Choice - v42 - i7 - March 2005 - p1268(1) [51-500]
Lam Bk Rpt - v13 - i4-5 - Nov-Dec 2004 - p33(2) [501+]

Moon, Elizabeth - *Marque and Reprisal*
BL - v101 - i1 - Sept 1 2004 - p75(1) [51-500]
Ent W - i790 - Oct 29 2004 - p71 [501+]
KR - v72 - i14 - July 15 2004 - p666(1) [51-500]
PW - v251 - i31 - August 2 2004 - p56(1) [501+]
Trading in Danger
Analog - v124 - i3 - March 2004 - p132(2) [501+]

Moon, Fabio - *Ursula*
PW - v251 - i36 - Sept 6 2004 - p48(1) [51-500]

Moon, Juno Who - *Yongbi the Invincible, Vol. 1*
PW - v251 - i37 - Sept 13 2004 - p60(1) [501+]

Moon, Nicola - *Tick-Tock, Drip-Drop!: A Bedtime Story (Illus. by Taylor, Eleanor)*
c SLJ - v50 - i11 - Nov 2004 - p113(1) [51-500]

Moon, Patrick - *Virgile's Vineyard: A Year in the Languedoc Wine Country*
KR - v72 - i15 - August 1 2004 - p729(1) [501+]
LJ - v129 - i13 - August 2004 - p106(1) [51-500]

Mooney, Amy M. - *Archibald J. Motley Jr.*
Black Iss - v6 - i6 - Nov-Dec 2004 - p42(1) [501+]

Mooney, Julie - *Encyclopedia of the Bizarre*
Bwatch - March 2005 - pNA [51-500]

Moor, James H. - *The Turning Test: The Elusive Standard of Artificial Intelligence*
Choice - v41 - i7 - March 2004 - p1329(1) [501+]

Moor, Margriet de - *The Kreutzer Sonata*
BL - v101 - i9-10 - Jan 1 2005 - p813(1) [1-50]
KR - v72 - i22 - Nov 15 2004 - p1060(1) [501+]
LJ - v130 - i2 - Feb 1 2005 - p67(1) [51-500]
NYTBR - Feb 13 2005 - p14 [501+]
PW - v252 - i2 - Jan 10 2005 - p38(1) [51-500]

Mooradian, John K. - *Disproportionate Confinement of African-American Juvenile Delinquents*
R&R Bk N - v19 - i1 - Feb 2004 - p145(1) [51-500]

Moorcock, Michael - *New Worlds: An Anthology*
KR - v72 - i20 - Oct 15 2004 - p990(1) [501+]
LJ - v129 - i19 - Nov 15 2004 - p55(1) [501+]

Moore, A.W. - *Noble in Reason, Infinite in Faculty: Themes and Variations in Kant's Moral and Religious Philosophy*
TLS - i5293 - Sept 10 2004 - p10-11 [501+]

Moore, Alan - *Across the Universe: The DC Universe Stories of Alan Moore*
LibMed - v22 - i6 - March 2004 - p69(1) [501+]
LibMed - v22 - i6 - March 2004 - p69(1) [501+]
Terra Obscura
BL - v101 - i1 - Sept 1 2004 - p78(1) [501+]
Tom Strong: Book Four
y BL - v101 - i9-10 - Jan 1 2005 - p836(1) [51-500]
Tom Strong Collected Edition
BL - v101 - i1 - Sept 1 2004 - p78(1) [501+]

Moore, Alasdair - *La Mortola: In the Footsteps of Thomas Hanbury*
TLS - i5293 - Sept 10 2004 - p25(1) [501+]

Moore, Andrew - *Realism and Christian Faith: God, Grammar, and Meaning*
JR - v84 - i4 - Oct 2004 - p642(2) [501+]
Rel St - v40 - i4 - Dec 2004 - p503(5) [501+]
TT - v61 - i2 - July 2004 - p260(3) [501+]

Moore, Ann - *'Til Morning Light*
y Kliatt - v39 - i1 - Jan 2005 - p16(1) [501+]
BL - v101 - i9-10 - Jan 1 2005 - p820(2) [51-500]

Moore, Anne-Elizabeth - *Hey, Kidz! Buy This Book: A Radical Primer on Corporate and Governmental Propaganda and Artistic Activism for Short People (Illus. by Kelso, Megan)*
y SLJ - v50 - i12 - Dec 2004 - p164(2) [51-500]

Moore, B. Winfred - *Warm Ashes: Issues in Southern History at the Dawn of the Twenty-first Century, Proceedings*
R&R Bk N - v19 - i3 - August 2004 - p73(1) [51-500]

Moore, Billy - *Little Brother Real Snake*
c Roundup M - v12 - i1 - Oct 2004 - p31(1) [51-500]
c SLJ - v50 - i7 - July 2004 - p110(1) [51-500]

Moore, Brenda L. - *Serving Our Country: Japanese American Women in the Military During World War II*
JAH - v91 - i2 - Sept 2004 - p685(2) [501+]

Moore, Charles B. - *Cemetery Records, the Town of Easton, Washington County, New York*
EFHM - v58 - i3 - May-June 2004 - p59(1) [51-500]

Moore, Charles E. - *Provocations: Spiritual Writings of Kierkegaard*
TT - v61 - i2 - July 2004 - p283(1) [501+]

Moore, Charlotte - *George and Sam*
TLS - i5291 - August 27 2004 - p10-11 [501+]

Moore, Christopher (b. 1950 -) - *Champlain (Illus. by Back, Francis)*
c BL - v101 - i4 - Oct 15 2004 - p402(1) [51-500]
c Globe & Mail - Sept 11 2004 - pD13 [51-500]
c Res Links - v10 - i1 - Oct 2004 - p26(1) [51-500]
c SLJ - v50 - i11 - Nov 2004 - p170(1) [51-500]

Moore, Christopher (b. 1952 -) - *Fighting for America: Black Soldiers--the Unsung Heroes of World War II*
BL - v101 - i7 - Dec 1 2004 - p628(1) [51-500]
LJ - v130 - i1 - Jan 1 2005 - p129(1) [51-500]
PW - v251 - i44 - Nov 1 2004 - p54(1) [501+]

Moore, Christopher (b. 1957 -) - *Fluke: or, I Know Why the Winged Whale Sings*
Globe & Mail - July 17 2004 - pD13 [1-50]
The Stupidest Angel: A Heartwarming Tale of Christmas Terror (Read by Roberts, Tony). Audiobook Review
PW - v251 - i49 - Dec 6 2004 - p20(1) [51-500]
The Stupidest Angel: A Heartwarming Tale of Christmas Terror
BL - v101 - i3 - Oct 1 2004 - p318(2) [51-500]
Ent W - i796 - Dec 10 2004 - p98 [51-500]
PW - v251 - i40 - Oct 4 2004 - p70(1) [51-500]
LJ - v129 - i19 - Nov 15 2004 - p51(1) [501+]

Moore, Christopher G. - *Waiting for the Lady*
BIC - v33 - i2 - March 2004 - p8(2) [501+]

Moore, Christopher J. - *In Other Words: A Language Lover's Guide to the Most Intriguing Words around the World*
y Globe & Mail - Dec 4 2004 - pD37 [51-500]

Moore, Clive - *New Guinea: Crossing Boundaries and History*
AHS - v35 - i124 - Oct 2004 - p388(2) [501+]

Moore, Deborah Dash - *GI Jews: How World War II Changed a Generation*
LJ - v129 - i13 - August 2004 - p94(2) [501+]
PW - v251 - i29 - July 19 2004 - p151(1) [501+]

Moore, Ellen K. - *Navajo Beadwork: Architectures of Light*
Am Ind CRJ - v28 - i2 - Spring 2004 - p164(3) [501+]

Moore, Gareth - *A Question of Truth: Christianity and Homosexuality*
Lam Bk Rpt - v13 - i4-5 - Nov-Dec 2004 - p30(3) [501+]

Moore, George - *Parnell and His Land*
LJ - v129 - i19 - Nov 15 2004 - p103(1) [51-500]

Moore, Harker - *A Mourning in Autumn*
LJ - v129 - i12 - July 2004 - p63(1) [51-500]

Moore, Harry R. - *Spanish Steps: One Man and His Ass on the Pilgrim Way to Santiago*
TLS - i5299 - Oct 22 2004 - p30-31 [51-500]
Travels with My Donkey: One Man and His Ass on a Pilgrimage to Santiago.
KR - v72 - i24 - Dec 15 2004 - p1187(2) [501+]
LJ - v129 - i20 - Dec 1 2004 - p147(1) [51-500]
PW - v251 - i48 - Nov 29 2004 - p29(1) [51-500]

Moore, Heidi - *Ida B. Wells-Barnett*
c SLJ - v50 - i11 - Nov 2004 - p128(2) [51-500]
A Mob of Meerkats
c CCB-B - v57 - i11 - July-August 2004 - p475(1) [501+]
c SLJ - v50 - i9 - Sept 2004 - p190(1) [51-500]

Moore, Hugh - *Sports Jokes*
c SLJ - v50 - i10 - Oct 2004 - p144(1) [51-500]

Moore, Jacqueline - *Management and Administration of Correctional Health*
SciTech - v28 - i4 - Dec 2004 - p10(1) [1-50]

Moore, James - *Bush's War for Reelection: Iraq, the White House, and the People*
R&R Bk N - v19 - i3 - August 2004 - p71(1) [51-500]

Moore, James F. - *Post-Shoah Dialogues: Re-Thinking Our Texts Together*
Choice - v42 - i3 - Nov 2004 - p501(1) [51-500]
R&R Bk N - v19 - i3 - August 2004 - p26(1) [1-50]

Moore, James P., Jr. - *One Nation under God: The History of Prayer in America*
LJ - v130 - i1 - Jan 1 2005 - p118(1) [51-500]

Moore, Jeffrey - *The Memory Artists*
BIC - v33 - i8 - Nov 2004 - p13(2) [501+]
Globe & Mail - Nov 27 2004 - pD31 [501+]
TLS - i5294 - Sept 17 2004 - p22(1) [501+]

Moore, Jeffrey M. - *Spies for Nimitz: Joint Military Intelligence in the Pacific War*
J Mil H - v68 - i3 - July 2004 - p1006-1008 [501+]

Moore, John A. - *From Genesis to Genetics: The Case of Evolution and Creationism*
Isis - v95 - i2 - June 2004 - p337(2) [501+]

Moore, John Norton - *Solving the War Puzzle: Beyond the Democratic Peace*
Choice - v42 - i2 - Oct 2004 - p369(1) [51-500]

Moore, Judith - *Fat Girl: A True Story*
y BL - v101 - i7 - Dec 1 2004 - p622(1) [51-500]
Ent W - i809 - March 4 2005 - p78 [51-500]
KR - v72 - i21 - Nov 1 2004 - p1039(1) [51-500]
LJ - v130 - i2 - Feb 1 2005 - p93(2) [51-500]
NW - March 7 2005 - p55 [51-500]
PW - v251 - i42 - Oct 18 2004 - p54(1) [51-500]

Moore, Laurence R. - *The American Century in Europe*
AHR - v109 - i2 - April 2004 - p489(3) [501+]

Moore, Lilian - *Mural on Second Avenue: And Other City Poems (Illus. by Karas, Roma)*
c PW - v252 - i11 - March 14 2005 - p69(2) [51-500]

Moore, Lisa Lynne - *Dangerous Intimacies*
Eight-C St - v36 - i2 - Winter 2003 - p275 [501+]

Moore, Liz - *Zizi and Tish (Illus. by Milkau, Liz)*
c CBRA - Annual 2003 - p460(1) [51-500]

Moore, Lloyd - *The Great Plague: The Story of London's Most Deadly Year*
HER - v119 - i483 - Sept 2004 - p1058(1) [1-50]

Moore, Lorrie - *The Best American Short Stories, 2004*
BL - v101 - i4 - Oct 15 2004 - p388(1) [51-500]
KR - v72 - i16 - August 15 2004 - p769(1) [501+]
PW - v251 - i40 - Oct 4 2004 - p68(1) [51-500]

Moore, Lucy - *Into the Canyon: Seven Years in Navajo Country*
Roundup M - v12 - i3 - Feb 2005 - p20(1) [51-500]
Maharanis: The Extraordinary Tale of Four Indian Queens and Their Journey from Purdah to Parliament
BL - v101 - i6 - Nov 15 2004 - p549(1) [51-500]
KR - v72 - i21 - Nov 1 2004 - p1039(1) [501+]
LJ - v130 - i2 - Feb 1 2005 - p98(1) [51-500]
PW - v252 - i1 - Jan 3 2005 - p49(1) [51-500]
Maharanis: The Lives and Times of Three Generations of Indian Princesses
Spec - v296 - i9189 - Sept 18 2004 - p55(2) [501+]
TLS - i5300 - Oct 29 2004 - p36(1) [501+]

Moore, Marianne - *Becoming Marianne Moore: The Early Poems, 1907-1924*
AL - v76 - i2 - June 2004 - p400(3) [501+]

Moore, Michael - *Dude, Where's My Country?*
R&R Bk N - v19 - i1 - Feb 2004 - pNA [51-500]
Objectivity in Ethics and Law
R&R Bk N - v19 - i3 - August 2004 - p11(1) [1-50]
The Official Fahrenheit 9/11 Reader
Globe & Mail - Oct 16 2004 - pD29 [501+]
Spec - v296 - i9199 - Nov 27 2004 - p47(2) [501+]
Will They Ever Trust Us Again?: Letters from the War Zone
Globe & Mail - Oct 16 2004 - pD29 [501+]
Spec - v296 - i9199 - Nov 27 2004 - p47(2) [501+]

Moore, Michele - *The Only Menopause Guide You'll Ever Need. 2nd Ed.*
PW - v251 - i45 - Nov 8 2004 - p47(1) [501+]

Moore, Mike - *A World Without Walls: Freedom, Development, Free Trade and Global Governance*
AJES - v63 - i3 - July 2004 - p753(4) [501+]

Moore, Oliver J. - *Rituals of Recruitment in Tang China: Reading an Annual Programme in the Collected Statements by Wang Dingbao*
R&R Bk N - v19 - i4 - Nov 2004 - p157(1) [501+]

Moore, Patrick - *Beyond Shame: Reclaiming the Abandoned History of Radical Gay Sexuality*
G&L Rev W - v11 - i6 - Nov-Dec 2004 - p40(2) [501+]
Firefly Atlas of the Universe
Sci Teach - v71 - i6 - July 2004 - p63-63 [501+]
SciTech - v28 - i1 - March 2004 - p43(1) [51-500]

Stars of Destiny
New Sci - v184 - i2476 - Dec 4 2004 - p54(1) [501+]

Moore, Peter - *Caught in the Act*
y HB - v81 - i2 - March-April 2005 - p206(1) [51-500]
y KR - v73 - i5 - March 1 2005 - p292(1) [51-500]

Moore, R. Laurence - *The American Century in Europe*
JAH - v91 - i3 - Dec 2004 - p1116(2) [501+]
Touchdown Jesus: The Mixing of Sacred and Secular in America History
J Ch St - v46 - i3 - Summer 2004 - p664(2) [501+]

Moore, Richard - *Boneyard*
BL - v101 - i9-10 - Jan 1 2005 - p836(1) [51-500]

Moore, Richard (b. 1960 -) - *Faces from the Flood: Hurricane Floyd Remembered*
Kliatt - v38 - i4 - July 2004 - p41(1) [51-500]

Moore, Richard W. - *Training That Works: Lessons from California's Employment Training Panel Program*
JEL - v42 - i1 - March 2004 - p281(2) [501+]

Moore, Robert M., III - *The Quality and Quantity of Contact: African Americans and Whites on College Campuses*
CS - v33 - i1 - Jan 2004 - p102-103 [501+]

Moore, Schuyler M. - *Taxation of the Entertainment Industry, 2004 Ed.*
R&R Bk N - v19 - i1 - Feb 2004 - pNA [51-500]

Moore, Sean - *Always Run Up the Stairs*
c CBRA - Annual 2003 - p360(1) [51-500]

Moore, Stephen D. - *New Testament Masculinities*
Intpr - v58 - i3 - July 2004 - p336(1) [51-500]
R&R Bk N - v19 - i3 - August 2004 - p24(1) [1-50]

Moore, Susanna - *One Last Look*
y Kliatt - v39 - i1 - Jan 2005 - p16(1) [51-500]

Moore, Terry - *Strangers in Paradise Treasury Edition*
PW - v251 - i46 - Nov 15 2004 - p43(2) [51-500]

Moore, Tim - *Spanish Steps*
Globe & Mail - Feb 19 2005 - pT7 [501+]

Moore, Wendy - *The Knife Man*
New Sci - v185 - i2489 - March 5 2005 - p57(1) [501+]
NS - v134 - i4728 - Feb 21 2005 - p51(1) [501+]
Spec - v297 - i9212 - Feb 26 2005 - p38(2) [501+]
TimHES - v0 - i1680 - Feb 25 2005 - p29(1) [501+]

Moore, Winfred B. - *Warm Ashes: Issues in Southern History at the Dawn of the Twenty-First Century*
HNet - Sept 2004 - pNA [501+]
JSH - v71 - i1 - Feb 2005 - p219(3) [501+]

Moorehead, Caroline - *Gellhorn: A Twentieth-Century Life*
NYTBR - Oct 24 2004 - p30 [501+]
Human Cargo: A Journey among Refugees
Econ - v374 - i8414 - Feb 19 2005 - p81US [501+]
KR - v72 - i24 - Dec 15 2004 - p1188(1) [501+]
NS - v134 - i4727 - Feb 14 2005 - p47(2) [501+]
PW - v252 - i3 - Jan 17 2005 - p42(1) [51-500]
Spec - v297 - i9210 - Feb 12 2005 - p39(2) [501+]
Iris Origo: Marchesa of Val d'Orcia
NYTBR - July 18 2004 - p20 [501+]
Martha Gellhorn: A Life
Globe & Mail - August 7 2004 - pD14 [1-50]
Lon R Bks - v26 - i17 - Sept 2 2004 - p26(3) [501+]

Moores, Phil - *Alisdair Gray: Critical Appreciations and a Bibliography*
SFS - v31 - i2 - July 2004 - p315-319 [501+]

Moores, Ted - *Kayaks You Can Build: An Illustrated Guide to Plywood Construction*
LJ - v129 - i20 - Dec 1 2004 - p157(1) [51-500]

Moorhead, Sue - *Nursing Outcomes Classification (NOC), 3rd Ed.*
SciTech - v28 - i1 - March 2004 - p126(1) [1-50]

Moote, A. Lloyd - *The Great Plague: The Story of London's Most Deadly Year*
Choice - v42 - i3 - Nov 2004 - p518(1) [1-50]
E-Streams - Nov 2004 - pNA [501+]
HER - v119 - i483 - Sept 2004 - p1058(2) [501+]
HNet - Oct 2004 - pNA [501+]

Mooz, Hal - *Communicating Project Management: The Integrated Vocabulary of Project Management and Systems*
SciTech - v28 - i1 - March 2004 - p134(1) [51-500]

Mora, Frank O. - *Latin American and Caribbean Foreign Policy*
Choice - v41 - i11-12 - July-August 2004 - p2117(1) [501+]
R&R Bk N - v19 - i1 - Feb 2004 - p67(1) [501+]

Moraga, Cherrie - *Watsonville/Circle in the Dirt*
Theat J - v56 - i3 - Oct 2004 - p523-525 [501+]

Morais, J. - *Integration of Advanced Micro- and Nanoelectronic Devices -- Critical Issues and Solutions: Proceedings*
SciTech - v28 - i4 - Dec 2004 - p156(1) [51-500]

The Moral of the Story (Illus. by Ward, Helen)
c PW - v251 - i36 - Sept 6 2004 - p65(1) [51-500]

Morales, Alfonso - *Renascent Pragmatism: Studies in Law and Social Science*
R&R Bk N - v19 - i1 - Feb 2004 - pNA [51-500]

Morales, Armando T. - *Social Work: A Profession of Many Faces, 10th Ed.*
R&R Bk N - v19 - i1 - Feb 2004 - p136(1) [51-500]

Morales, Erik E. - *Promoting Academic Resilience in Multicultural America: Factors Affecting Student Success*
R&R Bk N - v19 - i4 - Nov 2004 - p192(1) [501+]

Morales, Rodney - *When the Shark Bites*
Cont Pac - v16 - i2 - Fall 2004 - p438(3) [501+]

Moran, Bruce T. - *Distilling Knowledge: Alchemy, Chemistry, and the Scientific Revolution*
BL - v101 - i7 - Dec 1 2004 - p630(2) [51-500]
KR - v72 - i22 - Nov 15 2004 - p1081(1) [501+]

Moran, Daniel - *The People in Arms: Military Myth and National Mobilization Since the French Revolution*
HNet - August 2004 - pNA [501+]

Moran, Gerard - *Sending out Ireland's Poor: Assisted Emigration to North America in the Nineteenth Century*
R&R Bk N - v19 - i3 - August 2004 - p66(1) [51-500]
Sending out Ireland's Poor: Assisted Emigration to North America in the Nineteenth Century
Choice - v42 - i5 - Jan 2005 - p921(1) [1-50]

Moran, Katherine J. - *Diabetes: The Ultimate Teen Guide (Illus. by Merriman, Lisa P.)*
c SLJ - v50 - i8 - August 2004 - p140(1) [51-500]

Moran, Leslie J. - *Law's Moving Image*
TimHES - v0 - i1678 - Feb 11 2005 - p28(1) [501+]

Moran, Lindsay - *Blowing My Cover: My Life as a CIA Spy*
BL - v101 - i9-10 - Jan 1 2005 - p790(1) [1-50]
KR - v72 - i23 - Dec 1 2004 - p1136(2) [501+]
LJ - v130 - i1 - Jan 1 2005 - p124(1) [51-500]
PW - v251 - i51 - Dec 20 2004 - p50(1) [501+]

Moran, Mark - *Weird U.S.: Your Travel Guide to America's Local Legends and Best Kept Secrets*
LJ - v129 - i17 - Oct 15 2004 - p79(1) [51-500]

Moran, Michael - *Beyond the Coral Sea*
NS - v133 - i4716 - Nov 29 2004 - p42(1) [51-500]

Moran, Rachel F. - *Interracial Intimacy: The Regulation of Race and Romance*
Can Lit - i182 - Autumn 2004 - p160(3) [501+]

Moran, Ricardo - *Escaping the Poverty Trap: Investing in Children in Latin America*
R&R Bk N - v19 - i3 - August 2004 - p95(1) [51-500]

Moran, Richard - *Executioner's Current: Thomas Edison, George Westinghouse, and the Invention of the Electric Chair*
BHR - v78 - i1 - Spring 2004 - p116(4) [501+]

Moran, Robbin C. - *A Natural History of Ferns*
BL - v101 - i3 - Oct 1 2004 - p289(1) [51-500]
Choice - v42 - i6 - Feb 2005 - p1048(1) [51-500]
New Sci - v184 - Dec 25 2004 - p76(1) [501+]

Moran, Ronald - *Saying These Things*
South CR - v37 - i1 - Fall 2004 - p189-191 [501+]

Moran, Theodore H. - *International Political Risk Management: The Brave New World*
JEL - v42 - i1 - March 2004 - p268(1) [501+]
Reforming OPIC for the Twenty-First Century
JEL - v41 - i4 - Dec 2003 - p1361(1) [501+]

Moran, Thomas - *Anja the Liar*
NYTBR - Jan 23 2004 - p28 [501+]

Morana, Mabel - *Nuevas perspectivas desde/sobre America Latina: El desafio de los estudios culturales*
Hisp R - v72 - i2 - Spring 2004 - p332-334 [501+]

Morantz-Sanchez, Regina - *Conduct Unbecoming A Woman: Medicine on Trial in Turn-of-the-Century Brooklyn*
JWH - v16 - i3 - Autumn 2004 - p206(7) [501+]

Morata, Olympia Fulvia - *The Complete Writings of an Italian Heretic*
CHR - v90 - i3 - July 2004 - p552(2) [501+]

Moravcsik, Julius M.E. - *The Ties That Bind*
R&R Bk N - v20 - i1 - Feb 2005 - p10(1) [51-500]

Moravia, Alberto - *Boredom*
LJ - v129 - i16 - Oct 1 2004 - p121(1) [51-500]
Contempt
LJ - v129 - i16 - Oct 1 2004 - p121(1) [51-500]

Moraviec, Malgorzata - *Vision Europa: Deutsche und polnische Foderationsplane des 19. und fruhen 20. Jahrhunderts*
CEH - v37 - i3 - Summer 2004 - p440(3) [501+]

Morawetz, T - *Der Demos als tyrann und Banause. Aspekte antidemokratischer Polemik im Athen des 5. und 4. Jahrhunderts v. Chr*
Class R - v53 - i2 - Nov 2003 - p402-403 [501+]

Moray Eels
c SB - v40 - i3 - May-June 2004 - p133(1) [501+]

Morck, Irene - *Tough Trails*
c CBRA - Annual 2003 - p506(2) [51-500]

Mordaunt, Jason - *Welcome to Coolsville*
KR - v73 - i2 - Jan 15 2005 - p78(1) [501+]

Mordden, Ethan - *The Happiest Corpse I've Ever Seen: The Last Twenty-Five Years of the Broadway Musical*
BL - v101 - i5 - Nov 1 2004 - p460(1) [51-500]
The Happiest Corpse I've Ever Seen: The Last Twenty Five Years of the Broadway Musical
Choice - v42 - i6 - Feb 2005 - p1031(1) [51-500]
The Happiest Corpse I've Ever Seen: The Last Twenty-Five Years of the Broadway Musical
LJ - v129 - i18 - Nov 1 2004 - p86(2) [501+]
ON - v69 - i6 - Dec 2004 - p93(1) [501+]

Morden, Tony - *Principles of Management*
R&R Bk N - v19 - i3 - August 2004 - p103(1) [1-50]

Mordike, John - *'We Should Do This Thing Quietly': Japan and the Great Deception in Australian Defence Policy, 1911-1914*
AHS - v35 - i123 - April 2004 - p198-198 [501+]

Mordsley, Jessica - *Ghosts of the Old Year: New Welsh Short Fiction*
WLT - v78 - i3-4 - Sept-Dec 2004 - p155(1) [501+]

Mordue, Mark - *Dastgah: Diary of a Headtrip*
Globe & Mail - Jan 22 2005 - pT11 [501+]
LJ - v129 - i20 - Dec 1 2004 - p147(1) [51-500]

More Keep 'Em Reading Bulletin Boards: Year-Round Designs for the Library and Classroom (Illus. by Tusan, Stan)
c SLJ - v50 - i7 - July 2004 - p135(1) [51-500]

More, Thomas, Sir - *Thomas More: Utopia*
Six Ct J - v35 - i1 - Spring 2004 - p215(2) [501+]

Moreau, Joseph - *Schoolbook Nation: Conflicts over American History Textbooks from the Civil War to the Present*
Choice - v42 - i1 - Sept 2004 - p176(1) [501+]
TES - v0 - i4586 - June 4 2004 - psss19(1) [501+]

Moreau, Lynda - *Sweetly Southern: Delicious Desserts from the Sons of Confederate Veterans*
Bwatch - v26 - i8 - August 2004 - p3(1) [51-500]

Moreau, P. - *Incestus et prohibitae nuptiae. Conception romaine de l'inceste et histoire des prohibitions matrimoniales pour cause de parente dans la Rome antique*
Class R - v54 - i1 - May 2004 - p203(3) [501+]

Morecambe, Gary - *Cary Grant: In Name Only*
NYRB - v51 - i20 - Dec 16 2004 - p44(4) [501+]

Morecroft, Richard - *Zoo Album (Illus. by Lloyd-Diviny, Karen)*
c BL - v101 - i7 - Dec 1 2004 - p666(1) [51-500]
c SB - v40 - i6 - Nov-Dec 2004 - p271(1) [51-500]
c SLJ - v51 - i2 - Feb 2005 - p150(1) [51-500]

Morek, Irene - *Old Bird (Illus. by Wood, Muriel)*
c CBRA - Annual 2003 - p460(1) [51-500]

Morel, Lucas E. - *Ralph Ellison and the Raft of Hope: A Political Companion to Invisible Man*
Choice - v41 - i11-12 - July-August 2004 - p2046(1) [501+]

Moreland, Milton C. - *Between Text and Artifact: Integrating Archaeology in Biblical Studies Teaching*
Intpr - v58 - i3 - July 2004 - p336(1) [51-500]
R&R Bk N - v19 - i3 - August 2004 - p22(1) [1-50]

Morell, Abelardo - *Camera Obscura*
Globe & Mail - Dec 18 2004 - pD14 [1-50]

Morell, Samuel - *Studies in the Judicial Methodology of Rabbi David Ibn Abi Zimra*
R&R Bk N - v19 - i3 - August 2004 - p16(1) [1-50]

Moremen, Grace E. - *Adolphus Frederick, Duke of Cambridge--Steadfast Son of King George III, 1774-1850.*
Albion - v36 - i1 - Spring 2004 - p144(2) [501+]

Moreno, Barry - *Encyclopedia of Ellis Island*
LJ - v129 - i17 - Oct 15 2004 - p89(1) [51-500]

Moreno, Jonathan D. - *In the Wake of Terror: Medicine and Morality in a Time of Crisis*
AJPS - v39 - i2 - July 2004 - p469(469) [501+]
Ethics - v115 - i1 - Oct 2004 - p148(3) [501+]

Moreno, Julio - *Yankee Don't Go Home!: Mexican Nationalism, American Business Culture, and the Shaping of Modern Mexico, 1920-1950*
AHR - v109 - i4 - Oct 2004 - p1279-1280 [501+]
Ams - v61 - i2 - Oct 2004 - p298(3) [501+]

Moreno, Robyn - *Border-Line Personalities: A New Generation of Latinas Dish on Sex, Sass & Cultural Shifting*
BL - v100 - i21 - July 2004 - p1804(1) [1-50]

Morewitz, Stephen J. - *Domestic Violence and Maternal Child Health*
R&R Bk N - v19 - i3 - August 2004 - p166(1) [501+]

Morey, Anne - *Hollywood Outsiders: The Adaptation of the Film Industry, 1913-1934*
JouAmCul - v27 - i3 - Sept 2004 - p341(2) [501+]

Morey, Kathy - *Mau'i Trails: Walks, Strolls and Treks on the Valley Island, 3rd Ed.*
R&R Bk N - v19 - i1 - Feb 2004 - p51(1) [51-500]

Morford, M. - *The Roman Philosphers from the Time of Cato the Censor to the Death of Marcus Aurelius*
Class R - v53 - i2 - Nov 2003 - p349-350 [501+]

Morgan, Alisa - *Naked Fruit: Getting Honest about the Fruit of the Spirit*
PW - v251 - i30 - July 26 2004 - p50(1) [501+]

Morgan, Allen - *Quackadack Duck (Illus. by Beder, John)*
c CBRA - Annual 2003 - p461(1) [51-500]

Morgan, April L. - *Ethics and Global Politics: The Active Learning Sourcebook*
R&R Bk N - v19 - i3 - August 2004 - p159(1) [501+]

Morgan, Ben - *DK Guide to Mammals*
c LibMed - v22 - i5 - Feb 2004 - p59(1) [501+]
Gases
c SB - v40 - i4 - July-August 2004 - p173(1) [51-500]
Gravity
c SB - v40 - i4 - July-August 2004 - p173(1) [51-500]
Liquids
c SB - v40 - i4 - July-August 2004 - p173(1) [51-500]
Magnetism
c LibMed - v23 - i1 - August-Sept 2004 - p79(1) [51-500]
c SB - v40 - i4 - July-August 2004 - p173(1) [51-500]
Motion
c SB - v40 - i4 - July-August 2004 - p173(1) [51-500]
Solids
c SB - v40 - i4 - July-August 2004 - p173(1) [51-500]

Morgan, David W. - *Whips and Whipmaking, 2nd Ed.*
R&R Bk N - v19 - i4 - Nov 2004 - p250(1) [501+]

Morgan, Diane - *The Buddhist Experience in America*
LJ - v130 - i3 - Feb 15 2005 - p160(1) [51-500]

Morgan, Edmund - *The Meaning of Independence: John Adams, George Washington, and Thomas Jefferson*
Atl - v295 - i2 - March 2005 - p104(1) [51-500]

Morgan, Edmund Sears - *American Slavery, American Freedom: The Ordeal of Colonial Virginia*
R&R Bk N - v19 - i3 - August 2004 - p67(1) [51-500]
The Meaning of Independence: John Adams, George Washington, and Thomas Jefferson
R&R Bk N - v19 - i3 - August 2004 - p67(1) [51-500]

Morgan, Edwin - *Beowulf*
Lon R Bks - v26 - i22 - Nov 18 2004 - p26(2) [501+]
Cathures
Lon R Bks - v26 - i22 - Nov 18 2004 - p26(2) [501+]

Morgan, Forrest E. - *Compellence and the Strategic Culture of Imperial Japan: Implications for Coercive Diplomacy in the Twenty-First Century*
Choice - v41 - i11-12 - July-August 2004 - p2101(2) [501+]

Morgan, Gwenda - *Eighteenth-Century Criminal Transportation: The Formation of the Criminal Atlantic*
Choice - v42 - i4 - Dec 2004 - p713(1) [1-50]

Morgan, Hiram - *The Battle of Kinsale*
J Mil H - v68 - i4 - Oct 2004 - p1245-1247 [501+]

Morgan, Hywel - *Electrostatics 2003: Proceedings*
SciTech - v28 - i4 - Sept 2004 - p50(1) [51-500]

Morgan, James - *Chasing Matisse: A Year in France Living My Dream*
PW - v252 - i8 - Feb 21 2005 - p166(1) [51-500]

Morgan, Jeff - *The Working Parents Cookbook*
Time - v164 - i3 - July 19 2004 - p83 [501+]

Morgan, Jennifer L. - *Laboring Women: Reproduction and Gender in New World Slavery*
Choice - v42 - i5 - Jan 2005 - p917(1) [1-50]

Morgan, John D. - *Death and Bereavement around the World, vol. 3*
R&R Bk N - v19 - i3 - August 2004 - p13(1) [1-50]

Morgan, Kathleen O'Leary - *State Trends: Measuring Change in the 50 United States*
Choice - v42 - i5 - Jan 2005 - p839(1) [1-50]

Morgan, Kenneth - *The British Transatlantic Slave Trade, Vols. 1-4*
R&R Bk N - v19 - i3 - August 2004 - p157(1) [51-500]

Morgan, M. Granger - *Science and Technology Advice for Congress*
SciTech - v28 - i4 - Dec 2004 - p13(1) [1-50]

Morgan, Mark - *Obstetrics and Gynecology, 5th Ed.*
SciTech - v28 - i3 - Sept 2004 - p116(1) [51-500]

Morgan, Michael - *The Space between Our Ears: How the Brain Represents Visual Space*
TimHES - v0 - i1660 - Oct 1 2004 - p29(1) [501+]
TLS - i5286 - July 23 2004 - p27(1) [501+]

Morgan, Michaela - *Brave, Brave Mouse (Illus. by Cartlidge, Michelle)*
c BL - v101 - i9-10 - Jan 1 2005 - p872(1) [51-500]
c SLJ - v50 - i11 - Nov 2004 - p113(1) [51-500]

Morgan, Nicola - *Chicken Friend*
y KR - v73 - i4 - Feb 15 2005 - p234(1) [51-500]
Fleshmarket
y CCB-B - v58 - i2 - Oct 2004 - p92(1) [51-500]
HB - v80 - i5 - Sept-Oct 2004 - p594(1) [51-500]
y KR - v72 - i14 - July 15 2004 - p691(1) [51-500]
y SLJ - v50 - i9 - Sept 2004 - p213(1) [51-500]

Morgan, Patrick M. - *Deterrence Now*
VQR - v80 - i1 - Wntr 2004 - p267-268 [501+]

Morgan, Philippa - *Chaucer and the House of Fame*
BL - v101 - i1 - Sept 1 2004 - p70(1) [501+]
KR - v72 - i15 - August 1 2004 - p717(1) [51-500]
PW - v251 - i31 - August 2 2004 - p55(1) [501+]

Morgan, Richard - *Market Forces*
PW - v252 - i4 - Jan 24 2005 - p226(1) [501+]

Morgan, Richard K. - *Broken Angels*
BW - v34 - i12 - March 21 2004 - p13(1) [501+]
Market Forces
BL - v101 - i9-10 - Jan 1 2005 - p834(1) [1-50]
LJ - v130 - i3 - Feb 15 2005 - p123(1) [51-500]
Ent W - i810 - March 11 2005 - p108 [51-500]

Morgan, Ruth P. - *Governance by Decree: The Impact of the Voting Rights Act in Dallas*
Choice - v42 - i3 - Nov 2004 - p565-2 [1-50]

Morgan, Sue - *Women, Religion, and Feminism in Britain, 1750-1900*
HNet - Sept 2004 - pNA [501+]

Morgan, Ted - *Reds: McCarthyism in Twentieth-Century America*
Choice - v42 - i2 - Oct 2004 - p357(1) [501+]
JAH - v91 - i3 - Dec 2004 - p1081(2) [501+]

Morgan, Thomas D. - *Professional Responsibility: Problems and Materials, 8th Ed.*
R&R Bk N - v19 - i3 - August 2004 - p196(1) [1-50]

Morgan, W. John - *Law and Opinion in Twentieth-Century Britain and Ireland*
AHR - v109 - i3 - June 2004 - p981(2) [501+]

Morgan, William - *American Country Churches*
CC - v121 - i25 - Dec 14 2004 - p23(1) [51-500]

Morgenroth, Kate - *Jude*
y BL - v101 - i6 - Nov 15 2004 - p584(2) [51-500]
y Kliatt - v38 - i6 - Nov 2004 - p10(1) [51-500]
c KR - v72 - i18 - Sept 15 2004 - p916(1) [51-500]
y PW - v251 - i47 - Nov 22 2004 - p60(2) [51-500]
y SLJ - v50 - i11 - Nov 2004 - p150(1) [51-500]
y VOYA - v27 - i5 - Dec 2004 - p386(1) [51-500]

Morgenstern, Dan - *Living with Jazz*
BL - v101 - i5 - Nov 1 2004 - p461(1) [51-500]
KR - v72 - i18 - Sept 15 2004 - p905(1) [51-500]
NYTBR - Dec 19 2004 - p9 [501+]
PW - v251 - i42 - Oct 18 2004 - p58(1) [501+]

Morgenstern, Julie - *Making Work Work: New Strategies for Surviving and Thriving at the Office*
HR Mag - v50 - i2 - Feb 2005 - pS3(1) [501+]

Morgenstern, Scott - *Patterns of Legislative Politics: Roll-Call Voting in Latin America and United States*
Choice - v42 - i5 - Jan 2005 - p928(1) [51-500]

Morgenstierne, Christopher Munthe - *Denmark and the National Liberation in Southern Africa*
IJAHS - v37 - i1 - Wntr 2004 - p190-190 [501+]

Morgenthaler, Jefferson - *River Has Never Divided Us: A Border History of La Junta de los Rios*
Roundup M - v12 - i1 - Oct 2004 - p24(1) [51-500]

Morgolis, Joseph - *Reinventing Pragmatism: American Philosophy at the End of the Twentieth Century*
CS - v33 - i2 - March 2004 - p250-252 [501+]

Morhardt, Sia - *California Desert Flowers: An Introduction to Families, Genera, and Species (Illus. by Morhardt, Sia)*
QRB - v79 - i4 - Dec 2004 - p428(2) [501+]
California Desert Flowers: An Introduction to Families, Genera, and Species (Illus. by Morhardt, Emil)
Choice - v42 - i5 - Jan 2005 - p880(1) [1-50]

Mori, Gianluca - *Bayle Philosophe*
Eight-C St - v37 - i3 - Spring 2004 - p510-520 [501+]

Mori, Kyoko - *Polite Lies and the Dream of Water*
Globe & Mail - Dec 24 2004 - pD3 [1-50]

Moriarty, Catherine - *The Sculpture of Gilbert Ledward*
R&R Bk N - v19 - i3 - August 2004 - p242(1) [51-500]

Moriarty, J.T. - *Frontier Hero*
c SLJ - v50 - i12 - Dec 2004 - p126(1) [51-500]
The Rise of American Capitalism: The Growth of American Banks
y SLJ - v50 - i11 - Nov 2004 - p160(1) [501+]

Moriarty, Jaclyn - *The Year of Secret Assignments*
y BL - v101 - i9-10 - Jan 1 2005 - p772(1) [51-500]
HB - v81 - i1 - Jan-Feb 2005 - p15(2) [51-500]
LibMed - v22 - i7 - April-May 2004 - p63(63) [501+]

Moriarty, Laura - *Self-Destruction*
PW - v251 - i38 - Sept 20 2004 - p59(1) [51-500]

Moriarty, Michael - *Early Modern French Thought*
TLS - i5298 - Oct 15 2004 - p6(1) [501+]

Moriarty, Sinead - *The Baby Trail*
KR - v73 - i4 - Feb 15 2005 - p193(1) [501+]

Moriarty, Thomas A. - *Finding the Words: A Rhetorical History of South Africa's Transistion from Apartheid and Democracy*
R&R Bk N - v19 - i1 - Feb 2004 - p51(1) [51-500]

Morimoto, Rand - *Microsoft Windows Server 2003 Unleashed*
Bwatch - v26 - i8 - August 2004 - p6(1) [51-500]

Morin, Isobel V. - *Politics, American Style: Political Parties in American History*
c SLJ - v50 - i8 - August 2004 - p49(1) [51-500]

Morina, Domenico Maria - *Argonauti di via telegrafo*
WLT - v78 - i3-4 - Sept-Dec 2004 - p132(1) [501+]

Morita, Ken - *Economic Reforms and Capital Markets in Central Europe*
R&R Bk N - v19 - i4 - Nov 2004 - p119(1) [51-500]

Moritz, A.F. - *Early Poems*
CBRA - Annual 2003 - p226(2) [51-500]
Night Street Repairs
BIC - v33 - i9 - Dec 2004 - p34(3) [501+]
Poet - v185 - i2 - Nov 2004 - p139(2) [501+]

Moriyama, Yukiko - *Favourite Japanese Dishes*
y Kliatt - v39 - i1 - Jan 2005 - p37(1) [51-500]
A Taste of Tofu
y Kliatt - v39 - i1 - Jan 2005 - p37(1) [51-500]

Mork, Geir - *Den reflekterte latteren: Pa spor etter Arne Garborgs ironi*
Scan St - v76 - i4 - Winter 2004 - p552(3) [501+]

Morkes, Andrew - *College Exploration on the Internet: A Student and Counselor's Guide to More than 500 Web Sites*
y VOYA - v27 - i4 - Oct 2004 - p322(2) [51-500]

Morkot, Robert G. - *Historical Dictionary of Ancient Egyptian Warfare*
R&R Bk N - v19 - i1 - Feb 2004 - p50(1) [51-500]

Morland, Dave - *Political Issues for the Twenty-First Century*
R&R Bk N - v19 - i4 - Nov 2004 - p150(1) [501+]

Morley, G. David - *Explorations in Functional Syntax: A New Framework for Lexicogrammatical Analysis*
R&R Bk N - v19 - i4 - Nov 2004 - p213(1) [501+]

Morley, Georgina - *John Macquarrie's Natural Theology: The Grace of Being*
R&R Bk N - v19 - i1 - Feb 2004 - p25(1) [51-500]

Morley, Simon - *Writing on the Wall: Word and Image in Modern Art*
TLS - i5268 - March 19 2004 - p18-18 [501+]

Morley, Vincent - *Irish Opinion and the American Revolution, 1760-1783*
HER - v119 - i483 - Sept 2004 - p995(2) [501+]

Morman, Edward T. - *Catalog of the Robert L. Sadoff Library of Forensic Psychiatry and Legal Medicine*
SciTech - v28 - i3 - Sept 2004 - p87(1) [51-500]

Morneau, Robert F. - *Waiting in Joyful Hope: Daily Reflections for Advent & Christmas, 2004-2005*
LJ - v129 - i12 - July 2004 - p89(2) [51-500]

Morone, James A. - *Hellfire Nation: The Politics of Sin in American History*
AHR - v109 - i3 - June 2004 - p893(2) [501+]
HM - v309 - i1854 - Nov 2004 - p91(6) [501+]
JAH - v91 - i2 - Sept 2004 - p597(2) [501+]
JIH - v35 - i1 - Summer 2004 - p145-146 [501+]

Morone, James S. - *Hillfire Nation: The Politics of Sin in American History*
Am St - v45 - i1 - Spring 2004 - p135-136 [501+]

Morpurgo, Michael - *Dolphin Boy*
c   KR - v73 - i1 - Jan 1 2005 - p55(1) [51-500]
Little Albatross
c   Sch Lib - v52 - i4 - Winter 2004 - p188(1) [51-500]
Private Peaceful
y   BL - v101 - i3 - Oct 1 2004 - p326(1) [51-500]
y   BL - v101 - i9-10 - Jan 1 2005 - p772(1) [51-500]
y   CCB-B - v58 - i4 - Dec 2004 - p177(1) [51-500]
c   HB - v80 - i6 - Nov-Dec 2004 - p713(2) [501+]
c   Kliatt - v38 - i6 - Nov 2004 - p10(1) [51-500]
y   KR - v72 - i18 - Sept 15 2004 - p916(1) [51-500]
c   LibMed - v23 - i3 - Nov-Dec 2004 - p71(1) [51-500]
y   PW - v251 - i49 - Dec 6 2004 - p60(1) [51-500]
y   Sch Lib - v52 - i4 - Winter 2004 - p211(1) [51-500]
y   SLJ - v50 - i11 - Nov 2004 - p150(1) [51-500]
Sir Gawain and the Green Knight (Illus. by Foreman, Michael)
c   BL - v101 - i5 - Nov 1 2004 - p480(1) [51-500]
c   KR - v72 - i20 - Oct 15 2004 - p1011(1) [51-500]
c   PW - v251 - i50 - Dec 13 2004 - p69(2) [501+]
c   SLJ - v50 - i10 - Oct 2004 - p172(2) [51-500]

Morrall, Clare - *Astonishing Splashes of Colour*
BL - v101 - i1 - Sept 1 2004 - p63(1) [501+]
KR - v72 - i13 - July 1 2004 - p600(1) [501+]
LJ - v129 - i12 - July 2004 - p72(2) [51-500]
NYTBR - Jan 30 2005 - p14 [501+]

Morre, A.W. - *Noble in Reason, Infinite in Faculty: Themes and Variations in Kant's Moral and Religious Philosophy*
Choice - v41 - i7 - March 2004 - p1311(1) [501+]

Morre, E.A. - *Metal-Ligand Bonding*
Choice - v41 - i11-12 - July-August 2004 - p2074(1) [501+]

Morrell, David - *Nightscape*
PW - v251 - i29 - July 19 2004 - p149(1) [51-500]

Morrell, Ernest - *Becoming Critical Researchers: Literacy and Empowerment for Urban Youth*
R&R Bk N - v19 - i4 - Nov 2004 - p193(1) [501+]
Linking Literacy and Popular Culture: Finding Connections for Lifelong Learning
c   LibMed - v23 - i3 - Nov-Dec 2004 - p91(1) [51-500]

Morren, Ruth Axtell - *Wild Rose*
BL - v101 - i3 - Oct 1 2004 - p300(1) [501+]

Morris, Adalaide - *How to Live/What to Do: H.D.'s Cultural Poetics*
Choice - v41 - i7 - March 2004 - p1298(1) [501+]

Morris, Andrew D. - *Marrow of the Nation: A History of Sports and Physical Culture in Republican China*
Choice - v42 - i7 - March 2005 - p1266(1) [51-500]

Morris, Ann - *That's Our School (Illus. by Linenthal, Peter)*
c   LibMed - v23 - i1 - August-Sept 2004 - p83(2) [51-500]

Morris, Arthur - *Art of Bird Photography: The Complete Guide to Professional Field Techniques*
SciTech - v28 - i1 - March 2004 - p175(1) [51-500]

Morris, Benny - *The Birth of the Palestinian Refugee Problem Revisited*
Atl - v294 - i5 - Dec 2004 - p123(1) [501+]
CR - v285 - i1662 - July 2004 - p64(1) [51-500]
JPR - v41 - i5 - Sept 2004 - p642-643 [501+]
The Road to Jerusalem: Glubb Pasha, Palestine and the Jews
A Aff - v35 - i2 - July 2004 - p211-212 [501+]
IJMES - v36 - i3 - August 2004 - p495-496 [501+]

Morris, Betty J. - *Administering the School Library Media Center. 4th Ed.*
BL - v101 - i9-10 - Jan 1 2005 - p909(1) [501+]

Morris, Bob - *Bahamarama*
BL - v101 - i1 - Sept 1 2004 - p69(1) [51-500]
KR - v72 - i17 - Sept 1 2004 - p840(1) [51-500]
LJ - v129 - i14 - Sept 1 2004 - p121(1) [51-500]
PW - v251 - i38 - Sept 20 2004 - p47(1) [51-500]

Morris, Brian - *Insects and Human Life*
Choice - v42 - i5 - Jan 2005 - p878(2) [1-50]
Kropotkin: The Politics of Community
R&R Bk N - v19 - i3 - August 2004 - p172(1) [501+]

Morris, Colin - *Pilgrimage: The English Experience from Becket to Bunyan*
HER - v119 - i483 - Sept 2004 - p987(3) [501+]

Morris, Edmund - *Ten Acres Enough*
LJ - v130 - i2 - Feb 1 2005 - p126(1) [1-50]

Morris, Errol - *The Fog of War: Eleven Lessons from the Life of Robert S. McNamara*
Bks & Cult - v10 - i4 - July-August 2004 - p36(3) [501+]

Morris, Evan - *Making Whoopee: Words of Love for Lovers of Words*
y   VOYA - v27 - i3 - August 2004 - p240(1) [1-50]

Morris, Gerald - *Parsifal's Page*
y   Kliatt - v38 - i4 - July 2004 - p31(1) [51-500]
The Savage Damsel and the Dwarf
c   Kliatt - v38 - i4 - July 2004 - p31(1) [51-500]

Morris, Gilbert - *The Virtuous Woman*
LJ - v130 - i2 - Feb 1 2005 - p64(1) [51-500]

Morris, Ian Macgregor - *Themistocles: Defender of Greece*
y   SLJ - v50 - i9 - Sept 2004 - p230(1) [51-500]

Morris, Irwin L. - *Politics from Anarchy to Democracy: Rational Choice in Political Science*
Pers PS - v33 - i4 - Fall 2004 - p249(2) [501+]
R&R Bk N - v19 - i3 - August 2004 - p172(1) [501+]

Morris, Jackie - *The Seal Children (Illus. by Morris, Jackie)*
c   CCB-B - v58 - i2 - Oct 2004 - p92(2) [51-500]
c   SLJ - v50 - i7 - July 2004 - p83(1) [51-500]

Morris, James M. - *Historical Dictionary of Utopianism*
Choice - v42 - i3 - Nov 2004 - p467(1) [1-50]
R&R Bk N - v19 - i3 - August 2004 - p171(1) [501+]

Morris, Jennifer - *Come, Llamas*
c   CCB-B - v58 - i5 - May 2004 - p221(2) [51-500]
c   KR - v73 - i2 - Jan 15 2005 - p123(1) [51-500]
c   PW - v252 - i11 - March 14 2005 - p67(2) [51-500]
c   SLJ - v51 - i1 - Jan 2005 - p134(1) [51-500]

Morris, Keith - *The Greyhound God*
South CR - v37 - i1 - Fall 2004 - p186-189 [501+]

Morris, Larry E. - *The Fate of the Corps: What Became of the Lewis and Clark Explorers After the Expedition*
Bwatch - March 2005 - pNA [51-500]
Choice - v42 - i6 - Feb 2005 - p1082(1) [51-500]

Morris, Larry E - *The Fate of the Corps: What Became of the Lewis and Clark Explorers After the Expedition*
LJ - v129 - i13 - August 2004 - p95(1) [501+]

Morris, Mary - *Revenge*
BL - v101 - i1 - Sept 1 2004 - p63(1) [501+]
KR - v72 - i15 - August 1 2004 - p708(1) [501+]
LJ - v129 - i16 - Oct 1 2004 - p72(1) [51-500]

Morris, Mary McGarry - *A Hole in the Universe (Read by Culp, Jason). Audiobook Review*
y   Kliatt - v38 - i5 - Sept 2004 - p61(2) [51-500]
The Lost Mother
y   BL - v101 - i7 - Dec 1 2004 - p618(2) [51-500]
KR - v72 - i23 - Dec 1 2004 - p1110(1) [501+]
NYTBR - March 6 2005 - p17 [501+]
PW - v252 - i1 - Jan 3 2005 - p34(1) [51-500]

Morris, Monica - *Falling in Love Again: The Mature Woman's Guide to Finding Romantic Fulfillment*
LJ - v130 - i1 - Jan 1 2005 - p135(1) [51-500]

Morris, Neil - *Illustrated History of the World: From the Big Bang to the Third Millennium*
y   VOYA - v27 - i4 - Oct 2004 - p328(1) [51-500]
Landscapes and People
LibMed - v22 - i7 - April-May 2004 - p69(1) [501+]

Morris, Pam - *Conduct Literature for Women, 1720-1770, Vols. 1-6*
R&R Bk N - v19 - i4 - Nov 2004 - p13(1) [51-500]
Imagining Inclusive Society in Nineteenth-Century Novels: The Code of Sincerity in the Public Sphere
Choice - v42 - i7 - March 2005 - p1230(1) [51-500]

Morris, Richard - *Last Sorcerers: The Parth from Alchemy to the Periodic Table*
SciTech - v28 - i1 - March 2004 - p53(1) [51-500]

Morris, Robert Lee - *Robert Lee Morris: The Power of Jewelry*
Choice - v42 - i6 - Feb 2005 - p1010(1) [51-500]
Globe & Mail - Dec 18 2004 - pD14 [1-50]
R&R Bk N - v19 - i4 - Nov 2004 - p210(1) [501+]

Morris, Rod - *South Sea Islands: A Natural History*
SB - v40 - i6 - Nov-Dec 2004 - p245(1) [51-500]

Morris, Roy, Jr. - *Fraud of the Century: Rutherford B. Hayes, Samuel Tilden, and the Stolen Election of 1876*
CLR - v104 - i6 - Oct 2004 - p1732-1763 [501+]

Morris, S. Brent - *American Masonic Periodicals, 1811-2001: A Bibliography of the Library of the Supreme Council, 33 Degrees, S.J.*
R&R Bk N - v19 - i1 - Feb 2004 - p133(1) [51-500]

Morris, Simon Conway - *In Life's Solution: Inevitable Humans in a Lonely Universe*
New Sci - v185 - i2489 - March 5 2005 - p57(1) [51-500]
Life's Solution: Inevitable Humans in a Lonely Universe
Bks & Cult - v10 - i6 - Nov-Dec 2004 - p42(1) [501+]
TimHES - v0 - i1649 - July 16 2004 - p24(2) [501+]
TLS - i5262 - Feb 6 2004 - p6(1) [501+]

Morris, Tee - *Billibub Baddings and the Case of the Singing Sword*
ChrSFF&H - v26 - i10 - Oct 2004 - p26(1) [51-500]

Morris, Theodore - *Florida's Lost Tribes*
Bwatch - Feb 2005 - pNA [51-500]

Morris, Thomas V. - *The Stoic Art of Living: Inner Resilience and Outer Results*
R&R Bk N - v19 - i3 - August 2004 - p3(1) [1-50]

Morris, Tracy L. - *Anxiety Disorders in Children and Adolescents, 2nd Ed.*
SciTech - v28 - i3 - Sept 2004 - p118(1) [51-500]

Morris, Virginia - *Talking about Death*
R&R Bk N - v19 - i3 - August 2004 - p11(1) [1-50]

Morris, Wright - *The Home Place*
Afterimage - v30 - Winter 2003 - p10 [501+]

Morrisey, Tom - *Deep Blue: A Beck Easton Adventure*
PW - v251 - i48 - Nov 29 2004 - p24(1) [51-500]

Morrisey, Will - *Self-Government, the American Theme: Presidents of the Founding and Civil War*
Pers PS - v33 - i4 - Fall 2004 - p231(1) [501+]
R&R Bk N - v19 - i1 - Feb 2004 - pNA [51-500]

Morrison, Andrea Marie - *International Government Information and Country Information: A Subject Guide*
R&R Bk N - v19 - i4 - Nov 2004 - p260(1) [501+]
BL - v101 - i5 - Nov 1 2004 - p520(1) [501+]

Morrison, Dane Anthony - *Salem: Place, Myth and Memory*
Bwatch - v26 - i9 - Sept 2004 - p8(1) [51-500]
Choice - v42 - i5 - Jan 2005 - p918(1) [1-50]
R&R Bk N - v19 - i3 - August 2004 - p72(1) [51-500]

Morrison, David - *The Gush: Center of Modern Religious Zionism*
R&R Bk N - v19 - i3 - August 2004 - p52(1) [51-500]

Morrison, David A. - *Marketing to the Campus Crowd: Everything You Need To Know To Capture the $200 Billion College Market*
LJ - v129 - i12 - July 2004 - p95(1) [51-500]
R&R Bk N - v19 - i3 - August 2004 - p221(1) [1-50]

Morrison, Dorothy - *Everyday Sun Magic*
Bwatch - March 2005 - pNA [51-500]

Morrison, Gordon - *Nature in the Neighborhood (Illus. by Morrison, Gordon)*
c   BL - v101 - i7 - Dec 1 2004 - p666(2) [51-500]
c   KR - v72 - i20 - Oct 15 2004 - p1011(1) [51-500]
c   SLJ - v50 - i10 - Oct 2004 - p146(1) [51-500]

Morrison, Grant - *The Filth*
BL - v100 - i21 - July 2004 - p1831(1) [1-50]
BW - v34 - i29 - July 18 2004 - p8(1) [501+]
The Painting That Ate Paris
y   BL - v101 - i7 - Dec 1 2004 - p644(1) [51-500]
Sebastian O (Illus. by, Yeowell, Steve)
BL - v101 - i3 - Oct 1 2004 - p320(1) [51-500]

Morrison, Helen - *My Life among the Serial Killers: Inside the Minds of the World's Most Notorious Murderers (Read by Morrison, Helen). Audiobook Review*
LJ - v129 - i19 - Nov 15 2004 - p98(1) [51-500]
My Life Among the Serial Killers: Inside the Minds of the World's Most Notorious Murderers
BW - v34 - i30 - July 25 2004 - p13(1) [501+]

Morrison, Ian - *Australian Almanacs, 1806-1930: A Bibliography*
ALJ - v53 - i3 - August 2004 - p317(2) [501+]

Morrison, Katherine L. - *Canadians Are Not Americans: Myths and Literary Traditions*
CBRA - Annual 2003 - p257(2) [501+]

Muir, John Kenneth - *Best in Show: The Films of Christopher Guest and Company*
    Choice - v42 - i7 - March 2005 - p1235(1) [51-500]
    Globe & Mail - Dec 18 2004 - pD25 [51-500]
    PW - v251 - i43 - Oct 25 2004 - p35(1) [51-500]
    The Encyclopedia of Superheroes on Film and Television
    y LibMed - v23 - i3 - Nov-Dec 2004 - p85(2) [51-500]
    c SLJ - v50 - i8 - August 2004 - p58(1) [501+]
    The Unseen Force: The Films of Sam Raimi
    R&R Bk N - v19 - i4 - Nov 2004 - p225(1) [501+]

Muir, Richard - *Landscape Encyclopaedia: A Reference Guide to the Historic Landscape*
    R&R Bk N - v19 - i4 - Nov 2004 - p35(1) [51-500]
    Landscape Encyclopedia: A Reference Guide to the Historic Lanscape
    Choice - v42 - i4 - Dec 2004 - p642(1) [1-50]

Muir, Robin - *Norman Parkinson: Portraits in Fashion*
    Atl - v294 - i3 - Oct 2004 - p161(2) [501+]
    LJ - v129 - i19 - Nov 15 2004 - p57(1) [51-500]
    Lon R Bks - v26 - i18 - Sept 23 2004 - p28(1) [501+]

Muirden, James - *Shakespeare Well-Versed: A Rhyming Guide to All His Plays*
    BL - v101 - i2 - Sept 15 2004 - p194(1) [501+]

Muirhead, Russell - *Just Work*
    LJ - v129 - i16 - Oct 1 2004 - p84(1) [51-500]
    PW - v251 - i33 - August 16 2004 - p53(2) [51-500]

Mujib, Abdul - *In Vitro Application in Crop Management*
    SciTech - v28 - i3 - Sept 2004 - p128(1) [51-500]

Mujumdar, Arun S. - *Dehydration of Products of Biological Origin*
    SciTech - v28 - i4 - Dec 2004 - p171(1) [51-500]

Mukbaniani, O.V. - *Cyclolinear Organosilicon Copolymers: Synthesis, Properties, Application*
    SciTech - v28 - i1 - March 2004 - p55(1) [51-500]

Mukerjee, Madhusree - *The Land of Naked People: Encounters with Stone Age Islanders*
    Choice - v41 - i7 - March 2004 - p1337(1) [501+]
    TimHES - v0 - i1678 - Feb 11 2005 - p22(1) [501+]

Mukherjee, Bharati - *The Tree Bride*
    Globe & Mail - August 28 2004 - pD14 [501+]
    LJ - v129 - i13 - August 2004 - p69(1) [51-500]
    y NYTBR - Sept 26 2004 - p24 [501+]
    PW - v251 - i33 - August 16 2004 - p41(1) [51-500]

Mukherjee, Upamanyu Pablo - *Crime and Empire: The Colony in Nineteenth-Century Fictions of Crime*
    Choice - v41 - i11-12 - July-August 2004 - p2045(2) [501+]

Mukhopadhyay, S. - *Citrus: Production, Postharvest, Disease and Pest Management*
    SciTech - v28 - i3 - Sept 2004 - p129(1) [51-500]

Mukum Mbaku, John - *Africa at the Crossroads: Between Regionalism and Globalization*
    R&R Bk N - v19 - i3 - August 2004 - p91(1) [501+]
    R&R Bk N - v19 - i4 - Nov 2004 - p91(1) [501+]

Mulcahy, David E. - *Order-Fulfillment and Across-the-Dock Concepts, Design, and Operations Handbook*
    R&R Bk N - v19 - i2 - May 2004 - p114(1) [51-500]

Mulcahy, Kathryn - *Diabetes Ready Reference Guide for Health Professionals, 2nd Ed.*
    SciTech - v28 - i4 - Dec 2004 - p102(2) [51-500]

Mulder-Bakker, Anneke B. - *Seeing and Knowing: Women and Learning in Medieval Europe, 1200-1550*
    R&R Bk N - v19 - i4 - Nov 2004 - p132(1) [51-500]

Muldoon, James - *Identity on the Medieval Irish Frontier: Degenerate Englishmen, Wild Irishmen, Middle Nations*
    AHR - v109 - i3 - June 2004 - p962(2) [501+]
    HER - v119 - i483 - Sept 2004 - p1029(2) [501+]
    HER - v119 - i483 - Sept 2004 - p1029(2) [501+]

Muldoon, James P. - *The Architecture of Global Governance: An Introduction to the Study of International Organizations*
    R&R Bk N - v19 - i1 - Feb 2004 - pNA [501+]

Muldoon, Paul - *Moy Sand and Gravel*
    South R - v39 - Winter 2003 - p219 [501+]

Mulfinger, Dale - *The Getaway Home: Discovering Your Home Away from Home*
    BL - v101 - i9-10 - Jan 1 2005 - p800(1) [51-500]
    PW - v251 - i45 - Nov 8 2004 - p47(2) [501+]

Mulgan, Aurelia George - *Japan's Failed Revolution: Koizumi and the Politics of Economic Reform*
    A Aff - v35 - i2 - July 2004 - p258-260 [501+]

Mulhall, Douglas - *The Calcium Bomb: The Nanobacteria Link to Heart Disease and Cancer*
    Fut - v38 - i6 - Nov-Dec 2004 - p60(1) [51-500]

Mulholland, Andrew - *Official Butterfly.net Game Developer's Guide*
    SciTech - v28 - i4 - Dec 2004 - p27(1) [51-500]

Mulholland, Kate - *Class, Gender, and the Family Business*
    R&R Bk N - v19 - i1 - Feb 2004 - p92(1) [1-50]

Mulholland, Maureen - *Judicial Tribunals in England and Europe, 1200-1700: The Trial in History*
    AHR - v109 - i4 - Oct 2004 - p1300-1301 [501+]

Mulholland, Neil - *The Cultural Devolution: Art in Britain in the Late Twentieth Century*
    R&R Bk N - v19 - i1 - Feb 2004 - p199(1) [51-500]

Mulisch, Harry - *Siegfried*
    BIC - v33 - i5 - August 2004 - p08(2) [501+]

Mulke, C. - *Solons Politische Elegien und Lamben*
    Class R - v53 - i2 - Nov 2003 - p278-279 [501+]

Mullally, Evelyn - *The Deeds of the Normans in Ireland-La Geste des Engleis en Yrlande*
    FS - v58 - i2 - April 2004 - p238(2) [501+]

Mullard, Maurice - *Democracy Citizenship and Globalisation*
    R&R Bk N - v19 - i1 - Feb 2004 - p106(1) [51-500]

Mullen, Bill V. - *Left of the Color Line: Race, Radiacalism and Twentieth Century Literature of the United States*
    VQR - v80 - i2 - Spring 2004 - p258-258 [501+]

Mullen, Brendan - *Whores: An Oral Biography of Perry Farrell and Jane's Addiction*
    PW - v252 - i11 - March 14 2005 - p56(1) [51-500]

Mullen, Carol A. - *Climbing the Himalayas of School Leadership; the Socialization of Early Career Adminstrators*
    R&R Bk N - v19 - i3 - August 2004 - p220(1) [1-50]

Mullen, Laurie - *Digital Portfolios in Teacher Education*
    R&R Bk N - v19 - i4 - Nov 2004 - p179(1) [501+]

Mullen, Mary Catherine - *Childhood and Adolescent Overweight: The Health Professional's Guide to Identification, Treatment, and Prevention*
    SciTech - v28 - i1 - March 2004 - p118(1) [51-500]

Mullen, Megan - *The Rise of Cable Programming in the United States.*
    BHR - v78 - i1 - Spring 2004 - p146(3) [501+]

Mullen, Roderic L. - *The Expansion of Christianity: A Gazetteer of Its First Three Centuries*
    Choice - v42 - i2 - Oct 2004 - p268(1) [501+]
    R&R Bk N - v19 - i3 - August 2004 - p20(1) [1-50]

Mullener, Elizabeth - *War Stories*
    VQR - v79 - i1 - Winter 2003 - p18 [51-500]

Muller, Agnus C. - *German Pop Culture: How "American" Is It?*
    Choice - v42 - i7 - March 2005 - p1212(1) [51-500]

Muller, Andreas, P. - *Communication in Organizations: Structures and Practices*
    R&R Bk N - v19 - i1 - Feb 2004 - p86(1) [1-50]

Muller, Bertrand - *Lucien Febvre, Lecteur et Critique*
    Lib & Cul - v39 - i3 - Summer 2004 - p293(20) [501+]

Muller, Birte - *Felipa and the Day of the Dead*
    c SLJ - v50 - i12 - Dec 2004 - p114(1) [501+]

Muller-Brockmann, Josef - *History of the Poster*
    CR - v286 - i1669 - Feb 2005 - p122(1) [51-500]
    LJ - v129 - i16 - Oct 1 2004 - p121(1) [1-50]
    R&R Bk N - v19 - i4 - Nov 2004 - p206(1) [501+]

Muller, Carol A. - *South African Music: A Century of Traditions in Transformation*
    Choice - v42 - i4 - Dec 2004 - p671(2) [1-50]

Muller, Christian - *Money Demand in Europe: An Empirical Approach*
    JEL - v42 - i1 - March 2004 - p255(1) [501+]

Muller-Ebeling, Claudia - *Witchcraft Medicine: Healing Arts, Shamanic Practices, and Forbidden Plants*
    R&R Bk N - v19 - i1 - Feb 2004 - p71(1) [1-50]

Muller, Gerard L. - *Nala and Damayanti: A Tale of Love, Gambling, and Adventure in Ancient India*
    R&R Bk N - v19 - i3 - August 2004 - p257(1) [51-500]

Muller, Gerd B. - *Origination of Organismal Form: Beyond the Gene in Developmental and Evolutionary Biology*
    QRB - v79 - i4 - Dec 2004 - p425(2) [501+]

Muller, Gunter - *Lipases and Phospholipases in Drug Developement: From Biochemistry to Molecular Pharmacology*
    SciTech - v28 - i3 - Sept 2004 - p72(1) [51-500]

Muller, Jan-Werner - *A Dangerous Mind: Carl Schmitt in Post-War European Thought*
    AHR - v109 - i4 - Oct 2004 - p1333-1333 [501+]
    Choice - v41 - i11-12 - July-August 2004 - p2124(1) [501+]
    Memory and Power in Post-War Europe: Studies in the Presence of the Past
    JIH - v35 - i2 - Autumn 2004 - p293(2) [501+]

Muller, Jerry Z. - *The Mind and the Market: Capitalism in Modern Europe Thought*
    JIH - v35 - i2 - Autumn 2004 - p291(2) [501+]

Muller, Katharina - *Privatising Old-Age Security: Latin America and Eastern Europe Compared*
    R&R Bk N - v19 - i1 - Feb 2004 - p101(1) [51-500]

Muller, Marcia - *The Dangerous Hour (Read by Ericksen, Susan). Audiobook Review*
    y Kliatt - v39 - i2 - March 2005 - p51(1) [51-500]

Muller, Markus - *Die Christlieh-Nationale Bauern- und Landvolkpartei, 1928-1933*
    JMH - v76 - i4 - Dec 2004 - p992(4) [501+]

Muller, Richard A. - *After Calvin: Studies in the Development of a Theological Tradition*
    Theol St - v66 - i1 - March 2005 - p225(2) [501+]

Muller-Sievers, Helmut - *Desorientierung. Anatomie und Dichtung bei Georg Biichner*
    GSR - v27 - i1 - Feb 2004 - p148-149 [501+]

Muller-Ueltzhoffer, Bettina - *Der 500jahrige Rechtsstreit des Klosters Neresheim um die Erlangung der Reichsunmittelbarkeit*
    HNet - Oct 2004 - pNA [501+]

Muller, Werner - *Die Geschichte der SPD in Mecklenburg und Vorpommern*
    HNet - Oct 2004 - pNA [501+]

Mulligan, Sheila - *What Flows through Me That You Call Time*
    New ER - v24 - i4 - Fall 2003 - p139-148 [501+]

Mullin, Glenn H. - *Female Buddhas: Women of Enlightenment in Tibetan Mystical Art*
    R&R Bk N - v19 - i1 - Feb 2004 - p201(1) [51-500]

Mullin, Katherine - *James Joyce, Sexuality and Social Purity*
    ELT - v47 - i4 - Fall 2004 - p476(5) [501+]

Mullin, Robert Bruce - *The Puritan as Yankee: A Life of Horace Bushell*
    AHR - v109 - i2 - April 2004 - p522(2) [501+]

Mullineux, Andrew W. - *Handbook of International Banking*
    JEL - v41 - i4 - Dec 2003 - p1367(1) [501+]

Mulling, Leith - *Stress and Resilience: The Social Context of Reproduction in Central Harlem*
    MAQ - v18 - i4 - Dec 2004 - p515(2) [501+]

Mullins, John W. - *The New Business Road Test: What Enterpreneurs and Executives Should Do Before Writing a Business Plan*
    Choice - v42 - i7 - March 2005 - p1275(1) [51-500]

Mullins, Laurie J. - *Management and Organisational Behaviour, 7th Ed.*
    TimHES - v0 - i1680 - Feb 25 2005 - pVIII(1) [501+]

Mullins, Norman D. - *Mountain Boy: The Adventures of Orion Saddler*
    y Kliatt - v38 - i5 - Sept 2004 - p24(2) [51-500]

Mullis, Tony R. - *Peacekeeping on the Plains: Army Operations in Bleeding Kansas*
    Bwatch - v26 - i8 - August 2004 - p9(1) [51-500]
    R&R Bk N - v19 - i4 - Nov 2004 - p67(1) [51-500]

Mulloy, Darren J. - *American Extremism: History, Politics and the Militia Movement*
    TimHES - v0 - i1659 - Sept 24 2004 - p28(2) [501+]

Mulongoy, Kalemani Jo - *Protected Areas and Biodiversity: An Overview of Key Issues*
    SciTech - v28 - i4 - Dec 2004 - p123 [51-500]

Mulrooney, Margaret M. - *Black Powder, White Lace: The du Pont Irish and Cultural Identity in Nineteenth-Century America*
    JAH - v91 - i3 - Dec 2004 - p1015(1) [501+]

Mulroy, D. - *The Complete Poetry of Catullus*
    Class R - v54 - i1 - May 2004 - p246(1) [501+]

Mulryan, Lenore Hoag - *Ceramic Trees of Life: Popular Art from Mexico*
    Ceram Mo - v52 - i7 - Sept 2004 - p80(2) [501+]

Multifunctionality: The Policy Implications
    JEL - v42 - i1 - March 2004 - p329(1) [501+]

Murray, Martine - *Henrietta, There's No One Better*
  c Magpies - v19 - i5 - Nov 2004 - p30(1) [501+]
The Slightly True Story of Cedar B. Hartley
  c PW - v251 - i31 - August 2 2004 - p73(1) [51-500]
  c BL - v101 - i6 - Nov 15 2004 - p599(1) [501+]
  y Kliatt - v38 - i5 - Sept 2004 - p24(2) [51-500]
  y Teach Lib - v32 - i1 - Oct 2004 - p18(1) [51-500]

Murray, Maya - *The Queen Jade*
  PW - v252 - i3 - Jan 17 2005 - p36(1) [51-500]

Murray, Michael - *Critical Health Psychology*
  SciTech - v28 - i3 - Sept 2004 - p78(1) [51-500]

Murray, Michele - *Playing a Jewish Game: Gentile Christian Judaizing in the First and Second Centuries CE*
  R&R Bk N - v19 - i3 - August 2004 - p19(1) [1-50]

Murray, Miki - *Teaching Mathematics Vocabulary in Context: Windows, Doors, and Secret Passageways*
  SB - v40 - i4 - July-August 2004 - p157(2) [51-500]

Murray, Nicholas - *Aldous Huxley, A Biography*
  Parabola - v28 - i4 - Winter 2003 - p90-94 [501+]
Kafka
  BL - v101 - i4 - Oct 15 2004 - p377(1) [51-500]
  BW - v34 - i38 - Sept 19 2004 - p15(1) [51-500]
  CR - v286 - i1669 - Feb 2005 - p116(2) [501+]
  LJ - v129 - i14 - Sept 1 2004 - p43(1) [51-500]
  LJ - v129 - i18 - Nov 1 2004 - p85(1) [51-500]
  Nation - v279 - i12 - Oct 18 2004 - p34 [501+]
  PW - v251 - i36 - Sept 6 2004 - p59(1) [51-500]
  Wil Q - v28 - i4 - Autumn 2004 - p121(2) [501+]

Murray, Patrick R. - *Pocket Guide to Clinical Microbiology, 3rd ed.*
  E-Streams - Dec 2004 - pNA [501+]
  SciTech - v28 - i3 - Sept 2004 - p73(1) [51-500]

Murray, Paul - *An Evening of Long Goodbyes*
  BL - v101 - i6 - Nov 15 2004 - p558(1) [51-500]
  BL - v101 - i9-10 - Jan 1 2005 - p770(1) [51-500]
  Ent W - i778 - August 13 2004 - p95 [51-500]
  LJ - v129 - i15 - Sept 15 2004 - p50(1) [51-500]
  NYTBR - Sept 5 2004 - p6 [501+]
  NYTBR - Sept 19 2004 - p22 [501+]
From the Shadow of Dracula: A Life of Bram Stoker
  CR - v286 - i1669 - Feb 2005 - p114(2) [501+]
  Lon R Bks - v26 - i23 - Dec 2 2004 - p28(1) [501+]
  TimHES - v0 - i1666 - Nov 12 2004 - p32(1) [501+]
  TLS - i5292 - Sept 3 2004 - p36(1) [501+]

Murray, Peter - *The Saga of Sydney Opera House: The Dramatic Story of the Design and Construction of the Icon of Modern Australia*
  Choice - v42 - i1 - Sept 2004 - p91(1) [501+]

Murray, Peter C. - *Methodists and the Crucible of Race, 1930-1975*
  R&R Bk N - v19 - i3 - August 2004 - p66(1) [51-500]
Methodists and the Crucible of the Race, 1930-1975
  Choice - v42 - i5 - Jan 2005 - p918(1) [1-50]

Murray, Peter F. - *Magnificent Mihirungs: The Colossal Flightless Birds of the Australian Dreamtime*
  Choice - v42 - i2 - Oct 2004 - p320(1) [51-500]
  QRB - v79 - i4 - Dec 2004 - p411(2) [501+]

Murray, Raymond C. - *Evidence from the Earth; Forensic Geology and Criminal Investigation*
  SciTech - v28 - i3 - Sept 2004 - p55(1) [1-50]
Evidence from the Earth: Forsenic Geology and Criminal Investigation
  Choice - v42 - i3 - Nov 2004 - p513(1) [1-50]

Murray, Robert Bruce - *Legal Cases of the Civil War*
  JSH - v70 - i4 - Nov 2004 - p924(2) [501+]

Murray, Rose - *Hungry for Comfort: The Pleasures of Home Cooking*
  CBRA - Annual 2003 - p134(2) [51-500]

Murray, Sabina - *A Carnivore's Inquiry (Read by Hoopes, Wendy). Audiobook Review*
  Kliatt - v38 - i6 - Nov 2004 - p42(1) [51-500]
  PW - v251 - i36 - Sept 6 2004 - p25(2) [51-500]
A Carnivore's Inquiry
  NYTBR - July 11 2004 - p17 [501+]

Murray, Simon - *Jacques Lecoq*
  TimHES - v0 - i1655 - August 27 2004 - p26(1) [501+]

Murray, Susan - *Reality TV: Remaking Television Culture*
  Choice - v42 - i2 - Oct 2004 - p287(1) [501+]

Murray, Sylvie - *The Progressive Housewife: Community Activism in Suburban Queens, 1945-1965*
  HNet - Sept 2004 - pNA [501+]
  JAH - v91 - i2 - Sept 2004 - p702(2) [501+]

Murray, Watson - *Being English in Scotland*
  Choice - v42 - i6 - Feb 2005 - p1087(1) [51-500]

Murray, William - *City of the Soul: A Walk in Rome (Read by Gardner, Grover). Audiobook Review*
  y LJ - v129 - i15 - Sept 2004 - p67(2) [51-500]
  LJ - v129 - i17 - Oct 15 2004 - p98(1) [51-500]

Murray, Williamson - *The Iraq War: A Military History*
  APJ - v18 - i4 - Winter 2004 - p114(3) [501+]
  Choice - v41 - i7 - March 2004 - p1353(1) [501+]
  J Mil H - v68 - i2 - April 2004 - p661(2) [501+]
  Mar Crp G - v88 - i3 - March 2004 - p60(2) [501+]
  SPA - v60 - i5 - Sept-Oct 2004 - p63(4) [501+]

Murray, Yxta Maya - *The Queen Jade*
  BL - v101 - i9-10 - Jan 1 2005 - p821(1) [501+]
  KR - v72 - i24 - Dec 15 2004 - p1161(1) [501+]
  LJ - v130 - i3 - Feb 15 2005 - p120(1) [51-500]

Murrell, Deborah - *The Best Book of Ancient Rome*
  c KR - v72 - i16 - August 15 2004 - p810(1) [51-500]
  c SLJ - v51 - i2 - Feb 2005 - p124(1) [51-500]

Murrills, Angela - *Hot Sun Cool Shadow: Savouring the Food, History, and Mystery of the Languedoc (Illus. by Matthews, Peter)*
  Globe & Mail - Nov 27 2004 - pD27 [501+]

Murrin, John M. - *Liberty, Equality, Power: A History of the American People, 4th Ed.*
  R&R Bk N - v19 - i3 - August 2004 - p64(1) [51-500]

Murrow, David - *Why Men Hate Going to Church*
  PW - v252 - i9 - Feb 28 2005 - p62(1) [51-500]

Murshid, Ghulam - *Lured by Hope: A Biography of Michael Madhusudan Dutt*
  JAS - v63 - i3 - August 2004 - p830-831 [501+]

Muscari, Mary E. - *Pediatric nursing, 4th Ed.*
  SciTech - v28 - i4 - Dec 2004 - p112(1) [1-50]

Muse, Lamar - *Southwest Passage: The Inside Story of Southwest Airlines' Formative Years*
  SHQ - v107 - i3 - Jan 2004 - p495(2) [501+]

Musgrave, Michael - *George Grove, Music and Victorian Culture*
  MT - v145 - i1888 - Autumn 2004 - p95-99 [501+]
  Notes - v61 - i3 - March 2005 - p732(3) [501+]

Musgrave, Susan - *Certain Things About My Mother: Daughters Speak*
  y CBRA - Annual 2003 - p533(1) [51-500]
Perfectly Secret: The Hidden Lives of Seven Teen Girls
  c Globe & Mail - Jan 15 2005 - pD16 [51-500]
  y KR - v72 - i22 - Nov 15 2004 - p1092(1) [51-500]
  y Res Links - v10 - i2 - Dec 2004 - p45(2) [51-500]
  y SLJ - v50 - i12 - Dec 2004 - p166(1) [51-500]

Mushtaq, Faiza - *Fathlines: Muslim Conceptions of Islam and Society*
  CS - v33 - i5 - Sept 2004 - p553-554 [501+]

Musicplay for Kindergarten
  c Teach Mus - v12 - i2 - Oct 2004 - p71(1) [51-500]

Musisi, Nakanyike B. - *Makerere University in Transition 1993-2000: Opportunites and Challenges*
  TimHES - v0 - i1676 - Jan 28 2005 - p26(1) [501+]

Muske-Dukes, Carol - *Sparrow: Poems*
  NYTBR - Nov 21 2004 - p36 [501+]
  WLT - v78 - i3-4 - Sept-Dec 2004 - p101(2) [501+]

Musleah, Rahel - *Apples and Pomegranates: A Family Seder for Rosh Hashanah. (Illus. by Jarrett, Judy)*
  c SLJ - v50 - i12 - Dec 2004 - p135(1) [51-500]
Big Red Tub (Illus. by Reynolds, Adrian)
  c KR - v72 - i24 - Dec 15 2004 - p1203(1) [51-500]

Musolf, Gil Richard - *Structure and Agency in Everyday Life: An Introduction to Social Psychology*
  CS - v33 - i5 - Sept 2004 - p625-625 [501+]

Mussa, Michael - *Argentina and the Fund: From Triumph to Tragedy*
  JEL - v41 - i4 - Dec 2003 - p1291(3) [501+]

Musser, Elizabeth - *The Dwelling Place*
  PW - v252 - i10 - March 7 2005 - p52(1) [51-500]

Musslewhite, Lynn - *One Woman's Political Journey: Kate Barnard and Social Reform, 1875-1930*
  JSH - v71 - i1 - Feb 2005 - p183(2) [501+]

Mussulman, Joseph A. - *Discovering Lewis and Clark from the Air (Illus. by Wark, Jim)*
  y Kliatt - v38 - i5 - Sept 2004 - p50(3) [51-500]
  R&R Bk N - v19 - i3 - August 2004 - p74(1) [51-500]

Mustard, David B. - *Racial Justice in America: A Reference Handbook*
  R&R Bk N - v19 - i1 - Feb 2004 - p58(1) [51-500]

Musto, Ronald G. - *Apocalypse in Rome: Cola di Rienzo and the Politics of the New Age*
  AHR - v109 - i3 - June 2004 - p993(2) [501+]

Musumeci, Francesco - *Energy and Information Transfer in Biological Systems: How Physics Could Enrich Biological Understanding, Proceedings*
  SciTech - v28 - i4 - Dec 2004 - p62(1) [51-500]

Mutale, Emmanuel - *The Management of Urban Development in Zambia*
  R&R Bk N - v19 - i3 - August 2004 - p156(1) [51-500]

Mutalib, Hussin - *Parties and Politics: A Study of Opposition Parties and the PAP in Singapore*
  Pac A - v77 - i2 - Summer 2004 - p372(2) [501+]
  R&R Bk N - v19 - i1 - Feb 2004 - p48(1) [51-500]

Muten, Burleigh - *Goddesses: A World of Myth and Magic (Illus. by Guay, Rebecca)*
  c SLJ - v50 - i7 - July 2004 - p126(2) [51-500]
Grandfather Mountain: Stories of Gods and Heroes from Many Cultures (Illus. by Bailey, Sian)
  c BL - v101 - i6 - Nov 15 2004 - p576(1) [51-500]
  c SLJ - v51 - i1 - Jan 2005 - p113(1) [51-500]

Muth, Joerg - *Flucht aus dem militaerischen Alltag: Ursachen und individuelle Auspraegung der Desertion in der Armee Friedrichs des Grossen*
  HNet - Sept 2004 - pNA [501+]

Muth, Jon J. - *Zen Shorts*
  c KR - v73 - i3 - Feb 1 2005 - p179(1) [51-500]
  c PW - v252 - i9 - Feb 28 2005 - p66(2) [51-500]
  c SLJ - v51 - i2 - Feb 2005 - p108(1) [51-500]

Muth, Jorg - *Flucht aus dem militarischen Attlag. Ursachen und individuelle Auspragung der Desertion in der Armee Friedrichs des Groben. Mit besonderer Bucksichtigung der Infanterie-Regimenter der Postdamer Garnison*
  J Mil H - v68 - i2 - April 2004 - p589(2) [501+]

Muthwii, Margaret Jepkirui - *New Language Bearings in Africa: A Fresh Quest*
  R&R Bk N - v19 - i3 - August 2004 - p257(1) [51-500]

Mutimer, David - *Canadian Annual Review of Politics and Public Affairs, 1997*
  CBRA - Annual 2003 - p304(1) [501+]
  R&R Bk N - v19 - i1 - Feb 2004 - p68(1) [501+]

Mutten, Burleigh - *Goddesses: A World of Myth and Magic (Illus. by Guay, Rebecca)*
  c LibMed - v22 - i5 - Feb 2004 - p82(1) [501+]

Mutter, Davida W. - *School Money Matters: A Handbook for Principals*
  R&R Bk N - v19 - i3 - August 2004 - p223(1) [1-50]
  TCR - v107 - i2 - Feb 2005 - p243(4) [501+]

Mutton, Paul - *IRC Hacks*
  Bwatch - Feb 2005 - pNA [501+]
  SciTech - v28 - i4 - Dec 2004 - p31(1) [51-500]

Mutton Soup: More Adventures of Johnny Mutton
  c BooChiTr - April 18 2004 - p3(1) [501+]

My Day/In Motion and Play
  c SLJ - v50 - i11 - Nov 2004 - p84(1) [51-500]

My Favorite Writer
  c LibMed - v23 - i3 - Nov-Dec 2004 - p79(1) [51-500]

My First Animal Book
  c RT - v57 - Oct 2003 - p170 [1-50]

My First Britannica, Vols. 1-13
  c BL - v101 - i1 - Sept 1 2004 - p174(1) [501+]

My Pig Amarillo
  c LibMed - v22 - i4 - Jan 2004 - p58(1) [501+]

My Unbrilliant Career
  y Kliatt - v39 - i2 - March 2005 - p3(2) [51-500]

Myant, Martin - *The Rise and Fall of Czech Capitalism: Economic Development in the Czech Republic Since 1989*
  JEL - v41 - i4 - Dec 2003 - p1429(1) [501+]
  Slav R - v63 - i2 - Summer 2004 - p383(2) [501+]

Myasnikov, A. G. - *Group Theory, Statistics, and Cryptography: Proceedings*
  SciTech - v28 - i4 - Dec 2004 - p35(1) [51-500]

Mychajlyszyn, Natalie L. - *The Evolution of Civil-Military Relations in East-Central Europe and the Former Soviet Union*
  R&R Bk N - v19 - i3 - August 2004 - p182(1) [501+]

Myer, Rick A. - *CD-ROM and Workbook for Crisis Intervention*
  SciTech - v28 - i4 - Dec 2004 - p96(1) [51-500]

Myers, Amy - *The Wickenham Murders*
  BL - v101 - i2 - Sept 15 2004 - p214(1) [51-500]
  LJ - v129 - i18 - Nov 1 2004 - p58(1) [51-500]

Myers, Anna - *Hoggee*
  KR - v72 - i17 - Sept 1 2004 - p871(1) [51-500]
  y SLJ - v50 - i11 - Nov 2004 - p150(1) [51-500]

Myers, Beverle Graves - *Painted Veil: A Baroque Mystery*
  KR - v73 - i2 - Jan 15 2005 - p87(1) [51-500]
  PW - v252 - i9 - Feb 28 2005 - p46(1) [51-500]

Myers, Bill - *Soul Tracker*
>   BL - v101 - i3 - Oct 1 2004 - p300(1) [501+]
>   LJ - v129 - i14 - Sept 1 2004 - p132(1) [51-500]
>   PW - v251 - i33 - August 16 2004 - p43(1) [51-500]

Myers, David G. - *Psychology, 7th Ed.*
>   SciTech - v28 - i4 - Dec 2004 - p1(1) [1-50]
>   *Psychology. 7th Ed.*
>   TimHES - v0 - i1668 - Nov 26 2004 - pXVIII(2) [501+]

Myers, David N. - *Resisting History: Historicism and Its Discontents in German-Jewish Thought*
>   Bks & Cult - v11 - i1 - Jan-Feb 2005 - p34(2) [501+]
>   Choice - v42 - i1 - Sept 2004 - p181(1) [501+]
>   New R - August 2 2004 - p30 [501+]

Myers, Doris T. - *Bareface: A Guide to C.S. Lewis's Last Novel*
>   Choice - v41 - i11-12 - July-August 2004 - p2046(1) [501+]

Myers, Edward - *When Will I Stop Hurting: Teens, Loss and Grief (Illus. by Adams, Kelly)*
>   R&R Bk N - v19 - i3 - August 2004 - p10(1) [1-50]
>   *When Will I Stop Hurting?: Teens, Loss, and Grief (Illus. by Adams, Kelly)*
>   y SLJ - v50 - i11 - Nov 2004 - p170(1) [51-500]
>   y VOYA - v27 - i4 - Oct 2004 - p334(1) [51-500]

Myers, Edward A. - *Turnaround: Musings on the Earth's Future*
>   SciTech - v28 - i4 - Dec 2004 - p7(1) [1-50]

Myers, Garth Andrew - *Verandahs of Power: Colonialism and Space in Urban Africa*
>   IJAHS - v37 - i1 - Wntr 2004 - p123-125 [501+]
>   J Hist G - v30 - i1 - Jan 2004 - p187(2) [501+]

Myers, Glenford J. - *Art of Software Testing, 2nd Ed.*
>   SciTech - v28 - i3 - Sept 2004 - p20(1) [501+]

Myers, Howard - *Cloud Chamber*
>   MFSF - v107 - i3 - Sept 2004 - p162(1) [501+]

Myers, Jack - *How Dogs Came from Wolves*
>   c CH Bwatch - Jan 2005 - pNA [51-500]

Myers, Judith H. - *Ecology and Control of Introduced Plants*
>   Choice - v41 - i7 - March 2004 - p1322(1) [501+]

Myers, K. Jaguar - *Sports Market Place Directory, 2003 Ed.*
>   R&R Bk N - v19 - i1 - Feb 2004 - p73(1) [1-50]

Myers, Kathleen Ann - *Neither Saints nor Sinners: Writing the Lives of Women in Spanish America*
>   Choice - v42 - i4 - Dec 2004 - p666(1) [1-50]

Myers, Kenneth John - *Mr. Whistler's Gallery: Pictures at an 1884 Exhibition*
>   R&R Bk N - v19 - i2 - May 2004 - p195(1) [51-500]

Myers, Laurie - *Lewis and Clark and Me (Illus. by Dooling, Michael)*
>   c RT - v57 - Nov 2003 - p274 [51-500]
>   *Surviving Brick Johnson (Read by Leffert, Joel). Audiobook Review*
>   c BL - v101 - i1 - Sept 1 2004 - p148(1) [51-500]

Myers, Lois E. - *Rock beneath the Sand: Country Churches in Texas (Illus. by Baker, Clark G.)*
>   JR - v85 - i1 - Jan 2005 - p118(3) [501+]
>   JSH - v71 - i1 - Feb 2005 - p228(2) [501+]

Myers, Norman - *The New Consumers: The Influence of Affluence on the Environment*
>   LJ - v129 - i13 - August 2004 - p115(1) [51-500]

Myers, Rob - *Heart Disease: Everything You Need to Know*
>   E-Streams - Oct 2004 - pNA [501+]
>   *Woman Who Swallowed a Toothbrush and Other Bizarre Medical Cases*
>   CBRA - Annual 2003 - p432(1) [51-500]

Myers, Susan E. - *Friars and Jews in the Middle Ages and Renaissance*
>   R&R Bk N - v19 - i4 - Nov 2004 - p46(1) [51-500]

Myers, Tamar - *Assault and Pepper: A Pennsylvania Dutch Mystery with Recipes*
>   KR - v72 - i24 - Dec 15 2004 - p1168(1) [501+]
>   LJ - v130 - i1 - Jan 1 2005 - p84(1) [51-500]
>   PW - v252 - i4 - Jan 24 2005 - p226(1) [51-500]

Myers, Tim - *Basho and the River Stones (Illus. by Han, Oki S.)*
>   c BL - v101 - i5 - Nov 1 2004 - p490(1) [51-500]
>   c CCB-B - v58 - i3 - Nov 2004 - p135(2) [501+]
>   c KR - v72 - i15 - August 1 2004 - p746(1) [51-500]
>   c NYTBR - Oct 17 2004 - p21 [501+]
>   c SLJ - v50 - i10 - Oct 2004 - p125(1) [51-500]

Myers, Walter Dean - *Antarctica: Journeys to the South Pole*
>   y BL - v101 - i6 - Nov 15 2004 - p573(1) [51-500]
>   c CCB-B - v58 - i4 - Dec 2004 - p177(2) [501+]
>   y KR - v72 - i21 - Nov 1 2004 - p1045(1) [51-500]
>   y SLJ - v50 - i12 - Dec 2004 - p166(1) [51-500]
>   *Bad Boy, a Memoir*
>   c SLJ - v50 - i11 - Nov 2004 - p66(1) [51-500]
>   *The Beast*
>   JAAL - v48 - i4 - Dec 2004 - p347(1) [51-500]
>   *Blues Journey (Illus. by Myers, Christopher)*
>   c SLJ - v50 - i11 - Nov 2004 - p65(1) [51-500]
>   SLJ - v50 - i12 - Dec 2004 - p61(1) [501+]
>   *The Blues of Flats Brown*
>   SLJ - v50 - i12 - Dec 2004 - p61(1) [501+]
>   *The Dream Bearer*
>   Kliatt - v38 - i6 - Nov 2004 - p19(2) [51-500]
>   *Here in Harlem: Poems in Many Voices*
>   y BL - v101 - i5 - Nov 1 2004 - p480(1) [51-500]
>   c Black Iss - v7 - i2 - March-April 2005 - p66(2) [501+]
>   y CCB-B - v58 - i4 - Dec 2004 - p178(1) [51-500]
>   y KR - v72 - i22 - Nov 15 2004 - p1092(1) [51-500]
>   y SLJ - v50 - i12 - Dec 2004 - p166(1) [51-500]
>   *I've Seen the Promised Land: The Life of Dr. Martin Luther King, Jr. (Illus. by Jenkins, Leonard)*
>   BooChiTr - Jan 18 2004 - p5(1) [501+]
>   LibMed - v23 - i1 - August-Sept 2004 - p72(1) [51-500]

Patrol: An American Soldier in Vietnam (Illus. by Grifalconi, Ann)
>   c RT - v57 - Oct 2003 - p174 [1-50]
>   *Patrol: An American Soldier in Vietnam (Illus. by Grifalcony, Ann)*
>   c PW - v252 - i1 - Jan 3 2005 - p58(1) [51-500]
>   *Patrol: An American Soldier in Vietnam*
>   y Kliatt - v39 - i1 - Jan 2005 - p28(1) [51-500]
>   *Shooter (Read by Coleman, Chad). Audiobook Review*
>   y BL - v101 - i6 - Nov 15 2004 - p608(1) [501+]
>   y BL - v101 - i9-10 - Jan 1 2005 - p778(1) [1-50]
>   y Kliatt - v38 - i6 - Nov 2004 - p50(2) [51-500]
>   y SLJ - v50 - i9 - Sept 2004 - p79(1) [51-500]
>   *Shooter*
>   c Black Iss - v6 - i4 - July-August 2004 - p60(1) [51-500]
>   c Globe & Mail - July 31 2004 - pD11 [51-500]
>   y NYTBR - Sept 19 2004 - p16 [51-500]
>   *USS Constellation: Pride of the American Navy*
>   c BL - v100 - i21 - July 2004 - p1841(1) [1-50]
>   y CCB-B - v58 - i1 - Sept 2004 - p32(2) [51-500]
>   c CH Bwatch - v14 - i7 - July 2004 - p8(1) [51-500]
>   c HB - v80 - i4 - July-August 2004 - p469(2) [51-500]
>   c SLJ - v50 - i8 - August 2004 - p140(1) [51-500]
>   y VOYA - v27 - i3 - August 2004 - p240(1) [1-50]

Myerson, Joel - *Ralph Waldo Emerson, 1803-1882: A Bicentenary Exhibition from the Joel Myerson Collection of Nineteenth-Century American Literature.*
>   BSA-P - v98 - i1 - March 2004 - p128-128 [501+]

Mykkanen, Juri - *Inventing Politics: A New Political Anthropology of the Hawaiian Kingdom*
>   Pac A - v77 - i3 - Fall 2004 - p613(2) [501+]

Mykytiuk, Lawrence J. - *Identifying Biblical Persons in Northwest Semitic Inscriptions of 1200-539 B.C.E.*
>   R&R Bk N - v19 - i4 - Nov 2004 - p21(1) [51-500]

Myller, Rolf - *Palmerston and the Politics of Foreign Policy, 1846-55*
>   Albion - v36 - i2 - Summer 2004 - p334(3) [501+]

Mylonas, Christos - *Serbian Orthodox Fundamentals: The Quest for an Eternal Identity*
>   AHR - v109 - i3 - June 2004 - p1001(2) [501+]

Myracle, Lauren - *Kissing Kate*
>   LibMed - v22 - i4 - Jan 2004 - p68(1) [501+]
>   *Rhymes with Witches*
>   y Kliatt - v39 - i2 - March 2005 - p14(2) [51-500]
>   KR - v73 - i5 - March 1 2005 - p292(1) [51-500]

Myrdal, Gunnar - *An American Dilemma: The Negro Problem and American Democracy*
>   Comw - v132 - i3 - Feb 11 2005 - p11(2) [501+]

Myrick, Florence - *Nursing Preceptorship: Connecting Practice and Education*
>   SciTech - v28 - i3 - Sept 2004 - p126(1) [51-500]

Myrtek, Michael - *Heart and Emotion: Ambulatory Monitoring Studies in Everyday Life*
>   SciTech - v28 - i3 - Sept 2004 - p68(1) [51-500]

Mysliwiec, Karol - *Eros on the Nile*
>   HRNB - v33 - i1 - Fall 2004 - p37(1) [501+]

Myss, Caroline M. - *Invisible Acts of Power: Personal Choices That Create Miracles*
>   PW - v251 - i35 - August 30 2004 - p51(2) [501+]

Mysterious You
>   LibMed - v22 - i6 - March 2004 - p77(1) [501+]

Mythology A to Z
>   LibMed - v23 - i1 - August-Sept 2004 - p78(1) [51-500]

N

Na, Ye-Ri - *50 Rules For Teenagers: Volume 1 (Illus. by Na, Ye-Ri)*
  PW - v251 - i37 - Sept 13 2004 - p60(1) [501+]
  y SLJ - v50 - i11 - Nov 2004 - p179(1) [51-500]
Naam, Ramez - *More than Human: Embracing the Promise of Biological Enhancement.*
  KR - v73 - i1 - Jan 1 2005 - p39(1) [501+]
  PW - v252 - i6 - Feb 7 2005 - p54(1) [51-500]
Naar-King, Sylvie - *Assessing Children's Well-Being: A Handbook of Measures*
  E-Streams - August 2004 - pNA [501+]
Naas, Michael - *Taking on the Tradition: Jacques Derrida and the Legacies of Deconstruction*
  Dal R - v83 - i3 - Autumn 2003 - p458-460 [501+]
Naber, Gregory - *The Geometry of Minkowski Spacetime: An Introduction to the Mathematics of the Special Theory of Relativity*
  SciTech - v28 - i3 - Sept 2004 - p46(1) [1-50]
Nabhan, Gary Paul - *Why Some Like It Hot: Food, Genes, and Cultural Diversity*
  BL - v101 - i1 - Sept 1 2004 - p27(1) [51-500]
  BW - v34 - i46 - Nov 14 2004 - p12(1) [1-50]
  Nature - v431 - i7011 - Oct 21 2004 - p907(2) [501+]
  PW - v251 - i31 - August 2 2004 - p63(1) [51-500]
  SciTech - v28 - i4 - Dec 2004 - p61(1) [51-500]
Nablis, Mustapha K. - *Better Governance for Development in the Middle East and North Africa: Enhancing Inclusiveness and Accountability*
  JEL - v42 - i1 - March 2004 - p313(2) [501+]
Nabokov, Peter - *A Forest of Time: American Indian Ways of History*
  Am St - v45 - i1 - Spring 2004 - p139-140 [501+]
  WestFolk - v62 - i3 - Summer 2003 - p225-227 [501+]
  Restoring a Presence: American Indians and Yellowstone National Park
  LJ - v129 - i16 - Oct 1 2004 - p96(1) [501+]
Nabokov, Vladimir - *Pale Fire: A Novel*
  JPC - v36 - i3 - Winter 2003 - p480 [501+]
Nabokov, Vladimir Vladimirovich - *Despair: A Novel*
  JPC - v36 - i3 - Winter 2003 - p480 [501+]
  Lolita
  BL - v101 - i2 - Sept 15 2004 - p224(1) [501+]
Nabors, Murray W. - *Introduction to Botany*
  SciTech - v28 - i1 - March 2004 - p66(1) [51-500]
Nace, Ted - *Gangs of America: The Rise of Corporate Power and the Disabling of Democracy*
  Per Psy - v57 - i3 - Autumn 2004 - p780(4) [501+]
Nachman, Gerald - *Seriously Funny: The Rebel Comedians of the 1950s and 1960s*
  NYTBR - Nov 7 2004 - p30 [501+]
  R&R Bk N - v19 - i4 - Nov 2004 - p226(1) [501+]
Nadasdy, Paul - *Hunters and Bureaucrats: Power, Knowledge, and Aboriginal-State Relations in the Southwest Yukon*
  R&R Bk N - v19 - i1 - Feb 2004 - p52(1) [51-500]
Nadeau, Jean-Benoit - *Sixty Million Frenchmen Can't Be Wrong*
  NS - v133 - i4716 - Nov 29 2004 - p42(1) [51-500]
Nadeau, Kathleen M. - *Liberation Theology in the Philipines: Faith in a Revolution*
  JAS - v63 - i3 - August 2004 - p854-855 [501+]
Nadeau, Robert L. - *The Wealth of Nature: How Mainstream Economics Has Failed the Environment*
  JEL - v41 - i4 - Dec 2003 - p1434(1) [501+]
  QRB - v79 - i4 - Dec 2004 - p452(1) [501+]
  TLS - i5286 - July 23 2004 - p30(1) [501+]
Nadel, Barbara - *The Ottoman Cage*
  KR - v72 - i24 - Dec 15 2004 - p1169(1) [501+]

Nadel, Barbara A. - *Building Security: Handbook for Architectural Planning and Design*
  Choice - v42 - i3 - Nov 2004 - p515(1) [1-50]
Nadel, Ira B. - *Ezra Pound: A Literary Life*
  Choice - v42 - i5 - Jan 2005 - p854(1) [1-50]
  CR - v285 - i1665 - Oct 2004 - p245(3) [501+]
Nadell, Martha Jane - *Enter the New Negroes: Images of Race in American Culture*
  Choice - v42 - i7 - March 2005 - p1230(2) [51-500]
Naden, Corinne J. - *Mormonism*
  y SLJ - v50 - i11 - Nov 2004 - p170(1) [51-500]
Nader, Ralph - *The Good Fight: Declare Your Independence and Close the Democracy Gap*
  NYTBR - Sept 19 2004 - p9 [501+]
  In Pursuit of Justice: Collected Writings 2000-2003
  NYTBR - Sept 19 2004 - p9 [501+]
  R&R Bk N - v19 - i4 - Nov 2004 - p124(1) [51-500]
Nadler, Gerald - *Smart Questions: Learn to Ask the Right Questions for Powerful Results*
  R&R Bk N - v19 - i3 - August 2004 - p102(1) [501+]
Nadler, John - *Searching for Sofia: A Tale of Obsession, Murder and War*
  CBRA - Annual 2003 - p295(2) [501+]
Nadler, Steven - *Rembrandt's Jews*
  Apo - v159 - i509 - July 2004 - p67(2) [501+]
  BooChiTr - March 28 2004 - p1(4) [501+]
Nadon, C. - *Xenophon's Price: Republic and Empire in the Cyropaedia*
  Class R - v54 - i2 - Nov 2004 - p324-326 [501+]
Naef, Weston - *Photographers of Genius at the Getty*
  Choice - v42 - i2 - Oct 2004 - p286(2) [501+]
  LJ - v129 - i12 - July 2004 - p79(2) [51-500]
Naess, Arne - *Life's Philosophy: Reason and Feeling in a Deeper World*
  R&R Bk N - v19 - i1 - Feb 2004 - p10(1) [51-500]
Naff, Clay Ferris - *Vaccines*
  y BL - v101 - i7 - Dec 1 2004 - p665(1) [51-500]
Nafisi, Azar - *Reading Lolita in Tehran: A Memoir in Books (Read by Lecat, Lisette). Audiobook Review*
  LJ - v130 - i3 - Feb 15 2005 - p170(1) [51-500]
Nagabhushanam, R. - *Biotechnology of Aquatic Animals*
  SciTech - v28 - i4 - Dec 2004 - p164(1) [51-500]
Nagai, Nobuhito - *Les conseillers municipaux de Paris sous la Troisieme Republique, 1871-1914.*
  JMH - v77 - i1 - March 2005 - p199(3) [501+]
Nagami, Pamela - *Bitten: True Medical Stories of Bites and Stings*
  BL - v100 - i21 - July 2004 - p1808(1) [1-50]
  Globe & Mail - July 31 2004 - pD12 [1-50]
  Globe & Mail - Sept 25 2004 - pD29 [501+]
Nagatake, Takeshi - *Classic Japanese Porcelain: Imari and Kakiemon*
  Ceram Mo - v52 - i3 - March 2004 - p34(2) [501+]
Nagatomo, Haruno - *Draw Your Own Manga: All the Basics*
  y VOYA - v27 - i5 - Dec 2004 - p416(1) [51-500]
Nagda, Ann Whitehead - *A Home for Panda (Illus. by Effler, Jim)*
  c CE - v81 - i1 - Fall 2004 - p48(1) [51-500]
  Polar Bear Math: Learning about Fractions from Klondike and Snow (Illus. by Bickel, Cindy)
  c BL - v101 - i1 - Sept 1 2004 - p118(1) [1-50]
  c KR - v72 - i14 - July 15 2004 - p691(1) [51-500]
  c SLJ - v50 - i9 - Sept 2004 - p190(2) [51-500]
Nagel, Joane - *Race, Ethnicity, and Sexuality: Intimate Interactions, Forbidden Frontiers*
  JPC - v38 - i1 - August 2004 - p221(3) [501+]

Nagel, Susan - *Mistress of the Elgin Marbles: A Biography of Mary Nisbet, Countess of Elgin*
  People - v62 - i7 - August 16 2004 - p52 [51-500]
Naggar, Carole - *George Rodger: An Adventure in Photography, 1908-1995*
  R&R Bk N - v19 - i1 - Feb 2004 - p251(1) [51-500]
Nagin, Carl - *Because Writing Matters*
  TCR - v106 - i5 - May 2004 - p898(3) [501+]
Nagl-Docekal, Herta - *Feminist Philosophy*
  Choice - v42 - i4 - Dec 2004 - p675(1) [1-50]
  Wom R Bks - v21 - i10-11 - July 2004 - p28(1) [51-500]
Nagl, John A. - *Counterinsurgency Lessons from Malaya and Vietnam: Learning to Eat Soup with a Knife*
  Parameters - v34 - i3 - Autumn 2004 - p166(3) [501+]
Nagpaul, S.R. - *Topics in Applied Abstract Algebra*
  SciTech - v28 - i4 - Dec 2004 - p34(1) [51-500]
Nagurney, Anna - *Innovations in Financial and Economic Networks*
  R&R Bk N - v19 - i2 - May 2004 - p121 [51-500]
Nagyszalanczy, Sandor - *Tools Rare and Ingenious; Celebrating the World's Most Amazing Tools*
  SciTech - v28 - i4 - Dec 2004 - p147(1) [501+]
Nahin, Paul J. - *When Least Is Best: How Mathematicians Discovered Many Clever Ways to Make Things as Small (or as Large) as Possible*
  Choice - v42 - i5 - Jan 2005 - p889(1) [1-50]
  SB - v40 - i4 - July-August 2004 - p158(1) [51-500]
Nahm, Andrew C. - *Historical Dictionary of the Republic of Korea, 2nd Ed.*
  Choice - v42 - i4 - Dec 2004 - p642(1) [1-50]
  Choice - v42 - i4 - Dec 2004 - p642(1) [1-50]
  R&R Bk N - v19 - i4 - Nov 2004 - p50(1) [1-50]
Nahuis, Richard - *Knowledge, Inequality, and Growth in the New Economy*
  R&R Bk N - v19 - i3 - August 2004 - p96(1) [51-500]
Naib, Sudhir - *Disinvestment in India: Policies, Procedures, Practices*
  R&R Bk N - v19 - i3 - August 2004 - p138(1) [51-500]
Naidoo, Beverley - *Baba's Gift*
  c Sch Lib - v52 - i3 - Autumn 2004 - p132(1) [501+]
  Web of Lies
  y Sch Lib - v52 - i4 - Winter 2004 - p216(1) [51-500]
Naidu,Subbaram D. - *A First Course in Fuzzy and Neural Control*
  SIAM Rev - v46 - i1 - March 2004 - p176-179 [501+]
Naifeh, Ted - *Courtney Crumrin and the Night Things*
  y Teach Lib - v32 - i1 - Oct 2004 - p17(2) [501+]
  How Loathsome
  BL - v100 - i21 - July 2004 - p1831(1) [1-50]
Naimark, Norman M. - *Yugoslavia and Its Historians: Understanding the Balkan Wars of the 1990s*
  AHR - v109 - i2 - April 2004 - p644(2) [501+]
  Yugoslavia and Its Historians: Understanding the Balkan Wars of the 1990's
  Slav R - v63 - i2 - Summer 2004 - p388(2) [501+]
Naipaul, V.S. - *Literary Occasions: Essays*
  CR - v285 - i1663 - August 2004 - p123(1) [501+]
  NYTBR - Oct 10 2004 - p26 [501+]
  TLS - i5292 - Sept 3 2004 - p10-11 [501+]

Nattel, Lilian - *The Singing Fire. Audiobook Review*
Globe & Mail - Jan 22 2005 - pD13 [51-500]

Nattrass, Nicoli - *The Moral Economy of AIDS in South Africa*
For Aff - v83 - i5 - Sept-Oct 2004 - p164 [501+]
TLS - i5288 - August 6 2004 - p5-6 [501+]

Natural Gas Information, 2003 Ed.
JEL - v42 - i1 - March 2004 - p334(1) [501+]
SciTech - v28 - i3 - Sept 2004 - p8(1) [501+]

Natural Wonders
y LibMed - v23 - i1 - August-Sept 2004 - p74(1) [51-500]

Nature of Healing: Writings from the World's Spiritual Traditions.
SciTech - v28 - i3 - Sept 2004 - p4(1) [501+]

Nature of Science
LibMed - v22 - i6 - March 2004 - p92(1) [501+]

Nau, Henry R. - *At Home Abroad: Identity and Power in American Foreign Policy*
AJPS - v39 - i3 - Nov 2004 - p672(2) [501+]

Naughtie, James - *The Accidental American: Tony Blair and the Presidency*
NS - v133 - i4709 - Oct 11 2004 - p51(2) [501+]
PW - v251 - i35 - August 30 2004 - p46(1) [51-500]
SPA - v61 - i2 - March-April 2005 - p69(1) [51-500]

Naughton, Leonie - *That Was the Wild East: Film Culture, Unification and the "New" Germany*
GSR - v27 - i2 - May 2004 - p441-442 [501+]

Nault, Jennifer - *Judy Blume*
c SLJ - v50 - i10 - Oct 2004 - p139(2) [51-500]
Project Polar Bear
c SLJ - v50 - i12 - Dec 2004 - p135(2) [501+]

Naumkin, Vitaly V. - *Red Wolves of Yemen: The Struggle for Independence*
A Aff - v35 - i2 - July 2004 - p218-219 [501+]

Nauta Dutilh - *Dealing with Dominance: The Experience of National Competition Authorities*
R&R Bk N - v19 - i3 - August 2004 - p193(1) [501+]

Navari, Leonora - *Greek Civilization through the Eyes of Travellers and Scholars: From the Collection of Dimitris Contominas*
R&R Bk N - v19 - i4 - Nov 2004 - p257(1) [501+]

Navarra, Tova - *Encyclopedia of Asthma and Respiratory Disorders*
E-Streams - July 2004 - pNA [501+]
Encyclopedia of Complementary and Alternative Medicine
E-Streams - Nov 2004 - pNA [501+]
SciTech -, v28 - i1 - March 2004 - p79(1) [51-500]
The Encyclopedia of Vitamins, Minerals, and Supplements, 2nd Ed.
Choice - v42 - i6 - Feb 2005 - p998(1) [51-500]
SciTech - v28 - i3 - Sept 2004 - p73(1) [51-500]
The Encyclopedia of Vitamins, Minerals, and Supplements. 2nd Ed.
BL - v101 - i8 - Dec 15 2004 - p757(1) [501+]

Navarro, Dave - *Don't Try This at Home*
Ent W - i789 - Oct 22 2004 - p99 [501+]
PW - v251 - i41 - Oct 11 2004 - p69(1) [51-500]
PW - v251 - i49 - Dec 6 2004 - p39(1) [1-50]
Time - v164 - i18 - Nov 1 2004 - p83 [501+]

Navarro, Julio - *Malangatana Valente Ngwenya*
IJAHS - v37 - i2 - Spring 2004 - p357-359 [501+]

Navarro, Perez - *El ultimo dia de verano/The Last Day of Summer*
c BL - v100 - i22 - August 2004 - p1950(1) [501+]

Navarro, Vicente - *Political and Economic Determinants of Population Health and Well-Being: Controversies and Developments*
SciTech - v28 - i4 - Dec 2004 - p81(1) [51-500]
The Political and Social Contexts of Health
SciTech - v28 - i4 - Dec 2004 - p81(1) [51-500]

Navasky, Victor S. - *A Matter of Opinion*
KR - v73 - i4 - Feb 15 2005 - p217(1) [501+]

Naveh, Eyal - *Reinhold Niebuhr and Non-Utopian Liberalism: Beyond Illusion and Despair*
JR - v84 - i4 - Oct 2004 - p638(2) [501+]

Naveh, Hannah - *Gender and Israeli Society: Women's Time*
R&R Bk N - v19 - i1 - Feb 2004 - p132(1) [51-500]
Israeli Family and Community: Women's Time
R&R Bk N - v19 - i1 - Feb 2004 - p133(1) [51-500]

Naves, Elaine Kalman - *Shoshanna's Story: A Mother, a Daughter, and the Shadows of History*
Globe & Mail - March 5 2005 - pD17 [51-500]

Navratilova, Hana - *Egyptian Revival in Bohemia 1850-1920: Orientalism and Egyptomania in Czech Lands*
R&R Bk N - v19 - i4 - Nov 2004 - p29(1) [501+]

Nay, W. Robert - *Taking Charge of Anger: How to Resolve Conflict, Sustain Relationships, and Express Yourself Without Losing Control*
R&R Bk N - v19 - i3 - August 2004 - p9(1) [1-50]

Naya, Seiji F. - *The Asian Development Experience: Overcoming Crises and Adjusting to Change*
JEL - v41 - i4 - Dec 2003 - p1411(2) [501+]

Nayar, Kamala Elizabeth - *Hayagriva in South India: Complexity and Selectivity of a Pan-Indian Hindu Deity*
R&R Bk N - v19 - i3 - August 2004 - p14(1) [1-50]
The Sikh Diaspora in Vancouver: Three Generations Amid Tradition, Modernity, and Multiculturalism
R&R Bk N - v19 - i3 - August 2004 - p54(1) [51-500]

Nayder, Lillian - *Unequal Partners: Charles Dickens, Wilkie Collins, and Victorian Authorship*
RES - v55 - i221 - Sept 2004 - p632(2) [501+]

Nayfeh, Ali H. - *Linear and Nonlinear Structural Mechanics*
SciTech - v28 - i3 - Sept 2004 - p141(1) [51-500]

Naylor, Clare - *The Goddess Rules*
PW - v252 - i6 - Feb 7 2005 - p43(1) [51-500]

Naylor, Phyllis Reynolds - *Alice: Alice in Blunderland*
c PW - v252 - i11 - March 14 2005 - p70(1) [51-500]
Girls Rule!
c BL - v101 - i7 - Dec 1 2004 - p653(1) [51-500]
c CH Bwatch - v14 - i11 - Nov 2004 - pNA [51-500]
c SLJ - v50 - i10 - Oct 2004 - p173(1) [51-500]
Including Alice
c CH Bwatch - v14 - i7 - July 2004 - p7(1) [51-500]
y HB - v80 - i4 - July-August 2004 - p458(1) [51-500]
y VOYA - v27 - i3 - August 2004 - p223(1) [1-50]
Lovingly Alice
c BL - v101 - i5 - Nov 1 2004 - p486(1) [51-500]
c CH Bwatch - Feb 2005 - pNA [51-500]
c HB - v80 - i6 - Nov-Dec 2004 - p714(1) [501+]
c SLJ - v50 - i9 - Sept 2004 - p213(2) [51-500]
Patiently Alice
c Kliatt - v38 - i6 - Nov 2004 - p20(1) [51-500]
Simply Alice
c RT - v57 - Oct 2003 - p177 [1-50]

Naylor, R.T. - *Wages of Crime: Black Markets, Illegal Finance, and the Underworld Economy*
CBRA - Annual 2003 - p317(1) [501+]

Nayyar, Deepak - *Governing Globalization: Issues and Institutions*
JEL - v42 - i1 - March 2004 - p183(3) [501+]

Nazer, Mende - *Slave: My True Story*
BW - v34 - i12 - March 21 2004 - p5(1) [501+]
R&R Bk N - v19 - i1 - Feb 2004 - p135(1) [51-500]

Nazri, Gholam-Abbas - *Lithium Batteries: Science and Technology*
SciTech - v28 - i1 - March 2004 - p152(1) [51-500]

NCAA March Madness: Cinderellas, Superstars, and Champions from the NCAA Men's Final Four
BL - v101 - i1 - Sept 1 2004 - p45(1) [501+]

NCEO - Incentive Compensation and Employee Ownership: 5th Ed.
HR Mag - v49 - i7 - July 2004 - pS7(1) [51-500]

Ndege, George Oduor - *Health, State, and Society in Kenya: Faces of Contact and Change*
JIH - v34 - i4 - Spring 2004 - p670-671 [501+]

Ndegwa, David - *Main Issues in Mental Health and Race*
SciTech - v28 - i1 - March 2004 - p96(1) [51-500]

NDiaye, Marie - *Les Serpents*
WLT - v79 - i1 - Jan-April 2005 - p97(1) [501+]
Tous mes amis
TLS - i5285 - July 16 2004 - p28(1) [501+]
WLT - v79 - i1 - Jan-April 2005 - p97(1) [501+]

Nead, Lynda - *Victorian Babylon*
VS - v45 - i2 - Winter 2003 - p319 [501+]

Neal, Charles M., Jr. - *Valor Across the Lone Star: The Congressional Medal of Honor in Frontier Texas*
WHQ - v35 - i2 - Summer 2004 - p237-238 [501+]

Neal, Connie - *The Gospel According to Harry Potter: Spirituality in the Stories of the World's Most Famous Seeker*
Bks & Cult - v11 - i1 - Jan-Feb 2005 - p16(2) [501+]

Neal, David S. - *Mosaics of Britain, Vol. 1*
TimHES - v0 - i1654 - August 20 2004 - p30(1) [501+]

Neal, Moreton - *Remembering Bill Neal: Favorite Recipes from a Life in Cooking*
LJ - v129 - i19 - Nov 15 2004 - p80(2) [51-500]

Neal, Steve - *HST: Memories of the Truman Years*
PSQ - v119 - i3 - Fall 2004 - p524(3) [501+]

Neale, Jonathan - *Himalaya*
c CCB-B - v58 - i3 - Nov 2004 - p136(1) [501+]
c Kliatt - v38 - i4 - July 2004 - p10(2) [51-500]
y KR - v72 - i13 - July 1 2004 - p634(1) [51-500]
y PW - v251 - i34 - August 23 2004 - p56(1) [501+]
c SLJ - v50 - i10 - Oct 2004 - p173(1) [51-500]
y VOYA - v27 - i4 - Oct 2004 - p306(1) [51-500]
Lost at Sea
y Kliatt - v38 - i5 - Sept 2004 - p24(2) [51-500]
A People's History of the Vietnam War
Choice - v41 - i7 - March 2004 - p1347(1) [501+]

Neale, Mark - *William Gibson: No Maps for These Territories*
MFSF - v108 - i4 - April 2005 - p28(3) [501+]

Neale, Naomi - *Calendar Girl*
BL - v101 - i9-10 - Jan 1 2005 - p821(1) [501+]

Neame, Christopher - *A Take on British TV Drama: Stories from the Golden Years*
R&R Bk N - v19 - i4 - Nov 2004 - p222(1) [501+]

Neapolitan, Jane E. - *Traditions, Standards, and Transformations: A Model for Professional Development School Networks*
R&R Bk N - v19 - i3 - August 2004 - p220(1) [1-50]

Neatby, Blair - *Creating Carleton: The Shaping of a University*
Can Lit - i182 - Autumn 2004 - p129(2) [501+]

Neate, Patrick - *Where You're At: Notes from the Frontline of a Hip-Hop Planet*
BL - v100 - i21 - July 2004 - p1809(1) [1-50]
BW - v34 - i36 - Sept 5 2004 - p9(1) [501+]
LJ - v129 - i12 - July 2004 - p84(1) [51-500]
PW - v251 - i27 - July 5 2004 - p47(2) [51-500]

Neave, Airey - *Saturday at M.I.9: A History of Underground Escape Lines in the North-West Europe in 1940-5 by Leading Organiser at M.I.9*
R&R Bk N - v19 - i3 - August 2004 - p34(1) [51-500]

Nebelkopf, Ethan - *Healing and Mental Health for Native Americans: Speaking in Red*
SciTech - v28 - i4 - Dec 2004 - p95(1) [51-500]

Nebenzahl, Kenneth - *Mapping the Silk Road and Beyond: 2,000 Years of Exploring the East*
BL - v101 - i9-10 - Jan 1 2005 - p804(2) [51-500]
LJ - v129 - i20 - Dec 1 2004 - p168(1) [51-500]

Necessary Dreams: Ambition in Women's Changing Lives
Wom R Bks - v22 - i2 - Nov 2004 - p4(2) [501+]

Necipòglu, Gulru - *Muqarnas: An Annual on the Visual Culture of the Islamic World, Vol. 20*
R&R Bk N - v19 - i1 - Feb 2004 - p199(1) [51-500]

Nedeltchev, Plamen - *Troubleshooting Remote Access Networks*
SciTech - v28 - i3 - Sept 2004 - p159(1) [51-500]

Neder, Christina - *Transformation! Innovation?: Perspectives on Taiwan Culture*
R&R Bk N - v19 - i3 - August 2004 - p142(1) [51-500]

Nederman, Cary J. - *Political Thought in Early Fourteenth-Century England: Treatises of Walter of Milemete, William of Pagula, and William of Ockham*
Med R - June 2004 - pNA [501+]

Nedkov, Vesselin - *57 Hours: A Survivor's Account of the Moscow Hostage Drama*
CBRA - Annual 2003 - p296(1) [501+]

Nedzel, Nadia E. - *Legal Reasoning, Research, and Writing for International Graduate Students*
R&R Bk N - v19 - i3 - August 2004 - p196(1) [1-50]

Needle, Jan - *Dracula (Illus. by Blythe, Gary)*
y Magpies - v19 - i5 - Nov 2004 - p20(4) [501+]

Needleman, Ruth - *Black Freedom Fighters in Steel: The Struggle for Democratic Unionism*
AHR - v109 - i4 - Oct 2004 - p1252(1) [501+]
Choice - v41 - i7 - March 2004 - p1339(2) [501+]
JAH - v91 - i1 - June 2004 - p318-320 [501+]
JEL - v41 - i4 - Dec 2003 - p1383(1) [501+]

Needles, Dan - *With Axe and Flask: The History of Persephone Township from Pre-Cambrian Times to the Present*
CBRA - Annual 2003 - p179(2) [501+]

Neel, Carol - *Medieval Families: Perspectives on Marriage, Household, and Children*
R&R Bk N - v19 - i3 - August 2004 - p149(1) [51-500]

Neely, Carol Thomas - *Distracted Subjects: Madness and Gender in Shakespeare and Early Modern Culture*
Choice - v42 - i4 - Dec 2004 - p661(1) [1-50]
TLS - i5290 - August 20 2004 - p29(1) [51-500]
Neenan, Colin - *Idiot!*
c CH Bwatch - Oct 2004 - pNA [51-500]
y Kliatt - v39 - i2 - March 2005 - p21(2) [51-500]
Nees, Lawrence - *Early Medieval Art*
Specu - v79 - i3 - July 2004 - p805-807 [501+]
Neff, Heather - *Accident of Birth*
BL - v101 - i6 - Nov 15 2004 - p562(1) [51-500]
Black Iss - v6 - i6 - Nov-Dec 2004 - p72(1) [501+]
LJ - v129 - i18 - Nov 1 2004 - p76(1) [501+]
PW - v251 - i44 - Nov 1 2004 - p42(2) [501+]
Neff, Lyle - *Full Magpie Dodge*
Can Lit - i182 - Autumn 2004 - p116(3) [501+]
Neff, Thomas J. - *You're in Charge, Now What?*
Bus W - i3922 - Feb 28 2005 - p25 [501+]
LJ - v129 - i20 - Dec 1 2004 - p132(2) [51-500]
Time - v165 - i4 - Jan 24 2005 - pB5 [501+]
You're in Charge--Now What?: The 8-Point Plan
PW - v251 - i48 - Nov 29 2004 - p33(1) [501+]
Negri, Antonio - *Empire*
NYRB - v51 - i17 - Nov 4 2004 - p38(4) [501+]
Time for Revolution
R&R Bk N - v19 - i3 - August 2004 - p175(1) [501+]
Tikkun - v20 - i1 - Jan-Feb 2005 - p68(4) [501+]
Negrin, Micol - *The Italian Grill*
PW - v252 - i11 - March 14 2005 - p61(1) [51-500]
Negrino, Tom - *Creating a Presentation in PowerPoint: Visual QuickProject Guide*
LJ - v130 - i1 - Jan 1 2005 - p148(1) [501+]
JavaScript for the World Wide Web, 5th Ed.
CBRA - Annual 2003 - p21(1) [1-50]
SciTech - v28 - i4 - Dec 2004 - p21(1) [51-500]
Mac OS X Unwired: A Guide for Home, Office, and the Road
SciTech - v28 - i3 - Sept 2004 - p26(1) [51-500]
Negron-Muntaner, Frances - *Boricua Pop: Puerto Ricans and the Latinization of American Culture*
Choice - v42 - i3 - Nov 2004 - p573(1) [1-50]
Negus, Christopher - *Linux Troubleshooting Bible*
SciTech - v28 - i3 - Sept 2004 - p26(1) [51-500]
Red Hat Fedora Linux 2 Bible
SciTech - v28 - i3 - Sept 2004 - p28(1) [51-500]
Nehlen, Don - *American Football Coaches Association: Complete Guide to Special Teams*
LJ - v130 - i3 - Feb 15 2005 - p136(2) [51-500]
Nehlig, Astrid - *Coffee, Tea, Chocolate, and the Brain*
SciTech - v28 - i3 - Sept 2004 - p73(1) [51-500]
Nehring, Radine Trees - *A Treasure to Die For*
LJ - v130 - i2 - Feb 1 2005 - p64(1) [51-500]
Neiberg, Michael S. - *Fighting the Great War: A Global History*
KR - v73 - i2 - Jan 15 2005 - p106(1) [501+]
LJ - v130 - i2 - Feb 1 2005 - p98(2) [51-500]
Warfare and Society in Europe, 1898 to the Present
J Mil H - v68 - i3 - July 2004 - p971-973 [501+]
Warfare and World History
J Mil H - v68 - i3 - July 2004 - p971-973 [501+]
Neich, Roger - *Pacific Jewelry and Adornment*
Bwatch - Jan 2005 - pNA [51-500]
Choice - v42 - i6 - Feb 2005 - p1010(2) [51-500]
R&R Bk N - v19 - i4 - Nov 2004 - p210(1) [501+]
Neichly, Patrick - *The Supernaturalists*
PW - v251 - i44 - Nov 1 2004 - p46(1) [501+]
Neidhart, Christoph - *Russia's Carnival: The Smells, Sights, and Sounds of Transition*
Slav R - v63 - i2 - Summer 2004 - p430(2) [501+]
Neighly, Patrick - *Texarkana*
PW - v251 - i35 - August 30 2004 - p34(1) [501+]
Neillands, Robin - *Eighth Army: The Triumphant Desert Army That Held the Axis at Bay from North Africa to the Alps, 1939-45*
CR - v285 - i1663 - August 2004 - p117(2) [501+]
The Old Contemptibles: The British Expeditionary Force, 1914
CR - v286 - i1668 - Jan 2005 - p63(1) [51-500]
TLS - i5295 - Sept 24 2004 - p26(1) [501+]
The Travelling Historian's Guide to France
LJ - v129 - i19 - Nov 15 2004 - p78(1) [501+]
Neils, Jenifer - *Coming of Age in Ancient Greece: Images of Childhood from the Classical Past*
JIH - v35 - i2 - Autumn 2004 - p284(2) [501+]
Striving for Excellence: Ancient Greek Childhood and the Olympic Spirit
Choice - v42 - i1 - Sept 2004 - p86(1) [501+]
Neilsen, Peter E. - *Pseudo-Peptides in Drug Discovery*
SciTech - v28 - i4 - Dec 2004 - p120(1) [1-50]
Neilson, Shane - *The Beaten-Down Elegies*
BIC - v33 - i5 - August 2004 - p33(2) [501+]
Neiman, Susan - *Evil in Modern Thought: An Alternative History of Philosophy*
CC - v121 - i25 - Dec 14 2004 - p20(1) [501+]
Globe & Mail - Sept 11 2004 - pD23 [501+]
Theol St - v65 - i3 - Sept 2004 - p669(2) [501+]
Neipris, Janet - *Jeremy and the Thinking Machine*
c Sch Lib - v52 - i4 - Winter 2004 - p211(1) [51-500]
Neisuler, Susan G. - *Justice at the City Gate: Social Policy, Social Services, and the Law*
Choice - v41 - i7 - March 2004 - p1377(1) [501+]
Neisworth, John T. - *The Autism Encyclopedia*
LJ - v129 - i20 - Dec 1 2004 - p168(1) [51-500]
Neitzel, Soenke - *Kriegsaubruch: Deutschlands Weg in die Katastrophe 1900-1914*
HNet - July 2004 - pNA [501+]
Neiwert, David A. - *Death on the Fourth of July: A Killing, a Trial, and Hate Crime in America*
BL - v100 - i21 - July 2004 - p1805(1) [51-500]
Nekes, Werner - *Eyes, Lies and Illusions Drawn from the Werner Nekes Collection*
Sci - v306 - i5701 - Nov 26 2004 - p1480(1) [501+]
Nel, Philip - *The Avante-Garde and American Postmodernity: Small Incisive Shocks*
MFSF - v50 - i2 - Summer 2004 - p488-490 [501+]
Democratizing Foreign Policy?: Lessons from South Africa
Choice - v42 - i3 - Nov 2004 - p556(2) [1-50]
Dr. Seuss: American Icon
Choice - v42 - i2 - Oct 2004 - p295(1) [501+]
Nelis, D. - *Vergil's Aeneid and the Arginautica of Apollonius Rhodius*
Class R - v54 - i2 - Nov 2004 - p374(3) [501+]
Nell, Edward J. - *Reinventing Functional Finance: Transformational Growth and Full Employment*
R&R Bk N - v19 - i1 - Feb 2004 - p120(1) [51-500]
Nelles, H.V. - *A Little History of Canada*
Beav - v85 - i1 - Feb-March 2005 - p46(1) [501+]
CG - v124 - i5 - Sept-Oct 2004 - p112(1) [501+]
Nelles, Jurgen - *Bucher uber Bucher. Das Medium Buch in Romanen des 18. und 19. Jahrhunderts*
Ger Q - v77 - i4 - Fall 2004 - p499-500 [501+]
Nelscott, Kris - *War at Home*
KR - v73 - i2 - Jan 15 2005 - p87(1) [51-500]
PW - v252 - i9 - Feb 28 2005 - p46(1) [51-500]
Ent W - i812 - March 25 2005 - p76 [51-500]
Nelso, Sarah - *So Many Books, So Little Time: A Year of Passionate Reading*
Globe & Mail - Nov 27 2004 - pD49 [51-500]
Nelson, Alan H. - *Monstrous Adversary: The Life of Edward de Vere, 17th Earl of Oxford*
Choice - v41 - i7 - March 2004 - p1298(1) [501+]
Ren Q - v57 - i4 - Winter 2004 - p1529(2) [501+]
R&R Bk N - v19 - i1 - Feb 2004 - p235(1) [51-500]
Nelson, Blake - *The New Rules of High School*
y LibMed - v22 - i5 - Feb 2004 - p72(1) [501+]
c PW - v251 - i37 - Sept 13 2004 - p81(1) [51-500]
Rock Star Superstar
y BL - v101 - i5 - Nov 1 2004 - p476(1) [51-500]
y CCB-B - v58 - i4 - Dec 2004 - p179(1) [51-500]
y KR - v72 - i15 - August 1 2004 - p746(1) [51-500]
y PW - v251 - i38 - Sept 20 2004 - p63(1) [51-500]
y SLJ - v50 - i10 - Oct 2004 - p173(1) [51-500]
y VOYA - v27 - i4 - Oct 2004 - p306(1) [51-500]
Nelson, Cary - *The Wound and the Dream: Sixty Years of American Poems about the Spanish Civil War*
S&S - v68 - i3 - Fall 2004 - p386(1) [501+]
Nelson, Claudia - *Little Strangers: Portrayals of Adoption and Foster Care in America, 1850-1929*
AHR - v109 - i3 - June 2004 - p923(2) [501+]
Soc Ser R - v78 - i4 - Dec 2004 - p690(2) [501+]
Nelson, Daniel - *Northern Landscapes: The Struggle for Wilderness Alaska*
SciTech - v28 - i4 - Dec 2004 - p58(1) [51-500]
Nelson, Dave - *The Incredible Payback: Innovative Sourcing Solutions That Deliver Extraordinary Results*
Bwatch - Feb 2005 - pNA [501+]
Nelson, David - *The Penguin Dictionary of Mathematics, 3rd Ed.*
Choice - v42 - i2 - Oct 2004 - pNA [501+]
Nelson, David L. - *Lehninger Principles of Biochemistry, 4th Ed.*
TimHES - v0 - i1680 - Feb 25 2005 - pXIV(1) [501+]
Nelson, Dorothy - *Tar and Feathers*
BL - v101 - i7 - Dec 1 2004 - p637(1) [51-500]
KR - v72 - i20 - Oct 15 2004 - p981(1) [51-500]
LJ - v129 - i20 - Dec 1 2004 - p101(2) [51-500]
PW - v251 - i51 - Dec 20 2004 - p38(1) [51-500]
Nelson, Edward W. - *Blueprints Q & A Step 2: Surgery, 2nd Ed.*
SciTech - v28 - i4 - Dec 2004 - p107(1) [51-500]
Blueprints Q & A Step 3: Surgery, 2nd Ed.
SciTech - v28 - i4 - Dec 2004 - p107(1) [51-500]
Nelson, Emmanuel S. - *Contemporary Gay American Poets and Playwrights: An A-to-Z Guide*
Lam Bk Rpt - v13 - i4-5 - Nov-Dec 2004 - p21(2) [501+]
Nelson, Eric - *The Greek Tradition in Republican Thought*
Choice - v42 - i3 - Nov 2004 - p562(1) [1-50]
Nelson, J.G. - *Protected Areas and the Regional Planning Imperative in North America*
CBRA - Annual 2003 - p410(2) [501+]
Nelson, James L. - *Thieves of Mercy: A Novel of the Civil War at Sea*
KR - v73 - i2 - Jan 15 2005 - p78(1) [501+]
LJ - v130 - i2 - Feb 1 2005 - p70(1) [51-500]
PW - v252 - i8 - Feb 21 2005 - p157(1) [51-500]
Nelson, James Lindemann - *Rationing Sanity: Ethical Issues in Managed Mental Health Care*
SciTech - v28 - i3 - Sept 2004 - p86(1) [501+]
Nelson, Jennifer - *Women of Color and the Reproductive Rights Movement*
CS - v33 - i4 - July 2004 - p473(2) [501+]
JAH - v91 - i2 - Sept 2004 - p729(2) [501+]
Nelson, Jenny - *The Physics of Solar Cells*
Phys Today - v57 - i12 - Dec 2004 - p71-72 [501+]
Nelson-Jones, Richard - *Cognitive Humanistic Therapy: Buddhism, Christianity and Being Fully Human*
Choice - v42 - i4 - Dec 2004 - p739(1) [1-50]
SciTech - v28 - i3 - Sept 2004 - p99(1) [51-500]
Nelson, Joseph S. - *Common and Scientific Names of Fishes from the United States, Canada and Mexico, 6th Ed.*
SciTech - v28 - i4 - Dec 2004 - p65(1) [51-500]
Nelson, Julianne - *Women Working It Out: Career Plans and Business Decisions*
JEL - v41 - i4 - Dec 2003 - p1384(1) [501+]
Nelson, Kristin L. - *The Washington Monument*
c LibMed - v22 - i4 - Jan 2004 - p82(1) [501+]
Nelson, Lawrence J. - *Rumors of Indiscretion: The University of Missouri "Sex Questionanaire" Scandal in the Jazz Age*
JAH - v91 - i1 - June 2004 - p280-281 [501+]
Rumors of Indiscretion: The University of Missouri "Sex Questionnaire" Scandal in Jazz Age
AHR - v109 - i2 - April 2004 - p549(2) [501+]
Nelson, Lyle Emerson - *American Presidents: Year by Year, Vols. 1-3*
R&R Bk N - v19 - i1 - Feb 2004 - p55(1) [51-500]
Nelson, Margaret - *Saving Body & Soul: The Mission of Mary Jo Copeland (Illus. by Pickett, Keri)*
People - v62 - i17 - Oct 25 2004 - p52 [51-500]
Nelson, Marilyn - *Carver: A Life in Poems*
y HR - v55 - i4 - Winter 2003 - p671 [501+]
c SLJ - v50 - i11 - Nov 2004 - p67(1) [51-500]
Fortune's Bones: The Manumission Requiem
y BL - v101 - i6 - Nov 15 2004 - p573(1) [51-500]
CC - v121 - i25 - Dec 14 2004 - p24(1) [51-500]
y CCB-B - v58 - i6 - Feb 2005 - p259(1) [51-500]
y HB - v81 - i1 - Jan-Feb 2005 - p105(1) [51-500]
KR - v72 - i20 - Oct 15 2004 - p1011(1) [51-500]
y NYTBR - Nov 14 2004 - p43 [501+]
y SLJ - v50 - i12 - Dec 2004 - p166(1) [51-500]
A Wreath for Emmett Till (Illus. by Lardy, Philippe)
y KR - v73 - i5 - March 1 2005 - p292(1) [51-500]
Nelson, Maxine F. - *The Collectible Vernon Kilns 2nd Ed.*
Ant&CM - v109 - i1 - March 2004 - p16(1) [501+]
Nelson, Michael - *The Evolving Presidency: Addresses, Cases, Essays, Letters, Reports, Resolutions, Transcripts, and Other Landmark Documents, 1787-2004, 2nd Ed.*
R&R Bk N - v19 - i3 - August 2004 - p178(1) [501+]
The Presidency A to Z
BL - v101 - i3 - Oct 1 2004 - p358(1) [501+]
Nelson, Pete - *Left for Dead*
c RT - v57 - Nov 2003 - p277 [51-500]
Treehouses of the World (Illus. by Kurzaj, Radek)
PW - v251 - i41 - Oct 11 2004 - p73(1) [51-500]
Nelson, Philip Charles - *Biological Physics: Energy, Information, Life*
Phys Today - v57 - i11 - Nov 2004 - p63-64 [501+]
SciTech - v28 - i3 - Sept 2004 - p60(1) [1-50]

Nelson, Phillip J. - *Signaling Goodness: Social Rules and Public Choice*
 Choice - v42 - i1 - Sept 2004 - p146(1) [501+]
Nelson, Robert H. - *Economics as Religion: From Samuelson to Chicago and Beyond*
 JR - v85 - i1 - Jan 2005 - p170(3) [501+]
Nelson, Robert S. - *Hagia Sophia, 1850-1950: Holy Wisdom Modern Monument*
 Choice - v42 - i4 - Dec 2004 - p652(1) [1-50]
Nelson, Sandra - *Creating Policies for Results: From Chaos to Clarity*
 ALJ - v53 - i3 - August 2004 - p318(2) [501+]
Nelson, Sarah M. - *Gender in Archaeology: Analyzing Power and Prestige, 2nd Ed.*
 R&R Bk N - v19 - i3 - August 2004 - p29(1) [1-50]
Nelson, Sharon H. - *This Flesh These Words*
 CBRA - Annual 2003 - p227(2) [501+]
Nelson, Sue - *How to Clone the Perfect Blonde: Using Science to Make Your Wildest Dreams Come True*
 Am Sci - v93 - i2 - March-April 2005 - p178(1) [51-500]
 PW - v251 - i35 - August 30 2004 - p39(2) [501+]
Nelson, W. Dale - *Interpreters with Lewis and Clark*
 Bwatch - Dec 2004 - pNA [51-500]
Nelson, William - *New Jersey Biographical and Genealogical Notes*
 EFHM - v58 - i3 - May-June 2004 - p59(1) [1-50]
Nelson, William M. - *Agricultural Applications in Green Chemistry*
 SciTech - v28 - i3 - Sept 2004 - p127(1) [51-500]
Nemati, Hamid R. - *Organizational Data Mining: Leveraging Enterprise Data Resources for Optimal Performance*
 R&R Bk N - v19 - i1 - Feb 2004 - p87(1) [51-500]
Nemeth, Neil - *News Ombudsmen in North America: Assessing an Experiment in Social Responsibility*
 R&R Bk N - v19 - i1 - Feb 2004 - p229(1) [51-500]
Nemiro, Jill E. - *Creativity in Virtual Teams: Key Components for Success*
 R&R Bk N - v19 - i3 - August 2004 - p108(1) [51-500]
Neocleous, Mark - *Imagining the State*
 TimHES - v0 - i1668 - Nov 26 2004 - pVIII(1) [501+]
Nepo, Mark - *The Exquisite Risk: Daring to Live an Authentic Life*
 LJ - v130 - i2 - Feb 1 2005 - p104(1) [51-500]
Neporent, Liz - *The Fat-Free Truth: Real Answers to the Fitness and Weight-Loss Questions You Wonder about Most*
 LJ - v130 - i1 - Jan 1 2005 - p144(3) [501+]
Nerius, Maria Given - *Digital Scrapbooking*
 PetPho - v33 - i11 - March 2005 - p22(1) [501+]
Nersesian, Arthur - *Suicide Casanova*
 LJ - v130 - i2 - Feb 1 2005 - p70(1) [51-500]
 Unlubricated
 KR - v72 - i16 - August 15 2004 - p769(2) [51-500]
 NYTBR - Oct 24 2004 - p12 [501+]
 PW - v251 - i29 - July 19 2004 - p141(1) [51-500]
Nersesian, Roy L. - *Corporate Financial Risk Management: A Computer-Based Guide for Nonspecialists*
 R&R Bk N - v19 - i2 - May 2004 - p122 [51-500]
Neruda, Pablo - *100 Love Sonnets*
 Globe & Mail - August 28 2004 - pD10 [501+]
 Twenty Love Poems and a Song of Despair
 NS - v133 - i4700 - August 9 2004 - p38(2) [501+]
Nesadurai, Helen E.S. - *Globalisation, Domestic Politics and Regionalism: The ASEAN Free Trade Area*
 JEL - v42 - i1 - March 2004 - p261(1) [501+]
Nesbet, Anne - *Savage Junctures: Sergei Eisenstein and the Scope of Thinking*
 Slav R - v63 - i4 - Winter 2004 - p910(2) [501+]
Nesbit, Jeff - *Ryun's Story*
 VOYA - v27 - i5 - Dec 2004 - p378(1) [501+]
Nesbitt, Eleanor M. - *Intercultural Education: Ethnographic and Religious Approaches*
 R&R Bk N - v19 - i4 - Nov 2004 - p13(1) [51-500]
Nesbitt, Francis Njubi - *Race for Sanctions: African Americans Against Apartheid, 1964-1994*
 Choice - v42 - i6 - Feb 2005 - p1082(2) [51-500]
Nesbitt, John D. - *West of Rock River*
 Roundup M - v12 - i3 - Feb 2005 - p28(1) [51-500]
Nesbitt, John W. - *Byzantine Authors: Literary Activities and Preoccupations*
 Med R - Oct 2004 - pNA [501+]

Ness, Bryan D. - *Encyclopedia of Genetics, Rev. Ed., Vols. 1-2*
 BL - v101 - i1 - Sept 1 2004 - p168(1) [501+]
 Choice - v42 - i1 - Sept 2004 - p68(1) [501+]
 LJ - v129 - i12 - July 2004 - p116(1) [51-500]
 Ref Rev - July 2004 - pNA [501+]
 SB - v40 - i5 - Sept-Oct 2004 - p211(1) [51-500]
 SLJ - v50 - i12 - Dec 2004 - p86(1) [501+]
Ness, Immanuel - *Encyclopedia of American Social Movements, Vols. 1-4*
 Choice - v42 - i6 - Feb 2005 - p1002(1) [51-500]
 LJ - v130 - i1 - Jan 1 2005 - p152(1) [51-500]
 R&R Bk N - v19 - i4 - Nov 2004 - p124(1) [51-500]
Ness, Molly - *Lessons to Learn: Voices from the Front Lines of Teach for America*
 R&R Bk N - v19 - i3 - August 2004 - p220(1) [1-50]
Ness, Patrick - *Topics about Which I Know Nothing*
 TLS - i5285 - July 16 2004 - p23(1) [501+]
Nesselrath, Heinz-Gunther - *Platon und die Erfindung von Atlantis*
 Class R - v54 - i1 - May 2004 - p243(1) [501+]
Nester, Daniel - *God Save My Queen II: The Show Must Go On*
 ABR - v26 - i2 - Jan-Feb 2005 - p1(2) [501+]
Nesterov, Yurii - *Introductory Lectures on Convex Optimization: A Basic Course*
 SciTech - v28 - i1 - March 2004 - p40(1) [51-500]
Nesteruk, Alexei B. - *Light from the East: Theology, Science, and the Eastern Orthodox Tradition*
 TT - v61 - i1 - April 2004 - p122-126 [501+]
Neto, Jose R. Maia - *Skepticism in Renaissance and Post-Renaissance Thought: New Interpretations*
 R&R Bk N - v19 - i3 - August 2004 - p4(1) [1-50]
Nett, Mary T. - *Water Quality Assessments in the Mississippi Delta: Regional Solutions and National Scope*
 SciTech - v28 - i3 - Sept 2004 - p145(1) [51-500]
Nettler, Gwynn - *Boundaries of Competence: How Social Studies Make Feeble Science*
 Choice - v41 - i7 - March 2004 - p1377(1) [501+]
Nettleton, Pamela Hill - *Bend and Stretch: Learning about Your Bones and Muscles (Illus. by Shipe, Becky)*
 c SB - v40 - i4 - July-August 2004 - p181(2) [51-500]
 Benjamin Franklin, Writer, Inventor, Statesman (Illus. by Yesh, Jeff)
 c LibMed - v23 - i1 - August-Sept 2004 - p71(2) [51-500]
 Breathe In, Breath Out: Learning about Your Lungs (Illus. by Shipe, Becky)
 c SB - v40 - i4 - July-August 2004 - p181(2) [51-500]
 Breathe In, Breathe Out: Learning about Your Lungs (Illus. by Shipe, Becky)
 c SLJ - v50 - i11 - Nov 2004 - p130(1) [51-500]
 Gurgle and Growls: Learning about Your Stomach (Illus. by Shipe, Becky)
 c SB - v40 - i4 - July-August 2004 - p181(2) [51-500]
 Is That True?: Kids Talk about Honesty (Illus. by Muehlenhardt, Amy Bailey)
 c SLJ - v51 - i2 - Feb 2005 - p124(2) [51-500]
 Let's Get Along: Kids Talk about Tolerance (Illus. by Muehlenhardt, Amy Bailey)
 c SLJ - v51 - i2 - Feb 2005 - p124(2) [51-500]
 Look, Listen, Taste, Touch, Smell: Learning about Your Five Senses (Illus. by Shipe, Becky)
 c SB - v40 - i4 - July-August 2004 - p181(2) [51-500]
 Pitch In!: Kids Talk about Cooperation (Illus. by Muehlenhardt, Amy Bailey)
 c SLJ - v51 - i2 - Feb 2005 - p124(2) [51-500]
 Think, Think, Think: Learning about Your Brain (Illus. by Shipe, Becky)
 c SB - v40 - i4 - July-August 2004 - p181(2) [51-500]
 c SLJ - v50 - i11 - Nov 2004 - p130(1) [51-500]
 Thump-Thump: Learning about Your Heart (Illus. by Shipe, Becky)
 c SB - v40 - i4 - July-August 2004 - p181(2) [51-500]
Network Computing and Applications: Proceedings
 SciTech - v28 - i4 - Dec 2004 - p152(1) [51-500]
Network Protocols: Proceedings
 SciTech - v28 - i4 - Dec 2004 - p152(1) [51-500]
Networking Fundamentals Courseware; Release 3
 SciTech - v28 - i1 - March 2004 - p157(1) [51-500]
 SciTech - v28 - i1 - March 2004 - p157(1) [51-500]

Netz, Reviel - *The Transformation of Mathematics in the Early Mediterranean World: From Problems to Equations*
 Choice - v42 - i6 - Feb 2005 - p1058(2) [51-500]
Netzer, Dick - *The Property Tax, Land Use, and Land Use Regulation*
 R&R Bk N - v19 - i1 - Feb 2004 - p121(1) [51-500]
Neu, Dean - *Accounting for Genocide: Canada's Bureaucratic Assault on Aboriginal People*
 CBRA - Annual 2003 - p368(1) [51-500]
Neubauer, David N. - *Understanding Sleeplessness: Perspectives on Insomnia*
 SciTech - v28 - i3 - Sept 2004 - p101(1) [51-500]
Neubauer, David W. - *America's Courts and the Criminal Justice System, 8th Ed.*
 R&R Bk N - v19 - i4 - Nov 2004 - p173(1) [501+]
Neubecker, Robert - *Wow! City!*
 c BL - v101 - i5 - Nov 1 2004 - p480(1) [51-500]
 c KR - v72 - i17 - Sept 1 2004 - p871(1) [51-500]
 c PW - v251 - i38 - Sept 20 2004 - p61(1) [51-500]
 c SLJ - v50 - i9 - Sept 2004 - p176(1) [51-500]
Neuberger, John - *Variational Methods: Open Problems, Recent Progress, and Numerical Algorithms*
 SciTech - v28 - i4 - Dec 2004 - p41(1) [51-500]
Neuberger, Julia - *Dying Well: A Guide to Enabling a Good Death, 2nd Ed.*
 R&R Bk N - v19 - i4 - Nov 2004 - p132(1) [51-500]
Neuberger, Roy R. - *The Passionate Collector: Eighty Years in the World of Art*
 R&R Bk N - v19 - i1 - Feb 2004 - p199(1) [51-500]
Neubert, Gloria A. - *Putting It All Together: The Directed Reading Lesson in the Secondary Content Classroom*
 R&R Bk N - v19 - i1 - Feb 2004 - p183(1) [51-500]
Neuburger, Mary - *The Orient Within: Muslim Minorities and the Negotiation of Nationhood in Modern Bulgaria*
 Choice - v42 - i3 - Nov 2004 - p543(1) [1-50]
Neudecker, Reinhard - *The Voice of God on Mount Sinai: Rabbinic Commentaries on Exodus 20:1 in the Light of Sufi and Zen-Buddhist Texts*
 BCS - v24 - Annual 2004 - p278(6) [501+]
Neufeld, Josh - *A Few Perfect Hours and Other Stories from Southeast Asia and Central Europe*
 y BL - v101 - i2 - Sept 15 2004 - p217(1) [51-500]
 PW - v251 - i43 - Oct 25 2004 - p30(1) [51-500]
Neufeldt, Leonard N. - *Before We Were the Land's: Yarrow, British Columbia -- Mennonite Promise*
 CBRA - Annual 2003 - p336(1) [51-500]
 Village of Unsettled Yearnings: Yarrow, British Columbia -- Mennonite Promise
 CBRA - Annual 2003 - p336(1) [51-500]
Neugebauer, Wolfgang - *Zentralprovinz im Absolutismus: Brandenburg im 17. und 18. Jahrhundert*
 HNet - June 2004 - pNA [501+]
Neugeboren, Jay - *News from the New American Diaspora: And Other Tales of Exile*
 KR - v73 - i5 - March 1 2005 - p254(1) [501+]
Neugroschl, Judith - *Blueprints Notes and Cases: Behavioral Science and Epidemiology*
 SciTech - v28 - i1 - March 2004 - p97(1) [51-500]
Neuharth-Pritchett, Stacey - *Perspectives on Elementary Education: A Casebook for Critically Analyzing Issues of Diversity*
 R&R Bk N - v19 - i1 - Feb 2004 - p191(1) [51-500]
Neuhaus, Jessamyn - *Manly Meals and Mom's Home Cooking: Cookbooks and Gender in Modern America*
 J Soc H - v38 - i2 - Winter 2004 - p515(3) [501+]
 JAH - v91 - i1 - June 2004 - p308-309 [501+]
 JPC - v38 - i1 - August 2004 - p323(1) [501+]
Neuhoff, John G. - *Ecological Psychoacoustics*
 Choice - v42 - i6 - Feb 2005 - p1100(2) [51-500]
Neumann, Bruce R. - *Using Financial Accounting: An Introduction, 2nd Ed.*
 R&R Bk N - v19 - i1 - Feb 2004 - p112(1) [51-500]
Neumann, John - *Theory of Games and Economic Behavior: Sixtieth-Anniversary Edition*
 Nature - v431 - i7008 - Sept 30 2004 - p509(2) [501+]
Neumark, Heidi B. - *Breathing Space: A Journey in the South Bronx*
 TT - v61 - i3 - Oct 2004 - p396(2) [501+]
Neumayer, Eric - *The Pattern of Aid Giving: The Impact of Good Governance on Development Assistance*
 Choice - v42 - i2 - Oct 2004 - p339(2) [51-500]
 Weak versus Strong Sustainability: Exploring the Limits of Two Opposing Paradigms, 2nd Ed.
 JPR - v41 - i5 - Sept 2004 - p643-644 [501+]
 R&R Bk N - v19 - i1 - Feb 2004 - p95(1) [51-500]

Nezu, Arthur M. - *Cognitive-Behavioral Case Formulation and Treatment Design: A Problem-Solving Approach*
SciTech - v28 - i3 - Sept 2004 - p99(1) [51-500]

Ng, Hock Min - *GaN and Related Alloys-2003: Proceedings*
SciTech - v28 - i3 - Sept 2004 - p160(1) [51-500]

Ng, Janet - *The Experience of Modernity: Chinese Autobiography of the Early Twentieth Century*
JAS - v63 - i3 - August 2004 - p773-775 [501+]

Ng, Rick - *Drugs: From Discovery to Approval*
Choice - v41 - i11-12 - July-August 2004 - p2078(2) [501+]

Ng, Virginia - *Psychiatric Neuroimaging*
SciTech - v28 - i4 - Dec 2004 - p96(1) [51-500]

Ngai, Mae M. - *Impossible Subjects: Illegal Aliens and the Making of Modern America*
Choice - v42 - i2 - Oct 2004 - p357(1) [51-500]
HNet - Sept 2004 - pNA [501+]

Ngaosyvathn, Mayoury - *Breaking New Ground in Lao History: Essays on the Seventh to Twentieth Centuries*
JAS - v63 - i2 - May 2004 - p560(3) [501+]

Ngo, Dung - *Bent Ply: The Art of Plywood Furniture*
Am Craft - v64 - i1 - Feb-March 2004 - p24(1) [501+]

Ngor, Haing - *Survival in the Killing Fields*
LJ - v129 - i15 - Sept 15 2004 - p91(1) [1-50]

Nguyen, Anh V. - *Colloidal Science of Flotation*
SciTech - v28 - i1 - March 2004 - p57(1) [51-500]

Nguyen, Kien - *Le Colonial: A Novel*
BL - v101 - i2 - Sept 15 2004 - p209(2) [501+]
BW - v34 - i38 - Sept 19 2004 - p6(2) [51+]
KR - v72 - i14 - July 15 2004 - p653(1) [501+]
LJ - v129 - i14 - Sept 1 2004 - p141(1) [51-500]
PW - v251 - i35 - August 30 2004 - p34(1) [501+]

Nguyen, N.T. - *Thermal Analysis of Welds*
SciTech - v28 - i3 - Sept 2004 - p171(1) [51-500]

Nguyen, Thi Phuong Hoa - *Foreign Direct Investment and Its Contributions to Economic Growth and Poverty Reduction in Vietnam*
R&R Bk N - v19 - i4 - Nov 2004 - p119(1) [51-500]

Nhema, Alfred G. - *The Quest for Peace in Africa: Democracy and Public Policy*
Choice - v42 - i2 - Oct 2004 - p366(2) [51-500]

Nhial, Abraham - *Lost Boy No More: A True Story of Survival and Salvation*
PW - v251 - i41 - Oct 11 2004 - p76(1) [51-500]

Ni, Chuilleanain Eilean - *The Wilde Legacy*
ILS - v24 - i1 - Fall 2004 - p20(1) [501+]

Ni, Zhen - *Memoirs from the Beijing Film Academy: The Genesis of China's Fifth Generation*
FQ - v57 - i4 - Summer 2004 - p59(3) [501+]

Niall, Brenda - *Martin Boyd: A Life*
Quad - v48 - i9 - Sept 2004 - p91(2) [501+]
TLS - i5300 - Oct 29 2004 - p21(5) [501+]

Niazi, Sarfaraz K. - *Handbook of Pharmaceutical Manufacturing Formulations, Vols. 1-6*
SciTech - v28 - i3 - Sept 2004 - p125(1) [51-500]

Nice, David - *Prokofiev: From Russia to the West, 1891-1935*
Slav R - v63 - i2 - Summer 2004 - p447(2) [501+]

Nichills, Stan - *The Covenant Rising*
PW - v251 - i49 - Dec 6 2004 - p48(1) [51-500]

Nichol, Barbara - *Beethoven Lives Upstairs (Illus. by Cameron, Scott)*
c SLJ - v50 - i11 - Nov 2004 - p64(1) [51-500]
Safe and Sound (Illus. by Reichel, Anja)
c CBRA - Annual 2003 - p461(1) [51-500]
Tales of Don Quixote
c Globe & Mail - Dec 11 2004 - pD28 [51-500]

Nichol, James W. - *Midnight Cab*
BL - v101 - i6 - Nov 15 2004 - p557(1) [51-500]
KR - v72 - i19 - Oct 1 2004 - p934(2) [501+]
PW - v251 - i47 - Nov 22 2004 - p38(1) [51-500]

Nichol, John - *The Last Escape: The Untold Story of Allied Prisoners of War in Europe, 1944-45*
Sew R - v112 - i1 - Wntr 2004 - pXI-XIV [501+]
Tail-End Charlies
Spec - v296 - i9201 - Dec 11 2004 - p38(1) [501+]

Nicholas, David - *Urban Europe, 1100-1700*
J Hist G - v30 - i3 - July 2004 - p572(2) [501+]

Nicholas, J.B. - *The Waving Girl (Illus. by Waites, Joan C.)*
c SLJ - v50 - i12 - Dec 2004 - p116(1) [501+]

Nicholas, Kristin - *Kids' Embroidery (Illus. by Gruen, John)*
c LJ - v129 - i20 - Dec 1 2004 - p111(1) [51-500]
c PW - v252 - i2 - Jan 10 2005 - p58(1) [51-500]

Nicholas, Liza - *Imagining the Big Open: Nature, Identity, and Play in the New West*
WHQ - v35 - i3 - Autumn 2004 - p374(1) [501+]

Nicholas, Nick - *An Entertaining Tale of Quadrupeds*
TLS - i5264 - Feb 20 2004 - p30-30 [501+]

Nicholl, Charles - *Leonardo da Vinci: Flights of the Mind*
BL - v101 - i5 - Nov 1 2004 - p461(1) [51-500]
BW - v34 - i48 - Nov 28 2004 - p10(1) [51+]
Econ - v373 - i8405 - Dec 11 2004 - p81US [501+]
Globe & Mail - Jan 8 2005 - pD8 [501+]
KR - v72 - i19 - Oct 1 2004 - p950(1) [501+]
NS - v133 - i4708 - Oct 4 2004 - p50(2) [501+]
NYTBR - Dec 5 2004 - p9 [501+]
PW - v251 - i41 - Oct 11 2004 - p65(1) [51-500]
Spec - v296 - i9200 - Dec 4 2004 - p38(1) [501+]
Leonardo Da Vinci: The Flights of the Mind
TLS - i5300 - Oct 29 2004 - p4-6 [501+]

Nicholls, David - *A Question of Attraction (Read by Steele, Erik). Audiobook Review*
Kliatt - v38 - i5 - Sept 2004 - p64(2) [51-500]
A Question of Attraction
BL - v101 - i9-10 - Jan 1 2005 - p771(1) [51-500]

Nicholls, Mark - *Scorcese's Men: Melancholia and the Mob*
Arena - i74 - Dec 2004 - p38(2) [501+]

Nicholls, Stan - *The Covenant Rising*
ChrSFF&H - v26 - i10 - Oct 2004 - p26(2) [51-500]
LJ - v129 - i17 - Oct 15 2004 - p57(1) [51-500]

Nichols, Aidan - *Discovering Aquinas: An Introduction to His Life, Work, and Influence*
JR - v84 - i3 - July 2004 - p481(2) [501+]
Six Ct J - v35 - i3 - Fall 2004 - p881-883 [501+]

Nichols, Bruce - *Guerilla Warfare in Civil War Missouri, 1862*
R&R Bk N - v19 - i3 - August 2004 - p68(1) [51-500]

Nichols, C. Allen - *Thinking Outside the Book: Alternatives for Today's Teen Library Collections*
BL - v101 - i1 - Sept 1 2004 - p165(1) [51-500]
y Teach Lib - v32 - i1 - Oct 2004 - p38(2) [501+]
y VOYA - v27 - i4 - Oct 2004 - p340(1) [51-500]

Nichols, Catherine - *Medical Marvels: A Chapter Book*
c BL - v101 - i7 - Dec 1 2004 - p668(1) [51-500]
c SLJ - v51 - i2 - Feb 2005 - p146(1) [51-500]
Record Breakers: A Chapter Book
c SLJ - v51 - i1 - Jan 2005 - p148(1) [51-500]

Nichols, Heidi L. - *The Fashioning of Middle-Class America: Sartain's Union Magazine of Literature and Art and Antebellum Culture*
R&R Bk N - v19 - i1 - Feb 2004 - p242(1) [501+]

Nichols, Jack - *The Tomcat Chronicles: Erotic Adventures of a Gay Liberation Pioneer*
LJ - v129 - i13 - August 2004 - p90(1) [501+]

Nichols, Jeffrey - *Prostitution, Polygamy, and Power: Salt Lake City, 1847-1918*
AHR - v109 - i3 - June 2004 - p929(2) [501+]
JIH - v34 - i4 - Spring 2004 - p658-659 [501+]

Nichols, John - *Against the Beast: A Documentary History of American Rebellion*
Atl - v295 - i3 - April 2005 - p97(2) [501+]
LJ - v130 - i1 - Jan 1 2005 - p131(1) [51-500]
Dick: The Man Who Is President
BW - v34 - i35 - August 2004 - p3(2) [501+]
LJ - v129 - i15 - Sept 15 2004 - p70(1) [51-500]
PW - v251 - i32 - August 9 2004 - p244(1) [51-500]

Nichols, Linda - *At the Scent of Water*
LJ - v129 - i14 - Sept 1 2004 - p134(1) [51-500]

Nichols, Mark - *Book Sense Best Books: 125 Favorite Books Recommended by Independent Booksellers*
PW - v251 - i40 - Oct 4 2004 - p84(1) [51-500]

Nichols, Peter - *Evolution's Captain: The Story of the Kidnapping That Led to Charles Darwin's Voyage Aboard the ''Beagle''*
NYTBR - Oct 10 2004 - p26 [501+]
Evolution's Captain: The Tragic Fate of Robert Fitzroy, the Man Who Sailed Charles Darwin around the World
TLS - i5268 - March 19 2004 - p32-32 [501+]

Nichols, Peter M. - *The New York Times Guide to the Best 1,000 Movies Ever Made*
Globe & Mail - Dec 10 2004 - pR21 [1-50]

Nichols, Roger L. - *American Indians in U.S. History*
y Kliatt - v38 - i4 - July 2004 - p42(1) [51-500]
Roundup M - v12 - i1 - Oct 2004 - p25(1) [51-500]
SHQ - v108 - i1 - July 2004 - p108-109 [501+]

Nichols, Sharon L. - *America's Teenagers--Myths and Realities: Media Images, Schooling, and the Social Costs of Careless Indifference*
R&R Bk N - v19 - i3 - August 2004 - p161(1) [501+]
TCR - v106 - i12 - Dec 2004 - p2361(3) [501+]

Nichols, Thomas M. - *Winning the World: Lessons for America's Future from the Cold War*
NWCR - v57 - Autumn 2004 - p147(4) [501+]

Nichols, William C. - *Family Therapy around the World: A Festschrift for Florence W. Kaslow*
Adoles - v39 - i154 - Summer 2004 - p402(2) [51-500]

Nicholson, Barbara L. - *E-Portfolios for Educational Leaders: An ISLLC-Based Framework for Self-Assessment*
R&R Bk N - v19 - i3 - August 2004 - p216(1) [1-50]

Nicholson, Colin - *Edwin Morgan: Inventions of Modernity*
Lon R Bks - v26 - i22 - Nov 18 2004 - p26(2) [501+]

Nicholson, Deborah - *Evening the Score*
y BL - v101 - i4 - Oct 15 2004 - p393(1) [51-500]
KR - v72 - i22 - Nov 15 2004 - p1071(1) [51-500]

Nicholson, Ernest - *A Century of Theological and Religious Studies in Britain, 1902-2002*
TimHES - v0 - i1674 - Jan 14 2005 - p24(1) [501+]

Nicholson, Helen J. - *The Crusades*
R&R Bk N - v20 - i1 - Feb 2005 - p31(1) [501+]
y SLJ - v51 - i1 - Jan 2005 - p150(1) [51-500]
Love, War, and the Grail: Templars, Hospitallers, and Teutonic Knights in Medieval Epic and Romance
R&R Bk N - v19 - i3 - August 2004 - p259(1) [51-500]
Medieval Warfare: Theory and Practice of War in Europe, 300-1500
Choice - v42 - i2 - Oct 2004 - p362(1) [51-500]

Nicholson, Joy - *The Road to Esmeralda*
KR - v73 - i5 - March 1 2005 - p254(1) [501+]

Nicholson, Lorna Schultz - *See Fox Run*
Globe & Mail - Oct 2 2004 - pD18 [51-500]

Nicholson, Philip Yale - *Labor's Story in the United States*
Choice - v42 - i3 - Nov 2004 - p530(1) [1-50]
CS - v33 - i5 - Sept 2004 - p625-625 [501+]

Nicholson, Scott - *The Manor*
ChrSFF&H - v26 - i9 - Sept 2004 - p36(1) [51-500]

Nicholson, Steve - *The Censorship of British Drama 1900-1968*
Albion - v36 - i2 - Summer 2004 - p344(3) [501+]

Nicholson, Stuart - *Ella Fitzgerald: The Complete Biography*
Black Iss - v6 - i6 - Nov-Dec 2004 - p40(2) [501+]
Bwatch - v26 - i9 - Sept 2004 - p3(1) [51-500]
Globe & Mail - July 17 2004 - pD13 [1-50]

Nicholson, Walter - *Microeconomic Theory: Basic Principles and Extensions, 9th Ed.*
R&R Bk N - v19 - i3 - August 2004 - p93(1) [51-500]

Nicholson, William - *Firesong: An Adventure*
y Kliatt - v38 - i4 - July 2004 - p32(1) [501+]
Slaves of the Mastery: An Adventure
y Kliatt - v38 - i4 - July 2004 - p32(1) [501+]
The Society of Others
NYTBR - Feb 13 2005 - p13 [501+]

Nicholson, William (British writer and movie director) - *Firesong (Read by West, Samuel). Audiobook Review*
c Kliatt - v38 - i4 - July 2004 - p51(1) [51-500]
The Society of Others
BL - v101 - i9-10 - Jan 1 2005 - p821(1) [501+]
KR - v72 - i20 - Oct 15 2004 - p981(1) [501+]
LJ - v129 - i18 - Nov 1 2004 - p76(1) [51-500]
NYT - Jan 20 2005 - pE11 [501+]
PW - v252 - i3 - Jan 17 2005 - p36(2) [501+]
The Wind Singer: An Adventure
y Kliatt - v38 - i4 - July 2004 - p32(1) [501+]

Nicholson, William C. - *Emergency Response and Emergency Management Law: Cases and Materials*
R&R Bk N - v19 - i1 - Feb 2004 - pNA [51-500]

Nichter, Mark - *New Horizons in Medical Anthropology: Essays in Honour of Charles Leslie*
MAQ - v18 - i4 - Dec 2004 - p509(3) [501+]

Nickalaus, Keith - *Marriage Fictions in Old French Secular Narratives, 1170-1250: A Critical Re-Evaluation of the Courtly Love Debate*
Specu - v79 - i3 - July 2004 - p810-811 [501+]

Nickel, Norbert H. - *Hydrogen in Semiconductors*
SciTech - v28 - i4 - Dec 2004 - p156(1) [51-500]

Nickelsburg, George W.E. - *Ancient Judaism and Christian Origins: Diversity, Continuity, and Transformation*
Intpr - v58 - i4 - Oct 2004 - p432(1) [501+]
JR - v84 - i4 - Oct 2004 - p626(3) [501+]

Nickerson, Raymond S. - *Cognition and Chance: The Psychology of Probabilistic Reasoning*
R&R Bk N - v19 - i4 - Nov 2004 - p7(1) [51-500]

Nikolchina, Miglena - *Matricide in Language: Writing Theory in Kristeva and Woolf*
Choice - v42 - i1 - Sept 2004 - p96(1) [501+]
R&R Bk N - v19 - i3 - August 2004 - p258(1) [51-500]

Nikomo, Stella M. - *Applications in Human Resource management, 5th Ed.*
R&R Bk N - v19 - i2 - May 2004 - p117 [51-500]

Nikzentaitis, Alvydas - *The Vanished World of Lithuanian Jews*
R&R Bk N - v19 - i3 - August 2004 - p52(1) [51-500]

Niles, Steve - *Criminal Macabre*
KR - v72 - i19 - Oct 1 2004 - pNA [501+]

Nilsen, Anna - *The Great Art Scandal*
LibMed - v22 - i6 - March 2004 - p74(1) [501+]

Nilson, Ingela - *Erotic Pathos, Rhetorical Pleasure: Narrative Technique and Mimesis in Eumathios Makrembolites "Hysmine & Hysminias"*
Specu - v79 - i3 - July 2004 - p811-813 [501+]

Nilsson, Per - *Heart's Delight*
y BL - v101 - i2 - Sept 15 2004 - p236(1) [51-500]
y LibMed - v22 - i6 - March 2004 - p68(1) [501+]

Nilsson, Sven A. - *De stora krigens tid: Om Sverige som militarstat och bondesamhalle*
Scan St - v76 - i3 - Fall 2004 - p385(34) [501+]
Pa vag mot militarstaten: Krigsbefalets etablering i den aldre vasatidens Sverige
Scan St - v76 - i3 - Fall 2004 - p385(34) [501+]

Nimmo, Arlo H. - *The Andrews Sisters: A Biography and Career Record*
Choice - v41 - i11-12 - July-August 2004 - p2054(2) [501+]

Nimmo, Jenny - *Charlie Bone and the Invisible Boy*
c BL - v100 - i22 - August 2004 - p1936(1) [51-500]
c CCB-B - v58 - i1 - Sept 2004 - p33(2) [51-500]
c PW - v251 - i28 - July 12 2004 - p65(2) [501+]
c SLJ - v50 - i8 - August 2004 - p127(1) [51-500]
y VOYA - v27 - i3 - August 2004 - p232(1) [1-50]
Charlie Bone and the Time Twister
c CE - v80 - i5 - Mid-Summer 2004 - p274(1) [51-500]

Nimni, Ephrain - *The Challenge of Post-Zionism: Alternative to Israeli Fundamentalist Politics*
AJPS - v39 - i2 - July 2004 - p453(454) [501+]

Nimtz, August H. - *Marx, Tocqueville, and Race in America: The Absolute Democracy or Defiled Republic*
R&R Bk N - v19 - i1 - Feb 2004 - p59(1) [51-500]

Ninemeier, Jack D. - *Planning and Control for Food and Beverage Operations, 6th Ed.*
R&R Bk N - v19 - i4 - Nov 2004 - p251(1) [501+]

Niobium 2001 Symposium - *Niobium Science and Technology: Proceedings*
SciTech - v28 - i1 - March 2004 - p139(1) [51-500]

Nir, Rivkah - *Destruction of Jerusalem and the Idea of Redemption in the Syriac Apocalypse of Baruch*
JR - v85 - i1 - Jan 2005 - p155(3) [501+]
R&R Bk N - v19 - i1 - Feb 2004 - p20(1) [51-500]

Nirahara, Naomi - *Gasa-Gasa Girl*
PW - v252 - i9 - Feb 28 2005 - p45(2) [51-500]

Niro, Brian - *Race*
R&R Bk N - v19 - i1 - Feb 2004 - p234(1) [1-50]

Nisbet, R.G.M. - *A Commentary on Horace: Odes, Book III*
Choice - v42 - i6 - Feb 2005 - p1020(1) [51-500]
TLS - i5297 - Oct 8 2004 - p8-9 [501+]

Nishida, Mieko - *Slavery and Identity: Ethnicity, Gender, and Race in Salvador, Brazil, 1808-1888*
AHR - v109 - i2 - April 2004 - p580(2) [501+]
J Soc H - v38 - i2 - Winter 2004 - p536(2) [501+]

Nishida, S.I. - *Macro and Microscopic Approach to Fracture*
SciTech - v28 - i4 - Dec 2004 - p134 [51-500]

Niskanen, William A. - *Autocratic, Democratic, and Optimal Government: Fiscal Choices and Economic Outcomes*
R&R Bk N - v19 - i2 - May 2004 - p125 [51-500]

Nisonger, Thomas E. - *Evaluation of Library Collections, Access, and Electronic Resources: A Literature Guide and Annotated Bibliography*
R&R Bk N - v19 - i1 - Feb 2004 - p260(1) [51-500]

Nissanke, Machiko - *Comparative Development Experiences of Sub-Saharan Africa and East Asia: An Institutional Approach*
JEL - v42 - i1 - March 2004 - p310(1) [501+]

Nissen, Thisbe - *Osprey Island*
BW - v34 - i33 - August 15 2004 - p6(1) [501+]
PW - v251 - i27 - July 5 2004 - p37(1) [51-500]

Nissenbaum, Helen - *Academy and the Internet*
R&R Bk N - v19 - i2 - May 2004 - p128 [51-500]

Nissinen, Martti - *Prophecy in Its Ancient Near Eastern Context: Mesopotamian, Biblical, and Arabian Perspectives*
JNES - v63 - i4 - Oct 2004 - p298(2) [501+]
Prophets and Prophecy in the Ancient Near East
R&R Bk N - v19 - i1 - Feb 2004 - p9(1) [51-500]

Nitz, Kristin Wolden - *Defending Irene*
c SLJ - v50 - i9 - Sept 2004 - p214(1) [51-500]

Niven, Jennifer - *Ada Blackjack: A True Story of Survival in the Arctic*
Globe & Mail - Nov 6 2004 - pD25 [51-500]
y Kliatt - v39 - i2 - March 2005 - p34(1) [51-500]

Niven, Larry - *Ringworld's Children*
Analog - v124 - i11 - Nov 2004 - p134(6) [501+]
BL - v100 - i21 - July 2004 - p1829(1) [51-500]

Niven, William - *Politics and Culture in Twentieth-Century Germany*
GSR - v27 - i2 - May 2004 - p446-447 [501+]

Nives, Dolsak - *The Commons in the New Millennium: Challenges and Adaptation*
JEL - v42 - i3 - Sept 2004 - p886(3) [501+]

Nivre, Elisabeth Waghall - *Women and Family Life in Early Modern German Literature*
Choice - v41 - i11-12 - July-August 2004 - p2048(2) [501+]

Nix, Garth - *Abhorsen*
y Kliatt - v39 - i1 - Jan 2005 - p20(1) [51-500]
Grim Tuesday (Read by Corduner, Allan). Audiobook Review
c BL - v100 - i21 - July 2004 - p1857(1) [1-50]
Grim Tuesday
c JAAL - v48 - i2 - Oct 2004 - p178(1) [501+]
c Kliatt - v38 - i4 - July 2004 - p32(1) [51-500]
c SLJ - v50 - i8 - August 2004 - p127(1) [51-500]
y VOYA - v27 - i3 - August 2004 - p233(1) [1-50]
Mister Monday
y LibMed - v22 - i7 - April-May 2004 - p62(1) [501+]
c Sch Lib - v52 - i3 - Autumn 2004 - p147(1) [501+]

Nixon, Joan Lowery - *Laugh Till You Cry*
c CH Bwatch - Feb 2005 - pNA [50-500]
c Kliatt - v38 - i6 - Nov 2004 - p10(1) [51-500]
y KR - v72 - i21 - Nov 1 2004 - p1046(1) [51-500]
c SLJ - v51 - i2 - Feb 2005 - p139(1) [51-500]

Nixon, Jude V. - *Victorian Religious Discourse: New Directions in Criticism*
Choice - v42 - i6 - Feb 2005 - p1025(1) [51-500]

Nixon, Marion - *The Brains and Lives of Cephalopods*
QRB - v79 - i4 - Dec 2004 - p434(1) [501+]
SciTech - v28 - i1 - March 2004 - p69(1) [51-500]

Nixon, Sean - *Advertising Cultures: Gender, Commerce, Creativity*
R&R Bk N - v19 - i2 - May 2004 - p120 [51-500]

Nnadozie, Emmanuel - *African Economic Development*
JEL - v42 - i1 - March 2004 - p235(1) [501+]

Noah's Ark
c LibMed - v22 - i4 - Jan 2004 - p92(1) [501+]

Noakes, Jeremy - *Britain and Germany in Europe 1949-1990*
GSR - v27 - i2 - May 2004 - p429-430 [501+]

Noakes, Jonathan - *Iris Murdoch: The Essential Guide*
c SLJ - v50 - i8 - August 2004 - p142(1) [51-500]

Noakes, Vivien - *The Poems and Plays of Isaac Rosenberg*
CR - v285 - i1667 - Dec 2004 - p378(2) [501+]

Noam, E. - *Television Via the Internet: New Directions*
J Broadcst - v48 - i3 - Sept 2004 - p513(5) [501+]

Nobart, Nuchine - *Books and Periodicals Online: A Directory of Online Publications, 2003 ed., 2 volumes*
R&R Bk N - v19 - i1 - Feb 2004 - p260(1) [51-500]

Nobel, Philip - *Sixteen Acres: Architecture and the Outrageous Struggle for the Future of Ground Zero*
KR - v72 - i22 - Nov 15 2004 - p1081(2) [501+]
NYTBR - Jan 30 2005 - p25 [501+]
PW - v251 - i49 - Dec 6 2004 - p54(1) [51-500]

Nobes, Christopher W. - *Developments in International Accounting: General Issues and Classification, 2nd Ed.*
R&R Bk N - v19 - i3 - August 2004 - p132(1) [51-500]
Developments in the International Harmonisation of Accounting
R&R Bk N - v19 - i3 - August 2004 - p131(1) [51-500]

Nobisso, Josephine - *Josephine Nobisso's Show, Don't Tell!: Secrets of Writing (Illus. by Montanari, Eva)*
c CH Bwatch - v14 - i9 - Sept 2004 - p1(1) [51-500]
Josepine Nobisso's Show, Don't Tell!: Secrets of Writing (Illus. by Montanari, Eva)
c SLJ - v50 - i10 - Oct 2004 - p146(1) [51-500]

Noble, David Grant - *In Search of Chaco: New Approaches to an Archaeological Enigma*
R&R Bk N - v19 - i4 - Nov 2004 - p55(1) [51-500]

Noble, David W. - *The Death of the Nation: American Culture and the End of Exceptionalism*
AHR - v109 - i2 - April 2004 - p473(2) [501+]

Noble, Diane - *The Last Storyteller*
LJ - v129 - i14 - Sept 1 2004 - p134(1) [51-500]

Noble, Elizabeth - *The Reading Group*
KR - v72 - i22 - Nov 15 2004 - p1064(1) [501+]
LJ - v130 - i1 - Jan 1 2005 - p99(2) [51-500]
PW - v251 - i46 - Nov 15 2004 - p38(1) [51-500]
BL - v101 - i9-10 - Jan 1 2005 - p821(1) [501+]

Noble, Jean Bobby - *Masculinities Without Men?: Female Masculinity in Twentieth-Century Fictions*
CBRA - Annual 2003 - p259(1) [501+]
Choice - v41 - i11-12 - July-August 2004 - p2030(1) [501+]

Noble, Phil - *Beyond the Burning Bus: The Civil Rights Revolution in a Southern Town*
R&R Bk N - v19 - i1 - Feb 2004 - p64(1) [501+]

Noble, Suzanne - *Decision-Making for the Periodontal Team*
SciTech - v28 - i1 - March 2004 - p120(1) [51-500]

Nobleman, Marc Tyler - *Election Day*
c BL - v101 - i4 - Oct 15 2004 - p426(1) [51-500]
Martin Luther King Jr. Day
c SLJ - v51 - i1 - Jan 2005 - p113(1) [51-500]
The Television
c SLJ - v51 - i1 - Jan 2005 - p110(1) [51-500]

Nochimson, Martha P. - *Screen Couple Chemistry: The Power of 2*
FQ - v58 - i1 - Fall 2004 - p74(3) [501+]

Noda, Takayo - *Dear World*
c PW - v252 - i5 - Jan 31 2005 - p70(1) [501+]

Noddings, Nel - *Happiness and Education*
Choice - v41 - i7 - March 2004 - p1344(1) [501+]
TCR - v107 - i2 - Feb 2005 - p250(5) [501+]

Noe, Robert - *Fundamentals of Human Resource Management*
HR Mag - v49 - i7 - July 2004 - pS32(1) [501+]

Noel, Brook - *Surviving Holidays, Birthdays and Anniversaries*
Bwatch - Dec 2004 - pNA [51-500]

Noel, Francoise - *Family Life and Sociability in Upper and Lower Canada, 1780-1870: A View from Diaries and Family Correspondence*
AHR - v109 - i3 - June 2004 - p891(2) [501+]
CBRA - Annual 2003 - p388(1) [501+]
JIH - v35 - i1 - Summer 2004 - p168-169 [501+]

Noel, Gerard - *Miles*
Spec - v296 - i9200 - Dec 4 2004 - p43(1) [501+]

Noel, Michel - *Good for Nothing*
y BL - v101 - i9-10 - Jan 1 2005 - p846(1) [1-50]
Kliatt - v38 - i6 - Nov 2004 - p10(2) [51-500]
y SLJ - v51 - i1 - Jan 2005 - p134(1) [51-500]

Noelker, Frank - *Captive Beauty: 200 Protraits*
Am Sci - v92 - i4 - July-August 2004 - p381(1) [501+]

Noggle, James - *The Skeptical Sublime: Aesthetic Ideology in Pope and the Tory Satirists*
MP - v102 - i1 - August 2004 - p126(4) [501+]

Nogmanov, Aidar - *Tatary Srednego povolzh'ia i Priural'ia v Rossiiskom Zakonodatel'stve Vtoroi Poloviny XVI--XVIII vv*
Russ Rev - v63 - i3 - July 2004 - pNA [501+]
Tatary srednego povolzh'ia v rossiiskom zaonodatel'stve vtoroi poloviny XVI-XVIIIvv
Slav R - v63 - i4 - Winter 2004 - p885(3) [501+]

Nogowski, John - *Last Time Out: Big-League Farewells of Baseball's Greats*
PW - v251 - i50 - Dec 13 2004 - p56(2) [51-500]

Noguera, Pedro - *City Schools and the American Dream: Reclaiming the Promise of Public Education*
HER - v74 - i4 - Winter 2004 - p467-470 [501+]
NYRB - v51 - i19 - Dec 2 2004 - p29(4) [501+]

Nohl, Frederick - *Luther: Biography of a Reformer*
Six Ct J - v35 - i3 - Fall 2004 - p795-809 [501+]

Noire - *G-Spot: An Urban Erotic Tale*
KR - v72 - i21 - Nov 1 2004 - p1027(1) [51-500]
PW - v251 - i50 - Dec 13 2004 - p46(1) [51-500]

Noire G-Spot: An Urban Erotic Tale
BL - v101 - i6 - Nov 15 2004 - p557(2) [51-500]

Nojeim, Michael J. - *Gandhi and King: The Power of Nonviolent Resistance*
R&R Bk N - v19 - i3 - August 2004 - p145(1) [51-500]

Nolan, Brian - *Donald Brittain: Man of Film*
Globe & Mail - Jan 15 2005 - pD5 [501+]

Nolan, Cathal J. - *Ethics and Statecraft: The Moral Dimension of International Affairs, 2nd Ed.*
    R&R Bk N - v19 - i3 - August 2004 - p186(1) [501+]
Power and Responsibility in World Affairs: Reformation versus Transformation
    Choice - v42 - i6 - Feb 2005 - p1096(1) [51-500]
    R&R Bk N - v19 - i3 - August 2004 - p187(1) [501+]
Nolan, Godfrey - *Decompiling Java*
    SciTech - v28 - i3 - Sept 2004 - p21(1) [51-500]
Nolan, Jerdine - *Hewitt Anderson's Great Big Life (Illus. by Nelson, Kadir)*
    c PW - v252 - i4 - Jan 24 2005 - p243(1) [51-500]
Nolan, Lucy - *Down Girl and Sit: Smarter than Squirrels (Illus. by Reed, Mike)*
    c BL - v101 - i5 - Nov 1 2004 - p493(1) [51-500]
    c CCB-B - v58 - i3 - Nov 2004 - p137(1) [51-500]
    c KR - v72 - i15 - August 1 2004 - p747(1) [51-500]
    c SLJ - v50 - i11 - Nov 2004 - p113(1) [51-500]
Nolan, Mary - *Der Produktive Blick: Wahrnemung Amerikanischer und Japanishcher Management und Productionmethoden durch Deitsche Unternehmer, 1950-1985*
    BHR - v77 - i4 - Winter 2003 - p805(807) [501+]
Nolan, Peter - *China at the Crossroads*
    Choice - v41 - i11-12 - July-August 2004 - p2094(1) [501+]
Nolan, Riali W. - *Anthropology in Practice: Building a Career Outside the Academy*
    JRAI - v10 - i4 - Dec 2004 - p924(2) [501+]
Nold, Patrick - *Pope John XXII and His Franciscan Cardinal: Bertrand de la Tour and the Apostolic Poverty Controversy*
    CHR - v90 - i4 - Oct 2004 - p773(2) [501+]
Nold, Robert - *Columbines: Aquilegia, Paraquilegia, and Semiaquilegia*
    Choice - v41 - i7 - March 2004 - p1322(1) [501+]
    E-Streams - June 2004 - pNA [501+]
Nolen, Jerdine - *Hewitt Anderson's Great Big Life (Illus. by Nelson, Kadir)*
    c Black Iss - v7 - i2 - March-April 2005 - p66(2) [501+]
    c CCB-B - v58 - i6 - Feb 2005 - p260(2) [51-500]
    c KR - v72 - i24 - Dec 15 2004 - p1206(1) [51-500]
In My Momma's Kitchen (Illus. by Bootman, Colin)
    c SLJ - v51 - i2 - Feb 2005 - p58(1) [51-500]
Plantzilla (Illus. by Catrow, David)
    c RT - v57 - Oct 2003 - p174 [1-50]
Nolen, Stephanie - *Promised the Moon: The Untold Story of the First Women in the Space Race*
    Analog - v124 - i1-2 - Jan-Feb 2004 - p234(2) [51-500]
    CBRA - Annual 2003 - p388(2) [501+]
Nolen-Weathington, Eric - *Modern Masters. Volume 3, Bruce Timm*
    y BL - v101 - i4 - Oct 15 2004 - p373(1) [51-500]
Noles, James L., Jr. - *Twenty-Three Minutes to Eternity: The Final Voyage of the Escort Carrier U.S.S Liscome Bay*
    HRNB - v33 - i1 - Fall 2004 - p12(1) [501+]
Noll, A. Michael - *Crisis Communications: Lessons from September 11*
    R&R Bk N - v19 - i1 - Feb 2004 - p211 [51-500]
Noll, Mark A. - *America's God: From Jonathan Edwards to Abraham Lincoln*
    JAH - v91 - i2 - Sept 2004 - p595(3) [501+]
    RAH - v32 - i1 - March 2004 - p7(7) [501+]
    W&M Q - v61 - i3 - July 2004 - p539-544 [501+]
The Rise of Evangelicalism: The Age of Edwards, Whitefield and the Wesleys
    Bks & Cult - v10 - i4 - July-August 2004 - p29(1) [501+]
    J Ch St - v46 - i4 - Autumn 2004 - p897(2) [501+]
Nollen, Scott Allen - *Louis Armstrong: The Life, Music, and Screen Career*
    Choice - v42 - i6 - Feb 2005 - p1028(1) [51-500]
Nollet, Leo M.L. - *Handbook of Food Analysis, 2nd Ed., Vols. 1-3*
    Choice - v42 - i6 - Feb 2005 - p996(1) [51-500]
    SciTech - v28 - i4 - Dec 2004 - p171(1) [51-500]
Nolte, Claire E. - *The Sokol in the Czech Lands to 1914: Training for the Nation*
    HNet - Sept 2004 - pNA [501+]
    JMH - v76 - i4 - Dec 2004 - p999(2) [501+]
Nomani, Asra Q. - *Standing Alone in Mecca: An American Woman's Struggle for the Soul of Islam*
    BL - v101 - i9-10 - Jan 1 2005 - p789(1) [1-50]
    PW - v252 - i3 - Jan 17 2005 - p52(1) [51-500]
The Non-Profit Sector in a Changing Economy
    JEL - v41 - i4 - Dec 2003 - p1392(1) [501+]

Nonaka, Eiji - *Cromartie High School, Vol. 1*
    PW - v252 - i7 - Feb 14 2005 - p55(2) [51-500]
Noonan, Wesley J. - *Hardening Network Infrastructure*
    SciTech - v28 - i3 - Sept 2004 - p31(1) [51-500]
Noort, Ed - *Sodom's Sin: Genesis 18-19 and Its Interpretation*
    R&R Bk N - v19 - i4 - Nov 2004 - p22(1) [51-500]
Nooteboom, B. - *The Trust Process in Organizations: Empirical Studies of the Determinants and the Process of Trust Development*
    Econ J - v114 - i499 - Nov 2004 - pF556-F557 [501+]
Norberg, Dag - *An Introduction to the Study of Medieval Latin Versification*
    Med R - Nov 2004 - pNA [501+]
Norberg, Johan - *In Defense of Global Capitalism*
    JEL - v42 - i1 - March 2004 - p323(2) [501+]
    JPR - v41 - i5 - Sept 2004 - p644-644 [501+]
Norburn, Roger - *A James Joyce Chronology*
    Choice - v42 - i4 - Dec 2004 - p628(2) [1-50]
Nordholm, Gayle - *The Rainbow Tiger (Illus. by Frohwerk, Jennifer)*
    c CH Bwatch - Feb 2005 - pNA [51-500]
Nordquist, Myron H. - *Legal and Scientific Aspects of Continental Shelf Limits*
    SciTech - v28 - i3 - Sept 2004 - p10(1) [501+]
Norena, Carlos G. - *The Rise and Demise of the UC Santa Cruz Colleges*
    R&R Bk N - v19 - i4 - Nov 2004 - p193(1) [501+]
Noreng, Oysteng - *Crude Power: Politics and the Oil Market.*
    En Jnl - v25 - i1 - Jan 2004 - p107(3) [501+]
Norfolk, Bobby - *Dunbar out Loud (Read by Norfolk, Bobby). Audiobook Review*
    c BL - v101 - i2 - Sept 15 2004 - p260(2) [51-500]
Norgren, Jill - *Cherokee Cases: Two Landmark Federal Decisions in the Fight for Sovereignty*
    Roundup M - v12 - i1 - Oct 2004 - p25(1) [51-500]
Norkunas, Martha - *Monuments and Memory: History and Representation in Lowell, Massachusetts*
    Pub Hist - v26 - i2 - Spring 2004 - p84(86) [501+]
Norm, Zeigler - *Rivers of Shadow, Rivers of Sun: A Fly Fisherman's European Journal*
    LJ - v129 - i13 - August 2004 - p89(1) [501+]
Norman, Andrew - *Robert Mugabe and the Betrayal of Zimbabwe*
    HNet - August 2004 - pNA [501+]
Norman, Andrew G. - *Self-Organized Processes in Semiconductor Heteroepitaxy*
    SciTech - v28 - i3 - Sept 2004 - p161(1) [501+]
Norman, Diana - *Taking Liberties*
    y Kliatt - v38 - i5 - Sept 2004 - p25(2) [51-500]
Norman, Donald A. - *Emotional Design: Why We Love (or Hate) Everyday Things*
    Choice - v41 - i11-12 - July-August 2004 - p2127(1) [501+]
    Har Bus R - v82 - i2 - Feb 2004 - p39(1) [501+]
Norman, Edward - *Anglican Difficulties: A New Syllabus of Errors*
    TLS - i5284 - July 9 2004 - p24(1) [501+]
Norman, George - *Market Structure and Competition Policy: Game-Theoretic Approaches*
    JEL - v42 - i1 - March 2004 - p206(3) [501+]
Norman, Howard - *The Haunting of L*
    Can Lit - i182 - Autumn 2004 - p89(2) [501+]
In Fond Remembrance of Me
    Ent W - i808 - Feb 25 2005 - p106 [51-500]
    KR - v73 - i4 - Feb 15 2005 - p218(1) [501+]
Norman, Howard A. - *Between Heaven and Earth: Bird Tales from around the World (Illus. by Dillon, Leo)*
    c BL - v101 - i5 - Nov 1 2004 - p487(1) [51-500]
    c CCB-B - v58 - i5 - Jan 2005 - p222(1) [51-500]
    c KR - v72 - i19 - Oct 1 2004 - p966(1) [51-500]
    PW - v251 - i44 - Nov 1 2004 - p61(2) [501+]
Between Heaven and Earth: Bird Tales from around the World. (Illus. by Dillon, Leo)
    SLJ - v50 - i12 - Dec 2004 - p136(1) [501+]
Norman, Howard E. - *Between Heaven and Earth: Bird Tales from Around the World (Illus. by Dillon, Leo)*
    c HB - v80 - i6 - Nov-Dec 2004 - p721(2) [501+]
Norman, Katharine - *Sounding Art: Eight Literary Excursions through Electronic Music*
    R&R Bk N - v19 - i2 - May 2004 - p192(1) [51-500]
Norman, Michael - *Canadian Hauntings*
    y Res Links - v10 - i3 - Feb 2005 - p26(1) [51-500]
Norman, Pettit - *The Heart Renewed: Assurance of Salvation in New England Spiritual Life*
    Choice - v42 - i5 - Jan 2005 - p871(1) [1-50]

Norman, Philip - *Shout!: The Beatles in Their Generation*
    LJ - v130 - i2 - Feb 1 2005 - p81(1) [51-500]
Norman, Richard - *On Humanism*
    R&R Bk N - v19 - i4 - Nov 2004 - p16(1) [51-500]
    TLS - i5304 - Nov 26 2004 - p32(1) [51-500]
Norman, Tyler - *The Banjoman/El hombre del banjo (Illus. by Perez, Jose S.)*
    c SLJ - v51 - i1 - Jan 2005 - p121(1) [51-500]
Normant, Serge - *Metamorphosis*
    LJ - v129 - i13 - August 2004 - p74(1) [51-500]
    Time - v164 - i12 - Sept 20 2004 - p80 [51-500]
Norminton, Gregory - *Arts and Wonders*
    TLS - i5265 - Feb 27 2004 - p22-22 [501+]
Norris, Andrew - *Touchstone*
    c Sch Lib - v52 - i3 - Autumn 2004 - p147(1) [501+]
Norris, Chuck - *Against All Odds: My Story*
    PW - v251 - i30 - July 26 2004 - p52(1) [51-500]
Norris, Deborrah - *Clinical Research Coordinator Handbook, 3rd Ed.*
    SciTech - v28 - i3 - Sept 2004 - p79(1) [51-500]
Norris, Frances - *Blue Plate Special: A Novel of Love, Loss, and Food*
    BL - v101 - i6 - Nov 15 2004 - p558(1) [51-500]
    KR - v72 - i20 - Oct 15 2004 - p981(1) [501+]
    LJ - v130 - i1 - Jan 1 2005 - p100(1) [51-500]
    PW - v251 - i47 - Nov 22 2004 - p38(1) [51-500]
Norris, Frank - *Alaska Substitute: A National Park Service Management History*
    Pub Hist - v26 - i1 - Wntr 2004 - p173(3) [501+]
Norris, Gunilla - *Inviting Silence: Universal Principles of Meditation*
    PW - v251 - i33 - August 16 2004 - p59(1) [51-500]
Norris, Ken - *Way Life Should Be*
    CBRA - Annual 2003 - p228(1) [51-500]
Norris, Margot - *Suspicious Readings of Joyce's 'Dubliners'*
    ELT - v47 - i3 - Summer 2004 - p357(4) [501+]
Norris, Pat Wastell - *High Boats: A Century of Salmon Remembered*
    CBRA - Annual 2003 - p414(2) [501+]
Norris, Pippa - *Electoral Engineering: Voting Rules and Political Behavior*
    Choice - v42 - i2 - Oct 2004 - p373(1) [51-500]
Sacred and Secular: Religion and Politics Worldwide
    Choice - v42 - i7 - March 2005 - p1243(1) [51-500]
    Fut - v39 - i2 - March-April 2005 - p61(1) [51-500]
Norris, Ray P. - *Bioastronomy 2002: Life among the Stars*
    SciTech - v28 - i3 - Sept 2004 - p43(1) [1-50]
Norris, Richard A., Jr. - *The Church's Bible*
    Comw - v132 - i1 - Jan 14 2005 - p26(4) [501+]
The Song of Songs
    Comw - v132 - i1 - Jan 14 2005 - p26(4) [501+]
Norskov, Vinnie - *Greek Vases in New Contexts. The Collecting and Trading of Greek Vases: An Aspect of the Modern Reception of Antiquity*
    Class R - v54 - i1 - May 2004 - p232(2) [501+]
North American and Alaskan Cruises
    R&R Bk N - v19 - i4 - Nov 2004 - p73(1) [51-500]
North American Indians Today
    y LibMed - v23 - i3 - Nov-Dec 2004 - p84(2) [51-500]
North American Serials Interest Group Conference (18th: 2003: Portland State University) - *Serials in the Park*
    R&R Bk N - v19 - i4 - Nov 2004 - p257(1) [501+]
North American Waste to Energy
    SciTech - v28 - i3 - Sept 2004 - p147(1) [51-500]
North Carolina D.A.R. - *Roster of Soldiers from North Carolina in the American Revolution*
    EFHM - v58 - i3 - May-June 2004 - p60(1) [51-500]
North, John - *The Ambassadors' Secret: Holbein and the World of the Renaissance*
    Isis - v95 - i3 - Sept 2004 - p487(2) [501+]
North, John David - *The Ambassadors' Secret: Holbein and the World of the Renaissance*
    Six Ct J - v34 - i4 - Winter 2003 - p1192-1194 [501+]
North, Marcy L. - *The Anonymous Renaissance: Cultures of Discretion in Tudor-Stuart England*
    Albion - v36 - i2 - Summer 2004 - p299(2) [501+]
    Clio - v33 - i4 - Summer 2004 - p463(5) [501+]
    Ren Q - v57 - i3 - Fall 2004 - p1134(3) [501+]
The Anonymous Renaissance: Cultures of Discretion in Tudor-Stuart England
    RES - v55 - i221 - Sept 2004 - p617(2) [501+]

Nuland, Sherwin B. - *Doctors' Plague: Germs, Childbed Fever, and the Strange Story of Ignac Semmelweis*
SciTech - v28 - i1 - March 2004 - p117(1) [51-500]

Lost in America: A Journey with My Father
y Kliatt - v38 - i5 - Sept 2004 - p42(2) [51-500]

Null, Gary - *Gary Null's Perfect Health System. How to Think, Look and Feel Younger Now!*
LJ - v130 - i3 - Feb 15 2005 - p171(1) [51-500]

Null, J. Wesley - *A Disciplined Progressive Educator: The Life and Career of William Chandler Bagley*
R&R Bk N - v19 - i1 - Feb 2004 - pNA [51-500]

Numai, Takahiro - *Fundamentals of Semiconductor Lasers*
Choice - v41 - i11-12 - July-August 2004 - p2076(1) [501+]

Numbers, Ronald L. - *Disseminating Darwinism*
VS - v45 - i2 - Winter 2003 - p305 [501+]

Numeroff, Laura - *Beatrice Doesn't Want To (Illus. by Munsinger, Lynn)*
c BL - v101 - i7 - Dec 1 2004 - p661(2) [51-500]
c CCB-B - v58 - i3 - Nov 2004 - p138(1) [501+]
c KR - v72 - i20 - Oct 15 2004 - p1012(1) [51-500]
c SLJ - v50 - i11 - Nov 2004 - p113(2) [51-500]

If You Give a Mouse a Cookie (Illus. by Bond, Felicia)
c RT - v57 - Sept 2003 - p98 [1-50]

If You Take a Mouse to School (Illus. by Bond, Felicia)
c RT - v57 - Oct 2003 - p169 [1-50]

Laura Numeroff's 10-Step Guide to Living with Your Monster (Illus. by Evans, Nate)
c RT - v57 - Oct 2003 - p169 [1-50]

What Aunts Do Best/What Uncles Do Best (Illus. by Munsinger, Lynn)
c SLJ - v50 - i10 - Oct 2004 - p126(1) [51-500]

Nun, Jose - *Democracy: Government of the People or Government of the Politicians?*
Choice - v41 - i7 - March 2004 - p1370(1) [501+]
Choice - v41 - i7 - March 2004 - p1370(2) [501+]

Nunberg, Geoffrey - *Going Nucular: Language, Politics, and Culture in Confrontational Times*
BW - v34 - i29 - July 18 2004 - p5(1) [1-50]
Bwatch - v26 - i9 - Sept 2004 - p11(2) [501+]
TLS - i5291 - August 27 2004 - p28(1) [51-500]

Nuncius, Biblioteca - *De Figura Umana: Fisiognomica, Anatomia e Arte in Leonardo*
Six Ct J - v34 - i4 - Winter 2003 - p1210-1212 [501+]

Nunes, Ann - *Winter Fire*
PW - v252 - i3 - Jan 17 2005 - p36(1) [51-500]

Nunes, Julia - *Beyond Crazy: Journeys through Mental Illness*
CBRA - Annual 2003 - p432(1) [501+]

Nunes, Paul - *Mass Affluence: Seven New Rules of Marketing to Today's Consumer*
Bwatch - Jan 2005 - pNA [51-500]
Choice - v42 - i7 - March 2005 - p1275(1) [501+]
R&R Bk N - v19 - i4 - Nov 2004 - p110(1) [51-500]

Nunes, Paulo A.L.D. - *The Ecological Economics of Biodiversity: Methods and Policy Applications*
JEL - v41 - i4 - Dec 2003 - p1436(2) [501+]

Nunes, Pedro - *Translation and Commentary on the Lectures on Greek Rhetoric by Pedro Nunes (1502-1578): The Art of Public Speaking, Bk. 1*
R&R Bk N - v19 - i4 - Nov 2004 - p227(1) [501+]

Translation and Commentary on the Lectures on Greek Rhetoric by Pedro Nunes (1502-1578): The Art of Public Speaking, Bk. 2
R&R Bk N - v19 - i4 - Nov 2004 - p227(1) [501+]

Nunes, Rachel Ann - *Winter Fire*
LJ - v130 - i2 - Feb 1 2005 - p64(1) [51-500]

Nunn, Brett - *Panic Rising: True-Life Survivor Tales from the Great Outdoors*
R&R Bk N - v19 - i1 - Feb 2004 - p69(1) [501+]

Nunn, Bruce - *Magical Christmas Light of Old Nova Scotia (Illus. by Poplawska, Yolanda)*
c CBRA - Annual 2003 - p462(1) [51-500]

Nunn, Frederick M. - *Collisions with History: Latin American and Social Science from "El Boom" to the New World Order*
HAHR - v84 - i4 - Nov 2004 - p722(2) [501+]

Nunnally, Brian K. - *Prions and Mad Cow Disease*
E-Streams - August 2004 - pNA [501+]

Nunuk, David - *Natural Light: Visions of British Columbia*
CBRA - Annual 2003 - p119(1) [51-500]

Nurbhai, Saleel - *George Eliot, Judaism and the Novels: Jewish Myth and Mysticism*
VS - v46 - i4 - Summer 2004 - p692(3) [501+]

Nuridsany, Michel - *China: Art Now*
Choice - v42 - i2 - Dec 2004 - p282(1) [501+]

Nurk, Enn - *Mathematics 6: An Award-Winning Textbook from Russia*
SciTech - v28 - i3 - Sept 2004 - p16(1) [51-500]

Nurkse, D. - *Burnt Island*
LJ - v130 - i1 - Jan 1 2005 - p117(1) [501+]
PW - v252 - i4 - Jan 24 2005 - p236(2) [51-500]

Nurse, Donna Bailey - *What's a Black Critic to Do?: Interviews, Profiles and Reviews of Black Writers*
CBRA - Annual 2003 - p260(1) [51-500]

Nurse Practitioner's Quick Reference to Clinical Facts
SciTech - v28 - i3 - Sept 2004 - p126(1) [51-500]

Nursing 2005 Drug Handbook
SciTech - v28 - i3 - Sept 2004 - p121(1) [51-500]

Nursing Pharmacology Made Incredibly Easy
SciTech - v28 - i4 - Dec 2004 - p115(1) [1-50]

Nursing Rapid-fire Drug Facts
SciTech - v28 - i4 - Dec 2004 - p116(1) [1-50]

Nury, Fabien - *I Am Legion: The Dancing Faun*
Kliatt - v38 - i6 - Nov 2004 - p27(1) [51-500]

Nusinovich, Gregory S. - *Introduction to the Physics of Gyrotrons*
SciTech - v28 - i3 - Sept 2004 - p48(1) [1-50]

Nussbaum, Felicity A. - *The Global Eighteenth Century*
J Hist G - v30 - i3 - July 2004 - p574(2) [501+]
R&R Bk N - v19 - i1 - Feb 2004 - p28(1) [51-500]

The Limits of the Human: Fictions of Anomaly, Race, and Gender in the Long Eighteenth Century
TSWL - v23 - i1 - Spring 2004 - p135-137 [501+]

Nussbaum, Martha C. - *Hiding from Humanity: Disgust, Shame, and the Law*
Choice - v42 - i3 - Nov 2004 - p562(1) [1-50]
Law&PolBR - Sept 2004 - pNA [501+]
Lon R Bks - v26 - i14 - July 22 2004 - p24(2) [501+]
TLS - i5301 - Nov 5 2004 - p13(1) [501+]

Poetic Justice: The Literary Imagination and Public Life
Globe & Mail - Sept 25 2004 - pD31 [501+]

The Sleep of Reason: Erotic Experience and Sexual Ethics in Ancient Greece and Rome
Class R - v54 - i1 - May 2004 - p77(4) [501+]

Nussenblatt, Robert B. - *Uveitis: Fundamentals and Clinical Practice, 3rd Ed.*
SciTech - v28 - i1 - March 2004 - p114(1) [51-500]

Nutbeam, Don - *Theory in a Nutshell: A Practical Guide to Health Promotion Theories, 2nd Ed.*
SciTech - v28 - i3 - Sept 2004 - p83(1) [501+]

Nutt, Gary J. - *Distributed Virtual Machines: Inside the Rotor CLI*
SciTech - v28 - i4 - Dec 2004 - p30(1) [51-500]

Nuttall, A.D. - *Why Does Tragedy Give Pleasure?*
RES - v55 - i218 - Feb 2004 - p108-112 [501+]

Nuttall, Ena Vazquez - *Assessing and Screening Preschoolers: Psychological and Educational Dimensions, 2nd Ed.*
R&R Bk N - v19 - i4 - Nov 2004 - p11(1) [51-500]

Nuttall, Mark - *Encyclopedia of the Arctic. 3v.*
LJ - v129 - i20 - Dec 1 2004 - p164(1) [51-500]

Encyclopedia of the Arctic, Vols. 1-3
BL - v101 - i9-10 - Jan 1 2005 - p902(1) [501+]

Encyclopedia of the Arctic, Vols. 1-3
R&R Bk N - v20 - i1 - Feb 2005 - p81(1) [51-500]

Encylcopedia of the Arctic, Vols. 1-3
BL - v101 - i9-10 - Jan 1 2005 - p779(1) [1-50]

Nuttall, Paula - *From Flanders to Florence: The Impact of Netherlandish Painting, 1400-1500*
Apo - v161 - i516 - Feb 2005 - p74(2) [501+]
LJ - v130 - i1 - Jan 1 2005 - p108(1) [51-500]
R&R Bk N - v19 - i4 - Nov 2004 - p207(1) [501+]

Nutton, Vivian - *Ancient Medicine*
TimHES - v0 - i1680 - Feb 25 2005 - p28(1) [501+]

Nuys, Frank Van - *Americanizing the West: Race, Immigrants, and Citizenship, 1890-1930*
AHR - v109 - i4 - Oct 2004 - p1242(2) [501+]
J Am St - v38 - i1 - April 2004 - p173-173 [501+]

Nwachuku, Levi A. - *Troubled Journey: Nigeria Since the Civil War*
R&R Bk N - v19 - i3 - August 2004 - p59(1) [501+]

Nwafor, John Chidi - *Church and State: The Nigerian Experience*
J Ch St - v46 - i3 - Summer 2004 - p654(2) [501+]

Nwanna, Gladson I. - *Weapons of Mass Destruction, What You Should Know: A Citizen's Guide to Biological, Chemical, and Nuclear and Radiological Agents and Weapons*
SciTech - v28 - i3 - Sept 2004 - p172(1) [51-500]

Nwolisa Okanga, Eloka C.P. - *Njepu Amaka--Migration Is Rewarding: A Sociocultural Anthropological Study of Global Economic Migration...the Igbo of Eastern Nigeria*
R&R Bk N - v19 - i1 - Feb 2004 - p51(1) [51-500]

Nyala, Hannah - *Cry Last Heard*
DroRevMy - v24 - i4 - July-August 2004 - p12(2) [51-500]

Nyamuya Jackson, Maogoto - *War Crimes and Realpolitik: International Justice from World War I to the 21st Century*
R&R Bk N - v19 - i3 - August 2004 - p194(1) [501+]

Nyce, Ben - *Scorsese Up Close: A Study of the Films*
R&R Bk N - v19 - i3 - August 2004 - p264(1) [51-500]

Nyce, David S. - *Linear Position Sensors: Theory and Application*
SciTech - v28 - i1 - March 2004 - p162(1) [51-500]

Nye, Andrea - *Feminism and Modern Philosophy: An Introduction*
R&R Bk N - v20 - i1 - Feb 2005 - p3(1) [51-500]

Nye, Christopher - *The Old Shepherd's Tale (Illus. by Sorensen, Henry)*
c PW - v251 - i39 - Sept 27 2004 - p63(1) [51-500]

Nye, David E. - *America as Second Creation: Technology and Narratives of New Beginnings*
AHR - v109 - i4 - Oct 2004 - p1220(1) [501+]
Isis - v95 - i3 - Sept 2004 - p513(2) [501+]
J Am St - v38 - i1 - April 2004 - p155-156 [501+]
JIH - v35 - i2 - Autumn 2004 - p307(2) [501+]

Nye, Edward - *Literary and Linguistic Theories in Eighteenth-Century France: From Nuances to Impertinence*
MP - v102 - i1 - August 2004 - p129(5) [501+]

Nye, Jody Lynn - *The Lady and the Tiger*
y Kliatt - v38 - i4 - July 2004 - p32(1) [51-500]

Nye, Joseph S. - *The Power Game: A Washington Novel*
BW - v34 - i45 - Nov 7 2004 - p13(1) [501+]
KR - v72 - i17 - Sept 1 2004 - p829(1) [501+]
PW - v251 - i39 - Sept 27 2004 - p35(2) [51-500]

Soft Power: The Means to Success in World Politics
AM - v191 - i3 - August 2 2004 - p23 [501+]
PSQ - v119 - i4 - Winter 2004 - p680(2) [501+]

Understanding International Conflicts: An Introduction to Theory and History, 5th Ed.
R&R Bk N - v19 - i3 - August 2004 - p159(1) [501+]

Nye, Lydia Rider - *The Journal of a Sea Captain's Wife, 1841-1845: During a Passage and Sojourn in Hawaii and of a Trading Voyage in Oregon and California*
Roundup M - v12 - i3 - Feb 2005 - p20(1) [51-500]

Nye, Mary Jo - *Blackett: Physics, War, and Politics in the Twentieth Century*
Am Sci - v93 - i2 - March-April 2005 - p186(2) [501+]
New Sci - v184 - Dec 25 2004 - p76(2) [501+]
TimHES - v0 - i1676 - Jan 28 2005 - p27(1) [501+]

Nye, Naomi Shihab - *19 Varieties of Gazelle: Poems of the Middle East*
y PW - v252 - i11 - March 14 2005 - p70(1) [51-500]

Going Going
y PW - v252 - i11 - March 14 2005 - p69(1) [51-500]

Habibi
c BL - v101 - i7 - Dec 1 2004 - p647(1) [51-500]

Is This Forever, or What?: Poems and Paintings from Texas
y Teach Lib - v32 - i1 - Oct 2004 - p10(1) [51-500]
y Teach Lib - v32 - i1 - Oct 2004 - p30(1) [501+]

Is This Forever, or What?: Poems & Paintings from Texas
y BL - v100 - i21 - July 2004 - p1842(2) [1-50]
y HB - v80 - i4 - July-August 2004 - p464(1) [51-500]
c LibMed - v23 - i3 - Nov-Dec 2004 - p75(1) [51-500]
c SLJ - v50 - i7 - July 2004 - p127(1) [51-500]
c VOYA - v27 - i4 - Oct 2004 - p327(1) [51-500]

A Maze Me: Poems for Girls (Illus. by Maher, Terre)
y BL - v101 - i9-10 - Jan 1 2005 - p852(1) [1-50]
y KR - v73 - i3 - Feb 1 2005 - p179(1) [51-500]
y PW - v252 - i11 - March 14 2005 - p69(1) [51-500]

Nyengele, Mpyana Fulgence - *African Women's Theology, Gender Relations, and Family Systems Theory: Pastoral Theological Considerations and Guidelines for Care and Counseling*

R&R Bk N - v19 - i4 - Nov 2004 - p25(1) [501+]

Nyingpo, Yudra - *The Great Image: The Life Story of Vairochana the Translator*

LJ - v129 - i20 - Dec 1 2004 - p125(1) [51-500]

Nyiri, Pal - *Globalizing Chinese Migration: Trends in Europe and Asia*

CS - v33 - i1 - Jan 2004 - p129-129 [501+]

Nylen, William R. - *Participatory Democracy Versus Elitist Democracy: Lessons from Brazil*

Choice - v41 - i11-12 - July-August 2004 - p2117(1) [501+]

Nyman, John A. - *The Theory of Demand for Health Insurance*

JEL - v42 - i1 - March 2004 - p188(2) [501+]

Nyman, Jopi - *Postcolonial Animal Tale from Kipling to Coetzee*

ELT - v47 - i3 - Summer 2004 - p367(2) [501+]

Nys-Mazure, Colette - *Celebration of the Everyday*

R&R Bk N - v19 - i4 - Nov 2004 - p230(1) [501+]

Nyswaner, Ron - *Blue Days, Black Nights: A Memoir*

BL - v101 - i2 - Sept 15 2004 - p194(1) [501+]

Ent W - i785 - Sept 24 2004 - p112 [51-500]

Lam Bk Rpt - v13 - i4-5 - Nov-Dec 2004 - p52(2) [501+]

PW - v251 - i34 - August 23 2004 - p45(1) [51-500]

O

O Croinin, Daibhi - *Early Irish History and Chronology*
 Med R - July 2004 - pNA [501+]
O Holy Night
 c   KR - v72 - i21 - Nov 1 2004 - p1053(1) [51-500]
O Siochan, Stamas - *The Eyes of Another Race*
 ILS - v24 - i1 - Fall 2004 - p32(1) [51-500]
Oakes, Elizabeth H. - *American Writers*
 BL - v101 - i2 - Sept 15 2004 - p275(1) [501+]
Social Science Resources in the Electronic Age, Vol. 5
 R&R Bk N - v19 - i3 - August 2004 - p90(1) [51-500]
Social Science Resources in the Electronic Age, Vols. 1-5
 LJ - v129 - i15 - Sept 15 2004 - p82(1) [51-500]
Social Science Resources in the Electronic Age, Vols. 1-5
 R&USQ - v44 - i2 - Winter 2004 - p173(2) [501+]
 VOYA - v27 - i5 - Dec 2004 - p423(1) [51-500]
Oakes, Michael E. - *Bad Foods: Changing Attitudes about What We Eat*
 Choice - v42 - i3 - Nov 2004 - p526(1) [1-50]
Oakeshott, Michael - *What Is History? and Other Essays*
 Quad - v48 - i6 - June 2004 - p86(3) [501+]
Oaklander, L. Nathan - *The Ontology of Time*
 R&R Bk N - v20 - i1 - Feb 2005 - p6(1) [51-500]
Oakley, Ann - *Gender on Planet Earth*
 JGS - v13 - i2 - July 2004 - p168-169 [501+]
Private Complaints and Public Health: Richard Titmuss on the National Health Service
 SciTech - v28 - i4 - Dec 2004 - p81(1) [51-500]
Oakley, Francis - *Governance, Accountability, and the Future of the Catholic Church*
 Theol St - v65 - i4 - Dec 2004 - p885(2) [501+]
Oakley, Mark - *Memory and Amnesia: The Role of the Spanish Civil War in the Transition to Democracy*
 JMH - v76 - i4 - Dec 2004 - p980(3) [501+]
Oaks, Scott - *Java Threads, 3rd Ed.*
 CBRA - Annual 2003 - p21(1) [1-50]
 SciTech - v28 - i4 - Dec 2004 - p21(1) [51-500]
Oaksey, John - *An Evening with Oaksey. Audiobook Review*
 Spec - v297 - i9204 - Jan 1 2005 - p24(1) [501+]
Oates, David - *Excavations at Tell Brak. Vol. 2. Nagar in the Third Millennium BC*
 JNES - v63 - i4 - Oct 2004 - p307(4) [501+]
Paradise Wild: Reimagining American Nature
 Lam Bk Rpt - v13 - i1-2 - August-Sept 2004 - p18(2) [501+]
Oates, Joyce Carol - *Big Mouth and Ugly Girl (Read by Swank, Hillary). Audiobook Review*
 y   VOYA - v27 - i5 - Dec 2004 - p371(1) [501+]
The Faith of a Writer: Life, Craft, Art
 Sew R - v112 - i3 - Summer 2004 - p427-438 [501+]
The Falls (Read by Fields, Anna). Audiobook Review
 BL - v101 - i9-10 - Jan 1 2005 - p882(2) [501+]
The Falls
 BW - v34 - i37 - Sept 12 2004 - p6(1) [501+]
 Globe & Mail - Oct 16 2004 - pD4 [501+]
 NYTBR - Sept 19 2004 - p7 [501+]
 People - v62 - i15 - Oct 11 2004 - p53 [51-500]
 PW - v251 - i27 - July 5 2004 - p35(1) [501+]
 Spec - v296 - i9188 - Sept 11 2004 - p46(1) [501+]
 TLS - i5295 - Sept 24 2004 - p21(1) [501+]
Freaky Green Eyes (Read by Nielsen, Stina). Audiobook Review
 Kliatt - v38 - i6 - Nov 2004 - p47(1) [501+]
 y   SLJ - v50 - i9 - Sept 2004 - p79(1) [51-500]
 VOYA - v27 - i5 - Dec 2004 - p371(1) [501+]

Freaky Green Eyes
 BooChiTr - Jan 11 2004 - p5(1) [501+]
 y   LibMed - v22 - i6 - March 2004 - p68(1) [501+]
Sexy
 y   HB - v81 - i2 - March-April 2005 - p206(2) [51-500]
 y   Kliatt - v39 - i2 - March 2005 - p15(1) [51-500]
 KR - v73 - i4 - Feb 15 2005 - p235(1) [51-500]
 y   PW - v252 - i6 - Feb 7 2005 - p61(1) [51-500]
Uncensored: Views & (Re)Views.
 KR - v72 - i24 - Dec 15 2004 - p1188(2) [501+]
Oates, Wallace E. - *Environmental Policy and Fiscal Federalism: Selected Essays of Wallace E. Oates*
 R&R Bk N - v19 - i3 - August 2004 - p98(1) [51-500]
Obama, Barack - *Dreams from My Father: A Story of Race and Inheritance*
 Black Iss - v6 - i6 - Nov-Dec 2004 - p63(1) [501+]
 NYTBR - August 29 2004 - p20 [501+]
Obeidi, Mahdi - *The Bomb in My Garden: The Secrets of Saddam's Nuclear Mastermind*
 BW - v34 - i42 - Oct 17 2004 - p5(1) [501+]
 NYTBR - Oct 31 2004 - p21 [501+]
 PW - v251 - i38 - Sept 20 2004 - p58(1) [51-500]
Obeng, Samuel Gyasi - *Language in African Social Interaction: Indirectness in Akan Communication*
 R&R Bk N - v19 - i4 - Nov 2004 - p200(1) [501+]
Ober, K. Patrick - *Mark Twain and Medicine: "Any Mummery Will Cure"*
 R&R Bk N - v19 - i1 - Feb 2004 - p244(1) [51-500]
Oberdorfer, Don - *Senator Mansfield: The Extraordinary Life of a Great American Statesman and Diplomat*
 BW - v34 - i1 - Jan 4 2004 - p10(1) [501+]
 Mar Crp G - v88 - i6 - June 2004 - p64(3) [501+]
Oberg, Britt-Marie - *Changing Worlds and the Ageing Subject: Dimensions in the Study of Ageing and Later Life*
 R&R Bk N - v19 - i4 - Nov 2004 - p131(1) [51-500]
Oberg, Erik - *Machinery's Handbook: A Reference Book for the Mechanical Engineer, Designer, Manufacturing Engineer, Draftsman, Toolmaker, and Machinist, 27th Ed.*
 E-Streams - Nov 2004 - pNA [501+]
 SciTech - v28 - i3 - Sept 2004 - p149(1) [51-500]
Oberg, Michael Leroy - *Uncas: First of the Mohegans*
 Am Ind CRJ - v27 - i4 - Fall 2003 - p181-183 [501+]
 Clio - v33 - i3 - Spring 2004 - p357(5) [501+]
 JAH - v91 - i1 - June 2004 - p210-211 [501+]
 W&M Q - v61 - i3 - July 2004 - p559-562 [501+]
Oberg, P.A. - *Sensors in Medicine and Health Care*
 SciTech - v28 - i4 - Dec 2004 - p79(1) [51-500]
Oberhauser, Karen S. - *The Monarch Butterfly: Biology & Conservation*
 Choice - v42 - i5 - Jan 2005 - p881(1) [1-50]
 LJ - v129 - i12 - July 2004 - p114(1) [51-500]
 SciTech - v28 - i4 - Dec 2004 - p66(1) [51-500]
Oberhelman, Steven M. - *Prose Rhythm in Latin Literature of the Roman Empire: First Century B.C. to Fourth Century A.D.*
 R&R Bk N - v19 - i1 - Feb 2004 - p214 [51-500]
Oberlin, Cliff - *Building a High-End Financial Services Practice: Proven Techniques for Planners, Wealth Managers, and Other Advisors*
 R&R Bk N - v19 - i3 - August 2004 - p133(1) [51-500]
Oberman, Sheldon - *Island of the Minotaur: Greek Myths of Ancient Crete (Illus. by Drawson, Blair)*
 c   CBRA - Annual 2003 - p529(1) [51-500]
 c   LibMed - v23 - i1 - August-Sept 2004 - p78(1) [51-500]

Obeyesekere, Gananath - *Imagining Karma, Ethical Transformation in Amerindian, Buddhist, and Greek Rebirth*
 BCS - v24 - Annual 2004 - p303(4) [501+]
Obeyesekere, Ranjini - *Portraits of Buddhist Women*
 BCS - v24 - Annual 2004 - p289(5) [501+]
Obingny, Robert D. - *Le Conte de Floire et Blanchefleur*
 FS - v58 - i3 - July 2004 - p393-393 [501+]
Obiols, Anna - *Dali and the Path of Dreams (Illus. by Subirana, Joan)*
 c   SLJ - v50 - i8 - August 2004 - p90(2) [51-500]
Oblath, Michael D. - *The Exodus Itinerary Sites: Their Locations from the Perspective of the Biblical Sources*
 R&R Bk N - v19 - i3 - August 2004 - p23(1) [1-50]
Obmascik, Mark - *The Big Year: A Tale of Man, Nature and Fowl Obsession (Read by Wyman, Oliver). Audiobook Review*
 c   Kliatt - v38 - i4 - July 2004 - p59(1) [51-500]
The Big Year: A Tale of Man, Nature, and Fowl Obsession
 CG - v124 - i3 - May-June 2004 - p131(1) [501+]
 Globe & Mail - Dec 24 2004 - pD3 [1-50]
 Globe & Mail - March 5 2005 - pD17 [51-500]
Oborne, Peter - *Alistair Campbell*
 Spec - v295 - i9178 - July 3 2004 - p36(1) [501+]
Basil D'Oliveira: Cricket and Conspiracy: The Untold Story
 Econ - v372 - i8385 - July 24 2004 - p78US [501+]
 Lon R Bks - v26 - i24 - Dec 16 2004 - p33(2) [501+]
O'Braien, Michael J. - *Cladistics and Archeology*
 Choice - v41 - i11-12 - July-August 2004 - p2087(1) [501+]
O'Brian, Patrick - *21: The Final Unfinished Voyage of Jack Aubrey*
 BL - v101 - i4 - Oct 15 2004 - p390(1) [51-500]
 HT - v55 - i2 - Feb 2005 - p57(1) [501+]
 KR - v72 - i16 - August 15 2004 - p770(1) [501+]
 NYTBR - Oct 31 2004 - p25 [501+]
 PW - v251 - i35 - August 30 2004 - p31(1) [501+]
 Spec - v296 - i9196 - Nov 6 2004 - p60(2) [501+]
 LJ - v129 - i19 - Nov 15 2004 - p51(1) [501+]
O'Brien, Charles - *Noble Blood*
 LJ - v129 - i16 - Oct 1 2004 - p62(1) [51-500]
 PW - v251 - i41 - Oct 11 2004 - p60(1) [51-500]
O'Brien, D.P. - *The Classical Economists Revisited*
 Choice - v42 - i7 - March 2005 - p1277(1) [51-500]
O'Brien, Dan - *The Indian Agent*
 KR - v72 - i16 - August 15 2004 - p770(1) [501+]
 PW - v251 - i40 - Oct 4 2004 - p68(1) [51-500]
 Roundup M - v12 - i3 - Feb 2005 - p29(1) [51-500]
O'Brien, David (b. 1962 -) - *Beyond East and West: Seven Transnational Artists*
 Choice - v42 - i5 - Jan 2005 - p842(1) [1-50]
 LJ - v130 - i1 - Jan 1 2005 - p105(1) [51-500]
O'Brien, David J. - *Rural Reform in Post-Soviet Russia*
 CS - v33 - i6 - Nov 2004 - p747(2) [1-50]
O'Brien, David M. - *Animal Sacrifice and Religious Freedom: Church of the Lukumi Babalu Aye v. City of Hialeah*
 CHE - v50 - i26 - March 5 2004 - pA16-A16 [501+]
 Choice - v42 - i2 - Oct 2004 - p373(1) [51-500]
 Law&PolBR - June 2004 - p501(7) [501+]
O'Brien, Edna - *Triptych*
 Am Theat - v21 - i8 - Oct 2004 - p139(4) [51-500]

O'Brien, Eileen - *Usborne Internet Linked Introduction to Music*
    LibMed - v22 - i6 - March 2004 - p82(1) [501+]
O'Brien, Eugene - *Seamus Heaney: Searches for Answers*
    Choice - v41 - i11-12 - July-August 2004 -
    p2046(1) [501+]
O'Brien, Flann - *At War*
    ABR - v25 - i6 - Sept-Oct 2004 - p17(3) [501+]
    The Various Lives of Keats and Chapman, and The Brother
    Globe & Mail - March 12 2005 - pD12 [501+]
    KR - v73 - i1 - Jan 1 2005 - p15(1) [501+]
O'Brien, Geoffrey - *Sonata for Jukebox: Pop Music, Memory, and the Imagined Life*
    New York - v37 - i11 - April 5 2004 - p54(1) [501+]
    NS - v133 - i4695 - July 5 2004 - p54(2) [501+]
O'Brien, George Dennis - *The Idea of a Catholic University*
    JR - v85 - i1 - Jan 2005 - p143(3) [501+]
O'Brien, Greg - *Choctaws in a Revolutionary Age, 1750-1830*
    Am Ind CRJ - v28 - i2 - Spring 2004 - p147(4) [501+]
O'Brien, Jim - *School Leadership*
    R&R Bk N - v19 - i3 - August 2004 - p227(1) [1-50]
O'Brien, John (b. 1953 -) - *The Beach Patrol (Illus. by O'Brien, John)*
    c BL - v100 - i21 - July 2004 - p1848(1) [1-50]
    c SLJ - v50 - i7 - July 2004 - p95(1) [51-500]
O'Brien, Kathryn - *I'd Be Your Princess*
    c CH Bwatch - v14 - i8 - August 2004 - p5(1) [51-500]
O'Brien, Liam - *Software Technology and Engineering Practice (STEP 2003).*
    SciTech - v28 - i4 - Dec 2004 - p28(1) [51-500]
O'Brien, Lora - *Witchcraft from an Irish Witch*
    Bwatch - Feb 2005 - pNA [501+]
O'Brien, Mary Elizabeth - *A Nurse's Handbook of Spiritual Care: Standing on Holy Ground*
    E-Streams - August 2004 - pNA [501+]
O'Brien, Michael, (1943 -) - *John F. Kennedy: A Biography*
    KR - v72 - i22 - Nov 15 2004 - p1082(1) [501+]
O'Brien, Michael (1948 -) - *Conjectures of Order: Intellectual Life and the American South, 1810-1860*
    Choice - v42 - i3 - Nov 2004 - p550(1) [1-50]
O'Brien, Michael (b. 1943 -) - *John F. Kennedy: A Biography*
    LJ - v129 - i20 - Dec 1 2004 - p130(1) [51-500]
    PW - v252 - i1 - Jan 3 2005 - p44(2) [51-500]
O'Brien, Michael (b. 1948 -) - *Conjectures of Order: Intellectual Life and the American South, 1810-1860*
    AS - v74 - i1 - Wntr 2005 - p122(5) [501+]
    TLS - i5293 - Sept 10 2004 - p8(1) [501+]
O'Brien, Michael J. - *Cladistics and Archaeology*
    R&R Bk N - v19 - i1 - Feb 2004 - p26(1) [51-500]
O'Brien, Patrick (b. 1960 -) - *Fantastic Flights: One Hundred Years of Flying on the Edge*
    c LibMed - v22 - i4 - Jan 2004 - p77(1) [501+]
O'Brien, Patrick Karl - *Two Hegemonies: Britain 1846-1914 and the United States 1941-2001*
    Albion - v36 - i1 - Spring 2004 - p172(3) [501+]
O'Brien, Phillips Payson - *Technology and Naval Combat in the Twentieth Century and Beyond*
    J Mil H - v68 - i3 - July 2004 - p1026-1027 [501+]
O'Brien, Robert - *Global Unions? Theory and Strategies of Organized Labour in the Global Political Economy*
    AJES - v63 - i4 - Oct 2004 - p946(6) [501+]
O'Brien, Robert C. - *The Silver Crown*
    c Teach Lib - v32 - i1 - Oct 2004 - p14(1) [51-500]
O'Brien, Ruth - *Voices from the Edge: Narratives about the Americans with Disabilities Act*
    Law&PolBR - July 2004 - p579(4) [501+]
O'Brien, Sean Michael - *In Bitterness and in Tears: Andrew Jackson's Destruction of the Creeks and Seminoles*
    Am Ind CRJ - v28 - i1 - Winter 2004 - p101-102 [501+]
    Choice - v41 - i7 - March 2004 - p1357(1) [501+]
    HNet - June 2004 - pNA [501+]
O'Brien, Sharon - *The Family Silver: A Memoir of Depression and Inheritance*
    LJ - v129 - i12 - July 2004 - p105(2) [51-500]
O'Brien, Thomas W. - *John Courtney Murray in a Cold War Context*
    R&R Bk N - v19 - i3 - August 2004 - p28(1) [1-50]

O'Byrne, Darren J. - *The Dimensions of Global Citizenship: Political Identity Beyond the Nation-State*
    R&R Bk N - v19 - i1 - Feb 2004 - pNA [51-500]
O'Callaghan, Conor - *Seatown and Earlier Poems*
    Sew R - v111 - i3 - Summer 2003 - p486-492 [501+]
O'Callaghan, John P. - *Thomist Realism and the Linguistic Turn: Toward a More Perfect Form of Existence*
    Theol St - v66 - i1 - March 2005 - p220(3) [501+]
O'Callaghan, Paul - *The Christological Assimilation of the Apocalypse: An Essay on Fundamental Eschatology*
    R&R Bk N - v19 - i3 - August 2004 - p25(1) [1-50]
O'Callaghan, William G. - *Thinking Outside the Box: How Educational Leaders Can Safely Navigate the Rough Waters of Change*
    R&R Bk N - v19 - i3 - August 2004 - p223(1) [1-50]
O'Callahan, Jay - *Island (Read by O'Callahan, Jay). Audiobook Review*
    y BL - v101 - i4 - Oct 15 2004 - p433(1) [51-500]
Ocampo, Jose Antonio - *A Decade of Light and Shadow: Latin America and the Caribbean in the 1990s*
    Choice - v41 - i11-12 - July-August 2004 -
    p2091(1) [501+]
    Globalization and Development: A Latin American and Caribbean Perspective
    JEL - v42 - i1 - March 2004 - p310(1) [501+]
    R&R Bk N - v19 - i1 - Feb 2004 - p82(1) [51-500]
Ocasio, Rafael - *Literature of Latin America*
    Choice - v42 - i6 - Feb 2005 - p1026(2) [51-500]
    R&R Bk N - v19 - i4 - Nov 2004 - p232(1) [501+]
Oceans of the World
    c LibMed - v23 - i3 - Nov-Dec 2004 - p80(1) [51-500]
OCED Reviews of Health Care Systems: Korea
    JEL - v41 - i4 - Dec 2003 - p1375(1) [501+]
Ochiai, Akiko - *Harvesting Freedom: African American Agrarianism in Civil War Era South Carolina*
    Choice - v42 - i4 - Dec 2004 - p723(1) [1-50]
Ochiltree, Dianne - *Sixteen Runaway Pumpkins (Illus. by Lanquetin, Anne-Sophie)*
    c KR - v72 - i15 - August 1 2004 - p747(1) [51-500]
    c SLJ - v50 - i10 - Oct 2004 - p126(1) [51-500]
Ochoa, Annette Pina - *Night Is Gone, Day Is Still Coming: Stories and Poems by American Indian Teens and Young Adults*
    LibMed - v22 - i4 - Jan 2004 - p68(1) [51-500]
Ochs, Sidney - *History of Nerve Functions: From Animal Spirits to Molecular Mechanisms*
    SciTech - v28 - i4 - Dec 2004 - p70(1) [51-500]
Ochs, Vanessa L. - *Sarah Laughed: Modern Lessons from the Wisdom & Stories of Biblical Women*
    LJ - v129 - i12 - July 2004 - p90(1) [51-500]
    PW - v251 - i33 - August 16 2004 - p60(2) [51-500]
Ochsenbein, F. - *Astronomical Data Analysis Software and Systems: Proceedings*
    SciTech - v28 - i4 - Dec 2004 - p45(1) [51-500]
Ochsner, Gina - *People I Wanted to Be: Stories*
    KR - v73 - i5 - March 1 2005 - p254(1) [501+]
Ockendon, Hilary - *Waves and Compressible Flow*
    Choice - v42 - i5 - Jan 2005 - p888(1) [501+]
Ocker, Christopher - *Biblical Poetics Before Humanism and the Reformation*
    TT - v61 - i1 - April 2004 - p126-127 [501+]
Ockey, James - *Making Democracy: Leadership, Class, Gender, and Political Participation in Thailand*
    Choice - v42 - i6 - Feb 2005 - p1093(1) [51-500]
    R&R Bk N - v19 - i4 - Nov 2004 - p157(1) [501+]
O'Collins, Maev - *An Uneasy Relationship: Norfolk Island and the Commonwealth of Australia*
    AHS - v35 - i123 - April 2004 - p197-197 [501+]
O'Connell, Bill - *Handbook of Solution-Focused Therapy*
    E-Streams - August 2004 - pNA [501+]
    SciTech - v28 - i1 - March 2004 - p100(1) [51-500]
O'Connell, Brian - *Free Yourself from Student Loan Debt: Get Out from Under Once and for All*
    R&R Bk N - v19 - i3 - August 2004 - p221(1) [1-50]
O'Connell, Carol - *Dead Famous. Audiobook Review*
    Globe & Mail - Dec 4 2004 - pD38 [1-50]
    Winter House
    BL - v101 - i4 - Oct 15 2004 - p393(1) [51-500]
    PW - v251 - i39 - Sept 27 2004 - p36(1) [51-500]
O'Connell, Claire Babcock - *Comprehensive Review for the Certification and Recertification Examinations of Physicians Assistants, 2nd Ed.*
    SciTech - v28 - i1 - March 2004 - p79(1) [51-500]
O'Connell, Jennifer - *Dress Rehearsal*
    BL - v101 - i9-10 - Jan 1 2005 - p832(1) [1-50]

O'Connell, Mark - *The Good Father: On Men, Masculinity, and Life in the Family*
    LJ - v19 - i19 - Nov 15 2004 - p81(1) [501+]
    PW - v251 - i46 - Nov 15 2004 - p50(2) [51-500]
O'Connell, Nicholas - *On Sacred Ground: The Spirit of Place in Pacific Northwest Literature*
    Choice - v41 - i7 - March 2004 - p1298(1) [501+]
    PHR - v73 - i3 - August 2004 - p498(499) [501+]
O'Connell, Patrick - *Patrick O'Connell's Refined American Cuisine: The Inn at Little Washington (Illus. by Turner, Tim)*
    PW - v251 - i35 - August 30 2004 - p47(1) [501+]
O'Connell, Sanjida - *Sugar: The Grass That Changed the World*
    New Sci - v185 - i2481 - Jan 8 2005 - p50(1) [501+]
O'Connell, Tyne - *Pulling Princes*
    y CCB-B - v58 - i3 - Nov 2004 - p138(2) [501+]
        Kliatt - v38 - i6 - Nov 2004 - p11(1) [51-500]
        KR - v72 - i20 - Oct 15 2004 - p1012(1) [51-500]
    y PW - v251 - i40 - Oct 4 2004 - p88(2) [51-500]
    y Sch Lib - v52 - i3 - Autumn 2004 - p161(1) [501+]
    y SLJ - v50 - i12 - Dec 2004 - p152(1) [51-500]
    The Sex Was Great But ...
    BL - v100 - i22 - August 2004 - p1910(1) [51-500]
O'Connor, Alan - *Community Radio in Bolivia: The Miner's Radio Station*
    R&R Bk N - v19 - i3 - August 2004 - p116(1) [51-500]
O'Connor, Barbara - *Leonardo Da Vinci: Renaissance Genius*
    y Teach Lib - v32 - i1 - Oct 2004 - p30(1) [501+]
    Taking Care of Moses
    c BL - v100 - i22 - August 2004 - p1936(2) [51-500]
    c CCB-B - v58 - i3 - Nov 2004 - p139(1) [501+]
    c HB - v80 - i6 - Nov-Dec 2004 - p715(1) [501+]
    c KR - v72 - i19 - Oct 1 2004 - p966(1) [51-500]
    c SLJ - v50 - i10 - Oct 2004 - p173(2) [51-500]
O'Connor, Brendon - *A Political History of the American Welfare System: When Ideas Have Consequences*
    R&R Bk N - v19 - i1 - Feb 2004 - p136(1) [51-500]
O'Connor, Brian Clark - *Hunting and Gathering on the Information Savanna: Conversations on Modeling Human Search Abilities*
    R&R Bk N - v19 - i1 - Feb 2004 - p258(1) [51-500]
    Photo Provocations: Thinking in, with, and about Photographs
    R&R Bk N - v19 - i4 - Nov 2004 - p248(1) [501+]
O'Connor, David B. - *Ancient Egypt in Africa*
    R&R Bk N - v19 - i1 - Feb 2004 - p50(1) [51-500]
    TimHES - v0 - i1671 - Dec 17 2004 - p24(1) [501+]
    Mysterious Lands
    R&R Bk N - v19 - i1 - Feb 2004 - p50(1) [51-500]
    TimHES - v0 - i1671 - Dec 17 2004 - p24(1) [501+]
O'Connor, David E. - *Basics of Economics*
    R&R Bk N - v19 - i4 - Nov 2004 - p83(1) [51-500]
O'Connor, Francis G. - *Sports Medicine: Just the Facts*
    SciTech - v28 - i4 - Dec 2004 - p106(1) [51-500]
O'Connor, George - *Kapow! (Illus. by O'Connor, George)*
    c KR - v72 - i13 - July 1 2004 - p635(1) [51-500]
    c PW - v251 - i29 - July 19 2004 - p160(1) [51-500]
    c SLJ - v50 - i8 - August 2004 - p92(1) [51-500]
O'Connor, Isabel A. - *A Forgotten Community: The Mudejar Aljama of Xativa, 1240-1327*
    IJMES - v36 - i4 - Nov 2004 - p694(2) [501+]
    Med R - Dec 2004 - pNA [501+]
O'Connor, Jane - *The Emperor's Silent Army*
    c RT - v57 - Nov 2003 - p276 [51-500]
    If the Walls Could Talk: Family Life at the White House (Illus. by Hovland, Gary)
    c BL - v100 - i22 - August 2004 - p1939(1) [51-500]
    c KR - v72 - i15 - August 1 2004 - p747(1) [51-500]
    c NYTBR - Oct 17 2004 - p20 [501+]
    c PW - v251 - i37 - Sept 13 2004 - p78(2) [51-500]
    c SLJ - v50 - i9 - Sept 2004 - p191(1) [51-500]
O'Connor, Kevin - *The History of the Baltic States*
    R&R Bk N - v19 - i1 - Feb 2004 - p39(1) [1-50]
O'Connor, Patricia T. - *Woe Is I: The Grammarphobe's Guide to Better English in Plain English*
    y Kliatt - v38 - i5 - Sept 2004 - p38(2) [51-500]
O'Connor Rachel - *Construction Worker*
    c LibMed - v23 - i3 - Nov-Dec 2004 - p80(1) [51-500]
O'Connor, Richard - *Undoing Perpetual Stress: The Missing Connection Between Depression, Anxiety and 21st-Century Illness*
    PW - v252 - i7 - Feb 14 2005 - p69(1) [51-500]

O'Meally, Robert G. - *Uptown Conversation: The New Jazz Studies*
Choice - v42 - i7 - March 2005 - p1237(1) [51-500]

O'Meara, D.J. - *Plantonipolis: Platonic Political Philiosophy in Late Antiquity*
Class R - v54 - i2 - Nov 2004 - p351(2) [501+]

O'Meara, David - *The Vicinity*
BIC - v33 - i2 - March 2004 - p37(2) [501+]
CBRA - Annual 2003 - p2289(1) [51-500]

O'Meara, Kerry Ann - *Scholarship Unbound: Assessing Service as Scholarship for Promotion and Tenure*
J Hi E - v75 - i4 - July-August 2004 - p481(3) [501+]

O'Meara, Thomas F. - *A Theologian's Journey*
Theol St - v65 - i3 - Sept 2004 - p677(1) [501+]

Omer, Haim - *Non-Violent Resistance: A New Approach to Violent and Self-Destructive Children*
TCR - v106 - i8 - August 2004 - p1589(3) [501+]

Omer-Sherman, Ranen - *Diaspora and Zionism in Jewish American Literature: Lazarus, Syrkin, Reznikoff, and Roth*
AL - v76 - i2 - June 2004 - p402(3) [501+]

Omohundro, Ellen - *Living in a Contaminated World: Community Structures, Environmental Risks, and Decision Frameworks*
R&R Bk N - v20 - i1 - Feb 2005 - p82(1) [51-500]

Omoto, Charlotte K. - *Genes and DNA: A Beginner's Guide to Genetics and Its Applications*
Choice - v42 - i3 - Nov 2004 - p507(2) [1-50]
E-Streams - Oct 2004 - pNA [501+]
y SB - v40 - i5 - Sept-Oct 2004 - p211(1) [51-500]

On the Land
y VOYA - v27 - i4 - Oct 2004 - p334(1) [51-500]

O'Nan, Stewart - *Faithful: Two Diehard Boston Red Sox Fans Chronicle the Historic 2004 Season (Read by King, Stephen). Audiobook Review*
PW - v252 - i6 - Feb 7 2005 - p35(1) [501+]
Faithful: Two Diehard Boston Red Sox Fans Chronicle the Historic 2004 Season
Globe & Mail - Dec 18 2004 - pD10 [501+]
LJ - v129 - i20 - Dec 1 2004 - p126(1) [51-500]
The Good Wife
KR - v73 - i2 - Jan 15 2005 - p79(1) [501+]
LJ - v130 - i4 - March 1 2005 - p80(1) [51-500]
PW - v252 - i9 - Feb 28 2005 - p40(1) [51-500]
Ent W - i812 - March 25 2005 - p79 [51-500]
The Night Country
NYTBR - Oct 31 2004 - p26 [501+]

Once Upon a Poem: Favorite Poems That Tell Stories (Illus. by Bailey, Peter)
y BL - v101 - i9-10 - Jan 1 2005 - p849(2) [1-50]
c PW - v251 - i50 - Dec 13 2004 - p69(2) [501+]

Ondaatje, Michael - *Coming through Slaughter*
Globe & Mail - July 3 2004 - pD15 [501+]
The Conversations: Walter Murch and the Art of Editing Film
Globe & Mail - Nov 20 2004 - pD29 [1-50]
Running in the Family
Globe & Mail - Jan 29 2005 - pD15 [501+]

O'Neal, Bill - *The Johnson County War*
Bwatch - Oct 2004 - pNA [51-500]

O'Neal, Tatum - *A Paper Life*
PW - v251 - i41 - Oct 11 2004 - p68(2) [51-500]

O'Neil, Dennis - *Green Lantern/Green Arrow Collection, Vol. 1 (Illus. by Neal Adams)*
y LJ - v129 - i18 - Nov 1 2004 - p67(1) [501+]
Green Lantern/Green Arrow Collection, Vol. 2 (Illus. by Adams, Neal)
y BL - v101 - i2 - Sept 15 2004 - p216(2) [51-500]
y SLJ - v50 - i10 - Oct 2004 - p29(1) [51-500]

O'Neil, Edward - *Two Little Boys*
ILS - v24 - i1 - Fall 2004 - p32(1) [51-500]

O'Neil, Maryvelma Smith - *Giovanni Baglione: Artistic Reputation in Baroque Rome*
Six Ct J - v34 - i4 - Winter 2003 - p1165-1167 [501+]

O'Neil, Patrick M. - *Great World Writers: Twentieth Century, Vols. 1-3*
y Ref Rev - May 2004 - pNA [501+]
Great World Writers: Twentieth Century, Vols. 1-13
R&R Bk N - v19 - i1 - Feb 2004 - p222(1) [51-500]

O'Neill, Alexis - *The Recess Queen*
c SLJ - v50 - i7 - July 2004 - p43(1) [51-500]

O'Neill, Charles E. - *Diccionario Historico de la Compania de Jesus: Biografico-tematico*
Ren Q - v57 - i3 - Fall 2004 - p1055(4) [501+]

O'Neill, Dan - *The Last Giant of Beringia: The Mystery of the Bering Land Bridge*
Choice - v42 - i6 - Feb 2005 - p1065(1) [51-500]
NH - v113 - i8 - Oct 2004 - p68(2) [501+]
TimHES - v0 - i1682 - March 11 2005 - p30(1) [501+]
TLS - i5300 - Oct 29 2004 - p31(1) [51-500]

O'Neill, Dorothy P. - *Smoke Cover*
BL - v101 - i2 - Sept 15 2004 - p214(1) [51-500]

O'Neill, Edward L. - *Introduction to Statistical Optics*
SciTech - v28 - i3 - Sept 2004 - p47(1) [1-50]

O'Neill, James A., Jr. - *Principles of Pediatric Surgery, 2nd Ed.*
SciTech - v28 - i1 - March 2004 - p111(1) [51-500]

O'Neill, Jamie - *Disturbance*
KR - v72 - i24 - Dec 15 2004 - p1161(1) [501+]
PW - v251 - i49 - Dec 6 2004 - p41(1) [51-500]
BL - v101 - i9-10 - Jan 1 2005 - p821(2) [501+]
Kilbrack
KR - v72 - i24 - Dec 15 2004 - pS5(1) [501+]

O'Neill, Jennifer - *Your're Not Alone: Healing through God's Grace After Abortion*
Ch Today - v49 - i3 - March 2005 - p85(1) [51-500]

O'Neill, John - *Civic Capitalism: The State of Childhood*
R&R Bk N - v19 - i4 - Nov 2004 - p131(1) [51-500]
Five Bodies: Re-Figuring Relationships
R&R Bk N - v19 - i3 - August 2004 - p142(1) [51-500]

O'Neill, John E. - *Unfit for Command: Swift Boat Veterans Speak Out Against John Kerry*
NYTBR - Oct 10 2004 - p12 [501+]

O'Neill, Kaney - *Dream and Reach*
y Teach Lib - v32 - i1 - Oct 2004 - p20(1) [51-500]

O'Neill, Michael - *Devolution and British Politics*
CR - v285 - i1664 - Sept 2004 - p188(1) [51-500]

O'Neill, Mora Dianne - *The Artists' Halifax: Portraits of the Town and Harbour through 250 Years*
Can Hist R - v85 - i4 - Dec 2004 - p814(3) [501+]
CBRA - Annual 2003 - p119(1) [51-500]

O'Neill, Terry - *Haunted Houses*
c SLJ - v50 - i8 - August 2004 - p142(1) [501+]
Mysterious Monsters
c SLJ - v50 - i8 - August 2004 - p142(1) [501+]

O'Neill, Tom - *Shark Tank*
LJ - v129 - i13 - August 2004 - p61(1) [501+]
BL - v100 - i21 - July 2004 - p1826(1) [1-50]
DroRevMy - v24 - i3 - May-June 2004 - p12(1) [1-50]

O'Neill, William L. - *Coming Apart: An Informal History of America in the 1960s*
LJ - v130 - i3 - Feb 15 2005 - p172(1) [51-500]

Oneroad, Amos E. - *Being Dakota: Tales and Traditions of the Sisseton and Wahpeton*
Am Ind CRJ - v27 - i4 - Fall 2003 - p147-148 [501+]

Oness, Elizabeth - *Departures*
Kliatt - v38 - i5 - Sept 2004 - p25(2) [51-500]

Oney, Steve - *And the Dead Shall Rise: The Lynching of Leo Frank*
BooChiTr - Jan 11 2004 - p1(2) [501+]

Ong, Aihwa - *Buddha Is Hiding: Refugees, Citizenship, the New America*
CS - v33 - i6 - Nov 2004 - p684(2) [501+]

Ong, Han - *The Disinherited*
KR - v72 - i15 - August 1 2004 - p709(1) [501+]
LJ - v129 - i12 - July 2004 - p73(1) [51-500]
PW - v251 - i27 - July 5 2004 - p34(1) [51-500]

Ong, Lance O. - *From F to Phi Beta Kappa: Supercharge Your Study Skills*
y VOYA - v27 - i5 - Dec 2004 - p416(1) [51-500]

Ongaro, Giulio - *Music of the Renaissance*
R&R Bk N - v19 - i1 - Feb 2004 - p195(1) [51-500]

Onians, John - *Atlas of World Art*
Art Bull - v86 - i4 - Dec 2004 - p783(5) [501+]
LJ - v129 - i12 - July 2004 - p115(1) [51-500]
R&R Bk N - v19 - i3 - August 2004 - p80(1) [51-500]
SLJ - v50 - i12 - Dec 2004 - p86(1) [501+]
BL - v101 - i5 - Nov 1 2004 - p518(1) [501+]

Onis, Ziya - *The Turkish Economy in Crisis*
R&R Bk N - v19 - i1 - Feb 2004 - p85(1) [51-500]

Onkvisit, Sak - *International Marketing: Analysis and Strategy, 4th Ed.*
TimHES - v0 - i1680 - Feb 25 2005 - pIX(1) [501+]

Onley, Toni - *Flying Colours: The Toni Onley Story*
CBRA - Annual 2003 - p62(1) [501+]

Online Training Solutions (Firm) - *Microsoft Windows XP Step by Step, 2nd Ed.*
Bwatch - Oct 2004 - pNA [51-500]
SciTech - v28 - i4 - Dec 2004 - p26(1) [51-500]

Online Training Solutions, Inc. - *Microsoft Windows XP Step by Step, Deluxe 2nd Ed.*
SciTech - v28 - i4 - Dec 2004 - p26(1) [51-500]

Ono, Kent A. - *Shifting Borders: Rhetoric, Immigration, and California's Proposition*
CS - v33 - i1 - Jan 2004 - p63-64 [501+]

Onsman, Andrys - *Defining Indigeneity in the Twenty-First Century: A Case Study of the Free Frisians*
R&R Bk N - v19 - i4 - Nov 2004 - p41(1) [51-500]

O'Nuallain, Sean - *Being Human: The Search for Order, 2nd Ed.*
R&R Bk N - v19 - i4 - Nov 2004 - p74(1) [51-500]

Onuki, Hideo - *Undulators, Wigglers and Their Applications*
E-Streams - Dec 2004 - pNA [501+]

Onwuegbuzie, Anthony J. - *Library Anxiety: Theory, Research, and Applications*
A Lib - v35 - i7 - August 2004 - p86(1) [501+]
LJ - v129 - i13 - August 2004 - p124(1) [51-500]

Onwumechili, Chuka - *Reform, Organizational Players, and Technological Development in African Telecommunications - An Update*
R&R Bk N - v19 - i2 - May 2004 - p109(1) [51-500]

Onyefulu, Ifeoma - *Here Comes Our Bride!: An African Wedding Story*
c BL - v101 - i1 - Sept 1 2004 - p128(1) [1-50]
HB - v80 - i5 - Sept-Oct 2004 - p607(1) [51-500]
c Sch Lib - v52 - i4 - Winter 2004 - p188(1) [51-500]
Welcome Dede!: An African Naming Ceremony (Illus. by Onyefulu, Ifeoma)
c CCB-B - v58 - i6 - Feb 2005 - p261(2) [51-500]

Ooi, Shirley - *Guide to the Essentials in Emergency Medicine*
SciTech - v28 - i4 - Dec 2004 - p90(1) [51-500]

Oommen, T.K. - *Nation, Civil Society and Social Movements: Essays in Political Sociology*
R&R Bk N - v19 - i3 - August 2004 - p174(1) [501+]

Opel, Andy - *Micro Radio and the FCC: Media Activism and the Struggle over Broadcast Policy*
Choice - v42 - i6 - Feb 2005 - p1017(1) [51-500]
R&R Bk N - v19 - i3 - August 2004 - p122(1) [51-500]
Representing Resistance: Media, Civil Disobedience, and the Global Justice Movement
R&R Bk N - v19 - i1 - Feb 2004 - pNA [501+]

Operating Grants for Nonprofit Organizations, 2004
R&R Bk N - v19 - i3 - August 2004 - p133(1) [51-500]

Opgenort, Jean Robert - *A Grammar of Wambule: Grammar, Lexicon, Texts and Cultural Survey of a Kiranti Tribe of Eastern Nepal*
R&R Bk N - v19 - i4 - Nov 2004 - p220(1) [501+]

Ophiel - *Art and Practice of Caballa Magic*
Bwatch - v26 - i8 - August 2004 - p12(1) [51-500]

Opie, Clive - *Doing Educational Research: A Guide to First-Time Researchers*
R&R Bk N - v19 - i3 - August 2004 - p215(1) [1-50]

Opila, E. - *High Temperature Corrosion and Materials Chemistry IV: Proceedings*
SciTech - v28 - i1 - March 2004 - p142(1) [51-500]

Opler, Paul - *Butterflies of North America*
c CH Bwatch - v14 - i8 - August 2004 - p5(1) [51-500]

Oppel, Kenneth - *Airborn*
y BIC - v33 - i2 - March 2004 - p44(2) [501+]
y BL - v101 - i1 - Sept 1 2004 - p121(1) [501+]
y CBRA - Annual 2003 - p507(1) [51-500]
y CCB-B - v57 - i11 - July-August 2004 - p477(1) [501+]
ChrSFF&H - v26 - i10 - Oct 2004 - p25(1) [51-500]
Airborn. Audiobook Review
c Globe & Mail - Dec 11 2004 - pD53 [1-50]
Airborn
y HB - v80 - i4 - July-August 2004 - p459(1) [51-500]
Mac - v117 - i49 - Dec 6 2004 - p62(1) [501+]
y SLJ - v50 - i7 - July 2004 - p110(1) [51-500]
SLJ - v50 - i10 - Oct 2004 - pS54(1) [51-500]
Emma's Emu (Illus. by LaFave, Kim)
y Can CL - i111-112 - Fall-Winter 2003 - p134(6) [501+]
Peg and the Yeti (Illus. by Reid, Barbara)
c Globe & Mail - Sept 25 2004 - pD26 [51-500]

Book Review Index 2005 Cumulation **ORGANISATION • 457**

Oppenheim, A.K. - *Combustion in Piston Engines: Technology, Evolution, Diagnosis and Control*
Choice - v42 - i2 - Oct 2004 - p324(1) [51-500]
Oppenheim, Shulamith Levey - *Rescuing Einstein's Compass (Illus. by Juhasz, George)*
c CBRA - Annual 2003 - p462(1) [51-500]
Oppenheimer, Amy - *Investigating Workplace Harassment: How to Be Fair, Thorough, and Legal*
HR Mag - v50 - i2 - Feb 2005 - pS12(1) [501+]
Oppenheimer, Jerry - *Front Row: Anna Wintour, the Cool Life and Hot Times of Vogue's Editor in Chief*
BL - v101 - i8 - Dec 15 2004 - p690(1) [51-500]
Globe & Mail - Feb 7 2005 - pR1 [501+]
KR - v72 - i24 - Dec 15 2004 - p1189(1) [501+]
PW - v252 - i4 - Jan 24 2005 - p234(1) [501+]
Oppenheimer, Mark - *Knocking on Heaven's Door: American Religion in the Age of Counterculture*
BL - v101 - i3 - Oct 1 2004 - p302(1) [51-500]
HNet - August 2004 - pNA [501+]
JAH - v91 - i2 - Sept 2004 - p718(2) [501+]
Oppenheimer, Paul - *Rubens: A Portrait*
Ren Q - v57 - i4 - Winter 2004 - p1491(2) [501+]
Oppenheimer, Priscilla - *Top-Down Network Design*
Bwatch - v26 - i8 - August 2004 - p6(1) [51-500]
Oppenheimer, Stephen - *Out of Eden: The Peopling of the World*
TLS - i5268 - March 19 2004 - p23-23 [501+]
The Real Eve: Modern Man's Journey Out of Africa
Choice - v41 - i7 - March 2004 - p1337(1) [501+]
Opperman, Hal - *Birder's Guide to Washington*
SciTech - v28 - i1 - March 2004 - p70(1) [51-500]
Opposing Viewpoints in World History
LibMed - v23 - i1 - August-Sept 2004 - p77(1) [51-500]
O'Pray, Michael - *Film, Form, and Phantasy: Adrian Stokes and Film Aesthetics*
Choice - v42 - i5 - Jan 2005 - p860(1) [1-50]
Optical Fiber Communications Conference: Postconference Digest
SciTech - v28 - i3 - Sept 2004 - p154(1) [51-500]
Oram, Gerard Christopher - *Military Executions During World War I*
J Mil H - v68 - i3 - July 2004 - p978-979 [501+]
Oram, Hiawyn - *The Best Party of Them All (Illus. by Su, Lucy)*
c SLJ - v50 - i7 - July 2004 - p83(1) [51-500]
Busy-Busy Bears
c Sch Lib - v52 - i4 - Winter 2004 - p188(1) [51-500]
Rubbaduck and Ruby Roo (Illus. by Lucas, David)
c KR - v73 - i3 - Feb 1 2005 - p180(1) [51-500]
c PW - v252 - i10 - March 7 2005 - p67(1) [51-500]
Oram, William A. - *Spenser Studies: A Renaissance Poetry Annual, Vol. 19*
R&R Bk N - v19 - i4 - Nov 2004 - p235(1) [501+]
Orange, Vincent - *Tedder: Quietly in Command*
APJ - v18 - i4 - Winter 2004 - p112(2) [501+]
Orbach, Ann - *Counselling Older Clients*
Choice - v41 - i7 - March 2004 - p1375(1) [501+]
Orban, Christine - *One Day My Sister Disappeared*
BL - v100 - i21 - July 2004 - p1811(1) [1-50]
Orbanes, Philip E. - *The Game Makers: The Story of Parker Brothers from Tiddledy Winks to Trivial Pursuit*
BL - v101 - i4 - Oct 15 2004 - p387(1) [51-500]
R&R Bk N - v19 - i1 - Feb 2004 - p103(1) [51-500]
Orchard, Andy - *A Critical Companion to 'Beowulf'*
RES - v55 - i221 - Sept 2004 - p606(3) [501+]
Pride and Prodigies: Studies in the Monsters of the Beowulf-Manuscript
CBRA - Annual 2003 - p260(1) [51-500]
Orchard, Kate - *Exploring Villages*
c Sch Lib - v52 - i4 - Winter 2004 - p209(1) [51-500]
Orchard, Nicholas - *The Leofric Missal*
CHR - v90 - i4 - Oct 2004 - p749(3) [501+]
Orchid, Christina - *Christina's Cookbook: Recipes and Tales from a Northwest Island Kitchen*
PW - v251 - i41 - Oct 11 2004 - p72(2) [51-500]
Orchid, Nicholas - *The Leofric Missal*
Specu - v79 - i3 - July 2004 - p817-819 [501+]
Orcutt, James D. - *Drugs, Alcohol, and Social Problems*
R&R Bk N - v19 - i1 - Feb 2004 - p140(1) [51-500]
Ord, Douglas - *The National Gallery of Canada: Ideas, Art, Architecture*
Can Hist R - v85 - i3 - Sept 2004 - p561(4) [501+]
CBRA - Annual 2003 - p120(1) [51-500]
Orders, P.G.A. - *Britain, Australia, New Zealand and the Challenge of the United States, 1839-46: A Study in International History*
Albion - v36 - i2 - Summer 2004 - p362(2) [501+]
Britain, Australia, New Zealand and the Challenge of the United States, 1939-46: A Study in International History
AHR - v109 - i3 - June 2004 - p875(2) [501+]
Ordover, Nancy - *American Eugenics: Race, Queer Anatomy, and the Science of Nationalism*
AHR - v109 - i4 - Oct 2004 - p1257(2) [501+]
JIH - v35 - i1 - Summer 2004 - p163-164 [501+]
Soc Ser R - v78 - i3 - Sept 2004 - p525(1) [51-500]
Orebaugh, Angela - *Ethereal Packet Sniffing*
Bwatch - v26 - i7 - July 2004 - p8(1) [51-500]
O'Regan, Cyril - *Gnostic Apocalypse: Jacob Boehme's Haunted Narrative*
JR - v85 - i1 - Jan 2005 - p115(3) [501+]
O'Regan, David - *Auditor's Dictionary: Terms, Concepts, Processes, and Regulations*
R&R Bk N - v19 - i4 - Nov 2004 - p114(1) [51-500]
Oregon Genealogical Society - *Oregon Pioneers, Vol. 4*
EFHM - v58 - i2 - March-April 2004 - p90(1) [1-50]
O'Reilly, Andrea - *Toni Morrison and Motherhood: A Politics of the Heart*
Choice - v42 - i3 - Nov 2004 - p486(1) [1-50]
O'Reilly, Bill - *The O'Reilly Factor for Kids: A Survival Guide for America's Families*
y BL - v100 - i22 - August 2004 - p1867(2) [51-500]
Globe & Mail - Sept 4 2004 - pR3 [501+]
O'Reilly, Bill (American television broadcaster) - *The O'Reilly Factor for Kids: A Survival Guide for America's Families*
NYTBR - Nov 7 2004 - p22 [501+]
y SLJ - v50 - i11 - Nov 2004 - p170(1) [51-500]
O'Reilly, Gary - *The Handbook of Clinical Intervention with Young People Who Sexually Abuse*
SciTech - v28 - i4 - Dec 2004 - p114(1) [1-50]
O'Reilly, Gillian - *Slangalicious: Where We Got That Crazy Lingo (Illus. by Johnson, Krista)*
c BL - v101 - i8 - Dec 15 2004 - p740(1) [51-500]
c Globe & Mail - August 28 2004 - pD12 [501+]
y SLJ - v51 - i1 - Jan 2005 - p153(1) [51-500]
O'Reilly, Jacqueline - *Regulating Working-Time Transitions in Europe*
R&R Bk N - v19 - i1 - Feb 2004 - p99(1) [51-500]
O'Reilly, Kathleen - *The Diva's Guide to Selling Your Soul*
KR - v73 - i3 - Feb 1 2005 - p149(1) [51-500]
Orel, Vladimir - *A Handbook of Germanic Etymology*
R&R Bk N - v19 - i1 - Feb 2004 - p215(1) [51-500]
Orelove, Fred P. - *Educating Children with Multiple Disabilities: A Collaborative Approach, 4th Ed.*
R&R Bk N - v19 - i4 - Nov 2004 - p192(1) [501+]
Oren, Ido - *Our Enemies and US: America Rivalries and the Making of Political Science*
JAH - v91 - i1 - June 2004 - p297-298 [501+]
Oren, Michael B. - *Reunion, a Novel*
y Kliatt - v38 - i5 - Sept 2004 - p25(2) [501+]
Oren, Tasha G - *Demon in the Box: Jews, Arabs, Politics and Culture in the Making of Israeli Television*
CHE - v50 - i45 - July 16 2004 - pA18(2) [501+]
Oren, Tasha G. - *Demon in the Box: Jews, Arabs, Politics, and Culture in the Making of Israeli Televison*
Choice - v42 - i7 - March 2005 - p1222(2) [51-500]
Orend, Brian - *Human Rights: Concept and Context*
CBRA - Annual 2003 - p310(1) [501+]
Orengo, Christine - *Bioinformatics: Genes, Proteins and Computers*
E-Streams - Oct 2004 - pNA [501+]
Orens, John Richard - *Stewart Headlam's Radical Anglicanism: The Mass, the Masses, and the Music Hall*
Bks & Cult - v11 - i1 - Jan-Feb 2005 - p18(2) [501+]
TLS - i5284 - July 9 2004 - p29(1) [501+]
CHR - v90 - i3 - July 2004 - p559(2) [501+]
Orenstein, Catherine - *Little Red Riding Hood Uncloaked: Sex, Morality, and the Evolution of a Fairy Tale*
WestFolk - v62 - i4 - Fall 2003 - p305(2) [501+]
Orenstein, David M. - *Cystic Fibrosis: A Guide for Patient and Family, 3rd Ed.*
SciTech - v28 - i1 - March 2004 - p118(1) [51-500]
Orenstein, Denise Gosliner - *Unseen Companion*
y SLJ - v50 - i10 - Oct 2004 - pS68(1) [51-500]
Orenstein, Vik - *Photographer's Market Guide to Building Your Photography Business*
PetPho - v33 - i10 - Feb 2005 - p18(1) [51-500]
Orent, Wendy - *Plague: The Mysterious Past and Terrifying Future of the World's Most Dangerous Disease*
Bwatch - Nov 2004 - pNA [51-500]
Nature - v430 - i6996 - July 8 2004 - p145(2) [501+]
SciTech - v28 - i3 - Sept 2004 - p91(1) [51-500]
Orff, Joel - *Waterwise*
BL - v101 - i1 - Sept 1 2004 - p78(1) [51-500]
PW - v251 - i31 - August 2 2004 - p54(2) [501+]
Orford, Anne - *Reading Humanitarian Intervention: Human Rights and the Use of Force in International Law*
Law&PolBR - June 2004 - p363(11) [501+]
Organ, Betty - *My Newfoundland and Labrador Counting Book (Illus. by Carter, Dana)*
c Res Links - v10 - i3 - Feb 2005 - p7(2) [501+]
Organisation for Economic Co-operation and Development - *2002 Reports Related to the OECD Model Tax Convention*
JEL - v41 - i4 - Dec 2003 - p1373(1) [501+]
Agricultural Policies in OECD Countries: Monitoring and Evaluation 2003
JEL - v42 - i1 - March 2004 - p329(1) [501+]
Agriculture and Rural Development Policies in the Baltic Countries
JEL - v42 - i1 - March 2004 - p329(1) [501+]
Assessing the Solvency of Insurance Companies
JEL - v42 - i1 - March 2004 - p268(1) [501+]
Financing Education: Investments and Returns: Analysis of the World Education Indicators
JEL - v41 - i4 - Dec 2003 - p1379(1) [501+]
Financing Strategies of Water and Environmental Infrastructure
JEL - v41 - i4 - Dec 2003 - p1434(1) [501+]
Finland: A New Consensus for Change
JEL - v42 - i1 - March 2004 - p288(1) [501+]
Geographical Distribution of Financial Flows to Aid Recipients: Disbursements, Commitments, Country Indicators, 1998-2002
R&R Bk N - v19 - i3 - August 2004 - p139(1) [51-500]
Global Economic Prospects 2004: Realizing the Development Promise of the Doha Agenda
JEL - v42 - i1 - March 2004 - p314(1) [501+]
Organisation for Economic Co-Operation and Development - *Harmonising Donor Practices for Effective Aid Delivery*
JEL - v41 - i4 - Dec 2003 - p1361(1) [501+]
Harnessing Markets for Biodiversity: Towards Conservation and Sustainable Use
JEL - v41 - i4 - Dec 2003 - p1431(1) [501+]
Organisation for Economic Co-operation and Development - *Labour Force Statistics/Statistiques de la Population Active: 1982-2002*
JEL - v42 - i1 - March 2004 - p282(1) [501+]
Measuring Knowledge Management in the Business Sector: First Steps
R&R Bk N - v19 - i3 - August 2004 - p102(1) [501+]
Norway: Preparing for the Future Now
R&R Bk N - v19 - i1 - Feb 2004 - p98(1) [1-50]
OECD Agricultural Outlook: 2003-2008
JEL - v42 - i1 - March 2004 - p329(2) [501+]
OECD Code of Liberalisation of Capital Movements, 2003
JEL - v41 - i4 - Dec 2003 - p1361(2) [501+]
OECD Codes of Liberalisation of Capital Movements and of Current Invisible Operations: User's Guide
JEL - v42 - i1 - March 2004 - p266(1) [501+]
OECD Communications Outlook 2003
JEL - v42 - i1 - March 2004 - p293(1) [501+]
OECD Economic Surveys: Canada 2002-2003
JEL - v42 - i1 - March 2004 - p321(1) [501+]
OECD Economic Surveys: Czech Republic 2002-2003
JEL - v42 - i1 - March 2004 - p321(1) [501+]
OECD Economic Surveys: Denmark 2002-2003
JEL - v42 - i1 - March 2004 - p321(1) [501+]
OECD Economic Surveys: Iceland 2002-2003
JEL - v41 - i4 - Dec 2003 - p1424(1) [501+]
OECD Economic Surveys: Ireland 2002-2003
JEL - v42 - i1 - March 2004 - p321(2) [501+]
OECD Economic Surveys: Italy 2002-2003
JEL - v42 - i1 - March 2004 - p322(1) [501+]
OECD Economic Surveys: Spain 2002-2003
JEL - v41 - i4 - Dec 2003 - p1424(1) [501+]
OECD Employment Outlook, 2003 ed.: Towards More and Better Jobs
R&R Bk N - v19 - i1 - Feb 2004 - p98(1) [1-50]
OECD Employment Outlook: Towards More and Better Jobs
JEL - v42 - i1 - March 2004 - p254(1) [501+]
OECD Guiding Principles for Chemical Accident Prevention, Preparedness and Response: Guidance Industry (Including Management and Lobor), Public Authorities, Communities, and Other Stakeholders
JEL - v41 - i4 - Dec 2003 - p1437(1) [501+]
OECD Investment Policy Reviews: China: Progress and Reform Challenges

JEL - v42 - i1 - March 2004 - p326(2) [501+]
OECD Statistics on International Trade in Services: Detailed Tables by Service Category 1993-2004
R&R Bk N - v19 - i3 - August 2004 - p121(1) [51-500]
OECD Statistics on International Trade in Services/Statisques de L'OCDE Sur Les Echanges Internationaux de Services: 1992-2001
JEL - v41 - i4 - Dec 2004 - p1354(1) [501+]
OECD Territorial Reviews: Helsinki, Finland
JEL - v41 - i4 - Dec 2003 - p1441(1) [501+]
Organic Agriculture: Sustainability, Markets and Policies
JEL - v41 - i1 - March 2004 - p330(1) [501+]
Quantifying the Benefits of Liberalising Trade in Services
JEL - v41 - i4 - Dec 2003 - p1354(2) [501+]
Review of Fisheries in OECD Countries: Country Statistics: 1990-2001/Examen des Pecheries Dans les Pays De L'OCDE: Statisques Nationales: 1999-2001
JEL - v42 - i1 - March 2004 - p331(1) [501+]
Review of Fisheries in OECD Countries: Policies and Summary Statistics
JEL - v42 - i1 - March 2004 - p331(2) [501+]
Rural Finance and Credit Infrastructure in China
R&R Bk N - v19 - i3 - August 2004 - p139(1) [51-500]
Social Issues in the Provision and Pricing of Water Services
JEL - v42 - i1 - March 2004 - p332(1) [501+]
Taxing Wages: Special Feature: Taxing Families/Les Impots Sur les Salaires: Etude Speciale: Les Impots des Familles: 2001-2002
JEL - v42 - i1 - March 2004 - p271(1) [501+]

Organisation for Economic Co-operation and Development, Nuclear Energy Agency - *Public Confidence in the Management of Radioactive Waste: The Canadian Context, Proceedings*
SciTech - v28 - i3 - Sept 2004 - p147(1) [51-500]
Organisation of Economic Co-operation and Development - *Privacy Online: OECD Guidance on Policy and Practice*
SciTech - v28 - i3 - Sept 2004 - p9(1) [501+]
Private Finance and Economic Development: City and Regional Investment
JEL - v42 - i1 - March 2004 - p343(1) [501+]
Organization for Economic Co-operation and Development - *The Future of Rural Policy: From Sectoral to Place-Based Policies in Rural Areas, Proceedings*
R&R Bk N - v19 - i3 - August 2004 - p145(1) [51-500]
Insurance Statistics Yearbook 1994-2001, 2003 ed.
R&R Bk N - v19 - i1 - Feb 2004 - p119(1) [51-500]
OECD Handbook for Internationally Comparative Education Statistics: Concepts, Standards, Definitions and Classifications
R&R Bk N - v19 - i3 - August 2004 - p224(1) [1-50]
Reforming Public Pensions: Sharing the Experiences of Transition and OECD Countries
R&R Bk N - v19 - i3 - August 2004 - p117(1) [51-500]
Regionalism and the Multilateral Trading System
JEL - v42 - i1 - March 2004 - p261(1) [501+]
Organization for Economic Co-Operation and Development - *Structural Statistics for Industry and Services/Statistiques des Structures de L'Industrie et des Services*
JEL - v42 - i1 - March 2004 - p290(1) [501+]
Organization for Economic Cooperation and Development - *Foodborne Disease in OECD Countries: Present State and Economic Costs*
SciTech - v28 - i3 - Sept 2004 - p75(1) [51-500]
Mammalian Embryo Genomics
SciTech - v28 - i3 - Sept 2004 - p60(1) [1-50]
Orgel, Doris - *The Bremen Town Musicians and Other Animal Tales from Grimm (Illus. by Kitchen, Bert)*
c BL - v101 - i9-10 - Jan 1 2005 - p866(1) [51-500]
c HB - v81 - i1 - Jan-Feb 2005 - p103(2) [51-500]
The Bremen Town Musicians: and Other Animal Tales from Grimm (Illus. by Kitchen, Bert)
c KR - v72 - i18 - Sept 15 2004 - p917(1) [51-500]
PW - v251 - i45 - Nov 8 2004 - p55(2) [51-500]
The Bremen Town Musicians and Other Animal Tales from Grimm (Illus. by Kitchen, Bert)
c SLJ - v50 - i12 - Dec 2004 - p136(1) [501+]
Orgel, Stephen - *Imagining Shakespeare: A History of Texts and Visions*
Ren Q - v57 - i4 - Winter 2004 - p1526(2) [501+]
Orgill, Roxane - *Shout, Sister, Shout!: Ten Girl Singers Who Shaped a Century*
y SLJ - v50 - i12 - Dec 2004 - p61(1) [501+]

Origo, Iris - *War in Val D'Orcia: An Italian War Diary 1943-1944*
Comw - v131 - i21 - Dec 3 2004 - p26(2) [501+]
Oring, Elliott - *Engaging Humor*
Folkl - v115 - i3 - Dec 2004 - p381(2) [501+]
Orlean, Susan - *My Kind of Place: Travel Stories from a Woman Who's Been Everywhere*
BL - v101 - i2 - Sept 15 2004 - p178(1) [51-500]
Ent W - i787 - Oct 8 2004 - p121 [501+]
Globe & Mail - Nov 13 2004 - pD8 [501+]
KR - v72 - i15 - August 1 2004 - p730(1) [501+]
LJ - v129 - i16 - Oct 1 2004 - p102(1) [51-500]
PW - v251 - i33 - August 16 2004 - p49(1) [51-500]
Orloff, Alvin - *Gutterboys*
G&L Rev W - v12 - i1 - Jan-Feb 2005 - p44(1) [501+]
Orloff, Erica - *Mafia Chic*
BL - v101 - i2 - Sept 15 2004 - p225(1) [51-500]
Orloff, Judith - *Positive Energy (Read by Fields, Anna). Audiobook Review*
LJ - v129 - i15 - Sept 15 2004 - p90(1) [51-500]
Orloff, Karen Kaufman - *I Wanna Iguana (Illus. by Catrow, David)*
c KR - v72 - i16 - August 15 2004 - p811(1) [51-500]
c SLJ - v50 - i10 - Oct 2004 - p126(1) [51-500]
Orlow, Dietrich - *Common Destiny: A Comparative History of the Dutch, French, and German Social Democratic Parties, 1945-1969*
HNet - Oct 2004 - pNA [501+]
Orman, Lorraine - *Cross Tides*
y Magpies - v19 - i5 - Nov 2004 - p7S(1) [501+]
Orman, Suze - *The Money Book for the Young, Fabulous and Broke*
NW - March 21 2005 - p36 [501+]
PW - v252 - i7 - Feb 14 2005 - p66(1) [51-500]
Orme, Antony - *The Physical Geography of North America*
GJ - v170 - i3 - Sept 2004 - p283(2) [501+]
GJ - v170 - i4 - Dec 2004 - p384(1) [501+]
Orme, Nicholas - *Medieval Children*
Specu - v79 - i3 - July 2004 - p819-821 [501+]
Ormerod, Jan - *Emily and Albert (Illus. by Slonim, David)*
c Sch Lib - v52 - i3 - Autumn 2004 - p132(1) [501+]
c SLJ - v50 - i7 - July 2004 - p83(2) [51-500]
The Frog Princess (Illus. by Damon, Emma)
c KR - v72 - i24 - Dec 15 2004 - p1206(1) [51-500]
Ormrod, David - *The Rise of Commercial Empires: England and the Netherlands in the Age of Mercantilism, 1650-1770*
AHR - v109 - i4 - Oct 2004 - p1304-1305 [501+]
JIH - v35 - i1 - Summer 2004 - p125-127 [501+]
Ornstein, Allan C. - *Curriculum: Foundations, Principles, and Issues, 4th Ed.*
R&R Bk N - v19 - i1 - Feb 2004 - p187(1) [51-500]
K-8 Instructional Methods: A Literacy Perspective
R&R Bk N - v19 - i4 - Nov 2004 - p182(1) [501+]
Teaching and Schooling in America: Pre- and Post-September 11
R&R Bk N - v19 - i1 - Feb 2004 - p190(1) [51-500]
Teaching and Schooling in America Pre- and Post-September 11
TCR - v106 - i2 - Feb 2004 - p375-378 [501+]
Ornston, L. Nicholas - *Annual Review of Microbiology, Vol. 57*
SciTech - v28 - i1 - March 2004 - p75(1) [51-500]
Oropesa, Salvador A. - *The Contemporaneos Group: Rewriting Mexico In The Thirties And Forties*
Hisp R - v72 - i3 - Summer 2004 - p456-460 [501+]
O'Rourke, Michael - *Snow Loads: A Guide to the Use and Understanding of the Snow Load Provisions of ASCE 7-02*
SciTech - v28 - i3 - Sept 2004 - p141(1) [51-500]
O'Rourke, P.J. - *Peace Kills: America's Fun New Imperialism*
Globe & Mail - Oct 9 2004 - pD6 [501+]
O'Rourke, Timothy J. - *Catholic Families of Southern Maryland: Records of Catholic Residents of St. Mary's County in the 18th Century*
EFHM - v58 - i3 - May-June 2004 - p59(1) [51-500]
Orovio, Helio - *Cuban Music from A to Z*
Choice - v42 - i1 - Sept 2004 - p62(5) [501+]
Orozco, Gabriel - *Gabriel Orozco: Photographs*
LJ - v129 - i20 - Dec 1 2004 - p113(1) [51-500]
Orr, Clarissa Campbell - *Queenship in Europe, 1660-1815: The Role of the Consort*
TLS - i5307 - Dec 17 2004 - p32(1) [501+]

Orr, David W. - *Earth in Mind: On Education, Environment, and the Human Prospect*
Env - v47 - i1 - Jan-Feb 2005 - p42(2) [501+]
R&R Bk N - v19 - i4 - Nov 2004 - p74(1) [51-500]
The Last Refuge: Patriotism, Politics, and the Environment in an Age of Terror
Choice - v42 - i3 - Nov 2004 - p556(1) [1-50]
E Mag - v15 - i5 - Sept-Oct 2004 - p63(1) [51-500]
Env - v46 - i7 - Sept 2004 - p41(1) [501+]
R&R Bk N - v19 - i3 - August 2004 - p179(1) [501+]
Orr, Elaine Neil - *Gods of Noonday: A White Girl's African Life*
R&R Bk N - v19 - i1 - Feb 2004 - p27(1) [51-500]
Orr, Gregory - *Poetry as Survival*
South R - v39 - Winter 2003 - p219 [501+]
Orr, John - *The Cinema of Andrej Wajda: The Art of Irony and Defiance*
Choice - v42 - i4 - Dec 2004 - p668(1) [1-50]
Orr, Robert C. - *Winning the Peace: An American Strategy for Post-Conflict Reconstruction*
R&R Bk N - v19 - i4 - Nov 2004 - p63(1) [51-500]
Orr, Tamra - *Alan Shepard: The First American in Space*
y SLJ - v51 - i1 - Jan 2005 - p142(1) [51-500]
Life in the Arctic
c SB - v40 - i6 - Nov-Dec 2004 - p269(2) [51-500]
The Salem Witch Trials
y SLJ - v50 - i9 - Sept 2004 - p228(2) [51-500]
Slovenia
c SLJ - v50 - i7 - July 2004 - p126(1) [51-500]
The Telescope
c SLJ - v51 - i2 - Feb 2005 - p148(1) [51-500]
Violence in Our Schools: Halls of Hope, Halls of Fear
SLJ - v50 - i10 - Oct 2004 - pS60(1) [51-500]
Orrell, Martin - *Cane: Camberwell Assessment of Need for the Elderly, a Needs Assessment for Older Mental Health Service Users*
SciTech - v28 - i4 - Dec 2004 - p95(1) [51-500]
Orren, Karen - *The Search for American Political Development*
Choice - v42 - i5 - Jan 2005 - p936(1) [51-500]
Orrenh, Ido - *Our Enemies and US. America's Rivalries and the Making of Political Science*
J Am St - v38 - i1 - April 2004 - p156-157 [501+]
Orser, Charles E., Jr. - *Race and Practice in Archaeological Interpretation*
Choice - v42 - i1 - Sept 2004 - p148(1) [501+]
Orsi, Richard J. - *Sunset Limited: The Southern Pacific Railroad and the Development of the American West, 1850-1930*
PW - v252 - i11 - March 14 2005 - p55(1) [51-500]
Orsi, Robert - *Gods of the City: Religion and the Urban Landscape*
J Urban H - v31 - i2 - Jan 2005 - p249-257 [501+]
Orsi, Roberta A. - *Between Heaven and Earth: The Religious Worlds People Make and the Scholars Who Study Them*
PW - v251 - i51 - Dec 20 2004 - p56(1) [51-500]
Ortberg, John - *God Is Closer than You Think*
PW - v252 - i7 - Feb 14 2005 - p71(1) [51-500]
Ortego, Jose Antonio Serrano - *Jerarquia Territorial y Transicion Politica: Guanajuato, 1790-1836*
Ams - v61 - i2 - Oct 2004 - p287(3) [501+]
Ortel, Jo - *Woodland Reflections: The Art of the Truman Lowe*
Choice - v42 - i5 - Jan 2005 - p844(1) [1-50]
Orth, John V. - *Due Process of Law: A Brief History*
HNet - Sept 2004 - pNA [501+]
Orth, Maureen - *The Importance of Being Famous*
CJR - v43 - i2 - July-August 2004 - p48(4) [501+]
Ortigao, J.A.R. - *Handbook of Slope Stabilisation*
Choice - v42 - i3 - Nov 2004 - p514(1) [1-50]
Ortino, Federico - *The WTO Dispute Settlement System, 1995-2003*
R&R Bk N - v19 - i3 - August 2004 - p193(1) [501+]
Ortiz Cofer, Judith - *Call Me Maria: A Novel*
y BL - v101 - i7 - Dec 1 2004 - p647(2) [51-500]
y CCB-B - v58 - i3 - Nov 2004 - p116(1) [501+]
y HB - v81 - i1 - Jan-Feb 2005 - p90(1) [51-500]
y KR - v72 - i20 - Oct 15 2004 - p1003(1) [51-500]
y SLJ - v50 - i11 - Nov 2004 - p138(1) [51-500]
Riding Low on the Streets of Gold: Latino Literature for Young Adults
y VOYA - v27 - i4 - Oct 2004 - p330(1) [51-500]
Ortiz, Domingo - *La incorporacion de las Indias al mundo occidental en el siglo XVI*
Six Ct J - v35 - i1 - Spring 2004 - p239(3) [501+]

Otawa, Toru - *Maximizing the Power of Geographical Information Systems (GIS) in Applied Land Informatics*
   R&R Bk N - v19 - i4 - Nov 2004 - p71(1) [51-500]

Otfinoski, Steven - *Afghanistan*
   SLJ - v50 - i10 - Oct 2004 - pS58(1) [51-500]
The Baltic Republics
   y SLJ - v51 - i1 - Jan 2005 - p153(1) [51-500]
The Czech Republic. 2nd Ed
   y BL - v101 - i7 - Dec 1 2004 - p645(1) [51-500]

Otnes, Cele C. - *Contemporary Consumption Rituals: A Research Anthology*
   R&R Bk N - v19 - i1 - Feb 2004 - p80(1) [51-500]

O'Toole, Christopher - *The New Encyclopedia of Insects and Their Allies*
   TLS - i5292 - Sept 3 2004 - p28(1) [501+]

O'Toole, Fintan - *Critical Moments On Modern Irish Theatre*
   ILS - v24 - i1 - Fall 2004 - p24(2) [501+]

O'Toole, James M. - *Habits of Devotion: Catholic Religious Practice in Twentieth-Century America*
   AM - v192 - i8 - March 7 2005 - p22 [501+]
   LJ - v129 - i12 - July 2004 - p90(1) [51-500]
Passing for White: Race, Religion, and the Healy Family, 1820-1920
   AHR - v109 - i3 - June 2004 - p922(2) [501+]
Passing for White--Race, Religion, and the Healy Family 1820-1920
   CHR - v90 - i4 - Oct 2004 - p820(4) [501+]

O'Toole, Michael P. - *The Payroll Source*
   HR Mag - v49 - i7 - July 2004 - pS8(1) [51-500]

O'Toole, Patricia - *Shaping Sound Musicians: An Innovative Approach to Teaching Comprehensive Musicianship through Performance*
   M Ed J - v91 - i1 - Sept 2004 - p61(1) [501+]
When Trumpets Call: Theodore Roosevelt After the White House
   KR - v73 - i1 - Jan 1 2005 - p39(1) [501+]
   LJ - v130 - i2 - Feb 1 2005 - p99(1) [51-500]
   PW - v252 - i2 - Jan 10 2005 - p45(1) [51-500]

Otoshi, Kathryn - *Simon and the Sock Monster (Illus. by Otoshi, Kathryn)*
   c SLJ - v50 - i10 - Oct 2004 - p126(1) [51-500]

Otsuka, Michael - *Libertarianism without Inequality*
   Ethics - v115 - i1 - Oct 2004 - p158(3) [501+]
   Reason - v36 - i8 - Jan 2005 - p56(4) [501+]

Ott, John - *Die Macht der Weisheit: Das Bild des Bischofs in der Vita Augustini des Possidius und andere spaetantiken und fruehmittelalterlichen Bischofsviten*
   Med R - Dec 2004 - pNA [501+]

Ott, Katherine - *Artificial Parts, Practical Lives: Modern Histories of Prosthetics*
   T&C - v45 - i4 - Oct 2004 - p899(3) [501+]

Ott, Martin - *Die Entdeckung des Altertums: Der Umgang mit der romischen Vergangenheit Suddeutschlands im 16. Jahrhundert*
   Ren Q - v57 - i3 - Fall 2004 - p1041(2) [501+]

Ottaviani, Jim - *Suspended in Language: Niels Bohr's Life, Discoveries, and the Century He Shaped. (Illus. by Purvis, Leland)*
   BL - v100 - i22 - August 2004 - p1916(1) [501+]
Suspended in Language: Niels Bohr's Life, Discoveries, and the Century He Shaped (Illus. by Purvis, Leland)
   Choice - v42 - i4 - Dec 2004 - pNA684-1 [1-50]
   LJ - v129 - i18 - Nov 1 2004 - p66(1) [501+]
Suspended in language: Niels Bohr's life, discoveries, and the century he shaped
   y VOYA - v27 - i5 - Dec 2004 - p416(1) [51-500]

Ottaway, Marina - *Democracy Challenged: The Rise of Semi-Authoritarianism*
   JPR - v41 - i4 - July 2004 - p522-523 [501+]

Ottaway, Susan - *Violette Szabo*
   R&R Bk N - v19 - i1 - Feb 2004 - p30(1) [51-500]

Otte, C. - *Galen: De plenitudine*
   Class R - v53 - i2 - Nov 2003 - p337-338 [501+]

Otte, Marinus L. - *Wetlands of Ireland: Distribution, Ecology, Uses and Economic Value*
   Choice - v41 - i11-12 - July-August 2004 - p2071(2) [501+]

Otterness, Philip - *Becoming German: The 1709 Palatine Migration to New York*
   W&M Q - v62 - i1 - Jan 2005 - p133-3 [501+]

Otteson, James R. - *Adam Smith's Market Place of Life*
   IndRev - v9 - i3 - Wntr 2005 - p466(4) [501+]

Ottinger, Didier - *Jean Helion*
   Apo - v161 - i516 - Feb 2005 - p16(1) [501+]

Ottmann, Goetz Frank - *Lost for Words?: Brazilian Liberationism in the 1990s*
   CS - v33 - i6 - Nov 2004 - p748(1) [1-50]

Otto, Carolyn B. - *Spiders*
   c RT - v57 - Oct 2003 - p170 [1-50]

Otto, Catherine M. - *Textbook of Clinical Echocardiography, 3rd Ed.*
   SciTech - v28 - i4 - Dec 2004 - p103(1) [51-500]
Valvular Heart Disease, 2nd Ed.
   SciTech - v28 - i1 - March 2004 - p105(1) [51-500]

Otto, Henrik - *Vor und fruhreformatorische Tauler-Rezeption*
   HNet - Oct 2004 - pNA [501+]

Otto, Shirley E. - *Oncology Nursing Clinical Reference*
   SciTech - v28 - i1 - March 2004 - p90(1) [51-500]

Ouchi, William G. - *Making Schools Work: A Revolutionary Plan to Get Your Children the Education They Need*
   Choice - v41 - i7 - March 2004 - p1344(1) [501+]

Oudolf, Piet - *Planting the Natural Garden*
   E-Streams - June 2004 - pNA [501+]
   SciTech - v28 - i3 - Sept 2004 - p129(1) [51-500]

Oudshoorn, Nelly - *How Users Matter: The Co-Construction of Users and Technology*
   Am Sci - v92 - i5 - Sept-Oct 2004 - p482(2) [501+]
The Male Pill: A Biography of a Technology in the Making
   AJS - v110 - i1 - July 2004 - p273(3) [501+]
   Choice - v41 - i7 - March 2004 - p1327(1) [501+]

Ouguergouz, Fatsah - *The African Charter on Human and Peoples' Rights: A Comprehensive Agenda for Human Dignity and Sustainable Democracy in Africa*
   R&R Bk N - v19 - i4 - Nov 2004 - p152(1) [501+]

Ouimet, Francis - *A Game of Golf*
   LJ - v129 - i18 - Nov 1 2004 - p134(1) [1-50]
   R&R Bk N - v19 - i4 - Nov 2004 - p81(1) [1-50]

Ouimnet, David - *Dare to be Scared: Thirteen Stories to Chill and Thrill*
   LibMed - v22 - i5 - Feb 2004 - p70(1) [51-500]

Our Cultural Heritage
   c LibMed - v22 - i7 - April-May 2004 - p74(1) [51-500]

Our Documents: 100 Milestone Documents from the National Archives
   y R&R Bk N - v19 - i1 - Feb 2004 - p55(1) [51-500]

Oura, K - *Surface Science: An Introduction*
   Phys Today - v57 - i10 - Oct 2004 - p79-80 [501+]

Ouriou, Susan - *Damselfish*
   CBRA - Annual 2003 - p180(2) [51-500]

Ousager, Asger - *Plotinus on Selfhood, Freedom and Politics*
   R&R Bk N - v20 - i1 - Feb 2005 - p2(1) [51-500]

Ousterhout, Anne M. - *The Most Learned Woman in America: A Life of Elizabeth Graeme Fergusson*
   Choice - v42 - i2 - Oct 2004 - p358(1) [51-500]
   W&M Q - v61 - i4 - Oct 2004 - p770-773 [501+]

Out Of This World
   LibMed - v22 - i7 - April-May 2004 - p79(1) [501+]

Outland, Orland - *A Serious Person*
   BL - v101 - i2 - Sept 15 2004 - p210(1) [501+]
   PW - v251 - i41 - Oct 11 2004 - p55(1) [51-500]

Outman, James L. - *U.S. Immigration and Migration: Almanac, Vols. 1-2*
   Choice - v42 - i5 - Jan 2005 - p839(1) [1-50]
U.S. Immigration and Migration: Biographies, Vols. 1-2
   Choice - v42 - i5 - Jan 2005 - p839(1) [1-50]
   y Ref Rev - Oct 2004 - pNA [501+]
   R&R Bk N - v19 - i3 - August 2004 - p185(1) [501+]
   y R&USQ - v44 - i2 - Winter 2004 - p176(1) [501+]
   y SLJ - v51 - i2 - Feb 2005 - p82(1) [501+]
U.S. Immigration and Migration: Primary Sources
   y Ref Rev - Oct 2004 - pNA [501+]
   R&R Bk N - v19 - i3 - August 2004 - p185(1) [501+]
U.S. Immigration and Migration Primary Sources
   y SLJ - v51 - i2 - Feb 2005 - p82(1) [501+]

Outside Magazine - *Hip-Hop Hares and Other Moments of Epic Silliness*
   New Sci - v184 - i2476 - Dec 4 2004 - p54(1) [501+]

Outwater, Myra Yellin - *Garden Ornaments and Antiques*
   Ant&CM - v108 - i6 - August 2003 - p16(1) [501+]

Outwitting the Enemy: Stories from the Second World War
   LibMed - v22 - i5 - Feb 2004 - p80(1) [51-500]

Ouyang Xiu - *Historical Records of the Five Dynasties*
   Med R - Oct 2004 - pNA [501+]

Over, Joan - *Newfoundland and Labrador Seafood Cookbook*
   CBRA - Annual 2003 - p135(2) [51-500]

Over, William - *World Peace, Mass Culture, and National Policies*
   Choice - v42 - i4 - Dec 2004 - p733(2) [1-50]
   R&R Bk N - v19 - i3 - August 2004 - p188(1) [501+]

Overbeck, Wayne - *Major Principles of Media Law, 2005 Ed.*
   R&R Bk N - v19 - i4 - Nov 2004 - p168(1) [501+]

Overbye, Einar - *Pensions, Challenges and Reforms*
   R&R Bk N - v19 - i3 - August 2004 - p117(1) [51-500]

Overcamp, David - *Electrician*
   c SLJ - v50 - i7 - July 2004 - p120(2) [51-500]

Overman, Larry E. - *Organic Reactions: Vol. 64*
   SciTech - v28 - i4 - Dec 2004 - p56(1) [51-500]

Overmyer, Daniel L. - *Ethnography in China Today: A Critical Assessment of Methods and Results*
   Ch Rev Int - v10 - i2 - Fall 2003 - p431(2) [501+]

Overton, Rick - *Now You Know Zire*
   LJ - v129 - i14 - Sept 1 2004 - p182(1) [51-500]

Overy, Richard - *The Dictators: Hitler's Germany, and Stalin's Russia*
   BL - v101 - i1 - Sept 1 2004 - p42(2) [51-500]
The Dictators: Hitler's Germany and Stalin's Russia
   CR - v286 - i1668 - Jan 2005 - p63(2) [501+]
   HT - v54 - i11 - Nov 2004 - p79(1) [501+]
   KR - v72 - i14 - July 15 2004 - p677(1) [501+]
   LJ - v129 - i16 - Oct 1 2004 - p95(1) [51-500]
   New R - Dec 27 2004 - p29 [501+]
   NS - v133 - i4696 - July 12 2004 - p51(3) [501+]
   NS - v133 - i4716 - Nov 29 2004 - p45(2) [51-500]
   NYTBR - Dec 26 2004 - p15 [501+]
   PW - v251 - i30 - July 26 2004 - p45(2) [501+]
   TimHES - v0 - i1679 - Feb 18 2005 - p22(2) [501+]
   TLS - i5299 - Oct 22 2004 - p8-9 [501+]

Ovid - *The Golden Ass*
   R&R Bk N - v19 - i1 - Feb 2004 - p214 [51-500]
Ovid, Metamorphoses: A New Translation
   Sew R - v112 - i3 - Summer 2004 - p463-467 [501+]
Ovid: Metamorphoses
   Sew R - v112 - i3 - Summer 2004 - p463-467 [501+]
Ovid's Metamorphoses
   Sew R - v112 - i3 - Summer 2004 - p463-467 [501+]

Ovitz, Lori - *Facing the Mirror with Cancer: A Guide to Using Makeup To Make a Difference*
   LJ - v129 - i14 - Sept 1 2004 - p184(2) [501+]

Owe, Olaf - *From Object-Orientation to Formal Methods: Essays in Memory of Ole-Johan Dahl*
   TimHES - v0 - i1677 - Feb 4 2005 - p34(1) [501+]

Owen, Alex - *The Place of Enchantment: British Occultism and the Culture of the Modern*
   Choice - v42 - i4 - Dec 2004 - p701(1) [501+]
   New Sci - v183 - i2455 - July 10 2004 - p49(1) [501+]
   TLS - i5288 - August 6 2004 - p22(1) [501+]

Owen, Carol - *Crafting Personal Shrines: Using Photos, Mementos and Treasures to Create Artful Displays*
   LJ - v130 - i3 - Feb 15 2005 - p126(2) [51-500]

Owen, Cheryl - *Quick and Easy Glass Painting*
   Bwatch - Oct 2004 - pNA [501+]

Owen, David - *Copies in Seconds: How a Lone Inventor and Unknown Company Created the Biggest Communication Breakthrough since Gutenberg-Chester Carlson and the Birth of the Xerox Machine*
   Choice - v42 - i5 - Jan 2005 - p875(1) [1-50]
Final Frontier: Voyages into Outer Space
   y Kliatt - v39 - i2 - March 2005 - p42(1) [51-500]
   c SLJ - v51 - i2 - Feb 2005 - p150(2) [51-500]
Spies: The Undercover World of Secrets, Gadgets and Lies
   y PW - v251 - i36 - Sept 6 2004 - p65(1) [51-500]
   y SLJ - v50 - i10 - Oct 2004 - p193(1) [51-500]

Owen, David (b. 1948 -) - *Hume's Reason*
   Phil R - v112 - i4 - Oct 2003 - p572(4) [501+]

Owen, David (b. 1955 -) - *Copies in Seconds: How a Lone Inventor and an Unknown Company Created the Biggest Communication Breakthrough Since Gutenberg--Chester Carlson and the Birth of the Xerox Machine*
   LJ - v129 - i17 - Oct 15 2004 - p70(1) [51-500]
   NYTBR - Oct 3 2004 - p35 [501+]
   Wil Q - v28 - i4 - Autumn 2004 - p114(2) [501+]

Copies in Seconds: How a Lone Inventor and an Unknown Company Created the Biggest Communication Breakthrough Since Gutenberg:Chester Carlson and the Birth of the Xerox Machine
  y BL - v100 - i22 - August 2004 - p1885(1) [51-500]
    Bus W - i3896 - August 16 2004 - p16 [51-500]
Owen, David (b. 1956 -) - *Tasmanian Tiger: The Tragic Tale of How the World Lost its Most Mysterious Predator*
    SciTech - v28 - i3 - Sept 2004 - p66(1) [51-500]
    VQR - v80 - i3 - Summer 2004 - p272(1) [1-50]
Owen, Elizabeth - *Facts on File Dictionary of Evolutionary Biology*
    SciTech - v28 - i1 - March 2004 - p62(1) [51-500]
Owen, Glenn - *Using QuickBooks Pro for Accounting 2004*
    R&R Bk N - v19 - i4 - Nov 2004 - p115(1) [51-500]
Owen, James - *The Voices Of War*
    Spec - v296 - i9193 - Oct 16 2004 - p63(1) [501+]
Owen, Jim - *The Hidden History of the Historic Fundamentalists, 1933-1948: Reconsidering the Historic Fundamentalists' Response to the Upheavals, Hardships ... 1930s and 1940s*
    R&R Bk N - v20 - i1 - Feb 2005 - p11(1) [51-500]
Owen, June Duncan - *Mixed Matches: Interracial Marriage in Australia*
    AHS - v35 - i124 - Oct 2004 - p408(3) [501+]
Owen, Nancy E. - *Rookwood Pottery at the Philadelphia Museum of Art: The Gerald and Virginia Gordon Collection*
    Ceram Mo - v52 - i10 - Dec 2004 - p68(1) [501+]
Owen, Roger - *Lord Cromer: Victorian Imperialist, Edwardian Proconsul*
    HRNB - v33 - i1 - Fall 2004 - p20(1) [501+]
    Lon R Bks - v26 - i22 - Nov 18 2004 - p15(2) [501+]
    TimHES - v0 - i1650 - July 23 2004 - p26(2) [501+]
    TLS - i5287 - July 30 2004 - p7(1) [501+]
Owen, Tim Buckley - *Success at the Enquiry Desk: Successful Enquiry Answering--Every Time*
    ALJ - v53 - i3 - August 2004 - p320(1) [501+]
Owens, Agnes - *Bad Attitudes: Two Novellas*
    KR - v72 - i14 - July 15 2004 - p653(1) [501+]
Owens, Ann Maureen - *The Kids Book of Canadian Exploration*
  c Res Links - v10 - i2 - Dec 2004 - p28(2) [501+]
Owens, Eric - *America's Best Value Colleges, 2005 Ed.*
    Kliatt - v38 - i6 - Nov 2004 - p35(1) [51-500]
Owens, Irene - *Strategic Marketing in Library and Information Science*
    R&R Bk N - v19 - i1 - Feb 2004 - p260(1) [51-500]
Owens, Judith - *Enabling Engagements: Edmund Spenser and the Poetics of Patronage*
    Six Ct J - v35 - i1 - Spring 2004 - p253(2) [501+]
Owens, Kenneth N. - *Riches for All: The California Gold Rush and the World*
    Ams - v61 - i2 - Oct 2004 - p303(2) [501+]

Owens, Robert E. - *Language Development: An Introduction, 6th Ed.*
    R&R Bk N - v19 - i4 - Nov 2004 - p213(1) [501+]
Language Disorders: A Functional Approach to Assessment and Intervention, 4th Ed.
    R&R Bk N - v19 - i1 - Feb 2004 - p249(1) [51-500]
Owens, Sharon - *The Tea House on Mulberry Street*
    KR - v73 - i1 - Jan 1 2005 - p15(1) [501+]
    LJ - v130 - i2 - Feb 1 2005 - p70(1) [51-500]
    PW - v252 - i3 - Jan 17 2005 - p34(1) [51-500]
    BL - v101 - i9-10 - Jan 1 2005 - p822(1) [501+]
Owings, Alison - *Hey Waitress!: The USA from the Other Side of the Tray*
    JPC - v38 - i3 - Feb 2005 - p598(2) [501+]
Hey, Waitress!: The USA from the Other Side of the Tray
    NS - v133 - i4703 - August 30 2004 - p40(1) [501+]
Oxbridge Directory of Newsletters, 2004
    R&R Bk N - v19 - i3 - August 2004 - p1(1) [1-50]
Oxenbury, Helen - *The Helen Oxenbury Nursery Collection*
  c BL - v101 - i7 - Dec 1 2004 - p657(1) [501+]
  c PW - v251 - i38 - Sept 20 2004 - p65(1) [51-500]
  c SLJ - v50 - i12 - Dec 2004 - p117(1) [501+]
Oxfam International - *Rigged Rules and Double Standards: Trade, Globalization, and the Fight Against Poverty*
    Dis - v51 - i3 - Summer 2004 - p105(5) [501+]
Oxford, Amy - *Hooked Rugs Today*
    Ant&CM - v109 - i11 - Jan 2005 - p16(1) [501+]
Oxford Atlas of the World, 11th Ed.
    LibMed - v23 - i1 - August-Sept 2004 - p73(1) [51-500]
Oxford Atlas of the World, 11th ed.
    R&R Bk N - v19 - i1 - Feb 2004 - p69(1) [501+]
Oxford Atlas of the World, 12th Ed.
    LJ - v130 - i1 - Jan 1 2005 - p150(1) [51-500]
    R&R Bk N - v20 - i1 - Feb 2005 - p82(1) [51-500]
Oxford, Connie - *Screen Saviors: Hollywood Fictions of Whiteness*
    CS - v33 - i5 - Sept 2004 - p567-568 [501+]
Oxford Large Print Thesaurus
    LJ - v129 - i17 - Oct 15 2004 - p90(1) [51-500]
Oxhorn, Philip - *Decentralization, Democratic Governance, and Civil Society in Comparative Perspective: Africa, Asia, and Latin America*
    Choice - v42 - i6 - Feb 2005 - p1091(1) [51-500]
    R&R Bk N - v19 - i4 - Nov 2004 - p157(1) [501+]
Oxlade, Chris - *Energy: Present Knowledge: Future Trends*
  y Sch Lib - v52 - i3 - Autumn 2004 - p164(1) [501+]
How We Use Cotton
    Sch Lib - v52 - i3 - Autumn 2004 - p151(1) [501+]
Oxley, Michael G. - *Economics, Planning, and Housing*
    Choice - v42 - i2 - Oct 2004 - p340(1) [51-500]
Oxoby, Marc - *The 1990s*
  c SLJ - v50 - i8 - August 2004 - p59(1) [501+]

Oz, Amos - *A Tale of Love and Darkness*
    BL - v101 - i4 - Oct 15 2004 - p378(1) [51-500]
    BW - v34 - i45 - Nov 7 2004 - p3(1) [501+]
    KR - v72 - i14 - July 15 2004 - p677(1) [501+]
    LJ - v129 - i13 - August 2004 - p80(1) [501+]
    New R - Dec 27 2004 - p37 [501+]
    NYRB - v51 - i20 - Dec 16 2004 - p22(2) [501+]
    NYTBR - Dec 12 2004 - p16 [501+]
    PW - v251 - i46 - Nov 15 2004 - p56(1) [501+]
    Spec - v296 - i9188 - Sept 11 2004 - p47(2) [501+]
    TLS - i5294 - Sept 17 2004 - p8-9 [501+]
Ozcan, Sabire - *Diabetes Mellitus: Methods and Protocols*
    E-Streams - Sept 2004 - pNA [501+]
Ozdemir, Levent - *North American Tunneling: Proceedings*
    SciTech - v28 - i3 - Sept 2004 - p142(1) [51-500]
Ozer, Jan - *Guide to Digital Video, PC Magazine*
    SciTech - v28 - i4 - Dec 2004 - p155(1) [51-500]
Ozersky, Josh - *Archie Bunker's America: TV in an Era of Change, 1968-1978*
    AHR - v109 - i2 - April 2004 - p562(2) [501+]
    JAH - v91 - i1 - June 2004 - p334-335 [501+]
Ozick, Cynthia - *Heir to the Glimmering World*
    BIC - v33 - i9 - Dec 2004 - p3(2) [501+]
    BL - v100 - i21 - July 2004 - p1800(1) [501+]
    BL - v101 - i9-10 - Jan 1 2005 - p770(1) [51-500]
    BW - v34 - i39 - Sept 26 2004 - p6(1) [501+]
    Ent W - i781 - Sept 3 2004 - p80 [51-500]
    Globe & Mail - Sept 4 2004 - pD4 [501+]
    Globe & Mail - Nov 27 2004 - pD3 [51-500]
    KR - v72 - i13 - July 1 2004 - p600(2) [501+]
    LJ - v129 - i12 - July 2004 - p73(1) [51-500]
    Ms - v14 - i4 - Winter 2004 - p90(2) [501+]
    New R - Oct 18 2004 - p34 [501+]
    New York - v37 - i31 - Sept 13 2004 - p75(1) [501+]
    NY - v80 - i27 - Sept 20 2004 - p102(1) [51-500]
    NYTBR - Sept 5 2004 - p12 [501+]
    NYTBR - Sept 19 2004 - p22 [501+]
    PW - v251 - i32 - August 9 2004 - p228(1) [51-500]
    Wom R Bks - v22 - i2 - Nov 2004 - p3(2) [501+]
Ozieblo, Barbara - *Staging a Cultural Paradigm: The Political and the Personal in American Drama*
    Theat J - v56 - i1 - March 2004 - p147(2) [501+]
Ozkan, Cengiz S. - *Biomicroelectromechanical Systems (BioMEMS): Proceedings*
    SciTech - v28 - i1 - March 2004 - p163(1) [51-500]
Ozment, Steven - *A Mighty Fortress: A New History of the German People*
    R&R Bk N - v19 - i3 - August 2004 - p43(1) [51-500]
Ozoglu, Hakan - *Kurdish Notables and the Ottoman State: Evolving Identities, Competing Loyalties, and Shifting Boundaries*
    Choice - v42 - i2 - Oct 2004 - p352(1) [51-500]

P

Palmer, Lloyd M. - *Steam Towards the Sunset: The Railroads of Lincoln County, 3rd Ed.*
R&R Bk N - v19 - i4 - Nov 2004 - p247(1) [501+]

Palmer, Louis J. - *Encyclopedia of DNA and the United States Criminal Justice System*
E-Streams - Sept 2004 - pNA [501+]
Ref Rev - August 2004 - pNA [501+]
R&R Bk N - v19 - i1 - Feb 2004 - p249(1) [51-500]
SciTech - v28 - i1 - March 2004 - p85(1) [51-500]

Palmer, Mark - *Breaking the Real Axis of Evil: How to Oust the World's Last Dictators by 2025*
Fut - v38 - i5 - Sept-Oct 2004 - p62(1) [51-500]
MEQ - v11 - i4 - Fall 2004 - p75(1) [501+]
TimHES - v0 - i1676 - Jan 28 2005 - p30(2) [501+]

Palmer, Martin - *Faith in Conservation: New Approaches to Religions and the Environment*
JEL - v42 - i1 - March 2004 - p343(2) [501+]

Palmer, Michael - *The Society (Read by Charles, J.). Audiobook Review*
y Kliatt - v39 - i1 - Jan 2005 - p50(1) [51-500]
The Society
BL - v100 - i22 - August 2004 - p1871(1) [51-500]
DroRevMy - v24 - i4 - July-August 2004 - p13(1) [51-500]
KR - v72 - i14 - July 15 2004 - p654(1) [51-500]
PW - v251 - i32 - August 9 2004 - p232(2) [51-500]

Palmer, Michael A. - *Command at Sea: Naval Command and Control Since the Sixteenth Century*
PW - v252 - i3 - Jan 17 2005 - p45(1) [51-500]

Palmer, Michele - *Toile: The Storied Fabrics of Europe and America*
Ant&CM - v108 - i11 - Jan 2004 - p16(1) [501+]

Palmer, Monte - *At the Heart of Terror: Islam, Jihadists, and America's War on Terrorism*
NYTBR - Feb 6 2005 - p28 [501+]

Palmer, Parker J. - *A Hidden Wholeness: The Journey Toward an Undivided Life*
PW - v251 - i28 - July 12 2004 - p59(1) [51-500]

Palmer, R. Barton - *Joel and Ethan Coen*
Choice - v42 - i6 - Feb 2005 - p1029(1) [51-500]

Palmer, Robert C. - *Selling the Church: The English Parish in Law, Commerce, and Religion, 1350-1550*
Albion - v36 - i2 - Summer 2004 - p286(2) [501+]
HER - v119 - i483 - Sept 2004 - p993(3) [501+]
HER - v119 - i483 - Sept 2004 - p993(995) [501+]

Palmer, Steven - *From Popular Medicine to Medical Populism: Doctors, Healers, and Public Power in Costa Rica, 1800-1940*
AHR - v109 - i3 - June 2004 - p949(2) [501+]
HAHR - v84 - i2 - May 2004 - p366(3) [501+]

Palmer, Stuart - *The Puzzle of the Blue Banderilla*
LJ - v129 - i15 - Sept 15 2004 - p91(1) [1-50]

Palmer, Susan J. - *Aliens Adored: Rael's UFO Religion*
BL - v101 - i3 - Oct 1 2004 - p305(1) [51-500]
Globe & Mail - Jan 1 2005 - pD8 [501+]
PW - v251 - i46 - Nov 15 2004 - pS17(1) [51-500]

Palmer, Thomas - *Landscape with Reptile: Rattlesnakes in an Urban World*
Kliatt - v38 - i4 - July 2004 - p45(1) [51-500]

Palmer, Tim - *Endangered Rivers and the Conservation Movement*
Choice - v42 - i3 - Nov 2004 - p509(1) [1-50]

Palmer, Trevor - *Perilous Planet Earth: Catastrophes and Catastrophism through the Ages*
Choice - v41 - i7 - March 2004 - p1324(1) [501+]
TimHES - v0 - i1653 - August 13 2004 - p24(2) [501+]

Palmeri, Frank - *Satire, History, Novel: Narrative Forms, 1665-1815*
R&R Bk N - v19 - i1 - Feb 2004 - p230(1) [51-500]

Palmier-Chatrlain, Marie-Elise - *L'Orient des Femmes*
FS - v58 - i2 - April 2004 - p295(2) [501+]

Palmini, William G., Jr. - *Murder on the Rails: The True Story of the Detective Who Unlocked the Shocking Secrets of the Boxcar Serial Killer*
PW - v251 - i41 - Oct 11 2004 - p64(2) [501+]

Palmisano, Richard - *Overshadows: An Investigation into a Terrifying Modern Canadian Haunting*
CBRA - Annual 2003 - p98(1) [51-500]

Paloma, David - *El pollito repetido*
Inst - v114 - i3 - Oct 2004 - p74(2) [501+]

Palomares, Cristina - *The Quest for Survival After Franco: Moderate Francoism and the Slow Journey to the Polls, 1964-1977*
Choice - v42 - i6 - Feb 2005 - p1093(1) [501+]
R&R Bk N - v19 - i3 - August 2004 - p47(1) [51-500]

Palsson, Sigurour - *Ljootimavagn*
WLT - v79 - i1 - Jan-April 2005 - p102(1) [501+]

Palta, Mari - *Quantitative Methods in Population Health: Extensions of Ordinary Regression*
E-Streams - August 2004 - pNA [501+]

Paluch, Beily - *I Am a Torah*
c CH Bwatch - Oct 2004 - pNA [51-500]

Paluch, James - *A Life for a Life: Life Imprisonment, America's Other Death Penalty*
R&R Bk N - v19 - i3 - August 2004 - p170(1) [501+]

Palumbo, Arthur E. - *The Dead Sea Scrolls and the Personages of Earliest Christianity*
LJ - v129 - i19 - Nov 15 2004 - p66(1) [501+]

Palumbo, Donald - *Chaos Theory, Asimov's Foundations and Robots*
SFS - v31 - i1 - March 2004 - p153-156 [501+]

Palumbo, Patrizia - *A Place in the Sun: Africa in Italian Colonial Culture from Post-Unification to the Present*
IJAHS - v37 - i2 - Spring 2004 - p367-368 [501+]

Pampel, Fred C. - *Progress Against Heart Disease*
Bwatch - Jan 2005 - pNA [51-500]
SciTech - v28 - i4 - Dec 2004 - p102(1) [51-500]
Racial Profiling
Choice - v42 - i7 - March 2005 - p1203(1) [51-500]
Tobacco Industry and Smoking
Choice - v42 - i3 - Nov 2004 - p467(2) [1-50]
y LibMed - v23 - i3 - Nov-Dec 2004 - p89(1) [51-500]

Pamphile, Leon D. - *Haitians and African Americans: A Heritage of Tragedy and Hope*
HNet - Sept 2004 - pNA [501+]

Pamuk, Orhan - *Snow*
Bks & Cult - v10 - i6 - Nov-Dec 2004 - p36(2) [501+]
BW - v34 - i35 - August 2004 - p6(1) [501+]
Econ - v372 - i8388 - August 14 2004 - p75US [501+]
Ent W - i784 - Sept 17 2004 - p84 [51-500]
Globe & Mail - August 21 2004 - pD2 [501+]
Globe & Mail - Nov 27 2004 - pD3 [51-500]
HM - v309 - i1851 - August 2004 - p75(2) [501+]
LJ - v129 - i12 - July 2004 - p73(1) [51-500]
Lon R Bks - v26 - i15 - August 5 2004 - p30(3) [501+]
NL - v87 - i4 - July-August 2004 - p28(2) [501+]
NW - Sept 6 2004 - p69 [501+]
NYT - August 10 2004 - pE6(L) [501+]
NYTBR - August 15 2004 - p1 [501+]
NYTBR - August 22 2004 - p18 [501+]
NYTBR - Sept 5 2004 - p18 [501+]
PW - v251 - i29 - July 19 2004 - p144(2) [51-500]
WLT - v79 - i1 - Jan-April 2005 - p109(1) [501+]
NYTBR - August 29 2004 - p18 [501+]
People - v62 - i11 - Sept 13 2004 - p55 [501+]

Pan, Yihong - *Tempered in the Revolutionary Furnace: China's Youth in the Rustication Movement*
Ch Rev Int - v11 - i1 - Spring 2004 - p158(4) [501+]

Panarello, Melissa - *100 Strokes of the Brush Before Bed*
Ent W - i790 - Oct 29 2004 - p70 [501+]
People - v62 - i18 - Nov 1 2004 - p49 [501+]

Pancaldi, Giuliano - *Volta: Science and Culture in the Age of Enlightenment*
T&C - v45 - i2 - April 2004 - p420-421 [501+]

Panchyk, Richard - *American Folk Art for Kids: With 21 Activities*
y BL - v101 - i5 - Nov 1 2004 - p495(1) [51-500]
y Kliatt - v38 - i6 - Nov 2004 - p40(1) [501+]
y SLJ - v50 - i11 - Nov 2004 - p170(1) [51-500]

Pancrazio, James J. - *The Logic of Fetishism: Alejo Carpentier and the Cuban Tradition*
Choice - v42 - i4 - Dec 2004 - p667(1) [1-50]

Pande, Pete - *What Is Design for Six Sigma?*
HR Mag - v49 - i7 - July 2004 - pS52(1) [51-500]

Pandell, Karen - *Where's Stretch?: A Lift-the-Flap Book (Illus. by McElmurry, Jill)*
c PW - v251 - i41 - Oct 11 2004 - p82(1) [501+]

Pandey, Ashok - *Concise Encyclopedia of Bioresource Technology*
Choice - v42 - i7 - March 2005 - p1198(2) [51-500]
E-Streams - Dec 2004 - pNA [501+]
SB - v40 - i6 - Nov-Dec 2004 - p253(1) [51-500]
SciTech - v28 - i3 - Sept 2004 - p167(1) [51-500]

Pandey, Janak - *Psychology in India Revisited: Developments in the Discipline, Vol. 3*
R&R Bk N - v19 - i3 - August 2004 - p8(1) [1-50]

Pandiscio, Herbert F. - *Job Hunting in Education: An Insider's Guide*
R&R Bk N - v19 - i3 - August 2004 - p220(1) [1-50]

Pandy, Awadh B. - *Affordable Metal Matrix Composites for High Performance Applications: Proceedings*
SciTech - v28 - i1 - March 2004 - p143(1) [51-500]

Pandya, Raj - *Introduction to WLLs: Application and Deployment for Fixed and Broadband Services*
SciTech - v28 - i1 - March 2004 - p154(1) [51-500]

Paneak, Simon - *In a Hungry Country: Essays by Simon Paneak*
Choice - v42 - i7 - March 2005 - p1271(1) [51-500]
R&R Bk N - v19 - i4 - Nov 2004 - p55(1) [1-50]

Panebianco, Stefania - *A New Euro-Mediterranean Cultural Identity*
R&R Bk N - v19 - i1 - Feb 2004 - p31(1) [1-50]

Panek, Richard - *The Invisible Century: Einstein, Freud, and the Search for Hidden Universes*
Nature - v430 - i7000 - August 5 2004 - p615(1) [501+]
New Sci - v183 - i2461 - August 21 2004 - p51(1) [501+]
SciTech - v28 - i3 - Sept 2004 - p14(1) [501+]
Choice - v42 - i5 - Jan 2005 - p875(1) [1-50]

Panel to Review the 2000 Census - *The 2000 Census: Counting under Adversity*
R&R Bk N - v19 - i3 - August 2004 - p92(1) [51-500]

Panera Bread (Cafe) - *The Panera Bread Cookbook: Breadmaking Essentials and Recipes from America's Favorite Bakery-Cafe*
LJ - v129 - i19 - Nov 15 2004 - p83(1) [51-500]

Pang, Guek-Cheng - *Canada, 2nd Ed.*
c SLJ - v51 - i2 - Feb 2005 - p151(1) [51-500]

Pangborn, Edgar - *Davy*
LJ - v129 - i19 - Nov 15 2004 - p103(1) [501+]
A Mirror for Observers
LJ - v129 - i19 - Nov 15 2004 - p103(1) [501+]

Pangle, Thomas L. - *Political Philosophy and the God of Abraham*
R&R Bk N - v19 - i1 - Feb 2004 - p19(1) [1-50]

Panic, M. - *Globalization and National Economic Welfare*
JEL - v41 - i4 - Dec 2003 - p1350(2) [501+]

Panksepp, Jaak - *Textbook of Biological Psychiatry*
SciTech - v28 - i1 - March 2004 - p92(1) [51-500]

Panno, Joseph - *Aging: Theories and Potential Therapies*
c SLJ - v51 - i2 - Feb 2005 - p84(1) [51-500]
Animal Cloning: The Science of Nuclear Transfer
c SLJ - v51 - i2 - Feb 2005 - p84(1) [51-500]
Cancer: The Role of Genes, Lifestyle, and Environment
c SLJ - v51 - i2 - Feb 2005 - p84(1) [51-500]
The Cell: Evolution of the First Organism
c SLJ - v51 - i2 - Feb 2005 - p84(1) [51-500]
Gene Therapy: Treating Disease by Repairing Genes
c SLJ - v51 - i2 - Feb 2005 - p84(1) [51-500]
Stem Cell Research: Medical Applications and Ethical Controversy
y BL - v101 - i9-10 - Jan 1 2005 - p841(1) [51-500]
c SLJ - v51 - i2 - Feb 2005 - p84(1) [51-500]

Panova, L.G. - *"Mir," "Prostranstvo," "Vremia" v Poezii Opsipa Mandel'shtama*
Slav R - v63 - i4 - Winter 2004 - p905(2) [501+]

Pansini, Anthony J. - *Transmission Line Reliability and Security*
SciTech - v28 - i3 - Sept 2004 - p152(1) [51-500]

Panter, Gary - *Jimbo in Purgatory*
PW - v251 - i33 - August 16 2004 - p45(1) [51-500]

Panton, Kenneth - *London: A Historical Companion*
BL - v101 - i5 - Nov 1 2004 - p522(1) [501+]

Pantry, Sheila - *Creating a Successful E-Information Services, Rev. Ed.*
R&R Bk N - v19 - i1 - Feb 2004 - p104(1) [51-500]
Your Essential Guide to Career Success
ALJ - v53 - i4 - Nov 2004 - p419(2) [501+]

Panych, Morris - *Girl in the Goldfish Bowl*
BIC - v33 - i9 - Dec 2004 - p24(3) [501+]
CBRA - Annual 2003 - p240(2) [51-500]

Panzer, Nora - *Celebrate America: In Poetry and Art*
c SLJ - v51 - i2 - Feb 2005 - p65(1) [54-500]

Panzeri, Peter, Jr. - *Little Big Horn 1876: Custer's Last Stand*
R&R Bk N - v19 - i4 - Nov 2004 - p53(1) [51-500]

Panzner, Michael J. - *The New Laws of the Stock Market Jungle: An Insider's Guide to Successful Investing in a Changing World*
LJ - v129 - i16 - Oct 1 2004 - p92(1) [51-500]

Panzram, S. - *Stadtbild und Elite: Tarraco, Corduba und Augusta Emerita Zwischen Republik und Spatantike*
Class R - v54 - i2 - Nov 2004 - p516-517 [501+]

Paolera, Gerardo della - *Straining at the Anchor: The Argentine Currency Board and the Search for Macroeconomic Stability, 1880-1935*
JEL - v42 - i1 - March 2004 - p187(2) [501+]

Paoli, Letizia - *Mafia Brotherhoods: Organized Crime, Italian Style*
Choice - v41 - i11-12 - July-August 2004 - p2130(1) [501+]

Paolin, Giovanna - *Inquisizioni: Percorsi di ricerca*
Six Ct J - v35 - i3 - Fall 2004 - p932-934 [501+]

Paolini, Christopher - *Eragon (Read by Doyle, Gerard).*
Audiobook Review
People - v62 - i4 - July 26 2004 - p48 [51-500]
SLJ - v50 - i10 - Oct 2004 - pS68(1) [501+]
Eragon
LibMed - v22 - i6 - March 2004 - p68(1) [501+]
PW - v251 - i34 - August 23 2004 - p56(1) [51-500]

Paolo, Charles De - *Human Prehistory in Fiction*
SFS - v31 - i1 - March 2004 - p141-143 [501+]

Papa, Anthony - *15 to Life: How I Painted My Way to Freedom*
PW - v251 - i47 - Nov 22 2004 - p53(1) [51-500]

Papa, Ariella - *Bundle of Joy*
BL - v101 - i9-10 - Jan 1 2005 - p832(1) [1-50]

Papa, Carrie - *Mile Deep and Black as Pitch: An Oral History of the Franklin and Sterling Hill Mines*
SciTech - v28 - i3 - Sept 2004 - p165(1) [51-500]

Papadakis, Maxine A. - *Current Consult: Medicine, 2005*
SciTech - v28 - i4 - Dec 2004 - p89(1) [51-500]

Papanikolaou, Polina - *Unique, Monique*
LibMed - v22 - i5 - Feb 2004 - p66(1) [501+]

Papazian, Mary Arshagouni - *John Donne and the Protestant Reformation: New Perspectives*
Ren Q - v57 - i3 - Fall 2004 - p1168(3) [501+]

Pape, Gordon - *Quizmas: Christmas Trivia Family Fun*
c Globe & Mail - Dec 11 2004 - pD43 [51-500]

Paper & Paint
y LibMed - v22 - i5 - Feb 2004 - pNA [501+]

Paperny, Vladimir - *Architecture in the Age of Stalin: Culture Two*
Russ Rev - v63 - i2 - April 2004 - pNA [501+]

Papiernik, Charles - *Unbroken: From Auschwitz to Buenos Aires*
HNet - Sept 2004 - pNA [501+]

Papineau, David - *Western Philosophy: An Illustrated Guide*
R&R Bk N - v20 - i1 - Feb 2005 - p6(1) [51-500]

Papini, Robert - *The Catechism of the Nazarites and Related Writings*
IJAHS - v37 - i1 - Wntr 2004 - p137-139 [501+]

Paplewis, Rosemary - *Leadership on Purpose: Promising Practices for African American and Hispanic Students*
Adoles - v39 - i156 - Winter 2004 - p835(2) [51-500]

Pappalardo, Umberto - *Domus: Wall Painting in the Roman House (Illus. by Romano, Luciano)*
PW - v251 - i50 - Dec 13 2004 - p61(1) [51-500]

Paprocki, Joe - *God's Library: A Catholic Introduction to the World's Greatest Book*
PW - v251 - i48 - Nov 29 2004 - p37(1) [51-500]

Papush, Howard - *When's Recess?: Playing Your Way through the Stresses of Life*
LJ - v130 - i3 - Feb 15 2005 - p143(1) [51-500]

Paquet, Sandra Pouchet - *Caribbean Autobiography: Cultural Identity and Self-Representation*
Can Lit - i182 - Autumn 2004 - p163(3) [501+]

Paquette, Larry - *The Sourcing Solution: A Step-by-Step Guide to Creating a Successful Purchasing Program*
R&R Bk N - v19 - i1 - Feb 2004 - p109(1) [51-500]

Paquette, Laure - *Bioterrorism in Medical and Healthcare Administration*
SciTech - v28 - i4 - Dec 2004 - p84(1) [51-500]

Paquette, Leo A. - *Handbook of Reagents for Organic Synthesis: Vol. 5, Chiral Reagents for Asymmetric Synthesis*
SciTech - v28 - i1 - March 2004 - p54(1) [51-500]

Paquette, Penny Hutchins - *Asthma: The Ultimate Teen Guide*
y LibMed - v22 - i5 - Feb 2004 - p79(1) [501+]
y SLJ - v50 - i10 - Oct 2004 - pS64(1) [501+]

Paquin, Paul R. - *Metals in Aquatic Systems: A Review of Exposure, Bioaccumulation, and Toxicity Models*
SciTech - v28 - i1 - March 2004 - p65(1) [51-500]

Para, Adam - *Neutrino Factories and Superbeams: Proceedings*
SciTech - v28 - i4 - Dec 2004 - p52(1) [51-500]

Paracelsus - *The Archidoxes of Magic*
Bwatch - Jan 2005 - pNA [51-500]

Paraday, Michael - *Experimental Researches in Electricity*
SciTech - v28 - i4 - Dec 2004 - p50(1) [51-500]

Paradis, Michel - *A Neurolinguistic Theory of Bilingualism*
Choice - v42 - i6 - Feb 2005 - p1018(2) [51-500]

Paradis, Peter - *Nasty Business: One Biker Gang's Bloody War Against the Hell's Angels*
CBRA - Annual 2003 - p317(2) [501+]

Paradiz, Valerie - *Clever Maids: The Secret History of the Grimm Fairy Tales.*
KR - v72 - i23 - Dec 1 2004 - p1137(1) [501+]
LJ - v130 - i2 - Feb 1 2005 - p80(1) [51-500]
PW - v251 - i48 - Nov 29 2004 - p31(1) [51-500]

Parallel and Distributed Processing: Proceedings
SciTech - v28 - i3 - Sept 2004 - p20(1) [501+]

Parallel and Distributed Simulation, PADS 2004: Proceedings
SciTech - v28 - i3 - Sept 2004 - p20(1) [501+]

Parallel Processing: Proceedings
SciTech - v28 - i4 - Dec 2004 - p19(1) [1-50]

Paratore, Coleen - *26 Big Things Small Hands Do (Illus. by Reed, Mike)*
c SLJ - v51 - i2 - Feb 2005 - p126(1) [51-500]

Paratore, Coleen Murtagh - *How Prudence Proovit Proved the Truth about Fairy Tales (Illus. by Petrosino, Tamara)*
c CCB-B - v57 - i11 - July-August 2004 - p478(1) [501+]
c PW - v251 - i27 - July 5 2004 - p55(1) [51-500]
c SLJ - v50 - i7 - July 2004 - p84(1) [51-500]
The Wedding Planner's Daughter
c CCB-B - v58 - i6 - Feb 2005 - p262(1) [51-500]
y Kliatt - v39 - i1 - Jan 2005 - p10(1) [51-500]
c KR - v73 - i3 - Feb 1 2005 - p180(1) [51-500]
y PW - v252 - i7 - Feb 14 2005 - p77(1) [51-500]

Pardew, Les - *Game Art for Teens*
SciTech - v28 - i3 - Sept 2004 - p136(1) [51-500]

Pardey, Philip G. - *What's Economics Worth?: Valuing Policy Research*
R&R Bk N - v19 - i4 - Nov 2004 - p84(1) [51-500]

Pare, Jean - *Chinese Cooking*
CBRA - Annual 2003 - p136(1) [51-500]
Decadent Desserts
CBRA - Annual 2003 - p136(2) [51-500]
Garden Greens
CBRA - Annual 2003 - p137(1) [501+]
Heart-Friendly Cooking
CBRA - Annual 2003 - p137(1) [51-500]
Most Loved Appetizers
CBRA - Annual 2003 - p138(1) [51-500]
Pork Book
CBRA - Annual 2003 - p136(1) [51-500]
Weekend Cooking
CBRA - Annual 2003 - p138(1) [501+]
Year-Round Grilling
CBRA - Annual 2003 - p137(1) [501+]

Parekh, Sarad R. - *The GMO Handbook; Genetically Modified Animals, Microbes, and Plants in Biotechnology*
SciTech - v28 - i3 - Sept 2004 - p60(1) [1-50]

Parent, Anthony S. - *Foul Means: The Formation of a Slave Society in Virginia, 1660-1740*
JAH - v91 - i3 - Dec 2004 - p990(1) [501+]
JEL - v42 - i1 - March 2004 - p301(2) [501+]
JSH - v71 - i1 - Feb 2005 - p138(3) [501+]

Parent, Laurence - *Texas Mountains*
SHQ - v107 - i4 - April 2004 - p636(2) [501+]

Parent, Wayne - *Inside the Carnival: Unmasking Louisiana Politics*
Choice - v42 - i4 - Dec 2004 - p737(2) [1-50]

Parenti, Christian - *The Freedom: Shadows and Hallucinations in Occupied Iraq*
PW - v251 - i42 - Oct 18 2004 - p59(1) [51-500]
The Soft Cage: Surveillance in America from Slavery to the Patriot Act
R&R Bk N - v19 - i1 - Feb 2004 - p126(1) [51-500]

Parham, Claire Puccia - *From Great Wilderness to Seaway Towns: A Comparative History of Cornwall, Ontario, and Massena, New York, 1784-2001*
Choice - v42 - i2 - Oct 2004 - p358(1) [51-500]

Parham, P. - *The Immune System, 2nd Ed.*
SciTech - v28 - i3 - Sept 2004 - p74(1) [51-500]

Parham, Thomas A. - *Counseling Persons of African Descent: Raising the Bar of Practitioner Competence*
Adoles - v39 - i156 - Winter 2004 - p836(1) [51-500]

Pariani, Laura - *La straduzione*
WLT - v79 - i1 - Jan-April 2005 - p103(1) [501+]
Quando Dio ballava il tango
WLT - v78 - i3-4 - Sept-Dec 2004 - p132(1) [501+]

Parillo, Mark P. - *We Were in the Big One: Experiences of the World War II Generation*
J Mil H - v68 - i2 - April 2004 - p643(2) [501+]

Parini, Jay - *The Art of Teaching*
BL - v101 - i9-10 - Jan 1 2005 - p792(1) [51-500]
PW - v251 - i49 - Dec 6 2004 - p53(1) [51-500]
British Writers
R&R Bk N - v19 - i1 - Feb 2004 - p233(1) [51-500]
One Matchless Time: A Life of William Faulkner
BL - v101 - i5 - Nov 1 2004 - p455(1) [51-500]
BL - v101 - i9-10 - Jan 1 2005 - p766(1) [51-500]
BW - v34 - i43 - Oct 24 2004 - p2(1) [501+]
Comw - v131 - i18 - Oct 22 2004 - p34(3) [501+]
Globe & Mail - Nov 27 2004 - pD39 [501+]
HM - v309 - i1855 - Dec 2004 - p87(2) [501+]
KR - v72 - i17 - Sept 1 2004 - p852(1) [501+]
LJ - v129 - i19 - Nov 15 2004 - p60(1) [501+]
The Oxford Encyclopedia of American Literature
Choice - v41 - i11-12 - July-August 2004 - p2018(1) [501+]
Ref Rev - June 2004 - pNA [501+]
R&USQ - v44 - i1 - Fall 2004 - p93(2) [501+]
World Writers in English, Vols. 1-2
R&R Bk N - v19 - i1 - Feb 2004 - p240(1) [51-500]

Paris, Joel - *The Fall of an Icon: Psychoanalysis and Academic Psychiatry*
Globe & Mail - March 19 2005 - pD11 [501+]

The Paris Review Book for Planes, Trains, Elevators, and Waiting Rooms
Globe & Mail - August 28 2004 - pD10 [501+]
NYTBR - Oct 17 2004 - p31 [501+]

Paris, Roland - *At War's End: Building Peace After Civil Conflict*
Choice - v42 - i6 - Feb 2005 - p1095(1) [51-500]
For Aff - v84 - i1 - Jan-Feb 2005 - p162 [501+]

Paris, Timothy J. - *Britain, the Hashemites and Arab Rule 1920-1925: The Sherifian Solution*
A Aff - v35 - i2 - July 2004 - p212-213 [501+]

Pariser, Harry S. - *Explore the Virgin Islands, 6th Ed.*
Bwatch - Jan 2005 - pNA [51-500]

Parish, Helen - *Religion and Superstition in Reformation Europe*
CHR - v90 - i4 - Oct 2004 - p784(3) [501+]

Parish, Herman - *Happy Haunting, Amelia Bedelia (Illus. by Sweat, Lynn)*
c SLJ - v50 - i8 - August 2004 - p92(1) [51-500]

Parisi, Grace M. - *Get Saucy: Make Dinner a New Way Every Day*
LJ - v130 - i3 - Feb 15 2005 - p153(1) [51-500]

Parisi, Joseph - *The Poetry Anthology, 1912-2002: Ninety Years of America's Most Distinguished Verse Magazine*
NYTBR - Oct 17 2004 - p26 [501+]
Sew R - v111 - i3 - Summer 2003 - p463-470 [501+]

Parisi, Philip - *The Texas Post Office Murals: Art for the People*
Choice - v42 - i4 - Dec 2004 - p647(1) [1-50]

Park, Alison - *British Social Attitudes: The 20th Report: Continuity and Change over Two Decades*
Choice - v42 - i1 - Sept 2004 - p77(1) [501+]

Park, Barbara - *Junie B., First Grader (Illus. by Brunkus, Denise)*
c SLJ - v50 - i7 - July 2004 - p44(1) [51-500]
Junie B., First Grader: Shipwrecked (Illus. by Brunkus, Denise)
c SLJ - v50 - i9 - Sept 2004 - p176(1) [51-500]

Park, Chan E. - *Voices from the Straw Mat: Toward an Ethnography of Korean Story Singing*
JAS - v63 - i2 - May 2004 - p523(2) [501+]

Park, Chung-shin - *Protestantism and Politics in Korea*
CH - v73 - i4 - Dec 2004 - p905(3) [501+]
IBMR - v28 - i3 - July 2004 - p139(2) [501+]

Park, Clara C. - *Asian American Identities, Families and Schooling*
R&R Bk N - v19 - i3 - August 2004 - p228(1) [1-50]

Park, Eung Chun - *Either Jew or Gentile: Paul's Unfolding Theology of Inclusivity*
Intpr - v58 - i3 - July 2004 - p319(1) [501+]

Park, Frances - *Goodbye, 382 Shin Dang Dong*
c RT - v57 - Dec 2003 - p395 [51-500]

Park, Kyong-ni - *The Curse of Kim's Daughters*
BL - v100 - i21 - July 2004 - p1819(1) [1-50]

Parr, Adrian - *Exploring the Work of Leonardo da Vinci Within the Context of Contemporary Philosophical Thought and Art: From Bergson to Deleuze*
R&R Bk N - v19 - i1 - Feb 2004 - p200(1) [501+]

Parr, Todd - *The Family Book (Illus. by Parr, Todd)*
c SLJ - v50 - i10 - Oct 2004 - pS24(1) [1-50]
Otto Has a Birthday Party (Illus. by Parr, Todd)
c SLJ - v50 - i10 - Oct 2004 - p126(2) [51-500]
The Peace Book (Illus. by Parr, Todd)
c BL - v101 - i2 - Sept 15 2004 - p253(1) [51-500]
c SLJ - v50 - i11 - Nov 2004 - p114(1) [51-500]

Parra, Nicanor - *Antipoems: How to Look Better and Feel Great*
LJ - v129 - i15 - Sept 15 2004 - p61(2) [51-500]

Parramons Editorial Team - *Light and Color: Instruction in Methods and Materials When Creating Special Light and Color Effects in Finished Artworks*
LJ - v129 - i19 - Nov 15 2004 - p58(1) [501+]

Parrat, John - *An Introduction to Third World Theologies*
Intpr - v59 - i1 - Jan 2005 - p110(1) [51-500]

Parratt, Catriona M. - *More than Mere Amusement: Working-Class Women's Leisure in England, 1750-1914*
HER - v119 - i483 - Sept 2004 - p1078(2) [501+]
HER - v119 - i483 - Sept 2004 - p1078(2) [501+]

Parrillo, Vincent N. - *Contemporary Social Problems, 6th Ed.*
R&R Bk N - v19 - i3 - August 2004 - p141(1) [51-500]
Understanding Race and Ethnic Relations, 2nd Ed.
R&R Bk N - v19 - i3 - August 2004 - p158(1) [51-500]

Parrish, Michael - *Sacrifice of the Generals: Soviet Senior Officer Losses, 1939-1953*
R&R Bk N - v19 - i4 - Nov 2004 - p41(1) [51-500]

Parrish, P.J. - *Island of Bones*
y SLJ - v50 - i8 - August 2004 - p146(1) [501+]
A Killing Rain
PW - v252 - i2 - Jan 10 2005 - p44(1) [51-500]

Parrish, Richard Henry - *Defining Drugs*
Bwatch - Dec 2004 - pNA [51-500]

Parrish, Thomas - *The Submarine: A History*
Bwatch - v26 - i7 - July 2004 - p11(1) [51-500]
Choice - v42 - i5 - Jan 2005 - p907(1) [1-50]

Parrish, William Real - *History of Missouri, Vol. 1*
R&R Bk N - v19 - i4 - Nov 2004 - p67(1) [51-500]

Parrott, John B. - *Being Like God: How American Elites Abuse Politics and Power*
R&R Bk N - v19 - i1 - Feb 2004 - p127(1) [51-500]

Parry, Aaron - *The Complete Idiot's Guide to the Talmud*
LJ - v129 - i14 - Sept 1 2004 - p157(1) [51-500]

Parry, Bronwyn - *Trading the Genome: Investigating the Commodification of Bio-Information*
New Sci - v185 - i2489 - March 5 2005 - p57(1) [501+]

Parry, Donald W. - *The Dead Sea Scrolls Reader, Pt. 1*
R&R Bk N - v19 - i3 - August 2004 - p16(1) [1-50]
The Dead Sea Scrolls Reader, Pt. 2
R&R Bk N - v19 - i3 - August 2004 - p16(1) [1-50]
The Dead Sea Scrolls Reader, Pt. 4
R&R Bk N - v19 - i3 - August 2004 - p16(1) [1-50]

Parry, Graham - *Milton and the Terms of Liberty*
Six Ct J - v34 - i4 - Winter 2003 - p1138-1140 [501+]

Parry, Linda - *Textiles of the Arts and Crafts Movement*
LJ - v130 - i3 - Feb 15 2005 - p172(1) [51-500]

Parry, Owen - *Rebels of Babylon*
KR - v73 - i1 - Jan 1 2005 - p16(1) [501+]
PW - v252 - i9 - Feb 28 2005 - p42(2) [51-500]
Strike the Harp!: American Christmas Tales
BL - v101 - i6 - Nov 15 2004 - p562(1) [51-500]
Ent W - i796 - Dec 10 2004 - p101 [51-500]
KR - v72 - i17 - Sept 1 2004 - p830(1) [501+]

Parry, William T. - *All Veins, Lodes, and Ledges Throughout Their Entire Depth: Geology and the Apex Law in Utah Mines*
R&R Bk N - v19 - i4 - Nov 2004 - p174(1) [501+]

Parson, Ann B. - *The Proteus Effect: Stem Cells and Their Promise for Medicine*
Bwatch - Dec 2004 - pNA [51-500]
LJ - v129 - i15 - Sept 15 2004 - p80(1) [51-500]
Nature - v431 - i7011 - Oct 21 2004 - p905(2) [501+]
PW - v251 - i30 - July 26 2004 - p46(2) [501+]
SciTech - v28 - i4 - Dec 2004 - p63(1) [51-500]

Parson, Keith M. - *Great Dinosaur Controversy: A Guide to the Debates*
E-Streams - August 2004 - pNA [501+]

Parsons, Alexander - *In the Shadows of the Sun*
KR - v73 - i3 - Feb 1 2005 - p143(1) [501+]
LJ - v130 - i3 - Feb 15 2005 - p120(1) [51-500]
PW - v252 - i11 - March 14 2005 - p43(1) [51-500]

Parsons, Alexandra - *Victoria Romantic Window Style*
LJ - v129 - i15 - Sept 15 2004 - p56(1) [51-500]

Parsons, Andrew F. - *Keynotes in Organic Chemistry*
J Chem Ed - v81 - i5 - May 2004 - p651-652 [501+]

Parsons, Craig - *A Certain Idea of Europe*
JEL - v42 - i1 - March 2004 - p259(2) [501+]

Parsons, Deborah L. - *Streetwalking the Metropolis*
VS - v45 - i2 - Winter 2003 - p319 [501+]

Parsons, Elaine Frantz - *Manhood Lost: Fallen Drunkards and Redeeming Women in the Nineteenth-Century United States*
AHR - v109 - i4 - Oct 2004 - p1236(2) [501+]
J Soc H - v38 - i1 - Fall 2004 - p236(4) [501+]
JAH - v91 - i3 - Dec 2004 - p1018(2) [501+]

Parsons, Garry - *Billy's Bucket*
LibMed - v22 - i5 - Feb 2004 - p64(1) [501+]

Parsons, Gerald - *Siena, Civil Religion, and the Sienese*
Choice - v42 - i6 - Feb 2005 - p1088(2) [51-500]
R&R Bk N - v19 - i4 - Nov 2004 - p26(1) [501+]

Parsons, K.C. - *Human Thermal Environments: The Effects of Hot, Moderate, and Cold Environments on Human Health, 2nd ed.*
E-Streams - July 2004 - pNA [501+]

Parsons, Matthew - *Female Urinary Incontinence in Practice*
SciTech - v28 - i4 - Dec 2004 - p110(1) [51-500]

Parsons, Michael - *Luther and Calvin on Old Testament Narratives: Reformation Thought and Narrative Text*
R&R Bk N - v19 - i3 - August 2004 - p23(1) [1-50]

Parsons, Patricia J. - *Ethics in Public Relations: A Guide to Best Practice*
Choice - v42 - i6 - Feb 2005 - p1067(1) [51-500]

Parsons, Richard - *The School Counselor as Consultant: An Integrated Model for School-Based Consultation*
R&R Bk N - v19 - i4 - Nov 2004 - p178(1) [501+]

Parsons, Robert C. - *Wind and Wave: Sea Tales from around Our Coast*
CBRA - Annual 2003 - p346(1) [51-500]

Parsons, Susan Frank - *The Ethics of Gender*
Theol St - v65 - i4 - Dec 2004 - p881(3) [501+]

Parsons, Timothy H. - *The 1964 Army Mutinies and the Making of Modern East Africa*
J Mil H - v68 - i4 - Oct 2004 - p1313-1314 [501+]

Parsons, Tony - *The Family Way*
NS - v133 - i4698 - July 26 2004 - p54(2) [501+]

Parthasarathi, Prasannan - *The Transition to a Colonial Economy: Weavers, Merchants and Kings in South India, 1720-1800*
JIH - v34 - i4 - Spring 2004 - p678-679 [501+]

Partidge, Christopher - *New Religious: A Guide: New Religious Movements, Sects and Alternative Spiritualities*
Choice - v42 - i3 - Nov 2004 - p450(1) [1-50]

Partington, Alan - *Corpora and Discourse*
R&R Bk N - v19 - i4 - Nov 2004 - p214(1) [501+]

Partington, John S. - *Building Cosmopolis: The Political Thought of H.G. Wells*
R&R Bk N - v19 - i1 - Feb 2004 - p239(1) [51-500]

Partington, Jonathan R. - *Linear Operators and Linear Systems: An Analytical Approach to Control Theory*
SciTech - v28 - i4 - Dec 2004 - p40(1) [51-500]

Partlow, Thomas - *Chancery Court Records of Cannon County, Tennessee, 1840-1880*
EFHM - v58 - i3 - May-June 2004 - p61(1) [51-500]

Partner, Simon - *Toshie: A Story of Village Life in Twentieth-Century Japan*
Choice - v42 - i3 - Nov 2004 - p541(2) [1-50]

Parton, Sarah - *Cleisthenes: Founder of Athenian Democracy*
y SLJ - v50 - i9 - Sept 2004 - p230(1) [51-500]

Partridge, Elizabeth - *This Land Was Made for You and Me: The Life and Songs of Woody Guthrie*
c SLJ - v50 - i11 - Nov 2004 - p66(1) [51-500]
y SLJ - v50 - i12 - Dec 2004 - p61(1) [501+]

Partridge, Eric - *Dictionary of Americanisms: A Glossary of Words and Phrases, Usually Regarded as Peculiar to the United States*
R&R Bk N - v19 - i1 - Feb 2004 - p217(1) [1-50]
A Dictionary of Slang and Unconventional English, 8th Ed.
R&R Bk N - v19 - i1 - Feb 2004 - p217(1) [51-500]

Parson, Keith M. - *Great Dinosaur Controversy: A Guide to the Debates*

Pasachoff, Jay M. - *The Complete Idiot's Guide to the Sun*
y SB - v41 - i1 - Jan-Feb 2005 - p25(2) [501+]
S&T - v108 - i1 - July 2004 - p116(3) [501+]

Pasachoff, Naomi - *Linus Pauling: Advancing Science, Advocating Peace*
c SB - v40 - i6 - Nov-Dec 2004 - p267(1) [51-500]

Pascal, Elizabeth - *Defining Russian Federalism*
R&R Bk N - v19 - i1 - Feb 2004 - pNA [501+]

Pascal, Francine - *The Ruling Class*
y BL - v101 - i9-10 - Jan 1 2005 - p846(1) [1-50]
y CCB-B - v58 - i4 - Dec 2004 - p179(2) [51-500]
c PW - v251 - i48 - Nov 29 2004 - p41(1) [51-500]
y SLJ - v50 - i12 - Dec 2004 - p152(1) [51-500]
y VOYA - v27 - i5 - Dec 2004 - p392(1) [51-500]

Paschoud, F. - *Histoire Auguste. Tome V, 2eme partie. Vies de Probus, Firmus, Saturnin, Proclus et Bonose, Carus, Numerien et Carin*
Class R - v54 - i1 - May 2004 - p120(5) [501+]

Pasco, Rebecca J. - *Capital and Opportunity: A Critical Ethnography of Students-at-Risk*
R&R Bk N - v19 - i1 - Feb 2004 - p193(1) [51-500]

Pascoe, Elaine - *The Ecosystem of a Fallen Tree*
c LibMed - v22 - i5 - Feb 2004 - p58(1) [501+]
The Ecosystem of a Grassy Field
c LibMed - v22 - i5 - Feb 2004 - p58(1) [501+]
The Ecosystem of a Milkweed Patch
c LibMed - v22 - i5 - Feb 2004 - p58(1) [501+]
The Ecosystem of a Stream
c LibMed - v22 - i5 - Feb 2004 - p58(1) [501+]
The Ecosystem of an Apple Tree (Illus. by Kuhn, Dwight)
c LibMed - v22 - i5 - Feb 2004 - p58(1) [501+]
Into Wild Louisiana
c SB - v40 - i6 - Nov-Dec 2004 - p272(1) [51-500]
Plant Clones
c SB - v40 - i5 - Sept-Oct 2004 - p213(1) [51-500]

Paseman, Floyd L. - *A Spy's Journey: A CIA Memoir*
LJ - v130 - i1 - Jan 2005 - p129(1) [51-500]

Pasko, Thomas - *Physician Characteristics and Distribution in the US, 2004 ed.*
SciTech - v28 - i1 - March 2004 - p77(1) [51-500]

Paskow, Alan - *The Paradoxes of Art: A Phenomenological Investigation*
Choice - v42 - i3 - Nov 2004 - p497(1) [1-50]

Pasmore, William A. - *Research in Organizational Change and Development*
JEL - v41 - i4 - Dec 2003 - p1340(1) [501+]

Pasnau, Robert - *The Philosophy of Aquinas*
Choice - v41 - i11-12 - July-August 2004 - p2059(1) [501+]

Pasquale, Gianluigi - *La Storia Della Salvezza: Dio Signore Del Tempo E Della Storia*
Theol St - v66 - i1 - March 2005 - p202(3) [501+]
La teologia della storia della salvezza nel secolo xx
Theol St - v66 - i1 - March 2005 - p202(3) [501+]

Pasquaretta, Paul - *Gambling and Survival in Native North America*
Am Ind CRJ - v28 - i2 - Spring 2004 - p153(3) [501+]
R&R Bk N - v19 - i1 - Feb 2004 - p53(1) [51-500]

Pasquier, Nicolas - *Le Gentilhomme*
Ren Q - v57 - i4 - Winter 2004 - p1436(2) [501+]

Pasricha, Harpreet - *Designing Networks with Cisco*
SciTech - v28 - i4 - Dec 2004 - p151(1) [51-500]

Passages: Welcome Home to Canada
Can Lit - i182 - Autumn 2004 - p90(3) [501+]

Passarella, John - *Wither's Legacy*
ChrSFF&H - v26 - i10 - Oct 2004 - p27(1) [51-500]

Passe, Daniel - *The River between Us (Read by Patel, Lina). Audiobook Review*
y VOYA - v27 - i5 - Dec 2004 - p370(1) [501+]

Passen, Lisa - *The Abominable Snow Teacher (Illus. by Passen, Lisa)*
c BL - v101 - i1 - Sept 1 2004 - p135(1) [51-500]
c KR - v72 - i14 - July 15 2004 - p691(1) [51-500]
c SLJ - v50 - i10 - Oct 2004 - p128(1) [51-500]

Passer, Michael W. - *Psychology: The Science of Mind and Behaviour. 2nd Ed.*
TimHES - v0 - i1668 - Nov 26 2004 - pXVIII(2) [501+]

Passet, Joanne E. - *Sex Radicals and the Quest for Women's Equality*
JAH - v91 - i1 - June 2004 - p241-242 [501+]
Lib & Cul - v39 - i3 - Summer 2004 - p334(2) [501+]

Passin, Thomas B. - *Explorer's Guide to the Semantic Web*
Choice - v42 - i5 - Jan 2005 - p887(2) [1-50]
SciTech - v28 - i4 - Dec 2004 - p151(1) [51-500]

Passman, Frederick J. - *Fuel and Fuel System Microbiology: Fundamentals, Diagnosis, and Contamination Control*
    SciTech - v28 - i1 - March 2004 - p75(1) [51-500]

Passmann, Dirk F. - *The Library and Reading of Jonathan Swift: A Bio-Bibliographical Handbook; Part One: Swift's Library in Four Volumes*
    TLS - i5293 - Sept 10 2004 - p3-4 [501+]

Passmore, Kevin - *Women, Gender and Fascism in Europe, 1919-45*
    AHR - v109 - i3 - June 2004 - p969(3) [501+]

Passonneau, Joseph R. - *Washington through Two Centuries*
    BW - v34 - i38 - Sept 19 2004 - p11(1) [1-50]

Pastan, Amy - *Martin Luther King, Jr.*
    y Kliatt - v39 - i1 - Jan 2005 - p29(2) [51-500]

Paster, Gail Kern - *Humoring the Body: Emotions and the Shakespearean Stage*
    Choice - v42 - i6 - Feb 2005 - p1023(1) [51-500]

Pasternak, Harley - *5-Factor Fitness: The Diet and Fitness Secret of Hollywood's A-List*
    LJ - v130 - i1 - Jan 1 2005 - p144(3) [501+]

Pastor, James F. - *The Privatization of Police in America: An Analysis and Case Study*
    R&R Bk N - v19 - i1 - Feb 2004 - p145(1) [51-500]

Pastor, Manuel - *Numerical Modelling in Geomechanics*
    E-Streams - Oct 2004 - pNA [501+]

Pastor-Satorras, Romualdo - *Evolution and Structure of the Internet: A Statistical Physics Approach*
    TimHES - v0 - i1677 - Feb 4 2005 - p33(1) [501+]

Pastourmatzi, Domna - *Biotechnological and Medical Themes in Science Fiction*
    SFS - v31 - i1 - March 2004 - p156-161 [501+]

Pasveer, Juliette M. - *The Djief Hunters: 26,000 Years of Rainforest Exploitation on the Bird's Head of Papua, Indonesia*
    SciTech - v28 - i3 - Sept 2004 - p55(1) [1-50]

Pasztor, Suzanne B. - *The Spirit of Hidalgo: The Mexican Revolution in Coahuila*
    HAHR - v84 - i4 - Nov 2004 - p752(2) [501+]
    WHQ - v35 - i1 - Spring 2004 - p95-96 [501+]

Patankar, Manoj S. - *Applied Human Factors in Aviation Maintenance*
    SciTech - v28 - i4 - Dec 2004 - p161(1) [51-500]

Patarca-Montero, Roberto - *Chronic Fatigue Syndrome, Genes, and Infection: The Eta-1/Op Paradigm*
    SciTech - v28 - i1 - March 2004 - p87(1) [51-500]
Handbook of Cancer-Related Fatigue
    SciTech - v28 - i3 - Sept 2004 - p91(1) [51-500]

Pataux, Agnes - *Dogon: People of the Cliffs*
    Black Iss - v6 - i5 - Sept-Oct 2004 - p32(1) [501+]
    LJ - v129 - i16 - Oct 1 2004 - p78(1) [51-500]
    R&R Bk N - v19 - i3 - August 2004 - p59(1) [51-500]

Patchen, Martin - *Making Our Schools More Effective: What Matters and What Works*
    R&R Bk N - v19 - i3 - August 2004 - p223(1) [1-50]

Patchett, Ann - *Bel Canto*
    Globe & Mail - Oct 30 2004 - pD31 [501+]
Truth & Beauty: A Friendship (Read by Patchett, Ann). Audiobook Review
    LJ - v129 - i17 - Oct 15 2004 - p98(1) [51-500]
    BL - v101 - i5 - Nov 1 2004 - p506(1) [51-500]
Truth & Beauty: A Friendship
    y SLJ - v50 - i9 - Sept 2004 - p236(2) [501+]
    TLS - i5297 - Oct 8 2004 - p26(1) [501+]
    Wom R Bks - v22 - i1 - Oct 2004 - p4(2) [501+]

Pate, C. Marvin - *Deliverance New and Not Yet: The New Testament and the Great Tribulation*
    R&R Bk N - v19 - i4 - Feb 2004 - p21(1) [51-500]

Patel, Alka - *Building Communities in Gujarat: Architecture and Society During the Twelfth through Fourteenth Centuries*
    R&R Bk N - v19 - i3 - August 2004 - p241(1) [51-500]

Patel, Bimal N. - *The World Court Reference Guide: Judgments, Advisory Opinions, and Orders of the Permanent Court of International Justice and the International Court of Justice*
    R&R Bk N - v19 - i3 - August 2004 - p210(1) [1-50]

Patel, Kiran Klaus - *"Soldiers of Work": Work Programs in Germany and the USA, 1933-1945*
    JAH - v91 - i3 - Dec 2004 - p1069(2) [501+]

Pateman, Roy - *Chaos and Dancing Star: Wagner's Politics, Wagner's Legacy*
    GSR - v27 - i1 - Feb 2004 - p169-170 [501+]

Patenaude, Andrea Farkas - *Genetic Testing for Cancer: Psychological Approaches for Helping Patients and Families*
    SciTech - v28 - i3 - Sept 2004 - p92(1) [51-500]

Patenaude, Bertrand M. - *The Big Show in Bololand: The American Relief Expedition to Soviet Russia in the Famine of 1921*
    AHR - v109 - i3 - June 2004 - p871(2) [501+]
    JMH - v76 - i4 - Dec 2004 - p1009(3) [501+]

Patent, Dorothy Hinshaw - *Fabulous Fluttering: Tropical Butterflies (Illus. by Jubb, Kendhal Jan)*
    c LibMed - v22 - i5 - Feb 2004 - p60(1) [501+]
Garden of the Spirit Bear: Life in the Great Northern Rainforest (Illus. by Milton, Deborah)
    c KR - v72 - i14 - July 15 2004 - p692(1) [51-500]
    c SLJ - v50 - i10 - Oct 2004 - p147(1) [51-500]
The Lewis and Clark Trail (Illus. by Munoz, William)
    c RT - v57 - Nov 2003 - p275 [51-500]
White-Tailed Deer
    c BL - v101 - i8 - Dec 15 2004 - p740(1) [51-500]

Patera, T. - *A Concordance to the Poetry of Joseph Brodsky, Bk. 6*
    R&R Bk N - v19 - i1 - Feb 2004 - p218(1) [1-50]

Paterson, Don - *The Book of Shadows*
    Spec - v296 - Dec 18 2004 - p79(2) [501+]
    TLS - i5304 - Nov 26 2004 - p7(1) [501+]
Landing Light
    LJ - v129 - i20 - Dec 1 2004 - p122(1) [51-500]
New British Poetry
    ABR - v26 - i2 - Jan-Feb 2005 - p10(1) [501+]
    BIC - v33 - i5 - August 2004 - p36(2) [501+]
    Globe & Mail - Dec 24 2004 - pD3 [1-50]

Paterson, Frances R.A. - *Democracy and Intolerance: Christian School Curricula, School Choice, and Public Policy*
    R&R Bk N - v19 - i1 - Feb 2004 - p16(1) [51-500]

Paterson, John - *Blueberries for the Queen (Illus. by Jeffers, Susan)*
    c BL - v100 - i21 - July 2004 - p1849(1) [1-50]
    c CCB-B - v58 - i2 - Oct 2004 - p94(1) [51-500]
    c NYTBR - July 11 2004 - p19 [51-500]
    c SLJ - v50 - i7 - July 2004 - p84(1) [51-500]

Paterson, Katherine - *Bridge to Terabithia*
    c RT - v57 - Sept 2003 - p98 [1-50]
The Same Stuff as Stars (Read by Bresnahan, Alyssa). Audiobook Review
    c BL - v101 - i2 - Sept 15 2004 - p261(1) [51-500]
    y Kliatt - v38 - i5 - Sept 2004 - p64(2) [51-500]
The Same Stuff as Stars
    c RT - v57 - Nov 2003 - p278 [51-500]

Patey, Cecil - *A Companion to the Eucharist of the Church*
    CI - v12 - i10 - Nov 2004 - p42(1) [501+]

Patnaik, Pradyot - *Dean's Analytical Chemistry Handbook*
    Choice - v42 - i3 - Nov 2004 - p512(1) [1-50]

Patneaude, David - *Thin Wood Walls*
    y BL - v101 - i2 - Sept 15 2004 - p234(2) [51-500]
    c CCB-B - v58 - i2 - Oct 2004 - p94(2) [51-500]
    c KR - v72 - i17 - Sept 1 2004 - p872(1) [51-500]
    c SLJ - v50 - i10 - Oct 2004 - p175(1) [51-500]
    c VOYA - v27 - i5 - Dec 2004 - p392(1) [51-500]

Paton, B.E. - *Space: Technologies, Materials, Structures*
    E-Streams - June 2004 - pNA [501+]
    SciTech - v28 - i1 - March 2004 - p142(1) [51-500]

Paton, Priscilla - *Abandoned New England: Landscape in the Works of Homer, Frost, Hopper, Wyeth , and Bishop*
    JAH - v91 - i2 - Sept 2004 - p663(1) [501+]

Paton Walsh, Jill - *The Emperor's Winding Sheet*
    c PW - v251 - i31 - August 2 2004 - p73(1) [51-500]

Paton-Walsh, Margaret - *Our War Too: American Women Against the Axis*
    JIH - v35 - i1 - Summer 2004 - p164-166 [501+]

Patric, James H. - *To War in a Tin Can: A Memoir of World War II Aboard a Destroyer*
    R&R Bk N - v19 - i4 - Nov 2004 - p33(1) [51-500]

Patrick, Denise Lewis - *Ma Dear's Old Green House (Illus. by Sadler, Sonia Lynn)*
    c SLJ - v51 - i1 - Jan 2005 - p96(1) [51-500]

Patrick, Graham L. - *Organic Chemistry, 2nd Ed.*
    E-Streams - Dec 2004 - pNA [501+]
    SciTech - v28 - i3 - Sept 2004 - p51(1) [1-50]

Patrick, Jean - *Dolley Madison*
    c CH Bwatch - v14 - i7 - July 2004 - p2(2) [501+]

Patrizzi, Barbara - *O Is for Oystercatcher: A Book of Seaside ABCs*
    c PW - v251 - i34 - August 23 2004 - p56(2) [501+]

Patrouch, Joseph F. - *A Negotiated Settlement: The Counter-Reformation in Upper Austria under the Habsburgs*
    Six Ct J - v34 - i4 - Winter 2003 - p1145-1146 [501+]

Pattakos, Alex - *Prisoners of Our Thoughts: Viktor Frankl's Principles at Work*
    PW - v251 - i46 - Nov 15 2004 - p55(1) [501+]
    SciTech - v28 - i4 - Dec 2004 - p94(1) [51-500]

Patte, Daniel - *The Gospel of Matthew: A Contextual Introduction for Group Study*
    Intpr - v58 - i4 - Oct 2004 - p440(1) [501+]

Patten, Bernard M. - *Truth, Knowledge, or Just Plain Bull: How to Tell the Difference, a Handbook of Practical Logic and Clear Thinking*
    R&R Bk N - v20 - i1 - Feb 2005 - p3(1) [1-50]

Patten, Michael A. - *Birds of the Salton Sea: Status, Biogeography, and Ecology*
    QRB - v79 - i3 - Sept 2004 - p318(1) [501+]

Pattengale, Paula - *Tasks for the Veterinary Assistant*
    SciTech - v28 - i3 - Sept 2004 - p132(1) [51-500]

Patterson, Ann - *Landmark Buildings*
    Bwatch - Oct 2004 - pNA [51-500]

Patterson, Annabel - *Nobody's Perfect: A New Whig Interpretation of History*
    AHR - v109 - i3 - June 2004 - p860(2) [501+]
    HNet - June 2004 - pNA [501+]
The Prose Works of Andrew Marvell
    TLS - i5306 - Dec 10 2004 - p3-4 [501+]

Patterson, Annie - *Whale Snow*
    LibMed - v22 - i5 - Feb 2004 - p64(1) [501+]

Patterson, Brad - *Thr Irish in New Zealand: Historical Contexts and Perspectives*
    AHS - v35 - i123 - April 2004 - p171-172 [501+]

Patterson, Bruce D. - *The Lions of Tsavo: Exploring the Legacy of Africa's Notorious Man-Eaters*
    Choice - v42 - i1 - Sept 2004 - p132(1) [501+]

Patterson, Dennis - *Wittgenstein and Law*
    R&R Bk N - v19 - i4 - Nov 2004 - p161(1) [51-500]

Patterson, Don - *Landing Light*
    Lon R Bks - v26 - i5 - March 4 2004 - p25(3) [501+]

Patterson, Freeman - *The Garden*
    CBRA - Annual 2003 - p120(1) [501+]

Patterson, Gordon - *The Mosquito Wars: A History of Mosquito Control in Florida*
    HNet - Oct 2004 - pNA [501+]

Patterson, H.W. - *Small Boat Building*
    Bwatch - v26 - i8 - August 2004 - p11(1) [51-500]

Patterson, Heather - *A Poppy Is to Remember*
    Res Links - v10 - i2 - Dec 2004 - p29(2) [51-500]

Patterson, James - *3rd Degree (Read by McCormick, Carolyn). Audiobook Review*
    LJ - v129 - i13 - August 2004 - p129(1) [51-500]
Honeymoon
    Globe & Mail - March 19 2005 - pD15 [51-500]
    PW - v252 - i5 - Jan 31 2005 - p50(1) [51-500]
London Bridges (Read by Fernandez, Peter J.). Audiobook Review
    PW - v252 - i1 - Jan 3 2005 - p22(1) [51-500]
London Bridges
    Globe & Mail - Dec 4 2004 - pD35 [51-500]
    PW - v251 - i45 - Nov 8 2004 - p37(1) [501+]
Maximum Ride: The Angel Experiment
    y Kliatt - v39 - i2 - March 2005 - p15(1) [51-500]
Sam's Letters to Jennifer (Read by Heche, Anne). Audiobook Review
    y Kliatt - v39 - i1 - Jan 2005 - p49(1) [51-500]
    LJ - v130 - i4 - March 1 2005 - p122(2) [51-500]
    PW - v251 - i36 - Sept 6 2004 - p26(1) [51-500]
Sam's Letters to Jennifer
    BL - v100 - i21 - July 2004 - p1799(2) [51-500]
Santakid (Illus. by Garland, Michael)
    c PW - v251 - i39 - Sept 27 2004 - p60(1) [51-500]

Patterson, Jean - *Cooking Outside the Pizza Box: Easy Recipes for Today's College Student*
    Kliatt - v38 - i5 - Sept 2004 - p51(2) [51-500]
Handbook of the Norton Simon Museum
    R&R Bk N - v19 - i2 - May 2004 - p194(1) [51-500]

Patterson, JoEllen - *Mental Health Professionals in Medical Settings: A Primer*
    Adoles - v39 - i156 - Winter 2004 - p836(2) [51-500]

Patterson, Kerry - *Crucial Conversations: Tools for Talking When Stakes Are High*
    HR Mag - v50 - i2 - Feb 2005 - pS8(1) [501+]

Patterson, Kevin - *Country of Cold*
    y Kliatt - v38 - i4 - July 2004 - p34(1) [51-500]

Patterson, Lewis E. - *Counseling Process: A Multitheoretical Integrative Approach, 6th ed.*
    SciTech - v28 - i3 - Sept 2004 - p3(1) [501+]

Patterson, Michael - *Women's Medical Work in Early Modern France*
    TLS - i5300 - Oct 29 2004 - p30(1) [51-500]

Payne, Geoff - *Key Concepts in Social Research*
Choice - v42 - i4 - Dec 2004 - p643(1) [1-50]
R&R Bk N - v19 - i3 - August 2004 - p90(1) [51-500]

Payne, Holly - *The Sound of Blue*
BL - v101 - i4 - Oct 15 2004 - p391(1) [51-500]
LJ - v129 - i18 - Nov 1 2004 - p76(1) [501+]
PW - v251 - i50 - Dec 13 2004 - p44(2) [51-500]

Payne, Ian - *The Almain in Britain, c. 1549-c. 1675: A Dance Manual from Manuscript Sources*
Ren Q - v57 - i4 - Winter 2004 - p1537(2) [501+]

Payne, J. Mark - *Democracies in Development: Politics and Reform in Latin America*
JEL - v41 - i4 - Dec 2003 - p1412(1) [501+]

Payne, James L. - *A History of Force: Exploring the Worldwide Movement Against Habits of Coercion, Bloodshed, and Mayhem*
Choice - v41 - i11-12 - July-August 2004 - p2122(1) [501+]

Payne, John - *Catalonia: History and Culture*
TLS - i5294 - Sept 17 2004 - p31(1) [501+]

Payne, Leigh A. - *Uncivil Movements: The Armed Right Wing and Democracy in Latin America*
JTWS - v21 - i1 - Spring 2004 - p307(4) [501+]

Payne, Mathew J. - *Stalin's Railroad: Turksib and the Building of Socialism*
E-A St - v56 - i3 - May 2004 - p479(3) [501+]

Payne, Richard K. - *Approaching the Land of Bliss: Religious Praxis in the Cult of Amitabha*
R&R Bk N - v19 - i1 - Feb 2004 - p16(1) [1-50]

Payne, Ruby K. - *Crossing the Tracks for Love: What to Do When You and Your Partner Grew Up in Different Worlds*
LJ - v130 - i1 - Jan 1 2005 - p135(1) [51-500]

Payne, Sheila - *Palliative Care Nursing: Principles and Evidence for Practice, 1st Ed.*
TimHES - v0 - i1680 - Feb 25 2005 - pXV(1) [501+]

Payne, Stanley G. - *The Spanish Civil War, the Soviet Union, and Communism*
Choice - v42 - i5 - Jan 2005 - p907(1) [1-50]
For Aff - v83 - i5 - Sept-Oct 2004 - p164 [501+]
HRNB - v33 - i1 - Fall 2004 - p31(1) [501+]
What History Tells: George L. Mosse and the Culture of Modern Europe
R&R Bk N - v19 - i4 - Nov 2004 - p31(1) [51-500]

Payne, Thomas B. - *Les organa a deux voix du manuscrit de Wolfenbuttel, Herzog August Bibliothek, Cod. Guelf. 1099 Hemst*
Notes - v61 - i1 - Sept 2004 - p215(5) [501+]

Payne, Tony - *The Hippo-Not-Amus (Illus. by Parker-Rees, Guy)*
c SLJ - v50 - i9 - Sept 2004 - p177(1) [51-500]
Oh No, Annie!
c Sch Lib - v52 - i3 - Autumn 2004 - p133(2) [501+]
Plummet (Illus. by Bolam, Emily)
c Sch Lib - v52 - i4 - Winter 2004 - p188(1) [51-500]
c SLJ - v51 - i2 - Feb 2005 - p108(1) [51-500]

Payr, Sabine - *Agent Culture: Human-Agent Interaction in a Multicultural World*
SciTech - v28 - i3 - Sept 2004 - p29(1) [51-500]

Payton, Philip - *Cornish Studies: Eleven*
R&R Bk N - v19 - i3 - August 2004 - p39(1) [51-500]

Paz, Mario - *Structural Dynamics: Theory and Computation, 5th ed.*
SciTech - v28 - i1 - March 2004 - p143(1) [51-500]

Peabody, Bo - *Lucky or Smart? Secrets to an Entrepreneurial Life*
BL - v101 - i7 - Dec 1 2004 - p623(1) [51-500]

Peabody Essex Museum - *Geisha: Beyond the Painted Smile*
Choice - v42 - i3 - Nov 2004 - p541(1) [1-50]

Peabody, Sue - *The Color of Liberty: Histories of Race in France*
CS - v33 - i1 - Jan 2004 - p129-129 [51-500]

Peace, David - *GB84*
Lon R Bks - v26 - i18 - Sept 23 2004 - p25(2) [501+]

Peace, William J. - *Leslie A. White: Evolution and Revolution in Anthropology*
Choice - v42 - i6 - Feb 2005 - p1065(1) [51-500]

Peacey, Jason - *Politicians and Pamphleteers: Propaganda During the English Civil Wars and Interregnum*
R&R Bk N - v19 - i3 - August 2004 - p37(1) [51-500]

Peach, Lucinda - *Legislating Morality: Pluralism and Religious Identity in Law-making*
JAAR - v72 - i3 - Sept 2004 - p792-794 [501+]

Peach-Pit - *DearS*
PW - v252 - i6 - Feb 7 2005 - p44(1) [51-500]

Peackock, Graham - *Geology*
y SB - v40 - i5 - Sept-Oct 2004 - p193(1) [51-500]

Peacock, Carol Antoinette - *Pilgrim Cat (Illus. by Ettlinger, Doris)*
c BL - v101 - i3 - Oct 1 2004 - p336(1) [51-500]
c KR - v72 - i16 - August 15 2004 - p811(1) [51-500]
c SLJ - v50 - i9 - Sept 2004 - p177(1) [51-500]

Peacock, Shane - *Monster in the Mountains*
c CBRA - Annual 2003 - p508(2) [51-500]

Peacocke, Arthur - *Evolution: The Disguised Friend of Faith?*
PW - v251 - i45 - Nov 8 2004 - p52(1) [51-500]

Peacocke, Christopher - *The Realm of Reason*
TLS - i5298 - Oct 15 2004 - p8-9 [501+]

Peake, Jocelyn - *How to Start a Home-Based Antiques Business*
Bwatch - March 2005 - pNA [51-500]

Peake, Thomas H. - *Cinema and Life Development: Healing Lives and Training Therapists*
SciTech - v28 - i3 - Sept 2004 - p99(1) [51-500]

Peakman, Julie - *Lascivious Bodies: A Sexual History of the Eighteenth Century*
Spec - v296 - i9190 - Sept 25 2004 - p56(2) [501+]
TimHES - v0 - i1679 - Feb 18 2005 - p24(1) [501+]

The Peanut Man
c SLJ - v50 - i11 - Nov 2004 - p84(1) [51-500]

Pearce, Craig L. - *Shared Leadership: Reframing the How and Whys of Leadership*
Per Psy - v57 - i3 - Autumn 2004 - p802(3) [501+]

Pearce, Edward - *Reform*
TLS - i5263 - Feb 13 2004 - p25-25 [501+]

Pearce, George F. - *Pensacola During the Civil War: A Thorn in the Side of the Confederacy*
HNet - August 2004 - pNA [501+]

Pearce, Jacqueline - *Reunion*
y Can CL - i111-112 - Fall-Winter 2003 - p139(8) [501+]

Pearce, Jonathan - *John-Browne's Body & Sole: A Semester of Life*
y Kliatt - v38 - i4 - July 2004 - p23(1) [51-500]

Pearce, Joseph - *C.S. Lewis and the Catholic Church*
Bks & Cult - v10 - i6 - Nov-Dec 2004 - p30(4) [501+]

Pearce, Joseph Chilton - *The Biology of Transcendence: A Blueprint of the Human Spirit*
Parabola - v28 - i3 - Fall 2003 - p94(5) [501+]

Pearce, Margaret W. - *Exploring Human Geography with Maps*
R&R Bk N - v19 - i1 - Feb 2004 - p70(1) [501+]

Pearce, Michael - *A Cold Touch of Ice*
BL - v100 - i22 - August 2004 - p1907(1) [51-500]
KR - v72 - i13 - July 1 2004 - p607(1) [51-500]
PW - v251 - i29 - July 19 2004 - p148(2) [51-500]
A Dead Man in Trieste
Globe & Mail - Feb 5 2005 - pD15 [51-500]
KR - v72 - i19 - Oct 1 2004 - p943(1) [501+]
LJ - v129 - i18 - Nov 1 2004 - p58(1) [51-500]
NYTBR - Dec 26 2004 - p22 [501+]
PW - v251 - i40 - Oct 4 2004 - p73(1) [501+]
The Face in the Cemetery
BL - v101 - i8 - Dec 15 2004 - p712(1) [51-500]
Bwatch - Feb 2005 - pNA [51-500]
KR - v72 - i22 - Nov 15 2004 - p1071(2) [51-500]
NYTBR - Dec 26 2004 - p22 [501+]
PW - v251 - i45 - Nov 8 2004 - p39(2) [501+]
The Last Cut
DroRevMy - v24 - i3 - May-June 2004 - p5(2) [501+]
The Point in the Market
KR - v73 - i5 - March 1 2005 - p263(1) [51-500]

Pearce, Philippa - *The Little Gentleman (Illus. by Pohrt, Tom)*
c BL - v100 - i22 - August 2004 - p1937(1) [51-500]
c CCB-B - v58 - i4 - Dec 2004 - p180(2) [51-500]
c HB - v80 - i5 - Sept-Oct 2004 - p594(2) [51-500]
c KR - v72 - i14 - July 15 2004 - p692(1) [51-500]
c PW - v251 - i45 - Nov 8 2004 - p56(1) [51-500]
c Sch Lib - v52 - i4 - Winter 2004 - p203(1) [51-500]
c SLJ - v50 - i9 - Sept 2004 - p177(1) [51-500]

Pearce, Q.L. - *Experiments You Can Do in Your Backyard*
c LibMed - v22 - i5 - Feb 2004 - p61(1) [501+]
c SLJ - v50 - i10 - Oct 2004 - pS40(1) [51-500]

Pearce, Thomas - *Advances in Abrasive Technology 6*
SciTech - v28 - i1 - March 2004 - p152(1) [51-500]

Pearl, Nancy - *Book Lust: Recommended Reading for Every Mood, Moment, and Reason*
R&R Bk N - v19 - i1 - Feb 2004 - p261(1) [51-500]
More Book Lust: Recommended Reading for Every Mood, Moment, and Reason
PW - v252 - i9 - Feb 28 2005 - p54(1) [51-500]

Pearlman, Bobby - *Passover Is Here! (Illus. by Desmoinaux, Christel)*
c PW - v252 - i7 - Feb 14 2005 - p81(1) [51-500]

Pearlman, Edith - *How to Fall*
PW - v252 - i3 - Jan 17 2005 - p34(1) [51-500]

Pearlman, Laura - *Tibetan Sacred Dance: A Journey into the Religious and Folk Traditions*
Parabola - v28 - i3 - Fall 2003 - p104(3) [501+]

Pearlstein, Richard M. - *Fatal Future? Transnational Terrorism and the New Global Disorder*
MEJ - v58 - i4 - Autumn 2004 - p707(1) [501+]
Pers PS - v33 - i4 - Fall 2004 - p244(2) [501+]

Pearman, Alan - *Transport Projects, Programmes, and Policies: Evaluation Needs and Capabilities*
R&R Bk N - v19 - i2 - May 2004 - p108(1) [51-500]

Pearman, Hugh - *Airports: A Century of Architecture*
Choice - v42 - i6 - Feb 2005 - p1015(2) [51-500]
LJ - v129 - i20 - Dec 1 2004 - p113(1) [51-500]
PW - v251 - i48 - Nov 29 2004 - p35(1) [51-500]

Pears, Angela - *Feminist Christian Encounters: The Methods and Strategies of Feminist Informed Christian Theologies*
R&R Bk N - v19 - i4 - Nov 2004 - p24(1) [51-500]

Pears, Iain - *The Portrait*
KR - v73 - i3 - Feb 1 2005 - p144(1) [501+]
LJ - v129 - i20 - Dec 1 2004 - p88(1) [1-50]
LJ - v130 - i4 - March 1 2005 - p80(1) [51-500]
PW - v252 - i3 - Jan 17 2005 - p33(1) [51-500]

Pearse, Lesley - *Remember Me (Read by Beaton, Eilidh). Audiobook Review*
Kliatt - v38 - i6 - Nov 2004 - p49(1) [51-500]

Pearse, Meic - *Why the Rest Hates the West: Understanding the Roots of Global Rage*
Ch Today - v49 - i3 - March 2005 - p83(2) [501+]

Pearson, Debora - *Animachines (Illus. by Hilb, Nora)*
c CBRA - Annual 2003 - p464(1) [51-500]

Pearson, Geoffrey - *Seize the Day: Lester B. Pearson and Crisis Diplomacy*
Globe & Mail - Nov 27 2004 - pD51 [501+]

Pearson, Jacqueline - *Women's Reading in Britain 1750-1835*
Eight-C St - v36 - i2 - Winter 2003 - p289 [501+]

Pearson, Michael - *Red Sky in the Morning; The Battle of the Barents Sea, 1942*
APJ - v18 - i3 - Fall 2004 - p123(2) [501+]

Pearson, Patricia - *Area Woman Blows Gasket: And Other Tales from the Domestic Frontier*
KR - v73 - i3 - Feb 1 2005 - p169(1) [501+]

Pearson, Philip - *Keeping Well at Work, 2nd ed.*
TES - v0 - i4587 - June 11 2004 - psss19(1) [501+]

Pearson, Richard - *W.M. Thackeray and the Mediated Text*
VS - v45 - i2 - Winter 2003 - p348 [501+]

Pearson, Ridley - *The Body of David Hayes (Read by Hill, Dick). Audiobook Review*
Kliatt - v38 - i6 - Nov 2004 - p42(1) [51-500]
The Body of David Hayes
DroRevMy - v24 - i3 - May-June 2004 - p13(1) [1-50]
Cut and Run (Read by Hill, Dick). Audiobook Review
LJ - v129 - i20 - Dec 1 2004 - p182(1) [501+]
Cut and Run
PW - v252 - i11 - March 14 2005 - p46(1) [51-500]

Pearson, Robin - *Insuring the Industrial Revolution: Fire Insurance in Great Britain, 1700-1850*
R&R Bk N - v19 - i3 - August 2004 - p139(1) [51-500]

Pearson, Susan - *Squeal and Squawk: Barnyard Talk (Illus. by Slonim, David)*
c LibMed - v23 - i3 - Nov-Dec 2004 - p75(1) [51-500]

Pearson, T.R. - *Glad News of the Natural World*
KR - v73 - i5 - March 1 2005 - p255(1) [501+]
True Cross
VQR - v80 - i2 - Spring 2004 - p260-260 [501+]

Pearson, Tracey Campbell - *Hector Protector (Illus. by Pearson, Tracey Campbell)*
c BL - v100 - i22 - August 2004 - p1944(1) [51-500]
Little Bo-Peep (Illus. by Pearson, Tracey Campbell)
c BL - v100 - i22 - August 2004 - p1944(1) [51-500]

Book Review Index 2005 Cumulation **PELLEGRINO • 471**

Pearson, Will - *Mental Floss Presents Condensed Knowledge*
y VOYA - v27 - i5 - Dec 2004 - p416(1) [51-500]
Pease, Allison - *Modernism, Mass Culture, and the Aesthetics of Obscenity*
MP - v102 - i1 - August 2004 - p151(5) [501+]
Pease, Donald E. - *The Future of American Studies*
J Am St - v38 - i1 - April 2004 - p158-159 [501+]
Tikkun - v19 - i5 - Sept-Oct 2004 - p70(3) [501+]
Pease, William H. - *The Roman Years of a South Carolina Artist: Caroline Carson's Letters Home, 1872-1892*
JSH - v70 - i4 - Nov 2004 - p943(2) [501+]
Peat, John P. - *The Daylily: A Guide for Gardeners*
BL - v101 - i3 - Oct 1 2004 - p290(1) [51-500]
Peay, Pythia - *Mercury Retrograde: Its Myth and Meaning*
LJ - v129 - i12 - July 2004 - p107(1) [51-500]
Peccoud, Dominique - *Philosophical and Spiritual Perspectives on Decent Work*
ILR - v143 - i3 - Autumn 2004 - p290(2) [51-500]
Pechere, J.C. - *Streptococcal Pharyngitis: Optimal Management*
SciTech - v28 - i1 - March 2004 - p90(1) [1-50]
Pechilis, Karen - *The Graceful Guru: Hindu Female Gurus in India and the United States*
Choice - v42 - i6 - Feb 2005 - p1037(1) [51-500]
Peck, Bryan T. - *The Baltic States, Education, and the European Union*
R&R Bk N - v19 - i1 - Feb 2004 - pNA [51-500]
Peck, Dale - *Hatchet Jobs: Writings on Contemporary Fiction*
Atl - v294 - i1 - July-August 2004 - p144(1) [51-500]
BW - v34 - i27 - July 4 2004 - p7(1) [501+]
NYRB - v51 - i12 - July 15 2004 - p43(4) [501+]
NYTBR - July 18 2004 - p10 [501+]
Spec - v295 - i9182 - July 31 2004 - p27(2) [501+]
TLS - i5286 - July 23 2004 - p7-9 [501+]
Peck, Jan - *Way Down Deep in the Deep Blue Sea (Illus. by Petrone, Valeria)*
c SLJ - v50 - i7 - July 2004 - p84(2) [51-500]
Peck, M. Scott - *Glimpses of the Devil: A Psychiatrist's Personal Accounts of Possession, Exorcism, and Redemption*
BL - v101 - i7 - Dec 1 2004 - p618(1) [51-500]
PW - v252 - i1 - Jan 3 2005 - p48(1) [51-500]
Peck, Richard - *Past Perfect, Present Tense: New and Collected Stories*
c LibMed - v23 - i3 - Nov-Dec 2004 - p71(1) [51-500]
The River between Us (Read by Patel, Lina). Audiobook Review
c BL - v101 - i1 - Sept 1 2004 - p148(1) [51-500]
The River between Us
c Five Owls - v18 - i1 - Fall 2004 - p25(1) [51-500]
c LibMed - v22 - i4 - Jan 2004 - p66(1) [501+]
c RT - v58 - i3 - Nov 2004 - p291(1) [501+]
c SLJ - v50 - i8 - August 2004 - p78(1) [51-500]
The Teacher's Funeral: A Comedy in Three Parts
c BL - v101 - i3 - Oct 1 2004 - p326(1) [51-500]
y BW - v34 - i43 - Oct 24 2004 - p11(1) [51-500]
c CCB-B - v58 - i3 - Nov 2004 - p140(2) [501+]
y HB - v80 - i5 - Sept-Oct 2004 - p595(1) [51-500]
y Kliatt - v38 - i5 - Sept 2004 - p14(3) [51-500]
c KR - v72 - i19 - Oct 1 2004 - p966(1) [51-500]
y SLJ - v50 - i11 - Nov 2004 - p152(1) [51-500]
c VOYA - v27 - i5 - Dec 2004 - p392(1) [51-500]
Peck, Richard E. - *Dead Pawn*
Roundup M - v12 - i1 - Oct 2004 - p32(1) [51-500]
Peck, Robert Newton - *Bro (Read by Shina, Scott). Audiobook Review*
y Kliatt - v39 - i1 - Jan 2005 - p38(2) [51-500]
Bro
c Kliatt - v38 - i4 - July 2004 - p11(2) [51-500]
c PW - v251 - i28 - July 12 2004 - p65(2) [501+]
c SLJ - v50 - i8 - August 2004 - p128(1) [51-500]
Pecklers, Keith - *Dynamic Equivalence: The Living Language of Christian Worship*
Theol St - v66 - i1 - March 2005 - p218(3) [501+]
Worship: A Primer in Christian Ritual
Theol St - v66 - i1 - March 2005 - p218(3) [501+]
Peden, A.M. - *Abbo of Fleury and Ramsey: Commentary on the Calculus of Victorius of Aquitaine*
Med R - Sept 2004 - pNA [501+]
Peden, Ann H. - *Comparative Health Information Management, 2nd Ed.*
SciTech - v28 - i4 - Dec 2004 - p86(1) [51-500]
Pedersen, Jean Elisabeth - *Legislating the French Family: Feminism, Theatre, and Republican Politics, 1870-1920*
AHR - v109 - i4 - Oct 2004 - p1323(2) [501+]
Pedersen, Maggie Campbell - *Gem and Ornamental Materials of Organic Origin*
Choice - v41 - i11-12 - July-August 2004 - p2075(1) [501+]
Pedersen, Olof - *Archives and Libraries in the Ancient Near East 1500-300 b.c.*
Lib & Cul - v39 - i3 - Summer 2004 - p322(2) [501+]
Pedersen, Soren - *The Shadow Economy in Germany, Great Britain and Scandinavia: A Measurement Based on Questionnaire Surveys*
JEL - v42 - i1 - March 2004 - p254(2) [501+]
Pedersen, Susan - *Eleanor Rathbone and the Politics of Conscience*
Choice - v42 - i6 - Feb 2005 - p1086(2) [51-500]
CR - v285 - i1664 - Sept 2004 - p187(2) [51-500]
LJ - v129 - i13 - August 2004 - p90(1) [501+]
Lon R Bks - v26 - i13 - July 8 2004 - p19(3) [501+]
TimHES - v0 - i1657 - Sept 10 2004 - p34(1) [501+]
Pederson, Paul B. - *110 Experiences for Multicultural Learning*
R&R Bk N - v19 - i4 - Nov 2004 - p191(1) [501+]
Pederson, William D. - *Franklin D. Roosevelt and Abraham Lincoln*
Pres St Q - v34 - i3 - Sept 2004 - p698(3) [501+]
Pediatric Nursing Made Incredibly Easy
SciTech - v28 - i3 - Sept 2004 - p117(1) [51-500]
Pedley, Paul - *Essential Law for Information Professionals*
ALJ - v53 - i3 - August 2004 - p312(2) [501+]
Pedrick, Cherry - *Obsessive-Compulsive Disorder*
Sci Teach - v71 - i4 - April 2004 - p73-73 [501+]
Peebles-Kleiger, Mary Jo - *Beginnings: The Art and Science of Planning Psychotherapy*
Adoles - v39 - i154 - Summer 2004 - p403(2) [501+]
Peek, Charles A. - *A Companion to Faulkner Studies*
Choice - v42 - i5 - Jan 2005 - p851(1) [1-50]
R&R Bk N - v19 - i4 - Nov 2004 - p242(1) [501+]
Peek, Ian Denys - *One Fourteenth of an Elephant: A Memoir of Life and Death on the Burma-Thailand Railway*
Spec - v296 - i9193 - Oct 16 2004 - p68(1) [501+]
Peek, Philip M. - *African Folklore: An Encylcopedia*
R&USQ - v44 - i1 - Fall 2004 - p80(1) [501+]
Peeke, Pamela - *Body for Life for Women : A Woman's Plan for Physical and Mental Transformation*
PW - v252 - i5 - Jan 31 2005 - p65(1) [501+]
Peel, Mark - *The Lowest Rung: Voices of Australian Poverty*
AHS - v35 - i124 - Oct 2004 - p389(2) [501+]
Peele, Gillian - *Governing the UK: British Politics in the 21st Century, 4th Ed.*
R&R Bk N - v19 - i3 - August 2004 - p182(1) [501+]
TimHES - v0 - i1668 - Nov 26 2004 - pIII(1) [501+]
Peerenboom, Randall - *Asian Discourses of Rule of Law: Theories and Implementation of Rule of Law in Twelve Asian Countries, France and the United States*
Law&PolBR - July 2004 - p572(4) [501+]
Peers, Laura - *My First Years in the Fur Trade: The Journals of 1802-1804*
Can Hist R - v85 - i3 - Sept 2004 - p546(4) [501+]
Peery, Angela B. - *Deep Change: Professional Development from the Inside Out*
R&R Bk N - v19 - i3 - August 2004 - p219(1) [1-50]
TCR - v107 - i2 - Feb 2005 - p329(4) [501+]
Pefers, Ed - *Asia's Best Hotels and Resorts*
R&R Bk N - v19 - i1 - Feb 2004 - p253(1) [51-500]
Peffer, George Anthony - *If They Don't Bring Their Women Here: Chinese Female Immigration before Exclusion*
Wom HR - v13 - i1 - Spring 2004 - p139(4) [501+]
Pegg, Bruce - *Brown Eyed Handsome Man: The Life and Hard Times of Chuck Berry: An Unauthorized Biography*
Am St - v45 - i1 - Spring 2004 - p169-170 [501+]
Pegg, Nicholas - *The Complete David Bowie*
LJ - v129 - i19 - Nov 15 2004 - p86(1) [51-500]
Pegolotti, James A. - *Deems Taylor: A Biography*
R&R Bk N - v19 - i1 - Feb 2004 - p196(1) [51-500]
Peifer, Douglas C. - *The Three German Navies: Dissolution, Transition and New Beginings, 1945-1960*
GSR - v27 - i2 - May 2004 - p427-428 [501+]
The Three German Navies: Dissolution, Transition, and New Beginnings, 1945-1960
AHR - v109 - i2 - April 2004 - p636(2) [501+]
Peikari, Cyrus - *Security Warrior*
LJ - v129 - i12 - July 2004 - p112(1) [501+]
Peimani, Hooman - *Falling Terrorism and Rising Conflicts: The Afghan "Contribution" to Polarization and Confrontation in West and South Asia*
R&R Bk N - v19 - i1 - Feb 2004 - p46(1) [51-500]
Peirce, Hayford - *Black Hole Planet*
Analog - v124 - i5 - May 2004 - p132(142) [501+]
Peissel, Michel - *Tibet: The Secret Continent*
R&R Bk N - v19 - i3 - August 2004 - p57(1) [51-500]
Pejanovic, Mirko - *Through Bosnian Eyes: The Political Memoir of a Bosnian Serb*
R&R Bk N - v19 - i4 - Nov 2004 - p43(1) [51-500]
Pekar, Harvey - *American Splendor: Our Movie Year*
PW - v252 - i6 - Feb 7 2005 - p44(1) [51-500]
Pekic, Borislav - *How to Quiet a Vampire*
RCF - v24 - i3 - Fall 2004 - p135(1) [501+]
Pekkanen, Saadia M. - *Picking Winners? From Technology Catch-Up to the Space Race in Japan*
JEL - v42 - i1 - March 2004 - p289(1) [501+]
Pekov, Igor V. - *Kukisvumchorr Deposit: Mineralogy of Alkaline Pegmatites and Hydrothermalites*
RocksMiner - v80 - i2 - March-April 2005 - p133(1) [501+]
Pelan, John - *Off the Sand Road*
BW - v34 - i44 - Oct 31 2004 - p15(1) [501+]
What Shadows We Pursue
BW - v34 - i44 - Oct 31 2004 - p15(1) [501+]
Pelc, Milan - *Illustrium Imagines: Das Portratbuch der Renaissance*
Six Ct J - v35 - i1 - Spring 2004 - p198(2) [501+]
Pelecanos, George - *Drama City*
KR - v73 - i2 - Jan 15 2005 - p79(1) [51-500]
PW - v252 - i8 - Feb 21 2005 - p158(1) [51-500]
Ent W - i812 - March 25 2005 - p78 [51-500]
Hard Revolution (Read by Canada, Charles). Audiobook Review
BL - v101 - i1 - Sept 1 2004 - p144(1) [51-500]
y Kliatt - v38 - i5 - Sept 2004 - p60(3) [51-500]
LJ - v129 - i18 - Nov 1 2004 - p130(1) [51-500]
Hard Revolution
BooChiTr - April 4 2004 - p3(1) [501+]
Peletz, Michael G. - *Islamic Modern: Religious Courts and Cultural Politics in Malaysia*
Choice - v41 - i11-12 - July-August 2004 - p2118(1) [501+]
JAAR - v72 - i4 - Dec 2004 - p1056(3) [501+]
Pelevin, Viktor - *The Dialectics of the Transition Period from Nowhere to Nothing*
NYRB - v51 - i20 - Dec 16 2004 - p65(6) [501+]
Dialektika Perekhodnogo Perioda iz Niotkuda v Nikuda: Izbrannye proizvedeniia
WLT - v78 - i3-4 - Sept-Dec 2004 - p138(1) [501+]
Pelias, Ronald J. - *A Methodology of the Heart: Evoking Academic and Daily Life*
R&R Bk N - v19 - i4 - Nov 2004 - p183(1) [501+]
Pelikan, Jaroslav - *Credo: Historical and Theological Guide to Creeds and Confessions of Faith in the Christian Tradition*
TT - v61 - i3 - Oct 2004 - p398(3) [501+]
Interpreting the Bible and the Constitution
AM - v191 - i20 - Dec 20 2004 - p23 [501+]
Choice - v42 - i5 - Jan 2005 - p871(1) [1-50]
Whose Bible Is It?: A History of the Scriptures through the Ages
KR - v73 - i1 - Jan 1 2005 - p40(1) [501+]
PW - v252 - i3 - Jan 17 2005 - p51(1) [51-500]
Pelikan, Pavel - *The Evolutionary Analysis of Economic Policy*
JEL - v41 - i4 - Dec 2003 - p1338(1) [501+]
Pelinka, Anton - *Democracy Indian Style: Subhas Chandra Bose and the Creation of India's Political Culture*
Choice - v41 - i7 - March 2004 - p1366(1) [501+]
Pell, Ed - *John Winthrop: Governor of the Massachusetts Bay Colony*
c SLJ - v50 - i8 - August 2004 - p133(1) [501+]
Pellegrin, Nicole - *Veufs, veuves et veuvage dans la France d'Ancien Regime: Actes du Colloque de Poitiers*
Ren Q - v57 - i4 - Winter 2004 - p1419(2) [501+]
Pellegrini, Anthony D. - *Observing Children in Their Natural Worlds: A Methodological Primer, 2nd Ed.*
R&R Bk N - v19 - i3 - August 2004 - p10(1) [1-50]
Pellegrino, Charles R. - *Ghosts of Vesuvius: A New Look at the Last Days of Pompeii, How the Towers Fell, and Other Strange Connections*
R&R Bk N - v19 - i4 - Nov 2004 - p40(1) [51-500]

Penslar, Derek J. - *Shylock's Children: Economics and Jewish Identity in Modern Europe*
JIH - v34 - i3 - Wntr 2004 - p444-3 [501+]
JMH - v76 - i3 - Sept 2004 - p669(2) [501+]

Penz, Francois - *Space: In Science, Art, and Society*
Choice - v42 - i3 - Nov 2004 - p504(1) [1-50]

Penzel, Klaus - *The German Education of Christian Scholar Philip Schaff: The Formative Years, 1819-1844*
R&R Bk N - v19 - i4 - Nov 2004 - p19(1) [51-500]

Penzler, Otto - *Best American Crime Writing, 2004*
BL - v100 - i21 - July 2004 - p1804(1) [1-50]
PW - v251 - i27 - July 5 2004 - p50(1) [51-500]
Dangerous Women
BL - v101 - i6 - Nov 15 2004 - p564(1) [51-500]
Globe & Mail - Jan 22 2005 - pD12 [51-500]
KR - v72 - i19 - Oct 1 2004 - p943(1) [501+]
PW - v251 - i46 - Nov 15 2004 - p44(1) [51-500]

Peoples of North America
LibMed - v22 - i4 - Jan 2004 - p79(1) [501+]

Peot, Margaret - *Make Your Mark: Explore Your Creativity and Discover Your Inner Artist*
LJ - v129 - i12 - July 2004 - p81(1) [51-500]

Peperzak, Adriaan T. - *Elements of Ethics*
R&R Bk N - v19 - i1 - Feb 2004 - p10(1) [1-50]

Pepin, Jacques - *The Apprentice: My Life in the Kitchen*
y Kliatt - v39 - i1 - Jan 2005 - p30(2) [501+]
Fast Food My Way (Illus. by Fink, Ben)
LJ - v129 - i15 - Sept 15 2004 - p78(1) [51-500]
PW - v251 - i35 - August 30 2004 - p47(1) [501+]
Jacques Pepin's Fast Food My Way (Illus. by Fink, Ben)
Globe & Mail - Nov 27 2004 - pD26 [51-500]

Pepler, Debra J. - *The Development and Treatment of Girlhood Aggression*
SciTech - v28 - i4 - Dec 2004 - p113(1) [1-50]

Pepper, Laurie - *Straight Life: The Story of Art Pepper*
Atl - v294 - i2 - Sept 2004 - p139(1) [501+]

Pepper, William F. - *An Act of State: The Execution of Martin Luther King*
JSH - v70 - i4 - Nov 2004 - p969(2) [501+]

Peppers, Don - *Managing Customer Relationships: A Strategic Framework*
R&R Bk N - v19 - i3 - August 2004 - p127(1) [51-500]

Pepys, Samuel - *The Diary of Samuel Pepys: 1660-1663, Vol. 1. Audiobook Review*
Globe & Mail - Dec 18 2004 - pD25 [1-50]

Pequignot, Jean-Marc - *Chemoreception: From Cellular Signalling to Functional Plasticity, Proceedings*
SciTech - v28 - i1 - March 2004 - p73(1) [51-500]

Peragamins Del Monestir Benedicti de Sant Pau del Camp de Barcelona, De l' Arxiu de la Corona d'Arago
HER - v119 - i483 - Sept 2004 - p1033(1) [501+]

Perakh, Mark - *Unintelligent Design*
QRB - v79 - i3 - Sept 2004 - p302(1) [51-500]
R&R Bk N - v19 - i1 - Feb 2004 - p11(1) [51-500]

Perali, Federico - *The Behavioral and Welfare Analysis of Consumption: The Cost of Children, Equity, and Poverty in Colombia*
R&R Bk N - v19 - i1 - Feb 2004 - p83(1) [51-500]

Percheron, Rene - *Matisse: From Color to Architecture*
LJ - v130 - i1 - Jan 1 2005 - p110(1) [51-500]

Perciaccante, Marianne - *Calling Down Fire: Charles Grandison Finney and Revivalism in Jefferson County*
JAH - v91 - i1 - June 2004 - p226-227 [501+]

Percival, Robert V. - *Environmental Law: Statutory and Case Supplement with Internet Guide, 2004-2005*
R&R Bk N - v19 - i4 - Nov 2004 - p170(1) [501+]

Percy, Martyn - *The Character of Wisdom: Essays in Honour of Wesley Carr*
R&R Bk N - v19 - i4 - Nov 2004 - p27(1) [51-500]

Percy, Walker - *The Moviegoer*
Globe & Mail - Sept 4 2004 - pD19 [501+]

Perdomo, Willie - *Smoking Lovely*
ABR - v25 - i5 - July-August 2004 - p24(1) [501+]

Perdue, Theda - *"Mixed Blood" Indians: Racial Reconstruction in the Early South*
JIH - v35 - i1 - Summer 2004 - p148-149 [501+]

Perec, Georges - *Entretiens et conferences*
WLT - v78 - i3-4 - Sept-Dec 2004 - p121(1) [501+]

Peregrine, Peter N. - *Encyclopedia of Prehistory*
Lat Ant - v15 - i3 - Sept 2004 - p364(2) [501+]

Perenne, Marie-Helene - *Le verbe en action: Grammaire contrastive des temps verbaux*
FS - v58 - i1 - Jan 2004 - p153(2) [501+]

Perera, Ajith H. - *Emulating Natural Forest Landscape Disturbances: Concepts and Applications*
Choice - v42 - i5 - Jan 2005 - p879(1) [1-50]
SB - v41 - i1 - Jan-Feb 2005 - p22(1) [501+]
SciTech - v28 - i3 - Sept 2004 - p130(1) [51-500]

Peress, Maurice - *Dvorak to Duke Ellington: A Conductor Explores America's Music and Its African American Roots*
ABR - v26 - i2 - Jan-Feb 2005 - p25(1) [501+]
Choice - v42 - i3 - Nov 2004 - p492(1) [51-500]

Peretz, Eyal - *Literature, Disaster and the Enigma of Power: A Reading of Moby-Dick*
MFSF - v50 - i3 - Fall 2004 - p795-797 [501+]

Perez, Bertha - *Becoming Biliterate: A Study of Two-Way Bilingual Immersion Education*
Choice - v42 - i1 - Sept 2004 - p159(1) [501+]
R&R Bk N - v19 - i1 - Feb 2004 - p191(1) [51-500]

Perez, David M. Callejo - *Pedagogy of Place: Seeing Space as Cultural Education*
R&R Bk N - v19 - i1 - Feb 2004 - p189(1) [51-500]

Perez, Garcia Rafael D. - *Reforma y Resistencia: Manuel de Flon y la Intendencia de Puebla*
Ams - v61 - i2 - Oct 2004 - p262(1) [501+]

Perez, George - *Wonder Woman: Gods and Mortals*
LJ - v129 - i14 - Sept 1 2004 - p128(2) [51-500]

Perez, Janet - *The Feminist Encyclopedia of Spanish Literature*
TLS - i5286 - July 23 2004 - p34(1) [501+]

Perez, Joseph - *The Spanish Inquisition: A History*
CR - v286 - i1698 - Feb 2005 - p123(2) [51-500]
TLS - i5306 - Dec 10 2004 - p33(1) [501+]

Perez, Louis A. Jr. - *Winds of Change: Hurricanes and the Transformation of Nineteenth-Century Cuba*
JTWS - v21 - i1 - Spring 2004 - p314(3) [501+]

Perez, Maria Jose Osorio - *Transtiendas de la cultura: Librerias y libreros en la Granada del siglo XVI*
Six CtJ - v35 - i1 - Spring 2004 - p242(1) [501+]

Perez, Marlene - *Unexpected Development*
y BL - v101 - i6 - Nov 15 2004 - p598(1) [51-500]
y CCB-B - v58 - i2 - Oct 2004 - p95(1) [51-500]
y KR - v72 - i17 - Sept 1 2004 - p872(1) [51-500]
y PW - v251 - i36 - Sept 6 2004 - p64(1) [51-500]
y SLJ - v50 - i10 - Oct 2004 - p175(2) [51-500]
VOYA - v27 - i5 - Dec 2004 - p392(1) [51-500]

Perez-Mejia, Angela - *A Geography of Hard Times: Narratives about Travel to South America, 1780-1849*
Biomag - v27 - i4 - Fall 2004 - p853(3) [501+]

Perez-Reverte, Arturo - *The Queen of the South (Read by Patel, Lina). Audiobook Review*
BL - v101 - i5 - Nov 1 2004 - p505(1) [51-500]
The Queen of the South
NYTBR - August 1 2004 - p13 [501+]
TLS - i5286 - July 23 2004 - p22(1) [501+]

Peri, Yoram - *Telepopulism: Media and Politics in Israel*
MEJ - v58 - i4 - Autumn 2004 - p691(2) [501+]
Pers PS - v33 - i4 - Fall 2004 - p240(1) [501+]
R&R Bk N - v19 - i3 - August 2004 - p260(1) [51-500]

Peric, T.S. - *Wacky Days: How to Get Millions of $$$ in Free Publicity by Creating a "Real" Holilday and Other Tactics Used by Media Experts*
Bwatch - v26 - i8 - August 2004 - p8(1) [51-500]

Perica, Vjekoslav - *Balkan Idols: Religion and Nationalism in Yugoslav State*
JAAR - v72 - i4 - Dec 2004 - p1059(3) [501+]

Pericles
TLS - i5289 - August 13 2004 - p8-9 [501+]

Pericoli, Matteo - *See the City: the Journey of Manhattan Unfurled (Illus. by Pericoli, Matteo)*
c KR - v72 - i13 - July 1 2004 - p635(1) [51-500]
c PW - v251 - i33 - August 16 2004 - p63(2) [51-500]
c SLJ - v50 - i12 - Dec 2004 - p136(1) [51-500]

Perion, Joachim - *Dialogues de l'origine du francais et de sa parente avec le grec*
FS - v58 - i3 - July 2004 - p401-401 [501+]

Perisse, Bernard R. - *Solitude and the Quest for Happiness in Vladimir Nabokov's American Works and Tahar Ben Jelloun's Novels*
R&R Bk N - v19 - i1 - Feb 2004 - p245(1) [51-500]

Perito, John E. - *Contemporary Catholic Sexuality: What Is Taught and What Is Practiced*
Cons - v25 - i3 - Winter 2004 - p49(4) [501+]

Perker, Alexander S. - *Innovations in Health Services Delivery: The Corporatization of Public Hospitals*
JEL - v41 - i4 - Dec 2003 - p1375(2) [501+]

Perkins, Barbara Bridgman - *The Medical Delivery Business: Health Reform, Childbirth, and the Economic Order*
Choice - v42 - i1 - Sept 2004 - p139(1) [501+]

Perkins, D.H. - *Particle Astrophysics*
New Sci - v184 - i2475 - Nov 27 2004 - p50(1) [501+]
SciTech - v28 - i3 - Sept 2004 - p43(1) [1-50]

Perkins, David - *Romanticism and Animal Rights*
Nine-C Lit - v58 - i4 - March 2004 - p547(550) [501+]

Perkins, Dawson - *The Team*
BL - v100 - i21 - July 2004 - p1819(1) [1-50]
Black Iss - v6 - i4 - July-August 2004 - p44(2) [501+]

Perkins, Diane - *The Improper Wife*
BL - v101 - i6 - Nov 15 2004 - p568(2) [51-500]
PW - v251 - i42 - Oct 18 2004 - p53(1) [51-500]

Perkins, Donald - *Particle Astrophysics*
Phys Today - v57 - i12 - Dec 2004 - p67-68 [501+]

Perkins, John - *Confessions of an Economic Hit Man*
Bwatch - March 2005 - pNA [51-500]
Globe & Mail - Dec 18 2004 - pD22 [501+]
LJ - v130 - i1 - Jan 1 2005 - p126(1) [51-500]

Perkins, Lynne Rae - *Snow Music*
HB - v81 - i1 - Jan-Feb 2005 - p18(1) [51-500]
LibMed - v22 - i6 - March 2004 - p58(1) [501+]

Perkins, Mary Anne - *Nation and Word, 1770-1850: Religious and Metaphysical Language in European National Consciousness*
CH - v73 - i4 - Dec 2004 - p866(3) [501+]

Perkins, Mitali - *Monsoon Summer*
y CCB-B - v58 - i1 - Sept 2004 - p34(1) [51-500]
y HB - v80 - i6 - Nov-Dec 2004 - p715(2) [501+]
y Kliatt - v38 - i4 - July 2004 - p12(1) [501+]
y KR - v72 - i14 - July 15 2004 - p692(1) [51-500]
y PW - v251 - i34 - August 23 2004 - p55(2) [501+]
y SLJ - v50 - i9 - Sept 2004 - p215(1) [51-500]

Perkins, Wendy - *Animals Building Homes*
c SB - v40 - i4 - July-August 2004 - p179(1) [51-500]
Animals Finding Food
c SB - v40 - i4 - July-August 2004 - p179(1) [51-500]
Animals Raising Offspring
c SB - v40 - i4 - July-August 2004 - p179(1) [51-500]
Animals Sleeping
c SB - v40 - i4 - July-August 2004 - p179(1) [51-500]

Perkmann, Markus - *Globalization, Regionalization and Cross-Border Regions*
PG - v23 - i5 - June 2004 - p637-639 [501+]

Perkowitz, Sidney - *Digital People: From Bionic Humans to Androids*
Choice - v42 - i3 - Nov 2004 - p515(1) [1-50]
SciTech - v28 - i3 - Sept 2004 - p149(1) [51-500]

Perks, Peggy J. - *The Internet*
c SB - v40 - i5 - Sept-Oct 2004 - p217(1) [51-500]

Perkyns, Dorothy - *Last Days in Africville*
y CBRA - Annual 2003 - p509(1) [51-500]

Perl, Andras - *Autoimmunity: Methods and Protocols*
SciTech - v28 - i4 - Dec 2004 - p102(1) [51-500]

Perl, Erica, S. - *Chicken Bedtime Is Really Early (Illus. by Bates, George)*
c PW - v252 - i8 - Feb 21 2005 - p173(1) [51-500]

Perl, Lila - *The Ancient Egyptians*
c SLJ - v51 - i2 - Feb 2005 - p148(1) [51-500]
Terrorism
y SLJ - v50 - i7 - July 2004 - p123(2) [51-500]

Perlina, Nina - *Olga Freidenberg's Works and Days*
Slav R - v63 - i2 - Summer 2004 - p443(2) [501+]

Perlman, Elliot - *Seven Types of Ambiguity*
BL - v101 - i5 - Nov 1 2004 - p443(1) [51-500]
Ent W - i797 - Dec 17 2004 - p88 [501+]
KR - v72 - i18 - Sept 15 2004 - p888(1) [501+]
LJ - v129 - i17 - Oct 15 2004 - p55(1) [51-500]
NW - Dec 13 2004 - p72 [501+]
NYTBR - Jan 16 2005 - p11 [501+]
People - v63 - i1 - Jan 10 2005 - p45 [51-500]
PW - v251 - i40 - Oct 4 2004 - p66(1) [51-500]
TLS - i5290 - August 20 2004 - p19(1) [501+]
Esq - v143 - i2 - Feb 2005 - p38(1) [501+]

Perlman, Janet - *The Penguin and the Pea*
c KR - v72 - i20 - Oct 15 2004 - p1012(1) [51-500]
c Res Links - v10 - i2 - Dec 2004 - p9(2) [51-500]

Perlmann, Joel - *The New Race Question: How the Census Counts Multiracial Individuals*
JEL - v42 - i1 - March 2004 - p201(2) [501+]

Perlmutter, David - *The Better Brain Book: The Best Tools for Improving Memory and Sharpness, and Preventing Aging of the Brain*
c PW - v251 - i35 - August 30 2004 - p47(2) [51-500]

Perlmutter, Richard - *Beethoven's Wig 2 More Singalong Symphonies (Read by Perlmutter, Richard). Audiobook Review*
c BL - v100 - i21 - July 2004 - p1856(1) [1-50]

Peterson, Nadene - *The Role of Work in People's Lives: Applied Career Counseling and Vocational Psychology, 2nd Ed.*
R&R Bk N - v19 - i4 - Nov 2004 - p109(1) [51-500]

Peterson, Paul E. - *The Future of School Choice*
Choice - v42 - i2 - Oct 2004 - p343(1) [51-500]
No Child Left Behind? The Politics and Practice of School Accountability
Choice - v41 - i11-12 - July-August 2004 - p2097(1) [501+]
TCR - v106 - i8 - August 2004 - p1623(5) [501+]

Peterson, Peter G. - *Running on Empty: How the Democratic and Republican Parties Are Bankrupting Our Future and What Americans Can Do about It*
BL - v100 - i22 - August 2004 - p1881(1) [51-500]
Bus W - i3897 - August 30 2004 - p28 [501+]
BW - v34 - i29 - July 18 2004 - p3(1) [1-50]
NYT - August 12 2004 - pE9 [501+]

Peterson, Randall S. - *Leading and Managing People in the Dynamic Organization*
NACEJou - v64 - i2 - Wntr 2004 - p14(1) [501+]
Per Psy - v57 - i4 - Winter 2004 - p1052(4) [501+]

Peterson, Susan - *Feat of Clay: Five Decades of Jerry Rothman*
Am Craft - v64 - i2 - April-May 2004 - p30(1) [501+]
Ceram Mo - v52 - i6 - June-August 2004 - p30(1) [501+]
Shoji Hamada: A Potter's Way and Work
Ceram Mo - v52 - i7 - Sept 2004 - p78(2) [501+]

Peterson, Tiffany - *Greek Americans*
c SLJ - v50 - i11 - Nov 2004 - p126(1) [51-500]
Japanese Americans
c SLJ - v50 - i11 - Nov 2004 - p126(1) [51-500]

Peterson's Graduate Programs in Business, Education, Health, Information Studies, Law and Social Work, 2003, 37th Ed.,
R&R Bk N - v19 - i1 - Feb 2004 - pNA [51-500]

Peterson's Graduate Programs in Business, Health, Information Studies, Law and Social Work, 2004, 38th Ed.,
R&R Bk N - v19 - i1 - Feb 2004 - pNA [1-50]

Peterson's Nursing Programs 2005
SciTech - v28 - i4 - Dec 2004 - p121 [51-500]

Petey-Girard, Bruno - *Les Meditations chretiennes d'un parlementaire: Etude sur les premieres oeuvres de piete de Guillaume du Vair*
Ren Q - v57 - i3 - Fall 2004 - p1021(2) [501+]

Pething, Rudiger - *Challenges to the World Economy: Festschrift for Horst Siebert*
JEL - v41 - i4 - Dec 2003 - p1336(1) [501+]

Petie-Roulet, Philippe - *Music Is*
LibMed - v22 - i4 - Jan 2004 - p79(2) [501+]

Petit, Jorge R. - *Handbook of Emergency Psychiatry*
SciTech - v28 - i1 - March 2004 - p98(1) [51-500]

Petkov, Kiril - *The Kiss of Peace: Ritual, Self, and Society in the High and Late Medieval West*
CHR - v90 - i4 - Oct 2004 - p753(2) [501+]

Petkovic, Milan - *Content-Based Video Retrieval: A Database Perspective*
SciTech - v28 - i1 - March 2004 - p145(1) [51-500]

Petman, Jarna - *Nordic Cosmopolitanism: Essays in International Law for Martti Koskenniemi*
R&R Bk N - v19 - i3 - August 2004 - p211(1) [1-50]

Petraco, Nicholas - *Color Atlas and Manual of Microscopy for Criminalists, Chemists, and Conservators*
SciTech - v28 - i1 - March 2004 - p60(1) [51-500]

Petrakis, Harry Mark - *The Orchards of Ithaca*
BL - v100 - i22 - August 2004 - p1901(1) [501+]
KR - v72 - i13 - July 1 2004 - p601(1) [51-500]
LJ - v129 - i13 - August 2004 - p69(1) [51-500]

Petrarca, Francesco - *My Secret Book*
YR - v92 - i3 - July 2004 - p143-159 [501+]
Petrarch's Guide to the Holy Land: Itinerary to the Sepulcher of Our Lord Jesus Christ
YR - v92 - i3 - July 2004 - p143-159 [501+]
The Poetry of Petrarch
LJ - v129 - i12 - July 2004 - p88(1) [51-500]
YR - v92 - i3 - July 2004 - p143-159 [501+]

Petras, James - *The New Development Politics: The Age of Empire Building and New Social Movements*
Choice - v41 - i7 - March 2004 - p1369(1) [501+]
R&R Bk N - v19 - i1 - Feb 2004 - p82(1) [1-50]

Petrella, Ivan - *The Future of Liberation Theology: An Argument and Manifesto*
Choice - v42 - i6 - Feb 2005 - p1040(1) [51-500]
R&R Bk N - v19 - i4 - Nov 2004 - p24(1) [51-500]

Petri, Fabio - *General Equilibrium: Problems and Prospects*
JEL - v42 - i4 - Dec 2004 - p1125(2) [501+]

Petri, Gail G. - *American Memory Collection from A-Z: Grade 4-6*
LibMed - v22 - i5 - Feb 2004 - p84(1) [501+]
American Memory Collection from A-Z: Grade 7-9
LibMed - v22 - i5 - Feb 2004 - p84(1) [501+]

Petri, Gyorgy - *Petri Gyorgy osszegyujtott munkai I: Versek*
WLT - v78 - i3-4 - Sept-Dec 2004 - p107(2) [501+]

Petridis, Constantine - *South of the Sahara: Selected Works of African Art*
Choice - v41 - i11-12 - July-August 2004 - p2032(2) [501+]

Petrie, Kristin - *The Food Pyramid*
c SLJ - v50 - i10 - Oct 2004 - pS24(1) [1-50]
Nutrition Anyone?
c SLJ - v50 - i10 - Oct 2004 - pS24(1) [1-50]
Vitamins Are Vital
c SLJ - v50 - i10 - Oct 2004 - pS24(1) [1-50]

Petrina, Alessandra - *Cultural Politics in Fifteenth-Century England: The Case of Humphrey, Duke of Gloucester*
Choice - v42 - i3 - Nov 2004 - p554(1) [1-50]

Petro, Joseph - *Standing Next to History: An Agent's Life Inside the Secret Service*
BL - v101 - i9-10 - Jan 1 2005 - p792(1) [1-50]
LJ - v130 - i1 - Jan 1 2005 - p129(1) [51-500]
PW - v251 - i46 - Nov 15 2004 - p51(2) [51-500]

Petronella, Mary Melvin - *Victorian Boston Today: Twelve Walking Tours*
R&R Bk N - v19 - i4 - Nov 2004 - p64(1) [51-500]

Petroski, Henry - *Pushing the Limits: New Adventures in Engineering*
BL - v100 - i22 - August 2004 - p1885(1) [51-500]
BW - v34 - i42 - Oct 17 2004 - p8(2) [501+]
KR - v72 - i13 - July 1 2004 - p621(1) [501+]
LJ - v129 - i13 - August 2004 - p115(1) [51-500]
New Sci - v183 - i2465 - Sept 18 2004 - p47(1) [51-500]
PW - v251 - i28 - July 12 2004 - p56(1) [51-500]
y SB - v40 - i6 - Nov-Dec 2004 - p263(1) [51-500]

Petrovic, Rastko - *Prepiska: Priredila i komentare napisala Radmila Suljagic*
WLT - v78 - i3-4 - Sept-Dec 2004 - p140(1) [501+]

Petrovna, Tanya - *The Native Foods Restaurant Cookbook*
Veg J - v23 - i4 - July-August 2004 - p31(1) [51-500]

Petrucci, Ottaviano - *Motetti de Passione, de Cruce, de Sacramento, de Beata Virgine et huiusmodi B, Venice, 1503*
Notes - v61 - i1 - Sept 2004 - p222(5) [501+]

Petry, Yvonne - *Gender, Kabbalah, and the Reformation: The Mystical Theology of Guillaume Postel, 1510-1581*
R&R Bk N - v19 - i3 - August 2004 - p21(1) [1-50]

Petti, Ken - *Zenda and the Gazing Ball*
c SLJ - v50 - i9 - Sept 2004 - p215(2) [51-500]

Pettigrew, Mark - *Planet Earth*
c BL - v101 - i7 - Dec 1 2004 - p668(1) [51-500]

Pettit, Alexander - *Eighteenth-Century British Erotica II*
Choice - v42 - i2 - Oct 2004 - p292(1) [501+]
Eight-C St - v37 - i3 - Spring 2004 - p474-478 [501+]

Pettit, Norman - *The Heart Renewed: Assurance of Salvation in New England Spiritual Life*
R&R Bk N - v19 - i4 - Nov 2004 - p20(1) [51-500]

Pettitt, Clare - *Patent Inventions: Intellectual Property and the Victorian Novel*
TLS - i5300 - Oct 29 2004 - p28(1) [501+]

Pettman, Ralph - *Reason, Culture, Religion: The Metaphysics of World Politics*
Choice - v42 - i4 - Dec 2004 - p734(1) [1-50]

Petty, Grant W. - *A First Course in Atmospheric Radiation*
Choice - v42 - i1 - Sept 2004 - p523(1) [1-50]

Petty, Kate - *Makeover*
y Sch Lib - v52 - i3 - Autumn 2004 - p161(1) [501+]

Petuch, Edward J. - *Cenozoic Seas: The View from Eastern North America*
Choice - v42 - i1 - Sept 2004 - p135(1) [501+]
SciTech - v28 - i1 - March 2004 - p57(1) [51-500]

Petz, Lawrence D. - *Immune Hemolytic Anemia, 2nd Ed.*
SciTech - v28 - i1 - March 2004 - p103(1) [51-500]

Petz, Moritz - *The Bad Mood! (Illus. by Jackowski, Amelie)*
c SLJ - v50 - i11 - Nov 2004 - p114(1) [51-500]
Mona the Monster Girl (Illus. by James, J. Alison)
c SLJ - v51 - i2 - Feb 2005 - p108(1) [51-500]

Peurifoy, Reneau Z. - *Anxiety, Phobias, and Panic: A Step-by-Step Program for Regaining Control of Your Life*
LJ - v129 - i20 - Dec 1 2004 - p143(2) [51-500]

Peursen, W.Th. van - *The Verbal System in the Hebrew Text of Ben Sira*
R&R Bk N - v19 - i2 - May 2004 - pNA [501+]

Pevsner, Jonathan - *Bioinformatics and Functional Genomics*
Choice - v41 - i7 - March 2004 - p1320(1) [501+]
SciTech - v28 - i1 - March 2004 - p63(1) [51-500]

Peyre, Yves - *Art Deco Bookbindings: The Work of Pierre Legrain and Rose Adler*
R&R Bk N - v19 - i4 - Nov 2004 - p254(1) [501+]

Peyton, K.M. - *Blind Beauty (Read by Paull, Nicki). Audiobook Review*
y Kliatt - v39 - i2 - March 2005 - p48(1) [51-500]
VOYA - v27 - i5 - Dec 2004 - p372(1) [501+]
Blind Beauty
c SLJ - v50 - i8 - August 2004 - p77(1) [51-500]
Stealaway (Illus. by Wyatt, David)
c CCB-B - v58 - i4 - Dec 2004 - p180(1) [51-500]
c KR - v72 - i16 - August 15 2004 - p811(1) [51-500]
SLJ - v50 - i12 - Dec 2004 - p117(1) [501+]

Pezer, Vera - *Stone Age: A Social History of Curling on the Prairies*
CBRA - Annual 2003 - p145(1) [51-500]

Pezzimenti, Rocco - *The Political Thought of Lord Acton: The English Catholics in the Nineteenth Century*
MA - v46 - i3 - Summer 2004 - p255(7) [501+]

Pfaff, Christopher A. - *The Architecture of the Classical Temple of Hera*
R&R Bk N - v19 - i1 - Feb 2004 - p201(1) [51-500]

Pfaff, Francoise - *Focus on African Films*
Choice - v42 - i6 - Feb 2005 - p1029(1) [51-500]

Pfaff, William - *The Bullet's Song: Romantic Violence and Utopia*
BL - v101 - i4 - Oct 15 2004 - p369(1) [51-500]
Globe & Mail - Jan 1 2005 - pD5 [501+]
KR - v72 - i18 - Sept 15 2004 - p905(1) [501+]
Nation - v279 - i21 - Dec 20 2004 - p31 [501+]
PW - v251 - i40 - Oct 4 2004 - p79(1) [51-500]

Pfaffenberger, Brian - *HTML, XHTML, and CSS Bible, 3rd Ed.*
SciTech - v28 - i3 - Sept 2004 - p26(1) [51-500]

Pfannestiel, Todd J. - *Rethinking the Red Scare: The Lusk Committee and New York's Crusade Against Radicalism, 1919-1923*
JAH - v91 - i3 - Dec 2004 - p1066(2) [501+]

Pfarrer, Donald - *The Fearless Man: A Novel of Vietnam*
KR - v72 - i16 - August 15 2004 - p771(1) [51-500]
NYTBR - Nov 7 2004 - p23 [501+]
PW - v251 - i41 - Oct 11 2004 - p57(1) [51-500]
TLS - i5305 - Dec 3 2004 - p22(1) [501+]
LJ - v129 - i18 - Nov 1 2004 - p77(1) [501+]

Pfeffer, Wendy - *From Seed to Pumpkin (Illus. by Hale, James Graham)*
c BL - v101 - i3 - Oct 1 2004 - p332(1) [51-500]
c SLJ - v50 - i10 - Oct 2004 - p147(1) [51-500]
The Shortest Day: Celebrating the Winter Solstice
LibMed - v22 - i7 - April-May 2004 - p79(1) [501+]
Wiggling Worms at Work
c CE - v81 - i2 - Winter 2004 - p109(1) [1-50]
c SB - v40 - i3 - May-June 2004 - p133(1) [501+]

Pfeifer, Jeff - *High Pressure Technology 2004: Innovations and Advances in High Pressure Technology: Proceedings*
SciTech - v28 - i4 - Dec 2004 - p163(1) [51-500]

Pfeifer, Michael J. - *Rough Justice: Lynching and American Society, 1874-1947*
Choice - v42 - i6 - Feb 2005 - p1083(1) [51-500]
Law&PolBR - Nov 2004 - pNA [501+]

Pfeiffer, Raymond S. - *Ethics on the Job: Cases and Strategies, 3rd Ed.*
R&R Bk N - v19 - i2 - May 2004 - p113(1) [51-500]

Pfeiffer, Ronald P. - *Concepts of Athletic Training, 4th Ed.*
SciTech - v28 - i4 - Dec 2004 - p106(1) [51-500]

Pfenninger, John L. - *Pfenninger and Fowler's Procedures for Primary Care, 2nd Ed.*
SciTech - v28 - i1 - March 2004 - p88(1) [51-500]

Pfiffner, James P. - *The Character Factor: How We Judge America's Presidents*
　　Choice - v42 - i3 - Nov 2004 - p566-1 [1-50]
　　Pres St Q - v34 - i4 - Dec 2004 - p894(3) [501+]
　　PSQ - v119 - i3 - Fall 2004 - p528(2) [501+]
The Modern Presidency, 4th Ed.
　　R&R Bk N - v19 - i3 - August 2004 - p178(1) [501+]

Pfister, Joel - *Individuality Incorporated: Indians and the Multicultural Modern*
　　Choice - v42 - i4 - Dec 2004 - p723(1) [1-50]

Pfisterer, Ulrich - *Donatello und die Entdeckung der Stile 1430-1445*
　　Ren Q - v57 - i3 - Fall 2004 - p989(3) [501+]

Pfitzer, Gregory M. - *Picturing the Past: Illustrated Histories and the American Imagination, 1840-1900*
　　JAH - v91 - i2 - Sept 2004 - p645(2) [501+]

Pflaum, William D. - *The Technology Fix: The Promise and Reality of Computers in Our Schools*
　　Adoles - v39 - i155 - Fall 2004 - p625(2) [51-500]
　　Choice - v42 - i2 - Oct 2004 - p345(1) [51-500]

Pflugfelder, Stephen C. - *Dry Eye and Ocular Surface Disorders*
　　SciTech - v28 - i4 - Dec 2004 - p109(1) [51-500]

Pfragner, Roswitha - *Culture of Human Tumor Cells*
　　E-Streams - August 2004 - pNA [501+]
　　SciTech - v28 - i1 - March 2004 - p90(1) [51-500]

Phaedrus - *Aesop's Human Zoo: Roman Stories about Our Bodies*
　　TLS - i5298 - Oct 15 2004 - p36(1) [501+]

The Phaidon Atlas of Contemporary World Architecture
　　Globe & Mail - July 17 2004 - pD8 [501+]
　　TLS - i5300 - Oct 29 2004 - p9(1) [501+]

Pham, John-Peter - *Heirs of the Fisherman: Behind the Scenes of Papal Death and Succession*
　　BW - v35 - i4 - Jan 30 2005 - p1(2) [501+]
　　KR - v72 - i21 - Nov 1 2004 - p1040(1) [501+]
　　LJ - v129 - i20 - Dec 1 2004 - p125(2) [51-500]
　　PW - v251 - i48 - Nov 29 2004 - p37(1) [51-500]
Liberia: Portrait of a Failed State
　　Choice - v42 - i3 - Nov 2004 - p558(1) [1-50]
　　For Aff - v83 - i5 - Sept-Oct 2004 - p164 [501+]
　　Wil Q - v28 - i4 - Autumn 2004 - p118(3) [501+]

Pham, LeUyen - *Twenty-one Elephants*
　c　KR - v72 - i19 - Oct 1 2004 - p956(1) [501+]

Pham, Quang X. - *A Sense of Duty: My Father, My American Journey*
　　KR - v73 - i5 - March 1 2005 - p280(1) [501+]
　　PW - v252 - i11 - March 14 2005 - p60(1) [51-500]

Phan, Aimee - *We Should Never Meet*
　　BL - v101 - i2 - Sept 15 2004 - p210(1) [501+]
　　KR - v72 - i15 - August 1 2004 - p709(1) [501+]
　　PW - v251 - i35 - August 30 2004 - p31(1) [501+]

Phan, Peter C. - *The Asian Synod: Texts and Commentaries*
　　Theol St - v65 - i3 - Sept 2004 - p679(2) [501+]
Christianity with an Asian Face: Asian American Theology in the Making
　　JAAR - v72 - i4 - Dec 2004 - p1062(3) [501+]
　　Theol St - v65 - i4 - Dec 2004 - p870(2) [501+]
　　TT - v60 - i4 - Jan 2004 - p592-594 [501+]

Phares, Don - *Metropolitan Governance Without Metropolitan Government?*
　　R&R Bk N - v19 - i4 - Nov 2004 - p158(1) [501+]

Pharr, Mary - *Fantastic Odysseys: Selected Essays from the Twenty-Second International Conference on the Fantastic in the Arts*
　　Ext - v45 - i2 - Summer 2004 - p205(4) [501+]

Pheffer, Wendy - *Dolphin Talk: Whistles, Clicks, and Clapping Jaws (Illus. by Davie, Helen)*
　c　LibMed - v22 - i6 - March 2004 - p72(1) [501+]

Phegley, Jennifer - *Educating the Proper Woman Reader: Victorian Family Literary Magazines and the Cultural Health of the Nation*
　　Choice - v42 - i5 - Jan 2005 - p855(1) [1-50]

Phelan, James - *Living to Tell about It: A Rhetoric and Ethics of Character Narration*
　　Choice - v42 - i6 - Feb 2005 - p1019(1) [51-500]

Phelan, Twist - *Family Claims*
　　BooChiTr - March 7 2004 - p3(1) [501+]

Phelps, Michael E. - *PET: Molecular Imaging and Its Biological Applications*
　　TimHES - v0 - i1680 - Feb 25 2005 - p29(1) [501+]

Phelps, Ned - *Celebrating Ned*
　　JEL - v42 - i3 - Sept 2004 - p811(11) [501+]

Phelps, Nicholas - *The New Competition for Inward Investment: Companies, Institutions and Territorial Development*
　　JEL - v42 - i1 - March 2004 - p263(1) [501+]
　　R&R Bk N - v19 - i1 - Feb 2004 - p117(1) [51-500]

Phelps, W. Chris - *Charlestonians in War: The Charleston Battalion*
　　R&R Bk N - v19 - i4 - Nov 2004 - p62(1) [51-500]

Phenix, Jo - *Reading Teacher's Handbook*
　　CBRA - Annual 2003 - p395(2) [51-500]
Writing Teacher's Handbook
　　CBRA - Annual 2003 - p395(2) [51-500]

Phenix, Patricia - *Eatonians: The Story of the Family Behind the Family*
　　CBRA - Annual 2003 - p332(1) [51-500]

Phifer, Paul - *College Majors and Careers: A Resource Guide for Effective Life Planning, 5th Ed.*
　　R&R Bk N - v19 - i2 - May 2004 - p113(1) [1-50]

Phil, Bradley - *The Advanced Internet Searcher's Handbook, 3rd Ed.*
　　Choice - v42 - i6 - Feb 2005 - p989(1) [51-500]

Philander, S. George - *Our Affair with El Nino: How We Transformed an Enchanting Peruvian Current into a Global Climate Hazard*
　　Am Sci - v92 - i4 - July-August 2004 - p388(1) [501+]
　　Choice - v42 - i4 - Dec 2004 - p687(2) [1-50]
　　Nature - v429 - i6992 - June 10 2004 - p605(2) [501+]
　　NH - v113 - i6 - July-August 2004 - p56(2) [501+]
　y　SB - v40 - i4 - July-August 2004 - p165(2) [51-500]
　　SB - v40 - i6 - Nov-Dec 2004 - p242(1) [51-500]
　　TimHES - v0 - i1659 - Sept 24 2004 - p25(1) [501+]

Philaretou, Andreas G. - *Perils of Masculinity: An Analysis of Male Sexual Anxiety, Sexual Addiction, and Relational Abuse*
　　SciTech - v28 - i3 - Sept 2004 - p96(1) [51-500]

Philbrick, Nathaniel - *Revenge of the Whale: The True Story of the Whaleship Essex (Read by Mali, Taylor). Audiobook Review*
　y　PW - v252 - i2 - Jan 10 2005 - p24(1) [51-500]
Sea of Glory: America's Voyage of Discovery: The U.S. Exploring Expedition, 1838-1842
　　BIC - v33 - i2 - March 2004 - p18(4) [501+]
　　NYTBR - Jan 9 2005 - p22 [501+]

Philbrick, Stephen - *Three*
　　Ga R - v58 - i1 - Spring 2004 - p167-178 [501+]

Philbrick, W.R. - *The Young Man and the Sea*
　y　LibMed - v22 - i7 - April-May 2004 - p62(1) [501+]
　　SLJ - v50 - i10 - Oct 2004 - pS54(1) [51-500]
　y　VOYA - v27 - i3 - August 2004 - p224(1) [1-50]

Philip, Bennett E. - *The Cycle of Guillaume d'Orange or Grain de Molglane: A Critical Bibliography*
　　Choice - v42 - i5 - Jan 2005 - p824(1) [51-500]

Philip, Franklin - *Michael, Prince of Greece*
　　BL - v101 - i2 - Sept 15 2004 - p209(1) [501+]

Philip, Graham - *Ceramics and Change in the Early Bronze Age of the Southern Levant*
　　JNES - v63 - i4 - Oct 2004 - p319(2) [501+]

Philip, John - *Contested Empire: Peter Skene Ogdene and the Snake River Expeditions*
　　WHQ - v35 - i2 - Summer 2004 - p249-250 [501+]

Philip, Kavita - *Civilizing Natures: Race, Resources, and Modernity in Colonial South India*
　　SciTech - v28 - i3 - Sept 2004 - p13(1) [501+]

Philip, Neil - *Mythology of the World (Illus. by Palin, Nicki)*
　y　BL - v101 - i7 - Dec 1 2004 - p645(2) [51-500]
　y　SLJ - v50 - i10 - Oct 2004 - p193(1) [51-500]

Philip, Robert - *Performing Music in the Age of Recording*
　　Choice - v42 - i3 - Nov 2004 - p493(1) [51-500]
　　MT - v145 - i1889 - Winter 2004 - p98-100 [501+]

Philippo, Susanna - *Silent Witness: Racine's Non-Verbal Annotations of Euripides*
　　FS - v58 - i3 - July 2004 - p408-409 [501+]

Philippon, Daniel J. - *Conserving Words: How American Nature Writers Shaped the Environmental Movement*
　　Choice - v41 - i11-12 - July-August 2004 - p2066(1) [501+]

Philippot, Pierre - *The Regulation of Emotion*
　　Choice - v42 - i6 - Feb 2005 - p1103(1) [51-500]
　　SciTech - v28 - i3 - Sept 2004 - p2(1) [501+]

Philips, John - *Jivin' Johnny's Reel Talk 1...Making the Movie Magic Last*
　　CBRA - Annual 2003 - p105(2) [51-500]
Jivin' Johnny's Reel Talk 2...Making the Movie Magic Last
　　CBRA - Annual 2003 - p105(2) [51-500]

Philipson, Sandra J. - *Max's Rules*
　c　CH Bwatch - v14 - i11 - Nov 2004 - pNA [51-500]

Phillips, Alan - *Chess: 60 Years on with Caissa and Friends*
　　Spec - v297 - i9206 - Jan 15 2005 - p62(1) [501+]

Phillips, Alastair - *City of Darkness, City of Light: Emigre Filmmakers in Paris 1929-1939*
　　TimHES - v0 - i1674 - Jan 14 2005 - p27(1) [501+]

Phillips, Arthur - *The Egyptologist*
　　BW - v34 - i39 - Sept 26 2004 - p11(1) [1-50]
　　BW - v34 - i40 - Oct 3 2004 - p6(1) [501+]
　　Ent W - i781 - Sept 3 2004 - p80 [51-500]
　　Esq - v142 - i3 - Sept 2004 - p90(1) [51-500]
　　KR - v72 - i15 - August 1 2004 - p710(1) [501+]
　　LJ - v129 - i12 - July 2004 - p73(1) [51-500]
　　People - v62 - i9 - August 30 2004 - p49 [51-500]
　　People - Dec 27 2004 - p63 [501+]
　　PW - v251 - i27 - July 5 2004 - p35(1) [51-500]
　　NYTBR - Sept 12 2004 - p8(L) [501+]

Phillips, Barbara - *Obstructive Sleep Apnea*
　　SciTech - v28 - i3 - Sept 2004 - p107(1) [51-500]

Phillips, Brigitte M. - *American Dictionary of Writer's Guidelines*
　　Bwatch - Feb 2005 - pNA [51-500]

Phillips, Bruce - *Proceedings of the Third World Fisheries Congress: Feeding the World with Fish in the Next Millenium--The Balance between Production and Environment*
　　QRB - v79 - i3 - Sept 2004 - p321(3) [501+]
　　SciTech - v28 - i1 - March 2004 - p132(1) [51-500]

Phillips, Carl - *Coin of the Realm: Essays on the Life and Art of Poetry*
　　Black Iss - v6 - i6 - Nov-Dec 2004 - p46(1) [51-500]
　　Lam Bk Rpt - v13 - i4-5 - Nov-Dec 2004 - p14(2) [501+]
The Rest of Love
　　NYTBR - Jan 30 2005 - p24 [501+]
　　Poet - v184 - i5 - Sept 2004 - p387(2) [51-500]

Phillips, Carlene - *Marie Antoinette and the Decline of French Monarchy*
　y　SLJ - v50 - i12 - Dec 2004 - p163(1) [51-500]

Phillips, Carly - *Hot Stuff*
　　PW - v251 - i28 - July 12 2004 - p49(1) [51-500]
Stroke of Midnight
　　PW - v251 - i36 - Sept 6 2004 - p51(1) [51-500]
Under the Boardwalk
　　BW - v34 - i43 - Oct 24 2004 - p13(1) [501+]

Phillips, Caryl - *A Distant Shore*
　　HR - v57 - i2 - Summer 2004 - p311-316 [501+]

Phillips, Charles - *Encyclopedia of Wars, Vols. 1-3*
　　LJ - v130 - i4 - March 1 2005 - p114(1) [51-500]

Phillips, Christopher - *Six Questions of Socrates: A Modern-Day Journey of Discovery through World Philosophy*
　y　SLJ - v50 - i7 - July 2004 - p134(1) [51-500]

Phillips, Clifford H. - *The Lady Named Thunder: A Biography of Dr. Ethel Margaret Phillips*
　　CBRA - Annual 2003 - p63(1) [501+]
　　IBMR - v28 - i4 - Oct 2004 - p185(2) [501+]

Phillips, D.C. - *Prespectives of Learning*
　　TCR - v106 - i8 - August 2004 - p1592(4) [501+]

Phillips, Dana - *The Truth of Ecology: Nature, Culture, and Literature in America*
　　AL - v76 - i2 - June 2004 - p409(3) [501+]
　　NEQ - v77 - i2 - June 2004 - p300-307 [501+]

Phillips, Dave - *Center Field on Fire: An Umpire's Life with Pine Tar Bats, Spitballs, and Corked Personalities*
　　BooChiTr - May 9 2004 - p4(1) [501+]

Phillips, David J. - *Sport and Festival in the Ancient Greek World*
　　R&R Bk N - v19 - i4 - Nov 2004 - p80(1) [51-500]

Phillips, Debra - *Too Much Drama*
　　KR - v73 - i3 - Feb 1 2005 - p144(1) [501+]

Phillips, Donald T. - *Character in Action: The U.S. Coast Guard on Leadership*
　　NWCR - v57 - Autumn 2004 - p166(2) [501+]

Phillips, Dwayne - *The Software Project Manager's Handbook: Principles That Work at Work, 2nd Ed.*
　　SciTech - v28 - i3 - Sept 2004 - p28(1) [51-500]

Phillips, Edward O. - *A Voyage on Sunday*
　　Globe & Mail - July 10 2004 - pD6 [501+]

Book Review Index 2005 Cumulation **PIMLICO • 479**

Pickering, Sam - *Letters to a Teacher*
BL - v101 - i5 - Nov 1 2004 - p448(1) [51-500]
KR - v72 - i19 - Oct 1 2004 - p951(1) [501+]
LJ - v130 - i1 - Jan 1 2005 - p126(1) [51-500]
PW - v251 - i48 - Nov 29 2004 - p30(1) [51-500]
Pickering, Sharon - *Clinical Governance and Best Value: Meeting the Modernisation Agenda*
SciTech - v28 - i1 - March 2004 - p81(1) [51-500]
Pickett, Frieda - *The Medical History: Clinical Implications and Emergency Prevention in Dental Settings*
SciTech - v28 - i4 - Dec 2004 - p114(1) [1-50]
Pickett, R. Stewart - *Pickett's Charge*
Globe & Mail - Nov 6 2004 - pD27 [501+]
Pickett, Rex - *Sideways*
Globe & Mail - Feb 26 2005 - pD13 [1-50]
Pickett, S.T.A. - *The Ecology of Natural Disturbances and Patch Dynamics*
Globe & Mail - Jan 1 2005 - pD15 [501+]
Pickles, Katie - *Female Imperialism and National Identity: Imperial Order Daughters of the Empire*
Albion - v36 - i2 - Summer 2004 - p389(2) [501+]
Pickles, Tim - *New Orleans 1815: Andrew Jackson Crushes the British*
R&R Bk N - v19 - i4 - Nov 2004 - p60(1) [51-500]
Pickover, Clifford A. - *Calculus and Pizza: A Cookbook for the Hungry Mind*
Math T - v97 - i4 - April 2004 - p300-300 [501+]
Pickvance, Chris - *Local Environmental Regulation in Post-Socialism: A Hungarian Case Study*
AJS - v110 - i3 - Nov 2004 - p799(2) [501+]
R&R Bk N - v19 - i1 - Feb 2004 - p84(1) [51-500]
Picoult, Jodi - *My Sister's Keeper: A Novel*
BL - v101 - i9-10 - Jan 1 2005 - p771(1) [51-500]
y SLJ - v51 - i1 - Jan 2005 - p159(1) [51-500]
y VOYA - v27 - i5 - Dec 2004 - p392(1) [51-500]
My Sister's Keeper. Audiobook Review
c BL - v101 - i5 - Nov 1 2004 - p504(2) [51-500]
y Kliatt - v39 - i2 - March 2005 - p55(1) [51-500]
LJ - v130 - i1 - Jan 1 2005 - p168(1) [51-500]
Vanishing Acts
KR - v73 - i1 - Jan 1 2005 - p16(1) [501+]
People - v63 - i11 - March 21 2005 - p59 [51-500]
PW - v252 - i6 - Feb 7 2005 - p43(1) [51-500]
Ent W - i809 - March 4 2005 - p79 [51-500]
Picthall, Chez - *My First Canadian Trucks*
c CBRA - Annual 2003 - p464(1) [51-500]
My First Canadian Words
c CBRA - Annual 2003 - p464(1) [51-500]
Pidd, Michael - *Systems Modelling: Theory and Practice*
R&R Bk N - v19 - i3 - August 2004 - p102(1) [501+]
Pidgeon, Nick F. - *The Social Amplification of Risk*
CS - v33 - i5 - Sept 2004 - p626-626 [501+]
Piedmont, Ralph L. - *Research in the Social Scientific Study of Religion*
R&R Bk N - v19 - i1 - Feb 2004 - p11(1) [51-500]
Piel, Jean - *Entre communidad nacion: La historia de Guatemala revisitada desde lo local y lo regional*
HAHR - v84 - i4 - Nov 2004 - p754(2) [501+]
Pienkowski, Jan - *The First Noel: A Christmas Carousel (Illus. by Pienkowski, Jan)*
HB - v80 - i6 - Nov-Dec 2004 - p662(1) [51-500]
Piepenbrink, K. - *Philosophie und Lebenswelt in der Ankite*
Class R - v54 - i2 - Nov 2004 - p423(3) [501+]
Pieper, Hans-Joachim - *Musils Philosophie. Essayismus und Dichtung im Spannungsfeld der Theorien Nietzsches und Machs*
MLN - v119 - i3 - April 2004 - p630-634 [501+]
Piepho, Lee - *Holofernes' Mantuan: Italian Humanism in Early Modern England*
Six Ct J - v35 - i1 - Spring 2004 - p275(2) [501+]
Pier, Gerald B. - *Immunology, Infection and Immunity*
SciTech - v28 - i3 - Sept 2004 - p74(1) [51-500]
Pierangelo, Roger - *The Special Educator's Survival Guide, 2nd Ed.*
R&R Bk N - v19 - i4 - Nov 2004 - p192(1) [501+]
Pierce, Christine - *Immovable Laws, Irresistible Rights: Natural Law, Moral Rights, and Feminist Ethics*
Ethics - v114 - i4 - July 2004 - p862(1) [501+]
Pierce, Hazel - *Margaret Pole, Countess of Salisbury, 1473-1541: Loyalty, Lineage and Leadership*
Ren Q - v57 - i3 - Fall 2004 - p1111(2) [501+]
TLS - i5266 - March 5 2004 - p4-6 [501+]
Pierce, J. Kingston - *Eccentric Seattle: Pillars and Pariahs Who Made the City Not Such a Boring Place After All*
R&R Bk N - v19 - i1 - Feb 2004 - p65(1) [501+]
Pierce, John R. - *Yellow Jack: How Yellow Fever Ravaged America and Walter Reed Discovered Its Deadly Secrets*
PW - v252 - i3 - Jan 17 2005 - p41(1) [51-500]
Pierce, Karen - *Yoga Bear: Yoga for Youngsters (Illus. by Brinkman, Paula)*
c SLJ - v51 - i1 - Jan 2005 - p113(1) [51-500]
Pierce, Mary - *Confessions of a Prayer Wimp: My Fumbling, Faltering Foibles in Faith*
c PW - v251 - i48 - Nov 29 2004 - p37(1) [51-500]
Pierce, Meredith Ann - *Waters Luminous and Deep: Shorter Fictions*
y VOYA - v27 - i3 - August 2004 - p233(1) [1-50]
Pierce, Patrick A. - *Gambling Politics: State Government and the Business of Betting*
Choice - v42 - i6 - Feb 2005 - p1099(1) [51-500]
Pierce, Tamora - *Briar's Book. Audiobook Review*
y BL - v101 - i7 - Dec 1 2004 - p678(1) [1-50]
y Kliatt - v39 - i2 - March 2005 - p50(1) [51-500]
Daja's Book: Circle of Magic. Audiobook Review
c Kliatt - v38 - i4 - July 2004 - p50(1) [51-500]
The Immortals Quartet
y Sch Lib - v52 - i4 - Winter 2004 - p212(1) [51-500]
Lady Knight
y Kliatt - v38 - i6 - Nov 2004 - p22(1) [51-500]
Trickster's Choice
y Kliatt - v38 - i6 - Nov 2004 - p22(2) [51-500]
y PW - v251 - i40 - Oct 4 2004 - p90(1) [51-500]
c SLJ - v50 - i8 - August 2004 - p78(1) [51-500]
Trickster's Queen (Read by Alvarado, Tina). Audiobook Review
y SLJ - v51 - i1 - Jan 2005 - p78(2) [51-500]
Trickster's Queen
y BL - v101 - i3 - Oct 1 2004 - p324(1) [51-500]
y CCB-B - v58 - i2 - Oct 2004 - p95(1) [51-500]
y Kliatt - v38 - i5 - Sept 2004 - p15(2) [51-500]
y KR - v72 - i17 - Sept 1 2004 - p872(1) [51-500]
y SLJ - v50 - i9 - Sept 2004 - p216(1) [51-500]
Pierce, Valerie - *Countdown to College: 21 "To Do" Lists for High School*
LibMed - v22 - i5 - Feb 2004 - p78(1) [501+]
Piercy, Marge - *Hannah Senesh: Her Life and Diary*
PW - v251 - i43 - Oct 25 2004 - p34(2) [51-500]
Pierlot, Holly - *A Mother's Rule of Life: How to Bring Order to Your Home and Peace to Your Soul*
CI - v12 - i9 - Oct 2004 - p44(1) [501+]
Pieroth, Doris H. - *The Hutton Settlement: A Home for One Man's Family*
WHQ - v35 - i4 - Winter 2004 - p516-516 [501+]
Pieroth, Doris Hinson - *Seattle's Women Teachers of the Interwar Years: Shapers of a Livable City*
Choice - v42 - i5 - Jan 2005 - p905(2) [1-50]
Pierre, D.B.C. - *Vernon God Little*
Globe & Mail - July 17 2004 - pD13 [1-50]
Pierre, Hadot - *What Is Ancient Philosophy?*
RM - v58 - i1 - Sept 2004 - p180(2) [501+]
Pierson, Christopher - *The Modern State, 2nd Ed.*
TimHES - v0 - i1668 - Nov 26 2004 - pVIII(1) [501+]
Pierson, Jan - *Goodbye God, I'm Going to Bodie*
CH Bwatch - v14 - i8 - August 2004 - p2(1) [51-500]
Pierson, Michael D. - *Free Hearts and Free Homes: Gender and American Antislavery Politics*
AHR - v109 - i4 - Oct 2004 - p1231(2) [501+]
HNet - Oct 2004 - pNA [501+]
JAH - v91 - i2 - Sept 2004 - p627(2) [501+]
JSH - v71 - i1 - Feb 2005 - p154(3) [501+]
Pietri, Annie - *Orange Trees of Versailles*
c CH Bwatch - v14 - i7 - July 2004 - p7(2) [501+]
Pietromarchi, Luca - *Les Anges sauvages: la 'Quete de joie' de Patrice de La Tour du Pin*
FS - v58 - i1 - Jan 2004 - p136(1) [501+]
Pietrusza, David - *Rothestein: The Life, Times and Murder of the Criminal Genius Who Fixed the 1919 World Series*
VQR - v80 - i2 - Spring 2004 - p264-264 [501+]
Pietrzyk, Leslie - *A Year and a Day*
y VOYA - v27 - i3 - August 2004 - p224(1) [1-50]
Pietrzyk, Mark E. - *International Order and Individual Liberty: Effects of War and Peace on the Development of Governments*
APJ - v18 - i3 - Fall 2004 - p124(2) [501+]
Pietschmann, Horst - *Atlantic History: History of the Atlantic System, 1580-1830*
HAHR - v84 - i4 - Nov 2004 - p719(2) [501+]
Piggott, Jan - *Palace of the People: The Crystal Palace at Sydenham, 1854-1936*
R&R Bk N - v19 - i4 - Nov 2004 - p204(1) [501+]
Piggott, Joan R. - *Women and Confucian Cultures in Premodern China, Korea, and Japan*
Ch Rev Int - v11 - i1 - Spring 2004 - p15(7) [501+]
Pigler, A. - *Plotin: une metaphysique de l'amour, L'amour comme structure du monde intelligible*
Class R - v54 - i2 - Nov 2004 - p347(3) [501+]
Pignone, Charles - *The Sinatra Treasures: Intimate Photos, Mementos, and Music from the Sinatra Family Collection*
Ent W - i788 - Oct 15 2004 - p78 [51-500]
PW - v251 - i28 - July 12 2004 - p50(2) [51-500]
Pigott, Charles - *A Political Dictionary Explaining the True Meaning of Words: A Facsimile of the 1795 Edition*
R&R Bk N - v19 - i3 - August 2004 - p38(1) [51-500]
Pigram, John J. - *Encyclopedia of Leisure and Outdoor Recreation*
Choice - v42 - i2 - Oct 2004 - p261(2) [51-500]
Pihlstrom, Sami - *Naturalizing the Transcendental: A Pragmatic View*
R&R Bk N - v19 - i1 - Feb 2004 - p5(1) [51-500]
Pike, Christopher - *Alosha*
y CCB-B - v58 - i1 - Sept 2004 - p34(2) [51-500]
y Kliatt - v38 - i4 - July 2004 - p12(1) [51-500]
y LJ - v129 - i12 - July 2004 - p76(1) [51-500]
c SLJ - v50 - i10 - Oct 2004 - p176(1) [51-500]
y VOYA - v27 - i4 - Oct 2004 - p318(1) [51-500]
Pike, Jeffrey A. - *Neck Injury: The Use of X-Rays, CTs, and MRIs to Study Crash-Related Injury Mechanisms*
SciTech - v28 - i1 - March 2004 - p111(1) [51-500]
Pike, Sarah M. - *New Age and Neopagan Religions in America*
Choice - v42 - i7 - March 2005 - p1243(2) [51-500]
NH - v113 - i9 - Nov 2004 - p46(5) [501+]
Pilard, Georges - *Pardon My French! Pocket French Slang Dictionary: French-English/English-French*
FS - v58 - i3 - July 2004 - p448-449 [501+]
Pilarz, Scott R. - *Robert Southwell and the Mission of Literature, 1561-1595: Writing Reconciliation*
Choice - v42 - i4 - Dec 2004 - p662(1) [1-50]
Pilbeam, Bruce - *Conservatism in Crisis? Anglo-American Conservative Ideology After the Cold War*
R&R Bk N - v19 - i1 - Feb 2004 - p149(1) [51-500]
Pilbeam, Pamela - *Madame Tussaud and the History of Waxworks*
AHR - v109 - i2 - April 2004 - p630(1) [501+]
Pilcher, Jane - *Fifty Key Concepts in Gender Studies*
Choice - v42 - i3 - Nov 2004 - p446(1) [1-50]
R&R Bk N - v19 - i3 - August 2004 - p152(1) [51-500]
Pilcher, Jeffery M. - *The Human Tradition in Mexico*
HAHR - v84 - i4 - Nov 2004 - p721(2) [501+]
Pile, John F. - *A History of Interior Design, 2nd Ed.*
R&R Bk N - v19 - i4 - Nov 2004 - p209(1) [501+]
Pilegard, Virginia Walton - *The Warlord's Kites (Illus. by Debon, Nicolas)*
c BL - v101 - i6 - Nov 15 2004 - p591(1) [51-500]
c SLJ - v51 - i2 - Feb 2005 - p108(1) [51-500]
The Warlord's Puppeteers (Illus. by Debon, Nicolas)
c TC Math - v11 - i4 - Nov 2004 - p239(1) [501+]
Pilkey, Dav - *The Adventures of Super Diaper Baby (Illus. by Pilkey, Dav)*
c RT - v57 - Oct 2003 - p173 [1-50]
Ricky Ricotta's Mighty Robot vs. the Mecha-Monkeys from Mars (Illus. by Ontiveros, Martin)
c RT - v57 - Oct 2003 - p174 [1-50]
Pilkey, Orrin H. - *A Celebration of the World's Barrier Islands*
TimHES - v0 - i1648 - July 9 2004 - p30(1) [501+]
Pilkey, Walter D. - *Formulas for Stress, Strain, and Structural Matrices, 2nd Ed.*
SciTech - v28 - i4 - Dec 2004 - p133 [51-500]
Pilkington, Andrew - *Racial Disadvantage and Ethnic Diversity in Britain*
Albion - v36 - i2 - Summer 2004 - p368(2) [501+]
CS - v33 - i4 - July 2004 - p424(3) [501+]
Pilkington, John - *The Mapmaker's Daughter*
BL - v101 - i9-10 - Jan 1 2005 - p828(1) [1-50]
KR - v73 - i3 - Feb 1 2005 - p154(1) [51-500]
PW - v252 - i9 - Feb 28 2005 - p45(1) [51-500]
Pilkington, Thomas - *The Ramage Hawk*
BL - v100 - i22 - August 2004 - p1907(1) [51-500]
Pillai, Rajnandini - *Teaching, Leadership: Innovative Approaches for the 21st Century*
R&R Bk N - v19 - i1 - Feb 2004 - p90(1) [1-50]
Pilling, Marilyn Gear - *Field Next to Love*
CBRA - Annual 2003 - p228(2) [501+]
Pillow, Kirk - *Sublime Understanding*
JAAC - v61 - Winter 2003 - p74 [501+]
Pimentel, Maria da Graca Campos - *WebMedia and LA-Web 2004: Proceedings: 12-15 October 2004, Ribeirao Preto-SP, Brazil*
SciTech - v28 - i4 - Dec 2004 - p33(1) [51-500]
Pimlico, Diana Pearce - *The Diaries of Charles Greville*
Spec - v297 - i9205 - Jan 8 2005 - p30(2) [501+]

Pimlico, Nicholas Roe - *Fiery Heart*
    Spec - v297 - i9211` - Feb 19 2005 - p35(2) [501+]
Pimm, Nancy Roe - *Indy 500: The Inside Track*
    c   BL - v101 - i6 - Nov 15 2004 - p578(1) [51-500]
    c   CH Bwatch - v14 - i9 - Sept 2004 - p2(1) [51-500]
Pinault, G.-J - *Musiqueet et poesie dans l' Antiquite*
    Class R - v53 - i2 - Nov 2003 - p463-464 [501+]
Pinault, Lewis - *Play Zone*
    Bwatch - v26 - i8 - August 2004 - p8(1) [51-500]
Pinch, Trevor - *Analog Days: The Invention and Impact of the Moog Synthesizer*
    CS - v33 - i1 - Jan 2004 - p46-47 [501+]
Pinchuk, Amy Ruth - *The Best Books of Bikes*
    y   LibMed - v22 - i4 - Jan 2004 - p82(1) [501+]
Pinckney, Josephine - *Great Mischief*
    MFSF - v107 - i2 - August 2004 - p162(1) [51-500]
Pincus, Debra - *Small Bronzes in the Renaissance*
    Six Ct J - v34 - i4 - Winter 2003 - p1269-1271 [501+]
Pincus, Fred L. - *Reverse Discrimination: Dismantling the Myth*
    CS - v33 - i5 - Sept 2004 - p536-537 [501+]
Pindar, Ian - *Joyce*
    TLS - i5294 - Sept 17 2004 - p30(1) [501+]
Pinderhughes, Raquel - *Alternative Urban Futures: Planning for Sustainable Development in Cities Throughout the World*
    R&R Bk N - v19 - i3 - August 2004 - p156(1) [51-500]
Pine, Lisa - *Nazi Family Policy, 1933-1945*
    GSR - v27 - i1 - Feb 2004 - p173-174 [501+]
Pine, Red - *The Heart Sutra: The Womb of Buddhas*
    BL - v101 - i3 - Oct 1 2004 - p306(1) [51-500]
    Poems of the Masters: China's Classic Anthology of T'ang and Sung Dynasty Verse
    Choice - v41 - i11-12 - July-August 2004 - p2040(2) [501+]
Pineau, Gisele - *Exile According to Julia*
    Choice - v42 - i1 - Sept 2004 - p106(1) [501+]
Pineda, F.D. - *Sustainable Tourism: Proceedings*
    R&R Bk N - v19 - i4 - Nov 2004 - p72(1) [51-500]
Pinedo, Encarnacion - *Encarnacions Kitchen: Mexican Recipes from Nineteenth-Century California*
    PHR - v73 - i3 - August 2004 - p511(512) [501+]
Pinello, Daniel R. - *Gay Rights and American Law*
    PSQ - v119 - i2 - Summer 2004 - p387(2) [501+]
Pineo, Barry - *Acting That Matters*
    LJ - v129 - i20 - Dec 1 2004 - p120(1) [51-500]
Pines, Yuri - *Foundations of Confucian Thought: Intellectual Life in the Chunqiu Period, 772-453*
    JAS - v63 - i3 - August 2004 - p775-777 [501+]
Ping, Alvin Leong - *Theme and Rheme: An Alternative Account*
    R&R Bk N - v19 - i4 - Nov 2004 - p213(1) [51-500]
Pingree, David - *Catalogue of Jyotisa Manuscripts in the Wellcome Library: Sanskrit Astral and Mathematical Literature*
    SciTech - v28 - i1 - March 2004 - p43(1) [51-500]
    Descriptive Catalogue of the Sanskrit Astronomical Manuscripts Preserved at the Maharaja Man Singh II Museum in Jaipur, India
    SciTech - v28 - i1 - March 2004 - p42(1) [51-500]
Pinguilly, Yves - *Cuentos y leyendas del cuerno de Africa/Tales and Legends from the Horn of Africa*
    c   BL - v100 - i22 - August 2004 - p1950(1) [501+]
Pini, Giorgio - *Categories and Logic in Duns Scotus: An Interpretation of Aristotle's Categories in the Late Thirteenth Century*
    Specu - v79 - i4 - Oct 2004 - p1126(2) [501+]
Pini, Wendy - *Elfquest: The Searcher and the Sword (Illus. by Pini, Wendy)*
    y   BL - v100 - i22 - August 2004 - p1920(1) [51-500]
        ChrSFF&H - v26 - i10 - Oct 2004 - p30(1) [51-500]
    y   LJ - v129 - i18 - Nov 1 2004 - p66(1) [501+]
        PW - v251 - i27 - July 5 2004 - p40(2) [51-500]
Pinker, Steven - *The Best American Science and Nature Writing, 2004*
    y   BL - v101 - i3 - Oct 1 2004 - p289(1) [51-500]
        PW - v251 - i35 - August 30 2004 - p41(1) [51-500]
Pinkerton, Jan - *Encyclopedia of the Chicago Literary Renaissance*
    BL - v101 - i1 - Sept 1 2004 - p170(1) [501+]
    Choice - v42 - i2 - Oct 2004 - p268(1) [501+]
    SLJ - v50 - i12 - Oct 2004 - p86(2) [501+]
Pinkett Smith, Jada - *Girls Hold Up This World*
    c   KR - v73 - i1 - Jan 1 2005 - p57(1) [51-500]

Pinkney, Andrea Davis - *Ella Fitzgerald: The Tale of a Vocal Virtuosa (Illus. by Pinkney, Brian)*
    c   SLJ - v50 - i12 - Dec 2004 - p60(1) [501+]
    Fishing Day (Illus. by Evans, Shane W.)
    c   SLJ - v50 - i10 - Oct 2004 - p65(2) [51-500]
    Let It Shine: Stories of Black Women Freedom Fighters (Illus. by Alcorn, Stephen)
    c   SLJ - v50 - i10 - Oct 2004 - p66(1) [51-500]
    Sleeping Cutie (Illus. by Pinkney, Brian)
    c   BL - v101 - i2 - Sept 15 2004 - p254(1) [51-500]
    c   KR - v72 - i17 - Sept 1 2004 - p873(1) [51-500]
    c   SLJ - v50 - i11 - Nov 2004 - p114(1) [51-500]
Pinkster, Matthew - *Lincoln's Sanctuary: Abraham Lincoln and the Soldiers' Home*
    J Mil H - v68 - i3 - April 2004 - p605-606 [501+]
Pinkwater, Daniel - *Bad Bears in the Big City: An Irving & Muktuk Story (Illus. by Pinkwater, Jill)*
    c   BooChiTr - April 18 2004 - p3(1) [501+]
    c   LibMed - v23 - i3 - Nov-Dec 2004 - p67(2) [51-500]
    Cone Kong (Illus. by Pinkwater, Jill)
    c   RT - v57 - Oct 2003 - p168 [1-50]
    The Education of Robert Nifkin
    y   Kliatt - v39 - i2 - March 2005 - p22(1) [51-500]
    Looking for Bobowicz: A Hoboken Chicken Story (Read by Pinkwater, Daniel). Audiobook Review
    c   BL - v101 - i7 - Dec 1 2004 - p679(1) [1-50]
    Looking for Bobowicz: A Hoboken Chicken Story (Illus. by Pinkwater, Jill)
    c   BooChiTr - June 6 2004 - p2(1) [501+]
    c   BW - v34 - i29 - July 18 2004 - p11(1) [1-50]
    c   CCB-B - v57 - i11 - July-August 2004 - p478(2) [501+]
    c   SLJ - v50 - i7 - July 2004 - p110(2) [51-500]
    The Picture of Morty and Ray (Illus. by Davis, Jack E.)
    LibMed - v22 - i6 - March 2004 - p58(1) [501+]
Pinn, Anthony B. - *Noise and Spirit: The Religious Sensibilities of Rap Music*
    Choice - v42 - i4 - Dec 2004 - p672(1) [1-50]
    Terror and Triumph: The Nature of Black Religion
    Intpr - v59 - i1 - Jan 2005 - p100(1) [501+]
    JAAR - v72 - i3 - Sept 2004 - p795-797 [501+]
    Theol St - v65 - i4 - Dec 2004 - p900(2) [501+]
    TT - v61 - i2 - July 2004 - p235(1) [501+]
Pinnau, Ingo - *Advanced Materials for Membrane Separations*
    SciTech - v28 - i3 - Sept 2004 - p167(1) [51-500]
Pinney, Christopher - *Photography's Other Histories*
    JRAI - v10 - i3 - Sept 2004 - p725(2) [501+]
    'Photos of the Gods': The Printed Image and Political Struggle in India
    Choice - v42 - i1 - Sept 2004 - p86(2) [501+]
    TimHES - v0 - i1669 - Dec 3 2004 - p27(1) [501+]
Pinney, Thomas - *The Letters of Rudyard Kipling, Vol. 5*
    Spec - v296 - Dec 18 2004 - p89(2) [501+]
    The Letters of Rudyard Kipling, Vol. 6.
    Choice - v42 - i5 - Jan 2005 - p853(1) [1-50]
    Spec - v296 - Dec 18 2004 - p89(2) [501+]
Pinnick, Cassandra L. - *Scrutinizing Feminist Epistemology: An Examination of Gender in Science*
    QRB - v79 - i3 - Sept 2004 - p291(2) [501+]
    Wom R Bks - v22 - i1 - Oct 2004 - p7(2) [501+]
Pinsker, Matthew - *Lincoln's Sanctuary: Abraham Lincoln and the Soldiers' Home*
    JSH - v71 - i1 - Feb 2005 - p169(2) [501+]
Pinsky, Mark I. - *The Gospel According to Disney: Faith, Trust, and Pixie Dust*
    Bks & Cult - v11 - i1 - Jan-Feb 2005 - p16(2) [501+]
    CC - v121 - i23 - Nov 16 2004 - p22(3) [501+]
    Comw - v131 - i19 - Nov 5 2004 - p54(2) [501+]
    LJ - v129 - i14 - Sept 1 2004 - p160(1) [51-500]
    PW - v251 - i28 - July 12 2004 - p60(1) [51-500]
    The Gospel According to The Simpsons: The Spiritual Life of the World's Most Animated Family
    Bks & Cult - v11 - i1 - Jan-Feb 2005 - p16(2) [501+]
Pinsky, Michael - *Future Present: Ethics and/as Science Fiction*
    SFS - v31 - i1 - March 2004 - p161-163 [501+]
Pinsky, Robert - *Invitation to Poetry*
    LJ - v129 - i13 - August 2004 - p86(1) [501+]
Pinson, Linda - *Keeping the Books: Basic Recordkeeping and Accounting for the Successful Small Business, 6th Ed.*
    R&R Bk N - v19 - i3 - August 2004 - p131(1) [1-50]
    Steps to Small Business Start-Up: Everything You Need to Know to Turn Your Idea Into a Successful Business, 5th Ed.
    R&R Bk N - v19 - i1 - Feb 2004 - p93(1) [1-50]

Pinson, Patricia - *The Art of Walter Anderson*
    ABR - v25 - i5 - July-August 2004 - p5(2) [501+]
Pintabona, Don - *The Shared Table: Cooking with Spirit for Family and Friends*
    PW - v252 - i1 - Jan 3 2005 - p51(1) [51-500]
Pintak, Larry - *Seeds of Hate: How America's Flawed Middle East Policy Ignited the Jihad*
    R&R Bk N - v19 - i1 - Feb 2004 - p42(1) [51-500]
Pinti, Pietro - *Pietro's Book: The Story of a Tuscan Peasant*
    LJ - v129 - i12 - July 2004 - p92(2) [51-500]
    R&R Bk N - v19 - i4 - Nov 2004 - p41(1) [51-500]
Pinto, Jim - *Automation Unplugged: Pinto's Perspectives, Pointers and Prognostications*
    SciTech - v28 - i1 - March 2004 - p176(1) [51-500]
Piotrovsky, M.B. - *Heaven on Earth: Art from Islamic Lands: Works from the State Hermitage Museum and the Khalili Collection*
    Choice - v42 - i4 - Dec 2004 - p646(1) [1-50]
Piotrowski, Tadeusz - *The Polish Deportees of World War II: Recollections of Removal to the Soviet Union and Dispersal Throughout the World.*
    HRNB - v33 - i1 - Fall 2004 - p30(1) [501+]
    R&R Bk N - v19 - i3 - August 2004 - p35(1) [51-500]
Piott, Steven L. - *Giving Voters a Voice: The Origins of the Initiative and Referendum in America*
    JAH - v91 - i1 - June 2004 - p270-271 [501+]
    PSQ - v119 - i2 - Summer 2004 - p377(3) [501+]
Pipe, Jim - *Sun*
    c   BL - v101 - i4 - Oct 15 2004 - p424(1) [51-500]
    Weather
    c   BL - v101 - i4 - Oct 15 2004 - p424(1) [51-500]
Piper, Evelyn - *Bunny Lake Is Missing*
    LJ - v129 - i14 - Sept 1 2004 - p204(1) [51-500]
    BW - v34 - i46 - Nov 14 2004 - p12(1) [1-50]
Piper, James - *Handbook of Facility Assessment*
    SciTech - v28 - i3 - Sept 2004 - p148(1) [51-500]
Piper, John - *Don't Waste Your Life*
    Ch Today - v49 - i1 - Jan 2005 - p71(1) [51-500]
Piper, Karen - *Cartographic Fictions: Maps, Race and Identity*
    MFSF - v50 - i2 - Summer 2004 - p526-528 [501+]
Pipes, Daniel - *Militant Islam Reaches America*
    R&R Bk N - v19 - i3 - August 2004 - p17(1) [1-50]
Pipes, Richard - *Vixi: Memoirs of a Non-Belonger*
    Am Spect - v37 - i1 - Feb 2004 - p56(3) [501+]
    BW - v34 - i1 - Jan 4 2004 - p10(1) [501+]
    Lon R Bks - v26 - i16 - August 19 2004 - p7(4) [501+]
    Sew R - v112 - i1 - Wntr 2004 - pXVII-XXI [501+]
Pipkin, Turk - *The Old Man and the Tee: How I Took Ten Strokes Off My Game and Learned to Love Golf All Over Again*
    BL - v101 - i1 - Sept 1 2004 - p50(1) [51-500]
    LJ - v129 - i12 - July 2004 - p91(1) [51-500]
Pippin, Robert B. - *Hegel on Ethics and Politics*
    Pers PS - v33 - i4 - Fall 2004 - p249(1) [501+]
Piquard, Michelle - *L'edition pour la jeunesse en France de 1945 a 1980*
    c   Bkbird - v42 - i3 - July 2004 - p48(1) [501+]
Piragino, Maria Teresa - *Indios, Mujeres y Ciudadanos: Legislacion y Ejercicio de la Ciudadania en Bolivia (Siglo XIX).*
    HAHR - v84 - i2 - May 2004 - p383(3) [501+]
Pirandello, Luigi - *The Late Mattia Pascal*
    Globe & Mail - Jan 1 2005 - pD14 [1-50]
    LJ - v130 - i2 - Feb 1 2005 - p126(1) [1-50]
Pirckheimers, Willibald - *Willibald Pirckheimers Briefwechsel*
    Six Ct J - v35 - i1 - Spring 2004 - p193(3) [501+]
Piroch, Sigrid - *The Magic of Handweaving: The Basics and Beyond*
    LJ - v129 - i20 - Dec 1 2004 - p111(1) [51-500]
Pironello, Valerio - *Solid State Astrochemistry: Proceedings*
    SciTech - v28 - i1 - March 2004 - p43(1) [51-500]
Pirsos, Rena J. - *Your Paycheck*
    HR Mag - v49 - i7 - July 2004 - pS9(1) [51-500]
Pirto, Jane - *Understanding Creativity*
    R&R Bk N - v19 - i3 - August 2004 - p8(1) [1-50]
Pisani, Donald J. - *Water and American Government: The Reclamation Bureau, National Water Policy, and the West, 1902-1935*
    WHQ - v35 - i1 - Spring 2004 - p75-75 [501+]
Pisano, Dominick A. - *The Airplane in American Culture*
    J Mil H - v68 - i2 - April 2004 - p646(2) [501+]

Pisano, Douglas J. - *FDA Regulatory Affairs: A Guide for Prescription Drugs, Medical Devices and Biologics*
SciTech - v28 - i1 - March 2004 - p121(1) [51-500]

Pisano, Etta D. - *Digital Mammography*
SciTech - v28 - i1 - March 2004 - p116(1) [51-500]

Piscopo, Maria - *The Graphic Designer's and Illustrator's Guide to Marketing and Promotion*
R&R Bk N - v19 - i4 - Nov 2004 - p206(1) [501+]

Piskurich, George M. - *The AMA Handbook of E-Learning: Effective Design, Implementation, and Technology Solutions*
Per Psy - v57 - i3 - Autumn 2004 - p813(6) [501+]

Pistone, Joseph D. - *The Way of the Wiseguy: True Stories from the FBI's Most Famous Undercover Agent*
NYTBR - Oct 31 2004 - p20 [501+]

Piszkiewicz, Dennis - *Terrorism's War with America: A History*
Choice - v42 - i2 - Oct 2004 - p369(1) [51-500]
R&R Bk N - v19 - i1 - Feb 2004 - p142(1) [51-500]

Pit, Mirna - *How to Express Yourself with a Causal Connective: Subjectivity and Causal Connectives in Dutch, German and French*
R&R Bk N - v19 - i1 - Feb 2004 - p209(1) [51-500]

Pitaevskii, Lev - *Bose-Einstein Condensation*
Phys Today - v57 - i10 - Oct 2004 - p74-76 [501+]

Pitchall, Chez - *Mon Premier Livre de Mots*
c Res Links - v10 - i3 - Feb 2005 - p58(2) [501+]

Pitcher, Caroline - *The Gods Are Watching*
c Sch Lib - v52 - i4 - Winter 2004 - p203(2) [51-500]
Lord of the Forest (Illus. by Frances, Morris)
c KR - v72 - i15 - August 1 2004 - p748(1) [51-500]
The Winter Dragon (Illus. by Williams, Sophy)
c BL - v101 - i4 - Oct 15 2004 - p411(1) [51-500]
c KR - v72 - i22 - Nov 15 2004 - p1092(1) [51-500]
c SLJ - v51 - i1 - Jan 2005 - p96(1) [51-500]

Pitcher, Edward W.R. - *The American Magazine and Historical Chronical (Boston, 1743-1746): An Annotated Catalog of the Prose*
R&R Bk N - v19 - i1 - Feb 2004 - p242(1) [501+]
The New American Magazine (Woodbridge, New Jersey, January 1758-March 1760): An Annotated Catalogue of the Literary Contents with an Appendix on The Instructor (New York, March 6-May 10, 1755).
R&R Bk N - v19 - i4 - Nov 2004 - p2(1) [51-500]

Pitcher, John - *Medieval and Renaissance Drama in England, Vol. 16*
R&R Bk N - v19 - i1 - Feb 2004 - p236(1) [51-500]

Pitcher, Sharon M. - *Collaborating for Real Literacy: Librarian, Teacher, and Principal*
LibMed - v23 - i1 - August-Sept 2004 - p87(1) [51-500]
SLJ - v50 - i10 - Oct 2004 - p202(1) [51-500]
Teach Lib - v32 - i2 - Dec 2004 - p36(1) [501+]

Pitches, Jonathan - *Vsevolod Meyerhold*
TimHES - v0 - i1655 - August 27 2004 - p26(1) [501+]

Piterberg, Gabriel - *An Ottoman Tragedy: History and Historiography at Play*
JIH - v35 - i2 - Autumn 2004 - p334(3) [501+]

Pitkin, Joan - *Obstetrics and Gynaecology: An Illustrated Colour Text*
SciTech - v28 - i1 - March 2004 - p115(1) [51-500]

Pitkin, Linda M. - *Journey under the Sea*
c LibMed - v22 - i5 - Feb 2004 - p60(1) [501+]

Pitson, A.E. - *Hume's Philosophy of the Self*
RM - v58 - i2 - Dec 2004 - p462(2) [501+]

Pitt-Brooke, David - *Chasing Clayoquot: A Wilderness Almanac*
CG - v124 - i3 - May-June 2004 - p132(1) [501+]
Globe & Mail - Nov 27 2004 - pD3 [51-500]
PW - v252 - i10 - March 7 2005 - p57(2) [51-500]
Res Links - v10 - i1 - Oct 2004 - p40(1) [51-500]

Pitt, Steve - *Rain Tonight: A Story of Hurricane Hazel (Illus. by Collins, Heather)*
c Globe & Mail - Sept 25 2004 - pD26 [51-500]
Res Links - v10 - i2 - Dec 2004 - p30(1) [501+]

Pittau, Francesco - *ABC: A Lift-the-Flap Alphabet Book*
c PW - v251 - i41 - Oct 11 2004 - p82(1) [501+]

Pitti, Stephen J. - *The Devil in Silicon Valley: Northern California, Race, and Mexican Americans*
AHR - v109 - i2 - April 2004 - p542(3) [501+]
JAH - v91 - i1 - June 2004 - p343-344 [501+]
WHQ - v35 - i4 - Winter 2004 - p509-510 [501+]

Pittman, Al - *Down by Jim Long's Stage: Rhymes for Children and Young Fish (Illus. by Hall, Pam)*
c Can Lit - i182 - Autumn 2004 - p125(3) [501+]

Pitts, Winfred E. - *A Victory of Sorts: Desegregation in a Southern Community*
JSH - v70 - i4 - Nov 2004 - p968(2) [501+]
TCR - v106 - i5 - May 2004 - p982(4) [501+]

Pitzer, Chris - *Project: Superior*
PW - v252 - i11 - March 14 2005 - p47(1) [51-500]

Pitzer, Kurt - *The Bomb in my Garden: The Secrets of Saddam's Nuclear Mastermind*
People - v62 - i15 - Oct 11 2004 - p58 [51-500]

Pitzer, Marjorie W. - *I Can, Can You? (Illus. by Pitzer, Marjorie W.)*
c CH Bwatch - Oct 2004 - pNA [51-500]
c SLJ - v50 - i10 - Oct 2004 - p147(1) [51-500]

Pitzl, Gerald R. - *Encyclopedia of Human Geography*
Choice - v42 - i1 - Sept 2004 - p81(2) [501+]
E-Streams - Oct 2004 - pNA [51-500]

Piven, Frances Fox - *The War at Home: The Domestic Causes and Consequences of Bush's Militarism*
KR - v72 - i16 - August 15 2004 - p794(2) [501+]
PW - v251 - i34 - August 23 2004 - p47(1) [51-500]

Piven, Hanoch - *What Presidents Are Made Of (Illus. by Piven, Hanoch)*
c BL - v100 - i22 - August 2004 - p1926(2) [51-500]
c NYTBR - Oct 17 2004 - p20 [501+]
c PW - v251 - i31 - August 2 2004 - p70(1) [51-500]
c SLJ - v50 - i8 - August 2004 - p112(1) [51-500]

Piven, Jerry S. - *The Madness and Perversion of Yukio Mishima*
Choice - v42 - i4 - Dec 2004 - p657(1) [1-50]
R&R Bk N - v19 - i3 - August 2004 - p256(1) [51-500]
The Psychology of Death in Fantasy and History
Choice - v42 - i3 - Nov 2004 - p569(1) [51-500]
R&R Bk N - v19 - i3 - August 2004 - p10(1) [1-50]

Pizarnik, Alejandra - *From the Forbidden Garden: Letters from Alejandra Pizarnik to Antonio Beneyto*
Choice - v41 - i11-12 - July-August 2004 - p2050(1) [501+]

Pizzi, Matthew - *Macromedia Flash MX Unleashed*
SciTech - v28 - i1 - March 2004 - p175(1) [51-500]

Pizzigati, Sam - *Greed and Good: Understanding and Overcoming the Inequality That Limits Our Lives*
Choice - v42 - i7 - March 2005 - p1277(2) [51-500]

Place, Robert M. - *The Tarot: History, Symbolism, and Divination*
LJ - v130 - i2 - Feb 1 2005 - p101(1) [51-500]

Places in American History
c LibMed - v23 - i3 - Nov-Dec 2004 - p83(1) [51-500]

Places Online
LibMed - v22 - i7 - April-May 2004 - p91(1) [501+]

Placide, Jaira - *Fresh Girl*
c Kliatt - v38 - i6 - Nov 2004 - p20(1) [51-500]
c PW - v251 - i37 - Sept 13 2004 - p81(1) [51-500]

Plain, Belva - *The Sight of the Stars (Read by Dunne, Bernadette). Audiobook Review*
LJ - v129 - i12 - July 2004 - p124(1) [51-500]

Plakida, N.M. - *Spectroscopy of High-Tec Superconductors: A Theoretical View*
SciTech - v28 - i1 - March 2004 - p50(1) [51-500]

Plamondon, Martin - *Lewis and Clark Trail Maps: A Cartographic Reconstruction, Vol. 3*
R&R Bk N - v19 - i4 - Nov 2004 - p74(1) [51-500]

Plancher, Kevin D. - *MasterCases: Hand and Wrist Surgery*
SciTech - v28 - i3 - Sept 2004 - p112(1) [51-500]

Planel, Hubert - *Space and Life: An Introduction to Space Biology and Medicine*
SciTech - v28 - i3 - Sept 2004 - p58(1) [1-50]

Planet3 Wireless - *CWAP Certified Wireless Analysis Professional Official Study Guide*
SciTech - v28 - i4 - Dec 2004 - p149(1) [51-500]

Planinc, Zdravko - *Plato through Homer: Poetry and Philosophy in the Cosmological Dialogues*
Choice - v41 - i7 - March 2004 - p1311(1) [501+]

Plant, I.M. - *Women Writers of Ancient Greece and Rome: An Anthology*
Choice - v42 - i7 - March 2005 - p1225(2) [51-500]

Plant, Nick - *Molecular Toxicology*
E-Streams - Oct 2004 - pNA [501+]

Plante, David - *American Ghosts*
BL - v101 - i5 - Nov 1 2004 - p454(2) [51-500]
Comw - v132 - i2 - Jan 28 2005 - p36(3) [501+]
G&L Rev W - v12 - i2 - March-April 2005 - p36(2) [501+]
Globe & Mail - Jan 8 2005 - pD7 [501+]
KR - v72 - i19 - Oct 1 2004 - p951(1) [501+]
LJ - v129 - i13 - August 2004 - p80(1) [501+]
NYTBR - Jan 16 2005 - p6 [501+]
PW - v251 - i29 - July 19 2004 - p151(1) [51-500]

Plante, Raymond - *Le Temple De Xeros*
Res Links - v10 - i1 - Oct 2004 - p54(1) [501+]
Marilou Cries Wolf (Illus. by Favreau, Marie-Claude)
y Can CL - i111-112 - Fall-Winter 2003 - p134(6) [501+]

Plante, Thomas G. - *Sin Against the Innocents: Sexual Abuse by Priests and the Role of the Catholic Church*
R&R Bk N - v19 - i3 - August 2004 - p28(1) [1-50]

Plantec, Peter M. - *Virtual Humans: A Build-It-Yourself Kit, Complete with Software and Step-by-Step Instructions*
B Ent - v35 - i4 - Nov 2004 - p64(1) [501+]
E-Streams - July 2004 - pNA [501+]

Plasa, Carl - *Charlotte Bronte*
CR - v285 - i1665 - Oct 2004 - p245(3) [501+]

Plate, Brent - *Re-viewing the Passion: Mel Gibson's Film and its Critics*
PW - v251 - i41 - Oct 11 2004 - p77(1) [51-500]

Plater, Zygmunt J.B. - *Environmental Law and Policy: Nature, Law, and Society, 3rd Ed.*
R&R Bk N - v19 - i3 - August 2004 - p200(1) [1-50]

Plath, Sylvia - *Ariel: The Restored Edition*
y BL - v101 - i4 - Oct 15 2004 - p382(1) [51-500]
Econ - v373 - i8404 - Dec 4 2004 - p85US [501+]
LJ - v129 - i18 - Nov 1 2004 - p89(1) [51-500]
TLS - i5304 - Nov 26 2004 - p6(1) [501+]

Plato - *Plato's Sophist: A Translation with a Detailed Account of Its Theses and Arguments*
R&R Bk N - v19 - i1 - Feb 2005 - p2(1) [51-500]

Platt, Colin - *Marks of Opulence: The Why, When and Where of Western Art 1000-1914*
NS - v133 - i4673 - Feb 2 2004 - p50(2) [501+]

Platt, David S. - *Microsoft Platform Ahead*
SciTech - v28 - i4 - Dec 2004 - p26(1) [51-500]

Platt, Ellen Spector - *Easy and Elegant Rose Design: Beyond the Garden (Illus. by Detrick, Alan)*
LJ - v130 - i3 - Feb 15 2005 - p128(1) [51-500]

Platt, Frederic W. - *Field Guide to the Difficult Patient Review, 2nd Ed.*
SciTech - v28 - i3 - Sept 2004 - p90(1) [51-500]

Platt, Jennifer - *The British Sociological Association: A Sociological History*
CS - v33 - i4 - July 2004 - p444(3) [501+]

Platt, Len - *Musical Comedy on the West End Stage, 1890-1939*
Choice - v42 - i3 - Nov 2004 - p493(1) [51-500]

Platt, Richard - *Communication: From Hieroglyphs to Hyperlinks*
c BL - v101 - i1 - Sept 1 2004 - p116(1) [501+]
y SLJ - v50 - i11 - Nov 2004 - p158(1) [51-500]
Crime Scene: The Ultimate Guide to Forensic Science
LibMed - v22 - i5 - Feb 2004 - p60(1) [501+]
Eureka! Great Inventions and How They Happened
c LibMed - v22 - i6 - March 2004 - p80(1) [501+]

Platt, Rutherford H. - *Land Use and Society: Geography, Law, and Public Policy, Rev. Ed.*
R&R Bk N - v19 - i3 - August 2004 - p204(1) [1-50]

Platts, Linda - *Forest Fires*
y SB - v40 - i5 - Sept-Oct 2004 - p216(1) [51-500]

Plaut, S. Michael - *Sexual Dysfunction*
SciTech - v28 - i3 - Sept 2004 - p102(1) [1-50]

Play Ball: A Tribute to our National Pastime. Audiobook Review
BL - v101 - i1 - Sept 1 2004 - p144(1) [51-500]

Play Ball: A Tribute to Our National Pastime. Audiobook Review
LJ - v130 - i1 - Jan 1 2005 - p170(1) [51-500]

Player, Ian - *Zulu Wilderness*
Bwatch - Nov 2004 - pNA [51-500]

Pleasant Company Publications - *Room Crafts: Add Some Simple Style to Your Space*
c PW - v251 - i37 - Sept 13 2004 - p81(1) [51-500]

Pleasants, Julian M. - *Hanging Chads: The Inside Story of the 2000 Presidential Recount in Florida*
LJ - v129 - i15 - Sept 15 2004 - p70(2) [51-500]

The Pleasures of Bibliophily: Fifty Years of The Book Collector--An Anthology
ALJ - v53 - i3 - August 2004 - p321(2) [501+]
BSA-P - v98 - i1 - March 2004 - p111-112 [501+]

Pleij, Herman - *Colors Demonic and Divine: Shades of Meaning in the Middle Ages and After*
Choice - v42 - i4 - Dec 2004 - p739(2) [1-50]
R&R Bk N - v19 - i3 - August 2004 - p10(1) [1-50]

Pleiter, Allie - *Bad Heiress Day*
LJ - v130 - i2 - Feb 1 2005 - p64(1) [51-500]

Pleket, H.W. - *Supplementum Epigraphicum Graecum*
Class R - v54 - i2 - Nov 2004 - p536(2) [501+]

Plekon, Michael - *Living Icons: Persons of Faith in the Eastern Church*
TT - v61 - i1 - April 2004 - p127-130 [501+]
Tradition Alive: On the Church and the Christian Life in Our Time/Readings from the Eastern Church
R&R Bk N - v19 - i1 - Feb 2004 - p24(1) [1-50]

Pleskovic, Boris - *Annual World Conference on Development Economics 2003: The New Reform Agenda*
JEL - v41 - i4 - Dec 2003 - p1412(2) [501+]

Pliggon, Philip - *The Sea: Exploring Life on an Ocean Planet*
LibMed - v22 - i6 - March 2004 - p85(1) [501+]

Plimpton, George - *As Told at the Explorers Club: More than Fifty Gripping Tales of Adventure, Vol. 1*
R&R Bk N - v19 - i1 - Feb 2004 - pNA69(1) [501+]
Ernest Shackleton
R&R Bk N - v19 - i4 - Nov 2004 - p74(1) [51-500]
The Man in the Flying Lawn Chair and Other Excursions and Observations
BL - v101 - i1 - Sept 1 2004 - p40(1) [51-500]
BW - v34 - i40 - Oct 3 2004 - p14(1) [501+]
KR - v72 - i15 - August 1 2004 - p731(1) [501+]
LJ - v129 - i19 - Nov 15 2004 - p61(1) [501+]
NYTBR - Jan 2 2005 - p17 [501+]
PW - v251 - i31 - August 2 2004 - p62(1) [501+]

Plisson, Philip - *The Sea: Exploring Life on an Ocean Planet*
y SLJ - v50 - i10 - Oct 2004 - pS62(1) [501+]

Ploger, Bonnie J. - *Exploring Animal Behavior in Laboratory and Field*
New Sci - v185 - i2486 - Feb 12 2005 - p48(1) [501+]

Plokhy, Serhii - *Religion and Nation in Modern Ukraine*
CBRA - Annual 2003 - p98(2) [501+]
J Ch St - v46 - i3 - Summer 2004 - p657(2) [501+]
Slav R - v63 - i4 - Winter 2004 - p873(2) [501+]
CHR - v90 - i3 - July 2004 - p563(3) [501+]
Tsars and Cossacks: A Study in Iconography
Slav R - v63 - i2 - Summer 2004 - p394(2) [501+]

Plomp, Tjeerd - *Cross-National Information and Communication Technology Policies and Practices in Education*
R&R Bk N - v19 - i1 - Feb 2004 - pNA [51-500]

Plotkin, Fred - *Classical Music 101: A Complete Guide to Learning and Loving Classical Music (Read by Plotkin, Fred). Audiobook Review*
y Kliatt - v39 - i1 - Jan 2005 - p54(1) [501+]
Classical Music Unbuttoned: A Complete Guide to Learning and Loving Classical Music
MT - v145 - i1888 - Autumn 2004 - p106-108 [501+]

Plotkin, Mariano - *Argentina on the Couch: Psychiatry, State, and Society, 1880 to the Present*
HAHR - v84 - i4 - Nov 2004 - p762(2) [501+]

Plotnik, Rod - *Introduction to Psychology, 7th Ed.*
SciTech - v28 - i3 - Sept 2004 - p1(1) [501+]

Plourde, Lynn - *Dad, Aren't You Glad? (Illus. by Dutton, Amy Wummer)*
c KR - v73 - i3 - Feb 1 2005 - p180(1) [51-500]
Pajama Day (Illus. by Wickstrom, Thor)
c BL - v101 - i9-10 - Jan 1 2005 - p874(1) [51-500]
c KR - v72 - i24 - Dec 15 2004 - p1207(1) [51-500]
c PW - v252 - i6 - Feb 7 2005 - p61(2) [501+]
c SLJ - v51 - i2 - Feb 2005 - p108(1) [51-500]

Plum-Ucci, Carol - *What Happened to Lani Garver*
c CH Bwatch - v14 - i7 - July 2004 - p6(1) [51-500]
y Kliatt - v38 - i4 - July 2004 - p23(1) [51-500]

Plume, Ilse - *The Farmer in the Dell*
c BL - v101 - i2 - Sept 15 2004 - p247(1) [51-500]
c KR - v72 - i17 - Sept 1 2004 - p873(1) [51-500]
c SLJ - v50 - i12 - Dec 2004 - p128(1) [51-500]

Plumer, Eric - *Augustine's Commentary on Galatians*
Class R - v54 - i1 - May 2004 - p128(2) [501+]
Intpr - v58 - i4 - Oct 2004 - p430(2) [501+]
JR - v84 - i3 - July 2004 - p480(2) [501+]

Plumley, Sue - *Home Networking Bible, 2nd Ed.*
LJ - v129 - i12 - July 2004 - p112(1) [51-500]

Plumly, Stanley - *Now That My Father Lies Down Beside Me: New and Selected Poems, 1970-2000*
Sew R - v111 - i3 - Summer 2003 - p470-479 [501+]

Plummer, Brenda Gayle - *Window on Freedom: Race, Civil Rights, and Foreign Affairs*
CS - v33 - i1 - Jan 2004 - p129-129 [501+]

Plummer, Ken - *Intimate Citizenship: Private Decisions and Public Dialogues*
R&R Bk N - v19 - i1 - Feb 2004 - p133(1) [51-500]

Plummer, Mary - *GarageBand*
LJ - v129 - i14 - Sept 1 2004 - p182(1) [501+]

Plunkett, John - *Queen Victoria: First Media Monarch*
ELT - v47 - i4 - Fall 2004 - p446(4) [501+]
VS - v46 - i3 - Spring 2004 - p520(3) [501+]

Plunkett, Warren R. - *Management: Meeting and Exceeding Customer Expectations*
R&R Bk N - v19 - i3 - August 2004 - p103(1) [1-50]

Plutarch - *Greek Lives (Read by Farrell, Nicholas). Audiobook Review*
y Kliatt - v39 - i1 - Jan 2005 - p52(2) [51-500]

Poallota, Jerry - *The Beetle Alphabet Book*
c SB - v40 - i3 - May-June 2004 - p133(1) [501+]

Poarch, Candice - *Loving Delilah*
y BL - v101 - i6 - Nov 15 2004 - p569(1) [51-500]

Pobst, Sandra - *Virginia*
c BL - v101 - i8 - Dec 15 2004 - p740(1) [51-500]

Pocock, J.G.A. - *Barbarism and Religion, Vol. 3*
AHR - v109 - i2 - April 2004 - p470(2) [501+]
Ren Q - v57 - i3 - Fall 2004 - p1065(2) [501+]

Pocock, Tom - *Stopping Napoleon: War and Intrigue in the Mediterranean*
Spec - v295 - i9180 - July 17 2004 - p35(2) [501+]
TLS - i5286 - July 23 2004 - p28(1) [501+]

A Pod of Orcas
c Can Lit - i181 - Summer 2004 - p131-132 [501+]

Podair, Jerald E. - *The Strike That Changed New York: Blacks, Whites, and the Ocean Hill-Brownsville Crisis*
AHR - v109 - i2 - April 2004 - p561(2) [501+]
J Urban H - v31 - i2 - Jan 2005 - p269-277 [501+]

Podeh, Elie - *The Arab-Israeli Conflict in Israeli History Textbooks, 1948-2000*
MEQ - v12 - i1 - Wntr 2005 - p92(1) [501+]
Rethinking Nasserism: Revolution and Historical Memory in Modern Egypt
MEJ - v58 - i4 - Autumn 2004 - p705(1) [501+]

Podhoretz, John - *Bush Country: How George W. Bush Became the First Great Leader of the 21st Century-While Driving Liberals Insane*
NYTBR - March 13 2005 - p32 [501+]

Podnieks, Andrew - *Lord Stanley's Cup*
Globe & Mail - Oct 30 2004 - pD25 [51-500]

Podwal, Mark H. - *A Sweet Year: A Taste of Jewish Holidays*
LibMed - v22 - i6 - March 2004 - p87(1) [501+]

Poe, Edgar Allan - *Edgar Allan Poe's Tales of Mystery and Madness (Illus. by Grimly, Gris)*
y BL - v101 - i4 - Oct 15 2004 - p405(1) [51-500]
c Globe & Mail - Oct 23 2004 - pD22 [51-500]
c SLJ - v50 - i10 - Oct 2004 - p176(1) [51-500]
c BIC - v33 - i8 - Nov 2004 - p35(2) [501+]
Eureka
Choice - v42 - i7 - March 2005 - p1231(1) [51-500]
The Selected Writings of Edgar Allan Poe: Authoritative Texts, Backgrounds and Contexts, Criticism
R&R Bk N - v19 - i4 - Nov 2004 - p242(1) [501+]
Tales of Edgar Allen Poe
LibMed - v22 - i6 - March 2004 - p93(1) [501+]

Poe, Harry Lee - *See No Evil: The Existence of Sin in an Age of Relativism*
PW - v251 - i39 - Sept 27 2004 - p55(1) [51-500]

Poe, Marshall T. - *The Russian Moment in World History*
JPR - v41 - i5 - Sept 2004 - p644-645 [501+]
Slav R - v63 - i4 - Winter 2004 - p880(2) [501+]
South CR - v36 - i2 - Spring 2004 - p182-184 [501+]

Poeschke, Joachim - *Wandmalereien der Giottozeit in Italien 1280-1400*
HNet - Oct 2004 - pNA [501+]

The Poetry of Petrarch
AM - v191 - i4 - August 16 2004 - p25 [501+]

Poetter, Thomas S. - *Critical Perspectives on the Curriculum of Teacher Education*
R&R Bk N - v19 - i4 - Nov 2004 - p182(1) [501+]

Poffo, Lanny - *Limericks from the Heart*
c CH Bwatch - Jan 2005 - pNA [51-500]

Pogorelsky, Antony - *Little Black Hen (Illus. by Spirin, Gennady)*
c CBRA - Annual 2003 - p529(2) [51-500]

Pogue, David - *GarageBand: The Missing Manual*
SciTech - v28 - i4 - Dec 2004 - p25(1) [51-500]
iLife '04; the missing manual
SciTech - v28 - i4 - Dec 2004 - p18(1) [1-50]
Iphoto 4: The Missing Manual
SciTech - v28 - i3 - Sept 2004 - p168(1) [1-50]

Pohl, Frances K. - *Framing America: A Social History of American Art*
Am Q - v56 - i2 - June 2004 - p421(8) [501+]

Pohl, Frederik - *The Boy Who Would Live Forever*
y BL - v101 - i2 - Sept 15 2004 - p216(1) [51-500]
ChrSFF&H - v26 - i10 - Oct 2004 - p24(2) [51-500]
Ent W - i795 - Dec 3 2004 - p94 [501+]
KR - v72 - i16 - August 15 2004 - p782(1) [51-500]
LJ - v129 - i15 - Sept 15 2004 - p52(1) [51-500]
NYTBR - Nov 14 2004 - p51 [501+]
PW - v251 - i32 - August 9 2004 - p235(1) [51-500]

Pohl-Weary, Emily - *A Girl Like Sugar*
Globe & Mail - Nov 20 2004 - pD14 [501+]
Girls Who Bite Back
Globe & Mail - August 7 2004 - pD15 [501+]

Pohlman, H.L. - *Constitutional Debate in Action: Governmental Powers, 2nd Ed.*
R&R Bk N - v19 - i4 - Nov 2004 - p171(1) [501+]

Poignant, Roslyn - *Professional Savages: Captive Lives and Western Spectacle*
R&R Bk N - v19 - i4 - Nov 2004 - p77(1) [51-500]
TLS - i5287 - July 30 2004 - p30(1) [501+]

Pointer, Dennis Dale - *Essentials of Health Care Organization Finance: A Primer for Board Members*
SciTech - v28 - i4 - Dec 2004 - p86(1) [1-50]
Health Care Industry: A Primer for Board Members
SciTech - v28 - i1 - March 2004 - p81(1) [1-50]

Poirier, Mark Jude - *Modern Ranch Living*
Advocate - Nov 23 2004 - p96(1) [51-500]
BL - v101 - i1 - Sept 1 2004 - p64(1) [51-500]
KR - v72 - i15 - August 1 2004 - p710(1) [501+]
PW - v251 - i30 - July 26 2004 - p35(1) [501+]

Poirion, Daniel - *Le Livre Du Graal, II: Lancelot*
TLS - i5291 - August 27 2004 - p8(1) [501+]

Poirot, Luis - *Pablo Neruda: Absence and Presence*
LJ - v129 - i17 - Oct 15 2004 - p63(1) [51-500]

Poisel, Richard A. - *Modern Communications Jamming Principles and Techniques*
SciTech - v28 - i1 - March 2004 - p179(1) [51-500]
Target Acquisition in Communication Electronic Warfare Systems
SciTech - v28 - i4 - Dec 2004 - p172(1) [51-500]

Poisson, Catherine - *Sartre et Beauvoir: du je au nous*
FS - v58 - i1 - Jan 2004 - p137(2) [501+]

Poitras, Jacques - *The Right Fight: Bernard Lord and the Conservative Dilemma*
Globe & Mail - Oct 30 2004 - pD17 [501+]

Pojman, Louis P. - *Environmental Ethics: Reading in Theory and Application, 4th Ed.*
SciTech - v28 - i4 - Dec 2004 - p6(1) [1-50]
How Should We Live?: An Introduction to Ethics
R&R Bk N - v20 - i1 - Feb 2005 - p9(1) [51-500]

Poku, Nana K. - *Global Health and Governance: HIV/AIDS*
SciTech - v28 - i3 - Sept 2004 - p84(1) [501+]

Polacco, Patricia - *G Is for Goat*
LibMed - v22 - i5 - Feb 2004 - p65(2) [501+]
John Philip Duck (Illus. by Polacco, Patricia)
c BL - v100 - i22 - August 2004 - p1944(1) [51-500]
c CCB-B - v58 - i2 - Oct 2004 - p96(1) [51-500]
c PW - v251 - i27 - July 5 2004 - p56(1) [51-500]
Mommies Say Shhh!
c KR - v73 - i2 - Jan 15 2005 - p124(1) [51-500]
c PW - v252 - i6 - Feb 7 2005 - p58(1) [51-500]
Oh Look!
c LibMed - v23 - i3 - Nov-Dec 2004 - p68(1) [51-500]
An Orange for Frankie
c BL - v101 - i7 - Dec 1 2004 - p662(1) [51-500]
c KR - v72 - i21 - Nov 1 2004 - p1052(1) [51-500]
c PW - v251 - i39 - Sept 27 2004 - p63(1) [51-500]
Thank You, Mr. Falker
c SLJ - v50 - i7 - July 2004 - p44(1) [51-500]

Polachek, Solomon W. - *Worker Well-Being and Public Policy*
JEL - v41 - i4 - Dec 2003 - p1384(2) [501+]

Polak, J.M. - *Introduction to Immunocytochemistry, 3rd Ed.*
E-Streams - Oct 2004 - pNA [501+]

Polak, Monique - *Flip Turn*
Res Links - v10 - i3 - Feb 2005 - p20(1) [501+]
No More Pranks
y Kliatt - v39 - i1 - Jan 2005 - p17(1) [51-500]
y Res Links - v10 - i3 - Feb 2005 - p39(1) [51-500]
Polakoff, Serge - *Symbols in Art: The Hidden Keys to Love, Balance and Renewal*
R&R Bk N - v19 - i1 - Feb 2004 - p201(1) [51-500]
Polakow, Amy - *Daisy Bates: Civil Rights Crusader*
c LibMed - v22 - i5 - Feb 2004 - p77(1) [501+]
Pole, Graeme - *Classic Hikes in the Canadian Rockies*
CBRA - Annual 2003 - p26(1) [501+]
Pole, Reginald - *The Correspondence of Reginald Pole, Vol. 1 Book)*
Six Ct J - v35 - i1 - Spring 2004 - p192(2) [501+]
Polhemus, Robert M. - *Lot's Daughters: Sex, Redemption, and Women's Quest for Authority*
LJ - v130 - i2 - Feb 1 2005 - p105(1) [51-500]
NYTBR - Jan 30 2005 - p7 [501+]
PW - v252 - i1 - Jan 3 2005 - p49(1) [51-500]
Polian, Pavel - *Against Their Will: The History and Geography of Forced Migrations in the USSR*
Choice - v41 - i11-12 - July-August 2004 - p2102(1) [501+]
Policies for Distributed Systems and Networks: Proceedings
SciTech - v28 - i3 - Sept 2004 - p32(1) [51-500]
Polidoro, Massimo - *Secrets of the Psychics: Investigating Paranormal Claims*
R&R Bk N - v19 - i1 - Feb 2004 - p8(1) [51-500]
Polikoff, Barbara - *Why Does the Coqui Sing?*
VOYA - v27 - i5 - Dec 2004 - p392(1) [51-500]
Polin, Richard A. - *Fetal and Neonatal Physiology, 3rd Ed., Vols. 1-2*
SciTech - v28 - i1 - March 2004 - p116(1) [51-500]
Poliner, Elizabeth - *Mutual Life & Casualty*
KR - v72 - i23 - Dec 1 2004 - p1110(2) [501+]
PW - v252 - i2 - Jan 10 2005 - p38(1) [51-500]
Poling, James Newton - *Understanding Male Violence: Pastoral Care Issues*
Intpr - v58 - i4 - Oct 2004 - p439(1) [501+]
Poling, Jim, Sr. - *Tom Thomson: The Life and Mysterious Death of the Famous Canadian Painter*
CBRA - Annual 2003 - p63(2) [51-500]
Polis, Ben - *Only a Mother Could Love Him: My Life with and Triumph over ADD*
y BL - v101 - i7 - Dec 1 2004 - p625(1) [51-500]
LJ - v129 - i19 - Nov 15 2004 - p77(1) [501+]
PW - v251 - i44 - Nov 1 2004 - p54(1) [51-500]
Polisi, Joseph W. - *The Artist as Citizen*
Bwatch - March 2005 - pNA [51-500]
Politi, Mauro - *The International Criminal Court and the Crime of Aggression: Proceedings*
R&R Bk N - v19 - i3 - August 2004 - p212(1) [1-50]
Political Writings
Eight-C St - v37 - i3 - Spring 2004 - p504-507 [501+]
Politico, John Redwood - *Singing The Blues*
Spec - v296 - i9193 - Oct 16 2004 - p77(1) [501+]
Politkovskaya, Anna - *A Dirty War: A Russian Reporter in Chechnya*
Globe & Mail - Feb 26 2005 - pD13 [1-50]
Putin's Russia
NS - v133 - i4711 - Oct 25 2004 - p51(2) [501+]
Polito, Roberto - *The Sceptical Road: Aenesidemus' Appropriation of Heraclitus*
R&R Bk N - v19 - i3 - August 2004 - p3(1) [1-50]
Polizzotto, Carolyn - *Trumpet's Kittens (Illus. by Duke, Marion)*
c CH Bwatch - Feb 2005 - pNA [51-500]
Poljak, Dragan - *Human Exposure to Electromagnetic Fields*
SciTech - v28 - i4 - Dec 2004 - p69(1) [51-500]
Time Domain Techniques in Computational Electromagnetics
SciTech - v28 - i4 - Dec 2004 - p51(1) [51-500]
Polk, James K. - *Correspondence of James K. Polk, Vol. 10*
R&R Bk N - v19 - i3 - August 2004 - p67(1) [51-500]
Polk, William R. - *Understanding Iraq: The Whole Sweep of Iraqi History from Genghis Khan's Mongols to the Ottoman Turks to the British Mandate to the American Occupation*
KR - v73 - i5 - March 1 2005 - p280(1) [501+]
Polke, Sigmar - *Sigmar Polke: History of Everything: Paintings and Drawings, 1998-2003*
Choice - v42 - i1 - Sept 2004 - p90(1) [501+]

Polkinghorne, John - *Faith, Science and Understanding*
Zygon - v39 - i4 - Dec 2004 - pNA [501+]
Science and the Trinity: The Christian Encounter with Reality
BL - v101 - i3 - Oct 1 2004 - p305(2) [51-500]
LJ - v129 - i19 - Nov 15 2004 - p66(1) [501+]
PW - v251 - i35 - August 30 2004 - p52(1) [51-500]
Pollach, Irene - *Communicating Corporate Ethics on the World Wide Web: A Disclosure Analysis of Selected Company Web Sites*
R&R Bk N - v19 - i1 - Feb 2004 - p107(1) [51-500]
Pollack, Eileen - *Woman Walking Ahead: In Search of Catherine Weldon and Sitting Bull*
Am Ind CRJ - v27 - i2 - Spring 2003 - p149-150 [501+]
Pollack, John - *Cork Boat (Read by Pollack, John). Audiobook Review*
c Kliatt - v38 - i4 - July 2004 - p59(2) [501+]
Pollack, Kenneth M. - *The Persian Puzzle: The Conflict between Iran and America*
BL - v101 - i7 - Dec 1 2004 - p622(2) [51-500]
BW - v34 - i48 - Nov 28 2004 - p3(2) [501+]
Nation - v280 - i8 - Feb 28 2005 - p26 [501+]
NYTBR - Dec 12 2004 - p8 [501+]
PW - v251 - i48 - Nov 29 2004 - p33(2) [501+]
Pollack, Pam - *Halloween Night on Shivermore Street (Illus. by DuBurke, Randy)*
c KR - v72 - i20 - Oct 15 2004 - p1012(1) [51-500]
c PW - v251 - i32 - August 9 2004 - p248(1) [51-500]
c SLJ - v50 - i8 - August 2004 - p92(1) [51-500]
Pollack, William S. - *Real Boys' Voices*
CC - v121 - i18 - Sept 7 2004 - p48(3) [501+]
Pollak, Barbara - *Our Community Garden (Illus. by Pollak, Barbara)*
CH Bwatch - Oct 2004 - pNA [51-500]
c SLJ - v50 - i11 - Nov 2004 - p114(1) [51-500]
Pollak, Ellen - *Incest and the English Novel, 1684-1814*
TSWL - v23 - i2 - Fall 2004 - p371(3) [501+]
Pollan, Stephen M. - *Fire Your Boss: Work for the Money and the Love Will Follow*
Globe & Mail - Sept 4 2004 - pF6 [1-50]
Pollard, A.J. - *Imagining Robin Hood*
HT - v55 - i1 - Jan 2005 - p56(1) [501+]
LJ - v130 - i2 - Feb 1 2005 - p80(1) [51-500]
Pollard, Alton B., III - *"How Long This Road": Race, Religion, and the Legacy of C. Eric Lincoln*
Choice - v42 - i1 - Sept 2004 - p120(1) [501+]
Pollard, N. - *Soldiers, Cities, and Civilians in Roman Syria*
Class R - v53 - i2 - Nov 2003 - p431-433 [501+]
Pollard, Patrick - *Repertoire des lectures d'Andre Gide II. Lectures anglaises*
TLS - i5283 - July 2 2004 - p29(1) [501+]
Pollard, Thomas D. - *Cell Biology*
SciTech - v28 - i4 - Dec 2004 - p63(1) [51-500]
Pollard, Vincent Kelly - *Globalization, Democratization, and Asian Leadership: Power Sharing, Foreign Policy, and Society in the Philippines and Japan*
R&R Bk N - v19 - i3 - August 2004 - p160(1) [51-500]
Polleross, Friedrich - *Reiselust and Kunstgenuss: Barockes Bohmen, Mahren und Osterreich*
HNet - Sept 2004 - pNA [501+]
Pollet, Alison - *Nobody Was Here: 7th Grade in the Life of Me, Penelope*
c JAAL - v48 - i4 - Dec 2004 - p349(1) [501+]
c BL - v100 - i22 - August 2004 - p1937(1) [51-500]
y KR - v72 - i14 - July 15 2004 - p692(1) [51-500]
c NYT - Nov 7 2004 - p5 [501+]
c PW - v251 - i29 - July 19 2004 - p162(1) [51-500]
c SLJ - v50 - i9 - Sept 2004 - p216(1) [51-500]
Polletta, Francesca - *Freedom Is an Endless Meeting: Democracy in American Social Movements*
CS - v33 - i1 - Jan 2004 - p73-74 [501+]
S&S - v68 - i2 - Summer 2004 - p244-246 [501+]
Polliack, Meira - *Karaite Judaism: A Guide to Its History and Literacy Sources*
R&R Bk N - v19 - i3 - August 2004 - p16(1) [1-50]
Pollin, Robert - *Contours of Descent: U.S. Economic Fractures and the Landscape of Global Austerity*
Comw - v131 - i13 - July 16 2004 - p32(2) [501+]
R&R Bk N - v19 - i1 - Feb 2004 - p81(1) [1-50]
Pollington, Stephen - *The Mead Hall: The Feasting Tradition in Anglo-Saxon England*
R&R Bk N - v19 - i1 - Feb 2004 - p32(1) [1-50]

Pollock, Allyson M. - *NHS plc: The Privatisation of Our Health Care*
SciTech - v28 - i4 - Dec 2004 - p80(1) [51-500]
NHS plc: The Privatisation of Our Healthcare
NS - v133 - i4706 - Sept 20 2004 - p50(2) [501+]
Pollock, Clifford B. - *Integrated Photonics*
SciTech - v28 - i1 - March 2004 - p144(1) [51-500]
Pollock, Jeffrey T. - *Adaptive Information: Improving Business through Semantic Interoperability, Grid Computing, and Enterprise Integration*
SciTech - v28 - i4 - Dec 2004 - p23(1) [51-500]
Pollock, Jocelyn M. - *Prisons and Prison Life: Costs and Consequences*
R&R Bk N - v19 - i3 - August 2004 - p170(1) [501+]
Pollock, John - *Kitchener: The Road to Omdurman and Saviour of the Nation*
HER - v119 - i483 - Sept 2004 - p1087(2) [501+]
Pollock, Mary Sanders - *Elizabeth Barrett and Robert Browning: A Creative Partnership*
TLS - i5283 - July 2 2004 - p9-10 [501+]
Pollock, Mica - *Colormute: Race Talk Dilemmas in an American School*
LJ - v129 - i14 - Sept 1 2004 - p165(2) [51-500]
Pollock, Sheldon - *Literary Cultures in History: Reconstructions from South Asia*
Lib & Cul - v39 - i3 - Summer 2004 - p335(2) [501+]
WLT - v79 - i1 - Jan-April 2005 - p86(2) [501+]
Pollotta, Nick - *That Darn Squid God*
Analog - v124 - i4 - April 2004 - p138(1) [501+]
ChrSFF&H - v26 - i10 - Oct 2004 - p25(1) [51-500]
Polmar, Norman - *Cold War Submarines: The Design and Construction of U.S. and Soviet Submarines*
Choice - v42 - i1 - Sept 2004 - p163(1) [501+]
SciTech - v28 - i1 - March 2004 - p179(1) [51-500]
One Hundred Years of World Military Aircraft
SciTech - v28 - i1 - March 2004 - p179(1) [51-500]
Spy Book: The Encyclopedia of Espionage
R&R Bk N - v19 - i4 - Nov 2004 - p154(1) [501+]
Poloma, Margaret M. - *Main Street Mystics: The Toronto Blessing and Reviving Pentecostalism*
R&R Bk N - v19 - i1 - Feb 2004 - p17(1) [501+]
Polonsky, Michael Jay - *Designing and Managing a Research Project: A Business Student's Guide*
R&R Bk N - v19 - i4 - Nov 2004 - p92(1) [501+]
Polsby, Nelson W. - *Annual Review of Political Science, Vol. 6*
R&R Bk N - v19 - i1 - Feb 2004 - p147(1) [51-500]
Annual Review of Political Science, Vol. 7
R&R Bk N - v19 - i4 - Nov 2004 - p150(1) [501+]
How Congress Evolves: Social Bases of Institutional Change
Choice - v41 - i11-12 - July-August 2004 - p2126(1) [501+]
Presidential Elections: Strategies and Structures of American Politics, 11th Ed.
R&R Bk N - v19 - i1 - Feb 2004 - pNA [51-500]
Polsky, Howard W. - *From Custodialism to Community: A Theory Based Manual for Transforming Institutions*
R&R Bk N - v19 - i1 - Feb 2004 - p127(1) [51-500]
Polster, Burkard - *Q.E.D.: Beauty in Mathematical Proof*
SB - v40 - i6 - Nov-Dec 2004 - p248(2) [501+]
SciTech - v28 - i3 - Sept 2004 - p16(1) [501+]
Poluha, Eve - *Contesting 'Good' Governance: Crosscultural Perspectives on Representation, Accountability and Public Space*
JRAI - v10 - i4 - Dec 2004 - p933(1) [501+]
Polya, Gideon - *Biochemical Targets of Plant Bioactive Compounds: A Pharmacological Reference Guide to Sites of Action and Biological Effects*
E-Streams - July 2004 - pNA [501+]
Polyanin, Andrei D. - *Handbook of Nonlinear Partial Differential Equations*
E-Streams - Oct 2004 - pNA [501+]
SciTech - v28 - i4 - Dec 2004 - p39(1) [51-500]
Polycarpou, Andreas A. - *Magnetic Storage Symposium: Frontiers of Magnetic Hard Disk Drive Tribology and Technology: Proceedings*
SciTech - v28 - i1 - March 2004 - p165(1) [51-500]
Pomel, Fabrienne - *Les Voies de l'Au-dela et l'Essor de l'Allegorie au Moyen Age*
Specu - v79 - i3 - July 2004 - p825-827 [501+]

Pomerance, Murray - *Enfant Terrible*
FQ - v57 - i4 - Summer 2004 - p53(2) [501+]
Johnny Depp Starts Here
PW - v252 - i7 - Feb 14 2005 - p62(1) [51-500]
Popping Culture
R&R Bk N - v19 - i3 - August 2004 - p262(1) [51-500]

Pomerleau, Janne - *Corvees et quetes. Un parcours au Canada francais*
Can Hist R - v85 - i3 - Sept 2004 - p586(3) [501+]

Pomeroy, S.B. - *Spartan Women*
Class R - v54 - i2 - Nov 2004 - p465(3) [501+]

Pomfret, David M. - *Young People and the European City: Age Relations in Nottingham and Saint-Etienne, 1890-1940*
R&R Bk N - v19 - i4 - Nov 2004 - p136(1) [51-500]

Pomfret, Richard - *Constructing a Market Economy: Diverse Paths from Central Planning in Asia and Europe*
JEL - v41 - i4 - Dec 2003 - p1328(2) [501+]
Economic Analysis of Regional Trading Arrangements
JEL - v42 - i1 - March 2004 - p261(1) [501+]

Pomper, Gerald M. - *The Future of American Democratic Politics: Principles and Practices*
Choice - v41 - i7 - March 2004 - p1372(1) [501+]

Pomplun, Tom - *Graphic Classics: Edgar Allan Poe*
y SLJ - v50 - i8 - August 2004 - p149(1) [501+]
y VOYA - v27 - i3 - August 2004 - p229(1) [1-50]
Graphic Classics: Robert Louis Stevenson
ChrSFF&H - v26 - i9 - Sept 2004 - p37(1) [51-500]
y Kliatt - v38 - i5 - Sept 2004 - p36(2) [501+]

Pon, Lisa - *Raphael, Durer, and Marcantonio Raimondi: Copying and the Italian Renaissance Print*
Choice - v42 - i2 - Oct 2004 - pNA [501+]
R&R Bk N - v19 - i4 - Nov 2004 - p208(1) [501+]

Poncelet, Eric C. - *Partnering for the Environment: Multistakeholder Collaboration in a Changing World*
R&R Bk N - v19 - i3 - August 2004 - p81(1) [51-500]

Poncini, Gina - *Discursive Strategies in Multicultural Business Meetings*
R&R Bk N - v19 - i3 - August 2004 - p132(1) [51-500]

Poncio, John Henry - *Girocho: A GI's Story of Bataan and Beyond*
VQR - v80 - i1 - Wntr 2004 - p263-263 [501+]

Pond, Steve - *The Big Show: High Times and Dirty Dealings Backstage at the Academy Awards*
Ent W - i803 - Jan 28 2005 - p89 [51-500]
Globe & Mail - Feb 26 2005 - pD13 [51-500]
KR - v72 - i21 - Nov 1 2004 - p1040(1) [501+]
LJ - v129 - i20 - Dec 1 2004 - p120(2) [51-500]
PW - v251 - i47 - Nov 22 2004 - p49(1) [51-500]
USNews & Wrld Rpt - v138 - i6 - Feb 21 2005 - p75 [1-50]

Pond, Wilson G. - *Encyclopedia of Animal Science*
Bwatch - Jan 2005 - pNA [51-500]
LJ - v130 - i3 - Feb 15 2005 - p156(2) [51-500]

Poneman, Debra Halperin - *What, No Meat?!: What to Do When Your Kid Becomes a Vegetarian*
CBRA - Annual 2003 - p138(2) [51-500]

Ponessa, Joseph - *"Come and See Catholic Bible Study": Prophets and Apostles*
CI - v12 - i9 - Oct 2004 - p44(1) [501+]

Ponge, Francis - *Oeuvres Completes, II*
TLS - i5286 - July 23 2004 - p11(1) [501+]

Poniatowska, Elena - *The Skin of the Sky*
BL - v101 - i2 - Sept 15 2004 - p208(1) [501+]
KR - v72 - i16 - August 15 2004 - p771(1) [501+]
LJ - v129 - i15 - Sept 15 2004 - p50(1) [51-500]
PW - v251 - i38 - Sept 20 2004 - p45(2) [501+]

Pons, Silvio - *Stalin and the Inevitable War, 1936-1941*
E-A St - v56 - i7 - Nov 2004 - p1081(1093) [501+]

Ponsford, Jennie - *Cognitive and Behavioral Rehabilitation: From Neurobiology to Clinical Practice*
SciTech - v28 - i4 - Dec 2004 - p100(1) [51-500]

Ponti, Claude - *DeZert Isle*
c SLJ - v50 - i8 - August 2004 - p92(1) [51-500]

Ponting, Clive - *The Crimean War: The Truth Behind the Myth*
CR - v285 - i1665 - Oct 2004 - p250(1) [501+]
TimHES - v0 - i1657 - Sept 10 2004 - p31(1) [501+]

Pontremoli, Alessandro - *La Lingua e le Lingue di Machiavelli. Atti del Convegno internazionale di studi Torino*
Six Ct J - v34 - i4 - Winter 2003 - p1209-1210 [501+]

Pontuso, James F. - *Vaclav Havel: Civic Responsibility in the Postmodern Age*
R&R Bk N - v19 - i4 - Nov 2004 - p150(1) [501+]

Pook, Les - *Flexagons Inside Out*
Math T - v98 - i1 - August 2004 - p62-63 [501+]
SIAM Rev - v46 - i3 - Sept 2004 - p563(2) [501+]

Pool, Gail - *Other People's Mail: An Anthology of Letter Stories*
LJ - v130 - i1 - Jan 1 2005 - p174(1) [501+]

Poole, Adrian - *Shakespeare and the Victorians*
TLS - i5266 - March 5 2004 - p12-12 [501+]

Poole, Amy Lowry - *The Pea Blossom*
c KR - v73 - i3 - Feb 1 2005 - p180(1) [51-500]
c PW - v252 - i8 - Feb 21 2005 - p174(2) [51-500]

Poole, Charles P., Jr. - *Encyclopedia Dictionary of Condensed Matter Physics*
Choice - v42 - i5 - Jan 2005 - p830(1) [1-50]
Introduction to Nanotechnology
Phys Today - v57 - i9 - Sept 2004 - p62-63 [501+]

Poole, Josephine - *Jack and the Beanstalk (Illus. by Hess, Paul)*
c SLJ - v51 - i1 - Jan 2005 - p107(2) [51-500]

Poole, Matthew - *Best Places Northern California*
Bwatch - Nov 2004 - pNA [51-500]

Poole, Peter A. - *Europe Unites: The EU's Eastern Enlargement*
PSQ - v119 - i2 - Summer 2004 - p366(3) [501+]

Poole, Randall A. - *Problems of Idealism: Essays in Russian Social Philosophy*
Slav R - v63 - i2 - Summer 2004 - p434(3) [501+]

Poole-Robb, Stuart - *Risky Business: Corruption, Fraud, Terrorism and Other Threats to Global Business*
R&R Bk N - v19 - i4 - Nov 2004 - p118(1) [51-500]

Poole, Robert M. - *Explorers House: National Geographic and the World it Made*
Econ - v373 - i8397 - Oct 16 2004 - p82US [501+]
BL - v101 - i3 - Oct 1 2004 - p295(1) [51-500]
KR - v72 - i17 - Sept 1 2004 - p852(2) [501+]
LJ - v130 - i2 - Feb 1 2005 - p94(1) [51-500]
PW - v251 - i37 - Sept 13 2004 - p68(1) [51-500]

Poole, Stafford - *Juan de Ovando: Governing the Spanish Empire in the Reign of Philip II*
NYRB - v51 - i17 - Nov 4 2004 - p47(5) [501+]

Poole, W. Scott - *Never Surrender: Confederate Memory and Conservatism in the South Carolina Upcountry*
JouAmCul - v27 - i3 - Sept 2004 - p347(2) [501+]
Pub Hist - v26 - i4 - Fall 2004 - p118(2) [501+]
R&R Bk N - v19 - i3 - August 2004 - p73(1) [51-500]

Pooler, Jim - *Why We Shop: Emotional Rewards and Retail Strategies*
R&R Bk N - v19 - i1 - Feb 2004 - p109(1) [51-500]

Poor, Sara S. - *Mechthild of Magdeburg and Her Book: Gender and the Making of Textual Authority*
Choice - v42 - i6 - Feb 2005 - p1025(1) [51-500]

Poore, Gary C.B. - *Marine Decapod Crustacea of Southern Australia: A Guide to Identification*
Choice - v42 - i7 - March 2005 - p1254(1) [51-500]

Poorten, Alf van der - *High Primes and Misdemeanours: Lectures in Honour of the 60th Brithday of Hugh Cowie Williams*
SciTech - v28 - i3 - Sept 2004 - p36(1) [51-500]

Poorter, L. - *Biodiversity of West African Forests: An Ecological Atlas of Woody Plant Species*
Choice - v42 - i3 - Nov 2004 - p509(2) [1-50]

Poortmans, J.R. - *Principles of Exercise Biochemistry, 3rd Ed.*
SciTech - v28 - i1 - March 2004 - p72(1) [51-500]

Pope, Al - *Bad Latitudes*
Globe & Mail - Sept 4 2004 - pD16 [501+]

Pope, Alice - *2005 Children's Writer's and Illustrator's Market*
Bwatch - Dec 2004 - pNA [51-500]

Pope, Carl - *Strategic Ignorance: Why the Bush Administratin Is Recklessly Destroying a Century of Environmental Progress*
E Mag - v15 - i5 - Sept-Oct 2004 - p62(2) [51-500]
Strategic Ignorance: Why the Bush Administration Is Recklessly Destroying a Century of Environmental Progress
TimHES - v0 - i1677 - Feb 4 2005 - p30(2) [501+]

Pope-Davis, Donald B. - *Handbook of Multicultural Competencies in Counseling & Psychology*
Choice - v41 - i7 - March 2004 - p1374(1) [501+]

Pope, Dudley - *The Battle of the River Plate*
LJ - v129 - i20 - Dec 1 2004 - p184(1) [51-500]

Pope, Harrison G. - *The Adonis Complex: How to Identify, Treat, and Prevent Body Obsession in Men and Boys*
CC - v121 - i18 - Sept 7 2004 - p48(3) [501+]

Pope, William Henry - *Leading from the Front: The War Memoirs of Harry Pope*
J Mil H - v68 - i2 - April 2004 - p650(2) [501+]

Popescu, Alexandru D. - *Petre Tutea: Between Sacrifice and Suicide*
R&R Bk N - v19 - i3 - August 2004 - p6(1) [1-50]

Popescu, Mihail - *Applied Hydraulic Transients for Hydropower Plants and Pumping Stations*
SciTech - v28 - i1 - March 2004 - p138(1) [51-500]

Popham, W. James - *America's "Failing" Schools: How Parents and Teachers Can Cope with No Child Left Behind*
TCR - v106 - i12 - Dec 2004 - p2327(4) [501+]
Classroom Assessment: What Teachers Need to Know, 4th Ed.
R&R Bk N - v19 - i3 - August 2004 - p225(1) [1-50]
Test Better, Teach Better: The Instructional Role of Assessment
Choice - v42 - i1 - Sept 2004 - p159(1) [501+]

Popkin, Jeremy D. - *Press, Revolution, and Social Identities in France, 1830-1835*
JMH - v76 - i3 - Sept 2004 - p696(3) [501+]

Poplau, Ronald W. - *The Doer of Good Becomes Good: A Primer for Volunteerism*
R&R Bk N - v19 - i3 - August 2004 - p228(1) [1-50]

Poplawski, Paul - *Encyclopedia of Literary Modernism*
BL - v100 - i21 - July 2004 - p1862(2) [501+]
Choice - v41 - i11-12 - July-August 2004 - p2016(1) [501+]
Ref Rev - May 2004 - pNA [501+]
y SLJ - v50 - i8 - August 2004 - p59(1) [51-500]

Popoff, Martin - *Top 500 Heavy Metal Songs of All Time*
CBRA - Annual 2003 - p108(1) [51-500]

Popov, Linda Kavelin - *A Pace of Grace: The Virtues of a Sustainable Life*
LJ - v129 - i12 - July 2004 - p107(1) [51-500]

Popov, Oliver Blagoj - *Creative and Innovative Network Management*
SciTech - v28 - i4 - Dec 2004 - p151(1) [51-500]

Popovic, R.S. - *Hall Effect Devices, 2nd Ed.*
E-Streams - Dec 2004 - pNA [501+]

Popp, Marcia S. - *The Man Who Became a School*
R&R Bk N - v19 - i4 - Nov 2004 - p177(1) [501+]

Popular Woodworking - *Popular Woodworking Complete Book of Tips, Tricks and Techniques*
LJ - v129 - i14 - Sept 1 2004 - p180(1) [51-500]

Porch, Douglas - *Hitler's Mediterranean Gamble: The North African and Mediterranean Campaigns in World War II*
Spec - v295 - i9180 - July 17 2004 - p33(1) [501+]
TLS - i5292 - Sept 3 2004 - p21(1) [501+]
The Path to Victory: The Mediterranean Theater in World War II
J Mil H - v68 - i4 - Oct 2004 - p1294-1295 [501+]
Choice - v42 - i5 - Jan 2005 - p924(1) [1-50]

Porche, Demetrius James - *Public and Community Health Nursing Practice: A Population-Based Approach*
SciTech - v28 - i1 - March 2004 - p126(1) [51-500]

Porche, Jean - *Angels Help Us: Discovering Divine Guidance*
CBRA - Annual 2003 - p99(1) [51-500]

Pories, Kathy - *The M Word: Writers on Same-Sex Marriage*
BL - v101 - i3 - Oct 1 2004 - p287(1) [51-500]
M Word: Writes on Same-Sex Marriage
Advocate - Nov 23 2004 - p97(1) [51-500]

Pormann, Peter E. - *The Oriental Tradition of Paul of Aegina's Pragmeteia*
SciTech - v28 - i3 - Sept 2004 - p77(1) [51-500]

Porot, Daniel - *101 Toughest Interview Questions: And Answers That Win the Job*
HR Mag - v50 - i2 - Feb 2005 - pS10(1) [501+]

Porret, Michel - *Le Temps de Montesquieu*
FS - v58 - i2 - April 2004 - p259(1) [501+]

Porritt, Vernon L. - *The Rise and Fall of Communism in Sarawak 1940-1990*
R&R Bk N - v19 - i3 - August 2004 - p55(1) [51-500]

Portable RN 2005: The All-in-One Nursing Reference
SciTech - v28 - i4 - Dec 2004 - p121 [51-500]

Portale, Alfred - *Simple Pleasures: Home Cooking from the Gotham Bar and Grill's Acclaimed Chef*
BL - v101 - i3 - Oct 1 2004 - p291(1) [51-500]
Globe & Mail - Nov 27 2004 - pD26 [51-500]
PW - v251 - i39 - Sept 27 2004 - p51(1) [51-500]

Porte, Joel - *Consciousness and Culture: Emerson and Thoreau Reviewed*
Choice - v42 - i5 - Jan 2005 - p855(1) [1-50]

Porteffield, Jason - *Treasure Island and the Pirates of the 18th Century*
BL - v101 - i6 - Nov 15 2004 - p573(1) [51-500]

Portela, Carols - *Deicide: Path of the Dead, Book 1*
Kliatt - v38 - i6 - Nov 2004 - p28(1) [501+]

Porter, Andrew - *The Imperial Horizons of British Protestant Missions, 1880-1914*
CH - v73 - i4 - Dec 2004 - p870(3) [501+]
IJAHS - v37 - i1 - Wntr 2004 - p169-172 [501+]

Porter, Ann - *Gendered States: Women, Unemployment Insurance, and the Political Economy of the Welfare State in Canada, 1945-1997*
JEL - v42 - i1 - March 2004 - p280(1) [501+]
Soc Ser R - v78 - i4 - Dec 2004 - p683(3) [501+]

Porter, Barbara Nevling - *One God or Many? Concepts of Divinity in the Ancient World*
JNES - v63 - i4 - Oct 2004 - p297(2) [501+]

Porter, Catherine - *Collecting Modern Books*
ALJ - v53 - i4 - Nov 2004 - p420(3) [501+]

Porter, Cheryl - *Gross Grub: Wretched Recipes That Look Yucky but Taste Yummy*
c SLJ - v51 - i2 - Feb 2005 - p58(1) [51-500]

Porter, David L. - *Latino and African American Athletes Today: A Biographical Dictionary*
BL - v100 - i22 - August 2004 - p1980(1) [51-500]
Choice - v42 - i2 - Oct 2004 - p262(1) [51-500]
R&R Bk N - v19 - i3 - August 2004 - p87(1) [51-500]
SLJ - v50 - i8 - August 2004 - p59(1) [501+]

Porter, David W. - *Excerptiones de Prisciano*
Med R - June 2004 - pNA [501+]

Porter, Eric - *What Is This Thing Called Jazz? African American Musicians as Artists, Critics and Activists*
Am M - v22 - i2 - Summer 2004 - p323-326 [501+]

Porter, Gary A. - *Financial Accounting: The Impact on Decision Makers, the Alternative to Debits and Credits, 4th Ed.*
R&R Bk N - v19 - i2 - May 2004 - p119 [51-500]

Porter, Glenn - *Raymond Loewy: Designs for a Consumer Culture*
T&C - v45 - i4 - Oct 2004 - p854(2) [501+]

Porter, Horace A. - *Jazz Country: Ralph Ellison in America*
Am St - v45 - i1 - Spring 2004 - p163-164 [501+]

Porter, Joe Ashby - *Touch Wood: Short Stories*
Sew R - v112 - i3 - Summer 2004 - p456-463 [501+]

Porter, Kay - *The Mental Athlete*
R&R Bk N - v19 - i1 - Feb 2004 - p74(1) [51-500]

Porter, Lawrence M. - *Gustave Flaubert's 'Madame Bovary': A Reference Guide*
FS - v58 - i3 - July 2004 an p424-424 [501+]

Porter, Lynette R. - *Developing an Online Educational Curriculum: Techniques and Technologies*
R&R Bk N - v19 - i1 - Feb 2004 - pNA [51-500]

Porter, M.A. - *Design and Analysis of Pressure Vessels, Heat Exchangers, and Piping Components: Proceedings*
SciTech - v28 - i4 - Dec 2004 - p162(1) [51-500]

Porter, Norman - *The Elusive Quest: Reconciliation in Northern Ireland*
AJPS - v39 - i2 - July 2004 - p454(455) [501+]

Porter-O'Grady, Timothy - *Quantum Leadership: A Textbook of New Leadership*
R&R Bk N - v19 - i1 - Feb 2004 - p90(1) [1-50]

Porter, Pamela - *Courtly Love in Medieval Manuscripts*
c Med R - August 2004 - pNA [501+]
Sky (Illus. by Gerber, Mary Jane)
c CCB-B - v58 - i4 - Dec 2004 - p181(1) [51-500]
y HB - v81 - i1 - Jan-Feb 2005 - p97(1) [51-500]
c Res Links - v10 - i3 - Feb 2005 - p20(1) [501+]

Porter, Peter - *Afterburner*
Spec - v296 - i9200 - Dec 4 2004 - p40(1) [501+]

Porter, Randy - *The Best in Tent Camping Virginia*
Bwatch - Nov 2004 - pNA [501+]

Porter, Richard C. - *The Economics of Waste*
JEL - v42 - i1 - March 2004 - p230(2) [501+]

Porter, Roy - *Blood And Guts: A Short History of Medicine*
Kliatt - v38 - i6 - Nov 2004 - p40(1) [51-500]
Bodies Politics: Disease, Death and Doctors in Britain, 1650-1900
JIH - v34 - i3 - Wntr 2004 - p452-2 [501+]
The Confinement of the Insane: International Perspectives, 1800-1965
AHR - v109 - i3 - June 2004 - p867(2) [501+]
Isis - v95 - i2 - June 2004 - p348(2) [51-500]

Flesh in the Age of Reason
BL - v101 - i9-10 - Jan 1 2005 - p767(1) [51-500]
Choice - v42 - i6 - Feb 2005 - p1063(1) [51-500]
Isis - v95 - i3 - Sept 2004 - p493(2) [501+]

Porter, Stanley E. - *Concept of the Covenant in the Second Temple Period*
R&R Bk N - v19 - i1 - Feb 2004 - p14(1) [51-500]
The Pauline Canon
R&R Bk N - v19 - i4 - Nov 2004 - p23(1) [51-500]

Porter, Susie S. - *Working Women in Mexico City: Public Discourses and Material Conditions*
Hisp R - v72 - i3 - Summer 2004 - p460-463 [501+]

Porter, Theodore M. - *The Cambridge History of Science, Vol. 7*
Choice - v41 - i7 - March 2004 - p1315(2) [501+]
J Hist G - v30 - i3 - July 2004 - p575(4) [501+]
Karl Pearson: The Scientific Life in a Statistical Age
Am Sci - v92 - i4 - July-August 2004 - p386(2) [501+]
Choice - v42 - i1 - Sept 2004 - p126(1) [501+]
Nature - v430 - i6999 - July 29 2004 - p507(2) [501+]
SB - v40 - i5 - Sept-Oct 2004 - p202(1) [51-500]

Porterfield, James D. - *From the Dining Car: The Recipes and Stories Behind Today's Greatest Rail Dining Experiences*
LJ - v129 - i19 - Nov 15 2004 - p83(1) [51-500]

Porterfield, Jason - *Annie Oakley: Wild West Sharpshooter*
c BL - v101 - i2 - Sept 15 2004 - p238(1) [51-500]

Porterfield, Nolan - *Exploring Roots Music: Twenty Years of JEMF Quarterly*
R&R Bk N - v19 - i2 - May 2004 - p192(1) [51-500]

Porterfield, Todd - *The Allure of Empire: Art in the Service of French Imperialism 1798-1836*
Art Bull - v86 - i3 - Sept 2004 - p603(7) [501+]

Portis-Winner, Irene - *Semiotics of Peasants in Transition: Slovene Villagers and Their Ethnic Relatives in America*
Slav R - v63 - i2 - Summer 2004 - p386(2) [501+]

Portman, Ronald J. - *Pediatric Hypertension*
SciTech - v28 - i4 - Dec 2004 - p112(1) [1-50]

Portmann, John - *Bad for Us: The Lure of Self-Harm*
R&R Bk N - v19 - i3 - August 2004 - p9(1) [1-50]
Sex and Heaven: Catholics in Bed and at Prayer
Lam Bk Rpt - v13 - i1-2 - August-Sept 2004 - p34(3) [501+]

Portney, Kent E. - *Taking Sustainable Cities Seriously: Economic Development, the Environment, and Quality of Life in American Cities*
NRJ - v44 - i3 - Summer 2004 - p907-916 [501+]

Portnoy, Mindy Avra - *Where Do People Go When They Die? (Illus. by Haas, Shelly O.)*
c BL - v100 - i21 - July 2004 - p1849(1) [1-50]
c SLJ - v50 - i7 - July 2004 - p86(1) [51-500]

Porto, Brian L. - *A New Season: Using Title IX to Reform College Sports*
Choice - v41 - i7 - March 2004 - p1333(1) [501+]

Porto, Tony - *Blue Aliens!: An Adventure in Color*
BooChiTr - Jan 18 2004 - p5(1) [501+]

Ports, Michael A. - *Watershed Management: Proceedings*
SciTech - v28 - i1 - March 2004 - p146(1) [51-500]

Portsmouth, Amy Kaler. - *Running After Pills: Politics, Gender and Contraception in Colonial Zimbabwe*
AJS - v110 - i3 - Nov 2004 - p822(2) [501+]

Portugali, J. - *Self-Organization and the City*
PG - v23 - i8 - Nov 2004 - p1063-1065 [501+]

Portzamparc, Christian de - *Voir ecrire*
WLT - v78 - i3-4 - Sept-Dec 2004 - p122(1) [501+]

Posamentier, Alfred S. - *Math Charmers: Tantalizing Tidbits for the Mind*
Math T - v97 - i3 - March 2004 - p222-222 [501+]
Pi: A Biography of the World's Most Mysterious Number
Choice - v42 - i5 - Jan 2005 - p889(2) [1-50]
y SB - v41 - i1 - Jan-Feb 2005 - p25(1) [501+]
Sci - v306 - i5703 - Dec 10 2004 - p1894(1) [501+]
SciTech - v28 - i4 - Dec 2004 - p42(1) [51-500]

Poser, Charles M. - *History of Tropical Neurology: Nutritional Disorders*
SciTech - v28 - i1 - March 2004 - p90(1) [51-500]

Posey, Sam - *Playing with Trains: A Passion beyond Scale*
BL - v100 - i22 - August 2004 - p1885(1) [51-500]
Bwatch - March 2005 - pNA [501+]
Globe & Mail - Sept 11 2004 - pD22 [1-50]
KR - v72 - i13 - July 1 2004 - p621(1) [51-500]
LJ - v129 - i15 - Sept 15 2004 - p64(1) [51-500]
PW - v251 - i31 - August 2 2004 - p61(1) [501+]

Poskanzer, Steven G. - *Higher Education Law: The Faculty*
J Hi E - v75 - i4 - July-August 2004 - p474(3) [501+]

Posner, Elieser - *Wheat Flour Milling, 2nd Ed.*
SciTech - v28 - i4 - Dec 2004 - p170(1) [51-500]

Posner, Michael - *The Last Honest Man: Mordecai Richler, An Oral Biography*
Globe & Mail - Nov 27 2004 - pD3 [51-500]

Posner, Richard A. - *Catastrophe: Risk and Response*
HLR - v118 - i4 - Feb 2005 - p1339-1346 [501+]
NYTBR - Jan 2 2005 - p12 [501+]
PW - v251 - i42 - Oct 18 2004 - p57(1) [51-500]
Sci - v307 - i5713 - Feb 25 2005 - p1205(1) [501+]
Law, Pragmatism, and Democracy
JEL - v42 - i1 - March 2004 - p202(3) [501+]

Possanza, D. Mark - *Translating the Heavens: Aratus, Germanicus, and the Poetics of Latin Translation*
R&R Bk N - v19 - i1 - Feb 2004 - p214 [51-500]

Posset, Franz - *Front-Runner of the Catholic Reformation: The Life and Works of Johann von Staupitz*
HNet - Sept 2004 - pNA [501+]

Post, P. - *Disaster Ritual: Explorations of an Emerging Ritual Repertoire*
R&R Bk N - v19 - i1 - Feb 2004 - p12(1) [1-50]

Post, Peggy - *Emily Post's Etiquette, 17th Ed.*
BL - v101 - i2 - Sept 15 2004 - p184(1) [51-500]
Emily Post's The Guide to Good Manners for Kids (Illus. by Bjorkman, Steve)
y BL - v101 - i9-10 - Jan 1 2005 - p854(1) [1-50]
c SLJ - v50 - i12 - Dec 2004 - p168(1) [51-500]

Post, Stephen G. - *Chaos and Life: Complexity and Order in Evolution and Thought*
SciTech - v28 - i1 - March 2004 - p61(1) [51-500]
Encyclopedia of Bioethics, 3rd Ed.
y Ref Rev - July 2004 - pNA [501+]
Human Nature and the Freedom of Public Religious Expression
Choice - v41 - i7 - March 2004 - p1314(1) [501+]
J Ch St - v46 - i3 - Summer 2004 - p661(2) [501+]
JR - v84 - i4 - Oct 2004 - p654(2) [501+]

Postel, Philippe - *Victor Segalen et la statuaire chinoise: archeologie et poetique*
FS - v58 - i1 - Jan 2004 - p129(2) [501+]

Postel, Sandra - *Rivers for Life: Managing Water for People and Nature*
Choice - v41 - i7 - March 2004 - p1324(1) [501+]
SB - v40 - i3 - May-June 2004 - p112(1) [51-500]

Postgate, Carolyn - *The Excavations at Tell al Rimah: The Pottery*
JNES - v64 - i1 - Jan 2005 - p65(4) [501+]

Postle, Martin - *Art of the Garden*
LJ - v130 - i2 - Feb 1 2005 - p74(1) [51-500]

Postlewate, Marisa Herrera - *How and Why I Write: Redefining Women's Writing and Experience*
R&R Bk N - v19 - i1 - Feb 2004 - p232(1) [51-500]

Postma, Johannes - *The Atlantic Slave Trade*
SLJ - v50 - i10 - Oct 2004 - pS58(1) [51-500]

Postma, Obe - *What the Poet Must Know: An Anthology*
WLT - v79 - i1 - Jan-April 2005 - p102(1) [501+]

Poterba, James M. - *Tax Policy and the Economy*
JEL - v42 - i1 - March 2004 - p271(1) [501+]

Potoker, Elaine S. - *Managing Diverse Working Styles: The Leadership Competitive Advantage*
R&R Bk N - v19 - i3 - August 2004 - p105(1) [1-50]

Pottage, Alain - *Law, Anthropology, and the Constitution of the Social: Making Persons and Things*
Choice - v42 - i6 - Feb 2005 - p1063(1) [51-500]

Potten, Christopher - *Apoptosis: The Life and Death of Cells*
Choice - v42 - i7 - March 2005 - p1251(1) [51-500]

Potter, Alexandra - *Do You Come Here Often?*
Globe & Mail - Feb 12 2005 - pD6 [501+]
BL - v101 - i9-10 - Jan 1 2005 - p832(1) [1-50]

Potter, Bruce - *802.11 Security*
SciTech - v28 - i3 - Sept 2004 - p154(1) [51-500]

Potter, David - *Un Homme de guerre au temps de la Renaissance: La Vie et les lettres d'Oudart du Biez, Marechal de France, Gouverneur de Boulogne et de Picardie*
Six Ct J - v34 - i4 - Winter 2003 - p1114-1115 [501+]

Potter, Ellen - *Olivia Kidney and the Exit Academy (Illus. by Reynolds, Peter H.)*
  y HB - v81 - i2 - March-April 2005 - p207(1) [51-500]
Olivia Kidney (Illus. by Reynolds, Peter H.)
  y LibMed - v22 - i4 - Jan 2004 - p66(1) [501+]
  y Sch Lib - v52 - i3 - Autumn 2004 - p161(1) [501+]

Potter, Franklin - *Mad about Modern Physics*
  New Sci - v184 - i2476 - Dec 4 2004 - p54(1) [501+]

Potter, Gary W. - *Philadelphia's "Black Mafia": A Social and Political History*
  CS - v33 - i5 - Sept 2004 - p596-597 [501+]

Potter, Giselle - *Chloe's Birthday ... and Me (Illus. by Potter, Giselle)*
  c CCB-B - v57 - i11 - July-August 2004 - p479(1) [501+]
  c HB - v80 - i4 - July-August 2004 - p441(1) [51-500]
  c NYTBR - July 11 2004 - p18 [501+]
  c PW - v251 - i27 - July 5 2004 - p54(2) [51-500]
  c SLJ - v50 - i7 - July 2004 - p86(1) [51-500]

Potter, Julian - *Stephen Potter at the BBC: "Features" in War and Peace*
  TLS - i5288 - August 6 2004 - p29(1) [51-500]

Potter, Mark - *Corps and Clienteles: Public Finance and Political Change in France, 1688-1715*
  R&R Bk N - v19 - i2 - May 2004 - p125 [51-500]

Potter, Michael - *Set Theory and Its Philosophy: A Critical Introduction*
  Choice - v42 - i4 - Dec 2004 - p674(1) [501+]

Potter, Miriam Clark - *Just Mrs. Goose*
  c CH Bwatch - Oct 2004 - pNA [51-500]

Potter, Pitman B. - *From Leninist Discipline to Socialist Legalism: Peng Zhen on Law and Political Authority in the PRC*
  AHR - v109 - i3 - June 2004 - p885(2) [501+]

Potter, Thomas D. - *Handbook of Weather, Climate, and Water, Vols. 1-2*
  Choice - v41 - i7 - March 2004 - p1332(1) [501+]

Potthast, Thomas - *Die Evolution und der Naturschutz: Zum Verhaltnis von Evolutionsbiologie, Okologie und Naturethik*
  Isis - v95 - i3 - Sept 2004 - p540(2) [501+]

Pottle, Frederick Albert - *Boswell's London Journal 1762-1763*
  Globe & Mail - Sept 18 2004 - pD26 [1-50]

Potts, Denys - *Saint-Evremond: A Voice from Exile: Newly Discovered Letter to Madame de Gourville and the Abbe de Hautefeuille*
  FS - v58 - i1 - Jan 2004 - p105(2) [501+]

Potts, Jeannette M. - *Essential Urology: A Guide to Clinical Practice*
  E-Streams - Dec 2004 - pNA [501+]

Potts, Michele A. - *Maryland Employer's Guide, 12th Ed.*
  R&R Bk N - v19 - i4 - Nov 2004 - p169(1) [501+]
Virginia Employer's Guide, 10th Ed.
  R&R Bk N - v19 - i4 - Nov 2004 - p169(1) [501+]

Potts, Stephen - *Sams Teach Yourself Web Services in 24 Hours*
  SciTech - v28 - i1 - March 2004 - p158(1) [51-500]
The Ship Thief
  c Sch Lib - v52 - i4 - Winter 2004 - p204(1) [51-500]

Potworowski, Christophe - *Contemplation and Incarnation: The Theology of Marie-Dominique Chenu*
  Theol St - v65 - i3 - Sept 2004 - p651(2) [501+]

Pouey-Mounou, Anne-Pascale - *L'Imaginaire Cosmologique de Ronsard*
  FS - v58 - i1 - Jan 2004 - p89(2) [501+]
  Six Ct J - v35 - i1 - Spring 2004 - p226(3) [501+]

Pough, Gwendolyn D. - *Check It While I Wreck It: Black Womanhood, Hip Hop Culture, and the Public Sphere*
  Choice - v42 - i4 - Dec 2004 - p723(1) [1-50]
  R&R Bk N - v19 - i4 - Nov 2004 - p59(1) [51-500]

Poulet, Anne L. - *Jean-Antonie Houdon: Sculptor of the Enlightenment*
  Choice - v42 - i6 - Feb 2005 - p1014(1) [51-500]

Poulsen, David A. - *Last Sam's Cage*
  y Globe & Mail - Dec 11 2004 - pD42 [501+]

Poulson, Louise - *Learning to Read Critically in Teaching and Learning*
  R&R Bk N - v19 - i1 - Feb 2004 - p188(1) [51-500]

Pouncey, Peter - *Rules for Old Men Waiting (Read by Vance, Simon). Audiobook Review*
  KR - v73 - i4 - Feb 15 2005 - p194(1) [501+]
Rules for Old Men Waiting
  LJ - v129 - i20 - Dec 1 2004 - p88(1) [1-50]

Pound, Dick - *Inside the Olympics: A Behind-the-Scenes Look at the Politics, the Scandals, and the Glory of the Games*
  y BW - v34 - i34 - August 22 2004 - p8(2) [501+]
  Econ - v372 - i8386 - July 31 2004 - p70US [501+]
  Globe & Mail - August 14 2004 - pD15 [501+]

Pound, Richard W. - *Fitzhenry and Whiteside Book of Canadian Facts and Dates, 3rd Ed.*
  Globe & Mail - Dec 18 2004 - pD14 [1-50]

Pountain, Dick - *The Penguin Concise Dictionary of Computing*
  Choice - v42 - i1 - Sept 2004 - p72(1) [501+]
  SciTech - v28 - i3 - Sept 2004 - p19(1) [501+]

Pournelle, Jerry - *1001 Computer Words You Need to Know*
  Choice - v42 - i5 - Jan 2005 - p828(1) [1-50]
  SciTech - v28 - i4 - Dec 2004 - p18(1) [1-50]

Povey, Karen - *Centipede*
  c SLJ - v50 - i12 - Dec 2004 - p135(1) [51-500]

Povich, Shirley - *All Those Mornings--at the Post: The Twentieth Century in Sports from Famed Washington Post Columnist Shirley Povich*
  KR - v73 - i3 - Feb 1 2005 - p169(1) [501+]
  PW - v252 - i10 - March 7 2005 - p59(2) [51-500]

Pow, Tom - *Tell Me One Thing, Dad*
  c Sch Lib - v52 - i3 - Autumn 2004 - p134(1) [501+]

Powe, Bruce Allen - *Aldershot 1945*
  Globe & Mail - Sept 18 2004 - pD22 [51-500]
  Globe & Mail - Dec 24 2004 - pD3 [1-50]

Powel. Jane - *Bungalow: The Ultimate Arts and Crafts Home*
  LJ - v130 - i1 - Jan 1 2005 - p107(1) [51-500]

Powell, Alan - *The Third Force: ANGAU's New Guinea War, 1942-46*
  J Mil H - v68 - i4 - Oct 2004 - p1291-1292 [501+]

Powell, Anthony - *The Fisher King*
  Globe & Mail - Dec 24 2004 - pD14 [501+]

Powell, Ardal - *The Flute*
  Notes - v61 - i1 - Sept 2004 - p150(3) [501+]

Powell, Barry B. - *Homer*
  R&R Bk N - v19 - i1 - Feb 2004 - p214 [51-500]
Writing and the Origins of Greek Literature
  AJP - v125 - i1 - Spring 2004 - p135-140 [501+]

Powell, Consie - *Amazing Apples*
  c CE - v81 - i2 - Winter 2004 - p108(1) [51-500]

Powell, D.A. - *Cocktails*
  NYTBR - August 22 2004 - p18 [501+]
  NYTBR - August 29 2004 - p18 [501+]
  Ant R - v62 - i4 - Fall 2004 - p776(2) [501+]

Powell, David - *Nationhood and Identity: The British State Since 1800*
  Albion - v36 - i1 - Spring 2004 - p162(2) [501+]

Powell, David J. - *Clinical Supervision in Alcohol and Drug Abuse Counseling: Principles, Models, Methods*
  R&R Bk N - v19 - i3 - August 2004 - p162(1) [501+]

Powell, Eileen - *Gardener's A-Z Guide to Growing Flowers from Seed to Bloom*
  Bwatch - v26 - i8 - August 2004 - p10(1) [51-500]
  SciTech - v28 - i1 - March 2004 - p129(1) [51-500]

Powell, Elfreda - *The Letters of Vincent van Gogh to His Brother and Others 1872-1890*
  CR - v285 - i1663 - August 2004 - p118(2) [501+]

Powell, Eric - *The Goon: Heaps of Ruination*
  PW - v252 - i10 - March 7 2005 - p52(2) [51-500]
The Goon: My Murderous Childhood
  LJ - v129 - i12 - July 2004 - p62(1) [51-500]

Powell, Eve M. Troutt - *A Different Shade of Colonialism: Egypt, Great Britain, and the Mastery of the Sudan*
  HNet - Sept 2004 - pNA [501+]

Powell, Gary N. - *Managing a Diverse Workforce: Learning Activities, 2nd Ed.*
  R&R Bk N - v19 - i4 - Nov 2004 - p113(1) [51-500]

Powell, Gerald A., Jr. - *A Rhetoric of Symbolic Identity: An Analysis of Spike Lee's X and Bamboozled*
  R&R Bk N - v19 - i3 - August 2004 - p263(1) [51-500]

Powell, Gus - *The Company of Strangers*
  Afterimage - v32 - i3 - Nov-Dec 2004 - p14(1) [501+]

Powell, H. Jefferson - *A Community Built in Words: The Constitution in History and Politics*
  JIH - v34 - i3 - Wntr 2004 - p474(3) [501+]

Powell, James M. - *The Deeds of Pope Innocent III*
  Choice - v42 - i3 - Nov 2004 - p498(1) [1-50]
  CHR - v90 - i4 - Oct 2004 - p763(2) [501+]

Powell, Jefferson H. - *A Community Built on Words: The Constitution in History and Politics*
  AHR - v109 - i2 - April 2004 - p517(2) [501+]

Powell, Jillian - *Izzie's Idea (Illus. by Shearing, Leonie)*
  c SLJ - v51 - i1 - Jan 2005 - p90(1) [51-500]
Moving
  c BL - v101 - i5 - Nov 1 2004 - p487(1) [51-500]
  c CH Bwatch - Feb 2005 - pNA [51-500]

Powell, Jim - *FDR's Folly: How Roosevelt and His New Deal Prolonged the Great Depression*
  Am Spect - v37 - i3 - April 2004 - p60(3) [501+]
  Reason - v36 - i5 - Oct 2004 - p59(5) [501+]
Wilson's War: How Woodrow Wilson's Great Blunder Led to Hitler, Lenin, Stalin, and World War II
  KR - v73 - i2 - Jan 15 2005 - p109(1) [501+]
  PW - v252 - i11 - March 14 2005 - p58(1) [51-500]

Powell, John - *Dictionary of Literary Influences: The Twentieth Century, 1914-2000*
  R&USQ - v44 - i2 - Winter 2004 - p166(2) [501+]

Powell, John Wesley - *Canyons of the Colorado*
  NRJ - v44 - i1 - Wntr 2004 - p319-332 [501+]
Down the Colorado: Diary of the First Trip Through the Grand Canyon
  NRJ - v44 - i1 - Wntr 2004 - p319-332 [501+]

Powell, Kenneth - *Culture of Building: The Architecture of John McAslan and Partners*
  Choice - v42 - i4 - Dec 2004 - p653(1) [1-50]

Powell, Kerry - *The Cambridge Companion to Victorian and Edwardian Theatre*
  Choice - v42 - i2 - Oct 2004 - p304(1) [51-500]

Powell, Lynn - *The Zones of Paradise*
  ABR - v25 - i5 - July-August 2004 - p1(2) [501+]
  PSQ - v78 - i4 - Winter 2004 - p193(2) [501+]

Powell, Mark Allan - *Encyclopedia of Contemporary Christian Music*
  CH - v73 - i3 - Sept 2004 - p707(1) [501+]

Powell, Martyn J. - *Britain and Ireland in the Eighteenth Century Crisis of Empire*
  Albion - v36 - i2 - Summer 2004 - p309(2) [501+]

Powell, Nate - *It Disappears (Illus. by Powell, Nate)*
  y BL - v101 - i2 - Sept 15 2004 - p217(1) [501+]

Powell, Neil - *George Crabbe: An English Life, 1754-1832*
  Choice - v42 - i4 - Dec 2004 - p662(1) [1-50]
  KR - v72 - i16 - August 15 2004 - p795(1) [501+]
A Halfway House
  TLS - i5293 - Sept 10 2004 - p27(1) [501+]

Powell, O. - *On the Properties of Foodstuffs. Introduction, Translation and Commentary*
  Class R - v54 - i1 - May 2004 - p244(2) [501+]

Powell, Robert G. - *Classroom Communication and Diversity: Enhancing Institutional Practice*
  R&R Bk N - v19 - i3 - August 2004 - p228(1) [1-50]

Powell, Russell A. - *Introduction to Learning and Behavior, 2nd Ed.*
  R&R Bk N - v20 - i1 - Feb 2005 - p7(1) [51-500]

Powell, Susan - *New Perspectives on Middle English Texts: A Festschrift for R.A. Waldron*
  JEGP - v103 - i3 - July 2004 - p388-390 [501+]

Powell, Thomas - *JavaScript: The Complete Reference, 2nd Ed.*
  CBRA - Annual 2003 - p21(1) [1-50]
  SciTech - v28 - i4 - Dec 2004 - p21(1) [501+]

Powell, Walter L. - *Benedict Arnold: Revolutionary War Hero and Traitor*
  c SLJ - v50 - i7 - July 2004 - p126(1) [51-500]

Power, John - *Italy: The Essential Guide to Viewing Italian Renaissance Art*
  R&R Bk N - v19 - i1 - Feb 2004 - p200(1) [51-500]

Power, Margaret - *Right-Wing Women in Chile: Feminine Power and the Struggle Against Allende, 1964-1973*
  CS - v33 - i6 - Nov 2004 - p748(1) [1-50]

Power, Nani - *The Sea of Tears*
  BL - v101 - i8 - Dec 15 2004 - p709(1) [51-500]
  KR - v72 - i23 - Dec 1 2004 - p1111(1) [51-500]
  LJ - v130 - i1 - Jan 1 2005 - p100(1) [51-500]
  NYTBR - Feb 6 2005 - p23 [501+]
  PW - v251 - i48 - Nov 29 2004 - p24(1) [51-500]

Power, Paul W. - *Families Living with Chronic Illness and Disability: Interventions, Challenges, and Opportunities*
  SciTech - v28 - i4 - Dec 2004 - p91(1) [51-500]

Power, Susan C. - *Early Art of the Southeastern Indians: Feathered Serpents and Winged Beings*
  Choice - v42 - i4 - Dec 2004 - p647(1) [1-50]

Powers, Alan - *Children's Book Covers*
  ALJ - v53 - i4 - Nov 2004 - p420(3) [501+]
Front Cover
  ALJ - v53 - i4 - Nov 2004 - p420(3) [501+]
The Twentieth Century House in Britain from the Archives of Country Life
  Apo - v161 - i515 - Jan 2005 - p68(2) [501+]

Powers, Ann - *Tori Amos: Piece by Piece*
  NYTBR - Feb 27 2005 - p22 [501+]

Powers, Charles H. - *Making Sense of Social Theory: A Practical Introduction*
R&R Bk N - v19 - i3 - August 2004 - p141(1) [51-500]

Powers, David S. - *Law, Society, and Culture in the Maghrib, 1300-1500*
AHR - v109 - i3 - June 2004 - p1018(2) [501+]
JR - v84 - i4 - Oct 2004 - p668(2) [501+]

Powers, Dennis M. - *The Raging Sea: The Heroic Story of America's Worst Tidal Wave*
c PW - v252 - i6 - Feb 7 2005 - p57(1) [51-500]

Powers, John - *Sore Winners (And the Rest of Us) in George Bush's America*
BL - v100 - i21 - July 2004 - p1813(1) [51-500]
BW - v34 - i31 - August 1 2004 - p2(1) [501+]
NYTBR - Sept 12 2004 - p24 [501+]

Powers, Katherine - *Musica Spirituale, Libro Primo (Venice, 1563).*
Notes - v61 - i2 - Dec 2004 - p553(4) [501+]

Powers, Kemp - *The Shooting: A Memoir*
LJ - v129 - i20 - Dec 1 2004 - p140(1) [51-500]
BL - v101 - i6 - Nov 15 2004 - p533(1) [51-500]
KR - v72 - i22 - Nov 15 2004 - p1083(1) [501+]
PW - v251 - i41 - Oct 11 2004 - p63(1) [501+]

Powers, Lyall Harris - *Alien Heart: The Life and Work of Margaret Laurence*
CBRA - Annual 2003 - p64(1) [501+]
CWS - v23 - i3-4 - Spring-Summer 2004 - p215(3) [501+]

Powers, Michael D. - *Asperger Syndrome and Your Child: A Parent's Guide*
NYT - August 10 2004 - pF7(L) [501+]

Powers, Richard - *The Time of Our Singing*
WLT - v79 - i1 - Jan-April 2005 - p91(2) [501+]

Powers, Richard Gid - *Broken: The Troubled Past and Uncertain Future of the FBI*
BL - v101 - i2 - Sept 15 2004 - p184(1) [51-500]
BW - v34 - i44 - Oct 31 2004 - p6(1) [501+]
Bwatch - Dec 2004 - pNA [51-500]
CHE - v51 - i20 - Jan 21 2005 - pB12-B14 [501+]
KR - v72 - i15 - August 1 2004 - p731(1) [501+]
LJ - v129 - i15 - Sept 15 2004 - p69(1) [51-500]
NYTBR - Oct 24 2004 - p18 [501+]
PW - v251 - i32 - August 9 2004 - p238(1) [51-500]

Powers, Thomas - *Intelligence Wars: American Secret History from Hitler to Al Qaeda*
TLS - i5301 - Nov 5 2004 - p4-6 [501+]

Powers, Tom - *The Call of God: Women Doing Theology in Peru*
Theol St - v66 - i1 - March 2005 - p226(2) [501+]

Powers, William - *Blue Clay People: Seasons on Africa's Fragile Edge*
y BL - v101 - i8 - Dec 15 2004 - p695(1) [51-500]
KR - v72 - i21 - Nov 1 2004 - p1041(1) [501+]
PW - v251 - i46 - Nov 15 2004 - p48(1) [501+]

Powers, William Douglas - *An Eliadean Interpretation of Frank G. Speck's Account of the Cherokee Booger Dance*
R&R Bk N - v19 - i1 - Feb 2004 - p53(1) [51-500]

Powers, William F. - *Tar Heel Catholics: A History of Catholicism in North Carolina*
CHR - v90 - i4 - Oct 2004 - p817(3) [501+]
R&R Bk N - v19 - i1 - Feb 2004 - p24(1) [1-50]

Powlson, David S. - *Interactions in the Root Environment: An Integrated Approach, Proceedings*
SciTech - v28 - i1 - March 2004 - p67(1) [51-500]

Pownall, Frances - *Lessons from the Past: The Moral Use of History in Fourth-Century Prose*
Choice - v42 - i1 - Sept 2004 - p165(1) [51-500]

Pownell, David - *Administrative Solutions for Handheld Technology in Schools*
LibMed - v22 - i4 - Jan 2004 - p86(1) [501+]

Powning, Beth - *The Hatbox Letters*
Globe & Mail - August 21 2004 - pD5 [501+]
Globe & Mail - Nov 27 2004 - pD3 [51-500]
KR - v73 - i2 - Jan 15 2005 - p79(1) [501+]

Powrie, Phil - *French Cinema: A Student's Guide*
FS - v58 - i1 - Jan 2004 - p150(2) [501+]

Poydar, Nancy - *Brave Santa (Illus. by Poydar, Nancy)*
c CCB-B - v58 - i4 - Dec 2004 - p181(1) [51-500]
c KR - v72 - i21 - Nov 1 2004 - p1053(1) [51-500]

Pozefsky, Peter C. - *The Nihilist Imagination: Dmitrii Pisarev and the Cultural Origins of Russian Radicalism*
Slav R - v63 - i4 - Winter 2004 - p889(3) [501+]

Practical Money Skills for Life
LibMed - v22 - i6 - March 2004 - p91(1) [501+]

Prado, C.G. - *House Divided: Comparing Analytic and Continental Philosophy*
R&R Bk N - v19 - i1 - Feb 2004 - p2(1) [51-500]

Prados de la Escosura, Leandro - *Exceptionalism and Industrialisation: Britain and Its European Rivals, 1688-1815*
TLS - i5291 - August 27 2004 - p24(1) [501+]

Prados, John - *Hoodwinked: The Documents That Reveal How Bush Sold Us a War*
PSQ - v119 - i4 - Winter 2004 - p677(4) [501+]
SPA - v61 - i1 - Jan-Feb 2005 - p65(3) [501+]
Inside the Pentagon Papers
Law&PolBR - July 2004 - p543(3) [501+]
Lost Crusador: The Secret Wars of CIA Director William Colby
JAH - v91 - i1 - June 2004 - p326-326 [501+]
White House Tapes: Eavesdropping on the President
SLJ - v50 - i10 - Oct 2004 - pS57(1) [51-500]

Praeger Illustrated Military History - *American Civil War, Vols. 1-12*
R&R Bk N - v19 - i4 - Nov 2004 - p61(1) [51-500]

Praeger, Michele - *The Imaginary Caribbean and Caribbean Imaginary*
Choice - v42 - i1 - Sept 2004 - p106(1) [501+]

Praetorius, Michael - *Syntagma Musicum III*
Choice - v42 - i3 - Nov 2004 - p493(1) [51-500]

Prager, Charles - *World Commodity Survey: 2003-2004: Markets, Trends and the World Economic Environment*
JEL - v41 - i4 - Dec 2003 - p1365(1) [501+]

Prager, Ellen J. - *Furious Earth: The Science and Nature of Earthquakes, Volcanoes and Tsunamis*
Globe & Mail - Jan 1 2005 - pD15 [501+]

Prague, Cary N. - *Access 2003 Bible*
SciTech - v28 - i3 - Sept 2004 - p29(1) [51-500]

Prahalad, C.K. - *The Fortune at the Bottom of the Pyramid: Eradicating Poverty through Profits*
Econ - v372 - i8389 - August 21 2004 - p54US [501+]
The Future of Competition: Co-Creating Unique Value with Customers
Choice - v41 - i11-12 - July-August 2004 - p2090(1) [501+]

Prahlad, Swami Anand - *Reggae Wisdom: Proverbs in Jamaican Music*
Col Lit - v32 - i1 - Wntr 2005 - p201(5) [501+]

Prakash, Anand - *Water Resources Engineering: Handbook of Essential Methods and Design*
SciTech - v28 - i1 - March 2004 - p146(1) [51-500]

Prakash, Chandra - *A Therapeutic Guide to Common Problems in Gastroenterology*
SciTech - v28 - i3 - Sept 2004 - p107(1) [51-500]

Prakash, Nirmala - *Mathematical Perspectives on Theoretical Physics: A Journey from Black Holes to Superstrings*
SciTech - v28 - i1 - March 2004 - p45(1) [51-500]

Prange, Sally Bowen - *Sally Bowen Prange*
Ceram Mo - v52 - i2 - Feb 2004 - p32(1) [501+]

Pranger, M.B. - *The Artficiality of Christianity: Essays on the Poetics of Monasticism*
Specu - v79 - i3 - July 2004 - p827-829 [501+]
The Artificiality of Christianity: Essays on the Poetics of Monasticism
JR - v85 - i1 - Jan 2005 - p180(2) [501+]

Prasad, Rajendra - *Dharmakirti's Theory of Inference: Revaluation and Reconstruction*
HNet - Sept 2004 - pNA [501+]

Prasad, Ramjee - *OFDM for Wireless Communications Systems*
SciTech - v28 - i4 - Dec 2004 - p149(1) [51-500]

Prasad, S. Benjamin - *Global Firms and Emerging Markets in an Age of Anxiety*
R&R Bk N - v19 - i3 - August 2004 - p108(1) [51-500]

Prasso, Sheridan - *The Asian Mystique: Dragon Ladies, Geisha Girls, and Our Fantasies of the Exotic Orient*
KR - v73 - i5 - March 1 2005 - p280(1) [501+]

Pratchett, Terry - *Going Postal: A Novel of Discworld*
BL - v101 - i1 - Sept 1 2004 - p6(1) [51-500]
Econ - v373 - i8400 - Nov 6 2004 - p90US [501+]
KR - v72 - i17 - Sept 1 2004 - p830(1) [51-500]
MFSF - v108 - i2 - Feb 2005 - p44(6) [501+]
PW - v251 - i36 - Sept 6 2004 - p51(1) [51-500]
SLJ - v51 - i2 - Feb 2005 - p157(1) [51-500]
Hat Full of Sky (Read by Briggs, Stephen). Audiobook Review
y BL - v101 - i4 - Oct 15 2004 - p433(1) [51-500]
A Hat Full of Sky
c BW - v34 - i27 - July 4 2004 - p12(1) [501+]
c ChrSFF&H - v26 - i9 - Sept 2004 - p32(1) [51-500]
y HB - v80 - i4 - July-August 2004 - p460(1) [51-500]
c HB - v81 - i1 - Jan-Feb 2005 - p16(1) [51-500]
y Sch Lib - v52 - i3 - Autumn 2004 - p161(1) [51-500]
c SLJ - v50 - i7 - July 2004 - p111(1) [51-500]
The Wee Free Men
y Kliatt - v38 - i4 - July 2004 - p32(2) [501+]
The Wee Free Men. Audiobook Review
y CH Bwatch - v14 - i9 - Sept 2004 - p6(1) [51-500]

Pratt, Dorothy O. - *Shipshewana: An Indiana Amish Community*
PW - v251 - i46 - Nov 15 2004 - pS17(1) [51-500]

Pratt, Douglas - *Doug Pratt's DVD: Movies, Television, Music, Art, Adult, and More*
Choice - v42 - i5 - Jan 2005 - p828(1) [1-50]
LJ - v129 - i17 - Oct 15 2004 - p88(1) [51-500]

Pratt, Michael E. - *Mid-Century Modern Dinnerware: A Pictorial Guide: Red Wing to Winfield*
Ceram Mo - v52 - i6 - June-August 2004 - p34(2) [501+]

Pratt, Michael W. - *Family Stories and the Life Course: Across Time and Generations*
R&R Bk N - v19 - i3 - August 2004 - p150(1) [51-500]

Pratt, Minnie Bruce - *Crime Against Nature*
Lam Bk Rpt - v13 - i4-5 - Nov-Dec 2004 - p55(1) [501+]

Pratt, Richard Henry - *Battlefield and Classroom: Four Decades with the American Indian, 1867-1904*
Roundup M - v12 - i1 - Oct 2004 - p26(1) [51-500]

Pratt, Robert A. - *We Shall Not Be Moved: The Desegregation of the University of Georgia*
HNet - June 2004 - pNA [501+]

Pratt, William - *The Imagist Poem: Modern Poetry in Miniature*
South CR - v37 - i1 - Fall 2004 - p201-203 [501+]

Praver, Frances Cohen - *Crossroads at Midlife: Your Aging Parents, Your Emotions, and Your Self*
BL - v101 - i4 - Oct 15 2004 - p369(1) [51-500]
LJ - v129 - i19 - Nov 15 2004 - p77(1) [501+]
R&R Bk N - v19 - i4 - Nov 2004 - p131(1) [1-50]

Pray, W. Steven - *History of Nonprescription Product Regulation*
E-Streams - July 2004 - pNA [501+]

Prazmowska, Anita - *A History of Poland*
Choice - v42 - i5 - Jan 2005 - p911(1) [1-50]
CR - v285 - i1667 - Dec 2004 - p377(1) [51-500]

Preble, Christopher - *Exiting Iraq: Why the U.S. Must End the Military Occupation and Renew the War Against Al Qaeda*
MEQ - v11 - i4 - Fall 2004 - p77(2) [501+]
Exiting Iraq: Why the U.S. Must End the Military Occupation and Renew the War Against Al Quaeda
Bwatch - Oct 2004 - pNA [51-500]

Precin, Pat - *Surviving 9/11: Impact and Experiences of Occupational Therapy Practitioners*
SciTech - v28 - i3 - Sept 2004 - p123(1) [51-500]

Preddy, Shan - *How to Market Design Consultancy Services: Finding, Winning, Keeping and Developing Clients, 2nd Ed.*
R&R Bk N - v19 - i3 - August 2004 - p244(1) [51-500]

Predelli, Nyhagen - *Issues of Gender, Race, and Class in the Norwegian Missionary Society in Nineteenth Century Norway and Madagascar*
IBMR - v28 - i4 - Oct 2004 - p182(2) [501+]

Predictions
LibMed - v22 - i6 - March 2004 - p62(1) [501+]

Preece, David - *Technological Change and Organisational Action*
JEL - v41 - i4 - Dec 2003 - p1419(2) [501+]

Preedy, Victor R. - *Reviews in Food and Nutrition Toxicity: Vol. 1*
SciTech - v28 - i1 - March 2004 - p179(1) [51-500]
Reviews in Food and Nutrition Toxicity, Vol. 2
SciTech - v28 - i4 - Dec 2004 - p170(1) [51-500]

Prehistoric Animals Series
c LibMed - v23 - i3 - Nov-Dec 2004 - p87(2) [51-500]

Prehistoric Life Series
c LibMed - v23 - i3 - Nov-Dec 2004 - p64(1) [51-500]

Preissl, Brigitte - *The Dynamics of Clusters and Innovation: Beyond Systems and Networks*
JEL - v42 - i1 - March 2004 - p319(2) [501+]

Prejean, Helen - *The Death of Innocents: An Eyewitness Account of Wrongful Executions*
AM - v192 - i8 - March 7 2005 - p23 [501+]
BL - v101 - i8 - Dec 15 2004 - p690(1) [51-500]
Globe & Mail - March 5 2005 - pD3 [501+]
KR - v72 - i23 - Dec 1 2004 - p1137(2) [501+]
LJ - v130 - i3 - Feb 15 2005 - p146(1) [51-500]
NYTBR - Jan 23 2005 - p29 [501+]
PW - v251 - i49 - Dec 6 2004 - p55(1) [51-500]

Preker, Alexander S. - *Health Financing for Poor People: Resource Mobilization and Risk Sharing*
SciTech - v28 - i3 - Sept 2004 - p82(1) [501+]

Prelutsky, Jack - *The Frog Wore Red Suspenders*
  c PW - v252 - i6 - Feb 7 2005 - p62(1) [51-500]
If Not for the Cat (Illus. by Rand, Ted)
  c BL - v101 - i3 - Oct 1 2004 - p336(1) [51-500]
  c CCB-B - v58 - i4 - Dec 2004 - p181(2) [51-500]
  c HB - v80 - i6 - Nov-Dec 2004 - p723(2) [501+]
  c HB - v81 - i1 - Jan-Feb 2005 - p16(2) [51-500]
  c KR - v72 - i18 - Sept 15 2004 - p917(1) [51-500]
  c PW - v251 - i42 - Oct 18 2004 - p62(1) [51-500]
  c SLJ - v50 - i10 - Oct 2004 - p147(2) [51-500]
It's Raining Pigs and Noodles (Illus. by Stevenson, James)
  c PW - v252 - i11 - March 14 2005 - p70(1) [51-500]
Wild Witches' Ball (Illus. by Asbury, Kelly)
  c BL - v100 - i22 - August 2004 - p1944(1) [51-500]
  c KR - v72 - i14 - July 15 2004 - p692(1) [51-500]
  c SLJ - v50 - i8 - August 2004 - p92(2) [51-500]

Premack, David - *Original Intelligence: Unlocking the Mystery of Who We Are*
  TLS - i5300 - Oct 29 2004 - p32(1) [501+]

Prendergast, Catherine - *Literacy and Racial Justice: The Politics of Learning after Brown v. Board of Education*
  Afr Am R - v38 - i3 - Fall 2004 - p537(3) [501+]

Prendergast, William E. - *Treating Sex Offenders: A Guide to Clinical Practice with Adults, Clerics, Children, and Adolescents, 2nd ed.*
  E-Streams - July 2004 - pNA [501+]
  SciTech - v28 - i1 - March 2004 - p101(1) [51-500]

Prentice, Steven - *Cool Time and the Two-Pound Bucket: Time Management for the 24-Hour Person*
  CBRA - Annual 2003 - p16(2) [51-500]

Prentiss, William C. - *Complex Hunter-Gatherers: Evolution and Organization of Prehistoric Communities on the Plateau of Northwestern North America*
  R&R Bk N - v19 - i4 - Nov 2004 - p53(1) [51-500]

Preparing Reading Professionals: A Collection from the International Reading Association
  R Today - v22 - i1 - August-Sept 2004 - p32(1) [51-500]

Prerau, David - *Seize the Daylight: The Curious and Contentious Story of Daylight Saving Time*
  KR - v73 - i2 - Jan 15 2005 - p109(1) [501+]

Prescott, Andrew - *The Benedictional of St. Aethelwold: A Masterpiece of Anglo-Saxon Art: A Facsimile*
  R&R Bk N - v19 - i1 - Feb 2004 - p206(1) [51-500]

Prescott, Michael - *Dangerous Games*
  PW - v251 - i50 - Dec 13 2004 - p51(1) [51-500]

Presidential Leaders
  LibMed - v22 - i6 - March 2004 - p75(1) [501+]

President's Council on Bioethics - *Beyond Therapy: Biotechnology and the Pursuit of Happiness*
  Choice - v42 - i3 - Nov 2004 - p509(1) [1-50]
  SciTech - v28 - i1 - March 2004 - p71(1) [51-500]

Preskill, Hallie S. - *Building Evaluation Capacity: 72 Activities for Teaching and Training*
  R&R Bk N - v20 - i1 - Feb 2005 - p2(1) [51-500]

Presnell, Daniel - *Mermaids of the Saluda*
  South CR - v36 - i2 - Spring 2004 - p161-163 [501+]

Press, Bill - *Bush Must Go: The Top Ten Reasons Why George Bush Doesn't Deserve a Second Term*
  NYTBR - Sept 12 2004 - p24 [501+]
  R&R Bk N - v19 - i4 - Nov 2004 - p64(1) [51-500]

Press, Daniel - *Saving Open Space: The Politics of Local Preservation in California*
  Pub Hist - v26 - i1 - Wntr 2004 - p164(3) [501+]

Press, Joseph Henry - *Degress Kelvin: A Tale of Genius, Invention, and Tragedy*
  Sci - v305 - i5689 - Sept 3 2004 - p1406(1) [501+]

Presser, Harriet B. - *Working in a 24/7 Economy: Challenges for American Families*
  Choice - v41 - i11-12 - July-August 2004 - p2130(1) [501+]
  Soc Ser R - v78 - i4 - Dec 2004 - p681(3) [501+]

Pressfield, Steven - *The Virtues of War: A Novel of Alexander the Great*
  BL - v101 - i2 - Sept 15 2004 - p210(1) [501+]
  BW - v34 - i46 - Nov 14 2004 - p8(1) [501+]
  KR - v72 - i15 - August 1 2004 - p710(2) [501+]
  LJ - v129 - i16 - Oct 1 2004 - p72(1) [51-500]
  Mar Crp G - v88 - i11 - Nov 2004 - p88(1) [501+]
  PW - v251 - i41 - Oct 11 2004 - p57(1) [501+]

Pressler, Mirjam - *Malka*
  y PW - v252 - i4 - Jan 24 2005 - p246(1) [51-500]

Pressley, Brian - *Physics Jeopardy*
  Sci Teach - v72 - i3 - March 2005 - p81(1) [51-500]

Pressley, Michael - *Motivating Primary-Grade Students*
  SLJ - v50 - i10 - Oct 2004 - pS74(1) [51-500]

Pressman, David - *Patent It Yourself, 10th Ed.*
  SciTech - v28 - i3 - Sept 2004 - p11(1) [501+]

Prest, Wilfred - *The Wakefield Companion to South Australian History*
  AHS - v35 - i123 - April 2004 - p179-181 [501+]

Preston, Alison - *Cherry Bites*
  Globe & Mail - Feb 19 2005 - pD15 [501+]

Preston, Anne E. - *Leaving Science: Occupational Exit from Scientific Careers*
  Fut - v38 - i6 - Nov-Dec 2004 - p60(1) [51-500]
  Choice - v42 - i5 - Jan 2005 - p874(1) [1-50]

Preston, Carol - *Jump Back in Time: A Living History Resource*
  c LibMed - v23 - i3 - Nov-Dec 2004 - p91(1) [51-500]

Preston, David Seth - *Virtual Learning and Higher Education*
  R&R Bk N - v19 - i3 - August 2004 - p230(1) [1-50]

Preston, Diana - *Before the Fallout: From Marie Curie to Hiroshima*
  KR - v73 - i2 - Jan 15 2005 - p109(2) [501+]
  LJ - v130 - i4 - March 1 2005 - p109(1) [51-500]
  PW - v252 - i5 - Jan 31 2005 - p55(1) [501+]

Preston, Douglas - *Brimstone (Read by Brick, Scott). Audiobook Review*
  y Kliatt - v39 - i2 - March 2005 - p50(1) [51-500]
Brimstone
  LJ - v129 - i12 - July 2004 - p73(1) [51-500]
  PW - v251 - i27 - July 5 2004 - p36(1) [51-500]
  SLJ - v50 - i11 - Nov 2004 - p177(1) [51-500]
The Codex (Read by Brick, Scott). Audiobook Review
  Kliatt - v38 - i6 - Nov 2004 - p44(1) [51-500]
  LJ - v129 - i20 - Dec 1 2004 - p180(2) [51-500]

Preston-Dunlop, Valerie - *Dance and the Performative: A Choreological Perspective: Laban and Beyond*
  Dance RJ - v35 - i2 - Winter 2003 - p173-175 [501+]

Preston, John - *Kings of the Roundhouse*
  TLS - i5292 - Sept 3 2004 - p32(1) [501+]

Preston, Julia - *Opening Mexico: The Making of a Democracy*
  ABR - v25 - i6 - Sept-Oct 2004 - p7(2) [501+]
  Choice - v42 - i3 - Nov 2004 - p544(1) [1-50]
  Econ - v372 - i8385 - July 24 2004 - p78US [501+]

Preston, Lydia - *Breaking Out: A Woman's Guide to Coping with Acne at Any Age*
  LJ - v129 - i13 - August 2004 - p108(1) [51-500]

Preston, Michael - *A Pirate of Exquisite Mind: The Life of William Dampier--Explorer, Naturalist and Buccaneer*
  Econ - v372 - i8386 - July 31 2004 - p73US [501+]
  Spec - v295 - i9185 - August 21 2004 - p31(2) [501+]

Preston, Paul - *Doves of War: Four Women of Spain*
  AHR - v109 - i4 - Oct 2004 - p1318(2) [501+]
Juan Carlos: A People's King
  CR - v285 - i1667 - Dec 2004 - p378(1) [51-500]
  TLS - i5289 - August 13 2004 - p6(1) [501+]
Juan Carlos: Steering Spain from Dictatorship to Democracy
  BW - v34 - i28 - July 11 2004 - p6(2) [501+]
  R&R Bk N - v19 - i4 - Nov 2004 - p42(1) [51-500]
Palomas de Guerra: Cinco Mujeres Marcadas por el Enfrentamiento Belico
  S&S - v68 - i3 - Fall 2004 - p379-381 [501+]

Preston, Peter W. - *Political Change in East Asia, Vols. 1-2*
  JEL - v42 - i1 - March 2004 - p251(1) [501+]
  R&R Bk N - v19 - i1 - Feb 2004 - pNA [501+]

Preston, Zoe - *The Crystallization of the Iraqi State: Geopolitical Function and Form*
  R&R Bk N - v19 - i1 - Feb 2004 - p42(1) [51-500]

Prestopnik, Thomas J. - *Gabriel's Journey*
  c CH Bwatch - Jan 2005 - pNA [51-500]

Pretti-Frontczak, Kristie - *An Activity-Based Approach to Early Intervention, 3rd Ed.*
  R&R Bk N - v19 - i3 - August 2004 - p229(1) [1-50]

Preus, Anthony - *Before Plato*
  Class R - v54 - i2 - Nov 2004 - p291-292 [501+]

Preusse, Heinz Gert - *The New American Regionalism*
  Choice - v42 - i4 - Dec 2004 - p708(1) [1-50]
  R&R Bk N - v19 - i3 - August 2004 - p97(1) [51-500]

Prevas, John - *Envy of the Gods: Alexander the Great's Ill-Fated Journey Across Asia*
  BL - v101 - i6 - Nov 15 2004 - p538(1) [51-500]
  KR - v72 - i22 - Nov 15 2004 - p1083(1) [501+]
  LJ - v130 - i1 - Jan 1 2005 - p130(1) [51-500]
  PW - v251 - i49 - Dec 6 2004 - p54(2) [501+]

Preve, Francis - *Power Tools: Software for Loop Music: Essential Desktop Production Techniques*
  R&R Bk N - v19 - i4 - Nov 2004 - p199(1) [501+]

Preves, Sharon E. - *Intersex and Identity: The Contested Self*
  CS - v33 - i4 - July 2004 - p487(2) [501+]

Prevost, Antoine Francois - *Manon Lescaut*
  Bwatch - v26 - i9 - Sept 2004 - p1(1) [51-500]
  TLS - i5285 - July 16 2004 - p20(1) [501+]

Preziosi, Donald - *Grasping the World: The Idea of the Museum*
  Apo - v159 - i510 - August 2004 - p76(2) [501+]
  R&R Bk N - v19 - i3 - August 2004 - p1(1) [1-50]

Price, Annie - *The Middle Ages in Literature for Youth: A Guide and Resource Book*
  Teach Lib - v32 - i2 - Dec 2004 - p39(1) [501+]

Price, B. Byron - *Fine Art of the West*
  PW - v251 - i45 - Nov 8 2004 - p49(2) [501+]
  LJ - v129 - i20 - Dec 1 2004 - p115(1) [51-500]

Price, Bronwen - *Francis Bacon's New Atlantis: New Interdisciplinary Essays*
  Ren Q - v57 - i3 - Fall 2004 - p1108(2) [501+]

Price, Christopher - *Britain, America, and Rearmament in the 1930s: The Cost of Failure*
  JMH - v77 - i1 - March 2005 - p183(3) [501+]
Britain, America, and Rearmament in the 1930s: The Cost of Failure
  AHR - v109 - i2 - April 2004 - p488(2) [501+]

Price, Christopher P. - *Point-of-Care Testing, 2nd Ed.*
  SciTech - v28 - i4 - Dec 2004 - p90(1) [51-500]

Price, Daniel - *Slick*
  BL - v100 - i22 - August 2004 - p1901(2) [501+]

Price, Daniel J. - *Karl Barth's Anthropology in Light of Modern Thought*
  Intpr - v59 - i1 - Jan 2005 - p97(1) [501+]

Price, David A. - *Love and Hate in Jamestown: John Smith, Pocahontas, and the Heart of a New Nation*
  Bwatch - v26 - i7 - July 2004 - p10(1) [51-500]
  Choice - v41 - i7 - March 2004 - p1357(1) [501+]
  CR - v285 - i1665 - Oct 2004 - p251(1) [501+]
  JAH - v91 - i2 - Sept 2004 - p602(2) [501+]
  NYTBR - Jan 23 2005 - p28 [501+]
  RAH - v32 - i3 - Sept 2004 - p317-328 [501+]

Price, David H. - *Threatening Anthropology: McCarthyism and the FBI's Surveillance of Activist Anthropologists*
  Choice - v42 - i5 - Jan 2005 - p897(1) [1-50]
  HRNB - v33 - i1 - Fall 2004 - p11(1) [501+]

Price, Derek V. - *Borrowing Inequality: Race, Class and Student Loans*
  CS - v33 - i5 - Sept 2004 - p626-626 [501+]
Borrowing Inequality: Race, Class, and Student Loans
  R&R Bk N - v19 - i1 - Feb 2004 - p185(1) [51-500]
  TCR - v106 - i12 - Dec 2004 - p2294(4) [501+]

Price, Donald D. - *Psychological Methods of Pain Control: Basic Science and Clinical Perspectives*
  SciTech - v28 - i3 - Sept 2004 - p89(1) [51-500]

Price, Geoffrey L. - *Advances in Quantum Dynamics: Proceedings*
  SciTech - v28 - i1 - March 2004 - p47(1) [51-500]

Price, John - *Not Just Any Land: A Personal and Literary Journey into the American Grasslands*
  Choice - v42 - i3 - Nov 2004 - p486(1) [1-50]

Price, Kenneth M. - *To Walt Whitman, America*
  Choice - v42 - i2 - Oct 2004 - p295(1) [501+]

Price, Lisa - *Success Never Smelled So Sweet: How I Followed My Nose and Found My Passion*
  Black Iss - v6 - i5 - Sept-Oct 2004 - p28(1) [501+]

Price, Monroe E. - *Public Service Broadcasting in Transition: A Documentary Reader*
  R&R Bk N - v19 - i1 - Feb 2004 - p105(1) [51-500]

Price, Reynolds - *The Complete Stories of Truman Capote*
  NYTBR - Dec 5 2004 - p15 [501+]

Price, Richard - *United Arab Emirates Court of Cassation Judgments, 1989-1997*
  R&R Bk N - v19 - i3 - August 2004 - p209(1) [1-50]

Price, Roger - *People and Politics in France, 1848-1870*
  Choice - v42 - i5 - Jan 2005 - p924(1) [1-50]

Price, Ruth - *The Lives of Agnes Smedley*
  LJ - v130 - i1 - Jan 1 2005 - p124(1) [51-500]
  PW - v252 - i5 - Jan 31 2005 - p64(1) [501+]

Prokes, Mary Timothy - *At the Interface: Theology and Virtual Reality*
    CI - v13 - i2 - Feb 2005 - p38(2) [501+]
Prokofiev, Sergei - *Sergei Prokofiev's Peter and the Wolf (Illus. by Malone, Peter)*
    c KR - v72 - i16 - August 15 2004 - p811(1) [51-500]
    PW - v251 - i45 - Nov 8 2004 - p54(1) [51-500]
    c SLJ - v50 - i10 - Oct 2004 - p128(1) [51-500]
Pronger, Brian - *Body Fascism: Salvation in the Technology of Physical Fitness*
    R&R Bk N - v19 - i1 - Feb 2004 - p73(1) [1-50]
Pronzini, Bill - *Burgade's Crossing*
    Roundup M - v12 - i3 - Feb 2005 - p29(1) [51-500]
    Demons (Read by Sullivan, Nick). Audiobook Review
    c Kliatt - v38 - i4 - July 2004 - p50(1) [51-500]
    Nightcrawlers: A Nameless Detective Novel
    KR - v73 - i3 - Feb 1 2005 - p154(1) [51-500]
    PW - v252 - i8 - Feb 21 2005 - p161(1) [51-500]
The Prophet Outcast: Trotsky, 1929-1940
    Lon R Bks - v26 - i13 - Dec 2 2004 - p3(3) [501+]
Prosch, Susanna - *New Aspects of CMV-Related Immunopathology: Proceedings*
    SciTech - v28 - i1 - March 2004 - p90(1) [51-500]
Prose, Francine - *After*
    y Kliatt - v38 - i4 - July 2004 - p23(1) [51-500]
    Best New American Voices 2005
    BL - v101 - i2 - Sept 15 2004 - p205(2) [501+]
    KR - v72 - i15 - August 1 2004 - p711(1) [501+]
    LJ - v129 - i16 - Oct 1 2004 - p75(1) [51-500]
    PW - v251 - i40 - Oct 4 2004 - p68(1) [51-500]
    A Changed Man
    y BL - v101 - i7 - Dec 1 2004 - p619(1) [51-500]
    Ent W - i810 - March 11 2005 - p106 [501+]
    KR - v73 - i1 - Jan 1 2005 - p17(1) [51-500]
    LJ - v130 - i1 - Jan 1 2005 - p100(1) [51-500]
    People - v63 - i9 - March 7 2005 - p51 [501+]
    PW - v251 - i51 - Dec 20 2004 - p34(1) [501+]
    Gluttony
    HM - v310 - i1856 - Jan 2005 - p96(6) [501+]
    Sew R - v112 - i3 - Summer 2004 - pLXXVI-LXXIX [501+]
Prosek, James - *A Good Day's Fishing (Illus. by Prosek, James)*
    c SLJ - v50 - i10 - Oct 2004 - pS26(1) [1-50]
Prothero, Stephen - *American Jesus: How the Son of God Became a National Icon*
    AM - v191 - i2 - July 19 2004 - p28 [501+]
    CC - v121 - i14 - July 13 2004 - p30(2) [501+]
    CHR - v90 - i4 - Oct 2004 - p816(2) [501+]
    JR - v85 - i1 - Jan 2005 - p129(2) [501+]
    NYTBR - Nov 7 2004 - p30 [501+]
    OS - v40 - i4 - July-August 2004 - p40(1) [501+]
    RAH - v32 - i3 - Sept 2004 - p439-446 [501+]
    VQR - v80 - i2 - Spring 2004 - p267-267 [501+]
Prothrow-Stith, Deborah - *Murder Is No Accident: Understanding and Preventing Youth Violence in America*
    R&R Bk N - v19 - i3 - August 2004 - p151(1) [51-500]
Proudhon, Pierre-Joseph - *General Idea of the Revolution in the Nineteenth Century*
    Bwatch - v26 - i9 - Sept 2004 - p2(1) [51-500]
    R&R Bk N - v19 - i3 - August 2004 - p144(1) [51-500]
Proulx, Annie - *Bad Dirt: Wyoming Stories 2*
    BL - v101 - i3 - Oct 1 2004 - p283(1) [51-500]
    BW - v34 - i51 - Dec 19 2004 - p4(1) [501+]
    Econ - v374 - i8408 - Jan 8 2005 - p76US [501+]
    Ent W - i795 - Dec 3 2004 - p92 [501+]
    Globe & Mail - Jan 15 2005 - pD13 [501+]
    KR - v72 - i19 - Oct 1 2004 - p935(1) [501+]
    LJ - v129 - i18 - Nov 1 2004 - p79(1) [501+]
    NL - v87 - i6 - Nov-Dec 2004 - p31(3) [501+]
    NS - v134 - i4721 - Jan 10 2005 - p56(1) [501+]
    NYTBR - Dec 5 2004 - p46 [501+]
    People - v62 - i24 - Dec 13 2004 - p53 [51-500]
    PW - v251 - i40 - Oct 4 2004 - p67(2) [501+]
    Spec - v296 - Dec 18 2004 - p92(1) [501+]
    Time - v164 - i23 - Dec 6 2004 - p109 [501+]
    TLS - i5305 - Dec 3 2004 - p21(1) [501+]
    That Old Ace in the Hole
    Comw - v131 - i21 - Dec 3 2004 - p26(2) [501+]
Proulx, Craig - *Reclaiming Aboriginal Justice, Identity, and Community*
    CBRA - Annual 2003 - p368(2) [501+]

Proust, Marcel - *Finding Time Again*
    Lon R Bks - v27 - i1 - Jan 6 2005 - p18(3) [501+]
    The Guermantes Way
    Lon R Bks - v27 - i1 - Jan 6 2005 - p18(3) [501+]
    In the Shadow of Young Girls in Flower
    Lon R Bks - v27 - i1 - Jan 6 2005 - p18(3) [501+]
    Pleasures and Days
    TLS - i5304 - Nov 26 2004 - p32(1) [51-500]
    Remembrance of Things Past
    Lon R Bks - v27 - i1 - Jan 6 2005 - p18(3) [501+]
    Sodom and Gomorrah
    KR - v72 - i16 - August 15 2004 - p778(1) [51-500]
    Lon R Bks - v27 - i1 - Jan 6 2005 - p18(3) [501+]
    The Way by Swann's
    Lon R Bks - v27 - i1 - Jan 6 2005 - p18(3) [501+]
Prout, Ebenezer - *The Orchestra: Orchestral Techniques and Combinations*
    M Ed J - v91 - i3 - Jan 2005 - p64(1) [51-500]
Prouty, Olive Higgins - *Now, Voyager*
    LJ - v129 - i14 - Sept 1 2004 - p204(1) [51-500]
    BW - v34 - i46 - Nov 14 2004 - p12(1) [1-50]
Prove, Ralf - *Wissen ist Macht: Herrschaft und Kommunikation in Brandenburg-Preussen, 1600-1850*
    CEH - v37 - i3 - Summer 2004 - p438(3) [501+]
Provencher, Jean - *Quebec City: A Visual Testimony (Illus. by Paquet, Jocelyn)*
    Globe & Mail - Dec 11 2004 - pT9 [51-500]
Provencher, Rose-Marie - *Slithery Jake (Illus. by Carter, Abby)*
    CE - v81 - i1 - Fall 2004 - p47(1) [51-500]
Provoost, Anne - *In the Shadow of the Ark (Read by Gavin, Marguerite). Audiobook Review*
    y Kliatt - v39 - i2 - March 2005 - p53(1) [51-500]
    In the Shadow of the Ark
    c BL - v101 - i3 - Oct 1 2004 - p345(1) [51-500]
    y CCB-B - v58 - i2 - Oct 2004 - p96(2) [51-500]
    y KR - v72 - i13 - July 1 2004 - p635(1) [51-500]
    c LibMed - v23 - i3 - Nov-Dec 2004 - p73(1) [51-500]
    y NYTBR - Sept 19 2004 - p16 [51-500]
    y PW - v251 - i43 - Oct 25 2004 - p49(1) [51-500]
    y Sch Lib - v52 - i3 - Autumn 2004 - p161(1) [501+]
    y SLJ - v50 - i10 - Oct 2004 - p193(1) [51-500]
    y VOYA - v27 - i3 - August 2004 - p224(1) [1-50]
Prud'homme, Alex - *The Cell Game: Sam Waksal's Fast Money and False Promises--and the Fate of ImClone's Cancer Drug*
    R&R Bk N - v19 - i3 - August 2004 - p119(1) [51-500]
Prue, Sally - *Cold Tom*
    y Kliatt - v38 - i5 - Sept 2004 - p32(2) [51-500]
    c PW - v251 - i28 - July 12 2004 - p66(1) [51-500]
    The Devil's Toenail
    y CCB-B - v58 - i1 - Sept 2004 - p35(1) [51-500]
    y PW - v251 - i28 - July 12 2004 - p65(1) [51-500]
    y VOYA - v27 - i3 - August 2004 - p233(1) [1-50]
    c SLJ - v50 - i8 - August 2004 - p128(1) [51-500]
    Goldkeeper
    c Magpies - v19 - i5 - Nov 2004 - p36(1) [501+]
    c Sch Lib - v52 - i4 - Winter 2004 - p204(1) [51-500]
Pruett, Jon - *The Music Festival Guide: For Music Lovers and Musicians*
    Choice - v41 - i11-12 - July-August 2004 - p2018(2) [501+]
Pruitt, Kristin A. - *Gender and the Power of Relationship: "United as one Individual Soul" in Paradise Lost*
    Choice - v41 - i7 - March 2004 - p1299(1) [501+]
    R&R Bk N - v19 - i1 - Feb 2004 - p237(1) [51-500]
Prunty, Jacinta - *Maps and Map-Making in Local History*
    R&R Bk N - v19 - i4 - Nov 2004 - p74(1) [51-500]
Prusiner, Stanley B. - *Prion Biology and Diseases, 2nd Ed.*
    SciTech - v28 - i1 - March 2004 - p77(1) [51-500]
Pryde, Philip R. - *San Diego: An Introduction to the Region, 4th Ed.*
    R&R Bk N - v19 - i4 - Nov 2004 - p68(1) [51-500]
Pryer, Jane A. - *Poverty and Vulnerability in Dhaka Slums: The Urban Livelihoods Study*
    JEL - v42 - i1 - March 2004 - p310(2) [501+]
Pryor, Francis - *Britain BC: Life in Britain and Ireland before the Romans*
    TimHES - v0 - i1654 - August 20 2004 - p29(1) [501+]
Pryor, Michael - *Quentaris in Flames (Read by Macauley, Rebecca). Audiobook Review*
    c Kliatt - v38 - i4 - July 2004 - p55(1) [51-500]

Przeworski, Adam - *States and Markets: A Primer in Political Economy*
    JEL - v41 - i4 - Dec 2003 - p1334(2) [501+]
    PSQ - v119 - i4 - Winter 2004 - p709(2) [501+]
Przybos, Julia - *Zoom sur les decadents*
    NCFS - v32 - i3-4 - Spring-Summer 2004 - p386(3) [501+]
Psychology, 2nd ed.
    TimHES - v0 - i1668 - Nov 26 2004 - pXVIII(2) [501+]
Ptak, Carol A. - *ERP: Tools Techniques, and Applications for Integrating the Supply Chain, 2nd Ed.*
    SciTech - v28 - i1 - March 2004 - p176(1) [51-500]
Ptak, Roderich - *China, the Portuguese, and the Nanyang: Oceans and Routes, Regions and Trade 1000-1600*
    R&R Bk N - v19 - i3 - August 2004 - p125(1) [501+]
Ptashne, Mark - *A Genetic Switch: Phage Lambda Revisited, 3rd Ed.*
    QRB - v79 - i4 - Dec 2004 - p427(2) [501+]
    SciTech - v28 - i3 - Sept 2004 - p76(1) [51-500]
    A Genetic Switch: Phage Lamda Revisited, 3rd Ed.
    Sci - v305 - i5682 - July 16 2004 - p345(1) [501+]
Publishers Resource Group - *APA's Payroll Practice Fundamentals*
    HR Mag - v49 - i7 - July 2004 - pS6(1) [51-500]
Puchta, Claudia - *Focus Group Practice*
    R&R Bk N - v19 - i3 - August 2004 - p89(1) [51-500]
Puck, Wolfgang - *Wolfgang Puck Makes it Easy: Deliciously Simple Recipes for Restaurant-Quality Food from Your Kitchen*
    LJ - v129 - i17 - Oct 15 2004 - p82(1) [51-500]
Puddington, Arch - *Lane Kirkland: Champion of American Labor*
    BL - v101 - i9-10 - Jan 1 2005 - p792(2) [501+]
Puech, B. - *Orateurs et sophistes grecs dans les inscriptions d'epoque imperiale*
    Class R - v54 - i2 - Nov 2004 - p496-498 [501+]
Puerto Rico. 3rd Rev. Ed.
    R&R Bk N - v19 - i1 - Feb 2004 - p67(1) [501+]
Puett, Michael J. - *To Become a God: Cosmology, Sacrifice, and Self-Divinization in Early China*
    HJAS - v64 - i2 - Dec 2004 - p465-479 [501+]
    To Become a God: Cosmology, Sacrifice, and Self-Divinization in Early China
    HJAS - v64 - i2 - Dec 2004 - p465-479 [501+]
Pufall, Peter B. - *Rethinking Childhood*
    Choice - v42 - i2 - Oct 2004 - p377(1) [501+]
    TCR - v107 - i2 - Feb 2005 - p272(6) [501+]
Puff, Helmut - *Sodomy in Reformation Germany and Switzerland, 1400-1600*
    AHR - v109 - i2 - April 2004 - p633(2) [501+]
    CH - v73 - i4 - Dec 2004 - p853(1) [51-500]
    Choice - v41 - i7 - March 2004 - p1377(2) [501+]
    GSR - v27 - i3 - Oct 2004 - p605(2) [501+]
    HNet - Oct 2004 - pNA [501+]
    J Soc H - v38 - i1 - Fall 2004 - p265(3) [501+]
Puffer, Sheila M. - *International Management: Insights from Fiction and Practice*
    Choice - v42 - i5 - Jan 2005 - p899(1) [1-50]
Pugatch, Meir Perez - *The International Political Economy of Intellectual Property Rights*
    R&R Bk N - v19 - i4 - Nov 2004 - p161(1) [501+]
Pugesek, Bruce H. - *Structural Equation Modeling: Applications in Ecological and Evolutionary Biology*
    QRB - v79 - i3 - Sept 2004 - p330(1) [501+]
Pugh, David - *Schiller's Early Dramas: A Critical History*
    Eight-C St - v37 - i3 - Spring 2004 - p487-491 [501+]
Pugh, Derek S. - *International Business and Management, Vols. 1-4*
    R&R Bk N - v19 - i1 - Feb 2004 - p92(1) [51-500]
Pugh, Lyndon - *Practical Training Techniques*
    R&R Bk N - v19 - i1 - Feb 2004 - pNA [51-500]
Pugh, Michael - *The United Nations and Regional Security: Europe and Beyond*
    R&R Bk N - v19 - i1 - Feb 2004 - p209(1) [51-500]
    War Economies in a Regional Context: Challenges of Transformation
    Choice - v42 - i2 - Oct 2004 - p340(2) [51-500]
Pugliatti, Paola - *Beggary and Theatre in Early Modern England*
    Ren Q - v57 - i4 - Winter 2004 - p1510(2) [501+]
Pugliese, Stanislao - *The Political Legacy of Margaret Thatcher*
    Choice - v42 - i3 - Nov 2004 - p558(2) [1-50]
Pugsley, Michael K. - *Cardiac Drug Development Guide*
    E-Streams - Oct 2004 - pNA [501+]

Puhalla, Jim - *Baseball and Softball Fields: Design, Construction, Renovation, and Maintenance*
    R&R Bk N - v19 - i1 - Feb 2004 - p74(1) [51-500]
Puhn, Laurie - *Instant Persuasion: How to Change Your Words to Change Your Life*
    LJ - v130 - i2 - Feb 1 2005 - p104(1) [51-500]
    PW - v252 - i4 - Jan 24 2005 - p236(1) [501+]
Pujo, Bernard - *Vincent de Paul: The Trailblazer*
    Ren Q - v57 - i4 - Winter 2004 - p1416(2) [501+]
Pulera, Dominic J. - *Sharing the Dream: White Males in Multicultural America*
    LJ - v129 - i19 - Nov 15 2004 - p77(1) [501+]
Pulford, Elizabeth - *Daisy Doll (Illus. by Durkin, Denise)*
  c Magpies - v19 - i5 - Nov 2004 - p6S(1) [501+]
Pulitano, Elvira - *Toward a Native American Critical Theory*
    Choice - v42 - i2 - Oct 2004 - p295(2) [501+]
    WLT - v79 - i1 - Jan-April 2005 - p111(1) [501+]
Pulley, Brett - *The Billion Dollar BET: Robert Johnson and the Inside Story of Black Entertainment Television*
    Black Iss - v6 - i4 - July-August 2004 - p50(1) [501+]
Pullinger, Kate - *A Little Stranger*
    Globe & Mail - Nov 27 2004 - pD42 [501+]
Pullman, Philip - *The Golden Compass*
  c WLT - v79 - i1 - Jan-April 2005 - p69(4) [501+]
Pullman, Philip Nicholas - *The Golden Compass (Read by Pullman, Philip Nicholas and a full cast). Audiobook Review*
  c CH Bwatch - Feb 2005 - pNA [51-500]
The Golden Compass
    BW - v34 - i40 - Oct 3 2004 - p16(1) [501+]
The Ruby in the Smoke (Read by Lesser, Anton). Audiobook Review
  y BL - v101 - i7 - Dec 1 2004 - p679(1) [1-50]
  y Kliatt - v39 - i2 - March 2005 - p55(2) [51-500]
  y VOYA - v27 - i5 - Dec 2004 - p370(1) [501+]
The Ruby in the Smoke
    HB - v80 - i5 - Sept-Oct 2004 - p610(1) [51-500]
The Shadow in the North (Read by Lesser, Anton). Audiobook Review
  y HB - v81 - i2 - March-April 2005 - p221(1) [51-500]
Pullmen, Philip - *The Ruby in the Smoke*
    SLJ - v50 - i12 - Dec 2004 - p78(1) [501+]
Pulse, Simon - *The Nine Lives of Chloe King*
    PW - v251 - i30 - July 26 2004 - p56(1) [51-500]
Pulsiano, Phillip - *Old English Glossed Psalters: Psalms 1-50*
    JEGP - v103 - i1 - Jan 2004 - p131-134 [501+]
Pummer, Reinhard - *Early Christian Authors on Samaritans and Samaritanism: Texts, Translations and Commentary*
    Theol St - v65 - i3 - Sept 2004 - p636(2) [501+]
Punchinello and the Most Marvelous Gift
  c BL - v101 - i6 - Nov 15 2004 - p605(1) [501+]
Punnett, Betty Jane - *International Perspectives on Organizational Behavior and Human Resource Management*
    Choice - v42 - i5 - Jan 2005 - p900(1) [1-50]
    R&R Bk N - v19 - i3 - August 2004 - p106(1) [1-50]
Punter, David - *The Gothic*
    TLS - i5266 - March 5 2004 - p30-30 [501+]
Punter, John - *Vancouver Achievement: Urban Planning and Design*
    CBRA - Annual 2003 - p347(1) [51-500]
Purcell, Hugh - *The Last English Revolutionary: A Biography of Tom Wintringham*
    NS - v133 - i4708 - Oct 4 2004 - p53(2) [501+]
Purcell, Sarah J. - *The Early National Period*
    R&R Bk N - v19 - i3 - August 2004 - p67(1) [51-500]
    SLJ - v50 - i12 - Dec 2004 - p87(1) [501+]
Purdie, Rhiannon - *Ipomadon*
    JEGP - v103 - i4 - Oct 2004 - p540-542 [501+]
Purdum, Todd S. - *A Time of Our Choosing: America's War in Iraq*
    Lon R Bks - v26 - i7 - April 1 2004 - p15(2) [501+]
    NYTBR - Nov 7 2004 - p30 [501+]
Purdy, Al - *Yours, Al: The Collected Letters of Al Purdy*
    Globe & Mail - Dec 18 2004 - pD18 [501+]
Purdy, Daniel L. - *The Tyranny of Elegance: Consumer Cosmopolitanism in the Era of Goethe*
    GSR - v27 - i1 - Feb 2004 - p143-144 [501+]

Purdy, James - *Moe's Villa and Other Stories*
    BL - v101 - i6 - Nov 15 2004 - p562(2) [501+]
    KR - v72 - i17 - Sept 1 2004 - p831(1) [501+]
    PW - v251 - i40 - Oct 4 2004 - p67(1) [51-500]
Purdy, Jedediah - *Being America: Liberty, Commerce, and Violence in an American World*
    R&R Bk N - v19 - i1 - Feb 2004 - pNA [51-500]
Puri, Jyoti - *Encountering Nationalism*
    R&R Bk N - v19 - i1 - Feb 2004 - p148(1) [51-500]
Purinton, Jamie Crelly - *Voices of the Land*
    SciTech - v28 - i3 - Sept 2004 - p56(1) [1-50]
Purkayastha, Bandana - *The Power of Women's Informal Networks: Lessons in Social Change from South Asia and West Africa*
    R&R Bk N - v19 - i4 - Nov 2004 - p135(1) [51-500]
Purkis, Sally - *Tudor Children*
    Sch Lib - v52 - i3 - Autumn 2004 - p151(1) [501+]
Purmell, Ann - *Where Wild Babies Sleep (Illus. by Siomades, Lorianne)*
    CE - v81 - i1 - Fall 2004 - p47(1) [51-500]
Purnell, Larry D. - *Guide to Culturally Competent Health Care*
    SciTech - v28 - i4 - Dec 2004 - p81(1) [51-500]
Purpel, David E. - *Refelctions on the Moral and Spiritual Crisis in Education*
    R&R Bk N - v19 - i3 - August 2004 - p214(1) [1-50]
Pursell, Brennan C. - *The Winter King: Frederick V of the Palatinate and the Coming of the Thirty Years' War*
    HNet - Oct 2004 - pNA [501+]
    Ren Q - v57 - i3 - Fall 2004 - p1061(2) [501+]
    R&R Bk N - v19 - i1 - Feb 2004 - p35(1) [1-50]
Purser, Ann - *Theft on Thursday*
    BL - v101 - i6 - Nov 15 2004 - p565(2) [51-500]
    KR - v73 - i1 - Jan 1 2005 - p24(1) [51-500]
Pursley, Michael B. - *Introduction to Digital Communications*
    SciTech - v28 - i4 - Dec 2004 - p149(1) [51-500]
Purves, Dale - *Neuroscience, 3rd Ed.*
    SciTech - v28 - i3 - Sept 2004 - p70(1) [51-500]
Purvis, Alston W. - *Pacific Jewelry and Adornment*
    Choice - v42 - i6 - Feb 2005 - p1011(1) [51-500]
Purvis, June - *Emmeline Pankhurst: A Biography*
    VS - v46 - i3 - Spring 2004 - p515(4) [501+]
Purvis, Leland - *Outdoor Human Comfort and Its Assessment: State of the Art*
    SciTech - v28 - i3 - Sept 2004 - p141(1) [51-500]
Purvis, Martin - *Exploring Sustainable Development: Geographical Perspectives*
    R&R Bk N - v19 - i4 - Nov 2004 - p87(1) [51-500]
Puschner, Uwe - *Die volkische Bewegung im wilhelminischen Kaiserreich: Sprache- Rasse- Religion*
    CEH - v37 - i2 - Spring 2004 - p307(3) [501+]
Pusey, Brad - *Freshwater Fishes of North-Eastern Australia*
    SciTech - v28 - i4 - Dec 2004 - p66(1) [51-500]
Pusey, Michael - *The Experience of Middle Australia: The Dark Side of Economic Reform*
    Pac A - v77 - i3 - Fall 2004 - p610(3) [501+]
Pusser, Brian - *Burning Down the House: Politics, Governance, and Affirmative Action at the University of California*
    Choice - v42 - i4 - Dec 2004 - p700(2) [1-50]
    TCR - v106 - i12 - Dec 2004 - p2378(4) [501+]
Putman, Daniel - *Psychological Courage*
    R&R Bk N - v19 - i4 - Nov 2004 - p13(1) [51-500]
Putman, Richard E. - *Industrial Energy Systems: Analysis, Optimization, and Control*
    SciTech - v28 - i3 - Sept 2004 - p149(1) [51-500]
Putnam, Elizabeth Redfern - *Auriel Rising*
    KR - v72 - i24 - Dec 15 2004 - pS5(1) [501+]
Putnam, Hilary - *The Collapse of the Fact/Value Dichotomy and Other Essays*
    S&S - v68 - i4 - Winter 2004 - p483-10 [501+]
Putnam, James - *The Ancient Egypt Pop-Up Book*
    SLJ - v50 - i10 - Oct 2004 - pS34(1) [501+]
Putnam, Lara - *Foundation of Despotism: Peasants, the Trujillo Regime, and Modernity in Dominican History.*
    JIH - v34 - i3 - Wntr 2004 - p493(2) [501+]

Putnam, Robert D. - *Better Together: Restoring the American Community*
    CS - v33 - i6 - Nov 2004 - p704(2) [501+]
    VQR - v80 - i1 - Wntr 2004 - p265-265 [501+]
Bowling Alone: The Collapse and Revival of American Community
    Globe & Mail - March 5 2005 - pD19 [501+]
Putney, Diane T. - *Airpower Advantage: Planning the Gulf War Air Campaign, 1989-1991*
    APJ - v18 - i4 - Winter 2004 - p116(2) [501+]
Putney, Mary Jo - *A Kiss of Fate*
    PW - v251 - i27 - July 5 2004 - p38(2) [51-500]
  y SLJ - v50 - i11 - Nov 2004 - p177(1) [51-500]
Twist of Fate (Read by Jenner, James). Audiobook Review
    LJ - v129 - i18 - Nov 1 2004 - p130(1) [51-500]
Puttkamer, Joachim von - *Schulalltag und nationale Integration in Ungarn: Slowaken, Rumanen und Sieben-burger Sachsen in der Auseinandersetzung mit der ungarischen Staatsidee, 1867-1914*
    AHR - v109 - i3 - June 2004 - p997(2) [501+]
Puttlitz, Karl J. - *Handbook of Lead-Free Solder Technology for Microelectronic Assemblies*
    E-Streams - Nov 2004 - pNA [501+]
Puttock, Simon - *The Day the Baby Blew Away (Illus. by Gale, Cathy)*
  c Sch Lib - v52 - i4 - Winter 2004 - p190(1) [51-500]
  c SLJ - v50 - i7 - July 2004 - p86(1) [51-500]
Horsey
  c Sch Lib - v52 - i4 - Winter 2004 - p190(1) [51-500]
Squeaky Clean (Illus. by McQuillan, Mary)
  c RT - v57 - Oct 2003 - p167 [1-50]
You're Too Big! (Illus. by Bolam, Emily)
  c KR - v72 - i13 - July 1 2004 - p635(1) [51-500]
You're Too Big (Illus. by Bolam, Emily)
  c Sch Lib - v52 - i4 - Winter 2004 - p187(1) [51-500]
You're Too Big! (Illus. by Bolam, Emily)
  c SLJ - v50 - i12 - Dec 2004 - p118(1) [501+]
Putzier, John - *Weirdos in the Workplace: The New Normal--Thriving in the Age of the Individual*
    BL - v101 - i2 - Sept 15 2004 - p186(1) [51-500]
    HR Mag - v50 - i1 - Jan 2005 - p104(1) [501+]
    HR Mag - v50 - i2 - Feb 2005 - pS9(1) [501+]
Puzo, Mario - *The Godfather Returns*
    Ent W - i793 - Nov 19 2004 - p86 [501+]
Pybus, Cassandra - *American Citizens, British Slaves: Yankee Political Prisoners in an Australian Penal Colony*
    AHR - v109 - i2 - April 2004 - p481(2) [501+]
Pye, David - *Practical Nitriding and Ferritic Nitrocarburizing*
    SciTech - v28 - i1 - March 2004 - p171(1) [51-500]
Pye, Frances - *Sharing Sean*
    BL - v100 - i21 - July 2004 - p1819(1) [1-50]
Pyers, Greg - *Coral Reef Explorer*
    Sch Lib - v52 - i3 - Autumn 2004 - p151(1) [501+]
Pyle, Andrew - *Malebranche*
    TLS - i5298 - Oct 15 2004 - p6(1) [501+]
Pyle, Richard - *Lost Over Laos: A True Story of Tragedy, Mystery, and Friendship*
  y Kliatt - v38 - i4 - July 2004 - p42(1) [501+]
Pylyshyn, Zenon - *Seeing and Visualizing: It's Not What You Think*
    Choice - v42 - i2 - Oct 2004 - p375(1) [51-500]
Pym, David J. - *Reductive Logic and Proof-Search: Proof Theory, Semantics, and Control*
    SciTech - v28 - i3 - Sept 2004 - p16(1) [501+]
Reductive Logic and Proof-Search: Proof Theory, Sematics, and Control
    Choice - v42 - i3 - Nov 2004 - p522(1) [1-50]
Pymm, Bob - *Learn Library Management*
    R&R Bk N - v19 - i1 - Feb 2004 - p259(1) [51-500]
Pyne, Stephen J. - *Tending Fire: Coping With America's Wildland Fires*
    Aud - v106 - i5 - Nov-Dec 2004 - p96(1) [51-500]
    BL - v101 - i5 - Nov 1 2004 - p448(2) [51-500]
    Nature - v432 - i7017 - Dec 2 2004 - p555(2) [501+]
Pyper, Andrew - *The Trade Mission*
    Can Lit - i182 - Autumn 2004 - p165(2) [501+]
Pywell, Sharon - *What Happened to Henry*
    BL - v100 - i21 - July 2004 - p1819(1) [1-50]
Pyysiainen, Ilkka - *Magic, Miracles, and Religion: A Scientist's Perspective*
    R&R Bk N - v19 - i3 - August 2004 - p12(1) [1-50]

Q R

Qasim ibn Sallam, Abu Ubayd al- - *The Book of Revenue: Kitab al-Amwal*
R&R Bk N - v19 - i1 - Feb 2004 - p114(1) [51-500]

Qian, Ning - *Chinese Students Encounter America*
Ch Rev Int - v11 - i1 - Spring 2004 - p158(4) [501+]

Qian, Zhaoming - *Erza Pound and China*
JAS - v63 - i3 - August 2004 - p778-779 [501+]

Qiu, Xiaolong - *When Red Is Black*
BW - v34 - i31 - August 1 2004 - p9(1) [501+]

Qu, Gang - *Intellectual Property Protection in VLSI Designs: Theory and Practice*
SciTech - v28 - i1 - March 2004 - p162(1) [51-500]

Qu, Lei Lei - *The Simple Art of Chinese Brush Painting*
LJ - v130 - i3 - Feb 15 2005 - p128(1) [51-500]

Quadagno, Jill - *One Nation, Uninsured: Why the U.S. Has No National Health Insurance*
KR - v73 - i4 - Feb 15 2005 - p218(1) [501+]

Quah, Jon S.T. - *Curbing Corruption in Asia: A Comparative Study of Six Countries*
R&R Bk N - v19 - i1 - Feb 2004 - pNA [501+]

Quah, Stella R. - *Home and Kin: Families in Asia*
AJS - v110 - i3 - Nov 2004 - p803(2) [501+]
Choice - v42 - i2 - Oct 2004 - p377(1) [51-500]
R&R Bk N - v19 - i2 - May 2004 - p134 [51-500]

Quah, Sy Ren - *Gao Xingjian and Transcultural Chinese Theater*
R&R Bk N - v19 - i3 - August 2004 - p257(1) [51-500]

Quaid, Maeve - *Workfare: Why Good Social Policy Ideas go Bad*
CS - v33 - i1 - Jan 2004 - p78-80 [501+]

Qualey, Marsha - *One Night*
c   RT - v57 - Oct 2003 - p177 [1-50]
Too Big a Storm
y   SLJ - v50 - i7 - July 2004 - p111(2) [51-500]
y   VOYA - v27 - i3 - August 2004 - p224(1) [1-50]

Quammen, David - *Monster of God: The Man-Eating Predator in the Jungles of History and the Mind*
HM - v310 - i1858 - March 2005 - p95(7) [501+]
NYTBR - Oct 10 2004 - p26 [501+]
SB - v40 - i6 - Nov-Dec 2004 - p243(1) [51-500]
TLS - i5292 - Sept 3 2004 - p29(1) [501+]
VQR - v80 - i1 - Wntr 2004 - p275-275 [501+]

Quandt, Richard E. - *The Changing Landscape in Eastern Europe: A Personal Perspective on Philanthropy and Technology Transfer*
JEL - v41 - i4 - Dec 2003 - p1429(1) [501+]

Quantic, Diane D. - *A Great Plain Reader*
VQR - v80 - i1 - Wntr 2004 - p263-264 [501+]

Quantitative Evaluation of Systems: Proceedings
SciTech - v28 - i4 - Dec 2004 - p153(1) [51-500]

Quaratiello, Arlene R. - *Rachel Carson: A Biography*
SciTech - v28 - i4 - Dec 2004 - p58(1) [51-500]

Quarrington, Paul - *Galveston*
Globe & Mail - Nov 27 2004 - pD3 [51-500]
Mac - v117 - i45 - Nov 8 2004 - p58(1) [51-500]

Quart, Alissa - *Branded: The Buying and Selling of Teenagers*
Kliatt - v38 - i4 - July 2004 - p41(2) [501+]

Quarteroni, Alfio - *Scientific Computing with MATLAB*
Choice - v41 - i7 - March 2004 - p1329(1) [501+]

Quashie, Kevin Everod - *Black Women, Identity, and Cultural Theory: (Un)becoming the Subject*
Choice - v42 - i1 - Sept 2004 - p103(2) [501+]

Quattlebaum, Mary - *Jackson Jones and Mission Greentop*
c   CCB-B - v58 - i1 - Sept 2004 - p35(2) [51-500]
c   HB - v80 - i5 - Sept-Oct 2004 - p595(2) [501+]
c   KR - v72 - i13 - July 1 2004 - p636(1) [51-500]
c   SLJ - v50 - i11 - Nov 2004 - p116(1) [51-500]

Quattrochi, Dale A. - *Thermal Remote Sensing in Land Surface Processes*
SciTech - v28 - i3 - Sept 2004 - p5(1) [501+]

Quayum, M.A. - *Saul Bellow and American Transcendentalism*
R&R Bk N - v19 - i4 - Nov 2004 - p242(1) [501+]

Queen, Jay Allen - *The Block Scheduling Handbook*
SLJ - v50 - i10 - Oct 2004 - pS74(1) [51-500]
The Frazzled Teacher's Wellness Plan: A Five-Step Program for Reclaiming Time, Managing Stress, and Creating a Healthy Lifestyle
R&R Bk N - v19 - i4 - Nov 2004 - p189(1) [501+]

Queen, William - *Under and Alone: The True Story of the Undercover Agent Who Infiltrated America's Most Violent Outlaw Motorcycle Gang*
KR - v73 - i2 - Jan 15 2005 - p110(1) [501+]

Queenan, Joe - *Queenan Country: A Reluctant Anglophile's Pilgrimage to the Mother Country*
BL - v101 - i3 - Oct 1 2004 - p295(1) [51-500]
Globe & Mail - Nov 13 2004 - pD21 [501+]
KR - v72 - i17 - Sept 1 2004 - p853(1) [501+]
NYTBR - Dec 26 2004 - p10 [501+]
PW - v251 - i28 - July 12 2004 - p50(1) [51-500]
True Belivers: The Tragic Inner Life of Sports Fans
NYTBR - July 18 2004 - p20 [501+]

The Queer Movie Poster Book
Advocate - Dec 21 2004 - p51(1) [51-500]

Quezel, P. - *Etudes de botanique antique*
Class R - v54 - i2 - Nov 2004 - p534(3) [501+]

Quick, Amanda - *The Paid Companion*
y   BL - v101 - i2 - Sept 15 2004 - p222(1) [51-500]
Wait Until Midnight
PW - v252 - i3 - Jan 17 2005 - p40(1) [51-500]

Quick, Jennifer - *Magnificent Objects from the University of Pennsylvania Museum of Archaeology and Anthropology*
Choice - v42 - i4 - Dec 2004 - p646(2) [1-50]

Quigg, Chris - *Annual Review of Nuclear and Particle Science: Vol. 53, 2003*
SciTech - v28 - i1 - March 2004 - p51(1) [51-500]

Quigley, David - *Second Founding: New York City, Reconstruction and the Making of American Democracy*
Choice - v42 - i4 - Dec 2004 - p724(1) [1-50]

Quigley, Marian - *Information Security and Ethics: Social and Organizational Issues*
Choice - v42 - i6 - Feb 2005 - p1057(1) [51-500]
SciTech - v28 - i4 - Dec 2004 - p128 [51-500]

Quigley, Mary W. - *Going Back to Work: A Survival Guide for Comeback Moms*
BL - v100 - i22 - August 2004 - p1881(2) [51-500]
HR Mag - v49 - i11 - Nov 2004 - p145(1) [51-500]

Quill, Timothy E. - *Physician-Assisted Dying: The Case for Palliative Care and Patient Choice*
SciTech - v28 - i4 - Dec 2004 - p77(1) [51-500]

Quilley, Denis - *Happiness Indeed: An Actor's Life*
TLS - i5297 - Oct 8 2004 - p30-31 [51-500]

Quilley, Geoff - *An Economy of Colour: Visual Culture and the Atlantic World 1660-1830*
J Hist G - v30 - i1 - Jan 2004 - p179(3) [501+]
William Hodges 1744-1797: First Artist of Empire
TimHES - v0 - i1660 - Oct 1 2004 - p22(1) [501+]
William Hodges 1744-1797: The Art of Exploration
Choice - v42 - i6 - Feb 2005 - p1015(1) [51-500]
LJ - v129 - i20 - Dec 1 2004 - p112(2) [51-500]

Quilliam, Susan - *Body Language: Learning to Read and Use the Body's Secret Signals*
LJ - v130 - i3 - Feb 15 2005 - p143(1) [51-500]

Quilter, Jeffery - *Cobble Circles and Standing Stones: Archaeology at the Rivas Site, Costa Rica*
Choice - v42 - i3 - Nov 2004 - p528(1) [1-50]

Quinan, Jack - *Frank Lloyd Wright's Martin House: Architecture as Portraiture*
LJ - v130 - i1 - Jan 1 2005 - p110(1) [51-500]

Quindlen, Anna - *Being Perfect*
LJ - v129 - i20 - Dec 1 2004 - p92(1) [1-50]
Imagined London: A Tour of the World's Greatest Fictional City
BL - v101 - i2 - Sept 15 2004 - p201(2) [501+]
KR - v72 - i13 - July 1 2004 - p622(1) [501+]
LJ - v129 - i13 - August 2004 - p106(1) [51-500]
Loud and Clear (Read by Quindlen, Anna). Audiobook Review
BL - v100 - i22 - August 2004 - p1953(1) [51-500]
Kliatt - v38 - i4 - July 2004 - p60(2) [51-500]
LJ - v129 - i16 - Oct 1 2004 - p120(1) [51-500]

Quinet, Emile - *Principles of Transport Economics*
Choice - v42 - i2 - Oct 2004 - p341(1) [51-500]
R&R Bk N - v19 - i2 - May 2004 - p108(1) [51-500]

Quinion, Michael - *Ballyhoo, Buckaroo and Spuds: Ingenious Tales of Words and Their Origins*
BL - v101 - i3 - Oct 1 2004 - p289(1) [51-500]
LJ - v129 - i19 - Nov 15 2004 - p61(1) [501+]
Posh: Port Out, Starboard Home and Other Language Myths
Spec - v295 - i9182 - July 31 2004 - p32(1) [501+]
TimHES - v0 - i1678 - Feb 11 2005 - p24(1) [501+]

Quinlan, David - *Quinlan's Character Stars*
Choice - v42 - i3 - Nov 2004 - p454(1) [1-50]
LJ - v129 - i14 - Sept 1 2004 - p190(2) [51-500]

Quinlan, Mary Lou - *Time Off for Good Behavior: How Hardworking Women Can Take a Break and Change Their Lives*
BL - v101 - i8 - Dec 15 2004 - p696(1) [501+]
LJ - v130 - i1 - Jan 1 2005 - p134(1) [51-500]
PW - v251 - i49 - Dec 6 2004 - p52(2) [51-500]

Quinlin, Michael - *Irish Boston*
Bwatch - Oct 2004 - pNA [51-500]

Quinn, Antoinette - *Patrick Kavanagh: A Poet's Country*
LJ - v129 - i19 - Nov 15 2004 - p60(1) [501+]

Quinn, Charlotte A. - *Pride, Faith, and Fear: Islam in Sub-Saharan Africa*
JR - v84 - i3 - July 2004 - p491(2) [501+]

Quinn, Danny - *Just Say Uncle!. Audiobook Review*
c   SLJ - v50 - i9 - Sept 2004 - p82(1) [51-500]

Quinn, Edward - *History in Literature: A Reader's Guide to 20th-Century History and the Literature It Inspired*
Choice - v41 - i11-12 - July-August 2004 - p2020(1) [501+]
R&USQ - v44 - i1 - Fall 2004 - p90(2) [501+]

Quinn, Eithne - *Nuthin' but a "G" Thang: The Culture and Commerce of Gangsta Rap*
LJ - v129 - i18 - Nov 1 2004 - p88(1) [51-500]

Quinn, James - *Soul on Fire: A Life of Thomas Russell*
Albion - v36 - i2 - Summer 2004 - p385(2) [501+]

Quinn-Judge, Sophie - *Ho Chi Minh: The Missing Years 1919-1941*
AHR - v109 - i2 - April 2004 - p499(1) [501+]
TLS - i5266 - March 5 2004 - p9-10 [501+]

Quinn, Karen - *The Ivy Chronicles*
BL - v101 - i9-10 - Jan 1 2005 - p822(1) [501+]
KR - v72 - i23 - Dec 1 2004 - p1111(1) [51-500]
PW - v251 - i49 - Dec 6 2004 - p43(1) [51-500]

Quinn, Mark - *The King of Spring: The Life and Times of Peter O'Connor*
LJ - v130 - i3 - Feb 15 2005 - p137(1) [51-500]

Quinn, Martin - *Grass Scapes: Gardening with Ornamental Grasses*
CBRA - Annual 2003 - p422(1) [51-500]

Quinn, William H. - *Family Solutions for Youth at Risk: Applications to Juvenile Delinquency, Truancy, and Behavior Problems*
Adoles - v39 - i156 - Winter 2004 - p837(1) [51-500]

Quinn, William P. - *Shipwrecks Along the Atlantic Coast: A Remarkable Collection of Photographs of Maritime Accidents from Maine to Florida*
R&R Bk N - v20 - i1 - Feb 2005 - p81(1) [51-500]

Quinones, Karen E. - *Ida B.*
Black Iss - v6 - i5 - Sept-Oct 2004 - p51(1) [51-500]

Quinones, Sam - *True Tales from Another Mexico: The Lynch Mob, the Popsicle Kings, Chalino, and the Bronx*
Aztlan - v29 - i2 - Fall 2004 - p215-218 [501+]

Quinonez, Ernesto - *Chango's Fire*
BL - v100 - i22 - August 2004 - p1902(1) [501+]
KR - v72 - i16 - August 15 2004 - p772(1) [501+]
LJ - v129 - i14 - Sept 1 2004 - p141(1) [51-500]
PW - v251 - i32 - August 9 2004 - p228(1) [51-500]

Quint, David - *Cervantes's Novel of Modern Times: A New Reading of Don Quijote*
Choice - v41 - i7 - March 2004 - p1302(1) [501+]

Quint, Emanuel - *A Restatement of Rabbinic Civil Law, Vols. 1-9*
R&R Bk N - v19 - i1 - Feb 2004 - pNA [1-50]

Quintana, Leroy - *La Promesa and Other Stories*
WLT - v78 - i3-4 - Sept-Dec 2004 - p96(1) [501+]

Quintero, Elizabeth P. - *Problem-Posing with Multicultural Children's Literature: Developing Critical Early Childhood Curricula*
R&R Bk N - v19 - i4 - Nov 2004 - p190(1) [501+]

Quirina, Fiona - *Sex, a Mystery, 1st Ed.*
LJ - v130 - i4 - March 1 2005 - p71(1) [51-500]
PW - v252 - i6 - Feb 7 2005 - p46(1) [51-500]

Quiring, David M. - *CCF Colonialism in Northern Saskatchewan: Battling Parish Priests, Bootleggers, and Fur Sharks*
Choice - v42 - i5 - Jan 2005 - p918(1) [1-50]
HNet - Oct 2004 - pNA [501+]
R&R Bk N - v19 - i3 - August 2004 - p78(1) [51-500]

Quisqueya en el Hudson: Dominican Music in New York City
Teach Mus - v12 - i1 - August 2004 - p61(2) [501+]

Quisumbing, Agnes R. - *Household Decisions, Gender, and Development: A Synthesis of Recent Research*
R&R Bk N - v19 - i3 - August 2004 - p154(1) [51-500]
Land and Schooling: Transferring Wealth Across Generations
Choice - v42 - i1 - Sept 2004 - p156(1) [501+]

Qureshi, Emran - *The New Crusades: Constructing the Muslim Enemy*
Choice - v41 - i11-12 - July-August 2004 - p2121(2) [501+]
R&R Bk N - v19 - i1 - Feb 2004 - p31(1) [1-50]

Quyang, Xiu - *Historical Records of the Five Dynasties*
Choice - v42 - i3 - Nov 2004 - p541(1) [1-50]

Qvortrup, Mads - *The Political Philosophy of Jean-Jacques Rousseau: The Impossibility of Reason*
Choice - v42 - i3 - Nov 2004 - p563(1) [1-50]

Raab, Evelyn - *Clueless in the Kitchen: A Cookbook for Teens*
y SLJ - v51 - i2 - Feb 2005 - p59(1) [51-500]

Raab, L. Mark - *Prehistoric California: Archaeology and the Myth of Paradise*
Choice - v42 - i6 - Feb 2005 - p1065(1) [51-500]
R&R Bk N - v19 - i3 - August 2004 - p61(1) [51-500]

Raabe, Dierk - *Continuum Scale Simulation of Engineering Materials: Fundamentals-Microstructures-Process Applications*
SciTech - v28 - i4 - Dec 2004 - p134 [51-500]

Raabe, William A. - *West Federal Taxation: Advanced Business Entity Taxation, 2005 Ed.*
R&R Bk N - v19 - i4 - Nov 2004 - p172(1) [501+]

Raaflaub, Kurt - *The Discovery of Freedom in Ancient Greece*
Choice - v42 - i1 - Sept 2004 - p187(2) [501+]

Raat, W. Dirk - *Mexico and the United States: Ambivalent Vistas, 3rd Ed.*
R&R Bk N - v19 - i3 - August 2004 - p65(1) [51-500]

Raatma, Lucia - *Safety for Babysitters*
c SLJ - v50 - i12 - Dec 2004 - p168(1) [51-500]
Safety in Your Neighborhood
c SLJ - v50 - i12 - Dec 2004 - p168(1) [51-500]
Safety on the Internet
c SLJ - v50 - i12 - Dec 2004 - p168(1) [51-500]

Rabassa, Gregory - *If This Be Treason: Translation and Its Dyscontents: A Memoir*
KR - v73 - i4 - Feb 15 2005 - p219(1) [501+]

Rabate, Jean-Michel - *Palgrave Advances in James Joyce Studies*
Choice - v42 - i3 - Nov 2004 - p486(1) [1-50]

Rabb, Jonathan - *Rosa: A Novel*
BL - v101 - i7 - Dec 1 2004 - p619(1) [51-500]
KR - v73 - i2 - Jan 15 2005 - p87(2) [51-500]
LJ - v130 - i3 - Feb 15 2005 - p124(1) [51-500]
PW - v252 - i6 - Feb 7 2005 - p41(1) [51-500]
HM - v310 - i1858 - March 2005 - p89(2) [501+]

Rabb, M.E. - *The Rose Queen: Missing Persons Book One*
y PW - v251 - i30 - July 26 2004 - p56(1) [51-500]

Rabben, Linda - *Brazil's Indians and the Onslaught of Civilization: The Yanomami and the Kayapo*
Choice - v42 - i2 - Oct 2004 - p352(1) [51-500]
R&R Bk N - v19 - i1 - Feb 2004 - p67(1) [501+]

Rabe, Barry G. - *Statehouse and Greenhouse: The Emerging Politics of American Climate Change Policy*
Choice - v42 - i3 - Nov 2004 - p566(1) [1-50]

Rabe, Jean - *The Finest Creation*
y BL - v101 - i5 - Nov 1 2004 - p471(1) [51-500]
LJ - v129 - i15 - Sept 15 2004 - p53(1) [51-500]
PW - v251 - i41 - Oct 11 2004 - p61(1) [51-500]

Rabehl, Bernd - *Revolutionar im geteilten Deutschland*
TLS - i5264 - Feb 20 2004 - p29-29 [501+]

Rabelais, Francois - *Gargantua*
HM - v309 - i1853 - Oct 2004 - p93(8) [501+]
TLS - i5263 - Feb 13 2004 - p27-27 [501+]
Pantagruel
HM - v309 - i1853 - Oct 2004 - p93(8) [501+]
TLS - i5263 - Feb 13 2004 - p27-27 [501+]

Rabenau, Holger, F. - *Prions: A Challenge for Science, Medicine, and Public Health System. 2nd Rev.Ed.*
SciTech - v28 - i3 - Sept 2004 - p75(1) [51-500]

Rabi, Barbara - *Arztliche Ethik-eine Frage der Ehre? Die Prozesse und Urteile der arztlichen Ethrengerichtshofe in Preuben und Sachsen 1918-1933*
GSR - v27 - i2 - May 2004 - p394-395 [501+]

Rabin, Alan A. - *Monetary Theory*
R&R Bk N - v19 - i3 - August 2004 - p134(1) [51-500]

Rabin, Claire Low - *Understanding Gender and Culture in the Helping Process: Practitioners' Narratives from Global Perspectives*
R&R Bk N - v19 - i4 - Nov 2004 - p9(1) [51-500]

Rabin, Staton - *Betsy and the Emperor*
y BL - v101 - i6 - Nov 15 2004 - p598(2) [51-500]
c CCB-B - v58 - i3 - Nov 2004 - p141(1) [501+]
c KR - v72 - i19 - Oct 1 2004 - p967(1) [51-500]
y PW - v251 - i50 - Dec 13 2004 - p69(1) [51-500]
y SLJ - v50 - i11 - Nov 2004 - p152(2) [51-500]
y VOYA - v27 - i5 - Dec 2004 - p393(1) [51-500]

Rabinovich, Itamar - *Waging Peace: Israel and the Arabs, 1948-2003*
Comw - v131 - i19 - Nov 5 2004 - p44(3) [501+]
For Aff - v83 - i5 - Sept-Oct 2004 - p164 [501+]
NYRB - v51 - i12 - July 15 2004 - p26(4) [501+]

Rabinovitz, Lauren - *Comparing Media Systems: Three Models of Media and Politics*
Choice - v42 - i3 - Nov 2004 - p477(1) [1-50]

Rabinow, Paul - *A Machine to Make a Future Biotech Chronicles*
Sci - v307 - i5714 - March 4 2005 - p1414(1) [501+]

Rabinowitch, Alexander - *The Bolsheviks Come to Power*
HNet - Oct 2004 - pNA [501+]

Rabinowitz, Alan - *Urban Economics and Land Use in America: The Transformation of Cities in the Twentieth Century*
Choice - v42 - i4 - Dec 2004 - p742(2) [1-50]
R&R Bk N - v19 - i3 - August 2004 - p157(1) [51-500]

Rabinowitz, Mitchell - *The Design of Instruction and Evaluation: Affordances of Using Media and Technology*
R&R Bk N - v19 - i4 - Nov 2004 - p179(1) [501+]

Rabinowitz, N. - *Among Women. From the Homosocial to the Homoerotic in the Ancient World*
Class R - v54 - i1 - May 2004 - p160(3) [501+]

Rabinowitz, Paula - *Black & White & Noir: America's Pulp Modernism*
Am Q - v56 - i2 - June 2004 - p471(10) [501+]
FQ - v57 - i4 - Summer 2004 - p66(3) [501+]

Rabkin, Jeremy A. - *The Case for Sovereignty: Why the World Should Welcome American Independence*
Pers PS - v33 - i4 - Fall 2004 - p243(2) [501+]
R&R Bk N - v19 - i3 - August 2004 - p188(1) [501+]

Raboteau, Emily - *The Professor's Daughter*
KR - v72 - i23 - Dec 1 2004 - p1111(1) [501+]
LJ - v130 - i3 - Feb 15 2005 - p120(1) [51-500]
Black Iss - v7 - i2 - March-April 2005 - p48(1) [51-500]

Racaut, Luc - *Hatred in Print: Catholic Propaganda and Protestant Identity during the French wars of Religion*
Six Ct J - v34 - i4 - Winter 2003 - p1118-1120 [501+]

Rachamimov, Alon - *POWs and the Great War: Captivity on the Eastern Front*
CEH - v37 - i3 - Summer 2004 - p478(3) [501+]
GSR - v27 - i2 - May 2004 - p389-391 [501+]

Rachel, T. Cole - *Bend, Don't Shatter: Poets on the Beginning of Desire*
y CCB-B - v57 - i11 - July-August 2004 - p479(2) [501+]
Lam Bk Rpt - v13 - i1-2 - August-Sept 2004 - p42(1) [501+]
y SLJ - v51 - i1 - Jan 2005 - p153(2) [51-500]

Racher, James F. - *Integrity Matters*
Bwatch - v26 - i7 - July 2004 - p4(1) [51-500]

Rachewiltz, Igor de - *The Secret History of the Mongols: A Mongolian Epic Chronicle of the Thirteenth Century*
Choice - v42 - i1 - Sept 2004 - p167(2) [501+]

Rachlis, Michael - *Prescription for Excellence: How Innovation Is Saving Canada's Health Care System*
Globe & Mail - March 5 2005 - pD17 [51-500]

Rachman, Arnold William - *Psychotherapy of Difficult Cases: Flexibility and Responsiveness in Contemporary Practice*
SciTech - v28 - i1 - March 2004 - p98(1) [51-500]

Rachmaninoff, Sergei - *Sergei Rachmaninoff Piano Works*
Am MT - v54 - i2 - Oct-Nov 2004 - p86(1) [501+]

Racine, Jean-Francois - *The Text of Matthew in the Writings of Basil of Caesarea*
R&R Bk N - v19 - i3 - August 2004 - p24(1) [1-50]

Racine, Jean-Luc - *La question identitaire en Asie du sud*
JRAI - v10 - i4 - Dec 2004 - p911(2) [501+]

Racine, Karen - *Francisco the Miranda: A Transatlantic Life in the Age of Revolution*
W&M Q - v62 - i1 - Jan 2005 - p113-5 [501+]

Rackers, Mark - *The Arab-Israeli Conflict*
y SLJ - v50 - i12 - Dec 2004 - p168(1) [51-500]

Raczka, Bob - *More Than Meets the Eye: Seeing Art With All Five Senses*
c LibMed - v22 - i7 - April-May 2004 - p65(1) [501+]
No One Saw
c RT - v57 - Nov 2003 - p273 [51-500]

Radbruch, Don - *Dirt Track Auto Racing, 1919-1941: A Pictorial History*
R&R Bk N - v19 - i3 - August 2004 - p89(1) [51-500]

Raddant, Gloria R. - *Grandmother's Bible*
EFHM - v58 - i3 - May-June 2004 - p57(1) [51-500]

Radden, Jennifer - *The Philosophy of Psychiatry: A Companion*
Choice - v42 - i7 - March 2005 - p1261(1) [51-500]

Radding, Charles M. - *Theology, Rhetoric, and Politics in the Eucharistic Controversy, 1078-1079: Alberic of Monte Cassino against Berengar of Tours*
CH - v73 - i3 - Sept 2004 - p688(3) [501+]
Theol St - v65 - i4 - Dec 2004 - p896(1) [501+]

Radecka, Katarzyna - *Verification by Error Modeling: Using Testing Techniques in Hardware Verification*
SciTech - v28 - i1 - March 2004 - p163(1) [51-500]

Radell, Judith - *Clara Kathleen Rogers*
Notes - v61 - i1 - Sept 2004 - p241(2) [501+]

Rader, Dean - *Speak to Me Words: Essays on Contemporary American Indian Poetry*
R&R Bk N - v19 - i1 - Feb 2004 - p241(1) [501+]

Rader, Karen A. - *Making Mice: Standardizing Animals for American Biomedical Research, 1900-1955*
Am Sci - v93 - i1 - Jan-Feb 2005 - p85(2) [501+]
Choice - v42 - i2 - Oct 2004 - p320(1) [51-500]
Nature - v431 - i7004 - Sept 2 2004 - p22(1) [501+]

Radevsky, Anton - *Architecture Pop-Up Book*
Globe & Mail - Dec 18 2004 - pD14 [1-50]

Radford, Andrew - *Thomas Hardy and the Survivals of Time*
R&R Bk N - v19 - i1 - Feb 2004 - p238(1) [51-500]

Radford, Benjamin - *Media Mythmakers: How Journalists, Activists, and Advertisers Mislead Us*
PW - v251 - i44 - Nov 1 2004 - p53(1) [501+]
R&R Bk N - v19 - i1 - Feb 2004 - p211 [51-500]

Radford, Gary P. - *On the Philosophy of Communication*
R&R Bk N - v19 - i4 - Nov 2004 - p212(1) [501+]

Radford, Irene - *Guardian of the Freedom: Merlin's Descendants, Vol. 5*
PW - v252 - i11 - March 14 2005 - p50(2) [51-500]

Radford, Sheri - *Penelope and the Humongous Burp (Illus. by Tripp, Christine)*
c   SLJ - v50 - i9 - Sept 2004 - p177(1) [51-500]

Radhi, Hassan Ali - *Judiciary and Arbitration in Bahrain: Historical and Analytical Study*
R&R Bk N - v19 - i4 - Nov 2004 - p175(1) [501+]

Radical Harmonies
LJ - v129 - i14 - Sept 1 2004 - p198(2) [51-500]

Radin, Lisa - *What If It's Not Alzheimer's?: A Caregiver's Guide to Dementia*
SciTech - v28 - i1 - March 2004 - p100(1) [51-500]

Radish, Kris - *Dancing Naked at the Edge of Dawn*
BL - v101 - i6 - Nov 15 2004 - p563(1) [51-500]
KR - v72 - i21 - Nov 1 2004 - p1027(1) [501+]

Radner, Ephraim - *Spirit and Nature: The Saint-Medard Miracles and 18th-Century Jansenism*
Theol St - v66 - i1 - March 2005 - p194(3) [501+]

Radnoti, Miklos - *Forced March*
WLT - v78 - i3-4 - Sept-Dec 2004 - p108(1) [501+]

Radocy, Rudolf E. - *Psychological Foundations of Musical Behavior, 4th Ed.*
M Ed J - v91 - i1 - Sept 2004 - p60(2) [501+]

Radojcic, Natasha - *You Don't Have to Live Here*
KR - v73 - i2 - Jan 15 2005 - p80(1) [501+]
PW - v252 - i5 - Jan 31 2005 - p46(2) [51-500]

Radosh, Ronald - *Spain Betrayed: The Soviet Union in the Spanish Civil War*
S&S - v68 - i3 - Fall 2004 - p364-368 [501+]

Radu, Kenneth - *The Purest of Human Pleasures*
Globe & Mail - Jan 29 2005 - pD7 [501+]

Radulescu, Raluca L. - *The Gentry Context for Malory's Morte Darthur*
Med R - July 2004 - pNA [501+]

Radunsky, Vladimir - *The Mighty Asparagus (Illus. by Radunsky, Vladimir)*
c   NYTBR - Oct 17 2004 - p21 [501+]
c   SLJ - v50 - i7 - July 2004 - p86(1) [51-500]
What Does Peace Feel Like?
c   PW - v251 - i51 - Dec 20 2004 - p57(1) [51-500]
What Does Peace Feel Like? (Illus. by Radunsky, Vladimir)
c   BL - v101 - i5 - Nov 1 2004 - p487(1) [51-500]
c   Globe & Mail - Nov 20 2004 - pD26 [51-500]
c   KR - v72 - i21 - Nov 1 2004 - p1046(1) [51-500]
c   SLJ - v51 - i1 - Jan 2005 - p113(1) [51-500]

Radway, Richard - *Germany 1918-45*
y   TES - v0 - i4586 - June 4 2004 - psssss14(2) [501+]

Rae, Douglas W. - *City: Urbanism and Its End*
JEL - v42 - i1 - March 2004 - p304(2) [501+]
Soc Ser R - v79 - i1 - March 2005 - p186(4) [501+]

Rae, Heather - *State Identities and the Homogenisation of Peoples*
JPR - v41 - i4 - July 2004 - p523-523 [501+]

Rae, Ian - *Singular and Different: Business in China Past, Present, and Future*
Choice - v42 - i3 - Nov 2004 - p530(2) [1-50]

Rae, Nicol C. - *Impeaching Clinton: Partisan Strife on Capitol Hill*
Choice - v42 - i2 - Oct 2004 - p373(1) [51-500]

Raeburn, Daniel - *Chris Ware*
BL - v101 - i6 - Nov 15 2004 - p541(2) [51-500]
Choice - v42 - i7 - March 2005 - p1216(1) [51-500]

Rafalovich, Adam - *Framing ADHD Children: Critical Examination of the History, Discourse, and Everyday Experience of Attention Deficit/Hyperactivity disorder*
SciTech - v28 - i4 - Dec 2004 - p114(1) [1-50]

Raffaele, Herbert - *Birds of the West Indies (Illus. by Pedersen, Tracy)*
E-Streams - Oct 2004 - pNA [501+]

Raffaelli, Tiziano - *Marshall's Evolutionary Economics*
JEL - v42 - i1 - March 2004 - p241(2) [501+]

Raffel, Burton - *Pure Pagan: Seven Centuries of Greek Poems and Fragments*
BL - v100 - i21 - July 2004 - p1812(1) [1-50]

Raffi - *This Little Light of Mine (Illus. by Schuett, Stacey)*
c   Globe & Mail - August 14 2004 - pD16 [51-500]
c   Res Links - v10 - i1 - Oct 2004 - p9(1) [51-500]
c   SLJ - v50 - i7 - July 2004 - p95(1) [51-500]

Raffield, Paul - *Images and Cultures of Law in Early Modern England: Justice and Political Power, 1558-1660*
TLS - i5296 - Oct 1 2004 - p29(1) [501+]
Choice - v42 - i5 - Jan 2005 - p921(1) [1-50]

Raffles, Hugh - *In Amazonia: A Natural History*
Isis - v95 - i3 - Sept 2004 - p481(2) [501+]

Rafuse, Ethan S. - *George Gordon Meade and the War in the East*
J Mil H - v68 - i4 - Oct 2004 - p1264-1266 [501+]
R&R Bk N - v19 - i3 - August 2004 - p68(1) [51-500]
A Single Grand Victory: The First Campaign and Battle of Manassas
J Mil H - v68 - i3 - July 2004 - p962-963 [501+]

Ragaini, R. - *International Seminar on Nuclear War and Planetary Emergencies: Proceedings*
SciTech - v28 - i4 - Dec 2004 - p6(1) [1-50]

Ragan, Christopher - *Is the Debt War Over?: Dispatches from Canada's Fiscal Frontline*
R&R Bk N - v19 - i3 - August 2004 - p140(1) [51-500]

Ragen, Naomi - *The Covenant*
BL - v101 - i3 - Oct 1 2004 - p311(1) [51-500]
KR - v72 - i7 - Sept 1 2004 - p831(1) [501+]
LJ - v129 - i18 - Nov 1 2004 - p77(1) [501+]
PW - v251 - i44 - Nov 1 2004 - p43(1) [501+]

Ragionieri, Pina - *Michelangelo: Drawings and Other Treasures from the Casa Buonarroti, Florence*
HNet - Sept 2004 - pNA [501+]

Ragland, Ellie - *Lacan: Topologically Speaking*
Choice - v42 - i5 - Jan 2005 - p938(1) [51-500]
The Logic of Sexuation: From Aristotle to Lacan
Choice - v42 - i1 - Sept 2004 - p193(1) [501+]

Ragsdale, Hugh - *The Soviets, the Munich Crisis, and the Coming of World War II*
Choice - v42 - i1 - Sept 2004 - p169(1) [501+]
HRNB - v33 - i1 - Fall 2004 - p30(2) [501+]

Ragsdale, Lyn - *Vital Statistics on the Presidency*
BL - v101 - i3 - Oct 1 2004 - p358(1) [501+]

Raguin, Virginia Chieffo - *The History of Stained Glass: The Art of Light, Medieval to Contemporary*
TimHES - v0 - i1654 - August 20 2004 - p25(1) [501+]
Stained Glass: From Its Origins to the Present
Am Craft - v64 - i2 - April-May 2004 - p29(1) [501+]

Raha, Raria - *Cinderella's Big Score: Women of the Punk and Indie Underground*
y   BL - v101 - i9-10 - Jan 1 2005 - p799(2) [51-500]

Raham, Gary - *Teaching Science Fact with Science Fiction (Illus. by Raham, Gary)*
Kliatt - v38 - i6 - Nov 2004 - p35(2) [51-500]
y   SB - v41 - i1 - Jan-Feb 2005 - p24(2) [501+]
c   SciTech - v28 - i4 - Dec 2004 - p13(1) [1-50]

Raheb, Mitri - *Bethlehem Besieged: Stories of Hope in Times of Trouble*
Tikkun - v19 - i6 - Nov-Dec 2004 - p74(1) [501+]

Rahman, M. - *Advances in Fluid Mechanics V: Proceedings*
SciTech - v28 - i3 - Sept 2004 - p137(1) [51-500]

Rahnejat, Homer - *Multi-Body Dynamics: Monitoring and Simulation Techniques: Proceedings*
SciTech - v28 - i4 - Dec 2004 - p160(1) [51-500]

Rai, Bali - *Rani and Sukh*
y   Sch Lib - v52 - i3 - Autumn 2004 - p162(1) [501+]

Rai, Gurcharan S. - *Medical Ethics and the Elderly, 2nd Ed.*
SciTech - v28 - i3 - Sept 2004 - p77(1) [51-500]

Rai, Milan - *Regime Unchanged: Why the War on Iraq Changed Nothing*
BW - v34 - i1 - Jan 4 2004 - p4(1) [501+]

Rai, Mridu - *Hindu Rulers, Muslim Subjects: Islam, Rights, and the History of Kashmir*
HRNB - v33 - i1 - Fall 2004 - p34(2) [501+]
NS - v133 - i4703 - August 30 2004 - p36(2) [501+]

Raichlen, Steven - *Raichlen's Indoor! Grilling: 270 Recipes Just for Grill Pans, Countertop Grills, Grilling Machines, Stovetop Grills, Rotisseries & Fireplaces*
y   Kliatt - v39 - i2 - March 2005 - p44(1) [51-500]
People - v62 - i3 - Nov 22 2004 - p63 [51-500]
PW - v251 - i45 - Nov 8 2004 - p47(1) [501+]

Raimond, Michel - *Sur trois pieces de Jean Giraudoux: ' La Guerre de Troie n' aura pas lieu', 'Electre', 'Ondine'*
FS - v58 - i2 - April 2004 - p279(2) [501+]

Raimondo, Joyce - *Imagine That!: Activities and Adventures in Surrealism*
c   BL - v101 - i7 - Dec 1 2004 - p649(1) [51-500]
c   LibMed - v23 - i3 - Nov-Dec 2004 - p77(1) [51-500]
y   SLJ - v50 - i9 - Sept 2004 - p192(1) [51-500]
Picture This!: Activities and Adventures in Impressionism
y   KR - v72 - i16 - August 15 2004 - p812(1) [51-500]
c   SLJ - v51 - i1 - Jan 2005 - p113(2) [51-500]

Rain, Patricia - *Vanilla: The Cultural History of the World's Favorite Flavor and Fragrance*
BL - v101 - i3 - Oct 1 2004 - p290(1) [51-500]
KR - v72 - i17 - Sept 1 2004 - p853(1) [501+]
LJ - v129 - i19 - Nov 15 2004 - p81(1) [501+]
PW - v251 - i39 - Sept 27 2004 - p45(2) [51-500]
SciTech - v28 - i4 - Dec 2004 - p124 [51-500]
Vanilla: The Cultural History of the World's Most Popular Flavor and Fragrance
NYTBR - Dec 19 2004 - p31 [501+]

Raina, Dhruv - *Images and Contexts: The Historiography of Science and Modernity in India*
T&C - v45 - i2 - April 2004 - p467-468 [501+]

Raina, Lalit - *Non-Bank Financial Institutions and Capital Markets in Turkey*
JEL - v41 - i4 - Dec 2003 - p1415(1) [501+]

Rainbow, John D. - *Where to Weekend around Washington, D.C.*
LJ - v129 - i15 - Sept 15 2004 - p73(1) [51-500]

Rainer, Thom S. - *Breakout Churches: Discover How to Make the Leap*
PW - v252 - i3 - Jan 17 2005 - p52(1) [51-500]

Raines, J. Patrick - *The Economic Institutions of Higher Education: Economic Theories of University Behaviour*
JEL - v42 - i1 - March 2004 - p276(1) [501+]
R&R Bk N - v19 - i1 - Feb 2004 - p189(1) [501+]

Rainey, Buck - *The Strong, Silent Type: Over 100 Screen Cowboys, 1903-1930*
R&R Bk N - v19 - i1 - Feb 2004 - p225(1) [51-500]

Rainey, Larry B. - *Space Modeling and Simulation: Roles and Applications Throughout the System Lifecycle*
SciTech - v28 - i4 - Dec 2004 - p162(1) [51-500]

Rainford, Jenni - *Ripley's Believe It or Not*
KR - v72 - i23 - Dec 1 2004 - pNA [501+]

Rainsberger, J.B. - *JUnit Recipes: Practical Methods for Programmer Testing*
CBRA - Annual 2003 - p21(1) [51-500]
SciTech - v28 - i4 - Dec 2004 - p21(1) [51-500]

Rainsford, Dominic - *Literature, Identity and the English Channel: Narrow Seas Expanded*
FS - v58 - i1 - Jan 2004 - p118(2) [501+]

Rainwater, Dorothy T. - *Encyclopedia of American Silver Manufacturers, 5th Rev. Ed.*
R&R Bk N - v19 - i4 - Nov 2004 - p210(1) [501+]

Rainwater, Lee - *Poor Kids in a Rich Country: America's Children in Comparative Perspective*
Choice - v41 - i11-12 - July-August 2004 - p2085(1) [501+]

Raisinghani, Mahesh - *Business Intelligence in the Digital Economy: Opportunities, Limitations and Risks*
R&R Bk N - v19 - i3 - August 2004 - p103(1) [1-50]

Raiten-D'Antonio, Toni - *The Velveteen Principles: A Guide to Becoming Real*
LJ - v129 - i19 - Nov 15 2004 - p76(1) [501+]

Raj, Selva J. - *Popular Christianity in India: Riting between the Lines*
JRAI - v10 - i3 - Sept 2004 - p734(2) [501+]

Rajagopal, Indhu - *Hidden Academics: Contract Faculty in Canadian Universities*
R&R Bk N - v19 - i1 - Feb 2004 - p185(1) [51-500]

Rajan, Rajeswari Sunder - *The Scandal of the State: Women, Law, and Citizenship in Postcolonial India*
HNet - Sept 2004 - pNA [501+]

Rajan, Ramkishen - *Sustaining Competitiveness in the New Global Economy: The Experience of Singapore*
R&R Bk N - v19 - i2 - May 2004 - p111(1) [501+]

Rajan, Supritha - *Seven-Star Bird*
CQ - v56 - i2-3 - Spring-Summer 2004 - p82(2) [501+]

Rajan, Tilottama - *After Postconstructuralism: Writing the Intellectual History of Theory*
CBRA - Annual 2003 - p280(1) [501+]
Clio - v33 - i3 - Spring 2004 - p287(17) [501+]
Deconstruction and the Remainders of Phenomenology
Clio - v33 - i3 - Spring 2004 - p287(17) [501+]

Rajs, Jake - *These United States*
R&R Bk N - v19 - i1 - Feb 2004 - p54(1) [51-500]

Raju, C.K. - *Eleven Pictures of Time: The Physics, Philosophy, and Politics of Time Beliefs*
R&R Bk N - v19 - i1 - Feb 2004 - p7(1) [51-500]

Rak, Julie - *Negotiated Memory: Doukhobor Autobiographical Discourse*
R&R Bk N - v19 - i3 - August 2004 - p77(1) [51-500]

Rakel, Robert E. - *Conn's Current Therapy: Latest Approved Methods of Treatment for the Practicing Physician 2004*
SciTech - v28 - i1 - March 2004 - p120(1) [51-500]

Rakich, Jonathon - *Cases in Health Services Management, 4th Ed.*
SciTech - v28 - i1 - March 2004 - p85(1) [51-500]

Rakov, Vladimir A. - *Lightning: Physics and Effects*
Phys Today - v57 - i12 - Dec 2004 - p63-64 [501+]
TimHES - v0 - i1658 - Sept 17 2004 - p29(1) [501+]

Raleigh, Debbie - *How to Marry a Duke*
LJ - v130 - i1 - Jan 1 2005 - p92(1) [51-500]

Raleigh, Donald J. - *Experiencing Russia's Civil War: Politics, Society, and Revolutionary Culture in Saratov, 1917-1922*
AHR - v109 - i2 - April 2004 - p649(2) [501+]
HNet - Sept 2004 - pNA [501+]
JMH - v77 - i1 - March 2004 - p258(2) [501+]
Provincial Landscapes: Local Dimensions of Soviet Power, 1917-1953
Slav R - v63 - i2 - Summer 2004 - p410(3) [501+]

Rall, Ted - *Attitude 2: The New Subversive Alternative Cartoonists*
LJ - v129 - i12 - July 2004 - p62(1) [51-500]

Rallings, Colin - *British Elections and Parties Review, Vol. 13*
R&R Bk N - v19 - i1 - Feb 2004 - pNA [501+]

Rallison, Janette - *Life, Love, and the Pursuit of Free Throws*
c BL - v101 - i5 - Nov 1 2004 - p486(1) [51-500]
y KR - v72 - i15 - August 1 2004 - p748(1) [51-500]
y SLJ - v50 - i11 - Nov 2004 - p153(1) [51-500]

Ralph, Edwin G. - *Pursuing Instructional Effectiveness in Higher Education: It's about Time!*
R&R Bk N - v19 - i4 - Nov 2004 - p184(1) [501+]

Ralph, Ruth O. - *Recovery in Mental Illness: Broadening Our Understanding of Wellness*
SciTech - v28 - i4 - Dec 2004 - p94(1) [51-500]

Ralston, Anthony - *Encyclopedia of Computer Science, 4th Ed.*
E-Streams - July 2004 - pNA [501+]

Ralston, Aron - *Between a Rock and a Hard Place. (Read by Ralston, Aron). Audiobook Review*
PW - v251 - i44 - Nov 1 2004 - p28(1) [501+]
Between a Rock and a Hard Place
y BL - v100 - i22 - August 2004 - p1867(1) [51-500]
BW - v34 - i39 - Sept 26 2004 - p9(1) [501+]
NS - v133 - i4711 - Oct 25 2004 - p52(2) [501+]
PW - v251 - i32 - August 9 2004 - p242(2) [51-500]
SLJ - v51 - i2 - Feb 2005 - p159(1) [51-500]
Time - v164 - i14 - Oct 4 2004 - p95 [1-50]

Ram, Dass - *Paths to God: Living the Bhagavad Gita*
LJ - v129 - i16 - Oct 1 2004 - p86(1) [51-500]

Ram, Harsha - *The Imperial Sublime: A Russian Poetics of Empire*
Choice - v42 - i5 - Jan 2005 - p859(1) [1-50]

Ramachandran, V.K. - *Agrarian Studies: Essays on Agrarian Relations in Less-Developed Countries*
R&R Bk N - v19 - i1 - Feb 2004 - p96(1) [51-500]

Ramachandran, V.S. - *A Brief Tour of Human Consciousness: From Impostor Poodles to Purple Numbers*
Choice - v42 - i6 - Feb 2005 - p1102(1) [51-500]
LJ - v129 - i13 - August 2004 - p115(1) [51-500]

Ramachandran, Vimala - *Getting Children Back to School: Case Studies in Primary Education*
R&R Bk N - v19 - i1 - Feb 2004 - pNA [51-500]

Ramadan, Hisham M. - *Reconstructiong Jury Instructions in Homicide Offenses: Rethinking Homicide Law*
R&R Bk N - v19 - i4 - Nov 2004 - p173(1) [501+]

Ramadan, Tariq - *Western Muslims and the Future of Islam*
MEJ - v59 - i1 - Wntr 2005 - p158(4) [501+]
MEQ - v12 - i1 - Wntr 2005 - p71(8) [501+]
TLS - i5288 - August 6 2004 - p3-4 [501+]

Ramage, Jan - *Eyes in the Night*
c CH Bwatch - v14 - i12 - Dec 2004 - pNA [51-500]

Raman, Shanker - *Framing" India": The Colonial Imaginary in Early Modern Culture*
Six Ct J - v34 - i4 - Winter 2003 - p1232-1233 [501+]

Ramanna, Mridula - *Western Medicine and Public Health in Colonial Bombay, 1845-1895*
T&C - v45 - i1 - Jan 2004 - p179(2) [501+]

Ramawat, K.G. - *Biotechnology of Medicinal Plants: Vitalizer and Therapeutic*
SciTech - v28 - i4 - Dec 2004 - p119(1) [1-50]

Rambally, Rae Tucker - *Practice Imperfect: Reflections on a Career in Social Work*
CBRA - Annual 2003 - p64(2) [51-500]

Rambaud, Patrick - *The Retreat*
KR - v72 - i17 - Sept 1 2004 - p831(1) [501+]
LJ - v129 - i19 - Nov 15 2004 - p51(1) [501+]
PW - v251 - i41 - Oct 11 2004 - p54(1) [51-500]
TLS - i5291 - August 27 2004 - p21(1) [501+]

Ramchand, Kenneth - *The West Indian Novel and Its Background*
Choice - v42 - i4 - Dec 2004 - p662(1) [1-50]

Ramesh, Randeep - *The War We Could Not Stop: The Real Story of the Battle for Iraq*
R&R Bk N - v19 - i3 - August 2004 - p50(1) [51-500]

Ramet, Sabrina P. - *Kazaam! Splat! Ploof! The American Impact on European Popular Culture Since 1945*
HNet - Nov 2004 - pNA [501+]

Ramey, David W. - *Complementary and Alternative Veterinary Medicine Considered*
SciTech - v28 - i1 - March 2004 - p131(1) [51-500]

Raming, Ida - *The Priestly Office of Women: God's Gift to a Renewed Church, 2nd Ed.*
R&R Bk N - v19 - i3 - August 2004 - p26(1) [1-50]

Ramirez, Antonio - *Napi (Illus. by Groundwood, Domi)*
c BL - v101 - i6 - Nov 15 2004 - p591(1) [51-500]
c KR - v72 - i18 - Sept 15 2004 - p918(1) [51-500]
c SLJ - v50 - i9 - Sept 2004 - p177(1) [51-500]

Ramirez, Juan Antonio - *Architecture for the Screen: A Critical Study of Set Design in Hollywood's Golden Age*
R&R Bk N - v19 - i3 - August 2004 - p261(1) [51-500]

Ramirez, Maria Himelda - *Las mujeres y la sociedad colonial de Santa Fe de Bogota, 1750-1810*
HAHR - v84 - i4 - Nov 2004 - p738(2) [501+]

Ramlogan, Rajendra - *Developing World and the Environment: Making the Case for Effective Protection of the Global Environment*
R&R Bk N - v20 - i1 - Feb 2005 - p82(1) [51-500]

Ramond, Pierre - *Journeys Beyond the Standard Model*
SciTech - v28 - i1 - March 2004 - p52(1) [51-500]

Ramos, Denise Gimenez - *The Psyche of the Body: A Jungian Approach to Psychosomatics*
SciTech - v28 - i4 - Dec 2004 - p89(1) [51-500]

Ramos-Garcia, Luis A. - *The State of Latino Theatre in the United States.*
Theat J - v56 - i3 - Oct 2004 - p518-520 [501+]

Ramos, Jorge - *Dying to Cross: The Worst Immigrant Tragedy in American History (Read by Davis, Jonathan). Audiobook Review*
LJ - v129 - i20 - Dec 1 2004 - p182(1) [501+]
The Latino Wave: How Hispanics Will Elect the Next American President
BW - v34 - i29 - July 18 2004 - p5(1) [1-50]

Ramos, Manuel Joao - *The Indigenous and the Foreign in Christian Ethiopian Art: On Portuguese-Ethiopian Contacts in the 16th-17th Centuries*
R&R Bk N - v19 - i4 - Nov 2004 - p201(1) [501+]

Ramos, Mario - *Soy el mas fuerte!/I Am the Strongest*
c BL - v100 - i22 - August 2004 - p1950(1) [501+]

Ramos-Zayas, Ana Y. - *National Performances: The Politics of Class, Race, and Space in Puerto Rican Chicago*
CS - v33 - i6 - Nov 2004 - p662(3) [501+]
JRAI - v10 - i3 - Sept 2004 - p746(2) [501+]

Rampling Blair - *Windows Server 2003 Security Bible*
SciTech - v28 - i3 - Sept 2004 - p29(1) [51-500]

Rampuri. Baba - *Baba: Autobiography of a Blue-Eyed Yogi*
LJ - v130 - i1 - Jan 1 2005 - p119(1) [51-500]

Rampuri, Yogi - *Baba: Autobiography of a Blue-Eyed Yogi*
PW - v251 - i48 - Nov 29 2004 - p38(1) [51-500]

Ramsamy, Sam - *Reflections on a Life in Sport*
Lon R Bks - v26 - i24 - Dec 16 2004 - p33(2) [501+]

Ramsay, Caird - *Landscape and Building Design for Bushfire Areas*
SciTech - v28 - i3 - Sept 2004 - p131(1) [51-500]

Ramsay, Frederick - *Artscape*
BL - v100 - i21 - July 2004 - p1825(1) [1-50]
LJ - v129 - i12 - July 2004 - p64(1) [51-500]

Ramsay, Raylene L. - *French Women in Politics: Writing Power, Paternal Legitimization, and Maternal Legacies*
HNet - Oct 2004 - pNA [501+]

Ramsden, John - *The Dam Busters*
R&R Bk N - v19 - i1 - Feb 2004 - p226(1) [51-500]
Man of the Century: Winston Churchill and His Legend since 1945 (Read by Ramsden, John). Audiobook Review
LJ - v130 - i3 - Feb 15 2005 - p170(1) [51-500]
Man of the Century: Winston Churchill and His Legend since 1945
R&R Bk N - v19 - i1 - Feb 2004 - p32(1) [1-50]

Ramsey, Guthrie P., Jr. - *Race Music: Black Cultures from Bebop to Hip-Hop*
JAH - v91 - i2 - Sept 2004 - p709(2) [501+]

Ramsey, Russell W. - *Essays on Latin American Security: The Collected Writings of a Scholar-Implementer*
HAHR - v84 - i3 - August 2004 - p566(2) [501+]

Ramseyer, J. Mark - *Measuring Judicial Independence: The Political Economy of Judging in Japan*
Pac A - v77 - i2 - Summer 2004 - p336(2) [501+]

Ran, Shulamit - *Fanfare for 2 Trumpets, 2 Horns, and Trombone*
Notes - v61 - i3 - March 2005 - p870(5) [501+]

Ranan, David - *In Search of a Magic Flute: The Public Funding of Opera: Dilemmas and Decision Making*
R&R Bk N - v19 - i1 - Feb 2004 - p197(1) [51-500]

Ranchod-Nilsson, Sita - *Women, States, and Nationalism: At Home in the Nation?*
Signs - v30 - i2 - Wntr 2005 - p1683(6) [501+]

Rancic, Bill - *You're Hired: How to Succeed in Business and Life*
BL - v101 - i4 - Oct 15 2004 - p386(2) [51-500]
PW - v251 - i39 - Sept 27 2004 - p50(2) [51-500]

Ranciere, Jacques - *The Flesh of Words: The Politics of Writing*
R&R Bk N - v19 - i4 - Nov 2004 - p222(1) [501+]

Rancourt, Suzane S. - *Billboard in the Clouds*
LJ - v129 - i13 - August 2004 - p86(1) [501+]

Rand, Gloria - *Mary Was a Little Lamb (Illus. by Rand, Ted)*
c CCB-B - v57 - i11 - July-August 2004 - p480(1) [501+]

Rand, Salvatore J. - *Significance of Tests for Petroleum Products, 7th Ed.*
SciTech - v28 - i1 - March 2004 - p174(1) [51-500]

Randal, Allison - *Perl 6 and Parrot Essentials, 2nd Ed.*
SciTech - v28 - i4 - Dec 2004 - p22(1) [51-500]

Randal, Jonathan - *Osama: The Making of a Terrorist*
BL - v100 - i21 - July 2004 - p1796(1) [51-500]
Bus W - i3898 - Sept 6 2004 - p24 [501+]
BW - v34 - i34 - August 22 2004 - p6(1) [501+]
KR - v72 - i13 - July 1 2004 - p622(1) [501+]
LJ - v129 - i13 - August 2004 - p90(2) [501+]
NYTBR - Oct 3 2004 - p24 [501+]
PW - v251 - i28 - July 12 2004 - p58(1) [501+]

Randall, Alice - *Pushkin and the Queen of Spades (Read by Pitts, Lisa Renee). Audiobook Review*
BL - v101 - i3 - Oct 1 2004 - p351(1) [51-500]
LJ - v129 - i19 - Nov 15 2004 - p97(2) [51-500]
Pushkin and the Queen of Spades
Wom R Bks - v21 - i10-11 - July 2004 - p5(2) [501+]

Randall, Bernard - *Solon: The Lawmaker of Athens*
y SLJ - v50 - i9 - Sept 2004 - p230(1) [51-500]

Randall, David - *Clovermead: In the Shadow of the Bear*
y BL - v100 - i21 - July 2004 - p1834(1) [1-50]
c CH Bwatch - v14 - i7 - July 2004 - p7(1) [51-500]
y ChrSFF&H - v26 - i9 - Sept 2004 - p31(1) [51-500]
y PW - v251 - i31 - August 2 2004 - p71(1) [51-500]
c SLJ - v50 - i7 - July 2004 - p112(1) [51-500]
y VOYA - v27 - i3 - August 2004 - p233(1) [1-50]

Randall, Jeff - *Adventure Travel in the Third World: Everything You Need to Know to Survive in Remote and Hostile Destinations*
R&R Bk N - v19 - i1 - Feb 2004 - p68(1) [501+]

Randel, Don Michael - *The Harvard Dictionary of Music, 4th Ed.*
Notes - v61 - i3 - March 2005 - p741(3) [501+]

Randisi, Robert J. - *Invitation to a Hanging*
Roundup M - v12 - i3 - Feb 2005 - p29(1) [51-500]
The Sons of Daniel Shaye: Leaving Epitaph
Roundup M - v12 - i3 - Feb 2005 - p29(1) [51-500]

Randl, Chad - *A-Frame*
R&R Bk N - v19 - i3 - August 2004 - p242(1) [1-50]

Randle, Kristen D. - *Slumming. Audiobook Review*
c Kliatt - v38 - i4 - July 2004 - p56(1) [51-500]

Randle, Mechael - *Challenge to Nonviolence*
JPR - v41 - i5 - Sept 2004 - p645-645 [501+]

Rando, Daniela - *Dai Margini la Memoria: Johannes Hinderbach*
    HER - v119 - i483 - Sept 2004 - p1043(2) [501+]
    HER - v119 - i483 - Sept 2004 - p1043(2) [501+]
Randolph, Joanne - *Let's Draw a Horse with Rectangles/Vamos a dibujar un caballo usando rectangulos (Illus. by Muschinske, Emily)*
    c   SLJ - v50 - i9 - Sept 2004 - p195(1) [1-50]
What I Look Like When I Am Confused/Como me veo cuando estoy confundido
    y   SLJ - v50 - i7 - July 2004 - p94(1) [51-500]
    c   SLJ - v50 - i9 - Sept 2004 - p197(1) [51-500]
What I Look Like When I Am Sad/Como me veo cuando estoy triste
    c   SLJ - v50 - i8 - August 2004 - p110(1) [51-500]
    c   SLJ - v50 - i9 - Sept 2004 - p197(1) [51-500]
Randolph, John - *Environmental Land Use Planning and Management*
    NRJ - v44 - i2 - Spring 2004 - p621-651 [501+]
Randolph, Lewis A. - *Rights for a Season: The Politics of Race, Class, and Gender in Richmond, Virginia*
    JSH - v70 - i3 - August 2004 - p717(2) [501+]
Randolph, Mary - *The Excutor's Guide: Settling a Loved One's Estate or Trust*
    R&R Bk N - v19 - i3 - August 2004 - p197(1) [1-50]
Random, Kenneth M. Pollack - *The Persian Puzzle: The Conflict between Iran and America*
    NL - v87 - i6 - Nov-Dec 2004 - p22(2) [501+]
Rands, Bernard - *Fanfare for Brass Quintet*
    Notes - v61 - i3 - March 2005 - p870(5) [501+]
Rangell, Leo - *My Life in Theory*
    Choice - v42 - i4 - Dec 2004 - p740(1) [1-50]
    SciTech - v28 - i3 - Sept 2004 - p95(1) [1-50]
Rank, Mark Robert - *One Nation, Underprivileged: Why American Poverty Affects Us All*
    Choice - v42 - i4 - Dec 2004 - p743(1) [1-50]
    R&R Bk N - v19 - i3 - August 2004 - p159(1) [51-500]
    SF - v83 - i1 - Sept 2004 - p439(2) [501+]
Rank, Otto - *The Myth of the Birth of the Hero: A Psychological Exploration of Myth, Updated Ed.*
    R&R Bk N - v19 - i4 - Nov 2004 - p14(1) [51-500]
Ranke, Michael B. - *Diagnostics of Endocrine Function in Children and Adolescents, 3d Rev. Ed.*
    SciTech - v28 - i1 - March 2004 - p118(1) [51-500]
Rankin, David C. - *Diary of a Christian Soldier: Rufus Kinsley and the Civil War*
    JR - v85 - i1 - Jan 2005 - p133(2) [501+]
Rankin, Ian - *Fleshmarket Alley: An Inspector Rebus Novel (Read by MacPherson, James). Audiobook Review*
    PW - v252 - i10 - March 7 2005 - p26(1) [51-500]
Fleshmarket Alley: An Inspector Rebus Novel
    BL - v101 - i7 - Dec 1 2004 - p619(1) [51-500]
    Ent W - Feb 4 2005 - p137 [51-500]
    KR - v72 - i24 - Dec 15 2004 - p1169(1) [501+]
    LJ - v130 - i1 - Jan 1 2005 - p85(2) [51-500]
    PW - v252 - i2 - Jan 10 2005 - p41(2) [51-500]
    NYTBR - Feb 6 2005 - p25 [501+]
Fleshmarket Close
    Globe & Mail - Oct 9 2004 - pD5 [501+]
    Globe & Mail - Dec 24 2004 - pD3 [1-50]
    NS - v133 - i4708 - Oct 4 2004 - p54(2) [501+]
    TLS - i5296 - Oct 1 2004 - p22(1) [501+]
A Question of Blood
    Globe & Mail - August 28 2004 - pD13 [51-500]
Witch Hunt
    BL - v100 - i22 - August 2004 - p1871(2) [51-500]
    BW - v34 - i39 - Sept 26 2004 - p10(1) [501+]
    LJ - v129 - i14 - Sept 1 2004 - p142(1) [501+]
    NYTBR - Oct 3 2004 - p30 [501+]
    PW - v251 - i34 - August 23 2004 - p38(1) [51-500]
Rankin, Ian Niall - *Doomsday Just Ahead*
    Spec - v295 - i9186 - August 28 2004 - p34(2) [501+]
Rankin, Katharine Neilson - *Cultural Politics of Markets: Economic Liberalization and Social Change in Nepal*
    R&R Bk N - v19 - i4 - Nov 2004 - p47(1) [51-500]
Rankin, Laura - *Swan Harbor: A Nature Counting Book*
    LibMed - v22 - i5 - Feb 2004 - p82(1) [501+]
Rankin, Robert - *The Witches of Chiswick (Read by Rankin, Robert). Audiobook Review*
    Kliatt - v38 - i6 - Nov 2004 - p53(1) [51-500]
Ranlet, Philip - *Richard B. Morris and American History in the Twentieth Century*
    R&R Bk N - v19 - i4 - Nov 2004 - p56(1) [1-50]

Ransby, Barbara - *Ella Baker and the Black Freedom Movement: A Radical Democratic Vision*
    AHR - v109 - i4 - Oct 2004 - p1254(2) [501+]
    JSH - v70 - i4 - Nov 2004 - p966(2) [501+]
Lost Prophet: The Life and Times of Bayard Rustin
    JAH - v91 - i2 - Sept 2004 - p708(1) [501+]
Ransford, Sandy - *The Kingfisher Illustrated Horse and Pony Encyclopedia*
    y   SLJ - v51 - i1 - Jan 2005 - p154(1) [51-500]
Ransom, Candice - *John Hancock*
    c   SLJ - v51 - i1 - Jan 2005 - p101(1) [51-500]
Liberty Street (Illus. by Velasquez, Eric)
    RT - v58 - i3 - Nov 2004 - p289(1) [1-50]
Ransom, Roger - *The Confederate States of America: What Might Have Been*
    KR - v73 - i3 - Feb 1 2005 - p169(2) [501+]
    LJ - v130 - i4 - March 1 2005 - p98(1) [51-500]
Ransome, Hilda M. - *Sacred Bee in Ancient Times and Folklore*
    R&R Bk N - v19 - i4 - Nov 2004 - p77(1) [51-500]
Ranta, Judith A. - *The Life and Writings of Betty Chamberlain: Native American Mill Worker*
    NEQ - v77 - i4 - Dec 2004 - p672-675 [501+]
Rao, C.N.R. - *The Chemistry of Nanomaterials: Synthesis, Properties and Applications*
    Choice - v42 - i1 - Sept 2004 - p133(1) [501+]
    E-Streams - Nov 2004 - pNA [501+]
Rao, Madanmohan - *News Media and New Media*
    R&R Bk N - v19 - i1 - Feb 2004 - p210(1) [51-500]
Rao, Sirish - *Sophocles' Oedipus the King*
    y   BL - v101 - i9-10 - Jan 1 2005 - p841(1) [51-500]
Rao, Velcheru Narayana - *Hibiscus on the Lake: Twentieth-Century Telugu Poetry from India*
    JAS - v63 - i3 - August 2004 - p832-833 [501+]
Rao, Vijayendra - *Culture and Public Action*
    Pers PS - v34 - i1 - Wntr 2005 - p61(2) [501+]
Rapaport, Herman - *Later Derrida: Reading the Recent Work*
    RM - v58 - i2 - Dec 2004 - p463(3) [501+]
Rapatzikou, Tatiani G. - *Gothic Motifs in the Fiction of William Gibson*
    R&R Bk N - v19 - i4 - Nov 2004 - p234(1) [501+]
Raper, Arthur Franklin - *The Tragedy of Lynching*
    Bwatch - v26 - i9 - Sept 2004 - p2(1) [51-500]
    R&R Bk N - v19 - i3 - August 2004 - p165(1) [501+]
Raphael, Frederic - *Rough Copy: Personal Terms, II*
    Spec - v295 - i9184 - August 14 2004 - p35(1) [501+]
    TLS - i5283 - July 2 2004 - p30(1) [501+]
Raphael, Jody - *Listening to Olivia: Violence, Poverty, and Prostitution*
    Choice - v42 - i6 - Feb 2005 - p1106(1) [51-500]
    R&R Bk N - v19 - i3 - August 2004 - p149(1) [1-50]
Raphael, Jordan - *Stan Lee and the Rise and Fall of the American Comic Book*
    LibMed - v22 - i4 - Jan 2004 - p69(1) [501+]
    y   VOYA - v27 - i5 - Dec 2004 - p417(1) [51-500]
Raphael, Lev - *Tropic of Murder: A Nick Hoffman Mystery*
    BL - v101 - i1 - Sept 1 2004 - p69(1) [51-500]
    KR - v72 - i14 - July 15 2004 - p663(1) [51-500]
    Lam Bk Rpt - v13 - i3 - Oct 2004 - p28(2) [501+]
    LJ - v129 - i13 - August 2004 - p59(2) [501+]
Raphael, Ray - *Founding Myths: Stories That Hide Our Patriotic Past*
    y   BL - v101 - i1 - Sept 1 2004 - p43(1) [51-500]
    LJ - v129 - i16 - Oct 1 2004 - p95(1) [51-500]
    y   SLJ - v51 - i1 - Jan 2005 - p161(1) [51-500]
Rapley, John - *Globalization and Inequality: Neoliberalism's Downward Spiral*
    Choice - v42 - i4 - Dec 2004 - p735(1) [1-50]
    R&R Bk N - v19 - i3 - August 2004 - p174(1) [501+]
Rapley, Mark - *Quality of Life Research: A Critical Introduction*
    R&R Bk N - v19 - i2 - May 2004 - p130 [51-500]
The Social Construction of Intellectual Disability
    Choice - v42 - i4 - Dec 2004 - p740(1) [1-50]
Rapley, Ralph - *Molecular Analysis and Genome Discovery*
    SciTech - v28 - i3 - Sept 2004 - p88(1) [51-500]
Rapoport, Chaim - *Judaism and Homosexuality: An Authentic Orthodox View*
    R&R Bk N - v19 - i3 - August 2004 - p17(1) [1-50]
Rapoport, Nessa - *House on the River: A Summer Journey*
    BW - v34 - i39 - Sept 26 2004 - p8(1) [501+]
    Globe & Mail - August 14 2004 - pD5 [501+]

Rapp, Adam - *Under the Wolf, Under the Dog*
    y   BL - v101 - i6 - Nov 15 2004 - p585(1) [51-500]
    y   CCB-B - v58 - i4 - Dec 2004 - p182(1) [51-500]
    y   HB - v81 - i1 - Jan-Feb 2005 - p79(1) [51-500]
    y   Kliatt - v38 - i5 - Sept 2004 - p15(3) [51-500]
    y   KR - v72 - i18 - Sept 15 2004 - p918(1) [51-500]
    y   SLJ - v50 - i10 - Oct 2004 - p176(1) [51-500]
    VOYA - v27 - i5 - Dec 2004 - p394(1) [51-500]
Rappaport, Doreen - *Free at Last!: Stories and Songs of Emancipation (Illus. by Evans, Shane W.)*
    c   CCB-B - v57 - i11 - July-August 2004 - p480(2) [501+]
    c   CH Bwatch - v14 - i8 - August 2004 - p5(1) [51-500]
    c   SLJ - v50 - i10 - Oct 2004 - pS32(1) [51-500]
In the Promised Land: Lives of Jewish Americans (Illus. by Van Wright, Cornelius)
    BL - v101 - i9-10 - Jan 1 2005 - p854(1) [1-50]
    KR - v73 - i3 - Feb 1 2005 - p181(1) [51-500]
John's Secret Dreams: The Life of John Lennon (Illus. by Collier, Bryan)
    c   BL - v101 - i4 - Oct 15 2004 - p402(1) [51-500]
    c   CCB-B - v58 - i5 - Jan 2005 - p224(2) [51-500]
    c   HB - v80 - i5 - Sept-Oct 2004 - p607(2) [51-500]
    c   KR - v72 - i18 - Sept 15 2004 - p918(1) [51-500]
    c   NYTBR - March 13 2005 - p21 [501+]
    y   SLJ - v50 - i12 - Dec 2004 - p168(2) [51-500]
The Secret Seder (Illus. by McCully, Emily Arnold)
    c   BL - v101 - i9-10 - Jan 1 2005 - p860(2) [1-50]
    c   PW - v252 - i7 - Feb 14 2005 - p79(1) [51-500]
    c   SLJ - v51 - i2 - Feb 2005 - p108(2) [51-500]
Rappaport, Erika Diane - *Shopping for Pleasure*
    VS - v45 - i2 - Winter 2003 - p319 [501+]
Rappaport, Jill - *People We Know, Horses They Love (Illus. by Solomon, Linda)*
    Globe & Mail - Dec 18 2004 - pD14 [1-50]
Rappolt, Mark - *Gehry Draws*
    New Sci - v185 - i2484 - Jan 29 2005 - p50(1) [501+]
    PW - v252 - i9 - Feb 28 2005 - p58(1) [51-500]
Rarick, Ethan - *California Rising: The Life and Times of Pat Brown*
    LJ - v129 - i20 - Dec 1 2004 - p137(2) [51-500]
    PW - v251 - i47 - Nov 22 2004 - p51(1) [51-500]
Rasch, Manfred - *August Thyssen und Hugo Stinnes: ein Briefwechsel, 1898-1912*
    BHR - v78 - i2 - Summer 2004 - p359(4) [501+]
Raschka, Chris - *Boy Meets Girl/Girl Meets Boy (Illus. by Radunsky, Vladimir)*
    c   KR - v72 - i15 - August 1 2004 - p748(1) [51-500]
    c   PW - v251 - i35 - August 30 2004 - p53(1) [51-500]
    c   SLJ - v50 - i11 - Nov 2004 - p116(1) [51-500]
Raschke, Carl - *The Next Reformation: Why Evangelicals Must Embrace Postmodernity*
    LJ - v130 - i1 - Jan 1 2005 - p119(1) [51-500]
Raschke, Carl A. - *The Digital Revolution and the Coming of the Postmodern University*
    T&C - v45 - i2 - April 2004 - p473-475 [501+]
    TCR - v106 - i2 - Feb 2004 - p276-280 [501+]
Raschle, C.R. - *Pestes Harenae. Die Schlangenepisode in Lucans Pharsalia*
    Class R - v54 - i1 - May 2004 - p104(3) [501+]
Rascol, Sabina - *The Impudent Rooster (Illus. by Berry, Holly)*
    c   Five Owls - v18 - i1 - Fall 2004 - p18(1) [51-500]
    c   LibMed - v23 - i3 - Nov-Dec 2004 - p74(1) [51-500]
Rasenberger, Jim - *High Steel: The Daring Men Who Built the World's Greatest Skyline*
    Choice - v42 - i4 - Dec 2004 - p693(2) [1-50]
    KR - v72 - i24 - Dec 15 2004 - pS6(1) [501+]
    SciTech - v28 - i3 - Sept 2004 - p148(1) [51-500]
Raser, Timothy - *Peripheries of Nineteenth-Century French Studies: Views from the Edge*
    FS - v58 - i3 - July 2004 - p418-419 [501+]
Rash, Ron - *One Foot in Eden*
    S Liv - v39 - i3 - March 2004 - p121(1) [501+]
Saints at the River
    BL - v100 - i21 - July 2004 - p1819(1) [1-50]
    Ent W - i777 - August 6 2004 - p84 [501+]
    PW - v251 - i28 - July 12 2004 - p43(2) [51-500]
    S Liv - v39 - i8 - August 2004 - p205(1) [501+]
Rashad, Inas - *The Economics of Obesity*
    Wil Q - v28 - i4 - Autumn 2004 - p104(1) [501+]
Rasinski, T.V. - *The Fluent Reader: Oral Reading Strategies for Building Word Recognition, Fluency, and Comprehension*
    TCR - v106 - i5 - May 2004 - p891(4) [501+]

Raskin, Jamin B. - *Overruling Democracy: The Supreme Court vs. the American People*
BW - v34 - i38 - Sept 19 2004 - p11(1) [51-500]
R&R Bk N - v19 - i4 - Nov 2004 - p172(1) [501+]

Raskin, Marcus G. - *Liberalism: The Genius of American Ideals*
R&R Bk N - v19 - i1 - Feb 2004 - p149(1) [51-500]

Rasmussen, R. Kent - *Mark Twain for Kids: His Life and Times--21 Activities*
c BL - v101 - i2 - Sept 15 2004 - p239(1) [51-500]
c Cur R - v44 - i2 - Oct 2004 - p11(1) [501+]
c Kliatt - v38 - i6 - Nov 2004 - p29(1) [51-500]
c SLJ - v50 - i9 - Sept 2004 - p232(1) [51-500]

Rasmussen, William M.S. - *Old Virginia: The Pursuit of a Pastoral Ideal*
JAH - v91 - i1 - June 2004 - p282-283 [501+]

Raso, Tommaso - *Boezio abruzzese del XV secolo: Testo latino-Volgare per l'insegnamento della sintassi latina*
Specu - v79 - i3 - July 2004 - p829-829 [501+]

Rasporich, Beverly Jean - *Magic Off Main: The Art of Esther Warkov*
BIC - v33 - i8 - Nov 2004 - p22(2) [501+]
R&R Bk N - v19 - i1 - Feb 2004 - p199(1) [51-500]

Rastogi, Rajeev - *Data Mining ICDM 2004: Proceedings*
SciTech - v28 - i4 - Dec 2004 - p30(1) [51-500]

Rath, Eric C. - *The Ethos of Noh: Actors and Their Art*
Choice - v42 - i5 - Jan 2005 - p864(1) [1-50]

Rath, Richard Cullen - *How Early America Sounded*
Choice - v42 - i1 - Sept 2004 - p177(1) [501+]
HNet - Sept 2004 - pNA [501+]
RAH - v32 - i2 - June 2004 - p144-7 [501+]
W&M Q - v61 - i4 - Oct 2004 - p745-747 [501+]

Rath, Tom - *How Full Is Your Bucket? Positive Strategists for Work and Life*
HR Mag - v50 - i2 - Feb 2005 - pS3(1) [501+]

Rathbone, Andy - *TiVo for Dummies*
LJ - v129 - i16 - Oct 1 2004 - p104(1) [51-500]

Rathbone, Richard - *Nkrumah and the Chiefs: The Politics of Chieftaincy in Ghana 1951-60*
AHR - v109 - i3 - June 2004 - p1021(2) [501+]

Rathbun, A.J. - *Party Drinks!: 50 Classic Cocktails and Lively Libations*
LJ - v129 - i15 - Sept 15 2004 - p79(1) [51-500]

Rather, Rebecca - *The Pastry Queen*
People - v62 - i21 - Nov 22 2004 - p60 [51-500]

Rathmann, Peggy - *Good Night, Gorilla*
c PW - v251 - i38 - Sept 20 2004 - p64(1) [51-500]
Ruby the Copycat (Illus. by Rathmann, Peggy)
c SLJ - v50 - i7 - July 2004 - p44(1) [51-500]

Rathmell, James P. - *Regional Anesthesia: The Requisites in Anesthesiology*
SciTech - v28 - i3 - Sept 2004 - p111(1) [51-500]

Rathore, T.S. - *Digital Measurement Techniques, 2nd Ed.*
SciTech - v28 - i4 - Dec 2004 - p158(1) [51-500]

Rathus, Jill H. - *Assessment of Partner Violence: A Handbook for Researchers and Practitioners*
Choice - v42 - i3 - Nov 2004 - p569(1) [51-500]
SciTech - v28 - i3 - Sept 2004 - p102(1) [51-500]

Rathvon, Natalie - *Early Reading Assessment: A Practitioner's Handbook*
R&R Bk N - v19 - i4 - Nov 2004 - p181(1) [501+]

Ratliff, Gerald Lee - *Young Women's Monologs from Contemporary Plays: Professional Auditions for Aspiring Actresses*
Choice - v42 - i6 - Feb 2005 - p1028(1) [51-500]

Ratnasingam, Pauline - *Inter-Organizational Trust in Business-to-Business E-Commerce*
JEL - v41 - i4 - Dec 2003 - p1394(2) [501+]

Ratner, Lorman A. - *Fanatics and Fire-Eaters: Newspapers and the Coming of the Civil War*
JAH - v91 - i1 - June 2004 - p246-247 [501+]
JSH - v71 - i1 - Feb 2005 - p157(2) [501+]

Ratner, Michael - *Guantanamo: What the World Should Know*
Nation - v280 - i5 - Feb 7 2005 - p23 [501+]

Ratner, Peter - *Mastering 3D Animation, 2nd Ed.*
R&R Bk N - v19 - i4 - Nov 2004 - p249(1) [501+]

Ratsimbaharison, Adrien M. - *The Failure of the United Nations Development Programs for Africa*
R&R Bk N - v19 - i3 - August 2004 - p99(1) [51-500]

Rattan, Suresh I.S. - *Modulating Aging and Longevity*
SciTech - v28 - i1 - March 2004 - p71(1) [51-500]

Rattenbury, Richard C. - *The Art of American Arms Makers: Marketing Guns, Ammunition, and Western Adventure During the Golden Age of Illustration*
Roundup M - v12 - i3 - Feb 2005 - p21(1) [51-500]

Rattigan, Dermot - *Theatre of Sound: Radio and the Dramatic Imagination*
Theat J - v56 - i2 - May 2004 - p338(2) [501+]

Rattigan, Jama Kim - *Dumpling Soup (Illus. by Hsu-Flanders, Lillian)*
c SLJ - v51 - i2 - Feb 2005 - p58(1) [51-500]

Raty, Jukka - *UV-Visible Reflection Spectroscopy of Liquids*
Choice - v42 - i2 - Oct 2004 - p331(1) [51-500]

Ratzan, Lee - *Understanding Information Systems: What They Do and Why We Need Them*
BL - v100 - i21 - July 2004 - p1859(1) [501+]
Choice - v42 - i1 - Sept 2004 - p140(1) [51-500]
LibMed - v23 - i3 - Nov-Dec 2004 - p91(1) [51-500]

Ratzinger, Joseph, Cardinal - *Truth and Tolerance: Christian Belief and World Religions*
CI - v13 - i2 - Feb 2005 - p39(1) [501+]

Rau, Dana Meachen - *Antarctica*
y LibMed - v23 - i1 - August-Sept 2004 - p73(1) [51-500]
Chess
c Teach Lib - v32 - i3 - Feb 2005 - p30(1) [51-500]
My Bones and Muscles
c SLJ - v51 - i2 - Feb 2005 - p126(1) [51-500]
My Heart and Blood
c SLJ - v51 - i2 - Feb 2005 - p126(1) [51-500]
My Stomach
c SLJ - v51 - i2 - Feb 2005 - p126(1) [51-500]
Tired of Waiting (Illus. by Fitzpatrick, Brad)
c SLJ - v51 - i2 - Feb 2005 - p94(1) [51-500]

Rauchway, Eric - *Murdering McKinley: The Making of Theodore Roosevelt's America*
RAH - v32 - i3 - Sept 2004 - p399-406 [501+]
JAH - v91 - i2 - Sept 2004 - p657(2) [501+]

Raudenbush, Bryan - *Statistics for the Behavioral Sciences: A Short Course and Student Manual*
R&R Bk N - v19 - i3 - August 2004 - p91(1) [51-500]

Rauer, Christine - *Beowulf and the Dragon: Parallels and Analogues*
JEGP - v103 - i1 - Jan 2004 - p127-131 [501+]

Raugh, Harold E., Jr. - *The Victorians at War, 1985-1914: An Encyclopedia of British Military History*
Choice - v42 - i7 - March 2005 - p1208(1) [51-500]

Raum, Elizabeth - *Alice Paul*
c SLJ - v50 - i11 - Nov 2004 - p128(2) [51-500]
Jane Addams
c SLJ - v50 - i11 - Nov 2004 - p128(2) [51-500]
Julia Ward Howe
c SLJ - v50 - i11 - Nov 2004 - p128(2) [51-500]
Roger Williams
c SLJ - v51 - i2 - Feb 2005 - p119(2) [51-500]

Raus, Erhard - *Panzer Operations: The Eastern Front Memoir of General Raus, 1941-1945*
Choice - v41 - i11-12 - July-August 2004 - p2099(1) [501+]
HNet - Sept 2004 - pNA [501+]

Rausand, Marvin - *System Reliability Theory: Models, Statistical Methods and Applications, 2d ed.*
SciTech - v28 - i1 - March 2004 - p137(1) [51-500]

Rausch, Thomas P. - *Who is Jesus? An Introduction to Christology*
Choice - v42 - i1 - Sept 2004 - p122(1) [501+]

Raushenbush, Paul B. - *Teen Spirit: One World, Many Paths*
LJ - v129 - i12 - July 2004 - p90(1) [51-500]

Rausing, Sigrid - *History, Memory, and Identity in Post-Soviet Estonia: The End of a Collective Farm*
NYRB - v51 - i15 - Oct 7 2004 - p39(3) [501+]

Rausla, Jed - *Syncopations: The Stress of Innovation in Contemporary American Poetry*
Choice - v42 - i7 - March 2005 - p1231(1) [51-500]

Ravage, Barbara - *Burn Unit: Saving Lives After the Flames*
SB - v40 - i5 - Sept-Oct 2004 - p206(1) [51-500]

Ravas, Tammy - *Peter Schickele: A Bio-Bibliography*
R&R Bk N - v19 - i4 - Nov 2004 - p194(1) [501+]

Ravel, Edeet - *Look for Me*
Globe & Mail - Sept 4 2004 - pD7 [501+]
LJ - v129 - i12 - July 2004 - p73(2) [51-500]
The Thousand Lovers
BIC - v33 - i2 - March 2004 - p13(1) [501+]

Ravel, Maurice - *A Ravel Reader: Correspondence, Articles, Interviews*
R&R Bk N - v19 - i1 - Feb 2004 - p196(1) [51-500]

Raven, James - *Lost Libraries: The Destruction of Great Book Collections Since Antiquity*
CR - v286 - i1668 - Jan 2005 - p60(1) [51-500]
TLS - i5285 - July 16 2004 - p30(1) [501+]

Raven, Margot Theis - *Circle Unbroken (Illus. by Lewis, E.B.)*
c BL - v101 - i9-10 - Jan 1 2005 - p776(1) [1-50]
Mercedes and the Chocolate Pilot
c RT - v57 - Oct 2003 - p174 [1-50]

Ravenal, John B. - *Robert Lazzarini*
R&R Bk N - v19 - i2 - May 2004 - p195(1) [1-50]

Ravenel, Shannon - *New Stories from the South: The Year's Best, 2003*
Ga R - v57 - i4 - Winter 2003 - p888-890 [501+]
New Stories from the South: The Year's Best, 2004
ABR - v25 - i5 - July-August 2004 - p1(2) [501+]
Kliatt - v38 - i4 - July 2004 - p34(2) [51-500]

Ravetz, Alison - *Council Housing and Culture: The History of a Social Experiment*
J Urban H - v31 - i2 - Jan 2005 - p241-248 [501+]

Ravid, Benjamin - *Studies on the Jews of Venice, 1382-1797*
R&R Bk N - v19 - i1 - Feb 2004 - p44(1) [51-500]

Raviele, Antonio - *Cardiac Arrhythmias 2003: Proceedings*
SciTech - v28 - i3 - Sept 2004 - p106(1) [51-500]

Ravin, Judy - *Lose Your Accent in 28 Days*
Bwatch - Nov 2004 - pNA [51-500]

Raviola, Blythe Alice - *Il Monferrato gonzaghesco: Istituzioni ed elites di un micro-stato*
Ren Q - v57 - i4 - Winter 2004 - p1379(2) [501+]

Ravishankar, Anushka - *Anything but a Grabooberry (Illus. by Ramanathan, Rathna)*
c KR - v72 - i18 - Sept 15 2004 - p918(1) [51-500]
c PW - v251 - i42 - Oct 18 2004 - p63(1) [51-500]
Excuse Me, Is This India? (Illus. by Leutwiler, Anita)
c PW - v251 - i31 - August 2 2004 - p70(1) [51-500]
One, Two, Tree! (Illus. by Bai, Durga)
c SLJ - v50 - i10 - Oct 2004 - p128(1) [51-500]
Tiger on a Tree
c BooChiTr - May 30 2004 - p2(1) [501+]

Ravitch, Diane - *Kid Stuff: Marketing Sex and Violence to America's Children*
R&R Bk N - v19 - i2 - May 2004 - p131(1) [51-500]
The Language Police: How Pressure Groups Restrict what Students Learn
Kliatt - v38 - i5 - Sept 2004 - p45(2) [501+]
TLS - i5294 - Sept 17 2004 - p7-8 [501+]

Rawicz, Piotr - *Blood from the Sky*
TLS - i5298 - Oct 15 2004 - p24(1) [501+]

Rawles, Nancy - *My Jim*
y BL - v101 - i6 - Nov 15 2004 - p563(1) [51-500]
KR - v72 - i22 - Nov 15 2004 - p1065(1) [51-500]
LJ - v129 - i20 - Dec 1 2004 - p102(1) [51-500]
NYTBR - Jan 30 2005 - p26 [501+]
People - v63 - i7 - Feb 21 2005 - p51 [501+]
PW - v251 - i48 - Nov 29 2004 - p22(2) [501+]
Black Iss - v7 - i2 - March-April 2005 - p50(1) [501+]
Ent W - i802 - Jan 21 2005 - p93 [51-500]

Rawley, James A. - *London, Metropolis of the Slave Trade*
HNet - Sept 2004 - pNA [501+]
JSH - v71 - i1 - Feb 2005 - p137(2) [501+]

Rawlings, Helen - *Church, Religion and Society in Early Modern Spain*
Six Ct J - v34 - i4 - Winter 2003 - p1220-1222 [501+]

Rawlings, Irene - *Portable Houses*
LJ - v129 - i15 - Sept 15 2004 - p57(1) [51-500]

Rawlings, Laura - *Evaluating Social Funds: A Cross-Country Analysis of Community Interventions*
R&R Bk N - v19 - i2 - May 2004 - p130 [51-500]

Rawlinson, Julia - *A Surprise for Rosie (Illus. by Warnes, Tim)*
c KR - v73 - i5 - March 1 2005 - p294(1) [51-500]
c PW - v252 - i7 - Feb 14 2005 - p75(1) [51-500]

Rawnsley, Gary D. - *Political Communications in Greater China: The Construction and Reflection of Identity*
Ch Rev Int - v11 - i1 - Spring 2004 - p162(4) [501+]
Choice - v41 - i7 - March 2004 - p1366(1) [501+]

Raworth, Tom - *Collected Poems*
Lon R Bks - v26 - i16 - August 19 2004 - p27(3) [501+]

Rawson, Andrew - *Remagan Bridge: 9th Armoured Division*
R&R Bk N - v19 - i4 - Nov 2004 - p33(1) [1-50]

Rawson, Beryl - *Children and Childhood in Roman Italy*
TLS - i5297 - Oct 8 2004 - p10(1) [501+]

Rawson, Claude - *God, Gulliver and Genocide: Barbarism and the European Imagination, 1492-1945*
RES - v55 - i219 - April 2004 - p278-279 [501+]

Ray, Celeste - *Southern Heritage on Display: Public Ritual and Ethnic Diversity within Southern Regionalism*
JouAmCul - v27 - i3 - Sept 2004 - p357(2) [501+]

Ray, Deborah Kogan - *The Flower Hunter: William Bartram, America's First Naturalist*
c BooChiTr - June 6 2004 - p2(1) [501+]
c LibMed - v23 - i3 - Nov-Dec 2004 - p79(1) [51-500]
c SB - v40 - i6 - Nov-Dec 2004 - p270(1) [51-500]

Ray, Deborah S. - *UNIX, 2nd Ed.*
SciTech - v28 - i3 - Sept 2004 - p28(1) [51-500]

Ray, Donald I. - *Grassroots Governance? Chiefs in Africa and the Afro-Caribbean*
Choice - v41 - i7 - March 2004 - p1365(1) [501+]

Ray, G. Carleton - *Coastal-Marine Conservation: Science and Policy (Illus. by Smith, Robert L.)*
QRB - v79 - i4 - Dec 2004 - p447(1) [501+]

Ray, Jane - *Adam and Eve and the Garden of Eden (Illus. by Ray, Jane)*
c CCB-B - v58 - i6 - Feb 2005 - p263(1) [51-500]
c KR - v73 - i1 - Jan 1 2005 - p55(1) [51-500]
c PW - v252 - i7 - Feb 14 2005 - p78(1) [51-500]

Ray, Krishnendu - *The Migrant's Table: Meals and Memories in Bengali-American Households'*
CHE - v51 - i14 - Nov 26 2004 - pA16-A16 [501+]

Ray, Kurt - *Amerigo Vespucci: Italian Explorer of the Americas*
VOYA - v27 - i5 - Dec 2004 - p419(1) [51-500]
A Historical Atlas of Kuwait
c SLJ - v50 - i10 - Oct 2004 - p193(2) [51-500]

Ray, Marcella Ridlen - *The Changing and Unchanging Face of U.S. Civil Society*
CS - v33 - i2 - March 2004 - p226-227 [501+]

Ray, Mary Lyn - *Welcome, Brown Bird*
y NYTBR - Sept 19 2004 - p16 [501+]

Ray, Paul H. - *The Cultural Creatives*
Parabola - v28 - i3 - Fall 2003 - p107(4) [501+]

Ray, Rachael - *Rachael Ray's 30-Minute Get Real Meals: Eat Healthy without Going to Extremes*
PW - v252 - i11 - March 14 2005 - p62(1) [51-500]

Ray, Rajat Kanta - *The Felt Community: Commonalty and Mentality Before the Emergence of Indian Nationalism*
AHR - v109 - i2 - April 2004 - p503(1) [501+]
HNet - August 2004 - pNA [501+]
JAS - v63 - i2 - May 2004 - p538(3) [501+]

Ray, Ramon - *Technology Solutions for Growing Businesses*
B Ent - v35 - i1 - August 2004 - p61(1) [501+]

Ray, Stephen G., Jr. - *Do No Harm: Social Sin and Christian Responsibility*
TT - v61 - i2 - July 2004 - p266(1) [501+]

Ray, Subash C. - *Data Envelopment Analysis: Theory and Techniques for Economics and Operations Research*
R&R Bk N - v19 - i4 - Nov 2004 - p83(1) [51-500]

Ray, Susan - *Beyond Nihilism: Gottfried Benn's Postmodernist Poetics*
R&R Bk N - v19 - i1 - Feb 2004 - p247(1) [51-500]

Raya, Manuel Jimenez - *Differentiation in the Modern Languages Classroom*
R&R Bk N - v19 - i1 - Feb 2004 - p210(1) [51-500]

Rayban, Chloe - *Drama Queen*
y Sch Lib - v52 - i3 - Autumn 2004 - p156(1) [501+]

Raybon, Patricia - *I Told the Mountain to Move*
PW - v252 - i4 - Jan 24 2005 - p239(1) [501+]

Raye, Kimberly - *Sometimes Naughty, Sometimes Nice*
PW - v251 - i39 - Sept 27 2004 - p43(1) [501+]

Rayel, Michael G. - *First Aid to Mental Illness: A Practical Guide for Patients and Caregivers*
CBRA - Annual 2003 - p433(1) [51-500]

Rayfield, Donald - *Stalin and His Hangmen: An Authoritative Portrait of a Tyrant and Those Who Served Him*
CR - v285 - i1664 - Sept 2004 - p190(1) [51-500]
TLS - i5301 - Nov 5 2004 - p10(1) [501+]
Stalin and His Hangmen: The Tyrant and Those Who Killed for Him
LJ - v130 - i1 - Jan 1 2005 - p130(1) [51-500]
NL - v87 - i6 - Nov-Dec 2004 - p19(3) [501+]
PW - v251 - i50 - Dec 13 2004 - p59(1) [51-500]

Rayfuse, Rosemary Gail - *Non-Flag State Enforcement in High Seas Fisheries*
R&R Bk N - v19 - i3 - August 2004 - p193(1) [501+]

Raymaker, John - *A Buddhist-Christian Logic of the Heart: Nishida's Kyoto School and Lonergan's "Spiritual Genome" as World Bridge*
BCS - v24 - Annual 2004 - p271(6) [501+]
Empowering the Lonely Crowd: Pope John Paul II, Lonergan and Japanese Buddhism
R&R Bk N - v19 - i1 - Feb 2004 - p16(1) [1-50]

Rayment-Pickard, Hugh - *Impossible God: Derrida's Theology*
R&R Bk N - v19 - i1 - Feb 2004 - p21(1) [1-50]

Raymo, Chet - *Climbing Brandon: Science and Faith on Ireland's Holy Mountain*
R&R Bk N - v19 - i3 - August 2004 - p41(1) [51-500]
Intimate Look at the Night Sky
CBRA - Annual 2003 - p426(1) [501+]

Raymo, Robert R. - *The Mirroure of the Worlde: A Middle English Translation of 'Le miroir du monde'*
R&R Bk N - v19 - i1 - Feb 2004 - p231(1) [51-500]
Specu - v79 - i3 - July 2004 - p830-831 [501+]

Raymond, Alex - *Alex Raymond's Flash Gordon: Volume 2*
y BL - v101 - i3 - Oct 1 2004 - p320(1) [51-500]
y PW - v251 - i40 - Oct 4 2004 - p72(1) [51-500]

Raymond, Joad - *Pamphlets and Pamphleteering in Early Modern Britain*
AHR - v109 - i2 - April 2004 - p608(2) [501+]
Ren Q - v57 - i3 - Fall 2004 - p1131(2) [501+]
RES - v55 - i219 - April 2004 - p272-273 [501+]

Raymond, Leigh - *Private Rights in Public Resources: Equity and Property Allocation in Market-Based Environmental Policy*
Pers PS - v33 - i4 - Fall 2004 - p250(1) [501+]
R&R Bk N - v19 - i3 - August 2004 - p205(1) [501+]

Raymond, Michele - *Halifax's Northwest Arm: An Illustrated History*
Can Hist R - v85 - i4 - Dec 2004 - p814(3) [501+]

Raymond, Steve - *Blue Upright: The Flies of a Lifetime*
LJ - v129 - i13 - August 2004 - p89(1) [501+]

Rayner, Jay - *Eating Crow*
BL - v100 - i22 - August 2004 - p1902(1) [501+]
NYTBR - August 1 2004 - p11 [501+]
NYTBR - August 8 2004 - p18 [501+]
PW - v251 - i33 - August 16 2004 - p44(1) [51-500]

Rayner, Matthew - *Cat*
c SLJ - v50 - i8 - August 2004 - p112(1) [51-500]
Dog
c SLJ - v50 - i8 - August 2004 - p112(1) [51-500]
Hamster
c SLJ - v50 - i8 - August 2004 - p112(1) [51-500]
Rabbit
c SLJ - v50 - i8 - August 2004 - p112(1) [51-500]

Rayner, Michael - *English Battlefields: An Illustrated Encyclopedia*
Choice - v42 - i6 - Feb 2005 - p1005(2) [51-500]

Rayner, Richard - *The Devil's Wind*
KR - v72 - i21 - Nov 1 2004 - p1027(1) [51-500]
LJ - v130 - i1 - Jan 1 2005 - p100(1) [51-500]
PW - v252 - i2 - Jan 10 2005 - p39(1) [51-500]

Rayner, Robert - *Just for Kicks*
c Res Links - v10 - i2 - Dec 2004 - p22(1) [51-500]
Suspended
y Res Links - v10 - i3 - Feb 2005 - p39(2) [51-500]

Rayno, Don - *Paul Whiteman: Pioneer in American Music. Volume I: 1890-1930*
Notes - v61 - i1 - Sept 2004 - p114(3) [501+]

Rayport, Jeffrey F. - *Best Face Forward: Why Companies Must Improve Their Service Interfaces with Customers*
LJ - v130 - i2 - Feb 1 2005 - p94(2) [501+]

Rays
c SB - v40 - i3 - May-June 2004 - p133(1) [501+]

Raz, Aviad E. - *Emotions at Work: Normative Control, Organizations, and Culture in Japan and America*
AJS - v110 - i3 - Nov 2004 - p837(2) [501+]
Pac A - v77 - i3 - Fall 2004 - p580(2) [501+]

Raz, Joseph - *The Practice of Value*
Choice - v41 - i7 - March 2004 - p1311(1) [501+]

Razack, Sherene H. - *Dark Threats and White Knights: The Somalia Affair, Peacekeeping, and the New Imperialism*
BIC - v33 - i6 - Sept 2004 - p15(1) [501+]

Razavi, Shahra - *Agrarian Change, Gender, and Land Rights*
Choice - v42 - i1 - Sept 2004 - p181(1) [501+]

Razza, Nancy J. - *Healing Trauma: The Power of Group Treatment for People with Intellectual Disabilities*
SciTech - v28 - i4 - Dec 2004 - p95(1) [51-500]

Razzaque, Jona - *Public Interest Environmental Litigation in India, Pakistan, and Bangladesh*
R&R Bk N - v19 - i3 - August 2004 - p209(1) [1-50]

Razzell, Mary - *Haida Quest*
y Can CL - i111-112 - Fall-Winter 2003 - p153(6) [501+]

Read and Do Science Discovery Library
LibMed - v22 - i7 - April-May 2004 - p79(1) [501+]

Read, Anthony - *The Devil's Disciples: Hitler's Inner Circle*
Choice - v42 - i3 - Nov 2004 - p555(1) [1-50]
R&R Bk N - v19 - i3 - August 2004 - p42(1) [51-500]
VQR - v80 - i3 - Summer 2004 - p254(1) [501+]

Read, David - *Temperate Conquests: Spenser and the Spanish New World*
MP - v102 - i1 - August 2004 - p107(4) [501+]

Read, Donald - *A Manchester Boyhood in the Thirties and Forties-Growing Up in War and Peace*
R&R Bk N - v19 - i1 - Feb 2004 - p33(1) [1-50]

Read, Gardner - *Orchestral Combinations: The Science and Art of Tone-Color*
M Ed J - v91 - i3 - Jan 2005 - p64(1) [51-500]
R&R Bk N - v19 - i1 - Feb 2004 - p198(1) [51-500]

Read, Jacinda - *The New Avengers: Feminism, Femininity and the Rape-Revenge Cycle*
Signs - v30 - i2 - Wntr 2005 - p1700(4) [501+]

Read, Jen'nan Ghazal - *Culture, Class, and Work Among Arab-American Women*
R&R Bk N - v19 - i3 - August 2004 - p65(1) [51-500]

Read, John Hinton - *Young Man in Movieland*
R&R Bk N - v19 - i1 - Feb 2004 - p239(1) [51-500]

Read, Peter L. - *The Martian Climate Revisited : Atmosphere and Environment of a Desert Planet*
Choice - v42 - i2 - Oct 2004 - p315(1) [51-500]

Read, Stick and Learn about Animals (Illus. by Boos, Andre)
c CH Bwatch - March 2005 - pNA [51-500]

Read, Veronica M. - *Hippeastrum: The Gardener's Amaryllis*
Bwatch - Jan 2005 - pNA [51-500]
E-Streams - Oct 2004 - pNA [501+]
SciTech - v28 - i3 - Sept 2004 - p129(1) [51-500]

Reade, John B. - *Calculus with Complex Numbers*
Choice - v41 - i7 - March 2004 - p1331(1) [501+]

Reader, Simon M. - *Animal Innovation*
SciTech - v28 - i1 - March 2004 - p70(1) [51-500]

Reader's Digest - *Complete Do-It-Yourself Manual, Completely Rev. and Updated*
PW - v252 - i11 - March 14 2005 - p62(1) [51-500]

Reader's Digest Association - *Beginner's Guide to Gardening: Creating a Beautiful Garden from the Ground Up*
LJ - v129 - i18 - Nov 1 2004 - p111(1) [51-500]

Reader's Digest Illustrated World Atlas
Choice - v42 - i5 - Jan 2005 - p839(1) [1-50]
SLJ - v50 - i12 - Dec 2004 - p84(2) [501+]

Reagan, Michael - *Reflections on the Nature of God*
SEP - v277 - i2 - March-April 2005 - p45(1) [501+]

Reagan, Ron - *If You Had Five Minutes with the President: 5 Minutes, 55 Personalities, 1 President*
PW - v251 - i31 - August 2 2004 - p65(1) [51-500]

Reagan, Ronald - *The Long Goodbye*
Ent W - i793 - Nov 19 2004 - p88 [51-500]
Reagan's Path to Victory: The Shaping of Ronald Reagan's Vision: Selected Writings. Audiobook Review
LJ - v129 - i20 - Dec 1 2004 - p142(1) [51-500]

Reagan, Timothy G. - *Non-Western Educational Traditions: Indigenous Approaches to Educational Thought and Practice, 3rd Ed.*
R&R Bk N - v19 - i4 - Nov 2004 - p178(1) [501+]

Real People: Teens, Family and Stress
SLJ - v50 - i12 - Dec 2004 - p66(1) [501+]

Real, Terrence - *How Can I Get Through to You? Reconnecting Men and Women*
OOB - v34 - i9-10 - Sept-Oct 2004 - p51(2) [501+]
I Don't Want to Talk About It
Globe & Mail - August 21 2004 - pD15 [501+]

Reales, Catas - *The Catalan Rule of the Templars: Edition and Translation of Barcelona, Archivo de la Corona de Aragon*
HER - v119 - i483 - Sept 2004 - p1036(2) [501+]

Reamer, Frederic G. - *Criminal Lessons: Case Studies and Commentary on Crime and Justice*
   R&R Bk N - v19 - i1 - Feb 2004 - p141(1) [51-500]
   Soc Ser R - v79 - i1 - March 2005 - p203(4) [501+]
Social Work Malpractice and Liability: Strategies for Prevention, 2nd Ed.
   R&R Bk N - v19 - i1 - Feb 2004 - pNA [51-500]
Reardon, Joan - *Poet of the Appetites: The Lives and Loves of M.F.K. Fisher*
   BL - v101 - i4 - Oct 15 2004 - p373(1) [501+]
   KR - v72 - i17 - Sept 1 2004 - p853(2) [501+]
   NYTBR - Dec 12 2004 - p29 [501+]
   PW - v251 - i36 - Sept 6 2004 - p57(2) [51-500]
Reardon, Lisa - *The Mercy Killers*
   BW - v34 - i39 - Sept 26 2004 - p10(1) [501+]
   KR - v72 - i14 - July 15 2004 - p654(1) [501+]
   NYTBR - Dec 19 2004 - p23 [501+]
   PW - v251 - i37 - Sept 13 2004 - p59(1) [51-500]
Reardon, Mark J. - *Victory at Mortain: Stopping Hitler's Panzer Counteroffensive*
   J Mil H - v68 - i3 - July 2004 - p1005-1006 [501+]
Reaves, Michael - *Battle Surgeons*
   ChrSFF&H - v26 - i10 - Oct 2004 - p25(2) [51-500]
Reavill, Gil - *Smut: A Sex Industry Insider (and Concerned Father) Says Enough Is Enough*
   KR - v73 - i4 - Feb 15 2005 - p219(1) [501+]
Rebenich, Stefan - *Jerome*
   Class R - v54 - i1 - May 2004 - p126(2) [501+]
   J Ch St - v46 - i3 - Summer 2004 - p656(2) [501+]
Theodor Mommsen. Eine Biographie
   Class R - v53 - i2 - Nov 2003 - p497-481 [501+]
Rebenschied, Shane - *Macromedia Flash MX 2004 Beyond the Basics: Hands-On Training*
   SciTech - v28 - i3 - Sept 2004 - p169(1) [51-500]
Rebholz, Ronald A. - *Shakespeare's Philosophy of History Revealed in a Detailed Analysis of 'Henry V' and Examined in Other History Plays*
   R&R Bk N - v19 - i1 - Feb 2004 - p237(1) [51-500]
Rebick, Judy - *Ten Thousand Roses: The Making of a Feminist Revolution*
   Globe & Mail - Feb 26 2005 - pD9 [501+]
Rebold Benton, Janetta - *Medieval Mischief: Wit and Humour in the Art of the Middle Ages*
   CR - v285 - i1666 - Nov 2004 - p315(1) [501+]
Rech, Lindsay Faith - *Joyride*
   BL - v101 - i4 - Oct 15 2004 - p394(1) [51-500]
Rechner, Amy - *Out and About at the Aquarium (Illus. by Shipe, Becky)*
   c SB - v40 - i4 - July-August 2004 - p179(2) [51-500]
Rechy, John - *Beneath the Skin: The Collected Essays of John Rechy*
   LJ - v130 - i4 - March 1 2005 - p101(1) [51-500]
   PW - v252 - i3 - Jan 17 2005 - p45(1) [51-500]
Recinella, Dale S. - *The Biblical Truth about America's Death Penalty*
   BL - v101 - i6 - Nov 15 2004 - p534(1) [51-500]
   LJ - v129 - i17 - Oct 15 2004 - p68(1) [51-500]
Reck-Malleczewen, Friedrich - *Diary of a Man in Despair*
   Quad - v48 - i11 - Nov 2004 - p83(3) [501+]
Reclus, Elisee - *Anarchy, Geography, Modernity: The Radical Social Thought of Elisee Reclus*
   R&R Bk N - v19 - i3 - August 2004 - p171(1) [501+]
Record, Jeffrey - *Dark Victory: America's Second War against Iraq*
   Choice - v42 - i4 - Dec 2004 - p738(1) [1-50]
   J Mil H - v68 - i4 - Oct 2004 - p1328-1329 [501+]
Dark Victory: America's Second War against Iraq. (Read by Record, Jeffrey)
   R&R Bk N - v19 - i3 - August 2004 - p49(1) [51-500]
Making War, Thinking History: Munich, Vietnam, and Presidential Uses of Force from Korea to Kosovo
   Mar Crp G - v88 - i6 - June 2004 - p62(2) [501+]
Recorvits, Helen - *My Name is Yoon (Illus. by Swiatkowska, Gabi)*
   c SLJ - v50 - i7 - July 2004 - p44(1) [51-500]
Rector, Anne Elizabeth - *Anne Elizabeth's Diary: A Young Artist's True Story (Illus. by Rector, Anne Elizabeth)*
   c PW - v251 - i31 - August 2 2004 - p73(1) [51-500]
   c SLJ - v50 - i9 - Sept 2004 - p192(1) [51-500]
Redclift, Michael - *Chewing Gum: The Fortunes of Taste*
   Bwatch - Oct 2004 - pNA [51-500]
   Globe & Mail - July 17 2004 - pD14 [1-50]

Redding, Gordon - *Cross-Cultural Management, Volume 1: The Theory of Culture*
   Per Psy - v57 - i3 - Autumn 2004 - p795(4) [501+]
Cross-Cultural Management, Volume 2: Managing Cultural Differences
   Per Psy - v57 - i3 - Autumn 2004 - p795(4) [501+]
Redding, Kent - *Making Race, Making Power: North Carolina's Road to Disfranchisement*
   CS - v33 - i6 - Nov 2004 - p706(2) [501+]
   HNet - Sept 2004 - pNA [501+]
   JAH - v91 - i3 - Dec 2004 - p1027(2) [501+]
   JSH - v70 - i4 - Nov 2004 - p954(2) [501+]
Redding, Kimberly A. - *Growing Up in Hitler's Shadow: Remembering Youth in Postwar Berlin*
   R&R Bk N - v19 - i4 - Nov 2004 - p131(1) [1-50]
Reddy, A. Venugopal - *Investigation of Aeronautical and Engineering Component Failures*
   SciTech - v28 - i3 - Sept 2004 - p164(1) [51-500]
Reddy, Indra K. - *Essential Math and Calculations for Pharmacy Technicians*
   SciTech - v28 - i1 - March 2004 - p123(1) [1-50]
Reddy, J.N. - *Mechanics of Laminated Composite Plates and Shells: Theory and Analysis, 2nd Ed.*
   SciTech - v28 - i3 - Sept 2004 - p142(1) [51-500]
Reddy, Maureen T. - *Traces, Codes and Clues: Reading Race in Crime Fiction*
   MFSF - v0 - i3 - Fall 2004 - p791-792 [501+]
Redei, George P. - *Encyclopedic Dictionary of Genetics, Genomics, and Proteomics, 2nd Ed.*
   SciTech - v28 - i1 - March 2004 - p62(1) [51-500]
Redekop, Benjamin W. - *Power, Authority, and the Anabaptist Tradition*
   CHR - v90 - i4 - Oct 2004 - p734(3) [501+]
Redfern, Elizabeth - *Auriel Rising*
   NYTBR - July 4 2004 - p16 [51-500]
Redfield, James M. - *The Locrian Maidens: Love and Death in Greek Italy*
   Choice - v42 - i2 - Oct 2004 - p348(1) [51-500]
Redford, Donald B. - *Excavations at Mendes, Vol.1*
   R&R Bk N - v19 - i4 - Nov 2004 - p51(1) [51-500]
From Slave to Pharaoh: The Black Experience of Ancient Egypt
   R&R Bk N - v19 - i4 - Nov 2004 - p51(1) [51-500]
Redhead, Steve - *Paul Virilio: Theorist for an Accelerated Culture*
   R&R Bk N - v19 - i4 - Nov 2004 - p121(1) [51-500]
Redhill, Michael - *Fidelity*
   CBRA - Annual 2003 - p203(1) [51-500]
Rediker, Marcus - *Villains of All Nations: Atlantic Pirates in the Golden Age*
   Choice - v42 - i3 - Nov 2004 - p538(2) [1-50]
   Econ - v372 - i8386 - July 31 2004 - p73US [501+]
   NS - v133 - i4705 - Sept 13 2004 - p53(2) [501+]
   R&R Bk N - v19 - i3 - August 2004 - p72(1) [51-500]
   TLS - i5291 - August 27 2004 - p24(1) [501+]
Reding, Jean-Paul - *Comparative Essays in Early Greek and Chinese Rational Thinking*
   R&R Bk N - v19 - i3 - August 2004 - p2(1) [1-50]
Redlich, Monica - *The Nice Girl's Guide to Good Behavior*
   LJ - v129 - i17 - Oct 15 2004 - p99(1) [51-500]
Redman, Charles L. - *The Archaeology of Global Change: The Impact of Humans on Their Environment*
   Choice - v42 - i5 - Jan 2005 - p894(1) [1-50]
   R&R Bk N - v19 - i3 - August 2004 - p29(1) [1-50]
Redmond, Bairbre - *Reflection in Action: Developing Reflective Practice in Health and Social Services*
   SciTech - v28 - i3 - Sept 2004 - p79(1) [51-500]
Redmond, Diane - *Joshua Cross and the Queen's Conjuror*
   y Sch Lib - v52 - i3 - Autumn 2004 - p162(1) [501+]
Redmond, Sean - *Studying Blade Runner*
   TES - v0 - i4587 - June 11 2004 - psssss19(1) [501+]
Redmond, Shirley Raye - *The Dog That Dug for Dinosaurs: A True Story (Illus. by Sullivan, Simon)*
   c SLJ - v50 - i10 - Oct 2004 - p148(1) [51-500]
Redner, Harry - *Conserving Cultures: Technology, Globalization, and the Future of Local Cultures*
   R&R Bk N - v19 - i3 - August 2004 - p142(1) [51-500]
Redonet, F. Lillo - *Palabras contra el dolor: La consolacion filosofica latina de Ciceron a Fronton*
   Class R - v53 - i2 - Nov 2003 - p347-348 [501+]
Redoute, Pierre-Joseph - *Choix des Plus Belles Fleurs*
   LJ - v129 - i17 - Oct 15 2004 - p88(2) [51-500]

Redpath, Peter A. - *A Thomistic Tapestry*
   RM - v58 - i1 - Sept 2004 - p187(2) [501+]
Reduced Shakespeare Company - *The Reduced Shakespeare Company Radio Show (Read by Long, Adam, and others). Audiobook Review*
   LJ - v129 - i19 - Nov 15 2004 - p98(2) [51-500]
Redwall, Brian Jacques - *Loamhedge (Read by Jacques, Brian, and others). Audiobook Review*
   SLJ - v50 - i10 - Oct 2004 - p84(1) [51-500]
Redworth, Glyn - *The Prince and the Infanta: The Cultural Politics of the Spanish Match*
   Choice - v42 - i2 - Oct 2004 - p347(1) [51-500]
   Lon R Bks - v26 - i17 - Sept 2 2004 - p24(2) [501+]
   Ren Q - v57 - i4 - Winter 2004 - p1499(3) [501+]
Ree, Paul - *Basic Writings*
   Choice - v41 - i7 - March 2004 - p1311(1) [501+]
Reece, E. Albert - *Diabetes in Women: Adolescence, Pregnancy, and Menopause, 3rd Ed.*
   SciTech - v28 - i3 - Sept 2004 - p105(1) [51-500]
Reece, Helen - *Divorcing Responsibly*
   R&R Bk N - v19 - i1 - Feb 2004 - pNA [51-500]
Reece, Spencer - *The Clerk's Tale*
   ABR - v26 - i2 - Jan-Feb 2005 - p23(1) [501+]
   LJ - v129 - i12 - July 2004 - p88(1) [1-50]
Reece, William O. - *Functional Anatomy and Physiology of Domestic Animals, 3rd Ed.*
   SciTech - v28 - i3 - Sept 2004 - p132(1) [51-500]
Reed, Ananya Mukherjee - *Corporate Capitalism in Contemporary South Asia: Conventional Wisdoms and South Asian Realities*
   R&R Bk N - v19 - i1 - Feb 2004 - p117(1) [51-500]
Reed, Arden - *Manet, Flaubert, and the Emergence of Modernism: Blurring Genre Boundaries*
   Art Bull - v86 - i3 - Sept 2004 - p609(6) [501+]
Reed, Betty Jamerson - *The Brevard Rosenwald School: Black Education and Community Building in a Southern Appalachian Town, 1920-1966*
   R&R Bk N - v19 - i3 - August 2004 - p229(1) [1-50]
Reed, Carrie E. - *A Tang Miscellany: An Introduction to Youyang Zazu*
   R&R Bk N - v19 - i1 - Feb 2004 - p48(1) [51-500]
Reed, Cheryl - *New Directions for Writers, Vol. 2*
   R&R Bk N - v19 - i1 - Feb 2004 - p216(1) [51-500]
Reed, Cheryl L. - *Unveiled: The Hidden Lives of Nuns*
   Cons - v25 - i3 - Winter 2004 - p47(2) [501+]
Reed, Christopher A. (b. 1954 -) - *Gutenberg in Shanghai: Chinese Print Capitalism, 1876-1937*
   R&R Bk N - v19 - i4 - Nov 2004 - p254(1) [501+]
Reed, Christopher (b. 1961 -) - *Bloomsbury Rooms: Modernism, Subculture and Domesticity*
   Apo - v160 - i511 - Sept 2004 - p104(2) [501+]
Bloomsbury Rooms: Modernism, Subculture, and Domesticity
   Choice - v42 - i3 - Nov 2004 - p472(1) [1-50]
Reed, David - *Mortgages 101: Quick Answers to over 250 Critical Questions about Your Home Loan*
   Bwatch - Feb 2005 - pNA [501+]
   LJ - v129 - i16 - Oct 1 2004 - p92(1) [51-500]
   R&R Bk N - v19 - i4 - Nov 2004 - p116(1) [51-500]
Reed, Emmala - *Faithful Heart: The Journals of Emmala Reed, 1865 and 1866*
   R&R Bk N - v19 - i4 - Nov 2004 - p62(1) [51-500]
Reed, Fred A. - *Shattered Images: The Rise of Militant Iconoclasm in Syria*
   CBRA - Annual 2003 - p297(1) [51-500]
Reed, Henry (American critic) - *The United States Capitol: Its Architecture and Decoration (Illus. by Day, Anne)*
   PW - v251 - i50 - Dec 13 2004 - p60(1) [51-500]
Reed, Jan - *Health, Well-Being and Older People*
   R&R Bk N - v19 - i3 - August 2004 - p161(1) [501+]
Reed, John - *The Whole*
   KR - v72 - i22 - Nov 15 2004 - p1066(1) [51-500]
Reed, John Shelton - *Minding the South*
   JSH - v71 - i1 - Feb 2005 - p229(2) [501+]
Reed, Kit - *Thinner Than Thou*
   People - v62 - i1 - July 5 2004 - p47 [51-500]
   y VOYA - v27 - i4 - Oct 2004 - p287(1) [501+]
Reed, Liz - *Bigger than Gallipoli: War, History and Memory in Australia*
   R&R Bk N - v19 - i4 - Nov 2004 - p52(1) [51-500]

Reed, Maureen Gail - *Taking Stands: Gender and the Sustainablity of Rural Communities*
R&R Bk N - v19 - i3 - August 2004 - p154(1) [51-500]

Reed, Nathan - *My Little Toolbox*
c PW - v252 - i4 - Jan 24 2005 - p246(1) [51-500]

Reed, Nelson A. - *The Caste War of Yucatan*
Lat Ant - v15 - i3 - Sept 2004 - p366(1) [501+]

Reed, Paul F. - *Foundations of Anasazi Culture: The Basketmaker-Pueblo Transition*
Am Ant - v70 - i1 - Jan 2005 - p199(2) [501+]

Reed, Robert - *The Well of Stars*
KR - v73 - i5 - March 1 2005 - p267(2) [51-500]

Reed, Sally Gardner - *101+ Great Ideas for Libraries and Friends*
A Lib - v35 - i7 - August 2004 - p87(1) [501+]

Reed, Stephanie - *Across the Wide River*
y Kliatt - v39 - i2 - March 2005 - p22(2) [51-500]

Reed, Terry - *The Full Cleveland*
BL - v101 - i9-10 - Jan 1 2005 - p822(1) [501+]
KR - v72 - i22 - Nov 15 2004 - p1066(1) [501+]
LJ - v129 - i17 - Oct 15 2004 - p55(2) [51-500]
PW - v251 - i49 - Dec 6 2004 - p43(1) [51-500]

Reed, Thomas C. - *At the Abyss: An Insider's History of the Cold War*
Choice - v42 - i3 - Nov 2004 - p550(1) [1-50]
Parameters - v34 - i4 - Winter 2004 - p143(3) [501+]

Reed, Vicki A. - *An Introduction to Children with Language Disorders, 3rd Ed.*
SciTech - v28 - i4 - Dec 2004 - p113(1) [1-50]

Reeder, Jurgen - *Hate and Love in Psychoanalytical Institutions: The Dilemma of a Profession*
SciTech - v28 - i4 - Dec 2004 - p99(1) [51-500]

Reef, Catherine - *African Americans in the Military*
BL - v100 - i21 - July 2004 - p1860(1) [501+]
Alone in the World: Orphans and Orphanages in America
y KR - v73 - i5 - March 1 2005 - p294(1) [51-500]
John Steinbeck
y Kliatt - v38 - i5 - Sept 2004 - p42(2) [501+]
William Grant Still: African American Composer
LibMed - v22 - i5 - Feb 2004 - p77(1) [501+]

Reekie, Jocelyn - *The Week of the Horse*
y CH Bwatch - Oct 2004 - pNA [51-500]

Rees, Celia - *Pirates! (Read by Wiltsie, Jennifer). Audiobook Review*
y BL - v101 - i9-10 - Jan 1 2005 - p778(1) [1-50]
y Kliatt - v38 - i4 - July 2004 - p54(1) [51-500]
Pirates!
y BL - v101 - i1 - Sept 1 2004 - p121(1) [501+]
y HB - v80 - i4 - July-August 2004 - p475(1) [51-500]
y Sch Lib - v52 - i4 - Winter 2004 - p214(1) [51-500]
Witch Child
y VOYA - v27 - i3 - August 2004 - p181(1) [1-50]

Rees, Dai - *The New Brain Sciences: Perils and Prospects*
TimHES - v0 - i1684 - March 25 2005 - p26(2) [501+]

Rees, David - *Get Your War on II*
BL - v101 - i1 - Sept 1 2004 - p78(1) [501+]
PW - v251 - i34 - August 23 2004 - p39(1) [51-500]

Rees, Douglas - *Grandy Thaxter's Helper (Illus. by Schindler, S.D.)*
c CCB-B - v58 - i2 - Oct 2004 - p97(1) [51-500]
c HB - v80 - i6 - Nov-Dec 2004 - p700(1) [51-500]
c KR - v72 - i18 - Sept 15 2004 - p919(1) [51-500]
c NYTBR - March 13 2005 - p20 [51-500]
c PW - v251 - i38 - Sept 20 2004 - p61(2) [51-500]
c SLJ - v50 - i11 - Nov 2004 - p116(1) [51-500]
Smoking Mirror: An Encounter with Paul Gauguin
KR - v73 - i1 - Jan 1 2005 - p56(1) [51-500]
Vampire High
y LibMed - v22 - i6 - March 2004 - p65(1) [51-500]

Rees, Douglas C. - *Annual Review of Biophysics and Biomolecular Structure, Vol. 33*
QRB - v79 - i4 - Dec 2004 - p409(1) [501+]
SciTech - v28 - i3 - Sept 2004 - p60(1) [1-50]

Rees, E.A. - *Centre-Local Relations in the Stalinist State, 1928-1941*
Russ Rev - v63 - i2 - April 2004 - pNA [501+]
Slav R - v63 - i4 - Winter 2004 - p894(2) [501+]
The Nature of Stalin's Dictatorship: The Politburo, 1924-1953
E-A St - v56 - i8 - Dec 2004 - p1259(2) [501+]

Rees, Elizabeth - *An Essential Guide to Celtic Sites and Their Saints*
R&R Bk N - v19 - i3 - August 2004 - p20(1) [1-50]

Rees, Gwyneth - *Cosmo and the Magic Sneeze (Illus. by Hearn, Samuel)*
c Sch Lib - v52 - i4 - Winter 2004 - p204(1) [51-500]

Rees, Helen - *Echoes of History: Nazi Music in Modern China*
Ch Rev Int - v10 - i2 - Fall 2003 - p433(4) [501+]

Rees, Jonathan - *Managing the Mills: Labor Policy in the American Steel Industry During the Nonunion Era*
R&R Bk N - v19 - i2 - May 2004 - p106(1) [51-500]
The Voice of the People: Primary Sources on the History of American Labor, Industrial Relations, and Working-Class Culture
R&R Bk N - v19 - i2 - May 2004 - p106(1) [51-500]

Rees, Laurence - *Auschwitz: A New History*
BL - v101 - i9-10 - Jan 1 2005 - p809(1) [1-50]
Globe & Mail - Feb 19 2005 - pD13 [501+]
LJ - v130 - i3 - Feb 15 2005 - p145(1) [51-500]
PW - v252 - i2 - Jan 10 2005 - p50(1) [51-500]

Rees, Matt - *Cain's Field: Faith, Fratricide, and Fear in the Middle East*
PW - v251 - i44 - Nov 1 2004 - p57(1) [501+]

Rees, Peter - *Killing Juanita: A True Story of Murder and Corruption*
TLS - i5283 - July 2 2004 - p28(1) [501+]

Rees, R. - *Layers of Loyalty in Latin Panegyric*
Class R - v54 - i1 - May 2004 - p118(3) [501+]

Rees, Ronald - *Historic St. Croix: St. Stephen-Calais*
CBRA - Annual 2003 - p348(1) [501+]

Rees, Ruth - *A New Era in Educational Leadership - One Principal, Two Schools: Twinning*
R&R Bk N - v19 - i1 - Feb 2004 - p187(1) [51-500]

Rees, Sir Martin - *Our Final Hour: A Scientist's Warning*
y Kliatt - v38 - i5 - Sept 2004 - p50(2) [51-500]

Reese, Charles D. - *Office Building Safety and Health*
SciTech - v28 - i4 - Dec 2004 - p128 [51-500]

Reese, George - *Java Database Best Practices*
SciTech - v28 - i3 - Sept 2004 - p16(1) [501+]

Reese, Laura A. - *Critical Evaluations of Economic Development Policies*
Choice - v42 - i2 - Oct 2004 - p338(1) [51-500]

Reese, Renford - *American Paradox: Young Black Men*
Choice - v42 - i2 - Oct 2004 - p377(1) [501+]

Reese, Scott S. - *The Transmission of Learning in Islamic Africa*
R&R Bk N - v19 - i3 - August 2004 - p17(1) [1-50]

Reeser, Tim - *Citrix Metaframe Access Suite for Windows Server 2003: The Official Guide*
Bwatch - v26 - i8 - August 2004 - p6(1) [51-500]

Reeson, J. - *Heroides 11, 13 and 14: A Commentary*
Class R - v54 - i2 - Nov 2004 - p388(3) [501+]

Reeve, Andrew - *Real Libertarianism Assessed: Political Theory after Van Parijs*
Ethics - v114 - i4 - July 2004 - p830(7) [501+]

Reeve, C.D.C. - *Love's Confusions*
PW - v252 - i3 - Jan 17 2005 - p45(1) [51-500]

Reeve, John - *The Face of Naval Battle: The Human Experience of modern War at Sea*
J Mil H - v68 - i3 - July 2004 - p973-974 [501+]
NWCR - v57 - Autumn 2004 - p164(3) [501+]

Reeve, Philip - *Mortal Engines*
c Kliatt - v38 - i6 - Nov 2004 - p24(1) [501+]
c PW - v251 - i37 - Sept 13 2004 - p81(1) [51-500]
Predator's Gold
y BL - v100 - i22 - August 2004 - p1920(1) [51-500]
y CCB-B - v58 - i3 - Nov 2004 - p141(2) [501+]
y HB - v80 - i5 - Sept-Oct 2004 - p596(1) [501+]
y Kliatt - v38 - i5 - Sept 2004 - p16(2) [51-500]
y KR - v72 - i16 - August 15 2004 - p812(1) [51-500]
y PW - v251 - i33 - August 16 2004 - p64(1) [51-500]
y Sch Lib - v52 - i4 - Winter 2004 - p212(1) [51-500]
y SLJ - v50 - i9 - Sept 2004 - p216(1) [51-500]
y VOYA - v27 - i4 - Oct 2004 - p318(1) [51-500]

Reeve, William C. - *Peter M. Pringle: Master Decoy Maker*
Am Craft - v64 - i1 - Feb-March 2004 - p40(1) [501+]

Reeves, Adrienne Ellis - *Cherished*
BL - v101 - i6 - Nov 15 2004 - p569(1) [51-500]

Reeves, Anne R. - *Adolescents Talk About Reading: Exploring Resistance to and Engagement with Text*
y VOYA - v27 - i4 - Oct 2004 - p339(2) [51-500]

Reeves, John C. - *Bible and Qur'an: Essays in Scriptural Intertextuality*
R&R Bk N - v19 - i3 - August 2004 - p21(1) [1-50]

Reeves, M. Francis - *Platonic Engagements: A Contemporary Dialogue on Morality, Justice and the Business World*
R&R Bk N - v19 - i3 - August 2004 - p107(1) [1-50]

Regan, Geoffrey - *First Crusader: Byzantium's Holy Wars*
IJMES - v36 - i4 - Nov 2004 - p689(2) [501+]

Regan, John J. - *Atlas of Minimal Access Spine Surgery, 2nd Ed.*
SciTech - v28 - i3 - Sept 2004 - p112(1) [51-500]

Regan, Tom - *Animal Rights, Human Wrongs: An Introduction to Moral Philosophy*
Choice - v42 - i2 - Oct 2004 - p307(1) [51-500]
R&R Bk N - v19 - i1 - Feb 2004 - p139(1) [51-500]
The Case for Animal Rights
Globe & Mail - Nov 13 2004 - pD21 [51-500]
Empty Cages: Facing the Challenge of Animal Rights
Ethics - v115 - i1 - Oct 2004 - p160(4) [501+]

Rege, Sameer R. - *Applied General Equilibrium Analysis of India's Tax and Trade Policy*
R&R Bk N - v19 - i1 - Feb 2004 - p120(1) [51-500]

Rege, Sharmila - *Sociology of Gender: The Challenge of Feminist Sociological Knowledge*
R&R Bk N - v19 - i1 - Feb 2004 - p133(1) [51-500]

Regelski, Thomas A. - *Teaching General Music in Grades 4-8: A Musicianship Approach*
M Ed J - v91 - i2 - Nov 2004 - p55(3) [501+]

Regev, Motti - *Popular Music and National Culture in Israel*
Choice - v42 - i2 - Oct 2004 - p303(1) [51-500]

Regier, Willis Goth - *Book of the Sphinx*
BL - v101 - i4 - Oct 15 2004 - p365(1) [51-500]
HM - v309 - i1853 - Oct 2004 - p92(1) [501+]

Regis, Pamela - *A Natural History of the Romance Novel*
VQR - v80 - i1 - Wntr 2004 - p269-269 [501+]
VQR - v80 - i1 - Wntr 2004 - p269-269 [501+]

Regnat, Karl-Heinz - *Dornier Do 335: An Illustrated History*
SciTech - v28 - i4 - Dec 2004 - p161(1) [51-500]

Regnier, Philippe - *Etudes saint-simoniennes*
NCFS - v33 - i1-2 - Fall-Winter 2004 - p187(4) [501+]

Reguigne, Christine - *Spot the Differences: Animals: 50 Mind-Bending Photographic Puzzles*
c SLJ - v50 - i11 - Nov 2004 - p172(1) [51-500]
Spot the Differences: Vehicles: 50 Mind-Bending Photographic Puzzles
c SLJ - v50 - i11 - Nov 2004 - p172(1) [51-500]

Rehder, Ben - *Flat Crazy: A Blanco County Mystery*
KR - v72 - i15 - August 1 2004 - p717(1) [51-500]
PW - v251 - i33 - August 16 2004 - p46(1) [51-500]

Rehder, John B. - *Appalachian Folkways*
Choice - v42 - i7 - March 2005 - p1271(1) [51-500]
R&R Bk N - v19 - i4 - Nov 2004 - p77(1) [51-500]

Rehm, R. - *The Play of Space: Spatial Transformation in Greek Tragedy*
Class R - v53 - i2 - Nov 2003 - p282-284 [501+]

Rehnquist, William H. - *Centennial Crisis: The Disputed Election of 1876*
Choice - v42 - i3 - Nov 2004 - p550(1) [1-50]
CLR - v104 - i6 - Oct 2004 - p1732-1763 [501+]

Rehr, Louis S. - *Marauder: Memoir of a B-26 Pilot in Europe in World War II*
R&R Bk N - v19 - i1 - Feb 2004 - p30(1) [51-500]

Reibel, Carl-Wilhelm - *Das Fundament der Diktatur: Die NSDAP-Ortsgruppen 1932-1945*
GSR - v27 - i2 - May 2004 - p418-419 [501+]

Reiboldt, Max - *Buying, Selling, and Owning the Medical Practice, 2nd Ed.*
SciTech - v28 - i1 - March 2004 - p78(1) [51-500]

Reich, Bernard - *A Brief History of Israel*
y BL - v101 - i7 - Dec 1 2004 - p628(1) [51-500]

Reich, Howard - *The Life, Music, and Redemption of Jelly Roll Morton*
World&I - v19 - i3 - March 2004 - p215 [501+]

Reich, Jacqueline - *Beyond the Latin Lover: Marcello Mastroianni, Masculinity, and Italian Cinema*
Choice - v42 - i2 - Oct 2004 - p301(1) [51-500]

Reich, Lee - *Uncommon Fruits for Every Garden, 2nd Ed.* *(Illus. by Arlein, Vicki Herzfeld)*
E-Streams - Nov 2004 - pNA [501+]
Weedless Gardening
Bwatch - v26 - i7 - July 2004 - p4(1) [51-500]

Reich, Robert - *Bridging Liberalism and Multiculturalism in American Education*
Ethics - v114 - i4 - July 2004 - p863(1) [501+]
Reason: Why Liberals Will Win the Battle for America
NYTBR - July 18 2004 - p9 [501+]

Reich, S. - *Carbon Nanotubes: Basic Concepts and Physical Properties*
E-Streams - Oct 2004 - pNA [501+]

Reichardt, Mary R. - *Encyclopedia of Catholic Literature, Vols.1-2.*
LJ - v129 - i20 - Dec 1 2004 - p164(1) [51-500]

Reiche, Danyel - *Handbook of Renewable Energies in the European Union: Case Studies of all Member States in Collaboration with Stefan Lange, Stefan Korner, Mischa Bechberger and Graham Johnson*
SciTech - v28 - i3 - Sept 2004 - p150(1) [51-500]
Handbook of Renewable Energies in the European Union II: Case Studies of All Accession States
SciTech - v28 - i4 - Dec 2004 - p146(1) [501+]

Reiche, Dietlof - *I, Freddy (Illus. by Cepeda, Joe)*
c PW - v252 - i11 - March 14 2005 - p70(1) [51-500]

Reichert, David - *Chasing the Devil: My Twenty-Year Quest to Capture the Green River Killer*
KR - v72 - i16 - August 15 2004 - p795(1) [501+]

Reichert, Mickey Zucker - *The Return of Nightfall*
BL - v101 - i1 - Sept 1 2004 - p75(1) [501+]
PW - v251 - i34 - August 23 2004 - p41(2) [51-500]

Reichl, Karl - *Singing the Past: Turkic and Medieval Heroic Poetry*
Specu - v79 - i3 - July 2004 - p831-833 [501+]

Reichl, Ruth - *Garlic and Sapphires: The Secret Life of a Critic in Disguise*
KR - v73 - i3 - Feb 1 2005 - p170(1) [501+]
LJ - v129 - i20 - Dec 1 2004 - p92(1) [51-500]
PW - v252 - i7 - Feb 14 2005 - p60(1) [51-500]
The Gourmet Cookbook: More than 1000 Recipes
BL - v101 - i6 - Nov 15 2004 - p530(1) [51-500]
Globe & Mail - Nov 27 2004 - pD26 [51-500]
LJ - v129 - i17 - Oct 15 2004 - p82(2) [51-500]
NW - Dec 6 2004 - p88 [501+]
People - v62 - i21 - Nov 22 2004 - p55 [51-500]
PW - v251 - i31 - August 2 2004 - p67(1) [51-500]
Time - v164 - i13 - Sept 27 2004 - p81 [501+]

Reichold, Klaus - *Palaces that Changed the World*
Ant&CM - v108 - i9 - Nov 2003 - p16(1) [501+]

Reichs, Kathy - *Monday Mourning*
Globe & Mail - Dec 24 2004 - pD3 [1-50]

Reid, Alastair J. - *United We Stand: A History of Britain's Trade Unions*
CR - v285 - i1665 - Oct 2004 - p250(2) [501+]
HT - v54 - i7 - July 2004 - p57(1) [501+]
TLS - i5298 - Oct 15 2004 - p27(1) [501+]

Reid, Andrew M. - *African Historical Archaeologies*
R&R Bk N - v19 - i1 - Feb 2004 - p49(1) [51-500]

Reid, Audrey Weldon - *Athabasca Seasons: A Memoir*
CBRA - Annual 2003 - p65(1) [501+]

Reid, Barbara - *Read Me a Book*
c Res Links - v10 - i3 - Feb 2005 - p8(1) [501+]
Subway Mouse
c CBRA - Annual 2003 - p464(2) [501+]

Reid, Catherine - *Coyote: Seeking the Hunter in Our Midst*
y BL - v101 - i2 - Sept 15 2004 - p187(1) [51-500]
KR - v72 - i15 - August 1 2004 - p732(1) [51-500]
PW - v251 - i31 - August 2 2004 - p59(1) [51-500]

Reid, Charles - *Hurricanes over London*
Can Lit - i182 - Autumn 2004 - p135(2) [501+]

Reid, Christina - *The Gift of the Gab*
c Sch Lib - v52 - i4 - Winter 2004 - p211(1) [51-500]

Reid, Christopher - *Legends from Darkwood: The Unicorn Hunters*
PW - v251 - i39 - Sept 27 2004 - p40(1) [501+]

Reid, Constance - *A Long Way from Euclid*
SciTech - v28 - i4 - Dec 2004 - p16(1) [1-50]

Reid, Daniel G. - *The IVP Dictionary of the New Testament: A One-Volume Compendium of Contemporary Biblical Scholarship*
Choice - v42 - i4 - Dec 2004 - p628-1 [1-50]

Reid, David A. - *Fundamentals of Business Marketing Research*
Choice - v41 - i11-12 - July-August 2004 - p2089(1) [501+]
R&R Bk N - v19 - i2 - May 2004 - p114(1) [51-500]

Reid, Dennis - *Art Gallery of Ontario and the National Gallery of Canada*
Can Lit - i182 - Autumn 2004 - p174(3) [501+]

Reid, Elwood - *D. B.*
BL - v100 - i21 - July 2004 - p1819(1) [1-50]
NYTBR - August 8 2004 - p9 [501+]

Reid, Escott - *Radical Mandarin: The Memoirs of Escott Reid*
Globe & Mail - Nov 27 2004 - pD51 [501+]

Reid, Gilbert - *So This is Love: Lollipop and Other Stories*
Globe & Mail - Oct 16 2004 - pD21 [501+]
Globe & Mail - Nov 27 2004 - pD3 [51-500]

Reid, Jack - *Watercolor for the Fun of It: Easy Landscapes*
LJ - v129 - i12 - July 2004 - p81(1) [51-500]

Reid, John G. - *The "Conquest" of Acadia, 1710: Imperial, Colonial, and Aboriginal Constructions*
Choice - v42 - i2 - Oct 2004 - p353(2) [51-500]

Reid, John Phillip - *Controlling the Law: Legal Politics in Early National New Hampshire*
Choice - v42 - i2 - Oct 2004 - p358(1) [51-500]
Law&PolBR - June 2004 - p377(6) [501+]
Rule of Law: The Jurisprudence of Liberty in the Seventeenth and Eighteenth Centuries
Law&PolBR - Oct 2004 - pNA [501+]

Reid, Margaret - *Cultural Secrets as Narrative Form: Storytelling in Nineteenth-Century America*
Choice - v42 - i2 - Oct 2004 - p296(1) [501+]

Reid, Martine J. - *Paddling Where I Stand: Agnes Alferd, Qwiqwasutinuxw Nobelwomen*
Choice - v42 - i7 - March 2005 - p1271(1) [51-500]

Reid, Richard J. - *Political Power in Pre-Colonial Buganda: Economy, Society and Warfare in the Nineteenth Century*
AHR - v109 - i3 - June 2004 - p1022(2) [501+]
JEL - v42 - i1 - March 2004 - p303(1) [501+]

Reid, Rob - *Cool Story Programs for the School-Age Crowd*
CCB-B - v58 - i6 - Feb 2005 - p274(1) [51-500]
SLJ - v51 - i1 - Jan 2005 - p162(1) [51-500]

Reid, Robert - *Central America on a Shoestring, 5th Ed.*
Bwatch - Feb 2005 - pNA [51-500]
Two Hundred Years of Pushkin, Vol. 2
R&R Bk N - v19 - i1 - Feb 2004 - p217(1) [51-500]

Reid, Suzanne Elizabeth - *Virginia Euwer Wolff: Capturing the Music of Young Voices*
R&R Bk N - v19 - i1 - Feb 2004 - p247(1) [51-500]

Reid, T.R. - *The United States of Europe: The New Superpower and the End of American Supremacy*
BL - v101 - i3 - Oct 1 2004 - p287(1) [51-500]
KR - v72 - i16 - August 15 2004 - p796(1) [501+]
LJ - v129 - i15 - Sept 15 2004 - p71(1) [51-500]
NL - v87 - i6 - Nov-Dec 2004 - p15(3) [501+]
NYRB - v52 - i2 - Feb 10 2005 - p37(5) [501+]

Reid, Thomas - *Thomas Reid: Essays on the Intellectual Powers of Man*
Dialogue - v43 - i2 - Spring 2004 - p393(2) [501+]

Reid, Van - *Fiddler's Green: Or, A Wedding, a Ball, and the Singular Adventures of Sundry Moss*
BL - v100 - i21 - July 2004 - p1819(2) [1-50]

Reid, W. Darlene - *Clinical Management Notes and Case Histories in Cardiopulmonary Physical Therapy*
SciTech - v28 - i3 - Sept 2004 - p106(1) [51-500]

Reidel, James - *Vanished Act: The Life and Art of Weldon Kees*
TLS - i5286 - July 23 2004 - p9-10 [501+]

Reider, Rob - *Operational Review Workbook: Case Studies, Forms, and Exercises*
R&R Bk N - v19 - i2 - May 2004 - p119 [51-500]

Reif, Linda C. - *The Ombudsman, Good Governance, and the International Human Rights System*
R&R Bk N - v19 - i3 - August 2004 - p177(1) [501+]

Reigns, Steven - *Your Dead Body Is My Welcome Mat*
Lam Bk Rpt - v13 - i4-5 - Nov-Dec 2004 - p20(1) [501+]

Reiland, Rachel - *Get Me Out of Here: My Recovery from Borderline Personality Disorder*
LJ - v129 - i14 - Sept 1 2004 - p172(2) [51-500]

Reill, Peter Hanns - *Encyclopedia of the Enlightenment*
BL - v101 - i9-10 - Jan 1 2005 - p903(1) [501+]
LJ - v129 - i19 - Nov 15 2004 - p86(2) [51-500]

Reilly, Edwin D. - *Milestones in Computer Science and Information Technology*
LibMed - v22 - i7 - April-May 2004 - p68(1) [501+]

Reilly, James A. - *A Small Town in Syria: Ottoman Hama in the Eighteenth and Nineteenth Centuries*
IJMES - v36 - i1 - Feb 2004 - p128-129 [501+]

Reilly, Matthew - *Ice Station (Read by Mangan, Scan). Audiobook Review*
y Kliatt - v38 - i5 - Sept 2004 - p61(2) [51-500]
Scarecrow (Read by Sowers, Scott). Audiobook Review
c Kliatt - v38 - i4 - July 2004 - p56(1) [51-500]

Reilly, Patrick - *The Dark Landscape of Modern Fiction*
R&R Bk N - v19 - i1 - Feb 2004 - p228(1) [1-50]

Reilly, Philip R. - *Is It in Your Genes?: The Influence of Genes on Common Disorders and Diseases That Affect You and Your Family*
Choice - v42 - i3 - Nov 2004 - p518(1) [1-50]
SciTech - v28 - i3 - Sept 2004 - p89(1) [51-500]

Reiman, Erika - *Schumann's Piano Cycles and the Novels of Jean Paul*
Choice - v42 - i2 - Oct 2004 - p303(1) [51-500]
Notes - v61 - i3 - March 2005 - p785(3) [501+]

Reimpell, Jornsen - *Automotive Chassis: Engineering Principles*
SciTech - v28 - i1 - March 2004 - p168(1) [51-500]

Rein, Martin - *Rethinking the Welfare State: The Political Economy of Pension Reform*
R&R Bk N - v19 - i3 - August 2004 - p117(1) [51-500]

Reinalter, Helmut - *Die Franzoesische Revolution und das Projekt der Moderne*
HNet - June 2004 - pNA [501+]

Reinberger, Mark - *Utility and Beauty: Robert Wellford and Composition Ornament in America*
Choice - v42 - i1 - Sept 2004 - p87(1) [501+]
Mag Antiq - v166 - i1 - July 2004 - p50(1) [501+]

Reinecke, Gerhard - *Policies for Small Enterprises: Creating the Right Environment for Good Jobs*
ILR - v143 - i3 - Autumn 2004 - p291(1) [1-50]

Reiner, Carl - *My Anecdotal Life: A Memoir*
TV Q - v34 - i2 - Wntr 2004 - p70-72 [501+]

Reinert, Kenneth A. - *Windows on the World Economy: An Introduction to International Economics*
R&R Bk N - v19 - i2 - May 2004 - p111(1) [1-50]

Reinhardt, Robert - *Macromedia Flash MX 2004 Bible*
SciTech - v28 - i3 - Sept 2004 - p169(1) [51-500]

Reinhart, Joseph R. - *Two Germans in the Civil War: The Diary of John Daeuble and the Letters of Gottfried Rentschler, 6th Kentucky Volunteer Infantry*
R&R Bk N - v19 - i4 - Nov 2004 - p62(1) [51-500]

Reinhart, Matthew - *The Ark (Illus. by Reinhart, Matthew)*
c SLJ - v51 - i2 - Feb 2005 - p126(1) [51-500]
Young Naturalist's Handbook Insect-Lo-Pedia
c LibMed - v22 - i5 - Feb 2004 - p60(2) [501+]

Reinhart, Richard C. - *The Consequence of Sex*
G&L Rev W - v11 - i4 - July-August 2004 - p41(1) [501+]

Reinheimer, Brent A. - *USMLE Step 1 Recall: Buzzwords for the Boards, 2nd Ed.*
SciTech - v28 - i3 - Sept 2004 - p79(1) [51-500]

Reinhold, Natalya - *Woolf Across Cultures*
Wom R Bks - v21 - i10-11 - July 2004 - p28(1) [51-500]

Reinking, Dan L. - *Oklahoma Breeding Bid Atlas*
Choice - v42 - i7 - March 2005 - p1254(1) [51-500]

Reis, Joao Jose - *Death Is a Festival: Funeral Rites and Rebellion in Nineteenth-Century Brazil*
CS - v33 - i1 - Jan 2004 - p129-129 [501+]

Reisberg, Daniel - *Memory and Emotion*
R&R Bk N - v19 - i1 - Feb 2004 - p8(1) [1-50]

Reisler, Jim - *Babe Ruth: Launching the Legend*
NYTBR - July 18 2004 - p16 [501+]
Guys, Dolls, and Curveballs: Damon Runyon on Baseball
KR - v73 - i2 - Jan 15 2005 - p110(1) [501+]

Reisman, David A. - *Schumpeter's Market: Enterprise and Evolution*
R&R Bk N - v19 - i3 - August 2004 - p93(1) [51-500]

Reisman, Nancy - *The First Desire*
BL - v101 - i1 - Sept 1 2004 - p64(1) [51-500]
BW - v34 - i43 - Oct 24 2004 - p4(1) [501+]
Ent W - i784 - Sept 17 2004 - p84 [501+]
KR - v72 - i14 - July 15 2004 - p654(2) [501+]
LJ - v129 - i13 - August 2004 - p69(1) [51-500]
NYTBR - Sept 12 2004 - p17(L) [501+]
PW - v251 - i29 - July 19 2004 - p141(1) [51-500]
People - v62 - i16 - Oct 18 2004 - p50 [51-500]

Reisner, Gavriel - *The Death-Ego and the Vital Self: Romances of Desire in Literature and Psychoanalysis*
R&R Bk N - v19 - i1 - Feb 2004 - p234(1) [51-500]

Reiss, Benjamin - *The Showman and the Slave: Race, Death, and Memory in Barnum's America*
Theat J - v56 - i2 - May 2004 - p334(2) [501+]

Reiss, Jana - *What Would Buffy Do? The Vampire Slayer as Spiritual Guide*
CC - v121 - i23 - Nov 16 2004 - p22(3) [501+]

Reiss, Kathryn - *Dreadful Sorry*
c CH Bwatch - v14 - i7 - July 2004 - p6(1) [51-500]
c CH Bwatch - v14 - i9 - Sept 2004 - p4(1) [51-500]
Sweet Miss Honeywell's Revenge: A Ghost Story
y CCB-B - v57 - i11 - July-August 2004 - p481(1) [501+]
c CH Bwatch - v14 - i7 - July 2004 - p6(1) [51-500]
c JAAL - v48 - i3 - Nov 2004 - p266(2) [501+]
c SLJ - v50 - i8 - August 2004 - p128(1) [51-500]

Reiss, Tom - *The Orientalist: Solving the Mystery of a Strange and Dangerous Life*
Ent W - i807 - Feb 18 2005 - p81 [501+]
Econ - v374 - i8413 - Feb 12 2005 - p84US [501+]
Globe & Mail - Feb 12 2005 - pD13 [1-50]
KR - v72 - i24 - Dec 15 2004 - p1190(2) [501+]
LJ - v130 - i1 - Jan 1 2005 - p124(1) [51-500]
NW - Feb 14 2005 - p59 [501+]
NYTBR - Feb 27 2005 - p13 [501+]

Reiterer, Albert F. - *Cyprus: Case Study about a Failure of Ethno-National Understanding*
R&R Bk N - v19 - i1 - Feb 2004 - p41(1) [51-500]

Reith, Gerda - *Gambling: Who Wins? Who Loses?*
Choice - v41 - i7 - March 2004 - p1334(1) [501+]

Reitman, Charles A. - *Management of Thorocolumbar Fractures*
SciTech - v28 - i4 - Dec 2004 - p109(1) [51-500]

Reitz, Joan M. - *Dictionary for Liberary and Information Science*
Choice - v42 - i3 - Nov 2004 - p446(1) [1-50]
Dictionary for Library and Information Science
LJ - v129 - i14 - Sept 1 2004 - p195(1) [501+]

Rejwan, Nissim - *The Last Jews in Baghdad: Remembering a Lost Homeland*
MEJ - v59 - i1 - Wntr 2005 - p145(2) [501+]

Relano, Francesc - *The Shaping of Africa: Cosmographic Discourse and Cartographic Science in Late Medieval and Early Modern Europe*
J Hist G - v30 - i1 - Jan 2004 - p200(2) [501+]
Six Ct J - v35 - i1 - Spring 2004 - p191(2) [501+]

Religiones del mundo
BL - v101 - i6 - Nov 15 2004 - p612(1) [501+]

Relihan, Constance C. - *Prose Fiction and Early Modern Sexuality in England, 1580-1640*
Choice - v41 - i11-12 - July-August 2004 - p2046(1) [501+]

Rem, Tore - *Dickens, Melodrama, and the Parodic Imagination*
VS - v46 - i3 - Spring 2004 - p541(2) [501+]

Remaud, Michel - *Israel, Servant of God*
Theol St - v66 - i1 - March 2005 - p229(1) [501+]

Remer, Keith - *In the Midst of Wolves*
PW - v251 - i36 - Sept 6 2004 - p47(1) [51-500]

Remick, Elizabeth J. - *Building Local States: China During the Republican and Post-Mao Eras*
Choice - v42 - i4 - Dec 2004 - p708(1) [1-50]
Pers PS - v33 - i4 - Fall 2004 - p241(1) [501+]

Remington, Mary Rose - *Quest: A Practical and Spiritual Guide to Finding Your Life's Passion*
CI - v13 - i1 - Jan 2005 - p44(2) [501+]

Remington, Thomas F. - *Politics in Russia, 3rd Ed.*
R&R Bk N - v19 - i1 - Feb 2004 - pNA [501+]

Reminick, Gerald - *No Surrender: True Stories of the U.S. Navy Armed Guard in World War II*
R&R Bk N - v20 - i1 - Feb 2005 - p33(1) [51-500]

Remkiewicz, Frank - *Less than Zero*
TC Math - v11 - i4 - Nov 2004 - p237(1) [501+]

Remley, George A. - *Southern Sons, Northern Soldiers: The Civil War Letters of the Remley Brothers, 22nd Iowa Infantry*
R&R Bk N - v19 - i1 - Feb 2004 - p59(1) [51-500]

Rempel, David G. - *A Mennonite Family in Tsarist Russia and the Soviet Union, 1789-1923*
Russ Rev - v63 - i3 - July 2004 - pNA [501+]

Remshardt, Ralf - *Staging the Salvage God: The Grotesque in Performance*
Choice - v42 - i5 - Jan 2005 - p864(1) [1-50]

Remy, Steven P. - *The Heidelberg Myth: The Nazification and Denazification of a German University*
GSR - v27 - i3 - Oct 2004 - p645(2) [501+]

Renato, Barahona - *Sex Crimes, Honour, and the Law in Early Modern Spain: Vizcaya, 1528-1735*
R&R Bk N - v19 - i2 - May 2004 - p132 [51-500]

Renaud, Anne - *A Bloom of Friendship: The Story of the Canadian Tulip Festival (Illus. by Spires, Ashley)*
y Res Links - v10 - i3 - Feb 2005 - p27(1) [51-500]

Rendell, Matt - *A Significant Other: Riding the Centenary Tour de France with Lance Armstrong*
TLS - i5287 - July 30 2004 - p32(1) [501+]

Rendell, Ruth - *The Rottweiler*
Ent W - i793 - Nov 19 2004 - p88 [51-500]
NYTBR - Dec 12 2004 - p26 [501+]
Thirteen Steps Down
BIC - v33 - i9 - Dec 2004 - p13(1) [501+]
Globe & Mail - Nov 20 2004 - pD23 [501+]
NS - v133 - i4708 - Oct 4 2004 - p54(2) [501+]
TLS - i5302 - Nov 12 2004 - p22(1) [501+]

Rendell, Susan - *In the Chambers of the Sea*
CBRA - Annual 2003 - p203(2) [51-500]

Rendina, Laura Cooper - *Managing Fish: Ten Case Studies from Canada's Pacific Coast*
Choice - v42 - i1 - Sept 2004 - p129(1) [501+]

Rendon, Juan Carlos Velez - *Los Pueblos Allende el rio Cauca: La Formacion del Suroeste y la Cohesion del Espacio en Antioquia, 1830-1877*
HAHR - v84 - i3 - August 2004 - p552(2) [501+]

Renehan, Edward J. - *The Kennedys at War, 1937-1945 (Read by Forbes, Kate). Audiobook Review*
LJ - v129 - i19 - Nov 15 2004 - p100(1) [51-500]

Renevey, Denis - *Language, Self and Love: Hermeneutics in the Writings of Richard Rolle and the Commentaries on the Song of Songs*
Specu - v79 - i4 - Oct 2004 - p1127(3) [501+]

Renfrew, Donald L. - *Atlas of Spine Injection*
SciTech - v28 - i1 - March 2004 - p94(1) [51-500]

Renfrow, Kenon D. - *Alfred's Group Piano for Adults: Teacher Handbook, Book 1, 2nd Ed.*
Am MT - v54 - i4 - Feb-March 2005 - p104(2) [501+]

Rengel, Marian - *Pakistan: A Primary Source Cultural Guide*
SLJ - v50 - i9 - Sept 2004 - p232(1) [51-500]

Renn, Jurgen - *Galileo in Context*
HNet - August 2004 - pNA [501+]

Renne, Elisha P. - *Population and Progress in a Yoruba Town*
Choice - v41 - i7 - March 2004 - p1337(1) [501+]

Renner, Elmer - *Sea of Sharks: A Sailor's World War II Shipwreck Survival Story*
y BL - v101 - i4 - Oct 15 2004 - p384(1) [51-500]
LJ - v129 - i20 - Dec 1 2004 - p138(1) [51-500]

Rennie, Doug - *Berkeley: Creative Arts Book Company*
Ga R - v57 - i4 - Winter 2003 - p891-892 [501+]

Rennings, Klaus - *Employment Impacts of Cleaner Production*
JEL - v42 - i1 - March 2004 - p338(1) [501+]

Rennison, Louise - *Angus, Thongs and Full-Frontal Snogging: Confessions of Georgia Nicolson*
c WLT - v79 - i1 - Jan-April 2005 - p69(4) [501+]
Away Laughing on a Fast Camel: Even More Confessions of Georgia Nicolson (Read by Rennison, Louise). Audiobook Review
y Kliatt - v39 - i1 - Jan 2005 - p38(1) [51-500]
Away Laughing on a Fast Camel: Even More Confessions of Georgia Nicolson
y BL - v101 - i1 - Sept 1 2004 - p109(1) [1-50]
y HB - v80 - i5 - Sept-Oct 2004 - p596(2) [501+]
y Kliatt - v38 - i4 - July 2004 - p12(1) [51-500]
y SLJ - v50 - i11 - Nov 2004 - p153(1) [51-500]
y VOYA - v27 - i4 - Oct 2004 - p306(1) [51-500]
Confessions of Georgia Nicolson
PW - v251 - i34 - August 23 2004 - p56(1) [51-500]
Knocked Out by My Nunga-Nungas
y VOYA - v27 - i3 - August 2004 - p180(1) [1-50]

Renov, Michael - *The Subject of Documentary*
Choice - v42 - i6 - Feb 2005 - p1029(1) [51-500]
R&R Bk N - v19 - i4 - Nov 2004 - p224(1) [501+]

Renshaw, Patrick - *Franklin D. Roosevelt, 1st Ed.*
Choice - v42 - i3 - Nov 2004 - p551(1) [1-50]
TimHES - v0 - i1680 - Feb 25 2005 - pX(1) [501+]

Renteln, Alison Dundes - *The Cultural Defense*
Choice - v41 - i11-12 - July-August 2004 - p2124(1) [501+]

Renton, Linda - *Pinter and the Object of Desire*
FS - v58 - i2 - April 2004 - p289(2) [501+]

Renton, Tim - *Chief Whip: People, Power and Patronage in Westminster*
TLS - i5295 - Sept 24 2004 - p32(1) [501+]

Renwick, Roger deV. - *Recentering Anglo/American Folksong: Sea Crabs and Wicked Youths*
Folkl - v115 - i3 - Dec 2004 - p376(2) [501+]

Renzi, Thomas C. - *H.G. Wells: Six Scientific Romances Adapted for Film, 2nd Ed.*
ChrSFF&H - v26 - i9 - Sept 2004 - p37(1) [51-500]
R&R Bk N - v19 - i4 - Nov 2004 - p237(1) [501+]

Repka, Janice - *The Stupendous Dodgeball Fiasco (Illus. by Dibley, Glin)*
c BL - v101 - i8 - Dec 15 2004 - p742(1) [51-500]
c KR - v72 - i19 - Oct 1 2004 - p967(1) [51-500]
c SLJ - v50 - i12 - Dec 2004 - p152(1) [51-500]

Reppetto, Thomas - *American Mafia: A History of Its Rise to Power*
BW - v34 - i3 - Jan 18 2004 - p13(1) [501+]
TLS - i5283 - July 2 2004 - p6-7 [501+]
VQR - v80 - i3 - Summer 2004 - p267(1) [1-50]

Reppy, John H. - *The Standard ML Basis Library*
Choice - v42 - i6 - Feb 2005 - p1057(1) [51-500]

Republic of Ireland. E-book Review
c SLJ - v50 - i8 - August 2004 - p53(1) [51-500]

Requemore, Sylvie - *Les Tyrans de la mer: pirates, corsaires et flibustiers a l'age classique*
FS - v58 - i1 - Jan 2004 - p92(2) [501+]

Res, Janus - *Environment-Friendly Techniques of Rock Breaking*
SciTech - v28 - i1 - March 2004 - p144(1) [51-500]

Rescher, Nicholas - *Fairness: Theory and Practice of Distributive Justice*
RM - v58 - i1 - Sept 2004 - p188(3) [501+]

Resende, Mauricio G.C. - *Metaheuristics: Computer Decision-Making*
SciTech - v28 - i1 - March 2004 - p134(1) [51-500]

Reserve Bank of India - *Macroeconomic and Monetary Developments in 2002-03*
JEL - v41 - i4 - Dec 2003 - p1348(1) [501+]

Reserve Bank of India. Central Board of Directors - *Annual Report: 2002-03: Report of the Central Board of Directors on the Working of the Reserve Bank of India for the Year Ended June 30, 2003 Submitted to the Central Government in Terms of Section 53(2) of the Reserve Bank of India Act, 1934*
JEL - v42 - i1 - March 2004 - p258(1) [501+]

Reshef, Yonatan - *Unions in the Time of Revolution: Government Restructuring in Alberta and Ontario*
HNet - July 2004 - pNA [501+]
HNet - Sept 2004 - pNA [501+]
R&R Bk N - v19 - i1 - Feb 2004 - p101(1) [51-500]

Resina, Joan Ramon - *Disremembering the Dictatorship: The Politics of Memory in the Spanish Transition to Democracy*
R&R Bk N - v19 - i1 - Feb 2004 - p40(1) [1-50]

Resner, Andre - *Just Preaching: Prophetic Voices for Economic Justice*
Intpr - v58 - i4 - Oct 2004 - p436(2) [501+]

Resnick, Irven Michael - *Albert the Great: A Selectively Annotated Bibliography*
Choice - v42 - i4 - Dec 2004 - p626(1) [1-50]
R&R Bk N - v19 - i4 - Nov 2004 - p259(1) [501+]

Resnikoff, Ned - *Fool's Tavern*
y VOYA - v27 - i5 - Dec 2004 - p410(1) [51-500]

Resources for Learning
LibMed - v22 - i6 - March 2004 - p91(1) [501+]

Ressa, Maria A. - *Seeds of Terror: An Eyewitness Account of Al-Qaeda's Newest Center of Operations in Southeast Asia*
BW - v34 - i1 - Jan 4 2004 - p5(2) [501+]

Restak, Richard M. - *The New Brain: How the Modern Age Is Rewiring Your Mind*
Fut - v39 - i2 - March-April 2005 - p13(1) [501+]
Fut - v39 - i2 - March-April 2005 - p61(1) [51-500]
Poe's Heart and the Mountain Climber: Exploring the Effect of Anxiety on Our Brains and Our Culture
BL - v101 - i3 - Oct 1 2004 - p284(1) [51-500]
KR - v72 - i17 - Sept 1 2004 - p854(1) [51-500]
PW - v251 - i42 - Oct 18 2004 - p57(1) [51-500]

Restall, Mathew - *Seven Myths of the Spanish Conquest*
AHR - v109 - i4 - Oct 2004 - p1271-1272 [501+]

Restrepo, Laura - *A Tale of the Dispossessed*
KR - v72 - i13 - July 1 2004 - p601(1) [51-500]
LJ - v129 - i13 - August 2004 - p69(2) [51-500]

Retallack, James - *Saxony in German History: Culture, Society, and Politics, 1830-1933*
CEH - v37 - i3 - Summer 2004 - p442(3) [501+]

Retallack, Joan - *The Poethical Wager*
Choice - v42 - i1 - Sept 2004 - p96(1) [501+]

Retat, Pierre - *La Gazette d'Amsterdam: Miroir de l'Europe au XVIIIe Siecle*
Eight-C St - v37 - i3 - Spring 2004 - p483-486 [501+]

Retcher, Ralph - *Gross Me Out! 50 Nasty Projects to Disgust Your Friends & Repulse Your Family (Illus. by Meyer, Clay)*
c   PW - v251 - i28 - July 12 2004 - p66(1) [501+]

Reti, Gyorgy - *Hungarian-Italian Relations in the Shadow of Hitler's Germany, 1933-1940*
Slav R - v63 - i4 - Winter 2004 - p862(1) [501+]

Rettig, Michael D. - *From Rigorous Standards into Student Achievement: A Practical Process*
R&R Bk N - v19 - i1 - Feb 2004 - p189(1) [51-500]

Rettig, Perry Richard - *Practicing Principals: Case Studies, In-Baskets and Policy Analysis*
R&R Bk N - v19 - i3 - August 2004 - p224(1) [1-50]

Reuben, Shelly - *Weeping (Read by Fields, Anna).* Audiobook Review
BL - v101 - i8 - Dec 15 2004 - p752(1) [1-50]
y   Kliatt - v39 - i2 - March 2005 - p57(2) [51-500]

Reuland, Random - *Semiautomatic*
NYT - August 8 2004 - p10 [501+]

Reus-Smit, Christian - *American Power and World Order*
TimHES - v0 - i1668 - Nov 26 2004 - pV(1) [501+]
TLS - i5301 - Nov 5 2004 - p4-6 [501+]

Reuss, Martin - *Designing the Bayous: The Control of Water in the Atchafalaya Basin, 1800-1995*
Choice - v42 - i7 - March 2005 - p1258(1) [51-500]

Reuss, Richard A. - *American Folk Music and Left-Wing Politics, 1927-1957*
WestFolk - v62 - i4 - Fall 2003 - p293(5) [501+]

Reuter, Christoph - *My Life Is a Weapon: A Modern History of Suicide Bombing*
CC - v121 - i19 - Sept 21 2004 - p44(3) [501+]
For Aff - v83 - i5 - Sept-Oct 2004 - p164 [501+]
Lon R Bks - v26 - i21 - Nov 4 2004 - p21(3) [501+]

Reuter, Lars - *Modern Biotechnology in Postmodern Times?: A Reflection on European Policies and Human Agency*
SciTech - v28 - i1 - March 2004 - p173(1) [51-500]

Reuter, Thomas - *The House of Our Ancestors: Precedence and Dualism in Highland Balinese Society*
JAS - v63 - i3 - August 2004 - p850-854 [501+]

Reutter, Werner - *Germany on the Road to "Normalcy": Policies and Politics of the Red-Green Federal Government*
Choice - v42 - i6 - Feb 2005 - p1092(1) [51-500]

Reutzel, D. Ray - *Strategies for Reading Assessment and Instruction: Helping Every Child Succeed, 2nd Ed.*
R Today - v22 - i1 - August-Sept 2004 - p32(1) [51-500]

Reuvid, Jonathan - *Doing Business with Slovenia*
R&R Bk N - v19 - i3 - August 2004 - p125(1) [51-500]
A Handbook of World Trade: A Strategic Guide to Trading Internationally
Choice - v42 - i3 - Nov 2004 - p533(1) [1-50]
R&R Bk N - v19 - i3 - August 2004 - p124(1) [51-500]

Revard, Stella P. - *Pindar and the Renaissance Hymn-Ode, 1450-1700*
RES - v55 - i218 - Feb 2004 - p138-140 [501+]

Revel, Jean-Francois - *Anti-Americanism*
Bks & Cult - v10 - i4 - July-August 2004 - p26(3) [501+]
R&R Bk N - v19 - i1 - Feb 2004 - p61(1) [501+]

Revell, Donald - *Pennyweight Windows: New and Selected Poems*
LJ - v130 - i2 - Feb 1 2005 - p83(2) [51-500]

ReVelle, Jack B. - *Quality Essentials: A Reference Guide from A to Z*
SciTech - v28 - i3 - Sept 2004 - p170(1) [51-500]

Reveron, Derek S. - *America's Viceroys: The Military and U.S. Foreign Policy*
Choice - v42 - i5 - Jan 2005 - p933(1) [51-500]

Reverte, Arturo Perez - *Queen of the South (Read by Patel, Lina). Audiobook Review*
y   Kliatt - v38 - i5 - Sept 2004 - p64(2) [51-500]

Revie, Linda L. - *The Niagara Companion: Explorers, Artists, and Writers of the Falls; From Discovery through the Twentieth Century*
R&R Bk N - v19 - i1 - Feb 2004 - p63(1) [501+]

Revsine, Lawrence - *Financial Reporting and Analysis*
IJCM - v14 - i3-4 - Fall-Winter 2004 - p92(3) [501+]

Rew, Lynn - *Adolescent Health: A Multidisciplinary Approach to Theory, Research, and Intervention*
SciTech - v28 - i4 - Dec 2004 - p112(1) [1-50]

Rex, John - *Governance in Multicultural Societies*
R&R Bk N - v19 - i3 - August 2004 - p145(1) [51-500]

Rex, Michael - *Dunk Skunk*
c   KR - v73 - i3 - Feb 1 2005 - p181(1) [51-500]
The Mud Monster's Halloween (Illus. by Rex, Michael)
c   RT - v57 - Oct 2003 - p167 [1-50]
Truck Duck
c   PW - v252 - i5 - Jan 31 2005 - p69(2) [51-500]

Rex, Richard - *Elizabeth I: Fortune's Bastard: A Short Account of the Long Life of Elizabeth I*
TLS - i5266 - March 5 2004 - p4-6 [501+]
The Lollards
Specu - v79 - i4 - Oct 2004 - p1129(3) [501+]
The Tudors
y   BL - v100 - i22 - August 2004 - p1893(2) [51-500]
Choice - v42 - i6 - Feb 2005 - p1087(1) [51-500]
Six Ct J - v35 - i1 - Spring 2004 - p286(2) [501+]

Rey, Del - *Othello Satomi Ikezawa*
PW - v251 - i36 - Sept 6 2004 - p47(1) [51-500]

Rey, H.A. - *Curious George*
c   RT - v57 - Sept 2003 - p99 [51-500]

Rey, Margret - *Bill's Picture (Illus. by Rey, H.A.)*
c   PW - v251 - i36 - Sept 6 2004 - p64(1) [51-500]

Reycraft, Sean - *One Good Marriage*
BIC - v33 - i9 - Dec 2004 - p24(3) [501+]

Reydams, Luc - *Universal Jurisdiction: International and Municipal Perspectives*
TLS - i5295 - Sept 24 2004 - p6-7 [501+]

Reydams-Schils, Gretchen J. - *Plato's Timaeus as Cultural Icon*
Class R - v54 - i2 - Nov 2004 - p317-320 [501+]
Six Ct J - v35 - i1 - Spring 2004 - p305(2) [501+]

Reyerson, Kathryn L. - *Jacques Coeur: Entrepreneur and King's Bursar*
R&R Bk N - v19 - i4 - Nov 2004 - p120(1) [51-500]
Medieval Notaries and Their Acts: The 1327-1328 Register of Jean Holanie
Med R - August 2004 - pNA [501+]
R&R Bk N - v19 - i3 - August 2004 - p208(1) [1-50]

Reyes, Angelita - *Mothering Across Cultures: Postcolonial Representations*
Can Lit - i182 - Autumn 2004 - p112(3) [501+]

Reyes, Lawney L. - *White Frizzly Bear's Legacy: Learning to Be Indian*
WHQ - v35 - i1 - Spring 2004 - p86-87 [501+]

Reyher, Ken - *Wilderness Wanderers: The 1776 Expedition of Dominguez and Escalante*
R&R Bk N - v19 - i1 - Feb 2004 - p65(1) [501+]

Reyhner, Jon - *American Indian Education: A History*
Choice - v42 - i6 - Feb 2005 - p1073(1) [51-500]
Roundup M - v12 - i3 - Feb 2005 - p22(1) [51-500]

Reymond, Eric D. - *Innovations in Hebrew Poetry: Parellelism and the Poems of Sirach*
R&R Bk N - v19 - i3 - August 2004 - p24(1) [1-50]

Reynolds, Adrian - *Jarman, Julia. Big Red Tub (Illus. by Reynolds, Adrian)*
c   SLJ - v50 - i12 - Dec 2004 - p110(2) [501+]

Reynolds, Alastair - *Absolution Group*
Bwatch - v26 - i7 - July 2004 - p5(2) [51-500]
Diamond Dogs, Turquoise Days
KR - v72 - i23 - Dec 1 2004 - p1126(1) [501+]
LJ - v130 - i1 - Jan 1 2005 - p103(1) [51-500]
PW - v251 - i48 - Nov 29 2004 - p27(1) [51-500]

Reynolds, Andrew - *Peirce's Scientific Metaphysics: The Philosophy of Chance, Law and Evolution*
MLN - v118 - i5 - Dec 2003 - p1329-1332 [501+]
Understanding Development: Theory and Practice in the Third World
JPR - v41 - i5 - Sept 2004 - p645-646 [501+]

Reynolds, Ann - *Robert Smithson: Learning from New Jersey and Elsewhere*
Afterimage - v32 - i4 - Jan-Feb 2005 - p15(1) [1-50]

Reynolds, Anna Maria - *Showing of Love: Extant Texts and Translation*
Specu - v79 - i4 - Oct 2004 - p1103(3) [501+]

Reynolds, Bill - *Cousy: His Life, Career, and the Birth of Big-Time Basketball*
BL - v101 - i9-10 - Jan 1 2005 - p801(1) [51-500]
KR - v72 - i23 - Dec 1 2004 - p1138(1) [501+]
LJ - v129 - i20 - Dec 1 2004 - p126(2) [51-500]
PW - v251 - i50 - Dec 13 2004 - p57(1) [51-500]

Reynolds, Bryan - *Performing Transversally: Reimagining Shakespeare and the Critical Future, 1st Ed.*
Ren Q - v57 - i4 - Winter 2004 - p1527(3) [501+]
R&R Bk N - v19 - i1 - Feb 2004 - p237(1) [51-500]

Reynolds, Calvin - *Guide to Global Compensation and Benefits, 2nd Ed.*
HR Mag - v49 - i7 - July 2004 - pS12(1) [51-500]

Reynolds, Craig J. - *National Identity and Its Defenders: Thailand Today*
A Aff - v35 - i2 - July 2004 - p243-244 [501+]

Reynolds, David - *In Command Of History*
Spec - v296 - i9197 - Nov 13 2004 - p49(2) [501+]

Reynolds, David B. - *Partnering for Change: Unions and Community Groups Build Coalitions for Economic Justice*
R&R Bk N - v19 - i3 - August 2004 - p118(1) [51-500]

Reynolds, David S. - *John Brown, Abolitionist: The Man Who Killed Slavery, Sparked the Civil War, and Seeded Civil Rights*
KR - v73 - i3 - Feb 1 2005 - p170(1) [501+]
LJ - v130 - i3 - Feb 15 2005 - p140(1) [51-500]
PW - v252 - i6 - Feb 7 2005 - p50(1) [51-500]
Walt Whitman
BL - v101 - i6 - Nov 15 2004 - p546(1) [51-500]
KR - v72 - i20 - Oct 15 2004 - p995(2) [501+]
LJ - v130 - i3 - Feb 15 2005 - p130(1) [51-500]

Reynolds, Frank E. - *The Life of Buddhism*
HNet - Sept 2004 - pNA [501+]

Reynolds, Henry - *North of Capricorn: The Untold Story of Australia's North*
AHS - v35 - i124 - Oct 2004 - p410(2) [501+]
AJPS - v39 - i3 - Nov 2004 - p666(2) [501+]

Reynolds, Jack - *Merleau-Ponty and Derrida: Intertwining Embodiment and Alterity*
R&R Bk N - v20 - i1 - Feb 2005 - p4(1) [1-50]
Understanding Derrida
R&R Bk N - v19 - i4 - Nov 2004 - p5(1) [51-500]

Reynolds, John E., III - *Dolphins, Whales, and Manatees of Florida: A Guide to Sharing Their World*
E-Streams - July 2004 - pNA [501+]
QRB - v79 - i4 - Dec 2004 - p440(1) [51-500]

Reynolds, John Lawrence - *Haunted Hearts*
CBRA - Annual 2003 - p182(1) [501+]
The Naked Investor: Why Almost Everybody But You Gets Rich on Your RRSP
Globe & Mail - Jan 29 2005 - pD13 [1-50]

Reynolds, John Mark - *Toward a Unified Platonic Human Psychology*
R&R Bk N - v19 - i4 - Nov 2004 - p3(1) [51-500]

Reynolds, Larry T. - *Handbook of Symbolic Interpretation*
R&R Bk N - v19 - i1 - Feb 2004 - p122(1) [51-500]

Reynolds, Margaret - *A.S. Byatt: The Essential Guide*
c   SLJ - v50 - i8 - August 2004 - p142(1) [51-500]
Roddy Doyle: The Essential Guide
y   SLJ - v51 - i2 - Feb 2005 - p151(1) [51-500]
Roddy Doyle: The Essential Guide to Contemporary Literature
LJ - v129 - i19 - Nov 15 2004 - p60(1) [501+]
The Sappho History
Lon R Bks - v26 - i1 - Jan 8 2004 - pNA [501+]

Reynolds, Marilyn - *I Won't Read and You Can't Make Me: Reaching Reluctant Teen Readers*
VOYA - v27 - i3 - August 2004 - p250(1) [1-50]

Reynolds, Marilynn - *Goodbye to Griffith Street (Illus. by Benoit, Renne)*
c   Globe & Mail - Sept 25 2004 - pD26 [51-500]
c   PW - v251 - i50 - Dec 13 2004 - p67(1) [51-500]
c   Res Links - v10 - i1 - Oct 2004 - p9(1) [51-500]
c   SLJ - v51 - i1 - Jan 2005 - p96(2) [51-500]
The Name of the Child (Illus. by Kilby, Don)
c   Can Lit - i182 - Autumn 2004 - p166(2) [501+]

Reynolds, Marjorie - *The Starlite Drive-In*
LJ - v129 - i18 - Nov 1 2004 - p135(1) [51-500]

Reynolds, Matthew - *The Realms of Verse, 1830-1870: English Poetry in a Time of Nation-Building*
MP - v102 - i1 - August 2004 - p137(5) [501+]
VS - v45 - i2 - Winter 2003 - p387 [501+]

Reynolds, Max M. - *Hospital Joint Ventures Legal Handbook*
R&R Bk N - v19 - i3 - August 2004 - p201(1) [1-50]

Reynolds, Nancy - *No Fixed Points: Dance in the Twentieth Century*
Choice - v41 - i11-12 - July-August 2004 - p2055(2) [501+]

Reynolds, Paul - *Lock, Stock and Barrel: A Political Biography of Mike Ahern*
R&R Bk N - v19 - i1 - Feb 2004 - pNA [501+]

Reynolds, Peter H. - *The Dot (Illus. by Reynolds, Peter H.)*
  c SLJ - v50 - i7 - July 2004 - p44(1) [51-500]
  c TES - v0 - i4577 - April 2 2004 - p35(1) [501+]
Ish (Illus. by Reynolds, Peter H.)
  c Black Iss - v7 - i1 - Jan-Feb 2005 - p70(2) [501+]
  c KR - v72 - i14 - July 15 2004 - p693(1) [51-500]
  c PW - v251 - i41 - Oct 11 2004 - p79(2) [51-500]
  c SLJ - v51 - i1 - June 2005 - p97(1) [51-500]

Reynolds, Roger E. - *The Collectio canonum Casinensis duodecimi seculi*
  CHR - v90 - i4 - Oct 2004 - p761(2) [501+]

Reynolds, William M. - *Expanding Curriculum Theory: Dis/Positions and Lines of Flight*
  Choice - v42 - i3 - Nov 2004 - p536(1) [1-50]
  R&R Bk N - v19 - i3 - August 2004 - p222(1) [1-50]

Reyto, Susanne M. - *Pursuit of Freedom: A True Story of the Enduring Power of Hope and Dreams*
  Bwatch - v26 - i8 - August 2004 - p5(2) [51-500]

Rhatigan, Joe - *The Kids' Guide to Nature Adventures: 80 Great Activities for Exploring the Outdoors*
  c SLJ - v50 - i10 - Oct 2004 - pS40(1) [51-500]
Out-of-This-World Astronomy: 50 Amazing Activities and Projects
  c SB - v40 - i3 - May-June 2004 - p130(1) [501+]
  c SLJ - v50 - i10 - Oct 2004 - pS42(1) [51-500]
Prize-Winning Science Fair Projects for Curious Kids
  c BL - v101 - i7 - Dec 1 2004 - p668(2) [51-500]
  y SLJ - v51 - i1 - Jan 2005 - p154(1) [51-500]
Run, Jump, Hide, Slide, Splash: The 200 Best Outdoor Games Ever
  c SLJ - v50 - i10 - Oct 2004 - p148(1) [51-500]

Rhea, Gordon C. - *Carrying the Flag: The Story of Private Charles Whilden, the Confederacy's Most Unlikely Hero*
  R&R Bk N - v19 - i3 - August 2004 - p68(1) [51-500]

Rhees, Rush - *In Dialogue with the Greeks, Vol. 1*
  R&R Bk N - v20 - i1 - Feb 2005 - p2(1) [51-500]
In Dialogue with the Greeks, Vol. 2
  R&R Bk N - v20 - i1 - Feb 2005 - p2(1) [51-500]
Life of Jesus of Nazareth, Rev. Ed.
  R&R Bk N - v19 - i1 - Feb 2004 - p22(1) [51-500]

Rheims, Bettina - *Bettina Rheims: More Trouble*
  LJ - v130 - i2 - Feb 1 2005 - p78(1) [51-500]

Rheingold, Howard - *Smart Mobs: The Next Social Revolution*
  CS - v33 - i6 - Nov 2004 - p681(2) [501+]

Rheinheimer, Kurt - *Little Criminals*
  BL - v101 - i5 - Nov 1 2004 - p465(1) [51-500]

Rho, Jong M. - *Epilepsy: Scientific Foundations of Clinical Practice*
  SciTech - v28 - i3 - Sept 2004 - p94(1) [51-500]
  SciTech - v28 - i3 - Sept 2004 - p94(1) [51-500]

Rhoades, Dawna L. - *Evolution of International Aviation: Phoenix Rising*
  JEL - v42 - i1 - March 2004 - p293(1) [501+]
  R&R Bk N - v19 - i1 - Feb 2004 - p105(1) [51-500]

Rhoades, J.D. - *The Devil's Right Hand*
  BL - v101 - i6 - Nov 15 2004 - p564(1) [51-500]
  KR - v72 - i21 - Nov 1 2004 - p1031(1) [51-500]
  PW - v251 - i51 - Dec 20 2004 - p37(2) [51-500]

Rhoads, Steven E. - *Taking Sex Differences Seriously*
  CI - v12 - i9 - Oct 2004 - p44(1) [51-500]
  R&R Bk N - v19 - i3 - August 2004 - p152(1) [51-500]

Rhode, Deborah - *Access to Justice*
  BL - v101 - i3 - Oct 1 2004 - p287(2) [51-500]

Rhodes, Dan - *Timoleon Vieta Come Home: A Sentimental Journey (Illus. by Thuc, Vien)*
  NYTBR - Nov 7 2004 - p30 [501+]
  WLT - v78 - i3-4 - Sept-Dec 2004 - p97(1) [501+]

Rhodes, Danuta de - *The Little White Car*
  Ent W - i784 - Sept 17 2004 - p84 [501+]
  PW - v251 - i35 - August 30 2004 - p31(1) [501+]

Rhodes, Edward - *Presence, Prevention, and Persuasion: A Historical Analysis of Military Force and Political Influence*
  Choice - v41 - i11-12 - July-August 2004 - p2122(1) [501+]

Rhodes, Gary D. - *Horror at the Drive-In: Essays in Popular Culture*
  J POP F&TV - v32 - i3 - Fall 2004 - p143(2) [501+]

Rhodes, Glen - *Macromedia Flash MX 2004 Game Development*
  SciTech - v28 - i4 - Dec 2004 - p25(1) [51-500]

Rhodes, James A. - *Poetry Does Theology: Chaucer, Grosseteste, and the Pearl-Poet*
  JR - v85 - i1 - Jan 2005 - p185(2) [501+]

Rhodes, Jewel Parker - *Douglass' Women*
  BW - v34 - i5 - Feb 1 2004 - p13(1) [501+]

Rhodes, Linda Colvin - *Complete Idiot's Guide to Caring for Aging Parents*
  Bwatch - Oct 2004 - pNA [51-500]

Rhodes, Lorna A. - *Total Confinement: Madness and Reason in the Maximum Security Prison*
  Choice - v42 - i3 - Nov 2004 - p573(1) [1-50]
  Law&PolBR - June 2004 - p485(4) [501+]

Rhodes, Neil - *King James VI and I; Selected Writings*
  R&R Bk N - v19 - i1 - Feb 2004 - p32(1) [1-50]
Shakespeare and the Origin of English
  Choice - v42 - i7 - March 2005 - p1231(1) [51-500]

Rhodes, P.J. - *Ancient Democracy and Modern Ideology*
  Class R - v54 - i2 - Nov 2004 - p460(2) [501+]

Rhodes, R.A.W. - *Decentralizing the Civil Service: From Unitary State to Differentiated Polity in the United Kingdom*
  R&R Bk N - v19 - i1 - Feb 2004 - pNA [501+]

Rhodes, Richard - *John James Audubon: The Making of an American*
  Am Sci - v93 - i1 - Jan-Feb 2005 - p74(3) [501+]
  Aud - v106 - i5 - Nov-Dec 2004 - p94(4) [501+]
  BL - v100 - i22 - August 2004 - p1886(1) [51-500]
  BL - v101 - i9-10 - Jan 1 2005 - p766(1) [51-500]
  BW - v34 - i42 - Oct 17 2004 - p9(1) [501+]
  Econ - v372 - i8387 - August 7 2004 - p69US [501+]
  Ent W - i788 - Oct 15 2004 - p78 [51-500]
  LJ - v129 - i15 - Sept 15 2004 - p80(1) [51-500]
  NYTBR - Oct 31 2004 - p16 [501+]
  SciTech - v28 - i4 - Dec 2004 - p65(1) [51-500]

Rhodes, Shane - *Holding Pattern*
  Can Lit - i182 - Autumn 2004 - p167(3) [501+]

Rhyno, Art - *Using Open Source Systems for Digital Libraries*
  BL - v100 - i21 - July 2004 - p1859(1) [501+]
  SciTech - v28 - i1 - March 2004 - p180(1) [51-500]

Rhys, Jean - *Wide Sargasso Sea*
  Critq - v44 - Winter 2003 - p157 [501+]

Riaz, Ali - *God Willing: The Politics of Islamism in Bangladesh*
  Choice - v42 - i5 - Jan 2005 - p928(1) [51-500]
  R&R Bk N - v19 - i3 - August 2004 - p53(1) [51-500]

Riaz, Mian N. - *Halal Food Production*
  SciTech - v28 - i1 - March 2004 - p174(1) [51-500]

Riback, Estelle - *The Intimate Landscape*
  Bwatch - Jan 2005 - pNA [51-500]

Ribas, William B. - *Teacher Evaluation That Works, 2nd Ed.*
  R&R Bk N - v19 - i4 - Nov 2004 - p187(1) [501+]

Ribbens, William B. - *Understanding Automotive Electronics, 6th Ed.*
  SciTech - v28 - i1 - March 2004 - p168(1) [51-500]

Ribeiro, Marc - *Limiting Arbitrary Power: The Vagueness Doctrine in Canadian Constitutional Law*
  Law&PolBR - Nov 2004 - p882(7) [501+]
  R&R Bk N - v19 - i3 - August 2004 - p195(1) [501+]

Ribke, Simone T. - *The Shapes We Eat*
  c SLJ - v50 - i11 - Nov 2004 - p130(1) [51-500]

Ricahrdson, Adele - *Amphibians*
  c SB - v40 - i6 - Nov-Dec 2004 - p272(1) [51-500]

Ricard, Francois - *Agnes's Final Afternoon: An Essay on the Work of Milan Kundera*
  R&R Bk N - v19 - i1 - Feb 2004 - p218(1) [51-500]
  TLS - i5264 - Feb 20 2004 - p30-31 [501+]

Ricard, Matthieu - *Rainbows Appear: Tibetan Poems of Shabkar*
  Parabola - v29 - i2 - Summer 2004 - p100-106 [501+]

Ricardo, Catherine M. - *Databases Illuminated*
  SciTech - v28 - i4 - Dec 2004 - p30(1) [51-500]

Ricca, Ezio - *Bacterial Spore Formers: Probiotics and Emerging Applications*
  SciTech - v28 - i4 - Dec 2004 - p72(1) [51-500]

Ricci, David M. - *Good Citizenship in America*
  Choice - v42 - i6 - Feb 2005 - p1099(1) [51-500]

Ricciardelli, Marina - *Globalization and Multicultural Societies: Some Views from Europe*
  JEL - v41 - i4 - Dec 2003 - p1351(1) [501+]

Ricciardi, Alessia - *The Ends of Mourning: Psychoanalysis, Literature, Film*
  R&R Bk N - v19 - i1 - Feb 2004 - p220(1) [51-500]

Rice, Alan - *Radical Narratives of the Black Atlantic*
  J Am St - v38 - i1 - April 2004 - p159-160 [501+]

Rice, Albert R. - *The Clarinet in the Classical Period*
  Choice - v42 - i1 - Sept 2004 - p111(2) [501+]

Rice, Anne (b 1941 -) - *Blood Canticle (Read by Pittu, David). Audiobook Review*
  BL - v101 - i9-10 - Jan 1 2005 - p777(1) [1-50]

Rice, Anne P. - *Witnessing Lynching: American Writers Respond*
  R&R Bk N - v19 - i1 - Feb 2004 - p243(1) [51-500]

Rice, Chris - *Grace Matters: A True Story of Race, Friendship, and Faith in the Heart of the South*
  CC - v121 - i25 - Dec 14 2004 - p21(1) [51-500]

Rice, Christopher - *Light before Day*
  BL - v101 - i9-10 - Jan 1 2005 - p784(1) [1-50]
  KR - v73 - i1 - Jan 1 2005 - p17(1) [501+]
  LJ - v130 - i4 - March 1 2005 - p80(1) [51-500]
  PW - v252 - i7 - Feb 14 2005 - p54(1) [51-500]

Rice, H. William - *Ralph Ellison and the Politics of the Novel*
  R&R Bk N - v19 - i1 - Feb 2004 - p246(1) [51-500]

Rice, Hugh L. - *Construction Accounting Deskbook 2004: Financial, Tax, Accounting, Management, and Legal Answers, 5th Ed.*
  R&R Bk N - v19 - i2 - May 2004 - p120 [51-500]

Rice, John A. - *Empress Marie Therese and Music at the Viennese Court, 1792-1807*
  Choice - v41 - i7 - March 2004 - p1307(1) [501+]
  MT - v145 - i1886 - Spring 2004 - p112-116 [501+]
  TLS - i5292 - Sept 3 2004 - p27(1) [501+]

Rice, Luanne - *Beach Girls*
  y BL - v100 - i22 - August 2004 - p1910(1) [51-500]
Dance with Me (Read by Ziemba, Karen). Audiobook Review
  LJ - v130 - i3 - Feb 15 2005 - p169(1) [51-500]
Silver Bells: A Holiday Tale
  y BL - v101 - i4 - Oct 15 2004 - p394(1) [51-500]
  KR - v72 - i19 - Oct 1 2004 - p939(1) [501+]
  PW - v251 - i43 - Oct 25 2004 - p28(2) [501+]

Rice, Mabel L. - *Developmental Language Disorders: From Phenotypes to Etiologies*
  SciTech - v28 - i3 - Sept 2004 - p118(1) [51-500]

Rice, Patricia - *This Magic Moment*
  BL - v100 - i22 - August 2004 - p1910(1) [51-500]
  LJ - v129 - i13 - August 2004 - p56(1) [501+]

Rice, Prance Liamputtong - *Hmong Women and Reproduction*
  MAQ - v18 - i4 - Dec 2004 - p511(5) [501+]

Rice, Sean H. - *Evolutionary Theory; Mathematical and Conceptual Foundations*
  SciTech - v28 - i3 - Sept 2004 - p59(1) [1-50]

Rice, Stephen P. - *Minding the Machine: Languages of Class in Early Industrial America*
  Bwatch - Feb 2005 - pNA [51-500]

Rice, Stuart A. - *Advances in Chemical Physics, Vol. 128*
  SciTech - v28 - i1 - March 2004 - p55(1) [51-500]

Rich, Adrienne - *The School Among the Ruins: Poems, 2000-2004*
  BL - v100 - i22 - August 2004 - p1892(1) [51-500]
  BL - v101 - i9-10 - Jan 1 2005 - p768(1) [51-500]
  Lam Bk Rpt - v13 - i4-5 - Nov-Dec 2004 - p17(2) [501+]
  LJ - v129 - i13 - August 2004 - p86(1) [501+]
  Prog - v69 - i2 - Feb 2005 - p46(3) [501+]

Rich, Andrew - *Think Tanks, Public, and the Politics of Expertise*
  Choice - v42 - i2 - Oct 2004 - p373(1) [501+]

Rich, Lani Diane - *Time Off for Good Behavior*
  BL - v101 - i1 - Sept 1 2004 - p64(1) [51-500]

Rich, Mari - *World Authors 1995-2000*
  LibMed - v23 - i1 - August-Sept 2004 - p72(1) [51-500]

Rich, Norman - *Great Power Diplomacy since 1914*
  CEH - v37 - i3 - Summer 2004 - p472(3) [501+]

Rich, Norman M. - *Vascular Trauma, 2nd Ed.*
  SciTech - v28 - i3 - Sept 2004 - p113(1) [51-500]

Rich, Ronda - *What Southern Women Know*
  PW - v252 - i4 - Jan 24 2005 - p114(1) [501+]

Richard Bausch, Andrew Meier - *Black Earth: A Journey through Russia after the Fall*
  CR - v285 - i1663 - August 2004 - p126(1) [501+]

Richard, C.E. - *Louisiana: An Illustrated History*
  SHQ - v107 - i4 - April 2004 - p640(2) [501+]

Richard, Carl J. - *The Battle for the American Mind: A Brief History of a Nation's Thought*
  LJ - v129 - i16 - Oct 1 2004 - p95(1) [51-500]

Richard, Suzanne - *Near Eastern Archaeology: A Reader*
  Choice - v41 - i11-12 - July-August 2004 - p2100(1) [501+]

Richter, Kent E. - *Understanding Religion in a Global Society*
 R&R Bk N - v20 - i1 - Feb 2005 - p11(1) [51-500]

Richter, Ludwig - *Die Deutsche Volkspartei, 1918-1933*
 JMH - v76 - i4 - Dec 2004 - p992(4) [501+]

Richter, Melvin - *Dictatorship in History and Theory: Bonapartism, Caesarism, and Totalitarianism*
 HRNB - v33 - i1 - Fall 2004 - p27(1) [501+]

Richter, Ralph W. - *Alzheimer's Disease: A Physician's Guide to Practical Management*
 SciTech - v28 - i1 - March 2004 - p101(1) [51-500]

Richter, Thomas - *Self's Punishment*
 TLS - i5307 - Dec 17 2004 - p23(1) [501+]

Richter, William L. - *Historical Dictionary of the Civil War and Reconstruction*
 Choice - v42 - i3 - Nov 2004 - p468(1) [1-50]
 R&R Bk N - v19 - i3 - August 2004 - p68(1) [51-500]
 BL - v101 - i8 - Dec 15 2004 - p757(2) [501+]

Richter, Wolfgang - *Althebraische Inschriften transkribiert*
 JNES - v63 - i4 - Oct 2004 - p299(2) [501+]
Materialien einer althebraischen Datenbank: Wortfugungen.
 JNES - v63 - i4 - Oct 2004 - p300(2) [501+]

Rickard, John - *The Castle Community: The Personnel of English and Welsh Castles, 1272-1422*
 Albion - v36 - i1 - Spring 2004 - p88(3) [501+]

Rickard, John Nelson - *Patton at Bay: The Lorraine Campaign, 1944*
 R&R Bk N - v19 - i4 - Nov 2004 - p33(1) [51-500]

Ricke, Helmut - *Art Nouveau Glass: The Gerda Koepff Collection*
 Choice - v42 - i3 - Nov 2004 - p470(1) [1-50]
 LJ - v129 - i18 - Nov 1 2004 - p80(1) [501+]

Ricker, Joseph H. - *Differential Diagnosis in Adult Neuropsychological Assessment*
 SciTech - v28 - i1 - March 2004 - p94(1) [51-500]

Rickerl, Diane - *Agroecosystems Analysis*
 Choice - v42 - i2 - Oct 2004 - p316(1) [51-500]

Ricketts, Mark - *Lazarus Jack*
 PW - v251 - i45 - Nov 8 2004 - p38(1) [501+]

Ricketts, Shannon - *A Guide to Canadian Architectural Styles, 2nd Ed.*
 Choice - v41 - i11-12 - July-August 2004 - p2036(2) [501+]
 R&R Bk N - v19 - i3 - August 2004 - p241(1) [51-500]

Rickford, Russell J. - *Betty Shabazz: A Remarkable Story of Survival and Faith Before and After Malcolm X*
 R&R Bk N - v19 - i1 - Feb 2004 - p15(1) [51-500]

Ricklef, James - *Tarot: Get the Whole Story*
 Bwatch - Feb 2005 - pNA [51-500]

Rickman, Gregg - *The Science Fiction Film Reader*
 R&R Bk N - v19 - i3 - August 2004 - p263(1) [51-500]

Rickman, H.P. - *The Riddle of the Sphinx: Interpreting the Human World*
 R&R Bk N - v19 - i3 - August 2004 - p7(1) [1-50]

Rickman, Phil - *The Prayer of the Night Shepherd: The Sixth Merrily Watkins Mystery*
 KR - v72 - i17 - Sept 1 2004 - p841(1) [51-500]
 LJ - v129 - i16 - Oct 1 2004 - p65(1) [51-500]

Rico, Herminio, S.J. - *John Paul H. and the Legacy of "Dignitatis Humanae"*
 JR - v84 - i3 - July 2004 - p462(2) [501+]

Ricoeur, Paul - *Memory, History, Forgetting*
 LJ - v129 - i18 - Nov 1 2004 - p88(1) [51-500]

Riconda, Harry P. - *Prisoners of War in American Conflicts*
 Choice - v41 - i7 - March 2004 - p1358(1) [501+]

Ricou, Laurence - *Arbutus/Madrone Files: Reading the Pacific Northwest*
 CBRA - Annual 2003 - p261(1) [501+]

Riddell, Peter - *Hug Them Close: Blair, Clinton, Bush and the 'Special Relationship'*
 R&R Bk N - v19 - i3 - August 2004 - p38(1) [51-500]

Ridderbos, Katinka - *Time*
 Bwatch - Jan 2005 - pNA [51-500]

Riddick-Grisham, Susan - *Pediatric Life Care Planning and Case Management*
 SciTech - v28 - i4 - Dec 2004 - p112(1) [1-50]

Riddle, Peter H. - *American Musical: History and Development*
 CBRA - Annual 2003 - p109(1) [51-500]

Ride, Sally - *Exploring Our Solar System*
 LibMed - v22 - i7 - April-May 2004 - p79(1) [501+]
 c Sci Teach - v71 - i3 - March 2004 - p57-64 [501+]

Rideout, Vanda - *Continentalizing Canadian Telecommunications: The Politics of Regulatory Reform*
 R&R Bk N - v19 - i3 - August 2004 - p122(1) [51-500]

Rider, Alister McGrath - *The Twilight of Atheism: The Rise and Fall of Disbelief in the Modern World*
 Spec - v296 - i9192 - Oct 9 2004 - p52(1) [501+]

Ridgway, B.S. - *Hellenistic Sculpture III: The Styles of ca. 100-31 B.C.*
 Class R - v54 - i1 - May 2004 - p228(2) [501+]

Ridgway, Keith - *The Parts*
 Lam Bk Rpt - v13 - i1-2 - August-Sept 2004 - p29(2) [501+]

Riding, Leslie - *Dunton-Downer*
 c SLJ - v50 - i8 - August 2004 - p56(1) [51-500]

Ridinger, Robert B. - *Speaking for Our Lives: Historic Speeches and Rhetoric for Gay and Lesbian Rights: 1892-2000*
 Choice - v42 - i1 - Sept 2004 - p82(1) [501+]
 R&R Bk N - v19 - i2 - May 2004 - p133 [51-500]

Ridler, Anne - *Memories*
 Spec - v296 - i9194 - Oct 23 2004 - p55(1) [501+]

Ridley, Anne - *Cell Motility: From Molecules to Organisms*
 QRB - v79 - i4 - Dec 2004 - p416(2) [51-500]

Ridley, Glynis - *Clara's Grand Tour: Travels with a Rhinoceros in Eighteenth-Century Europe*
 y BL - v101 - i9-10 - Jan 1 2005 - p794(2) [51-500]
 Ent W - i810 - March 11 2005 - p107 [51-500]
 KR - v72 - i23 - Dec 1 2004 - p1138(2) [501+]
 LJ - v130 - i3 - Feb 15 2005 - p155(1) [51-500]
 New Sci - v183 - i2461 - August 21 2004 - p51(1) [501+]
 NS - v133 - i4696 - July 12 2004 - p54(2) [501+]
 PW - v251 - i49 - Dec 6 2004 - p49(1) [51-500]
 TLS - i5288 - August 6 2004 - p29(1) [51-500]

Ridley, Jane - *The Early Novels of Benjamin Disraeli, Vols. 1-6*
 TLS - i5304 - Nov 26 2004 - p24(1) [501+]

Ridley, Mark - *Evolution*
 QRB - v79 - i4 - Dec 2004 - p422(2) [501+]

Ridley, Matt - *The Agile Gene: How Nature Turns on Nurture*
 SciTech - v28 - i4 - Dec 2004 - p150(1) [51-500]

Ridley, Matthew - *How to Invest in Hedge Funds: An Investment Professional's Guide*
 R&R Bk N - v19 - i4 - Nov 2004 - p118(1) [51-500]

Ridley, Philip - *Daffodil Scissors*
 c Sch Lib - v52 - i4 - Winter 2004 - p211(1) [51-500]

Ridley, Ronald T. - *The Emperor's Retrospect: Augustus' Res gestai in Epigraphy, Historiography, and Commentary*
 R&R Bk N - v19 - i3 - August 2004 - p44(1) [51-500]

Ridpath, Ian - *Firefly Astronomy Dictionary, 3rd Rev. Ed.*
 SciTech - v28 - i1 - March 2004 - p42(1) [51-500]

Rieder, Jonathan - *The Fractious Nation?: Unity and Division in Contemporary American Life*
 CS - v33 - i6 - Nov 2004 - pNA [501+]

Riedmann, Bettina - *"Ich Bin Jude, Osterreicher, Deutscher." Judentum in Arthur Schnitzlers Tagebuchern und Briefen*
 GSR - v27 - i3 - Oct 2004 - p626(2) [501+]

Rieff, David - *At the Point of a Gun: Democratic Dreams and Armed Intervention*
 KR - v73 - i1 - Jan 1 2005 - p41(1) [501+]
 PW - v252 - i7 - Feb 14 2005 - p67(1) [51-500]

Rieffel, Lex - *"Indonesia's Quiet Revolution"*
 Wil Q - v29 - i1 - Wntr 2005 - p106(3) [501+]
Restructuring Sovereign Debt: The Case for Ad Hoc Machinery
 R&R Bk N - v19 - i1 - Feb 2004 - p121(1) [51-500]

Riegel, Christian - *Writing Grief: Margaret Laurence and the Work of Mourning*
 CBRA - Annual 2003 - p262(1) [501+]
 CWS - v23 - i3-4 - Spring-Summer 2004 - p215(3) [501+]

Rieger, Angelica - *Alter ego: Der Maler als Schatten des Schriftstellers in der franzosischen Erzahlliteratur von der Romantik bis zum fin de siecle*
 NCFS - v32 - i3-4 - Spring-Summer 2004 - p388(3) [501+]

Rieger, Joerg - *God and the Excluded: Visions and Blindspots in Contemporary Theology*
 JAAR - v72 - i4 - Dec 2004 - p1064(3) [501+]
Opting for the Margins: Postmodernity and Liberation in Christian Theology
 Intpr - v59 - i1 - Jan 2005 - p111(1) [51-500]

Riegl, Alois - *Historical Grammar of the Visual Arts*
 Afterimage - v32 - i4 - Jan-Feb 2005 - p15(1) [51-500]

Riegle, Rosalie G. - *Dorothy Day: Portraits by Those Who Knew Her*
 Comw - v132 - i1 - Jan 14 2005 - p26(4) [501+]
 TT - v61 - i3 - Oct 2004 - p426(1) [501+]

Riehl, Gene - *Sleeper*
 BL - v101 - i9-10 - Jan 1 2005 - p828(1) [51-500]
 KR - v73 - i1 - Jan 1 2005 - p17(1) [51-500]
 PW - v252 - i6 - Feb 7 2005 - p42(1) [501+]

Reilly, Edward J. - *Baseball and American Culture: Across the Diamond*
 Choice - v41 - i7 - March 2004 - p1332(1) [501+]

Reilly, Robin L. - *Karate for Kids (Illus. by Tok, Stephanie)*
 c BL - v101 - i1 - Sept 1 2004 - p111(1) [501+]
 c CH Bwatch - v14 - i8 - August 2004 - p1(1) [51-500]
 c PW - v251 - i28 - July 12 2004 - p66(1) [501+]
 c SLJ - v51 - i2 - Feb 2005 - p151(1) [51-500]

Rienner, Lynne - *Mexico under Fox*
 LJ - v129 - i12 - July 2004 - p104(1) [51-500]

Rienstra, Debra - *So Much More: An Invitation to Christian Spirituality*
 LJ - v130 - i4 - March 1 2005 - p94(1) [51-500]
 PW - v252 - i4 - Jan 24 2005 - p239(1) [501+]

Ries, Al - *The Origin of Brands: Discover the Natural Laws of Product Innovation and Business Survival*
 Bwatch - v26 - i8 - August 2004 - p8(1) [51-500]
 Choice - v42 - i6 - Feb 2005 - p1067(1) [51-500]
 Har Bus R - v82 - i10 - Oct 2004 - p32(1) [501+]

Ries, Laura - *Fall of Advertising and the Rise of PR*
 Bwatch - v26 - i8 - August 2004 - p8(1) [51-500]

Ries, Lori - *Super Sam! (Illus. by Rama, Sue)*
 c PW - v251 - i27 - July 5 2004 - p54(1) [51-500]
 c SLJ - v50 - i9 - Sept 2004 - p177(1) [51-500]

Rieser, Andrew C. - *The Chautauqua Moment: Protestants, Progressives, and the Culture of Modern Liberalism*
 Choice - v41 - i11-12 - July-August 2004 - p2109(2) [501+]
 JAH - v91 - i3 - Dec 2004 - p1047(1) [501+]
 JouAmCul - v27 - i3 - Sept 2004 - p358(2) [501+]
 R&R Bk N - v19 - i1 - Feb 2004 - p194(1) [51-500]

Riess, Jana - *What Would Buffy Do?*
 ChrSFF&H - v26 - i9 - Sept 2004 - p37(1) [51-500]

Rietveld, Piet - *Urban Transport*
 R&R Bk N - v19 - i3 - August 2004 - p121(1) [51-500]

Rifbjerg, Klaus - *Alea: En tilfaeldighedsroman*
 WLT - v79 - i1 - Jan-April 2005 - p101(1) [501+]

Rifert, V.G. - *Condensation Heat Transfer Enhancement*
 SciTech - v28 - i3 - Sept 2004 - p47(1) [1-50]

Riffenburgh, Beau - *Nimrod: Ernest Shackleton and the Extraordinary Story of the 1907-09 British Antarctic Expedition*
 TLS - i5304 - Nov 26 2004 - p32-33 [51-500]
Shackleton's Forgotten Expedition: The Voyage of the Nimrod
 y BL - v101 - i4 - Oct 15 2004 - p382(1) [51-500]
 KR - v72 - i18 - Sept 15 2004 - p906(1) [501+]
 PW - v251 - i39 - Sept 27 2004 - p46(1) [51-500]
 R&R Bk N - v20 - i1 - Feb 2005 - p81(1) [51-500]

Rifkin, Jeremy - *The European Dream: How Europe's Vision of the Future Is Quietly Eclipsing the American Dream*
 BL - v101 - i1 - Sept 1 2004 - p30(2) [51-500]
 Bus W - i3899 - Sept 13 2004 - p22 [51-500]
 BW - v34 - i41 - Oct 10 2004 - p6(1) [501+]
 Fut - v38 - i5 - Sept-Oct 2004 - p62(1) [51-500]
 Fut - v38 - i6 - Nov-Dec 2004 - p60(1) [51-500]
 Globe & Mail - Sept 4 2004 - pD10 [501+]
 Har Bus R - v82 - i9 - Sept 2004 - p26(1) [501+]
 NYRB - v52 - i2 - Feb 10 2005 - p37(5) [501+]
 PW - v251 - i28 - July 12 2004 - p56(2) [501+]
 Tikkun - v20 - i1 - Jan-Feb 2005 - p72(2) [501+]

Rifkin, L. - *The Nine Lives of Romeo Crumb: Life One (Illus. by Hartman, Kurt)*
 c SLJ - v51 - i1 - Jan 2005 - p135(2) [51-500]

Rigakos, George S. - *New Parapolice: Risk Markets and Commodified Social Control*
 CBRA - Annual 2003 - p318(2) [501+]

Rigby, S.H. - *A Companion to Britain in the Later Middle Ages*
 Albion - v36 - i1 - Spring 2004 - p94(2) [501+]

Rigden, John S. - *Einstein 1905: The Standard of Greatness*
  AS - v74 - i1 - Wntr 2005 - p127(3) [501+]
  y BL - v101 - i7 - Dec 1 2004 - p631(1) [51-500]
  Globe & Mail - Jan 15 2005 - pD9 [501+]
  PW - v251 - i45 - Nov 8 2004 - p42(1) [501+]
Rigg, Bryan Mark - *Hitler's Jewish Soldiers: The Untold Story of Nazi Racial Laws and Men of Jewish Descent in the German Military*
  HNet - August 2004 - pNA [501+]
  Rescued from the Reich: How One of Hitler's Solciers Saved the Lubavitcher Rebbe
  Lon R Bks - v26 - i21 - Nov 4 2004 - p12(1) [1-50]
  Rescued from the Reich: How One of Hitler's Soldiers Saved the Lubavitcher Rebbe
  BL - v101 - i5 - Nov 1 2004 - p456(1) [51-500]
  LJ - v129 - i19 - Nov 15 2004 - p71(1) [501+]
  PW - v251 - i42 - Oct 18 2004 - p57(1) [51-500]
Riggins, Stephen Harold - *Pleasures of Time: Two Men, a Life*
  CBRA - Annual 2003 - p66(2) [501+]
Riggs, Cliff - *Network Perimeter Security: Building Defense In-Depth*
  SciTech - v28 - i1 - March 2004 - p150(1) [51-500]
Riggs, Cynthia - *The Paperwhite Narcissus*
  KR - v73 - i5 - March 1 2005 - p264(1) [51-500]
  PW - v252 - i10 - March 7 2005 - p53(1) [51-500]
Riggs, David - *The World of Christopher Marlowe*
  NL - v87 - i6 - Nov-Dec 2004 - p37(3) [501+]
  BL - v101 - i9-10 - Jan 1 2005 - p802(1) [51-500]
  Globe & Mail - March 19 2005 - pD13 [501+]
  KR - v72 - i20 - Oct 15 2004 - p996(1) [501+]
  LJ - v130 - i1 - Jan 1 2005 - p112(1) [501+]
  Lon R Bks - v26 - i16 - August 19 2004 - p11(4) [501+]
  NYTBR - Jan 2 2005 - p8 [501+]
  PW - v251 - i43 - Oct 25 2004 - p34(1) [51-500]
Riggs, Henry E. - *Financial and Economic Analysis for Engineering and Technology Management, 2nd Ed.*
  R&R Bk N - v19 - i3 - August 2004 - p131(1) [51-500]
Righter, William - *American Memory in Henry James: Void and Value*
  ELT - v48 - i2 - Spring 2005 - p104(5) [501+]
  TLS - i5295 - Sept 24 2004 - p3-4 [501+]
Rigolot, Francois - *L'Erreur de la Renaissance*
  FS - v58 - i2 - April 2004 - p245(2) [501+]
Rigsbee, David - *The Dissolving Island*
  South CR - v36 - i2 - Spring 2004 - p184-187 [501+]
Rihtman-Augustin, Dunja - *Ethnology, Myth and Politics: Anthropologizing Croatian Ethnology*
  R&R Bk N - v19 - i4 - Nov 2004 - p42(1) [51-500]
Rijker, Roelof - *Nuclear Physics, Large and Small: Proceedings*
  SciTech - v28 - i4 - Dec 2004 - p51(1) [51-500]
Rijn, Guido van - *The Truman and Eisenhower Blues: African-American Blues and Gospel Songs, 1945-1960*
  Choice - v42 - i5 - Jan 2005 - p862(1) [1-50]
Riles, Annelise - *The Network Inside Out*
  Cont Pac - v16 - i2 - Fall 2004 - p443(3) [501+]
Riley, Barbara - *Grow Grow Grow*
  c CH Bwatch - v14 - i12 - Dec 2004 - pNA [51-500]
Riley, Charles A., II - *The Jazz Age in France*
  NYTBR - Dec 5 2004 - p58 [501+]
Riley, Christopher - *Hollywood Standard: The Complete and Authoritative Guide to Script Format and Style*
  PW - v252 - i6 - Feb 7 2005 - p56(1) [51-500]
Riley, Glenda - *Taking Land, Breaking Land: Women Colonizing the American West and Kenya, 1840-1940*
  Choice - v41 - i11-12 - July-August 2004 - p2099(1) [501+]
  Wild Women of the Old West
  SHQ - v107 - i4 - April 2004 - p634(2) [501+]
Riley, James C. - *Rising Life Expectancy: A Global History*
  JIH - v35 - i1 - Summer 2004 - p114-115 [501+]
Riley, Jeni - *Learning in the Early Years: A Guide for Teachers of Children 3-7*
  R&R Bk N - v19 - i1 - Feb 2004 - p183(1) [51-500]
Riley, Lee W. - *Molecular Epidemiology of Infectious Diseases: Principles and Practices*
  SciTech - v28 - i3 - Sept 2004 - p83(1) [501+]
Riley, Mary - *Indigenous Intellectual Property Rights: Legal Obstacles and Innovative Solutions*
  R&R Bk N - v19 - i4 - Nov 2004 - p165(1) [501+]
Riley, Nano - *Florida's Farmworkers in the Twenty-First Century (Illus. by Johns, Davida)*
  JSH - v70 - i3 - August 2004 - p711(2) [501+]

Riley, Naomi Schaefer - *God on the Quad: How Religious Colleges and the Missionary Generation Are Changing America*
  BL - v101 - i9-10 - Jan 1 2005 - p792(1) [1-50]
  KR - v72 - i22 - Nov 15 2004 - p1083(2) [501+]
  PW - v251 - i48 - Nov 29 2004 - p38(1) [51-500]
Riley, Noel - *The Elements of Design*
  Ant&CM - v108 - i11 - Jan 2004 - p16(1) [501+]
Riley, Peter D. - *Animals*
  c SLJ - v50 - i7 - July 2004 - p95(1) [51-500]
  Habitats
  c SLJ - v50 - i7 - July 2004 - p95(1) [51-500]
  Life Cycles
  c SLJ - v50 - i7 - July 2004 - p95(1) [51-500]
Riley, Robert Q. - *Alternative Cars in the Twenty-First Century: A New Personal Transportation Paradigm, 2nd Ed.*
  SciTech - v28 - i1 - March 2004 - p166(1) [51-500]
Riley, Robin - *Film, Faith, and Cultural Conflict: The Case of Martin Scorsese's 'The Last Temptation of Christ'*
  R&R Bk N - v19 - i1 - Feb 2004 - p226(1) [1-50]
Rilke, Rainer Maria - *Auguste Rodin*
  NYTBR - August 1 2004 - p12 [51-500]
  The Poet's Guide to Life: The Wisdom of Rilke
  LJ - v130 - i4 - March 1 2005 - p86(1) [51-500]
  Sonnets to Orpheus
  AM - v191 - i4 - August 16 2004 - p25 [501+]
Rimbaud, Arthur - *I Promise to Be Good: The Letters of Arthur Rimbaud*
  Globe & Mail - Dec 24 2004 - pD3 [1-50]
  Oeuvres completes, Tome IV: Fac-similes
  NCFS - v33 - i1-2 - Fall-Winter 2004 - p216(3) [501+]
  Rimbaud Complete
  TLS - i5268 - March 19 2004 - p8-9 [501+]
Rimell, Victoria - *Petronius and the Anatomy of Fiction*
  AJP - v125 - i1 - Spring 2004 - p152-155 [501+]
  Class R - v54 - i2 - Nov 2004 - p403(3) [501+]
Rimer, J. Thomas - *Art of the Japanese Postcard: The Leonard A. Lauder Collection at the Museum of Fine Arts, Boston*
  LJ - v129 - i14 - Sept 1 2004 - p146(2) [51-500]
Rimes, LeAnn - *Jag's New Friend (Illus. by Bernal, Richard)*
  c SLJ - v51 - i2 - Feb 2005 - p109(1) [51-500]
Rimington, Stella - *At Risk*
  Ent W - i801 - Jan 14 2005 - p92 [51-500]
  KR - v72 - i22 - Nov 15 2004 - p1066(1) [501+]
  LJ - v129 - i20 - Dec 1 2004 - p102(1) [51-500]
  People - v63 - i1 - Jan 10 2005 - p46 [51-500]
  PW - v251 - i48 - Nov 29 2004 - p24(1) [51-500]
  Time - v165 - i7 - Feb 14 2005 - p58 [501+]
Rinaldi, Ann - *Brooklyn Rose*
  Kliatt - v38 - i6 - Nov 2004 - p11(1) [501+]
  KR - v72 - i24 - Dec 15 2004 - p1207(1) [51-500]
  y PW - v252 - i2 - Jan 10 2005 - p56(1) [51-500]
  y SLJ - v51 - i1 - Jan 2005 - p129(1) [51-500]
  The Fifth of March: A Story of the Boston Massacre (Illus. by Hughes, Melissa). Audiobook Review
  y BL - v101 - i3 - Oct 1 2004 - p352(1) [51-500]
  Nine Days a Queen: The Short Life and Reign of Lady Jane Grey
  y BL - v101 - i7 - Dec 1 2004 - p648(1) [51-500]
  y CCB-B - v58 - i6 - Feb 2005 - p263(2) [51-500]
  y KR - v73 - i1 - Jan 1 2005 - p56(1) [51-500]
  Or Give Me Death: A Novel of Patrick Henry's Family
  y Kliatt - v38 - i5 - Sept 2004 - p25(3) [501+]
Rinaldi, Harriette - *Born at the Battlefield of Gettysburg*
  Bwatch - Nov 2004 - pNA [501+]
Rinaldi, Nicholas - *Between Two Rivers*
  LJ - v129 - i12 - July 2004 - p74(1) [51-500]
  Time - v164 - i10 - Sept 6 2004 - p87 [501+]
Rinck, Maranke - *The Prince Child (Illus. by Linden, Martijn van der)*
  c KR - v72 - i19 - Oct 1 2004 - p967(1) [51-500]
  c PW - v252 - i2 - Jan 10 2005 - p54(1) [51-500]
  Rinck, Maranke. The Prince Child (Illus. by Linden, Martijn van der)
  SLJ - v50 - i12 - Dec 2004 - p118(1) [501+]
Rindermann, Georg - *Venture Capitalist Participation and the Performance of IPO Firms: Empirical Evidence from France, Germany, and the UK*
  R&R Bk N - v19 - i3 - August 2004 - p136(1) [51-500]
Rinear, Davis L. - *Stage, Page, Scandals, and Vandals: William E. Burton and Nineteenth-Century American Theatre*
  Choice - v42 - i4 - Dec 2004 - p673(1) [1-50]
Rinehart, Robert E. - *To the Extreme: Alternative Sports, Inside and Out*
  SSJ - v21 - i1 - March 2004 - p108-110 [501+]

Rinehart, Steven - *Built in a Day: A Novel*
  Kliatt - v38 - i6 - Nov 2004 - p20(1) [51-500]
Rinehart, Susie - *Eliza and the Dragonfly (Illus. by Hovemann, Anisa Claire)*
  c SB - v40 - i4 - July-August 2004 - p180(1) [51-500]
Ring, Jim - *Riviera: The Rise and Rise of the Cote d'Azur*
  CR - v285 - i1667 - Dec 2004 - p380(1) [51-500]
  TLS - i5288 - August 6 2004 - p25(1) [501+]
Ring, Susan - *Earth*
  c SB - v40 - i6 - Nov-Dec 2004 - p266(1) [51-500]
  Election Connection: The Official Nick Guide to Electing the President
  c PW - v251 - i28 - July 12 2004 - p66(1) [51-500]
  Jupiter
  c SB - v40 - i6 - Nov-Dec 2004 - p266(1) [51-500]
  Mars
  c SB - v40 - i6 - Nov-Dec 2004 - p266(1) [51-500]
  Mercury
  c SB - v40 - i6 - Nov-Dec 2004 - p266(1) [51-500]
  Neptune
  c SB - v40 - i6 - Nov-Dec 2004 - p266(1) [51-500]
  Pluto
  c SB - v40 - i6 - Nov-Dec 2004 - p266(1) [51-500]
  Project Orangutan
  c SB - v40 - i4 - July-August 2004 - p180(1) [51-500]
  Saturn
  c SB - v40 - i6 - Nov-Dec 2004 - p266(1) [51-500]
  Uranus
  c SB - v40 - i6 - Nov-Dec 2004 - p266(1) [51-500]
  Venus
  c SB - v40 - i6 - Nov-Dec 2004 - p266(1) [51-500]
Ringdal, Nils - *Love for Sale: A Global History of Prostitution*
  Spec - v297 - i9206 - Jan 15 2005 - p41(2) [501+]
Ringgold, Faith - *If a Bus Could Talk: The Story of Rosa Parks (Illus. by Ringgold, Faith)*
  c SLJ - v50 - i10 - Oct 2004 - p66(1) [51-500]
  O Holy Night: Christmas with the Boys Choir of Harlem
  c PW - v251 - i39 - Sept 27 2004 - p60(1) [51-500]
Ringo, John - *Cally's War*
  Bwatch - Dec 2004 - pNA [501+]
Ringrose, Kathryn M. - *The Perfect Servant: Eunuchs and the Social Construction of Gender in Byzantium*
  AHR - v109 - i2 - April 2004 - p585(2) [501+]
  Choice - v41 - i7 - March 2004 - p1353(1) [501+]
  J Soc H - v38 - i2 - Winter 2004 - p522(3) [501+]
  VQR - v80 - i1 - Wntr 2004 - p261-262 [501+]
Ringuest, Jeffrey L. - *Models and Methods for Project Selection: Concepts from Management Science, Finance, and Information Technology*
  R&R Bk N - v19 - i1 - Feb 2004 - p94(1) [1-50]
Rinke, Wolf J. - *Don't Oil the Squeaky Wheel: And 19 Other Contrarian Ways to Improve Your Leadership Effectiveness*
  HR Mag - v50 - i2 - Feb 2005 - pS8(1) [501+]
Rio, Nela - *During Nights That Undress Other Nights*
  CBRA - Annual 2003 - p229(1) [51-500]
Riordan, James - *The Gift*
  y Sch Lib - v52 - i3 - Autumn 2004 - p162(1) [501+]
Riordan, Jan - *Breastfeeding and Human Lactation, 3rd Ed.*
  SciTech - v28 - i3 - Sept 2004 - p117(1) [51-500]
Riordan, Rebecca M. - *Seeing Data: Designing User Interfaces for Database Systems Using .NET*
  SciTech - v28 - i4 - Dec 2004 - p33(1) [51-500]
Riordan, Rick - *Southtown*
  BooChiTr - May 2 2004 - p3(1) [501+]
Riordan, Teresa - *Inventing Beauty: A History of the Innovations That Have Made Us Beautiful*
  BL - v101 - i2 - Sept 15 2004 - p184(1) [51-500]
  Globe & Mail - Jan 15 2005 - pL2 [501+]
  LJ - v129 - i14 - Sept 1 2004 - p174(1) [51-500]
  NYTBR - Dec 12 2004 - p21 [501+]
  PW - v251 - i30 - July 26 2004 - p45(1) [501+]
Rios-Font, Wadda C. - *The Canon and the Archive: Configuring Literature in Modern Spain*
  Choice - v42 - i6 - Feb 2005 - p1027(1) [51-500]
  R&R Bk N - v19 - i4 - Nov 2004 - p231(1) [501+]
Rip, Michael Russell - *The Precision Revolution: GPS and the Future of Aerial Warfare*
  T&C - v45 - i4 - Oct 2004 - p883(2) [501+]
Ripken, Cal, Jr. - *Play Baseball the Ripken Way*
  c BW - v34 - i35 - August 2004 - p11(1) [1-50]
Ripley, Tim - *The Wehrmacht: The German Army in World War II 1939-1945*
  GSR - v27 - i3 - Oct 2004 - p648(2) [501+]
Rippe, James M. - *Weight Watchers Weight Loss That Lasts: Break through the 10 Big Diet Myths*
  LJ - v130 - i1 - Jan 1 2005 - p144(3) [501+]
  PW - v252 - i3 - Jan 17 2005 - p49(1) [51-500]

Rippin, Sally - *Gezani and the Tricky Baboon*
　LibMed - v22 - i5 - Feb 2004 - p64(1) [501+]

Ripple, Dean C. - *Temperature: Its Measurement and Control in Science and Industry, Proceedings, Vol. 7*
　SciTech - v28 - i1 - March 2004 - p48(1) [51-500]

Rippley, L.J. - *Trail by Fire and Battle in Medieval German Literature*
　Choice - v42 - i5 - Jan 2005 - p857(1) [1-50]

Rips, Michael - *The Face of a Naked Lady: An Omaha Family Mystery*
　BL - v101 - i9-10 - Jan 1 2005 - p809(2) [1-50]
　Esq - v143 - i3 - March 2005 - p60(1) [1-50]
　KR - v73 - i1 - Jan 1 2005 - p41(1) [51-500]
　NYT - March 12 2005 - pB7 [501+]
　PW - v252 - i8 - Feb 21 2005 - p170(1) [51-500]

Risby, Bonnie - *Analogy Roundup*
　c Cur R - v44 - i6 - Feb 2005 - p13(1) [501+]

Rischin, Rebecca - *For the End of Time: The Story of the Messiaen Quartet*
　HNet - Nov 2004 - pNA [501+]
　MT - v145 - i1886 - Spring 2004 - p91-96 [501+]
　Notes - v61 - i2 - Dec 2004 - p423(3) [501+]
　TLS - i5288 - August 6 2004 - p18(1) [501+]

Riser, John - *Democracy: An Alternate View*
　R&R Bk N - v19 - i3 - August 2004 - p175(1) [501+]

Rishinevsky, Vera - *Russian Immigrants in the United States: Adapting to American Culture*
　R&R Bk N - v19 - i4 - Nov 2004 - p59(1) [51-500]

Rising, Marsha Hoffman - *The Family Tree Problem Solver: Proven Methods for Scaling the Inevitable Brick Wall*
　BL - v101 - i9-10 - Jan 1 2005 - p810(1) [1-50]

Riskin, Jessica - *Science in the Age of Sensibility: The Sentimental Empiricists of the French Enlightenment*
　AHR - v109 - i2 - April 2004 - p627(2) [501+]
　JIH - v35 - i1 - Summer 2004 - p130-131 [501+]
　JMH - v77 - i1 - March 2005 - p195(3) [501+]

Risley, Judy S. - *Unknown Man*
　Roundup M - v11 - i6 - August 2004 - p29(1) [501+]

Risoluti, Piero - *Nuclear Waste: A Technological and Political Challenge*
　Choice - v41 - i11-12 - July-August 2004 - p2076(1) [501+]

Risso, Eduardo - *100 Bullets: First Shot, Last Call*
　KR - v72 - i19 - Oct 1 2004 - pNA [501+]

Rist, John M. - *Real Ethics: Rethinking the Foundations of Morality*
　Ethics - v115 - i1 - Oct 2004 - p189(1) [501+]

Risteau, Delores - *American Payroll Association Basic Guide to Payroll: 2004, Rev. Ed.*
　R&R Bk N - v19 - i4 - Nov 2004 - p170(1) [501+]

Ritchey, David A. - *Innovative Ideas for School Business Officials: Best Practices from ASBO's Pinnacle Awards*
　R&R Bk N - v19 - i3 - August 2004 - p223(1) [1-50]

Ritchie, Brent W. - *Sport Tourism: Interrelationships, Impacts and Issues*
　R&R Bk N - v19 - i4 - Nov 2004 - p72(1) [51-500]

Ritchie, Donald A. - *The Congress of the United States: A Student Companion*
　c SLJ - v50 - i8 - August 2004 - p50(1) [51-500]
　Executive Sessions of the Senate Permanent Subcommittee on Investigations of the Committee on Government Operations
　Pub Hist - v26 - i3 - Summer 2004 - p86(90) [501+]
　Reporting from Washington: The History of the Washington Press Corps
　CJR - v43 - i5 - Jan-Feb 2005 - p58(4) [501+]
　KR - v73 - i1 - Jan 1 2005 - p41(1) [501+]
　PW - v252 - i5 - Jan 31 2005 - p57(1) [51-500]

Ritchie, John - *Australian Dictionary of Biography, Vol. 16*
　AHS - v35 - i123 - April 2004 - p181-182 [501+]

Ritchie, Nigel - *The Civil Rights Movement*
　LibMed - v22 - i4 - Jan 2004 - p76(1) [501+]
　c SLJ - v50 - i10 - Oct 2004 - p67(1) [51-500]

Ritchie, Pamela E. - *Mary of Guise in Scotland, 1548-1560: A Political Career*
　AHR - v109 - i2 - April 2004 - p606(2) [501+]
　Albion - v36 - i1 - Spring 2004 - p187(3) [501+]
　Six Ct J - v35 - i1 - Spring 2004 - p293(3) [501+]

Ritchie, Robert - *Historical Atlas of the Renaissance*
　y R&R Bk N - v19 - i4 - Nov 2004 - p29(1) [501+]
　y SLJ - v51 - i2 - Feb 2005 - p84(2) [51-500]
　y VOYA - v27 - i5 - Dec 2004 - p419(1) [51-500]

Ritschel, Wolfgang A. - *Handbook of Basic Pharmacokinetics: Including Clinical Application, 6th Ed.*
　E-Streams - Dec 2004 - pNA [501+]
　SciTech - v28 - i3 - Sept 2004 - p122(1) [51-500]

Rittenberg, Larry E. - *Auditing Concepts for a Changing Environment, 5th Ed.*
　R&R Bk N - v19 - i4 - Nov 2004 - p114(1) [51-500]

Ritter, Archibald R.M. - *The Cuban Economy*
　Choice - v42 - i4 - Dec 2004 - p708(1) [1-50]

Ritter, Erika - *The Great Big Book of Guys: Alphabetical Encounters with Men*
　Globe & Mail - Oct 30 2004 - pD14 [501+]

Ritter, Gerhard A. - *Geschichte des deutschen Parlamentarismus*
　JMH - v76 - i4 - Dec 2004 - p988(3) [501+]

Ritter, Hellmut - *The Ocean of the Soul: Men, the World and God in the Stories of Farid al-Din Attar*
　HNet - Sept 2004 - pNA [501+]

Ritter, John H. - *The Boy Who Saved Baseball (Read by Ramirez, Robert). Audiobook Review*
　c Kliatt - v38 - i4 - July 2004 - p48(1) [51-500]

Ritter, Kurt - *Presidential Speechwriting: From the New Deal to the Reagan Revolution and Beyond*
　JAH - v91 - i2 - Sept 2004 - p721(3) [501+]

Ritter, R.M. - *The Oxford Style Manual*
　R&R Bk N - v19 - i1 - Feb 2004 - p221(1) [51-500]

Rittgers, Ronald K. - *The Reformation of the Keys: Confession, Conscience, and Authority in Sixteenth-Century Germany*
　CH - v73 - i4 - Dec 2004 - p855(3) [501+]
　Choice - v42 - i3 - Nov 2004 - p501(1) [501+]

Rittner, Carol - *Genocide in Rwanda: Complicity of the Churches*
　Choice - v42 - i7 - March 2005 - p1242(1) [51-500]
　R&R Bk N - v19 - i4 - Nov 2004 - p52(1) [1-50]

Rittner, Don - *Encyclopedia of Biology*
　Choice - v42 - i6 - Feb 2005 - p1000(1) [501+]
　SciTech - v28 - i4 - Dec 2004 - p60(1) [51-500]

Ritzer, George - *The Blackwell Companion to Major Classical Social Theorists*
　CS - v33 - i1 - Jan 2004 - p129-129 [501+]
　The Blackwell Companion to Major Contemporary Social Theorists
　CS - v33 - i1 - Jan 2004 - p129-130 [501+]
　Enchanting a Disenchanted World: Revolutionalizing the Means of Consumption, 2nd Ed.
　R&R Bk N - v19 - i4 - Nov 2004 - p89(1) [51-500]
　Encyclopedia of Social Theory, Vols. 1-2
　Choice - v42 - i7 - March 2005 - p1207(1) [51-500]
　LJ - v130 - i1 - Jan 1 2005 - p154(1) [51-500]
　R&R Bk N - v19 - i4 - Nov 2004 - p82(1) [51-500]
　The McDonaldization of Society, Rev. New Century Ed.
　Choice - v42 - i3 - Nov 2004 - p573(1) [1-50]
　JouAmCul - v27 - i3 - Sept 2004 - p359(2) [501+]
　R&R Bk N - v19 - i2 - May 2004 - p127 [51-500]

Rivas, Mim Eichler - *Beautiful Jim Key: The Lost History of a Horse and a Man Who Changed the World*
　Ent W - i806 - Feb 11 2005 - p68 [51-500]
　KR - v73 - i1 - Jan 1 2005 - p42(1) [501+]
　LJ - v130 - i1 - Jan 1 2005 - p138(1) [51-500]
　PW - v252 - i2 - Jan 10 2005 - p48(1) [51-500]

River, Uncle - *Prometheus: The Autobiography*
　y Analog - v124 - i6 - June 2004 - p132(6) [501+]

Rivera-Garza, Cristina - *No One Will Sea Me Cry*
　WLT - v78 - i3-4 - Sept-Dec 2004 - p146(2) [501+]

Rivera, Raquel Z. - *New York Ricans from the Hip Hop Zone*
　CS - v33 - i1 - Jan 2004 - p130-130 [501+]

Rivera, Roberto - *A Study of Liberation Discourse: The Semantics of Opposition in Freire and Gutierrez*
　R&R Bk N - v19 - i1 - Feb 2004 - p4(1) [51-500]

Rivero, Albert J. - *The Eighteenth-Century Novel, Vol. 3*
　R&R Bk N - v19 - i1 - Feb 2004 - p235(1) [51-500]

Rivero, Horacio Chiong - *The Rise of Pseudo-Historical Fiction: Fray Antonio de Guevara's Novelizations*
　R&R Bk N - v19 - i4 - Nov 2004 - p231(1) [501+]

Rivero Marin, Rosanna - *Janus Identities and Forked Tongues: Two Caribbean Writers in the United States*
　R&R Bk N - v19 - i1 - Feb 2004 - p246(1) [51-500]

Rivers, Francine - *A Voice in the Wind (Read by Ferrone, Richard). Audiobook Review*
　LJ - v130 - i4 - March 1 2005 - p124(1) [51-500]
　The Warrior
　LJ - v130 - i2 - Feb 1 2005 - p62(1) [51-500]

Rivers in American Life and Times
　c LibMed - v23 - i3 - Nov-Dec 2004 - p83(1) [51-500]

Rivers, Karen - *Gold Diggers Club*
　y Can CL - i111-112 - Fall-Winter 2003 - p139(8) [501+]
　The Healing Time of Hickeys
　y BL - v100 - i22 - August 2004 - p1920(1) [51-500]
　y CBRA - Annual 2003 - p509(2) [51-500]
　y VOYA - v27 - i3 - August 2004 - p224(1) [1-50]

Rivers, R.W. - *Basic Physics: Notes for Traffic Crash Investigators and Reconstructionists: An Introduction for Some, a Review for Others*
　R&R Bk N - v19 - i3 - August 2004 - p168(1) [501+]

Rivers, Reggie - *4th and Fixed*
　BL - v100 - i21 - July 2004 - p1820(1) [1-50]
　PW - v251 - i34 - August 23 2004 - p38(1) [51-500]

Rivers, Vickie - *The Branch Librarians' Handbook*
　LJ - v130 - i1 - Jan 1 2005 - p160(1) [51-500]

Rivers, Victor - *A Private Family Matter: A Memoir*
　KR - v73 - i2 - Jan 15 2005 - p111(1) [501+]
　PW - v252 - i9 - Feb 28 2005 - p51(1) [51-500]

Rivett, Bess Burrows - *Looking West*
　CBRA - Annual 2003 - p67(1) [51-500]

Riviere, Francois - *Voyage into the Deep*
　y VOYA - v27 - i3 - August 2004 - p233(1) [1-50]

Riviere, William - *By the Grand Canal*
　BL - v101 - i9-10 - Jan 1 2005 - p822(2) [501+]
　KR - v72 - i23 - Dec 1 2004 - p1112(1) [501+]
　LJ - v130 - i2 - Feb 1 2005 - p70(1) [51-500]
　PW - v252 - i1 - Jan 3 2005 - p33(1) [51-500]
　Spec - v296 - i9190 - Sept 25 2004 - p52(1) [501+]
　TLS - i5301 - Nov 5 2004 - p24(1) [501+]

Rivkin, Steve - *The Making of a Name: The Inside Story of the Brands We Buy*
　LJ - v130 - i1 - Jan 1 2005 - p126(1) [51-500]
　PW - v252 - i1 - Jan 3 2005 - p50(1) [51-500]

Rivlin, Ray - *Shalom Ireland: A Social History of Jews in Modern Ireland*
　ILS - v24 - i1 - Fall 2004 - p7(1) [501+]
　TLS - i5265 - Feb 27 2004 - p33-33 [501+]

Rivoli, Pietra - *The Travels of a T-Shirt in the Global Economy: An Economist Examines the Markets, Power and Politics of World Trade*
　PW - v252 - i11 - March 14 2005 - p61(1) [51-500]
　Time - v165 - i13 - March 28 2005 - pA4 [501+]

Rizakis, A.D. - *La cite de Patras: epigraphie et histoire*
　Class R - v54 - i1 - May 2004 - p222(2) [501+]
　Roman Peloponnese I. Roman Personal Names in their Social Context
　Class R - v54 - i1 - May 2004 - p138(2) [501+]

Rizcallah, Marcel - *I.D.A.P. Directories*
　SciTech - v28 - i1 - March 2004 - p157(1) [51-500]

Rizi, Fabio Fernando - *Benedetto Croce and Italian Fascism*
　CBRA - Annual 2003 - p67(2) [51-500]

Rizzi, Anthony - *The Science Before Science: A Guide to Thinking in the 21st Century*
　Choice - v42 - i6 - Feb 2005 - p1042(1) [51-500]
　RM - v58 - i1 - Sept 2004 - p190(1) [501+]

Rizzo, Matthew - *Principles and Practice of Behavioral Neurology and Neuropsychology*
　SciTech - v28 - i1 - March 2004 - p94(1) [51-500]

Rmachandran, V.S. - *A Brief Tour of Human Consciousness*
　SB - v41 - i1 - Jan-Feb 2005 - p16(1) [501+]

Ro, Ronin - *Tales to Astonish: Jack Kirby, Stan Lee, and the American Comic Book Revolution*
　Bwatch - Feb 2005 - pNA [51-500]
　Ent W - i774 - July 16 2004 - p82 [501+]
　R&R Bk N - v19 - i4 - Nov 2004 - p229(1) [501+]

Roach, Kent - *September 11: Consequences for Canada*
　CBRA - Annual 2003 - p297(1) [501+]

Roach, Marilynne K. - *In the Days of the Salem Witchcraft Trials*
　Kliatt - v38 - i4 - July 2004 - p42(1) [51-500]

Roach, Mary - *Stiff: The Curious Lives of Human Cadavers*
　Kliatt - v38 - i6 - Nov 2004 - p40(1) [51-500]

Roberts, Gregory David - *Shantaram*
　BL - v101 - i1 - Sept 1 2004 - p6(2) [51-500]
　KR - v72 - i15 - August 1 2004 - p711(1) [501+]
　LJ - v129 - i13 - August 2004 - p70(1) [51-500]
　NYTBR - Dec 26 2004 - p17 [501+]
　People - v62 - i19 - Nov 8 2004 - p57 [51-500]
　PW - v251 - i34 - August 23 2004 - p35(1) [501+]
Roberts, Hugh - *The Battlefield Algeria, 1988-2002: Studies in a Broken Polity*
　JPR - v41 - i4 - July 2004 - p523-523 [501+]
　S&S - v68 - i1 - Spring 2004 - p105-107 [501+]
Roberts, J. Timmons - *Trouble in Paradise: Globalization and Environmental Crises in Latin America*
　JEL - v41 - i4 - Dec 2003 - p1413(1) [501+]
　T&C - v45 - i3 - July 2004 - p636-638 [501+]
Roberts, James R. - *Clinical Procedures in Emergency Medicine, 4th Ed.*
　SciTech - v28 - i1 - March 2004 - p89(1) [51-500]
Roberts, Jeffery J. - *The Origins of Conflict in Afghanistan*
　APJ - v18 - i3 - Fall 2004 - p119(3) [501+]
　Choice - v42 - i1 - Sept 2004 - p167(1) [501+]
　MEJ - v58 - i4 - Autumn 2004 - p678(2) [501+]
Roberts, Jennifer L. - *Mirror-Travels: Robert Smithson and History*
　TLS - i5300 - Oct 29 2004 - p12(1) [501+]
Roberts, Jennifer T. - *The Ancient Greek World*
　y Ref Rev - August 2004 - pNA [501+]
　c SLJ - v50 - i8 - August 2004 - p142(1) [51-500]
Roberts, Jeremy - *Chinese Mythology A to Z*
　c SLJ - v50 - i10 - Oct 2004 - p95(2) [51-500]
Japanese Mythology A to Z
　SLJ - v50 - i10 - Oct 2004 - pS62(1) [51-500]
Roberts, John Richard - *John Donne: An Annotated Bibliography of Modern Criticism, 1979/1995.*
　Choice - v42 - i6 - Feb 2005 - p994(1) [51-500]
　R&R Bk N - v19 - i4 - Nov 2004 - p234(1) [501+]
Roberts, Jonathan - *Coordinated and Multiple Views in Exploratory Visualization (CMV 2004): Proceedings*
　SciTech - v28 - i3 - Sept 2004 - p143(1) [51-500]
Roberts, Ken - *The Leisure Industries*
　Choice - v42 - i4 - Dec 2004 - p699(1) [1-50]
Roberts, Luise - *1000 Great Quilting Designs for Hand or Machine Stitching*
　LJ - v129 - i13 - August 2004 - p79(1) [51-500]
Roberts, Mark - *Tomorrow Belongs to Me*
　y Sch Lib - v52 - i3 - Autumn 2004 - p162(1) [501+]
Roberts, Mark D. - *No Holds Barred: Wrestling with God in Prayer*
　PW - v252 - i9 - Feb 28 2005 - p62(2) [51-500]
Roberts, Mary Louise - *Disruptive Acts: The New Woman in Fin-de-siecle France*
　FS - v58 - i1 - Jan 2004 - p127(2) [501+]
　JMH - v76 - i3 - Sept 2004 - p702(3) [501+]
Roberts, Michael - *Snowman in Paradise (Illus. by Roberts, Michael)*
　c PW - v251 - i39 - Sept 27 2004 - p62(1) [51-500]
　c SLJ - v51 - i1 - Jan 2005 - p97(1) [51-500]
Roberts, Michael C. - *Handbook of Pediatric Psychology, 3rd Ed.*
　SciTech - v28 - i1 - March 2004 - p117(1) [51-500]
Roberts, Michael J. - *Signals and Systems: Analysis Using Transform Methods and MATLAB. 1st Ed.*
　TimHES - v0 - i1668 - Nov 26 2004 - pXV(1) [501+]
Roberts, Michele - *Reader, I Married Him*
　NS - v134 - i4724 - Jan 24 2005 - p53(2) [501+]
Roberts-Miller, Patricia - *Deliberate Conflict: Argument, Political Theory, and Composition Classes*
　Choice - v42 - i4 - Dec 2004 - p656(1) [1-50]
Roberts, Noel Keith - *From Piltdown Man to Point Omega: The Evolutionary Theory of Tellhard De Chardin*
　Isis - v95 - i3 - Sept 2004 - p514(1) [501+]
Roberts, Nora - *Blue Dahlia*
　y BL - v101 - i5 - Nov 1 2004 - p471(1) [51-500]
　LJ - v129 - i19 - Nov 15 2004 - p46(2) [501+]
　PW - v251 - i43 - Oct 25 2004 - p33(1) [51-500]
Divided in Death (Read by Ericksen, Susan). Audiobook Review
　c Kliatt - v38 - i4 - July 2004 - p50(2) [51-500]
Divided in Death
　ChrSFF&H - v26 - i10 - Oct 2004 - p25(1) [51-500]
Immortal in Death (Read by Ericksen, Susan). Audiobook Review
　PW - v252 - i1 - Jan 3 2005 - p22(1) [51-500]
The Key of Valor
　y BL - v101 - i2 - Sept 15 2004 - p222(1) [51-500]
Moon Shadows
　LJ - v129 - i13 - August 2004 - p56(1) [501+]
　PW - v251 - i39 - Sept 27 2004 - p43(1) [51-500]

Naked in Death (Read by Ericksen, Susan). Audiobook Review
　Kliatt - v38 - i4 - July 2004 - p53(1) [51-500]
Northern Lights
　BL - v101 - i1 - Sept 1 2004 - p7(1) [51-500]
　BW - v34 - i43 - Oct 24 2004 - p13(1) [51-500]
　KR - v72 - i17 - Sept 1 2004 - p832(1) [51-500]
　LJ - v129 - i16 - Oct 1 2004 - p72(2) [51-500]
　NYTBR - Oct 10 2004 - p10 [501+]
　PW - v251 - i36 - Sept 6 2004 - p44(1) [51-500]
Remember When (Read by Ericksen, Susan). Audiobook Review
　c Kliatt - v38 - i4 - July 2004 - p55(1) [51-500]
Visions in Death (Read by Ericksen, Susan). Audiobook Review
　y Kliatt - v39 - i1 - Jan 2005 - p51(1) [51-500]
Visions in Death
　KR - v72 - i13 - July 1 2004 - p601(1) [51-500]
　PW - v251 - i30 - July 26 2004 - p39(1) [501+]
Roberts, Paul - *The End of Oil: On the Edge of a Perilous New World*
　Choice - v42 - i1 - Sept 2004 - p156(1) [501+]
　Globe & Mail - July 10 2004 - pD4 [501+]
　R&R Bk N - v19 - i3 - August 2004 - p119(1) [51-500]
Roberts, Paul William - *A War Against the Truth: An Intimate Account of Invasion of Iraq*
　Globe & Mail - Oct 2 2004 - pD4 [501+]
Roberts, Phil - *A Penny for the Governor, a Dollar for Uncle Sam: Income Taxation in Washington*
　AHR - v109 - i2 - April 2004 - p541(2) [501+]
　JAH - v91 - i1 - June 2004 - p287-287 [501+]
　WHQ - v35 - i2 - Summer 2004 - p252-253 [501+]
Roberts, Philip - *Industrial Brazing Practice*
　Choice - v41 - i11-12 - July-August 2004 - p2076(2) [501+]
　SciTech - v28 - i1 - March 2004 - p178(1) [51-500]
Roberts, Randy - *The Rock, the Curse, and the Hub: A Random History of Boston Sports*
　KR - v73 - i1 - Jan 1 2005 - p42(1) [51-500]
　PW - v252 - i3 - Jan 17 2005 - p41(2) [51-500]
Roberts, Robert North - *Encyclopedia of Presidential Campaigns, Slogans, Issues, and Platforms*
　BL - v100 - i22 - August 2004 - p1972(2) [501+]
　Choice - v42 - i2 - Oct 2004 - p276(1) [501+]
　y LibMed - v23 - i3 - Nov-Dec 2004 - p83(1) [51-500]
　Ref Rev - June 2004 - pNA [501+]
　R&R Bk N - v19 - i3 - August 2004 - p63(1) [51-500]
　y SLJ - v50 - i10 - Oct 2004 - p96(1) [51-500]
Roberts, Russell - *The Invisible Heart: An Economic Romance*
　Bks & Cult - v11 - i1 - Jan-Feb 2005 - p26(4) [501+]
Philo T. Farnsworth: The Life of Television's Forgotten Inventor
　y SB - v40 - i3 - May-June 2004 - p129(1) [501+]
Roberts, Sam - *Who We Are Now: The Changing Face of America in the Twenty-First Century*
　y BL - v101 - i1 - Sept 1 2004 - p43(1) [51-500]
　KR - v72 - i14 - July 15 2004 - p678(1) [51-500]
　LJ - v129 - i20 - Dec 1 2004 - p145(2) [51-500]
　NYTBR - Nov 28 2004 - p21 [501+]
Roberts, Tim S. - *Online Collaborative Learning: Theory and Practice*
　R&R Bk N - v19 - i1 - Feb 2004 - p181(1) [51-500]
Roberts, Warren - *A Bibliography of D.H. Lawrence*
　RES - v55 - i220 - June 2004 - p482-483 [501+]
Roberts, Wendy - *Dating Can Be Deadly*
　PW - v252 - i4 - Jan 24 2005 - p225(1) [501+]
Roberts, William H. - *Civil War Ironclads: The U.S. Navy and Industrial Mobilization*
　BHR - v78 - i1 - Spring 2004 - p111(4) [501+]
　JAH - v91 - i1 - June 2004 - p247-248 [501+]
　T&C - v45 - i1 - Jan 2004 - p188(2) [501+]
Roberts, William J. - *France: A Reference Guide from the Renaissance to the Present*
　Choice - v42 - i6 - Feb 2005 - p1006(1) [501+]
　LJ - v129 - i19 - Nov 15 2004 - p86(1) [51-500]
　R&R Bk N - v19 - i4 - Nov 2004 - p38(1) [51-500]
Roberts, Willo Davis - *Blood on His Hands*
　y CCB-B - v58 - i1 - Sept 2004 - p36(1) [51-500]
　y Kliatt - v38 - i4 - July 2004 - p12(1) [51-500]
　c SLJ - v50 - i8 - August 2004 - p128(1) [51-500]
　y VOYA - v27 - i5 - Dec 2004 - p394(1) [51-500]
Robertson, Aileen - *Food and Health in Europe: A New Basis for Action*
　SciTech - v28 - i3 - Sept 2004 - p84(1) [501+]

Robertson, Brewster Milton - *A Posturing of Fools*
　PW - v251 - i32 - August 9 2004 - p231(2) [51-500]
Robertson, C.K. - *Religion and Alcohol: Sobering Thoughts*
　R&R Bk N - v19 - i3 - August 2004 - p162(1) [501+]
Religion as Entertainment
　JouAmCul - v27 - i4 - Dec 2004 - p460(2) [501+]
Robertson, Christopher T. - *Printed Circuit Board Designer's Reference*
　SciTech - v28 - i1 - March 2004 - p160(1) [51-500]
Robertson, Claire C. - *Trouble Showed the Way: Women, Men and Trade in the Nairobi Area, 1890-1990*
　JTWS - v21 - i1 - Spring 2004 - p300(3) [501+]
Robertson, D. Gordon - *Research Methods in Biomechanics*
　SciTech - v28 - i3 - Sept 2004 - p70(1) [51-500]
Robertson, David M. - *A Passionate Pilgrim: A Biography of Bishop James A. Pike*
　BL - v101 - i1 - Sept 1 2004 - p24(1) [51-500]
　PW - v251 - i30 - July 26 2004 - p50(1) [501+]
Robertson, Heather - *Magical, Mysterious Lake of the Woods*
　Beav - v84 - i4 - August-Sept 2004 - p44(2) [501+]
Robertson, Ian - *Tyranny under the Mantle of St Peter: Pope Paul II and Bologna*
　CHR - v90 - i3 - July 2004 - p537(3) [501+]
Robertson, J. Craig - *The Kids' Building Workshop: 15 Woodworking Projects for Kids and Parents to Build Together*
　c SLJ - v51 - i2 - Feb 2005 - p151(2) [51-500]
Robertson, James - *Requirements-Led Project Management: Discovering David's Slingshot*
　SciTech - v28 - i4 - Dec 2004 - p132 [51-500]
Robertson, Linda R. - *The Dream of Civilized Warfare: World War I Flying Aces and the American Imagination*
　Choice - v41 - i11-12 - July-August 2004 - p2110(1) [501+]
　J Mil H - v68 - i3 - July 2004 - p982-983 [501+]
Robertson, M.P. - *The Great Dragon Rescue (Illus. by Robertson, M.P.)*
　c BL - v101 - i7 - Dec 1 2004 - p662(1) [51-500]
　c KR - v72 - i18 - Sept 15 2004 - p919(1) [51-500]
　c SLJ - v51 - i1 - Jan 2005 - p97(1) [51-500]
The Moon in Swampland
　KR - v72 - i20 - Oct 15 2004 - p1013(1) [51-500]
Robertson, Oscar - *The Big O*
　BL - v101 - i1 - Sept 1 2004 - p46(1) [51-500]
Robertson, Patrisha - *Cirque Du Soleil: Parade of Colors*
　LibMed - v22 - i7 - April-May 2004 - p58(1) [501+]
　c Teach Lib - v32 - i3 - Feb 2005 - p20(1) [51-500]
Robertson, R. Garcia Y. - *White Rose*
　ChrSFF&H - v26 - i10 - Oct 2004 - p24(1) [51-500]
　LJ - v129 - i16 - Oct 1 2004 - p73(1) [51-500]
Robertson, Robert J. - *Perceived Exertion for Practitioners: Rating Effort with OMNI Picture System*
　SciTech - v28 - i3 - Sept 2004 - p69(1) [51-500]
Robertson, William C. - *Light*
　SciTech - v28 - i1 - March 2004 - p49(1) [51-500]
Robida, Albert - *The Twentieth Century*
　Choice - v41 - i11-12 - July-August 2004 - p2050(1) [501+]
Robin, Corey - *Fear: The History of a Political Idea*
　Globe & Mail - Nov 6 2004 - pD9 [501+]
　KR - v72 - i15 - August 1 2004 - p732(1) [501+]
　LJ - v129 - i17 - Oct 15 2004 - p76(1) [51-500]
　NS - v133 - i4714 - Nov 15 2004 - p53(2) [501+]
　NYRB - v51 - i17 - Nov 4 2004 - p38(4) [501+]
　NYTBR - Nov 28 2004 - p31 [501+]
　PW - v251 - i34 - August 23 2004 - p47(1) [51-500]
Robin, Ron - *Scandals and Scoundrels: Seven Cases That Shook the Academy*
　BW - v34 - i46 - Nov 14 2004 - p4(1) [501+]
Robins, Charles Edward - *New York Voices: The Trauma of 9/11*
　SciTech - v28 - i1 - March 2004 - p101(1) [51-500]
Robins, Corinne - *One Thousand Years*
　ABR - v26 - i2 - Jan-Feb 2005 - p26(2) [501+]
Robins, Deri - *Special Effects*
　c BL - v101 - i5 - Nov 1 2004 - p497(1) [51-500]
Robins, Lauren - *The Palette of Breath*
　c CH Bwatch - Jan 2005 - pNA [51-500]
　c CH Bwatch - Feb 2005 - pNA [51-500]

Robins, Madeleine E. - *Petty Treason: A Sarah Tolerance Mystery*
  KR - v72 - i17 - Sept 1 2004 - p841(1) [51-500]
  LJ - v129 - i14 - Sept 1 2004 - p126(1) [501+]
  PW - v251 - i33 - August 16 2004 - p46(1) [51-500]

Robins, Natalie - *Copeland's Cure: Homeopathy and the War between Conventional and Alternative Medicine.*
  KR - v72 - i24 - Dec 15 2004 - p1191(1) [501+]
  PW - v251 - i50 - Dec 13 2004 - p55(1) [501+]

Robins, Nicholas A. - *Genocide and Millennialism in Upper Peru: The Great Rebellion of 1780-82*
  Ams - v61 - i2 - Oct 2004 - p321(2) [501+]

Robins, Philip - *A History of Jordan*
  MEJ - v58 - i4 - Autumn 2004 - p692(3) [501+]
  Suits and Uniforms: Turkish Foreign Policy since the Cold War
  IJMES - v36 - i4 - Nov 2004 - p700(3) [501+]

Robinson, Alan G. - *Ideas Are Free: How the Idea Revolution Is Liberating People and Transforming Organizations*
  R&R Bk N - v19 - i3 - August 2004 - p129(1) [51-500]

Robinson, Andy - *Grassroots Grants: An Activist's Guide to Grantseeking, 2nd Ed.*
  R&R Bk N - v19 - i3 - August 2004 - p133(1) [51-500]

Robinson, Annabel - *The Life and Work of Jane Ellen Harrison*
  ELT - v47 - i3 - Summer 2004 - p342(5) [501+]

Robinson, Armstead L. - *Bitter Fruits of Bondage: The Demise of Slavery and the Collapse of the Confederacy, 1861-1865*
  LJ - v129 - i18 - Nov 1 2004 - p108(1) [51-500]

Robinson, Barbara - *The Best Halloween Ever (Read by Stritch, Elaine). Audiobook Review*
  c PW - v251 - i37 - Sept 13 2004 - p36(1) [51-500]
  The Best Halloween Ever
  c CCB-B - v58 - i1 - Sept 2004 - p36(2) [51-500]
  c HB - v80 - i5 - Sept-Oct 2004 - p597(1) [501+]
  c PW - v251 - i32 - August 9 2004 - p250(1) [51-500]
  c SLJ - v50 - i8 - August 2004 - p93(1) [51-500]
  c SLJ - v50 - i10 - Oct 2004 - pS29(1) [51-500]
  he Best Halloween Ever (Read by Stritch, Elaine). Audiobook Review
  c BL - v100 - i22 - August 2004 - p1937(1) [51-500]

Robinson, C. Kelly - *The Strong, Silent Type*
  BL - v100 - i8 - Dec 15 2004 - p709(1) [51-500]

Robinson, Charles Frank, II - *Dangerous Liaisons: Sex and Love in the Segregated South*
  HNet - Dec 2004 - pNA [501+]
  JAH - v91 - i3 - Dec 2004 - p1044(2) [501+]
  JSH - v71 - i1 - Feb 2005 - p178(2) [501+]

Robinson, Charles M., III - *Texas and the Mexican War: A History and a Guide*
  Bwatch - v26 - i8 - August 2004 - p10(1) [51-500]
  Roundup M - v11 - i6 - August 2004 - p25(2) [501+]

Robinson, Colin - *Energy in a Competitive Market: Essays in Honour of Colin Robinson*
  JEL - v41 - i4 - Dec 2003 - p1435(1) [501+]

Robinson, David M. - *Natural Life: Thoreau's Worldly Transcendentalism*
  AS - v74 - i1 - Wntr 2005 - p132(3) [501+]
  Choice - v42 - i6 - Feb 2005 - p1024(1) [501+]
  Wil Q - v29 - i1 - Wntr 2005 - p125(2) [501+]

Robinson, David Maurice - *Muslim Societies in African History*
  IJAHS - v37 - i2 - Spring 2004 - p393-395 [501+]

Robinson, Dean E. - *Black Nationalism in American Politics and Thought*
  JSH - v70 - i4 - Nov 2004 - p918(2) [501+]

Robinson, E.W. - *Ancient Greek Democracy. Readingsand Sources*
  Class R - v54 - i2 - Nov 2004 - p458(3) [501+]

Robinson, Elisabeth - *The True and Outstanding Adventures of the Hunt Sisters (Read by Emond, Linda). Audiobook Review*
  LJ - v129 - i12 - July 2004 - p125(1) [51-500]
  The True and Outstanding Adventures of the Hunt Sisters
  LJ - v130 - i1 - Jan 1 2005 - p174(1) [501+]

Robinson, Eugene - *Last Dance in Havana: The Final Days of Fidel and the Start of the New Cuban Revolution*
  BL - v100 - i21 - July 2004 - p1812(1) [1-50]
  BW - v34 - i29 - July 18 2004 - p7(1) [501+]
  Nation - v279 - i13 - Oct 25 2004 - p36 [501+]

Robinson, Fay - *Halloween Crafts*
  c SLJ - v50 - i7 - July 2004 - p95(1) [51-500]

Robinson, Fiona - *The Useful Moose: A Truthful, Moose-Full Tale (Illus. by Robinson, Fiona)*
  c PW - v251 - i43 - Oct 25 2004 - p47(2) [51-500]
  c Sch Lib - v52 - i4 - Winter 2004 - p190(1) [51-500]
  c SLJ - v51 - i1 - Jan 2005 - p97(1) [51-500]

Robinson, Frank M. - *Great Divide*
  ChrSFF&H - v26 - i10 - Oct 2004 - p27(1) [51-500]

Robinson, H.R. - *A Modern de Quincey: Autobiography of an Opium Addict*
  TLS - i5288 - August 6 2004 - p28(1) [501+]

Robinson, Hilary - *E-mail: Jesus@Bethlehem*
  c TES - v0 - i4576 - March 26 2004 - pssss18(2) [501+]

Robinson, J. Jill - *Residual Desire*
  CBRA - Annual 2003 - p204(2) [51-500]

Robinson, James - *Grand Guignol*
  y BL - v101 - i7 - Dec 1 2004 - p644(1) [51-500]
  Leave It to Chance, Vol. 1: Shaman's Rain
  y Teach Lib - v32 - i1 - Oct 2004 - p17(2) [501+]

Robinson, James C. - *An Introduction to Ordinary Differential Equations*
  Choice - v42 - i1 - Sept 2004 - p142(1) [501+]
  TimHES - v0 - i1668 - Nov 26 2004 - pXVI(1) [501+]

Robinson, Jane - *Mary Seacole: The Charismatic Black Nurse Who Became a Heroine of the Crimea*
  NS - v134 - i4722 - Jan 17 2005 - p48(2) [501+]
  Mary Seacole: The Most Famous Black Woman of the Victorian Age
  KR - v72 - i21 - Nov 1 2004 - p1041(1) [501+]

Robinson, Jeffrey - *Sink: Crime, Terror, and Dirty Money in the Offshore World*
  CBRA - Annual 2003 - p319(1) [501+]

Robinson, Kim Stanley - *Forty Signs of Rain*
  BW - v34 - i40 - Oct 3 2004 - p17(1) [501+]
  MFSF - v107 - i4-5 - Oct-Nov 2004 - p39(8) [501+]
  SLJ - v50 - i9 - Sept 2004 - p235(1) [51-500]

Robinson, Lillian S. - *Wonder Women: Feminisms and Superheroes*
  Globe & Mail - August 7 2004 - pD15 [501+]
  Wom R Bks - v22 - i1 - Oct 2004 - p13(2) [501+]

Robinson, Linda - *Masters of Chaos: The Secret History of the Special Forces*
  BW - v34 - i42 - Oct 17 2004 - p13(1) [501+]
  NYTBR - Nov 14 2004 - p60 [501+]
  PW - v251 - i39 - Sept 27 2004 - p48(2) [51-500]

Robinson, Lynne - *The Complete Book of Paint: 70 Techniques, Finishes, and Designs for Your Home*
  LJ - v130 - i4 - March 1 2005 - p109(1) [51-500]

Robinson, Marguerite S. - *The Microfinance Revolution: Sustainable Finance for the Poor*
  JEL - v41 - i4 - Dec 2003 - p1325(3) [501+]

Robinson, Marilynne - *Gilead*
  Atl - v294 - i5 - Dec 2004 - p135(4) [501+]
  BL - v100 - i22 - August 2004 - p1874(1) [51-500]
  BL - v101 - i9-10 - Jan 1 2005 - p770(1) [51-500]
  BW - v34 - i47 - Nov 21 2004 - p15(1) [501+]
  CC - v122 - i3 - Feb 8 2005 - p40(2) [501+]
  Ch Today - v49 - i3 - March 2005 - p84(1) [51-500]
  Comw - v132 - i4 - Feb 25 2005 - p22(2) [501+]
  Econ - v374 - i8409 - Jan 15 2005 - p77US [501+]
  Globe & Mail - Nov 20 2004 - pD4 [501+]
  HM - v309 - i1855 - Dec 2004 - p87(2) [501+]
  KR - v72 - i16 - August 15 2004 - p772(1) [501+]
  Ms - v14 - i4 - Winter 2004 - p89(1) [501+]
  New York - v37 - i43 - Dec 6 2004 - p82(2) [501+]
  NW - Dec 6 2004 - p87 [501+]
  NYTBR - Nov 28 2004 - p1 [501+]
  People - Nov 29 2004 - p55 [51-500]
  People - Dec 27 2004 - p63 [501+]
  PW - v251 - i39 - Sept 27 2004 - p36(1) [51-500]
  Wom R Bks - v22 - i3 - Dec 2004 - p19(1) [501+]
  Ent W - i793 - Nov 19 2004 - p87 [501+]

Robinson, Matt - *How We Play at It*
  CBRA - Annual 2003 - p229(2) [51-500]
  A Ruckus of Awkward Stacking
  Can Lit - i182 - Autumn 2004 - p167(3) [501+]

Robinson, Michael D. - *The Storms of Providence: Navigating the Waters of Calvinism, Arminianism, and Open Theism*
  R&R Bk N - v19 - i3 - August 2004 - p28(1) [1-50]

Robinson, Monique - *Longing for Daddy: Healing from the Pain of an Absent or Emotionally Distant Father*
  Black Iss - v6 - i5 - Sept-Oct 2004 - p38(1) [501+]

Robinson, Neal - *Discovering the Qur'an: A Contemporary Approach to a Veiled Text, 2nd Ed.*
  R&R Bk N - v19 - i3 - August 2004 - p17(1) [1-50]

Robinson, Neil - *Secrets of Intellectual Property: A Guide for Small and Medium-Sized Exporters*
  R&R Bk N - v19 - i4 - Nov 2004 - p108(1) [501+]

Robinson, O.F. - *The Register of Walter Bronescombe, Bishop of Exeter, 1258-1280*
  HER - v119 - i483 - Sept 2004 - p1035(2) [501+]
  HER - v119 - i483 - Sept 2004 - p1035(2) [501+]

Robinson, Patrick - *Scimitar SL-2*
  PW - v251 - i31 - August 2 2004 - p53(1) [501+]

Robinson, Paul - *Just War in Comparative Perspective*
  R&R Bk N - v19 - i1 - Feb 2004 - p253(1) [51-500]
  Queer Wars: The New Gay Right and Its Critics
  LJ - v130 - i1 - Jan 1 2005 - p136(1) [51-500]

Robinson, Peter - *The First Cut*
  DroRevMy - v24 - i4 - July-August 2004 - p13(1) [51-500]
  KR - v72 - i14 - July 15 2004 - p663(2) [51-500]
  LJ - v129 - i12 - July 2004 - p65(1) [51-500]
  PW - v251 - i30 - July 26 2004 - p36(2) [501+]
  No Cure for Love. Audiobook Review
  Globe & Mail - August 14 2004 - pD13 [1-50]
  Not Safe After Dark
  Globe & Mail - Nov 27 2004 - pD16 [51-500]
  Playing with Fire (Read by Keith, Ron). Audiobook Review
  LJ - v129 - i12 - July 2004 - p125(1) [51-500]
  Playing with Fire. Audiobook Review
  Globe & Mail - Jan 8 2005 - pD13 [1-50]
  The Return of Inspector Banks
  Globe & Mail - August 21 2004 - pD13 [1-50]
  Strange Affair
  Globe & Mail - Jan 22 2005 - pD11 [501+]
  KR - v72 - i24 - Dec 15 2004 - p1169(1) [501+]
  LJ - v129 - i16 - Oct 1 2004 - p64(1) [501+]
  LJ - v130 - i2 - Feb 1 2005 - p58(1) [51-500]
  NYTBR - Feb 20 2005 - p21 [501+]
  PW - v252 - i3 - Jan 17 2005 - p35(1) [501+]
  Summer That Never Was
  CBRA - Annual 2003 - p182(2) [51-500]

Robinson, Peter M. - *Time Series with Long Memory*
  JEL - v42 - i1 - March 2004 - p245(1) [501+]

Robinson, Phillip T. - *Life at the Zoo: Behind the Scenes with the Animal Doctors*
  y BL - v101 - i1 - Sept 1 2004 - p32(2) [51-500]
  LJ - v129 - i13 - August 2004 - p115(1) [51-500]
  New Sci - v184 - i2472 - Nov 6 2004 - p53(1) [51-500]
  SB - v40 - i6 - Nov-Dec 2004 - p243(1) [51-500]
  y SB - v40 - i6 - Nov-Dec 2004 - p261(1) [51-500]

Robinson, R. Clark - *An Introduction to Dynamical Systems: Continuous and Discrete*
  SciTech - v28 - i3 - Sept 2004 - p41(1) [1-50]

Robinson, Randall - *Quitting America: The Departure of a Black Man From His Native Land*
  Black Iss - v6 - i4 - July-August 2004 - p54(1) [51-500]

Robinson, Rowena - *Christians of India*
  JRAI - v10 - i3 - Sept 2004 - p736(2) [501+]
  Pac A - v77 - i3 - Fall 2004 - p599(2) [501+]
  R&R Bk N - v19 - i1 - Feb 2004 - p17(1) [51-500]
  Religious Conversions in India: Modes, Motivations, and Meanings
  JRAI - v10 - i4 - Dec 2004 - p940(2) [501+]
  Sociology of Religion in India
  R&R Bk N - v19 - i3 - August 2004 - p15(1) [1-50]

Robinson, Roxana - *A Perfect Stranger and Other Stories*
  KR - v73 - i5 - March 1 2005 - p256(1) [501+]
  PW - v252 - i11 - March 14 2005 - p44(1) [51-500]

Robinson, Sharon - *Promises to Keep: How Jackie Robinson Changed America*
  LibMed - v23 - i1 - August-Sept 2004 - p72(1) [51-500]
  c SLJ - v50 - i10 - Oct 2004 - pS32(1) [1-50]

Robinson, Solveig C. - *A Serious Occupation: Literary Criticism by Victorian Women Writers*
  R&R Bk N - v19 - i4 - Nov 2004 - p233(1) [501+]

Robinson, Stephanie Nicole - *History of Immigrant Female Students in Chicago Public Schools, 1900-1950*
  R&R Bk N - v19 - i3 - August 2004 - p229(1) [1-50]

Robinson, Sue - *Bear in the Barnyard (Illus. by Morris, Tony)*
  c SLJ - v50 - i9 - Sept 2004 - p178(1) [51-500]

Rodionoff, Enrique Breccia - *Lovecraft*
　　MFSF - v107 - i1 - July 2004 - p27(4) [51-500]
Rodman, Robert - *Winnicott: Life and Work*
　　Lon R Bks - v26 - i5 - March 4 2004 - p12(2)
　　[501+]
Rodogno, Davide - *nuovo ordine mediterraneo: Le politiche di occupazione dell'Italia fascista in Europa, 1940-1943*
　　JMH - v76 - i4 - Dec 2004 - p976(3) [501+]
Rodowsky, Colby F. - *Not Quite a Stranger*
　　y LibMed - v22 - i6 - March 2004 - p65(1) [501+]
Rodrick, Anne B. - *Self-Help and Civic Culture: Citizenship in Victorian Birmingham*
　　R&R Bk N - v19 - i3 - August 2004 - p184(1)
　　[501+]
Rodrick, Scott - *Equity-Based Compensation for Multinational Corporations: Using Stock Options and Other Equity Plans to Reward a Global Workforce, 6th Ed.*
　　HR Mag - v49 - i7 - July 2004 - pS7(1) [51-500]
Rodrigues, Maria Joao - *European Policies for a Knowledge Economy*
　　R&R Bk N - v19 - i2 - May 2004 - p128 [51-500]
Rodriguez, Alberto J. - *Preparing Mathematics and Science Teachers for Diverse Classrooms: Promising Strategies for Transformative Pedagogy*
　　SciTech - v28 - i4 - Dec 2004 - p15(1) [1-50]
Rodriguez-Bachiller, Agustin - *Expert Systems and Geographic Information Systems for Impact Assessment*
　　SciTech - v28 - i4 - Dec 2004 - on p5(1) [1-50]
Rodriguez, Douglas - *Latin Flavors on the Grill*
　　Time - v164 - i6 - August 9 2004 - p99 [51-500]
Rodriguez-Duarte, Alexis - *Presenting Celia Cruz*
　　People - v62 - i25 - Dec 20 2004 - p61 [51-500]
Rodriguez, Felix V. Matos - *Women in San Fuan, 1820-1868*
　　HAHR - v84 - i2 - May 2004 - p347(2) [501+]
Rodriguez, Ferdinand - *Principles of Polymer Systems*
　　Choice - v41 - i7 - March 2004 - p1326(1) [501+]
Rodriguez, Judith Green - *Qualitative Methods for Health Research*
　　SciTech - v28 - i3 - Sept 2004 - p93(1) [51-500]
Rodriguez, Martha Pachon - *Objectos Rituales*
　　Ceram Mo - v52 - i6 - June-August 2004 - p30(1)
　　[501+]
Rodriguez, Orlando - *The Last Masquerade*
　　PW - v252 - i10 - March 7 2005 - p51(1) [51-500]
Rodriguez, Victoria E. - *Women in Contemporary Mexican Politics*
　　Pers PS - v33 - i4 - Fall 2004 - p237(1) [501+]
Rodriguz-Mangual, Edna M. - *Lydia Cabrera and the Construction of an Afro-Cuban Cultural Identity*
　　Choice - v42 - i5 - Jan 2005 - p858(1) [1-50]
Rodrik, Dani - *In Search of Prosperity: Analytic Narratives on Economic Growth*
　　Econ J - v114 - i499 - Nov 2004 - pF547-F548
　　[501+]
　　JEL - v41 - i4 - Dec 2003 - p1421(1) [501+]
　　JEL - v42 - i3 - Sept 2004 - p881(2) [501+]
Rodska, Christian - *Viking!: Myths of Gods & Monsters (Read by Rodska, Christian). Audiobook Review*
　　SLJ - v50 - i10 - Oct 2004 - pS37(1) [51-500]
Rodwell, J.F. - *Essentials of Aviation Management: A Guide for Aviation Service Businesses, 6th Ed.*
　　R&R Bk N - v19 - i2 - May 2004 - p110(1) [51-500]
Roe, Caroline - *Consolation for an Exile*
　　Globe & Mail - Nov 27 2004 - pD16 [51-500]
　　PW - v251 - i40 - Oct 4 2004 - p73(1) [51-500]
Roe, John - *Lectures on Coarse Geometry*
　　SciTech - v28 - i1 - March 2004 - p41(1) [51-500]
Roe, Nicholas - *Fiery Heart: The First Life of Leigh Hunt*
　　Econ - v374 - i8411 - Jan 29 2005 - p81US [501+]
Roeckelein, Jon E. - *Imagery in Psychology: A Reference Guide*
　　SciTech - v28 - i3 - Sept 2004 - p2(1) [51-500]
Roedel, Christian - *Krieger, Denker, Amateure: Alfred von Tirpitz und Das Seekriegsbild vor dem Ersten Weltkrieg*
　　HNet - Nov 2004 - pNA [501+]
Roediger-Schluga, Thomas - *The Porter Hypothesis and the Economic Consequences of Environmental Regulation, a Neo-Schumpeterian Appeoach*
　　R&R Bk N - v19 - i3 - August 2004 - p97(1) [51-500]
Roegner, Harry R. - *Butterfly Trails*
　　South CR - v36 - i2 - Spring 2004 - p171-172
　　[501+]
Roehl-Anderson, Janice M. - *Controllership: The Work of the Managerial Accountant, 7th Ed.*
　　R&R Bk N - v19 - i3 - August 2004 - p136(1)
　　[51-500]

Roehner, Bertrand M. - *Pattern and Repertoire in History*
　　JEL - v42 - i1 - March 2004 - p211(2) [501+]
Patterns of Speculation: A Study in Observational Econophysics
　　JEL - v42 - i3 - Sept 2004 - p838(3) [501+]
Roehrig, Alysia D. - *Stories of Beginning Teachers: First-year Challenges and Beyond*
　　CE - v80 - i5 - Mid-Summer 2004 - p277(2)
　　[501+]
　　TCR - v106 - i5 - May 2004 - p1034(4) [501+]
Roemer, Heidi - *Come to My Party and Other Shape Poems (Illus. by Takahashi, Hideko)*
　　c LibMed - v23 - i3 - Nov-Dec 2004 - p75(1) [51-500]
Roensch, Greg - *The Lindbergh Baby Kidnapping Trial: A Primary Source Account*
　　c SLJ - v50 - i8 - August 2004 - p142(1) [51-500]
Roeper, Richard - *Schlock Value: Hollywood at Its Worst*
　　LJ - v130 - i2 - Feb 1 2005 - p81(1) [51-500]
　　PW - v252 - i2 - Jan 10 2005 - p49(1) [51-500]
Roepstorff, Andreas - *Imagining Nature: Practices of Cosmology and Identity*
　　JRAI - v10 - i3 - Sept 2004 - p747(2) [501+]
Roese, Neal - *If Only: How to Turn Regret into Opportunity*
　　LJ - v129 - i18 - Nov 1 2004 - p110(1) [51-500]
　　PW - v251 - i40 - Oct 4 2004 - p76(1) [51-500]
Roetzel, Calvin J. - *Paul--A Jew on the Margins*
　　Intpr - v58 - i3 - July 2004 - p321(2) [501+]
Rofes, Eric - *Queer Man on Campus: A History of Non-Hetrosexual college Men, 1945 to 2000*
　　CS - v33 - i5 - Sept 2004 - p602-603 [501+]
Rogak, Lisa - *Dr. Robert Atkins: The True Story of the Man Behind the War on Carbohydrates*
　　LJ - v130 - i3 - Feb 15 2005 - p151(1) [51-500]
　　PW - v251 - i51 - Dec 20 2004 - p50(2) [51-500]
Rogan, James E. - *Rough Edges: My Unlikely Road from Welfare to Washington*
　　BL - v100 - i22 - August 2004 - p1882(1) [51-500]
　　BW - v34 - i31 - August 1 2004 - p3(2) [501+]
Rogel, Carole - *The Breakup of Yugoslavia and Its Aftermath, Rev. Ed.*
　　R&R Bk N - v19 - i3 - August 2004 - p47(1) [51-500]
Roger Nichols - *Henri Dutilleux: Music, Mystery and Memory. Conversations with Claude Glayman.*
　　Notes - v61 - i2 - Dec 2004 - p425(4) [501+]
Roger, Philippe - *L'ennemi Americain: Genealogie de L'antiamericanisme Francais*
　　World&I - v19 - i2 - Feb 2004 - p235 [501+]
Rogers, Allan - *Peonies*
　　SciTech - v28 - i4 - Dec 2004 - p125 [51-500]
Rogers, Anna - *While You're Away: New Zealand Nurses at War 1899-1948*
　　AHS - v35 - i124 - Oct 2004 - p405(2) [501+]
Rogers-Barnett, Cheryl - *Cowboy Princess: Life with My Parents Roy Rogers and Dale Evans*
　　Bwatch - v26 - i7 - July 2004 - p10(1) [51-500]
Rogers, Benedict - *A Land without Evil: Stopping the Genocide of Burma's Karen People*
　　TimHES - v0 - i1648 - July 9 2004 - p26(1)
　　[501+]
Rogers, Bill - *Behaviour Recovery, 2nd Ed.*
　　R&R Bk N - v19 - i3 - August 2004 - p225(1)
　　[1-50]
Rogers, Bruce Holland - *Thirteen Ways to Water and Other Stories*
　　ChrSFF&H - v26 - i10 - Oct 2004 - p26(1) [51-500]
Rogers, Byron - *The Last Human Cannonball*
　　Spec - v296 - i9201 - Dec 11 2004 - p41(1) [501+]
Rogers, Carole Garibaldi - *Fasting: Exploring a Great Spiritual Practice*
　　PW - v251 - i30 - July 26 2004 - p51(2) [501+]
Rogers, Connie - *The Illustrated Encyclopedia of British Willow Ware*
　　Ceram Mo - v52 - i5 - May 2004 - p36(1) [501+]
Rogers-Dillon, Robin - *The Welfare Experiments: Politics and Policy Evaluation*
　　Choice - v42 - i6 - Feb 2005 - p1106(1) [51-500]
Rogers, Donald W. - *Computational Chemistry Using the PC, 3rd Ed.*
　　J Chem Ed - v81 - i10 - Oct 2004 - p1423(2)
　　[501+]
Rogers, G.A.J. - *Leviathan*
　　TLS - i5305 - Dec 3 2004 - p3-4 [501+]
Rogers, Geoff - *Focus on Freshwater Aquarium Fish*
　　Globe & Mail - Dec 18 2004 - pD14 [1-50]
　　SciTech - v28 - i4 - Dec 2004 - p126 [51-500]

Rogers, Gregory - *The Boy, the Bear, the Baron, the Bard (Illus. by Rogers, Gregory)*
　　c BL - v101 - i3 - Oct 1 2004 - p336(1) [51-500]
　　c CCB-B - v58 - i4 - Dec 2004 - p182(2) [51-500]
　　c CH Bwatch - Feb 2005 - pNA [51-500]
　　c HB - v80 - i6 - Nov-Dec 2004 - p701(1) [51-500]
　　c KR - v72 - i18 - Sept 15 2004 - p919(1) [51-500]
　　c NYTBR - Oct 17 2004 - p21 [501+]
　　c PW - v251 - i38 - Sept 20 2004 - p62(1) [51-500]
　　c SLJ - v50 - i12 - Dec 2004 - p118(2) [501+]
Rogers, Henry - *Writing Systems: A Linguistic Approach, 1st Ed.*
　　TimHES - v0 - i1668 - Nov 26 2004 - pXII(1)
　　[501+]
Rogers, Jacqueline - *Dodi's Prince*
　　c LibMed - v22 - i4 - Jan 2004 - p63(1) [501+]
Kindergarten Count to 100
　　c LibMed - v23 - i3 - Nov-Dec 2004 - p84(1) [51-500]
　　c SLJ - v50 - i8 - August 2004 - p93(1) [501+]
Rogers, Jane - *The Voyage Home*
　　BW - v34 - i33 - August 15 2004 - p6(1) [501+]
　　MHR - v30 - i2 - Dec 2004 - p106(2) [501+]
　　PW - v251 - i27 - July 5 2004 - p37(1) [51-500]
Rogers, Jerry R. - *Water Resources and Environmental History: Proceedings*
　　SciTech - v28 - i3 - Sept 2004 - p144(1) [51-500]
Rogers, Jim - *Hot Commodities: How Anyone Can Invest Profitably in the World's Best Market*
　　BL - v101 - i9-10 - Jan 1 2005 - p794(1) [51-500]
　　LJ - v130 - i2 - Feb 1 2005 - p95(1) [51-500]
Rogers, John C. - *Task-Oriented Processes in Care (TOPIC) Model in Ambulatory Care*
　　SciTech - v28 - i3 - Sept 2004 - p79(1) [51-500]
Rogers, John J.W. - *Continents and Supercontinents*
　　Choice - v42 - i7 - March 2005 - p1257(1) [51-500]
　　SciTech - v28 - i4 - Dec 2004 - p57(1) [51-500]
Rogers, Jonathan - *The Bark of the Bog Owl: Book One of the Wilderking Trilogy (Illus. by Goolsby, Abe)*
　　c PW - v251 - i31 - August 2 2004 - p51(2) [501+]
　　c SLJ - v51 - i2 - Feb 2005 - p140(1) [501+]
Rogers, Kimberly Ann - *Preventing and Responding to Violence at Work*
　　ILR - v143 - i3 - Autumn 2004 - p292(1) [51-500]
Rogers, L. Edna - *Rational Communication: An Interactional Perspective to the Study of Process and Form*
　　R&R Bk N - v19 - i1 - Feb 2004 - p124(1) [51-500]
Rogers, Lesley J. - *Comparative Vertebrate Cognition: Are Primates Superior to Non-Primates?*
　　SciTech - v28 - i1 - March 2004 - p71(1) [51-500]
Spirit of the Wild Dog: The World of Wolves, Coyotes, Foxes, Jackals, Dingoes
　　LibMed - v22 - i5 - Feb 2004 - p61(1) [501+]
Rogers, Linda - *Al Purdy: Essays on His Works*
　　CBRA - Annual 2003 - p251(2) [501+]
Bill Bissett: Essays on His Works
　　CBRA - Annual 2003 - p252(2) [51-500]
Bursting Test
　　CBRA - Annual 2003 - p230(1) [501+]
Rogers, Lisa Waller - *The Great Storm: The Hurricane Diary of J.T. King*
　　SHQ - v107 - i3 - Jan 2004 - p498(2) [501+]
Rogers, Miller - *Everyday Dairy-Free Cookbook*
　　CBRA - Annual 2003 - p139(1) [51-500]
Rogers, Pat - *The Alexander Pope Encyclopedia*
　　Choice - v42 - i2 - Oct 2004 - p268(1) [501+]
　　TLS - i5294 - Sept 17 2004 - p26(1) [501+]
Rogers, Penelope Walton - *The Roman Textile Industry and Its Influence: A Birthday Tribute to John Peter Wild*
　　JNES - v63 - i3 - July 2004 - p224(2) [501+]
Rogers, Richard George - *Information Politics on the Web*
　　New Sci - v185 - i2484 - Jan 29 2005 - p50(1)
　　[501+]
Rogers, Robert - *How Parliament Works*
　　CR - v285 - i1662 - July 2004 - p57(2) [501+]
Rogers, Robert M. - *Applied Mathematics in Integrated Navigation Systems, 2nd Ed.*
　　SciTech - v28 - i1 - March 2004 - p169(1) [51-500]
Rogers, Robin D. - *Lonic Liquids as Green Solvents: Progress and Prospects*
　　Choice - v41 - i11-12 - July-August 2004 - p2074(1) [501+]
Rogers, Robyn - *Use Your Words: A Child's Struggle to Understand the Concept of War*
　　c CH Bwatch - v14 - i8 - August 2004 - p1(1) [51-500]
　　c SLJ - v50 - i10 - Oct 2004 - p148(1) [51-500]

Rogers, Rosemary - *Jewel of My Heart*
  BL - v101 - i8 - Dec 15 2004 - p714(1) [51-500]

Rogers, Susan Fox - *Going Alone: Women's Adventures in the Wild*
  Globe & Mail - July 31 2004 - pT7 [51-500]

Rogers, Thomas - *Jerry Engels*
  KR - v73 - i1 - Jan 1 2005 - p18(1) [501+]

Rogers, Tony - *Newswriting on Deadline*
  R&R Bk N - v19 - i1 - Feb 2004 - p229(1) [51-500]

Rogers, William Elford - *Interpretation in Piers Plowman*
  RES - v55 - i220 - June 2004 - p446-447 [501+]
  Specu - v79 - i4 - Oct 2004 - p1131(3) [501+]

Rogers, William Warren - *Transition to the Twentieth Century: Thomas County, Georgia, 1900-1920*
  JSH - v70 - i3 - August 2004 - p706(2) [501+]

Rogge, Jorg - *Hochadlige Herrschaft im mitteldeutschen Raum. Formen-Legitimation-Representation*
  GSR - v27 - i2 - May 2004 - p367-368 [501+]

Rogoff, Edward G. - *Bankable Business Plans*
  R&R Bk N - v19 - i1 - Feb 2004 - p86(1) [1-50]

Rogov, Daniel - *Rogov's Guide to Israeli Wine 2005*
  NYT - Nov 7 2004 - p14 [51-500]

Rogow, Sally M. - *Faces of Courage: Young Heroes of World War II*
  y CBRA - Annual 2003 - p540(2) [51-500]

Rohmann, Eric - *Pumpkinhead*
  c LibMed - v22 - i6 - March 2004 - p58(1) [501+]

Rohmer, Richard - *Generally Speaking: The Memoirs of Major-General Richard Rohmer*
  Globe & Mail - Feb 5 2005 - pD14 [501+]
  Raleigh on the Rocks: The Canada Shipwreck of HMS Raleigh
  CBRA - Annual 2003 - p442(1) [501+]

Rohrbacher, D. - *The Historians of Late Antiquity*
  Class R - v53 - i2 - Nov 2003 - p389-391 [501+]

Rohrer, Glenn E. - *Mental Health in Literature; Literary Luancy and Lucidity*
  SciTech - v28 - i4 - Dec 2004 - p12(1) [1-50]

Roid, Gale H. - *Essentials of Stanford-Binet Intelligence Scales (SB5) Assessment*
  SciTech - v28 - i4 - Dec 2004 - p3(1) [1-50]

Roisman, H.M. - *Essays on Homeric Epic*
  Class R - v54 - i2 - Nov 2004 - p281-282 [501+]

Roisman, J. - *Brill's Companion to Alexander the Great*
  Class R - v54 - i2 - Nov 2004 - p469(4) [501+]

Rojavin, Marina - *A Guide to Russian Words and Expressions That Cause Difficulties*
  R&R Bk N - v19 - i4 - Nov 2004 - p217(1) [501+]

Rokhlin, L.L. - *Magnesium Alloys Containing Rare Earth Metals: Structure and Properties*
  E-Streams - Oct 2004 - pNA [501+]

Roland, Charles P. - *My Odyssey through History: Memoirs of War and Academe*
  J Mil H - v68 - i2 - April 2004 - p644(3) [501+]

Roland, John F. - *CCSP Cisco Secure VPN Exam Certification Guide*
  SciTech - v28 - i3 - Sept 2004 - p155(1) [51-500]

Rolcik, Karen Ann - *The Complete Living Trust Kit*
  LJ - v129 - i17 - Oct 15 2004 - p75(1) [51-500]

Rolde, Neil - *Unsettled Past Unsettled Future: The Story of Maine Indians*
  R&R Bk N - v19 - i3 - August 2004 - p61(1) [51-500]

Roleff, Tamara L. - *The Oklahoma City Bombing*
  y SLJ - v50 - i11 - Nov 2004 - p172(1) [51-500]

Rolfe, Jim - *Camellias*
  Bwatch - Jan 2005 - pNA [51-500]

Rolheiser, Ronald - *Forgotten among the Lilies: Learning to Love Beyond Our Fears*
  PW - v252 - i9 - Feb 28 2005 - p61(1) [51-500]

Rolingson, Martha Ann - *Historical Perspectives on Midsouth Archeology*
  Am Ant - v69 - i3 - July 2004 - p589(2) [501+]

Roll, Bob - *The Tour de France Companion: A Nuts, Bolts and Spokes Guide to the Greatest Race in the World*
  R&R Bk N - v19 - i3 - August 2004 - p89(1) [51-500]

Rollason, David - *Northumbria 500-1100: Creation and Destruction of a Kingdom*
  Choice - v41 - i11-12 - July-August 2004 - p2112(1) [501+]

Rolleston, James - *A Companion to the Works of Franz Kafka*
  GSR - v27 - i2 - May 2004 - p408-409 [501+]

Rollin, Catherine - *Pathways to Artistry: A Method for Comprehensive Technical and Musical Development; Technique 2 and Repertoire 2.*
  Am MT - v54 - i1 - August-Sept 2004 - p103(2) [501+]

Rollings, Willard Hughes - *Unaffected by the Gospel: Osage Resistance to the Christian Invasion, 1673-1906: A Cultural Victory*
  Roundup M - v12 - i3 - Feb 2005 - p22(1) [51-500]

Rollins, Barbara B. - *Ballistics*
  c SLJ - v50 - i8 - August 2004 - p142(1) [51-500]
  Blood Evidence
  c SLJ - v50 - i8 - August 2004 - p142(1) [51-500]
  Cause of Death
  c SLJ - v50 - i8 - August 2004 - p142(1) [51-500]
  Fingerprint Evidence
  c SLJ - v50 - i8 - August 2004 - p142(1) [51-500]

Rollins, James - *Map of Bones*
  PW - v252 - i4 - Jan 24 2005 - p26(1) [501+]
  Sandstorm
  y SLJ - v50 - i11 - Nov 2004 - p177(1) [51-500]

Rollins, Joe - *AIDS and the Sexuality of Law: Ironic Jurisprudence*
  Choice - v42 - i1 - Sept 2004 - p190(1) [501+]
  SciTech - v28 - i3 - Sept 2004 - p11(1) [501+]

Rollins, Peter C. - *The Columbia Companion to American History on Film: How the Movies Have Portrayed the American Past*
  Choice - v42 - i3 - Nov 2004 - p490(1) [51-500]
  R&R Bk N - v19 - i3 - August 2004 - p261(1) [51-500]
  y SLJ - v50 - i10 - Oct 2004 - p200(1) [51-500]
  TimHES - v0 - i1674 - Jan 14 2005 - p28(2) [501+]
  Hollywood's White House: The American Presidency in Film and History
  JPC - v38 - i2 - Nov 2004 - p433(2) [501+]
  The West Wing: The American Presidency as Television Drama
  JPC - v38 - i1 - August 2004 - p219(3) [501+]

Rollyson, Carl - *Notable Playwrights, Vols. 1-3*
  y BL - v101 - i9-10 - Jan 1 2005 - p906(1) [51-500]
  y LJ - v130 - i1 - Jan 1 2005 - p156(1) [51-500]
  y SLJ - v51 - i2 - Feb 2005 - p86(1) [51-500]

Roma Sottarnea
  LibMed - v22 - i7 - April-May 2004 - p91(1) [501+]

Romain, Lothar - *Peter Basseler*
  R&R Bk N - v19 - i4 - Nov 2004 - p200(1) [501+]

Roman, Eric - *Austria-Hungary and the Successor States: A Reference Guide from the Renaissance to the Present*
  R&R Bk N - v19 - i1 - Feb 2004 - p34(1) [1-50]

Roman, Peter - *People's Power: Cuba's Experience with Representative Government, Rev. Ed.*
  R&R Bk N - v19 - i1 - Feb 2004 - pNA [501+]

Romanek, Trudee - *Achoo!: The Most Interesting Book You'll Ever Read about Germs (Illus. by Cowles, Rose)*
  y CBRA - Annual 2003 - p562(1) [51-500]
  c SB - v40 - i6 - Nov-Dec 2004 - p273(2) [51-500]
  Achoo!: The Most Interesting Book You'll Ever Read about Germs (Illus. by Crowles, Rose)
  y LibMed - v22 - i6 - March 2004 - p77(1) [501+]
  Aha!: The Most Interesting Book You'll Ever Read about Intelligence (Illus. by Cowles, Rose)
  y SB - v40 - i4 - July-August 2004 - p161(1) [51-500]
  Wow!: The Most Interesting Book You'll Ever Read about the Five Senses (Illus. by Cowles, Rose)
  KR - v72 - i20 - Oct 15 2004 - p1013(1) [51-500]
  y Res Links - v10 - i3 - Feb 2005 - p27(1) [51-500]
  Zzz...: The Most Interesting Book You'll Ever Read about Sleep (Illus. by Cowles, Rose)
  c RT - v57 - Oct 2003 - p178 [1-50]

Romani, Roberto - *National Character and Public Spirit in Britain and France, 1750-1914*
  JMH - v76 - i3 - Sept 2004 - p656(3) [501+]

Romano, Amy - *Germ Warfare*
  y SLJ - v51 - i1 - Jan 2005 - p146(1) [51-500]
  A Historical Atlas of Jordan
  c SLJ - v50 - i10 - Oct 2004 - p193(2) [51-500]
  A Historical Atlas of the United Arab Emirates
  c BL - v101 - i7 - Dec 1 2004 - p649(1) [51-500]

Romano, Ray - *Raymie, Dickie, and the Bean: Why I Love and Hate My Brothers (Illus. by Locke, Gary)*
  c KR - v73 - i5 - March 1 2005 - p294(1) [51-500]
  c PW - v252 - i9 - Feb 28 2005 - p65(2) [51-500]

Romano, Renee C. - *Race Mixing: Black-White Marriage in Postwar America*
  AHR - v109 - i4 - Oct 2004 - p1256(2) [501+]
  JAH - v91 - i1 - June 2004 - p314-316 [501+]
  JSH - v71 - i1 - Feb 2005 - p209(2) [501+]
  Soc Ser R - v78 - i4 - Dec 2004 - p697(1) [51-500]

Romano, Rossana Barragan - *Indios, Mujeres y Ciudadanos: Legislacion y Ejercicio de la Ciudadania en Bolivia*
  HAHR - v84 - i2 - May 2004 - p381(3) [501+]

Romanuk, Paul - *Hockey Superstars 2003-2004*
  c CBRA - Annual 2003 - p559(1) [51-500]
  Hockey Superstars, 2004-2005
  c Res Links - v10 - i3 - Feb 2005 - p27(2) [51-500]

Romberg, Raquel - *Witchcraft and Welfare: Spiritual Capital and the Business of Magic in Modern Puerto Rico*
  JR - v84 - i3 - July 2004 - p506(2) [501+]

Romberg, Thomas A. - *Standards-Based Mathematics Assessment in Middle School: Rethinking Classroom Practice*
  SciTech - v28 - i4 - Dec 2004 - p16(1) [1-50]

Rombke, Jorg - *Effects of Plant Protection Products on Functional Endpoints in Soil (EPFES): Proceedings*
  SciTech - v28 - i1 - March 2004 - p65(1) [51-500]

Rome, Dennis - *Black Demons: Media's Depiction of the African American Male Criminal Stereotype*
  R&R Bk N - v19 - i4 - Nov 2004 - p212(1) [501+]

Rome, Richard - *Fine Art Metal Casting: An Illustrated Guide to Mould Making and Lost Wax Processes*
  Choice - v42 - i3 - Nov 2004 - p472(2) [1-50]

Romeny, Bart M. ter Haar - *Front-End Vision and Multi-Scale Image Anlaysis: Multi-Scale Computer Vision Theory and Applications, Written in Mathematica*
  SciTech - v28 - i1 - March 2004 - p80(1) [51-500]

Romkey, Michael - *American Gothic*
  ChrSFF&H - v26 - i9 - Sept 2004 - p36(1) [51-500]

Romm, Joseph J. - *The Hype about Hydrogen: Fact and Fiction in the Race to Save the Climate*
  Choice - v42 - i3 - Nov 2004 - p515(1) [1-50]
  Env - v46 - i7 - Sept 2004 - p40(2) [501+]
  New Sci - v182 - i2450 - June 5 2004 - p54(2) [51-500]
  SB - v40 - i5 - Sept-Oct 2004 - p200(2) [51-500]
  SB - v41 - i1 - Jan-Feb 2005 - p16(2) [501+]
  SPA - v60 - i4 - July-August 2004 - p65(3) [501+]

Romm, Sharon - *Dating After 50: Negotiating the Minefields of Midlife Romance*
  LJ - v130 - i1 - Jan 1 2005 - p135(1) [51-500]

Romney, Jonathan - *Atom Egoyan*
  Si & So - v14 - i8 - August 2004 - p38(2) [501+]

Romney, Mitt - *Turnaround: Crisis, Leadership, and the Olympic Games*
  PW - v251 - i31 - August 2 2004 - p64(1) [51-500]

Rompkey, Bill - *Story of Labrador*
  CBRA - Annual 2003 - p349(1) [501+]

Rompkey, Ronald - *The Labrador Memoir of Dr. Harry Paddon, 1912-1938.*
  Can Hist R - v85 - i4 - Dec 2004 - p866(3) [501+]

Ron, James - *Frontier and Ghettos: State Violence in Serbia and Israel*
  CS - v33 - i6 - Nov 2004 - p714(2) [501+]

Ronald, Ann - *Reader of the Purple Sage: Essays on Western Writers and Environmental Literature*
  AL - v76 - i2 - June 2004 - p409(3) [501+]

Ronald, Susan - *The Sancy Blood Diamond: Power, Greed, and the Cursed History of One of the World's Most Coveted Gems*
  BL - v101 - i2 - Sept 15 2004 - p191 [51-500]
  PW - v251 - i34 - August 23 2004 - p43(1) [51-500]

Ronch, Judah L. - *Culture Change in Long-Term Care*
  SciTech - v28 - i1 - March 2004 - p85(1) [51-500]

Ronchi, Stefano - *The Internet and the Customer-Supplier Relationship*
  R&R Bk N - v19 - i1 - Feb 2004 - p89(1) [51-500]

Ronco, Claudio - *Hemodialysis Vascular Access and Peritoneal Dialysis Access*
  SciTech - v28 - i4 - Dec 2004 - p105(1) [51-500]
  Peritoneal Dialysis Today
  SciTech - v28 - i1 - March 2004 - p106(1) [51-500]

Ronczkowski, Michael R. - *Terrorism and Hate Crime: Intelligence Gathering, Analysis, and Investigation*
  R&R Bk N - v19 - i1 - Feb 2004 - p144(1) [51-500]

Ronda, James P. - *Beyond Lewis and Clark: The Army Explores the West*
  J Mil H - v68 - i3 - July 2004 - p960-961 [501+]

Rondeau, Amanda - *Do Something in Your Community*
  c BL - v101 - i5 - Nov 1 2004 - p487(1) [51-500]
  Do Something in Your Family
  c BL - v101 - i5 - Nov 1 2004 - p487(1) [51-500]

Rose, Steven - *The 21st-Century Brain: Explaining, Mending and Manipulating the Mind*
    Econ - v374 - i8416 - March 5 2005 - p83US [501+]

Rose, Sylvia - *Rise Up: A Call to Leadership for African American Women*
    Black Iss - v6 - i5 - Sept-Oct 2004 - p36(1) [501+]

Rose, Warner - *I'm Watching You*
    PW - v251 - i38 - Sept 20 2004 - p51(1) [51-500]

Rosebury, Brian - *Tolkien: A Cultural Phenomenon*
    Analog - v124 - i4 - April 2004 - p138(2) [501+]

Rosedale, Ron - *The Rosedale Diet: Turn Off Your "Hunger Switch" for Quick, Healthy and Lasting Weight Loss*
    PW - v251 - i27 - July 5 2004 - p53(1) [51-500]

Roseman, Curtis C. - *Grand Excursions on the Upper Mississippi River: Places, Landscapes, and Regional Identity After 1854*
    Choice - v42 - i6 - Feb 2005 - p1081(2) [51-500]

Roseman, Ellen - *Money 201: More Personal Finance Advice for Every Canadian*
    CBRA - Annual 2003 - p31(1) [51-500]

Rosen, Aaron - *Developing Practice Guidelines for Social Work Intervention: Issues, Methods, and Research Agenda*
    R&R Bk N - v19 - i1 - Feb 2004 - p135(1) [51-500]

Rosen, Alice J. - *The Feeding Ourselves Method: A Guide to Achieving a Healthy Relationship with Food (Read by Rosen, Alice J.). Audiobook Review*
    LJ - v130 - i2 - Feb 1 2005 - p124(1) [51-500]

Rosen, Andrew - *The Transformation of British Life, 1950-2000: A Social History*
    Choice - v42 - i3 - Nov 2004 - p554(1) [1-50]
    CR - v285 - i1664 - Sept 2004 - p192(1) [51-500]

Rosen, Charley - *The Pivotal Season: How the 1971-72 Los Angeles Lakers Changed the NBA*
    LJ - v130 - i1 - Jan 1 2005 - p122(1) [51-500]

Rosen, Christine - *Preaching Eugenics: Religious Leaders and the American Eugenics Movement*
    Bks & Cult - v10 - i4 - July-August 2004 - p7(1) [501+]
    CC - v121 - i22 - Nov 2 2004 - p24(5) [501+]
    Choice - v42 - i4 - Dec 2004 - p680(1) [1-50]

Rosen, Daniel - *Independence Now: The American Revolution 1763-1783*
    c BL - v100 - i22 - August 2004 - p1926(1) [51-500]

Rosen, David - *Words on Music: Essays in Honour of Andrew Porter on the Occasion of His Seventy-Fifth Birthday*
    TLS - i5288 - August 6 2004 - p18(1) [501+]

Rosen, Fred - *Case Studies in Immunology: A Clinical Companion, 4th Ed.*
    SciTech - v28 - i3 - Sept 2004 - p103(1) [51-500]
    Cremation in America
    R&R Bk N - v19 - i3 - August 2004 - p86(1) [51-500]

Rosen, Harvey S. - *Public Finance, 7th Ed.*
    R&R Bk N - v19 - i2 - May 2004 - p125 [51-500]

Rosen, Jeffrey - *The Naked Crowd: Reclaiming Security and Freedom in an Anxious Age*
    NYRB - v51 - i18 - Nov 18 2004 - p56(5) [501+]

Rosen, Jeremy - *Understanding Judaism*
    R&R Bk N - v19 - i3 - August 2004 - p16(1) [1-50]

Rosen, Joe - *Encyclopedia of Physics*
    Choice - v42 - i5 - Jan 2005 - p832(1) [1-50]
    SciTech - v28 - i3 - Sept 2004 - p45(1) [1-50]
    BL - v101 - i7 - Dec 1 2004 - p685(2) [501+]

Rosen, Jonathan - *Joy Comes in the Morning*
    BL - v100 - i22 - August 2004 - p1902(1) [501+]
    BW - v34 - i47 - Nov 21 2004 - p6(2) [501+]
    KR - v72 - i14 - July 15 2004 - p655(1) [51-500]
    LJ - v129 - i14 - Sept 1 2004 - p141(1) [51-500]
    NYTBR - Sept 26 2004 - p19 [501+]
    PW - v251 - i28 - July 12 2004 - p43(1) [51-500]
    Tikkun - v20 - i1 - Jan-Feb 2005 - p74(1) [501+]

Rosen, Joseph - *Encyclopedia of Physics*
    SLJ - v50 - i12 - Dec 2004 - p87(1) [501+]

Rosen, Lawrence - *The Culture of Islam: Changing Aspects of Contemporary Muslim Life*
    IJMES - v36 - i3 - August 2004 - p501-503 [501+]

Rosen, Michael - *Howler (Illus. by Layton, Neal)*
    c SLJ - v50 - i8 - August 2004 - p93(1) [51-500]
    Michael Rosen's Sad Book (Illus. by Blake, Quentin)
    KR - v73 - i2 - Jan 15 2005 - p125(1) [51-500]
    y Magpies - v19 - i5 - Nov 2004 - p32(1) [501+]
    Oww!
    c Sch Lib - v52 - i4 - Winter 2004 - p187(1) [51-500]
    Shakespeare's Romeo and Juliet (Illus. by Ray, Jane)
    y LibMed - v22 - i7 - April-May 2004 - p73(1) [501+]
    y SLJ - v50 - i10 - Oct 2004 - pS50(1) [51-500]
    y VOYA - v27 - i3 - August 2004 - p241(1) [1-50]
    Shakespeare's Romeo & Juliet (Illus. by Ray, Jane)
    c Teach Lib - v32 - i3 - Feb 2005 - p21(1) [51-500]
    A Spider Bought a Bicycle: And Other Poems for Young Children (Illus. by Moore, Inca)
    c PW - v252 - i11 - March 14 2005 - p70(1) [51-500]

Rosen, Michael J. - *Baking from the Heart: Our Nation's Best Bakers Share Cherished Recipes for the Great American Bake Sale*
    LJ - v129 - i15 - Sept 15 2004 - p78(1) [51-500]
    May Contain Nuts: A Very Loose Canon of American Humor
    People - v62 - i17 - Oct 25 2004 - p52 [51-500]

Rosen, Milton J. - *Surfactants and Interfacial Phenomena, 3rd Ed.*
    Choice - v42 - i5 - Jan 2005 - p884(1) [1-50]
    SciTech - v28 - i3 - Sept 2004 - p168(1) [51-500]

Rosen, R.M. - *Andreia. Studies in Manliness and Courage in Classical Antiquity*
    Class R - v54 - i2 - Nov 2004 - p437(3) [501+]

Rosen, Richard - *Yoga for 50+: Modified Poses & Techniques for a Safe Practice*
    LJ - v129 - i18 - Nov 1 2004 - p116(1) [51-500]

Rosen, Robert H. - *Global Literacies: Lessons on Business Leadership and National Cultures*
    HR Mag - v49 - i7 - July 2004 - pS11(1) [51-500]

Rosen, Robyn L. - *Reproductive Health, Reproductive Rights: Reformers and the Politics of Maternal Welfare, 1917-1940*
    Isis - v95 - i2 - June 2004 - p331(2) [501+]
    JAH - v91 - i3 - Dec 2004 - p1067(2) [501+]

Rosen, Steven M. - *Dimensions of Apeiron: A Topological Phenomenology of Space, Time, and Individuation*
    R&R Bk N - v19 - i3 - August 2004 - p4(1) [1-50]

Rosen-Zvi, Issachar - *Taking Space Seriously: Law, Space and Society in Contemporary Israel*
    Law&PolBR - Sept 2004 - pNA [501+]
    R&R Bk N - v19 - i3 - August 2004 - p209(1) [1-50]

Rosenau, James N. - *Distant Proximities: Dynamics Beyond Globalization*
    JEL - v41 - i4 - Dec 2003 - p1351(1) [501+]

Rosenauer, Kenneth L. - *Storycrafting: A Process Approach to Writing News*
    Choice - v42 - i4 - Dec 2004 - p654(2) [1-50]
    R&R Bk N - v19 - i4 - Nov 2004 - p227(1) [501+]

Rosenbaum, Jonathan - *Essential Cinema: On the Necessity of Film Canons*
    Choice - v42 - i2 - Oct 2004 - p301(1) [51-500]
    R&R Bk N - v19 - i4 - Nov 2004 - p223(1) [501+]
    TimHES - v0 - i1654 - August 20 2004 - p28(1) [501+]

Rosenbaum, S. P. - *Georgian Bloomsbury: The Early Literary History of the Bloomsbury Group, 1910-1914*
    ELT - v48 - i1 - Wntr 2005 - p232(4) [501+]

Rosenbaum, Steve - *Learning Paths: Increase Profits by Reducing the Time It Takes for Employees to Get Up-to-Speed*
    R&R Bk N - v19 - i4 - Nov 2004 - p103(1) [51-500]

Rosenbaum, Stuart - *Pragmatism and Religion*
    VQR - v80 - i2 - Spring 2004 - p268-269 [501+]

Rosenberg, Aaron - *The Yore Kippur War*
    y SLJ - v51 - i1 - Jan 2005 - p142(1) [51-500]

Rosenberg, Charles E. - *Right Living: An Anglo-American Tradition of Self-Help Medicine and Hygiene*
    AHR - v109 - i4 - Oct 2004 - p1198-1199 [501+]

Rosenberg, David - *The Book of J (Read by Bloom, Claire). Audiobook Review*
    Globe & Mail - Jan 22 2005 - pD13 [51-500]

Rosenberg, Emily S. - *A Date Which Will Live: Pearl Harbor in American Memory*
    Choice - v41 - i11-12 - July-August 2004 - p2110(1) [501+]
    Pac A - v77 - i3 - Fall 2004 - p616(2) [501+]
    Pub Hist - v26 - i3 - Summer 2004 - p61(63) [501+]
    RAH - v32 - i2 - June 2004 - p239-8 [501+]

Rosenberg, Howard - *Not So Prime Time: Chasing the Trivial on American Television*
    BL - v100 - i22 - August 2004 - p1889(1) [51-500]
    Choice - v42 - i5 - Jan 2005 - p847(1) [1-50]
    Globe & Mail - August 21 2004 - pD13 [501+]
    KR - v72 - i13 - July 1 2004 - p622(1) [501+]
    R&R Bk N - v19 - i4 - Nov 2004 - p222(1) [501+]
    TLS - i5304 - Nov 26 2004 - p33(1) [51-500]

Rosenberg, Jay F. - *Thinking about Knowing*
    TLS - i5286 - July 23 2004 - p27(1) [501+]

Rosenberg, Joel - *Paladins*
    y BL - v101 - i2 - Sept 15 2004 - p216(1) [51-500]
    ChrSFF&H - v26 - i10 - Oct 2004 - p25(1) [51-500]

Rosenberg, Margot - *The Care and Feeding of Books Old and New: A Simple Repair Manual for Booklovers*
    Ant&CM - v108 - i9 - Nov 2003 - p16(1) [501+]

Rosenberg, Nancy Taylor - *Sullivan's Law (Read by Burr, Sandra). Audiobook Review*
    LJ - v129 - i18 - Nov 1 2004 - p130(1) [51-500]

Rosenberg, Pam - *Dinosaur Jokes (Illus. by Girouard, Patrick)*
    c SLJ - v50 - i10 - Oct 2004 - p148(1) [51-500]
    Knock-Knock Jokes (Illus. by Girouard, Patrick)
    c SLJ - v50 - i10 - Oct 2004 - p148(1) [51-500]
    Tongue Twisters (Illus. by Girouard, Patrick)
    c SLJ - v50 - i10 - Oct 2004 - p148(1) [51-500]

Rosenberg, Paul - *Audel Practical Electricity, 5th Ed.*
    SciTech - v28 - i3 - Sept 2004 - p151(1) [51-500]

Rosenberg, Robert - *This Is Not Civilization*
    BL - v100 - i21 - July 2004 - p1820(1) [1-50]

Rosenberg, Rosalind - *Changing the Subject: How the Women of Columbia Shaped the Way We Think about Sex and Politics*
    KR - v72 - i19 - Oct 1 2004 - p951(2) [501+]
    LJ - v129 - i19 - Nov 15 2004 - p72(2) [501+]

Rosenberg, Saralee - *Claire Voyant*
    LJ - v129 - i16 - Oct 1 2004 - p73(1) [51-500]

Rosenberg, Scott - *Historical Dictionary of Lesotho, 2nd Ed.*
    Choice - v41 - i11-12 - July-August 2004 - p2029(1) [501+]
    HNet - June 2004 - pNA [501+]

Rosenberry, Vera - *Vera Rides a Bike (Illus. by Rosenberry, Vera)*
    c SLJ - v50 - i7 - July 2004 - p86(2) [51-500]
    Vera's Baby Sister (Illus. by Rosenberry, Vera)
    c HB - v81 - i2 - March-April 2005 - p193(1) [51-500]

Rosenblatt, Naomi Harris - *After the Apple: Women in the Bible: Timeless Stories of Love, Lust, and Longing*
    KR - v73 - i1 - Jan 1 2005 - p43(1) [501+]
    LJ - v130 - i4 - March 1 2005 - p93(1) [51-500]
    PW - v252 - i7 - Feb 14 2005 - p72(1) [51-500]

Rosenblith, Walter A. - *Jerry Wiesner: Scientist, Statesman, Humanist-Memories and Memoirs*
    Phys Today - v57 - i8 - August 2004 - p55-56 [501+]

Rosenbloom, Joshua L. - *Looking for Work, Searching for Workers: American Labor Markets During Industrialization*
    JEL - v42 - i1 - March 2004 - p212(2) [501+]

Rosenblum, Mort - *Chocolate: A Bittersweet Saga of Dark and Light*
    KR - v72 - i22 - Nov 15 2004 - p1084(1) [501+]
    LJ - v130 - i1 - Jan 1 2005 - p142(1) [51-500]
    PW - v251 - i50 - Dec 13 2004 - p57(1) [51-500]

Rosenfarb, Chava - *Survivors*
    Globe & Mail - July 10 2004 - pD7 [501+]
    The Tree of Life: On the Brink of the Precipice
    LJ - v130 - i3 - Feb 15 2005 - p172(1) [51-500]

Rosenfeld, Barry - *Assisted Suicide and the Right to Die: The Interface of Social Science, Public Policy, and Medical Ethics*
    SciTech - v28 - i3 - Sept 2004 - p77(1) [51-500]

Rosenfeld, Dana - *The Changing of the Guard: Lesbian and Gay Elders, Identity, and Social Change*
    CS - v33 - i5 - Sept 2004 - p544-546 [501+]
    Peacocks, Chameleons, Centaurs: Gay Suburbia and Grammar of Social Identity
    CS - v33 - i5 - Sept 2004 - p552-553 [501+]

Rosenfeld, David M. - *Unhappy Soldier: Hino Ashihei and Japanese World War II Literature*
    JAS - v63 - i3 - August 2004 - p802-803 [501+]

Rosenfeld, Maya - *Confronting the Occupation: Work, Education, and Political Activism of Palestinian Families in a Refugee Camp*
    Choice - v42 - i2 - Oct 2004 - p352(1) [51-500]
    MEJ - v58 - i4 - Autumn 2004 - p695(2) [501+]
    R&R Bk N - v19 - i3 - August 2004 - p125(1) [51-500]

Ross, Michael A. - *Justice of Shattered Dreams: Samuel Freeman Miller and the Supreme Court During the Civil War Era*
  HNet - June 2004 - pNA [501+]
  JAH - v91 - i3 - Dec 2004 - p1029(2) [501+]
Ross, Michael Elsohn - *Salvador Dali and the Surrealists: Their Lives and Ideas: 21 Activities*
  c LibMed - v22 - i5 - Feb 2004 - p75(2) [501+]
  c SLJ - v50 - i10 - Oct 2004 - pS50(1) [51-500]
  What's the Matter in Mr. Whiskers' Room? (Illus. by Meisel, Paul)
  c KR - v72 - i16 - August 15 2004 - p812(1) [51-500]
  c SLJ - v50 - i10 - Oct 2004 - p148(1) [51-500]
Ross, Nicola - *Dufferin County*
  CBRA - Annual 2003 - p349(2) [51-500]
Ross, Richard - *Waiting for the End of the World*
  R&R Bk N - v19 - i4 - Nov 2004 - p248(1) [501+]
Ross, Robert R. - *Antisocial Drivers: Prosocial Driver Training for Prevention and Rehabilitation*
  R&R Bk N - v19 - i4 - Nov 2004 - p247(1) [501+]
Ross, Robert S. - *Re-Examining the Cold War: U.S.-China Diplomacy, 1954-1973*
  Ch Rev Int - v10 - i2 - Fall 2003 - p436(5) [501+]
Ross, Rosetta E. - *Witnessing and Testifying: Black Women, Religion, and Civil Rights*
  CH - v73 - i3 - Sept 2004 - p703(2) [501+]
  TT - v61 - i2 - July 2004 - p235(4) [501+]
Ross, Sharon - *Decorative Painting and Faux Finishes*
  LJ - v130 - i3 - Feb 15 2005 - p128(1) [51-500]
Ross, Stephen - *Conard and Empire*
  Choice - v42 - i2 - Oct 2004 - p296(1) [501+]
Ross, Stephen L. - *The Color of Credit: Mortgage Discrimination, Research Methodology, and Fair Lending Enforcement*
  CS - v33 - i2 - March 2004 - p166-167 [501+]
  Econ J - v114 - i499 - Nov 2004 - pF541-F543 [501+]
  JEL - v42 - i1 - March 2004 - p190(2) [501+]
  Discrimination in Metropolitian Housing Markets: National Results from Phase 1 Housing Discrimination Study 2000
  CS - v33 - i1 - Jan 2004 - p21-23 [501+]
Ross, Stewart - *The Collapse of Communism*
  y Sch Lib - v52 - i4 - Winter 2004 - p218(1) [51-500]
  y SLJ - v51 - i1 - Jan 2005 - p154(1) [51-500]
  Monarchs
  c BL - v101 - i4 - Oct 15 2004 - p424(2) [51-500]
  Wolfgang Amadeus Mozart: Musical Genius
  c SLJ - v51 - i1 - Jan 2005 - p110(1) [51-500]
Ross, Stuart - *Diabetes and Related Disorders*
  SciTech - v28 - i3 - Sept 2004 - p105(1) [51-500]
Ross, Stuart (b. 1959 -) - *Hey, Crumbling Balcony!: Poems New and Selected*
  CBRA - Annual 2003 - p230(2) [51-500]
Ross, Tamar - *Expanding the Palace of Torah: Orthodoxy and Feminism*
  Choice - v42 - i6 - Feb 2005 - p1040(1) [51-500]
Ross, Tony - *Don't Let Go!*
  LibMed - v22 - i5 - Feb 2004 - p66(1) [501+]
  I Don't Want To Go to Bed! (Illus. by Ross, Tony)
  c SLJ - v50 - i12 - Dec 2004 - p120(1) [51-500]
  I Want My Pacifier (Illus. by Ross, Tony)
  c SLJ - v50 - i12 - Dec 2004 - p120(1) [51-500]
Ross, Val - *The Road to There: Mapmakers and Their Stories*
  c BIC - v33 - i5 - August 2004 - p44(1) [501+]
  The Road to There: Mapmakers and Their Stories
  y CBRA - Annual 2003 - p541(1) [51-500]
  y CG - v124 - i2 - March-April 2004 - p101(1) [501+]
  y VOYA - v27 - i3 - August 2004 - p241(1) [1-50]
Ross, Veronica - *Brain*
  c SB - v40 - i6 - Nov-Dec 2004 - p274(1) [51-500]
  Lungs
  c SB - v40 - i6 - Nov-Dec 2004 - p274(1) [51-500]
Ross, William O.K. - *In Quest of Fur: The Travel Journal of William O.K. Ross, 1909*
  CBRA - Annual 2003 - p68(1) [51-500]
Rossa, O'Donovan - *Rossa's Recollections, 1838-1898: Memoirs of an Irish Revolutionary*
  R&R Bk N - v19 - i3 - August 2004 - p40(1) [501+]
Rossabi, Morris - *Governing China's Multiethnic Frontiers*
  R&R Bk N - v19 - i3 - August 2004 - p183(1) [501+]
  Choice - v42 - i4 - Dec 2004 - p732(2) [1-50]
Rosser, J. Barkley - *Complexity in Economics, Vols. 1-3*
  R&R Bk N - v19 - i4 - Nov 2004 - p84(1) [51-500]

Rosser, Sue V. - *Science Glass Ceiling: Academic Women Scientists and the Struggle to Succeed*
  SciTech - v28 - i3 - Sept 2004 - p13(1) [501+]
Rossholm, Goran - *To Be and Not to Be: On Interpretation, Iconicity and Fiction*
  R&R Bk N - v19 - i3 - August 2004 - p258(1) [501+]
  R&R Bk N - v19 - i4 - Nov 2004 - p221(1) [501+]
Rossi, Andreola - *Context of War: Manipulation of Genre in Virgilian Battle Narrative*
  Choice - v41 - i11-12 - July-August 2004 - p2041(1) [501+]
Rossi, John V. - *Snakes of the United States and Canada: Natural History and Care in Captivity*
  QRB - v79 - i4 - Dec 2004 - p437(1) [501+]
Rossi, Laura Mottioli - *Boccioni's Materia: A Futurist Masterpiece and the Avant-Garde in Milan*
  Choice - v42 - i2 - Oct 2004 - p283(1) [501+]
Rossi, Peter H. - *Evaluation : A Systematic Approach, 7th Ed.*
  R&R Bk N - v19 - i1 - Feb 2004 - p76(1) [51-500]
Rossi, Richard Michael - *Waiting To Die: Life on Death Row*
  LJ - v129 - i20 - Dec 1 2004 - p140(2) [51-500]
Rossignol, Marie-Jeanne - *The Nationalist Ferment: The Origins of U.S. Foreign Policy, 1789-1812*
  Choice - v42 - i1 - Sept 2004 - p177(1) [501+]
Rossing, Barbara R. - *The Rapture Exposed: The Message of Hope in the Book of Relevation*
  Choice - v42 - i3 - Nov 2004 - p501(1) [501+]
Rossino, Alexander - *Hitler Strikes Poland. Blitzkrieg, Ideology, and Atrocity*
  GSR - v27 - i3 - Oct 2004 - p649(2) [501+]
Rossiter, Diane E. - *Leadership Skills*
  y VOYA - v27 - i4 - Oct 2004 - p332(2) [51-500]
Rossiter, Sean - *Chosen Ones: Canada's Test Pilots in Action*
  CBRA - Annual 2003 - p442(2) [51-500]
Rossiter, Walter J., Jr. - *Roofing Research and Standards Development: 5th Volume, Proceedings*
  SciTech - v28 - i1 - March 2004 - p149(1) [51-500]
Rossler, Beate - *Privacies: Philosophical Evaluations*
  Law&PolBR - June 2004 - p489(4) [501+]
Rosslyn, Wendy - *Women and Gender in 18th-Century Russia*
  Slav R - v63 - i4 - Winter 2004 - p888(2) [501+]
Rossman, Allan - *Investigating Statistical Concepts, Applications, and Methods*
  SciTech - v28 - i4 - Dec 2004 - p36(1) [51-500]
Rossman, R. Louis - *TIPS: Discipline in the Music Classroom*
  M Ed J - v91 - i1 - Sept 2004 - p13(1) [501+]
Rossman, Vadim - *Russian Intellectual Antisemitism in the Post-Communist Era*
  Russ Rev - v63 - i2 - April 2004 - pNA [501+]
Rossotti, Charles O. - *Many Unhappy Returns: One Man's Quest to Turn Around the Most Unpopular Organization in America*
  PW - v252 - i4 - Jan 24 2005 - p232(1) [51-500]
Rostad, Lee - *Grace Stone Coates: Her Life in Letters*
  Roundup M - v12 - i3 - Feb 2005 - p22(1) [51-500]
Rostoker-Gruber, Karen - *Rooster Can't Cock-a-Doodle-Doo (Illus. by Tagyos, Paul Ratz de)*
  c HB - v80 - i4 - July-August 2004 - p441(2) [51-500]
  c SLJ - v50 - i7 - July 2004 - p88(1) [51-500]
Rostow, Cary D. - *A Handbook for Psychological Fitness-For-Duty Evaluations in Law Enforcement*
  R&R Bk N - v19 - i4 - Nov 2004 - p147(1) [501+]
Rostow, Walt - *Concept and Controversy: Sixty Years of Taking Ideas to Market*
  JEL - v41 - i4 - Dec 2003 - p1337(1) [501+]
Roszler, Janis - *The Secrets to Living and Loving with Diabetes*
  Bwatch - Jan 2005 - pNA [51-500]
Rotberg, Iris C. - *Balancing Change and Tradition in Global Education Reform*
  R&R Bk N - v19 - i4 - Nov 2004 - p178(1) [501+]
Rotella, Carlo - *Cut Time: An Education at the Fights*
  BL - v101 - i1 - Sept 1 2004 - p52(1) [501+]
Rotella, Guy - *Castings: Monuments and Monumentality in Poems by Elizabeth Bishop, Robert Lowell, James Merrill, Derek Walcott, and Seamus Heaney*
  Choice - v42 - i3 - Nov 2004 - p487(1) [1-50]
Rotella, Mark - *Stolen Figs and Other Adventures in Calabria*
  BooChiTr - Jan 4 2004 - p2(1) [501+]
Rotenberg, David - *Hua Shan Hospital Murders*
  CBRA - Annual 2003 - p183(1) [51-500]

Rotgers, Frederick - *Treating Substance Abuse: Theory and Technique, 2nd Ed.*
  E-Streams - Oct 2004 - pNA [501+]
  SciTech - v28 - i1 - March 2004 - p102(1) [51-500]
Roth, Benita - *Separate Roads to Feminism: Black, Chicana, and White Feminist Movements in America's Second Wave*
  HNet - Sept 2004 - pNA [501+]
  Wom R Bks - v22 - i2 - Nov 2004 - p20(2) [501+]
Roth, Jeffrey D. - *Group Psychotherapy and Recovery from Addiction: Carrying the Message*
  SciTech - v28 - i3 - Sept 2004 - p103(1) [51-500]
Roth, Joseph - *Right and Left*
  BIC - v33 - i7 - Oct 2004 - p10(2) [501+]
  The White Cities: Reports From France
  Spec - v296 - i9199 - Nov 27 2004 - p42(2) [501+]
Roth, Ken - *Successful Landlord*
  Bwatch - Oct 2004 - pNA [51-500]
Roth, Laurence - *Inspecting Jews: American Jewish Detective Stories*
  Choice - v41 - i11-12 - July-August 2004 - p2047(1) [501+]
Roth, Matthue - *Never Mind the Goldbergs*
  KR - v73 - i2 - Jan 15 2005 - p125(1) [51-500]
  y PW - v252 - i10 - March 7 2005 - p68(2) [51-500]
Roth, Mitchel P. - *Crime and Punishment: A History of the Criminal Justice System*
  R&R Bk N - v19 - i3 - August 2004 - p170(1) [501+]
Roth, Philip - *The Plot Against America (Read by Silver, Ron). Audiobook Review*
  y Kliatt - v39 - i2 - March 2005 - p55(1) [51-500]
  PW - v251 - i49 - Dec 6 2004 - p19(2) [51-500]
  The Plot Against America
  BIC - v33 - i9 - Dec 2004 - p4(2) [501+]
  BL - v100 - i22 - August 2004 - p1874(1) [51-500]
  BL - v101 - i9-10 - Jan 1 2005 - p770(1) [51-500]
  BW - v34 - i40 - Oct 3 2004 - p2(2) [501+]
  CC - v121 - i25 - Dec 14 2004 - p22(1) [51-500]
  Comw - v131 - i21 - Dec 3 2004 - p26(2) [501+]
  Econ - v373 - i8396 - Oct 9 2004 - p80US [501+]
  Ent W - i787 - Oct 8 2004 - p118 [501+]
  Globe & Mail - Oct 2 2004 - pD11 [501+]
  Globe & Mail - Nov 27 2004 - pD3 [51-500]
  Globe & Mail - Dec 24 2004 - pD3 [1-50]
  KR - v72 - i14 - July 15 2004 - p655(2) [501+]
  LJ - v129 - i15 - Sept 15 2004 - p50(1) [51-500]
  Lon R Bks - v26 - i21 - Nov 4 2004 - p3(3) [501+]
  Mac - v117 - i46 - Nov 15 2004 - p129(3) [501+]
  Nation - v279 - i17 - Nov 22 2004 - p23 [501+]
  NS - v133 - i4709 - Oct 11 2004 - p48(2) [501+]
  NS - v133 - i4716 - Nov 29 2004 - p46(1) [51-500]
  NW - Sept 20 2004 - p56 [501+]
  NY - v80 - i27 - Sept 20 2004 - p096 [501+]
  NYRB - v51 - i18 - Nov 18 2004 - p4(3) [501+]
  NYTBR - Oct 3 2004 - p1 [501+]
  People - v62 - i14 - Oct 4 2004 - p57 [51-500]
  People - Dec 27 2004 - p63 [501+]
  PW - v251 - i28 - July 12 2004 - p44(1) [501+]
  SLJ - v50 - i11 - Nov 2004 - p177(2) [51-500]
  Spec - v296 - i9195 - Oct 30 2004 - p57(2) [501+]
  Time - v164 - i13 - Sept 27 2004 - p67 [501+]
  TLS - i5297 - Oct 8 2004 - p21-22 [501+]
  Atl - v294 - i4 - Nov 2004 - p143(5) [501+]
  NL - v87 - i5 - Sept-Oct 2004 - p28(3) [501+]
Roth, Ralf - *City and the Railway in Europe*
  SciTech - v28 - i1 - March 2004 - p149(1) [51-500]
Roth, Seigmar - *One-Dimensional Metals: Conjugated Polymers, Organic Crystals, Carbon Nanotubes, 2nd Rev. Ed.*
  SciTech - v28 - i3 - Sept 2004 - p52(1) [1-50]
Roth, Silke - *Building Movement Bridges: The Coalition of Labor Union Women*
  CS - v33 - i4 - July 2004 - p479(2) [501+]
  Die Konigsmutter des Alten Agypten von der Fruhzeit bis zum Ende der 12. Dynastie
  JNES - v63 - i3 - July 2004 - p219(3) [501+]
Roth, Susan L. - *Hanukkah, Oh Hanukkah (Illus. by Roth, Susan L.)*
  c BL - v101 - i1 - Sept 1 2004 - p130(1) [501+]
  c HB - v80 - i6 - Nov-Dec 2004 - p663(1) [51-500]
  c KR - v72 - i21 - Nov 1 2004 - p1053(1) [51-500]
  c PW - v251 - i39 - Sept 27 2004 - p59(1) [501+]
  Hard Hat Area (Illus. by Roth, Susan L.)
  c BL - v101 - i5 - Nov 1 2004 - p493(2) [51-500]
  c CCB-B - v58 - i5 - Jan 2005 - p225(1) [51-500]
  c HB - v81 - i1 - Jan-Feb 2005 - p110(2) [51-500]
  c KR - v72 - i16 - August 15 2004 - p812(1) [51-500]
  c PW - v251 - i44 - Nov 1 2004 - p61(1) [501+]
  c SLJ - v50 - i9 - Sept 2004 - p178(1) [51-500]

Roth, Timothy P. - *Equality, Rights, and the Autonomous Self: Toward a Conservative Economics*
Choice - v42 - i2 - Oct 2004 - p341(1) [51-500]
R&R Bk N - v19 - i3 - August 2004 - p92(1) [51-500]
The Ethics and the Economics of Minimalist Government
Soc Ser R - v78 - i4 - Dec 2004 - p697(2) [51-500]

Roth, Wolff-Michael - *Rethinking Scientific Literacy*
TCR - v107 - i2 - Feb 2005 - p255(4) [501+]

Rothbart, Davy - *Found: The Best Lost, Tossed, and Forgotten Items from around the World*
Globe & Mail - July 3 2004 - pD3 [501+]
y SLJ - v50 - i11 - Nov 2004 - p179(1) [51-500]

Rothberg, Robert I. - *Patterns of Social Capital: Stability and Change in Historical Perspective*
JTWS - v21 - i1 - Spring 2004 - p336(3) [501+]
When States Fail: Causes and Consequences
Choice - v41 - i11-12 - July-August 2004 - p2123(1) [501+]

Rothenberg, David - *Why Birds Sing: A Journey through the Mystery of Bird Song*
KR - v73 - i3 - Feb 1 2005 - p170(2) [501+]
LJ - v130 - i4 - March 1 2005 - p109(1) [51-500]
PW - v252 - i8 - Feb 21 2005 - p167(1) [51-500]

Rothenberg, Jerome - *Writing Through: Translations and Variations*
LJ - v129 - i12 - July 2004 - p86(1) [51-500]

Rothenberg, Laura - *Breathing for a Living: A Memoir*
BooChiTr - Jan 4 2004 - p2(1) [501+]
Parabola - v29 - i3 - Fall 2004 - p136-2 [501+]

Rothfels, Nigel - *Savages and Beasts: The Birth of the Modern Zoo*
Comw - v131 - i16 - Sept 24 2004 - p32(2) [501+]
JMH - v76 - i3 - Sept 2004 - p665(3) [501+]

Rothfuss, Joan - *Past Things and Present: Jasper Johns Since 1983*
R&R Bk N - v19 - i2 - May 2004 - p195(1) [51-500]

Rothko, Mark - *The Artsits's Reality: Philosophies of Art*
Choice - v42 - i7 - March 2005 - p1218(1) [51-500]

Rothman, Adam - *Slave Country: American Expansion and the Origins of the Deep South*
PW - v252 - i2 - Jan 10 2005 - p45(1) [51-500]

Rothman, Barbara Katz - *Weaving a Family: Untangling Race and Adoption*
KR - v73 - i4 - Feb 15 2005 - p220(1) [501+]

Rothman, David - *The Pursuit of Perfection: The Promise and Perils of Medical Enhancement*
Dis - v51 - i3 - Summer 2004 - p95(8) [501+]

Rothman, Hal K. - *The Culture of Tourism, the Tourism of Culture: Selling ther Past to the Present in the American Southwest*
WHQ - v35 - i4 - Winter 2004 - p508-509 [501+]
Encyclopedia of American National Parks
Choice - v42 - i7 - March 2005 - p1191(1) [51-500]
Encyclopedia of American National Parks, Vols. 1-2
LJ - v129 - i20 - Dec 1 2004 - p162(2) [51-500]
The Grit Beneath the Glitter: Tales of the Real Las Vegas
J Urban H - v31 - i2 - Jan 2005 - p258-268 [501+]
The New Urban Park: Golden Gate National Recreation Area and Civic Environmentalism
Choice - v42 - i2 - Oct 2004 - p358(1) [51-500]
PHR - v73 - i4 - Nov 2004 - p692(3) [501+]

Rothman, Jack - *Hollywood in Wide Angle: How Directors View Filmmaking*
LJ - v130 - i2 - Feb 1 2005 - p81(2) [501+]

Rothman, Joshua D. - *Notorious in the Neighborhood: Sex and Families Across the Color Line in Virginia, 1787-1861*
JAH - v91 - i1 - June 2004 - p231-231 [501+]
JSH - v71 - i1 - Feb 2005 - p143(2) [501+]
RAH - v32 - i1 - March 2004 - p20(7) [501+]

Rothman, Tony - *Everything's Relative: And Other Fables from Science and Technology*
Choice - v41 - i11-12 - July-August 2004 - p2065(1) [501+]
Phys Today - v57 - i11 - Nov 2004 - p63-63 [501+]

Rothschild, Emma - *Economic Sentiments: Adam Smith, Condorcet, and the Enlightenment*
JMH - v76 - i3 - Sept 2004 - p658(3) [501+]

Rothschild, Lynn J. - *Evolution on Planet Earth: The Impact of the Physical Environment*
Choice - v41 - i7 - March 2004 - p1320(1) [501+]

Rothschild, Rose - *A Rose Blooms Again: A Survivor's Story*
R&R Bk N - v19 - i1 - Feb 2004 - p44(1) [51-500]

Rothstein, Mark A. - *Genetics and Life Insurance: Medical Underwriting and Social Policy*
Choice - v42 - i7 - March 2005 - p1259(1) [51-500]

Rothstein, Richard - *Class and Schools: Using Social, Economic, and Educational Reform to Close The Black-White Achievement Gap*
Dis - v51 - i4 - Fall 2004 - p93(4) [501+]
TCR - v107 - i2 - Feb 2005 - p311(4) [501+]

Rothstein, William G. - *Public Health and the Risk Factor: A History of an Uneven Medical Revolution*
JAH - v91 - i3 - Dec 2004 - p1060(2) [501+]

Rothwell, Geoffrey - *Electricity Economics: Regulation and Deregulation*
JEL - v42 - i3 - Sept 2004 - p868(2) [501+]

Rothwell, Phillip - *A Postmodern Nationalist: Truth, Orality, and Gender in the Work of Mia Couto*
Choice - v42 - i4 - Dec 2004 - p656(2) [1-50]

Rothwell, William J. - *Mastering the Instructional Design Process: A Systematic Approach*
R&R Bk N - v19 - i3 - August 2004 - p130(1) [51-500]
Strategic Development of Talent: A Framework for Using Talent to Support Your Organizational Strategy
HR Mag - v50 - i2 - Feb 2005 - pS17(1) [501+]

Rotker, Susana - *Captive Women: Oblivion and Memory in Argentina*
Biomag - v27 - i4 - Fall 2004 - p859(4) [501+]

Rotman, Deborah L. - *Shared Spaces and Divided Places: Material Dimensions of Gender Relations and the American Historical Landscape*
JAH - v91 - i3 - Dec 2004 - p1004(2) [501+]

Rotner, Shelley - *Lots of Feelings*
c SLJ - v50 - i10 - Oct 2004 - pS24(1) [1-50]

Rotskoff, Lori - *Love on the Rocks: Men, Women, and Alcohol in Postwar America*
Am Q - v56 - i2 - June 2004 - p489(9) [501+]

Rotter, Ekkehart - *Die Zeit Wenzels 1376-1387*
Six Ct J - v34 - i4 - Winter 2003 - p1134-1135 [501+]

Rottman, S.L. - *Slalom*
y BL - v101 - i1 - Sept 1 2004 - p110(1) [1-50]
y CCB-B - v58 - i4 - Dec 2004 - p183(1) [51-500]
y Kliatt - v38 - i5 - Sept 2004 - p16(2) [51-500]
y KR - v72 - i18 - Sept 15 2004 - p919(1) [51-500]
y SLJ - v50 - i11 - Nov 2004 - p153(1) [51-500]
y VOYA - v27 - i4 - Oct 2004 - p306(1) [51-500]

Rouch, Lawrence L. - *The Vernor's Story: From Gnomes to Now*
JEL - v42 - i1 - March 2004 - p304(1) [501+]

Rouda, Bill - *Nashville's Lower Broad: The Street thet Music Made*
R&R Bk N - v19 - i3 - August 2004 - p74(1) [51-500]

Roudaut, Francois - *Le Livre au XVIe siecle: Elements de bibliographie materielle et d'histoire*
Ren Q - v57 - i4 - Winter 2004 - p1444(3) [501+]

Rougeau, Remy - *All We Know of Heaven*
Comw - v131 - i21 - Dec 3 2004 - p29(2) [501+]

Rouget, Francois - *Cite des hommes, cite de Dieu: Travaux sur la litterature de la Renaissance en l'honneur de Daniel Menager*
Ren Q - v57 - i3 - Fall 2004 - p1073(3) [501+]

Roughan, Howard - *The Promise of a Lie (Read by Dean, Robertson). Audiobook Review*
BL - v100 - i22 - August 2004 - p1954(1) [51-500]
Kliatt - v38 - i5 - Sept 2004 - p64(2) [51-500]
LJ - v129 - i17 - Oct 15 2004 - p96(1) [51-500]

Roughgarden, Joan - *Evolution's Rainbow: Diversity, Gender, and Sexuality in Nature and People*
Am Sci - v92 - i5 - Sept-Oct 2004 - p464(4) [501+]
BW - v34 - i27 - July 4 2004 - p7(1) [501+]
Choice - v42 - i3 - Nov 2004 - p509(1) [1-50]
G&L Rev W - v11 - i4 - July-August 2004 - p38(2) [501+]
Globe & Mail - July 10 2004 - pD13 [501+]
Globe & Mail - July 10 2004 - pD9 [501+]
Nature - v429 - i6987 - May 6 2004 - p19(2) [501+]
PW - v251 - i49 - Dec 6 2004 - p32(2) [51-500]
TimHES - v0 - i1668 - Nov 26 2004 - p24(2) [501+]
TLS - i5287 - July 30 2004 - p5(1) [501+]

Rougier, A. - *Electrochromic Materials and Applications: Proceedings*
SciTech - v28 - i1 - March 2004 - p146(1) [51-500]

Roukes, Nicholas - *Artful Jesters: Innovators of Visual Wit and Humor*
Choice - v42 - i2 - Oct 2004 - p282 [501+]

Roulis, Eleni - *Transforming Learning for the Workplace of the New Millennium: Students and Workers as Critical Learners, Bk. 3*
R&R Bk N - v19 - i1 - Feb 2004 - p191(1) [51-500]

Rounce, Adam - *Charles Churchill: Selected Poetry*
TLS - i5288 - August 6 2004 - p28(1) [51-500]

Rounds, Charles E. - *Loring: A Trustee's Handbook, 2004 Ed.*
R&R Bk N - v19 - i4 - Nov 2004 - p166(1) [501+]

Roundy, Shad - *Energy Scavenging for Wireless Sensor Networks: With Special Focus on Vibrations*
SciTech - v28 - i1 - March 2004 - p162(1) [51-500]

Rountree, Helen C. - *Before and After Jamestown: Virginia's Powhatans and Their Predecessors*
Am Ind CRJ - v27 - i2 - Spring 2003 - p106-108 [501+]

Rourke, Constance - *American Humor: A Study of the National Character*
JPC - v38 - i3 - Feb 2005 - p600(2) [501+]

Rouse, Carolyn Moxley - *Engaged Surrender: African American Women and Islam*
Choice - v42 - i2 - Oct 2004 - p377(2) [501+]
JR - v84 - i4 - Oct 2004 - p592(12) [501+]

Rouse, Joseph - *How Scientific Practices Matter: Reclaiming Philosophical Naturalism*
RM - v58 - i1 - Sept 2004 - p191(4) [501+]

Rousmaniere, John - *Sleek: Classic Images from the Rosenfeld Collection*
R&R Bk N - v19 - i4 - Nov 2004 - p253(1) [501+]

Rouss, Sylvia - *The Littlest Frog*
c CH Bwatch - v14 - i8 - August 2004 - p4(1) [51-500]
Reach for the Stars: A Little Torah's Journey (Illus. by Ofer, Rosalie)
c SLJ - v50 - i8 - August 2004 - p112(2) [51-500]
Tali's Jerusalem Scrapbook (Illus. by Oppenheimer, Nancy)
c BL - v101 - i7 - Dec 1 2004 - p647(1) [51-500]

Roussas, George G. - *An Introduction to Measure-Theoretic Probability*
Choice - v42 - i7 - March 2005 - p1263(2) [51-500]

Rousseau, George - *Yourcenar*
TLS - i5293 - Sept 10 2004 - p27(1) [501+]

Routh, Kristina - *Down Syndrome*
c SLJ - v51 - i2 - Feb 2005 - p147(1) [51-500]
Tuberculosis
y Sch Lib - v52 - i3 - Autumn 2004 - p165(1) [501+]

Routledge - *Journal of Chinese Economics and Business Studies*
JEL - v41 - i4 - Dec 2003 - p1447(1) [501+]
Review of Middle East Economics and Finance
JEL - v41 - i4 - Dec 2003 - p1448(1) [501+]

Routledge's Encyclopedia of the Arctic
BL - v101 - i9-10 - Jan 1 2005 - p908(1) [51-500]

Roux, Nicolas Le - *La Faveur du Roi*
Six Ct J - v34 - i4 - Winter 2003 - p1170-1172 [501+]

Rovin, Jeff - *Tom Clancy's Op Center: Call To Treason (Read by Kramer, Michael). Audiobook Review*
y Kliatt - v39 - i1 - Jan 2005 - p51(1) [51-500]

Rovner, Julie - *Health Care Policy and Politics A to Z, 2nd Ed.*
SciTech - v28 - i1 - March 2004 - p81(1) [51-500]

Row, Jess - *The Train to Lo Wu: Stories*
Ent W - i803 - Jan 28 2005 - p86 [501+]
KR - v72 - i24 - Dec 15 2004 - p1161(1) [501+]
PW - v252 - i1 - Jan 3 2005 - p34(1) [51-500]

Rowan, Roy - *Chasing the Dragon: A Veteran Journalist's Firsthand Account of the 1949 Chinese Revolution*
Ent W - i806 - Feb 11 2005 - p67 [51-500]
People - v62 - i19 - Nov 8 2004 - p60 [51-500]
R&R Bk N - v19 - i4 - Nov 2004 - p49(1) [1-50]

Rowan, Yorke - *Marketing Heritage: Archaeology and the Consumption of the Past*
R&R Bk N - v19 - i4 - Nov 2004 - p30(1) [501+]

Rowe, Dorothy - *Representing Berlin: Sexuality and the Big City in Imperial and Weimar Germany*
GSR - v27 - i2 - May 2004 - p401-403 [501+]

Rowe-Finkbeiner, Kristin - *The F Word: Feminism in Jeopardy; Women, Politics, and the Future*
LJ - v129 - i16 - Oct 1 2004 - p102(1) [51-500]

Rowe, Fiona - *Clinical Orthoptics, 2nd Ed.*
SciTech - v28 - i1 - Sept 2004 - p115(1) [51-500]

Rowe, Greg - *Princes and Political Cultures: The New Tiberian Senatorial Decrees*
AHR - v109 - i3 - June 2004 - p956(2) [501+]
Class R - v54 - i1 - May 2004 - p180(3) [501+]

Rowe, John - *Amazing Animal Hide and Seek*
  c Sch Lib - v52 - i4 - Winter 2004 - p187(1) [51-500]

Rowe, John A. - *The Emperor's New Clothes*
  c BW - v34 - i39 - Sept 26 2004 - p11(1) [501+]

Rowe, Lisa - *Don't Cramp My Style*
  c BooChiTr - May 16 2004 - p3(1) [501+]

Rowe, Mary Ellen - *Bulwark of the Republic: The American Militia in the Antebellum West*
  JAH - v91 - i3 - Dec 2004 - p1020(2) [501+]
  R&R Bk N - v19 - i1 - Feb 2004 - p64(1) [501+]

Rowe, Michael - *Collaboration and Resistance in Napoleonic Europe: State-Formation in an Age of Upheaval, c. 1800-1815*
  J Soc H - v38 - i1 - Fall 2004 - p221(3) [501+]
From Reich to State: The Rhineland in the Revolutionary Age, 1780-1830
  AHR - v109 - i4 - Oct 2004 - p1325(2) [501+]
Policing, Race and Racism
  Law&PolBR - Sept 2004 - pNA [501+]
  R&R Bk N - v19 - i3 - August 2004 - p169(1) [501+]
Queer Fear II: Gay Horror Fiction
  CBRA - Annual 2003 - p248(1) [51-500]

Rowe, Ray C. - *Pharmaceutical Excipients 2004 Single-user Version*
  SciTech - v28 - i4 - Dec 2004 - p119(1) [1-50]

Rowe, Victoria - *A History of Armenian Women's Writing, 1880-1992*
  Choice - v42 - i3 - Nov 2004 - p479(1) [1-50]

Rowitz, Louis - *Public Health Leadership: Putting Principles into Practice*
  SciTech - v28 - i1 - March 2004 - p82(1) [51-500]

Rowland, Debran - *The Boundaries of Her Body: The Troubling History of Women's Rights in America*
  Black Iss - v7 - i2 - March-April 2005 - p55(1) [501+]
  Choice - v42 - i5 - Jan 2005 - p940(1) [51-500]
  KR - v72 - i14 - July 15 2004 - p678(1) [501+]
  LJ - v129 - i13 - August 2004 - p98(1) [501+]
  R&R Bk N - v19 - i4 - Nov 2004 - p166(1) [501+]

Rowland, Herbert - *Goethe, Chaos, and Complexity*
  Ger Q - v77 - i1 - Wntr 2004 - p96(3) [501+]
  Ger Q - v77 - i1 - Wntr 2004 - p102(1) [501+]

Rowland, Ingrid D. - *The Scarith of Scornello: A Tale of Renaissance Forgery*
  LJ - v130 - i3 - Feb 15 2005 - p145(1) [51-500]
  NYTBR - Jan 16 2005 - p22 [501+]
  Spec - v296 - i9198 - Nov 20 2004 - p43(1) [501+]

Rowland, Susan - *Jung: A Feminist Revision*
  Col Lit - v32 - i1 - Wntr 2005 - p177(10) [501+]
  JGS - v13 - i1 - March 2004 - p83-85 [501+]

Rowlands, Alison - *Witchcraft Narratives in Germany: Rothenburg 1561-1652*
  R&R Bk N - v19 - i1 - Feb 2004 - p9(1) [51-500]

Rowlands, Betty - *Deadly Obsession*
  BL - v101 - i7 - Dec 1 2004 - p640(1) [51-500]

Rowlands, Guy - *The Dynastic State and the Army under Louis XIV: Royal Service and Private Interest, 1661-1701.*
  JIH - v34 - i3 - Wntr 2004 - p459(3) [501+]
  JMH - v77 - i1 - March 2005 - p189(3) [501+]

Rowlands, Mark - *The Philosopher at the End of the Universe: Philosophy Explained Through Science Fiction Films*
  Analog - v124 - i11 - Nov 2004 - p134(6) [501+]
  y BL - v100 - i22 - August 2004 - p1889(1) [51-500]
  LJ - v129 - i12 - July 2004 - p85(2) [51-500]

Rowley, Charles Kershaw - *The Encyclopedia of Public Choice*
  JEL - v42 - i1 - March 2004 - p251(1) [501+]
  R&R Bk N - v19 - i1 - Feb 2004 - p75(1) [51-500]

Rowley, Daniel James - *Academic Planning: The Heart and Soul of the Academic Strategic Plan*
  R&R Bk N - v19 - i3 - August 2004 - p221(1) [1-50]

Rowley, Mari-Lou - *Viral Suite*
  Globe & Mail - July 17 2004 - pD12 [501+]

Rowling, J.K. - *Harry Potter and the Order of the Phoenix*
  c BW - v34 - i35 - August 2004 - p11(1) [1-50]
Harry Potter and the Order of the Phoenix. Audiobook Review
  c Globe & Mail - Dec 11 2004 - pD53 [1-50]
Harry Potter and the Sorcerer's Stone
  c TCR - v106 - i2 - Feb 2004 - p267-270 [501+]
  c WLT - v79 - i1 - Jan-April 2005 - p69(4) [501+]

Rowse, A. L. - *The Expansion of Elizabethan England, 2d ed.*
  R&R Bk N - v19 - i4 - Nov 2004 - p36(1) [51-500]

Rowse, Tim - *Nugget Coombs: A Reforming Life*
  BHR - v78 - i2 - Summer 2004 - p371(3) [501+]
  JEH - v64 - i1 - March 2004 - p260(3) [501+]

Roxburgh, David J. - *Turks: A Journey of a Thousand Years, 600-1600*
  TimHES - v0 - i1682 - March 11 2005 - p24(2) [501+]

Roy, Ananya - *Urban Informality: Transnational Perspectives from the Middle East, Latin America, and South Asia*
  R&R Bk N - v19 - i1 - Feb 2004 - p134(1) [51-500]

Roy, Arundhati - *An Ordinary Person's Guide to Empire*
  R&R Bk N - v19 - i4 - Nov 2004 - p64(1) [1-50]
  Wom R Bks - v21 - i12 - Sept 2004 - p16(2) [501+]

Roy, Denny - *Taiwan: A Political History*
  Ch Rev Int - v10 - i2 - Fall 2003 - p440(4) [501+]

Roy, F. Hampton - *Master Techniques in Cataract and Refractive Surgery*
  SciTech - v28 - i3 - Sept 2004 - p115(1) [51-500]

Roy, James - *Billy Mack's War*
  y Magpies - v19 - i5 - Nov 2004 - p36(2) [501+]

Roy, Louis - *Mystical Consciousness: Western Perspectives and Dialogue with Japanese Thinkers*
  JR - v84 - i4 - Oct 2004 - p651(2) [501+]
  Theol St - v65 - i4 - Dec 2004 - p903(1) [501+]

Roy, Michael J. - *Physician's Guide to Terrorist Attack*
  E-Streams - July 2004 - pNA [501+]
  SciTech - v28 - i1 - March 2004 - p89(1) [51-500]

Roy, Olivier - *Globalized Islam: The Search for a New Ummah*
  Econ - v373 - i8397 - Oct 16 2004 - p80US [501+]
  For Aff - v84 - i1 - Jan-Feb 2005 - p148 [501+]
  Globe & Mail - Nov 20 2004 - pD16 [501+]
  MEJ - v59 - i1 - Wntr 2005 - p161(3) [501+]
  NYTBR - Feb 6 2005 - p28 [501+]

Roy, Patricia E. - *The Oriental Question: Consolidating a White Man's Province, 1914-41*
  Can Hist R - v85 - i4 - Dec 2004 - p793(4) [501+]
  CBRA - Annual 2003 - p357(2) [501+]
  R&R Bk N - v19 - i1 - Feb 2004 - p68(1) [501+]

Roy, Ranjan - *Chronic Pain, Loss, and Suffering*
  SciTech - v28 - i4 - Dec 2004 - p88(1) [501+]

Roy, Rob - *Sauna: A Complete Guide to the Construction, Use, and Benefits of the Finnish Bath*
  Bwatch - March 2005 - pNA [51-500]

Roy, Robert L. - *Timber Framing for the Rest of Us: A Guide to Contemporary Post and Beam Construction*
  LJ - v129 - i20 - Dec 1 2004 - p158(1) [51-500]

Royal, Brandon - *The Little Red Writing Book: 20 Powerful Principles of Structure, Style & Readability*
  LJ - v129 - i13 - August 2004 - p91(1) [501+]

The Royal Canadian Geographic Society - *The Canadian Atlas*
  Globe & Mail - Sept 18 2004 - pT6 [501+]

Royal Canadian Geographical Society - *The Canadian Atlas: Our Nation, Environment and People*
  c Globe & Mail - Jan 15 2005 - pD16 [501+]

Royal, Priscilla - *Tyrant of the Mind*
  BL - v101 - i8 - Dec 15 2004 - p712(1) [51-500]

Royal, Priscilla J. - *Tyrant Of The Mind*
  Bwatch - Feb 2005 - pNA [51-500]
  LJ - v129 - i18 - Nov 1 2004 - p60(1) [51-500]
  PW - v251 - i46 - Nov 15 2004 - p44(1) [51-500]

Royal Society of Chemistry - *100 Years of Physical Chemistry*
  Choice - v42 - i3 - Nov 2004 - p511(1) [1-50]

Royalle, Candida - *How to Tell a Naked Man What to Do: Sex Advice from a Woman Who Knows*
  LJ - v129 - i15 - Sept 15 2004 - p71(1) [51-500]

Royce, Anya Peterson - *Anthropology of the Performing Arts: Artistry, Virtuosity, and Interpretation in a Cross-Cultural Perspective*
  Choice - v42 - i6 - Feb 2005 - p1065(2) [51-500]
  R&R Bk N - v19 - i3 - August 2004 - p260(1) [501+]

Royeen, Charlotte Brasic - *Pediatric Issues in Occupational Therapy: A Compendium of Leading Scholarship*
  SciTech - v28 - i4 - Dec 2004 - p111(1) [1-50]

Royle, Nicholas - *Derrida in and out of Context: On the Necessity to Know "Why Derrida?"*
  MLN - v118 - i5 - Dec 2003 - p1298-1310 [501+]

Royle, Trevor - *The British Civil War: The Wars of the Three Kingdoms, 1638-1660*
  Choice - v42 - i6 - Feb 2005 - p1087(1) [51-500]
Civil War: The Wars of the Three Kingdoms 1638-1660
  CR - v285 - i1664 - Sept 2004 - p189(1) [51-500]

Royston, Angela - *Asthma*
  c SLJ - v50 - i12 - Dec 2004 - p137(1) [501+]
Eat Well
  c SB - v40 - i4 - July-August 2004 - p150(1) [51-500]
Healthy Body
  c SB - v40 - i4 - July-August 2004 - p150(1) [51-500]
It's Not Catching -- Tooth Decay
  c Sch Lib - v52 - i3 - Autumn 2004 - p134(1) [1-50]
My Amazing Body -- Moving
  c Sch Lib - v52 - i3 - Autumn 2004 - p134(1) [501+]
Why Do Bones Break? And Other Questions about Movement
  c SB - v40 - i4 - July-August 2004 - p150(2) [51-500]
Why Do Bruises Change Color? And Other Questions about Blood
  c SB - v40 - i4 - July-August 2004 - p150(2) [51-500]
Why Do I Get a Toothache? And Other Questions about the Nervous System
  c SB - v40 - i4 - July-August 2004 - p150(2) [51-500]
Why Do I Get Sunburned? And Other Questions about Skin
  c SB - v40 - i4 - July-August 2004 - p150(2) [51-500]
Why Do I Sneeze? And Other Questions about Breathing
  c SB - v40 - i4 - July-August 2004 - p150(2) [51-500]
Why Do I Vomit? And Other Questions about Digestion
  c SB - v40 - i4 - July-August 2004 - p150(2) [51-500]
Why Do My Eyes Itch? And Other Questions about Allergies
  c SB - v40 - i4 - July-August 2004 - p150(2) [51-500]
Why Does my Body Smell? And Other Questions about Hygiene
  c SB - v40 - i4 - July-August 2004 - p150(2) [51-500]

Roza, Greg - *The Incredible Story of Aircraft Carriers*
  c SLJ - v51 - i2 - Feb 2005 - p128(1) [501+]
The Incredible Story of Computers and the Interact
  c SLJ - v51 - i2 - Feb 2005 - p128(1) [501+]
The Incredible Story of Skyscrapers
  c SLJ - v51 - i2 - Feb 2005 - p128(1) [501+]
The Incredible Story of Telescopes
  c SLJ - v51 - i2 - Feb 2005 - p128(1) [501+]

Rozan, S.J. - *Absent Friends*
  BL - v101 - i1 - Sept 1 2004 - p7(1) [51-500]
  Globe & Mail - Oct 2 2004 - pD18 [51-500]
  KR - v72 - i17 - Sept 1 2004 - p832(1) [501+]
  LJ - v129 - i15 - Sept 15 2004 - p50(1) [51-500]
  People - v62 - i16 - Oct 18 2004 - p49 [51-500]
  PW - v251 - i36 - Sept 6 2004 - p45(2) [51-500]
  Ent W - i812 - March 25 2005 - p76 [501+]

Rozek, Barbara J. - *Come to Texas: Attracting Immigrants, 1865-1915*
  Choice - v41 - i7 - March 2004 - p1358(1) [501+]
  SHQ - v107 - i4 - April 2004 - p637(2) [501+]
  WHQ - v35 - i3 - Autumn 2004 - p396(2) [501+]

Rozell, Mark - *Executive Privilege: Presidential Power, Secrecy, and Accountability*
  Pres St Q - v34 - i4 - Dec 2004 - p893(2) [501+]

Rozelle, Scott D. - *Agricultural Trade and Policy in China: Issues, Analysis and Implications*
  R&R Bk N - v19 - i1 - Feb 2004 - p85(1) [1-50]

Rozema, Vicki - *Cherokee Voices: Early Accounts of Cherokee Life in the East*
  Am Ind CRJ - v27 - i2 - Spring 2003 - p108-110 [501+]

Rozen, Beti - *A Heart Alone in the Land of Darkness*
  c CH Bwatch - v14 - i8 - August 2004 - p6(1) [51-500]

Rozenberg, Jacques J. - *Bioethical and Ethical Issues Surrounding the Trials and Code of Nuremberg: Nuremberg Revisited*
  R&R Bk N - v19 - i1 - Feb 2004 - pNA [51-500]

Rozenberg, Joshua - *Privacy and the Press*
  HLR - v118 - i3 - Jan 2005 - p1097(1) [1-50]
  Law&PolBR - Sept 2004 - pNA [501+]
  TimHES - v0 - i1665 - Nov 5 2004 - p24(1) [501+]

Rozenberg, Ronald H. - *Psychology Builds a Healthy World: Opportunities for Research and Practice*
  SciTech - v28 - i1 - March 2004 - p78(1) [51-500]

Rozewicz, Tadeusz - *They Came to See a Poet*
  TLS - i5292 - Sept 3 2004 - p25(1) [501+]

Rozman, Gilbert - *Northeast Asia's Stunted Regionalism: Bilateral Distrust in the Shadow of Globalization*
Choice - v42 - i5 - Jan 2005 - p931(1) [51-500]
Rozwadowski, Helen M. - *Fathoming the Ocean: The Discovery and Exploration of the Deep Sea*
LJ - v129 - i20 - Dec 1 2004 - p157(2) [51-500]
PW - v252 - i3 - Jan 17 2005 - p44(1) [51-500]
Rrenban, Monad - *Wild, Unforgettable Philosophy: In Early Works of Walter Benjamin*
R&R Bk N - v20 - i1 - Feb 2005 - p5(1) [51-500]
Rsenault, Elaine - *Doggie in the Window (Illus. by Fanny)*
c Res Links - v10 - i3 - Feb 2005 - p2(1) [51-500]
RSM McGladrey, Inc. - *Mandated Benefits 2004 Compliance Guide*
HR Mag - v49 - i7 - July 2004 - pS7(1) [51-500]
Ruane, Janet M. - *Essentials of Research Methods: A Guide to Social Science Research, 1st Ed.*
TimHES - v0 - i1680 - Feb 25 2005 - pVI(1) [501+]
Second Thoughts: Seeing Conventional Wisdom through the Sociological Eye, 3rd Ed.
R&R Bk N - v19 - i3 - August 2004 - p141(1) [1-50]
Ruane, Joseph - *Europe's Old States in the New World Order: The Politics of Transition in Britian, France and Spain*
Choice - v42 - i4 - Dec 2004 - p730(1) [1-50]
Ruane, Kevin - *To Kill a Priest: The Murder of Father Popieluszko and the Fall of Communism*
CR - v285 - i1667 - Dec 2004 - p368(2) [501+]
NS - v133 - i4697 - July 19 2004 - p49(3) [501+]
Spec - v295 - i9179 - July 10 2004 - p34(1) [501+]
Rubel, Janet - *101 Complaint Letters that Get Results*
R&R Bk N - v19 - i1 - Feb 2004 - p114(1) [51-500]
Rubel, Nicole - *Twice as Nice: What It's Like to Be a Twin (Illus. by Rubel, Nicole)*
c BL - v101 - i6 - Nov 15 2004 - p578(1) [51-500]
c KR - v72 - i19 - Oct 1 2004 - p967(1) [51-500]
c SLJ - v50 - i11 - Nov 2004 - p130(1) [51-500]
Ruben, Brent D. - *Pursuing Excellence in Higher Education: Eight Fundamental Challenges*
R&R Bk N - v19 - i1 - Feb 2004 - pNA [51-500]
Ruben, David-Hillel - *Action and Its Explanation*
TLS - i5295 - Sept 24 2004 - p22(1) [501+]
Rubens, Bernice - *The Sergeants' Tale*
KR - v73 - i1 - Jan 1 2005 - p18(1) [501+]
Rubenstein, Jeffrey L. - *The Culture of the Babylonian Talmud*
Choice - v41 - i11-12 - July-August 2004 - p2063(1) [501+]
Rubenstein, Lorne - *Mike Weir: The Road to the Masters*
CBRA - Annual 2003 - p68(1) [501+]
Rubenstein, Meridel - *Belonging: Los Alamos to Vietnam*
LJ - v130 - i4 - March 1 2005 - p83(2) [51-500]
Rubenstein, Rheta N. - *Perspectives on the Teaching of Mathematics, Sixty-Sixth Yearbook*
SciTech - v28 - i3 - Sept 2004 - p17(1) [501+]
Rubenstein, Richard E. - *Aristotle's Children: How Christians, Muslims, and Jews Rediscovered Ancient Wisdom and Illuminated the Dark Ages*
CC - v121 - i14 - July 13 2004 - p40(2) [501+]
R&R Bk N - v19 - i1 - Feb 2004 - p2(1) [1-50]
VQR - v80 - i2 - Spring 2004 - p268-268 [501+]
Rubenzer, Steven J. - *Personality, Character, and Leadership in the White House: Psychologists Assets the Presidents*
Choice - v42 - i6 - Feb 2005 - p1099(2) [51-500]
Rubery, Jill - *The Organisation of Employment: An International Perspective*
CS - v33 - i4 - July 2004 - p441(2) [501+]
Rubin, Allen - *Research Methods for Social Work, 5th Ed.*
R&R Bk N - v19 - i4 - Nov 2004 - p137(1) [51-500]
Rubin, Barnett R. - *Blood on the Doorstep: The Politics of Preventive Action*
JAS - v63 - i3 - August 2004 - p764-765 [501+]
Rubin, Barry - *Hating America: A History*
BL - v101 - i6 - Nov 15 2004 - p550(1) [51-500]
PW - v251 - i33 - August 16 2004 - p55(2) [51-500]
The Tragedy of the Middle East
Pers PS - v33 - i4 - Fall 2004 - p240(2) [501+]
Yasir Arafat: A Political Biography
BW - v34 - i1 - Jan 4 2004 - p5(1) [501+]
MEQ - v11 - i3 - Summer 2004 - p94(2) [501+]
Rubin, Beth C. - *Critical Voices in School Reform: Students Living through Change*
AJE - v110 - i4 - August 2004 - p407(5) [501+]
Rubin, Bruce K. - *Therapy for Mucus-clearance Disorders*
SciTech - v28 - i3 - Sept 2004 - p69(1) [51-500]

Rubin, Carole - *How to Get Your Lawn and Garden Off Drugs: A Basic Guide to Pesticide-Free Gardening in North America*
CBRA - Annual 2003 - p422(2) [51-500]
Rubin, Emanuel - *Pathology: Clinicopathologic Foundations of Medicine, 4th ed.*
SciTech - v28 - i3 - Sept 2004 - p88(1) [51-500]
Rubin, Emanuel (b. 1935 -) - *The English Glee in the Reign of George III: Participatory Art Music for an Urban Society*
Choice - v41 - i11-12 - July-August 2004 - p2055(1) [501+]
R&R Bk N - v19 - i2 - May 2004 - p192(1) [51-500]
Rubin, Harriet - *Dante in Love: The World's Greatest Poem and How It Made History*
Choice - v42 - i2 - Oct 2004 - p298(1) [501+]
Rubin, Richard - *Foundations of Library and Information Science, 2nd Ed.*
R&R Bk N - v19 - i4 - Nov 2004 - p255(1) [501+]
Rubin, Ron - *Success @ Life: How to Catch and Live Your Dream*
NACEJou - v64 - i2 - Wntr 2004 - p13(2) [501+]
Rubin, Susan Goldman - *Art Against the Odds: From Slave Quilts to Prison Paintings*
c LibMed - v23 - i1 - August-Sept 2004 - p71(1) [51-500]
Degas and the Dance: The Painter and the Petits Rats, Perfecting Their Art
c SLJ - v50 - i11 - Nov 2004 - p66(1) [51-500]
L'Chaim! To Jewish Life in America! Celebrating from 1654 until Today
y BL - v101 - i5 - Nov 1 2004 - p474(1) [51-500]
c CCB-B - v58 - i5 - Jan 2005 - p225(1) [51-500]
y KR - v72 - i22 - Nov 15 2004 - p1092(1) [51-500]
y PW - v251 - i47 - Nov 22 2004 - p61(2) [51-500]
y SLJ - v51 - i1 - Jan 2005 - p154(1) [51-500]
Searching for Anne Frank: Letters from Amsterdam to Iowa
LibMed - v22 - i4 - Jan 2004 - p78(1) [501+]
Rubinfien, Leo - *Shomei Tomatsu: Skin of the Nation*
Afterimage - v32 - i3 - Nov-Dec 2004 - p14(1) [501+]
LJ - v129 - i20 - Dec 1 2004 - p113(1) [51-500]
Rubington, Earl - *Deviance: The Interactionist Perspective, 9th Ed.*
R&R Bk N - v19 - i3 - August 2004 - p143(1) [51-500]
Rubinov, Aleksandr - *Lagrange-Type Functions in Constrained Non-Convex Optimization*
SciTech - v28 - i1 - March 2004 - p40(1) [51-500]
Rubinstein, Annette - *I Vote My Conscience: Debates, Speeches and Writings of Vito Marcantonio*
S&S - v68 - i1 - Spring 2004 - p108-110 [501+]
Rubinstein, Gillian - *Across the Nightingale Floor*
c Analog - v124 - i1-2 - Jan-Feb 2004 - p230(2) [501+]
Brilliance of the Moon
y SLJ - v50 - i10 - Oct 2004 - p198(2) [51-500]
Grass for His Pillow
y VOYA - v27 - i4 - Oct 2004 - p315(1) [51-500]
Jake and Pete (Read by King, Alan). Audiobook Review
c SLJ - v50 - i12 - Dec 2004 - p74(2) [501+]
Rubinstein, Julian - *Ballad of the Whiskey Robber: A True Story of Bank Heists, Ice Hockey, Transylvanian Pelt Smuggling, Moonlighting Detectives, and Broken Hearts*
BL - v100 - i22 - August 2004 - p1882(1) [51-500]
Ent W - i786 - Oct 1 2004 - p78 [51-500]
Globe & Mail - Oct 9 2004 - pD22 [501+]
Globe & Mail - Nov 27 2004 - pD3 [51-500]
KR - v72 - i14 - July 15 2004 - p679(1) [501+]
LJ - v129 - i13 - August 2004 - p98(1) [501+]
NYTBR - Nov 14 2004 - p53(L) [501+]
PW - v251 - i34 - August 23 2004 - p51(2) [51-500]
Rubinstein, William D. - *Twentieth-Century Britain: A Political History*
Albion - v36 - i2 - Summer 2004 - p363(2) [501+]
Rubio, Luis - *Mexico Under Fox*
Choice - v42 - i3 - Nov 2004 - p558(1) [1-50]
R&R Bk N - v19 - i3 - August 2004 - p76(1) [51-500]
Rubio, Mary H. - *The Selected Journals of L.M. Montgomery, Vol. V*
BIC - v33 - i9 - Dec 2004 - p18(1) [501+]
Rublack, Ulinka - *Gender in Early Modern German History*
Six Ct J - v35 - i1 - Spring 2004 - p209(3) [501+]
Ruble, Blair A - *Second Metropolis: Pragmatic Pluralism in Gilded Age Chicago, Silver Age Moscow, and Meiji Osaka*
J Soc H - v38 - i2 - Winter 2004 - p557(3) [501+]

Ruble, Blaire A. - *Fragmented Space in the Russian Federation*
E-A St - v56 - i3 - May 2004 - p471(3) [501+]
Rubsamen-Waigmann, Helga - *Viral Infections and Treatment*
E-Streams - July 2004 - pNA [501+]
Ruby, Laura - *Lily's Ghosts*
LibMed - v22 - i4 - Jan 2004 - p66(1) [501+]
Rucka, Greg - *Down to Earth*
y BL - v101 - i4 - Oct 15 2004 - p396(1) [51-500]
A Gentleman's Game: A Queen & Country Novel
BL - v101 - i1 - Sept 1 2004 - p7(1) [51-500]
Ent W - i786 - Oct 1 2004 - p77 [51-500]
KR - v72 - i16 - August 15 2004 - p772(2) [501+]
LJ - v129 - i14 - Sept 1 2004 - p142(1) [501+]
PW - v251 - i36 - Sept 6 2004 - p45(1) [51-500]
In the Line of Duty
BL - v100 - i21 - July 2004 - p1831(1) [1-50]
Ruckenstein, Lelia - *Everything Irish*
ILS - v24 - i1 - Fall 2004 - p32(1) [51-500]
Ruckenstein, Michael J. - *Comprehensive Review of Otolaryngology*
SciTech - v28 - i3 - Sept 2004 - p115(1) [51-500]
Rucker, Rudy - *Frek and the Elixir*
Bwatch - v26 - i7 - July 2004 - p6(1) [51-500]
y VOYA - v27 - i4 - Oct 2004 - p286(1) [501+]
NYTBR - Sept 12 2004 - p22 [501+]
Rudacille, Deborah - *The Riddle of Gender: Science, Activism, and Transgender Rights*
PW - v252 - i3 - Jan 17 2005 - p47(1) [51-500]
Rudan, Vedrana - *Night*
BL - v101 - i7 - Dec 1 2004 - p637(1) [51-500]
LJ - v129 - i20 - Dec 1 2004 - p102(1) [51-500]
Rudanko, Juhani - *The Forging of Freedom of Speech: Essays on Argumentation in Congressional Debates on the Bill of Rights and on the Sedition Act*
R&R Bk N - v19 - i1 - Feb 2004 - pNA [501+]
James Madison and Freedom of Speech: Major Debates in the Early Republic
R&R Bk N - v19 - i3 - August 2004 - p67(1) [51-500]
Rudas, Tamas - *Probability Theory: A Primer*
SciTech - v28 - i3 - Sept 2004 - p36(1) [1-50]
Rudd, Anthony - *Expressing the World: Skepticism, Wittgenstein, and Heidegger*
R&R Bk N - v19 - i1 - Feb 2004 - p3(1) [51-500]
Ruddell, Robert B. - *Theoretical Models and Processes of Reading, 5th Ed.*
R&R Bk N - v19 - i4 - Nov 2004 - p180(1) [501+]
Ruddy, T. Michael - *The Alger Hiss Espionage Case*
R&R Bk N - v19 - i3 - August 2004 - p69(1) [51-500]
Ruden, S. - *Aristophanes: Lysistrata. Translated, with Notes and Topical Commentaries*
Class R - v54 - i2 - Nov 2004 - p563-564 [501+]
Rudes, Blair A. - *Essays in Algonquian. Catawban and Siouan Linguistics in Memory of Frank T. Siebert. Jr.*
CBRA - Annual 2003 - p363(1) [501+]
Rudich, Steven - *Computational Complexity Theory*
SciTech - v28 - i4 - Dec 2004 - p36(1) [51-500]
Rudiger, Gunther - *Magnetic Universe: Geophysical and Astrophysical Dynamo Theory*
SciTech - v28 - i4 - Dec 2004 - p53(1) [51-500]
Rudin, Ronald - *Founding Fathers: The Celebration of Champlain and Laval in the Streets of Quebec, 1878-1908*
AHR - v109 - i4 - Oct 2004 - p1217(2) [501+]
Archiv - i56 - Fall 2003 - p424(4) [501+]
Can Hist R - v85 - i4 - Dec 2004 - p780(4) [501+]
CBRA - Annual 2003 - p278(1) [501+]
Choice - v41 - i7 - March 2004 - p1358(1) [501+]
Rudnick, Ben - *Blast Off*
c PW - v251 - i45 - Nov 8 2004 - p25(1) [51-500]
Rudnicki, Marek - *Optimization and Inverse Problems in Electromagnetism*
SciTech - v28 - i1 - March 2004 - p51(1) [51-500]
Rudnytsky, Peter L. - *Reading Psychoanalysis: Freud, Rank, Ferenczi, Groddeck*
Isis - v95 - i3 - Sept 2004 - p516(2) [501+]
Rudolf, Joseph - *Encyclopedia of Modern Ethnic Conflicts*
LibMed - v22 - i4 - Jan 2004 - p81(1) [501+]
Rudolph, Conrad - *Pilgrimage to the End of the World*
Spec - v295 - i9183 - August 7 2004 - p33(2) [501+]
Rudolph, Julia - *Revolution by Degrees: James Tyrrell and Whig Political Thought in the Late Seventeenth Century*
AHR - v109 - i3 - June 2004 - p973(2) [501+]
Albion - v36 - i2 - Summer 2004 - p377(2) [501+]
JMH - v77 - i1 - March 2005 - p174(3) [501+]

522 • RUDRAPPA Book Review Index 2005 Cumulation

Rudrappa, Sharmila - *Ethnic Routes to Becoming American: Indian Immigrants and the Cultures of Citizenship*
Choice - v42 - i5 - Jan 2005 - p940(1) [51-500]
Rudwick, Martin J.S. - *The New Science of Geology: Studies in the Earth Sciences in the Age of Revolution*
SciTech - v28 - i3 - Sept 2004 - p54(1) [1-50]
Rudy, Gordon - *Mystical Language of Sensation in the Later Middle Ages*
JR - v84 - i3 - July 2004 - p463(2) [501+]
Rudy, John G. - *Romanticism and Zen Buddhism*
Choice - v42 - i5 - Jan 2005 - p855(1) [1-50]
Rudy, Willis - *Building America's Schools: The Federal Contribution*
TCR - v106 - i8 - August 2004 - p1620(3) [501+]
Rue, Leonard Lee, III - *The Encyclopedia of Deer: Your Guide to the World's Deer Species, Including Whitetails, Mule Deer, Caribou, Elk, Moose, and More*
SciTech - v28 - i3 - Sept 2004 - p66(1) [51-500]
Rue, Loyal D. - *Religion Is Not About God: How Spiritual Traditions Nurture Our Biological Nature and What to Expect When They Fail*
R&R Bk N - v20 - i1 - Feb 2005 - p11(1) [51-500]
Rue, Nancy - *Sophie's World*
c BL - v101 - i3 - Oct 1 2004 - p345(2) [51-500]
c SLJ - v51 - i2 - Feb 2005 - p140(1) [51-500]
Ruefle, Mary - *Tristimania*
ABR - v26 - i2 - Jan-Feb 2005 - p17(1) [501+]
Ruelle, Karen Gray - *Just in Time for New Year's!: A Harry and Emily Adventure (Illus. by Ruelle, Karen Gray)*
c SLJ - v50 - i10 - Oct 2004 - p128(1) [51-500]
Rueschmann, Eva - *Moving Pictures, Migrating Identities*
Choice - v41 - i7 - March 2004 - p1303(1) [501+]
Ruether, Sue E. - *Understanding Pathophysiology, 3rd Ed.*
SciTech - v28 - i1 - March 2004 - p87(1) [51-500]
Ruf, Francois - *From Slash-and-Burn to Replanting: Green Revolutions in the Indonesian Uplands*
SciTech - v28 - i3 - Sept 2004 - p127(1) [51-500]
Ruff, Martin - *Set this House in Order*
Lon R Bks - v26 - i1 - Jan 8 2004 - pNA [501+]
Ruffin, Frances E. - *Cats/Gatos*
c SLJ - v50 - i9 - Sept 2004 - p196(2) [1-50]
Whales/Ballenas
c SLJ - v50 - i9 - Sept 2004 - p196(2) [1-50]
Ruffing, Janet K. - *Mysticism and Social Transformation*
BCS - v24 - Annual 2004 - p264(5) [501+]
Ruffini, Remo - *Nonlinear Gravitodynamics: The Lense-Thirring Effect, a Documentary Introduction to Current Research*
SciTech - v28 - i1 - March 2004 - p48(1) [51-500]
Ruffley, David L. - *Children of Victory: Young Specialists and the Evolution of Soviet Society*
Slav R - v63 - i2 - Summer 2004 - p420(2) [501+]
Rufin, Carlos - *The Political Economy of Institutional Change in the Electricity Supply Industry: Shifting Currents*
R&R Bk N - v19 - i2 - May 2004 - p107(1) [51-500]
Rufin, Jean-Christophe - *Brazil Red*
BL - v100 - i22 - August 2004 - p1902(1) [501+]
KR - v72 - i13 - July 1 2004 - p602(1) [501+]
LJ - v129 - i12 - July 2004 - p74(1) [51-500]
PW - v251 - i27 - July 5 2004 - p36(2) [51-500]
TLS - i5307 - Dec 17 2004 - p23(1) [501+]
Rugeley, Terry - *Of Wonders and Wise Men: Religion and Popular Cultures in Southeast Mexico, 1800-1876*
HAHR - v84 - i2 - May 2004 - p357(2) [501+]
Ruggero, Ed - *Combat Jump: The Young Men Who Led the Assault into Fortress Europe, July 1943*
R&R Bk N - v19 - i1 - Feb 2004 - p29(1) [51-500]
Ruggiero, Adriane - *The Great Depression*
c SLJ - v51 - i2 - Feb 2005 - p152(1) [501+]
Ruggiero, Guido - *A Companion to the Worlds of the Renaissance*
Six Ct J - v35 - i3 - Fall 2004 - p840-842 [501+]
Ruggiero, Kristin - *Modernity in the Flesh: Medicine, Law, and Society in Turn-of-the-Century Argentina*
Choice - v42 - i2 - Oct 2004 - p378(1) [501+]
Ruggles, Jeffrey - *The Unboxing of Henry Brown*
Choice - v41 - i7 - March 2004 - p1358(1) [501+]
JSH - v70 - i4 - Nov 2004 - p917(2) [501+]
Rugh, Susan Sessions - *Our Common Country: Family Farming, Culture, and Community in the Nineteenth-Century Midwest*
JAH - v91 - i3 - Dec 2004 - p1010(2) [501+]
Rugh, William - *Arab Mass Media: Newspapers, Radio, and Television in Arab Politics*
Choice - v42 - i5 - Jan 2005 - p847(1) [1-50]
Rugimbana, Robert - *Cross-Cultural Marketing*
TimHES - v0 - i1666 - Nov 12 2004 - p26(1) [501+]
Rugman, Alan M. - *Alliance Capitalism for the New American Economy*
R&R Bk N - v19 - i1 - Feb 2004 - p89(1) [51-500]
Ruh, Brian - *Stray Dog of Anime: The Films of Mamoru Oshii*
Choice - v42 - i4 - Dec 2004 - p669(1) [1-50]
Ruhle, Ray - *Entstehung von politischer Offentlichkeit in der DDR in den 1980er Jahren am Beispiel von Leipzig*
HNet - July 2004 - pNA [501+]
Ruhlman, Michael - *House: A Memoir*
KR - v73 - i1 - Jan 1 2005 - p43(1) [501+]
PW - v252 - i9 - Feb 28 2005 - p51(1) [51-500]
Ruijsenaars, Heijo - *Character Merchandising in Europe*
R&R Bk N - v19 - i1 - Feb 2004 - pNA [51-500]
Ruiter, David - *Shakespeare's Festive History: Feasting, Fasting, and Lent in the Second Henriad*
R&R Bk N - v19 - i1 - Feb 2004 - p237(1) [51-500]
Ruiz, Dorothy S. - *Amazing Grace: African American Grandmothers as Caregivers and Conveyers of Traditional Values*
R&R Bk N - v19 - i3 - August 2004 - p150(1) [51-500]
Ruiz, Gregory M. - *Invasive Species: Vectors and Management Strategies*
QRB - v79 - i3 - Sept 2004 - p328(1) [501+]
SciTech - v28 - i3 - Sept 2004 - p58(1) [1-50]
Ruiz, Teofilo F. - *From Heaven to Earth: The Reordering of Castilian Society, 1150-1350*
Choice - v42 - i2 - Oct 2004 - p363(1) [51-500]
Med R - Sept 2004 - pNA [501+]
Ruiz, Victor Peralta - *En defensa de la autoridad: Politica y cultura bajo el gobierno del virrey Abascal Peru, 1806-1816*
HAHR - v84 - i4 - Nov 2004 - p741-3 [501+]
Ruiz Zafon, Carlos - *The Shadow of the Wind (Read by Davis, Jonathan). Audiobook Review*
BL - v101 - i2 - Sept 15 2004 - p259(1) [51-500]
The Shadow of the Wind
BooChiTr - April 18 2004 - p6(1) [501+]
Globe & Mail - Dec 24 2004 - pD3 [1-50]
The Shadow of the Wind (Read by Davis, Jonathan). Audiobook Review
Globe & Mail - Feb 5 2005 - pD17 [1-50]
The Shadow of the Wind
TLS - i5283 - July 2 2004 - p21(1) [501+]
Rukhsana, Khan - *The Roses in My Carpets*
c RT - v57 - Dec 2003 - p393 [51-500]
Rule, Ann - *Green River, Running Red: The Real Story of the Green River Killer--America's Deadliest Serial Murderer (Read by Pawk, Michele). Audiobook Review*
Globe & Mail - Jan 22 2005 - pD13 [51-500]
Green River, Running Red: The Real Story of the Green River Killer--America's Deadliest Serial Murderer
BL - v101 - i2 - Sept 15 2004 - p179(1) [51-500]
People - v62 - i20 - Nov 15 2004 - p50 [51-500]
PW - v251 - i35 - August 30 2004 - p42(2) [51-500]
Kiss Me, Kill Me: And Other True Cases
PW - v251 - i48 - Nov 29 2004 - p28(1) [51-500]
Rule, James T. - *Ethical Questions in Dentistry, 2nd Ed.*
SciTech - v28 - i3 - Sept 2004 - p119(1) [51-500]
Rule, Leslie - *Ghosts Among Us: True Stories Of Spirit Encounters*
Bwatch - March 2005 - pNA [51-500]
Rule, Rebecca - *The Best Revenge: Short Stories*
y Kliatt - v38 - i5 - Sept 2004 - p37(2) [51-500]
Rumaker, Michael - *Black Mountain Days*
Lam Bk Rpt - v13 - i1-2 - August-Sept 2004 - p19(1) [501+]
Rumbaugh, Duane M. - *Intelligence of Apes and Other Rational Beings*
QRB - v79 - i3 - Sept 2004 - p335(1) [501+]
Sci - v306 - i5695 - Oct 15 2004 - p413(2) [501+]
Rumble, Coral - *Breaking the Rules and Other Poems (Illus. by Baines, Nigel)*
c Sch Lib - v52 - i4 - Winter 2004 - p210(2) [51-500]
Rumble, Walker - *The Swifts: Printers in the Age of Typesetting Races*
AHR - v109 - i3 - June 2004 - p936(2) [501+]
BSA-P - v98 - i1 - March 2004 - p128-129 [501+]
Rumer, Boris - *Central Asia: A Gathering Storm?*
Slav R - v63 - i3 - Fall 2004 - p646-647 [501+]
Rumford, James - *Dog-of-the-Sea-Waves: In English & Hawaiian*
c LibMed - v23 - i3 - Nov-Dec 2004 - p68(1) [51-500]
Dog-of-the-Sea-Waves: In English & Hawaiian (Illus. by Rumford, James)
c SLJ - v50 - i10 - Oct 2004 - p128(2) [51-500]
Nine Animals and the Well
LibMed - v22 - i4 - Jan 2004 - p61(1) [501+]
Sequoyah: The Cherokee Man Who Gave His People Writing (Illus. by Rumford, James)
c BL - v101 - i4 - Oct 15 2004 - p402(1) [51-500]
c CCB-B - v58 - i5 - Jan 2005 - p225(2) [51-500]
c HB - v81 - i1 - Jan-Feb 2005 - p17(1) [51-500]
c KR - v72 - i20 - Oct 15 2004 - p1013(1) [51-500]
c PW - v251 - i45 - Nov 8 2004 - p55(1) [51-500]
c SLJ - v50 - i10 - Oct 2004 - p150(1) [51-500]
HB - v80 - i6 - Nov-Dec 2004 - p730(2) [501+]
Rummonds, Richard-Gabriel - *Nineteenth-Century Printing Practices and the Iron Handpress, with Selected Readings, Vols. 1-2*
R&R Bk N - v19 - i4 - Nov 2004 - p254(1) [501+]
Rumpf, L. - *Naturekenntnis und Naturerfahrung Zur Reflexion epikureischer Theorie bei Lukrez*
Class R - v54 - i2 - Nov 2004 - p370(2) [501+]
Rumph, Stephen C. - *Beethoven After Napoleon: Political Romanticism inthe Late Works*
Choice - v42 - i4 - Dec 2004 - p672(1) [1-50]
Rumphius, Georgius Everhardus - *Rumphius' Orchids: Orchid Texts from 'The Ambonese Herbal'*
E-Streams - Sept 2004 - pNA [501+]
Rumsey, David - *Cartographica Extraordinaire: The Historical Map Transformed*
BL - v101 - i2 - Sept 15 2004 - p202(1) [501+]
Choice - v42 - i5 - Jan 2005 - p907(1) [1-50]
R&R Bk N - v19 - i3 - August 2004 - p80(1) [51-500]
Runciman, W.G. - *Hutton and Butler: Lifting the Lid on the Workings of Power*
Spec - v296 - i9199 - Nov 27 2004 - p45(2) [501+]
Rune Poem
ANQ:QJ - v16 - i1 - Winter 2003 - p3 [501+]
Runge, C. Ford - *Ending Hunger in Our Lifetime: Food Security and Globalization*
JEL - v41 - i4 - Dec 2003 - p1381(1) [501+]
JEL - v42 - i4 - Dec 2004 - p1142(2) [501+]
Runia, David T. - *Laws Stamped with the Seals of Nature: Law and Nature in Hellenistic Philosophy and Philo of Alexandria*
R&R Bk N - v19 - i1 - Feb 2004 - p2(1) [51-500]
Philo of Alexandria: On the Creation of the Cosmos According to Moses. Introduction, Translation and Commentary
Class R - v54 - i1 - May 2004 - p50(51) [501+]
Runion, Meryl - *How to Use Power Phrases to Say What You Mean, Mean What You Say, and Get What You Want*
HR Mag - v49 - i7 - July 2004 - pS3(1) [51-500]
Runowicz, Carolyn D. - *The Answer to Cancer: Stop It Before It Starts, Arrest It in Its Earliest Stages, and Keep It from Coming Back*
LJ - v129 - i15 - Sept 15 2004 - p74(2) [51-500]
PW - v251 - i31 - August 2 2004 - p68(1) [51-500]
Runton, Andy - *Owly: The Way Home and the Bittersweet Summer*
c PW - v251 - i35 - August 30 2004 - p34(1) [501+]
c SLJ - v50 - i12 - Dec 2004 - p25(1) [51-500]
Runyon, Brent - *The Burn Journals*
c CCB-B - v58 - i3 - Nov 2004 - p14(1) [501+]
y HB - v80 - i6 - Nov-Dec 2004 - p731(2) [501+]
y KR - v72 - i14 - July 15 2004 - p693(1) [51-500]
y PW - v251 - i41 - Oct 11 2004 - p81(1) [51-500]
y SLJ - v50 - i11 - Nov 2004 - p172(1) [51-500]
y VOYA - v27 - i4 - Oct 2004 - p330(2) [51-500]
Runzo, Joseph - *The Meaning of Life in the World Religions*
IBMR - v28 - i3 - July 2004 - p140(2) [501+]
Ruocco, Ilario - *Il Platone latino. Il Parmenide: Giorgio di Trebisonda e il cardinale Cusano*
Ren Q - v57 - i4 - Winter 2004 - p1360(3) [501+]
Rupnik, Jacques - *International Perspectives on the Balkans*
R&R Bk N - v19 - i1 - Feb 2004 - p40(1) [1-50]
Rupp, Leila J. - *Drag Queens at the 801 Cabaret*
G&L Rev W - v11 - i4 - July-August 2004 - p42(2) [501+]
Rupp, Rebecca - *The Waterstone*
c RT - v57 - Oct 2003 - p178 [1-50]
Weather!: Watch How Weather Works (Illus. by Sweet, Melissa)
RT - v58 - i3 - Nov 2004 - p289(2) [1-50]
SLJ - v50 - i10 - Oct 2004 - pS42(1) [51-500]

Rust, Val D. - *Radical Origins: Early Mormom Converts and their Colonial Ancestors*
　Choice - v42 - i5 - Jan 2005 - p872(1) [1-50]
Rustad, Martha E.H. - *Foxes and Their Dens*
　c　SLJ - v51 - i2 - Feb 2005 - p128(1) [51-500]
Prairie Dogs and Their Burrows
　c　SLJ - v51 - i2 - Feb 2005 - p128(1) [51-500]
Squirrels and Their Nests
　c　SLJ - v51 - i2 - Feb 2005 - p128(1) [51-500]
Rustage, Alan - *Blackstone and the Golden Egg*
　BL - v101 - i9-10 - Jan 1 2005 - p828(1) [1-50]
　KR - v73 - i4 - Feb 15 2005 - p203(1) [51-500]
Rusth, Glenn - *Canadian Prairies Crosswords*
　CBRA - Annual 2003 - p18(1) [51-500]
Ruszcznski, A. - *Stochastic Programming*
　JEL - v42 - i1 - March 2004 - p245(1) [501+]
Ruth, Amy - *Herbert Hoover*
　y　SLJ - v51 - i1 - Jan 2005 - p140(1) [51-500]
Ruth, Elizabeth - *Bent on Writing: Contemporary Queen Tales*
　CBRA - Annual 2003 - p242(1) [51-500]
Ruth, Henry - *The Challenge Of Crime: Rethinking Our Response*
　Soc Ser R - v78 - i3 - Sept 2004 - p525(1) [51-500]
Ruth, Nick - *The Dark Dreamweaver*
　c　CH Bwatch - Oct 2004 - pNA [51-500]
Rutherdale, Myra - *Women and the White Man's God: Gender and Race in the Canadian Mission Field*
　Can Lit - i182 - Autumn 2004 - p98(3) [501+]
Rutherford, Danilyn - *Raiding the Land of the Foreigners: The Limits of the Nation on an Indonesian Frontier*
　Cont Pac - v17 - i1 - Spring 2005 - p243(3) [501+]
Rutherford, Edward - *The Princes of Ireland: The Dublin Saga, Part One (Read by Keating, John). Audiobook Review*
　Kliatt - v38 - i6 - Nov 2004 - p49(1) [51-500]
The Princess of Ireland (Read by Matthews, Richard). Audiobook Review
　BL - v101 - i1 - Sept 1 2004 - p144(1) [51-500]
Rutherford, Janice Williams - *Selling Mrs. Consumer: Christine Frederick and the Rise of Household Efficiency*
　AHR - v109 - i4 - Oct 2004 - p1249(2) [501+]
　T&C - v45 - i4 - Oct 2004 - p906(2) [501+]
Rutherford, Kenneth R. - *Reframing the Agenda: The Impact of NGO and Middle Power Cooperation in International Security Policy*
　R&R Bk N - v19 - i1 - Feb 2004 - pNA [51-500]
Rutherford, Malcolm - *The Emergence of a National Economy: The United States from Independence to the Civil War, Vols. 1-6*
　Choice - v42 - i7 - March 2005 - p1276(1) [51-500]
　R&R Bk N - v19 - i4 - Nov 2004 - p84(1) [51-500]
Rutherford, Paul - *Weapons of Mass Persuasion: Marketing the War Against Iraq*
　R&R Bk N - v19 - i3 - August 2004 - p50(1) [51-500]
Rutherford, Richard B. - *Classical Literature: A Concise History*
　R&R Bk N - v19 - i4 - Nov 2004 - p214(1) [501+]
Rutherfurd, Jonathan - *A Tale of Two Global Cities: Comparing the Territoralities of Telecommunications Developments in Paris and London*
　R&R Bk N - v19 - i2 - May 2004 - p109(1) [1-50]
Ruthven, Malise - *Fundamentalism: The Search for Meaning*
　CR - v285 - i1665 - Oct 2004 - p240(2) [501+]
　TimHES - v0 - i1679 - Feb 18 2005 - p22(2) [501+]
　TLS - i5284 - July 9 2004 - p28(1) [501+]
Historical Atlas of Islam
　CC - v121 - i25 - Dec 14 2004 - p23(1) [51-500]
　Choice - v42 - i6 - Feb 2005 - p1006(1) [51-500]
　MEJ - v58 - i4 - Autumn 2004 - p709(1) [501+]
　NS - v133 - i4716 - Nov 29 2004 - p44(2) [51-500]
Ruting, Torsten - *Pavlov und der neue Mensch: Diskurse uber Disziplinierung in Sowjetrussland*
　Slav R - v63 - i2 - Summer 2004 - p409(2) [501+]
Rutkosky, Nita - *Microsoft Excel 2003: Specialist and Expert*
　R&R Bk N - v19 - i2 - May 2004 - p116(1) [1-50]
Microsoft Excel 2003: Specialist
　R&R Bk N - v19 - i1 - Feb 2004 - p110(1) [51-500]
Microsoft Office 2003
　R&R Bk N - v19 - i2 - May 2004 - p116(1) [1-50]

Microsoft Office 2003: Specialist
　R&R Bk N - v19 - i1 - Feb 2004 - p110(1) [51-500]
Microsoft Office Brief Edition: 2003
　R&R Bk N - v19 - i2 - May 2004 - p116(1) [1-50]
Microsoft PowerPoint 2003 Specialist
　SciTech - v28 - i1 - March 2004 - p135(1) [51-500]
Microsoft Word 2003
　R&R Bk N - v19 - i4 - Nov 2004 - p254(1) [501+]
Microsoft Word 2003 Expert
　R&R Bk N - v19 - i1 - Feb 2004 - p257(1) [51-500]
Microsoft Word 2003: Specialist and Expert
　R&R Bk N - v19 - i1 - Feb 2004 - p258(1) [51-500]
Rutkow, Ira M. - *Bleeding Blue and Gray: Civil War Surgery and the Evolution of American Medicine*
　KR - v73 - i1 - Jan 1 2005 - p43(1) [501+]
　PW - v252 - i8 - Feb 21 2005 - p164(1) [51-500]
Bleeding Blue and Gray: The Untold Story of Civil War Medicine
　LJ - v130 - i2 - Feb 1 2005 - p109(1) [51-500]
Rutledge, Fleming - *The Seven Last Words from the Cross*
　Ch Today - v49 - i2 - Feb 2005 - p89(1) [51-500]
　LJ - v130 - i4 - March 1 2005 - p94(1) [51-500]
Rutt, Val - *The Race for the Lost Keystone*
　c　Sch Lib - v52 - i4 - Winter 2004 - p204(1) [51-500]
Rutten, Roel - *Economic Geography of Higher Education: Knowledge Infrastructure and Learning Regions*
　JEL - v41 - i4 - Dec 2003 - p1439(1) [501+]
Ruud, Arild, Engelsen - *Poetics of Village Politics: The Making of West Bengal's Rural Communism*
　CS - v33 - i6 - Nov 2004 - p748(1) [1-50]
Ruud, Brandon K. - *Karl Bodmer's North American Prints*
　BL - v101 - i3 - Oct 1 2004 - p293(1) [51-500]
Ruurs, Margriet - *Wild Babies (Illus. by Kiss, Andrew)*
　c　CBRA - Annual 2003 - p569(1) [51-500]
Ruvalcaba, Zak - *Macromedia Dreamweaver MX 2004 Unleashed*
　Bwatch - Dec 2004 - pNA [51-500]
Ruvinsky, A. - *The Genetics of the Dog*
　QRB - v79 - i4 - Dec 2004 - p439(1) [501+]
Ruy-Sanchez, Byalbero - *Tequila: A Traditional Art of Mexico*
　PW - v251 - i48 - Nov 29 2004 - p35(1) [51-500]
Ruymbeke, Bertrand Van - *Memory and Identity: The Huguenots in France and the Atlantic Diaspora*
　AHR - v109 - i3 - June 2004 - p863(2) [501+]
Ruzova, Jirina - *Catalogue of the Library of the Czech Institute of Egyptology*
　R&R Bk N - v19 - i4 - Nov 2004 - p51(1) [51-500]
Ryabchikova, Elena I. - *Ebola and Marburg Viruses: A View of Infection Using Electron Microscopy*
　E-Streams - August 2004 - pNA [501+]
　SciTech - v28 - i1 - March 2004 - p76(1) [51-500]
Ryan, Beth - *What is Invisible*
　CBRA - Annual 2003 - p205(1) [51-500]
Ryan, Brittney - *The Legend of Holly Claus (Illus. by Long, Laurel)*
　c　BL - v101 - i3 - Oct 1 2004 - p330(1) [51-500]
　y　KR - v72 - i21 - Nov 1 2004 - p1053(1) [51-500]
　c　PW - v251 - i44 - Nov 1 2004 - p62(1) [51-500]
　c　SLJ - v50 - i12 - Dec 2004 - p152(1) [51-500]
　y　VOYA - v27 - i5 - Dec 2004 - p410(1) [51-500]
Ryan, Cheryl - *Christmas Morning (Illus. by Mattheson, Jenny)*
　c　PW - v251 - i39 - Sept 27 2004 - p60(1) [51-500]
Ryan, Christopher K. - *Harry Gunnison Brown: an Orthodox Economist and His Contributions*
　Isis - v95 - i3 - Sept 2004 - p517(2) [501+]
Ryan, Daniel J. - *Job Search Handbook for People with Disabilities*
　NACEJou - v64 - i4 - Summer 2004 - p11-12 [501+]
Ryan, Darlene - *Rules for Life*
　y　CCB-B - v58 - i6 - Feb 2005 - p264(264) [51-500]
　y　Kliatt - v39 - i2 - March 2005 - p23(1) [51-500]
Ryan, David - *The United States and Europe in the Twentieth Century, 1st Ed.*
　TimHES - v0 - i1680 - Feb 25 2005 - pX(1) [501+]
Ryan, Edward - *Napoleon's Shield and Guardian: The Unconquerable General Daumesnil*
　Parameters - v34 - i4 - Winter 2004 - p148(2) [501+]
Ryan, Frank - *Darwin's Blind Spot: Evolution Beyond Natural Selection*
　QRB - v79 - i3 - Sept 2004 - p304(1) [501+]

Ryan, Gordon - *A Question of Consequence*
　BL - v101 - i3 - Oct 1 2004 - p303(1) [51-500]
Ryan, James - *Natural Affinities*
　Parameters - v34 - i4 - Winter 2004 - p129(2) [501+]
Ryan, James P. - *Physiology: PreTest Self-Assessment and Review, 11th Ed.*
　SciTech - v28 - i4 - Dec 2004 - p68(1) [51-500]
Ryan, Joan - *Little Girls in Pretty Boxes*
　BL - v101 - i1 - Sept 1 2004 - p53(1) [51-500]
Ryan, Louise - *Gender Identity and the Irish Press, 1922-1937: Embodying the Nation*
　Wom HR - v13 - i2 - Summer 2004 - p319-321 [501+]
Ryan, Mark A. - *Chinese Warfighting: The PLA Experience Since 1949*
　Pac A - v77 - i2 - Summer 2004 - p330(2) [501+]
Ryan, Matt - *Mystic: Master Class*
　LibMed - v22 - i4 - Jan 2004 - p69(1) [501+]
Mystic: Out All Night
　LibMed - v22 - i4 - Jan 2004 - p69(1) [501+]
Ryan, Meda - *Tom Barry: Irish Freedom Fighter*
　ILS - v24 - i1 - Fall 2004 - p8(1) [501+]
Ryan, Michael - *New and Selected Poems*
　VQR - v80 - i3 - Summer 2004 - p272(1) [1-50]
Ryan, Mike - *Baghdad or Bust: The Inside Story of Gulf War 2*
　APH - v51 - i4 - Winter 2004 - p54(1) [501+]
Ryan, Pam Munoz - *Becoming Naomi Leon*
　c　BL - v101 - i2 - Sept 15 2004 - p245(1) [51-500]
　　CC - v121 - i25 - Dec 14 2004 - p24(1) [51-500]
　c　CCB-B - v58 - i2 - Oct 2004 - p97(2) [51-500]
　c　HB - v80 - i5 - Sept-Oct 2004 - p598(1) [51-500]
　c　KR - v72 - i17 - Sept 1 2004 - p873(1) [51-500]
　c　NYTBR - March 13 2005 - p21 [501+]
　c　PW - v251 - i37 - Sept 13 2004 - p79(1) [51-500]
　y　SLJ - v50 - i9 - Sept 2004 - p216(2) [51-500]
　　VOYA - v27 - i5 - Dec 2004 - p394(1) [51-500]
When Marian Sang (Illus. by Selznick, Brian)
　c　SLJ - v50 - i12 - Dec 2004 - p60(1) [501+]
Ryan, Paul - *Never Apologise: The Collected Writings of Lindsay Anderson*
　Spec - v296 - i9201 - Dec 11 2004 - p39(3) [501+]
Ryan, Peter - *Brief Lives*
　Quad - v48 - i12 - Dec 2004 - p93(2) [501+]
Ryan, Regina Sara - *Only God: A Biography of Yogi Ramsuratkumar*
　LJ - v129 - i20 - Dec 1 2004 - p126(1) [51-500]
Ryan, Susan M. - *The Grammar of Good Intentions: Race and the Antebellum Culture of Benevolence*
　HNet - June 2004 - pNA [501+]
　JAH - v91 - i2 - Sept 2004 - p625(2) [501+]
　NEQ - v77 - i4 - Dec 2004 - p659-662 [501+]
　RAH - v32 - i1 - March 2004 - p27(6) [501+]
Ryan, Thomas F. - *Thomas Aquinas as Reader of the Psalms*
　Theol St - v65 - i3 - Sept 2004 - p642(3) [501+]
Ryang, Sonia - *Koreans in Japan: Critical Voices from the Margin*
　JRAI - v10 - i3 - Sept 2004 - p748(2) [501+]
Ryavec, Karl W. - *Russian Bureaucracy: Power and Pathology*
　Choice - v42 - i2 - Oct 2004 - p367(1) [51-500]
　R&R Bk N - v19 - i1 - Feb 2004 - pNA [501+]
Rybski, Melinda - *Kinesiology for Occupational Therapy*
　SciTech - v28 - i3 - Sept 2004 - p69(1) [51-500]
Rychen, Dominique Simone - *Key Competencies for a Successful Life and a Well-Functioning Society*
　R&R Bk N - v19 - i1 - Feb 2004 - p133(1) [51-500]
Rychlewski, Jacek - *Explicitly Correlated Wave Functions in Chemistry and Physics: Theory and Applications*
　SciTech - v28 - i1 - March 2004 - p47(1) [51-500]
Rychlik, Mike - *13 Ways of Looking at Student Teaching: A Guide for First-Time English Teachers*
　R&R Bk N - v19 - i1 - Feb 2004 - p185(1) [51-500]
Ryden, Barbara - *Introduction to Cosmology*
　Phys Today - v57 - i10 - Oct 2004 - p77-78 [501+]
Ryden, Lennart - *The Life of St Philaretos the Merciful Written by His Grandson Niketas*
　Specu - v79 - i4 - Oct 2004 - p1121(2) [501+]
Ryder, S.D. - *Dark Matter in Galaxies: Proceedings*
　SciTech - v28 - i3 - Sept 2004 - p44(1) [1-50]
Rye, Gill - *Women's Writing in Contemporary France: New Writers, New Literatures in the 1990s*
　FS - v58 - i2 - April 2004 - p291(2) [501+]
Rye, Terry L. - *Fresh Ideas in Dried Flowers*
　LJ - v129 - i17 - Oct 15 2004 - p63(1) [51-500]
Rygh, Jayne L. - *Treating Generalized Anxiety Disorder*
　Bwatch - Dec 2004 - pNA [51-500]

Rylant, Cynthia - *God Went to Beauty School*
  c Five Owls - v18 - i1 - Fall 2004 - p22(2) [51-500]
  c HB - v81 - i1 - Jan-Feb 2005 - p30(1) [51-500]
  c LibMed - v22 - i5 - Feb 2004 - p75(1) [501+]
The High-Rise Private Eyes: The Case of the Baffled Bear (Illus. by Karas, G. Brian)
  c BL - v100 - i21 - July 2004 - p1852(1) [1-50]
  c HB - v80 - i5 - Sept-Oct 2004 - p599(1) [51-500]
  c SLJ - v50 - i9 - Sept 2004 - p178(1) [51-500]
If You'll Be My Valentine (Illus. by Kosaka, Fumi)
  c BL - v101 - i8 - Dec 15 2004 - p747(1) [1-50]
  c SLJ - v51 - i2 - Feb 2005 - p109(1) [51-500]
If You'll Be My Valentine
    KR - v72 - i24 - Dec 15 2004 - p1207(1) [51-500]
The Lighthouse Family: The Eagle (Illus. by McDaniels, Preston)
  c SLJ - v50 - i11 - Nov 2004 - p117(1) [51-500]
The Lighthouse Family: The Turtle (Illus. by McDaniels, Preston)
  c KR - v73 - i5 - March 1 2005 - p294(1) [51-500]
Long Night Moon (Illus. by Siegel, Mark)

  c BL - v101 - i6 - Nov 15 2004 - p591(2) [51-500]
    KR - v72 - i22 - Nov 15 2004 - p1093(1) [51-500]
  c PW - v252 - i3 - Jan 17 2005 - p54(1) [51-500]
  c SLJ - v50 - i12 - Dec 2004 - p120(1) [51-500]
Mr. Putter & Tabby Write the Book (Illus. by Howard, Arthur)
  c SLJ - v50 - i9 - Sept 2004 - p178(1) [51-500]
Rylatt, Alastair - *Winning the Knowledge Game: A Smarter Strategy for Better Business in Australia and New Zealand*
    ALJ - v53 - i3 - August 2004 - p323(2) [501+]
Rylatt, Margaret - *The Archaeology of the Medieval Cathedral and Priory of St. Mary, Coventry*
    R&R Bk N - v19 - i4 - Nov 2004 - p35(1) [51-500]
Ryman, Geoff - *Air*
    MFSF - v108 - i4 - April 2005 - p33(8) [501+]
Rymarczyk, Jutta - *In Search of the Active Learner: Untersuchungen zu Fremdsprachenunterricht, Bilingualen und Interdisziplinaren Kontexten*

    R&R Bk N - v19 - i1 - Feb 2004 - p209(1) [51-500]
Rymer, Cyndy Lyle - *Photo Fun*
    Bwatch - v26 - i7 - July 2004 - p7(1) [51-500]
Rymsza, Guy A. - *County Longford Residents Prior to the Famine: A Transcription and Complete Index of the Tithe Applotment Books of County Longford, Ireland*
    R&R Bk N - v19 - i3 - August 2004 - p41(1) [51-500]
Ryn, Claes G. - *America the Virtuous: The Crisis of Democracy and the Quest for Empire*
    Choice - v41 - i11-12 - July-August 2004 - p2122(1) [501+]
Common Human Ground: Universality and Particularity in a Multicultural World
    R&R Bk N - v19 - i1 - Feb 2004 - p7(1) [51-500]
Ryrie, Alec - *The Gospel and Henry VIII: Evangelicals in the Early English Reformation*
    Ren Q - v57 - i4 - Winter 2004 - p1493(3) [501+]

S

Sa, Jorge Alberto Sousa de Vasconcellos - *The Neglected Firm: Every Manager Must Manage Two Firms: The Present One and the Future One*
JEL - v41 - i4 - Dec 2003 - p1400(1) [501+]

Sa, Shan - *The Girl Who Played Go*
y Kliatt - v39 - i2 - March 2005 - p23(1) [51-500]

Saadi, Suhayl - *Psychoraag*
NS - v133 - i4716 - Nov 29 2004 - p48(1) [51-500]
TLS - i5299 - Oct 22 2004 - p22(1) [501+]

Saarikoski, Pentti - *Trilogy*
WLT - v78 - i3-4 - Sept-Dec 2004 - p112(2) [501+]

Sabahi, Farian - *The OSCE and the Multiple Challenges of Transition: The Caucasus and Central Asia*
R&R Bk N - v19 - i3 - August 2004 - p211(1) [1-50]

Saban, Nick - *How Good Do You Want to Be? A Champion's Tips on How to Lead and Succeed at Work and in Life*
PW - v251 - i49 - Dec 6 2004 - p56(1) [51-500]

Sabanovic, Asif - *Variable Structure Systems: From Principles to Implementation*
TimHES - v0 - i1681 - March 4 2005 - p28(1) [501+]

Sabaratnam, Lakshmanan - *Ethnic Attachments in Sri Lanka: Social Change and Cultural Continuity*
CS - v33 - i1 - Jan 2004 - p90-91 [501+]

Sabatini, Massimo - *Cartilage and Osteoarthritis: Vol. 1*
SciTech - v28 - i4 - Dec 2004 - p69(1) [51-500]
Cartilage and Osteoarthritis: Vol. 2
SciTech - v28 - i4 - Dec 2004 - p69(1) [51-500]

Sabatini, Sandra - *Making Babies: Infants in Canadian Fiction*
Can CL - i113/114 - Spring-Summer 2004 - p131(3) [501+]
CBRA - Annual 2003 - p262(2) [501+]
The One with the News
Can Lit - i182 - Autumn 2004 - p173(2) [501+]

Sabatino, Colleen A. - *The Play of Your Life: Your Program for Finding the Career of Your Dreams--and a Step-by-Step Guide to Making It a Reality*
BL - v100 - i21 - July 2004 - p1807(1) [1-50]

Sabbagh, Karl - *The Riemann Hypothesis: The Greatest Unsolved Problem in Mathematics*
Phys Today - v57 - i6 - June 2004 - p63-64 [501+]

Saberhagen, Fred - *Berserker Man*
Bwatch - Dec 2004 - pNA [501+]
Rogue Berserker
BL - v101 - i9-10 - Jan 1 2005 - p835(1) [1-50]

Sabin, E. Rose - *When the Beast Ravens*
y BL - v101 - i9-10 - Jan 1 2005 - p835(1) [1-50]
y Kliatt - v39 - i1 - Jan 2005 - p10(1) [51-500]

Sabina, Maria - *Selections*
ABR - v25 - i5 - July-August 2004 - p19(2) [501+]

Sabine, Maureen - *Maxine Hong Kingston's Broken Book of Life: An Intertextual Study of The Woman Warrior and China Men*
Choice - v42 - i4 - Dec 2004 - p662(1) [1-50]

Sabloff, Jeremy A. - *Tikal: Dynasties, Foreigners, and Affairs of State, Advancing Maya Archaeology*
JRAI - v10 - i3 - Sept 2004 - p715(2) [501+]

Sabol, Steven - *Russian Colonization and the Genesis of Kazak National Consciousness*
Slav R - v63 - i3 - Fall 2004 - p645-646 [501+]

Sabuda, Robert - *America the Beautiful (Illus. by Sabuda, Robert)*
c BL - v101 - i6 - Nov 15 2004 - p578(1) [51-500]
c KR - v72 - i19 - Oct 1 2004 - p968(1) [51-500]
c PW - v251 - i37 - Sept 13 2004 - p77(1) [501+]
c SLJ - v50 - i11 - Nov 2004 - p130(1) [51-500]

Sacco, Joe - *War's End: Profiles from Bosnia 1995-96*
PW - v252 - i10 - March 7 2005 - p52(1) [51-500]

Sachar, Louis - *More Sideways Arithmetic from Wayside School*
c Sch Lib - v52 - i3 - Autumn 2004 - p151(1) [51-500]
Sideways Arithmetic from Wayside School
c Sch Lib - v52 - i3 - Autumn 2004 - p151(1) [51-500]
Sideways Stories from Wayside School
y Kliatt - v39 - i2 - March 2005 - p31(2) [51-500]

Sacharov, Eliyahu - *Out of the Limelight: Events Operations, Missions and Personalitites in Israeli History*
R&R Bk N - v19 - i4 - Nov 2004 - p45(1) [51-500]

Sachatello-Sawyer, Bonnie - *Adult Museum Programs: Designing Meaningful Experiences*
Pub Hist - v26 - i2 - Spring 2004 - p98(100) [501+]

Sachdev, P.L. - *Shock Waves and Explosions*
SciTech - v28 - i4 - Dec 2004 - p41(1) [51-500]

Sachedina, Abdulaziz - *The Islamic Roots of Democratic Pluralism*
JR - v85 - i1 - Jan 2005 - p172(3) [501+]

Sacher, John M. - *A Perfect War of Politics: Parties, Politicians, and Democracy in Louisiana, 1824-1861*
AHR - v109 - i4 - Oct 2004 - p1228(2) [501+]
JAH - v91 - i1 - June 2004 - p237-238 [501+]
JSH - v70 - i3 - August 2004 - p666(3) [501+]

Sachhi, Sergio - *Etudes sur les 'Illuminations' de Rimbaud*
FS - v58 - i3 - July 2004 - p424-425 [501+]

Sachleben, Mark - *Seeing the Bigger Picture: Understanding Politics through Film and Television*
R&R Bk N - v19 - i1 - Feb 2004 - p225(1) [51-500]

Sachs, Angeli - *Jewish Identity in Contemporary Architecture*
Choice - v42 - i4 - Dec 2004 - p652(1) [1-50]

Sachs, David H. - *The Life and Work of the Twentieth Century Louisiana Architect, A. Hays Town*
R&R Bk N - v19 - i1 - Feb 2004 - p202(1) [51-500]

Sachs, Jeffrey D. - *The End of Poverty: Economic Possibilities for Our Time*
Econ - v374 - i8418 - March 19 2005 - p87US [501+]
KR - v73 - i2 - Jan 15 2005 - p111(1) [501+]
PW - v252 - i6 - Feb 7 2005 - p51(1) [51-500]

Sachs, Marilyn - *Lost in America*
y Kliatt - v39 - i2 - March 2005 - p15(2) [51-500]
y KR - v73 - i5 - March 1 2005 - p295(1) [51-500]

Sachs, Mendel - *Quantum Mechanics and Gravity*
Choice - v41 - i11-12 - July-August 2004 - p2082(2) [501+]

Sachs, Sid - *Yvonne Rainer: Radical Juxtapositions 1961-2002*
TDR - v48 - i2 - Summer 2004 - p181(2) [501+]

Sack, Ronald H. - *Images of Nebuchadnezzar: The Emergence of a Legend, 2nd Ed.*
R&R Bk N - v19 - i1 - Feb 2004 - p41(1) [51-500]

Sackett, Hannah Kate - *Animal Faces at Night (Illus. by Camm, Martin)*
c LibMed - v22 - i4 - Jan 2004 - p70(1) [501+]

Sackett, Paul R. - *Evaluating Military Advertising and Recruiting: Theory and Methodology*
R&R Bk N - v19 - i4 - Nov 2004 - p252(1) [501+]

Sackheim, George I. - *Introduction to Chemistry for Biology Students, 8th ed.*
SciTech - v28 - i3 - Sept 2004 - p50(1) [1-50]

Sackmann, Rosemarie - *Identity and Integration: Migrants in Western Europe*
R&R Bk N - v19 - i1 - Feb 2004 - pNA [501+]

Sacks, Adam - *Salmon Doubts (Illus. by Sacks, Adam)*
y BL - v101 - i9-10 - Jan 1 2005 - p846(1) [1-50]
y SLJ - v50 - i12 - Dec 2004 - p177(1) [51-500]

Sacks, David - *The Alphabet*
TLS - i5265 - Feb 27 2004 - p29-29 [501+]
Language Visible: Unraveling the Mystery of the Alphabet from A to Z
CBRA - Annual 2003 - p271(1) [51-500]
Letter Perfect: The A-to-Z History of Our Alphabet
Globe & Mail - August 28 2004 - pD13 [51-500]

Sacks, Gerald E. - *Mathematical Logic in the 20th Century*
SciTech - v28 - i4 - Dec 2004 - p15(1) [1-50]

Sacks, Janet - *The Human Body*
c SB - v40 - i5 - Sept-Oct 2004 - p224(2) [51-500]
Little Box of Wizard Tricks: Over 80 Tricks to Amaze Your Friends
c PW - v251 - i43 - Oct 25 2004 - p50(1) [51-500]
Nations of the Southwest
c CBRA - Annual 2003 - p533(2) [51-500]

Sacks, Kenneth S. - *Understanding Emerson: "The American Scholar" and His Struggle for Self-Reliance*
AL - v76 - i2 - June 2004 - p391(3) [501+]
J Am St - v38 - i1 - April 2004 - p161-162 [501+]
JAH - v91 - i1 - June 2004 - p240-241 [501+]
Pub Hist - v26 - i3 - Summer 2004 - p91(93) [501+]

Sacks, Oliver - *The Best American Science Fiction Writing 2003*
y VOYA - v27 - i3 - August 2004 - p236(1) [1-50]

Sadat-Akhavi, Seyed Ali - *Methods of Resolving Conflicts between Treaties*
R&R Bk N - v19 - i3 - August 2004 - p210(1) [1-50]

Saddow, Stephen E. - *Advances in Silicon Carbide Processing and Applications*
SciTech - v28 - i3 - Sept 2004 - p160(1) [51-500]

Sadgrove, Judy - *Exercise*
y SB - v40 - i4 - July-August 2004 - p151(1) [51-500]

Sadie, Stanley - *The Billboard Encyclopedia of Classical Music*
BL - v100 - i21 - July 2004 - p1861(1) [501+]
The Billboard Illustrated Encyclopedia of Opera
LJ - v129 - i19 - Nov 15 2004 - p86(1) [51-500]

Sadiki, Larbi - *The Search for Arab Democracy: Discourses and Counter-Discourses*
Choice - v42 - i5 - Jan 2005 - p932(1) [51-500]
R&R Bk N - v19 - i3 - August 2004 - p183(1) [501+]

Sadlek, Gregory M. - *Idleness Working: The Discourse of Love's Labor from Ovid through Chaucer and Gower*
Choice - v42 - i5 - Jan 2005 - p848(1) [1-50]

Sadler, Judy Ann - *Christmas Crafts from Around the World*
c CBRA - Annual 2003 - p555(2) [51-500]
c LibMed - v22 - i6 - March 2004 - p76(1) [501+]
Embroidery (Illus. by Bradford, June)
c SLJ - v50 - i8 - August 2004 - p144(1) [51-500]
Simply Sewing (Illus. by Kurisu, Jane)
c BL - v101 - i8 - Dec 15 2004 - p748(1) [51-500]
c Res Links - v10 - i2 - Dec 2004 - p29(1) [51-500]
y SLJ - v50 - i11 - Nov 2004 - p172(1) [51-500]

Sadler, Rosemary - *Kids Book of Black Canadian History (Illus. by Quijun, Wang)*
c CBRA - Annual 2003 - p541(1) [51-500]

Sadowski, Michael - *Adolescents at School: Perspectives on Youth, Identity, and Education*
TCR - v106 - i2 - Feb 2004 - p386-389 [501+]

Sadowski, Piotr - *Dynamism of Character in Shakespeare's Mature Tragedies*
Choice - v42 - i2 - Oct 2004 - p296(1) [501+]
TLS - i5296 - Oct 1 2004 - p31(1) [51-500]

Saeed, Abdullah - *Freedom of Religion, Apostasy and Islam*
R&R Bk N - v19 - i4 - Nov 2004 - p17(1) [51-500]
Choice - v42 - i5 - Jan 2005 - p872(1) [1-50]

Saenz, Benjamin Alire - *Sammy and Juliana in Hollywood.*
y BL - v101 - i3 - Oct 1 2004 - p324(1) [51-500]
y CCB-B - v58 - i1 - Sept 2004 - p37(2) [51-500]
y SLJ - v50 - i9 - Sept 2004 - p217(1) [51-500]
y VOYA - v27 - i5 - Dec 2004 - p395(1) [51-500]

Saenz, Eugenia Rodriguez - *Hijas Novias Esposas: Familia, Matrimonio y Violencia Domestica en el Valle Central de Costa Rica*
HAHR - v84 - i4 - Nov 2004 - p735(2) [501+]
Mujeres, Genero e Historia en America Central Durante Los Siglos XVIII, XIX y XX
HAHR - v84 - i2 - May 2004 - p341(2) [501+]
Un Siglo de Luchas Femeninas en America Latina
HAHR - v84 - i2 - May 2004 - p339(2) [501+]

Saez, Castan Javier - *The Three Hedgehogs*
c Res Links - v10 - i1 - Oct 2004 - p2(2) [51-500]
c SLJ - v50 - i7 - July 2004 - p68(1) [51-500]

Saez, Lawrence - *Federalism without a Centre: The Impact of Political and Economic Reform on India's Federal System*
JAS - v63 - i3 - August 2004 - p835-837 [501+]

Safety Evaluation of Certain Food Additives: Proceedings
SciTech - v28 - i1 - March 2004 - p179(1) [51-500]

Safety of Genetically Engineered Foods: Approaches to Assessing Unintended Health Effects
SciTech - v28 - i4 - Dec 2004 - p165(1) [51-500]

Saffell, David C. - *The Encyclopedia of U.S. Presidential Elections*
c SLJ - v50 - i8 - August 2004 - p49(1) [51-500]
c SLJ - v50 - i10 - Oct 2004 - p96(1) [51-500]

Saffer, Barbara - *Anthrax*
y SLJ - v50 - i10 - Oct 2004 - p194(1) [51-500]
Kenya
c HNet - Sept 2004 - pNA [501+]
Smallpox
c CH Bwatch - Feb 2005 - pNA [51-500]

Safi, Omid - *Progressive Muslims. On Justice, Gender, and Pluralism*
Theol St - v65 - i3 - Sept 2004 - p665(3) [501+]

Safranski, Rudiger - *Schiller Oder die Erfindung des Deutschen Idealismus*
TLS - i5306 - Dec 10 2004 - p8-o [501+]

Sagan, Nick - *Edenborn*
BL - v101 - i1 - Sept 1 2004 - p75(2) [51-500]
KR - v72 - i14 - July 15 2004 - p666(1) [501+]
MFSF - v108 - i4 - April 2005 - p33(8) [501+]
NYTBR - August 29 2004 - p12 [501+]
PW - v251 - i37 - Sept 13 2004 - p59(1) [501+]
Idlewild
y Kliatt - v39 - i1 - Jan 2005 - p20(2) [501+]

Sagar, Keith - *D.H. Lawrence's Paintings*
ELT - v48 - i1 - Wntr 2005 - p244(5) [501+]
Stud Hum - v31 - i1 - June 2004 - p105(2) [501+]
The Life of D.H. Lawrence: An Illustrated Biography
LJ - v129 - i14 - Sept 1 2004 - p150(1) [51-500]

Sagard, Gabriel - *Le Grand Voyage Du Pays Des Hurons ...*
Essays CW - Winter 2003 - p137 [501+]

Sagaris, Lake - *Bone and Dream: Into the World's Driest Desert*
Can Lit - i181 - Summer 2004 - p103-104 [501+]

Sagas, Ernesto - *The Dominican People: A Documentary History.*
HAHR - v84 - i3 - August 2004 - p518(2) [501+]

Sagasti, Francisco R. - *Knowledge and Innovation for Development: The Sisyphus Challenge of the 21st Century*
SciTech - v28 - i3 - Sept 2004 - p13(1) [501+]

Sage, Angie - *Magyk (Illus. by Zug, Mark)*
c CCB-B - v58 - i6 - Feb 2005 - p264(2) [51-500]
c KR - v73 - i2 - Jan 15 2005 - p125(1) [51-500]

Sage, Victor - *Le Fanu's Gothic: The Rhetoric of Darkness*
Choice - v41 - i11-12 - July-August 2004 - p2047(1) [501+]

Sageman, Marc - *Understanding Terror Networks*
BW - v34 - i32 - August 8 2004 - p10(1) [501+]
Choice - v42 - i4 - Dec 2004 - p734(1) [1-50]
MEJ - v58 - i4 - Autumn 2004 - p709(1) [501+]
Parameters - v34 - i4 - Winter 2004 - p129(2) [501+]
Pers PS - v34 - i1 - Wntr 2005 - p58(1) [501+]
Prog - v68 - i8 - August 2004 - p45(4) [501+]

Sager, Lawrence G. - *Justice in Plainclothes: A Theory of American Constitutional Practice*
HLR - v118 - i4 - Feb 2005 - p1395(1) [501+]
R&R Bk N - v19 - i4 - Nov 2004 - p171(1) [501+]

Sagoff, Mark - *Price, Principle, and the Environment*
Choice - v42 - i6 - Feb 2005 - p1071(1) [51-500]

Sagolla, Lisa Jo - *The Girl Who Fell Down: A Biography of Joan McCracken*
R&R Bk N - v19 - i1 - Feb 2004 - p75(1) [1-50]
Theat J - v56 - i4 - Dec 2004 - p722-723 [501+]

Sagona, Antonio - *A View from the Highlands: Archaeological Studies in Honour of Charles Burney*
R&R Bk N - v19 - i3 - August 2004 - p47(1) [51-500]

Sagona, Claudia - *Punic Antiquities of Malta and Other Ancient Artefacts Held in Ecclesiastic and Private Collections*
R&R Bk N - v19 - i1 - Feb 2004 - p38(1) [1-50]

Sagona, Marina - *I Call My Hand Gentle*
LibMed - v22 - i4 - Jan 2004 - p58(1) [501+]

Sagui, Pat - *Landscaping with Stone: Create Patios, Walkways, Walls, and Other Landscape Features*
LJ - v130 - i4 - March 1 2005 - p109(1) [51-500]

Saguy, Abigail C. - *What Is Sexual Harassment?: From Capitol Hill to the Sorbonne*
CS - v33 - i6 - Nov 2004 - p719(2) [501+]

Saha, Badal C. - *Fermentation Biotechnology*
SciTech - v28 - i1 - March 2004 - p172(1) [51-500]
Lignocellulose Biodegradation
SciTech - v28 - i4 - Dec 2004 - p164(1) [51-500]

Sahadi, Lou - *Johnny Unitas: America's Quarterback*
BL - v101 - i1 - Sept 1 2004 - p50(1) [51-500]
LJ - v129 - i16 - Oct 1 2004 - p90(1) [51-500]

Sahajwalla, Chandrahas G. - *New Drug Developments: Regulatory Paradigms for Clinical Pharmacology and Biopharmaceutics*
SciTech - v28 - i3 - Sept 2004 - p122(1) [501+]

Sahlins, Marshall - *Apologies to Thucydides: Understanding History as Culture and Vice Versa*
Lon R Bks - v26 - i21 - Nov 4 2004 - p6(1) [1-50]
Lon R Bks - v27 - i2 - Jan 20 2005 - p31(1) [51-500]

Sahlins, Peter - *Unnaturally French: Foreign Citizens in the Old Regime and After*
Choice - v42 - i3 - Nov 2004 - p555(1) [1-50]

Said, Edward W. - *Culture and Resistance: Conversations with Edward W. Said*
WLT - v79 - i1 - Jan-April 2005 - p112(1) [501+]
Freud and the Non-European
WLT - v78 - i3-4 - Sept-Dec 2004 - p158(1) [501+]
From Oslo to Iraq and the Road Map
BL - v100 - i22 - August 2004 - p1882(1) [51-500]
BW - v34 - i33 - August 15 2004 - p1(2) [501+]
For Aff - v83 - i5 - Sept-Oct 2004 - p164 [501+]
Humanism and Democratic Criticism
Choice - v42 - i4 - Dec 2004 - p644(1) [1-50]
R&R Bk N - v19 - i3 - August 2004 - p4(1) [1-50]
TimHES - v0 - i1648 - July 9 2004 - p27(1) [501+]
Power, Politics and Culture: Interviews with Edward W. Said
TimHES - v0 - i1648 - July 9 2004 - p27(1) [501+]
Power, Politics and Culture:Interviews with Edward W. Said
NS - v133 - i4716 - Nov 29 2004 - p44(1) [51-500]

Said, S.F. - *Varjak Paw (Read by Guidall, George).* Audiobook Review
y Kliatt - v38 - i5 - Sept 2004 - p65(2) [51-500]
c SLJ - v50 - i12 - Dec 2004 - p76(1) [501+]

Saidel, Rochelle G. - *The Jewish Women of Ravensbruck Concentration Camp*
Choice - v42 - i3 - Nov 2004 - p556(1) [1-50]
Wom R Bks - v21 - i12 - Sept 2004 - p24(2) [501+]

Saigo, M. - *H-Transforms: Theory and Applications*
SciTech - v28 - i3 - Sept 2004 - p39(1) [51-500]

Saikal, Amin - *Democratization in the Middle East: Experiences, Struggles, Challenges*
Choice - v42 - i3 - Nov 2004 - p556(1) [1-50]

Sailnger, Lawrence M. - *Encyclopedia of White-Collar and Corporate Crime*
Choice - v42 - i6 - Feb 2005 - p1002(1) [51-500]

Saindon, Ed - *Berklee Practice Method: Vibraphone: Get Your Band Together*
Teach Mus - v12 - i1 - August 2004 - p60(1) [501+]

SAINT 2004 Workshops: 2004 International Symposium on Applications and the Internet: Workshops
SciTech - v28 - i1 - March 2004 - p155(1) [51-500]

Saint-Jacques, Denis - *Love, Always and Again*
Can Lit - i181 - Summer 2004 - p171-173 [501+]

Sainz, Juan Pablo Perez - *Communities in Globalization: The Invisibile Mayan Nahual*
R&R Bk N - v19 - i1 - Feb 2004 - p82(1) [1-50]

Saito, Fumihiko - *Decentralization and Development Partnerships: Lessons from Uganda*
JEL - v42 - i1 - March 2004 - p311(1) [501+]

Sajatovic, Martha - *Rating Scales in Mental Health, 2d Ed.*
SciTech - v28 - i1 - March 2004 - p97(1) [51-500]

Saje, Natasha - *Bend*
Wom R Bks - v21 - i10-11 - July 2004 - p18(2) [501+]

Sajo, Andras - *Human Rights with Modesty: The Problem of Universalism*
R&R Bk N - v19 - i3 - August 2004 - p192(1) [501+]
Judicial Integrity
R&R Bk N - v19 - i3 - August 2004 - p192(1) [501+]

Saka, Ayse - *Cross-National Appropriation of Work Systems: Japanese Firms in the UK*
R&R Bk N - v19 - i1 - Feb 2004 - p119(1) [51-500]

Sakai, Stan - *Usagi Yojimbo: Travels with Jotaro (Illus. by Sakai, Stan)*
y BL - v101 - i2 - Sept 15 2004 - p235(1) [51-500]
y SLJ - v50 - i10 - Oct 2004 - p201(1) [51-500]

Sakamoto, Kerri - *One Hundred Million Hearts.* Audiobook Review
Globe & Mail - July 24 2004 - pD13 [51-500]

Sakany, Lois - *Women Civil War Spies of the Union*
y SLJ - v50 - i12 - Dec 2004 - p162(1) [51-500]

Sakenfeld, Katharine Doob - *Just Wives? Stories of Power and Survival in the Old Testament and Today*
TT - v61 - i3 - Oct 2004 - p400(2) [501+]

Saktanber, Ayse - *Living Islam: Women, Religion and the Politicization of Culture in Turkey*
IJMES - v36 - i3 - August 2004 - p516-517 [501+]

Sakwa, Richard - *Putin: Russia's Choice*
CR - v285 - i1664 - Sept 2004 - p185(1) [51-500]

Sala, Barbara - *Celestine and the Magical Geranium*
c CH Bwatch - Oct 2004 - pNA [51-500]

Sala, Richard - *Maniac Killer Strikes Again*
c SLJ - v50 - i8 - August 2004 - p149(1) [501+]

Sala, Sharon - *Missing*
PW - v251 - i45 - Nov 8 2004 - p41(1) [501+]

Salacuse, Jeswald W. - *The Global Negotiator: Making, Managing, and Mending Deals around the World in the Twenty-First Century*
R&R Bk N - v19 - i1 - Feb 2004 - p91(1) [1-50]

Salah, Trish - *Wanting in Arabic*
Can Lit - i182 - Autumn 2004 - p167(3) [501+]

Salak, Kira - *The Cruelest Journey: 600 Miles to Timbuktu*
y BL - v101 - i6 - Nov 15 2004 - p574(1) [51-500]
LJ - v129 - i19 - Nov 15 2004 - p78(1) [501+]
PW - v251 - i42 - Oct 18 2004 - p58(1) [51-500]

Salama, Mamdouh - *Offshore Mechanics and Arctic Engineering (OMAE 2003): Proceedings, Vol. 3, Materials Technology, Ocean Engineering, Polar and Arctic Sciences and Technology Workshops*
SciTech - v28 - i1 - March 2004 - p171(1) [51-500]

Salamon, Lester M. - *The Resilient Sector: The State of Nonprofit America*
R&R Bk N - v19 - i1 - Feb 2004 - p98(1) [1-50]

Salamon, Michael J. - *Home or Nursing Home: Making the Right Choices, 2d Ed.*
SciTech - v28 - i1 - March 2004 - p84(1) [51-500]

Salamone, Frank A. - *Encyclopedia of Religious Rites, Rituals, and Festivals*
Choice - v42 - i5 - Jan 2005 - p826(1) [1-50]
LJ - v129 - i15 - Sept 15 2004 - p81(1) [51-500]
y SLJ - v50 - i12 - Dec 2004 - p87(2) [501+]
BL - v101 - i3 - Oct 1 2004 - p354(2) [51-500]

Salanie, Bernard - *The Economics of Taxation*
JEL - v41 - i4 - Dec 2003 - p1370(1) [501+]

Salant, Richard - *Salant, CBS, and the Battle for the Soul of Broadcast Journalism: The Memoirs of Richard S. Salant*
HNet - Sept 2004 - pNA [501+]

Salary Budget Survey 2004-2005
HR Mag - v50 - i2 - Feb 2005 - pS5(1) [501+]

Salazar-Carrillo, Jorge - *Oil and Development in Venezuela During the 20th Century*
R&R Bk N - v19 - i3 - August 2004 - p119(1) [51-500]

Saldana-Portillo, Maria Josefina - *The Revolutionary Imagination in the Americas and the Age of Development*
    AHR - v109 - i3 - June 2004 - p876(2) [501+]
    Ams - v61 - i2 - Oct 2004 - p327(2) [501+]
    Choice - v41 - i11-12 - July-August 2004 - p2118(1) [501+]

Saldern, Adelheid von - *The Challenge of Modernity: German Social and Cultural Studies, 1890-1960*
    GSR - v27 - i1 - Feb 2004 - p220-221 [501+]
    J Soc H - v38 - i1 - Fall 2004 - p217(3) [501+]

Sale, J. Timothy - *Advances in International Accounting*
    JEL - v42 - i1 - March 2004 - p298(1) [501+]

Sale, Teel - *Drawing: A Contemporary Approach, 5th Ed.*
    R&R Bk N - v19 - i1 - Feb 2004 - p205(1) [51-500]

Saleem, Hiner - *My Father's Rifle: A Childhood in Kurdistan*
    y BL - v101 - i6 - Nov 15 2004 - p550(1) [51-500]
       KR - v72 - i20 - Oct 15 2004 - p996(1) [501+]
       PW - v251 - i41 - Oct 11 2004 - p63(1) [51-500]

Salem, Elise - *Constructing Lebanon: A Century of Literary Narratives*
    MFSF - v50 - i3 - Fall 2004 - p800-801 [501+]

Salem Press - *Magill's Medical Guide, 3rd Rev. Ed., Vols. 1-4*
    SciTech - v28 - i4 - Dec 2004 - p89(1) [51-500]

Salemenkivi, E. - *Cartonnage Papyri in Context. New Ptolemaic Documents from Abu Sir al-Malaq*
    Class R - v54 - i1 - May 2004 - p223(2) [501+]

Salerno, Roger A. - *Beyond the Enlightenment: Lives and Thoughts of Social Theorists*
    R&R Bk N - v19 - i4 - Nov 2004 - p121(1) [51-500]

Salerno, Steven - *Coco the Carrot*
    c PW - v252 - i10 - March 7 2005 - p67(2) [51-500]

Saletan, William - *Bearing Right: How Conservatives Won the Abortion War*
    Am St - v45 - i1 - Spring 2004 - p175-176 [501+]
    Choice - v41 - i7 - March 2004 - p1373(1) [501+]
    JAH - v91 - i3 - Dec 2004 - p1104(2) [501+]
    Slate's Field Guide to the Candidates 2004
    R&R Bk N - v19 - i4 - Nov 2004 - p64(1) [51-500]

Salevao, Iutisone - *Legitimation in the Letter to the Hebrews: the Construction and Maintenance of a Symbolic Universe*
    Theol St - v65 - i3 - Sept 2004 - p672(1) [501+]

Salgado, Sebastiao - *Sahel: The End of the Road*
    PW - v251 - i41 - Oct 11 2004 - p74(1) [51-500]
    TimHES - v0 - i1683 - March 18 2005 - p26(1) [501+]

Salhi, Kamal - *Francophone Post-Colonial Cultures: Critical Essays*
    Choice - v41 - i7 - March 2004 - p1301(1) [501+]
    HNet - Sept 2004 - pNA [501+]

Saliba, John A. - *Understanding New Religious Movements, 2nd Ed.*
    R&R Bk N - v19 - i1 - Feb 2004 - p15(1) [51-500]

Saliba, Robert - *Beirut City Center Recovery: The Foch-Allenby and Etoile Conservation Area*
    LJ - v129 - i13 - August 2004 - p74(1) [51-500]

Saliba, Therese - *Gender, Politics, and Islam*
    HNet - Nov 2004 - pNA [501+]
    JAAR - v72 - i4 - Dec 2004 - p1067(3) [501+]

Saliers, Don - *A Song to Sing, a Life to Live: Reflections on Music as Spiritual Practice*
    BL - v101 - i5 - Nov 1 2004 - p445(2) [51-500]
    PW - v251 - i39 - Sept 27 2004 - p55(1) [51-500]

Salih, M.A. Mohamed - *African Political Parties: Evolution, Institutionalisation and Governance*
    Choice - v41 - i7 - March 2004 - p1363(1) [501+]

Salih, Ruba - *Gender in Transnationalism: Home, Longing and Belonging Among Moroccan Migrant Women*
    HNet - Nov 2004 - pNA [501+]

Salinas, Jaime - *Travesias: Memorias*
    WLT - v78 - i3-4 - Sept-Dec 2004 - p145(2) [501+]

Salinas, Moises F. - *The Politics of Stereotype: Psychology and Affirmative Action*
    R&R Bk N - v19 - i1 - Feb 2004 - p190(1) [51-500]

Saline, Carol - *Sisters*
    Globe & Mail - Dec 18 2004 - pD14 [1-50]

Salinger, Lawrence M. - *Encyclopedia of White-Collar and Corporate Crime, Vols. 1-2*
    LJ - v130 - i1 - Jan 1 2005 - p154(1) [51-500]

Salinger, Sharon V. - *Taverns and Drinking in Early America*
    BHR - v78 - i1 - Spring 2004 - p106(4) [501+]
    JSH - v70 - i3 - August 2004 - p644(2) [501+]

Salisbury, David - *Educational Freedom in Urban America: Brown v. Board after Half a Century*
    Choice - v42 - i6 - Feb 2005 - p1072(1) [51-500]
    R&R Bk N - v19 - i3 - August 2004 - p230(1) [1-50]

Salisbury, Jan - *Investigating Harassment and Discrimination Complaints: A Practical Guide*
    R&R Bk N - v19 - i1 - Feb 2004 - p99(1) [51-500]

Salisbury, Joyce E. - *Encyclopedia of Women in the Ancient World*
    Wom HR - v13 - i2 - Summer 2004 - p317-319 [501+]
    The Greenwood Encyclopedia of Daily Life: A Tour through History from Ancient Times to the Present, Vols. 1-6
    BL - v101 - i1 - Sept 1 2004 - p163(1) [501+]
    LJ - v129 - i13 - August 2004 - p118(1) [51-500]
    The Greenwood Encyclopedia of Daily Life: A Tour through History from Ancient Times to the Present, Vols. 1-6
    R&R Bk N - v19 - i4 - Nov 2004 - p77(1) [51-500]
    The Greenwood Encyclopedia of Daily Life: A Tour through History from Ancient Times to the Present, Vols. 1-6. E-book Review
    BL - v101 - i9-10 - Jan 1 2005 - p780(1) [51-500]

Salisbury, Laney - *The Cruellest Miles: The Heroic Story of Dogs and Men in a Race Against an Epidemic*
    TLS - i5300 - Oct 29 2004 - p32(1) [501+]

Salisbury, Martin - *Illustrating Children's Books: Creating Pictures for Publication*
    y Magpies - v19 - i5 - Nov 2004 - p45(1) [501+]
       SLJ - v51 - i2 - Feb 2005 - p160(1) [501+]

Salisbury, Wendy - *Move Over, Mrs. Robinson: The Vibrant Guide to Dating, Mating, and Relating for Women of a Certain Age*
    LJ - v129 - i19 - Nov 15 2004 - p76(1) [51-500]

Salivarova, Zdena - *Ashes, Ashes, All Fall Down*
    Sew R - v112 - i2 - Spring 2004 - pXLIV-XLVII [501+]

Salkind, Neil J. - *An Introduction to Theories of Human Development*
    Adoles - v39 - i156 - Winter 2004 - p837(2) [51-500]

Salkintzis, Apostolis K. - *Mobile Internet: Enabling Technologies and Services*
    SciTech - v28 - i3 - Sept 2004 - p154(1) [51-500]

Sallares, Robert - *Malaria and Rome: A History of Malaria in Ancient Italy*
    AHR - v109 - i4 - Oct 2004 - p1287-1288 [501+]
    JIH - v35 - i1 - Summer 2004 - p117-118 [501+]

Sallee, Shelley - *The Whiteness of Child Labor Reform in the New South*
    R&R Bk N - v19 - i3 - August 2004 - p116(1) [51-500]

Salley, Alexander S. - *Marriage Notices in the South-Carolina Gazette and Its Successors, 1732-1801*
    EFHM - v58 - i3 - May-June 2004 - p61(1) [1-50]

Salley, Coleen - *Epossumondas (Illus. by Stevens, Janet)*
    c RT - v57 - Oct 2003 - p169 [1-50]
    Why Epossumondas Has No Hair on His Tail (Illus. by Stevens, Janet)
    c BL - v101 - i1 - Sept 1 2004 - p135(1) [51-500]
    c CCB-B - v58 - i2 - Oct 2004 - p98(1) [51-500]
    c HB - v81 - i1 - Jan-Feb 2005 - p85(1) [51-500]
    c KR - v72 - i15 - August 1 2004 - p748(1) [51-500]
    c NYTBR - March 13 2005 - p21 [501+]
    c SLJ - v50 - i9 - Sept 2004 - p179(1) [51-500]

Sallis, Eva - *The City of Sealions*
    KR - v73 - i3 - Feb 1 2005 - p145(1) [501+]
    Mahjar
    KR - v73 - i4 - Feb 15 2005 - p194(1) [501+]

Sallis, James - *A City Equal to My Desire*
    BL - v101 - i4 - Oct 15 2004 - p391(1) [51-500]

Salloum, Alison - *Group Work with Adolescents after Violent Death: A Manual for Practitioners*
    SciTech - v28 - i4 - Dec 2004 - p118(1) [51-500]

Salman, Ton - *Imaging the Andes: Shifting Margins of a Marginal World*
    Ams - v61 - i2 - Oct 2004 - p319(2) [501+]

Salmen, Walter - *Spielfrauen im Mittelalter*
    Specu - v79 - i3 - July 2004 - p835-837 [501+]

Salminen, Ari - *Governing Networks: EGPA Yearbook*
    R&R Bk N - v19 - i3 - August 2004 - p182(1) [501+]

Salminen, Seppo - *Lactic Acid Bacteria: Microbiological and Functional Aspects, 3rd Rev. Ed.*
    SciTech - v28 - i4 - Dec 2004 - p75(1) [51-500]

Salmon, Philip - *Electoral Reform at Work: Local Politics and National Parties, 1832-1841*
    Albion - v36 - i1 - Spring 2004 - p153(2) [501+]
    HNet - Sept 2004 - pNA [501+]

Salmon, Trevor C. - *Toward a European Army: A Military Power in the Making?*
    Choice - v42 - i1 - Sept 2004 - p183(2) [501+]

Salmond, Anne - *The Trial of the Cannibal Dog: Captain Cook in the South Seas*
    Cont Pac - v17 - i1 - Spring 2005 - p224(9) [501+]

Salmond, John A. - *The General Textile Strike of 1934: From Maine to Alabama*
    J Am St - v38 - i1 - April 2004 - p163-165 [501+]
    Southern Struggles: The Southern Labor Movement and the Civil Struggle
    Choice - v42 - i4 - Dec 2004 - p724(1) [1-50]

Salmond, Noel A. - *Hindu Iconoclasts: Rammohun Roy, Dayananda Sarasvati, and Nineteenth-Century Polemics Against Idolatry*
    Choice - v42 - i7 - March 2005 - p1244(1) [51-500]
    R&R Bk N - v19 - i4 - Nov 2004 - p15(1) [51-500]

Salomies, O. - *The Greek East in the Roman Context: Proceedings of a Colloquium Organized by Finnish Institute at Athens*
    Class R - v54 - i2 - Nov 2004 - p503-504 [501+]

Salomon, Alice - *Character Is Destiny: The Autobiography of Alice Salomon*
    Choice - v42 - i5 - Jan 2005 - p925(1) [1-50]

Salomon, Antoine - *Vuillard*
    TLS - i5263 - Feb 13 2004 - p18-19 [501+]

Salomon, Nanette - *Shifting Priorities: Gender and Genre in Seventeenth-Century Dutch Painting*
    R&R Bk N - v19 - i4 - Nov 2004 - p207(1) [501+]

Salomone, Rosemary C. - *Same, Different, Equal: Rethinking Single-Sex Schooling*
    CS - v33 - i1 - Jan 2004 - p130-130 [501+]
    HER - v74 - i2 - Summer 2004 - p224-227 [501+]

Salomone, William - *Inside Writing: A Writer's Workbook; Form B, 5th Ed.*
    R&R Bk N - v19 - i4 - Nov 2004 - p221(1) [501+]

Salowey, Christina A. - *Great Lives from History: The Ancient World, Prehistory-476 C.E., Vols. 1-2*
    BL - v101 - i4 - Oct 15 2004 - p438(1) [501+]
    Choice - v42 - i4 - Dec 2004 - p638(2) [1-50]
    y Ref Rev - Sept 2004 - pNA [501+]
    R&R Bk N - v19 - i3 - August 2004 - p30(1) [1-50]

Salten, Felix - *Bambi*
    c Sch Lib - v52 - i3 - Autumn 2004 - p134(1) [501+]

Salter, James - *Gods of Tin: The Flying Years*
    BL - v101 - i3 - Oct 1 2004 - p298(1) [51-500]
    PW - v251 - i33 - August 16 2004 - p53(1) [51-500]
    Last Night
    KR - v73 - i4 - Feb 15 2005 - p195(1) [501+]
    PW - v252 - i7 - Feb 14 2005 - p51(1) [51-500]

Salter, John - *Wine Labels, 1730-2003: A Worldwide History*
    Mag Antiq - v167 - i1 - Jan 2005 - p128(1) [51-500]
    Mag Antiq - v167 - i2 - Feb 2005 - p54(1) [51-500]

Salter, Mark B. - *Rights of Passage: The Passport in International Relations*
    Choice - v41 - i7 - March 2004 - p1369(1) [501+]

Salton, George Lucius - *The 23rd Psalm: A Holocaust Memoir*
    Kliatt - v38 - i6 - Nov 2004 - p34(1) [51-500]

Saltzberg, Barney - *Crazy Hair Day*
    c LibMed - v22 - i6 - March 2004 - p59(1) [501+]

Saltzman, Mark - *X-Play Insider's Guide to Gaming*
    Bwatch - March 2005 - pNA [501+]

Salutin, Rick - *The Womanizer: A Man of His Time*
    Can Lit - i182 - Autumn 2004 - p133(3) [501+]
    Womanizer: A Man of His Time
    CBRA - Annual 2003 - p183(1) [51-500]

Salvadori, Mario - *Math Games for Middle School*
    c SLJ - v50 - i9 - Sept 2004 - p59(1) [51-500]

Salvadori, Neri - *Old and New Growth Theories: An Assessment*
    JEL - v41 - i4 - Dec 2003 - p1421(2) [501+]
    The Theory of Economic Growth: A 'Classical' Perspective
    JEL - v41 - i4 - Dec 2003 - p1422(1) [501+]

Salvan, Genevieve - *Seduction et Dialogue dans l'Oeuvre de Crebillon*
    FS - v58 - i1 - Jan 2004 - p111(2) [501+]

Salvatore, Armando - *Public Islam and the Common Good*
    R&R Bk N - v19 - i3 - August 2004 - p18(1) [1-50]

Salvatore, Dominick - *The Dollarization Debate*
    JEL - v41 - i4 - Dec 2003 - p1362(1) [501+]

Sanchez, Norma G. - *Early Universe and the Cosmic Microwave Background: Theory and Observations*
   SciTech - v28 - i1 - March 2004 - p45(1) [51-500]
Sanchez, P. - *L'Amphictionie des Pyles et de Delphes: Recherches sur Son Role Historique des Origines au IIe Siecle de Notre Ere*
   Class R - v54 - i1 - May 2004 - p146(3) [501+]
Sanchez-Walsh, Arlene M. - *Latino Pentecostal Identity*
   R&R Bk N - v19 - i1 - Feb 2004 - p17(1) [51-500]
Sand, Christophe - *Edward W. Gifford and Richard Shutler Jr.'s Archaeological Expedition to New Caledonia in 1952*
   Cont Pac - v16 - i2 - Fall 2004 - p461(2) [501+]
Sand, G.W. - *Defending the West: The Truman-Churchill Correspondence, 1945-1960*
   R&R Bk N - v19 - i3 - August 2004 - p69(1) [51-500]
Sand, Jordan - *House and Home in Modern Japan: Architecture, Domestic Space and Bourgeois Culture, 1880-1930*
   Choice - v42 - i1 - Sept 2004 - p91(1) [501+]
Sandage, Scott A. - *Born Losers: A History of Failure in America*
   Atl - v295 - i1 - Jan-Feb 2005 - p159(2) [501+]
   BW - v35 - i4 - Jan 30 2005 - p2(1) [501+]
   Esq - v143 - i2 - Feb 2005 - p38(1) [501+]
   KR - v72 - i20 - Oct 15 2004 - p996(2) [501+]
   LJ - v129 - i16 - Oct 1 2004 - p95(2) [51-500]
   PW - v251 - i44 - Nov 1 2004 - p52(1) [501+]
Sandberg, K. - *Magistrates and Assemblies: A Study of Legislative Practice in Republican Rome*
   Class R - v54 - i1 - May 2004 - p171(2) [501+]
Sandberg, Mark B. - *Living Pictures, Missing Persons: Mannequins, Museums, and Modernity*
   Scan St - v76 - i3 - Fall 2004 - p436(3) [501+]
Sandbrook, Dominic - *Eugene McCarthy: The Rise and Fall of Postwar American Liberalism*
   BooChiTr - March 28 2004 - p3(1) [501+]
Sande, Pamela - *Quick Reference to COBRA Compliance, 2003*
   R&R Bk N - v19 - i1 - Feb 2004 - pNA [51-500]
   Quick Reference to COBRA Compliance, 2004
   R&R Bk N - v19 - i4 - Nov 2004 - p170(1) [501+]
   Quick reference to HIPAA compliance, 2004
   SciTech - v28 - i4 - Dec 2004 - p11(1) [1-50]
Sandelands, Lloyd E. - *Thinking About Social Life*
   R&R Bk N - v19 - i1 - Feb 2004 - p122(1) [51-500]
Sander, Gordon F. - *The Frank Family that Survived: A Twentieth-Century Odyssey*
   CR - v286 - i1669 - Feb 2005 - p124(1) [51-500]
Sander, Heather - *Make Mine with Everything*
   c Res Links - v10 - i1 - Oct 2004 - p15(2) [51-500]
   Robbie Packford--Alien Monster (Illus. by Revell, Cindy)
   c CBRA - Annual 2003 - p510(1) [51-500]
   c SLJ - v50 - i9 - Sept 2004 - p217(2) [51-500]
Sandercock, Josie - *Peace Under Fire: Israel/Palestine and the International Solidarity Movement*
   MEJ - v59 - i1 - Wntr 2005 - p167(1) [51-500]
   MEQ - v12 - i1 - Wntr 2005 - p94(2) [501+]
Sanders, Bruce - *Talking About Bullying*
   y TES - v0 - i4586 - June 4 2004 - pssss19(1) [501+]
   Talking About Death and Dying
   Sch Lib - v52 - i3 - Autumn 2004 - p151(2) [501+]
Sanders, Charles J. - *The Boys of Winter: Life and Death in the U. S. Ski Troops during the Second World War*
   BL - v101 - i8 - Dec 15 2004 - p703(1) [51-500]
Sanders, Cheryl E. - *Bullying: Implications for the Classroom*
   Choice - v42 - i6 - Feb 2005 - p1071(1) [51-500]
Sanders, Harry M. - *Story Behind Alberta Names: How Cities, Towns, Villages and Hamlets Got Their Names*
   CBRA - Annual 2003 - p350(1) [501+]
Sanders, James E. - *Contentious Republicans: Popular Politics, Race, and Class in Nineteenth-Century Colombia*
   Choice - v42 - i5 - Jan 2005 - p192(2) [1-50]
Sanders, Lauren - *With or Without You*
   PW - v252 - i8 - Feb 21 2005 - p158(1) [51-500]
   Ent W - i811 - March 18 2005 - p72 [1-50]
Sanders, Lawrence - *McNally's Bluff*
   BL - v100 - i22 - August 2004 - p1872(1) [51-500]
   McNally's Chance (Read by Henderson, Adam). Audiobook Review
   LJ - v129 - i16 - Oct 1 2004 - p119(1) [51-500]
   McNally's Risk (Read by Henderson, Adam). Audiobook Review
   LJ - v129 - i16 - Oct 1 2004 - p119(1) [51-500]

Sanders, Lynn Moss - *Howard W. Odum's Folklore Odyssey: Transformation to Tolerance through African American Folk Studies*
   JSH - v71 - i1 - Feb 2005 - p196(2) [501+]
   R&R Bk N - v19 - i3 - August 2004 - p85(1) [51-500]
Sanders, Marcus - *Dante's Inferno (Illus. by Birk, Sandow)*
   Lon R Bks - v26 - i13 - July 8 2004 - p32(2) [501+]
Sanders, Mark - *Your Right to Vote*
   c SLJ - v50 - i8 - August 2004 - p48(1) [51-500]
Sanders, Michael S. - *Families of the Vine: Seasons Among the Winemakers of Southwest France*
   KR - v73 - i5 - March 1 2005 - p281(1) [501+]
Sanders, Pete - *Drinking Alcohol*
   y Sch Lib - v52 - i3 - Autumn 2004 - p165(1) [501+]
Sanders, Robert - *Sibling Relationships: Theory and Issues for Practice*
   Choice - v42 - i3 - Nov 2004 - p569(2) [51-500]
   SciTech - v28 - i3 - Sept 2004 - p4(1) [501+]
Sanders, Tim - *The Likeability Factor: How to Boost Your L Factor and Achieve Your Life's Dreams*
   PW - v252 - i8 - Feb 21 2005 - p165(1) [51-500]
Sanderson, Douglas - *Pure Sweet Hell/ Catch a Fallen Starlet*
   BL - v101 - i5 - Nov 1 2004 - p468(2) [51-500]
Sanderson, Jim - *Nevin's History: A Novel of Texas*
   Roundup M - v11 - i6 - August 2004 - p29(2) [501+]
Sanderson, Margaret H. B. - *A Kindly Place? Living in Sixteenth-Century Scotland*
   Six Ct J - v35 - i1 - Spring 2004 - p292(2) [501+]
Sanderson, Ruth - *Cinderella*
   c RT - v57 - Oct 2003 - p168 [1-50]
   The Snow Princess (Illus. by Sanderson, Ruth)
   c KR - v72 - i20 - Oct 15 2004 - p1013(1) [51-500]
   c SLJ - v50 - i12 - Dec 2004 - p120(1) [51-500]
Sanderson, Terry - *The Gay Man's Kama Sutra*
   G&L Rev W - v11 - i6 - Nov-Dec 2004 - p42(1) [501+]
Sandford, John - *Hidden Prey (Read by Ferrone, Richard). Audiobook Review*
   y Kliatt - v39 - i1 - Jan 2005 - p44(1) [51-500]
   LJ - v129 - i20 - Dec 1 2004 - p182(1) [51-500]
Sandham, William - *Geophysical Applications of Artificial Neural Networks and Fuzzy Logic*
   SciTech - v28 - i1 - March 2004 - p58(1) [51-500]
Sandhu, Ranvinder Singh - *Urbanization in India: Sociological Perspectives*
   R&R Bk N - v19 - i1 - Feb 2004 - p134(1) [51-500]
Sandhu, Sukhdev - *London Calling: How Black and Asian Writers Imagined a City*
   Lon R Bks - v26 - i22 - Nov 18 2004 - p21(2) [501+]
Sandi, Lefaucheur - *The Secret Shelter*
   SLJ - v51 - i1 - Jan 2005 - p132(1) [51-500]
Sandiford, Robert Edison - *Sand for Snow: A Caribbean-Canadian Chronicle*
   CBRA - Annual 2003 - p69(1) [51-500]
Sandin, Joan - *Coyote School News*
   c LibMed - v22 - i5 - Feb 2004 - p68(1) [51-500]
Sandler, Irving - *A Sweeper-Up After Artists*
   TimHES - v0 - i1651 - July 30 2004 - p27(1) [501+]
Sandler, Karen - *Chocolate Magic*
   BL - v101 - i2 - Sept 15 2004 - p228(1) [51-500]
Sandler, Martin W. - *Flying over the USA: Airplanes in American Life*
   c Cur R - v44 - i1 - Sept 2004 - p12(1) [51-500]
   Galloping Across the U.S.A.: Horses in American Life
   c LibMed - v22 - i4 - Jan 2004 - p78(1) [501+]
   Island of Hope: The Story of Ellis Island and the Journey to America
   c LibMed - v23 - i3 - Nov-Dec 2004 - p83(2) [51-500]
   On the Waters of the USA: Ships and Boats in American Life
   c SLJ - v50 - i7 - July 2004 - p127(1) [51-500]
Sandler, Nick - *Preserved*
   NW - Dec 6 2004 - p88 [501+]
Sandler, Stanley - *Ground Warfare: An International Encyclopedia*
   J Mil H - v68 - i3 - July 2004 - p945-946 [501+]
Sandler, Stephanie - *Commemorating Pushkin: Russia's Myth of a National Poet*
   TLS - i5300 - Oct 29 2004 - p28(1) [501+]
Sandler, Todd - *The Economics of Conflict*
   JPR - v41 - i5 - Sept 2004 - p646-646 [501+]

Sandner, David - *Fantastic Literature: A Critical Reader*
   ChrSFF&H - v26 - i10 - Oct 2004 - p30(1) [51-500]
   R&R Bk N - v19 - i4 - Nov 2004 - p221(1) [501+]
Sandole-Staroste, Ingrid - *Women in Transition: Between Socialism and Capitalism*
   CS - v33 - i1 - Jan 2004 - p27-28 [501+]
Sandor, Marjorie - *Portrait of My Mother, Who Posed Nude in Wartime*
   Ga R - v58 - i3 - Fall 2004 - p685-696 [501+]
Sandos, James A. - *Converting California: Indians and Franciscans in the Missions*
   Choice - v42 - i6 - Feb 2005 - p1083(2) [51-500]
   HRNB - v33 - i1 - Fall 2004 - p17(1) [501+]
Sandoval-Garcia, Carlos - *Threatening Others: Nicaraguans and the Formation of National Identities in Costa Rica*
   R&R Bk N - v19 - i4 - Nov 2004 - p70(1) [51-500]
Sandoval, Lynda - *Unsettling*
   BW - v34 - i28 - July 11 2004 - p13(1) [501+]
   Who's Your Daddy
   y Kliatt - v38 - i5 - Sept 2004 - p26(2) [51-500]
   y Kliatt - v39 - i1 - Jan 2005 - p17(1) [51-500]
   y PW - v251 - i51 - Dec 20 2004 - p60(1) [51-500]
Sandoz, Jeff - *Exploring the Spiritual Experience in the 12 Step Program of Alcoholics Anonymous: Spiritus Contra Spiritum*
   R&R Bk N - v19 - i4 - Nov 2004 - p14(1) [51-500]
Sandoz, Mari - *Crazy Horse: The Strange Man of the Oglalas*
   LJ - v129 - i19 - Nov 15 2004 - p103(1) [51-500]
Sandpoint, James L. Payne - *A History of Force: Exploring the Worldwide Movement Against Habits of Coercion, Bloodshed, and Mayhem*
   IndRev - v9 - i2 - Fall 2004 - p283(4) [501+]
Sands, Emily - *Egyptology: Search for the Tomb of Osiris, Being the Journal of Miss Emily Sands, November 1926 (Illus. by Andrew, Ian)*
   y PW - v251 - i42 - Oct 18 2004 - p65(2) [51-500]
Sands, Katharine - *Making the Perfect Pitch: How to Catch a Literary Agent's Eye*
   Bwatch - v26 - i7 - July 2004 - p11(1) [51-500]
   Bwatch - Feb 2005 - pNA [51-500]
   R&R Bk N - v19 - i3 - August 2004 - p258(1) [51-500]
Sands, Lynsay - *The Chase*
   BL - v101 - i8 - Dec 15 2004 - p714(1) [51-500]
Sandweiss, Eric - *St. Louis in the Century of Henry Shaw: A View Beyond the Garden Wall*
   AHR - v109 - i2 - April 2004 - p534(2) [501+]
   JSH - v70 - i3 - August 2004 - p676(3) [501+]
   WHQ - v34 - i4 - Winter 2003 - p523 [501+]
Sandweiss, Martha A. - *Print the Legend: Photography and the American West*
   J Am St - v38 - i1 - April 2004 - p165-167 [501+]
   Pub Hist - v26 - i4 - Fall 2004 - p121(3) [501+]
   WHQ - v35 - i4 - Winter 2004 - p501-501 [501+]
Sandwell, Isabella - *Culture and Society in Later Roman Antioch: Papers From a Colloquium, London 15th December 2001*
   R&R Bk N - v19 - i3 - August 2004 - p52(1) [51-500]
Sandy, Robert - *The Economics of Sport: An International Prespective*
   Choice - v42 - i2 - Oct 2004 - p331(1) [51-500]
Saner, Raymond - *The Expert Negotiator: Strategy, Tactics, Motivation, Behaviour, Leadership, 2nd Ed.*
   R&R Bk N - v20 - i1 - Feb 2005 - p7(1) [51-500]
Sanfilippo, Matteo - *L'Affermazione del Cattolicesimo nel Nord America: Elite, Emigranti e Chiesa Cattolica negli Stati Uniti e in Canada, 1750-1920*
   CHR - v90 - i4 - Oct 2004 - p813(2) [501+]
Sanford, George - *Democratic Government in Poland: Constitutional Politics Since 1989*
   E-A St - v56 - i6 - Sept 2004 - p919(920) [501+]
   Historical Dictionary of Poland, 2nd Ed.
   R&R Bk N - v19 - i1 - Feb 2004 - p39(1) [1-50]
Sanford, Victoria - *Buried Secrets: Truth and Human Rights in Guatemala*
   Ams - v61 - i2 - Oct 2004 - p328(3) [501+]
Sang, Tze-lan D. - *The Emerging Lesbian: Female Same-Sex Desire in Modern China*
   Ch Rev Int - v11 - i1 - Spring 2004 - p166(3) [501+]
   Pac A - v77 - i2 - Summer 2004 - p327(2) [501+]
Sanga, Jaina C. - *South Asian Literature in English: An Encyclopedia*
   Choice - v42 - i4 - Dec 2004 - p630(1) [1-50]
   BL - v101 - i9-10 - Jan 1 2005 - p908(2) [501+]

Sarna, Jonathan D. - *American Judaism: A History*
  Choice - v42 - i3 - Nov 2004 - p501(1) [51-500]
Sarnecki, Judith Holland - *Subversive Subjects: Reading Marguerite Yourcenar*
  Choice - v42 - i2 - Oct 2004 - p299(1) [51-500]
Sarno, Lucio - *The Economics of Exchange Rates*
  Econ J - v114 - i499 - Nov 2004 - pF551-F552 [501+]
Sarra-Bournet, Michel - *Les nationalismes au Quebec, du XIXe au XXIe Siecle*
  Can Hist R - v85 - i3 - Sept 2004 - p541(4) [501+]
Sarra, Janis - *Corporate Governance in Global Capital Markets*
  R&R Bk N - v19 - i1 - Feb 2004 - p97(1) [1-50]
Sarrantonio, Al - *Hornets and Others*
  PW - v251 - i35 - August 30 2004 - p37(2) [501+]
Sarrinikolaou, George - *Facing Athens*
  NY - v80 - i24 - August 30 2004 - p97(1) [1-50]
Sarris, Nikos - *3D Modeling and Animation: Synthesis and Analysis Techniques for the Human Body*
  SciTech - v28 - i4 - Dec 2004 - p167(1) [51-500]
Sarsfield, Mairuth - *No Crystal Stair. Audiobook Review*
  c Globe & Mail - Dec 11 2004 - pD53 [1-50]
Sarti, Raffaella - *Europe at Home: Family and Material Culture, 1500-1800*
  CR - v285 - i1664 - Sept 2004 - p183(2) [501+]
  JMH - v76 - i4 - Dec 2004 - p936(2) [501+]
  Six Ct J - v34 - i4 - Winter 2003 - p1271-1272 [501+]
Sarti, Roland - *Italy: A Reference Guide from the Renaissance to the Present*
  Choice - v42 - i7 - March 2005 - p1208(2) [51-500]
  LJ - v129 - i19 - Nov 15 2004 - p86(1) [51-500]
  R&R Bk N - v19 - i4 - Nov 2004 - p40(1) [51-500]
Sartre, Maurice - *The Middle East Under Rome*
  PW - v252 - i8 - Feb 21 2005 - p164(1) [51-500]
Sartwell, Crispin - *Extreme Virtue: Truth and Leadership in Five Great American Lives*
  Biomag - v27 - i3 - Summer 2004 - p625(4) [501+]
  Choice - v42 - i1 - Sept 2004 - p116(1) [501+]
Sarty, Roger - *No Higher Purpose: The Official Operational History of the Royal Canadian Navy in the Second World War, 1939-1943*
  Can Hist R - v85 - i3 - Sept 2004 - p566(3) [501+]
  Saint John Fortifications, 1630-1956.
  Can Hist R - v85 - i4 - Dec 2004 - p816(3) [501+]
  CBRA - Annual 2003 - p350(2) [501+]
Sasaki, Chikara - *Descartes's Mathematical Thought*
  Choice - v42 - i1 - Sept 2004 - p142(1) [501+]
Sasser, Charles - *Dark Planet*
  PW - v252 - i9 - Feb 28 2005 - p47(1) [51-500]
Sassi, Maria Michela - *The Science of Man in Ancient Greece*
  Isis - v95 - i3 - Sept 2004 - p483(2) [501+]
Sasso, Len - *Emagic Logic: Tips and Tricks*
  SciTech - v28 - i1 - March 2004 - p164(1) [51-500]
Sasson, Jean - *Mayada, Daughter of Iraq: One Woman's Survival under Saddam Hussein*
  BW - v34 - i1 - Jan 4 2004 - p6(1) [501+]
Sassower, Raphael - *Confronting Disaster: An Existential Approach to Technoscience*
  Choice - v42 - i4 - Dec 2004 - p682(1) [1-50]
  SciTech - v28 - i4 - Dec 2004 - p128 [51-500]
Sateren, Shelley Swanson - *Michelangelo*
  Sch Lib - v52 - i3 - Autumn 2004 - p153(1) [501+]
Saterstrom, Selah - *The Pink Institution*
  ABR - v26 - i2 - Jan-Feb 2005 - p5(1) [501+]
Sather, Clifford - *Seeds of Play, Words of Power: An Ethnographic Study of Iban Shamanic Chants*
  JRAI - v10 - i4 - Dec 2004 - p941(2) [501+]
Satin, Mark - *Radical Middle: The Politics We Need Now*
  Fut - v39 - i1 - Jan-Feb 2005 - p45(3) [501+]
  Fut - v39 - i1 - Jan-Feb 2005 - p49(1) [501+]
Satloff, Robert - *Policy Focus*
  LJ - v129 - i12 - July 2004 - p120(1) [51-500]
Sato, Barbara - *Colonizing Sex: Sexology and Social Control in Modern Japan*
  AHR - v109 - i4 - Oct 2004 - p1211-1211 [501+]
  The New Japanese Woman: Modernity, Media, and Women in Interwar Japan
  J Soc H - v38 - i2 - Winter 2004 - p548(3) [501+]
  JAS - v63 - i2 - May 2004 - p511(3) [501+]
  Pac A - v77 - i3 - Fall 2004 - p578(2) [501+]

Sato, Hiroshi - *The Growth of Market Relations in Post-Reform Rural China: A Micro-Analysis of Peasants, Migrants and Peasant Entrepreneurs*
  AJS - v110 - i2 - Sept 2004 - p499(3) [501+]
  Ch Rev Int - v11 - i1 - Spring 2004 - p151(7) [501+]
Satow, Roberta - *Doing the Right Thing: Taking Care of Your Elderly Parents Even if They Didn't Take Care of You*
  PW - v252 - i5 - Jan 31 2005 - p65(1) [501+]
Satran, Pamela Redmond - *Babes in Captivity*
  BL - v100 - i22 - August 2004 - p1902(1) [501+]
Satrapi, Marjane - *Embroideries*
  KR - v73 - i3 - Feb 1 2005 - p148(1) [501+]
  LJ - v129 - i20 - Dec 1 2004 - p92(1) [1-50]
  PW - v252 - i10 - March 7 2005 - p52(1) [51-500]
  Persepolis 2: The Story of a Return
  y BL - v100 - i22 - August 2004 - p1916(1) [51-500]
  BL - v101 - i9-10 - Jan 1 2005 - p771(1) [51-500]
  Ent W - i781 - Sept 3 2004 - p81 [51-500]
  Globe & Mail - Sept 4 2004 - pD6 [501+]
  Globe & Mail - Nov 27 2004 - pD3 [51-500]
  LJ - v129 - i14 - Sept 1 2004 - p129(1) [501+]
  NYTBR - August 22 2004 - p7 [501+]
  NYTBR - Sept 5 2004 - p18 [501+]
  SLJ - v50 - i12 - Dec 2004 - p177(1) [51-500]
  Time - v164 - i8 - August 23 2004 - p74 [501+]
  Wom R Bks - v21 - i12 - Sept 2004 - p8(2) [501+]
  Persepolis: The Story of a Childhood
  Globe & Mail - July 31 2004 - pD14 [1-50]
  y Kliatt - v38 - i5 - Sept 2004 - p42(3) [501+]
Satter, David - *Darkness at Dawn: The Rise of the Russian Criminal State*
  BW - v34 - i42 - Oct 17 2004 - p12(1) [501+]
  Slav R - v63 - i2 - Summer 2004 - p426(2) [501+]
Satterfield, George - *Princes, Posts and Partisans: The Army of Louis XIV and Partisan Warfare in the Netherlands 1653-1678*
  R&R Bk N - v19 - i1 - Feb 2004 - p35(1) [1-50]
Satterfield, Jay - *The World's Best Book: Taste, Culture, and the Modern Library*
  AHR - v109 - i2 - April 2004 - p551(2) [501+]
Satterfield, Terre - *What's Nature Worth? Narrative Expressions of Environmental Values*
  Choice - v42 - i1 - Sept 2004 - p104(1) [501+]
  Env - v47 - i1 - Jan-Feb 2005 - p42(1) [501+]
Satterly, Faye - *Where Have All the Nurses Gone?: The Impact of the Nursing Shortage on American Healthcare*
  SciTech - v28 - i1 - March 2004 - p126(1) [51-500]
Satterthwait, Walter - *Cavalcade*
  KR - v72 - i23 - Dec 1 2004 - p1123(1) [501+]
  PW - v252 - i1 - Jan 3 2005 - p39(2) [51-500]
Satterthwaite, Ann - *Going Shopping: Consumer Choices and Community Consequences*
  J Am St - v38 - i1 - April 2004 - p167-168 [501+]
Sattin, Anthony - *The Gates of Africa: Death, Discovery, and the Search for Timbuktu*
  BL - v101 - i9-10 - Jan 1 2005 - p805(1) [51-500]
  KR - v72 - i24 - Dec 15 2004 - p1191(1) [501+]
  LJ - v130 - i1 - Jan 1 2005 - p130(1) [51-500]
  TimHES - v0 - i1649 - July 16 2004 - p24(1) [501+]
Sattler, Friederike - *Wirtschaftsordnung im Ubergang: Politik, Organisation und Funktion der KPD/SED im Land Brandenburg bei der Etablierung der Zentralen Planwirtschaft in der SBZ/DDR 1945-52*
  HNet - Nov 2004 - pNA [501+]
Satz, Ronald N. - *American Indian Policy in the Jacksonian Era*
  HNet - Sept 2004 - pNA [501+]
Sauer, David K. - *David Mamet: A Research and Production Sourcebook*
  R&R Bk N - v19 - i1 - Feb 2004 - p246(1) [51-500]
Sauer, Walter - *Der Struwwelpeter und sein Schopfer Dr. Heinrich Hoffman: Bibliographie der Secundarliteratur*
  BSA-P - v98 - i1 - March 2004 - p129-129 [501+]
Sauers, Michael P. - *Neal-Schuman Directory of Management Software for Public Access Computers*
  LibMed - v22 - i7 - April-May 2004 - p89(1) [501+]
  R&R Bk N - v19 - i1 - Feb 2004 - p259(1) [51-500]
Sauers, Richard A. - *Gettysburg: The Meade-Sickles Controversy*
  AHR - v109 - i4 - Oct 2004 - p1234(2) [501+]
Sauerwein, Leigh - *Song for Eloise*
  LibMed - v22 - i6 - March 2004 - p65(1) [501+]
  LibMed - v22 - i6 - March 2004 - p65(1) [501+]

Saukko, Paula - *Doing Research in Cultural Studies: An Introduction to Classical and New Methodological Approaches*
  R&R Bk N - v19 - i1 - Feb 2004 - p121(1) [51-500]
Saul, E. Wendy - *Crossing Borders in Literacy and Science Instruction: Perspectives on Theory and Practice*
  Sci Teach - v71 - i7 - Sept 2004 - p86-88 [501+]
Saul, John - *Black Creek Crossing (Read by Hill, Dick). Audiobook Review*
  Kliatt - v38 - i6 - Nov 2004 - p42(1) [51-500]
Saul, Norman E. - *War and Revolution: The United States and Russia, 1914-1921*
  HNet - Sept 2004 - pNA [501+]
Saul, Scott - *Freedom Is, Freedom Ain't: Jazz and the Making of the Sixties*
  JAH - v91 - i3 - Dec 2004 - p1090(2) [501+]
Saulnier, Beth - *The Fourth Wall*
  KR - v73 - i4 - Feb 15 2005 - p202(2) [51-500]
  Reliable Sources
  BL - v101 - i1 - Sept 1 2004 - p69(1) [51-500]
Saulsberry, Rodney - *You Can Bank on Your Voice: Your Guide to a Successful Career in Voice-Overs*
  BL - v100 - i21 - July 2004 - p1809(1) [1-50]
  Bwatch - Feb 2005 - pNA [51-500]
Saum, Steven Boyd - *Each a Mighty Voice: A Century of Speeches from the Commonwealth Club of California*
  R&R Bk N - v19 - i4 - Nov 2004 - p241(1) [501+]
Saums, Mary - *When the Last Magnolia Weeps*
  DroRevMy - v24 - i3 - May-June 2004 - p13(1) [1-50]
  DroRevMy - v24 - i4 - July-August 2004 - p13(1) [51-500]
Saunders, Alan - *Beyond the Locket*
  c CH Bwatch - v14 - i12 - Dec 2004 - pNA [51-500]
Saunders, Barbara - *Theories, Technologies, Instrumentalities of Color: Anthropological and Historiographic Perspectives*
  JRAI - v10 - i3 - Sept 2004 - p707(2) [501+]
  Whither Multiculturalism? A Politics of Dissensus
  R&R Bk N - v19 - i2 - May 2004 - p130(1) [51-500]
Saunders, Frances Stonor - *Hawkwood: Diabolical Englishman*
  NS - v133 - i4713 - Nov 8 2004 - p50(2) [501+]
Saunders, Frances Stonor - *Hawkwood: Diabolical Englishman*
  Spec - v296 - i9201 - Dec 11 2004 - p37(2) [501+]
Saunders, Gary L. - *So Much Weather!: Facts, Phenomena and Weather Lore from Atlantic Canada*
  CBRA - Annual 2003 - p427(2) [51-500]
Saunders, Graham - *Love Me or Kill Me: Sarah Kane and the Theatre of Extremes*
  Theat J - v56 - i1 - March 2004 - p153(2) [501+]
Saunders, Judith P. - *The Poetry of Charles Tomlinson: Border Lines*
  ANQ:QJ - v17 - i4 - Fall 2004 - p45(3) [501+]
Saunders, Kevin W. - *Saving our Children from the First Amendment*
  Choice - v41 - i11-12 - July-August 2004 - p2126(1) [51-500]
Saunders, Nicholas - *Divine Action and Modern Science*
  JR - v84 - i4 - Oct 2004 - p648(2) [501+]
Saunders, Nicholas J. - *Trench Art: Materialities and Memories of War*
  y TimHES - v0 - i1652 - August 6 2004 - p24(2) [501+]
Saunders, Nigel - *Energy Essentials: Fossil Fuels*
  c Sch Lib - v52 - i4 - Winter 2004 - p209(1) [51-500]
  Uranium and the Lanthanides and Actinides
  y Sch Lib - v52 - i3 - Autumn 2004 - p165(1) [501+]
Saunders, Peter - *Wine Label Language*
  R&R Bk N - v19 - i4 - Nov 2004 - p248(1) [501+]
Saunders, Richard - *Main Lines: Rebirth of the North American Railroads, 1970-2002*
  BHR - v78 - i2 - Summer 2004 - p321(3) [501+]
  R&R Bk N - v19 - i1 - Feb 2004 - p104(1) [51-500]
Saunders, Tim - *Juno Beach, 3rd Canadian and 79th Armoured Divisions*
  R&R Bk N - v19 - i4 - Nov 2004 - p33(1) [51-500]
Saunders, W.B. - *Physical Rehabilitation of the Injured Athlete, 3d Ed.*
  SciTech - v28 - i3 - Sept 2004 - p111(1) [51-500]
Sauppe, Eberhard - *Dictionary of Librarianship Including a Selection from the Terminology of Information Science, Bibliology, Reprography, Higher Education and Data Processing. German-English, English-German. 3rd Ed., Rev and Enl*
  ALJ - v53 - i3 - August 2004 - p324(1) [501+]

Scarborough, Elizabeth Ann - *Cleopatra 7.2.*
  PW - v251 - i46 - Nov 15 2004 - p45(1) [51-500]
  LJ - v129 - i20 - Dec 1 2004 - p104(1) [51-500]

Scarborough, Joe - *Rome Wasn't Burnt in a Day: The Real Deal on How Politicians, Bureaucrats, and Other Washington Barbarians Are Bankrupting America*
  PW - v251 - i37 - Sept 13 2004 - p71(1) [501+]

Scarborough, Rowan - *Rumsfeld's War: The Untold Story of America's Antiterrorist Commander*
  NWCR - v57 - Autumn 2004 - p156(3) [501+]
  R&R Bk N - v19 - i3 - August 2004 - p70(1) [51-500]

Scarborough, Vernon L. - *Flow of Power: Ancient Water Systems and Landscapes*
  R&R Bk N - v19 - i4 - Nov 2004 - p77(1) [51-500]
Heterarchy, Political Economy, and the Ancient Maya: The Three Rivers Region of the East-Central Yucatan Peninsula
  Lat Ant - v15 - i4 - Dec 2004 - p456(3) [501+]
  R&R Bk N - v19 - i1 - Feb 2004 - p67(1) [501+]

Scarborough, William Kauffman - *Masters of the Big House: Elite Slaveholders of the Mid-Nineteenth-Century South*
  HNet - Sept 2004 - pNA [501+]
  JAH - v91 - i3 - Dec 2004 - p1005(2) [501+]

Scardino, Barrie - *Ephemeral City: Cite Looks at Houston*
  JSH - v70 - i4 - Nov 2004 - p991(1) [501+]

Scarf, Maggie - *Secrets, Lies, Betrayals: How the Body Holds the Secrets of a Life, and How to Unlock Them*
  Choice - v42 - i3 - Nov 2004 - p570(1) [1-50]

Scarfone, Jay - *The Wizardry Of Oz: The Artistry and Magic of the 1939 M-G-M Classic*
  Bwatch - Dec 2004 - pNA [51-500]
  R&R Bk N - v19 - i4 - Nov 2004 - p224(1) [501+]

Scarlett, Mel - *The Great Rip-Off in American Education: Undergrads Underserved*
  R&R Bk N - v19 - i3 - August 2004 - p214(1) [1-50]

Scarpetta, Kay - *Trace*
  NYTBR - Sept 19 2004 - p15 [501+]

Scarr, Deryck - *A History of the Pacific Islands: Passages through Tropical Time*
  PHR - v73 - i4 - Nov 2004 - p661(3) [501+]

Scarratt, William L.H. - *Lives and Work at Sea: Herbert Holdsworth, Colin Hannah and the Ship Ladakh*
  R&R Bk N - v19 - i3 - August 2004 - p122(1) [51-500]

Scarre, Geoffrey - *After Evil: Responding to Wrongdoing*
  R&R Bk N - v19 - i4 - Nov 2004 - p13(1) [51-500]

Scarrow, Simon - *The Eagle's Prey*
  Globe & Mail - Oct 30 2004 - pD26 [51-500]

Scarry, Richard - *The Rooster Struts*
  c PW - v251 - i38 - Sept 20 2004 - p64(1) [51-500]

Scarsbrook, Richard - *Cheeseburger Subversive*
  y CBRA - Annual 2003 - p510(2) [51-500]

Scetti, Aurelio - *Journal of Aurelio Scetti: A Florentine Galley Slave at Lepanto*
  R&R Bk N - v19 - i4 - Nov 2004 - p41(1) [51-500]

Schaaf, Gregory - *Franklin, Jefferson, and Madison: On Religion and the State*
  Bwatch - v26 - i9 - Sept 2004 - p7(1) [51-500]

Schaaf, Phil - *Sports Inc.: 100 Years of Sports Business*
  R&R Bk N - v19 - i1 - Feb 2004 - p74(1) [51-500]

Schaap, Ella B. - *Delft Ceramics at the Philadelphia Museum of Art*
  Ceram Mo - v52 - i4 - April 2004 - p32(1) [501+]

Schaberg, Jane - *On the Cutting Edge: The Study of Women in Biblical Worlds, Essays in Honor of Elisabeth Schussler Fiorenza*
  R&R Bk N - v19 - i1 - Feb 2004 - p18(1) [1-50]

Schabert, Ina - *Imaginationen des Anderen im 16. und 17. Jahrhundert*
  Ren Q - v57 - i3 - Fall 2004 - p1070(3) [501+]

Schachnow, Sid - *Hope and Honor*
  BW - v34 - i44 - Oct 31 2004 - p5(2) [501+]

Schacht, Charles A. - *Refractories Handbook*
  SciTech - v28 - i4 - Dec 2004 - p165(1) [51-500]

Schachter, Esty - *Anya's Echoes*
  y Kliatt - v38 - i5 - Sept 2004 - p26(2) [51-500]

Schachter, Madeleine - *Informational and Decisional Privacy*
  R&R Bk N - v19 - i1 - Feb 2004 - pNA [51-500]

Schachter-Shalomi, Zalman - *Jewish with Feeling: A Guide to Meaningful Jewish Practice*
  LJ - v130 - i4 - March 1 2005 - p94(1) [51-500]
  PW - v252 - i9 - Feb 28 2005 - p64(1) [51-500]

Schackel, Sandra K. - *Western Women's Lives: Continuity and Change in the Twentieth Century*
  R&R Bk N - v19 - i1 - Feb 2004 - p132(1) [51-500]

Schad, John - *Queer Fish: Christian Unreason from Darwin to Derrida*
  Choice - v42 - i7 - March 2005 - p1212(1) [51-500]
  R&R Bk N - v19 - i4 - Nov 2004 - p19(1) [51-500]

Schaebler, Birgit - *Globalization and the Muslim World: Culture, Religion, and Modernity*
  R&R Bk N - v19 - i4 - Nov 2004 - p43(1) [51-500]

Schaechter, Moselio - *The Desk Encyclopedia of Microbiology*
  Choice - v42 - i3 - Nov 2004 - p458(1) [1-50]
  E-Streams - Oct 2004 - pNA [501+]

Schaefer, Carole Lexa - *The Biggest Soap* (Illus. by Dressen-McQueen, Stacey)
  c BL - v101 - i3 - Oct 1 2004 - p326(1) [51-500]
  c HB - v80 - i5 - Sept-Oct 2004 - p574(1) [51-500]
  c KR - v72 - i17 - Sept 1 2004 - p873(1) [51-500]
  c SLJ - v50 - i9 - Sept 2004 - p179(1) [51-500]
Cool Time Song (Illus. by Morgan, Pierr)
  c CCB-B - v58 - i6 - Feb 2005 - p265(1) [51-500]
  c KR - v73 - i3 - Feb 1 2005 - p181(1) [51-500]
Someone Says (Illus. by Morgan, Pierr)
  c Five Owls - v18 - i1 - Fall 2004 - p17(1) [51-500]

Schaefer, Hartmut - *Richard Strauss: Autographen, Portrats, Buhnenbilder. Ausstellung zum 50. Todestag*
  Notes - v61 - i2 - Dec 2004 - p435(3) [501+]

Schaefer, Heike - *Mary Austin's Regionalism: Reflections on Gender, Genre, and Geography*
  Choice - v42 - i4 - Dec 2004 - p662(1) [1-50]
  R&R Bk N - v19 - i4 - Nov 2004 - p242(1) [+1]

Schaefer, Henry F. - *Quantum Chemistry; The Development of 'Ab Initio' Methods in Molecular Electronic Structure Theory*
  SciTech - v28 - i3 - Sept 2004 - p53(1) [1-50]

Schaefer, Lola M. - *Aircraft*
  c LibMed - v22 - i5 - Feb 2004 - p88(2) [501+]
Armadillos
  c SLJ - v51 - i1 - Jan 2005 - p114(1) [51-500]
Arms, Elbows, Hands, and Fingers
  c LibMed - v22 - i5 - Feb 2004 - p57(1) [501+]
Arrowhawk (Illus. by Swiatkowska, Gabi)
  c CCB-B - v57 - i11 - July-August 2004 - p482(1) [501+]
Javelinas
  c SLJ - v51 - i1 - Jan 2005 - p114(1) [51-500]
Loose Tooth (Illus. by Wickstrom, Sylvie)
  c BL - v100 - i22 - August 2004 - p1944(1) [51-500]
My Neck and Shoulders
  c LibMed - v22 - i5 - Feb 2004 - p57(1) [501+]
Roadrunners
  c SLJ - v51 - i1 - Jan 2005 - p114(1) [51-500]
Tiny-Spiny Animals Series
  c LibMed - v23 - i1 - August-Sept 2004 - p71(1) [51-500]

Schaeffer, Frank - *Faith of Our Sons*
  Mar Crp G - v88 - i5 - May 2004 - p89(1) [501+]
Voices from the Front: Letters Home from America's Military Family
  y BL - v101 - i4 - Oct 15 2004 - p384(1) [51-500]
Zermatt (Read by James, Lloyd). Audiobook Review
  y Kliatt - v38 - i5 - Sept 2004 - p66(2) [51-500]
  LJ - v130 - i1 - Jan 1 2005 - p168(1) [51-500]

Schaeffer, Mary S. - *Accounts Payable Best Practices*
  R&R Bk N - v19 - i3 - August 2004 - p132(1) [51-500]

Schaer, Frank - *The Three Kings of Cologne*
  JEGP - v103 - i2 - April 2004 - p265-267 [501+]

Schafer, Antje - *Vergils Eklogen 3 und 7 in der Tradition der Lateinischen Streitdichtung: Eine Darstellung Anhand Ausgewahlter Texte der Antike und des Mittelalters*
  Class R - v54 - i1 - May 2004 - p94(2) [501+]

Schafer, Daniel L. - *Anna Madgigine Jai Kingsley: African Princess, Florida Slave, Plantation Slaveowner*
  AHR - v109 - i4 - Oct 2004 - p1228(1) [501+]
  JAH - v91 - i1 - June 2004 - p230-230 [501+]
  JSH - v70 - i3 - August 2004 - p662(2) [501+]

Schafer, Hans J. - *Encyclopedia of Electrochemistry, Vol. 8*
  SciTech - v28 - i4 - Dec 2004 - p56(1) [51-500]

Schafer, John R. - *Advanced Interviewing Techniques: Proven Strategies for Law Enforcement, Military, and Security Personnel*
  R&R Bk N - v19 - i3 - August 2004 - p168(1) [501+]

Schafer, Judith Kelleher - *Becoming Free, Remaining Free: Manumission and Enslavement in New Orleans, 1846-1862*
  AHR - v109 - i4 - Oct 2004 - p1229(2) [501+]
  JAH - v91 - i3 - Dec 2004 - p1007(1) [501+]
  JSH - v71 - i1 - Feb 2005 - p151(2) [501+]

Schafer, Peter - *The Bar Kokhba War Reconsidered*
  J Mil H - v68 - i2 - April 2004 - p582-584 [501+]
Mirror of His Beauty: Feminine Images of God from the Bible to the Early Kabbalah
  CH - v73 - i4 - Dec 2004 - p844(2) [501+]
  JR - v84 - i4 - Oct 2004 - p658(2) [501+]
  Specu - v79 - i4 - Oct 2004 - p1136(3) [501+]

Schaffer, David - *Iraq*
  SLJ - v50 - i10 - Oct 2004 - pS58(1) [51-500]

Schaffer, Jeffrey P. - *Desolation Wilderness and the South Lake Tahoe Basin, 4th Ed.*
  R&R Bk N - v19 - i1 - Feb 2004 - p73(1) [1-50]

Schaffer, Matthew - *Djinns, Stars, and Warriors: Mandinka Legends from Pakao, Senegal*
  R&R Bk N - v19 - i1 - Feb 2004 - p72(1) [1-50]

Schaffer, Richard - *International Business Law and its Environment, 6th Ed.*
  R&R Bk N - v19 - i3 - August 2004 - p190(1) [501+]

Schaffer, Robert K. - *Understanding Globalization: The Social Consequences of Political, Economic, and Environmental Change*
  CS - v33 - i5 - Sept 2004 - p626-626 [501+]

Schaffer, Talia - *The Forgotten Female Aesthetes*
  VS - v45 - i2 - Winter 2003 - p370 [501+]

Schaffner, Alain - *Le Porte-Plume Souvenir: Alexandre Vialatte Romancier*
  FS - v58 - i2 - April 2004 - p282(2) [501+]

Schaffter, Peter - *The Schumann Proof*
  Globe & Mail - Nov 27 2004 - pD16 [51-500]

Schafly, Phyllis - *The Supremacists: The Tyranny of Judges and How to Stop It*
  R&R Bk N - v19 - i4 - Nov 2004 - p172(1) [501+]

Schaie, K. Warner - *Religious Influences on Health and Well-Being in the Elderly*
  SciTech - v28 - i4 - Dec 2004 - p4(1) [1-50]

Schaik, Carel Van - *Among Orangutans: Red Apes and the Rise of Human Culture*
  New Sci - v185 - i2483 - Jan 22 2005 - p51(1) [1-50]

Schaler, Jeffrey A. - *Szasz Under Fire: A Psychiatric Abolitionist Faces His Critics*
  SciTech - v28 - i4 - Dec 2004 - p94(1) [51-500]

Schanilec, Gaylord - *Magnificent Mayflies*
  Nature - v429 - i6989 - May 20 2004 - p246(1) [501+]

Schank, Roger C. - *Making Minds Less Well Educated than Our Own*
  Choice - v42 - i4 - Dec 2004 - p711(1) [1-50]
  R&R Bk N - v19 - i3 - August 2004 - p214(1) [1-50]

Schanke, Robert A. - *"That Furious Lesbian": The Story of Mercedes de Acosta*
  Lam Bk Rpt - v13 - i3 - Oct 2004 - p21(2) [501+]
  Theat J - v56 - i4 - Dec 2004 - p723-725 [501+]
  TLS - i5293 - Sept 10 2004 - p18(1) [501+]
Women in Turmoil: Six Plays by Mercedes de Acosta
  Lam Bk Rpt - v13 - i3 - Oct 2004 - p21(2) [501+]
  Theat J - v56 - i4 - Dec 2004 - p723-725 [501+]

Schanker, D.R. - *A Criminal Appeal*
  LJ - v129 - i18 - Nov 1 2004 - p135(1) [501+]

Schanzer, Rosalyn - *George vs. George: The American Revolution as Seen from Both Sides* (Illus. by Schanzer, Rosalyn)
  c BL - v101 - i6 - Nov 15 2004 - p578(2) [51-500]
  c CCB-B - v58 - i5 - Jan 2005 - p226(1) [51-500]
  c HB - v81 - i1 - Jan-Feb 2005 - p107(2) [51-500]
  c SLJ - v50 - i10 - Oct 2004 - p194(1) [51-500]
How Ben Franklin Stole the Lightning (Illus. by Schanzer, Rosalyn)
  c RT - v58 - i3 - Nov 2004 - p288(1) [1-50]

Schaps, David M. - *The Invention of Coinage and the Monetization of Ancient Greece*
  Choice - v41 - i11-12 - July-August 2004 - p2100(1) [501+]

Scharf, Gian Paolo G. - *Borgo San Sepolcro a Meta del Quattrocento: Istituzioni e Societa 1440-1460*
  Ren Q - v57 - i4 - Winter 2004 - p1374(3) [501+]

Scharff, Virginia - *Seeing Nature through Gender*
  PHR - v73 - i4 - Nov 2004 - p670(2) [501+]
  WHQ - v35 - i4 - Winter 2004 - p504-505 [501+]

Schieder, Wolfgang - *Adolf Butenandt und die Kaiser-Wilhelm-Gesellschaft: Wissenschaft, Industrie und Politik im "Dritten Reich"*
Nature - v431 - i7006 - Sept 16 2004 - p246(1) [501+]

Schieffer, Bob - *Face the Nation: My Favorite Stories from the First 50 Years of the Award-Winning News Broadcast*
AJR - v26 - i5 - Oct-Nov 2004 - p102(1) [501+]
y BL - v101 - i1 - Sept 1 2004 - p3(1) [51-500]
LJ - v129 - i18 - Nov 1 2004 - p98(1) [51-500]
PW - v251 - i33 - August 16 2004 - p50(1) [51-500]

Schienstock, Gerd - *Embracing the Knowledge Economy; the Dynamic Transformation of the Finnish Innovation System*
R&R Bk N - v19 - i3 - August 2004 - p101(1) [501+]

Schier, Steven E. - *High Risk amd Big Ambition: The Presidency of George W. Bush*
Choice - v42 - i5 - Jan 2005 - p935(1) [51-500]

Schier, Tracy - *Catholic Women's Colleges in America*
HNet - Nov 2004 - pNA [501+]

Schiff, Stacy - *A Great Improvisation: Franklin, France, and the Birth of America*
KR - v73 - i2 - Jan 15 2005 - p111(1) [501+]
LJ - v129 - i20 - Dec 1 2004 - p92(1) [1-50]
NW - March 28 2005 - p53 [501+]
PW - v252 - i6 - Feb 7 2005 - p50(1) [51-500]

Schiffauer, Werner - *Civic Enculturation: Nation-State, Schools and Ethnic Difference in Four European Countries*
R&R Bk N - v19 - i4 - Nov 2004 - p190(1) [501+]

Schiffer, Michael Brain - *Draw the Lightning Down: Benjamin Franklin and Electrical Technology in the Age of Enlightenment*
JAH - v91 - i3 - Dec 2004 - p993(2) [501+]
T&C - v45 - i4 - Oct 2004 - p840(3) [501+]

Schiffer, Nancy N. - *The World of Bertoia*
Am Craft - v64 - i2 - April-May 2004 - p36(1) [501+]

Schiffer, Stephen - *The Things We Mean*
Choice - v41 - i11-12 - July-August 2004 - p2059(1) [501+]

Schiffhorst, Lynn B. - *It's Great to Be A Ghost!*
c CH Bwatch - March 2005 - pNA [51-500]

Schiffman, Stephan - *The Young Entrepreneur's Guide to Business Terms*
y LibMed - v22 - i6 - March 2004 - p87(1) [501+]
y SLJ - v50 - i7 - July 2004 - p127(2) [51-500]

Schiffrin, Anya - *Covering Globalization: A Handbook For Reporters*
CJR - v43 - i6 - March-April 2005 - p63(1) [51-500]

Schifllett, Samuel - *Scaled Worlds: Development, Validation, and Applications*
R&R Bk N - v19 - i3 - August 2004 - p90(1) [51-500]

Schildgen, Brenda Deen - *Dante and the Orient*
Dal R - v83 - i3 - Autumn 2003 - p451-453 [501+]
Ren Q - v57 - i3 - Fall 2004 - p972(3) [501+]

Schildt, Herbert - *The Art of C++*
LJ - v129 - i16 - Oct 1 2004 - p104(1) [51-500]

Schilhung, Rene - *Kriegsheldon. Deutungsmuster heroischer Mannlichkeit in Deutschland 1813-1945*
GSR - v27 - i2 - May 2004 - p393-394 [501+]

Schiller, Dieter - *Der verweigerte Dialog: Zum Verhaltnis von Parteifuhrung der SED und Schriftstellern im Krisenjahr 1956*
HNet - Sept 2004 - pNA [501+]

Schiller, Jochen H. - *Mobile Communications. 2nd Ed.*
SciTech - v28 - i3 - Sept 2004 - p159(1) [51-500]

Schilling, Govert - *Evolving Cosmos*
New Sci - v185 - i2481 - Jan 8 2005 - p50(1) [51-500]

Schillinger, Liesl - *Good Girl Wants It Bad*
BW - v34 - i34 - August 22 2004 - p4(1) [501+]

Schimitzek, Peter - *The Efficient Enterprise: Increased Corporate Success With Industry-specific Information Technology and Knowledge Management*
R&R Bk N - v19 - i1 - Feb 2004 - p87(1) [1-50]

Schindehette, Susan - *Between Good and Evil*
People - v63 - i11 - March 21 2005 - p60 [51-500]

Schindel, John - *Busy Kitties (Illus. by Franzen, Sean)*
c PW - v251 - i31 - August 2 2004 - p72(1) [51-500]

Schindler, Dietrich - *The Laws of Armed Conflicts: A Collection of Conventions, Resolutions, and Other Documents, 4th Rev. Ed.*
R&R Bk N - v19 - i4 - Nov 2004 - p176(1) [501+]

Schindler, Nina - *An Order of Amelie, Hold the Fries (Illus. by Barrett, Robert)*
y BL - v101 - i9-10 - Jan 1 2005 - p847(1) [1-50]
y KR - v72 - i22 - Nov 15 2004 - p1093(1) [51-500]
c Res Links - v10 - i2 - Dec 2004 - p39(1) [51-500]
y SLJ - v51 - i1 - Jan 2005 - p136(1) [51-500]

Schindler, Norbert - *Rebellion, Community and Custom in Early Modern Germany*
GSR - v27 - i1 - Feb 2004 - p139-140 [501+]
Ren Q - v57 - i3 - Fall 2004 - p1042(3) [501+]

Schine, Cathleen - *She is Me*
NYTBR - Oct 24 2004 - p30 [501+]

Schintz, Mike - *Alequiers: The History of a Homestead*
CBRA - Annual 2003 - p69(2) [51-500]

Schinzinger, Roland - *Conformal Mapping: Methods and Applications*
SciTech - v28 - i1 - March 2004 - p137(1) [51-500]

Schipper, Mineke - *Never Marry a Woman with Big Feet: Women in Proverbs from Around the World*
LJ - v129 - i12 - July 2004 - p92(1) [51-500]
Lon R Bks - v27 - i4 - Feb 17 2005 - p19(2) [501+]

Schippers, Jan C. - *Integrated Membrane Systems*
SciTech - v28 - i3 - Sept 2004 - p146(1) [51-500]

Schirato, Tony - *Understanding the Visual*
R&R Bk N - v20 - i1 - Feb 2005 - p9(1) [51-500]

Schirm, Stefan A. - *New Rules for Global Markets: Public and Private Governance in the World Economy*
Choice - v42 - i2 - Oct 2004 - p340(1) [51-500]

Schirmer, Jennifer - *The Guatemalan Military Project: A Violence Called Democracy*
Ams - v61 - i2 - Oct 2004 - p331(3) [501+]

Schiro, Michael Stephen - *Oral Storytelling and Teaching Mathematics: Pedagogical and Multicultural Perspectives*
Choice - v42 - i6 - Feb 2005 - p1073(2) [501+]

Schissel, Bernard - *Legacy of School for Aboriginal People: Education, Oppression, and Emancipation*
CBRA - Annual 2003 - p369(1) [501+]

Schittich, Christian - *Architectural Details 2003: Annual Selected Edition from Detail Review of Architecture*
E-Streams - Dec 2004 - pNA [501+]

Schivelbusch, Wolfgang - *The Culture of Defeat: On National Trauma, Mourning, and Recovery*
AHR - v109 - i2 - April 2004 - p486(2) [501+]

Schjonning, P. - *Managing Soil Quality: Challenges in Modern Agriculture*
QRB - v79 - i4 - Dec 2004 - p449(2) [501+]

Schladweiler, Kief - *The Foundation Center's Guide to Grantseeking on the Web, 2003 ed.*
R&R Bk N - v19 - i3 - August 2004 - p158(1) [51-500]

Schlager, Neil - *St. James Encyclopedia of Labor History Worldwide: Major Events in Labor History and Their Impact*
Ref Rev - Oct 2004 - pNA [501+]

Schlaucht, Wolfgang - *In Amerikanischer Kriegsgefangenschaft: Berichte Deutscher Soldaten aus dem Zweiten Weltkrieg*
J Mil H - v68 - i2 - April 2004 - p635(2) [501+]

Schlee, Guenther - *Imagined Differences: Hatred and the Construction of Identity*
CS - v33 - i6 - Nov 2004 - p749(1) [1-50]

Schleiermacher, Friedrich - *Fifteen Sermons of Friedrich Schleiermacher Delivered to Celebrate the Beginning of a New Year*
R&R Bk N - v19 - i1 - Feb 2004 - p23(1) [51-500]
Friedrich Schleiermacher on creeds, Confessions and Church Union: That They May Be One
R&R Bk N - v19 - i3 - August 2004 - p27(1) [1-50]

Schlein, Miriam - *Little Raccoon's Big Question (Illus. by Schoenherr, Ian)*
c NYTBR - August 8 2004 - p16 [501+]

Schlesinger, Arthur M., Jr. - *The Election of 2000 and the Administration of George W. Bush*
y SLJ - v50 - i8 - August 2004 - p50(1) [51-500]
War and the American Presidency
BL - v100 - i22 - August 2004 - p1882(1) [51-500]
BW - v34 - i51 - Dec 19 2004 - p7(1) [51-500]
Econ - v373 - i8396 - Oct 9 2004 - p80US [501+]
Hum - v65 - i2 - March-April 2005 - p45(3) [501+]
KR - v72 - i13 - July 1 2004 - p623(1) [501+]
LJ - v129 - i12 - July 2004 - p104(2) [51-500]
Nation - v279 - i11 - Oct 11 2004 - p42 [501+]
NL - v87 - i5 - Sept-Oct 2004 - p23(2) [501+]
NYRB - v51 - i15 - Oct 7 2004 - p15(4) [501+]
NYTBR - Sept 5 2004 - p22 [501+]
Spec - v296 - i9195 - Oct 30 2004 - p50(3) [501+]

Schlesinger, Erica - *Addressing the World: National Identity and Internet Country Code Domains*
SciTech - v28 - i1 - March 2004 - p155(1) [51-500]

Schlesinger, James R. - *Final Report of the Independent Panel to Review DoD Detention Operations*
NYRB - v51 - i15 - Oct 7 2004 - p44(7) [501+]

Schlessinger, Laura - *Woman Power: Transform Your Man, Your Marriage, Your Life*
PW - v251 - i31 - August 2 2004 - p64(1) [51-500]

Schlight, John - *Help from Above: Air Force Close Air Support of the Army, 1946-1973*
J Mil H - v68 - i4 - Oct 2004 - p1304-1305 [501+]

Schloen, J. David - *The House of the Father as Fact and Symbol: Patrimonialism in Ugarit and the Ancient Near East*
JNES - v63 - i3 - July 2004 - p232(3) [501+]

Schloss, Joseph G. - *Making Beats: The Art of Sample-Based Hip-Hop*
Choice - v42 - i5 - Jan 2005 - p862(1) [1-50]

Schlosser, Gerhard - *Modularity in Development and Evolution*
Nature - v430 - i7003 - August 26 2004 - p970(1) [501+]
New Sci - v183 - i2463 - Sept 4 2004 - p47(1) [51-500]
Sci - v306 - i5697 - Oct 29 2004 - p814(2) [501+]

Schlosser, Peter - *Jurisdiction and International Judicial and Administrative Co-operation*
R&R Bk N - v19 - i4 - Nov 2004 - p159(1) [501+]

Schlow, Michael - *It's About Time: Great Recipes for Everyday Life*
PW - v252 - i5 - Jan 31 2005 - p64(1) [501+]

Schluter-Ahrens, Regina - *Der Volkswirt Jens Jessen. Leben und Werk*
GSR - v27 - i3 - Oct 2004 - p636(1) [501+]

Schmadel, Lutz D. - *Dictionary of Minor Planet Names, Fifth Edition*
S&T - v107 - i1 - Jan 2004 - p76(1) [501+]

Schmal, S. - *Sallust*
Class R - v54 - i1 - May 2004 - p93(2) [501+]

Schmalbeck, Richard L. - *Federal Income Taxation*
R&R Bk N - v19 - i3 - August 2004 - p204(1) [1-50]

Schmandt-Besserat, Denise - *The History of Counting (Illus. by Hays, Michael)*
c SLJ - v50 - i9 - Sept 2004 - p58(1) [51-500]

Schmeller, Erik S. - *Perceptions of Race and Nation in English and American Travel Writers, 1833-1914*
R&R Bk N - v19 - i4 - Nov 2004 - p234(1) [501+]

Schmid, Gunter - *Nanoparticles: From Theory to Application*
E-Streams - Nov 2004 - pNA [501+]
SciTech - v28 - i3 - Sept 2004 - p46(1) [1-50]

Schmid, Mark-Daniel - *The Richard Strauss Companion*
R&R Bk N - v19 - i1 - Feb 2004 - p196(1) [51-500]

Schmid, Michael - *Der "Eiserne Kanzler" und Die Generale. Deutsche Rustungspolitik in Der Ara Bismarck*
GSR - v27 - i3 - Oct 2004 - p624(2) [501+]

Schmid, Peter - *1803: Wende in Europas Mitte: Vom Feudalen zum Buergerlichen Zeitalter*
HNet - July 2004 - pNA [501+]

Schmid, Robert - *Tribal Asia: Ceremonies, Rituals and Dress*
LJ - v129 - i15 - Sept 15 2004 - p54(2) [51-500]
R&R Bk N - v19 - i3 - August 2004 - p84(1) [51-500]
TimHES - v0 - i1669 - Dec 3 2004 - p29(1) [501+]

Schmid, Stephan G. - *Petra, Ez Zantur II: Ergebnisse der schweizerisch-liechtensteinischen Ausgrabungen, Teil 1: Die Feinkeramik der Nabataer: Typologie, Chronologie und kulturhistorische Hintergrunde*
JNES - v63 - i3 - July 2004 - p230(3) [501+]

Schmid, Vernon - *Houlihans and Horse Sense*
Roundup M - v12 - i3 - Feb 2005 - p22(1) [51-500]
Showdown at Chalk Creek: A Novel of the Old West
Roundup M - v11 - i6 - August 2004 - p30(1) [501+]
Roundup M - v12 - i1 - Oct 2004 - p32(1) [51-500]

Schmid, Wolfgang - *Durer als Unternehmer: Kunst, Humanismus und Okonomie in Nurnberg um 1500*
Ren Q - v57 - i3 - Fall 2004 - p1036(3) [501+]

Schmider, Klaus - *Partisanenkrieg in Jugoslawien 1941-1944*
J Mil H - v68 - i3 - July 2004 - p994-996 [501+]
Slav R - v63 - i3 - Fall 2004 - p633-634 [501+]

Schoch, Irene - *The Cat's Vacation*
c SLJ - v50 - i8 - August 2004 - p93(1) [51-500]
Schoch, Richard W. - *Not Shakespeare: Bardolatry and Burlesque in the Nineteenth Century*
Shakes Q - v55 - i1 - Spring 2004 - p107-108 [501+]
Theat J - v56 - i2 - May 2004 - p325(2) [501+]
VS - v46 - i3 - Spring 2004 - p544(4) [501+]
Queen Victoria and the Theatre of Her Age
Choice - v42 - i3 - Nov 2004 - p495(1) [51-500]
CR - v285 - i1665 - Oct 2004 - p253(1) [501+]
Schock, Peter A. - *Romantic Satanism: Myth and the Historical Moment in Blake, Shelley, and Byron*
Choice - v41 - i7 - March 2004 - p1299(1) [501+]
Schockenhoff, Eberhard - *Natural Law and Human Dignity: Universal Ethics in an Historical World*
Theol St - v65 - i4 - Dec 2004 - p880(2) [501+]
Schodt, Frederik L. - *Native American in the Land of the Shogun: Ranald MacDonald and the Opening of Japan*
Can Hist R - v85 - i3 - Sept 2004 - p621(2) [501+]
JAS - v63 - i2 - May 2004 - p513(2) [501+]
Schoell, William - *H.P. Lovecraft: Master of Weird Fiction*
y VOYA - v27 - i5 - Dec 2004 - p421(1) [51-500]
Mystery and Terror: The Story of Edgar Allan Poe
y BL - v101 - i3 - Oct 1 2004 - p321(1) [51-500]
y CH Bwatch - v14 - i11 - Nov 2004 - pNA [51-500]
y SLJ - v50 - i12 - Dec 2004 - p169(1) [51-500]
y VOYA - v27 - i5 - Dec 2004 - p421(1) [51-500]
Schoeman, Roy H. - *"Salvation Is from the Jews": The Role of Judaism in Salvation History from Abraham to the Second Coming*
IBMR - v28 - i4 - Oct 2004 - p184(2) [501+]
Schoemperlen, Diane - *Names of the Dead: An Elegy for the Victims of September 11*
Globe & Mail - Nov 27 2004 - pD3 [51-500]
Schoenberg, Jane - *My Bodyworks (Illus. by Fisher, Cynthia)*
c KR - v73 - i5 - March 1 2005 - p295(1) [51-500]
Schoenberner, Gerhard - *The Yellow Star: The Persecutions of the Jews in Europe, 1933-1945*
Bwatch - March 2005 - pNA [51-500]
LJ - v130 - i3 - Feb 15 2005 - p172(1) [51-500]
Schoenfeld, Steven A. - *Active Index Investing: Maximizing Portfolio Performance and Minimizing Risk Through Global Index Strategies*
R&R Bk N - v19 - i4 - Nov 2004 - p118(1) [51-500]
Schoepflin, Rennie B. - *Christian Science on Trial: Religious Healing in America*
AHR - v109 - i2 - April 2004 - p538(2) [501+]
CH - v73 - i3 - Sept 2004 - p701(2) [501+]
Isis - v95 - i3 - Sept 2004 - p518(1) [501+]
Schoeser, Mary - *World Textiles: A Concise History*
Am Craft - v64 - i1 - Feb-March 2004 - p40(1) [501+]
Schofield, Jennifer - *Animal Babies in Polar Lands*
c SLJ - v50 - i10 - Oct 2004 - p150(1) [51-500]
Animal Babies in Ponds and Rivers
c SLJ - v50 - i10 - Oct 2004 - p150(1) [51-500]
Animal Babies in Rain Forests
c SLJ - v50 - i10 - Oct 2004 - p150(1) [51-500]
Schofield, Phillipp R. - *Credit and Debt in Medieval England, 1180-1350*
JIH - v34 - i4 - Spring 2004 - p627-628 [501+]
Peasant and Community in Medieval England, 1200-1500
Med R - Oct 2004 - pNA [501+]
Schogt, Henry G. - *Curtain: Witness and Memory in Wartime Holland*
CBRA - Annual 2003 - p70(1) [51-500]
Schoiswohl, Michael - *Status and (Human Rights) Obligations of Non-Recognized De Facto Regimes in International Law: The Case of 'Somaliland', the Resurrection of Somaliland Against All International 'Odds'...*
R&R Bk N - v19 - i4 - Nov 2004 - p163(1) [501+]
Scholastic, Inc. - *Scholastic Children's Encyclopedia*
c BL - v101 - i4 - Oct 15 2004 - p439(1) [51-500]
Scholastic Reference (Firm) - *Scholastic Atlas of Weather*
c LibMed - v23 - i3 - Nov-Dec 2004 - p88(1) [51-500]
Scholem, Gershom Gerhard - *Es Gibt Ein Geheimnis in Der Welt: Tradition und Sakularisation*
TLS - i5265 - Feb 27 2004 - p7-7 [501+]
The Fullness of Time
TLS - i5265 - Feb 27 2004 - p7-7 [501+]
Scholl, Elizabeth J. - *Praying Mantis*
c SLJ - v50 - i12 - Dec 2004 - p135(1) [51-500]
Scholl, Tim - *Sleeping Beauty, a Legend in Progress*
Choice - v42 - i3 - Nov 2004 - p495(1) [51-500]
Schollgen, Gregor - *Der Auftritt: Deutschlands Ruckkehr auf die Weltbuhne*
HNet - Sept 2004 - pNA [501+]

Scholten, Frits - *Willem van Tetrode, Sculptor, (c. 1525-1580): Guglielmo Fiammingo Scultore*
Ren Q - v57 - i3 - Fall 2004 - p1028(5) [501+]
Scholtz, Gerhard - *Evolutionary Developmental Biology of Crustacea*
E-Streams - June 2004 - pNA [501+]
SciTech - v28 - i1 - March 2004 - p69(1) [51-500]
Schom, Alan - *The Eagle and the Rising Sun: The Japanese-American War, 1941-1943, Pearl Harbour Through Guadalcanal*
Choice - v41 - i11-12 - July-August 2004 - p2102(1) [501+]
Liberty on the Waterfront: America Maritime Culture in the Age of Revolution
VQR - v80 - i3 - Summer 2004 - p258(1) [501+]
Schom, Isabel - *Best of Latino Heritage, 1996-2002: A Guide to the Best Juvenile Books about Latino People and cultures*
LibMed - v22 - i4 - Jan 2004 - p86(1) [501+]
Schomp, Virginia - *The Ancient Chinese*
c SLJ - v51 - i2 - Feb 2005 - p148(1) [51-500]
Schon, Marbeth - *Modernist Jewelry 1930-1960: The Wearable Art Movement*
R&R Bk N - v19 - i4 - Nov 2004 - p210(1) [501+]
Schonberg, Karl K. - *Pursuing the National Interest: Moments of Transition in Twentieth-Century American Foreign Policy*
R&R Bk N - v19 - i1 - Feb 2004 - p61(1) [501+]
Schonfeld, Roger C. - *JSTOR: A History*
JEL - v41 - i4 - Dec 2003 - p1395(1) [501+]
JEL - v42 - i3 - Sept 2004 - p869(2) [501+]
TimHES - v0 - i1676 - Jan 28 2005 - p26(1) [501+]
Schonherr, Johannes - *Trashfilm Roadshows: On the Road with Subversive Movies*
FQ - v57 - i2 - Winter 2003 - p63(1) [501+]
Schonsleben, Paul - *Integral Logistics Management: Planning and Control of Comprehensive Supply Chains, 2nd Ed.*
R&R Bk N - v19 - i1 - Feb 2004 - p88(1) [1-50]
Schonstein, Patricia - *A Time of Angels*
BL - v101 - i4 - Oct 15 2004 - p391(1) [51-500]
KR - v72 - i19 - Oct 1 2004 - p935(2) [51-500]
LJ - v129 - i20 - Dec 1 2004 - p102(2) [51-500]
People - v62 - i24 - Dec 13 2004 - p54 [51-500]
PW - v251 - i43 - Oct 25 2004 - p26(1) [51-500]
Schonthal, Axel H. - *Checkpoint Controls and Cancer, Vol 1: Reviews and Model Systems*
SciTech - v28 - i3 - Sept 2004 - p91(1) [51-500]
Checkpoint Controls and Cancer, Vol. 2: Activation and Regulation Protocols
SciTech - v28 - i3 - Sept 2004 - p91(1) [51-500]
Schooch, Irene - *The Cat's Vacation*
y NYTBR - Sept 19 2004 - p16 [501+]
Schoolcraft, Ralph - *Romain Gary: The Man Who Sold His Shadow*
FS - v58 - i2 - April 2004 - p286(2) [501+]
Schooley, Kerry J. - *Revenge*
Globe & Mail - Oct 30 2004 - pD26 [51-500]
Schoolfield, George C. - *A Baedeker of Decadence: Charting a Literary Fashion*
Sew R - v112 - i3 - Summer 2004 - pLXXXII-LXXXIV [501+]
Schoonmaker, Sara - *High-Tech Trade Wars: U.S. -Brazilian Conflicts in the Global Economy*
T&C - v45 - i1 - Jan 2004 - p217(3) [501+]
Schoonover, Thomas - *Uncle Sam's War of 1898 and the Origins of Globalization*
JAH - v91 - i3 - Dec 2004 - p1048(2) [501+]
PHR - v73 - i3 - August 2004 - p516(518) [501+]
Schopenhauer, Arthur - *The Art of Always Being Right: Thirty Eight Ways to Win When You Are Defeated*
Spec - v297 - i9204 - Jan 1 2005 - p26(1) [501+]
Schoppa, R. Keith - *Twentieth Century China: A History in Documents*
Cur R - v44 - i6 - Feb 2005 - p12(2) [501+]
Schor, Esther - *The Cambridge Companion to Mary Shelley*
Choice - v41 - i11-12 - July-August 2004 - p2042(2) [501+]
Schor, Juliet - *Born to Buy: The Commercialized Child and the New Consumer Culture*
Bus W - i3901 - Sept 27 2004 - p26 [501+]
BW - v34 - i46 - Nov 14 2004 - p5(1) [1-50]
NYTBR - Oct 24 2004 - p26 [501+]
Pub Int - i158 - Wntr 2005 - p125(6) [501+]

Schories, Pat - *Breakfast for Jack (Illus. by Schories, Pat)*
c HB - v81 - i1 - Jan-Feb 2005 - p86(1) [51-500]
c KR - v72 - i19 - Oct 1 2004 - p968(1) [51-500]
c PW - v251 - i51 - Dec 20 2004 - p57(1) [51-500]
c SLJ - v50 - i11 - Nov 2004 - p117(2) [51-500]
Jack and the Missing Piece (Illus. by Schories, Pat)
c HB - v81 - i1 - Jan-Feb 2005 - p86(1) [51-500]
c PW - v251 - i51 - Dec 20 2004 - p57(1) [51-500]
c SLJ - v50 - i11 - Nov 2004 - p117(2) [51-500]
Schorlemmer, Friedrich - *Hier stehe ich: Martin Luther*
Six Ct J - v35 - i3 - Fall 2004 - p795-809 [501+]
Schorman, Rob - *Selling Style: Clothing and Social Change at the Turn of the Century*
JAH - v91 - i2 - Sept 2004 - p655(2) [501+]
Schott, Ben - *Schott's Food & Drink Miscellany*
Globe & Mail - July 31 2004 - pD13 [51-500]
Schott's Original Miscellany
Globe & Mail - July 31 2004 - pD13 [51-500]
Schott, Jeffrey J. - *Free Trade Agreements: US Strategies and Priorities*
Choice - v42 - i3 - Nov 2004 - p532(1) [1-50]
R&R Bk N - v19 - i3 - August 2004 - p125(1) [51-500]
Schou, Mogens - *Lithium Treatment of Mood Disorders: A Practical Guide, 6th Rev. Ed.*
SciTech - v28 - i3 - Sept 2004 - p98(1) [51-500]
Schouls, Tim - *Shifting Boundaries: Aboriginal Identity, Pluralist Theory, and the Politics of Self-Government*
CBRA - Annual 2003 - p369(2) [501+]
R&R Bk N - v19 - i1 - Feb 2004 - p52(1) [51-500]
Schousboe, Arne - *Molecular Neuropharmacology: Strategies and Methods*
SciTech - v28 - i1 - March 2004 - p73(1) [51-500]
Schouwenburg, Henri C. - *Counseling the Procrastinator in Academic Settings*
R&R Bk N - v19 - i3 - August 2004 - p222(1) [1-50]
Schrader, Abby M. - *Languages of the Lash: Corporal Punishment and Identity in Imperial Russia*
JMH - v77 - i1 - March 2005 - p255(3) [501+]
Schraff, Anne - *Dr. Charles Drew: Blood Bank Innovator*
c Sci Teach - v71 - i4 - April 2004 - p73-73 [501+]
Wilma Rudolph: The Greatest Woman Sprinter in History
c SLJ - v50 - i8 - August 2004 - p144(1) [51-500]
Schrafstetter, Susanna - *Avoiding Armageddon: Europe, the United States, and the Struggle for Nuclear Nonproliferation, 1945-1970*
R&R Bk N - v19 - i3 - August 2004 - p189(1) [501+]
Schrag, Peter - *Final Test: The Battle for Adequacy in American's Schools*
NYRB - v51 - i19 - Dec 2 2004 - p29(4) [501+]
Schram, Sanford F. - *Praxis for the Poor: Piven and Cloward and the Future of Social Science in Social Welfare*
AJS - v110 - i2 - Sept 2004 - p533(2) [501+]
CS - v33 - i1 - Jan 2004 - p77-78 [501+]
Soc Ser R - v78 - i4 - Dec 2004 - p700(1) [51-500]
Race and the Politics of Welfare Reform
CS - v33 - i6 - Nov 2004 - p707(2) [501+]
Schrank, William E. - *The Cost of Fisheries Management*
JEL - v42 - i1 - March 2004 - p332(1) [501+]
Schrecker, Ellen - *Cold War Triumphalism: The Misuse of History After the Fall of Communism*
For Aff - v83 - i5 - Sept-Oct 2004 - p164 [501+]
Cold War Triumphalism: The Politics of American History after the Fall of Communism
Choice - v42 - i5 - Jan 2005 - p914(2) [1-50]
Schreiber, Brad - *What Are You Laughing At?: How To Write Funny Screenplays, Stories, & More*
Bwatch - Feb 2005 - pNA [51-500]
Schreiber, Carolin - *King Alfred's Old English Translation of Pope Gregory the Great's "Regula pastoralis" and Its Cultural Context*
Specu - v79 - i4 - Oct 2004 - p1138(3) [501+]
Schreiber, Ellen - *Comedy Girl*
y Kliatt - v38 - i4 - July 2004 - p13(1) [51-500]
y KR - v72 - i13 - July 1 2004 - p636(1) [51-500]
y PW - v251 - i37 - Sept 13 2004 - p79(2) [51-500]
y SLJ - v50 - i9 - Sept 2004 - p218(1) [51-500]
Vampire Kisses
LibMed - v22 - i5 - Feb 2004 - p70(1) [501+]
Schreiber, Marion - *The Twentieth Train: The True Story of the Ambush of the Death Train to Auschwitz*
BW - v34 - i12 - March 21 2004 - p2(1) [501+]
Schreiber, Mark - *Dreams of the Solo Trapeze: Offstage with the Cirque du Soleil*
PW - v251 - i47 - Nov 22 2004 - p52(1) [51-500]
Schreiber, Mordecai - *The Shengold Jewish Encyclopedia, 3rd Ed.*
R&R Bk N - v19 - i1 - Feb 2004 - p42(1) [51-500]

Schreier, Iris - *Exquisite Little Knits: Knitting with Luxurious Specialty Yarns*
  BL - v101 - i5 - Nov 1 2004 - p453(1) [51-500]
  LJ - v129 - i20 - Dec 1 2004 - p111(1) [51-500]
Schreiner, Mark - *Rural Microfinance in Argentina: After the Tequila Crisis*
  R&R Bk N - v19 - i3 - August 2004 - p133(1) [51-500]
Schreyer, Ray - *The Best 100 Web Sites for HR Professionals*
  HR Mag - v49 - i7 - July 2004 - pS32(1) [501+]
Schrieber, Ellen - *Teenage Mermaid*
  c LibMed - v22 - i5 - Feb 2004 - p70(1) [501+]
Schriesheim, Chester A. - *New Directions in Human Resource Management*
  R&R Bk N - v19 - i2 - May 2004 - p118 [51-500]
Schrift, Melissa - *Biography of a Chairman Mao Badge: The Creation and Mass Consumption of a Personality Cult*
  Ch Rev Int - v11 - i1 - Spring 2004 - p1(8) [501+]
Schrijver, Nico - *International Law and Sustainable Development: Principles and Practice*
  R&R Bk N - v19 - i4 - Nov 2004 - p163(1) [501+]
Schriver, Joe M. - *Human Behavior and the Social Environment: Shifting Paradigms in Essential Knowledge for Social Work, 4th Ed.*
  R&R Bk N - v19 - i1 - Feb 2004 - p124(1) [51-500]
Schroedel, Jenny - *The Blackbird's Nest*
  c CH Bwatch - v14 - i8 - August 2004 - p4(2) [51-500]
Schroeder, Alan - *Celebrity-in-Chief: How Show Business Took over the White House*
  Choice - v42 - i1 - Sept 2004 - p147(1) [501+]
Schroeder, Andreas - *Scams!*
  y Kliatt - v38 - i5 - Sept 2004 - p47(2) [501+]
  c SLJ - v50 - i8 - August 2004 - p144(1) [51-500]
  y VOYA - v27 - i4 - Oct 2004 - p332(1) [51-500]
Schroeder, Brock E. - *Ecstasy*
  SB - v40 - i3 - May-June 2004 - p127(1) [501+]
Schroeder, Holly - *New Zealand ABCs: A Book about the People and Places of New Zealand (Illus. by Wolf, Claudia)*
  c SLJ - v50 - i8 - August 2004 - p108(1) [51-500]
Schroeder, Lars - *Slave to the Body: Black Bodies, White No-Bodies, and the Regulative Dualism of Body-Politics in the Old South*
  JSH - v70 - i4 - Nov 2004 - p908(2) [501+]
  R&R Bk N - v19 - i1 - Feb 2004 - p122(1) [51-500]
Schroeder, Patricia R. - *Robert Johnson, Mythmaking, and Contemporary American culture*
  Choice - v42 - i5 - Jan 2005 - p862(1) [1-50]
Schroeder, Paul E. - *Systems, Stability, and Statecraft: Essays on the International History of Modern Europe*
  R&R Bk N - v20 - i1 - Feb 2005 - p31(1) [51-500]
Schroeder, Peter W. - *Six Million Paper Clips: The Making of a Children's Holocaust Memorial*
  y BL - v101 - i9-10 - Jan 1 2005 - p854(2) [1-50]
Schroeder, Sandi - *Software for Indexing*
  R&R Bk N - v19 - i4 - Nov 2004 - p257(1) [501+]
Schroen, Gary - *First In: An Insider's Account of How the CIA Spearheaded the War on Terror in Afghanistan*
  PW - v252 - i8 - Feb 21 2005 - p163(1) [51-500]
Schroer, Silvia - *Feminist Interpretation of the Bible and the Hermeneutics of Liberation*
  R&R Bk N - v19 - i3 - August 2004 - p22(1) [1-50]
Schroeter, Daniel J. - *The Sultan's Jew: Morocco and the Sephardi World*
  JIH - v35 - i1 - Summer 2004 - p174-175 [501+]
Schroth, Gotz - *Fundamentals of Astrometry*
  Choice - v42 - i6 - Feb 2005 - p1045(1) [51-500]
Schroth, Raymond A. - *Fordham: A History and Memoir*
  CHR - v90 - i3 - July 2004 - p576(3) [501+]
Schubert, Blaine W. - *Ice Age Cave Faunas of North America*
  Choice - v41 - i11-12 - July-August 2004 - p2075(1) [501+]
  QRB - v79 - i3 - Sept 2004 - p299(2) [501+]
Schubert, E. Fred - *Light-Emitting Diodes*
  Phys Today - v57 - i11 - Nov 2004 - p64-66 [501+]
Schubert, Frank N. - *Voices Of the Buffalo Soldiers: Records, Reports, and Recollections of Military Life and Services in the West*
  WHQ - v35 - i2 - Summer 2004 - p238-239 [501+]
Schubert, Ingrid - *Hammer Soup (Illus. by Schubert, Ingrid)*
  c BL - v101 - i1 - Sept 1 2004 - p135(2) [51-500]
  c SLJ - v50 - i9 - Sept 2004 - p179(1) [51-500]

Schubert, Karl - *CIO Survival Guide; the Roles and Responsibilities of the Chief Information Officer*
  R&R Bk N - v19 - i3 - August 2004 - p101(1) [501+]
Schuckett, Sandy - *Political Advocacy for School Librarians: You Have the Power!*
  SLJ - v50 - i12 - Dec 2004 - p179(1) [51-500]
Schuerkens, Ulrike - *Global Forces and Local Life-Worlds: Social Transformations*
  R&R Bk N - v19 - i3 - August 2004 - p143(1) [51-500]
Schuette, Sarah L. - *I Am Polite*
  c SLJ - v50 - i12 - Feb 2004 - p137(1) [501+]
Schuetze, Hans G. - *Integrating School and Workplace Learning in Canada: Principles and Practices of Alternative Education and Training*
  R&R Bk N - v19 - i3 - August 2004 - p228(1) [1-50]
Schuiten, Francois - *The Book of Schuiten*
  BL - v101 - i4 - Oct 15 2004 - p374(1) [51-500]
  The Invisible Frontier. Vol. 2
  y BL - v101 - i3 - Oct 1 2004 - p320(1) [51-500]
  PW - v251 - i43 - Oct 25 2004 - p30(1) [51-500]
Schuiten, Luc - *The Hollow Grounds*
  BL - v101 - i4 - Oct 15 2004 - p396(1) [51-500]
Schuld, J. Joyce - *Foucault and Augustine: Reconsidering Power and Love*
  JAAR - v72 - i4 - Dec 2004 - p1070(3) [501+]
  TT - v61 - i2 - July 2004 - p272(2) [501+]
Schuler, Charles - *Digital Signal Processing: A Hands-On Approach. 1st Ed.*
  TimHES - v0 - i1668 - Nov 26 2004 - pXV(1) [501+]
Schuler, Heinz - *AMI: Achievement Motivation Inventory, Technical and User's Manual*
  R&R Bk N - v20 - i1 - Feb 2005 - p8(1) [51-500]
Schuler, Stanley - *Architectural Details from Victorian Homes*
  R&R Bk N - v19 - i1 - Feb 2004 - p204(1) [51-500]
Schulke, Flip - *Witness to Our Times*
  LibMed - v22 - i4 - Jan 2004 - p72(1) [501+]
Schulkin, Jay - *Allostasis, Homeostasis, and the Costs of Physiological Adaption*
  SciTech - v28 - i4 - Dec 2004 - p68(1) [501+]
Schuller, Marianne - *Mikrologien. Literarische und Philosophische Figuren des Kleinen*
  MLN - v119 - i3 - April 2004 - p614-619 [501+]
Schuller, Robert - *Don't Throw Away Tomorrow: Living God's Dream for Your Life*
  LJ - v130 - i4 - March 1 2005 - p94(1) [51-500]
  Hours of Power: My Daily Book of Motivation and Inspiration
  LJ - v129 - i13 - August 2004 - p88(1) [501+]
Schullery, Paul - *Myth and History in the Creation of Yellowstone National Park*
  Isis - v95 - i3 - Sept 2004 - p518(2) [501+]
  Pub Hist - v26 - i3 - Summer 2004 - p75(77) [501+]
  Yellowstone Wolf: A Guide and Sourcebook
  SciTech - v28 - i1 - March 2004 - p70(1) [51-500]
Schulman, Grace - *The Poems of Marianne Moore*
  BW - v34 - i5 - Feb 1 2004 - p10(1) [501+]
Schulman, Janet - *Sergei Prokofiev's Peter and the Wolf*
  c BL - v101 - i7 - Dec 1 2004 - p662(1) [51-500]
Schulman, Lisa - *The Matzo Ball Boy (Illus. by Litzinger, Rosanne)*
  c PW - v252 - i7 - Feb 14 2005 - p79(1) [51-500]
Schulman, Mark - *Big Cat*
  c PW - v251 - i38 - Sept 20 2004 - p64(1) [51-500]
  Foxy Fox
  c PW - v251 - i38 - Sept 20 2004 - p64(1) [51-500]
Schulman, Michael - *Play the Scene: The Ultimate Collection of Contemporary and Classic Scenes and Monologues*
  Am Theat - v21 - i8 - Oct 2004 - p139(4) [501+]
Schulte, Francisco Raymond - *Mexican Spirituality: Its Sources and Mission in the Earliest Guadalupan Sermons*
  Theol St - v65 - i4 - Dec 2004 - p903(2) [501+]
Schulte, Jan Erik - *Zwangsarbeit und Vernichtung: Das Wirtschaftsimperium der SS. Oswald Pohl und das SS-Wirtschafts-Verwaltungshauptant 1933-1945*
  GSR - v27 - i2 - May 2004 - p415-416 [501+]
Schulte-Markwort, Michael - *Cross-Walks: ICD 1 - DSM-IV-TR: A Synopsis of Classifications of Mental Disorders*
  SciTech - v28 - i1 - March 2004 - p96(1) [51-500]
Schulte, Peter - *Complex IT Project Management: 16 Steps to Success*
  SciTech - v28 - i1 - March 2004 - p134(1) [51-500]

Schulten, Susan - *The Geographical Imagination in America, 1880-1950*
  Isis - v95 - i3 - Sept 2004 - p519(2) [501+]
Schultes, Richard Evan - *Vine of the Soul: Medicine Men, Their Plants and Rituals in the Colombian Amazonia*
  y SB - v40 - i4 - July-August 2004 - p169(1) [51-500]
Schulthess, G.K. von - *Diseases of the Brain, Head and Neck, Spine: Diagnostic Imaging and Interventional Techniques, Proceedings*
  SciTech - v28 - i3 - Sept 2004 - p93(1) [51-500]
Schultz, Bart - *Henry Sidgwick, Eye of the Universe: An Intellectual Biography*
  Choice - v42 - i5 - Jan 2005 - p867(2) [1-50]
  LJ - v129 - i12 - July 2004 - p94(1) [51-500]
Schultz, David A. - *Encyclopedia of Public Administration and Public Policy*
  R&R Bk N - v19 - i1 - Feb 2004 - pNA [501+]
  Lights, Camera, Campaign! Media, Politics, and Political Advertising
  R&R Bk N - v19 - i4 - Nov 2004 - p154(1) [501+]
Schultz, Debra L. - *Going South: Jewish Women in the Civil Rights Movement*
  Signs - v30 - i2 - Wntr 2005 - p1670(4) [501+]
Schultz, Duane P. - *Theories of Personality, 8th Ed.*
  SciTech - v28 - i4 - Dec 2004 - p3(1) [1-50]
Schultz, Gwen M. - *Wisconsin's Foundations: A Review of the State's Geology and Its Influence on Geography and Human Activity*
  SciTech - v28 - i4 - Dec 2004 - p57(1) [51-500]
Schultz, Jane E. - *Women at the Front: Hospital Workers in Civil War America*
  Choice - v42 - i6 - Feb 2005 - p1084(1) [51-500]
Schultz, Judith M. - *Lippincott's Manual of Psychiatric Nursing Care Plans, 7th Ed.*
  SciTech - v28 - i4 - Dec 2004 - p94(1) [51-500]
Schultz, Katherine - *Listening: A Framework for Teaching Across Differences*
  Choice - v42 - i2 - Oct 2004 - p345(1) [51-500]
  TCR - v106 - i5 - May 2004 - p904(4) [501+]
Schultz, Ken - *Ken Schultz's Field Guide to Freshwater Fish*
  E-Streams - Sept 2004 - pNA [501+]
Schultz, Lois - *Cataloging Sheet Music: Guidelines for Use with AACR2 and the MARC Format*
  LRTS - v48 - i3 - July 2004 - p229(3) [501+]
Schultz Nicholson, Lorna - *Interference*
  Res Links - v10 - i3 - Feb 2005 - p20(2) [501+]
Schultz, Sam - *Animal Antics: The Beast Jokes Ever! (Illus. by Gable, Brian)*
  c LibMed - v22 - i5 - Feb 2004 - p81(1) [501+]
Schultze, Quentin J. - *Christianity and the Mass Media in America: Toward a Democratic Accommodation*
  AHR - v109 - i4 - Oct 2004 - p1269-1270 [501+]
  JouAmCul - v27 - i3 - Sept 2004 - p350(4) [501+]
  R&R Bk N - v19 - i3 - August 2004 - p26(1) [1-50]
  Habits of the High-Tech Heart: Living Virtuously in the Information Age
  Intpr - v59 - i1 - Jan 2005 - p103(2) [501+]
  Lib & Cul - v39 - i4 - Fall 2004 - p452(9) [501+]
Schulz, Armin - *Die Seichen Des Korpers Und Der Liebe: "Paris Und Vienna" In Der Jiddischen Fassung Des Ella Levita*
  JEGP - v103 - i3 - July 2004 - p413-415 [501+]
Schulz, Charles M. - *The Complete Peanuts: 1953 to 1954 (Illus. by Schulz, Charles)*
  y BL - v101 - i4 - Oct 15 2004 - p396(1) [51-500]
  PW - v251 - i38 - Sept 20 2004 - p48(1) [51-500]
  It's Only a Game
  PW - v251 - i45 - Nov 8 2004 - p37(1) [501+]
  Peanuts: A Pop-up Celebration
  c PW - v251 - i36 - Sept 6 2004 - p64(2) [51-500]
Schulz, Helena Lindholm - *The Palestinian Diaspora: Formation of Identifies and Politics of Homeland*
  MEJ - v59 - i1 - Wntr 2005 - p149(2) [501+]
Schulz, Kristina - *Der lange Atem der Provokation: Die Frauenbewegung in der Bundesrepublik und in Frankreich 1968-1976*
  HNet - Sept 2004 - pNA [501+]
Schulz, William F. - *Tainted Legacy: 9/11 and the Ruin of Human Rights*
  R&R Bk N - v19 - i1 - Feb 2004 - p149(1) [51-500]
Schulze, Hagen - *Die radikale Herausforderung: Die politische Kultur der englischen Konservativen zwischen landlicher Tradition und industrieller Moderne, 1846-1868.*
  JMH - v77 - i1 - March 2005 - p176(3) [501+]

Schulze, Ralf - *Meta-Analysis: A Comparison of Approaches*
R&R Bk N - v19 - i4 - Nov 2004 - p83(1) [51-500]

Schulzinger, Robert D. - *A Companion to American Relations*
Choice - v41 - i7 - March 2004 - p1354(1) [501+]

Schumacher, Claude - *Staging the Holocaust: The Shoah In Drama and Performance*
Bks & Cult - v10 - i6 - Nov-Dec 2004 - p41(1) [501+]

Schumacher, Julie - *The Chain Letter*
c KR - v73 - i2 - Jan 15 2005 - p125(1) [51-500]
Grass Angel
c BooChiTr - May 16 2004 - p3(1) [501+]
c LibMed - v22 - i7 - April-May 2004 - p62(1) [501+]
y VOYA - v27 - i4 - Oct 2004 - p308(1) [51-500]

Schumacher, Rod - *Habits and Love*
CBRA - Annual 2003 - p206(1) [51-500]

Schumacher, Randall E. - *Beginner's Guide to Structural Equation Modeling, 2nd Ed.*
SciTech - v28 - i4 - Dec 2004 - p37(1) [51-500]

Schuman, David - *A Preface to Politics, 6th Ed.*
R&R Bk N - v19 - i1 - Feb 2004 - pNA [51-500]

Schuman, Joel S. - *Optical Coherence Tomography of Ocular Diseases, 2nd Ed.*
E-Streams - Dec 2004 - pNA [501+]
SciTech - v28 - i3 - Sept 2004 - p115(1) [51-500]

Schumann, John H. - *The Neurobiology of Learning, Perspectives from Second Language Acquisition*
SciTech - v28 - i3 - Sept 2004 - p70(1) [51-500]

Schumm, Bruce - *Deep Down Things*
New Sci - v185 - i2482 - Jan 15 2005 - p50(2) [51-500]

Schumm, Sandra - *Reflections In Sequence: Novels By Spanish Women, 1944-1988*
Hisp R - v72 - i3 - Summer 2004 - p463-464 [501+]

Schuster, Henry - *Hunting Eric Rudolph*
PW - v252 - i8 - Feb 21 2005 - p171(1) [51-500]

Schuster, Leslie A. - *A Workforce Divided: Community, Labor, and the State in Saint-Nazaire's Shipbuilding Industry, 1880-1910*
J Soc H - v38 - i1 - Fall 2004 - p253(2) [501+]

Schuster, Lynda - *A Burning Hunger: One Family's Struggle against Apartheid*
TLS - i5293 - Sept 10 2004 - p22(1) [501+]

Schuster, Shlomit C. - *The Philosopher's Autobiography: A Qualitative Study*
Biomag - v27 - i3 - Summer 2004 - p602(4) [501+]

Schutjer, Karin - *Narrating Community after Kant: Schiller, Goethe, and Holderlin*
GSR - v27 - i1 - Feb 2004 - p150-151 [501+]

Schutte, Elaine - *Tissue Engineered Medical Products (TEMPs): Proceedings*
SciTech - v28 - i3 - Sept 2004 - p80(1) [51-500]

Schutte, Kimberly - *A Biography of Margaret Douglas, Countess of Lennox (1515-1578): Niece of Henry VIII and Mother-in-Law of Mary, Queen of Scots*
Albion - v36 - i2 - Summer 2004 - p296(2) [501+]

Schutyser, Sebastian - *Banco: Adobe Mosques of the Inner Niger Delta*
R&R Bk N - v19 - i1 - Feb 2004 - p202(1) [51-500]

Schutz, Benjamin M. - *The Mongol Reply*
BL - v101 - i3 - Oct 1 2004 - p314(1) [51-500]
LJ - v129 - i18 - Nov 1 2004 - p62(1) [51-500]
PW - v251 - i38 - Sept 20 2004 - p49(1) [51-500]

Schutz, Bernard - *Gravity from the Ground Up*
Choice - v42 - i1 - Sept 2004 - p143(1) [501+]

Schutz, Herbert - *The Carolingians in Central Europe, Their History, Arts and Architecture: A Cultural History of Central Europe, 750-900*
Choice - v42 - i1 - Sept 2004 - p169(1) [501+]

Schutz, Susan Polis - *Blue Mountain: Turning Dreams into Reality*
PW - v251 - i33 - August 16 2004 - p56(1) [51-500]

Schuyler, Dean - *Cognitive Therapy: A Practical Guide*
E-Streams - August 2004 - pNA [501+]

Schuyler, Nina - *The Painting*
BL - v100 - i22 - August 2004 - p1902(2) [501+]
KR - v72 - i16 - August 15 2004 - p773(1) [501+]
LJ - v129 - i14 - Sept 1 2004 - p142(1) [51-500]
PW - v251 - i34 - Oct 4 2004 - p68(1) [51-500]

Schwab, Brian - *AI Game Engine Programming*
SciTech - v28 - i4 - Dec 2004 - p24(1) [51-500]

Schwab, Irina - *Fluchtlinge und Vertriebene in Sachsen 1945-1952: Die Rolle der Kries und Stadtverwaltungen bei Aufnahme und Integration*
GSR - v27 - i1 - Feb 2004 - p193-194 [501+]

Schwab, Peter - *Designing West Africa: Prelude to 21st-Century Calamity*
Choice - v42 - i4 - Dec 2004 - p731(1) [1-50]

Schwabauer, Daniel - *Runt The Brave*
c CH Bwatch - Oct 2004 - pNA [51-500]
c KR - v72 - i19 - Oct 1 2004 - p968(1) [51-500]
c Teach Lib - v32 - i3 - Feb 2005 - p54(1) [1-50]
y VOYA - v27 - i4 - Oct 2004 - p318(1) [51-500]

Schwalbach, Eileen M. - *Value and Validity in Action Research: A Guidebook for Reflective Practitioners*
R&R Bk N - v19 - i1 - Feb 2004 - p181(1) [51-500]

Schwandt, Stephen - *Siren Song*
PW - v251 - i34 - August 23 2004 - p40(2) [51-500]

Schwantes, Carlos Arnaldo - *Going Places: Transportation Redefines the Twentieth-Century West*
AHR - v109 - i4 - Oct 2004 - p1243(2) [501+]
SHQ - v107 - i4 - April 2004 - p631(2) [501+]

Schwar, Harriet D. - *Arab-Israeli Crisis and War, 1967*
MEJ - v58 - i4 - Autumn 2004 - p681(4) [501+]

Schwarcz, Joe - *The Fly in the Ointment: 70 Fascinating Commentaries on the Science of Everyday Life*
Choice - v42 - i7 - March 2005 - p1246(1) [51-500]
That's the Way the Cookie Crumbles: 62 All-New Commentaries on the Fascinating Chemistry of Everyday Life
CBRA - Annual 2003 - p427(1) [51-500]

Schwartz, Alan - *SpamAssassin*
Bwatch - Feb 2005 - pNA [501+]
SciTech - v28 - i4 - Dec 2004 - p153(1) [51-500]

Schwartz, Amy - *Glorious Day (Illus. by Schwartz, Amy)*
c CCB-B - v58 - i2 - Oct 2004 - p98(2) [51-500]
Things I Learned in Second Grade
c BL - v100 - i22 - August 2004 - p1948(1) [51-500]
c NYTBR - Sept 19 2004 - p16 [51-500]
c SLJ - v50 - i8 - August 2004 - p93(1) [51-500]

Schwartz, Anna L. - *Cancer Fitness: Exercise Programs for Cancer Patients and Survivors*
LJ - v129 - i12 - July 2004 - p109(2) [51-500]

Schwartz, Arthur E. - *Endocrine Surgery*
SciTech - v28 - i1 - March 2004 - p112(1) [51-500]

Schwartz, Barry - *The Paradox of Choice: Why More is Less*
CC - v121 - i14 - July 13 2004 - p18(4) [501+]
TimHES - v0 - i1660 - Oct 1 2004 - p27(1) [501+]

Schwartz, Bonnie D. - *Raising a Reader: Simple and Fun Activities for Parents to Foster Reading Success*
R&R Bk N - v19 - i1 - Feb 2004 - p183(1) [51-500]

Schwartz, Daniel R. - *Reading the Modern British and Irish Novel, 1890-1930*
TLS - i5306 - Dec 10 2004 - p32(1) [51-500]

Schwartz, David G. - *Suburban Xanadu: The Casino Resort on the Las Vegas Strip and Beyond*
WHQ - v35 - i4 - Winter 2004 - p507-508 [501+]

Schwartz, David M. - *G Is for Googol: A Math Alphabet Book*
c SLJ - v50 - i9 - Sept 2004 - p59(1) [51-500]
How Much Is a Million? (Illus. by Kellogg, Steven)
c SLJ - v50 - i9 - Sept 2004 - p58(1) [51-500]

Schwartz, David T. - *Art, Education, and the Democratic Commitment*
JAAC - v61 - Winter 2003 - p87 [501+]

Schwartz, Dov - *Studies on Astral Magic in Medieval Jewish Thought*
R&R Bk N - v20 - i1 - Feb 2005 - p8(1) [51-500]

Schwartz, Ellen - *I Love Yoga: A Guide for Kids and Teens*
SLJ - v50 - i10 - Oct 2004 - p64(1) [51-500]

Schwartz, Erika - *The Teen Weight-Loss Solution: The Safe and Effective Path to Health and Self-Confidence*
LJ - v129 - i15 - Sept 15 2004 - p75(1) [51-500]
PW - v251 - i27 - July 5 2004 - p53(1) [51-500]

Schwartz, Frank J. - *The State of Civil Society in Japan*
Choice - v41 - i11-12 - July-August 2004 - p2119(1) [501+]
Pac A - v77 - i2 - Summer 2004 - p337(3) [501+]

Schwartz, Herbert F. - *Patent Law and Practice, 4th Ed.*
R&R Bk N - v19 - i1 - Feb 2004 - pNA [51-500]

Schwartz, Howard - *Tree of Souls: The Mythology of Judaism*
BL - v101 - i3 - Oct 1 2004 - p306(1) [51-500]
LJ - v129 - i14 - Sept 1 2004 - p160(1) [51-500]

Schwartz, Joan M. - *Picturing Place: Photography and the Geographical Imagination*
Archiv - i56 - Fall 2003 - p417(3) [501+]

Schwartz, Joanne - *Charms and Charm Bracelets: The Complete Guide*
LJ - v130 - i3 - Feb 15 2005 - p128(1) [51-500]

Schwartz, Kathryn Carlisle - *Baptist Faith in Action: The Private Writings of Maria Baker Taylor, 1813-1895*
JSH - v70 - i4 - Nov 2004 - p911(2) [501+]

Schwartz, Leslie - *Angels Crest*
BW - v34 - i27 - July 4 2004 - p6(1) [501+]

Schwartz, Linda Smoak - *The Wadsworth Guide to MLA Documentation, 2nd Ed.*
R&R Bk N - v19 - i1 - Feb 2004 - p221(1) [51-500]

Schwartz, Lita Linzer - *Welcome Home: An International and Nontraditional Adoption Reader*
R&R Bk N - v19 - i1 - Feb 2004 - p137(1) [51-500]

Schwartz, Lynell - *Purse Masterpieces Identification & Value Guide*
Ant&CM - v108 - i12 - Feb 2004 - p16(1) [501+]

Schwartz, Lynne Sharon - *Referred Pain: And Other Stories*
KR - v72 - i24 - Dec 15 2004 - pS6(1) [501+]
Wom R Bks - v21 - i10-11 - July 2004 - p13(1) [501+]

Schwartz, Mark D. - *Phenology: An Integrative Environmental Science*
Choice - v42 - i1 - Sept 2004 - p130(1) [501+]
SciTech - v28 - i1 - March 2004 - p65(1) [51-500]

Schwartz, Mark S. - *Biofeedback: A Practitioner's Guide, 3rd Ed.*
SciTech - v28 - i1 - March 2004 - p99(1) [51-500]

Schwartz, Martha - *The Vanguard Landscapes and Gardens of Martha Schwartz*
LJ - v129 - i14 - Sept 1 2004 - p147(1) [51-500]

Schwartz, Maxime - *How the Cows Turned Mad: Unlocking the Mysteries of Mad Cow Disease*
SciTech - v28 - i4 - Dec 2004 - p84(1) [51-500]

Schwartz, Mortimer D. - *Problems in Legal Ethics, 6th Ed.*
R&R Bk N - v19 - i1 - Feb 2004 - pNA [51-500]

Schwartz, Peter - *Inevitable Surprises: Thinking Ahead in a Time of Turbulence*
NWCR - v57 - Autumn 2004 - p151(3) [501+]

Schwartz, Robert A. - *Equity Markets in Action: The Fundamentals of Liquidity, Market Structure and Trading*
R&R Bk N - v19 - i4 - Nov 2004 - p118(1) [51-500]

Schwartz, Robert M. - *Tocqueville and Beyond: Essays on the Old Regime in Honor of David D. Bien*
R&R Bk N - v19 - i1 - Feb 2004 - p35(1) [1-50]

Schwartz, Roslyn - *The Complete Adventures of the Mole Sisters (Illus. by Schwartz, Roslyn)*
c Globe & Mail - August 28 2004 - pD12 [501+]
c Res Links - v10 - i2 - Dec 2004 - p10(1) [51-500]
Mole Sisters and the Fairy Ring
c CBRA - Annual 2003 - p466(1) [51-500]
Mole Sisters and the Way Home
c CBRA - Annual 2003 - p466(1) [51-500]

Schwartz, Ruth L. - *Dear Good Naked Morning*
LJ - v130 - i2 - Feb 1 2005 - p84(1) [51-500]
Edgewater
PSQ - v78 - i2 - Summer 2004 - p190(2) [501+]

Schwartz, Sanford - *William Nicholson*
Choice - v42 - i5 - Jan 2005 - p845(1) [1-50]
NYRB - v51 - i17 - Nov 4 2004 - p22(4) [501+]

Schwartz, Seth - *Imperialism and Jewish Society, 200 B.C.E. to 640 C.E*
Class R - v54 - i2 - Nov 2004 - p506-508 [501+]

Schwartz, Steven H. - *Visual Perception: A Clinical Orientation, 3rd Ed.*
SciTech - v28 - i3 - Sept 2004 - p70(1) [51-500]

Schwartz, Stuart B. - *Tropical Babylons: Sugar and the Making of the Atlantic World, 1450-1680*
HNet - Nov 2004 - pNA [501+]

Schwartz, Sue - *The New Language of Toys: Teaching Communication Skills to Children with Special Needs*
Bwatch - v26 - i7 - July 2004 - p6(1) [51-500]

Schwartz, Susan - *Hostile Takeover*
BL - v101 - i6 - Nov 15 2004 - p571(1) [51-500]

Schwartz, Susan L. - *Rasa: Performing the Divine in India*
Dance - v79 - i3 - March 2005 - p73(1) [51-500]

Schwartz, Thomas Alan - *Lyndon Johnson and Europe: In the Shadow of Vietnam*
BHR - v77 - i4 - Winter 2003 - p779(780) [501+]
JAH - v91 - i2 - Sept 2004 - p712(2) [501+]

Schwartz, Virginia Frances - *Initiation*
y CBRA - Annual 2003 - p511(1) [51-500]

Schwartzberg, Steven - *Democracy and U.S. Policy in Latin America during the Truman Years*
Ams - v61 - i2 - Oct 2004 - p324(2) [501+]
Choice - v41 - i11-12 - July-August 2004 - p2122(2) [501+]

Schwartzkopf, William - *Calculating Lost Labor Productivity in Construction Claims*
  R&R Bk N - v19 - i3 - August 2004 - p120(1) [51-500]

Schwarz, Alan - *The Numbers Game: Baseball's Lifelong Fascination with Statistics*
  y BW - v34 - i34 - August 22 2004 - p8(2) [501+]
  NYTBR - August 15 2004 - p10 [501+]

Schwarz, Cindy - *Charmed, I'm Sure-Tales from the Subatomic Zoo: Stories and Poems about Subatomic Particles by Students at Vassar College*
  Physics T - v42 - i3 - March 2004 - p192-192 [501+]

Schwarz, James A. - *Dekker Encyclopedia of Nanoscience and Nanotechnology*
  Choice - v42 - i5 - Jan 2005 - p830(1) [501+]
  E-Streams - Sept 2004 - pNA [501+]
  SB - v41 - i1 - Jan-Feb 2005 - p20(1) [501+]

Schwarz, Martin - *A Church History of Denmark*
  Six Ct J - v34 - i4 - Winter 2003 - p1121-1122 [501+]

Schwarz, Maureen Trudelle - *Blood and Voice: Navajo Women Ceremonial Practitioners*
  JRAI - v10 - i4 - Dec 2004 - p942(2) [501+]

Schwarz, Michelle - *The Best Restaurant in the World (Illus. by Harvey, Roland)*
  c SLJ - v50 - i10 - Oct 2004 - p129(1) [51-500]

Schwarz, Renee - *Funky Junk*
  c CBRA - Annual 2003 - p556(2) [51-500]

Schwarz, Robin - *Night Swimming*
  BW - v34 - i31 - August 1 2004 - p10(1) [51-500]

Schwarz, Ted - *Joseph P. Kennedy: The Mogul, the Mob, the Statesman and the Making of an American Myth*
  R&R Bk N - v19 - i1 - Feb 2004 - p61(1) [501+]

Schwarzbein, Diana - *The Schwarzbein Principle: The Program: Losing Weight the Healthy Way: An Easy, 5-Step, No-Nonsense Approach*
  LJ - v130 - i1 - Jan 1 2005 - p144(3) [501+]
  PW - v251 - i43 - Oct 25 2004 - p41(2) [501+]

Schwarzenbach, Sibyl - *Women and the United States Constitution; history, interpretation, and practice*
  R&R Bk N - v19 - i3 - August 2004 - p197(1) [1-50]

Schwarzkopf, Jutta - *Unpicking Gender: The Social Construction of Gender in the Lancashire Cotton Weaving Industry, 1880-1914*
  R&R Bk N - v19 - i3 - August 2004 - p116(1) [51-500]

Schwarzschild, Edward - *Responsible Men*
  BL - v101 - i9-10 - Jan 1 2005 - p823(1) [501+]
  KR - v73 - i2 - Jan 15 2005 - p80(1) [501+]
  PW - v252 - i4 - Jan 24 2005 - p218(1) [501+]

Schweber, Simone - *Making Sense of the Holocaust: Lessons from Classroom Practice*
  Choice - v42 - i5 - Jan 2005 - p906(1) [1-50]

Schweickart, Patrocinio P. - *Reading Sites: Social Difference and Reader Response*
  R&R Bk N - v19 - i3 - August 2004 - p258(1) [51-500]

Schweid, Richard - *Che's Chevrolet, Fidel's Oldsmobile: On the Road in Cuba*
  LJ - v129 - i12 - July 2004 - p99(1) [51-500]
  PW - v251 - i28 - July 12 2004 - p53(1) [51-500]

Schweiger, Beth Barton - *Religion in the American South: Protestants and Others in History and Culture*
  PW - v251 - i39 - Sept 27 2004 - p55(1) [51-500]

Schweiker, William - *Having: Property and Possession in Religious and Social Life*
  Intpr - v59 - i1 - Jan 2005 - p110(1) [51-500]
  Theological Ethics and Global Dynamics: In the Time of Many Worlds
  R&R Bk N - v19 - i3 - August 2004 - p12(1) [1-50]

Schweinfurth, Kay Parker - *Prayer on Top of the Earth: The Spiritual Universe of the Plains Apaches*
  Am Ind CRJ - v27 - i2 - Spring 2003 - p138-141 [501+]

Schweitzer, Albert - *The African Sermons*
  TT - v61 - i2 - July 2004 - p287(1) [501+]

Schweitzer, Darrell - *Innsmouth Tabernacle Choir Hymnal*
  ChrSFF&H - v26 - i10 - Oct 2004 - p30(1) [51-500]

Schweitzer, F. - *Brownian Agents and Active Particles: Collective Dynamics in the Natural and Social Sciences*
  SIAM Rev - v46 - i2 - June 2004 - p372-374 [501+]

Schweitzer, Philip A. - *Encyclopedia of Corrosion Technology, 2nd Ed.*
  E-Streams - Nov 2004 - pNA [501+]

Schweitzer, Richard - *The Cross and the Trenches: Religious Faith and Doubt Among British and American Great War Soldiers*
  HER - v119 - i483 - Sept 2004 - p1091(2) [501+]
  J Soc H - v38 - i2 - Winter 2004 - p520(3) [501+]

Schweizerischer Apotheker-Verein - *Index Nominum, International Drug Directory, 18th Ed.*
  SciTech - v28 - i3 - Sept 2004 - p123(1) [51-500]

Schweizer, Peter - *The Bushes: Portrait of a Dynasty (Read by Dean, Robertson). Audiobook Review*
  BL - v101 - i1 - Sept 1 2004 - p146(1) [1-50]
  LJ - v130 - i4 - March 1 2005 - p125(1) [51-500]
  The Bushes: Portrait of a Dynasty
  CJR - v43 - i3 - Sept-Oct 2004 - p62(2) [501+]

Schwemer, Daniel - *Wettergottgestalten Mesopotamiens und Nordsyriens im Zeitalter der Keilschriftkulturen: Materialien und Studien nach den schriftlichen Quellen*
  JNES - v63 - i3 - July 2004 - p212(3) [501+]

Schwing, Ned - *2004 Standard Catalogue of Firearms: Collector's Price and Reference Guide*
  SciTech - v28 - i4 - Dec 2004 - p171(1) [51-500]

Schwoerer, Lois G. - *The Ingenious Mr. Henry Care: London's First Spin Doctor*
  TLS - i5289 - August 13 2004 - p28(1) [501+]

Schyffert, Bea Uusma - *The Man Who Went to the Far Side of the Moon: The Story of Apollo 11 Astronaut Michael Collins*
  c HB - v81 - i1 - Jan-Feb 2005 - p24(1) [51-500]

Sciarra, Daniel T. - *School Counseling: Foundations and Contemporary Issues*
  R&R Bk N - v19 - i1 - Feb 2004 - pNA [51-500]

Sciban, Shu-ning - *Dragonflies: Fiction by Chinese Women in the Twentieth Century*
  Ch Rev Int - v11 - i1 - Spring 2004 - p169(3) [501+]

Science and Technology Dept., Carnegie Library of Pittsburg - *The Handy Science Answer Book: Thoroughly Revised and Greatly Expanded*
  Sci Teach - v71 - i5 - May 2004 - p68-69 [501+]

Science Matters Series
  c LibMed - v23 - i1 - August-Sept 2004 - p80(1) [51-500]

Science on the Edge Series
  c LibMed - v22 - i6 - March 2004 - p86(1) [501+]

Science Photo Library - *Photographic Atlas of the Body*
  LJ - v130 - i1 - Jan 1 2005 - p147(1) [501+]

Science Resources in the Electronic Age
  LibMed - v23 - i1 - August-Sept 2004 - p87(1) [51-500]

Science Toys
  LibMed - v22 - i6 - March 2004 - p91(1) [501+]

Scientific and Statistical Database Management: Proceedings
  SciTech - v28 - i3 - Sept 2004 - p33(1) [51-500]

Scienze Regionali: Italian Journal of Regional Science
  JEL - v42 - i1 - March 2004 - p345(2) [501+]

Scieszka, Jon - *Da Wild, Da Crazy, da Vinci (Illus. by McCauley, Adam)*
  c BL - v100 - i22 - August 2004 - p1937(1) [51-500]
  c SLJ - v50 - i12 - Dec 2004 - p122(1) [51-500]
  Guys Write for Guys Read
  c PW - v252 - i8 - Feb 21 2005 - p176(2) [51-500]
  Knights of the Kitchen Table
  c Storyworks - v12 - i2 - Oct 2004 - p6(1) [51-500]
  Math Curse (Illus. by Smith, Lane)
  c SLJ - v50 - i9 - Sept 2004 - p58(2) [51-500]
  Me Oh Maya (Illus. by McCauley, Adam)
  c SLJ - v50 - i10 - Oct 2004 - p530(1) [51-500]
  Science Verse (Illus. by Smith, Lane)
  c BL - v100 - i21 - July 2004 - p1843(1) [1-50]
  c BL - v101 - i7 - Dec 1 2004 - p670(1) [51-500]
  c BW - v34 - i41 - Oct 10 2004 - p12(1) [51-500]
  c CCB-B - v58 - i3 - Nov 2004 - p143(1) [501+]
  c Globe & Mail - Dec 11 2004 - pD28 [51-500]
  c HB - v80 - i5 - Sept-Oct 2004 - p574(2) [51-500]
  c KR - v72 - i16 - August 15 2004 - p813(1) [51-500]
  c NH - v113 - i10 - Dec 2004 - p50 [501+]
  c PW - v251 - i31 - August 2 2004 - p70(1) [51-500]
  c PW - v251 - i37 - Sept 13 2004 - p36(1) [51-500]
  c Sci - v306 - i5704 - Dec 17 2004 - p2044(1) [51-500]
  c SLJ - v50 - i9 - Sept 2004 - p179(2) [51-500]

Scigliano, Eric - *Love, War and Circuses: The Age-Old Relationship between Elephants and Humans*
  TLS - i5265 - Feb 27 2004 - p31-31 [501+]

Scime, Anthony - *Web Mining: Applications and Techniques*
  Choice - v42 - i6 - Feb 2005 - p1057(1) [51-500]
  SciTech - v28 - i4 - Dec 2004 - p28(1) [51-500]

Sclafani, Joseph D. - *The Educated Parent: Recent Trends in Raising Children*
  Choice - v42 - i6 - Feb 2005 - p1063(2) [501+]
  LJ - v129 - i13 - August 2004 - p110(1) [51-500]
  R&R Bk N - v19 - i4 - Nov 2004 - p129(1) [51-500]

Sclippa, Norbert - *Le Jeu de la Sphinge: Sade et la Philosophie des Lumieres*
  Eight-C St - v37 - i3 - Spring 2004 - p469-474 [501+]

Scobell, Andrew - *China's Use of Military Force: Beyond the Great Wall and the Long March*
  Ch Rev Int - v11 - i1 - Spring 2004 - p171(3) [501+]
  Parameters - v34 - i3 - Autumn 2004 - p159(2) [501+]

Scobey, Joan - *The Fannie Farmer Junior Cookbook (Illus. by Brewster, Patience)*
  y SLJ - v51 - i2 - Feb 2005 - p59(1) [51-500]

Scobie, Charles H.H. - *The Ways of Our God: An Approach to Biblical Theology*
  JR - v84 - i3 - July 2004 - p482(3) [501+]

Scobie, Stephen - *Alias Bob Dylan Revisited*
  CBRA - Annual 2003 - p109(1) [51-500]

Scodel, R. - *Listening to Homer: Tradition, Narrative, and Audience*
  Class R - v54 - i1 - May 2004 - p18(3) [501+]

Scofield, Sandra - *Occasions of Sin: A Memoir*
  BooChiTr - Jan 25 2004 - p1(3) [501+]
  VQR - v80 - i2 - Spring 2004 - p261-262 [501+]

Scoresby, William - *The Arctic Whaling Journals of William Scoresby the Younger, vol. 1: The Voyages of 1811, 1812 and 1813*
  R&R Bk N - v19 - i3 - August 2004 - p76(1) [51-500]

Scotchie, Virginia - *Setting Up Your Ceramic Studio: Ideas and Plans From Working Artists*
  Ceram Mo - v52 - i3 - March 2004 - p38(1) [501+]

Scott, A. Hugh - *Computer and Intellectual Property Crime: Federal and State Law, with 2002 Supplement, Vols. 1-2*
  R&R Bk N - v19 - i1 - Feb 2004 - pNA [51-500]

Scott, Allen - *Sontagliche Evangelien*
  Notes - v61 - i2 - Dec 2004 - p548(4) [501+]

Scott, Alwyn - *Nonlinear Science: Emergence and Dynamics of Coherent Structures, 2nd Ed.*
  SciTech - v28 - i4 - Dec 2004 - p42(1) [51-500]

Scott, Amanda - *Highland Princess*
  BL - v101 - i5 - Nov 1 2004 - p471(1) [51-500]

Scott, Andrew - *Painter, Paddler: The Art and Adventures of Stewart Marshall*
  CBRA - Annual 2003 - p70(1) [51-500]
  R&R Bk N - v19 - i3 - August 2004 - p243(1) [51-500]

Scott-Cameron, Nancy - *Choices for Teenagers*
  y TES - v0 - i4586 - June 4 2004 - pssss18(2) [501+]

Scott, Carole - *Astronomy*
  c LibMed - v22 - i6 - March 2004 - p86(1) [501+]

Scott, Chic - *Summits and Icefields: Canadian Rockies Alpine Ski Tours*
  CBRA - Annual 2003 - p146(1) [501+]
  Summits and Icefields: Columbia Mountains Alpine Ski Tours
  CBRA - Annual 2003 - p146(1) [501+]

Scott-Clark, Catherine - *The Amber Room: The Fate of the World's Greatest Lost Treasure*
  BW - v34 - i29 - July 18 2004 - p13(1) [1-50]
  Globe & Mail - July 31 2004 - pD16 [501+]
  R&R Bk N - v19 - i4 - Nov 2004 - p209(1) [501+]
  y SLJ - v50 - i11 - Nov 2004 - p179(1) [51-500]
  The Amber Room: The Untold Story of the Greatest Hoax of the Twentieth Century
  Apo - v159 - i510 - August 2004 - p80(1) [501+]
  TLS - i5291 - August 27 2004 - p22(1) [501+]

Scott, Clive - *Channel Crossings: French and English Poetry in Dialogue, 1550-2000*
  FS - v58 - i3 - July 2004 - p446-447 [501+]

Scott, David - *Politics and War in the Three Stuart Kingdoms, 1637-49*
  Choice - v42 - i1 - Sept 2004 - p179(1) [501+]
  HNet - Oct 2004 - pNA [501+]

Scott, David (b. 1961 -) - *A Revolution of Love: The Meaning of Mother Teresa*
  LJ - v130 - i3 - Feb 15 2005 - p136(1) [51-500]
  PW - v251 - i51 - Dec 20 2004 - p54(1) [51-500]

Scott, David H.T. - *Semiologies of Travel: From Gautier to Baudrillard*
  TLS - i5302 - Nov 12 2004 - p30(1) [51-500]

Scott, David Logan - *David Scott's Guide to Investing in Bonds*
R&R Bk N - v19 - i3 - August 2004 - p138(1) [1-50]

David Scott's Guide to Investing in Mutual Funds
R&R Bk N - v19 - i3 - August 2004 - p137(1) [1-50]

Scott, Derek - *Off Whitehall: A View from Downing Street by Tony Blair's Adviser*
NS - v133 - i4710 - Oct 18 2004 - p53(2) [501+]
TimHES - v0 - i1667 - Nov 19 2004 - p22(2) [501+]

Scott, Derek B. - *From the Erotic to the Demonic: On Critical Musicology*
Notes - v61 - i1 - Sept 2004 - p140(3) [501+]

Scott, Elaine - *Poles Apart: Why Penguins and Polar Bears Will Never Be Neighbors*
c   BL - v101 - i7 - Dec 1 2004 - p670(1) [51-500]
y   HB - v81 - i1 - Jan-Feb 2005 - p114(2) [51-500]
y   KR - v72 - i18 - Sept 15 2004 - p920(1) [51-500]
y   SLJ - v50 - i12 - Dec 2004 - p169(2) [51-500]

Scott, Eugenie Carol - *Evolution vs. Creationism: An Introduction*
Bwatch - v26 - i9 - Sept 2004 - p8(1) [51-500]
SciTech - v28 - i3 - Sept 2004 - p59(1) [1-50]

Scott, Geoffrey - *The Architecture of Humanism: A Study in the History of Taste*
NYRB - v51 - i16 - Oct 21 2004 - p30(3) [501+]

Scott, Graham - *Essential Animal Behavior*
SciTech - v28 - i4 - Dec 2004 - p67(1) [51-500]

Scott, Grant - *Hippie*
Reason - v36 - i7 - Dec 2004 - p55(4) [501+]

Scott, H.M. - *The Emergence of the Eastern Powers, 1756-1775*
Russ Rev - v63 - i3 - July 2004 - pNA [501+]

Scott, Janus - *Audio in the 21st Century*
SciTech - v28 - i3 - Sept 2004 - p162(1) [51-500]

Scott, John A. - *Understanding Dante*
LJ - v129 - i13 - August 2004 - p80(1) [501+]

Scott, John (b. 1950 -) - *Shiva's Really Scary Gifts*
BIC - v33 - i2 - March 2004 - p25(2) [501+]

Scott, John Beldon - *Architecture for the Shroud: Relic and Ritual in Turin*
Ren Q - v57 - i4 - Winter 2004 - p1396(3) [501+]

Scott, John H. - *Witness to the Truth: My Struggle for Human Rights in Louisiana*
HNet - June 2004 - pNA [501+]

Scott, John T. - *Environmental Research and Development: US Industrial Research, the Clean Air Act, and Environmental Damage*
JEL - v41 - i4 - Dec 2003 - p1434(1) [501+]

Scott, Kathleen L. - *Dated and Datable English Manuscript Borders, c. 1395-1499*
Specu - v79 - i4 - Oct 2004 - p1140(3) [501+]

Scott, Kenneth (b. 1900 -) - *Early New York Naturalizations: Abstracts of Naturalization Records from Federal, State, and Local Courts, 1792-1840*
EFHM - v58 - i2 - March-April 2004 - p90(1) [1-50]

Scott, Kenneth (b. 1967 -) - *Take Action!: How To Meet Women and Get Dates*
LJ - v129 - i19 - Nov 15 2004 - p76(1) [501+]

Scott, Kieran - *I Was a Non-Blonde Cheerleader*
y   BL - v101 - i9-10 - Jan 1 2005 - p847(1) [1-50]
y   Kliatt - v39 - i1 - Jan 2005 - p10(2) [501+]
KR - v73 - i1 - Jan 1 2005 - p56(1) [51-500]
y   PW - v252 - i9 - Feb 28 2005 - p68(1) [51-500]

Scott, Linda M. - *Fresh Lipstick: Redressing Fashion and Feminism*
LJ - v130 - i2 - Feb 1 2005 - p105(2) [501+]
PW - v251 - i51 - Dec 20 2004 - p47(2) [501+]

Scott, Malcolm - *Chercheurs d'absolu: Mauriac et de Gaulle, Chroniques et discours, 1945-1948*
FS - v58 - i2 - April 2004 - p284(2) [501+]

Scott, Martin - *Death and Thraxas*
y   Kliatt - v39 - i2 - March 2005 - p29(1) [51-500]

Scott, Mary Ann - *New Girl*
y   CBRA - Annual 2003 - p511(1) [51-500]

Scott, Michael D. - *Licensing and Intellectual Property Law Desk Reference, 2004 Ed.*
R&R Bk N - v19 - i1 - Feb 2004 - pNA [51-500]
Telecommunications Law Desk Reference, 2nd Ed.
SciTech - v28 - i4 - Dec 2004 - p10(1) [1-50]

Scott, Patrick - *The Joseph Heller Papers: An Exhibition*
BSA-P - v98 - i1 - March 2004 - p129-129 [501+]

Scott, Peter (b. 1961 -) - *The Blackwell Companion to Political Theology*
TT - v61 - i3 - Oct 2004 - p426(2) [501+]

Scott, Peter Dale - *Minding the Darkness*
PSQ - v78 - i4 - Winter 2004 - p195(3) [501+]

Scott, Peter J. - *Perl Medic: Transforming Legacy Code*
SciTech - v28 - i3 - Sept 2004 - p23(1) [51-500]

Scott, Phil - *Wrong Stuff?*
SciTech - v28 - i3 - Sept 2004 - p163(1) [51-500]

Scott, Shirley V. - *International Law in World Politics: An Introduction*
Choice - v42 - i3 - Nov 2004 - p561(1) [1-50]
The Political Interpretation of Multilateral Treaties
R&R Bk N - v19 - i3 - August 2004 - p159(1) [501+]

Scott-Smith, Giles - *The Cultural Cold War in Western Europe, 1945-1960*
R&R Bk N - v19 - i1 - Feb 2004 - p54(1) [51-500]

Scott, Susan - *Return of the Black Death: The World's Greatest Serial Killer*
Nature - v430 - i6996 - July 8 2004 - p145(2) [501+]

Scott, Walter - *The Heart of Mid-Lothian*
Choice - v42 - i4 - Dec 2004 - p663(1) [1-50]
Ivanhoe (Read by Lee, Christopher). Audiobook Review
y   Kliatt - v39 - i2 - March 2005 - p54(1) [51-500]

Scott, Whitney - *Things That Go Bump in the Night*
y   BL - v101 - i2 - Sept 15 2004 - p185(1) [51-500]

Scott, William - *Sustainable Development and Learning: Framing the Issues*
TCR - v106 - i12 - Dec 2004 - p2301(4) [501+]

Scotti, R.A. - *The Sudden Sea: The Great Hurricane of 1938*
Globe & Mail - Jan 1 2005 - pD15 [501+]

Scowen, Peter - *Rogue Nation: The America the Rest of the World Knows*
CBRA - Annual 2003 - p311(2) [501+]

Scrase, Timothy J. - *Globalization, Culture and Inequality in Asia*
R&R Bk N - v19 - i1 - Feb 2004 - p106(1) [501+]

Scraton, Phil - *Hillsborough: The Truth*
NS - v133 - i4716 - Nov 29 2004 - p42(2) [501+]

Scrimger, Richard - *The Boy from Earth*
c   Res Links - v10 - i3 - Feb 2005 - p21(2) [501+]
Eugene's Story (Illus. by Johnson, Gillian)
c   CBRA - Annual 2003 - p466(1) [501+]
Noses Are Red
y   Can CL - i111-112 - Fall-Winter 2003 - p134(6) [501+]

Scriver, Phil - *Lewis and Clark Passed Here: New Perspectives Beyond the Adventure*
Bwatch - v26 - i8 - August 2004 - p9(2) [51-500]

Scroggins, Deborah - *Emma's War: A True Story*
Kliatt - v38 - i4 - July 2004 - p38(1) [51-500]

Scruton, Roger - *Death-Devoted Heart: Sex and the Sacred in Wagner's Tristan and Isolde*
Notes - v61 - i3 - March 2005 - p763(4) [501+]
ON - v69 - i4 - Oct 2004 - p84(1) [501+]
The Meaning of Conservatism, 3rd Ed.
MA - v46 - i3 - Summer 2004 - p264(5) [501+]
The West and the Rest: Globalization and the Terrorist Threat
IBMR - v29 - i1 - Jan 2005 - p42(2) [501+]

Scully, Helen - *In the Hope of Rising Again*
BL - v100 - i21 - July 2004 - p1820(1) [1-50]
NYT - July 19 2004 - pE6 [501+]
PW - v251 - i27 - July 5 2004 - p38(1) [51-500]

Sea and Stars
c   LibMed - v22 - i4 - Jan 2004 - p93(1) [501+]

Sea Stars
c   SB - v40 - i3 - May-June 2004 - p133(1) [501+]

Sea Through
c   LibMed - v22 - i7 - April-May 2004 - p72(1) [501+]

Seabright, Paul - *The Company of Strangers: A Natural History of Economic Life*
Choice - v42 - i3 - Nov 2004 - p533(2) [1-50]
Econ - v372 - i8388 - August 14 2004 - p69US [501+]
Nature - v431 - i7006 - Sept 16 2004 - p245(2) [501+]
TimHES - v0 - i1662 - Oct 15 2004 - p26(2) [501+]

Seabrooke, Brenda - *Stonewolf*
c   CCB-B - v58 - i6 - Feb 2005 - p265(2) [51-500]
c   KR - v73 - i3 - Feb 1 2005 - p181(1) [51-500]

Seafarers International Research Centre - *The Global Seafarer: Living and Working Conditions in a Globalized Industry*
ILR - v143 - i3 - Autumn 2004 - p294(1) [51-500]

Seager, Spencer L. - *Chemistry for Today: General, Organic, and Biochemistry, 5th Ed.*
SciTech - v28 - i1 - March 2004 - p53(1) [51-500]
Introductory Chemistry for Today, 5th Ed.
SciTech - v28 - i1 - March 2004 - p53(1) [51-500]

Seagle, Steven T. - *It's a Bird-- (Illus. by Kristiansen, Teddy)*
BW - v34 - i30 - July 25 2004 - p15(1) [51-500]
LJ - v129 - i14 - Sept 1 2004 - p129(1) [51-500]
MFSF - v107 - i4-5 - Oct-Nov 2004 - p37(2) [51-500]

Seagrave, John - *The Hudson's Bay Boy: From Cabbagetown to Rupert's Land*
Globe & Mail - Sept 11 2004 - pD22 [1-50]

Seagraves, Theresa - *Quick! Show Me Your Value*
HR Mag - v50 - i2 - Feb 2005 - pS15(1) [501+]

Seal, Graham - *Inventing Anzac: The Digger and National Mythology*
R&R Bk N - v19 - i4 - Nov 2004 - p77(1) [51-500]

Sealander, Judith - *The Failed Century of the Child: Governing America's Young in the Twentieth Century*
JAH - v91 - i3 - Dec 2004 - p1100(2) [501+]

Seale, Clive - *Qualitative Research Practice*
Choice - v42 - i4 - Dec 2004 - p701(1) [1-50]
R&R Bk N - v19 - i3 - August 2004 - p158(1) [51-500]
Researching Society and Culture, 2nd Ed.
R&R Bk N - v19 - i4 - Nov 2004 - p120(1) [51-500]

Seaman, Amanda C. - *Bodies of Evidence: Women, Society, and Detective Fiction in 1990's Japan*
R&R Bk N - v19 - i3 - August 2004 - p256(1) [51-500]

Seaman, Ann Rowe - *America's Most Hated Woman: The Life and Gruesome Death of Madalyn Murray O'Hair*
LJ - v130 - i3 - Feb 15 2005 - p140(2) [51-500]

Seamon, Hollis - *Flesh: A Suzanne LaFleshe Mystery*
LJ - v130 - i4 - March 1 2005 - p71(1) [51-500]

Seamon, Mary Ploski - *Technology Timesavers: Simple Steps to Increasing Classroom Productivity*
SLJ - v50 - i10 - Oct 2004 - pS74(1) [51-500]

Seamon, Tobias - *The Magician's Study: A Guided Tour of the Life, Times, and Memorabilia of Robert "The Great" Rouncival*
BL - v101 - i3 - Oct 1 2004 - p312(1) [51-500]

Search It! Science: the Books You Need at Lightning Speed.
SLJ - v50 - i12 - Dec 2004 - p92(1) [501+]

Searcy, Edwin - *Awed To Heaven, Rooted in Earth: Prayers of Walter Brueggemann*
CC - v121 - i21 - Oct 19 2004 - p35(1) [501+]

Searle, G.R. - *A New England?: Peace and War, 1886-1918*
Choice - v42 - i6 - Feb 2005 - p1087(1) [51-500]
A New England? Peace and War 1886-1918
TLS - i5264 - Feb 20 2004 - p11-12 [501+]

Searle, John R. - *Mind: A Brief Introduction*
Comw - v131 - i18 - Oct 22 2004 - p40(3) [501+]
KR - v72 - i17 - Sept 1 2004 - p854(2) [501+]
LJ - v129 - i17 - Oct 15 2004 - p66(1) [51-500]
Sci - v306 - i5698 - Nov 5 2004 - p979(2) [501+]

Searles, John - *Strange but True*
BL - v100 - i21 - July 2004 - p1820(1) [1-50]
KR - v72 - i13 - July 1 2004 - p602(1) [501+]
PW - v251 - i27 - July 5 2004 - p37(2) [51-500]

Sears, Stephen W. - *Gettysburg*
JSH - v70 - i4 - Nov 2004 - p927(2) [501+]

Sears, Susan - *Contexting Teaching and Learning: A Primer for Effective Instruction*
TCR - v106 - i2 - Feb 2004 - p397-400 [501+]

Sears, William - *Eat Healthy, Feel Great*
c   SB - v40 - i4 - July-August 2004 - p151(1) [51-500]

Seasholes, Nancy S. - *Gaining Ground: A History of Landmaking in Boston*
JAH - v91 - i3 - Dec 2004 - p1054(1) [501+]
JEH - v64 - i1 - March 2004 - p264(2) [501+]
Gaining Ground: A History of Landmaking in Boston
T&C - v45 - i4 - Oct 2004 - p844(3) [501+]

Seaver, Barry W. - *A True Politician: Rebecca Browning Rankin, Municipal Reference Librarian of the City of New York, 1920-1952*
ALJ - v53 - i4 - Nov 2004 - p424(2) [501+]
R&R Bk N - v19 - i1 - Feb 2004 - p261(1) [51-500]

Seaver, Jeannette - *My New Mediterranean Cookbook: Eat Better, Live Longer by Following the Mediterranean Diet*
PW - v251 - i47 - Nov 22 2004 - p54(2) [51-500]

Seaver, Kirsten A. - *Maps, Myths, and Men: The Story of the Vinland Map*
LJ - v129 - i13 - August 2004 - p95(1) [501+]
PW - v251 - i27 - July 5 2004 - p49(1) [51-500]
R&R Bk N - v20 - i1 - Feb 2005 - p82(1) [51-500]
Sci - v307 - i5714 - March 4 2005 - p1413(2) [501+]

Seidler, Tor - *The Dulcimer Boy (Illus. by Selznick, Brian)*
c PW - v251 - i47 - Nov 22 2004 - p62(1) [501+]
Toes (Illus. by Beddows, Eric)
c BW - v34 - i29 - July 18 2004 - p11(1) [1-50]
c CCB-B - v58 - i1 - Sept 2004 - p38(1) [51-50]
c SLJ - v50 - i7 - July 2004 - p112(1) [51-500]
Seidman, David - *Jerry Spinelli*
y SLJ - v50 - i9 - Sept 2004 - p226(1) [51-500]
Seidman, Leslie F. - *2004 Miller Financial Instruments: A Comprehensive Guide to Accounting and Reporting*
R&R Bk N - v19 - i2 - May 2004 - p119 [51-500]
Seidman, Michael - *The Imaginary Revolution: Parisian Students and Workers in 1968*
R&R Bk N - v19 - i4 - Nov 2004 - p38(1) [51-500]
Republic of Egos: A Social History of the Spanish Civil War
J Soc H - v38 - i2 - Winter 2004 - p528(3) [501+]
JMH - v76 - i4 - Dec 2004 - p978(3) [501+]
Seidman, Steven - *The Social Construction of Sexuality*
R&R Bk N - v19 - i2 - May 2004 - p132 [51-500]
Seidt, Hans-Ulrich - *Berlin, Kabul, Moskau: Oskar Ritter von Niedermayer und Deutschlands Geopolitik*
CEH - v37 - i2 - Spring 2004 - p304(3) [501+]
Seierstad, Asne - *The Bookseller of Kabul (Read by David, Joanna). Audiobook Review*
y Kliatt - v38 - i5 - Sept 2004 - p67(2) [51-500]
The Bookseller of Kabul
CR - v285 - i1662 - July 2004 - p54(2) [501+]
TLS - i5266 - March 5 2004 - p31-31 [501+]
A Hundred and One Days
KR - v73 - i4 - Feb 15 2005 - p220(1) [501+]
PW - v252 - i11 - March 14 2005 - p60(2) [51-500]
Seife, Charles - *Alpha and Omega: The Search for the Beginning and End of the Universe*
VQR - v80 - i1 - Wntr 2004 - p276-277 [501+]
Zero: The Biography of a Dangerous Idea (Read by Seife, Charles). Audiobook Review
Kliatt - v38 - i4 - July 2004 - p62(1) [51-500]
Zero: The Biography of a Dangerous Idea
Isis - v95 - i2 - June 2004 - p279(2) [501+]
Seiffert, Rachel - *Field Study*
BL - v100 - i22 - August 2004 - p1903(1) [501+]
Ent W - i775 - July 23 2004 - p82 [51-500]
SLJ - v51 - i2 - Feb 2005 - p157(1) [51-500]
TLS - i5267 - March 12 2004 - p20-20 [501+]
Seifried, Richard D. - *The Warrior Angels*
Roundup M - v11 - i6 - August 2004 - p30(1) [501+]
Seigal, Larry J. - *Introduction to criminal justice, 10th Ed*
R&R Bk N - v19 - i3 - August 2004 - p206(1) [501+]
Seigel, Andrea - *Like the Red Panda*
y BL - v101 - i9-10 - Jan 1 2005 - p771(1) [51-500]
Seindells, Robert E. - *Blitzed (Read by Rodska, Christian). Audiobook Review*
y SLJ - v51 - i1 - Jan 2005 - p78(1) [51-500]
Seiple, Robert A. - *Religion and Security: The New Nexus in International Relations*
R&R Bk N - v20 - i1 - Feb 2005 - p11(1) [51-500]
Seitel, Peter - *The Powers of Genre: Interpreting Haya Oral Literature*
WestFolk - v62 - i3 - Summer 2003 - p219-221 [501+]
Seitz, Neil - *Capital Budgeting and Long-Term Financing Decision*
R&R Bk N - v19 - i2 - May 2004 - p123 [51-500]
Seiver, Ellen - *Linux in a Nutshell, 4th Ed.*
SciTech - v28 - i3 - June 2004 - p26(1) [51-500]
Seixas, Peter - *Theorizing Historical Consciousness*
R&R Bk N - v20 - i1 - Feb 2005 - p31(2) [51-500]
Sejour, Victor - *The Fortune-Teller*
NCFS - v33 - i1-2 - Fall-Winter 2004 - p190(2) [501+]
The Jew of Seville
NCFS - v33 - i1-2 - Fall-Winter 2004 - p190(2) [501+]
Selborne, Joanna - *Gwen Raverat, Wood Engraver*
R&R Bk N - v19 - i1 - Feb 2004 - p207(1) [51-50]
Selden, George - *The Genie of Sutton Place*
c BL - v101 - i2 - Sept 15 2004 - p233(1) [51-500]
Seldon, Anthony - *Blair*
Econ - v372 - i8382 - July 3 2004 - p71US [501+]
NS - v133 - i4695 - July 5 2004 - p50(2) [501+]
TimHES - v0 - i1667 - Nov 19 2004 - p22(2) [501+]
TLS - i5290 - August 20 2004 - p9(1) [501+]
The Conservative Party: An Illustrated History
CR - v286 - i1669 - Feb 2005 - p125(1) [51-500]

Seldon, Arthur - *The Virtues of Capitalism*
Bwatch - Dec 2004 - pNA [51-500]
Selengut, Charles - *Sacred Fury: Understanding Religious Violence*
Choice - v41 - i11-12 - July-August 2004 - p2085(1) [501+]
R&R Bk N - v19 - i1 - Feb 2004 - p11(1) [51-500]
Self, David - *Struggling with Forgiveness: Stories from People and Communities*
CBRA - Annual 2003 - p100(1) [51-500]
Self, Jonathan - *Self Abuse: Love, Loss and Fatherhood*
PW - v252 - i4 - Jan 24 2005 - p234(1) [501+]
Self, Robert O. - *American Babylon: Race and the Struggle for Postwar Oakland*
Black Iss - v7 - i2 - March-April 2005 - p40(2) [501+]
Choice - v41 - i11-12 - July-August 2004 - p2110(1) [501+]
JAH - v91 - i3 - Dec 2004 - p1091(1) [501+]
PHR - v73 - i3 - August 2004 - p514(515) [501+]
RAH - v32 - i4 - Dec 2004 - p552-557 [501+]
Selfridge, Benjamin - *A Kid's Guide to Creating Web Pages for Home and School*
c SLJ - v51 - i2 - Feb 2005 - p152(1) [51-500]
Seligman, Craig - *Sontag & Kael: Opposites Attract Me*
Atl - v294 - i1 - July-August 2004 - p159(5) [501+]
Lam Bk Rpt - v13 - i3 - Oct 2004 - p20(2) [501+]
Seligman, Linda - *Diagnosis and Treatment Planning in Counseling, 3rd Ed.*
SciTech - v28 - i4 - Dec 2004 - p96(1) [51-500]
Seligman, Martin E.P. - *Authentic Happiness: Using the New Positive Psychology to Realize Your Potential for Lasting Fulfillment*
Adoles - v39 - i156 - Winter 2004 - p838(2) [51-500]
Seligmann, Linda J. - *Peruvian Street Lives: Culture, Power, and Economy among Market Women of Cuzco*
Choice - v42 - i5 - Jan 2005 - p897(1) [1-50]
Seligson, Michelle - *Bringing Yourself to Work: A Guide to Successful Staff Development in After-School Programs*
y VOYA - v27 - i3 - August 2004 - p251(1) [1-50]
Selin, Helaine - *Nature across Cultures: Views of Nature and the Environment in Non-Western Cultures*
R&R Bk N - v19 - i1 - Feb 2004 - p70(1) [501+]
Sell, Alan P.F. - *Confessing and Commending the Faith: Historic Witness and Apologetic Method*
TT - v60 - i4 - Jan 2004 - p596-598 [501+]
Mill on God: The Pervasiveness and Elusiveness of Mill's Religious Thought
R&R Bk N - v19 - i4 - Nov 2004 - p5(1) [51-500]
Philosophy, Dissent and Nonconformity: 1689-1920
CH - v73 - i4 - Dec 2004 - p872(2) [501+]
Sell, Louis - *Slobodan Milosevic and the Destruction of Yugoslavia*
JPR - v41 - i4 - July 2004 - p524-524 [501+]
Sell, Stewart - *Stem Cells Handbook*
E-Streams - Sept 2004 - pNA [501+]
SciTech - v28 - i1 - March 2004 - p66(1) [51-500]
Sellato, Bernard - *Innermost Borneo: Studies in Dayak Cultures*
JRAI - v10 - i3 - Sept 2004 - p749(2) [501+]
Sellers, Heather - *Spike and Cubby's Ice Cream Island Adventure (Illus. by Young, Amy L.)*
c KR - v72 - i19 - Oct 1 2004 - p969(1) [51-500]
c SLJ - v50 - i11 - Nov 2004 - p118(1) [51-500]
Sellick, Douglas R.G. - *Castaway: Remarkable True Stories of Survival*
R&R Bk N - v19 - i1 - Feb 2004 - p64(1) [51+]
Sellier, Andre - *A History of the Dora Camp*
VQR - v80 - i1 - Wntr 2004 - p261-261 [501+]
Sellier, Philippe - *Pascal: New Trends in Port-Royal Studies: Actes du 33 congres annuel de la North American Society for Seventeenth-Century French Literature*
FS - v58 - i1 - Jan 2004 - p101(2) [501+]
Sells, Chris - *Windows Forms Programming in Visual Basic .NET*
SciTech - v28 - i3 - Sept 2004 - p29(1) [51-500]
Selm, Joanne van - *The Refugee Convention at Fifty: A View from Forced Migration Studies*
HNet - Sept 2004 - pNA [501+]
Selman, Robert - *The Promotion of Social Awareness: Powerful Lessons from the Partnership of Developmental Theory and Classroom Practice*
HER - v74 - i4 - Winter 2004 - p463-465 [501+]
Selmi, Daniel P. - *Land Use Regulation: Cases and Materials, 2nd Ed.*
R&R Bk N - v19 - i3 - August 2004 - p204(1) [1-50]

Selth, Andrew - *Burma's Armed Forces: Power without Glory*
Pac A - v77 - i3 - Fall 2004 - p600(2) [501+]
Selvadurai, Shyam - *Story-Wallah*
Globe & Mail - Sept 11 2004 - pD8 [501+]
Selvaraj, Henry - *Digital System Design: Proceedings*
SciTech - v28 - i4 - Dec 2004 - p155(1) [51-500]
Selwyn, Douglas - *History in the Present Tense: Engaging Students Through Inquiry and Action.*
R&R Bk N - v19 - i1 - Feb 2004 - p76(1) [51-500]
Selznik, Philip - *The Communitarian Persuasion*
RM - v58 - i1 - Sept 2004 - p194(2) [501+]
Semans, Anne - *The Many Joys of Sex Toys: The Ultimate How-To Handbook for Couples and Singles*
LJ - v129 - i14 - Sept 1 2004 - p173(1) [51-500]
Sembach, Kenneth R. - *Hubble's Science Legacy: Future Optical/Ultraviolet Astronomy From Space, Proceedings*
SciTech - v28 - i1 - March 2004 - p44(1) [51-500]
Sember, Brette McWhorter - *Seniors' Rights: Your Legal Guide to Living Life to the Fullest*
BL - v101 - i1 - Sept 1 2004 - p31(1) [51-500]
Semel, Eleanor - *Understanding Williams Syndrome: Behavioral Patterns and Interventions*
Lang Soc - v33 - i4 - Sept 2004 - p612-616 [501+]
Semenza, Gregory M. Colon - *Sport, Politics, and Literature in the English Renaissance*
TLS - i5303 - Nov 19 2004 - p10-11 [501+]
Semes, Steven W. - *The Architecture of the Classical Interior*
R&R Bk N - v19 - i4 - Nov 2004 - p203(1) [501+]
Seminar on the British Book Trade - *Light on the Book Trade: Essays in Honour of Peter Isaac; Proceedings*
R&R Bk N - v19 - i4 - Nov 2004 - p255(1) [501+]
Seminet, Philippe - *Sade in His Own Name: An Analysis of 'Les Crimes de l'Amour'*
R&R Bk N - v19 - i1 - Feb 2004 - p231(1) [51-50]
Semmel, Stuart - *Napoleon and the British*
Lon R Bks - v26 - i21 - Nov 4 2004 - p12(1) [1-50]
Spec - v296 - Dec 18 2004 - p83(3) [501+]
Semmens, P.W.B. - *How Steam Locomotives Really Work*
SciTech - v28 - i4 - Dec 2004 - p146(1) [501+]
Semmens, Richard - *Bals Publics at the Paris Opera in the Eighteenth Century*
R&R Bk N - v19 - i4 - Nov 2004 - p82(1) [51-50]
Semmerling, Tim Jon - *Israeli and Palestinian Postcards: Presentations of National Self*
TLS - i5295 - Sept 24 2004 - p12(1) [501+]
Semmler, Josef - *Der Dynastiewechsel von 751 und die frankische Konigssalbung*
HNet - June 2004 - pNA [501+]
Semmler, Willi - *Asset Prices, Booms and Recessions: Financial Market, Economic Activity and the Macroeconomy*
JEL - v42 - i1 - March 2004 - p255(1) [501+]
Semmlow, John L. - *Biosignal and Biomedical Image Processing: MATLAB-Based Applications*
E-Streams - July 2004 - pNA [501+]
Semple, Andrea - *The Ex-Factor*
BL - v101 - i2 - Sept 15 2004 - p228(1) [51-500]
Semprun, Jorge - *Veinte anos y un dia*
WLT - v78 - i3-4 - Sept-Dec 2004 - p144(1) [501+]
Sen, Amartya - *Elements of a Theory of Human Rights*
Wil Q - v29 - i1 - Wntr 2005 - p97(2) [501+]
Sen, Asim - *Democratic Management: The Path to Total Quality With Total Liberty and Equality*
R&R Bk N - v19 - i1 - Feb 2004 - p86(1) [1-50]
Sen, Colleen Taylor - *Food Culture in India*
SciTech - v28 - i4 - Dec 2004 - p171(1) [51-500]
Sen, Geeti - *India: A National Culture?*
R&R Bk N - v19 - i1 - Feb 2004 - p46(1) [51-500]
Sen, Ilina - *A Space Within the Struggle: Women's Participation in People's Movements*
CS - v33 - i6 - Nov 2004 - p648(4) [501+]
Sen, Sudipta - *Distant Sovereignty: National Imperialism and the Origins of British India*
HER - v119 - i483 - Sept 2004 - p1064(2) [501+]
HER - v119 - i483 - Sept 2004 - p1064(2) [501+]
Sen, Tansen - *Buddhism, Diplomacy, and Trade: The Realignment of Sino-Indian Relations, 600-1400.*
Ch Rev Int - v10 - i2 - Fall 2003 - p447(3) [501+]
Senagore, Anthony J. - *Gale Encyclopedia of Surgery: A Guide for Patients and Caregivers*
SciTech - v28 - i1 - March 2004 - p109(1) [51-500]
Senate, Melissa - *Whose Wedding Is It Anyway?*
BL - v101 - i6 - Nov 15 2004 - p569(1) [51-500]

Senay, Emily - *From Boys to Men: A Woman's Guide to the Health of Husbands, Partners, Sons, Fathers, and Brothers*
   NYT - July 20 2004 - pF7(L) [501+]

Senba, Takasi - *Applied Analysis: Mathematical Methods in Natural Science*
   SciTech - v28 - i4 - Dec 2004 - p39(1) [51-500]

Sendak, Maurice - *Brundibar*
  c LibMed - v22 - i5 - Feb 2004 - p67(2) [501+]
  c Sch Lib - v52 - i3 - Autumn 2004 - p16(3) [501+]
  Pincus and the Pig: A Klezmer Tale
  c PW - v252 - i2 - Jan 10 2005 - p25(1) [51-500]
  Where the Wild Things Are (Illus. by Sendak, Maurice)
  c RT - v57 - Sept 2003 - p101 [51-500]

Seneca, Michael J. - *The Fairmount Park Motor Races, 1908-1911*
   R&R Bk N - v19 - i1 - Feb 2004 - p75(1) [1-50]

Senftleben, M. R. F. - *Copyright, Limitations and the Three-Step Test: An Analysis of the Three-Step Test in International and EC Copyright Law*
   R&R Bk N - v19 - i3 - August 2004 - p191(1/5) [501+]

Senger, Jeffrey M. - *Federal Dispute Resolution: Using ADR in United States Government*
   R&R Bk N - v19 - i3 - August 2004 - p204(1) [1-50]

Sengstack, Jeff - *Sams Teach Yourself Adobe Premiere Pro in 24 Hours*
   SciTech - v28 - i3 - Sept 2004 - p170(1) [1-50]

Sengupta, Anita - *The Formation of the Uzbek Nation-State: A Study in Transition*
   Choice - v42 - i1 - Sept 2004 - p184(1) [501+]
   R&R Bk N - v19 - i1 - Feb 2004 - p39(1) [1-50]

Sengupta, Jati K. - *New Efficiency Theory: With Applications of Data Envelopment Analysis*
   JEL - v42 - i1 - March 2004 - p248(1) [501+]

Senior, Donald P. - *1 Peter, Jude, and 2 Peter*
   Theol St - v66 - i1 - March 2005 - p181(2) [501+]

Senior, Olive - *Encyclopedia of Jamaican Heritage*
   Choice - v42 - i4 - Dec 2004 - p643(1) [1-50]

Senk, Sharon L. - *Standards-Based School Mathematics Curricula: What Are They? What Do Students Learn?*
   Math T - v97 - i4 - April 2004 - p302-302 [501+]

Senker, Cath - *The Arab-Israeli Conflict*
  y Sch Lib - v52 - i4 - Winter 2004 - p219(1) [51-500]
  c SLJ - v51 - i2 - Feb 2005 - p152(1) [51-500]
  Relationships
  c Sch Lib - v52 - i4 - Winter 2004 - p190(1) [51-500]
  Why Are People Refugees?
  c SLJ - v51 - i2 - Feb 2005 - p152(2) [51-500]
  Winter
  c BL - v101 - i6 - Nov 15 2004 - p575(1) [51-500]

Sennett, Frank - *Nash, Metropolitan*
   BL - v101 - i3 - Oct 1 2004 - p314(2) [51-500]

Sennott, R. Steven - *Encyclopedia of 20th-Century Architecture, Vols. 1-3*
   Ref Rev - Oct 2004 - pNA [501+]

Sensbach, Jon - *Rebecca's Revival: Creating Black Christianity in the Atlantic World*
   PW - v252 - i3 - Jan 17 2005 - p50(1) [51-500]

The Senses
   LibMed - v22 - i7 - April-May 2004 - p80(1) [501+]

Sentance, Bryan - *Ceramics: A World Guide to Traditional Techniques*
   Ceram Mo - v52 - i10 - Dec 2004 - p66(2) [501+]
   Choice - v42 - i6 - Feb 2005 - p1011(1) [51-500]

Sentilles, Renee M. - *Performing Menken: Adah Isaacs Menken and the Birth of American Celebrity*
   AHR - v109 - i4 - Oct 2004 - p1238(1) [501+]
   JAH - v91 - i2 - Sept 2004 - p629(2) [501+]
   Legacy - v21 - i2 - June 2004 - p247(3) [501+]
   Theat J - v56 - i4 - Dec 2004 - p709-710 [501+]

Seo, Danny - *Generation React: Activism for Beginners*
  y SLJ - v50 - i8 - August 2004 - p50(1) [51-500]

Sept, J. Duane - *Common Wildflowers of British Columbia*
   CBRA - Annual 2003 - p405(2) [51-500]

Sepulveda, Juan A. - *The Life and Times of Willie Velaquez: su voto es su vos*
   R&R Bk N - v19 - i3 - August 2004 - p65(1) [51-500]

Sepulveda, Luis - *The Story of a Seagull and the Cat Who Taught Her to Fly (Illus. by Sheban, Chris)*
   LibMed - v22 - i6 - March 2004 - p62(1) [501+]

Serafin, Bruce - *Colin's Big Thing: A Sequence*
   BIC - v33 - i6 - Sept 2004 - p29(2) [501+]
   Globe & Mail - Oct 2 2004 - pD15 [501+]
   Globe & Mail - Nov 27 2004 - pD3 [51-500]

Serafini, Frank - *Reading Aloud and Beyond: Fostering the Intellectual Life with Older Readers*
   JAAL - v48 - i2 - Oct 2004 - p183(2) [51-500]

Serafini, Luigi - *Codex Seraphinianus*
   MFSF - v108 - i4 - April 2005 - p162(1) [51-500]

Serageldin, Samia - *The Cairo House*
   Econ - v372 - i8384 - July 17 2004 - p81US [501+]

Seranella, Barbara - *Unwilling Accomplice*
   BooChiTr - June 6 2004 - p4(1) [501+]

Serb, Ioan - *Antologia basmului cult romanesc: anthologie*
  c Bkbird - v42 - i3 - July 2004 - p50(1) [501+]

Serfini, Frank - *Audiobooks & Literacy: An Educator's Guide to Utilizing Audiobooks in the Classroom*
   SLJ - v50 - i10 - Oct 2004 - pS9(1) [51-500]

Sergeant, John - *Maggie: Her Fatal Legacy*
   NS - v134 - i4728 - Feb 21 2005 - p50(1) [501+]

Sergi, Bruno S. - *Economic Dynamics in Transitional Economies: The Four-P Governments, the EU Enlargement, and the Bruxelles Consensus*
   R&R Bk N - v19 - i1 - Feb 2004 - p83(1) [51-500]

Sergiovanni, Thomas J. - *Strengthening the Heartbeat: Leading and Learning Together in Schools*
   R&R Bk N - v19 - i4 - Nov 2004 - p186(1) [501+]

Serials Publications - *International Journal of Applied Business and Economic Research*
   JEL - v41 - i4 - Dec 2003 - p1446(1) [501+]

Serim, Ferdi - *Information Technology for Learning: No School Left Behined*
   LibMed - v22 - i7 - April-May 2004 - p89(1) [501+]

Serio, John - *Poetry for Young People: Wallace Stevens (Illus. by Steele, Robert Gantt)*
  c PW - v252 - i5 - Jan 31 2005 - p70(1) [501+]

Serjeantson, Richard - *Generall Learning: A Seventeenth-Century Treatise on the Formation of the General Scholar by Meric Casaubon*
   Six Ct J - v35 - i3 - Fall 2004 - p925-927 [501+]

Serota, Nicholas - *Donald Judd*
   Choice - v42 - i1 - Sept 2004 - p88(2) [501+]

Serper, Mark R. - *Psychotic Violence: Methods, Motives, Madness*
   SciTech - v28 - i1 - March 2004 - p102(1) [51-500]

Serretti, Massimo - *The Uniqueness and Universality of Jesus Christ: In Dialogue with the Religions*
   R&R Bk N - v19 - i3 - August 2004 - p25(1) [1-50]

Servadio, Gaia - *Rossini*
   Choice - v41 - i7 - March 2004 - p1307(1) [501+]

Servaes, Jan - *The European Information Society: A Reality Check*
   R&R Bk N - v19 - i2 - May 2004 - p128 [51-500]

Service, Robert - *Russia: Experiment with a People*
   Slav R - v63 - i3 - Fall 2004 - p667-668 [51-500]
  Stalin: A Biography
   NS - v133 - i4710 - Oct 18 2004 - p50(2) [501+]
   PW - v252 - i8 - Feb 21 2005 - p164(1) [51-500]
   Spec - v296 - i9200 - Dec 4 2004 - p49(2) [501+]

Serway, Raymond A. - *Physics for Scientists and Engineers with Modern Physics. 6th Ed.*
   TimHES - v0 - i1668 - Nov 26 2004 - pXIV(2) [501+]

Sesame Street Music Zone
   SLJ - v50 - i12 - Dec 2004 - p63(1) [501+]

Seshadri, Vijay - *The Long Meadow*
   Poet - v184 - i5 - Sept 2004 - p385(2) [501+]

Setala, P. - *Women, Wealth and Power in the Roman Empire*
   Class R - v53 - i2 - Nov 2003 - p423-424 [501+]

Seth, Clyde - *Fans: Book One*
   LJ - v129 - i18 - Nov 1 2004 - p67(1) [501+]

Seth, Laurel - *Folk Art Journey: Florence D. Bartlett and the Museum of International Folk Art, Featuring the Florence Dibell Bartlett Collection*
   R&R Bk N - v19 - i4 - Nov 2004 - p208(1) [501+]

Seth, Vikram - *A Suitable Boy*
   Comw - v131 - i21 - Dec 3 2004 - p30(2) [501+]

Seto, Kan-ichi - *Atlas of Oral and Maxillofacial Rehabilitation*
   SciTech - v28 - i3 - Sept 2004 - p120(1) [51-500]

Setright, L.J.K. - *Drive On!: A Social History of the Motor Car*
   Choice - v42 - i4 - Dec 2004 - p684(1) [1-50]

Setterfield, Gwenlyn - *Niki Goldschmidt: A Life in Canadian Music*
   Can Hist R - v85 - i3 - Sept 2004 - p626(3) [501+]
   CBRA - Annual 2003 - p70(2) [501+]

Setterfield, Mark - *The Economics of Demand-Led Growth: Challenging the Supply-Side Vision of the Long Run*
   JEL - v42 - i1 - March 2004 - p223(2) [501+]

Setterington, Ken - *Mom and Mum are Getting Married! (Illus. by Priestley, Alice)*
  c KR - v73 - i1 - Jan 1 2005 - p57(1) [51-500]
  c Res Links - v10 - i3 - Feb 2005 - p8(2) [51-500]
  The Wild Swans (Illus. by Hofer, Nelly)
  c CBRA - Annual 2003 - p466(2) [51-500]

Settersten, Richard A., Jr. - *Advances in Life Course Research, Vol. 7*
   CS - v33 - i4 - July 2004 - p431(3) [501+]

Settle, Mary Lee - *Spanish Recognitions: The Roads to the Present*
   R&R Bk N - v19 - i4 - Nov 2004 - p42(1) [51-500]

Setzer, Claudia - *Resurrection of the Body in Early Judaism and Early Christianity: Doctrine, Community, and Self-Definition*
   R&R Bk N - v19 - i4 - Nov 2004 - p25(1) [501+]

Seuling, Barbara - *Flick a Switch: How Electricity Gets to Your Home (Illus. by Tobin, Nancy)*
  c LibMed - v22 - i7 - April-May 2004 - p80(1) [501+]
  Robert and the Back-to-School Special (Illus. by Brewer, Paul)
  c SLJ - v50 - i7 - July 2004 - p44(1) [51-500]
  Robert Takes a Stand (Illus. by Brewer, Paul)
  c HB - v80 - i4 - July-August 2004 - p460(2) [51-500]
  Whose House? (Illus. by Chorao, Kay)
  c SLJ - v50 - i8 - August 2004 - p93(2) [51-500]

Seuront, Laurent - *Handbook of Scaling Methods in Aquatic Ecology: Measurement, Analysis, Simulation*
   E-Streams - Sept 2004 - pNA [501+]
   SciTech - v28 - i1 - March 2004 - p65(1) [51-500]

Sever, David M. - *Reproductive Biology and Phylogeny of Urodela*
   QRB - v79 - i4 - Dec 2004 - p437(2) [501+]

Severs, Aysan - *Fleeing the House of Horrors: Women Who Have Left Abusive Partners*
   CWS - v23 - i3-4 - Spring-Summer 2004 - p213(1) [501+]

Severson, Marilyn S. - *Masterpieces of French Literature*
   LJ - v129 - i12 - July 2004 - p83(1) [51-500]

Severy, Beth - *Augustus and the Family at the Birth of the Roman Empire*
   TLS - i5297 - Oct 8 2004 - p10(1) [501+]

Sew News - *All about Machine Arts: Decorative Techniques from A to Z*
   Bwatch - v26 - i7 - July 2004 - p7(1) [51-500]
   LJ - v129 - i13 - August 2004 - p77(1) [501+]

Seward, Desmond - *Eugenie and Her Empire*
   CR - v285 - i1664 - Sept 2004 - p186(2) [51-500]

Sewell, Marilyn - *Breaking Free: Women of Spirit at Mid-Life and Beyond*
   LJ - v129 - i15 - Sept 15 2004 - p72(2) [51-500]

Sewell, Robert C. - *The Book as Art, Literature, and History*
   BSA-P - v98 - i1 - March 2004 - p130-130 [501+]

Sewing, Werner - *Architecture: Sculpture*
   Choice - v42 - i3 - Nov 2004 - p476(1) [1-50]
   LJ - v129 - i14 - Sept 1 2004 - p147(2) [51-500]

Sexton, Brenda - *It's Easter! (Illus. by Sexton, Brenda)*
  c PW - v252 - i7 - Feb 14 2005 - p79(2) [501+]

Sexton-Radek, Kathy - *Sleep Quality in Young Adults*
   SciTech - v28 - i1 - March 2004 - p84(1) [51-500]
  Violence in Schools: Issues, Consequences, and Expressions
   BL - v101 - i8 - Dec 15 2004 - p695(1) [51-500]

Sexton, Robert F. - *Mobilizing Citizens for Better Schools*
   TCR - v106 - i12 - Dec 2004 - p2332(4) [501+]

Sexton, Robert L. - *Exploring Economics, 3rd Ed.*
   R&R Bk N - v19 - i3 - August 2004 - p93(1) [51-500]
  Exploring Microeconomics, 3d Ed.
   R&R Bk N - v19 - i4 - Nov 2004 - p85(1) [51-500]

Seydel, Rudiger - *Tools for Computational Finance*
   SIAM Rev - v46 - i4 - Dec 2004 - p756-757 [501+]

Seyfried, Gerhard - *Herero*
   WLT - v78 - i3-4 - Sept-Dec 2004 - p126(1) [501+]

Seyler, Dorothy U. - *Patterns of Reflection: A Reader, 5th Ed*
   R&R Bk N - v19 - i1 - Feb 2004 - p216(1) [51-500]

Seyller, John - *Pearls of the Parrot of India: The Walter's Art Museum Khamsa of Amir Khusraw of Delhi*
   Six Ct J - v34 - i4 - Winter 2003 - p1256-1258 [501+]

Seymour, Claire - *The Operas of Benjamin Britten: Expression and Evasion*
Choice - v42 - i7 - March 2005 - p1237(1) [51-500]

Seymour, Craig - *Luther: The Life and Longing of Luther Vandross*
LJ - v129 - i12 - July 2004 - p84(1) [51-500]

Seymour, Gerald - *Traitor's Kiss (Read by Kay, Christopher). Audiobook Review*
LJ - v130 - i2 - Feb 1 2005 - p123(2) [51-500]
The Unknown Soldier
Ent W - i809 - March 4 2005 - p77 [501+]
KR - v72 - i24 - Dec 15 2004 - p1162(1) [501+]
LJ - v130 - i2 - Feb 1 2005 - p70(1) [51-500]
PW - v252 - i2 - Jan 10 2005 - p37(1) [51-500]

Seymour, Michel - *The Fate of the Nation-State*
R&R Bk N - v19 - i3 - August 2004 - p173(1) [501+]

Seymour, Mike - *Educating for Humanity: Rethinking the Purposes of Education*
R&R Bk N - v19 - i4 - Nov 2004 - p191(1) [501+]

Seymour, Miranda - *Bugatti Queen: In Search of a French Racing Legend*
BL - v101 - i6 - Nov 15 2004 - p545(1) [51-500]
KR - v72 - i20 - Oct 15 2004 - p997(1) [501+]
LJ - v129 - i19 - Nov 15 2004 - p67(1) [51-500]
NYTBR - Dec 26 2004 - p12 [501+]
PW - v251 - i42 - Oct 18 2004 - p56(1) [51-500]
The Bugatti Queen: In Search of a Motor-Racing Legend
TLS - i5265 - Feb 27 2004 - p26-26 [501+]

Seymour-Ure, Colin - *Prime Ministers and the Media: Issues of Power and Control, 1st Ed.*
TimHES - v0 - i1668 - Nov 26 2004 - pIII(1) [501+]

Seymour, Victoria - *Court in the Act*
NS - v133 - i4716 - Nov 29 2004 - p48(2) [51-500]

Seynaeve, Katrien - *Borders*
y   VOYA - v27 - i3 - August 2004 - p181(1) [1-50]

Sfar, Joann - *Dungeon, Vol. 1*
y   BL - v101 - i7 - Dec 1 2004 - p648(1) [51-500]
PW - v251 - i46 - Nov 15 2004 - p43(1) [51-500]
Dungeon, Vol. 2
PW - v252 - i10 - March 7 2005 - p52(1) [51-500]

Sforzi, Fabio - *The Institutions of Local Development*
JEL - v42 - i1 - March 2004 - p340(1) [501+]

Sfraga, Michael - *Bradford Washburn: A Life of Exploration*
Choice - v42 - i4 - Dec 2004 - p699(1) [1-50]
R&R Bk N - v19 - i3 - August 2004 - p86(1) [51-500]

SFS Kids: Fun with Music
SLJ - v50 - i12 - Dec 2004 - p63(1) [501+]

Sgaramella, Vittorio - *Mammalian Artificial Chromosomes: Methods and Protocols*
SciTech - v28 - i1 - March 2004 - p66(1) [51-500]

Sgaravatti, Mariella - *Tuscan Artists' Gardens (Read by Mario Ciampi)*
LJ - v129 - i19 - Nov 15 2004 - p79(1) [501+]

Shaara, Jeff - *Rise to Rebellion*
y   Kliatt - v38 - i5 - Sept 2004 - p26(2) [51-500]
To the Last Man: A Novel of the First World War
BL - v101 - i2 - Sept 15 2004 - p180(1) [51-500]
KR - v72 - i18 - Sept 15 2004 - p888(1) [501+]
LJ - v129 - i16 - Oct 1 2004 - p73(2) [51-500]
PW - v251 - i41 - Oct 11 2004 - p54(1) [51-500]

Shaara, Michael - *The Killer Angels (Read by Hoye, Stephen). Audiobook Review*
y   Kliatt - v39 - i1 - Jan 2005 - p45(1) [51-500]

Shabazz, Amilcar - *Advancing Democracy: African Americans and the Struggle for Access and Equity in Higher Education in Texas*
Black Iss - v6 - i5 - Sept-Oct 2004 - p40(2) [51-500]
HNet - August 2004 - pNA [501+]
RAH - v32 - i3 - Sept 2004 - p422-430 [501+]

Shabetai, Ralph - *Pericardium, 2nd Ed.*
SciTech - v28 - i1 - March 2004 - p105(1) [51-500]

Shabtai, Yaakov - *Uncle Peretz Takes Off: Short Stories*
KR - v72 - i15 - August 1 2004 - p711(2) [501+]
PW - v251 - i35 - August 30 2004 - p32(1) [501+]

Shachman, Maurice - *The Soft Drink Companion: A Technical Handbook for the Beverage Industry*
SciTech - v28 - i4 - Dec 2004 - p165(1) [51-500]

Shachnow, Sid - *Hope and Honor*
KR - v72 - i15 - August 1 2004 - p733(1) [51-500]
LJ - v129 - i15 - Sept 15 2004 - p65(1) [51-500]

Shackel, Paul A. - *Memory in Black and White: Race, Commemoration, and the Post-Bellum Landscape*
JAH - v91 - i2 - Sept 2004 - p675(2) [501+]
Pub Hist - v26 - i2 - Spring 2004 - p90(92) [501+]

Shackelford, George T.M. - *Gauguin Tahiti*
Choice - v41 - i11-12 - July-August 2004 - p2035(1) [501+]

Shackelford, Jole - *William Harvey and the Mechanics of the Heart*
y   SB - v40 - i4 - July-August 2004 - p169(1) [51-500]

Shackelford, Ron - *Married to an Opposite: Making Personality Differences Work for You*
R&R Bk N - v19 - i1 - Feb 2004 - p129(1) [51-500]

Shackleford, Jim - *Allegiance*
y   SLJ - v51 - i1 - Jan 2005 - p136(1) [51-500]

Shackleton, Michael - *Operation Vietnam: A New Zealand Surgical First*
SciTech - v28 - i3 - Sept 2004 - p4(1) [501+]

Shadbolt, Doris - *The Seven Journeys of Emily Carr*
Can Lit - i182 - Autumn 2004 - p174(3) [501+]
Seven Journeys: The Sketchbooks of Emily Carr
CBRA - Annual 2003 - p121(1) [501+]

Shade, Eric - *Eyesores*
Ga R - v58 - i3 - Fall 2004 - p685-696 [501+]

Shade, William G. - *American Presidential Campaigns and Elections*
LibMed - v22 - i5 - Feb 2004 - p79(1) [501+]
BL - v101 - i3 - Oct 1 2004 - p358(1) [501+]

Shadoian, Jack - *Dreams and Dead Ends: The American Gangster Film*
JPC - v38 - i3 - Feb 2005 - p583(2) [501+]

Shafak, Elif - *The Saint of Incipient Insanities*
BL - v101 - i2 - Sept 15 2004 - p209(1) [501+]
BW - v34 - i44 - Oct 31 2004 - p8(1) [501+]
Econ - v372 - i8388 - August 14 2004 - p75US [501+]
KR - v72 - i16 - August 15 2004 - p773(2) [501+]
LJ - v129 - i17 - Oct 15 2004 - p56(1) [51-500]
MEJ - v58 - i4 - Autumn 2004 - p706(2) [501+]
PW - v251 - i37 - Sept 13 2004 - p56(2) [501+]

Shafer, Harry J. - *Mimbres Archaeology at the NAN Ranch Ruin*
Choice - v42 - i1 - Sept 2004 - p148(1) [501+]

Shafer, Judith Kelleher - *Becoming Free, Remaining Free: Manumission and Enslavement in New Orleans, 1846-1862*
JIH - v35 - i2 - Autumn 2004 - p312(2) [501+]

Shafer-Landau, Russ - *Moral Realism: A Defence*
Choice - v41 - i11-12 - July-August 2004 - p2059(1) [501+]

Shaffer, David R. - *Social and Personality Development, 5th Ed.*
R&R Bk N - v19 - i4 - Nov 2004 - p11(1) [51-500]

Shaffer, Donald R. - *After the Glory: The Struggles of Black Civil War Veterans*
HNet - Nov 2004 - pNA [501+]

Shaffer, Gregory C. - *Defending Interests: Public-Private Partnerships in WTO Litigation*
PSQ - v119 - i3 - Fall 2004 - p541(2) [501+]

Shaffer, Jay - *The MacAddict Guide to Making Music with GarageBand*
LJ - v129 - i14 - Sept 1 2004 - p182(1) [51-500]

Shaffer, John W. - *Clash of Loyalties: A Border County in the Civil War*
R&R Bk N - v19 - i1 - Feb 2004 - p63(1) [501+]

Shaffer, Karen - *Ancient Spirit, Modern Voice: The Mythic Journeys Art Exhibition*
MFSF - v107 - i6 - Dec 2004 - p29(3) [501+]

Shaffer, Marguerite S. - *See America First: Tourism and National Identity, 1880-1940*
Am Q - v56 - i4 - Dec 2004 - p1089(9) [501+]

Shaffer, Ron - *Community Economics: Linking Theory and Practice, 2nd Ed.*
R&R Bk N - v19 - i3 - August 2004 - p157(1) [51-500]

Shaffer, Susan Morris - *Why Boys Don't Talk and Why It Matters: A Parent's Survival Guide to Connecting with Your Teen*
BL - v101 - i7 - Dec 1 2004 - p623(1) [51-500]
LJ - v129 - i20 - Dec 1 2004 - p154(1) [51-500]
Why Girls Talk - and What They're Really Saying: A Parent's Survival Guide to Connecting with Your Teen
BL - v101 - i7 - Dec 1 2004 - p623(1) [51-500]
PW - v251 - i43 - Oct 25 2004 - p42(1) [51-500]

Shaffner, George - *In the Land of Second Chances*
BL - v100 - i22 - August 2004 - p1903(1) [501+]
KR - v72 - i15 - August 1 2004 - p712(1) [501+]
Ent W - i789 - Oct 22 2004 - p99 [51-500]
PW - v251 - i37 - Sept 13 2004 - p57(2) [501+]

Shafritz, Jay M. - *Introducing Public Administration, 4th Ed.*
R&R Bk N - v19 - i4 - Nov 2004 - p153(1) [501+]

Shagan, Ethan H. - *Popular Politics and the English Reformation*
Albion - v36 - i1 - Spring 2004 - p109(3) [501+]
JIH - v34 - i4 - Spring 2004 - p629-630 [501+]
Ren Q - v57 - i3 - Fall 2004 - p1117(3) [501+]
CHR - v90 - i3 - July 2004 - p546(4) [501+]

Shagena, Jack L. - *Who Really Invented the Steamboat? Fulton's Clermont Coup*
Choice - v42 - i6 - Feb 2005 - p1044(1) [501+]
SciTech - v28 - i4 - Dec 2004 - p172(1) [51-500]

Shah, Anup - *Circle of Life: Wildlife on the African Savannah*
SB - v40 - i4 - July-August 2004 - p160(1) [51-500]
SB - v40 - i6 - Nov-Dec 2004 - p245(1) [51-500]
SciTech - v28 - i1 - March 2004 - p68(1) [51-500]

Shah, Ghanshyam - *Social Movements in India: A Review of Literature, 2nd Ed.*
R&R Bk N - v19 - i3 - August 2004 - p147(1) [51-500]

Shah, Hemant - *Newspaper Coverage of Interethnic Conflict: Competing Visions of America*
R&R Bk N - v19 - i1 - Feb 2004 - p230(1) [51-500]

Shah, R.K. - *Fuel Cell Science, Engineering and Technology; Proceedings*
SciTech - v28 - i3 - Sept 2004 - p152(1) [51-500]

Shah, Saira - *The Storyteller's Daughter: One Woman's Return to Her Lost Homeland*
Globe & Mail - Oct 16 2004 - pD31 [501+]
y   Kliatt - v39 - i1 - Jan 2005 - p31(1) [51-500]
NYTBR - Jan 30 2005 - p24 [501+]

Shah, Samir S. - *Blueprints Pediatric Infectious Diseases*
SciTech - v28 - i4 - Dec 2004 - p112(1) [1-50]

Shah, Sonia - *Crude: The Story of Oil*
SciTech - v28 - i4 - Dec 2004 - p162(1) [51-500]

Shah, Tahir - *House of the Tiger King*
Globe & Mail - Nov 3 2004 - pT1 [501+]
Trail Of Feathers
Bwatch - March 2005 - pNA [51-500]

Shahan, Sherry - *Spicy Hot Colors/Colores Picantes (Illus. by Barragan, Paula)*
c   BL - v101 - i2 - Sept 15 2004 - p247(1) [51-500]
c   CH Bwatch - Oct 2004 - pNA [51-500]
c   KR - v72 - i15 - August 1 2004 - p749(1) [51-500]
c   PW - v251 - i46 - Nov 15 2004 - p58(1) [501+]
c   SLJ - v50 - i11 - Nov 2004 - p130(1) [51-500]

Shaheen, Mohammad - *E.M. Forster and the Politics of Imperialism*
Choice - v42 - i5 - Jan 2005 - p855(1) [1-50]

Shahideh, Laleh - *The Power of Iranian Narratives: A Thousand Years of Healing*
R&R Bk N - v19 - i3 - August 2004 - p255(1) [51-500]

Shahrani, M. Nazif - *The Kirghiz and Wakhi of Afghanistan: Adaptation to Closed Frontiers and War*
IJMES - v36 - i3 - August 2004 - p503-504 [501+]
JAS - v63 - i3 - August 2004 - p795-796 [501+]

Shahrokh, Narriman C. - *American Psychiatric Glossary, 8th Ed.*
E-Streams - July 2004 - pNA [501+]

Shahwan, Usamah - *Public Administration in Palestine Past and Present*
R&R Bk N - v19 - i4 - Nov 2004 - p45(1) [51-500]

Shai, Shaul - *The Shahids: Islam and Suicide Attacks*
Choice - v42 - i5 - Jan 2005 - p928(1) [51-500]

Shainberg, Catherine - *Kabbalah and the Power of Dreaming: Awakening the Visionary Life*
PW - v252 - i11 - March 14 2005 - p64(2) [51-500]

Shaine, Laura - *Sleeping Arrangements*
Spec - v297 - i9205 - Jan 8 2005 - p33(1) [501+]

Shaker, Bonnie James - *Coloring Locals: Racial Formation in Kate Chopin's Youth's Companion Stories*
Legacy - v21 - i2 - June 2004 - p255(2) [501+]

Shakespeare, Nicholas - *In Tasmania*
Spec - v296 - i9198 - Nov 20 2004 - p42(2) [501+]
Snowleg
BL - v101 - i1 - Sept 1 2004 - p64(1) [51-500]
BW - v34 - i42 - Oct 17 2004 - p7(1) [501+]
KR - v72 - i13 - July 1 2004 - p602(1) [501+]
LJ - v129 - i13 - August 2004 - p70(1) [51-500]
NYTBR - Nov 7 2004 - p23 [501+]
PW - v251 - i36 - Sept 6 2004 - p45(1) [51-500]

Shakespeare, William - *The Taming of the Shrew*
Shakes Q - v55 - i2 - Summer 2004 - p214-217 [501+]
To Sleep Perchance to Dream: A Child's Book of Rhymes (Illus. by Mayhew, James)
c   Teach Lib - v32 - i3 - Feb 2005 - p21(1) [51-500]

Shapiro, Karl - *Creative Glut: Selected Essays*
TLS - i5292 - Sept 3 2004 - p24(1) [501+]
Essay on Rime with Trial of a Poet
Sew R - v111 - i3 - Summer 2003 - p455-462
[501+]
Selected Poems
TLS - i5292 - Sept 3 2004 - p24(1) [501+]

Shapiro, Lawrence A. - *The Mind Incarnate*
Choice - v42 - i5 - Jan 2005 - p868(1) [1-50]
TLS - i5302 - Nov 12 2004 - p32(1) [501+]

Shapiro, Lawrence E. - *Arnold Gets Angry*
c CH Bwatch - v14 - i12 - Dec 2004 - pNA [51-500]
Debra Doesn't Take the Dare (Illus. by Harpster, Steve)
c CH Bwatch - March 2005 - pNA [51-500]

Shapiro, Michael - *A Sense of Place: Great Travel Writers Talk about Their Craft, Lives and Inspirations*
Globe & Mail - Dec 4 2004 - pT12 [501+]

Shapiro, Moshe - *Principles of the Quantum Control of Molecular Processes*
Phys Today - v57 - i9 - Sept 2004 - p59-60 [501+]

Shapiro, Norman R. - *Creole Echoes: The Francophone Poetry of Nineteenth-Century Louisiana*
Choice - v42 - i1 - Sept 2004 - p105(1) [501+]

Shapiro, Stephen - *Hoodwinked: Deception and Resistance (Illus. by Craig, David)*
y BL - v101 - i9-10 - Jan 1 2005 - p841(1) [1-50]
y Res Links - v10 - i3 - Feb 2005 - p49(1) [501+]
y SLJ - v51 - i1 - Jan 2005 - p154(2) [51-500]
Ultra Hush-Hush: Espionage and Special Missions (Illus. by Craig, David)
c CBRA - Annual 2003 - p542(1) [51-500]
Ultra Hush-Hush: Espionage and Special Missions
LibMed - v22 - i5 - Feb 2004 - p80(1) [51-500]

Shapiro, Susan - *Lighting Up: How I Stopped Smoking, Drinking and Everything Else I Loved in Life Except Sex*
KR - v72 - i20 - Oct 15 2004 - p997(1) [501+]
NYTBR - March 13 2005 - p26 [501+]
PW - v251 - i50 - Dec 13 2004 - p59(1) [51-500]

Shapiro, Susan G. - *The Curtain Rises: Oral Histories of the Fall of Communism in Eastern Europe*
R&R Bk N - v19 - i2 - May 2004 - p131 [51-500]

Shapiro, Walter - *One Car Caravan: On the Road with the 2004 Democrats before America Tunes In*
R&R Bk N - v19 - i3 - August 2004 - p71(1) [51-500]

Sharan, Shlomo - *Israel and the Post-Zionists: A Nation at Risk*
Choice - v41 - i11-12 - July-August 2004 - p2117(1) [501+]

Sharansky, Natan - *The Case for Democracy: The Power of Freedom to Overcome Tyranny and Terror*
Globe & Mail - Jan 1 2005 - pD4 [501+]
NYT - Feb 12 2005 - pB7 [501+]
PW - v251 - i46 - Nov 15 2004 - p55(1) [501+]

Share, Don - *Union*
PSQ - v78 - i3 - Fall 2004 - p177(7) [501+]

Sharf, Robert H. - *Coming to Terms with Chinese Buddhism: A Reading of the "Treasure Store Treatise"*
JAAR - v72 - i4 - Dec 2004 - p1073(4) [501+]

Shargel, Leon - *Applied Biopharmaceutics and Pharmacokinetics, 5th Ed.*
SciTech - v28 - i4 - Dec 2004 - p116(1) [1-50]

Sharif, Mohammed - *Work Behavior of the World's Poor: Theory, Evidence, and Policy*
JEL - v42 - i1 - March 2004 - p282(1) [501+]
JEL - v42 - i4 - Dec 2004 - p1146(2) [501+]

Sharkansky, Ira - *Coping with Terror: An Israeli Perspective*
R&R Bk N - v19 - i1 - Feb 2004 - p142(1) [51-500]
Politics and Policymaking: In Search of Simplicity
PG - v23 - i4 - May 2004 - p500-502 [501+]

Sharkey, Heather J. - *Living with Colonialism: Nationalism and Culture in the Anglo-Egyptian Sudan*
AHR - v109 - i2 - April 2004 - p656(2) [501+]
HNet - August 2004 - pNA [501+]

Sharma, Arun Kumar - *Plant Genome: Biodiversity and Evolution (Illus. by Sharma, Arun Kumar)*
QRB - v79 - i3 - Sept 2004 - p305(2) [501+]

Sharma, Arvind - *Goddesses and Women in the Indic Religious Tradition*
R&R Bk N - v20 - i1 - Feb 2005 - p12(1) [51-500]
Hinduism and Its Sense of History
Choice - v42 - i1 - Sept 2004 - p122(1) [501+]
The Study of Hinduism
Choice - v41 - i7 - March 2004 - p1314(1) [501+]

Sharma, Chetan - *Wireless Data Services: Technologies, Business Models and Global Markets*
E-Streams - August 2004 - pNA [501+]

Sharma, Dinesh - *Childhood, Family, and Sociocultural Change in India: Reinterpreting the Inner World*
R&R Bk N - v19 - i2 - May 2004 - p135 [51-500]

Sharma, Hari D. - *Geoenvironmental Engineering: Site Remediation, Waste Containment, and Emerging Waste Management Technologies*
SciTech - v28 - i3 - Sept 2004 - p144(1) [51-500]

Sharma, Jyotirmaya - *Hindutva: Exploring the Idea of Hindu Nationalism*
R&R Bk N - v19 - i4 - Nov 2004 - p15(1) [51-500]

Sharma, Kapil - *Professional Red Hat Enterprise Linux 3*
SciTech - v28 - i4 - Dec 2004 - p27(1) [1-50]

Sharma, Mukul - *Improving People's Lives: Lessons in Empowerment from Asia*
R&R Bk N - v19 - i1 - Feb 2004 - p85(1) [1-50]

Sharman, Gundula M. - *Twentieth-Century Reworkings of German Literature: An Analysis of Six Fictional Reinterpretations from Geothe to Thomas Mann*
GSR - v27 - i3 - Oct 2004 - p675(2) [501+]

Sharmat, Marjorie Weinman - *Nate the Great and the Mushy Valentine (Illus. by Simont, Marc)*
c PW - v251 - i49 - Dec 6 2004 - p61(2) [501+]
Nate the Great Collected Stories (Read by Lavelle, John). Audiobook Review
c SLJ - v50 - i10 - Oct 2004 - pS30(1) [1-50]
Nate the Great on the Owl Express (Illus. by Weston, Martha)
c SLJ - v50 - i10 - Oct 2004 - pS30(1) [1-50]

Sharon, Michael - *Nutrients A to Z: A User's Guide to Foods, Herbs, Vitamins, Minerals and Supplements, 3rd Ed.*
Choice - v42 - i2 - Oct 2004 - p272(1) [501+]
E-Streams - Oct 2004 - pNA [501+]

Sharot, Scott - *New Mexico Chow: Restaurants for the Rest of Us*
Bwatch - v26 - i8 - August 2004 - p2(1) [51-500]

Sharot, Stephen - *A Comparative Sociology of World Religions: Virtuosos, Priests and Popular Religion*
JR - v85 - i1 - Jan 2005 - p188(2) [501+]

Sharp, Adrienne - *White Swan, Black Swan*
BL - v101 - i5 - Nov 1 2004 - p458(1) [51-500]

Sharp, David W.A. - *The Penguin Dictionary of Chemistry*
Choice - v42 - i1 - Sept 2004 - p72(1) [501+]

Sharp, Kevin - *A Wilder Image Bright: Hudson River School Paintings from the Manoogian Collection*
Choice - v42 - i4 - Dec 2004 - p651(1) [1-50]

Sharp, Margery - *The Eye of Love*
Spec - v295 - i9184 - August 14 2004 - p35(2) [501+]

Sharp, Nonie - *Saltwater People: The Waves of Memory*
AHS - v35 - i124 - Oct 2004 - p413(2) [501+]
R&R Bk N - v19 - i1 - Feb 2004 - p71(1) [1-50]

Sharp, Robert T. - *No Dogs in Heaven?: Scenes from the Life of a Country Veterinarian*
KR - v73 - i4 - Feb 15 2005 - p220(1) [501+]

Sharp, Rosalie Wise - *Ceramics Ethics & Scandal*
Ceram Mo - v52 - i3 - March 2004 - p36(2) [501+]

Sharpe, Charles C. - *Frauds Against the Elderly*
R&R Bk N - v19 - i3 - August 2004 - p163(1) [501+]

Sharpe, James - *Dick Turpin: The Myth of the English Highwayman*
CR - v285 - i1663 - August 2004 - p127(2) [501+]
Lon R Bks - v27 - i3 - Feb 3 2005 - p21(2) [501+]
TLS - i5267 - March 12 2004 - p8-8 [501+]
English Witchcraft, 1560-1736
JIH - v35 - i1 - Summer 2004 - p105-111 [501+]

Sharpe, Jenny - *Ghosts of Slavery: A Literary Archaeology of Black Women's Lives*
Biomag - v27 - i4 - Fall 2004 - p865(3) [501+]
JAH - v91 - i2 - Sept 2004 - p641(2) [501+]

Sharpe, Kevin - *Reading, Society, and Politics in Early Modern England*
Critm - v46 - i2 - Spring 2004 - p281(18) [501+]
Ren Q - v57 - i3 - Fall 2004 - p1128(4) [501+]
TLS - i5264 - Feb 20 2004 - p26-26 [501+]

Sharpe, Lesley - *The Cambridge Companion to Goethe*
GSR - v27 - i2 - May 2004 - p376-378 [501+]

Sharpe, Matthew - *Slavoj Zizek: A Little Piece of the Real*
R&R Bk N - v20 - i1 - Feb 2005 - p5(1) [501+]

Sharpe, Pamela - *Population and Society in an East Devon Parish: Reproducing Colyton, 1540-1840*
J Soc H - v38 - i1 - Fall 2004 - p257(3) [501+]

Sharpes, Donald K. - *Advanced Educational Foundations for Teachers: The History, Philosophy, and Culture of Schooling*
TCR - v107 - i2 - Feb 2005 - p322(3) [501+]

Sharples, Joseph - *Liverpool*
Choice - v42 - i4 - Dec 2004 - p653(1) [1-50]

Sharples, R.W. - *Perspectives on Greek Philosophy: S.V. Keeling Memorial Lectures in Ancient Philosophy, 1992-2002*
R&R Bk N - v19 - i1 - Feb 2004 - p1(1) [1-50]
Supplement to On the Soul
Choice - v42 - i6 - Feb 2005 - p1033(1) [51-500]

Sharratt, Mary - *The Real Minerva*
BL - v101 - i1 - Sept 1 2004 - p64(2) [51-500]
BW - v34 - i38 - Sept 19 2004 - p10(1) [501+]
KR - v72 - i16 - August 15 2004 - p774(1) [51-500]
PW - v251 - i36 - Sept 6 2004 - p47(1) [51-500]

Sharratt, Nick - *You Choose*
c TES - v0 - i4577 - April 2 2004 - p35(1) [501+]

Shattschneider, Doris - *Visions of Symmetry*
y Sch Lib - v52 - i4 - Winter 2004 - p220(1) [51-500]

Shattuck, Jessica - *The Hazards of Good Breeding*
Kliatt - v38 - i4 - July 2004 - p24(1) [51-500]

Shattuck, John - *Freedom on Fire: Human Rights Wars and America's Response*
Choice - v41 - i11-12 - July-August 2004 - p2123(1) [501+]

Shattuck, Roger - *The Innocent Eye: On Modern Literature and the Arts*
R&R Bk N - v19 - i1 - Feb 2004 - p242(1) [501+]
Proust's Way: A Field Guide to "In Search of Lost Time"
Sew R - v112 - i2 - Spring 2004 - p294-300 [501+]

Shatz, Adam - *Prophets Outcast: A Century of Dissident Jewish Writing About Zionism and Israel*
ABR - v26 - i2 - Jan-Feb 2005 - p27(2) [501+]

Shatz, David - *Mind, Body and Judaism: The Interaction of Jewish Law With Psychology and Biology*
SciTech - v28 - i3 - Sept 2004 - p4(1) [501+]

Shaughnessy, Dan - *The Legend of the Curse of the Bambino (Illus. by Payne, C.F.)*
c PW - v252 - i6 - Feb 7 2005 - p59(1) [51-500]
Reversing the Curse: Inside the 2004 Boston Red Sox
PW - v252 - i9 - Feb 28 2005 - p57(1) [51-500]

Shaughnessy, J. Michael - *Navigating through Probability in Grades 9-12*
SciTech - v28 - i3 - Sept 2004 - p36(1) [51-500]

Shaughnessy, Michael F. - *Education in the New Millenium: Not Like Your Grandmother's Schoolhouse*
R&R Bk N - v19 - i3 - August 2004 - p214(1) [1-50]

Shaughnessy, Robert - *The Shakespeare Effect: A History of Twentieth-Century Performance*
Shakes Q - v55 - i1 - Spring 2004 - p105-107 [501+]

Shavarini, Mitra K. - *Educating Immigrants: Experiences of Second-Generation Iranians*
R&R Bk N - v19 - i4 - Nov 2004 - p58(1) [51-500]

Shavelson, Richard J. - *Scientific Research in Education*
TCR - v106 - i2 - Feb 2004 - p329-337 [501+]

Shaver, Robert - *Rational Egoism*
Ethics - v115 - i1 - Oct 2004 - p191(1) [501+]

Shavinina, Larisa V. - *Beyond Knowledge: Extracognitive Aspects of Developing High Ability*
R&R Bk N - v19 - i3 - August 2004 - p8(1) [1-50]

Shaviro, Daniel - *Who Should Pay for Medicine*
Choice - v42 - i4 - Dec 2004 - p695(1) [1-50]

Shaviro, Steven - *Connected, or What It Means to Live in the Network Society*
ABR - v25 - i6 - Sept-Oct 2004 - p21(3) [501+]

Shaw, Allyson - *The Bon-Bon and Love Token*
Ant R - v63 - i1 - Wntr 2005 - p192(1) [51-500]

Shaw, Carolyn M. - *Cooperation, Conflict, and Consequences in the Organization of American States*
Choice - v42 - i5 - Jan 2005 - p931(2) [51-500]

Shaw, Catherine - *The Three-Body Problem*
BooChiTr - June 6 2004 - p4(1) [501+]

Shaw, Daniel - *Dark Thoughts: Philosophic Reflections on Cinematic Horror*
R&R Bk N - v19 - i1 - Feb 2004 - p225(1) [1-50]

Shaw, Dave (b. 1966 -) - *Here Comes the Roar*
VQR - v80 - i3 - Summer 2004 - p263(1) [1-50]

Shaw, David W. - *America's Victory: The Heroic Story of a Team of Ordinary Americans, and How They Won the Greatest Yacht Race Ever (Read by Cullen, Patrick). Audiobook Review*
Kliatt - v38 - i6 - Nov 2004 - p54(1) [51-500]
America's Victory: The Heroic Story of a Team of Ordinary Americans, and How They Won the Greatest Yacht Race Ever
R&R Bk N - v19 - i3 - August 2004 - p88(1) [51-500]

Shaw, Deborah - *Contemporary Cinema of Latin America: Ten Key Films*
Choice - v41 - i7 - March 2004 - p1303(1) [501+]

Shaw, George Bernard - *A Misalliance (Read by Stolz, Eric). Audiobook Review*
  LJ - v130 - i1 - Jan 1 2005 - p168(1) [501+]
Shaw, Gordon - *Keeping Mozart in Mind*
  M Ed J - v91 - i2 - Nov 2004 - p57(2) [501+]
Shaw, Harley G. - *Stalking the Big Bird: A Tale of Turkeys, Biologists, and Bureaucrats*
  E-Streams - Nov 2004 - pNA [501+]
  SciTech - v28 - i3 - Sept 2004 - p65(1) [51-500]
Shaw, Ian - *Constructions of Health and Illness: European Perspectives*
  SciTech - v28 - i3 - Sept 2004 - p82(1) [501+]
Shaw, Ian J. - *High Calvinists in Action: Calvinism and the City, Manchester and London, c. 1810-1860*
  CH - v73 - i4 - Dec 2004 - p868(3) [501+]
Shaw, Jane S. - *Energy*
  y SB - v40 - i4 - July-August 2004 - p161(2) [51-500]
Shaw, Jennifer L. - *Dream States: Puvis de Chavannes, Modernism, and the Fantasy of France*
  Art Bull - v86 - i3 - Sept 2004 - p609(6) [501+]
  NCFS - v32 - i3-4 - Spring-Summer 2004 - p379(2) [501+]
Shaw, Leon L. - *Processing and Properties of Structural Nanomaterials: Proceedings*
  SciTech - v28 - i1 - March 2004 - p141(1) [51-500]
Shaw, Leslee J. - *Coronary Disease in Women: Evidence-Based Diagnosis and Treatment*
  SciTech - v28 - i1 - March 2004 - p105(1) [51-500]
Shaw, Louise Grace - *The British Political Elite and the Soviet Union, 1937-1939*
  J Mil H - v68 - i3 - July 2004 - p987-988 [501+]
Shaw, Maria - *Maria Shaw's Book of Love: Horoscopes, Palmistry, Numbers, Candles, Genstones and Colors*
  c SLJ - v51 - i2 - Feb 2005 - p153(1) [51-500]
Shaw, Mark - *Book Report: Publishing Strategies, Writing Tips, and 101 Literary Ideas for Aspiring Authors and Poets*
  SLJ - v51 - i2 - Feb 2005 - p159(1) [501+]
  Grammar Report: Basic Writing Tools for Aspiring Authors and Poets
  SLJ - v51 - i2 - Feb 2005 - p159(1) [501+]
Shaw, Mark (b. 1969-) - *Crime and Policing in Post-Apartheid South Africa: Transforming Under Fire*
  HNet - August 2004 - pNA [501+]
Shaw, Mary - *Brady Brady and the MVP (Illus. by Temple, Chuck)*
  c Res Links - v10 - i2 - Dec 2004 - p10(1) [51-500]
Shaw, Matthew - *Great Scots! How the Scots Created Canada*
  Beav - v84 - i6 - Dec 2004 - p45(2) [501+]
  Mac - Feb 2 2004 - p55(1) [51-500]
Shaw, Maura D. - *Black Elk: Native Man of Spirit (Illus. by Marchesi, Stephen)*
  c BL - v101 - i8 - Dec 15 2004 - p742(1) [51-500]
  Dorothy Day: A Catholic Life of Action (Illus. by Marchesi, Stephen)
  c BL - v101 - i3 - Oct 1 2004 - p346(1) [51-500]
  Gandhi: India's Great Soul (Illus. by Marchesi, Stephen)
  c SLJ - v50 - i9 - Sept 2004 - p192(1) [51-500]
  The Keeners
  c PW - v252 - i6 - Feb 7 2005 - p40(1) [501+]
  Thich Nhat Hanh: Buddhism in Action (Illus. by Marchesi, Stephen)
  c SLJ - v50 - i9 - Sept 2004 - p192(1) [51-500]
Shaw, Milton C. - *Metal Cutting Principles. 2nd Ed.*
  SciTech - v28 - i3 - Sept 2004 - p151(1) [51-500]
Shaw, Nicola T. - *Computerization and Going Paperless in Canadian Primary Care*
  SciTech - v28 - i4 - Dec 2004 - p79(1) [51-500]
Shaw, Robert - *Classic Guitars*
  Bwatch - Jan 2005 - pNA [51-500]
  The Epidemic: The Rot of American Culture, Absentee and Permissive Parenting, and the Resultant Plague of Joyless, Selfish Children
  TES - v0 - i4587 - June 11 2004 - psss19(1) [501+]
Shaw, Rosalind - *Memories of the Slave Trade: Ritual and the Historical Imagination*
  JR - v84 - i4 - Oct 2004 - p672(2) [501+]
Shaw, Seyfarth - *Understanding the Federal Wage and Hour Laws: What Employees Must Know about the FLSA and Its Overtime Regulations*
  HR Mag - v50 - i2 - Feb 2005 - pS12(1) [501+]
  Understanding the Federal Wage & Hour Laws: What Employees Must Know about the FLSA and Its Overtime Regulations
  HR Mag - v49 - i11 - Nov 2004 - p145(1) [501+]

Shaw-Smith, David - *Traditional Crafts of Ireland*
  Am Craft - v64 - i2 - April-May 2004 - p36(1) [501+]
  Am Craft - v64 - i2 - April-May 2004 - p36(1) [501+]
Shaw, Stephen (b. 1950 -) - *Airline Marketing and Management*
  R&R Bk N - v19 - i3 - August 2004 - p122(1) [51-500]
Shaw, Stephen K. - *Franklin D. Roosevelt and the Transformation of the Supreme Court*
  Choice - v41 - i11-12 - July-August 2004 - p2125(1) [501+]
  R&R Bk N - v19 - i1 - Feb 2004 - pNA [51-500]
Shaw, Susan - *The Boy from the Basement*
  y BL - v101 - i6 - Nov 15 2004 - p574(1) [51-500]
  c CCB-B - v58 - i3 - Nov 2004 - p144(1) [501+]
  c CH Bwatch - Feb 2005 - pNA [51-500]
  y Kliatt - v38 - i5 - Sept 2004 - p16(2) [51-500]
  y KR - v72 - i18 - Sept 15 2004 - p920(1) [51-500]
  y SLJ - v50 - i11 - Nov 2004 - p154(1) [51-500]
  y VOYA - v27 - i5 - Dec 2004 - p396(1) [51-500]
Shaw, Susannah - *Stop Motion: Craft Skills for Model Animation*
  TimHES - v0 - i1647 - July 2 2004 - p28(1) [501+]
Shaw, Tony - *British Cinema and the Cold War: The State, Propaganda, and Consensus*
  J POP F&TV - v32 - i3 - Fall 2004 - p144(1) [501+]
Shaw, Tucker - *Confessions of a Backup Dancer*
  y PW - v251 - i31 - August 2 2004 - p72(1) [51-500]
  c SLJ - v50 - i8 - August 2004 - p115(1) [501+]
  Flavor of the Week
  y SLJ - v51 - i2 - Feb 2005 - p59(1) [51-500]
Shaw, Victor N. - *Substance Use and Abuse: Sociological Perspectives*
  CS - v33 - i2 - March 2004 - p257-259 [501+]
Shaw, Wendy M.K. - *Possessors and Possessed: Museums, Archaeology, and the Visualization of History in the Late Ottoman Empire*
  AHR - v109 - i2 - April 2004 - p652(2) [501+]
  Possessors and Possessed: Museums, Archaeology and the Visualization of History in the Late Ottoman Empire
  T&C - v45 - i3 - July 2004 - p666-668 [501+]
Shaw, William H. - *Business Ethics*
  R&R Bk N - v19 - i3 - August 2004 - p126(1) [51-500]
  Social and Personal Ethics, 5th Ed.
  R&R Bk N - v19 - i3 - August 2004 - p11(1) [1-50]
Shawcross, John T. - *The Arms of the Family: The Significance of John Milton's Relatives and Associates*
  Ren Q - v57 - i4 - Winter 2004 - p1532(2) [501+]
Shawcross, William - *Allies*
  TLS - i5263 - Feb 13 2004 - p6-6 [501+]
Shay, Anthony - *Choreographic Politics: State Folk Dance Companies, Representation and Power*
  Dance RJ - v35 - i2 - Winter 2003 - p200-203 [501+]
Shay, Kathryn - *On the Line*
  BL - v100 - i21 - July 2004 - p1827(1) [51-500]
Shay, William A. - *Understanding Data Communications and Networks, 3rd Ed.*
  SciTech - v28 - i1 - March 2004 - p158(1) [51-500]
Shaylor, Andrew - *Hell's Angels Motorcycle Club*
  PetPho - v33 - i10 - Feb 2005 - p18(1) [51-500]
Shaywitz, Sally - *Overcoming Dyslexia: A New and Complete Science-Based Program for Reading Problems at Any Level (Read by Fields, Anna). Audiobook Review*
  y Kliatt - v39 - i1 - Jan 2005 - p53(1) [51-500]
Shcheboleva, E.G. - *Svod pamiatnikov arkhitektury i monumental'nogo iskusstva Rossii: Ivanovskaia oblast'*
  Russ Rev - v63 - i3 - July 2004 - pNA [501+]
Shea, Kevin - *Barilko: Without a Trace*
  Globe & Mail - Oct 30 2004 - pD25 [51-500]
Shea, Kitty - *Cesar Chavez*
  c SLJ - v51 - i1 - Jan 2005 - p112(1) [51-500]
  Out and About at the Science Center (Illus. by Shipe, Becky)
  c SB - v40 - i4 - July-August 2004 - p172(1) [51-500]
  c SLJ - v50 - i12 - Dec 2004 - p137(1) [51-500]
  Out and About at the Vet Clinic (Illus. by Shipe, Becky)
  c SB - v40 - i4 - July-August 2004 - p182(1) [51-500]
  The Wright Brothers
  c SLJ - v51 - i1 - Jan 2005 - p112(1) [51-500]

Shea, Pegi Deitz - *The Carpet Boy's Gift (Illus. by Morin, Leane)*
  c CE - v81 - i1 - Fall 2004 - p47(1) [51-500]
  Tangled Threads: A Hmong Girl's Story
  y CE - v80 - i5 - Mid-Summer 2004 - p274(2) [51-500]
  Ten Mice for Tet (Illus. by Trang, Ngoc)
  c SLJ - v50 - i10 - Oct 2004 - pS22(1) [1-50]
  The Whispering Cloth
  c RT - v57 - Dec 2003 - p392 [51-500]
Shea, Renee H. - *Marcia Myers/Twenty Years: Paintings and Works on Paper*
  R&R Bk N - v19 - i3 - August 2004 - p243(1) [51-500]
Shea, William L. - *Vickburg is the Key: The Struggle for the Mississippi River*
  J Mil H - v68 - i3 - April 2004 - p608-609 [501+]
Shea, William M. - *The Lion and the Lamb: Evangelicals and Catholics in America*
  AM - v191 - i8 - Sept 27 2004 - p26 [501+]
  Choice - v42 - i4 - Dec 2004 - p680(2) [1-50]
  TT - v61 - i3 - Oct 2004 - p428(1) [501+]
Shea, William R. - *Galileo in Rome: The Rise and Fall of a Troublesome Genius*
  Ren Q - v57 - i3 - Fall 2004 - p1102(3) [501+]
Sheafer, Silvia Anne - *Aimee Semple McPherson*
  y SLJ - v50 - i10 - Oct 2004 - p190(1) [51-500]
Shean, Glenn D. - *Understanding and Treating Schizophrenia: Contemporary Research, Theory, and Practice*
  Choice - v41 - i11-12 - July-August 2004 - p2079(1) [501+]
  E-Streams - August 2004 - pNA [501+]
  What is Schizophrenia and How Can We Fix It?
  SciTech - v28 - i3 - Sept 2004 - p100(1) [51-500]
Sheard, Sally - *Body and City: Histories of Urban Public Health*
  J Urban H - v31 - i2 - Jan 2005 - p241-248 [501+]
Shearer, Alex - *The Fugitives*
  y Sch Lib - v52 - i3 - Autumn 2004 - p162(1) [501+]
  Lost
  y Magpies - v19 - i5 - Nov 2004 - p41(2) [501+]
  Sea Legs
  y Kliatt - v39 - i2 - March 2005 - p16(1) [51-500]
  y KR - v73 - i4 - Feb 15 2005 - p235(1) [51-500]
  c PW - v252 - i11 - March 14 2005 - p68(1) [51-500]
Shearer, Benjamin F. - *The United States: The Story of Statehood for the Fifty United States*
  BL - v101 - i6 - Nov 15 2004 - p615(1) [501+]
  The Uniting States: The Story of Statehood for the Fifty United States, Vols. 1-3
  LJ - v129 - i20 - Dec 1 2004 - p172(1) [51-500]
  R&R Bk N - v19 - i4 - Nov 2004 - p155(1) [51-500]
Shearer, Cynthia - *The Celestial Jukebox*
  BL - v101 - i7 - Dec 1 2004 - p637(1) [51-500]
  KR - v72 - i21 - Nov 1 2004 - p1028(1) [51-500]
  LJ - v129 - i20 - Dec 1 2004 - p103(1) [51-500]
Shearing, George - *Lullaby of Birdland*
  Choice - v42 - i2 - Oct 2004 - p303(1) [51-500]
Sheckels, Theodore F. - *The Island Motif in the Fiction of L.M. Montgomery, Margaret Laurence, Margaret Atwood, and Other Canadian Women Novelists*
  R&R Bk N - v19 - i1 - Feb 2004 - p240(1) [51-500]
Shecter, Lara - *Now and Then: The Coolest Scrapbook for School-Aged Children*
  c Res Links - v10 - i1 - Oct 2004 - p27(1) [501+]
Shecter, Relli - *Transitions in Domestic Consumption and Family Life in the Modern Middle East: Houses in Motion*
  MEJ - v58 - i4 - Autumn 2004 - p708(2) [501+]
Shectman, Jonathan - *Groundbreaking Scientific Experiments, Inventions, and Discoveries of the 18th Century*
  R&R Bk N - v19 - i1 - Feb 2004 - p248(1) [51-500]
Shedletsky, Leonard J. - *Human Communication on the Internet*
  R&R Bk N - v19 - i1 - Feb 2004 - p123(1) [51-500]
Sheehan, Arthur - *Father Damien and the Bells*
  c CI - v12 - i11 - Dec 2004 - p23(1) [501+]
Sheehan, Brett - *Trust in Troubled Times: Money, Banks, and State-Society Relations in Republican Tian-jin*
  AHR - v109 - i3 - June 2004 - p881(2) [501+]
Sheehan, Helena - *The Continuing Story of Irish Television Drama: Tracking the Tiger*
  R&R Bk N - v19 - i4 - Nov 2004 - p222(1) [501+]

Shoemperlen, Diane - *Names of the Dead: An Elegy for the Victims of September 11*
Globe & Mail - August 28 2004 - pD2 [501+]

Shogan, Robert - *The Battle of Blair Mountain: The Story of America's Largest Labor Uprising*
R&R Bk N - v19 - i3 - August 2004 - p115(1) [51-500]
Constant Conflict: Politics, Culture, and the Struggle for America's Future
R&R Bk N - v19 - i3 - August 2004 - p63(1) [51-500]

Shogren, Jason F. - *Experiments in Environmental Economics*
JEL - v42 - i1 - March 2004 - p338(1) [501+]

Shoham, Shlomo G. - *Tradition and Innovation in Crime and Criminal Justice*
R&R Bk N - v19 - i4 - Nov 2004 - p147(1) [501+]

Shojai, Slamack - *The Virtuous Vice: Globalization*
R&R Bk N - v19 - i3 - August 2004 - p123(1) [51-500]

Shoji, Toshiaki - *Representation Theory of Algebraic Groups and Quantum Groups; Proceedings*
SciTech - v28 - i3 - Sept 2004 - p41(1) [1-50]

Shollar, Leah Perl - *The Key under the Pillow (Illus. by Klineman, Harvey)*
c CH Bwatch - v14 - i7 - July 2004 - p2(1) [51-500]

Shone, Rob - *Harriet Tubman: The Life of an African-American Abolitionist*
PW - v252 - i9 - Feb 28 2005 - p44(1) [51-500]

Shone, Tom - *Blockbuster: How Hollywood Learned to Stop Worrying and Love the Summer*
BL - v101 - i6 - Nov 15 2004 - p538(1) [51-500]
Ent W - i795 - Dec 3 2004 - p97 [51-500]
KR - v72 - i18 - Sept 15 2004 - p906(1) [501+]
NS - v133 - i4709 - Oct 11 2004 - p50(2) [501+]
PW - v251 - i39 - Sept 27 2004 - p44(1) [51-500]
Spec - v296 - i9192 - Oct 9 2004 - p49(1) [501+]
TLS - i5304 - Nov 26 2004 - p36(1) [501+]

Shooting Star Comics - *Shooting Star Comics Anthology #4*
Bwatch - v26 - i7 - July 2004 - p12(1) [51-500]

Shoquist, Jennifer - *The Encyclopedia of Sexually Transmitted Diseases*
Choice - v41 - i11-12 - July-August 2004 - p2023(1) [501+]
E-Streams - August 2004 - pNA [501+]
SciTech - v28 - i1 - March 2004 - p90(1) [51-500]

Shore, Diane Z. - *Rosa Loves to Read (Illus. by Day, Larry)*
c SLJ - v50 - i8 - August 2004 - p90(1) [51-500]

Shore, Kenneth - *Elementary Teacher's Discipline Problem Solver: A Practical A-Z Guide for Managing Classroom Behavior Problems*
R&R Bk N - v19 - i3 - August 2004 - p225(1) [1-50]

Shores, Christopher - *Those Other Eagles: A Tribute to the British, Commonwealth and Free European Fighter Pilots Who Claimed between Two and Four Victories in Aerial Combat, 1939-1982*
CR - v286 - i1668 - Jan 2005 - p64(1) [51-500]

Shorris, Earl - *The Life and Times of Mexico*
BL - v100 - i21 - July 2004 - p1813(2) [51-500]
PW - v251 - i27 - July 5 2004 - p49(1) [51-500]

Short, Clare - *An Honourable Deception?: New Labour, Iraq and the Misuse of Power*
NS - v133 - i4714 - Nov 15 2004 - p52(2) [501+]

Short, Geoffrey - *Issues in Holocaust Education*
R&R Bk N - v19 - i4 - Nov 2004 - p34(1) [51-500]

A Short History of Progress
Globe & Mail - March 5 2005 - pD17 [51-500]

Short, John Rennie - *Making Space: Revisioning the World, 1475-1600*
Choice - v42 - i4 - Dec 2004 - p713(1) [1-50]
R&R Bk N - v19 - i3 - August 2004 - p80(1) [51-500]

Short, Philip - *In Pursuit of Plants: Experiences of Nineteenth and Early Twentieth Century Plant Collectors*
SciTech - v28 - i3 - Sept 2004 - p61(1) [51-500]
Pol Pot: Anatomy of a Nightmare
BL - v101 - i8 - Dec 15 2004 - p703(1) [51-500]
HM - v310 - i1857 - Feb 2005 - p83(2) [51-500]
KR - v72 - i22 - Nov 15 2004 - p1084(1) [501+]
LJ - v129 - i20 - Dec 1 2004 - p138(1) [51-500]
NYTBR - Feb 27 2005 - p8 [501+]
Pol Pot: The History of a Nightmare
Econ - v373 - i8400 - Nov 6 2004 - p90US [501+]
Spec - v296 - i9193 - Oct 16 2004 - p75(1) [501+]
TimHES - v0 - i1680 - Feb 25 2005 - p26(2) [501+]

Short, Robert L. - *The Gospel According to Peanuts, 35th Anniversary Ed.*
Bks & Cult - v11 - i1 - Jan-Feb 2005 - p16(2) [501+]

Short, T.A. - *Electric Power Distribution Handbook*
E-Streams - Sept 2004 - pNA [501+]
SciTech - v28 - i1 - March 2004 - p152(1) [51-500]

Shortle, James S. - *Irrigated Agriculture and the Environment*
NRJ - v44 - i2 - Spring 2004 - p654-656 [501+]

Shorto, Russell - *The Island at the Center of the World: The Epic Story of Dutch Manhattan and the Forgotten Colony That Shaped America*
AM - v191 - i1 - July 5 2004 - p26 [501+]
Choice - v42 - i4 - Dec 2004 - p724(2) [1-50]
New York - v37 - i17 - May 17 2004 - p52(4) [501+]
NYRB - v51 - i17 - Nov 4 2004 - p35(3) [501+]
The Island at the Center of the World: The Epic Story of Dutch Manhattan and the Forgotten Colony That Shaped America (Read by Ganser, L.J.). Audiobook Review
PW - v251 - i40 - Oct 4 2004 - p32(1) [51-500]
The Island at the Centre of the World: The Untold Story of Dutch Manhattan and the Founding of New York
TLS - i5292 - Sept 3 2004 - p23(1) [501+]

Shortridge, James R. - *Cities on the Plains: The Evolution of Urban Kansas*
Choice - v42 - i6 - Feb 2005 - p1084(1) [51-500]

Shortt, Colette - *Handbook of Functional Dairy Products*
E-Streams - Sept 2004 - pNA [501+]
SciTech - v28 - i3 - Sept 2004 - p69(1) [51-500]

Shostak, Arthur B. - *In the Shadow of War*
y SLJ - v50 - i11 - Nov 2004 - p172(1) [51-500]
Making War/Making Peace
y SLJ - v50 - i11 - Nov 2004 - p172(1) [51-500]
Trade Towers/War Clouds
y SLJ - v50 - i11 - Nov 2004 - p172(1) [51-500]

Shostak, Debra B. - *Philip Roth: Countertexts, Counterlives*
Choice - v42 - i5 - Jan 2005 - p855(2) [1-50]
R&R Bk N - v19 - i4 - Nov 2004 - p244(1) [501+]
TLS - i5303 - Nov 19 2004 - p37(1) [51-500]

Shostak, Seth - *Cosmic Company: The Search for Life in the Universe*
QRB - v79 - i4 - Dec 2004 - p410(2) [501+]

Shotter, David - *Rome and Her Empire*
Class R - v54 - i2 - Nov 2004 - p572(2) [501+]
R&R Bk N - v19 - i3 - August 2004 - p44(1) [51-500]

Shotwell, David J. - *Glass A to Z*
R&R Bk N - v19 - i1 - Feb 2004 - p207(1) [51-500]

Should I Say Anything? How to Decide
SLJ - v50 - i12 - Dec 2004 - p66(1) [501+]

Showalter, Dennis E. - *Patton and Rommel: Men of War in the Twentieth Century*
PW - v252 - i10 - March 7 2005 - p63(1) [51-500]
Tannenberg: Clash of Empires, 1914
R&R Bk N - v19 - i3 - August 2004 - p32(1) [51-500]
The Wars of German Unification
TLS - i5301 - Nov 5 2004 - p12(1) [501+]

Showers, Paul - *A Drop of Blood (Illus. by Miller, Edward)*
c BL - v100 - i22 - August 2004 - p1939(2) [51-500]
c SB - v40 - i5 - Sept-Oct 2004 - p225(2) [51-500]
c SLJ - v50 - i7 - July 2004 - p96(1) [51-500]

Shraer-Petrov, David - *Forma liubvi: Izbrannaia lirika*
WLT - v78 - i3-4 - Sept-Dec 2004 - p138(2) [501+]

Shrawan, Kumar - *Muscle Strength*
SciTech - v28 - i3 - Sept 2004 - p70(1) [51-500]

Shreeve, James - *The Genome War: How Craig Venter Tried to Capture the Code of Life and Save the World (Read by Gardner, Grover). Audiobook Review*
Kliatt - v38 - i6 - Nov 2004 - p56(1) [51-500]
The Genome War: How Craig Venter Tried to Capture the Code of Life and Save the World
Am Sci - v92 - i4 - July-August 2004 - p376(3) [501+]
Choice - v42 - i1 - Sept 2004 - p130(1) [501+]
Globe & Mail - Sept 11 2004 - pD21 [1-50]
KR - v72 - i24 - Dec 15 2004 - pS5(1) [501+]
SB - v40 - i3 - May-June 2004 - p115(1) [501+]
SB - v40 - i6 - Nov-Dec 2004 - p242(1) [51-500]

Shreiner, David - *OpenGL Programming Guide: The Official Guide to Learning OpenGL, Version 1.4, 4th Ed.*
SciTech - v28 - i3 - Sept 2004 - p136(1) [51-500]

Shrestha, Anil - *Cropping Systems: Trends and Advances*
Choice - v42 - i1 - Sept 2004 - p128(1) [501+]

Shrestha, Nanda R. - *Historical Dictionary of Nepal*
R&R Bk N - v19 - i1 - Feb 2004 - p47(1) [51-500]

Shreve, Anita - *Light on Snow*
y BL - v100 - i22 - August 2004 - p1872(2) [51-500]
BW - v34 - i45 - Nov 7 2004 - p10(1) [51-500]
Ent W - i788 - Oct 15 2004 - p78 [51-500]
KR - v72 - i15 - August 1 2004 - p712(1) [501+]
LJ - v129 - i15 - Sept 15 2004 - p50(2) [51-500]
NYTBR - Dec 19 2004 - p23 [501+]
People - v62 - i19 - Nov 8 2004 - p57 [51-500]
PW - v251 - i38 - Sept 20 2004 - p44(1) [51-500]
SLJ - v50 - i12 - Dec 2004 - p175(1) [51-500]

Shreve, Porter - *Drives Like a Dream*
BL - v101 - i2 - Sept 15 2004 - p210(1) [501+]
KR - v72 - i24 - Dec 15 2004 - p1162(1) [501+]
LJ - v130 - i1 - Jan 1 2005 - p92(1) [51-500]

Shreve, Susan - *Under the Watsons' Porch*
c BL - v100 - i21 - July 2004 - p1843(1) [1-50]
y BL - v101 - i2 - Sept 15 2004 - p236(1) [51-500]
c CCB-B - v57 - i11 - July-August 2004 - p483(2) [501+]
c CH Bwatch - v14 - i8 - August 2004 - p2(1) [51-500]
c PW - v251 - i29 - July 19 2004 - p162(1) [51-500]
c SLJ - v50 - i8 - August 2004 - p128(2) [51-500]
y VOYA - v27 - i5 - Dec 2004 - p396(1) [51-500]

Shriver, Gary - *Unfaithful: Rebuilding Trust After Infidelity*
PW - v252 - i11 - March 14 2005 - p63(1) [51-500]

Shriver, Maria - *What's Happening to Grandpa? (Illus. by Speidel, Sandra)*
c BL - v100 - i22 - August 2004 - p1943(1) [501+]
c SLJ - v50 - i8 - August 2004 - p94(1) [51-500]

Shrm Information Center - *Preventing Harassment: Federal Employment Law, Vol. III*
HR Mag - v49 - i7 - July 2004 - pS31(1) [501+]

Shrock, Cheryl R. - *Exercise Workbook for Beginning AutoCAD: 2005*
SciTech - v28 - i4 - Dec 2004 - p130 [51-500]

Shrock, Joel - *The Gilded Age*
BL - v101 - i9-10 - Jan 1 2005 - p888(1) [501+]
R&R Bk N - v19 - i3 - August 2004 - p63(1) [51-500]

Shropshire, Mike - *When the Tuna Went Down to Texas: How Bill Parcells Led the Cowboys Back to the Promised Land*
PW - v251 - i32 - August 9 2004 - p246(1) [51-500]

Shrum, L.J. - *The Psychology of Entertainment Media: Blurring the Lines Between Entertainment and Persuasion*
R&R Bk N - v19 - i1 - Feb 2004 - p114(1) [51-500]

Shryock, Andrew - *Off Stage/On Display: Intimacy and Ethnography in the Age of Public Culture*
R&R Bk N - v19 - i4 - Nov 2004 - p76(1) [51-500]

Shteir, Rachel - *Striptease: The Untold History of the Girlie Show*
BW - v34 - i51 - Dec 19 2004 - p2(1) [501+]
Globe & Mail - Jan 22 2005 - pD8 [501+]
KR - v72 - i18 - Sept 15 2004 - p907(1) [501+]
NY - v81 - i2 - Feb 28 2005 - p086 [501+]
PW - v251 - i43 - Oct 25 2004 - p36(1) [51-500]

Shtern, Ludmila - *Brodsky: A Personal Memoir*
BL - v101 - i4 - Oct 15 2004 - p379(2) [51-500]
BW - v34 - i47 - Nov 21 2004 - p13(1) [501+]
NY - v80 - i33 - Nov 1 2004 - pNA105(1) [1-50]
PW - v251 - i36 - Sept 6 2004 - p56(1) [51-500]

Shtromas, Aleksandras - *Totalitarianism and the Prospects for World Order: Closing the Door on the Twentieth Century*
R&R Bk N - v19 - i1 - Feb 2004 - p149(1) [51-500]

Shtub, Avraham - *Project Management: Processes, Methodologies, and Economics, 2nd Ed.*
SciTech - v28 - i4 - Dec 2004 - p132 [51-500]

Shu, Jennifer - *Baby and Child Health*
BL - v101 - i7 - Dec 1 2004 - p684(1) [1-50]

Shuck, Glenn W. - *Marks of the Beast: The Left Behind Novels and the Struggle for Evangelical Identity*
PW - v251 - i45 - Nov 8 2004 - p53(1) [51-500]

Shugart, H.H. - *How the Earthquake Bird Got Its Name and Other Tales of an Unbalanced Nature*
BL - v101 - i9-10 - Jan 1 2005 - p796(1) [51-500]
New Sci - v185 - i2490 - March 12 2005 - p50(2) [501+]
PW - v251 - i48 - Nov 29 2004 - p31(2) [51-500]

Shuger, Debora Kuller - *Political Theologies in Shakespeare's England: The Sacred and the State in Measure for Measure*
Six Ct J - v35 - i1 - Spring 2004 - p269(2) [501+]

Shukman, Harold - *Redefining Stalinism*
R&R Bk N - v19 - i1 - Feb 2004 - p38(1) [1-50]

Shukman, Henry - *Darien Dogs*
Spec - v295 - i9186 - August 28 2004 - p29(2) [501+]

Shuldham-Shaw, Patrick - *The Greig-Duncan Folk Song Collection. Volume 8*
Folkl - v115 - i3 - Dec 2004 - p379(2) [501+]

Shulevitz, Uri - *The Travels of Benjamin of Tudela: Through Three Continents in the Twelfth Century (Illus. by Shulevitz, Uri)*
c HB - v81 - i2 - March-April 2005 - p217(1) [501+]
c KR - v73 - i5 - March 1 2005 - p295(1) [51-500]

Shull, Jodie A. - *Georgia O'Keeffe: Legendary American Painter*
c BL - v101 - i5 - Nov 1 2004 - p495(1) [51-500]

Shulman, Joey - *Winning the Food Fight: Every Parent's Guide to Raising a Healthy Happy Child*
CBRA - Annual 2003 - p434(1) [501+]

Shulman, Lee S. - *Teaching as Community Property: Essays on Higher Education*
TCR - v106 - i12 - Dec 2004 - p2297(4) [501+]
The Wisdom of Practice: Essays on Teaching, Learning, and Learning to Teach
Choice - v42 - i3 - Nov 2004 - p536(2) [1-50]
R&R Bk N - v19 - i3 - August 2004 - p215(1) [1-50]

Shulman, Lisa - *The Matzo Ball Boy (Illus. by Litzinger, Rosanne)*
c HB - v81 - i2 - March-April 2005 - p212(1) [51-500]
c KR - v73 - i1 - Jan 1 2005 - p57(1) [51-500]
Old MacDonald Had a Woodshop (Illus. by Wolff, Ashley)
c PW - v251 - i48 - Nov 29 2004 - p42(1) [51-500]

Shulman, Mark - *Attack of the Killer Video Book: Tips and Tricks for Young Directors (Illus. by Newbigging, Martha)*
y VOYA - v27 - i3 - August 2004 - p242(1) [1-50]
Fillmore and Geary Take Off! (Illus. by Fickling, Phillip)
c KR - v72 - i19 - Oct 1 2004 - p969(1) [51-500]
c PW - v251 - i50 - Dec 13 2004 - p67(1) [51-500]

Shulman, Nicola - *A Rage for Rock Gardening: The Story of Reginald Farrer: Gardener, Writer, and Plant Collector*
BL - v101 - i4 - Oct 15 2004 - p372(1) [51-500]
PW - v251 - i38 - Sept 20 2004 - p55(1) [51-500]

Shulman, Polly - *The Curse of the Pharaohs: My Adventures with Mummies*
Arch - v57 - i5 - Sept-Oct 2004 - p53-53 [501+]
Hidden Treasures of Ancient Egypt
Arch - v57 - i5 - Sept-Oct 2004 - p53-53 [501+]

Shulman, Seth - *Scientific Integrity in Policymaking: An Investigation into the Bush Administration's Misuse of Science*
NYRB - v51 - i18 - Nov 18 2004 - p38(3) [501+]

Shults, F. LeRon - *Reforming Theological Anthropology: After the Philosophical Turn to Relationality*
Theol St - v65 - i4 - Dec 2004 - p900(1) [501+]
TT - v61 - i3 - Oct 2004 - p428(2) [501+]

Shultz, Kenneth S. - *Measurement Theory in Action: Case Studies and Exercises*
R&R Bk N - v19 - i4 - Nov 2004 - p9(1) [51-500]

Shumaker, Robert W. - *Primates in Question: The Smithsonian Answer Book (Illus. by Ellis, Gerry)*
QRB - v79 - i4 - Dec 2004 - p442(1) [501+]
SciTech - v28 - i1 - March 2004 - p70(1) [51-500]

Shumaker, Terence M. - *AutoCAD and Its Applications, Comprehensive 2004 Ed.*
SciTech - v28 - i1 - March 2004 - p135(1) [51-500]

Shuman, Carol - *Jenny Is Scared!*
c CH Bwatch - v14 - i12 - Dec 2004 - pNA [51-500]

Shuman, Daniel W. - *Law and Mental Health Professionals: Texas, 3rd Ed.*
SciTech - v28 - i3 - Sept 2004 - p12(1) [501+]

Shumate, David - *High Water Mark*
NYTBR - Jan 9 2005 - p19 [501+]

Shumovsky, A.S. - *Quantum Communication and Information Technologies*
SciTech - v28 - i1 - March 2004 - p154(1) [51-500]

Shumway, David R. - *Modern Love: Romance, Intimacy, and the Marriage Crisis*
JAH - v91 - i3 - Dec 2004 - p1101(2) [501+]
JAH - v91 - i3 - Dec 2004 - p1101(2) [501+]

Shurei, Kouyu - *Alichino, Vol. 1*
PW - v252 - i7 - Feb 14 2005 - p56(1) [51-500]

Shushkevich, Val - *The Real Winnie: A One-of-a-Kind Bear*
Beav - v84 - i4 - August-Sept 2004 - p48(2) [51-500]
CBRA - Annual 2003 - p406(1) [501+]

Shuster, Carl N., Jr. - *The American Horseshoe Crab*
Choice - v42 - i1 - Sept 2004 - p131(1) [501+]

Shuster, Stephen M. - *Mating Systems and Strategies*
QRB - v79 - i3 - Sept 2004 - p333(3) [501+]

Shuster, William George - *Legacy of Leadership: A History of the Gemological Institute of America*
Choice - v41 - i11-12 - July-August 2004 - p2066(1) [501+]

Shusterman, Neal - *Full Tilt: A Novel*
y Kliatt - v38 - i5 - Sept 2004 - p32(2) [51-500]
The Schwa Was Here
y BL - v101 - i7 - Dec 1 2004 - p648(1) [51-500]
y CCB-B - v58 - i4 - Dec 2004 - p184(1) [51-500]
y Kliatt - v38 - i5 - Sept 2004 - p16(2) [51-500]
y KR - v72 - i19 - Oct 1 2004 - p969(1) [51-500]
y SLJ - v50 - i10 - Oct 2004 - p176(2) [51-500]
y VOYA - v27 - i4 - Oct 2004 - p320(1) [51-500]

Shusterman, Richard - *Performing Live: Aesthetic Alternatives for the Ends of Art*
JAAC - v62 - i3 - Summer 2004 - p300-302 [501+]

Shut Up and Listen: The Truth about How to Communicate at Work (
Bwatch - March 2005 - pNA [51-500]

Shuter, Jane - *Cycle Power: Two-Wheeled Travel Past and Present*
Sch Lib - v52 - i3 - Autumn 2004 - p153 [501+]

Shutt, Timothy B. - *Monsters, Gods and Heroes: Approaching the Epic in Literature. Audiobook Review*
BL - v101 - i6 - Nov 15 2004 - p606(1) [501+]
BL - v101 - i6 - Nov 15 2004 - p606(1) [501+]

Shuttleworth, Antony - *And in Our Time: Vision, Revision, and British Writing of the 1930's*
RES - v55 - i221 - Sept 2004 - p639(2) [501+]

Shuzo, Kuki - *The Structure of Detachment: The Aesthetic Vision of Kuki Shuzo*
R&R Bk N - v19 - i3 - August 2004 - p6(1) [1-50]

Shwartz, Ronald B. - *For the Love of Books: 115 Celebrated Writers on the Books They Love Most*
Globe & Mail - Nov 27 2004 - pD49 [51-500]

Shwartz, Susan - *Hostile Takeover*
KR - v72 - i19 - Oct 1 2004 - p944(1) [501+]
PW - v251 - i47 - Nov 22 2004 - p43(1) [51-500]
LJ - v129 - i20 - Dec 1 2004 - p105(1) [51-500]

Shweder, Richard - *Engaging Cultural Differences: The Multicultural Challenge in Liberal Democracies*
CS - v33 - i6 - Nov 2004 - p749(1) [1-50]

Si, Jennie - *Handbook of Learning and Approximate Dynamic Programming*
SciTech - v28 - i4 - Dec 2004 - p128 [51-500]

Siafakas, Nikos M. - *Acute Exacerbations of Chronic Obstructive Pulmonary Disease*
SciTech - v28 - i1 - March 2004 - p105(1) [51-500]

Siamon, Sharon - *Brave Horse*
c Res Links - v10 - i1 - Oct 2004 - p20(1) [51-500]

Sibberson, Franki - *Still Learning to Read: Teaching Students in Grades 3-6*
SLJ - v50 - i10 - Oct 2004 - pS75(1) [51-500]

Sibeon, Roger - *Rethinking Social Theory*
Choice - v42 - i4 - Dec 2004 - p743(1) [1-50]
R&R Bk N - v19 - i3 - August 2004 - p91(1) [51-500]

Sibinga, C.Th. Smit - *Cellular Engineering and Cellular Therapies: Proceedings*
SciTech - v28 - i1 - March 2004 - p87(1) [51-500]

Sibley, Brian - *The Maps of Tolkien's Middle-Earth, Vols. 1-2 (Illus. by Howe, John)*
R&R Bk N - v19 - i1 - Feb 2004 - p240(1) [51-500]

Sibley, Frank - *Approach to Aesthetics: Collected Papers on Philosophical Aesthetics*
Phil R - v112 - i4 - Oct 2003 - p580(7) [501+]

Sibley, Katherine A.S. - *Red Spies in America: Stolen Secrets and the Dawn of the Cold War*
LJ - v129 - i17 - Oct 15 2004 - p75(1) [51-500]

Sibly, W.A. - *The Chronicle of William of Puylaurens: The Albigensian Crusade and its Aftermath*
HER - v119 - i483 - Sept 2004 - p1033(2) [501+]
HER - v119 - i483 - Sept 2004 - p1033(2) [501+]
Med R - July 2004 - pNA [501+]

Sica, Alan - *Max Weber: A Comprehensive Bibliography*
Choice - v42 - i1 - Sept 2004 - p82(1) [501+]
Max Weber & the New Century
Choice - v42 - i1 - Sept 2004 - p82(1) [501+]

Sicher, Efraim - *Holocaust Novelists*
Choice - v42 - i7 - March 2005 - p1196(1) [51-500]
Rereading the City/Rereading Dickens: Representation, the Novel, and Urban Realism
RES - v55 - i219 - April 2004 - p291-292 [501+]

Sicile-Kira, Chantal - *Autism Spectrum Disorders*
LJ - v129 - i15 - Sept 15 2004 - p71(1) [51-500]

Siciliano, Rocco C. - *Walking on Sand: The Story of an Immigrant Son and the Forgotten Art of Public Service*
R&R Bk N - v19 - i4 - Nov 2004 - p63(1) [1-50]

Sickels, Robert J. - *The 1940s*
R&R Bk N - v19 - i3 - August 2004 - p62(1) [51-500]

Sicker, Martin - *The Rise and Fall of Ancient Israeli States*
R&R Bk N - v19 - i1 - Feb 2004 - p43(1) [51-500]

Sicking, Louis - *Neptune and the Netherlands: State, Economy, and War at Sea in the Renaissance*
R&R Bk N - v19 - i3 - August 2004 - p45(1) [51-500]

Siddiqi, Asif A. - *The Soviet Space Race with Apollo*
Russ Rev - v63 - i3 - July 2004 - pNA [501+]
Sputnik and the Soviet Space Challenge
Russ Rev - v63 - i3 - July 2004 - pNA [501+]

Siddons, Anne Rivers - *Islands (Read by Fleming, Kate). Audiobook Review*
BL - v101 - i3 - Oct 1 2004 - p351(1) [51-500]

Sidebottom, Charles - *International Labeling Requirements for Medical Devices, Medical Equipment, and Diagnostic Products, 2nd Ed.*
SciTech - v28 - i1 - March 2004 - p81(1) [51-500]

Sidebottom, Harry - *Ancient Warfare: A Very Short Introduction*
CR - v286 - i1669 - Feb 2005 - p121(1) [51-500]

Sider, Gerald - *Between History and Tomorrow: Making and Breaking Everyday Life in Rural Newfoundland*
CBRA - Annual 2003 - p351(2) [501+]
Living Indian Histories: Lumbee and Tuscaroa People in North Carolina
CS - v33 - i5 - Sept 2004 - p626-627 [501+]
Living Indian Histories: Lumbee and Tuscarora People in North Carolina
JSH - v70 - i4 - Nov 2004 - p987(1) [501+]

Sider, Ronald J. - *The Scandal of the Evangelical Conscience: Why Are Christians Living Just Like the Rest of the World?*
Ch Today - v49 - i3 - March 2005 - p84(1) [51-500]
PW - v252 - i3 - Jan 17 2005 - p53(1) [51-500]

Sideri, Simona - *Let's Look at Eyes (Illus. by Noble, Sheilagh)*
c BL - v101 - i9-10 - Jan 1 2005 - p866(1) [51-500]

Sideris, Lisa H. - *Environmental Ethics, Ecological Theology, and Natural Selection*
Env - v46 - i9 - Nov 2004 - p41(2) [501+]

Siderits, Mark - *Personal Identity and Buddhist Philosophy: Empty Persons*
R&R Bk N - v19 - i1 - Feb 2004 - p6(1) [51-500]

Sides, Josh - *L.A. City Limits: African American Los Angeles from the Great Depression to the Present*
Black Iss - v7 - i2 - March-April 2005 - p40(2) [501+]
Choice - v42 - i2 - Oct 2004 - p353(1) [501+]
HNet - Sept 2004 - pNA [501+]
PHR - v73 - i4 - Nov 2004 - p686(2) [501+]
RAH - v32 - i4 - Dec 2004 - p545-551 [501+]
Soc Ser R - v79 - i1 - March 2005 - p193(5) [501+]

Sidi, A. - *Practical Extrapolation Methods, Theory and Applications*
SIAM Rev - v46 - i2 - June 2004 - p360-362 [501+]

Sidlow, Edward I. - *Challenging the Incumbent: An Underdog's Undertaking*
R&R Bk N - v19 - i1 - Feb 2004 - pNA [51-500]

Sidman, Joyce - *The World According to Dog: Poems and Teen Voices*
y Teach Lib - v32 - i1 - Oct 2004 - p10(1) [51-500]

Sidney, Mara S. - *Unfair Housing: How National Policy Shapes Community Action*
Soc Ser R - v79 - i1 - March 2005 - p181(5) [501+]

Sidor, Steven - *Skin River*
LJ - v129 - i13 - August 2004 - p60(1) [501+]
BL - v100 - i22 - August 2004 - p1907(1) [51-500]
KR - v72 - i14 - July 15 2004 - p664(1) [51-500]

Sidorenko, Alexandra - *Regulation and Market Access*
R&R Bk N - v19 - i3 - August 2004 - p100(1) [51-500]

Sie, Maureen - *Reasons of One's Own*
R&R Bk N - v19 - i4 - Nov 2004 - p3(1) [51-500]

Siebels, Don - *The Quality Improvement Glossary*
Choice - v42 - i6 - Feb 2005 - p1006(1) [51-500]
R&R Bk N - v19 - i3 - August 2004 - p108(1) [51-500]

Siebenschuh, William R. - *The Struggle for Education in Modern Tibet: The Three Thousand Children of Tashi Tsering*
R&R Bk N - v19 - i1 - Feb 2004 - pNA [51-500]

Silver, Timothy - *Mount Mitchell and the Black Mountains: An Environmental History of the Highest Peaks in Eastern America*
> AHR - v109 - i4 - Oct 2004 - p1227(2) [501+]
> Hist Geo - v32 - Annual 2004 - p217(2) [501+]

Silvera, Makeda - *The Heart Does Not Bend*
> Can Lit - i181 - Summer 2004 - p175-176 [501+]

Silverberg, Robert - *Legends II: New Short Novels by the Masters of Modern Fantasy*
> y   VOYA - v27 - i4 - Oct 2004 - p316(1) [51-500]
> *Star of the Gypsies*
> LJ - v130 - i3 - Feb 15 2005 - p172(1) [1-50]

Silverman, Erica - *Sholom's Treasure: How Sholom Aleichem Became a Writer (Illus. by Gerstein, Mordicai)*
> c   HB - v81 - i2 - March-April 2005 - p218(1) [51-500]
> c   KR - v73 - i3 - Feb 1 2005 - p182(1) [51-500]
> *When the Chickens Went on Strike*
> LibMed - v22 - i6 - March 2004 - p59(1) [501+]

Silverman, Franklin - *Collegiality and Service for Tenure and Beyond: Acquiring a Reputation as a Team Player*
> R&R Bk N - v19 - i1 - Feb 2004 - p185(1) [51-500]

Silverman, Helaine - *Ancient Nasca Settlement and Society*
> Lat Ant - v15 - i4 - Dec 2004 - p470(3) [501+]
> *Andean Archeology*
> Choice - v42 - i7 - March 2005 - p1268(2) [51-500]

Silverman, Jeff - *Yuk Yuk's Joke Books, Vol. 1*
> CBRA - Annual 2003 - p87(1) [51-500]
> *Yuk Yuk's Joke Books, Vol. 2*
> CBRA - Annual 2003 - p87(1) [51-500]
> *Yuk Yuk's Joke Books, Vol. 3*
> CBRA - Annual 2003 - p87(1) [51-500]

Silverman, Kenneth - *Lightning Man: The Accursed Life of Samuel F.B. Morse*
> Bwatch - v26 - i7 - July 2004 - p10(1) [501+]
> SciTech - v28 - i1 - March 2004 - p158(1) [51-500]

Silverman, Sydel - *Totems and Tachers: Key Figures in the History of Anthropology, 2nd Ed.*
> R&R Bk N - v19 - i1 - Feb 2004 - p71(1) [1-50]

Silvers, Robert B. - *Striking Terror: America's New War*
> HNet - June 2004 - pNA [501+]

Silversides, Ann - *AIDS Activist: Michael Lynch and the Politics of Community*
> CBRA - Annual 2003 - p434(2) [501+]

Silverstein, Clara - *White Girl: A Story of School Desegregation*
> LJ - v129 - i14 - Sept 1 2004 - p166(1) [51-500]
> PW - v251 - i29 - July 19 2004 - p154(1) [51-500]

Silverstein, Ken - *The Radioactive Boy Scout: The True Story of a Boy and His Backyard Nuclear Reactor*
> BL - v101 - i9-10 - Jan 1 2005 - p771(1) [51-500]
> New Sci - v183 - i2461 - August 21 2004 - p50(1) [501+]
> y   SLJ - v50 - i10 - Oct 2004 - p200(2) [51-500]

Silverstein, Shel - *Runny Babbit: A Billy Sook (Illus. by Silverstein, Shel)*
> c   KR - v73 - i5 - March 1 2005 - p295(1) [51-500]
> c   PW - v252 - i3 - Jan 17 2005 - p54(1) [51-500]

Silverthorne, Judith - *Dinosaur Breakout*
> c   Kliatt - v38 - i6 - Nov 2004 - p24(1) [501+]
> *Dinosaur Hideout*
> c   CBRA - Annual 2003 - p512(2) [501+]
> *Five Stars for Emily*
> c   Res Links - v10 - i1 - Oct 2004 - p20(1) [51-500]

Silvertown, Jonathan - *Integrating Ecology and Evolution in a Spatial Context*
> QRB - v79 - i3 - Sept 2004 - p331(1) [501+]

Silvester, Jeremy - *Words Cannot Be Found. German Colonial Rule in Namibia: An Annotated Report of the 1918 Blue Book*
> IJAHS - v37 - i1 - Wntr 2004 - p125-127 [501+]

Silvey, Anita - *100 Best Books for Children*
> BL - v100 - i21 - July 2004 - p1802(1) [1-50]
> CCB-B - v58 - i1 - Sept 2004 - p50(1) [51-500]
> HB - v80 - i4 - July-August 2004 - p473(1) [51-500]
> SLJ - v51 - i2 - Feb 2005 - p160(1) [51-500]

Silvey, Le Anne E. - *Ordinal Position and Role Development of the Firstborn American Indian Daughter Within Her Family of Origin*
> R&R Bk N - v19 - i3 - August 2004 - p61(1) [51-500]

Silvis, Randall - *Heart So Hungry: The Extraordinary Expedition of Mina Hubbard into the Labrador Wilderness*
> Beav - v84 - i6 - Dec 2004 - p50(2) [501+]
> Globe & Mail - Nov 13 2004 - pD3 [501+]

Sim, Valerie - *Tarot Outside the Box*
> Bwatch - Jan 2005 - pNA [501+]
> Bwatch - Feb 2005 - pNA [501+]

Sima, Judy - *Raising Voices: Creating Youth Storytelling Groups and Troupes*
> LibMed - v22 - i5 - Feb 2004 - p85(1) [501+]
> VOYA - v27 - i4 - Oct 2004 - p267(1) [51-500]

Simak, Clifford D. - *Way Station*
> LJ - v129 - i19 - Nov 15 2004 - p103(1) [501+]

Simerka, Barbara A. - *Discourses of Empire: Counter-Epic Literature in Early Modern Spain*
> Ren Q - v57 - i3 - Fall 2004 - p1010(3) [501+]
> VQR - v80 - i1 - Wntr 2004 - p268-269 [501+]
> VQR - v80 - i1 - Wntr 2004 - p268-269 [501+]

Simester, A.P. - *Criminal Law: Theory and Doctrine, 2nd Ed.*
> R&R Bk N - v19 - i1 - Feb 2004 - pNA [51-500]

Simic, Charles - *The Metaphysician in the Dark*
> TLS - i5266 - March 5 2004 - p11-11 [501+]
> *My Noiseless Entourage*
> PW - v252 - i4 - Jan 24 2005 - p236(1) [501+]
> *The Voice at 3:00 A.M.: Selected Late and New Poems*
> TLS - i5266 - March 5 2004 - p11-11 [501+]
> WLT - v79 - i1 - Jan-April 2005 - p90(1) [51-500]

Simic, Goran - *A Severe Elsewhere*
> BIC - v33 - i6 - Sept 2004 - p31(1) [501+]

Simm, G. - *Farm Animal Genetic Resources*
> SciTech - v28 - i4 - Dec 2004 - p126 [51-500]

Simmie, Lois - *What I'm Trying to Say Is Goodbye*
> BIC - v33 - i2 - March 2004 - p9(1) [501+]

Simmon, Scott - *The Invention of the Western Film: A Cultural History of the Genre's First Half-Century*
> Choice - v41 - i7 - March 2004 - p1304(1) [501+]
> FQ - v58 - i1 - Fall 2004 - p68(3) [501+]

Simmonds, Posy - *Gemma Bovery.*
> KR - v72 - i23 - Dec 1 2004 - p1117(1) [501+]
> People - v63 - i8 - Feb 28 2005 - p57 [51-500]
> PW - v251 - i48 - Nov 29 2004 - p25(1) [51-500]
> Ent W - i807 - Feb 18 2005 - p82 [51-500]

Simmons, Curt - *How to Do Everything with Your BlackBerry, 2nd Ed.*
> LJ - v129 - i14 - Sept 1 2004 - p182(1) [501+]

Simmons, Donald C. Jr. - *Confederate Settlements in British Honduras*
> JTWS - v21 - i1 - Spring 2004 - p312(3) [501+]

Simmons, Edwin H. - *The United States Marines: A History, 4th Ed.*
> Mar Crp G - v88 - i1 - Jan 2004 - p60(1) [501+]

Simmons, I.G. - *The Moorlands of England and Wales: An Environmental History*
> HER - v119 - i483 - Sept 2004 - p1108(2) [501+]

Simmons, Jane - *Pog and the Birdies*
> c   Magpies - v19 - i5 - Nov 2004 - p27(1) [501+]

Simmons, Louise - *Welfare, the Working Poor, and Labor*
> Choice - v42 - i1 - Sept 2004 - p157(1) [501+]
> R&R Bk N - v19 - i2 - May 2004 - p106(1) [51-500]

Simmons, Marc - *Kit Carson and His Three Wives: A Family History*
> R&R Bk N - v19 - i1 - Feb 2004 - p64(1) [501+]

Simmons, Michael - *Pool Boy (Read by Lowe, Chad). Audiobook Review*
> c   BL - v100 - i22 - August 2004 - p1954(1) [51-500]
> c   SLJ - v50 - i7 - July 2004 - p61(1) [51-500]
> SLJ - v50 - i10 - Oct 2004 - pS68(1) [501+]

Simmons, Sylvie - *Serge Gainsbourg: A Fistful of Gitanes: Requiem for a Twister*
> R&R Bk N - v19 - i1 - Feb 2004 - p197(1) [51-500]
> *Too Weird for Ziggy*
> Ent W - i791 - Nov 5 2004 - p85 [501+]
> KR - v72 - i18 - Sept 15 2004 - p889(1) [501+]
> LJ - v129 - i14 - Sept 1 2004 - p145(1) [501+]
> PW - v251 - i36 - Sept 6 2004 - p43(1) [51-500]

Simmons, T.M. - *Dead Man Talking*
> LJ - v129 - i20 - Dec 1 2004 - p95(1) [51-500]

Simmons, Tracy Lee - *Climbing Parnassus: A New Apologia for Greek and Latin*
> Dal R - v83 - i3 - Autumn 2003 - p449-451 [501+]

Simmons, Walter - *Voices in the Wilderness: Six American Neo-Romantic Composers*
> Choice - v42 - i1 - Sept 2004 - p112(1) [501+]

Simms, Norman - *Crypto-Judaism, Madness, and the Female Quixote: Charlotte Lennox as Marrana in Mid-Eighteenth Century England*
> Choice - v42 - i1 - Sept 2004 - p104(1) [501+]

Simms, Phil - *Sunday Morning Quarterback: Going Deep on the Strategies, Myths, & Mayhem of Football*
> LJ - v129 - i20 - Dec 1 2004 - p127(1) [51-500]
> PW - v251 - i44 - Nov 1 2004 - p56(1) [501+]

Simms, Rob - *The Repertoire of Iraqi Maqam*
> R&R Bk N - v19 - i2 - May 2004 - p192(1) [51-500]

Simo, Melanie - *Forest and Gardens: Traces of Wildness in a Modernizing Land, 1897-1949*
> PHR - v73 - i3 - August 2004 - p503(504) [501+]

Simon, Albert F. - *Appleton and Lange's Outline Review for the Physician Assistant Examination. 2nd Ed.*
> SciTech - v28 - i1 - March 2004 - p78(1) [51-500]

Simon, Barbara Brooks - *Escape to Freedom: The Underground Railroad Adventures of Callie and William*
> c   SLJ - v50 - i8 - August 2004 - p144(1) [51-500]

Simon, Bart - *Undead Science: Science Studies and the Afterlife of Cold Fusion*
> T&C - v45 - i2 - April 2004 - p462-463 [501+]

Simon, Charnan - *The Mighty Mississippi*
> c   SLJ - v50 - i12 - Dec 2004 - p137(2) [501+]
> *The Noble Yangtze*
> c   SLJ - v51 - i1 - Jan 2005 - p114(1) [51-500]

Simon, David R. - *Tony Soprano's America: The Criminal Side of the American Dream*
> R&R Bk N - v19 - i3 - August 2004 - p146(1) [51-500]

Simon, Ilana - *125 Best Indoor Grill Recipes*
> LJ - v129 - i19 - Nov 15 2004 - p83(1) [51-500]

Simon, Jacqueline Albert - *A Century of Artists' Letters: Notes to Family, Friends, and Dealers: Delacroix to Leger*
> R&R Bk N - v19 - i2 - May 2004 - p195(1) [51-500]

Simon, Jeffrey - *Hungary and NATO: Problems in Civil-Military Relations*
> R&R Bk N - v19 - i1 - Feb 2004 - p34(1) [1-50]
> *NATO and the Czech and Slovak Republics: A Comparative Study in Civil-Military Relations*
> Pers PS - v33 - i4 - Fall 2004 - p246(2) [501+]
> R&R Bk N - v19 - i1 - Feb 2004 - p35(1) [1-50]
> *Poland and NATO: A Study in Civil-Military Relations*
> Pers PS - v33 - i4 - Fall 2004 - p246(1) [501+]

Simon, Jeffrey Frank - *Bad Publicity*
> KR - v72 - i24 - Dec 15 2004 - pS3(1) [501+]

Simon, Jinjer L. - *Excel Data Analysis: Your Visual Blueprint for Creating and Analyzing Data, Charts, and PivotTables*
> SciTech - v28 - i3 - Sept 2004 - p8(1) [501+]

Simon, Julian L. - *A Life Against the Grain: The Autobiography of an Unconventional Economist*
> JEL - v42 - i1 - March 2004 - p242(1) [501+]

Simon, Linda - *Dark Light: Electricity and Anxiety from the Telegraph to the X-Ray*
> BL - v100 - i21 - July 2004 - p1805(1) [1-50]
> Choice - v42 - i4 - Dec 2004 - p684(1) [1-50]
> SciTech - v28 - i3 - Sept 2004 - p151(1) [51-500]

Simon, Michael - *Dirty Sally*
> LJ - v129 - i13 - August 2004 - p61(2) [501+]

Simon, Reeva Spector - *Iraq Between the Two World Wars: The Militarist Origins of Tyranny, Rev. Ed.*
> R&R Bk N - v19 - i3 - August 2004 - p49(1) [51-500]

Simon, Rita J. - *Global Perspectives on Social Issues: Education*
> R&R Bk N - v19 - i1 - Feb 2004 - pNA [501+]

Simon, Robert I. - *Assessing and Managing Suicide Risk: Guidelines for Clinically Based Risk Management*
> E-Streams - Sept 2004 - pNA [501+]
> SciTech - v28 - i1 - March 2004 - p102(1) [51-500]

Simon, Roger I. - *Between Hope and Despair: Pedagogy and the Remembrance of Historical Trauma*
> HNet - June 2004 - pNA [501+]

Simon, Seymour - *Hurricanes*
> c   CE - v81 - i2 - Winter 2004 - p109(1) [51-500]
> c   SB - v40 - i5 - Sept-Oct 2004 - p219(1) [51-500]
> c   SLJ - v50 - i10 - Oct 2004 - pS42(1) [51-500]
> *The Moon*
> c   SLJ - v50 - i10 - Oct 2004 - pS23(1) [1-50]
> *Pyramids & Mummies*
> c   SLJ - v50 - i12 - Dec 2004 - p138(1) [501+]
> *Spiders*
> c   LibMed - v23 - i1 - August-Sept 2004 - p80(2) [51-500]
> c   SB - v40 - i5 - Sept-Oct 2004 - p223(2) [501+]
> c   SLJ - v50 - i10 - Oct 2004 - pS42(1) [51-500]
> y   Teach Lib - v32 - i1 - Oct 2004 - p44(1) [51-500]

Simon, Sunka - *Mail-Orders: The Fiction of Letters in Postmodern Culture*
> GSR - v27 - i1 - Feb 2004 - p219-220 [501+]

Simonds, Dawn - *Best Food in Town*
> Bwatch - Dec 2004 - pNA [51-500]

Simonds, Merilyn - *The Holding*
> BIC - v33 - i5 - August 2004 - p06(2) [501+]
> Globe & Mail - March 19 2005 - pD17 [1-50]

Small, Gail - *Joyful Learning: No One Ever Wants to Go to Recess!*
   R&R Bk N - v19 - i1 - Feb 2004 - p182(1) [51-500]

Small, Helen - *Literature, Science, Psychoanalysis, 1830-1970: Essays in Honour of Gillian Beer*
   Nine-C Lit - v59 - i1 - June 2004 - p132(136) [501+]
   VS - v46 - i4 - Summer 2004 - p698(3) [501+]

Small, J.P. - *The Parallel Worlds of Classical Art and Text*
   Class R - v54 - i2 - Nov 2004 - p539(3) [501+]

Small, Melvin - *At the Water's Edge: American Politics and the Vietnam War*
   KR - v73 - i2 - Jan 15 2005 - p112(1) [501+]
   LJ - v130 - i3 - Feb 15 2005 - p145(1) [51-500]

Small, Nora Pat - *Beauty and Convenience: Architecture and Order in the New Republic*
   JouAmCul - v27 - i3 - Sept 2004 - p338(2) [501+]
   R&R Bk N - v19 - i1 - Feb 2004 - p204(1) [51-500]

Small, Stephen - *Political Thought in Ireland, 1776-1798: Republicanism, Patriotism, and Radicalism*
   Albion - v36 - i2 - Summer 2004 - p383(2) [501+]

Smalley, Greg - *The Marriage You've Always Dreamed Of*
   LJ - v130 - i1 - Jan 1 2005 - p135(1) [51-500]

Smalls, Carla - *The Full Spectrum: Essays on Staff Diversity in Corrections*
   R&R Bk N - v19 - i4 - Nov 2004 - p149(1) [501+]

Smalls, Irene - *I Can't Take a Bath! (Illus. by Boyd, Aaron)*
   c SLJ - v51 - i2 - Feb 2005 - p97(1) [51-500]

Smallwood, Philip - *Critical Pasts: Writing Criticism, Writing History*
   Choice - v42 - i7 - March 2005 - p1223(2) [51-500]
   Johnson's Critical Presence: Image, History, Judgment
   TLS - i5283 - July 2 2004 - p27(1) [501+]

Smallwood, Robert - *Players of Shakespeare 6: Essays in the Performance of Shakespeare's History Plays*
   TLS - i5299 - Oct 22 2004 - p31(1) [51-500]

Smarandache, Florentin - *Advances and Applications of DSmT for Information Fusion*
   SciTech - v28 - i4 - Dec 2004 - p35(1) [51-500]

Smarr, Janet Levarie - *Italian Women and the City*
   MLN - v119 - i1 - Jan 2004 - p197-199 [501+]

Smart about History
   LibMed - v22 - i4 - Jan 2004 - p74(1) [501+]

Smart, Lesley - *The Third Dimension*
   J Chem Ed - v81 - i3 - March 2004 - p337-342 [501+]

Smart, Mary Ann - *Mimomania: Music and Gesture in Nineteenth-Century Opera*
   Choice - v42 - i3 - Nov 2004 - p493(2) [51-500]

Smart, Nick - *British Strategy and Politics during the Phony War: Before the Balloon Went Up*
   Albion - v36 - i2 - Summer 2004 - p354(3) [501+]
   J Mil H - v68 - i3 - July 2004 - p992-993 [501+]

Smart, Phil - *The Real Angels Among Us*
   Bwatch - Jan 2005 - pNA [501+]

Smart, Tom - *Alex Colville: Return*
   CBRA - Annual 2003 - p122(2) [51-500]

Smead, Robert N. - *Cowboy Talk: A Dictionary of Spanish Terms from the American West*
   Roundup M - v12 - i3 - Feb 2005 - p23(1) [51-500]

Smedley, Brian D. - *In the Nation's Compelling Interest: Ensuring Diversity in the Health Care Workforce*
   Choice - v42 - i6 - Feb 2005 - p1055(1) [51-500]
   SciTech - v28 - i4 - Dec 2004 - p78(1) [51-500]

Smeets, Marc - *Huysmans l'Inchange: Histoire d'une Conversion*
   NCFS - v33 - i1-2 - Fall-Winter 2004 - p209(3) [501+]

Smerconish, Michael A. - *Flying Blind: How Political Correctness Continues to Compromise Airline Security Post-9/11*
   PW - v251 - i35 - August 30 2004 - p45(1) [51-500]

Smethurst, Mae J. - *The Noh Ominameshi: A Flower Viewed from Many Directions*
   R&R Bk N - v19 - i1 - Feb 2004 - p228(1) [51-500]

Smil, Vaclav - *Energy at the Crossroads: Global Perspectives and Uncertainties*
   JEL - v42 - i1 - March 2004 - p335(1) [501+]

Smiley, Gene - *Rethinking the Great Depression: A New View of Its Causes and Consequences*
   BHR - v78 - i1 - Spring 2004 - p134(3)] [501+]

Smiley, Jan Bode - *Focus on Batiks*
   Bwatch - v26 - i7 - July 2004 - p7(1) [51-500]

Smiley, Jane - *A Year at the Races: Reflections on Horses, Humans, Love, Money, and Luck*
   BL - v101 - i1 - Sept 1 2004 - p46(1) [501+]
   Econ - v371 - i8380 - June 19 2004 - p81US [501+]
   Spec - v296 - i9197 - Nov 13 2004 - p60(2) [501+]

Smiley, Patricia - *False Profits*
   BL - v101 - i1 - Sept 1 2004 - p71(1) [51-500]
   Ent W - i794 - Nov 26 2004 - p125 [51-500]
   KR - v72 - i17 - Sept 1 2004 - p841(2) [51-500]
   PW - v251 - i40 - Oct 4 2004 - p73(1) [51-500]

Smiley, Tavis - *Keeping the Faith: Stories of Love, Courage, Healing, and Hope from Black America*
   Kliatt - v38 - i6 - Nov 2004 - p32(1) [51-500]

Smit, Johan J. - *High Voltage Engineering: Proceedings*
   SciTech - v28 - i1 - March 2004 - p152(1) [51-500]

Smith, A.D. - *The Problem of Perception*
   J Phil - v101 - i1 - Jan 2004 - p44-53 [501+]
   J Phil - v101 - i2 - Feb 2004 - p44-10 [501+]

Smith, Aaron - *The Sport Business Future*
   Choice - v42 - i6 - Feb 2005 - p1060(2) [51-500]

Smith, Abby - *New-Model Scholarship: How Will It Survive ?*
   ALJ - v53 - i4 - Nov 2004 - p426(2) [501+]

Smith, Adrian B. - *The God Shift: Our Changing Perception of the Ultimate Mystery*
   LJ - v130 - i1 - Jan 1 2005 - p121(1) [51-500]

Smith, Alexander McCall - *At the Villa of Reduced Circumstances*
   LJ - v130 - i1 - Jan 1 2005 - p101(1) [51-500]
   At the Villa of Reduced Circumstances (Illus. by McIntosh, Iain)
   KR - v72 - i23 - Dec 1 2004 - p1113(1) [501+]
   NYTBR - March 13 2005 - p34 [501+]
   The Finer Points of Sausage Dogs (Illus. by McIntosh, Iain)
   KR - v72 - i23 - Dec 1 2004 - p1113(1) [501+]
   LJ - v130 - i1 - Jan 1 2005 - p101(1) [51-500]
   NYTBR - March 13 2005 - p34 [501+]
   The Full Cupboard of Life (Read by Lecat, Lisette). Audiobook Review
   BL - v101 - i9-10 - Jan 1 2005 - p777(1) [1-50]
   y Kliatt - v39 - i2 - March 2005 - p52(1) [51-500]
   LJ - v129 - i19 - Nov 15 2004 - p98(1) [51-500]
   The Full Cupboard of Life
   y SLJ - v50 - i10 - Oct 2004 - p199(1) [51-500]
   The Girl Who Married a Lion and Other Tales from Africa
   LJ - v130 - i1 - Jan 1 2005 - p123(1) [51-500]
   y PW - v251 - i43 - Oct 25 2004 - p26(1) [51-500]
   In the Company of Cheerful Ladies: More from the No. 1 Ladies' Detective Agency
   LJ - v129 - i20 - Dec 1 2004 - p96(1) [51-500]
   PW - v252 - i7 - Feb 14 2005 - p51(1) [51-500]
   Kalahari Typing School for Men: More from the No. 1 Ladies' Detective Agency
   CBRA - Annual 2003 - p186(2) [501+]
   Portuguese Irregular Verbs
   KR - v72 - i23 - Dec 1 2004 - p1113(1) [501+]
   LJ - v130 - i1 - Jan 1 2005 - p101(1) [51-500]
   NYTBR - March 13 2005 - p34 [501+]
   The Sunday Philosophy Club
   Ent W - i786 - Oct 1 2004 - p76 [501+]

Smith, Alice Bilari - *Under a Bilari Tree I Born*
   AHS - v35 - i123 - April 2004 - p196-196 [501+]

Smith, Alison - *Name All the Animals: A Memoir*
   BL - v101 - i9-10 - Jan 1 2005 - p771(1) [51-500]
   Lam Bk Rpt - v13 - i1-2 - August-Sept 2004 - p20(2) [501+]
   NYTBR - March 13 2005 - p32 [501+]
   People - Dec 27 2004 - p63 [501+]
   SLJ - v51 - i2 - Feb 2005 - p159(1) [51-500]

Smith, Allison Chandler - *The Girls' World Book of Bath & Beauty: Fresh Ideas & Fun Recipes for Hair, Skin, Nails & More*
   c SLJ - v50 - i8 - August 2004 - p144(1) [51-500]

Smith, Andrew Brodie - *Shooting Cowboys and Indians: Silent Western Films, American Culture, and the Birth of Hollywood*
   Choice - v42 - i1 - Sept 2004 - p110(1) [51-500]
   PHR - v73 - i4 - Nov 2004 - p675(2) [501+]
   Victorian Demons: Medicine, Masculinity and the Gothic at the Fin de Siecle
   Choice - v42 - i2 - Oct 2004 - p296(1) [501+]

Smith, Andrew F. - *The Oxford Encyclopedia of Food and Drink in America, Vols. 1-2*
   BL - v101 - i7 - Dec 1 2004 - p687(1) [501+]
   BL - v101 - i9-10 - Jan 1 2005 - p780(1) [1-50]
   LJ - v130 - i3 - Feb 15 2005 - p160(1) [501+]
   PW - v251 - i45 - Nov 8 2004 - p45(1) [501+]

Popped Culture: A Social History of Popcorn in America
   HNet - Sept 2004 - pNA [501+]
Pure Ketchup: A History of America's National Condiment
   HNet - Sept 2004 - pNA [501+]

Smith, Anna Deavere - *House Arrest and Piano*
   Kliatt - v38 - i6 - Nov 2004 - p30(1) [51-500]

Smith, Anthony D. - *Chosen Peoples: Sacred Sources of National Identity*
   Choice - v42 - i2 - Oct 2004 - p333(1) [51-500]
   TimHES - v0 - i1676 - Jan 28 2005 - p28(2) [501+]

Smith, Art - *Kitchen Life: Real Food for Real Families--Even Yours!*
   BL - v101 - i2 - Sept 15 2004 - p189(2) [51-500]
   LJ - v129 - i15 - Sept 15 2004 - p79(1) [51-500]
   PW - v251 - i37 - Sept 13 2004 - p71(2) [501+]

Smith, Barbara - *Animal Phantoms*
   y Res Links - v10 - i3 - Feb 2005 - p28(1) [51-500]
   Ghost Riders: True Ghost Stories of Planes, Trains and Automobiles
   y Res Links - v10 - i3 - Feb 2005 - p28(1) [501+]
   Ghost Stories of the Rocky Mountains, Vol. 2
   CBRA - Annual 2003 - p268(1) [51-500]
   Horribly Haunted Houses
   y Res Links - v10 - i3 - Feb 2005 - p28(2) [51-500]
   Monkey Wrench
   Bwatch - v26 - i7 - July 2004 - p6(1) [51-500]

Smith, Barbara L. - *Learning Communities: Reforming Undergraduate Education*
   R&R Bk N - v19 - i4 - Nov 2004 - p184(1) [501+]

Smith, Brad - *Busted Flush*
   BL - v101 - i9-10 - Jan 1 2005 - p823(1) [1-50]
   Globe & Mail - Feb 5 2005 - pD6 [501+]
   KR - v73 - i1 - Jan 1 2005 - p19(1) [501+]
   PW - v251 - i47 - Nov 22 2004 - p36(1) [51-500]

Smith, Brian H. - *Sommelier's Guide to Wine: A Primer for Selecting, Serving, and Savoring Wine*
   SciTech - v28 - i1 - March 2004 - p174(1) [1-50]

Smith, Carl - *Chancellorsville 1863: Jackson's Lightning Strike*
   R&R Bk N - v19 - i4 - Nov 2004 - p62(1) [51-500]
   Fredericksburg, 1862: "Clear the Way"
   R&R Bk N - v19 - i4 - Nov 2004 - p62(1) [51-500]
   Gettysburg 1863: High Tide of the Confederacy
   R&R Bk N - v19 - i4 - Nov 2004 - p62(1) [51-500]

Smith, Carl B., II. - *No Longer Jews: The Search for Gnostic Origins*
   LJ - v129 - i13 - August 2004 - p88(1) [501+]

Smith, Carter - *Presidents Every Question Answered: Everything you Could Possibly Want to Know About the Nation's Chief Executives*
   R&R Bk N - v19 - i3 - August 2004 - p63(1) [51-500]
   Student Almanac of Hispanic American History
   y VOYA - v27 - i3 - August 2004 - p247(1) [1-50]

Smith, Cat Bowman - *The Rosie Stories*
   LibMed - v22 - i6 - March 2004 - p63(1) [501+]

Smith, Charles D. - *Palestine and the Arab-Israeli Conflict: A History with Documents*
   MEJ - v59 - i1 - Wntr 2005 - p167(1) [51-500]

Smith, Charles David - *Ecology, Civil Society and the Informal Economy in North West Tanzania*
   GJ - v170 - i3 - Sept 2004 - p283(1) [501+]

Smith, Charles R. - *Diamond Life: Baseball Sights, Sounds, and Swings 1st Ed.*
   LibMed - v22 - i7 - April-May 2004 - p85(1) [501+]

Smith, Charles R., Jr. - *Hoop Kings*
   LibMed - v23 - i1 - August-Sept 2004 - p70(1) [51-500]
   SLJ - v50 - i10 - Oct 2004 - pS52(1) [51-500]
   Hoop Queens: Poems
   LibMed - v22 - i6 - March 2004 - p71(1) [501+]
   LibMed - v22 - i6 - March 2004 - p71(1) [501+]
   I Am America
   y Teach Lib - v32 - i1 - Oct 2004 - p20(1) [51-500]
   Let's Play Basketball! (Illus. by Widener, Terry)
   c BL - v101 - i1 - Sept 1 2004 - p114(1) [51-500]
   c PW - v251 - i36 - Sept 6 2004 - p65(1) [51-500]

Smith, Charles W.G. - *The Weather-Resilient Garden: A Defensive Approach to Planning and Landscaping*
   R&R Bk N - v19 - i4 - Nov 2004 - p246(1) [501+]

Smith, Charlotte Turner - *The Collected Letters of Charlotte Smith*
   Choice - v41 - i7 - March 2004 - p1299(1) [501+]

Smith, Christian - *Moral, Believing Animals: Human Personhood and Culture*
 CS - v33 - i6 - Nov 2004 - p677(2) [501+]
 SF - v83 - i2 - Dec 2004 - p865(3) [501+]
The Secular Revolution: Power, Interests, and Conflict in the Secularization of American Public Life
 CH - v73 - i4 - Dec 2004 - p897(3) [501+]
Soul Searching: The Religious and Spiritual Lives of American Teenagers
 PW - v252 - i4 - Jan 24 2005 - p238(2) [501+]

Smith, Colleen M. - *Marks' Basic Medical Biochemistry: A Clinical Approach, 2nd Ed.*
 SciTech - v28 - i4 - Dec 2004 - p71(1) [51-500]

Smith, Connie Macdonald - *Pea Soup Fog (Illus. by Cart, Jen)*
 c CH Bwatch - Feb 2005 - pNA [51-500]

Smith, Cotton - *The Thirteenth Bullet*
 Roundup M - v11 - i6 - August 2004 - p30(1) [501+]

Smith, Craig B. - *How the Great Pyramid Was Built*
 BL - v101 - i7 - Dec 1 2004 - p632(1) [51-500]
 LJ - v130 - i2 - Feb 1 2005 - p100(1) [51-500]
 PW - v251 - i48 - Nov 29 2004 - p32(2) [51-500]

Smith, D. Gordon - *Business Organizations: Cases, Problems, and Case Studies*
 R&R Bk N - v19 - i4 - Nov 2004 - p167(1) [501+]

Smith, D. James - *The Boys of San Joaquin*
 c CCB-B - v58 - i6 - Feb 2005 - p266(1) [51-500]
 y KR - v73 - i3 - Feb 1 2005 - p182(1) [51-500]
 y SLJ - v51 - i1 - Jan 2005 - p136(1) [51-500]
My Brother's Passion
 KR - v72 - i16 - August 15 2004 - p774(1) [51-500]

Smith, D.L - *The Miracles of Santo Fico (Read by Hope, William). Audiobook Review*
 y Kliatt - v38 - i5 - Sept 2004 - p63(2) [51-500]

Smith, D. Vance - *Arts of Possession: The Middle English Household Imaginary*
 AHR - v109 - i4 - Oct 2004 - p1299-1299 [501+]

Smith, Dale - *What the Orangutan Told Alice: A Rain Forest Adventure*
 y Kliatt - v38 - i4 - July 2004 - p33(1) [51-500]

Smith, Damian - *The Book of Deeds of James I of Aragon: A Translation of the Medieval Catalan Llibre dels Fets*
 HER - v119 - i483 - Sept 2004 - p985(986) [501+]

Smith, Dana Kessimakis - *A Wild Cowboy (Illus. by Freeman, Laura)*
 c Black Iss - v6 - i4 - July-August 2004 - p61(1) [51-500]
 c LibMed - v23 - i1 - August-Sept 2004 - p65(1) [51-500]

Smith, Darren L. - *Parks Directory of the United States*
 Choice - v42 - i3 - Nov 2004 - p468(1) [1-50]

Smith, David - *Hinduism and Modernity*
 IBMR - v28 - i3 - July 2004 - p133(1) [501+]

Smith, David Andrew - *George S. Patton: A Biography*
 J Mil H - v68 - i3 - July 2004 - p1009(1) [501+]

Smith, David E. - *The Canadian Senate in Bicameral Perspective*
 PSQ - v119 - i3 - Fall 2004 - p553(3) [501+]

Smith, David Eugene - *History of Japanese Mathematics*
 SciTech - v28 - i3 - Sept 2004 - p17(1) [501+]

Smith, David G. - *Entitlement Politics: Medicare and Medicaid, 1995 to 2001*
 CS - v33 - i1 - Jan 2004 - p80-81 [501+]

Smith, David J. - *If the World Were a Village (Illus. by Armstrong, Shelagh)*
 c RT - v57 - Oct 2003 - p173 [1-50]
 c RT - v57 - Nov 2003 - p274 [51-500]

Smith, David Livingstone - *Why We Lie: The Evolutionary Roots of Deception and the Unconscious Mind*
 BL - v100 - i21 - July 2004 - p1802(1) [51-500]
 Choice - v42 - i6 - Feb 2005 - p1036(1) [51-500]
 Globe & Mail - Feb 19 2005 - pD14 [501+]
 LJ - v129 - i12 - July 2004 - p114(1) [51-500]
 New Sci - v183 - i2464 - Sept 11 2004 - p46(2) [501+]
 R&R Bk N - v19 - i3 - August 2004 - p9(1) [1-50]
 SB - v40 - i5 - Sept-Oct 2004 - p200(1) [51-500]

Smith, David R. - *Digital Transmission Systems. 3rd Ed.*
 SciTech - v28 - i1 - March 2004 - p153(1) [51-500]

Smith, Dee - *Poking, Pinching, and Pretending: Documenting Toddlers' Explorations with Clay*
 R&R Bk N - v19 - i3 - August 2004 - p150(1) [51-500]

Smith, Dennis E. - *From Symposium to Eucharist: The Banquet in the Early Christian World*
 Intpr - v58 - i3 - July 2004 - p328(1) [501+]
 Theol St - v66 - i1 - March 2005 - p186(2) [501+]
 TT - v61 - i3 - Oct 2004 - p406(2) [501+]

Smith-Doerr, Laurel - *Women's Work: Gender Equality vs. Hierarchy in the Life Sciences*
 Choice - v42 - i6 - Feb 2005 - p1047(1) [51-500]
 SciTech - v28 - i4 - Dec 2004 - p59(1) [51-500]

Smith, Donald A. - *Heroes of the Revolution*
 LibMed - v22 - i6 - March 2004 - p78(1) [501+]

Smith, Donald E. - *American Printmakers of the Twentieth Century: A Bibliography*
 Choice - v42 - i3 - Nov 2004 - p454(1) [1-50]
 R&R Bk N - v19 - i4 - Nov 2004 - p208(1) [501+]

Smith, Douglas - *Decade of the Wolf: Returning the Wild to Yellowstone*
 PW - v252 - i9 - Feb 28 2005 - p54(1) [51-500]
Managing White Supremacy: Race, Politics and Citizenship in Jim Crow Virginia
 JAH - v91 - i1 - June 2004 - p287-288 [501+]

Smith Duff, Dorothy - *Dekalb County, Alabama Marriage Index 1836-1916*
 EFHM - v58 - i2 - March-April 2004 - p89(1) [51-500]

Smith, E. Brian - *Basic Chemical Thermodynamics, 5th Ed.*
 Choice - v42 - i4 - Dec 2004 - p692(1) [1-50]
 SciTech - v28 - i3 - Sept 2004 - p53(1) [1-50]

Smith, Efrem - *Raising Up Young Heroes: Developing a Revolutionary Youth Ministry*
 Black Iss - v6 - i6 - Nov-Dec 2004 - p18(1) [51-500]

Smith, Elliott - *From a Basement on the Hill*
 New York - v37 - i41 - Nov 22 2004 - p97(1) [501+]

Smith, Elwood - *Raise the Roof!*
 LibMed - v22 - i4 - Jan 2004 - p61(1) [501+]

Smith, Eric Ledell - *African American Theater Buildings: An Illustrated Historical Directory, 1900-1955*
 R&R Bk N - v19 - i1 - Feb 2004 - p227(1) [51-500]

Smith, Frank - *Understanding Reading: A Psycholinguistic Analysis of Reading and Learning to Read, 6th Ed.*
 R&R Bk N - v19 - i3 - August 2004 - p217(1) [1-50]
Unspeakable Acts, Unnatural Practices: Flaws and Fallacies in "Scientific" Reading Instruction
 R&R Bk N - v19 - i1 - Feb 2004 - p182(1) [51-500]

Smith, Frank Dabba - *Elsie's War: A Story of Courage in Nazi Germany (Illus. by Lincoln, France)*
 c BL - v101 - i7 - Dec 1 2004 - p650(1) [51-500]

Smith, Gary Alden - *State and National Boundaries of the United States*
 BL - v101 - i6 - Nov 15 2004 - p615(1) [501+]

Smith, Gary Allen - *Epic Films: Casts, Credits, and Commentary on Over 350 Historical Spectacle Movies, 2nd Ed.*
 BL - v100 - i22 - August 2004 - p1976(1) [51-500]
 R&R Bk N - v19 - i3 - August 2004 - p261(1) [51-500]

Smith, Gerald J. - *Agrarian Letters: The Correspondence of John Donald Wade and Donald Davidson, 1930-1939*
 Sew R - v112 - i3 - Summer 2004 - pXCVI-XCVII [501+]

Smith, Gina - *The Genomics Age: How DNA Technology Is Transforming the Way We Live and Who We Are*
 SB - v41 - i1 - Jan-Feb 2005 - p20(2) [501+]

Smith, Graham - *Deliberative Democracy and the Environment*
 Env - v46 - i6 - July-August 2004 - p43(1) [501+]

Smith, Greg Leitich - *Ninjas, Piranhas, and Galileo (Read by Paris, Andy). Audiobook Review*
 Kliatt - v38 - i4 - July 2004 - p53(1) [501+]
Ninjas, Piranhas and Galileo. Audiobook Review
 c SLJ - v50 - i7 - July 2004 - p59(1) [51-500]

Smith, Greg M. - *Film Structure and the Emotion System*
 J Film & Vid - v56 - i1 - Spring 2004 - p53-54 [501+]

Smith, Hal L. - *Differential Equations and Mathematical Biology*
 SIAM Rev - v46 - i1 - March 2004 - p183-184 [501+]

Smith, Haywood - *The Red Hat Club (Read by Gartlan, Anne). Audiobook Review*
 BL - v100 - i21 - July 2004 - p1856(1) [1-50]
The Red Hat Club Rides Again
 KR - v73 - i2 - Jan 15 2005 - p81(1) [501+]
 LJ - v129 - i20 - Dec 1 2004 - p88(1) [51-500]
 LJ - v130 - i4 - March 1 2005 - p80(1) [51-500]
 PW - v252 - i9 - Feb 28 2005 - p43(1) [51-500]

Smith-Hefner, Nancy J. - *Khmer American: Identity and Moral Education in a Diasporic Community*
 Amerasia J - v30 - i1 - Spring 2004 - p249-251 [501+]

Smith, Helmut Walser - *The Butcher's Tale: Murder and Anti-Semitism in a German Town*
 AHR - v109 - i2 - April 2004 - p634(2) [501+]
 GSR - v27 - i3 - Oct 2004 - p625(2) [501+]

Smith, Henrietta M. - *The Coretta Scott King Awards: 1970-2004, 3rd Ed.*
 Adoles - v39 - i156 - Winter 2004 - p839(1) [51-500]
 CCB-B - v58 - i2 - Oct 2004 - p105(1) [51-500]
 R&R Bk N - v19 - i4 - Nov 2004 - p258(1) [501+]
 Teach Lib - v32 - i2 - Dec 2004 - p38(1) [501+]

Smith, Henry Nash - *Virgin Land: The American West as Symbol and Myth*
 CHE - v51 - i23 - Feb 11 2005 - pB4-1 [501+]

Smith, Hugh - *The Strategists*
 AJPS - v39 - i2 - July 2004 - p455(456) [501+]

Smith, Ian - *The Blackbird Papers (Read by Jennings, Brent). Audiobook Review*
 Kliatt - v38 - i6 - Nov 2004 - p41(2) [51-500]
The Blackbird Papers
 NYTBR - July 4 2004 - p16 [51-500]
Emily and the Intergalactic Lemonade Stand
 c CH Bwatch - v14 - i9 - Sept 2004 - p4(1) [51-500]
 c VOYA - v27 - i5 - Dec 2004 - p375(1) [501+]

Smith, Icy - *Voices of Healing: Spirit and Unity After 9/11 in the Asian American and Pacific Islander Community*
 y VOYA - v27 - i3 - August 2004 - p242(2) [1-50]

Smith, J. Douglas - *Managing White Supremacy: Race, Politics, and Citizenship in Jim Crow Virginia*
 HNet - June 2004 - pNA [501+]
 JIH - v35 - i1 - Summer 2004 - p161-163 [501+]

Smith, J.H. - *African American Miners and Migrants: The Eastern Kentucky Social Club*
 Choice - v42 - i3 - Nov 2004 - p525(1) [1-50]

Smith, J.S. - *Script and Seals and Inscriptions*
 Class R - v54 - i1 - May 2004 - p212(2) [501+]

Smith, J. Scott - *Food Processing: Principles and Applications*
 SciTech - v28 - i3 - Sept 2004 - p167(1) [51-500]

Smith, Jada Pinkett - *Girls Hold Up This World*
 c PW - v252 - i8 - Feb 21 2005 - p177(1) [501+]

Smith, James Bryan - *Room of Marvels*
 Ch Today - v48 - i7 - July 2004 - p66(1) [51-500]

Smith, James E. - *Taxation of Business Entities, 2005 Ed.*
 R&R Bk N - v19 - i3 - August 2004 - p205(1) [501+]

Smith, James K. - *David Thompson*
 c CBRA - Annual 2003 - p542(2) [51-500]

Smith, Jane - *Matchbox Labels: Over 2,000 Elegant Examples from All over the World*
 Globe & Mail - Dec 18 2004 - pD14 [1-50]

Smith, Janna Malamud - *A Potent Spell: Mother Love and the Power of Fear*
 NYTBR - July 11 2004 - p24 [501+]

Smith, Jedwin - *Our Brother's Keeper: My Family's Journey through Vietnam to Hell and Back*
 PW - v252 - i4 - Jan 24 2005 - p231(1) [501+]

Smith, Jeff - *The Complete Bone Adventures (Illus. by Smith, Jeff)*
 y BL - v101 - i4 - Oct 15 2004 - p396(1) [51-500]
 Ent W - i785 - Sept 24 2004 - p117 [51-500]
 LJ - v129 - i18 - Nov 1 2004 - p67(1) [501+]
 Time - v164 - i15 - Oct 11 2004 - p103 [501+]
Crown of Horns (Illus. by Smith, Jeff)
 BL - v101 - i1 - Sept 1 2004 - p77(1) [501+]
Out from Boneville
 y Kliatt - v39 - i2 - March 2005 - p31(1) [51-500]
 PW - v252 - i6 - Feb 7 2005 - p44(1) [51-500]

Smith, Jeffrey Chipps - *The Northern Renaissance*
 Apo - v161 - i515 - Jan 2005 - p65(2) [501+]
 Choice - v42 - i5 - Jan 2005 - p842(1) [1-50]
 R&R Bk N - v19 - i4 - Nov 2004 - p199(1) [501+]
 TLS - i5297 - Oct 8 2004 - p31(1) [51-500]
Sensuous Worship: Jesuits and the Art of the Early Catholic Reformation in Germany
 Ren Q - v57 - i3 - Fall 2004 - p1033(3) [501+]

Smith, Jennifer - *The Gay Rights Movement*
 LibMed - v22 - i5 - Feb 2004 - p86(1) [501+]

Smith, Jeremy - *The Fall of the Berlin Wall*
 c SLJ - v50 - i7 - July 2004 - p116(1) [51-500]

Smith, Jessie Carney - *Black Heroes*
 Choice - v41 - i11-12 - July-August 2004 - p2029 [501+]

Smith, Jim - *A Practical Guide for the Law Enforcement and Security Manager: A Theoretical and Experiential Approach*
 R&R Bk N - v19 - i3 - August 2004 - p167(1) [501+]
Technology of Reduced Additive Foods, 2nd Ed.
 SciTech - v28 - i4 - Dec 2004 - p165(1) [51-500]

564 • SMITH Book Review Index 2005 Cumulation

Smith, Roy C. - *Global Banking*
JEL - v42 - i1 - March 2004 - p269(1) [501+]
Smith, Russell - *Muriella Pent*
BIC - v33 - i5 - August 2004 - p04(2) [501+]
Globe & Mail - Nov 27 2004 - pD3 [51-500]
Globe & Mail - Dec 24 2004 - pD3 [1-50]
Princess and the Whisk Heads: A Fable
CBRA - Annual 2003 - p187(1) [51-500]
The Princess and the Whiskheads: A Fable
Can Lit - i181 - Summer 2004 - p176-178 [501+]
Smith, S.A. - *Like Cattle and Horses: Nationalism and Labor in Shagai, 1895-1927*
JIH - v34 - i4 - Spring 2004 - p675-678 [501+]
Smith, Sally Bedell - *Grace and Power: The Private World of the Kennedy White House*
Globe & Mail - Nov 27 2004 - pD3 [51-500]
NYTBR - July 25 2004 - p9 [501+]
Spec - v295 - i9180 - July 17 2004 - p36(1) [501+]
Smith, Sarah Harrison - *The Fact Checker's Bible: A Guide to Getting It Right*
LJ - v129 - i15 - Sept 15 2004 - p66(1) [51-500]
Smith, Sebastian - *Southern Winds: Escaping to the Heart of the Mediterranean*
TLS - i5287 - July 30 2004 - p28(1) [51-500]
Smith, Shawn A. - *The HR Answer Book: An Indispensable Guide for Managers and Human Resources Professionals*
HR Mag - v49 - i7 - July 2004 - pS33(1) [501+]
HR Mag - v49 - i8 - August 2004 - p141(2) [501+]
HR Answer Book: An Indispensable Guide for Managers and Human Resources Professionals
HR Mag - v50 - i2 - Feb 2005 - pNA [501+]
HR Mag - v50 - i2 - Feb 2005 - pS14(1) [501+]
Smith, Shawn Michelle - *Photography on the Color Line: W.E.B. Du Bois, Race and Visual Culture*
Bl S - v34 - i3 - Fall 2004 - p75-75 [501+]
Smith, Sherry L. - *The Future of the Southern Plains*
JSH - v71 - i1 - Feb 2005 - p224(2) [501+]
Reimagining Indians: Native Americans through Anglo Eyes, 1880-1940
WestFolk - v62 - i3 - Summer 2003 - p228-230 [501+]
Smith, Sheryl S. - *Neurosteroid Effects in the Central Nervous System: The Role of the GABA-A Receptor*
SciTech - v28 - i1 - March 2004 - p72(1) [51-500]
Smith, Stephen (b. 1961-) - *Underground London: Travels Beneath the City Streets*
CR - v285 - i1664 - Sept 2004 - p191(1) [51-500]
Smith, Stephen Samuel - *Boom for Whom?: Education, Desegregation, and Development in Charlotte*
Choice - v42 - i5 - Jan 2005 - p936(1) [51-500]
Smith, Stephen W. (b. 1955 -) - *Labour Economics*
JEL - v42 - i1 - March 2004 - p236(2) [501+]
Smith, Steven G. - *Worth Doing*
Choice - v42 - i3 - Nov 2004 - p497(1) [1-50]
Smith, Steven W. Dr. - *Shakespeare's Last Plays: Essays in Literature and Politics*
Six Ct J - v35 - i1 - Spring 2004 - p249(2) [501+]
Smith, Stu - *Goldilocks and the Three Martians (Illus. by Garland, Michael)*
c BW - v34 - i39 - Sept 26 2004 - p11(1) [501+]
c SLJ - v50 - i8 - August 2004 - p94(1) [51-500]
My School's a Zoo! (Illus. by Catrow, David)
c SLJ - v50 - i10 - Oct 2004 - p129(2) [51-500]
Smith, Sybil D. - *Parish Nursing: A Handbook for the New Millennium*
Choice - v41 - i7 - March 2004 - p1327(1) [501+]
SciTech - v28 - i1 - March 2004 - p127(1) [51-500]
Smith, Sylvia K. - *A Gathering of Garrisons: The Ancestors, Family, and Descendents of Lot Garrison and Margaret Erwin*
EFHM - v58 - i2 - March-April 2004 - p88(1) [51-500]
Smith, T.W. - *Revaluing Ethics: Aristotle's Dialectical Pedagogy*
Class R - v54 - i2 - Nov 2004 - p327-329 [501+]
Smith, Tara Bray - *West of Then: A Mother, a Daughter, and a Journey Past Paradise*
y BL - v101 - i1 - Sept 1 2004 - p27(1) [51-500]
KR - v72 - i15 - August 1 2004 - p733(1) [51-500]
LJ - v129 - i15 - Sept 15 2004 - p65(1) [51-500]
NYTBR - Nov 28 2004 - p26 [501+]
People - v62 - i16 - Oct 18 2004 - p50 [51-500]
Smith, Timothy B. - *Creating the Welfare State in France, 1880-1940*
JIH - v35 - i2 - Autumn 2004 - p300(2) [501+]
This Great Battlefield of Shiloh: History, Memory, and the Establishment of a Civil War National Military Park
Wil Q - v29 - i1 - Wntr 2005 - p123(2) [501+]
Smith, Truman - *The Wrong Stuff: The Adventures and Misadventures of an 8th Air Force Aviator*
APH - v51 - i4 - Winter 2004 - p62(2) [501+]
Smith, Vicki - *Crossing the Great Divide: Worker Risk, Uncertainty and Opportunity in the New Economy*
SF - v83 - i2 - Dec 2004 - p874(3) [501+]
Smith, W. Ramsay - *Myths and Legends of the Australian Aborigines*
R&R Bk N - v19 - i1 - Feb 2004 - p72(1) [1-50]
Smith, W. Thomas., Jr. - *Encyclopedia of the Central Intelligence Agency*
LibMed - v22 - i5 - Feb 2004 - p88(1) [501+]
Smith, Wallace - *Garden of the Sun: A History of the San Joaquin Valley, 1772-1939, 2nd Ed.*
R&R Bk N - v19 - i3 - August 2004 - p75(1) [51-500]
Smith, Walter E. - *Anthony Trollope: A Bibliography of His First American Editions, 1859-1884, with Photographic Reproductions of Bindings and Titlepages; A Supplement to Michael Sadleir's "Trollope: A Bibliography"*
BSA-P - v98 - i2 - June 2004 - p244-246 [501+]
Smith, Wesley J. - *Consumer's Guide to a Brave New World*
Choice - v42 - i7 - March 2005 - p1246(1) [51-500]
PW - v251 - i46 - Nov 15 2004 - p56(1) [501+]
Smith, Will - *Maximum PC Guide to Building a Dream PC*
LJ - v130 - i2 - Feb 1 2005 - p110(1) [51-500]
Smith, William (b. 1769-1839) - *A Delineation of the Strata of England and Wales with Part of Scotland*
New Sci - v183 - i2457 - July 24 2004 - p54(2) [501+]
Smith, William G. - *Plato and Popcorn: A Philosopher's Guide to 75 Thought-Provoking Movies*
R&R Bk N - v19 - i3 - August 2004 - p263(1) [51-500]
Smith, William L. - *Irish Priests in the United States: A Vanishing Subculture*
R&R Bk N - v19 - i4 - Nov 2004 - p13(1) [51-500]
Smith, Woodruff - *Consumption and the Making of Respectability, 1600-1800*
J Soc H - v38 - i2 - Winter 2004 - p513(3) [501+]
Smithers, A.J. - *The Tangier Campaign: The Birth of the British Army*
J Mil H - v68 - i2 - April 2004 - p587(2) [501+]
Smithers, Brian - *Nuendo Power!*
SciTech - v28 - i4 - Dec 2004 - p159(1) [51-500]
Sonar 3 Ignite!
SciTech - v28 - i1 - March 2004 - p164(1) [51-500]
Smithin, John - *Controversies in Monetary Economics*
JEL - v41 - i4 - Dec 2003 - p1346(1) [501+]
Smithsonian Jazz Class
SLJ - v50 - i12 - Dec 2004 - p63(1) [501+]
Smitten, Susan - *Canadian Ghost Stories, Vol. 2*
CBRA - Annual 2003 - p268(1) [51-500]
Smock, David R. - *Interfaith Dialogue and Peacebuilding*
J Ch St - v46 - i3 - Summer 2004 - p651(2) [501+]
Smock, William - *The Bauhaus Ideal Then and Now: An Illustrated Guide to Modernist Design*
BL - v101 - i2 - Sept 15 2004 - p191(1) [51-500]
The Bauhaus Ideal, Then and Now: An Illustrated Guide to Modernist Design
Choice - v42 - i6 - Feb 2005 - p1011(1) [51-500]
Smol, John P. - *Pollution of Lakes and Rivers: A Paleoenvironmental Perspective*
GJ - v170 - i3 - Sept 2004 - p284(1) [501+]
Smolan, Rick - *New Hampshire 24/7: Amazing Photographs of an Extraordinary State*
PW - v251 - i39 - Sept 27 2004 - p53(2) [51-500]
Smolens, John - *Fire Point*
BL - v100 - i22 - August 2004 - p1904(1) [501+]
KR - v72 - i15 - August 1 2004 - p712(2) [501+]
PW - v251 - i30 - July 26 2004 - p36(1) [501+]
Smoley, Richard - *Inner Christianity: A Guide to the Esoteric Tradition*
Parabola - v28 - i3 - Fall 2003 - p86(2) [501+]
Smolinski, Mark S. - *Microbial Threats to Health: Emergence, Detection, and Response*
SciTech - v28 - i1 - March 2004 - p83(1) [51-500]
Smollett, Tobias - *The Life and Adventures of Sir Launcelot Greaves*
Eight-C St - v37 - i4 - Summer 2004 - p673-677 [501+]
Smothers, Ethel - *The Hard Times Jar*
c LibMed - v22 - i6 - March 2004 - p59(1) [501+]
Smothers, Ethel Footman - *The Hard-Times Jar (Illus. by Holyfield, John)*
c SLJ - v50 - i7 - July 2004 - p45(1) [51-500]
Smucker, Philip - *Al Qaeda's Great Escape: The Military and the Media on Terror's Trail*
R&R Bk N - v19 - i3 - August 2004 - p164(1) [501+]
Smutny, Joan Franklin - *Gifted Education: Promising Practices*
TCR - v106 - i5 - May 2004 - p909(3) [501+]
Smyth, Adam - *"Profit and Delight": Printed Miscellanies in England, 1640-1682*
TLS - i5299 - Oct 22 2004 - p25(1) [501+]
Smyth, Alfred P. - *The Medieval Life of King Alfred the Great: A Translation and Commentary on the Text Attributed to Asser*
Albion - v36 - i1 - Spring 2004 - p86(3) [501+]
Specu - v79 - i4 - Oct 2004 - p1144(2) [501+]
Smyth, Nancy J. - *Women and Girls in the Social Environment: Behavioral Perspectives*
R&R Bk N - v19 - i4 - Nov 2004 - p133(1) [1-50]
Smythe, Dion C. - *Strangers to Themselves: The Byzantine Outsider*
Specu - v79 - i4 - Oct 2004 - p1145(3) [501+]
Smythe, Ted Curtis - *The Gilded Age Press, 1865-1900*
JAH - v91 - i2 - Sept 2004 - p644(2) [501+]
Smythe, Theresa - *Snowbear's Christmas Countdown (Illus. by Smythe, Theresa)*
c BL - v101 - i2 - Sept 15 2004 - p254(1) [51-500]
c HB - v80 - i6 - Nov-Dec 2004 - p663(2) [51-500]
c KR - v72 - i21 - Nov 1 2004 - p1054(1) [51-500]
Smythe, William - *Studies of How the Mind Publicly Enfolds into Being*
R&R Bk N - v19 - i4 - Nov 2004 - p11(1) [51-500]
Snakepit, Ben - *The Snake Pit Book (Illus. by Snakepit, Ben)*
BL - v100 - i22 - August 2004 - p1915(1) [501+]
Snape, M.F. - *The Church of England in Industrialising Society: the Lancashire Parish of Whalley in the Eighteenth Century*
CH - v73 - i4 - Dec 2004 - p868(1) [501+]
HNet - Oct 2004 - pNA [501+]
Snedaker, Susan - *Best Damn Windows Server 2003 Book Period*
SciTech - v28 - i3 - Sept 2004 - p25(1) [51-500]
How to Cheat at Managing Windows Small Business Server 2003
Bwatch - March 2005 - pNA [51-500]
SciTech - v28 - i4 - Dec 2004 - p31(1) [51-500]
Snedecker, George - *The Politics of Critical Theory: Language/Discourse/Society*
R&R Bk N - v19 - i3 - August 2004 - pNA [51-500]
Sneed, Brad - *Thumbelina*
c BL - v101 - i2 - Sept 15 2004 - p254(1) [51-500]
c KR - v72 - i18 - Sept 15 2004 - p920(1) [51-500]
Snell, Clarke - *The Good House Book: A Common-Sense Guide to Alternative Homebuilding*
LJ - v129 - i14 - Sept 1 2004 - p180(1) [51-500]
Snell, Gordon - *Further Fabulous Canadians! Hysterically Historical Rhymes*
Globe & Mail - Nov 20 2004 - pD30 [51-500]
Snelling, Lauraine - *The Way of Women*
BL - v101 - i9-10 - Jan 1 2005 - p818(1) [501+]
Snelson, John - *Andrew Lloyd Webber*
Choice - v42 - i6 - Feb 2005 - p1032(1) [51-500]
LJ - v129 - i17 - Oct 15 2004 - p65(1) [51-500]
Snicket, Lemony - *The Grim Grotto (Read by Curry, Tim). Audiobook Review*
c Globe & Mail - Dec 11 2004 - pD53 [1-50]
The Grim Grotto (Illus. by Helquist, Brett)
c BL - v101 - i6 - Nov 15 2004 - p586(2) [51-500]
c Ent W - i785 - Sept 24 2004 - p112 [51-500]
y Magpies - v19 - i5 - Nov 2004 - p37(1) [501+]
y PW - v251 - i42 - Oct 18 2004 - p66(1) [501+]
A Series of Unfortunate Events: The Bad Beginning, The Reptile Room, and The Wide Window
Ent W - i801 - Jan 14 2005 - p92 [501+]
Snider, Marvin - *Compatibility Breeds Success: How to Manage Your Relationship with Your Business Partner*
R&R Bk N - v19 - i1 - Feb 2004 - p93(1) [1-50]
Snijders, H. - *E-Commerce Law: National and Transnational Topics and Perspectives*
R&R Bk N - v19 - i1 - Feb 2004 - pNA [51-500]
Snodgrass, Catherine S. - *Super Silly Sayings That Are over Your Head: A Children's Illustrated Book of Idioms (Illus. by Snodgrass, Catherine S.)*
c SLJ - v51 - i1 - Jan 2005 - p114(1) [51-500]
Snodgrass, Mary Ellen - *Encyclopedia of Gothic Literature*
LJ - v130 - i4 - March 1 2005 - p116(1) [51-500]
Encyclopedia of Kitchen History
Choice - v42 - i6 - Feb 2005 - p1006(2) [51-500]
World Epidemics: A Cultural Chronology of Disease from Prehistory to the Era of SARS
E-Streams - Sept 2004 - pNA [501+]

Snodgrass, Michael - *Los indios del valle de Mexico y la construccion de una nueva sociabilidad politica, 1770-1835*
    AHR - v109 - i3 - June 2004 - p948(2) [501+]
Snodgrass, Philip J. - *Ornithine Transcarbamylase: Basic Science and Clinical Considerations*
    SciTech - v28 - i1 - March 2004 - p103(1) [51-500]
Snoe, Eboni - *When Everything's Said and Done*
    PW - v251 - i42 - Oct 18 2004 - p47(2) [51-500]
Snoeijer, Wim - *Agapanthus: A Revision of the Genus*
    SciTech - v28 - i4 - Dec 2004 - p65(1) [51-500]
Snook, I. Donald, Jr. - *Hospitals: What They Are and How They Work. 2nd Ed.*
    SciTech - v28 - i1 - March 2004 - p84(1) [51-500]
Snooks, Graeme Donald - *The Collapse of Darwinism, or, The Rise of a Realist Theory of Life*
    JEL - v42 - i1 - March 2004 - p344(2) [501+]
Snow, Alan - *How Santa Really Works (Illus. by Snow, Alan)*
    c BL - v101 - i6 - Nov 15 2004 - p587(1) [51-500]
    c CCB-B - v58 - i3 - Nov 2004 - p145(1) [501+]
Snow, Albert Lee - *More Practical Advice for Principals*
    R&R Bk N - v19 - i3 - August 2004 - p224(1) [1-50]
Snow, Constance - *The Rustic Table: Simple Fare from the World's Kitchens*
    LJ - v130 - i3 - Feb 15 2005 - p153(1) [51-500]
    PW - v252 - i9 - Feb 28 2005 - p59(1) [51-500]
Snow, David A. - *The Blackwell Companion to Social Movements*
    Choice - v42 - i3 - Nov 2004 - p570(2) [1-50]
Snow, Edward Rowe - *Pirates and Buccaneers of the Atlantic Coast*
    R&R Bk N - v19 - i3 - August 2004 - p72(1) [51-500]
Snow, Judith E. - *How It Feels to Have a Gay or Lesbian Parent: A Book by Kids for Kids of All Ages*
    y BL - v101 - i9-10 - Jan 1 2005 - p856(1) [1-50]
    c SLJ - v50 - i10 - Oct 2004 - p194(1) [51-500]
Snow, Michael - *The Nightfisherman: Selected Letters of W.S. Graham*
    Poet - v185 - i4 - Jan 2005 - p309(11) [501+]
Snow, Nancy E. - *Stem Cell Research: New Frontiers in Science and Ethics*
    Choice - v42 - i1 - Sept 2004 - p130(1) [501+]
    Theol St - v66 - i1 - March 2005 - p232(2) [501+]
    TLS - i5267 - March 12 2004 - p11-11 [501+]
Snow, Philip - *The Fall of Hong Kong: Britain, China and the Japanese Occupation*
    A Aff - v35 - i2 - July 2004 - p248-249 [501+]
Snow, Robert L. - *Deadly Cults: The Crimes of True Believers*
    R&R Bk N - v19 - i1 - Feb 2004 - p11(1) [51-500]
Snyder, Douglas K. - *Treating Difficult Couples: Helping Clients with Coexisting Mental and Relationship Disorders*
    SciTech - v28 - i1 - March 2004 - p99(1) [51-500]
Snyder, Gary - *Danger on Peaks*
    BL - v101 - i1 - Sept 1 2004 - p40(1) [51-500]
    LJ - v129 - i19 - Nov 15 2004 - p64(1) [501+]
    NYTBR - Nov 21 2004 - p8 [501+]
    PW - v251 - i42 - Oct 18 2004 - p61(1) [51-500]
Snyder, Graydon F. - *Ante Pacem: Archaeological Evidence of Church Life Before Constantine, Rev. Ed.*
    R&R Bk N - v19 - i1 - Feb 2004 - p16(1) [1-50]
Snyder, Inez - *Apples*
    SLJ - v50 - i12 - Dec 2004 - p138(1) [501+]
Snyder, Jeffrey B. - *Canes and Walking Sticks: A Stroll through Time and Place*
    R&R Bk N - v19 - i4 - Nov 2004 - p210(1) [501+]
Snyder, Kerala J. - *The Organ as a Mirror of Its Time: North European Reflections, 1610-2000*
    JIH - v34 - i4 - Spring 2004 - p623-625 [501+]
Snyder, Larry - *Molecular Genetics of Bacteria*
    QRB - v79 - i3 - Sept 2004 - p308(1) [501+]
Snyder, Susan - *Shakespeare: A Wayward Journey*
    Six Ct J - v34 - i4 - Winter 2003 - p1242-1243 [501+]
Snyder, Terri L. - *Brabbling Women: Disorderly Speech and the Law in Early Virginia*
    AHR - v109 - i2 - April 2004 - p515(2) [501+]
    JSH - v70 - i4 - Nov 2004 - p891(2) [501+]
Snyder, Zilpha Keatley - *Unlocking the Employment Potential in the Middle East and North Africa: Toward a New Social Contract*
    R&R Bk N - v19 - i3 - August 2004 - p115(1) [51-500]
So, Irene - *Investing in Greater China*
    CBRA - Annual 2003 - p31(2) [51-500]

So, Meilo - *Gobble, Gobble, Slip, Slop: A Tale of a Very Greedy Cat (Illus. by So, Meilo)*
    c LibMed - v22 - i7 - April-May 2004 - p58(1) [501+]
    c SLJ - v50 - i10 - Oct 2004 - pS27(1) [1-50]
So-Un, Kim - *Korean Children's Favorite Stories (Illus. by Kyoung-Sim, Jeong)*
    c BL - v100 - i22 - August 2004 - p1928(1) [51-500]
    c SLJ - v50 - i11 - Nov 2004 - p130(2) [51-500]
Soaba, Russell - *Kwamra: A Season of Harvest*
    Cont Pac - v17 - i1 - Spring 2005 - p260(5) [501+]
Soames, Scott - *Philosophical Analysis in the 20th Century, Vol. 1*
    Choice - v41 - i7 - March 2004 - p1311(1) [501+]
    VQR - v80 - i1 - Wntr 2004 - p276-277 [501+]
Philosophical Analysis in the 20th Century, Vol. I
    Lon R Bks - v27 - i2 - Jan 20 2005 - p12(2) [501+]
Philosophical Analysis in the 20th Century, Vol. II
    Lon R Bks - v27 - i2 - Jan 20 2005 - p12(2) [501+]
    VQR - v80 - i3 - Summer 2004 - p271(2) [1-50]
Soanes, Catherine - *Consise Oxford English Dictionary*
    Choice - v42 - i5 - Jan 2005 - p823(1) [51-500]
Soares, Joseph A. - *Critical Visions: New Direction in Social Theory*
    CS - v33 - i5 - Sept 2004 - p613-614 [501+]
The Decline of Privilege: The Modernization of Oxford University
    CS - v33 - i1 - Jan 2004 - p101-102 [501+]
Soares-Prabhu, George - *The Dharma of Jesus*
    Theol St - v65 - i4 - Dec 2004 - p871(3) [501+]
Sobel, Dava - *The Best American Science Writing, 2004*
    y BL - v101 - i2 - Sept 15 2004 - p186(1) [51-500]
Sobel, David - *Place-Based Education: Connecting Classrooms and Communities*
    CE - v81 - i2 - Winter 2004 - p116(1) [51-500]
Sobel, Jack - *Marine Reserves: A Guide to Science, Design, and Use*
    SciTech - v28 - i4 - Dec 2004 - p59(1) [51-500]
Sobel, Robert - *The United States Executive Branch: A Biographical Directory of Heads Of State and Cabinet Officials*
    LibMed - v22 - i7 - April-May 2004 - p68(1) [501+]
    LibMed - v22 - i7 - April-May 2004 - p68(1) [501+]
Sobel, Sylvan - *Presidential Elections and Other Cool Facts*
    c SLJ - v50 - i8 - August 2004 - p48(1) [51-500]
Sober, Elliott - *Likelihood, Model Selection, and the Duhem-Quine Problem*
    RM - v58 - i1 - Sept 2004 - p219(1) [501+]
Soble, Alan - *Pornography, Sex and Feminism*
    Wom HR - v13 - i1 - Spring 2004 - p148(4) [501+]
Sobol, Donald J. - *Encyclopedia Brown Mysteries, Vol. 1 (Read by Harris, Jason). Audiobook Review*
    c SLJ - v50 - i12 - Dec 2004 - p73(1) [501+]
Sobol, Julie Macfie - *Lake Erie: A Pictorial History*
    Bwatch - Nov 2004 - pNA [51-500]
    CG - v124 - i5 - Sept-Oct 2004 - p114(1) [501+]
    R&R Bk N - v19 - i3 - August 2004 - p78(1) [51-500]
Sobol, Richard - *Adelina's Whales (Illus. by Sobol, Richard)*
    c LibMed - v22 - i5 - Feb 2004 - p75(1) [501+]
An Elephant in the Backyard (Illus. by Sobol, Richard)
    c CCB-B - v58 - i1 - Sept 2004 - p39(2) [51-500]
    c SLJ - v50 - i7 - July 2004 - p96(1) [51-500]
Sobre, Judith Berg - *San Antonio on Parade: Six Historic Festivals*
    JAH - v91 - i1 - June 2004 - p275-275 [501+]
    JSH - v71 - i1 - Feb 2005 - p227(2) [501+]
Sobrino, Francisco - *Foot and Mouth Disease: Current Perspectives*
    SciTech - v28 - i4 - Dec 2004 - p127 [501+]
Sobti, R.C. - *Advanced Flow Cytometry: Applications in Biological Research*
    SciTech - v28 - i1 - March 2004 - p65(1) [51-500]
Society for Human Resource Management - *Graduate Programs in Human Resource Management, 2nd Ed.*
    HR Mag - v49 - i7 - July 2004 - pS3(1) [51-500]
    HR Mag - v50 - i2 - Feb 2005 - pS3(1) [501+]
Understanding COBRA, 2nd Ed.
    HR Mag - v49 - i7 - July 2004 - pS31(1) [501+]
Understanding FMLA
    HR Mag - v49 - i7 - July 2004 - pS31(1) [501+]
Understanding HIPAA
    HR Mag - v49 - i7 - July 2004 - pS31(1) [501+]

Society of Autimtive Engineers - *42 Volt Technology 2003: Proceedings*
    SciTech - v28 - i1 - March 2004 - p168(1) [51-500]
Lean Engine NOx Control: Proceedings
    SciTech - v28 - i1 - March 2004 - p166(1) [51-500]
Socio-Economic Security Programme - *Economic Security for a Better World*
    ILR - v143 - i3 - Autumn 2004 - p288(2) [51-500]
Soda, Masahito - *Firefighter! Daigo of Fire Company M*
    y VOYA - v27 - i4 - Oct 2004 - p288(1) [51-500]
Soderbaum, Fredrik - *Regionalism and Uneven Development in Southern Africa: The Case of the Maputo Development Corridor*
    R&R Bk N - v19 - i1 - Feb 2004 - p86(1) [1-50]
Soderberg, Nancy - *The Superpower Myth: The Use and Misuse of American Might*
    KR - v72 - i23 - Dec 1 2004 - p1139(1) [501+]
    LJ - v130 - i3 - Feb 15 2005 - p147(1) [51-500]
    PW - v251 - i49 - Dec 6 2004 - p49(1) [51-500]
Soderman, Anne Keil - *Scaffolding Emergent Literacy: A Child-Centered Approach for Preschool Through Grade 5, 2nd Ed.*
    R&R Bk N - v19 - i4 - Nov 2004 - p181(1) [501+]
Soderquist, Larry D. - *Securities Regulation, 5th Ed.*
    R&R Bk N - v19 - i4 - Nov 2004 - p168(1) [501+]
Soderqvist, Thomas - *Science as Autobiography: The Troubled Life of Niels Jerne*
    Isis - v95 - i2 - June 2004 - p329(2) [501+]
Soderstrom, Mary - *After Surfing Ocean Beach*
    BIC - v33 - i8 - Nov 2004 - p16(3) [501+]
    Globe & Mail - August 14 2004 - pD11 [501+]
Sodini, Carla - *L'Ercole Tirreno: Guerra e Dinastia Medicea Nella Prima Meta del '600*
    Six Ct J - v35 - i3 - Fall 2004 - p908-909 [501+]
Sofer, Andrew - *The Stage Life of Props*
    Choice - v41 - i7 - March 2004 - p1308(1) [501+]
    Theat J - v56 - i2 - May 2004 - p327(2) [501+]
Sofer, Catherine - *Human Capital over the Lifecycle: A European Perspective*
    R&R Bk N - v19 - i3 - August 2004 - p115(1) [51-500]
Sofer, Morry - *The Translator's Handbook, 5th Rev. Ed.*
    R&R Bk N - v19 - i4 - Nov 2004 - p214(1) [501+]
Sofield, Shannon - *Paypal Hacks*
    Bwatch - Feb 2005 - pNA [501+]
Sogrin, Vladimir V. - *The Political History of the USA, 17th to 20th Centuries*
    JAH - v91 - i3 - Dec 2004 - p988(2) [501+]
Sohail, Muhammad - *Gene Silencing by RNA Interference: Technology and Application*
    SciTech - v28 - i4 - Dec 2004 - p62(1) [51-500]
Sohm, Philip - *Style in the Art Theory of Early Modern Italy*
    HNet - Nov 2004 - pNA [501+]
Sohn, Alan - *Parenting Your Asperger Child: Individualized Solutions for Teaching Your Child Practical Skills*
    LJ - v130 - i3 - Feb 15 2005 - p154(1) [51-500]
    PW - v252 - i1 - Jan 3 2005 - p52(1) [51-500]
Sohn, Amy - *My Old Man*
    BL - v101 - i1 - Sept 1 2004 - p65(1) [51-500]
    KR - v72 - i14 - July 15 2004 - p657(2) [501+]
    NYTBR - Sept 19 2004 - p20 [501+]
    People - v62 - i14 - Oct 4 2004 - p57 [501+]
    PW - v251 - i29 - July 19 2004 - p142(1) [51-500]
Sohn, Ho-Min - *Selected Readings in Korean*
    R&R Bk N - v19 - i2 - May 2004 - p218(1) [501+]
Soister, John T. - *Up from the Vault: Rare Thrillers of the 1920's and 1930's*
    R&R Bk N - v19 - i3 - August 2004 - p263(1) [51-500]
Sokal, Alan - *The Sokal Hoax: The Sham that Shook the Academy*
    Sew R - v112 - i3 - Summer 2004 - p444-455 [501+]
Sokol, B.J. - *Shakespeare, Law, and Marriage*
    TLS - i5285 - July 16 2004 - p28-29 [501+]
Sokolove, Michael - *The Ticket Out: Darryl Strawberry and the Boys of Crenshaw*
    BooChiTr - May 9 2004 - p4(1) [501+]
Sokolow, Jayme A. - *The Great Encounter: Native Peoples and European Settlers in the Americas, 1492-1800*
    Am Ind CRJ - v27 - i4 - Fall 2003 - p153-155 [501+]
    HAHR - v84 - i3 - August 2004 - p520(2) [501+]
Sokolow, Michael - *Charles Benson: Mariner of Color in the Age of Sail*
    R&R Bk N - v19 - i1 - Feb 2004 - p69(1) [501+]

Sonne, Wolfgang - *Representing the State: Capital City Planning in the Early Twentieth Century*
Choice - v42 - i1 - Sept 2004 - pNA [501+]

Sonnemann, Guido - *Integrated Life-Cycle and Risk Assessment for Industrial Processes*
SciTech - v28 - i3 - Sept 2004 - p170(1) [51-500]

Sonnenberg, Joel - *Joel*
PW - v251 - i28 - July 12 2004 - p61(1) [51-500]

Sonnenblick, Jordan - *Drums, Girls and Dangerous Pie*
c SLJ - v50 - i10 - Oct 2004 - p178(1) [51-500]
y VOYA - v27 - i5 - Dec 2004 - p396(1) [51-500]

Sonnendrucker, Eric - *Three Courses on Partial Differential Equations*
SciTech - v28 - i1 - March 2004 - p39(1) [51-500]
SciTech - v28 - i1 - March 2004 - p39(1) [51-500]

Sonnet, Anne - *Aging and Employment Policies*
JEL - v41 - i4 - Dec 2003 - p1384(1) [501+]

Sontag, Susan - *Regarding the Pain of Others*
Afterimage - v32 - i4 - Jan-Feb 2005 - p8(2) [501+]
CC - v122 - i2 - Jan 25 2005 - p6(2) [51-500]

Sontheimer, Gunther-Dietz - *Essays on Religion, Literature, and Law*
R&R Bk N - v19 - i4 - Nov 2004 - p15(1) [51-500]

Sood, V.K. - *Operation in Parakram: The War Unfinished*
R&R Bk N - v19 - i1 - Feb 2004 - p47(1) [51-500]

Soon, Willie - *The Maunder Minimum and the Variable Sun-Earth Connection*
Choice - v42 - i2 - Oct 2004 - p316(1) [51-500]

Soonok, Chun - *They Are Not Machines: Korean Women Workers and Their Fight for Democratic Trade Unionism in the 1970s*
JAS - v63 - i3 - August 2004 - p813-814 [501+]
R&R Bk N - v19 - i1 - Feb 2004 - p100(1) [1-50]

Soos, Troy - *Burning Bridges*
SLJ - v50 - i12 - Dec 2004 - p175(1) [51-500]

Soper-Cook, JoAnne - *Opium Lady*
CBRA - Annual 2003 - p187(1) [51-500]

Soper, Mark Edward - *Absolute Beginner's Guide to Home Networking*
LJ - v130 - i2 - Feb 1 2005 - p110(1) [501+]

The Sopranos
New R - Dec 13 2004 - p40 [501+]

Sora, Steven - *The Lost Colony of the Templars: Verrazano's Secret Mission to America*
PW - v251 - i48 - Nov 29 2004 - p33(1) [51-500]
Treasures of Heaven: Relics from Noah's Ark to the Shroud of Turin
KR - v72 - i23 - Dec 1 2004 - p1139(2) [501+]
PW - v251 - i50 - Dec 13 2004 - p62(1) [51-500]

Soranus, of Ephesus - *Maladies des Femmes. Tome IV, Livre 4*
Class R - v53 - i2 - Nov 2003 - p338-339 [501+]

Sorby, Sheryl A. - *Solid Modeling with I-DEAS, 2nd Ed.*
SciTech - v28 - i3 - Sept 2004 - p137(1) [51-500]

Sorelius, Gunnar - *Shakespeare and Scandinavia: A Collection of Nordic Essays*
Six Ct J - v35 - i3 - Fall 2004 - p942-943 [501+]

Sorell, Tom - *Leviathan after 350 Years*
CR - v285 - i1667 - Dec 2004 - p379(1) [51-500]

Sorensen, Andre - *Towards Sustainable Cities: East Asian, North American, and European Perspectives on Managing Urban Regions*
R&R Bk N - v19 - i3 - August 2004 - p156(1) [51-500]

Sorensen, Eric - *Possession and Exorcism in the New Testament and Early Christianity*
JR - v84 - i3 - July 2004 - p450(2) [501+]

Sorensen, Lene Bogh - *Fascism, Liberalism, and Social Democracy in Central Europe: Past and Present*
Slav R - v63 - i2 - Summer 2004 - p379(2) [501+]

Sorensen, Roy - *A Brief History of the Paradox: Philosophy and the Labyrinths of the Mind*
Choice - v41 - i11-12 - July-August 2004 - p2059(1) [501+]

Sorenson, Randall Lehmann - *Minding Spirituality*
Choice - v42 - i3 - Nov 2004 - p502(1) [51-500]

Sorenstam, Annika - *Golf Annika's Way: How I Elevated My Game to Be the Best, and How You Can, Too*
y BL - v101 - i4 - Oct 15 2004 - p376(1) [51-500]

Sorin, Gerald - *Irving Howe: A Life of Passionate Dissent*
JAH - v91 - i1 - June 2004 - p327-328 [501+]

Sornette, Didier - *Why Stock Markets Crash: Critical Events in Complex Financial Systems*
Phys Today - v57 - i3 - March 2004 - p78-80 [501+]

Soroka, Stuart N. - *Agenda-Setting Dynamics in Canada*
CBRA - Annual 2003 - p312(1) [501+]

Sorokie, Alyce M. - *Gut Wisdom: Understanding and Improving Your Digestive Health*
BL - v101 - i3 - Oct 1 2004 - p290(1) [51-500]

Sorokin, Vladimir - *Ice*
NYRB - v51 - i20 - Dec 16 2004 - p65(6) [501+]

Soros, George - *The Alchemy of Finance*
R&R Bk N - v19 - i3 - August 2004 - p136(1) [51-500]
The Bubble of American Supremacy: Correcting the Misuse of American Power
R&R Bk N - v19 - i1 - Feb 2004 - p60(1) [51-500]
The Bubble of American Supremacy: The Costs of Bush's War in Iraq
BW - v34 - i42 - Oct 17 2004 - p12(1) [501+]
Underwriting Democracy: Encouraging Free Enterprise and Democratic Reform Among the Soviets and in Eastern Europe
R&R Bk N - v19 - i3 - August 2004 - p160(1) [51-500]

Soros, Susan Weber - *Castellani and Italian Archaeological Jewelry*
Mag Antiq - v167 - i1 - Jan 2005 - p128(1) [51-500]
Mag Antiq - v167 - i2 - Feb 2005 - p54(1) [51-500]
Mag Antiq - v167 - i3 - March 2005 - p58(1) [501+]

Sorrel, Christian - *Liberalisme et modernisme: Mgr Lacroix (1855-1922): Enquete sur un suspect*
Theol St - v65 - i3 - Sept 2004 - p647(3) [501+]

Sorrells, Audrey McCray - *Critical Issues in Special Education: Access, Diversity, and Accountability*
R&R Bk N - v19 - i1 - Feb 2004 - p193(1) [51-500]

Sorrenti, Francesca - *Water Culture*
Aud - v106 - i3 - July-August 2004 - p66(2) [51-500]

Sorrentino, Gilbert - *Lunar Follies*
PW - v252 - i7 - Feb 14 2005 - p50(2) [51-500]
The Moon in Its Flight
ABR - v26 - i2 - Jan-Feb 2005 - p21(2) [501+]
RCF - v24 - i3 - Fall 2004 - p129(1) [501+]

Sorrentino, Steven - *Luncheonette: A Memoir*
Ent W - i806 - Feb 11 2005 - p69 [51-500]
KR - v72 - i24 - Dec 15 2004 - p1192(2) [501+]
LJ - v130 - i1 - Jan 1 2005 - p124(1) [51-500]
PW - v251 - i48 - Nov 29 2004 - p29(1) [51-500]

Soseki, Natsume - *The Tower of London*
Spec - v297 - i9207 - Jan 22 2005 - p35(1) [501+]

Sosik, John J. - *The Dream Weavers: Strategy-Focused Leadership in Technology-Driven Organizations*
R&R Bk N - v19 - i3 - August 2004 - p104(1) [1-50]

Soskin, Eileen - *Rudiments of Music for Music Majors with CD-ROM*
R&R Bk N - v19 - i4 - Nov 2004 - p198(1) [501+]

Sosnowski, David - *Vamped*
BL - v100 - i22 - August 2004 - p1914(1) [501+]
Ent W - i777 - August 6 2004 - p85 [51-500]
NYTBR - Oct 31 2004 - p18 [501+]
People - v62 - i9 - August 30 2004 - p50 [51-500]
PW - v251 - i28 - July 12 2004 - p48(2) [51-500]
USNews & Wrld Rpt - v137 - i4 - August 9 2004 - p58 [51-500]

Sossaman, Stephen - *Writing Your First Play*
Theat J - v56 - i1 - March 2004 - p145(3) [501+]

Soto, Gary - *The Afterlife (Read by Ramirez, Robert). Audiobook Review*
Kliatt - v38 - i6 - Nov 2004 - p41(1) [51-500]
y SLJ - v50 - i9 - Sept 2004 - p79(1) [51-500]
One Kind of Faith
WLT - v78 - i3-4 - Sept-Dec 2004 - p102(1) [501+]
Worlds Apart: Traveling with Fernie and Me (Illus. by Clarke, Greg)
c KR - v73 - i4 - Feb 15 2005 - p235(1) [51-500]

Soto, Michael - *The Modernist Nation: Generation, Renaissance, and Twentieth-Century American Literature*
Choice - v42 - i5 - Jan 2005 - p856(1) [1-50]

Souaid, Carolyn Marie - *Snow Formations*
CBRA - Annual 2003 - p232(1) [51-500]

Souayah, Nizar - *Neurology: Examination and Board Review*
SciTech - v28 - i4 - Dec 2004 - p93(1) [51-500]

Souder, William - *Under a Wild Sky: John James Audubon and the Making of The Birds of America*
Am Sci - v93 - i1 - Jan-Feb 2005 - p74(3) [501+]
Aud - v106 - i5 - Nov-Dec 2004 - p94(4) [501+]
BL - v100 - i22 - August 2004 - p1886(1) [51-500]
BooChiTr - May 30 2004 - p1(2) [501+]
Econ - v372 - i8387 - August 7 2004 - p69US [501+]
LJ - v129 - i13 - August 2004 - p112(1) [51-500]

Soueif, Ahdaf - *Baghdad Burning: Girl Blog from Iraq*
PW - v252 - i6 - Feb 7 2005 - p49(1) [51-500]

Souhami, Diana - *Wild Girls: Paris, Sappho and Art: The Lives and Loves of Natalie Barney and Romaine Brooks*
Lon R Bks - v26 - i20 - Oct 21 2004 - p31(3) [501+]

Soulieres, Robert - *L'epingle De La Reine*
Res Links - v10 - i1 - Oct 2004 - p54(1) [51-500]

Soumerai, Eve Nussbaum - *Voice from the Holocaust*
R&R Bk N - v19 - i1 - Feb 2004 - p30(1) [51-500]

Souster, Raymond - *Take Me Out to the Ballgame*
CBRA - Annual 2003 - p232(1) [51-500]

South-Paul, Jeannette E. - *Current Diagnosis and Treatment in Family Medicine*
SciTech - v28 - i3 - Sept 2004 - p95(1) [51-500]

Southam, Nancy - *Pierre: Colleagues and Friends Talk about the Trudeau They Knew*
Globe & Mail - March 12 2005 - pD6 [501+]

Southby-Tailyour, Ewen - *Reasons in Writing: A Commando's View of the Falklands War*
R&R Bk N - v19 - i3 - August 2004 - p77(1) [51-500]

Southerden, Louise - *Surf's Up: The Girl's Guide to Surfing*
LJ - v130 - i2 - Feb 1 2005 - p87(1) [51-500]

Southern, Nile - *The Candy Men: The Rollicking Life and Times of the Notorious Novel Candy*
ABR - v26 - i2 - Jan-Feb 2005 - p13(2) [501+]

Southerton, Simon G. - *Losing a Lost Tribe: Native Americans, DNA, and the Mormon Church*
Ch Today - v48 - i10 - Oct 2004 - p20(1) [501+]
PW - v251 - i30 - July 26 2004 - p50(1) [501+]

Southey, Robert - *Robert Southey: Poetical Works, 1793-1810, 5 Vols.*
R&R Bk N - v19 - i4 - Nov 2004 - p237(1) [501+]

Southgate, Beverley - *Postmodernism in History: Fear or Freedom?*
TimHES - v0 - i1655 - August 27 2004 - p24(1) [501+]

Southwick, Frederick S. - *Infectious Disease Quick Glance*
SciTech - v28 - i4 - Dec 2004 - p91(1) [51-500]

Southworth, Samuel A. - *U.S. Armed Forces Arsenal: A Guide to Modern Combat Hardware*
SciTech - v28 - i3 - Sept 2004 - p172(1) [51-500]

Souvestre, Emile - *The World As It Shall Be*
ChrSFF&H - v26 - i9 - Sept 2004 - p31(1) [51-500]
Fut - v38 - i6 - Nov-Dec 2004 - p61(1) [51-500]
LJ - v129 - i16 - Oct 1 2004 - p74(1) [51-500]

Souvestre, Emile - *The World As It Shall Be*
NYTBR - Oct 10 2004 - p13 [501+]

Souza-Santos, Marcio L. De - *Solid Fuels Combustion and Gasification; Modeling, Simulation, and Equipment Operation*
SciTech - v28 - i3 - Sept 2004 - p53(1) [1-50]

Sova, Dawn B. - *Banned Plays: Censorship Histories of 125 Stage Dramas*
Choice - v42 - i1 - Sept 2004 - p66(1) [501+]
LJ - v129 - i12 - July 2004 - p84(1) [51-500]
R&R Bk N - v19 - i3 - August 2004 - p264(1) [51-500]
SLJ - v50 - i8 - August 2004 - p60(1) [501+]

Sovada, Marsha A. - *Swift Fox: Ecology and Conservation of Swift Foxes in a Changing World*
CBRA - Annual 2003 - p411(1) [501+]

Sovak, Jan - *Dinosaurs A to Z: The Ultimate Dinosaur Encyclopedia*
LibMed - v22 - i5 - Feb 2004 - p58(1) [501+]

Sowell, Kirk H. - *The Arab World: An Illustrated History*
Choice - v42 - i5 - Jan 2005 - p193(2) [1-50]
R&R Bk N - v19 - i3 - August 2004 - p48(1) [51-500]

Sowell, Mike - *The Pitch That Killed*
BooChiTr - May 9 2004 - p4(1) [501+]

Sowell, Thomas - *Affirmative Action Around the World: An Empirical Study*
Choice - v42 - i3 - Nov 2004 - p526(1) [1-50]
Econ - v371 - i8380 - June 19 2004 - p80US [501+]
Soc Ser R - v78 - i4 - Dec 2004 - p699(1) [51-500]
Applied Economics: Thinking Beyond Stage One
Choice - v42 - i1 - Sept 2004 - p156(2) [501+]
R&R Bk N - v19 - i3 - August 2004 - p92(1) [51-500]
Basic Economics: A Citizen's Guide to the Economy Rev. and Expanded Ed.
Choice - v42 - i2 - Oct 2004 - p341(2) [51-500]
Basic Economics: A Citizen's Guide to the Economy, Rev. and Expanded Ed.
R&R Bk N - v19 - i3 - August 2004 - p93(1) [51-500]

Soyer, Alexis - *Food, Cookery and Dining in Ancient Times: Alexis Soyer's Pantropheon*
Bwatch - v26 - i9 - Sept 2004 - p2(1) [51-500]

Soyer, Refik - *Mathematical Reliability: An Expository Perspective*
SciTech - v28 - i1 - March 2004 - p177(1) [51-500]

Soyinka, Wole - *Climate of Fear: The Quest for Dignity in a Dehumanized World*
KR - v72 - i24 - Dec 15 2004 - p1193(1) [501+]

Sozzani, Franca - *Kartell: 150 Items, 150 Artworks*
Esq - v140 - i3 - Sept 2003 - p66 [51-500]

Space Science
y LibMed - v23 - i3 - Nov-Dec 2004 - p88(1) [51-500]

Space Technology
LibMed - v22 - i6 - March 2004 - p86(1) [501+]

Spack, Ruth - *America's Second Tongue: American Indian Education and the Ownership of English, 1860-1900*
Am Ind CRJ - v28 - i2 - Spring 2004 - p137(3) [501+]

Spackman, Devin - *Enterprise Integration Solutions*
SciTech - v28 - i4 - Dec 2004 - p129 [51-500]

Spada, James - *The Bush Family: Four Generations of History in Photographs*
BL - v100 - i22 - August 2004 - p1894(1) [51-500]

Spada, Stefania - *Directory of Approved Biopharmaceutical Products*
SciTech - v28 - i4 - Dec 2004 - p120(1) [1-50]

Spagna, Ana Maria - *Now Go Home: Wilderness, Belonging, and the Crosscut Saw*
Wom R Bks - v22 - i3 - Dec 2004 - p29(1) [501+]

Spain, Amber - *The International Political Economy of Investment Bubbles*
R&R Bk N - v19 - i4 - Nov 2004 - p119(1) [51-500]

Spain, Philip - *Analysis I: Convergence, Elementary Functions*
Choice - v42 - i2 - Oct 2004 - p329(1) [501+]

Spain, Rufus B. - *At Ease in Zion: A Social History of Southern Baptists, 1865-1900*
HNet - Sept 2004 - pNA [501+]

Spainhour, Stephen - *Webmaster in a Nutshell, 3rd Ed.*
SciTech - v28 - i1 - March 2004 - p158(1) [51-500]

Spalding, A.G. - *America's National Game*
BooChiTr - May 9 2004 - p1(1) [501+]

Spalding, Andrea - *Dance of the Stones*
y CBRA - Annual 2003 - p514(1) [51-500]
Klondike Ring
c CBRA - Annual 2003 - p514(1) [51-500]
Most Beautiful Kite in the World (Illus. by Watts, Leslie)
c CBRA - Annual 2003 - p468(1) [51-500]

Spalding, Julian - *The Poetic Museums: Reviving Historic Collections*
JAAC - v62 - i3 - Summer 2004 - p304-306 [501+]

Spalding, Mark D. - *Guide to the Coral Reefs of the Caribbean*
SciTech - v28 - i4 - Dec 2004 - p59(1) [51-500]

Spang, Michael - *Omnia homini simula sunt: Eine Interpretation von Giordano Brunos Artificium perorandi*
Ren Q - v57 - i3 - Fall 2004 - p1098(4) [501+]

Spangenburg, Ray - *African Americans in Science, Math, and Invention*
Sci Teach - v71 - i3 - March 2004 - p88-90 [501+]
The Birth of Science: Ancient Times to 1699.
SLJ - v50 - i12 - Dec 2004 - p88(1) [501+]
The Life and Death of Stars
y SB - v41 - i1 - Jan-Feb 2005 - p25(2) [501+]
A Look at Comets
y SB - v41 - i1 - Jan-Feb 2005 - p25(2) [501+]
Observing the Universe
y SB - v41 - i1 - Jan-Feb 2005 - p25(2) [501+]
Teen Fads: Fun, Foolish, or Fatal?
LibMed - v22 - i4 - Jan 2004 - p73(1) [501+]

Spangler, Lynn C. - *Television Women from Lucy to Friends: Fifty Years of Sitcoms and Feminism*
R&R Bk N - v19 - i1 - Feb 2004 - p225(1) [51-500]
TV Q - v34 - i3-4 - Spring-Summer 2004 - p77-78 [501+]

Spann, Edward - *Democracy's Children: The Young Rebels of the 1960s and the Power of Ideals*
PHR - v73 - i3 - August 2004 - p523(524) [501+]

Spann, Edward K. - *Democracy's Children: The Young Rebels of the 1960s and the Power of Ideals*
JAH - v91 - i3 - Dec 2004 - p1088(2) [501+]
R&R Bk N - v19 - i1 - Feb 2004 - p126(1) [51-500]

Spanos, Pol D. - *Computational Stochastic Mechanics: Proceedings*
SciTech - v28 - i1 - March 2004 - p47(1) [51-500]

Spanoudakis, K. - *Philitas of Cos*
Class R - v53 - i2 - Nov 2003 - p311-312 [501+]

Spanyol, Jessica - *Carlo and the Really Nice Librarian (Illus. by Spanyol, Jessica)*
c BL - v101 - i1 - Sept 1 2004 - p137(1) [51-500]
c CH Bwatch - Feb 2005 - pNA [1-50]
c KR - v72 - i13 - July 1 2004 - p637(1) [51-500]
c SLJ - v50 - i10 - Oct 2004 - p135(1) [51-500]
Carlo and the Realy Nice Librarian
c Sch Lib - v52 - i4 - Winter 2004 - p190(1) [51-500]

Spargo, Tamsin - *Wanted Man: The Forgotten Story of an American Outlaw*
BL - v101 - i5 - Nov 1 2004 - p448(1) [51-500]
KR - v72 - i18 - Sept 15 2004 - p907(1) [501+]

Spark, Muriel - *All the Poems of Muriel Spark*
Spec - v296 - i9191 - Oct 2 2004 - p45(2) [501+]
TLS - i5290 - August 20 2004 - p5(1) [501+]
The Driver's Seat
Atl - v294 - i4 - Nov 2004 - p150(7) [501+]
The Finishing School
BL - v100 - i21 - July 2004 - p1800(1) [51-500]
KR - v72 - i14 - July 15 2004 - p658(1) [51-500]
LJ - v129 - i13 - August 2004 - p70(1) [51-500]
NYRB - v51 - i18 - Nov 18 2004 - p21(3) [501+]
NYTBR - Sept 19 2004 - p26 [501+]
PW - v251 - i33 - August 16 2004 - p42(1) [51-500]
SLJ - v51 - i2 - Feb 2005 - p157(1) [51-500]
Atl - v294 - i4 - Nov 2004 - p150(7) [501+]
People - v62 - i17 - Oct 25 2004 - p55 [501+]
The Girls of Slender Means
Atl - v294 - i4 - Nov 2004 - p150(7) [501+]
The Only Problem
Atl - v294 - i4 - Nov 2004 - p150(7) [501+]
The Prime of Miss Jean Brodie
Atl - v294 - i4 - Nov 2004 - p150(7) [501+]

Sparkes, Randy J. - *The Two Princes of Calabar: An Eighteenth Century Atlantic Odyssey*
TimHES - v0 - i1675 - Jan 21 2005 - p24(1) [501+]

Sparkes, Stephen - *The House in Southeast Asia: A Changing Social, Economic and Political Domain*
TimHES - v0 - i1669 - Dec 3 2004 - p28(1) [501+]

Sparks, Allister - *Beyond the Miracle: Inside the New South Africa*
TimHES - v0 - i1653 - August 13 2004 - p26(1) [501+]

Sparks, Nicholas - *Three Weeks with My Brother: A Memoir (Read by Leyva, Henry). Audiobook Review*
LJ - v130 - i3 - Feb 15 2005 - p170(2) [51-500]
Three Weeks with My Brother (Read by Leyva, Henry). Audiobook Review
BL - v101 - i2 - Sept 15 2004 - p259(1) [501+]
True Believer (Read by Baker, David Aaron). Audiobook Review
LJ - v129 - i20 - Dec 1 2004 - p88(1) [501+]
Sparky
LibMed - v22 - i7 - April-May 2004 - p57(1) [501+]

Sparrow, Andrew P. - *The Law of Internet and Mobile Communications: The EU and US Contrasted*
R&R Bk N - v19 - i4 - Nov 2004 - p166(1) [501+]

Spatz, Chris - *Basic Statistics: Tales of Distributions, 8th Ed.*
SciTech - v28 - i4 - Dec 2004 - p36(1) [51-500]

Spaul, John - *The Evidence for and a Short History of the Auxiliary Infantry Units of the Imperial Roman Army*
CJ - v99 - i4 - April-May 2004 - p441-449 [501+]

Spaulding, Amy E. - *The Wisdom of Storytelling in an Information Age: A Collection of Talks*
R&R Bk N - v19 - i4 - Nov 2004 - p227(1) [501+]
SLJ - v51 - i1 - Jan 2005 - p162(1) [51-500]

Spaulding, Malcolm L. - *Estuarine and Coastal Modeling: Proceedings*
SciTech - v28 - i4 - Dec 2004 - p6(1) [1-50]

Spaulding, W.D. - *Treatment and Rehabilitation of Severe Mental Illness*
J Rehab - v70 - i3 - July-Sept 2004 - p51(2) [501+]

Speake, Jennifer - *Encyclopedia of the Renaissance and the Reformation, Rev. Ed.*
BL - v100 - i22 - August 2004 - p1974(2) [501+]
Choice - v42 - i2 - Oct 2004 - p274(1) [501+]
R&R Bk N - v19 - i3 - August 2004 - p29(1) [1-50]
The Oxford Dictionary of Proverbs
y BL - v101 - i4 - Oct 15 2004 - p438(1) [51-500]

Spearing, Elizabeth - *Medieval Writings on Female Spirituality*
Specu - v79 - i4 - Oct 2004 - p1148(2) [501+]

Spears, Heather - *The Flourish: Murder in the Family*
BIC - v33 - i8 - Nov 2004 - p16(3) [501+]

Spears, Larry C. - *Practicing Servant-Leadership: Succeeding Through Trust, Bravery, and Forgiveness*
R&R Bk N - v19 - i4 - Nov 2004 - p124(1) [51-500]

Spears, Rick - *Teenagers from Mars*
PW - v252 - i5 - Jan 31 2005 - p51(1) [51-500]

Speca, Robert - *The Championship Domino Toppling Book and Gift Set*
c PW - v251 - i43 - Oct 25 2004 - p50(1) [51-500]

Speck, Bruce W. - *Service Learning: History, Theory, and Issues*
R&R Bk N - v19 - i4 - Nov 2004 - p190(1) [501+]

Speck, Frank G. - *Ethnology of the Yuchi Indians*
Roundup M - v12 - i1 - Oct 2004 - p26(1) [51-500]

Spector, Craig - *Underground*
KR - v73 - i5 - March 1 2005 - p257(1) [501+]

Spector, Norman - *Chronicle of a War Foretold: How Mideast Peace Became America's Fight*
CBRA - Annual 2003 - p298(1) [501+]

Spector, Sheila A. - *Glorious Incomprehensible*
Eight-C St - v36 - i2 - Winter 2003 - p294 [501+]
Wonders Divine
Eight-C St - v36 - i2 - Winter 2003 - p294 [501+]

The Speed of Light
LibMed - v22 - i4 - Jan 2004 - p67(1) [501+]

Speegle, Darren - *Gothic Wine*
MFSF - v107 - i4-5 - Oct-Nov 2004 - p36(1) [501+]

Speelman, Patrick J. - *Henry Lloyd and the Military Enlightenment of Eighteenth-Century Europe*
Albion - v36 - i1 - Spring 2004 - p141(2) [501+]

Speerstra, Joel - *Bach and the Pedal Clavichord: An Organist's Guide*
Choice - v42 - i1 - Sept 2004 - p112(1) [501+]
Notes - v61 - i3 - March 2005 - p760(4) [501+]

Speichert, C. Greg - *Encyclopedia of Water Garden Plants*
Bwatch - v26 - i8 - August 2004 - p10(1) [51-500]
Choice - v41 - i11-12 - July-August 2004 - p2023(1) [501+]
E-Streams - Sept 2004 - pNA [501+]
Ref Rev - May 2004 - pNA [501+]
SciTech - v28 - i3 - Sept 2004 - p129(1) [51-500]

Speight, Charlotte F. - *Hands in Clay*
Ceram Mo - v52 - i4 - April 2004 - p28(1) [501+]

Speirs, Gill - *The Donkey and the Golden Light (Illus. by Speirs, John)*
c SLJ - v50 - i8 - August 2004 - p94(1) [51-500]

Spektorowski, Alberto - *The Origins of Argentina's Revolution of the Right*
AHR - v109 - i3 - June 2004 - p954(1) [501+]
HAHR - v84 - i4 - Nov 2004 - p765(2) [501+]

Speller, Elizabeth - *Athens: A New Guide*
LJ - v129 - i12 - July 2004 - p108(1) [51-500]
TLS - i5284 - July 9 2004 - p7(1) [501+]

Spellman, Frank R. - *Mathematics Manual for Water and Wastewater Treatment Plant Operators*
SciTech - v28 - i3 - Sept 2004 - p146(1) [51-500]
Stormwater Discharge Management: A Practical Guide to Compliance
SciTech - v28 - i1 - March 2004 - p148(1) [51-500]

Spellman, Paul N. - *Captain John H. Rogers, Texas Ranger*
SHQ - v107 - i3 - Jan 2004 - p483(2) [501+]

Spence, June - *Change Baby*
BL - v101 - i1 - Sept 1 2004 - p65(1) [51-500]
LJ - v129 - i14 - Sept 1 2004 - p143(1) [51-500]
NYTBR - Oct 10 2004 - p20 [501+]
PW - v251 - i32 - August 9 2004 - p229(1) [51-500]

Spence, Pam - *Sun Observer's Guide*
y BL - v101 - i5 - Nov 1 2004 - p451(1) [51-500]

Spence, Stephen - *The Parting of the Ways: The Roman Church as a Case Study*
R&R Bk N - v19 - i4 - Nov 2004 - p20(1) [51-500]

Spencer, A.J. - *Excavations at Tell El-Balamun: 1999-2001*
R&R Bk N - v19 - i3 - August 2004 - p58(1) [51-500]

Spencer, Adam - *Adam Spencer's Book of Numbers*
Choice - v42 - i3 - Nov 2004 - p522(2) [1-50]
y SB - v40 - i4 - July-August 2004 - p162(1) [51-500]

Spencer, Ann - *And Round Me Rings: Bell Tales and Folklore (Illus. by Grater, Lindsay)*
c CBRA - Annual 2003 - p530(1) [51-500]

c BL - v101 - i4 - Oct 15 2004 - p411(1) [51-500]
c Globe & Mail - Dec 11 2004 - pD43 [51-500]
c KR - v72 - i16 - August 15 2004 - p813(1) [51-500]
c SLJ - v50 - i9 - Sept 2004 - p181(1) [51-500]
The Perfect Thanksgiving (Illus. by Adinolfi, JoAnn)
c LibMed - v22 - i6 - March 2004 - p59(1) [501+]
While You Are Away
c LibMed - v23 - i1 - August-Sept 2004 - p66(1) [51-500]

Spinelli, Henry M. - *Atlas of Aesthetic Eyelid and Periocular Surgery*
SciTech - v28 - i1 - March 2004 - p110(1) [51-500]

Spinelli, Jerry - *Milkweed*
c JAAL - v48 - i1 - Sept 2004 - p80(2) [501+]
c LibMed - v22 - i5 - Feb 2004 - p70(2) [501+]
Stargirl
c SLJ - v50 - i11 - Nov 2004 - p65(1) [51-500]

Spinello, Richard A. - *Intellectual Property Rights in a Networked World: Theory and Practice*
R&R Bk N - v19 - i4 - Nov 2004 - p162(1) [501+]

Spinner, Stephanie - *Quicksilver*
y HB - v81 - i2 - March-April 2005 - p207(2) [51-500]
y Kliatt - v39 - i2 - March 2005 - p16(1) [51-500]

Spinosaurus
c SLJ - v51 - i2 - Feb 2005 - p120(1) [51-500]

Spinrad, Norman - *Bug Jack Barron*
ChrSFF&H - v26 - i10 - Oct 2004 - p27(1) [51-500]
The Druid King
y Kliatt - v39 - i1 - Jan 2005 - p22(1) [51-500]

Spires, Elizabeth - *Now the Green Blade Rises*
Poet - v184 - i5 - Sept 2004 - p378(3) [501+]

Spirin, Gennadiji - *The Story of Noah and the Ark: According to the Book of Genesis: From the King James Bible (Illus. by Spirin, Gennadii)*
c HB - v80 - i4 - July-August 2004 - p471(1) [51-500]

Spirit of America: Our Thirteen Colonies
LibMed - v22 - i7 - April-May 2004 - p72(1) [501+]

Spirn, Michele Sobel - *I Am the Turkey (Illus. by Allen, Joy)*
c BL - v100 - i22 - August 2004 - p1945(1) [51-500]
c KR - v72 - i16 - August 15 2004 - p813(1) [51-500]
c SLJ - v51 - i1 - Jan 2005 - p98(1) [51-500]

Spitalnic, Stuart - *Bringing Back Eight*
KR - v72 - i13 - July 1 2004 - p604(1) [501+]

Spiteri, Raymond - *Surrealism, Politics, and Culture*
R&R Bk N - v19 - i1 - Feb 2004 - p209(1) [51-500]

Spittell, John A., Jr. - *Peripheral Vascular Disease for Cardiologists: A Clinical Approach*
SciTech - v28 - i1 - March 2004 - p105(1) [51-500]

Spitzer, Daniel William - *Variable Speed Drives: Principles and Applications for Energy Cost Savings, 3rd Ed.*
SciTech - v28 - i1 - March 2004 - p151(1) [51-500]

Spitzer, John - *The Birth of the Orchestra: History of an Institution, 1650-1815*
Choice - v42 - i6 - Feb 2005 - p1032(1) [51-500]
MT - v145 - i1889 - Winter 2004 - p85-89 [501+]

Spitzer, Michael - *Metaphor and Musical Thought*
Choice - v42 - i1 - Sept 2004 - p112(1) [501+]

Spitzer, Robert L. - *Treatment Companion to the DSM-IV-TR Casebook*
SciTech - v28 - i3 - Sept 2004 - p97(1) [51-500]

Spivey, Donald - *Fire from the Soul: A History of the African-American Struggle*
R&R Bk N - v19 - i1 - Feb 2004 - p57(1) [51-500]

Spivey, Nigel Jonathan - *The Ancient Olympics*
Choice - v42 - i5 - Jan 2005 - p892(1) [1-50]
NYTBR - August 8 2004 - p8 [501+]
TLS - i5284 - July 9 2004 - p3-4 [501+]

A Splendor of Letters: The Permanence of Books in an Impermanent War
Sew R - v112 - i3 - Summer 2004 - pLXX-LXXIV [501+]

Spohn, Kate - *By Word of Mouse (Illus. by Spohn, Kate)*
c CCB-B - v58 - i3 - Nov 2004 - p145(1) [501+]
c PW - v251 - i30 - July 26 2004 - p54(1) [51-500]
c SLJ - v50 - i7 - July 2004 - p88(1) [51-500]

Spolsky, Joel - *Joel on Software: And on Diverse and Occasionally Related Matters ...*
SciTech - v28 - i4 - Dec 2004 - p25(1) [51-500]

Spongberg, Mary - *Writing Women's History Since the Renaissance*
HNet - July 2004 - pNA [501+]

Spooner, Rick - *The Spirit of Semper Fidelis: Reflections from the Bottom of an Old Canteen Cup*
Mar Crp G - v89 - i1 - Jan 2005 - p68(1) [501+]

Spoor, Max - *Transition Institutions and the Rural Sector*
JEL - v41 - i4 - Dec 2003 - p1429(2) [501+]

Sports Machines
c LibMed - v23 - i3 - Nov-Dec 2004 - p64(2) [51-500]

Spotila, James R. - *Sea Turtles: A Complete Guide to Their Biology, Behavior, and Conservation*
Am Sci - v93 - i2 - March-April 2005 - p175(1) [51-500]
y BL - v101 - i7 - Dec 1 2004 - p632(2) [51-500]
LJ - v130 - i2 - Feb 1 2005 - p112(1) [51-500]
Sci - v307 - i5707 - Jan 14 2005 - p211(1) [501+]

Spoto, Donald - *In Silence: Why We Pray*
BL - v101 - i3 - Oct 1 2004 - p306(1) [51-500]
c PW - v251 - i41 - Oct 11 2004 - p77(1) [51-500]

Spotted Eagle, Douglas - *Vegas 5 Editing Workshop, 2nd Ed.*
SciTech - v28 - i4 - Dec 2004 - p155(1) [51-500]

Spotts, Frederic - *Hitler and Power of Aesthetics*
GSR - v27 - i3 - Oct 2004 - p638(2) [501+]

Spradlin, Michael P. - *Spy Goddess, Bk. 1*
KR - v73 - i3 - Feb 1 2005 - p182(1) [51-500]

Spragg, Mark - *An Unfinished Life (Read by Amendola, Tony). Audiobook Review*
y Kliatt - v39 - i2 - March 2005 - p57(1) [51-500]
PW - v251 - i40 - Oct 4 2004 - p31(1) [51-500]
An Unfinished Life
BL - v100 - i22 - August 2004 - p1901(1) [501+]
BL - v101 - i9-10 - Jan 1 2005 - p770(1) [51-500]
NYTBR - Nov 7 2004 - p23 [501+]
PW - v251 - i32 - August 9 2004 - p231(1) [51-500]
Spec - v296 - i9201 - Dec 11 2004 - p41(2) [501+]
Where Rivers Change Direction
A Lib - v35 - i7 - August 2004 - p88(1) [501+]

Spraggon, Julie - *Puritan Iconoclasm during the English Civil War*
Albion - v36 - i2 - Summer 2004 - p304(2) [501+]
HNet - June 2004 - pNA [501+]

Sprague, Ralph H. - *System Sciences: Abstracts and CD-ROM of Full Papers 2004: Proceedings*
SciTech - v28 - i1 - March 2004 - p165(1) [51-500]

Spratford, Becky Siegel - *The Horror Readers' Advisory: The Librarian's Guide to Vampires, Killer Tomatoes, and Haunted Houses*
y Kliatt - v38 - i4 - July 2004 - p36(1) [501+]
y LJ - v129 - i14 - Sept 1 2004 - p195(1) [51-500]
c SLJ - v50 - i7 - July 2004 - p135(1) [51-500]
y Teach Lib - v32 - i1 - Oct 2004 - p38(2) [501+]
y VOYA - v27 - i3 - August 2004 - p252(1) [1-50]

Spratto, George - *PDR Nurse's Drug Handbook: The Information Standard for Prescription Drugs and Nursing Considerations*
Choice - v42 - i4 - Dec 2004 - p634(2) [1-50]

Spray, Sharon L. - *Loss of Biodiversity*
Choice - v41 - i11-12 - July-August 2004 - p2070(1) [501+]
SciTech - v28 - i1 - March 2004 - p59(1) [51-500]
Wetlands
Choice - v42 - i4 - Dec 2004 - p688(1) [1-50]

Spree, Reinhard - *Geschichte der deutschen Wirtschaft im 20. Jahrhundert*
HNet - June 2004 - pNA [501+]

Spretnak, Charlene - *Missing Mary: The Queen of Heaven and Her Re-Emergence in the Modern Church*
Choice - v42 - i2 - Oct 2004 - p312(1) [51-500]

Sprigg, Peter - *Getting It Straight: What the Research Shows about Homosexuality*
CI - v12 - i9 - Oct 2004 - p45(1) [501+]

Spring, Joel - *Educating the Consumer-Citizen: A History of the Marriage of Schools, Advertising, and Media*
HNet - Nov 2004 - pNA [501+]
How Educational Ideologies are Shaping Global Society: Intergovernmental Organizations, NGO's and the Nationstate
Choice - v42 - i4 - Dec 2004 - p712(1) [1-50]

Springer, Caroline J. - *Suicide Gene Therapy: Methods and Reviews*
SciTech - v28 - i1 - March 2004 - p91(1) [51-500]

Springer, Nancy - *Outlaw Princess of Sherwood: A Tale of Rowan Hood. (Read by Gray, Emily). Audiobook Review*
c Kliatt - v38 - i4 - July 2004 - p54(1) [51-500]
Wild Boy: A Tale of Rowan Hood
c SLJ - v50 - i8 - August 2004 - p129(1) [51-500]
y VOYA - v27 - i4 - Oct 2004 - p320(1) [51-500]

Springer, Robert - *The Lyrics in African American Popular Music*
PMS - v27 - i3 - Oct 2004 - p375(2) [501+]

Springhouse Corporation - *Anatomy and Physiology Made Incredibly Easy, 2nd Ed.*
SciTech - v28 - i3 - Sept 2004 - p68(1) [51-500]

Springhouse Nurse's Drug Guide 2005, 6th Ed.
SciTech - v28 - i3 - Sept 2004 - p122(1) [51-500]

Spritzler, John - *The People as Enemy: The Leader's Hidden Agenda in World War Two*
CBRA - Annual 2003 - p298(1) [51-500]
The People as Enemy: The Leaders' Hidden Agenda in World War Two
R&R Bk N - v19 - i3 - August 2004 - p32(1) [51-500]

Sprott, Duncan - *The Ptolemies*
KR - v72 - i24 - Dec 15 2004 - pS7(1) [501+]

Sprout, Jerry - *Hawai'i, the Big Island Trailblazer: Where to Hike, Snorkel, Surf, Bike, Drive*
R&R Bk N - v19 - i1 - Feb 2004 - p51(1) [51-500]

Spruill, Matt - *Storming the Heights: A Guide to the Battle of Chattanooga*
R&R Bk N - v19 - i1 - Feb 2004 - p59(1) [51-500]

Spufford, Francis - *I May Be Some Time: Ice and the English Imagination*
Globe & Mail - Feb 5 2005 - pD19 [501+]

Spufford, Peter - *Power and Profit: The Merchant in Medieval Europe*
R&R Bk N - v19 - i1 - Feb 2004 - p107(1) [51-500]

Spulber, Nicolas - *Russia's Economic Transitions: From Late Tsarism to the New Millennium.*
BHR - v78 - i2 - Summer 2004 - p368(4) [501+]
JEL - v42 - i1 - March 2004 - p324(2) [501+]
Russ Rev - v63 - i3 - July 2004 - pNA [501+]

Spurkland, Kristin - *Knits from the Heart: Quick Projects for Generous Giving*
LJ - v129 - i13 - August 2004 - p79(1) [501+]

Spurling, Laurence - *Introduction to Psychodynamic Counselling*
SciTech - v28 - i3 - Sept 2004 - p100(1) [51-500]

Spurr, Elizabeth - *The Peterkins' Christmas (Illus. by Halperin, Wendy Anderson)*
c HB - v80 - i6 - Nov-Dec 2004 - p664(2) [51-500]
c PW - v251 - i39 - Sept 27 2004 - p63(1) [51-500]

Spuybroek, Lars - *NOX: Machining Architecture*
BL - v101 - i9-10 - Jan 1 2005 - p800(1) [51-500]

Squier, Susan Merrill - *Communities of the Air: Radio Century, Radio Culture*
JAH - v91 - i2 - Sept 2004 - p700(2) [501+]

Squires, E.J. - *Applied Animal Endocrinology*
SciTech - v28 - i1 - March 2004 - p132(1) [51-500]

Squires, Gregory D. - *Organizing Access to Capital: Advocacy and the Democratization of Financial Institutions*
CS - v33 - i4 - July 2004 - p480(3) [501+]

Sreenivasan, Govind P. - *The Peasants of Ottobeuren, 1487-1726: A Rural Society in Early Modern Europe*
Choice - v42 - i6 - Feb 2005 - p1089(1) [51-500]

Srigley, Susan - *Flannery O'Connor's Sacramental Art*
Wil Q - v29 - i1 - Wntr 2005 - p114(3) [501+]

Srikanth, Ranjini - *The World Next Door: South Asian American Literature and the of America*
Choice - v42 - i6 - Feb 2005 - p1024(1) [51-500]

Srimani, Pradip K. - *Information Technology: Coding and Computing: Proceedings, 2 Vols*
SciTech - v28 - i3 - Sept 2004 - p135(1) [51-500]

Sriram, Chandra Lekha - *Exploring Subregional Conflict: Opportunities for Conflict Prevention*
R&R Bk N - v19 - i4 - Nov 2004 - p123(1) [1-50]

Srivastava, Sanjay - *Sexual Sites, Seminal Attitudes: Sexualities, Masculinities, and Culture in South Asia*
R&R Bk N - v19 - i3 - August 2004 - p148(1) [51-500]

Srivastava, Sheela - *Understanding Bacteria*
SciTech - v28 - i1 - March 2004 - p76(1) [51-500]

Srode, Molly - *Keeping Spiritual Balance as We Grow Older: More than 65 Ways to Use Purpose, Prayer, and the Power of Spirit to Build a Meaningful Retirement*
PW - v251 - i45 - Nov 8 2004 - p50(1) [51-500]

Ssorin-Chaikov, Nikolai V. - *The Social Life of the State in Subarctic Siberia*
AHR - v109 - i2 - April 2004 - p651(1) [501+]
Russ Rev - v63 - i3 - July 2004 - pNA [501+]
Slav R - v63 - i3 - Fall 2004 - p677-678 [501+]

St. Amant, Mark - *Committed: Confessions of a Fantasy Football Junkie*
y BL - v101 - i1 - Sept 1 2004 - p52(1) [51-500]
LJ - v129 - i16 - Oct 1 2004 - p90(1) [51-500]
PW - v251 - i31 - August 2 2004 - p60(1) [501+]

St. Antoine, Sara - *The Great North American Prairie*
  c CH Bwatch - March 2005 - pNA [51-500]
St. Aubyn, Edward - *Some Hope: A Trilogy*
  Globe & Mail - Nov 27 2004 - pD3 [51-500]
St. Clair, Archer - *Carving as Craft: Palatine East and the Greco-Roman Bone and Ivory Carving Tradition*
  R&R Bk N - v19 - i1 - Feb 2004 - p208(1) [51-500]
St. Clair, Guy - *Beyond Degrees: Professional Learning for Knowledge Services*
  ALJ - v53 - i3 - August 2004 - p325(1) [501+]
  R&R Bk N - v19 - i1 - Feb 2004 - p102(1) [51-500]
St. Clair, Robert N. - *Literary Structures, Character Development, and Dramaturgical Scenarios in Framing the Category Novel*
  R&R Bk N - v19 - i4 - Nov 2004 - p227(1) [501+]
St. Clair, William - *The Reading Nation in the Romantic Period*
  Choice - v42 - i6 - Feb 2005 - p1008(1) [51-500]
  Lon R Bks - v27 - i2 - Jan 20 2005 - p26(3) [501+]
  TLS - i5286 - July 23 2004 - p3-4 [501+]
St. Claire, Rocki - *Hit Reply*
  BL - v101 - i1 - Sept 1 2004 - p74(1) [51-500]
  KR - v72 - i20 - Oct 15 2004 - p984(2) [51-500]
St. Claire, Roxanne - *Killer Curves*
  BL - v101 - i7 - Dec 1 2004 - p642(1) [51-500]
  PW - v252 - i1 - Jan 3 2005 - p41(1) [51-500]
St. George, Judith - *So You Want to Be an Inventor?* (Illus. by Small, David)
  c RT - v57 - Nov 2003 - p275 [51-500]
Take the Lead, George Washington (Illus. by Powers, Daniel)
  c BL - v101 - i7 - Dec 1 2004 - p650(1) [51-500]
  c CCB-B - v58 - i4 - Dec 2004 - p184(2) [51-500]
  c KR - v72 - i24 - Dec 15 2004 - p1208(1) [51-500]
  c SLJ - v51 - i1 - Jan 2005 - p114(1) [51-500]
You're on Your Way, Teddy Roosevelt (Illus. by Faulkner, Matt)
  c BL - v101 - i5 - Nov 1 2004 - p478(1) [501+]
  c CCB-B - v58 - i4 - Dec 2004 - p184(2) [51-500]
  c HB - v80 - i5 - Sept-Oct 2004 - p608(1) [51-500]
  c KR - v72 - i16 - August 15 2004 - p813(1) [51-500]
  c PW - v251 - i37 - Sept 13 2004 - p78(1) [51-500]
  c SLJ - v50 - i10 - Oct 2004 - p150(1) [51-500]
St. Giles, Jennifer - *The Mistress of Trevelyan*
  LJ - v129 - i13 - August 2004 - p56(2) [501+]
  PW - v251 - i29 - July 19 2004 - p150(1) [51-500]
St. James, Rebecca - *She: The Woman You're Made to Be*
  PW - v251 - i39 - Sept 27 2004 - p55(1) [51-500]
St. John, Edward P. - *Public Funding of Higher Education: Changing Contexts and New Rationales*
  R&R Bk N - v19 - i4 - Nov 2004 - p185(1) [501+]
Public Policy and College Access: Investigating the Federal and State Roles in Equalizing Postsecondary Opportunity
  R&R Bk N - v19 - i4 - Nov 2004 - p190(1) [501+]
Refinancing the College Dream: Access, Equal Opportunity, and Justice for Taxpayers
  R&R Bk N - v19 - i1 - Feb 2004 - p186(1) [51-500]
St. John, Warren - *Rammer Jammer Yellow Hammer: A Journey into the Heart of Fan Mania* (Read by St. John, Warren). Audiobook Review
  PW - v251 - i40 - Oct 4 2004 - p32(1) [51-500]
Rammer Jammer Yellow Hammer: A Journey into the Heart of Fan Mania
  BL - v100 - i21 - July 2004 - p1810(1) [1-50]
  BL - v101 - i1 - Sept 1 2004 - p46(1) [51-500]
  LJ - v129 - i12 - July 2004 - p91(1) [51-500]
  SLJ - v51 - i2 - Feb 2005 - p159(1) [51-500]
Rammer Jammer Yellow Hammer
  Ent W - i778 - August 13 2004 - p93 [51-500]
Staake, Bob - *Hello, Robots* (Illus. by Staake, Bob)
  c BL - v101 - i7 - Dec 1 2004 - p662(2) [51-500]
  c KR - v72 - i15 - August 1 2004 - p749(1) [51-500]
  c SLJ - v50 - i12 - Dec 2004 - p122(1) [51-500]
Stabenow, Dana - *Powers of Detection: Stories of Mystery and Fantasy*
  ChrSFF&H - v26 - i10 - Oct 2004 - p48(2) [501+]
  PW - v251 - i35 - August 30 2004 - p37(1) [501+]
A Taint in the Blood
  BL - v101 - i1 - Sept 1 2004 - p70(1) [51-500]
  KR - v72 - i14 - July 15 2004 - p664(1) [51-500]
  PW - v251 - i35 - August 30 2004 - p35(2) [501+]
Wild Crimes
  y Kliatt - v39 - i1 - Jan 2005 - p26(1) [51-500]
Stabile, Susan M. - *Memory's Daughters: The Material Culture of Remembrance in Eighteenth-Century America*
  Choice - v42 - i3 - Nov 2004 - p551(1) [1-50]

Stabiner, Karen - *My Girl: Adventures with a Teen in Training*
  KR - v73 - i2 - Jan 15 2005 - p112(1) [501+]
Stableford, Brian - *Historical Dictionary of Science Fiction Literature*
  BL - v101 - i4 - Oct 15 2004 - p438(1) [51-500]
  New Sci - v184 - i2469 - Oct 16 2004 - p53(1) [51-500]
Stabler, Jane - *Byron, Poetics and History*
  Nine-C Lit - v58 - i4 - March 2004 - p553(555) [501+]
  RES - v55 - i221 - Sept 2004 - p630(3) [501+]
Staccioli, Romolo Augusto - *The Roads of the Romans*
  Choice - v42 - i5 - Jan 2005 - p875(1) [1-50]
Stace, Wesley - *Misfortune*
  KR - v73 - i1 - Jan 1 2005 - p19(1) [501+]
  LJ - v129 - i20 - Dec 1 2004 - p88(1) [51-500]
  LJ - v130 - i2 - Feb 1 2005 - p71(1) [51-500]
  PW - v252 - i5 - Jan 31 2005 - p47(1) [501+]
Stacey, Lyndon - *Deadfall*
  KR - v73 - i2 - Jan 15 2005 - p88(1) [51-500]
Stacey, Sarah - *Total Beauty*
  People - v63 - i1 - Jan 10 2005 - p49 [51-500]
  PW - v251 - i49 - Dec 6 2004 - p57(1) [51-500]
Stacey, Sarah Alyn - *Culture and Conflict in Seventeenth-Century France and Ireland*
  R&R Bk N - v19 - i3 - August 2004 - p41(1) [51-500]
Stachel, John - *Einstein from "B" to "Z."*
  Isis - v95 - i3 - Sept 2004 - p535(2) [501+]
Stachiw, Jerry D. - *Handbook of Acrylics for Submersibles, Hyperbaric Chambers and Aquaria*
  SciTech - v28 - i1 - March 2004 - p174(1) [51-500]
Stack, Laura - *Leave the Office Earlier: The Productivity Pro Shows You How to Do More in Less Time--and Feel Great about It*
  LJ - v129 - i12 - July 2004 - p107(1) [51-500]
Stackhouse, Max L. - *God and Globalization, Vol. 3*
  IBMR - v28 - i3 - July 2004 - p133(1) [501+]
Stackpole, Michael A. - *A Secret Atlas*
  KR - v72 - i24 - Dec 15 2004 - p1171(1) [501+]
  LJ - v130 - i3 - Feb 15 2005 - p123(1) [51-500]
  PW - v252 - i6 - Feb 7 2005 - p47(1) [51-500]
Stadiem, William - *Dear Senator: A Memoir by the Daughter of Strom Thurmond*
  PW - v252 - i1 - Jan 3 2005 - p48(2) [51-500]
Stadler, Alexander - *Beverly Billingsly Can't Catch* (Illus. by Stadler, Alexander)
  c BooChiTr - April 11 2004 - p2(1) [501+]
  c SLJ - v50 - i10 - Oct 2004 - pS26(1) [1-50]
Beverly Billingsly Takes the Cake (Illus. by Stadler, Alexander)
  c KR - v73 - i4 - Feb 15 2005 - p236(1) [51-500]
  c PW - v252 - i5 - Jan 31 2005 - p69(2) [51-500]
Duncan Rumplemeyer's Bad Birthday (Illus. by Stadler, Alexander)
  c CCB-B - v58 - i4 - Dec 2004 - p185(1) [51-500]
  c KR - v72 - i15 - August 1 2004 - p749(1) [51-500]
  c PW - v251 - i33 - August 16 2004 - p62(1) [51-500]
  c SLJ - v50 - i10 - Oct 2004 - p135(1) [51-500]
Stadler, John - *Take Me Out to the Ball Game*
  c PW - v252 - i4 - Jan 24 2005 - p46(1) [51-500]
Stadler, Ulrich - *Der Technisierte Blick. Optische Instrumente und der Status von Literatur. Ein Kulturhistorisches Museum*
  MLN - v119 - i3 - April 2004 - p610-614 [501+]
Staeger, Rob - *Asylees*
  y SLJ - v50 - i11 - Nov 2004 - p158(1) [51-500]
Deported Aliens
  y SLJ - v50 - i11 - Nov 2004 - p158(1) [51-500]
Stafford, Matthew - *Signaling and Switching for Packet Telephony*
  SciTech - v28 - i4 - Dec 2004 - p153(1) [51-500]
Stafford, Philip B. - *Gray Areas: Ethnographic Encounters with Nursing Home Culture*
  MAQ - v18 - i4 - Dec 2004 - p519(2) [501+]
Stafford, Tom - *Mind Hacks*
  New Sci - v185 - i2485 - Feb 5 2005 - p53(1) [501+]
Stafford, William - *English Feminists and Their Opponents in the 1790s: Unsex'd and Proper Females*
  Albion - v36 - i2 - Summer 2004 - p312(2) [501+]
  HER - v119 - i483 - Sept 2004 - p997(2) [501+]
  HER - v119 - i483 - Sept 2004 - p997(2) [501+]
Stafstrom, Carl E. - *Epilepsy and the Ketogenic Diet*
  SciTech - v28 - i4 - Dec 2004 - p93(1) [51-500]
Stagg, J.C.A. - *Papers of James Madison: 10 July 1812-7 February 1813*
  R&R Bk N - v19 - i4 - Nov 2004 - p60(1) [51-500]

Stagni, Pellegrino - *View from Rome: Archbishop Stagni's 1915 Reports on the Ontario Bilingual Schools Question*
  CBRA - Annual 2003 - p396(1) [51-500]
Stahl, Ann B. - *Making History in Banda: Anthropological Visions of Africa's Past*
  JRAI - v10 - i3 - Sept 2004 - p708(2) [501+]
Stahl, David C. - *The Burdens of Survival: Ooka Shohei's Writings on the Pacific War*
  HNet - July 2004 - pNA [501+]
Stahl, Hans-Peter - *Thucydides: Man's Place in History*
  Choice - v42 - i1 - Sept 2004 - p165(1) [501+]
Stahl, Jerry - *I, Fatty*
  Ent W - i775 - July 23 2004 - p80 [501+]
  KR - v72 - i24 - Dec 15 2004 - pS10(1) [501+]
  NYTBR - August 8 2004 - p14 [51-500]
  People - v62 - i9 - August 30 2004 - p50 [51-500]
Stahl, Julie Muller - *Dish: International Design for the Home*
  PW - v251 - i50 - Dec 13 2004 - p60(1) [51-500]
Stahl, Michael J. - *Encyclopedia of Health Care Management*
  E-Streams - August 2004 - pNA [501+]
  R&R Bk N - v19 - i1 - Feb 2004 - p249(1) [51-500]
  SciTech - v28 - i1 - March 2004 - p85(1) [51-500]
Stahl, Saul - *Introduction to Topology and Geometry*
  SciTech - v28 - i4 - Dec 2004 - p42(1) [51-500]
Stahler, David, Jr. - *Truesight*
  y Kliatt - v39 - i1 - Jan 2005 - p22(1) [51-500]
  PW - v251 - i51 - Dec 20 2004 - p62(1) [501+]
Stahr, Walter - *John Jay: Founding Father*
  PW - v252 - i5 - Jan 31 2005 - p58(2) [501+]
Stainton, Sue - *The Lighthouse Cat* (Illus. by Mortimer, Anne)
  c BL - v100 - i22 - August 2004 - p1945(2) [51-500]
  c KR - v72 - i13 - July 1 2004 - p637(1) [51-500]
  c SLJ - v50 - i9 - Sept 2004 - p181(1) [51-500]
Stake, Robert E. - *Standards-Based and Responsive Evaluation*
  R&R Bk N - v19 - i1 - Feb 2004 - p76(1) [1-50]
Stalcup, Ann - *Leo Politi: Artist of the Angels*
  KR - v72 - i24 - Dec 15 2004 - p1208(1) [51-500]
Stalcup, Brenda - *Women's Suffrage*
  c SLJ - v50 - i8 - August 2004 - p50(1) [51-500]
Stald, G. - *Global Encounters: Media and Cultural Transformation*
  J Broadcst - v48 - i3 - Sept 2004 - p518(7) [501+]
Staley, David J. - *Computers, Visualization and History: How New Technology Will Transform Our Understanding of the Past*
  JAH - v91 - i1 - June 2004 - p344-345 [501+]
Staley, Kent W. - *The Evidence for the Top Quark: Objectivity and Bias in Collaborative Experimentation*
  Choice - v42 - i3 - Nov 2004 - p523(1) [1-50]
Stalin - *Stalin's Holy War: Religion, Nationalism, and Alliance Politics, 1941-1945*
  JMH - v76 - i4 - Dec 2004 - p1011(3) [501+]
Stall, Sam - *The Encyclopedia of Guilty Pleasures*
  PW - v251 - i38 - Sept 20 2004 - p52(1) [51-500]
Stallard, Patricia Y. - *Fanny Dunbar Corbusier: Recollections of Her Army Life, 1869-1908*
  J Mil H - v68 - i3 - April 2004 - p613-614 [501+]
  WHQ - v35 - i4 - Winter 2004 - p526-527 [501+]
Staller, Natasha - *A Sum of Destructions: Picasso's Cultures and the Creation of Cubism*
  Art Bull - v86 - i3 - Sept 2004 - p614(7) [501+]
Stamaty, Mark Alan - *Alia's Mission: Saving the Books of Iraq: Inspired by a True Story* (Illus. by Stamary, Mark Alan)
  KR - v73 - i1 - Jan 1 2005 - p57(1) [51-500]
Alia's Mission: Saving the Books of Iraq: Inspired by a True Story (Illus. by Stamaty, Mark Alan)
  c CCB-B - v58 - i6 - Feb 2005 - p266(2) [51-500]
  c Globe & Mail - Dec 11 2004 - pD43 [51-500]
  c HB - v81 - i2 - March-April 2005 - p218(1) [51-500]
  c PW - v251 - i51 - Dec 20 2004 - p59(1) [51-500]
Stambaugh, Joan - *The Formless Self*
  BCS - v24 - Annual 2004 - p300(4) [501+]
Stambovsky, Phillip - *Myth and the limits of reason, Rev. Ed.*
  R&R Bk N - v19 - i3 - August 2004 - p13(1) [1-50]
Philosophical Conceptualization and Literary Art: Inference, Ereignis, and Conceptual Attunement to the Work of Poetic Genius
  R&R Bk N - v19 - i4 - Nov 2004 - p240(1) [501+]
Stamen, Jessica - *Self-Destruction Handbook: 8 Simple Steps to an Unhealthy You*
  NYTBR - Jan 2 2005 - p19 [501+]
Stamm, Peter - *Unformed Landscape*
  KR - v73 - i2 - Jan 15 2005 - p81(1) [501+]

Sterling, Dorothy - *Close to My Heart*
 BL - v101 - i4 - Oct 15 2004 - p380(1) [51-500]
Sterling-Hellenbrand, Alexandra - *Topographies of Gender in Middle High German Arthurian Romance*
 GSR - v27 - i2 - May 2004 - p363-364 [501+]
Stern, Bonnie - *Essentials of Home Cooking*
 CBRA - Annual 2003 - p140(1) [501+]
Stern, Claudio D. - *Gastrulation: From Cells to Embryo*
 Choice - v42 - i7 - March 2005 - p1251(1) [51-500]
 SciTech - v28 - i4 - Dec 2004 - p67(1) [51-500]
Stern, Daniel - *A Little Street Music*
 BL - v101 - i7 - Dec 1 2004 - p638(1) [51-500]
Stern, Dave - *Daedalus*
 c Kliatt - v38 - i4 - July 2004 - p33(1) [51-500]
Stern, Ellen - *Threads: My Life Behind the Seams in the High-Stakes World of Fashion*
 KR - v72 - i19 - Oct 1 2004 - p945(1) [501+]
Stern, Gary H. - *Too Big to Fail: The Hazards of Bank Bailouts*
 R&R Bk N - v19 - i3 - August 2004 - p135(1) [51-500]
Stern, Gerald - *What I Can't Bear Losing: Notes From a Life*
 APR - v34 - i1 - Jan-Feb 2005 - p45(6) [501+]
 R&R Bk N - v19 - i1 - Feb 2004 - p247(1) [51-500]
Stern, Gray H. - *Too Big to Fail: The Hazards of Bank Bailouts*
 Choice - v42 - i2 - Oct 2004 - p342(1) [51-500]
Stern, Harold P.E. - *Communication Systems: Analysis and Design*
 SciTech - v28 - i1 - March 2004 - p153(1) [51-500]
Stern, Herbert J. - *Trying Cases to Win: Evidence, Weapons for Winning, Vol. 3: Lay Witness and Expert Opinion*
 R&R Bk N - v19 - i3 - August 2004 - p206(1) [51-500]
Stern, Jessica - *Terror in the Name of God: Why Religious Militants Kill*
 BooChiTr - Jan 25 2004 - p3(1) [501+]
 JPR - v41 - i5 - Sept 2004 - p648-648 [501+]
 NYTBR - August 22 2004 - p20 [501+]
Stern, Joel M. - *Against the Grain: How to Succeed in Business by Peddling Heresy*
 R&R Bk N - v19 - i1 - Feb 2004 - p116(1) [51-500]
Stern, Judith - *QuickTime 6 for Macintosh and Windows*
 SciTech - v28 - i1 - March 2004 - p176(1) [51-500]
Stern, Lise - *How to Keep Kosher: A Comprehensive Guide to Understanding Jewish Dietary Laws*
 BL - v100 - i22 - August 2004 - p1878(1) [51-500]
 LJ - v129 - i13 - August 2004 - p111(1) [51-500]
Stern, Madeleine B. - *Behind a Mask: The Unknown Thrillers of Louisa May Alcott*
 LJ - v129 - i14 - Sept 1 2004 - p204(1) [51-500]
Stern, Mark J. - *The Divided Welfare State: The Battle over Public and Private Social Benefits in the United States*
 BHR - v77 - i4 - Winter 2003 - p766(768) [501+]
Stern, Nancy - *101 Stupid Things Trainers Do to Sabotage Success*
 HR Mag - v50 - i2 - Feb 2005 - pS8(1) [501+]
Stern, Nora - *Controlling Illegal Drugs: A Comparative Study*
 Choice - v42 - i2 - Oct 2004 - p333(1) [51-500]
Stern, Pamela R. - *Historical Dictionary of the Inuit*
 Choice - v42 - i6 - Feb 2005 - p1007(1) [51-500]
 R&R Bk N - v19 - i4 - Nov 2004 - p54(1) [51-500]
Stern, Richard G. - *What Is What Was: Essays, Stories, Poems*
 Sew R - v111 - i3 - Summer 2003 - pLXXIX-LXXXI [501+]
Stern, Robert M. - *Japan's Economic Recovery: Commercial Policy, Monetry Policy, and Corporate Governance*
 JEL - v41 - i4 - Dec 2003 - p1425(1) [501+]
Stern, S. Alan - *Worlds Beyond: The Thrill of Planetary Exploration*
 S&T - v107 - i1 - Jan 2004 - p76(1) [501+]
Stern, Sacha - *Time and Process in Ancient Judaism*
 R&R Bk N - v19 - i1 - Feb 2004 - p141(1) [51-500]
Stern, Sheldon M. - *Averting "The Final Failure": John F. Kennedy and the Secret Cuban Missile Crisis Meetings*
 Choice - v41 - i7 - March 2004 - p1359(1) [501+]
 J Mil H - v68 - i2 - April 2004 - p651(2) [501+]
 JAH - v91 - i2 - Sept 2004 - p696(2) [501+]

Averting "The Final Failure": John F. Kennedy and the Secret Cuban Missile Crisis Mettings
 RAH - v32 - i2 - June 2004 - p262-266 [501+]
Stern, Steve (b. 1947) - *The Angel of Forgetfulness*
 KR - v72 - i24 - Dec 15 2004 - p1163(1) [501+]
Stern, Steve J. - *Remembering Pinochet's Chile: On the Eve of London, 1998*
 TLS - i5284 - July 9 2004 - p29(1) [501+]
Stern, Theodore A. - *Facing Cancer: A Complete Guide for People with Cancer, Their Families, and Caregivers*
 SciTech - v28 - i1 - March 2004 - p92(1) [51-500]
 Massachusetts General Hospital Guide to Primary Care Psychiatry, 2nd Ed.
 SciTech - v28 - i1 - March 2004 - p97(1) [51-500]
Sternberg, Guy - *Native Trees for North American Landscapes: From the Atlantic to the Rockies*
 Choice - v42 - i1 - Sept 2004 - p131(1) [501+]
 E-Streams - Sept 2004 - pNA [501+]
 QRB - v79 - i4 - Dec 2004 - p448(1) [501+]
 Ref Rev - July 2004 - pNA [501+]
 SciTech - v28 - i1 - March 2004 - p130(1) [51-500]
Sternberg, Libby - *Finding the Forger*
 KR - v72 - i24 - Dec 15 2004 - p1209(1) [51-500]
Sternberg, Ricardo - *Bamboo Church*
 CBRA - Annual 2003 - p232(2) [501+]
Sternberg, Robert J. - *Creativity: From Potential to Realization*
 SciTech - v28 - i3 - Sept 2004 - p2(1) [501+]
 Culture and Competence: Contexts of Life Success
 Choice - v41 - i11-12 - July-August 2004 - p2126(1) [501+]
 The Psychology of Abilities, Competencies, and Expertise
 TCR - v106 - i2 - Feb 2004 - p299-305 [501+]
 Unity in Psychology: Possibility or Pipedream?
 Choice - v42 - i6 - Feb 2005 - p1103(1) [51-500]
 SciTech - v28 - i3 - Sept 2004 - p1(1) [501+]
 Wisdom, Intelligence and Creativity Synthesized
 TCR - v106 - i8 - August 2004 - p1583(3) [501+]
Sterne, Evelyn Savidge - *Ballots and Bibles: Ethnic Politics and the Catholic Church in Providence*
 Am St - v45 - i1 - Spring 2004 - p147-148 [501+]
 Choice - v42 - i1 - Sept 2004 - p177(1) [501+]
 CHR - v90 - i4 - Oct 2004 - p823(2) [501+]
Sterne, Jonathan - *The Audible Past: Cultural Origins of Sound Reproduction*
 AHR - v109 - i4 - Oct 2004 - p1200-1201 [501+]
 BHR - v77 - i4 - Winter 2003 - p770(772) [501+]
 CS - v33 - i4 - July 2004 - p457(3) [501+]
 JAH - v91 - i1 - June 2004 - p269-270 [501+]
 T&C - v45 - i2 - April 2004 - p441-442 [501+]
Sterne, Melvin - *Thanksgiving*
 South CR - v36 - i2 - Spring 2004 - p137-153 [501+]
Sterneckert, Alan B. - *Critical Incident Management*
 R&R Bk N - v19 - i1 - Feb 2004 - p91(1) [1-50]
Sterner, Thomas - *Policy Instruments for Environmental and Natural Resource Management*
 R&R Bk N - v19 - i3 - August 2004 - p80(1) [51-500]
Sternheimer, Karen - *It's Not the Media: The Truth about Pop Culture's Influence on Children*
 CC - v122 - i1 - Jan 11 2005 - p22(4) [501+]
Sternlicht, Sanford - *Student Companion to Elie Wiesel*
 R&R Bk N - v19 - i1 - Feb 2004 - p232(1) [51-500]
Sterrett, Andrew - *101 Careers in Mathematics, 2nd Ed.*
 Math T - v97 - i3 - March 2004 - p222-222 [501+]
Sterritt, David - *Screening the Beats: Media Culture and the Beat Sensibility*
 Choice - v42 - i2 - Oct 2004 - p279(1) [501+]
Sterry, Paul - *Birds of the Mediterranean: A Photographic Guide*
 QRB - v79 - i4 - Dec 2004 - p438(2) [501+]
Stetson, Emily - *Kids' Easy-to-Create Wildlife Habitats (Illus. by Stone, J. Susan)*
 c BL - v101 - i7 - Dec 1 2004 - p670(1) [51-500]
Stetson, Jeff - *Blood on the Leaves*
 Globe & Mail - August 21 2004 - pD12 [51-500]
 LJ - v129 - i13 - August 2004 - p70(1) [51-500]
Stetter, Hans J. - *Numerical Polynomial Algebra*
 SciTech - v28 - i3 - Sept 2004 - p34(1) [51-500]
Steuer, Max - *The Scientific Study of Society*
 Choice - v41 - i11-12 - July-August 2004 - p2085(1) [501+]
Steuer, Sharon - *The Adobe Illustrator CS Wow! Book*
 SciTech - v28 - i4 - Dec 2004 - p130 [51-500]
Steuerle, C. Eugene - *Contemporary U.S. Tax Policy*
 Choice - v42 - i3 - Nov 2004 - p534(1) [1-50]
 R&R Bk N - v19 - i3 - August 2004 - p140(1) [1-50]

Steuver, Hank - *Off Ramp*
 Ent W - i775 - July 23 2004 - p81 [51-500]
Steven, Geoffrey - *The Player: The Life and Times of Dalton Camp*
 BIC - v33 - i2 - March 2004 - p33(2) [501+]
Steven, Graeme C.S. - *Counterterrorism: A Reference Handbook*
 c SLJ - v51 - i2 - Feb 2005 - p82(1) [51-500]
Stevenot, Ted - *Prospect Factory*
 Bwatch - v26 - i8 - August 2004 - p8(1) [51-500]
Stevens, Anthony - *Jung: A Very Short Introduction (Read by Pigott-Smith, Tim). Audiobook Review*
 Kliatt - v38 - i4 - July 2004 - p60(1) [51-500]
 Private Myths: Dreams and Dreaming
 Globe & Mail - Dec 24 2004 - pD3 [1-50]
 The Roots of War and Terror
 R&R Bk N - v19 - i3 - August 2004 - p26(1) [1-50]
Stevens, Brian L. - *Aircraft Control and Simulation, 2nd Ed.*
 SciTech - v28 - i1 - March 2004 - p169(1) [51-500]
Stevens, Brooke - *Kissing Your Ex*
 BL - v100 - i21 - July 2004 - p1823(1) [1-50]
 BW - v34 - i28 - July 11 2004 - p13(1) [501+]
Stevens, Camilla - *Family and Identity in Contemporary Cuban and Puerto Rican Drama*
 Choice - v42 - i2 - Oct 2004 - p298(2) [51-500]
Stevens, Carla - *Who's Knocking at the Door? (Illus. by Chapman, Lee)*
 c SLJ - v50 - i8 - August 2004 - p94(1) [51-500]
Stevens, Elizabeth C. - *Elizabeth Buffum Chace and Lillie Chace Wyman: A Century of Abolitionist, Suffragist and Workers' Rights*
 R&R Bk N - v19 - i1 - Feb 2004 - p132(1) [51-500]
Stevens, Francis - *The Nightmare and Other Tales of Dark Fantasy*
 BW - v34 - i44 - Oct 31 2004 - p15(1) [501+]
Stevens, Gareth - *Brain, Nerves and Stenses*
 c CH Bwatch - Feb 2005 - pNA [51-500]
 Digestion and Reproduction
 c CH Bwatch - Feb 2005 - pNA [51-500]
 Heart, Blood and Lungs
 c CH Bwatch - Feb 2005 - pNA [51-500]
 Skin, Muscles and Bones
 c CH Bwatch - Feb 2005 - pNA [51-500]
 Understanding the Human Body
 c CH Bwatch - Feb 2005 - pNA [51-500]
Stevens, Geoffrey - *Player: The Life and Times of Dalton Camp*
 CBRA - Annual 2003 - p73(1) [51-500]
Stevens, Lewis - *Composers of Classical Music of Jewish Descent*
 Notes - v61 - i2 - Dec 2004 - p444(4) [501+]
Stevens, Marcus - *Useful Girl: A novel*
 y VOYA - v27 - i5 - Dec 2004 - p397(1) [51-500]
Stevens, Mark - *De Kooning: An American Master*
 Art N - v104 - i2 - Feb 2005 - p104(1) [501+]
 BL - v101 - i5 - Nov 1 2004 - p461(1) [51-500]
 BW - v34 - i48 - Nov 28 2004 - p9(1) [501+]
 Globe & Mail - Jan 15 2005 - pR7 [501+]
 LJ - v130 - i3 - Feb 15 2005 - p126(2) [51-500]
 NW - Nov 22 2004 - p71 [501+]
 NY - v80 - i40 - Dec 20 2004 - p176 [501+]
 NYT - Nov 8 2004 - pE1 [501+]
 NYTBR - Dec 12 2004 - p10 [501+]
 People - v62 - i23 - Dec 6 2004 - p58 [51-500]
 PW - v251 - i41 - Oct 11 2004 - p65(1) [51-500]
 Time - v164 - i21 - Nov 22 2004 - p86 [501+]
Stevens, Michael J. - *Handbook of International Psychology*
 Choice - v42 - i6 - Feb 2005 - p1101(1) [51-500]
 SciTech - v28 - i4 - Dec 2004 - p1(1) [1-50]
Stevens, Mitchell L. - *Kingdom of Children: Culture and Controversy in the Homeschooling Movement*
 TCR - v106 - i2 - Feb 2004 - p357-362 [501+]
Stevens, Norman - *Antietam 1862: The Civil War's Bloodiest Day*
 R&R Bk N - v19 - i4 - Nov 2004 - p61(2) [51-500]
Stevens, Robert - *The English Judges: Their Role in the Changing Constitution*
 Law Q Rev - v120 - Jan 2004 - p179-183 [501+]
Stevens, Roger - *The Monster That Ate the Universe*
 c Sch Lib - v52 - i3 - Autumn 2004 - p154(1) [501+]
Stevens, Serita - *Forensic Nurse: The New Role of the Nurse in Law Enforcement*
 BL - v101 - i2 - Sept 15 2004 - p189(1) [51-500]
 LJ - v129 - i15 - Sept 15 2004 - p75(1) [51-500]
 PW - v251 - i31 - August 2 2004 - p62(1) [501+]

Stevenson, D. - *1914-1918: The History of the First World War*
> HT - v54 - i11 - Nov 2004 - p73(1) [501+]

Cataclysm: The First World War as Political Tragedy
> Atl - v294 - i5 - Dec 2004 - p123(1) [501+]
> Choice - v42 - i6 - Feb 2005 - p1075(1) [51-500]
> Globe & Mail - August 28 2004 - pD8 [501+]
> Globe & Mail - Nov 27 2004 - pD3 [51-500]
> Lon R Bks - v26 - i23 - Dec 2 2004 - p10(2) [501+]
> R&R Bk N - v20 - i1 - Feb 2005 - p31(1) [51-500]

Stevenson, David, Ph.D. - *The Hunt for Rob Roy: The Man and the Myths*
> Spec - v295 - i9179 - July 10 2004 - p32(2) [501+]

Stevenson, Fanny Van de Grift - *The Cruise of the "Janet Nichol" Among the South Sea Islands: A Diary*
> Choice - v42 - i1 - Sept 2004 - p104(1) [501+]

Stevenson, George B. - *Veg Out: Vegetarian Guide to Seattle and Portland*
> E Mag - v16 - i2 - March-April 2005 - p62(1) [501+]

Stevenson, Howard C. - *Playing with Anger: Teaching Coping Skills to African American Boys through Athletics and Culture*
> Choice - v41 - i11-12 - July-August 2004 - p2085(1) [501+]
> R&R Bk N - v19 - i1 - Feb 2004 - p58(1) [51-500]

Stevenson, James (American writer and illustrator) -
Corn Chowder
> LibMed - v22 - i4 - Jan 2004 - p70(1) [501+]

No Laughing, No Smiling, No Giggling (Illus. by Stevenson, James)
> c BL - v100 - i22 - August 2004 - p1946(1) [51-500]
> c CCB-B - v58 - i2 - Oct 2004 - p100(1) [51-500]
> c HB - v80 - i6 - Nov-Dec 2004 - p701(1) [51-500]
> c KR - v72 - i14 - July 15 2004 - p694(1) [51-500]
> c SLJ - v50 - i8 - August 2004 - p94(2) [51-500]

Stevenson, Jane - *Early Modern Women Poets: An Anthology*
> Ren Q - v57 - i4 - Winter 2004 - p1506(2) [501+]

The Empress of the Last Days
> BL - v101 - i4 - Oct 15 2004 - p391(1) [51-500]
> BL - v101 - i9-10 - Jan 1 2005 - p770(1) [51-500]
> KR - v72 - i19 - Oct 1 2004 - p936(1) [501+]
> LJ - v129 - i19 - Nov 15 2004 - p52(1) [501+]
> PW - v251 - i42 - Oct 18 2004 - p48(1) [51-500]
> NYTBR - Jan 23 2005 - p27 [501+]

Stevenson, Jennifer - *Trash Sex Magic*
> BW - v34 - i40 - Oct 3 2004 - p17(1) [501+]

Stevenson, John - *Japanese Kite Prints: Selections from the Skinner Collection*
> Choice - v42 - i7 - March 2005 - p1218(1) [51-500]

Stevenson, John - *Japanese Kite Prints: Selections from the Skinner Collection*
> PW - v251 - i45 - Nov 8 2004 - p48(1) [501+]

Stevenson, John - *Japanese Kite Prints: Selections from the Skinner Collections*
> R&R Bk N - v19 - i4 - Nov 2004 - p208(1) [501+]

Stevenson, Michael D. - *Canada's Greatest Wartime Muddle: National Selective Service and the Mobilization of Human Resources during World War II*
> Can Hist R - v85 - i4 - Dec 2004 - p841(3) [501+]

Stevenson, Patrick - *Language and German Disunity: A Sociolinguistic History of East and West Germany, 1945-2000*
> GSR - v27 - i3 - Oct 2004 - p672(2) [501+]

Stevenson, Randall - *The Last of England?*
> CR - v285 - i1664 - Sept 2004 - p186(1) [51-500]
> LJ - v129 - i13 - August 2004 - p79(2) [501+]
> TimHES - v0 - i1650 - July 23 2004 - p26(2) [501+]

Stevenson, Richard - *Live Evil: A Homage to Miles Davis*
> Can Lit - i181 - Summer 2004 - p96-97 [501+]

Stevenson, Robert Louis - *A Child's Garden of Verses*
> c RT - v57 - Sept 2003 - p97 [51-500]

Graphic Classics: Robert Louis Stevenson
> y BL - v101 - i2 - Sept 15 2004 - p235(1) [51-500]

Kidnapped (Illus. by Wyeth, N.C.)
> c SLJ - v51 - i1 - Jan 2005 - p137(1) [51-500]

Strange Case of Dr. Jekyll and Mr. Hyde
> SFS - v31 - i2 - July 2004 - p319-324 [501+]

Stevenson, Talitha - *An Empty Room*
> BooChiTr - May 9 2004 - p2(1) [501+]
> Globe & Mail - July 24 2004 - pD6 [501+]

Stevenson, Tom - *The Relationship Advantage: Become a Trusted Advisor and Create Clients for Life*
> R&R Bk N - v19 - i1 - Feb 2004 - p108(1) [51-500]

Stevermer, Caroline - *A Scholar of Magics*
> MFSF - v107 - i3 - Sept 2004 - p34(5) [501+]
> y VOYA - v27 - i5 - Dec 2004 - p410(1) [51-500]

Steward, David L. - *Doing Business by the Good Book: 52 Lessons on Success Straight from the Bible*
> B Ent - v35 - i1 - August 2004 - p125(1) [501+]
> Black Iss - v6 - i4 - July-August 2004 - p31(1) [51-500]

Steward, E.G. - *Fourier Optics; An Introduction, 2nd Ed.*
> SciTech - v28 - i3 - Sept 2004 - p48(1) [1-50]

Steward, Sid - *PDF Hacks*
> Bwatch - Feb 2005 - pNA [501+]
> LJ - v130 - i2 - Feb 1 2005 - p110(1) [51-500]
> SciTech - v28 - i4 - Dec 2004 - p27(1) [51-500]

Stewart, Amy - *The Earth Moved: On the Remarkable Achievements of Earthworms*
> y SB - v40 - i3 - May-June 2004 - p125(2) [501+]
> SB - v40 - i6 - Nov-Dec 2004 - p243(1) [51-500]
> y SciTech - v28 - i1 - March 2004 - p68(1) [51-500]
> y SLJ - v50 - i10 - Oct 2004 - pS63(1) [501+]

Stewart, Barbara (b. 1960) - *Women's Soccer: The Passionate Game*
> CBRA - Annual 2003 - p146(2) [51-500]

Stewart, Barbara J. - *The Sleeping Boy: A Novel*
> CBRA - Annual 2003 - p187(1) [51-500]

Stewart, C. Neal - *Genetically Modified Planet: Environmental Impacts of Genatically Engineered Plants*
> Choice - v42 - i6 - Feb 2005 - p1049(2) [51-500]

Genetically Modified Planet: Environmental Impacts of Genetically Engineered Plants
> SciTech - v28 - i4 - Dec 2004 - p124 [51-500]

Stewart, D.H. - *Kipling's America: Travel Letters, 1889-1895*
> ELT - v47 - i3 - Summer 2004 - p331(5) [501+]

Stewart, David - *InsidersChoice to the Candidate's Guide to (CFA) Chartered Financial Analyst 2004 Level 1 Learning Outcome Statements*
> SciTech - v28 - i3 - Sept 2004 - p9(1) [501+]

Stewart, David A. - *Sign Language Interpreting: Exploring Its Art and Science, 2nd Ed.*
> R&R Bk N - v19 - i1 - Feb 2004 - p139(1) [51-500]

Stewart, David R. - *The Literature of Theology: A Guide for Students and Pastors*
> TT - v61 - i2 - July 2004 - p287(2) [501+]

Stewart, Frank - *Romare Bearden*
> Black Iss - v7 - i1 - Jan-Feb 2005 - p42(1) [501+]

Stewart, Gail B. - *Life under the Taliban*
> y SLJ - v51 - i1 - Jan 2005 - p156(1) [51-500]

SARS
> y SLJ - v50 - i10 - Oct 2004 - p194(1) [51-500]

Stewart, Iain W. - *Static and Dynamic Continuum Theory of Liquid Crystals: A Mathematical Introduction*
> SciTech - v28 - i4 - Dec 2004 - p56(1) [51-500]

Stewart, Ian - *Ambushed: A War Reporter's Life on the Line*
> CBRA - Annual 2003 - p81(1) [51-500]

The Colors of Infinity
> Bwatch - Nov 2004 - pNA [501+]

The Colours of Infinity
> New Sci - v183 - i2465 - Sept 18 2004 - p46(2) [51-500]

The Mahathir Legacy: A Nation Divided, a Region at Risk
> R&R Bk N - v19 - i1 - Feb 2004 - p48(1) [501+]

Stewart, James B. - *Disney War*
> Bus W - i3922 - Feb 28 2005 - p24 [501+]
> Econ - v374 - i8415 - Feb 26 2005 - p84US [501+]
> Ent W - i808 - Feb 25 2005 - p104 [501+]
> People - v63 - i8 - Feb 28 2005 - p57 [501+]
> PW - v252 - i7 - Feb 14 2005 - p61(1) [501+]
> Time - v165 - i8 - Feb 21 2005 - p39 [501+]

Stewart, Jennifer J. - *Close Encounters of a Third-World Kind*
> c CCB-B - v58 - i5 - Jan 2005 - p228(1) [51-500]
> c KR - v72 - i21 - Nov 15 2004 - p1093(1) [51-500]
> c SLJ - v50 - i12 - Dec 2004 - p153(1) [51-500]

Stewart, Jim - *The County Decoys: The Fine Old Decoys of Prince Edward County, Ontario*
> Ant&CM - v109 - i6 - August 2004 - p16(1) [501+]

Stewart, Joel - *Tales of Hans Christian Andersen*
> SLJ - v50 - i12 - Dec 2004 - p96(1) [501+]

Stewart, John W. - *Charles Hodge Revisited: A Critical Appraisal of His Life and Work*
> TT - v60 - i4 - Jan 2004 - p598-602 [501+]

Stewart, Jon - *America: A Citizen's Guide to Democracy Inaction*
> Fortune - v150 - i6 - Sept 20 2004 - p60 [51-500]

America: A Citizen's Guide to Democracy Inaction (Read by Stewart, Jon). Audiobook Review
> PW - v251 - i40 - Oct 4 2004 - p32(1) [501+]

America: A Citizen's Guide to Democracy Inaction
> BW - v34 - i41 - Oct 10 2004 - p1(1) [501+]
> Econ - v373 - i8400 - Nov 6 2004 - p90US [501+]
> Ent W - i786 - Nov 4 2004 - p78 [51-500]
> Globe & Mail - Oct 9 2004 - pD6 [501+]
> NYTBR - Oct 3 2004 - p20 [501+]
> People - Dec 27 2004 - p63 [501+]
> PW - v251 - i36 - Sept 6 2004 - p59(1) [501+]

America (the Book): A Citizen's Guide to Democracy Inaction
> BL - v101 - i5 - Nov 1 2004 - p450(1) [501+]

Kierkegaard and His Contemporaries: The Culture of Golden Age Denmark
> Scan St - v76 - i4 - Winter 2004 - p562(5) [501+]

Kierkegaard's Relations to Hegel Reconsidered
> RM - v58 - i2 - Dec 2004 - p469(3) [501+]

Stewart, Kelly - *Gorillas: Natural History and Conservation*
> SciTech - v28 - i1 - March 2004 - p70(1) [51-500]

Stewart, Kenneth G. - *Introduction to Applied Econometrics*
> R&R Bk N - v19 - i4 - Nov 2004 - p84(1) [51-500]

Stewart, Linda McK. - *25 Months: A Memoir*
> KR - v72 - i15 - August 1 2004 - p734(1) [501+]
> LJ - v129 - i17 - Oct 15 2004 - p80(1) [51-500]

Stewart, Marcia - *Every Landlord's Legal Guide, 6th Ed.*
> R&R Bk N - v19 - i1 - Feb 2004 - p71(1) [1-50]

Stewart, Mart A. - *"What Nature Suffers to Groe": Life, Labor, and Landscape on the Georgia Coast, 1680-1920*
> R&R Bk N - v19 - i1 - Feb 2004 - p71(1) [1-50]

Stewart, Matthew - *Monturiol's Dream: The Extraordinary Story of the Submarine Inventor Who Wanted to Save the World*
> Am Sci - v92 - i5 - Sept-Oct 2004 - p478(2) [501+]
> Choice - v42 - i3 - Nov 2004 - p505(1) [1-50]
> Globe & Mail - July 10 2004 - pD16 [51-500]
> LJ - v129 - i12 - July 2004 - p114(1) [501+]

Stewart, Melissa - *Animals All Around*
> c SB - v40 - i4 - July-August 2004 - p180(2) [51-500]
> c SLJ - v50 - i10 - Oct 2004 - p150(2) [51-500]

Down to Earth
> c SB - v40 - i4 - July-August 2004 - p175(2) [51-500]
> c SB - v40 - i5 - Sept-Oct 2004 - p192(2) [51-500]
> c SLJ - v50 - i10 - Oct 2004 - p150(2) [51-500]

Fun with the Sun
> c SB - v40 - i4 - July-August 2004 - p172(2) [51-500]

Maggots, Grubs, and More: The Secret Lives of Young Insects
> c SLJ - v50 - i10 - Oct 2004 - pS43(1) [51-500]

Parade of Plants
> c SB - v40 - i4 - July-August 2004 - p176(1) [51-500]

Stewart, Mike - *A Perfect Life*
> PW - v251 - i50 - Dec 13 2004 - p51(1) [51-500]

Stewart, Omer C. - *Forgotten Fires: Native Americans and the Transient Wilderness*
> WHQ - v35 - i2 - Summer 2004 - p244-245 [501+]

Stewart, Pamela J. - *Landscape, Memory, and History: Anthropological Perspectives*
> R&R Bk N - v19 - i1 - Feb 2004 - p53(1) [51-500]

Remaking the World: Myth, Mining, and Ritual Change Among the Duna of Papua New Guinea
> JRAI - v10 - i4 - Dec 2004 - p956(2) [501+]

Stewart, Paul - *Beyond the Deepwoods*
> c CH Bwatch - v14 - i7 - July 2004 - p7(2) [501+]

Beyond the Deepwoods (Illus. by Riddell, Chris)
> c BL - v100 - i21 - July 2004 - p1844(2) [1-50]
> y CCB-B - v58 - i1 - Sept 2004 - p40(1) [51-500]
> c KR - v72 - i13 - July 1 2004 - p637(1) [51-500]
> c SLJ - v50 - i9 - Sept 2004 - p218(1) [51-500]

The Curse of the Gloamglozer (Illus. by Stewart, Paul)
> y SLJ - v51 - i2 - Feb 2005 - p140(2) [51-500]

Fergus Crane
> c Sch Lib - v52 - i4 - Winter 2004 - p204(1) [51-500]

Free Lance and the Field of Blood
> y Sch Lib - v52 - i4 - Winter 2004 - p216(1) [51-500]

Lake of Skulls (Illus. by Riddell, Chris)
> c CCB-B - v58 - i3 - Nov 2004 - p146(1) [501+]
> c SLJ - v50 - i9 - Sept 2004 - p218(1) [51-500]

Midnight over Sanctaphrax (Illus. by Riddell, Chris)
> c BL - v101 - i1 - Sept 1 2004 - p125(1) [1-50]
> y SLJ - v50 - i10 - Oct 2004 - p178(1) [51-500]

Stormchaser (Illus. by Riddell, Chris)
> c BL - v100 - i22 - August 2004 - p1925(1) [51-500]
> y CCB-B - v58 - i1 - Sept 2004 - p40(1) [51-500]
> c CH Bwatch - v14 - i7 - July 2004 - p7(2) [501+]
> c SLJ - v50 - i9 - Sept 2004 - p218(1) [51-500]

Vox
> c Sch Lib - v52 - i4 - Winter 2004 - p212(1) [51-500]

Stewart, Peter - *Statues in Roman Society: Representation and Response*
> TLS - i5297 - Oct 8 2004 - p10(1) [501+]

Stewart, Richard - *Leper Priest of Moloka'i: The Father Damien Story*
CHR - v90 - i3 - July 2004 - p581(2) [501+]
Stewart, Robert Armistead - *Index to Printed Virginia Genealogies, Including Key and Bibliography*
EFHM - v58 - i3 - May-June 2004 - p61(1) [51-500]
Stewart, Rory - *The Places in Between*
NS - v133 - i4697 - July 19 2004 - p52(1) [501+]
Spec - v295 - i9185 - August 21 2004 - p30(2) [501+]
TLS - i5290 - August 20 2004 - p32(1) [501+]
Stewart, Sally - *A Time to Dance*
BL - v101 - i1 - Sept 1 2004 - p65(2) [51-500]
Stewart, Sarah - *The Friend (Illus. by Small, David)*
c BL - v100 - i22 - August 2004 - p1945(1) [501+]
c CCB-B - v58 - i3 - Nov 2004 - p146(2) [501+]
c HB - v80 - i5 - Sept-Oct 2004 - p575(2) [51-500]
c KR - v72 - i13 - July 1 2004 - p637(1) [51-500]
c SLJ - v50 - i8 - August 2004 - p96(1) [51-500]
The Gardener
c Sch Lib - v52 - i4 - Winter 2004 - p191(1) [51-500]
Stewart, Sean - *Dark Rendezvous*
y BL - v101 - i8 - Dec 15 2004 - p715(2) [51-500]
Perfect Circle
BW - v34 - i28 - July 11 2004 - p10(1) [501+]
MFSF - v107 - i3 - Sept 2004 - p34(5) [501+]
Stewart, Shannon - *Sea Crow (Illus. by Milkau, Liz)*
c Globe & Mail - July 31 2004 - pD11 [51-500]
Stewart, Sharon - *Raven Quest*
y CBRA - Annual 2003 - p515(1) [51-500]
Stewart, Stan - *Distribution Switchgear*
SciTech - v28 - i4 - Dec 2004 - p148(1) [501+]
Stewart, Stanley - *Frontiers of Heaven: A Journey to the End of China*
Globe & Mail - Nov 3 2004 - pT1 [501+]
LJ - v129 - i12 - July 2004 - p108(1) [51-500]
R&R Bk N - v19 - i3 - August 2004 - p56(1) [51-500]
Stewart, Susan - *Columbarium*
Poet - v184 - i4 - August 2004 - p305(12) [501+]
Poet - v185 - i1 - Oct 2004 - p53(9) [501+]
Poetry and the Fate of the Senses
Comp L - v56 - i3 - Summer 2004 - p276-274 [501+]
Stewart, Walter - *Life and Political Times of Tommy Douglas*
CBRA - Annual 2003 - p73(2) [51-500]
Stewig, John Warren - *Making Plum Jam (Illus. by O'Malley, Kevin)*
c SLJ - v51 - i2 - Feb 2005 - p58(1) [51-500]
Whuppity Stoorie (Illus. by McDaniels, Preston)
c NYTBR - July 11 2004 - p18 [501+]
Steyaert, Chris - *New Movements in Entrepreneurship (Illus. by Hjorth, Daniel)*
R&R Bk N - v19 - i1 - Feb 2004 - p79(1) [51-500]
Steyn, Frances Caroline - *Medieval and Renaissance Manuscripts in the Grey Collection of the National Library of South Africa, Cape Town*
Specu - v79 - i3 - July 2004 - p842-844 [501+]
Steyn, Mark - *Mark Steyn from Head to Toe: An Anatomical Anthology*
Am Spect - v37 - i7 - Sept 2004 - p63(3) [501+]
Stieber, Mary - *The Poetics of Appearance in the Attic Korai*
TLS - i5294 - Sept 17 2004 - p29(1) [501+]
Stiegemeyer, Julie - *Bright Easter Day*
c PW - v252 - i7 - Feb 14 2005 - p79(2) [501+]
Stielow, Frederick - *Building Digital Archives, Descriptions, and Displays: A How-to-Do-It Manual for Archivistsand Librarians*
R&R Bk N - v19 - i1 - Feb 2004 - p26(1) [51-500]
Stien, Phyllis T. - *Psychological Trauma and the Developing Brain: Neurologically Based Interventions for Troubled Children*
E-Streams - Sept 2004 - pNA [501+]
SciTech - v28 - i1 - March 2004 - p119(1) [51-500]
Stier, Oren Baruch - *Committed to Memory: Cultural Mediations of the Holocaust*
Biomag - v27 - i3 - Summer 2004 - p654(4) [501+]
Stigler, George J. - *Memoirs of an Unregulated Economist*
JEL - v41 - i4 - Dec 2003 - p1337(1) [501+]
Stiglitz, Joseph E. - *Economics for an Imperfect World: Essays in Honor of Joseph E. Stiglitz*
JEL - v42 - i1 - March 2004 - p252(1) [501+]
The Roaring Nineties: A New History of the World's Most Prosperous Decade
R&R Bk N - v19 - i1 - Feb 2004 - p81(1) [51-500]
Towards a New Paradigm in Monetary Economics
JEL - v42 - i1 - March 2004 - p255(2) [501+]

Stigum, Bernt P. - *Econometrics and the Philosophy of Economics: Theory-Data Confrontations in Economics*
JEL - v41 - i4 - Dec 2003 - p1338(1) [501+]
Stilgoe, John R. - *Shallow Water Dictionary: A Grounding in Estuary English*
SciTech - v28 - i3 - Sept 2004 - p13(1) [501+]
Still, Joanne - *The Smart Approach to Baby Rooms*
PW - v251 - i39 - Sept 27 2004 - p52(1) [51-500]
Still, Judith Anne - *William Grant Still: A Voice High-Sounding*
R&R Bk N - v19 - i1 - Feb 2004 - p196(1) [51-500]
Stille, Alexander - *The Sack of Rome: How Silvio Berlusconi Took over Italy*
Har Bus R - v83 - i2 - Feb 2005 - p57(1) [1-50]
Stille, Darlene R. - *Air: Outside, Inside, and all Around (Illus. by Boyd, Sheree)*
c SB - v40 - i4 - July-August 2004 - p175(1) [51-500]
Cheetahs
c SLJ - v51 - i1 - Jan 2005 - p108(2) [51-500]
Electricity: Bulbs, Batteries and Sparks (Illus. by Boyd, Sheree)
c SB - v40 - i4 - July-August 2004 - p173(1) [51-500]
Energy
c BL - v101 - i5 - Nov 1 2004 - p478(1) [51-500]
Energy: Heat, Light, and Fuel (Illus. by Boyd, Sheree)
c SB - v40 - i4 - July-August 2004 - p173(1) [51-500]
I Am a Seal: The Life of an Elephant Seal (Illus. by Ouren, Todd)
c SLJ - v51 - i1 - Jan 2005 - p116(1) [51-500]
I Am a Shark: The Life of a Hammerhead Shark (Illus. by Ouren, Todd)
c SLJ - v51 - i1 - Jan 2005 - p116(1) [51-500]
I Am a Whale: The Life of a Humpback Whale (Illus. by Ouren, Todd)
c SLJ - v51 - i1 - Jan 2005 - p116(1) [51-500]
Matter: See It, Touch It, Taste It, Smell It (Illus. by Boyd, Sheree)
c SB - v40 - i4 - July-August 2004 - p173(1) [51-500]
Motion: Push and Pull, Fast and Slow (Illus. by Boyd, Sheree)
c SB - v40 - i4 - July-August 2004 - p173(1) [51-500]
Solids, Liquids, and Gases
c BL - v101 - i5 - Nov 1 2004 - p478(1) [51-500]
Temperature: Heating Up and Cooling Down (Illus. by Boyd, Sheree)
c SB - v40 - i4 - July-August 2004 - p173(1) [51-500]
Stillerman, Joel - *Free Trade and Uneven Development : The North American Apparel Industry After NAFTA*
CS - v33 - i5 - Sept 2004 - p550-551 [501+]
Stillinger, Doug - *The Klutz Book of Ball Games*
c PW - v252 - i4 - Jan 24 2005 - p246(1) [501+]
Stillman, Yedida Kalfon - *Arab Dress: A Short History, from the Dawn of Islam to Modern Times, 2nd Rev. Ed.*
R&R Bk N - v19 - i1 - Feb 2004 - p73(1) [51-500]
Stillwell, John - *Elements of Number Theory*
SIAM Rev - v46 - i2 - June 2004 - p358-360 [501+]
Stilton, Geronimo - *The Curse of the Cheese Pyramid (Illus. by Wolf, Matt)*
c SLJ - v50 - i8 - August 2004 - p96(1) [501+]
Geronimo Stilton Books 1-3 (Read by Herrmann, Edward). Audiobook Review
c PW - v251 - i50 - Dec 13 2004 - p24(1) [51-500]
Lost Treasure of the Emerald Eye (Illus. by Wolf, Matt)
c SLJ - v50 - i8 - August 2004 - p96(1) [51-500]
Paws Off, Cheddarface! (Illus. by Nithael, Mark)
c SLJ - v50 - i9 - Sept 2004 - p181(1) [51-500]
Red Pizzas for a Blue Count (Illus. by Wolf, Matt)
c SLJ - v50 - i9 - Sept 2004 - p181(1) [51-500]
Stim, Richard - *License Your Invention, 4th ed*
R&R Bk N - v19 - i3 - August 2004 - p200(1) [1-50]
Patent Pending in 24 Hours, 2nd Ed.
R&R Bk N - v19 - i1 - Feb 2004 - pNA [51-500]
Stimpson, Jeff - *Alex: The Fathering of a Preemie*
BL - v101 - i7 - Dec 1 2004 - p625(1) [51-500]
KR - v72 - i19 - Oct 1 2004 - p952(1) [51-500]
LJ - v129 - i20 - Dec 1 2004 - p144(1) [51-500]
PW - v251 - i45 - Nov 8 2004 - p43(1) [501+]
Stimpson, Michelle - *Boaz Brown*
Black Iss - v6 - i6 - Nov-Dec 2004 - p74(1) [51-500]

Stinchcomb, Dawn F. - *The Development of Literary Blackness in the Dominican Republic*
Choice - v41 - i11-12 - July-August 2004 - p2051(1) [501+]
Stine, Allison - *Lot of My Sister*
Ga R - v58 - i1 - Spring 2004 - p167-178 [501+]
Stine, Catherine - *Refugees*
KR - v73 - i1 - Jan 1 2005 - p57(1) [51-500]
Stine, G. Harry - *Handbook of Model Rocketry, 7th Ed.*
SciTech - v28 - i3 - Sept 2004 - p165(1) [51-500]
Stine, James E. - *Digital Computer Arithmetic Datapath Design Using Verilog HDL*
SciTech - v28 - i1 - March 2004 - p160(1) [51-500]
Stine, R.L. - *Have You Met My Ghoulfriend?*
c SLJ - v50 - i10 - Oct 2004 - p178(1) [51-500]
The Taste of Night
y BL - v101 - i1 - Sept 1 2004 - p109(1) [1-50]
c SLJ - v50 - i8 - August 2004 - p129(2) [51-500]
y VOYA - v27 - i4 - Oct 2004 - p321(1) [51-500]
Who Let the Ghosts Out?
c PW - v251 - i35 - August 30 2004 - p55(2) [51-500]
c SLJ - v50 - i10 - Oct 2004 - p178(1) [51-500]
Sting - *Broken Music: A Memoir. Audiobook Review*
Globe & Mail - Feb 5 2005 - pD17 [1-50]
Stingley, Diane - *I'm with Cupid*
BL - v101 - i9-10 - Jan 1 2005 - p832(1) [1-50]
PW - v251 - i50 - Dec 13 2004 - p44(1) [51-500]
Stinson, David - *The Traynor Legacy*
KR - v73 - i5 - March 1 2005 - p264(1) [51-500]
Stinson, Kathy - *Becoming Ruby*
y CBRA - Annual 2003 - p515(2) [51-500]
Marie Claire, Bk. 3
c CBRA - Annual 2003 - p516(1) [51-500]
Marie-Claire, Bk. 4
c Res Links - v10 - i2 - Dec 2004 - p22(2) [51-500]
Stinson, Susan - *Venus of Chalk*
Lam Bk Rpt - v13 - i4-5 - Nov-Dec 2004 - p35(2) [501+]
Wom R Bks - v22 - i3 - Dec 2004 - p22(2) [501+]
Stinton, Diane B. - *Jesus of Africa: Voices of Contemporary African Christology*
Choice - v42 - i1 - Sept 2004 - p122(1) [501+]
Stipe, Margo - *Frank Lloyd Wright: The Interactive Portfolio*
PW - v251 - i39 - Sept 27 2004 - p53(1) [51-500]
Stipe, Robert E. - *A Richer Heritage: Historic Preservation in the Twenty-First Century*
Pub Hist - v26 - i3 - Summer 2004 - p78(80) [501+]
Stirewalt, M. Luther, Jr. - *Paul, the Letter Writer*
Intpr - v58 - i3 - July 2004 - p322(2) [501+]
Stirling, S.M. - *Dies the Fire*
BL - v100 - i22 - August 2004 - p1914(1) [501+]
LJ - v129 - i12 - July 2004 - p75(1) [51-500]
PW - v251 - i27 - July 5 2004 - p42(1) [51-500]
Stirzaker, David - *Elementary Probability*
JEL - v42 - i1 - March 2004 - p237(1) [501+]
Stitt, Frank - *Frank Stitt's Southern Table: Recipes and Gracious Traditions from Highlands Bar and Grill (Illus. by Hirsheimer, Christopher)*
LJ - v129 - i17 - Oct 15 2004 - p84(1) [51-500]
People - v62 - i21 - Nov 22 2004 - p55 [51-500]
PW - v251 - i43 - Oct 25 2004 - p41(1) [51-500]
Stitt-Gohdes, Wanda - *Business and Industry*
c SLJ - v50 - i8 - August 2004 - p56(1) [51-500]
Stittle, John - *Annual Reports: Delivering Your Corporate Message to Stakeholders*
R&R Bk N - v19 - i1 - Feb 2004 - p116(1) [51-500]
Stivers, Richard - *Shades of Loneliness: Pathologies of a Technological Society*
R&R Bk N - v19 - i3 - August 2004 - p144(1) [51-500]
Stobart, Jon - *The First Industrial Region: North-West England, c. 1700-60*
CR - v285 - i1664 - Sept 2004 - p189(1) [51-500]
Choice - v42 - i5 - Jan 2005 - p921(1) [1-50]
Stock, Jan van der - *Early Prints: The Print Collection of the Royal Library of Belgium*
Six Ct J - v35 - i3 - Fall 2004 - p846-847 [501+]
Stockdale, Margaret S. - *The Psychology and Management of Workplace Diversity*
Choice - v42 - i1 - Sept 2004 - p151(1) [501+]
Per Psy - v57 - i4 - Winter 2004 - p1041(4) [501+]
Stockdale, Susan - *Carry Me!: Animal Babies on the Move (Illus. by Stockdale, Susan)*
c KR - v73 - i4 - Feb 15 2005 - p236(1) [51-500]

Book Review Index 2005 Cumulation STONE • 579

Stockdill, Brett C. - *Activism Against AIDS: At the Intersections of Sexuality, Race, Gender, and Class*
AJS - v110 - i1 - July 2004 - p275(3) [501+]
CS - v33 - i4 - July 2004 - p482(2) [501+]
Stockel, H. Henrietta - *On the Bloody Road to Jesus: Christianity and the Chiricahua Apaches*
R&R Bk N - v19 - i3 - August 2004 - p62(1) [51-500]
Shame and Endurances: The Untold Story of the Chiricahua Apache Prisoners of War
R&R Bk N - v19 - i4 - Nov 2004 - p55(1) [51-500]
Stocker, Barry - *Post-Analytic 'Tractatus'*
R&R Bk N - v19 - i4 - Nov 2004 - p6(1) [51-500]
Stocker, Frederick T. - *I Pay, You Pay, We All Pay: How the Growing Tort Crisis Undermines the U.S. Economy and the American System of Justice*
JEL - v41 - i4 - Dec 2003 - p1390(1) [501+]
Stockford, Marjorie A. - *The Bellwomen: The Story of the Landmark AT&T Sex Discrimination Case*
Choice - v42 - i5 - Jan 2005 - p900(1) [1-50]
HRNB - v33 - i1 - Fall 2004 - p8(1) [501+]
Stocking, Scott - *Mosby's Dental Dictionary*
SciTech - v28 - i1 - March 2004 - p119(1) [51-500]
Stockley, Philippa - *A Factory of Cunning*
KR - v73 - i1 - Jan 1 2005 - p20(1) [501+]
LJ - v129 - i20 - Dec 1 2004 - p88(1) [51-500]
LJ - v130 - i4 - March 1 2005 - p81(1) [51-500]
PW - v252 - i6 - Feb 7 2005 - p38(1) [51-500]
Stockwell, Foster - *A Sourcebook for Genealogical Research: Resources Alphabetically by Type and Location*
Choice - v42 - i3 - Nov 2004 - p446(1) [1-50]
LJ - v129 - i15 - Sept 15 2004 - p82(2) [51-500]
R&R Bk N - v19 - i3 - August 2004 - p29(1) [1-50]
Stockwell, Peter - *The Poetics of Science Fiction*
SFS - v31 - i1 - March 2004 - p122-126 [501+]
Stoddard, Barstow - *"I Believe I Shall Die an Impenetrable Secret": The Writings of Elizabeth Barstow Stoddard*
Legacy - v21 - i2 - June 2004 - p249(2) [501+]
Stoddard Holmes, Martha - *Fictions of Affliction: Physical Disability in Victorian Culture*
Choice - v42 - i3 - Nov 2004 - p487(1) [1-50]
Stoddard, Kathryn - *The Narrative Voice in the Theogony of Hesiod*
R&R Bk N - v19 - i4 - Nov 2004 - p214(1) [501+]
Stoer, Stephen R. - *Theories of Social Exclusion*
R&R Bk N - v19 - i2 - May 2004 - p129 [51-500]
Stoessinger, John G. - *Why Nations Go to War, 9th Ed.*
R&R Bk N - v19 - i3 - August 2004 - p30(1) [1-50]
Stoff, Joshua - *Building Moonships*
Astron - v32 - i12 - Dec 2004 - p104 [51-500]
Stoffman, Daniel - *Who Gets In: What's Wrong with Canada's Immigration Program - and How to Fix It*
CBRA - Annual 2003 - p313(1) [501+]
Stohlman, Nancy - *Live from Palestine: International and Palestinian Direct Action Against the Israeli Occupation*
R&R Bk N - v19 - i4 - Nov 2004 - p45(1) [51-500]
Stohner, Anu - *Santa's Littlest Helper (Illus. by Wilson, Henrike)*
c PW - v251 - i39 - Sept 27 2004 - p62(1) [51-500]
Stohr, Greg - *A Black and White Case: How Affirmative Action Survived Its Greatest Legal Challenge*
BL - v101 - i2 - Sept 15 2004 - p184(1) [51-500]
LJ - v129 - i17 - Oct 15 2004 - p75(2) [51-500]
PW - v251 - i33 - August 16 2004 - p55(1) [51-500]
R&R Bk N - v19 - i4 - Nov 2004 - p165(1) [501+]
Stoianoff, Natalie P. - *Accessing Biological Resources: Complying with the Convention on Biological Diversity*
SciTech - v28 - i3 - Sept 2004 - p56(1) [1-50]
Stoick, Jean - *Winter Friends (Illus. by Sams, Carl R., III)*
c Res Links - v10 - i3 - Feb 2005 - p9(2) [501+]
Stojkovic, Stan - *The Administration and Management of Criminal Justice Organizations: A Book of Readings, 4th Ed.*
R&R Bk N - v19 - i3 - August 2004 - p167(1) [501+]
Stoker, Donald J. - *Britain, France, and the Naval Arms Trade in the Baltic, 1919-1939: Grand Strategy and Failure*
R&R Bk N - v19 - i1 - Feb 2004 - p28(1) [51-500]
Girding for Battle: The Arms Trade in a Global Perspective, 1815-1940
J Mil H - v68 - i3 - April 2004 - p617-618 [501+]
Stokes, Ben - *The Heritage Trees of Britain and Northern Ireland*
Spec - v296 - i9200 - Dec 4 2004 - p49(1) [501+]
Stokes, David - *Testing Computer Systems for FDA/MHRA Compliance*
SciTech - v28 - i4 - Dec 2004 - p119(1) [1-50]
Stokes, E.B. - *State-of-the-Art Program on Compound Semiconductors XXXVIII and Wide Bandgap Semiconductors for Photonic and Electronic Devices and Sensors III: Proceedings*
SciTech - v28 - i1 - March 2004 - p162(1) [51-500]
Stokes, Lawrence D. - *Der Eutiner Dichterkreis und der Nationalsozialismus 1936-1945*
GSR - v27 - i3 - Oct 2004 - p639(2) [501+]
Stokes, Martin - *Celtic Modern: Music at the Global Fringe*
Notes - v61 - i2 - Dec 2004 - p473(4) [501+]
R&R Bk N - v19 - i1 - Feb 2004 - p197(1) [51-500]
Stokes, Melvyn - *The State of U.S History*
JAH - v91 - i1 - June 2004 - p204-205 [501+]
Stokes, Philip - *Philosophy 100 Essential Thinkers*
SLJ - v50 - i10 - Oct 2004 - pS62(1) [51-500]
Stokes, Simon - *Art and Copyright, Rev. Ed.*
R&R Bk N - v19 - i1 - Feb 2004 - pNA [51-500]
Stokstad, Marilyn - *Medieval Art, 2nd Ed.*
Med R - July 2004 - pNA [501+]
Stokvis, Willemijn - *Cobra: The Last Avant-Garde Movement of the Twentieth Century*
Choice - v42 - i6 - Feb 2005 - p1011(1) [51-500]
Stoler, Ann Laura - *Carnal Knowledge and Imperial Power: Race and the Intimate in Colonial Rule*
HNet - August 2004 - pNA [501+]
JMH - v76 - i3 - Sept 2004 - p667(3) [501+]
JRAI - v10 - i3 - Sept 2004 - p709(2) [501+]
Stoler, Mark A. - *Major Problems in the History of World War II: Documents and Essays*
J Mil H - v68 - i4 - Oct 2004 - p1301-1302 [501+]
Stolfi, R.H.S. - *German Panzers on the Offensive: Russian Front, North Africa, 1941-1942*
J Mil H - v68 - i4 - Oct 2004 - p1282-1283 [501+]
Stoll, O. - *Zwischen Intergration und Abgrenzung. Die Religion des romischen Heeres im Nahen Osten*
Class R - v53 - i2 - Nov 2003 - p429-431 [501+]
Stoll, Steven - *Larding the Lean Earth: Soil and Society in Nineteenth-Century America*
HNet - June 2004 - pNA [501+]
Stoller, David W. - *Diagnostic Imaging: Orthopaedics*
SciTech - v28 - i1 - March 2004 - p107(1) [51-500]
Stoller, Debbie - *Stitch 'n Bitch Nation*
BL - v101 - i8 - Dec 15 2004 - p706(1) [501+]
BL - v101 - i8 - Dec 15 2004 - p706(1) [51-500]
PW - v251 - i43 - Oct 25 2004 - p42(2) [51-500]
Stoller, Paul - *Stranger in the Village of the Sick: A Memoir of Cancer, Sorcery, and Healing*
Bwatch - Oct 2004 - pNA [51-500]
Choice - v42 - i4 - Dec 2004 - p695(1) [1-50]
Stolls, Amy - *Palms to the Ground*
y Kliatt - v39 - i2 - March 2005 - p16(1) [51-500]
Stolovitch, Harold D. - *Engineering Effective Learning Toolkit*
R&R Bk N - v19 - i1 - Feb 2004 - p111(1) [51-500]
Stolper, Wolfgang - *Inside Independent Nigeria: Diaries of Wolfgang Stolper, 1960-1962*
JEL - v42 - i1 - March 2004 - p316(1) [501+]
Stoltenberg, John - *The End of Manhood: A Book for Men of Conscience*
OOB - v34 - i9-10 - Sept-Oct 2004 - p51(2) [501+]
Stoltz, J.F. - *Mechanobiology: Cartilage and Chondrocyte, Vol. 2*
SciTech - v28 - i3 - Sept 2004 - p68(1) [51-500]
Stoltzenberg, Dietrich - *Fritz Haber: Chemist, Nobel Laureate, German, Jew*
SB - v40 - i6 - Nov-Dec 2004 - p251(1) [501+]
Stoltzfus, Nathan - *Widerstand des Herzens. Der Aufstand der Berliner Frauen in der Rosenstrabe-1943. Mit einem Vorwort von Joschka Fischer*
GSR - v27 - i1 - Feb 2004 - p181-182 [501+]
Stolz, Joelle - *The Shadows of Ghadames*
y BL - v101 - i7 - Dec 1 2004 - p652(1) [51-500]
y BL - v101 - i9-10 - Jan 1 2005 - p774(1) [1-50]
c CCB-B - v58 - i3 - Nov 2004 - p147(1) [501+]
y HB - v81 - i1 - Jan-Feb 2005 - p98(2) [51-500]
c Inst - v114 - i5 - Jan-Feb 2005 - p73(2) [501+]
y KR - v72 - i19 - Oct 1 2004 - p970(1) [51-500]
y SLJ - v50 - i11 - Nov 2004 - p154(1) [51-500]
Stolz, Karen - *Fanny and Sue*
y Kliatt - v38 - i4 - July 2004 - p24(1) [51-500]
Stolz, Mary - *Belling the Tiger (Illus. by Pratt, Pierre)*
c BL - v101 - i1 - Sept 1 2004 - p125(1) [1-50]
c KR - v72 - i13 - July 1 2004 - p638(1) [51-500]
c PW - v251 - i36 - Sept 6 2004 - p64(1) [51-500]
c SLJ - v50 - i9 - Sept 2004 - p181(2) [51-500]
Emmett's Pig (Illus. by Williams, Garth)
c BL - v101 - i5 - Nov 1 2004 - p494(1) [51-500]
c PW - v251 - i37 - Sept 13 2004 - p80(2) [51-500]
Stolze, Joachim - *Quantum Computing: A Short Course from Theory to Experiment*
SciTech - v28 - i4 - Dec 2004 - p29(1) [51-500]
Stommel, Manfred - *Clinical Research: Concepts and Principles for Advanced Practice Nurses*
SciTech - v28 - i4 - Dec 2004 - p121 [51-500]
Stone, Alva T. - *The LCSH-Century: One Hundred Years with the Library of Congress Subject Headings System*
LRTS - v48 - i3 - July 2004 - p232(1) [501+]
Stone, Amy - *Creek*
y SLJ - v51 - i1 - Jan 2005 - p156(1) [51-500]
Dorothea Lange
LibMed - v22 - i4 - Jan 2004 - p72(1) [501+]
Maya Lin
LibMed - v22 - i4 - Jan 2004 - p72(1) [501+]
Stone, Andrea - *Heart of Creation: The Mesoamerican World and the Legacy of Linda Schele*
Lat Ant - v15 - i4 - Dec 2004 - p462(3) [501+]
Stone, Bailey - *Reinterpreting the French Revolution: A Global-Historical Perspective*
JMH - v76 - i4 - Dec 2004 - p964(2) [501+]
Stone, Biz - *Who Let the Blogs Out?: A Hyperconnected Peek at the World of Weblogs*
BL - v101 - i6 - Nov 15 2004 - p533(1) [51-500]
LJ - v129 - i20 - Dec 1 2004 - p148(1) [51-500]
PW - v251 - i44 - Nov 1 2004 - p54(2) [501+]
Stone, C. Ketih - *Current Emergency Diagnosis and Treatment, 5th Ed.*
SciTech - v28 - i1 - March 2004 - p89(1) [51-500]
Stone, Carol Leth - *The Basics of Biology*
Ref Rev - Nov 2004 - pNA [501+]
SciTech - v28 - i4 - Dec 2004 - p59(1) [51-500]
Stone, Charles R. - *The Fountainhead of Chinese Erotica: The Lord of Perfect Satisfaction*
Ch Rev Int - v10 - i2 - Fall 2003 - p457(4) [501+]
Stone, Dan - *Breeding Superman: Nietzsche, Race and Eugenics in Edwardian and Interwar Britain*
RES - v55 - i218 - Feb 2004 - p145-147 [501+]
The Historiography of the Holocaust
Choice - v42 - i4 - Dec 2004 - p728(1) [1-50]
Responses to Nazism in Britain, 1933-1939: Before War and Holocaust
Choice - v42 - i1 - Sept 2004 - p179(1) [501+]
Stone, David Lee - *The Illmoor chronicles: The Ratastrophe Catastrophe*
c VOYA - v27 - i5 - Dec 2004 - p410(1) [51-500]
The Ratastrophe Catastrophe (Read by Llewellyn, Robert). Audiobook Review
c SLJ - v51 - i2 - Feb 2005 - p74(2) [501+]
The Ratastrophe Catastrophe (Illus. by Lea, Bob)
c BL - v101 - i5 - Nov 1 2004 - p486(1) [51-500]
y HB - v81 - i1 - Jan-Feb 2005 - p99(1) [51-500]
c Kliatt - v38 - i6 - Nov 2004 - p11(2) [51-500]
y KR - v72 - i18 - Sept 15 2004 - p921(1) [51-500]
c PW - v251 - i45 - Nov 8 2004 - p56(1) [51-500]
y SLJ - v51 - i1 - Jan 2005 - p137(1) [51-500]
The Ratastrphe Catastrophe (Illus. by Lea, Bob)
y CCB-B - v58 - i5 - Jan 2005 - p228(1) [51-500]
The Yowler Foul-Up
y Sch Lib - v52 - i4 - Winter 2004 - p216(1) [51-500]
Stone, DeWitt Boyd - *Wandering to Glory: Confederate Veterans Remember Evans' Brigade*
JSH - v70 - i3 - August 2004 - p686(2) [501+]
Stone, Diane - *Think Tank Traditions: Policy Research and the Politics of Ideas*
Choice - v42 - i5 - Jan 2005 - p929(1) [51-500]
CR - v285 - i1666 - Nov 2004 - p318(1) [501+]
Stone, Douglas - *Difficult Conversations: How to Discuss What Matters Most*
HR Mag - v50 - i2 - Feb 2005 - pS2(1) [501+]
Real College: The Essential Guide to Student Life
NYTBR - August 22 2004 - p10 [501+]
Stone, Eric - *Wrong Side of the Wall: The Life of Blackie Schwamb, the Greatest Prison Baseball Player of All Time*
LJ - v130 - i2 - Feb 1 2005 - p87(1) [51-500]
Stone, Florence M. - *The Essential New Manager's Kit*
R&R Bk N - v19 - i3 - August 2004 - p103(1) [1-50]
The Mentoring Advantage: Creating the Next Generation of Leaders
HR Mag - v50 - i3 - March 2005 - p127(2) [501+]

Stone, Geoffrey R. - *Perilous Times*
　　NY - v80 - i31 - Oct 18 2004 - p203(1) [51-500]
　　Perilous Times: Free Speech in Wartime from the
　　Sedition Act of 1798 to the War on Terrorism
　　　BL - v101 - i5 - Nov 1 2004 - p449(1) [51-500]
　　　BW - v34 - i47 - Nov 21 2004 - p1(2) [501+]
　　　CJR - v43 - i4 - Nov-Dec 2004 - p65(2) [501+]
　　　KR - v72 - i16 - August 15 2004 - p797(1) [501+]
　　　Law&PolBR - Nov 2004 - p896(4) [501+]
　　　Nation - v279 - i19 - Dec 6 2004 - p36 [501+]
　　　New R - Feb 28 2005 - p31 [501+]
　　　NYT - Nov 5 2004 - pE35 [501+]
　　　NYTBR - Nov 7 2004 - p8 [501+]
　　　PW - v251 - i37 - Sept 13 2004 - p70(2) [501+]
Stone, Gleen - *Fathering at Risk*
　　R&R Bk N - v19 - i4 - Nov 2004 - p130(1) [51-500]
Stone, Greg C. - *Electrical Insulation for Rotating*
　Machines: Design, Evaluation, Aging, Testing, and
　Repair
　　SciTech - v28 - i1 - March 2004 - p152(1) [51-500]
Stone, Jean - *Once Upon a Bride*
　　PW - v252 - i2 - Jan 10 2005 - p44(1) [51-500]
Stone, Jeff - *Tiger*
　c CCB-B - v58 - i6 - Feb 2005 - p267(1) [51-500]
　y KR - v73 - i4 - Feb 15 2005 - p236(1) [51-500]
　y PW - v252 - i4 - Jan 24 2005 - p244(1) [51-500]
　y SLJ - v51 - i2 - Feb 2005 - p142(1) [51-500]
Stone, Karen - *Image and Spirit: Finding Meaning in*
　Visual Art
　　Intpr - v58 - i3 - July 2004 - p330(2) [501+]
Stone, Katherine V. W. - *From Widgets to Digits:*
　Employment Regulation for the Changing Workplace
　　Choice - v42 - i6 - Feb 2005 - p1067(1) [51-500]
Stone, Lynn M. - *Giant Pandas (Illus. by Su, Keren)*
　c SB - v40 - i4 - July-August 2004 - p181(1) [51-500]
Stone-Mediatore, Shari - *Reading Across Borders:*
　Storytelling and Knowledges of Resistance
　　R&R Bk N - v19 - i4 - Feb 2004 - p72(1) [1-50]
Stone, Randi - *Best Teaching Practices for Reaching all*
　Learners: What Award-Winning Classroom Teachers Do
　　Choice - v42 - i3 - Nov 2004 - p537(1) [1-50]
Stone, Rob - *The Flamenco Tradition in the Works of*
　Federico Garcia Lorca and Carlos Saura: The Wounded
　Throat
　　R&R Bk N - v19 - i4 - Nov 2004 - p231(1) [501+]
Stone, Robert - *Bay of Souls*
　　Lon R Bks - v26 - i6 - March 18 2004 - pNA
　　[501+]
　　Outerbridge Reach
　　　BL - v101 - i3 - Oct 1 2004 - p360(1) [501+]
Stone, Robin D. - *No Secrets, No Lies: How Black*
　Families Can Heal from Sexual Abuse
　　Black Iss - v6 - i5 - Sept-Oct 2004 - p44(1) [501+]
Stone, Ronald H. - *Resistance and Theological Ethics*
　　R&R Bk N - v19 - i4 - Nov 2004 - p29(1) [501+]
Stone, Ruth - *In the Dark*
　　BL - v101 - i2 - Sept 15 2004 - p196(1) [501+]
　　LJ - v129 - i13 - August 2004 - p87(1) [501+]
　　Poems
　　　BW - v34 - i45 - Nov 7 2004 - p12(1) [501+]
Stone, Ruth M. - *Music in West Africa: Experiencing*
　Music, Expressing Culture
　　Am MT - v54 - i4 - Feb-March 2005 - p114(2)
　　[501+]
Stone, Tiffany - *Floyd the Flamingo and His Flock of*
　Friends
　　Res Links - v10 - i2 - Dec 2004 - p10(2) [51-500]
Stone, William S. - *Early Clinical Intervention and*
　Prevention in Schizophrenia
　　SciTech - v28 - i1 - March 2004 - p100(1) [51-500]
Stonebanks, Roger - *Fighting for Dignity: The Ginger*
　Goodwin Story
　　Beav - v85 - i1 - Feb-March 2005 - p48(2) [51-500]
　　Can Hist R - v85 - i4 - Dec 2004 - p864(3) [501+]
Stonehill, Judith - *Brooklyn: A Journey through the City of*
　Dreams
　　R&R Bk N - v19 - i3 - August 2004 - p73(1) [51-500]
Stonehouse, Bernard - *How Animals Live: The Amazing*
　World of Aminals in the Wild (Illus. by Francis, John)
　　c LibMed - v23 - i3 - Nov-Dec 2004 - p77(1) [51-500]
　　How Animals Live: The Amazing World of Animals in the
　　Wild (Illus. by Francis, John)
　　　c CH Bwatch - Jan 2005 - pNA [51-500]
　　　y SLJ - v51 - i1 - Jan 2005 - p156(1) [51-500]

Stonehouse, Roger - *The Architecture of the British*
　Library at St Pancras
　　Spec - v296 - i9193 - Oct 16 2004 - p71(2) [501+]
　　TimHES - v0 - i1667 - Nov 19 2004 - p26(2)
　　[501+]
Stoneman, Richard - *A Traveller's History of Athens*
　　TLS - i5284 - July 9 2004 - p7(1) [501+]
Stonich, Sarah - *The Ice Chorus*
　　BL - v101 - i9-10 - Jan 1 2005 - p823(1) [1-50]
　　KR - v72 - i24 - Dec 15 2004 - p1163(1) [501+]
　　PW - v252 - i2 - Jan 10 2005 - p38(1) [51-500]
　　LJ - v129 - i20 - Dec 1 2004 - p103(1) [51-500]
Stookey, Lorena Laura - *Thematic Guide to World*
　Mythology
　　Choice - v42 - i3 - Nov 2004 - p454(1) [1-50]
　　LJ - v129 - i15 - Sept 15 2004 - p83(1) [51-500]
　　R&R Bk N - v19 - i3 - August 2004 - p13(1)
　　[1-50]
Stople, J. - *A Primer of Analytic Number Thoery*
　　SIAM Rev - v46 - i4 - Dec 2004 - p757-758
　　[501+]
Stoppard, Miriam - *Healthy Weight Loss*
　　c SB - v40 - i4 - July-August 2004 - p151(1) [51-500]
Stoppato, Marco C. - *Deserts*
　　E-Streams - July 2004 - pNA [501+]
　　Sci Teach - v71 - i7 - Sept 2004 - p96-97 [501+]
Storad, Conrad J. - *The Circulatory System*
　　c BL - v101 - i4 - Oct 15 2004 - p424(1) [51-500]
　　c SLJ - v51 - i2 - Feb 2005 - p114(1) [51-500]
Storaro, Vittorio - *Writing with Light*
　　FQ - v58 - i1 - Fall 2004 - p77(2) [501+]
Storck, Peter L. - *Journey to the Ice Age: Discovering an*
　Ancient World
　　Choice - v42 - i5 - Jan 2005 - p897(1) [1-50]
　　R&R Bk N - v19 - i3 - August 2004 - p61(1) [51-500]
Storey, Arthur G. - *Prairie Harvest*
　　CBRA - Annual 2003 - p188(1) [51-500]
Storey, David - *Thin-Ice Skater*
　　NS - v133 - i4716 - Nov 29 2004 - p42(1) [51-500]
　　TLS - i5264 - Feb 20 2004 - p23-23 [501+]
Storey, Ian C. - *Eupolis: Poet of Old Comedy*
　　TLS - i5287 - July 30 2004 - p22(1) [501+]
Storey, John - *Cultural Studies and the Study of Popular*
　Culture, 2nd Ed.
　　R&R Bk N - v19 - i3 - August 2004 - p142(1)
　　[51-500]
Storey, Kenneth B. - *Functional Metabolism: Regulation*
　and Adaptation
　　SciTech - v28 - i4 - Dec 2004 - p70(1) [51-500]
Storey, Margaret M. - *Loyalty and Loss: Alabama's*
　Unionists in the Civil War and Reconstruction
　　Choice - v42 - i5 - Jan 2005 - p919(1) [1-50]
Storey, Michael L. - *Representing the Troubles in Irish*
　Short Fiction
　　Choice - v42 - i3 - Nov 2004 - p487(1) [1-50]
Storey, P.J. - *Conservation and Improvement of Sloping*
　Land: A Manual of Soil and Water Conservation and Soil
　Improvement on Sloping Land, Vol. 3
　　SciTech - v28 - i1 - March 2004 - p127(1) [51-500]
Storhoff, Gary - *Understanding Charles Johnson*
　　Choice - v42 - i7 - March 2005 - p1232(1) [51-500]
Stori, Mary - *Beading Basics: 30 Embellishing Techniques*
　for Quilters
　　LJ - v129 - i13 - August 2004 - p79(1) [501+]
Stories, Elizabeth - *All This Heavenly Glory*
　　Ent W - i812 - March 25 2005 - p79 [51-500]
Storm, Howard - *My Descent into Death: A Second*
　Chance at Life
　　PW - v251 - i48 - Nov 29 2004 - p37(1) [51-500]
Stormer, Nathan - *Articulating Life's Memory: U.S.*
　Medical Rhetoric about Abortion in the Nineteenth
　Century
　　JAH - v91 - i3 - Dec 2004 - p1017(2) [501+]
Storr, Anthony - *Freud: A Very Short Introduction (Read*
　by Jason, Neville). Audiobook Review
　　y Kliatt - v38 - i5 - Sept 2004 - p67(3) [51-500]
　　Solitude
　　　Globe & Mail - Nov 20 2004 - pD31 [501+]
Storr, Virgil Henry - *Enterprising Slaves and Master*
　Pirates: Understanding Economic Life in the Bahamas
　　R&R Bk N - v19 - i3 - August 2004 - p98(1) [51-500]
Storti, Craig - *Americans at Work: A Cultural Guide to the*
　Can-Do People
　　R&R Bk N - v19 - i4 - Nov 2004 - p104(1) [51-500]

Story, Derrick - *Digital Photography Pocket Guide*
　　SciTech - v28 - i1 - March 2004 - p174(1) [1-50]
Story, Jonathan - *China: The Race to Market*
　　A Aff - v35 - i2 - July 2004 - p251-252 [501+]
The Story of Flight
　　c LibMed - v22 - i5 - Feb 2004 - p80(1) [501+]
Story, Rosalyn - *More than You Know*
　　BL - v101 - i2 - Sept 15 2004 - p210(1) [51-500]
　　Black Iss - v6 - i6 - Nov-Dec 2004 - p70(1) [51-500]
　　BW - v34 - i44 - Oct 31 2004 - p8(1) [501+]
　　KR - v72 - i17 - Sept 1 2004 - p835(1) [51-500]
　　LJ - v129 - i18 - Nov 1 2004 - p78(1) [501+]
　　PW - v251 - i34 - August 23 2004 - p37(1) [501+]
Stossel, John - *Give Me a Break: How I Exposed*
　Hucksters, Cheats and Scam Artists and Became the
　Scourge of the Liberal Media...
　　Am Spect - v37 - i4 - May 2004 - p58(2) [501+]
Stossel, Scott - *Sarge: The Life and Times of Sargent*
　Shriver
　　AM - v191 - i8 - Sept 27 2004 - p24 [501+]
　　Comw - v131 - i13 - July 16 2004 - p27(3) [501+]
　　R&R Bk N - v19 - i3 - August 2004 - p70(1) [51-500]
Stott, Anne - *Hannah More: The First Victorian*
　　AHR - v109 - i3 - June 2004 - p975(2) [501+]
　　Lon R Bks - v26 - i24 - Dec 16 2004 - p15(2)
　　[501+]
　　RES - v55 - i219 - April 2004 - p287-289 [501+]
Stott, Annette - *Holland Mania: The Unknown Dutch*
　Period in American Art and Culture
　　NYRB - v51 - i17 - Nov 4 2004 - p35(3) [501+]
Stott, Jim - *Stonewall Kitchen Harvest: Celebrating the*
　Bounty of the Seasons (Illus. by Kauck, Jeff)
　　LJ - v129 - i19 - Nov 15 2004 - p83(1) [51-500]
Stott, Rebecca - *Darwin and the Barnacle*
　　y SB - v40 - i3 - May-June 2004 - p123(1) [501+]
Stouck, David - *Ethel Wilson: A Critical Biography*
　　CBRA - Annual 2003 - p74(1) [501+]
　　CWS - v23 - i3-4 - Spring-Summer 2004 - p217(3)
　　[501+]
Stough, Roger - *Transport and Information Systems*
　　JEL - v41 - i4 - Dec 2003 - p1440(1) [501+]
Stourton, Edward - *In the Footsteps of Saint Paul*
　　TLS - i5287 - July 30 2004 - p27(1) [501+]
Stourton, James - *Great Smaller Museums of Europe*
　　TimHES - v0 - i1648 - July 9 2004 - p28(2)
　　[501+]
Stouse, Karen G. - *Customer-Centered Telecommunications*
　Services Marketing
　　SciTech - v28 - i4 - Dec 2004 - p9(1) [1-50]
Stout, A. Kathryn - *Social Problems, Law, and Society*
　　R&R Bk N - v19 - i4 - Nov 2004 - p161(1) [501+]
Stout, Chris E. - *Evidence-Based Practice: Methods,*
　Models, and Tools for Mental Health Professionals
　　SciTech - v28 - i4 - Dec 2004 - p77(1) [51-500]
　　Psychology of Terrorism: Coping with the Continuing
　　Threat, Condensed Ed.
　　　LJ - v129 - i16 - Oct 1 2004 - p101(1) [51-500]
Stout, Glenn - *The Best American Sports Writing 2004*
　　y BL - v101 - i5 - Nov 1 2004 - p453(1) [51-500]
　　PW - v251 - i37 - Sept 13 2004 - p67(1) [51-500]
　　The Dodgers: 120 Years of Dodgers Baseball
　　　BL - v101 - i1 - Sept 1 2004 - p52(2) [51-500]
　　　PW - v251 - i34 - August 23 2004 - p49(1) [51-500]
Stout, Jeffrey - *Democracy and Tradition*
　　Choice - v42 - i2 - Oct 2004 - p312(1) [51-500]
　　Ethics - v115 - i1 - Oct 2004 - p169(7) [501+]
Stout, Joseph Allen - *Schemers and Dreamers:*
　Filibustering in Mexico, 1848-1921
　　Ams - v61 - i2 - Oct 2004 - p301(2) [501+]
　　HAHR - v84 - i4 - Nov 2004 - p772(1) [501+]
Stout, Martha - *The Sociopath Next Door: The Ruthless*
　versus the Rest of Us
　　Globe & Mail - Feb 19 2005 - pD14 [501+]
　　KR - v72 - i21 - Nov 1 2004 - p1042(1) [501+]
　　LJ - v129 - i20 - Dec 1 2004 - p144(1) [51-500]
　　NYTBR - March 6 2005 - p10 [501+]
　　PW - v251 - i51 - Dec 20 2004 - p44(1) [51-500]
Stout, Mary - *Blackfoot*
　　y SLJ - v51 - i1 - Jan 2005 - p156(1) [51-500]
Stout, Maureen - *The Feel-Good Curriculum: The*
　Dumbing Down of America's Kids in the Name of
　Self-Esteem
　　MA - v46 - i3 - Summer 2004 - p268(4) [501+]
Stovall, Tyler - *French Civilization and Its Discontents:*
　Nationalism, Colonialism, Race
　　R&R Bk N - v19 - i1 - Feb 2004 - p35(1) [1-50]
Stover, Bernd - *Die Bundesrepublik Deutschland*
　　GSR - v27 - i1 - Feb 2004 - p199-200 [501+]

Stover, Johnnie M. - *Rhetoric and Resistance in Black Women's Autobiography*
  Choice - v41 - i7 - March 2004 - p1299(1) [501+]
  JSH - v71 - i1 - Feb 2005 - p152(2) [501+]

Stover, Lois Thomas - *Jacqueline Woodson: The Real Thing*
  R&R Bk N - v19 - i1 - Feb 2004 - p247(1) [1-50]

Stover, Matthew Woodring - *Star Wars: Episode III, Revenge of the Sith (Read by Davis, Jonathan). Audiobook Review*
  LJ - v130 - i1 - Jan 1 2005 - p168(1) [501+]

Stow, Kenneth - *Theater of Acculturation: The Roman Ghetto in the Sixteenth Century*
  HNet - Oct 2004 - pNA [501+]

Stowe, David W. - *How Sweet the Sound: Music in the Spiritual Lives of Americans*
  Choice - v42 - i2 - Oct 2004 - p304(1) [51-500]

Stowell, Fred - *Principles of Foam Fire Fighting, 2nd Ed.*
  SciTech - v28 - i1 - March 2004 - p150(1) [51-500]

Stowell, Robin - *The Cambridge Companion to the String Quartet*
  Choice - v41 - i11-12 - July-August 2004 - p2053(1) [501+]
  Notes - v61 - i2 - Dec 2004 - p456(3) [501+]

Stower, Adam - *Two Left Feet (Illus. by Stower, Adam)*
  c KR - v72 - i13 - July 1 2004 - p638(1) [51-500]
  c PW - v251 - i32 - August 9 2004 - p250(1) [51-500]
  c SLJ - v50 - i10 - Oct 2004 - p135(1) [51-500]

Stoynoff, Natasha - *Final Beginnings*
  People - v62 - i15 - Oct 11 2004 - p58 [51-500]

Stozek, H.G. - *The Edge*
  Res Links - v10 - i3 - Feb 2005 - p41(1) [501+]

Stozier, Charles R. - *Heinz Kohut: The Making of a Psychoanalyst*
  SciTech - v28 - i4 - Dec 2004 - p1(1) [1-50]

Strachan, Alan - *Secret Dreams: A Biography of Michael Redgrave*
  Globe & Mail - July 10 2004 - pD16 [51-500]
  Lon R Bks - v26 - i15 - August 5 2004 - p14(2) [501+]
  TLS - i5291 - August 27 2004 - p18(1) [501+]

Strachan, Hew - *The First World War*
  y SLJ - v50 - i9 - Sept 2004 - p237(1) [51-500]
  y TimHES - v0 - i1652 - August 6 2004 - p24(2) [501+]

Strachan, Isabella - *Emma, the Twice-Crowned Queen: England in the Viking Age*
  BL - v101 - i9-10 - Jan 1 2005 - p810(1) [1-50]

Strachan, Tom - *Human Molecular Genetics 3*
  QRB - v79 - i4 - Dec 2004 - p464(1) [501+]

Straczynski, J. Michael - *Amazing Spider-Man. Vol. 6*
  LJ - v129 - i14 - Sept 1 2004 - p129(1) [51-500]

Strade, Helmut - *Simple Lie Algebras over Fields of Positive Characteristic, Vol. 1*
  SciTech - v28 - i3 - Sept 2004 - p36(1) [51-500]

Stradley, Randy - *Star Wars Panel to Panel: From the Pages of Dark Horse Comics to a Galaxy Far, Far Away, 1st Ed.*
  SLJ - v51 - i2 - Feb 2005 - p25(1) [51-500]

Stradling, David - *Conservation in the Progressive Era: Classic Texts*
  SciTech - v28 - i3 - Sept 2004 - p56(1) [1-50]

Stradling, Julie - *Educating for the Good Life: Democratic Schooling and Its Dilemmas*
  R&R Bk N - v19 - i4 - Nov 2004 - p176(1) [501+]

Strain, Ellen - *Public Places, Private Journeys: Ethnography, Entertainment, and the Tourist Gaze*
  Choice - v41 - i7 - March 2004 - p1336(1) [501+]

Straley, Dona S. - *The Undergraduate's Companion to Arab Writers and Their Web Sites*
  R&R Bk N - v19 - i4 - Nov 2004 - p258(1) [501+]

Strand, Ginger - *Flight*
  KR - v73 - i5 - March 1 2005 - p258(1) [501+]

Strang, G. Bruce - *On the Fiery March: Mussolini Prepares for War*
  HNet - July 2004 - pNA [501+]

Strang, Heather - *Restorative Justice and Family Violence*
  CS - v33 - i1 - Jan 2004 - p96-98 [501+]

Strangio, Paul - *Keeper of the Faith: A Biography of Jim Cairns*
  AHS - v35 - i124 - Oct 2004 - p387(2) [501+]
  AJPS - v39 - i3 - Nov 2004 - p668(1) [501+]

Strasser, Judith - *Black eye; escaping a marriage, writing a life*
  R&R Bk N - v19 - i3 - August 2004 - p30(1) [1-50]

Strasser, Steven - *The 9/11 Investigations: Staff Reports of the 9/11 Commission: Excerpts from the House-Senate Joint Inquiry Report on 9/11*
  For Aff - v83 - i5 - Sept-Oct 2004 - p164 [501+]
  R&R Bk N - v19 - i3 - August 2004 - p165(1) [501+]

The Abu Ghraib Investigations: The Official Report of the Independent Panel and Pentagon on the Shocking Prisoner Abuse in Iraq
  NYTBR - Jan 23 2005 - p1 [501+]

The Abu Ghraib Investigations: The Official Reports of the Independent Panel and the Pentagon on the Shocking Prisoner Abuse in Iraq
  Nation - v280 - i5 - Feb 7 2005 - p23 [501+]

Strasser, Todd - *Can't Get There from Here*
  y CCB-B - v57 - i11 - July-August 2004 - p485(2) [501+]
  c LibMed - v23 - i3 - Nov-Dec 2004 - p73(1) [51-500]

Cut Back
  y BL - v100 - i21 - July 2004 - p1835(1) [1-50]
  y Kliatt - v39 - i2 - March 2005 - p23(1) [51-500]

Take Off
  y BL - v100 - i21 - July 2004 - p1835(1) [1-50]
  c SLJ - v50 - i8 - August 2004 - p130(1) [51-500]

Thief of Dreams
  LibMed - v22 - i4 - Jan 2004 - p63(1) [501+]

Strasser, Ulrike - *State of Virginity: Gender, Religion, and Politics in an Early Modern Catholic State*
  Choice - v42 - i2 - Oct 2004 - p312(1) [51-500]

Stratford, Philip - *Pelagie: The Return to Acadie*
  Globe & Mail - July 3 2004 - pD13 [1-50]

Strathern, Andrew - *Empowering the Past, Confronting the Future: The Duna People of Papua New Guinea*
  Choice - v42 - i7 - March 2005 - p1272(1) [51-500]

Strathern, Paul - *Brief History of Economic Genius*
  R&R Bk N - v19 - i4 - Nov 2004 - p84(1) [51-500]

Dostoevsky in 90 Minutes
  y Kliatt - v39 - i1 - Jan 2005 - p27(1) [51-500]

Stratton, Allan - *Chanda's Secrets*
  y BL - v100 - i21 - July 2004 - p1843(1) [1-50]
  y BL - v101 - i9-10 - Jan 1 2005 - p773(1) [51-500]
  c CCB-B - v58 - i2 - Oct 2004 - p100(2) [51-500]
  y Kliatt - v38 - i4 - July 2004 - p24(1) [51-500]
  c LibMed - v23 - i3 - Nov-Dec 2004 - p73(1) [51-500]
  y Magpies - v19 - i5 - Nov 2004 - p42(1) [501+]
  y SLJ - v50 - i7 - July 2004 - p112(1) [51-500]
  y VOYA - v27 - i5 - Dec 2004 - p397(1) [51-500]

Stratton, Arthur - *Form and Design in Classic Architecture*
  R&R Bk N - v19 - i4 - Nov 2004 - p202(1) [51-500]

Stratton, Kathleen - *Immunization Safety Review: Influenza Vaccines and Neurological Complications*
  SciTech - v28 - i4 - Dec 2004 - p75(1) [51-500]

Stratton-Lake, Philip - *Ethical Intuitionism: Re-evaluations*
  Ethics - v115 - i1 - Oct 2004 - p175(3) [501+]

Stratton, W.K. - *Chasing the Rodeo: on Wild Rides and Big Dreams, Broken Hearts and Broken Bones, and One Man's Search for the West*
  KR - v73 - i4 - Feb 15 2005 - p221(1) [501+]
  PW - v252 - i10 - March 7 2005 - p57(1) [51-500]

Straub, Katrin - *Creating a Newsletter in InDesign: Visual QuickProject Guide*
  LJ - v130 - i1 - Jan 1 2005 - p148(1) [501+]

Straub, Peter - *In the Night Room*
  BL - v101 - i4 - Oct 15 2004 - p363(1) [51-500]
  Ent W - i789 - Oct 22 2004 - p101 [51-500]
  KR - v72 - i18 - Sept 15 2004 - p890(1) [501+]
  NYTBR - Jan 23 2005 - p19 [501+]
  PW - v251 - i40 - Oct 4 2004 - p70(1) [51-500]

Strauch, Katina - *The Charleston Conference Proceedings 2001*
  ALJ - v53 - i3 - August 2004 - p326(1) [501+]

Straus, Ulrich - *The Anguish of Surrender: Japanese POWs of World War II*
  Choice - v42 - i3 - Nov 2004 - p542(1) [1-50]

Strauss, Barry - *The Battle of Salamis: The Naval Encounter That Saved Greece--and Western Civilization*
  BW - v34 - i28 - July 11 2004 - p5(1) [501+]
  Choice - v42 - i6 - Feb 2005 - p1076(1) [51-500]

The Battle of Salamis: The Naval Encounter That Saved Greece--and Western Civilization
  Globe & Mail - August 21 2004 - pD11 [501+]

The Battle of Salamis: The Naval Encounter That Saved Greece--and Western Civilization
  y SLJ - v51 - i1 - Jan 2005 - p161(1) [501+]

Strauss, Botho - *Die Nacht mit Alice, als Julia ums Haus schlich*
  WLT - v78 - i3-4 - Sept-Dec 2004 - p126(1) [501+]

Strauss, Claudia - *Talking to Anxiety: simple Ways to Support Someone in Your Life Who Suffers from Anxiety*
  LJ - v129 - i20 - Dec 1 2004 - p143(2) [51-500]

Strauss, Jerome F. - *Yen and Jaffe's Reproductive Endocrinology: Physiology, Pathophysiology, and Clinical Management, 5th ed.*
  SciTech - v28 - i4 - Dec 2004 - p70(1) [51-500]

Strauss, Leo - *Gesammelte Schriften, vols. 1-3*
  NYRB - v51 - i16 - Oct 21 2004 - p58(3) [501+]

Leo Strauss: The Early Writings, 1921-1932
  NYRB - v51 - i16 - Oct 21 2004 - p58(3) [501+]

Strauss, Linda Leopold - *Really, Truly, Everything's Fine*
  c SLJ - v50 - i7 - July 2004 - p112(2) [51-500]

Strauss, Michael B. - *Diving Science*
  SciTech - v28 - i3 - Sept 2004 - p109(1) [51-500]

Strauss, Rochelle - *Tree of Life: The Incredible Biodiversity of Life on Earth (Illus. by Thompson, Margot)*
  c BL - v101 - i7 - Dec 1 2004 - p670(2) [51-500]
  c KR - v72 - i16 - August 15 2004 - p813(1) [51-500]
  c PW - v251 - i38 - Sept 20 2004 - p64(2) [51-500]
  c Res Links - v10 - i2 - Dec 2004 - p30(2) [51-500]
  c SLJ - v50 - i10 - Oct 2004 - p194(2) [51-500]

Strauss, Steven H. - *The Bioengineered Forest: Challenges for Science and Society*
  Choice - v42 - i7 - March 2005 - p1252(1) [51-500]

Strausser, Jeffrey - *Painless American Strategy*
  y VOYA - v27 - i3 - August 2004 - p242(1) [1-50]

Straussner, Shulamith Lala Ashenberg - *Understanding Mass Violence: A Social Work Perspective*
  R&R Bk N - v19 - i1 - Feb 2004 - p136(1) [51-500]

Stravitz, David - *New York, Empire City, 1920-1945*
  R&R Bk N - v19 - i4 - Nov 2004 - p248(1) [501+]

Strawser, Cornelia J. - *Business Statistics of the United States, 9th Ed.*
  Choice - v42 - i1 - Sept 2004 - p77(1) [501+]
  R&R Bk N - v19 - i2 - May 2004 - p110(1) [51-500]

Strawson, P.F. - *Logico-Linguistic Papers, rev. ed.*
  R&R Bk N - v19 - i4 - Nov 2004 - p7(1) [51-500]

Subject and Predicate in Logic and Grammar, rev. ed.
  R&R Bk N - v19 - i4 - Nov 2004 - p5(1) [51-500]

Stray, Christopher - *The Classical Association: The First Century, 1903-2003*
  TLS - i5285 - July 16 2004 - p24(1) [501+]

Strazny, Philipp - *Encyclopedia of Linguistics. 2 vols.*
  LJ - v130 - i2 - Feb 1 2005 - p114(1) [51-500]

Streatfeild, Noel - *Ballet Shoes. Audiobook Review*
  c PW - v252 - i11 - March 14 2005 - p26(1) [501+]

Ballet Shoes
  c Sch Lib - v52 - i4 - Winter 2004 - p203(1) [51-500]

Dancing Shoes (Read by Sastre, Elizabeth). Audiobook Review
  c PW - v252 - i11 - March 14 2005 - p26(1) [501+]

Strecker, Trey - *Dead Balls and Double Curves: An Anthology of Early Baseball Fiction*
  ABR - v26 - i2 - Jan-Feb 2005 - p24(1) [501+]

Streckfus, Peter - *Cuckoo*
  LJ - v129 - i12 - July 2004 - p88(1) [51-500]

Streeck, Wolfgang - *The Origins of Nonliberal Capitalism: Germany and Japan in Comparison*
  JEL - v42 - i3 - Sept 2004 - p885(2) [501+]

Street, Bill - *2004 Conservation Directory: The Guide to Worldwide Environmental Organizations, 49th ed.*
  SciTech - v28 - i1 - March 2004 - p65(1) [51-500]

Street, Richard Steven - *Beasts of the Field: A Narrative History of California Farmworkers 1769-1913*
  R&R Bk N - v19 - i3 - August 2004 - p111(1) [51-500]

Photographing Farmworkers in California
  LJ - v129 - i13 - August 2004 - p105(1) [51-500]

Strege, Mark A. - *Capillary Electrophoresis of Proteins and Peptides*
  SciTech - v28 - i3 - Sept 2004 - p71(1) [51-500]

Streiber, Anne - *The Invisible Woman*
  KR - v72 - i18 - Sept 15 2004 - p895(1) [501+]

Streifer, Philip A. - *Tools and Techniques for Effective Data-Driven Decision Making*
  R&R Bk N - v19 - i4 - Nov 2004 - p188(1) [501+]

Streissguth, Michael - *Johnny Cash at Folsom Prison: The Making of a Masterpiece*
  BL - v101 - i1 - Sept 1 2004 - p37(2) [51-500]
  Bwatch - Feb 2005 - pNA [51-500]
  Econ - v372 - i8393 - Sept 18 2004 - p88US [501+]
  LJ - v129 - i14 - Sept 1 2004 - p153(1) [501+]
  PW - v251 - i34 - August 23 2004 - p51(1) [51-500]
Songwriting Success: How to Write Songs for Fun and (Maybe) Profit
  Bwatch - v26 - i9 - Sept 2004 - p9(1) [51-500]

Streissguth, Thomas - *Combating the Global Terrorist Threat*
  y BL - v100 - i22 - August 2004 - p1918(1) [51-500]

Streissguth, Tom - *Benjamin Franklin*
  c SLJ - v51 - i2 - Feb 2005 - p153(1) [51-500]

Strek, Andrea - *Renouncing the World Yet Leading the Church: The Monk-Bishop in Late Antiquity*
  Choice - v42 - i3 - Nov 2004 - p502(1) [51-500]

Stren, Patti - *Un calin, s.v.p.*
  Res Links - v10 - i2 - Dec 2004 - p57(1) [51-500]

Strenski, Ivan - *Contesting Sacrifice: Religion, Nationalism, and Social Thought in France*
  JAAR - v72 - i3 - Sept 2004 - p798-799 [501+]
Dictionnaire des femmes libraires en France: 1470-1870
  FS - v58 - i3 - July 2004 - p445-446 [501+]
Theology and the First Theory of Sacrifice
  R&R Bk N - v19 - i1 - Feb 2004 - p22(1) [51-500]

Streshinsky, Shirley - *Audubon: Life and Art in the American Wilderness*
  BL - v100 - i22 - August 2004 - p1886(1) [51-500]

Stretch, John J. - *Practicing Social Justice*
  Fam in Soc - v85 - i4 - Oct-Dec 2004 - p593(3) [501+]
  R&R Bk N - v19 - i1 - Feb 2004 - p136(1) [51-500]

Strete, Craig - *The Rattlesnake Who Went to School (Illus. by Cravath, Lynne)*
  c BL - v100 - i22 - August 2004 - p1948(2) [51-500]
  c CCB-B - v58 - i1 - Sept 2004 - p40(2) [51-500]
  c SLJ - v50 - i7 - July 2004 - p88(2) [51-500]

Strichartz, Robert S. - *Guide to Distribution Theory and Fourier Transforms*
  SciTech - v28 - i4 - Dec 2004 - p39(1) [51-500]

Strick, Candace Eisner - *Quilter's Quick Reference Guide*
  Bwatch - v26 - i9 - Sept 2004 - p10(2) [51-500]

Strick, James E. - *Sparks of Life*
  VS - v45 - i2 - Winter 2003 - p305 [501+]

Strickland, Bobby - *Adeline (Illus. by Rathke, Kathryn)*
  c SLJ - v51 - i1 - Jan 2005 - p98(1) [51-500]

Strickland, Brad - *Marooned!*
  c SLJ - v50 - i10 - Oct 2004 - p178(1) [51-500]

Strickland, Debra Higgs - *Saracens, Demons, and Jews: Making Monsters in Medieval Art*
  JR - v84 - i4 - Oct 2004 - p614(2) [501+]
  Specu - v79 - i4 - Oct 2004 - p1155(4) [501+]

Strickland, Dorothy S. - *Bridging the Literacy Achievement Gap, Grades 4-12*
  Choice - v42 - i3 - Nov 2004 - p535(1) [1-50]
  TCR - v107 - i2 - Feb 2005 - p292(4) [501+]
Learning about Print in Preschool: Working with Letters, Words, and Beginning Links with Phonemic Awareness
  R Today - v22 - i1 - August-Sept 2004 - p12(1) [501+]
  R Today - v22 - i1 - August-Sept 2004 - p32(1) [51-500]

Strickland, Ruth Ann - *Restorative Justice*
  R&R Bk N - v19 - i3 - August 2004 - p169(1) [501+]

Strieber, Anne - *An Invisible Woman*
  LJ - v130 - i1 - Jan 1 2005 - p101(1) [51-500]
  PW - v251 - i41 - Oct 11 2004 - p56(1) [51-500]

Striff, Erin - *Performance Studies*
  Theat J - v56 - i3 - Oct 2004 - p537-539 [501+]

Striffler, Steve - *Banana Wars: Power, Production, and History in the Americas*
  Choice - v42 - i1 - Sept 2004 - p151(1) [501+]
  JRAI - v10 - i4 - Dec 2004 - p934(1) [501+]
Bantana Wars: Power, Production, and History in the Americas
  Ams - v61 - i2 - Oct 2004 - p300(2) [501+]

Stright, Barbara R. - *Maternal Newborn Nursing, 4th Ed.*
  SciTech - v28 - i4 - Dec 2004 - p111(1) [1-50]

Strindberg, August - *The Chamber Plays*
  TLS - i5303 - Nov 19 2004 - p37(1) [51-500]
A Madman's Manifesto
  Atl - v294 - i2 - Sept 2004 - p139(1) [501+]

Stringer, John - *Nations of the Western Great Lakes*
  c CBRA - Annual 2003 - p534(1) [51-500]

Stringer, Lee - *Sleepaway School: Stories from a Boy's Life*
  BW - v34 - i27 - July 4 2004 - p6(2) [501+]
  y SLJ - v50 - i11 - Nov 2004 - p179(1) [51-500]

Stringham, Jim - *Unemployment Survival Guide*
  Bwatch - v26 - i8 - August 2004 - p1(1) [51-500]

Stripling, Barbara K. - *Curriculum Connections through the Library*
  LibMed - v23 - i1 - August-Sept 2004 - p84(1) [51-500]
  R&R Bk N - v19 - i1 - Feb 2004 - p186(1) [51-500]
  Teach Lib - v32 - i2 - Dec 2004 - p37(1) [501+]

Strittmatter, Beate - *Identifying and Treating Blockages to Healing: New Approaches to Therapy-Resistant Patients*
  SciTech - v28 - i3 - Sept 2004 - p126(1) [51-500]

Strobel, Alison - *Worlds Collide*
  PW - v252 - i8 - Feb 21 2005 - p159(1) [51-500]

Strober, Deborah H. - *The Nixon Presidency: An Oral History of the Era*
  R&R Bk N - v19 - i1 - Feb 2004 - p62(1) [501+]
The Reagan Presidency: An Oral History of the Era. Rev. Ed.
  R&R Bk N - v19 - i1 - Feb 2004 - p62(1) [501+]

Stroby, Wallace - *The Heartbreak Lounge*
  BL - v101 - i6 - Nov 15 2004 - p566(1) [51-500]
  KR - v72 - i23 - Dec 1 2004 - p1124(1) [51-500]
  LJ - v130 - i1 - Jan 1 2005 - p84(1) [51-500]
  PW - v251 - i49 - Dec 6 2004 - p46(1) [51-500]

Strogatz, Steven - *Sync: The Emerging Science of Spontaneous Order*
  Phys Today - v57 - i6 - June 2004 - p59-60 [501+]

Strohm, Christoph - *Martin Bucer und das Recht: Beitrage zum internationalen Symposium vom 1. bis 3. Marz 2001 in der Johannes a Lasco Bibliothek Emden*
  Ren Q - v57 - i3 - Fall 2004 - p1050(2) [501+]
  Six Ct J - v34 - i4 - Winter 2003 - p1185-1186 [501+]

Strohm, Paul - *Theory and the Premodern Text*
  JEGP - v103 - i3 - July 2004 - p385-386 [501+]

Strohmeier, Martin - *Crucial Images in the Presentation of a Kurdish National Identity: Heroes and Patriots; Traitors and Foes*
  MEJ - v58 - i4 - Autumn 2004 - p694(2) [501+]

Strohmer, Michael - *Von Hexen, Ratsherren und Juristen: Die Rezeption der Peinlichen Halsgerichtsordnung Kaiser Karls V. in den fruhen Hexenprozessen der Hansestadt Lemgo 1583-1621*
  HNet - July 2004 - pNA [501+]

Strohmeyer, Sarah - *Bubbles Betrothed*
  KR - v72 - i24 - Dec 15 2004 - p1169(2) [501+]
  LJ - v129 - i20 - Dec 1 2004 - p96(1) [51-500]
  LJ - v130 - i4 - March 1 2005 - p71(1) [51-500]
  PW - v252 - i7 - Feb 14 2005 - p56(1) [51-500]

Stroll, Mary - *Calixtus II (1119-1124): A Pope Born to Rule*
  R&R Bk N - v19 - i4 - Nov 2004 - p26(1) [501+]

Strom, Claire - *Profiting from the Plains: The Great Northern Railway and Corporate Development of the American West*
  BHR - v78 - i3 - Autumn 2004 - p528(3) [501+]
  JAH - v91 - i3 - Dec 2004 - p1055(1) [501+]

Strom, Robert G. - *Exploring Mercury: The Iron Planet*
  S&T - v108 - i1 - July 2004 - p118(1) [501+]

Stroman, James - *Administrative Assistant's and Secretary's Handbook, 2d ed.*
  R&R Bk N - v19 - i1 - Feb 2004 - p109(1) [51-500]

Stromberg, Gary - *The Harder They Fall: Celebrities Tell Their Real-Life Stories of Addiction and Recovery*
  PW - v252 - i5 - Jan 31 2005 - p55(1) [51-500]

Stromquist, Annie - *Simple Screenprinting: Basic Techniques and Creative Projects*
  LJ - v130 - i3 - Feb 15 2005 - p128(1) [51-500]

Stromseth, Jane E. - *Accountability for Atrocities: National and International Responses*
  R&R Bk N - v19 - i3 - August 2004 - p193(1) [501+]

Stronach, Ian - *Educational Research: Difference and Diversity*
  R&R Bk N - v19 - i4 - Nov 2004 - p179(1) [501+]

Strong, Jeremy - *Liar, Liar Pants on Fire!*
  c Sch Lib - v52 - i4 - Winter 2004 - p192(1) [51-500]

Strong, John S. - *Relics of the Buddha*
  Choice - v42 - i6 - Feb 2005 - p1040(1) [51-500]

Strong, Robert A. - *Derivatives: An Introduction, 2nd Ed.*
  R&R Bk N - v19 - i4 - Nov 2004 - p119(1) [51-500]

Strong, Roy - *Feast: A History of Grand Eating*
  NYRB - v51 - i12 - July 15 2004 - p30(3) [501+]
  R&R Bk N - v19 - i1 - Feb 2004 - p253(1) [51-500]
  VQR - v80 - i2 - Spring 2004 - p262-262 [501+]

Strong, Terence - *Cold Monday*
  Econ - v373 - i8395 - Oct 2 2004 - p84US [501+]

Strong, Thomas - *Furthering Talk: Advances in the Discursive Therapies*
  SciTech - v28 - i1 - March 2004 - p97(1) [51-500]

Stronge, James H. - *Handbook on Educational Specialist Evaluation: Assessing and Improving Performance*
  R&R Bk N - v19 - i1 - Feb 2004 - p187(1) [51-500]

Stronge, W.L. - *Impact Biomechanics*
  SciTech - v28 - i1 - March 2004 - p72(1) [51-500]

Stroninska, Magda - *Exile, Language and Identity: Proceedings*
  R&R Bk N - v19 - i1 - Feb 2004 - p221(1) [51-500]

Stross, Charles - *The Atrocity Archives*
  BW - v34 - i28 - July 11 2004 - p10(1) [501+]
The Family Trade
  y BL - v101 - i6 - Nov 15 2004 - p572(1) [51-500]
  LJ - v129 - i19 - Nov 15 2004 - p54(2) [501+]
  PW - v251 - i45 - Nov 8 2004 - p40(1) [501+]
Iron Sunrise
  Analog - v125 - i1-2 - Jan-Feb 2005 - p230(6) [501+]
  BL - v100 - i21 - July 2004 - p1829(2) [1-50]
  LJ - v129 - i12 - July 2004 - p75(1) [51-500]
  y VOYA - v27 - i4 - Oct 2004 - p287(1) [501+]
Singularity Sky
  Analog - v124 - i1-2 - Jan-Feb 2004 - p231(1) [501+]
  New Sci - v183 - i2463 - Sept 4 2004 - p47(1) [51-500]
  y VOYA - v27 - i4 - Oct 2004 - p287(1) [51-500]

Stroud, Bettye - *The Patchwork Path: A Quilt Map to Freedom (Illus. by Bennett, Erin Susanne)*
  c CCB-B - v58 - i5 - Jan 2005 - p229(1) [51-500]
  c KR - v72 - i24 - Dec 15 2004 - p1209(1) [51-500]
  c PW - v252 - i1 - Jan 3 2005 - p55(1) [51-500]
  c SLJ - v51 - i1 - Jan 2005 - p98(1) [51-500]

Stroud, Jonathan - *The Amulet of Samarkand*
  c BL - v101 - i2 - Sept 15 2004 - p233(1) [51-500]
  c HB - v81 - i1 - Jan-Feb 2005 - p30(1) [51-500]
  y Kliatt - v39 - i1 - Jan 2005 - p22(1) [51-500]
  c LibMed - v22 - i5 - Feb 2004 - p71(1) [501+]
The Golem's Eye (Read by Jones, Simon). Audiobook Review
  c HB - v81 - i1 - Jan-Feb 2005 - p122(1) [51-500]
The Golem's Eye
  y BL - v100 - i22 - August 2004 - p1920(2) [51-500]
  y CCB-B - v58 - i3 - Nov 2004 - p148(1) [501+]
  c HB - v80 - i5 - Sept-Oct 2004 - p599(2) [501+]
  y KR - v72 - i15 - August 1 2004 - p749(1) [51-500]
  y Magpies - v19 - i5 - Nov 2004 - p38(1) [501+]
  c PW - v251 - i33 - August 16 2004 - p64(1) [51-500]
  c SLJ - v50 - i10 - Oct 2004 - p178(2) [51-500]
  y VOYA - v27 - i4 - Oct 2004 - p321(1) [51-500]

Stroud, K.A. - *Differential Equations*
  SciTech - v28 - i4 - Dec 2004 - p40(1) [51-500]

Stroud, Mark - *Extreme Weather: A Guide and Record Book*
  PW - v251 - i31 - August 2 2004 - p58(2) [501+]

Stroud, Mike - *Survival of the Fittest: Anatomy of Peak Physical Performance*
  TLS - i5300 - Oct 29 2004 - p32(1) [501+]

Stroud, Robert M. - *Annual Review of Biophysics and Biomolecular Structure: Vol. 32, 2003*
  SciTech - v28 - i1 - March 2004 - p63(1) [51-500]

Stroux, Sigrid - *US and EC Oligopoly Control*
  R&R Bk N - v19 - i4 - Nov 2004 - p164(1) [501+]

Strozier, Robert M. - *Foucault, Subjectivity, and Identity: Historical Constructions of Subject and Self*
  Six Ct J - v35 - i3 - Fall 2004 - p951-953 [501+]

Strudwick, Leslie - *Inuit*
  c CH Bwatch - v14 - i7 - July 2004 - p5(2) [51-500]
  c SLJ - v50 - i7 - July 2004 - p94(1) [51-500]
Laura Ingalls Wilder
  c SLJ - v50 - i10 - Oct 2004 - p139(2) [51-500]

Strudwick, Nigel - *The Theban Necropolis: Past, Present and Future*
  R&R Bk N - v19 - i3 - August 2004 - p58(1) [51-500]

Struek, William - *Rethinking the Korean War: A New Diplomatic and Strategic History*
  J Am St - v38 - i1 - April 2004 - p170-170 [501+]

Struge, M.D. - *Statistical and Thermal Physics: Fundamentals and Applications*
Choice - v41 - i7 - March 2004 - p1332(1) [501+]

Struk, Janina - *Photographing the Holocaust: Interpretations of the Evidence*
Choice - v42 - i1 - Sept 2004 - p93(1) [501+]
Lon R Bks - v26 - i21 - Nov 4 2004 - p7(6) [501+]

Struve, Edgar - *Die Grenzen der Nationen: Identitdtenwandel in Oberschlesien in der Neuzeit*
HNet - June 2004 - pNA [501+]

Stuart, Andrea - *Rose of Martinique: A Life of Napoleon's Josephine*
BW - v34 - i32 - August 8 2004 - p8(1) [501+]

Stuart, Anne - *Hidden Honor*
LJ - v129 - i13 - August 2004 - p58(1) [501+]

The Stuart Court in Rome: The Legacy of Exile
R&R Bk N - v19 - i1 - Feb 2004 - p34(1) [1-50]

Stuart, David - *Dangerous Garden: The Quest for Plants to Change Our Lives*
Choice - v42 - i6 - Feb 2005 - p1049(1) [51-500]
TimHES - v0 - i1649 - July 16 2004 - p28(1) [501+]

Stuart-Fox, David J. - *Pura Besakih: Temple, Religion, and Society in Bali*
JAS - v63 - i3 - August 2004 - p855-856 [501+]

Stuart-Fox, Martin - *A Short History of China and Southeast Asia: Tribute, Trade and Influence*
R&R Bk N - v19 - i1 - Feb 2004 - p48(1) [51-500]

Stuart, Gary L. - *Miranda: The Story of America's Right to Remain Silent*
BL - v101 - i1 - Sept 1 2004 - p31(1) [51-500]

Stuart, Granville - *Forty Years on the Frontier*
LJ - v130 - i1 - Jan 1 2005 - p172(1) [1-50]

Stuart, Guy - *Discriminating Risk: The U.S. Mortgage Lending Industry in the Twentieth Century*
JEL - v41 - i4 - Dec 2003 - p1367(1) [501+]

Stuart, Nancy Rubin - *The Reluctant Spiritualist: the Life of Maggie Fox*
KR - v72 - i23 - Dec 1 2004 - p1140(1) [501+]
PW - v252 - i3 - Jan 17 2005 - p53(1) [51-500]

Stubbendieck, James - *North American Wildland Plants: A Field Guide (Illus. by Hays, Kelly L. Rhodes)*
E-Streams - July 2004 - pNA [501+]
QRB - v79 - i3 - Sept 2004 - p312(1) [501+]

Stubbs, Jean - *I'm a Stranger Here Myself*
BL - v101 - i6 - Nov 15 2004 - p569(1) [51-500]

Stubbs, Richard - *Heart and Minds in Guerrilla Warfare: The Malayan Emergency, 1948-1960*
R&R Bk N - v19 - i4 - Nov 2004 - p49(1) [51-500]

Stuckenschmidt, Heiner - *The Ontology and Modelling of Real Estate Transactions*
R&R Bk N - v19 - i1 - Feb 2004 - pNA [51-500]

Stucky, Nathan - *Teaching Performance Studies*
Theat J - v56 - i3 - Oct 2004 - p536-539 [501+]

Student Workshop--Taunting, Gossiping, Hazing: It's Harassment
SLJ - v50 - i12 - Dec 2004 - p66(2) [501+]

Student's Guide to Earth Science
y E-Streams - Sept 2004 - pNA [501+]

Studer, Brigitte - *Parler de soi sous Staline: La construction identitaire dans le communisme des annees trente*
Russ Rev - v63 - i2 - April 2004 - pNA [501+]

Studia Borromaica: Saggi e documenti di storia religiosa e civile della prima eta moderna, Vols. 14-15
Six Ct J - v35 - i3 - Fall 2004 - p836-838 [501+]

Stuebner, Stephen - *Salmon River Country (Illus. by Lisk, Mark)*
LJ - v130 - i4 - March 1 2005 - p102(1) [51-500]

Stueck, William - *The Korean War in World History*
APH - v51 - i4 - Winter 2004 - p63(1) [501+]
Choice - v42 - i5 - Jan 2005 - p907(1) [1-50]
HNet - Sept 2004 - pNA [501+]
J Mil H - v68 - i4 - Oct 2004 - p1306-1308 [501+]
Rethinking the Korean War: A New Diplomatic and Strategic History
AHR - v109 - i4 - Oct 2004 - p1203-1204 [501+]

Stuever, Hank - *Off Ramp: Adventures and Heartaches in the American Elsewhere*
BL - v100 - i21 - July 2004 - p1814(1) [51-500]

Stukas, David - *Biceps of Death*
PW - v251 - i31 - August 2 2004 - p55(1) [501+]

Stukenbrock, Kai - *The Stability of Currency Boards*
R&R Bk N - v19 - i4 - Nov 2004 - p116(1) [51-500]

Stull, William J. - *The School-to-Work Movement: Origins and Destinations*
JEL - v41 - i4 - Dec 2003 - p1385(1) [501+]

Stump, Eleonore - *Aquinas*
JR - v85 - i1 - Jan 2005 - p104(7) [501+]
RM - v58 - i1 - Sept 2004 - p196(2) [501+]

Sturdee, David W. - *Facts of Hormone Therapy for Menopausal Women*
SciTech - v28 - i1 - March 2004 - p116(1) [51-500]

Sturdevant, Louis - *Changemaker: W. Harry Davis*
R&R Bk N - v19 - i1 - Feb 2004 - p65(1) [501+]

Sturgeon, Stephen C. - *The Politics of Western Water: The Congressional Career of Wayne Aspinall*
HNet - June 2004 - pNA [501+]

Sturges, Jock - *Jock Sturges: Notes*
Bwatch - March 2005 - pNA [51-500]

Sturges, Philemon - *I Love School! (Illus. by Halpern, Shari)*
c BL - v100 - i22 - August 2004 - p1949(1) [51-500]
c SLJ - v50 - i8 - August 2004 - p96(1) [51-500]
She'll Be Comin' 'round the Mountain (Illus. by Wolff, Ashley)
c BL - v100 - i22 - August 2004 - p1940(1) [51-500]
c CH Bwatch - v14 - i7 - July 2004 - p4(1) [51-500]
c SLJ - v50 - i7 - July 2004 - p96(1) [51-500]
c SLJ - v50 - i12 - Dec 2004 - p59(1) [501+]
Waggers (Illus. by Ishikawa, Jim)
c KR - v73 - i5 - March 1 2005 - p296(1) [51-500]
c PW - v252 - i9 - Feb 28 2005 - p65(1) [51-500]

Sturges, Robert S. - *Chaucer's Pardoner and Gender Theory: Bodies of Discourse*
Specu - v79 - i4 - Oct 2004 - p1158(3) [501+]

Sturgess, Kim C. - *Shakespeare and the American Nation*
Choice - v42 - i4 - Dec 2004 - p663(1) [1-50]

Sturgis, Amy H. - *Presidents from Hayes Through McKinley: Debating the Issues in Pro and Con Primary Documents*
R&R Bk N - v19 - i1 - Feb 2004 - p60(1) [51-500]

Sturgis, Ingrid - *Aunties: Thirty-Five Writers Celebrate Their Other Mother*
y Kliatt - v38 - i5 - Sept 2004 - p40(2) [51-500]

Sturgis, Matthew - *Walter Sickert:A Life*
Spec - v297 - i9210 - Feb 12 2005 - p36(2) [501+]

Sturken, Marita - *Technological Visions: The Hopes and Fears that Shape New Technologies*
Choice - v42 - i4 - Dec 2004 - p682(1) [1-50]

Sturm, Terry - *Literary Culture and Female Authorship in Canada 1760-2000*
R&R Bk N - v19 - i1 - Feb 2004 - p240(1) [51-500]

Sturma, Michael - *South Sea Maidens: Western Fantasy and Sexual Politics in the South Pacific*
AHR - v109 - i4 - Oct 2004 - p1215-1216 [501+]

Sturman, Jennifer - *The Pact*
c BL - v101 - i5 - Nov 1 2004 - p469(1) [51-500]
PW - v251 - i43 - Oct 25 2004 - p30(2) [51-500]

Sturt, Charles - *The Central Australian Expedition 1844-1846*
R&R Bk N - v19 - i1 - Feb 2004 - p66(1) [501+]

Stutely, Richard - *The Definitive Guide to Managing the Numbers: The Executive's Fast-Track to Mastering Spreadsheets, Budgets, Forecasts, Investment Metrics...*
Choice - v42 - i2 - Oct 2004 - p337(1) [51-500]

Stutley, Richard - *Numbers Guide: The Essentials of Business Numeracy, 5th ed.*
R&R Bk N - v19 - i2 - May 2004 - p120 [51-500]

Stutz, Michael - *Linux Cookbook: Tips and Techniques for Everyday Use, 2nd Ed., Completely Rev. and Expanded*
Choice - v42 - i7 - March 2005 - p1262(1) [51-500]
SciTech - v28 - i4 - Dec 2004 - p25(1) [51-500]
Linux Cookbook: Tips and Techniques for Everyday Use, 2nd Ed., Completely Revised and Expanded
Bwatch - Dec 2004 - pNA [51-500]

Stuve-Bodeen, Stephanie - *Babu's Song (Illus. by Boyd, Aaron)*
c SLJ - v50 - i10 - Oct 2004 - pS22(1) [1-50]
Elizabeti's School (Illus. by Hale, Christy)
c SLJ - v50 - i7 - July 2004 - p45(1) [51-500]

Stux, Erica - *Enrico Fermi: Trailblazer in Nuclear Physics*
y SB - v40 - i3 - May-June 2004 - p121(1) [501+]

Styf, Jorma - *Compartment Syndromes: Diagnosis, Treatment, and Complications*
SciTech - v28 - i3 - Sept 2004 - p109(1) [51-500]

Stygall, Gail - *Reading Context*
R&R Bk N - v19 - i4 - Nov 2004 - p216(1) [501+]

Styne, Dennis M. - *Pediatric Endocrinology*
SciTech - v28 - i1 - March 2004 - p118(1) [51-500]

Su, Di - *Evolution in Reference and Information Services: The Impact of the Internet*
ALJ - v53 - i3 - August 2004 - p322(2) [501+]

Su-Kennedy, Hui Hui - *What Do I Do? (Read by Su-Kennedy, Hui Hui)*
c CH Bwatch - v14 - i12 - Dec 2004 - pNA [51-500]
What Do I Do? (Illus. by Su-Kennedy, Hui Hui)
c BL - v100 - i22 - August 2004 - p1946(1) [51-500]
c PW - v251 - i27 - July 5 2004 - p54(1) [51-500]
c SLJ - v50 - i8 - August 2004 - p96(1) [51-500]

Su Tong - *My Life as Emperor*
KR - v72 - i24 - Dec 15 2004 - p1163(1) [501+]
LJ - v130 - i2 - Feb 1 2005 - p71(1) [51-500]
PW - v252 - i5 - Jan 31 2005 - p50(1) [51-500]

Suarez-Balcazar, Yolanda - *Empowerment and Participatory Evaluation in Community Intervention: Multiple Benefits*
R&R Bk N - v19 - i3 - August 2004 - p158(1) [51-500]

Suarez, Francisco - *A Commentary on Aristotle's Metaphysics or, A Most Ample Index to The Metaphysics of Aristotle*
R&R Bk N - v19 - i3 - August 2004 - p3(1) [1-50]
On Creation, Conservation, and Concurrence: Metaphysical Disputations 20, 21 and 22
Theol St - v65 - i4 - Dec 2004 - p888(2) [501+]

Suarez, Jose I. - *Critical Care Neurology and Neurosurgery*
SciTech - v28 - i1 - March 2004 - p93(1) [51-500]

Suarez-Rivas, Maite - *An Illustrated Treasury Of Latino Read-Aloud Stories*
c CH Bwatch - Feb 2005 - pNA [51-500]
c SLJ - v51 - i1 - Jan 2005 - p121(1) [51-500]

Suarez, Thomas - *Early Mapping of the Pacific: The Epic Story of Seafarers, Adventurers, and Cartographers Who Mapped the Earth's Greatest Ocean*
BIC - v33 - i6 - Sept 2004 - p38(2) [501+]

Suberu, Rotimi T. - *Federalism and Ethnic Conflict in Nigeria*
JTWS - v21 - i1 - Spring 2004 - p296(5) [501+]

Subiotto, Romano - *Antitrust Developments in Europe, 2003*
R&R Bk N - v19 - i4 - Nov 2004 - p175(1) [51-500]

Sublett, Michael D. - *Township: Diffusion and Persistence of Grassroots Government in Illinois, 1850-2000*
R&R Bk N - v19 - i4 - Nov 2004 - p158(1) [51-500]

Sublette, Ned - *Cuba and Its Music: From the First Drums to the Mambo*
BW - v34 - i29 - July 18 2004 - p7(1) [501+]
Choice - v42 - i3 - Nov 2004 - p494(1) [51-500]
LJ - v129 - i12 - July 2004 - p85(1) [51-500]
Nation - v279 - i13 - Oct 25 2004 - p36 [501+]
NYTBR - Oct 31 2004 - p31 [501+]

Subrenat, Jean-Jacques - *Estonia: Identity and Independence*
R&R Bk N - v19 - i3 - August 2004 - p46(1) [51-500]

Subrin, Stephen N. - *Federal Rules of Civil Procedure with Resources for Study: 2004*
R&R Bk N - v19 - i4 - Nov 2004 - p172(1) [501+]

Subsea Control and Data Acquisition: Proceedings
SciTech - v28 - i3 - Sept 2004 - p166(1) [51-500]

The Subtle Knife (Read by Pullman, Philip). Audiobook Review
c CH Bwatch - Feb 2005 - pNA [51-500]

Suburg, Lilli - *Kogutud kirjatood*
WLT - v78 - i3-4 - Sept-Dec 2004 - p110(1) [501+]

Suchoff, Benjamin - *Bela Bartok: A Celebration*
R&R Bk N - v19 - i1 - Feb 2004 - p196(1) [501+]

Suchting-Hanger, Andrea - *Das "Gewissen der Nation": Nationales Engagement und politisches Handeln konservativer Frauenorganisationen 1900 bis 1937.*
JMH - v77 - i1 - March 2005 - p224(3) [501+]

Suchy, Sherene - *Leading with Passion: Change Management in the 21st Century Museums*
R&R Bk N - v19 - i2 - May 2004 - p194(1) [51-500]

Sudarsanam, Sudi - *Creating Value from Mergers and Acquisitions: The Challenges*
TimHES - v0 - i1666 - Nov 12 2004 - p29(1) [501+]

Sudarshan, Hindupur V. - *Seamless Sky*
SciTech - v28 - i1 - March 2004 - p169(1) [51-500]

Suder, Gabriele G.S. - *Terrorism and the International Business Environment: The Security Business Nexus*
Choice - v42 - i6 - Feb 2005 - p1067(1) [51-500]

Suderburg, Robert - *Entertainment--Sets (Chamber Music X) for Brass Quintet*
Notes - v61 - i3 - March 2005 - p870(5) [501+]

Sudhir, Dixit - *Content Networking in the Mobile Internet*
SciTech - v28 - i4 - Dec 2004 - p149(1) [51-500]

Sudo, Shoichi - *New Photonics Technologies for the Information Age: The Dream of Ubiquitous Services*
SciTech - v28 - i4 - Dec 2004 - p159(1) [51-500]

Sue, Darryl Y. - *Current Essentials of Critical Care*
SciTech - v28 - i4 - Dec 2004 - p90(1) [51-500]

Suen, Anastasia - *Subway (Illus. by Katz, Karen)*
c NYTBR - August 8 2004 - p17 [51-500]

Suess, Bernhard J. - *Mastering Black-and-White Photography: From Camera to Darkroom, Rev Ed.*
R&R Bk N - v19 - i1 - Feb 2004 - p251(1) [51-500]

Suettinger, Robert L. - *Beyond Tiananmen: The Politics of U.S.-China Relations, 1989-2000*
Choice - v41 - i7 - March 2004 - p1369(1) [501+]
Pac A - v77 - i2 - Summer 2004 - p316(3) [501+]
Parameters - v34 - i3 - Autumn 2004 - p156(3) [501+]
SPA - v60 - i4 - July-August 2004 - p67(3) [501+]
Beyond Tiananmen: The Politics of U.S.-China Relations, 1998-2000
E-A St - v56 - i6 - Sept 2004 - p931(932) [501+]

Sugamura, Kazuo - *Two Decades of Adult T-Cell Leukemia and HTLV-1 Research*
SciTech - v28 - i3 - Sept 2004 - p104(1) [51-500]

Sugano, Alan - *The Real-World Network Troubleshooting Manual: Tools, Techniques, and Scenarios*
Bwatch - Dec 2004 - pNA [51-500]
SciTech - v28 - i4 - Dec 2004 - p153(1) [51-500]

Suganuma, Katsuaki - *Lead-Free Soldering in Electronics: Science, Technology, and Environmental Impact*
SciTech - v28 - i1 - March 2004 - p160(1) [51-500]

Sugarman, Leonie - *Counselling and the Life Course*
R&R Bk N - v19 - i3 - August 2004 - p9(1) [1-50]

Sugars, Cynthia - *Home-Work: Postcolonialism, Pedagogy, and Canadian Literature*
R&R Bk N - v19 - i4 - Nov 2004 - p239(1) [501+]
Unhomely States: Theorizing English-Canadian Postcolonialism
R&R Bk N - v19 - i4 - Nov 2004 - p239(1) [501+]

Sugawara, Katsuhiko - *Rock Stress: Proceedings*
SciTech - v28 - i1 - March 2004 - p144(1) [51-500]

Sugden, John - *Nelson: A Dream of Glory, 1758-1797*
BL - v101 - i5 - Nov 1 2004 - p449(1) [51-500]
BL - v101 - i9-10 - Jan 1 2005 - p766(1) [51-500]
HT - v54 - i12 - Dec 2004 - p55(2) [501+]
LJ - v129 - i18 - Nov 1 2004 - p96(1) [51-500]
NS - v133 - i4716 - Nov 29 2004 - p45(2) [51-500]
PW - v251 - i42 - Oct 18 2004 - p59(1) [51-500]
Spec - v296 - i9192 - Oct 9 2004 - p56(1) [501+]
TimHES - v0 - i1673 - Jan 7 2005 - p20(2) [501+]

Sugden, John Peter - *Power Games: A Critical Sociology of Sport*
SSJ - v21 - i3 - Sept 2004 - p344-345 [501+]

Sugden, Roger - *Urban and Regional Prosperity in a Globalised New Economy: Proceedings*
R&R Bk N - v19 - i1 - Feb 2004 - p134(1) [51-500]

Suggs, Welch - *A Place on the Team: The Triumph and Tragedy of Title IX*
LJ - v130 - i3 - Feb 15 2005 - p137(1) [51-500]

Sugisaki, Yukiru - *D.N. Angel. Vol. 1*
Kliatt - v38 - i6 - Nov 2004 - p28(1) [51-500]
Lagoon Engine, Vol. 1
PW - v252 - i8 - Feb 21 2005 - p160(1) [51-500]

Suh, Sharon A. - *Being Buddhist in a Christian World: Gender and Community in a Korean American Temple*
HNet - Oct 2004 - pNA [51-500]
Being Buddist in a Christian World: Gender and Community in a Korean American Temple
Choice - v42 - i5 - Jan 2005 - p872(1) [1-50]

Suk, Julie - *The Dark Takes Aim*
ABR - v25 - i5 - July-August 2004 - p7(1) [501+]

Sukhanova, Ekaterina - *Voicing the Distant: Shakespeare and Russian Modernist Poetry*
Choice - v42 - i5 - Jan 2005 - p859(1) [1-50]
R&R Bk N - v19 - i4 - Nov 2004 - p218(1) [501+]

Sukumar, Raman - *The Living Elephants: Evolutionary Ecology, Behavior, and Conservation*
Choice - v41 - i7 - March 2004 - p1322(1) [501+]

Suleiman, Ezra - *Dismantling Democratic States*
VQR - v80 - i2 - Spring 2004 - p256-256 [501+]

Suleiman, Susan Rubin - *Contemporary Jewish Writing in Hungary: An Anthology*
WLT - v78 - i3-4 - Sept-Dec 2004 - p107(1) [501+]

Suleiman, Yasir - *A War of Words: Language and Conflict in the Middle East*
MEJ - v59 - i1 - Wntr 2005 - p156(3) [501+]

Suli, E. - *An Introduction to Numerical Analysis*
SIAM Rev - v46 - i3 - Sept 2004 - p561(2) [501+]

Sull, Donald - *Made in China: What Western Managers Can Learn from Trail-Blazing Chinese Entrepreneurs*
Har Bus R - v83 - i2 - Feb 2005 - p57(1) [1-50]

Sullivan, Arthur - *The Chieftain: A Comic Opera in Two Acts*
Notes - v61 - i2 - Dec 2004 - p532(5) [501+]

Sullivan, Ceri - *The Rhetoric of Credit: Merchants in Early Modern Writing*
RES - v55 - i218 - Feb 2004 - p121-122 [501+]

Sullivan, Cheryl Granade - *How to Mentor in the Midst of Change, 2nd Ed.*
Adoles - v39 - i155 - Fall 2004 - p626(1) [51-500]

Sullivan, Eugene - *The Majority Rules*
KR - v72 - i23 - Dec 1 2004 - p1114(1) [501+]

Sullivan, George - *Photography on the Color Line: W.E.B. Du Bois, Race, and Visual Culture*
Choice - v42 - i3 - Nov 2004 - p476(2) [1-50]

Sullivan, Jenny - *Brochures: Making a Strong Impression*
Bwatch - v26 - i9 - Sept 2004 - p1(1) [51-500]
Nowhere Again
y Sch Lib - v52 - i3 - Autumn 2004 - p162(2) [501+]

Sullivan, Jerry - *Hunting for Frogs on Elston: And Other Tales from Field and Street (Illus. by Sutton, Bobby)*
E-Streams - July 2004 - pNA [501+]

Sullivan, John - *Rethinking Strategic HR*
HR Mag - v49 - i11 - Nov 2004 - p146(2) [501+]
HR Mag - v50 - i2 - Feb 2005 - pS15(1) [501+]

Sullivan, John Jeremiah - *Blood Horses: Notes of a Sportswriter's Son*
Econ - v371 - i8380 - June 19 2004 - p81US [501+]
Globe & Mail - Dec 24 2004 - pD3 [1-50]

Sullivan, Keith - *Bullying in Secondary Schools: What It Looks Like and How to Manage it*
Choice - v42 - i1 - Sept 2004 - p160(1) [501+]
R&R Bk N - v19 - i1 - Feb 2004 - p188(1) [51-500]

Sullivan, Kevin P. - *Wrestling with Angels: A Study of the Relationship Between Angels and Humans in Ancient Jewish Literature and the New Testament*
R&R Bk N - v19 - i3 - August 2004 - p26(1) [1-50]

Sullivan, Larry E. - *Bandits & Bibles: Convict Literature in Nineteenth-Century America*
R&R Bk N - v19 - i1 - Feb 2004 - p243(1) [51-500]

Sullivan, Luke - *Hey, Whipple, Squeeze This*
Globe & Mail - March 19 2005 - pD19 [501+]

Sullivan, Mary - *Ship sooner*
y VOYA - v27 - i5 - Dec 2004 - p397(1) [51-500]

Sullivan, Michael - *Algebra and Trigonometry: Graphing, Data, and Analysis. 3rd Ed.*
SciTech - v28 - i3 - Sept 2004 - p34(1) [51-500]
Precalculus: Graphing, Data, and Analysis. 3rd Ed.
SciTech - v28 - i3 - Sept 2004 - p39(1) [51-500]

Sullivan, Michael J., III - *American Adventurism Abroad: 30 Invasions, Interventions and Regime Changes since World War II*
TimHES - v0 - i1676 - Jan 28 2005 - p30(2) [501+]

Sullivan, Nancy A. - *Walking with a Shadow: Surviving Childhood Leukemia*
SciTech - v28 - i4 - Dec 2004 - p112(1) [1-50]

Sullivan, Patricia - *Freedom Writer: Virginia Foster Durr, Letters from the Civil Rights Years*
JSH - v70 - i4 - Nov 2004 - p965(2) [501+]

Sullivan, Paul - *Xuxub must Die: The Lost Histories of a Murder on the Yucatan*
Choice - v42 - i4 - Dec 2004 - p718(1) [1-50]
TLS - i5294 - Sept 17 2004 - p30(1) [501+]

Sullivan, Randall - *The Miracle Detective: An Investigation Of Holy Visions*
Bwatch - Feb 2005 - pNA [51-500]

Sullivan, Robert - *Captain Cook in the Underworld*
Cont Pac - v17 - i1 - Spring 2005 - p260(5) [501+]
Rats: A Year with New York's Most Unwanted Inhabitants
New Sci - v185 - i2490 - March 12 2005 - p51(1) [501+]
NS - v134 - i4722 - Jan 17 2005 - p54(2) [501+]
Spec - v297 - i9207 - Jan 22 2005 - p34(1) [501+]
Rats: Observations on the History and Habitat of the City's Most Unwanted Inhabitants, 1st U.S. Ed.
Choice - v42 - i6 - Feb 2005 - p1050(1) [51-500]
c SLJ - v50 - i9 - Sept 2004 - p237(1) [51-500]
y VOYA - v27 - i4 - Oct 2004 - p332(1) [51-500]

Sullivan, Roger J. - *Radar Foundations for Imaging and Advanced Concepts*
SciTech - v28 - i1 - March 2004 - p159(1) [51-500]

Sullivan, Rosemary - *Labyrinth of Desire: Women, Passion and Romantic Obsession*
Can Lit - i182 - Autumn 2004 - p100(3) [501+]

Sullivan, Terrence - *Preventing and Managing Disabling Injury at Work*
SciTech - v28 - i1 - March 2004 - p133(1) [51-500]

Sullivan, Thelma D. - *A Scattering of Jades: Stories, Poems, and Prayers of the Aztecs*
Lat Ant - v15 - i4 - Dec 2004 - p466(2) [501+]

Sullivan, Thomas - *Parisian Licentiates in Theology, A.D. 1373-1500: A Biographical Register*
CHR - v90 - i4 - Oct 2004 - p774(3) [501+]
R&R Bk N - v19 - i1 - Feb 2004 - p24(1) [51-500]

Sullivan, Thomas F.P. - *Environmental Law Handbook, 17th Ed.*
SciTech - v28 - i4 - Dec 2004 - p11(1) [1-50]

Sullivan, Vickie B. - *Machiavelli, Hobbes, and the Formation of a Liberal Republicanism in England*
Choice - v42 - i3 - Nov 2004 - p563(1) [1-50]

Sullivan, William M. - *Work and Integrity: The Crisis and Promise of Professionalism in America, 2d ed.*
SciTech - v28 - i2 - i1 - Feb 2005 - p10(1) [51-500]

Sultanik, Aaron - *Inventing Orders: An Essay and Critique in 20th Century American Literature*
R&R Bk N - v19 - i1 - Feb 2004 - p222(1) [51-500]

Sumbatyan, Mezhlum A. - *Equations of Mathematical Diffraction Theory*
SciTech - v28 - i4 - Dec 2004 - p50(1) [51-500]

Sumich, James L. - *Introduction to the Biology of Marine Life. 8th Ed.*
SciTech - v28 - i3 - Sept 2004 - p57(1) [1-50]

Summer, Jane - *Not the Only One: Lesbian and Gay Fiction for Teens*
y BL - v101 - i8 - Dec 15 2004 - p737(1) [51-500]
y Kliatt - v39 - i1 - Jan 2005 - p26(2) [51-500]

Summerhill, William R. - *Order Against Progress: Government, Foreign Investment, and Railroads in Brazil, 1854-1913*
Ams - v61 - i2 - Oct 2004 - p294(2) [501+]
JEL - v42 - i1 - March 2004 - p303(2) [501+]

Summers, B.J. - *Collectible Soda Pop Memorabilia*
Ant&CM - v109 - i1 - March 2004 - p16(1) [501+]

Summers, Claude J. - *The Queer Encyclopedia of the Visual Arts*
BL - v101 - i1 - Sept 1 2004 - p174(2) [501+]
Choice - v42 - i5 - Jan 2005 - p828(1) [1-50]
G&L Rev W - v11 - i6 - Nov-Dec 2004 - p45(2) [501+]
Lam Bk Rpt - v13 - i4-5 - Nov-Dec 2004 - p45(2) [501+]
LJ - v129 - i16 - Oct 1 2004 - p113(1) [501+]

Summers, David - *Real Spaces: World Art History and the Rise of Western Modernism*
R&R Bk N - v19 - i2 - May 2004 - p194(1) [51-500]
TLS - i5285 - July 16 2004 - p19(1) [501+]

Summers, James L. - *Dietary Supplement Labeling Compliance Review, 3rd Ed.*
SciTech - v28 - i3 - Sept 2004 - p172(1) [51-500]

Summers, Mark Wahlgren - *Party Games: Getting, Keeping, and Using Power in Gilded Age Politics*
Choice - v42 - i4 - Dec 2004 - p725(1) [1-50]

Summers, Robert S. - *Essays in Legal Theory*
Ethics - v114 - i4 - July 2004 - p843(3) [501+]

Sumner, Judith - *American Household Botany: A History of Useful Plants, 1620-1900*
BL - v101 - i2 - Sept 15 2004 - p187(1) [51-500]
Choice - v42 - i7 - March 2005 - p1253(1) [51-500]
SciTech - v28 - i4 - Dec 2004 - p123 [51-500]

Sumners, Cristina - *Crooked Heart*
CC - v121 - i21 - Oct 19 2004 - p24(5) [501+]
Thieves Break In
DroRevMy - v24 - i4 - July-August 2004 - p13(1) [51-500]

Sumption, Jonathan - *Age of Pilgrimage: The Medieval Journey to God*
R&R Bk N - v19 - i1 - Feb 2004 - p16(1) [51-500]

Sun, Changming - *Digital Image Computing: Techniques and Applications, Proceedings. Vols. 1-2*
SciTech - v28 - i3 - Sept 2004 - p143(1) [51-500]

Sun-pong Yuen - *Marriage, Gender, and Sex in a Contemporary Chinese Village*
Choice - v42 - i5 - Jan 2005 - p941(1) [51-500]

Sun, Yin - *Detection Technologies for Chemical Warfare Agents and Toxic Vapors*
SciTech - v28 - i4 - Dec 2004 - p171(1) [51-500]

Sunal, Dennis W. - *Reform in Undergraduate Science Teaching for the 21st Century*
SciTech - v28 - i4 - Dec 2004 - p14(1) [1-50]

Sundel, Martin - *Behavior Change in the Human Services: Behavioral and Cognitive Principles and Applications, 5th Ed.*
R&R Bk N - v19 - i4 - Nov 2004 - p10(1) [51-500]

Sunden, B. - *Advanced Computational Methods in Heat Transfer VIII: Proceedings*
SciTech - v28 - i3 - Sept 2004 - p47(1) [1-50]

Sunder Rajan, Rajeswari - *The Scandal of the State: Women, Law and Citizenship in Postcolonial India*
Pac A - v77 - i3 - Fall 2004 - p594(2) [501+]

Sunderland, Willard - *Taming the Wild Field: Colonization and Empire on the Russian Steppe*
NYRB - v51 - i15 - Oct 7 2004 - p39(3) [501+]

Sunseri, Thaddeus - *Vilimani: Labor Migration and Rural Change in Early Colonial Tanzania*
AHR - v109 - i2 - April 2004 - p660(2) [501+]

Sunshine, Glenn S. - *Reforming French Protestantism: The Development of Huguenot Ecclesiastical Institutions, 1557-1572*
Choice - v42 - i1 - Sept 2004 - p181(1) [501+]
Ren Q - v57 - i4 - Winter 2004 - p1418(2) [501+]

Sunshine, Linda - *All Things Alice: The Wit, Wisdom and Wonderland of Lewis Carroll*
Globe & Mail - Dec 18 2004 - pD14 [1-50]

Sunstein, Cass R. - *Animal Rights: Current Debates and New Directions*
Choice - v42 - i5 - Jan 2005 - p892(1) [1-50]
HLR - v118 - i3 - Jan 2005 - p1098(1) [1-50]
Sci - v306 - i5693 - Oct 1 2004 - p58(2) [501+]
The Second Bill of Rights: FDR's Unfinished Revolution and Why We Need It More than Ever
BW - v34 - i27 - July 4 2004 - p4(2) [501+]
HLR - v118 - i1 - Nov 2004 - p524(1) [1-50]
LJ - v129 - i13 - August 2004 - p98(2) [501+]
NYTBR - Sept 19 2004 - p23 [501+]
Why Societies Need Dissent
JEL - v42 - i1 - March 2004 - p284(2) [501+]

Suny, Ronald Grigor - *The Structure of Soviet History: Essays and Documents. 1st Ed.*
TimHES - v0 - i1668 - Nov 26 2004 - pVII(1) [501+]

Sunyaev, R.A. - *Zeldovich: Reminiscences*
SciTech - v28 - i4 - Dec 2004 - p47(1) [51-500]

Suomala, Karla R. - *Moses and God in Dialogue: Exodus 32-34 in Postbiblical Literature*
R&R Bk N - v19 - i3 - August 2004 - p23(1) [1-50]

Suoranta, Juha - *Children in the Information Society: The Case of Finland*
R&R Bk N - v19 - i3 - August 2004 - p143(1) [51-500]

Supeene, Shelagh Lynne - *My Name Is Mitch*
c CBRA - Annual 2003 - p516(2) [51-500]

Super Structures of the World
LibMed - v22 - i7 - April-May 2004 - p83(1) [501+]

Superko, H. Robert - *Before the Heart Attacks*
SciTech - v28 - i3 - Sept 2004 - p106(1) [1-50]

Supovitz, Frank - *Sports Event Management and Marketing Playbook*
R&R Bk N - v19 - i4 - Nov 2004 - p81(1) [51-500]

Supplee, Audra - *I Almost Love You, Eddie Clegg*
c SLJ - v50 - i8 - August 2004 - p130(1) [51-500]

Suprenant, Leon J. - *Faith Facts II: Answers to Catholic Questions*
CI - v12 - i9 - Oct 2004 - p44(1) [501+]

Supriya, K.E. - *Remembering Empire: Power, Memory, and Place in Postcolonial India*
R&R Bk N - v19 - i4 - Nov 2004 - p47(1) [51-500]

Supuran, Claudiu T. - *Carbonic Anhydrase: Its Inhibitors and Activators*
SciTech - v28 - i3 - Sept 2004 - p72(1) [51-500]

Surampaili, Rao Y. - *Advance in Water and Wastewater Treatment*
SciTech - v28 - i3 - Sept 2004 - p146(1) [51-500]

Surette, Leon - *Pound in Purgatory: From Economic Radicalism to Anti-Semitism*
JEL - v42 - i1 - March 2004 - p240(1) [501+]

Suri, Jeremi - *Power and Protest: Global Revolution and the Rise of Detente*
HNet - Sept 2004 - pNA [501+]
JAH - v91 - i2 - Sept 2004 - p711(2) [501+]
RAH - v32 - i2 - June 2004 - p255-7 [501+]

Surowiecki, James - *The Wisdom of Crowds: Why the Many Are Smarter than the Few and How Collective Wisdom Shapes Business, Economies, Societies, and Nations*
New Sci - v183 - i2462 - August 28 2004 - p51(1) [501+]
Bwatch - Oct 2004 - pNA [51-500]
Bwatch - Jan 2005 - pNA [51-500]
Choice - v42 - i3 - Nov 2004 - p526(1) [1-50]
Fut - v38 - i6 - Nov-Dec 2004 - p61(1) [51-500]
Globe & Mail - July 17 2004 - pD4 [501+]
JouAmCul - v27 - i4 - Dec 2004 - p462(2) [501+]
Lon R Bks - v26 - i15 - August 5 2004 - p19(3) [501+]
NS - v133 - i4695 - July 5 2004 - p52(2) [501+]
TimHES - v0 - i1650 - July 23 2004 - p30(1) [501+]

Surprenant, Aimee M. - *Coglab Reader*
SciTech - v28 - i3 - Sept 2004 - p2(1) [501+]

Surprise Heirs, Vol. 1
HAHR - v84 - i3 - August 2004 - p530(4) [501+]

Surrell, Jason - *Screenplay by Disney: Tips and Techniques to Bring Magic to Your Moviemaking*
y VOYA - v27 - i5 - Dec 2004 - p418(1) [51-500]

Survey of Economic and Social Developments in the ESCWA Region, 2002-2003
R&R Bk N - v19 - i3 - August 2004 - p50(1) [51-500]

Suryadinata, Leo - *Chinese Indonesians: State Policy, Monoculture and Multiculture*
R&R Bk N - v19 - i3 - August 2004 - p55(1) [51-500]

Surzycki, Stefan - *Human Molecular Biology Laboratory Manual*
QRB - v79 - i4 - Dec 2004 - p416(1) [501+]

Suskie, Linda - *Assessing Student Learning: A Common Sense Guide*
R&R Bk N - v19 - i4 - Nov 2004 - p188(1) [501+]

Suskin, Steven - *A Must See! Brilliant Broadway Artwork*
BL - v101 - i6 - Nov 15 2004 - p542(1) [51-500]
Choice - v42 - i6 - Feb 2005 - p1011(1) [51-500]

Suskind, Ron - *The Price of Loyalty: George W. Bush, the White House, and the Education of Paul O'Neill*
BW - v34 - i5 - Feb 1 2004 - p8(1) [501+]
NYTBR - Sept 26 2004 - p28 [501+]

Sussman, Ellen - *On a Night Like This (Read by Gough, Michael). Audiobook Review*
BL - v100 - i21 - July 2004 - p1856(1) [1-50]

Sussman, Leonard R. - *A Passion for Freedom: My Encounters with Extraordinary People*
R&R Bk N - v19 - i3 - August 2004 - p30(1) [1-50]

Sussman, Lyle - *Lost and Found: The Story of How One Man Discovered the Secrets of Leadership...Where He Wasn't Even Looking*
R&R Bk N - v19 - i3 - August 2004 - p105(1) [1-50]

Sussman, Robert W. - *Man The Hunted: Primates, Predators, and Human Evolution*
PW - v252 - i5 - Jan 31 2005 - p59(1) [501+]

Sustainable World
LibMed - v23 - i1 - August-Sept 2004 - p83(1) [51-500]

Sustein, Cass R. - *Risk and Reason: Law and the Environment*
AJPS - v39 - i2 - July 2004 - p427(430) [501+]

Sutcliffe, Andrea - *Steam: The Untold Story of America's First Great Invention*
Choice - v42 - i4 - Dec 2004 - p684(1) [1-50]

Sutcliffe, Jane - *Milton Hershey*
c CH Bwatch - v14 - i7 - July 2004 - p2(2) [51-500]
Paul Revere
c CH Bwatch - v14 - i7 - July 2004 - p2(2) [51-500]

Sutcliffe, Steven - *Children of the New Age: A History of Spiritual Practices*
TT - v61 - i2 - July 2004 - p274(3) [501+]
Religion: Empirical Studies
R&R Bk N - v20 - i1 - Feb 2005 - p10(1) [51-500]

Sutcliffe, W. Dean - *The Keyboard Sonatas of Domenico Scarlatti and Eighteenth-Century Musical Style*
Notes - v61 - i1 - Sept 2004 - p145(3) [501+]
TLS - i5263 - Feb 13 2004 - p10-10 [501+]

Sutela, Pekka - *The Russian Market Economy*
E-A St - v56 - i7 - Nov 2004 - p1094(1096) [501+]

Suter, A. - *The Narcissus and the Pomegranate: An Archaeology of the Homeric Hymn to Demeter*
Class R - v54 - i1 - Nov 2004 - p286-288 [501+]

Suter, Keith - *Global Order and Global Disorder: Globalization and the Nation-State*
AJPS - v39 - i2 - July 2004 - p457(458) [501+]

Sutherland, Bill - *Beautiful Models: 70 Years of Exactly Solved Quantum Many-Body Problems*
SciTech - v28 - i4 - Dec 2004 - p48(1) [51-500]

Sutherland, Bryony - *Uma Thurman: The Biography*
LJ - v130 - i2 - Feb 1 2005 - p82(1) [51-500]

Sutherland, John - *Stephen Spender: A Literary Life*
BL - v101 - i9-10 - Jan 1 2005 - p802(2) [51-500]
NYTBR - Feb 27 2005 - p16 [501+]
Stephen Spender: The Authorized Biography
Atl - v295 - i1 - Jan-Feb 2005 - p174(5) [501+]
CR - v286 - i1668 - Jan 2005 - p51(2) [501+]
Econ - v371 - i8380 - June 19 2004 - p82US [501+]
Globe & Mail - Dec 24 2004 - pD3 [1-50]
KR - v72 - i24 - Dec 15 2004 - p1193(2) [501+]
LJ - v130 - i1 - Jan 1 2005 - p112(1) [51-500]
Lon R Bks - v26 - i14 - July 22 2004 - p6(4) [501+]
TimHES - v0 - i1649 - July 16 2004 - p24(2) [501+]
TLS - i5289 - August 13 2004 - p3-6 [501+]

Sutherland, Jonathan - *Key Concepts in Operations Management*
SciTech - v28 - i3 - Sept 2004 - p170(1) [1-50]

Sutherland, Jonathan D. - *African Americans at War: An Encyclopedia*
BL - v100 - i21 - July 2004 - p1860(1) [501+]
Choice - v42 - i1 - Sept 2004 - p82(1) [501+]
J Mil H - v68 - i4 - Oct 2004 - p1302-1303 [501+]
y Ref Rev - May 2004 - pNA [501+]
African Americans at War: An Encyclopedia, Vols. 1-2
BL - v101 - i9-10 - Jan 1 2005 - p779(1) [1-50]

Sutherland, Keith - *The Party's Over: Blueprint for a Very English Revolution*
TimHES - v0 - i1659 - Sept 24 2004 - p28(1) [501+]

Sutherland, Peter D. - *Autograf: New York City's Graffiti Writers*
LJ - v129 - i14 - Sept 1 2004 - p148(1) [51-500]

Sutherland, Robert - *Adventures of Tommy Smith*
y Can CL - i111-112 - Fall-Winter 2003 - p139(8) [501+]

Sutherland-Smith, James - *In the Country of Birds*
TLS - i5295 - Sept 24 2004 - p24(1) [501+]

Sutherland, Tui T. - *This Must Be Love*
y CCB-B - v58 - i5 - Jan 2005 - p229(2) [51-500]
y KR - v72 - i18 - Sept 15 2004 - p921(1) [51-500]
PW - v251 - i41 - Oct 11 2004 - p80(2) [51-500]
y SLJ - v50 - i9 - Sept 2004 - p218(1) [51-500]

Sutphen, Roy F. - *Commercial Vehicle Accident Reconstruction and Investigation*
R&R Bk N - v19 - i3 - August 2004 - p168(1) [501+]

Sutter, Paul S. - *Driven Wild: How the Fight Against Automobiles Launched the Modern Wilderness Movement*
HNet - August 2004 - pNA [501+]

Suttles, Wayne - *Musqueam Reference Grammar*
Choice - v42 - i6 - Feb 2005 - p1019(1) [51-500]
R&R Bk N - v19 - i3 - August 2004 - p257(1) [51-500]

Sutton, Amy L. - *Pregnancy and Birth Sourcebook, 2nd Ed.*
Bwatch - v26 - i7 - July 2004 - p3(1) [51-500]
E-Streams - Oct 2004 - pNA [501+]

Sutton, Barbara - *The Send-Away Girl: Stories*
BL - v100 - i22 - August 2004 - p1898(1) [51-500]
KR - v72 - i15 - August 1 2004 - p713(1) [501+]
PW - v251 - i36 - Sept 6 2004 - p44(2) [51-500]

Sutton, Donald S. - *Steps of Perfection: Exorcistic Performers and Chinese Religion in Twentieth-Century Taiwan*
JAS - v63 - i3 - August 2004 - p783-785 [501+]

Sutton, Emma - *Aubrey Beardsley and British Wagnerism in the 1890s*
Nine-C Lit - v58 - i4 - March 2004 - p562(566) [501+]
VS - v46 - i3 - Spring 2004 - p532(3) [501+]

Sutton, Mark Q. - *Introduction to Cultural Ecology*
Choice - v42 - i5 - Jan 2005 - p897(1) [1-50]
R&R Bk N - v19 - i3 - August 2004 - p81(1) [51-500]

Sutton, R. Anderson - *Calling Back the Spirit: Music, Dance, and Cultural Politics in Lowland South Sulawesi*
JAS - v63 - i2 - May 2004 - p562(3) [501+]

Sutton, Richard Manliffe - *Demonstration Experiments in Physics*
Physics T - v42 - i4 - April 2004 - p256-256 [501+]

Sutton, Robert P. - *Communal Utopias and the American Experience: Secular Communities, 1824-2000*
HRNB - v33 - i1 - Fall 2004 - p5(2) [501+]
Choice - v42 - i3 - Nov 2004 - p551(1) [1-50]

Suwanaporn, Chodechai - *Determinants of Bank Landing in Thailand: An Empirical Examination for the Years 1992 to 1996*
R&R Bk N - v19 - i1 - Feb 2004 - p115(1) [51-500]

Suzanne, Claudia - *This Business of Books: A Complete Overview of the Industry from Concept through Sales, 4th Ed., Rev. and Updated for the 21st Century*
R&R Bk N - v19 - i4 - Nov 2004 - p255(1) [501+]

Suzuki, David - *The David Suzuki Reader*
CBRA - Annual 2003 - p377(1) [501+]
R&R Bk N - v19 - i3 - August 2004 - p81(1) [51-500]
Sacred Balance: A Visual Celebration of Our Place in Nature
R&R Bk N - v19 - i4 - Nov 2004 - p75(1) [51-500]
Salmon Forest (Illus. by Lott, Sheena)
c CBRA - Annual 2003 - p569(2) [51-500]
c CE - v80 - i5 - Mid-Summer 2004 - p275(1) [51-500]
Tree: A Life Story (Illus. by Bateman, Robert)
BL - v101 - i4 - Oct 15 2004 - p370(1) [51-500]
Bwatch - Nov 2004 - pNA [51-500]
Globe & Mail - Nov 6 2004 - pD8 [501+]
SB - v40 - i6 - Nov-Dec 2004 - p243(1) [51-500]
SB - v40 - i6 - Nov-Dec 2004 - p252(1) [51-500]

Suzuki, Hiroshige - *Advanced Ceramics and Composites: Proceedings*
SciTech - v28 - i1 - March 2004 - p174(1) [51-500]

Suzuki, Koji - *Dark Water*
PW - v251 - i41 - Oct 11 2004 - p58(1) [51-500]

Suzuki, Mihoko - *Debating Gender in Early Modern England, 1500-1700*
JGS - v13 - i1 - March 2004 - p82-83 [501+]
Subordinate Subjects: Gender, the Political Nation, and Literary Form in England, 1588-1688
Ren Q - v57 - i3 - Fall 2004 - p1142(3) [501+]

Suzuki, Yasuyuki - *Structure and Reactions of Light Exotic Nuclei*
SciTech - v28 - i1 - March 2004 - p52(1) [51-500]

Svare, Bruce B. - *Reforming Sports Before the Clock Runs Out: One Man's Journey through Our Runaway Sports Culture*
Choice - v42 - i2 - Oct 2004 - p331(1) [51-500]

Svarney, Thomas E. - *Handy Dinosaur Answer Book*
SciTech - v28 - i1 - March 2004 - p59(1) [51-500]

Svee, Gary - *The Peacemaker's Vengeance*
Roundup M - v11 - i6 - August 2004 - p30(2) [501+]

Svendsen, Allan - *Enzyme Functionality: Design, Engineering, and Screening*
SciTech - v28 - i1 - March 2004 - p172(1) [51-500]

Svendsen, Mark - *Ratface and Snake-Eyes*
c Sch Lib - v52 - i3 - Autumn 2004 - p147(2) [501+]

Svenson, Arne - *Sock Monkeys*
Ant&CM - v108 - i5 - July 2003 - p16(1) [501+]

Svenson, Peter - *Washed Up with a Broken Heart in Rock Hall*
KR - v72 - i20 - Oct 15 2004 - p982(1) [501+]
PW - v251 - i48 - Nov 29 2004 - p25(1) [51-500]
Wrongful Reconciliation
KR - v72 - i24 - Dec 15 2004 - p1164(1) [501+]

Svenson, Sonke - *Carrier-Based Drug Delivery*
SciTech - v28 - i3 - Sept 2004 - p125(1) [51-500]

Svenvold, Mark - *Elmer McCurdy: The Misadventures in Life and Afterlife of an American Outlaw*
JSH - v70 - i4 - Nov 2004 - p989(2) [501+]

Svetlicic, Marjan - *Facilitating Transition by Internationalization: Outward Direct Investment from Central Europe Economies in Transition*
R&R Bk N - v19 - i1 - Feb 2004 - p118(1) [51-500]

Svoboda, Jiri A. - *Stranska Skala: Origins of the Upper Paleolithic in the Brno Basin, Moravia, Czech Republic*
R&R Bk N - v19 - i3 - August 2004 - p84(1) [51-500]

Swaddling, Judith - *The Ancient Olympic Games*
HT - v54 - i9 - Sept 2004 - p56(1) [501+]

Swados, Elizabeth - *The Animal Rescue Store (Illus. by Wilson, Anne)*
c KR - v73 - i5 - March 1 2005 - p296(1) [51-500]

Swain, Bert L. - *CPA's Guide to Management Letter Comments, 2004*
R&R Bk N - v19 - i2 - May 2004 - p119 [51-500]

Swain, Carol - *Foodboy*
y VOYA - v27 - i4 - Oct 2004 - p308(1) [51-500]

Swain, Carol M. - *Contemporary Voices of White Nationalism in America*
CS - v33 - i2 - March 2004 - p157-159 [501+]
JSH - v70 - i3 - August 2004 - p725(2) [501+]
The New White Nationalism in America: Its Challange to Integration
Am St - v45 - i1 - Spring 2004 - p176-177 [501+]
The New White Nationalism in America: Its Challenge to Integration
AJPS - v39 - i2 - July 2004 - p458(459) [501+]
CS - v33 - i2 - March 2004 - p157-159 [501+]

Swain, Gwenyth - *Dred and Harriet Scott: A Family's Struggle for Freedom*
c SLJ - v50 - i7 - July 2004 - p128(1) [51-500]
Little Crow: Leader of the Dakota
c BL - v100 - i21 - July 2004 - p1832(2) [1-50]
c SLJ - v50 - i7 - July 2004 - p128(1) [51-500]

Swain, Heather - *Luscious Lemon*
BL - v101 - i2 - Sept 15 2004 - p210(2) [501+]
KR - v72 - i16 - August 15 2004 - p774(1) [501+]

Swain, James - *Loaded Dice (Read by Boehmer, Paul). Audiobook Review*
y Kliatt - v39 - i2 - March 2005 - p54(1) [51-500]
Loaded Dice
DroRevMy - v24 - i3 - May-June 2004 - p13(1) [1-50]
Mr. Lucky: A Novel
Ent W - i809 - March 4 2005 - p77 [51-500]
KR - v73 - i1 - Jan 1 2005 - p24(2) [51-500]
PW - v252 - i6 - Feb 7 2005 - p41(1) [51-500]

Swain, James - *Mr. Lucky*
Globe & Mail - March 5 2005 - pD15 [51-500]

Swain, John - *Disabling Barriers - Enabling Environments, 2nd Edition*
R&R Bk N - v19 - i3 - August 2004 - p161(1) [501+]

Swain, Martha H. - *Mississippi Women: Their Histories, Their Lives*
R&R Bk N - v19 - i3 - August 2004 - p30(1) [1-50]

Swain Monte R. - *Management Accounting, 3rd Ed.*
R&R Bk N - v19 - i2 - May 2004 - p119 [51-500]

Swain, Roger - *Saving Graces: Sojourns of a Backyard Biologist*
AS - v74 - i1 - Wntr 2005 - p10(2) [501+]

Swain, Ruth Freeman - *How Sweet It Is (and Was): The History of Candy*
c CH Bwatch - v14 - i11 - Nov 2004 - pNA [51-500]
c LibMed - v22 - i7 - April-May 2004 - p84(1) [501+]
How Tall? How Long? How Fast? How Big?
LibMed - v22 - i7 - April-May 2004 - p78(1) [501+]

Swainger, Jonathan - *People and Place: Historical Influences on Legal Culture*
Can Hist R - v85 - i4 - Dec 2004 - p856(3) [501+]
R&R Bk N - v19 - i1 - Feb 2004 - pNA [501+]

Swainston, Steph - *The Year of Our War*
KR - v72 - i24 - Dec 15 2004 - p1171(1) [501+]
LJ - v130 - i1 - Jan 1 2005 - p102(1) [51-500]
PW - v251 - i49 - Dec 6 2004 - p47(1) [501+]

Swan, Bill - *Corner Kick*
Res Links - v10 - i3 - Feb 2005 - p22(1) [501+]
Mud Run
c CBRA - Annual 2003 - p517(1) [51-500]

Swan, James - *The Librarian's Guide to Genealogical Services and Research*
R&R Bk N - v19 - i4 - Nov 2004 - p255(1) [501+]

Swan, John - *Proving Ground*
CBRA - Annual 2003 - p188(1) [51-500]
Sap: A Mystery
CBRA - Annual 2003 - p188(2) [51-500]

Swan, Mary - *Emma's Hands*
CBRA - Annual 2003 - p206(1) [501+]
Globe & Mail - Nov 27 2004 - pD3 [51-500]

Swan, Susan - *What Casanova Told Me*
BIC - v33 - i7 - Oct 2004 - p12(1) [501+]
Globe & Mail - Sept 18 2004 - pD6 [501+]
Globe & Mail - Nov 27 2004 - pD3 [51-500]

Swan, Wallace - *Handbook of Gay, Lesbian, Bisexual, and Transgender Administration and Policy*
R&R Bk N - v19 - i2 - May 2004 - p132 [51-500]

Swanee, Hunt - *This Was Not Our War: Bosnian Women Reclaiming the Peace*
PW - v251 - i49 - Dec 6 2004 - p53(2) [501+]

Swangviboonpong, Dusadee - *Thai Classical Singing: Its History, Musical Characteristics, and Transmission*
R&R Bk N - v19 - i4 - Nov 2004 - p197(1) [501+]

Swann, Brian - *Voices from Four Directions: Contemporary Translations of the Native Literatures of North America*
y Kliatt - v38 - i5 - Sept 2004 - p40(2) [51-500]
WLT - v79 - i1 - Jan-April 2005 - p109(2) [501+]

Swann, Julian - *Provincial Power and Absolute Monarchy: The Estates General of Burgundy, 1661-1790*
AHR - v109 - i3 - June 2004 - p985(2) [501+]

Swann, S. Andrew - *Broken Crescent*
y Kliatt - v38 - i5 - Sept 2004 - p32(3) [51-500]

Swann-Wright, Dianne - *A Way out of No Way: Claiming Family and Freedom in the New South*
HNet - Dec 2004 - pNA [501+]
JAH - v91 - i1 - June 2004 - p254-255 [501+]

Swanson, D.G. - *Plasma Waves, 2nd Ed.*
SciTech - v28 - i4 - Dec 2004 - p51(1) [51-500]

Swanson, Diane - *Alligators and Crocodiles*
c SLJ - v50 - i9 - Sept 2004 - p194(1) [51-500]
Balloon Sailors (Illus. by Lipka-Sztarballo, Krstyna)
c CBRA - Annual 2003 - p468(1) [51-500]
Frogs and Toads
c SLJ - v50 - i9 - Sept 2004 - p194(1) [51-500]
Hummingbirds
y SB - v40 - i3 - May-June 2004 - p126(1) [51-500]
Penguins
c SLJ - v50 - i9 - Sept 2004 - p194(1) [51-500]
Tunnels!: True Stories from the Edge (Illus. by MacEachern, Stephen)
c CBRA - Annual 2003 - p574(1) [51-500]
Turn It Loose: The Scientist in Absolutely Everybody (Illus. by Clark, Warren)
c SB - v40 - i5 - Sept-Oct 2004 - p218(1) [51-500]
y VOYA - v27 - i4 - Oct 2004 - p332(1) [51-500]

Swanson, Gerald - *Swanee's Silverton: A Firsthand Account of Silverton, Colorado from the 1930s to the Millennium*
R&R Bk N - v19 - i1 - Feb 2004 - p65(1) [501+]

Swanson, Heidi - *Cook 1.0: A Fresh Approach to the Vegetarian Kitchen*
LJ - v129 - i19 - Nov 15 2004 - p82(1) [51-500]

Swanson, Julie A. - *Going for the Record*
y BL - v101 - i1 - Sept 1 2004 - p110(1) [1-50]
y Kliatt - v38 - i4 - July 2004 - p24(2) [501+]
c SLJ - v50 - i8 - August 2004 - p130(1) [51-500]
y VOYA - v27 - i4 - Oct 2004 - p308(1) [51-500]

Swanson, Michael - *The NexStar UserEs Guide*
S&T - v108 - i6 - Dec 2004 - pNA [501+]

Swanson, Wayne - *Why the West Was Wild*
c BL - v100 - i22 - August 2004 - p1928(1) [51-500]

Swanson, Zane - *The Capital Structure Paradigm: Evolution of Debt / Equity Choices*
R&R Bk N - v19 - i1 - Feb 2004 - p116(1) [51-500]

Swanton, Christine - *Virtue Ethics: A Pluralistic View*
Choice - v41 - i7 - March 2004 - p1311(2) [501+]
Ethics - v115 - i2 - Jan 2005 - p430(5) [501+]

Sward, Robert - *The Collected Poems, 1957-2004*
Globe & Mail - Dec 4 2004 - pD34 [501+]

Swart, K.W. - *William of Orange and the Revolt of the Netherlands, 1572-84*
R&R Bk N - v19 - i3 - August 2004 - p38(1) [51-500]

Swarthout, Glendon Fred - *Bless the Beasts and Children (Read by Brick, Scott). Audiobook Review*
y Kliatt - v38 - i5 - Sept 2004 - p54(2) [51-500]
VOYA - v27 - i5 - Dec 2004 - p372(1) [501+]

Swartz, Clifford - *Back-of-the-Envelope Physics*
Physics T - v42 - i6 - Sept 2004 - p384-384 [501+]

Swartz, Judith L. - *Hip to Crochet: 23 Contemporary Projects for Today's Crocheter*
LJ - v129 - i13 - August 2004 - p79(1) [501+]

Swartz, Nancy Sohn - *How Did the Animals Help God? (Illus. by Hall, Melanie)*
c PW - v251 - i43 - Oct 25 2004 - p46(1) [501+]

Swedberg, Richard - *Principles of Economic Sociology*
Choice - v41 - i7 - March 2004 - p1378(1) [501+]
JEL - v41 - i4 - Dec 2003 - p1333(1) [501+]

Swee, Karen - *Life, Liberty and the Pursuit of Murder: A Revolutionary War Mystery*
y VOYA - v27 - i4 - Oct 2004 - p308(1) [51-500]

Sweeney, Douglas A. - *Nathaniel Taylor, New Haven Theology, and the Legacy of Jonathan Edwards*
TT - v60 - i4 - Jan 2004 - p602-605 [501+]
W&M Q - v61 - i3 - July 2004 - p562-564 [501+]

Sweeney, Gerald - *"Fighting for the Good Cause": Reflections on Francis Galton's Legacy to American Hereditarian Psychology*
Isis - v95 - i2 - June 2004 - p316(2) [501+]

Sweeney, Jon M. - *The Lure of Saints: A Protestant Experience of Catholic Tradition*
PW - v252 - i11 - March 14 2005 - p63(1) [51-500]

Sweeney, Joyce - *Takedown*
c BL - v101 - i4 - Oct 15 2004 - p406(1) [51-500]
y SLJ - v51 - i1 - Jan 2005 - p137(1) [51-500]
c KR - v72 - i19 - Oct 1 2004 - p970(1) [51-500]

Sweeney, Kep - *The New Restaurant Entrepreneur: An Inside Look at Restaurant Deal-Making and Other Tales from the Culinary Trenches*
R&R Bk N - v19 - i4 - Nov 2004 - p251(1) [501+]

Sweeney, Kevin - *Captors and Captives: The 1704 French and Indian Raid on Deerfield*
RAH - v32 - i2 - June 2004 - p151-8 [501+]

Sweeney, Matthew - *The Poetry Quarters, Vols. 8-9*
y Sch Lib - v52 - i4 - Winter 2004 - p220(1) [51-500]

Sweeney, Neal J. - *2004 Construction Law Update*
R&R Bk N - v19 - i3 - August 2004 - p198(1) [1-50]

Sweet, Anne Polselli - *Rethinking Reading Comprehension*
TCR - v106 - i12 - Dec 2004 - p2312(4) [501+]

Sweet, James H. - *Recreating Africa: Culture, Kinship, and Religion in the African Portuguese World, 1441-1770*
Ams - v61 - i2 - Oct 2004 - p314(2) [501+]

Sweet, Jill D. - *Dances of the Tewa Pueblo Indians: Expressions of New Life, 2nd Ed.*
R&R Bk N - v19 - i4 - Nov 2004 - p54(1) [51-500]

Sweet, John Wood - *Bodies Politic: Negotiating Race in the American North, 1730-1830*
Choice - v41 - i11-12 - July-August 2004 - p2110(1) [501+]
RAH - v32 - i3 - Sept 2004 - p347-351 [501+]

Sweet, Leonard - *Out of the Question ... into the Mystery: Getting Lost in the Godlife Relationship*
PW - v251 - i35 - August 30 2004 - p52(1) [51-500]

Sweet, Matthew - *Shepperton Babylon: The Lost Worlds of British Cinema*
NS - v134 - i4728 - Feb 21 2005 - p52(2) [501+]
Spec - v297 - i9212 - Feb 26 2005 - p42(1) [501+]

Sweet, Rosemary - *Antiquaries: The Discovery of the Past in Eighteenth-Century Britain*
Choice - v42 - i5 - Jan 2005 - p921(1) [1-50]

Sweet, William - *Philosophical Theory and the Universal Declaration of Human Rights*
R&R Bk N - v19 - i3 - August 2004 - p175(1) [501+]

Sweeten, Alan Richard - *Christianity in Rural China: Conflict and Accommodation in Jiangxi Province 1860-1900*
JAS - v63 - i3 - August 2004 - p785-786 [501+]

Sweetinburgh, Sheila - *The Role of the Hospital in Medieval England: Gift-giving and the Spiritual Economy*
R&R Bk N - v19 - i3 - August 2004 - p37(1) [51-500]

Sweetman, John - *Bomber Crew*
Spec - v296 - i9201 - Dec 11 2004 - p38(1) [501+]
A Dictionary of European Land Battles: From the Earliest Times to 1945
R&R Bk N - v19 - i3 - August 2004 - p31(1) [51-500]

Sweig, Julia E. - *Inside the Cuban Revolution: Fidel Castro and the Urban Underground*
HAHR - v84 - i1 - May 2004 - p351(2) [501+]

Swenson, James - *On Jean-Jacques Rousseau, Considered as One of the First Authors of the Revolution*
Eight-C St - v37 - i4 - Summer 2004 - p677-682 [501+]

Swers, Michael L. - *The Difference Women Make: The Policy Impact of Women in Congress*
CS - v33 - i1 - Jan 2004 - p1-3 [51-500]

Swerynski, Michal - *Collective Agreements and Individual Contracts of Employment*
R&R Bk N - v19 - i1 - Feb 2004 - pNA [51-500]

Swezey, Marilyn Pfeifer - *Faberge Flowers*
R&R Bk N - v19 - i4 - Nov 2004 - p210(1) [501+]

Swiac, Chris - *Where to Weekend around New York City*
LJ - v129 - i15 - Sept 15 2004 - p73(1) [51-500]

Swian, Simon - *Approaching Late Antiquity: The Transformation from Early to Late Empire*
Choice - v42 - i4 - Dec 2004 - p714(1) [1-50]

Swick, Thomas - *Way to See the World: From Texas to Transylvania with a Maverick Traveler*
R&R Bk N - v19 - i4 - Nov 2004 - p72(1) [51-500]

Swiderski, Frank - *Threat Modeling*
SciTech - v28 - i3 - March 2004 - p33(1) [51-500]

Swidler, Ann - *Talk of Love: How Culture Matters*
J Soc H - v38 - i1 - Fall 2004 - p229(3) [501+]

Swidler, Stephen A. - *Naturally Small: Teaching and Learning in the Last One-Room Schools*
R&R Bk N - v19 - i4 - Nov 2004 - p193(1) [501+]

Swierenga, Robert P. - *Dutch Chicago: A History of the Hollanders in the Windy City*
AHR - v109 - i3 - June 2004 - p937(2) [501+]

Swift, Amanda - *The Boys' Club*
c Sch Lib - v52 - i4 - Winter 2004 - p204(2) [51-500]

Swift, Charles I. - *Introduction To Stage Lighting: The Fundamentals Of Theatre Lighting Design*
Bwatch - Feb 2005 - pNA [501+]

Swift, Dan - *Roman Burials, Medieval Tenements and Suburban Growth: 201 Bishopsgate, City of London*
R&R Bk N - v19 - i4 - Nov 2004 - p37(1) [51-500]

Swift, E. Anthony - *Popular Theater and Society in Tsarist Russia*
JMH - v76 - i3 - Sept 2004 - p734(3) [501+]
Slav R - v63 - i2 - Summer 2004 - p403(2) [501+]

Swift, Earl - *Where They Lay: Searching for America's Lost Soldiers*
Mar Crp G - v88 - i11 - Nov 2004 - p90(1) [501+]

Swift, John N. - *Willa Cather and the American Southwest*
Roundup M - v12 - i1 - Oct 2004 - p26(1) [51-500]

Swift, Jonathan - *Gulliver (Illus. by Riddell, Chris)*
c KR - v73 - i4 - Feb 15 2005 - p229(1) [51-500]

Swift, Mark Stanley - *Biblical Subtexts and Religious Themes in Works of Anton Chekhov*
R&R Bk N - v19 - i1 - Feb 2004 - p217(1) [51-500]

Swift, Todd - *Cafe Alibi*
CBRA - Annual 2003 - p233(1) [51-500]
Rue du Regard
Globe & Mail - March 19 2005 - pD14 [501+]

Swift, Virginia - *Bye, Bye Love*
BL - v101 - i1 - Sept 1 2004 - p70(1) [51-500]
Bye, Bye, Love
LJ - v129 - i16 - Oct 1 2004 - p62(2) [51-500]
PW - v251 - i39 - Sept 27 2004 - p40(1) [51-500]

Swift, Will - *The Roosevelts and the Royals: Franklin and Eleanor, the King and Queen of England, and the Friendship That Changed History*
BL - v100 - i21 - July 2004 - p1814(1) [51-500]
LJ - v129 - i12 - July 2004 - p99(2) [51-500]

Swinburne, Richard - *The Resurrection of God Incarnate*
Rel St - v40 - i3 - Sept 2004 - p367(5) [501+]
Theol St - v65 - i3 - Sept 2004 - p677(2) [501+]
TT - v61 - i3 - Oct 2004 - p408(3) [501+]

Swinburne, Stephen R. - *Black Bear: North America's Bear*
c LibMed - v22 - i6 - March 2004 - p72(1) [501+]
What's a Pair? What's a Dozen? (Illus. by Swinburne, Stephen R.)
c SLJ - v50 - i9 - Sept 2004 - p59(1) [501+]

Swinchatt, Jonathan - *The Winemaker's Dance: Exploring Terroir in the Napa Valley*
BL - v101 - i1 - Sept 1 2004 - p36(1) [51-500]

Swindells, Robert - *Abomination (Read by Hulme, Amanda). Audiobook Review*
y Kliatt - v38 - i5 - Sept 2004 - p52(2) [51-500]
Blitzed (Read by Rodska, Christian). Audiobook Review
y Kliatt - v39 - i1 - Jan 2005 - p38(1) [51-500]
Ruby Tanya
c TES - v0 - i4587 - June 11 2004 - psssss18(2) [501+]

Swingrover, E.A. - *The Counterculture Reader*
R&R Bk N - v19 - i3 - August 2004 - p63(1) [51-500]

Swink Magazine
LJ - v129 - i12 - July 2004 - p120(1) [501+]

Swiontkowski, Gale - *Imagining Incest: Sexton, Plath, Rich, and Olds on Life with Daddy*
Choice - v41 - i11-12 - July-August 2004 - p2047(1) [501+]

Swischuk, Leonard E. - *Imaging of the Newborn, Infant, and Young Child. 5th Ed.*
SciTech - v28 - i1 - March 2004 - p117(1) [51-500]

Swisher, Clarice - *Understanding the Canterbury Tales*
LibMed - v22 - i5 - Feb 2004 - p81(1) [51-500]

Switched On: Renewable Energy Opportunities in the Tourism Industry
R&R Bk N - v19 - i1 - Feb 2004 - p69(1) [501+]

Swokowski, Earl William - *Fundamentals of College Algebra, 11th Ed.*
SciTech - v28 - i4 - Dec 2004 - p34(1) [1-50]

Swope, Sam - *I Am a Pencil: A Teacher, His Kids, and Their World of Stories*
BL - v100 - i22 - August 2004 - p1882(2) [51-500]
LJ - v129 - i15 - Sept 15 2004 - p67(1) [51-500]
Jack and the Seven Deadly Giants (Illus. by Cneut, Carll)
c CCB-B - v57 - i11 - July-August 2004 - p486(1) [501+]

Swozilek, Helmut - *Memorie Istoriche di Maria Angelica Kauffman Zucchi Riguardanti l'Arte della Pittura da lei Professata Scritte da G.C.Z.*
Eight-C St - v37 - i3 - Spring 2004 - p478-482 [501+]

Sycamore, Matt Bernstein - *Dangerous Families: Queer Writing on Surviving*
Lam Bk Rpt - v13 - i4-5 - Nov-Dec 2004 - p44(2) [501+]

Sydenham, Peter H. - *Systems Approach to Engineering Design*
SciTech - v28 - i1 - March 2004 - p137(1) [51-500]

Syed, Mohammad Ali - *The Position of Women in Islam: A Progressive View*
Choice - v42 - i6 - Feb 2005 - p1040(2) [51-500]

Sykes, Bryan - *Adam's Curse: A Future Without Men (Read by Kay, Christopher). Audiobook Review*
y Kliatt - v39 - i1 - Jan 2005 - p51(2) [51-500]
LJ - v129 - i20 - Dec 1 2004 - p183(1) [51-500]
Adam's Curse: A Future Without Men
Choice - v42 - i4 - Dec 2004 - p688(1) [1-50]
Fut - v39 - i2 - March-April 2005 - p9(2) [501+]
Fut - v39 - i2 - March-April 2005 - p60(1) [51-500]
y SB - v40 - i5 - Sept-Oct 2004 - p211(2) [51-500]
SB - v40 - i6 - Nov-Dec 2004 - p242(2) [51-500]

Sykes, Christopher Simon - *The Big House: The Story of a Country House and Its Family*
Spec - v295 - i9184 - August 14 2004 - p29(2) [501+]
TLS - i5303 - Nov 19 2004 - p40(1) [501+]

Sykes, Julie - *Bless You, Santa! (Illus. by Warnes, Tim)*
c KR - v72 - i21 - Nov 1 2004 - p1054(1) [51-500]

Sykes, Wanda - *Yeah, I Said It*
BL - v101 - i2 - Sept 15 2004 - p192(1) [51-500]
Black Iss - v7 - i1 - Jan-Feb 2005 - p69(1) [501+]
PW - v251 - i33 - August 16 2004 - p56(1) [51-500]

Sylvester, Christine - *Feminist International Relations: An Unfinished Journey*
CS - v33 - i1 - Jan 2004 - p29-31 [501+]

Sylvester, Kenneth Michael - *The Limits of Rural Capitalism: Family, Culture, and Markets in Montcalm, Manitoba, 1870-1940*
Can Hist R - v85 - i3 - Sept 2004 - p612(3) [501+]

Symanski, Richard - *Geography Inside Out: Space, Place, and Society*
Hist Geo - v32 - Annual 2004 - p181(5) [501+]

Symbols of America
LibMed - v22 - i7 - April-May 2004 - p84(1) [501+]

Symcox, Geoffrey - *Italian Reports on America 1493-1522: Accounts by Contemporary Observers*
Six Ct J - v35 - i1 - Spring 2004 - p196(3) [501+]

Symeonides, Symeon C. - *The American Choice-of-Law Revolution in the Courts: Today and Tomorrow*
R&R Bk N - v19 - i4 - Nov 2004 - p158(1) [501+]

Symeonidis, George - *The Effects of Competition: Cartel Policy and the Evolution of Strategy and Structure in British Industry*
JEL - v41 - i4 - Dec 2003 - p1313(3) [501+]

Symes, Ruth - *The Sheep Fairy*
LibMed - v22 - i5 - Feb 2004 - p66(1) [501+]

Symmes, Marilyn - *Impressions of New York: Prints from the New York Historical Society*
Choice - v42 - i7 - March 2005 - p1218(2) [51-500]
Mag Antiq - v167 - i1 - Jan 2005 - p128(1) [51-500]
Mag Antiq - v167 - i2 - Feb 2005 - p54(1) [51-500]

Symonds, E. Malcolm - *Essential Obstetrics and Gynaecology. 4th Ed.*
SciTech - v28 - i1 - March 2004 - p115(1) [51-500]

Symonds, Patricia V. - *Calling the Soul: Gender and the Cycle of Life in a Hmong Village*
Choice - v42 - i3 - Nov 2004 - p528(1) [1-50]

Symonides, Janusz - *Human Rights: International Protection, Monitoring, Enforcement*
Choice - v41 - i11-12 - July-August 2004 - p2120(1) [501+]
R&R Bk N - v19 - i1 - Feb 2004 - pNA [51-500]

Symposium on the Origins of Semiosis (2000: San Marino, Italy) - *In the Beginning: Origins of Semiosis*
R&R Bk N - v19 - i4 - Nov 2004 - p213(1) [501+]

Synder, Kirk - *Lavender Road to Success: The Career Guide for the Gay Community*
NACEJou - v64 - i4 - Summer 2004 - p10-11 [501+]

Synder, Terri L. - *Brabblinmg Women: Disorderly Speech and the Law in Early Virginia*
JAH - v91 - i3 - Dec 2004 - p991(1) [501+]

Szabados, Bela - *Hypocrisy: Ethical Investigations*
R&R Bk N - v20 - i1 - Feb 2005 - p10(1) [51-500]

Szanto, George - *Second Sight*
Globe & Mail - Oct 9 2004 - pD21 [501+]

Szapary, Gyorgy - *Monetary Strategies for Joining the Euro*
R&R Bk N - v19 - i3 - August 2004 - p134(1) [51-500]

Szasz, Thomas - *Pharmacracy: Medicine and Politics in America*
Choice - v41 - i7 - March 2004 - p1327(2) [501+]

Szatmari, Peter - *A Mind Apart: Understanding Children with Autism and Asperger Syndrome*
SciTech - v28 - i4 - Dec 2004 - p114(1) [1-50]

Szczerbiak, Aleks - *Poles Together? Emergence and Development of Political Parties in Post-Communist Poland*
E-A St - v56 - i5 - July 2004 - p767(2) [501+]

Szechenyi, Agnes - *Menedekhaz: Sarkozi Marta emlekkonyv*
WLT - v79 - i1 - Jan-April 2005 - p95(2) [501+]

Szego, Giorgio - *Risk Measures for the 21st Century*
R&R Bk N - v19 - i3 - August 2004 - p135(1) [51-500]

Szeker, Endre - *A stilusnaz iro*
WLT - v78 - i3-4 - Sept-Dec 2004 - p108(2) [501+]

Szeman, Imre - *Zones of Instability: Literature, Postcolonialism, and the Nation*
Choice - v42 - i2 - Oct 2004 - p297(1) [501+]

Szentes, Tamas - *The Political Economy of Development, Globalization and System Transformation*
E-A St - v56 - i6 - Sept 2004 - p924(926) [501+]
World Economics 2: The Political Economy of Development Globalization and System Transformation
Choice - v42 - i3 - Nov 2004 - p534(1) [1-50]

Szewczak, Edward J. - *Managing the Human Side of Information Technology: Challenges and Solutions*
JEL - v41 - i4 - Dec 2003 - p1420(1) [501+]

Szilard, Rudolph - *Theories and Applications of Plate Analysis: Classical, Numerical, and Engineering Methods*
SciTech - v28 - i1 - March 2004 - p144(1) [51-500]

Szmigin, Isabelle - *Understanding the Consumer*
R&R Bk N - v19 - i2 - May 2004 - p115(1) [51-500]

Szonyi, Michael - *Practicing Kinship: Lineage and Descent in Late Imperial China*
AHR - v109 - i2 - April 2004 - p491(2) [501+]
HJAS - v64 - i2 - Dec 2004 - p492-502 [501+]
HJAS - v64 - i2 - Dec 2004 - p492-502 [501+]
JIH - v34 - i4 - Spring 2004 - p674-675 [501+]

Szpakowska, Kaslia - *Behind Closed Eyes: Dreams and Nightmares in Ancient Egypt*
R&R Bk N - v19 - i1 - Feb 2004 - p49(1) [51-500]

Szpirglas, Jeff - *Gross Universe: Your Guide to All Disguising Things under the Sun (Illus. by Cho, Michael)*
y   SB - v40 - i4 - July-August 2004 - p167(1) [51-500]

Gross Universe: Your Guide to All Disguisting Things under the Sun (Illus. by Cho, Michael)
c   SLJ - v50 - i11 - Nov 2004 - p132(1) [501+]

Szuchman, Lenore T. - *Writing with Style: APA Style Made Easy, 3rd Ed.*
R&R Bk N - v19 - i3 - August 2004 - p8(1) [1-50]

Szulakowska, Urszula - *The Alchemy of Light: Geometry and Optics in Late Renaissance Alchemical Illustration*
Isis - v95 - i3 - Sept 2004 - p488(1) [501+]

Szymanski, Ann-Marie E. - *Pathways to Prohibition: Radicals, Moderates, and Social Movement Outcomes*
JAH - v91 - i3 - Dec 2004 - p1046(2) [501+]

Szymanski, Marianne M. - *Toy Tips: A Parent's Essential Guide to Smart Toy Choices*
LJ - v129 - i14 - Sept 1 2004 - p183(1) [51-500]

T

Tangredi, Sam J. - *Globalization and Maritime Power*
APJ - v18 - i3 - Fall 2004 - p116(2) [501+]
Tanguay, Daniel - *Leo Strauss: Une biographie intellectuelle*
NYRB - v51 - i16 - Oct 21 2004 - p58(3) [501+]
Tanguay, Ronald C. - *The Double Star Observer's Handbook, 2nd Ed.*
S&T - v107 - i1 - Jan 2004 - p76(1) [501+]
Taniar, David - *Web Information Systems*
Choice - v42 - i1 - Sept 2004 - p140(2) [501+]
Tanigawa, Takeshi - *Amerika Eiga to Senryo Seisaku*
JAH - v91 - i2 - Sept 2004 - p688(1) [501+]
Tanimoto, Yasuko - *A New Reading of The Wings of the Dove*
R&R Bk N - v19 - i4 - Nov 2004 - p241(1) [501+]
Tanizaki, Jun'ichiro - *The Key and Diary of an Old Man*
LJ - v130 - i1 - Jan 1 2005 - p172(1) [1-50]
Tankard, Judith B. - *Gardens of the Arts and Crafts Movement: Reality and Imagination*
BL - v101 - i6 - Nov 15 2004 - p542(1) [51-500]
Choice - v42 - i7 - March 2005 - p1216(2) [51-500]
R&R Bk N - v19 - i4 - Nov 2004 - p246(1) [501+]
Tanksley, Neeld - *Certified Macromedia Flash MX Developer Study Guide*
SciTech - v28 - i1 - March 2004 - p175(1) [1-50]
Tannenbaum, Nicola - *Founders' Cults in Southeast Asia: Ancestors, Polity, and Identity*
JRAI - v10 - i3 - Sept 2004 - p750(1) [501+]
Tanner, Bernard R. - *F. Scott Fitzgerald's Odyssey: A Reader's Guide to the Gospels in The Great Gatsby*
R&R Bk N - v19 - i1 - Feb 2004 - p245(1) [51-500]
Tanner, Duncan - *Labour's First Century*
JEH - v64 - i1 - March 2004 - p249(3) [501+]
Tanner, Heather J. - *Families, Friends and Allies: Boulogne and Politics in Northern France and England, c. 879-1160*
Choice - v42 - i1 - Sept 2004 - p181(1) [501+]
R&R Bk N - v19 - i3 - August 2004 - p42(1) [51-500]
Tanner, James T. - *Ivory-Billed Woodpecker*
SciTech - v28 - i1 - March 2004 - p70(1) [51-500]
Tanner, Janet - *Forgotten Destiny*
y BL - v101 - i3 - Oct 1 2004 - p317(2) [51-500]
Tanner, Marcus - *The Last of the Celts*
BW - v34 - i46 - Nov 14 2004 - p9(2) [501+]
Globe & Mail - Nov 6 2004 - pD18 [501+]
LJ - v129 - i19 - Nov 15 2004 - p73(1) [501+]
NS - v134 - i4719-20 - Jan 1 2005 - p88(2) [501+]
PW - v251 - i35 - August 30 2004 - p40(1) [501+]
Spec - v296 - i9198 - Nov 20 2004 - p44(3) [501+]
Wil Q - v29 - i1 - Wntr 2005 - p124(1) [501+]
Tanner, Michael - *The Poverty of Welfare: Helping Others in Civil Society*
IndRev - v9 - i2 - Fall 2004 - p302(4) [501+]
JEL - v42 - i1 - March 2004 - p277(1) [501+]
Social Security and Its Discontents: Perspectives on Choice
Bwatch - v26 - i9 - Sept 2004 - p12(1) [51-500]
Choice - v42 - i3 - Nov 2004 - p534(1) [1-50]
R&R Bk N - v19 - i3 - August 2004 - p117(1) [51-500]
Tanner, Mike - *Acting the Giddy Goat*
Can Lit - i181 - Summer 2004 - p100-102 [501+]
Tanner, Norman - *Is the Church Too Asian? Reflections on the Ecumenical Councils*
Theol St - v66 - i1 - March 2005 - p228(2) [501+]
Was the Church Too Democratic? Councils, Collegiality and the Church's Future
CHR - v90 - i3 - July 2004 - p589(2) [501+]
Tanner, Stephan - *Quotable Opera: Aria Ready for a Laugh? (Illus. by Taccola, Umberto)*
CBRA - Annual 2003 - p17(1) [51-500]
Tanner, Stephen - *The Wars of the Bushes: A Father and Son as Military Leaders*
BW - v34 - i35 - August 2004 - p3(2) [501+]
LJ - v129 - i13 - August 2004 - p100(1) [501+]
R&R Bk N - v19 - i4 - Nov 2004 - p64(1) [1-50]
Tanner, Suzy-Jane - *Tinyflock Nursery School*
c SLJ - v50 - i8 - August 2004 - p96(1) [51-500]
Tanning, Dorothea - *Chasm: A Weekend*
ChrSFF&H - v26 - i10 - Oct 2004 - p26(1) [51-500]
KR - v72 - i16 - August 15 2004 - p775(1) [501+]
Ent W - i789 - Oct 22 2004 - p101 [501+]
Table of Content
BW - v34 - i27 - July 4 2004 - p12(1) [51-500]

Tantillo, Astrida Orle - *The Will to Create: Goethe's Philosophy of Nature*
Ger Q - v77 - i1 - Wntr 2004 - p95(2) [501+]
Ger Q - v77 - i1 - Wntr 2004 - p102(1) [501+]
GSR - v27 - i3 - Oct 2004 - p610(1) [501+]
Tao Jie - *Holding Up Half the Sky: Chinese Women Past, Present, and Future*
Choice - v42 - i5 - Jan 2005 - p939(1) [51-500]
Taper, Mark L. - *The Nature of Scientific Evidence Statistical, Philosophical, and Empirical Considerations*
Sci - v306 - i5701 - Nov 26 2004 - p1478(1) [501+]
Tapp-McDougall, Caroline - *The Complete Canadian Eldercare Guide: Expert Solutions to Help You Make the Best Decisions for Your Loved Ones*
Globe & Mail - July 24 2004 - pF6 [51-500]
Tapper, Suzanne Cloud - *Voices from Slavery's Past: Yearning to Be Heard*
y SLJ - v50 - i12 - Dec 2004 - p156(1) [51-500]
Tapply, William G. - *Bitch Creek*
BL - v101 - i2 - Sept 15 2004 - p214(1) [51-500]
KR - v72 - i14 - July 15 2004 - p664(2) [51-500]
LJ - v129 - i14 - Sept 1 2004 - p121(1) [51-500]
PW - v251 - i33 - August 16 2004 - p46(1) [51-500]
Gone Fishin': Ruminations on Fly Fishing
BL - v101 - i4 - Oct 15 2004 - p376(1) [51-500]
PW - v251 - i40 - Oct 4 2004 - p82(1) [51-500]
Tappolet, Christine - *Emotions et valeurs*
Dialogue - v43 - i3 - Summer 2004 - p609-612 [501+]
Tapscott, Don - *Naked Corporation: How the Age of Transparency Will Revolutionize Business*
CBRA - Annual 2003 - p333(1) [51-500]
Taras, David - *How Candians Communicate*
CBRA - Annual 2003 - p376(1) [501+]
Tarbuck, Ed - *The Theory of Plate Tectonics*
Sci Teach - v71 - i5 - May 2004 - p69-69 [501+]
Targ, Russell - *Limitless Mind: A Guide to Remote Viewing and Transformation of Consciousness*
Choice - v41 - i11-12 - July-August 2004 - p2128(1) [501+]
Target
LibMed - v22 - i4 - Jan 2004 - p67(1) [501+]
Targoff, Ramie - *Common Prayer: The Language of Public Devotion in Early Modern England*
JAAR - v72 - i4 - Dec 2004 - p1076(3) [501+]
Targowski, Andrew S. - *Electronic Enterprise: Stratregy and Architecture*
JEL - v41 - i4 - Dec 2003 - p1420(1) [501+]
Tarlo, Emma - *Unsettling Memories: Narratives of the Emergency in Delhi*
Choice - v41 - i7 - March 2004 - p1350(1) [501+]
Tarnay, Laszlo - *Specificity Recognition and Social Cognition*
R&R Bk N - v19 - i3 - August 2004 - p8(1) [1-50]
Tarp, Finn - *Foreign Aid and Development: Lessons Learnt and Directions for the Future*
JEL - v41 - i4 - Dec 2003 - p1362(1) [501+]
Tarpley, Natasha - *Destiny's Gift (Illus. by Burrowes, Adjoa J.)*
c BL - v101 - i6 - Nov 15 2004 - p592(2) [51-500]
c KR - v72 - i20 - Oct 15 2004 - p1014(1) [51-500]
c PW - v252 - i1 - Jan 3 2005 - p55(2) [51-500]
c SLJ - v50 - i12 - Dec 2004 - p123(1) [51-500]
Tarr, Joel A. - *Devastation and Renewal: An Environmental History of Pittsburgh and Its Region*
BHR - v78 - i3 - Autumn 2004 - p540(3) [501+]
HNet - August 2004 - pNA [501+]
T&C - v45 - i3 - July 2004 - p640-641 [501+]
Tarr, Judith - *Rite of Conquest*
BL - v101 - i2 - Sept 15 2004 - p215(1) [51-500]
Bwatch - Dec 2004 - pNA [51-500]
LJ - v129 - i15 - Sept 15 2004 - p52(1) [51-500]
PW - v251 - i38 - Sept 20 2004 - p50(1) [51-500]
Tarrant, John - *Bring Me the Rhinoceros: And Other Zen Koans To Bring You Joy*
LJ - v130 - i1 - Jan 1 2005 - p121(1) [51-500]
Tarricone, Luciano - *Grid Computing for Electromagnetics*
SciTech - v28 - i4 - Dec 2004 - p31(1) [51-500]
Tartamella, Lisa - *Generation Extra Large: Rescuing Our Children from the Epidemic of Obesity*
LJ - v130 - i1 - Jan 1 2005 - p140(1) [51-500]
Taruskin, Richard - *The Oxford History of Western Music*
BW - v34 - i48 - Nov 28 2004 - p15(1) [501+]
Globe & Mail - Dec 11 2004 - pR1 [501+]
LJ - v130 - i3 - Feb 15 2005 - p132(3) [51-500]
Tas, Kenan - *Global Analysis and Applied Mathematics: Proceedings*
SciTech - v28 - i4 - Dec 2004 - p39(1) [51-500]

Taschen, Angelika - *Inside Africa (Illus. by Von Schaewen, Deidi)*
Black Iss - v6 - i4 - July-August 2004 - p32(1) [501+]
Tashiro, Takuya - *Najica Blitz Tactics, Vol. 1*
y VOYA - v27 - i5 - Dec 2004 - p411(1) [51-500]
Tashjian, Janet - *Fault Line (Read by Bryant, Clara). Audiobook Review*
y BL - v101 - i4 - Oct 15 2004 - p433(1) [51-500]
y Kliatt - v39 - i1 - Jan 2005 - p42(1) [51-500]
y SLJ - v50 - i11 - Nov 2004 - p82(1) [51-500]
Fault Line
y LibMed - v22 - i5 - Feb 2004 - p73(1) [501+]
The Gospel According to Larry (Read by Eisenberg, Jesse). Audiobook Review
y Kliatt - v38 - i5 - Sept 2004 - p60(2) [501+]
The Gospel According to Larry
HB - v80 - i5 - Sept-Oct 2004 - p610(1) [501+]
Vote for Larry (Read by Eisenberg, Jesse). Audiobook Review
y BL - v101 - i3 - Oct 1 2004 - p352(1) [51-500]
y Kliatt - v38 - i5 - Sept 2004 - p60(2) [501+]
y SLJ - v50 - i10 - Oct 2004 - p88(1) [51-500]
Vote for Larry
c BL - v101 - i3 - Oct 1 2004 - p327(1) [51-500]
y CCB-B - v58 - i1 - Sept 2004 - p41(1) [51-500]
y HB - v80 - i4 - July-August 2004 - p461(1) [51-500]
JAAL - v48 - i4 - Dec 2004 - p347(2) [501+]
y Teach Lib - v32 - i1 - Oct 2004 - p18(1) [51-500]
Tassoul, Jean Louis - *A Concise History of Solar and Stellar Physics*
Choice - v42 - i4 - Dec 2004 - p685(1) [1-50]
New Sci - v183 - i2459 - August 7 2004 - p48(1) [501+]
Tatalovich, Raymond - *The Presidency and Political Science: Two Hundred Years of Constitutional Debate*
JAH - v91 - i3 - Dec 2004 - p1094(2) [501+]
Pres St Q - v34 - i3 - Sept 2004 - p700(3) [501+]
R&R Bk N - v19 - i1 - Feb 2004 - pNA [51-500]
Tatar, Maria - *The Annotated Brothers Grimm*
NS - v133 - i4718 - Dec 13 2004 - p70(2) [501+]
Secrets Beyond the Door: The Story of Bluebeard and His Wives
AS - v74 - i1 - Wntr 2005 - p129(4) [501+]
HM - v310 - i1857 - Feb 2005 - p83(2) [51-500]
Tate, Allen - *Essays of Four Decades*
MA - v45 - i1 - Winter 2003 - p85 [501+]
Tate, Bruce A. - *Better, Faster, Ligther Java*
SciTech - v28 - i3 - Sept 2004 - p21(1) [51-500]
Tate, Greg - *Everything but the Burden: What White People Are Taking from Black Culture*
JPC - v38 - i3 - Feb 2005 - p577(3) [501+]
Tate, James - *Return to the City of White Donkeys*
BL - v101 - i5 - Nov 1 2004 - p455(1) [51-500]
LJ - v129 - i16 - Oct 1 2004 - p85(1) [51-500]
NYRB - v51 - i19 - Dec 2 2004 - p48(3) [501+]
PW - v251 - i47 - Nov 22 2004 - p56(1) [51-500]
Tate, Nikki - *Battle for Carnillo*
y CBRA - Annual 2003 - p517(1) [51-500]
Grandpaent's Day (Illus. by Laverdiere, Benoit)
c Res Links - v10 - i2 - Dec 2004 - p11(1) [51-500]
Tate, Una O'Farrell - *The Abridged English Metrical Brut: Edited from London, British Library MS Royal 12.C.XII*
JEGP - v103 - i2 - April 2004 - p263-265 [501+]
Tatham, Betty - *How Animals Communicate*
c SB - v40 - i5 - Sept-Oct 2004 - p224(1) [51-500]
How Animals Play
c SB - v40 - i5 - Sept-Oct 2004 - p224(1) [51-500]
Tati, Jacques - *Jour de Fete*
TimHES - v0 - i1674 - Jan 14 2005 - p28(2) [501+]
TimHES - v0 - i1674 - Jan 14 2005 - p28(2) [501+]
Les Vacances de M. Hulo
TimHES - v0 - i1674 - Jan 14 2005 - p28(2) [501+]
TimHES - v0 - i1674 - Jan 14 2005 - p28(2) [501+]
Mon Oncle
TimHES - v0 - i1674 - Jan 14 2005 - p28(2) [501+]
TimHES - v0 - i1674 - Jan 14 2005 - p28(2) [501+]
Playtime
TimHES - v0 - i1674 - Jan 14 2005 - p28(2) [501+]
TimHES - v0 - i1674 - Jan 14 2005 - p28(2) [501+]
Tatum, Becky L. - *Violence and Minority Youths*
Adoles - v39 - i154 - Summer 2004 - p405(1) [51-500]

Taub, Michael - *An Anthology of Israeli Drama for the New Millennium*
Choice - v42 - i7 - March 2005 - p1224(1) [51-500]

Tauber, Eliezer - *Personal Policy Making, Canada's Role in the Adoption of the Palestine Partition Resolution*
Can Hist R - v85 - i3 - Sept 2004 - p645(2) [501+]

Tauberschmidt, Gerhard - *Secondary Parallelism: A Study of Translation Technique in LXX Proverbs*
R&R Bk N - v19 - i4 - Nov 2004 - p21(1) [51-500]
R&R Bk N - v19 - i4 - Nov 2004 - p22(1) [51-500]

Taubman, Philip - *Secret Empire: Eisenhower, the CIA, and the Hidden Story of America's Space Espionage*
T&C - v45 - i1 - Jan 2004 - p204(3) [501+]

Taubman, William - *Khrushchev: The Man and His Era*
E-A St - v56 - i4 - June 2004 - p615(621) [501+]

Taus-Bolstad, Stacy - *Puerto Ricans in America*
c BL - v101 - i6 - Nov 15 2004 - p575(1) [51-500]

Taussig, Michael T. - *Law in a Lawless Land: Diary of a ""Limpieza"" in Colombia*
ABR - v25 - i5 - July-August 2004 - p19(2) [501+]
Nation - v279 - i5 - August 16 2004 - p31 [501+]
Law in a Lawless Land: Diary of a "Limpieza" in Columbia
R&R Bk N - v19 - i3 - August 2004 - p146(1) [51-500]

Tavares, Matt - *Mudball (Illus. by Tavares, Matt)*
c HB - v81 - i2 - March-April 2005 - p195(1) [51-500]
c PW - v252 - i6 - Feb 7 2005 - p60(1) [51-500]
Oliver's Game (Illus. by Tavares, Matt)
c LibMed - v23 - i1 - August-Sept 2004 - p66(1) [51-500]
c SLJ - v50 - i7 - July 2004 - p89(1) [51-500]

Tavidze, Albert - *Adean Regional Initiative*
R&R Bk N - v19 - i3 - August 2004 - p77(1) [51-500]

Tawancy, Hani M. - *Practical Engineering Failure Analysis*
SciTech - v28 - i4 - Dec 2004 - p132 [51-500]

Taxidou, Olga - *Tragedy, Modernity and Mourning*
Choice - v42 - i5 - Jan 2005 - p848(1) [1-50]

Tay, Simon S.C. - *The Enemy Within: Combating Corruption in Asia*
R&R Bk N - v19 - i1 - Feb 2004 - pNA [501+]

Tayfur, M. Faith - *Semiperipheral Development and Foreign Policy; the Cases of Greece and Spain*
R&R Bk N - v19 - i1 - Feb 2004 - p31(1) [1-50]

Tayler, Jeffrey - *Angry Wind: Through Muslim Black Africa by Truck, Bus, Boat, and Camel*
BL - v101 - i9-10 - Jan 1 2005 - p805(1) [51-500]
KR - v72 - i24 - Dec 15 2004 - p1194(1) [501+]
LJ - v130 - i1 - Jan 1 2005 - p137(1) [51-500]
PW - v251 - i47 - Nov 22 2004 - p45(1) [51-500]

Tayler, Yolanda - *Battling HIV/AIDS: A Decision Maker's Guide to the Procurement of Medicines and Related Supplies*
SciTech - v28 - i3 - Sept 2004 - p104(1) [51-500]

Taylor, Andrew - *Call the Dying*
Spec - v296 - i9194 - Oct 23 2004 - p58(1) [501+]
Textual Situations: Three Medieval Manuscripts and Their Readers
JEGP - v103 - i2 - April 2004 - p269-271 [501+]
RES - v55 - i221 - Sept 2004 - p610(2) [501+]
An Unpardonable Crime (Read by Vance, Simon). Audiobook Review
BL - v100 - i21 - July 2004 - p1856(1) [1-50]
An Unpardonable Crime
BooChiTr - March 7 2004 - p3(1) [501+]
The World of Gerard Mercator: The Mapmaker Who Revolutionalized Geography
Am Sci - v93 - i2 - March-April 2005 - p176(1) [51-500]
The World of Gerard Mercator: The Mapmaker Who Revolutionized Geography
BL - v101 - i4 - Oct 15 2004 - p370(1) [51-500]
KR - v72 - i19 - Oct 1 2004 - p952(2) [501+]
PW - v251 - i38 - Sept 20 2004 - p53(1) [51-500]
R&R Bk N - v20 - i1 - Feb 2005 - p82(1) [1-50]

Taylor, Andrew J. - *Flavour Perception*
SciTech - v28 - i4 - Dec 2004 - p71(1) [51-500]

Taylor, Angus - *Animals and Ethics*
CBRA - Annual 2003 - p101(1) [51-500]

Taylor, Anne L., M.D. - *The African American Woman's Guide to a Healthy Heart*
LJ - v129 - i16 - Oct 1 2004 - p106(1) [51-500]

Taylor, Arlene G. - *The Organization of Information, 2nd Ed.*
BL - v100 - i21 - July 2004 - p1859(1) [501+]
R&USQ - v44 - i2 - Winter 2004 - p177(2) [51-500]

Taylor, Avram - *Working Class Credit and Community Since 1918*
Albion - v36 - i2 - Summer 2004 - p346(2) [501+]

Taylor, Barbara (1950 -) - *Mary Wollstonecraft and the Feminist Imagination*
AHR - v109 - i4 - Oct 2004 - p1311-1312 [501+]
Albion - v36 - i2 - Summer 2004 - p316(2) [501+]
JGS - v13 - i2 - July 2004 - p177-178 [501+]

Taylor, Barbara (1954 -) - *Animal Giants*
c SB - v40 - i6 - Nov-Dec 2004 - p273(1) [51-500]
y SLJ - v50 - i11 - Nov 2004 - p158(1) [51-500]
Apes and Monkeys
c SB - v40 - i6 - Nov-Dec 2004 - p273(1) [51-500]

Taylor, Barbara Lea - *Old-Fashioned and David Austin Roses*
E-Streams - August 2004 - pNA [501+]

Taylor, Barry - *Foreign-Language Printing in London 1500-1900*
Lib & Cul - v39 - i3 - Summer 2004 - p329(2) [501+]
R&R Bk N - v19 - i1 - Feb 2004 - p258(1) [51-500]

Taylor, Bernard A. - *X Congress of the International Organization for Septuagint and Cognate Studies: Oslo, 1998.*
JNES - v64 - i1 - Jan 2005 - p60(1) [501+]

Taylor, Bill - *Industrial Relations in China*
R&R Bk N - v19 - i2 - May 2004 - p106(1) [51-500]

Taylor, Blaine - *Volkswagen Military Vehicles of the Third Reich: An Illustrated History*
R&R Bk N - v19 - i4 - Nov 2004 - p252(1) [501+]

Taylor, Brandon - *Collage: The Making of Modern Art*
Choice - v42 - i6 - Feb 2005 - p1011(2) [51-500]
LJ - v130 - i4 - March 1 2005 - p84(1) [51-500]

Taylor, Brian D. - *Politics and the Russian Army: Civil-Military Relations, 1689-2000*
AJS - v110 - i1 - July 2004 - p241(3) [501+]
Russ Rev - v63 - i3 - July 2004 - pNA [501+]
Slav R - v63 - i3 - Fall 2004 - p648-649 [501+]

Taylor, C.J. - *Peace Walker: The Legend of Hiawatha and Tekanawita*
c Globe & Mail - Sept 11 2004 - pD13 [51-500]
Res Links - v10 - i2 - Dec 2004 - p23(1) [501+]

Taylor, Charles - *Modern Social Imaginaries*
Choice - v41 - i11-12 - July-August 2004 - p2059(1) [501+]
Comw - v131 - i13 - July 16 2004 - p30(2) [501+]
Theol St - v65 - i4 - Dec 2004 - p907(1) [501+]

Taylor, Clare L. - *Women, Writing, and Fetishism 1890-1950: Female Cross-Gendering*
ELT - v47 - i4 - Fall 2004 - p455(5) [501+]

Taylor, Clarence - *Black Religious Intellectuals: The Fight for Inequality from Jim Crow to the Twenty-First Century*
CH - v73 - i4 - Dec 2004 - p828(6) [501+]

Taylor, Cora - *Angelique, Bk. 1*
y Can CL - i111-112 - Fall-Winter 2003 - p128(7) [501+]
Ghost Voyages III: Endeavour and Resolution
Res Links - v10 - i3 - Feb 2005 - p22(2) [501+]

Taylor, Cyril - *Excellence in Education: The Making of Great Schools*
NS - v134 - i4721 - Jan 10 2005 - p53(2) [501+]

Taylor, D.J. - *Orwell: The Life*
Nation - v279 - i19 - Dec 6 2004 - p40 [501+]
NYTBR - Dec 19 2004 - p30 [501+]

Taylor, Daniel - *In Search of Sacred Places: Looking for Wisdom on Celtic Holy Islands*
LJ - v130 - i2 - Feb 1 2005 - p107(1) [51-500]
PW - v252 - i3 - Jan 17 2005 - p51(1) [51-500]

Taylor, David - *The Brand Stretch: Why 1 in 2 Extensions Fail, and How to Beat the Odds*
R&R Bk N - v19 - i3 - August 2004 - p109(1) [51-500]
Policing the Victorian Town: The Development of the Police in Middlesbrough, c. 1840-1914.
JMH - v77 - i1 - March 2005 - p180(2) [501+]

Taylor, Debbie A. - *Sweet Music in Harlem (Illus. by Morrison, Frank)*
c Black Iss - v6 - i5 - Sept-Oct 2004 - p59(1) [51-500]
c SLJ - v50 - i7 - July 2004 - p89(1) [51-500]

Taylor-Di Bartolo, Laini - *The Drowned*
PW - v251 - i42 - Oct 18 2004 - p50(1) [51-500]

Taylor, Diana - *The Archive and the Repertoire: Performing Cultural Memory in the Americas*
Theat J - v56 - i3 - Oct 2004 - p520-520 [501+]
Holy Terrors: Latin American Women Perform
Choice - v41 - i11-12 - July-August 2004 - p2050(1) [501+]

Taylor, G.P. - *Shadowmancer (Read by Malcolm, Graeme). Audiobook Review*
y BL - v101 - i3 - Oct 1 2004 - p352(1) [51-500]
y Kliatt - v38 - i5 - Sept 2004 - p65(2) [51-500]
y SLJ - v50 - i10 - Oct 2004 - p86(2) [51-500]
Shadowmancer
c Bwatch - v26 - i7 - July 2004 - p5(1) [51-500]
y CCB-B - v57 - i11 - July-August 2004 - p486(2) [501+]
c CH Bwatch - v14 - i7 - July 2004 - p6(1) [51-500]
c HB - v80 - i4 - July-August 2004 - p461(2) [51-500]
Wormwood
y BL - v101 - i1 - Sept 1 2004 - p109(1) [1-50]
y CCB-B - v58 - i5 - Jan 2005 - p230(1) [51-500]
Ch Today - v49 - i1 - Jan 2005 - p71(1) [51-500]
y Kliatt - v38 - i5 - Sept 2004 - p16(3) [51-500]
KR - v72 - i17 - Sept 1 2004 - p874(1) [51-500]
PW - v251 - i33 - August 16 2004 - p64(1) [51-500]
y SLJ - v50 - i10 - Oct 2004 - p180(1) [51-500]
VOYA - v27 - i5 - Dec 2004 - p411(1) [51-500]

Taylor, Gary - *Buying Whiteness: Race, Culture, and Identity from Columbus to Hip-Hop*
LJ - v130 - i3 - Feb 15 2005 - p148(1) [51-500]

Taylor, George (1940 -) - *The French Revolution and the London Stage, 1789-1805*
RES - v55 - i221 - Sept 2004 - p626(3) [501+]

Taylor, George R. - *Practical Application of Social Learning Theories in Educating Young African-American Males*
R&R Bk N - v19 - i3 - August 2004 - p216(1) [1-50]
Youths Serving Youths in Drug Education Programs
y VOYA - v27 - i5 - Dec 2004 - p428(1) [51-500]

Taylor, George Rogers - *The American Railroad Network, 1861-1890*
Hist Geo - v32 - Annual 2004 - p200(3) [501+]

Taylor, J. Gary - *Smart Alliance: How a Global Corporation and Environmental Activists Transformed a Tarnished Brand*
Aud - v106 - i3 - July-August 2004 - p66(1) [51-500]
R&R Bk N - v19 - i3 - August 2004 - p118(1) [51-500]

Taylor, James - *Managing Information Technology Projects: Applying Project Management Strategies to Software, Hardware, and Integration Initiatives*
R&R Bk N - v19 - i1 - Feb 2004 - p94(1) [1-50]

Taylor, Janelle - *Dying to Marry*
y BL - v101 - i4 - Oct 15 2004 - p394(1) [51-500]

Taylor, Jean Gelman - *Indonesia: Peoples and Histories*
JIH - v35 - i2 - Autumn 2004 - p342(2) [501+]

Taylor, Jeannie - *Out at Home: A Novel*
y Kliatt - v39 - i2 - March 2005 - p23(1) [51-500]

Taylor, Joanne - *Making Room (Illus. by Rankin, Peter)*
c CH Bwatch - v14 - i12 - Dec 2004 - pNA [51-500]
c Globe & Mail - Sept 25 2004 - pD26 [51-500]
c KR - v72 - i18 - Sept 15 2004 - p921(1) [51-500]
c Res Links - v10 - i1 - Oct 2004 - p10(1) [51-500]
c SLJ - v50 - i11 - Nov 2004 - p118(1) [51-500]
There You Are: A Novel
y SLJ - v50 - i11 - Nov 2004 - p154(1) [51-500]

Taylor, John - *Paths to Contemporary French Literature*
Choice - v41 - i11-12 - July-August 2004 - p2051(1) [501+]

Taylor, John H. - *Mummy: The Inside Story*
c Kliatt - v38 - i6 - Nov 2004 - p37(2) [51-500]
c SLJ - v50 - i12 - Dec 2004 - p170(1) [51-500]

Taylor, John M. - *Semmes: Rebel Raider*
R&R Bk N - v19 - i1 - Feb 2004 - p59(1) [51-500]

Taylor, John R. - *Classical Mechanics*
SciTech - v28 - i4 - Dec 2004 - p47(1) [51-500]

Taylor, Joseph E. III - *Making Salmon: An Environmental History of the Northwest Fisheries Crisis*
Isis - v95 - i2 - June 2004 - p327(2) [501+]

Taylor, Julie - *Muslims in Medieval Italy: The Colony at Lucera*
AHR - v109 - i4 - Oct 2004 - p1295-1296 [501+]

Taylor, Kate - *Mme. Proust and the Kosher Kitchen*
Can Lit - i182 - Autumn 2004 - p156(3) [501+]

Taylor, Kathleen - *Brainwashing: The Science of Thought Control*
TimHES - v0 - i1684 - March 25 2005 - p31(1) [501+]

Taylor, Kevin - *Sociology for Pharmacists: An Introduction, 2d ed*
SciTech - v28 - i4 - Dec 2004 - p119(1) [1-50]
Sociology for Pharmacists: An Introduction, 2nd Ed.
E-Streams - August 2004 - pNA [501+]
SciTech - v28 - i1 - March 2004 - p123(1) [51-500]

Taylor, Marc - *Original Marvelettes: Motowns' Mystery Girl Group*
  Bwatch - v26 - i8 - August 2004 - p3(1) [51-500]
Taylor, Margie - *Displaced Persons*
  Globe & Mail - Jan 8 2005 - pD11 [51-500]
Taylor, Marianne - *Mountain Gorilla*
  y SLJ - v51 - i1 - Jan 2005 - p156(1) [51-500]
Taylor, Mark - *Shakespeare's Imitations*
  Shakes Q - v55 - i2 - Summer 2004 - p232-233 [501+]
  The Vietnam War in History, Literature and Film
  Am St - v45 - i1 - Spring 2004 - p170-172 [501+]
  Choice - v41 - i11-12 - July-August 2004 - p2030(1) [501+]
  The Vietnam War in History, Literature, and Film
  HNet - Sept 2004 - pNA [501+]
Taylor, Mark (b. 1939 -) - *Shakespeare's Imitations*
  Six Ct J - v35 - i1 - Spring 2004 - p302(2) [501+]
Taylor, Mark C. - *Confidence Games: Money and Markets in a World without Redemption*
  Lon R Bks - v26 - i21 - Nov 4 2004 - p6 [1-50]
  Lon R Bks - v27 - i2 - Jan 20 2005 - p31(1) [51-500]
Taylor, Michael J.H. - *"The Times" Aviators: A History in Photographia*
  SciTech - v28 - i4 - Dec 2004 - p161(1) [1-50]
Taylor, Michelle - *What's Happily Ever After, Anyway?*
  y SLJ - v51 - i2 - Feb 2005 - p142(1) [51-500]
Taylor, Mildred D. - *Roll of Thunder, Hear My Cry*
  c RT - v57 - Sept 2003 - p101 [51-500]
Taylor, Monique M. - *Harlem between Heaven and Hell*
  CS - v33 - i2 - March 2004 - p212-213 [501+]
  JIH - v35 - i1 - Summer 2004 - p167-168 [501+]
Taylor, Nancy - *Cousins in love; the letters of Lydia DuGard, 1665-1672; with a new edition of The marriages of cousin Germans by Samuel DuGard*
  R&R Bk N - v19 - i3 - August 2004 - p30(1) [1-50]
Taylor, Nikki M. - *Frontiers of Freedom: Cincinnati's Black Community, 1802-1868*
  Black Iss - v7 - i1 - Jan-Feb 2005 - p25(1) [501+]
Taylor, Nora Annesley - *Painters in Hanoi: An Ethnography of Vietnamese Art*
  Choice - v42 - i1 - Sept 2004 - p90(1) [501+]
Taylor, Paige - *Consider the Source: Finding Reliable Information on the Internet*
  Bwatch - March 2005 - pNA [51-500]
  Teach Lib - v32 - i2 - Dec 2004 - p38(1) [501+]
Taylor, Patrick - *The Apprenticeship of Doctor Laverty*
  Globe & Mail - Dec 18 2004 - pD12 [501+]
Taylor, Paul - *Jews and the Olympic Games: The Clash Between Sport and Politics: With a Complete Review of Jewish Olympic Medallists*
  Choice - v42 - i6 - Feb 2005 - p1061(1) [51-500]
  R&R Bk N - v19 - i4 - Nov 2004 - p80(1) [51-500]
Taylor, Philip - *Goddess on the Rise: Pilgrimage and Popular Religion in Vietnam*
  Choice - v42 - i2 - Oct 2004 - p333(2) [51-500]
  R&R Bk N - v19 - i3 - August 2004 - p15(1) [1-50]
Taylor, Porter - *From Anger to Zion: An Alphabet of Faith*
  LJ - v129 - i12 - July 2004 - p90(1) [51-500]
  PW - v251 - i30 - July 26 2004 - p49(2) [501+]
Taylor, Purcell - *Diagnosis and Treatment of Substance-Related Disorders: The DECLARE Model*
  SciTech - v28 - i4 - Dec 2004 - p101(1) [51-500]
Taylor, Quintard - *African American Women Confront the West, 1600-2000*
  JAH - v91 - i3 - Dec 2004 - p984(2) [501+]
  PHR - v73 - i3 - August 2004 - p496(498) [501+]
  SHQ - v107 - i4 - April 2004 - p629(2) [501+]
  WHQ - v35 - i4 - Winter 2004 - p511-512 [501+]
Taylor, R. - *Roman Builders: A Study in Architectural Process*
  Class R - v54 - i2 - Nov 2004 - p537(3) [501+]
Taylor, Rebe - *Unearthed: The Aboriginal Tasmanians of Kangaroo Island*
  AHS - v35 - i123 - April 2004 - p182-183 [501+]
Taylor, Richard L. - *First Flight: The Story of the Wright Brothers*
  c LibMed - v22 - i6 - March 2004 - p79(1) [501+]
Taylor, Robert - *Genetics*
  LibMed - v23 - i1 - August-Sept 2004 - p80(1) [51-500]
  y SB - v40 - i5 - Sept-Oct 2004 - p212(1) [51-500]
  SLJ - v50 - i10 - Oct 2004 - pS63(1) [501+]
Taylor, Rodney L. - *Confucianism*
  y SLJ - v50 - i9 - Sept 2004 - p232(1) [51-500]

Taylor, S. Caroline - *Court Licensed Abuse: Patriarchal Lore and the Legal Response to Intrafamilial Sexual Abuse of Children*
  R&R Bk N - v19 - i4 - Nov 2004 - p176(1) [501+]
Taylor, Sarah Stewart - *Mansions of the Dead*
  BW - v34 - i31 - August 1 2004 - p8(1) [51-500]
  LJ - v129 - i12 - July 2004 - p64(1) [51-500]
Taylor, Sean - *Boing! (Illus. by Ingman, Bruce)*
  c BL - v100 - i22 - August 2004 - p1946(1) [51-500]
  c PW - v251 - i28 - July 12 2004 - p63(1) [51-500]
  c SLJ - v50 - i8 - August 2004 - p96(2) [51-500]
  c TES - v0 - i4586 - June 4 2004 - p21(1) [501+]
  Small Bad Wolf (Illus. by Lewis, Jan)
  c SLJ - v50 - i8 - August 2004 - p86(1) [51-500]
Taylor, Stephen - *The Caliban Shore: The Fate of the Grosvenor Castaways*
  TLS - i5288 - August 6 2004 - p7(1) [501+]
  Caliban's Shore: The Wreck of the Grosvenor and the Strange Fate of Her Survivors
  LJ - v129 - i12 - July 2004 - p100(1) [51-500]
  NYTBR - July 18 2004 - p6 [501+]
  NYTBR - July 25 2004 - p18 [501+]
  R&R Bk N - v19 - i4 - Nov 2004 - p52(1) [51-500]
Taylor, Steve - *The A to X of Alternative Music*
  LJ - v129 - i13 - August 2004 - p120(1) [51-500]
Taylor, Steven - *Advances in the Treatment of Posttraumatic Stress Disorder: Cognitive-Behavioural Perspectives*
  SciTech - v28 - i4 - Dec 2004 - p99(1) [51-500]
  False Prophet: Fieldnotes from the Punk Underground
  Notes - v61 - i2 - Dec 2004 - p467(3) [501+]
  Treating Health Anxiety: A Cognitive-Behavioral Approach
  SciTech - v28 - i4 - Dec 2004 - p100(1) [51-500]
Taylor, Stewart - *Intel Integrated Performance Primitives: How to Optimze Software Applications Using Intel IPP*
  SciTech - v28 - i3 - Sept 2004 - p22(1) [1-50]
Taylor, Suzanne - *Inside Intuit: How the Makers of Quicken Beat Microsoft and Revolutionized an Entire Industry*
  R&R Bk N - v19 - i1 - Feb 2004 - p103(1) [51-500]
Taylor, Terry - *Techniques for Creating Altered Books, Boxes, Cards and More*
  y BL - v101 - i8 - Dec 15 2004 - p704(1) [51-500]
Taylor, Theodore - *The Cay*
  y Storyworks - v12 - i5 - Feb-March 2005 - p7(1) [51-500]
  Ice Drift
  c CCB-B - v58 - i6 - Feb 2005 - p267(2) [51-500]
  c KR - v72 - i24 - Dec 15 2004 - p1209(1) [51-500]
  c SLJ - v51 - i1 - Jan 2005 - p137(1) [51-500]
  Lord of the Kill
  y Kliatt - v38 - i5 - Sept 2004 - p26(2) [51-500]
Taylor, Therese - *Bernadette of Lourdes: Her Life, Death and Visions*
  R&R Bk N - v19 - i1 - Feb 2004 - p21(1) [51-500]
  CHR - v90 - i3 - July 2004 - p558(2) [501+]
Taylor, Timothy - *The Buried Soul: How Humans Invented Death*
  Arch - v57 - i4 - July-August 2004 - p60-60 [501+]
  AS - v73 - i4 - Autumn 2004 - p165(2) [501+]
  JRAI - v10 - i3 - Sept 2004 - p737(2) [501+]
Taylor, William (American government official) - *Blue Lawn*
  y Magpies - v19 - i5 - Nov 2004 - p8S(1) [501+]
Taylor, William L. - *The Passion of My Times: An Advocate's Fifty-Year Journey through the Civil Rights Revolution*
  BL - v101 - i5 - Nov 1 2004 - p449(1) [51-500]
  KR - v72 - i19 - Oct 1 2004 - p953(1) [501+]
  PW - v251 - i43 - Oct 25 2004 - p37(1) [51-500]
Tayob, Abdulkader - *Islam in South Africa: Mosques, Imams and Sermons, Religions of Africa*
  IJMES - v36 - i3 - August 2004 - p519-521 [501+]
Tayob, Abulkader - *Religion and Politics in South Africa*
  HNet - Oct 2004 - pNA [501+]
Tazon, Juan E. - *The Life and Times of Thomas Stukeley*
  TLS - i5285 - July 16 2004 - p28(1) [501+]
  Ren Q - v57 - i3 - Fall 2004 - p1120(2) [501+]
Tchak, Sami - *La fete des masques*
  WLT - v78 - i3-4 - Sept-Dec 2004 - p83(1) [501+]
Te Loo, Sanne - *Little Fish*
  c SLJ - v50 - i8 - August 2004 - p97(1) [51-500]

Tea, Michelle - *Rent Girl*
  Lam Bk Rpt - v13 - i3 - Oct 2004 - p11(1) [501+]
  Without a Net: The Female Experience of Growing Up Working Class
  OOB - v35 - Jan-Feb 2005 - p50(1) [501+]
  R&R Bk N - v19 - i4 - Nov 2004 - p103(1) [51-500]
Teachout, Terry - *All in the Dances: A Brief Life of George Balanchine*
  y BL - v101 - i5 - Nov 1 2004 - p459(1) [501+]
  BW - v34 - i48 - Nov 28 2004 - p7(1) [501+]
  Dance - v79 - i1 - Jan 2005 - p106(5) [501+]
  Ent W - i790 - Oct 29 2004 - p71 [51-500]
  KR - v72 - i19 - Oct 1 2004 - p953(1) [501+]
  LJ - v129 - i18 - Nov 1 2004 - p87(1) [501+]
  NYTBR - Nov 28 2004 - p16 [501+]
  PW - v251 - i41 - Oct 11 2004 - p72(1) [501+]
  The Skeptic: A Life of H.L. Mencken
  MA - v46 - i4 - Fall 2004 - p352(5) [501+]
Teaford, Jon C. - *The Rise of the States: Evolution of American State Government*
  AHR - v109 - i3 - June 2004 - p935(2) [501+]
  JAH - v91 - i2 - Sept 2004 - p676(2) [501+]
Teague, Mark - *Detective LaRue: Letters from the Investigation*
  c PW - v251 - i29 - July 19 2004 - p160(2) [51-500]
  Detective LaRue: Letters from the Investigation (Illus. by Teague, Mark)
  c BL - v101 - i4 - Oct 15 2004 - p411(1) [51-500]
  c Globe & Mail - Dec 11 2004 - pD43 [51-500]
  c KR - v72 - i16 - August 15 2004 - p814(1) [51-500]
  c SLJ - v50 - i10 - Oct 2004 - p135(1) [51-500]
Team, Cide - *Funny Cide (Read by Cashman, Dan). Audiobook Review*
  Kliatt - v38 - i6 - Nov 2004 - p55(2) [51-500]
Teams That Click
  R&R Bk N - v19 - i3 - August 2004 - p132(1) [1-50]
Teare, Brian - *The Room Where I Was Born*
  VQR - v80 - i3 - Summer 2004 - p264(1) [501+]
Teasdale, Wayne - *Catholicism in Dialogue: Conservation Across Traditions*
  Choice - v42 - i5 - Jan 2005 - p872(1) [1-50]
  The Mystic Hours: A Daybook of Interspiritual Wisdom and Devotion
  LJ - v130 - i1 - Jan 1 2005 - p121(1) [51-500]
Tebben, Karin - *Beruf Schriftstellerin: Schreibende Frauen im 18 und 19*
  GSR - v27 - i1 - Feb 2004 - p146-147 [501+]
Tebeau, Mark - *Eating Smoke: Fire in Urban America, 1800-1950*
  BHR - v78 - i3 - Autumn 2004 - p537(3) [501+]
  Choice - v41 - i11-12 - July-August 2004 - p2066(2) [501+]
  HNet - Dec 2004 - pNA [501+]
  SciTech - v28 - i3 - Sept 2004 - p149(1) [51-500]
TeBordo, Christian - *The Conviction and Subsequent Life of Savior Neck*
  KR - v72 - i22 - Nov 15 2004 - p1067(1) [51-500]
Technology in Education: A Twenty Year Retrospective
  LibMed - v23 - i1 - August-Sept 2004 - p87(1) [51-500]
Teckentrup, Britta - *Bumposaurus*
  LibMed - v22 - i5 - Feb 2004 - p65(1) [501+]
Tedlock, Dennis - *Rabinal Achi: A Mayan Drama of War and Sacrifice*
  Theat J - v56 - i3 - Oct 2004 - p517-518 [501+]
  TimHES - v0 - i1669 - Dec 3 2004 - p27(1) [501+]
Tedlow, Richard S. - *The Watson Dynasty: The Fiery Reign and Troubled Legacy of IBM's Founding Father and Son*
  BHR - v78 - i3 - Autumn 2004 - p535(3) [501+]
  R&R Bk N - v19 - i1 - Feb 2004 - p103(1) [1-50]
Teece, Geoff - *Buddhism*
  c BL - v101 - i3 - Oct 1 2004 - p346(1) [51-500]
  c CH Bwatch - Feb 2005 - pNA [51-500]
  Christianity
  c BL - v101 - i3 - Oct 1 2004 - p346(1) [51-500]
  c CH Bwatch - Feb 2005 - pNA [51-500]
Teegarden, David M. - *Polymer Chemistry: Introduction to an Indispensable Science*
  Choice - v42 - i3 - Nov 2004 - p512(1) [1-50]
  SB - v40 - i6 - Nov-Dec 2004 - p250(2) [501+]
  Polymer Chemistry; Introduction to an Indispensable Science
  SciTech - v28 - i3 - Sept 2004 - p52(1) [1-50]
Teel, Leonard Ray - *Ralph Emerson McGill: Voice of the Southern Conscience*
  HNet - Sept 2004 - pNA [501+]

Teele, James E. - *E. Franklin Frazier and "Black Bourgeoisie"*
J Am St - v38 - i2 - August 2004 - p366(2) [501+]

Teeter, Lawrence - *Forest Policy for Private Forestry: Global and Regional Challenges*
QRB - v79 - i3 - Sept 2004 - p325(2) [501+]

Teferra, Mengistu - *Capacity Building for a Reforming African Power Sector*
R&R Bk N - v19 - i1 - Feb 2004 - p102(1) [51-500]

Tefs, Wayne - *4 x 4*
Globe & Mail - Dec 11 2004 - pD15 [501+]

Tegen, Katherine - *The Story of the Easter Bunny (Illus. by Lambert, Sally Anne)*
c CCB-B - v58 - i6 - Feb 2005 - p268(1) [51-500]
c KR - v73 - i2 - Jan 15 2005 - p126(1) [51-500]
c PW - v252 - i7 - Feb 14 2005 - p79(2) [501+]
c SLJ - v51 - i2 - Feb 2005 - p110(1) [51-500]

Teicher, Hendel - *Trisha Brown: Dance and Art in Dialogue, 1961-2001*
TDR - v48 - i2 - Summer 2004 - p181(2) [501+]

Teichmann, Iris - *Expanding Industry*
y Sch Lib - v52 - i3 - Autumn 2004 - p165(1) [501+]

Teichova, Alice - *Business and Politics in Europe, 1900-1970: Essays in Honour of Alice Teichova*
JEL - v42 - i1 - March 2004 - p299(1) [501+]
Nation, State, and the Economy in History
BHR - v78 - i1 - Spring 2004 - p175(3) [501+]
JEL - v41 - i4 - Dec 2003 - p1404(2) [501+]

Teilhard de Chardin, Pierre - *The Divine Milieu*
R&R Bk N - v19 - i3 - August 2004 - p19(1) [1-50]

Teitelbaum, Jonathan E. - *In a Page Pediatric Signs and Symptoms*
SciTech - v28 - i4 - Dec 2004 - p111(1) [1-50]

Teitelbaum, Michael - *The U.S. Constitution*
c SLJ - v51 - i1 - Jan 2005 - p144(1) [51-500]

Teitell, Beth - *From Here to Maternity: The Education of a Rookie Mom*
LJ - v130 - i1 - Jan 1 2005 - p142(1) [51-500]
PW - v252 - i1 - Jan 3 2005 - p43(1) [51-500]

Teja, R. - *La Hispania del Siglo IV: Administracion Economia, Sociedad, Cristianizacion*
Class R - v54 - i2 - Nov 2004 - p518-519 [501+]

Tekavec, Heather - *Storm Is Coming (Illus. by Spengler, Margaret)*
c RT - v57 - Oct 2003 - p172 [1-50]
What's That AWFUL Smell?
c HB - v80 - i4 - July-August 2004 - p442(2) [51-500]

Tekippe, Terry J. - *Bernard Lonergan's Insight: A Comprehensive Commentary*
Theol St - v65 - i4 - Dec 2004 - p891(3) [501+]

Teleky, Richard - *Pack Up the Moon*
Can Lit - i181 - Summer 2004 - p179(1) [501+]

Telepan, Bill - *Inspired by Ingredients: Market Menus and Family Favorites from a Three-Star Chef*
LJ - v129 - i17 - Oct 15 2004 - p82(1) [51-500]
PW - v251 - i39 - Sept 27 2004 - p51(1) [51-500]

Telepchak, Michael J. - *Forensic and Clinical Applications of Solid Phase Extraction*
SciTech - v28 - i3 - Sept 2004 - p50(1) [1-50]

Teles, Gilberto Mendonca - *Hora aberta: Poemas reunidos*
WLT - v78 - i3-4 - Sept-Dec 2004 - p153(1) [501+]

Telesco, Patricia - *Kitchen Witch's Guide to Divination: Finding, Crafting and Using Fortune-Telling Tools from around Your Home*
Bwatch - Feb 2005 - pNA [501+]
Which Witch Is Which?: A Concise Guide to Wiccan and Neo-Pagan Paths and Traditions
Bwatch - Feb 2005 - pNA [501+]

Telford, Gillian Eades - *Making the Right Move*
Bwatch - v26 - i8 - August 2004 - p1(1) [501+]

Telhami, Shibley - *Identity and Foreign Policy in the Middle East*
PG - v23 - i4 - May 2004 - p497-500 [501+]

Teller, Edward - *Memoirs: A Twentieth-Century Journey in Science and Politics*
T&C - v45 - i2 - April 2004 - p460-461 [501+]

Telling, Glenn C. - *Prions and Prion Diseases: Current Perspectives*
SciTech - v28 - i3 - Sept 2004 - p76(1) [51-500]

Tellis, Gerard J. - *Effective Advertising: Understanding When, How, and Why Advertising Works*
R&R Bk N - v19 - i2 - May 2004 - p120 [51-500]

Telnaes, Ann - *Humor's Edge*
PW - v251 - i29 - July 19 2004 - p146(1) [51-500]

Telushkin, Joseph - *Heaven's Witness*
KR - v72 - i15 - August 1 2004 - p717(1) [51-500]
PW - v251 - i33 - August 16 2004 - p46(1) [51-500]

Temes, Peter S. - *Against School Reform*
CE - v81 - i1 - Fall 2004 - p50(1) [501+]
The Just War: An American Reflection on the Morality of War in Our Time
Mar Crp G - v88 - i3 - March 2004 - p61(2) [501+]

Temirbolat, S.E. - *Ill-Posed Boundary-Value Problems*
SciTech - v28 - i1 - March 2004 - p39(1) [51-500]

Temperley, Alan - *The Magician of Samarkand (Read by Sachs, Andrew). Audiobook Review*
c SLJ - v50 - i7 - July 2004 - p59(1) [51-500]

Temperley, Nicholas - *Bound for America: Three British Composers*
MT - v145 - i1888 - Autumn 2004 - p100-101 [501+]

Temperton, Vicky M. - *Assembly Rules and Restoration Ecology: Bridging the Gap Between Theory and Practice*
SciTech - v28 - i3 - Sept 2004 - p60(1) [1-50]

Temple, Bob - *Guyana*
LibMed - v22 - i4 - Jan 2004 - p74(1) [501+]

Temple, Michael - *The French Cinema Book*
TimHES - v0 - i1674 - Jan 14 2005 - p28(2) [501+]
TimHES - v0 - i1674 - Jan 14 2005 - p28(2) [501+]

Temple, Peter - *Identity Theory*
BL - v101 - i4 - Oct 15 2004 - p393(1) [51-500]
LJ - v129 - i16 - Oct 1 2004 - p74(1) [51-500]

Temple, Philip - *A Sort of Conscience: The Wakefields*
AHS - v35 - i123 - April 2004 - p170-171 [501+]

Temple-Plotz, Lana - *Practical Tools for Foster Parents*
Adoles - v39 - i156 - Winter 2004 - p839(2) [51-500]

Temple-Raston, Dina - *Justice on the Grass: Three Rwandan Journalists, Their Trial for War Crimes, and a Nation's Quest for Redemption*
KR - v73 - i1 - Jan 1 2005 - p44(1) [501+]
PW - v252 - i5 - Jan 31 2005 - p56(1) [51-500]

Temple, Richard - *Icons: Divine Beauty*
Choice - v42 - i2 - Oct 2004 - p282(1) [501+]
LJ - v129 - i14 - Sept 1 2004 - p148(1) [51-500]

Templeton, Nancy Smyth - *Gene and Cell Therapy: Therapeutic Mechanisms and Strategies, 2nd Ed., Rev. and Expanded*
SciTech - v28 - i1 - March 2004 - p87(1) [51-500]

Tenenbaum, Roberto A. - *Fundamentals of Applied Dynamics*
Choice - v41 - i11-12 - July-August 2004 - p2077(1) [501+]

Tenev, Stoyan - *Informality and the Playing Field in Vietnam's Business Sector*
JEL - v41 - i4 - Dec 2003 - p1431(1) [501+]

Teng, Emma Jinhua - *Taiwan's Imagined Geography: Chinese Colonial Travel Writing and Pictures, 1683-1895*
Choice - v42 - i6 - Feb 2005 - p1077(1) [501+]

Teng, J.G. - *Buckling of Thin Metal Shells*
SciTech - v28 - i1 - March 2004 - p142(1) [51-500]

Tengelyi, Laszlo - *The Wild Region in Life-History*
R&R Bk N - v19 - i3 - August 2004 - p7(1) [1-50]

Tennant, Alan - *On the Wing: To the Edge of the Earth with the Peregrine Falcon*
y BL - v101 - i1 - Sept 1 2004 - p32(1) [51-500]
BL - v101 - i7 - Dec 1 2004 - p632(1) [51-500]
BL - v101 - i9-10 - Jan 1 2005 - p768(1) [51-500]
BW - v34 - i39 - Sept 26 2004 - p8(2) [501+]
KR - v72 - i15 - August 1 2004 - p734(1) [51-500]
LJ - v129 - i14 - Sept 1 2004 - p185(1) [51-500]
NH - v113 - i8 - Oct 2004 - p66(2) [501+]
NYTBR - Sept 19 2004 - p6 [501+]
PW - v251 - i31 - August 2 2004 - p63(1) [501+]

Tenner, Edward - *Our Own Devices: The Past and Future of Body Technology*
SLJ - v50 - i10 - Oct 2004 - pS63(1) [501+]

Tennesen, Michael - *The Complete Idiot's Guide to Global Warming*
CG - v124 - i5 - Sept-Oct 2004 - p112(1) [501+]
y SB - v40 - i6 - Nov-Dec 2004 - p261(1) [51-500]

Tenney, Tommy - *Hadassah: The Girl Who Became Queen Esther*
c PW - v252 - i7 - Feb 14 2005 - p81(1) [51-500]

Tenney, William Jewett - *The Military and Naval History of the Rebellion in the United States: With Biographical Sketches of Deceased Officers*
NWCR - v57 - Autumn 2004 - p173(1) [501+]

Tenny-Brittian, William - *Prayer for People Who Can't Sit Still*
PW - v252 - i3 - Jan 17 2005 - p51(1) [51-500]

Tenopir, Carol - *Communication Patterns of Engineers*
E-Streams - July 2004 - pNA [501+]
SciTech - v28 - i1 - March 2004 - p136(1) [51-500]

Tenpas, Kathryn Dunn - *Presidents as Candidates: Inside the White House for Presidential Campaign*
Choice - v41 - i11-12 - July-August 2004 - p2126(1) [501+]

Tensen, Bonnie L. - *Research Strategies for a Digital Age*
R&R Bk N - v19 - i1 - Feb 2004 - p262(1) [51-500]

Tent, James F. - *In the Shadow of the Holocaust: Nazi Persecution of Jewish-Christian Germans*
GSR - v27 - i1 - Feb 2004 - p176-177 [501+]
JMH - v77 - i1 - March 2005 - p234(2) [501+]

Tent, Pam - *Midnight at the Palace: My Life as a Fabulous Cockette*
BL - v101 - i6 - Nov 15 2004 - p542(1) [51-500]
KR - v72 - i19 - Oct 1 2004 - p953(2) [501+]
PW - v251 - i43 - Oct 25 2004 - p35(1) [51-500]

Tenzing Norbu - *Secret of the Snow Leopard (Illus. by Tenzing Norbu)*
c Globe & Mail - July 31 2004 - pD11 [51-500]
Secret of the Snow Leopard (Illus. by Tenzing, Norbu)
c Res Links - v10 - i1 - Oct 2004 - p5(2) [501+]
Secret of the Snow Leopard (Illus. by Tenzing Norbu)
c SLJ - v50 - i8 - August 2004 - p97(1) [51-500]

Teo, Hsu-Ming - *Cultural History in Australia*
AHR - v109 - i2 - April 2004 - p504(2) [501+]

Teologia Senza Verita: Bayle Contro i "Rationaux"
Eight-C St - v37 - i3 - Spring 2004 - p510-520 [501+]

TeoraUSA, LLC - *1000 Games For Smart Kids*
c CH Bwatch - v14 - i9 - Sept 2004 - p1(1) [51-500]

Tepper, Sheri S. - *The Companions*
Analog - v124 - i4 - April 2004 - p134(2) [501+]

Ter Haar, Gerrie - *Bridge or Barrier: Religion, Violence, and Visions for Peace*
R&R Bk N - v20 - i1 - Feb 2005 - p11(1) [51-500]

Teran, Lisa St Aubin de - *Otto: A Novel*
NS - v134 - i4724 - Jan 24 2005 - p54(1) [501+]

Terborgh, John - *Requiem for Nature*
SciTech - v28 - i4 - Dec 2004 - p58(1) [51-500]

Terkel, Studs - *Hope Dies Last: Keeping Faith in Difficult Times*
R&R Bk N - v19 - i1 - Feb 2004 - p6(1) [51-500]

Terpening, Ron - *League of Shadows*
LJ - v129 - i20 - Dec 1 2004 - p103(2) [51-500]

Terpstra, John - *Disarmament*
CBRA - Annual 2003 - p233(1) [501+]
Hardening Linux
SciTech - v28 - i4 - Dec 2004 - p25(1) [51-500]

Terrace, Vincent - *Radio Program Openings and Closings, 1931-1972*
R&R Bk N - v19 - i1 - Feb 2004 - p223(1) [51-500]
The Television Crime Fighters Factbook: Over 9,800 Details from 301 Programs, 1937-2003
Ref Rev - Sept 2004 - pNA [501+]

Terraciano, Kevin - *The Mixtecs of Colonial Oaxaca: Nudzahui History, Sixteenth through Eighteenth Centuries*
HAHR - v84 - i3 - August 2004 - p529(2) [501+]

Terragni, Attilio - *The Terragni Atlas: Built Architecture*
LJ - v130 - i3 - Feb 15 2005 - p128(1) [51-500]

Terraroli, Valerio - *Monumental Sites*
Choice - v42 - i4 - Dec 2004 - p652(1) [1-50]
LJ - v129 - i16 - Oct 1 2004 - p97(1) [51-500]

Terreblanche, Sample - *A History of Inequality in South Africa, 1652-2002*
IJAHS - v37 - i1 - Wntr 2004 - p177-178 [501+]

Terrenoire, David - *Beneath a Panamanian Moon*
BL - v101 - i9-10 - Jan 1 2005 - p829(1) [1-50]
KR - v72 - i23 - Dec 1 2004 - p1124(1) [501+]
PW - v252 - i2 - Jan 10 2005 - p42(1) [51-500]

Terrien, Samuel - *The Psalms: Strophic Structure and Theological Commentary*
TT - v61 - i1 - April 2004 - p130-132 [501+]

Terrill, Ross - *The New Chinese Empire and What It Means for the United States*
Ch Rev Int - v11 - i1 - Spring 2004 - p182(4) [501+]

Terrorism and the Military: International Legal Implications, Proceedings
R&R Bk N - v19 - i1 - Feb 2004 - pNA [51-500]

Terrorism Coverage for Commercial Lines
R&R Bk N - v19 - i2 - May 2004 - p124 [51-500]

Terrorists Dossiers
LibMed - v22 - i7 - April-May 2004 - p84(1) [501+]

Terry, Fiona - *Condemned to Repeat? The Paradox of Humanitarian Action*
JPR - v41 - i5 - Sept 2004 - p647-647 [501+]

Terterov, Marat - *Doing Business with Croatia, 2nd Ed.*
R&R Bk N - v19 - i2 - May 2004 - p112(1) [51-500]
Doing Business with Kazakhstan
R&R Bk N - v19 - i4 - Nov 2004 - p109(1) [51-500]
Doing Business with Malta
R&R Bk N - v19 - i1 - Feb 2004 - p107(1) [51-500]
Doing Business with Serbia and Montenegro
R&R Bk N - v19 - i4 - Nov 2004 - p109(1) [51-500]

Teschke, Benno - *The Myth of 1648: Class, Geopolitics and the Making of Modern International Relations*
J Soc H - v38 - i1 - Fall 2004 - p213(3) [501+]

Tesich, Steve - *Karoo*
NYTBR - August 8 2004 - p20 [501+]

Teske, Paul - *Regulation in the States*
Choice - v42 - i4 - Dec 2004 - p729(2) [1-50]
Law&PolBR - June 2004 - p465(4) [501+]

Teslenko, Tatiana - *Feminist Utopian Novels of the 1970s: Joanna Russ & Dorothy Bryant*
SFS - v31 - i2 - July 2004 - p324-326 [501+]

Tessem, Bjornar - *Eighth Scandinavian Conference on Artificial Intelligence, SCAI'03: Proceedings*
SciTech - v28 - i3 - Sept 2004 - p15(1) [501+]

Tessier, Vanna - *Peppermint Night*
CBRA - Annual 2003 - p234(1) [51-500]

Tessitore, John - *Extraordinary American Writers*
y SLJ - v50 - i9 - Sept 2004 - p232(1) [51-500]

Testa, Bernard - *Hydrolosis in Drug and Prodrug Metabolism: Chemistry, Biochemistry, and Enzymology*
SciTech - v28 - i1 - March 2004 - p124(1) [51-500]

Testa, Carlo - *Masters of Two Arts: Re-Creation of European Literatures in Italian Cinema*
FQ - v57 - i2 - Winter 2003 - p58(2) [501+]
R&R Bk N - v19 - i1 - Feb 2004 - p224(1) [51-500]

Testa, David Del - *Global History: Cultural Encounters from Antiquity to the Present*
c LibMed - v23 - i3 - Nov-Dec 2004 - p82(1) [51-500]

Testa, Maria - *Becoming Joe DiMaggio (Illus. by Hunt, Scott)*
c RT - v57 - Oct 2003 - p176 [1-50]

Tester, Royston - *Summat Else*
Globe & Mail - Dec 11 2004 - pD49 [501+]

Testi, Arnaldo - *La formazione degli Stati Uniti*
JAH - v91 - i2 - Sept 2004 - p602(1) [501+]

Testing and Failure Analysis, ISTFA 03: Proceedings
SciTech - v28 - i1 - March 2004 - p137(1) [51-500]

Tetreault, Mary Ann - *Gods, Guns, and Globalization: Religious Radicalism and International Political Economy*
R&R Bk N - v19 - i4 - Nov 2004 - p108(1) [51-500]

Tetworth, Charles - *Wielding Power*
Parabola - v28 - i4 - Winter 2003 - p115-116 [501+]

Tetzner, Lisa - *The Black Brothers: A Novel in Pictures (Illus. by Binder, Hannes)*
y BL - v101 - i1 - Sept 1 2004 - p109(1) [1-50]
c CH Bwatch - v14 - i9 - Sept 2004 - p5(1) [51-500]
c KR - v72 - i19 - Oct 1 2004 - p970(1) [51-500]
y SLJ - v50 - i11 - Nov 2004 - p154(2) [51-500]

Teuscher, Christof - *Alan Turing: Life and Legacy of a Great Thinker*
TimHES - v0 - i1660 - Oct 1 2004 - p22(2) [501+]

Tew, Philip - *The Contemporary British Novel: From John Fowles to Zadie Smith*
TLS - i5294 - Sept 17 2004 - p30(1) [501+]

Tewinkel, Wim - *Salish Elders*
CBRA - Annual 2003 - p370(2) [501+]

Texley, Juliana - *Investigating Safely: A Guide for High School Teachers*
SB - v40 - i6 - Nov-Dec 2004 - p248(1) [501+]
SciTech - v28 - i3 - Sept 2004 - p14(1) [501+]

Tezuka, Osamu - *Buddha, Vol. 1 (Illus. by Tezuka, Osamu)*
Globe & Mail - August 14 2004 - pD6 [501+]
Buddha, Vol. 2 (Illus. by Tezuka, Osamu)
Globe & Mail - August 14 2004 - pD6 [501+]
Buddha, Vol. 3 (Illus. by Tezuka, Osamu)
Globe & Mail - August 14 2004 - pD6 [501+]
Buddha, Vol. 4 (Illus. by Tezuka, Osamu)
Globe & Mail - August 14 2004 - pD6 [501+]

Tguieff, Pierre-Andre - *Rising from the Muck: The New Anti-Semitism in Europe*
MEJ - v58 - i4 - Autumn 2004 - p708(1) [501+]

Thacher, Eric F. - *Solar Car Primer*
SciTech - v28 - i1 - March 2004 - p167(1) [51-500]

Thacker, Andrew - *Moving through Modernity: Space and Geography in Modernism*
RES - v55 - i221 - Sept 2004 - p637(3) [501+]

Thackeray, Frank W. - *Events that Changed Great Britain from 1066 to 1714*
Choice - v42 - i4 - Dec 2004 - p726(1) [1-50]

Thackeray, William Makepeace - *Barry Lyndon (Read by Cormack, John). Audiobook Review*
BL - v100 - i22 - August 2004 - p1952(1) [51-500]
c Kliatt - v38 - i4 - July 2004 - p48(1) [51-500]
The History of Henry Esmond (Illus. by Griffin, Gordon). Audiobook Review
y Kliatt - v39 - i1 - Jan 2005 - p44(1) [51-500]

Thackray, Arnold - *Arnold O. Beckman: One Hundred Years of Excellence*
BHR - v78 - i2 - Summer 2004 - p319(3) [501+]

Thackway, Melissa - *Africa Shoots Back: Alternative Perspective in Sub-Saharan Francophone African Film*
Choice - v41 - i11-12 - July-August 2004 - p2052(1) [501+]

Thaden, Louise - *High, Wide, and Frightened*
LJ - v129 - i13 - August 2004 - p131(1) [51-500]

Thai, Thuan - *.NET Framework Essentials, 3rd Ed.*
SciTech - v28 - i4 - Dec 2004 - p19(1) [51-500]

Thakur, Ramesh - *South Asia in the World: Problem Solving Perspectives on Security, Sustainable Development, and Good Governance*
R&R Bk N - v19 - i3 - August 2004 - p53(1) [51-500]

Thalmann, Philippe - *The Dynamics of Freight Transport Development: A UK and Swiss Comparison*
R&R Bk N - v19 - i3 - August 2004 - p121(1) [51-500]

Tham, Claire - *The Gunpowder Trail and Other Stories*
WLT - v78 - i3-4 - Sept-Dec 2004 - p90(1) [501+]

Thang, Leng Leng - *Generations in Touch: Linking the Old and Young in a Tokyo Neighborhood*
JAS - v63 - i2 - May 2004 - p514(3) [501+]
Old Challenges, New Strategies: Women, Work, and Family in Contemporary Asia
Choice - v42 - i4 - Dec 2004 - p742(1) [1-50]
R&R Bk N - v19 - i3 - August 2004 - p116(1) [51-500]

Thapa, Prem Jung - *Modelling the Efficiency of Family and Hired Labour: Illustrations from Nepalese Agriculture*
JEL - v42 - i1 - March 2004 - p312(1) [501+]

Thapar, Valmik - *Battling for Survival: India's Wilderness Over Two Centuries*
R&R Bk N - v19 - i1 - Feb 2004 - p47(1) [51-500]

Tharlet, Eve - *Nancy, the Little Gosling (Illus. by Tharlet, Eve)*
c KR - v72 - i24 - Dec 15 2004 - p1209(1) [51-500]
c PW - v252 - i5 - Jan 31 2005 - p68(1) [51-500]
c SLJ - v51 - i2 - Feb 2005 - p110(1) [51-500]

Tharoor, Shashi - *Nehru: The Invention of India*
BW - v34 - i1 - Jan 4 2004 - p2(1) [501+]
New R - Feb 14 2005 - p25 [501+]

Thatcher, Ian D. - *Trotsky*
Russ Rev - v63 - i3 - July 2004 - pNA [501+]

Thatcher, Mark - *The Politics of Delegation*
R&R Bk N - v19 - i1 - Feb 2004 - pNA [501+]

Thatcher, Murcia Rebecca - *E. B. White*
y SLJ - v51 - i1 - Jan 2005 - p140(1) [51-500]

Thathachar, M.A.L. - *Networks of Learning Automata: Techniques for Online Stochastic Optimization*
SciTech - v28 - i1 - March 2004 - p134(1) [51-500]

That's Life
LibMed - v23 - i3 - Nov-Dec 2004 - p65(1) [51-500]

Thay, Edrick - *Haunted Houses*
CBRA - Annual 2003 - p97(1) [51-500]

Thayer, Anne - *Penitence, Preaching and the Coming of the Reformation*
Six Ct J - v35 - i1 - Spring 2004 - p187(3) [501+]

Thayer, Cynthia - *A Brief Lunacy*
BL - v101 - i9-10 - Jan 1 2005 - p823(1) [1-50]
KR - v73 - i1 - Jan 1 2005 - p20(1) [501+]
LJ - v130 - i2 - Feb 1 2005 - p71(2) [51-500]
PW - v252 - i5 - Jan 31 2005 - p49(1) [51-500]

Thayer, Jane - *Part-Time Dog (Illus. by McCue, Lisa)*
c BL - v100 - i22 - August 2004 - p1946(1) [51-500]
c SLJ - v50 - i9 - Sept 2004 - p182(1) [51-500]

Thayer, Nancy - *The Hot Flash Club (Read by MacDuffie, Carrington). Audiobook Review*
BL - v100 - i21 - July 2004 - p1856(1) [1-50]
The Hot Flash Club Strikes Again
BL - v101 - i6 - Nov 15 2004 - p532(1) [51-500]
KR - v72 - i22 - Nov 15 2004 - p1068(1) [501+]
PW - v251 - i46 - Nov 15 2004 - p42(1) [51-500]

Thayer, Tanya - *Spending Money*
TC Math - v11 - i2 - Sept 2004 - p110(1) [51-500]

Theall, Donald F. - *The Virtual Marshall McLuhan*
Can Lit - i181 - Summer 2004 - p179-181 [501+]

Thede, Les - *Practical Analog and Digital Filter Design*
SciTech - v28 - i4 - Dec 2004 - p157(1) [51-500]

Thein, Myat - *Economic Development of Mayanmar*
Choice - v42 - i7 - March 2005 - p1277(1) [51-500]

Theisen, Bianca - *Silenced Facts: Media Montages in Contemporary Austrian Literature*
Ger Q - v77 - i1 - Wntr 2004 - p111(3) [501+]

Theissen, Gerd - *The Quest for the Plausible Jesus: the Question of Criteria*
TLS - i5264 - Feb 20 2004 - p32-32 [501+]

Thelen, Laurie - *Essentials of Elementary School Library Management*
LibMed - v22 - i5 - Feb 2004 - p85(1) [501+]

Thelen, Laurie Noble - *Essentials of Elementary Library Management*
Teach Lib - v32 - i3 - Feb 2005 - p38(2) [51-500]

Thelin, John R. - *A History of American Higher Eduaction*
Choice - v42 - i5 - Jan 2005 - p906(1) [1-50]
A History of American Higher Education
HRNB - v33 - i1 - Fall 2004 - p6(1) [501+]
R&R Bk N - v19 - i3 - August 2004 - p214(1) [1-50]
TCR - v107 - i2 - Feb 2005 - p284(4) [501+]

Themelis, Nikos - *I Analambi*
TLS - i5267 - March 12 2004 - p21-22 [501+]
I Anatropi
TLS - i5267 - March 12 2004 - p21-22 [501+]
I Anazitisi
TLS - i5267 - March 12 2004 - p21-22 [501+]

Themerson, Stefan - *Tom Harris*
Globe & Mail - Nov 13 2004 - pD21 [501+]
LJ - v129 - i19 - Nov 15 2004 - p103(1) [501+]

Theml, Harald - *Color Atlas of Hematology: Practical Microscopic and Clinical Diagnosis, 2nd. Rev. Ed.*
SciTech - v28 - i3 - Sept 2004 - p104(1) [51-500]

Thenaud, Jean - *Le Triumphe des vertuz*
FS - v58 - i1 - Jan 2004 - p84(1) [501+]

Thenell, Jan - *The Library's Crisis Communications Planner: A PR Guide for Handling Every Emergency*
LJ - v129 - i19 - Nov 15 2004 - p92(1) [51-500]
R&R Bk N - v19 - i4 - Nov 2004 - p256(1) [501+]

Theo - *Theo: Oscar and Hoo Forever (Illus. by Dudok de Wit, Michael)*
c KR - v73 - i2 - Jan 15 2005 - p126(1) [51-500]

Theobald, Theo - *Shut Up and Listen: The Truth about How to Communicate at Work*
R&R Bk N - v19 - i3 - August 2004 - p102(1) [501+]

Theobald, William F. - *Global Tourism, 3rd ed.*
Choice - v42 - i5 - Jan 2005 - p899(1) [1-50]

Theodoropoulos, David I. - *Invasion Biology: Critique of a Pseudoscience*
QRB - v79 - i3 - Sept 2004 - p328(2) [501+]

Theodoulou, Stella Z. - *The Art of the Game: Understanding American Public Policy Making*
R&R Bk N - v19 - i1 - Feb 2004 - pNA [501+]

Theoharis, Athan - *The FBI and American Democracy: A Brief Criticial History*
BW - v34 - i44 - Oct 31 2004 - p6(1) [501+]

Theoharis, Athan G. - *The FBI and American Democracy: A Brief Critical History*
CHE - v51 - i20 - Jan 21 2005 - pB12-B14 [501+]
LJ - v129 - i18 - Nov 1 2004 - p108(1) [51-500]

Theoharis, Jeanne - *Freedom North: Black Freedom Struggle Outside the South, 1940-1980*
JAH - v91 - i2 - Sept 2004 - p710(2) [501+]

Ther, Philipp - *Redrawing Nations: Ethnic Cleansing in East-Central Europe, 1944-1948*
CEH - v37 - i3 - Summer 2004 - p482(4) [501+]

Theret, Bruno - *Protection sociale et federalisme dans le miroir de l'Amerique du Nord*
Can Hist R - v85 - i3 - Sept 2004 - p558(4) [501+]

Therivel, Riki - *Strategic Environmental Assessment in Action*
SciTech - v28 - i3 - Sept 2004 - p145(1) [51-500]

Thernstrom, Abigail - *No Excuses: Closing the Racial Gap in Learning*
AJE - v111 - i1 - Nov 2004 - p127(5) [501+]
Inst - v114 - i4 - Nov-Dec 2004 - p9(1) [501+]
NYRB - v51 - i19 - Dec 2 2004 - p29(4) [501+]
Soc - v41 - i6 - Sept-Oct 2004 - p80(6) [501+]

Theroux, Paul - *Blinding Light*
KR - v73 - i5 - March 1 2005 - p258(1) [501+]
Stranger at the Palazzo D'Oro (Read by Nolan, Nathan). Audiobook Review
Kliatt - v38 - i5 - Sept 2004 - p65(2) [51-500]
Sunrise with Seamonsters
BW - v34 - i36 - Sept 5 2004 - p13(1) [501+]

Thesman, Jean - *Cattail Moon*
c SLJ - v50 - i11 - Nov 2004 - p65(2) [51-500]
Singer
y HB - v81 - i2 - March-April 2005 - p208(2) [51-500]
y Kliatt - v39 - i2 - March 2005 - p16(1) [51-500]

Theuerkorn, Fenix - *Lightweight Enterprise Architectures*
SciTech - v28 - i4 - Dec 2004 - p31(1) [51-500]

Thibodeau, Gary A. - *Structure and Function of the Body, 12th Ed.*
SciTech - v28 - i1 - March 2004 - p71(1) [51-500]

Thickett, D. - *Selection of Materials for the Storage or Display of Museum Objects*
R&R Bk N - v19 - i4 - Nov 2004 - p1(1) [501+]

Thiederman, Sondra - *Making Diversity Work: 7 Steps for Defeating Bias in the Workplace*
HR Mag - v50 - i2 - Feb 2005 - pS6(1) [501+]
R&R Bk N - v19 - i1 - Feb 2004 - p99(1) [1-50]

Thiel, R. - *Ammonius Hermeae: Commentaria in Quinque Voces Porphyrii. Ubersetzt von Pomponius Gauricus*
Class R - v54 - i2 - Nov 2004 - p569-569 [501+]

Thiele, Colin - *Twilight Ghost*
y Magpies - v19 - i5 - Nov 2004 - p37(1) [501+]

Thieman, William J. - *Introduction to Biotechnology*
Am Bio T - v66 - i8 - Oct 2004 - p580(1) [501+]

Thieme, Horst R. - *Mathematics in Population Biology*
SIAM Rev - v46 - i2 - June 2004 - p356-358 [501+]

Thieme, John - *Post-Colonial Studies: The Essential Glossary*
Choice - v41 - i11-12 - July-August 2004 - p2029(1) [501+]

Thieme, Richard - *Islands in the Clickstream: Reflections on Life in Virtual World*
SciTech - v28 - i4 - Dec 2004 - p129 [51-500]

Thiesing, Lisa - *The Aliens Are Coming! (Illus. by Thiesing, Lisa)*
c BL - v101 - i1 - Sept 1 2004 - p137(1) [51-500]
c CH Bwatch - v14 - i9 - Sept 2004 - p5(1) [51-500]
c KR - v72 - i14 - July 15 2004 - p694(1) [51-500]
c SLJ - v50 - i8 - August 2004 - p97(1) [51-500]

Thiessen, Diane - *Exploring Mathematics through Literature: Articles and Lessons for Prekindergarten through Grade 8*
TC Math - v11 - i4 - Nov 2004 - p239(1) [501+]

Thieves' Dozen
NYT - August 8 2004 - p10 [501+]

Thill, Mary Kay - *Wablenica: Tale of a Lakotah Orphan*
c CH Bwatch - v14 - i7 - July 2004 - p7(1) [501+]

Thimmesh, Catherine - *Madam President: The Extraordinary True (and Evolving) Story of Women in Politics*
c BL - v101 - i3 - Oct 1 2004 - p327(1) [501+]
Madam President: The Extraordinary, True (and Evolving) Story of Women in Politics (Illus. by Jones, Douglas B.)
c CCB-B - v58 - i3 - Nov 2004 - p111(2) [501+]
c KR - v72 - i13 - July 1 2004 - p638(1) [501+]
c NYTBR - Oct 17 2004 - p20 [501+]
c PW - v251 - i31 - August 2 2004 - p70(2) [501+]
y SLJ - v50 - i11 - Nov 2004 - p174(1) [51-500]
y VOYA - v27 - i4 - Oct 2004 - p332(1) [51-500]
The Sky's the Limit: Stories of Discovery by Women and Girls
y Kliatt - v39 - i2 - March 2005 - p34(2) [501+]

Thinking Reader 1.0
LibMed - v23 - i3 - Nov-Dec 2004 - p65(1) [51-500]

Thio, Alex - *Deviant Behavior, 7th Ed.*
R&R Bk N - v19 - i1 - Feb 2004 - p123(1) [51-500]

Thirlwall, A.P. - *Trade, Balance of Payments and Exchange Rate Policy in Developing Countries*
JEL - v41 - i4 - Dec 2003 - p1414(1) [501+]

Thirlwell, Angela - *William and Lucy: The Other Rossettis*
Nine-C Lit - v59 - i2 - Sept 2004 - p271(3) [501+]
Sew R - v112 - i3 - Summer 2004 - pXCIII-XCVI [501+]

Thirty Years of Adventure: A Celebration of Dungeons and Dragons
NW - Nov 22 2004 - p14 [1-50]

Thissen, W.A.H. - *Critical Infrastructures: State of the Art in Research and Application, Proceedings*
R&R Bk N - v19 - i1 - Feb 2004 - p80(1) [51-500]

Thivel, A. - *Le Normal et la Pathologique Dans la Collection Hippocratique. Actes du Xeme Colloque International Hippocratique*
Class R - v54 - i2 - Nov 2004 - p565-566 [501+]

Thom, James Alexander - *The Red Heart*
LJ - v129 - i18 - Nov 1 2004 - p135(1) [501+]

Thomas, Andrew Peyton - *The People v. Harvard Law: How America's Oldest Law School Turned Its Back on Free Speech*
PW - v252 - i9 - Feb 28 2005 - p57(1) [51-500]

Thomas, Beth - *Domestic Life in Wales. By S. Minwel Tibbott*
Folkl - v115 - i2 - August 2004 - p240(2) [501+]

Thomas, Brian - *Encyclopedia of Applied Plant Sciences*
E-Streams - June 2004 - pNA [501+]

Thomas, Cameron - *Mystery of the Lake (Illus. by Krystoforski, Andrej)*
c SLJ - v50 - i9 - Sept 2004 - p182(1) [51-500]
Shipwrecked on the Island of Skree (Illus. by Krystoforski, Andrej)
c SLJ - v50 - i9 - Sept 2004 - p182(1) [51-500]
The Utt Jungle Airline (Illus. by Krystoforski, Andrej)
c CH Bwatch - v14 - i7 - July 2004 - p5(1) [51-500]

Thomas, Carolyn - *Empires of Light: Edison, Tesla, Westinghouse and the Race to electricity the World*
T&C - v45 - i3 - July 2004 - p652-653 [501+]

Thomas, Christine M. - *The Acts of Peter, Gospel Literature, and the Ancient Novel: Rewriting the Past*
JR - v84 - i3 - July 2004 - p451(2) [501+]

Thomas, Claude Anshin - *At Hell's Gate: A Soldier's Journey from War to Peace*
PW - v251 - i30 - July 26 2004 - p48(1) [501+]

Thomas, Clive S. - *Research Guide to U.S. and International Interest Groups*
Choice - v42 - i4 - Dec 2004 - p643(1) [1-50]
Choice - v42 - i4 - Dec 2004 - p643(1) [1-50]
R&R Bk N - v19 - i3 - August 2004 - p179(1) [501+]

Thomas, Cullen - *U.S. National Debate Topic, 2004-2005: The United Nations*
y Ref Rev - Sept 2004 - pNA [501+]
R&R Bk N - v19 - i3 - August 2004 - p188(1) [501+]

Thomas, Daniel C. - *The Helsinki Effect: International Norms, Human Rights, and the Demise of Communism*
Slav R - v63 - i3 - Fall 2004 - p618-618 [501+]

Thomas, Dave (b. 1956 -) - *Pragmatic Version Control with CVS*
SciTech - v28 - i3 - Sept 2004 - p27(1) [1-50]
Programming Ruby: The Pragmatic Programmer's Guide, 2nd Ed.
Bwatch - Dec 2004 - pNA [51-500]

Thomas, David (1956 -) - *Programming Ruby: The Pragmatic Programmer's Guide, 2nd Ed.*
SciTech - v28 - i4 - Dec 2004 - p19(1) [1-50]

Thomas, David (b. 1948 -) - *A Faithful Presence: Essays for Kenneth Cragg*
IBMR - v28 - i4 - Oct 2004 - p180(2) [501+]

Thomas, David C. - *Cultural Intelligence: People Skills for Global Business*
HR Mag - v49 - i7 - July 2004 - pS10(1) [51-500]
R&R Bk N - v19 - i3 - August 2004 - p83(1) [51-500]

Thomas, David N. - *Frozen Oceans: The Floating World of Pack Ice*
TimHES - v0 - i1677 - Feb 4 2005 - p28(1) [501+]

Thomas, David Piers - *Reading Doctors' Writing: Race, Politics and Power in Indigenous Health Research, 1870-1969*
SciTech - v28 - i3 - Sept 2004 - p6(1) [501+]

Thomas, David Wayne - *Cultivating Victorians: Liberal Culture and the Aesthetic*
Choice - v41 - i11-12 - July-August 2004 - p2047(1) [501+]

Thomas De La Pena, Carolyn - *The Body Electric: How Strange Machines Built the Modern American*
AHR - v109 - i2 - April 2004 - p539(2) [501+]
Shooting Cowboys and Indians: Silent Western Films, American Culture, and the Birth of Hollywood
BHR - v78 - i3 - Autumn 2004 - p551(3) [501+]

Thomas, Deborah E. - *The Bramble Thicket*
c CH Bwatch - v14 - i8 - August 2004 - p7(1) [51-500]

Thomas, Donald - *The Enemy Within: Hucksters, Racketeers, Deserters, and Civilians During the Second World War*
Choice - v42 - i5 - Jan 2005 - p921(2) [1-50]

Thomas, Dylan - *A Child's Christmas in Wales (Illus. by Hyman, Trina Schart)*
c BW - v34 - i50 - Dec 12 2004 - p9(1) [501+]
A Child's Christmas in Wales (Illus. by Raschka, Chris)
c BL - v101 - i3 - Oct 1 2004 - p325(2) [51-500]
c Globe & Mail - Dec 11 2004 - pD28 [51-500]
c HB - v80 - i6 - Nov-Dec 2004 - p665(1) [51-500]
c KR - v72 - i21 - Nov 1 2004 - p1054(1) [51-500]
c PW - v251 - i39 - Sept 27 2004 - p60(1) [51-500]
c NYTBR - Nov 14 2004 - p28(L) [501+]

Thomas, Edwin W. - *Blighted Cliffs*
DroRevMy - v24 - i4 - July-August 2004 - p13(1) [51-500]

Thomas, Elisabeth Louise - *Emmanuel Levinas: Ethics, Justice, and the Human Beyond Being*
R&R Bk N - v20 - i1 - Feb 2005 - p4(1) [51-500]

Thomas, Eliza - *The Red Blanket (Illus. by Cepeda, Joe)*
c SLJ - v50 - i7 - July 2004 - p89(1) [51-500]

Thomas, Elizabeth Marshall - *The Tribe of Tiger: Cats and Their Culture*
HM - v310 - i1858 - March 2005 - p95(7) [501+]

Thomas, Evan - *Election 2004: How Bush Won and What You Can Expect in the Future*
LJ - v130 - i3 - Feb 15 2005 - p147(2) [51-500]
John Paul Jones: Sailor, Hero, Father of the American Navy
NYTBR - July 18 2004 - p20 [501+]

Thomas Food and Beverage Market Place, 3rd. Ed., Vols. 1-3
R&R Bk N - v19 - i1 - Feb 2004 - p253(1) [51-500]

Thomas, Garen Eileen - *Santa's Kwanzaa (Illus. by Francis, Guy)*
c BL - v101 - i2 - Sept 15 2004 - p254(1) [51-500]
c KR - v72 - i21 - Nov 1 2004 - p1054(1) [51-500]
c PW - v251 - i39 - Sept 27 2004 - p61(1) [51-500]

Thomas, Gareth - *Fundamentals of Medicinal Chemistry*
SciTech - v28 - i1 - March 2004 - p125(1) [1-50]
Medicinal Chemistry-An Introduction Fundamentals of Medicinal Chemistry
J Chem Ed - v81 - i9 - Sept 2004 - p1271-1272 [501+]

Thomas, Gerald Lamont - *African American Preaching: The Contribution of Dr. Gardner C. Taylor*
R&R Bk N - v19 - i3 - August 2004 - p27(1) [1-50]

Thomas-Graham, Pamela - *Orange Crushed: An Ivy League Mystery*
Black Iss - v6 - i5 - Sept-Oct 2004 - p50(2) [501+]

Thomas, Harry - *Talking with Poets*
South R - v39 - i1 - Winter 2003 - p219 [501+]

Thomas, Helen - *The Body, Dance, and Cultural Theory*
R&R Bk N - v19 - i1 - Feb 2004 - p75(1) [51-500]

Thomas, Hugh - *Rivers of Gold: The Rise of the Spanish Empire, from Columbus to Magellan*
BW - v34 - i30 - July 25 2004 - p4(1) [501+]
Bwatch - Nov 2004 - pNA [51-500]
Choice - v42 - i6 - Feb 2005 - p1078(1) [51-500]
HM - v309 - i1850 - July 2004 - p83(2) [501+]
LJ - v129 - i13 - August 2004 - p95(2) [501+]
NYRB - v51 - i17 - Nov 4 2004 - p47(5) [501+]
NYTBR - July 25 2004 - p10 [501+]
NYTBR - August 1 2004 - p14 [501+]
NYTBR - August 8 2004 - p18 [501+]

Thomas, Hugh M. - *The English and the Normans: Ethnic Hostility, Assimilation, and Identity, 1066-c. 1220*
Choice - v41 - i7 - March 2004 - p1360(1) [501+]
TLS - i5287 - July 30 2004 - p11(1) [501+]

Thomas, Jack Ward - *Jack Ward Thomas: The Journals of a Forest Service Chief*
E-Streams - July 2004 - pNA [501+]
SciTech - v28 - i3 - Sept 2004 - p130(1) [51-500]

Thomas, Jay C. - *Comprehensive Handbook of Psychological Assessment Volume 4: Industrial and Organizational Assessment*
Per Psy - v57 - i3 - Autumn 2004 - p837(5) [501+]

Thomas, Jeanette A. - *Echolocation in Bats and Dolphins*
E-Streams - July 2004 - pNA [501+]
QRB - v79 - i4 - Dec 2004 - p458(1) [51-500]

Thomas, Jeannie B. - *Naked Barbies, Warrior Joes and Other Forms of Visible Gender*
JPC - v38 - i2 - Nov 2004 - p438(2) [501+]
Naked Barbies, Warrior Joes, and Other Forms of Visible Gender
NWSA Jnl - v16 - i3 - Fall 2004 - p235(3) [501+]
Wom R Bks - v21 - i12 - Sept 2004 - p23(2) [501+]

Thomas, Jeffrey - *Everybody Scream*
  PW - v251 - i45 - Nov 8 2004 - p41(1) [501+]
Honey Is Sweeter Than Blood
  ChrSFF&H - v26 - i9 - Sept 2004 - p31(1) [51-500]

Thomas, Jodi - *Finding Mary Blaine*
  PW - v251 - i30 - July 26 2004 - p43(1) [501+]
A Texan's Luck
  y BL - v101 - i6 - Nov 15 2004 - p569(2) [51-500]
  PW - v251 - i41 - Oct 11 2004 - p61(2) [51-500]

Thomas, John Ira - *The Fairer Sex: A Tale of Shades and Angels, vol. 1.*
  y BL - v101 - i3 - Oct 1 2004 - p320(1) [51-500]
Man is Vox: Paingels (Illus. by Allen, Carter)
  y BL - v101 - i2 - Sept 15 2004 - p217(1) [501+]

Thomas, Joyce Carol - *The Gospel Cinderella (Illus. by Diaz, David)*
  c Black Iss - v6 - i4 - July-August 2004 - p61(1) [1-50]
Linda Brown, You Are Not Alone: The Brown v. Board of Education Decision: A Collection (Illus. by James, Curtis)
  y LibMed - v22 - i5 - Feb 2004 - p80(1) [501+]
  y SLJ - v50 - i10 - Oct 2004 - p68(1) [51-500]
The Skull Talks Back and Other Haunting Tales (Illus. by Jenkins, Leonard)
  c CCB-B - v58 - i1 - Sept 2004 - p42(1) [51-500]
What's the Hurry, Fox? And Other Animal Stories (Illus. by Collier, Bryan)
  c CCB-B - v57 - i11 - July-August 2004 - p487(1) [501+]

Thomas, Julian - *Archaeology and Modernity*
  R&R Bk N - v19 - i4 - Nov 2004 - p29(1) [501+]

Thomas, Kecia M. - *Diversity Dynamics in the Workplace*
  R&R Bk N - v19 - i4 - Nov 2004 - p216(1) [501+]

Thomas, Keltie - *Blades, Boards and Scooters (Illus. by Attoe, Steve)*
  c CBRA - Annual 2003 - p561(2) [51-500]
How Baseball Works (Illus. by Hall, Greg)
  c Globe & Mail - July 3 2004 - pD11 [501+]
  c LibMed - v23 - i3 - Nov-Dec 2004 - p88(1) [51-500]
  c SLJ - v50 - i11 - Nov 2004 - p174(1) [51-500]
The Kids Guide to Money Cent$
  c SLJ - v50 - i7 - July 2004 - p128(1) [51-500]

Thomas, Lorenzo - *Dancing on Main Street*
  Bl S - v34 - i3 - Fall 2004 - p75-75 [501+]
  Black Iss - v6 - i5 - Sept-Oct 2004 - p55(1) [501+]

Thomas, Marlo - *Thanks and Giving: All Year Long*
  c BL - v101 - i6 - Nov 15 2004 - p580(1) [51-500]
  c KR - v72 - i21 - Nov 1 2004 - p1046(1) [51-500]
  c PW - v251 - i47 - Nov 22 2004 - p58(1) [51-500]
  c SLJ - v51 - i2 - Feb 2005 - p128(2) [51-500]

Thomas, Martin - *The Artificial Horizon: Imaging the Blue Mountains*
  AHS - v35 - i124 - Oct 2004 - p416(2) [501+]

Thomas, Maureen - *Architectures of Illusion: From Motion Pictures to Navigable Interactive Environments*
  R&R Bk N - v19 - i1 - Feb 2004 - p202(1) [51-500]

Thomas, Michael A. - *Hat Dance*
  Roundup M - v12 - i1 - Oct 2004 - p32(2) [51-500]

Thomas, Nancy Pickering - *Information Literacy and Information Skills Instruction: Applying Research to Practice in the School Library Media Center, 2nd Ed.*
  R&R Bk N - v19 - i4 - Nov 2004 - p257(1) [501+]

Thomas, Neil - *'Diu Crone' and the Medieval Arthurian Cycle*
  FS - v58 - i1 - Jan 2004 - p78(2) [501+]

Thomas, Nicholas - *Cook*
  Bwatch - v26 - i7 - July 2004 - p11(1) [51-500]
Re-Orienting Australia-China Relations: 1972 to the Present
  R&R Bk N - v19 - i3 - August 2004 - p60(1) [51-500]

Thomas, Nick - *Protest Movements in 1960s West Germany: A Social History of Dissent and Democracy*
  AHR - v109 - i3 - June 2004 - p993(1) [501+]
  GSR - v27 - i3 - Oct 2004 - p663(2) [501+]

Thomas, Nicola - *Advanced Renal Care*
  SciTech - v28 - i4 - Dec 2004 - p105(1) [51-500]

Thomas, Norman E. - *International Mission Bibliography, 1960-2000*
  IBMR - v28 - i3 - July 2004 - p136(1) [501+]
  R&R Bk N - v19 - i1 - Feb 2004 - p22(1) [51-500]

Thomas, P.L. - *Numbers Games: Measuring and Mandating American Education*
  R&R Bk N - v19 - i4 - Nov 2004 - p188(1) [501+]

Thomas, Pat - *Is It Right to Fight?: A First Look at Conflict*
  y TES - v0 - i4586 - June 4 2004 - pssss19(1) [501+]
The Skin I'm In: A First Look At Racism
  y TES - v0 - i4586 - June 4 2004 - pssss19(1) [501+]

Thomas, Peter D.G. - *George III: King and Politicians, 1760-1770*
  AHR - v109 - i4 - Oct 2004 - p1310-1311 [501+]
  HNet - June 2004 - pNA [501+]

Thomas, R. Murray - *Comparing Theories of Child Development, 6th Ed.*
  SciTech - v28 - i3 - Sept 2004 - p3(1) [501+]

Thomas, R. Roosevelt - *Building a House for Diversity*
  HR Mag - v49 - i7 - July 2004 - pS10(1) [51-500]

Thomas, R. S. - *Collected Later Poems*
  Spec - v295 - i9186 - August 28 2004 - p35(1) [501+]

Thomas, Raju G.C. - *Yugoslavia Unraveled: Sovereignty, Self-Determination, Intervention*
  HNet - Sept 2004 - pNA [501+]

Thomas, Rebecca L. - *Popular Series Fiction for K-6 Readers*
  Cur R - v44 - i7 - March 2005 - p12(1) [51-500]

Thomas, Richard - *Counting People In: Changing the Way We Think About Membership and the Church*
  TLS - i5266 - March 5 2004 - p25-25 [501+]

Thomas, Richard K. - *Health Services Planning, 2nd Ed.*
  SciTech - v28 - i1 - March 2004 - p81(1) [51-500]
Society and Health: Sociology for Health Professionals
  SciTech - v28 - i1 - March 2004 - p82(1) [51-500]

Thomas, Rosalind - *Herodotus in Context: Ethnography, Science, and the Art of Persuasion.*
  Isis - v95 - i2 - June 2004 - p286(2) [501+]

Thomas, Scarlett - *Seaside: A Lily Pascale Mystery*
  LJ - v129 - i16 - Oct 1 2004 - p64(1) [51-500]

Thomas, Scott - *Shadows of Flesh*
  ChrSFF&H - v26 - i9 - Sept 2004 - p31(1) [51-500]

Thomas-Slayter, Barbara P. - *Southern Exposure: International Development and the Global South in the Twenty-First Century*
  Choice - v42 - i2 - Oct 2004 - p369(1) [51-500]
  R&R Bk N - v19 - i3 - August 2004 - p111(1) [51-500]

Thomas, Susanna - *Ahmose: Liberator of Egypt*
  c HNet - Oct 2004 - pNA [501+]
Akhenaten and Tutankhamen: The Religious Revolution
  c HNet - Oct 2004 - pNA [501+]
Rameses II: Pharaoh of the New Kingdom
  c HNet - Oct 2004 - pNA [501+]

Thomas, Thomas M. - *OSPF Network Design Solutions, 2nd Ed.*
  SciTech - v28 - i3 - Sept 2004 - p158(1) [501+]

Thomas, Verna - *Invisible Shadows: A Black Woman's Life in Nova Scotia*
  Can Lit - i182 - Autumn 2004 - p178(3) [501+]

Thomas, Volker - *Clinical Issues with Interracial Couples: Theories and Research*
  SciTech - v28 - i1 - March 2004 - p99(1) [51-500]

Thomas, Wes - *Down the Crawfish Hole*
  c SLJ - v50 - i8 - August 2004 - p97(1) [51-500]

Thomas, Will (1958 -) - *Some Danger Involved: A Novel*
  DroRevMy - v24 - i3 - May-June 2004 - p3(2) [501+]

Thomas, William J. - *Never Hitchhike on the Road Less Travelled*
  CBRA - Annual 2003 - p86(1) [51-500]

Thomas, Willie - *Cristoforo: Strange Tales of a Singular Traveller*
  Globe & Mail - Oct 2 2004 - pD24 [501+]

Thomas Yaccato, Joanne - *The 80Minority: Reaching the Real World of Women Consumers*
  CBRA - Annual 2003 - p390(1) [51-500]

Thomason-Carroll, Kristi L. - *Young Adult's Guide to Business Communications*
  c SLJ - v50 - i7 - July 2004 - p122(1) [51-500]
  y VOYA - v27 - i3 - August 2004 - p237(1) [1-50]

Thomasson, Amie L. - *Fiction and Metaphysics*
  Phil R - v112 - i3 - July 2003 - p427(5) [501+]

Thompkins, Toby - *The Real Lives of Strong Black Women: Transcending Myths, Reclaiming Joy*
  BL - v101 - i6 - Nov 15 2004 - p550(1) [51-500]

Thompson, A.K. - *Fruit and Vegetables: Harvesting, Handling and Storage*
  E-Streams - Sept 2004 - pNA [501+]

Thompson, Amy - *Storyteller*
  y Analog - v124 - i6 - June 2004 - p132(6) [501+]

Thompson, Brian - *Devastating Eden: The Search for Utopia in America*
  Spec - v295 - i9180 - July 17 2004 - p30(2) [501+]

Thompson, Bruce - *Exploratory and Confirmatory Factor Analysis: Understanding Concepts and Applications*
  SciTech - v28 - i3 - Sept 2004 - p1(1) [501+]

Thompson, C. Bradley - *Antislavery Political Writings, 1833-1860: A Reader*
  R&R Bk N - v19 - i1 - Feb 2004 - p58(1) [51-500]

Thompson, Chad W. - *Loving Homosexuals as Jesus Would: A Fresh Christian Approach*
  BL - v101 - i6 - Nov 15 2004 - p534(1) [51-500]

Thompson, Charles D. - *The Human Cost of Food: Farmworkers' Lives, Labor, and Advocacy*
  CS - v33 - i2 - March 2004 - p230-231 [501+]

Thompson, Clifford - *Current Biography Yearbook 2003*
  y Ref Rev - July 2004 - pNA [501+]
  R&R Bk N - v19 - i3 - August 2004 - p30(1) [1-50]
World Authors, 1995-2000
  Ref Rev - Sept 2004 - pNA [501+]
  R&R Bk N - v19 - i1 - Feb 2004 - p221(1) [51-500]
  R&USQ - v44 - i1 - Fall 2004 - p96(1) [501+]

Thompson, Colin - *The Great Montefiasco*
  KR - v72 - i24 - Dec 15 2004 - p1209(1) [51-500]
St. John of the Cross: Songs in the Night
  Theol St - v65 - i4 - Dec 2004 - p865(3) [501+]

Thompson, Colleen - *Fatal Error*
  y BL - v101 - i6 - Nov 15 2004 - p570(1) [51-500]
  LJ - v129 - i19 - Nov 15 2004 - p47(1) [501+]

Thompson, Craig - *Blankets*
  JAAL - v48 - i2 - Oct 2004 - p178(2) [501+]
Carnet de Voyage (Illus. by Thompson, Craig)
  BL - v101 - i6 - Nov 15 2004 - p572(1) [51-500]
  BW - v34 - i37 - Sept 12 2004 - p13(1) [501+]
  Kliatt - v38 - i6 - Nov 2004 - p38(1) [51-500]
  PW - v251 - i38 - Sept 20 2004 - p58(1) [51-500]
  c SLJ - v50 - i12 - Dec 2004 - p177(1) [51-500]

Thompson, D.R. - *The Big Ocean: An Underwater Naptime Adventure (Illus. by Thompson, D.R.)*
  c SLJ - v50 - i9 - Sept 2004 - p182(1) [51-500]

Thompson, Damian - *Loose Canon: A Portrait of Brian Brindley*
  Spec - v295 - i9179 - July 10 2004 - p36(1) [501+]

Thompson, Daniel Speed - *The Language of Dissent: Edward Schillenbeeckx on the Crisis of Authority in the Catholic Church*
  Choice - v41 - i7 - March 2004 - p1314(1) [501+]

Thompson, David G. - *The Norwegian Armed Forces and Defense Policy, 1905-1955*
  R&R Bk N - v19 - i4 - Nov 2004 - p252(1) [501+]

Thompson, Douglas N. - *The Real New Economy*
  JEL - v42 - i1 - March 2004 - p258(1) [501+]

Thompson, Dyble - *Cartwheel to the Moon: My Sicilian Childhood*
  LibMed - v22 - i5 - Feb 2004 - p74(1) [501+]

Thompson, F.M.L. - *Gentrification and the Enterprise Culture: Britain 1780-1980*
  J Soc H - v38 - i1 - Fall 2004 - p259(3) [501+]

Thompson, Frances M. - *Ready-to-Use Math Proficiency Lessons & Activities*
  TC Math - v11 - i2 - Sept 2004 - p111(1) [51-500]

Thompson, Gail L. - *Through Ebony Eyes: What Teachers Need to Know but Are Afraid to Ask about African American Students*
  R&R Bk N - v19 - i3 - August 2004 - p229(1) [1-50]
What African American Parents Want Educators to Know
  LibMed - v22 - i4 - Jan 2004 - p87(1) [501+]

Thompson, Graham - *The Business of America: The Cultural Production of a Post-war Nation*
  R&R Bk N - v19 - i3 - August 2004 - p83(1) [51-500]
Male Sexuality under Surveillance: The Office in American Literature
  J Am St - v38 - i1 - April 2004 - p171-172 [501+]

Thompson, Grahame F. - *Between Hierarchies and Markets: The Logic and Limits of Network Forms of Organization*
  AJS - v110 - i1 - July 2004 - p269(3) [501+]

Thompson, Hannah - *Naturalism Redressed: Identity and Clothing in the Novels of Emile Zola*
  TLS - i5301 - Nov 5 2004 - p35(1) [51-500]

Thompson, Harvey - *Who Stole My Customer? Winning Strategies for Creating and Sustaining Customer Loyalty*
  HR Mag - v49 - i8 - August 2004 - p143(2) [501+]

Thompson, Harvey - *Who Stole My Customer? Winning Strategies for Creating and Sustaining Customer Loyalty*
  HR Mag - v50 - i2 - Feb 2005 - pS4(1) [501+]

Thompson, Hunter S. - *Gonzo Redux*
NYTBR - March 13 2005 - p30 [501+]
Hey Rube: Blood Sport, the Bush Doctrine, and the Downward Spiral of Dumbness: Modern History from the Sports Desk
BL - v100 - i21 - July 2004 - p1796(1) [51-500]
LJ - v129 - i13 - August 2004 - p89(1) [501+]
PW - v251 - i28 - July 12 2004 - p58(1) [51-500]

Thompson, J. Kevin - *Handbook of Eating Disorders and Obesity*
SciTech - v28 - i1 - March 2004 - p101(1) [51-500]

Thompson, James - *Applied Theatre: Bewilderment and Beyond*
R&R Bk N - v19 - i1 - Feb 2004 - p228(1) [51-500]

Thompson, Janna - *Taking Responsibility for the Past: Reparations and Historical Justice*
AJPS - v39 - i2 - July 2004 - p469(470) [501+]

Thompson, Jean - *City Boy*
BooChiTr - Feb 1 2004 - p1(2) [501+]

Thompson, Jerry L. - *Truth and Photography: Notes on Looking and Photographing*
R&R Bk N - v19 - i1 - Feb 2004 - p251(1) [51-500]

Thompson, John O. - *Gates of Even*
CBRA - Annual 2003 - p234(1) [51-500]

Thompson, Julia F. - *Hard Time*
y LibMed - v22 - i7 - April-May 2004 - p63(63) [501+]

Thompson, Kate - *Annan Water*
y Sch Lib - v52 - i3 - Autumn 2004 - p163(1) [501+]

Thompson, Kathleen - *Power and Border Lordship in Midieval France: The Country of the Perche, 1000-1226*
Specu - v79 - i3 - July 2004 - p844-846 [501+]

Thompson, Kim - *Epileptic*
BL - v101 - i8 - Dec 15 2004 - p716(1) [51-500]

Thompson, Laura - *Life in a Cold Climate: A Portrait of a Contradictory Woman*
LJ - v129 - i18 - Nov 1 2004 - p85(2) [501+]
Life in a Cold Climate: Nancy Mitford: The Biography
KR - v72 - i15 - August 1 2004 - p735(1) [501+]

Thompson, Lauren - *Little Quack's Bedtime (Illus. by Anderson, Derek)*
c KR - v73 - i2 - Jan 15 2005 - p126(1) [51-500]
c PW - v252 - i7 - Feb 14 2005 - p80(2) [501+]
c SLJ - v51 - i2 - Feb 2005 - p110(1) [51-500]
Polar Bear Night (Illus. by Savage, Stephen)
c BL - v101 - i6 - Nov 15 2004 - p585(1) [51-500]
c HB - v80 - i6 - Nov-Dec 2004 - p703(1) [51-500]
KR - v72 - i20 - Oct 15 2004 - p1014(1) [51-500]
c PW - v251 - i47 - Nov 22 2004 - p59(1) [51-500]
c SLJ - v50 - i11 - Nov 2004 - p118(2) [51-500]

Thompson, Margaret - *Fox Winter*
c CBRA - Annual 2003 - p517(2) [51-500]
Knocking on the Moonlit Door: Reflections on Journeys to Europe and Other Destinations
Globe & Mail - Nov 3 2004 - pT1 [501+]

Thompson, Mary Anne - *The Global Resume and CV Guide*
HR Mag - v49 - i7 - July 2004 - pS12(1) [51-500]
Going Global: Country Career Guide: Your One-Stop Career Resource for 23 Countries
HR Mag - v50 - i2 - Feb 2005 - pS6(1) [501+]

Thompson, Michael - *The Pressured Child: Helping Your Child Find Success in School and Life*
BL - v100 - i22 - August 2004 - p1885(1) [51-500]
Globe & Mail - Sept 4 2004 - pF6 [1-50]

Thompson, Nato - *The Interventionists: Users' Manual for the Creative Disruption of Everyday Life*
Afterimage - v32 - i4 - Jan-Feb 2005 - p15(1) [51-500]

Thompson, Patricia J. - *Fatal Abstractions: The Parallogics of Everyday Life*
R&R Bk N - v19 - i1 - Feb 2004 - p131(1) [51-500]

Thompson, Paul S. - *An Historical Atlas of the Zulu Rebellion of 1906*
J Mil H - v68 - i3 - July 2004 - p974-975 [501+]

Thompson, Peter - *Explore Canada: The Adventurer's Guide*
Bwatch - Dec 2004 - pNA [51-500]

Thompson, Richard - *The Night Walker (Illus. by Springett, Martin)*
c Can Lit - i182 - Autumn 2004 - p125(3) [501+]

Thompson, Robert (1962 -) - *The Broadcast Journalism Handbook: A Television News Survival Guide*
R&R Bk N - v19 - i1 - Feb 2004 - p229(1) [51-500]

Thompson, Robert Bruce - *Building the Perfect PC*
LJ - v130 - i2 - Feb 1 2005 - p110(1) [51-500]

Thompson, Stacy - *Punk Productions: Unfinished Business*
Choice - v42 - i5 - Jan 2005 - p862(2) [1-50]

Thompson, Sue C. - *Reforming Middle Level Education: Considerations for Policy Makers*
R&R Bk N - v19 - i4 - Nov 2004 - p182(1) [501+]

Thompson, Thomas L. - *The Messiah Myth: The Near Eastern Roots of Jesus and David*
KR - v73 - i4 - Feb 15 2005 - p222(1) [501+]

Thompson, Vicki Lewis - *Nerd Gone Wild*
PW - v251 - i51 - Dec 20 2004 - p42(1) [51-500]
The Nerd Who Loved Me
BL - v100 - i22 - August 2004 - p1910(1) [51-500]

Thompson, William J. - *French XX Bibliography*
R&R Bk N - v19 - i1 - Feb 2004 - p230(1) [51-500]

Thoms, Peg - *Driven by Time: Time Orientation and Leadership*
R&R Bk N - v19 - i1 - Feb 2004 - p90(1) [1-50]

Thomsen, Ole - *Classica et Mediaevalia*
R&R Bk N - v19 - i1 - Feb 2004 - p27(1) [51-500]

Thomsen, Paul A. - *Rebel Chief: The Motley Life of Colonel William Holland Thomas, C.S.A.*
BL - v100 - i1 - Sept 1 2004 - p44(1) [51-500]

Thomsett, Michael C. - *The Landlord's Financial Tool Kit*
Bwatch - Feb 2005 - pNA [501+]
LJ - v129 - i17 - Oct 15 2004 - p70(2) [51-500]

Thomson, Alison - *Gene Targeting and Embryonic Stem Cells*
SciTech - v28 - i4 - Dec 2004 - p61(1) [51-500]

Thomson, Amy - *Storyteller*
y VOYA - v27 - i3 - August 2004 - p234(1) [1-50]

Thomson, Andrew - *Emergency Sex and Other Desperate Measures: A True Story from Hell on Earth*
NY - v80 - i40 - Dec 20 2004 - p042 [501+]

Thomson, Celia - *The Chosen*
y Kliatt - v39 - i1 - Jan 2005 - p24(1) [51-500]
The Fallen
y Kliatt - v38 - i5 - Sept 2004 - p33(2) [51-500]
y SLJ - v50 - i9 - Sept 2004 - p218(2) [51-500]
The Stolen
y SLJ - v50 - i11 - Nov 2004 - p155(1) [51-500]

Thomson, Colin - *The Great Montefiasco (Illus. by Redlich, Ben)*
c PW - v252 - i6 - Feb 7 2005 - p60(1) [51-500]

Thomson, David - *The New Biographical Dictionary of Film, Rev. and Expanded*
Globe & Mail - Dec 10 2004 - pR21 [1-50]
LJ - v129 - i16 - Oct 1 2004 - p110(1) [51-500]
Nation - v280 - i6 - Feb 14 2005 - p29 [501+]
The Whole Equation: A History of Hollywood
BL - v101 - i9-10 - Jan 1 2005 - p767(1) [51-500]
Ent W - i797 - Dec 17 2004 - p91 [51-500]
Globe & Mail - Dec 18 2004 - pD8 [501+]
NYTBR - Dec 19 2004 - p8 [501+]
Spec - v297 - i9015 - Feb 19 2005 - p41(1) [501+]

Thomson, David (English writer) - *The Whole Equation: A History of Hollywood*
BL - v101 - i6 - Nov 15 2004 - p543(1) [51-500]
KR - v72 - i19 - Oct 1 2004 - p954(1) [501+]
LJ - v129 - i19 - Nov 15 2004 - p63(1) [51-500]
PW - v251 - i41 - Oct 11 2004 - p63(2) [501+]

Thomson, Ernie - *The Discovery of the Materialist Conception of History in the Writings of the Young Karl Marx*
R&R Bk N - v20 - i1 - Feb 2005 - p5(1) [51-500]

Thomson, Garrett - *On Modern Philosophy*
R&R Bk N - v19 - i1 - Feb 2004 - p2(1) [51-500]

Thomson, Hugh - *Nanda Devi: A Journey to the Last Sanctuary*
LJ - v130 - i2 - Feb 1 2005 - p107(1) [51-500]

Thomson, June - *The Secret Notebooks of Sherlock Holmes*
PW - v251 - i29 - July 19 2004 - p149(1) [51-500]

Thomson, Keith - *Pirates of Pensacola*
KR - v73 - i3 - Feb 1 2005 - p146(1) [51-500]
PW - v252 - i7 - Feb 14 2005 - p52(1) [51-500]

Thomson Learning's Certified Business Manager: CBM Examination Preparation Guide, Vol. 5, Pt. 3
R&R Bk N - v19 - i1 - Feb 2004 - p112(1) [51-500]

Thomson Learning's Certified Business Manager: CRM Examination Preparation Guide, Vol. 6, Pt. 3
R&R Bk N - v19 - i1 - Feb 2004 - p113(1) [51-500]

Thomson, Ruth - *Creatures*
c SLJ - v50 - i9 - Sept 2004 - p194(1) [51-500]
Families
c SLJ - v50 - i9 - Sept 2004 - p194(1) [51-500]
Places
c SLJ - v50 - i9 - Sept 2004 - p194(1) [51-500]
Portraits
c SLJ - v50 - i9 - Sept 2004 - p194(1) [51-500]

Thomson, Sarah L. - *Amazing Whales!*
c SLJ - v51 - i1 - Jan 2005 - p116(1) [51-500]
Imagine a Day (Illus. by Gonsalves, Rob)
c BL - v101 - i9-10 - Jan 1 2005 - p862(1) [1-50]
c KR - v73 - i1 - Jan 1 2005 - p58(1) [51-500]
Stars and Stripes: The Story of the American Flag
y Teach Lib - v32 - i1 - Oct 2004 - p20(1) [51-500]
Tigers
c BL - v100 - i21 - July 2004 - p1852(1) [51-500]
c KR - v72 - i14 - July 15 2004 - p694(1) [51-500]
c SLJ - v50 - i9 - Sept 2004 - p194(1) [51-500]

Thomson, Sinclair - *We Alone Will Rule: Native Andean Politics in the Age of Insurgency*
AHR - v109 - i2 - April 2004 - p577(2) [501+]
HAHR - v84 - i3 - August 2004 - p533(3) [501+]

Thomson, T. - *Polyurethanes as Specialty Chemicals: Principles and Applications*
SciTech - v28 - i4 - Dec 2004 - p166(1) [51-500]

Thong, Roseanne - *Red Is a Dragon: A Book of Colors (Illus. by Lin, Grace)*
c Teach Lib - v32 - i3 - Feb 2005 - p20(1) [51-500]

Thonhoff, Robert H. - *Camp Kenedy, Texas*
SHQ - v107 - i4 - April 2004 - p626(2) [501+]

Thor, Jonas - *Icelanders in North America: The First Settlers*
Can Hist R - v85 - i3 - Sept 2004 - p610(3) [501+]

Thorburn, Matthew - *Subject to Change*
NYTBR - Nov 21 2004 - p26 [501+]

Thordarson, David B. - *Foot and Ankle*
SciTech - v28 - i3 - Sept 2004 - p112(1) [51-500]

Thoreau, Henry David - *Letters to a Spiritual Seeker*
BL - v100 - i22 - August 2004 - p1891(1) [51-500]
LJ - v129 - i13 - August 2004 - p80(2) [501+]
Walden, 150th Anniversary Illustrated Ed.
R&R Bk N - v19 - i4 - Nov 2004 - p242(1) [501+]
Walden: A Fully Annotated Edition
Choice - v42 - i5 - Jan 2005 - p856(1) [1-50]
Walden
Globe & Mail - July 3 2004 - pD13 [1-50]

Thorley, A.R. David - *Fluid Transients in Pipeline Systems: A Guide to the Control and Suppression of Fluid Transients in Liquids in Closed Conduits, 2nd Ed.*
SciTech - v28 - i3 - Sept 2004 - p138(1) [51-500]

Thorn, Alan - *DirectX 9 User Interfaces: Design and Implementation*
SciTech - v28 - i3 - Sept 2004 - p31(1) [51-500]

Thorn, John - *Total Baseball: The Ultimate Baseball Encyclopedia*
BL - v101 - i2 - Sept 15 2004 - p279(1) [501+]

Thorn, William J. - *Dorothy Day and the Catholic Worker Movement: Centenary Essays*
CHR - v90 - i4 - Oct 2004 - p828(3) [501+]

Thornburg, Linda - *Cool Careers for Girls in Cybersecurity and National Safety*
c SLJ - v51 - i10 - Oct 2004 - p196(1) [51-500]

Thorne, Brian - *Carl Rogers, 2nd Ed.*
SciTech - v28 - i3 - Sept 2004 - p93(1) [51-500]

Thorne, Matt - *Cherry*
NS - v133 - i4706 - Sept 20 2004 - p52(2) [501+]
Spec - v296 - i9188 - Sept 11 2004 - p48(1) [501+]
TLS - i5292 - Sept 3 2004 - p13(1) [501+]

Thorne, Tanis C. - *The World's Richest Indian: The Scandal over Jackson Barnett's Oil Fortune*
Choice - v42 - i1 - Sept 2004 - p177(1) [501+]

Thorne-Thomsen, Kathleen - *Greene and Greene for Kids*
c PW - v251 - i49 - Dec 6 2004 - p62(1) [51-500]
c SLJ - v50 - i12 - Dec 2004 - p170(1) [51-500]

Thornhill, Jan - *Over in the Meadow (Illus. by Thornhill, Jan)*
c Globe & Mail - Feb 26 2005 - pD11 [501+]
c Res Links - v10 - i2 - Dec 2004 - p11(1) [51-500]
c SLJ - v51 - i1 - Jan 2005 - p116(1) [51-500]

Thornhill, Jan - *The Wildlife ABC and 123: A Nature Alphabet and Counting Book (Illus. by Thornhill, Jan)*
c Globe & Mail - Sept 11 2004 - pD13 [51-500]

Thornhill, Jan - *The Wildlife ABC and 123: A Nature Alphabet and Counting Book (Illus. by Thornhill, Jan)*
c PW - v251 - i37 - Sept 13 2004 - p80(2) [51-500]
c Res Links - v10 - i2 - Dec 2004 - p11(2) [501+]

Thornton, Anna C. - *Variation Risk Management: Focusing Quality Improvements in Product Development and Production*
SciTech - v28 - i1 - March 2004 - p177(1) [51-500]

Thornton, Betsy - *Dead for the Winter*
BL - v101 - i3 - Oct 1 2004 - p315(1) [51-500]
KR - v72 - i18 - Sept 15 2004 - p895(2) [51-500]
LJ - v129 - i18 - Nov 1 2004 - p62(1) [51-500]
PW - v251 - i35 - August 30 2004 - p35(1) [501+]

Thornton, Bruce - *Searching for Joaquin*
Bwatch - Nov 2004 - pNA [51-500]

Thornton, Duncan - *The Star-Glass*
c CBRA - Annual 2003 - p518(1) [51-500]
c Kliatt - v38 - i6 - Nov 2004 - p24(1) [501+]

Thornton, George C. - *Developing Organizational Simulations: A Guide for Practitioners and Students*
R&R Bk N - v19 - i1 - Feb 2004 - p111(1) [51-500]

Thornton, J. Mills, III - *Dividing Lines: Municipal Politics and the Struggle for Civil Rights in Montgomery, Birmingham, and Selma*
HNet - Oct 2004 - pNA [501+]

Thornton, Jeremy - *Religious Intolerance: Jewish Immigrants Come to America*
c SLJ - v50 - i9 - Sept 2004 - p192(1) [51-500]

Thornton, Judith - *Russia's Far East: A Region at Risk*
E-A St - v56 - i5 - July 2004 - p772(3) [501+]

Thornton, Kim Campbell - *Your New Cat*
Bwatch - Nov 2004 - pNA [51-500]

Thornton, Lawrence - *Sailors on the Inward Sea*
BL - v100 - i22 - August 2004 - p1904(1) [501+]
BW - v34 - i36 - Sept 5 2004 - p13(1) [501+]
KR - v72 - i14 - July 15 2004 - p658(2) [501+]
LJ - v129 - i14 - Sept 1 2004 - p143(1) [51-500]
y NYTBR - Sept 26 2004 - p24 [501+]
PW - v251 - i37 - Sept 13 2004 - p58(1) [501+]

Thornton, Mark - *Tariffs, Blockades, and Inflation: The Economics of the Civil War*
R&R Bk N - v19 - i3 - August 2004 - p97(1) [51-500]

Thornton, Russell - *House Built to Rain*
BIC - v33 - i2 - March 2004 - p37(2) [501+]

Thorp, John - *Information Paradox: Realizing the Business Benefits of Information Technology*
CBRA - Annual 2003 - p333(2) [51-500]

Thorp, Simon - *Sport Matters*
Sch Lib - v52 - i4 - Winter 2004 - p222(1) [51-500]

Thorpe, Adam - *Ulverton*
Globe & Mail - Sept 18 2004 - pL3 [1-50]

Thorpe, Sara - *The Coaching Handbook: An Action Kit for Trainers and Managers*
R&R Bk N - v19 - i1 - Feb 2004 - p110(1) [1-50]

Those Ca-Way-Zee Crickets
HB - v81 - i1 - Jan-Feb 2005 - p68(2) [501+]

Thoss, Bruno - *Erster Weltkrieg. Zweiter Weltkrieg. Ein Vergleich. Krieg, Kriegserlebnis, Kriegsserfahrung in Deutschland*
GSR - v27 - i2 - May 2004 - p425-426 [501+]

Thoumi, Francisco E. - *Illegal Drugs, Economy, and Society in the Andes*
Choice - v42 - i6 - Feb 2005 - p1071(1) [51-500]

Thrall, Mary Anna - *Veterinary Hematology and Clinical Chemistry*
SciTech - v28 - i1 - March 2004 - p132(1) [51-500]

Thrane, Henrik - *Diachronic Settlement Studies in the Metal Ages: Proceedings*
R&R Bk N - v19 - i4 - Nov 2004 - p77(1) [51-500]
Excavations at Tepe Guran in Luristan: The Bronze Age and Iron Age Periods
JNES - v63 - i4 - Oct 2004 - p314(2) [501+]

Threinen-Pendarvis, Cher - *The Photoshop and Painter Artist Tablet Book: Creative Techniques in Digital Painting*
Bwatch - Jan 2005 - pNA [51-500]

Throne, James L. - *Thermoplastic Foam Extrusion: An Introduction*
SciTech - v28 - i4 - Dec 2004 - p166(1) [51-500]

Thrower, James - *The Religious History of Central Asia from the Earliest Times to the Present Day*
R&R Bk N - v19 - i4 - Nov 2004 - p17(1) [51-500]

Thruber, James - *The Thurber Letters: The Wit, Wisdom and Surprising Life of James Thurber*
TLS - i5265 - Feb 27 2004 - p11-11 [501+]

Thubten Chodron - *Taming the Mind*
LJ - v129 - i16 - Oct 1 2004 - p86(1) [51-500]

Thuillier, J.-P. - *Sport im antiken Rom*
Class R - v54 - i1 - May 2004 - p202(2) [501+]

Thumbelina
LibMed - v22 - i6 - March 2004 - p60(1) [501+]

Thumma, Scott - *Gay Religion*
PW - v251 - i48 - Nov 29 2004 - p36(1) [51-500]

Thunder and Glory: The 25 Most Memorable Races in NASCAR Winston Cup History
BL - v101 - i1 - Sept 1 2004 - p45(1) [501+]

Thunecke, Jorg - *B. Traven the Writer*
GSR - v27 - i2 - May 2004 - p412-413 [501+]

Thurley, Simon - *Hampton Court: A Social and Architectural History*
Choice - v41 - i11-12 - July-August 2004 - p2037(1) [501+]
TimHES - v0 - i1652 - August 6 2004 - p29(1) [501+]
TLS - i5306 - Dec 10 2004 - p25(1) [501+]
Lost Buildings of Britain
TLS - i5304 - Nov 26 2004 - p25(1) [501+]

Thurlo, David - *Blood Retribution*
y BL - v101 - i1 - Sept 1 2004 - p70(1) [51-500]
PW - v251 - i37 - Sept 13 2004 - p62(1) [51-500]
Thief in Retreat: A Sister Agatha Mystery
PW - v251 - i47 - Nov 22 2004 - p41(2) [501+]
White Thunder
KR - v73 - i5 - March 1 2005 - p264(2) [501+]

Thurlow, Crispin - *Computer Mediated Communication: Social Interaction and the Internet*
Choice - v42 - i2 - Oct 2004 - p328(1) [51-500]
R&R Bk N - v19 - i3 - August 2004 - p143(1) [51-500]

Thurmaier, Kurt - *Case Studies of City-County Consolidation: Reshaping the Local Government Landscape*
R&R Bk N - v19 - i4 - Nov 2004 - p157(1) [501+]

Thurman, Quint - *Contemporary Policing: Controversies, Challenges, and Solutions: An Anthology*
R&R Bk N - v19 - i3 - August 2004 - p169(1) [501+]
Police Problem Solving
R&R Bk N - v19 - i3 - August 2004 - p167(1) [501+]

Thurman, Robert A.F. - *Anger*
BL - v101 - i3 - Oct 1 2004 - p306(1) [51-500]
PW - v251 - i37 - Sept 13 2004 - p75(2) [501+]
The Jewel Tree of Tibet: The Enlightenment Engine of Tibetan Buddhism
PW - v252 - i4 - Jan 24 2005 - p240(1) [501+]

Thurman, Suzanne R. - *"O Sisters Ain't You Happy?" Gender, Family, and Community Among the Harvard and Shirley Shakers, 1781-1918*
JWH - v16 - i3 - Autumn 2004 - p187(10) [501+]

Thurman, Wallace Henry - *The Collected Writings of Wallace Thurman: A Harlem Renaissance Reader*
Choice - v41 - i7 - March 2004 - p1300(1) [501+]

Thurner, Mark - *After Spanish Rule: Postcolonial Predicaments of the Americas*
Ams - v61 - i2 - Oct 2004 - p267(2) [501+]

Thurow, Lester C. - *Fortune Favors the Bold: What We Must Do to Build a New and Lasting Global Prosperity*
R&R Bk N - v19 - i1 - Feb 2004 - p105(1) [51-500]

Thurston, Harry - *Island of the Blessed: The Secrets of Egypt's Everlasting Oasis*
BIC - v33 - i2 - March 2004 - p31(2) [501+]
CBRA - Annual 2003 - p298(2) [501+]
Place Between the Tides: A Naturalist's Reflections on the Salt Marsh
SciTech - v28 - i4 - Dec 2004 - p59(1) [51-500]

Thurston, Luke - *James Joyce and the Problem of Psychoanalysis*
TLS - i5295 - Sept 24 2004 - p27(1) [501+]

Thussu, Daya Kishan - *War and the Media: Reporting Conflict 24/7*
Pub Op Q - v68 - i4 - Winter 2004 - p644(5) [501+]

Thwaite, Anthony - *A Move in the Weather*
TLS - i5265 - Feb 27 2004 - p30-30 [501+]

Thwaites, Tony - *Joycean Temporalities: Debts, Promises, and Countersignatures*
MFSF - v50 - i2 - Summer 2004 - p503-504 [501+]

Tibi, Laurence - *La Lyre Desenchantee: l'Instrument de Musique et la Voix Humaine dans la Litterature Francaise du XIXe Siecle*
FS - v58 - i3 - July 2004 - p417-418 [501+]

Tibo, Gilles - *La Bataille Des Mots*
Res Links - v10 - i1 - Oct 2004 - p54(1) [51-500]
Too Many Books! (Illus. by St-Aubin, Bruno)
c CBRA - Annual 2003 - p468(1) [51-500]
c Globe & Mail - Dec 11 2004 - pD43 [51-500]

Tichi, Cecelia - *Embodiment of a Nation: Human Form in American Places*
Am Q - v56 - i4 - Dec 2004 - p1089(9) [501+]
JouAmCul - v27 - i4 - Dec 2004 - p441(1) [501+]
Exposes and Excess: Muckraking in America, 1900-2000
JAH - v91 - i3 - Dec 2004 - p1113(2) [501+]

Tick, Edward - *The Practice of Dream Healing: Bringing Ancient Greek Mysteries into Modern Medicine*
Parabola - v28 - i4 - Winter 2003 - p110-112 [501+]

Tickle, Phyllis A. - *Greed*
HM - v310 - i1856 - Jan 2005 - p96(6) [501+]

Tickoo, Sham - *AutoCAD 2005: A Problem-Solving Approach*
LJ - v129 - i18 - Nov 1 2004 - p114(1) [51-500]

Tidball, Eugene C. - *Soldier-Artist of the Great Reconnaissance: John C. Tidball and the 35th Parallel Pacific Railroad Survey*
Roundup M - v12 - i3 - Feb 2005 - p23(1) [51-500]
R&R Bk N - v19 - i4 - Nov 2004 - p67(1) [51-500]

Tidcombe, Marianne - *The Doves Press*
BSA-P - v98 - i3 - Sept 2004 - p367-369 [501+]
Lib & Cul - v39 - i3 - Summer 2004 - p327(2) [501+]

Tidler, Charles - *Going to New Orleans*
BIC - v33 - i9 - Dec 2004 - p38(2) [51-500]
Globe & Mail - August 21 2004 - pD10 [501+]

Tidrow, Rob - *Outlook 2003 Bible*
R&R Bk N - v19 - i4 - Nov 2004 - p112(1) [51-500]

Tielhof, Milja - *The "Mother of All Trades": The Baltic Grain Trade in Amsterdam from the Late 16th to the Early 19th Century*
Six Ct J - v34 - i4 - Winter 2003 - p1147-1148 [501+]

Tieman, Robert - *The Disney Treasures*
LibMed - v22 - i6 - March 2004 - p89(1) [501+]

Tier, Mark - *Visons of Liberty*
y Kliatt - v39 - i1 - Jan 2005 - p24(1) [51-500]

Tierney, John Lawrence - *A Perfect World*
y BL - v101 - i9-10 - Jan 1 2005 - p845(1) [1-50]

Tierney, Lawrence M. - *Current Medical Diagnosis and Treatment 2005, Digital Ed.*
SciTech - v28 - i4 - Dec 2004 - p89(1) [51-500]

Tierney, Ronald - *Nickel-Plated Soul*
BL - v101 - i6 - Nov 15 2004 - p566(1) [51-500]
KR - v72 - i24 - Dec 15 2004 - p1170(1) [501+]
LJ - v130 - i2 - Feb 1 2005 - p57(1) [51-500]

Tierney, William G. - *Competing Conceptions of Academic Governance: Negotiating the Perfect Storm*
R&R Bk N - v19 - i3 - August 2004 - p221(1) [1-50]

Tiersky, Ronald - *Europe Today: National Politics, European Integration, and European Security, 2nd Ed.*
R&R Bk N - v19 - i3 - August 2004 - p181(1) [501+]

Tiersten, Lisa - *Marianne in the Market: Envisioning Consumer Society in Fin-de-Siecle France*
Signs - v30 - i2 - Wntr 2005 - p1703(4) [501+]

Tietge, David J. - *Flash Effect: Science and the Rhetorical Origins of Cold War America*
Isis - v95 - i3 - Sept 2004 - p536(2) [501+]

Tiffany-Castiglioni, Evelyn - *In Vitro Neurotoxicology: Principles and Challenges*
SciTech - v28 - i1 - March 2004 - p93(1) [51-500]

Tiffany, Grace - *Will*
y SLJ - v51 - i1 - Jan 2005 - p159(1) [51-500]

Tiger Woods
y LibMed - v22 - i5 - Feb 2004 - p76(1) [501+]

Tight, Malcolm - *Key Concepts in Adult Education and Training*
TCR - v106 - i12 - Dec 2004 - p2261(3) [501+]

Tilden, Scott J. - *Architecture for Art: American Art Museums 1938-2008.*
LJ - v130 - i2 - Feb 1 2005 - p74(1) [51-500]

Tiles, Mary - *The Philosophy of Set Theory: An Historical Introduction to Cantor's Paradise*
SciTech - v28 - i4 - Dec 2004 - p14(1) [1-50]

Tilghman, Christopher - *Roads of the Heart*
BW - v34 - i28 - July 11 2004 - p2(1) [501+]
NYTBR - August 8 2004 - p14 [51-500]
World&I - v19 - i9 - Sept 2004 - pNA [501+]

Till, David W. - *The Recipe for Simple Business Improvement*
R&R Bk N - v19 - i1 - Feb 2004 - p91(1) [1-50]

Till, Geoffrey - *Seapower: A Guide for the Twenty-First Century*
J Mil H - v68 - i2 - April 2004 - p667(2) [501+]
R&R Bk N - v19 - i1 - Feb 2004 - p256(1) [51-500]

Tiller, Jerome - *Sammy's Day at the Fair*
c CH Bwatch - Jan 2005 - pNA [51-500]

Tillman, Barrett - *Brassey's D-Day Encyclopedia: The Normandy Invasion A - Z*
R&R Bk N - v19 - i3 - August 2004 - p32(1) [51-500]

Tillotson, Katherine - *Penguin and Little Blue*
LibMed - v22 - i6 - March 2004 - p58(1) [501+]

Tilly, Charles - *Contention and Democracy in Europe, 1650-2000*
  Choice - v42 - i2 - Oct 2004 - p367(1) [51-500]
The Politics of Collective Violence
  AHR - v109 - i2 - April 2004 - p474(2) [501+]
Social Movements, 1768-2004
  R&R Bk N - v19 - i2 - May 2004 - p128 [51-500]

Tilman, Rick - *The Legacy of Thorstein Veblen, Vols. 1-3*
  JEL - v42 - i1 - March 2004 - p242(1) [501+]
  R&R Bk N - v19 - i1 - Feb 2004 - p78(1) [51-500]
Thorstein Veblen, John Dewey, C. Wright Mills and the Generic Ends of Life
  R&R Bk N - v19 - i3 - August 2004 - p93(1) [51-500]

Tilney, Nicholas L. - *Transplant: From Myth to Reality*
  Choice - v41 - i7 - March 2004 - p1328(1) [501+]
  CR - v285 - i1662 - July 2004 - p59(2) [51-500]
  E-Streams - August 2004 - pNA [501+]

Tilove, Jonathan - *Along Martin Luther King: Travels on Black America's Main Street*
  Black Iss - v7 - i2 - March-April 2005 - p40(2) [501+]

Tilson, Donn James - *Toward the Common Good: Perspectives in International Public Relations*
  R&R Bk N - v19 - i1 - Feb 2004 - p125(1) [51-500]

Tilton, Buck - *Backcountry First Aid and Extended Care, 4th Ed.*
  SciTech - v28 - i4 - Dec 2004 - p91(1) [1-50]

Tilton, John E. - *On Borrowed Time? Assessing the Threat of Mineral Depletion*
  En Jnl - v25 - i1 - Jan 2004 - p111(3) [501+]
  NRJ - v44 - i2 - Spring 2004 - p652-654 [501+]

Timberg, Robert - *State of Grace: A Memoir of Twilight Time*
  BW - v34 - i44 - Oct 31 2004 - p5(2) [501+]
  PW - v251 - i36 - Sept 6 2004 - p58(1) [51-500]

Time and Tide: A Walk through Nantucket (Read by Gardner, Grover). Audiobook Review
  BL - v101 - i2 - Sept 15 2004 - p259(1) [501+]

Time Out Film Guide
  Globe & Mail - Dec 10 2004 - pR21 [1-50]

Timeline of Costume History
  LibMed - v22 - i6 - March 2004 - p91(1) [501+]

Timlin, Mark - *Answers from the Grave*
  LJ - v129 - i20 - Dec 1 2004 - p96(1) [51-500]

Timm, Bruce - *Catwoman: Nine Lives of a Feline Fatale*
  PW - v251 - i32 - August 9 2004 - p233(2) [51-500]

Timm, Larry M. - *The Soul of Cinema: An Appreciation of Film Music*
  Am M - v22 - i1 - Spring 2004 - p189-191 [501+]

Timm, Uwe - *In My Brother's Shadow: A Life and Death in the SS*
  KR - v73 - i2 - Jan 15 2005 - p113(1) [501+]
  LJ - v130 - i4 - March 1 2005 - p98(2) [51-500]
  PW - v252 - i5 - Jan 31 2005 - p55(2) [51-500]

Timmerman, John H. - *Jane Kenyon: A Literary Life*
  Sew R - v111 - i3 - Summer 2003 - pCI-CIII [501+]

Timmerman, Kenneth R. - *The French Betrayal of America*
  Am Spect - v37 - i5 - June 2004 - p64(2) [501+]
Preachers of Hate: Islam and the War on America
  R&R Bk N - v19 - i3 - August 2004 - p51(1) [51-500]

Timmermann, Heiner - *Deutsche Fragen: Von der Teilung Zur Einheit*
  GSR - v27 - i3 - Oct 2004 - p660(2) [501+]

Timmermans, Stefan - *The Gold Standard: The Challenge of Evidence-Based Medicine and Standardization in Health Care*
  AJS - v110 - i2 - Sept 2004 - p513(2) [501+]

Timmons, Deborah - *ExamInsight for Installing, Configuring, and Adminstering Microsft Windows XP Professional MCP/MCE Exam 70-270, 2nd Ed.*
  SciTech - v28 - i3 - Sept 2004 - p25(1) [51-500]
ExamWise for Windows XP Professional Certification Exam 70-270: Installing, Configuring, and Administering Microsoft Windows XP Professional. 2nd Ed.
  SciTech - v28 - i3 - Sept 2004 - p25(1) [51-500]
InsidersChoice to Microsoft Windows XP Professional MCP/MCSE exam 70-720, 2nd Ed.
  SciTech - v28 - i3 - Sept 2004 - p26(1) [51-500]

Timmons, Jeffry A. - *Business Plans that Work: A Guide for Small Business*
  Choice - v42 - i4 - Dec 2004 - p705(1) [1-50]
How to Raise Capital: Techniques and Strategies for Financing and Valuing Your Small Business
  Choice - v42 - i6 - Feb 2005 - p1067(2) [51-500]

Timney, Mary M. - *Power for the People: Protecting State's Energy Policy Interest in an Era of Deregulation*
  R&R Bk N - v19 - i3 - August 2004 - p119(1) [51-500]

Timonen, Virpi - *Restructuring the Welfare State: Globalization and Social Policy Reform in Finland and Sweden*
  JEL - v42 - i1 - March 2004 - p324(1) [501+]

Timoshenko, Alexandre - *Environmental Negotiator Handbook*
  R&R Bk N - v19 - i1 - Feb 2004 - pNA [51-500]

Timpson, William M. - *Concepts and Choices for Teaching: Meeting the Challenges in Higher Education*
  R&R Bk N - v19 - i4 - Nov 2004 - p184(1) [501+]

Tindale, Christopher W. - *Rhetorical Argumentation: Principles of Theory and Practice*
  R&R Bk N - v19 - i4 - Nov 2004 - p222(1) [501+]

Tindall, George Brown - *America: A Narrative History, 6th Ed.*
  R&R Bk N - v19 - i1 - Feb 2004 - p55(1) [51-500]

Tiner, John Hudson - *Airplanes*
  c SB - v40 - i3 - May-June 2004 - p135(1) [501+]

Ting-Xing Ye - *Throwaway Daughter*
  c TES - v0 - i4587 - June 11 2004 - pssss18(2) [501+]

Tingle, Rebecca - *Edge of the Sword*
  c CH Bwatch - v14 - i7 - July 2004 - p6(1) [51-500]
Far Traveler
  y KR - v73 - i4 - Feb 15 2005 - p236(1) [51-500]
  y SLJ - v51 - i2 - Feb 2005 - p142(1) [51-500]

Tingle, Tim - *Texas Ghost Stories: Fifty Favorites for the Telling*
  Roundup M - v12 - i1 - Oct 2004 - p33(1) [51-500]

Tinker, George E. - *Spirit and Resistance: Political Theology and American Indian Liberation*
  CC - v122 - i5 - March 8 2005 - p46(2) [501+]

Tinkham, Michael - *Introduction to Superconductivity, 2nd Ed.*
  SciTech - v28 - i4 - Dec 2004 - p50(1) [51-500]

Tinniswood, Adrian - *By Permission of Heaven: The True Story of the Great Fire of London*
  BW - v34 - i3 - Jan 18 2004 - p2(1) [501+]

Tinsley, Ian J. - *Chemical Concepts in Pollutant Behavior, 2nd Ed.*
  SciTech - v28 - i3 - Sept 2004 - p61(1) [51-500]

Tinsman, Heidi - *Partners in Conflict: The Politics of Gender, Sexuality, and Labor in the Chilean Agrarian Reform, 1950-1973*
  J Soc H - v38 - i1 - Fall 2004 - p239(3) [501+]
  JIH - v34 - i4 - Spring 2004 - pNA [501+]

Tipene, Tim - *Kura Toa: Warrior School*
  y Magpies - v19 - i5 - Nov 2004 - p7S(2) [501+]

Tipiotaka - *A Buddhist Reader: Selections from the Sacred Books*
  R&R Bk N - v19 - i4 - Nov 2004 - p18(1) [1-50]

Tipler, Paul A. - *Physics for Scientists and Engineers, 5th Ed.*
  TimHES - v0 - i1668 - Nov 26 2004 - pXIV(2) [501+]

Tippins, Sherill - *February House*
  BL - v101 - i9-10 - Jan 1 2005 - p803(1) [51-500]
  KR - v72 - i23 - Dec 1 2004 - p1140(2) [501+]
  LJ - v130 - i2 - Feb 1 2005 - p80(1) [51-500]
  NY - v81 - i3 - March 7 2005 - p078 [501+]
  NYTBR - Feb 6 2005 - p8 [501+]

Tipton, Charles M. - *Exercise Physiology: People and Ideas*
  Choice - v41 - i7 - March 2004 - p1320(1) [501+]

Tipton, Frank B. - *A History of Modern Germany Since 1815*
  HNet - Sept 2004 - pNA [501+]
  TimHES - v0 - i1669 - Dec 3 2004 - p25(1) [501+]

Tirole, Jean - *Financial Crisis, Liquidity, and the International Monetary System*
  JEL - v42 - i4 - Dec 2004 - p1095(3) [501+]

Tiryakioglu, M. - *Metallurgical Modeling for Aluminum Alloys: Proceedings*
  SciTech - v28 - i1 - March 2004 - p143(1) [51-500]

Tisch, Jonathan - *The Power of We: Succeeding through Partnerships*
  BL - v101 - i1 - Sept 1 2004 - p32(1) [51-500]
  PW - v251 - i32 - August 9 2004 - p245(1) [51-500]

Tischeler, Matthias M. - *Einharts "Vita Karoli": Studien zur Entstechung, Uberlieferung und Rezeption*
  Specu - v79 - i3 - July 2004 - p846-848 [501+]

Tischler, Henry L. - *Introduction to Sociology, 8th Ed.*
  R&R Bk N - v19 - i1 - Feb 2004 - p122(1) [51-500]

Tisdell, Clem - *Ecological and Environmental Economics: Selected Issues and Policy Responses*
  JEL - v41 - i4 - Dec 2003 - p1435(1) [501+]
Economic Globalisation: Social Conflicts, Labour and Environmental Issues
  R&R Bk N - v19 - i3 - August 2004 - p95(1) [51-500]
Economics and Ecology in Agriculture and Marine Production: Bioeconomics and Resource use
  JEL - v41 - i4 - Dec 2003 - p1432(1) [501+]

Tisdell, Elizabeth J. - *Exploring Spirituality and Culture in Adult and Higher Education*
  TCR - v106 - i2 - Feb 2004 - p225-227 [501+]

Tise, B. - *Imperialismo romano e imitatio Alexandri. Due studi di storia politica*
  Class R - v54 - i2 - Nov 2004 - p571(2) [501+]

Tishkov, Valery - *Chechnya: Life in a War-Torn Society*
  Choice - v42 - i6 - Feb 2005 - p1078(1) [51-500]
  For Aff - v83 - i5 - Sept-Oct 2004 - p164 [501+]
  PW - v251 - i49 - Dec 6 2004 - p32(2) [51-500]

Tishy, Cecelia - *Now You See Her*
  BL - v101 - i9-10 - Jan 1 2005 - p829(1) [1-50]
  KR - v72 - i24 - Dec 15 2004 - p1170(1) [51-500]
  PW - v252 - i1 - Jan 3 2005 - p39(1) [51-500]

Tismaneanu, Vladimir - *Stalinism for all Seasons: A Political History of Romanian Communism*
  Slav R - v63 - i4 - Winter 2004 - p864(1) [501+]
  TLS - i5266 - March 5 2004 - p7-7 [501+]

Tita, George - *Reducing Gun Violence: Results from an Intervention in East Los Angeles*
  R&R Bk N - v19 - i1 - Feb 2004 - p143(1) [51-500]

Titchkosky, Tanya - *Disability, Self, and Society*
  CS - v33 - i1 - Jan 2004 - p130-130 [501+]
  R&R Bk N - v19 - i1 - Feb 2004 - p138(1) [51-500]

Titon, Jeff Todd - *Worlds of Music: An Introduction to the Music of the World's Peoples, Shorter Version, 2nd Ed.*
  R&R Bk N - v19 - i4 - Nov 2004 - p198(1) [501+]

Titone, Connie - *Gender Equality in the Philosophy of Education: Catherine Macaulay's Forgotten Contribution*
  R&R Bk N - v19 - i3 - August 2004 - p214(1) [1-50]

Tittle, Peg - *Should Parents Be Licensed?*
  NYTBR - Oct 24 2004 - p26 [501+]
Should Parents be Licensed?: Debating the Issues
  R&R Bk N - v19 - i4 - Nov 2004 - p130(1) [51-500]
What If - : Collected Thought Experiments in Philosophy
  R&R Bk N - v19 - i4 - Nov 2004 - p8(1) [51-500]

Titus, Andrew - *Sweet Mother Prophesy*
  CBRA - Annual 2003 - p189(1) [51-500]

Titus-Carmel, Gerard - *Ici rien n'est present*
  WLT - v78 - i3-4 - Sept-Dec 2004 - p120(1) [501+]

Tjosvold, Dean - *Cross-Cultural Management: Foundations and Future*
  R&R Bk N - v19 - i1 - Feb 2004 - p88(1) [51-500]

Tlusty, B. Ann - *Bacchus and Civic Order: The Culture of Drink in Early Modern Germany*
  Six Ct J - v34 - i4 - Winter 2003 - p1258-1260 [501+]

Tobar, Hector - *Translation Nation: Defining a New American Identity in the Spanish Speaking United States*
  KR - v73 - i5 - March 1 2005 - p281(2) [501+]

Tober, Gillian - *Methadone Matters: Evolving Community Methadone Treatment of Opiate Addiction*
  SciTech - v28 - i3 - Sept 2004 - p103(1) [51-500]

Tobi, Yosef - *Proximity and Distance: Medieval Hebrew and Arabic Poetry*
  R&R Bk N - v19 - i4 - Nov 2004 - p218(1) [501+]

Tobias, Andrew - *The Only Investment Guide You'll Ever Need*
  NYT - Jan 9 2005 - pBU26 [501+]

Tobin, Brian - *All in Good Time*
  CBRA - Annual 2003 - p313(2) [501+]

Tobin, James, (1918 -) - *World Finance and Economic Stability: Selected Essays of James Tobin*
  JEL - v41 - i4 - Dec 2003 - p1362(1) [501+]

Tobin, James, (1956 -) - *To Conquer the Air: The Wright Brothers and the Great Race for Flight*
  JAH - v91 - i2 - Sept 2004 - p658(2) [501+]

Tobin, Joseph - *Pikachu's Global Adventure: The Rise and Fall of Pokemon*
  Choice - v41 - i11-12 - July-August 2004 - p2038(1) [501+]

Tobin, Thomas J. - *Pre-Raphaelitism in the Nineteenth-Century Press: A Biography*
  RES - v55 - i220 - June 2004 - p472-474 [501+]

Tocci, Salvatore - *Hydrogen and the Noble Gases*
  c BL - v101 - i7 - Dec 1 2004 - p672(1) [51-500]

Tocher, Michelle - *How to Ride a Dragon: Women with Breast Cancer Tell Their Stories*
  CBRA - Annual 2003 - p435(2) [51-500]

Tocher, Timothy - *Chief Sunrise, John McGraw, and Me (Illus. by Copeland, Greg)*
  c CCB-B - v57 - i11 - July-August 2004 - p451(2) [501+]
  c SLJ - v50 - i9 - Sept 2004 - p219(1) [51-500]

Tockey, Steve - *Return on Software: Maximizing the Return on Your Software Investment*
  SciTech - v28 - i4 - Dec 2004 - p28(1) [51-500]

Tocqueville, Alexis de - *Democracy in America and Two Essays on America*
  TLS - i5283 - July 2 2004 - p3-4 [501+]
  Oeuvres, III
  TLS - i5283 - July 2 2004 - p3-4 [501+]

Tocqueville Unveiled: The Historian and His Sources for "The Old Regime and the Revolution"
  TLS - i5283 - July 2 2004 - p3-4 [501+]

Toda, Fumio - *Separations and Reactions in Organic Supramolecular Chemistry*
  SciTech - v28 - i3 - Sept 2004 - p54(1) [1-50]

Todd, Barbara - *The Rainmaker (Illus. by Roge)*
  c CBRA - Annual 2003 - p469(1) [51-500]

Todd, Charles - *A Cold Treachery*
  Globe & Mail - March 5 2005 - pD15 [51-500]
  KR - v72 - i24 - Dec 15 2004 - p1170(1) [501+]
  LJ - v130 - i1 - Jan 1 2005 - p86(1) [51-500]
  PW - v251 - i49 - Dec 6 2004 - p46(1) [51-500]
  NYTBR - Feb 6 2005 - p25 [501+]

Todd, Emmanuel - *After the Empire: The Breakdown of the American Order*
  Choice - v41 - i11-12 - July-August 2004 - p2123(1) [501+]
  Dis - v51 - i2 - Spring 2004 - p104(5) [501+]
  NS - v133 - i4673 - Feb 2 2004 - p49(2) [501+]
  NYRB - v51 - i14 - Sept 23 2004 - p40(4) [501+]

Todd, Janet - *Daughters of Ireland: The Rebellious Kingsborough Sisters and the Making of a Modern Nation*
  Choice - v41 - i11-12 - July-August 2004 - p2047(2) [501+]
  Mary Wollstonecraft: A Revolutionary Life
  Signs - v30 - i2 - Wntr 2005 - p1719(4) [501+]

Todd, Malcolm - *A Companion to Roman Britain*
  Choice - v41 - i11-12 - July-August 2004 - p2112(1) [501+]

Todd, Margo - *The Culture of Protestantism in Early Modern Scotland*
  Albion - v36 - i2 - Summer 2004 - p375(3) [501+]

Todd, Marilyn - *Widow's Pique*
  LJ - v129 - i18 - Nov 1 2004 - p62(1) [51-500]

Todd, Olivier - *Malraux: A Life*
  BL - v101 - i9-10 - Jan 1 2005 - p803(1) [51-500]
  HM - v310 - i1858 - March 2005 - p89(2) [501+]
  KR - v72 - i24 - Dec 15 2004 - p1194(1) [501+]
  Nation - v280 - i8 - Feb 28 2005 - p23 [501+]
  PW - v251 - i50 - Dec 13 2004 - p53(1) [51-500]

Todd, Pamela - *The Arts and Crafts Companion*
  TimHES - v0 - i1667 - Nov 19 2004 - p26(1) [501+]

Todd, Paula - *A Quiet Courage: Inspiring Stories from All of Us*
  Globe & Mail - Nov 6 2004 - pD17 [501+]

Todd, R. Larry - *Mendelssohn: A Life in Music*
  CR - v285 - i1662 - July 2004 - p63(1) [51-500]
  NYRB - v51 - i17 - Nov 4 2004 - p44(3) [501+]
  TLS - i5268 - March 19 2004 - p4-3 [501+]

Todd, Robert B. - *The Dictionary of British Classicists. Vols. 1-3*
  LJ - v129 - i19 - Nov 15 2004 - p85(1) [51-500]

Todero, Giuseppe - *Le medaglie italiane del XVI secolo, Vols. 1-3*
  Ren Q - v57 - i3 - Fall 2004 - p1004(4) [501+]

Todhunter, Andrew - *A Meal Observed*
  NY - v80 - i25 - Sept 6 2004 - p163(1) [1-50]

Todono, Seiuchiroh - *Hymn for the Dead*
  PW - v251 - i44 - Nov 1 2004 - p46(1) [501+]

Todorov, Tzvetan - *Hope and Memory: Lessons from the Twentieth Century*
  Globe & Mail - July 17 2004 - pD10 [501+]
  Imperfect Gardens: The Legacy of Humanism
  Soc - v41 - i3 - March-April 2004 - p91(3) [501+]

Toews, Miriam - *A Complicated Kindness*
  Globe & Mail - March 5 2005 - pD17 [51-500]
  BIC - v33 - i5 - August 2004 - p16(1) [501+]
  BL - v101 - i2 - Sept 15 2004 - p210(1) [501+]
  Globe & Mail - Nov 27 2004 - pD3 [501+]
  KR - v72 - i16 - August 15 2004 - p775(1) [501+]
  People - v62 - i15 - Oct 11 2004 - p56 [51-500]
  PW - v251 - i29 - July 19 2004 - p141(1) [51-500]
  TLS - i5284 - July 9 2004 - p21(1) [501+]
  NYTBR - Jan 23 2005 - p18 [501+]

Tofel, Richard J. - *Vanishing Point: The Disappearance of Judge Crater, and the New York He Left Behind*
  KR - v72 - i15 - August 1 2004 - p735(1) [501+]

Toft, Albert - *Modelling and Sculpture: A Guide to Traditional Methods*
  R&R Bk N - v19 - i4 - Nov 2004 - p205(1) [501+]

Toft, Monica Duffy - *The Geography of Ethnic Violence: Identity, Interests, and the Indivisability of Territory*
  JPR - v41 - i5 - Sept 2004 - p648-648 [501+]
  VQR - v80 - i1 - Wntr 2004 - p265-265 [501+]

Tofte, Mavis - *Doogie Dork Meets Trouble*
  c CH Bwatch - v14 - i8 - August 2004 - p2(1) [51-500]

Tofts, Darren - *Prefiguring Cyberculture: An Intellectual History*
  T&C - v45 - i4 - Oct 2004 - p901(2) [501+]

Tofts, Paul - *Quantitative MRI of the Brain: Measuring Changes Caused by Disease*
  SciTech - v28 - i1 - March 2004 - p94(1) [51-500]

Tognetti, Sergio - *Un industria di lusso al servizio del grande commercio: Il mercato dei drappi serici e della seta nella Firenze del Quattrocento*
  Six Ct J - v34 - i4 - Winter 2003 - p1207-1208 [501+]

Toibin, Colm - *Lady Gregory's Toothbrush*
  Lon R Bks - v26 - i2 - Jan 22 2004 - p23(2) [501+]
  The Master
  BL - v101 - i9-10 - Jan 1 2005 - p770(1) [501+]
  BooChiTr - June 6 2004 - p1(2) [501+]
  G&L Rev W - v11 - i5 - Sept-Oct 2004 - p38(2) [501+]
  Globe & Mail - Nov 27 2004 - pD3 [51-500]
  Lam Bk Rpt - v13 - i1-2 - August-Sept 2004 - p31(1) [501+]
  Lon R Bks - v26 - i6 - March 18 2004 - pNA [501+]
  Nation - v279 - i14 - Nov 1 2004 - p34 [501+]
  New R - July 5 2004 - p39 [501+]
  NS - v133 - i4716 - Nov 29 2004 - p44(1) [51-500]
  NS - v133 - i4716 - Nov 29 2004 - p49(1) [51-500]
  NYRB - v51 - i12 - July 15 2004 - p18(2) [501+]
  NYTBR - July 4 2004 - p18 [501+]
  Sew R - v112 - i3 - Summer 2004 - pLXXXVII-XC [501+]
  NL - v87 - i5 - Sept-Oct 2004 - p31(3) [501+]

Toil, Monica Duffy - *The Geography of Ethnic Violence*
  PSQ - v119 - i4 - Winter 2004 - p714(3) [501+]

Toit, Johan T. - *The Kruger Experience: Ecology and Management of Savanna Heterogeneity*
  Nature - v429 - i6991 - June 3 2004 - p504(2w) [501+]

Toivonen, Ida - *Non-Projecting Words: A Case Study of Swedish Particles*
  R&R Bk N - v19 - i1 - Feb 2004 - p215(1) [51-500]

Tokarczuk, Olga - *House of Day, House of Night*
  CQ - v56 - i2-3 - Spring-Summer 2004 - p97(4) [501+]

Tokayer, Marvin - *The Fugu Plan: The Untold Story of the Japanese and the Jews During World War II*
  R&R Bk N - v19 - i4 - Nov 2004 - p33(1) [501+]

Toker, Franklin - *Fallingwater Rising: Frank Lloyd Wright, E.J. Kaufmann, and America's Most Extraordinary House*
  Choice - v42 - i1 - Sept 2004 - p92(1) [501+]

Toker, Leona - *Return from the Archipelago*
  MFSF - v50 - i2 - Summer 2004 - p532-534 [501+]

Tokeshi, Jinichi - *Kendo: Elements, Rules, and Philosophy*
  Choice - v41 - i7 - March 2004 - p1333(1) [501+]
  Pac A - v77 - i2 - Summer 2004 - p351(2) [501+]
  R&R Bk N - v19 - i1 - Feb 2004 - p75(1) [51-500]

Tokio, Marnelle - *More than You Can Chew*
  y CBRA - Annual 2003 - p518(1) [51-500]
  y VOYA - v27 - i3 - August 2004 - p225(1) [1-50]

Tokitsu, Kenji - *Miyamoto Musashi: His Life and Writings*
  LJ - v129 - i14 - Sept 1 2004 - p167(1) [51-500]
  R&R Bk N - v19 - i4 - Nov 2004 - p50(1) [51-500]

Tokoro, Mario - *The Future of Learning: Issues and Prospects*
  R&R Bk N - v19 - i4 - Nov 2004 - p180(1) [501+]

Tokuyama, Michio - *Slow Dynamics in Complex Systems: Proceedings*
  SciTech - v28 - i3 - Sept 2004 - p58(1) [1-50]

Tolan, Stephanie S. - *Bartholomew's Blessing (Illus. by Moore, Margie)*
  c KR - v72 - i21 - Nov 1 2004 - p1054(1) [51-500]
  c PW - v251 - i39 - Sept 27 2004 - p62(1) [51-500]
  Surviving the Applewhites
  c SLJ - v50 - i11 - Nov 2004 - p66(1) [51-500]

Tolchin, Susan J. - *Glass Houses: Congressional Ethics and the Politics of Venom*
  Choice - v42 - i1 - Sept 2004 - p190(1) [501+]

Toledo, Gregory - *The Hanging of Old Brown: A Story of Slaves, Statesmen, and Redemption*
  HNet - Oct 2004 - pNA [501+]

Tolen, Jane - *Odysseus in the Serpent's Maze*
  c Teach Lib - v32 - i1 - Oct 2004 - p14(1) [51-500]

Toliyat, Hamid A. - *DSP-Based Electomechanical Motion Control*
  SciTech - v28 - i1 - March 2004 - p151(1) [51-500]
  Handbook of Electric Motors, 2nd Ed., Rev. and Expanded
  E-Streams - Dec 2004 - pNA [501+]
  SciTech - v28 - i3 - Sept 2004 - p152(1) [51-500]

Tolkien, J.R.R. - *The Hobbit*
  c RT - v57 - Sept 2003 - p99 [51-500]
  The Return of the King
  c Ent W - i787 - Oct 8 2004 - p120 [51-500]
  The Silmarillion
  c LJ - v129 - i20 - Dec 1 2004 - p184(1) [501+]

Toll, Cathy A. - *The Literacy Coach's Survival Guide: Essential Questions and Practical Answers*
  R Today - v22 - i2 - Oct-Nov 2004 - p33(1) [501+]

Tolle, Eckhart - *The Power of Now: A Guide to Spiritual Enlightenment*
  PW - v251 - i34 - August 23 2004 - pS14(2) [501+]

Tollefsbol, Trygve O. - *Epigenetics Protocols*
  SciTech - v28 - i4 - Dec 2004 - p64(1) [51-500]

Tolley, Kemp - *Caviar and Commissars: The Experiences of a U.S. Naval Officer in Stalin's Russia*
  R&R Bk N - v19 - i3 - August 2004 - p33(1) [51-500]

Tollini, Frederick Paul - *Scene Design at the Court of Louis XIV: The Work of the Vigarani Family and Jean Berain*
  R&R Bk N - v19 - i1 - Feb 2004 - p227(1) [51-500]

Tolpin, Jim - *Woodworking Wit and Wisdom: Thirty Years of Lessons from the Trade*
  LJ - v129 - i20 - Dec 1 2004 - p158(1) [51-500]

Tolstoy, Leo - *The Death of Ivan Ilych: Master and Man*
  BL - v101 - i9-10 - Jan 1 2005 - p816(1) [501+]
  Walk in the Light and Twenty-Three Tales
  TT - v61 - i2 - July 2004 - p283(2) [501+]

Tolstoy, Nikolai - *Patrick O'Brian: The Making of a Novelist*
  HT - v55 - i2 - Feb 2005 - p57(1) [501+]
  Spec - v296 - i9196 - Nov 6 2004 - p60(2) [501+]

Tom, Reichert - *Sex in Advertising: Perspectives on the Erotic Appeal*
  TV Q - v34 - i2 - Wntr 2004 - p61-63 [501+]

Tomaiuolo, Nicholas G. - *The Web Library*
  Bwatch - Jan 2005 - pNA [51-500]

Tomalin, Claire - *Samuel Pepys: The Unequalled Self*
  HR - v57 - i2 - Summer 2004 - p234-248 [501+]
  Sew R - v111 - i4 - Fall 2003 - pcviii-cxvi [501+]

Toman, Michael A. - *Climate Change*
  SciTech - v28 - i4 - Dec 2004 - p53(1) [51-500]

Tomas, David - *Beyond the Image Machine: A History of Visual Technologies*
  Choice - v42 - i4 - Dec 2004 - p696(1) [1-50]
  SciTech - v28 - i3 - Sept 2004 - p20(1) [501+]

Tomas, Natalie R. - *The Medici Women: Gender and Power in Renaissance Florence*
  Choice - v41 - i11-12 - July-August 2004 - p2115(1) [501+]
  R&R Bk N - v19 - i1 - Feb 2004 - p37(1) [1-50]

Tomasello, Michael - *Constructing a Language: A Usage-Based Theory of Language Acquisition*
  QRB - v79 - i3 - Sept 2004 - p339(2) [501+]

Tomasevski, Katarina - *Education Denied: Costs and Remedies*
  TCR - v106 - i5 - May 2004 - p964(4) [501+]

Tomasi, Aldo - *Free Radicals, Nitric Oxide, and Inflammation: Molecular, Biochemical, and Clinical Aspects*
  SciTech - v28 - i3 - Sept 2004 - p89(1) [51-500]

Tomasi, Massimiliano - *Rhetoric in Modern Japan: Western Influences on the Development of Narrative and Oratorical Style*
  R&R Bk N - v19 - i4 - Nov 2004 - p219(1) [501+]

Tomasik, Piotr - *Chemical and Functional Properties of Food Saccharides*
SciTech - v28 - i1 - March 2004 - p174(1) [51-500]

Tomasivich, Jozo - *War and Revolution in Yugoslavia, 1941-1945: Occupation and Collaboration*
JIH - v34 - i3 - Wntr 2004 - p466(3) [501+]

Tomasula, Steve - *In and Oz*
ABR - v25 - i5 - July-August 2004 - p17(2) [501+]

Tomayko, James E. - *Human Aspects of Software Engineering*
SciTech - v28 - i3 - Sept 2004 - p24(1) [51-500]

Tomblin, Stephen G. - *Regionalism in a Global Society: Persistance and Change in Atlantic Canada and New England*
R&R Bk N - v19 - i3 - August 2004 - p146(1) [51-500]

Tombs, George - *Lord Black: The Biography*
Globe & Mail - Sept 18 2004 - pD18 [501+]
NYTBR - Jan 2 2005 - p13 [501+]

Tombs, Robert - *France 1814-1940*
FS - v58 - i3 - July 2004 - p417-417 [501+]

Tombs, Steve - *Unmasking the Crimes of the Powerful: Scrutinizing States and Corporations*
R&R Bk N - v19 - i1 - Feb 2004 - p142(1) [51-500]

Tomei, Lawrence A. - *A Challenges of Teaching with Technology Across the Curriculum: Issues and Solutions*
SLJ - v50 - i10 - Oct 2004 - pS76(1) [51-500]

Tomek, William G. - *Agricultural Product Prices*
JEL - v41 - i4 - Dec 2003 - p1335(1) [501+]

Tomes, Jason Hunter - *King Zon of Albania: Europe's Self-Made Muslim King*
Choice - v42 - i3 - Nov 2004 - p543(1) [1-50]

Tomes, Susan - *Beyond the Notes: Journeys with Chamber Music*
Choice - v42 - i4 - Dec 2004 - p672(1) [1-50]
TLS - i5293 - Sept 10 2004 - p27(1) [501+]

Tomich, Dale W. - *Through the Prism of Slavery: Labor, Capital, and World Economy*
Choice - v41 - i11-12 - July-August 2004 - p2094(2) [501+]

Tomida, Hiroko - *Hiratsuka Raicho and Early Japanese Feminism*
Choice - v42 - i2 - Oct 2004 - p349(2) [51-500]

Tomine, Adrian - *Scrapbook: Uncollected Work, 1990-2004*
BL - v101 - i1 - Sept 1 2004 - p78(1) [501+]
PW - v251 - i29 - July 19 2004 - p147(1) [51-500]

Tomizawa, Hitoshi - *Treasure Hunter: Eternal Youth (Illus. by Tomizawa, Hitoshi)*
y SLJ - v50 - i12 - Dec 2004 - p177(1) [51-500]

Tomkins, Adam - *Public Law*
Law Q Rev - v120 - Oct 2004 - p700-704 [501+]
Law&PolBR - June 2004 - p469(3) [501+]

Tomkins, Jasper - *Catwalk*
c PW - v251 - i47 - Nov 22 2004 - p58(2) [501+]

Tomlinson, Charles - *Metamorphosis: Poetry and Translation*
TLS - i5264 - Feb 20 2004 - p27-27 [501+]
Skywriting
TLS - i5287 - July 30 2004 - p25(1) [501+]

Tomlinson, Jim - *The Labour Governments 1964-1970, Vol. 3*
HER - v119 - i483 - Sept 2004 - p1018(3) [501+]

Tomlinson, Richard - *Emerging Johanesburg: Perspectives on the Postpartheid City*
JEL - v41 - i4 - Dec 2003 - p1414(1) [501+]

Tomlinson, Theresa - *Voyage of the Snake Lady*
y Sch Lib - v52 - i3 - Autumn 2004 - p163(1) [501+]

Tommasini, Anthony - *Opera: A Critic's Guide to the 100 Most Important Recordings*
y BL - v101 - i6 - Nov 15 2004 - p544(1) [51-500]
Opera: A Critic's Guide to the 100 Most Important Works and the Best Recordings
ON - v69 - i7 - Jan 2005 - p75(1) [51-500]

Tompert, Ann - *Grandfather Tang's Story (Illus. by Parker, Robert A.)*
c SLJ - v50 - i9 - Sept 2004 - p59(1) [51-500]
Saint Valentine (Illus. by Kasparavicius, Kestutis)
c KR - v72 - i22 - Nov 15 2004 - p1093(1) [51-500]
c SLJ - v50 - i12 - Dec 2004 - p138(1) [501+]

Tompkins, Cynthia - *Teen Life in Latin America and the Caribbean*
y Ref Rev - August 2004 - pNA [501+]
R&R Bk N - v19 - i3 - August 2004 - p152(1) [51-500]
y VOYA - v27 - i5 - Dec 2004 - p423(1) [51-500]

Tompkins, Gail E. - *Teaching Vocabulary: 50 Successful Strategies, Grades K-12*
R Today - v22 - i1 - August-Sept 2004 - p32(1) [51-500]

Tompkins, Phillip K. - *Apollo, Challenger, Columbia: The Decline of the Space Program: A Study in Organizational Communication*
SciTech - v28 - i4 - Dec 2004 - p161(1) [51-500]

Tomsak, Robert L. - *Handbook of Neuro-Ophthalmology and Orbital Disease: Diagnosis and Treatment, 2nd Ed.*
SciTech - v28 - i1 - March 2004 - p114(1) [51-500]

Tondeur, Louise - *The Haven Home for Delinquent Girls*
TLS - i5304 - Nov 26 2004 - p22(1) [501+]

Tone, Andrea - *Devices and Desires: A History of Contraceptives in America*
JWH - v16 - i4 - Winter 2004 - p215(11) [501+]

Toner, Jules - *Love and Friendship*
Theol St - v65 - i4 - Dec 2004 - p906(2) [501+]

Tones, Keith - *Health Promotion: Planning and Strategies*
SciTech - v28 - i3 - Sept 2004 - p83(1) [501+]

Tong, Benson - *Asian American Children: A Historical Handbook and Guide*
R&R Bk N - v19 - i4 - Nov 2004 - p57(1) [51-500]

Tong, Ng Suat - *Rosetta 2: A Comics Anthology*
SLJ - v50 - i12 - Dec 2004 - p177(1) [51-500]
Rosetta 2
BL - v101 - i7 - Dec 1 2004 - p644(1) [51-500]

Tong, Su - *My Life as Emperor*
BL - v101 - i9-10 - Jan 1 2005 - p823(2) [1-50]

Tonkin, Peter - *Titan 10*
BL - v100 - i22 - August 2004 - p1907(1) [51-500]

Tonnard, Patrick L. - *The MACS-Lift Short Scar Rhytidectomy*
SciTech - v28 - i3 - Sept 2004 - p111(1) [51-500]

Tonnensen, Hanne Hjorth - *Photostability of Drugs and Drug Formulations, 2nd Ed.*
SciTech - v28 - i4 - Dec 2004 - p120(1) [1-50]

Tonnet-Lacroix, Eliane - *La Litterature francaise et francophone de 1945 a l'm 2000*
FS - v58 - i3 - July 2004 - p440-441 [501+]

Tonry, Michael - *The Future of Imprisonment*
Choice - v42 - i6 - Feb 2005 - p1104(1) [51-500]
Law&PolBR - Nov 2004 - p870(4) [501+]
Punishment and Politics: Evidence and Emulation in the Making of English Crime Control Policy
R&R Bk N - v19 - i3 - August 2004 - p171(1) [501+]
TLS - i5304 - Nov 26 2004 - p9-10 [501+]
Thinking about Crime: Sense and Sensibility in American Penal Culture
Law&PolBR - June 2004 - p424(4) [501+]
TLS - i5304 - Nov 26 2004 - p9-10 [501+]

Tonsing, Betty K. - *The Quakers in South Africa: A Social Witness*
HNet - July 2004 - pNA [501+]

Tontti, Jarkko - *Right and Prejudice: Prolegoma to a Hermeneutical Philosophy of Law*
R&R Bk N - v19 - i4 - Nov 2004 - p161(1) [501+]

Tony, Jackson - *No Excuses: Closing the Racial Gap in Learning*
CS - v33 - i5 - Sept 2004 - p605-606 [501+]

Toobin, Jeffrey - *The Run of His Life: The People v. O.J. Simpson*
Globe & Mail - July 31 2004 - pD15 [51-500]

Toogood, James - *Incredible Light and Texture in Watercolor*
LJ - v129 - i12 - July 2004 - p80(1) [51-500]

Toohey, Peter - *Melancholy, Love, and Time: Boundaries of the Self in Ancient Literature*
Choice - v42 - i5 - Jan 2005 - p849(1) [1-50]

Tooker, D. K. - *Stand Well Clear*
APH - v51 - i3 - Fall 2004 - p54(1) [501+]

Tooks, Lance - *Lucifer's Garden of Verses, Vol. 1*
PW - v252 - i8 - Feb 21 2005 - p160(1) [51-500]

Tool, Marc R. - *Institutional Analysis and Economic Policy*
JEL - v42 - i1 - March 2004 - p243(2) [501+]

Toole, F.X. - *Million Dollar Baby*
Globe & Mail - March 12 2005 - pD17 [1-50]
Rope Burns
Ent W - i801 - Jan 14 2005 - p92 [501+]

Tooley, Hunt - *The Western Front: Battleground and Home Front in the First World War*
IndRev - v9 - i3 - Wntr 2005 - p433(5) [501+]
J Mil H - v68 - i3 - April 2004 - p622-623 [501+]

Tooley, James - *Government Failure: E. G. West on Education*
IndRev - v9 - i3 - Wntr 2005 - p445(4) [501+]
The Miseducation of Women
Choice - v42 - i1 - Sept 2004 - p160(1) [51-500]

Toor, Rachel - *The Pig and I: Why It's So Easy to Love an Animal, and So Hard to Live with a Man*
PW - v251 - i49 - Dec 6 2004 - p50(1) [51-500]

Toor, Will - *Transportation and Sustainable Campus Communities: Issues, Examples, Solutions*
R&R Bk N - v19 - i3 - August 2004 - p225(1) [1-50]

Toorn, Peter Van - *Moutain Tea*
BIC - v33 - i7 - Oct 2004 - p29(2) [501+]

Tope, Rebecca - *The Sting of Death*
BL - v100 - i22 - August 2004 - p1907(1) [51-500]
KR - v72 - i13 - July 1 2004 - p608(1) [51-500]

Topham, Sean - *Move House*
LJ - v129 - i15 - Sept 15 2004 - p57(1) [51-500]

Toplin, Robert Brent - *Reel History: In Defense of Hollywood*
FQ - v57 - i4 - Summer 2004 - p68(2) [501+]
Pub Hist - v26 - i2 - Spring 2004 - p94(96) [501+]
AHR - v109 - i4 - Oct 2004 - p1263(2) [501+]

Toporek, Chuck - *Inside .Mac*
Bwatch - v26 - i8 - August 2004 - p6(1) [51-500]
Mac OS X Panther in a Nutshell
SciTech - v28 - i4 - Dec 2004 - p26(1) [51-500]

Toporkov, Vasili - *Stanislavski in Rehearsal*
Am Theat - v21 - i8 - Oct 2004 - p139(4) [501+]

Topp, Elizabeth M. - *Journal of Pharmaceutical Sciences: Compendium of Reviews*
SciTech - v28 - i4 - Dec 2004 - p119(1) [1-50]

Topping, Rhea - *Rod Rage: The Polite Fly Fisher's Companion*
PW - v251 - i37 - Sept 13 2004 - p67(1) [51-500]

Torbiorn, Kjell M. - *Destination Europe: The Political and Economic Growth of a Continent*
Choice - v41 - i11-12 - July-August 2004 - p2119(1) [501+]

Torchia, Joseph - *The Kryptonite Kid*
Globe & Mail - August 7 2004 - pD15 [501+]

Torchinsky, Alberto - *Real-Variable Methods in Harmonic Analysis*
SciTech - v28 - i3 - Sept 2004 - p41(1) [1-50]

Torchio, M.C. - *Aristofane: Pluto*
Class R - v53 - i2 - Nov 2003 - p290-291 [501+]

Torey, Allysa - *More from Magnolia: Recipes from the World Famous Bakery and Allysa Torey's Home Kitchen*
BL - v101 - i2 - Sept 15 2004 - p190(1) [51-500]

Torgoff, Martin - *Can't Find My Way Home: America in the Great Stoned Age, 1945-2000*
Choice - v42 - i5 - Jan 2005 - p919(1) [1-50]

Toro-Morn, Maura I. - *Migration and Immigration: A Global View*
Choice - v42 - i5 - Jan 2005 - p838(1) [1-50]
R&R Bk N - v19 - i3 - August 2004 - p184(1) [501+]

Torok, George D. - *A Guide to Historic Coal Towns of the Big Sandy River Valley*
R&R Bk N - v19 - i3 - August 2004 - p74(1) [51-500]

Toropov, Brandon - *Manager's Portfolio of Model Performance Evaluations: Ready-to-Use Performance Appraisals Covering All Employee Functions*
HR Mag - v49 - i7 - July 2004 - p21(1) [51-500]

Toroticaguena, Gloria P. - *Identity, Culture, and Politics in the Basque Diaspora*
Choice - v42 - i1 - Sept 2004 - p163(1) [501+]

Torr, James D. - *Crime and Criminals*
y SLJ - v50 - i11 - Nov 2004 - p174(1) [51-500]
Is Military Action Justified Against Nations That Support Terrorism?
SLJ - v50 - i10 - Oct 2004 - pS60(1) [51-500]
Professional Sports
SLJ - v50 - i10 - Oct 2004 - pS66(1) [501+]
U.S. Policy Toward Rogue Nations
y SLJ - v50 - i11 - Nov 2004 - p164(1) [51-500]

Torrans, Lee Ann - *Law and Libraries: The Public Library*
BL - v101 - i9-10 - Jan 1 2005 - p911(1) [51-500]
R&R Bk N - v19 - i3 - August 2004 - p202(1) [1-50]

Torrans, Thomas - *Forging the Tortilla Curtain: Cultural Drift and Change along the United States-Mexico Border from the Spanish Era to the Present*
HAHR - v84 - i3 - August 2004 - p568(2) [501+]

Torras, Mariano - *Welfare Inequality, and Resource Depletion: A Reassessment of Brazilian Economic Growth*
JEL - v41 - i4 - Dec 2003 - p1425(1) [501+]
JEL - v41 - i4 - Dec 2003 - p1425(1) [501+]

Torrell, Jean-Pierre - *Recherches thomasiennes: Etudes revues et augumentees*
Theol St - v65 - i3 - Sept 2004 - p646(2) [501+]
Saint Thomas Aquinas, Vol. 2
Theol St - v66 - i1 - March 2005 - p204(2) [501+]

Torremans, Paul L.C. - *Copyright and Human Rights: Freedom of Expression, Intellectual Property, Privacy*
R&R Bk N - v19 - i4 - Nov 2004 - p162(1) [501+]

Torrens, James - *Uphill Running: A Jesuit Life*
AM - v192 - i1 - Jan 3 2005 - p22 [501+]

Torres, Daniel - *Rocco Vargas: A Game of Gods*
y VOYA - v27 - i4 - Oct 2004 - p321(1) [51-500]

Torres, Germano Lambert - *Advances in Intelligent Systems and Robotics, LAPTEC 2003: Proceedings*
SciTech - v28 - i3 - Sept 2004 - p15(1) [501+]

Torres, J. - *Teen Titans Go! Truth, Justice, Pizza*
c Teach Lib - v32 - i3 - Feb 2005 - p24(1) [51-500]

Torres, Laura - *Best Friends Forever! 199 Projects to Make and Share*
y SLJ - v51 - i2 - Feb 2005 - p153(1) [51-500]

Torres, Leyla - *The Kite Festival (Illus. by Torres, Leyla)*
c SLJ - v50 - i7 - July 2004 - p89(1) [51-500]

Torres, Maria de los Angeles - *By Heart/De Memoria: Cuban Women's Journeys in and out of Exile*
Ams - v61 - i2 - Oct 2004 - p279(2) [501+]
The Lost Apple: Operation Pedro Pan, Cuban Children in the U.S., and the Promise of a Better Future
Choice - v41 - i7 - March 2004 - p1347(2) [501+]

Torres, Sasha - *Black, White, and in Color: Television and Black Civil Rights*
FQ - v58 - i1 - Fall 2004 - p58(3) [501+]

Torres, Vasti - *Identity Development of Diverse Populations: Implications for Teaching and Administration in Higher Education*
J Hi E - v76 - i1 - Jan-Feb 2005 - p117(3) [501+]

Torrey, Michele - *To the Edge of the World*
y Kliatt - v39 - i2 - March 2005 - p23(2) [51-500]
Voyage of Ice: Chronicles of Courage
y SLJ - v50 - i7 - July 2004 - p113(1) [51-500]
y VOYA - v27 - i4 - Oct 2004 - p308(2) [51-500]

Torrez, Juliette - *Madness and Retribution*
Prog - v69 - i2 - Feb 2005 - p46(3) [501+]

Torstrick, Rebecca L. - *Culture and Customs of Israel*
R&R Bk N - v19 - i3 - August 2004 - p83(1) [51-500]

Tortajada, Ana - *The Silenced Cry: One Woman's Diary of a Journey to Afghanistan*
BL - v100 - i22 - August 2004 - p1892(1) [51-500]
LJ - v129 - i12 - July 2004 - p105(1) [51-500]

Tortes, J. - *Sidekicks, Vol. 1*
y Teach Lib - v32 - i3 - Feb 2005 - p58(1) [1-50]

Tortorelli, P.F. - *John Stringer Symposium on High Temperature Corrosion: Proceedings*
SciTech - v28 - i1 - March 2004 - p140(1) [51-500]

Tory, Leo - *The Twilight of the Old Unionism*
Choice - v42 - i2 - Oct 2004 - p337(1) [51-500]

Toscano, Filippo M. - *Sicily--A Literary and Cultural History: Ancient and Esoteric Voices*
R&R Bk N - v19 - i1 - Feb 2004 - p37(1) [1-50]

Toscano, Rodrigo - *To Leveling Swerve*
PW - v251 - i47 - Nov 22 2004 - p57(1) [51-500]

Tosco, Carlo - *Viaggio di Affrica e America Portughesa*
IJAHS - v37 - i1 - Wntr 2004 - p162-163 [501+]

Toseland, Ronald W. - *An Introduction to Group Work Practice, 5th Ed.*
R&R Bk N - v19 - i3 - August 2004 - p159(1) [51-500]

Tost, Tony - *Invisible Bride: Poems*
ABR - v25 - i5 - July-August 2004 - p5(2) [501+]
LJ - v129 - i12 - July 2004 - p88(1) [51-500]

Toth, Susan Allen - *Leaning Into the Wind: A Memoir of Midwest Weather*
BooChiTr - Jan 4 2004 - p2(1) [501+]

Totman, Conard - *Pre-Industrial Korea and Japan in Environmental Perspective*
Choice - v42 - i2 - Oct 2004 - p350(1) [51-500]

Totten, George E. - *Fuels and Lubricants Handbook: Technology, Properties, Performance, and Testing*
SciTech - v28 - i1 - March 2004 - p173(1) [51-500]
Handbook of Mechanical Alloy Design
E-Streams - Oct 2004 - pNA [501+]
SciTech - v28 - i1 - March 2004 - p170(1) [51-500]
Handbook of Metallurgical Process Design
SciTech - v28 - i3 - Sept 2004 - p165(1) [51-500]
Mechanical Tribology; Materials, Characterization, and Applications
SciTech - v28 - i3 - Sept 2004 - p150(1) [51-500]
Modeling and Simulation for Material Seclection and Mechanical Design
SciTech - v28 - i1 - March 2004 - p139(1) [51-500]
Surface Modification and Mechanisms: Friction, Stress, and Reaction Engineering
SciTech - v28 - i3 - Sept 2004 - p140(1) [51-500]

Totten, Samuel - *Hinduism and Modernity*
CS - v33 - i6 - Nov 2004 - p750(1) [1-50]
Teaching about the Holocaust: Essays by College and University Teachers
R&R Bk N - v19 - i3 - August 2004 - p34(1) [51-500]

Totton, Robin - *Song of the Outcasts: An Introduction to Flamenco*
Notes - v61 - i2 - Dec 2004 - p471(3) [501+]
R&R Bk N - v19 - i1 - Feb 2004 - p197(1) [51-500]

Totz, Colleen - *Floodplain Modeling Using HEC-RAS*
E-Streams - July 2004 - pNA [501+]

Toufique, Kazi Ali - *Hands Not Land: How Livelihoods Are Changing in Rural Bangladesh*
JEL - v42 - i1 - March 2004 - p312(1) [501+]

Toulmin, Stephen - *Return to Reason*
Isis - v95 - i3 - Sept 2004 - p541(2) [501+]

Toulouse-Lautrec, Henri de - *A Toulouse-Lautrec Sketchbook Introduction*
A Art - v68 - i746 - Sept 2004 - p75(1) [501+]

Toulouse, Mark G. - *Makers of Christian Theology in America*
TT - v61 - i1 - April 2004 - p132-134 [501+]

Toure (b. 1971 -) - *Soul City*
y BL - v101 - i1 - Sept 1 2004 - p66(1) [51-500]
Black Iss - v6 - i5 - Sept-Oct 2004 - p50(1) [1-50]
Ent W - i781 - Sept 3 2004 - p81 [51-500]
KR - v72 - i14 - July 15 2004 - p659(1) [51-500]
LJ - v129 - i16 - Oct 1 2004 - p74(1) [51-500]
PW - v251 - i32 - August 9 2004 - p231(1) [51-500]

Tournadre, Nicolas - *Manual of Standard Tibetan Language and Civilization: Introduction to Standard Tibetan (Spoken and Written) Followed by an Appendix on Classical Literary Tibetan*
R&R Bk N - v19 - i4 - Nov 2004 - p219(1) [501+]

Tournay, Audrey - *Beaver Tales: Audrey Tournay and the Aspen Valley Beavers*
CBRA - Annual 2003 - p406(1) [501+]

Tourniaire, Francoise - *Just Enough CRM*
R&R Bk N - v19 - i1 - Feb 2004 - p108(1) [51-500]

Tourondel, Laurent - *Go Fish: Fresh Ideas for American Seafood*
LJ - v129 - i17 - Oct 15 2004 - p83(1) [51-500]

Toussaint, Jean-Philippe - *Television*
BL - v101 - i8 - Dec 15 2004 - p709(1) [51-500]
KR - v72 - i19 - Oct 1 2004 - p937(1) [501+]
LJ - v129 - i18 - Nov 1 2004 - p78(1) [501+]
NYTBR - Jan 2 2005 - p11 [501+]
PW - v251 - i42 - Oct 18 2004 - p48(2) [501+]

Tout, Ken - *Roads to Falaise: 'Cobra' and 'Goodwood' Reassessed*
J Mil H - v68 - i2 - April 2004 - p637(2) [501+]

Toutonghi, Pauls - *Live Cargo*
Ga R - v58 - i3 - Fall 2004 - p685-696 [501+]

Tovani, Cris - *Comprehending Content: Reading Across the Curriculum, Grades 6-12*
SLJ - v50 - i10 - Oct 2004 - pS76(1) [51-500]
Do I Really Have to Teach Reading? Content Comprehension Grades 6-12
SLJ - v50 - i10 - Oct 2004 - pS76(1) [51-500]
Thoughtful Reading: Teaching Comprehension to Adolescents
SLJ - v50 - i10 - Oct 2004 - pS76(1) [51-500]

Tovey, Phillip - *Inculturation of Christian Worship: Exploring the Eucharist*
R&R Bk N - v19 - i3 - August 2004 - p27(1) [1-50]

Towe, L. Clarence - *American Azaleas*
BL - v100 - i22 - August 2004 - p1887(1) [51-500]
SciTech - v28 - i3 - Sept 2004 - p129(1) [51-500]

Tower, Jeremiah - *California Dish: What I Saw*
NYTBR - August 22 2004 - p20 [501+]

Towers, J. Tarin - *Macromedia Dreamweaver MX Advanced for Windows and Macintosh*
SciTech - v28 - i3 - Sept 2004 - p157(1) [51-500]

Towers, S. Mutchow - *Control of Religious Printing in Early Stuart England*
AHR - v109 - i4 - Oct 2004 - p1308-1309 [501+]

Towle, Michael J. - *Out of Touch: The Presidency and Public Opinion*
PSQ - v119 - i3 - Fall 2004 - p526(2) [501+]
Pub Op Q - v68 - i3 - Fall 2004 - p426(5) [501+]

Townley, Gemma - *Little White Lies: A Novel of Love and Good Intentions*
PW - v252 - i6 - Feb 7 2005 - p43(1) [51-500]

Townley, Roderick - *Sky: A Novel in Three Sets and an Encore*
y BL - v100 - i22 - August 2004 - p1921(1) [51-500]
y CCB-B - v58 - i1 - Sept 2004 - p42(1) [51-500]
y Kliatt - v38 - i4 - July 2004 - p13(1) [51-500]
y KR - v72 - i13 - July 1 2004 - p638(1) [51-500]
y PW - v251 - i35 - August 30 2004 - p56(2) [51-500]
y SLJ - v50 - i7 - July 2004 - p113(1) [51-500]
y VOYA - v27 - i3 - August 2004 - p225(1) [1-50]

Townsend, Ann - *The Coronary Garden*
LJ - v130 - i4 - March 1 2005 - p90(1) [51-500]

Townsend, Camilla - *Pocahontas and the Powhatan Dilemma*
HM - v309 - i1853 - Oct 2004 - p92(1) [501+]
KR - v72 - i16 - August 15 2004 - p797(2) [501+]

Townsend, Courtney M. - *Sabiston Textbook of Surgery: The Biological Basis of Modern Surgical Practice, 17th Ed.*
SciTech - v28 - i3 - Sept 2004 - p110(1) [51-500]

Townsend, Donna - *Apple Fractions*
c BL - v101 - i4 - Oct 15 2004 - p426(1) [51-500]

Townsend, Emily Rose - *Arctic Foxes*
c SLJ - v50 - i7 - July 2004 - p96(1) [51-500]
Owls
c SLJ - v50 - i8 - August 2004 - p114(1) [51-500]
Penguins
c SLJ - v50 - i7 - July 2004 - p96(1) [51-500]
Polar Bears
c SLJ - v50 - i7 - July 2004 - p96(1) [51-500]
Woodpeckers
c SLJ - v50 - i8 - August 2004 - p114(1) [51-500]

Townsend, John - *Mysterious Monsters*
c SLJ - v50 - i10 - Oct 2004 - p196(1) [51-500]
Mysterious Signs
y Sch Lib - v52 - i4 - Winter 2004 - p219(1) [51-500]
c SLJ - v50 - i10 - Oct 2004 - p196(1) [51-500]
Mysterious Urban Myths
c SLJ - v50 - i10 - Oct 2004 - p196(1) [51-500]

Townsend, Lindsay - *The English Daughter*
BL - v101 - i9-10 - Jan 1 2005 - p832(2) [1-50]

Townsend, Mary C. - *Nursing Diagnoses in Psychiatric Nursing: Care Plans and Psychotropic Medications, 6th Ed.*
SciTech - v28 - i1 - March 2004 - p95(1) [51-500]

Townsend, Richard F. - *Hero, Hawk, and Open Hand: American Indian Art of the Ancient Midwest and South*
Choice - v42 - i6 - Feb 2005 - p1010(1) [51-500]

Townsend, Sue - *Adrian Mole and the Weapons of Mass Destruction*
y Globe & Mail - Dec 11 2004 - pD40 [501+]
NS - v133 - i4711 - Oct 25 2004 - p54(1) [501+]
Spec - v296 - i9196 - Nov 6 2004 - p64(1) [501+]
TLS - i5300 - Oct 29 2004 - p23(1) [501+]

Townsend, Susanne Grayson - *How to Eat Like a Republican, or, Hold the Mayo, Muffy--I'm Feeling Miracle Whipped Tonight*
BL - v100 - i21 - July 2004 - p1808(2) [1-50]

Townsley, Nikki C. - *Postponing the Postmodern: Sociological Practices, Selves and Theories*
CS - v33 - i5 - Sept 2004 - p611-613 [501+]

Townson, Hazel - *Adventures of a Lottery Winner*
c Sch Lib - v52 - i3 - Autumn 2004 - p148(1) [501+]

Towse, Ruth - *A Handbook of Cultural Economics*
JEL - v41 - i4 - Dec 2003 - p1443(1) [501+]

Toy, Eugene C. - *Case Files: Emergency Medicine*
SciTech - v28 - i4 - Dec 2004 - p90(1) [51-500]
Case Files: General Surgery
SciTech - v28 - i1 - March 2004 - p109(1) [51-500]
Case Files; Internal Medicine
SciTech - v28 - i3 - Sept 2004 - p90(1) [51-500]

Toy Store
LibMed - v22 - i4 - Jan 2004 - p89(1) [501+]

Toye, John - *Trade and Development: Directions for the Twenty-First Century*
JEL - v41 - i4 - Dec 2003 - p1414(1) [501+]
The UN and Global Political Economy: Trade, Finance, and Development
Choice - v42 - i4 - Dec 2004 - p709(1) [1-50]

Toye, Richard - *The Labour Party and the Planned Economy, 1931-1951*
AHR - v109 - i2 - April 2004 - p618(2) [501+]
Albion - v36 - i2 - Summer 2004 - p360(2) [501+]
HER - v119 - i483 - Sept 2004 - p1014(3) [501+]
HER - v119 - i483 - Sept 2004 - p1014(3) [501+]

Tozer, E.P.J. - *Broadcast Engineer's Reference Book*
Choice - v42 - i2 - Oct 2004 - p322(1) [51-500]

Tracey, Rhian - *Isla and Luke: Make or Break*
y Sch Lib - v52 - i3 - Autumn 2004 - p163(1) [501+]

Tracey, William R. - *The Human Resources Glossary: The Complete Desk Reference for HR Executive, Managers, and Practitioners, 3rd Ed.*
 R&R Bk N - v19 - i2 - May 2004 - p118 [51-500]
The Human Resources Glossary: The Complete Desk Reference for HR Executives, Managers and Practitioners
 Choice - v41 - i11-12 - July-August 2004 - p2029(1) [501+]

Trachtenberg, Adam - *Upgrading to PHP 5*
 SciTech - v28 - i4 - Dec 2004 - p22(1) [51-500]

Trachtenberg, Alan - *Distinctly American*
 Afterimage - v30 - Winter 2003 - p10 [501+]
Shades of Hiawatha: Staging Indians, Making Americans, 1880-1930
 BW - v34 - i50 - Dec 12 2004 - p2(1) [501+]
 LJ - v129 - i16 - Oct 1 2004 - p96(1) [501+]
 PW - v251 - i35 - August 30 2004 - p43(1) [51-500]

Tracy Chevalier - *The Lady and the Unicorn (Read by Blumenfeld, Robert). Audiobook Review*
 c Kliatt - v38 - i4 - July 2004 - p52(1) [51-500]

Tracy, James D. - *Emperor Charles V, Impresario of War: Campaign Strategy, International Finance, and Domestic Politics*
 JIH - v34 - i4 - Spring 2004 - p648-650 [501+]
 JMH - v77 - i1 - March 2005 - p162(3) [501+]

Tracy, Kathleen - *John Steinbeck*
 y SLJ - v51 - i1 - Jan 2005 - p140(1) [51-500]
The Life and Times of Homer
 c BL - v101 - i4 - Oct 15 2004 - p415(1) [51-500]
 c SLJ - v50 - i12 - Dec 2004 - p170(1) [51-500]

Tracy, P.J. - *Dead Run (Read by Schirner, Buck). Audiobook Review*
 KR - v73 - i4 - Feb 15 2005 - p196(1) [51-500]
 LJ - v129 - i20 - Dec 1 2004 - p182(1) [501+]
Dead Run
 PW - v252 - i8 - Feb 21 2005 - p157(1) [51-500]
Live Bait (Read by Schirner, Buck). Audiobook Review
 y Kliatt - v39 - i1 - Jan 2005 - p46(2) [51-500]
Live Bait
 BooChiTr - May 23 2004 - p2(1) [501+]

Tracy, Paul E. - *Decision Making and Juvenile Justice: An Analysis of Bias in Case Processing*
 CS - v33 - i1 - Jan 2004 - p93-94 [501+]

Tracy, Robert - *Ailey Spirit: The Journey of an American Dance Company*
 Dance - v78 - i12 - Dec 2004 - p46(1) [501+]

Tracy, Sarah W. - *Altering American Consciousness: The History of Alcohol and Drug Use in the United States, 1800-2000*
 Choice - v42 - i5 - Jan 2005 - p892(1) [1-50]
 R&R Bk N - v19 - i3 - August 2004 - p162(1) [501+]

Tracy, Steven C. - *A Historical Guide to Langston Hughes*
 VQR - v80 - i3 - Summer 2004 - p261(1) [1-50]
A Historical Guide to Ralph Ellison
 Bl S - v34 - i3 - Fall 2004 - p75-75 [501+]
 Choice - v42 - i5 - Jan 2005 - p853(1) [1-50]

Trade and Development Report, 2003
 JEL - v42 - i1 - March 2004 - p313(1) [501+]
 R&R Bk N - v19 - i1 - Feb 2004 - p105(1) [51-500]

Trade, Investment, and Development in the Middle East and North Africa: Engaging with the World
 JEL - v42 - i1 - March 2004 - p314(2) [501+]

The Trade Policies in Russia: The Role of Local and Regional Governments
 JEL - v41 - i4 - Dec 2003 - p1431(1) [501+]

Trafficking in Persons: An Analysis of Afghanistan
 R&R Bk N - v19 - i4 - Nov 2004 - p151(1) [501+]

Tragardh, Lars - *After National Democracy: Rights, Law and Power in America and the New Europe*
 Law&PolBR - Nov 2004 - p867(3) [501+]

Trager, Oliver - *Keys to the Rain: The Definitive Bob Dylan Encyclopedia*
 Bwatch - Jan 2005 - pNA [51-500]
 Choice - v42 - i6 - Feb 2005 - p994(1) [51-500]
 LJ - v129 - i19 - Nov 15 2004 - p86(1) [51-500]
 NYTBR - Oct 24 2004 - p15 [501+]

Trahair, Richard C.S. - *Encyclopedia of Cold War Espionage, Spies, and Secret Operations*
 BL - v101 - i6 - Nov 15 2004 - p613(2) [501+]

Traig, Jennifer - *Devil in the Details: Scenes from an Obsessive Girlhood (Read by Wade, Melinda). Audiobook Review*
 y Kliatt - v39 - i2 - March 2005 - p58(2) [51-500]
Devil in the Details: Scenes from an Obsessive Girlhood
 y BL - v100 - i22 - August 2004 - p1883(1) [51-500]
 BL - v101 - i9-10 - Jan 1 2005 - p771(1) [51-500]
 Ent W - i784 - Sept 17 2004 - p86 [501+]
 LJ - v129 - i14 - Sept 1 2004 - p173(1) [51-500]
 PW - v251 - i35 - August 30 2004 - p45(2) [51-500]

Trail, Gayla - *You Grow Girl: The Groundbreaking Guide to Gardening*
 LJ - v130 - i4 - March 1 2005 - p104(1) [51-500]

Trailblazers Biographies
 LibMed - v22 - i7 - April-May 2004 - p68(1) [501+]

Trailblazers Biography
 LibMed - v22 - i7 - April-May 2004 - p68(1) [501+]

Trailblazers of the Modern World
 y Ref Rev - July 2004 - pNA [501+]

The Train of States
 PW - v251 - i37 - Sept 13 2004 - p79(1) [501+]

Train, Russell E. - *Politics, Pollution, and Pandas: An Environmental Memoir*
 Env - v46 - i9 - Nov 2004 - p40(2) [501+]
 SciTech - v28 - i3 - Sept 2004 - p5(1) [501+]

Traistaru, Iulia - *The Emerging Economic Geography in EU Accession Countries*
 R&R Bk N - v19 - i1 - Feb 2004 - p83(1) [51-500]

Tramble, Nichelle D. - *The Last King*
 BW - v34 - i29 - July 18 2004 - p10(1) [501+]

Trambouze, Pierre - *Chemical Reactors: From Design to Operation*
 Choice - v42 - i5 - Jan 2005 - p885(1) [1-50]
 SciTech - v28 - i3 - Sept 2004 - p166(1) [51-500]

Trammell, Jeremiah - *The Giant Cabbage: An Alaskan Folktale*
 LibMed - v22 - i5 - Feb 2004 - p73(1) [501+]

Tramonto, Rick - *Tru: A Cookbook from the Legendary Chicago Restaurant*
 LJ - v129 - i19 - Nov 15 2004 - p82(2) [51-500]

Tran-Nguyen, Anh-Nga - *Trade and Gender: Opportunities and Challenges for Developing Countries*
 R&R Bk N - v19 - i4 - Nov 2004 - p134(1) [51-500]

Tran, Truong - *Going Home, Coming Home*
 LibMed - v22 - i6 - March 2004 - p62(1) [501+]

Tran, Van Hoa - *Competition Policy and Global Competitiveness in Major Asian Economies*
 R&R Bk N - v19 - i2 - May 2004 - p112(1) [1-50]

Tranberg, Heidi - *Medical Records: Use and Abuse*
 SciTech - v28 - i3 - Sept 2004 - p80(1) [51-500]

Tranel, Virginia - *Ten Circles Upon the Pond; Reflections of a Prodigal Mother*
 y Kliatt - v38 - i4 - July 2004 - p38(1) [51-500]

Tranquilli, William J. - *Pain Management for the Small Animal Practitioner, 2nd Ed.*
 SciTech - v28 - i4 - Dec 2004 - p127 [51-500]

Transactions of the American Society of Civil Engineers, Vol 168
 SciTech - v28 - i3 - Sept 2004 - p137(1) [51-500]

Transfer of Technology for Successful Integration Into the Global Economy
 R&R Bk N - v19 - i3 - August 2004 - p97(1) [51-500]

Transforming Disability into Ability: Policies to Promote Work and Income Security for Disabled People
 R&R Bk N - v19 - i1 - Feb 2004 - p139(1) [51-500]

Transit, Roxanna P. - *Disciplining the Child Via the Discourse of the Professions*
 R&R Bk N - v19 - i4 - Nov 2004 - p130(1) [51-500]

Transparency International - *Global Corruption Report 2004*
 TimHES - v0 - i1651 - July 30 2004 - p23(1) [501+]

Transue, Emily R. - *On Call: A Doctor's Days and Nights in Residency*
 BL - v100 - i22 - August 2004 - p1885(1) [51-500]
 Ent W - i778 - August 13 2004 - p92 [501+]

Trapani, Iza - *Froggie Went A-Courtin' (Illus. by Trapani, Iza)*
 c RT - v57 - Oct 2003 - p165 [1-50]
The Itsy Bitsy Spider (Read by Stephens, Valerie). Audiobook Review
 c SLJ - v50 - i9 - Sept 2004 - p77(1) [51-500]
Row Row Row Your Boat
 c SLJ - v50 - i8 - August 2004 - p76(1) [51-500]
Twinkle, Twinkle, Little Star (Read by Stephens, Valerie). Audiobook Review
 c SLJ - v50 - i9 - Sept 2004 - p78(2) [51-500]

Trapeznik, Alexander - *Lenin's Legacy Down Under: New Zealand's Cold War*
 R&R Bk N - v19 - i3 - August 2004 - p60(1) [51-500]

Traphagan, John W. - *Democratic Change and the Family in Japan's Aging Society*
 CS - v33 - i1 - Jan 2004 - p131-131 [501+]

Trapiello, Andres - *Los amigos del crimen perfecto*
 WLT - v78 - i3-4 - Sept-Dec 2004 - p144(2) [501+]

Trapp, Michael B. - *Greek and Latin Letters: An Anthology with Translation*
 Class R - v54 - i2 - Nov 2004 - p335-337 [501+]

Trask, Haunani-Kay - *Night Is a Sharkskin Drum*
 Cont Pac - v16 - i2 - Fall 2004 - p436(3) [501+]

Trask, Michael - *Cruising Modernism: Class and Sexuality in American Literature and Social Thought*
 R&R Bk N - v19 - i1 - Feb 2004 - p242(1) [501+]

Traub, James - *The Devil's Playground: A Century of Pleasure and Profit in Times Square*
 BHR - v78 - i3 - Autumn 2004 - p507(3) [501+]
 Choice - v42 - i4 - Dec 2004 - p725(1) [1-50]

Traub, Valerie - *The Renaissance of Lesbianism in Early Modern England*
 JWH - v16 - i4 - Winter 2004 - p207(8) [501+]
 Shakes Q - v55 - i2 - Summer 2004 - p225-228 [501+]
 Six Ct J - v34 - i4 - Winter 2003 - p1167-1168 [501+]
 Theat J - v56 - i4 - Dec 2004 - p712-714 [501+]

Traugott, Michael W. - *The Voter's Guide to Election Polls, 3rd Ed.*
 R&R Bk N - v19 - i3 - August 2004 - p146(1) [51-500]

Trauner, Michael - *Molecular Pathogenesis of Cholestasis*
 SciTech - v28 - i1 - March 2004 - p106(1) [51-500]

Traupman, John C. - *Conversational Latin for Oral Proficiency: Phrase Book and Dictionary, 3d ed.*
 R&R Bk N - v19 - i1 - Feb 2004 - p214 [51-500]

Trauth, Stanley E. - *The Amphibians and Reptiles of Arkansas*
 Choice - v42 - i5 - Jan 2005 - p881(2) [1-50]
 SciTech - v28 - i4 - Dec 2004 - p67(1) [51-500]

Trautmann, Lutz - *Digital Sound Synthesis by Physical Modeling Using the Functional Transformation Method*
 SciTech - v28 - i1 - March 2004 - p162(1) [51-500]

Travel Atlas
 Bwatch - Nov 2004 - pNA [51-500]

The Travel Book: A Journey through Every Country in the World
 Globe & Mail - Nov 20 2004 - pT8 [501+]

Travers, Tony - *The Politics of London: Governing an Ungovernable City*
 Choice - v42 - i2 - Oct 2004 - p367(1) [51-500]

Traverso, Susan - *Welfare Politics in Boston, 1910-1940*
 JAH - v91 - i1 - June 2004 - p288-289 [501+]

Travis, Cheryl Brown - *Evolution, Gender, and Rape*
 CS - v33 - i4 - July 2004 - p498(2) [501+]

Travis, Doris Eaton - *The Days We Danced: The Story of My Theatrical Family from Florenz Ziegfeld to Arthur Murray and Beyond*
 M Ed J - v91 - i3 - Jan 2005 - p65(1) [501+]

Travis, Jeremy - *Prisoners Once Removed: The Impact of Incarceration and Reentry on Children, Families, and Communities*
 Choice - v42 - i2 - Oct 2004 - p377(1) [51-500]

Travis, Nora - *Haviland China: The Age of Elegance, 3rd Rev. Ed.*
 R&R Bk N - v19 - i4 - Nov 2004 - p209(1) [501+]

Travitsky, Betty S. - *Anne Killigrew*
 R&R Bk N - v19 - i1 - Feb 2004 - p191(1) [51-500]
The Early Modern Englishwoman: A Facsimile Library of Essential Works, Series 2, Vol. 2, Pt. 2
 R&R Bk N - v19 - i1 - Feb 2004 - p236(1) [51-500]
The Early Modern Englishwoman: A Facsimile Library of Essential Works, Series 2, Vol. 4, Pt. 2
 R&R Bk N - v19 - i1 - Feb 2004 - p236(1) [51-500]
The Early Modern Englishwoman: A Facsimile Library of Essential Works, Series 2, Vol. 6, Pt. 2
 R&R Bk N - v19 - i1 - Feb 2004 - p236(1) [51-500]
The Early Modern Englishwoman: A Facsimile Library of Essential Works, Series 2, Vol. 7, Pt. 2
 R&R Bk N - v19 - i1 - Feb 2004 - p236(1) [51-500]

Trawick, Paul B. - *The Struggle for Water in Peru: Comedy and Tragedy in the Andean Commons*
 JIH - v34 - i4 - Spring 2004 - p664-666 [501+]

Treadwell, Donald F. - *Public Relations Writing: Principles in Practice, Updated Ed.*
 R&R Bk N - v19 - i2 - May 2004 - p129 [51-500]

Treanor, Nick - *The Civil Rights Movement*
 y SLJ - v50 - i10 - Oct 2004 - p68(1) [1-50]

Eats, Shoots and Leaves: Cutting a Dash--the Radio Series That Inspired the Hit Book (Read by Truss, Lynne). Audiobook Review
  BL - v100 - i21 - July 2004 - p1855(1) [1-50]
Eats, Shoots and Leaves: Cutting a Dash--the Radio Series That Inspired the Hit Book. Audiobook Review
  People - v62 - i4 - July 26 2004 - p48 [51-500]
Eats, Shoots and Leaves: The Zero Tolerance Approach to Punctuation (Read by Truss, Lynne). Audiobook Review
  y   Kliatt - v39 - i1 - Jan 2005 - p52(1) [51-500]
Eats, Shoots and Leaves: The Zero Tolerance Approach to Punctuation
  CC - v121 - i17 - August 24 2004 - p6(1) [51-500]
  Globe & Mail - Nov 27 2004 - pD3 [51-500]
  PhiKapP - v84 - i3 - Summer 2004 - p46(1) [501+]
  y   SLJ - v50 - i8 - August 2004 - p147(1) [501+]

Trusted, Jennifer - *Physics and Metaphysics: Theories of Space and Time*
  Zygon - v39 - i4 - Dec 2004 - pNA [501+]

Trutnau, Ludwig - *Venomous Snakes*
  Bwatch - Oct 2004 - pNA [51-500]
  SciTech - v28 - i4 - Dec 2004 - p126 [51-500]

Tsai, Eugenie - *Robert Smithson*
  LJ - v129 - i20 - Dec 1 2004 - p112(1) [51-500]

Tsai, Ming-Yen - *From Adversaries to Partners? Chinese and Russian Military Cooperation After the Cold War*
  R&R Bk N - v19 - i1 - Feb 2004 - p255(1) [51-500]

Tsakalakos, T. - *Nanostructures: Synthesis, Functional Properties and Applications*
  SciTech - v28 - i1 - March 2004 - p141(1) [51-500]

Tsang, Steve - *A Modern History of Hong Kong*
  Choice - v42 - i4 - Dec 2004 - p715(2) [1-50]
  CR - v285 - i1665 - Oct 2004 - p253(1) [501+]

Tschannen-Moran, Megan - *Trust Matters: Leadership for Successful Schools*
  R&R Bk N - v19 - i4 - Nov 2004 - p187(1) [501+]

Tscharntke, Denise - *Re-Educating German Women: The Work of the Women's Affairs Section of the British Military Government 1946-1951*
  R&R Bk N - v19 - i1 - Feb 2004 - p133(1) [51-500]

Tschumi, Christian - *Mirei Shigemori: Modernizing the Japanese Garden (Illus. by Saito, Markuz Wernli)*
  PW - v252 - i9 - Feb 28 2005 - p60(1) [51-500]

Tsebelis, George - *Veto Players: How Political Institutions Work*
  IndRev - v9 - i2 - Fall 2004 - p297(3) [501+]

Tseng, Roy - *The Sceptical Idealist: Michael Oakeshott as a Critic of the Enlightenment*
  HER - v119 - i483 - Sept 2004 - p1010(3) [501+]
  HER - v119 - i483 - Sept 2004 - p1010(3) [501+]

Tseng, Wen-Shing - *Cultural Competence in Clinical Psychiatry*
  SciTech - v28 - i4 - Dec 2004 - p95(1) [51-500]
Cultural Competence in Forensic Mental Health: A Guide for Psychiatrists, Psychologists, and Attorneys
  SciTech - v28 - i3 - Sept 2004 - p87(1) [51-500]

Tsetskhladze, Gocha R. - *The Archaeology of Greek Colonisation: Essays Dedicated to Sir John Boardman*
  R&R Bk N - v19 - i4 - Nov 2004 - p39(1) [51-500]

Tsia, Eugene - *Robert Smithson*
  TLS - i5300 - Oct 29 2004 - p12(1) [501+]

Tsjeard, Bouta - *Women's Roles in Conflict Prevention, Conflict Resolution and Post-Conflict Reconstruction*
  JPR - v41 - i5 - Sept 2004 - p638-638 [501+]

Tsmimicalis, Stavros - *Fragments*
  CBRA - Annual 2003 - p235(1) [51-500]

Tsokos, George C. - *Complement in Autoimmunity*
  SciTech - v28 - i3 - Sept 2004 - p75(1) [51-500]

Tsokos, Michael - *Forensic Pathology Reviews, Vol. 1*
  SciTech - v28 - i3 - Sept 2004 - p87(1) [51-500]

Tsoukalis, Loukas - *What Kind of Europe?*
  Choice - v42 - i4 - Dec 2004 - p731(1) [1-50]
  PSQ - v119 - i3 - Fall 2004 - p547(2) [501+]
  TimHES - v0 - i1675 - Jan 21 2005 - p27(1) [501+]

Tsouna, Voula - *The Epistemology of the Cyrenaic School*
  Phil R - v112 - i3 - July 2003 - p409(5) [501+]

Tsouras, Peter G. - *Alexander: Invincible King of Macedonia*
  R&R Bk N - v19 - i3 - August 2004 - p43(1) [51-500]
Dixie Victorious: An Alternate History of the Civil War
  PW - v251 - i28 - July 12 2004 - p57(1) [51-500]

Tsuda, Masami - *Kare Kano*
  LibMed - v22 - i5 - Feb 2004 - p74(1) [501+]

Tsui, Bonnie - *She Went to the Field: Women Soldiers of the Civil War*
  R&R Bk N - v19 - i1 - Feb 2004 - p60(1) [51-500]

Tsui, Chia-Chi - *Robust Control System Design: Advanced State Space Techniques, 2nd Ed.*
  SciTech - v28 - i1 - March 2004 - p151(1) [51-500]

Tsur, Samuel A. - *Elsevier's Dictionary of Abbreviations, Acronyms, Synonyms, and Symbols Used in Medicine*
  Choice - v42 - i4 - Dec 2004 - p636(1) [1-50]

Tsur, Yacov - *Pricing Irrigation Water: Principles and Cases From Developing Countries*
  R&R Bk N - v19 - i3 - August 2004 - p112(1) [51-500]

Tsutsui, William - *Godzilla on My Mind: Fifty Years of the King of Monsters*
  LJ - v129 - i14 - Sept 1 2004 - p154(1) [51-500]
  Lon R Bks - v27 - i3 - Feb 3 2005 - p23(2) [501+]

Tsuya, Noriko O. - *Marriage, Work, and Family Life in Comparative Perspective: Japan, South Korea, and the United States*
  Choice - v42 - i2 - Oct 2004 - p377(1) [51-500]
  R&R Bk N - v19 - i2 - May 2004 - p134 [51-500]

Tsygankov, Andrei P. - *Whose World Order? Russia's Perception of American Ideas after the Cold War*
  Choice - v42 - i5 - Jan 2005 - p932(1) [51-500]
  Pers PS - v33 - i4 - Fall 2004 - p238(1) [501+]

Tsypkin, Leonid - *Summer in Baden-Baden*
  Sew R - v112 - i2 - Spring 2004 - p301-303 [501+]

Tubert, Silvia - *Women Without a Shadow: Maternal Desire and Assisted Reproductive Technologies*
  R&R Bk N - v19 - i4 - Nov 2004 - p130(1) [51-500]

Tuccille, Jerome - *Kingdom: The Story of the Hunt Family of Texas*
  R&R Bk N - v19 - i3 - August 2004 - p97(1) [51-500]
Trump: The Saga of America's Most Powerful Real Estate Baron
  R&R Bk N - v19 - i3 - August 2004 - p97(1) [51-500]

Tuck, Lily - *The News from Paraguay*
  Ent W - i795 - Dec 3 2004 - p94 [51-500]
  Time - v164 - i22 - Nov 29 2004 - p146 [501+]

Tuck, Robert - *Churches of Nova Scotia*
  CBRA - Annual 2003 - p123(1) [51-500]

Tuck, Stephen G.N. - *Beyond Atlanta: The Struggle for Racial Equality in Georgia, 1940-1980.*
  JSH - v71 - i1 - Feb 2005 - p203(2) [501+]

Tucker, Allen B. - *The Computer science Handbook, 2nd Ed.*
  SciTech - v28 - i4 - Dec 2004 - p16(1) [1-50]

Tucker, Dennis C. - *Pathways to Nursing: A Guide to Library and Online Research in Nursing and Allied Health*
  Bwatch - v26 - i7 - July 2004 - p2(1) [51-500]
  Choice - v42 - i6 - Feb 2005 - p1056(1) [51-500]
  SciTech - v28 - i3 - Sept 2004 - p126(1) [51-500]

Tucker, E.F. - *Otto Mears and the San Juans*
  R&R Bk N - v19 - i4 - Nov 2004 - p106(1) [51-500]

Tucker, George Hugo - *Homo Viator: Itineraries of Exile, Displacement and Writing in Renaissance Europe*
  Ren Q - v57 - i3 - Fall 2004 - p1086(2) [501+]

Tucker, Holly - *Pregnant Fictions: Childbirth and the Fairy Tale in Early-Modern France*
  Isis - v95 - i3 - Sept 2004 - p496(2) [501+]

Tucker, Janet G. - *Against Grain: Parody, Satire and Intertextuality in Russian Literature*
  Slav R - v63 - i3 - Fall 2004 - p681-682 [501+]

Tucker, Jeffrey Allen - *A Sense of Wonder: Samuel R. Delany, Race, Identity, and Difference*
  Bl S - v34 - i3 - Fall 2004 - p75-75 [501+]
  Choice - v42 - i6 - Feb 2005 - p1025(1) [51-500]

Tucker, Ken - *Kissing Bill O'Reilly, Roasting Miss Piggy: 100 Things to Love and Hate About TV*
  PW - v252 - i4 - Jan 24 2005 - p233(1) [501+]

Tucker, Lisa - *Shout Down the Moon*
  y   SLJ - v50 - i7 - July 2004 - p132(1) [51-500]

Tucker, Liz - *Infinite Secrets: The Genius of Archimedes. Audiobook Review*
  LJ - v129 - i14 - Sept 1 2004 - p199(1) [51-500]

Tucker, Mary Evelyn - *Buddhism and Ecology: The Interconnection of Dharma and Deeds*
  Parabola - v29 - i3 - Fall 2004 - p107(3) [501+]
Confucianism and Ecology: The Interrelation of Heaven, Earth and Humans
  Parabola - v29 - i3 - Fall 2004 - p107(3) [501+]
Religions of the World and Ecology
  Parabola - v29 - i3 - Fall 2004 - p107(3) [501+]

Tucker, Mike - *Hell Is Over: Voices of the Kurds after Saddam*
  PW - v251 - i44 - Nov 1 2004 - p58(1) [501+]

Tucker, Neely - *Love in the Driest Season: A Family Memoir (Read by Kramer, Michael). Audiobook Review*
  BL - v100 - i22 - August 2004 - p1953(2) [51-500]
  Kliatt - v38 - i4 - July 2004 - p61(1) [51-500]
Love in the Driest Season: A Family Memoir
  Black Iss - v6 - i4 - July-August 2004 - p54(2) [51-500]
  y   SLJ - v50 - i8 - August 2004 - p147(2) [501+]

Tucker, Nicholas - *Darkness Visible: Inside the World of Philip Pullman*
  TLS - i5265 - Feb 27 2004 - p31-31 [501+]

Tucker, Sarah - *The Last Year of Being Married*
  BL - v101 - i7 - Dec 1 2004 - p642(1) [51-500]

Tucker, Spencer C. - *Brigadier General John D. Imboden: Confederate Commander in the Shenandoah*
  JSH - v70 - i3 - August 2004 - p688(2) [501+]

Tucker, Tanya - *100 Ways to Beat the Blues*
  PW - v252 - i5 - Jan 31 2005 - p57(1) [51-500]

Tucker, Todd - *Notre Dame vs. the Klan: How the Fighting Irish Defeated the Ku Klux Klan*
  LJ - v129 - i16 - Oct 1 2004 - p97(1) [51-500]

Tucker, Tom - *Bolt of Fate: Benjamin Franklin and His Electric Kite Hoax*
  CR - v285 - i1665 - Oct 2004 - p255(1) [501+]
  T&C - v45 - i4 - Oct 2004 - p839(2) [501+]

Tucker, William H. - *The Funding of Scientific Racism: Wickliffe Draper and the Pioneer Fund*
  CS - v33 - i1 - Jan 2004 - p58-59 [501+]

Tufariello, Catherine - *Keeping My Name*
  BL - v101 - i9-10 - Jan 1 2005 - p768(1) [51-500]
  Poet - v185 - i5 - Feb 2005 - p403(1) [51-500]

Tuite, Clara - *Romantic Austen: Sexual Politics and the Literary Canon*
  Clio - v33 - i3 - Spring 2004 - p305(10) [501+]

Tulandi, Togas - *Endometriosis: Advances and Controversies*
  E-Streams - July 2004 - pNA [501+]
  SciTech - v28 - i1 - March 2004 - p116(1) [51-500]
Preservation of Fertility
  SciTech - v28 - i4 - Dec 2004 - p92(1) [51-500]

Tulchinsky, Karen X. - *The Five Books of Moses Lapinsky*
  Globe & Mail - August 21 2004 - pD13 [1-50]
Love and Other Ruins
  CBRA - Annual 2003 - p189(1) [501+]

Tulgan, Bruce - *H.O.T. Management: Hands-On Transactional*
  HR Mag - v50 - i2 - Feb 2005 - pS8(1) [51-500]

Tulliu, Steve - *Coming to Terms with Security: A Lexicon for Arms Control, Disarmament and Confidence-Building*
  R&R Bk N - v19 - i3 - August 2004 - p185(1) [501+]

Tulloch, Carol - *Black Style*
  Black Iss - v7 - i1 - Jan-Feb 2005 - p43(1) [51-500]

Tulloch, Mitch - *Windows Server Hacks*
  Bwatch - v26 - i7 - July 2004 - p7(1) [51-500]
  SciTech - v28 - i3 - Sept 2004 - p159(1) [51-500]

Tulloch, Richard - *Weird Stuff (Illus. by Nagle, Shane)*
  y   Magpies - v19 - i5 - Nov 2004 - p37(1) [501+]

Tullson, Diane - *Blue Highway*
  y   BL - v101 - i6 - Nov 15 2004 - p574(2) [51-500]
  y   Kliatt - v39 - i1 - Jan 2005 - p18(1) [51-500]
  Res Links - v10 - i3 - Feb 2005 - p41(1) [501+]
  SLJ - v50 - i12 - Dec 2004 - p154(1) [51-500]

Tumbauer, Lisa - *What Is a Thermometer?*
  c   SB - v40 - i3 - May-June 2004 - p130(1) [501+]

Tumber, Howard - *Media at War: The Iraq Crisis*
  Choice - v42 - i4 - Dec 2004 - p655(1) [1-50]
  R&R Bk N - v19 - i3 - August 2004 - p50(1) [51-500]

Tumielewicz, P.J. - *Summer Theatre Directory 2004*
  Choice - v42 - i3 - Nov 2004 - p454(1) [1-50]
  R&R Bk N - v19 - i4 - Nov 2004 - p226(1) [501+]

Tummala, Krishna K. - *Comparative Bureaucratic Systems*
  Choice - v41 - i7 - March 2004 - p1364(1) [501+]

Tumpel-Gugerell, Gertrude - *Economic Convergence and Divergence in Europe: Growth and Regional Development in an Enlarged European Union*
  JEL - v41 - i4 - Dec 2003 - p1422(1) [501+]

Tunasima, Sirou - *Jinki, Vol. 1*
  y   VOYA - v27 - i5 - Dec 2004 - p411(1) [51-500]

Tung, Lisa - *Anne Wilson: Unfoldings*
  Am Craft - v64 - i1 - Feb-March 2004 - p40(1) [501+]

Tungate, Mark - *Media Monoliths: How Great Media Brands Thrive and Survive*
  R&R Bk N - v19 - i4 - Nov 2004 - p212(1) [501+]

608 • TUNGODEN Book Review Index 2005 Cumulation

Tungoden, Bertil - *Toward Pro-Poor Policies: Aid, Institutions, and Globalization*
R&R Bk N - v19 - i3 - August 2004 - p110(1) [51-500]
Tunley, David - *Francois Couperin and the Perfection of Music*
Choice - v42 - i6 - Feb 2005 - p1032(1) [51-500]
R&R Bk N - v19 - i4 - Nov 2004 - p195(1) [501+]
Tunnell, Kenneth D. - *Pissing on Demand: Workplace Drug Testing and the Rise of the Detox Industry*
Choice - v42 - i3 - Nov 2004 - p526(1) [1-50]
Tunnell, Michael O. - *Wishing Moon*
y BL - v100 - i22 - August 2004 - p1921(1) [51-500]
c BL - v101 - i2 - Sept 15 2004 - p233(1) [51-500]
c CCB-B - v57 - i11 - July-August 2004 - p487(2) [501+]
c SLJ - v50 - i7 - July 2004 - p113(1) [51-500]
Tunney, Kelly Smith - *Memories of World War II: Photographs from the Archives of the Associated Press*
LJ - v129 - i14 - Sept 1 2004 - p169(1) [51-500]
R&R Bk N - v19 - i3 - August 2004 - p32(1) [51-500]
Tuns, Paul - *Jean Chretein: A Legacy of Scandel*
CI - v12 - i10 - Nov 2004 - p38(1) [501+]
Tuomanen, Elaine I. - *The Pneumococcus*
SciTech - v28 - i3 - Sept 2004 - p74(1) [51-500]
Tuominen, Mary C. - *We Are Not Babysitters: Family Childcare Providers Redefine Work and Care*
Choice - v41 - i7 - March 2004 - p1336(1) [501+]
Soc Ser R - v78 - i3 - Sept 2004 - p503(4) [501+]
Tupitsyn, Margarita - *Gustav Klutsis and Valentina Kulagina: Photography and Montage after Constructivism*
Choice - v42 - i1 - Sept 2004 - p93(1) [501+]
LJ - v129 - i18 - Nov 1 2004 - p80(2) [501+]
Tuplin, C.J. - *Science and Mathematics in Ancient Greek Culture*
AJP - v125 - i1 - Spring 2004 - p140-144 [501+]
Class R - v54 - i1 - May 2004 - p82(3) [501+]
Turan, Kenneth - *Never Coming to a Theater Near You: A Celebration of a Certain Kind of Movie*
BL - v101 - i4 - Oct 15 2004 - p374(2) [51-500]
KR - v72 - i16 - August 15 2004 - p800(1) [51-500]
LJ - v129 - i14 - Sept 1 2004 - p154(1) [51-500]
New R - Feb 7 2005 - p22 [501+]
PW - v251 - i29 - July 19 2004 - p152(1) [51-500]
R&R Bk N - v19 - i4 - Nov 2004 - p223(1) [501+]
Turch, Mary - *Healthy Eating for Weight Management*
y SB - v40 - i4 - July-August 2004 - p151(1) [51-500]
Turchi, Peter - *Maps of the Imagination*
BL - v101 - i2 - Sept 15 2004 - p193(1) [501+]
Choice - v42 - i6 - Feb 2005 - p1008(2) [51-500]
Turchin, Peter - *Complex Population Dynamics: A Theoretical/Empirical Synthesis*
QRB - v79 - i3 - Sept 2004 - p298(1) [501+]
Turck, Eva-Monika - *Lucien Clergue: Poesie Photographique*
Choice - v41 - i11-12 - July-August 2004 - p2037(1) [501+]
Turck, Mary C. - *The Civil Rights Movement for Kids: A History with 21 Activities*
c SLJ - v50 - i10 - Oct 2004 - p67(1) [51-500]
Mexico and Central America: A Fiesta of Cultures, Crafts, and Activities for Ages 8-12
c BL - v100 - i22 - August 2004 - p1928(1) [51-500]
c SLJ - v50 - i8 - August 2004 - p145(1) [501+]
Turcotte, Elise - *The Alien House*
Globe & Mail - Dec 11 2004 - pD11 [501+]
Turell, David J. - *Science vs. Religion: The 500-Year War: Finding God in the Heat of the Battle*
LJ - v129 - i14 - Sept 1 2004 - p161(1) [51-500]
Turi, Gabriele - *Stato educatore: Politica e intellettuali nell'Italia fascista*
JMH - v76 - i4 - Dec 2004 - p974(3) [501+]
Turill, David - *An Apology for Autumn*
BL - v101 - i1 - Sept 1 2004 - p55(1) [501+]
Turino, Thomas - *Identity and the Arts in Diaspora Communities*
R&R Bk N - v19 - i4 - Nov 2004 - p198(1) [501+]
Turits, Richard Lee - *Foundations of Despotism: Peasants, the Trujillo Regime, and Modernity in Dominican History*
HAHR - v84 - i3 - August 2004 - p543(2) [501+]
JIH - v34 - i3 - Wntr 2004 - p492(2) [501+]
Turk, Diana B. - *Bound by a Mighty Vow: Sisterhood and Women's Fraternities, 1870-1920*
Choice - v42 - i3 - Nov 2004 - p551(2) [1-50]
LJ - v129 - i12 - July 2004 - p100(1) [51-500]
Turkington, Carol - *The Encyclopedia of Children's Health and Wellness*
Choice - v42 - i6 - Feb 2005 - p1000(1) [51-500]
SciTech - v28 - i4 - Dec 2004 - p111(1) [1-50]
Encyclopedia of Deafness and Hearing Disorders, 2nd Rev. Ed.
SciTech - v28 - i1 - March 2004 - p115(1) [51-500]
The Encyclopedia of Infectious Diseases
LibMed - v22 - i4 - Jan 2004 - p74(1) [501+]
Turksen, Kursad - *Adult Stem Cells*
E-Streams - August 2004 - pNA [501+]
Turley, Paul - *Professional SQL Server Reporting Services*
SciTech - v28 - i3 - Sept 2004 - p33(1) [51-500]
Turmusani, Majid - *Disabled People and Economic Needs in the Developing World: A Political Perspective from Jordan*
JEL - v42 - i1 - March 2004 - p312(1) [501+]
Turnbull, Ann - *Josie under Fire*
c Sch Lib - v52 - i4 - Winter 2004 - p203(1) [1-50]
No Shame, No Fear
c BL - v101 - i3 - Oct 1 2004 - p340(1) [51-500]
c CCB-B - v58 - i3 - Nov 2004 - p149(1) [501+]
y Kliatt - v38 - i6 - Nov 2004 - p12(1) [51-500]
y KR - v72 - i19 - Oct 1 2004 - p971(1) [51-500]
y SLJ - v50 - i11 - Nov 2004 - p155(2) [51-500]
Turnbull, Peter - *The Dance Master*
BL - v100 - i21 - July 2004 - p1825(1) [1-50]
Turnbull, Stephen - *Samurai: The Story of Japan's Great Warriors*
LJ - v129 - i13 - August 2004 - p97(1) [501+]
Turner, Alan - *National Geographic Prehistoric Mammals (Illus. by Anton, Mauricio)*
c BL - v101 - i5 - Nov 1 2004 - p478(1) [51-500]
y SLJ - v51 - i1 - Jan 2005 - p156(2) [51-500]
Turner, Anderson - *Glazes: Materials, Recipes and Techniques*
Ceram Mo - v52 - i4 - April 2004 - p32(1) [501+]
Pottery Making Techniques
Ceram Mo - v52 - i2 - Feb 2004 - p26(2) [501+]
Studio Practices, Techniques and Tips: A Collection of Articles from Ceramics Monthly
Ceram Mo - v52 - i4 - April 2004 - p30(1) [501+]
Turner, Ann Warren - *Pumpkin Cat (Illus. by Bates, Amy)*
c BL - v100 - i22 - August 2004 - p1946(1) [51-500]
c CCB-B - v58 - i1 - Sept 2004 - p42(2) [51-500]
c KR - v72 - i13 - July 1 2004 - p639(1) [51-500]
c SLJ - v50 - i8 - August 2004 - p97(1) [51-500]
Pumpkin Cat (Illus. by Bates, Amy June)
c CH Bwatch - v14 - i11 - Nov 2004 - pNA [51-500]
Turner, Anne M. - *It Comes with the Territory: Handling Problem Situations in Libraries*
BL - v101 - i9-10 - Jan 1 2005 - p911(1) [51-500]
LJ - v129 - i19 - Nov 15 2004 - p92(1) [51-500]
Turner, Barrie Carson - *Ludwig Van Beethoven*
c CH Bwatch - v14 - i7 - July 2004 - p3(1) [51-500]
Wolfgang Amadeus Mozart
c CH Bwatch - v14 - i7 - July 2004 - p3(1) [51-500]
Turner, Barry - *Countdown to Victory: The Final European Campaigns of World War II*
BL - v101 - i7 - Dec 1 2004 - p628(1) [51-500]
R&R Bk N - v20 - i1 - Feb 2005 - p33(1) [51-500]
Turner, Betty Stagg - *Out of the Blue and into History: Women Airforce Service Pilots WWII*
HNet - Sept 2004 - pNA [501+]
Turner, Bryan - *The New Medical Sociology: Social Forms of Health and Illness*
SciTech - v28 - i4 - Dec 2004 - p81(1) [51-500]
Turner, Catherine - *Marketing Modernism Between the Two World Wars*
AHR - v109 - i2 - April 2004 - p550(2) [501+]
BSA-P - v98 - i1 - March 2004 - p124-126 [501+]
MFSF - v50 - i3 - Fall 2004 - p788-790 [501+]
MFSF - v50 - i3 - Fall 2004 - p788-790 [501+]
Turner, Chris - *Planet Simpson: How a Cartoon Masterpiece Defined a Generation*
y BL - v101 - i5 - Nov 1 2004 - p461(1) [51-500]
Globe & Mail - Oct 23 2004 - pD7 [501+]
LJ - v129 - i18 - Nov 1 2004 - p88(1) [51-500]
PW - v251 - i40 - Oct 4 2004 - p81(1) [51-500]
Planet Simpson: How a Cartoon Masterpiece Documented an Era and Defined a Generation
Spec - v296 - i9194 - Oct 23 2004 - p52(1) [501+]
Turner, David A. - *Theory of Education*
R&R Bk N - v19 - i4 - Nov 2004 - p178(1) [501+]
Turner, David M. - *Fashioning Adultery: Gender, Sex, and Civility in England, 1660-1740*
HNet - Sept 2004 - pNA [501+]
JIH - v34 - i4 - Spring 2004 - p633-634 [501+]
Six Ct J - v35 - i3 - Fall 2004 - p855-856 [501+]
Turner, Dennis A. - *Modern Neurosurgery: Clinical Translation of Neuroscience Advances*
SciTech - v28 - i4 - Dec 2004 - p108(1) [51-500]
Turner, E.S. - *Metro-Land: British Empire Exhibition Number*
Lon R Bks - v26 - i23 - Dec 2 2004 - p26(2) [501+]
Turner, Frank M. - *John Henry Newman: The Challenge to Evangelical Religion*
JMH - v76 - i3 - Sept 2004 - p680(2) [501+]
TT - v61 - i1 - April 2004 - p134-138 [501+]
Turner, Frederick - *In the Land of Temple Caves: Notes on Art and the Human Spirit*
LJ - v129 - i12 - July 2004 - p108(1) [51-500]
Turner, Gerard L'Estrange - *Renaissance Astrolabes and Their Makers*
Isis - v95 - i2 - June 2004 - p349(1) [51-500]
Turner, Ginger - *Abraham Lincoln: The Civil War President (Illus. by Tiwari, Saral)*
c SLJ - v50 - i7 - July 2004 - p128(2) [51-500]
Turner, J. Rodney - *Managing Web Projects: The Management of Large Projects and Programmes for Web-Space Delivery*
SciTech - v28 - i3 - Sept 2004 - p27(1) [51-500]
People in Project Management
R&R Bk N - v19 - i1 - Feb 2004 - p94(1) [1-50]
Turner, Jack - *Spice: The History of a Temptation*
BL - v100 - i21 - July 2004 - p1809(1) [1-50]
BW - v34 - i33 - August 15 2004 - p13(1) [501+]
New Sci - v183 - i2465 - Sept 18 2004 - p47(1) [51-500]
NS - v133 - i4705 - Sept 13 2004 - p51(2) [501+]
NY - v80 - i25 - Sept 6 2004 - p163(1) [1-50]
NYT - August 13 2004 - pE35(L) [501+]
NYTBR - Dec 19 2004 - p31 [501+]
R&R Bk N - v19 - i4 - Nov 2004 - p250(1) [501+]
The Spice Trade
BIC - v33 - i8 - Nov 2004 - p24(1) [501+]
Turner, James (b. 1946 -) - *Language, Religion, Knowledge: Past and Present*
JR - v84 - i4 - Oct 2004 - p630(2) [501+]
Turner, James (b. 1947 -) - *Libertines and Radicals in Early Modern London: Sexuality, Politics, and Literary Culture, 1630-1685*
Eight-C St - v37 - i3 - Spring 2004 - p474-478 [501+]
Six Ct J - v35 - i3 - Fall 2004 - p856-858 [501+]
Schooling Sex: Libertine Literature and Erotic Education in Italy, France, and England 1534-1685
Ren Q - v57 - i3 - Fall 2004 - p1083(3) [501+]
Turner, James T. - *Threat Assessment: A Risk Management Approach*
R&R Bk N - v19 - i1 - Feb 2004 - p92(1) [1-50]
Turner, Jamie Langston - *No Dark Valley*
BL - v101 - i1 - Sept 1 2004 - p55(1) [501+]
Turner, Janette - *North of Nowhere, South of Loss*
Ent W - i790 - Oct 29 2004 - p72 [501+]
Turner, Jeffrey S. - *Dating and Sexuality in America: A Reference Handbook*
R&R Bk N - v19 - i2 - May 2004 - p135 [51-500]
Infamous
c BL - v101 - i1 - Sept 1 2004 - p120(1) [1-50]
Turner, Jessica Baron - *Your Musical Child: Inspiring Kids to Play and Sing for Keeps*
Am MT - v54 - i4 - Feb-March 2005 - p115(2) [501+]
Turner, John Frayn - *Heroic Flights: The First 100 Years of Aviation*
APH - v51 - i3 - Fall 2004 - p54(1) [501+]
Turner, Jonathan H. - *Human Institutions: A Theory of Societal Evolution*
AJS - v110 - i3 - Nov 2004 - p806(3) [501+]
SF - v83 - i1 - Sept 2004 - p432(2) [501+]
Turner, Langston - *No Dark Valley*
PW - v251 - i27 - July 5 2004 - p37(1) [51-500]
Turner, Mark W. - *Backward Glances: Cruising the Queer Streets of New York and London*
G&L Rev W - v11 - i4 - July-August 2004 - p44(2) [501+]
Turner, Michael A. - *A Peculiar Prophet: William H. Willimon and the Art of Preaching*
CC - v121 - i25 - Dec 14 2004 - p21(1) [51-500]
Turner, Michael (b. 1962 -) - *The Pornographer's Poem*
LJ - v129 - i12 - July 2004 - p74(1) [51-500]
Turner, Michael J. - *Independent Radicalism in Early Victorian Britain*
R&R Bk N - v19 - i4 - Nov 2004 - p36(1) [51-500]
Pitt the Younger: A Life
TLS - i5297 - Oct 8 2004 - p36(1) [501+]

Turner, Nancy J. - *Plants of Haida Gwaii; Zaadaa Gwaay gud gina k'aws (Skidegate), Zaadaa Gwaayee guu ginn k'aws*
SciTech - v28 - i4 - Dec 2004 - p4(1) [1-50]

Turner, Pamela S. - *Hachiko: The True Story of a Loyal Dog (Illus. by Nascimbene, Yan)*
c BL - v101 - i9-10 - Jan 1 2005 - p776(1) [1-50]
c HB - v80 - i4 - July-August 2004 - p471(2) [51-500]

Turner, Paul Venable - *Mrs. Hoover's Pueblo Walls: The Primitive and the Modern in the Lou Henry Hoover House*
R&R Bk N - v19 - i4 - Nov 2004 - p204(1) [501+]

Turner, Pauline - *Crocheted Lace*
Bwatch - v26 - i7 - July 2004 - p7(1) [51-500]

Turner, Philip A. - *Helping Teachers Teach: A School Library Media Specialist's Role*
LibMed - v22 - i7 - April-May 2004 - p89(1) [501+]

Turner, Philip M. - *Helping Teachers Teach: A School Library Media Specialist's Role, 3rd Ed.*
R&R Bk N - v19 - i1 - Feb 2004 - p259(1) [51-500]

Turner, R. Kerry - *Managing Wetlands: An Ecological Economics Approach*
SciTech - v28 - i1 - March 2004 - p60(1) [51-500]

Turner, Ralph V. - *Magna Carta: Through the Ages*
CR - v285 - i1662 - July 2004 - p60(1) [51-500]
HER - v119 - i483 - Sept 2004 - p1031(3) [501+]
HER - v119 - i483 - Sept 2004 - p1031(3) [501+]
The Register of Walter Bronescombe, Bishop of Exerter, 1258-1280
HER - v119 - i483 - Sept 2004 - p1031(3) [501+]

Turner, Robert D. - *Thunder of Their Passing: A Tribute to the Denver and Rio Grande's Narrow Gauge and the Cumbres and Toltec Scenic Railroad*
R&R Bk N - v19 - i1 - Feb 2004 - p250(1) [51-500]

Turner, Rodney J. - *Contracting for Project Management*
R&R Bk N - v19 - i1 - Feb 2004 - p97(1) [1-50]

Turner, S.J. - *Distributed Simulation and Real-Time Applications: Proceedings*
SciTech - v28 - i4 - Dec 2004 - p30(1) [51-500]

Turner, Sandy - *Otto's Trunk*
LibMed - v22 - i6 - March 2004 - p59(1) [501+]

Turner, Sarah - *Indonesia's Small Entrepreneurs: Trading on the Margins*
Pac A - v77 - i2 - Summer 2004 - p378(2) [501+]

Turner, Steve - *Amazing Grace: The Story of America's Most Beloved Song*
HNet - June 2004 - pNA [501+]
I Was Only Asking: Poems about Big Questions
c Sch Lib - v52 - i3 - Autumn 2004 - p154(2) [501+]
The Man Called Cash: The Life, Love, and Faith of an American Legend
People - v62 - i13 - Sept 27 2004 - p58 [501+]
PW - v251 - i38 - Sept 20 2004 - p58(1) [51-500]

Turner, Trevor - *Schizophrenia: Your Questions Answered*
SciTech - v28 - i1 - March 2004 - p100(1) [51-500]

Turner, Walter R. - *Paving Tobacco Road: A Century of Progress by the North Carolina Department of Transportation*
JSH - v71 - i1 - Feb 2005 - p192(2) [501+]
Pub Hist - v26 - i4 - Fall 2004 - p127(3) [501+]

Turner, Wayne C. - *Energy Management Handbook, 5th Ed.*
SciTech - v28 - i4 - Dec 2004 - p145(1) [501+]

Turney, Jon - *Lovelock and Gaia: Signs of Life*
BL - v101 - i4 - Oct 15 2004 - p370(2) [51-500]
LJ - v129 - i15 - Sept 15 2004 - p80(1) [51-500]
y SB - v40 - i6 - Nov-Dec 2004 - p255(1) [51-500]

Turney, Mary Ann - *Tapping Diverse Talent in Aviation, Culture, Gender, and Diversity*
R&R Bk N - v19 - i3 - August 2004 - p117(1) [51-500]

Turning Science into Business: Patenting and Licensing at Public Research Organisations
JEL - v42 - i1 - March 2004 - p319(1) [501+]

Turow, Scott - *Ultimate Punishment (Read by Turow, Scott). Audiobook Review*
Kliatt - v38 - i4 - July 2004 - p62(1) [51-500]

Turpie, Irene D. - *Aging Issues in Cardiology*
SciTech - v28 - i1 - March 2004 - p104(1) [51-500]

Turrell, Kerry - *Tungsten*
y SB - v40 - i4 - July-August 2004 - p164(2) [51-500]

Turrill, David - *An Apology for Autumn*
BL - v101 - i3 - Oct 1 2004 - p303(1) [51-500]
KR - v72 - i16 - August 15 2004 - p775(1) [51-500]

Turteltaub, H.N. - *Owls to Athens*
KR - v72 - i20 - Oct 15 2004 - p983(1) [501+]

Turtledove, Harry - *3 x T*
ChrSFF&H - v26 - i10 - Oct 2004 - p24(1) [51-500]
Alternate Generals II
y Kliatt - v38 - i4 - July 2004 - p33(1) [51-500]
Curious Notions
BL - v101 - i4 - Oct 15 2004 - p395(1) [51-500]
Days of Infamy
y BL - v101 - i2 - Sept 15 2004 - p180(1) [51-500]
Bwatch - Dec 2004 - pNA [51-500]
LJ - v129 - i17 - Oct 15 2004 - p57(1) [51-500]
PW - v251 - i41 - Oct 11 2004 - p60(2) [51-500]
Gunpowder Empire
y Kliatt - v39 - i2 - March 2005 - p29(1) [51-500]
Homeward Bound
y BL - v101 - i4 - Oct 15 2004 - p363(1) [51-500]
KR - v72 - i21 - Nov 1 2004 - p1032(1) [501+]
PW - v251 - i48 - Nov 29 2004 - p27(1) [51-500]
LJ - v129 - i20 - Dec 1 2004 - p104(1) [51-500]
Settling Accounts: Return Engagement
BL - v100 - i21 - July 2004 - p1800(1) [51-500]
ChrSFF&H - v26 - i9 - Sept 2004 - p32(1) [51-500]
KR - v72 - i13 - July 1 2004 - p605(1) [51-500]
LJ - v129 - i13 - August 2004 - p72(1) [51-500]
PW - v251 - i29 - July 19 2004 - p149(1) [51-500]

Tushnet, Mark V. - *A Court Divided: The Rehnquist Court and the Future of Constitutional Law*
BL - v101 - i6 - Nov 15 2004 - p538(1) [51-500]
KR - v72 - i21 - Nov 1 2004 - p1042(1) [501+]
KR - v72 - i22 - Nov 15 2004 - p1085(1) [501+]
LJ - v129 - i20 - Dec 1 2004 - p141(1) [51-500]
New R - Dec 27 2004 - p32 [501+]
PW - v251 - i46 - Nov 15 2004 - p48(2) [51-500]
Slave Law in the American South: State v. Mann in History and Literature
HNet - Sept 2004 - pNA [501+]

Tusji, Masatsugu - *The Internet Revolution: A Global Prespective*
JEL - v41 - i4 - Dec 2003 - p1394(1) [501+]

Tuska, Jon - *Stories of the Golden West, Bk. Five*
Roundup M - v11 - i6 - August 2004 - p31(1) [501+]

Tuson, Penelope - *Playing the Game: Western Women in Arabia*
A Aff - v35 - i2 - July 2004 - p225-226 [501+]

Tussy, Alan S. - *Elementary Algebra, 3rd Ed.*
SciTech - v28 - i4 - Dec 2004 - p34(1) [51-500]

Tutorow, Norman E. - *Governor: The Life and Legacy of Leland Stanford, a California Colossus, Vols. 1-2*
R&R Bk N - v19 - i4 - Nov 2004 - p62(1) [51-500]

Tutschke, Wolfgang - *An Introduction to Complex Analysis: Classical and Modern Approaches*
Choice - v42 - i7 - March 2005 - p1264(1) [51-500]
SciTech - v28 - i4 - Dec 2004 - p39(1) [51-500]

Tuttle, Howard N. - *Human Life Is Radical Reality: An Idea Developed from the Conceptions of Dilthey, Heidegger, and Ortega y Gasset*
R&R Bk N - v20 - i1 - Feb 2005 - p6(1) [51-500]

Tuttle, Lisa - *The Mysteries*
KR - v73 - i1 - Jan 1 2005 - p20(1) [501+]
LJ - v130 - i3 - Feb 15 2005 - p123(1) [51-500]
PW - v252 - i3 - Jan 17 2005 - p38(2) [51-500]

Tuttle, Mark E. - *Structural Analysis of Polymeric Composite Materials*
SciTech - v28 - i1 - March 2004 - p142(1) [51-500]

Tutu, Desmond, Archbishop - *God Has a Dream: A Vision of Hope for Our Time*
Black Iss - v6 - i4 - July-August 2004 - p30(2) [501+]

Tutumluer, Erol - *Recent Advances in Materials Characterization and Modeling of Pavement Systems: Proceedings*
SciTech - v28 - i1 - March 2004 - p148(1) [51-500]

Tuuk, Alex van der - *Paramount's Rise and Fall: A History of Wisconsin Chair Company and Its Recording Activities*
R&R Bk N - v19 - i2 - May 2004 - p193(1) [51-500]

Tvedt, Terje - *The River Nile in the Age of the British: Political Ecology and the Quest for Economic Power*
Choice - v42 - i5 - Jan 2005 - p908(1) [1-50]
TLS - i5307 - Dec 17 2004 - p30(1) [1-50]

Tveten, John - *Our Life with Birds*
Bwatch - Nov 2004 - pNA [51-500]

Twagilimana, Aimable - *The Debris of Ham: Ethnicity, Regionalism, and the 1994 Rwandan Genocide*
Choice - v41 - i11-12 - July-August 2004 - p2119(1) [501+]

Twain, Mark - *Mark Twain's Letters from Hawaii (Read by Layne, McAvoy). Audiobook Review*
y Kliatt - v39 - i2 - March 2005 - p60(1) [51-500]
PW - v252 - i1 - Jan 3 2005 - p23(1) [51-500]

Tweedy, Jeff - *Adult Head*
JouAmCul - v27 - i4 - Dec 2004 - p432(2) [501+]

Twentieth Century Turning Points in U.S. History
y SLJ - v50 - i11 - Nov 2004 - p80(1) [51-500]

Twigg, Alan - *Intensive Care: A Memoir*
CBRA - Annual 2003 - p74(2) [51-500]

Twigg, Judyth - *Social Capital and Social Cohesion in Post-Soviet Russia*
R&R Bk N - v19 - i1 - Feb 2004 - p127(1) [51-500]

Twinam, Ann - *Private Lives, Public Secrets: Gender, Honor, Sexuality, and Illegitimacy in Colonial Spanish America*
AHR - v109 - i2 - April 2004 - p570(1) [51-500]

Twinem, Neecy - *Baby Coyote Counts/Bebe Coyote cuenta (Illus. by Twinem, Neecy)*
c SLJ - v51 - i1 - Jan 2005 - p121(1) [51-500]

Twining, William - *Bentham: Selected Writings of John Dinwiddy*
Law&PolBR - June 2004 - p357(6) [501+]

Twist, Clint - *Sharks and Other Sea Creatures A-Z*
c SB - v40 - i4 - July-August 2004 - p181(1) [51-500]

Twiston-Davies, David - *The Daily Telegraph Book of Military Obituaries*
CR - v285 - i1662 - July 2004 - p60(2) [51-500]

Twitchell, James B. - *Branded Nation: The Marketing of Megachurch, College, Inc., and Museumworld*
BL - v101 - i2 - Sept 15 2004 - p186(1) [51-500]
Choice - v42 - i7 - March 2005 - p1268(1) [51-500]
NYT - Nov 7 2004 - p10 [501+]
PW - v251 - i29 - July 19 2004 - p155(1) [51-500]

Twohig, Dorothy - *The Papers of George Washington: Presidential Series, Vols. 7-11*
JSH - v70 - i3 - August 2004 - p653(5) [501+]

Twombly, Robert - *Louis Kahn: Essential Texts*
R&R Bk N - v19 - i1 - Feb 2004 - p203(1) [51-500]

Twomey, David P. - *Anderson's Business Law and the Legal Environment, 19th Ed.*
R&R Bk N - v19 - i3 - August 2004 - p198(1) [1-50]

Twycross, Meg - *Masks and Masking in Medieval and Early Tudor England*
Specu - v79 - i4 - Oct 2004 - p1164(3) [501+]

Twyman, R.M. - *Principles of Proteomics*
SciTech - v28 - i4 - Dec 2004 - p72(1) [1-50]
TimHES - v0 - i1680 - Feb 25 2005 - pIII(1) [501+]

Twyman, Susan - *Papal Ceremonial at Rome in the Twelfth Century*
Specu - v79 - i4 - Oct 2004 - p1166(3) [501+]

Ty, Eleanor - *Asia North American Identities: Beyond the Hyphen*
Choice - v42 - i3 - Nov 2004 - p480(1) [1-50]

Tyack, David - *Seeking Common Ground: Public Schools in a Diverse Society*
Choice - v42 - i1 - Sept 2004 - p160(1) [501+]
TCR - v106 - i12 - Dec 2004 - p2359(3) [501+]

Tyacke, Nicholas - *Aspects of English Protestantism, c. 1530-1700*
JMH - v76 - i3 - Sept 2004 - p673(4) [501+]

Tyan, Nady - *Business Laws of the Middle East: Lebanon*
R&R Bk N - v19 - i4 - Nov 2004 - p175(1) [501+]

Tyburski, Genie - *Introduction to Online Legal, Regulatory and Intellectual Property Research*
R&R Bk N - v19 - i3 - August 2004 - p196(1) [1-50]

Tydeman, William - *The Medieval European Stage, 500-1550*
JEGP - v103 - i2 - April 2004 - p253-256 [501+]
Specu - v79 - i3 - July 2004 - p848-849 [501+]

Tye, Larry - *Rising from the Rails: Pullman Porters and the Making of the Black Middle Class*
Black Iss - v7 - i2 - March-April 2005 - p56(1) [501+]
BW - v34 - i28 - July 11 2004 - p12(1) [501+]
NYTBR - July 25 2004 - p15 [501+]
People - v62 - i6 - August 9 2004 - p48 [51-500]

Tye, Michael - *Consciousness and Persons: Unity and Identity*
  Choice - v42 - i1 - Sept 2004 - p116(1) [501+]
  QRB - v79 - i4 - Dec 2004 - p405(1) [501+]
  TLS - i5299 - Oct 22 2004 - p33(1) [501+]
Tyerman, Christopher - *Fighting for Christendom: Holy War and the Crusades*
  CR - v286 - i1669 - Feb 2005 - p126(1) [51-500]
  LJ - v129 - i20 - Dec 1 2004 - p138(1) [51-500]
  PW - v251 - i51 - Dec 20 2004 - p55(2) [51-500]
  Spec - v296 - i9194 - Oct 23 2004 - p51(2) [501+]
Tylawsky, E.I. - *Saturio's Inheritance: The Greek Ancestry of the Roman Comic Parasite*
  Class R - v54 - i2 - Nov 2004 - p360(3) [501+]
Tyldesley, Michael - *No Heavenly Delusion? A Comparative Study of Three Communal Movements*
  Choice - v42 - i2 - Oct 2004 - p378(1) [501+]
  R&R Bk N - v19 - i2 - May 2004 - p130 [51-500]
Tyldesley, William - *Michael William Balfe: His Life and His English Operas*
  Notes - v61 - i2 - Dec 2004 - p433(3) [501+]
  R&R Bk N - v19 - i1 - Feb 2004 - p196(1) [51-500]
Tyler, Anne - *The Amateur Marriage: A Novel (Read by Brown, Blair). Audiobook Review*
  LJ - v129 - i17 - Oct 15 2004 - p96(1) [51-500]
The Amateur Marriage: A Novel
  BooChiTr - Jan 18 2004 - p2(1) [501+]
  Lon R Bks - v26 - i6 - March 18 2004 - pNA [501+]
  Lon R Bks - v26 - i6 - March 18 2004 - pNA [501+]
  Ms - v14 - i1 - Spring 2004 - p87(3) [501+]
  S Liv - v39 - i3 - March 2004 - p121(1) [501+]
Tyler, Ben - *One Night Stand*
  PW - v251 - i43 - Oct 25 2004 - p26(1) [51-500]
Tyler, Christian - *Wild West China: The Taming of Xinjiang*
  For Aff - v83 - i4 - July-August 2004 - p136 [501+]
  TimHES - v0 - i1648 - July 9 2004 - p28(1) [501+]
Tyler, Daniel - *Silver Fox of the Rockies: Delphus E. Carpenter and Western Water Compacts*
  AHR - v109 - i4 - Oct 2004 - p1244(2) [501+]
  BHR - v78 - i1 - Spring 2004 - p123(4) [501+]
  JAH - v91 - i1 - June 2004 - p337-338 [501+]
  SHQ - v107 - i3 - Jan 2004 - p490(2) [501+]
  WHQ - v35 - i3 - Autumn 2004 - p387(1) [501+]
Tyler, Deidre - *Thrice-Told Tales: Married People Tell Their Stories*
  CS - v33 - i5 - Sept 2004 - p543-544 [501+]
Tyler, Gillian - *Froggy Went a-Courtin' (Illus. by Tyler, Gillian)*
  c BL - v101 - i9-10 - Jan 1 2005 - p866(2) [51-500]
  c KR - v72 - i24 - Dec 15 2004 - p1210(1) [51-500]
  c PW - v252 - i3 - Jan 17 2005 - p54(2) [51-500]
  c SLJ - v51 - i1 - Jan 2005 - p116(1) [51-500]

Tyler, William - *Star Lore*
  Bwatch - Feb 2005 - pNA [51-500]
Tymieniecka, Anna-Teresa - *Passions of the Soul in the Metamorphosis of Becoming*
  R&R Bk N - v19 - i1 - Feb 2004 - p2(1) [51-500]
Tymoczko, Maria - *Language and Tradition in Ireland: Continuities and Displacements*
  R&R Bk N - v19 - i3 - August 2004 - p40(1) [51-500]
Tymony, Cy - *Sneaky Uses for Everyday Things*
  Sci Teach - v71 - i7 - Sept 2004 - p85-86 [501+]
Tyner, Beverly - *Small-Group Reading Instruction: A Differentiated Teaching Model for Beginning and Struggling Readers*
  R&R Bk N - v19 - i4 - Nov 2004 - p182(1) [501+]
Tyrack, David B. - *The One Best System: A History of American Urban Education*
  CHE - v51 - i23 - Feb 11 2005 - pB4-1 [501+]
Tyres, Kathy - *Shivering World*
  y VOYA - v27 - i5 - Dec 2004 - p411(1) [51-500]
Tyrrel, Rebecca - *Camilla: An Intimate Portrait*
  Lon R Bks - v26 - i2 - Jan 22 2004 - p28(1) [501+]
Tyrrell, Avril - *Grandmother's Tree (Illus. by Tyrrell, Frances)*
  c CBRA - Annual 2003 - p470(1) [51-500]
Tyrrell, Patricia - *The Reckoning*
  Globe & Mail - July 31 2004 - pD4 [501+]
  TLS - i5287 - July 30 2004 - p21(1) [501+]
Tyrrell, R. Emmett, Jr. - *Madame Hillary: The Dark Road to the White House (Read by Rohan, Richard). Audiobook Review*
  LJ - v129 - i17 - Oct 15 2004 - p98(1) [51-500]
Tyrrell, William Blake - *Smell of Sweat: Greek Athletics, Olympics, and Culture*
  R&R Bk N - v19 - i4 - Nov 2004 - p79(1) [51-500]
Tysdahl, Bjorn - *English and Nordic Modernisms*
  Scan St - v76 - i3 - Fall 2004 - p421(5) [501+]
Tyson, Alan - *Jumpmetrics*
  R&R Bk N - v19 - i4 - Nov 2004 - p80(1) [51-500]
Tyson, Donald - *Necronomicon: The Wanderings of Alhazred*
  KR - v72 - i21 - Nov 1 2004 - p1028(1) [51-500]
  PW - v251 - i48 - Nov 29 2004 - p27(2) [51-500]
  LJ - v129 - i20 - Dec 1 2004 - p105(1) [51-500]
Tyson, Edith S. - *Orson Scott Card: Writer of the Terrible Choice*
  R&R Bk N - v19 - i1 - Feb 2004 - p246(1) [51-500]
Tyson, Janet - *Our Man in Judea: The Secret World of the First Gospel*
  CBRA - Annual 2003 - p101(1) [51-500]

Tyson, Leigh Ann - *An Interview with Harry the Tarantula (Illus. by Drescher, Henrik)*
  c LibMed - v22 - i5 - Feb 2004 - p66(1) [501+]
Tyson, Neil deGrasse - *Origins: Fourteen Billion Years of Cosmic Evolution*
  y BL - v101 - i1 - Sept 1 2004 - p33(1) [51-500]
  Fut - v38 - i6 - Nov-Dec 2004 - p61(1) [51-500]
  KR - v72 - i16 - August 15 2004 - p798(1) [51-500]
  LJ - v129 - i14 - Sept 1 2004 - p185(1) [51-500]
  New Sci - v185 - i2484 - Jan 29 2005 - p51(1) [501+]
  PW - v251 - i39 - Sept 27 2004 - p48(1) [501+]
The Sky Is Not the Limit: Adventures of an Urban Astrophysicist, 2nd Ed.
  Bl S - v34 - i3 - Fall 2004 - p75-75 [501+]
  Choice - v42 - i3 - Nov 2004 - p506(1) [1-50]
  SciTech - v28 - i3 - Sept 2004 - p43(1) [1-50]
The Sky Is Not the Limit: Adventures of an Urban Astrophysicist
  NYTBR - August 1 2004 - p12 [51-500]
Tyson, Timothy B. - *Blood Done Sign My Name (Read by Dean, Robertson). Audiobook Review*
  BL - v101 - i3 - Oct 1 2004 - p350(1) [51-500]
Blood Done Sign My Name
  BooChiTr - May 30 2004 - p1(2) [501+]
  CC - v121 - i22 - Nov 2 2004 - p37(2) [501+]
Tytell, John - *Ezra Pound: The Solitary Volcano*
  R&R Bk N - v19 - i4 - Nov 2004 - p243(1) [501+]
Tythacott, Louise - *Surrealism and the Exotic*
  JRAI - v10 - i4 - Dec 2004 - p925(2) [501+]
Tzanaki, Rosemary - *Mandeville's Medieval Audiences: A Study on the Reception of the Book of Sir John Mandeville*
  RES - v55 - i219 - April 2004 - p264-266 [501+]
Tze-lan D. Sang - *The Emerging Lesbian: Female Same-Sex Desire in Modern China*
  Comp L - v56 - i3 - Summer 2004 - p276-278 [501+]
Tzeng, Nian-Feng - *Parallel and Distributed Systems (ICPADS 2004): Proceedings*
  SciTech - v28 - i3 - Sept 2004 - p20(1) [501+]
Tziovas, Dimitris - *Greece and the Balkans: Identities, Perceptions and Cultural Encounters Since the Enlightenment*
  R&R Bk N - v19 - i1 - Feb 2004 - p40(1) [1-50]
Tzonis, Alexander - *Classical Greek Architecture: The Construction of the Modern*
  LJ - v129 - i20 - Dec 1 2004 - p113(1) [51-500]
New York, Empire City, 1920-1945
  Choice - v42 - i6 - Feb 2005 - p1016(1) [51-500]
Tzvelev, N.N. - *Flora of Russia: The European Part and Bordering Regions, Vol. 8*
  SciTech - v28 - i1 - March 2004 - p129(1) [51-500]

U

Ubaydli, Mohammad al- - *Handheld Computers for Doctors*
E-Streams - Nov 2004 - pNA [501+]

Uchida, Yoshiko - *Jar of Dreams*
RT - v57 - Sept 2003 - p102 [501+]

Uchino, Bert N. - *Social Support and Physical Health: Understanding the Health Consequences of Relationships*
Choice - v41 - i11-12 - July-August 2004 - p2079(1) [501+]

Uchmanowicz, Pauline - *Considering Cultural Difference*
R&R Bk N - v19 - i4 - Nov 2004 - p58(1) [51-500]

Ucinski, Dariusz - *Optimal Measurement Methods for Distributed Parameter System Identification*
SciTech - v28 - i4 - Dec 2004 - p42(1) [51-500]

Ucko, Peter - *The Wisdom of Egypt: Changing Visions through the Ages*
R&R Bk N - v19 - i1 - Feb 2004 - p50(1) [51-500]
TimHES - v0 - i1671 - Dec 17 2004 - p24(1) [501+]

Udall, Stewart L. - *The Forgotten Founders: Rethinking the History of the Old West*
WHQ - v35 - i1 - Spring 2004 - p73-73 [501+]

Udayakumar, S.P. - *Handcuffed to History: Narratives, Pathologies, and Violence in South Asia, 2001*
JTWS - v21 - i1 - Spring 2004 - p261(2) [501+]

Uden, Tony - *Learning's Not a Crime: Education and Training for Offenders and Ex-Offenders in the Community*
TES - v0 - i4586 - June 4 2004 - pss6(1) [501+]

Uderzo, Albert - *Asterix and the Class Act*
c PW - v251 - i31 - August 2 2004 - p73(1) [51-500]

Udias, Augustin - *Searching the Heavens and the Earth: The History of Jesuit Observatories*
SciTech - v28 - i1 - March 2004 - p43(1) [51-500]

Udogu, E. Ike - *The Issue of Political Ethnicity in Africa*
JTWS - v21 - i1 - Spring 2004 - p282(4) [501+]

Udpa, Satish S. - *Nondestructive Testing Handbook, 3rd Ed., Vol. 5*
SciTech - v28 - i3 - Sept 2004 - p139(1) [51-500]

Udubasa, Gheorghe - *Minerals of the Carpathians*
RocksMiner - v79 - i5 - Sept-Oct 2004 - p358(1) [501+]

Udwadia, Firdaus E. - *Dynamical Systems and Control*
SciTech - v28 - i3 - Sept 2004 - p42(1) [1-50]

Ueberschar, Gerd R. - *Der Deutsche Widerstand Gegen Hitler. Wahrnehmung und Wertung in Europa und den USA*
GSR - v27 - i3 - Oct 2004 - p655(2) [501+]

Ueda, Makoto - *Dew on the Grass: The Life and Poetry of Kobayashi Issa*
R&R Bk N - v19 - i3 - August 2004 - p256(1) [51-500]

Ueda, Reed - *Faces of Community: Immigrant Massachusetts, 1860-2000*
JAH - v91 - i2 - Sept 2004 - p668(3) [501+]
NEQ - v77 - i4 - Dec 2004 - p670-672 [501+]

Uegaki, Chieri - *Suki's Kimono (Illus. by Jorisch, Stephane)*
c CBRA - Annual 2003 - p470(1) [51-500]
c RT - v58 - i3 - Nov 2004 - p287(1) [51-500]

Uematsu, Ketzo - *Ceramic Interfaces: Properties and Applications, 5: Proceedings*
SciTech - v28 - i1 - March 2004 - p142(1) [51-500]

Ueno, Kenji - *Mathematical Gift, I: The Interplay between Topology Functions, Geometry, and Algebra*
SciTech - v28 - i1 - March 2004 - p40(1) [51-500]

Ueshiba, Kisshomaru - *The Art of Aikido: Principles and Essentials Techniques*
Choice - v42 - i6 - Feb 2005 - p1061(1) [51-500]

Ufford, Van - *A Moral Critique of Development: In Search of Global Responsibilities*
JRAI - v10 - i4 - Dec 2004 - p926(2) [501+]

Ugarteche, Oscar - *The False Dilemma - Globalization: Opportunity or Threat?*
JTWS - v21 - i1 - Spring 2004 - p321(3) [501+]

Ugaz, Cecilia - *Utility Privatization and Regulation: A Fair Deal for Consumers?*
JEL - v41 - i4 - Dec 2003 - p1397(1) [501+]

Uglesich, John - *Uglesich's Restaurant Cookbook*
New Or - v39 - i1 - Oct 2004 - p24(1) [501+]

Uglow, Jenny - *A Little History of British Gardening*
Am Sci - v92 - i4 - July-August 2004 - p369(1) [501+]
CR - v285 - i1666 - Nov 2004 - p316(1) [501+]
TimHES - v0 - i1649 - July 16 2004 - p27(1) [501+]
TLS - i5293 - Sept 10 2004 - p25(1) [501+]

The Lunar Men: Five Friends Whose Curiosity Changed the World
Sew R - v111 - i4 - Fall 2003 - pcxxi-cxxiv [501+]

Uhl, Christopher - *Developing Ecological Consciousness: Paths to a Sustainable Future*
Choice - v41 - i11-12 - July-August 2004 - p2071(1) [501+]
Env - v46 - i9 - Nov 2004 - p40(1) [51-500]

Uhl, Heidemarie - *Zivilisationsbruch und Gedaechtniskultur*
HNet - Dec 2004 - pNA [501+]

Uhlberg, Myron - *Dad, Jackie, and Me (Illus. by Bootman, Colin)*
c KR - v73 - i5 - March 1 2005 - p297(1) [51-500]
c PW - v252 - i6 - Feb 7 2005 - p59(1) [51-500]

Uhlenbrock, Detlev - *MR Imaging of the Spine and Spinal Cord*
SciTech - v28 - i3 - Sept 2004 - p114(1) [51-500]

Ulanski, Stan L. - *Science of Fly-Fishing*
SciTech - v28 - i1 - March 2004 - p133(1) [51-500]

Ulbrich, Claudia - *Shulamith and Margarete: Power, Gender, and Religion in a Rural Society in Eighteenth-Century Europe*
Choice - v42 - i6 - Feb 2005 - p1089(1) [51-500]
R&R Bk N - v19 - i3 - August 2004 - p52(1) [51-500]

Uldrich, Jack - *Into the Unknown: Leadership Lessons from Lewis and Clark's Daring Westward Expedition*
Bwatch - v26 - i9 - Sept 2004 - p8(1) [51-500]

Ulin, David L. - *The Myth of Solid Ground: Earthquakes, Prediction, and the Fault Line between Reason and Faith*
BL - v100 - i22 - August 2004 - p1884(1) [51-500]
Ent W - i775 - July 23 2004 - p82 [501+]
LJ - v129 - i13 - August 2004 - p115(1) [51-500]
SciTech - v28 - i3 - Sept 2004 - p55(1) [1-50]

Ulivi, Paolo - *Lunar Exploration: Human Pioneers and Robostic Surveyors*
Choice - v42 - i1 - Sept 2004 - p127(1) [501+]

Ullen, Magnus - *The Half-Vanished Structure: Hawthorne's Allegorical Dialectics*
R&R Bk N - v19 - i4 - Nov 2004 - p241(1) [501+]

Ullman, Ellen - *The Bug*
NYTBR - July 25 2004 - p20 [501+]

Ullman, Harlan - *Finishing Business: Ten Steps to Defeat Global Terror*
Parameters - v34 - i4 - Winter 2004 - p129(2) [501+]
PW - v251 - i32 - August 9 2004 - p241(1) [51-500]
R&R Bk N - v19 - i4 - Nov 2004 - p144(1) [501+]

Ullmann, Agnes - *Origins of Molecular Biology: A Tribute to Jacques Monod, Rev. Ed.*
QRB - v79 - i3 - Sept 2004 - p301(1) [501+]
SciTech - v28 - i3 - Sept 2004 - p56(1) [1-50]

Ullmann, Linn - *Grace*
BL - v101 - i9-10 - Jan 1 2005 - p824(1) [1-50]
KR - v72 - i22 - Nov 15 2004 - p1068(1) [501+]
NYTBR - Jan 30 2005 - p21 [501+]
PW - v251 - i49 - Dec 6 2004 - p42(1) [51-500]
LJ - v129 - i20 - Dec 1 2004 - p104(2) [51-500]

Stella Descending
BW - v34 - i32 - August 8 2004 - p11(1) [501+]

Ullmann, M. - *Worterbuch zu den Griechisch-Arabischen Ubersetzungen des 9. Jahrhunderts*
Class R - v54 - i1 - May 2004 - p252(1) [501+]

Ullmann, Walter - *A Short History of the Papacy in the Middle Ages*
R&R Bk N - v19 - i4 - Nov 2004 - p26(1) [501+]

Ullmann's Processes and Process Engineering, Vols. 1-3
E-Streams - Sept 2004 - pNA [501+]

Ulman, Jean G. - *Making Technology Work for Learners with Special Needs: Practical Skills for Teachers*
R&R Bk N - v19 - i3 - August 2004 - p230(1) [1-50]

Ulmer, Mike - *The Gift of the Inuksuk*
c Res Links - v10 - i3 - Feb 2005 - p10(1) [51-500]
The Gift of the Inuksuk (Illus. by Rose, Melanie)
c BL - v101 - i9-10 - Jan 1 2005 - p875(2) [51-500]

Ulmer, Torsten - *Passiflora: Passionflowers of the World*
Choice - v42 - i6 - Feb 2005 - p1049(1) [51-500]
SciTech - v28 - i4 - Dec 2004 - p125 [51-500]

Ulrich, David - *Human Resource Competencies Toolkit*
HR Mag - v50 - i2 - Feb 2005 - pS15(1) [501+]

Ulrich-Fuller, Laurie - *Photoshop Elements 2 Bible*
SciTech - v28 - i4 - Dec 2004 - p167(1) [51-500]

Ulrich, John M. - *GenXegesis: Essays on "Alternative" Youth (Sub)Culture*
R&R Bk N - v19 - i3 - August 2004 - p151(1) [51-500]

Ulrich, Laurel Thatcher - *The Age of Homespun: Objects and Stories in the Creation of an American Myth*
T&C - v45 - i1 - Jan 2004 - p186(3) [501+]
Yards and Gates: Gender in Harvard and Radcliffe History.
Choice - v42 - i4 - Dec 2004 - p725(1) [1-50]

Umansky, Kaye - *A Chair for Baby Bear (Illus. by Fisher, Chris)*
c PW - v251 - i46 - Nov 15 2004 - p58(1) [501+]
c SLJ - v51 - i2 - Feb 2005 - p110(1) [51-500]
Sophie and Abigail (Illus. by Currey, Anna)
c Sch Lib - v52 - i4 - Winter 2004 - p191(1) [51-500]
Sophie and the Wonderful Picture (Illus. by Currey, Anna)
c Sch Lib - v52 - i4 - Winter 2004 - p191(1) [51-500]

Umar, Asad - *The Applications of Bioinformatics in Cancer Detection*
SciTech - v28 - i4 - Dec 2004 - p92(1) [51-500]

Umbach, Maiken - *German Federalism: Past, Present, Future*
GSR - v27 - i1 - Feb 2004 - p205-206 [501+]

Umphlett, Wiley Lee - *The Visual Focus of American Media Culture in the Twentieth Century: The Modern Era, 1893-1945*
Choice - v42 - i2 - Oct 2004 - p288(1) [501+]

Umstatter, Jack - *Words, Words, Words! Ready-to-Use Games and Activities for Vocabulary Building, Grades 7-12*
R&R Bk N - v19 - i4 - Nov 2004 - p216(1) [501+]

Uslaner, Eric M. - *The Moral Foundations of Trust*
JC - v54 - i3 - Sept 2004 - p581(3) [501+]

Uslu, Nasuh - *The Turkish-American Relationship between 1947 and 2003: The History of a Distinctive Alliance*
R&R Bk N - v19 - i1 - Feb 2004 - p56(1) [51-500]
Turkish Foreign Policy in the Post-Cold War Period
R&R Bk N - v19 - i3 - August 2004 - p47(1) [51-500]

Usselman, Steven W. - *Regulating Railroad Innovation: Business, Technology, and Politics in America, 1840-1920*
JEL - v41 - i4 - Dec 2003 - p1319(3) [501+]
JIH - v34 - i3 - Wntr 2004 - p476(2) [501+]

Ustinov, Victor M. - *Quantum Dot Lasers*
SciTech - v28 - i1 - March 2004 - p163(1) [51-500]

Usui, Yoshito - *Crayon Shinchan, Vol. 8*
PW - v251 - i31 - August 2 2004 - p55(1) [501+]

Uta Hagen's Acting Class
Am Theat - v21 - i8 - Oct 2004 - p139(4) [51-500]

Utley, Robert M. - *After Lewis and Clark: Mountain Men and the Paths to the Pacific*
y Kliatt - v39 - i2 - March 2005 - p40(1) [51-500]
Lone Star Justice: The First Century of the Texas Rangers
SHQ - v108 - i1 - July 2004 - p106-107 [501+]

Uttal, William R. - *Dualism: The Original Sin of Cognitivism*
SciTech - v28 - i4 - Dec 2004 - p2(1) [1-50]

Utts, Jessica M. - *Seeing through Statistics, 3rd Ed.*
SciTech - v28 - i4 - Dec 2004 - p37(1) [51-500]
SciTech - v28 - i4 - Dec 2004 - p37(1) [51-500]

Uviller, H. Richard - *The Militia and the Right to Arms, or, How the Second Amendment Fell Silent*
J Am St - v38 - i1 - April 2004 - p174-175 [501+]
JSH - v70 - i4 - Nov 2004 - p970(2) [501+]

Uvin, Peter - *Human Rights and Development*
R&R Bk N - v19 - i3 - August 2004 - p175(1) [501+]

Uwazie, Ernest E. - *Conflict Resolution and Peace Education in Africa*
R&R Bk N - v19 - i1 - Feb 2004 - p49(1) [51-500]

Uyehara, Beth Maltbie - *The Zen of Genealogy: The Lighter Side of Genealogy*
EFHM - v58 - i2 - March-April 2004 - p88(1) [51-500]

Uzawa, Hirofumi - *Economic Theory and Global Warming*
JEL - v42 - i1 - March 2004 - p338(2) [501+]

Uzdavinys, Algis - *The Golden Chain*
Bwatch - Nov 2004 - pNA [51-500]

Uzochukwu, Godfrey A. - *Environmental Science and Technology: Proceedings*
SciTech - v28 - i1 - March 2004 - p147(1) [1-50]

V

Va'a, Leulu Felise - *Saili Matagi: Samoan Migrants in Australia*
 Cont Pac - v16 - i2 - Fall 2004 - p455(5) [501+]

Vaarst, M. - *Animal Health and Welfare in Organic Agriculture*
 Choice - v42 - i3 - Nov 2004 - p507(1) [1-50]

Vacca, Carolyn Summers - *A Reform Against Nature: Woman Suffrage and the Rethinking of American Citizenship, 1840-1920*
 R&R Bk N - v19 - i3 - August 2004 - p179(1) [501+]

Vacca, John R. - *Public Key Infrastructure: Building Trusted Applications and Web Services*
 SciTech - v28 - i3 - Sept 2004 - p33(1) [51-500]
The World's 20 Greatest Unsolved Problems
 Choice - v42 - i6 - Feb 2005 - p1043(1) [51-500]
 SciTech - v28 - i3 - Sept 2004 - p14(1) [501+]

Vaccaeus, Joannes - *Un Professeur-Poete Humaniste: Joannes Vaccaeus-La Sylve Parisienne*
 FS - v58 - i2 - April 2004 - p243(2) [501+]

Vaccaro, Laura - *Seeger Lemons Are Not Red (Illus. by Vaccaro, Laura)*
 c HB - v81 - i1 - Jan-Feb 2005 - p86(2) [51-500]

Vachon, John - *John Vachon's America: Photographs and Letters from the Depression to World War II*
 VQR - v80 - i3 - Summer 2004 - p268(2) [501+]

Vad, Janos - *Modelling Fluid Flow: The State of the Art*
 Choice - v42 - i7 - March 2005 - p1258(1) [51-500]

Vadali, Srinivas Rao - *John L. Junkins Astrodynamics Symposium: Proceedings*
 SciTech - v28 - i1 - March 2004 - p170(1) [51-500]

Vadim, Volkov - *Violent Entrepreneurs: The Use of Force in the Making of Russian Capitalism*
 E-A St - v56 - i5 - July 2004 - p768(3) [501+]

Vadnais, Chris - *Instant Boris Effects*
 SciTech - v28 - i4 - Dec 2004 - p167(1) [51-500]

Vagelos, P. Roy - *Medicine, Science and Merck*
 Choice - v42 - i3 - Nov 2004 - p518(1) [1-50]

Vaggi, Gianni - *A Concise History of Economic Thought: Form Mercantilism to Monetarism*
 AJPS - v39 - i2 - July 2004 - p470(471) [501+]

Vaid, Helen - *Branding*
 R&R Bk N - v19 - i1 - Feb 2004 - p93(1) [1-50]

Vaidhyanathan, Siva - *The Anarchist in the Library: How the Clash between Freedom and Control Is Hacking the Real World and Crashing the System*
 Choice - v42 - i6 - Feb 2005 - p1043(1) [51-500]
 R&R Bk N - v19 - i4 - Nov 2004 - p247(1) [501+]

Vail, Avi - *Never Mind!: A Twin Novel*
 c LibMed - v23 - i3 - Nov-Dec 2004 - p69(1) [51-500]

Vail, Jeffery W. - *The Literacy Relationship of Lord Byron and Thomas Moore*
 RES - v55 - i219 - April 2004 - p289-291 [501+]

Vail, Kathleen - *Homework Problems: How Much Is Too Much?*
 CE - v81 - i1 - Fall 2004 - p56(1) [501+]

Vail, Ken - *Dizzy Gillespie: The Bebop Years, 1937-1952*
 R&R Bk N - v19 - i1 - Feb 2004 - p196(1) [51-500]

Vail, Rachel - *Mama Rex and T: The Reading Champion (Illus. by Bjorkman, Steve)*
 c SLJ - v50 - i8 - August 2004 - p82(1) [51-500]

Vail, Tom - *Grand Canyon: A Different View*
 CC - v121 - i25 - Dec 14 2004 - p7(1) [501+]

Vailati, Ezio - *Leibniz and Clarke: A Study of Their Correspondence*
 Phil R - v112 - i4 - Oct 2003 - p570(3) [501+]

Vaillancourt, Luc - *La lettre familiere au XVIe siecle: Rhetorique humaniste de l'epistolaire*
 Ren Q - v57 - i4 - Winter 2004 - p1429(3) [501+]

Vaillant, Derek - *Sounds of Reform: Progressivism and Music in Chicago, 1873-1935*
 JAH - v91 - i3 - Dec 2004 - p1050(2) [501+]
 RAH - v32 - i3 - Sept 2004 - p407-412 [501+]

Vaillant, John - *The Golden Spruce: A True Story of Myth, Madness, and Greed*
 KR - v73 - i4 - Feb 15 2005 - p222(1) [501+]
 LJ - v130 - i3 - Feb 15 2005 - p155(1) [51-500]
 PW - v252 - i7 - Feb 14 2005 - p60(1) [51-500]

Vainker, Shelagh - *Chinese Silk: A Cultural History*
 TimHES - v0 - i1683 - March 18 2005 - p26(1) [501+]

Vaio, J - *The Mythiambi of Babrius. Notes on the Constitution of the Text*
 Class R - v54 - i2 - Nov 2004 - p342-343 [501+]

Vaitheeswaran, Vijay V. - *Power to the People: How the Coming Energy Revolution Will Transform an Industry, Change our Lives, and Maybe Save the Planet*
 SciTech - v28 - i1 - March 2004 - p150(1) [51-500]

Valadier, Paul - *La Condition Chretienne: Du Monde sans en Etre*
 Theol St - v65 - i3 - Sept 2004 - p685(1) [501+]

Valadka, Alex B. - *Neurotrauma: Evidence-Based Answers to Common Questions*
 SciTech - v28 - i4 - Dec 2004 - p108(1) [51-500]

Valantasis, Richard - *Centuries of Holiness: Ancient Spirituality for a Postmodern Age*
 LJ - v130 - i4 - March 1 2005 - p94(1) [51-500]

Valaoritis, Nanos - *An Anthology of Modern Greek Poetry*
 TLS - i5284 - July 9 2004 - p5(1) [501+]

Valavanis, Panos - *Games and Sanctuaries in Ancient Greece: Olympia, Delphi, Isthmia, Nemea, Athens*
 Bwatch - v26 - i9 - Sept 2004 - p3(1) [51-500]
 NYRB - v51 - i16 - Oct 21 2004 - p19(3) [501+]

Valbuena, Olga L. - *Subjects to the King's Divorce: Equivocation, Infidelity, and Resistance in Early Modern England*
 Ren Q - v57 - i3 - Fall 2004 - p1155(3) [501+]

Valcarcel, Maria del Carmen Hernandez - *El Cuento Espanol en los siglos de Oro: El Siglo XVI*
 Six Ct J - v35 - i3 - Fall 2004 - p938-939 [501+]

Valdes, Mario J. - *Literary Cultures of Latin America: A Comparative History, Vols. 1-3*
 Choice - v42 - i6 - Feb 2005 - p1026(1) [501+]
 LJ - v129 - i17 - Oct 15 2004 - p88(1) [51-500]
 Ref Rev - Nov 2004 - pNA [501+]
 R&R Bk N - v19 - i4 - Nov 2004 - p232(1) [501+]

Valdes-Rodriguez, Alisa - *Playing with Boys*
 Ent W - i781 - Sept 3 2004 - p79 [501+]
 KR - v72 - i15 - August 1 2004 - p713(1) [501+]
 LJ - v129 - i13 - August 2004 - p70(2) [51-500]
 People - Sept 20 2004 - p64 [51-500]
 PW - v251 - i35 - August 30 2004 - p31(2) [501+]

Valdez, Stephen - *An Introduction to Global Financial Markets*
 JEL - v42 - i1 - March 2004 - p237(1) [501+]

Vale, Brian - *The Audacious Admiral Cochrane: The True Life of a Naval Legend*
 TLS - i5300 - Oct 29 2004 - p31(1) [51-500]

Vale, Lawrence J. - *Reclaiming Public Housing: A Half Century of Struggle in Three Public Neighborhoods*
 AJS - v110 - i3 - Nov 2004 - p797(3) [501+]
 CS - v33 - i1 - Jan 2004 - p64-65 [501+]
 JAH - v91 - i1 - June 2004 - p333-334 [501+]

Vale, Thomas R. - *Fire, Native Peoples, and the Natural Landscape*
 WHQ - v35 - i3 - Autumn 2004 - p392(2) [501+]

Valence, Jean R. - *Architect's Essentials of Professional Development*
 R&R Bk N - v19 - i1 - Feb 2004 - p202(1) [51-500]

Valente, Catherynne M. - *The Labyrinth*
 PW - v251 - i29 - July 19 2004 - p149(2) [51-500]

Valente, Claire - *The Theory and Practice of Revolt in Medieval England*
 Albion - v36 - i2 - Summer 2004 - p283(2) [501+]
 Specu - v79 - i3 - July 2004 - p853-854 [501+]

Valenti, Diane C. - *Training Budget Step-by-Step: Complete Guide to Planning and Budgeting Strategically-Aligned Training*
 R&R Bk N - v19 - i1 - Feb 2004 - p111(1) [51-500]

Valenti, Patricia Dunlavy - *Sophia Peabody Hawthorne: A Life, Vol. 1*
 Choice - v42 - i4 - Dec 2004 - p663(1) [1-50]
 R&R Bk N - v19 - i4 - Nov 2004 - p241(1) [501+]

Valentine, Douglas - *The Strength of the Wolf: The Secret History of America's War on Drugs*
 Choice - v42 - i3 - Nov 2004 - p552(1) [1-50]
 R&R Bk N - v19 - i3 - August 2004 - p163(1) [501+]

Valentine, Ian - *Station 43: Audley End House and SOE's Polish Section*
 TLS - i5298 - Oct 15 2004 - p31(1) [51-500]

Valentine, James - *Jumpman Rule #1: Don't Touch Anything*
 c BL - v100 - i21 - July 2004 - p1845(1) [1-50]
 y CCB-B - v57 - i11 - July-August 2004 - p488(1) [501+]
 c CH Bwatch - v14 - i9 - Sept 2004 - p4(1) [51-500]
 y Kliatt - v38 - i4 - July 2004 - p13(1) [51-500]
 y SLJ - v50 - i7 - July 2004 - p113(1) [51-500]
 y VOYA - v27 - i3 - August 2004 - p234(1) [1-50]

Valentine, James W. - *On the Origin of Phyla*
 Choice - v42 - i4 - Dec 2004 - p688(1) [1-50]
 Nature - v430 - i6999 - July 29 2004 - p506(1) [501+]
 New Sci - v183 - i2464 - Sept 11 2004 - p46(1) [501+]
 Sci - v305 - i5684 - July 30 2004 - p613(2) [501+]

Valentine, Jean - *Door in the Mountain: New and Collected Poems*
 LJ - v129 - i19 - Nov 15 2004 - p64(1) [501+]
 PW - v251 - i42 - Oct 18 2004 - p60(1) [51-500]

Valentine, Kylie - *Psychoanalysis, Psychiatry and Modernist Literature*
 JGS - v13 - i1 - March 2004 - p88-90 [501+]

Valentino, Benjamin A. - *Final Solutions: Mass Killing and Genocide in the 20th Century*
 For Aff - v83 - i5 - Sept-Oct 2004 - p164 [501+]
 Wil Q - v28 - i4 - Autumn 2004 - p116(2) [501+]
Final Solutions: Mass Killing and Genocide in the Twentieth Century
 Choice - v42 - i2 - Oct 2004 - p369(2) [51-500]

Valenza, Joyce Kasman - *Power Tools Recharged: 125+ Essential Forms and Presentations for Your School Library Information Program*
 y Kliatt - v38 - i5 - Sept 2004 - p44(2) [51-500]

Valenzuela, Arturo - *Latin American Presidencies Interrupted*
 Wil Q - v29 - i1 - Wntr 2005 - p106(1) [501+]

Valenzuela, Jose - *The Complete Pro Tools Handbook*
 M Ed J - v91 - i2 - Nov 2004 - p61(2) [501+]

Valenzuela-Zapata, Ana Guadalupe - *Tequila: A Natural and Cultural History*
 Choice - v42 - i1 - Sept 2004 - p131(1) [501+]
 E-Streams - Nov 2004 - pNA [501+]
 NH - v113 - i9 - Nov 2004 - p52(1) [501+]

Valimaki, Tuomas - *Central Bank Tenders: Three Essays on Money Market Liquidity Auctions*
JEL - v41 - i4 - Dec 2003 - p1348(1) [501+]

Valis, Noel - *The Culture of Cursileria*
MA - v46 - i4 - Fall 2004 - p362(5) [501+]

Valiunas, Algis - *Churchill's Military Histories: A Rhetorical Study*
HNet - Sept 2004 - pNA [501+]

Valkenburg, Patti M. - *Children's Responses to the Screen: A Media Psychological Approach*
R&R Bk N - v19 - i3 - August 2004 - p151(1) [51-500]

Valle, Gonzalez Del - *La Canonizacion del Diablo. Baudelaire y la Estetica Moderna en Espana*
Hisp R - v72 - i2 - Spring 2004 - p329-331 [501+]

Vallely, Anne - *Guardians of the Transcendent: An Ethnography of a Jain Ascetic Community*
CBRA - Annual 2003 - p358(2) [501+]

Valliant, James Stevens - *The Passion of Ayn Rand's Critics*
KR - v73 - i4 - Feb 15 2005 - p223(1) [501+]

Valriu, Caterina - *Thumbelina/Pulgareita: Bilingual Book (Illus. by Max)*
c SLJ - v51 - i1 - Jan 2005 - p120(1) [51-500]

Valterra, Mikelann R. - *Why Women Earn Less: How to Make What You're Really Worth*
Wom R Bks - v22 - i2 - Nov 2004 - p4(2) [501+]

Valtin, Jan - *Out of the Night: Memoir of Richard Julius Herman Krebs Alias Jan Valtin*
R&R Bk N - v20 - i1 - Feb 2005 - p33(1) [51-500]

Valverde, Leonard A. - *Leaders of Color in Higher Education: Unrecognized Triumphs in Harsh Institutions*
Bl S - v34 - i3 - Fall 2004 - p75-75 [501+]

van Aaken, Anne - *Deliberation and Decision: Economics, Constitutional Theory and Deliberative Democracy*
R&R Bk N - v19 - i3 - August 2004 - p101(1) [501+]

Van Aken, Mauro - *Facing Home: Palestinian Belonging in a Valley of Doubt*
HNet - Sept 2004 - pNA [501+]

Van Alfen, Neal K. - *Annual Review of Pathopathology, Vol. 42*
SciTech - v28 - i4 - Dec 2004 - p125 [51-500]

Van Allsburg, Chris - *The Mysteries of Harris Burdick (Illus. by Van Allsburg, Chris)*
c SLJ - v50 - i11 - Nov 2004 - p64(2) [51-500]
The Polar Express (Illus. by Van Allsburg, Chris)
c RT - v57 - Sept 2003 - p103 [501+]

Van Andringa, W. - *La Religion en Gaule Romaine. Piete et Politique*
Class R - v54 - i2 - Nov 2004 - p519-520 [501+]

Van Arsdall, Anne - *Medieval Herbal Remedies: The "Old English Herbarium" and Anglo-Saxon Medicine*
Specu - v79 - i4 - Oct 2004 - p1168(3) [501+]

Van Bael, Ivo - *Anti-Dumping and Other Trade Protection Laws of the EC, 4th Ed.*
R&R Bk N - v19 - i4 - Nov 2004 - p175(1) [501+]

Van, Bart - *Spenser's Forms of History*
RES - v55 - i218 - Feb 2004 - p124-129 [501+]

Van Belkom, Edo - *Wolf Pack*
c Res Links - v10 - i1 - Oct 2004 - p35(1) [501+]
c SLJ - v50 - i10 - Oct 2004 - p180(1) [51-500]

Van Belle, Douglas A. - *Media Bureaucracies, and Foreign Aid: A Comparative Analysis of the United States, the United Kingdom, Canada, France, and Japan.*
Choice - v42 - i3 - Nov 2004 - p559(1) [1-50]

Van Belle, Gerald - *Biostatistics: A Methodology for the Health Sciences, 2nd Ed.*
SciTech - v28 - i3 - Sept 2004 - p57(1) [1-50]

Van Blerkom, Dianna L. - *College Reading and Study Strategies*
R&R Bk N - v19 - i3 - August 2004 - p222(1) [1-50]

van Boxsel, Matthijs - *The Encyclopaedia of Stupidity*
Quad - v49 - i1-2 - Jan-Feb 2005 - p115(3) [501+]

Van Cauwelaert, Didier - *Out of My Head*
KR - v72 - i18 - Sept 15 2004 - p890(1) [501+]
PW - v251 - i40 - Oct 4 2004 - p66(1) [51-500]

Van Cleave, Ryan G. - *Contemporary American Poetry: Behind the Scenes*
ANQ:QJ - v17 - i4 - Fall 2004 - p47(3) [501+]

Van Creveld, Martin L. - *Defending Israel: A Controversial Plan Toward Peace*
Atl - v294 - i3 - Oct 2004 - p162(2) [501+]
LJ - v129 - i20 - Dec 1 2004 - p142(1) [51-500]
MEQ - v11 - i4 - Fall 2004 - p76(2) [501+]
Moshe Dayan
Choice - v42 - i6 - Feb 2005 - p1079(1) [501+]
CR - v285 - i1663 - August 2004 - p114(3) [501+]

Van Dam, Harm-Jan - *Hugo Grotius. De Impererio Summarum Potestatum circa Sacra: Critical Edition with Introduction, English Translation and Commentary*
Six Ct J - v34 - i4 - Winter 2003 - p1143-1145 [501+]

Van Dam, Jacques - *Gastrointestinal Endoscopy*
SciTech - v28 - i3 - Sept 2004 - p107(1) [51-500]

Van Dam, Raymond - *Becoming Christian: The Conversion of Roman Cappadocia*
AHR - v109 - i3 - June 2004 - p957(3) [501+]
Families and Friends in Late Roman Cappadocia
AHR - v109 - i3 - June 2004 - p957(1) [501+]
Kingdom of Snow: Roman Rule and Greek Culture in Cappadocia
AHR - v109 - i3 - June 2004 - p957(1) [501+]
Class R - v53 - i2 - Nov 2003 - p435-436 [501+]

Van De Mieroop, Marc - *A History of the Ancient Near East c. 3000-323 BC, 1st Ed.*
TimHES - v0 - i1680 - Feb 25 2005 - pXII(1) [501+]

Van de Noort, Robert - *The Humber Wetlands: The Archaeology of a Dynamic Landscape*
SciTech - v28 - i4 - Dec 2004 - p4(1) [1-50]

Van Deburg, William L. - *Hoodlums: Black Villains and Social Bandits in American Life*
BL - v101 - i2 - Sept 15 2004 - p185(1) [51-500]

Van den Belt, Marjan - *Mediated Modeling: A System Dynamics Approach to Environmental Consensus Building*
Choice - v42 - i4 - Dec 2004 - p693(1) [1-50]
SciTech - v28 - i3 - Sept 2004 - p5(1) [501+]

Van Den Berg, Leo - *Social Challenges and Organising Capacity in Cities: Experiences in Eight European Cities*
JEL - v42 - i1 - March 2004 - p342(1) [501+]

van den Ham, Allert - *Shifting Logic in Area Development Practices*
R&R Bk N - v19 - i3 - August 2004 - p110(1) [51-500]

van den Hoonaard, Will C. - *Walking the Tightrope: Ethical Issues for Qualitative Researchers*
CBRA - Annual 2003 - p102(1) [501+]

Van Der Burg, Wibren - *The Importance of Ideals: Debating Their Relevance in Law, Morality, and Politics*
R&R Bk N - v19 - i3 - August 2004 - p2(1) [1-50]

Van der Hoeven, Rolph - *Perspectives on Growth and Poverty*
R&R Bk N - v19 - i1 - Feb 2004 - p95(1) [51-500]

van der Jagt, Marek - *The Story of My Baldness*
KR - v72 - i18 - Sept 15 2004 - p890(2) [501+]
PW - v251 - i41 - Oct 11 2004 - p56(1) [51-500]
Ent W - i789 - Oct 22 2004 - p102 [51-500]

Van der Linden, Frans P.G.M. - *Orthodontic Concepts and Strategies*
SciTech - v28 - i3 - Sept 2004 - p120(1) [51-500]

Van der Linden, Marcel - *Transnational Labour History: Explorations*
R&R Bk N - v19 - i1 - Feb 2004 - p99(1) [501+]

van der Linden, Peter - *Just Java 2, 6th Ed.*
SciTech - v28 - i4 - Dec 2004 - p21(1) [51-500]

Van der Merwe, C.G. - *Introduction to the Law of South Africa*
R&R Bk N - v19 - i4 - Nov 2004 - p176(1) [501+]

Van der Pluijm, Ben A. - *Earth Structure: An Introduction to Structural Geology and Tectonics, 2nd Ed.*
SciTech - v28 - i1 - March 2004 - p9(1) [51-500]

Van der Put, Klaartje - *Little Duck and Little Ladybug (Illus. by van der Put, Klaartje)*
c PW - v252 - i7 - Feb 14 2005 - p80(2) [501+]

Van der Vat, Dan - *D-Day: The Greatest Invasion: A People's History*
BIC - v33 - i5 - August 2004 - p41(1) [501+]

Van Deusen, Kira - *Singing Story, Healing Drum: Shamans and Storytellers of Turkic Siberia*
R&R Bk N - v19 - i3 - August 2004 - p15(1) [1-50]

Van Die, Marguerite - *Religion and Public Life in Canada: Historical and Comparative Perspectives*
Can Hist R - v85 - i3 - Sept 2004 - p630(3) [501+]

Van Draanen, Wendelin - *Attack of the Tagger (Illus. by Biggs, Brian)*
c BL - v101 - i1 - Sept 1 2004 - p125(2) [1-50]
y SLJ - v50 - i11 - Nov 2004 - p156(1) [51-500]
Flipped (Read by Paris, Andy). Audiobook Review
y Kliatt - v38 - i5 - Sept 2004 - p58(3) [51-500]
c SLJ - v50 - i7 - July 2004 - p58(1) [51-500]
Meet the Gecko (Illus. by Biggs, Brian)
c KR - v72 - i24 - Dec 15 2004 - p1210(1) [51-500]
c PW - v252 - i1 - Jan 3 2005 - p57(2) [501+]
c SLJ - v51 - i1 - Jan 2005 - p138(1) [51-500]
Sammy Keyes and the Art of Deception (Read by Sands, Tara). Audiobook Review
y BL - v101 - i7 - Dec 1 2004 - p679(1) [1-50]
c SLJ - v50 - i11 - Nov 2004 - p82(1) [51-500]
Sammy Keyes and the Psycho Kitty Queen.
c BL - v101 - i3 - Oct 1 2004 - p330(1) [51-500]

c SLJ - v50 - i10 - Oct 2004 - p180(2) [501+]
Sammy Keyes and the Search for Snake Eyes (Read by Sands, Tara). Audiobook Review
y BL - v101 - i9-10 - Jan 1 2005 - p887(1) [501+]
Shredderman: Attack of the Tagger (Illus. by Biggs, Brian)
c KR - v72 - i14 - July 15 2004 - p694(1) [51-500]
Shredderman: Secret Identity (Illus. by Biggs, Brian)
c BL - v101 - i9-10 - Jan 1 2005 - p774(1) [1-50]
c LibMed - v22 - i6 - March 2004 - p63(1) [501+]
Swear to Howdy (Read by Woodman, Jeff). Audiobook Review
Kliatt - v38 - i6 - Nov 2004 - p51(1) [51-500]
y SLJ - v50 - i10 - Oct 2004 - p86(1) [51-500]

Van Dulken, Stephen - *American Inventions: A History of Curious, Extraordinary, and Just Plain Useful Patents*
Choice - v41 - i11-12 - July-August 2004 - p2067(1) [501+]
JouAmCul - v27 - i3 - Sept 2004 - p335(1) [501+]

Van Eechoud, Mireille M.M. - *Choice of Law in Copyright and Related: Alternatives to the Lex Protectionis*
R&R Bk N - v19 - i1 - Feb 2004 - pNA [501+]

Van Eijck, Jan - *Logic colloquium '99: Proceedings*
SciTech - v28 - i4 - Dec 2004 - p15(1) [1-50]

Van Eikels, Kai - *Zeitlekturen*
Ger Q - v77 - i2 - Spring 2004 - p255-256 [501+]

Van Engen, John - *Educating People of Faith: Exploring the History of Jewish and Christian Communities*
CHR - v90 - i4 - Oct 2004 - p728(2) [501+]
R&R Bk N - v19 - i3 - August 2004 - p27(1) [1-50]
Religion in the History of the Medieval West
R&R Bk N - v19 - i4 - Nov 2004 - p20(1) [51-500]

Van Es, Bart - *Spenser's Forms of History*
Six Ct J - v35 - i3 - Fall 2004 - p918-920 [501+]

Van Esch, Kees - *A Framework for Freedom: Learner Autonomy in Foreign Language Teacher Education*
R&R Bk N - v19 - i1 - Feb 2004 - p210(1) [51-500]
New Insights into Foreign Language Learning and Teaching
R&R Bk N - v19 - i4 - Nov 2004 - p211(1) [501+]

Van Ess, Josef - *Der Fehltritt des Gelehrten: Die "Pest von Emmaus" und ihre theologischen Nachspiele*
Specu - v79 - i4 - Oct 2004 - p1066(4) [501+]

Van Gelder, Gordon - *In Lands That Never Were*
y BL - v101 - i1 - Sept 1 2004 - p75(1) [51-500]
ChrSFF&H - v26 - i9 - Sept 2004 - p32(2) [51-500]

Van Gelder, Sicco - *Global Brand Strategy: Unlocking Brand Potential Across Countries, Cultures and Markets*
R&R Bk N - v19 - i4 - Nov 2004 - p93(1) [1-50]

Van Gelderen, C.J. - *Encyclopedia of Hydrangeas*
R&R Bk N - v19 - i4 - Nov 2004 - p246(1) [501+]

van Gelderen, Martin - *Republicanism: A Shared European Heritage, Vols. 1-2*
JMH - v77 - i1 - March 2005 - p160(3) [501+]

Van Grembergen, Wim - *Strategies for Information Technology Governance*
R&R Bk N - v19 - i1 - Feb 2004 - p88(1) [51-500]

Van Greuning, Hennie - *Analysing and Managing Banking Risk: A Framework for Assessing Corporate Governance and Financial Risk*
JEL - v41 - i4 - Dec 2003 - p1366(1) [501+]

Van Gulik, Robert - *The Chinese Bell Murders*
LJ - v129 - i20 - Dec 1 2004 - p184(1) [501+]
The Chinese Gold Murders
LJ - v129 - i20 - Dec 1 2004 - p184(1) [501+]

van Gurp, Hetty - *Peaceful School: Models That Work*
CBRA - Annual 2003 - p397(1) [51-500]

Van Harn, Roger E. - *Exploring and Proclaiming the Apostles' Creed*
Intpr - v59 - i1 - Jan 2005 - p111(1) [51-500]

Van Hensbergen, Gijs - *Guernica: The Biography of a Twentieth-Century Icon*
BL - v101 - i5 - Nov 1 2004 - p461(1) [501+]
BW - v34 - i48 - Nov 28 2004 - p8(1) [501+]
KR - v72 - i19 - Oct 1 2004 - p954(1) [501+]
LJ - v130 - i3 - Feb 15 2005 - p128(2) [51-500]
Nation - v279 - i20 - Dec 13 2004 - p22(7) [501+]
PW - v251 - i51 - Dec 20 2004 - p51(1) [501+]

Van Herwaarden, Jan - *Between Saint James and Erasmus: Studies in Late-Medieval Religious Life: Devotion and Pilgrimage in the Netherlands*
Ren Q - v57 - i4 - Winter 2004 - p1485(3) [501+]

Van Hollen, Cecilia - *Birth on the Threshold: Childbirth and Modernity in South India*
SciTech - v28 - i4 - Dec 2004 - p110(1) [51-500]

Van Hook, Bailey - *The Virgin and Dynamo: Public Murals in American Architecture*
JAH - v91 - i2 - Sept 2004 - p664(2) [501+]
Van Horn, Carl E. - *Work in America: An Encyclopedia of History, Policy, and Society*
Ref Rev - Oct 2004 - pNA [501+]
R&R Bk N - v19 - i2 - May 2004 - p106(1) [51-500]
Van Huylenbroek, Guido - *Multifunctional Agriculture: A New Paradigm for European Agriculture and Rural Development*
R&R Bk N - v19 - i1 - Feb 2004 - p97(1) [51-500]
van Kampen, Vlasta - *It Couldn't Be Worse!*
c CBRA - Annual 2003 - p470(1) [51-500]
Van Kooten, G.C. - *Climate Change Economics: Why International Accords Fail*
Choice - v42 - i2 - Oct 2004 - p342(1) [51-500]
SciTech - v28 - i3 - Sept 2004 - p50(1) [1-50]
Van Leeuwen, Jean - *Cabin on Trouble Creek*
c SLJ - v50 - i7 - July 2004 - p113(2) [51-500]
y VOYA - v27 - i4 - Oct 2004 - p309(2) [51-500]
The Great Cheese Conspiracy (Read by Bostick, Daniel). Audiobook Review
c PW - v251 - i41 - Oct 11 2004 - p27(1) [501+]
c SLJ - v51 - i1 - Jan 2005 - p76(1) [51-500]
The Great Googlestein Museum Mystery (Illus. by Alley, R.W.)
c LibMed - v22 - i4 - Jan 2004 - p63(1) [501+]
Oliver the Mighty Pig (Illus. by Schweninger, Ann)
c SLJ - v50 - i10 - Oct 2004 - pS30(1) [1-50]
Van Lieshout, Elle - *The Nothing King (Illus. by Gerritsen, Paula)*
c SLJ - v51 - i1 - Jan 2005 - p98(1) [51-500]
Van Lustbader, Eric - *The Bourne Legacy*
BL - v100 - i21 - July 2004 - p1825(1) [1-50]
Van Maarsen, Jacqueline - *A Friend Called Anne: One Girl's Story of War, Peace, and a Unique Friendship with Anne Frank*
y HB - v81 - i2 - March-April 2005 - p214(1) [501+]
van Meene, Hellen - *Hellen van Meene: Portraits*
Bwatch - March 2005 - pNA [51-500]
Van Meter, Jonathan - *The Last Good Time*
TLS - i5302 - Nov 12 2004 - p30(1) [51-500]
van Meter, Karl M. - *Interrelation between Type of Analysis and Type of Interpretation*
R&R Bk N - v19 - i2 - May 2004 - p126 [51-500]
Van Minnen, Cornelis A. - *Nation on the Move: Mobility in U.S. History*
JAH - v91 - i1 - June 2004 - p208-209 [501+]
JSH - v70 - i4 - Nov 2004 - p888(2) [501+]
Van Nieuwenhove, Rik - *Jan van Ruusbroec, Mystical Theologian of the Trinity*
Theol St - v65 - i4 - Dec 2004 - p897(2) [501+]
Van Oss, Adriaan C. - *Church and Society in Spanish America*
Ams - v61 - i2 - Oct 2004 - p260(1) [501+]
van Poppel, Frans - *The Road to Independence: Leaving Home in Western and Eastern Societies, 16th-20th Centuries*
R&R Bk N - v19 - i2 - May 2004 - p134 [51-500]
Van Riper, A. Bowdoin - *Imagining Flight: Aviation and Popular Culture*
APH - v51 - i3 - Fall 2004 - p54(2) [501+]
T&C - v45 - i3 - July 2004 - p627-629 [501+]
van Rossum, Heleen - *Will You Carry Me?*
KR - v73 - i2 - Jan 15 2005 - p126(1) [51-500]
Van Rynbach, Iris - *Safely to Shore: America's Lighthouses*
LibMed - v22 - i5 - Feb 2004 - p88(1) [501+]
van Schaik, Carel - *Among Orangutans: Red Apes and the Rise of Human Culture (Illus. by van Duijnhoven, Perry)*
Globe & Mail - Dec 18 2004 - pD14 [1-50]
Van Schaik, Leon - *Ecocells: Landscapes and Masterplans by Hamzah and Yeang*
R&R Bk N - v19 - i4 - Nov 2004 - p203(1) [501+]
Van Scoyoc, Pam - *The Ballerina with Webbed Feet/La bailarina palmipeda (Illus. by Lewis, R.J.)*
c SLJ - v51 - i1 - Jan 2005 - p121(1) [51-500]
Van Sickle, Jan - *Basic GIS Coordinates*
SciTech - v28 - i3 - Sept 2004 - p5(1) [501+]
Van Sliedregt, E. - *The Criminal Responsibility of Individuals for Violations of International Humanitarian Law*
R&R Bk N - v19 - i1 - Feb 2004 - pNA [51-500]
Van Steenwyk, Elizabeth - *One Fine Day (Illus. by Farnsworth, Bill)*
c LibMed - v22 - i4 - Jan 2004 - p78(1) [501+]
Van 't Spijker, Ineke - *Fictions of the Inner Life: Religious Literature and Formation of the Self in the Eleventh and Twelfth Centuries*
R&R Bk N - v19 - i4 - Nov 2004 - p20(1) [51-500]
Van Tassel-Baska, Joyce - *Curriculum for Gifted and Talented Students*
Choice - v42 - i1 - Sept 2004 - p157(1) [501+]
van Turennout, Paola - *One Little Bug*
KR - v73 - i1 - Jan 1 2005 - p58(1) [51-500]
Van Vleet, Carmella - *How to Handle School Snafus*
LJ - v129 - i18 - Nov 1 2004 - p116(1) [51-500]
Van Wormer, Katherine S. - *Confronting Oppression, Restoring Justice: From Policy Analysis to Social Action*
R&R Bk N - v19 - i3 - August 2004 - p142(1) [51-500]
Van Wyhe, John - *Phrenology and the Origins of Victorian Scientific Naturalism*
SciTech - v28 - i3 - Sept 2004 - p4(1) [501+]
Van Wyk, Ben-Erik - *Medicinal Plants of the World: An Illustrated Scientific Guide to Important Medicinal Plants and Their Uses*
Bwatch - v26 - i7 - July 2004 - p3(1) [51-500]
Choice - v42 - i1 - Sept 2004 - p72(5) [501+]
E-Streams - August 2004 - pNA [501+]
QRB - v79 - i4 - Dec 2004 - p430(1) [501+]
Vanaik, Achin - *Globalization and South Asia: Multidimensional Perspectives*
Pac A - v77 - i3 - Fall 2004 - p596(2) [501+]
Vance, Daniela Geracitano - *Jade Book: A Stone of Hope*
CBRA - Annual 2003 - p124(1) [51-500]
Vance, Donald R. - *An Introduction to Classical Hebrew*
R&R Bk N - v19 - i4 - Nov 2004 - p218(1) [501+]
Vance, Jack - *Lurulu*
BL - v101 - i6 - Nov 15 2004 - p572(1) [51-500]
KR - v72 - i19 - Oct 1 2004 - p944(1) [501+]
PW - v251 - i41 - Oct 11 2004 - p60(1) [51-500]
VanCleave, Janice Pratt - *Earth Science for Every Kid: 101 Easy Experiments That Really Work*
y SB - v40 - i5 - Sept-Oct 2004 - p193(1) [51-500]
Janice VanCleave's A+ Projects in Physics: Winning Experiments for Science Fairs and Extra Credit
y Sci Teach - v71 - i6 - July 2004 - p65-65 [501+]
Janice VanCleave's Math for Every Kid
c SLJ - v50 - i9 - Sept 2004 - p59(1) [51-500]
Janice VanCleave's Rocks and Minerals: Mind-Boggling Experiments You Can Turn into Science Fair Projects
y SB - v40 - i5 - Sept-Oct 2004 - p193(1) [51-500]
y SB - v40 - i5 - Sept-Oct 2004 - p193(1) [51-500]
y SB - v40 - i5 - Sept-Oct 2004 - p193(1) [51-500]
y SB - v40 - i5 - Sept-Oct 2004 - p193(1) [51-500]
Janice VanCleave's Volcanoes: Mind-Boggling Experiments You Can Turn into Science Fair Projects
y SB - v40 - i5 - Sept-Oct 2004 - p193(1) [51-500]
Janice VanCleave's Weather: Mind-Boggling Experiments You Can Turn into Science Fair Projects
y SB - v40 - i5 - Sept-Oct 2004 - p193(1) [51-500]
Vancouver and Victoria, 4th Ed.
CBRA - Annual 2003 - p26(1) [501+]
Vancouver, Rebecca Johnson - *Taxing Choices: The Intersection of Class, Gender, Parenthood, and the Law*
CWS - v23 - i3-4 - Spring-Summer 2004 - p212(2) [501+]
Vande Kopple, William J. - *The Catch: Families, Fishing, and Faith*
Ch Today - v48 - i9 - Sept 2004 - p90(1) [51-500]
Vande Velde, Vivian - *Heir Apparent*
y Kliatt - v38 - i5 - Sept 2004 - p33(2) [51-500]
Now You See It...
y BL - v101 - i9-10 - Jan 1 2005 - p862(1) [1-50]
y CCB-B - v58 - i5 - Jan 2005 - p231(1) [51-500]
y Kliatt - v39 - i1 - Jan 2005 - p11(1) [51-500]
KR - v72 - i24 - Dec 15 2004 - p1210(1) [51-500]
y PW - v252 - i3 - Jan 17 2005 - p56(2) [51-500]
y SLJ - v51 - i1 - Jan 2005 - p138(1) [51-500]
Vandenberg, Dominiquie - *The Iron Circle: The True Life Story of Dominiquie Vandenberg*
BL - v101 - i1 - Sept 1 2004 - p53(1) [51-500]
PW - v251 - i30 - July 26 2004 - p48(1) [501+]
Vandepitte, J. - *Basic Laboratory Procedures in Clinical Bacteriology, 2nd Ed.*
SciTech - v28 - i3 - Sept 2004 - p74 [51-500]
SciTech - v28 - i3 - Sept 2004 - p74(1) [51-500]
Vander Zee, Ruth - *Mississippi Morning (Illus. by Cooper, Floyd)*
c BL - v101 - i4 - Oct 15 2004 - p406(1) [501+]
c KR - v72 - i18 - Sept 15 2004 - p921(1) [51-500]
c SLJ - v50 - i9 - Sept 2004 - p182(1) [51-500]
VanDerbeck, Edward J. - *Principles of Cost Accounting, 13th Ed.*
R&R Bk N - v19 - i2 - May 2004 - p120 [51-500]
R&R Bk N - v19 - i2 - May 2004 - p120 [51-500]
Vanderbilt, Gloria - *It Seemed Important at the Time: A Romance Memoir*
BL - v101 - i2 - Sept 15 2004 - p192(1) [51-500]
KR - v72 - i15 - August 1 2004 - p735(1) [501+]
LJ - v129 - i14 - Sept 1 2004 - p163(1) [51-500]
NYTBR - Nov 21 2004 - p31 [501+]
People - v62 - i15 - Oct 11 2004 - p58 [51-500]
PW - v251 - i28 - July 12 2004 - p51(2) [51-500]
Vanderbilt, Tom - *Survival City: Adventures among the Ruins of Atomic America*
T&C - v45 - i3 - July 2004 - p673-675 [501+]
Vanderhaeghe, Guy - *The Last Crossing (Read by Cox, John Henry). Audiobook Review*
BL - v101 - i5 - Nov 1 2004 - p504(1) [51-500]
The Last Crossing
CBRA - Annual 2003 - p190(1) [51-500]
NS - v133 - i4716 - Nov 29 2004 - p42(1) [51-500]
NYTBR - Feb 27 2005 - p24 [1-50]
PW - v251 - i49 - Dec 6 2004 - p32(2) [51-500]
Vanderhaeghe, Lorna R. - *Healthy Fats for Life: Preventing and Treating Common Health Problems with Essential Fatty Acids, Rev. 2nd Ed.*
SciTech - v28 - i4 - Dec 2004 - p74(1) [51-500]
Vanderlinden, Kathy - *Foot: A Playful Biography*
CBRA - Annual 2003 - p268(2) [51-500]
VanderMeer, Jeff - *Secret Life*
Bwatch - v26 - i7 - July 2004 - p6(1) [51-500]
The Thackery T. Lambshead Pocket Guide to Eccentric and Discredited Diseases
Analog - v124 - i3 - March 2004 - p136(2) [51-500]
TLS - i5305 - Dec 3 2004 - p30(1) [51-500]
Why Should I Cut Your Throat?
PW - v251 - i40 - Oct 4 2004 - p75(1) [1-50]
Vandervelde, Beatrice - *Home Ice*
Res Links - v10 - i3 - Feb 2005 - p23(1) [501+]
Vandervelde, Maryanne - *Retirement for Two: Everything You Need to Know to Thrive Together as Long as You Both Shall Live*
BL - v100 - i22 - August 2004 - p1884(1) [51-500]
Vanderwood, Paul J. - *Juan Soldado: Rapist, Murderer, Martyr, Saint*
CHE - v51 - i18 - Jan 7 2005 - pA30-A30 [501+]
PW - v251 - i45 - Nov 8 2004 - p44(1) [501+]
VanDevelder, Paul - *Coyote Warrior: One Man, Three Tribes, and the Trial That Forged a Nation*
Aud - v106 - i5 - Nov-Dec 2004 - p94(2) [51-500]
BL - v100 - i22 - August 2004 - p1883(1) [51-500]
Vandewiele, Agnes - *Whales and Dolphins*
c Sch Lib - v52 - i4 - Winter 2004 - p190(2) [51-500]
Vanel, S.G. - *The Astrological Karma of the U.S.A.*
Bwatch - Dec 2004 - pNA [51-500]
Vaney, Neil - *Christ in a Grain of Sand: An Ecological Journey with the Spiritual Exercises*
LJ - v129 - i16 - Oct 1 2004 - p87(1) [51-500]
Vangelisti, Anita L. - *Handbook of Family Communication*
R&R Bk N - v19 - i1 - Feb 2004 - p133(1) [51-500]
Vanhaelen, Angela - *Comic Print and Theatre in Early Modern Amsterdam: Gender, Childhood and the City*
Ren Q - v57 - i3 - Fall 2004 - p1027(2) [501+]
Vanhanen, Tatu - *Democratization: A Comparative Analysis of 170 Countries*
AJPS - v39 - i2 - July 2004 - p471(472) [501+]
JPR - v41 - i5 - Sept 2004 - p649-649 [501+]
Vanhoutte, Jacqueline - *Strange Communion: Motherland and Masculinity in Tudor Plays, Pamphlets, and Politics*
Ren Q - v57 - i4 - Winter 2004 - p1501(2) [501+]
R&R Bk N - v19 - i1 - Feb 2004 - p235(1) [51-500]
VanKatwyk, Peter L. - *Spiritual Care and Therapy: Integrative Perspectives*
R&R Bk N - v19 - i1 - Feb 2004 - p23(1) [1-50]
Vankin, Jonathan - *Based on a True Story: Fact and Fantasy in 100 Favorite Movies*
LJ - v130 - i3 - Feb 15 2005 - p134(1) [51-500]
PW - v252 - i1 - Jan 3 2005 - p47(1) [51-500]
Vankovska, Biljana - *Between Past and Future: Civil-Military Relations in the Post-Communist Balkans*
Slav R - v63 - i4 - Winter 2004 - p867(2) [501+]
Vanlandingham, Marta - *Transforming the State: King, Court and Political Culture in the Realms of Aragon*
Specu - v79 - i4 - Oct 2004 - p1170(2) [501+]
Vann, Barry - *Rediscovering the South's Celtic Heritage*
Bwatch - v26 - i8 - August 2004 - p9(1) [51-500]
Vann, Philip - *Face to Face: British Self-Portraits in the Twentieth Century*
Spec - v295 - i9179 - July 10 2004 - p31(2) [501+]
Vannatta, Dennis - *Lives of the Artists*
Ga R - v58 - i1 - Spring 2004 - p199-200 [501+]

Vanneman, Alan - *Sherlock Holmes and the Hapsburg Tiara (Read by Vance, Simon). Audiobook Review*
LJ - v130 - i4 - March 1 2005 - p125(1) [51-500]

Vannucci, Marta - *Mangrove Management and Conservation: Present and Future*
SciTech - v28 - i3 - Sept 2004 - p131(1) [51-500]

Vansina, Jan - *How Societies Are Born: Governance in West Central Africa Before 1600*
R&R Bk N - v19 - i4 - Nov 2004 - p52(1) [1-50]

Vanstiphout, Herman - *Epics of Sumerian Kings: The Matter of Aratta*
Choice - v42 - i1 - Sept 2004 - p97(1) [501+]

Vanstone, Maurice - *Supervising Offenders in the Community: A History of Probation Theory and Practice*
R&R Bk N - v19 - i4 - Nov 2004 - p149(1) [501+]

Vant Sant, John E. - *Mori Arinori's Life and Resources in America*
Choice - v42 - i1 - Sept 2004 - p167(1) [501+]

Vantrease, Brenda Rickman - *The Illuminator (Read by Jones, Simon). Audiobook Review*
LJ - v129 - i20 - Dec 1 2004 - p88(1) [51-500]
The Illuminator
KR - v73 - i2 - Jan 15 2005 - p82(1) [501+]
LJ - v130 - i4 - March 1 2005 - p81(1) [51-500]
PW - v252 - i6 - Feb 7 2005 - p41(1) [501+]

Vantrease, Norma - *Ants in My Pants (Illus. by Cox, Steve)*
c SLJ - v50 - i8 - August 2004 - p90(1) [51-500]

Vapnyar, Lara - *There are Jews in my House: Stories*
y Kliatt - v39 - i2 - March 2005 - p32(1) [51-500]

Varadarajan, V.S. - *Supersymmetry for Mathematicians: An Introduction*
SciTech - v28 - i3 - Sept 2004 - p35(1) [51-500]

Varando, Michael L. - *Soft Targets: A Woman's Guide to Survival*
Bwatch - March 2005 - pNA [51-500]

Vardalas, John N. - *The Computer Revolution in Canada: Building National Technological Competence*
T&C - v45 - i3 - July 2004 - p659-661 [501+]

Vardi, Yoav - *Misbehavior in Organizations: Theory, Research, and Management*
Per Psy - v57 - i3 - Autumn 2004 - p807(5) [501+]

Vardy, Steven Bela - *Ethnic Cleansing in Twentieth-Century Europe*
Choice - v42 - i1 - Sept 2004 - p162(1) [501+]

Varennes, Monique de - *The Sugar Child (Illus. by Gore, Leonid)*
c BL - v101 - i7 - Dec 1 2004 - p659(1) [51-500]
c KR - v72 - i19 - Oct 1 2004 - p959(1) [51-500]
c NYTBR - Oct 17 2004 - p21 [501+]
c PW - v251 - i51 - Dec 20 2004 - p58(1) [51-500]
c SLJ - v50 - i11 - Nov 2004 - p96(2) [51-500]

Varga, Andres E. - *Mariposas Argentinas: Guia Practica e Ilustrada Para la Identificacion de las Principales Mariposas Diurnas Nocturnas de la Provincia de Buenos Aires*
QRB - v79 - i3 - Sept 2004 - p315(2) [501+]

Vargas, Claudia Maria - *Caring for Children with Neurodevelopmental Disabilities and Their Families: An Innovative Approach to Interdisciplinary Practice*
SciTech - v28 - i4 - Dec 2004 - p113(1) [1-50]

Vargas, Fred - *Seeking Whom He May Devour*
Globe & Mail - Feb 19 2005 - pD15 [501+]

Vargas Llosa, Alvaro - *Liberty for Latin America: How to Undo Five Hundred Years of State Oppression*
BL - v101 - i9-10 - Jan 1 2005 - p810(1) [1-50]
KR - v72 - i22 - Nov 15 2004 - p1085(1) [501+]
LJ - v129 - i20 - Dec 1 2004 - p142(1) [51-500]

Vargas Llosa, Mario - *The Way to Paradise*
NYTBR - Oct 17 2004 - p26 [501+]

Vargas-Luna, Miguel - *Medical Physics: Proceedings*
SciTech - v28 - i4 - Dec 2004 - p80(1) [51-500]

Varghese, Baby - *West Syrian Liturgical Theology*
R&R Bk N - v19 - i4 - Nov 2004 - p26(1) [501+]

Variety: A Collection of Miscellanies in Verse and Prose, with Original Poetry and Fugitive Pieces, Vols. 1-2
ANQ:QJ - v16 - i1 - Winter 2003 - p22 [501+]

Varnava, George - *Stop Bullying in Your School*
y TES - v0 - i4586 - June 4 2004 - pssss19(1) [501+]

Varner, Collin - *Plants of the Gulf and San Juan Islands and Southern Vancouver Island*
CBRA - Annual 2003 - p407(2) [51-500]
Plants of the West Coast
CBRA - Annual 2003 - p407(2) [51-500]
Plants of the Whistler Region
CBRA - Annual 2003 - p407(2) [51-500]
Plants of Vancouver and the Lower Mainland
CBRA - Annual 2003 - p407(2) [51-500]

Varner, Eric R. - *Mutilation and Transformation: Damnatio Memoriae and Roman Imperial Portraiture*
R&R Bk N - v19 - i4 - Nov 2004 - p205(1) [501+]

Varnum, Robin - *The Language of Comics: Word and Image*
Col Lit - v32 - i1 - Wntr 2005 - p166(11) [501+]

Varon, Elizabeth R. - *Southern Lady, Yankee Spy: The True Story of Elizabeth Van Lew, A Union Agent in the Heart of the Confederacy*
JAH - v91 - i3 - Dec 2004 - p1023(2) [501+]
JSH - v70 - i4 - Nov 2004 - p936(3) [501+]

Varon, Jeremy - *Bringing the War Home: The Weather Underground, the Red Army Faction, and Revolutionary Violence in the Sixties and Seventies*
Choice - v42 - i5 - Jan 2005 - p908(1) [1-50]

Varouxakis, Georgios - *Victorian Political Thought on France and the French*
HNet - July 2004 - pNA [501+]

Varricchio, Claudette G. - *Cancer Source Book for Nurses, 8th Ed.*
SciTech - v28 - i3 - Sept 2004 - p91(1) [51-500]

Varsano, Paula M. - *Tracking the Banished Immortal: The Poetry of Li Bo and Its Critical Reception*
HJAS - v64 - i2 - Dec 2004 - p502-511 [501+]
HJAS - v64 - i2 - Dec 2004 - p502-511 [501+]
R&R Bk N - v19 - i1 - Feb 2004 - p219(1) [51-500]

Vasile, Albert J. - *Speak with Confidence: A Practical Guide, 9th Ed.*
R&R Bk N - v19 - i1 - Feb 2004 - p228(1) [1-50]

Vasil'ev, A.N. - *The Field Theoretic Renormalization Group in Critical Behavior Theory and Stochastic Dynamics*
SciTech - v28 - i3 - Sept 2004 - p45(1) [1-50]

Vasilev, Ren - *From Abbots to Zurich: New York State Placenames*
R&R Bk N - v19 - i3 - August 2004 - p72(1) [51-500]

Vasquez, Manuel A. - *Globalizing the Sacred: Religion Across the Americas*
CS - v33 - i6 - Nov 2004 - p687(2) [501+]

Vasquez, Mark G. - *Authority and Reform: Religious and Educational Discourses in Nineteenth-Century New England Literature*
CH - v73 - i4 - Dec 2004 - p882(3) [501+]

Vasquez, Vivian Maria - *Negotiating Critical Literacies with Young Children*
R&R Bk N - v19 - i4 - Nov 2004 - p181(1) [501+]

Vassanji, M.G. - *The In-Between World of Vikram Lall*
BL - v101 - i1 - Sept 1 2004 - p66(1) [51-500]
Can Lit - i182 - Autumn 2004 - p181(3) [501+]
CBRA - Annual 2003 - p190(2) [51-500]
KR - v72 - i15 - August 1 2004 - p713(2) [501+]
LJ - v129 - i13 - August 2004 - p71(1) [51-500]
Nation - v279 - i22 - Dec 27 2004 - p31 [501+]
NS - v133 - i4717 - Dec 6 2004 - p55(1) [501+]
NY - v80 - i32 - Oct 25 2004 - p91(1) [51-500]
PW - v251 - i30 - July 26 2004 - p37(1) [501+]
Spec - v296 - i9192 - Oct 9 2004 - p51(1) [501+]
TLS - i5291 - August 27 2004 - p20(1) [501+]

Vaswani, Neela - *Where the Long Grass Bends: Stories*
Choice - v42 - i4 - Dec 2004 - p663(2) [1-50]

Vaswani, Vikram - *MySQL: the Complete Reference*
LJ - v129 - i20 - Dec 1 2004 - p152(1) [51-500]

Vatnsdal, Caelum - *They Came from Within: A History of Canadian Horror Cinema*
Globe & Mail - August 14 2004 - pD2 [501+]

Vattimo, Gianni - *The Future of Religion*
LJ - v130 - i3 - Feb 15 2005 - p136(1) [51-500]
Nihilism and Emancipation: Ethics, Politics, and Law
LJ - v129 - i15 - Sept 15 2004 - p60(1) [51-500]

Vauchez, Andre - *Ermites de France et d'Italie*
CHR - v90 - i4 - Oct 2004 - p751(2) [501+]

Vaughan, Brian K. - *Ex Machina: The First Hundred Days*
PW - v252 - i7 - Feb 14 2005 - p56(1) [51-500]
Mystique: Dead Drop Gorgeous
PW - v251 - i39 - Sept 27 2004 - p39(1) [51-500]
Runaways, Vol.1
LJ - v129 - i14 - Sept 1 2004 - p129(1) [51-500]
y Teach Lib - v32 - i3 - Feb 2005 - p58(1) [51-500]
Y: The Last Man: Safeword
y BL - v101 - i9-10 - Jan 1 2005 - p836(1) [51-500]
PW - v251 - i41 - Oct 11 2004 - p58(1) [51-500]
Y: The Last Man: Unmanned
LibMed - v22 - i4 - Jan 2004 - p69(1) [501+]

Vaughan, Frederick - *The Canadian Federalist Experiment: From Defiant Monarchy to Reluctant Republic*
R&R Bk N - v19 - i3 - August 2004 - p180(1) [501+]

Vaughan, Hal - *Doctor to the Resistance: The Heroic True Story of an American Surgeon and His Family in Occupied Paris*
LJ - v129 - i12 - July 2004 - p100(1) [51-500]

Vaughan, R.M. - *Spells*
CBRA - Annual 2003 - p191(1) [51-500]

Vaughan, Robert - *Light of Hope*
KR - v72 - i19 - Oct 1 2004 - p940(1) [501+]

Vaughan-Whitehead, Daniel C. - *EU Enlargement versus Social Europe? The Uncertain Future of the European Social Model*
JEL - v42 - i1 - March 2004 - p260(1) [501+]

Vaughn, Ellen - *Radical Gratitude: Discovering Joy through Everyday Thankfulness*
PW - v252 - i11 - March 14 2005 - p64(1) [51-500]

Vaughn, Sharon - *Reading in the Classroom: Systems for the Observation of Teaching and Learning*
TCR - v106 - i5 - May 2004 - p875(2) [501+]
TCR - v106 - i8 - August 2004 - p1525(1) [501+]

Vaught, Susan - *Stormwitch*
KR - v72 - i24 - Dec 15 2004 - p1210(1) [51-500]

Vault - *The Vault College Career Bible, 2005 Ed.*
PW - v251 - i44 - Nov 1 2004 - p58(1) [501+]

Vaz, Mark Cotta - *The Art of the Incredibles*
y BL - v101 - i4 - Oct 15 2004 - p375(1) [51-500]
LJ - v130 - i3 - Feb 15 2005 - p133(1) [51-500]
Caught in the Web
ChrSFF&H - v26 - i9 - Sept 2004 - p37(1) [51-500]

Vazquez, Carmen Inoa - *Parenting with Pride--Latino Style: How to Help Your Child Cherish Your Cultural Values and Succeed in Today's World*
PW - v251 - i49 - Dec 6 2004 - p32(2) [501+]

Vazquez, Francisco H. - *Latino/a Thought: Culture, Politics, and Society*
CS - v33 - i6 - Nov 2004 - p750(1) [1-50]

Vazquez, Josefina Zoraida - *El Establecimiento del Federalismo en Mexico*
Ams - v61 - i2 - Oct 2004 - p286(2) [501+]

Veach, Theresa, A. - *Cancer and the Family Life Cycle: A Practitioner's Guide*
Adoles - v39 - i154 - Summer 2004 - p406(1) [51-500]

Vecchione, Glen - *100 Award-Winning Science Fair Projects*
SB - v40 - i5 - Sept-Oct 2004 - p191(1) [51-500]

Vecchione, Patrice - *Revenge and Forgiveness: An Anthology of Poems*
c SLJ - v50 - i7 - July 2004 - p129(1) [51-500]
y SLJ - v50 - i10 - Oct 2004 - pS68(1) [51-500]
y Teach Lib - v32 - i1 - Oct 2004 - p10(1) [51-500]

Veccia, Susan H. - *Uncovering Our History: Teaching with Primary Sources*
LibMed - v23 - i1 - August-Sept 2004 - p87(2) [51-500]
R&R Bk N - v19 - i3 - August 2004 - p63(1) [51-500]
R&USQ - v44 - i2 - Winter 2004 - p179(1) [501+]

Vedder, Richard K. - *Going Broke by Degree: Why College Costs Too Much*
R&R Bk N - v19 - i4 - Nov 2004 - p184(1) [501+]

Veeck, Mike - *Fun Is Good: How to Create Joy and Passion in Your Workplace and Career*
PW - v252 - i11 - March 14 2005 - p54(1) [51-500]

Veeser, Cyrus - *A World Safe for Capitalism: Dollar Diplomacy and America's Rise to Global Power*
BHR - v77 - i4 - Winter 2003 - p743(745) [501+]
HAHR - v84 - i2 - May 2004 - p385(2) [501+]

Vega, Denise - *Click Here to Find Out How I Survived the Seventh Grade*
c KR - v73 - i5 - March 1 2005 - p297(1) [51-500]

Vega, Ed - *The Lamentable Journey of Omaha Bigelow into the Impenetrable Loisaida Jungle*
BL - v101 - i5 - Nov 1 2004 - p465(2) [51-500]
KR - v72 - i19 - Oct 1 2004 - p937(1) [51-500]
LJ - v129 - i18 - Nov 1 2004 - p78(1) [501+]

Vega, Marta Moreno - *When the Spirits Dance Mambo: Growing Up Nuyorican in el Barrio*
y BL - v101 - i6 - Nov 15 2004 - p550(1) [51-500]
PW - v251 - i44 - Nov 1 2004 - p57(1) [501+]

Vega-Redondo, Fernando - *Economics and the Theory of Games*
JEL - v41 - i4 - Dec 2003 - p1339(2) [501+]

Vegetarian Resource Group - *Vegetarian Journal's Guide to Natural Foods Restaurants in the U.S. and Canada, 4th Ed.*
Veg J - v24 - i1 - Jan-Feb 2005 - p34(1) [501+]

Vegetarians of Washington - *Veg-Feasting in the Pacific Northwest: A Complete Guide for Vegetarians and the Curious*
Veg J - v23 - i4 - July-August 2004 - p31(1) [51-500]

Vehables, Stephen - *To the Top: The Story of Everest*
LibMed - v22 - i4 - Jan 2004 - p82(1) [501+]

Vesciunaite, Aldona - *Blykstelejimai: Simtmeciui baigiantis ir kiti netiketumai*
WLT - v79 - i1 - Jan-April 2005 - p96(1) [501+]

Vess, Charles - *The Book of Ballads*
BL - v101 - i7 - Dec 1 2004 - p644(1) [51-500]
Globe & Mail - Jan 1 2005 - pD7 [501+]
PW - v251 - i48 - Nov 29 2004 - p25(1) [51-500]

Vest, Charles M. - *Pursuing the Endless Frontier: Essays on MIT and the Role of Reseach Universities*
Choice - v42 - i7 - March 2005 - p1246(1) [51-500]

Vest, James M. - *Hitchcock and France: The Forging of an Auteur*
Choice - v41 - i11-12 - July-August 2004 - p2052(1) [501+]
R&R Bk N - v19 - i1 - Feb 2004 - p226(1) [51-500]

Vestergaard, Hope - *Hello, Snow! (Illus. by Westcott, Nadine Bernard)*
c BL - v101 - i5 - Nov 1 2004 - p494(1) [51-500]
c HB - v80 - i6 - Nov-Dec 2004 - p703(1) [51-500]
c KR - v72 - i19 - Oct 1 2004 - p971(1) [51-500]
c SLJ - v50 - i11 - Nov 2004 - p119(1) [51-500]

Veterans History Project - *Voices of War: Stories of Service from the Home Front and the Front Lines*
BL - v101 - i5 - Nov 1 2004 - p449(1) [51-500]

Vetter, Ingrid - *Lotte Reimers and Ceramic Art*
Ceram Mo - v52 - i1 - Jan 2004 - p26(2) [501+]

Via, Dan O. - *Homosexuality and the Bible: Two Views*
Intpr - v59 - i1 - Jan 2005 - p90(2) [501+]

Viader, Roland - *L'Andorre du IXe au XIVe siecle: Montagne, feodalite et communautes*
Med R - Oct 2004 - pNA [501+]

Vial, Theodore M. - *Liturgy Wars: Ritual Theory and Protestant Reform in Nineteenth-Century Zurich*
JR - v85 - i1 - Jan 2005 - p167(3) [501+]

Viano, David C. - *Role of the Seat in Rear Crash Safety*
SciTech - v28 - i1 - March 2004 - p168(1) [51-500]

Viardot, Eric - *Successful Marketing Strategy for High-tech Firms, 3rd Ed.*
R&R Bk N - v19 - i3 - August 2004 - p97(1) [51-500]

Vibert, Conor - *An Introduction to Online Competitive Intelligence Research: Search Strategies, Research Case Study, Research Problems, and Data Source Evaluations and Reviews*
Choice - v42 - i5 - Jan 2005 - p899(1) [1-50]

Vibrations in Rotaing Machinery: Proceedings
SciTech - v28 - i4 - Dec 2004 - p133 [51-500]

Vicari, L. - *Optical Applications of Liquid Crystals*
SciTech - v28 - i4 - Dec 2004 - p57(1) [51-500]

Vice, Sue - *Children Writing the Holocaust*
Choice - v42 - i4 - Dec 2004 - p656(1) [1-50]

Vicinus, Martha - *Intimate Friends: Women Who Loved Women*
NS - v133 - i4699 - August 2 2004 - p39(2) [501+]
LJ - v129 - i13 - August 2004 - p105(1) [51-500]

Vick-Westgate, Ann - *Nunavik: Inuit-Controlled Education in Arctic Quebec*
CBRA - Annual 2003 - p371(1) [51-500]

Vickers, Brian - *"Counterfeiting" Shakespeare: Evidence, Authorship and John Ford's Funerall Elegye*
Six Ct J - v34 - i4 - Winter 2003 - p1158-1160 [501+]
Shakespeare, Co-Author: A Historical Study of Five Collaborative Plays
Six Ct J - v35 - i3 - Fall 2004 - p913-914 [501+]

Vickers, Daniel - *A Companion to Colonial America*
J Am St - v38 - i1 - April 2004 - p173-174 [501+]
JSH - v70 - i4 - Nov 2004 - p885(4) [501+]

Vickers, Huco - *Beaton in the Sixties: The Cecil Beaton Diaries as He Wrote Them, 1965-1969*
PW - v251 - i38 - Sept 20 2004 - p52(1) [51-500]

Vickers, Rhiannon - *The Labour Party and the World, Vol. 1*
Choice - v42 - i4 - Dec 2004 - p726(1) [1-50]
CR - v286 - i1669 - Feb 2005 - p112(2) [501+]
HER - v119 - i483 - Sept 2004 - p1102(2) [501+]

Vickers, Salley - *Mr. Golightly's Holiday*
BW - v34 - i5 - Feb 1 2004 - p7(1) [501+]

Vickroy, Laurie - *Trauma and Survival in Contemporary Fiction*
MFSF - v50 - i2 - Summer 2004 - p522-524 [501+]

Vico, Giambattista - *Statecraft: The Deeds of Antonio Carafa*
R&R Bk N - v19 - i3 - August 2004 - p32(1) [501+]

Vico's Synopsis of Universal Law and on the One Principle and One End of Universal Law
R&R Bk N - v19 - i3 - August 2004 - p6(1) [1-50]

Victor, Barbara - *Army of Roses: Inside the World of Palestinian Women Suicide Bombers*
Lon R Bks - v26 - i21 - Nov 4 2004 - p21(3) [501+]

Victor, Clement J. - *Tamil-English, English-Tamil Dictionary and Phrasebook*
R&R Bk N - v19 - i4 - Nov 2004 - p220(1) [501+]

Victor, David G. - *Climate Change: Debating America's Policy Options*
Bwatch - Nov 2004 - pNA [51-500]
SciTech - v28 - i3 - Sept 2004 - p50(1) [1-50]
The Collapse of the Kyoto Protocol and the Struggle to Slow Global Warming
y Kliatt - v39 - i2 - March 2005 - p37(2) [51-500]

Victore, Hugo De - *De archa Noe, Libellus de Formationearche arche*
Specu - v79 - i3 - July 2004 - p773-775 [501+]

Victorian Sources of Fairy Tales, 1: A Collection of Researches, Vols. 1-5
Folkl - v115 - i3 - Dec 2004 - p371(3) [501+]

Vicziany, Marika - *Regional Security in the Asia Pacific: 9/11 and After*
R&R Bk N - v19 - i3 - August 2004 - p188(1) [501+]

Vida, Vendela - *And Now You Can Go*
BW - v34 - i40 - Oct 3 2004 - p15(1) [501+]
y Kliatt - v38 - i1 - Jan 2004 - p18(1) [51-500]
NYTBR - Sept 5 2004 - p20 [501+]

Vidal, Beatriz - *Federico and the Magi's Gift: A Latin American Christmas Story (Illus. by Vidal, Beatriz)*
c BL - v101 - i6 - Nov 15 2004 - p594(1) [51-500]
c HB - v80 - i6 - Nov-Dec 2004 - p665(2) [51-500]
c KR - v72 - i21 - Nov 1 2004 - p1055(1) [51-500]
c PW - v251 - i39 - Sept 27 2004 - p62(2) [51-500]

Vidal, Gore - *1876*
Globe & Mail - Oct 30 2004 - pD31 [501+]
The Best Man: A Play about Politics
BW - v34 - i39 - Sept 26 2004 - p4(1) [501+]
Imperial America: Reflections on the United States of Amnesia
Globe & Mail - July 24 2004 - pD8 [501+]
Imperial America: The Privatizing of the Presidential Election
LJ - v129 - i12 - July 2004 - p103(2) [51-500]
Inventing a Nation: Washington, Adams, Jefferson
BW - v34 - i1 - Jan 4 2004 - p7(1) [501+]
Lon R Bks - v26 - i18 - Sept 23 2004 - p32(2) [501+]
TLS - i5264 - Feb 20 2004 - p5-7 [501+]

Vidan, Aida - *Embroidered with Gold, Strung with Pearls: The Traditional Ballads of Bosnian Women*
Slav R - v63 - i4 - Winter 2004 - p871(2) [501+]

Vidhyasekaran, P. - *Concise Encyclopedia of Plant Pathology*
Choice - v42 - i3 - Nov 2004 - p459(1) [1-50]
E-Streams - Nov 2004 - pNA [501+]
QRB - v79 - i4 - Dec 2004 - p430(1) [501+]
SciTech - v28 - i3 - Sept 2004 - p130(1) [51-500]

Vidocq, Eugene-Francois - *Memoirs of Vidocq: Master of Crime*
Lon R Bks - v26 - i6 - March 18 2004 - pNA [501+]

Vidyamurthy, Ganapathy - *Pairs Trading: Quantitative Methods and Analysis*
R&R Bk N - v19 - i4 - Nov 2004 - p119(1) [51-500]

Viegas, Jennifer - *Parasites*
y SLJ - v51 - i1 - Jan 2005 - p146(1) [51-500]

Viehl, S.L. - *Bio Rescue*
Analog - v124 - i11 - Nov 2004 - p134(6) [501+]
BL - v100 - i21 - July 2004 - p1830(1) [51-500]
LJ - v129 - i12 - July 2004 - p75(1) [51-500]

Viehmann, Martha L. - *Improving American Indian Health Care: The Western Cherokee Experience*
Am Ind CRJ - v27 - i4 - Fall 2003 - p155-158 [501+]

Vieira, Mark A. - *Hollywood Horror: From Gothic to Cosmic*
Choice - v41 - i7 - March 2004 - p1304(1) [501+]

Vieira, Robert - *Professional SQL Server 2000 Programming*
SciTech - v28 - i3 - Sept 2004 - p32(1) [51-500]

Viera, Dave - *Lighting for Film and Digital Cinematography, 2nd Ed.*
R&R Bk N - v19 - i4 - Nov 2004 - p249(1) [501+]

Vierhaus, Rudolf - *Vergangenheit als Geschichte: Studien zum 19. und 20. Jahrhundert*
HER - v119 - i482 - June 2004 - p832(2) [501+]

Vierow, Wendy - *Africa*
c SLJ - v50 - i7 - July 2004 - p96(2) [51-500]
Asia
c SLJ - v50 - i7 - July 2004 - p96(2) [51-500]
The Assault on Fort Wagner: Black Union Soldiers Make a Stand in South Carolina Battle
c SLJ - v50 - i9 - Sept 2004 - p194(1) [51-500]
The Battle of Bull Run: Confederate Forces Overwhelm Union Troops
c SLJ - v50 - i9 - Sept 2004 - p194(1) [51-500]
The Capture of New Orleans: Union Fleet Takes Control of the Lower Mississippi River
c SLJ - v50 - i9 - Sept 2004 - p194(1) [51-500]
Shots Fired at Fort Sumter: Civil War Breaks Out!
c SLJ - v50 - i9 - Sept 2004 - p194(1) [51-500]
South America
c SLJ - v50 - i7 - July 2004 - p96(2) [51-500]

Viessman, Sara S. - *Appleton and Lange Review of Pediatrics, 6th Ed.*
SciTech - v28 - i3 - Sept 2004 - p117(1) [51-500]

The Vietnam War
LibMed - v23 - i1 - August-Sept 2004 - p76(1) [51-500]

Vietor, Richard H.K. - *Globalization and Growth: Case Studies in National Economic Strategies*
R&R Bk N - v19 - i3 - August 2004 - p110(1) [51-500]

Vigil, Arnold - *Forever New Mexico: Heartfelt Images from the Land of Enchantment*
Roundup M - v12 - i3 - Feb 2005 - p24(1) [51-500]

Vigneault, Guillaume - *Necessary Betrayals*
Can Lit - i182 - Autumn 2004 - p153(2) [501+]
CBRA - Annual 2003 - p191(1) [51-500]

Vigoda-Gadot, Eran - *Citizenship and Management in Public Administration: Integrating Behavioral Theories and Managerial Thinking*
R&R Bk N - v19 - i4 - Nov 2004 - p153(1) [501+]
Developments in Organizational Politics: How Political Dynamics Affect Employee Performance in Modern Work Sites
R&R Bk N - v19 - i2 - May 2004 - p113(1) [51-500]
Managing Collaboration in Public Administration: The Promise of Alliance among Governance, Citizens, and Businesses
Choice - v42 - i2 - Oct 2004 - p364(1) [51-500]
R&R Bk N - v19 - i1 - Feb 2004 - p150(1) [51-500]

Vigorita, T.S. - *Casta domus. Un seminario sulla legislazione auguste, 2nd Ed.*
Class R - v53 - i2 - Nov 2003 - p425-426 [501+]

Viguerie, Richard A. - *America's Right Turn: How Conservatives Used New and Alternative Media to Take Power*
R&R Bk N - v19 - i4 - Nov 2004 - p151(1) [501+]

Viguie, Debbie - *Scarlet Moon*
y Kliatt - v38 - i5 - Sept 2004 - p33(2) [51-500]
y VOYA - v27 - i3 - August 2004 - p234(1) [1-50]

Vikan, Gary - *Sacred Images and Sacred Power in Byzantium*
R&R Bk N - v19 - i1 - Feb 2004 - p201(1) [51-500]

Viking Discoveries
LibMed - v22 - i6 - March 2004 - p93(1) [501+]

Vila, Anne C. - *Enlightenment and Pathology*
Eight-C St - v36 - i2 - Winter 2003 - p259 [501+]

Vila-Matas, Enrique - *Bartleby and Co.*
Econ - v372 - i8384 - July 17 2004 - p80US [501+]
KR - v72 - i20 - Oct 15 2004 - p983(1) [501+]
Spec - v295 - i9186 - August 28 2004 - p30(1) [501+]

Vila, Pablo - *Ethnography at the Border*
CS - v33 - i6 - Nov 2004 - p697(2) [501+]
WHQ - v35 - i3 - Autumn 2004 - p395(2) [501+]

Vilagines, Jaume - *El paisatge, la societat i l'alimantaco al valles oriental, segles X-XII*
Specu - v79 - i3 - July 2004 - p858-860 [501+]

Vilaseca, David - *Hindsight and the Real: Subjectivity in Gay Hispanic Autobiography*
R&R Bk N - v19 - i1 - Feb 2004 - p233(1) [51-500]

Villalon, L.J. Andrew - *Crusaders, Condottieri, and Cannon: Medieval Warfare in Societies around the Mediterranean*
Six Ct J - v35 - i3 - Fall 2004 - p850-851 [501+]

Villamil, Victoria Etnier - *From Johnson's Kids to Lemonade Opera: The American Classical Singer Comes of Age*
BL - v101 - i6 - Nov 15 2004 - p543(1) [51-500]
ON - v69 - i5 - Nov 2004 - p86(2) [501+]

W

Waal, Edmund de - *Timeless Beauty: Traditional Japanese Art from the Montgomery Collection*
    Ant&CM - v108 - i9 - Nov 2003 - p16(1) [501+]

Waardenburg, Jacques - *Islam: Historical, Social, and Political Perspectives*
    JR - v84 - i3 - July 2004 - p499(2) [501+]

Wabuda, Susan - *Preaching during the English Reformation*
    Albion - v36 - i1 - Spring 2004 - p111(2) [501+]
    Six Ct J - v35 - i1 - Spring 2004 - p207(3) [501+]

Wachinger, Tobias A. - *Posing in-between: Postcolonial Englishness and the Commodification of Hybridity*
    R&R Bk N - v19 - i1 - Feb 2004 - p234(1) [51-500]

Wachsmann, Nikolaus - *Hitler's Prisons: Legal Terror in Nazi Germany*
    Choice - v42 - i6 - Feb 2005 - p1089(1) [51-500]
    CR - v285 - i1664 - Sept 2004 - p191(2) [51-500]
    HT - v55 - i3 - March 2005 - p3(1) [501+]
    TimHES - v0 - i1678 - Feb 11 2005 - p26(1) [501+]

Wachtel, Eleanor - *Original Minds: Conversations with CBC Radio's Eleanor Wachtel*
    BIC - v33 - i6 - Sept 2004 - p12(1) [501+]
    CBRA - Annual 2003 - p81(2) [51-500]

Wachtel, Howard - *Street of Dreams-Boulevard of Broken Hearts: Wall Street's First Century*
    BHR - v77 - i4 - Winter 2003 - p752(755) [501+]

Wacker, Mary B. - *Stories Trainers Tell: 55 Ready-to-Use Stories to Make Training Stick*
    HR Mag - v50 - i2 - Feb 2005 - pS16(1) [501+]

Wackers, Frans J. Th. - *Nuclear Cardiology: The Basics: How to Set Up and Maintain a Laboratory*
    E-Streams - Sept 2004 - pNA [501+]

Wacquant, Loic - *Body and Soul: Notebooks of an Apprentice Boxer*
    AJS - v110 - i2 - Sept 2004 - p505(3) [501+]

Wada, Yoko - *A Companion to Ancrene Wisse*
    Med R - Dec 2004 - pNA [501+]

Waddams, Stephen - *Dimensions of Private Law: Categories and Concepts in Anglo-American Legal Reasoning*
    Law Q Rev - v120 - Oct 2004 - p711-714 [501+]

Waddell, Martin - *It's Quacking Time! (Illus. by Barton, Jill)*
    c KR - v73 - i2 - Jan 15 2005 - p127(1) [51-500]
    c PW - v252 - i7 - Feb 14 2005 - p75(1) [51-500]
    Room for a Little One: A Christmas Tale (Illus. by Cockcroft, Jason)
    c BL - v101 - i7 - Dec 1 2004 - p663(2) [51-500]
    c KR - v72 - i21 - Nov 1 2004 - p1055(1) [51-500]
    c Magpies - v19 - i5 - Nov 2004 - p26(1) [501+]
    c PW - v251 - i39 - Sept 27 2004 - p61(1) [51-500]
    c R Today - v22 - i3 - Dec 2004 - p28(1) [501+]
    Tiny's Big Adventure (Illus. by Lawrence, John)
    c BooChiTr - May 30 2004 - p2(1) [501+]
    c Globe & Mail - July 17 2004 - pD11 [1-50]
    c HB - v80 - i4 - July-August 2004 - p443(1) [51-500]
    c HB - v81 - i1 - Jan-Feb 2005 - p14(1) [51-500]
    c Sch Lib - v52 - i3 - Autumn 2004 - p134(1) [501+]
    c SLJ - v50 - i7 - July 2004 - p89(1) [51-500]
    Who Do You Love? (Illus. by Ashforth, Camilla)
    c PW - v251 - i49 - Dec 6 2004 - p61(2) [501+]

Waddell, Patricia - *He Said Never*
    BL - v101 - i3 - Oct 1 2004 - p318(1) [501+]

Waddell, Terrie - *Cultural Expressions of Evil and Wickedness: Wrath, Sex, Crime*
    R&R Bk N - v19 - i1 - Feb 2004 - p10(1) [1-50]

Wadden, Paul - *Rhetoric of Self in Robert Bly and Adrienne Rich: Doubling and the Holotropic Urge*
    R&R Bk N - v19 - i1 - Feb 2004 - p246(1) [51-500]

Waddington, Keir - *Medical Education at St Bartholomew's Hospital 1123-1995*
    AHR - v109 - i3 - June 2004 - p976(2) [501+]

Wade, Barrie - *My Birthday Party*
    c Sch Lib - v52 - i4 - Winter 2004 - p191(1) [51-500]

Wade, Bonnie C. - *Thinking Musically: Experiencing Music, Expressing Culture*
    Am MT - v54 - i2 - Oct-Nov 2004 - p76(2) [501+]
    M Ed J - v91 - i2 - Nov 2004 - p52(1) [501+]

Wade, Harold L. - *Basic and Advanced Regulatory Control: System Design and Application, 2nd Ed.*
    SciTech - v28 - i3 - Sept 2004 - p149(1) [51-500]

Wade, Maria F. - *The Native Americans of the Texas Edwards Plateau, 1582-1799*
    Am Ind CRJ - v27 - i4 - Fall 2003 - p168-170 [501+]

Wade, Mary Dodson - *Joan Lowery Nixon: Masterful Mystery Writer*
    y SLJ - v50 - i11 - Nov 2004 - p174(1) [51-500]
    VOYA - v27 - i5 - Dec 2004 - p418(1) [51-500]

Wade, Peter - *Race, Nature and Culture: An Anthropological Perspective*
    JRAI - v10 - i4 - Dec 2004 - p927(2) [501+]

Wadsworth, Ginger - *Benjamin Banneker: Pioneering Scientist (Illus. by Orback, Craig)*
    c Sci Teach - v71 - i3 - March 2004 - p57-64 [501+]
    Words West: Voices of Young Pioneers
    c Five Owls - v18 - i1 - Fall 2004 - p27(1) [51-500]
    c JAAL - v48 - i3 - Nov 2004 - p268(2) [501+]
    c LibMed - v22 - i5 - Feb 2004 - p81(1) [501+]
    c SLJ - v50 - i10 - Oct 2004 - pS32(1) [51-500]
    y VOYA - v27 - i3 - August 2004 - p243(1) [1-50]

Waeche, Niko Marcel - *Internet Entrepreneurship in Europe: Venture Failure and the Timing of Telecommunications Reform*
    JEL - v41 - i4 - Dec 2003 - p1395(1) [501+]

Waetjen, Thembisa - *Workers and Warriors: Masculinity and the Struggle for Nation in South Africa*
    Choice - v42 - i5 - Jan 2005 - p908(1) [1-50]

Wagamese, Richard - *For Joshua: An Ojibway Father Teaches His Son*
    Can Lit - i182 - Autumn 2004 - p183(3) [501+]

Wagar, W. Warren - *H.G. Wells: Traversing Time*
    Fut - v39 - i1 - Jan-Feb 2005 - p48(1) [51-500]
    Fut - v39 - i2 - March-April 2005 - p60(1) [51-500]
    MFSF - v108 - i3 - March 2005 - p30(5) [501+]
    PW - v251 - i34 - August 23 2004 - p42(1) [51-500]

Waggoner, Tim - *Temple of the Dragonslayer (Illus. by Rams, Vinod)*
    c BL - v101 - i1 - Sept 1 2004 - p126(1) [1-50]
    y SLJ - v50 - i11 - Nov 2004 - p156(1) [51-500]
    c VOYA - v27 - i5 - Dec 2004 - p412(1) [501+]

Wagner, Bill - *Effective C#: 50 Specific Ways to Improve Your C#*
    Bwatch - March 2005 - pNA [51-500]

Wagner, Bruce - *The Chrysanthemum Palace*
    BL - v101 - i8 - Dec 15 2004 - p709(2) [51-500]
    KR - v72 - i22 - Nov 15 2004 - p1068(1) [501+]
    People - v63 - i9 - March 7 2005 - p51 [501+]
    PW - v252 - i1 - Jan 3 2005 - p33(2) [51-500]
    Time - v165 - i6 - Feb 7 2005 - p73 [501+]
    Ent W - Feb 4 2005 - p138 [501+]
    NYTBR - March 13 2005 - p27 [501+]
    Still Holding
    NYTBR - Oct 24 2004 - p30 [501+]

Wagner, Dave - *Blacklisted: The Film Lover's Guide to the Hollywood Blacklist*
    Tikkun - v19 - i5 - Sept-Oct 2004 - p72(2) [501+]

Wagner, E. Glenn - *God: An Honest Conversation for the Undecided*
    PW - v251 - i48 - Nov 29 2004 - p36(2) [51-500]

Wagner, Eduard - *Swords and Daggers: An Illustrated Handbook*
    R&R Bk N - v19 - i4 - Nov 2004 - p251(1) [501+]

Wagner, Fritz W. - *Human Capital Investment for Central City Revitalization*
    Choice - v41 - i7 - March 2004 - p1342(1) [501+]

Wagner, Gillian - *Thomas Coram, Gent, 1668-1751*
    TLS - i5286 - July 23 2004 - p25(1) [501+]

Wagner, Herbert - *At the Creation: Myth, Reality, and the Origin of the Harley-Davidson Motorcycle, 1901-1909*
    Choice - v41 - i7 - March 2004 - p1318(1) [501+]

Wagner, Hugh L. - *Physiological Psychology*
    SciTech - v28 - i4 - Dec 2004 - p70(1) [51-500]

Wagner, Jacques - *Roman et religion en France: 1713-1866*
    FS - v58 - i2 - April 2004 - p258(2) [501+]

Wagner-Martin, Linda - *Zelda Sayre Fitzgerald: An American Woman's Life*
    BL - v101 - i5 - Nov 1 2004 - p455(1) [51-500]
    KR - v72 - i18 - Sept 15 2004 - p908(1) [501+]
    LJ - v129 - i20 - Dec 1 2004 - p118(1) [51-500]
    PW - v251 - i43 - Oct 25 2004 - p39(2) [51-500]

Wagner, Matt - *Trinity*
    BL - v101 - i1 - Sept 1 2004 - p77(1) [501+]
    LJ - v129 - i18 - Nov 1 2004 - p67(1) [501+]

Wagner, Michael - *Dog Wars*
    y Magpies - v19 - i5 - Nov 2004 - p37(2) [501+]

Wagner, Ralph D. - *A History of the Farmington Plan*
    Lib & Cul - v39 - i4 - Fall 2004 - p473(3) [501+]

Wagner, Rob Leicester - *Red Ink, White Lies: The Rise and Fall of Los Angeles Newspapers, 1920-1962*
    HNet - June 2004 - pNA [501+]

Wagner, Scott A. - *Color Atlas of the Autopsy*
    SciTech - v28 - i1 - March 2004 - p86(1) [51-500]

Wagner-Tsukamoto, Sigmund - *Human Nature and Organization Theory: On the Economic Approach to Institutional Organization*
    JEL - v41 - i4 - Dec 2003 - p1340(2) [501+]

Wagstaff, Sheena - *Edward Hopper*
    LJ - v129 - i20 - Dec 1 2004 - p107(2) [51-500]
    R&R Bk N - v19 - i4 - Nov 2004 - p200(1) [501+]
    TimHES - v0 - i1654 - August 20 2004 - p26(1) [501+]
    TLS - i5287 - July 30 2004 - p16-17 [501+]

Wahl, Elizabeth Susan - *Invisible Relations*
    Eight-C St - v36 - i2 - Winter 2003 - p275 [501+]

Wahl, Hans Rudolf - *Die Religion des deutschen Nationalismus. Eine mentalitatsgeschichtliche Studie Zur Literatur des Kaiserreichs: Felix Dahn, Ernst von Wildenbrusch, Walter Flex*
    GSR - v27 - i2 - May 2004 - p384-385 [501+]

Wahl, Hans-Werner - *Annual Review of Gerontology and Geriatrics, Vol. 23*
    SciTech - v28 - i1 - March 2004 - p108(1) [51-500]

Wahl, Jan - *Candy Shop*
    c CH Bwatch - v14 - i12 - Dec 2004 - pNA [51-500]
    Knock! Knock! (Illus. by DePalma, Mary Newell)
    c BL - v101 - i7 - Dec 1 2004 - p664(1) [51-500]
    c CCB-B - v58 - i1 - Sept 2004 - p43(2) [51-500]
    c KR - v72 - i14 - July 15 2004 - p695(1) [51-500]
    c SLJ - v50 - i8 - August 2004 - p97(2) [51-500]

Wahnbaeck, Till - *Luxury and Public Happiness: Political Economy in the Italian Enlightenment.*
    HRNB - v33 - i1 - Fall 2004 - p30(1) [501+]

Wahrman, Dror - *The Age of Cultural Revolutions: Britain and France, 1750-1820*
    FS - v58 - i1 - Jan 2004 - p116(2) [501+]
Waid, Candace - *The Age of Innocence*
    CR - v285 - i1665 - Oct 2004 - p245(3) [501+]
Waid, Mark - *Fantastic Four, Vol. 2 (Illus. by Wieringo, Mike)*
    y Kliatt - v38 - i4 - July 2004 - p34(1) [51-500]
    Fantastic Four, Vol. 3 (Illus. by Porter, Howard)
    LJ - v129 - i14 - Sept 1 2004 - p129(1) [51-500]
    Superman: Birthright
    Ent W - i797 - Dec 17 2004 - p88 [501+]
    Superman: Birthright: The Origin of the Man of Steel
    BL - v101 - i9-10 - Jan 1 2005 - p835(2) [501+]
    Superman: Secret Identity (Illus. by Immonen, Stuart)
    BL - v101 - i9-10 - Jan 1 2005 - p835(2) [501+]
Wailoo, Keith - *Dying in the City of the Blues*
    JIH - v33 - i3 - Winter 2003 - p501 [51-500]
Wainer, Howard - *Graphic Discovery: A Trout in the Milk and Other Visual Adventures*
    Econ - v374 - i8408 - Jan 8 2005 - p75US [501+]
Waines, David - *An Introduction to Islam, 2nd Ed.*
    MEQ - v11 - i3 - Summer 2004 - p86(1) [501+]
Waiser, Bill - *All Hell Can't Stop Us: The On-to-Ottawa Trek and Regina Riot*
    CBRA - Annual 2003 - p352(1) [501+]
Wait, Lea - *Seaward Born*
    RT - v58 - i3 - Nov 2004 - p291(1) [501+]
    Shadows on the Ivy: An Antique Print Mystery
    BL - v100 - i22 - August 2004 - p1907(2) [51-500]
    DroRevMy - v24 - i4 - July-August 2004 - p13(1) [51-500]
    LJ - v129 - i13 - August 2004 - p60(1) [501+]
    NYTBR - August 22 2004 - p15 [501+]
    PW - v251 - i28 - July 12 2004 - p47(1) [51-500]
    Wintering Well
    c BL - v101 - i2 - Sept 15 2004 - p246(1) [51-500]
    c CCB-B - v58 - i2 - Oct 2004 - p101(1) [51-500]
    c CH Bwatch - Feb 2005 - pNA [51-500]
    c HB - v80 - i6 - Nov-Dec 2004 - p718(1) [51-500]
    c KR - v72 - i16 - August 15 2004 - p814(1) [51-500]
    y SLJ - v50 - i11 - Nov 2004 - p156(1) [51-500]
Waite, C. Kaha - *Mediation and the Communication Matrix*
    R&R Bk N - v19 - i1 - Feb 2004 - p125(1) [51-500]
Waite, Judy - *Shopaholic*
    y Kliatt - v39 - i1 - Jan 2005 - p18(1) [51-500]
    Trick of the Mind
    y Kliatt - v39 - i1 - Jan 2005 - p11(1) [51-500]
    KR - v73 - i1 - Jan 1 2005 - p58(1) [51-500]
    y PW - v252 - i5 - Jan 31 2005 - p69(1) [51-500]
Waiter, Mariko Namba - *Shamanism: An Encyclopedia of World Beliefs, Practices, and Culture.*
    LJ - v130 - i4 - March 1 2005 - p112(3) [501+]
Waitzkin, Howard - *At the Front Lines of Medicine: How the Health Care System Alienates Doctors and Mistreats Patients...and What We Can Do about It*
    SciTech - v28 - i4 - Dec 2004 - p81(1) [51-500]
Waiwaiole, Lono - *Wiley's Shuffle*
    DroRevMy - v24 - i3 - May-June 2004 - p13(1) [1-50]
Wajcman, Judy - *TechnoFeminism*
    Wom R Bks - v21 - i12 - Sept 2004 - p27(1) [501+]
Wakatsuki, Jeanne - *The Legend of Fire Horse Woman*
    Wom R Bks - v21 - i10-11 - July 2004 - p22(1) [501+]
Wakefield, Andrew H. - *Where to Live: The Hermeneutical Significance of Paul's Citations from Scripture in Galatians 3:1-14*
    R&R Bk N - v19 - i1 - Feb 2004 - p21(1) [51-500]
Wakefield, Thaddeus - *The Family in Twentieth-Century American Drama*
    R&R Bk N - v19 - i1 - Feb 2004 - p242(1) [51-500]
Wakelyn, Jon L. - *Birth of the Bill of Rights: Encyclopedia of the Antifederalists*
    LJ - v129 - i20 - Dec 1 2004 - p172(1) [51-500]
Wakeman, Dan - *Fortress of the Grizzlies: The Khutzeymateen Grizzly Bear Sanctuary*
    CBRA - Annual 2003 - p408(1) [501+]
Wakeman, Frederic E. - *Spymaster: Dai Li and the Chinese Secret Service*
    AHR - v109 - i3 - June 2004 - p882(2) [501+]
    HJAS - v64 - i2 - Dec 2004 - p448-455 [501+]
Wakeman, Rosemary - *Themes in Modern European History Since 1945, 1st Ed.*
    TimHES - v0 - i1668 - Nov 26 2004 - pV(1) [501+]

Walbank, F.W. - *Polybius, Rome and the Hellenistic World: Essays and Reflections*
    Class R - v54 - i1 - May 2004 - p166(2) [501+]
Walberg, Herbert J. - *Education and Capitalism: How Overcoming Our Fear of Markets and Economics Can Improve America's Schools*
    TCR - v106 - i8 - August 2004 - p1596(6) [501+]
Walch, Timothy - *Uncommon Americans: The Lives and Legacies of Herbert and Lou Henry Hoover*
    Pres St Q - v34 - i4 - Dec 2004 - p900(3) [501+]
    R&R Bk N - v19 - i1 - Feb 2004 - p61(1) [501+]
Walcott, Derek - *The Prodigal*
    BL - v101 - i2 - Sept 15 2004 - p195(1) [501+]
    BW - v34 - i47 - Nov 21 2004 - p12(1) [501+]
    Econ - v373 - i8400 - Nov 6 2004 - p89US [501+]
    LJ - v129 - i14 - Sept 1 2004 - p42(1) [51-500]
    LJ - v129 - i16 - Oct 1 2004 - p85(2) [51-500]
    NYTBR - Oct 31 2004 - p12 [501+]
    PW - v251 - i42 - Oct 18 2004 - p61(1) [51-500]
Walcott, Rinaldo - *Black Like Who?: Writing Black Canada*
    CBRA - Annual 2003 - p359(1) [501+]
Walcott, Susan M. - *Chinese Science and Industrial Technology Parks*
    SciTech - v28 - i1 - March 2004 - p134(1) [51-500]
Wald, Elijah - *Escaping the Delta: Robert Johnson and the Invention of the Blues*
    BL - v101 - i9-10 - Jan 1 2005 - p766(1) [51-500]
    BW - v34 - i12 - March 21 2004 - p8(2) [501+]
    JPC - v38 - i2 - Nov 2004 - p436(3) [501+]
    NYTBR - Oct 31 2004 - p31 [501+]
    NYTBR - Jan 30 2005 - p24 [501+]
Wald, Kenneth D. - *Religion and Politics in the United States*
    HNet - Sept 2004 - pNA [501+]
Wald, Noreen - *Ghostwriter*
    LJ - v129 - i14 - Sept 1 2004 - p207(1) [501+]
Waldau, Paul - *The Specter of Speciesism: Buddhist and Christian Views of Animals*
    BCS - v24 - Annual 2004 - p293(3) [501+]
Waldbauer, Gilbert - *Insights from Insects: What Bad Bugs Can Teach Us*
    New Sci - v185 - i2489 - March 5 2005 - p56(2) [501+]
    PW - v252 - i4 - Jan 24 2005 - p230(1) [501+]
Walde, C. - *Die Traumdarstellugen in der griechisch-romischen Dichtung*
    Class R - v53 - i2 - Nov 2003 - p341-344 [501+]
Walden, Raphael - *Racism and Human Rights*
    R&R Bk N - v19 - i3 - August 2004 - p192(1) [501+]
Waldinger, Roger - *Strangers at the Gates: New Immigrants in Urban America*
    Can Lit - i181 - Summer 2004 - p183-185 [501+]
Waldman, Alan S. - *Genetic Recombination: Reviews and Protocols*
    SciTech - v28 - i1 - March 2004 - p63(1) [51-500]
Waldman, Anne - *Civil Disobediences: Poetics and Politics in Action*
    LJ - v129 - i13 - August 2004 - p75(2) [501+]
Waldman, Carl - *Encyclopedia of Exploration, Vols. 1-2*
    BL - v101 - i8 - Dec 15 2004 - p756(1) [501+]
    BL - v101 - i9-10 - Jan 1 2005 - p779(1) [1-50]
    LJ - v130 - i2 - Feb 1 2005 - p118(1) [51-500]
    R&R Bk N - v19 - i4 - Nov 2004 - p71(1) [51-500]
    SLJ - v50 - i12 - Dec 2004 - p88(1) [501+]
Waldman, David L. - *Interventional Radiology Secrets*
    SciTech - v28 - i4 - Dec 2004 - p90(1) [51-500]
Waldman, Debby - *Your Child's Hearing Loss: What Parents Need to Know*
    PW - v252 - i9 - Feb 28 2005 - p60(1) [51-500]
Waldman, Louis A. - *Baccio Bandinelli and Art at the Medici Court: A Corpus of Early Modern Sources*
    R&R Bk N - v19 - i4 - Nov 2004 - p205(1) [501+]
Waldman, Neil - *The Snowflake: A Water Cycle Story*
    c CE - v80 - i5 - Mid-Summer 2004 - p276(1) [51-500]
Waldman, Nomi J. - *The Italian Renaissance*
    y SLJ - v51 - i2 - Feb 2005 - p153(2) [51-500]
Waldman, Paul - *Fraud: The Strategy Behind the Bush Lies and Why the Media Didn't Tell You*
    SPA - v60 - i5 - Sept-Oct 2004 - p63(4) [501+]
Waldman, Steven D. - *Atlas of Interventional Pain Management, 2nd Ed.*
    SciTech - v28 - i1 - March 2004 - p110(1) [51-500]
Waldman, Stuart - *We Asked for Nothing: The Remarkable Journey of Cabeza de Vaca (Illus. by McNeely, Tom)*
    SLJ - v50 - i10 - Oct 2004 - pS34(1) [51-500]

Waldorf, Heather - *Fighting the Current*
    Res Links - v10 - i2 - Dec 2004 - p40(2) [501+]
Waldram, James B. - *Revenge of the Windigo: The Construction of the Mind and Mental Health of North American Aboriginal Peoples*
    SciTech - v28 - i3 - Sept 2004 - p96(1) [51-500]
Waldrep, Christopher - *Local Matters: Race, Crime, and Justice in the Nineteenth-Century South*
    HNet - Sept 2004 - pNA [501+]
    The Many Faces of Judge Lynch: Extralegal Violence and Punishment in America
    Am St - v45 - i1 - Spring 2004 - p141-141 [501+]
Waldrep, G.C. - *Goldbeater's Skin*
    South CR - v36 - i2 - Spring 2004 - p184-187 [501+]
Waldrep, Shelton - *The Aesthetics of Self-Invention: Oscar Wilde to David Bowie*
    Choice - v42 - i7 - March 2005 - p1212(2) [51-500]
Waldron, Gerry - *Trees of the Carolinian Forest*
    Globe & Mail - July 17 2004 - pD15 [501+]
Waldron, Jeremy - *God, Locke, and Equality: Christian Foundations in Locke's Political Thought*
    JR - v84 - i4 - Oct 2004 - p646(3) [501+]
    TLS - i5302 - Nov 12 2004 - p32(1) [501+]
Waldron, Kathleen Cook - *Five Stars for Emily*
    c Res Links - v10 - i1 - Oct 2004 - p21(1) [501+]
Waldron, Scott A. - *Rural Development in China: Insights from the Beef Industry*
    Ch Rev Int - v11 - i1 - Spring 2004 - p186(4) [501+]
    R&R Bk N - v19 - i1 - Feb 2004 - p102(1) [51-500]
Waldroop, James - *The 12 Bad Habits That Hold Good People Back: Overcoming the Behavior Patterns That Keep You From Getting Ahead*
    HR Mag - v49 - i7 - July 2004 - pS2(1) [51-500]
Waldrop, Keith - *The Real Subject: Queries and Conjectures of Jacob Delafon, with Sample Poems*
    ABR - v26 - i2 - Jan-Feb 2005 - p3(2) [501+]
Waldrop, Rosmarie - *Blindsight*
    ABR - v25 - i6 - Sept-Oct 2004 - p22(3) [501+]
    Lavish Absence: Recalling and Rereading Edmond Jabes
    TLS - i5290 - August 20 2004 - p22(1) [501+]
Waldrup, Carole Chandler - *More Colonial Women: 25 Pioneers of Early America*
    R&R Bk N - v19 - i4 - Nov 2004 - p60(1) [51-500]
Waldstreicher, David - *Runaway America: Benjamin Franklin, Slavery, and the American Revolution*
    LJ - v129 - i12 - July 2004 - p94(1) [501+]
Wales, David J. - *Energy Landscapes Applications to Clusters, Biomolecules and Glasses*
    Sci - v305 - i5687 - August 20 2004 - p1108(2) [501+]
Wales, Lorene M. - *The People and Process of Film and Video Production: From Low Budget to High Budget*
    R&R Bk N - v19 - i4 - Nov 2004 - p223(1) [501+]
Walesh, Stuart G. - *Managing and Leading: 52 Lessons Learned for Engineers*
    SciTech - v28 - i1 - March 2004 - p137(1) [51-500]
Walia, Rajni - *Women and Self: Fictions of Jean Rhys, Barbara Pym, Anita Brookner*
    TSWL - v23 - i1 - Spring 2004 - p144-146 [501+]
Walkenbach, John - *Excel 2003 Formulas*
    R&R Bk N - v19 - i3 - August 2004 - p129(1) [51-500]
Walker, Alan - *The Death of Franz Liszt*
    Am MT - v54 - i1 - August-Sept 2004 - p98(2) [501+]
Walker, Alexander - *Icons in the Fire: The Rise and Fall of Almost Everybody in the British Film Industry, 1984-2000*
    TimHES - v0 - i1675 - Jan 21 2005 - p22(2) [501+]
    TLS - i5304 - Nov 26 2004 - p36(1) [501+]
Walker, Alice - *Her Blue Body Everything We Know*
    LJ - v129 - i12 - July 2004 - p127(1) [501+]
    In Search of Our Mother's Gardens
    LJ - v129 - i12 - July 2004 - p127(1) [501+]
    Now Is the Time To Open Your Heart (Read by Woodard, Alfre). Audiobook Review
    LJ - v129 - i20 - Dec 1 2004 - p182(1) [51-500]
    Now is the Time to Open Your Heart
    BooChiTr - May 2 2004 - p4(1) [501+]
    Globe & Mail - August 14 2004 - pD14 [501+]
    TLS - i5303 - Nov 19 2004 - p23(1) [501+]
Walker, Beth - *The Girls' Guide to AD/HD: Don't Lose This Book*
    c CH Bwatch - Jan 2005 - pNA [51-500]
    y SLJ - v51 - i2 - Feb 2005 - p154(1) [51-500]

Wallace, Harvey - *Family Violence: Legal, Medical, and Social Perspectives*
    R&R Bk N - v19 - i3 - August 2004 - p166(1) [501+]

Wallace, Ian - *The Man Who Walked the Earth*
    c CBRA - Annual 2003 - p471(2) [51-500]
    c CE - v81 - i2 - Winter 2004 - p108(1) [51-500]
    The Naked Lady
    c Can Lit - i181 - Summer 2004 - p109-110 [501+]

Wallace, Jennifer - *Digging the Dirt: The Archaeological Imagination*
    TimHES - v0 - i1654 - August 20 2004 - p29(1) [501+]

Wallace, John - *Hello Sunshine, Good Night Moonlight (Illus. by Wallace, John)*
    c SLJ - v50 - i7 - July 2004 - p93(2) [51-500]

Wallace, Joseph - *The Baseball Anthology: 125 Years of Stories, Poems, Articles, Photographs, Drawings, Interviews, Cartoons, and Other Memorabilia*
    LJ - v129 - i16 - Oct 1 2004 - p121(1) [1-50]

Wallace, Karen - *I Am a Tyrannosaurus (Illus. by Bostock, Mike)*
    c KR - v72 - i21 - Nov 1 2004 - p1046(1) [51-500]
    Marvin, the Blue Pig (Illus. by Williams, Lisa)
    c SLJ - v51 - i1 - Jan 2005 - p90(1) [51-500]
    Wendy (Read by Francis, Jan). Audiobook Review
    y Kliatt - v39 - i2 - March 2005 - p58(1) [51-500]
    Wendy
    c BooChiTr - March 7 2004 - p2(1) [501+]

Wallace, Lee - *Sexual Encounters: Pacific Texts, Modern Sexualities*
    HNet - Sept 2004 - pNA [501+]

Wallace, Linda K. - *Libraries, Mission, and Marketing: Writing Mission Statements That Work*
    ALJ - v53 - i4 - Nov 2004 - p428(1) [501+]
    y LibMed - v22 - i7 - April-May 2004 - p89(1) [501+]
    Teach Lib - v32 - i2 - Dec 2004 - p39(1) [501+]

Wallace, Linda L. - *After the Fires: The Ecology of Change in Yellowstone National Park*
    SciTech - v28 - i3 - Sept 2004 - p131(1) [51-500]

Wallace, Marianne D. - *America's Mountains*
    c LibMed - v22 - i7 - April-May 2004 - p69(1) [501+]

Wallace, Mark S. - *Pain Medicine and Management: Just the Facts*
    SciTech - v28 - i4 - Dec 2004 - p88(1) [51-500]

Wallace, Mary - *The Girls' Spa Book: 20 Dreamy Ways to Relax and Feel Great (Illus. by Davila, Claudia)*
    y Res Links - v10 - i2 - Dec 2004 - p46(1) [501+]
    y SLJ - v51 - i1 - Jan 2005 - p157(1) [51-500]

Wallace, Max - *The American Axis: Henry Ford, Charles Lindbergh, and the Rise of the Third Reich*
    Choice - v41 - i7 - March 2004 - p1359(1) [501+]

Wallace, Michael - *The Disaster Recovery Handbook: A Step-by-Step Plan to Ensure Business Continuity and Protect Vital Operations, Facilities, and Assets*
    Choice - v42 - i4 - Dec 2004 - p705(1) [1-50]
    R&R Bk N - v19 - i3 - August 2004 - p104(1) [1-50]

Wallace, Michele - *Dark Designs and Visual Culture*
    Black Iss - v7 - i1 - Jan-Feb 2005 - p67(2) [501+]
    Ms - v14 - i4 - Winter 2004 - p89(2) [501+]

Wallace, Nancy Elizabeth - *Seeds! Seeds! Seeds!*
    c LibMed - v23 - i3 - Nov-Dec 2004 - p85(1) [51-500]
    The Valentine Express (Illus. by Wallace, Nancy Elizabeth)
    c BL - v101 - i6 - Nov 15 2004 - p594(1) [51-500]
    c PW - v251 - i49 - Dec 6 2004 - p59(1) [51-500]
    c SLJ - v50 - i12 - Dec 2004 - p123(2) [501+]

Wallace, Patricia - *The Internet in the Workplace*
    Choice - v42 - i1 - Sept 2004 - p151(1) [501+]

Wallace, Randall - *Love and Honor*
    BL - v101 - i5 - Nov 1 2004 - p466(1) [501+]
    KR - v72 - i15 - August 1 2004 - p714(1) [501+]
    PW - v251 - i35 - August 30 2004 - p33(1) [501+]

Wallace, Rich - *Losing Is Not an Option: Stories*
    y LibMed - v22 - i6 - March 2004 - p68(1) [501+]
    Restless: A Ghost's Story
    y LibMed - v22 - i7 - April-May 2004 - p64(1) [501+]
    The Roar of the Crowd
    c BL - v101 - i1 - Sept 1 2004 - p111(2) [501+]
    c SLJ - v50 - i9 - Sept 2004 - p219(1) [51-500]
    Technical Foul
    c BL - v101 - i1 - Sept 1 2004 - p111(2) [501+]
    c SLJ - v50 - i10 - Oct 2004 - p181(1) [51-500]

Wallace, Stan W. - *Does God Exist?: The Craig-Flew Debate*
    R&R Bk N - v19 - i1 - Feb 2004 - p7(1) [51-500]

Wallace, Tom - *What Matters Blood*
    PW - v251 - i46 - Nov 15 2004 - p44(2) [51-500]

Wallace, William N. - *No Dogs Allowed!*
    c BL - v100 - i21 - July 2004 - p1845(1) [1-50]
    c SLJ - v50 - i8 - August 2004 - p130(1) [51-500]

Wallach, Lori - *Whose Trade Organization?: The Comprehensive Guide to the WTO*
    Choice - v42 - i2 - Oct 2004 - p342(1) [51-500]

Walle, Alf H. - *Path of Handsome Lake: A Model of Recovery for Native People*
    R&R Bk N - v19 - i4 - Nov 2004 - p54(1) [51-500]

Walle, Wille Vande - *The History of the Relations between the Low Countries and China in the Qing Era, 1644-1911*
    IBMR - v29 - i1 - Jan 2005 - p50(1) [501+]

Wallen, Ila - *A Team of One*
    c CH Bwatch - v14 - i12 - Dec 2004 - pNA [501+]

Wallengerger, Frederick T. - *Natural Fibers, Plastics and Composites*
    SciTech - v28 - i1 - March 2004 - p141(1) [51-500]

Wallenstein, Peter - *Blue Laws and Black Codes: Conflict, Courts, and Change in Twentieth-Century Virginia*
    Choice - v42 - i4 - Dec 2004 - p725(1) [1-50]
    HNet - Sept 2004 - pNA [501+]
    R&R Bk N - v19 - i3 - August 2004 - p207(1) [1-50]
    Tell the Court I Love My Wife: Race, Marriage, and Law: An American History
    JAH - v91 - i1 - June 2004 - p314-316 [501+]

Waller, Douglas C. - *A Question of Loyalty: Gen. Billy Mitchell and the Court-Martial that Gripped the Nation*
    APH - v51 - i3 - Fall 2004 - p44(2) [501+]
    BL - v101 - i1 - Sept 1 2004 - p28(1) [51-500]
    BL - v101 - i9-10 - Jan 1 2005 - p766(1) [51-500]
    BW - v34 - i44 - Oct 31 2004 - p5(1) [501+]
    KR - v72 - i14 - July 15 2004 - p679(1) [501+]
    LJ - v129 - i19 - Nov 15 2004 - p74(1) [501+]
    PW - v251 - i28 - July 12 2004 - p53(2) [51-500]

Waller, John - *The Discovery of the Germ: Twenty Years That Transformed the Way we Think about Disease*
    Choice - v41 - i7 - March 2004 - p1328(1) [501+]
    E-Streams - Sept 2004 - pNA [501+]
    SciTech - v28 - i1 - March 2004 - p87(1) [51-500]
    Leaps in the Dark
    New Sci - v184 - i2478 - Dec 18 2004 - p51(1) [501+]

Waller, Lance A. - *Applied Spatial Statistics for Public Health Data*
    SciTech - v28 - i3 - Sept 2004 - p83(1) [501+]

Waller, Maureen - *London 1945: Life in the Debris of War*
    KR - v73 - i3 - Feb 1 2005 - p172(1) [501+]
    LJ - v130 - i4 - March 1 2005 - p99(1) [51-500]
    TLS - i5284 - July 9 2004 - p32(1) [501+]

Waller, Maureen Rosamond - *My Baby's Father: Unmarried Parents and Paternal Responsibility*
    CS - v33 - i1 - Jan 2004 - p32-33 [501+]

Waller, Ralph - *John Wesley: A Personal Portrait*
    TT - v61 - i2 - July 2004 - p288(2) [501+]

Waller, William H. - *Galaxies and the Cosmic Frontier*
    Phys Today - v57 - i10 - Oct 2004 - p80-81 [501+]
    S&T - v107 - i3 - March 2004 - p71(4) [501+]

Wallerstein, Immanuel - *Alternatives: The United States Confronts the World*
    Fut - v39 - i2 - March-April 2005 - p60(1) [51-500]
    The Decline of American Power: The U.S. in a Chaotic World
    R&R Bk N - v19 - i1 - Feb 2004 - p61(1) [501+]

Walley, Christine J. - *Rough Waters: Nature and Development in an East African Marine Park*
    Choice - v42 - i5 - Jan 2005 - p908(2) [1-50]

Walliman, Nicholas - *Your Undergraduate Dissertation: The Essential Guide for Success*
    R&R Bk N - v19 - i4 - Nov 2004 - p185(1) [501+]

Walling, Donovan R. - *Virtual Schooling: Issues in the Development of E-Learning Policy*
    R&R Bk N - v19 - i1 - Feb 2004 - p194(1) [501+]

Wallis, David - *Killed: Great Journalism Too Hot to Print*
    LJ - v129 - i12 - July 2004 - p94(1) [51-500]

Wallis, Glenn - *The Dhammapada: Verses on the Way: A New Translation of the Teachings of the Buddha, with a Guide to Reading the Text*
    LJ - v129 - i17 - Oct 15 2004 - p67(2) [51-500]

Wallis, Jim - *God's Politics: Why the Right Gets It Wrong and the Left Doesn't Get It*
    LJ - v130 - i3 - Feb 15 2005 - p136(1) [51-500]
    Nation - v280 - i5 - Feb 7 2005 - p10 [501+]
    NYTBR - Feb 6 2005 - p14 [501+]

Wallis, Karen - *Washoe Seasons of Life: A Native American Story (Illus. by Saling, Lea)*
    c KR - v72 - i13 - July 1 2004 - p639(1) [51-500]
    c SLJ - v50 - i9 - Sept 2004 - p219(1) [51-500]

Wallis, W. David - *Regional Transmission Organizations: Restructuring Electricity Transmission in Canada*
    JEL - v41 - i4 - Dec 2003 - p1397(1) [501+]

Wallner, Alexandra - *Grandma Moses (Illus. by Wallner, Alexandra)*
    c HB - v80 - i4 - July-August 2004 - p470(2) [51-500]

Walls, Jeannette - *The Glass Castle: A Memoir*
    KR - v72 - i24 - Dec 15 2004 - p1195(1) [501+]
    LJ - v130 - i3 - Feb 15 2005 - p141(1) [51-500]
    NW - March 7 2005 - p55 [51-500]
    NYTBR - March 13 2005 - p1 [501+]
    PW - v252 - i3 - Jan 17 2005 - p41(1) [51-500]

Walls, Laura Dassow - *Emerson's Life in Science: The Culture of Truth*
    AL - v76 - i2 - June 2004 - p391(3) [501+]
    Isis - v95 - i2 - June 2004 - p302(1) [501+]
    JAH - v91 - i1 - June 2004 - p240-241 [501+]

Walls, Peter - *History, Imagination, and the Performance of Music*
    MT - v145 - i1887 - Summer 2004 - p107(4) [501+]
    Notes - v61 - i2 - Dec 2004 - p451(4) [501+]

Walmsley, Peter - *Locke's Essay and the Rhetoric of Science*
    Choice - v41 - i7 - March 2004 - p1312(1) [501+]

Walnum, Clayton - *Microsoft Direct3D Programming: Kick Start*
    SciTech - v28 - i1 - March 2004 - p135(1) [51-500]
    Pro Tools Recording Guide
    Bwatch - v26 - i8 - August 2004 - p7(1) [51-500]
    SciTech - v28 - i3 - Sept 2004 - p162(1) [51-500]

Walpole, Sharon - *The Literacy Coach's Handbook: A Guide to Research-Based Practice*
    R&R Bk N - v19 - i4 - Nov 2004 - p181(1) [501+]

Walser, Martin - *Der Augenblick der Liebe*
    TLS - i5296 - Oct 1 2004 - p23(1) [501+]

Walsh, Alice - *Pomiuk, Prince of the North (Illus. by Whitehead, Jerry)*
    c Globe & Mail - Jan 1 2005 - pD11 [51-500]
    c Res Links - v10 - i2 - Dec 2004 - p23(1) [51-500]

Walsh, Ann - *Beginnings: Stories of Canada's Past*
    c Can Lit - i182 - Autumn 2004 - p166(2) [501+]
    Winds through Time: An Anthology of Canadian Historical Young Adult Fiction
    c Can Lit - i182 - Autumn 2004 - p166(2) [501+]

Walsh, Anthony - *Race and Crime: A Biosocial Analysis*
    R&R Bk N - v19 - i3 - August 2004 - p167(1) [501+]

Walsh, Bill - *The Elephants of Style: A Trunkload of Tips on the Big Issues and Gray Areas of Contemporary American English*
    y Kliatt - v38 - i4 - July 2004 - p36(1) [51-500]

Walsh, Carl E. - *Monetary Theory and Policy*
    JEL - v41 - i4 - Dec 2003 - p1335(1) [501+]

Walsh, Caroline - *Stories from a New Ireland New York*
    ILS - v24 - i1 - Fall 2004 - p19(2) [501+]

Walsh, David Allen - *Why Do They Act That Way?: A Survival Guide to the Adolescent Brain for You and Your Teen*
    LJ - v129 - i13 - August 2004 - p110(1) [501+]

Walsh, David F. - *Musical Theater and American Culture*
    R&R Bk N - v19 - i1 - Feb 2004 - p198(1) [51-500]

Walsh, Froma - *Living Beyond Loss: Death in the Family*
    Adoles - v39 - i154 - Summer 2004 - p406(1) [51-500]

Walsh, Gary - *Biopharmaceuticals: Biochemistry and Biotechnology, 2nd Ed.*
    SciTech - v28 - i1 - March 2004 - p124(1) [51-500]
    Pell's Equation
    SIAM Rev - v46 - i1 - March 2004 - p184-185 [501+]

Walsh, George - *"Whip the Rebellion": Ulysses S. Grant's Rise to Command*
    LJ - v130 - i4 - March 1 2005 - p99(1) [51-500]

Walsh, Helen - *Brass*
    BL - v101 - i4 - Oct 15 2004 - p391(1) [51-500]
    KR - v72 - i17 - Sept 1 2004 - p836(1) [51-500]
    Ent W - i791 - Nov 5 2004 - p88 [51-500]
    LJ - v129 - i18 - Nov 1 2004 - p78(1) [501+]
    NYTBR - Jan 30 2005 - p14 [501+]
    PW - v251 - i37 - Sept 13 2004 - p56(1) [51-500]

Walsh, James - *Liberty in Troubled Times: A Libertarian Guide to Laws, Politics and Society in a Terrorized World*
R&R Bk N - v19 - i4 - Nov 2004 - p152(1) [501+]

Walsh, John F. - *The Indispensable Staff Manager: A Guide to Accountable, Effective Staff Ledership*
R&R Bk N - v19 - i2 - May 2004 - p118 [51-500]

Walsh, Judith E. - *Domesticity in Colonial India: What Women Learned When Men Gave Them Advice*
Choice - v42 - i5 - Jan 2005 - p910(1) [1-50]
HNet - Oct 2004 - pNA [501+]
R&R Bk N - v19 - i3 - August 2004 - p154(1) [51-500]

Walsh, Katherine Cramer - *Talking about Politics: Informal Groups and Social Identity in American Life*
Pub Op Q - v68 - i3 - Fall 2004 - p430(3) [501+]
Soc Ser R - v78 - i4 - Dec 2004 - p698(2) [51-500]
VQR - v80 - i3 - Summer 2004 - p259(2) [501+]

Walsh, Kiernan - *Countries in the News*
LibMed - v22 - i7 - April-May 2004 - p68(1) [501+]

Walsh, Marcie - *The Killing Club*
KR - v73 - i2 - Jan 15 2005 - p88(1) [51-500]
LJ - v129 - i16 - Oct 1 2004 - p64(1) [501+]
LJ - v130 - i2 - Feb 1 2005 - p57(1) [51-500]
PW - v252 - i4 - Jan 24 2005 - p220(1) [501+]

Walsh, Michael - *Warriors of the Lord: The Military Orders of Christendom*
CHR - v90 - i3 - July 2004 - p590(1) [501+]

Walsh, Patricia Noonan - *Women with Disabilities Aging Well: A Global View*
SciTech - v28 - i3 - Sept 2004 - p83(1) [501+]

Walsh, Peter - *How to Organize Just about Everything: More than 500 Step-by-Step Instructions for Everything from Organizing Your Closets to Planning a Wedding to Creating a Flawless Filing System*
BL - v101 - i9-10 - Jan 1 2005 - p796(1) [51-500]

Walsh, Philip P. - *Gas Turbine Performance, 2nd Ed.*
SciTech - v28 - i3 - Sept 2004 - p150(1) [51-500]

Walsh, Richard - *Reading the Gospels in the Dark: Portrayals of Jesus in Film*
Choice - v41 - i7 - March 2004 - p1304(1) [501+]
Intpr - v59 - i1 - Jan 2005 - p109(1) [51-500]

Walsh, Robb - *Are you Really Going to Eat That? Reflections of a Culinary Thrill Seeker*
y Kliatt - v39 - i2 - March 2005 - p44(1) [51-500]

Walsh, Sharon K. - *Civil Disobedience: A Wadsworth Casebook in Argument*
R&R Bk N - v19 - i4 - Nov 2004 - p216(1) [501+]

Walsh, Sheila - *Gigi, God's Little Princess (Illus. by Johnson, Meredith)*
c PW - v252 - i9 - Feb 28 2005 - p69(2) [51-500]

Walsh, Tommy - *Tommy Walsh Living Spaces DIY*
LJ - v130 - i4 - March 1 2005 - p109(1) [51-500]

Walsh, Vivian - *Olive, My Love (Illus. by Seibold, J. Otto)*
c KR - v72 - i20 - Oct 15 2004 - p1015(1) [51-500]
c PW - v251 - i42 - Oct 18 2004 - p62(1) [51-500]
c SLJ - v50 - i11 - Nov 2004 - p119(1) [51-500]

Walshaw, Margaret - *Mathematics Education Within the Postmodern*
SciTech - v28 - i4 - Dec 2004 - p15(1) [1-50]

Walter, James J. - *A Call to Fidelity: On the Moral Theology of Charles E. Curran*
TT - v60 - i4 - Jan 2004 - p605-606 [501+]

Walter, Jennifer K. - *Story of Bioethics: From Seminal Works to Contemporary Explorations*
SciTech - v28 - i1 - March 2004 - p62(1) [51-500]

Walter, Jess - *Citizen Vince*
BL - v101 - i6 - Nov 15 2004 - p566(1) [51-500]
KR - v72 - i17 - Sept 1 2004 - p836(1) [51-500]

Walter, Lynn - *The Greenwood Encyclopedia of Women's Issues Worldwide*
LibMed - v22 - i7 - April-May 2004 - p83(1) [501+]
Ref Rev - June 2004 - pNA [501+]
R&R Bk N - v19 - i1 - Feb 2004 - p133(1) [51-500]

Walter, Mildred Pitts - *Alec's Primer (Illus. by Johnson, Larry)*
c BL - v101 - i8 - Dec 15 2004 - p738(1) [51-500]

Walter, Virginia A. - *Teens and Libraries: Getting It Right*
LibMed - v22 - i6 - March 2004 - p89(1) [501+]

Walters, Barbara R. - *The Politics of Aesthetic Judgment*
R&R Bk N - v19 - i3 - August 2004 - p11(1) [1-50]

Walters, Eric - *Camp 30*
Res Links - v10 - i2 - Dec 2004 - p24(1) [51-500]
Death by Exposure
Res Links - v10 - i3 - Feb 2005 - p61(1) [501+]
Grind
y Kliatt - v39 - i1 - Jan 2005 - p18(1) [51-500]
Res Links - v10 - i3 - Feb 2005 - p41(1) [501+]
Off Season
y Can CL - i111-112 - Fall-Winter 2003 - p139(8) [501+]
c CBRA - Annual 2003 - p519(2) [51-500]
Overdrive
y VOYA - v27 - i4 - Oct 2004 - p310(1) [51-500]
Ricky
y Can CL - i111-112 - Fall-Winter 2003 - p153(6) [501+]
Royal Ransom
y Can CL - i111-112 - Fall-Winter 2003 - p139(8) [501+]
y CBRA - Annual 2003 - p520(1) [501+]
Run
y CBRA - Annual 2003 - p520(2) [51-500]
So Yesterday
y VOYA - v27 - i4 - Oct 2004 - p310(1) [51-500]
Underdog
c Res Links - v10 - i1 - Oct 2004 - p21(1) [51-500]

Walters, Guy - *The Occupation*
Globe & Mail - Jan 8 2005 - pD11 [51-500]

Walters, James W. - *Martin Buber and Feminist Ethics: The Priority of the Personal*
R&R Bk N - v19 - i1 - Feb 2004 - p4(1) [51-500]

Walters, John A. - *Hoop-Wrapped, Composite, Internally Pressurized Cylinders: Development and Application of a Design Theory*
SciTech - v28 - i1 - March 2004 - p144(1) [51-500]

Walters, Minette - *Disordered Minds*
Globe & Mail - Sept 18 2004 - pD26 [1-50]
LJ - v129 - i20 - Dec 1 2004 - p105(1) [51-500]
PW - v251 - i45 - Nov 8 2004 - p41(1) [501+]
Fox Evil (Read by Prebble, Simon). Audiobook Review
Kliatt - v38 - i4 - July 2004 - p51(1) [51-500]
The Tinder Box
Globe & Mail - Sept 18 2004 - pD22 [51-500]

Walters, Reece - *Deviant Knowledge: Criminology, Politics and Policy*
Law&PolBR - Nov 2004 - p893(3) [501+]

Walters, Rhodri - *How Parliament Works, 5th Ed.*
R&R Bk N - v19 - i4 - Nov 2004 - p156(1) [501+]

Walters, Ronald W. - *White Nationalists, Black Interest: Conservative Public Policy and the Black Community*
Choice - v42 - i1 - Sept 2004 - p190(2) [501+]

Walters, S.M. - *Darwin's Mentor: John Stevens Henslow, 1796-1861*
VS - v46 - i3 - Spring 2004 - p508(3) [501+]

Walters, Terrence - *Cycaad Classification: Concepts and Recommendations*
SciTech - v28 - i3 - Sept 2004 - p62(1) [51-500]

Walther, Eric H. - *The Shattering of the Union: America in the 1850s*
Choice - v41 - i11-12 - July-August 2004 - p2110(1) [51-500]

Waltman, Jerold L. - *The Case for the Living Wage*
Choice - v42 - i4 - Dec 2004 - p709(1) [1-50]
LJ - v129 - i17 - Oct 15 2004 - p71(1) [51-500]

Walton, Douglas N. - *Legal Argumentation and Evidence*
Dialogue - v43 - i3 - Summer 2004 - p607-609 [501+]
RM - v58 - i2 - Dec 2004 - p471(3) [501+]
Relevance in Argumentation
R&R Bk N - v19 - i1 - Feb 2004 - p6(1) [51-500]

Walton, Gary M. - *History of the American Economy, 10th Ed.*
R&R Bk N - v19 - i4 - Nov 2004 - p88(1) [51-500]

Walton, John - *The Failure of Planning: Permitting Sprawl in San Diego Suburbs, 1970 to 1999*
CS - v33 - i5 - Sept 2004 - p569-570 [501+]

Walton, Rick - *Alligator!: An Adverbial Tale (Illus. by Bradshaw, Jim)*
c SLJ - v50 - i11 - Nov 2004 - p120(1) [51-500]
Mrs. McMurphy's Pumpkin (Illus. by Bettoli, Delana)
c KR - v72 - i16 - August 15 2004 - p814(1) [51-500]
c SLJ - v50 - i8 - August 2004 - p103(1) [51-500]
Puzzle Crazy (Illus. by Peterson, Stacy)
c PW - v252 - i8 - Feb 21 2005 - p177(1) [501+]
A Very Hairy Scary Story (Illus. by Clark, David)
c KR - v72 - i13 - July 1 2004 - p639(1) [51-500]
c SLJ - v50 - i8 - August 2004 - p103(1) [51-500]

Walton, Simon - *Playing the Flute, Recorder and Other Woodwinds*
CH Bwatch - Feb 2005 - pNA [51-500]

Walvoord, Barbara E. - *Assessment Clear and Simple: A Practical Guide for Institutions, Departments and General Education*
R&R Bk N - v19 - i3 - August 2004 - p223(1) [1-50]

Walvoord, Linda - *Razzamadaddy (Illus. by Yoshikawa, Sachiko)*
c SLJ - v50 - i7 - July 2004 - p89(1) [51-500]
Rosetta, Rosetta, Sit by Me! (Illus. by Velasquez, Eric)
c BL - v101 - i6 - Nov 15 2004 - p587(1) [51-500]
c KR - v72 - i18 - Sept 15 2004 - p922(1) [51-500]
c SLJ - v50 - i11 - Nov 2004 - p120(1) [51-500]

Walz, Gene - *Canada's Best Features: Critical Essays on 15 Canadian Films*
Can Hist R - v85 - i4 - Dec 2004 - p875(5) [501+]
Can Lit - i181 - Summer 2004 - p185-186 [501+]

Walzer, Michael - *Arguing about War*
CC - v121 - i25 - Dec 14 2004 - p20(1) [501+]
Choice - v42 - i3 - Nov 2004 - p562(1) [1-50]
HLR - v118 - i1 - Nov 2004 - p524(1) [1-50]
LJ - v129 - i14 - Sept 1 2004 - p171(2) [51-500]
Nation - v279 - i20 - Dec 13 2004 - p50 [501+]
NS - v133 - i4697 - July 19 2004 - p48(2) [501+]
NYRB - v51 - i18 - Nov 18 2004 - p32(4) [501+]
Parameters - v34 - i4 - Winter 2004 - p133(3) [501+]

Walzog, David - *The New American Steakhouse Cookbook: It's Not Just Meat and Potatoes Anymore*
PW - v252 - i9 - Feb 28 2005 - p59(1) [51-500]

Wampler, Roy H. - *Supplement to the Derr Family 1750-1994 with Allied Families*
EFHM - v58 - i3 - May-June 2004 - p57(1) [51-500]

Wan, Henry Y. - *Economic Development in a Globalized Environment: East Asia Evidences*
R&R Bk N - v19 - i1 - Feb 2004 - p85(1) [1-50]

Wandel, Lee Palmer - *History Has Many Voices*
Ren Q - v57 - i3 - Fall 2004 - p1068(3) [501+]

Wanegffelen, Thierry - *De Michel de l'Hospital a l'Edit de Nantes: Politique et Religion Face aux Eglises*
Six Ct J - v35 - i3 - Fall 2004 - p924-925 [501+]

Wang, Anxing - *Studies of Chinese Bond Markets: An Empirical Approach*
R&R Bk N - v19 - i1 - Feb 2004 - p118(1) [51-500]

Wang, Aubrey H. - *Preparing Teachers around the World*
CE - v81 - i2 - Winter 2004 - p117(1) [51-500]

Wang, Chaohua - *One China, Many Paths*
Lon R Bks - v26 - i13 - July 8 2004 - p9(2) [501+]
R&R Bk N - v19 - i3 - August 2004 - p55(1) [51-500]

Wang, David Der-wei - *The Monster That Is History: History, Violence, and Fictional Writing in Twentieth-Century China*
Choice - v42 - i7 - March 2005 - p1225(1) [51-500]

Wang, Di - *Street Culture in Chengdu: Public Space, Urban Commoners, and Local Politics, 1870-1930*
AHR - v109 - i3 - June 2004 - p879(1) [501+]
Pac A - v77 - i2 - Summer 2004 - p325(3) [501+]

Wang, Hongyu - *The Call from the Stranger on a Journey Home: Curriculum in a Third Space*
R&R Bk N - v19 - i4 - Nov 2004 - p177(1) [501+]

Wang, Kesheng - *Intelligent Condition Monitoring and Diagnosis Systems: A Computational Intelligence Approach*
SciTech - v28 - i4 - Dec 2004 - p25(1) [51-500]

Wang, Lawrence K. - *Handbook of Industrial and Hazardous Wastes Treatment, 2nd Ed.*
Choice - v42 - i7 - March 2005 - p1202(1) [51-500]

Wang, Lingzhen - *Personal Matters: Women's Autobiographical Practice in Twentieth-Century China*
R&R Bk N - v19 - i4 - Nov 2004 - p30(1) [501+]

Wang, Oliver - *Classic Material: The Hip-Hop Album Guide*
CBRA - Annual 2003 - p104(1) [501+]

Wang, Robin R. - *Images of Women in Chinese Thought and Culture: Writings from the Pre-Qin Period through the Song Dynasty*
Ch Rev Int - v11 - i1 - Spring 2004 - p15(7) [501+]
R&R Bk N - v19 - i1 - Feb 2004 - p133(1) [51-500]

Wang, Rui - *Signal Transduction and the Gasotransmitters: NO, CO, and H2S in Biology and Medicine*
SciTech - v28 - i3 - Sept 2004 - p70(1) [51-500]

Wang, Shujen - *Framing Piracy: Globalization and Film Distribution in Greater China*
Choice - v41 - i7 - March 2004 - p1304(1) [501+]
R&R Bk N - v19 - i1 - Feb 2004 - p224(1) [51-500]

Wang, Wallace - *The Book of Nero 6 Ultra Edition: CD and DVD Burning Made Easy*
LJ - v129 - i18 - Nov 1 2004 - p114(1) [51-500]
SciTech - v28 - i4 - Dec 2004 - p159(1) [51-500]
Steal This File Sharing Book: What They Won't Tell You about File Sharing
SciTech - v28 - i4 - Dec 2004 - p153(1) [51-500]

Wang, Xiaodong - *Wireless Communication Systems: Advanced Techniques for Signal Reception*
SciTech - v28 - i1 - March 2004 - p155(1) [51-500]

Wang, Xu - *Mutual Empowerment of State and Peasantry: Village Self-Government in Rural China*
Pac A - v77 - i3 - Fall 2004 - p557(2) [501+]

Wang, Yan - *Chinese Legal Reform: The Case of Foreign Investment*
Ch Rev Int - v10 - i2 - Fall 2003 - p468(2) [501+]

Wang, Yong-Yi - *Flaw Evaluation, Service Experience, and Materials for Hydrogen Service: Proceedings*
SciTech - v28 - i4 - Dec 2004 - p159(1) [51-500]

Wang, Young-Yi - *Residual Stress, Fracture, and Stress Corrosion Cracking: Proceedings*
SciTech - v28 - i4 - Dec 2004 - p163(1) [51-500]

Wang, Zhen - *The Tao of War: The Martial Taote Ching*
Bwatch - Oct 2004 - pNA [51-500]

Wangenheim, Georg von - *Games and Public Administration: The Law and Economics of Regulation and Licensing*
R&R Bk N - v19 - i3 - August 2004 - p166(1) [501+]

Wanke, Christine A. - *Lipodystrophy Syndrome in HIV*
SciTech - v28 - i1 - March 2004 - p103(1) [51-500]
SciTech - v28 - i1 - March 2004 - p103(1) [51-500]

Wankel, Charles - *Educating Managers with Tomorrow's Technologies*
R&R Bk N - v19 - i1 - Feb 2004 - p87(1) [1-50]

Wanko, Cheryl - *Roles of Authority: Thespian Biography and Celebrity in Eighteenth-Century Britain*
Albion - v36 - i2 - Summer 2004 - p310(2) [501+]
Biomag - v27 - i3 - Summer 2004 - p609(3) [501+]

Wann, Marilyn - *Fat! So? Because You Don't Have to Apologize for Your Size*
OOB - v34 - Nov-Dec 2004 - p64(2) [501+]

Wanna, John - *Controlling the Public Expenditure: The Changing Roles of Central Budget Agencies-Better Guardians?*
R&R Bk N - v19 - i1 - Feb 2004 - p120(1) [51-500]

Wansbrough, John - *Quranic Studies: Sources and Methods of Scriptural Interpretation*
R&R Bk N - v19 - i4 - Nov 2004 - p17(1) [51-500]

Wanyeki, L. Muthoni - *Women and Land in Africa: Culture, Religion and Realizing Women's Rights*
R&R Bk N - v19 - i1 - Feb 2004 - p100(1) [1-50]

War Machines
LibMed - v23 - i3 - Nov-Dec 2004 - p65(1) [51-500]

The War of 1812
c SLJ - v50 - i7 - July 2004 - p56(1) [51-500]

Warburg, Gabriel - *Islam, Sectarianism, and Politics in Sudan since the Mahdiyya*
Choice - v41 - i7 - March 2004 - p1353(1) [501+]

Warburton, Eileen - *John Fowles: A Life in Two Worlds*
Choice - v42 - i5 - Jan 2005 - p856(1) [1-50]
CR - v285 - i1666 - Nov 2004 - p316(1) [501+]

Warburton, Nigel - *Erno Goldfinger: The Life of an Architect*
Lon R Bks - v26 - i7 - April 1 2004 - p25(1) [501+]
TLS - i5300 - Oct 29 2004 - p11(1) [501+]

Ward, Amanda Eyre - *How to Be Lost*
BL - v101 - i1 - Sept 1 2004 - p66(1) [51-500]
Ent W - i788 - Oct 15 2004 - p81 [51-500]
KR - v72 - i16 - August 15 2004 - p776(1) [501+]
People - v62 - i19 - Nov 8 2004 - p60 [51-500]
PW - v251 - i32 - August 9 2004 - p228(1) [51-500]

Ward, Bob - *Mr. Space: The Life of Wernher von Braun*
BL - v101 - i7 - Dec 1 2004 - p633(1) [51-500]

Ward, Bobby J. - *The Plant Hunter's Garden: The New Explorers and Their Discoveries*
BL - v101 - i4 - Oct 15 2004 - p371(1) [51-500]

Ward, Brian - *How Linux Works: What Every Superuser Should Know*
SciTech - v28 - i3 - Sept 2004 - p25(1) [51-500]
Radio and the Struggle for Civil Rights in the South
Choice - v42 - i4 - Dec 2004 - p655(1) [1-50]

Ward, Carlton - *The Edge of Africa*
R&R Bk N - v19 - i3 - August 2004 - p59(1) [51-500]

Ward, Chip - *Hope's Horizon: Three Visions for Healing the American Land*
Choice - v42 - i6 - Feb 2005 - p1048(1) [51-500]
SB - v41 - i1 - Jan-Feb 2005 - p17(1) [501+]
SciTech - v28 - i3 - Sept 2004 - p56(1) [1-50]

Ward, David - *Beneath the Mask*
y CBRA - Annual 2003 - p521(1) [51-500]

Ward, David C. - *Charles Willson Peale: Art and Selfhood in the Early Republic*
Choice - v42 - i5 - Jan 2005 - p845(1) [1-50]

Ward, Dayton - *A Time to Harvest*
Kliatt - v38 - i6 - Nov 2004 - p26(1) [51-500]
A Time to Sow
y Kliatt - v38 - i5 - Sept 2004 - p33(3) [51-500]

Ward, Douglas - *Ocean Cruises & Cruise Ships*
Globe & Mail - Nov 24 2004 - pR10 [1-50]

Ward, Elaine - *Old Testament Women*
c SLJ - v50 - i8 - August 2004 - p133(1) [51-500]

Ward, Evan R. - *Border Oasis: Water and the Political Ecology of the Colorado River Delta, 1940-1975*
WHQ - v35 - i1 - Spring 2004 - p78-79 [501+]

Ward, Fay E. - *The Cowboy at Work*
R&R Bk N - v19 - i1 - Feb 2004 - p64(1) [501+]

Ward, Geoffrey C. - *Unforgivable Blackness: The Rise and Fall of Jack Johnson*
LJ - v129 - i20 - Dec 1 2004 - p130(1) [51-500]
BL - v101 - i4 - Oct 15 2004 - p376(1) [51-500]
Black Iss - v7 - i1 - Jan-Feb 2005 - p67(1) [501+]
Bus W - i3909 - Nov 22 2004 - p32 [501+]
BW - v34 - i47 - Nov 21 2004 - p9(1) [501+]
Choice - v42 - i7 - March 2005 - p1266(1) [51-500]
KR - v72 - i17 - Sept 1 2004 - p855(1) [501+]
NW - Nov 8 2004 - p54 [501+]
NYRB - v51 - i18 - Nov 18 2004 - p25(4) [501+]
NYTBR - Nov 7 2004 - p32 [501+]
PW - v251 - i41 - Oct 11 2004 - p68(1) [51-500]

Ward, Helen - *Finding Christmas (Illus. by Anderson, Wayne)*
c BL - v101 - i3 - Oct 1 2004 - p338(1) [51-500]
c CCB-B - v58 - i4 - Dec 2004 - p186(2) [51-500]
c PW - v251 - i39 - Sept 27 2004 - p61(1) [51-500]
Unwitting Wisdom: An Anthology of Aesop's Animal Fables (Illus. by Ward, Helen)
c Sch Lib - v52 - i4 - Winter 2004 - p206(1) [51-500]
Unwitting Wisdom: An Anthology of Aesop's Fables (Illus. by Ward, Helen)
c BL - v101 - i2 - Sept 15 2004 - p242(1) [51-500]
c CCB-B - v58 - i3 - Nov 2004 - p149(2) [501+]
c KR - v72 - i18 - Sept 15 2004 - p922(1) [51-500]
c SLJ - v50 - i10 - Oct 2004 - p152(1) [51-500]

Ward, I.A. - *An Introduction to the Mechanical Properties of Solid Polymers*
Choice - v42 - i4 - Dec 2004 - p694(1) [1-50]

Ward, I.M. - *Introduction to the Mechanical Properties of Solid Polymers, 2d ed.*
SciTech - v28 - i3 - Sept 2004 - p140(1) [51-500]

Ward, J.T. - *W.B. Ferrand: "The Working Man's Friend," 1809-1889*
Albion - v36 - i2 - Summer 2004 - p319(2) [501+]
JMH - v76 - i4 - Dec 2004 - p951(3) [501+]

Ward, Jennifer - *The Seed and the Giant Saguaro (Illus. by Rangner, Mike)*
c CH Bwatch - v14 - i7 - July 2004 - p4(1) [51-500]
c LibMed - v22 - i7 - April-May 2004 - p74(1) [501+]

Ward, John Powell - *The Spell of the Song: Letters, Meaning, and English Poetry*
Choice - v42 - i4 - Dec 2004 - p664(1) [1-50]
R&R Bk N - v19 - i4 - Nov 2004 - p233(1) [501+]

Ward, Keith - *The Case for Religion*
TLS - i5284 - July 9 2004 - p24(1) [501+]
What the Bible Really Teaches: A Challenge for Fundamentalists
TLS - i5307 - Dec 17 2004 - p6-7 [501+]

Ward, L.B.B. - *Professor Angelicus Visits The Big Blue Ball*
c CH Bwatch - Oct 2004 - pNA [51-500]

Ward, Liza - *Outside Valentine*
BL - v100 - i22 - August 2004 - p1903(1) [501+]
BL - v101 - i6 - Nov 15 2004 - p558(1) [51-500]
BL - v101 - i9-10 - Jan 1 2005 - p770(1) [51-500]
BW - v34 - i38 - Sept 19 2004 - p10(1) [501+]
Globe & Mail - Sept 4 2004 - pD18 [501+]
KR - v72 - i13 - July 1 2004 - p604(2) [501+]
LJ - v129 - i14 - Sept 1 2004 - p143(1) [51-500]
NYTBR - Sept 26 2004 - p12 [501+]
People - v62 - i11 - Sept 13 2004 - p56 [51-500]
SLJ - v51 - i2 - Feb 2005 - p157(2) [51-500]

Ward, Lynd - *Gods' Man: a Novel in Woodcuts*
A Art - v68 - i748 - Nov 2004 - p75(1) [51-500]

Ward, Martha - *Voodoo Queen: The Spirited Lives of Marie Laveau*
BL - v101 - i3 - Oct 1 2004 - p302(1) [51-500]
Black Iss - v6 - i6 - Nov-Dec 2004 - p66(2) [501+]
Bwatch - Oct 2004 - pNA [51-500]
HNet - Sept 2004 - pNA [501+]

Ward, Matthew C. - *Breaking the Backcountry: The Seven Years' War in Virginia and Pennsylvania, 1754-1765*
Choice - v41 - i11-12 - July-August 2004 - p2110(2) [501+]
HNet - Sept 2004 - pNA [501+]
J Mil H - v68 - i3 - July 2004 - p955-956 [501+]
JAH - v91 - i2 - Sept 2004 - p605(2) [501+]
RAH - v32 - i4 - Dec 2004 - p471-477 [501+]

Ward, Michael - *Quantifying the World: UN Ideas and Statistics*
Choice - v42 - i2 - Oct 2004 - p334(1) [51-500]

Ward, Nick - *Come On, Baby Duck!*
c PW - v251 - i48 - Nov 29 2004 - p39(1) [51-500]
c Sch Lib - v52 - i4 - Winter 2004 - p191(1) [51-500]
c SLJ - v50 - i11 - Nov 2004 - p120(1) [51-500]
Don't Eat the Teacher! (Illus. by Ward, Nick)
c RT - v57 - Oct 2003 - p165 [1-50]
Squash the Spider!
c Sch Lib - v52 - i4 - Winter 2004 - p191(1) [51-500]

Ward, Robert - *London's New River*
Lon R Bks - v26 - i14 - July 22 2004 - p28(2) [501+]

Ward, Robert David - *Alabama's Response to the Penitentiary Movement, 1829-1865*
Choice - v41 - i11-12 - July-August 2004 - p2111(1) [501+]
JSH - v71 - i1 - Feb 2005 - p149(2) [501+]

Ward, Stephen V. - *Planning and Urban Change, 2d ed.*
R&R Bk N - v19 - i3 - August 2004 - p156(1) [51-500]

Ward, Steven L. - *Modernizing the Mind: Psychological Knowledge and the Remaking of Society*
CS - v33 - i5 - Sept 2004 - p557-558 [501+]

Ward, Thomas - *The Ethics of Destruction: Norms and Force in International Relations*
JPR - v41 - i5 - Sept 2004 - p649-650 [501+]

Ward, Thomas J. - *Black Physicians in the Jim Crow South*
Choice - v41 - i11-12 - July-August 2004 - p2079(1) [501+]
JSH - v71 - i1 - Feb 2005 - p184(2) [501+]
SciTech - v28 - i1 - March 2004 - p78(1) [51-500]

Ward, Timothy - *Word and Supplement: Speech Acts, Biblical Texts and the Sufficiency of Scripture*
TT - v61 - i1 - April 2004 - p138-140 [501+]

Wardlaw, Lee - *101 Ways to Bug Your Teacher*
c BL - v101 - i1 - Sept 1 2004 - p126(1) [1-50]
c SLJ - v50 - i8 - August 2004 - p132(1) [51-500]

Wardle, Bill - *Mounted Squad: An Illustrated History of the Toronto Mounted Police, 1886-2000*
CBRA - Annual 2003 - p320(1) [501+]

Wardle, Francis - *Meeting the Needs of Multiethnic and Multiracial Children in Schools*
R&R Bk N - v19 - i1 - Feb 2004 - p192(1) [51-500]

Wardle, Philip - *Forest Production Statistical Information of EU and EFTA*
R&R Bk N - v19 - i3 - August 2004 - p120(1) [51-500]

Wardrip-Fruin, Noah - *First Person: New Media as Story, Performance, and Game*
Choice - v42 - i2 - Oct 2004 - p278(1) [501+]

Ware, Chris - *The Acme Novelty Library*
LJ - v129 - i20 - Dec 1 2004 - p88(1) [1-50]
McSweeney's 13: The Comics Issue
Spec - v295 - i9186 - August 28 2004 - p31(1) [501+]
McSweeney's Quarterly Concern, No. 13
PW - v251 - i29 - July 19 2004 - p146(1) [51-500]

Ware, Ezell - *By Duty Bound: Survival and Redemption in a Time of War*
KR - v73 - i2 - Jan 15 2005 - p113(1) [501+]
PW - v252 - i6 - Feb 7 2005 - p56(1) [51-500]
Ware, Jim - *Investment Leadership: Building a Winning Culture for Long-Term Success*
R&R Bk N - v19 - i3 - August 2004 - p137(1) [51-500]
Ware, Linda P. - *Ideology and the Politics of (In)exclusion*
R&R Bk N - v19 - i4 - Nov 2004 - p191(1) [501+]
Ware, Martin - *Island in the Sky: Selected Poetry of Al Pittman*
BIC - v33 - i7 - Oct 2004 - p36(1) [501+]
Ware, Michael E. - *Veteran Motor Cars*
Bwatch - Feb 2005 - pNA [51-500]
Ware, Susan - *It's One O'Clock and Here Is Mary Margaret McBride*
BL - v101 - i9-10 - Jan 1 2005 - p801(1) [51-500]
CJR - v43 - i5 - Jan-Feb 2005 - p62(1) [51-500]
Wareham, Louise - *Since You Ask*
ABR - v25 - i6 - Sept-Oct 2004 - p12(2) [501+]
Waresquiel, Emmanuel De - *Talleyrand: Le Prince Immobile*
HER - v119 - i483 - Sept 2004 - p998(1000) [501+]
Warford, Malcolm L. - *Practical Wisdom: On Theological Teaching and Learning*
CC - v122 - i4 - Feb 22 2005 - p49(3) [501+]
R&R Bk N - v19 - i4 - Nov 2004 - p25(1) [501+]
Wargin, Kathy-Jo - *The Edmund Fitzgerald: The Song of The Bell*
LibMed - v22 - i7 - April-May 2004 - p72(1) [501+]
M Is for Melody: A Music Alphabet (Illus. by Larson, Katherine)
c SLJ - v51 - i2 - Feb 2005 - p130(1) [51-500]
Win One for the Gipper: America's Football Hero (Illus. by Langton, Bruce)
c PW - v251 - i48 - Nov 29 2004 - p40(1) [51-500]
c SLJ - v51 - i1 - Jan 2005 - p116(1) [51-500]
Wargon, Sylvia T. - *Demography in Canada in the Twentieth Century*
JIH - v34 - i4 - Spring 2004 - p662-664 [501+]
Wargus, Nanci - *All About Sound*
c SB - v40 - i5 - Sept-Oct 2004 - p219(1) [51-500]
Warhol, Andy - *Andy Warhol: The Late Work*
Choice - v42 - i3 - Nov 2004 - p473(1) [1-50]
Warhola, James - *Uncle Andy's: A Faabbbbulous Visit with Andy Warhol*
c Teach Lib - v32 - i1 - Oct 2004 - p16(1) [51-500]
Warhurst, John - *2001: The Centenary Election*
AJPS - v39 - i2 - July 2004 - p446(446) [501+]
R&R Bk N - v19 - i1 - Feb 2004 - pNA [501+]
Constitutional Politics: The Republic Referendum and the Future
R&R Bk N - v19 - i1 - Feb 2004 - pNA [501+]
Waring, Marilyn - *If Women Counted: A New Feminist Economics*
OOB - v35 - Jan-Feb 2005 - p47(2) [501+]
Wark, Jim - *Discovering Lewis and Clark From the Air*
Bwatch - v26 - i8 - August 2004 - p11(1) [51-500]
Wark, McKenzie - *A Hacker Manifesto*
Nation - v279 - i13 - Oct 25 2004 - p40 [501+]
New Sci - v184 - i2470 - Oct 23 2004 - p55(1) [51-500]
TimHES - v0 - i1661 - Oct 8 2004 - p31(1) [501+]
Warkentin, Germaine - *Decentring the Renaissance: Canada and Europe in Multidisciplinary Perspective 1500-1700*
Six Ct J - v35 - i1 - Spring 2004 - p312(3) [501+]
The Queen's Majesty's Passage and Related Documents
TLS - i5295 - Sept 24 2004 - p26(1) [501+]
Warkus, Matthias - *The Official Gnome 2 Developer's Guide*
SciTech - v28 - i3 - Sept 2004 - p32(1) [51-500]
Warleigh, Alex - *Democracy and the European Union: Theory, Practice, and Reform*
R&R Bk N - v19 - i4 - Nov 2004 - p155(1) [501+]
Warlick, Ashley - *Seek the Living*
BL - v101 - i5 - Nov 1 2004 - p466(1) [51-500]
KR - v72 - i19 - Oct 1 2004 - p938(1) [501+]
LJ - v129 - i18 - Nov 1 2004 - p78(1) [501+]
People - v63 - i3 - Jan 24 2005 - p50 [51-500]
PW - v251 - i47 - Nov 22 2004 - p37(1) [51-500]
Warlick, David - *Redefining Literacy for the 21st Century*
LibMed - v23 - i1 - August-Sept 2004 - p88(1) [51-500]
SLJ - v50 - i12 - Dec 2004 - p179(1) [51-500]
Teach Lib - v32 - i2 - Dec 2004 - p37(1) [501+]
Warman, Caroline - *Sade: From Materialism to Pornography*
Eight-C St - v37 - i3 - Spring 2004 - p469-474 [501+]
Warme, Gordon - *Cure of Folly: A Psychiatrist's Cautionary Tale*
CBRA - Annual 2003 - p436(1) [51-500]
Warmuzek, Malgorzata - *Aluminum-Silicon Casting Alloys: Atlas of Microfractographs*
SciTech - v28 - i3 - Sept 2004 - p165(1) [51-500]
Warncke, Carsten-Peter - *Theatre D'Amour: The Garden of Love and Its Delights: Rediscovery of a Lost Book from the Age of the Baroque*
PW - v252 - i9 - Feb 28 2005 - p58(1) [51-500]
Warner, Brian D. - *A Practical Guide to Lightcurve Photometry and Analysis*
Astron - v32 - i10 - Oct 2004 - p90 [51-500]
S&T - v107 - i1 - Jan 2004 - p76(1) [501+]
Warner, Carolyn M. - *Confessions of an Interest Group: The Catholic Church and Political Parties in Europe*
JR - v84 - i3 - July 2004 - p488(2) [501+]
Warner, Charles - *Media Selling: Broadcast, Cable, Print and Interactive, 3rd Ed.*
R&R Bk N - v19 - i1 - Feb 2004 - p109(1) [51-500]
Warner, Ding Xiang - *A Wild Deer Amid Soaring Phoenixes: The Opposition Poetics of Wang Ji*
R&R Bk N - v19 - i1 - Feb 2004 - p219(1) [1-50]
Warner, Janine - *50 Fast Dreamweaver MX Techniques*
SciTech - v28 - i1 - March 2004 - p155(1) [51-500]
Teach Yourself Visually: Dreamweaver MX 2004
LJ - v129 - i12 - July 2004 - p112(1) [501+]
Warner, Jessica - *Craze: Gin and Debauchery in an Age of Reason*
Albion - v36 - i1 - Spring 2004 - p139(2) [501+]
The Incendiary: The Misadventures of John the Painter, First Modern Terrorist
Globe & Mail - March 12 2005 - pD3 [501+]
John the Painter: Terrorist of the American Revolution
BL - v101 - i3 - Oct 1 2004 - p298(1) [51-500]
PW - v251 - i35 - August 30 2004 - p40(2) [51-500]
Warner, Judith - *Perfect Madness: Motherhood in the Age of Anxiety*
LJ - v130 - i3 - Feb 15 2005 - p149(1) [51-500]
NYTBR - Feb 20 2005 - p1 [501+]
PW - v252 - i5 - Jan 31 2005 - p61(1) [501+]
Warner, Julian - *Humanizing Information Technology*
LRTS - v49 - i1 - Jan 2005 - p59(2) [501+]
Warner, M. - *Liquid Crystal Elastomers*
SciTech - v28 - i1 - March 2004 - p47(1) [51-500]
Warner, Malcolm - *Stubbs and the Horse*
BL - v101 - i9-10 - Jan 1 2005 - p800(1) [51-500]
Warner, Roger - *Memoirs of a Twentieth Century Antique Dealer*
Apo - v161 - i515 - Jan 2005 - p69(1) [501+]
Warner, Sally - *Only Emma*
c KR - v73 - i5 - March 1 2005 - p297(1) [51-500]
Warnes, Andrew - *Hunger Overcome?: Food and Resistance in Tweenth-Century African American Literature*
Choice - v41 - i11-12 - July-August 2004 - p2048(1) [501+]
Warnes, Tim - *Mommy Mine (Illus. by Chapman, Jane)*
c KR - v73 - i4 - Feb 15 2005 - p237(1) [51-500]
Warrell, Ian - *Turner and Venice*
Choice - v42 - i3 - Nov 2004 - p475(1) [1-50]
R&R Bk N - v19 - i3 - August 2004 - p244(1) [51-500]
Warren, Alan - *This Is a Thriller: An Episode Guide, History and Analysis of the Classic 1960s Television Series*
R&R Bk N - v19 - i4 - Nov 2004 - p222(1) [501+]
Warren, Andrea - *Escape from Saigon: How a Vietnam War Orphan Became an American Boy*
y BL - v101 - i9-10 - Jan 1 2005 - p773(1) [51-500]
c CCB-B - v58 - i2 - Oct 2004 - p101(2) [51-500]
HB - v80 - i5 - Sept-Oct 2004 - p608(2) [51-500]
c KR - v72 - i15 - August 1 2004 - p750(1) [51-500]
c PW - v251 - i42 - Oct 18 2004 - p65(1) [51-500]
c SLJ - v50 - i10 - Oct 2004 - p196(1) [51-500]
VOYA - v27 - i5 - Dec 2004 - p418(1) [51-500]
We Rode the Orphan Trains
y Kliatt - v38 - i4 - July 2004 - p42(2) [51-500]
Warren, Carl S. - *Acounting, 21st Ed.*
R&R Bk N - v19 - i2 - May 2004 - p118 [51-500]
Corporate Financial Accounting, 8th Ed.
R&R Bk N - v19 - i2 - May 2004 - p121 [51-500]
Financial Accounting, 9th Ed.
R&R Bk N - v19 - i2 - May 2004 - p119 [51-500]
Financial and Managerial Accounting, 8th Ed.
R&R Bk N - v19 - i2 - May 2004 - p119 [51-500]
Warren, Dave - *Cisco Self-Study: Building Cisco Metro Optical Networks*
SciTech - v28 - i4 - Dec 2004 - p150(1) [51-500]
Warren, David H. - *Early Christian Voices: In Texts, Traditions, and Symbols, Essays in Honor of Francis Bovon*
R&R Bk N - v19 - i1 - Feb 2004 - p18(1) [51-500]
Warren, Deborah - *Zero Meridian*
BL - v101 - i3 - Oct 1 2004 - p295(1) [51-500]
Warren, Dianne - *Reckless Moon*
CBRA - Annual 2003 - p207(1) [51-500]
Warren, Elizabeth - *The Two-Income Trap: Why Middle-Class Mothers and Fathers are Going Broke*
Choice - v41 - i11-12 - July-August 2004 - p2095(1) [501+]
CS - v33 - i5 - Sept 2004 - p627-627 [501+]
Warren, Elizabeth F. - *Refining Common Sense: Moving from Data to Information*
R&R Bk N - v19 - i3 - August 2004 - p225(1) [1-50]
Warren, James - *Epicurus and Democritean Ethics: An Archaeology of Ataraxia*
Class R - v54 - i2 - Nov 2004 - p333-335 [501+]
RM - v58 - i1 - Sept 2004 - p199(2) [501+]
Facing Death: Epicurus and His Critics
TLS - i5297 - Oct 8 2004 - p11(1) [501+]
Warren, Jonathan W. - *Racial Revolutions: Antiracism and Indian Resurgence in Brazil*
HAHR - v84 - i2 - May 2004 - p372(2) [501+]
Warren, Kay B. - *Indigenous Movements and Their Critics: Pan-Maya Activism in Guatemala*
J Urban H - v31 - i1 - Nov 2004 - p124-132 [501+]
Warren, Kenneth W. - *So Black and Blue: Ralph Ellison and the Occasion of Criticism*
Choice - v41 - i7 - March 2004 - p1300(1) [501+]
Warren, Neil Clark - *Falling in Love for All the Right Reasons: How To Find Your Soul Mate*
LJ - v130 - i1 - Jan 1 2005 - p134(2) [501+]
Warren, Penn - *All the King's Men*
Globe & Mail - Oct 30 2004 - pD31 [501+]
Warren, Rick - *The Purpose Driven Life*
SEP - v277 - i2 - March-April 2005 - p45(1) [501+]
Warren, Rosanna - *Departure*
Poet - v184 - i4 - August 2004 - p305(12) [501+]
Warren, Susan May - *Flee the Night*
PW - v252 - i8 - Feb 21 2005 - p159(1) [51-500]
Warrick, Karen Clemens - *The Perilous Search for the Fabled Northwest Passage in American History*
c SLJ - v50 - i10 - Oct 2004 - p196(1) [51-500]
Warrick, Leanne - *Chillin' Trix for Cool Chix: Fab Recipes, Crafty Fun, Mystic Magic, and Super-Cool Quizzes*
y Kliatt - v39 - i2 - March 2005 - p44(1) [51-500]
Hair Trix for Cool Chix: The Real Girl's Guide to Great Hair (Illus. by Boon, Debbie)
c SLJ - v50 - i7 - July 2004 - p129(1) [51-500]
Warsh, Sylvia Maultash - *Find Me Again: A Rebecca Temple Mystery*
BIC - v33 - i8 - Nov 2004 - p16(3) [501+]
CBRA - Annual 2003 - p192(2) [51-500]
Warshaw, Hope S. - *Complete Guide to Carb Counting*
Bwatch - Nov 2004 - pNA [51-500]
Bwatch - March 2005 - pNA [51-500]
Warshaw, Matt - *The Encyclopedia of Surfing*
R&R Bk N - v19 - i1 - Feb 2004 - p74(1) [51-500]
Zero Break: An Illustrated Collection of Surf Writing
LJ - v129 - i20 - Dec 1 2004 - p127(1) [51-500]
Warshaw, Shirley Anne - *The Clinton Years*
y Choice - v42 - i7 - March 2005 - p1210(1) [51-500]
c SLJ - v51 - i2 - Feb 2005 - p86(1) [51-500]
Wartewig, Siegfried - *IR and Raman Spectroscopy: Fundamental Processing*
SciTech - v28 - i1 - March 2004 - p49(1) [51-500]
Warwaruk, Larry - *Andrei and the Snow Walker*
y Can CL - i111-112 - Fall-Winter 2003 - p128(7) [501+]
Sundog Highway: Writing from Saskatchewan
Can Lit - i181 - Summer 2004 - p186-189 [501+]
Warwick, Andrew - *Masters of Theory: Cambridge and the Rise of Mathematical Physics*
Phys Today - v57 - i9 - Sept 2004 - p58-58 [501+]
VS - v46 - i4 - Summer 2004 - p701(3) [501+]
Warwick, Dionne - *My Point of View*
Black Iss - v6 - i6 - Nov-Dec 2004 - p41(1) [51-500]
Warwick, Tony - *Synchrotron Radiation Instrumentation; Proceedings*
SciTech - v28 - i3 - Sept 2004 - p49(1) [1-50]

Wasa, Kiyotaka - *Thin Film Materials Technology: Sputtering of Compound Materials*
  SciTech - v28 - i3 - Sept 2004 - p171(1) [51-500]
Wasburn, Philo C. - *The Social Construction of International News: We're Talking about Them*
  CS - v33 - i2 - March 2004 - p198-199 [501+]
Waseem, M. - *On Becoming an Indian Muslim: French Essays on Aspects of Syncretism*
  JAS - v63 - i3 - August 2004 - p837-838 [501+]
Washburn, Bradford - *Washburn: Extraordinary Adventures of a Young Mountaineer*
  Bwatch - Nov 2004 - pNA [51-500]
Washburn, Dorothy K. - *Embedded Symmetries, Natural and Cultural*
  Am Sci - v93 - i2 - March-April 2005 - p180(3) [501+]
  Symmetry Comes of Age: The Role of Pattern in Culture
  Am Sci - v93 - i2 - March-April 2005 - p180(3) [501+]
  Choice - v42 - i5 - Jan 2005 - p842(1) [1-50]
Washburn, Jennifer - *University, Inc.: The Corporate Corruption of Higher Education*
  KR - v73 - i1 - Jan 1 2005 - p45(1) [501+]
  PW - v252 - i5 - Jan 31 2005 - p63(2) [501+]
Washington, Charles M. - *Principles and Practice of Radiation Therapy, 2d ed.*
  SciTech - v28 - i1 - March 2004 - p91(1) [51-500]
Washington, Donna L. - *A Little Shiver (Read by Washington, Donna L.). Audiobook Review*
  c BL - v101 - i3 - Oct 1 2004 - p352(1) [51-500]
  A Pride of African Tales (Illus. by Ransome, James)
  c CE - v81 - i2 - Winter 2004 - p109(1) [51-500]
  LibMed - v23 - i1 - August-Sept 2004 - p69(1) [51-500]
  c SLJ - v50 - i8 - August 2004 - p114(1) [51-500]
Washington Information Directory, 2004-2005
  R&R Bk N - v19 - i4 - Nov 2004 - p65(1) [51-500]
Washington, Jacqueline M. - *Neurologic Disorders in Pregnancy*
  SciTech - v28 - i1 - March 2004 - p116(1) [51-500]
Washington, La Trice M. - *The Veteran's Millennium Health Care Act of 1999: A Case Study of Role Orientations of Legislators, the President, and Interest Groups*
  R&R Bk N - v19 - i1 - Feb 2004 - pNA [51-500]
Washington, Lawrence C. - *Elliptic Curves: Number Theory and Cryptography*
  Choice - v41 - i7 - March 2004 - p1331(1) [501+]
Washington, Robert E. - *Confronting the American Dilemma of Race: The Second Generation Black American Sociologists*
  CS - v33 - i1 - Jan 2004 - p26-27 [501+]
  The Ideologies of African American Literature: From the Harlem Renaissance to the Black Nationalist Revolt: A Sociology of Literature Perspective
  CS - v33 - i5 - Sept 2004 - p558-559 [501+]
Washington-Williams, Essie Mae - *Dear Senator: A Memoir by the Daughter of Strom Thurmond*
  LJ - v130 - i3 - Feb 15 2005 - p148(1) [51-500]
Wasik, Barbara Hanna - *Handbook of Family Literacy*
  R&R Bk N - v19 - i3 - August 2004 - p227(1) [1-50]
Wasko, Janet - *How Hollywood Works*
  Choice - v42 - i2 - Oct 2004 - p301(1) [51-500]
Waskul, Dennis D. - *Net.seXXX: Readings on Sex, Pornography, and the Internet*
  R&R Bk N - v19 - i4 - Nov 2004 - p127(1) [51-500]
  Self-Games and Body-Play: Personhood in Online Chat and Cybersex
  CS - v33 - i6 - Nov 2004 - pNA [501+]
Wasser, Frederick - *Veni, Vidi, Video: The Hollywood Empire and the VCR*
  T&C - v45 - i1 - Jan 2004 - p211(2) [501+]
Wasserman, Bonnie S. - *Metaphors of Oppression in Lusophone Historical Drama*
  R&R Bk N - v19 - i1 - Feb 2004 - p233(1) [51-500]
Wasserman, Bryna - *The Naked Island*
  Globe & Mail - Oct 23 2004 - pD13 [501+]
Wasserman, Dale - *The Impossible Musical*
  R&R Bk N - v19 - i2 - May 2004 - p191(1) [51-500]
Wasserman, Debra - *Conveniently Vegan*
  Veg J - v24 - i1 - Jan-Feb 2005 - p33(1) [501+]
  Meatless Meals for Working People--Quick and Easy Vegetarian Recipes
  Veg J - v24 - i1 - Jan-Feb 2005 - p33(1) [501+]
  No Cholesterol Passover Recipes
  Veg J - v24 - i1 - Jan-Feb 2005 - p33(1) [501+]
  Simply Vegan
  Veg J - v24 - i1 - Jan-Feb 2005 - p33(1) [501+]
  Vegan Handbook
  Veg J - v24 - i1 - Jan-Feb 2005 - p33(1) [501+]

Wasserman, Jo Ann - *The Escape*
  LJ - v129 - i12 - July 2004 - p88(1) [51-500]
Wasserman, Mark - *Giraffes? Giraffes!*
  c Globe & Mail - Dec 11 2004 - pD28 [51-500]
  Your Disgusting Head: The Darkest Most Offensive -- And Most Moist -- Secrets of Your Ears, Mouth and Nose
  c Globe & Mail - Dec 11 2004 - pD28 [51-500]
Wasserman, Robert H. - *Tensors and Manifolds with Applications to Physics, 2nd Ed.*
  SciTech - v28 - i4 - Dec 2004 - p42(1) [51-500]
Wasserstein, Bernard - *Israelis and Palestinians: Why Do They Fight? Can They Stop?*
  MEQ - v11 - i4 - Fall 2004 - p80(2) [501+]
Wasserstrom, Wendy - *Sloth*
  BL - v101 - i8 - Dec 15 2004 - p692(1) [51-500]
  Globe & Mail - Jan 1 2005 - pD13 [51-500]
  HM - v310 - i1856 - Jan 2005 - p96(6) [501+]
  PW - v251 - i49 - Dec 6 2004 - p54(1) [51-500]
  LJ - v129 - i20 - Dec 1 2004 - p118(1) [51-500]
Wasserstrom, Jeffrey N. - *Twentieth-Century China: New Approaches*
  Pac A - v77 - i2 - Summer 2004 - p319(2) [501+]
Wasson, Barbara - *Designing for Change in Networked Learning Environments: Proceedings*
  R&R Bk N - v19 - i1 - Feb 2004 - p181(1) [51-500]
Wasson, John H. - *A-Z Common Symptom Answer Guide: A Family Medical Reference*
  SciTech - v28 - i4 - Dec 2004 - p89(1) [51-500]
Wasti, S. Tanvir - *Seismic Assessment and Rehabilitation of Existing Buildings: Proceedings*
  SciTech - v28 - i1 - March 2004 - p149(1) [51-500]
Wastvedt, Tricia - *The River*
  KR - v73 - i3 - Feb 1 2005 - p146(1) [501+]
  LJ - v130 - i3 - Feb 15 2005 - p121(1) [51-500]
  TLS - i5289 - August 13 2004 - p21(1) [501+]
Waswo, Ann - *Housing in Postwar Japan: A Social History*
  HNet - Sept 2004 - pNA [501+]
Watanabe, John M. - *Pluralizing Ethnography: Comparison and Representation in Maya Cultures, Histories, and Identities*
  R&R Bk N - v19 - i4 - Nov 2004 - p69(1) [501+]
Watase, Yu - *Imadoki! Dandelion, Vol. 1*
  y Kliatt - v39 - i1 - Jan 2005 - p25(2) [51-500]
Water Environment Federation. Control of Odors and Emissions from Wastewater Treatment Plants Task Force - *Control of Odors and Emissions from Wastewater Treatment Plants*
  SciTech - v28 - i3 - Sept 2004 - p145(1) [51-500]
Water, Mark - *The Encyclopedia of Prayer and Praise*
  Choice - v42 - i2 - Oct 2004 - p270(1) [501+]
Water Science Fair Projects: Using Ice Cubes, Super Soakers, and Other Wet Stuff
  c SLJ - v50 - i7 - July 2004 - p122(1) [51-500]
Waterbird Books - *Sculpting and Drama: Artistic Creations for Young Artists*
  y LibMed - v22 - i5 - Feb 2004 - pNA [51-500]
Watercolor
  R&R Bk N - v19 - i4 - Nov 2004 - p207(1) [501+]
Waterfield, Robin - *Athens: A History from Ancient Ideal to Modern City*
  Choice - v42 - i4 - Dec 2004 - p729(1) [1-50]
  CR - v285 - i1666 - Nov 2004 - p317(1) [501+]
  TLS - i5284 - July 9 2004 - p7(1) [501+]
  Wil Q - v28 - i4 - Autumn 2004 - p120(2) [501+]
Watergate
  LibMed - v22 - i6 - March 2004 - p93(1) [501+]
Waterhouse, Michael - *The Strange Death of British Birdsong*
  Spec - v296 - i9192 - Oct 9 2004 - p55(1) [501+]
Waterman, Laura - *Losing the Garden: The Story of a Marriage*
  LJ - v130 - i4 - March 1 2005 - p100(1) [51-500]
  PW - v252 - i6 - Feb 7 2005 - p52(1) [51-500]
Waterman, Richard W. - *Bureaucrats, Politics, and the Environment*
  Choice - v42 - i5 - Jan 2005 - p936(1) [51-500]
Waters, Anne - *American Indian Thought: Philosophical Essays*
  Choice - v41 - i11-12 - July-August 2004 - p2056(1) [501+]
Waters, Brent - *God and the Embryo: Religious Voices on Stem Cells and Cloning*
  Choice - v42 - i1 - Sept 2004 - p120(1) [501+]
Waters, Christopher P.M. - *Counsel in the Caucasus: Professionalization and Law in Georgia*
  R&R Bk N - v19 - i3 - August 2004 - p207(1) [1-50]

Waters, Claire M. - *Angels and Earthly Creatures: Preaching, Performance, and Gender in the Later Middle Ages*
  Choice - v42 - i1 - Sept 2004 - p122(2) [501+]
  CHR - v90 - i4 - Oct 2004 - p776(2) [501+]
Waters, Donald - *Global Logistics and Distribution Planning: Strategies for Management, 4th Ed.*
  R&R Bk N - v19 - i1 - Feb 2004 - p108(1) [51-500]
Waters, John - *Art: A Sex Book*
  Art N - v103 - i1 - Jan 2004 - p102(1) [501+]
  Lam Bk Rpt - v13 - i4-5 - Nov-Dec 2004 - p46(1) [501+]
  The Real Business of Web Design
  SciTech - v28 - i3 - Sept 2004 - p158(1) [51-500]
  The Real Business to Web Design
  Choice - v42 - i1 - Sept 2004 - p141(1) [501+]
Waters, Sarah - *Fingersmith*
  Globe & Mail - Dec 24 2004 - pD3 [1-50]
  Social Movements in France: Towards a New Citizenship
  R&R Bk N - v19 - i1 - Feb 2004 - p126(1) [51-500]
Waters, William - *Poetry's Touch: On Lyric Address*
  VQR - v80 - i3 - Summer 2004 - p262(1) [1-50]
Waterson, Michael - *Competition, Monopoly, and Corporate Governance: Essays in Honour of Keith Cowling*
  R&R Bk N - v19 - i1 - Feb 2004 - p105(1) [51-500]
Watkin, David - *The Architect King: George III and the Culture of the Enlightenment*
  Spec - v296 - i9195 - Oct 30 2004 - p59(2) [501+]
Watkin, William - *On Mourning: Theories of Loss in Modern Literature*
  Choice - v42 - i5 - Jan 2005 - p848(2) [1-50]
Watkins, Adam - *The Maya 6 Handbook*
  Bwatch - Feb 2005 - pNA [51-500]
Watkins, Clifford Edward - *Showman: The Life and Music of Perry George Lowery*
  Choice - v41 - i7 - March 2004 - p1303(1) [501+]
Watkins, George - *Stationary Steam Engines of Great Britian: The National Photographic Collection*
  T&C - v45 - i1 - Jan 2004 - p181(3) [501+]
Watkins, John - *Representing Elizabeth in Stuart England: Literature, History, Sovereignty*
  HER - v119 - i483 - Sept 2004 - p1055(2) [501+]
  HER - v119 - i483 - Sept 2004 - p1055(2) [501+]
  Representing Elizabeth in Stuart England: Literture, History, Sovereignty
  Six Ct J - v34 - i4 - Winter 2003 - p1162-1164 [501+]
Watkins, John J. - *Across the Board: The Mathematics of Chessboard Problems*
  Choice - v42 - i5 - Jan 2005 - p888(1) [501+]
  y SB - v40 - i4 - July-August 2004 - p162(2) [51-500]
  SB - v40 - i6 - Nov-Dec 2004 - p241(1) [51-500]
Watkins, Michael - *The First 90 Days: Critical Success Strategies for New Leaders at All Levels*
  HR Mag - v49 - i7 - July 2004 - pS3(1) [51-500]
  HR Mag - v50 - i2 - Feb 2005 - pS2(1) [501+]
  Mar Crp G - v89 - i1 - Jan 2005 - p57(1) [501+]
  Parameters - v34 - i3 - Autumn 2004 - p169(2) [501+]
  Per Psy - v57 - i4 - Winter 2004 - p1073(4) [501+]
Watkins, Paul - *Calm at Sunset, Calm at Dawn*
  BL - v101 - i3 - Oct 1 2004 - p360(1) [501+]
Watkins-Pitchford, Denys - *The Little Grey Men, By BB: A Story for the Young in Heart*
  c KR - v72 - i18 - Sept 15 2004 - p922(1) [51-500]
Watkins, William D. - *The Transforming Habits of a Growing Christian*
  Ch Today - v48 - i10 - Oct 2004 - p113(3) [501+]
Watkins, William J., Jr. - *Reclaiming the American Revolution: The Kentucky and Virginia Resolutions and Their Legacy*
  HRNB - v33 - i1 - Fall 2004 - p15(2) [501+]
  Law&PolBR - Nov 2004 - p849(3) [501+]
  R&R Bk N - v19 - i4 - Nov 2004 - p171(1) [51-500]
Watling, Roy - *Fungi*
  SciTech - v28 - i1 - March 2004 - p67(1) [51-500]
Watras, Joseph - *Philosophic Conflicts in American Education, 1893-2000*
  Choice - v42 - i1 - Sept 2004 - p160(2) [501+]
Watry, Maureen - *The Vale Press: Charles Ricketts, a Publisher in Earnest*
  R&R Bk N - v19 - i4 - Nov 2004 - p254(1) [501+]

Watsky, Andrew M. - *Chikubushima: Deploying the Sacred Arts in Momoyama Japan*
  Choice - v41 - i11-12 - July-August 2004 - p2033(1) [501+]
  R&R Bk N - v19 - i2 - May 2004 - p196(1) [51-500]

Watson, Christine - *Piercing the Ground: Balgo Women's Image Making and Relationship to Country*
  R&R Bk N - v19 - i1 - Feb 2004 - p200(1) [51-500]

Watson, Clyde - *Father Fox's Christmas Rhymes (Illus. by Watson, Wendy)*
  c LibMed - v22 - i6 - March 2004 - p71(1) [501+]

Watson, Don - *Death Sentence: The Decay of Public Language*
  Quad - v48 - i7-8 - July-August 2004 - p122(3) [501+]
  TLS - i5263 - Feb 13 2004 - p12-12 [501+]
Gobbledygook: How Cliches, Sludge and Management-Speak are Strangling Our Public Language
  NS - v133 - i4706 - Sept 20 2004 - p51(2) [501+]

Watson, Elwood - *"There She Is, Miss America": The Politics of Sex, Beauty, and Race in America's Most Famous Pageant*
  Choice - v42 - i6 - Feb 2005 - p1106(2) [51-500]
  LJ - v129 - i13 - August 2004 - p105(1) [51-500]

Watson, Gary - *The Cinema of Mike Leigh: A Sense of the Real*
  Choice - v42 - i4 - Dec 2004 - p669(2) [1-50]

Watson, Ian - *Inquisition War*
  ChrSFF&H - v26 - i10 - Oct 2004 - p26(1) [51-500]
Mockymen
  Analog - v124 - i4 - April 2004 - p136(2) [501+]

Watson, Iarfhlaith - *Broadcasting in Irish: Minority Language, Radio, Television and Identity*
  R&R Bk N - v19 - i1 - Feb 2004 - p221(1) [51-500]

Watson, James (b. 1936 -) - *Dictionary of Media and Communication Studies*
  Choice - v42 - i2 - Oct 2004 - p270(1) [501+]

Watson, James D. - *DNA: The Secret of Life*
  Am Bio T - v66 - i9 - Nov-Dec 2004 - p654(2) [501+]
  SciTech - v28 - i4 - Dec 2004 - p61(1) [1-50]
Molecular Biology of the Gene, 5th ed.
  SciTech - v28 - i1 - March 2004 - p64(1) [51-500]

Watson, Janet - *Odyssey VI and VII*
  Class R - v54 - i2 - Nov 2004 - p275-276 [501+]

Watson, Janet S.K. - *Fighting Different Wars: Experience, Memory, and the First World War in Britian*
  Choice - v42 - i4 - Dec 2004 - p726(1) [1-50]

Watson, Jean - *Caring Science as Sacred Science*
  SciTech - v28 - i4 - Dec 2004 - p121 [51-500]

Watson, Jennifer - *Swedish Novelist Selma Lagerlof, 1858-1940, and Germany at the Turn of the Century: O du Stern ob Meinem Garten*
  R&R Bk N - v19 - i4 - Nov 2004 - p244(1) [501+]

Watson, Jo Anna Holt - *A Taste of the Sweet Apple: A Memoir*
  KR - v72 - i17 - Sept 1 2004 - p856(1) [51-500]
  LJ - v129 - i20 - Dec 1 2004 - p118(2) [51-500]

Watson, Jude - *Premonitions*
  Kliatt - v38 - i6 - Nov 2004 - p26(1) [501+]

Watson, Jules - *The White Mare*
  KR - v73 - i2 - Jan 15 2005 - p90(1) [51-500]
  LJ - v130 - i3 - Feb 15 2005 - p123(1) [51-500]
  PW - v252 - i6 - Feb 7 2005 - p46(1) [51-500]

Watson, Kathy - *The Devil Kissed Her: The Story of Mary Lamb*
  KR - v72 - i14 - July 15 2004 - p680(1) [501+]
  LJ - v129 - i14 - Sept 1 2004 - p163(1) [51-500]
  NS - v133 - i4701 - August 16 2004 - p38(3) [501+]
  NYRB - v51 - i16 - Oct 21 2004 - p54(4) [501+]

Watson, L. - *Martial: Select Epigrams*
  Class R - v54 - i2 - Nov 2004 - p407(4) [501+]

Watson, Lindsay C. - *A Commentary on Horace's Epodes*
  Choice - v42 - i1 - Sept 2004 - p98(1) [501+]

Watson, Lucy - *Life Drawing Class*
  R&R Bk N - v19 - i1 - Feb 2004 - p205(1) [51-500]

Watson, Lyall - *The Whole Hog: Exploring the Extraordinary Potential of Pigs*
  BL - v101 - i6 - Nov 15 2004 - p539(1) [501+]
  New Sci - v184 - i2469 - Oct 16 2004 - p53(1) [51-500]
  NYTBR - Dec 19 2004 - p31 [501+]
  PW - v251 - i42 - Oct 18 2004 - p59(1) [51-500]

Watson, Marilyn - *Learning to Trust: Transforming Difficult Elementary Classrooms through Developmental Discipline*
  CE - v81 - i2 - Winter 2004 - p110(1) [501+]

Watson, Mark - *Bullet Points*
  TLS - i5264 - Feb 20 2004 - p22-22 [501+]

Watson, Oliver - *Ceramics from Islamic Lands*
  Choice - v42 - i2 - Oct 2004 - p282(1) [501+]
  LJ - v129 - i18 - Nov 1 2004 - p82(1) [501+]

Watson, Patrick - *Canadians: Biographies of a Nation, Vols. 1-3*
  CBRA - Annual 2003 - p75(2) [51-500]
This Hour has Seven Decades
  Globe & Mail - Nov 6 2004 - pD3 [501+]
  Globe & Mail - Nov 27 2004 - pD3 [51-500]

Watson, Richard Jesse - *The Magic Rabbit*
  c BL - v101 - i9-10 - Jan 1 2005 - p876(1) [51-500]
  KR - v72 - i24 - Dec 15 2004 - p1210(1) [51-500]

Watson, Robert P. - *American First Ladies*
  BL - v101 - i3 - Oct 1 2004 - p358(1) [501+]
Anticipating Madam President
  Choice - v41 - i7 - March 2004 - p1371(1) [501+]
Counting Votes: Lessons from the 2000 Presidential Election in Florida
  Choice - v42 - i5 - Jan 2005 - p934(1) [51-500]
The Presidential Companion: Readings on the First Ladies
  JAH - v91 - i1 - June 2004 - p321-324 [501+]
  JSH - v70 - i3 - August 2004 - p659(2) [501+]

Watson, Ronald R. - *Nutrition and Alcohol: Linking Nutrient Interactions and Dietary Intake*
  SciTech - v28 - i1 - March 2004 - p102(1) [51-500]

Watson, Ronald Ross - *AIDS and Heart Disease*
  SciTech - v28 - i4 - Dec 2004 - p103(1) [51-500]

Watson, Ruth - *'Civil Disorder Is the Disease of Ibadan': Chieftaincy & Civic Culture in a Yoruba City*
  R&R Bk N - v19 - i3 - August 2004 - p59(1) [51-500]

Watson, Stephanie - *Endocrine System*
  SciTech - v28 - i4 - Dec 2004 - p70(1) [51-500]
The Urinary System
  SciTech - v28 - i4 - Dec 2004 - p105(1) [51-500]

Watson, Steven - *Factory Made: Warhol and the Sixties*
  JPC - v38 - i2 - Nov 2004 - p431(3) [501+]

Watson, Thomas - *Italian Madrigals Englished*
  Notes - v61 - i2 - Dec 2004 - p551(3) [501+]

Watson, W. Marvin - *Chief of Staff: Lyndon Johnson and His Presidency*
  BL - v101 - i1 - Sept 1 2004 - p44(1) [51-500]
  BW - v34 - i38 - Sept 19 2004 - p5(1) [501+]
  LJ - v129 - i12 - July 2004 - p100(1) [51-500]

Watsuki, Nobuhiro - *Rurouni Kenshin, Vol. 8*
  PW - v252 - i2 - Jan 10 2005 - p41(1) [51-500]

Watt, Eva Tulene - *Don't Let the Sun Step over You: A White Mountain Apache Family Life, 1860-1975*
  y Kliatt - v39 - i1 - Jan 2005 - p31(1) [51-500]
  Roundup M - v12 - i3 - Feb 2005 - p23(1) [51-500]

Watt, Gavin K. - *"As Many Liars": The Story of the 1995 Manitoba Vote-Splitting Scandal*
  CBRA - Annual 2003 - p279(1) [501+]

Watt, Melanie - *The Alphabet with Wild Animals (Illus. by Watt, Melanie)*
  c CBRA - Annual 2003 - p471(1) [51-500]
  c Globe & Mail - March 12 2005 - pD14 [51-500]
Colors
  c CBRA - Annual 2003 - p471(1) [51-500]
Numbers
  c CBRA - Annual 2003 - p471(1) [51-500]
Opposites
  c CBRA - Annual 2003 - p471(1) [51-500]
Shapes
  c CBRA - Annual 2003 - p471(1) [51-500]

Wattenberg, Ben J. - *Fewer: How the New Demography of Depopulation Will Shape Our Future*
  Am Spect - v37 - i7 - Sept 2004 - p60(2) [501+]
  LJ - v129 - i17 - Oct 15 2004 - p78(1) [51-500]
  R&R Bk N - v19 - i4 - Nov 2004 - p86(1) [51-500]

Wattenberg, Jane - *Never Cry Woof! (Illus. by Wattenberg, Jane)*
  c KR - v73 - i2 - Jan 15 2005 - p127(1) [51-500]

Wattenberg, Laura - *The Baby Name Wizard: A Magical Method for Finding the Perfect Name for Your Baby*
  LJ - v130 - i2 - Feb 15 2005 - p160(1) [51-500]

Watters, Robert - *The Wholesale Candy Company*
  Bwatch - v26 - i9 - Sept 2004 - p4(1) [51-500]

Watts, Barrie - *Butterfly*
  c SB - v40 - i3 - May-June 2004 - p133(2) [501+]

Watts, David H. - *Bedside Manners: One Doctor's Reflections on the Oddly Intimate Encounters between Patient and Healer*
  KR - v72 - i24 - Dec 15 2004 - p1195(1) [501+]
  PW - v251 - i51 - Dec 20 2004 - p45(1) [51-500]

Watts, Duncan J. - *Six Degrees: The Science of a Connected Age*
  TLS - i5290 - August 20 2004 - p29(1) [51-500]

Watts, Frances - *This Dog Bruce (Illus. by Strevens-Marzo, Bridget)*
  c Magpies - v19 - i5 - Nov 2004 - p24(1) [501+]

Watts, Heather - *Halifax's Northwest Arm: An Illustrated History*
  CBRA - Annual 2003 - p352(2) [51-500]

Watts, Irene N. - *Finding Sophie: A Search for Belonging in Postwar Britain*
  y Can CL - i111-112 - Fall-Winter 2003 - p128(7) [501+]
A Telling Time (Illus. by Shoemaker, Kathryn E.)
  c PW - v252 - i7 - Feb 14 2005 - p81(1) [51-500]
  c Globe & Mail - March 12 2005 - pD14 [51-500]

Watts, Peter - *Behemoth: B-Max*
  BL - v100 - i21 - July 2004 - p1830(1) [1-50]
  LJ - v129 - i12 - July 2004 - p76(1) [51-500]
Behemoth: Seppuku
  BL - v101 - i9-10 - Jan 1 2005 - p835(1) [1-50]
  KR - v72 - i23 - Dec 1 2004 - p1126(1) [501+]
  LJ - v130 - i1 - Jan 1 2005 - p102(1) [51-500]
  PW - v251 - i50 - Dec 13 2004 - p50(1) [51-500]

Watts, Richard J. - *Politeness*
  TimHES - v0 - i1661 - Oct 8 2004 - p28(2) [501+]

Watts, Sarah - *Rough Rider in the White House: Theodore Roosevelt and the Politics of Desire*
  JAH - v91 - i3 - Dec 2004 - p1049(2) [501+]

Watts, Sharon - *A Style All Her Own*
  PW - v252 - i5 - Jan 31 2005 - p67(1) [501+]

Watts, Victor - *The Cambridge Dictionary of English Place-Names: Based on the Collections of the English Place-Name Society*
  Choice - v42 - i1 - Sept 2004 - p77(1) [501+]
  HNet - Sept 2004 - pNA [501+]

Wauer, Roland H. - *Birding the Southwestern National Parks (Illus. by Wolf, Mimi Hoppe)*
  E-Streams - Nov 2004 - pNA [501+]
Butterflies of the Lower Rio Grande Valley
  SciTech - v28 - i4 - Dec 2004 - p66(1) [51-500]

Waugh, Alexander - *Fathers and Sons: The Autobiography of a Family*
  Globe & Mail - Dec 4 2004 - pD8 [501+]
  Globe & Mail - Dec 24 2004 - pD3 [1-50]
  Spec - v296 - i9188 - Sept 11 2004 - p40(2) [501+]
  TLS - i5303 - Nov 19 2004 - p40(1) [501+]

Waugh, Billy - *Hunting the Jackal: A Special Forces and CIA Ground Soldier's Fifty-Year Career Hunting America's Enemies*
  BL - v100 - i21 - July 2004 - p1806(1) [51-500]

Waugh, Evelyn - *Waugh Abroad: Collected Travel Writing*
  WLT - v78 - i3-4 - Sept-Dec 2004 - p106(1) [501+]

Waugh, Louisa - *Hearing Birds Fly: A Nomadic Year in Mongolia*
  LJ - v129 - i14 - Sept 1 2004 - p175(1) [51-500]

Waugh, Russell F. - *On the Forefront of Educational Psychology*
  R&R Bk N - v19 - i1 - Feb 2004 - p182(1) [51-500]

Wauquelin, Jehan - *La Belle Helene De Constantinople: Mise en Prose D'une Chanson De Geste*
  Specu - v79 - i4 - Oct 2004 - p1175(3) [501+]

Wauthier, Jean-Luc - *Fruits de l'ombre*
  WLT - v78 - i3-4 - Sept-Dec 2004 - p120(2) [501+]

Wauzzinski, Robert A. - *The Transforming Story of Dwelling House Savings and Loan: A Pittsburgh Bank's Fight Against Urban Poverty*
  R&R Bk N - v19 - i1 - Feb 2004 - p115(1) [1-50]

Waverman, Lucy - *A Matter of Taste: Inspired Seasonal Menus with Wines and Spirits to Match*
  BIC - v33 - i9 - Dec 2004 - p26(2) [501+]
  Globe & Mail - Nov 27 2004 - pD26 [51-500]

Wawn, Andrew - *Approaches to Vinland: A Conference on the written and Archaeological Sources for the Norse Settlements in the North-Atlantic Region and Exploration of America*
  JEGP - v103 - i3 - July 2004 - p408-410 [501+]

Wawro, Geoffrey - *The Franco-Prussian War: The German Conquest of France in 1870-1871*
  HNet - Sept 2004 - pNA [501+]
  HRNB - v33 - i1 - Fall 2004 - p28(1) [501+]
  J Mil H - v68 - i3 - April 2004 - p612-613 [501+]
  TLS - i5301 - Nov 5 2004 - p12(1) [501+]

Weber, EdNah New Rider - *Rattlesnake Mesa: Stories from a Native American Childhood (Illus. by Renkun, Richela)*
  c BL - v101 - i8 - Dec 15 2004 - p733(2) [51-500]
  c CCB-B - v58 - i6 - Feb 2005 - p269(1) [51-500]
  y HB - v81 - i1 - Jan-Feb 2005 - p118(2) [51-500]
  c SLJ - v50 - i12 - Dec 2004 - p170(2) [51-500]

Weber, Edward P. - *Bringing Society Back In: Grassroots Ecosystem Management, Accountability, and Sustainable Communities*
  QRB - v79 - i4 - Dec 2004 - p453(1) [501+]

Weber, Ewald - *Invasive Plant Species of the World: A Reference Guide to Environmental Weeds*
  QRB - v79 - i3 - Sept 2004 - p314(1) [501+]
  SciTech - v28 - i1 - March 2004 - p130(1) [51-500]

Weber, Jurgen - *Germany, 1945-1990: A Parallel History*
  R&R Bk N - v19 - i4 - Nov 2004 - p39(1) [51-500]

Weber, Katherine - *The Little Women*
  VQR - v80 - i1 - Wntr 2004 - p270-271 [501+]
  VQR - v80 - i1 - Wntr 2004 - p271-271 [501+]

Weber, Lori - *Klepto*
  y Kliatt - v39 - i1 - Jan 2005 - p18(1) [501+]
  y SLJ - v51 - i1 - Jan 2005 - p138(1) [51-500]
  Res Links - v10 - i3 - Feb 2005 - p41(2) [501+]

Weber, Max - *The History of Commercial Partnerships in the Middle Ages*
  CS - v33 - i2 - March 2004 - p253-254 [501+]
  JEL - v41 - i4 - Dec 2003 - p1405(1) [501+]
  The Protestant Ethic and the Spirit of Capitalism
  NYTBR - March 13 2005 - p35 [501+]
  The Religion of China: Confucianism and Taoism
  NYTBR - March 13 2005 - p35 [501+]

Weber, Myles - *Middlebrow Annoyances: American Drama in the 21st Century*
  Sew R - v112 - i3 - Summer 2004 - pLXXXIV-LXXXV [501+]

Weber, Peter J. - *The National Directory to College and University Student Records: Verify Student Attendace, Degree, and Transcript Records at Accredited Post-Secondary Schools*
  Choice - v42 - i4 - Dec 2004 - p642(1) [1-50]

Weber, R.H. - *Homeland*
  LJ - v129 - i12 - July 2004 - p74(2) [51-500]
  Spec - v296 - i9201 - Dec 11 2004 - p44(2) [501+]

Weber, Rebecca - *The Body's Business*
  c SB - v40 - i4 - July-August 2004 - p182(1) [51-500]
  c SLJ - v51 - i1 - Jan 2005 - p116(2) [501+]
  The Cycle of Your Life
  c SB - v40 - i4 - July-August 2004 - p182(1) [51-500]
  c SLJ - v51 - i1 - Jan 2005 - p116(2) [501+]
  First Aid for You
  c SB - v40 - i4 - July-August 2004 - p182(1) [51-500]
  Foods from the Farm
  c SLJ - v51 - i1 - Jan 2005 - p116(2) [501+]
  Healthy Habits
  c SB - v40 - i4 - July-August 2004 - p182(1) [51-500]
  c SLJ - v51 - i1 - Jan 2005 - p116(2) [501+]
  Safety First
  c SB - v40 - i4 - July-August 2004 - p182(1) [51-500]

Weber, Richard - *Miss Gazillions*
  KR - v73 - i2 - Jan 15 2005 - p88(2) [51-500]
  PW - v252 - i9 - Feb 28 2005 - p45(1) [51-500]

Weber, Sandra - *Not Just Any Dress: Narratives of Memory, Body, and Identity*
  R&R Bk N - v19 - i3 - August 2004 - p85(1) [51-500]

Weber, Steven - *The Success of Open Source*
  New Sci - v183 - i2458 - July 31 2004 - p52(1) [51-500]

Weber, Steven A. - *Indus Ethnobiology: New Perspectives from the Field*
  R&R Bk N - v19 - i1 - Feb 2004 - p46(1) [51-500]

Weber, Steven (b. 1961 -) - *The Success of Open Source*
  Choice - v42 - i2 - Oct 2004 - p328(1) [51-500]

Weber, Timothy P. - *On the Road to Armageddon: How Evangelicals became Israel's Best Friend*
  Choice - v42 - i6 - Feb 2005 - p1040(2) [51-500]

Webgrammer
  LibMed - v22 - i7 - April-May 2004 - p92(1) [501+]

Webster, Chris - *Property Rights, Planning and Markets: Managing Spontaneous Cities*
  JEL - v41 - i4 - Dec 2003 - p1441(2) [501+]

Webster, Christine - *Mauna Loa: The Largest Volcano in the United Slates*
  c SLJ - v50 - i8 - August 2004 - p107(1) [51-500]
  Polynesians
  c CH Bwatch - v14 - i7 - July 2004 - p5(2) [51-500]
  c SLJ - v50 - i7 - July 2004 - p94(1) [51-500]
  Yanomam
  c SLJ - v50 - i7 - July 2004 - p94(1) [51-500]

Webster, Donovan - *Aftermath: The Remnants of War*
  Atl - v294 - i5 - Dec 2004 - p137(1) [501+]
  The Burma Road: The Epic Story of the China-Burma-India Theater in World War II
  J Mil H - v68 - i3 - July 2004 - p997-999 [501+]
  The Burma Road: The Epic Story of the China Burma-India Theater in World War II
  VQR - v80 - i2 - Spring 2004 - p254-254 [501+]

Webster, Edward D. - *A Year of Sundays: Taking the Plunge (and Our Cat) to Explore Europe*
  LJ - v129 - i13 - August 2004 - p106(1) [51-500]

Webster, Jean - *Daddy Long Legs and Dear Enemy*
  LJ - v130 - i3 - Feb 15 2005 - p172(1) [1-50]

Webster, John - *Holy Scripture: A Dogmatic Sketch*
  TT - v61 - i2 - July 2004 - p288(1) [501+]

Webster, John G. - *Bioinstrumentation*
  SciTech - v28 - i3 - Sept 2004 - p58(1) [1-50]

Webster, Laurie D. - *Collecting the Weaver's Art: The William Claflin Collection of Southwestern Textiles*
  R&R Bk N - v19 - i3 - August 2004 - p62(1) [51-500]

Webster, Mandy - *Data Protection for the HR Manager*
  R&R Bk N - v19 - i2 - May 2004 - p117 [51-500]

Webster, Sally - *Eve's Daughter/Modern Woman: A Mural by Mary Cassatt*
  Choice - v42 - i3 - Nov 2004 - p475(1) [1-50]

Wechsler, Robert T. - *Blueprints Notes and Cases: Neuroscience*
  SciTech - v28 - i1 - March 2004 - p93(1) [51-500]

Wecht, Cyril - *Mortal Evidence: The Forensics behind Nine Shocking Cases*
  TLS - i5292 - Sept 3 2004 - p28(1) [501+]

Wecht, Cyril H. - *Forensic Aspects of Chemical and Biological Terrorism*
  SciTech - v28 - i4 - Dec 2004 - p10(1) [1-50]

Weddle, Peter D. - *Weddle's 2005/6 Guide to Employment Sites on the Internet: For Corporate and Third Party Recruiters, Job Seekers and Career Activists*
  HR Mag - v50 - i2 - Feb 2005 - pS11(1) [51-500]
  Weddle's Recruiter's and Job Seeker's Directory of Employment-Related Internet Sites 2005/6
  HR Mag - v50 - i2 - Feb 2005 - pS11(1) [501+]

Wedel, Johan - *Santeria Healing: A Journey into the Afro-Cuban World of Divinities, Spirits, and Sorcery*
  Choice - v42 - i3 - Nov 2004 - p518(1) [1-50]
  MAQ - v18 - i4 - Dec 2004 - p521(3) [501+]

Wedeman, Andrew H. - *From Mao to Market: Rent Seeking, Local Protection, and Marketization in China*
  JAS - v63 - i3 - August 2004 - p787-789 [501+]

Wedlick, Dennis - *Good House Parts: Creating a Great Home Piece By Piece*
  R&R Bk N - v19 - i1 - Feb 2004 - p250(1) [51-500]

Weeber, Stan - *Militias in the New Millennium: A Test of Smelser's Theory of Collective Behavior*
  R&R Bk N - v19 - i4 - Nov 2004 - p82(1) [51-500]

Weedon, Alexis - *Victorian Publishing: The Economics of Book Production for a Mass Market 1836-1916*
  CR - v285 - i1662 - July 2004 - p60(1) [501+]

Weekes, Don - *Best and Worst of Hockey Firsts: The Unofficial Guide*
  CBRA - Annual 2003 - p147(2) [51-500]

Weekes, Trevor C. - *Very High Energy Gamma-Ray Astronomy*
  E-Streams - Dec 2004 - pNA [501+]
  Phys Today - v57 - i9 - Sept 2004 - p63-64 [501+]
  SciTech - v28 - i4 - Dec 2004 - p46(1) [51-500]

Weekley, Dallas - *Duet Repertoire: One Piano, Four Hands by Various Composers, Level Four*
  Am MT - v54 - i2 - Oct-Nov 2004 - p86(3) [501+]

Weeks, Albert Loren - *Russia's Life-Saver: Lend-lease Aid to the U.S.S.R. in World War II*
  R&R Bk N - v19 - i3 - August 2004 - p32(1) [51-500]
  Stalin's Other War: Soviet Grand Strategy, 1939-1941
  Russ Rev - v63 - i2 - April 2004 - pNA [501+]

Weeks, Gerald R. - *Treating Infidelity: Therapeutic Dilemmas and Effective Strategies*
  SciTech - v28 - i1 - March 2004 - p99(1) [51-500]

Weeks, Gregory - *The Military and Politics in Postauthoritarian Chile*
  J Mil H - v68 - i3 - July 2004 - p1019-1020 [501+]

Weeks, Jeffrey - *Sexuality*
  TimHES - v0 - i1656 - Sept 3 2004 - p29(1) [501+]

Weeks, Jim - *Gettysburg: Memory, Market, and an American Shrine*
  AHR - v109 - i3 - June 2004 - p918(2) [501+]
  Am St - v45 - i1 - Spring 2004 - p150-151 [501+]
  J Am St - v38 - i2 - August 2004 - p369(2) [501+]
  JAH - v91 - i1 - June 2004 - p249-250 [501+]

Weeks, John - *Unpopular Culture: The Ritual of Complaint in a British Bank*
  TimHES - v0 - i1666 - Nov 12 2004 - p26(1) [501+]

Weeks, Kent R. - *Atlas of the Valley of the Kings*
  Choice - v42 - i1 - Sept 2004 - p76(1) [501+]

Weeks, Lioyd R. - *Early Metallurgy of the Persian Gulf: Technology, Trade, and the Bronze Age World*
  R&R Bk N - v19 - i3 - August 2004 - p84(1) [51-500]

Weeks, Roger - *Linux Unwired*
  LJ - v130 - i1 - Jan 1 2005 - p148(1) [501+]
  SciTech - v28 - i3 - Sept 2004 - p19(1) [51-500]

Weeks, S. - *Not My Sister*
  c Sch Lib - v52 - i3 - Autumn 2004 - p148(1) [501+]

Weeks, Sarah - *Baa-Choo! (Illus. by Manning, Jane)*
  c BL - v100 - i22 - August 2004 - p1946(1) [51-500]
  c HB - v81 - i1 - Jan-Feb 2005 - p99(2) [51-500]
  c KR - v72 - i21 - Nov 1 2004 - p1047(1) [51-500]
  c SLJ - v51 - i1 - Jan 2005 - p98(1) [51-500]
  My Somebody Special (Illus. by Wolff, Ashley)
  c RT - v57 - Oct 2003 - p170 [1-50]
  Oh My Gosh, Mrs. McNosh! (Illus. by Westcott, Nadine Bernard)
  c RT - v57 - Oct 2003 - p167 [1-50]
  Paper Parade
  c HB - v80 - i4 - July-August 2004 - p443(2) [51-500]
  So B. It
  c BL - v101 - i9-10 - Jan 1 2005 - p774(1) [1-50]
  y CCB-B - v58 - i1 - Sept 2004 - p44(1) [51-500]
  y HB - v80 - i4 - July-August 2004 - p462(1) [51-500]
  c SLJ - v50 - i7 - July 2004 - p114(1) [51-500]
  c VOYA - v27 - i5 - Dec 2004 - p397(1) [51-500]
  Two Eggs, Please (Illus. by Lewin, Betsy)
  c BooChiTr - Jan 4 2004 - p5(1) [501+]
  c SLJ - v50 - i10 - Oct 2004 - pS28(1) [1-50]

Weeks, Thomas, III - *Even as Your Soul Prospers: Realize Your Purpose Release Your Blessings*
  Black Iss - v7 - i2 - March-April 2005 - p61(1) [51-500]

Weerahandi, Samaradasa - *Generalized Inference in Repeated Measures: Exact Methods in MANOVA and Mixed Models*
  SciTech - v28 - i4 - Dec 2004 - p37(1) [51-500]

Weeramantry, C.G. - *Universalising International Law*
  R&R Bk N - v19 - i3 - August 2004 - p211(1) [1-50]

Wegesin, Janice M. - *5500 Preparer's Manual: 2003 Plan Years*
  R&R Bk N - v19 - i4 - Nov 2004 - p170(1) [501+]

Wegman, David H. - *Health and Safety Needs of Older Workers*
  Choice - v42 - i4 - Dec 2004 - p704(1) [1-50]
  SciTech - v28 - i4 - Dec 2004 - p106(1) [51-500]

Wegman, William - *Dressup Batty*
  c Globe & Mail - Dec 11 2004 - pD43 [51-500]
  c PW - v251 - i51 - Dec 20 2004 - p62(1) [51-500]

Wegner, Gregory Paul - *Anti-Semitism and Schooling under the Third Reich*
  HNet - Nov 2004 - pNA [501+]

Wegren, Stephen K. - *Russia's Policy Challenges: Security, Stability, and Development*
  E-A St - v56 - i8 - Dec 2004 - p1249(4) [501+]
  Slav R - v63 - i2 - Summer 2004 - p421(2) [501+]

Wehbi, Samantha - *Community Organizing Against Homophobia and Heterosexism: The World through Rainbow-Colored Glasses*
  R&R Bk N - v19 - i3 - August 2004 - p148(1) [51-500]

Wehr, Gerhard - *Jung and Steiner: The Birth of a New Psychology*
  Parabola - v28 - i4 - Winter 2003 - p98-99 [501+]

Wei, Daming - *Computer and Information Technology: Proceedings*
  SciTech - v28 - i4 - Dec 2004 - p129 [51-500]

Wei Djao - *Being Chinese: Voices from the Diaspora*
  Globe & Mail - Oct 23 2004 - pD27 [501+]

Wei, Jie - *Beam Halo Dynamics, Diagnostics, and Collimatoin*
  SciTech - v28 - i1 - March 2004 - p51(1) [51-500]

Wei, Wei - *Leadership and Management Principles in Libraries in Developing Countries*
R&R Bk N - v19 - i4 - Nov 2004 - p257(1) [501+]
Scholarly Communication in Science and Engineering Research in Higher Education
Choice - v42 - i2 - Oct 2004 - p313(1) [51-500]
SciTech - v28 - i3 - Sept 2004 - p15(1) [501+]

Weibrecht, Isabella - *Projections 13: Women Film-makers on Film-making*
TimHES - v0 - i1654 - August 20 2004 - p28(1) [501+]

Weickmann, Dorion - *Der dressierte Leib: Kulturgeschichte des Balletts*
HNet - June 2004 - pNA [501+]

Weidenfeld, Charles Spencer - *Blenheim: Battle for Europe*
Spec - v295 - i9186 - August 28 2004 - p32(2) [501+]

Weidenfeld, John Coldstream - *Dirk Bogarde*
Spec - v296 - i9193 - Oct 16 2004 - p73(3) [501+]

Weidenfeld, R.W. Johnson - *South Africa: The First Man, The Last Nation*
Spec - v296 - i9197 - Nov 13 2004 - p48(2) [501+]

Weidensaul, Scott - *The Raptor Almanac: A Comprehensive Guide to Eagles, Hawks, Falcons, and Vultures*
Bwatch - Jan 2005 - pNA [51-500]
Kliatt - v38 - i6 - Nov 2004 - p40(1) [51-500]

Weidner, Marsha - *Cultural Intersections in Later Chinese Buddhism*
Ch Rev Int - v11 - i1 - Spring 2004 - p193(6) [501+]

Weier, John - *Violinmaker's Lament*
CBRA - Annual 2003 - p235(2) [51-500]

Weiermair, Klaus - *The Tourism and Leisure Industry: Shaping the Future*
Choice - v42 - i2 - Oct 2004 - p337(1) [51-500]
R&R Bk N - v19 - i3 - August 2004 - p78(1) [51-500]

Weiermair, Peter - *The Nude: Ideal and Reality Painting and Sculpture*
Choice - v42 - i5 - Jan 2005 - p844(1) [1-50]
LJ - v129 - i15 - Sept 15 2004 - p54(1) [51-500]

Weiers, Ronald M. - *Introduction to Business Statistics*
R&R Bk N - v19 - i3 - August 2004 - p123(1) [51-500]

Weigand, Bernhard - *Analytical Methods for Heat Transfer and Fluid Flow Problems*
Choice - v42 - i7 - March 2005 - p1265(1) [51-500]

Weigand, Debra - *Advancing Technology, Caring and Nursing*
CS - v33 - i5 - Sept 2004 - p609-610 [501+]

Weigel, George - *The Cube and the Cathedral: Europe, America, and Politics Without God*
KR - v73 - i2 - Jan 15 2005 - p114(1) [501+]
PW - v252 - i10 - March 7 2005 - p62(2) [51-500]
Letters to a Young Catholic
AM - v191 - i18 - Dec 6 2004 - p27 [501+]
Comw - v132 - i1 - Jan 14 2005 - p26(4) [501+]

Weigelt, Udo - *The Legendary Unicorn (Illus. by Gukova, Julia)*
c CH Bwatch - v14 - i12 - Dec 2004 - pNA [51-500]
c SLJ - v51 - i2 - Feb 2005 - p110(1) [51-500]

Weigert, Laura - *Weaving Sacred Stories: French Choir Tapestries and the Performance of Clerical Identity*
Med R - Nov 2004 - pNA [501+]

Weightman, Gavin - *Signor Marconi's Magic Box: The Most Remarkable Invention of the 19th Century & the Amateur Inventor whose Genius Sparked a Revolution*
Choice - v41 - i7 - March 2004 - p1318(1) [501+]

Weigley, Russell F. - *A Great Civil War: A Military and Political History, 1861-1865*
y Kliatt - v38 - i4 - July 2004 - p43(1) [51-500]

Weiglhofer, Werner S. - *Introduction to Complex Mediums for Optics and Electromagnetics*
SciTech - v28 - i1 - March 2004 - p49(1) [51-500]

Weigman, Robyn - *Women's Studies on Its Own: A Next Wave Reader in Institutional Change*
CS - v33 - i1 - Jan 2004 - p99-101 [501+]

Weikart, Richard - *From Darwin to Hitler: Evolutionary Ethics, Eugenics, and Racism in Germany*
Choice - v42 - i6 - Feb 2005 - p1089(2) [501+]

Weil, David - *Leaders of the Information Age*
Choice - v42 - i1 - Sept 2004 - p72(1) [501+]
y Ref Rev - June 2004 - pNA [501+]
Ref Rev - Dec 2004 - pNA [501+]

Weil, Ellen - *Harlan Ellison: The Edge of Forever*
Ext - v45 - i3 - Fall 2004 - p318(3) [501+]

Weil, Francois - *History of New York*
R&R Bk N - v19 - i4 - Nov 2004 - p65(1) [51-500]

Weil, Simone - *Simone Weil on Colonialism: An Ethic of the Other*
Choice - v41 - i7 - March 2004 - p1362(1) [501+]

Weil, Sylvie - *My Guardian Angel*
c BL - v101 - i5 - Nov 1 2004 - p486(1) [51-500]
c CCB-B - v58 - i2 - Oct 2004 - p102(1) [51-500]
c KR - v72 - i17 - Sept 1 2004 - p874(1) [51-500]
c SLJ - v50 - i10 - Oct 2004 - p181(2) [51-500]

Weiler, Bjorn K.U. - *England and Europe in the Reign of Henry III*
Albion - v36 - i1 - Spring 2004 - p95(2) [501+]

Weiler, J.H.H. - *European Constitutionalism Beyond the State*
Choice - v42 - i1 - Sept 2004 - p182(1) [501+]
Integration in an Expanding in an Expanding European Union: Reassessing the Funadamentals
AJPS - v39 - i2 - July 2004 - p460(461) [501+]

Weiler, Jonathan - *Human Rights in Russia: A Darker Side of Reform*
Choice - v42 - i3 - Nov 2004 - p559(1) [1-50]
R&R Bk N - v19 - i3 - August 2004 - p175(1) [501+]

Weiler, Todd - *NAFTA Investment Law and Arbitration: Past Issues, Current Practice, Future Prospects*
R&R Bk N - v19 - i3 - August 2004 - p195(1) [501+]

Weill, Alain - *Graphic Design: A History*
R&R Bk N - v19 - i4 - Nov 2004 - p205(1) [501+]

Weill, Gus - *The Cajuns*
BL - v100 - i22 - August 2004 - p1908(1) [51-500]
PW - v251 - i29 - July 19 2004 - p143(2) [51-500]

Weimer, Paul - *Petroleum Systems of Deepwater Settings*
SciTech - v28 - i4 - Dec 2004 - p162(1) [51-500]

Weinandy, T.G. - *The Theology of St Cyril of Alexandria: A Critical Appreciation*
TT - v61 - i2 - July 2004 - p288(2) [501+]

Weinberg, Dana Beth - *Code Green: Money-Driven Hospitals and the Dismantling of Nursing*
JEL - v41 - i4 - Dec 2003 - p1376(1) [501+]

Weinberg, Elizabeth A. - *Sociology in the Soviet Union and Beyond: Social Enquiry and Social Change*
R&R Bk N - v19 - i4 - Nov 2004 - p120(1) [51-500]

Weinberg, Eugene D. - *Exposing the Hidden Dangers of Iron: What Every Medical Professional Should Know about the Impact of Iron on the Disease Process*
SciTech - v28 - i4 - Dec 2004 - p102(1) [51-500]

Weinberg Founders Conference - *Between Hope and Challenge: The Bush Administration and the Middle East, 2003*
R&R Bk N - v19 - i4 - Nov 2004 - p44(1) [51-500]

Weinberg, H. Barbara - *Childe Hassam, American Impressionist*
BL - v101 - i1 - Sept 1 2004 - p38(1) [51-500]
Choice - v42 - i7 - March 2005 - p1219(1) [51-500]
NYRB - v51 - i12 - July 15 2004 - p10(2) [501+]
PW - v251 - i31 - August 2 2004 - p66(1) [51-500]
R&R Bk N - v19 - i4 - Nov 2004 - p200(1) [501+]

Weinberg, Raymond B. - *Certification Guide, 8th Ed.*
HR Mag - v50 - i2 - Feb 2005 - pS2(1) [501+]

Weinberg, Samantha - *Pointing from the Grave: A True Story of Murder and DNA*
TLS - i5292 - Sept 3 2004 - p28(1) [501+]

Weinberg, Steven - *The Discovery of Subatomic Particles, Rev. Ed.*
Choice - v41 - i7 - March 2004 - p1332(1) [501+]
E-Streams - July 2004 - pNA [501+]
Glory and Terror: The Growing Nuclear Danger
TimHES - v0 - i1662 - Oct 15 2004 - p24(2) [501+]

Weineck, Silk-Maria - *The Abyss above: Philosophy and Poetic Madness in Plato, Holderlin, and Nietzsche*
GSR - v27 - i1 - Feb 2004 - p151-152 [501+]

Weiner, Amir - *Landscaping the Human Garden: Twentieth-Century Population Management in a Comparative Framework*
AHR - v109 - i3 - June 2004 - p971(1) [501+]
CS - v33 - i1 - Jan 2004 - p131-131 [501+]

Weiner, Ellis - *The Big Boat to Bye-Bye*
KR - v73 - i2 - Jan 15 2005 - p89(1) [51-500]
PW - v252 - i9 - Feb 28 2005 - p45(1) [51-500]

Weiner, Howard L. - *Neurology, 7th Ed.*
SciTech - v28 - i4 - Dec 2004 - p93(1) [51-500]

Weiner, James F. - *Tree Leaf Talk: A Heideggerian Anthropology*
JRAI - v10 - i3 - Sept 2004 - p730(2) [501+]

Weiner, Jennifer - *American Girls about Town*
PW - v251 - i40 - Oct 4 2004 - p70(1) [51-500]
Little Earthquakes
BL - v101 - i1 - Sept 1 2004 - p66(1) [51-500]
Ent W - i785 - Sept 24 2004 - p112 [51-500]
KR - v72 - i14 - July 15 2004 - p659(2) [501+]
LJ - v129 - i13 - August 2004 - p71(1) [51-500]
People - v62 - i17 - Oct 25 2004 - p52 [501+]
PW - v251 - i44 - Nov 1 2004 - p26(2) [501+]
PW - v251 - i37 - Sept 13 2004 - p59(1) [501+]

Weiner, Jonathan - *The Beak of the Finch: A Stony of Evolution in Our Time*
AS - v74 - i1 - Wntr 2005 - p10(2) [501+]
His Brother's Keeper: A Story from the Edge of Medicine
Sci - v305 - i5685 - August 6 2004 - p780(2) [501+]

Weiner, Mark S. - *Black Trials: Citizenship from the Beginnings of Slavery to the End of Caste*
y BL - v101 - i3 - Oct 1 2004 - p288(1) [51-500]
KR - v72 - i17 - Sept 1 2004 - p856(1) [501+]
LJ - v129 - i18 - Nov 1 2004 - p108(1) [51-500]
New R - Nov 22 2004 - p29 [501+]
PW - v251 - i33 - August 16 2004 - p52(1) [51-500]

Weiner, Stephen - *Faster than a Speeding Bullet: The Rise of the Graphic Novel*
R&R Bk N - v19 - i1 - Feb 2004 - p230(1) [51-500]

Weiner, Tom - *Voices of War: Stories of Service from the Home Front and the Front Lines*
LJ - v129 - i19 - Nov 15 2004 - p74(1) [501+]
PW - v251 - i44 - Nov 1 2004 - p58(1) [501+]

Weiner, William J. - *Neurology for the Non-Neurologist, 5th ed.*
SciTech - v28 - i3 - Sept 2004 - p93(1) [51-500]

Weinert, Friedel - *The Scientist as Philosopher: Philosophical Consequences of Great Discoveries*
Choice - v42 - i4 - Dec 2004 - p682(1) [1-50]

Weinfeld, Moshe - *The Place of the Law in the Religion of Ancient Israel*
R&R Bk N - v19 - i3 - August 2004 - p51(1) [51-500]

Weingarten, Kaethe - *Common Shock: Witnessing Violence Every Day*
y Kliatt - v39 - i2 - March 2005 - p38(1) [51-500]

Weinhauer, Klaus - *Schutzpolizei in der Bundesrepublik: Zwischen Buergerkrieg und Innerer Sicherheit, Die turbulenten sechziger Jahre*
HNet - Sept 2004 - pNA [501+]

Weinke, Annette - *Die Verfolgung von NS-Tatern im geteilten Deuschland: Vergagenheitsbewaltigung 1949-1969, order: Eine deutsch deutsche Beziehungsgeschichte im Kalten Krieg*
GSR - v27 - i2 - May 2004 - p422-423 [501+]

Weinman, Brad - *The Postman Always Brings Mice (Illus. by Weinman, Brad)*
c PW - v251 - i30 - July 26 2004 - p55(1) [51-500]
To Scratch a Thief
KR - v72 - i18 - Sept 15 2004 - p914(1) [501+]

Weinmann, Barbara - *Eine andere Burgergesellschaft: Klassischer Republikanismus und Kommunalismus im Kanton Zurich im spaten 18. und 19. Jahrhundert*
JMH - v77 - i1 - March 2005 - p240(3) [501+]

Weinmann, Elaine - *Illustrator 10 for Windows and Macintosh, Student Edition*
LibMed - v22 - i5 - Feb 2004 - p77(2) [501+]
Illustrator 10 for Windows and Macintosh: Student Edition
SciTech - v28 - i1 - March 2004 - p135(1) [51-500]
Illustrator CS for Windows and Macintosh
Bwatch - v26 - i7 - July 2004 - p7(1) [51-500]

Weinstein, Art - *Handbook of Market Segmentation: Strategic Targeting for Business and Technology Firms*
R&R Bk N - v19 - i3 - August 2004 - p127(1) [501+]

Weinstein, Bruce - *The Ultimate Chocolate Cookie Book*
LJ - v129 - i15 - Sept 15 2004 - p79(1) [51-500]
The Ultimate Muffin Book: More Than 600 Recipes for Sweet and Savory Muffin
LJ - v129 - i13 - August 2004 - p113(1) [51-500]

Weinstein, Cindy - *The Cambridge Companion to Harriet Beecher Stowe*
Choice - v42 - i5 - Jan 2005 - p851(1) [1-50]

Weinstein, David - *The Forgotten Network: DuMont and the Birth of American Television*
Choice - v42 - i5 - Jan 2005 - p847(1) [1-50]
J Broadcst - v48 - i4 - Dec 2004 - p705(5) [501+]

Weinstein, Debra - *Apprentice to the Flower Poet Z: A Novel*
Poet - v185 - i5 - Feb 2005 - p405(1) [51-500]

Weinstein, Laurie - *Native Peoples of the Southwest: Negotiating Land, Water, and Ethnicities*
　　Hist Geo - v32 - Annual 2004 - p194(3) [501+]

Weinstein, Marc - *La geste russe: Comment les Russes ecrivent-ils l'historie au XXe siecle?*
　　Slav R - v63 - i2 - Summer 2004 - p438(2) [501+]

Weinstein, Matt - *Dogs Don't Bite When a Growl Will Do: What Your Dog Can Teach You about Living a Happy Life*
　　y　Kliatt - v39 - i2 - March 2005 - p36(1) [51-500]

Weinstein, Roni - *Marriage Rituals Italian Style: A Historical Anthropological Perspective on Early Modern Italian Jews*
　　R&R Bk N - v19 - i1 - Feb 2004 - p14(1) [51-500]

Weinstock, Jeffrey Andrew - *The Pedagogical Wallpaper: Teaching Charlotte Perkin's Gilman's "The Yellow Wall-paper"*
　　J Am St - v38 - i1 - April 2004 - p175-176 [501+]

Weinstock, Robert - *Gordimer Byrd's Reminder (Illus. by Weinstock, Robert)*
　　c　KR - v72 - i18 - Sept 15 2004 - p922(1) [51-500]
　　c　PW - v252 - i1 - Jan 3 2005 - p55(1) [51-500]
　　c　SLJ - v51 - i2 - Feb 2005 - p110(2) [51-500]

Weinthal, Susie - *Oy of Cooking: A Grandmother's Legacy of Food and Memories*
　　CBRA - Annual 2003 - p141(1) [501+]

Weintraub, Aileen - *Auto Mechanic*
　　c　SLJ - v50 - i7 - July 2004 - p120(2) [51-500]
Discovering Africa's Land, People, and Wildlife
　　y　SLJ - v50 - i11 - Nov 2004 - p158(1) [51-500]
Discovering Europe's Land, People, and Wildlife
　　c　SLJ - v50 - i8 - August 2004 - p137(1) [51-500]

Weintraub, E. Roy - *The Future of the History of Economics*
　　Isis - v95 - i3 - Sept 2004 - p482(2) [501+]
How Economics Became a Mathematical Science
　　JEL - v42 - i1 - March 2004 - p173(2) [501+]

Weintraub, Sidney - *Commentaries on International Political Economy: Constructive Irreverence*
　　R&R Bk N - v19 - i2 - May 2004 - p110(1) [1-50]
Free Trade in the Americas: Economic and Political Issues for Governments and Firms
　　R&R Bk N - v19 - i4 - Nov 2004 - p109(1) [51-500]

Weintraub, Stanley - *Emma Sutton, Aubrey Beardsley and British Wagnerism in the 1890s*
　　ELT - v47 - i4 - Fall 2004 - p493(3) [501+]
Iron Tears: America's Battle for Freedom, Britain's Quagmire, 1775-1783
　　BL - v101 - i8 - Dec 15 2004 - p703(1) [51-500]
　　KR - v72 - i22 - Nov 15 2004 - p1085(2) [501+]
　　LJ - v130 - i1 - Jan 1 2005 - p130(1) [51-500]
Iron Tears: America's Battle for Freedom, Britain's Quagmire: 1775-1783
　　PW - v251 - i48 - Nov 29 2004 - p31(1) [51-500]

Weintraub, William - *Tendon and Ligament Healing: A New Approach to Sports and Overuse Injury, 2d ed.*
　　SciTech - v28 - i1 - March 2004 - p112(1) [51-500]

Weir, Gary E. - *An Ocean in Common: American Naval Officers, Scientists, and the Ocean Environment*
　　J Mil H - v68 - i3 - July 2004 - p1011-1012 [501+]
Rising Tide: The Untold Story of the Russian Submarines that Fought the Cold War
　　J Mil H - v68 - i3 - July 2004 - p1016-1017 [501+]
　　y　Kliatt - v39 - i1 - Jan 2005 - p34(1) [501+]

Weir, Robert E. - *Historical Encyclopedia of American Labor*
　　BL - v100 - i22 - August 2004 - p1976(2) [501+]
　　Choice - v42 - i2 - Oct 2004 - p276(1) [501+]
　　Ref Rev - Oct 2004 - pNA [501+]
　　R&USQ - v44 - i2 - Winter 2004 - p172(2) [501+]
　　R&R Bk N - v19 - i3 - August 2004 - p118(1) [51-500]

Weir, Sara - *Voices of a New Generation: A Feminist Anthology*
　　R&R Bk N - v19 - i1 - Feb 2004 - p131(1) [51-500]

Weir, William - *The Encyclopedia of African American Military History*
　　Choice - v42 - i7 - March 2005 - p1210(1) [51-500]

Weis, Margaret - *The Dragon's Son*
　　BL - v100 - i21 - July 2004 - p1830(1) [1-50]
　　LJ - v129 - i12 - July 2004 - p75(1) [51-500]
　　y　VOYA - v27 - i4 - Oct 2004 - p321(1) [51-500]
Mistress of Dragons
　　Kliatt - v38 - i6 - Nov 2004 - p26(1) [501+]

Weisbard, Eric - *This Is Pop: In Search of the Elusive at Experience Music Project*
　　Choice - v42 - i3 - Nov 2004 - p494(1) [51-500]

Weisberg, Herbert F. - *Models of Voting in Presidential Elections: The 2000 U.S. Election*
　　Pres St Q - v34 - i3 - Sept 2004 - p691(3) [501+]
　　R&R Bk N - v19 - i1 - Feb 2004 - pNA [51-500]

Weisberg, Jeffrey - *Safe Medicine for Sober People: How to Avoid Relapsing on Pain, Sleep, Cold or Any Other Medication*
　　LJ - v129 - i20 - Dec 1 2004 - p151(1) [51-500]

Weisberger, Lauren - *The Devil Wears Prada (Read by Dunne, Bernadette). Audiobook Review*
　　BL - v101 - i6 - Nov 15 2004 - p607(1) [501+]
The Devil Wears Prada
　　NYT - July 11 2004 - pBU8 [501+]

Weisbrod, Eva - *A Student's Guide to F. Scott Fitzgerald*
　　c　CH Bwatch - Jan 2005 - pNA [51-500]
　　y　Teach Lib - v32 - i1 - Oct 2004 - p51(1) [51-500]
　　y　VOYA - v27 - i5 - Dec 2004 - p420(1) [51-500]

Weise, Donald - *Fresh Men: New Voices in Gay Fiction*
　　PW - v251 - i46 - Nov 15 2004 - p41(1) [51-500]

Weiser, Benjamin - *A Secret Life: The Polish Officer, His Covert Mission, and the Price He Paid to Save His Country*
　　Am Spect - v37 - i3 - April 2004 - p58(3) [501+]
　　TLS - i5283 - July 2 2004 - p24(1) [501+]

Weiser, Brian - *Charles II and the Politics of Access*
　　HER - v119 - i483 - Sept 2004 - p1058(1) [501+]
　　HER - v119 - i483 - Sept 2004 - p1058(2) [501+]

Weisgerber, Jean - *La Muse des jardins: Jardins de l'Europe litteraire*
　　Ren Q - v57 - i3 - Fall 2004 - p1087(2) [501+]

Weisgrau, Richard - *The Real Business of Photography*
　　PetPho - v33 - i11 - March 2005 - p22(1) [501+]
　　R&R Bk N - v19 - i4 - Nov 2004 - p249(1) [501+]

Weishampel, David B. - *Dinosaur Papers, 1676-1906*
　　SciTech - v28 - i1 - March 2004 - p59(1) [51-500]

Weisl, Angela Jane - *The Persistence of Medievalism: Narrative Adventures in Contemporary Cultures*
　　Med R - July 2004 - pNA [501+]

Weisman, Brent Richard - *Pioneer in Space and Time: John Mann Goggin and the Development of Florida Archaeology*
　　JSH - v71 - i1 - Feb 2005 - p225(2) [501+]

Weisman, Steve - *50 Ways To Protect Your Identity and Your Credit*
　　LJ - v129 - i19 - Nov 15 2004 - p74(1) [501+]

Weiss, Brad - *Producing African Futures: Ritual and Reproduction in a Neoliberal Age*
　　R&R Bk N - v19 - i4 - Nov 2004 - p16(1) [51-500]
Sacred Trees, Bitter Harvests: Globalizing Coffee in Northwest Tanzania
　　Choice - v41 - i7 - March 2004 - p1348(1) [501+]

Weiss, Daniel H. - *France and the Holy Land: Frankish Culture at the End of the Crusades*
　　CHR - v90 - i4 - Oct 2004 - p767(3) [501+]
　　HRNB - v33 - i1 - Fall 2004 - p32(2) [501+]
　　R&R Bk N - v19 - i3 - August 2004 - p31(1) [51-500]

Weiss, Donald H. - *Fair, Square, and Legal: Safe Hiring, Managing and Firing Practices to Keep You & Your Company Out of Court, 4th Ed.*
　　Bwatch - Feb 2005 - pNA [501+]
　　R&R Bk N - v19 - i3 - August 2004 - p200(1) [1-50]

Weiss, Doris - *Social Exclusion: An Approach to the Australian Case*
　　R&R Bk N - v19 - i2 - May 2004 - p132 [51-500]

Weiss, Ellen - *Twins Go To Bed (Illus. by Williams, Sanr)*
　　c　SLJ - v50 - i8 - August 2004 - p103(1) [51-500]
Twins Have A Fight (Illus. by Williams, Sanr)
　　c　SLJ - v50 - i8 - August 2004 - p103(1) [51-500]

Weiss, Gary R. - *Born to Steal: A Life Inside the Wall Street Mafia*
　　R&R Bk N - v19 - i3 - August 2004 - p138(1) [51-500]

Weiss, Herold - *A Day of Gladness: The Sabbath among Jews and Christians in Antiquity*
　　JR - v84 - i3 - July 2004 - p490(2) [501+]

Weiss, Idit - *Professional Ideologies and Preferences in Social Work: A Global Study*
　　Choice - v42 - i1 - Sept 2004 - p146(2) [501+]

Weiss, Jeffrey - *Picasso: The Cubist Portraits of Fernande Olivier*
　　Art Bull - v86 - i3 - Sept 2004 - p614(7) [501+]

Weiss, Jim - *Abraham Lincoln and the Heart of America. Audiobook Review*
　　c　CH Bwatch - Feb 2005 - pNA [51-500]
Abraham Lincoln and the Heart of America
　　c　PW - v251 - i45 - Nov 8 2004 - p25(1) [501+]
Famously Funny!. Audiobook Review
　　c　CH Bwatch - Feb 2005 - pNA [51-500]

Weiss, Jodi - *145 Things to be When you Grow up*
　　y　Kliatt - v38 - i5 - Sept 2004 - p44(2) [51-500]

Weiss, Kenneth M. - *Genetics and the Logic of Evolution*
　　E-Streams - August 2004 - pNA [501+]
　　QRB - v79 - i4 - Dec 2004 - p420(1) [501+]
　　SciTech - v28 - i1 - March 2004 - p62(1) [51-500]

Weiss, Meira - *The Chosen Body: The Politics of the Body in Israeli Society*
　　CS - v33 - i2 - March 2004 - p205-206 [501+]

Weiss, Paul - *Surrogates*
　　RM - v58 - i2 - Dec 2004 - p473(2) [501+]

Weiss, Philip - *American Taboo: A Murder in the Peace Corps*
　　Nation - v279 - i3 - July 19 2004 - p36 [501+]
　　NYTBR - July 4 2004 - p18 [501+]

Weiss, Roslyn - *Virtue in the Cave: Moral Inquiry in Plato's Meno*
　　Class R - v53 - i2 - Nov 2003 - p299-301 [501+]

Weiss, Timothy - *Translating Orients: Between Ideology and Utopia*
　　Choice - v42 - i3 - Nov 2004 - p479(1) [1-50]

Weissberger, Barbara - *Isabel Rules: Constructing Queenship, Wielding Power*
　　Biomag - v27 - i4 - Fall 2004 - p851(3) [501+]

Weissbort, Daniel - *Iraqi Poetry Today*
　　Choice - v42 - i1 - Sept 2004 - p96(1) [501+]

Weissbrod, Lilly - *Israeli Identity: In Search of a Successor to the Pioneer, Tsabar and Settler*
　　MEQ - v11 - i3 - Summer 2004 - p88(1) [501+]

Weissman, David - *Lost Souls: The Philosophical Origins of a Cultural Dilemma*
　　RM - v58 - i2 - Dec 2004 - p475(2) [501+]

Weissman, Fabrice - *In the Shadow of "Just Wars": Violence, Politics and Humanitarian Action*
　　JPR - v41 - i5 - Sept 2004 - p650-650 [501+]
　　LJ - v129 - i13 - August 2004 - p100(1) [501+]

Weissman, Gary - *Fantasies of Witnessing: Postwar Efforts to Experience the Holocaust*
　　LJ - v129 - i13 - August 2004 - p97(1) [501+]

Weissmark, Mona Sue - *Justice Matters: Legacies of the Holocaust and World War II*
　　Choice - v42 - i1 - Sept 2004 - p147(1) [501+]

Weisstein, Eric W. - *Featured Review: CRC Concise Encyclopedia of Mathematics. Second Edition*
　　SIAM Rev - v46 - i2 - June 2004 - p349-354 [501+]

Weiten, Wayne - *Psychology: Themes and Variations, Briefer Version, 6th ed.*
　　SciTech - v28 - i3 - Sept 2004 - p1(1) [501+]

Weithman, Paul J. - *Religion and the Obligations of Citizenship*
　　Soc - v41 - i3 - March-April 2004 - p75(5) [501+]

Weitsman, Patricia A. - *Dangerous Alliances: Proponents of Peace, Weapons of War*
　　J Mil H - v68 - i4 - Oct 2004 - p1271-1272 [501+]
　　PSQ - v119 - i3 - Fall 2004 - p540(2) [501+]

Weitz, Eric D. - *A Century of Genocide: Utopias of Race and Nation*
　　J Ch St - v46 - i3 - Summer 2004 - p660(2) [501+]
　　JMH - v77 - i1 - March 2005 - p171(2) [51-500]

Weitz, Jay - *Cataloger's Judgment: Music Cataloging Questions and Answers from the Music OCLC Users Group Newsletter*
　　R&R Bk N - v19 - i1 - Feb 2004 - p194(1) [51-500]
　　R&USQ - v44 - i1 - Fall 2004 - p96(2) [501+]

Weitz, Paul - *In Good Company*
　　LJ - v130 - i3 - Feb 15 2005 - p133(1) [51-500]

Weitzman, David - *Subway for New York*
　　c　BW - v34 - i31 - August 1 2004 - p11(1) [51-500]

Weitzman, Martin L. - *Income, Wealth, and the Maximum Principle*
　　JEL - v41 - i4 - Dec 2003 - p1335(1) [501+]

Weitzstein, Michael Eugene - *Microeconomic Theory: Conepts at Connections*
　　R&R Bk N - v19 - i3 - August 2004 - p94(1) [51-500]

Weizer, Paul I. - *How to Please the Court: A Moot Court Handbook*
　　Law&PolBR - Nov 2004 - p852(2) [501+]
　　R&R Bk N - v19 - i3 - August 2004 - p196(1) [1-50]

Wendlandt, Lisa - *Knowing Freedom: Epicurean Philosophy Beyond Atomism and the Swerve*
    RM - v58 - i1 - Sept 2004 - p238(2) [501+]

Wendt, Albert - *Whetu Moana: Contemporary Polynesian Poems in English*
    WLT - v78 - i3-4 - Sept-Dec 2004 - p89(2) [501+]

Wener, Louise - *Goodnight Steve McQueen*
    BL - v101 - i9-10 - Jan 1 2005 - p824(1) [1-50]
    KR - v73 - i1 - Jan 1 2005 - p21(1) [51-500]
    LJ - v130 - i1 - Jan 1 2005 - p101(1) [51-500]
    PW - v252 - i7 - Feb 14 2005 - p55(1) [51-500]
The Perfect Play
  y SLJ - v50 - i7 - July 2004 - p132(1) [51-500]

Wenger, Brahm - *Dewey Doo-It*
  c CH Bwatch - v14 - i8 - August 2004 - p6(1) [51-500]

Wenger, Jennifer - *Teen Knitting Club: Chill Out and Knit*
    BL - v101 - i8 - Dec 15 2004 - p748(1) [501+]
    CH Bwatch - Feb 2005 - pNA [51-500]
    SLJ - v51 - i2 - Feb 2005 - p154(1) [51-500]

Wenham, David - *Paul and Jesus: The True Story*
    TLS - i5264 - Feb 20 2004 - p32-32 [501+]

Weninger, Brigitte - *A Child Is a Child (Illus. by Tharlet, Eve)*
    KR - v72 - i20 - Oct 15 2004 - p1015(1) [51-500]
  c SLJ - v51 - i1 - Jan 2005 - p98(2) [51-500]
Davy in The Middle (Illus. by Tharlet, Eve)
  c CH Bwatch - v14 - i9 - Sept 2004 - p2(1) [51-500]
  c SLJ - v50 - i8 - August 2004 - p103(1) [51-500]
Good Bread -- A Book of Thanks
  c Sch Lib - v52 - i3 - Autumn 2004 - p134(1) [501+]
The Magic Crystal (Illus. by Ingpen, Robert)
  c BL - v101 - i5 - Nov 1 2004 - p494(1) [51-500]
  c BW - v34 - i39 - Sept 26 2004 - p11(1) [501+]
  c SLJ - v51 - i1 - Jan 2005 - p100(1) [51-500]
Miko: "No Bath! No Way!" (Illus. by Roehe, Stephanie)
    KR - v73 - i3 - Feb 1 2005 - p182(1) [51-500]

Wenk, Hans-Rudolf - *Minerals: Their Construction and Origin*
    Choice - v42 - i4 - Dec 2004 - p693(1) [1-50]

Wensky, Nora - *Secondary Stress in English Words*
    R&R Bk N - v19 - i4 - Nov 2004 - p213(1) [501+]

Wensveen, John G. - *Wheels Up: Airlines Business Plan Development*
    R&R Bk N - v19 - i2 - May 2004 - p109(1) [51-500]

Wente, Margaret - *An Accidental Canadian: Reflections On My Home and (Not) Native Land*
    Globe & Mail - Oct 23 2004 - pD16 [501+]

Wentworth, Nancy - *Integrating Information Technology into the Teacher Education Curriculum: Process and Products of Charge*
    Cur R - v44 - i6 - Feb 2005 - p12(1) [501+]

Wentzel, Gregor - *Quantum Theory of Fields*
    SciTech - v28 - i1 - March 2004 - p47(1) [51-500]

Wenzel, Amy - *Cognitive Methods and Their Application to Clinical Research*
    SciTech - v28 - i4 - Dec 2004 - p96(1) [51-500]

Wenzel, Gregory - *Feathered Dinosaurs of China*
  c LibMed - v23 - i3 - Nov-Dec 2004 - p88(1) [51-500]
  c SB - v40 - i5 - Sept-Oct 2004 - p220(2) [51-500]
Giant Dinosaurs of the Jurassic (Illus. by Wenzel, Gregory)
  c BL - v101 - i3 - Oct 1 2004 - p328(1) [51-500]
  c PW - v251 - i31 - August 2 2004 - p73(1) [51-500]
  c SLJ - v50 - i9 - Sept 2004 - p194(1) [51-500]

Werell, Kenneth P. - *Chasing the Silver Bullet: U.S Air Force Weapons Development from Vietnam to Desert Storm*
    T&C - v45 - i3 - July 2004 - p630-631 [501+]

Wergin, Jon F. - *Departments That Work: Building and Sustaining Cultures of Excellence in Academic Programs*
    R&R Bk N - v19 - i1 - Feb 2004 - p186(1) [501+]

Werin, Lars - *Economic Behavior and Legal Institutions: An Introductory Survey*
    JEL - v41 - i4 - Dec 2003 - p1389(2) [501+]

Werlin, Nancy - *Double Helix: A Novel*
  y SLJ - v50 - i10 - Oct 2004 - pS68(1) [501+]
Double Helix (Read by Shina, Scott). Audiobook Review
  y Kliatt - v38 - i5 - Sept 2004 - p58(2) [51-500]
  y SLJ - v50 - i8 - August 2004 - p77(1) [51-500]
Double Helix
  y BL - v101 - i9-10 - Jan 1 2005 - p773(1) [51-500]

Wermuth, Laurie - *Global Inequality and Human Needs: Health and Illness in an Increasingly Unequal World*
    CS - v33 - i1 - Jan 2004 - p105-106 [501+]

Werner, C.L. - *Blood of the Dragon*
    ChrSFF&H - v26 - i10 - Oct 2004 - p27(1) [51-500]

Werner, Craig - *Higher Ground: Stevie Wonder, Aretha Franklin, Curtis Mayfield, and the Rise and Fall of American Soul*
    BW - v34 - i12 - March 21 2004 - p8(1) [501+]
    Globe & Mail - July 10 2004 - pD10 [501+]
    Notes - v61 - i3 - March 2005 - p752(3) [501+]

Werner, Heinz - *Comparative Psychology of Mental Development*
    SciTech - v28 - i4 - Dec 2004 - p2(1) [1-50]

Werner, Jayne - *Gender, Household, State: doi moi in Viet Nam*
    Pac A - v77 - i2 - Summer 2004 - p370(2) [501+]

Werner, Richard A. - *Princes of the Yen: Japan's Central Bankers and the Transformation of the Economy*
    HNet - Dec 2004 - pNA [501+]
    Pac A - v77 - i2 - Summer 2004 - p333(2) [501+]

Werner, Sarah - *Shakespeare and Feminist Performance: Ideology On Stage*
    Theat J - v56 - i4 - Dec 2004 - p714-715 [501+]

Werner, Stephen - *The Comic Philosophers: Montesquieu, Voltaire, Diderot, Sade*
    FS - v58 - i1 - Jan 2004 - p109(2) [501+]

Werner, Winfried - *Fundamentaltheologie bei Karl Rahner: Denkwege und Paradigmen*
    Theol St - v65 - i3 - Sept 2004 - p652(3) [501+]

Werness, Hope B. - *The Continuum Encyclopedia of Animal Symbolism in Art*
    Choice - v42 - i1 - Sept 2004 - p66(1) [501+]
    R&R Bk N - v19 - i3 - August 2004 - p85(1) [51-500]

Werrell, Kenneth P. - *Chasing the Silver Bullet: U.S. Air Force Weapons Development from Vietnam to Desert Storm*
    J Mil H - v68 - i3 - July 2004 - p1015-1016 [501+]

Werstch, James V. - *The Stalin-Kaganovich Correspondence, 1931-36*
    Slav R - v63 - i3 - Fall 2004 - p665-665 [501+]

Wert, Jeffry D. - *The Sword of Lincoln: The Army of the Potomac*
    KR - v73 - i3 - Feb 1 2005 - p172(1) [501+]
    PW - v252 - i7 - Feb 14 2005 - p64(1) [51-500]

Werth, Margaret - *The Joy of Life: The Idyllic in French Art, circa 1900*
    FS - v58 - i1 - Jan 2004 - p128(2) [501+]

Werth, Paul W. - *At the Margins of Orthodoxy: Mission, Governance, and Confessional Politics in Russia's Volga-Kama Region, 1827-1905.*
    JMH - v77 - i1 - March 2005 - p248(4) [501+]
    Russ Rev - v63 - i3 - July 2004 - pNA [501+]

Wertheim, Albert - *Staging the War: American Drama and World War II*
    Choice - v42 - i2 - Oct 2004 - p297(1) [501+]

Wertheim, L. Jon - *Transition Game: How Hoosiers Went Hip-Hop*
    PW - v252 - i5 - Jan 31 2005 - p58(1) [51-500]
Venus Envy
    BL - v101 - i1 - Sept 1 2004 - p53(1) [51-500]

Wertheimer, Alan - *Consent to Sexual Relations*
    Ethics - v115 - i1 - Oct 2004 - p178(6) [501+]
    PSQ - v119 - i2 - Summer 2004 - p385(3) [501+]

Wertheimer, Albert I. - *International Drug Regulatory Mechanisms*
    SciTech - v28 - i4 - Dec 2004 - p80(1) [51-500]

Wertheimer, Elaine C. - *Honor, Love, and Religion in the Theater Before Lope de Vega*
    Ren Q - v57 - i3 - Fall 2004 - p1009(2) [501+]

Wertheimer, Molly Meijer - *Inventing a Voice: The Rhetoric of American First Ladies of the Twentieth Century*
    Choice - v42 - i1 - Sept 2004 - p94(1) [501+]
    R&R Bk N - v19 - i3 - August 2004 - p63(1) [51-500]

Wertkin, Gerard C. - *Encyclopedia of American Folk Art*
    Choice - v41 - i11-12 - July-August 2004 - p2014(3) [501+]
    JouAmCul - v27 - i4 - Dec 2004 - p442(2) [501+]
    R&USQ - v44 - i1 - Fall 2004 - p82(2) [501+]

Wertsch, James V. - *Voices of Collective Remembering*
    CS - v33 - i1 - Jan 2004 - p57-58 [501+]
    JMH - v76 - i3 - Sept 2004 - p743(2) [501+]
    Slav R - v63 - i3 - Fall 2004 - p665-667 [501+]

Weschler, Lawrence - *Mr. Wilson's Cabinet of Wonder*
    Ent W - i785 - Sept 24 2004 - p112 [51-500]
Vermeer in Bosnia: A Reader
    BIC - v33 - i6 - Nov 2004 - p16(1) [501+]
    BL - v100 - i21 - July 2004 - p1809(1) [1-50]
    BW - v34 - i38 - Sept 19 2004 - p11(1) [50+]
    Ent W - i773 - July 9 2004 - p95 [501+]
    Globe & Mail - August 7 2004 - pD3 [501+]
    Globe & Mail - Nov 27 2004 - pD3 [501+]

Wescoat, James L., Jr. - *Water for Life*
    TimHES - v0 - i1656 - Sept 3 2004 - p30(1) [501+]

Wesley, Crichlow - *Buller Men and Batty Bwoys: Hidden Men in Toronto and Halifax Black Communities*
    R&R Bk N - v19 - i2 - May 2004 - p133 [51-500]

Wesley, Marilyn C. - *Violent Adventure: Contemporary Fiction by American Men*
    Choice - v41 - i7 - March 2004 - p1300(1) [501+]
    R&R Bk N - v19 - i1 - Feb 2004 - p243(1) [51-500]

Wesley, Valerie Wilson - *Dying in the Dark: A Tamara Hayle Mystery*
  y BL - v101 - i1 - Sept 1 2004 - p70(1) [51-500]
    Black Iss - v7 - i2 - March-April 2005 - p48(1) [51-500]
How to Fish for Trouble (Illus. by Roos, Maryn)
  c Black Iss - v6 - i4 - July-August 2004 - p60(1) [51-500]
  c SLJ - v50 - i10 - Oct 2004 - p135(2) [51-500]

Wessel, James K. - *Handbook of Advanced Materials: Enabling New Designs*
    E-Streams - Nov 2004 - pNA [501+]
    SciTech - v28 - i3 - Sept 2004 - p138(1) [51-500]

Wesseling, H.L. - *The European Colonial Empires, 1815-1919*
    R&R Bk N - v19 - i4 - Nov 2004 - p31(1) [51-500]

Wessells, John - *Conversations with the Voiceless: Finding God's Love in Life's Hardest Questions*
    Ch Today - v49 - i1 - Jan 2005 - p70(1) [51-500]
    PW - v251 - i50 - Dec 13 2004 - p62(2) [51-500]

Wesselman, Hank - *Little Ruth Reddingford and the Wolf*
  c CH Bwatch - Feb 2005 - pNA [51-500]

Wessex Institute of Technology (UK) - *Computational Finance and Its Applications: Proceedings*
    R&R Bk N - v19 - i4 - Nov 2004 - p115(1) [51-500]

Wessler, Marlis - *South of the Border*
    Globe & Mail - Jan 1 2005 - pD12 [501+]

Wesson, Andrea - *Evangeline Mudd and the Golden Haired Apes of the Ikkinasti Jungle*
    LibMed - v22 - i7 - April-May 2004 - p58(1) [501+]

Wesson, Marianne - *Chilling Effect*
    LJ - v129 - i14 - Sept 1 2004 - p122(1) [51-500]
    PW - v251 - i32 - August 9 2004 - p235(1) [51-500]

West, Anthony James - *The Shakespeare First Folio: The History of the Book, vol. 2*
    TLS - i5289 - August 13 2004 - p11(1) [501+]

West, Bill - *Garagenous Zone: Innovative Ideas for the Garage*
    BL - v101 - i2 - Sept 15 2004 - p192(1) [51-500]

West, Bruce J. - *Biodynamics: Why the Wirewalker Doesn't Fall*
    E-Streams - June 2004 - pNA [501+]
    QRB - v79 - i3 - Sept 2004 - p337(1) [501+]
    SciTech - v28 - i1 - March 2004 - p63(1) [51-500]

West, Charles G. - *Evil Breed*
    Roundup M - v11 - i6 - August 2004 - p31(1) [501+]

West, Colin - *Moose and Mouse*
  c SLJ - v50 - i8 - August 2004 - p86(1) [51-500]

West, Cornel - *Democracy Matters: Winning the Fight against Imperialism*
    BL - v101 - i1 - Sept 1 2004 - p31(1) [51-500]
    Black Iss - v6 - i5 - Sept-Oct 2004 - p45(1) [51-500]
    LJ - v129 - i14 - Sept 1 2004 - p172(1) [51-500]
    NYTBR - Sept 12 2004 - p9 [501+]

West, David A. - *Fritz Muller: A Naturalist in Brazil*
    TLS - i5265 - Feb 27 2004 - p28-28 [501+]

West-Duran, Alan - *Latino and Latina Writers*
    R&R Bk N - v19 - i1 - Feb 2004 - p241(1) [501+]
    R&USQ - v44 - i1 - Fall 2004 - p91(2) [501+]

West, Harry G. - *Transparency and Conspiracy: Ethnographies of Suspicion in the New World Order*
    JRAI - v10 - i4 - Dec 2004 - p935(1) [501+]

West, Henry R. - *An Introduction to Mill's Utilitarian Ethics*
    Choice - v42 - i2 - Oct 2004 - p308(1) [501+]

West, James L.W. - *The Perfect Hour: The Romance of F. Scott Fitzgerald and Ginevra King, His First Love*
  y BL - v101 - i9-10 - Jan 1 2005 - p802(2) [51-500]
    Ent W - i807 - Feb 18 2005 - p83 [51-500]
    KR - v72 - i23 - Dec 1 2004 - p1142(1) [501+]
    LJ - v130 - i3 - Feb 15 2005 - p130(1) [51-500]
    PW - v251 - i50 - Dec 13 2004 - p54(1) [51-500]

West, Jim - *The Dog Who Sang at the Opera (Illus. by Oller, Erika)*
  c BL - v101 - i9-10 - Jan 1 2005 - p876(1) [51-500]
      KR - v72 - i20 - Oct 15 2004 - p1015(1) [51-500]
  c Sch Lib - v52 - i4 - Winter 2004 - p191(1) [51-500]
  c SLJ - v51 - i2 - Feb 2005 - p112(1) [51-500]

West, John B. - *Respiratory Physiology: The Essentials, 7th ed*
      SciTech - v28 - i3 - Sept 2004 - p68(1) [51-500]

West, Joseph A. - *Donovan's Dove*
      Roundup M - v12 - i3 - Feb 2005 - p29(1) [51-500]

    Johnny Blue and the Texas Rangers
      Roundup M - v12 - i3 - Feb 2005 - p30(1) [51-500]

West, Kathleene - *The Summer of the Sub-Comandante*
      PSQ - v78 - i3 - Fall 2004 - p174(4) [501+]

West, Kim - *Good Night, Sleep Tight: The Sleep Lady's Gentle Guide to Helping Your Child Go to Sleep, Stay Asleep, and Wake Up Happy*
      LJ - v130 - i3 - Feb 15 2005 - p151(4) [501+]

West, Lorane A. - *Color: Latino Voices in the Pacific Northwest*
      R&R Bk N - v19 - i4 - Nov 2004 - p68(1) [1-50]

West, M.L. - *Greek Epic Fragments from the Seventh to the Fifth Centuries B.C.*
      Class R - v54 - i2 - Nov 2004 - p283-286 [501+]
    Homeric Hymns, Homeric Apocrypha, Lives of Homer
      Class R - v54 - i2 - Nov 2004 - p283-286 [501+]

West, Mark I. - *A Children's Literature Tour of Great Britain*
      R&R Bk N - v19 - i1 - Feb 2004 - p233(1) [51-500]

West, Michael A. - *Building Team-Based Working: A Practical Guide to Organizational Transformation*
      Per Psy - v57 - i4 - Winter 2004 - p1048(5) [501+]
      R&R Bk N - v19 - i1 - Feb 2004 - p93(1) [51-500]
    Motivate Teams, Maximize Success: Effective Strategies for Realizing Your Goals
      HR Mag - v50 - i1 - Jan 2005 - p104(2) [501+]

West, Nathanael - *The Dream Life of Balso*
      LJ - v129 - i13 - August 2004 - p131(1) [51 500]

West, Patrick - *Conspicuous Compassion: Why Sometimes It Really is Cruel to be Kind*
      TLS - i5300 - Oct 29 2004 - p30(1) [51-500]

West, Paul - *The Immensity of the Here and Now: A Novel of 9.11*
      ABR - v25 - i5 - July-August 2004 - p8(1) [501+]
    The Very Rich Hours of Count von Stauffenberg
      HM - v309 - i1850 - July 2004 - p89(5) [501+]

West, Philip - *Henry Vaughan's Silex Scintillans: Scripture Uses*
      RES - v55 - i219 - April 2004 - p275-276 [501+]

West, Ray - *Dreamweaver MX 2004: The Complete Reference. 2d ed.*
      LJ - v129 - i12 - July 2004 - p112(1) [501+]

West, Rebecca, Dame - *Survivors in Mexico*
      ELT - v48 - i2 - Spring 2005 - p71(5) [501+]

West, Robert - *Smoking Cessation*
      SciTech - v28 - i4 - Dec 2004 - p101(1) [51-500]

West, Robin L. - *Re-Imagining Justice: Progressive Interpretations of Formal Equality, Rights, and the Rule of Law*
      Law&PolBR - July 2004 - p520(5) [501+]

West, Russell - *Subverting Masculinity: Hegemonic and Alternative Versions of Masculinity in Contemporary Culture*
      RES - v55 - i218 - Feb 2004 - p147-149 [501+]

West-Sooby, John - *Consuming Culture: The Arts of the French Table*
      R&R Bk N - v19 - i4 - Nov 2004 - p250(1) [501+]

West, Thomas G. - *Thinking Like Einstein: Returning to Our Visual Roots with the Emerging Revolution in Computer Information Visualization*
      LJ - v129 - i16 - Oct 1 2004 - p103(1) [51-500]
      R&R Bk N - v20 - i1 - Feb 2005 - p7(1) [51-500]

West, Thomas R. - *Signs of Struggle: The Rhetorical Politics of Cultural Difference*
      Col Lit - v31 - i4 - Fall 2004 - p181(7) [501+]

West Virginia Auditor's Office - *Sims Index to Land Grants in West Virginia*
      EFHM - v58 - i3 - May-June 2004 - p61(1) [51-500]

West, William N. - *Theatres and Encyclopedias in Early Modern Europe*
      Ren Q - v57 - i3 - Fall 2004 - p1159(2) [501+]
      Shakes Q - v55 - i1 - Spring 2004 - p100-102 [501+]
      Six Ct J - v35 - i3 - Fall 2004 - p865-866 [501+]

Westad, Odd Arne - *Decisive Encounters: The Chinese Civil War, 1946-1950*
      AHR - v109 - i3 - June 2004 - p883(1) [501+]
      Ch Rev Int - v10 - i2 - Fall 2003 - p470(3) [501+]
      Pac A - v77 - i2 - Summer 2004 - p324(2) [501+]

Westall, Robert - *Ghost Abbey*
  y Sch Lib - v52 - i4 - Winter 2004 - p214(1) [51-500]
    The Machine Gunners
  c WLT - v79 - i1 - Jan-April 2005 - p69(4) [501+]

Westbrook, Michael H. - *Electric and Hybrid-Electric Car*
      SciTech - v28 - i1 - March 2004 - p167(1) [51-500]

Westbrook, Raymond - *A History of Ancient Near Eastern Law, Vols. 1-2*
      R&R Bk N - v19 - i1 - Feb 2004 - pNA [51-500]

Westbrook, Vivienne - *Long Travail and Great Paynes: A Politics of Reformation Revision*
      CH - v73 - i3 - Sept 2004 - p692(2) [51-500]

Westby, Jody R. - *International Guide to Cyber Security*
      SciTech - v28 - i4 - Dec 2004 - p152(1) [51-500]

Westcott, Nadine Bernard - *Thanksgiving in the Barn*
  c PW - v251 - i39 - Sept 27 2004 - p59(1) [51-500]

Westcott, Patsy - *Diet and Nutrition*
      SB - v40 - i4 - July-August 2004 - p152(1) [51-500]

Weste, Neil H.E. - *CMOS VLSI Design: A Circuits and Systems Perspective, 3rd Ed.*
      SciTech - v28 - i4 - Dec 2004 - p158(1) [51-500]

Westen, Peter - *The Logic of Consent: The Diversity and Deceptiveness of Consent as a Defense to Criminal Conduct*
      R&R Bk N - v19 - i4 - Nov 2004 - p173(1) [501+]

Westerfeld, Scott - *The Killing of Worlds: Book Two of Succession*
      Analog - v124 - i5 - May 2004 - p132(142) [501+]
    The Secret Hour
  c LibMed - v23 - i3 - Nov-Dec 2004 - p73(2) [51-500]
    So Yesterday
  y BL - v101 - i2 - Sept 15 2004 - p235(1) [51-500]
  y CCB-B - v58 - i2 - Oct 2004 - p57(2) [501+]
  y HB - v81 - i1 - Jan-Feb 2005 - p101(2) [51-500]
  y Kliatt - v38 - i5 - Sept 2004 - p17(2) [51-500]
  c KR - v72 - i15 - August 1 2004 - p750(1) [51-500]
  y PW - v251 - i40 - Oct 4 2004 - p89(1) [51-500]
  y SLJ - v50 - i10 - Oct 2004 - p182(1) [51-500]
    Touching Darkness
  c KR - v73 - i3 - Feb 1 2005 - p182(1) [51-500]
    Uglies
  y CCB-B - v58 - i6 - Feb 2005 - p269(2) [51-500]
  y Kliatt - v39 - i2 - March 2005 - p29(1) [51-500]
  y KR - v73 - i4 - Feb 15 2005 - p237(1) [51-500]

Westerhoff, Caroline A. - *Good Fences: The Boundaries of Hospitality*
      Ch Today - v48 - i12 - Dec 2004 - p64(2) [501+]

Westerhoff, Gary P. - *The Evolving Water Utility: Pathways to Higher Performance*
      R&R Bk N - v19 - i3 - August 2004 - p115(1) [51-500]

Westerholm, Peter - *Practical Ethics in Occupational Health*
      SciTech - v28 - i3 - Sept 2004 - p109(1) [51-500]

Westerholm, Stephen - *Perspectives Old and New on Paul: The "Lutheran" Paul and His Critics*
      Choice - v42 - i3 - Nov 2004 - p502(2) [51-500]
      Intpr - v58 - i4 - Oct 2004 - p428(2) [501+]
    Understanding Paul, 2nd ed.
      Intpr - v58 - i3 - July 2004 - p276(1) [51-500]

Westerink, L.G. - *Damascius: Commentaire du Parmenide de Platon*
      Class R - v54 - i2 - Nov 2004 - p353(2) [501+]

Westerlund, John S. - *Arizona's War Town: Flagstaff, Navajo Ordnance Depot, and World War II*
      J Mil H - v68 - i3 - July 2004 - p996-997 [501+]

Westfahl, Gary - *No Cure for the Future: Disease and Medicine in Science Fiction and Fantasy*
      SFS - v31 - i1 - March 2004 - p156-161 [501+]

Westhues, Anne - *Canadian Social Policy: Issues and Perspectives, 3rd Ed.*
      CBRA - Annual 2003 - p374(1) [51-500]

Westlake, Donald E. - *Anarchaos*
      BL - v101 - i3 - Oct 1 2004 - p319(1) [51-500]
      LJ - v129 - i12 - July 2004 - p127(1) [1-50]
    Nobody Runs Forever
      BL - v101 - i1 - Sept 1 2004 - p7(1) [51-500]
      KR - v72 - i18 - Sept 15 2004 - p895(1) [51-500]
      LJ - v129 - i18 - Nov 1 2004 - p63(1) [51-500]
      PW - v251 - i41 - Oct 11 2004 - p59(1) [51-500]

    The Road to Ruin
      BooChiTr - April 18 2004 - p6(1) [501+]
      BW - v34 - i37 - Sept 12 2004 - p7(1) [51-500]
      DroRevMy - v24 - i3 - May-June 2004 - p4(2) [501+]
    Thieves' Dozen
      BooChiTr - April 18 2004 - p6(1) [501+]
      DroRevMy - v24 - i3 - May-June 2004 - p4(2) [501+]
    Watch Your Back! (Read by Dufris, William). Audiobook Review
      KR - v73 - i5 - March 1 2005 - p265(1) [51-500]
      LJ - v129 - i20 - Dec 1 2004 - p96(1) [51-500]
    Watch Your Back
      PW - v252 - i11 - March 14 2005 - p49(1) [51-500]

Westland, Stephen - *Computational Colour Science Using MATLAB*
      SciTech - v28 - i3 - Sept 2004 - p48(1) [1-50]

Westley, Frances R. - *Experiments in Consilience: Integrating Social and Science Responses to Save Endangered Species*
      SciTech - v28 - i1 - March 2004 - p68(1) [51-500]

Westmoreland, Susan - *Good Housekeeping Great American Classics Cookbook*
      BL - v101 - i5 - Nov 1 2004 - p453(1) [51-500]

Westney, William - *The Perfect Wrong Note: Learning to Trust Your Musical Self*
      M Ed J - v91 - i1 - Sept 2004 - p63(2) [501+]
      R&R Bk N - v19 - i1 - Feb 2004 - p197(1) [51-500]

Weston, Carol - *For Girls Only: Wise Words, Good Advice*
  y BL - v101 - i5 - Nov 1 2004 - p474(1) [51-500]
    Melanie in Manhattan
      KR - v73 - i1 - Jan 1 2005 - p59(1) [51-500]
  c SLJ - v51 - i1 - Jan 2005 - p138(1) [51-500]

Weston, Carrie - *Lucky Socks (Illus. by Middleton, Charlotte)*
  c RT - v57 - Oct 2003 - p170 [1-50]

Weston, Liz - *Your Credit Score: How to Fix, Improve, and Protect Your Credit for Life*
      LJ - v129 - i16 - Oct 1 2004 - p92(1) [51-500]

Weston, Martha - *Dr. Clock-sicle (Illus. by Weston, Martha)*
  c SLJ - v50 - i10 - Oct 2004 - p136(1) [51-500]

Weston, Timothy B. - *The Power of Position: Beijing University, Intellectuals, and Chinese Political Culture, 1898-1929*
      Choice - v42 - i3 - Nov 2004 - p542(1) [1-50]

Westover, Jeffery W. - *The Colonial Moment: Discoveries and Settlements in Modern American Poetry*
      Choice - v42 - i7 - March 2005 - p1232(1) [51-500]

Westwick, David T. - *Identification of Nonlinear Physiological Systems*
      SciTech - v28 - i1 - March 2004 - p71(1) [51-500]

Westwick, Peter J. - *The National Labs: Science in an American System, 1947-1974*
      AHR - v109 - i2 - April 2004 - p556(2) [501+]
      Isis - v95 - i2 - June 2004 - p324(2) [501+]
      JAH - v91 - i1 - June 2004 - p303-304 [501+]
      T&C - v45 - i2 - April 2004 - pNA [501+]

Westwood, James D. - *Medicine Meets Virtual Reality 11: NextMed, Health Horizon, Proceedings*
      SciTech - v28 - i3 - Sept 2004 - p80(1) [51-500]

Westwood, Robert - *Debating Organization: Point-Counterpoint in Organization Studies*
      CS - v33 - i4 - July 2004 - p443(2) [501+]

Wetherell, W.D. - *A Century of November*
      BL - v101 - i3 - Oct 1 2004 - p312(1) [51-500]
      PW - v251 - i42 - Oct 18 2004 - p49(1) [51-500]
      Ent W - i792 - Nov 12 2004 - p131 [51-500]

Wetscherek, Hugo - *Kafkas Letzter Freund*
      Ger Q - v77 - i4 - Fall 2004 - p511-512 [501+]

Wetsel, David - *La Spiritualite-L'Epistolaire-Le Merveilleux au Grand Siecle: Actes du 33 congres annuel de la NASSCFL*
      FS - v58 - i3 - July 2004 - p404-405 [501+]

Wetter, Bruce - *The Boy with the Lampshade on His Head*
  c CCB-B - v57 - i11 - July-August 2004 - p488(2) [501+]
  c SLJ - v50 - i8 - August 2004 - p132(1) [51-500]

Wetterhahn, Ralph - *The Last Flight of Bomber 31: Harrowing Tales of American and Japanese Pilots Who Fought in World War II's Arctic Air Campaign*
      BL - v101 - i1 - Sept 1 2004 - p44(1) [51-500]
      KR - v72 - i14 - July 15 2004 - p680(1) [501+]

Wettlaufer, Alexandra K. - *In the Mind's Eye: The Visual Impulse in Diderot, Baudelaire and Ruskin*
      R&R Bk N - v19 - i1 - Feb 2004 - p9(1) [51-500]

Wettstein, Howard - *The Magic Prism: An Essay in the Philosophy of Language*
Choice - v42 - i4 - Dec 2004 - p675(1) [1-50]

Wetzel, David - *A Duel of Giants: Bismarck, Napoleon III, and the Origins of the Franco-Prussian War*
HNet - Sept 2004 - pNA [501+]

Wetzel, Patricia J. - *Keigo in Modern Japan: Polite Language from Meiji to the Present*
Pac A - v77 - i3 - Fall 2004 - p589(2) [501+]

Wevadau, Ed - *Abstracts of Lancaster County, Pennsylvania Deed Records Including Areas now Comprising Dauphin and Lebanon Counties, 1770-1789*
EFHM - v58 - i3 - May-June 2004 - p60(1) [51-500]

Weverka, Peter - *Microsoft Office OneNote 2003 Step by Step*
SciTech - v28 - i4 - Dec 2004 - p11(1) [1-50]

Wexler, Laura - *Tender Violence: Domestic Visions in an Age of US Imperialism*
Wom HR - v13 - i2 - Summer 2004 - p324-327 [501+]

Wexler, Robert Freeman - *Circus of the Grand Design*
BL - v100 - i22 - August 2004 - p1914(1) [501+]
PW - v251 - i30 - July 26 2004 - p42(1) [501+]

Weyeneth, Robert R. - *Kapi'olani Park: A History*
Pub Hist - v26 - i1 - Wntr 2004 - p180(3) [501+]

Weygrandt Powell, Esther - *Early Ohio Tax Records: Reprinted with the Index to Early Ohio Tax Records*
EFHM - v58 - i3 - May-June 2004 - p60(1) [51-500]

Weyland, Kurt - *Learning from Foreign Models in Latin American Policy Reform*
Pers PS - v33 - i4 - Fall 2004 - p235(1) [501+]
R&R Bk N - v19 - i3 - August 2004 - p146(1) [51-500]

Weyler, Rex - *Greenpeace: An Insider's Account*
Globe & Mail - Sept 11 2004 - pD5 [501+]
New Sci - v184 - i2475 - Nov 27 2004 - p51(1) [501+]
NS - v133 - i4712 - Nov 1 2004 - p53(2) [501+]
Greenpeace: How a Group of Journalists, Ecologists and Visionaries Changed the World
BL - v101 - i4 - Oct 15 2004 - p368(1) [51-500]
KR - v72 - i17 - Sept 1 2004 - p856(1) [501+]
PW - v251 - i36 - Sept 6 2004 - p55(1) [51-500]

Weyman, Stanley John - *A Gentleman of France*
NS - v133 - i4716 - Nov 29 2004 - p51(2) [501+]

Weyn, Suzanne - *The Bar Code Tattoo*
y SLJ - v51 - i2 - Feb 2005 - p142(1) [51-500]

Weynand, Diana - *Final Cut Pro for Avid Editors: A Guide for Editors Making the Switch*
SciTech - v28 - i1 - March 2004 - p176(1) [51-500]

Weyr, Thomas - *The Setting of the Pearl: Vienna under Hitler*
KR - v72 - i24 - Dec 15 2004 - p1196(1) [501+]
LJ - v130 - i3 - Feb 15 2005 - p145(2) [51-500]
PW - v251 - i51 - Dec 20 2004 - p44(1) [51-500]

Whaley, Douglas J. - *Problems and Materials on the Sale and Lease of Goods, 4th Ed.*
R&R Bk N - v19 - i4 - Nov 2004 - p167(1) [501+]

Whaley, Preston - *Blows Like a Horn: Beat Writing, Jazz, Style and Markets in the Transformation of U.S. Culture*
Choice - v42 - i6 - Feb 2005 - p1009(1) [51-500]

Whaln, Thomas J. - *Dynasty's End: Bill Russell and the 1968-69 World Champion Boston Celtics*
R&R Bk N - v19 - i1 - Feb 2004 - p74(1) [1-50]

Whannel, Garry - *Media Sports Stars: Masculinities and Moralities*
JGS - v13 - i2 - July 2004 - p173-175 [501+]

Wharton, Calvin - *Three Songs by Hank Williams*
CBRA - Annual 2003 - p207(1) [501+]

Wharton, Edith - *The Cruise of the Vanadis*
NYRB - v51 - i17 - Nov 4 2004 - p42(2) [501+]
R&R Bk N - v19 - i3 - August 2004 - p36(1) [51-500]
The Fruit of the Tree
LJ - v129 - i19 - Nov 15 2004 - p103(1) [501+]

Wharton, Michael - *Peter Simple's Domain*
Quad - v48 - i10 - Oct 2004 - p92(3) [501+]

Wharton, Thomas - *The Logogryph: A Bibliography of Imaginary Books*
Globe & Mail - Nov 20 2004 - pD18 [501+]

What, Leslie - *Olympic Games*
Analog - v124 - i11 - Nov 2004 - p134(6) [501+]
LJ - v129 - i13 - August 2004 - p72(1) [51-500]
c MFSF - v107 - i2 - August 2004 - p35(6) [501+]

Whatley, Bruce - *Diary of a Wombat*
LibMed - v22 - i4 - Jan 2004 - p57(1) [501+]

Whayne, Susanne Santoro - *Petropolis* (Illus. by Santoro, Christopher)
c BL - v101 - i2 - Sept 15 2004 - p254(2) [501-500]
c SLJ - v50 - i12 - Dec 2004 - p124(1) [501+]

Wheal, Elizabeth-Anne - *Dictionary of the Second World War*
R&R Bk N - v19 - i3 - August 2004 - p32(1) [51-500]

Wheat, Joe Ben - *Blanket Weaving in the Southwest*
Am Craft - v64 - i1 - Feb-March 2004 - p47(1) [501+]
R&R Bk N - v19 - i4 - Nov 2004 - p54(1) [51-500]

Wheatcroft, Andrew - *Infidels: A History of the Conflict between Christendom and Islam*
BL - v101 - i3 - Oct 1 2004 - p302(1) [51-500]
BL - v101 - i9-10 - Jan 1 2005 - p767(1) [51-500]
Globe & Mail - August 14 2004 - pD8 [501+]
Globe & Mail - Nov 27 2004 - pD3 [501+]

Wheatcroft, Stephen G. - *Challenging Traditional Views of Russian History*
HNet - Sept 2004 - pNA [501+]

Wheatley, Abigail - *The Usborne Introduction to Archaeology: Internet-Linked*
c CH Bwatch - March 2005 - pNA [51-500]

Wheatley, Christopher - *Humanization of Social Life, Vol. 1*
R&R Bk N - v19 - i4 - Nov 2004 - p121(1) [51-500]

Wheatley, Denise N. - *I Wish I Never Met You*
PW - v251 - i28 - July 12 2004 - p44(1) [51-500]

Wheatley, Kim - *Romantic Periodicals and Print Culture*
R&R Bk N - v19 - i1 - Feb 2004 - p235(1) [51-500]

Wheaton, Wil - *Just A Geek*
Bwatch - Nov 2004 - pNA [51-500]
ChrSFF&H - v26 - i10 - Oct 2004 - p30(1) [51-500]

Whedon, Joss - *Astonishing X-men: Gifted*
PW - v252 - i9 - Feb 28 2005 - p44(1) [51-500]
Fray
y Teach Lib - v32 - i3 - Feb 2005 - p58(1) [1-50]
Tales of the Vampires
y BL - v101 - i9-10 - Jan 1 2005 - p847(1) [1-50]
PW - v252 - i1 - Jan 3 2005 - p38(2) [51-500]

Wheelan, Charles - *Naked Economics: Undressing the Dismal Science*
JEL - v41 - i4 - Dec 2003 - p1333(1) [501+]

Wheelan, Joseph - *Jefferson's Vendetta: The Pursuit of Aaron Burr and the Judiciary*
BL - v101 - i9-10 - Jan 1 2005 - p810(1) [1-50]
KR - v72 - i24 - Dec 15 2004 - p1196(1) [501+]
LJ - v130 - i2 - Feb 1 2005 - p101(1) [51-500]
PW - v252 - i2 - Jan 10 2005 - p47(1) [51-500]
Jefferson's War: America's First War on Terror, 1801-1805
Mar Crp G - v88 - i4 - April 2004 - p62(1) [501+]
R&R Bk N - v19 - i1 - Feb 2004 - p58(1) [51-500]

Wheelan, Susan A. - *Group Processes: A Developmental Perspective, 2nd Ed.*
R&R Bk N - v19 - i3 - August 2004 - p143(1) [51-500]

Wheeland, Craig M. - *Empowering the Vision: Community-Wide Strategic Planning in Rock Hill, South Carolina*
R&R Bk N - v19 - i3 - August 2004 - p155(1) [51-500]

Wheeler, Bonnie - *Eleanor of Aquitaine: Lord and Lady*
AHR - v109 - i4 - Oct 2004 - p1297-1298 [501+]

Wheeler, Graeme - *Sound Practice in Government Debt Management*
R&R Bk N - v19 - i3 - August 2004 - p140(1) [51-500]

Wheeler, Hoyt N. - *Workplace Justice Without Unions*
Choice - v42 - i6 - Feb 2005 - p1068(1) [51-500]
R&R Bk N - v19 - i4 - Nov 2004 - p103(1) [51-500]

Wheeler, Leigh Ann - *Against Obscenity: Reform and the Politics of Womanhood in America, 1873-1935*
R&R Bk N - v19 - i4 - Nov 2004 - p134(1) [51-500]
Choice - v42 - i5 - Jan 2005 - p919(2) [1-50]

Wheeler, Lesley - *The Poetics of Enclosure: American Women Poets from Dickinson to Dove*
TSWL - v23 - i1 - Spring 2004 - p143-144 [501+]

Wheeler, Lisa - *Bubble Gum, Bubble Gum* (Illus. by Huliska-Beith, Laura)
c CCB-B - v57 - i11 - July-August 2004 - p489(1) [501+]
Farmer Dale's Red Pickup Truck (Illus. by Bates, Ivan)
c BL - v101 - i5 - Nov 1 2004 - p494(1) [51-500]
c KR - v72 - i16 - August 15 2004 - p814(1) [51-500]
c PW - v251 - i40 - Oct 4 2004 - p86(1) [51-500]
c SLJ - v50 - i12 - Dec 2004 - p124(1) [501+]
Te Amo, Bebe, Little One (Illus. by Suarez, Maribel)
c BL - v100 - i22 - August 2004 - p1946(1) [51-500]
c BL - v101 - i3 - Oct 1 2004 - p339(1) [51-500]
Uncles and Antlers (Illus. by Floca, Brian)
c BL - v101 - i7 - Dec 1 2004 - p664(1) [51-500]
c KR - v72 - i21 - Nov 1 2004 - p1055(1) [51-500]
c PW - v251 - i39 - Sept 27 2004 - p60(1) [51-500]
Who's Afraid of Granny Wolf? (Illus. by Ansley, Frank)
c CCB-B - v58 - i1 - Sept 2004 - p44(2) [51-500]
c CH Bwatch - v14 - i9 - Sept 2004 - p5(1) [51-500]
c SLJ - v50 - i8 - August 2004 - p103(1) [51-500]

Wheeler, Richard S. - *Bounty Trail*
Roundup M - v12 - i1 - Oct 2004 - p33(1) [51-500]
An Obituary for Major Reno
PW - v251 - i49 - Dec 6 2004 - p45(1) [51-500]
Vengeance Valley
Roundup M - v12 - i3 - Feb 2005 - p30(1) [51-500]

Wheeler, Stephen M. - *The Sustainable Urban Development Reader*
NRJ - v44 - i3 - Summer 2004 - p907-916 [501+]
R&R Bk N - v19 - i3 - August 2004 - p155(1) [51-500]

Wheeler, Susan - *Ledger*
PW - v252 - i10 - March 7 2005 - p65(1) [51-500]

Wheeler, William J. - *Flying Under Fire, Volume 2: More Aviation Tales from the Second World War*
CBRA - Annual 2003 - p287(2) [51-500]

Wheeler, Winslow T. - *The Wastrals of Defense: How Congress Sabotages U.S. Security*
R&R Bk N - v19 - i4 - Nov 2004 - p120(1) [51-500]
Wastrels of Defense
Bwatch - March 2005 - pNA [51-500]

Wheelock, Arthur K., Jr. - *Gerard ter Borch*
LJ - v129 - i20 - Dec 1 2004 - p112(1) [51-500]

The Wheels on the Bus
c BL - v100 - i22 - August 2004 - p1952(1) [51-500]

Wheen, Francis - *How Mumbo-Jumbo Conquered the World*
NS - v133 - i4716 - Nov 29 2004 - p48(1) [51-500]
TLS - i5263 - Feb 13 2004 - p36-36 [501+]
Idiot Proof: Deluded Celebrities, Irrational Power Brokers, Media Morons, and the Erosion of Common Sense
R&R Bk N - v19 - i3 - August 2004 - p2(1) [1-50]

Whelan, Frederick G. - *Hume and Machiavelli: Political Realism and Liberal Thought*
R&R Bk N - v19 - i3 - August 2004 - p173(1) [501+]

Whelan, Gloria - *Burying the Sun*
c BL - v101 - i4 - Oct 15 2004 - p405(1) [51-500]
y BL - v101 - i5 - Nov 1 2004 - p496(1) [51-500]
y Kliatt - v38 - i5 - Sept 2004 - p17(2) [51-500]
c KR - v72 - i18 - Sept 15 2004 - p923(1) [51-500]
y PW - v251 - i42 - Oct 18 2004 - p66(1) [501+]
y SLJ - v50 - i11 - Nov 2004 - p156(1) [51-500]
y VOYA - v27 - i4 - Oct 2004 - p310(1) [51-500]
Chu Ju's House
c SLJ - v50 - i10 - Oct 2004 - pS37(1) [1-50]
y VOYA - v27 - i4 - Oct 2004 - p310(1) [51-500]
Friends on Freedom River
KR - v73 - i3 - Feb 1 2005 - p183(1) [51-500]
The Impossible Journey (Read by Dretzin, Julie). Audiobook Review
SLJ - v50 - i10 - Oct 2004 - pS54(1) [51-500]

Whelan, Ruth - *Toleration and Religious Identity: The Edict of Nantes and its Implications in France, Britain and Ireland*
FS - v58 - i3 - July 2004 - p403-403 [501+]

When Someone Dies: Understanding Grief
BL - v100 - i22 - August 2004 - p1952(1) [51-500]

Wherry, Timothy Lee - *Trademarks in the Digital Age*
R&R Bk N - v19 - i4 - Nov 2004 - p247(1) [501+]

Whigham, Thomas - *The Paraguayan War. Vol. 1, Causes and Early Conduct*
HAHR - v84 - i2 - May 2004 - p374(2) [501+]

Whincop, Michael J. - *From Bureaucracy to Business Enterprise: Legal and Policy Issues in the Transformation of Government Services*
    JEL - v42 - i1 - March 2004 - p288(1) [501+]
Whipperman, Bruce - *Moon Handbooks: Acapulco*
    Bwatch - Jan 2005 - pNA [51-500]
Whipple, George - *Fanfares*
    CBRA - Annual 2003 - p76(1) [51-500]
    Origins
    CBRA - Annual 2003 - p236(1) [501+]
Whipple, Laura - *A Snowflake Fell: Poems About Winter (Illus. by Huri, Hatsuki)*
    c LibMed - v22 - i4 - Jan 2004 - p70(1) [501+]
Whirlwind: A Novel
    Ent W - i789 - Oct 22 2004 - p101 [51-500]
Whisker, James B. - *Production of Military Arms in the Commonwealth of Virginia*
    R&R Bk N - v19 - i3 - August 2004 - p120(1) [51-500]
    U.S. and Confederate Arms and Armories During the American Civil War, Vol. 4
    R&R Bk N - v19 - i1 - Feb 2004 - p256(1) [51-500]
Whisman, Dale - *Friends, and Other Perishables*
    KR - v72 - i20 - Oct 15 2004 - p988(1) [51-500]
Whistler, James McNeill - *Whistler on Art: Selected Letters and Writings of James McNeill Whistler*
    TLS - i5307 - Dec 17 2004 - p30-31 [1-50]
Whiston, Susan C. - *Principles and Applications of Assessment in Counseling, 2nd Ed.*
    SciTech - v28 - i4 - Dec 2004 - p3(1) [1-50]
Whitaker, Albert Keith - *A Journey into Platonic Politics: Plato's Laws*
    R&R Bk N - v19 - i3 - August 2004 - p173(1) [501+]
Whitaker, Campbell - *The Metaphysics of Explanation: An Inquiry into the Nature and Philosophical Limits of Explanation*
    R&R Bk N - v19 - i3 - August 2004 - p7(1) [1-50]
Whitaker, Reg - *Canada and the Cold War*
    Can Hist R - v85 - i4 - Dec 2004 - p873(3) [501+]
    CBRA - Annual 2003 - p279(2) [501+]
Whitaker, Robert - *The Mapmaker's Wife: A True Tale of Love, Murder, and Survival in the Amazon*
    BL - v101 - i9-10 - Jan 1 2005 - p767(1) [51-500]
    Bwatch - Oct 2004 - pNA [51-500]
    The Mapmaker's Wife: A True Tale of Love, Murder, and Survival in the Amazon. Audiobook Review
    Globe & Mail - Jan 15 2005 - pD13 [1-50]
    The Mapmaker's Wife: A True Tale of Love, Murder, and Survival in the Amazon
    SB - v40 - i4 - July-August 2004 - p159(2) [51-500]
    SB - v40 - i6 - Nov-Dec 2004 - p242(1) [51-500]
    y SLJ - v50 - i8 - August 2004 - p148(1) [501+]
    TimHES - v0 - i1677 - Feb 4 2005 - p26(1) [501+]
    TLS - i5303 - Nov 19 2004 - p35(1) [51-500]
Whitcomb, Cynthia - *The Writer's Guide to Selling Your Screenplay: A Top-Selling Hollywood Writer Tells You How to Break Into the Business--and Stay There!*
    R&R Bk N - v19 - i4 - Nov 2004 - p224(1) [501+]
White, Alan - *Breaking Silence: The Case That Changed the Face of Human Rights*
    AM - v191 - i10 - Oct 11 2004 - p32 [501+]
White, Amanda - *Sand Sister (Illus. by Morales, Yuyi)*
    c SLJ - v50 - i10 - Oct 2004 - p136(1) [51-500]
White, Andrew - *Lancaster: A History*
    R&R Bk N - v19 - i1 - Feb 2004 - p33(1) [1-50]
White, Barbara A. - *The Beecher Sisters*
    NEQ - v77 - i2 - June 2004 - p311-315 [501+]
White, Cameron - *Mr. Nasty: A Confession*
    Globe & Mail - Oct 2 2004 - pD17 [501+]
White, Christopher - *Our Twelve Days Before Christmas*
    CBRA - Annual 2003 - p76(1) [51-500]
White, Curtis - *America's Magic Mountain*
    KR - v72 - i19 - Oct 1 2004 - p938(1) [51-500]
    LJ - v130 - i2 - Feb 1 2005 - p72(1) [51-500]
    NYTBR - Dec 26 2004 - p17 [501+]
    PW - v251 - i42 - Oct 18 2004 - p47(1) [51-500]
White, E.B. - *Charlotte's Web (Illus. by Williams, Garth)*
    c RT - v57 - Sept 2003 - p98 [1-50]
White, Edmund - *Arts and Letters*
    BW - v34 - i46 - Nov 14 2004 - p15(1) [501+]
    G&L Rev W - v12 - i1 - Jan-Feb 2005 - p44(2) [501+]
    Lam Bk Rpt - v13 - i4-5 - Nov-Dec 2004 - p27(1) [501+]
    LJ - v129 - i19 - Nov 15 2004 - p61(2) [501+]
    Fanny: A Fiction
    VQR - v80 - i2 - Spring 2004 - p260-260 [501+]
    World&I - v19 - i3 - March 2004 - p233 [501+]

Fresh Men: New Voices of Gay Fiction
    BL - v101 - i6 - Nov 15 2004 - p561(1) [51-500]
Marcel Proust
    Sew R - v112 - i2 - Spring 2004 - p294-300 [501+]
White, Eric Marshall - *Peter Shoeffer: Printer of Mainz; A Quincentenary Exhibition at Bridwell Library, 8 September - 8 December 2003*
    BSA-P - v98 - i2 - June 2004 - p229-231 [501+]
White, Evelyn C. - *Alice Walker: A Life*
    BL - v100 - i22 - August 2004 - p1891(1) [51-500]
    G&L Rev W - v11 - i6 - Nov-Dec 2004 - p39(1) [501+]
    KR - v72 - i13 - July 1 2004 - p624(1) [501+]
    LJ - v129 - i14 - Sept 1 2004 - p150(2) [51-500]
    NYTBR - Oct 24 2004 - p24 [501+]
White, Fred - *LifeWriting*
    Bwatch - Oct 2004 - pNA [51-500]
White, Gary - *Color Atlas of Dermatology, 3d ed.*
    SciTech - v28 - i1 - March 2004 - p120(1) [51-500]
White, Gary C. - *Equipment Theory for Respiratory Care, 4th Ed.*
    SciTech - v28 - i4 - Dec 2004 - p104(1) [51-500]
White, Gloria - *Death Notes*
    KR - v73 - i5 - March 1 2005 - p265(1) [51-500]
White, Graham - *2020 Vision: How Global Business Leaders See Australia's Future*
    JEL - v42 - i1 - March 2004 - p258(2) [501+]
White, Halbert - *New Perspectives in Econometric Theory: The Selected Works of Halbert White, Vol. 2*
    R&R Bk N - v19 - i3 - August 2004 - p93(1) [51-500]
White, Howard - *Raincoast Chronicles 19: Stories and History of the British Columbia Coast*
    CBRA - Annual 2003 - p347(1) [51-500]
White, James L. - *Ray: A Tribute to the Movie, the Music, and the Man*
    LJ - v130 - i3 - Feb 15 2005 - p133(1) [51-500]
White, James R. - *Scripture Alone: Exploring the Bible's Accuracy, Authority, and Authenticity*
    LJ - v129 - i19 - Nov 15 2004 - p66(1) [501+]
White, Jan V. - *Editing by Design: For Designers, Art Directors, and Editors: The Classic Guide to Winning Readers, Completely Rev. 3rd Ed.*
    R&R Bk N - v19 - i1 - Feb 2004 - p258(1) [51-500]
White, Jenny B. - *Islamist Mobilization in Turkey: A Study in Vernacular Politics*
    HNet - August 2004 - pNA [501+]
White, Jerry P. - *Aboriginal Conditions: Research as a Foundation for Public Policy*
    CBRA - Annual 2003 - p360(1) [501+]
White, Joseph F. - *High Frequency Techniques: An Introduction to RF and Microwave Engineering*
    SciTech - v28 - i1 - March 2004 - p164(1) [51-500]
White, Kate - *'Til Death Do Us Part (Read by White, Karen). Audiobook Review*
    Kliatt - v38 - i6 - Nov 2004 - p52(1) [51-500]
    LJ - v130 - i2 - Feb 1 2005 - p124(1) [51-500]
White, Kathryn - *The Nutty Nut Chase (Illus. by Cabban, Vanessa)*
    c Sch Lib - v52 - i4 - Winter 2004 - p191(1) [51-500]
    c SLJ - v51 - i1 - Jan 2005 - p100(1) [51-500]
White, Kerry - *Australian Children's Books: A Bibliography, Vol. 3*
    ALJ - v53 - i3 - August 2004 - p314(3) [501+]
White, L. Michael - *From Jesus to Christianity: How Four Generations of Visionaries and Storytellers Created the New Testament and the Christian Faith*
    LJ - v130 - i3 - Feb 15 2005 - p136(1) [51-500]
    PW - v251 - i45 - Nov 8 2004 - p52(2) [51-500]
White, Luise - *The Assassination of Herbert Chitepo: Texts and Politics in Zimbabwae*
    AHR - v109 - i4 - Oct 2004 - p1348-1349 [501+]
    The Assassination of Herbert Chitepo: Texts and Politics in Zimbabwe
    IJAHS - v37 - i2 - Spring 2004 - p345-347 [501+]
White, Mary - *Lettering on Ceramics*
    Ceram Mo - v52 - i2 - Feb 2004 - p26(1) [501+]
White, Mel - *Exploring the Great Texas Coastal Birding Trail: Highlights of a Birding Mecca*
    SciTech - v28 - i1 - March 2004 - p70(1) [51-500]
White, Merry Isaacs - *Perfectly Japanese: Making Families in an Era of Upheaval*
    JAS - v63 - i2 - May 2004 - p516(3) [501+]

White, Michael - *C.S. Lewis: A Life*
    KR - v72 - i15 - August 1 2004 - p736(1) [501+]
    LJ - v129 - i19 - Nov 15 2004 - p62(1) [501+]
    PW - v251 - i32 - August 9 2004 - p240(1) [51-500]
White, Mike - *Kings Canyon National Park*
    Bwatch - v26 - i7 - July 2004 - p1(1) [51-500]
White Nicholas P. - *Individual and Conflict in Greek Ethics*
    Class R - v54 - i1 - May 2004 - p80(2) [501+]
White, Nicholas P. - *Individual and Conflict in Greek Ethics*
    Ethics - v114 - i4 - July 2004 - p848(11) [501+]
    RM - v58 - i1 - Sept 2004 - p200(3) [501+]
White, Norman - *Hopkins in Ireland*
    RES - v55 - i221 - Sept 2004 - p633(3) [501+]
White, Osmar - *Conqueror's Road: An Eyewitness Report of Germany 1945*
    J Mil H - v68 - i3 - July 2004 - p1008-1009 [501+]
White, Pamela J. - *Corn: Chemistry and Technology, 2d ed.*
    SciTech - v28 - i3 - Sept 2004 - p128(1) [51-500]
White, Pat - *Ring around My Heart*
    BL - v101 - i1 - Sept 1 2004 - p74(1) [51-500]
White, Paul Whitfield - *Shakespeare and Theatrical Patronage in Early Modern England*
    Shakes Q - v55 - i2 - Summer 2004 - p219-221 [501+]
    Six Ct J - v34 - i4 - Winter 2003 - p1169-1170 [501+]
White, R.E. - *Computational Mathematics: Models, Methods, and Analysis with MATLAB and MPI*
    SIAM Rev - v46 - i3 - Sept 2004 - p571(2) [501+]
White, Randy Wayne - *Dead of Night (Read by Hill, Dick). Audiobook Review*
    KR - v73 - i4 - Feb 15 2005 - p203(1) [51-500]
    Tampa Burn. Audiobook Review
    BL - v101 - i5 - Nov 1 2004 - p502(1) [51-500]
    Tampa Burn (Read by Hill, Dick). Audiobook Review
    BL - v101 - i9-10 - Jan 1 2005 - p778(1) [51-500]
White, Richard Alan - *Breaking Silence: The Case That Changed the Face of Human Rights*
    TimHES - v0 - i1678 - Feb 11 2005 - p27(1) [501+]
White, Richard D., Jr. - *Roosevelt the Reformer: Theodore Roosevelt as Civil Service Commissioner, 1889-1895*
    Choice - v42 - i2 - Oct 2004 - p359(1) [51-500]
White, Ronald C. - *The Eloquent President: A Portrait of Lincoln through His Words*
    BL - v101 - i9-10 - Jan 1 2005 - p810(1) [1-50]
    LJ - v129 - i20 - Dec 1 2004 - p138(2) [501+]
    PW - v251 - i47 - Nov 22 2004 - p50(2) [51-500]
White, Ruth - *Belle Prater's Boy*
    y Kliatt - v39 - i2 - March 2005 - p24(1) [51-500]
    Buttermilk Hill
    c BL - v100 - i22 - August 2004 - p1937(1) [51-500]
    c CCB-B - v58 - i4 - Dec 2004 - p186(2) [51-500]
    HB - v80 - i5 - Sept-Oct 2004 - p600(2) [501+]
    c KR - v72 - i15 - August 1 2004 - p750(1) [51-500]
    PW - v251 - i45 - Nov 8 2004 - p56(2) [51-500]
    c SLJ - v50 - i9 - Sept 2004 - p219(2) [51-500]
    c VOYA - v27 - i5 - Dec 2004 - p397(1) [51-500]
    The Search for Belle Prater
    y Kliatt - v39 - i2 - March 2005 - p16(2) [51-500]
White, Samuel G. - *McKim, Mead & White: The Masterworks*
    R&R Bk N - v19 - i1 - Feb 2004 - p204(1) [51-500]
White, Stephen - *Blinded (Read by Hill, Dick). Audiobook Review*
    c Kliatt - v38 - i4 - July 2004 - p48(1) [51-500]
    Developments in Central and East European Politics 3
    Choice - v41 - i7 - March 2004 - p1364(2) [501+]
    Developments in Central and East European Politics
    Slav R - v63 - i3 - Fall 2004 - p622-623 [501+]
    Missing Persons
    BL - v101 - i8 - Dec 15 2004 - p691(1) [51-500]
    KR - v72 - i24 - Dec 15 2004 - p1164(1) [501+]
    LJ - v130 - i2 - Feb 1 2005 - p72(1) [51-500]
    PW - v251 - i49 - Dec 6 2004 - p41(1) [51-500]
White, Stephen K. - *What Is Political Theory?*
    R&R Bk N - v19 - i3 - August 2004 - p172(1) [501+]
White, Terry - *Justice Denoted: The Legal Thriller in American, British, and Continental Courtroom Literature*
    R&R Bk N - v19 - i1 - Feb 2004 - p228(1) [51-500]
    TLS - i5289 - August 13 2004 - p30(1) [501+]
White, Theodore H. - *The Making of the President, 1960*
    BW - v34 - i39 - Sept 26 2004 - p4(1) [501+]

Why Not?
KR - v72 - i17 - Sept 1 2004 - p826(1) [501+]
Whybrow, Ian - *Harry and the Dinosaurs Make a Christmas Wish* (Illus. by Reynolds, Adrian)
HB - v80 - i6 - Nov-Dec 2004 - p666(2) [51-500]
The Kingfisher Book of Classic Christmas Stories
c CH Bwatch - v14 - i12 - Dec 2004 - pNA [51-500]
Little Wolf, Terror of the Shivery Sea (Illus. by Ross, Tony)
c SLJ - v50 - i12 - Dec 2004 - p124(1) [51-500]
Whybrow, Peter C. - *American Mania: When More Is Not Enough*
KR - v72 - i20 - Oct 15 2004 - p998(1) [501+]
NYT - March 12 2005 - pB7(L) [501+]
PW - v251 - i44 - Nov 1 2004 - p51(1) [501+]
Whyman, Matt - *Boy Kills Man*
y Kliatt - v39 - i2 - March 2005 - p17(1) [51-500]
KR - v73 - i3 - Feb 1 2005 - p183(1) [51-500]
Whyman, Philip - *Analysis of the Economic Democracy Reforms in Sweden*
R&R Bk N - v19 - i4 - Nov 2004 - p90(1) [51-500]
Sweden and the "Third Way": A Macroeconomic Evaluation
JEL - v42 - i1 - March 2004 - p324(1) [501+]
Whynott, Douglas - *A Country Practice: Scenes from the Veterinary Life*
BL - v101 - i5 - Nov 1 2004 - p452(1) [51-500]
KR - v72 - i17 - Sept 1 2004 - p857(1) [501+]
PW - v251 - i39 - Sept 27 2004 - p45(1) [51-500]
Whyte, Christopher - *Modern Scottish Poetry*
TLS - i5290 - August 20 2004 - p4-5 [501+]
Whyte, Martin King - *China's Revolutions and Intergenerational Relations*
AJS - v110 - i3 - Nov 2004 - p801(2) [501+]
CS - v33 - i6 - Nov 2004 - p669(2) [501+]
Whyte, Nicholas - *Science, Colonialism, and Ireland*
Isis - v95 - i2 - June 2004 - p299(2) [501+]
Whyte, Susan Reynolds - *Social Lives of Medicines*
AJS - v110 - i1 - July 2004 - p277(3) [501+]
Whytock, Cherry - *My Cup Runneth Over: The Life of Angelica Cookson Potts* (Illus. by Whytock, Cherry)
c Kliatt - v38 - i6 - Nov 2004 - p21(1) [51-500]
LibMed - v22 - i6 - March 2004 - p65(1) [501+]
LibMed - v22 - i6 - March 2004 - p65(1) [51-500]
y PW - v251 - i42 - Oct 18 2004 - p66(1) [51-500]
My Scrumptious Scottish Dumplings: The Life of Angelica Cookson Potts
y BL - v101 - i9-10 - Jan 1 2005 - p847(1) [1-50]
c CH Bwatch - Feb 2005 - pNA [51-500]
c Kliatt - v38 - i5 - Sept 2004 - p17(2) [51-500]
c KR - v72 - i18 - Sept 15 2004 - p923(1) [51-500]
y PW - v251 - i42 - Oct 18 2004 - p66(1) [501+]
y SLJ - v51 - i1 - Jan 2005 - p138(1) [51-500]
Wiarda, Howard J. - *Authoritarianism and Corporatism in Latin America-Revisited*
Choice - v42 - i6 - Feb 2005 - p1090(2) [51-500]
Politics and Social Change in Latin America: Still a Distinct Tradition? 4th Ed.
R&R Bk N - v19 - i1 - Feb 2004 - pNA [501+]
Wible, Jean M. - *Pharmacology for Massage Therapy*
SciTech - v28 - i4 - Dec 2004 - p68(1) [51-500]
Wicham, Chris - *Courts and Conflict in Twelfth-Century Tuscany*
Choice - v42 - i2 - Oct 2004 - p363(1) [51-500]
Wichert, Sabine - *From the United Irishmen to Twentieth-Century Unionism: A Festschrift for A.T.Q. Stewart*
R&R Bk N - v19 - i4 - Nov 2004 - p37(1) [51-500]
Wichmann, Soren - *Linguistics of Maya Writing*
R&R Bk N - v19 - i4 - Nov 2004 - p69(1) [51-500]
Wick, Walter - *Can You See What I See? Cool Collections: Picture Puzzles to Search and Solve* (Illus. by Wick, Walter)
c BL - v101 - i7 - Dec 1 2004 - p657(1) [51-500]
c SLJ - v50 - i10 - Oct 2004 - p152(1) [51-500]
Can You See What I See? Dream Machine: A Picture Adventure to Search and Solve (Illus. by Wick, Walter)
c RT - v57 - Oct 2003 - p173 [1-50]
c SLJ - v50 - i10 - Oct 2004 - pS26(1) [51-500]
Seymour and the Juice Box Boat
c SLJ - v50 - i8 - August 2004 - p114(1) [51-500]
Wickens, G. Glen - *Thomas Hardy, Monism, and the Carnival Tradition: The One and the Many in The Dynasts*
CBRA - Annual 2003 - p264(2) [501+]
RES - v55 - i218 - Feb 2004 - p143-145 [501+]
Wicker, Jan Lee - *Those Funny Flamingos* (Illus. by Weaver, Steve)
c CH Bwatch - March 2005 - pNA [51-500]

Wickhan, Sara - *Sacred Cycles: The Spiral of Women's Well-Being*
SciTech - v28 - i4 - Dec 2004 - p110(1) [51-500]
Wickramasinghe, Chandra - *Fred Hoyle's Universe*
SciTech - v28 - i1 - March 2004 - p43(1) [51-500]
A Journey With Fred Boyle
New Sci - v184 - i2472 - Nov 6 2004 - p52(2) [501+]
Wickramasinghe, Nilmini - *Creating Knowledge-Based Healthcare Organizations*
SciTech - v28 - i4 - Dec 2004 - p85(1) [51-500]
Wicks, Susan - *Night Toad*
TLS - i5265 - Feb 27 2004 - p24-24 [501+]
Wickstrom, Thor - *Teacher Appreciation Day*
LibMed - v22 - i4 - Jan 2004 - p60(1) [501+]
Widdicombe, Toby - *Revisiting the Legacy of Edward Bellamy (1850-1898), American Author and Social Reformer*
SFS - v31 - i2 - July 2004 - p326-328 [501+]
Widdis, Emma - *Visions of a New Land: Soviet Film from the Revolution to the Second World War*
Slav R - v63 - i3 - Fall 2004 - p687-688 [501+]
Wideman, John Edgar - *God's Gym*
BL - v101 - i7 - Dec 1 2004 - p619(1) [51-500]
Ent W - i806 - Feb 11 2005 - p68 [51-500]
KR - v72 - i23 - Dec 1 2004 - p1115(1) [501+]
LJ - v130 - i1 - Jan 1 2005 - p104(1) [51-500]
People - v63 - i6 - Feb 14 2005 - p60 [501+]
PW - v252 - i2 - Jan 10 2005 - p36(1) [51-500]
Widess, Jim - *Complete Book of Gourd Carving*
LJ - v130 - i3 - Feb 15 2005 - p128(1) [51-500]
Widgren, Mats - *Islands of Intensive Agriculture in Eastern Africa: Past and Present*
SciTech - v28 - i4 - Dec 2004 - p123 [51-500]
Widmaier-Picasso, Olivier - *Picasso: The Real Family Story*
BL - v101 - i5 - Nov 1 2004 - p461(1) [501+]
Widmalm, Sven - *Vetenskapsbararna: Naturvetenskapen i det svenska samhallet, 1880-1950 [The Carriers of Science: Science in Swedish Society, 1880-1950]*
Isis - v95 - i3 - Sept 2004 - p520(3) [501+]
Widmer, Kirsten - *Workshops That Work! 30 Days of Mini-Lessons That Help Launch and Establish All-Important Routines for an Effective Reading and Writing Workshop*
SLJ - v50 - i10 - Oct 2004 - pS76(1) [51-500]
Widmer, Ted - *Martin Van Buren*
y BL - v101 - i7 - Dec 1 2004 - p628(1) [51-500]
KR - v72 - i22 - Nov 15 2004 - p1086(1) [501+]
NYTBR - Feb 27 2005 - p11 [501+]
PW - v251 - i46 - Nov 15 2004 - p47(2) [51-500]
Wiebe, Keith - *Land Quality, Agricultural Productivity, and Food Security: Biophysical Processes and Economic Choices at Local, Regional, and Global Levels*
SciTech - v28 - i1 - March 2004 - p127(1) [51-500]
Wiebe, M.G. - *Benjamin Disraeli Letters, Vol. 7*
R&R Bk N - v19 - i3 - August 2004 - p38(1) [51-500]
Wiebe, Phillip H. - *God and Other Spirits: Intimations of Transcendence in Christian Experience*
Choice - v42 - i4 - Dec 2004 - p681(1) [1-50]
Wiebe, Robert H. - *Who We Are: A History of Popular Nationalism*
JAH - v91 - i1 - June 2004 - p205-206 [501+]
Wiebe, Rudy - *Sweeter than All the World*
Can Lit - i182 - Autumn 2004 - p185(2) [501+]
Wiebe, Rudy Henry - *Hidden Buffalo* (Illus. by Lonechild, Michael)
c CBRA - Annual 2003 - p471(2) [51-500]
c SLJ - v50 - i7 - July 2004 - p97(1) [51-500]
The Mad Trapper
y Kliatt - v38 - i4 - July 2004 - p25(1) [501+]
Wiebe, Trina - *Max the Mighty Superhero* (Illus. by Flook, Helen)
c CBRA - Annual 2003 - p521(1) [51-500]
Max the Movie Director (Illus. by Flook, Helen)
c CBRA - Annual 2003 - p521(1) [51-500]
Wieck, Carl F. - *Lincoln's Quest for Equality: The Road to Gettysburg*
AHR - v109 - i4 - Oct 2004 - p1233(2) [501+]
Refiguring Huckleberry Finn
JouAmCul - v27 - i4 - Dec 2004 - p459(2) [501+]
Wieck, Michael - *A Childhood under Hitler and Stalin: Memoirs of a "Certified" Jew*
VQR - v80 - i1 - Wntr 2004 - p262-262 [501+]
Wiedemann, Thomas - *Representing the Body of the Slave*
IJAHS - v37 - i1 - Wntr 2004 - p153-155 [501+]
Wieder, Joy Nelkin - *The Secret Tunnel*
c CH Bwatch - Feb 2005 - pNA [51-500]

Wiederhold, Brenda K. - *Virtual Reality Therapy for Anxiety Disorders: Advances in Evaluation and Treatment*
SciTech - v28 - i4 - Dec 2004 - p99(1) [51-500]
Wiegand, Chris - *Federico Fellini: The Complete Films*
TimHES - v0 - i1647 - July 2 2004 - p26(1) [501+]
Wiegand, Patrick - *The Oxford Primary Atlas*
c Sch Lib - v52 - i4 - Winter 2004 - p209(1) [51-500]
Wielen, Lex van der - *International Cash Management: A Practical Guide to Managing Cash Flows, Liquidity, Working Capital and Short-Term Financial Risks*
JEL - v41 - i4 - Dec 2003 - p1358(1) [501+]
Wiencek, Henry - *An Imperfect God: George Washington, His Slaves, and the Creation of America*
CR - v285 - i1666 - Nov 2004 - p313(1) [501+]
JAH - v91 - i3 - Dec 2004 - p997(2) [501+]
VQR - v80 - i1 - Wntr 2004 - p261-261 [501+]
Wiener, Charles M. - *Harrison's Principles of Internal Medicine: Self-Assessment and Board Review, 16th Ed.*
SciTech - v28 - i4 - Dec 2004 - p89(1) [51-500]
Wiener, Jerry M. - *Textbook of Child and Adolescent Psychiatry, 3d ed.*
SciTech - v28 - i1 - March 2004 - p119(1) [51-500]
Wiener, Jon - *Historians in Trouble: Plagiarism, Fraud, and Politics in the Ivory Tower*
LJ - v130 - i2 - Feb 1 2005 - p100(1) [51-500]
Wiener, Martin J. - *Men of Blood: Violence, Manliness and Criminal Justice in Victorian England*
Choice - v42 - i4 - Dec 2004 - p726(2) [1-50]
CR - v285 - i1663 - August 2004 - p127(1) [501+]
TLS - i5292 - Sept 3 2004 - p23(1) [501+]
Wiener, Tom - *Off Hollywood Film Guide*
Globe & Mail - Dec 10 2004 - pR21 [1-50]
Wiergertjes, G. - *Host-Parasite Interactions*
SciTech - v28 - i4 - Dec 2004 - p67(1) [51-500]
Wierschowski, L. - *Fremde in Gallien-'Gallier' in der Fremde. Die epigraphisch bezeugte Mobilitat in, von und nach Gallien vom 1. bis 3. Jh. n. Chr*
Class R - v53 - i2 - Nov 2003 - p439-440 [501+]
Wiersma, G. Bruce - *Environmental Monitoring*
SciTech - v28 - i3 - Sept 2004 - p61 [51-500]
Wierzbicki, Susan - *Beyond the Immigrant Enclave: Network Change and Assimilation*
R&R Bk N - v19 - i3 - August 2004 - p65(1) [51-500]
Wiese, Andrew - *Places of their Own: African American Suburbanization in the Twentieth Century*
Choice - v42 - i2 - Oct 2004 - p359(1) [51-500]
HRNB - v33 - i1 - Fall 2004 - p6(2) [501+]
Wiese, Jim - *Head to Toe Science: Over 40 Eye-Popping, Spine-Tingling, Heart-Pounding Activities That Teach Kids about the Human Body*
c SB - v40 - i4 - July-August 2004 - p152(1) [51-500]
Wiesel, Elie - *Legends of Our Time*
R&R Bk N - v19 - i4 - Nov 2004 - p230(1) [501+]
Wiesen, S. Jonathan - *The East German Dictatorship: Problems and Perspectives in the Interpretation of the GDR*
Ger Q - v77 - i2 - Spring 2004 - p253-255 [501+]
West German Industry and the Challenge of the Nazi Past, 1945-1955
Ger Q - v77 - i2 - Spring 2004 - p252-253 [501+]
GSR - v27 - i1 - Feb 2004 - p191-192 [501+]
Wiesmann, Doris - *International Nutrition Index: Concept and Analyses of Food Insecurity and Undernutrition at Country Levels*
SciTech - v28 - i3 - Sept 2004 - p171(1) [51-500]
Wiesner, David - *The Loathsome Dragon* (Illus. by Wiesner, David)
c PW - v252 - i8 - Feb 21 2005 - p175(1) [51-500]
Wiesner, Eduardo - *Fiscal Federalism in Latin America: From Entitlements to Markets*
R&R Bk N - v19 - i1 - Feb 2004 - p82(1) [1-50]
Wiggers, Raymond - *The Amateur Geologist: Explorations and Investigations*
SB - v40 - i5 - Sept-Oct 2004 - p192(1) [51-500]
Wiggins, Arthur W. - *Five Biggest Unsolved Problems in Science*
SB - v40 - i6 - Nov-Dec 2004 - p240(1) [51-500]
Wiggins, David - *Neo-Aristotelian Reflections on Justice*
RM - v58 - i1 - Sept 2004 - p222(1) [501+]
Wiggins, Kerri L. - *Renal Care: Resources and Practical Applications*
SciTech - v28 - i1 - March 2004 - p107(1) [51-500]
Wiggins, Pamela - *Buying & Selling Antiques and Collectibles on eBay*
Ant&CM - v109 - i11 - Jan 2005 - p16(1) [501+]

Wiggs, Susan - *The Ocean between Us (Read by Ferrone, Richard). Audiobook Review*
    BL - v101 - i9-10 - Jan 1 2005 - p884(1) [51-500]

Wignall, Dennis L. - *The Internet in Everyday Life*
    JC - v54 - i3 - Sept 2004 - p571(4) [501+]

Wignall, Kevin - *For the Dogs*
    PW - v251 - i27 - July 5 2004 - p39(1) [51-500]

Wigoder, Geoffrey - *The Student's Encyclopedia of Judaism*
    Bwatch - Feb 2005 - pNA [51-500]
c   SLJ - v50 - i8 - August 2004 - p60(1) [501+]
    SLJ - v50 - i10 - Oct 2004 - pS62(1) [501+]
y   VOYA - v27 - i3 - August 2004 - p247(1) [1-50]
    BL - v101 - i2 - Sept 15 2004 - p278(1) [501+]

Wijaya, Made - *Architecture of Bali: A Source Book of Traditional and Modern Forms*
    JAS - v63 - i2 - May 2004 - p566(3) [501+]

Wijngaards, John - *No Women in Holy Orders? The Women Deacons of the Early Church*
    Theol St - v65 - i4 - Dec 2004 - p902(2) [501+]

Wik, Tom - *Memory Technology, Design and Testing: Proceedings*
    SciTech - v28 - i4 - Dec 2004 - p23(1) [51-500]

Wiktorowicz, Quintan - *Islamic Activism: A Social Movement Theory Approach*
    Choice - v41 - i11-12 - July-August 2004 - p2116(2) [501+]
The Name of the Enemy: Jihadi Salafis (Read by Gardner, Grover). Audiobook Review
y   Kliatt - v39 - i2 - March 2005 - p60(1) [51-500]

Wilbeck, Christopher W. - *Sledgehammers: Strengths and Flaws of Tiger Tank Battalions in World War II*
    J Mil H - v68 - i4 - Oct 2004 - p1283-1284 [501+]

Wilber, Ken - *The Simple Feeling of Being*
    Bwatch - Nov 2004 - pNA [501+]

Wilbour, Benjamin Franklin - *Little Compton Families, Vol. 1 and 2*
    EFHM - v58 - i3 - May-June 2004 - p60(1) [51-500]

Wilbur, J.R.H. - *Horse-Drawn Carriages and Sleighs: Elegant Vehicles from New England and New Brunswick*
    CBRA - Annual 2003 - p443(1) [51-500]

Wilbur, Jason K. - *Family Practice Examination and Board Review*
    SciTech - v28 - i4 - Dec 2004 - p89(1) [51-500]

Wilbur, Richard - *Collected Poems, 1943-2004*
    BL - v101 - i7 - Dec 1 2004 - p627(1) [51-500]
    BW - v34 - i48 - Nov 28 2004 - p15(1) [501+]
    PW - v251 - i51 - Dec 20 2004 - p52(1) [501+]
The Pig in the Spigot
c   PW - v251 - i45 - Nov 8 2004 - p58(1) [51-500]

Wilce, James M. Jr. - *Social and Cultural Lives of Immune Systems*
    AJS - v110 - i2 - Sept 2004 - p511(2) [501+]

Wilcockson, John - *23 Days in July: Inside Lance Armstrong's Record-Breaking Tour de France Victory*
    PW - v251 - i44 - Nov 1 2004 - p56(1) [501+]

Wilcox, Clifford - *Robert Redfield and The Development of American Anthropology*
    R&R Bk N - v19 - i3 - August 2004 - p82(1) [51-500]

Wilcox, James - *Heavenly Days*
    NYTBR - Jan 23 2005 - p28 [501+]

Wilcox, Jonathan - *Naked Before God: Uncovering the Body in Anglo-Saxon England*
    Med R - June 2004 - pNA [501+]

Wilcox, Leah - *Falling for Rapunzel (Illus. by Monks, Lydia)*
c   SLJ - v50 - i10 - Oct 2004 - pS27(1) [1-50]

Wilcox, Martin - *The CCL Guide to Leadership in Action: How Managers and Organizations Can Improve the Practice of Leadership*
    R&R Bk N - v19 - i3 - August 2004 - p104(1) [1-50]

Wilcox, Melissa M. - *Coming Out in Christianity: Religion, Identity and Community*
    CC - v121 - i16 - August 10 2004 - p39(2) [501+]
Coming Out in Christianity: Religion, Identity, and Community
    Lam Bk Rpt - v13 - i1-2 - August-Sept 2004 - p33(2) [501+]
Expressions of Ethography: Novel Approaches to Qualitative Methods
    CS - v33 - i5 - Sept 2004 - p618-620 [501+]

Wilcox, R. Turner - *Five Centuries of American Costume*
    LJ - v129 - i20 - Dec 1 2004 - p184(1) [51-500]
    R&R Bk N - v19 - i4 - Nov 2004 - p77(1) [51-500]

Wilcox, Ralph C. - *Sporting Dystopias. The Making and Meanings of Urban Sports Cultures*
    SSJ - v21 - i1 - March 2004 - p95-97 [501+]

Wilcox, Robert K. - *First Blue: The Story of WWII Ace Butch Voris and the Creation of the Blue Angels*
    BL - v101 - i3 - Oct 1 2004 - p288(2) [51-500]
    LJ - v129 - i18 - Nov 1 2004 - p98(1) [51-500]

Wilcox, Sue Ki - *Raku Beads*
    Ceram Mo - v52 - i5 - May 2004 - p32(1) [501+]

Wilcox, W. Bradford - *Soft Patriarchs, New Men: How Christianity Shapes Fathers and Husbands*
    CC - v122 - i1 - Jan 11 2005 - p18(3) [501+]

Wilcoxen, Chuck - *Niccolini's Song (Illus. by Buehner, Mark)*
    KR - v72 - i17 - Sept 1 2004 - p874(1) [51-500]
c   PW - v251 - i40 - Oct 4 2004 - p87(2) [51-500]
c   SLJ - v50 - i12 - Dec 2004 - p124(1) [51-500]

Wilczek, Annette - *Einkommen, Karriere, Versorgung: Das DDR-Kombinat und die Lebenslage seiner Beschaftigten*
    HNet - July 2004 - pNA [501+]

Wild, Alan - *Soils, Land and Food: Managing the Land During the Twenty-First Century*
    QRB - v79 - i4 - Dec 2004 - p450(1) [51-500]

Wild America Habitats
    LibMed - v22 - i5 - Feb 2004 - p82(1) [501+]

Wild, Antony - *Coffee: A Dark History*
    CR - v285 - i1666 - Nov 2004 - p319(1) [501+]

Wild, Margaret - *Little Humpty (Illus. by James, Ann)*
    KR - v72 - i24 - Dec 15 2004 - p1211(1) [51-500]
c   PW - v252 - i3 - Jan 17 2005 - p54(1) [51-500]
c   Res Links - v10 - i3 - Feb 2005 - p10(1) [51-500]
c   SLJ - v51 - i2 - Feb 2005 - p112(1) [51-500]
One Night
c   CH Bwatch - v14 - i7 - July 2004 - p7(2) [501+]
y   Sch Lib - v52 - i4 - Winter 2004 - p217(1) [51-500]
y   VOYA - v27 - i3 - August 2004 - p226(1) [1-50]

Wild, Trevor - *Village England: A Social History of the Countryside*
    Choice - v42 - i6 - Feb 2005 - p1087(1) [51-500]

Wildavsky, Aaron - *The New Politics of the Budgetary Process, 5th Ed.*
    R&R Bk N - v19 - i1 - Feb 2004 - p120(1) [51-500]

Wildavsky, Ben - *U.S. News Ultimate Guide to Becoming a Teacher*
    Choice - v42 - i5 - Jan 2005 - p839(1) [1-50]
    R&R Bk N - v19 - i4 - Nov 2004 - p183(1) [501+]

Wildberg, C. - *Hyperesie und Epiphanie. Ein Versuch uber die Bedeutung der Gotter in den Dramen des Euripides*
    Class R - v54 - i1 - May 2004 - p37(2) [501+]

Wilde, Oscar - *The Best of Oscar Wilde: Selected Plays and Writings*
    R&R Bk N - v19 - i4 - Nov 2004 - p237(1) [501+]
Fairy Tales of Oscar Wilde (Illus. by Russell, P. Craig)
    LJ - v129 - i18 - Nov 1 2004 - p66(2) [501+]
Intentions
    LJ - v129 - i17 - Oct 15 2004 - p99(1) [51-500]
Oscar Wilde's The Star Child (Illus. by Whelan, Olwyn)
y   Magpies - v19 - i5 - Nov 2004 - p20(4) [501+]

Wildenthal, Bryan H. - *Native American Sovereignty on Trial: A Handbook with Cases, Law, and Documents*
    NRJ - v44 - i3 - Summer 2004 - p924-926 [501+]

Wilder, Craig Steven - *A Covenant with Color: Race and Social Power in Brooklyn*
    J Urban H - v31 - i2 - Jan 2005 - p269-277 [501+]

Wilder, Gene - *Kiss Me Like A Stranger: My Search for Love and Art*
    Ent W - i811 - March 18 2005 - p72 [51-500]
    KR - v73 - i1 - Jan 1 2005 - p46(1) [501+]
    LJ - v130 - i4 - March 1 2005 - p89(1) [51-500]
    PW - v252 - i4 - Jan 24 2005 - p230(2) [501+]

Wilder, Laura Ingalls - *Farmer Boy (Read by Jones, Cherry). Audiobook Review*
c   BL - v100 - i22 - August 2004 - p1954(1) [51-500]

Wilder, Terry L. - *Pseudonymity, the New Testament, and Deception: An Inquiry into Intention and Reception*
    R&R Bk N - v19 - i3 - August 2004 - p24(1) [1-50]

Wildman, Beth G. - *Treating Children's Psychosocial Problems in Primary Care*
    SciTech - v28 - i3 - Sept 2004 - p119(1) [51-500]

Wilds, Mary - *I Dare Not Fail: Notable African American Women Educators*
c   SLJ - v50 - i10 - Oct 2004 - p196(1) [51-500]

Wildt, Michael - *Generation des Unbedingten: Das Fuehrungskorps des Reichssicherheitshauptamtes*
    HNet - Oct 2004 - pNA [501+]
Generation des Unbedingten: Das Fuhrungskorps des Reichssicherheitshauptamtes
    GSR - v27 - i2 - May 2004 - p419-421 [501+]

Wilensky, Amy - *The Weight of It: A Story of Two Sisters*
y   VOYA - v27 - i3 - August 2004 - p243(1) [1-50]

Wilensky, Harold L. - *Rich Democracies: Political Economy*
    CS - v33 - i1 - Jan 2004 - p74-76 [501+]

Wilentz, Sean - *The Rose and the Briar: Death, Love and Liberty in the American Ballad*
    BL - v101 - i6 - Nov 15 2004 - p542(1) [51-500]
    LJ - v129 - i17 - Oct 15 2004 - p65(1) [51-500]
    PW - v251 - i42 - Oct 18 2004 - p58(1) [51-500]

Wiles, Deborah - *Each Little Bird That Sings*
c   CCB-B - v58 - i6 - Feb 2005 - p270(1) [51-500]
y   HB - v81 - i2 - March-April 2005 - p209(2) [51-500]
c   KR - v73 - i4 - Feb 15 2005 - p237(1) [51-500]
    PW - v252 - i8 - Feb 21 2005 - p175(2) [51-500]
Freedom Summer (Illus. by Lagarrigue, Jerome)
c   PW - v252 - i1 - Jan 3 2005 - p58(1) [51-500]
c   SLJ - v50 - i10 - Oct 2004 - p66(1) [51-500]
Love, Ruby Lavender
c   PW - v252 - i11 - March 14 2005 - p70(1) [51-500]

Wiles, Jon - *Curriculum Essentials: A Resource for Educators, 2nd Ed.*
    R&R Bk N - v19 - i4 - Nov 2004 - p186(1) [501+]
Leaving School: Finding Education
    Fut - v38 - i6 - Nov-Dec 2004 - p60(1) [51-500]
    Fut - v39 - i1 - Jan-Feb 2005 - p49(1) [51-500]

Wiley, Keith - *On The Wild Side*
    Bwatch - v26 - i9 - Sept 2004 - p2(2) [51-500]

Wiley, Kristi L. - *Historical Dictionary of Jainism*
    Choice - v42 - i5 - Jan 2005 - p828(1) [1-50]

Wiley, T.S. - *Sex, Lies, and Menopause: The Shoking Truth about Hormone Replacement Therapy*
    Choice - v41 - i7 - March 2004 - p1328(1) [501+]

Wiley, Tatha - *Original Sin: Origins, Development, Contemporary Meanings*
    TT - v61 - i2 - July 2004 - p266-5 [501+]
Thinking of Christ: Proclamation, Explanation, Meaning
    Theol St - v65 - i3 - Sept 2004 - p662(2) [501+]

Wilford, Hugh - *The CIA, the British Left, and the Cold War: Calling the Tune?*
    Choice - v41 - i7 - March 2004 - p1348(1) [501+]

Wilhelm, Doug - *The Revealers*
    LibMed - v22 - i6 - March 2004 - p65(1) [501+]

Wilhelm, Hans - *With Lots of Love*
c   PW - v251 - i33 - August 16 2004 - p62(1) [51-500]

Wilhelm, Jeffrey D. - *Reading Is Seeing: Learning to Visualize Scenes, Characters, Ideas, and Text Worlds to Improve Comprehension and Reflective Reading*
    SLJ - v50 - i10 - Oct 2004 - pS76(1) [51-500]

Wilhelm, Kate - *The Unbidden Truth*
    BL - v101 - i2 - Sept 15 2004 - p214(1) [51-500]

Wilken, Robert Louis - *The Spirit of Early Christian Thought: Seeking the Face of God*
    CHR - v90 - i4 - Oct 2004 - p738(2) [501+]

Wilkes, Angela - *The Children's Step-by-Step Cookbook*
y   SLJ - v51 - i2 - Feb 2005 - p58(1) [51-500]

Wilkes, Gail M. - *Oncology Nursing Drug Handbook*
    E-Streams - Sept 2004 - pNA [501+]

Wilkes, John - *An Essay on Woman*
    Eight-C St - v37 - i3 - Spring 2004 - p474-478 [501+]

Wilkin, Eloise - *Prayers for Children (Illus. by Wilkin, Eloise)*
c   PW - v252 - i7 - Feb 14 2005 - p81(1) [501+]

Wilkins, Charles - *Walk to New York: A Journey out of the Wilds of Canada*
    Globe & Mail - Oct 9 2004 - pD10 [501+]
    Globe & Mail - Nov 3 2004 - pT1 [501+]
    Globe & Mail - Nov 27 2004 - pD3 [51-500]

Wilkins, David E. - *Uneven Ground: American Indian Sovereignty and Federal Law*
    Pub Hist - v26 - i3 - Summer 2004 - p90(91) [501+]

Wilkins, Esther M. - *Clinical Practice of the Dental Hygienist, 9th Ed.*
    SciTech - v28 - i3 - Sept 2004 - p119(1) [51-500]

Wilkins, Kim - *The Autumn Castle*
    ChrSFF&H - v26 - i9 - Sept 2004 - p32(1) [51-500]
    MFSF - v107 - i3 - Sept 2004 - p31(2) [501+]
    PW - v252 - i5 - Jan 31 2005 - p54(1) [51-500]

Wilkins, Maurice - *The Third Man of the Double Helix: The Autobiography of Muarice Wilkins*
    TLS - i5266 - March 5 2004 - p28-28 [501+]

Wilkins, Mira - *The History of Foreign Investment in the United States, 1914-1945*
    Choice - v42 - i3 - Nov 2004 - p534(1) [1-50]

Wilkins, Rose - *So Super Starry*
 y BL - v101 - i4 - Oct 15 2004 - p399(1) [51-500]
 y CCB-B - v58 - i3 - Nov 2004 - p151(1) [501+]
 y PW - v251 - i47 - Nov 22 2004 - p61(1) [51-500]
 y Sch Lib - v52 - i3 - Autumn 2004 - p163(1) [501+]
 y SLJ - v50 - i12 - Dec 2004 - p154(1) [51-500]
  VOYA - v27 - i5 - Dec 2004 - p397(1) [51-500]

Wilkinson, Anne - *Heresies: The Complete Poems of Anne Wilkinson, 1924-1961*
  CBRA - Annual 2003 - p236(2) [501+]

Wilkinson, Bruce - *Beyond Jabez: Expanding Your Borders*
  Ch Today - v49 - i3 - March 2005 - p85(1) [51-500]

Wilkinson, Carole - *Alexander the Great: Reckless Conqueror*
 y Magpies - v19 - i5 - Nov 2004 - p44(1) [501+]

Wilkinson, Charles - *The Working Director: How To Arrive, Thrive and Survive in the Director's Chair*
  LJ - v130 - i2 - Feb 1 2005 - p81(2) [51-500]
  PW - v251 - i40 - Oct 4 2004 - p76(1) [51-500]

Wilkinson, Charles F. - *Blood Struggle: The Rise of Modern Indian Nations*
  LJ - v130 - i1 - Jan 1 2005 - p130(1) [51-500]
  PW - v252 - i1 - Jan 3 2005 - p49(1) [51-500]

Wilkinson, Christopher - *Jazz on the Road: Don Albert's Musical Life*
  Am M - v22 - i2 - Summer 2004 - p323-326 [501+]

Wilkinson, Clive - *The British Navy and the State in the Eighteenth Century*
  Choice - v42 - i6 - Feb 2005 - p1087(2) [51-500]
  HNet - Dec 2004 - pNA [501+]

Wilkinson, David - *The Duke of Portland: Politics and Party in the Age of George III*
  Albion - v36 - i2 - Summer 2004 - p308(2) [501+]
  HNet - June 2004 - pNA [501+]

Wilkinson, Dean - *The Legend of Arthur King (Read by Pacy, Steven). Audiobook Review*
 c SLJ - v51 - i2 - Feb 2005 - p75(1) [501+]

Wilkinson, Glenn R. - *Depictions and Images of War in Edwardian Newspapers, 1899-1914*
  Albion - v36 - i2 - Summer 2004 - p343(2) [501+]

Wilkinson, J. Eric - *Early Childhood Education: The New Agenda*
  R&R Bk N - v19 - i3 - August 2004 - p226(1) [1-50]

Wilkinson, Lise - *Prevention and Cure: The London School of Hygiene and Tropical Medicine: A Twentieth-Century Quest for Global Public Health*
  Isis - v95 - i2 - June 2004 - p318(2) [501+]

Wilkinson, Philip - *Flight*
 c SLJ - v50 - i12 - Dec 2004 - p138(1) [501+]
  Thr Kingfisher student Atlas
  LibMed - v22 - March 2004 - p77(1) [501+]

Wilks, Brian - *Browsing Science Research at the Federal Level in Canada: History, Research Activities, and Publications*
  SciTech - v28 - i3 - Sept 2004 - p14(1) [501+]

Willan, Anne - *The Good Cook (Illus. by Harris, Alison)*
  LJ - v129 - i20 - Dec 1 2004 - p150(1) [51-500]

Willard, Nancy - *Cinderella's Dress (Illus. by Dyer, Jane)*
  LibMed - v22 - i4 - Jan 2004 - p68(1) [501+]
  In the Salt Marsh
  BL - v100 - i21 - July 2004 - p1812(1) [1-50]
  The Tale of Paradise Lost: Based on the Poem by John Milton (Illus. by Daly, Jude)
 y BL - v101 - i3 - Oct 1 2004 - p340(2) [51-500]
 y HB - v80 - i6 - Nov-Dec 2004 - p719(1) [51-500]
 y KR - v72 - i19 - Oct 1 2004 - p971(1) [51-500]
 y SLJ - v51 - i1 - Jan 2005 - p138(2) [51-500]
  The Tale of Paradise Lost (Illus. by Daly, Jude)
 y PW - v251 - i43 - Oct 25 2004 - p48(1) [51-500]

Willard, Stephen - *General Topology*
  SciTech - v28 - i3 - Sept 2004 - p41(1) [1-50]

Willard, Terry - *Mind-Body Harmony: How to Resist and Recover from Auto-Immune Diseases*
  CBRA - Annual 2003 - p436(1) [51-500]

Willbanks, James H. - *Abandoning Vietnam: How America Left and South Vietnam Lost Its War*
  HNet - Dec 2004 - pNA [501+]

Willcox, Ken - *Totality: Eclipses of the Sun, 2nd Ed.*
  Astron - v33 - i2 - Feb 2005 - p100 [501+]

Willcox, Merlin - *Traditional Medicinal Plants and Malaria*
  SciTech - v28 - i4 - Dec 2004 - p91(1) [51-500]

Wille, Stefan - *The American Demand for Household Furniture and Trends, 8th Ed.*
  R&R Bk N - v19 - i2 - May 2004 - p108(1) [51-500]
  The Canadian Demand for Office Furniture and Trends
  R&R Bk N - v19 - i3 - August 2004 - p120(1) [51-500]

The Demand and Trends for Canadian Household Furniture, 10th Ed.
  R&R Bk N - v19 - i2 - May 2004 - p108(1) [51-500]

Willeford, Charles Ray - *Miami Blues*
  LJ - v129 - i15 - Sept 15 2004 - p91(1) [51-500]
  New Hope for the Dead
  LJ - v129 - i15 - Sept 15 2004 - p91(1) [51-500]

Willems, Harco - *Temple of Shanhur, Vol. 1*
  R&R Bk N - v19 - i4 - Nov 2004 - p51(1) [51-500]

Willems, Mo - *A Cautionary Tale*
  HB - v80 - i5 - Sept-Oct 2004 - p576(2) [51-500]
  Don't Let the Pigeon Drive the Bus!
 c Sch Lib - v52 - i4 - Winter 2004 - p191(1) [51-500]
  Knuffle Bunny: A Cautionary Tale (Illus. by Willems, Mo)
 c BL - v101 - i2 - Sept 15 2004 - p241(1) [51-500]
 c CCB-B - v58 - i2 - Oct 2004 - p103(1) [51-500]
 c Globe & Mail - Oct 23 2004 - pD22 [51-500]
 c HB - v81 - i1 - Jan-Feb 2005 - p14(1) [51-500]
 c KR - v72 - i15 - August 1 2004 - p750(1) [51-500]
 c PW - v251 - i33 - August 16 2004 - p62(1) [51-500]
 c SLJ - v50 - i10 - Oct 2004 - p136(1) [51-500]
  The Pigeon Finds a Hot Dog! (Illus. by Willems, Mo)
 c BooChiTr - May 23 2004 - p5(1) [501+]
 c CCB-B - v57 - i11 - July-August 2004 - p489(2) [501+]
 c Globe & Mail - July 17 2004 - pD11 [1-50]
  Pigeon Finds a Hot Dog (Illus. by Willems, Mo)
 c LibMed - v23 - i1 - August-Sept 2004 - p66(2) [51-500]
  Pigeon Finds a Hot Dogs (Illus. by Willems, Mo)
 c LibMed - v23 - i1 - August-Sept 2004 - p67(1) [51-500]

Willes, Ed - *The Rebel League: The Short and Unruly Life of the World Hockey Association*
  Globe & Mail - Oct 30 2004 - pD18 [501+]

Willett, Edward - *J.R.R. Tolkien: Master of Imaginary Worlds*
 y BL - v101 - i5 - Nov 1 2004 - p474(1) [51-500]
 y CCB-B - v58 - i1 - Sept 2004 - p45(1) [51-500]
 y SLJ - v50 - i12 - Dec 2004 - p164(1) [51-500]
  VOYA - v27 - i5 - Dec 2004 - p418(1) [51-500]

Willett, Marcia - *The Children's Hour (Read by Barrie, June). Audiobook Review*
 y Kliatt - v39 - i2 - March 2005 - p50(1) [51-500]

Willett, Robert L. - *Russian Sideshow: America's Undeclared War, 1918-1920*
  Choice - v41 - i11-12 - July-August 2004 - p2099(1) [501+]
  R&R Bk N - v19 - i1 - Feb 2004 - p38(1) [1-50]

Willett, Sabin - *Present Value*
  World&I - v19 - i4 - April 2004 - p240 [501+]

Willey, Margaret - *Clever Beatrice and the Best Little Pony (Illus. by Solomon, Heather M.)*
 c CCB-B - v58 - i2 - Oct 2004 - p103(2) [51-500]
 c HB - v80 - i5 - Sept-Oct 2004 - p577(1) [51-500]
 c KR - v72 - i15 - August 1 2004 - p750(1) [51-500]
 c SLJ - v50 - i11 - Nov 2004 - p132(1) [51-500]

William, C. Becker - *Using Oxidants to Enhance Filter Performance*
  SciTech - v28 - i3 - Sept 2004 - p146(1) [51-500]

William, Gormley T., Jr. - *Bureaucracy and Democracy: Accountability and Performance*
  Choice - v41 - i11-12 - July-August 2004 - p2125(1) [501+]

William, Nancy S. - *Using Literature to Support Skills and Critical Discussion for Struggling Readers: Grades 3-9*
  Choice - v42 - i3 - Nov 2004 - p537(1) [1-50]

William, of Malmesbury - *Saints' Lives: Lives of SS. Wulfstan, Dunstan, Patrick, Benignus and Indract*
  Albion - v36 - i1 - Spring 2004 - p93(2) [501+]

Williams, Abigail R. - *Outpatient Department EMTALA Handbook 2004*
  SciTech - v28 - i1 - March 2004 - p82(1) [51-500]

Williams, Adam - *The Palace of Heavenly Pleasure*
  BL - v101 - i7 - Dec 1 2004 - p638(1) [51-500]
  PW - v252 - i1 - Jan 3 2005 - p37(2) [51-500]
  LJ - v129 - i19 - Nov 15 2004 - p53(1) [51-500]

Williams, Adrian - *Transdermal and Topical Drug Delivery: From Theory to Clinical Practice*
  E-Streams - Dec 2004 - pNA [501+]

Williams, Alan - *The Knight and the Blast Furnace: A History of the Metallurgy of Armour in the Middle Ages and the Early Modern Period*
  Ren Q - v57 - i3 - Fall 2004 - p1063(3) [501+]
  Six Ct J - v35 - i3 - Fall 2004 - p851-852 [501+]
  Specu - v79 - i4 - Oct 2004 - p1177(2) [501+]

Williams, Andrew - *The Battle of the Atlantic: The Allies' Submarine Fight Against Hitler's Gray Wolves of the Sea*
  HRNB - v33 - i1 - Fall 2004 - p25(1) [51-500]
 y Kliatt - v38 - i5 - Sept 2004 - p47(3) [501+]

Williams, Ann - *Domesday Book: A Complete Translation*
  R&R Bk N - v19 - i3 - August 2004 - p37(1) [51-500]
  Ethelred the Unready: The Ill-Counselled King
  Choice - v41 - i11-12 - July-August 2004 - p2113(1) [501+]
  TLS - i5264 - Feb 20 2004 - p12-12 [501+]

Williams, Anne - *Three Vampire Tales: Bram Stoker, Dracula; Sheridan Le Fanu, Carmilla; John Polidori, The Vampyre*
  SFS - v31 - i2 - July 2004 - p319-324 [501+]

Williams, Arlene - *Tales from the Dragon's Cave...Peacemaking Stories for Everyone (Illus. by Williams, Arlene)*
 c RT - v57 - Oct 2003 - p175 [1-50]

Williams, Barbara - *World War II: Pacific*
 c SLJ - v51 - i2 - Feb 2005 - p154(1) [51-500]

Williams, Belinda - *Closing the Achievement Gap: A Vision for Changing Beliefs and Practices, 2nd Ed.*
  R&R Bk N - v19 - i4 - Nov 2004 - p193(1) [501+]
  TCR - v106 - i12 - Dec 2004 - p2342(4) [501+]

Williams-Boyd, Pat - *Middle Grades Education: A Reference Handbook*
  R&R Bk N - v19 - i1 - Feb 2004 - p184(1) [51-500]

Williams, Brandy - *Practical Magic for Beginners: Techniques and Rituals to Focus Magical Energy*
  PW - v251 - i50 - Dec 13 2004 - p63(1) [51-500]

Williams, Buzz - *Spare Parts: A Marine Reservist's Journey from Campus to Combat in 38 Days*
  BL - v101 - i9-10 - Jan 1 2005 - p771(1) [1-50]

Williams, C.A. - *Roman Homosexuality: Ideologies of Masculinity in Classical Antiquity*
  Class R - v53 - i2 - Nov 2003 - p468-470 [501+]

Williams, C.G. - *Technology and the Dream: Reflections on the Black Experience at MIT, 1941-1999*
  Isis - v95 - i3 - Sept 2004 - p537(1) [501+]

Williams, C.K. - *The Singing*
  APR - v34 - i1 - Jan-Feb 2005 - p45(6) [501+]
  Poet - v185 - i1 - Oct 2004 - p53(9) [501+]
  The Singing: Poems
  NYTBR - Nov 21 2004 - p36 [501+]

Williams, Charlotte - *A Tolerant Nation?: Exploring Ethnic Diversity in Wales*
  CS - v33 - i6 - Nov 2004 - p664(2) [501+]

Williams, Christine L. - *Therapeutic Interaction in Nursing*
  SciTech - v28 - i3 - Sept 2004 - p126(1) [51-500]

Williams, Christopher - *Youth, Risk and Russian Modernity*
  Russ Rev - v63 - i3 - July 2004 - pNA [501+]

Williams, Cindy - *Filling the Ranks: Transforming the U.S. Military Personnel System*
  Pers PS - v34 - i1 - Wntr 2005 - p54(1) [501+]

Williams, Clois - *Aircrew Security: A Practical Guide*
  SciTech - v28 - i4 - Dec 2004 - p161(1) [51-500]

Williams, D.H. - *The Free Church and the Early Church: Bridging the Historical and Theological Divide*
  CH - v73 - i4 - Dec 2004 - p880(3) [501+]
  Retrieving the Tradition and Renewing Evangelicalism: A Primer for Suspicious Protestants
  CH - v73 - i4 - Dec 2004 - p880(3) [501+]

Williams, Dar - *Amalee*
 c HB - v80 - i4 - July-August 2004 - p462(2) [51-500]
 c PW - v251 - i30 - July 26 2004 - p55(2) [51-500]
 c SLJ - v50 - i10 - Oct 2004 - p182(1) [51-500]

Williams, David (b. 1959 -) - *Plain Folk in a Rich Man's War: Class and Dissent in Confederate Georgia*
  HNet - Sept 2004 - pNA [501+]

Williams, David Cratis - *Tales from the Sacred Wind: Coming of Age in Appalachia*
  JSH - v70 - i3 - August 2004 - p719(2) [501+]

Williams, David H. - *The Welsh Cistercians*
  Specu - v79 - i3 - July 2004 - p860-861 [501+]

Williams, David M. - *Milestones in Systematics*
  Choice - v42 - i6 - Feb 2005 - p1047(1) [51-500]
  SciTech - v28 - i3 - Sept 2004 - p56(1) [1-50]

Williams, David R. - *Sin Boldly! Dr. Dave's Guide to Writing the College Paper*
  Kliatt - v39 - i1 - Jan 2005 - p27(2) [501+]

Williams, Demetrius - *An End to This Strife: The Politics of Gender in African American Churches*
  Bl S - v34 - i3 - Fall 2004 - p76-76 [501+]

Williams, Donnie - *The Thunder of Angels: Behind the Scenes of Segregation*
  Black Iss - v6 - i5 - Sept-Oct 2004 - p11(1) [501+]

Williams, Drid - *Anthropology and the Dance: Ten Lectures*
  Choice - v42 - i5 - Jan 2005 - p864(1) [1-50]
Williams-Garcia, Rita - *No Laughter Here*
  LibMed - v23 - i1 - August-Sept 2004 - p69(1) [51-500]
Williams, George M. - *Handbook of Hindu Mythology*
  R&R Bk N - v19 - i1 - Feb 2004 - p13(1) [51-500]
Williams, Gerhild Scholz - *Paracelsian Moments: Science, Medicine, and Astrology in Early Modern Europe*
  Six Ct J - v35 - i1 - Spring 2004 - p287(3) [501+]
Williams, Glyn - *Voyages of Delusion: The Quest for the Northwest Passage*
  BIC - v33 - i2 - March 2004 - p18(4) [501+]
Williams, Godfried - *Synchronizing E-Security*
  SciTech - v28 - i1 - March 2004 - p158(1) [51-500]
Williams, Greg - *Boomtown*
  VQR - v80 - i3 - Summer 2004 - p263(1) [1-50]
Williams, Heather - *Mallarme's Ideas in Language*
  R&R Bk N - v19 - i4 - Nov 2004 - p230(1) [501+]
Parachutes, Patriots, and Partisans: The Special Operations Executive and Yugoslavia, 1941-1945
  Choice - v42 - i3 - Nov 2004 - p539(1) [1-50]
Williams, Howard - *The Ethics of Diet: A Catena of Authorities Deprecatory of the Practice of Flesh-Eating*
  Choice - v42 - i1 - Sept 2004 - p116(2) [501+]
Williams, Hugh E. - *Web Database Applications with PHP and MySQL*
  LJ - v129 - i20 - Dec 1 2004 - p152(1) [51-500]
Williams, Ira E. - *First Do No Harm: The Cure for Medical Malpractice*
  Bwatch - v26 - i7 - July 2004 - p2(1) [51-500]
Williams, Jack - *Entertaining the Nation: A Social History of British Television*
  HT - v54 - i8 - August 2004 - p57(2) [501+]
  TLS - i5296 - Oct 1 2004 - p24-25 [501+]
Williams, James R. - *Developing Performance Support for Computer Systems: A Strategy for Maximizing Usability and Learnability*
  SciTech - v28 - i3 - Sept 2004 - p18(1) [501+]
Williams, Jan R. - *2004 Miller GAAP Practice Manual: Restatement and Analysis of Other Current FASB, EITF, and AICPA Pronouncements*
  R&R Bk N - v19 - i1 - Feb 2004 - p112(1) [51-500]
Miller GAAP Guide, 2004: Restatement and Analysis of Current FASB Standards
  R&R Bk N - v19 - i1 - Feb 2004 - p112(1) [51-500]
Williams, Jean A. - *Sweet Expectations: Michele Hoskins' Recipe for Success*
  PW - v251 - i46 - Nov 15 2004 - p21(1) [501+]
Williams, Jean Calterone - *"A Roof over My Head": Homeless Women and the Shelter Industry*
  CS - v33 - i4 - July 2004 - p430(2) [501+]
Williams, Jeanne - *The Hidden Valley: A Frontier Story*
  Roundup M - v12 - i3 - Feb 2005 - p30(1) [51-500]
Williams, Jeffrey J. - *Critics at Work: Interviews 1993-2003*
  TLS - i5286 - July 23 2004 - p7-9 [501+]
The Institution of Literature
  Col Lit - v31 - i4 - Fall 2004 - p172(9) [501+]
Williams, Jerome D. - *Diversity in Advertising: Broadening the Scope of Research Directions*
  R&R Bk N - v19 - i3 - August 2004 - p132(1) [501+]
Williams, John - *The Illustrated Beatus: A Corpus of the Illustrations of the Commentary on the Apocalypse, vol. 5*
  Med R - August 2004 - pNA [501+]
Wales Half Welsh
  KR - v73 - i3 - Feb 1 2005 - p146(1) [501+]
  TLS - i5302 - Nov 12 2004 - p22(1) [501+]
Williams, John A. - *The Man Who Cried I Am*
  Bl S - v34 - i3 - Fall 2004 - p76-76 [501+]
Williams, John Alexander - *Appalachia: A History*
  Black Iss - v6 - i5 - Sept-Oct 2004 - p42(2) [501+]
Williams, Johnny E. - *African American Religion and the Civil Rights Movement in Arkansas*
  Choice - v41 - i7 - March 2004 - p1359(1) [501+]
  JSH - v71 - i1 - Feb 2005 - p211(2) [501+]
Williams, Jonathan - *Jubilant Thicket: New and Selected Poems*
  PW - v252 - i10 - March 7 2005 - p66(1) [51-500]
Williams, Joy - *Honored Guest: Stories*
  Atl - v294 - i5 - Dec 2004 - p123(1) [501+]
  Atl - v294 - i5 - Dec 2004 - p124(1) [501+]
y BL - v101 - i1 - Sept 1 2004 - p66(1) [501+]
  BL - v101 - i9-10 - Jan 1 2005 - p770(1) [501+]
  KR - v72 - i16 - August 15 2004 - p776(1) [501+]
  LJ - v129 - i14 - Sept 1 2004 - p145(1) [501+]
  NYTBR - Dec 19 2004 - p14 [501+]
  PW - v251 - i35 - August 30 2004 - p30(1) [501+]

Williams, Juan - *I'll Find a Way or Make One: A Tribute to Historically Black Colleges and Universities*
y BL - v101 - i4 - Oct 15 2004 - p370(1) [51-500]
  PW - v251 - i41 - Oct 11 2004 - p66(1) [51-500]
Williams, Judith - *Discovering Dinosaurs with a Fossil Hunter (Illus. by Skrepnick, Michael W.)*
c SLJ - v51 - i2 - Feb 2005 - p124(1) [51-500]
y SB - v40 - i6 - Nov-Dec 2004 - p260(1) [51-500]
Exploring the Rain Forest Treetops with a Scientist
c SLJ - v51 - i11 - Nov 2004 - p132(1) [51-500]
Saving Endangered Animals with a Scientist
c SLJ - v51 - i1 - Jan 2005 - p118(1) [51-500]
Searching for Stormy Weather with a Scientist
c SB - v40 - i6 - Nov-Dec 2004 - p268(1) [51-500]
Williams, Judy - *Dynamite Stories*
  CBRA - Annual 2003 - p353(2) [51-500]
Williams, Julie - *Escaping Tornado Season: A Story in Poems*
  LibMed - v23 - i1 - August-Sept 2004 - p69(1) [51-500]
A Smart Girl's Guide to Starting Middle School: Everything You Need to Know about Juggling More Homework, More Teachers, and More Friends! (Illus. by Martini, Angela)
c SLJ - v50 - i10 - Oct 2004 - p196(1) [51-500]
Williams, Karen Lynn - *Circles of Hope (Illus. by Saport, Linda)*
c KR - v73 - i2 - Jan 15 2005 - p127(1) [51-500]
c PW - v252 - i9 - Feb 28 2005 - p66(1) [51-500]
Williams, Karla A. - *Donor Focused Strategies for Annual Giving*
  R&R Bk N - v19 - i1 - Feb 2004 - p136(1) [51-500]
Williams, Kathleen Broome - *Grace Hopper: Admiral of the Cyber Sea*
  BL - v101 - i2 - Sept 15 2004 - p185(1) [51-500]
Williams, Kevin L. - *Microbial Contamination Control in Parneteral Manufacturing*
  SciTech - v28 - i3 - Sept 2004 - p124(1) [51-500]
Williams, Kim - *The Villas of Palladio (Illus. by Giaconi, Giovanni)*
  Choice - v42 - i1 - Sept 2004 - p92(1) [501+]
  R&R Bk N - v19 - i1 - Feb 2004 - p202 [51-500]
Williams, Kristian - *Our Enemies in Blue: Police and Power in America*
  PW - v251 - i50 - Dec 13 2004 - p56(1) [51-500]
Williams, Lillian Serece - *Strangers in the Land of Paradise: The Creation of an African American Community in Buffalo, New York, 1900-1940*
  J Urban H - v31 - i1 - Nov 2004 - p106-114 [501+]
Williams, Linda - *Porn Studies*
  Choice - v42 - i4 - Dec 2004 - p644(1) [1-50]
  Wom R Bks - v21 - i12 - Sept 2004 - p27(1) [501+]
Williams, Linda D. - *Backhoes*
c SLJ - v51 - i2 - Feb 2005 - p130(1) [51-500]
Bulldozers
c SLJ - v51 - i2 - Feb 2005 - p130(1) [51-500]
Dump Trucks
c SLJ - v51 - i2 - Feb 2005 - p130(1) [51-500]
Earthmovers
c SLJ - v51 - i2 - Feb 2005 - p130(1) [51-500]
Williams, Liz - *Banner of Souls*
  BL - v101 - i3 - Oct 1 2004 - p319(1) [51-500]
  Ent W - i790 - Oct 29 2004 - p71 [501+]
  LJ - v129 - i17 - Oct 15 2004 - p58(1) [51-500]
  PW - v251 - i34 - August 23 2004 - p42(1) [51-500]
The Banquet of the Lords of Night: And Other Stories
  PW - v251 - i33 - August 16 2004 - p47(1) [51-500]
Williams, Lori Aurelia - *Broken China*
y HB - v81 - i2 - March-April 2005 - p210(1) [51-500]
  KR - v73 - i3 - Feb 1 2005 - p183(1) [51-500]
Williams, Louise Blakeney - *Modernism and the Ideology of History: Literature, Politics, and the Past*
  AHR - v109 - i3 - June 2004 - p861(2) [501+]
  Clio - v33 - i2 - Wntr 2004 - p189(22) [501+]
Williams, Lucy - *Law and Poverty: The Legal System and Poverty Reduction*
  Choice - v42 - i2 - Oct 2004 - p366(1) [51-500]
Williams, Maiya - *The Golden Hour (Read by Free, Kevin R.). Audiobook Review*
y Kliatt - v39 - i1 - Jan 2005 - p42(1) [51-500]
c SLJ - v51 - i1 - Jan 2005 - p76(1) [51-500]
The Golden Hour
  Black Iss - v7 - i2 - March-April 2005 - p16(1) [51-500]
c NYTBR - August 8 2004 - p17 [51-500]

Williams, Marcia - *Bravo, Mr. William Shakespeare!*
c Teach Lib - v32 - i3 - Feb 2005 - p21(1) [51-500]
God and His Creations: Tales from the Old Testament (Illus. by Williams, Marcia)
  Sch Lib - v52 - i3 - Autumn 2004 - p153(1) [501+]
c TES - v0 - i4576 - March 26 2004 - pssss18(2) [501+]
Williams, Marianne - *Classical Music Without Fear: A Guide for General Audiences*
  MT - v145 - i1888 - Autumn 2004 - p106-108 [501+]
Williams, Mark London - *Ancient Fire*
c BL - v100 - i22 - August 2004 - p1937(1) [51-500]
c CH Bwatch - v14 - i7 - July 2004 - p7(1) [51-500]
y VOYA - v27 - i3 - August 2004 - p235(1) [1-50]
Dragon Sword
c CH Bwatch - v14 - i7 - July 2004 - p7(1) [51-500]
y VOYA - v27 - i3 - August 2004 - p235(1) [1-50]
Williams, Michael - *Deforesting the Earth: From Prehistory to Global Crisis*
  J Hist G - v30 - i1 - Jan 2004 - p208(3) [501+]
  QRB - v79 - i4 - Dec 2004 - p447(2) [501+]
Williams, Michael Ann - *Homeplace: The Social Use and Meaning of the Folk Dwelling in Southwestern North Carolina*
  R&R Bk N - v19 - i3 - August 2004 - p85(1) [51-500]
Williams, Nancy S. - *Using Literature to Support Skills and Critical Discussion for Struggling Readers: Grades 3-9*
  R&R Bk N - v19 - i3 - August 2004 - p217(1) [1-50]
Williams, Niall - *A Healing Force*
  Econ - v374 - i8411 - Jan 29 2005 - p80US [501+]
Williams, Nicholas M. - *Ideology and Utopia in the Poetry of William Blake*
  Eight-C St - v36 - i2 - Winter 2003 - p295 [501+]
Williams-Nickelson, Carol - *Internships in Psychology: An APAGS Workbook for Writing Successful Applications and Finding the Right Match, 2005-2006 Ed.*
  SciTech - v28 - i4 - Dec 2004 - p1(1) [1-50]
Williams, Norman - *One Unblinking Eye*
  Ant R - v63 - i1 - Wntr 2005 - p191(1) [501+]
Williams, Pat - *Coaching Your Kids to Be Leaders: The Keys to Unlocking Their Potential*
  BL - v101 - i6 - Nov 15 2004 - p534(1) [51-500]
  LJ - v129 - i19 - Nov 15 2004 - p81(1) [51-500]
  PW - v251 - i48 - Nov 29 2004 - p32(1) [51-500]
Williams, Patricia J. - *Open House of Family, Friends, Food, Piano Lessons and the Search for a Room of My Own*
y BL - v101 - i6 - Nov 15 2004 - p533(1) [51-500]
  Bl S - v34 - i3 - Fall 2004 - p76-76 [501+]
  Black Iss - v6 - i6 - Nov-Dec 2004 - p65(1) [501+]
  KR - v72 - i17 - Sept 1 2004 - p857(1) [501+]
  LJ - v130 - i1 - Jan 1 2005 - p114(1) [501+]
  People - v62 - i23 - Dec 6 2004 - p55 [51-500]
  PW - v251 - i36 - Sept 6 2004 - p54(1) [51-500]
Williams, Paul - *Performing Artist: 1986-1990 and Beyond*
  TLS - i5302 - Nov 12 2004 - p8-9 [501+]
The Unexpected Way: On Converting from Buddhism to Catholicism
  CC - v121 - i21 - Oct 19 2004 - p61(2) [501+]
  IBMR - v29 - i1 - Jan 2005 - p51(1) [501+]
Williams, Paul L. - *Osama's Revenge: The Next 9/11: What the Media and the Government Haven't Told You*
  Globe & Mail - July 24 2004 - pD14 [501+]
  MEJ - v58 - i4 - Autumn 2004 - p708(1) [501+]
  R&R Bk N - v19 - i4 - Nov 2004 - p145(1) [501+]
  SPA - v61 - i1 - Jan-Feb 2005 - p69(2) [501+]
Williams, Pepper - *Interactive Statistics for the Behavioral Sciences*
  Choice - v41 - i7 - March 2004 - p1331(1) [501+]
Williams, Peter - *The Life of Bach*
  Choice - v42 - i1 - Sept 2004 - p112(1) [501+]
  MT - v145 - i1886 - Spring 2004 - p116-118 [501+]
  Notes - v61 - i3 - March 2005 - p772(3) [501+]
The Organ Music of J.S. Bach
  Choice - v42 - i1 - Sept 2004 - p112(1) [501+]
  Notes - v61 - i2 - Dec 2004 - p430(3) [501+]
Williams, Philip F. - *The Great Wall of Confinement: The Chinese Prison Camp Through Contemporary Fiction and Reportage*
  TLS - i5291 - August 27 2004 - p11(1) [501+]
Williams, Philip Lee - *A Distant Flame: A Novel of the Civil War*
  KR - v72 - i14 - July 15 2004 - p660(1) [501+]

Williams, Raymond Leslie - *The Twentieth-Century Spanish American Novel*
  VQR - v80 - i1 - Wntr 2004 - p269-270 [501+]
  VQR - v80 - i1 - Wntr 2004 - p269-270 [501+]
Williams, Rhonda Y. - *The Politics of Public Housing: Black Women's Struggles Against Urban Inequality*
  LJ - v129 - i17 - Oct 15 2004 - p78(1) [51-500]
Williams, Robert - *Art Theory: An Historical Introduction*
  Choice - v42 - i1 - Sept 2004 - p87(1) [501+]
Williams, Robin - *The Robin Williams Mac OS X Book: Jaguar Ed.*
  SciTech - v28 - i4 - Dec 2004 - p28(1) [1-50]
  The Robin Williams Mac OS X book, Panther Ed.
  SciTech - v28 - i3 - Sept 2004 - p28(1) [1-50]
Williams, Robin Lynn - *The Assistants*
  BW - v34 - i33 - August 15 2004 - p6(1) [501+]
  People - v62 - i1 - July 5 2004 - p48 [51-500]
Williams, Robin Murphy - *The Wars Within: Peoples and States in Conflict*
  AJS - v110 - i1 - July 2004 - p232(2) [501+]
  CS - v33 - i4 - July 2004 - p476(2) [501+]
Williams, Roger - *The Bloudy Tenet of Persecution: For Cause of Conscience, Discussed in a Conference Between Truth and Peace*
  J Ch St - v46 - i3 - Summer 2004 - p665(2) [501+]
Williams, Rowan - *Anglican Identities*
  TLS - i5284 - July 9 2004 - p24(1) [501+]
  The Dwelling of the Light: Praying with Icons of Christ
  TLS - i5264 - Feb 20 2004 - p32-32 [501+]
  Silence and Honey Cakes: The Wisdom of the Desert
  TLS - i5264 - Feb 20 2004 - p32-32 [501+]
Williams, Sam - *Talk Peace (Illus. by Moriuchi, Mique)*
  c PW - v252 - i9 - Feb 28 2005 - p65(1) [51-500]
Williams, Sean - *The Resurrected Man*
  KR - v73 - i3 - Feb 1 2005 - p156(1) [51-500]
Williams, Serena - *Venus and Serena: Serving from the Hip*
  c PW - v252 - i8 - Feb 21 2005 - p177(1) [501+]
Williams, Shirley - *God and Caesar: Personal Reflections on Politics and Religion*
  Theol St - v65 - i3 - Sept 2004 - p684(2) [501+]
Williams, Simon - *Wagner and the Romantic Hero*
  Choice - v42 - i6 - Feb 2005 - p1032(1) [51-500]
Williams, Simon J. - *Medicine and the Body*
  SciTech - v28 - i4 - Dec 2004 - p81(1) [51-500]
Williams, Sonny - *Story Hour: Contemporary Narratives by American Poets*
  BL - v101 - i1 - Sept 1 2004 - p40(2) [51-500]
Williams, Susan - *The People's King: The True Story of the Abdication*
  Choice - v42 - i2 - Oct 2004 - p360(1) [51-500]
Williams, Susan G. - *Symbolic Dynamics and Its Applications; Proceedings*
  SciTech - v28 - i3 - Sept 2004 - p42(1) [1-50]
Williams, Susan H. - *Truth, Autonomy, and Speech: Feminist Theory and the First Amendment*
  Choice - v42 - i5 - Jan 2005 - p936(1) [51-500]
  Law&PolBR - Sept 2004 - pNA [501+]
Williams, Tad - *Shadowmarch. Vol. 1*
  BL - v101 - i4 - Oct 15 2004 - p395(1) [51-500]
  Kliatt - v38 - i6 - Nov 2004 - p12(1) [51-500]
  PW - v251 - i40 - Oct 4 2004 - p74(1) [51-500]
Williams, Tennessee - *Cat on a Hot Tin Roof*
  Am Theat - v21 - i8 - Oct 2004 - p139(4) [51-500]
  The Selected Letters of Tennessee Williams
  PW - v251 - i43 - Oct 25 2004 - p39(1) [51-500]
  A Streetcar Named Desire
  Am Theat - v21 - i8 - Oct 2004 - p139(4) [51-500]
Williams, Thomas - *The Cambridge Companion to Duns Scotus*
  Med R - Dec 2004 - pNA [501+]
Williams, Tony - *Body and Soul: The Cinematic Vision of Robert Aldrich*
  Choice - v42 - i6 - Feb 2005 - p1029(1) [51-500]
  R&R Bk N - v19 - i4 - Nov 2004 - p225(1) [501+]
Williams, Vera - *Amber Was Brave, Essie Was Smart*
  y Magpies - v19 - i5 - Nov 2004 - p38(1) [501+]
Williams. W. Larry - *Developmental Disabilities; Etiology, Assessment, Intervention, and Integration*
  SciTech - v28 - i3 - Sept 2004 - p96(1) [51-500]
Williams, Walter - *Reaganism and the Death of Representative Democracy*
  PSQ - v119 - i2 - Summer 2004 - p340(2) [501+]
  R&R Bk N - v19 - i1 - Feb 2004 - pNA [501+]
Williamson, Chilton - *The Conservative Bookshelf: Essential Works That Impact Today's Conservative Thinkers*
  BL - v101 - i5 - Nov 1 2004 - p449(1) [501+]
Williamson, Donald I. - *Origins of Larvae, rev. ed.*
  SciTech - v28 - i1 - March 2004 - p68(1) [51-500]

Williamson, Edwin - *Borges: A Life*
  Atl - v294 - i2 - Sept 2004 - p143(6) [501+]
  BL - v100 - i21 - July 2004 - p1811(1) [1-50]
  BW - v34 - i35 - August 2004 - p11(1) [1-50]
  BW - v34 - i32 - August 8 2004 - p15(1) [501+]
  Choice - v42 - i6 - Feb 2005 - p1027(1) [51-500]
  Econ - v372 - i8392 - Sept 11 2004 - p79US [501+]
  HM - v309 - i1852 - Sept 2004 - p87(4) [501+]
  LJ - v129 - i13 - August 2004 - p82(1) [501+]
  NYTBR - Nov 7 2004 - p10 [501+]
  Spec - v296 - i9197 - Nov 13 2004 - p47(1) [501+]
Williamson, Jack - *The Humanoids and with Folded Hands (Read by Rudnicki, Stefan). Audiobook Review*
  y Kliatt - v38 - i5 - Sept 2004 - p61(2) [51-500]
Williamson, Joy Ann - *Black Power on Campus: The University of Illinois, 1965-75*
  Choice - v41 - i7 - March 2004 - p1345(1) [501+]
  JAH - v91 - i2 - Sept 2004 - p714(2) [501+]
Williamson, Lamar - *Preaching the Gospel of John: Proclaiming the Living Word*
  Intpr - v58 - i4 - Oct 2004 - p426(2) [501+]
Williamson, Margaret Holmes - *Powhatan Lords of Life and Death: Command and Consent in Seventeenth-Century Virginia*
  Am Ind CRJ - v27 - i4 - Fall 2003 - pNA [501+]
  JAH - v91 - i1 - June 2004 - p211-212 [501+]
  JSH - v70 - i3 - August 2004 - p641(2) [501+]
Williamson, Marianne - *The Gift of Change: Spiritual Guidance for a Radically New Life*
  PW - v251 - i43 - Oct 25 2004 - p45(1) [51-500]
Williamson, Miryam Ehrlich - *Type 2*
  Bwatch - Dec 2004 - pNA [51-500]
Williamson, Nancy J. - *Knowledge Organization and Classification in International Information Retrieval*
  LJ - v129 - i13 - August 2004 - p124(1) [51-500]
  LRTS - v49 - i1 - Jan 2005 - p62(4) [501+]
Williamson, Paul - *Medieval and Renaissance Stained Glass in the Victoria and Albert Museum*
  TimHES - v0 - i1654 - August 20 2004 - p25(1) [501+]
Williamson, Ronald F. - *Bones of the Ancestors: The Archaeology and Osteobiography of the Moatfield Ossuary*
  CBRA - Annual 2003 - p362(1) [501+]
Williamson, Thad - *More than Just a Game: Why North Carolina Basketball Means So Much to So Many*
  SSJ - v21 - i2 - June 2004 - p230-237 [501+]
Williamson, Tom - *Shaping Medieval Landscapes: Settlement, Society, Environment, 2nd Ed.*
  R&R Bk N - v19 - i4 - Nov 2004 - p36(1) [51-500]
  Shaping Medieval Lanscapes: Settlement, Society, Environment, 2nd Ed.
  J Hist G - v30 - i1 - Jan 2004 - p211(2) [501+]
Willie, Charles Vert - *A New Look at Black Families*
  CS - v33 - i1 - Jan 2004 - p131-131 [501+]
  Student Diversity, Choice and School Improvement
  JNE - v73 - i1 - Wntr 2004 - p100-102 [501+]
Willie, Sarah Susannah - *Acting Black: College, Identity, and the Performance of Race*
  CS - v33 - i4 - July 2004 - p418(2) [501+]
  TCR - v106 - i2 - Feb 2004 - p262-266 [501+]
Willig, Lauren - *The Secret History of the Pink Carnation (Read by Reading, Kate). Audiobook Review*
  PW - v252 - i10 - March 7 2005 - p26(1) [51-500]
  The Secret History of the Pink Carnation
  y BL - v101 - i6 - Nov 15 2004 - p558(1) [51-500]
  KR - v72 - i21 - Nov 1 2004 - p1028(2) [51-500]
  LJ - v129 - i19 - Nov 15 2004 - p53(1) [51-500]
  PW - v252 - i4 - Jan 24 2005 - p223(1) [501+]
Willinger, Barbara I. - *A History of AIDS Social Work in Hospitals: A Daring Response to an Epidemic*
  SciTech - v28 - i1 - March 2004 - p83(1) [51-500]
  Soc Ser R - v78 - i4 - Dec 2004 - p698(1) [501+]
Willingham, Bill - *Storybook Love*
  BL - v100 - i21 - July 2004 - p1831(1) [1-50]
Willis, Clint - *The I Hate Dick Cheney, John Ashcroft, Donald Rumsfeld, Condi Rice . . . Reader: Behind the Bush Cabinet's War on America*
  Globe & Mail - August 14 2004 - pD12 [1-50]
Willis, David - *Notes on the Holiness of God*
  TT - v60 - i4 - Jan 2004 - p606-609 [501+]
Willis, James F. - *Macroeconomics*
  JEL - v42 - i1 - March 2004 - p237(1) [501+]
  Macroeconomics Study Guide
  JEL - v42 - i1 - March 2004 - p237(1) [501+]

Willis, Jeanne - *The Adventures of Jimmy Scar*
  c SLJ - v50 - i10 - Oct 2004 - p182(1) [51-500]
  Don't Let Go
  c CE - v80 - i5 - Mid-Summer 2004 - p275(1) [1-50]
  Dumb Creatures
  c Sch Lib - v52 - i4 - Winter 2004 - p206(1) [51-500]
  I Hate School (Illus. by Ross, Tony)
  c CH Bwatch - v14 - i7 - July 2004 - p4(1) [51-500]
  c SLJ - v50 - i8 - August 2004 - p104(1) [51-500]
  Naked without a Hat
  BL - v100 - i21 - July 2004 - p1835(2) [1-50]
  Never Too Little to Love (Illus. by Fearnley, Jan)
  c PW - v251 - i49 - Dec 6 2004 - p59(1) [51-500]
  Operation Itchy (Illus. by Dann, Penny)
  c PW - v251 - i48 - Nov 29 2004 - p41(2) [501+]
  Shhh!
  c Sch Lib - v52 - i4 - Winter 2004 - p191(1) [51-500]
  When Stephanie Smiled.... (Illus. by Jossen, Penelope)
  c SLJ - v50 - i9 - Sept 2004 - p182(1) [51-500]
Willis, Jim - *The Human Journalist: Reporters, Perspectives, and Emotions*
  R&R Bk N - v19 - i1 - Feb 2004 - p229(1) [51-500]
  The Religion Book: Places, Prophets, Saints, and Seers
  Choice - v42 - i2 - Oct 2004 - p270(1) [501+]
  y LibMed - v23 - i3 - Nov-Dec 2004 - p86(1) [51-500]
  R&R Bk N - v19 - i3 - August 2004 - p12(1) [1-50]
  R&USQ - v44 - i2 - Winter 2004 - p174(2) [501+]
  c SLJ - v50 - i8 - August 2004 - p60(1) [501+]
Willis, Resa - *FDR and Lucy: Lovers and Friends*
  LJ - v129 - i17 - Oct 15 2004 - p75(1) [51-500]
Willis, Robert - *Environmental Systems Engineering and Economics*
  SciTech - v28 - i1 - March 2004 - p147(1) [51-500]
Willis, Terri - *Democratic Republic of the Congo*
  c BL - v101 - i1 - Sept 1 2004 - p118(1) [1-50]
Willis, Thearon - *Beginning VB.NET 2003*
  SciTech - v28 - i3 - Sept 2004 - p21(1) [51-500]
Willmott, H.P. - *Battleship*
  R&R Bk N - v19 - i1 - Feb 2004 - p257(1) [51-500]
  World War II
  R&R Bk N - v20 - i1 - Feb 2005 - p32(1) [51-500]
Willms, Jon Douglas - *Vulnerable Children: Findings from Canada's National Longitudinal Survey of Children and Youth*
  CBRA - Annual 2003 - p378(1) [501+]
Willner-Pardo, Gina - *My Mom and Other Mysteries of the Universe*
  c BL - v101 - i5 - Nov 1 2004 - p486(1) [51-500]
  c CCB-B - v58 - i3 - Nov 2004 - p151(2) [501+]
  c KR - v72 - i19 - Oct 1 2004 - p971(1) [51-500]
  c SLJ - v50 - i10 - Oct 2004 - p182(1) [51-500]
Willrich, Michael - *City of Courts: Socializing Justice in Progressive Era Chicago*
  AHR - v109 - i2 - April 2004 - p548(2) [501+]
  JAH - v91 - i2 - Sept 2004 - p659(2) [501+]
Wills, David C. - *The First War on Terrorism: Counter-Terrorism Policy During the Reagan Administration*
  PSQ - v119 - i4 - Winter 2004 - p690(2) [501+]
  R&R Bk N - v19 - i1 - Feb 2004 - p141(1) [51-500]
Wills, Gregory A. - *Democratic Religion: Freedom, Authority, and Church Discipline in the Baptist South*
  J Ch St - v46 - i3 - Summer 2004 - p666(3) [501+]
Wills, Rebecca - *The Jacobites and Russia, 1715-1750*
  HER - v119 - i483 - Sept 2004 - p1063(2) [501+]
  HER - v119 - i483 - Sept 2004 - p1063(2) [501+]
Wills, Susan - *Meteorology: Predicting the Weather*
  c SLJ - v50 - i7 - July 2004 - p129(1) [51-500]
Willsdon, Clare A.P. - *In the Gardens of Impressionism*
  Choice - v42 - i7 - March 2005 - p1219(1) [51-500]
Willsher, James - *The Dedalus Book of English Decadence*
  TLS - i5295 - Sept 24 2004 - p26(1) [501+]
Willsher, Peter - *Fred Pontin: The Man and His Business*
  R&R Bk N - v19 - i1 - Feb 2004 - p73(1) [51-500]
Willson, Rachel Beckles - *Gyorgy Kurtag: The Sayings of Peter Bornemisza, Op. 7 (1963-68); A 'Concerto' for Soprano and Piano*
  R&R Bk N - v19 - i4 - Nov 2004 - p195(1) [501+]
Willughby, Francis - *Francis Willughby's Book of Games: A Seventeenth Century Treatise on Sports, Games, and Pastimes*
  R&R Bk N - v19 - i1 - Feb 2004 - p75(1) [51-500]

Wilmer, S.E. - *Theatre, Society and the Nation: Staging American Identities*
    Theat J - v56 - i1 - March 2004 - p148(3) [501+]
Writing and Rewriting: National Theatre Histories
    Choice - v42 - i6 - Feb 2005 - p1033(1) [51-500]

Wilmerding, John - *American Art in the Princeton University Art Museum, Volume 1: Drawings and Watercolors*
    LJ - v129 - i20 - Dec 1 2004 - p113(1) [51-500]
    Mag Antiq - v167 - i1 - Jan 2005 - p128(1) [51-500]
    Mag Antiq - v167 - i2 - Feb 2005 - p54(1) [51-500]
    Mag Antiq - v167 - i3 - March 2005 - p58(1) [501+]

Wilmot, Laurence F. - *Through the Hitler Line: Memoirs of an Infantry Chaplain*
    Can Hist R - v85 - i3 - Sept 2004 - p624(3) [501+]
    CBRA - Annual 2003 - p77(1) [51-500]

Wilner, Eleanor Rand - *The Girl with Bees in Her Hair*
    Poet - v185 - i6 - March 2005 - p463(13) [501+]

Wilshire, Bruce - *Fashionable Nihilism: A Critique of Analytic Philosophy*
    Parabola - v29 - i1 - Spring 2004 - p102(3) [501+]
    RM - v58 - i1 - Sept 2004 - p202(4) [501+]

Wilson, A.N. - *Iris Murdoch as I Knew Her*
    CR - v285 - i1662 - July 2004 - p51(2) [501+]
London: A History
    BW - v34 - i39 - Sept 26 2004 - p8(1) [501+]
    Globe & Mail - August 7 2004 - pD6 [501+]
London: A Short History
    CR - v285 - i1665 - Oct 2004 - p251(1) [501+]
My Name Is Legion
    KR - v73 - i5 - March 1 2005 - p259(1) [51-500]
    PW - v252 - i11 - March 14 2005 - p44(2) [51-500]
The Victorians
    MA - v46 - i4 - Fall 2004 - p366(4) [501+]

Wilson, A. Paula - *Library Web Sites: Creating Online Collections and Services*
    BL - v101 - i1 - Sept 1 2004 - p164(1) [1-50]

Wilson, Andrew - *Beautiful Shadow: A Life of Patricia Highsmith*
    Choice - v41 - i7 - March 2004 - p1300(1) [501+]

Wilson, Andrew R. - *Ambition and Identity: Chinese Merchant Elites in Colonial Manila, 1880-1916*
    Choice - v42 - i4 - Dec 2004 - p716(1) [1-50]
    R&R Bk N - v19 - i3 - August 2004 - p55(1) [51-500]

Wilson, Ara - *The Intimate Economies of Bangkok: Tomboys, Tycoons, and Avon Ladies in the Global City*
    Choice - v42 - i4 - Dec 2004 - p701(1) [1-50]

Wilson, Barbara A. - *Neuropsychological Rehabilitation: Theory and Practice*
    E-Streams - Dec 2004 - pNA [501+]

Wilson, Barbara Ker - *Maui and the Big Fish*
    c Sch Lib - v52 - i4 - Winter 2004 - p191(1) [51-500]

Wilson, Bee - *The Hive: The Story of the Honeybee and Us*
    Econ - v372 - i8393 - Sept 18 2004 - p87US [501+]
    Lon R Bks - v26 - i21 - Nov 4 2004 - p13(2) [501+]
    NS - v133 - i4710 - Oct 18 2004 - p52(2) [501+]
    NS - v133 - i4716 - Nov 29 2004 - p45(1) [51-500]

Wilson, Brandon - *Yak Butter Blues: A Tibetan Trek of Faith*
    LJ - v129 - i17 - Oct 15 2004 - p79(1) [51-500]

Wilson, Carolyn C. - *St. Joseph in Italian Renaissance Society and Art: New Directions and Interpretations*
    CHR - v90 - i4 - Oct 2004 - p781(2) [501+]

Wilson, Catherine - *Descartes's Meditations: An Introduction*
    Choice - v42 - i1 - Sept 2004 - p117(1) [501+]

Wilson, Chris - *Everyday America: Cultural Landscape Studies after J.B. Jackson*
    Pub Hist - v26 - i1 - Wntr 2004 - p157(3) [501+]
Hermesetas
    T&C - v45 - i4 - Oct 2004 - p859(2) [501+]

Wilson, Cintra - *Colors Insulting to Nature*
    BL - v100 - i21 - July 2004 - p1818(1) [1-50]

Wilson, Clyde N. - *The Papers of John C. Calhoun. Volume XXVII: 1849-1850. With Supplement*
    JSH - v70 - i4 - Nov 2004 - p920(2) [501+]

Wilson, Colin - *Dreaming to Some Purpose: An Autobiography*
    Spec - v295 - i9182 - July 31 2004 - p33(1) [501+]
    TLS - i5285 - July 16 2004 - p9(1) [501+]
The History of Murder
    LJ - v130 - i1 - Jan 1 2005 - p172(1) [1-50]

Wilson, D.F. - *Ransom, Revenge, and Heroic Identity in the Iliad*
    Class R - v54 - i2 - Nov 2004 - p277-278 [501+]

Wilson, Darlene Anderson - *Strategies for Classroom Management, K-6: Making Magic Happen*
    R&R Bk N - v19 - i4 - Nov 2004 - p188(1) [501+]

Wilson, David Sloan - *Darwin's Cathedral: Evolution, Religion, and the Nature of Society*
    JAAR - v72 - i3 - Sept 2004 - p800-802 [501+]

Wilson, Debbie - *Tiger in the Shadows: A Novel*
    Kliatt - v38 - i6 - Nov 2004 - p21(1) [51-500]

Wilson, Dede - *A Baker's Field Guide to Chocolate Chip Cookies*
    LJ - v129 - i15 - Sept 15 2004 - p79(1) [51-500]

Wilson, Derek - *The Nature of Rare Things*
    KR - v73 - i4 - Feb 15 2005 - p203(2) [51-500]
The Uncrowned Kings of England: The Black History of the Dudleys and the Tudor Throne
    KR - v72 - i18 - Sept 15 2004 - p908(1) [51-500]
    PW - v251 - i40 - Oct 4 2004 - p79(1) [51-500]

Wilson, Dolores J. - *Big Hair and Flying Cows*
    PW - v252 - i9 - Feb 28 2005 - p42(1) [51-500]

Wilson, Donna - *Ransom, Revenge and Heroic Identity in the Iliad*
    CJ - v99 - i3 - Feb-March 2004 - p349-353 [501+]

Wilson, Ed - *Microsoft Windows Scripting Self-Paced Learning Guide*
    SciTech - v28 - i3 - Sept 2004 - p27(1) [51-500]

Wilson, Edmund - *Axel's Castle: A Study of the Imaginative Literature of 1870-1930*
    AS - v73 - i4 - Autumn 2004 - p162(3) [501+]
    LJ - v130 - i1 - Jan 1 2005 - p172(1) [1-50]
Memoirs of Hecate County
    LJ - v130 - i2 - Feb 1 2005 - p126(1) [1-50]

Wilson, Edward O. - *On Human Nature*
    Bwatch - March 2005 - pNA [51-500]
Pheidole in the New World: A Dominant, Hyperdiverse Ant Genus
    TLS - i5287 - July 30 2004 - p3-4 [501+]

Wilson, Elizabeth - *Adorned in Dreams: Fashion and Modernity, Rev. Ed.*
    R&R Bk N - v19 - i1 - Feb 2004 - p73(1) [501+]

Wilson, Ellen Judy - *Encyclopedia of the Enlightenment, Rev. Ed.*
    Choice - v42 - i6 - Feb 2005 - p990(1) [501+]
    R&R Bk N - v19 - i4 - Nov 2004 - p4(1) [51-500]

Wilson, Emily Herring - *No One Gardens Alone: A Life of Elizabeth Lawrence*
    BL - v101 - i2 - Sept 15 2004 - p189(1) [51-500]
    KR - v72 - i15 - August 1 2004 - p736(1) [501+]
    LJ - v129 - i16 - Oct 1 2004 - p103(1) [51-500]
    PW - v251 - i32 - August 9 2004 - p240(2) [51-500]

Wilson, F. Paul - *Crisscross*
    ChrSFF&H - v26 - i10 - Oct 2004 - p24(1) [51-500]
    KR - v72 - i16 - August 15 2004 - p777(1) [501+]
    PW - v251 - i36 - Sept 6 2004 - p50(1) [51-500]

Wilson, Fiona - *Organisational Behaviour and Gender, 2nd Ed.*
    TimHES - v0 - i1680 - Feb 25 2005 - pVIII(1) [501+]

Wilson, Frank Harold - *Race, Class, and the Postindustrial City: William Julius Wilson and the Promise of Sociology*
    Bl S - v34 - i3 - Fall 2004 - p76-76 [501+]
    Choice - v42 - i6 - Feb 2005 - p1107(1) [51-500]

Wilson, Geoff - *Encyclopedia of Fishing Knots and Rigs*
    Bwatch - v26 - i8 - August 2004 - p4(1) [51-500]

Wilson, Gina - *Grandma's Bears (Illus. by Howard, Paul)*
    c KR - v72 - i22 - Nov 15 2004 - p1094(1) [51-500]
    c PW - v252 - i1 - Jan 3 2005 - p54(1) [51-500]
    c SLJ - v50 - i12 - Dec 2004 - p124(2) [51-500]

Wilson, Graham - *Macc and Other Islands*
    Spec - v296 - Dec 18 2004 - p94(1) [501+]

Wilson, H.T. - *The Vocation of Reason: Studies in Critical Theory and Social Science in the Age of Max Weber*
    R&R Bk N - v19 - i3 - August 2004 - p141(1) [51-500]

Wilson, Hap - *Canoeing and Hiking Wild Muskoka: An Eco-Adventure Guide*
    CBRA - Annual 2003 - p27(1) [501+]

Wilson, Harold S. - *Confederate Industry: Manufacturers and Quatermasters in the Civil War*
    AHR - v109 - i2 - April 2004 - p527(2) [501+]

Wilson, Howard B. - *Mathematical Methods for Scientists and Engineers*
    SIAM Rev - v46 - i3 - Sept 2004 - p549(13) [501+]

Wilson, Ian - *The Subtle Art of Strategy: Organizational Planning in Uncertain Times*
    R&R Bk N - v19 - i1 - Feb 2004 - p88(1) [1-50]

Wilson, Jacqueline - *Best Friends*
    c Sch Lib - v52 - i3 - Autumn 2004 - p148(1) [51-500]
Girls in Tears
    y Kliatt - v38 - i5 - Sept 2004 - p26(3) [501+]
The Illustrated Mum
    y BL - v101 - i9-10 - Jan 1 2005 - p862(2) [1-50]
    c CCB-B - v58 - i6 - Feb 2005 - p271(1) [51-500]
    c KR - v73 - i1 - Jan 1 2005 - p59(1) [51-500]
Midnight
    c Sch Lib - v52 - i4 - Winter 2004 - p203(1) [51-500]
Mr. Cool (Illus. by Lewis, Stephen)
    c BL - v100 - i21 - July 2004 - p1852(1) [51-500]
    c SLJ - v50 - i9 - Sept 2004 - p174(1) [51-500]

Wilson, Janet - *Lighthouse, A Story of Remembrance*
    LibMed - v22 - i4 - Jan 2004 - p60(1) [501+]

Wilson, Jeanne - *Strategic Partners: Russian-Chinese Relations in the Post-Soviet Era*
    R&R Bk N - v19 - i3 - August 2004 - p45(1) [51-500]

Wilson, John - *The Flags of War*
    y SLJ - v51 - i2 - Feb 2005 - p142(1) [51-500]

Wilson, John (b. 1951 -) - *And in the Morning*
    c CBRA - Annual 2003 - p521(2) [51-500]
Battle Scars
    y KR - v73 - i4 - Feb 15 2005 - p237(1) [51-500]
Dancing Elephants and Floating Continents: The Story of Canada Beneath Your Feet
    c CBRA - Annual 2003 - p570(1) [51-500]
The Flags of War
    c CCB-B - v58 - i5 - Jan 2005 - p232(1) [51-500]
    c Res Links - v10 - i3 - Feb 2005 - p42(1) [501+]
Flames of the Tiger
    c Can CL - i113/114 - Spring-Summer 2004 - p136(3) [501+]
    c CBRA - Annual 2003 - p522(1) [51-500]
    c LibMed - v22 - i6 - March 2004 - p69(1) [501+]

Wilson, John (b. 1954 -) - *The Official Razzie Movie Guide: Enjoying the Best of Hollywood's Worst*
    Globe & Mail - Dec 18 2004 - pD25 [51-500]
    LJ - v130 - i1 - Jan 1 2005 - p116(1) [51-500]

Wilson, John D. - *Magill's Literary Annual 2003: Essay-Reviews of 200 Outstanding Books Published in the United States During 2002, Vols. 1-2*
    R&R Bk N - v19 - i1 - Feb 2004 - p257(1) [51-500]

Wilson, John Frederick - *Industrial Cluster and Regional Business Networks in England 1750-1970*
    JEH - v64 - i1 - March 2004 - p247(2) [501+]
Religion and the American Nation: Historiography and History
    HNet - July 2004 - pNA [501+]
    VQR - v80 - i1 - Wntr 2004 - p279-279 [501+]

Wilson, John M. - *Moth and Flame*
    KR - v72 - i23 - Dec 1 2004 - p1124(2) [501+]
    LJ - v130 - i4 - March 1 2005 - p71(2) [501+]
    PW - v252 - i2 - Jan 10 2005 - p42(2) [501+]

Wilson, John P. - *Broken Spirits: The Treatment of Traumatized Asylum Seekers, Refugees, War and Torture Victims*
    SciTech - v28 - i4 - Dec 2004 - p99(1) [51-500]
Empathy in the Treatment of Trauma and PTSD
    SciTech - v28 - i4 - Dec 2004 - p100(1) [51-500]

Wilson, John S. - *Standards and Global Trade: A Voice for Africa*
    JEL - v41 - i4 - Dec 2003 - p1415(1) [501+]

Wilson, Jonathan - *An Ambulance Is on the Way: Stories of Men in Trouble*
    LJ - v130 - i1 - Jan 1 2005 - p104(1) [51-500]
    LJ - v130 - i2 - Feb 1 2005 - p73(1) [51-500]
    PW - v252 - i3 - Jan 17 2005 - p34(1) [51-500]
A Palestine Affair
    y NYTBR - August 1 2004 - p16 [501+]

Wilson, Karma - *Bear Hugs: Romantically Ridiculous Animal Rhymes*
    c PW - v251 - i49 - Dec 6 2004 - p61(2) [501+]
Bear Stays Up for Christmas (Illus. by Chapman, Jane)
    c KR - v72 - i21 - Nov 1 2004 - p1055(1) [51-500]
    c PW - v251 - i39 - Sept 27 2004 - p61(1) [51-500]
Dinos on the Go! (Illus. by Rader, Laura)
    c KR - v72 - i15 - August 1 2004 - p751(1) [51-500]
    c PW - v251 - i41 - Oct 11 2004 - p78(1) [51-500]
    c SLJ - v50 - i9 - Sept 2004 - p182(1) [51-500]
Mr. Murry and Thumbkin (Illus. by Hoyt, Ard)
    c SLJ - v50 - i9 - Sept 2004 - p184(1) [51-500]
Never, Ever Shout in a Zoo (Illus. by Cushman, Doug)
    c CH Bwatch - v14 - i7 - July 2004 - p4(1) [51-500]
    c CH Bwatch - v14 - i12 - Dec 2004 - pNA [51-500]

Wilson, Kathleen - *The Island Race: Englishness, Empire and Gender in the Eighteenth Century*
    Albion - v36 - i1 - Spring 2004 - p145(3) [501+]

Wilson, Kathleen W. - *Your Husband's Health: Simplify Your Worry List*
NYT - July 20 2004 - pF7(L) [501+]

Wilson, Keith P. - *Campfires of Freedom: The Camp Life of Black Soldiers during the Civil War*
JSH - v70 - i3 - August 2004 - p683(2) [501+]

Wilson, Kim - *Tea with Jane Austen*
BL - v101 - i6 - Nov 15 2004 - p546(2) [51-500]

Wilson, Kirt H. - *The Reconstruction Desegregation Debate: The Politics of Equality and the Rhetoric of Place, 1870-1875*
AHR - v109 - i3 - June 2004 - p920(1) [501+]

Wilson, Kristina - *Livable Modern: Interior Decorating and Design During the Great Depression*
LJ - v130 - i1 - Jan 1 2005 - p107(1) [51-500]

Wilson, Laird - *Industrial Safety and Risk Management*
CBRA - Annual 2003 - p436(2) [51-500]

Wilson, Lee - *Making It in the Music Business: The Business and Legal Guide for Songwriters and Performers, 3rd Ed.*
R&R Bk N - v19 - i2 - May 2004 - p192(1) [51-500]

Wilson, Linda Henshall - *Teaching 201: Traveling Beyond the Basics*
R&R Bk N - v19 - i3 - August 2004 - p224(1) [1-50]

Wilson, Liz - *The Living and the Dead: Social Dimensions of Death in South Asian Religions*
JAS - v63 - i3 - August 2004 - p838-840 [501+]

Wilson, Mathew - *The Land of War Elephants: Travels in Afghanistan, Pakistan, and India*
R&R Bk N - v19 - i1 - Feb 2004 - p46(1) [51-500]

Wilson, Matthew - *Whiteness in the Novels of Charles W. Chesnutt*
Black Iss - v6 - i6 - Nov-Dec 2004 - p68(1) [501+]

Wilson, Natashya - *Bats/Murcielagos*
c   SLJ - v50 - i9 - Sept 2004 - p196(2) [1-50]
Bears/Osos
c   SLJ - v50 - i9 - Sept 2004 - p196(2) [1-50]

Wilson, Paula A. - *Library Web Sites: Creating Online Collections and Services*
LibMed - v23 - i3 - Nov-Dec 2004 - p91(1) [51-500]
VOYA - v27 - i5 - Dec 2004 - p424(1) [501+]

Wilson, Peter - *The International Theory of Leonard Woolf: A Study in Twentieth-Century Idealism*
R&R Bk N - v19 - i1 - Feb 2004 - pNA [501+]
Young Minds in Our Schools: A Guide for Teachers and Others Working in Schools
TES - v0 - i4586 - June 4 2004 - psss17(1) [501+]

Wilson, Peter (b. 1948 -) - *The Essential Guide to Managing Small Business Growth*
R&R Bk N - v19 - i3 - August 2004 - p107(1) [1-50]

Wilson, Philip - *Kitaj*
Spec - v296 - i9193 - Oct 16 2004 - p67(1) [501+]

Wilson, R.L. - *Silk & Steel: Women at Arms*
Globe & Mail - Dec 4 2004 - pD39 [501+]

Wilson, Richard Guy - *The Colonial Revival House*
LJ - v130 - i1 - Jan 1 2005 - p107(1) [51-500]
A Guide to Popular U.S. Landmarks
LibMed - v22 - i6 - March 2004 - p77(1) [501+]
LibMed - v22 - i6 - March 2004 - p77(1) [501+]

Wilson, Robert - *The Vanished Hands*
BL - v101 - i9-10 - Jan 1 2005 - p829(1) [1-50]
KR - v72 - i23 - Dec 1 2004 - p1125(1) [501+]
LJ - v129 - i16 - Oct 1 2004 - p65(1) [51-500]
PW - v251 - i45 - Nov 8 2004 - p38(1) [501+]

Wilson, Robert A. - *Boundaries of the Mind: The Individual in the Fragile Sciences*
Choice - v42 - i5 - Jan 2005 - p868(1) [1-50]

Wilson, Robert Charles - *Spin*
KR - v73 - i2 - Jan 15 2005 - p90(1) [51-500]
PW - v252 - i5 - Jan 31 2005 - p53(1) [51-500]

Wilson, Robert H. - *State Growth Management and Open Space Preservation Policies*
R&R Bk N - v19 - i1 - Feb 2004 - p95(1) [1-50]

Wilson, Robley - *The World Still Melting*
BL - v101 - i8 - Dec 15 2004 - p710(1) [51-500]
KR - v72 - i23 - Dec 1 2004 - p1115(1) [51-500]
LJ - v130 - i2 - Feb 1 2005 - p72(1) [51-500]
PW - v252 - i4 - Jan 24 2005 - p221(1) [501+]

Wilson, Ruth - *Immigration*
y   Sch Lib - v52 - i4 - Winter 2004 - p219(1) [51-500]

Wilson, Ruth A. - *Special Educational Needs in the Early Years, 2nd Ed.*
R&R Bk N - v19 - i3 - August 2004 - p229(1) [1-50]

Wilson, Sondra Kathryn - *Meet Me at the Theresa: The Story of Harlem's Most Famous Hotel*
Black Iss - v6 - i4 - July-August 2004 - p52(1) [501+]

Wilson, Stephen G. - *Leaving the Fold: Apostates and Defectors in Antiquity*
Choice - v42 - i7 - March 2005 - p1245(1) [51-500]

Wilson, Steve - *Reptiles of Australia*
E-Streams - August 2004 - pNA [501+]

Wilson, Steven Harmon - *The Rise of Judicial Management in the U.S. District Court, Southern District of Texas, 1955-2000*
HNet - Dec 2004 - pNA [501+]
JAH - v91 - i1 - June 2004 - p316-316 [501+]
JSH - v70 - i3 - August 2004 - p720(4) [501+]

Wilson, Steven R. - *Seeking and Resisting Compliance: Why People Say What They Do When Trying To Influence Others*
JC - v54 - i3 - Sept 2004 - p566(2) [501+]

Wilson, Ted - *Beverages in Nutrition and Health*
E-Streams - July 2004 - pNA [501+]
SciTech - v28 - i1 - March 2004 - p72(1) [51-500]

Wilson, Terrie L. - *Twenty-First Century Art Librarian*
R&R Bk N - v19 - i1 - Feb 2004 - p259(1) [51-500]

Wilson, Thomas A. - *On Sacred Grounds: Culture, Society, Politics, and the Formation of the Cult of Confucius*
Ch Rev Int - v10 - i2 - Fall 2003 - p351(12) [501+]

Wilson, Timothy D. - *Strangers to Ourselves: Discovering the Adaptive Unconscious*
TLS - i5289 - August 13 2004 - p29(1) [501+]

Wilson, Van G. - *Sumoylation: Molecular Biology and Biochemistry*
SciTech - v28 - i3 - Sept 2004 - p71(1) [51-500]

Wilson, Wendell E. - *Masterpieces of the Mineral World: Treasures from the Houston Museum of Natural Science*
Ant&CM - v109 - i11 - Jan 2005 - p16(1) [501+]
Choice - v42 - i7 - March 2005 - p1256(1) [51-500]

Wilson, William - *Central Issues in Criminal Theory*
Law Q Rev - v120 - July 2004 - p522-524 [501+]

Wilson, William Scott - *The Lone Samurai: The Life of Miyamoto Musashi*
KR - v72 - i17 - Sept 1 2004 - p857(1) [51-500]
LJ - v129 - i14 - Sept 1 2004 - p167(1) [501+]
PW - v251 - i41 - Oct 11 2004 - p68(1) [51-500]

Wilt, Alan F. - *The Atlantic Wall: Rommel's Plan to Stop the Allied Invasion!*
J Mil H - v68 - i4 - Oct 2004 - p1297-1298 [501+]

Wilt, David E. - *The Mexican Filmography, 1916 through 2001*
R&R Bk N - v19 - i1 - Feb 2004 - p224(1) [51-500]

Wilt, Judith - *Making Humans: Mary Shelley, Frankenstein; H.G. Wells, The Island of Doctor Moreau*
SFS - v31 - i2 - July 2004 - p319-324 [501+]

Wilton, Paul - *Beginning JavaScript, 2nd Ed.*
SciTech - v28 - i3 - Sept 2004 - p21(1) [51-500]

Wimmel, Kenneth - *William Woodville Rockhill: Scholar-Diplomat of the Tibetan Highlands*
A Aff - v35 - i2 - July 2004 - p232-233 [501+]

Wimmer, Andreas - *Facing Ethnic Conflicts: Toward a New Realism*
Choice - v42 - i5 - Jan 2005 - p930(1) [51-500]

Wimmers, Inge Crosman - *Proust and Emotion: The Importance of Affect in 'A la Recherche du Temps Perdu'*
R&R Bk N - v19 - i1 - Feb 2004 - p232(1) [51-500]

Wincelowicz, Vincent C. - *The Police Culture and the Marginally Performing Employee*
R&R Bk N - v19 - i3 - August 2004 - p167(1) [501+]

Winch, Donald - *The Political Economy of the British Historical Experience*
Albion - v36 - i1 - Spring 2004 - p151(3) [501+]

Winch, John - *Two by Two (Illus. by Winch, John)*
c   BL - v101 - i3 - Oct 1 2004 - p346(1) [51-500]
c   CH Bwatch - v14 - i12 - Dec 2004 - pNA [51-500]
c   KR - v72 - i16 - August 15 2004 - p814(1) [51-500]
c   PW - v251 - i43 - Oct 25 2004 - p46(1) [51-500]
c   SLJ - v50 - i10 - Oct 2004 - p152(1) [51-500]

Winchester, Simon - *In Other Words: A Language Lover's Guide to the Most Intriguing Words around the World*
PW - v251 - i51 - Dec 20 2004 - p51(1) [501+]
Krakatoa; The Day the World Exploded, August 27, 1883
SciTech - v28 - i3 - Sept 2004 - p55(1) [1-50]
The Meaning of Everything: The Story of the Oxford English Dictionary
CR - v285 - i1666 - Nov 2004 - p308(2) [501+]
Kliatt - v38 - i6 - Nov 2004 - p29(2) [51-500]
Sew R - v112 - i2 - Spring 2004 - p312-316 [501+]

Outposts: Journeys to the Surviving Relics of the British Empire
Globe & Mail - August 28 2004 - pD13 [51-500]
Simon Winchester's Calcutta
BL - v101 - i2 - Sept 15 2004 - p202(1) [501+]
LJ - v129 - i17 - Oct 15 2004 - p79(1) [51-500]

Wind, Yoram Jerry - *Marketing Research and Modeling: Progress and Prospects, A Tribute to Paul E. Green*
R&R Bk N - v19 - i2 - May 2004 - p114(1) [51-500]

Windelspecht, Michael - *The Digestive System*
SciTech - v28 - i4 - Dec 2004 - p104(1) [51-500]
Groundbreaking Scientific Experiments, Inventions and Discoveries of 19th Century
LibMed - v22 - i5 - Feb 2004 - p56(1) [501+]
Human Body Systems, Vols. 1-10
c   SLJ - v51 - i2 - Feb 2005 - p86(1) [51-500]

Winder, Robert - *Bloody Foreigners: The Story of Immigration to Britain*
CR - v285 - i1667 - Dec 2004 - p380(2) [51-500]
HT - v54 - i9 - Sept 2004 - p57(1) [501+]
NS - v133 - i4716 - Nov 29 2004 - p48(1) [51-500]
TimHES - v0 - i1672 - Dec 24 2004 - p26(1) [501+]
TLS - i5288 - August 6 2004 - p27(1) [501+]

Winders, Richard Bruce - *Sacrificed at the Alamo: Tragedy and Triumph in the Texas Revolution*
Roundup M - v12 - i3 - Feb 2005 - p23(1) [51-500]
R&R Bk N - v19 - i3 - August 2004 - p74(1) [51-500]

Windh, Jacqueline - *The Wild Edge: Clayoquot, Long Beach & Barkley Sound*
Globe & Mail - Jan 15 2005 - pD14 [1-50]

Windham, Kathryn Tucker - *Ernest's Gift (Illus. by Hardy, Francis Joseph)*
A Lib - v35 - i8 - Sept 2004 - p78(1) [51-500]

Windler, Christian - *La Diplomatie comme experience de l'autre: Consuls Francais au Maghreb (1700-1840).*
JMH - v77 - i1 - March 2005 - p197(3) [501+]

Windrow, Martin - *The Last Valley: Dien Bien Phu and the French Defeat in Vietnam*
BL - v101 - i9-10 - Jan 1 2005 - p810(1) [1-50]
CR - v285 - i1664 - Sept 2004 - p192(1) [51-500]
LJ - v130 - i3 - Feb 15 2005 - p146(1) [51-500]

Windsor, Alan - *British Sculptors of the Twentieth Century*
R&R Bk N - v19 - i1 - Feb 2004 - p204(1) [51-500]

Wineapple, Brenda - *Hawthorne: A Life*
BooChiTr - Jan 4 2004 - p3(1) [501+]
Kliatt - v38 - i6 - Nov 2004 - p34(2) [51-500]
NEQ - v77 - i2 - June 2004 - p308-311 [501+]
New R - v231 - August 9 2004 - p31 [501+]
NYTBR - Sept 5 2004 - p20 [501+]

Winebrake, James J. - *Alternate Energy: Assessment and Implementation Reference Book*
E-Streams - August 2004 - pNA [501+]
SciTech - v28 - i1 - March 2004 - p151(1) [51-500]

Wineburg, Bob - *A Limited Partnership: The Politics of Religion, Welfare, and Social Service*
CC - v121 - i17 - August 24 2004 - p27(7) [501+]

Winegardner, Mark - *The Godfather Returns (Read by Grifasi, Joe). Audiobook Review*
PW - v251 - i49 - Dec 6 2004 - p19(1) [51-500]
The Godfather Returns
BL - v101 - i7 - Dec 1 2004 - p619(1) [51-500]
Ent W - i794 - Nov 26 2004 - p127 [501+]
LJ - v129 - i20 - Dec 1 2004 - p106(1) [51-500]
New R - Dec 13 2004 - p40 [501+]
NW - Nov 8 2004 - p55 [501+]
NYTBR - Dec 5 2004 - p8 [501+]
People - v62 - i23 - Dec 6 2004 - p56 [51-500]
PW - v251 - i44 - Nov 1 2004 - p42(1) [501+]
Time - v164 - i21 - Nov 22 2004 - p88 [501+]

Winerip, Michael - *Adam Canfield of the Slash*
CJR - v43 - i6 - March-April 2005 - p61(2) [501+]

Wing, Nathaniel - *Between Genders: Narrating Difference in Early French Modernism*
Choice - v42 - i1 - Sept 2004 - p106(1) [501+]

Wingard-Nelson, Rebecca - *Algebra I and Algebra II*
y   SB - v41 - i1 - Jan-Feb 2005 - p25(1) [51-500]

Wingate, Brian - *BMX Bicycle Racing: Techniques and Tricks*
Teach Lib - v32 - i3 - Feb 2005 - p30(1) [51-500]
Saddam Hussein
c   SLJ - v50 - i10 - Oct 2004 - p192(1) [51-500]

Wingate, Katherine - *The Intifadas*
y   BL - v101 - i5 - Nov 1 2004 - p474(1) [51-500]

Wohlforth, Charles - *The Whale and the Supercomputer: On the Northern Front of Climate Change*
Choice - v42 - i5 - Jan 2005 - p879(1) [1-50]
SB - v40 - i5 - Sept-Oct 2004 - p200(1) [51-500]
SB - v40 - i6 - Nov-Dec 2004 - p240(1) [51-500]

Wojak, Irmtrud - *Im Labyrinth der Schuld: Taeter, Opfer, Anklaeger*
HNet - Oct 2004 - pNA [501+]

Wojciechowski, Gene - *Cubs Nation: 162 Games, 162 Stories, 1 Addiction*
KR - v73 - i3 - Feb 1 2005 - p172(1) [501+]

Wojtkowski, Paul A. - *Landscape Agroecology*
Choice - v41 - i11-12 - July-August 2004 - p2072(1) [501+]
E-Streams - Oct 2004 - pNA [501+]
Env - v46 - i7 - Sept 2004 - p39(2) [501+]
SciTech - v28 - i1 - March 2004 - p127(1) [51-500]

Wolaner, Robin - *Naked in the Boardroom: A CEO Bares Her Secrets So You Can Transform Your Career*
Fortune - v151 - i7 - April 4 2005 - p32 [51-500]
LJ - v130 - i2 - Feb 1 2005 - p95(1) [51-500]
PW - v252 - i4 - Jan 24 2005 - p232(1) [501+]

Wolcott, Harry F. - *Sneaky Kid and Its Aftermath: Ethics and Intimacy in Fieldwork*
CS - v33 - i2 - March 2004 - p260-262 [501+]

Wolcott, James - *Attack Poodles and Other Media Mutants: The Looting of the News in a Time of Terror*
BL - v101 - i1 - Sept 1 2004 - p22(1) [51-500]
Globe & Mail - Sept 4 2004 - pD3 [501+]
KR - v72 - i14 - July 15 2004 - p680(1) [501+]
LJ - v129 - i20 - Dec 1 2004 - p132(1) [51-500]
NYTBR - August 29 2004 - p13 [501+]
PW - v251 - i30 - July 26 2004 - p49(1) [501+]

Wold, Gloria Hoffmann - *Basic Geriatric Nursing, 3rd Ed.*
SciTech - v28 - i1 - March 2004 - p108(1) [51-500]

Wolf, Allan - *The Blood-Hungry Spleen and Other Poems about Our Parts (Illus. by Clarke, Greg)*
c LibMed - v22 - i6 - March 2004 - p71(1) [501+]
New Found Land: Lewis and Clark's Voyage of Discovery
y BL - v101 - i4 - Oct 15 2004 - p398(2) [51-500]
y CCB-B - v58 - i2 - Oct 2004 - p104(1) [51-500]
c KR - v72 - i14 - July 15 2004 - p695(1) [51-500]
y PW - v251 - i44 - Nov 1 2004 - p63(1) [501+]
y SLJ - v50 - i9 - Sept 2004 - p220(1) [51-500]

Wolf, Beat - *Vademecum Medievale: Glossar Zur Hofischen Literatur des Deutschsprachigen Mittelalters*
Specu - v79 - i4 - Oct 2004 - p1179(1) [501+]

Wolf, Benjamin - *Sustainable Soils: The Place of Organic Matter in Sustaining Soils and Their Productivity*
Choice - v41 - i11-12 - July-August 2004 - p2072(1) [501+]
E-Streams - June 2004 - pNA [501+]
QRB - v79 - i3 - Sept 2004 - p313(1) [501+]
SciTech - v28 - i1 - March 2004 - p128(1) [51-500]

Wolf, Christa - *Ein Tag im Jahr 1960-2000 (Illus. by Hoffman, Martin)*
WLT - v78 - i3-4 - Sept-Dec 2004 - p127(1) [501+]
In the Flesh
BL - v101 - i9-10 - Jan 1 2005 - p824(1) [1-50]
KR - v72 - i23 - Dec 1 2004 - p1116(1) [501+]
LJ - v130 - i1 - Jan 1 2005 - p101(2) [51-500]
Wolves Eat Dogs
HM - v309 - i1854 - Nov 2004 - p83(2) [501+]

Wolf, Christian Norbert - *Streitbare Asthetik: Goethes Kunst- und Literatur- Theoretische Schriften 1771-1789*
GSR - v27 - i3 - Oct 2004 - p610(4) [501+]

Wolf, Eric R. - *Europe and the People Without History*
CHE - v51 - i14 - Nov 26 2004 - pB4-B4 [501+]

Wolf, Gita - *In the Dark*
KR - v72 - i20 - Oct 15 2004 - p1015(1) [501+]

Wolf, Hubert - *Rankes "Papste" auf dem Index. Dogma und Historie im Widerstreit*
CHR - v90 - i4 - Oct 2004 - p805(3) [501+]

Wolf, Jacqueline H. - *Don't Kill Your Baby: Public Health and the Decline of Breastfeeding in the Nineteenth and Twentieth Centuries*
JWH - v16 - i4 - Winter 2004 - p215(11) [501+]

Wolf, Joan - *White Horses*
BL - v100 - i22 - August 2004 - p1910(2) [51-500]

Wolf, John P. - *Foundation Vibration Analysis: A Strength-of-Materials Approach*
Choice - v42 - i1 - Sept 2004 - p136(1) [501+]

Wolf, Kenneth Baxter - *The Poverty of Riches: St. Francis of Assisi Reconsidered*
AHR - v109 - i2 - April 2004 - p592(2) [501+]
CH - v73 - i4 - Dec 2004 - p842(1) [501+]
Specu - v79 - i3 - July 2004 - p861-862 [501+]

Wolf, Kirsten - *Saga Heilagrar Onnu*
Scan St - v76 - i4 - Winter 2004 - p549(4) [501+]

Wolf-Knuts, Ulrika - *Input and Output: The Process of Fieldwork, Archiving and Research in Folklore*
Folkl - v115 - i2 - August 2004 - p247(1) [501+]

Wolf, Linda - *Kinsey: Public and Private*
PW - v251 - i49 - Dec 6 2004 - p56(1) [51-500]

Wolf, Maritta - *Sudden Rain*
PW - v252 - i8 - Feb 21 2005 - p154(1) [51-500]

Wolf, Martin - *Why Globalization Works*
Choice - v42 - i2 - Oct 2004 - p342(1) [51-500]
Econ - v372 - i8384 - July 17 2004 - p75US [501+]
For Aff - v83 - i5 - Sept-Oct 2004 - p146 [501+]
Globe & Mail - Oct 30 2004 - pD20 [501+]
NS - v133 - i4696 - July 12 2004 - p50(2) [501+]
R&R Bk N - v19 - i3 - August 2004 - p123(1) [51-500]

Wolf, Molly - *White China: Finding the Divine in the Everyday*
PW - v252 - i11 - March 14 2005 - p64(1) [51-500]

Wolf, Naomi - *The Treehouse: Eccentric Wisdom from My Father on How to Live, Love, and See*
KR - v73 - i4 - Feb 15 2005 - p224(1) [501+]
PW - v252 - i9 - Feb 28 2005 - p48(1) [501+]

Wolf, Peter - *Der Winterkonig: Friedrich V., der letzte Kurfurst aus der oberen Pfalz*
GSR - v27 - i2 - May 2004 - p362-363 [501+]

Wolf, Rachel Rubin - *Splash 8: Watercolor Discoveries*
LJ - v129 - i12 - July 2004 - p81(1) [51-500]

Wolf, Raoul L. - *Essential Pediatric Allergy, Asthma and Immunology*
SciTech - v28 - i3 - Sept 2004 - p117(1) [51-500]

Wolf, Shelby A. - *Interpreting Literature with Children*
R&R Bk N - v19 - i1 - Feb 2004 - p183(1) [51-500]

Wolf, Stacy - *A Problem Like Maria: Gender and Sexuality in the American Musical*
Lam Bk Rpt - v13 - i3 - Oct 2004 - p17(3) [501+]

Wolf-Wendel, Lisa - *The Two-Body Problem: Dual-Career-Couple Hiring Policies in Higher Education*
R&R Bk N - v19 - i3 - August 2004 - p220(1) [1-50]

Wolfart, Johannes - *Religion, Government and Political Culture in Early Modern Germany*
CEH - v37 - i3 - Summer 2004 - p434(3) [501+]

Wolfe, Alan - *Return to Greatness: How America Lost Its Sense of Purpose and What It Needs to Do to Recover It*
PW - v252 - i6 - Feb 7 2005 - p55(1) [51-500]
School Choice: The Moral Debate
CS - v33 - i6 - Nov 2004 - p723(2) [501+]
The Transformation of American Religion: How We Actually Live Our Faith
Choice - v42 - i2 - Oct 2004 - p312(2) [51-500]
TT - v61 - i2 - July 2004 - p280(3) [501+]

Wolfe, Art - *Northwest Wild; Celebrating Our Natural Heritage*
SciTech - v28 - i3 - Sept 2004 - p57(1) [1-50]

Wolfe, Cary - *Animal Rites: American Culture, the Discourse of Species, and Posthumanist Theory*
SFS - v31 - i1 - March 2004 - p163-167 [501+]
Animal Rites: American Culture, the Discourse of Species, and Postumanist Theory
Am Q - v56 - i4 - Dec 2004 - p1125(10) [501+]
Zoontologies: The Question of the Animal
Am Q - v56 - i4 - Dec 2004 - p1125(10) [501+]

Wolfe, Christopher - *That Eminent Tribunal: Judicial Supremacy and the Constitution*
Law&PolBR - Dec 2004 - p941(5) [501+]

Wolfe, Claire - *The Freedom Outlaw's Handbook: 179 Things to Do 'til the Revolution*
Bwatch - Oct 2004 - pNA [51-500]
R&R Bk N - v19 - i4 - Nov 2004 - p155(1) [501+]

Wolfe, Gene - *Innocents Aboard: New Fantasy Stories*
BW - v34 - i40 - Oct 3 2004 - p17(1) [501+]
Innocents Abroad: New Fantasy Stories
BL - v100 - i21 - July 2004 - p1830(1) [1-50]
The Knight
MFSF - v107 - i1 - July 2004 - p27(4) [51-500]
The Wizard
y BL - v101 - i5 - Nov 1 2004 - p472(1) [51-500]
KR - v72 - i20 - Oct 15 2004 - p990(1) [51-500]
PW - v251 - i41 - Oct 11 2004 - p61(1) [501+]

Wolfe, Gillian - *Look! Body Language in Art*
c BL - v101 - i4 - Oct 15 2004 - p498(1) [51-500]
Look!: Body Language in Art
c KR - v72 - i22 - Nov 15 2004 - p1094(1) [51-500]
c SLJ - v50 - i12 - Dec 2004 - p139(1) [501+]

Wolfe, Gregory - *Malcolm Muggeridge: A Biography*
Quad - v49 - i1-2 - Jan-Feb 2005 - p112(3) [501+]

Wolfe, Jessica - *Rewriting White: Race, Class, and Cultural Capital in Nineteenth-Century America*
Choice - v42 - i6 - Feb 2005 - p1025(1) [51-500]

Wolfe, Linda - *The Murder of Dr. Chapman: The Legendary Trials of Lucretia Chapman and Her Lover*
BooChiTr - March 14 2004 - p3(1) [501+]

Wolfe, Lisa M. - *Yoga Band: An Exciting and Challenging New Yoga Workout*
LJ - v129 - i15 - Sept 15 2004 - p75(2) [501+]

Wolfe, Pat - *Building the Reading Brain, PreK-3*
Teach Lib - v32 - i2 - Dec 2004 - p38(1) [501+]

Wolfe, Patricia - *Building The Reading Brain, PreK-3*
CE - v81 - i2 - Winter 2004 - p111(1) [501+]
R&R Bk N - v19 - i3 - August 2004 - p218(1) [1-50]

Wolfe, Richard - *Final Report of the External Evaluation of EQAQ's Assessment Processes*
BIC - v33 - i7 - Oct 2004 - p37(2) [501+]

Wolfe, Robert R. - *Isotope Tracers in Metabolic Research: Principles and Practice of Kinetic Analysis, 2nd Ed.*
SciTech - v28 - i4 - Dec 2004 - p71(1) [501+]

Wolfe, Suzanne M. - *Unveiling*
AM - v191 - i9 - Oct 4 2004 - p18 [501+]
Bks & Cult - v10 - i4 - July-August 2004 - p33(1) [501+]
BL - v101 - i3 - Oct 1 2004 - p303(1) [51-500]

Wolfe, Swain - *The Parrot Trainer*
y Kliatt - v38 - i5 - Sept 2004 - p27(2) [51-500]

Wolfe, Tom - *I Am Charlotte Simmons (Read by Baker, Dylan). Audiobook Review*
Globe & Mail - Nov 27 2004 - pD49 [1-50]
I Am Charlotte Simmons
BL - v101 - i8 - Dec 15 2004 - p691(1) [501+]
BW - v34 - i45 - Nov 7 2004 - p15(1) [501+]
Globe & Mail - Dec 4 2004 - pD6 [501+]
Lon R Bks - v27 - i1 - Jan 6 2005 - p21(2) [501+]
New York - v37 - i42 - Nov 29 2004 - p126(2) [501+]
NYRB - v51 - i20 - Dec 16 2004 - p38(4) [501+]
NYT - Nov 16 2004 - pA27 [501+]
NYTBR - Nov 28 2004 - p13 [501+]
Spec - v296 - i9197 - Nov 13 2004 - p42(2) [501+]
TLS - i5304 - Nov 26 2004 - p21-22 [501+]
Ent W - i792 - Nov 12 2004 - p127 [501+]
PW - v251 - i45 - Nov 8 2004 - p35(2) [501+]

Wolfe, William L. - *Optical Engineer's Desk Reference*
E-Streams - August 2004 - pNA [501+]
SciTech - v28 - i1 - March 2004 - p145(1) [51-500]

Wolfers, Melanie - *Theologische Ethik als Handlungsleitende Sinnwissenschaft: Der Fundamentalethische Entwurf von Klaus Demmer*
Theol St - v65 - i4 - Dec 2004 - p875(2) [501+]

Wolff, Edward N. - *What Has Happened to the Quality of Life in the Advanced Industrialized Nations?*
Choice - v42 - i5 - Jan 2005 - p904(1) [1-50]
R&R Bk N - v19 - i4 - Nov 2004 - p124(1) [51-500]

Wolff, Elana - *Birdheart*
Can Lit - i182 - Autumn 2004 - p167(3) [501+]

Wolff, Geoffrey - *The Art of Burning Bridges: A Life of John O'Hara*
Choice - v41 - i7 - March 2004 - p1300(2) [501+]
WLT - v78 - i3-4 - Sept-Dec 2004 - p105(1) [501+]

Wolff, H.J. - *Das Recht der griechischen Papyri Agyptens in der Zeit der Ptolemaer und des Prinzipats.*
Class R - v54 - i1 - May 2004 - p224(3) [501+]

Wolff, Justin - *Richard Caton Woodville: American Painter, Artful Dodger*
JAH - v91 - i1 - June 2004 - p239-240 [501+]

Wolff, Maritta - *Sudden Rain*
BL - v101 - i9-10 - Jan 1 2005 - p824(1) [1-50]
KR - v73 - i3 - Feb 1 2005 - p147(1) [501+]
LJ - v130 - i1 - Jan 1 2005 - p102(1) [51-500]
LJ - v129 - i20 - Dec 1 2004 - p90(1) [51-500]
Whistle Stop
LJ - v130 - i1 - Jan 1 2005 - p172(1) [1-50]

Wolff, Stefan - *Disputed Territories: The Transnational Dynamics of Ethnic Conflict Settlement*
Choice - v41 - i7 - March 2004 - p1366(1) [501+]

Wolff, Tobias - *Old School: A Novel (Read by Cashman, Dan). Audiobook Review*
BL - v101 - i6 - Nov 15 2004 - p607(1) [501+]
VOYA - v27 - i5 - Dec 2004 - p370(1) [501+]
Old School: A Novel
BW - v34 - i40 - Oct 3 2004 - p15(1) [501+]
Globe & Mail - Dec 24 2004 - pD3 [1-50]
HR - v57 - i2 - Summer 2004 - p311-316 [501+]
y Kliatt - v39 - i1 - Jan 2005 - p18(2) [501+]

Woods, Stuart - *Dirty Work (Read by Lawrence, Robert). Audiobook Review*
 LJ - v129 - i12 - July 2004 - p125(1) [51-500]
The Prince of Beverly Hills
 BL - v101 - i1 - Sept 1 2004 - p8(1) [51-500]
 KR - v72 - i17 - Sept 1 2004 - p837(1) [501+]
 LJ - v129 - i16 - Oct 1 2004 - p74(2) [51-500]
 PW - v251 - i38 - Sept 20 2004 - p45(1) [51-500]
Reckless Abandon (Read by Roberts, Tony). Audiobook Review
 Kliatt - v38 - i6 - Nov 2004 - p49(1) [51-500]
Two-Dollar Bill (Read by Roberts, Tony). Audiobook Review
 KR - v73 - i4 - Feb 15 2005 - p197(1) [501+]
 LJ - v129 - i20 - Dec 1 2004 - p90(1) [51-500]
Two-Dollar Bill
 PW - v252 - i9 - Feb 28 2005 - p41(1) [51-500]

Woods, Thomas E. - *The Church Confronts Modernity: Catholic Intellectuals And the Progressive Era*
 Bks & Cult - v10 - i6 - Nov-Dec 2004 - p30(2) [501+]
 Choice - v42 - i7 - March 2005 - p1245(1) [51-500]
 R&R Bk N - v19 - i3 - August 2004 - p28(1) [1-50]
The Politically Incorrect Guide to American History
 NYT - Jan 26 2005 - pA16 [501+]

Woods, Tim - *The Poetics of the Limit: Ethics and Politics in Modern and Contemporary American Poetry*
 Clio - v33 - i3 - Spring 2004 - p346(5) [501+]
 J Am St - v38 - i1 - April 2004 - p177-177 [501+]

Woodside, Arch G. - *Evaluating Marketing Actions and Outcomes*
 JEL - v42 - i1 - March 2004 - p297(1) [501+]

Woodson, Jacqueline - *Behind You*
 y SLJ - v50 - i10 - Oct 2004 - pS68(1) [51-500]
Coming on Home Soon (Illus. by Lewis, Earl B.)
 c BL - v100 - i22 - August 2004 - p1925(1) [51-500]
 c BL - v101 - i9-10 - Jan 1 2005 - p776(1) [1-50]
 c Black Iss - v7 - i1 - Jan-Feb 2005 - p70(2) [501+]
 c BW - v34 - i50 - Dec 12 2004 - p8(1) [501+]
 c CCB-B - v58 - i6 - Feb 2005 - p272(1) [51-500]
 c HB - v80 - i5 - Sept-Oct 2004 - p577(1) [51-500]
 c KR - v72 - i18 - Sept 15 2004 - p923(1) [51-500]
 c PW - v251 - i48 - Nov 29 2004 - p40(1) [51-500]
 c SLJ - v50 - i10 - Oct 2004 - p137(1) [51-500]
Locomotion
 c LibMed - v22 - i4 - Jan 2004 - p63(1) [501+]
The Other Side (Illus. by Lewis, E.B.)
 c SLJ - v50 - i10 - Oct 2004 - p66(1) [51-500]
Our Gracie Aunt (Illus. by Muth, Jon J.)
 c RT - v57 - Nov 2003 - p273 [51-500]

Woodward, Bob - *Plan of Attack*
 Am Spect - v37 - i5 - June 2004 - p58(3) [501+]
 Arena - i73 - Oct-Nov 2004 - p51(2) [501+]
 BW - v34 - i42 - Oct 17 2004 - p12(1) [501+]
 For Aff - v83 - i5 - Sept-Oct 2004 - p164 [501+]
 Globe & Mail - Nov 27 2004 - pD3 [51-500]
 NYTBR - Oct 17 2004 - p26 [501+]
 TLS - i5287 - July 30 2004 - p8-9 [501+]
 Wom R Bks - v21 - i12 - Sept 2004 - p10(1) [501+]

Woodward, Clive - *Winning (Read by Woodward, Clive). Audiobook Review*
 Spec - v297 - i9204 - Jan 1 2005 - p24(1) [501+]

Woodward, Gerard - *I'll Go to Bed at Noon*
 NS - v133 - i4716 - Nov 29 2004 - p49(1) [51-500]
 TLS - i5286 - July 23 2004 - p23(1) [501+]

Woodward, John - *Perfect Partners*
 Sch Lib - v52 - i3 - Autumn 2004 - p153(2) [501+]

Woodward, Peter - *The True Story of Alexander the Great*
 LJ - v129 - i20 - Dec 1 2004 - p178(1) [51-500]

Woodward, Rhonda - *Moonlight and Mischief*
 y BL - v101 - i6 - Nov 15 2004 - p570(1) [51-500]

Woodward, Susan L. - *Biomes of Earth: Terrestrial, Aquatic, and Human-Dominated*
 Choice - v41 - i11-12 - July-August 2004 - p2072(1) [501+]
 E-Streams - Sept 2004 - pNA [501+]
 y SB - v40 - i4 - July-August 2004 - p167(1) [501+]
 SciTech - v28 - i1 - March 2004 - p64(1) [51-500]

Woodworth, Chris - *When Ratboy Lived Next Door*
 y BL - v101 - i9-10 - Jan 1 2005 - p847(1) [1-50]
 c CCB-B - v58 - i6 - Feb 2005 - p272(1) [51-500]
 c KR - v73 - i4 - Feb 15 2005 - p238(1) [51-500]

Woodworth, George G. - *Biostatistics: A Bayesian Introduction*
 Choice - v42 - i7 - March 2005 - p1264(1) [51-500]
 SciTech - v28 - i4 - Dec 2004 - p38(1) [51-500]

Woodworth, Stephen - *Through Violet Eyes*
 MFSF - v108 - i2 - Feb 2005 - p40(2) [501+]
 PW - v251 - i28 - July 12 2004 - p49(1) [51-500]
With Red Hands
 PW - v251 - i48 - Nov 29 2004 - p28(1) [51-500]

Woodworth, Steven E. - *Beneath a Northern Sky: A Short History of the Gettysburg Campaign*
 HNet - Sept 2004 - pNA [501+]
 J Mil H - v68 - i4 - Oct 2004 - p1262-1264 [501+]
 JSH - v70 - i4 - Nov 2004 - p934(2) [501+]

Woody, Robert Henley - *Group Therapy An Integrative Cognitive Social-Learning Approach*
 SciTech - v28 - i3 - Sept 2004 - p99(1) [51-500]

Woof, Pamela - *Reading "Paradise Lost"*
 TLS - i5294 - Sept 17 2004 - p18-19 [501+]

Woof, Robert - *Paradise Lost: The Poem and Its Illustrators*
 TLS - i5294 - Sept 17 2004 - p18-19 [501+]

Wookiee World
 LibMed - v22 - i5 - Feb 2004 - p74(1) [501+]

Woolever, Cynthia - *Beyond the Ordinary: 10 Strengths of U.S. Congregations*
 CC - v121 - i24 - Nov 30 2004 - p40(5) [501+]

Wooley, Charles F. - *The Irritable Heart of Soldiers and the Origins of Anglo-American Cardiology: The U.S. Civil War 1861 to World War I 1918*
 Albion - v36 - i1 - Spring 2004 - p169(2) [501+]
 Isis - v95 - i3 - Sept 2004 - p522(1) [501+]

Woolf, Alex - *Are People Terrorists?*
 c SLJ - v51 - i2 - Feb 2005 - p154(1) [51-500]
Death and Disease
 c BL - v101 - i4 - Oct 15 2004 - p424(2) [51-500]
Fundamentalism
 c SLJ - v50 - i8 - August 2004 - p144(2) [501+]
Investigating Fakes and Hoaxes
 c SLJ - v50 - i10 - Oct 2004 - p189(1) [51-500]
Investigating History Mysteries
 y Sch Lib - v52 - i4 - Winter 2004 - p219(1) [51-500]

Woolf, D.R. - *Reading History in Early Modern England*
 AHR - v109 - i2 - April 2004 - p469(2) [501+]

Woolf, Daniel - *The Social Circulation of the Past: English Historical Culture, 1500-1730*
 Choice - v41 - i7 - March 2004 - p1360(1) [501+]

Woolf, Virginia - *Mrs. Dalloway*
 Globe & Mail - July 10 2004 - pD13 [501+]
 Globe & Mail - Sept 18 2004 - pL3 [1-50]

Woolfe, Angela - *Avril Crump and Her Amazing Clones*
 KR - v73 - i3 - Feb 1 2005 - p183(1) [51-500]
Avril Crump... and Her Amazing Clones
 c Sch Lib - v52 - i3 - Autumn 2004 - p148(1) [501+]

Woolfolk, Anita - *Educational Psychology, Active Learning, 9th Ed.*
 R&R Bk N - v19 - i4 - Nov 2004 - p180(1) [501+]

Woolfson, Jonathan - *Reassessing Tudor Humanism*
 Six Ct J - v34 - i4 - Winter 2003 - p1219-1220 [501+]

Woollen, Dick - *Fridays with Art: Insiders' Accounts of the Early Days of the TV Biz by Some of the Guys Who Made It Work*
 TV Q - v34 - i3-4 - Spring-Summer 2004 - p74-76 [501+]

Woolley, Adam - *Guide to Practical Toxicology: Evaluation, Prediction and Risk*
 SciTech - v28 - i1 - March 2004 - p86(1) [51-500]

Woolley, Benjamin - *Heal Thyself: Nicholas Culpeper and the Seventeenth-Century Struggle to Bring Medicine to the People*
 BL - v100 - i22 - August 2004 - p1885(2) [51-500]
 LJ - v129 - i12 - July 2004 - p110(1) [51-500]
The Herbalist: Nicholas Culpeper and the Fight for Medical Freedom
 CR - v285 - i1667 - Dec 2004 - p379(1) [51-500]

Woolley, David - *The Correspondence of Jonathan Swift; Vol. 3*
 TLS - i5293 - Sept 10 2004 - p3-4 [501+]

Woollins, J. Derek - *Inorganic Experiments, 2nd Ed.*
 J Chem Ed - v81 - i8 - August 2004 - p1122-1124 [501+]

Woolner, David B. - *FDR, the Vatican, and the Roman Catholic Church in America, 1933-1945*
 Pres St Q - v34 - i4 - Dec 2004 - p902(2) [501+]
 R&R Bk N - v19 - i1 - Feb 2004 - p61(1) [501+]

Woolrych, Austin - *Britain in Revolution, 1625-1660*
 Albion - v36 - i1 - Spring 2004 - p125(3) [501+]

Wools, Blanche - *The School Library Media Manager, 3rd Ed.*
 BL - v101 - i9-10 - Jan 1 2005 - p911(1) [501+]

Wooster, Robert - *Soldier, Surgeon, Scholar: The Memoirs of William Henry Corbusier, 1844-1930*
 WHQ - v35 - i4 - Winter 2004 - p526-527 [501+]
Soldier, Surgeon, Scholar: The Memoirs of William Henry Corbusier
 J Mil H - v68 - i3 - April 2004 - p613-614 [501+]
 SciTech - v28 - i1 - March 2004 - p109(1) [51-500]

Wooten, Jim - *We Are All the Same: A Story of a Boy's Courage and a Mother's Love*
 y BL - v101 - i1 - Sept 1 2004 - p3(1) [51-500]
 Ent W - i791 - Nov 5 2004 - p87 [51-500]
 KR - v72 - i17 - Sept 1 2004 - p858(1) [501+]
 LJ - v129 - i16 - Oct 1 2004 - p106(1) [51-500]
 NYT - Dec 4 2004 - pB9 [501+]
 People - Nov 29 2004 - p58 [51-500]
 PW - v251 - i36 - Sept 6 2004 - p54(1) [51-500]

Wootson, Alice - *Aloha Love*
 BL - v101 - i9-10 - Jan 1 2005 - p833(1) [1-50]

Worboys, Michael - *GIS: A Computing Perspective, 2nd Ed.*
 SciTech - v28 - i3 - Sept 2004 - p4(1) [501+]

Worbyt, John C. - *Teaching Kids to Care and to Be Careful: A Practical Guide for Teachers, Counselors, and Parents*
 R&R Bk N - v19 - i4 - Nov 2004 - p190(1) [501+]

Word, Brian R. - *Microscopic Life in the Garden*
 c CH Bwatch - Feb 2005 - pNA [51-500]
Microscopic Life in your Body
 c CH Bwatch - Feb 2005 - pNA [51-500]

Word Histories and Mysteries: From Abracadabra to Zeus
 LJ - v130 - i1 - Jan 1 2005 - p158(1) [51-500]

Worden, K. - *Smart Technologies*
 SciTech - v28 - i4 - Dec 2004 - p129 [51-500]

Words and Terms, Vol. 1
 y SB - v40 - i6 - Nov-Dec 2004 - p259(1) [51-500]

Words to the Wise: Tales of Wisdom from Many Cultures (Read by Farley, Tom). Audiobook Review
 c SLJ - v50 - i10 - Oct 2004 - p86(1) [51-500]

Wordsworth, William - *Early Poems and Fragments, 1785-1787*
 JEGP - v103 - i3 - July 2004 - p403-406 [501+]
Guide to the Lakes
 TLS - i5290 - August 20 2004 - p28-29 [501+]
Last Poems, 1821-1850
 JEGP - v103 - i3 - July 2004 - p403-406 [501+]

Work, James C. - *The Dead Ride Alone: A Keystone Ranch Story*
 Roundup M - v11 - i6 - August 2004 - p31(1) [501+]

The Work of the International Law Commission, 6th Ed., Vols. 1-2
 R&R Bk N - v19 - i3 - August 2004 - p210(1) [1-50]

Workentin, M.S. - *Organic Electrochemistry: Proceedings*
 SciTech - v28 - i1 - March 2004 - p55(1) [51-500]

Workman, Hawksley - *Hawksley Burns for Isadora*
 CBRA - Annual 2003 - p237(2) [51-500]

Workman, Lance - *Evolutionary Psychology: An Introduction, 1st ed.*
 TimHES - v0 - i1668 - Nov 26 2004 - pXVII(1) [501+]

Workplace Violence in Services Sectors and Measures to Combat This Phenomenon
 ILR - v143 - i3 - Autumn 2004 - p295(1) [51-500]

World Allergy Organization Congress - *Abstracts: World Allergy Congress - XVIII ICACI, Proceedings*
 SciTech - v28 - i3 - Sept 2004 - p103(1) [51-500]

World Almanac Biblioteca de los estados
 y Ref Rev - August 2004 - pNA [501+]

The World Almanac for Kids 2005
 c PW - v251 - i31 - August 2 2004 - p73(1) [51-500]

World Almanac Library of the Civil War
 c LibMed - v23 - i3 - Nov-Dec 2004 - p84(1) [51-500]

World Art And Culture
 LibMed - v22 - i7 - April-May 2004 - p84(1) [501+]

World at Work - *Salary Budget Survey 2004-2005.*
 HR Mag - v49 - i7 - July 2004 - p8(1) [51-500]

World Bank - *Agriculture in Nicaragua: Promoting Competitiveness and Stimulating Broad-Based Growth*
 JEL - v42 - i1 - March 2004 - p313(1) [501+]
The Bog People: Iron-Age Man Preserved
 Globe & Mail - Jan 22 2005 - pD15 [501+]
Global Development Finance, 2004, Vols. 1-2
 R&R Bk N - v19 - i3 - August 2004 - p134(1) [51-500]

Global Monitoring Report 2004: Policies and Actions for Achieving the Millennium Development Goals and Related Outcomes
R&R Bk N - v19 - i4 - Nov 2004 - p153(1) [501+]
A Guide to the World Bank
JEL - v42 - i1 - March 2004 - p266(1) [501+]
Labor Issues in Infrastructure Reform: A Toolkit Public/Private Infrastructure Advisory Facility
R&R Bk N - v19 - i3 - August 2004 - p114(1) [51-500]
Lifelong Learning in the Global Knowledge Economy: Challenges for Developing Countries
JEL - v41 - i4 - Dec 2003 - p1378(1) [501+]
Millenium Development Goals for Health: Rising to the Challenges
SciTech - v28 - i3 - Sept 2004 - p83(1) [501+]
Private Participation in Infrastructure: Trends in Developing Countries in 1990-2001
JEL - v42 - i1 - March 2004 - p273(1) [501+]
Private Solutions for Infrastructure in Mexico: Country Framework Report for Private Participation in Infrastructure
JEL - v41 - i4 - Dec 2003 - pNA [501+]
Public Expenditure Review of Armenia
JEL - v42 - i1 - March 2004 - p327(1) [501+]
R&R Bk N - v19 - i1 - Feb 2004 - p121(1) [51-500]
Reforming Public Institutions and Strengthening Governance: A World Bank Strategy Implementation Update
JEL - v41 - i4 - Dec 2003 - p1415(1) [501+]
Restoring Fiscal Discipline for Poverty Reduction in Peru: A Public Expenditure Review
JEL - v42 - i1 - March 2004 - p316(1) [501+]
Rural Poverty Alleviation in Brazil: Toward an Integrated Strategy
JEL - v42 - i1 - March 2004 - p314(1) [501+]
Slovak Republic--Joining the EU: A Development Policy Review
JEL - v42 - i1 - March 2004 - p327(2) [501+]
Sustaining Forests: A Development Strategy
SciTech - v28 - i3 - Sept 2004 - p131(1) [51-500]
SciTech - v28 - i3 - Sept 2004 - p131(1) [501+]
Teritary Education in Colombia: Paving the Way for Reform
JEL - v41 - i4 - Dec 2003 - p1378(2) [501+]
World Bank Annual Report 2003, Vol. 1
JEL - v42 - i1 - March 2004 - p266(1) [501+]
World Bank Annual Report 2003, Vol. 2
JEL - v42 - i1 - March 2004 - p266(2) [501+]
World Bank Atlas 2003
JEL - v41 - i4 - Dec 2003 - p1352(1) [501+]
World Bank Group - *The World Bank Group Directory, November 2003*
R&R Bk N - v19 - i3 - August 2004 - p136(1) [51-500]
The World Bank Research Program: Abstracts of Current Studies, 2002-03
R&R Bk N - v19 - i4 - Nov 2004 - p117(1) [51-500]
The World Book Encyclopedia
BL - v101 - i2 - Sept 15 2004 - p268(1) [501+]
World Book of America's Multicultural Heritage
LibMed - v22 - i4 - Jan 2004 - p79(1) [501+]
World Book Online Reference Center
BL - v101 - i2 - Sept 15 2004 - p272(1) [501+]
World Book's Biographical Encyclopedia of Scientists
LibMed - v22 - i5 - Feb 2004 - p62(1) [501+]
World Commission - *A Fair Globalization: Creating Opportunities for All*
ILR - v143 - i3 - Autumn 2004 - p285(1) [51-500]
World Development Indicators - *The Little Green Data Book 2003*
JEL - v41 - i4 - Dec 2003 - p1432(1) [501+]
World Development Indicators 2004
R&R Bk N - v19 - i3 - August 2004 - p96(1) [51-500]
World Development Report 2004: Making Services Work for Poor People
JEL - v42 - i1 - March 2004 - p315(1) [501+]
World Drug Report 2004, Vols. 1-2
SciTech - v28 - i4 - Dec 2004 - p10(1) [1-50]
World Energy Investment Outlook: 2003 Insights
SciTech - v28 - i3 - Sept 2004 - p8(1) [501+]
World Health Organization - *Global Tuberculosis Control: Surveillance, Planning, Financing WHO Report 2004*
SciTech - v28 - i3 - Sept 2004 - p93(1) [51-500]
Guidelines for Safe Recreational Water Environments, Vol. 1
SciTech - v28 - i1 - March 2004 - p147(1) [51-500]

Managing Complications in Pregnancy and Childbirth: A Guide for Midwives and Doctors
SciTech - v28 - i1 - March 2004 - p116(1) [51-500]
Neuroscience of Psychoactive Substance Use and Dependence
SciTech - v28 - i3 - Sept 2004 - p122(1) [51-500]
Public Health Response to Biological and Chemical Weapons: WHO Guidance, 2nd Ed.
SciTech - v28 - i3 - Sept 2004 - p91(1) [51-500]
Safe Blood and Blood Products: Distance Learning Materials, Rev. Ed., Vols. 1-5
SciTech - v28 - i1 - March 2004 - p121(1) [51-500]
WHO Model Formulary, 2004
SciTech - v28 - i3 - Sept 2004 - p122(1) [501+]
World Health Report 2004: Changing History
SciTech - v28 - i3 - Sept 2004 - p122(1) [501+]
World History: Ancient and Medieval Eras
LJ - v130 - i1 - Jan 1 2005 - p158(1) [51-500]
SLJ - v50 - i12 - Dec 2004 - p90(2) [501+]
World History. Audiobook Review
c SLJ - v50 - i11 - Nov 2004 - p80(1) [51-500]
World History: Lives and Times in Egypt, Greece and the Roman Empire. Audiobook Review
SLJ - v50 - i10 - Oct 2004 - pS34(2) [501+]
World Intellectual Property Association - *Secrets of Intellectual Property: A Guide for Small and Medium-Sized Exporters*
R&R Bk N - v19 - i4 - Nov 2004 - p108(1) [51-500]
World Investment Report 2003: FDI Policies for Development: National and International Perspectives
JEL - v42 - i1 - March 2004 - p264(1) [51-500]
World List of Universities and Other Institutions of Higher Education, 24th Ed.
Choice - v42 - i5 - Jan 2005 - p839(1) [1-50]
World Of Animals: Birds
LibMed - v22 - i7 - April-May 2004 - p65(1) [501+]
A World of Festivals
SLJ - v50 - i12 - Dec 2004 - p63(1) [501+]
The World of Paperbacks
CR - v285 - i1665 - Oct 2004 - p247(2) [501+]
World Peacemakers
LibMed - v23 - i1 - August-Sept 2004 - p72(2) [51-500]
World Press Photo 2004
LJ - v129 - i17 - Oct 15 2004 - p60(2) [51-500]
World Trade Review
JEL - v41 - i4 - Dec 2003 - p1448(1) [501+]
World Water Assessment Programme - *Water for People, Water for Life: A Joint Report by the Twenty-Three UN Agencies Concerned with Freshwater*
Choice - v41 - i7 - March 2004 - p1325(1) [501+]
The World's Hot Spots
LibMed - v23 - i1 - August-Sept 2004 - p77(1) [51-500]
Worldwatch Institute - *State of the World 2004*
y SB - v40 - i4 - July-August 2004 - p161(1) [51-500]
Worley, Matthew - *In Search of Revolution: International Communist Parties in the Third Period*
Choice - v42 - i4 - Dec 2004 - p713(1) [1-50]
Wormald, Peter-John - *Endoscopic Sinus Surgery: Anatomy, Three-Dimensional Reconstruction, and Surgical Technique*
SciTech - v28 - i4 - Dec 2004 - p110(1) [51-500]
Worman, Nancy - *The Cast of Character: Style in Greek Literature*
AJP - v125 - i1 - Spring 2004 - p145-147 [501+]
Wormell, Christopher - *The Big Ugly Monster and the Little Stone Rabbit (Illus. by Wormell, Christopher)*
c CCB-B - v58 - i1 - Sept 2004 - p3(2) [51-500]
c KR - v72 - i16 - August 15 2004 - p815(1) [51-500]
c PW - v251 - i43 - Oct 25 2004 - p48(1) [501+]
c SLJ - v50 - i9 - Sept 2004 - p184(1) [501+]
The New Alphabet of Animals
c PW - v251 - i34 - August 23 2004 - p56(2) [501+]
Teeth, Tails, and Tentacles: An Animal Counting Book (Illus. by Wormell, Christopher)
c BL - v101 - i3 - Oct 1 2004 - p326(1) [51-500]
c CCB-B - v58 - i1 - Sept 2004 - p47(2) [51-500]
c Globe & Mail - Dec 11 2004 - pD28 [51-500]
c KR - v72 - i14 - July 15 2004 - p695(1) [51-500]
c NYTBR - Nov 14 2004 - p21(L) [501+]
c SLJ - v50 - i12 - Dec 2004 - p139(1) [501+]
Worms
c SB - v40 - i3 - May-June 2004 - p132(1) [501+]

Wormsley, Diane P. - *Braille Literacy: A Functional Approach*
R&R Bk N - v19 - i3 - August 2004 - p162(1) [501+]
Worrall, Jay - *Sails on the Horizon: A Novel of the Napoleonic Wars*
KR - v73 - i3 - Feb 1 2005 - p148(1) [501+]
Worrall, John L. - *Criminal Procedure: From First Contact to Appeal*
R&R Bk N - v19 - i1 - Feb 2004 - pNA [51-500]
Worschech, Udo - *A Burial Cave at Umm Dimis North of el-Balu*
R&R Bk N - v19 - i1 - Feb 2004 - p45(1) [51-500]
Worsley, Giles - *The Architect King: George III and the Culture of Enlightenment*
Apo - v161 - i517 - March 2005 - p99(2) [501+]
John, 3rd Earl of Bute: Patron and Collector Francis Russell
Apo - v161 - i517 - March 2005 - p99(2) [501+]
Worster, Donald - *A River Running West: The Life of John Wesley Powell*
NRJ - v44 - i1 - Wntr 2004 - p319-332 [501+]
Worsthorne, Peregrine - *In Defence of Aristocracy*
TLS - i5286 - July 23 2004 - p36(1) [501+]
Worth, Michael J. - *New Strategies for Educational Fund Raising*
J Hi E - v76 - i1 - Jan-Feb 2005 - p110(2) [501+]
Worth, Richard - *Organization Skills, 2nd Ed.*
y VOYA - v27 - i4 - Oct 2004 - p332(2) [51-500]
Professional Ethics and Etiquette, 2nd Ed.
y SLJ - v51 - i1 - Jan 2005 - p144(1) [51-500]
Slave Life on the Plantation: Prisons beneath the Sun
y BL - v101 - i1 - Sept 1 2004 - p79(1) [501+]
c SLJ - v50 - i12 - Dec 2004 - p172(1) [51-500]
The Slave Trade in America: Cruel Commerce
c CH Bwatch - v14 - i7 - July 2004 - p5(1) [51-500]
c SLJ - v50 - i8 - August 2004 - p135(1) [501+]
South Carolina
c SLJ - v50 - i11 - Nov 2004 - p132(1) [51-500]
Wortham, Simon Morgan - *Samuel Weber: Acts of Reading*
R&R Bk N - v19 - i1 - Feb 2004 - p220(1) [51-500]
Wortham, Stanton - *Linguistic Anthropology of Education*
Lang Soc - v33 - i4 - Sept 2004 - p617-619 [501+]
Worthen, Dennis B. - *Dictionary of Pharmacy*
Bwatch - Nov 2004 - pNA [51-500]
Choice - v42 - i7 - March 2005 - p1200(1) [51-500]
SciTech - v28 - i4 - Dec 2004 - p118(1) [1-50]
Pharmacy in World War II
Choice - v42 - i5 - Jan 2005 - p887(1) [1-50]
SciTech - v28 - i3 - Sept 2004 - p123(1) [51-500]
Seabirds: A Natural History
SB - v41 - i1 - Jan-Feb 2005 - p21(2) [501+]
Worthen, W.B. - *Shakespeare and the Force of Modern Performance*
Ren Q - v57 - i3 - Fall 2004 - p1162(2) [501+]
Theat J - v56 - i2 - May 2004 - p322(2) [501+]
Worthington, Andy - *Stonehenge: Celebration and Subversion*
HT - v54 - i11 - Nov 2004 - p63(1) [501+]
Worthington, David - *Scots in Habsburg Service, 1618-1648*
J Mil H - v68 - i4 - Oct 2004 - p1248-1250 [501+]
Worthington, Diane Rossen - *The Taste of the Season: Inspired Recipes for Fall and Winter*
PW - v251 - i37 - Sept 13 2004 - p72(1) [1-50]
Worthington, Glenn W. - *A Thorough and Accurate History of Genuine Diamonds in Arkansas*
RocksMiner - v79 - i6 - Nov-Dec 2004 - p423(1) [501+]
Worthington, Ian - *Alexander the Great: A Reader*
Class R - v54 - i1 - May 2004 - p149(3) [501+]
Alexander the Great: Man and God
Choice - v42 - i1 - Sept 2004 - p165(1) [501+]
Worthington, Maulfry - *Children's Mathematics: Making Marks, Making Meaning.*
TC Math - v11 - i1 - August 2004 - p45(2) [501+]
Worthington, Sarah - *Commercial Law and Commercial Practice*
Law Q Rev - v121 - Jan 2005 - p161-163 [501+]
Worzel, Richard - *Who Owns Tomorrow?: 7 Secrets for the Future of Business*
CBRA - Annual 2003 - p334(2) [51-500]
Wosk, Julie - *Women and the Machine: Representations from the Spinning Wheel to the Electronic Age*
NWSA Jnl - v16 - i3 - Fall 2004 - p229(3) [501+]
Wom HR - v13 - i2 - Summer 2004 - p311-313 [501+]

Wouk, Herman - *A Hole in Texas: A Novel*
Nature - v429 - i6994 - June 24 2004 - p808(1) [501+]
Sci - v306 - i5696 - Oct 22 2004 - p615(1) [501+]
Marjorie Morningstar
BW - v34 - i27 - July 4 2004 - p13(1) [501+]

Woyshner, Christine - *Social Education in the Twentieth Century: Curriculum and Context for Citizenship*
R&R Bk N - v19 - i3 - August 2004 - p218(1) [1-50]

Wozencraft, Kim - *Wanted*
BL - v101 - i1 - Sept 1 2004 - p71(1) [51-500]
Ent W - Sept 10 2004 - p171 [51-500]
KR - v72 - i14 - July 15 2004 - p660(1) [51-500]
LJ - v129 - i14 - Sept 1 2004 - p144(1) [51-500]
People - v62 - i13 - Sept 27 2004 - p57 [501+]
PW - v251 - i35 - August 30 2004 - p33(1) [501+]

Wozniak, Danielle F. - *They're All My Children: Faster Mothering in America*
MAQ - v18 - i1 - March 2004 - p115(2) [501+]

Wrage, Stephen D. - *Immaculate Warfare: Participants Reflect on the Air Campaigns over Kosovo and Afghanistan*
R&R Bk N - v19 - i1 - Feb 2004 - p256(1) [51-500]

Wrathall, Mark A. - *Religion After Metaphysics*
TLS - i5307 - Dec 17 2004 - p4-6 [501+]

Wray, David - *Critical Literacy*
Sch Lib - v52 - i4 - Winter 2004 - p222(1) [51-500]

Wray, David L. - *Take Control with Your 401(k): An Employee's Guide to Maximizing Your Investments*
HR Mag - v49 - i7 - July 2004 - pS9(1) [51-500]

Wray, Randall L. - *Credit and State Theories of Money: The Contributions of A. Mitchell Innes*
R&R Bk N - v19 - i3 - August 2004 - p94(1) [51-500]

Wray, T.J. - *Grief Dreams: How They Help Heal Us After the Death of a Loved One*
LJ - v130 - i2 - Feb 1 2005 - p104(1) [51-500]

Wrede, Patricia C. - *The Grand Tour*
y   BL - v101 - i1 - Sept 1 2004 - p109(1) [1-50]
c   CCB-B - v58 - i3 - Nov 2004 - p153(1) [501+]
y   Kliatt - v38 - i5 - Sept 2004 - p17(2) [51-500]
y   KR - v72 - i17 - Sept 1 2004 - p875(1) [51-500]
y   SLJ - v50 - i11 - Nov 2004 - p156(2) [51-500]
y   VOYA - v27 - i5 - Dec 2004 - p412(1) [51-500]
Sorcery and Cecelia, or The Enchanted Chocolate Pot
y   Kliatt - v38 - i6 - Nov 2004 - p26(1) [51-500]

Wren, Benjamin Lee - *Teaching World Civilization with Joy and Enthusiasm*
R&R Bk N - v19 - i3 - August 2004 - p31(1) [51-500]

Wriggins, Howard - *Picking up the Pieces from Portugal to Palestine: Quaker Rufugee Relief in World War II: A Memoir*
R&R Bk N - v19 - i3 - August 2004 - p35(1) [51-500]

Wright, Amos J., Jr. - *Historic Indian Towns in Alabama, 1540-1838*
Am Ant - v69 - i4 - Oct 2004 - p791(2) [501+]

Wright, Bil - *One Foot in Love*
Lam Bk Rpt - v13 - i1-2 - August-Sept 2004 - p45(2) [501+]

Wright, Bradford W. - *Comic Book Nation: The Transformation of Youth Culture in America*
Col Lit - v32 - i1 - Wntr 2005 - p166(11) [501+]

Wright, C.D. - *Cooling Time: An American Poetry Vigil*
PW - v251 - i51 - Dec 20 2004 - p51(1) [501+]

Wright, Charles - *Snake Eyes*
TLS - i5303 - Nov 19 2004 - p34(1) [501+]

Wright, Clare - *Beyond the Ladies Lounge: Australia's Female Publicans*
AHS - v35 - i124 - Oct 2004 - p417(3) [501+]

Wright, Courtni - *Espresso for Two*
y   BL - v101 - i2 - Sept 15 2004 - p228(1) [51-500]

Wright, Craig - *The Maze and the Warrior: Symbols in Architecture, Theology, and Music*
CH - v73 - i4 - Dec 2004 - p899(3) [501+]

Wright, David - *Mental Disability in Victorian England: The Earlswood Asylum, 1847-1901*
JIH - v34 - i4 - Spring 2004 - p639-640 [501+]

Wright, David (b. 1939 -) - *Facts on File Children's Atlas, Updated Ed.*
c   LibMed - v22 - i7 - April-May 2004 - p69(1) [51-500]

Wright, Edward - *The Silver Face*
Globe & Mail - Sept 18 2004 - pD22 [51-500]
Globe & Mail - Nov 27 2004 - pD18 [1-50]

Wright, Eric - *Hemingway Caper*
CBRA - Annual 2003 - p193(1) [51-500]

Wright, Evan - *Generation Kill: Devil Dogs, Iceman, Captain America, and the New Face of American War*
Bus W - i3894 - August 2 2004 - p20 [501+]
Bus W - i3895 - August 9 2004 - p10 [501+]
NS - v133 - i4699 - August 2 2004 - p38(2) [501+]
NYRB - v51 - i20 - Dec 16 2004 - p8(3) [501+]
NYTBR - Nov 14 2004 - p60 [501+]
People - Dec 27 2004 - p63 [501+]

Wright, Franz - *Walking to Martha's Vineyard*
Poet - v185 - i1 - Oct 2004 - p53(9) [501+]

Wright, George - *The Legal Studies Reader: A Conversation and Readings about Law*
Law&PolBR - Sept 2004 - pNA [501+]
R&R Bk N - v19 - i3 - August 2004 - p189(1) [501+]

Wright, H. Stephen - *Film Music at the Piano: An Index to Piano Arrangements of Instrumental Film and Television Music in Anthologies and Collections*
R&R Bk N - v19 - i1 - Feb 2004 - p195(1) [51-500]

Wright, Hilary - *Biodynamic Gardening for Health and Flavour*
E-Streams - July 2004 - pNA [501+]

Wright, Jesse H. - *Cognitive-Behavior Therapy*
SciTech - v28 - i3 - Sept 2004 - p99(1) [1-50]

Wright, Jim - *Fixin' to Git: One Fan's Love Affair with NASCAR's Winston Cup*
SSJ - v21 - i1 - March 2004 - p113-115 [501+]

Wright, Joanne H. - *Origin Stories in Political Thought: Discourses on Gender, Power, and Citizenship*
R&R Bk N - v19 - i3 - August 2004 - p3(1) [1-50]

Wright, John (b. 1956 -) - *The Ethics of Economic Rationalism*
Choice - v41 - i7 - March 2004 - p1343(1) [501+]
JEL - v42 - i1 - March 2004 - p233(1) [501+]

Wright, John C. - *The Last Guardian of Everness*
LJ - v129 - i13 - August 2004 - p73(1) [51-500]
PW - v251 - i28 - July 12 2004 - p49(1) [501+]
Mists of Everness: Being the Second Part of the War of the Dreaming
KR - v73 - i4 - Feb 15 2005 - p204(1) [501+]
PW - v252 - i8 - Feb 21 2005 - p162(1) [51-500]

Wright, Jonathan - *God's Soldiers: Adventure, Politics, Intrigue, and Power: A History of the Jesuits*
CC - v121 - i21 - Oct 19 2004 - p62(3) [501+]
Choice - v42 - i5 - Jan 2005 - p908(1) [1-50]
Gustav Stresemann
Ger Q - v77 - i2 - Spring 2004 - p249-250 [501+]
The Jesuits: Missions, Myths and Histories
CR - v285 - i1663 - August 2004 - p126(2) [501+]
TLS - i5290 - August 20 2004 - p28(1) [51-500]

Wright, Julian - *The Regionalist Movement in France, 1890-1914: Jean Charles-Brun and French Political Thought*
HER - v119 - i483 - Sept 2004 - p1004(3) [501+]
HER - v119 - i483 - Sept 2004 - p1005(3) [501+]

Wright, Kate - *Screenwriting Is Storytelling: Creating an A-List Screenplay That Sells*
BL - v101 - i4 - Oct 15 2004 - p380(2) [51-500]

Wright, Lorraine M. - *Spirituality, Suffering, and Illnes: Ideas for Healing*
SciTech - v28 - i4 - Dec 2004 - p122 [51-500]

Wright, M.R. - *Reason and Necessity: Essays on Plato's Timaeus*
Class R - v54 - i2 - Nov 2004 - p316-317 [501+]

Wright, Margaret Nickelson - *Hopi Silver: The History and Hallmarks of Hopi Silversmithing*
Roundup M - v12 - i1 - Oct 2004 - p27(1) [51-500]

Wright, Margaret Robson - *An Introduction to Chemical Kinetics*
SciTech - v28 - i3 - Sept 2004 - p53(1) [1-50]

Wright, Mary C. - *More Voices, New Stories: King County, Washington's First 150 Years*
WHQ - v35 - i3 - Autumn 2004 - p403(2) [501+]

Wright, Maurice - *Japan's Fiscal Crisis: The Ministry of Finance and the Politics of Public Spending, 1975-2000*
Pac A - v77 - i2 - Summer 2004 - p331(3) [501+]

Wright, Michelle M. - *Becoming Black: Creating Identity in the African Diaspora*
Choice - v42 - i1 - Sept 2004 - p196(1) [501+]

Wright, N.T. - *The Resurrection of the Son of God*
JR - v84 - i4 - Oct 2004 - p636(2) [501+]
Theol St - v66 - i1 - March 2005 - p184(3) [501+]
TT - v61 - i3 - Oct 2004 - p412(3) [501+]

Wright, Nancy E. - *Women, Property, and the Letters of the Law in Early Modern England*
R&R Bk N - v19 - i4 - Nov 2004 - p164(1) [501+]

Wright, Nancy Means - *Mad Cow Nightmare*
KR - v73 - i4 - Feb 15 2005 - p204(1) [51-500]

Wright, Patricia C. - *Tarsiers: Past, Present, and Future*
QRB - v79 - i3 - Sept 2004 - p319(2) [501+]

Wright, Raymond S. - *Ancestors in German Archives: A Guide to Family History Sources*
Choice - v41 - i11-12 - July-August 2004 - p2023(2) [501+]
LJ - v129 - i13 - August 2004 - p120(1) [51-500]
BL - v101 - i7 - Dec 1 2004 - p684(1) [501+]

Wright, Rex A. - *Motivational Analyses of Social Behavior: Building on Jack Brehm's Contributions to Psychology*
R&R Bk N - v19 - i3 - August 2004 - p8(1) [1-50]

Wright, Richard (1908-1960) - *Black Boy. Audiobook Review*
Globe & Mail - Feb 19 2005 - pD17 [501+]

Wright, Richard B. - *Adultery*
Globe & Mail - Sept 25 2004 - pD4 [501+]
Globe & Mail - Nov 27 2004 - pD3 [51-500]

Wright, Robert E. - *Hamilton Unbound: Finance and the Creation of the American Republic*
AHR - v109 - i3 - June 2004 - p899(2) [501+]
JAH - v91 - i2 - Sept 2004 - p608(2) [501+]
The History of Corporate Finance: Development of Anglo-American Securities Markets, Financial Practices, Theories and Laws, Vols. 1-6
BHR - v78 - i2 - Summer 2004 - p378(1) [501+]
R&R Bk N - v19 - i4 - Nov 2004 - p117(1) [51-500]
The History of Corporate Governance: The Importance of Stakeholder Activism
BHR - v78 - i2 - Summer 2004 - p379(2) [501+]
The Wealth of Nations Rediscovered: Integration and Expansion in American Financial Markets, 1780-1850
AHR - v109 - i3 - June 2004 - p900(2) [501+]
JAH - v91 - i3 - Dec 2004 - p999(2) [501+]
JIH - v35 - i2 - Autumn 2004 - p308(2) [501+]

Wright, Ronald - *A Short History of Progress*
Globe & Mail - Nov 6 2004 - pD6 [501+]
Globe & Mail - Nov 27 2004 - pD3 [51-500]
KR - v73 - i4 - Feb 15 2005 - p224(1) [501+]

Wright, Russell O. - *Chronology of Transportation in the United States*
R&R Bk N - v19 - i3 - August 2004 - p121(1) [51-500]

Wright, T.R. - *Hardy and His Readers*
Choice - v41 - i7 - March 2004 - p1301(1) [501+]
VS - v46 - i3 - Spring 2004 - p538(4) [501+]

Wright, Teresa - *The Perils of Protest: State Repression and Student Activism in China and Taiwan*
Ch Rev Int - v10 - i2 - Fall 2003 - p473(4) [501+]

Wright, Thomas - *Early Travels in Palestine*
R&R Bk N - v19 - i1 - Feb 2004 - p42(1) [51-500]
A Traveller's Companion to London
R&R Bk N - v19 - i4 - Nov 2004 - p37(1) [51-500]

Wright, William M. - *Meuse-Argonne Diary: A Division Commander in World War 1*
Parameters - v34 - i4 - Winter 2004 - p145(2) [501+]

Wrightsman, Lawrence S. - *Forensic Psychology, 2nd Ed.*
SciTech - v28 - i4 - Dec 2004 - p87(1) [51-500]

Wrightson, Kellinde - *Fourteenth-Century Icelandic Verse on the Virgin Mary: Drapa af Mariugrat, Vitnisvisur af Mariu, Mariuvisur, I-III*
Specu - v79 - i3 - July 2004 - p862-863 [501+]

Wrigley, Colin - *Encyclopedia of Grain Science, Vols. 1-3*
Choice - v42 - i7 - March 2005 - p1200(1) [51-500]
LJ - v129 - i20 - Dec 1 2004 - p164(1) [51-500]

Wrigley, E.A. - *Poverty, Progress and Population*
TimHES - v0 - i1675 - Jan 21 2005 - p26(1) [501+]

Wrigley, Graham C. - *Facility Validation: Theory, Practice, and Tools*
SciTech - v28 - i3 - Sept 2004 - p124(1) [51-500]

Wrigley, Richard - *Politics of Appearances: Representations of Dress in Revolutionary France*
JMH - v76 - i4 - Dec 2004 - p966(2) [501+]

Wrigley, Robert - *Lives of the Animals*
Ga R - v58 - i2 - Summer 2004 - p484-501 [501+]

Wrobel, David M. - *Promised Lands: Promotion, Memory, and the Creation of The American West*
WHQ - v35 - i2 - Summer 2004 - p226-226 [501+]

Wroe, Ann - *Perfect Prince: Truth and Deception in Renaissance Europe*
Globe & Mail - Sept 25 2004 - pD30 [1-50]

Wrone, David R. - *The Zapruder Film: Reframing JFK's Assassination*
JAH - v91 - i3 - Dec 2004 - p1087(2) [501+]

Wrong, Michela - *I Didn't Do It for You: How the World Betrayed a Small African Nation*
　　NS - v134 - i4722 - Jan 17 2005 - p49(2) [501+]
　　PW - v252 - i11 - March 14 2005 - p53(1) [51-500]

Wu, Bang Ye - *Spanning Trees and Optimization Problems*
　　Choice - v42 - i3 - Nov 2004 - p521(1) [501+]

Wu, Chi-san - *Handbook of Size Exclusion Chromatography and Related Techniques, 2nd Ed.*
　　E-Streams - Dec 2004 - pNA [501+]
　　SciTech - v28 - i1 - March 2004 - p54(1) [51-500]

Wu, Chih - *Thermodynamic Cycles: Computer-Aided Design and Optimization*
　　SciTech - v28 - i1 - March 2004 - p152(1) [51-500]

Wu, Chung - *The Essentials of the Yi Jing*
　　Ch Rev Int - v11 - i1 - Spring 2004 - p198(8) [501+]
　　R&R Bk N - v19 - i1 - Feb 2004 - p219(1) [51-500]

Wu, Eleanor B. Morris - *From China to Taiwan: Historical, Anthropological, and Religious Perspectives*
　　R&R Bk N - v19 - i4 - Nov 2004 - p50(1) [51-500]

Wu, George Y. - *Internist's Illustrated Guide to Gastrointestinal Surgery*
　　E-Streams - August 2004 - pNA [501+]

Wu, Hequan - *Wireless and Mobile Communications II: Proceedings*
　　SciTech - v28 - i3 - Sept 2004 - p159(1) [51-500]

Wu, Norbert - *Under Antarctic Ice: The Photographs of Norbert Wu*
　y　BL - v101 - i4 - Oct 15 2004 - p375(1) [51-500]
　　LJ - v129 - i14 - Sept 1 2004 - p183(2) [51-500]
　　New Sci - v184 - i2468 - Oct 9 2004 - p49(1) [501+]
　　SciTech - v28 - i4 - Dec 2004 - p59(1) [51-500]

Wu, William - *Gene Giotechnology, 2nd Ed.*
　　SciTech - v28 - i1 - March 2004 - p63(1) [51-500]

Wu, Z.S. - *Structural Health Monitoring and Intelligent Infrastructure: Proceedings, Vols. 1-2*
　　SciTech - v28 - i1 - March 2004 - p143(1) [51-500]

Wubben, Emiel F.M. - *On Creating Competition and Strategic Restructuring: Regulatory Reform in Public Utilities*
　　JEL - v42 - i1 - March 2004 - p294(1) [501+]
　　R&R Bk N - v19 - i1 - Feb 2004 - p97(1) [1-50]

Wuketits, Franz M. - *Handbook of Evolution: The Evolution of Human Societies and Cultures*
　　Choice - v42 - i2 - Oct 2004 - p317(1) [51-500]

Wukovits, John - *Pacific Alamo: The Battle for Wake Island*
　　J Mil H - v68 - i4 - Oct 2004 - p1286-1287 [501+]
　　R&R Bk N - v19 - i1 - Feb 2004 - p29(1) [51-500]

Wullschlager, Jackie - *Hans Christian Andersen: The Life of a Storyteller*
　y　Scan St - v76 - i4 - Winter 2004 - p535(14) [501+]

Wunder, Heide - *Dynastie und Herrschaftssicherung in der Fruehen Neuzeit: Geschlechter und Geschlecht*
　　HNet - Dec 2004 - pNA [501+]

Wunderlich, Gene - *American Country Life: A Legacy*
　　R&R Bk N - v19 - i1 - Feb 2004 - p54(1) [51-500]

Wunderlich, Mark - *Voluntary Servitude*
　　Poet - v185 - i2 - Nov 2004 - p140(2) [51-500]
　　PW - v251 - i47 - Nov 22 2004 - p57(1) [51-500]

Wunnava, Phanindra V. - *The Changing Role of Unions: New Forms of Representation*
　　Choice - v42 - i7 - March 2005 - p1273(1) [51-500]
　　R&R Bk N - v19 - i4 - Nov 2004 - p103(1) [51-500]

Wunsch, A. David - *Complex Variables with Applications, 3rd Ed.*
　　SciTech - v28 - i4 - Dec 2004 - p40(1) [51-500]

Wunschiere, Robbe - *Computational Biology - Unix/Linux, Data Processing and Programming*
　　Choice - v42 - i4 - Dec 2004 - p696(1) [1-50]

Wurst, Spencer - *Descending from the Clouds: A Memoir of Combat in the 505 Parachute Infantry Regiment, 82d Airborne Division*
　　LJ - v129 - i20 - Dec 1 2004 - p140(1) [51-500]

Wushanley, Ying - *Playing Nice and Losing: The Struggle for Control of Women's Intercollegiate Athletics, 1960-2000*
　　Choice - v42 - i2 - Oct 2004 - p332(1) [51-500]
　　R&R Bk N - v19 - i3 - August 2004 - p87(1) [51-500]

Wust, Wolfgang - *Geistlicher Staat und Altes Reich: Fruhneuzeitliche Herrschaftsformen, Administration und Hofhaltung im Augsburger Furstbistum*
　　JMH - v76 - i3 - Sept 2004 - p711(2) [501+]

Wuthnow, Robert - *All in Sync: How Music and Art Are Revitalizing American Religion*
　　JR - v85 - i1 - Jan 2005 - p182(2) [501+]
　Saving America? Faith-Based Services and the Future of Civil Society
　　AM - v191 - i2 - July 19 2004 - p27 [501+]
　　Bks & Cult - v10 - i5 - Sept-Oct 2004 - p32(1) [501+]
　Saving America?: Faith-Based Services and the Future of Civil Society
　　Choice - v42 - i6 - Feb 2005 - p1107(1) [51-500]

Wyandt, Herman E. - *Atlas of Human Chromosome Heteromorphisms*
　　SciTech - v28 - i1 - March 2004 - p62(1) [51-500]

Wyatt-Brown, Bertram - *Hearts of Darkness: Wellsprings of a Southern Literary Tradition*
　　HNet - August 2004 - pNA [501+]

Wyatt, Jean - *Risking Difference: Identification, Race, and Community in Comtemporary Fiction and Feminism*
　　Choice - v42 - i4 - Dec 2004 - p665(1) [1-50]
　Risking Difference: Identification, Race, and Community in Contemporary Fiction and Feminism
　　Wom R Bks - v21 - i12 - Sept 2004 - p27(1) [501+]

Wyatt, Melissa - *Raising The Griffin*
　　LibMed - v22 - i7 - April-May 2004 - p62(1) [501+]

Wyatt, Michael G. - *Endovascular Intervention: Current Controversies*
　　SciTech - v28 - i4 - Dec 2004 - p109(1) [51-500]

Wyatt, Rachael - *Mona Lisa Smiled a Little*
　　Can Lit - i182 - Autumn 2004 - p173(2) [501+]

Wyatt, Time's - *Time's Reach*
　　Globe & Mail - Sept 18 2004 - pD13 [501+]

Wyatt, Valerie - *Inventions: Frequently Asked Questions (Illus. by Fernandes, Matthew)*
　c　CBRA - Annual 2003 - p574(1) [51-500]

Wyborny, Sheila - *The Aztec Empire*
　c　SLJ - v50 - i8 - August 2004 - p138(1) [501+]
　The Han Dynasty
　y　CH Bwatch - v14 - i7 - July 2004 - p5(1) [51-500]

Wyche, Thomas - *21 Special Places in the Carolinas: The Land Conservation Legacy of Duke Power*
　　NRJ - v44 - i2 - Spring 2004 - p621-651 [501+]

Wydoski, Richard S. - *Inland Fishes of Washington, 2nd Ed.*
　　E-Streams - June 2004 - pNA [501+]

Wye, Deborah - *Modern Means: Continuity and Change in Art, 1880 to the Present: Highlights from the Museum of Modern Art*
　　Choice - v42 - i4 - Dec 2004 - p647(1) [1-50]

Wyeth, Sharon Dennis - *Orphea Proud*
　y　BL - v101 - i5 - Nov 1 2004 - p476(1) [51-500]
　y　Black Iss - v7 - i2 - March-April 2005 - p16(1) [51-500]
　y　Kliatt - v38 - i6 - Nov 2004 - p12(2) [51-500]
　y　KR - v72 - i21 - Nov 1 2004 - p1047(1) [51-500]
　y　SLJ - v50 - i12 - Dec 2004 - p154(1) [51-500]
　y　VOYA - v27 - i5 - Dec 2004 - p398(1) [51-500]
　y　PW - v252 - i1 - Jan 3 2005 - p57(1) [51-500]
　Something Beautiful
　c　RT - v57 - Dec 2003 - p393 [51-500]

Wyile, Herb - *Speculative Fictions: Contemporary Canadian Novelists and the Writing of History*
　　CBRA - Annual 2003 - p266(1) [51-500]

Wyke, Maria - *The Roman Mistress: Ancient and Modern Representations*
　　Class R - v54 - i2 - Nov 2004 - p392(2) [501+]

Wylder, John - *Strategic Information Security*
　　SciTech - v28 - i3 - Sept 2004 - p158(1) [51-500]

Wylie, Betty Jane - *Write Track: How to Succeed as a Freelance Writer in Canada, 2nd Ed.*
　　CBRA - Annual 2003 - p19(1) [51-500]

Wylie, Neville - *Britain, Switzerland, and the Second World War*
　　HER - v119 - i483 - Sept 2004 - p1101(2) [501+]

Wyllie, Barbara - *Nabokov at the Movies: Film Perspectives in Fiction*
　　R&R Bk N - v19 - i1 - Feb 2004 - p217(1) [51-500]

Wyma, Keith David - *Crucible of Reason: Intentional Action, Practical Rationality, and Weakness of Will*
　　R&R Bk N - v20 - i1 - Feb 2005 - p2(1) [51-500]

Wyman, Carolyn - *Better Than Homemade: Amazing Foods That Changed the Way We Eat*
　　PW - v251 - i33 - August 16 2004 - p57(1) [51-500]

Wynbrandt, James - *Brief History of Saudi Arabia*
　　R&R Bk N - v19 - i4 - Nov 2004 - p47(1) [51-500]
　Flying Highs: How JetBlue Founder and CEO David Neeleman Beats the Competition ... Even in the World's Most Turbulent Industry
　　R&R Bk N - v19 - i4 - Nov 2004 - p107(1) [51-500]

Wyndham, Joan - *Dawn Chorus*
　　CR - v286 - i1669 - Feb 2005 - p124(1) [51-500]

Wyngaard, Amy S. - *From Savage to Citizen: The Invention of the Peasant in the French Enlightenment*
　　Choice - v42 - i7 - March 2005 - p1234(1) [51-500]
　　R&R Bk N - v19 - i4 - Nov 2004 - p230(1) [501+]

Wyngaard, Susan - *Digital Images and Art Libraries in the Twenty-First Century*
　　LJ - v129 - i12 - July 2004 - p119(1) [51-500]

Wynn, Neil A. - *Historical Dictionary from the Great War to the Great Depression*
　　R&R Bk N - v19 - i1 - Feb 2004 - p60(1) [51-500]

Wynne, Ben - *A Hard Trip: A History of the 15th Mississippi Infantry, C.S.A*
　　JSH - v70 - i4 - Nov 2004 - p929(2) [501+]

Wynne, Catherine - *The Colonial Conan Doyle: British Imperialism, Irish Nationalism, and the Gothic*
　　ELT - v48 - i1 - Wntr 2005 - p248(5) [501+]
　　VS - v46 - i4 - Summer 2004 - p694(3) [501+]

Wynne, Clive D.L. - *Do Animals Think?*
　　Am Sci - v92 - i5 - Sept-Oct 2004 - p481(2) [501+]
　　Choice - v42 - i3 - Nov 2004 - p511(1) [1-50]
　　Globe & Mail - August 14 2004 - pD12 [1-50]
　　Nature - v430 - i6996 - July 8 2004 - p148(1) [501+]
　　NS - v133 - i4705 - Sept 13 2004 - p52(2) [501+]
　　QRB - v79 - i4 - Dec 2004 - p431(2) [501+]
　　SB - v40 - i5 - Sept-Oct 2004 - p205(1) [501+]
　　SB - v40 - i6 - Nov-Dec 2004 - p243(1) [51-500]
　　TimHES - v0 - i1684 - March 25 2005 - p30(1) [501+]
　　TLS - i5288 - August 6 2004 - p32(1) [501+]

Wynne-Jones, Tim - *A Thief in the House of Memory*
　　Globe & Mail - Sept 11 2004 - pD9 [501+]
　　Res Links - v10 - i3 - Feb 2005 - p43(1) [501+]

Wynne, Lewis N. - *Florida in the Civil War*
　　HNet - Sept 2004 - pNA [501+]

Wynne, Patricia J. - *Birds: Nature's Magnificent Flying Machines*
　　LibMed - v22 - i5 - Feb 2004 - p54(1) [501+]

Wynot, Jennifer Jean - *Keeping the Faith: Russian Orthodox Monasticism in the Soviet Union, 1917-1939*
　　Choice - v42 - i5 - Jan 2005 - p911(1) [1-50]

Wynveen, Tim - *Balloon*
　　Can Lit - i182 - Autumn 2004 - p186(2) [501+]
　Sweeter Life
　　CBRA - Annual 2003 - p193(1) [51-500]

Wypych, George - *Handbook of Plasticizers*
　　E-Streams - Nov 2004 - pNA [501+]

Wyschogrod, Michael - *Abraham's Promise: Judaism and Jewish-Christian Relations*
　　LJ - v129 - i13 - August 2004 - p88(2) [501+]

X Y Z

Xambo-Descamps, Sebastian - *Block Error-Correcting Codes: A Computational Primer*
  Choice - v41 - i7 - March 2004 - p1329-1 [501+]

Xanthoudaki, Maria - *Researching Visual Arts Education in Museums and Galleries: An International Reader*
  R&R Bk N - v19 - i1 - Feb 2004 - p199(1) [51-500]

Xenophon - *Hero: A New Translation*
  R&R Bk N - v19 - i1 - Feb 2004 - p214 [51-500]

Xiaojuan, Jiang - *FDI in China: Contributions to Growth, Restructuring, and Competitiveness*
  R&R Bk N - v19 - i3 - August 2004 - p139(1) [51-500]

Xie, Yu - *Women in Science: Career Processes and Outcomes*
  JEL - v42 - i1 - March 2004 - p280(2) [501+]

Xinran - *Sky Burial*
  TLS - i5305 - Dec 3 2004 - p30(1) [51-500]

Xu, Jianzhong - *Case Studies of Families Doing Third-Grade Homework*
  CE - v81 - i1 - Fall 2004 - p57(1) [51-500]

Xu, Junming - *Theory and Application of Graphs*
  Choice - v42 - i1 - Sept 2004 - p142(1) [501+]

Xu, Quanyun A. - *Stability-Indicating HPLC Methods for Drug Analysis, 2nd Ed.*
  E-Streams - June 2004 - pNA [501+]

Xu, Wenying - *Ethics and Aesthetics of Freedom in American and Chinese Realism*
  R&R Bk N - v19 - i1 - Feb 2004 - p242(1) [501+]

Xu, Xiangming - *Epidemiology of Mycotoxin Producing Fungi: Under the Aegis of COST Action 835 "Agriculturally Important Toxigenic Fungi 1998-2003," EU Project*
  SciTech - v28 - i1 - March 2004 - p130(1) [51-500]

Xu, Xipeng - *Advances in Grinding and Abrasive Processes: Selected Papers*
  SciTech - v28 - i1 - March 2004 - p152(1) [51-500]

  Machining of Natural Stone Materials
  SciTech - v28 - i1 - March 2004 - p141(1) [51-500]

Xu, Yi-Chong - *The Governance of World Trade: International Civil Servants and the GATT/WTO*
  R&R Bk N - v19 - i4 - Nov 2004 - p108(1) [51-500]

Xue, Yongling - *The Influence of Religious Beliefs on Social Interaction*
  R&R Bk N - v19 - i4 - Nov 2004 - p127(1) [51-500]

XYZ, Emily - *The Emily XYZ Songbook: Poems for 2 Voices*
  PW - v252 - i4 - Jan 24 2005 - p237(1) [501+]

Yaakov, Juliette - *Senior High School Library Catalog. 16th Ed.*
  c SLJ - v50 - i8 - August 2004 - p62(1) [501+]

Yablonka, Hanna - *The State of Israel vs. Adolf Eichmann*
  Choice - v42 - i3 - Nov 2004 - p544(2) [51-500]

Yaccarino, Dan - *Dan Yaccarino's Mother Goose (Illus. by Yaccarino, Dan)*
  c BL - v101 - i4 - Oct 15 2004 - p409(1) [51-500]
  c KR - v72 - i17 - Sept 1 2004 - p875(1) [51-500]
  c NYTBR - March 13 2005 - p20 [501+]
  c PW - v251 - i36 - Sept 6 2004 - p61(1) [51-500]
  c SLJ - v50 - i10 - Oct 2004 - p152(1) [51-500]

  Five Little Ducks
  c PW - v252 - i7 - Feb 14 2005 - p80(2) [501+]

Yacobi, Haim - *Constructing a Sense of Place: Architecture and the Zionist Discourse*
  R&R Bk N - v19 - i3 - August 2004 - p156(1) [51-500]

Yacovone, Donald - *Freedom's Journey: African American Voices of the Civil War*
  Choice - v42 - i2 - Oct 2004 - p354(1) [51-500]
  Kliatt - v38 - i4 - July 2004 - p43(1) [501+]

Yadav, Alok - *Before the Empire of English: Literature, Provinciality, and Nationalism in Eighteenth-Century Britain*
  Choice - v42 - i5 - Jan 2005 - p856(1) [1-50]

Yafa, Stephen - *Big Cotton: How a Humble Fiber Created Fortunes, Wrecked Civilizations, and Put America on the Map*
  KR - v72 - i22 - Nov 15 2004 - p1086(1) [501+]
  PW - v251 - i50 - Dec 13 2004 - p58(1) [51-500]

  How a Humble Fiber Created Fortunes, Wrecked Civilizations, and Put America on the Map
  y BL - v101 - i8 - Dec 15 2004 - p695(1) [51-500]

Yager, Fred - *Career Opportunities in the Film Industry*
  R&R Bk N - v19 - i1 - Feb 2004 - p225(1) [51-500]

  Career Opportunities in the Publishing Industry
  PW - v251 - i49 - Dec 6 2004 - p53(1) [51-500]

Yager, Jan - *Who's That Sitting at My Desk?*
  Bwatch - v26 - i9 - Sept 2004 - p8(1) [51-500]

Yaghmour, Karim - *Building Embedded Linux Systems*
  SciTech - v28 - i3 - Sept 2004 - p24(1) [51-500]

Yakowicz, Susie - *Fire Runner*
  c CH Bwatch - v14 - i9 - Sept 2004 - p4(1) [51-500]

Yalciner, Ahmet C. - *Submarine Landslides and Tsunamis: Proceedings*
  SciTech - v28 - i1 - March 2004 - p59(1) [51-500]

Yale, Ronald Lightbown - *Carlo Crivelli*
  Spec - v296 - i9197 - Nov 13 2004 - p56(1) [501+]

Yale, Veronica Franklin Gould - *G.F.Watts: The Last Victorian*
  Spec - v297 - i9204 - Jan 1 2005 - p27(1) [501+]

Yale, Worsley - *The British Stable*
  Spec - v297 - i9205 - Jan 8 2005 - p36(1) [501+]

Yalom, Irvin D. - *The Schopenhauer Cure: A Novel*
  KR - v72 - i22 - Nov 15 2004 - p1069(1) [51-500]
  LJ - v129 - i18 - Nov 1 2004 - p78(1) [51-500]
  PW - v251 - i45 - Nov 8 2004 - p33(2) [501+]

Yalom, Marilyn - *Birth of the Chess Queen: A History*
  Econ - v372 - i8383 - July 10 2004 - p76US [501+]
  Globe & Mail - July 10 2004 - pD16 [51-500]
  TLS - i5307 - Dec 17 2004 - p32(1) [501+]

Yam, Philip - *The Pathological Protein: Mad Cow, Chronic Wasting, and Other Deadly Prion Diseases*
  Choice - v41 - i7 - March 2004 - p1328(1) [501+]

Yamada, Hironari - *Portable Synchrotron Light Sources and Advanced Applications: Proceedings*
  SciTech - v28 - i1 - March 2004 - p43(1) [51-500]

Yamaguchi, Billy - *Billy Yamaguchi Feng Shui Beauty*
  BL - v101 - i9-10 - Jan 1 2005 - p796(1) [51-500]
  LJ - v129 - i20 - Dec 1 2004 - p154(1) [51-500]
  PW - v251 - i45 - Nov 8 2004 - p47(1) [501+]

Yamaguchi, Takayuki - *Apocalypse Zero Vol. 1.*
  PW - v251 - i51 - Dec 20 2004 - p39(1) [51-500]

Yamamoto, Beverley - *Nationalism and Gender*
  Choice - v42 - i2 - Oct 2004 - p350(1) [51-500]

Yamamoto, Hisashi - *Main Group Metals in Organic Synthesis*
  E-Streams - Dec 2004 - pNA [501+]

Yamamoto, Kumiko - *The Oral Background of Persian Epics: Storytelling and Poetry*
  HNet - Dec 2004 - pNA [501+]

Yamamoto, Lani - *Albert (Illus. by Yamamoto, Lani)*
  c SLJ - v51 - i2 - Feb 2005 - p112(1) [51-500]
  c PW - v251 - i50 - Dec 13 2004 - p66(2) [51-500]

Yamamura, Kozo - *The End of Diversity? Prospects for German and Japanese Capitalism*
  JEL - v41 - i4 - Dec 2003 - p1425(2) [501+]

  The End of Diversity? Prospects for German and Japanese Capitalism
  Pac A - v77 - i3 - Fall 2004 - p573(2) [501+]

Yamanaka, Naoaki - *High-Performance Backbone Network Technology*
  E-Streams - Nov 2004 - pNA [501+]
  SciTech - v28 - i3 - Sept 2004 - p157(1) [51-500]

Yamarone, Richard - *The Trader's Guide to Key Economic Indicators*
  R&R Bk N - v19 - i3 - August 2004 - p98(1) [51-500]

Yamashita, Bruce I. - *Fighting Tradition: A Marine's Journey to Justice*
  R&R Bk N - v19 - i1 - Feb 2004 - p257(1) [51-500]

Yamashita, Keith - *Unstuck: A Tool for Yourself, Your Team, and Your World*
  HR Mag - v50 - i2 - Feb 2005 - pS9(1) [501+]

Yan, Bing - *Analysis and Purification Methods in Combinatorial Chemistry*
  SciTech - v28 - i1 - March 2004 - p125(1) [51-500]

Yan, Martin - *Martin Yan Quick and Easy*
  PW - v251 - i41 - Oct 11 2004 - p73(1) [51-500]

Yan, Yunxiang - *Private Life under Socialism: Love, Intimacy and Family Change in a Chinese Village, 1949-1999*
  CS - v33 - i4 - July 2004 - p433(2) [501+]
  JIH - v35 - i1 - Summer 2004 - p180-181 [501+]

Yan, Zhengyin - *Optimization in Drug Discovery: In Vitro Methods*
  SciTech - v28 - i4 - Dec 2004 - p119(1) [1-50]

Yancey, Diane - *Life During the Dust Bowl*
  y BL - v100 - i22 - August 2004 - p1918(1) [51-500]
  y SLJ - v50 - i8 - August 2004 - p145(1) [501+]
  y VOYA - v27 - i4 - Oct 2004 - p323(1) [51-500]

Yancey, George A. - *One Body, One Spirit: Principles of Successful Multiracial Churches*
  Ch Today - v48 - i8 - August 2004 - p60(1) [501+]

  What White Looks Like: African-American Philosophers on the Whiteness Question
  Choice - v42 - i5 - Jan 2005 - p868(1) [1-50]

  Who Is White? Latinos, Asians, and the New Black/Nonblack Divide
  CS - v33 - i2 - March 2004 - p195-196 [501+]

Yancey, Richard - *Confessions of a Tax Collector: One Man's Tour of Duty inside the IRS*
  BL - v101 - i4 - Oct 15 2004 - p387(1) [51-500]

Yanez, Rene - *Chicano Visions: American Painters on the Verge*
  Aztlan - v29 - i2 - Fall 2004 - p233-237 [501+]

Yang, Belle - *Hannah Is My Name*
  c BL - v101 - i2 - Sept 15 2004 - p255(1) [51-500]
  c BW - v34 - i50 - Dec 12 2004 - p8(1) [501+]
  c HB - v80 - i6 - Nov-Dec 2004 - p704(1) [51-500]
  c KR - v72 - i17 - Sept 1 2004 - p875(1) [51-500]
  c SLJ - v50 - i11 - Nov 2004 - p120(1) [51-500]

Yang, Dali L. - *Remaking the Chinese Leviation: Market Transition and the Politics of Governance in China*
  Choice - v42 - i5 - Jan 2005 - p904(1) [1-50]

Yang, James - *Joey and Jet (Illus. by Yang, James)*
  c BL - v101 - i9-10 - Jan 1 2005 - p876(1) [51-500]
  c HB - v81 - i1 - Jan-Feb 2005 - p87(2) [51-500]
  c KR - v72 - i15 - August 1 2004 - p751(1) [51-500]
  c PW - v251 - i40 - Oct 4 2004 - p86(1) [51-500]
  c SLJ - v50 - i10 - Oct 2004 - p137(2) [51-500]

Yemelianova, Galina M. - *Russia and Islam: A Historical Survey.*
E-A St - v56 - i5 - July 2004 - p775(2) [501+]

Yen, William M. - *Inorganic Phosphors: Compositions, Preparation, and Optical Properties*
SciTech - v28 - i4 - Dec 2004 - p50(1) [51-500]

Yeo-Jin, Yan - *Sainte Marie*
y VOYA - v27 - i4 - Oct 2004 - p288(2) [51-500]

Yeo, Kiat-Seng - *Low Voltage, Low Power VLSI*
SciTech - v28 - i4 - Dec 2004 - p158(1) [51-500]

Yeomans, Ellen - *Jubilee (Illus. by Ladwig, Tim)*
c SLJ - v50 - i7 - July 2004 - p90(1) [51-500]

Yeomans, Matthew - *Oil: Anatomy of an Industry*
BL - v100 - i22 - August 2004 - p1883(1) [51-500]
LJ - v129 - i13 - August 2004 - p92(1) [501+]
PW - v251 - i27 - July 5 2004 - p48(1) [51-500]

Yep, Gust A. - *Queer Theory and Communication: From Disciplining Queers to Queering the Discipline(s).*
R&R Bk N - v19 - i3 - August 2004 - p149(1) [51-500]

Yep, Laurence - *Dragonwings*
c RT - v57 - Sept 2003 - p101 [51-500]
Lady of Ch'iao Kuo: Warrior of the South, Southern China, A.D. 531
c Teach Lib - v32 - i3 - Feb 2005 - p14(1) [51-500]
The Tiger's Apprentice
y PW - v252 - i1 - Jan 3 2005 - p58(1) [51-500]
Tiger's Blood
y BL - v101 - i9-10 - Jan 1 2005 - p864(1) [1-50]
c KR - v72 - i24 - Dec 15 2004 - p1211(1) [51-500]
c PW - v252 - i1 - Jan 3 2005 - p57(2) [501+]
y SLJ - v51 - i2 - Feb 2005 - p142(2) [51-500]
The Traitor
y Kliatt - v39 - i1 - Jan 2005 - p19(1) [51-500]
y RT - v58 - i3 - Nov 2004 - p292(1) [501+]

Yes Magazine - *Amazing International Space Station (Illus. by Cowles, Rose)*
c CBRA - Annual 2003 - p570(2) [51-500]

Yeschke, Charles L. - *Interrogation: Achieving Confessions Using Permissible Persuasion*
R&R Bk N - v19 - i4 - Nov 2004 - p147(1) [501+]

Yesilada, Birol A. - *The Emerging European Union, 3rd Ed.*
R&R Bk N - v19 - i1 - Feb 2004 - pNA [501+]

Yetiv, Steve A. - *Crude Awakenings: Global Oil Security and American Foreign Policy*
MEJ - v59 - i1 - Wntr 2005 - p154(2) [501+]
Explaining Foreign Policy: U.S. Decision-Making and the Persian Gulf War
MEJ - v58 - i4 - Autumn 2004 - p708(1) [501+]
Pers PS - v33 - i4 - Fall 2004 - p234(1) [501+]
R&R Bk N - v19 - i3 - August 2004 - p49(1) [51-500]

Yeung, Godfrey - *Foreign Investment and Socio-Economic Development in China: The Case of Dongguan*
Ch Rev Int - v10 - i2 - Fall 2003 - p485(4) [501+]

Yezzi, David - *The Hidden Model*
Ant R - v62 - i4 - Fall 2004 - p777(1) [501+]

Yi, Eunjeong - *Guild Dynamics in Seventeeth-Century Istanbul: Fluidity and Leverage*
R&R Bk N - v19 - i1 - Feb 2004 - p100(1) [51-500]

Yifa - *The Origins of Buddhist Monastic Codes in China: An Annotated Translation and Study of the Chanyuan Qinggui*
Ch Rev Int - v11 - i1 - Spring 2004 - p206(5) [501+]

Yilmaz, Serdar - *Subnational Data Requirements for Fiscal Decentralization: Case Studies from Central and Eastern Europe*
R&R Bk N - v19 - i2 - May 2004 - p125 [51-500]

Yim, Denise - *Viotti and the Chinnerys: A Relationship Charted through Letters*
R&R Bk N - v19 - i4 - Nov 2004 - p196(1) [501+]

Yin, George - *Mathematics of Finance: Proceedings*
SciTech - v28 - i3 - July 2004 - p9(1) [501+]

Yin, Robert - *The Case Study Anthology*
R&R Bk N - v19 - i3 - August 2004 - p89(1) [51-500]

Yip, Mingmei - *Chinese Children's Favorite Stories*
c PW - v251 - i51 - Dec 20 2004 - p61(1) [501+]

Yngve, Victor H. - *Hard-Science Linguistics*
R&R Bk N - v19 - i4 - Nov 2004 - p213(1) [51-500]

Yochem, Angela - *J2EE Applications and BEA WebLogic Server, 2nd Ed.*
SciTech - v28 - i4 - Dec 2004 - p21(1) [51-500]

Yochum, Terry R. - *Yochum and Rowe's Essentials of Skeletal Radiology. 3rd Ed., Vols. 1-2*
SciTech - v28 - i3 - Sept 2004 - p108(1) [51-500]

Yocum, John - *Ecclesial mediation in Karl Barth*
R&R Bk N - v19 - i3 - August 2004 - p26(1) [1-50]

Yocum, Robin - *Dead Before Deadline ... and Other Tales from the Police Beat*
R&R Bk N - v19 - i3 - August 2004 - p167(1) [501+]

Yoda, Tomiko - *Gender and National Literature: Hein Texts in the Emergence of Japanese Modernity*
Choice - v42 - i5 - Jan 2005 - p849(1) [1-50]

Yoder, John C. - *Popular Political Culture, Civic Society, and State Crisis in Liberia*
R&R Bk N - v19 - i1 - Feb 2004 - pNA [501+]

Yoder, John Howard - *Jewish-Christian Schism Revisited*
R&R Bk N - v19 - i1 - Feb 2004 - p22(1) [1-50]

Yoder, Robert Stuart - *Youth Deviance in Japan: Class Reproduction of Non-Conformity*
Choice - v42 - i6 - Feb 2005 - p1107(1) [51-500]
R&R Bk N - v19 - i4 - Nov 2004 - p50(1) [51-500]

Yoder, Sharon - *Making the Most of Microsoft Office*
R&R Bk N - v19 - i1 - Feb 2004 - p110(1) [51-500]

Yoko, Hayami - *Between Hills and Plains: Power and Practice in Socio-Religious Dynamics among Karen*
Choice - v42 - i5 - Jan 2005 - p897(1) [1-50]
R&R Bk N - v19 - i3 - August 2004 - p32(1) [51-500]

Yokoyama, John - *When Fish Fly: Lessons for Creating a Vital and Energized Workplace from the World Famous Pike Place Fish Market*
BL - v100 - i22 - August 2004 - p1884(1) [51-500]

Yolen, Jane - *The Barefoot Book of Ballet Stories (Illus. by Guay, Rebecca)*
c BL - v101 - i5 - Nov 1 2004 - p498(1) [51-500]
c CH Bwatch - v14 - i12 - Dec 2004 - pNA [51-500]
c PW - v251 - i38 - Sept 20 2004 - p65(1) [51-500]
c SLJ - v50 - i12 - Dec 2004 - p172(1) [51-500]
Fine Feathered Friends: Poems for Young People (Illus. by Stemple, Jason)
c BL - v101 - i5 - Nov 1 2004 - p478(1) [51-500]
c SLJ - v50 - i12 - Dec 2004 - p172(1) [51-500]
How Do Dinosaurs Clean Their Rooms? (Illus. by Teague, Mark)
c Globe & Mail - Dec 11 2004 - pD43 [51-500]
How Do Dinosaurs Count to Ten? (Illus. by Teague, Mark)
c Globe & Mail - Jan 1 2005 - pD11 [51-500]
My Brothers' Flying Machine: Wilbur, Orville, and Me (Illus. by Burke, Jim)
c RT - v58 - i3 - Nov 2004 - p287(1) [51-500]
The Perfect Wizard: Hans Christian Andersen (Illus. by Nolan, Dennis)
c CCB-B - v58 - i6 - Feb 2005 - p273(1) [51-500]
c KR - v73 - i1 - Jan 1 2005 - p59(1) [51-500]
c PW - v252 - i8 - Feb 21 2005 - p175(1) [51-500]
Prince across the Water
y BL - v101 - i6 - Nov 15 2004 - p585(1) [51-500]
c HB - v80 - i6 - Nov-Dec 2004 - p720(1) [51-500]
c KR - v72 - i18 - Sept 15 2004 - p923(1) [51-500]
y SLJ - v50 - i12 - Dec 2004 - p154(2) [501+]
y VOYA - v27 - i4 - Oct 2004 - p311(1) [51-500]
The Salem Witch Trials: An Unsolved Mystery from History (Illus. by Roth, Roger)
c BL - v101 - i1 - Sept 1 2004 - p118(2) [1-50]
c KR - v72 - i16 - August 15 2004 - p815(1) [51-500]
y SLJ - v50 - i11 - Nov 2004 - p174(1) [51-500]
Sea King (Illus. by Czernecki, Stefan)
c CBRA - Annual 2003 - p530(2) [51-500]
Sword of the Rightful King: A Novel of King Arthur
c HB - v80 - i4 - July-August 2004 - p475(1) [51-500]
y Kliatt - v38 - i5 - Sept 2004 - p34(2) [51-500]
c SLJ - v50 - i8 - August 2004 - p76(1) [51-500]
Sword of the Rightful King (Read by Crossley, Steven). Audiobook Review
c BL - v101 - i1 - Sept 1 2004 - p148(1) [51-500]
c Kliatt - v38 - i4 - July 2004 - p57(1) [51-500]

Yonemoto, Marcia - *Mapping Early Modern Japan: Space, Place, and Culture in the Tokugawa Period, 1603-1868*
AHR - v109 - i2 - April 2004 - p495(2) [501+]
Mapping Early Modern Japan: Space, Place, and Culture in the Tokugawa Period 1603-1868
Hist Geo - v32 - Annual 2004 - p191(3) [501+]
Mapping Early Modern Japan: Space, Place, and Culture in the Tokugawa Period, 1603-1868
JIH - v35 - i2 - Autumn 2004 - p341(2) [501+]
Six Ct J - v35 - i3 - Fall 2004 - p939-941 [501+]
T&C - v45 - i1 - Jan 2004 - p175(2) [501+]

Yong, Amos - *Beyond the Impasse: Toward a Pneumatological Theology of Religions*
Intpr - v58 - i3 - July 2004 - p332(1) [501+]

Yongping Bao - *Phytochemicals in Health and Disease*
E-Streams - Nov 2004 - pNA [501+]

Yoo, Terry S. - *Insight into Images: Principles and Practice for Segmentation, Registration, and Image Analysis*
SciTech - v28 - i4 - Dec 2004 - p90(1) [51-500]

Yoon, Salina - *Animal Count*
c PW - v251 - i31 - August 2 2004 - p72(1) [51-500]
Easter Egg Surprise
c PW - v252 - i7 - Feb 14 2005 - p79(2) [501+]

York, Alissa - *Mercy*
BL - v101 - i2 - Sept 15 2004 - p211(1) [501+]
KR - v72 - i16 - August 15 2004 - p777(1) [501+]
LJ - v129 - i14 - Sept 1 2004 - p144(1) [501+]
PW - v251 - i40 - Oct 4 2004 - p67(1) [51-500]

York, Christina - *Dream House*
BL - v101 - i7 - Dec 1 2004 - p642(1) [51-500]

York, John - *Sharing the Night Sky*
Astron - v33 - i1 - Jan 2005 - p92 [51-500]

York, Michael - *Pagan Theology: Paganism as a World Religion*
TLS - i5266 - March 5 2004 - p25-25 [501+]

York, Neil Longley - *Turning the World Upside Down: The War of American Independence and the Problem of Empire*
JAH - v91 - i3 - Dec 2004 - p994(2) [501+]
R&R Bk N - v19 - i1 - Feb 2004 - p58(1) [51-500]

York, Pat - *The Moon*
c SLJ - v50 - i8 - August 2004 - p105(1) [51-500]

York, Rebecca - *Crimson Moon*
BL - v101 - i9-10 - Jan 1 2005 - p833(1) [1-50]
Immortal Bad Boys
BL - v101 - i2 - Sept 15 2004 - p214(2) [501+]

York, Sherry - *Children's and Young Adult Literature by Latino Writers*
RT - v57 - Nov 2003 - p296 [501+]

Yorks, Lyle - *Strategic Human Resource Development*
HR Mag - v49 - i7 - July 2004 - pS52(1) [51-500]
R&R Bk N - v19 - i3 - August 2004 - p106(1) [1-50]

Yosef, Raz - *Beyond Flesh: Queer Masculinities and Nationalism in Israeli Cinema*
Choice - v42 - i7 - March 2005 - p1235(1) [51-500]

Yoshida, Hiroyuki - *Absolute CM-Periods*
SciTech - v28 - i1 - March 2004 - p40(1) [51-500]

Yoshida, Makoto - *Lesson Study: A Japanese Approach to Improving Mathematics Teaching and Learning*
SciTech - v28 - i3 - Sept 2004 - p34(1) [51-500]

Yoshida, Michihiro - *Vaizard, Vol. 1*
PW - v251 - i50 - Dec 13 2004 - p47(1) [51-500]

Yoshida, Shigeru - *Ultra-High Energy Particle Astrophysics*
Phys Today - v57 - i9 - Sept 2004 - p62-62 [501+]

Yoshihara, Mari - *Embracing the East: White Women and American Orientalism*
HNet - August 2004 - pNA [501+]

Yoshimi, Maeno - *The Acquisition of the Japanese Oral Narrative Style by Native English-Speaking Bilinguals*
R&R Bk N - v19 - i3 - August 2004 - p255(1) [51-500]

Yoshitomi, Akihito - *Ray, Vol. 1*
PW - v251 - i49 - Dec 6 2004 - p45(1) [51-500]

Yoshizaki, Mine - *Sgt. Frog*
y Kliatt - v38 - i4 - July 2004 - p34(1) [51-500]
y VOYA - v27 - i4 - Oct 2004 - p288(1) [51-500]

Yoshizmni, Carol - *Snooze-a-Palooza! More than 100 Slumber Party Ideas (Illus. by Yoshizmni, Carol)*
c PW - v252 - i8 - Feb 21 2005 - p177(1) [51-500]

Yosipovitch, Gil - *Itch: Basic Mechanisms and Therapy*
SciTech - v28 - i1 - March 2004 - p120(1) [51-500]

Yost, Jeffrey R. - *A Bibliographic Guide to Resources in Scientific Computing, 1945-1975*
Isis - v95 - i2 - June 2004 - p334(1) [501+]

Youmans, Marly - *The Curse of the Raven Mocker*
c LibMed - v22 - i6 - March 2004 - p69(1) [501+]
LibMed - v22 - i6 - March 2004 - p69(1) [501+]

Youme - *Selavi, That Is Life: A Haitian Story of Hope (Illus. by Youme)*
c BL - v100 - i21 - July 2004 - p1848(1) [1-50]
c CCB-B - v58 - i1 - Sept 2004 - p48(1) [51-500]
c CH Bwatch - v14 - i11 - Nov 2004 - pNA [51-500]

Young, Adam L. - *Malicious Cryptography: Exposing Cryptovirology*
TimHES - v0 - i1661 - Oct 8 2004 - p30(1) [51-500]

Young, Alan N. - *Justice Defiled: Perverts, Potheads, Serial Killers and Lawyers*
CBRA - Annual 2003 - p320(2) [501+]

Young, Alfred Fabian - *Masquerade: The Life and Times of Deborah Sampson, Continental Soldier*
BooChiTr - May 23 2004 - p2(1) [501+]
RAH - v32 - i4 - Dec 2004 - p493-498 [501+]

Young, Amy - *Belinda in Paris*
  c BL - v101 - i9-10 - Jan 1 2005 - p876(1) [51-500]
  c KR - v73 - i2 - Jan 15 2005 - p127(1) [51-500]
  c PW - v252 - i6 - Feb 7 2005 - p61(2) [501+]
Young, Audrey - *What Patients Taught Me: A Medical Student's Journey*
    BL - v101 - i1 - Sept 1 2004 - p34(1) [51-500]
    KR - v72 - i16 - August 15 2004 - p799(1) [501+]
    People - v62 - i20 - Nov 15 2004 - p48 [51-500]
Young, Biloine Whiting - *Cahokia: The Great Native American Metropolis*
    J Urban H - v30 - i4 - May 2004 - p594-604 [501+]
Young, Brian - *A Short History of Quebec*
    Can Hist R - v85 - i4 - Dec 2004 - p808(4) [501+]
Young, Carl - *Carl Young's Adobe Acrobat 6.0: Getting Professional Results from Your PDFs*
    SciTech - v28 - i4 - Dec 2004 - p24(1) [51-500]
Young, Christine Ellen - *A Bitter Brew: Faith, Power, and Poison in a Small New England County*
    PW - v252 - i8 - Feb 21 2005 - p165(1) [51-500]
Young, D. - *Mind over Magma: The Story of Igneous Petrology*
    J Hist G - v30 - i3 - July 2004 - p569(2) [501+]
Young, David - *Our Islands, Our Selves; A History of Conservation in New Zealand*
    SciTech - v28 - i4 - Dec 2004 - p7(1) [1-50]
Young, David W. - *Management Accounting in Health Care Organizations*
    R&R Bk N - v19 - i1 - Feb 2004 - p113(1) [51-500]
Young, Dean - *Elegy on Toy Piano*
    PW - v252 - i4 - Jan 24 2005 - p236(1) [501+]
Skid
    PSQ - v78 - i2 - Summer 2004 - p193(3) [501+]
Young, Don - *Having Their Cake...How the City and Big Bosses Are Consuming UK Business*
    R&R Bk N - v19 - i2 - May 2004 - p123 [51-500]
    TimHES - v0 - i1666 - Nov 12 2004 - p30(1) [501+]
Young, Ed - *I, Doko: The Tale of a Basket (Illus. by Young, Ed)*
  c BL - v101 - i7 - Dec 1 2004 - p652(1) [51-500]
  c BW - v34 - i50 - Dec 12 2004 - p8(1) [501+]
  c HB - v80 - i6 - Nov-Dec 2004 - p704(2) [51-500]
  c KR - v72 - i22 - Nov 15 2004 - p1095(1) [51-500]
  c PW - v251 - i45 - Nov 8 2004 - p54(2) [51-500]
  c SLJ - v50 - i11 - Nov 2004 - p120(1) [51-500]
The Sons of the Dragon King: A Chinese Legend (Illus. by Young, Ed)
  c CCB-B - v57 - i11 - July-August 2004 - p490(1) [501+]
The Sons of the Dragon King: A Chinese Legend (Illus. by Young, Ed)
  c LibMed - v23 - i3 - Nov-Dec 2004 - p74(1) [51-500]
Young, Edward - *The Complaint, and the Consolation, or, Night Thoughts. E-book Review*
    LJ - v129 - i15 - Sept 15 2004 - p83(2) [51-500]
Young, Grace - *The Breath of a Wok: Unlocking the Secrets of Chinese Wok Cooking through Recipes and Lore (Illus. by Richardson, Alan)*
    BL - v100 - i22 - August 2004 - p1887(1) [51-500]
    LJ - v129 - i13 - August 2004 - p112(1) [51-500]
Young, H. Darrell - *Leadership under Construction: Creating Paths Toward Transformation*
    R&R Bk N - v19 - i3 - August 2004 - p105(1) [1-50]
Young, Hugh D. - *Sears and Zemansky's University Physics with Modern Physics, 11th Ed.*
    SciTech - v28 - i1 - March 2004 - p46(1) [51-500]
Young, Iris Marion - *Inclusion and Democracy*
    Signs - v30 - i2 - Wntr 2005 - p1674(4) [501+]
Young, James V. - *Eye on Korea: An Insider Account of Korean-American Relations*
    J Mil H - v68 - i2 - April 2004 - p662(2) [501+]
Young, Jeff C. - *The Fathers of American Presidents: From Augustine Washington to William Blythe and Roger Clinton.*
    BL - v101 - i3 - Oct 1 2004 - p358(1) [501+]
Young, John W. - *International Relations Since 1945: A Global History, 1st Ed.*
    CR - v285 - i1665 - Oct 2004 - p249(1) [501+]
    TimHES - v0 - i1668 - Nov 26 2004 - pVII(1) [501+]
Young, Julian - *Heidegger's Philosophy of Art*
    Phil R - v112 - i4 - Oct 2004 - p575(6) [501+]
Young, Karen Romano - *Cobwebs*
  y BL - v101 - i9-10 - Jan 1 2005 - p864(2) [1-50]
    Kliatt - v38 - i6 - Nov 2004 - p13(1) [51-500]
    KR - v72 - i20 - Oct 15 2004 - p1015(1) [51-500]
  y SLJ - v51 - i1 - Jan 2005 - p139(1) [51-500]

Young, Kevin - *Black Maria*
    Black Iss - v7 - i2 - March-April 2005 - p34(1) [51-500]
    Ent W - i810 - March 11 2005 - p109 [51-500]
    LJ - v130 - i3 - Feb 15 2005 - p135(1) [51-500]
    PW - v251 - i51 - Dec 20 2004 - p52(1) [501+]
Young, Linda - *Middle-Class Culture in the Nineteenth Century: America, Australia and Britian*
    AHR - v109 - i2 - April 2004 - p480(2) [501+]
Young, Lucie - *Eva Zeisel*
    Am Craft - v64 - i1 - Feb-March 2004 - p20(1) [501+]
    Am Craft - v64 - i1 - Feb-March 2004 - p20(1) [501+]
Young, Lynne - *Systemic Functional Linguistics and Critical Discourse Analysis: Studies in Social Change*
    R&R Bk N - v19 - i4 - Nov 2004 - p211(1) [501+]
Young, Matt - *Why Intelligent Design Fails: A Scientific Critique of the New Creationism*
    Choice - v42 - i5 - Jan 2005 - p872(2) [1-50]
    New Sci - v183 - i2456 - July 17 2004 - p47(1) [501+]
Young, Michael R. - *The Financial Reporting Handbook*
    R&R Bk N - v19 - i2 - May 2004 - p120 [51-500]
Young, Michael W. - *Malinowski: Odyssey of an Anthropologist, 1884-1920*
    LJ - v129 - i20 - Dec 1 2004 - p130(1) [51-500]
    Lon R Bks - v26 - i19 - Oct 7 2004 - p29(2) [501+]
    New Sci - v183 - i2466 - Sept 25 2004 - p48(1) [51-500]
    R&R Bk N - v19 - i4 - Nov 2004 - p76(1) [51-500]
Young, Miriam - *Miss Suzy: 40th Anniversary Edition (Illus. by Lobel, Arnold)*
  c PW - v251 - i37 - Sept 13 2004 - p80(1) [51-500]
Young Person's Occupational Outlook Handbook
  y VOYA - v27 - i5 - Dec 2004 - p418(1) [51-500]
Young, Peter - *Tortise*
    Choice - v41 - i11-12 - July-August 2004 - p2064(1) [501+]
Young, Philip H. - *The Printed Homer: A 3,000 Year Publishing and Translation History of 'The Iliad' and 'The Odyssey'*
    R&R Bk N - v19 - i1 - Feb 2004 - p214 [51-500]
Young, Ralph F. - *Dissent in America, Vol. 1*
    R&R Bk N - v19 - i4 - Nov 2004 - p57(1) [51-500]
Young, Regina - *Romantic and Transcendental Quests of Ralph Waldo Emerson and Victor-Marie Hugo*
    R&R Bk N - v19 - i1 - Feb 2004 - p244(1) [51-500]
Young, Richard - *Echoes from Calvary: Meditations on Franz Joseph Haydn's The Seven Last Words of Christ*
    LJ - v130 - i1 - Jan 1 2005 - p120(1) [51-500]
Young, Robert J. - *Marketing Marianne: French Propaganda in America, 1900-1940*
    Choice - v42 - i2 - Oct 2004 - p347(1) [51-500]
    J Mil H - v68 - i3 - July 2004 - p988-990 [501+]
Young-Sanchez, Margaret - *Tiwanaku: Ancestors of the Inca*
    BL - v101 - i9-10 - Jan 1 2005 - p810(1) [1-50]
    Globe & Mail - Dec 18 2004 - pD14 [1-50]
Young, Stephen - *Moral Capitalism: Reconciling Private Interest with the Public Good*
    R&R Bk N - v19 - i1 - Feb 2004 - p78(1) [51-500]
Multinationals and Public Policy
    R&R Bk N - v19 - i3 - August 2004 - p113(1) [51-500]
Young, Steve - *Winchell Mink: The Misadventure Begins*
  c CCB-B - v58 - i1 - Sept 2004 - p48(2) [51-500]
Young, Sue - *Solutions to Bullying*
  y TES - v0 - i4586 - June 4 2004 - psssss19(1) [501+]
Young, Susan - *The Hacker's Handbook: The Strategy Behind Breaking into and Defending Networks*
    E-Streams - Sept 2004 - pNA [501+]
The Hacker's Handbook: The Strategy Behind Breaking into Defending Networks
    SciTech - v28 - i3 - Sept 2004 - p31(1) [51-500]
Young, Terence - *Building San Francisco's Parks, 1850-1930*
    Choice - v41 - i11-12 - July-August 2004 - p2111(1) [501+]
    PHR - v73 - i4 - Nov 2004 - p689(2) [501+]
Young, Terrell A. - *Happily Ever After: Sharing Folk Literature with Elementary and Middle School Students*
  y SLJ - v50 - i10 - Oct 2004 - p202(1) [51-500]
  c SLJ - v50 - i10 - Oct 2004 - pS76(1) [51-500]
Young, Thomas - *Thomas Young's Life and Works*
    TimHES - v0 - i1647 - July 2 2004 - p30(1) [501+]

Young, William H. - *The 1950s.*
    R&R Bk N - v19 - i3 - August 2004 - p62(1) [51-500]
Youngquist, Paul - *Monstrosities: Bodies and British Romanticism*
    Nine-C Lit - v59 - i2 - Sept 2004 - p254(4) [501+]
Youngren, William H. - *C.P.E. Bach and the Rebirth of the Strophic Song*
    R&R Bk N - v19 - i1 - Feb 2004 - p196(1) [51-500]
Yount, David - *Celebrating the Rest of Your Life: A Baby Boomer's Guide to Spirituality*
    PW - v252 - i7 - Feb 14 2005 - p72(1) [51-500]
Yount, Lisa - *Animal Rights*
    Choice - v42 - i3 - Nov 2004 - p459(1) [1-50]
    R&R Bk N - v19 - i3 - August 2004 - p162(1) [501+]
Biotechnology and Genetic Engineering, Rev. Ed.
    SciTech - v28 - i4 - Dec 2004 - p163(1) [51-500]
    SLJ - v51 - i2 - Feb 2005 - p86(1) [51-500]
Virtual Reality
  y BL - v101 - i9-10 - Jan 1 2005 - p856(1) [1-50]
Yourdon, Ed - *Outsource: Competing in the Global Productivity Race*
    PW - v251 - i33 - August 16 2004 - p54(1) [51-500]
Yourgrau, Barry - *My Curious Uncle Dudley (Illus. by Auth, Tony)*
  c BL - v101 - i2 - Sept 15 2004 - p246(1) [51-500]
  c CCB-B - v58 - i2 - Oct 2004 - p104(1) [51-500]
  c KR - v72 - i14 - July 15 2004 - p695(1) [51-500]
  c PW - v251 - i30 - July 26 2004 - p55(1) [51-500]
  c SLJ - v51 - i1 - Jan 2005 - p100(1) [51-500]
Yourgrau, Palle - *A World Without Time: The Forgotten Legacy of Godel and Einstein*
    BL - v101 - i9-10 - Jan 1 2005 - p786(1) [1-50]
    BW - v35 - i4 - Jan 30 2005 - p8(2) [501+]
    KR - v72 - i23 - Dec 1 2004 - p1142(1) [501+]
    PW - v252 - i2 - Jan 10 2005 - p50(2) [51-500]
Youssoupoff, Felix - *Lost Splendor: The Amazing Memoirs of the Man Who Killed Rasputin*
    R&R Bk N - v19 - i1 - Feb 2004 - p38(1) [1-50]
Youth in the UNECE Region: Realities, Challenges, and Opportunities
    R&R Bk N - v19 - i1 - Feb 2004 - p138(1) [51-500]
Youth With Special Needs
    LibMed - v23 - i3 - Nov-Dec 2004 - p65(1) [51-500]
Ypma, Herbert - *Hip Hotels: Beach*
    R&R Bk N - v19 - i4 - Nov 2004 - p250(1) [501+]
Yu, Chun - *Little Green: Growing Up During the Cultural Revolution*
  y BL - v101 - i9-10 - Jan 1 2005 - p842(1) [51-500]
  c HB - v81 - i2 - March-April 2005 - p219(1) [51-500]
  c KR - v73 - i2 - Jan 15 2005 - p118(1) [51-500]
  c PW - v252 - i10 - March 7 2005 - p70(1) [51-500]
Yu, Guangyuan - *Deng Xiaoping Shakes the World: An Eyewitness Account of China's Party Work Conference and the Third Plenum*
    R&R Bk N - v19 - i3 - August 2004 - p183(1) [501+]
Yu, Jiyuan - *Structure of Being in Aristotle's 'Metaphysics'*
    R&R Bk N - v19 - i1 - Feb 2004 - p2(1) [51-500]
Yuan, Margaret Speaker - *The Royal Gorge Bridge*
  c SLJ - v50 - i7 - July 2004 - p123(1) [1-50]
Yudice, George - *The Expediency of Culture: Uses of Culture in the Global Era*
    Choice - v42 - i3 - Nov 2004 - p563(1) [1-50]
Yudofsky, Stuart C. - *Essentials of Neuropsychiatry and Clinical Neurosciences*
    SciTech - v28 - i1 - March 2004 - p92(1) [51-500]
Neuropsychiatric Assessment
    SciTech - v28 - i3 - Sept 2004 - p97(1) [51-500]
Yuen, Sun-pong - *Marriage, Gender, and Sex in a Contemporary Chinese Village*
    R&R Bk N - v19 - i4 - Nov 2004 - p134(1) [51-500]
Yufit, Robert I. - *Assessment, Treatment, and Prevention of Suicidal Behavior*
    SciTech - v28 - i4 - Dec 2004 - p101(1) [51-500]
Yukio, Yamane - *Kenkoku Daigaku no Kenkyu: Nihon Teigoku Shugi no Ichidanmen*
    JAS - v63 - i2 - May 2004 - p518(2) [501+]
Yukl, Gary - *Flexible Leadership: Creating Value by Balancing Multiple Challenges and Choices*
    HR Mag - v49 - i12 - Dec 2004 - p122(1) [501+]
    Per Psy - v57 - i4 - Winter 2004 - p1055(4) [501+]
    R&R Bk N - v19 - i3 - August 2004 - p104(1) [1-50]

Yuli, Liu - *The Unity of Rule and Virtue: A Critique of a Supposed Parallel between Confucian Ethics and Virtue Ethics*
R&R Bk N - v19 - i4 - Nov 2004 - p12(1) [51-500]

Yunesuk'o Han'guk Wiwonhoe - *Korean History: Discovery of Its Characteristics and Developments*
Choice - v42 - i4 - Dec 2004 - p715(1) [1-50]

Yunker, James A. - *Capital Management Effort: Theory and Applications*
R&R Bk N - v19 - i3 - August 2004 - p94(1) [51-500]

Yunque, Edgardo Vega - *The Lamentable Journey of Omaha Bigelow into the Impenetrable Loisaida Jungle*
PW - v251 - i41 - Oct 11 2004 - p55(1) [51-500]

Yunxiang Yan - *Private Life under Socialism: Love, Intimacy, and Family Change in a Chinese Village, 1949-1999*
AHR - v109 - i2 - April 2004 - p493(2) [501+]
Pac A - v77 - i3 - Fall 2004 - p555(3) [501+]

Yurkievich, Saul - *Background Noise/Ruido de Fondo*
WLT - v78 - i3-4 - Sept-Dec 2004 - p147(1) [501+]

Yusa, Michiko - *Zen and Philosophy: An Intellectual Biography of Nishida Kitaro*
BCS - v24 - Annual 2004 - p268(4) [501+]

Yust, Karen Marie - *Real Kids, Real Faith: Practices for Nurturing Children's Spiritual Lives*
CC - v121 - i14 - July 13 2004 - p33(3) [501+]

Yusuf, Abdulqawi A. - *African Yearbook of International Law/Annuaire african de droit international, Vol. 10, 202*
R&R Bk N - v19 - i3 - August 2004 - p210(1) [1-50]

Yusuf, Shahid - *Global Change and East Asian Policy Initiatives*
R&R Bk N - v19 - i4 - Nov 2004 - p91(1) [501+]
Global Production Networking and Technological Change in East Asia
R&R Bk N - v19 - i4 - Nov 2004 - p105(1) [51-500]

Zabel, Barbara Beth - *Assembling Art: The Machine and the American Avant-garde*
Choice - v42 - i2 - Oct 2004 - p283(1) [501+]

Zabel, Darcy - *The (Underground) Railroad in African American Literature*
R&R Bk N - v19 - i4 - Nov 2004 - p239(1) [501+]

Zaborowski, Marcin - *Poland: A New Power in Transatlantic Security*
Choice - v41 - i11-12 - July-August 2004 - p2118(1) [501+]

Zaccaro, Edward - *Challenge Math for the Elementary and Middle School Student*
c SLJ - v50 - i9 - Sept 2004 - p59(1) [51-500]

Zach, Kim K. - *Reproductive Technology*
c SLJ - v50 - i7 - July 2004 - p129(1) [51-500]

Zacharia, Katerina - *Converging Truths: Euripides' Ion and the Athenian Quest for Self-Definition*
Class R - v54 - i2 - Nov 2004 - p308-309 [501+]

Zachariah, Benjamin - *Nehru*
Lon R Bks - v26 - i13 - July 8 2004 - p6(3) [501+]
TimHES - v0 - i1659 - Sept 24 2004 - p31(1) [501+]

Zacharias, Gary - *The Bill of Rights*
SLJ - v50 - i10 - Oct 2004 - pS57(1) [51-500]

Zacharias, Karen Spears - *Hero Mama: A Daughter Remembers the Father She Lost in Vietnam--and the Mother Who Held Her Family Together*
BL - v101 - i8 - Dec 15 2004 - p703(1) [51-500]
LJ - v129 - i20 - Dec 1 2004 - p130(2) [51-500]
PW - v251 - i46 - Nov 15 2004 - p50(1) [51-500]

Zacharius, Walter - *Songbird*
KR - v72 - i14 - July 15 2004 - p660(1) [51-500]
LJ - v129 - i15 - Sept 15 2004 - p51(2) [51-500]
PW - v251 - i30 - July 26 2004 - p37(1) [51-500]

Zachary, G. Pascal - *Cheap Chickens: Feeding Africa's Poor*
Wil Q - v29 - i1 - Wntr 2005 - p108(1) [501+]

Zackrisson, Mats - *Measuring Your Company's Environmental Impact: Templates and Tools for a Complete ISO 14001 Initial Review*
SciTech - v28 - i4 - Dec 2004 - p168(1) [51-500]

Zadooran, Michael - *Second Hand: A Novel*
BL - v101 - i6 - Nov 15 2004 - p556(1) [501+]

Zaehringer, Alfred J. - *Rocket Science: Rocket Science in the Second Millennium*
Choice - v42 - i7 - March 2005 - p1248(1) [51-500]

Zaeske, Susan - *Signatures of Citizenship: Petitioning, Antislavery, and Women's Political Identity*
AHR - v109 - i3 - June 2004 - p908(2) [501+]

Zafirovski, Milan - *Market and Society: Two Theoretical Frameworks*
R&R Bk N - v19 - i2 - May 2004 - p126 [51-500]

Zafon, Carlos Ruiz - *The Shadow of the Wind (Read by Davis, Jonathan). Audiobook Review*
Kliatt - v38 - i6 - Nov 2004 - p50(1) [51-500]
The Shadow of the Wind
Econ - v371 - i8369 - April 3 2004 - p88US [501+]
Spec - v295 - i9183 - August 7 2004 - p33(1) [501+]
Time - v165 - i11 - March 14 2005 - p68 [501+]

Zafran, Eric - *Renaissance to Rococo: Masterpieces from the Wadsworth Atheneum Museum of Art*
Choice - v42 - i1 - Sept 2004 - p90(1) [501+]

Zafris, Nancy - *Lucky Strike*
PW - v252 - i11 - March 14 2005 - p45(1) [51-500]

Zagajewski, Adam - *A Defense of Ardor*
BL - v101 - i4 - Oct 15 2004 - p381(1) [51-500]
LJ - v129 - i17 - Oct 15 2004 - p64(1) [51-500]
Powrot
WLT - v79 - i1 - Jan-April 2005 - p104(1) [501+]

Zagelmeyer, Stefan - *Governance Structures and the Employment Relationship: Determinants of Employer Demand for Collective Bargaining in Britain*
R&R Bk N - v19 - i3 - August 2004 - p118(1) [501+]

Zager, Dianne Berkell - *Autism Spectrum Disorders; Identification, Education, and Treatment, 3rd Ed.*
SciTech - v28 - i4 - Dec 2004 - p113(1) [1-50]

Zagoria, Donald S. - *Breaking the China-Taiwan Impasse*
R&R Bk N - v19 - i1 - Feb 2004 - p49(1) [51-500]

Zagorin, Perez - *How the Idea of Religious Toleration Came to the West*
AHR - v109 - i2 - April 2004 - p477(2) [501+]
Choice - v41 - i7 - March 2004 - p1314(1) [501+]
J Ch St - v46 - i4 - Autumn 2004 - p896(2) [501+]
TT - v61 - i3 - Oct 2004 - p416(3) [501+]

Zahab, Mariam Abhou - *Islamist Networks: The Afghan-Pakistan Connection*
BW - v34 - i32 - August 8 2004 - p10(1) [501+]

Zahariadis, Nikolaos - *Ambiguity and Choice in Public Policy: Political Decision Making in Modern Democracies*
Pers PS - v34 - i1 - Wntr 2005 - p56(2) [501+]
R&R Bk N - v19 - i1 - Feb 2004 - p76(1) [1-50]

Zahi, Hawass - *Curse of the Pharaohs: My Adventures with Mummies*
c CCB-B - v57 - i11 - July-August 2004 - p468(1) [501+]

Zahl, Paul F.M. - *The First Christian: Universal Truth in the Teachings of Jesus*
BL - v101 - i3 - Oct 1 2004 - p302(1) [51-500]
Five Women of the English Reformation
Six Ct J - v35 - i1 - Spring 2004 - p237(2) [501+]

Zahn, Timothy - *Dragon and Soldier: The Second Dragonback Adventure*
y BL - v100 - i22 - August 2004 - p1921(1) [51-500]
y VOYA - v27 - i5 - Dec 2004 - p412(1) [51-500]
Dragon and Thief
c Kliatt - v38 - i4 - July 2004 - p33(1) [51-500]
The Green and the Gray
ChrSFF&H - v26 - i10 - Oct 2004 - p24(1) [51-500]
LJ - v129 - i15 - Sept 15 2004 - p53(1) [51-500]
PW - v251 - i32 - August 9 2004 - p235(1) [51-500]

Zahniser, Marvin R. - *Then Came Disaster: France and the United States, 1918-1940*
J Mil H - v68 - i3 - July 2004 - p988-990 [501+]
JAH - v91 - i1 - June 2004 - p289-291 [501+]

Zaho, Margaret Ann - *'Imago Triumphalis': The Function and Significance of Triumphal Imagery for Italian Renaissance Rulers*
R&R Bk N - v19 - i2 - May 2004 - p196(1) [501+]

Zaidel, Eran - *The Parallel Brain: the Cognitive Neuroscience of the Corpus Callosum.*
QRB - v79 - i4 - Dec 2004 - p456(2) [501+]

Zaikov, Gennadii Efremovich - *Chemical Reactions in Liquid and Solid Phase: Kinetics and Thermodynamics*
SciTech - v28 - i1 - March 2004 - p57(1) [51-500]
Homolytic and Heterolytic Reactions: Problems and Solutions
SciTech - v28 - i3 - Sept 2004 - p70(1) [51-500]

Zailckas, Koren - *Smashed: Story of a Drunken Girlhood*
KR - v72 - i21 - Nov 1 2004 - p1042(1) [501+]
LJ - v129 - i19 - Nov 15 2004 - p77(1) [501+]
NYTBR - Feb 27 2005 - p22 [501+]
People - v63 - i5 - Feb 7 2005 - p49 [501+]
PW - v251 - i49 - Dec 6 2004 - p50(1) [51-500]
PW - v252 - i8 - Feb 21 2005 - p16(1) [51-500]

Zailen, Rubin M. - *Engineering Considerations for Lift-Slab Construction*
SciTech - v28 - i1 - March 2004 - p149(1) [51-500]

Zajc, Dane - *Barren Harvest: Selected Poems*
LJ - v129 - i12 - July 2004 - p88(1) [51-500]
WLT - v78 - i3-4 - Sept-Dec 2004 - p141(1) [501+]

Zak, Albin J. - *The Poetics of Rock: Cutting Tracks, Making Records*
T&C - v45 - i2 - April 2004 - p442-444 [501+]

Zakai, Avihu - *Jonathan Edwards' Philosophy of History: The Re-Enchantment of the World in the Age of Enlightenment*
TT - v61 - i3 - Oct 2004 - p420(2) [501+]
JR - v85 - i1 - Jan 2005 - p121(3) [501+]
Jonathan Edwards' Philosophy of History: The Re-Enchantment of the World in the Age of Enlightment
JAH - v91 - i1 - June 2004 - p217-218 [501+]

Zakim, Michael - *Ready-Made Democracy: A History of Men's Dress in the American Republic*
BHR - v78 - i3 - Autumn 2004 - p517(3) [501+]

Zalambani, Maria - *La Morte del romanzo: Dall'avanguardia al realismo socialista*
Slav R - v63 - i3 - Fall 2004 - p684-685 [501+]

Zalben, Jane Breskin - *Baby Babka: The Gorgeous Genius (Illus. by Chess, Victoria)*
c CCB-B - v58 - i3 - Nov 2004 - p153(2) [501+]
c KR - v72 - i17 - Sept 1 2004 - p875(1) [51-500]
c SLJ - v50 - i11 - Nov 2004 - p120(2) [51-500]
Hey, Mama Goose (Illus. by Chollat, Emilie)
c KR - v73 - i3 - Feb 1 2005 - p183(1) [51-500]
c PW - v252 - i7 - Feb 14 2005 - p75(1) [51-500]
c SLJ - v51 - i2 - Feb 2005 - p112(2) [51-500]
Saturday Night at the Beastro (Illus. by Zalben, Jane Breskin)
c BL - v101 - i2 - Sept 15 2004 - p255(1) [51-500]
c KR - v72 - i13 - July 1 2004 - p639(1) [51-500]
c PW - v251 - i32 - August 9 2004 - p250(1) [51-500]
c SLJ - v50 - i8 - August 2004 - p104(1) [51-500]

Zaleski, Irma - *Who Is God?: The Soul's Road Home*
CBRA - Annual 2003 - p102(1) [51-500]

Zaleski, Philip - *The Best American Spiritual Writing 2004*
Comw - v131 - i19 - Nov 5 2004 - p56(2) [501+]
LJ - v130 - i1 - Jan 1 2005 - p120(1) [51-500]
PW - v251 - i39 - Sept 27 2004 - p56(1) [51-500]

Zalkind, Paola - *Global Perspectives on Social Issues: Juvenile Justice Systems*
Choice - v42 - i6 - Feb 2005 - p1107(1) [51-500]
R&R Bk N - v19 - i4 - Nov 2004 - p148(1) [501+]

Zaller, John R. - *The Nature and Origins of Mass Opinion*
Pub Op Q - v68 - i3 - Fall 2004 - p437(1) [51-500]

Zaloga, Steven J. - *Red Army Handbook, 1939-1945*
J Mil H - v68 - i3 - July 2004 - p994(1) [501+]

Zalot, Jozef D. - *The Roman Catholic Church and Economic Development in Sub-Saharan Africa: Voices Yet Unheard in a Listening World*
Theol St - v66 - i1 - March 2005 - p235(1) [501+]

Zamagni, Stefano - *Time in Economic Theory, Vols. 1-3*
R&R Bk N - v19 - i3 - August 2004 - p93(1) [51-500]

Zaman, Muhammad Qasim - *The Ulama in Contemporary Islam: Custodians of Change*
JR - v84 - i3 - July 2004 - p492(4) [501+]

Zammett, Erin - *My (So-Called) Normal Life: How I Learned to Balance Love, Work, Family, Friends...and Cancer at 23*
KR - v73 - i5 - March 1 2005 - p282(1) [501+]
PW - v252 - i10 - March 7 2005 - p58(1) [51-500]

Zammito, John H. - *Kant, Herder, and the Birth of Anthropology*
Ethics - v115 - i1 - Oct 2004 - p183(4) [501+]
JMH - v76 - i4 - Dec 2004 - p984(3) [501+]
A Nice Derangement of Epistemes: Post-Positivism in the Study of Science from Quine to Latour
AHR - v109 - i4 - Oct 2004 - p1194-1194 [501+]
Choice - v42 - i3 - Nov 2004 - p498(1) [1-50]

Book Review Index 2005 Cumulation ZENGOTITA • 663

Zamoyski, Adam - *1812: Napoleon's Fatal March on Moscow*
CR - v285 - i1665 - Oct 2004 - p254(2) [501+]
Moscow 1812: Napoleon's Fatal March
BL - v100 - i21 - July 2004 - p1814(1) [51-500]
BW - v34 - i32 - August 8 2004 - p9(1) [501+]
NYRB - v51 - i19 - Dec 2 2004 - p41(3) [501+]
Zanden, J.L. van - *The Strictures of Inheritence: The Dutch Economy in the Nineteenth Century*
Choice - v42 - i3 - Nov 2004 - p535(1) [1-50]
Zanders, Be - *Gargoyles, Girders & Glass Houses: Magnificent Master Builders (Illus. by Munro, Roxie)*
c HB - v80 - i6 - Nov-Dec 2004 - p732(2) [501+]
Zandstra, Matt - *Sams Teach Yourself PHP in 24 Hours, 3rd Ed.*
SciTech - v28 - i3 - Sept 2004 - p23(1) [51-500]
Zane, Alexander - *The Wheels on the Race Car (Illus. by Warhola, James)*
c KR - v73 - i2 - Jan 15 2005 - p127(1) [51-500]
Zaner, Richard M. - *Conversations on the Edge: Narratives of Ethics and Illness*
Choice - v42 - i2 - Oct 2004 - p327(1) [51-500]
E-Streams - Dec 2004 - pNA [501+]
SciTech - v28 - i1 - March 2004 - p78(1) [51-500]
Zanes, Dan - *Hello, Hello (Illus. by Saaf, Donald)*
c PW - v251 - i31 - August 2 2004 - p72(2) [501+]
c SLJ - v50 - i10 - Oct 2004 - p152(1) [51-500]
Zanetta, Cecilia - *The Influence of the World Bank on National Housing and Urban Policies: A Case of Mexico and Argentina During the 1990's*
R&R Bk N - v19 - i3 - August 2004 - p156(1) [51-500]
Zanger, Mark - *American History Cookbook*
Bwatch - v26 - i8 - August 2004 - p2(1) [51-500]
LibMed - v22 - i4 - Jan 2004 - p78(1) [501+]
Zanglein, Jayne E. - *ERISA Litigation*
R&R Bk N - v19 - i3 - August 2004 - p200(1) [1-50]
Zaniello, Tom - *Working Stiffs, Union Maids, Reds, and Riffraff: An Expanded Guide to Films about Labor*
JEL - v42 - i1 - March 2004 - p284(1) [501+]
Zanjani, Sally - *Sarah Winnemucca*
y Kliatt - v39 - i1 - Jan 2005 - p31(1) [51-500]
Zanker, Graham - *Modes of Viewing in Hellenistic Poetry and Art*
Choice - v42 - i4 - Dec 2004 - p657(2) [1-50]
Zanlonghi, Giovanna - *Teatri di formazione: Actio, parola e immagine nella scena gesuitica del Sei-Settecento a Milano*
CHR - v90 - i4 - Oct 2004 - p801(2) [501+]
Zannos, Susan - *Dmitri Mendeleyev and the Periodic Table*
c BL - v101 - i4 - Oct 15 2004 - p415(1) [51-500]
y SB - v40 - i6 - Nov-Dec 2004 - p258(1) [51-500]
y SLJ - v50 - i12 - Dec 2004 - p157(2) [51-500]
The Life and Times of Archimedes
c SLJ - v50 - i12 - Dec 2004 - p170(1) [51-500]
The Life and Times of Socrates
c SLJ - v50 - i12 - Dec 2004 - p170(1) [51-500]
Michael Faraday and the Discovery of Electromagnetism
c SLJ - v51 - i2 - Feb 2005 - p154(1) [51-500]
Zanre, Domenico - *Cultural Non-Conformity in Early Modern Florence*
CR - v285 - i1667 - Dec 2004 - p377(1) [51-500]
R&R Bk N - v19 - i3 - August 2004 - p44(1) [51-500]
Zapp, Anna - *The Zapp Method of Couture Sewing: Tailor Garments Easily Using Any Pattern.*
LJ - v129 - i13 - August 2004 - p79(1) [501+]
Zarankin, Andres - *Modern Society Archaeology in South America: Material Culture, Discourses and Practices*
Lat Ant - v15 - i4 - Dec 2004 - p473(3) [501+]
Zarb, George A. - *Prosthodontic Treatment for Edentulous Patients: Complete Dentures and Implant-Supported Prostheses, 12th Ed.*
SciTech - v28 - i1 - March 2004 - p120(1) [51-500]
Zard, Samir Z. - *Radical Reactions in Organic Synthesis*
J Chem Ed - v81 - i12 - Dec 2004 - p1718-1720 [501+]
Zaretsky, Eli - *Secrets of the Soul: A Social and Cultural History of Psychoanalysis*
BooChiTr - June 6 2004 - p1(2) [501+]
Choice - v42 - i4 - Dec 2004 - p740(1) [1-50]
Globe & Mail - July 31 2004 - pD12 [1-50]
NYTBR - Sept 5 2004 - p9 [501+]
Zaretsky, Robert - *Cock and Bull Stories: Folco de Baroncelli and the Invention of the Camargue.*
HRNB - v33 - i1 - Fall 2004 - p27(1) [501+]
Zarian, Beth Bartleson - *Around the World with Historical Fiction and Folktales: Highly Recommended and Award-Winning Books, Grades K-8*
R&R Bk N - v19 - i4 - Nov 2004 - p258(1) [501+]
Zarimpas, Nicholas - *Transparency in Nuclear Warheads and Materials: The Political and Technical Dimensions*
SPA - v61 - i1 - Jan-Feb 2005 - p70(2) [501+]
Zarkin, Michael J. - *Social Learning and the History of U.S. Telecommunications Policy, 1900-1996: Creating the Telecommunications Act of 1996*
R&R Bk N - v19 - i1 - Feb 2004 - p104(1) [51-500]
Zarowski, Christopher J. - *An Introduction to Numerical Analysis for Electrical and Computer Engineers*
Choice - v42 - i2 - Oct 2004 - p324(1) [51-500]
Zarri, Gabriella - *Ordini religiosi, santita e culti: prospettive di ricerca tra Europa e America Latina. Atti del Seminario di Roma 21-22 giugno 2001*
CHR - v90 - i4 - Oct 2004 - p830(2) [501+]
Zarsky, Lyuba - *Human Rights & the Environment: Conflicts and Norms in a Globalizing World*
JPR - v41 - i4 - July 2004 - p524-525 [501+]
Zarzycki, Daryl Davis - *Mia Hamm: Soccer Star*
c BL - v101 - i6 - Nov 15 2004 - p576(1) [51-500]
Zarzyski, Paul - *Wolf Tracks on the Welcome Mat*
JouAmCul - v27 - i3 - Sept 2004 - p363(3) [501+]
Zaslau, Stanley - *Blueprints Urology*
SciTech - v28 - i3 - Sept 2004 - p107(1) [51-500]
Zaslavsky, Claudia - *More Math Games and Activities from around the World*
SLJ - v50 - i10 - Oct 2004 - pS43(1) [51-500]
Zastrow, Claus von - *Academic Atrophy: The Condition of the Liberal Arts in America's Public Schools*
BIC - v33 - i7 - Oct 2004 - p37(2) [501+]
Zasurskii, Ivan - *Media and Power in Post-Soviet Russia*
R&R Bk N - v19 - i1 - Feb 2004 - p211 [51-500]
Zaunders, Bo - *Gargoyles, Girders and Glass Houses: Magnificent Master Builders (Illus. by Munro, Roxie)*
c BL - v101 - i5 - Nov 1 2004 - p498(1) [51-500]
c CCB-B - v58 - i5 - Jan 2005 - p233(1) [51-500]
c KR - v72 - i22 - Nov 15 2004 - p1095(1) [51-500]
c SLJ - v50 - i12 - Dec 2004 - p172(1) [51-500]
The Great Bridge-Building Contest (Illus. by Munro, Roxie)
c BL - v101 - i7 - Dec 1 2004 - p672(1) [51-500]
Zawawi, Sharifa M. - *Arabic for English Speaking Medics*
SciTech - v28 - i4 - Dec 2004 - p12(1) [1-50]
Zawia, Nasser H. - *Molecular Neurotoxicology: Environmental Agents and Transcription-Transduction Coupling*
SciTech - v28 - i3 - Sept 2004 - p93(1) [51-500]
Zawodny, Jeremy D. - *High Performance MySQL: Optimization, Backups, Replication and Load Balancing*
LJ - v129 - i20 - Dec 1 2004 - p152(1) [51-500]
SciTech - v28 - i3 - Sept 2004 - p22(1) [1-50]
Zayyat, Montasser al- - *The Road to Al-Qaeda: The Story of Bin Laden's Right-Hand Man*
MEQ - v11 - i3 - Summer 2004 - p93(1) [501+]
Zdanowicz, Irena - *Fred Williams: An Australian Vision*
R&R Bk N - v19 - i4 - Nov 2004 - p201(1) [501+]
Zdunkowski, Wilford - *Thermodynamics of the Atmosphere: Course in Theoretical Meteorology*
Choice - v42 - i4 - Dec 2004 - p698(1) [1-50]
Zea, Leopoldo - *El 98 y su Impacto en Latinoamerica*
HAHR - v84 - i3 - August 2004 - p509(2) [501+]
Zeballos, Estanislao E. - *La conquista de quince mil leguas: Estudio sobre la traslacion de la frontera sur de la Republica al Rio Negro*
HAHR - v84 - i4 - Nov 2004 - p760(2) [501+]
Zebrowski, George - *Synergy SF: New Science Fiction*
BL - v101 - i2 - Sept 15 2004 - p216(1) [51-500]
NYTBR - Nov 14 2004 - p51 [501+]
Zebrun, Gary - *Someone You Know*
Lam Bk Rpt - v13 - i3 - Oct 2004 - p31(2) [501+]
Zee, Ruth Vander - *Erika's Story (Illus. by Innocenti, Roberto)*
y Magpies - v19 - i5 - Nov 2004 - p31(1) [501+]
Zeev, Maoz - *Bound by Struggle: The Strategic Evolution of Enduring International Rivalries*
JPR - v41 - i4 - July 2004 - p521-521 [501+]
Zehetbauer, Michael - *Nanomaterials by Severe Plastic Deformation: Proceedings*
SciTech - v28 - i3 - Sept 2004 - p144(1) [51-500]
Zeidel, Robert F. - *Immigrants, Progressives, and Exclusion Politics: The Dillingham Commission, 1900-1927*
R&R Bk N - v19 - i3 - August 2004 - p185(1) [501+]
Choice - v42 - i3 - Nov 2004 - p552(1) [1-50]
Zeigler, Norm - *Rivers of Shadow, Rivers of Sun*
Bwatch - v26 - i9 - Sept 2004 - p7(1) [51-500]
Zeiler, Lorne - *Hearts of Gold: Stories of Courage, Dedication and Triumph from Canadian Olympic Athletes*
c Res Links - v10 - i1 - Oct 2004 - p40(2) [501+]
Zeiler, Thomas W. - *Unconditional Defeat: Japan, America, and the End of World War II*
J Mil H - v68 - i2 - April 2004 - p642(2) [501+]
R&R Bk N - v19 - i1 - Feb 2004 - p29(1) [51-500]
Zeitein, Maurice - *Political Power and Social Theory, Vol 15*
CS - v33 - i5 - Sept 2004 - p622-622 [501+]
Zeitel, Sarah - *The Firebird's Vengeance: A Novel of Isavalta*
PW - v251 - i28 - July 12 2004 - p49(1) [501+]
Zeitlin, Michael - *Soldier Talk: The Vietnam War in Oral Narrative*
R&R Bk N - v19 - i4 - Nov 2004 - p48(1) [51-500]
Zeldin, Richard P. - *Business Forms on File, 2004 Ed.*
R&R Bk N - v19 - i4 - Nov 2004 - p109(1) [51-500]
Personal Forms on File, 2004 Ed.
R&R Bk N - v19 - i4 - Nov 2004 - p115(1) [51-500]
Zelenitz, Alan - *Alien Legion: Footsloggers*
PW - v252 - i9 - Feb 28 2005 - p44(1) [51-500]
Zelensky, Elizabeth - *Windows to Heaven: Introducing Icons to Protestants and Catholics*
PW - v251 - i50 - Dec 13 2004 - p62(1) [51-500]
Zelikow, Philip - *The 9/11 Commission Report*
Econ - v372 - i8387 - August 7 2004 - p69US [501+]
Zelin, Madeleine - *Contract and Property in Early Modern China*
HRNB - v33 - i1 - Fall 2004 - p35(1) [501+]
R&R Bk N - v19 - i3 - August 2004 - p209(1) [1-50]
Zelizer, Julian E. - *On Capitol Hill: The Struggle to Reform Congress and Its Consequences, 1948-2000*
Choice - v42 - i3 - Nov 2004 - p566(2) [1-50]
Zell, Hans M. - *The African Studies Companion: A Guide to Information Sources, 3rd Rev. Ed.*
R&R Bk N - v19 - i3 - August 2004 - p57(1) [51-500]
Zeller, Manfred - *The Triangle of Microfinance: Financial Sustainability, Outreach, and Impact*
JEL - v41 - i4 - Dec 2003 - p1415(2) [501+]
Zeller, Thomas - *Strasse, Bahn, Panorama: Verkehrswege und Landschaftsveranderung in Deutschland von 1930 bis 1990*
HNet - June 2004 - pNA [501+]
Zellers, Carolyn M. - *Computer Activities: Making Slide Shows and Simple Web Pages*
LibMed - v22 - i5 - Feb 2004 - p84(1) [501+]
Computer Activities: Teaching with Spreadsheets
LibMed - v22 - i5 - Feb 2004 - p84(1) [501+]
Zelnick, Robert - *Swing Dance: Justice O'Connor and the Michigan Muddle*
Choice - v42 - i6 - Feb 2005 - p1100(1) [51-500]
R&R Bk N - v19 - i3 - August 2004 - p205(1) [501+]
Zeltzer, Lonnie K. - *Conquering Your Child's Chronic Pain: A Pediatrician's Guide for Reclaiming a Normal Childhood*
LJ - v130 - i1 - Jan 1 2005 - p140(1) [51-500]
Zemach-Bersin, Kaethe - *Just Enough and Not Too Much*
c LibMed - v22 - i4 - Jan 2004 - p62(1) [501+]
Zeman, Ludmila - *Le secret de Sinbad*
c Res Links - v10 - i2 - Dec 2004 - p57(1) [501+]
Sinbad's Secret
c CBRA - Annual 2003 - p472(1) [51-500]
Zeman, Scott C. - *Atomic Culture: How We Learned to Stop Worrying and Love the Bomb*
SPA - v61 - i1 - Jan-Feb 2005 - p67(3) [501+]
Zemitzov, Boris - *The Merry Baker of Riga*
Bwatch - v26 - i7 - July 2004 - p3(1) [51-500]
Zemke, Deborah - *D Is for Doodle: A Step-by-Step Drawing Book*
c PW - v251 - i31 - August 2 2004 - p72(2) [501+]
c SLJ - v50 - i12 - Dec 2004 - p139(1) [51-500]
Zeng, Hong - *A Deconstructive Reading of Chinese Natural Philosophy in Literature and the Arts: Taoism and Zen Buddhism*
R&R Bk N - v19 - i4 - Nov 2004 - p221(1) [501+]
Zeng, Ka - *Trade Threats, Trade Wars: Bargaining, Retaliation, and American Coercive Diplomacy*
Choice - v42 - i4 - Dec 2004 - p709(2) [1-50]
For Aff - v83 - i5 - Sept-Oct 2004 - p164 [501+]
Fut - v38 - i6 - Nov-Dec 2004 - p61(1) [51-500]
PSQ - v119 - i3 - Fall 2004 - p537(2) [501+]
Zengotita, Thomas - *Mediated: How the Media Shapes Your World and the Way You Live in It*
PW - v252 - i7 - Feb 14 2005 - p66(1) [51-500]

GSR - v27 - i2 - May 2004 - p409-410 [501+]

HNet - Sept 2004 - pNA [501+]

Zilkha, Bettina - *Ultimate Style: The Best of the Best-Dressed List*

Globe & Mail - Dec 18 2004 - pL5 [1-50]

Zill, Dennis G. - *First Course in Differential Equations with Modeling Applications, 8th Ed.*

SciTech - v28 - i4 - Dec 2004 - p40(1) [51-500]

Zimbardo, Rose A. - *Understanding the Lord of the Rings: The Best of Tolkien Criticism*

LibMed - v22 - i5 - Feb 2004 - p81(1) [501+]

LJ - v129 - i12 - July 2004 - p83(1) [51-500]

Zimdahl, Robert L. - *Weed-Crop Competition: A Review*

QRB - v79 - i4 - Dec 2004 - p449(1) [501+]

Zimmer, Annette - *Strategy Mix for Nonprofit Organisations: Vehicles for Social and Labour Market Integration*

R&R Bk N - v19 - i3 - August 2004 - p114(1) [51-500]

Zimmer, Carl - *Soul Made Flesh: The Discovery of the Brain--and How It Changed the World*

Choice - v42 - i4 - Dec 2004 - p689(1) [1-50]

CR - v285 - i1666 - Nov 2004 - p317(1) [501+]

QRB - v79 - i3 - Sept 2004 - p290(1) [501+]

y SB - v40 - i3 - May-June 2004 - p128(1) [501+]

SB - v40 - i6 - Nov-Dec 2004 - p244(1) [51-500]

Zimmer, Dave - *Four Way Street: The Crosby, Stills, Nash and Young Reader*

Bwatch - v26 - i8 - August 2004 - p4(1) [51-500]

Zimmer, Don - *The Zen of Zim: Baseballs, Beanballs, and Bosses*

BL - v100 - i22 - August 2004 - p1891(1) [51-500]

LJ - v129 - i12 - July 2004 - p91(1) [51-500]

Zimmer, Marc - *Glowing Genes: A Revolution in Biotechnology*

BL - v101 - i9-10 - Jan 1 2005 - p796(1) [51-500]

PW - v251 - i50 - Dec 13 2004 - p55(2) [501+]

Zimmer, Oliver - *A Contested Nation: History, Memory and Nationalism in Switzerland, 1761-1891*

HNet - Sept 2004 - pNA [501+]

Zimmerer, Karl S. - *Political Ecology: An Integrative Approach to Geography and Environment-Development Studies*

Choice - v41 - i11-12 - July-August 2004 - p2098(2) [501+]

Zimmerli, Walther - *The Fiery Throne: The Prophets and Old Testament Theology*

Intpr - v59 - i1 - Jan 2005 - p109(1) [51-500]

Zimmerman, Andrea - *Dig! (Illus. by Rosenthal, Marc)*

c NYTBR - Sept 19 2004 - p16 [51-500]

c SLJ - v50 - i7 - July 2004 - p90(1) [51-500]

Zimmerman, David A. - *Comic Book Character: Unleashing the Hero in Us All*

PW - v251 - i45 - Nov 8 2004 - p51(1) [51-500]

Zimmerman, Dean W. - *Oxford Studies in Metaphysics, Vol. 1*

Choice - v42 - i4 - Dec 2004 - p675(1) [1-50]

Zimmerman, Joseph F. - *Interstate Economic Relations*

Choice - v42 - i6 - Feb 2005 - p1071(1) [51-500]

Zimmerman, Karl R. - *Steam Locomotives: Whistling, Chugging, Smoking Iron Horses of the Past (Illus. by Zimmerman, Karl R.)*

c LibMed - v23 - i3 - Nov-Dec 2004 - p84(1) [51-500]

Zimmerman, M. - *Apuleius Madaraurensis: Book X. Text, Introduction and Commentary*

Class R - v53 - i2 - Nov 2003 - p381-383 [501+]

Zimmerman, Robert - *Leaving Earth: Space Stations, Rival Superpowers, and the Quest for Interplanetary Travel*

Choice - v41 - i7 - March 2004 - p1319(1) [501+]

Zimmerman, Robert M. - *Boards That Love Fundraising: A How-to Guide for Your Board*

R&R Bk N - v19 - i3 - August 2004 - p133(1) [51-500]

Zimmerman, Steven M. - *Statistical Quality Control Using Excel. 2nd Ed.*

SciTech - v28 - i3 - Sept 2004 - p170(1) [51-500]

Zimmermann, Hubert - *Money and Security: Troops, Monetary Policy and West Germany's Relations with the United States and Britain, 1950-1971*

GSR - v27 - i2 - May 2004 - p428-429 [501+]

Zimmermann, Karl-Heinz - *Introduction to Protein Informatics*

SciTech - v28 - i1 - March 2004 - p74(1) [51-500]

Zimmermann, Karl R. - *Steam Locomotives: Whistling, Chugging, Smoking Iron Horses of the Past (Illus. by Zimmermann, Karl R.)*

c SLJ - v50 - i7 - July 2004 - p129(1) [51-500]

Zimmermann, Oskar - *Escape by Troika: The World War II Chronicle of a Bessarabian German*

R&R Bk N - v19 - i4 - Nov 2004 - p34(1) [51-500]

Zimmermann, Roukayatou - *Biotechnology and Value-Added Traits in Food Crops: Relevance for Developing Countries and Economic Analysis*

R&R Bk N - v19 - i4 - Nov 2004 - p104(1) [51-500]

Zimnik, Reiner - *The Crane (Illus. by Zimnik, Reiner)*

c Sch Lib - v52 - i4 - Winter 2004 - p201(1) [51-500]

Zimpher, Nancy L. - *University Leadership in Urban School Renewal*

R&R Bk N - v19 - i3 - August 2004 - p221(1) [1-50]

Zimring, Franklin E. - *An American Travesty: Legal Responses to Adolescent Sex Offending*

Law&PolBR - Oct 2004 - pNA [501+]

The Contradictions of American Capital Punishment

CS - v33 - i2 - March 2004 - p235-237 [501+]

Soc Ser R - v78 - i4 - Dec 2004 - p688(3) [501+]

Zine, Magubane - *Bringing the Empire Home: Race, Class, and Gender in Britain and Colonial South Africa*

JRAI - v10 - i4 - Dec 2004 - p910(2) [501+]

Zingg, Robert M. - *Behind the Mexican Mountains*

HAHR - v84 - i2 - May 2004 - p361(2) [501+]

Huichol Mythology

R&R Bk N - v19 - i4 - Nov 2004 - p69(1) [51-500]

Zinguer, Ilana - *Les Deux Reformes Chretiennes: Propagation et Diffusion*

R&R Bk N - v19 - i4 - Nov 2004 - p20(1) [51-500]

Zink, Rui - *The Boy Who Did Not Like Television (Illus. by Ramos, Manuel Joao)*

c PW - v251 - i51 - Dec 20 2004 - p58(1) [51-500]

Zink, Wilbur A. - *It All Started with a Tornado: Memories of My Home Town: "The Prairie Queen," Appleton City, Missouri, St. Clair County*

Roundup M - v12 - i3 - Feb 2005 - p24(1) [51-500]

Zinn, Holger - *Zwischen Republik und Diktatur: Die Studentenschaft der Philipps Universitat Marburg in den Jahren von 1925 bis 1945*

GSR - v27 - i2 - May 2004 - p398-399 [501+]

Zinn, Howard - *A People's History of the United States 1492-Present*

CR - v285 - i1662 - July 2004 - p59(1) [51-500]

Terrorism and War

IJMES - v36 - i3 - August 2004 - p530-533 [501+]

Voices of a People's History of the United States

y Kliatt - v39 - i1 - Jan 2005 - p34(2) [51-500]

Zinn, Maxine Baca - *Diversity in Families, 7th Ed.*

R&R Bk N - v19 - i4 - Nov 2004 - p129(1) [1-50]

Zinnen, Linda - *The Dragons of Spratt, Ohio*

c BL - v101 - i6 - Nov 15 2004 - p587(1) [51-500]

c CCB-B - v58 - i4 - Dec 2004 - p187(2) [51-500]

y KR - v72 - i22 - Nov 15 2004 - p1095(1) [51-500]

y SLJ - v50 - i12 - Dec 2004 - p155(1) [51-500]

Zinner, Ira D. - *Implant Dentistry: From Failure to Success*

SciTech - v28 - i1 - March 2004 - p120(1) [51-500]

Zinsmeister, Karl - *Dawn over Baghdad: How the U.S. Military Is Using Bullets and Ballots to Remake Iraq*

Bwatch - v26 - i9 - Sept 2004 - p6(1) [51-500]

NYTBR - Nov 14 2004 - p60 [501+]

R&R Bk N - v19 - i3 - August 2004 - p49(1) [51-500]

Zinzius, Brigit - *Doing Business with the New China: A Handbook and Guide*

Choice - v42 - i7 - March 2005 - p1275(1) [51-500]

Ziolkowski, Margaret - *Tale of Boiarynia Morozova: A Seventeenth-Century Religious Life*

HNet - Oct 2004 - pNA [501+]

Ziolkowski, Theodore - *Berlin: Aufstieg einer Kulturmetropole um 1810*

Ger Q - v77 - i2 - Spring 2004 - p234-235 [501+]

Hesitant Heroes: Private Inhibition, Cultural Crisis

Choice - v41 - i11-12 - July-August 2004 - p2040(1) [501+]

Zionkowski, Linda - *Men's Work: Gender, Class, and the Professionalization of Poetry, 1660-1784*

MP - v102 - i1 - August 2004 - p120(3) [501+]

Zipes, Douglas P. - *Cardiac Electrophysiology: From Cell to Bedside, 4th Ed.*

SciTech - v28 - i3 - Sept 2004 - p106(1) [51-500]

Zipes, Jack - *The Oxford Companion to Fairy Tales*

Can Lit - i181 - Summer 2004 - p190-191 [501+]

Ziporyn, Brook - *The Penumbra Unbound: The Neo-Taoist Philosophy of Guo Xiang*

JAS - v63 - i2 - May 2004 - p502(3) [501+]

Zipper, Yaacov - *The Journals of Yaacov Zipper, 1950-1982: The Struggle for Yiddishkeit*

R&R Bk N - v19 - i3 - August 2004 - p78(1) [51-500]

Ziran, Bruce H. - *Fractures of the Upper Extremity*

SciTech - v28 - i1 - March 2004 - p112(1) [51-500]

Ziring, Lawrence - *Pakistan: At the Crosscurrent of History*

Choice - v41 - i11-12 - July-August 2004 - p2119(1) [501+]

Zirker, J.B. - *Sunquakes: Probing the Interior of the Sun*

Sci Teach - v71 - i7 - Sept 2004 - p95-96 [501+]

SciTech - v28 - i1 - March 2004 - p44(1) [51-500]

TLS - i5264 - Feb 20 2004 - p31-31 [501+]

Zischler, Hanns - *Kafka Goes to the Movies*

Lon R Bks - v26 - i5 - March 4 2004 - p27(2) [501+]

Zisserman-Brodsky, Dina - *Constructing Ethnopolitics in the Soviet Union: Samizdat, Deprivation and the Rise of Ethnic Nationalism*

Choice - v41 - i7 - March 2004 - p1367(1) [501+]

Zitser, Ernest A. - *The Transfigured Kingdom: Sacred Parody and Charismatic Authority at the Court of Peter the Great*

TLS - i5299 - Oct 22 2004 - p10-11 [501+]

Zittrain, Jonathan - *The Torts Game: Defending Mean Joe Greene*

R&R Bk N - v19 - i4 - Nov 2004 - p167(1) [501+]

Zizek, Slavoj - *Conversations with Zizek*

TLS - i5285 - July 16 2004 - p25(1) [501+]

Iraq: The Borrowed Kettle

PW - v251 - i31 - August 2 2004 - p64(1) [51-500]

Tikkun - v20 - i1 - Jan-Feb 2005 - p71(2) [501+]

The Puppet and the Dwarf: The Perverse Core of Christianity

Choice - v41 - i7 - March 2004 - p1312(1) [501+]

CS - v33 - i5 - Sept 2004 - p563-564 [501+]

TLS - i5299 - Oct 22 2004 - p32(1) [501+]

Zlaoui, Leila - *Bulgaria--Public Expenditure Issues and Directions for Reform*

JEL - v42 - i1 - March 2004 - p327(1) [501+]

Zmuda, Allison - *Transforming Schools: Creating a Culture of Continuous Improvement*

R&R Bk N - v19 - i4 - Nov 2004 - p183(1) [501+]

Znamenski, Andrei A. - *Through Orthodox Eyes: Russian Missionary Narratives of Travels to the Denaina and Ahtna, 1850s-1930s*

Russ Rev - v63 - i2 - April 2004 - p317-320 [501+]

Zoba, Wendy Murray - *On Broken Legs: A Shattered Life, a Search for God, a Miracle That Met Me in a Cave in Assisi*

PW - v251 - i33 - August 16 2004 - p59(1) [51-500]

Zobel, Melissa Tantaquidgeon - *Oracles*

Roundup M - v12 - i1 - Oct 2004 - p33(1) [51-500]

Zoch, Paul A. - *Doomed to Fail: The Built-in Defects of American Education*

Choice - v42 - i6 - Feb 2005 - p1074(1) [51-500]

R&R Bk N - v19 - i4 - Nov 2004 - p177(1) [501+]

Zoch, Paula A. - *Doomed to Fail: The Built-in Defects of American Education*

PW - v251 - i29 - July 19 2004 - p156(1) [51-500]

Zoehfeld, Kathleen Weidner - *Apples, Apples (Illus. by Santoro, Christopher)*

c PW - v251 - i31 - August 2 2004 - p72(1) [51-500]

Did Dinosaurs Have Feathers? (Illus. by Washburn, Lucia)

LibMed - v23 - i1 - August-Sept 2004 - p81(1) [51-500]

c SLJ - v50 - i10 - Oct 2004 - pS23(1) [51-500]

Zofia, Burr - *Of Women, Poetry, and Power: Strategies of Address in Dickinson, Miles, Brooks, Lorede, and Angelou*

Callaloo - v27 - i2 - Spring 2004 - p575(579) [501+]

Zohar, Danah - *Spiritual Capital: Wealth We Can Live By*

R&R Bk N - v19 - i3 - August 2004 - p106(1) [1-50]

Zolf, Rachel - *Masque*

Globe & Mail - March 5 2005 - pD14 [501+]

Zoller, Curt J. - *Annotated Bibliography of Works about Sir Winston S. Churchill*

Choice - v42 - i1 - Sept 2004 - p76(1) [501+]

Zoller, Uri - *Handbook of Detergents, Part B*

SciTech - v28 - i4 - Dec 2004 - p166(1) [51-500]

A

Alzheimer's Disease — *Doka, Kenneth J.*

Alzheimer's Disease Sourcebook: Basic Consumer Health Information about Alzheimer's Disease, Other Dementias, and Related Disorders..., 3rd Ed. — *Bellenir, Karen*

Am I Not Your Lord? Human Meaning in Divine Question — *Cragg, Kenneth*

Am I Still a Woman?: Hysterectomy and Gender Identity — *Elson, Jean*

Ama: A Story of the Atlantic Slave Trade — *Herbstein, Manu*

The AMA Handbook of E-Learning: Effective Design, Implementation, and Technology Solutions — *Piskurich, George M.*

y   Amagansett — *Mills, Mark*

Amakudari: The Hidden Fabric of Japan's Economy — *Colignon, Richard A.*

c   Amalee — *Williams, Dar*

Amarillo Slim in a World of Fat People — *Amarillo Slim*

y   Amaryllis — *Crist-Evans, Craig*

The Amateur Geologist: Explorations and Investigations — *Wiggers, Raymond*

The Amateur Marriage: A Novel (Read by Brown, Blair). Audiobook Review — *Tyler, Anne*

The Amateur Marriage: A Novel — *Tyler, Anne*

The Amateur Meteorologist: Explorations and Investigations — *Mogil, H. Michael*

c   Amazement Park: 12 Wild Mazes (Illus. by Munro, Roxie) — *Munro, Roxie*

y   The Amazing Adventures of the Escapist. Vol. 1 — *Chabon, Michael*

c   Amazing Animal Facts — *Bailey, Jacqui*

c   Amazing Animal Hide and Seek — *Rowe, John*

c   Amazing Apples — *Powell, Consie*

c   Amazing Flights: The Golden Age — *Hansen, Ole Steen*

Amazing Grace: African American Grandmothers as Caregivers and Conveyers of Traditional Values — *Ruiz, Dorothy S.*

Amazing Grace: An Anthology of Poems about Slavery — *Basker, James G.*

Amazing Grace: The Story of America's Most Beloved Song — *Turner, Steve*

The Amazing Hot Air Balloon (Illus. by Ventura, Marco) — *Ventura, Marco*

c   The Amazing International Space Station — *Cowles, Rose*

c   Amazing International Space Station (Illus. by Cowles, Rose) — *Yes Magazine*

c   Amazing Machines Jigsaw Book — *Mitton, Tony*

Amazing Medical Stories — *Burden, George*

c   The Amazing Mr. Franklin, or, The Boy Who Read Everything — *Ashby, Ruth*

c   Amazing Octopus (Illus. by Reiach, Margaret Amy) — *Kalman, Bobbie*

c   Amazing Schemes Within Your Genes (Illus. by Rolph, Mic) — *Balkwill, Frances R.*

Amazing Science

Amazing Science: Weather

Amazing Spider-Man. Vol. 6 — *Straczynski, J. Michael*

c   Amazing Things Animals Do (Illus. by Caron, Romi) — *Baillie, Marilyn*

c   Amazing Whales! — *Thomson, Sarah L.*

y   Amazon River — *Fitzpatrick, Anne*

c   The Amazon River — *Graf, Mike*

c   Amazon River Rescue (Illus. by McIntyre, Sarah) — *Lumry, Amanda*

Amazonia: Five Years at the Epicenter of the Dot.com Juggernaut — *Marcus, James*

Amazonian Dark Earths: Explorations in Space and Time — *Glaser, Bruno*

Amazons, Savages, and Machiavels: Travel and Colonial Writing in English, 1550-1630 — *Hadfield, Andrew*

Ambassadors of Christ: Commemorating 150 Years of Theological Education in Cuddesdon, 1854-2004 — *Chapman, Mark D.*

The Ambassadors' Secret: Holbein and the World of the Renaissance — *North, John*

The Ambassadors' Secret: Holbein and the World of the Renaissance — *North, John David*

The Ambassador's Son — *Hickam, Homer*

y   The Amber Room: The Fate of the World's Greatest Lost Treasure — *Scott-Clark, Catherine*

The Amber Room: The Untold Story of the Greatest Hoax of the Twentieth Century — *Scott-Clark, Catherine*

c   Amber: The Story of a Red Fox (Illus. by Godkin, Celia) — *Woods, Shirley*

y   Amber Was Brave, Essie Was Smart — *Williams, Vera*

Ambient Intelligence: Impact on Embedded System Design — *Basten, Twan*

Ambiguity and Choice in Public Policy: Political Decision Making in Modern Democracies — *Zahariadis, Nikolaos*

The Ambiguity of Teaching to the Test: Standards, Assessment, and Educational Reform — *Firestone, William A.*

Ambiguity, Tension, and Multiplicity in Deutero-Isaiah — *Kim, Hyun Chul Paul*

Ambiguous Images: Gender and Rock Art — *Hays-Gilpin, Kelley A.*

Ambition and Identity: Chinese Merchant Elites in Colonial Manila, 1880-1916 — *Wilson, Andrew R.*

The Ambitions of Curiosity: Understanding the World in Ancient Greece and China — *Lloyd, G.E.R.*

Ambivalence, a Love Story: Portrait of a Marriage — *Donatich, John*

Ambivalence and the Postcolonial Subject: The Strategic Alliance of Juan Francisco Manzano and Richard Robert Madden — *Burton, Gera C.*

The Ambivalent Alliance: Konrad Adenauer, the CDU/CSU, and the West, 1949-1966 — *Granieri, Ronald J.*

Ambivalent Europeans: Ritual, Memory and the Public Sphere in Malta — *Mitchell, Jon P.*

Ambrose Bierce and the Ace of Shoots — *Hall, Oakley*

An Ambulance Is on the Way: Stories of Men in Trouble — *Wilson, Jonathan*

Ambulatory Care Procedures for the Nurse Practitioner, 2nd Ed. — *Colyar, Margaret R.*

Ambushed: A War Reporter's Life on the Line — *Stewart, Ian*

The Ambushed Grand Jury: How the Justice Department Covered Up Government Nuclear Crimes and How We Caught Them Red Handed — *McKinley, Wes*

Amchitka and the Bomb — *Kohlhoff, Dean W.*

c   Amelia Rules! What Makes You Happy — *Gownley, Jimmy*

c   Amelia's Show-and-Tell Fiesta/Amelia y la fiesta de "muestra y cuenta." (Illus. by Aviles, Martha) — *Chapra, Mimi*

The Amending Process in Congress — *Bach, Stanley*

America: A Citizen's Guide to Democracy Inaction — *Stewart, Jon*

America: A Citizen's Guide to Democracy Inaction (Read by Stewart, Jon). Audiobook Review — *Stewart, Jon*

America: A Citizen's Guide to Democracy Inaction — *Stewart, Jon*

America: A Narrative History, 6th Ed. — *Tindall, George Brown*

c   America: A Patriotic Primer (Illus. by Glasser, Robin Preiss) — *Cheney, Lynne*

America Alone: The Neo-Conservatives and the Global Order — *Halper, Stefan*

America and the Armenian Genocide of 1915 — *Winter, Jay*

America as Empire: Global Leader or Rogue Power? — *Garrison, Jim*

America as Second Creation: Technology and Narratives of New Beginnings — *Nye, David E.*

America Attacks Japan — *Maga, Timothy P.*

America Behind the Color Line: Dialogues with African Americans — *Gates, Henry Louis, Jr.*

America beyond Capitalism: Reclaiming Our Wealth, Our Liberty, and Our Democracy — *Alperovitz, Gar*

America Discovered: A Historical Atlas of North American Exploration — *Hayes, Derek*

y   America from the Air: An Aviator's Story — *Langewiesche, Wolfgang*

y   America in the 1960s — *Kronenwetter, Michael*

America in Words and Song

y   America, My New Home (Illus. by Condon, Ken) — *Gunning, Monica*

America on Trial: Inside the Legal Battles That Transformed our Nation — *Dershowitz, Alan M.*

America Right or Wrong: An Anatomy of American Nationalism — *Lieven, Anatol*

c   America, the Beautiful (Illus. by Minor, Wendell) — *Bates, Katharine Lee*

c   America the Beautiful (Illus. by Sabuda, Robert) — *Sabuda, Robert*

c   America the Beautiful (Illus. by Gall, Chris) — *Bates, Katharine Lee*

America (the Book): A Citizen's Guide to Democracy Inaction — *Stewart, Jon*

America, the Vietnam War, and the World: Comparative and International Perspectives — *Daum, Andreas W.*

America the Virtuous: The Crisis of Democracy and the Quest for Empire — *Ryn, Claes G.*

America the Vulnerable: How Our Government Is Failing to Protect Us from Terrorism — *Flynn, Stephen*

America to Nikka Kowa — *En, Kokukin*

America Unbound: The Bush Revolution in Foreign Policy — *Daalder, Ivo H.*

America Votes 25: A Handbook of Contemporary American Election Statistics, 2001-2002 — *Scammon, Richard M.*

c   America Votes: How Our President Is Elected (Illus. by Bjorkman, Steve) — *Granfield, Linda*

American Adonis: Tony Sansone, the First Male Physique Icon — *Massey, John*

The American Adventure

American Adventurism Abroad: 30 Invasions, Interventions and Regime Changes since World War II — *Sullivan, Michael J., III*

American Agriculture in the Twentieth Century: How It Flourished and What It Cost — *Gardner, Bruce L.*

American Architectural History: A Contemporary Reader — *Eggener, Keith L.*

American Art at the Flint Institute of Arts — *Gerdts, William H.*

American Art Deco: An Illustrated Survey — *Leonard, R.L.*

American Art in the Princeton University Art Museum, Volume 1: Drawings and Watercolors — *Wilmerding, John*

The American Axis: Henry Ford, Charles Lindbergh, and the Rise of the Third Reich — *Wallace, Max*

American Azaleas — *Towe, L. Clarence*

American Babylon: Race and the Struggle for Postwar Oakland — *Self, Robert O.*

The American Ballot Box in the Mid-Nineteenth — *Bensel, Richard Franklin*

American Bird Conservancy Guide to the 500 Most Important Bird Areas in the United States: Key Sites for Birds and Birding in All 50 States — *Chipley, Robert M.*

The American Black Chamber — *Yardley, Herbert O.*

American Book Trade Directory, 2004-2005, 50th Ed. — *Information Today*

American Brutus: John Wilkes Booth and the Lincoln Conspiracies — *Kauffman, Michael W.*

American Cancer Society's Complete Guide to Prostate Cancer — *Bostwick, David G.*

American Capitalism, 1945-2000: Continuity and Change from Mass Production to the Information Society — *Wells, Wyatt*

American Cars, 1960 to 1972: Every Model Year by Year — *Flory, J. Kelly*

American Cars in Prewar England: A Pictorial Survey — *Goodman, Bryan*

American Catholics, American Culture: Tradition and Resistance — *Steinfels, Margaret O'Brien*

American Catholics and Civic Engagement: A Distinctive Voice — *Steinfels, Margaret O'Brien*

The American Century in Europe — *Moore, Laurence R.*

The American Century in Europe — *Moore, R. Laurence*

The American Child: A Cultural Studies Reader — *Levander, Caroline F.*

An American Childhood — *Dillard, Annie*

The American Choice-of-Law Revolution in the Courts: Today and Tomorrow — *Symeonides, Symeon C.*

The American Church Experience: A Concise History — *Askew, Thomas A.*

American Cinema's Transitional Era: Audiences, Institutions, Practices — *Keil, Charlie*

American Citizens, British Slaves: Yankee Political Prisoners in an Australian Penal Colony — *Pybus, Cassandra*

c   The American Civil Rights Movement: The African-American Struggle for Equality — *Altman, Linda Jacobs*

The American Civil War through British Eyes: Dispatches from British Diplomats — *Barnes, James J.*

American Civil War, Vols. 1-12 — *Praeger Illustrated Military History*

The American College Novel: An Annotated Bibliography — *Kramer, John E.*

The American Colonial State in the Philippines: Global Perspectives — *Go, Julian*

American Congo: The African American Freedom Struggle in the Delta — *Woodruff, Nan Elizabeth*

B

The Bog People: Iron-Age Man Preserved — *World Bank*

Boiling Point: How Politicians, Big Oil and Coal, Journalists, and Activists are Fueling the Climate Crisis--and What We Can Do to Avert Disaster — *Gelbspan, Ross*

c Boing! (Illus. by Bruel, Nick) — *Bruel, Nick*

c Boing!

c Boing! (Illus. by Ingman, Bruce) — *Taylor, Sean*

y Bold, Brave and Born to Lead — *Fryer, Mary Beacock*

Bold Entrepreneur: A Life of James B. Duke — *Durden, Robert F.*

Bold Journey: West with Lewis and Clark: A Novel — *Bohner, Charles*

y Bold Spirit: Helga Estby's Forgotten Walk Across Victorian America — *Hunt, Linda Lawrence*

The Bolero School — *Grut, Marina*

Bolivia — *Gelletly, LeeAnne*

y Bollywood Babes — *Dhami, Narinder*

Bolo! — *Weber, David*

The Bolsheviks Come to Power — *Rabinowitch, Alexander*

Bolt of Fate: Benjamin Franklin and His Electric Kite Hoax — *Tucker, Tom*

The Bomb: A Life — *DeGroot, Gerard J.*

The Bomb in My Garden: The Secrets of Saddam's Nuclear Mastermind — *Obeidi, Mahdi*

The Bomb in my Garden: The Secrets of Saddam's Nuclear Mastermind — *Pitzer, Kurt*

Bomber Crew — *Sweetman, John*

The Bon-Bon and Love Token — *Shaw, Allyson*

Bon Po Hidden Treasures: A Catalogue of gTer ston BDe chen gling pa's Collected Revelations — *Archard, Jean-Luc*

Bonagratia von Bergamo: Franziskanerjurist und Wortfuhrer seines Ordens im Streit mit Papst Johannes XXII. — *Wittneben, Eva Luise*

A Bond with Death — *Crider, Bill*

Bondi Classic — *Freeman, Paul*

Bonds and Bondholders: British Investors and Mexico's Foreign Debt, 1824-1888 — *Costeloe, Michael P.*

Bonds of Imperfection: Christian Politics, Past and Present — *O'Donovan, Oliver*

Bone and Dream: Into the World's Driest Desert — *Sagaris, Lake*

The Bone Beneath the Pulp: Drawings by Wyndham Lewis (Illus. by Lewis, Wyndham) — *Klein, Jacky*

c Bone Collector's Son (Illus. by Juhasz, George) — *Yee, Paul*

The Bone Flute — *Bow, Patricia*

Bone Graft Substitutes — *Laurencin, Cato T.*

The Bone House — *Armstrong, Luanne*

Bone to Pick: Of Forgiveness, Reconciliation, Reparation, and Revenge — *Cose, Ellis*

y The Bone Vault (Read by Brown, Blair). Audiobook Review — *Fairstein, Linda*

The Bone Woman: A Forensic Anthropologist's Search for Truth in the Mass Graves of Rwanda, Bosnia, Croatia, and Kosovo — *Koff, Clea*

y Bonecrack. Audiobook Review — *Francis, Dick*

c Bones and the Big Yellow Mystery (Illus. by Newman, Barbara Johansen) — *Adler, David A.*

c Bones and the Dog Gone Mystery (Illus. by Newman, Barbara Johansen) — *Adler, David A.*

The Bones — *Greenland, Seth*

Bones of the Ancestors: The Archaeology and Osteobiography of the Moatfield Ossuary — *Williamson, Ronald F.*

The Bones of the Earth — *Mansfield, Howard*

y Bones Rock!: Everything You Need to Know to Be a Paleontologist — *Larson, Peter*

Bones, Stones, and Molecules: "Out of Africa" and Human Rights — *Cameron, David W.*

Boneyard — *Moore, Richard*

Bonfire of Creeds: The Essential Ashis Nandy — *Nandy, Ashis*

Bonhoeffer as Martyr: Social Responsibility and Modern Christian Commitment — *Slane, Craig J.*

The Bonhoeffer Phenomenon: Portraits of a Protestant Saint — *Haynes, Stephen R.*

Bonjour, Monsieur Courbet!: The Bruyas Collection from the Musee Fabre, Montpellier — *Lees, Sarah*

Bonne Nuit, Beaux Reves — *Apperley, Dawn*

Bonnie and Clyde: A Twenty-First-Century Update — *Knight, James R.*

The Bonus Army: An American Epic — *Dickson, Paul*

c Bonz Inside-Out! A Rhythm, Rhyme, and Reason Bonz-anza! (Illus. by Glaser, Byron) — *Glaser, Byron*

c Boo! (Illus. by Martchenko, Michael) — *Munsch, Robert*

Boo Who — *Guttteridge, Rene*

c BooBoo (Illus. by Dunrea, Olivier) — *Dunrea, Olivier*

c Boogaloo on 2nd Avenue: A Novel of Pastry, Guilt, and Music — *Kurlansky, Mark*

c Boogers are Blessings (Illus. by Ross, Bill) — *McDermott, Michael*

Boogers Are Blessings (Illus. by Ross, Bill) — *Parker, Michael McDermott*

A Book about Myself: Newspaper Days — *Dreiser, Theodore*

The Book Against God — *Wood, James*

The Book as Art, Literature, and History — *Sewell, Robert C.*

c The Book Bunch: Developing Book Clubs for Beginning Readers — *Smith, Laura J.H.*

Book Doctor — *Cohen, Esther*

Book Lust: Recommended Reading for Every Mood, Moment, and Reason — *Pearl, Nancy*

The Book Nobody Read: Chasing the Revolutions of Nicolaus Copernicus — *Gingerich, Owen*

The Book of Ash — *Flint, James*

The Book of Ballads — *Vess, Charles*

y The Book of Broken Hours — *Doherty-Wayne, C.H.*

Book of Clouds — *Day, John A.*

The Book of Corrections: Reflections on the National Crisis During the Japanese Invasion of Korea, 1592-1598 — *Song-nyong, Yu*

The Book of Customs: A Complete Handbook for the Jewish Year — *Kosofsky, Scott-Martin*

y The Book of Dead Days — *Sedgwick, Marcus*

The Book of Deeds of James I of Aragon: A Translation of the Medieval Catalan Llibre dels Fets — *Smith, Damian*

y The Book of Dreams — *Melling, O.R.*

The Book of Edible Nuts — *Rosengarten, Frederic*

The Book of Evidence — *Achinstein, Peter*

The Book of Fire, 2nd Ed. — *Cottrell, William H.*

The Book of Hebrew Script: History, Palaeography, Script Styles, Calligraphy and Design — *Yardeni, Ada*

A Book of Hours: Music, Literature, and Life: A Memoir — *Lee, M. Owen*

Book of Ifs and Buts — *Maharaj, Rabindranath*

y The Book of Inventions — *Harrison, Ian*

The Book of J (Read by Bloom, Claire). Audiobook Review — *Rosenberg, David*

The Book of Job: A Contest of Moral Imaginations — *Newsom, Carol A.*

The Book of Joe (Read by Brick, Scott). Audiobook Review — *Tropper, Jonathan*

The Book of John Mandeville: An Edition of the Pynson Text with commentary on the Defective Version — *Kohanski, Tamarah*

The Book of John Mandeville: An Edition of the Pyson Text with Commentary on the Defective Version — *Kohanski, Tamarah*

Book of Jon — *Sikelianos, Eleni*

The Book of Kehls — *O'Hagan, Christine Kehl*

The Book of Lancelot: The Middle Dutch "Lancelot" Compilation and the Medieval Tradition of Narrative Cycles — *Besamusca, Bart*

The Book of Letters. Audiobook Review

The Book of Light — *Blake, Michelle*

The Book of Love Letters: Canadian Kinship, Friendship, and Romance — *Grescoe, Paul*

The Book of Nero 6 Ultra Edition: CD and DVD Burning Made Easy — *Wang, Wallace*

c The Book of Nonsense — *Lear, Edward*

The Book of Proper Names — *Nothomb, Amelie*

The Book of Ralph: A Fiction — *McNally, John*

The Book of Revenue: Kitab al-Amwal — *Qasim ibn Sallam, Abu Ubayd al-*

The Book of Roasting — *Egan, Jeanette*

y The Book of Rock Stars: 24 Musical Icons That Shine through History — *Krull, Kathleen*

The Book of Rule: How the World Is Governed

A Book of Scattered Leaves: Poetry of Poverty in Broadside Ballads of Nineteenth-Century England — *Hepburn, James*

The Book of Schuiten — *Schuiten, Francois*

The Book of Secrets: Unlocking the Hidden Dimensions of Your Life — *Chopra, Deepak*

The Book of Shadows — *Paterson, Don*

The Book of Skin — *Connor, Steven*

The Book of Small — *Carr, Emily*

The Book of Spies: An Anthology of Literary Espionage — *Furst, Alan*

Book of Spirit Communications — *Buckland, Raymond*

The Book of Ten Nights and a Night — *Barth, John*

The Book of the Film of the Story of My Life — *Brandt, William*

The Book of the Sage — *Mills, J.C.*

Book of the Sphinx — *Regier, Willis Goth*

The Book of War Letters — *Grescoe, Audrey*

c The Book of ZZZs (Illus. by Alda, Arlene) — *Alda, Arlene*

The Book on Bush: How George W. (Mis)Leads America — *Alterman, Eric*

Book Report: Publishing Strategies, Writing Tips, and 101 Literary Ideas for Aspiring Authors and Poets — *Shaw, Mark*

Book Sense Best Books: 125 Favorite Books Recommended by Independent Booksellers — *Nichols, Mark*

The Book That Changed My Life — *Osen, Diane*

Bookbinding Materials and Techniques, 1700-1920 — *Lock, Margaret*

Booked to Die — *Dunning, John*

Bookends: The Changing Media Environment of American Classrooms — *Cassidy, Margaret*

Booker T. Washington and Black Progress: Up from Slavery 100 Years Later — *Brundage, W. Fitzhugh*

Bookkeepers' Boot Camp: Get a Grip on Accounting Basics — *Mohr, Angie*

Bookmaking: Editing, Design, Production — *Lee, Marshall*

The Bookman's Promise (Read by Guidall, George). Audiobook Review — *Dunning, John*

Booknotes: On American Character — *Lamb, Brian*

Books and Bombs in Buenos Aires: Bergers, Gerchunoff, and Argentine-Jewish Writing — *Aizenberg, Edna*

Books and Periodicals Online: A Directory of Online Publications, 2003 ed., 2 volumes — *Nobart, Nuchine*

y Books for the Journey: A Guide to the World of Reading — *Fenner, Pamela J.*

Books, Friends, and Bibliophilia: Reminiscences of an Antiquarian Bookseller — *Gerits, Anton*

c Books in Bloom: Creative Patterns & Props That Bring Stories to Life — *Faurot, Kimberly K.*

Books, Maps, and Politics: A Cultural History of the Library of Congress, 1783-1861 — *Ostrowski, Carl*

Books of Definition in Islamic Philosophy: The Limits of Works — *Kennedy-Day, Kiki*

Books on the Frontier: Print Culture in the American West, 1763-1875 — *Clement, Richard W.*

Books to Grow With: A Guide to Using the Best Children's Fiction for Everyday Issues and Tough Challenges — *Coon, Cheryl F.*

y The Bookseller of Kabul (Read by David, Joanna). Audiobook Review — *Seierstad, Asne*

The Bookseller of Kabul — *Seierstad, Asne*

A Bookshelf of Our Own: Works That Changed Women's Lives — *Felder, Deborah G.*

The Bookshop at 10 Curzon Street: Letters between Nancy Mitford and Heywood Hill, 1952-1973 — *Mitford, Nancy*

BookSource: Nonfiction[TM]

The Booktalker's Bible: How to Talk about the Books You Love to Any Audience — *Langemack, Chapple*

The Boom and the Bubble: The US in the World Economy — *Brenner, Robert*

Boom for Whom?: Education, Desegregation, and Development in Charlotte — *Smith, Stephen Samuel*

Boomer Nation: The Largest and Richest Generation Ever, and How it Changed America — *Gillon, Steven M.*

Boomer Shock: Preparing Communities for the Retirement Generation — *Haan, Ellen de*

Boomtown — *Williams, Greg*

Bootcamp 360: A Complete Fitness Programs for Brides: The Few, the Proud, the Fit — *Kleinberg, Tamara*

The Bootlegger's Other Daughter — *Cimarolli, Mary*

Booty Nomad (Read by Feverstein, Michael). Audiobook Review — *Mebus, Scott*

Booze: A Distilled History — *Heron, Craig*

c The Bora Boys and the Last Big Door — *Feeney, Michael J.*

Bordeaux and Its Wines — *Joseph, Robert*

Border, Bindings & Edges — *Collins, Sally*

The Border: Canada, the U.S. and Dispatches from the 49th Parallel — *Laxer, James*

Border-Line Personalities: A New Generation of Latinas Dish on Sex, Sass & Cultural Shifting — *Moreno, Robyn*

Border Lines: The Partition of Judaeo-Christianity — *Boyarin, Daniel*

Border Oasis: Water and the Political Ecology of the Colarado River Delta, 1940-1975 — *Ward, Evan R.*

Border of Death, Valley of Life: An Immigrant Journey of Heart and Spirit — *Groody, Daniel G.*

y Borderlines: A Memoir — *Kraus, Caroline*

Butterflies — *Mitchell, Melanie*

Butterflies — *Mozetic, Brane*

Butterflies: Ecology and Evalution Taking Flight — *Boggs, Carol L.*

c **Butterflies of North America** — *Opler, Paul*

Butterflies of Oklahoma, Kansas, and North Texas — *Dole, John M.*

Butterflies of the Lower Rio Grande Valley — *Wauer, Roland H.*

c **Butterfly** — *Watts, Barrie*

y **The Butterfly Handbook** — *Miller, Jacueline Y.*

Butterfly Trails — *Roegner, Harry R.*

c **Buttermilk Hill** — *White, Ruth*

c **The Button Box: Stories about Mama (Read by McBride-Smith, Barbara). Audiobook Review** — *McBride-Smith, Barbara*

Button Man — *Lyons, Paul*

c **Buttons and Bo** — *Itaya, Satoshi*

The Buwayhid Dynasty in Iraq 334 H./945 to 403 H./1012: Shaping Institutions for the Future — *Donohue, John J.*

Buying a Fishing Rod for My Grandfather — *Gao, Xingjian*

Buying and Contracting for Resources and Services: A How-to-Do-It Manual for Librarians — *Anderson, Rick*

Buying and Owning Your Own Airplane, 3rd Ed. — *Ellis, James E.*

Buying Information Systems: Selecting, Implementing and Assessing Off-the-Shelf Systems — *James, David*

The Buying of the President 2004: Who's Really Bankrolling Bush and His Democratic Challengers--and What They Expect in Return — *Chideya, Farai*

The Buying of the President 2004: Who's Really Bankrolling Bush and His Democratic Challengers--And What They Expect in Return — *Lewis, Charles*

Buying, Selling, and Owning the Medical Practice, 2nd Ed. — *Reiboldt, Max*

Buying & Selling Antiques and Collectibles on eBay — *Wiggins, Pamela*

Buying Time and Getting By: The Voluntary Simplicity Movement — *Grigsby, Mary*

Buying Whiteness: Race, Culture, and Identity from Columbus to Hip-Hop — *Taylor, Gary*

Buyways: Billboards, Automobiles, and the American Landscape — *Gudis, Catherine*

Buzz Riff — *Hill, Sam*

Buzz: The Intimate Bond Between Humans and Insects (Illus. by Steger, Volker) — *Glausiusz, Josie*

Buzzed: The Straight Facts about the Most Used and Abused Drugs from Alcohol to Ecstasy — *Kuhn, Cynthia*

By a Spider's Thread (Read by Rosenblat, Barbara). Audiobook Review — *Lippman, Laura*

By a Spider's Thread — *Lippman, Laura*

By a Thread: How Child Care Centers Hold on to Teachers, How Teachers Build Lasting Careers — *Whitebook, Marcy*

By Bread Alone — *Lynch, Sarah-Kate*

By Duty Bound: Survival and Redemption in a Time of War — *Ware, Ezell*

By Heart/De Memoria: Cuban Women's Journeys in and out of Exile — *Torres, Maria de los Angeles*

c **By My Brother's Side (Illus. by Root, Barry)** — *Barber, Tiki*

By Myself and Then Some — *Bacall, Lauren*

By Order of the Kaiser: Otto von Diederichs and the Rise of the Imperial German Navy, 1865-1902 — *Gottschall, Terrell D.*

By Order of the President — *Griffin, W.E.B.*

By Permission of Heaven: The True Story of the Great Fire of London — *Tinniswood, Adrian*

By Summer's End — *Morsi, Pamela*

By the Grand Canal — *Riviere, William*

c **By the Great Horn Spoon! (Read by Lape, Willard E.). Audiobook Review** — *Fleischman, Sid*

c **By the Great Horn Spoon!**

c **By the Great Spoon!**

By the Hand of Mormon: The American Scripture That Launched a New World Religion — *Givens, Terry L.*

By Their Deeds Alone: America's Combat Commanders on the Art of War — *Atkinson, Rick*

c **By Word of Mouth (Illus. by Spohn, Kate)** — *Spohn, Kate*

Bye Bye Bertie: A Joe LaFlam Mystery — *Dewhurst, Rick*

Bye, Bye Love — *Swift, Virginia*

Bye, Bye, Love — *Swift, Virginia*

Byline: Mickey Spillane — *Spillane, Mickey*

Byrdcliffe: An American Arts and Crafts Colony — *Denker, Ellen Paul*

Byron and Place: History, Translation, Nostalgia — *Cheeke, Stephen*

Byron, Poetics and History — *Stabler, Jane*

Byron: The Flawed Angel — *Grosskurth, Phyllis*

Byron's Othered Self and Voice: Contextualizing the Homographic Signature — *Keegan, Abigail F.*

Byzantine Authors: Literary Activities and Preoccupations — *Nesbitt, John W.*

Byzantine Monuments of Istanbul — *Freely, John*

Byzantine and the Crusades — *Harris, Jonathan*

y **Byzantium** — *Loverance, Rowena*

Byzantium: Faith and Power (1261-1557). — *Evans, Helen C.*

Byzantium Rediscovered: The Byzantine Revival in Europe and America — *Bullen, J.B.*

C

C# Concisely — *Bishop, Judith*

C.F. Martin and His Guitars, 1796-1873 — *Gura, Philip F.*

C++ for Dummies — *Davis, Stephen Randy*

C.G. Jung's Complex Dynamics and the Clinical Relationship: One Map for Mystery — *Donahue, Brenda*

c C Is for Chinook: An Alberta Alphabet (Illus. by Bennett, Lorna) — *Welykochy, Dawn*

C# .Net illuminated — *Gittleman, Art*

C.P.E. Bach and the Rebirth of the Strophic Song — *Youngren, William H.*

C.S. Lewis: A Life — *White, Michael*

C.S. Lewis and the Catholic Church — *Pearce, Joseph*

C.T. Hsia on Chinese Literature — *Hsia, C.T.*

C3: Nuclear Command, Control Cooperation — *Yarynich, Valery E.*

The Cabaret — *Appignanesi, Lisa*

y Cabbagehead — *Lesynski, Loris*

Cabiers Voltaire, I: revue annuelle de la Societe Voltaire — *Kolving, Ulla*

Cabin Kitchens and Baths — *Schmidt, Franklin*

y Cabin on Trouble Creek — *Van Leeuwen, Jean*

y Cactus Soup (Illus. by Huling, Paul) — *Kimmel, Eric A.*

c Cactus Soup (Illus. by Huling, Phil) — *Kimmel, Eric A.*

The Caddie Was a Reindeer: And Other Tales of Extreme Recreation — *The Caddie Was a Reindeer: And Other Tales of Extreme Recreation (Book)*

The Caddie Was a Reindeer: And Other Tales of Extreme Recreation — *Rushin, Steve*

Cadillac Story: The Postwar Years — *Bonsall, Thomas E.*

c Cadoc — *Malone, Geoffrey*

Caesar Against Liberty? Perspectives on His Autocracy — *Cairns, Francis*

c Caesar Rodney's Ride: The Story of an American Patriot (Illus. by Lippincott, Gary) — *Cheripko, Jan*

The Caesarean — *Odent, Michel*

Caesar's Hours: My Life in Comedy, with Love and Laughter — *Caesar, Sid*

Caetana Says No: Women's Stories from a Brazilian Slave Society — *Graham, Sandra Lauderdale*

Cafe Alibi — *Swift, Todd*

Caffey's Pediatric Diagnostic Imaging. 10th Ed. — *Kuhn, Jerald P.*

c The Caged Birds of Phnom Penh — *Lipp, Frederick*

y Caged — *Freud, S.A.*

Cage's Bend — *Coleman, Carter*

Cahiers Patrice de La Tour du Pin, 18: Correspondance

Cahokia and the Hinterlands: Middle Mississippian Cultures of the Midwest — *Emerson, Thomas E.*

y Cahokia Mounds — *Pauketat, Timothy*

Cahokia: The Great Native American Metropolis — *Young, Biloine Whiting*

Cain's Field: Faith, Fratricide, and Fear in the Middle East — *Rees, Matt*

y Cairo: A Cultural History — *Beattie, Andrew*

Cairo City of Sand — *Golia, Maria*

The Cairo House — *Serageldin, Samia*

c Cajita Musica de Crayola!

y The Cajun Cowboy — *Hill, Sandra*

The Cajuns: Americanization of a People — *Bernard, Shane K.*

The Cajuns — *Weill, Gus*

The Calabrian Charlatan, 1598-1603: Messianic Nationalism in Early Modern Europe — *Olsen, H. Eric R.*

Calamity and Other Stories — *Kalotay, Daphne*

The Calamity Papers: Western Myths and Cold Cases — *Walker, Dale L.*

c Calavera Abecedario: A Day of the Dead Alphabet Book — *Winter, Jeanette*

Calaveras Gold: The Impact Of Mining on a Mother Lode Country — *Limbaugh, Ronald H.*

The Calcium Bomb: The Nanobacteria Link to Heart Disease and Cancer — *Mulhall, Douglas*

Calcium Channel Pharmacology — *McDonough, Stefan I.*

Calculating Lost Labor Productivity in Construction Claims — *Schwartzkopf, William*

Calculating the Value of the Union: Slavery, Property Rights, and the Economic Origins of the Civil War — *Huston, James L.*

Calculation of NMR and EPR Parameters: Theory and Applications — *Kaupp, Martin*

Calculus 1 — *Harnett, Gerald*

Calculus and Pizza: A Cookbook for the Hungry Mind — *Pickover, Clifford A.*

The Calculus of Variations — *Brunt, Bruce Van*

Calculus with Complex Numbers — *Reade, John B.*

Calder: Gravity and Grace — *Giminez, Carmen*

Calder, Miro — *Calder, Alexander*

Calder Miro — *Hutton, Elizabeth*

Calendar Girl — *Neale, Naomi*

The Caliban Shore: The Fate of the Grosvenor Castaways — *Taylor, Stephen*

Caliban's Reason: Introducing Afro-Caribbean Philosophy — *Henry, Paget*

Caliban's Shore: The Wreck of the Grosvenor and the Strange Fate of Her Survivors — *Frankel, Boris*

Caliban's Shore: The Wreck of the Grosvenor and the Strange Fate of Her Survivors — *Taylor, Stephen*

Calico — *Hastings, Michael*

c Calie's Gift (Illus. by Vavak, S. Dean) — *Arroyo, Madeline*

Califia's Daughters — *Richards, Leigh*

California Desert Flowers: An Introduction to Families, Genera, and Species (Illus. by Morhardt, Sia) — *Morhardt, Sia*

California Desert Flowers: An Introduction to Families, Genera, and Species (Illus. by Morhardt, Emil) — *Morhardt, Sia*

California Dish: What I Saw — *Tower, Jeremiah*

California Dreamin': Camera Clubs in the Pictorial Photography Tradition — *McCarroll, Stacey*

California Earthquakes: Science, Risk, and the Politics of Hazard Mitigation — *Geschwind, Carl-Henry*

The California Electricity Crisis: Causes and Policy Options — *Weare, Christopher*

California Girl — *Parker, T. Jefferson*

California Jews — *Kahn, Ava F.*

The California Poem — *Sikelianos, Eleni*

The California Republic: Institutions, Statesmanship, and Policies — *Janiskee, Brian P.*

California Rising: The Life and Times of Pat Brown — *Rarick, Ethan*

Caliphs and Kings: The Art and Influence of Islamic Spain — *Ecker, Heather*

Calixtus II (1119-1124): A Pope Born to Rule — *Stroll, Mary*

Call for the Dead — *Le Carre, John*

The Call from the Stranger on a Journey Home: Curriculum in a Third Space — *Wang, Hongyu*

y Call Me Maria: A Novel — *Ortiz Cofer, Judith*

The Call of God: Women Doing Theology in Peru — *Powers, Tom*

Call of the Desert: The Sahara — *Bourseiller, Philippe*

Call of the Mall — *Underhill, Paco*

c The Call of the Osprey (Illus. by Harrison-Lever, Brian) — *Jorgensen, Norman*

Call the Dying — *Taylor, Andrew*

y A Call to Arms (Read by Graham, Errick). Audiobook Review — *Mallinson, Allan*

A Call to Fidelity: On the Moral Theology of Charles E. Curran — *Walter, James J.*

A Call to Piety: St. Bonaventure's Collations on the Six Days — *Anderson, C. Colt*

The Call-Up: A History of National Service — *Hickman, Tom*

Callgirl — *Angell, Jeannette L.*

The Calligrapher — *Docx, Edward*

y Calligraphy for Kids — *Winters, Eleanor*

The Calligraphy Shop — *Downing, Ben*

Calling Back the Spirit: Music, Dance, and Cultural Politics in Lowland South Sulawesi — *Sutton, R. Anderson*

Calling Down Fire: Charles Grandison Finney and Revivalism in Jefferson County — *Perciaccante, Marianne*

Calling Home — *Sanger, Richard*

Calling the Soul: Gender and the Cycle of Life in a Hmong Village — *Symonds, Patricia V.*

Cally's War — *Ringo, John*

Calm at Sunset, Calm at Dawn — *Watkins, Paul*

Calvet's Web: Enlightenment and the Republic of Letters in Eighteenth-Century France — *Brockliss, L.W.B.*

Calvin: Biographie und Theologie — *Spijker, Willem Van't*

Calvinism and Religious Toleration in the Dutch Golden Age — *Hsia, R. Po-Chia*

Calvinism in the Las Vegas Airport:Making Connections in Today's World — *Mouw, Richard J.*

Camaldolese Extraordinary: The Life, Doctrine, and Rule of Blessed Paul Giustiniani — *Leclercq, Dom Jean*

Camber: Selected Poems, 1983-2000 — *McKay, Don*

Cambodia After the Khmer Rouge: Inside the Politics of Nation Building — *Gottesman, Evan*

Cambodia — *Freeman, Michael*

The Cambrian Fossils of Chengjiang, China: The Flowering of Early Animal Life — *Hou, Xianguang*

The Cambrian Fossils of Chengjiang, China: The Flowering of Early Animal Life — *Hou Xianguang*

The Cambrian Fossils of Chengjiang, China: The Flowering of Early Animal Life — *Hou, Xianguang*

Cambridge: A Cultural and Literary History — *Garrett, Martin*

The Cambridge Aerospace Dictionary — *Gunston, Bill*

The Cambridge Ancient History. 2nd Ed. — *Cameron, A.*

The Cambridge Companion to Quine — *Gibson, Roger F., Jr.*

Cambridge Companion to Canadian Literature — *Kroller, Eva-Marie*

The Cambridge Companion to Chaucer — *Boitani, Piero*

The Cambridge Companion to Christopher Marlowe — *Cheney, Patrick*

The Cambridge Companion to Conducting — *Bowen, Jose Antonio*

The Cambridge Companion to Darwin — *Hodge, Jonathan*

The Cambridge Companion to David Mamet — *Bigsby, Christopher*

The Cambridge Companion to Debussy — *Trezise, Simon*

The Cambridge Companion to Duns Scotus — *Williams, Thomas*

Case Studies in Breastfeeding: Problem-Solving Skills and Strategies — *Cadwell, Karin*

Case Studies in Constructivist Leadership and Teaching — *Shapiro, Arthur*

Case Studies in Environmental Ethics — *Derr, Patrick George*

Case Studies in Estate Planning: with Abridged Student Forms — *Gazur, Wayne M.*

Case Studies in Genes and Disease: A Primer for Clinicians — *Bergeron, Bryan P.*

Case Studies in Immunology: A Clinical Companion, 4th Ed. — *Rosen, Fred*

Case Studies in Japanese Negotiating Behavior — *Blaker, Michael*

Case Studies in School Leadership: Keys to a Successful Principalship — *Hessel, Karen M.*

Case Studies in Sport Communication — *Brown, Robert S.*

Case Studies of City-County Consolidation: Reshaping the Local Government Landscape — *Thurmaier, Kurt*

Case Studies of Families Doing Third-Grade Homework — *Xu, Jianzhong*

Case Studies of U.S. Economic Sanctions: The Chinese, Cuban, and Iranian Experience — *Askari, Hossein G.*

Case Studies on Educational Administration, 4th Ed. — *Kowalski, Theodore J.*

The Case Study Anthology — *Yin, Robert*

Casenote Legal Briefs: Administrative Law, Keyed to Gellhorn and Byse's Administrative Law, 10th Rev. Ed.

Casenote Legal Briefs: Agency and Partnership; Keyed to Hynes and Loewenstein's Agency, Partnership, and the LLC, 6th Ed.

Casenote Legal Briefs: Business Organizations

Casenote Legal Briefs: Business Organizations, Keyed to 'O'Kelley and Thompson's Corporations and Other Business Associations, Cases and Materials'

Casenote Legal Briefs: Civil Procedure; Keyed to Field, Kaplan, and Clermont's Civil Procedure: Materials for a Basic Course, 8th Ed.

Casenote Legal Briefs: Community Property, Keyed to Blumberg's 'Community Property in California'

Casenote Legal Briefs: Constitutional Law, Keyed to Farber, Eskridge, and Frickey's 'Constitutional Law, Themes for the Constitutions's Third Century'

Casenote Legal Briefs: Contracts, Keyed to Dawson, Harvey, and Henderson's 'Contracts, Cases and Materials'

Casenote Legal Briefs: Contracts; Keyed to Murphy, Speidel, and Ayres's Studies in Contract Law, 6th Ed.

Casenote Legal Briefs: Criminal Procedures; Keyed to Weaver, Abramson, Bacigal, Burkoff, Hancock, and Lively's Criminal Procedure

Casenote Legal Briefs: Evidence Keyed to Sklansky's 'Evidence: Cases, Commentary, and Problems'

Casenote Legal Briefs: Health Care Law, Keyed to Hall, Bobinski, and Orentlicher's 'Health Care Law and Ethics'

Casenote Legal Briefs: Patent Law, Keyed to Adelman, Rader, Thomas, and Wagner's 'Cases and Materials on Patent Law'

Cases and Materials on Environmental Law, 6th Ed. — *Findley, Roger W.*

Cases and Materials on Torts, 8th Ed. — *Epstein, Richard Allen*

Cases and Text on Property, 5th Ed. — *Casner, A. James*

Cases in Health Services Management, 4th Ed. — *Rakich, Jonathon*

Cases in Human Parasitology — *Heelan, Judith Stephenson*

Cases, Problems, and Materials on Contracts, 4th Ed. — *Crandall, Thomas D.*

The Cash Nexus: Money and Power in the Modern World, 1700-2000 — *Ferguson, Niall*

Cashing in on Pay Equity? Supermarket Restructuring and Gender Equality — *Kainer, Jan*

Cassandra at the Wedding — *Baker, Dorothy*

Cassandra French's Finishing School for Boys — *Garcia, Eric*

Cassiar, a Jewel in the Wilderness — *Leblanc, Suzanne*

c Cassie and the Kiss Soldier — *Rose, Marion*

Cast Iron Toy Cook Stoves and Ranges — *Ford, Dick*

The Cast of Character: Style in Greek Literature — *Worman, Nancy*

Cast of Shadows — *Guilfoile, Kevin*

Casta domus. Un seminario sulla legislazione auguste, 2nd Ed. — *Vigorita, T.S.*

Casta Painting: Images of Race in Eighteenth-Century Mexico — *Katzew, Ilona*

Castaway: Remarkable True Stories of Survival — *Sellick, Douglas R.G.*

c Castaways: Stories of Survival — *Hausman, Gerald*

The Caste War of Yucatan — *Reed, Nelson A.*

Castellani and Italian Archaeological Jewelry — *Soros, Susan Weber*

Castings: Monuments and Monumentality in Poems by Elizabeth Bishop, Robert Lowell, James Merrill, Derek Walcott, and Seamus Heaney — *Rotella, Guy*

The Castle Community: The Personnel of English and Welsh Castles, 1272-1422 — *Rickard, John*

y Castle in the Sky — *Miyazaki, Hayao*

c Castle of Llyr (Read by Langton, James). Audiobook Review — *Alexander, Lloyd*

c The Castle of the Cats (Illus. by Krenina, Katya) — *Kimmel, Eric A.*

The Castlemaine Murders: A Phryne Fisher Mystery — *Greenwood, Kerry*

c Castles — *Sheehan, Sean*

y Castles Burning: A Child's Life in War — *Denes, Magda*

Castles of God: Fortified Religious Buildings of the World — *Harrison, Peter*

y Castles of Steel: Britain, Germany, and the Winning of the Great War at Sea — *Massie, Robert K.*

Castro: A Beginner's Guide — *Connolly, Sean*

y Castro's Cuba — *Carey, Charles W.*

The Casualty Issue″ in American Military Practice: The Impact of World War I — *Huelfer, Evan Andrew*

Casualty of War: The Bush Administration's Assault on a Free Press — *Amherst, David Dadge*

Casualty of War: The Bush Administration's Assault on a Free Press — *Dadge, David*

c The Cat Ate My Gymsuit (Read by Danziger, Paula). Audiobook Review — *Danziger, Paula*

c Cat — *Rayner, Matthew*

c Cat Chat — *Phillips, Meredith*

Cat Cross Their Graves: A Joe Grey Mystery — *Murphy, Shirley Rousseau*

The Cat Fanciers' Association Complete Cat Book — *Siegal, Mordecai*

Cat in an Orange Twist: A Midnight Louie Mystery — *Douglas, Carole Nelson*

c The Cat in the Hat — *Geisel, Theodore Seuss*

The Cat in the Hat's Learning Library

Cat on a Hot Tin Roof — *Williams, Tennessee*

c Cat on the Hill (Illus. by Foreman, Michael) — *Foreman, Michael*

c Cat Poems (Illus. by Petrosino, Tamara) — *Crawley, Dave*

c Cat Trap! — *Gormley, Greg*

Cat vs. Cat: Keeping Peace When You Have More Than One Cat — *Johnson-Bennett, Pam*

The Cat Who Came in from the Cold: A Fable — *Masson, Jeffrey Moussaieff*

The Cat Who Went Bananas — *Braun, Lilian Jackson*

Cataclysm: The First World War as Political Tragedy — *Stevenson, D.*

Cataclysm: The First World War as Political Tragedy — *Wood, Michael*

The Catalan Rule of the Templars — *Upton-Ward, Judi*

The Catalan Rule of the Templars: Edition and Translation of Barcelona, Archivo de la Corona de Aragon — *Reales, Catas*

y Catalina Magdalena Hoopensteiner Wallendiner Hogan Logan Bogan Was Her Name (Illus. by Arnold, Tedd) — *Arnold, Tedd*

A Catalog of Folk Song Settings for Wind Band — *Aldrich, Mark*

Catalog of the Robert L. Sadoff Library of Forensic Psychiatry and Legal Medicine — *Morman, Edward T.*

Cataloger's Judgment: Music Cataloging Questions and Answers from the Music OCLC Users Group Newsletter — *Weitz, Jay*

Cataloging and Classification for Library Technicians — *Kao, Mary Liu*

Cataloging Sheet Maps: The Basics — *Andrew, Paige G.*

Cataloging Sheet Music: Guidelines for Use with AACR2 and the MARC Format — *Schultz, Lois*

Cataloging with AACR2 and MARC21: For Books, Electronic Resources, Sound Recordings, Videorecordings, and Serials — *Fritz, Deborah A.*

Catalogue of European Armour at the Fitzwilliam Museum — *Eaves, Ian*

Catalogue of Jyotisa Manuscripts in the Wellcome Library: Sanskrit Astral and Mathematical Literature — *Pingree, David*

Catalogue of Medieval and Renaissance Manuscripts in the Beinecke Rare Book and Manuscript Library Yale University, Vol. 4 — *Babcock, Robert G.*

Catalogue of the Greek inscriptions in the Sudan National Museum of Khartoum — *Lajtar, Adam*

Catalogue of the Library of the Czech Institute of Egyptology — *Ruzova, Jirina*

Catalogue of the Spanish Collection of the General Land Office, Part I — *Greaser, Galen D.*

Catalogue of the Spanish Collection of the General Land Office, Part II — *Greaser, Galen D.*

Catalonia: History and Culture — *Payne, John*

Catalysis from A to Z: A Concise Encyclopedia. 2nd Ed. — *Cornils, Boy*

Cataract Canyon: A Human and Environmental History of the Rivers in Canyonlands — *Webb, Robert H.*

Cataract Surgery: Techniques, Complications and Management, 2nd Ed. — *Steinert, Roger F.*

Catastrophe and Culture: The Anthropology of Disaster — *Hoffman, Susanna M.*

The Catastrophe of Modernity: Tragedy and the Nation in Latin American Literature — *Dove, Patrick*

Catastrophe: Risk and Response — *Posner, Richard A.*

Catastrophe Theory, 2nd Ed. — *Castrigiano, Domenico P.L.*

Catastrophes and Lesser Calamities: The Causes of Mass Extinctions — *Cressler, W.L., III*

Catastrophes and Lesser Calamities: The Causes of Mass Extinctions — *Hallam, Tony*

Catawba Indian Pottery: The Survival of a Folk Tradition — *Blumer, Thomas John*

Catch-22 — *Heller, Joseph*

Catch And Release: Trout Fishing and the Meaning of Life — *Kingwell, Mark*

The Catch: Families, Fishing, and Faith — *Vande Kopple, William J.*

y Catch Us If You Can — *MacPhail, Catherine*

Catching Fireflies — *Rocca, Tony*

Catching Light: Looking for God in the Movies — *Anker, Roy M.*

c Catching Spring — *Olsen, Sylvia*

The Catechism of the Nazarites and Related Writings — *Papini, Robert*

Categories and Logic in Duns Scotus: An Interpretation of Aristotle's Categories in the Late Thirteenth Century — *Pini, Giorgio*

A Catered Murder — *Crawford, Isis*

A Catered Wedding: A Mystery with Recipes — *Crawford, Isis*

c Caterpillar Dance (Illus. by McBee, Scott) — *Grace, Will*

Catfish, Fiddles, Mules, and More: Missouri's State Symbols — *Fisher, John C.*

Catfishes, Vols. 1-2 — *Arratia, Gloria*

Catharine Maria Sedgwick: Critical Perspectives — *Damon-Bach, Lucinda L.*

c Catharine Parr Traill: Backwoods Pioneer — *Martin, Carol*

Cathedral of the Black Madonna: The Druids and the Mysteries of Chartres — *Markale, Jean*

y Catherine de' Medici and the Protestant Reformation — *Whitelaw, Nancy*

Catherine de Medici: Renaissance Queen of France — *Frieda, Leonie*

y Catherine the Great and the Enlightenment in Russia — *Whitelaw, Nancy*

The Catholic Church and Russia: Popes, Patriarchs, Tsars, and Commissars — *Dunn, Dennis J.*

The Catholic Ethic and Global Capitalism — *Fields, Bryan*

Catholic Families of Southern Maryland: Records of Catholic Residents of St. Mary's County in the 18th Century — *O'Rourke, Timothy J.*

Catholic for a Reason 111: Scripture & the Mystery of the Mass — *Hahn, Scott*

Catholic Higher Education in Protestant America: The Jesuits and Harvard in the Age of the University — *Mahoney, Kathleen A.*

A Catholic New Deal: Religion and Reform in Depression Pittsburgh — *Heineman, Kenneth J.*

Catholic Perspectives on Peace and War — *Massaro, Thomas J.*

The Catholic Revival in English Literature, 1845-1961 — *Ker, I.T.*

Chasing the Dragon — *Stansberry, Domenic*
Chasing the Molecule — *Buckingham, John*
Chasing the Rodeo: on Wild Rides and Big Dreams, Broken Hearts and Broken Bones, and One Man's Search for the West — *Stratton, W.K.*
y Chasing the Sea: Being a Narrative of a Journey through Uzbekistan...the Aral Sea, the World's Worst Man-Made Ecological Catastrophe — *Bissell, Tom*
Chasing the Silver Bullet: U.S Air Force Weapons Development from Vietnam to Desert Storm — *Werell, Kenneth P.*
Chasing the Silver Bullet: U.S. Air Force Weapons Development from Vietnam to Desert Storm — *Werrell, Kenneth P.*
Chasing Tornadoes — *Lindop, Laurie*
y Chasing Vermeer (Illus. by Helquist, Brett) — *Balliett, Blue*
y Chasing Vermeer — *Balliett, Blue*
c Ch'askin: A Legend of the Sechelt People (Illus. by Jeffries, Jamie) — *Joe, Donna*
Chasm: A Weekend — *Tanning, Dorothea*
Chassis Design: Principles and Analysis, Based on Previously Unpublished Technical Notes by Maurice Olley — *Milliken, William F.*
Chateaubriand: Poesie et terreur — *Fumaroli, Marc*
The Chatham House Version and Other Middle-Eastern Studies — *Kedourie, Elie*
Chattanooga Choo Choo: The Life and Times of the World Famous Glenn Miller Orchestra — *Grudens, Richard*
Chattel House Blues: Making of a Democractic Society in Barbados — *Beckles, Hilary*
Chatter: Dispatches from the Secret World of Global Eavesdropping — *Keefe, Patrick Radden*
Chaucer and Boccaccio: Antiquity and Modernity — *Edwards, Robert R.*
Chaucer and the Challenges of Medievalism: Studies in Honour of H.A. Kelly — *Minkova, Donka*
Chaucer and the House of Fame — *Morgan, Philippa*
Chaucer and the Jews: Sources, Contexts, Meanings — *Delany, Sheila*
Chaucer as Children's Literature: Retellings from the Victorian and Edwardian Eras — *Richmond, Velma Bourgeois*
Chaucer — *Ackroyd, Peter*
Chaucer's Body: The Anxiety of Circulation in the Canterbury Tales — *Shoaf, R. Allen*
Chaucer's Cultural Geography — *Lynch, Kathryn L.*
Chaucer's Pardoner and Gender Theory: Bodies of Discourse — *Sturges, Robert S.*
The Chautauqua Moment: Protestants, Progressives, and the Culture of Modern Liberalism — *Rieser, Andrew C.*
Cheap Chickens: Feeding Africa's Poor — *Zachary, G. Pascal*
Cheap Laffs: The Art of the Novelty Item — *Newgarden, Mark*
Cheapskates — *Stella, Carmelo*
Cheat and Charmer — *Frank, Elizabeth*
Cheat and Charmer — *Novel, Elizabeth Frank*
The Cheating Culture — *Callahan, Avid*
y The Cheating Culture: Why More Americans are Doing Wrong to Get Ahead — *Callahan, David*
Chechnya: Life in a War-Torn Society — *Tishkov, Valery*
Chechnya: To the Heart of a Conflict — *Meier, Andrew*
Check It While I Wreck It: Black Womanhood, Hip Hop Culture, and the Public Sphere — *Pough, Gwendolyn D.*
The Checkbook and the Cruise Missile: Conversations with Arundhati Roy — *Barsamian, David*
Checkered Courage: Chuckwagon Racing's Glass Family — *Mikkelsen, Glen*
Checking Executive Power: Presidential Impeachment in Comparative Perspective — *Baumgartner, Jody C.*
Checkpoint — *Baker, Nicholson*
Checkpoint Controls and Cancer, Vol 1: Reviews and Model Systems — *Schonthal, Axel H.*
Checkpoint Controls and Cancer, Vol. 2: Activation and Regulation Protocols — *Schonthal, Axel H.*
Chee Chee: A Study of Aboriginal Suicide — *Evans, Al*
c Cheerleading in Action (Illus. by Rouse, Bonna) — *Crossingham, John*
y Cheeseburger Subversive — *Scarsbrook, Richard*
c Cheetahs — *Estigarribia, Diana*
c Cheetahs — *Stille, Darlene R.*
Chef in Your Backpack — *Bassett, Nicole*
Chekhov: Scenes from a Life — *Bartlett, Rosamund*

Chekhov's Doctors: A Collection of Chekhov's Medical Tales — *Coulehan, J.*
c Chelsea Morning (Illus. by Froud, Brian) — *Mitchell, Joni*
Chemical Analysis Based on Nonlinearity — *Nakata, Satoshi*
y Chemical and Biological Warfare — *Judson, Karen*
Chemical and Functional Properties of Food Saccharides — *Tomasik, Piotr*
Chemical Concepts in Pollutant Behavior, 2nd Ed. — *Tinsley, Ian J.*
Chemical Consequences: Environmental Mutagens, Scientist Activism, and the Rise of Genetic Toxicology — *Frickel, Scott*
Chemical Genomics — *Darvas, Ferenc*
Chemical Micro Process Engineering — *Hessel, Volker*
Chemical Pesticides: Mode of Action and Toxicology — *Stenersen, Jorgen*
Chemical Process Research: The Art of Practical Organic Synthesis — *Abdel-Magid, Ahmed F.*
Chemical Protective Clothing, 2nd Ed. — *Daniel, H. Anna*
y Chemical Reactions — *Baldwin, Carol*
Chemical Reactions in Liquid and Solid Phase: Kinetics and Thermodynamics — *Zaikov, Gennadii Efremovich*
Chemical Reactors: From Design to Operation — *Trambouze, Pierre*
Chemical Vapor Deposition Polymerization: The Growth and Properties of Parylene Thin Films — *Fortin, Jeffrey B.*
Chemical Vapor Deposition XVI and EUROCVD 14, Vols. 1-2 — *Allendorf, Mark Donald*
Chemistry: A Project of the American Chemical Society — *Bell, Jerry A.*
Chemistry and Politics: The History of Huls Chemical Works, 1938-1979 — *Lorentz, Bernhard*
Chemistry! Best Science Projects
Chemistry for Today: General, Organic, and Biochemistry, 5th Ed. — *Seager, Spencer L.*
Chemistry: Foundation and Applications. Vol. 4
y Chemistry: Foundations and Applications — *Lagowski, J.J.*
y Chemistry: Foundations and Applications. Vol. 1-4 — *Logowski, J.J.*
Chemistry in Alternative Reaction Media — *Adams, Dave J.*
The Chemistry Must Be Right: The Privatization of Buna Sow Leuna Olefinverbund GmbH — *Karlsch, Rainer*
The Chemistry of Explosives, 2nd Ed. — *Akhavan, Jacqueline*
The Chemistry of Nanomaterials: Synthesis, Properties and Applications — *Rao, C.N.R.*
Chemistry Resources in the Electronic Age — *Bazler, Judith A.*
y Chemistry Science Fair Projects Using Acids, Bases, Metals, Salts, and Inorganic Stuff — *Gardner, Robert*
Chemistry: The Science in Context, 1st Ed. — *Gilbert, Thomas R.*
Chemoinformatics: Concepts, Methods, and Tools for Drug Discovery — *Bajorath, Jurgen*
Chemometrics from Basics to Wavelet Transform — *Chau, Foo-Tim*
Chemoreception: From Cellular Signalling to Functional Plasticity, Proceedings — *Pequignot, Jean-Marc*
c Chemotherapy — *Bardhan-Quallen, Sudipta*
Chemotherapy for Gynecological Neoplasms: Current Therapy and Novel Approaches — *Angioli, Roberto*
Chemoton Theory — *Ganti, Tibor*
Chercheurs d'absolu: Mauriac et de Gaulle, Chroniques et discours, 1945-1948 — *Scott, Malcolm*
Cherchez lebon pain: Guide des Meilleurs Boulangeries de Paris — *Kaplan, Steven L.*
Cherished — *Reeves, Adrienne Ellis*
Cherished Possessions: A New England Legacy — *Carlisle, Nancy*
y The Chernagor Pirates — *Chernenko, Dan*
Cherokee Cases: Two Landmark Federal Decisions in the Fight for Sovereignty — *Norgren, Jill*
Cherokee Voices: Early Accounts of Cherokee Life in the East — *Rozema, Vicki*
Cherokee Women in Crisis: Trail of Tears, Civil War, and Allotment, 1838-1907 — *Johnston, Carolyn Ross*
Cherries in the Snow — *Forrest, Emma*
c Cherry Bites — *Preston, Alison*
Cherry — *Thorne, Matt*
c The Cherry Tree Egg — *Birchall, Mark*

Che's Chevrolet, Fidel's Oldsmobile: On the Road in Cuba — *Schweid, Richard*
Chesapeake Bay Buyboats — *Chowning, Larry S.*
Chesley Awards — *Humphrey, Elizabeth*
Chess: 60 Years on with Caissa and Friends — *Phillips, Alan*
The Chess Artist: Genius, Obsession, and the World's Oldest Game — *Hallman, J.C.*
A Chess Biography by Richard Forster — *Burn, Amos*
c Chess — *Rau, Dana Meachen*
Chester Alan Arthur — *Karabell, Zachary*
c Chestnut (Illus. by Whyte, Mary) — *McGeorge, Constance W.*
c Chestnut (Illus. by Whyte, Mary) — *MeGeorge, Constance W.*
Chewing Gum: The Fortunes of Taste — *Redclift, Michael*
c Chewing the Seatbelt — *Daddo, Andrew*
Chez Charlotte and Fin-De-Siecle Montparnasse — *Crombie, John*
The Chicago Guide to Communicating Science — *Montgomery, Scott L.*
The Chicago Guide to Writing about Numbers — *Mller, Jane E.*
Chicana Feminisms: A Critical Reader — *Arredondo, Gabriela F.*
Chicana/o Identity in a Changing U.S Society: Quien Soy?, Quienes Somos? — *Hurtado, Aida*
Chicano Visions: American Painters on the Verge — *Yanez, Rene*
c Chicka Chicka 1, 2, 3 (Illus. by Ehlert, Lois) — *Martin, Bill, Jr.*
Chickamauga 1863: The River of Death — *Arnold, James R.*
c Chicken Bedtime Is Really Early (Illus. by Bates, George) — *Perl, Erica, S.*
Chicken Dreaming Corn — *Hoffman, Roy*
y Chicken Friend — *Morgan, Nicola*
c Chicken in the Kitchen (Illus. by Taylor, Eleanor) — *Johnston, Tony*
Chicken Soup for the African American Soul: Celebrating and Sharing Our Culture One Story at a Time — *Canfield, Jack*
Chicken Soup for the African American Soul: Celebrating and Sharing Our Culture One Story at a Time — *Hansen, Mark Victor*
Chicken Soup for the Girlfriend's Soul: Stories Celebrating the Magic of Friendship — *Canfield, Jack*
Chicken Soup for the Recovering Soul: Your Personal, Portable Support Group with Stories of Healing, Hope, Love and Resilience — *Canfield, Jack*
Chief Daniel Bread and the Oneida Nation of Indians of Wisconsin — *Hauptman, Laurence M.*
c Chief Joseph, 1840-1904 — *Englar, Mary*
Chief Justice Cornelius of Pakistan: An Analysis with Letters and Speeches — *Braibanti, Ralph*
A Chief Lieutenant of the Tuskegee Machine: Charles Banks of Mississippi — *Jackson, David H., Jr.*
Chief of Staff: Lyndon Johnson and His Presidency — *Watson, W. Marvin*
c Chief Red Cloud, 1822-1909 — *Monroe, Judy*
c Chief Sunrise, John McGraw, and Me (Illus. by Copeland, Greg) — *Tocher, Timothy*
c Chief: The Life of Peter J. Ganci, a New York City Firefighter — *Ganci, Chris*
Chief Whip: People, Power and Patronage in Westminster — *Renton, Tim*
The Chieftain: A Comic Opera in Two Acts — *Sullivan, Arthur*
c Chien-Shiung Wu: Pioneering Physicist and Atomic Researcher — *Macbain, Jennifer*
Chiffon Saris — *Jussawalla, Feroza*
c Chiggers — *Jarrow, Gail*
Chikubushima: Deploying the Sacred Arts in Momoyama Japan — *Watsky, Andrew M.*
Child Abuse Sourcebook — *Matthews, Dawn D.*
Child and Adolescent Development: A Behavioral Systems Approach — *Novak, Gary*
Child and Adolescent Mental Health — *Kaye, David L.*
Child and Family Assessment in Social Work Practice — *Holland, Sally*
Child Care & Inequality: Rethinking Carework for Children and Youth — *Cancian, Francesca M.*
The Child Care Problem: An Economic Analysis — *Blau, David*
Child Development through Sports — *Humphrey, James Harry*
y The Child Goddess — *Marley, Louise*
Child Guidance through Play: Teaching Positive Social Behaviors — *Wolfgang, Charles H.*

y Cities — *Bowden, Rob*

Cities — *Crowther, Peter*

Cities in the International Marketplace: The Political Economy of Urban Development in North America and Western Europe — *Savitch, H.V.*

y Cities of Blood — *Ackroyd, Peter*

Cities of Ideas: Civil Society and Urban Governance in Britain 1800-2000, Essays in Honour of David Reader (i.e. Reeder). — *Colls, Robert*

Cities of Words: Pedagogical Letters on a Register of the Moral Life — *Cavell, Stanley*

Cities on the Plains: The Evolution of Urban Kansas — *Shortridge, James R.*

Cities, Sin, and Social Reform in Imperial Germany — *Lees, Andrew*

The Cities, the Towns, the Crowds: The Paintings of Robert Spencer — *Peterson, Brian H.*

Citizen Bachae: Women's Ritual Practice in Ancient Greece — *Goff, Barbara*

Citizen — *Feld, Andrew*

Citizen Cyborg: Why Democratic Societies Must Respond to the Redesigned Human of the Future — *Hughes, James H.*

Citizen Democracy: Political Activists in a Cynical Age, 2nd Ed. — *Frantzich, Stephen E.*

y Citizen Girl — *McLaughlin, Emma*

Citizen Girl — *Nicola, Kraus*

Citizen Girl — *McLaughlin, Emma*

Citizen Hobo: How a Century of Homelessness Shaped America. — *DePastino, Todd*

Citizen Labillardiere: A Naturalist's Life in Revolution and Exploration — *Duyker, Edward*

Citizen Labillardiere: A Naturalist's Life in Revolution and Exploration — *Edward, Duyker*

Citizen of the Galaxy (Read by James, Lloyd). Audiobook Review — *Heinlein, Robert A.*

Citizen Vince — *Walter, Jess*

Citizens and Aliens: Foreigners and the Law in Britain and the German States 1789-1870 — *Fahrmeir, Andreas*

Citizens and Citoyens: Republicans and Liberals in America and France — *Hulliung, Mark*

Citizens — *Gidengil, Elisabeth*

Citizens of the Empire: The Struggle to Claim our Humanity — *Jensen, Robert*

Citizens on Stage: Comedy and Political Culture in the Athenian Democracy — *McGlew, James F.*

The Citizen's Voice: Twentieth-Century Politics and Literature — *Keren, Michael*

Citizens Without Shelter: Homelessness, Democracy, and Political Exclusion — *Feldman, Leonard C.*

Citizenship and Management in Public Administration: Integrating Behavioral Theories and Managerial Thinking — *Vigoda-Gadot, Eran*

Citizenship and the Environment — *Dobson, Andrew*

Citizenship: Feminist Perspectives — *Lister, Ruth*

Citizenship in European Cities: Immigrants, Local Politics, and Integration Policies — *Penninx, Rinus*

Citizenship in Transformation in Canada — *Hebert, Yvonne M.*

Citizenship Papers — *Berry, Wendell*

Citizenship: Personal Lives and Social Policy — *Lewis, Gail*

Citizenship Revisited: Threats or Opportunities of Shifting Boundaries — *Herrmann, Peter*

Citrix Metaframe Access Suite for Windows Server 2003: The Official Guide — *Reeser, Tim*

Citrus: Production, Postharvest, Disease and Pest Management — *Mukhopadhyay, S.*

c City 123 (Illus. by Milich, Zoran) — *Milich, Zoran*

The City: A Global History — *Kotkin, Joel*

c The City ABC Book — *Milich, Zoran*

City and Enterprise: Corporate Community Involvement in European and US Cities — *Berg, Leo van den*

City and the Railway in Europe — *Roth, Ralf*

The City and the Theatre: The History of New York Playhouses: A 250 Year Journey from Bowling Green to Times Square — *Henderson, Mary C.*

c City Angel (Illus. by Brooker, Kyrsten) — *Spinelli, Eileen*

c City Angel (Illus. by Pederson, Janet) — *Spinelli, Eileen*

The City at Stake: Secession, Reform, and the Battle for Los Angeles — *Sonenshein, Raphael J.*

c City Bear — *Dixon, Dougal*

City — *Baricco, Alessandro*

The City — *Hinds, Kathryn*

City Boy — *Thompson, Jean*

City-County Consolidation and Its Alternatives: Reshaping the Local Government Landscape — *Carr, Jered B.*

A City Equal to My Desire — *Sallis, James*

The City in Roman Byzantine Egypt — *Alston, R.*

City in the Sky: The Rise and Fall of the World Trade Center — *Glanz, James*

City Matters: Competitiveness, Cohesion and Urban Governance — *Boddy, Martin*

City Merchants and the Arts 1670-1720 — *Galinou, Mireille*

City of Courts: Socializing Justice in Progressive Era Chicago — *Willrich, Michael*

City of Darkness, City of Light: Emigre Filmmakers in Paris 1929-1939 — *Phillips, Alastair*

c The City of Ember. Audiobook Review — *DuPrau, Jeanne*

c The City of Ember — *DuPrau, Jeanne*

c The City of Ember — *DuPrau, Jeanne*

A City of Gardens — *Seeber, Barbara*

y City of Glass — *Auster, Paul*

City of Glass (Illus. by Mazzucchelli, David) — *Karasik, Paul*

City of Glass — *Mazzucchelli, David*

City of Light: The Story of Fiber Optics, Rev. Ed. — *Hecht, Jeff*

The City of Musical Memory: Salsa, Record Grooves, and Popular Culture in Cali, Colombia — *Waxer, Lise A.*

y City of One: Young Writers Speak to the World — *DeDonato, Colette*

City of Quarters: Urban Villages in the Contemporary City — *Bell, David*

The City of Sardis: Approaches in Graphic Recording — *Greenewalt, Crawford H., Jr.*

The City of Sealions — *Sallis, Eva*

c City of Snow: The Great Blizzard of 1888 (Illus. by Filippucci, Laura) — *High, Linda Oatman*

y City of the Soul: A Walk in Rome (Read by Gardner, Grover). Audiobook Review — *Murray, William*

City Politics: Private Power and Public Policy, 4th Ed. — *Judd, Dennis R.*

City Profiles U.S.A. 2005: A Traveler's Guide to Major U.S. Cities, 7th ed.

The City Reader, 3rd Ed. — *LeGates, Richard T.*

City Room — *Gelb, Arthur*

City Schools and the American Dream: Reclaiming the Promise of Public Education — *Noguera, Pedro*

City: Urbanism and Its End — *Rae, Douglas W.*

Civic Capitalism: The State of Childhood — *O'Neill, John*

Civic Culture and Urban Change: Governing Dallas — *Hanson, Royce*

Civic Enculturation: Nation-State, Schools and Ethnic Difference in Four European Countries — *Schiffauer, Werner*

Civic Revolutionaries: Igniting the Passion for Change in America's Communities — *Henton, Douglas*

Civic Service: What Difference Does It Make? — *Perry, James L.*

Civil and Uncivil Violence in Lebanon: A History of the Internationalization of Communal Conflict — *Khalaf, Samir*

Civil Disobedience: A Wadsworth Casebook in Argument — *Walsh, Sharon K.*

Civil Disobedience — *Falcon y Tella, Maria Jose*

y Civil Disobedience — *Kirk, Andrew*

Civil Disobediences: Poetics and Politics in Action — *Waldman, Anne*

'Civil Disorder Is the Disease of Ibadan': Chieftaincy & Civic Culture in a Yoruba City — *Watson, Ruth*

Civil Gang Abatement: The Effectiveness and Implications of Policing by Injunction — *Allan, Edward L.*

c Civil Liberties — *Ojeda, Auriana*

y Civil Liberties in America: A Reference Handbook — *Walker, Samuel*

Civil-Military Relations, Nation Building, and National Identity: Comparative Perspectives — *Danopoulos, Constantine P.*

Civil Procedure, 2nd Ed. — *Emanuel, Steven L.*

y The Civil Rights Act of 1964 — *Mayer, Robert H.*

Civil Rights Chronicle: The American Struggle for Freedom — *Bauerlein, Mark*

Civil Rights Crossroads: Nation, Community, and the Black Freedom Struggle — *Lawson, Steven F.*

y The Civil Rights Movement — *Dunn, John M.*

c The Civil Rights Movement — *Kallen, Stuart*

Civil Rights Movement — *Newman, Mark*

The Civil Rights Movement — *Ritchie, Nigel*

y The Civil Rights Movement — *Treanor, Nick*

c The Civil Rights Movement — *Venable, Rose*

c The Civil Rights Movement for Kids: A History with 21 Activities — *Turck, Mary C.*

y The Civil Rights Movement in America from 1865 to the Present — *McKissack, Patricia*

Civil Rights Unionism: Tobacco Workers and the Struggle for Democracy in the Mid-Twentieth Century South — *Korstad, Robert Rodgers*

Civil Rights Unionism: Tobacco Workers and the Struggle for Democracy in the Mid-Twentieth-Century South — *Korstad, Robert Rodgers*

Civil Rights Unionism: Tobacco Workers and the Struggle for Democracy in the Mid-Twentieth Century South — *Rodgers, Robert*

Civil Service Systems in Anglo-American Countries — *Halligan, John*

Civil Society in the Baltic Sea Region — *Gotz, Norbert*

c Civil War A to Z — *Bolotin, Norman*

Civil War America: Making a Nation, 1848-1877 — *Cook, Robert*

c The Civil War at Sea — *Anderson, Dale*

c The Civil War

y The Civil War — *Tackach, James*

Civil War Heavy Explosive Ordnance: A Guide to Large Artillery Projectiles, Torpedoes, and Mines. — *Bell, Jack*

c The Civil War in the East

c The Civil War in the West

Civil War Ironclads: The U.S. Navy and Industrial Mobilization — *Roberts, William H.*

Civil War on Race Street: The Civil Rights Movement in Cambridge, Maryland — *Levy, Peter B.*

Civil War Pharmacy: A History of Drugs, Drug Supply and Provision, and Therapeutics for the Union and Confederacy — *Flannery, Michael A.*

The Civil War Research Guide — *McManus, Stephen*

Civil War: The Wars of the Three Kingdoms 1638-1660 — *Royle, Trevor*

The Civil War. Vols. 1-10

Civil Wars: A Battle for Gay Marriage — *Moats, David*

Civilising Subjects: Colony and Metropole in the English Imagination, 1830-1867 — *Hall, Catherine*

Civilising Subjects: Metropole and Colony in the English Imagination, 1830-1867 — *Hall, Catherine*

Civility in the City: Blacks, Jews, and Koreans in Urban America — *Lee, Jennifer*

Civilization and Its Enemies: The Next Stage of History — *Harris, Lee*

Civilization in Dispute: Historical Questions and Theoretical Traditions — *Arnason, Johann P.*

The Civilization of the Holocaust in Italy: Poets, Artists, Saints, Anti-Semites — *Feinstein, Wiley*

Civilizations of Africa: A History to 1800 — *Ehret, Christopher*

Civilizing Natures: Race, Resources, and Modernity in Colonial South India — *Philip, Kavita*

c Clabbernappers — *Bailey, Len*

Cladistics and Archaeology — *O'Brien, Michael J.*

Cladistics and Archeology — *O'Braien, Michael J.*

Claiming Knowledge: Strategies of Epistemology from Theosophy to the New Age — *Hammer, Olav*

The Claims of Kinfolk: African American Property and Community in the Nineteenth-Century South — *Penningroth, Dylan C.*

Claire Denis — *Beugnet, Martine*

Claire Voyant — *Rosenberg, Saralee*

Claire's Head — *Bush, Catherine*

Clara Collet, 1860-1948: An Educated Working Woman — *McDonald, Deborah*

Clara Kathleen Rogers — *Radell, Judith*

y Clara's Grand Tour: Travels with a Rhinoceros in Eighteenth-Century Europe — *Ridley, Glynis*

c Clare and Francis — *Visconte, Guido*

c Clarice Bean Spells Trouble — *Child, Lauren*

The Clarinet in the Classical Period — *Rice, Albert R.*

The Clarinet Polka — *Maillard, Keith*

Clarke's Analysis of Drugs and Poisons in Pharmaceuticals, Body Fluids and Postmortem Material, 3rd Ed. — *Moffat, Anthony C.*

Clash of Globalizations? The Politics of International Labor Rights in the United States — *Greven, Thomas*

c A Clash of Kings (Read by Dotrice, Roy). Audiobook Review — *Martin, George R.R.*

Clash of Loyalties: A Border County in the Civil War — *Shaffer, John W.*

The Clash of Orthodoxies: Law, Religion and Morality in Crisis — *George, Robert P.*

Clash of Titans: How the Unbridled Ambition of Ted Turner and Rupert Murdoch Has Created Global Empires That Control What We Read and Watch Each Day — *Hack, Richard*

Class and News — *Heider, Don*

Communicative Competence for Individuals Who Use AAC from Research to Effective Practice — *Light, Janice C.*

The Communist Takeover of Hangzhou: The Transformation of City and Cadre, 1949-1954 — *Gao, James Zheng*

The Communitarian Constitution — *Breslin, Beau*

The Communitarian Moment: The Radical Challenge of the Northampton Association — *Clark, Christopher*

The Communitarian Persuasion — *Selznik, Philip*

The Communitarian Reader: Beyond the Essentials — *Etzioni, Amitai*

The Communitarian Third Way: Alexandre Marc's Ordre Nouveau, 1930-2000 — *Hellman, John*

Communities in Globalization: The Invisibile Mayan Nahual — *Sainz, Juan Pablo Perez*

Communities of Informed Judgement: Newman's Illative and Accounts of Rationality — *Aquino, Frederick D.*

Communities of the Air: Radio Century, Radio Culture — *Squier, Susan Merrill*

Communities of Work: Rural Restructuring in Local and Global Contexts — *Falk, William W.*

Communities of Work: Rural Restructuring in Local and Global Contexts — *Faulk, William W.*

Community and Conscience: The Jews in Apartheid South Africa — *Shimoni, Gideon*

Community and the World: Participating in Social Change — *Dickinson, Torry D.*

Community as Partner: Theory and Practice in Nursing, 4th Ed. — *Anderson, Elizabeth T.*

Community-Based Health Research: Issues and Methods — *Blumenthal, Daniel S.*

Community — *Delanty, Gerard*

A Community Built in Words: The Constitution in History and Politics — *Powell, H. Jefferson*

A Community Built on Words: The Constitution in History and Politics — *Powell, Jefferson H.*

Community Colleges: A Model for Latin America? — *de Moura Castro, Claudio*

Community Diaries: Arkansas Newspapering, 1819-2002 — *Dougan, Michael B.*

Community Economics: Linking Theory and Practice, 2nd Ed. — *Shaffer, Ron*

A Community for Children?: Children, Citizenship, and Internal Migration in the EU. — *Ackers, Louise*

Community in The Digital Age: Philosophy and Practice — *Feenberg, Andrew*

Community Interventions to Create Change in Children — *London, Lorna H.*

Community of the Cross: Moravian Piety in Colonial Bethlehem — *Atwood, Craig D.*

Community Organizing Against Homophobia and Heterosexism: The World through Rainbow-Colored Glasses — *Wehbi, Samantha*

Community Policing: Partnerships for Problem Solving, 4th Ed. — *Miller, Linda S.*

Community Practice: Theories and Skills for Social Workers, 2nd Ed. — *Hardcastle, David A.*

Community: Pursuing the Dream, Living the Reality — *Keller, Suzanne*

Community Radio in Bolivia: The Miner's Radio Station — *O'Connor, Alan*

Community Social Action for School Reform — *Baum, Howell S.*

Como bestia que duerme — *Cela Conde, Camilo Jose*

Compact Handbook of Computational Biology — *Konopka, Andrzej K.*

A Companion for Owls: Being the Commonplace Book of D. Boone, Long Hunter, Back Woodsman — *Manning, Maurice*

A Companion Guide to the Folklore, Myths & Customs of Britain — *Alexander, Marc*

Companion Handbook to the Chemotherapy Sourcebook, 2nd Ed. — *Perry, Michael C.*

A Companion to 20th-Century America — *Whitfield, Stephen J.*

A Companion to African Philosophy — *Wiredu, Kwasi*

A Companion to American Relations — *Schulzinger, Robert D.*

A Companion to Ancrene Wisse — *Wada, Yoko*

A Companion to Archaeology — *Bintliff, John*

A Companion to Britain in the Later Middle Ages — *Rigby, S.H.*

A Companion to Colonial America — *Vickers, Daniel*

A Companion to Cultural Geography — *Duncan, James S.*

A Companion to Faulkner Studies — *Peek, Charles A.*

A Companion to Gender History — *Meade, Teresa A.*

A Companion to German Realism, 1848-1900 — *Kontje, Todd*

A Companion to Gower — *Echard, Sian*

An Companion to Linguistic Anthropology — *Duranti, Alessandro*

The Companion to Little Dorrit — *Philpotts, Trey*

Companion to Medieval Arms and Armour — *Nicolle, David*

A Companion to Petronius — *Courtney, E.*

A Companion to Philosophy in the Middle Ages — *Gracia, Jorge J.E.*

A Companion to Qualitative Research — *Flick, Uwe*

A Companion to Rhetoric and Rhetorical Criticism — *Jost, Walter*

A Companion to Roman Britain — *Todd, Malcolm*

A Companion to Shakespeare's Works — *Dutton, Richard*

A Companion to the Anthropology of Politics — *Nugent, David*

A Companion to the Eucharist of the Church — *Patey, Cecil*

A Companion to the Fairy Tale — *Davidson, Hilda Ellis*

A Companion to the Hellenistic World — *Erskine, Andrew*

A Companion to the History of Economic Thought — *Samuels, Warren J.*

A Companion to the Lancelot-Grail Cycle — *Dover, Carol*

A Companion to the Literature and Culture of the American South — *Gray, Richard*

A Companion to the Reformation World — *Hsia, R. Po-Chia*

A Companion to the Regional Literatures of America — *Crow, Charles L.*

A Companion to the Victorian Novel — *Brantlinger, Patrick*

A Companion to the Works of Arthur Schnitzler — *Lorenz, Dagmar C.G.*

A Companion to the Works of Elias Canetti — *Lorenz, Dagmar C.G.*

A Companion to the Works of Franz Kafka — *Rolleston, James*

A Companion to the Works of Heinrich Heine — *Cook, Roger F.*

A Companion to the Works of Heinrich von Kleist — *Fischer, Bernd*

A Companion to the Works of Thomas Mann — *Lehnert, Herbert*

A Companion to the Worlds of the Renaissance — *Ruggiero, Guido*

A Companion to Tourism — *Lew, Alan A.*

The Companions — *Tepper, Sheri S.*

The Company Doctor: Risk, Responsibility, and Corporate Professionalism — *Draper, Elaine*

Company Man (Read by Brick, Scott). Audiobook Review — *Finder, Joseph*

Company Man — *Finder, Joseph*

Company of Adventurers: How the Hudson's Bay Empire Determined the Destiny of a Continent — *Newman, Peter C.*

A Company of Fools — *Ellis, Deborah*

Company of Rebels — *Lord, Elizabeth*

The Company of Strangers: A Natural History of Economic Life — *Seabright, Paul*

The Company of Strangers — *Powell, Gus*

The Company of the Future: Meeting the Management Challenges of the Communications Revolutions — *Cairncross, Frances*

Company Towns of the Pacific Northwest — *Carlson, Linda*

The Company You Keep — *Gordon, Neil*

Comparative Biomechanics: Life's Physical World — *Vogel, Steven*

Comparative Bureaucratic Systems — *Tummala, Krishna K.*

Comparative Constitutionalism and Good Governance in the Commonwealth: An Eastern and Southern African Perspective — *Hatchard, Johan*

Comparative Development Experiences of Sub-Saharan Africa and East Asia: An Institutional Approach — *Nissanke, Machiko*

Comparative Education: Continuing Traditions, New Challenges, and New Paradigms — *Bray, Mark*

Comparative Education: The Dialectic of the Global and the Local, 2nd Ed. — *Arnove, Robert F.*

Comparative Essays in Early Greek and Chinese Rational Thinking — *Reding, Jean-Paul*

A Comparative Glossary of Cypriot Maronite Arabic (Arabic-English): With an Introductory Essay — *Borg, Alexander*

Comparative Health Information Management, 2nd Ed. — *Peden, Ann H.*

Comparative Health Policy — *Blank, Robert H.*

Comparative Historical Analysis in the Social Sciences — *Mahoney, James*

Comparative Income Taxation: A Structural Analysis, 2nd Ed. — *Ault, Hugh J.*

Comparative Labour Law and Industrial Relations in Industrialized Market Economies, 8th Ed. — *Blanpain, R.*

Comparative Law and Economics — *Geest, Gerrit de*

Comparative Law in the Courtroom and Classroom: The Story of the Last Thirty-Five Years — *Markesinis, Basil*

Comparative Politics Using MicroCase ExplorIt, 3rd Ed. — *Le Roy, Michael K.*

Comparative Psychology of Mental Development — *Werner, Heinz*

Comparative Regional Integration: Theoretical Perspectives — *Laursen, Finn*

A Comparative Sociology of World Religions: Virtuosos, Priests and Popular Religion — *Sharot, Stephen*

A Comparative Study of Longinus and Al-Jurjani: The Interrelationships Between Medieval Arabic Literary Criticism and Graeco-Roman Poetics — *Abdulla, Adnan K.*

A Comparative Study of Six City-State Cultures: An Investigation — *Hansen, M.H.*

Comparative Theology: Essays for Keith Ward — *Bartel, T.W.*

Comparative Vertebrate Cognition: Are Primates Superior to Non-Primates? — *Rogers, Lesley J.*

Comparing Cultures: Dimensions of Culture in a Comparative Perspective — *Vinken, Henk*

Comparing Empires: European Colonialism from Portuguese Expansion to the Spanish-American War — *Hart, Jonathan*

Comparing Media Systems: Three Models of Media and Politics — *Hallin, Daniel C.*

Comparing Media Systems: Three Models of Media and Politics — *Rabinovitz, Lauren*

Comparing Theories of Child Development, 6th Ed. — *Thomas, R. Murray*

Comparing Welfare Capitalism: Social Policy and Political Economy in Europe, Japan, and the United States — *Ebbinghaus, Bernhard*

Compartment Syndromes: Diagnosis, Treatment, and Complications — *Styf, Jorma*

Compass: A Story of Exploration and Innovation — *Gurney, Alan*

Compassionate Canadians: Civic Leaders Discuss Human Rights — *Howard-Hassmann, Rhoda E.*

A Compassionate Conservative: A Political Biography of Joseph W. Martin, Jr., Speaker of the U.S. House of Representatives — *Kenneally, James J.*

Compassionate Respect: A Feminist Approach to Medical Ethics and Other Questions — *Farley, Margaret A.*

Compassion's Way: A Doctor's Quest into the Soul of Medicine — *Crawshaw, Ralph (b. 1921 -)*

Compatibility Breeds Success: How to Manage Your Relationship with Your Business Partner — *Snider, Marvin*

Compatible Forest Management — *Monserud, Robert A.*

Compellence and the Strategic Culture of Imperial Japan: Implications for Coercive Diplomacy in the Twenty-First Century — *Morgan, Forrest E.*

The Compendium of American Genealogy — *Filby, P. William*

Compendium of Intra-African and Related Foreign Trade Statistics, 2003 ed — *Economic Commission for Africa*

Compendium of Intra-African and Related Foreign Trade Statistics, 2003 Ed. — *United Nations Publications*

Compendium of Learning and Development Quizzes — *Cook, Sarah*

Compendium of Ornamental Palm Diseases and Disorders — *Elliott, M.L.*

Compensation and Benefits: Vital Statistics for Your Veterinary Practice. 3rd Ed.

The Compensation Handbook: A State-of-the-Art Guide to Compensation Strategy and Design. 4th Ed. — *Berger, Lance A.*

Compensation Management in a Knowledge-Based World — *Henderson, Richard I.*

Competency-Based Human Resource Management — *Dubois, David D.*

Competing Devotions: Career and Family among Women Executives — *Blair-Loy, Mary*

Creating the American Mind: Intellect and Politics in the Colonial Colleges — *Hoeveler, J. David*

Creating the "Divine" Artist: From Dante to Michelangelo — *Emison, Patricia A.*

Creating the Welfare State in France, 1880-1940 — *Smith, Timothy B.*

Creating Their Own Image: The History of African-American Women Artists — *Farrington, Lisa E.*

Creating Value from Mergers and Acquisitions: The Challenges — *Sudarsanam, Sudi*

Creation: A Reader — *Astley, Jeff*

Creation — *Govier, Katherine*

Creation

c Creation — *McDermott, Gerald*

The Creation of Quaker Theory: Insider Perspectives — *Dandelion, Pink*

The Creation of the Media: Political Origins of Modern Communications — *Starr, Paul*

A Creation-Order Theodicy: God and Gratuitous Evil — *Little, Bruce A.*

Creation out of Nothing: A Biblical, Philosophical, and Scientific Exploration — *Copan, Paul*

Creative Activities for the School Year — *Callihan, Joanna*

Creative and Innovative Network Management — *Popov, Oliver Blagoj*

c Creative Arts and Activities

Creative Book Reports: Fun Projects With Rubrics for Fiction and Nonfiction — *Feber, Jane*

Creative Crocheted Dolls: 50 Whimsical Designs — *Crone-Findlay, Noreen*

Creative Destruction: How Globalization Is Changing the World's Cultures — *Cowen, Tyler*

Creative Glut: Selected Essays — *Shapiro, Karl*

Creative Perseverance: Sustaining Life-Giving Ministry in Today's Church — *Goulding, Gill*

Creative Photoshop Lighting Techniques — *Huggins, Barry*

Creative Scarecrows — *Miller, Marcianne*

Creative Social Research: Rethinking Theories and Methods — *Giri, Ananta Kumar*

Creative Strategy in Advertising, 8th Ed. — *Jewler, A. Jerome*

Creative Women of Korea: The Fifteenth through the Twentieth Centuries — *Kim-Renaud, Young-Key*

Creative Women of Korea: The Fifteenth through the Twentieth Century — *Kim-Renaud, Young-Key*

y Creative Writing the Easy Way — *Hirschi, Heather L.*

Creativity: From Potential to Realization — *Sternberg, Robert J.*

Creativity in Psychotherapy: Reaching New Heights with Individuals, Couples, and Families — *Carson, David K.*

Creativity in Science: Chance, Logic, Genius, and Zeitgeist — *Simonton, Dean Keith*

Creativity in the Classroom: Schools of Curious Delight, 3rd Ed. — *Starko, Alane Jordan*

Creativity in Virtual Teams: Key Components for Success — *Nemiro, Jill E.*

Creature — *Harp, Jerry*

c Creatures — *Thomson, Ruth*

Creatures of Empire: How Domestic Animals Transformed Early America — *Anderson, Virginia DeJohn*

Creatures of Fiction, Myth, and Imagination — *Caplan, Ben*

Creatures of the Night — *Gaiman, Neil*

Credible Signs of Christ Alive: Case Studies from the Catholic Campaign for Human Development — *Hogan, John P.*

Credit and Debt in Medieval England, 1180-1350 — *Schofield, Phillipp R.*

Credit and State Theories of Money: The Contributions of A. Mitchell Innes — *Wray, Randall L.*

Credit Management Handbook, 5th Ed. — *Edwards, Burt*

The Credit Repair Kit, 4th Ed. — *Ventura, John*

Credit Reporting Systems and the International Economy — *Miller, Margaret J.*

Credit Risk, Capital Structure, and the Pricing of Equity Options — *Hanke, Michael*

Credit Risk, Capital Structure, and the Pricing of Equity Options — *Hasan, Iftekhar*

Credit Scoring for Risk Managers: The Handbook for Lenders — *Mays, Elizabeth*

Credit to the Community: Community Reinvestment and Fair Lending Policy in the United States — *Immergluck, Daniel*

Credo: Historical and Theological Guide to Creeds and Confessions of Faith in the Christian Tradition — *Pelikan, Jaroslav*

y The Creek: A Novel of Suspense — *Holm, Jennifer L.*

y Creek — *Stone, Amy*

Creek Country: The Creek Indians and Their World — *Ethridge, Robbie*

y Creepers — *Gray, Keith*

Creeping Conformity: How Canada Became Suburban, 1900-1960 — *Harris, Richard (b. 1952 -)*

c Creepy Crawly Calypso (Illus. by Hatter, Debbie) — *Langham, Tony*

Cremation in America — *Rosen, Fred*

Creole Echoes: The Francophone Poetry of Nineteenth-Century Louisiana — *Shapiro, Norman R.*

Creole Gentlemen: The Maryland Elite, 1691-1776 — *Burnard, Trevor*

Creole Nouvelle: Contemporary Creole Cookery — *Carey, Joseph*

Creole Religions of the Caribbean: An Introduction from Vodou and Santeria to Obeah and Espiritismo — *Fernandez Olmos, Margarite*

Creole Transformation from Slavery to Freedom: Historical Archaelogy of the East End Community, St. John, Virgin Islands — *Armstrong, Douglas V.*

The Cretaceous World — *Skelton, Peter W.*

Crete Beyond the Palaces: Proceedings — *Day, Preston Leslie*

Crete on the Half Shell — *Ayanoglu, Byron*

Cretesi — *Euripides*

c Creutzfeldt-Jakob Disease — *Margulies, Phillip*

Crewel Yule — *Ferris, Monica*

c Cricket — *Miller, Heather*

The Cries of Dublin Drawn from the Life by Hugh Douglas Hamilton, 1760 — *Laffan, William*

Crime Against Nature — *Pratt, Minnie Bruce*

y Crime and Criminals — *Torr, James D.*

Crime and Empire: The Colony in Nineteenth-Century Fictions of Crime — *Mukherjee, Upamanyu Pablo*

Crime and Employment: Critical Issues in Crime Reduction for Corrections — *Krienert, Jessie L.*

Crime and Policing in Post-Apartheid South Africa: Transforming Under Fire — *Shaw, Mark (b. 1969 -)*

Crime and Punishment: A History of the Criminal Justice System — *Roth, Mitchel P.*

y Crime and Punishment. Audiobook Review — *Dostoevsky, Fyodor*

Crime and Punishment in the Royal Navy of the Seven Years' War, 1755-1763 — *Eder, Marcus*

Crime and Violence in Latin America: Citizen Security, Democracy, and the State — *Fruhling, Hugo*

Crime, Compliance and Control — *McBarnet, Doreen J.*

Crime Films — *Leitch, Thomas*

Crime, Gender and Social Order in Early Modern England — *Walker, Garthine*

Crime, Justice, and Discretion in England 1740-1820 — *King, Peter*

Crime on the Border: Immigration and Homicide in Urban Communities — *Lee, Matthew T.*

Crime Scene: The Ultimate Guide to Forensic Science — *Platt, Richard*

Crime School: Money Laundering: True Crime Meets the World of Business and Finance — *Mathers, Chris*

Crime, Victims and Justice: Essays on Principles and Practice — *Kaptein, Hendrik*

Crimean Journals of the Sisters of Mercy, 1854-56 — *Luddy, Maria*

The Crimean War: A Clash of Empires — *Fletcher, Ian*

The Crimean War: The Truth Behind the Myth — *Ponting, Clive*

Crimes and Punishments?: Retaliation under the WTO — *Lawrence, Robert Z.*

Crimes of Hate: Selected Readings — *Gerstenfeld, Phyllis B.*

The Criminal Anthropological Writings of Cesare Lombroso Published in English Language Periodical Literature during the Late 19th and Early 20th Centuries: With Bibliographic Appendices of Books — *Lombroso, Cesare*

A Criminal Appeal — *Schanker, D.R.*

Criminal Evidence: Principles and Cases, 5th Ed. — *Gardner, Thomas J.*

Criminal Investigation: A Method for Reconstructing the Past, 4th Ed. — *Osterburg, James W.*

Criminal Investigation: An Analytical Perpsective — *Brandl, Steven G.*

Criminal Justice and Criminology: A Career Guide to Local, State, Federal, and Academic Positions — *Anderson, James F.*

Criminal Justice and Political Cultures: National and International Dimensions of Crime Control — *Newburn, Tim*

Criminal Justice: Concepts and Issues, an Anthology, 4th Ed. — *Eskridge, Chris W.*

Criminal Justice Ethics: Theory and Practice — *Banks, Cyndi*

Criminal Justice History: Themes and Controversies from Pre-Independence Ireland — *O'Donnell, Ian*

Criminal Justice Internships: Theory into Practice, 5th ed. — *Gordon, Gary R.*

Criminal Justice: Retribution vs. Restoration — *Judah, Eleanor Hannon*

Criminal Law, 7th Ed. — *Klotter, John C.*

Criminal Law, 8th Ed. — *Samaha, Joel*

Criminal Law: Cases and Materials, 5th Ed. — *Kaplan, John (b. 1929 - 1989)*

Criminal Law: Theory and Doctrine, 2nd Ed. — *Simester, A.P.*

Criminal Lessons: Case Studies and Commentary on Crime and Justice — *Reamer, Frederic G.*

Criminal Macabre — *Niles, Steve*

Criminal — *Jacob, Gregory*

Criminal Procedure, 3rd Ed. — *Emanuel, Steven L.*

Criminal Procedure, 24th Ed. — *Emanuel, Steven L.*

Criminal Procedure: Examples and Explanations, 4th Ed. — *Bloom, Robert M.*

Criminal Procedure for the Criminal Justice Professional, 9th ed. — *Ferdico, John N.*

Criminal Procedure: From First Contact to Appeal — *Worrall, John L.*

The Criminal Responsibility of Individuals for Violations of International Humanitarian Law — *Van Sliedregt, E.*

Criminal Visions: Media Representations of Crime and Justice — *Mason, Paul*

Criminological Theories: Introduction, Evaluation, and Application, 4th Ed. — *Akers, Ronald L.*

Criminology: A Sociological Introduction, 1st Ed. — *Carrabine, Eamonn*

Criminology: Explaining Crime and Its Context, 5th Ed. — *Brown, Stephen E.*

y Crimpy's Fishing for Kids — *Crimp, Daryl*

Crimson Moon — *York, Rebecca*

The Cripple and His Talismans — *Irani, Anosh*

Crisis and Innovation in Asian Technology — *Keller, William W.*

Crisis and Renewal in Twentieth Century Banking: Exploring History and Archives of Banking at Times of Political and Social Stress — *Green, Edwin*

A Crisis Call for New Preventive Medicine: Emerging Effects of Lifestyle on Morbidity and Mortality — *Knight, Joseph A.*

Crisis Communications: Lessons from September 11 — *Noll, A. Michael*

Crisis in American Institutions, 12th Ed. — *Skolnick, Jerome H.*

The Crisis in Tax Administration — *Aaron, Henry J.*

Crisis Intervention Strategies, 5th Ed. — *James, Richard K.*

A Crisis of Governance: Zimbabwe — *Chikuhwa, Jacob*

The Crisis of Islam: Holy War and Unholy Terror — *Lewis, Bernard*

Crisis on the Korean Peninsula: How to Deal with a Nuclear North Korea — *O'Hanlon, Michael E.*

Crisis on the Stinking Water — *Cheek, Roland*

Crisis: The Anatomy of Two Major Foreign Policy Crises — *Kissinger, Henry A.*

The Crisis: The President, the Prophet, and the Shah--1979 and the Coming of Militant Islam — *Harris, David*

y Crispin: The Cross of Lead — *Avi*

c Crispus Attucks: Hero of the Boston Massacre/Heroe de la Masacre de Boston — *Beier, Anne*

y Criss Cross, Double Cross: Sophie, Alias Star Girl, to the Rescue — *Charles, Norma*

Crisscross — *Wilson, F. Paul*

Cristoforo: Strange Tales of a Singular Traveller — *Thomas, Willie*

Cristologia Primitiva: Dalla Teofania del Sinai all'Io Sono Giovanneo — *Binni, Walther*

Critical Beings: Law, Nation, and the Global Subject — *Fitzpatrick, Peter*

Critical Care Neurology and Neurosurgery — *Suarez, Jose I.*

A Critical Companion to 'Beowulf' — *Orchard, Andy*

Critical Condition — *Birkerts, Sven*

Critical Condition: How Health Care in America Became Big Business--and Bad Medicine — *Barlett, Donald L.*

Critical Criminology at the Edge: Postmodern Perspectives, Integration, and Application — *Simons, Glenna L.*

Critical Edition of Andres de Li's Summa de Paciencia, 1505 — *Li, Andres de*

A Critical Edition of Penelope Aubin's Translation of Mme Gillot de Beaucour's The Adventures of the Prince of Clermont and Madam de Ravezan 1722 — *Gillot de Beaucour, Louise-Genevieve de Gomes de Vasconcellos*

Critical Essays on Bessie Head — *Sample, Maxine*

Critical Essays on Contemporary European Culture and Society — *Beitter, Ursula E.*

Critical Essays on Ronald Firbank, English Novelist, 1886-1926 — *Davies, Gill*

Critical Essays on the Bondwoman's Narrative — *Gates, Henry Louis, Jr.*

Critical Evaluations of Economic Development Policies — *Reese, Laura A.*

Critical Fictions: Sentiment and the American Market, 1780-1870 — *Fichtelberg, Joseph*

Critical Health Pyschology — *Murray, Michael*

A Critical History of Television's The Red Skelton Show, 1951-1971 — *Hyatt, Wesley*

Critical Incident Management — *Sterneckert, Alan B.*

Critical Infrastructures: State of the Art in Research and Application, Proceedings — *Thissen, W.A.H.*

Critical Interfacial Issues in Thin-Film Optoelectronic and Energy Conversion Devices: Proceedings — *Grinley, David S.*

A Critical Introduction to Law, 3rd Ed. — *Mansell, Wade*

Critical Issues in Child Welfare — *Shireman, Joan*

Critical Issues in Rural Health — *Glasgow, Nina*

Critical Issues in Social Studies Teacher Education — *Adler, Susan*

Critical Issues in Special Education: Access, Diversity, and Accountability — *Sorrells, Audrey McCray*

Critical Issues in Weather Modification Research

Critical Literacy — *Wray, David*

Critical Literacy: Enhancing Students' Comprehension of Text — *McLaughlin, Maureen*

Critical Mass: How Nazi Germany Surrendered Enriched Uranium for the United States — *Hydrick, Carter*

Critical Mass: How One Thing Leads to Another — *Bali, Philip*

Critical Mass: How One Thing Leads to Another — *Ball, Philip*

Critical Moments On Modern Irish Theatre — *O'Toole, Fintan*

Critical Pasts: Writing Criticism, Writing History — *Smallwood, Philip*

Critical Pedagogy Primer — *Kincheloe, Joe L.*

The Critical Pedagogy Reader — *Darder, Antonia*

Critical Perspective on Classicism in Japanese Painting, 1600-1700 — *Lillehoj, Elizabeth*

Critical Perspectives on the Curriculum of Teacher Education — *Poetter, Thomas S.*

Critical Race Theory Perspectives on the Social Studies: The Profession, Policies, and Curriculum — *Ladson-Billings, Gloria*

Critical Realism: The Difference That It Makes — *Steinmetz, George*

Critical Reasoning and Philosophy: A Concise Guide to Reading, Writing, and Writing Philosophical Works — *Holowchak, M. Andrew*

The Critical Response to John Irving — *Davis, Todd F.*

Critical Response to Marianne Moore — *Gregory, Elizabeth*

The Critical Response to Robert Musil's The Man Without Qualities — *Mehigan, Tim*

Critical Social Issues in American Education: Democracy and Meaning in a Globalizing World, 3rd Ed. — *Shapiro, H. Svi*

Critical Social Theory: Culture, Society and Critique — *Dant, Tim*

Critical Theory after Habermas — *Freundlieb, Dieter*

Critical Theory — *How, Alan*

Critical Theory Since Plato, 3rd Ed. — *Adams, Hazard*

Critical Thinking and Everyday Argument — *Verlinden, Jay*

Critical Thinking and Learning: An Encyclopedia for Parents and Teachers — *Kincheloe, Joe L.*

Critical Thinking and the Bible in the Age of New Media — *Ess, Charles M.*

Critical Thinking in Nursing: A Cognitive Skills Workbook — *Lipe, Saundra K.*

Critical Visions: New Direction in Social Theory — *Soares, Joseph A.*

Critical Voices in School Reform: Students Living through Change — *Rubin, Beth C.*

Critics at Work: Interviews 1993-2003 — *Williams, Jeffrey J.*

Critique of Practical Reason — *Kant, Immanuel*

Critiques of Capital in Modern Britain and America: Transatlantic Exchanges 1800 to the Present Day — *Bevir, Mark*

c Critter Riddles (Illus. by Parker, Eric) — *Helmer, Marilyn*

CRM at the Speed of Light: Essential Customer Strategies for the 21st Century, 3rd Ed. — *Greenberg, Paul*

CRM Unplugged: Releasing CRM's Strategic Value — *Bligh, Philip*

Croatia: Travels in Undiscovered Country — *Fabijancic, Tony*

Crocheted Lace — *Turner, Pauline*

c Crocheting (Illus. by Melo, Esperanca) — *Kinsler, Gwen Glakely*

Crocheting School: A Complete Course

c Crocodile (Illus. by Mendez, Simon) — *Llewellyn, Claire*

c Crocodiles — *Markle, Sandra*

Cromartie High School, Vol. 1 — *Nonaka, Eiji*

The Cromwellian Protectorate — *Coward, Barry*

Cronica Walliae — *Llwyd, Humphrey*

Crooked Heart — *Sumners, Cristina*

Crop Management and Postharvest Handling of Horticultural Products, Vol. 4 — *Dris, Ramdane*

Cropping Systems: Trends and Advances — *Shrestha, Anil*

The Croquet Player — *Wells, H.G.*

The Cross and the Crescent: Christianity and Islam from Muhammad to the Reformation — *Fletcher, Richard*

The Cross and the River: Ethiopia and the Nile — *Erlich, Haggai*

The Cross and the Trenches: Religious Faith and Doubt Among British and American Great War Soldiers — *Schweitzer, Richard*

Cross Channel Currents: 100 Years of the Entente Cordiale — *Mayne, Richard*

Cross-Cultural Adoption: How to Answer Questions from Family, Friends, and Community — *Coughlin, Amy*

Cross-Cultural Biotechnology — *Brannigan, Michael C.*

Cross-Cultural Management: Foundations and Future — *Tjosvold, Dean*

Cross-Cultural Management, Volume 1: The Theory of Culture — *Redding, Gordon*

Cross-Cultural Management, Volume 2: Managing Cultural Differences — *Redding, Gordon*

Cross-Cultural Marketing — *Rugimbana, Robert*

Cross-Cultural Travel: Papers from the Royal Irish Academy International Symposium on Literature and Travel; Proceedings — *Conroy, Jane*

Cross Current — *Kling, Christine*

The Cross in Our Context; Jesus and the Suffering World — *Hall, Douglas John*

Cross-National Appropriation of Work Systems: Japanese Firms in the UK — *Saka, Ayse*

Cross-National Information and Communication Technology Policies and Practices in Education — *Plomp, Tjeerd*

Cross-Platform .NET Development — *Easton, M.J.*

Cross-Shattered Christ: Meditations on Christ's Seven Last Words — *Hauerwas, Stanley*

y Cross Tides — *Orman, Lorraine*

Cross-Walks: ICD 1 - DSM-IV-TR: A Synopsis of Classifications of Mental Disorders — *Schulte-Markwort, Michael*

Cross Your Heart and Hope to Die: A Blackbird Sisters Mystery — *Martin, Nancy*

Crosscurrents at Century's End: Selections from the Neuberger Berman Art Collection

Crossing Borderlands: Composition and Postcolonial Studies — *Lunsford, Andrea A.*

Crossing Borders in Literacy and Science Instruction: Perspectives on Theory and Practice — *Saul, E. Wendy*

Crossing Borders: Re-Mapping Women's Movements at the Turn of the 21st Century — *Christensen, Hilda Romer*

y Crossing California — *Langer, Adam*

Crossing Fields in Modern Spanish Culture — *Bonaddio, Federico*

c Crossing Philip Booth

Crossing the Digital Divide: Race, Writing, and Technology in the Classroom — *Monroe, Barbara*

Crossing the Equator: New and Selected Poems, 1972-2004 — *Christopher, Nicholas*

Crossing the Great Divide: Worker Risk, Uncertainty and Opportunity in the New Economy — *Smith, Vicki*

Crossing the Line — *Baratz-Logsted, Lauren*

c Crossing the Panther's Path — *Alder, Elizabeth*

Crossing the Rubicon: Ronald Reagan and US Policy in the Middle East — *Laham, Nicholas*

Crossing the Rubicon: The Shaping of India's New Foreign Policy — *Mohan, C. Raja*

Crossing the Tracks for Love: What to Do When You and Your Partner Grew Up in Different Worlds — *Payne, Ruby K.*

y The Crossley Baby — *Carey, Jacqueline*

Crossroads at Midlife: Your Aging Parents, Your Emotions, and Your Self — *Praver, Frances Cohen*

Crossroads of Freedom: Antietam — *McPherson, James M.*

Crossroads: Tales of the Southern Literary Fantastic — *Cox, F. Brett*

Crossroads to Islam: The Origins of the Arab Religion and the Arab State — *Nevo, Yehuda D.*

Crossways — *Kohler, Sheila*

Crow — *Sax, Boria*

c The Crow-Girl: The Children of Crow Cove — *Bredsdorff, Bodil*

The Crow Indians — *Lowie, Robert H.*

Crow Lake — *Lawson, Mary*

Crown, Church and Episcopate under Louis XIV — *Bergin, Joseph*

Crown Fire — *Annandale, David*

c Crown Me! — *Lay, Kathryn*

Crown of Horns (Illus. by Smith, Jeff) — *Smith, Jeff*

The Crown of the Continent: Glacier National Park

c Crows — *Johnson, Sylvia*

Crucial Confrontations: Tools for Broken Promises, Violated Expectations and Bad Behavior — *Peterson, Kerry*

Crucial Conversations: Tools for Talking When Stakes Are High — *Patterson, Kerry*

Crucial Images in the Presentation of a Kurdish National Identity: Heroes and Patriots; Traitors and Foes — *Strohmeier, Martin*

y Crucible — *Kress, Nancy*

Crucible of American Democracy: The Struggle to Fuse Egalitarianism and Capitalism in Jeffersonian Pennsylvania — *Shankman, Andrew*

Crucible of Reason: Intentional Action, Practical Rationality, and Weakness of Will — *Wyma, Keith David*

The Crucified God in the Carolingian Era — *Chazelle, Celia*

Crude Awakenings: Global Oil Security and American Foreign Policy — *Yetiv, Steve A.*

Crude Power: Politics and the Oil Market. — *Noreng, Oysteng*

Crude: The Story of Oil — *Shah, Sonia*

Cruel and Unusual: Bush/Cheney's New World Order — *Miller, Mark Crispin*

Cruel and Unusual: Punishment and US Culture — *Jarvis, Brian*

Cruel Delight: Enlightenment Culture and the Inhuman — *Steintrager, James A.*

y The Cruelest Journey: 600 Miles to Timbuktu — *Salak, Kira*

The Cruellest Miles: The Heroic Story of Dogs and Men in a Race Against an Epidemic — *Salisbury, Laney*

y Cruise Control — *Trueman, Terry*

The Cruise of the "Janet Nichol" Among the South Sea Islands: A Diary — *Stevenson, Fanny Van de Grift*

The Cruise of the Vanadis — *Wharton, Edith*

Cruisers — *Nova, Craig*

Cruising Modernism: Class and Sexuality in American Literature and Social Thought — *Trask, Michael*

Cruising the Anime City: An Otaku Guide to Neo Tokyo — *Macias, Patrick*

Crusade and Conversion on the Baltic Frontier, 1150-1500 — *Murray, Alan V.*

Crusade: Chronicles of an Unjust War — *Carroll, James*

Crusaders, Condottieri, and Cannon: Medieval Warfare in Societies around the Mediterranean — *Villalon, L.J. Andrew*

y The Crusades — *Nicholson, Helen J.*

Crusades: The Illustrated History — *Madden, Thomas F.*

Crusading and the Crusader States — *Jotischky, Andrew*

D

D. B. — *Reid, Elwood*
D-Branes — *Johnson, Clifford V.*
The D-Day Atlas: Anatomy of the Normandy
  Campaign — *Messenger, Charles*
y The D-Day Companion: Leading Historians Explore
  History's Greatest Amphibious Assault — *Penrose,
  Jane*
D-Day: The Greatest Invasion: A People's History
  — *Van der Vat, Dan*
c D-Day: They Fought to Free Europe from Hitler's
  Tyranny (Illus. by Craig, David) — *Tanaka, Shelley*
D.H. Lawrence and Italian Futurism: A Study of
  Influence — *Harrison, Andrew*
D.H. Lawrence: Paul Morel — *Baron, Helen*
D.H. Lawrence's Paintings — *Sagar, Keith*
c D Is for Democracy: A Citizen's Alphabet (Illus. by
  Juhasz, Victor) — *Grodin, Elissa*
c D Is for Democracy: A Citizen's Alphabet — *Grodin,
  Elissa*
c D Is for Doodle: A Step-by-Step Drawing Book
  — *Zemke, Deborah*
c D Is for Drums: A Colonial Williamsburg ABC (Illus.
  by Chorao, Kay) — *Chorao, Kay*
D.N. Angel. Vol. 1 — *Sugisaki, Yukiru*
Da Capo Best Music Writing, 2004: The Year's Finest
  Writing on Rock, Hip-Hop, Jazz, Pop, Country,
  and More — *Hart, Mickey*
The Da Vinci Code — *Brown, Dan*
Da Vinci Decoded: Discovering the Spiritual Secrets of
  Da Vinci's Seven Principles — *Gelb, Michael J.*
c Da Wild, Da Crazy, da Vinci (Illus. by McCauley,
  Adam) — *Scieszka, Jon*
c Dad, Aren't You Glad? (Illus. by Dutton, Amy
  Wummer) — *Plourde, Lynn*
c Dad, Jackie, and Me (Illus. by Bootman, Colin)
  — *Uhlberg, Myron*
c Dad Runs Away with the Circus (Illus. by Modan,
  Rutu) — *Keret, Etgar*
c Dad Runs Away with the Circus (Illus. by Modan,
  Rutu) — *Kerret, Etgar*
c Daddy I Wanna Be a Lawyer — *Goldfarb, Larry*
Daddy Long Legs and Dear Enemy — *Webster, Jean*
c Daddy's Girl (Illus. by Glasser, Robin Preiss)
  — *Keillor, Garrison*
c Daddy's Scratchy Face (Illus. by Kunhardt, Edith)
  — *Kunhardt, Edith*
c Daedalus — *Stern, Dave*
Daewoo — *Bon, Francois*
c Daffodil (Illus. by Bogacki, Tomek) — *Jenkins, Emily*
c Daffodil Scissors — *Ridley, Philip*
The Daguerreotype — *Gregory, Patrick*
Dahlia Cassidy — *Cameron, Anne*
Dai Margini la Memoria: Johannes Hinderbach
  — *Rando, Daniela*
Daily and Nocturnal Hemodialysis — *Lindsay, Robert
  M.*
The Daily Drucker: 365 Days of Insight and
  Motivation for Getting the Right Things Done
  — *Drucker, Peter F.*
y Daily Life — *Chrisp, Peter*
c Daily Life — *Elgin, Kathy*
y Daily Life During the American Revolution — *Volo,
  Dorothy Denneen*
c Daily Life in Ancient and Modern Cairo
  — *Barghusen, Joan D.*
Daily Life in Biblical Times — *Borowski, Oded*
Daily Life in the United States, 1920-1940: How
  Americans Lived through the "Roaring Twenties"
  and the Great Depression — *Kyvig, David E.*
Daily Meditations on Golden Texts of the Bible
  — *Gariepy, Henry*

The Daily Telegraph: 80 Years of Cryptic Crosswords
  — *Gilbert, Val*
The Daily Telegraph Book of Military Obituaries
  — *Twiston-Davies, David*
The Daily Telegraph Book of Naval Obituaries
  — *Davies, David Twiston*
The 'Daily Telegraph' Book of the Weather: Past and
  Future Climate Changes Explained — *Eden, Philip*
Dairy of a Newlywed Poet: A Bilingual Edition of
  Diario de un Poeta Reciencasado — *Harter, Hugh
  A.*
c Daisy Bates: Civil Rights Crusader — *Polakow, Amy*
c Daisy Comes Home — *Brett, Jan*
c Daisy Doll (Illus. by Durkin, Denise) — *Pulford,
  Elizabeth*
c Daisy, the Cripple Creek Donkey — *Bezek, Lyn*
c Daja's Book: Circle of Magic. Audiobook Review
  — *Pierce, Tamora*
Dakota Cross-Bearer: The Life and World of a Native
  American Bishop — *Cochran, Mary E.*
c Dali and the Path of Dreams (Illus. by Subirana,
  Joan) — *Obiols, Anna*
Dali: Master of Fantasies — *Gaillemin, Jean-Louis*
Dalit Women in India: Issues and Perspectives
  — *Jogdand, P.G.*
The Dam Busters — *Ramsden, John*
Dam Politics: Restoring America's Rivers — *Lowry,
  William R.*
Dam Removal Research: Status and Prospects
  — *Graf, William L.*
Damage and Fracture Mechanics VIII: Computer
  Aided Assessment and Control: Proceedings
  — *Brebbia, C.A.*
Damage Done by the Storm — *Hodgins, Jack*
Damages — *Bazhe*
The Damascened Blade — *Cleverly, Barbara*
Damascius: Commentaire du Parmenide de Planton
  — *Westerink, L.G.*
Damned: An Illustrated History of the Devil
  — *Muchembled, Robert*
Damned for Their Difference: The Cultural
  Construction of Deaf People as Disabled
  — *Branson, Jan*
Damned If I Do — *Everett, Percival L.*
Damon Family of Scituate, Massachusettes.
  Genealogy, 2000, One of 3 Separate Colonial
  Families Massachusettes Damon Families
  — *Damon, Richard A., Jr.*
Damp Indoor Spaces and Health — *Institute of
  Medicine (U.S.). Committee on Damp Indoor Spaces
  and Health*
Damselfish — *Ouriou, Susan*
y Damsels Not in Distress: The True Story of Women in
  Medieval Times — *Hopkins, Andrea*
Dan Flavin: A Retrospective — *Govan, Michael*
Dan Flavin: The Complete Lights 1961-1996
  — *Govan, Michael*
Dan Rice: The Most Famous Man You've Never
  Heard Of — *Carlyon, David*
c Dan Yaccarino's Mother Goose (Illus. by Yaccarino's,
  Dan) — *Yaccarino, Dan*
Dance and the Performative: A Choreological
  Perspective: Laban and Beyond — *Preston-Dunlop,
  Valerie*
Dance Hall Days: Intimacy and Leisure among
  Working-Class Immigrants in the United States
  — *McBee, Randy D.*
The Dance Master — *Turnbull, Peter*
Dance/Movement Therapists in Action: A Working
  Guide to Research Options — *Cruz, Robyn Flaum*
Dance Naked: A Stripper's Guide to Life — *Conrad,
  Jessica*

Dance of Days: Two Decades of Punk in the Nation's
  Capital — *Andersen, Mark*
A Dance of Life and Death — *Carbyn, Lu*
Dance of the Dialectic: Steps in Marx's Method
  — *Ollman, Bertell*
y Dance of the Stones — *Spalding, Andrea*
Dance of the Thunder Dogs — *Mitchell, Kirk*
c Dance Performance: From Rehearsal to Opening
  Night — *Kessel, Kristin*
Dance, Space and Subjectivity — *Briginshaw, Valerie*
Dance with Me (Read by Ziemba, Karen). Audiobook
  Review — *Rice, Luanne*
Dancer. Audiobook Review — *McCann, Colum*
Dancer — *McCann, Colum*
The Dancer Defects: The Struggle for Cultural
  Supremacy During the Cold War — *Caute, David*
Dances of the Tewa Pueblo Indians: Expressions of
  New Life, 2nd Ed. — *Sweet, Jill D.*
Dancing at the Dead Sea: Tracking the World's
  Environmental Hotspots — *Mitchell, Alanna*
c Dancing Elephants and Floating Continents: The
  Story of Canada Beneath Your Feet — *Wilson, John
  (b. 1951 -)*
Dancing Girls, Loose Ladies, and Women of the
  Cloth: The Women in Jesus' Life — *Spencer, F.
  Scott*
Dancing in Odessa — *Kaminsky, Ilya*
y Dancing in Red Shoes Will Kill You — *Cirrone,
  Dorian*
Dancing in the Dharma: The Life and Teachings of
  Ruth Denison — *Boucher, Sandy*
Dancing in the Margins: Meditations for People Who
  Struggle with Their Churches — *Coffey, Kathy*
y Dancing in the Streets of Brooklyn — *Lurie, April*
Dancing Many Drums: Excavations in African
  American Dance — *DeFrantz, Thomas*
Dancing Naked at the Edge of Dawn — *Radish, Kris*
Dancing on Main Street — *Thomas, Lorenzo*
A Dancing People: Powwow Culture on the Southern
  Plains — *Ellis, Clyde*
Dancing Revelations: Alvin Ailey's Embodiment of
  African American Culture — *DeFrantz, Thomas*
c Dancing Shoes (Read by Sastre, Elizabeth). Audiobook
  Review — *Streatfeild, Noel*
Dancing the Self: Personhood and Performance in the
  Pandav Lila of Garhwal — *Sax, William S.*
Dancing to the Concertina's Tune: A Prison Teacher's
  Memoir — *Walker, Jan*
Dancing with a Tiger: Poems, 1941-1998 — *Friend,
  Robert*
Dancing with Cuba: A Memoir of the Revolution
  — *Guillermoprieto, Alma*
Dancing with Death — *Coggin, Joan*
Dancing with Saddam: The Strategic Tango of
  Jordanian-Iraqi Relations — *Schenker, David*
Dancing with Strangers — *Clendinnen, Inga*
Dancing with the Sacred: Evolution, Ecology, and God
  — *Peters, Karl E.*
Dancing with the Virgin: Body and Faith in the Fiesta
  of Tortugas, New Mexico — *Sklar, Deidre*
y Danger at the Landings — *Citra, Becky*
Danger-Close — *Merz, Jon F.*
c Danger, Dynamite! — *Capeci, Anne*
The Danger of Dreams: German and American
  Imperialism in Latin America — *Mitchell, Nancy*
Danger on Peaks — *Snyder, Gary*
Dangerous Alliances: Civil Society, the Media and
  Democratic Transition in North Africa — *Garon,
  Lise*
Dangerous Alliances: Proponents of Peace, Weapons
  of War — *Weitsman, Patricia A.*

Dictionary of Physics — *Coleman, Larry*
Dictionary of Pseudonyms: 11,000 Assumed Names and Their Origins — *Room, Adrian*
Dictionary of Public Health Promotion and Education: Terms and Concepts, 2nd Ed. — *Modeste, Naomi N.*
Dictionary of Real Estate Terms — *Friedman, Jack P.*
Dictionary of Saints — *Delaney, John D.*
A Dictionary of Slang and Unconventional English, 8th Ed. — *Partridge, Eric*
Dictionary of Smoky Mountain English — *Montgomery, Michael B.*
Dictionary of Strategy: Strategic Management A-Z — *Kelly, Louise*
Dictionary of the Earth — *Farndon, John*
Dictionary of the Ecumenical Movement — *Lossky, Nicholas*
Dictionary of the Second World War — *Wheal, Elizabeth-Anne*
Dictionary of Toys and Games in American Popular Culture — *Augustyn, Frederick J.*
Dictionnaire Berlioz — *Citron, Pierre*
Dictionnaire des femmes libraires en France: 1470-1870 — *Strenski, Ivan*
Did Babe Ruth Call His Shot? and Other Unsolved Baseball Mysteries — *Aron, Paul (b. 1956)*
Did Dinosaurs Have Feathers? (Illus. by Washburn, Lucia) — *Zoehfeld, Kathleen Weidner*
c Did I Tell You I Love You Today? (Illus. by Evans, Shane) — *Jordan, Deloris*
Did I Tell You I Love You Today? — *Jordan, Deloris*
c Did I Tell You I Love You Today? (Illus. by Evans, Shane) — *Jordon, Deloris*
c Did You See Chip? — *Yee, Wong Herbert*
Didactic Literature in England 1500-1800 — *Glaisyer, Natasha*
Diderot: l'ordre et le devenir — *Chernl, Amor*
Didn't You Used to Be What's His Name? — *Miller, Denny*
Dido's Daughters: Literacy, Gender, and Empire in Early Modern England and France — *Ferguson, Margaret W.*
Die a Little — *Abbott, Megan*
Die Abenteuer des Ritters Theuerdank — *Maximilian, Kaiser I.*
Die Aehrenthals: Eine Familie in ihrer Korrespondenz 1872-1911 — *Adlgasser, Franz*
Die alevitische Religion: Traditionslinien und Neubestimmungen — *Dressler, Markus*
Die arabischen Dialekte der Cukurova (Sudturkei), Semitica Viva 27 — *Prochazka, Stephan*
Die Argonautika des Apollonios Rhodios. Das zweite Zorn-Epos der griechischen Literatur — *Drager, P.*
Die Bibliothek Konard Peutingers. Edition der historischen Kataloge und Rekonstrucktion der Bestande. Band I: Die autographen Kataloge Peutinges. Der nicht-juristische Bibliotheksteil — *Kunast, Hans-Jorg*
Die Buchholzschnitte Hans Brosamers zu den Frankfurter "Volksbuch": Ausgaben und ihre Wiederverwendungen — *Gotzkowsky, Bodo*
Die Bundesrepublik Deutschland — *Stover, Bernd*
Die Chemnitzer Auto Union AG und die "Demokratisierung" der Wirtschaft in der Sowjetischen Besatzungszone von 1945 bis 1948 — *Kukowski, Martin*
Die Christlich-Nationale Bauern- und Landvolkpartei, 1928-1933 — *Muller, Markus*
Die Chronik ueber Don Juan de Austria — *Del Rio, Martin Antoine*
Die Damonen: Die Damonologie der Israelitisch-Judischen und Fruhchristlichen Literatur im Kontext ihrer Umwelt = Demons: The Demonology of Israelite-Jewish and Early Christian Literature in Context of Their Environment — *Lange, Armin*
Die DDR--ein Sozialstaat? Sozialpolitik in der Ara Honecker — *Bouvier, Beatrix*
Die DDR unter Ulbricht: Gewaltsame Neuordnung und gescheiterte Modernisierung — *Hoffmann, Dierk*
Die Denkbewegung von Leo Strauss: Die Geschichte der Philosophie und die Intentionen des Philosophen — *Meier, Heinrich*
Die Deutsche Volkspartei, 1918-1933 — *Richter, Ludwig*
Die Deutschen in der Moskauer Gesellschaft. Symbiose und Konflikte — *Donninghaus, Victor*
Die doppelte Konfessionalisierung in Irland: Konflikt und Koexistenz im 16. Jahrhundert und in der ersten Halfte des 17. Jahrhunderts — *Lotz-Heumann, Ute*

Die Einblattdrucke der Universitatsbibliothek Erlangen-Nurnberg — *Hofmann-Randall, Christina*
Die Entdeckung der Evolution: Eine revolutionare Theorie und ihre Geschichte — *Junker, Thomas*
Die Entdeckung des Altertums: Der Umgang mit der romischen Vergangenheit Suddeutschlands im 16. Jahrhundert — *Ott, Martin*
Die Evolution und der Naturschutz: Zum Verhaltnis von Evolutionsbiologie, Okologie und Naturethik — *Potthast, Thomas*
Die fernen Inseln — *Boldl, Klaus*
Die Franzoesische Revolution und das Projekt der Moderne — *Reinalter, Helmut*
Die Geschichte der SPD in Mecklenburg und Vorpommern — *Muller, Werner*
Die Gestapo im Zweiten Weltkrieg: "Heimatfront" und besetztes Europa — *Paul, Gerhard*
Die Gleichschaltung der Deutschen Volksgruppe in Rumanien und das 'Dritte Reich' 1941-1944 — *Bohm, Johann*
Die Grenzen der Nationen: Identitdtenwandel in Oberschlesien in der Neuzeit — *Struve, Kai*
Die Grundung der Republic Estland und das "Einen und unteilbaren Rubland": Die Petrograder FRront des Russischen Burgerkrieges, 1918-1920 — *Bruggemann, Karsten*
Die Herren Journalisten: Die Elite der deutschen Presse nach 1945 — *Hachmeister, Lutz*
Die historische Meisterezahlung: Deutungslinien der deutschen Nationalgeschichte nach 1945 — *Jarausch, Konrad H.*
Die holprige Siegeszug des Automobils, 1895-1930 — *Merki, Christoph*
Die Hussitische Revolution — *Smahel, Frantisek*
Die If You Must: Brazilian Indians in the Twentieth Century — *Hemming, John*
Die If You Must: Brazilian Indians in the Twentieth Century — *Macmillan, John Hemming*
Die Institutionalisierung der Rumanischen Monarchie Unter Carol I: 1866-1881 — *Binder-Iijima, Edda*
Die Inszenierung der Vergangenheit im Mittelalter: Die Kloster Glastonbury und Saint-Denis — *Albrecht, Stephan*
Die Kaiserinnen Roms. Von Livia bis Theodora — *Vitzthum, H. Temporini-Grafin*
Die Konfliktgemeinschaft: Tschechen und Deutsche, 1780-1918 — *Kren, Jan*
Die Konigsmutter des Alten Agypten von der Fruhzeit bis zum Ende der 12. Dynastie — *Roth, Silke*
Die Krankengeschichten der Epidemienbucher des Corpus Hippocraticum. Medizinhistorische Bedeutung und Moglichkeiten der retrospektiven Diagnose — *Graumann, L.A.*
Die Kulturgeschichte des Zoos — *Dittrich, Lothar*
Die lateinischen Patriarchen von Jerusalem: Von der Eroberung der Heiligen Stadt durch die Kreuzfahrer 1099 bis zum Ende der Kreuzfahrerstaaten 1291 — *Kirstein, Klaus-Peter*
Die Macht der Dinge: Geschichte und Theorie sakraler Objekte — *Kohl, Karl-Heinz*
Die Macht der Toene: Musik als Mittel politischer Identitaetsstiftung im 20 Jahrhundert — *Bendikowski, Tillmann*
Die Macht der Weisheit: Das Bild des Bischofs in der Vita Augustini des Possidius und andere spaetantiken und fruehmittelalterlichen Bischofsviten — *Ott, John*
Die Maler von Florenz: zu Beginn der Renaissance — *Jacobsen, Werner*
Die Nacht mit Alice, als Julia ums Haus schlich — *Strauss, Botho*
Die pidreks saga im Kontext der altnorwegischen Literatur — *KramarzBein, Susanne*
Die radikale Herausforderung: Die politische Kultur der englischen Konservativen zwischen landlicher Tradition und industrieller Moderne, 1846-1868. — *Schulze, Hagen*
Die Religion des deutschen Nationalismus. Eine mentalitatsgeschichtliche Studie Zur Literatur des Kaiserreichs: Felix Dahn, Ernst von Wildenbrusch, Walter Flex — *Wahl, Hans Rudolf*
Die Religionspolitik Marc Aurels — *Motschmann, C.*
Die romische Nobilitat im Ersten Punischen Krieg. Untersuchungen zur aristokratischen Konkurrenz in der Republik — *Bleckmann, B.*
Die Rote Hilfe: Die Geschichte der internationalen kommunistischen "Wohlfahrtsorganisation" und ihrer sozialen Aktivitaten in Deutschland — *Hering, Sabine*
Die Seichen Des Korpers Und Der Liebe: "Paris Und Vienna" in Der Jiddischen Fassung Des Ella Levita — *Schulz, Armin*

Die technologische Fachliteratur der Antike. Struktur, Uberlieferung und Wirkung technischen Wissens in der Antike — *Meissner, B.*
Die Traumdarstellugen in der griechisch-romischen Dichtung — *Walde, C.*
Die Unfahigkeit, sich zu Erkennen: Sophokles' Tragodien — *Lefevre, Eckard*
Die Verfolgung von NS-Tatern im geteilten Deuschland: Vergagenheitsbewaltigung 1949-1969, order: Eine deutsch deutsche Beziehungsgeschichte im Kalten Krieg — *Weinke, Annette*
Die volkische Bewegung im wilhelminischen Kaiserreich: Sprache- Rasse- Religion — *Puschner, Uwe*
Die Weimarer Republik: Portrait einer Epoche in Biographien — *Frohlich, Michael*
Die Werke von Daniel Bernoulli. Volume 5: Hydrodynamik II — *Bernoulli, Daniel*
Die westfaelische Veme im Bild: Geschichte, Verbreitung und Einfluss der westfaelischen Vemegerichtbarkeit — *Fricke, Eberhard*
Die Zeit Wenzels 1376-1387 — *Rotter, Ekkehart*
Die Zentralen Rategremien in Bayern 1918/19: Legitimation-Organisation-Funktion — *Koglmeier, Georg*
Died Blonde: A Bad Hair Day Mystery — *Cohen, Nancy J.*
c Diego Velazquez (Illus. by Venezia, Mike) — *Venezia, Mike*
Dielectric Phenomena in Solids: With Emphasis on Physical Concepts of Electronic Processes — *Kwan Chi Kao*
Dielectrics in Emerging Technologies: Proceedings of the International Symposium — *Misra, D.*
Dies the Fire — *Stirling, S.M.*
Diesel Particulate Emissions: Landmark Research, 1994-2001 — *Johnson, John H.*
Diet and Human Immune Function — *Hughes, David A.*
Diet and Nutrition — *Westcott, Patsy*
Diet for a Dead Planet: How the Food Industry Is Killing Us — *Cook, Christopher D.*
Dietary Fibre: Bio-active Carbohydrates for Food and Feed — *Kamp, J.W. van der*
Dietary Proteins and Atherosclerosis — *Debry, Gerard*
Dietary Reference Intakes: Applications in Dietary Planning — *Institute of Medicine (U.S.)*
Dietary Supplement Labeling Compliance Review, 3rd Ed. — *Summers, James L.*
Dietary Supplements of Plant Origin: A Nutrition and Health Approach — *Maffei, Massimo*
Dieter Roth: Books + Multiples: Catalogue Raisonne — *Dobke, Dirk*
The Dietician's Guide to Vegetarian Diets: Issues and Applications, 2nd Ed. — *Mangels, Reed*
Diez Anos de Publicaciones de Filologia Griega en Espana — *Somolinos, H. Rodriguez*
The Diezmo — *Bass, Rick*
The Difference a Day Makes: 365 Ways to Change Your World in Just 24 Hours — *Jones, Karen M.*
Difference and Differential Equations: Proceedings — *International Conference on Difference Equations and Aplications*
The Difference Satire Makes: Rhetoric and Reading from Jonson to Byron — *Bogel, Fredric V.*
Difference Schemes with Operator Factors — *Samarskii, A.A.*
The Difference Women Make: The Policy Impact of Women in Congress — *Swers, Michael L.*
A Different Jesus?: The Christ of the Latter-Day Saints — *Millet, Robert*
y A Different Kind of Beauty — *McNicoll, Sylvia*
A Different Shade of Colonialism: Egypt, Great Britain, and the Mastery of the Sudan — *Powell, Eve M. Troutt*
A Different Universe: Reinventing Physics from the Bottom Down — *Laughlin, Robert B.*
Differential Diagnosis in Adult Neurophological Assessment — *Ricker, Joseph H.*
Differential Equations: An Introduction to Basic Concepts, Results and Applications — *Vrabie, Ioan I.*
Differential Equations and Boundary Value Problems: Computing and Modeling, 3rd Ed. — *Edwards, C. Henry*
Differential Equations and Mathematical Biology — *Smith, Hal L.*
Differential Equations — *Cushing, J.M.*
Differential Equations — *Stroud, K.A.*
Differential Equations Demystified — *Krantz, Steven G.*

E

The Encyclopedia of African American Military History — *Weir, William*

Encyclopedia of African-American Politics — *Smith, Robert C.*

Encyclopedia of African American Society, 2 Vols. — *Jaynes, Gerald David*

Encyclopedia of African History. Vols. 1-3 — *Shillington, Kevin*

Encyclopedia of Agricultural, Food, and Biological Engineering — *Heldman, Dennis R.*

y Encyclopedia of Air — *Newton, David E.*

y Encyclopedia of American Business — *Folsom, W. Davis*

Encyclopedia of American Folk Art — *Wertkin, Gerard C.*

Encyclopedia of American Foreign Policy — *Hastedt, Glenn*

y Encyclopedia of American Historical Documents — *Rosenfeld, Susan C.*

Encyclopedia of American Historical Documents, Vol. 3 — *Rosenfeld, Susan*

Encyclopedia of American Historical Documents, Vols. 1-3 — *Rosenfeld, Susan*

Encyclopedia of American National Parks — *Rothman, Hal K.*

Encyclopedia of American National Parks, Vols. 1-2 — *Rothman, Hal K.*

Encyclopedia of American Silver Manufacturers, 5th Rev. Ed. — *Rainwater, Dorothy T.*

Encyclopedia of American Social Movements, Vols. 1-4 — *Ness, Immanuel*

Encyclopedia of an Ordinary Life — *Rosenthal, Amy Krouse*

y Encyclopedia of Ancient Asian Civilizations — *Higham, Charles F.W.*

The Encyclopedia of Angels — *Guiley, Rosemary Ellen*

Encyclopedia of Animal Science — *Pond, Wilson G.*

The Encyclopedia of Animals: A Complete Visual Guide

Encyclopedia of Animals: A Complete Visual Guide — *Goodwin, Stephanie*

The Encyclopedia of Animals: A Complete Visual Guide — *McKay, George*

The Encyclopedia of Animals: A Complete Visual Guide

Encyclopedia of Applied Plant Sciences — *Thomas, Brian*

Encyclopedia of Applied Psychology — *Spielberger, Charles D.*

Encyclopedia of Aquarium and Pond Fish — *Alderton, David*

Encyclopedia of Arthritis — *Stein, C. Michael*

Encyclopedia of Asthma and Respiratory Disorders — *Navarra, Tova*

y Encyclopedia of Bioethics, 3rd Ed. — *Post, Stephen G.*

Encyclopedia of Biology — *Rittner, Don*

Encyclopedia of Biomaterials and Biomedical Engineering — *Wnek, Gary E.*

Encyclopedia of British Writers: 19th and 20th Centuries

The Encyclopedia of Buddhism, Vols. 1-2. — *Buswell, Robert*

The Encyclopedia of Canadian Organized Crime: From Captain Kidd to Mom Boucher — *Edwards, Peter*

Encyclopedia of Capitalism — *Hussain, Syed B.*

Encyclopedia of Capitalism, Vols. 1-3 — *Hussain, Syed B.*

Encyclopedia of Catholic Literature, Vols.1-2. — *Reichardt, Mary R.*

Encyclopedia of Caves and Karst Science — *Gunn, John*

y The Encyclopedia of Celtic Mythology and Folklore — *Monaghan, Patricia*

The Encyclopedia of Chicago — *Grossman, James R.*

Encyclopedia of Chicago

The Encyclopedia of Chicago — *Grossman, James R.*

Encyclopedia of Children and Childhood: In History and Society, Vols. 1-3 — *Fass, Paula S.*

The Encyclopedia of Children's Health and Wellness — *Turkington, Carol*

Encyclopedia of Chinese Philosophy — *Cua, Antonio S.*

Encyclopedia of Christian Theology — *Lacoste, Jean-Yves*

Encyclopedia of Clothing and Fashion — *Steele, Valerie*

Encyclopedia of Cold War Espionage, Spies, and Secret Operations — *Trahair, Richard C.S.*

Encyclopedia of Community: From the Village to the Virtual World — *Christensen, Karen*

Encyclopedia of Complementary and Alternative Medicine — *Navarra, Tova*

Encyclopedia of Computer Science, 4th Ed. — *Ralston, Anthony*

Encyclopedia of Contemporary Christian Music — *Powell, Mark Allan*

Encyclopedia of Corrosion Technology, 2nd Ed. — *Schweitzer, Philip A.*

Encyclopedia of Cuban-United States Relations — *Leonard, Thomas M.*

Encyclopedia of Dahlias — *McClaren, Bill*

Encyclopedia of Deafness and Hearing Disorders, 2nd Rev. Ed. — *Turkington, Carol*

The Encyclopedia of Deer: Your Guide to the World's Deer Species, Including Whitetails, Mule Deer, Caribou, Elk, Moose, and More — *Rue, Leonard Lee, III*

Encyclopedia of Distributed Learning — *DiStefano, Anna*

Encyclopedia of DNA and the United States Criminal Justice System — *Palmer, Louis J.*

The Encyclopedia of Elder Care — *Mezey, Mathy D.*

Encyclopedia of Electrochemistry, Vol. 8 — *Bard, Allen J.*

Encyclopedia of Electrochemistry, Vol. 8 — *Schafer, Hans J.*

Encyclopedia of Ellis Island — *Moreno, Barry*

Encyclopedia of Energy, Vols. 1-6 — *Cleveland, Cutler J.*

Encyclopedia of Espionage, Intelligence, and Security — *Lerner, K. Lee*

Encyclopedia of Evaluation — *Mathison, Sandra*

The Encyclopedia of Exercise, Sport and Health — *Brukner, Peter*

Encyclopedia of Exploration 1800-1850 — *Howgego, Raymond John*

Encyclopedia of Exploration, 1800 to 1850 — *John, Raymond*

Encyclopedia of Exploration to 1800 — *Howgego, Raymond John*

Encyclopedia of Exploration, Vols. 1-2 — *Waldman, Carl*

Encyclopedia of Federal Agencies and Commissions — *Hill, Kathleen Thompson*

Encyclopedia of Feminist Literature — *Whitson, Kathy J.*

Encyclopedia of Fishing Knots and Rigs — *Wilson, Geoff*

Encyclopedia of Folk Medicine: Old World and New World Traditions — *Hatfield, Gabrielle*

Encyclopedia of Forensic Science — *Bell, Suzanne*

Encyclopedia of Forest Sciences — *Burley, Jeffery*

Encyclopedia of Gastroenterology — *Johnson, Leonard R.*

Encyclopedia of Genetics, Rev. Ed., Vols. 1-2 — *Ness, Bryan D.*

Encyclopedia of Geomorphology — *Goudie, A.S.*

Encyclopedia of Gothic Literature — *Snodgrass, Mary Ellen*

Encyclopedia of Government and Politics — *Hawkesworth, Mary*

Encyclopedia of Grain Science, Vols. 1-3 — *Wrigley, Colin*

The Encyclopedia of Guilty Pleasures — *Stall, Sam*

Encyclopedia of Health & Behavior — *Anderson, Norman B.*

Encyclopedia of Health Care Management — *Stahl, Michael J.*

The Encyclopedia of High-Tech Crime and Crime Fighting — *Newton, Michael*

The Encyclopedia of High-Tech Crime and Crime-Fighting — *Newton, Michael*

The Encyclopedia of Hollywood: An A-to-Z Guide to the Stars, Stories, and Secrets of Hollywood — *Siegel, Scott*

Encyclopedia of Homelessness — *Levinson, David*

Encyclopedia of Homelessness, Vols. 1-2 — *Levinson, David*

Encyclopedia of Human Geography — *Pitzl, Gerald R.*

Encyclopedia of Hydrangeas — *Gelderen, C.J. van*

Encyclopedia of Hydrangeas — *Van Gelderen, C.J.*

The Encyclopedia of Infectious Diseases — *Turkington, Carol*

The Encyclopedia of Ireland — *Lalor, Brian*

Encyclopedia of Irish History and Culture — *Donnelly, James S., Jr.*

y Encyclopedia of Islam and the Muslim World — *Martin, Richard C.*

Encyclopedia of Jamaican Heritage — *Senior, Olive*

Encyclopedia of Kitchen History — *Snodgrass, Mary Ellen*

An Encyclopedia of Kitchen Science, History and Culture — *McGee, Harold*

Encyclopedia of Latin American Theater — *Cortes, Eladio*

Encyclopedia of Latino Popular Culture, Vols. 1-2 — *Chavez, Cordelia*

Encyclopedia of Leadership — *Goethals, George R.*

Encyclopedia of Leadership. Vol. 4 — *Burns, James MacGregor*

Encyclopedia of Leadership, Vols. 1-4 — *Goethals, George R.*

Encyclopedia of Leisure and Outdoor Recreation — *Jenkins, John M.*

Encyclopedia of Leisure and Outdoor Recreation — *Pigram, John J.*

Encyclopedia of Lesbian, Gay, Bisexual, and Transgender History in America, Vol. 1-3 — *Stein, Marc*

Encyclopedia of Lesbian, Gay, Bisexual, and Transgender History in America, Vols. 1-3 — *Stein, Marc*

Encyclopedia of Library and Information Science, 2nd Ed. — *Drake, Miriam A.*

c Encyclopedia of Life Sciences, 2nd Ed., Vols. 1-13 — *O'Daly, Anne*

Encyclopedia of Linguistics. 2 vols. — *Strazny, Philipp*

y Encyclopedia of Literary Modernism — *Poplawski, Paul*

Encyclopedia of Meat Sciences — *Devine, Carrick*

Encyclopedia of Military Technology and Innovation — *Bull, Stephen*

Encyclopedia of Modern Ethnic Conflicts — *Rudolf, Joseph*

Encyclopedia of Modern Everyday Inventions — *Cole, David John*

Encyclopedia of Modern French Thought — *Dunmore, 4th Earl of*

Encyclopedia of Modern French Thought — *Murray, Christopher John*

Encyclopedia of Modern Greek Literature — *Merry, Bruce*

Encyclopedia of Modern Mexico — *Dent, David W.*

y Encyclopedia of Modern Worldwide Extremists and Extremist Groups — *Atkins, Stephen E.*

Encyclopedia of Mongolia and the Mongol Empire — *Atwood, Christopher P.*

Encyclopedia of Mosiac — *Goodwin, Elaine M.*

Encyclopedia of Murder and Violent Crime — *Hickey, Eric W.*

Encyclopedia of Nanoscience and Nanotechnology — *Nalwa, Hari Singh*

Encyclopedia of New Jersey — *Lurie, Maxine N.*

Encyclopedia of Opera on Screen: A Guide to More than 100 Years of Opera Films, Videos, and DVDs — *Wlaschin, Ken*

The Encyclopedia of Parkinson's Disease — *Mosley, Anthony D.*

Encyclopedia of Physics — *Rosen, Joe*

Encyclopedia of Physics — *Rosen, Joseph*

Encyclopedia of Physics — *Rosen, Joe*

Encyclopedia of Plant and Crop Science — *Goodman, Robert M.*

The Encyclopedia of Prayer and Praise — *Water, Mark*

Encyclopedia of Prehistory — *Peregrine, Peter N.*

y Encyclopedia of Presidential Campaigns, Slogans, Issues, and Platforms — *Roberts, Robert North*

The Encyclopedia of Protestantism — *Hillerbrand, Hans Joachim*

Encyclopedia of Public Administration and Public Policy — *Schultz, David A.*

The Encyclopedia of Public Choice — *Rowley, Charles Kershaw*

Encyclopedia of Race and Ethnic Studies — *Cashmore, Ernest*

Encyclopedia of Rape — *Smith, Merril D.*

Encyclopedia of Recorded Sound, 2nd Ed. — *Hoffman, Frank W.*

Encyclopedia of Recorded Sound, 2nd Ed., Vols. 1-2 — *Hoffmann, Frank W.*

Encyclopedia of Recreation and Leisure in America, Vols. 1-2 — *Cross, Gary S.*

y Encyclopedia of Religion and War — *Palmer-Fernandez, Gabriel*

y Encyclopedia of Religious Rites, Rituals, and Festivals — *Salamone, Frank A.*

Encyclopedia of Retirement and Finance — *Vitt, Lois A.*

Encyclopedia of Rose Science — *Roberts, Andrew V.*

y Encyclopedia of Russian History — *Millar, James R.*

The Encyclopedia of Sculpture, Vols. 1-3 — *Bostrom, Antonia*

The Enemy — *Child, Lee*

Enemy Within — *Beckett, Francis*

The Enemy Within: Combating Corruption in Asia — *Tay, Simon S.C.*

The Enemy Within: Hucksters, Racketeers, Deserters, and Civilians During the Second World War — *Thomas, Donald*

Energy and Geometry: An Introduction to Deformed Special Relativity — *Cardone, Fabio*

Energy and Information Transfer in Biological Systems: How Physics Could Enrich Biological Understanding, Proceedings — *Musumeci, Francesco*

Energy and the Unexpected — *Laidler, Keith James*

Energy at the Crossroads: Global Perspectives and Uncertainties — *Smil, Vaclav*

Energy Balances of Non-OECD Countries 2000-2001

Energy Balances of OECD Countries 2000-2001

y   Energy — *Bowden, Rob*

y   Energy — *Shaw, Jane S.*

c   Energy — *Stille, Darlene R.*

Energy-Efficient Electric Motors, 3rd Rev. Ed. — *Emadi, Ali*

c   Energy Essentials: Fossil Fuels — *Saunders, Nigel*

c   Energy: Heat, Light, and Fuel (Illus. by Boyd, Sheree) — *Stille, Darlene R.*

Energy in a Competitive Market: Essays in Honour of Colin Robinson — *Hunt, Lester C.*

Energy in a Competitive Market: Essays in Honour of Colin Robinson — *Robinson, Colin*

Energy Landscapes Applications to Clusters, Biomolecules and Glasses — *Wales, David J.*

Energy Management Handbook, 5th Ed. — *Turner, Wayne C.*

Energy Policies of IEA Countries: 2003 Review

Energy Policies of IEA Countries: Austria: 2002 Review

Energy Policies of IEA Countries: Hungary: 2003 Review

Energy Policies of IEA Countries: Switzerland: 2003 Review

Energy Policy and Regulation in the People's Republic of China — *Andrews-Speed, Phillip*

y   Energy: Present Knowledge: Future Trends — *Oxlade, Chris*

Energy Scavenging for Wireless Sensor Networks: With Special Focus on Vibrations — *Roundy, Shad*

Energy Statistics of Non-OECD Countries: 2000-2001

Energy Statistics of Non-OECD Countries 2000-2001

Energy Statistics of OECD Countries/Statistiques de L'Energie des Pays de L'OCDE, 2000-2001

Energy Statistics Yearbook 2001

Energy Systems and Sustainability: Power for a Sustainable Future — *Boyle, Godfrey*

Enfant Terrible — *Pomerance, Murray*

Enfermedades y trastornos de la salud — *Izenberg, Neil*

The Enforcement of Directors' Duties in Britain and Germany: A Comparative Study with Particular Reference to Large Companies — *Hirt, Hans C.*

Engaged Surrender: African American Women and Islam — *Rouse, Carolyn Moxley*

An Engagement with Plato's Republic: A Companion to the Republic — *Mitchell, B.*

Engaging Africa: Washington and the Fall of Portugal's Colonial Empire — *Schneidman, Witney W.*

Engaging Cultural Differences: The Multicultural Challenge in Liberal Democracies — *Shweder, Richard*

Engaging Eurasia's Separatist States: Unresolved Conflicts and de Facto States — *Lynch, Dov*

Engaging Film Criticism: Film History and Contemporary American Cinema — *Metz, Walter*

Engaging Humor — *Oring, Elliott*

Engaging India: Diplomacy, Democracy, and the Bomb — *Talbott, Strobe*

Engaging Modernity: Methods and Cases for Studying African Independent Churches in South Africa — *Venter, Dawid J.*

Engaging Modernity: Readings in Irish Politics, Culture and Literature at the Turn of the Century — *Boss, Michael*

Engaging Schools for Fostering High School Students' Motivation to Learn

Engaging Schools: Fostering High School Students' Motivation to Learn — *National Research Council (U.S.). Committee on Increasing High School Students' Engagement and Motivation to Learn*

Engaging Teachers: Towards a Radical Democratic Agenda for Schooling — *Gale, Trevor*

Engaging Young Children in Mathematics: Standards for Early Childhood Mathematics Education — *Clements, Douglas H.*

Engendering Church: Women, Power, and the AME Church — *Schmidt, Kimberley D.*

Engendering Psychology: Women and Gender Revisted, 2nd Ed. — *Denmark, Florence*

Engineering Acoustics: An Introduction to Noise Control — *Michael, Moser*

Engineering: An Endless Frontier — *Auyang, Sunny Y.*

Engineering Architecture: The Vision of Fazlur R. Khan — *Khan, Yasmin Sabina*

Engineering Considerations for Lift-Slab Construction — *Zailen, Rubin M.*

Engineering Design for Wear, 2nd Ed. — *Bayer, Raymond G.*

Engineering Effective Learning Toolkit — *Stolovitch, Harold D.*

Engineering Ethics: Concepts and Cases, 3rd Ed. — *Harris, Charles E.*

Engineering Geology and Construction — *Bell, F.G.*

Engineering Graphics, 2nd Ed. — *Chandra, A.M.*

Engineering Graphics with AutoCAD, 2004 — *Bethune, James D.*

The Engineering Handbook, 2nd Ed. — *Dorf, Richard C.*

Engineering Is Elementary: Engineering and Technology Lessons for Children

Engineering Materials Science: Properties, Uses, Degradation and Remediation — *McArthur, Hugh*

Engineering Materials Technology: Structures, Processing, Properties and Selection. 5th Ed. — *Jacobs, James A.*

Engineering Mechanics: Statics and Dynamics, 4th Ed. — *Bedford, Anthony*

The Engineering of Chemical Reactions, 2nd Ed. — *Schmidt, Lanny D.*

Engineering of Computer-Based Systems (ECBS 2004): Proceedings — *Dvorak, V.*

Engineering Systems Design and Analysis, Vol. 1

Engineering Systems Design and Analysis, Vol. 2

Engineering Systems Design and Analysis, Vol. 3

Engines of Our Ingenuity: An Engineer Looks at Technology and Culture — *Lienhard, John H.*

England and Europe in the Reign of Henry III — *Weiler, Bjorn K.U.*

c   England — *Dahl, Michael*

England Eats Out: A Social History of Eating Out in England From 1830 to the Present — *Burnett, John*

c   England, the Culture — *Banting, Erinn*

c   England, the Land — *Banting, Erinn*

c   England, the People — *Banting, Erinn*

England's Elizabeth: An Afterlife in Fame and Fantasy — *Dobson, Michael*

English and French Medieval Stained Glass in the Collection of the Metropolitan Museum of Art, Vols. 1-2 — *Hayward, Jane*

English and Nordic Modernisms — *Tysdahl, Bjorn*

The English and Scottish Popular Ballads: In Five Volumes, Vol. 1 — *Child, Francis James*

The English and Scottish Popular Ballads: In Five Volumes, Vol. 3 — *Child, Francis James*

The English and Scottish Popular Ballads: In Five Volumes, Vol. 4 — *Child, Francis James*

The English and the Normans: Ethnic Hostility, Assimilation, and Identity, 1066-c. 1220 — *Thomas, Hugh M.*

English Aristocratic Women, 1450-1550: Marriage and Family, Property and Careers — *Harris, Barbara J.*

English as a Second Language — *Crane, Megan*

English Battlefields: An Illustrated Encyclopedia — *Rayner, Michael*

English Children's Costume — *Brooke, Iris*

English Civic Pageantry, 1558-1642, Rev. Ed. — *Bergeron, David Moore*

The English Cookery Book: Historical Essays — *Leeds Symposium on Food History (16th: 2001)*

English Costume of the Later Middle Ages: Fourteenth-Fifteenth Century, Rev. 3rd Ed. — *Brooke, Iris*

The English Daughter — *Townsend, Lindsay*

English Diplomatic Practice in the Middle Ages — *Chaplais, Pierre*

English Dramatic Interludes, 1300-1580: A Reference Guide — *Grantley, Darryll*

English Episcopal Acta. London: 1189-1228 — *Johnson, D.P.*

English Ethnicity and Race in Early Modern Drama — *Floyd-Wilson, Mary*

The English Experience in France 1450-1558: War, Diplomacy and Cultural Exchange — *Grummitt, David*

English Feminists and Their Opponents in the 1790s: Unsex'd and Proper Females — *Stafford, William*

An English Gentleman — *Gilbert, Sky*

The English Glee in the Reign of George III: Participatory Art Music for an Urban Society — *Rubin, Emanuel (b. 1935 -)*

The English House: English Country Houses and Interiors — *Griffiths, Sally*

English Hymns of the Nineteenth Century: An Anthology — *Arnold, Richard*

The English in Australia — *Jupp, James*

The English Jacobin Novel on Rights, Property, and the Law: Critiquing the Contract — *Johnson, Nancy E.*

The English Judges: Their Role in the Changing Constitution — *Stevens, Robert*

English Language Teaching in East Asia Today: Changing Policies and Practices, 2nd Ed. — *Ho, Wah Kam*

English Lawyers between Market and State: The Politics of Professionalism — *Abel, Richard L.*

English Lessons: The Pedagogy of Imperialism in Nineteenth-Century China — *Hevia, James L.*

English Literature and Ancient Languages — *Haynes, Kenneth*

The English Manor c. 1200-1500 — *Bailey, Mark (b. 1960 -)*

English Modality in Perspective: Genre Analysis and Contrastive Studies — *Facchinetti, Roberta*

The English Novel: An Introduction — *Eagleton, Terry*

English Political Culture in the Fifteenth Century — *Hicks, Michael*

The English Prose Treatises of Richard Rolle — *McIlroy, Claire Elizabeth*

English Public Law — *Feldman, David*

English Public Opinion and the American Civil War — *Campbell, Duncan Andrew*

The English Radical Imagination: Culture, Religion, and Revolution, 1630-1660 — *McDowell, Nicholas*

The English Romance in Time: Transforming Motifs from Geoffrey of Monmouth to the Death of Shakespeare — *Cooper, Helen (b. 1947 -)*

English Romanticism and the Celtic World — *Carruthers, Gerard*

English Shops and Shopping: An Architectural History — *Morrison, Kathryn A.*

English Society and the Prison: Time, Culture, and Politics in the Development of the Modern Prison, 1850-1920 — *Brown, Alyson*

English-Spanish Real Estate Dictionary — *Olmos, Nora*

An English Translation of Bachofen's Mutterrecht (Mother Right) (1861): A Study of the Religious and Juridical Aspects of Gynecocracy in the Ancient World — *Bachofen, Johann Jakob*

An English Translation of Fa-Tsang's 'Commentary on the Awakening of Faith' — *Fazang*

English Witchcraft, 1560-1736 — *Sharpe, James*

Englishmen Transplanted: The English Colonization of Barbados, 1627-1660 — *Gragg, Larry*

Enhanced Transition through Outward Internationalization: Outward FDI by Slovenian Firms — *Jaklic, Andreja*

Enhancing LAN Performance, 4th Ed. — *Held, Gilbert*

Enhancing Our Way to Happiness?: Aristotle Versus Bacon on the Nature of True Happiness — *McReynolds, Kathy*

Enhancing Urban Management in East Asia — *Freire, Mila*

Enigma: How the Poles Broke the Nazi Code — *Kozaczuk, Wadysaw*

The Enigma of Comparative Law: Variations on a Theme for the Twenty-First Century — *Orucu, Esin*

Enlightened Networking: Import and Export of Enlightenment in 18th Century Denmark — *Bredsdorff, Thomas*

Enlightening the British: Knowledge, Discovery and the Museum in the Eighteenth Century: Proceedings — *Anderson, R.G.W.*

Enlightenment and Pathology — *Vila, Anne C.*

The Enlightenment and Religion: The Myths of Modernity — *Barnett, S.J.*

Enlightenment and Revolution: Essays in Honour of Norman Hampson — *Crook, Malcolm*

The Enlightenment and the Intellectual Foundations of Modern Culture — *Dupre, Louis*

The Enlightenment and the Intellectual Foundations of Modern Culture — *Louis, Dupre*

Enlightenment Blues: My Years with an American Guru — *Braak, Andre*

Title Index

F

The First Female Stars: Women of the Silent Era
— *Menefee, David W.*
c First Flight: The Story of the Wright Brothers
— *Taylor, Richard L.*
First Globalization: The Eurasian Exchange
1500-1800 — *Gunn, Geoffrey C.*
First Hand — *Bierds, Linda*
y The First Humans — *Diagram Group*
The First Idea: How Symbols, Language, and
Intelligence Evolved from Our Primate Ancestors
to Modern Humans — *Greenspan, Stanley I.*
The First Idea: How Symbols, Language, and
Intelligence Evolved in Early Primates and
Humans — *Greenspan, Stanley I.*
y First Impressions: What You Don't Know about How
Others See You — *Demarais, Ann*
First In: An Insider's Account of How the CIA
Spearheaded the War on Terror in Afghanistan
— *Schroen, Gary*
The First Industrial Region: North-West England, c.
1700-60 — *Stobart, Jon*
The First Jewish Revolt: Archaeology, History, and
Ideology — *Berlin, Andrea M.*
c A First Look at Art
First Look at ASP.NET v.2.0 — *Homer, Alex*
First Look at SQL Server 2005 for Developers
— *Beauchemin, Bob*
First Loves — *Solotaroff, Ted*
c The First Man in Space — *Cullen, David*
c The First Moon Landing — *Crewe, Sabrina*
First Mountain Man: Preacher's Justice — *Johnstone,
William W.*
The First New Nation: The United States in Historical
and Comparative Perspective — *Lipset, Seymour
Martin*
First Nights at the Opera — *Kelly, Thomas Forrest*
The First Noel: A Christmas Carousel (Illus. by
Pienkowski, Jan) — *Pienkowski, Jan*
First Note — *MENC*
c First Painter — *Lasky, Kathryn*
y The First Part Last (Read by Oldjohn, Khalipa).
Audiobook Review — *Johnson, Angela*
y The First Part Last — *Johnson, Angela*
First Peoples in Canada — *McMillan, Alan D.*
First Person: New Media as Story, Performance, and
Game — *Wardrip-Fruin, Noah*
c First Phonics — *Shannon, Rosemarie*
The First Poets: Lives of the Ancient Greek Poets
— *Schmidt, Michael*
c First Science Experiments: Mighty Machines (Illus. by
Harpster, Steve) — *Levine, Shar*
y The First Stone — *Aker, Don*
c The First "Test-Tube Baby." — *MacDonald, Fiona*
The First Texas Legion During the American Civil
War — *Hatley, Allen G.*
First Time Director: How to Make Your Breakthrough
Movie — *Bettman, Gil*
c First Time: Set 2
First to Fight — *Mihesuah, Henry*
c First to Fly (Illus. by Craig, David) — *Busby, Peter*
The First War on Terrorism: Counter-Terrorism
Policy During the Reagan Administration — *Wills,
David C.*
y The First World War — *Strachan, Hew*
First World War.com — *Duffy, Michael*
The First World War: The Essential Guide to Sources
in the UK National Archives — *Beckett, I.F.W.*
The First-Year Principal — *Hall, Peter A.*
Fiscal and Generational Imbalances: New Budget
Measures for New Budget Priorities — *Gokhale,
Jagadeesh*
Fiscal Federalism in Latin America: From
Entitlements to Markets — *Wiesner, Eduardo*
Fiscal Federalism in Unitary States — *Molander, Per*
Fiscal Policies in Federal States — *Braun, Dietmar*
Fischer in Frankfurt. Karriere eines aubenseiters
— *Kraushaar, Wolfgang*
Fish: A Novel (Read by Lamia, Jenna). Audiobook
Review — *Matthews, L.S.*
Fish and Fish Dishes of Laos — *Davidson, Alan*
Fish and Seafood — *Jaros, Patrik*
c Fish (Read by Lamia, Jenna). Audiobook Review
— *Matthews, L.S.*
c Fish — *Bendry, Christa*
y Fish — *Matthews, L.S.*
c Fish — *Richardson, Adele*
Fish, Flesh and Good Red Herring: A Gallimaufry
— *Ellis, Alice Thomas*
Fish for All: An Oral History of Multiple Claims and
Dividend Sentiment on Lake Michigan
— *Chiarappa, Michael*
c The Fish in Room 11 — *Dyer, Heather*

Fish of Alberta — *Joynt, Amanda*
Fish Versus Power: An Environmental History of the
Fraser River — *Evenden, Matthew*
The Fisher King — *Powell, Anthony*
The Fisherman's Net: The Influence of the Popes on
History — *Collins, Michael (b. 1960 -)*
c Fishing Day (Illus. by Evans, Shane W.) — *Pinkney,
Andrea Davis*
Fishing Lure Collectibles, Volume Two — *Murphy,
Dudley*
Fishing the Massachusetts Coast — *Gribb, John*
c Fishing with Balloons — *DiMucci, Dion*
Fiske Guide to Colleges, 2005 — *Fiske, Edward B.*
Fiske New SAT Insider's Guide — *Fiske, Edward B.*
Fiskerton: An Iron Age Timber Causeway with Iron
Age and Roman Votive Offerings, the 1981
Excavations — *Field, Naomi*
A Fistful of Fig Newtons — *Shepherd, Jean*
The Fit — *Hensher, Philip*
Fitness for Service, Life Extension, Remediation,
Repair, and Erosion / Corrosion Issues for Pressure
Vessels and Components: Proceedings — *Takagi,
Yoshio*
Fitness Information for Teens: Health Tips about
Exercise, Physical Well-Being, and Health
Maintenance, Including Facts about Aerobic and
Anaerobic Conditioning, Stretching, Body Shape
and Body Image... — *Bellenir, Karen*
y Fitness Information for Teens: Health Tips about
Exercise, Physical Well-Being, and Health
Maintenance Including Facts about Aerobic and
Anaerobic Conditioning, Stretching, Body Shape
and Body Image... — *Bellenir, Karen*
The Fitness Kitchen: Recipes for a Fad-Free Lifestyle
— *Sinton, Shelly*
Fitting Models to Biological Data Using Linear and
Nonlinear Regression; A Practical Guide to Curve
Fitting — *Motulsky, Harvey*
Fitzhenry and Whiteside Book of Canadian Facts and
Dates, 3rd Ed. — *Pound, Richard W.*
Fitzpatrick's War — *Judson, Theodore*
FitzRoy: The Remarkable Story of Darwin's Captain
and the Invention of the Weather Forecast
— *Gribbin, John*
y FitzRoy: The Remarkable Story of Darwin's Captain
and the Invention of the Weather Forecast
— *Gribbin, John R.*
Five Biggest Unsolved Problems in Science
— *Wiggins, Arthur W.*
Five Bodies: Re-Figuring Relationships — *O'Neill,
John*
The Five Books of Moses: A Translation with
Commentary — *Alter, Robert*
The Five Books of Moses Lapinsky — *Tulchinsky,
Karen X.*
Five Centuries of American Costume — *Wilcox, R.
Turner*
c Five Creatures (Illus. by Bogacki, Tomek) — *Jenkins,
Emily*
Five Gentlemen of Japan: The Portrait of a Nation's
Character — *Gibney, Frank*
c Five Little Ducks — *Yaccarino, Dan*
c Five Little Monkeys Play Hide-and-Seek (Illus. by
Christelow, Eileen) — *Christelow, Eileen*
c Five-Minutes Bible Stories (Illus. by Johnson,
Richard) — *Rock, Lois*
Five Minutes to a Great Real Estate Sales Meeting
— *Mayfield, John D.*
Five Quarts: A Personal and Natural History of Blood
— *Hayes, Bill*
Five Roses: Guide to Good Cooking — *Driver,
Elizabeth*
y Five Seasons of Angel: Science Fiction and Fantasy
Writers Discuss Their Favorite Vampire — *Yeffeth,
Glenn*
c Five Stars for Emily — *Silverthorne, Judith*
c Five Stars for Emily — *Waldron, Kathleen Cook*
Five Talents or One? The Shocking Secret of
Inequality — *Efimov, Igor Markovich*
Five Thousand Days: Press Photography in a
Changing World — *British Press Photographer's
Association*
Five Thousand Days: Press Photography in a
Changing World Members of The British Press
Association — *Evans, Harold*
Five Women of the English Reformation — *Zahl, Paul
F.M.*
The Fix Is In: A History of Baseball Gambling and
Game Fixing Scandals — *Ginsburg, Daniel E.*
Fix-It and Forget-It Diabetic Cookbook: Slow Cooker
Favorites--to Include Everyone! — *Pellman, Phyllis*

Fix It Before It Breaks: Seasonal Checklist Guide to
Home Maintenance — *Kennedy, Terry*
Fixed Point Theory — *Granas, Andrzej*
Fixin' to Git: One Fan's Love Affair with NASCAR's
Winston Cup — *Wright, Jim*
Fixing African Economies: Policy Research for
Development — *Phillips, Lucie Colvin*
Fixing Intelligence: For a More Secure America
— *Marion, Forrest L.*
Fixing Intelligence: For a More Secure America
— *Odom, William E.*
y Fizz, Bubble and Flash! Element Explorations and
Atom Adventures for Hands-On Science Fun!
— *Brandolini, Anita*
c Flag Day — *Kaplan, Leslie C.*
y The Flags of War — *Wilson, John*
c The Flags of War — *Wilson, John (b. 1951 -)*
A Flame in Hali — *Bradley, Marion Zimmer*
y The Flame Keepers (Read by Marosz, Jonathan).
Audiobook Review — *Handy, Ned*
y The Flame Tree — *Lewis, Richard*
The Flamenco Tradition in the Works of Federico
Garcia Lorca and Carlos Saura: The Wounded
Throat — *Stone, Rob*
c Flames of the Tiger — *Wilson, John (b. 1951 -)*
Flaming Iguanas — *Lopez, Erika*
The Flaming Luau of Death: A Madeline Bean Novel
— *Farmer, Jerrilyn*
Flammability and Sensitivity of Materials in
Oxygen-Enriched Atmospheres, Vol. 10
— *Steinberg, Theodore A.*
Flanimals — *Gervais, Ricky*
Flannery O'Connor: A Life — *Cash, Jean*
Flannery O'Connor and the Christ-Haunted South
— *Wood, Ralph C.*
Flannery O'Connor's Sacramental Art — *Srigley,
Susan*
Flash And Crash Days: Brazilian Theatre in the
Post-Dictatorship — *George, David*
y Flash — *Modesitt, L.E.*
The Flash: Crossfire — *Geoff, Johns*
Flash Effect: Science and the Rhetorical Origins of
Cold War America — *Tietge, David J.*
Flash Hacks — *Bhangal, Sham*
The Flash of Capital — *Cazdyn, Eric M.*
Flash Remoting: The Definitive Guide — *Muck, Tom*
Flash Smelting: Analysis, Control and Optimization.
2nd Ed. — *Davenport, W.G.*
Flashpoint (Read by Ewbank, Melanie). Audiobook
Review — *Brockmann, Suzanne*
Flat — *MacDonald, Mark*
Flat Crazy: A Blanco County Mystery — *Rehder, Ben*
c Flat Stanley Audio Collection (Read by Pinkwater,
Daniel). Audiobook Review — *Brown, Jeff*
Flaubert and Madame Bovary — *Steegmuller, Francis*
Flaubert's 'Salammbo': The Ancient Orient as a
Political Allegory of Nineteenth-Century France
— *Durr, Volker*
y Flavor of the Week — *Shaw, Tucker*
Flavour Perception — *Taylor, Andrew J.*
Flaw Evaluation, Service Experience, and Materials
for Hydrogen Service: Proceedings — *Wang,
Yong-Yi*
The Flawed Architect: Henry Kissinger and American
Foreign Policy — *Hanhimaki, Jussi*
Flaws and Fallacies in Statistical Thinking
— *Campbell, Stephen K.*
The Flayed Dog — *Saprjanov, Chanadon Christo*
y FLCL, Vol 1. Art (Illus. by Ueda, Hajime) — *Gainax*
Flee the Night — *Warren, Susan May*
Fleeing for Freedom: Stories of the Underground
Railroad — *Hendrick, George*
Fleeing the House of Horrors: Women Who Have Left
Abusive Partners — *Severs, Aysan*
Fleet Fire: Thomas Edison and the Pioneers of the
Electric Revolution — *Davis, L.J.*
Fleeting Rome: In Search of "La Dolce Vita" — *Levi,
Carlo*
Fleming's Arts & Ideas, 10th Ed., Vol. 1 — *Marien,
Mary Warner*
Fleming's Arts & Ideas, 10th Ed., Vol. 2 — *Marien,
Mary Warner*
Flemish Art and Architecture 1585-1700 — *Vlieghe,
Hans*
Flemish Illuminated Manuscripts, 1400-1550
— *McKendrick, Scot*
Flesers' Reagents for Organic Synthesis: Vol. 22
— *Ho, Tse-Lok*
Flesh: A Suzanne LaFleshe Mystery — *Seamon, Hollis*
Flesh and Blood (Read by Griffin, Gordon).
Audiobook Review — *Harvey, John*
Flesh and Blood — *Harvey, John*

Food and Health in Europe: A New Basis for Action
— Robertson, Aileen

y Food and Nutrition

c Food Chains — Ganeri, Anita

Food, Cookery and Dining in Ancient Times: Alexis
Soyer's Pantropheon — Soyer, Alexis

Food Culture in China — Newman, Jacqueline M.

Food Culture in India — Sen, Colleen Taylor

Food Culture in Japan — Ashkenazi, Michael

Food Emulsions. 4th Ed., Rev. and Expanded
— Friberg, Stig E.

Food Emulsions, 4th Ed., Rev. and Expanded
— Friberg, Stig E.

Food Fights over Free Trade: How International
Institutions Promote Agricultural Trade
Liberalization — Davis, Christina L.

Food for the Soul: Selections from the Holy Apostles
Soup Kitchen Writers Workshop — Maxwell,
Elizabeth

Food for Thought: The Complete Book of Concepts
for Growing Minds — Freymann, Saxton

Food for Thought: The Debate Over Eating Meat
— Sapontzis, Steve F.

Food History Comes of Age — Davidson, Alan

c Food — Hosack, Karen

Food in Early Modern Europe — Albala, Ken

Food in the Ancient World from A to Z — Dalby,
Andrew

Food, Inc.: From Mendel to Monsanto--The Promises
and Perils of the Biotech Harvest — Pringle, Peter

Food Microbiology Laboratory — McLandsborough,
Lynne Ann

Food Nations: Selling Taste in Consumer Societies
— Belasco, Warren

The Food of Love — Capella, Anthony

Food Policy Old and New — Maxwell, Simon

Food Processing: Principles and Applications
— Smith, J. Scott

c The Food Pyramid — Petrie, Kristin

Food Regulation and Trade: Toward a Safe and Open
Global Food System — Josling, Timothy Edward

c Food Rules! The Stuff You Munch, Its Crunch, and
Why You Sometimes Lose Your Lunch — Haduck,
Bill

Food Wars: The Global Battle for Mouths, Minds and
Markets — Lang, Tim

Foodborne Disease in OECD Countries: Present State
and Economic Costs — Organization for Economic
Cooperation and Development

y Foodboy — Swain, Carol

c Foods from the Farm — Weber, Rebecca

Foods of the Americas: Native Recipes and Traditions
— Divina, Fernando

A Fool and His Forty Acres: Conjuring a Vineyard
Three Thousand Miles from Burgundy
— Heinricks, Geoff

Fooled by Randomness: The Hidden Role of Chance
in Life and in the Markets, 2nd Ed. — Taleb,
Nassim Nicholas

Fool's Curtain (Read by Bennett, Judy). Audiobook
Review — Lorrimer, Claire

Fools in the Field — Bailo, Ben M.

Fool's Paradise: Remembering the Thousand Islands
— Malo, Paul

Fools Rush In: Steve Case, Jerry Levin, and the
Unmaking of AOL Time Warner — Munk, Nina

The Fool's Tale: A Novel — Galland, Nicole

y The Fool's Tale — Garland, Nicole

y Fool's Tavern — Resnikoff, Ned

Fooly Booked! Reader Development and the
Secondary School LRC — Armstrong, Eileen

Foot: A Playful Biography — Vanderlinden, Kathy

Foot and Ankle — Thordarson, David B.

Foot and Mouth Disease: Current Perspectives
— Sobrino, Francisco

y Football and Its Followers — May, Pete

The Football Game I'll Never Forget: 100 NFL Stars'
Stories — McDonell, Chris

Football in Africa — Armstrong, Gary

Football Lexicon: A Dictionary of Usage in Football
Journalism and Commentary — Leigh, John

Footnotes — Cole, Kenneth

Footprints of the Lion: Isaac Newton at Work
— Mandelbrote, Scott

Footprints on the Sands of Time: RAF Bomber
Command Prisoners-of-War in Germany,
1939-1945 — Clutton-Brock, Oliver

Footprints: The Life and Work of Wayne Shorter
— Mercer, Michelle

Footsteps — Mills, Diann

Foozlers — Osborne, Tom

For All These Rights: Business, Labor, and the
Shaping of America's Public-Private Welfare State
— Klein, Jennifer

For Anatole's Tomb — Mallarme, Stephane

For Better or Worse?: How Political Consultants Are
Changing Elections in the United States — Dulio,
David A.

For Ethical Politics — Blunden, Andy

For Fear of the Fire: Joan of Arc and the Limits of
Subjectivity — Meltzer, Francoise

For Free Press and Equal Rights: Republican
Newspapers in the Reconstruction South — Abbott,
Richard H.

"For Freedom Alone": The Declaration of Arbroath,
1320 — Cowan, Edward J.

y For Freedom: The Story of a French Spy — Bradley,
Kimberly Brubaker

y For Girls Only: Wise Words, Good Advice — Weston,
Carol

For Joshua: An Ojibway Father Teaches His Son
— Wagamese, Richard

For Keeps: 30 Years at the Movies — Kael, Pauline

For Love and Money: A Novel of Stocks and Robbers
— Glass, Leslie

For Love of Insects — Eisner, Thomas

For Our Navajo People: Dine Letters, Speeches and
Petitions, 1990-1960 — Iverson, Peter

For Patients of Moderate Means: A Social History of
the Voluntary Public General Hospital in Canada,
1890-1950 — Gagan, David

For Race and Country: The Life and Career of
Colonel Charles Young — Kilroy, David P.

For Shade and for Comfort: Democratizing
Horticulture in the Nineteenth-Century Midwest
— Cheryl, Lyon-Jenness

c For Sure! For Sure! (Illus. by Czernecki, Stefan)
— Andersen, Hans Christian

For the Common Good: A Critical Examination of
Law and Social Control — Miller, R. Robin

For the Common Good? American Civic Life and the
Golden Age of Fraternity — Kaufman, Jason

For the Common Good: Popular Politics in Barcelona,
1580-1640 — Corteguera, Luis R.

For the Dogs — Wignall, Kevin

For the End of Time: The Story of the Messiaen
Quartet — Rischin, Rebecca

For the Glory of God: How Monotheism Led to
Reformations, Science, Witch-Hunts, and the End
of Slavery — Stark, Rodney

For the Good of the Company: The History of the
McCrory Corporation — Barmash, Isadore

For the Love of Books: 115 Celebrated Writers on the
Books They Love Most — Shwartz, Ronald B.

For the Love of Knitting: A Celebration of the
Knitter's Art — Cornell, Kari A.

For the Love of Reading: Books to Build Lifelong
Readers — Bouchard, David

For the Love of the Game: Amateur Sport in
Small-town Ontario, 1838-1895 — Bouchier, Nancy

For the Love of Women — Kirtsoglou, Elisabeth

For the Record: A Documentary History of America,
2nd Ed., Vol. 1 — Shi, David E.

For the Sake of Argument: Practical Reasoning,
Character, and the Ethics of Belief — Garver,
Eugene

For the Sake of Heaven and Earth: The New
Encounter Between Judaism and Christianity
— Greenberg, Irving

For the Sake of Heaven and Earth: The New
Encounter between Judaism and Christianity
— Greenberg, Irving

For the Survival of Democracy: Franklin Roosevelt
and the World Crisis of the 1930s — Hamby,
Alonzo

y For Those About to Rock: A Road Map to Being in a
Band — Bidini, Dave

For Those Who Fell — Dietz, William C.

For What Tomorrow: A Dialogue — Derrida, Jacques

Forbidden Acts: Pioneering Gay and Lesbian Plays of
the Twentieth Century — Hodges, Ben

Forbidden Animation: Censored Cartoons and
Blacklisted Animators in America — Cohen, Karl F.

Forbidden — Wall, Wilma

Forbidden Dance, Vol. 4 — Ashihara, Hinako

Forbidden Fruit: Love Stories from the Underground
Railroad and Beyond — Deramus, Betit

Forbidden Fruit: Love Stories from the Underground
Railroad. — De Ramus, Betty

Forbidden Territory and Realms of Strife: The
Memoirs of Juan Goytisolo — Goytisolo, Juan

The Force of Art — Ziarek, Krzysztof

The Force of Culture: Vincent Massey and Canadian
Sovereignty — Finlay, Karen A.

A Force Profonde: The Power, Politics, and Promise of
Human Rights — Kolodziej, Edward A.

Force Protection — Kent, Gordon

Forced March — Radnoti, Miklos

y Forces and Motion Science Fair Projects: Using Water
Balloons, Pulleys and Other Stuff — Fardner,
Robert

Forces of Labor: Workers' Movements and
Globalization since 1870 — Silver, Beverly J.

y Forces of Nature: The Awesome Power of Volcanoes,
Earthquakes, and Tornadoes — Grace, Catherine
O'Neill

Fordham: A History and Memoir — Schroth, Raymond
A.

The Fords: An American Epic — Collier, Peter

Foreign Aid and Development: Lessons Learnt and
Directions for the Future — Tarp, Finn

Foreign Babes in Beijing: Behind the Scenes of a New
China — DeWoskin, Rachel

Foreign Direct Investment and Its Contributions to
Economic Growth and Poverty Reduction in
Vietnam — Nguyen, Thi Phuong Hoa

Foreign Direct Investment and Performance
Requirements: New Evidence from Selected
Countries — United Nations Conference on Trade
and Development

Foreign Direct Investment in Central and Eastern
Europe — Marinova, Svetla Trifonova

Foreign Direct Investment in Central Asian and
Caucasian Economies: Policies and Issues: Papers
and Proceedings — United Nations

Foreign Direct Investment in Kazakhstan:
Politico-Legal Aspects of Post-Communist
Transition — Dosmukhamedov, E.K.

y A Foreign Field — Chan, Gillian

A Foreign Field — Mayhew, Margaret

Foreign Films in America: A History — Segrave,
Kerry

Foreign Investment and Socio-Economic Development
in China: The Case of Dongguan — Yeung, Godfrey

Foreign-Language Printing in London 1500-1900
— Taylor, Barry

The Foreign Missionary Enterprise at Home:
Explorations in North American Cultural History
— Bays, Daniel H.

y Foreign Oil Dependence — Haley, James (b. 1968 -)

Foreign Trade Statistics of Asia and the Pacific
1996-2000, 2001-2002 Ed. — United Nations

Foreigners in Their Native Land: Historical Roots of
the Mexican Americans — Weber, David J.

Forensic Analysis: Weighing Bullet Lead Evidence
— National Research Council

Forensic and Clinical Applications of Solid Phase
Extraction — Telepchak, Michael J.

Forensic Aspects of Chemical and Biological
Terrorism — Wecht, Cyril H.

The Forensic Casebook — Genge, N.E.

y Forensic Crime Solvers

Forensic Linguistics: An Introduction to Language,
Crime, and the Law — Olsson, John

Forensic Linguistics: An Introduction to Language,
Crime and the Law — Olsson, John

Forensic Materials Engineering: Case Studies
— Lewis, Peter Rhys

Forensic Nurse: The New Role of the Nurse in Law
Enforcement — Stevens, Serita

Forensic Pathology Reviews, Vol. 1 — Tsokos, Michael

Forensic Psychology, 2nd Ed. — Wrightsman, Lawrence
S.

Forensic Science, 1st Ed. — Jackson, Andrew R.W.

Forensic Science: An Illustrated Dictionary
— Brenner, John C.

Forest and Gardens: Traces of Wildness in a
Modernizing Land, 1897-1949 — Simo, Melanie

Forest Biodiversity: Lessons from History for
Conservation — Honnay, O.

Forest Conservation Policy: A Reference Handbook
— Sample, V. Alaric

c Forest Explorer: A Life-Size Field Guide — Bishop,
Nic

Forest Farmsteads: A Millennium of Human
Occupation at Winding Stair in the Ouachita
Mountains — Early, Ann M.

y Forest Fires — Platts, Linda

The Forest for the Trees: How Humans Shaped the
North Woods — Forester, Jeff

Forest Futures: Science, Politics, and Policy for the
Next Century — Arabas, Karen

y The Forest Lover (Read by White, Karen). Audiobook
Review — Vreeland, Susan

The Fountain at the Center of the World — *Newman, Robert*

The Fountainhead of Chinese Erotica: The Lord of Perfect Satisfaction — *Stone, Charles R.*

c Four Boys Named Jordan (Illus. by King, Tara Calahan) — *Harper, Jessica*

Four Corners — *Bloomfield, Debra*

Four Creations: An Epic Story of the Chiapas Mayas — *Gossen, Gary H.*

Four Cultures of the West — *O'Malley, John W.*

Four Decades of Transformation: Land Use in Singapore, 1960-2000 — *Wong, Tai-Chee*

The Four Faces of Nuclear Terrorism — *Ferguson, Charles D.*

c Four Friends in Autumn (Illus. by DePaola, Tomie) — *DePaola, Tomie*

c Four Friends in the Garden (Illus. by Heap, Sue) — *Heap, Sue*

The Four Horsemen of the Apocalypse: Religion, War, Famine and Death in Reformation Europe — *Cunningham, Andrew*

Four Illusions: Candrakirti's Advice to Travelers on the Bodhisattva Path — *Lang, Karen C.*

Four Pictures — *Carr, Emily*

c Four Pictures by Emily Carr — *Debon, Nicolas*

y Four Seasons Make a Year (Illus. by Halsey, Megan) — *Rockwell, Anne*

Four Seminars — *Heidegger, Martin*

Four Souls — *Erdrich, Louise*

Four Spirits — *Naslund, Sena Jeter*

Four Surprises in Global Demography — *Eberstadt, Nicholas*

Four Tenths of an Acre: Reflections on a Gardening Life — *Lisle, Laurie*

Four Trials — *Edwards, John (b. 1953 -)*

Four Trials — *Edwards, John (b. 1953 -)*

Four Way Street: The Crosby, Stills, Nash and Young Reader — *Zimmer, Dave*

Fourbodings — *Crowther, Peter*

Fourier and Laplace Transforms. 1st Ed. — *Beerends, R.J.*

Fourier Optics; An Introduction, 2nd Ed. — *Steward, E.G.*

Fourier-Transform Spectroscopy Instrumentation Engineering — *Saptari, Vidi*

The Fourteenth and Fifteenth Centuries — *Griffiths, Ralph*

Fourteenth Century England II — *Given-Wilson, Chris*

Fourteenth-Century Icelandic Verse on the Virgin Mary: Drapa at Mariugrat, Vitnisvisur of Mariu, Mariuvisur, I-III — *Wrightson, Kellinde*

The Fourth Crusade and the Sack of Constantinople — *Phillips, Jonathan*

The Fourth Crusade: Event and Context — *Angold, Michael*

c Fourth-Grade Fuss (Illus. by Hammond, Andy) — *Hurwitz, Johanna*

Fourth International Conference on Peer-to-Peer Computing — *Caronni, Germano*

The Fourth Network: How Fox Broke the Rules and Reinvented Television — *Kimmel, Daniel M.*

The Fourth Power: A Grand Strategy for the United States in the Twenty-First Century — *Hart, Gary*

The Fourth R: Conflicts over Religion in America's Public Schools — *DelFattore, Joan*

The Fourth Wall — *Saulnier, Beth*

Fox Evil (Read by Prebble, Simon). Audiobook Review — *Walters, Minette*

The Fox in the Cupboard: A Memoir — *Shilling, Jane*

c Fox on the Ice (Illus. by Deines, Brian) — *Highway, Tomson*

c Fox Winter — *Thompson, Margaret*

c Foxes and Their Dens — *Rustad, Martha E.H.*

Foxfire 12 — *Collins, Kaye Carver*

y Foxmask — *Marillier, Juliet*

The Fox's Walk — *Davis-Goff, Annabel*

c Foxy Fox — *Schulman, Mark*

Fra Regola e Licenza: Chiesa e Vita Religiosa, Feste e Beneficenza a Napoli e in Campania — *Barletta, Laura*

The Fractal Murders — *Cohen, Mark*

Fractals and Chaos: The Mandelbrot Set and Beyond — *Mandelbrot, Benoit B.*

c Fraction Action — *Leedy, Loreen*

The Fractious Nation?: Unity and Division in Contemporary American Life — *Rieder, Jonathan*

Fracture Methodologies and Manufacturing Processes: Proceedings — *Lam, Poh-Sang*

The Fracture of Good Order: Christian Antiliberalism and the Challenge to American Politics — *Bivins, Jason C.*

Fractures of the Upper Extremity — *Ziran, Bruce H.*

Fragmented Space in the Russian Federation — *Ruble, Blaire A.*

Fragmented Ties: Salvadoran Immigrant Networks in America — *Menjivar, Cecilia*

Fragments — *Tsmimicalis, Stavros*

Fragments of Grace: My Search for Meaning in the Strife of South Asia — *Constable, Pamela*

Frame Work in Language and Literacy: How Theory Informs Practice — *Duchan, Judith Felson*

Framed: America's Art Dealer to the Stars Tells All — *Volpe, Tod*

Framed! Labor and the Corporate Media — *Martin, Christopher R.*

A Framework for Freedom: Learner Autonomy in Foreign Language Teacher Education — *Van Esch, Kees*

Framing a National Narrative: The Legend Collections of Peter Christen Asbjornsen — *Hult, Marte Hvam*

Framing ADHD Children: Critical Examination of the History, Discourse, and Everyday Experience of Attention Deficit/Hyperactivity disorder — *Rafalovich, Adam*

Framing America: A Social History of American Art — *Pohl, Frances K.*

Framing American Divorce: From the Revolutionary Generation to the Victorians — *Basch, Norma*

Framing Europe: Attitudes to European Integration in Germany, Spain, and the United Kingdom — *Diez Medrano, Juan*

Framing Europe: Attitudes to European Integration in Germany, Spain, and the United Kingdom — *Medrano, Juan Diez*

Framing Financial Structure in an Information Environment — *Courchene, Thomas J.*

Framing" India": The Colonial Imaginary in Early Modern Culture — *Raman, Shanker*

Framing Piracy: Globalization and Film Distribution in Greater China — *Wang, Shujen*

Framing the Bride: Globalizing Beauty and Romance in Taiwan's Bridal Industry — *Adrian, Bonnie*

Framing the Polish Home: Postwar Cultural Constructions of Hearth, Nation, and Self — *Shallcross, Bozena*

France, 1715-1804: Power and the People — *Lewis, Gwynne*

France 1814-1940 — *Tombs, Robert*

France, a Love Story: Women Write about the French Experience — *Cusumano, Camille*

France: A Reference Guide from the Renaissance to the Present — *Roberts, William J.*

France and the Cult of the Sacred Heart — *Jonas, Raymond*

France and the Grand Tour — *Black, Jeremy*

France and the Great War, 1914-1918 — *Smith, Leonard V.*

France and the Holy Land: Frankish Culture at the End of the Crusades — *Weiss, Daniel H.*

France and the Nazi Threat: The Collapse of French Diplomacy, 1932-1939 — *Duroselle, Jean-Baptiste*

France: The Essential Guide to Viewing Art in Paris and Its Surrounds — *Hannan, Bill*

Frances Burney and the Female Bildungsroman: An Interpretation of The Wanderer, or Female Difficulties — *Gemmeke, Mascha*

Frances Hodgson Burnett: The Unexpected Life of the Author of The Secret Garden — *Gerzina, Gretchen Holbrook*

Frances Hodgson Burnett: The Unexpected Life of the Author of 'The Secret Garden' — *Gerzina, Gretchen Holbrook*

Frances Hodgson Burnett: The Unexpected Life of the Author of The Secret Garden — *Gerzina, Gretchen Holbrook*

Frances Power Cobbe: Victorian Feminist, Journalist, Reformer — *Mitchell, Sally*

c Francesca and the Magic Bike — *Nugent, Cynthia*

Francesco D'Adamo: Iqbal (Read by Moore, Christina). Audiobook Review — *Leonori, Ann*

Francis Bacon e a fundamentacao de ciencia como tecnologia — *Oliveira, Bernardo Jefferson De*

Francis Bacon: The Logic of Sensation — *Deleuze, Gilles*

Francis Bacon's New Atlantis: New Interdisciplinary Essays — *Price, Bronwen*

Francis Ford Coppola: Interviews — *Phillips, Gene D.*

Francis Galton: Pioneer of Heredity and Biometry — *Bulmer, Michael G.*

Francis of Assisi: History, Hagiography and Hermeneutics in the Early Documents — *Hammond, Jay M.*

Francis of Assisi: Performing the Gospel Life — *Cunningham, Lawrence S.*

Francis Willughby's Book of Games: A Seventeenth-Century Treatise on Sports, Games and Pastimes — *Cram, David*

Francis Willughby's Book of Games: A Seventeenth Century Treatise on Sports, Games, and Pastimes — *Willughby, Francis*

c Francisca Alvarez: The Angel of Goliad/El angel de Goliad — *Egan, Tracie*

Francisco Goya: A Life — *Connell, Evan S.*

Francisco the Miranda: A Transatlantic Life in the Age of Revolution — *Racine, Karen*

The Franco-Prussian War: The German Conquest of France in 1870-1871 — *Wawro, Geoffrey*

Francois Boucher: Seductive Visions — *Hedley, Jo*

Francois Couperin and the Perfection of Music — *Tunley, David*

Francois LeVaillant and the Birds of Africa — *Rookmaker, L.C.*

Francois Valle and His World: Upper Louisiana before Lewis and Clark — *Ekberg, Carl J.*

Francophone Post-Colonial Cultures: Critical Essays — *Salhi, Kamal*

Francophone Studies: The Essential Glossary — *Majumdar, Margaret*

The Frank Family that Survived: A Twentieth-Century Odyssey — *Sander, Gordon F.*

Frank Hardy and the Literature of Commitment — *Adams, Paul*

Frank Lloyd Wright: A Bio-Bibliography — *Langmead, Donald*

Frank Lloyd Wright and the Johnson Wax Buildings — *Lipman, Jonathan*

Frank Lloyd Wright — *Huxtable, Ada Louise*

c Frank Lloyd Wright — *Ingram, Scott*

c Frank Lloyd Wright — *Mayo, Gretchen Will*

Frank Lloyd Wright: The Interactive Portfolio — *Stipe, Margo*

Frank Lloyd Wright's Martin House: Architecture as Portraiture — *Quinan, Jack*

Frank Stitt's Southern Table: Recipes and Gracious Traditions from Highlands Bar and Grill (Illus. by Hirsheimer, Christopher) — *Stitt, Frank*

The Frankenfood Myth: How Protest and Politics Threaten the Biotech Revolution — *Miller, Henry I.*

The Frankenstein Archive: Essays on the Monster, the Myth, the Movies, and More — *Glut, Donald F.*

Frankenstein: Penetrating the Secrets of Nature — *Lederer, Susan E.*

Frankie — *Dettori, Frankie*

Frankie Howerd — *McCann, Graham*

Frankland: A Novel — *Whorton, James*

The Franklin Affair — *Lehrer, Jim*

c Franklin and Eleanor — *Harness, Cheryl*

c Franklin and the New Teacher — *Jennings, Sharon*

Franklin and Winston: An Intimate Portrait of an Epic Friendship — *Meacham, Jon*

c Franklin Annual — *Jennings, Sharon*

Franklin D. Roosevelt, 1st Ed. — *Renshaw, Patrick*

Franklin D. Roosevelt and Abraham Lincoln — *Pederson, William D.*

Franklin D. Roosevelt and the Transformation of the Supreme Court — *Shaw, Stephen K.*

c Franklin D. Roosevelt — *Mara, Wil*

Franklin Delano Roosevelt: Champion of Freedom — *Black, Conrad*

Franklin, Jefferson, and Madison: On Religion and the State — *Schaaf, Gregory*

c Franklin Says I Love You (Illus. by Clark, Brenda) — *Bourgeois, Paulette*

c Franklin Stays Up (Illus. by Jeffrey, Sean) — *Jennings, Sharon*

c Franklin the Detective — *Jennings, Sharon*

c Franklin's Big Life-and-Learn Book — *Jeffey, Sean*

c Franklin's Big Search-and-Solve Flap Book (Illus. by Jeffrey, Sean) — *Jeffrey, Sean*

c Franklin's Christmas: A Sticker Activity Book

c Franklin's Family Treasury (Illus. by Clark, Brenda) — *Bourgeois, Paulette*

c Franklin's Nickname (Illus. by Lei, John) — *Jennings, Sharon*

Franklin's Passage — *Solway, David*

c Franklin's Picture Dictionary — *Shannon, Rosemarie*

c Franklin's Pumpkin — *Jennings, Sharon*

c Franklin's Reading Club (Illus. by Koren, Mark) — *Jennings, Sharon*

c Franklin's Surprise (Illus. by Jeffrey, Sean) — *Jennings, Sharon*

c Franklin's Trading Cards (Illus. by Jeffrey, Sean) — *Jennings, Sharon*

The Franz Josef Land Archipelago: E.B. Baldwin's Journal of the Wellman Polar Expedition, 1898-1899 — *Baldwin, Evelyn Briggs*

Franz Kafka: The Jewish Patient — *Gilman, Sander L.*

Franz Kafka: The Necessity of Form — *Corngold, Stanley*

Franz Kafka's The Trial: Four Stage Adaptations — *Malone, Paul M.*

Fraternal Capital: Peasant-Workers, Self-Made, and Globalization in Provincial India — *Chari, Sharad*

Fraternity: A Journey in Search of Five Presidents — *Greene, Bob*

A Fraternity of Arms: America and France in the Great War — *Bruce, Robert A.*

A Fraternity of Arms: America and France in the Great War — *Bruce, Robert B.*

Fratricide in the Holy Land: A Psychoanalytic View of the Arab-Israeli Conflict — *Falk, Avner*

Fraud and Corruption in Public Services: A Guide to Risk and Prevention — *Jones, P.C.*

Fraud of the Century: Rutherford B. Hayes, Samuel Tilden, and the Stolen Election of 1876 — *Morris, Roy, Jr.*

Fraud: The Strategy Behind the Bush Lies and Why the Media Didn't Tell You — *Waldman, Paul*

Frauds Against the Elderly — *Sharpe, Charles C.*

Frauen fur die Front: Gesprdche mit Wehrmachtshelferinnen — *Killius, Rosemarie*

Frauen in der Pharmazie: Die Geschiehte eines Frauenberufs — *Beisswanger, Gabriele*

Frauen und Migration — *Krauss, Marita*

Frauen und Widerstand. — *Leichsenring, Jana*

Frauen in der Mannschaft: Sozialdemokratinnen im Parlamentarischen Rat und im Deutschen Bundestag — *Notz, Gisela*

y Fray — *Whedon, Joss*

The Frazzled Teacher's Wellness Plan: A Five-Step Program for Reclaiming Time, Managing Stress, and Creating a Healthy Lifestyle — *Queen, Jay Allen*

Freakonomics: A Rogue Economist Explores the Hidden Side of Everything — *Levitt, Steven D.*

Freaks, Geeks, and Cool Kids: American Teenagers, Schools, and the Culture of Consumption — *Milner, Murray, Jr.*

y Freaky Green Eyes (Read by Nielsen, Stina). Audiobook Review — *Oates, Joyce Carol*

y Freaky Green Eyes — *Oates, Joyce Carol*

Fred Harris: His Journey from Liberalism to Populism — *Lowitt, Richard*

Fred Hoyle's Universe — *Wickramasinghe, Chandra*

Fred Pontin: The Man and His Business — *Willsher, Peter*

y Fred the Clown — *Langridge, Roger*

Fred Williams: An Australian Vision — *Zdanowicz, Irena*

c Freddy and the Space Ship (Read by McDonough, John). Audiobook Review — *Brooks, Walter R.*

Fredericksburg, 1862: "Clear the Way" — *Smith, Carl*

Fredericton Flashbacks: Stories and Photography from the Past — *Jones, Ted*

Frederik II and the Protestant Cause: Denmark's Role in the Wars of Religion, 1559-1596 — *Lockhart, Paul Douglas*

y Fred's Halloween Adventure (Illus. by St-Aubin, Bruno) — *Croteau, Marie-Danielle*

Free at Last! Stop Smoking: How I Did It, How You Can Too — *Keelan, Brian*

c Free at Last!: Stories and Songs of Emancipation (Illus. by Evans, Shane W.) — *Rappaport, Doreen*

Free Black Heads of Households in the New York States Federal Census, 1790-1830 — *Eichholz, Alice*

The Free Church and the Early Church: Bridging the Historical and Theological Divide — *Williams, D.H.*

Free Culture: How Big Media Uses Technology and the Law to Lock Down Culture and Control Creativity — *Lessig, Lawrence*

Free Energy Relationships in Organic and Bio-Organic Chemistry — *Pagni, Richard*

Free Enterprise: A Novel of Mary Ellen Pleasant — *Cliff, Michelle*

Free Hearts and Free Homes: Gender and American Antislavery Politics — *Pierson, Michael D.*

Free Jazz and Free Improvisation: An Encyclopedia, Vols. 1-2 — *Jenkins, Todd S.*

Free L.A. — *Corley, Troy*

y Free Lance and the Field of Blood — *Stewart, Paul*

Free Market Democracy and the Chilean and Mexican Countryside — *Kurtz, Marcus J.*

Free Movement of Goods and Services Within the European Community — *Woods, Lorna*

Free/Open Source Software Development — *Koch, Stefan*

Free Press vs. Fair Trials: Examining Publicity's Role in Trial Outcomes — *Bruschke, Jon*

Free Prize Inside! — *Godin, Seth*

Free Radical: New Century Essays — *Benn, Tony*

Free Radicals: American Poets Before Their First Books — *Davis, Jordan*

Free Radicals, Nitric Oxide, and Inflammation: Molecular, Biochemical, and Clinical Aspects — *Tomasi, Aldo*

Free Radicals of the Left in Postwar Melbourne — *McLaren, John*

The Free Sea — *Grotius, Hugo*

y The Free Speech Movement — *Steffens, Bradley*

The Free Speech Movement: Reflections on Berkley in the 1960s — *Cohen, Robert*

Free State or Republic — *Boyle, John F.*

Free Time: Towards a Theology of Leisure — *Neville, Graham*

Free Trade Agreements: US Strategies and Priorities — *Schott, Jeffrey J.*

Free Trade and Uneven Development : The North American Apparel Industry After NAFTA — *Stillerman, Joel*

Free Trade in the Americas: Economic and Political Issues for Governments and Firms — *Weintraub, Sidney*

Free World: America, Europe, and the Surprising Future of the West — *Ash, Timothy Garton*

Free World: America, Europe, and the Surprising Future of the West — *Garton Ash, Timothy*

Free World: Why a Crisis of the West Reveals the Opportunity of Our Time — *Garton Ash, Timothy*

Free World: Why a Crisis of the West Reveals the Opportunity of Our Time — *Graton Ash, Timothy*

Free Yourself from Student Loan Debt: Get Out from Under Once and for All — *O'Connell, Brian*

Freedom and Orthodoxy: Islam and Difference in the Post-Andalusian Age — *Majid, Anouar*

Freedom and Security and the Consequences for Democracies Using Emergency Powers to Fight Terror — *Freeman, Michael (b. 1973 -)*

Freedom as Responsibility: The Social Market Economy in the Light of Catholic Social Teaching for the Nigerian Society — *Ezumezu, Nwokedi Francis*

Freedom from Fear: The American People In Depression and War, 1929-1945 — *Kennedy, David (1954-)*

Freedom from Want: American Liberalism and the Idea of the Consumer — *Donohue, Kathleen G.*

Freedom Is an Endless Meeting: Democracy in American Social Movements — *Polletta, Francesca*

Freedom Is, Freedom Ain't: Jazz and the Making of the Sixties — *Saul, Scott*

Freedom North: Black Freedom Struggle Outside the South, 1940-1980 — *Theoharis, Jeanne*

y Freedom of Association: Rights and Liberties under the Law — *Bresler, Robert J.*

Freedom of Commercial Expression — *Shiner, Roger A.*

Freedom of Expression in El Salvador: The Struggle for Human Rights and Democracy — *Ladutke, Lawrence Michael*

Freedom of Expression: Overzealous Copyright Bozos and Other Enemies of Creativity — *McLeod, Kembrew*

Freedom of Religion, Apostasy and Islam — *Saeed, Abdullah*

Freedom of Speech — *Allport, Alan*

Freedom on Fire: Human Rights Wars and America's Response — *Shattuck, John*

c Freedom on the Menu: The Greensboro Sit-Ins (Illus. by Lagarrigue, Jerome) — *Weatherford, Carole Boston*

The Freedom Outlaw's Handbook: 179 Things to Do 'til the Revolution — *Wolfe, Claire*

c The Freedom Riders — *Kent, Deborah*

Freedom Rising: Washington in the Civil War — *Furgurson, Ernest B.*

c Freedom School, Yes — *Littlesugar, Amy*

The Freedom: Shadows and Hallucinations in Occupied Iraq — *Parenti, Christian*

c Freedom Summer (Illus. by Lagarrigue, Jerome) — *Wiles, Deborah*

Freedom to Play: We Made Our Own Fun — *Lewis, Norah L.*

Freedom-Treason-Revolution: Uncollected Sources of the Political and Legal Culture of the London Treason Trials — *Houswitschka, Christoph*

Freedom, Union, and Power: Lincoln and his Party During the Civil War — *Green, Michael S.*

Freedom Walk: Mississippi or Bust — *Stanton, Mary*

Freedom Writer: Virginia Foster Durr, Letters from the Civil Rights Years — *Durr, Virginia Foster*

Freedom Writer: Virginia Foster Durr, Letters from the Civil Rights Years — *Sullivan, Patricia*

Freedom's Cause: Lives of the Suffragettes — *Abrams, Fran*

y Freedom's Children: Young Civil Rights Activists Tell Their Own Stories — *Levine, Ellen*

Freedom's Journey: African American Voices of the Civil War — *Yacovone, Donald*

Freeing God's Children: The Unlikely Alliance for Global Human Rights — *Hertzke, Allen D.*

Freemasonry in Context: History, Ritual, Controversy — *de Hoyos, Arturo*

Freethinkers: A History of American Secularism — *Jacoby, Susan*

Freewalker — *Foon, Dennis*

Freie Bearbeitungen, IV — *Liszt, Franz*

Freie Bearbeitungen, IX — *Liszt, Franz*

Freie Bearbeitungen, VI — *Liszt, Franz*

Freie Bearbeitungen, X — *Liszt, Franz*

Freie Buerger und Freimaurerinnen: Lokalpolitik am Ende des 20. Jahrhunderts — *Lanik, Monika*

Freiheit und Offentlichkeit: Politischer Samisdat in der DDR 1985-1989, Eine Dokumentation — *Kowalczuk, Ilko-Sascha*

y Frek and the Elixir — *Rucker, Rudy*

Fremde in Gallien-'Gallier' in der Fremde. Die epigraphisch bezeugte Mobilitat in, von und nach Gallien vom 1. bis 3. Jh. n. Chr — *Wierschowski, L.*

French and Francophone: The Challenge of Expanding Horizons — *Laroussi, Farid*

The French and Italian Communist Parties: Comrades and Culture — *Guiat, Cyrille*

The French Army, 1750-1820: Careers, Talent, Merit — *Blaufarb, Rafe*

The French Betrayal of America — *Timmerman, Kenneth R.*

The French Canadians of Michigan: Their Contribution to the Development of the Saginaw Valley and the Keweenaw Peninsula, 1840-1914 — *Lamarre, Jean (b. 1958-)*

French Cinema: A Student's Guide — *Powrie, Phil*

The French Cinema Book — *Temple, Michael*

French Civilization and Its Discontents: Nationalism, Colonialism, Race — *Stovall, Tyler*

French Gay Modernism — *Schehe, Lawerance R.*

A French Genocide: The Vendee — *Secher, Reynald*

French Hegel: From Surrealism to Postmodernism — *Baugh, Bruce*

The French in Texas: History, Migration, Culture — *Lagarde, Francois*

French Negotiating Behavior: Dealing with La Grande Nation — *Cogan, Charles*

French Painting in the Golden Age — *Allen, Christopher*

French Paintings from the Musee Fabre, Montpellier — *Hilaire, Michel*

The French Party System — *Evans, Jocelyn*

French Popular Culture: An Introduction — *Dauncey, Hugh*

The French Presidential and Legislative Elections of 2002 — *Gaffney, John*

The French Revolution and the London Stage, 1789-1805 — *Taylor, George (1940-)*

The French Revolution and the People — *Andress, David*

French Salons: High Society and Political Sociability from the Old Regime to the Revolution of 1848 — *Kale, Steven D.*

French Thru Art — *Gardner, Jenny*

French Thru Verbs — *Gardner, Jenny*

French Women Don't Get Fat: The Secret of Eating for Pleasure — *Guiliano, Mireille*

French Women in Politics: Writing Power, Paternal Legitimization, and Maternal Legacies — *Ramsay, Raylene L.*

French XX Bibliography — *Thompson, William J.*

Fresh and Tired Metaphors — *Andrew, Meredith*

Fresh from the Past: Recipes and Revelations from Moll Flanders's Kitchen — *Sherman, Sandra*

c Fresh Girl — *Placide, Jaira*

Fresh Ideas in Dried Flowers — *Rye, Terry L.*

Fresh Lipstick: Redressing Fashion and Feminism — *Scott, Linda M.*

Fresh Men: New Voices in Gay Fiction — *Weise, Donald*

Fresh Men: New Voices of Gay Fiction — *White, Edmund*

G

Gender in Transnationalism: Home, Longing and Belonging Among Moroccan Migrant Women — *Salih, Ruba*

Gender Indicators for Monitoring the Implementation of the Beijing Platform for Action on Women in the ESCAP Region — *Economic and Social Commission for Asia and the Pacific*

Gender, Kabbalah, and the Reformation: The Mystical Theology of Guillaume Postel, 1510-1581 — *Petry, Yvonne*

The Gender Knot — *Johnson, Allan G.*

Gender, Language and Discourse — *Weatherall, Ann*

The Gender of Freedom: Fictions of Liberalism and the Literary Public Sphere — *Dillon, Elizabeth Maddock*

Gender on Planet Earth — *Oakley, Ann*

Gender, Peace and Conflict — *Skjelsbaek, Inger*

Gender, Place and Memory in the Modern Jewish Experience: Re-Placing Ourselves — *Baumel, Judith Tydor*

Gender, Place and the Labour Market — *Jenkins, Sarah*

Gender, Politics, and Islam — *Saliba, Therese*

Gender: Psychological Perspectives. 4th Ed. — *Brannon, Linda*

Gender, Race, and Religion: Nordic Missions, 1860-1940 — *Okkenhaug, Inger Marie*

Gender Reconstructions: Pornography and Perversions in Literature and Culture — *Carlson, Cindy L.*

Gender, Religion, and Diversity; Cross-Cultural Perspectives — *King, Ursula*

Gender — *Connell, R.W.*

Gender, Theatre, and the Origins of Criticism, from Dryden to Manley — *Frank, Marcie*

Gendercide and Genocide — *Jones, Adam*

Gendered Freedoms: Race, Rights, and the Politics of Household in the Delta, 1861-1875 — *Bercaw, Nancy*

Gendered Futures in Higher Education: Critical Perspectives for Change — *Ropers-Huilman, Becky*

Gendered Justice: Addressing Female Offenders — *Bloom, Barbara E.*

Gendered Lives: Communication, Gender, and Culture, 6th Ed. — *Wood, Julia T.*

Gendered Nations: Nationalisms and Gender Order in the Long Nineteenth Century — *Blom, Ida*

Gendered Pasts: Historical Essays in Femininity and Masculinity in Canada — *McPherson, Kathryn*

Gendered States: Women, Unemployment Insurance, and the Political Economy of the Welfare State in Canada, 1945-1997 — *Porter, Ann*

Gene and Cell Therapy: Therapeutic Mechanisms and Strategies, 2nd Ed., Rev. and Expanded — *Templeton, Nancy Smyth*

Gene Delivery to Mammalian Cells, Vol. 1 — *Heiser, William C.*

Gene Giotechnology, 2nd Ed. — *Wu, William*

Gene Silencing by RNA Interference: Technology and Application — *Sohail, Muhammad*

Gene Targeting and Embryonic Stem Cells — *Thomson, Alison*

c Gene Therapy: Treating Disease by Repairing Genes — *Panno, Joseph*

Gene Vincent — *Farren, Mick*

Genealogical Gazetter of Galicia: Expanded Data Edition — *Lenius, Brian J.*

Genealogical Guide to East and West Prussia — *Brandt, Edward R.*

Genealogist's Internet — *Christian, Peter*

Genealogy Is Destiny — *Cadwalladr, Carole*

The Genealogy of Violence: Reflections on Creation, Freedom and Evil — *Bellinger, Charles K.*

General and Madame de Lafayette: Partners in Liberty's Cause in the American and French Revolution — *Lane, Jason*

General Equilibrium Analysis: Existence and Optimality Properties of Equilibria — *Florenzano, Monique*

General Equilibrium: Problems and Prospects — *Petri, Fabio*

General Idea of the Revolution in the Nineteenth Century — *Proudhon, Pierre-Joseph*

General Ike: A Personal Reminiscence — *Eisenhower, John S.D.*

General Index to the Collected Courses of the Hague Academy of International Law, Vols. 201-250 (1987-1994)/ Index General du Recueil des Cours ...

General John Bratton: Sumter to Appomattox, in Letters to His Wife — *Austin, J. Luke*

General Stores of Canada: Merchants and Memories — *Fleming, R.B.*

General Studies of Charles Dickens and His Writings and Collected Editions of His Works: An Annotated Bibliography — *DeVries, Duane*

The General Textile Strike of 1934: From Maine to Alabama — *Salmond, John A.*

A General Theory of Entrepreneurship: The Individual-Opportunity Nexus — *Shane, Scott*

General Topology — *Willard, Stephen*

Generalissimo: Chiang Kai-shek and the China He Lost — *Fenby, Jonathan*

Generalist Medicine and the U.S. Health Care System — *Isaacs, Stephen L.*

The Generality Constraint and Categorial Restrictions — *Camp, Elizabeth*

Generalized Anxiety Disorder: Advances in Research and Practice — *Heimberg, Richard G.*

Generalized Inference in Repeated Measures: Exact Methods in MANOVA and Mixed Models — *Weerahandi, Samaradasa*

Generalized Inverse Operators and Fredholm Boundary-Value Problems — *Boichuk, A.A.*

Generalized Latent Variable Modeling: Multilevel, Longitudinal, and Structural Equation Models — *Skrondal, Anders*

Generall Learning: A Seventeenth-Century Treatise on the Formation of the General Scholar by Meric Casaubon — *Serjeantson, Richard*

Generally Speaking: The Memoirs of Major-General Richard Rohmer — *Rohmer, Richard*

Generals Die in Bed — *Harrison, Charles Yale*

Generals in Blue and Gray — *Jones, Wilmer L.*

Generating and Sustaining Nonprofit Earned Income: A Guide to Successful Enterprise Strategies — *Oster, Sharon M.*

Generating Images of Stratification: A Formal Theory — *Fararo, Thomas J.*

Generation and Effector Functions of Regulatory Lymphocytes: Proceedings — *Bock, Gregory*

Generation Deluxe: Consumerism and Philanthropy of the New Super-Rich — *Nowell, Iris*

Generation des Unbedingten: Das Fuehrungskorps des Reichssicherheitshauptamtes — *Wildt, Michael*

Generation des Unbedingten: Das Fuhrungskorps des Reichssicherheitshauptamtes — *Wildt, Michael*

Generation Extra Large: Rescuing Our Children from Obesity — *Herscher, Elaine*

Generation Extra Large: Rescuing Our Children from the Epidemic of Obesity — *Tartamella, Lisa*

Generation Kill: Devil Dogs, Iceman, Captain America, and the New Face of American War — *Wright, Evan*

y Generation React: Activism for Beginners — *Seo, Danny*

Generation X: Americans Born 1965 to 1976, 4th Ed. — *New Strategist Editors*

Generation X: Americans Born 1965 to 1976

Generations in Touch: Linking the Old and Young in a Tokyo Neighborhood — *Thang, Leng Leng*

y Generations of Captivity: A History of African-American Slaves — *Berlin, Ira*

Generous Enemies: Patriots and Loyalists in Revolutionary New York — *Buskirk, Judith L. Van*

y Genes and DNA: A Beginner's Guide to Genetics and Its Applications — *Omoto, Charlotte K.*

Gene's Corner and Other Nooks and Crannies: Perspectives on Math — *Maier, Eugene A.*

Genes in the Environment — *Hails, Rosie S.*

Genes, Trade, and Regulation: The Seeds of Conflict in Food Biotechnology — *Bernauer, Thomas*

Genese d'une morale materialiste: les passions et le controle de soi chez Diderot — *Ida, Hisashi*

Genesis — *Cotter, David W.*

Genesis — *Crace, Jim*

Genesis Force — *Vornholt, John*

Genesis — *Crace, Jim*

Genesis of an American Playwright — *Foote, Horton*

The Genesis of Napoleonic Propaganda, 1796 to 1799 — *Hanley, Wayne*

Genesis, Structure, and Meaning in Gray Snyder's Mountains and Rivers Without End — *Hunt, Anthony*

Genesis: The Evolution of Biology — *Sapp, Jan*

Genetic and Cultural Evolution of Cooperation — *Hammerstein, Peter*

Genetic Nature/Culture: Anthropology and Science Beyond the Two-Culture Divide — *Goodman, Alan H.*

A Genetic Puzzle: The Search for a Solution, Sects. 1-5, Student Book & Teacher Guide

Genetic Recombination: Reviews and Protocols — *Waldman, Alan S.*

A Genetic Switch: Phage Lambda Revisited, 3rd Ed. — *Ptashne, Mark*

A Genetic Switch: Phage Lamda Revisited, 3rd Ed. — *Ptashne, Mark*

Genetic Testing for Cancer: Psychological Approaches for Helping Patients and Families — *Patenaude, Andrea Farkas*

Genetically Modified Crops — *Halford, Nigel G.*

Genetically Modified Crops: Their Development, Uses, and Risks — *Liang, G.H.*

Genetically Modified Planet: Environmental Impacts of Genetically Engineered Plants — *Stewart, C. Neal*

Genetics: Analysis of Genes and Genomes, 6th Ed. — *Hartl, Daniel L.*

Genetics and Ethics: An Interdisciplinary Study — *Magill, Gerard*

Genetics and Life Insurance: Medical Underwriting and Social Policy — *Rothstein, Mark A.*

Genetics and Society: A Sociology of Disease — *Kerr, Anne*

Genetics and the Logic of Evolution — *Weiss, Kenneth M.*

y Genetics — *Taylor, Robert*

Genetics, Evolution and Biological Control — *Ehler, L.E.*

Genetics for Healthcare Professionals: A Lifestage Approach — *Skirton, Heather*

Genetics of Pain — *Mogil, Jeffrey S.*

Genetics of Subpolar Fish and Invertebrates — *Gharett, Anthony J.*

The Genetics of the Dog — *Ruvinsky, A.*

Genevieve (Read by Allen, Richard). Audiobook Review — *Dickey, Eric Jerome*

y Genghis Khan and Mongol Rule — *Lane, George*

y Genghis Khan and the Making of the Modern World — *Weatherford, Jack*

Genghis Khan: Life, Death and Resurrection — *Man, John*

c The Genie in the Book (Illus. by Alley, R.W.) — *Trumbore, Cindy*

c The Genie of Sutton Place — *Selden, George*

Genital Dermatology Atlas — *Edwards, Libby*

The Genius in the Design: Bernini, Borromini, and the Rivalry That Transformed Rome. — *Morrissey, Jake*

The Genius of Language: Fifteen Writers Reflect on Their Mother Tongues — *Lesser, Wendy*

The Genius of Rome, 1592-1623 — *Brown, Beverly Louise*

The Genizah at the House of Shepher — *Yellin, Tamar*

The Genocidal Temptation: Auschwitz, Hiroshima, Rwanda, and Beyond — *Frey, Robert S.*

Genocide: A History — *Robinstein, William D.*

Genocide and Millennialism in Upper Peru: The Great Rebellion of 1780-82 — *Robins, Nicholas A.*

Genocide in Rwanda: Complicity of the Churches — *Rittner, Carol*

Genocide, War Crimes and the West: History and Complicity — *Jones, Adam*

The Genome War: How Craig Venter Tried to Capture the Code of Life and Save the World (Read by Gardner, Grover). Audiobook Review — *Shreeve, James*

The Genome War: How Craig Venter Tried to Capture the Code of Life and Save the World — *Shreeve, James*

Genomic and Molecular Neuro-Oncology — *Zhang, Wei*

The Genomics Age: How DNA Technology Is Transforming the Way We Live and Who We Are — *Smith, Gina*

Genomics and Proteomics in Nutrition — *Berdanier, Carolyn D.*

Genomics: Applications in Human Biology — *Primrose, Sandy B.*

Genomics, Proteomics, and Clinical Bacteriology: Methods and Reviews — *Woodford, Neil*

Genomics, Proteomics and Vaccines — *Grandi, Guido*

Genre, Myth and Convention in the French Cinema: 1929-1939 — *Crisp, Colin*

Genteel Rebel: The Life of Mary Greenhow Lee — *Phipps, Sheila R.*

A Gentle Jesuit: Philip Caraman, SJ, 1911-1998 — *Rockett, June*

A Gentle Priest: Philip Caraman, SJ, 1911-1998 — *Rockett, June*

The Gentle World of Childhood: Starting School in England — *Stephens, William*

A Gentleman of France — *Weyman, Stanley John*

German-Irish Corporate Relationships: The Cultural Dimension — *O'Mahoney, Niamh*

German Language Varieties Worldwide: Internal and External Perspectives — *Keel, William D.*

German Literature of the Early Middle Ages — *Murdoch, Brian*

German Panzers on the Offensive: Russian Front, North Africa, 1941-1942 — *Stolfi, R.H.S.*

German Parliamentary Debates, 1848-1933 — *Allen, Mitchell*

The German Polity, 8th Ed. — *Conradt, David P.*

German Pop Culture: How "American" Is It? — *Muller, Agnus C.*

German-Speaking Officers in the U.S. Colored Troops, 1863-1867 — *Ofele, Martin W.*

German-Speaking Officers in the United States Colored Troops, 1863-1867 — *Ofele, Martin W.*

German Students' War Letters — *Witkop, Philipp*

German Women in Cameroon: Travelogues from Colonial Times — *Schestokat, Karin U.*

German Writers and the Politics of Culture: Dealing with the Stasi — *Cooke, Paul*

Germans and Indians: Fantasies, Encounters, Projections — *Calloway, Colin G.*

Germans, Jews and the Claims of Modernity — *Hess, Jonathan M.*

Germans or Foreigners? Attitudes Toward Ethnic Minorities in Post-Reunification Germany — *Alba, Richard*

Germans to America, vol. 6 — *Glazier, Ira A.*

y Germany 1918-45 — *Radway, Richard*

y Germany 1918-1945: A Study in Depth — *Banham, Dale*

y Germany 1918-1945 — *Boxer, Andrew*

y Germany 1918-1945 — *Cloake, J.A.*

y Germany 1918-1945 — *Grey, Paul*

y Germany 1918-1945 — *Lacey, Greg*

y Germany 1918-1945: Democracy and Dictatorship — *Brooman, Josh*

Germany, 1945-1990: A Parallel History — *Weber, Jurgen*

Germany and America — *Friedrich, Wolfgang-Uwe*

Germany Calling: A Personal Biography of William Joyce, Lord Haw-Haw — *Kenny, Mary*

Germany, Europe, and the Politics of Constraint — *Dyson, Kenneth*

Germany on the Road to "Normalcy": Policies and Politics of the Red-Green Federal Government — *Reutter, Werner*

Germany's Northern Challenge: The Holy Roman Empire and the Scandinavian Struggle for Baltic, 1563-1576 — *Lavery, Jason*

Germany's Transient Pasts: Preservation and National Memory in the Twentieth Century — *Koshar, Rudy*

Germany's War and the Holocaust: Disputed Histories — *Bartov, Omer*

Germs: A Memoir of Childhood — *Wollheim, Richard*

c Germs — *Collins, Ross*

c Geronimo Stilton!

c Geronimo Stilton Books 1-3 (Read by Herrmann, Edward). Audiobook Review — *Stilton, Geronimo*

Gerontological Nursing: Promoting Successful Aging with Older Adults, 3rd Ed. — *Stanley, Mickey*

Gertrude Bell — *Winstone, H.V.F.*

c Gertrude Elion: Nobel Prize Winner in Physiology and Medicine — *Cooperman, Stephanie H.*

Gesammelte Schriften, vols. 1-3 — *Strauss, Leo*

Geschichte der Baustatik — *Kurrer, Karl-Eugen*

Geschichte der deutschen Wirtschaft im 20. Jahrhundert — *Spree, Reinhard*

Geschichte der Grosselternrollen vom 16 bis zum 20 — *Chvojka, Erhard*

Geschichte der Sowjetunion 1917-1991 — *Hildermeier, Manfred*

Geschichte des deutschen Parlamentarismus — *Ritter, Gerhard A.*

Geschichte des judischen Alltags in Deutschland vom 17 Jahrhundert bis 1945 — *Kaplan, Marion*

Geschichte des Mittelalters für unsere Zeit — *Ballof, Rolf*

Geschichtsssschreibung und nationale Identitat: Probleme und Leistungen der osterreichischen Geschichtswissenschaft — *Fellner, Fritz*

Geschosse zu Wassertropfen Sozio-religiose Aspekte des maji-Maji-Krieges in Deutsch-Ostafika — *Beez, Jigal*

Gestures and Looks in Medieval Narrative — *Burrow, J.A.*

Gestures: Essays in Ancient History, Literature, and Philosophy Presented to Alan L. Boegehold on the Occasion of His Retirement and His Seventy-Fifth Birthday — *Bakewell, Geoffrey W.*

Gestures: The Do's and Taboos of Body Language Around the World — *Axtell, Roger E.*

Gesungene Innigkeit: Studien zu einer Musikhandschrift der Devotio Moderna (Utrecht, Universiteitsbibliotheek, MS. 16 H 34, Olim B 113), Mit einer Edition der Gesange. — *Hascher-Burger, Ulrike*

Get Bunny Love — *Long, Kathleen*

c Get Busy, Beaver! (Illus. by Bynum, Janie) — *Crimi, Carolyn*

y Get In!: How to Market Yourself and Become Successful at a Young Age — *Harbeke, Dan*

c Get It Together! Math Problems for Groups Grades 4-12 — *Erickson, Tim*

Get Me Out of Here: My Recovery from Borderline Personality Disorder — *Reiland, Rachel*

Get Out or Die — *Finnis, Jane*

Get Out the Vote: How to Increase Voter Turnout — *Green, Donald P.*

Get over It and on with It — *Hammond, Michelle McKinney*

Get Rich Quick — *Doyle, Peter*

c The Get Rich Quick Club (Read by Goethals, Angela). Audiobook Review — *Gutman, Dan*

c The Get Rich Quick Club (Illus. by Gutman, Dan) — *Gutman, Dan*

Get Rommel: The Secret British Mission to Kill Hitler's Greatest General — *Asher, Michael*

Get Saucy: Make Dinner a New Way Every Day — *Parisi, Grace M.*

Get Serious about Getting Married: 365 Proven Ways To Find Love in Less Than a Year — *Spindel, Janis*

Get Up Off Your Knees: Preaching the U2 Catalog — *Whitely, Raewynne J.*

Get Your War on II — *Rees, David*

The Getaway Home: Discovering Your Home Away from Home — *Mulfinger, Dale*

Gettering and Defect Engineering in Semiconductor Technology GADEST 2003: Proceedings — *Richter, H.*

Getting a Life: How to Find Your True Vocation — *LaReau, Renee M.*

Getting Along with Others — *Baroff, Michael*

Getting Around: Exploring Transportation History — *Grant, Roger*

Getting Away with Murder: The True Story of the Emmett Till Case — *Crowe, Chris*

Getting Children Back to School: Case Studies in Primary Education — *Ramachandran, Vimala*

Getting Closer: A Dancer's Perspective — *O'Connor, Rosalie*

Getting Down to Business — *Horsley, Lorraine*

c Getting Enough Sleep — *Salzmann, Mary Elizabeth*

Getting Garbo — *Ludwig, Jerry*

y Getting Graphic! Using Graphic Novels to Promote Literacy with Preteens and Teens — *Gorman, Michele*

Getting Graphic!: Using Graphic Novels to Promote Literacy with Preteens and Teens — *Gorman, Michele*

Getting Graphic! Using Graphic Novels to Promote Literacy with Preteens and Teens — *Gorman, Michele*

Getting in on Online: Cyberspace, Gay Male Sexuality, and Embodied Identity — *Campbell, John Edward*

y Getting in the Game — *Fitzgerald, Dawn*

Getting It Straight: What the Research Shows about Homosexuality — *Sprigg, Peter*

Getting Marriage Right: Realistic Counsel for Saving & Strengthening Relationships — *Gushee, David P.*

Getting Paid: How to Collect from Bankrupt Debtors — *Elias, Stephen*

Getting Personal — *Manby, Chris*

Getting Publicity — *Fletcher, Tana*

Getting Published: A Guide for Lecturers and Researchers — *Wellington, Jerry J.*

Getting Science Grants: Effective Strategies for Funding Success — *Blackburn, Thomas R.*

Getting Started: An Introduction to Dynamic Psychotherapy — *Kotin, Joel*

Getting Started in Communication: A Practical Guide for Activists and Organisations — *Norton, Michael*

Getting the Gospels: Understanding the New Testament Accounts of Jesus' Life — *Bridge, Steven L.*

Getting to Excellent: How to Create Better Schools — *Langer, Judith A.*

Getting to Grips with Grammar — *Manser, Martin H.*

Getting Used to Being Shot At: The Spence Family Civil War Letters — *Christ, Mark K.*

Getting What You Deserve: The Adverntures of Goldhawk Fights Back — *Goldhawk, Dale*

Getting Wiser to Teens: More Insights into Marketing to Teenagers — *Zollo, Peter*

Gettysburg 1863: High Tide of the Confederacy — *Smith, Carl*

Gettysburg: A Novel of the Civil War — *Gingrich, Newt*

Gettysburg: A Testing of Courage — *Trudeau, Noah Andre*

Gettysburg — *Sears, Stephen W.*

c Gettysburg (Illus. by Craig, David) — *Tanaka, Shelley*

Gettysburg: Memory, Market, and an American Shrine — *Weeks, Jim*

Gettysburg: The Meade-Sickles Controversy — *Sauers, Richard A.*

Gewerkschaften, Arbeitslosigkeit und Politische Stabilitat — *Kaiser, Claudia*

Gewerkschaften, Arbeitslosigkeit und Politische Stabilitat — *Steininger, Rolf*

Gezani and the Tricky Baboon — *Rippin, Sally*

y Ghost Abbey — *Westall, Robert*

c Ghost Fever: Mal de Fantasma — *Hayes, Joe*

Ghost Girl — *Gertsler, Amy*

Ghost Hotel — *Slade, Arthur G.*

A Ghost in the Machine: A Chief Inspector Barnaby Mystery — *Graham, Caroline*

Ghost in the Shell 2: Man-Made Interface — *Masamune, Shirow*

Ghost in the Shell — *Masamune, Shirow*

Ghost of a Chance — *Fitzpatrick, Flo*

The Ghost of Cutler Creek — *DeFelice, Cynthia C.*

y Ghost Riders: True Ghost Stories of Planes, Trains and Automobiles — *Smith, Barbara*

c Ghost Ship: The Mysterious Trite Story of the Mary Celeste and Her Missing Crew — *Hicks, Brian*

Ghost Ships: A Surrealist Love Triangle — *McNab, Robert*

Ghost Stories of Michigan — *Asfar, Dan*

Ghost Stories of the Old West — *Asfar, Dan*

Ghost Stories of the Rocky Mountains, Vol. 2 — *Smith, Barbara*

y Ghost Story — *Litt, Toby*

c Ghost Train (Illus. by Capeci, Anne) — *Capeci, Anne*

Ghost Voyages III: Endeavour and Resolution — *Taylor, Cora*

Ghost Wars: The Secret History of the CIA, Afghanistan, and bin Laden, from the Soviet Invasion to September 10, 2001 — *Coll, Steve*

The Ghost Writer — *Harwood, John*

Ghosting: A Double Life — *Erdal, Jennie*

Ghosting: A Memoir — *Erdal, Jennie*

c Ghostly Beasts — *Aiken, Joan*

Ghosts Among Us: True Stories Of Spirit Encounters — *Rule, Leslie*

Ghosts — *Fuller, John*

Ghosts in Medicine: Women's Voices in Research with Technology — *Yelland, Nicola*

Ghosts in the Garden: Reflections on Endings, Beginnings, and the Unearthing of Self — *Kephart, Beth*

y Ghosts of Albion: Astray (Illus. by Nieto, Jose R.) — *Benson, Amber*

Ghosts of Eden — *Gray, T.M.*

The Ghosts of Medak Pocket: The Story of Canada's Secret War — *Off, Carol*

Ghosts of Slavery: A Literary Archaeology of Black Women's Lives — *Sharpe, Jenny*

c Ghosts of the Nile (Illus. by Harness, Cheryl) — *Harness, Cheryl*

Ghosts of the Old Year: New Welsh Short Fiction — *Mordsley, Jessica*

Ghosts of Vesuvius: A New Look at the Last Days of Pompeii, How the Towers Fell, and Other Strange Connections — *Pellegrino, Charles R.*

Ghosts of Vesuvius: A New Look at the Last Days of Pompeii, How Towers Fall, and Other Strange Connections — *Pellegrino, Charles R.*

Ghostwriter — *Wald, Noreen*

Ghouls, Gimmicks, and Gold: Horror Films and the American Movie Business, 1953-1968 — *Heffernan, Kevin*

GI Jews: How World War II Changed a Generation — *Moore, Deborah Dash*

Giacomo Puccini: Catalogue of the Works — *Schickling, Dieter*

Giancarlo de Carlo: Layered Places — *McKean, John*

c The Giant and the Beanstalk (Illus. by Stanley, Diane) — *Stanley, Diane*

The Giant Cabbage: An Alaskan Folktale — *Trammell, Jeremiah*

Title Index

c Gracie's Baby Chub Chop (Illus. by Johnson, Gillian)
— *Johnson, Gillian*

Grade Inflation: A Crisis in College Education
— *Johnson, Valen E.*

Grade Power: The Complete Guide to Improving
Your Grades through Self-Hypnosis — *Alderson,
Kevin*

Gradebusters: How Parents Can End the Bad Grades
Battle — *Schmitz, Stephen*

Graduate Medical Education Directory: 2004-2005
— *American Medical Association*

Graduate Programs in Human Resource Management,
2nd Ed. — *Society for Human Resource Management*

Graduate Programs in the Humanities, Arts and
Social Sciences, 2003, 37th Ed.

Graduate Study in Psychology, 2005 25th Ed.
— *American Psychological Association*

Graduate Study in Psychology, 2005 25th Ed.

Graeci und Suriani im Palastina der Kreuzfahrerzeit.
Beitrage und Quellen zur Geschichte des
griechisch-orthodoxen Patriarchats von Jerusalem.
Berliner Historische Studien — *Pahlitzsch,
Johannes*

Graffiti: New Poems in Translation — *DesRuisseaux,
Pierre*

Graffiti World: Street Art from Five Continents
— *Ganz, Nicholas*

Graffiti World: Street Art from the Five Continents
— *Granz, Nicholas*

Grafters and Goo Goos: Corruption and Reform in
Chicago, 1833-2003 — *Merriner, James L.*

Grafting Helen: The Abduction of the Classical Past
— *Gumpert, Matthew*

Grain Size Control — *Gladman, T.*

A Grammar of Egyptian Aramaic, 2nd Ed.
— *Muraoka, Takamitsu*

The Grammar of Good Intentions: Race and the
Antebellum Culture of Benevolence — *Ryan, Susan
M.*

A Grammar of Old Turkic — *Erdal, Marcel*

A Grammar of Wambule: Grammar, Lexicon, Texts
and Cultural Survey of a Kiranti Tribe of Eastern
Nepal — *Opgenort, Jean Robert*

Grammar Report: Basic Writing Tools for Aspiring
Authors and Poets — *Shaw, Mark*

Grammarians and Grammatical Theory in the
Medieval Arabic Tradition — *Baalbaki, Ramzi*

c Grampa and Julie: Shark Hunters — *Czekaj, Jef*

Gramsci, Culture and Anthropology — *Crehan, Kate*

Granada: A Novel — *Ashour, Radwa*

Grand Canyon: A Different View — *Vail, Tom*

c The Grand Canyon: The Largest Canyon in the
United States — *Lomberg, Michelle*

Grand Excursion: Antebellum America Discovers the
Upper Mississippi — *Keillor, Steven J.*

Grand Excursions on the Upper Mississippi River:
Places, Landscapes, and Regional Identity After
1854 — *Roseman, Curtis C.*

y Grand Guignol — *Robinson, James*

The Grand Idea: George Washington's Potomac and
the Race to the West — *Achenbach, Joel*

The Grand Masters of Maine Gardening: And Some
of Their Disciples — *Lamb, Jane*

Grand Old Party: A History of the Republicans
— *Gould, Lewis L.*

Grand Rapids — *Flynn, Gillian*

The Grand Slam: Bobby Jones, America, and the
Story of Golf — *Frost, Mark*

A Grand Strategy for America — *Art, Robert J.*

Grand Strategy in the War Against Terrorism
— *Mockaitis, Thomas R.*

Grand Strategy in the War Against Terrrorism
— *Mockaitis, Thomas R.*

The Grand Strategy of the Russian Empire, 1650-1831
— *LeDonne, John P.*

y The Grand Tour — *Wrede, Patricia C.*

Grandchild of Empire - About Irony, Mainly in the
Commonwealth — *New, W.H.*

c Grandfather Mountain: Stories of Gods and Heroes
from Many Cultures (Illus. by Bailey, Sian)
— *Muten, Burleigh*

c Grandfather Tang's Story (Illus. by Parker, Robert A.)
— *Tompert, Ann*

Grandma Elephant's in Charge — *Baktes, Ivan*

c Grandma Lena's Big Ol' Turnip (Illus. by Urbanovic,
Jackie) — *Hester, Denia Lewis*

c Grandma Moses (Illus. by Wallner, Alexandra)
— *Wallner, Alexandra*

c Grandma's Beach — *Beardshaw, Rosalind*

c Grandma's Bears (Illus. by Howard, Paul) — *Wilson,
Gina*

c Grandma's General Store: The Ark (Illus. by Allen,
Thomas B.) — *Carter, Dorothy*

Grandma's Kitchen: Comfort Cooking from Canadian
Grandmas — *Hrechuk, Irene*

c Grandmother Winter (Illus. by Krommes, Beth)
— *Root, Phyllis*

Grandmother's Bible — *Raddant, Gloria R.*

The Grandmothers — *Lessing, Doris*

c Grandmother's Tree (Illus. by Tyrrell, Frances)
— *Tyrrell, Avril*

c Grandpa and Me on Tu B'Shevat (Illus. by Evans,
Leslie) — *Gold-Vukson, Marji E.*

Grandparenting in Divorced Families — *Ferguson,
Neil*

Grandparents: A New Look at the Supporting
Generation — *Falk, Ursula Adler*

c Grandparent's Day (Illus. by Laverdiere, Benoit)
— *Tate, Nikki*

c Grandpa's Surprise — *Beardshaw, Rosalind*

c Grandy Thaxter's Helper (Illus. by Schindler, S.D.)
— *Rees, Douglas*

Granita Magic — *Roden, Nadia*

Granny Made Me an Anarchist — *Christie, Stuart*

c Granny Torrelli Makes Soup (Read by Murphy,
Donna). Audiobook Review — *Creech, Sharon*

y Granny Torrelli Makes Soup — *Creech, Sharon*

y Grant and Twain: The Story of a Friendship That
Changed America — *Perry, Mark*

Grant Comes East: A Novel of the Civil War
— *Gingrich, Newt*

Granting and Renegotiating Infrastructure
Concessions: Doing It Right — *Guasch, J. Luis*

Grant's Atlas of Anatomy, 11th Ed. — *Argur, Anne
M.R.*

y Grants for School Libraries — *Hall-Ellis, Sylvia D.*

The Grants Register 2005, 23rd Ed.

Grape Thief — *Franklin, Kristine L.*

Graph Colorings — *Kubale, Marek*

Graphic Agitation 2: Social and Political Graphics in
the Digital Age — *McQuiston, Liz*

y Graphic Classics: Edgar Allan Poe — *Pomplun, Tom*

y Graphic Classics: Robert Louis Stevenson
— *Pomplun, Tom*

y Graphic Classics: Robert Louis Stevenson
— *Stevenson, Robert Louis*

Graphic Design: A History — *Weill, Alain*

Graphic Design, Print Culture, and the
Eighteenth-Century Novel — *Barchas, Janine*

The Graphic Designer's and Illustrator's Guide to
Marketing and Promotion — *Piscopo, Maria*

Graphic Discovery: A Trout in the Milk and Other
Visual Adventures — *Wainer, Howard*

Graphic Modernism: Selections from the Francey and
Dr. Martin L. Gecht Collection at the Art Institute
of Chicago — *Druick, Douglas W.*

Graphic Novels 101: Selecting and Using Graphic
Novels to Promote Literacy for Children and
Young Adults, A Resource Guide for School
Librarians and Educators — *Crawford, Philip
Charles*

y Graphic Novels in Your Media Center: A Definitive
Guide. — *Lyga, Allyson A.W.*

Graphics Interface Proceedings — *Heidrich, Wolfgang*

Graphics Programming Methods — *Lander, Jeff*

y Grasp the Stars — *Wingert, Jennifer*

Grasping the World: The Idea of the Museum
— *Preziosi, Donald*

y Grass Angel — *Schumacher, Julie*

y Grass for His Pillow — *Rubinstein, Gillian*

Grass Scapes: Gardening with Ornamental Grasses
— *Quinn, Martin*

c Grasshopper Pie and Other Poems (Illus. by Sinnott,
Adrian) — *Steinberg, David*

Grassroots: A Field Guide for Feminist Activism
— *Baumgardner, Jennifer*

Grassroots Governance? Chiefs in Africa and the
Afro-Caribbean — *Ray, Donald I.*

Grassroots Grants: An Activist's Guide to
Grantseeking, 2nd Ed. — *Robinson, Andy*

Grave Endings — *Krich, Rochelle*

Grave Injustice: The American Indian Repatriation
Movement and NAGPRA — *Fine-Dare, Kathleen S.*

Grave New World: Security Challenges in the 21st
Century — *Brown, Michael E.*

y The Gravedigger's Cottage — *Lynch, Chris*

Graven Images — *Geisler, Barbara Reichmuth*

Gravity — *Cathcart, James*

c Gravity — *Morgan, Ben*

Gravity from the Ground Up — *Schutz, Bernard*

Gravity Wells: Speculative Fiction Stories — *Gardner,
James Alan*

Gravity's Shadow: The Search for Gravitational
Waves — *Collins, Harry*

The Gravy Train. — *Bushill-Matthews, Philip*

Gray Areas: Ethnographic Encounters with Nursing
Home Culture — *Stafford, Philip B.*

c Gray Wolves — *Becker, John E.*

Grazer philosophische studien; internationale
Zeitschrift fur analytische philosophie;Vol. 67
— *Brandl, Johannes L.*

y The Great American History Fact-Finder: The Who,
What, Where, When and Why of American
History, 2nd Ed. — *Cornelison, Pam*

Great and Glorious Days: Marlborough's Battles,
1704-09 — *Falkner, James*

A Great and Noble Scheme: The Expulsion of the
French Acadians — *Faragher, John Mack*

c A Great and Terrible Beauty (Read by Bailey,
Josephine). Audiobook Review — *Bray, Libba*

c A Great and Terrible Beauty — *Bray, Libba*

The Great Art Scandal — *Nilsen, Anna*

Great Basin Riparian Area: Ecology, Management,
and Restoration — *Chambers, Jeanne C.*

Great Battles through the Ages

The Great Betrayal: Fraud in Science — *Judson,
Horace Freeland*

y The Great Beyond: Higher Dimensions, Parallel
Universes, and the Extraordinary Search for a
Theory of Everything — *Halpern, Paul*

The Great Big Book of Guys: Alphabetical Encounters
with Men — *Ritter, Erika*

c The Great Big Little Red Train — *Blathwayt, Ben*

The Great Book of Tattoo — *Webb, Spider*

y Great Books for High School Kids: A Teacher's Guide
to Books That Can Change Teens' Lives — *Ayers,
Rick*

c The Great Bridge-Building Contest (Illus. by Munro,
Roxie) — *Zaunders, Bo*

The Great Bridge: The Epic Story of the Building of
the Brooklyn Bridge (Read by Herrmann,
Edward). Audiobook Review — *McCullough, David*

Great Britain and the Holy See: The Diplomatic
Relations Question, 1846-1852 — *Flint, James P.*

Great Britain, Germany and the Soviet Union:
Rapallo and After, 1922-1934 — *Salzmann,
Stephanie C.*

Great Canadian Speeches — *Gruending, Dennis*

c The Great Castle of Marshmangle — *Doyle, Malachy*

The Great Catastrophe of My Life: Divorce in the Old
Dominion — *Buckley, Thomas E.*

c The Great Cheese Conspiracy (Read by Bostick,
Daniel). Audiobook Review — *Leeuwen, Jean Van*

c The Great Cheese Conspiracy (Read by Bostick,
Daniel). Audiobook Review — *Van Leeuwen, Jean*

Great Chef's Cook at Barbara-Jo's — *McIntosh,
Barbara-Jo*

y The Great Chicago Fire of 1871 — *Marx, Christy*

Great Chiefs — *Hollihan, Tony*

Great Children's Illustrators, 1880-1930 — *Heppner,
Darrell*

y Great Cities of the World

y A Great Civil War: A Military and Political History,
1861-1865 — *Weigley, Russell F.*

The Great Confrontation: Europe and Islam Through
the Centuries — *Gaiduk, Ilya V.*

The Great Deception: A Secret History of the
European Union — *Booker, Christopher*

The Great Depression

c The Great Depression — *Ruggiero, Adriane*

Great Dinosaur Controversy: A Guide to the Debates
— *Parson, Keith M.*

c Great Dinosaur Expeditions and Discoveries:
Adventures with the Fossil Hunters — *Holmes,
Thom*

y Great Discoveries and Amazing Adventures: The
Stories of Hidden Marvels and Lost Treasures
— *Llewellyn, Claire*

c The Great Divide: A Mathematical Marathon (Illus.
by Mitchell, Tracy) — *Dodds, Dayle Ann*

Great Divide — *Robinson, Frank M.*

The Great Divide: Retro vs. Metro America
— *Sperling, John*

Great Divide: The Rocky Mountains in the American
Mind — *Ferguson, Gary*

c The Great Dragon Rescue (Illus. by Robertson, M.P.)
— *Robertson, M.P.*

c The Great Easter Egg Hunt — *Garland, Michael*

The Great Encounter: Native Peoples and European
Settlers in the Americas, 1492-1800 — *Sokolow,
Jayme A.*

y Great Events from History: The Ancient World,
Prehistory-476 C.E., Vols. 1-2 — *Chavalas, Mark W.*

The Green Agenda in American Politics: New Strategies for the Twenty-First Century — *Duffy, Robert J.*

Green and Pleasant Land: English Culture and the Romantic Countryside — *Gilroy, Amanda*

The Green and the Gray — *Zahn, Timothy*

y Green Angel — *Hoffman, Alice*

Green Buildings Pay, 2nd Ed. — *Edwards, Brian (b. 1944 -)*

Green by Design: Creating a Home for Sustainable Living — *Dean, Angela M.*

Green Chemistry Using Liquid and Supercritical Carbon Dioxide — *DeSimone, Joseph M.*

Green Crescent over Nazareth: The Displacement of Christians by Muslims in the Holy Land, Israeli History, Politics and Society — *Israeli, Raphael*

Green Desire: Imagining Early Modern English Gardens — *Bushnell, Rebecca*

Green Dragon, Sombre Warrior: A Journey Around China's Symbolic Frontiers — *Brown, Liam D'Arcy*

Green Empire: The St. Joe Company and the Remaking of Florida's Panhandle — *Ziewitz, Kathryn*

The Green Lantern: A Romance of Stalinist Russia — *Charyn, Jerome*

Green Lantern: Brother's Keeper — *Winick, Judd*

y Green Lantern/Green Arrow Collection, Vol. 1 (Illus. by Neal Adams) — *O'Neil, Dennis*

y Green Lantern/Green Arrow Collection, Vol. 2 (Illus. by Adams, Neal) — *O'Neil, Dennis*

Green MiniAtlas

Green Park (Reading Business Park): Phase 2 Excavations 1995, Neolitich and Bronze Age Sites — *Brossler, Adam*

Green River, Running Red: The Real Story of the Green River Killer--America's Deadliest Serial Murderer (Read by Pawk, Michele). Audiobook Review — *Rule, Ann*

Green River, Running Red: The Real Story of the Green River Killer--America's Deadliest Serial Murderer — *Rule, Ann*

y Green Sea Turtles — *Becker, John E.*

c Green Sea Turtles — *Blomquist, Christopher*

The Green State: Rethinking Democracy and Sovereignty — *Eckersley, Robyn*

Green Suede Shoes: An Irish-American Odyssey — *Kirwan, Larry*

Green Thumb — *McInerny, Ralph*

Green versus Gold: Sources in California's Environmental History — *Merchant, Carolyn*

Greene and Greene: Creating a Style — *Makinson, Randell L.*

c Greene and Greene for Kids — *Thorne-Thomsen, Kathleen*

Greenhouse Gas Emissions Trading and Project-Based Mechanisms — *OECD Global Forum on Sustainable Development*

Greening NAFTA: The North American Commission for Environmental Cooperation — *Markell, David L.*

The Greening of Georgia: The Improvement of the Environment in the Twentieth Century — *Brown, R. Harold*

Greenpeace: An Insider's Account — *Weyler, Rex*

Greenpeace: How a Group of Journalists, Ecologists and Visionaries Changed the World — *Weyler, Rex*

The Greenpeace to Amchitka: An Environmental Odyssey — *Hunter, Robert*

The Greenstone Grail — *Hemingway, Amanda*

c Greenwillow — *Hannigan, Katherine*

Greenwood Daily Life Online. E-book Review

The Greenwood Dictionary of Education — *Collins, John W., III*

y The Greenwood Encyclopedia of African American Civil Rights: From Emancipation to the Twenty-first Century — *Lowery, Charles D.*

The Greenwood Encyclopedia of Daily Life: A Tour through History from Ancient Times to the Present, Vols. 1-6 — *Salisbury, Joyce E.*

The Greenwood Encyclopedia of Daily Life: A Tour through History from Ancient Times to the Present, Vols. 1-6 — *Salisbury, Joyce E.*

The Greenwood Encyclopedia of Daily Life: A Tour through History from Ancient Times to the Present, Vols. 1-6. E-book Review — *Salisbury, Joyce E.*

The Greenwood Encyclopedia of Women's Issues Worldwide — *Walter, Lynn*

y Gregor and the Prophecy of Bane — *Collins, Suzanne*

y Gregor Mendel and the Discovery of the Gene — *Bankston, John*

Gregor Mendel and the Roots of Genetics — *Edelson, Edward.*

c Gregor the Overlander — *Collins, Suzanne*

Gregor VII: Papst Zwischen Canossa und Kirchenreform — *Blumenthal, Uta-Renate*

The "Gregorian" Dialogues and the Origins of Benedictine Monasticism — *Clark, Francis*

c Gregory and Alexander (Illus. by LaFave, Kim) — *Barringer, William*

Gregory Peck: A Charmed Life — *Haney, Lynn*

A Gregory Treasury 1 (Illus. by Hempel, Marc) — *Hempel, Marc*

y A Gregory Treasury 2 (Illus. by Hempel, Marc) — *Hempel, Marc*

The Greig-Duncan Folk Song Collection. Volume 8 — *Shuldham-Shaw, Patrick*

The Grenadillo Box — *Gleeson, Janet*

Grenze und ungleiche regionale Entwicklung: Binnenmarkt und Migration in der Habsburgermonarchie — *Komlosy, Andrea*

c Gretchen: The Bicycle Dog — *Heyman, Anita*

Grey House Homeland Security Directory, 2004 ed.

Grey Knights — *Counter, Ben*

The Greyhound God — *Morris, Keith*

Grid Computing for Electromagnetics — *Tarricone, Luciano*

y Gridlinked — *Asher, Neal*

Grief and Loss: Understanding the Journey — *Freeman, Stephen J.*

Grief Dreams: How They Help Heal Us After the Death of a Loved One — *Wray, T.J.*

y Grierson's Raid: A Daring Cavalry Strike through the Heart of the Confederacy — *Lalicki, Tom*

Grievance Guide, 11th Ed. — *Bureau of National Affairs*

Griffin and Sabine: An Extraordinary Correspondence — *Bantock, Nick*

Griffin & Sabine: An Extraordinary Correspondence — *Bantock, Nick*

Grifter's Game — *Block, Lawrence*

Grilling — *Treuille, Eric*

Grim Fairy Tales: The Rhetorical Construction of American Welfare Policy — *Gring-Pemble, Lisa M.*

c The Grim Grotto (Read by Curry, Tim). Audiobook Review — *Snicket, Lemony*

y The Grim Grotto (Illus. by Helquist, Brett) — *Snicket, Lemony*

c Grim Tuesday (Read by Corduner, Allan). Audiobook Review — *Nix, Garth*

y Grim Tuesday — *Nix, Garth*

y Grind — *Walters, Eric*

The Grit Beneath the Glitter: Tales of the Real Las Vegas — *Rothman, Hal K.*

Gritos: Essays — *Gilb, Dagoberto*

The Grizzly Almanac — *Busch, Robert H.*

Grizzly Seasons: Life with the Brown Bears of Kamchatka — *Russell, Charlie*

Grolier Multimedia Encyclopedia

Grolier Online

c Grolier Student Encyclopedia

The Groo Odyssey — *Aragones, Sergio*

y Gross and Gory — *Laskey, Elizabeth*

c Gross Grub: Wretched Recipes That Look Yucky but Taste Yummy — *Porter, Cheryl*

c Gross Me Out! 50 Nasty Projects to Disgust Your Friends & Repulse Your Family (Illus. by Meyer, Clay) — *Retcher, Ralph*

y Gross Universe: Your Guide to All Disgusting Things under the Sun (Illus. by Cho, Michael) — *Szpirglas, Jeff*

c Gross Universe: Your Guide to All Disgusting Things under the Sun (Illus. by Cho, Michael) — *Szpirglas, Jeff*

The Ground beneath Our Feet: A Factor in Urban Planning — *United Nations. Economic and Social Commission for Asia and the Pacific*

Ground Floor Magazine — *Hirsch, Jeffrey A.*

Ground Warfare: An International Encyclopedia — *Sandler, Stanley*

Ground Water — *Hollis, Matthew*

Groundbreaking Scientific Experiments, Inventions and Discoveries of 19th Century — *Windelspecht, Michael*

Groundbreaking Scientific Experiments, Inventions, and Discoveries of the 18th Century — *Shectman, Jonathan*

Groundbreaking Scientific Experiments, Inventions, and Discoveries of the Ancient World — *Krebs, Robert E.*

Groundbreaking Scientific Experiments, Inventions, and Discoveries of the Middle Ages and the Renaissance — *Krebs, Robert E.*

"Groundhog Day" — *Gilbey, Ryan*

c The Groundhog Day Book of Facts and Fun (Illus. by Billin-Frye, Paige) — *Old, Wendie*

Grounds for Agreement: The Political Economy of the Coffee Commodity Chain — *Talbot, John M.*

The Grounds of Ethical Judgement: New Transcendental Arguments in Moral Philosophy — *Illies, Christian*

Grounds to Play: Culture-specific Ideals in the Upbringing of Children in France, Germany, and the Netherlands — *Gram, Malene*

Groundwater Recharge in a Desert Environment: The Southwestern United States — *Hogan, James F.*

Group 24; Physical and Mathematical Aspects of Symmetries — *Gazeau, J.P.*

Group Creativity: Music, Theater, Collaboration — *Sawyer, R. Keith*

Group of Seven and Tom Thomson — *Silcox, David P.*

Group Processes: A Developmental Perspective, 2nd Ed. — *Wheelan, Susan A.*

Group Psychotherapy and Recovery from Addiction: Carrying the Message — *Roth, Jeffrey D.*

Group Theory, Statistics, and Cryptography: Proceedings — *Myasnikov, A. G.*

Group Therapy An Integrative Cognitive Social-Learning Approach — *Woody, Robert Henley*

Group Work with Adolescents after Violent Death: A Manual for Practitioners — *Salloum, Alison*

Groups in Music: Strategies from Music Therapy — *Pavlicevic, Mercedes*

c Grow Grow Grow — *Riley, Barbara*

Growing and Knowing: A Selection Guide for Children's Literature — *Trim, Mary*

Growing Orchids in Your Garden — *Friend, Robert G.M.*

Growing Public: Social Spending and Economic Growth since the Eighteenth Century. Vol. 1 — *Lindert, Peter H.*

Growing Public: Social Spending and Economic Growth since the Eighteenth Century, Vol. 1 — *Lindert, Peter H.*

Growing Public: Social Spending and Economic Growth since the Eighteenth-Century. Vol. 2 — *Lindert, Peter H.*

Growing Up Abolitionist: The Story of the Garrison Children — *Alonso, Harriet Hyman*

Growing Up Fast — *Lipper, Joanna*

Growing Up in Hitler's Shadow: Remembering Youth in Postwar Berlin — *Redding, Kimberly A.*

y Growing up King: An Intimate Memoir — *King, Dexter*

Growing Up Palestinian: Israeli Occupation and the Intifada Generation — *Bucaille, Laetitia*

Growing up with Lucy: How to Build an Android in Twenty Easy Steps — *Grand, Steve*

Growing Your Musician: A Practical Guide for Band and Orchestra Parents — *Bancroft, Tony*

Growth and Development across the Lifespan: A Health Promotion Focus — *Leifer, Gloria*

Growth, Distribution, and Effective Demand: Alternatives to Economic Orthodoxy: Essays in Honor of Edward J. Nell — *Argyrous, George*

Growth, Industrial Organization and Economic Generalities — *Baumol, William J.*

Growth, Industrial Organization and Economic Generalities — *Buamol, William J.*

The Growth of Market Relations in Post-Reform Rural China: A Micro-Analysis of Peasants, Migrants and Peasant Entrepreneurs — *Sato, Hiroshi*

Growth of the American Revolution: 1766-1775 — *Knollenberg, Bernhard*

c The Gruffalo's Child (Illus. by Scheffler, Axel) — *Donaldson, Julia*

c Grumblebunny (Illus. by Clark, David) — *Clark, David*

Grzimek's Animal Life Encyclopedia, 2nd Ed. — *Grzimek, Bernhard*

GSM, GPRS and EDGE Performance: Evolution Towards 3G/UMTS, 2nd Ed. — *Halonen, Timo*

Guantanamo: The War on Human Rights — *Rose, David*

Guantanamo: What the World Should Know — *Ratner, Michael*

The Guarani under Spanish Rule in the Rio de la Plata — *Ganson, Barbara*

Guardian of the Freedom: Merlin's Descendants, Vol. 5 — *Radford, Irene*

Guardian of the Horizon (Read by Rosenblat, Barbara) — *Mertz, Barbara*

Guardian of the Horizon (Read by Rosenblat, Barbara). Audiobook Review — *Mertz, Barbara*

H

Hawthorns and Medlars — *Phipps, James B.*

Hay una vaca entre las coies — *Beaton, Claire*

Hayagriva in South India: Complexity and Selectivity of a Pan-Indian Hindu Deity — *Nayar, Kamala Elizabeth*

Hayek's Challenge: An Intellectual Biography of F.A. Hayek — *Caldwell, Bruce*

Hayek's Journey: The Mind of Friedrich Hayek — *Ebenstein, Alan*

Haymarket — *Duberman, Martin*

The Hazards of Good Breeding — *Shattuck, Jessica*

The Hazards of Sleeping Alone — *Juska, Elise*

c Hazel Nutt, Alien Hunter (Illus. by Kelley, True) — *Elliott, David*

Hazel Wolf: Fighting the Establishment — *Starbuck, Susan*

c he Best Halloween Ever (Read by Stritch, Elaine). Audiobook Review — *Robinson, Barbara*

He Had It Coming — *Spencer, Camika*

He-Motions: Even Strong Men Struggle — *Jakes, T.D.*

He Paves the Road with Iron Bars — *Knox, Caroline*

He Said Never — *Waddell, Patricia*

He Who Fears the Wolf — *Fossum, Karin*

Head and Neck Cancer: A Multidisciplinary Approach, 2nd Ed. — *Harrison, Louis B.*

Head First Java — *Sierra, Kathy*

Head First Servlets and JSP — *Basham, Bryan*

y Head Games — *Fredericks, Mariah*

c Head Lice Up Close — *Birch, Robin*

The Head Negro in Charge Syndrome: The Dead End of Black Politics — *Kelley, Norman*

The Head Start Debates — *Zigler, Edward*

c Head to Toe Science: Over 40 Eye-Popping, Spine-Tingling, Heart-Pounding Activities That Teach Kids about the Human Body — *Wiese, Jim*

Headache: A Guide for the Primary Care Physician — *Loder, Elizabeth W.*

Headhunters: Matchmaking in the Labor Market — *Finlay, William*

Headlines From History: The Civil War

The Headmaster's Wife — *Haddam, Jane*

Headquarters USA: A Directory of Contact Information for Headquarters and Other Central Offices of Major Business and Organizations in the US and in Canada, 2004, vols. 1-2, 26th ed.

Heads up: How to Anticipate Business Surprises and Seize Opportunities First — *McGee, Kenneth G.*

Heads You Win — *Mount, Ferdinand*

Heal the Ocean: Solutions for Saving Our Seas — *Fujita, Rod*

Heal Thyself: Nicholas Culpeper and the Seventeenth-Century Struggle to Bring Medicine to the People — *Woolley, Benjamin*

Healed Without Scars — *Evans, David G.*

Healers and Heroes: Ordinary People in Extraordinary Times — *Cleaveland, Clif*

y The Healer's Keep — *Hanley, Victoria*

Healing America: The Life of Senate Majority Leader William H. Frist, M.D., and the Issues That Shape Our Time — *Martin, Charles*

Healing and Mental Health for Native Americans: Speaking in Red — *Nebelkopf, Ethan*

The Healing Art: A Doctor's Black Bag of Poetry — *Campo, Rafael*

The Healing Arts: Health, Disease and Society in Europe 1500-1800, 1st Ed. — *Elmer, Peter*

Healing by Heart: Clinical and Ethical Case Stories of Hmong Families and Western Providers — *Culhane-Pera, Kathleen A.*

A Healing Force — *Williams, Niall*

Healing from the Trauma of Childhood Sexual Abuse: The Journey for Women — *Duncan, Karen A.*

Healing Identities: Black Feminist Thought and the Politics of Groups — *Burack, Cynthia*

Healing Plots: The Narrative Basis of Psychotherapy — *Lieblich, Amia*

Healing Power of Horses: Lessons from the Lakota Indians (Illus. by Vinitsky, Hope) — *Baker, Wendy*

Healing the Heart of Conflict: 8 Crucial Steps to Making Peace with Yourself and Others — *Gopin, Marc*

y The Healing Time of Hickeys — *Rivers, Karen*

The Healing Tradition: Reviving the Soul of Western Medicine — *Greaves, David*

Healing Trauma: The Power of Group Treatment for People with Intellectual Disabilities — *Razza, Nancy J.*

Healing Violent Men: A Model for Christian Communities — *Livingston, David J.*

Health and Labor Force Participation over the Life Cycle: Evidence from the Past — *Costa, Dora L.*

Health and Safety Needs of Older Workers — *Wegman, David H.*

The Health and Social Care Divide: The Experiences of Older People, 2nd Ed. — *Glasby, Jon*

Health and Social Justice: Politics, Ideology, and Inequity in the Distribution of Disease, a Public Health Reader — *Hofrichter, Richard*

Health and Wellness: Life Stages and Reproduction — *Anderson, P.F.*

Health as International Politics: Combating Communicable Diseases in the Baltic Sea Region — *Honneland, Geir*

Health Care Administration: Planning, Implementing, and Managing Organized Delivery Systems, 4th Ed. — *Wolper, Lawrence F.*

Health Care Ethics for Psychologists: A Casebook — *Hanson, Stephanie L.*

Health Care Ethics: Lessons from Intensive Care — *Melia, Kath*

Health Care Fraud and Abuse: Practical Perspectives, 2003 Supplement — *Baumann, Linda A.*

Health Care Industry: A Primer for Board Members — *Pointer, Dennis Dale*

Health Care Matters: Pharmaceuticals, Obesity, and the Quality of Life — *Miller, Richard D.*

Health Care Policy and Politics A to Z, 2nd Ed. — *Rovner, Julie*

Health Care Reform in Central America: NGO-Government Collaboration in Guatemala and El Salvador — *Cardelle, Alberto Jose Frick*

Health Care Systems of the Developed World: How the United States' System Remains an Outlier — *Matcha, Duane A.*

Health Consequences of Abuse in the Family: A Clinical Guide for Evidence-Based Practice — *Kendall-Tackett, Kathleen A.*

Health, Disease and Society in Europe 1500-1800: A Source Book, 1st Ed. — *Elmer, Peter*

Health, Disease and Society in Europe 1800-1930: A Source Book, 1st ed. — *Brunton, Deborah*

Health Financing for Poor People: Resource Mobilization and Risk Sharing — *Preker, Alexander S.*

Health Hazards Manual for Artists, 5th Rev. Ed. — *McCann, Michael*

Health in America: A Multicultural Perspective, 2nd Ed. — *Nakamura, Raymond M.*

Health Literacy: A Prescription to End Confusion — *Nielsen-Bohlman, Lynn*

Health Literacy from A to Z: Practical Ways to Communicate Your Health Message — *Osborne, Helen*

Health Policy and the Uninsured — *McLaughlin, Catherine G.*

Health Policy in a Globalising World — *Fustukian, Suzanne*

Health Promotion: Planning and Strategies — *Tones, Keith*

Health Promotion Practice: Power and Empowerment — *Laverack, Glenn*

Health Psychology Handbook: Practical Issues for the Behavioral Medicine Specialist — *Cohen, Lee M.*

Health Services Planning, 2nd Ed. — *Thomas, Richard K.*

Health, Sickness, Medicine and the Friars in the Thirteenth and Fourteenth Centuries — *Montford, Angela*

Health, State, and Society in Kenya: Faces of Contact and Change — *Ndege, George Oduor*

Health, Well-Being and Older People — *Reed, Jan*

Healthcare Engineering - Latest Developments and Applications: Proceedings

y Healthcare Reform in America: A Reference Handbook — *Kronenfeld, Jennie Jacobs*

c Healthy Body — *Royston, Angela*

y The Healthy Body Cookbook: Over 50 Fun Activities and Delicious Recipes for Kids (Illus. by Cash-Walsh, Tina) — *D'Amico, Joan*

Healthy Children Sourcebook: Basic Consumer Health Information about the Physical and Mental Development of Children Between the Ages of 3 and 2 ... — *Kimball, Chad T.*

Healthy Cities and Urban Policy Research — *Takano, Takehito*

y Healthy Eating for Weight Management — *Turch, Mary*

Healthy Fats for Life: Preventing and Treating Common Health Problems with Essential Fatty Acids, Rev. 2nd Ed. — *Vanderhaeghe, Lorna R.*

c Healthy Habits — *Weber, Rebecca*

Healthy Sexuality — *Blonna, Richard*

c Healthy Weight Loss — *Stoppard, Miriam*

Hear Me Talking to You — *Craig, David*

y Hear My Sorrow: The Diary of Angela Denoto, a Shirtwaist Worker — *Hopkinson, Deborah*

Hear No Evil (Read by Sullivan, Nick). Audiobook Review — *Grippando, James*

Hear No Evil — *Grippando, James*

c Hear That Train Whistle Blow!: How the Railroad Changed the World — *Meltzer, Milton*

Hear the Wind Blow — *Hahn, Mary Downing*

Hear Us Out: Conversations with Gay Novelists — *Canning, Richard*

Hearing America's Youth: Social Identities in Uncertain Times — *Cornbleth, Catherine*

Hearing Birds Fly: A Nomadic Year in Mongolia — *Waugh, Louisa*

Hearing Gesture: How Our Hands Help Us Think — *Goldin-Meadow, Susan*

Hearing God's Call: Ways of Discernment for Laity and Clergy — *Johnson, Ben Campbell*

Hearing Is Believing: How Words Can Make or Break Our Kids — *Medhus, Elisa*

c A Heart Alone in the Land of Darkness — *Rozen, Beti*

c Heart and Blood — *Ballard, Carol*

Heart and Emotion: Ambulatory Monitoring Studies in Everyday Life — *Myrtek, Michael*

Heart and Head: Black Theology - Past, Present, and Future — *Hopkins, Dwight, N.*

Heart and Minds in Guerrilla Warfare: The Malayan Emergency, 1948-1960 — *Stubbs, Richard*

c Heart, Blood and Lungs — *Stevens, Gareth*

Heart Disease: Everything You Need to Know — *Myers, Rob*

c A Heart Divided — *Bennett, Cherie*

The Heart Does Not Bend — *Silvera, Makeda*

Heart Failure: Providing Optimal Care — *Jessup, Mariell*

Heart-Friendly Cooking — *Pare, Jean*

The Heart Is a Lonely Hunter. Audiobook Review — *McCullers, Carson*

The Heart Is a Lonely Hunter — *McCullers, Carson*

The Heart Laid Bare — *Tremblay, Michel*

Heart of a Stranger — *Laurence, Margaret*

Heart of Creation: The Mesoamerican World and the Legacy of Linda Schele — *Stone, Andrea*

A Heart of Devotion — *McCullors, Tia*

The Heart of Mid-Lothian — *Scott, Walter*

Heart of the Hunter — *Meyer, Deon*

y The Heart of the Matter (Read by Kitchen, Michael). Audiobook Review — *Greene, Graham*

The Heart of the Sound — *Holleman, Marybeth*

c Heart of the Tiger (Illus. by Chapman, Gaye) — *Millard, Glenda*

The Heart of the World: A Journey to the Last Secret Place — *Baker, Ian*

The Heart of Thornton Creek — *Leon, Bonnie*

The Heart of War: On Power, Conflict and Obligation in the Twenty-First Century — *Prins, Gwyn*

y Heart on My Sleeve — *Wittlinger, Ellen*

The Heart Renewed: Assurance of Salvation in New England Spiritual Life — *Norman, Pettit*

The Heart Renewed: Assurance of Salvation in New England Spiritual Life — *Pettit, Norman*

Heart So Hungry: The Extraordinary Expedition of Mina Hubbard into the Labrador Wilderness

Heart So Hungry: The Extraordinary Expedition of Mina Hubbard into the Labrador Wilderness — *Silvis, Randall*

Heart Sounds Made Incredibly Easy — *Labus, Diane*

The Heart Sutra: The Womb of Buddhas — *Pine, Red*

c Heart to Heart: New Poems Inspired by Twentieth-Century American Art — *Greenberg, Jan*

y Heartbeat (Read by Siegfried, Mandy). Audiobook Review — *Creech, Sharon*

c Heartbeat — *Creech, Sharon*

The Heartbreak Lounge — *Stroby, Wallace*

Heartbreakers: Women and Violence in Contemporary Culture and Literature — *Hendin, Josephine G.*

Heartland: A Prairie Sampler (Illus. by Moore, Yvette) — *Bannatyne-Cugnet, Jo*

y Heart's Delight — *Nilsson, Per*

Hearts of Darkness: Wellsprings of a Southern Literary Tradition — *Wyatt-Brown, Bertram*

Hearts of Darkness: White Women Write Race — *Marcus, Jane*

c Hearts of Gold: Stories of Courage, Dedication and Triumph from Canadian Olympic Athletes — *Zeiler, Lorne*

HeartSmart Nutrition: Shopping on the Run — *Leighton, Myriam*

Heartwood: The First Generation of Theravada Buddhism in America — *Cadge, Wendy*

Henologie, Ontologie et Ereignis — *Narbonne, Jean-Marc*

Henri Dutilleux: Music, Mystery and Memory. Conversations with Claude Glayman. — *Roger Nichols*

Henri Dutilleux: Music, Mystery and Memory — *Glayman, Claude*

Henri Irenee Marrou: Historien Engage — *Riche, Pierre*

c Henrietta, There's No One Better — *Murray, Martine*

c Henry and Edsel: The Creation of the Ford Empire — *Bak, Richard*

c Henry and Pawl and the Round Yellow Ball — *Casmer, Tom*

c Henry and the Kite Dragon (Illus. by Low, William) — *Hall, Bruce Edward*

Henry de Montherland (1895-1972): A Philosophy of Failure — *O'Flaherty, Patricia*

Henry F. Gilbert: A Bio-Bibliography — *Martin, Sherrill V.*

c Henry Fickle and the Secret Laboratory — *Mack, Michele*

Henry Handel Richardson: A Life — *Ackland, Michael*

Henry Hastings Sibley: Divided Heart — *Gilman, Rhoda R.*

Henry IV, Part 1 — *Kastan, David Scott*

Henry IV: The Establishment of the Regime, 1399-1406 — *Dodd, Gwilym*

Henry IV: The Establishment of the Regime, 1399-1406 — *Dood, Gwilym*

Henry James and the Suspense of Masculinity — *Person, Leland S.*

Henry Lloyd and the Military Enlightenment of Eighteenth-Century Europe — *Speelman, Patrick J.*

Henry Maudslay and the Pioneers of the Machine Age — *Cantrell, John*

Henry Oldenburg: Shaping the Royal Society — *Hall, Marie Boas*

Henry Sidgwick, Eye of the Universe: An Intellectual Biography — *Schultz, Bart*

Henry Timrod: A Biography — *Cisco, Walter Brian*

Henry Vaughan's Silex Scintillians: Scripture Uses — *West, Philip*

Henry VI: Critical Essays — *Pendleton, Thomas A.*

Henry VI — *Martin, Randall*

Henry VIII: A Study in Kingship — *Graves, Michael A.R.*

Henry VIII, the League of Schmalkalden, and the English Reformation — *McEntegart, Rory*

A Henry Wadsworth Longfellow Companion — *Gale, Robert L.*

c Henry Works (Illus. by Johnson, D.B.) — *Johnson, D.B.*

c Henry Works (Illus. by Johnson, D.B.) — *Johnson, D.B. (American illustrator)*

c Henry's 100 Days of Kindergarten — *Carlson, Nancy*

c Henry's 100 Days of Kindergarten

c Henry's Amazing Machine (Illus. by Brooker, Kyrsten) — *Dodds, Dayle Ann*

c Henry's Show and Tell (Illus. by Carlson, Nancy) — *Carlson, Nancy*

c Hepcat — *Bramhall, William*

Her Blue Body Everything We Know — *Walker, Alice*

Her First American — *Segal, Lore*

y Her Husband: Hughes and Plath--A Marriage (Read by Dunne, Bernadette). Audiobook Review — *Middlebrook, Diane Wood*

Her Husband: Hughes and Plath--A Marriage — *Middlebrook, Diane Wood*

Her Husband: Ted Hughes & Sylvia Plath -- A Marriage — *Middlebrook, Diane Wood*

Her Name Was Lola — *Hoban, Russell*

Her Other Thief — *Garland, Glenda*

Her Place at the Table: A Woman's Guide to Negotiating Five Key Challenges to Leadership Success — *Kolb, Deborah M.*

Her Scandalous Affair — *Hern, Candice*

Heraclius: Emperor of Byzantium — *Kaegi, Walter E.*

The Herbaceous Layer in Forests of Eastern North America — *Gilliam, Frank S.*

Herbal and Traditional Medicine: Molecular Aspects of Health — *Packer, Lester*

Herbal-Drug Interactions and Adverse Effects: An Evidence-Based Quick Reference Guide — *Philp, Richard B.*

Herbal Drugs and Phytopharmaceuticals: A Handbook for Practice on a Scientific Basis, 3rd Ed. — *Michtl, Max*

The Herbalist: Nicholas Culpeper and the Fight for Medical Freedom — *Woolley, Benjamin*

Herbert Butterfield: Historian as Dissenter — *McIntire, C.T.*

y Herbert Hoover — *Ruth, Amy*

Herbert Spencer — *Jones, Greta*

Herding Cats: Multiparty Mediation in a Complex World — *Crocker, Chester A.*

Here Am I Lord ... Send Somebody Else!: How God Uses Ordinary People to do Extraordinary Things — *Briscoe, Jill*

Here Be Dragons: Telling Tales of People, Passion and Power — *Newman, Peter C.*

Here Beneath Low-Flying Planes — *Feitell, Merrill*

c Here Comes Our Bride!: An African Wedding Story — *Onyefulu, Ifeoma*

Here Comes the Roar — *Shaw, Dave (b. 1966 -)*

y Here in Harlem: Poems in Many Voices — *Myers, Walter Dean*

y Here Is Greenwood — *Nasu, Yukie*

Here, There and Everywhere — *Roberson, Chris*

c Here They Come! (Illus. by Costello, David) — *Costello, David*

y Here Today (Read by Kaye, Judy). Audiobook Review — *Martin, Ann M.*

y Here Today — *Martin, Ann M.*

Herero — *Seyfried, Gerhard*

Heresies — *Gray, John (b. 1948 -)*

Heresies: The Complete Poems of Anne Wilkinson 1924-61 — *Irvine, Dean*

Heresies: The Complete Poems of Anne Wilkinson, 1924-1961 — *Wilkinson, Anne*

The Heretic in Darwin's Court: The Life of Alfred Russel Wallace — *Palmer, Douglas*

The Heretic in Darwin's Court: The Life of Alfred Russel Wallace — *Slotten, Ross A.*

Heribert Muhlen: His Theology and Praxis: A New Profile of the Church — *Vondey, Wolfgang*

Heritage Houses of Nova Scotia — *Archibald, Stephen*

A Heritage of Holy Wood: The Legend of the True Cross in Text and Image — *Baert, Barbara*

A Heritage of Light: Lamps and Lighting in the Early Canadian Home — *Russell, Loris S.*

The Heritage Trees of Britain and Northern Ireland — *Stokes, Ben*

Herman Bang: Morkvordige losninger. Toogfirs tableauer — *Heede, Dag*

Herman Classics, Vol. 1 — *Unger, Jim*

Herman Melville's Whaling Years — *Heflin, Wilson L.*

Hermanitos Comanchitos — *Lamadrid, Enrique R.*

Hermanitos Comanchitos: Indo-Hispano Rituals of Captivity and Redemption — *Lamadrid, Enrique R.*

Hermann Broch, Visionary in Exile: The 2001 Yale Symposium — *Lutzeler, Paul Michael*

Hermann Hesse: Between the Perils of Politics and the Allure of the Orient — *Mileck, Joseph*

Hermeneutical Apprenticeships: Essays, Epigrams, Verse — *Loewen, G.V.*

Hermeneutics, Faith, and Relations between Cultures: Lecutres in Qom, Iran — *McLean, George F.*

The Hermeneutics of the Subject: Lectures at the College de France, 1981-82 — *Foucault, Michel*

Hermesetas — *Wilson, Chris*

Hermine: An Animal Life — *Beig, Maria*

c Hermit Crabs — *Binns, Tristan Boyer*

Hermit in Paris: Autobiographical Writings — *Calvino, Italo*

Hernia Infections: Pathophysiology, Diagnosis, Treatment, Prevention — *Deysine, Maximo*

Hero: A New Translation — *Xenophon*

The Hero and His Shadow: Psychopolitical Aspects of Myth and Reality in Israel, Rev. Ed. — *Shalit, Erel*

c Hero — *Attema, Martha*

c Hero Dogs: Courageous Canines in Action — *Jackson, Donna M.*

Hero, Hawk, and Open Hand: American Indian Art of the Ancient Midwest and South — *Townsend, Richard F.*

Hero Mama: A Daughter Remembers the Father She Lost in Vietnam--and the Mother Who Held Her Family Together — *Zacharias, Karen Spears*

Hero Myths: A Reader — *Segal, Robert A.*

y Hero Returns (Illus. by Nightow, Yasuhiro) — *Nightow, Yasuhiro*

c Herobear and the Kid: The Inheritance — *Kunkel, Mike*

Herodotus and His World: Essays from a Conference in Memory of George Forrest — *Derow, Peter*

Herodotus and Religion in the Persian Wars — *Mikalson, Jon D.*

Herodotus and the War for Greek Freedom: Selections from the Histories — *Shirley, Samuel*

Herodotus Book — *McQueen, E.I.*

Herodotus in Context: Ethnography, Science, and the Art of Persuasion. — *Thomas, Rosalind*

y Heroes and She-roes: Poems of Amazing and Everyday Heroes (Illus. by Cooke, Jim) — *Lewis, J. Patrick*

Heroes at Home: Help & Hope for America's Military Families (Read by Kay, Ellie). Audiobook Review — *Kay, Ellie*

Heroes Never Die: Warriors and Warfare in World War II — *Blumenson, Martin*

c Heroes of the Revolution — *Adler, David A.*

Heroes of the Revolution — *Smith, Donald A.*

Heroes or Traitors: The German Replacement Army, the July Plot, and Adolf Hitler — *Dunn, Walter S., Jr.*

Heroes, Saints, and Ordinary Morality — *Flescher, Andrew Michael*

Heroes: Saviours, Traitors And Supermen — *Hughes-Hallett, Lucy*

Heroic Adventures of Donny Coyote — *Mithcell, Ken*

The Heroic Adventures of Hercules Amsterdam — *Haber, Melissa*

Heroic Efforts: The Emotional Culture of Search and Rescue Volunteers — *Lois, Jennifer*

Heroic Flights: The First 100 Years of Aviation — *Turner, John Frayn*

Heroic Leadership: Best Practices from a 450-Year-Old Company That Changed the World — *Lowney, Chris*

Heroic Rescues at Sea: True Stories of the Canadian Coast Guard — *Matthews, Carolyn*

The Heroic Story of the United States Merchant Marine — *Herbert, Brian*

Heroides 11, 13 and 14: A Commentary — *Reeson, J.*

Heroines and History: Representations of Madeleine de Vercheres and Laura Secord — *Coates, Colin M.*

c Herons — *Hall, Margaret*

Hero's Journey: Joseph Campbell on His Life and Work, Centennial Ed. — *Campbell, Joseph*

Heros of Empire: The British Imperial Protagonist in America, 1596-1764 — *Frohock, Richard*

Herrschaft und Widerstand im augusteischen Principat. Die Konkurrenz zwischen res publica und und domus Augusta — *Dettenhoffer, M.H.*

Herrscherideologie in der Spatantike — *Kolb, F.*

The Herschel Partnership: As Viewed by Caroline — *Hoskin, Michael*

c The Hershey's Milk Chocolate Multiplication Book (Illus. by Bolster, Rob) — *Pallotta, Jerry*

Herspace: Women, Writing, and Solitude — *Malin, Jo*

He's Just Not That into You: The No-Excuses Truth to Understanding Guys — *Behrendt, Greg*

Hesiod's Ascra — *Edwards, Anthony T.*

Hesiod's Cosmos — *Clay, Jenny Strauss*

Hesitant Heroes: Private Inhibition, Cultural Crisis — *Ziolkowski, Theodore*

Hester. Fascicule 1. Introduction — *Haelewyck, Jean-Claude*

Heterarchy, Political Economy, and the Ancient Maya: The Three Rivers Region of the East-Central Yucatan Peninsula — *Scarborough, Vernon L.*

Heterodoxy in Late Imperial China — *Liu, Kwang-Ching*

Heterogender Homosexuality in Honduras — *Alemany-Fernandez, Manuel*

Hetty: The Genius and Madness of America's First Female Tycoon — *Slack, Charles*

Hewett Cottrell Watson: Victorian Plant Ecologist and Evolutionist — *Egerton, Frank N.*

c Hewitt Anderson's Great Big Life (Illus. by Nelson, Kadir) — *Nolan, Jerdine*

c Hewitt Anderson's Great Big Life (Illus. by Nelson, Kadir) — *Nolen, Jerdine*

Hey, Crumbling Balcony!: Poems New and Selected — *Ross, Stuart (b. 1959 -)*

c Hey Diddle Diddle — *Collins, Heather*

y Hey, Kidz! Buy This Book: A Radical Primer on Corporate and Governmental Propaganda and Artistic Activism for Short People (Illus. by Kelso, Megan) — *Moore, Anne-Elizabeth*

c Hey, Mama Goose (Illus. by Chollat, Emilie) — *Zalben, Jane Breskin*

Hey Nostradamus! — *Coupland, Douglas*

c Hey, Picasso — *Harper, Jessica*

Hey Rube: Blood Sport, the Bush Doctrine, and the Downward Spiral of Dumbness: Modern History from the Sports Desk — *Thompson, Hunter S.*

Hey, Waitress!: The USA from the Other Side of the Tray — *Owings, Alison*

Hey, Waitress!: The USA from the Other Side of the Tray — *Owings, Alison*

Hey, Whipple, Squeeze This — *Sullivan, Luke*

Hey Ya!: The Unauthorized Biography of OutKast — *Nickson, Chris*

Hindu Bioethics for the Twenty-First Century
— Crawford, S. Cromwell

Hindu Iconoclasts: Rammohun Roy, Dayananda
Sarasvati, and Nineteenth-Century Polemics
Against Idolatry — Salmond, Noel A.

Hindu Rulers, Muslim Subjects: Islam, Rights, and
the History of Kashmir — Mridu, Raj

Hindu Rulers, Muslim Subjects: Islam, Rights, and
the History of Kashmir — Rai, Mridu

Hinduism and Its Sense of History — Sharma, Arvind

Hinduism and Modernity — Smith, David

Hinduism and Modernity — Totten, Samuel

Hinduism: Past and Present — Michaels, Axel

Hindutva: Exploring the Idea of Hindu Nationalism
— Sharma, Jyotirmaya

y The Hip Handbag Book: 25 Easy-to-Make Totes,
Purses, and Bags — Haab, Sherri

Hip-Hop Hares and Other Moments of Epic Silliness
— Outside Magazine

y Hip-Hop Poetry and the Classics for the Classroom
— Sitomer, Alan Lawrence

Hip Hotels: Beach — Ypma, Herbert

y Hip: The History — Leland, John

Hip to Crochet: 23 Contemporary Projects for
Today's Crocheter — Swartz, Judith L.

Hip to Stitch: 20 Contemporary Projects Embellished
with Thread — Barta, Melinda A.

HIPAA Privacy Source Book: A Collection of Practical
Samples — Hubbartt, William S.

HIPAA Transactions: A Nontechnical Business Guide
for Health Care — Jones, Edward D.

Hippeastrum: The Gardener's Amaryllis — Read,
Veronica M.

y Hippie — Miles, Barry

Hippie — Scott, Grant

Hippie Crafts: Creating a Hip New Look Using
Groovy '60s Crafts — O'Sullivan, Joanne

Hippie Dictionary — McCleary, John Bassett

y The Hippie House — Holubitsky, Katherine

c The Hippo-Not-Amus (Illus. by Parker-Rees, Guy)
— Payne, Tony

Hippocrates — Jouanna, Jacques

The Hippocratic Oath and the Ethics of Medicine
— Miles, Steven H.

Hippocratic Oaths: Medicine and Its Discontents
— Tallis, Raymond

Hippolytus — Euripides

Hiratsuka Raicho and Early Japanese Feminism
— Tomida, Hiroko

Hiring Source Book: A Collection of Practical Samples
— Fyock, Catherine D.

y Hiroshima: The Story of the First Atom Bomb
— Lawton, Clive A.

Hirschfeld's Harlem — Hirschfeld, Al

His Brother's Keeper: A Story from the Edge of
Medicine — Weiner, Jonathan

y His Excellency: George Washington — Ellis, Joseph J.

His Majesty's Enemies: Great Britain's War against
Holocaust Victims and Survivors — Levin, Itamar

His Religion and Hers: A Study of the Faith of Our
Fathers and the Work of Our Mothers — Gilman,
Charlotte Perkins

HISCO: Historical International Standard
Classification of Occupations — Leeuwen, Marco
H.D. van

The Hispanic Connection: Spanish and
Spanish-American Literature in the Arts of the
World — DaSilva, Zenia Sacks

The Hispanic Databook: Detailed Statistics and
Rankings on the Hispanic Population, 2nd Ed.
— Garoogian, David

The Hispanic Databook: Detailed Statistics and
Rankings on the Hispanic Population, Including 23
Ethnic Backgrounds from Argentinian to
Venezuelan, for 1,266 U.S. Counties and Cities
— Garoogian, David

Hispanic Literature of the United States: A
Comprehensive Reference — Kanellos, Nicolas

Hissy Fit — Andrews, Mary Kay

Histoire Auguste. Tome V, 2eme partie. Vies de
Probus, Firmus, Saturnin, Proclus et Bonose,
Carus, Numerien et Carin — Paschoud, F.

Histoire des Routes et des Transports en Europe: Des
Chemins de Saint-Jacques a l'age d'or des
Diligences — Livet, George

Histoire sociale des idees au Quebec — Lamonde, Yvan

Histoire universelle de la chastete et du celibat
— Abbott, Elizabeth

Histopathology and Seed-Borne Infection — Singh,
Dalbir

Historia corporis humani sive Anatomice — Benedetti,
Alessandro

Historia de la Ciudad de Mexico en los fines de siglo
— Medina, Manuel Ramos

Historia Economica e Historia De Empresas
— Brazilian Association of Researches in Economic
History

The Historian — Kostova, Elizabeth

Historians in Trouble: Plagiarism, Fraud, and Politics
in the Ivory Tower — Wiener, Jon

The Historians of Late Antiquity — Rohrbacher, D.

The Historic Imaginary: Politics of History in Facist
Italy — Fogu, Claudio

Historic Indian Towns in Alabama, 1540-1838
— Wright, Amos J., Jr.

Historic St. Croix: St. Stephen-Calais — Rees, Ronald

Historic Wolfville: Grand Pre and Countryside
— Sheppard, Tom

A Historical Archaeology of Delaware: People,
Contexts, and the Cultures of Agriculture — De
Cunzo, Lu Ann

Historical Aspects of Cataloging and Classification
— Joachim, Martin D.

Historical Atlas of Ancient Mesopotamia — Hunt,
Norman Bancroft

c Historical Atlas of Azerbaijan — Liberman, Sherri

y A Historical Atlas of Azerbaijan — Liberman, Sherri

Historical Atlas of Canada: Canada's History
Illustrated with Original Maps — Hayes, Derek

Historical Atlas of Central Europe — Magocsi, Paul
Robert

Historical Atlas of Islam — Ruthven, Malise

c A Historical Atlas of Jordan — Romano, Amy

c A Historical Atlas of Kuwait — Ray, Kurt

y A Historical Atlas of Kyrgyzstan — Khan, Aisha

c A Historical Atlas of Lebanon — Skahill, Carolyn M.

Historical Atlas of North Yorkshire — Butlin, R. A.

Historical Atlas of North Yorkshire — Slaley, Nick

Historical Atlas of the Ancient Greece — Hayes, Derek

Historical Atlas of the Arctic — Hayes, Derek

Historical Atlas of the Holy Land — Farrington,
Karen

Historical Atlas of the Holy Lands

y Historical Atlas of the Islamic World — Nicolle, David

Historical Atlas of the Napoleonic Era — Konstam,
Angus

y Historical Atlas of the Renaissance — Ritchie, Robert

c A Historical Atlas of the United Arab Emirates
— Romano, Amy

An Historical Atlas of the Zulu Rebellion of 1906
— Thompson, Paul S.

Historical Atlases: The First Three Hundred Years,
1570-1870 — Goffart, Walter A.

The Historical Austen — Galperin, William H.

Historical Dictionary from the Great War to the Great
Depression — Wynn, Neil A.

Historical Dictionary of Afghanistan, 3rd Ed.
— Adamec, Ludwig W.

Historical Dictionary of Albania, 2nd Ed. — Elsie,
Robert

Historical Dictionary of American Propaganda
— Manning, Martin J.

Historical Dictionary of Ancient and Medieval Nubia
— Lobban, Richard A., Jr.

Historical Dictionary of Ancient Egyptian Warfare
— Morkot, Robert G.

Historical Dictionary of Ancient Israel — Lemche,
Niels Peter

Historical Dictionary of Angola — James, W. Martin

Historical Dictionary of Angola, Rev. Ed. — Martin,
James W.

Historical Dictionary of Bangladesh, 3rd Ed.
— Baxter, Craig

Historical Dictionary of Brussels — State, Paul F.

Historical Dictionary of Cambodia — Corfield, Justin

Historical Dictionary of Descartes and Cartesian
Philosophy — Ariew, Roger

Historical Dictionary of Egypt, 3rd. Ed.
— Goldschmidt, Arthur

Historical Dictionary of Estonia — Miljan, Toivo

Historical Dictionary of Ethiopia — Shinn, David
Hamilton

Historical Dictionary of Feminism, 2nd Ed. — Boles,
Janet K.

Historical Dictionary of Indonesia, 2nd Ed. — Cribb,
R.B.

Historical Dictionary of Iraq — Ghareeb, Edmund A.

Historical Dictionary of Jainism — Wiley, Kristi L.

Historical Dictionary of Kyrgyzstan — Abazov, Rafis

Historical Dictionary of Lesotho, 2nd Ed.
— Rosenberg, Scott

Historical Dictionary of Mozambique, 2nd Ed.
— Azevedo, Mario

Historical Dictionary of Nepal — Shrestha, Nanda R.

Historical Dictionary of New England — Holloran,
Peter C.

Historical Dictionary of Organized Labor 2nd Ed.
— Docherty, James C

Historical Dictionary of Poland, 2nd Ed. — Sanford,
George

Historical Dictionary of Schopenhauer's Philosophy
— Cartwright, David E.

Historical Dictionary of Science Fiction Literature
— Stableford, Brian

Historical Dictionary of Syria, 2nd Ed. — Commins,
David Dean

Historical Dictionary of Syria. 2nd Ed. — Commins,
David Dean

Historical Dictionary of Syria, 2nd Ed. — Commins,
David Dean

Historical Dictionary of the Civil War and
Reconstruction — Richter, William L.

Historical Dictionary of the Crusades — Slack, Corliss
K.

Historical Dictionary of the "Dirty Wars". — Kohut,
David R.

Historical Dictionary of the French Revolution
— Hanson, Paul R.

Historical Dictionary of the Hittites — Burney, Charles

Historical Dictionary of the Inuit — Stern, Pamela R.

Historical Dictionary of the Kurds — Gunter, Michael
M.

Historical Dictionary of the Republic of Korea, 2nd
Ed. — Nahm, Andrew C.

Historical Dictionary of the Vikings — Holman,
Katherine

Historical Dictionary of Unitarian Universalism
— Harris, Mark W.

Historical Dictionary of Utopianism — Morris, James
M.

Historical Dictionary of Witchcraft — Bailey, Michael
D.

Historical Dictionary of Wittgenstein's Philosophy
— Richter, Duncan

Historical Documents Index 1972-2002

Historical Encyclopedia of American Labor — Weir,
Robert E.

Historical Grammar of the Visual Arts — Riegl, Alois

A Historical Guide to F. Scott Fitzgerald — Curnutt,
Kirk

A Historical Guide to Langston Hughes — Tracy,
Steven C.

A Historical Guide to Ralph Ellison — Tracy, Steven
C.

Historical Linguistics: An Introduction. 2nd Ed.
— Campbell, Lyle

Historical Perspectives on Midsouth Archeology
— Rolingson, Martha Ann

The Historical Practice of Diversity: Transcultural
Interaction from the Early Modern Mediterranean
to the Postcolonial World — Hoerder, Dirk

Historical Records of the Five Dynasties — Ouyang,
Xiu

Historical Records of the Five Dynasties — Quyang,
Xiu

Historical Review of Developments Relating to
Aggression

Historically Black Colleges and Universities: A
Reference Handbook — Jackson, Cynthia L.

Histories and Historicities in Amazonia — Whitehead,
Neil L.

Histories. Book 1 — Damon, Cynthia

The Histories of Herodotus — Herodotus

Histories of the Hanged: Britain's Dirty War in Kenya
and the End of the Empire — Anderson, David

Histories of the Hanged: The Dirty War in Kenya and
the End of Empire — Anderson, David

Historiography at the Court of Christian IV
— Skovgaard-Petersen, Karen

The Historiography of the Holocaust — Stone, Dan

Historische Anstobe: Festschrift fur Wolfgang
Reinhard zum 65. Geburtstag am 10. April 2002
— Burschel, Peter

Historische Debatten und Kontroversen im 19. und
20. Jahrhundert. Jubilaumstagung der
Ranke-Gesellschaft in Essen, 2001 — Elvert, Jurgen

Historische Humanoekologie: Interdisziplinaere
Zugaenge zu Menschen und Ihrer Umwelt
— Winiwarter, Verena

History After Apartheid: Visual Culture and Public
Memory in a Democratic South Africa — Coombes,
Annie E.

History and Historians in the Twentieth Century
— Burke, Peter

History and Literature of Byzantium in the 9th-10th
Centuries — Markopoulos, Athanasios

Holy Day, Holiday: The American Sunday
— McCrossen, Alexis
The Holy Family and Its Legacy: Religious
Imagination from the Gospels to Star Wars
— Koschorke, Albrecht
Holy Fools — Harris, Joanne
The Holy Grail: Imagination and Belief — Barber,
Richard
Holy Ground: A Liturgical Cosmology — Lathrop,
Gordon W.
The Holy Machine — Beckett, Chris
The Holy Reich: Nazi Conceptions of Christianity,
1919-1945 — Steigmann-Gall, Richard
Holy Scripture: A Dogmatic Sketch — Webster, John
Holy Scripture Speaks: The Production and Reception
of Erasmus's Paraphrases on the New Testament
— Pabel, Hilmar M.
Holy Scripture Speaks: The ProductionReception of
Erasmus' Paraphrases on the New Testment
— Pabel, Hilmar M.
Holy Skirts — Steinke, Rene
Holy Tears, Holy Blood: Women, Catholicism, and the
Culture of Suffering in France, 1840-1970
— Burton, Richard D.E.
Holy Terrors: Latin American Women Perform
— Taylor, Diana
Holy Terrors: Thinking about Religion after
September 11 — Lincoln, Bruce
The Holy Thief: A Con Man's Journey from Darkness
to Light — Borovitz, Mark
Holy War, Holy Peace: How Religion Can Bring Peace
to the Middle East — Gopin, Marc
Holy War in China: The Muslim Rebellion and State
in Chinese Central Asia, 1864-1877 — Kim,
Ho-dong
Holy War in China: The Muslim Rebellion and State
in Chinese Central Asia, 1864-1877 — Kim, Hodong
Home-Alone America: The Hidden Toll of Day Care,
Behavioral Drugs, and Other Parent Substitutes
— Eberstadt, Mary
Home and Kin: Families in Asia — Quah, Stella R.
A Home at the End of the World. Audiobook Review
— Cunningham, Michael
y A Home at the End of the World (Read by Farrell,
Colin). Audiobook Review — Cunningham, Michael
A Home at the End of the World — Cunningham,
Michael
Home Away from Home — Cook, Lorna J.
c Home — Baker, Jeannie
Home Bound: Filipino American Lives Across
Cultures, Communities, and Countries — Espiritu,
Yen Le
Home Cheap Home: A Room-by-Room Guide to
Great Decorating — Budget Living Magazine
Home Fires Burning: Married to the Military, for
Better or Worse — Houppert, Karen
c A Home for Panda (Illus. by Effler, Jim) — Nagda,
Ann Whitehead
Home from the Vinyl Cafe: A Year of Stories
— McLean, Stuart
Home Front: New Deveopment in Housing
— Bullivant, Lucy
c The Home Fronts in the Civil War — Anderson, Dale
Home Gardens and Agrobiodiversity — Eyzaguirre,
Pablo B.
Home-Grown Hate: Gender and Organized Racism
— Ferber, Abby L.
Home Hacking Projects for Geeks — Northrup, Tony
Home Health Care for Children Who Are Technology
Dependent — Fleming, Juanita W.
Home Ice — Vandervelde, Beatrice
Home in Hollywood: The Imaginary Geography of
Cinema — Bronfen, Elisabeth
y A Home in the Heart: The Story of Sandra Cisneros
(Illus. by Reynolds, Morgan) — Brackett, Virginia
Home Is Everything: The Latino Baseball Story
— Breton, Marcos
Home Land — Lipsyte, Sam
c Home Life in Ancient Egypt — Kaplan, Leslie C.
c Home Life in Ancient Greece — Apel, Melanie Ann
Home Networking: A Visual Do-It-Yourself Guide
— Underdahl, Brian
Home Networking Bible, 2nd Ed. — Plumley, Sue
Home Office and the Dangerous Trades: Regulating
Occupational Disease in Victorian and Edwardian
Britain — Bartrip, Peter W.J.
c Home on the Range (Illus. by Ajhar, Brian) — Ajhar,
Brian
Home or Nursing Home: Making the Right Choices,
2d Ed. — Salamon, Michael J.
The Home Place — Morris, Wright

Home Plate Cooking: Everyday Southern Cuisine with
a Healthy Twist — Woods, Marvin
Home Rule: An Irish History — Jackson, Alvin
The Home Run Horse: Inside America's Billion-Dollar
Racehorse Industry and the High-Stakes Dreams
That Fuel It — Cain, Glenye
Home Schooling: Educating with Head, Heart, and
Hand — Higgins, J. Brian
Home Team — MacGregor, Roy
Home Theater Hacks — McLaughlin, Brett
y Home to the Sea — Aaron, Chester
Home-Work: Postcolonialism, Pedagogy, and
Canadian Literature — Sugars, Cynthia
Homegirls in the Public Sphere — Miranda, Marie
Keta
Homegrown Democrat: A Few Plain Thoughts from
the Heart of America — Keillor, Garrison
Homegrown Democrat: A Few Plain Thoughts from
the Heart of America (Read by Keillor, Garrison).
Audiobook Review — Keillor, Garrison
Homegrown Democrat: A Few Plain Thoughts from
the Heart of America — Keillor, Garrison
Homegrown Music: Discovering Bluegrass — Ledgin,
Stephanie P.
Homeland — Maharidge, Dale
Homeland — Mazza, Cris
Homeland — Weber, R.H.
y Homeland Security — Smith, Norris
Homeland Security Techniques and Technologies
— Mena, Jesus
Homeland Security Versus Constitutional Rights
— Gottfried, Ted
Homeland Security Versus Constitutional Rights
— Gottfried, Theodore Mark
c The Homeless Pooch (Read by Erickson, John R.).
Audiobook Review — Erickson, John R.
"Homemaker's" Menu of the Month Cookbook
— McCauley, Dana
Homeopathy: How It Really Works — Shelton, Jay W.
Homeplace: The Social Use and Meaning of the Folk
Dwelling in Southwestern North Carolina
— Williams, Michael Ann
Homer — Powell, Barry B.
Homer, Eakins,and Anshutz: The Search for American
Identity in the Gilded Age — Griffin, Randall C.
The Homeric Hymns — Homer
Homeric Hymns, Homeric Apocrypha, Lives of Homer
— Homer
Homeric Hymns, Homeric Apocrypha, Lives of Homer
— West, M.L.
Homeric Megathemes: War-Homilia-Homecoming
— Maronites, D.N.
Homescaping: Designing Your Landscape to Match
Your Home — Halpin, Anne
Homeschooling High School: Planning Ahead for
College Admission, 2nd Ed. — Dennis, Jeanne
Gowen
Homeschooling: Take a Deep Breath-- You Can Do
This! — Bittner, Terrie Lynn
y Homeward Bound — Turtledove, Harry
Homewood House — Arthur, Catherine Rogers
Homework Problems: How Much Is Too Much?
— Vail, Kathleen
Homicide My Own — Argula, Anne
Homicide Special — Corwin, Miles
Homo Promo
Homo Viator: Itineraries of Exile, Displacement and
Writing in Renaissance Europe — Harrigan,
Michael
Homo Viator: Itineraries of Exile, Displacement and
Writing in Renaissance Europe — Tucker, George
Hugo
Homocide: A Sociological Explanation — Cooney,
Mark
Homoerotic Space: The Poetics of Loss in Renaissance
Literature — Guy-Bray, Stephen
Homolytic and Heterolytic Reactions: Problems and
Solutions — Zaikov, Gennadii Efremovich
Homosexuality and the Bible: Two Views — Via, Dan
O.
Homosexuality & Civilization — Crompton, Louis
Homosexuality in Greece and Rome. A Sourcebook of
Basic Documents — Hubbard, T.K
c Honest Pretzels: and 64 Other Amazing Recipes for
Cooks Ages 8 and Up. — Katzen, Mollie
An Honest Writer: The Life and Times of James T.
Farrell — Landers, Robert K.
c Honey Baby Sugar Child — Duncan, Alice Faye
y Honey, Baby, Sweetheart — Caletti, Deb
c Honey Biscuits — Bartlett, Allison
Honey Is Sweeter Than Blood — Thomas, Jeffrey
c Honey Sandwich — Honey, Elizabeth

y Honey, We Lost the Kids: Re-Thinking Childhood in
the Multimedia Age — McDonnell, Kathleen
Honeymoon — Patterson, James
Honeymoon Suite — Michaels, Lynn
Honeymoon Wilderness — Di Cicco, Pier Giorgio
Honeymoon with My Brother: A Memoir — Wisner,
Franz
c Honeysuckle House — Cheng, Andrea
Hong Kong Arbitration: A User's Guide — Moser,
Michael J.
Hong Kong Cinema: A Cross-Cultural View — Kar,
Law
Honor Among Nations?: Treaties and Agreements with
Indigenous People — Langton, Marcia
Honor Killing: How the Infamous "Massie Affair"
Transformed Hawai'i — Stannard, David E.
Honor, Love, and Religion in the Theater Before Lope
de Vega — Wertheimer, Elaine C.
An Honorable Murderer — Gooden, Philip
y Honored Guest: Stories — Williams, Joy
Honoring God and the City: Music at the Venetian
Confraterities, 1260-1807 — Glixon, Jonathan
Honoring God and the City: Music at the Venetian
Confraternities, 1260-1807 — Glixon, Jonathan
Honoring Sergeant Carter — Carter, Allene G.
Honoring the Trust: Quality and Cost Containment in
Higher Education — Massy, William F.
y Honour Earth Mother — Johnston, Basil
An Honourable Deception?: New Labour, Iraq and
the Misuse of Power — Short, Clare
Hoodlums: Black Villains and Social Bandits in
American Life — Van Deburg, William L.
y Hoodwinked: Deception and Resistance (Illus. by
Craig, David) — Shapiro, Stephen
Hoodwinked: The Documents That Reveal How Bush
Sold Us a War — Prados, John
The Hoof Peninsula, County Wexford — Colfer, Billy
Hooked and Heroin : Drugs and Drifters in a
Globalized World — Lalander, Philip
Hooked!: Buddhist Writings on Greed, Desire, and the
Urge to Consume — Kaza, Stephanie
Hooked On Growth — Jacobsen, Kurt
Hooked on Growth: Economic Addictions and the
Environment — Booth, Douglas E.
Hooked Rugs Today — Oxford, Amy
The Hookup Handbook: A Single Girl's Guide to
Living It Up — Lavinthal, Andrea
c Hooligan Wreckit, Goldfisherman (Illus. by Gerrard,
Liam) — Dickson, Liz
The Hooligan's Return: A Memoir — Manea, Norman
Hoop Kings — Smith, Charles R., Jr.
Hoop Queens: Poems — Smith, Charles R., Jr.
Hoop-Wrapped, Composite, Internally Pressurized
Cylinders: Development and Application of a
Design Theory — Walters, John A.
The Hoopster — Sitomer, Alan Lawrence
c Hooray for Ballet! (Illus. by Haley, Amanda) — Frith,
Margaret
c Hooray, I'm Five Today! (Illus. by Freeman, Tor)
— Freeman, Tor
y Hoot — Hiaasen, Carl
c The Hoover Dam — DuTemple, Leslie A.
c Hooway for Wodney Wat (Illus. by Munsinger, Lynn).
Audiobook Review — Lester, Helen
c Hop! and Quack! (Illus. by Meade, Holly) — Root,
Phyllis
Hope and Danger in the New South City:
Working-Class Women and Urban Development in
Atlanta, 1890-1940 — Hickey, Georgina
Hope and Dread in Montana Literature — Egan, Ken
Hope and Honor — Schachnow, Sid
Hope and Honor — Shachnow, Sid
Hope and Memory: Lessons from the Twentieth
Century — Todorov, Tzvetan
Hope Dies Last: Keeping Faith in Difficult Times
— Terkel, Studs
The Hope, Hype and Reality of Genetic Engineering:
Remarkable Stories from Agriculture, Industry,
Medicine, and the Environment — Arise, John C.
The Hope, Hype, and Reality of Genetic Engineering:
Remarkable Stories from Agriculture, Industry,
Medicine, and the Environment — Avise, John C.
Hope in Hell: Inside the World of Doctors without
Borders — Bortolotti, Dan
Hope in the Dark — Solnit, Rebecca
Hope Restored: The American Revolution and the
Founding of New Brunswick — Dallison, Robert L.
Hopeful Girls, Troubled Boys: Race and Gender
Disparity in Urban Education — Lopez, Nancy
Hope's Horizon: Three Visions for Healing the
American Land — Ward, Chip

I

The Image and Influence of the Oklahoma Prairie in Washington Irving's Tour of the West — *Steele, Linda L.*

Image and Remembrance: Representation and the Holocaust. — *Hornstein, Shelley*

Image and Spirit: Finding Meaning in Visual Art — *Stone, Karen*

Image Comics Presents: Flight, vol. 1

The Image Factory: Consumer Culture, Photography and the Visual Content Industry — *Frosh, Paul*

The Image of the Jew in European Liberal Culture, 1789-1914 — *Cheyette, Brian*

Image, Text and Audience: The Taishokan Narrative in Visual Representations of the Early Modern Period in Japan — *Trede, Melanie*

Imagerie des Anderen im Weimarer Kino — *Kabatek, Wolfgang*

Imagery in Psychology: A Reference Guide — *Roeckelein, Jon E.*

Imagery of Colour & Shining in Catullus, Propertius, & Horace — *Clarke, Jacqueline*

Images and Contexts: The Historiography of Science and Modernity in India — *Raina, Dhruv*

Images and Cultures of Law in Early Modern England: Justice and Political Power, 1558-1660 — *Raffield, Paul*

Images and Empires: Visuality in Colonial and Postcolonial Africa — *Landau, Paul S.*

Images from Science, An Exhibition of Scientific Photography

Images in the Heavens, Patterns on the Earth: The I Ching — *Russek, Janet*

Images of Ancestors — *Hojte, J.M.*

c Images of Australia: A History of Australian Children's Literature, 1941-1970 — *Saxby, Maurice*

Images of Cult and Devotion: Function and Reception of Christian Images in Medieval and Post-Medieval Europe — *Kaspersen, Soren*

Images of Idiocy: The Idiot Figure in Modern Fiction and Film — *Halliwell, Martin*

Images of Myths in Classical Antiquity — *Woodford, S.*

Images of Nebuchadnezzar: The Emergence of a Legend, 2nd Ed. — *Sack, Ronald H.*

Images of Redemption: Art, Literature and Salvation — *Sherry, Patrick*

Images of Terror: What We Can and Can't Know about Terrorism — *Jenkins, Philip*

Images of the Outcast: The Urban Poor in the Cries of London — *Shesgreen, Sean*

Images of the Woman Reader in Victorian British and American Fiction — *Golden, Catherine J.*

Images of Women in Chinese Thought and Culture: Writings from the Pre-Qin Period through the Song Dynasty — *Wang, Robin R.*

Images That Injure: Pictorial Stereotypes in the Media, 2nd Ed. — *Lester, Paul Martin*

The Imaginary Caribbean and Caribbean Imaginary — *Praeger, Michele*

The Imaginary in the Writing of Latin American Author Amanda Labarca Hubertson (1886-1975): Supplements to a Feminist Critique — *Boschetto-Sandoval, Sandra M.*

The Imaginary Revolution: Parisian Students and Workers in 1968 — *Seidman, Michael*

Imaginary States: Studies in Cultural Transnationalism — *Hitchcock, Peter*

Imagination of a Monarchy. Studies in Polemaic Propaganda — *Hazzard, R.A.*

Imaginationen des Anderen im 16. und 17. Jahrhundert — *Schabert, Ina*

Imaginative Horizans: An Essay in Literary-Philosophical Anthropology — *Crapanzano, Vincent*

c Imagine a Day (Illus. by Thomson, Sarah) — *Gonsalves, Rob*

c Imagine a Day (Illus. by Gonsalves, Rob) — *Thomson, Sarah L.*

Imagine a House: A Journey to Fascinating houses around the World

y Imagine That!: Activities and Adventures in Surrealism — *Raimondo, Joyce*

Imagine There's No Country: Poverty, Inequality, and Growth in the Era of Globalization — *Bhalla, Surjit S.*

Imagined Corners: Exploring the World's First Atlas — *Binding, Paul*

Imagined Differences: Hatred and the Construction of Identity — *Schlee, Guenther*

Imagined London: A Tour of the World's Greatest Fictional City — *Quindlen, Anna*

Imaging In Trauma and Critical Care, 2nd Ed. — *Mirvis, Stuart E.*

Imaging of the Newborn, Infant, and Young Child. 5th Ed. — *Swischuk, Leonard E.*

Imaging Strategies for the Shoulder — *Maeurer, Juergen*

Imaging the Andes: Shifting Margins of a Marginal World — *Salman, Ton*

Imaging Zion: Dreams, Designs, and Realities in a Century of Jewish Settlement — *Troen, S. Ilan*

Imagining America: Influence and Images in Twentieth-Century Russia — *Ball, Alan M.*

Imagining Biblical Worlds: Studies in Spatial, Social, and Historical Constructs in Honor of James W. Flanagan — *Gunn, David M.*

Imagining Bodies; Merleau-Ponty's Philosophy of Imagination — *Steeves, James R.*

Imagining Flight: Aviation and Popular Culture — *Van Riper, A. Bowdoin*

Imagining Ground Zero: Official and Unofficial Proposals for the World Trade Center Site — *Stephens, Suzanne*

Imagining Identity in New Spain: Race, Linage, and the Colonial Body in Portraiture and Casts Paintings — *Carrera, Magali M.*

Imagining Incest: Sexton, Plath, Rich, and Olds on Life with Daddy — *Swiontkowski, Gale*

Imagining Inclusive Society in Nineteenth-Century Novels: The Code of Sincerity in the Public Sphere — *Morris, Pam*

Imagining Karma, Ethical Transformation in Amerindian, Buddhist, and Greek Rebirth — *Obeyesekere, Gananath*

Imagining London: Postcolonial Fiction and the Transnational Metropolis — *Ball, John Clement*

Imagining Media: Rhodessa Jones and Theater for Incarcerated Women — *Fraden, Rena*

Imagining Nature: Practices of Cosmology and Identity — *Roepstorff, Andreas*

Imagining Robin Hood — *Pollard, A.J.*

Imagining Shakespeare: A History of Texts and Visions — *Orgel, Stephen*

Imagining the American Policy: Political Science and the Discourse of Democracy — *Gunnell, John G.*

Imagining the Big Open: Nature, Identity, and Play in the New West — *Nicholas, Liza*

Imagining the Nation in Nature: Landscape Preservation and German Identity, 1885-1945 — *Lekan, Thomas M.*

Imagining the Real: Essays on Politics, Ideology, and Literature — *Grant, Robert (b. 1945 -)*

Imagining the Sciences: Expressions of New Knowledge in the Long Eighteenth Century — *Leitz, Robert C.*

Imagining the Self, Imagining the Other: Visual Representations and Jewish-Christian Dynamics in the Middle Ages and Early Modern Period — *Frojmovic, Eva*

Imagining the State — *Neocleous, Mark*

The Imagist Poem: Modern Poetry in Miniature — *Pratt, William*

'Imago Triumphalis': The Function and Significance of Triumphal Imagery for Italian Renaissance Rulers — *Zaho, Margaret Ann*

An Imam in Paris: Al-Tahtawi's Visit to France — *Tahtawi, Rifaa al-Rafi al-*

Imbreviature: I Registro — *Notaio, Ser Matteo Di Biliotto*

The IMF and Economic Development — *Vreeland, James Raymond*

IMF Essays from a Time of Crisis: The International Financial System, Stabilization, and Development — *Fischer, Stanley*

Imhotep Today: Egyptianizing Architecture — *Humbert, Jean-Marcel*

Imitation and Politics, Redesigning Modern Germany — *Jacoby, Wade*

Imitation of Life — *Hurst, Fannie*

Imitation of Life: How Biology Is Inspiring Computing — *Forbes, Nancy*

Immaculate Warfare: Participants Reflect on the Air Campaigns over Kosovo and Afghanistan — *Wrage, Stephen D.*

Immediacy and Reflection in Kierkegaard's Thought — *Cruysberghs, Paul*

The Immensity of the Here and Now: A Novel of 9.11 — *West, Paul*

Immigrant Mothers: Narratives of Races and Maternity, 1890-1925 — *Irving, Katrina*

Immigrant Women Tell Their Stories — *Berger, Roni*

Immigrants and the American Dream: Remaking the Middle Class — *Clark, William A.V.*

Immigrants, Progressives, and Exclusion Politics: The Dillingham Commission, 1900-1927 — *Zeidel, Robert F.*

Immigration and Ethnic Formation in a Deeply Divided Society: The Case of the 1990's Immigrants from the Former Soviet Union in Israel — *Al-Haj, Majid*

Immigration and Integration: The Irish in Wales, 1798-1922 — *O'Leary, Paul*

y Immigration and Migration: Primary Sources, Vols. 1-2

Immigration and Political Economy of Home: West Indian Brooklyn and American Indian Minneapolis, 1945-1992 — *Buff, Rachel*

Immigration and Politics in the New Europe: Reinventing Borders — *Lahav, Gallya*

y Immigration — *Wilson, Ruth*

Immigration, Colonisation et Propagande: Du Reve American au Reve Colonial — *Courville, Serge*

c Immigration, Migration, and the Growth of the American City — *Sioux, Tracee*

Immortal Bad Boys — *York, Rebecca*

The Immortal Count: The Life and Films of Bela Lugosi — *Lening, Arthur*

The Immortal Dinner — *Hughes-Hallett, Penelope*

The Immortal Highlander — *Moning, Karen Marie*

Immortal in Death (Read by Ericksen, Susan). Audiobook Review — *Roberts, Nora*

Immortal Wishes: Labor and Transcendence on a Japanese Sacred Mountain — *Schattschneider, Ellen*

The Immortals — *Gunn, James*

y The Immortals Quartet — *Pierce, Tamora*

Immovable Laws, Irresistible Rights: Natural Law, Moral Rights, and Feminist Ethics — *Pierce, Christine*

Immune Hemolytic Anemia, 2nd Ed. — *Petz, Lawrence D.*

The Immune System, 2nd Ed. — *Parham, P.*

Immunization Safety Review: Influenza Vaccines and Neurological Complications — *Stratton, Kathleen*

Immunobiology: The Immune System in Health and Disease, 6th Ed. — *Janeway, Charles A., Jr.*

Immunology, Infection and Immunity — *Pier, Gerald B.*

Immunology of Behcet's Disease — *Zierhut, Manfred*

The Imp of the Mind: Exploring the Silent Epidemic of Obsessive Bad Thoughts — *Baer, Lee*

Impact Biomechanics — *Stronge, W.L.*

The Impact of African-American Antecedents on the Baptist Foreign Missionary Movement, 1782-1825 — *Ballew, Christopher Brent*

The Impact of Black Nationalist Ideology on American Jazz Music of the 1960s and 1970s — *Baskerville, John D.*

The Impact of Buddhism on Chinese Material Culture — *Kieschnick, John*

The Impact of Economic Policies on Poverty and Income Distribution: Evaluation Techniques and Tools — *Bourguignon, Francois*

The Impact of Electronic Mail on Business Processes and the Relevance of Proper English in This Context — *Beer, Alexander*

The Impact of Information and Communication Technolgies (ICTs) on Rural Households: A Holistic Approach Applied to the Case of Lao People's Democratic Republic — *Song, Gi-Soon*

The Impact of International Television: A Paradigm Shift — *Elasmar, M.*

The Impact of Race: Theatre and Culture — *King, Woodie, Jr.*

The Impact of the English Civil War on the Economy of London, 1642-50 — *Coates, Ben*

The Impact of the Railway on Society in Britain: Essays in Honor of Jack Simmons — *Evans, A.K.B.*

The Impact of Trade Agreements: Effect of the Tokyo Round, U.S.-Israel FTA, U.S.-Canada FTA, NAFTA, and the Uruguay Round on the U.S. Economy

The Impact of Trade on Labor: Issues, Perspectives, and Experiences from Developing Asia — *Hasan, Rana*

Impact of World War II on the Economy of Vietnam, 1939-45 — *Hung, Le Manh*

The Impact on Philosophy of Semiotics: The Quasi-Error of the External World with a Dialogue between a 'Semiotist' and a 'Realist' — *Deely, John N.*

Impacts of a Warming Arctic: Arctic Climate Impact Assessment

The Impartial Recorder — *Sansom, Ian*

Impeaching Clinton: Partisan Strife on Capitol Hill — *Rae, Nicol C.*

J

The J.A.P. Chronicles — *Rose, Isabel*
J-Holomorphic Curves and Symplectic Topology
— *McDuff, Dusa*
J R — *Gaddis, William*
y J.R.R. Tolkien — *Levine, Stuart*
c J.R.R. Tolkien: Creator of Languages and Legends
— *Lynch, Doris*
y J.R.R. Tolkien: Master of Imaginary Worlds
— *Willett, Edward*
J. Robert Oppenheimer and the American Century
— *Cassidy, David C.*
c J. Roger's School for Pirates. Audiobook Review
— *Gallagher, John*
J2EE 1.4: The Big Picture — *Haugland, Solveig*
J2EE Applications and BEA WebLogic Server, 2nd
Ed. — *Yochem, Angela*
The J2EE Architect's Handbook: How to Be a
Successful Technical Architect for J2EE
Applications — *Ashmore, Derek C.*
J2EE Tutorial, 2nd Ed. — *Bodoff, Stephanie*
J2EE Web Services — *Monson-Haefel, Richard*
y Jabberwocky (Illus. by Jorisch, Stephane) — *Carroll,
Lewis*
Jabez — *McKie, David*
Jack Absolute: A Novel — *Humphreys, C.C.*
c Jack Adrift: Fourth Grade Without a Clue — *Gantos,
Jack*
c Jack and Jill — *Collins, Heather*
Jack and Jill — *Kirk, Daniel*
Jack and Other New Poems — *Kumin, Maxine*
c Jack and the Beanstalk (Illus. by Hess, Paul)
— *Poole, Josephine*
c Jack and the Beanstalk (Illus. by Kurtz, John)
c Jack and the Missing Piece (Illus. by Schories, Pat)
— *Schories, Pat*
c Jack and the Seven Deadly Giants (Illus. by Cneut,
Carll) — *Swope, Sam*
Jack Aubrey Commands: An Historical Companion to
the Naval World of Patrick O'Brian — *Lavery,
Brian*
Jack Fish — *Milligan, J.*
Jack Lenor Larsen: Creator and Collector — *Larsen,
Jack Lenor*
Jack, the Great Seducer: The Life and Many Loves of
Jack Nicholson — *Douglas, Edward*
Jack the Ripper and the London Press — *Curtis, L.
Perry, Jr.*
c Jack: The Story of a Beaver (Illus. by Godkin, Celia)
— *Woods, Shirley*
Jack Ward Thomas: The Journals of a Forest Service
Chief — *Thomas, Jack Ward*
Jackass — *Cliver, Sean*
y Jackie and Me: A Baseball Card Adventure (Read by
Heller, Johnny). Audiobook Review — *Gutman,
Dan*
c Jackie's Wild Seattle (Read by Nielsen, Stina).
Audiobook Review — *Hobbs, Will*
Jackie's Wild Seattle — *Hobbs, Will*
Jacking into the Matrix Franchise: Cultural Reception
and Interpretation — *Kapell, Matthew*
c Jack's Kite (Illus. by Jagtenberg, Yvonne)
— *Jagtenberg, Yvonne*
c Jack's New Power: Stories from a Caribbean Year
— *Gantos, Jack*
c Jackson Jones and Mission Greentop — *Quattlebaum,
Mary*
A Jackson Man: Amos Kendall and the Rise of
American Democracy — *Cole, Donald B.*
Jackson Square Jazz — *Herren, Greg*
Jacksonville: The Consolidation Story, from Civil
Rights to the Jaguars — *Crooks, James B.*

Jacob Burckhardt and the Crisis of Modernity
— *Hinde, John R.*
The Jacobin Republic under Fire: The Federalist
Revolt in the French Revolution — *Hanson, Paul R.*
The Jacobites and Russia, 1715-1750 — *Wills, Rebecca*
Jacob's Ladder: The History of the Human Genome
— *Gee, Henry*
Jacob's Wound: A Search for the Spirit of Wildness
— *Herriot, Trevor*
Jacquard's Web: How a Hand-Loom Led to the Birth
of the Information Age — *Essinger, James*
Jacqueline Kennedy: First Lady of the New Frontier
— *Perry, Barbara A.*
Jacqueline Woodson: The Real Thing — *Stover, Lois
Thomas*
c Jacques and Spock (Illus. by Tilley, Debbie) — *Slater,
David Michael*
Jacques Coeur: Entrepreneur and King's Bursar
— *Reyerson, Kathryn L.*
Jacques Derrida: Critical Thought — *Maclachlan, Ian*
Jacques-Emile Ruhlmann: The Designer's Archives,
Vol. 1 — *Breon, Emmanuel*
Jacques-Emile Ruhlmann: The Designer's Archives,
Vol. 2 — *Breon, Emmanuel*
Jacques-Emile Ruhlmann: The Designer's Archives.
Vol. 2 — *Breon, Emmanuel*
Jacques Lecoq — *Murray, Simon*
Jacques Marquette and Louis Jolliet: Explorers of the
Mississippi — *Larkin, Tanya*
Jacques Offenbach and the Paris of His Time
— *Kracauer, Siegfried*
Jacques Pepin's Fast Food My Way (Illus. by Fink,
Ben) — *Pepin, Jacques*
Jade Book: A Stone of Hope — *Vance, Daniela
Geracitano*
The Jade Cat — *Brogger, Suzanne*
Jade Coast: The Ecology of the North Pacific Ocean
— *Butler, Robert*
The Jade Peony — *Choy, Wayson*
Jagnje i vuk: Basne za veliku i malu decu
— *Mihailovich, Vasa D.*
c Jag's New Friend (Illus. by Bernal, Richard)
— *Rimes, LeAnn*
The Jaguar Knights: A Chronicle of the King's Blades
— *Duncan, Dave*
J'ai nom sans bruit — *Jarry, Isabelle*
Jailbait: The Politics of Statutory Rape Laws in the
United States — *Cocca, Carolyn E.*
c Jake and Pete (Read by King, Alan). Audiobook
Review — *Rubinstein, Gillian*
y Jake — *Montgomery, Arch*
c Jake, Reinvented (Read by Colby, Jim). Audiobook
Review — *Korman, Gordon Richard*
c Jake, Reinvented — *Korman, Gordon Richard*
y Jamari's Drum (Illus. by Diakite, Baba Wague)
— *Bynum, Eboni*
c Jambalaya: Stories with Louisiana Flavor (Read by
Casas, Dianne de las). Audiobook Review — *Casas,
Dianne de las*
Jambands: The Complete Guide to the Players, Music
& Scene — *Budnick, Dean*
Jamblich: Itepi Toy Ityoatopeioy Bioy. Pythagoras:
Legende-Lehre-Lebensgestaltung — *Albrecht, M.
von*
James Agee, Omnibus, and Mr. Lincoln: The Culture
of Liberalism and the Challenge of Television,
1952-1953 — *Hughes, William C.*
James Agee, Omnibus, and Mr. Lincoln: The Culture
of Liberalism and the Challenge of Television,
1952-1953 — *Hughes, William C.*
James Baldwin: African-American Writer and Activist
— *Cannarella, Deborah*

James Baldwin's God: Sex, Hope, and Crisis in Black
Holiness Culture — *Hardy, Clarence E., III*
James Bond 007: Goldfinger — *Fleming, Ian*
James — *Hartin, Patrick J.*
James Bowdoin and the Patriot Philosophers
— *Manuel, Frank E.*
James Buchanan — *Baker, Jean H.*
James Burnham and the Struggle for the World: A
Life — *Kelly, Daniel*
James Burnham — *Francis, Samuel*
James Cameron's Aliens of the Deep — *MacInnis,
Joseph*
James Castle: His Life and Art — *Trusky, Tom*
The James Deans: A Moe Prager Mystery
— *Coleman, Reed Farrel*
James Hanley: Modernism and the Working Class
— *Fordham, John*
James Ivory in Conversation: How Merchant Ivory
Makes Its Movies — *Emmet, Robert Long*
James Ivory in Conversation: How Merchant Ivory
Makes Its Movies — *Long, Robert Emmet*
James Joyce and the Problem of Psychoanalysis
— *Thurston, Luke*
James Joyce and Victims: Reading the Logic of
Exclusion — *Murphy, Sean P.*
A James Joyce Chronology — *Norburn, Roger*
James Joyce, Sexuality and Social Purity — *Mullin,
Katherine*
James Joyce: The Complete Recordings — *Joyce,
James*
James Joyce's A Portrait of the Artist as a Young Man
— *Wollaeger, Mark*
James Joyce's Dublin: A Topographical Guide to the
Dublin of Ulysses — *Hart, Clive*
James Joyce's 'Ulysses': A Casebook — *Attridge,
Derek*
James Joyce's Ulysses: A Reference Guide
— *McKenna, Bernard*
James Maclaren: Arts and Crafts Pioneer — *Calder,
Alan*
James Madison and Freedom of Speech: Major
Debates in the Early Republic — *Rudanko, Juhani*
c James Madison: Creating a Nation — *Kent, Zachary*
James Madison: The Theory and Practice of
Republican Government — *Kernell, Samuel*
James Stirling, Admiral and Founding Governor of
Western Australia — *Statham-Drew, Pamela*
c James the Dancing Dog (Illus. by Johnson, Gillian)
— *Maybarduk, Linda*
The James Tiptree Award Anthology 1 — *Fowler,
Karen Joy*
Jamesland — *Huneven, Michelle*
Jamie's Dinners — *Oliver, Jamie*
Jamie's Dinners — *Oliver, Jamie*
The Jamlady Cookbook — *Alfeld, Beverly Ellen
Schoonmaker*
Jan Karon's Mitford Cookbook and Kitchen Reader
— *Karon, Jan*
Jan van Ruusbroec, Mystical Theologian of the Trinity
— *Nieuwenhove, Rik Van*
Jan van Ruusbroec, Mystical Theologian of the Trinity
— *Van Nieuwenhove, Rik*
The Janacek Opera Libretti, Vol. 2 — *Janacek, Leoes*
Jane Addams: A Writer's Life — *Joslin, Katherine*
c Jane Addams — *Raum, Elizabeth*
Jane and His Lordship's Legacy: Being a Jane Austen
Mystery — *Barron, Stephanie*
Jane and His Lordship's Legacy — *Barron, Stephanie*
Jane Austen and the Morality of Conversation
— *Tandon, Bharat*
Jane Austen — *Jones, Darryl*
Jane Austen — *Shields, Carol*

K

L

c Little Hands Celebrate America!: Learning about the U.S.A. through Crafts and Activities (Illus. by Kline, Michael) — *Hauser, Jill Frankel*

c Little Hands Create!: Art & Activities for Kids Ages 3 to 6 — *Dall, Mary Doerfler*

A Little History of British Gardening — *Uglow, Jenny*

A Little History of Canada — *Nelles, H.V.*

c Little Horse on His Own (Illus. by McPhail, David) — *Byars, Betsy*

c Little House, Little Town — *Beck, Scott*

Little Humpty (Illus. by James, Ann) — *Wild, Margaret*

Little Known History of the Texas Big Bend: Documented Chronicles from Cabeza de Vaca to the Era of the Pancho Villa — *Justice, Glenn*

A Little Learning Is a Murderous Thing — *Allin, Lou*

c The Little Mermaid (Illus. by Zwerger, Lisbeth) — *Andersen, Hans Christian*

c The Little Mermaid (Illus. by Zwerger, Lisbeth) — *Bell, Anthea*

c Little Miss Muffet — *Collins, Heather*

The Little Monster: Growing Up with ADHD — *Jergen, Robert*

c Little Mook and Dwarf Longnose (Illus. by Pak, Boris) — *Hauff, Wilhelm*

c Little Mouse (Illus. by Grobler, Piet) — *Dijkstra, Linda*

c Little Mouse (Illus. by Grobler, Piet) — *Dijkstra, Lida*

c Little Numbers: And Pictures That Show Just How Little They Are (Illus. by Murdocca, Salvatore) — *Packard, Edward*

c Little One, God Loves You (Illus. by Thompson, Carol) — *Hilliker, Amy Warren*

c Little One, God Made You (Illus. by Thompson, Carol) — *Hilliker, Amy Warren*

c Little Owl — *Harper, Piers*

A Little Parliament: The Virginia General Assembly in the Seventeenth Century — *Billings, Warren M.*

c Little Quack's Bedtime (Illus. by Anderson, Derek) — *Thompson, Lauren*

c Little Rabbit Goes to School (Illus. by Horse, Harry) — *Horse, Harry*

c Little Raccoon's Big Question (Illus. by Schoenherr, Ian) — *Schlein, Miriam*

c Little Red Riding Hood: A Newfangled Prairie Tale — *Ernst, Lisa Campbell*

c Little Red Riding Hood (Illus. by Ceccoli, Nicoletta) — *Evetts-Secker, Josephine*

c Little Red Riding Hood (Illus. by Chichester-Clark, Emma) — *McBratney, Sam*

y Little Red Riding Hood in the Big Bad City — *Greenberg, Martin H.*

Little Red Riding Hood Uncloaked: Sex, Morality, and the Evolution of a Fairy Tale — *Orenstein, Catherine*

c Little Red Riding Wolf (Illus. by Robins, Arthur) — *Anholt, Laurence*

The Little Red Writing Book: 20 Powerful Principles of Structure, Style & Readability — *Royal, Brandon*

c Little Ruth Reddingford and the Wolf — *Wesselman, Hank*

Little Savage — *Fragos, Emily*

y Little Scarlet (Read by Boatman, Michael). Audiobook Review — *Mosley, Walter*

Little Scarlet — *Mosley, Walter*

c A Little Shiver (Read by Washington, Donna L.). Audiobook Review — *Washington, Donna L.*

c The Little Sleepyhead (Illus. by Gore, Leonid) — *Manushkin, Fran*

c A Little Story about a Big Turnip (Illus. by Antonenkov, Evgeny) — *Zunshine, Tatiana*

A Little Stranger — *Pullinger, Kate*

Little Strangers: Portrayals of Adoption and Foster Care in America, 1850-1929 — *Nelson, Claudia*

A Little Street Music — *Stern, Daniel*

Little Sugar Addicts — *Desmaisons, Kathleen*

Little Things in a Big Country: An Artist and Her Dog on the Rocky Mountain Front — *Hinchman, Hannah*

Little Vera — *Beardow, Frank*

The Little White Car — *De Rhodes, Danuta*

The Little White Car — *Rhodes, Danuta de*

Little White Lies: A Novel of Love and Good Intentions — *Townley, Gemma*

c Little Wolf, Terror of the Shivery Sea (Illus. by Ross, Tony) — *Whybrow, Ian*

c Little Women (Read by Radio Theatre Performers). Audiobook Review — *Alcott, Louisa May*

The Little Women — *Weber, Katharine*

Little Women; Little Men; Jo's Boys — *Alcott, Louisa May*

c Little Women — *Alcott, Louisa May*

A Little Work: Behind the Doors of a Park Avenue Plastic Surgeon — *Lorenc, Z. Paul*

c Little Yau (Illus. by Cannon, Janell) — *Cannon, Janell*

c The Littlest Frog — *Rouss, Sylvia*

c The Littlest Wolf (Illus. by Aruego, Jose) — *Brimner, Larry Dane*

Litt's Pocketbook of Drug Eruptions and Interactions, 3rd Ed. — *Litt, Jerome Z.*

The Liturgy of Motherhood: Moments of Grace — *Finley, Kathleen*

Liturgy Wars: Ritual Theory and Protestant Reform in Nineteenth-Century Zurich — *Vial, Theodore M.*

Livable Modern: Interior Decorating and Design During the Great Depression — *Wilson, Kristina*

Live at 10:00, Dead at 10:15 — *Klensch, Elsa*

y Live at the Apollo — *Wolk, Douglas*

y Live Bait (Read by Schirner, Buck). Audiobook Review — *Tracy, P.J.*

Live Bait — *Tracy, P.J.*

Live Cargo — *Toutonghi, Pauls*

Live Cell Imaging: A Laboratory Manual — *Goldman, Robert D.*

Live Evil: A Homage to Miles Davis — *Stevenson, Richard*

Live from New York, It's Lena Sharpe — *Litz, Courtney*

Live from Palestine: International and Palestinian Direct Action Against the Israeli Occupation — *Stohlman, Nancy*

Live Well on Less Than You Think: The New York TImes Guide to Achieving Your Financial Freedom — *Brock, Fred*

Liverpool — *Sharples, Joseph*

Lives Across Cultures: Cross-Cultural Human Development, 3rd Ed. — *Gardiner, Harry W.*

The Lives and Times of the Great Composers — *Steen, Michael*

Lives and Work at Sea: Herbert Holdsworth, Colin Hannah and the Ship Ladakh — *Scarratt, William L.H.*

Lives for Sale: Biographers' Tales — *Bostridge, Mark*

"Lives Full of Struggle and Triumph": Southern Women, Their Institutions, and Their Communities — *Clayton, Bruce L.*

Lives in Spirit: Precursors and Dilemmas of a Secular Western Mysticism — *Hunt, Harry T.*

Lives in the Law — *Sarat, Austin*

The Lives of Agnes Smedley — *Price, Ruth*

y The Lives of Christopher Chant (Read by Doyle, Gerard). Audiobook Review — *Jones, Diana Wynne*

Lives of Lesbian Elders: Looking Back, Looking Forward — *Clunis, D. Merilee*

Lives of the Animals — *Wrigley, Robert*

y Lives of the Artists

Lives of the Artists — *Vannatta, Dennis*

Lives of the Laureates: Eighteen Nobel Economists — *Breit, William*

c Lives of the Musicians: Good Times, Bad Times, and What the Neighbors Thought (Illus. by Hewitt, Kathryn) — *Krull, Kathleen*

Lives of the Philadelphia Engineers: Capital, Class and Revolution, 1830-1890 — *Dawson, Andrew*

Livia: First Lady of Imperial Rome — *Barrett, Anthony*

Livin' Large: African American Sisters Confront Obesity — *Mitchell, Stacy Ann*

Living Among Meat Eaters: The Vegetarian's Survival Handbook — *Adams, Carol J.*

The Living and the Dead: Social Dimensions of Death in South Asian Religions — *Wilson, Liz*

c Living and Working Aboard the International Space Station — *Holden, Henry M.*

The Living Art of Greek Tragedy — *McDonald, Marianne*

Living at the Edge of Thai Society: The Karen in the Highlands of Northern Thailand — *Delang, Claudio O.*

Living Beyond Loss — *Froma Walsh*

Living Beyond Loss: Death in the Family — *Walsh, Froma*

Living Dangerously in Korea: The Western Experience, 1900-1950 — *Clark, Donald N.*

Living, Dreaming, Dying: Practical Wisdom from the Tibetan Book of the Dead — *Nairn, Rob*

The Living Elephants: Evolutionary Ecology, Behavior, and Conservation — *Sukumar, Raman*

Living Fully with Shyness and Social Anxiety: A Comprehensive Guide to Gaining Social Confidence — *Hilliard, Bukkfalvi*

y Living Habitats

Living Icons: Persons of Faith in the Eastern Church — *Plekon, Michael*

Living in a Contaminated World: Community Structures, Environmental Risks, and Decision Frameworks — *Omohundro, Ellen*

y Living in Ancient Egypt — *Nardo, Don*

y Living in Ancient Greece — *Nardo, Don*

y Living in Ancient Rome — *Nardo, Don*

y Living in Nazi Germany — *Halleck, Elaine*

Living in Prison: A History of the Correctional System with an Insider's View — *Stanko, Stephen*

c Living in Space — *Whitehouse, Patricia*

Living in the environment: Principles, Connections, and Solutions, 14th Ed. — *Miller, G. Tyler, Jr.*

Living in the Land of Death: The Choctaw Nation, 1830-1860 — *Akers, Donna L.*

Living in Translation: Polish Writers in America — *Stephan, Halina*

Living Indian Histories: Lumbee and Tuscaroa People in North Carolina — *Sider, Gerald*

Living Indian Histories: Lumbee and Tuscarora People in North Carolina — *Sider, Gerald*

Living Islam: Women, Religion and the Politicization of Culture in Turkey — *Saktanber, Ayse*

Living Justice: Love, Justice, and the Making of The Exonerated — *Blank, Jessica*

Living on the Edge: Nuu-Chah-Nulth History from an Ahousaht Chief's Perspective — *George, Earl Maquinna*

Living on Wilderness Time — *Walker, Melissa*

Living Pictures, Missing Persons: Mannequins, Museums, and Modernity — *Sandberg, Mark B.*

The Living Prism: Itineraries in Comparative Literature — *Kushner, Eva*

c Living Rain Forest: An Animal Alphabet — *Kratter, Paul*

Living Safer Sexual Lives--A Training & Resource Pack for People with Learning Disabilities & Those Who Support Them — *Frawley, Patsie*

The Living Soil: Fundamentals of Soil Science and Soil Biology — *Gobat, Jean-Michel*

Living Spirit, Living Practice: Poetics, Politics, Epistemology — *Frankenberg, Ruth*

Living the G.I. Diet: Delicious Recipes and Real Life Strategies to Lose Weight and Keep it Off — *Gallp, Rick*

Living through Breast Cancer: What a Harvard Doctor Wants You to Know about Getting the Best Care while Preserving Your Self-Image — *Kaelin, Carolyn M.*

Living to Tell about It: A Rhetoric and Ethics of Character Narration — *Phelan, James*

Living to Tell the Tale — *Garcia Marquez, Gabriel*

Living to Tell the Tale. Audiobook Review — *Garcia Marquez, Gabriel*

y Living to Tell the Tale — *Garcia Marquez, Gabriel*

The Living Universe: NASA and the Development of Astrobiology — *Dick, Steven J.*

The Living Unknown Soldier: A Story of Grief and the Great War — *Le Naour, Jean-Yves*

Living with a Writer — *Salwak, Dale*

Living with Colonialism: Nationalism and Culture in the Anglo-Egyptian Sudan — *Sharkey, Heather J.*

Living with Dying: A Handbook for End-of-Life Healthcare Practitioners — *Berzoff, Joan*

Living with Florida's Atlantic Beaches: Coastal Hazards from Amelia Island to Key West — *Bush, David M.*

Living with Fred — *Whittington, Brad*

Living with Jazz — *Morgenstern, Dan*

Living with Languages: The Contemporary Swiss Model — *Charnley, Joy*

Living with Spinal Cord Injury: A Wellness Approach — *Cristian, Adrian*

Living with the Aftermath: Trauma, Nostalgia and Grief in Post-War Australia — *Damousi, Joy*

Living with the Genie: Essays on Technology and the Quest for Human Mastery — *Lightman, Alan*

Living with Wildlife in the Pacific Northwest — *Link, Russell*

Living Your Strengths: Discover Your God-Given Talents and Inspire Your Community — *Winseman, Albert L.*

c Lizard Walinsky — *Baker, Roberta*

Lizards: Windows to the Evolution of Diversity — *Pianka, Eric R.*

y Lizzie Bright and the Buckminster Boy — *Schmidt, Gary D.*

Lizzie Siddal: The Tragedy of a Pre-Raphaelite Supermodel — *Hawksley, Lucinda*

c Lizzie's Storm (Illus. by Wood, Muriel) — *Fitz-Gibbon, Sally*

The Lowest Rung: Voices of Australian Poverty
— *Peel, Mark*
Lowji Discovers America — *Fleming, Candace*
The Lowland Maya Area: Three Millennia at the
Human-Wildland Interface — *Gomez-Pompa,
Arturo*
Lowly Origin: Where, When and Why Our Ancestors
First Stood Up — *Kingdon, Jonathan*
Loyal Soldiers in the Cocaine Kingdom: Tales of
Drugs, Mules and Gunmen — *Molano, Alfred*
Loyal to the Land: The Legendary Parker Ranch,
750-1950 — *Bergin, Billy*
Loyalty and Loss: Alabama's Unionists in the Civil
War and Reconstruction — *Storey, Margaret M.*
Loyalty on the Frontier: or, Sketches of Union Men of
the South-West with Incidents and Adventures in
Rebellion on the Border — *Bishop, Albert Webb*
Loyola's Bees: Ideology and Industry in Jesuit Latin
Didactic Poetry — *Haskell, Yasmin Annabel*
y Loz & Al — *Lawrinson, Julia*
LSC 2001, Advances in Liquid Scintillation
Spectrometry — *Mobius, Siegurd*
c Lu and the Swamp Ghost (Illus. by Catrow, David)
— *Carville, James*
Lubrication and Lubricant Selection: A Practical
Guide, 3rd Ed. — *Lansdown, A.R.*
Luc Leestemaker (Illus. by Leestemaker, Luc)
— *Frank, Peter*
Luca Marenzio: The Career of a Musician between
the Renaissance and the Counter-Reformation
— *Bizzarini, Marco*
Luca Marenzio: The Career of a Musician between
the Renaissance and the Counter-Reformation
— *Chater, James*
y Lucas (Read by Nielsen, Stina). Audiobook Review
— *Brooks, Kevin*
c Lucas (Read by Nielson, Stina). Audiobook Review
— *Brooks, Kevin*
Lucas Cranach d. A. und der deutsche Humanismus:
Tafelmalerei im Kontext von Rhetorik, Chroniken
und Furstenspiegeln — *Bierende, Edgar*
Lucasville: the Untold Story of a Prison Uprising
— *Lynd, Staughton*
Luce Irigaray: Dialogues around Her Work
— *Irigaray, Luce*
Luce Irigaray: Key Writings — *Irigaray, Luce*
Lucia Joyce: To Dance in the Wake — *Loeb, Carol*
Lucia Joyce: To Dance in the Wake — *Shloss, Carol
Loeb*
Lucia, Lucia (Read by Campbell, Cassandra).
Audiobook Review — *Trigiani, Adriana*
Lucian: On the Syrian Goddess — *Lightfoot, J.L.*
Lucien Clergue: Poesie Photographique — *Turck,
Eva-Monika*
Lucien Febvre, Lecteur et Critique — *Muller, Bertrand*
Lucifer Ascending: The Occult in Folklore and
Popular Culture — *Ellis, Bill*
Lucifer's Garden of Verses, Vol. 1 — *Tooks, Lance*
Lucifer's Shadow — *Dewson, David*
Lucifer's Shadow — *Hewson, David*
c Lucille Camps In (Illus. by Hafner, Marilyn) — *Lasky,
Kathryn*
Lucille Lortel: The Queen of Off Broadway
— *Greene, Alexis*
c Lucinda's Secret and The Ironwood Tree (Read by
Hamill, Mark). Audiobook Review — *DiTerlizzi,
Tony*

Luckiest Man: The Life and Death of Lou Gehrig
— *Eig, Jonathan*
y Lucky — *De Oliveira, Eddie*
Lucky Child: A Daughter of Cambodia Reunites with
the Sister She Left Behind — *Ung, Loung*
c Lucky Days with Mr. and Mrs. Green — *Baker, Keith*
Lucky Girls: Stories — *Freudenberger, Nell*
c Lucky Leaf (Illus. by O'Malley, Kevin) — *O'Malley,
Kevin*
c Lucky Leaf — *O'Malley, Kevin*
Lucky Leonardo — *Canter, Jonathan D.*
The Lucky Ones — *Cusk, Rachel*
Lucky or Smart? Secrets to an Entrepreneurial Life
— *Peabody, Bo*
c Lucky Socks (Illus. by Middleton, Charlotte)
— *Weston, Carrie*
Lucky Stiff: A Lillian Byrd Crime Story — *Sims,
Elizabeth*
Lucky Strike — *Zafris, Nancy*
Lucretius on the Gates of Horn and Ivory: A
Psychophysical Challenge to Prophecy by Dreams
— *Holowchak, Andrew*
Lucrezia Borgia: Life, Love and Death in Renaissance
Italy — *Bradford, Sarah*
Lucy and Desi: A Real-Life Scrapbook of America's
Favorite TV Couple — *Edwards, Elizabeth*
c Lucy and the Big Bad Wolf — *Jungman, Ann*
c Lucy Rose: Here's the Thing about Me (Illus. by Rex,
Adam) — *Kelly, Katy*
c Lucy's Quiet Book (Illus. by Ernst, Lisa Campbell)
— *Medearis, Angela Shelf*
c Lucy's Secret — *Levert, Mireille*
c Ludmila's Way — *Chase, Andra*
c Ludmila's Way (Illus. by Chase, Audra) — *Talley,
Linda*
Ludus Danielis — *Levchin, Rafael*
c Ludwig Van Beethoven — *Turner, Barrie Carson*
Luftverkehr zwischen Markt und Macht (1919-1937):
Lufthansa, Verkehrsflug und der Kampf ums
Monopol — *Fischer, Albert*
Luftwaffe over America: The Secret Plans to Bomb
the United States in World War II — *Griehl,
Manfred.*
c Luke Goes to Bat (Illus. by Isadora, Rachel)
— *Isadora, Rachel*
Lullaby of Birdland — *Shearing, George*
Lumbar Interbody Fusion Techniques: Cages, Dowels
and Grafts — *Haid, Regis W.*
The Lumber: A River Heritage: The Story of North
Carolina's Lumber River
Lumiere Light: Recipes from the Tasting Bar
— *Feenie, Rob*
y Luna — *Peters, Julie Anne*
y Luna-C — *Goetze, Jutta*
Lunacies — *Cesereanu, Ruxandra*
Lunacy and the Arrangement of Books — *Belanger,
Terry*
Lunar Exploration: Human Pioneers and Robostic
Surveyors — *Ulivi, Paolo*
Lunar Follies — *Sorrentino, Gilbert*
The Lunar Men: Five Friends Whose Curiosity
Changed the World — *Uglow, Jenny*
c Lunch Munch: Step-by-Step Healthy Recipes for Kids
— *Kalman, Bobbie*
Lunch with Lady Eaton: Inside the Dining Rooms of
a Nation — *Anderson, Carol*
Luncheonette: A Memoir — *Sorrentino, Steven*
c Lunchroom Lizard — *Kirk, Daniel*

Lung Cancer Myths, Facts, Choices--and Hope
— *Henschke, Claudia I.*
Lung Volume Reduction Surgery for Emphysema
— *Fessler, Henry E.*
c Lungs — *Ross, Veronica*
c Lungs: Injury, Illness and Health — *Bullard, Carol*
c Lupe: A Wolf Pup's First Year (Illus. by Cox, Daniel
J.) — *Grambo, Rebecca L.*
The Lure of Saints: A Protestant Experience of
Catholic Tradition — *Sweeney, Jon M.*
Lured by Hope: A Biography of Michael Madhusudan
Dutt — *Murshid, Ghulam*
Lures — *Goyette, Sue*
Lurulu — *Vance, Jack*
Luscious Lemon — *Swain, Heather*
Lust — *Blackburn, Simon*
Luther and Calvin on Old Testament Narratives:
Reformation Thought and Narrative Text
— *Parsons, Michael*
Luther: Biography of a Reformer — *Nohl, Frederick*
Luther — *Dieckmann, Guido*
Luther on Women: A Sourcebook — *Karant-Nunn,
Susan C.*
Luther P. Jackson and a Life for Civil Rights
— *Dennis, Michael*
Luther: The Life and Longing of Luther Vandross
— *Seymour, Craig*
Luthers Bild und Lutherbilder: Ein Rundgang durch
die Wirkungsgeschichte — *Joestel, Volkmar*
c Luther's Halloween (Illus. by Petrone, Valeria)
— *Meister, Cari*
Luther's Rhetoric: Strategies and Style from the
Invocavit Sermons — *Leroux, Neil R.*
L'Utopie reactionnaire: Epuration et modernisation de
l'etat dans l'Espange de la fin de l'Ancien Regime
— *Luis, Jean-Philippe*
Luuletused 1968-2002 — *Liiv, Toomas*
Lux — *Flook, Maria*
Luxury and Public Happiness: Political Economy in
the Italian Enlightenment. — *Wahnbaeck, Till*
Lviv: A City in the Crosscurrents of Culture
— *Czaplicka, John*
Lydia Cabrera and the Construction of an
Afro-Cuban Cultural Identity — *Rodriguz-Mangual,
Edna M.*
Lying: An Augustinian Theology of Duplicity
— *Griffiths, Paul J.*
Lying Together: My Russian Affair — *Cohen, Jennifer
Beth*
Lyme Borreliosis: Biology, Epidemiology and Control
— *Gray, J.S.*
Lymphatic System — *McDowell, Julie*
Lymphoma of the Nervous System — *Batchelor, Tracy*
Lynching in Colorado, 1859-1919 — *Leonard, Stephen
J.*
Lyndon Johnson and Europe: In the Shadow of
Vietnam — *Schwartz, Thomas Alan*
Lyndon Johnson Remembered: An Intimate Portrait
of a Presidency — *Cowger, Thomas W.*
Lyon College, 1872-2002: The Perseverance and
Promise of an Arkansas College — *Blevins, Brooks*
Lyotard and Greek Thought: Sophistry — *Crome,
Keith*
Lyric Generations: Poetry and the Novel in the Long
Eighteenth Century — *Starr, G. Gabrielle*
Lyrics, 1962-2001 — *Dylan, Bob*
The Lyrics in African American Popular Music
— *Springer, Robert*
Lytton Strachey and the Search for Modern Sexual
Identity: The Last Eminent Victorian — *Taddeo,
Julie Anne*

M

Makran, Oman, and Zanzibar: Three-Terminal
   Cultural Corridor in the Western Indian Ocean
   — *Nicolini, Beatrice*
Malachy McCourt's History of Ireland — *McCourt,
   Malachy*
Maladies des Femmes. Tome IV, Livre 4 — *Soranus,
   of Ephesus*
The Malady of Islam — *Meddeb, Abdelwahab*
Malangatana Valente Ngwenya — *Navarro, Julio*
Malaria and Rome: A History of Malaria in Ancient
   Italy — *Sallares, Robert*
The Malaspina Expedition 1789-1794: Journal of the
   Voyage by Aleyandro Malaspina, Vol. 2 — *David,
   Andrew*
Malaysia: The Making of a Nation — *Kheng, Cheah
   Boon*
Malcolm Muggeridge: A Biography — *Wolfe, Gregory*
c Malcolm X — *Crushshon, Theresa*
The Male Biological Clock: The Startling News about
   Aging and Fertility in Men — *Fisch, Harry*
Male Bodies: A Photographic History of the Nude
   — *Cooper, Emmanuel*
The Male Body at War: American Masculinity During
   World War II — *Jarvis, Christina S.*
y Male/Female Roles — *Ojeda, Auriana*
Male Hypogonadism: Basic, Clinical, and Therapeutic
   Principles — *Winters, Stephen J.*
The Male Ideal: Lon of New York and the Masculine
   Physique — *Massengill, Reed*
The Male Pill: A Biography of a Technology in the
   Making — *Oudshoorn, Nelly*
Male Sexuality under Surveillance: The Office in
   American Literature — *Thompson, Graham*
Male Witches in Early Modern Europe — *Apps, Lara*
Malebranche — *Pyle, Andrew*
Malen, Schreiben und Beten: Die spatmittelalterliche
   Handschriftenproduktion im Doppelkloster
   Engelberg — *Marti, Susan*
The Maleness of God — *Baker, Brenda*
c Mali: Land of Gold and Glory — *Masoff, Joy*
Malicious Cryptography: Exposing Cryptovirology
   — *Young, Adam L.*
Malick Sidibe: Photographs Hasselblad Center/Steidl
   March 2004 (Illus. by Sidibe, Malick)
Malinowski: Odyssey of an Anthropologist, 1884-1920
   — *Young, Michael W.*
y Malka — *Pressler, Mirjam*
Mall Maker: Victor Gruen, Architect of an American
   Dream — *Hardwick, M. Jeffrey*
c Mallards — *Hall, Margaret*
Mallarme's Ideas in Language — *Williams, Heather*
y Mallets Aforethought (Read by Ellison, Lindsay).
   Audiobook Review — *Graves, Sarah*
The Malleus Maleficarum and the Construction of
   Witchcraft: Theology and Popular Belief
   — *Broedel, Hans Peter*
c Mallory on the Move (Illus. by Schmitz, Tamara)
   — *Friedman, Laurie*
c Mallory vs. Max (Illus. by Schmitz, Tamara)
   — *Friedman, Laurie*
Malory's 'Morte Darthur': Remaking Arthurian
   Tradition — *Batt, Catherine*
Malraux: A Life — *Todd, Olivier*
Malraux: L'Espoir — *Boak, Denis*
The Maltese Falcon (Read by Dufris, WIlliam).
   Audiobook Review — *Hammett, Dashiell*
The Maltese Falcon — *Hammett, Dashiell*
c Mama Don't Allow — *Hurd, Thacher*
c Mama Goose: A Latino Nursery Treasury/Un Tesoro
   de Rimas Infantiles (Illus. by Suarez, Maribel)
   — *Ada, Alma Flor*
c Mama Loves (Illus. by Brown, Kathryn) — *Dotlich,
   Rebecca Kai*
c Mama Loves Me from Away (Illus. by Caple, Laurie)
   — *Brisson, Pat*
c Mama Panya's Pancakes: A Village Tale from Kenya
   (Illus. by Cairns, Julia) — *Chamberlin, Mary*
c Mama Rex and T: The Reading Champion (Illus. by
   Bjorkman, Steve) — *Vail, Rachel*
Mamaka Kaiao: A Modern Hawaiian Vocabulary, a
   Compilation of Hawaiian Words That Have Been
   Created, Collected, and Approved by the Hawaiian
   Lexicon Committee from 1987 through 2000
   — *Huaolelo, Komike*
Mamaphonic: Balancing Motherhood and Other
   Creative Acts — *Lavender, Bee*
Mambo Italiano — *Galluccio, Steve*
Mambo Peligroso — *Chao, Patricia*
Mamma Mia! Good Italian Girls Talk Back
   — *McLean, Maria Coletta*
Mammalian Artificial Chromosomes: Methods and
   Protocols — *Sgaramella, Vittorio*

Mammalian Embryo Genomics — *Organization for
   Economic Cooperation and Development*
Mammalian TRP Channels as Molecular Targets:
   Proceedings — *Novartis Foundation*
c Mammals — *Richardson, Adele*
Mammals of California (Illus. by Jameson, E.W., Jr.)
   — *Jameson, E.W., Jr.*
Mammals of North America — *Bowers, Nora*
Mammals of the World: A Checklist — *Duff, Andrew*
Mammon's Music: Literature and Economics in the
   Age of Milton — *Hoxby, Blair*
y The Mammoth Cheese — *Holman, Sheri*
c Mammoths: Ice-Age Giants — *Agenbroad, Larry D.*
Man and Wife in America: A History — *Hartog,
   Hendrik*
Man Bites Log: The Unlikely Adventures of a City
   Guy in the Woods. — *Alexander, Max*
The Man Called Cash: The Life, Love, and Faith of
   an American Legend — *Turner, Steve*
The Man from Clear Lake: Earth Day Founder
   Gaylord Nelson — *Christofferson, Bill*
The Man in a Kilt — *Blair, Sandy*
The Man in My Basement (Read by Hudson, Ernie).
   Audiobook Review — *Mosley, Walter*
The Man in My Basement — *Mosley, Walter*
The Man in the Flying Lawn Chair and Other
   Excursions and Observations — *Plimpton, George*
A Man Inspired — *Jackson, Derek*
y Man is Vox: Paingels (Illus. by Allen, Carter)
   — *Thomas, John Ira*
The Man Jesus Loved — *Jennings, Theodore W., Jr.*
Man-Kzin Wars X: The Wunder War — *Colebatch,
   Hal*
Man-Made Disasters Series
Man O' War — *Cooper, Page*
A Man of Faith: The Spiritual Journey of George W.
   Bush. Audiobook Review — *Aikman, David*
The Man of Fifty — *Goethe, Johann Wolfgang von*
Man of the Century: Winston Churchill and His
   Legend since 1945 (Read by Ramsden, John).
   Audiobook Review — *Ramsden, John*
Man of the Century: Winston Churchill and His
   Legend since 1945 — *Ramsden, John*
A Man of Three Words: Samuel Pallache, a moroccan
   Jew in Catholic and Protestant Europe
   — *Gracia-Arenal, Mercedes*
Man on the Border — *Austin, Dave*
c Man on the Moon (Illus. by Bartram, Simon)
   — *Bartram, Simon*
Man The Hunted: Primates, Predators, and Human
   Evolution — *Sussman, Robert W.*
The Man Who Ate the 747 — *Sherwood, Ben*
The Man Who Became a School — *Popp, Marcia S.*
The Man Who Changed China: The Life and Legacy
   of Jiang Zemin — *Kuhn, Robert Lawrence*
Man Who Could Work Miracles: A Critical Text
   — *Wells, H.G.*
The Man Who Cried I Am — *Williams, John A.*
The Man Who Had All the Luck — *Miller, Arthur*
The Man Who Hated Emily Bronte — *Smith, Ray*
The Man Who Invented the Chromosome: The Life of
   Cyril Darlington — *Harman, Oren Solomon*
c The Man Who Made Time Travel — *Lasky, Kathryn*
The Man Who Mapped the Arctic: The Intrepid Life
   of George Back, Frankins Lieutenant — *Steele,
   Peter*
y The Man Who Mapped the Arctic: The Intrepid Life
   of George Back, Franklin's Lieutenant — *Steele,
   Peter*
The Man Who Outgrew His Prison Cell: Confessions
   of a Bank Robber — *Loya, Joe (b. 1961 -)*
The Man Who Saved Kabuki: Faubion Bowers and
   Theatre Censorship in Occupied Japan
   — *Okamoto, Shiro*
The Man Who Saw the Future — *Forrester, Andrew*
The Man Who Shocked the World: The Life and
   Legacy of Stanley Milgram — *Blass, Thomas*
The Man Who Tried to Get Away — *Donaldson,
   Stephen R.*
The Man Who Walked between the Towers
   — *Gerstein, Mordicai*
c The Man Who Walked the Earth — *Wallace, Ian*
The Man Who Was Cyrano: A Life of Edmond
   Rostand, Creator of "Cyrano de Bergerac"
   — *Lloyd, Sue*
c The Man Who Went to the Far Side of the Moon: The
   Story of Apollo 11 Astronaut Michael Collins
   — *Schyffert, Bea Uusma*
The Man Who Would Be Kipling: The Colonial
   Fiction and the Frontiers of Exile — *Hagiioannu,
   Andrew*

Managed Care and Monopoly Power: The Antitrust
   Challenge — *Haa-Wilson, Deborah*
Management Accounting, 3rd Ed. — *Swain Monte R.*
Management Accounting, 7th Ed. — *Hansen, Don R.*
Management Accounting in Health Care
   Organizations — *Young, David W.*
Management Accounting in the Digital Economy
   — *Bhimani, Alnoor*
Management and Administration of Correctional
   Health — *Moore, Jacqueline*
The Management and Control of Quality, 6th Ed.
   — *Evans, James R.*
Management and Organisational Behaviour, 1st Ed.
   — *Bloisi, Wendy*
Management and Organisational Behaviour, 7th Ed.
   — *Mullins, Laurie J.*
Management Dynamics: Merging Constraints
   Accounting to Drive Improvement — *Caspari, John
   A.*
Management for Nurses and Health Professionals:
   Theory into Practice — *Hewison, Alistair*
Management Guidelines for Nurse Practitioners
   Working with Adults, 2nd Ed. — *Dunphy, Lynne M.
   Hektor*
Management Guidelines for Nurse Practitioners
   Working with Women, 2nd Ed. — *Brown, Kathleen
   M. Pelletier*
Management in Tourism — *Jesenko, Joze*
Management: Inventing and Delivering Its Future
   — *Kochan, Thomas A.*
Management Knowledge and the New Employee
   — *Hodgson, Damian E.*
Management: Meeting and Exceeding Customer
   Expectations — *Plunkett, Warren R.*
Management of Benign Prostatic Hypertrophy
   — *McVary, Kevin T.*
Management of Cerebral Aneurysms — *Le Roux,
   Peter D.*
Management of Combined Sewer Overflows — *Field,
   Richard*
The Management of Genital Warts in Primary Care
   — *Stanley, Margaret*
Management of Off-Highway Plant and Equipment
   — *Edwards, David J.*
Management of Patients with Neuromuscular Disease
   — *Bach, John R.*
Management of Prostate Cancer, 2nd Ed. — *Klein,
   Eric A.*
Management of Thorocolumbar Fractures — *Reitman,
   Charles A.*
The Management of Urban Development in Zambia
   — *Mutale, Emmanuel*
Management, Organisation, and Ethics in the Public
   Sector — *Bishop, Patrick*
Management Risk: The Bottleneck Is at the Top of the
   Bottle — *Chorafas, Dimitris N.*
Manager of Choice: 5 Competencies for Cultivating
   Top Talent — *Ahlrichs, Nancy S.*
Managerial and Supervisory Principles for Physical
   Therapists, 2nd Ed. — *Nosse, Larry J.*
Managerial Economics for Decision Making
   — *Adams, John*
The Manager's Guide to Competitive Intelligence
   — *McGonagle, John J.*
Managers Make the Difference: Managing vs. Leading
   in Our Schools — *Leiding, Darlene*
Managers, Not MBAs: A Hard Look at the Soft
   Practice of Managing and Management
   Development — *Mintzberg, Henry*
Manager's Portfolio of Model Performance
   Evaluations: Ready-to-Use Performance Appraisals
   Covering All Employee Functions — *Toropov,
   Brandon*
Managing a Diverse Workforce: Learning Activities,
   2nd Ed. — *Powell, Gary N.*
Managing a Public Speaker Bureau: A Manual for
   Health and Human Services Organizations
   — *Gambescia, Stephen F.*
Managing and Leading: 52 Lessons Learned for
   Engineers — *Walesh, Stuart G.*
Managing and Securing a Cisco Structured
   Wireless-Aware Network — *Wall, David*
Managing Bank Conversions: The Guide to
   Organizing, Controlling, and Implementing
   Systems Conversions — *Belasco, Kent S.*
Managing Beverage Service — *Kotschevar, Lendal H.*
Managing Business with SAP: Planning,
   Implementation and Evaluation — *Lau, Linda K.*
Managing Chronic Illness Using the Four-Phase
   Treatment Approach: A Mental Health
   Professional's Guide to Helping Chronically Ill
   People — *Fennell, Patricia A.*

Masculinity, Power, and Technology: A Malaysian Ethnography — *Mellstrom, Ulf*

The Mask of Red Death: An Edgar Allen Poe Mystery — *Schechter, Harold*

Masking Terror: How Women Contain Violence in Southern Sri Lanka — *Argenti-Pillen, Alex*

Masks and Masking in Medieval and Early Tudor England — *Twycross, Meg*

Mason County, West Virginia Marriages, 1806-1915 — *Hesson, Julie Chapin*

y The Mason-Dixon Line — *Davenport, John C.*

Mason Moves Away: Mason Se Muda — *Mommaerts, Robb*

Masque — *Zolf, Rachel*

Masquerade: Queer Poetry in America to the End of World War II — *Elledge, Jim*

Masquerade: The Life and Times of Deborah Sampson, Continental Soldier — *Young, Alfred Fabian*

Mass Affluence: Seven New Rules of Marketing to Today's Consumer — *Nunes, Paul*

Mass Communications and American Social Thought: Key Texts, 1919-1968 — *Durham, John*

Mass Conservatism: The Conservatives and the Public since the 1880s — *Ball, Stuart*

Mass Immigration and the National Interest: Policy Directions for the New Century — *Briggs, Vernon M., Jr.*

Mass Media and the Shaping of American Feminism, 1963-1975 — *Bradley, Patricia*

Mass Media in a Mass Society: Myth and Reality — *Hoggart, Richard*

Mass Migration to the United States: Classical and Contemporary Periods — *Min, Pyong Gap*

Mass Persuasion: The Social Psychology of a War Bond Drive — *Merton, Robert K.*

Mass Spectrometry: A Textbook — *Gross, Jurgen H.*

Massachusetts Breeding Bird Atlas (Illus. by Sill, John) — *Petersen, Wayne R.*

Massachusetts, California, Timbuktu (Read by Taylor, Jen). Audiobook Review — *Rosenfeld, Stephanie*

Massachusetts, California, Timbuktu — *Rosenfeld, Stephanie*

The Massachusetts Eye and Ear Infirmary Illustrated Manual of Ophthalmology, 2d ed. — *Kaiser, Peter K.*

Massachusetts General Hospital Guide to Primary Care Psychiatry, 2nd Ed. — *Stern, Theodore A.*

Massage for the Hospital Patient and Medically Frail Client — *MacDonald, Gayle*

Massive Change: The Future of Global Design — *Mau, Bruce*

Mastabas at Saqqara: Kaiemheset, Kaipunesut, Kaiemsenu, Sehetepu and Others — *McFarlane, Ann*

The Master — *Toibin, Colm*

Master Built Pools and Patios: An Inspiring Portfolio of Design Ideas — *Skinner, Tina*

Master Math: Geometry-Including Everything From Triangles, Polygons, Proofs, and Deductive Resoning to Circles, Solids, Similarity, and Coordinate Geometry — *Ross, Debra Anne*

The Master — *Toibin, Colm*

Master of None — *Wood, Lee*

y Master of the Cauldron — *Drake, David*

Master Techniques in Cataract and Refractive Surgery — *Roy, F. Hampton*

MasterCases: Hand and Wrist Surgery — *Plancher, Kevin D.*

Masterful Women: Slaveholding Widows from the American Revolution through the Civil War — *Wood, Kirsten E.*

Mastering 3D Animation, 2nd Ed. — *Ratner, Peter*

Mastering Black-and-White Photography: From Camera to Darkroom, Rev Ed. — *Suess, Bernhard J.*

Mastering Import and Export Management — *Cook, Thomas A.*

Mastering JavaServer Faces — *Dudney, Bill*

Mastering Management Skills: A Manager's Toolkit — *Aldag, Ramon J.*

Mastering MATLAB 7 — *Hanselman, Duane C.*

Mastering Mentoring and Coaching with Emotional Intelligence: Increase Your Job EQ — *Merlevede, Patrick E.*

Mastering Networks: An Internet Lab Manual — *Liebeherr, Jorg*

Mastering Oracle SQL, 2nd Ed. — *Mishra, Sanjay*

Mastering Real Estate Principles — *Cortesi, Gerald R.*

Mastering the Financial Dimension of Your Practice: The Definitive Resource for Private Practice Development and Financial Planning — *Cole, Peter H.*

Mastering the Instructional Design Process: A Systematic Approach — *Rothwell, William J.*

Mastering the Merger: Four Critical Decisions That Make or Break the Deal — *Harding, David*

Mastering the Ultimate High Ground: Next Steps in the Military Uses of Space — *Lambeth, Benjamin S.*

Mastering Unreal Technology: The Art of Level Design — *Busby, Jason*

Mastering Visual Studio .NET — *Griffiths, Ian*

Mastering Weave Structures: Transforming Ideas into Great Cloth — *Alderman, Sharon*

Masterpieces of Chicago Architecture — *Zukowsky, John*

Masterpieces of French Literature — *Severson, Marilyn S.*

Masterpieces of Kabuki: Eighteen Plays on Stage — *Brandon, James R.*

Masterpieces of the Mineral World: Treasures from the Houston Museum of Natural Science — *Wilson, Wendell E.*

Masterplots II: Drama Series, Rev. Ed., Vols. 1-4 — *Moe, Christian H.*

y Masterplots II: Short Story Series, Rev. Ed., Vols. 1-8 — *May, Charles E.*

Masters of All They Surveyed: Exploration, Geography, and a British El Dorado — *Burnett, D. Graham*

Masters of Chaos: The Secret History of the Special Forces — *Robinson, Linda*

Masters of Deception: Escher, Dali, and the Artists of Optical Illusion — *Seckel, Al*

y Masters of Fantasy — *Fawcett, Bill*

Masters of Functional Orthodontics — *Levrini, Aurelio*

Masters of Movement: Portraits of America's Great Choreographers — *Eichenbaum, Rose*

Masters of the Big House: Elite Slaveholders of the Mid-Nineteenth-Century South — *Scarborough, William Kauffman*

Masters of the Mind: Exploring the Story of Mental Illness from Ancient Times to the New Millennium — *Millon, Theodore*

Masters of Theory: Cambridge and the Rise of Mathematical Physics — *Warwick, Andrew*

Masters of Two Arts: Re-Creation of European Literatures in Italian Cinema — *Testa, Carlo*

Masters of War: Latin American and United States Aggression from the Cuban Revolution through the Clinton Years — *Nieto, Clara*

Masterworks — *Illetschko, Georgia*

Masterworks of Technology: The Story of Creative Engineering, Architecture, and Design — *Lewis, E.E.*

Masterworks of the Jewish Museum — *Berger, Maurice*

Masterworks: The Arts and Crafts of Traditional Buildings in Northern Europe — *Pennick, Nigel*

Mastery, Tyranny, and Desire: Thomas Thistlewood and His Slaves in the Anglo-Jamaican World — *Burnard, Trevor*

Masturbation: The History of a Great Terror — *Stenger, Jean*

Matadora — *Gambito, Sarah*

Matchbook: The Diary of a Modern-Day Matchmaker — *Daniels, Samantha*

Matchbox Labels: Over 2,000 Elegant Examples from All over the World — *Cox, Ida Prather*

Matchbox Labels: Over 2,000 Elegant Examples from All over the World — *Smith, Jane*

Matched Pairs: Gender and Intertextual Dialogue in Eighteenth-Century Fiction — *Bartolomeo, Joseph F.*

c Mateo's Progress: Jornadas de Mateo: Cuentos para ninos de todas las edades/Tales for Children of All Ages (Illus. by Lorenzo, Alejandro) — *Lorenzo, Alejandro*

Material Culture and Sacred Landscape:The Anthropology of the Siberian Khanty — *Jordan, Peter*

The Material Culture of Sex, Procreation and Marriage in Premodern Europe — *McClanan, Anne L.*

Material Modernism: The Politics of the Page — *Bornstein, George*

Material Strategies: Dress and Gender in Historical Perspective — *Burman, Barbara*

The Material, The Real, and the Fractured Self: Subjectivity and Representation from Rimbaud to Reda — *Harrow, Susan*

Material Virtue: Ethics and the Body in Early China — *Csikszentmihalyi, Mark*

Materialien einer althebraischen Datenbank: Wortfugungen. — *Richter, Wolfgang*

Materials and Devices for Smart Systems — *Furuya, Yasubumi*

y Materials — *Lauw, Darlene*

Materials for Electrical and Electronic Contacts: Processing, Properties, and Applications — *Joshi, P.B.*

Materials, Integration and Packaging Issues for High-Frequency Devices: Proceedings — *Muralt, P.*

Materials Matter: Toward a Sustainable Materials Policy — *Geiser, Kenneth*

Materials Processing and Design: Modeling, Simulation and Applications (NUMIFORM 2004): Proceedings — *Ghosh, Somnath*

Materials Science

Materials, Technology and Reliability for Advanced Interconnects and Low-K Dielectrics 2003: Proceedings — *McKerrow, Andrew J.*

Materials, Technology and Reliability for Advanced Interconnects and Low-K Dielectrics -- 2004: Proceedings — *Carter, R.J.*

Maternal Body and Voice in Toni Morrison, Bobbie Ann Mason and Lee Smith — *Eckard, Paula Gallant*

Maternal Desire: On Children, Love, and the Inner Life — *De Marneffe, Daphne*

Maternal Newborn Nursing, 4th Ed. — *Stright, Barbara R.*

c Mates, Dates, and Mad Mistakes — *Hopkins, Cathy*

y Mates, Dates, and Sequin Smiles — *Hopkins, Cathy*

Math and My World Series

Math and the Mona Lisa: The Art and Science of Leonardo da Vinci — *Atalay, Bulent*

c Math behind the Science: Classroom Set — *Johnson, Rebecca L.*

Math Charmers: Tantalizing Tidbits for the Mind — *Posamentier, Alfred S.*

c Math Curse (Illus. by Smith, Lane) — *Scieszka, Jon*

c Math for All Seasons (Illus. by Briggs, Harry) — *Tang, Greg*

Math for Teachers: An Exploratory Approach — *Stein, Robert*

c Math Games for Middle School — *Salvadori, Mario*

Math Magic: How to Master Everyday Math Problems, Rev. Ed. — *Flansburg, Scott*

Math Matters Series

c Math Mini-Mysteries — *Markle, Sandra*

c Math Rashes: And Other Classroom Tales (Illus. by Di Fiori, Larry) — *Evans, Douglas*

c Math Stories: Addition — *Shannon, Rosemarie*

c Math Stories: Subtraction — *Shannon, Rosemarie*

Math-terpieces: The Art of Problem-Solving (Illus. by Paprocki, Greg) — *Tang, Greg*

Math through the Ages: A Gentle History for Teachers and Others — *Berlinghoff, William P.*

Mathematica 5.0 — *Carter, J.D.*

The Mathematica Guidebook: Programming — *Trott, Michael*

y Mathematical Adventures for Students and Amateurs — *Hayes, David F.*

Mathematical Analysis I — *Cooke, Roger*

Mathematical Analysis II — *Cooke, Roger*

Mathematical Analysis, Vols. 1-2 — *Zorich, V.A.*

Mathematical and Computational Methods for Compressible Flow — *Feistauer, M.*

Mathematical and Quantitative Methods — *Fair, Ray C.*

Mathematical Biology I: An introduction, 3rd Ed. — *Murray, J.D.*

Mathematical Biology II: Spatial Models and Biomedical Applications, 3rd Ed. — *O'Malley, Robert E. Jr.*

A Mathematical Bridge: An Intuitive Journey in Higher Mathematics, 1st Ed. — *Hewson, Stephen Fletcher*

The Mathematical Century: The 30 Greatest Problems of the Last 100 Years — *Odifreddi, Piergiorgio*

Mathematical Circles Adieu and Return to Mathematical Circles — *Eves, Howard W.*

A Mathematical Companion for Differential Equations — *Hollis, Selwyn L.*

Mathematical Constants — *Finch, Steven R.*

Mathematical Delights — *Honsberger, Ross*

Mathematical Development in Young Children: Exploring Notations — *Brizuela, Barbara M.*

Mathematical Foundation of Classical Statistical Mechanics: Continous Systesms. Second Edition — *Illner, Reinhard*

Mathematical Foundation of Quantum Mechanics
— *Mackey, George Whitelaw*

Mathematical Gift, I: The Interplay between Topology Functions, Geometry, and Algebra — *Ueno, Kenji*

Mathematical Logic in the 20th Century — *Sacks, Gerald E.*

Mathematical Methods for Scientists and Engineers — *McQuarrie, Donald A.*

Mathematical Methods for Scientists and Engineers — *Wilson, Howard B.*

Mathematical methods for scientists and engineers; linear and nonlinear systems — *Kahn, Peter B.*

Mathematical Methods of Many-Body Quantum Field Theory — *Lehmann, Detlef*

Mathematical Modeling for Polymer Processing: Polymerization, Crystalization, Manufacturing — *Matheij, Robert M.M.*

Mathematical Olympiads 2000-2001: Problems and Solutions from around the World — *Andreescu, Titu*

A Mathematical Passage: Strategies for Promoting Inquiry in Grades 4-6 — *Whitin, David J.*

Mathematical Perspectives on Theoretical Physics: A Journey from Black Holes to Superstrings — *Prakash, Nirmala*

Mathematical Physics Research at the Cutting Edge — *Benton, Charles V.*

Mathematical Physiology — *Keener, James*

Mathematical Puzzles: A Connoisseur's Collection — *Winkler, Peter*

Mathematical Reliability: An Expository Perspective — *Soyer, Refik*

Mathematical Statistics — *Shao, Jun*

Mathematical Theory of Elasticity — *Hetnarski, Richard B.*

y A Mathematician Plays the Stock Market — *Paulos, John Allen*

Mathematicians under the Nazis — *O'Maley, Robert E.*

Mathematicians Under the Nazis — *Segal, Sanford L.*

c Mathematickles (Illus. by Salerno, Steven) — *Franco, Betsy*

Mathematics 6: An Award-Winning Textbook from Russia — *Nurk, Enn*

Mathematics and Sex — *Cresswell, Clio*

Mathematics by Experiment: Plausible Reasoning in the 21st Century — *Borwein, Jonathan M.*

Mathematics Content for Elementary Teachers — *Brumbaugh, Douglas K.*

Mathematics Education in the United States, 2004: A Capsule Summary Fact Book Written for the Tenth International Congress on Mathematical Education — *Usiskin, Zalman*

Mathematics Education Within the Postmodern — *Walshaw, Margaret*

Mathematics Elsewhere: An Exploration of Ideas Across Cultures — *Ascher, Marcia*

Mathematics for Engineers. 2nd Ed. — *Croft, Anthony*

Mathematics for Engineers and Scientists, 6th Ed. — *Jeffrey, Alan*

Mathematics in Nature: Modeling Patterns in the Natural World — *Adam, John A.*

Mathematics in Population Biology — *Thieme, Horst R.*

Mathematics Manual for Water and Wastewater Treatment Plant Operators — *Spellman, Frank R.*

Mathematics of Finance: Proceedings — *Yin, George*

The Mathematics of Marriage Dynamic Nonlinear Models — *Gottman, John M.*

Mathis Lussy: A Pioneer in Studies of Expressive Performance — *Dogantan, Mine*

Maths for Chemists, Vol. 1 — *Cockett, Martin*

Maths for Chemists, Vol. 2 — *Cockett, Martin*

Matilda of Scotland: A Study in Medieval Queenship — *Huneycutt, Lois L.*

Matilda of Scotland: A Study of Medieval Queenship — *Huneycutt, Lois L.*

The Mating Season — *Brunkhorst, Alex*

Mating Systems and Strategies — *Shuster, Stephen M.*

Matisse at Villa le Reve (Illus. by Adant, Helene) — *Boyer, Marie-France*

Matisse: From Color to Architecture — *Percheron, Rene*

Matricide in Language: Writing Theory in Kristeva and Woolf — *Nikolchina, Miglena*

Matrimoni di antico regime — *Lombardi, Daniela*

Matrimoni in dubbio: Unioni controverse e nozze clandestine in Italia dal XIV al XVIII secolo — *Menchi, Silvana Seidel*

A Matrix of Meanings: Finding God in Pop Culture — *Detweiler, Craig*

Matrix Riccati Equations in Control and Systems Theory — *Abu-Kandil, Abu*

c Matt the Rat and His Magic Cloud/A Day at School/Raton Mateo y su nube Magica/Un dia de escuela (Illus. by Torres, Irving) — *Liberto, Lorenzo*

c Matt The Rat And His Magic Cloud — *Liberto, Lorenzo*

c Matt the Rat and His Sister Maggie/When I Grow Up/Raton Mateo y su Hermana Maggie/Cuando yo Crezca (Illus. by Torres, Irving) — *Liberto, Lorenzo*

A Matter of Character: Inside the White House of George W. Bush — *Kessler, Ronald*

A Matter of Fate: The Concept of Fate in the Arab World as Reflected in Modern Arabic Literature — *Cohen-Mor, Dalya*

The Matter of Identity in Medieval Romance — *Hardman, Phillipa*

A Matter of Motive — *Hachey, Michael*

A Matter of Opinion — *Navasky, Victor S.*

A Matter of Taste: Inspired Seasonal Menus with Wines and Spirits to Match — *Waverman, Lucy*

c Matter: See It, Touch It, Taste It, Smell It (Illus. by Boyd, Sheree) — *Stille, Darlene R.*

Matters of Consequence — *Macdonald, Copthorne*

Matters of Gravity: Special Effects and Supermen in the 20th Century — *Bukatman, Scott*

Matters of Life and Longing: Female Sterilisation in Northeast Brazil — *Dalsgaard, Anne Line*

Matthew J. Perry: The Man, His Times, and His Legacy — *Burke, W. Lewis*

c Mattimeo — *Jacques, Brian*

c The Matzo Ball Boy (Illus. by Litzinger, Rosanne) — *Schulman, Lisa*

c The Matzo Ball Boy (Illus. by Litzinger, Rosanne) — *Shulman, Lisa*

Matzo Balls for Breakfast: And Other Memories of Growing Up Jewish — *King, Alan*

Mau Mau and Nationhood: Arms, Authority and Narration — *Odhiambo, E.S. Atieno*

c Maui and the Big Fish — *Wilson, Barbara Ker*

Mau'i Trails: Walks, Strolls and Treks on the Valley Island, 3rd Ed. — *Morey, Kathy*

c Mauna Loa: The Largest Volcano in the United States — *Webster, Christine*

The Maunder Minimum and the Variable Sun-Earth Connection — *Soon, Willie*

Maurice Merleau-Ponty's Phenomenology of Perception: A Basis For Sharing the Earth — *Gordon, Haim*

The Maverick Room — *Ellis, Thomas Sayers*

Maverick Voices: Conversations with Political and Cultural Rebels — *Booth, Douglas*

Maverick Voices: Conversations with the Political and Cultural Rebels — *Jacobsen, Kurt*

Mavericks and Other Traditions in American Music — *Broyles, Michael*

Max and Sven — *Bouden, Tom*

Max Beerbohm: A Kind of a Life — *Hall, N. John*

The Max Chronicles Presents the Storyteller — *Carwile, Ernie*

c Max for President — *Krosoczka, Jarrett*

Max Planck Yearbook of United Nations Law, Vol. 7 — *Bogdandy, Armin von*

Max Reger and Karl Straube: Perspectives on an Organ Performing Tradition — *Anderson, Christopher*

c Max the Mighty Superhero (Illus. by Flook, Helen) — *Wiebe, Trina*

c Max the Movie Director (Illus. by Flook, Helen) — *Wiebe, Trina*

Max Weber: A Comprehensive Bibliography — *Sica, Alan*

Max Weber & the New Century — *Sica, Alan*

Max Weber's Politics of Civil Society — *Kim, Sung Ho*

Maximizing Intelligence — *Armor, David J.*

Maximizing the Power of Geographical Information Systems (GIS) in Applied Land Informatics — *Otawa, Toru*

Maxims — *La Rochefoucauld*

Maximum City: Bombay Lost and Found — *Mehta, Suketu*

Maximum Dreamweaver: 85 Add-Ons to Supercharge Your Development — *Doyle, Michael (b. 1957 -)*

Maximum Likelihood Estimation with Stata — *Gould, William*

Maximum PC Guide to Building a Dream PC — *Smith, Will*

y Maximum Ride: The Angel Experiment — *Patterson, James*

Maximum Sail Power: The Complete Guide to Sails, Sail Technology, and Performance — *Hancock, Brian*

Maximum Security — *Connors, Rose*

Maximus the Confessor and His Companions: Documents from Exile — *Allen, Pauline*

Maxine Hong Kingston's Broken Book of Life: An Intertextual Study of The Woman Warrior and China Men — *Sabine, Maureen*

c Max's Rules — *Philipson, Sandra J.*

c Maxx Comedy — *Korman, Gordon Richard*

y The Maxx, Vol. 3 — *Kieth, Sam*

May and Amy: A True Story of Family, Forbidden Love, and the Secret Lives of May Gaskell, Her Daughter Amy, and Sir Edward Burne-Jones — *Dimbleby, Josceline*

May Contain Nuts: A Very Loose Canon of American Humor — *Rosen, Michael J.*

May Her Likes Be Multiplied: Biography and Gender Politics in Egypt — *Booth, Marilyn*

May the Best Man Win: Sport, Masculinity, and the Nationalism in Great Britain and the Empire, 1880-1935 — *McDevitt, Patrick F.*

The Maya 6 Handbook — *Watkins, Adam*

The Maya and Teotihuacan: Reinterpreting Early Classic Interaction — *Braswell, Geoffrey E.*

Maya Hair Sashes Backstrap Woven in Jacaltenango, Gutemala, 2nd Ed. — *Ventura, Carol*

Maya Lin — *Stone, Amy*

The Maya of Morganton: Work and Community in the Nuevo New South — *Fink, Leon*

Maya Palaces and Elite Residences: An Interdisciplinary Approach — *Christie, Jessica Joyce*

y Maya Running — *Banerjee, Anjali*

Mayada, Daughter of Iraq: One Woman's Survival under Saddam Hussein — *Sasson, Jean*

Mayan Lives, Mayan Utopias: The Indigenous Peoples in Chiapas and the Zapatista Rebellion — *Rus, Jan*

Maybe Baby — *Darlington, Tenaya*

The Mayday: A Jack Merchant and Sarah Ballard Novel — *Eidson, Bill*

c Mayday! Mayday! A Coast Guard Rescue (Illus. by Demarest, Chris L.) — *Demarest, Chris L.*

Mayflower 1620: A New Look at a Pilgrim Voyage — *Arenstam, Peter*

y Mayflower Bastard: A Stranger Among the Pilgrims — *Lindsay, David (English writer)*

c The Mayflower Compact — *Armentrout, David*

c Mayfly (Illus. by Jocelyn, Marthe) — *Jocelyn, Marthe*

Mayo Clinic Guide to Women's Cancers — *Hartmann, Lynn C.*

Mayo Clinic Guide to Women's Cancers — *Mayo Clinic*

Mayo Clinic Health Information

Mayo Clinic Images in Internal Medicine: Self-Assessment for Board Exam Review — *McDonald, Furman S.*

Mayors in the Middle: Politics, Race, and Mayoral Control of Urban Schools — *Henig, Jeffrey R.*

The Maze and the Warrior: Symbols in Architecture, Theology, and Music — *Wright, Craig*

y A Maze Me: Poems for Girls (Illus. by Maher, Terre) — *Nye, Naomi Shihab*

c Mazescapes (Illus. by Munro, Roxie) — *Munro, Roxie*

Mazzini and Marx: Thoughts Upon Democracy in Europe — *Mastellone, Salvo*

MBA in a Box: The Practical Guide to the Big Ideas of Business — *Kurtzman, Joel*

MCAD/MCSD Self-Paced Training Kit: Implementing Security for Applications with Microsoft Visual Basic .NET and Microsoft Visual C# .NET — *Northrup, Anthony*

The McDonaldization of Society, Rev. New Century Ed. — *Ritzer, George*

MCDST self-paced training kit (exam 70-270); supporting users and troubleshooting a Microsoft Windows XP operating system — *Glenn, Walter*

MCDST Self-Paced Training Kit (Exam 70-272): Supporting Users and Troubleshooting Desktop Applications on a Microsoft Windows XP Operating System — *Glenn, Walter*

c McDuff's Wild Romp (Illus. by Jeffers, Susan) — *Wells, Rosemary*

c McGillycuddy Could! (Illus. by Porter, Sue) — *Edwards, Pamela Duncan*

McGraw-Hill Concise Encyclopedia of Chemistry

McGraw-Hill Dictionary of Electrical and Computer Engineering

The McKannahs — *Magers, Rick*

The McKenzie Artifact — *Kent, Alison*

McKim, Mead & White: The Masterworks — *White, Samuel G.*

McLuhan for Managers: New Tools for New Thinking — *Federman, Mark*

McMinn's Color Atlas of Head and Neck Anatomy
— *Logan, Bari M.*

McNally's Bluff — *Lardo, Vincent*

McNally's Bluff — *Sanders, Lawrence*

McNally's Chance (Read by Henderson, Adam).
Audiobook Review — *Sanders, Lawrence*

McNally's Risk (Read by Henderson, Adam).
Audiobook Review — *Sanders, Lawrence*

MCSE Self-Paced Training Kit (Exam 70-298):
Designing Security for a Microsoft Windows Server
2003 Network — *Bragg, Roberta*

McSweeney's 13: The Comics Issue — *Ware, Chris*

McSweeney's Enchanted Chamber of Astonishing
Stories — *Chabon, Michael*

McSweeney's Quarterly Concern, No. 13 — *Ware,
Chris*

y Me and Billy — *Collier, James Lincoln*

Me and Emma — *Flock, Elizabeth*

c Me and My Cat? — *Kitamura, Satoshi*

c Me and Neesie (Illus. by Gilchrist, Jan Spivey)
— *Greenfield, Eloise*

Me and Orson Welles — *Kaplow, Robert*

c Me Oh Maya (Illus. by McCauley, Adam) — *Scieszka,
Jon*

Me to We: Turning Self-Help on Its Head
— *Kielburger, Marc*

c Me Too! — *Harper, Jamie*

The Mead Hall: The Feasting Tradition in
Anglo-Saxon England — *Pollington, Stephen*

Meadows — *Lee, Christopher*

Meadows — *Lloyd, Cristopher*

Meagher, Gummow and Lehane's Doctrines and
Remedies, 4th Ed. — *Meagher, R.P.*

A Meal Observed — *Todhunter, Andrew*

c Mean Chicks, Cliques, and Dirty Tricks: A Real Girl's
Guide to Getting through the Day with Smarts and
Style — *Karres, Erika V. Shearin*

Mean Season — *Cochran, Heather*

Mean Streets: Confessions of a Nighttime Taxi Driver
— *McSherry, Peter*

Meaning in Spinoza's Method — *Garrett, Aaron*

The Meaning in the Miracles — *Eerdmans, Jeffrey
John*

The Meaning of Byzantium in the Poetry and Prose of
W.B. Yeats: The Artifice of Eternity — *Murphy,
Russell E.*

The Meaning of Conservatism, 3rd Ed. — *Scruton,
Roger*

The Meaning of Everything: The Story of the Oxford
English Dictionary — *Winchester, Simon*

The Meaning of Ichiro: The New Wave From Japan
and the Transformation of Our National Pastime
— *Whiting, Robert*

The Meaning of Independence: John Adams, George
Washington, and Thomas Jefferson — *Morgan,
Edmund*

The Meaning of Independence: John Adams, George
Washington, and Thomas Jefferson — *Morgan,
Edmund Sears*

The Meaning of Life in the World Religions — *Runzo,
Joseph*

The Meaning of Relativity. Audiobook Review
— *Einstein, Albert*

The Meaning of Sports: Why Americans Watch
Baseball, Football, and Basketball and What They
See When They Do — *Mandelbaum, Michael*

The Meaning of Wife — *Kingston, Anne*

y The Meanwhile Adventures (Illus. by Ajhar, Brian)
— *Doyle, Roddy*

Meanwhile: The Critical Writings of bpNichol
— *Miki, Roy*

c Measle and the Dragodon — *Ogilvy, Ian*

c Measle and the Wrathmonk — *Ogilvy, Ian*

Measure for Measure: The Story of Imperial, Metric,
and Other Units — *Hebra, Alex*

Measure of a Man — *Byrd, Adrianne*

A Measure of Endurance: The Unlikely Triumph of
Steven Sharp — *Mishler, William*

The Measure of International Law: Effectiveness,
Fairness and Validity — *Canadian Council*

The Measure of Multitude: Population in Medieval
Thought — *Biller, Peter*

The Measure of STAR: Review of the U.S.
Environmental Protection Agency's Science to
Achieve Results (STAR) Research Grants Program
— *National Research Council (U.S.). Committee to
Review EPA's Research Grant Program*

A Measure of Undoing — *Kos, David*

c Measurement — *Shannon, Rosemarie*

Measurement Theory in Action: Case Studies and
Exercises — *Shultz, Kenneth S.*

Measures of the Holy Commonwealth in
Seventeenth-Century England — *Barbour, Reid*

Measuring America: How an Untamed Wilderness
Shaped the United States and Fulfilled the Promise
of Democracy — *Linklater, Andro*

Measuring Biological Diversity — *Magurran, Anne E.*

Measuring for Results: The Dimensions of Public
Library Effectiveness — *Matthews, Joseph R.*

Measuring Human Capital: Converting Workplace
Behavior into Dollars — *Kravetz, Dennis J.*

Measuring Judicial Independence: The Political
Economy of Judging in Japan — *Ramseyer, J. Mark*

Measuring Knowledge Management in the Business
Sector: First Steps — *Organisation for Economic
Co-operation and Development*

Measuring the Cosmos: How Scientists Discovered the
Dimensions of the Universe — *Clark, David H.*

Measuring the Costs of Protection in Europe:
European Commercial Policy in the 2000s
— *Messerlin, Patrick A.*

Measuring the Gains from Medical Research: An
Economic Approach — *Murphy, Kevin M.*

Measuring Up: Educational Assessment Challenges
and Practices for Psychology — *Dunn, Dana S.*

Measuring What Matters: Allocation, Planning, and
Quality Assessment for the Ryan White Care Act
— *Institute of Medicine (U.S.). Committee on the
Ryan White CARE Act*

Measuring Your Company's Environmental Impact:
Templates and Tools for a Complete ISO 14001
Initial Review — *Zackrisson, Mats*

Meat Harry — *Jordan, Harry*

The Meat You Eat: Corporate Farming and the
Decline of the American Diet — *Midkiff, Ken*

Meatless Meals for Working People--Quick and Easy
Vegetarian Recipes — *Wasserman, Debra*

Mebyon Kernow and Cornish Nationalism — *Deacon,
Bernard*

c Mecca — *Ross, Mandy*

Mechanical Tolerance Stackup and Analysis
— *Fischer, Bryan R.*

Mechanical Tribology; Materials, Characterization,
and Applications — *Totten, George E.*

Mechanical Wear Fundamentals and Testing. 2nd Ed.
— *Bayer, Raymond G.*

Mechanics of Elastic Composites — *Cristescu, N.*

Mechanics of Laminated Composite Plates and Shells:
Theory and Analysis, 2nd Ed. — *Reddy, J.N.*

Mechanics of Materials, 6th Ed. — *Gere, James M.*

Mechanistic and Synthetic Aspects of Organic and
Biological Electrochemistry: Proceedings — *Peters,
D.G.*

Mechanizing Proof: Computing, Risk, and Trust
— *MacKenzie, Donald*

Mechanobiology: Cartilage and Chondrocyte, Vol. 2
— *Stoltz, J.F.*

Mechthild of Magdeburg and Her Book: Gender and
the Making of Textual Authority — *Poor, Sara S.*

y Medalon — *Fallon, Jennifer*

Medea's Daughters: Forming and Performing the
Woman Who Kills — *Jones, Jennifer (b. 1961 -)*

Media Access: Social and Psychological Dimensions of
New Technology Use — *Bucy, Erik P.*

Media Analysis Techniques, 3rd Ed. — *Berger, Arthur
Asa*

y Media and American Courts: A Reference Handbook
— *Alexander, S.L.*

Media and Crime — *Jewkes, Yvonne*

Media and Democracy in Africa — *Hyden, Goran*

Media and Politics in Pacific Asia — *McCargo,
Duncan*

Media and Power in Post-Soviet Russia — *Zasurskii,
Ivan*

Media and Society: A Critical Perspective — *Berger,
Arthur Asa*

Media and the Path to Peace — *Wolfsfeld, Gadi*

Media and the Restyling of Politics: Consumerism,
Celebrity and Cynicism — *Corner, John*

Media at War: The Iraq Crisis — *Tumber, Howard*

Media Bureaucracies, and Foreign Aid: A
Comparative Analysis of the United States, the
United Kingdom, Canada, France, and Japan.
— *Van Belle, Douglas A.*

Media Democracy: How the Media Colonize Politics
— *Meyer, Thomas*

Media Economics: Theory and Practice, 3rd Ed.
— *Alexander, Alison*

Media Economics: Understanding Markets, Industries
and Concepts — *Albarran, Alan Brett*

Media/Impact: An Introduction to Mass Media, 7th
Ed. — *Biagi, Shirley*

Media in a Terrorized World: Reflections in the Wake
of 9/11 — *Venkatraman, S.*

The Media in Europe — *Kelly, Mary*

Media Literacy: Activities For Understanding the
Scripted world — *Endich, Roberta Solomon*

Media Man: Ted Turner's Improbable Empire
— *Auletta, Ken*

Media Management in the Age of Giants: Business
Dynamics of Journalism — *Herrick, Dennis F.*

Media Monoliths: How Great Media Brands Thrive
and Survive — *Tungate, Mark*

Media Mythmakers: How Journalists, Activists, and
Advertisers Mislead Us — *Radford, Benjamin*

Media Relations for Public Safety Professionals
— *Brown, Leo M.*

Media Representations of September 11th
— *Chermak, Steve*

Media Selling: Broadcast, Cable, Print and
Interactive, 3rd Ed. — *Warner, Charles*

Media Sports Stars: Masculinities and Moralities
— *Whannel, Garry*

Media, Technology, and Copyright: Integrating Law
and Economics — *Einhorn, Michael A.*

Media Unlimited: How the Torrent of Images and
Sounds Overwhelms Our Lives — *Gitlin, Todd*

Media Violence and Children: A Complete Guide for
Parents and Professionals — *Gentile, Douglas A.*

Media Violence — *Gerdes, Louise I.*

Mediate, Don't Litigate — *Lovenheim, Peter*

Mediated: How the Media Shapes Your World and the
Way You Live in It — *De Zengotita, Thomas*

Mediated: How the Media Shapes Your World and the
Way You Live in It — *Zengotita, Thomas*

Mediated Modeling: A System Dynamics Approach to
Environmental Consensus Building — *Van den Belt,
Marjan*

Mediated Modeling: System Dynamics Approach to
Environmental Consensus Building — *Belt, Marjan
Van Den*

Mediation and the Communication Matrix — *Waite,
C. Kaha*

Mediation Theory and Practice — *McCorkle, Suzanne*

Medical and Bioengineering Aspects of Electrical
Injuries — *Fish, Raymond M.*

Medical Confidentiality and Crime — *Michalowski,
Sabine*

Medical Conflicts in Early Modern London:
Patronage, Physicians, and Irregular Practitioners,
1550-1640. — *Pelling, Margaret*

The Medical Delivery Business: Health Reform,
Childbirth, and the Economic Order — *Perkins,
Barbara Bridgman*

Medical Directives and Powers of Attorney for
California, 2nd Ed. — *Irving, Shae*

Medical Education at St Bartholomew's Hospital
1123-1995 — *Waddington, Keir*

Medical Entomology: A Textbook on Public Health
and Veterinary Problems Caused by Arthropods,
Rev. Ed. — *Eldridge, Bruce F.*

Medical Epidemiology, 4th ed. — *Greenberg, Raymond
S.*

Medical Errors and Litigation: Investigation and Case
Preparation — *Abele, Jon R.*

Medical Ethics and the Elderly, 2nd Ed. — *Rai,
Gurcharan S.*

y Medical Firsts: From Hippocrates to the Human
Genome — *Adler, Robert E.*

The Medical History: Clinical Implications and
Emergency Prevention in Dental Settings
— *Pickett, Frieda*

Medical-Legal Aspects of Alcohol, 4th Ed. — *Garriott,
James C.*

The Medical Library Association Encyclopedic Guide
to Searching and Finding Health Information on
the Web, Vols. 1-3 — *Anderson, P.F.*

Medical Malpractice: A Physician's Sourcebook
— *Anderson, Richard E.*

Medical Management of Infectious Disease — *Grace,
Christopher*

c Medical Marvels: A Chapter Book — *Nichols,
Catherine*

Medical Meanings: A Glossary of Word Origins, 2nd
Ed. — *Haubrich, William S.*

Medical Microbiology and Immunology: Examination
and Board Review — *Levinson, Warren*

Medical Microbiology and Infection at a Glance. 2d
Ed. — *Gillespie, Stephen H.*

Medical Office Practice, 7th Ed. — *Atkinson, Phillip S.*

Medical Physics: Proceedings — *Vargas-Luna, Miguel*

Medical Records: Use and Abuse — *Tranberg, Heidi*

Medical-Surgical Care Planning, 4th Ed. — *Holloway,
Nancy M.*

Metallica: This Monster Lives: The Inside Story of Some Kind of Monster — *Berlinger, Joe*

Metallurgical Modeling for Aluminum Alloys: Proceedings — *Tiryakioglu, M.*

Metals and Chemical Change — *Johnson, D.A.*

Metals in Aquatic Systems: A Review of Exposure, Bioaccumulation, and Toxicity Models — *Paquin, Paul R.*

Metamorphoses de la dialectique dans les dialogues de Platon — *Dixsaut, Monique*

The Metamorphoses of Don Juan's Women: Early Parity to Late Modern Pathology — *Davies, Ann*

The Metamorphoses of Ovid — *Simpson, Michael*

Metamorphoses — *Martin, Charles*

Metamorphoses: Towards a Material Theory of Becoming — *Braidotti, Rosi*

Metamorphosis — *Normant, Serge*

Metamorphosis of the Private Sphere: Gardens and Objects in Tang-Song Poetry — *Allen, Joseph R.*

Metamorphosis of the Private Sphere: Gardens and Objects in Tang-Song Poetry — *Yang, Xiaoshan*

Metamorphosis: Poetry and Translation — *Tomlinson, Charles*

Metaphor, Allegory, and the Classical Tradition: Ancient Thought and Modern Revisions — *Boys-Stones, G.R.*

Metaphor and Musical Thought

Metaphor and Musical Thought — *Spitzer, Michael*

Metaphors of Oppression in Lusophone Historical Drama — *Wasserman, Bonnie S.*

Metaphysical Techniques That Really Work — *Davis, Audrey Craft*

The Metaphysician in the Dark — *Simic, Charles*

Metaphysics: Classic and Contemporary Readings, 2nd Ed. — *Hoy, Ronald*

The Metaphysics of Autonomy: The Reconciliation of Ancient and Modern Ideals of the Person — *Coeckelbergh, Mark*

The Metaphysics of Explanation: An Inquiry into the Nature and Philosophical Limits of Explanation — *Whitaker, Campbell*

The Metaphysics of the Incarnation: Thomas Aquinas to Duns Scotus — *Cross, Richard*

Metaprogramming GPUs with Sh — *McColl, Michael*

Metaromanticism, Aesthetics, Literature, Theory — *Hamilton, Paul*

Meteorites: A Petrologic, Chemical and Isotopic Synthesis — *Hutchison, Robert*

Meteorites, Ice, and Antarctica — *Cassidy, W.A.*

c Meteorology: Predicting the Weather — *Wills, Susan*

Methadone Matters: Evolving Community Methadone Treatment of Opiate Addiction — *Tober, Gillian*

Methodists and the Crucible of Race, 1930-1975 — *Murray, Peter C.*

Methodists and the Crucible of the Race, 1930-1975 — *Murray, Peter C.*

A Methodology of the Heart: Evoking Academic and Daily Life — *Pelias, Ronald J.*

Methods of Applied Mathematics with a MATLAB Overview — *Davis, J.H.*

Methods of Meta-Analysis: Correcting Error and Bias in Research Findings, 2nd Ed. — *Hunter, John E.*

Methods of Resolving Conflicts between Treaties — *Sadat-Akhavi, Seyed Ali*

Methods of Social Movements Research — *Klandermans, Bert*

The Metre of Beowulf: A Constraint-Based Approach — *Getty, Michael*

Metro Girl — *Evanovich, Janet*

Metro-Land: British Empire Exhibition Number — *Turner, E.S.*

Metroland — *Barnes, Julian*

The Metrology Handbook — *Bucher, Jay L.*

Metropolis and Nature on the American Frontier: From Indian Non-Cities to Thoreau's City, from Industrial Metropolises to the Ecological City — *Sioli, Marco*

Metropolis — *Gaffney, Elizabeth*

Metropolitan Area WDM Networks: An AWG Based Approach — *Maier, Martin*

Metropolitan Governance Without Metropolitan Government? — *Phares, Don*

Metropolitan Railways: Rapid Transit in America — *Middleton, William D. (b. 1928 -)*

Metrum De Praelio Apud Bannockburn — *Baston, Robert*

Meuse-Argonne Diary: A Division Commander in World War 1 — *Wright, William M.*

y The Mexican American Experience: An Encyclopedia — *Meier, Matt S.*

Mexican Americans and the Law: El Pueblo Unido Jamas Sera Vencido! — *Anaya Valencia, Reynaldo*

The Mexican Economy, 1870-1930: Essays on the Economic History of Institutions, Revolution, and Growth — *Bortz, Jeffrey L.*

The Mexican Filmography, 1916 through 2001 — *Wilt, David E.*

Mexican Immigration — *Gelletly, LeeAnne*

Mexican Masculinities — *Irwin, Robert McKee*

Mexican Spirituality: Its Sources and Mission in the Earliest Guadalupan Sermons — *Schulte, Francisco Raymond*

Mexican Workers and American Dreams: Immigration, Repatriation, and California Farm Labor: 1900-1939 — *Guerin-Gonzales, Camille*

Mexicana Encounters: The Making of Social Identities on the Borderlands — *Fregoso, Rosa Linda*

Mexico: An Encyclopedia of Contemporary Culture and History — *Coerver, Don M.*

c Mexico and Central America: A Fiesta of Cultures, Crafts, and Activities for Ages 8-12 — *Turck, Mary C.*

Mexico and the United States: Ambivalent Vistas, 3rd Ed. — *Raat, W. Dirk*

The Mexico City Reader — *Gallo, Ruben*

Mexico under Fox — *Rienner, Lynne*

Mexico Under Fox — *Rubio, Luis*

Mexico under Siege: Popular Resistance to Presidential Despotism — *Hodges, Donald*

Mexico's Pivotal Democracy Election: Candidates, Voters, Campaign Effects, and the Presidential Campaign of 2000 — *Dominguez, Jorge I.*

Mexoamerican Lithic Technology: Experimentation and Interpretation: Proceedings — *Hirth, Kenneth G.*

"Mi Raza Primero" (My People First): Nationalism, Identity and Insurgency in the Chicano Movement in Los Angeles--1966-1978 — *Chavez, Ernesto*

MI5 and Ireland, 1939-1945: The Official History — *O'Halpin, Eunan*

c Mia Hamm: Soccer Star — *Zarzycki, Daryl Davis*

Mia Tells It Like It Is — *Cabot, Meg*

Miami and the Siege of Chicago — *Mailer, Norman*

Miami Blues — *Willeford, Charles Ray*

Micah: A New Translation with Introduction and Commentary — *Andersen, Francis I.*

Michael Chekhov — *Chamberlain, Franc*

The Michael Eric Dyson Reader — *Dyson, Michael Eric*

c Michael Faraday and the Discovery of Electromagnetism — *Zannos, Susan*

Michael Faraday and the Electrical Century — *Morus, Iwan Rhys*

Michael Finney's Consumer Confidential: The Money-Saving Secrets They Don't Want You to Know — *Finney, Michael*

Michael Mann — *Steensland, Mark*

Michael Moore Is a Big Fat Stupid White Man — *Hardy, David T.*

Michael Oakeshott on Hobbes — *Tregenza, Ian*

Michael, Prince of Greece — *Philip, Franklin*

y Michael Rosen's Sad Book (Illus. by Blake, Quentin) — *Rosen, Michael*

Michael Servetus: Intellectual Giant, Humanist, and Martyr — *Hillar, Marian*

Michael William Balfe: His Life and His English Operas — *Tyldesley, William*

Michaelangelo — *Langley, Andrew*

The Michaels Book of Arts and Crafts — *Cusik, Dawn*

Michel de Cereau: Le marcheur blesse — *Dosse, Francois*

Michel de Montaigne: Accidental Philosopher — *Hartle, Ann*

Michel Foucault: Form and Power — *Beer, Dan*

Michel Saint-Denis and the Shaping of the Modern Actor — *Baldwin, Jane*

Michelangelo and the Finger of God — *Barolsky, Paul*

Michelangelo and the Reinvention of the Human Body — *Hall, James (b. 1963 -)*

c Michelangelo — *Richmond, Robin*

Michelangelo — *Sateren, Shelley Swanson*

c Michelangelo — *Stanley, Diane*

Michelangelo: Drawings and Other Treasures from the Casa Buonarroti, Florence — *Ragionieri, Pina*

Michelangelo & the Pope's Ceiling — *King, Ross*

The Michelin Men: Driving an Empire — *Lottman, Herbert R.*

Michigan Trees: A Guide to the Trees of the Great Lakes Region, Rev. and Updated Ed. — *Barnes, Burton V.*

c Mickey Mantle — *Marlin, John*

Micro--and Nanosystems: Proceedings — *La Van, David A.*

Micro Energy Systems — *Knowles, M.*

Micro Radio and the FCC: Media Activism and the Struggle over Broadcast Policy — *Opel, Andy*

Microarray Gene Expression Data Analysis: A Beginner's Guide — *Causton, Helen C.*

Microarrays and Microplates: Applications in Biomedical Sciences — *Day, S. Ye*

Microbial Biofilms — *Ghannoum, Mahmoud*

Microbial Contamination Control in Parneteral Manufacturing — *Williams, Kevin L.*

Microbial Diversity and Bioprospecting — *Bull, Alan T.*

Microbial Genomes — *Fraser, Claire M.*

The Microbial Models of Molecular Biology: From Genes to Genomes — *Davis, Rowland H.*

Microbial Threats to Health: Emergence, Detection, and Response — *Smolinski, Mark S.*

Microbiological Contamination Control in Pharmaceutical Clean Rooms — *Halls, Nigel*

Microbiology: PreTest Self-Assessment and Review, 11th Ed. — *Kettering, James D.*

Microbiology Recall — *Diallo, Alfa Omar*

Microchannels and Minichannels: Proceedings — *Kandlikar, Satish G.*

Microeconomic Theory: Basic Principles and Extensions, 9th Ed. — *Nicholson, Walter*

Microeconomic Theory: Conepts at Connections — *Weitzstein, Michael Eugene*

Microeconomics: Behavior, Institutions and Evolution — *Bowles, Samuel*

Microeconomics for Public Decisions — *Steinmann, Anne C.*

Microelectrode Recording in Movement Disorder Surgery — *Israel, Zvi*

Microelectronic Circuit Design. 2nd Ed. — *Blalock, Travis N.*

Microelectronic Circuits. 5th Ed. — *Sedra, Adel S.*

Microelectronics Technology and Devices: Proceedings — *Martino, J.A.*

Microfacies of Carbonatre Rocks: Analysis, Interpretaion and Application — *Flugel, Erik*

Microfinance Poverty Assessment Tool — *Henry, Carla*

The Microfinance Revolution: Sustainable Finance for the Poor — *Robinson, Marguerite S.*

Microhabitats, Set 2

Micronutrient Deficiencies in the First Months of Life: Proceedings — *Delange, Francois M.*

Microresonators ad Building Blocks for VLSI Photonics: Proceedings — *International School of Quantum Electronics*

y Microscopic Life — *Walker, Richard*

c Microscopic Life in the Garden — *Word, Brian R.*

c Microscopic Life in your Body — *Word, Brian R.*

Microscopy of Semiconducting Materials 2003: Proceedings — *Midgley, P.A.*

Microsoft Biztalk Server 2004 Unleashed — *Woodgate, Scott*

Microsoft Direct3D Programming: Kick Start — *Walnum, Clayton*

Microsoft Excel 2003: Specialist and Expert — *Rutkosky, Nita*

Microsoft Excel 2003: Specialist — *Rutkosky, Nita*

Microsoft Frontpage For Windows 2002 — *Hester, Nolan*

Microsoft IIS 6.0 Administrator's Pocket Consultant — *Stanek, William R.*

Microsoft Manual of Style for Technical Publications — *Microsoft Corporation*

Microsoft .NET Distributed Applications: Integrating XML Web Services and .NET Remoting — *MacDonald, Matthew*

Microsoft Office 2003 — *Rutkosky, Nita*

Microsoft Office 2003: Specialist — *Rutkosky, Nita*

Microsoft Office Brief Edition: 2003 — *Rutkosky, Nita*

Microsoft Office OneNote 2003 Step by Step — *Weverka, Peter*

Microsoft Office Outlook 2003 Inside Out — *Boyce, Jim*

Microsoft Office Visio 2003 Inside Out — *Walker, Mark H.*

Microsoft Office Visio 2003 Step by Step — *Lemke, Judy*

Microsoft Office Word 2003 for Windows — *Langer, Maria*

Microsoft Platform Ahead — *Platt, David S.*

Microsoft PowerPoint 2003 Specialist — *Rutkosky, Nita*

Microsoft Rebooted: How Bill Gates and Steve Ballmer Reinvented Their Company — *Slater, Robert*

Microsoft Reporting Services in Action — *Lachev, Teo*

Microsoft SQL Server 2000 Reporting Services Step by Step — *Misner, Stacia*

Microsoft Windows Command-Line Administrator's Pocket Consultant — *Stanek, William R.*

Microsoft Windows Movie Maker 2: Do Amazing Things — *Buechler, John*

Microsoft Windows Scripting Self-Paced Learning Guide — *Wilson, Ed*

Microsoft Windows Server 2003 Inside Out — *Stanek, William R.*

Microsoft Windows Server 2003 PKI and Certificate Security — *Komar, Brian*

Microsoft Windows Server 2003 Unleashed — *Morimoto, Rand*

Microsoft Windows XP Inside Out, 2nd Ed. — *Bott, Ed*

Microsoft Windows XP Inside Out Deluxe, 2nd Ed. — *Bott, Ed*

Microsoft Windows XP Plain and Simple, 2nd Ed. — *Joyce, Jerry*

Microsoft Windows XP Step by Step, 2nd Ed. — *Online Training Solutions (Firm)*

Microsoft Windows XP Step by Step, Deluxe 2nd Ed. — *Online Training Solutions, Inc.*

Microsoft Word 2003 — *Rutkosky, Nita*

Microsoft Word 2003 Expert — *Rutkosky, Nita*

Microsoft Word 2003: Specialist and Expert — *Rutkosky, Nita*

Microstrip and Printed Antenna Design — *Bancroft, Randy*

Microstructure of Martensite: Why It Forms and How It Gives Rise to the Shape-Memory Effect — *Bhattacharya, Kaushik*

Microsystems Technology: Fabrication, Test and Reliability — *Boussey, Jumana*

Microwave and Radio Frequency Applications: Proceedings — *Folz, Diane C.*

Microwave Passive Direction Finding — *Lipsky, Stephen E.*

Microwave Ring Circuits and Related Structures. 2nd Ed. — *Chang, Kai*

Mid-Century Modern Dinnerware: A Pictorial Guide: Red Wing to Winfield — *Pratt, Michael E.*

Mid-Century Modern Dinnerware: A Pictorial Guide Redwing to Winfield — *Hardbound, Michael Pratt*

Mid-Ocean Ridges: Hydrothermal Interactions Between the Lithosphere and Oceans — *German, Christopher R.*

c A Mid-Semester Night's Dream — *Meacham, Margaret*

Midas (Read by Lawlor, Patrick G.). Audiobook Review — *Andrews, Russell*

Midas — *Andrews, Midas*

c The Middle Ages

y Middle Ages in Literature for Youth: A Guide and Resource Book — *Barnhouse, Rebecca*

The Middle Ages in Literature for Youth: A Guide and Resource Book — *Price, Annie*

c Middle and Junior High School Library Catalog, 8th Ed. — *Barnhouse, Rebecca*

The Middle-Class City: Transforming Space and Time in Philadelphia, 1876-1926 — *Hepp, John Henry*

The Middle-Class City: Transforming Space and Time in Philadelphia, 1876-1926 — *Hepp, John Henry*

Middle-Class Culture in the Nineteenth Century: America, Australia and Britian — *Young, Linda*

Middle Class Identity and Education: A Review Essay — *Brantlinger, Ellen*

Middle Ear and Mastoid Surgery — *Haberman, Rex S.*

Middle Ear Surgery: Recent Advances and Future Directions — *Jahnke, Klaus*

Middle Earth — *Cole, Henri*

Middle East Illusions: Including Peace in the Middle East?, Reflections on Justice and Nationhood — *Chomsky, Noam*

The Middle East Under Rome — *Sartre, Maurice*

The Middle East, Vol. 5 — *Creative Media Applications*

The Middle East Water Question: Hydropolitics and the Global Economy — *Allan, J.A.*

A Middle English Chronicle of the First Crusade: The Caxton Eracles — *Cushing, Dana*

Middle English Poetry: Texts and Traditions: Essays in Honour of Derek Pearsall — *Minnis, A.J.*

Middle Grades Education: A Reference Handbook — *Williams-Boyd, Pat*

The Middle of Everything: Memoirs of Motherhood — *Herman, Michelle*

Middle Path in Math Instruction: Solutions for Improving Math Education — *An, Shuhua*

Middle School Science with Calculators: Science Experiments Using Vernier Sensors with the LabPro or the CBL2 — *Volz, Don*

Middlebrow Annoyances: American Drama in the 21st Century — *Weber, Myles*

Middlebrow Moderns: Popular American Women Writers of the 1920s — *Botshon, Lisa*

Middlesex — *Eugenides, Jeffrey*

The Middling Sort and the Politics of Social Reformation: Colchester, 1570-1640 — *Smith, Richard Dean (b. 1950-)*

Midgic — *Lochhead, Douglas*

Midnight Assassin: A Murder in America's Heartland — *Bryan, Patricia L.*

Midnight Assassin: Murder in America's Heartland — *Bryan, Patricia L.*

Midnight at the Dragon Cafe — *Bates, Judy Fong*

Midnight at the Palace: My Life as a Fabulous Cockette — *Tent, Pam*

Midnight (Read by Charles, J.). Audiobook Review — *Koontz, Dean*

y The Midnight Band of Mercy — *Blaine, Michael*

Midnight Blue — *Fisk, Pauline*

c Midnight — *Wilson, Jacqueline*

Midnight Cab — *Nichol, James W.*

The Midnight Disease: The Drive to Write, Writer's Block, and the Creative Brain — *Flaherty, Alice W.*

y Midnight over Sanctaphrax (Illus. by Riddell, Chris) — *Stewart, Paul*

Midnight Pass (Read by Brick, Scott). Audiobook Review — *Kaminsky, Stuart M.*

c The Midnight Ship — *Impey, Rose*

Midnight Thirsts — *Herren, Greg*

The Midshipman Culture and Educational Reform: The U.S. Naval Academy 1946-76 — *Forney, Todd A.*

A Midsummer Night's Scream: A Jane Jeffry Mystery — *Churchill, Jill*

y Midwinter Nightingale — *Aiken, Joan*

Midwiving Subjects in Shakespeare's England — *Bicks, Caroline*

c Miffy's Happy New Year! — *Bruna, Dick*

c The Mighty Asparagus (Illus. by Radunsky, Vladimir) — *Radunsky, Vladimir*

The Mighty Experiment: Free Labor versus Slavery in British Emancipation — *Drescher, Seymour*

A Mighty Fortress: A New History of the German People — *Ozment, Steven*

c Mighty Jackie: The Strike-Out Queen — *Moss, Marissa*

c Mighty Maddie (Illus. by Lum, Bernice) — *Murphy, Stuart J.*

c The Mighty Mississippi — *Simon, Charnan*

The Mighty Niagara: One River, Two Frontiers — *Jackson, John N.*

The Mighty Niagra: One River, Two Frontiers — *Jackson, John N.*

Migraine and Other Headaches — *Silberstein, Stephen D.*

Migrants and Militants: Fun and Urban Violence in Pakistan — *Verkaaik, Oskar*

The Migrant's Table: Meals and Memories in Bengali-American Households' — *Ray, Krishnendu*

Migration and Immigration: A Global View — *Toro-Morn, Maura I.*

Migration between States and Markets — *Entzinger, Han*

Migration, Common Property, Resources and Environmental Degradation: Interlinkages in India's Arid and Semi-arid Regions — *Gulati, S.C.*

Migration in the Asia Pacific: Population, Settlement and Citizenship Issues — *Hawksley, Charles*

Migration, Mujercitas, and Medicine Men: Living in Urban Mexico — *Napolitano, Valentina*

Migration: New and Selected Poems — *Merwin, W.S.*

The Migration of Butterflies — *Malyon, Carol*

Migration Policies in Flux: Changing Patterns of Inclusion and Exclusion — *Boswell, Christina*

Migration: The Boundaries of Equality and Justice — *Jordan, Bill*

The Mikado in Full Score — *Gilbert, W. S.*

The Mikado: Vocal score — *Gilbert, W. S.*

Mike, Mike, and Me — *Markham, Wendy*

c Mike Mulligan and His Steam Shovel (Read by Ross, Rod). Audiobook Review — *Burton, Virginia Lee*

c Mike Mulligan and His Steam Shovel (Read by Simon, Stephen). Audiobook Review — *Burton, Virginia Lee*

c Mike Mulligan and His Steam Shovel (Read by Ross, Rod). Audiobook Review — *Burton, Virginia Lee*

Mike Weir: The Road to the Masters — *Rubenstein, Lorne*

Miko: "No Bath! No Way!" (Illus. by Roehe, Stephanie) — *Weninger, Brigitte*

Mikrologien. Literarische und Philosophische Figuren des Kleinen — *Schuller, Marianne*

Milady's Revenge — *Herries, Anne*

Milady's Standard Fundamentals for Estheticians, 9th Ed. — *Gerson, Joel*

Milch und Acker. Koperliche und Sexuelle Aspekte der Religiosen Erfahrung. Am Besipiel der Bussdidaxe des Strickers — *Dworschak, Helmut*

c Mildew on the Wall — *Henshon, Suzanna E.*

Mile Deep and Black as Pitch: An Oral History of the Franklin and Sterling Hill Mines — *Papa, Carrie*

c Mile-High Apple Pie (Illus. by Gardiner, Lindsey) — *Langston, Laura*

Miles — *Noel, Gerard*

Miles Gone By: A Literary Autobiography — *Buckley, William F., Jr.*

Milestones in Computer Science and Information Technology — *Reilly, Edwin D.*

Milestones in Systematics — *Williams, David M.*

c The Milestones Project: Celebrating Childhood around the World — *Steckel, Richard*

Milicia General en la Edad Moderna: 'El Batallon' de Don Rafael de la Barreda y Figueroa — *Hernan, Enrique Garcia*

Militant Islam Reaches America — *Pipes, Daniel*

The Militant Suffrage Movement: Citizenship and Resistance in Britain, 1860-1930 — *Mayhall, Laura E. Nym*

The Militarization and Weaponization of Space — *Mowthorpe, Matthew*

Militarization, Democracy and Development: The Perils of Praetorianism in Latin America — *Bowman, Kirk S.*

c Military Aircraft of WW I — *Hansen, Ole Steen*

c Military Aircraft of WW II — *Hansen, Ole Steen*

The Military and Naval History of the Rebellion in the United States: With Biographical Sketches of Deceased Officers — *Tenney, William Jewett*

The Military and Politics in Africa: From Engagement to Democratic and Constitutional Control — *Kieh, George Klay*

The Military and Politics in Postauthoritarian Chile — *Weeks, Gregory*

Military and Society in Russia, 1450-1917 — *Lohr, Eric*

Military Aviation — *Ader, Clement*

The Military Balance, 2003-2004 — *Langton, Christopher*

Military Commanders: The 100 Greatest Throughout History — *Cawthorne, Nigel*

Military Executions During World War I — *Oram, Gerard Christopher*

Military History of Ancient Israel — *Gabriel, Richard A.*

The Military History of the Soviet Union — *Higham, Robin*

The Military History of Tsarist Russia — *Higham, Robin*

Military Intervention: Cases in Context for the Twenty-First Century — *Lahneman, William J.*

Military Politics and Democratization in Indonesia — *Honna, Jun*

The Militia and the Right to Arms, or, How the Second Amendment Fell Silent — *Uviller, H. Richard*

Militias in the New Millennium: A Test of Smelser's Theory of Collective Behavior — *Weeber, Stan*

Milk and Honey--But no Gold: Postwar Migration to Western Australia, 1945-1964 — *Peters, Nonja*

Milk — *Steinke, Darcey*

Milk: Its Remarkable Contribution to Human Health and Well-Being — *Patton, Stuart*

Milk — *Steinke, Darcey*

c Milk Snakes — *Feldman, Heather*

c Milkweed — *Spinelli, Jerry*

Mill Girls and Strangers: Single Women's Independent Migration in England, Scotland, and the United States, 1850-1881 — *Gordon, Wendy M.*

The Mill House — *McCusker, Paul*

Mill on God: The Pervasiveness and Elusiveness of Mill's Religious Thought — *Sell, Alan P.F.*

c The Mill on the Floss (Read by Watson, Emily). Audiobook Review — *Eliot, George*

Millard Fillmore, Mon Amour — *Blumenthal, John*

Millenium Development Goals for Health: Rising to the Challenges — *World Bank*

Millennial Ecuador: Critical Essays on Cultural Transformations and Social Dynamics — *Whitten, Norman E., Jr.*

The Millennials: Americans Born 1977 to 1994, 2nd Ed. — *New Strategist Editors*

The Millennium Election: Communicaiton in the 2000 Campaign — *Kaid, Lynda Lee*

Title Index

Mon Oncle — *Tati, Jacques*

c Mon Premier Livre de Mots — *Pitchall, Chez*

Mona Lisa Smiled a Little — *Wyatt, Rachael*

c Mona the Monster Girl (Illus. by James, J. Alison)
— *Petz, Moritz*

Monaca, Moglie, Serva, Cortigiana: Vita e immagine
delle donne tra Rinascimento e Controriforma
— *Matthews-Grieco, Sara F.*

The Monarch Butterfly: Biology & Conservation
— *Oberhauser, Karen S.*

The Monarchia Controversy: An Historical Study with
Accompanying Translations of Dante Alighieri's
Monarchia, Guido Vernani's Refutation of the
Monarchia Composed by Dante, and Pope John
XXII's Bull, Si Fratrum — *Cassell, Anthony K.*

The Monarchia Controversy: An Historical Study with
Accompanying Translations of Dante Alighieri's
Monarchia, Guido Vernani's Refutation of the
Monarchia Composed by Dante, and Pope John
XXII's Bull Si Fratrum — *Cassell, Anthony K.*

Monarchies, States Generals and Parliaments: The
Netherlands in the Fifteenth and Sixteenth
Centuries — *Koenigsberger, H.G.*

c Monarchs — *Ross, Stewart*

The Monarchy of England, Vol. 1 — *Starkey, David*

Monastic Life in Medieval Daoism: A Cross-Cultural
Perspective — *Kohn, Livia*

Monday Mourning — *Reichs, Kathy*

Mondo Homo: Your Essential Guide to Queer Pop
Culture — *Andreoli, Richard*

The Monetary History of Gold: A Documentary
History, 1660-1999 — *Duckenfield, Mark*

Monetary Policy in the Euro Area: Strategy and
Decision-Making at the European Central Bank
— *Issing, Otmar*

Monetary Policy Report: January 2003

Monetary Policy: Rules and Transmission Mechanisms
— *Loayza, Norman*

Monetary Strategies for Joining the Euro — *Szapary,
Gyorgy*

Monetary Theory and Policy — *Walsh, Carl E.*

Monetary Theory — *Rabin, Alan A.*

The Monetary Theory of Production — *Graziani,
Augusto*

Monetary Union in South America: Lessons from
EMU — *Arestis, Philip*

Money 201: More Personal Finance Advice for Every
Canadian — *Roseman, Ellen*

Money: A Suicide Note — *Amis, Martin*

Money and Security: Troops, Monetary Policy and
West Germany's Relations with the United States
and Britain, 1950-1971 — *Zimmermann, Hubert*

Money and the Age of Shakespeare: Essays in New
Economic Criticism — *Woodbridge, Linda*

Money and the Nation State: The Financial
Revolution, Government and the World Monetary
System — *Dowd, Kevin*

The Money Book for the Young, Fabulous and Broke
— *Orman, Suze*

Money, Credit, and the Role of the State: Essays in
Honour of Augusto Graziani — *Arena, Richard*

Money Demand in Europe: An Empirical Approach
— *Muller, Christian*

Money for the Nothing: Real Wealth, Financial
Fantasies, and the Economy of the Future
— *Bootle, Roger P.*

Money in Their Own Name: The Feminist Voice in
Poverty Debate in Canada, 1970-1995 — *McKeen,
Wendy*

The Money Is the Gravy: Finding the Career That
Nourishes You — *Clark, John*

Money Laundering Counter-Measures in the
European Union: A New Paradigm of Security
Governance Versus Fundamental Legal Principles
— *Mitsilegas, Valsamis*

Money Markets and Politics: A Study of European
Financial Integration and Monetary Policy Options
— *Forssbaeck, Jens*

Money Matters: Essays in Honour of Alan Walters
— *Minford, Patrick*

y Money, Money, Money: Where It Comes from, How
to Save It, Spend It, and Make It (Illus. by Davila,
Claudia) — *Drobot, Eve*

Money, Politics and Health Care: Reconstructing the
Federal-Provincial Partnership — *Lazar, Harvey*

The Money Primary: The New Politics of the Early
Presidential Nomination Process — *Goff, Michael J.*

y Money Sense for Kids! — *Harman, Hollis Page*

The Money Shot: Trash, Class, and the Making of TV
Talk Shows — *Grindstaff, Laura*

Money Troubles: Legal Strategies to Cope with Your
Debts, 9th Ed. — *Leonard, Robin*

Moneyball: The Art of Winning an Unfair Game
(Read by Brick, Scott). Audiobook Review
— *Lewis, Michael*

Moneyball: The Art of Winning an Unfair Game
— *Lewis, Michael*

Moneymaker: How an Amateur Poker Player Turned
$40 into $2.5 Million at the World Series of Poker
— *Moneymaker, Chris*

y Mongo: Adventures in Trash — *Botha, Ted*

The Mongol Reply — *Schutz, Benjamin M.*

Monitoring Educational Performance in the
Caribbean — *Di Gropello, Emanuela*

Monitoring Sweatshops: Workers, Consumers, and the
Global Apparel Industry — *Esbenshade, Jill*

c A Monkey among Us (Illus. by Horowitz, Dave)
— *Horowitz, Dave*

c A Monkey Baby Grows Up (Illus. by Hewett, Richard)
— *Hewett, Joan*

c Monkey Business — *Edwards, Wallace*

Monkey Business — *Mlynowski, Sarah*

y Monkey Dancing: A Father, Two Kids, and a Journey
to the Ends of the Earth — *Glick, Daniel*

Monkey Dancing — *Glick, Daniel*

c Monkey-Man — *Glover, Sandra*

Monkey See, Monkey Do — *Anderson, Michael*

Monkey Trap — *Denning, Lee*

Monkey Wrench — *Smith, Barbara*

The Monkey Wrench Gang — *Abbey, Edward*

The Monkey's Mask: Identity, Memory, Narrative and
Voice — *Kearney, Chris*

Monkology: 13 Stories from the World of Private Eye
Ivan Monk — *Phillips, Gary*

Monkology — *McMillan, Dennis*

Mono: A Developer's Notebook — *Dumbill, Edd*

Monochrome Memories: Nostalgia and Style in Retro
America — *Grainge, Paul*

The Monotheists: Jews, Christians, and Muslims in
Conflict and Competition — *Peters, F.E.*

c The Monroe Doctrine: An End to European Colonies
in America — *Alagna, Magdalena*

Monsieur Levy — *Villemain, Marc*

Monsieur Proust — *Albaret, Celeste*

Monsoon — *Akib, Jamel*

y Monsoon Summer — *Perkins, Mitali*

c Monster Bones: The Story of a Dinosaur Fossil (Illus.
by Lilly, Matthew) — *Bailey, Jacqui*

c Monster Bones: The Story of a Dinosaur Fossil
— *Bailey, Jacui*

The Monster Book of Canadian Monsters
— *Colombo, John Robert*

Monster: Gay Adventures in American Machismo
— *Bouldrey, Brian*

c Monster in the Mountains — *Peacock, Shane*

c The Monster Mall and Other Spooky Poems (Illus. by
Sinnott, Adrian C.) — *Steinberg, David*

Monster of God: The Man-Eating Predator in the
Jungles of History and the Mind — *Quammen,
David*

c The Monster Show: Everything You Never Knew
about Monsters (Illus. by Harper, Charise Mericle)
— *Harper, Charise Mericle*

c The Monster That Ate the Universe — *Stevens, Roger*

The Monster That Is History: History, Violence, and
Fictional Writing in Twentieth-Century China
— *Wang, David Der-wei*

c The Monster Trap (Illus. by Morrissey, Dean)
— *Morrissey, Dean*

Monsters and Angels: Surviving a Career in Music
— *Bernstein, Seymour*

Monsters and Grotesques in Medieval Manuscripts
— *Bovey, Alixe*

c Monsters — *Herbst, Judith*

Monsters: Evil Beings, Mythical Beasts, and All
Manners of Imaginary Terrors — *Gilmore, David*

Monsters, Gods and Heroes: Approaching the Epic in
Literature. Audiobook Review — *Shutt, Timothy B.*

Monsters: Human Freaks in America's Gilded Age:
The Photographs of Chas. Eisenmann — *Mitchell,
Michael*

c Monsters Party All Night Long — *Lane, Adam J.B.*

Monstrosities: Bodies and British Romanticism
— *Youngquist, Paul*

Monstrous Adversary: The Life of Edward de Vere,
17th Earl of Oxford — *Nelson, Alan H.*

The Montana Frontier: One Woman's West — *Litz,
Joyce*

Monte Alban: Settlement Patterns at the Ancient
Zapotec Capital — *Blanton, Richard E.*

Monte Carlo Method in the Physical Sciences:
Celebrating the 50th Anniversary of the Metropolis
Algorithm: Proceedings — *Gubernatis, James E.*

Monterey, Carmel, Big Sur, Santa Cruz — *Harris,
Richard (b. 1947 -)*

Montesquieu and the Spirit of Modernity
— *Carrithers, David W.*

Montesquieu — *Auger, Catherine Volpilhac*

The Montessori Method: The Origins of an
Educational Innovation, Including an Abridged and
Annotated Edition of Maria Montessori's "The
Montessori Method" — *Gutek, Gerald Lee*

Monteverdi's Musical Theatre — *Carter, Tim*

c The Montgomery Bus Boycott — *Stein, R. Conrad*

Montgomery County, Missouri, Vol. 15 — *Weant,
Kenneth*

y Montmorency on the Rocks: Doctor, Aristocrat,
Murderer? — *Updale, Eleanor*

y Montmorency: Thief, Liar, Gentleman? (Read by Fry,
Stephen). Audiobook Review — *Updale, Eleanor*

Montmorency: Thief, Liar, Gentleman? — *Updale,
Eleanor*

The Montreal Massacre: A Story of Membership
Categorization Analysis — *Eglin, Peter*

Montreal Protocol on Substances that Deplete the
Ozone Layer: Report of the Technology and
Economic Assessment Panel, April 2002, vols. 1-3

Montreal Stories — *Blaise, Clark*

Monturiol's Dream: The Extraordinary Story of the
Submarine Inventor Who Wanted to Save the
World — *Stewart, Matthew*

The Monument: Art and Vulgarity in Saddam
Hussein's Iraq — *Makiya, Kanan*

Monumental Melville: The Formation of a Literary
Career — *Dryden, Edgar A.*

Monumental Propaganda — *Voinovich, Vladimir*

Monumental Sites — *Terraroli, Valerio*

Monuments and Memory: History and Representation
in Lowell, Massachusetts — *Norkunas, Martha*

Monuments of Progress: Modernization and Public
Health in Mexico City, 1876-1910 — *Agostoni,
Claudia*

Monuments to the Lost Cause: Women, Art, and the
Landscapes of Southern Memory — *Mills, Cynthia
(b. 1947 -)*

c Moo! (Illus. by Sharp, Melanie) — *Dolan, Penny*

c Moo Who? (Illus. by Graves, Keith) — *Palatini,
Margie*

The Moody Pews: A 52 Week Devotional for the
Flower Child/Baby Boomer — *Brown, Sandra L.*

c The Moon — *Simon, Seymour*

c The Moon — *York, Pat*

c The Moon Came Down on Milk Street (Illus. by
Gralley, Jean) — *Gralley, Jean*

Moon Handbooks: Acapulco — *Whipperman, Bruce*

The Moon in Its Flight — *Sorrentino, Gilbert*

The Moon in Our Hands — *Dyja, Thomas*

The Moon in Swampland — *Robertson, M.P.*

y Moon Observer's Guide — *Grego, Peter*

The Moon Pool — *Marritt, A.*

The Moon Pool — *Merritt, A.*

c Moon Runner — *Marsden, Carolyn*

Moon Shadows — *Roberts, Nora*

c Moondog (Illus. by Heo, Yumi) — *Hoffman, Alice*

y Moonlight and Mischief — *Woodward, Rhonda*

Moonrush: Improving Life on Earth with the Moon's
Resources — *Wingo, Dennis*

Moons and Planets, 5th Ed. — *Hartmann, William K.*

c Mooove Over!: A Book about Counting by Twos
(Illus. by Meisel, Paul) — *Beil, Karen Magnuson*

The Moorlands of England and Wales: An
Environmental History — *Simmons, I.G.*

c Moose and Mouse — *West, Colin*

c Moosekitos: A Moose Family Reunion (Illus. by Cole,
Henry) — *Palatini, Margie*

The Moral Advantage: How to Succeed in Business by
Doing the Right Thing — *Damon, William*

Moral and Political Reasoning in Environmental
Practice — *Light, Andrew*

Moral, Believing Animals: Human Personhood and
Culture — *Smith, Christian*

The Moral Capital of Leaders: Why Virtue Matters
— *Sison, Alejo Jose G.*

Moral Capitalism: Reconciling Private Interest with
the Public Good — *Young, Stephen*

The Moral Circle and the Self: Chinese and Western
Approaches — *Chong, Kim Chong*

Moral Circle and the Self: Chinese and Western
Approaches — *Chong, Kim Chong*

Moral Courage: Ethics in Action — *Kidder, Rushworth
M.*

A Moral Critique of Development: In Search of
Global Responsibilities — *Ufford, Van*

Moral Development, Self, and Identity — *Lapsley,
Daniel K.*

Murder on the Rails: The True Story of the Detective Who Unlocked the Shocking Secrets of the Boxcar Serial Killer — *Palmini, William G., Jr.*

Murder on the Reservation: American Indian Crime Fiction: Aims and Achievements — *Browne, Ray Broadus*

Murder on the Salsette — *Allen, Conrad*

The Murder Room (Read by Jayston, Michael). Audiobook Review — *James, P.D.*

The Murder Room — *James, P.D.*

Murder, She Wrote: A Vote for Murder — *Bain, Donald*

Murder Suicide — *Ablow, Keith*

Murder Two: The Second Casebook of Forensic Detection — *Evans, Colin*

Murder Walks the Plank (Read by Reading, Kate). Audiobook Review — *Hart, Carolyn*

The Murderer Next Door: Why the Mind Is Designed to Kill — *Buss, David*

Murdering Holiness: The Trials of Franz Creffield and George Mitchell — *Phillips, Jim*

Murdering McKinley: The Making of Theodore Roosevelt's America — *Rauchway, Eric*

y Murdering Mr. Lincoln: A New Detection of the 19th Century's Most Famous Crime (Read by Cashman, Dan). Audiobook Review — *Higham, Charles*

Murders and Other Confusions — *Emerson, Kathy Lynn*

Muriel Rukeyser's "The Book of the Dead" — *Dayton, Tim*

Muriella Pent — *Smith, Russell*

y Murkmere — *Elliott, Patricia*

Murphy's Favorite Channels — *Dunmore, 4th Earl of Murphy's Favourite Channels — *Flambard, John Murray*

Musashi #9: Vol. 1 — *Miyaki, Takahashi*

Muscle — *Hotten, Jon*

Muscle Strength — *Shrawan, Kumar*

Muscles, Bones, and Skin, 2nd Ed. — *Knight, Sian*

c Muscles — *Fitzpatrick, Anne*

Muscular Dystrophy Sourcebook — *Shannon, Joyce Brennfleck*

Muscular System — *Adams, Amy*

c Muscular System — *Gray, Susan H.*

c The Muscular System — *Johnson, Rebecca L.*

Musculoskeletal Procedures: Diagnostic and Therapeutic — *Hodge, Jacqueline C.*

Muse in the Machine: American Fiction and Publicity — *Conroy, Mark*

Museum Administration: An Introduction — *Genoways, Hugh H.*

The Museum Called Canada: 25 Rooms of Wonder — *Gray, Charlotte*

The Museum Called Canada — *Angel, Sara*

The Museum of Broadcast Communications Encyclopedia of Radio. 3v. — *Sterling, Christopher H.*

The Museum of Broadcast Communications Encyclopedia of Radio — *Sterling, Christopher*

y The Museum of Broadcast Communications Encyclopedia of Radio — *Sterling, Christopher H.*

Museum Politics: Power Plays at the Exhibition — *Luke, Timothy W.*

Museum Studies: An Anthology of Contexts — *Carbonell, Bettina Messias*

Museum und Film — *Eberl, Hans-Christian*

Museums and the Future of Collecting, 2nd Ed. — *Knell, Simon J.*

Museums and the Interpretation of Visual Culture — *Hooper-Greenhill, Eilean*

Mushrooms: Cultivation, Nutritional Value, Medicinal Effect, and Environmental Impact. 2nd Ed. — *Chang, Shu-Ting*

Music Analysis in Britain in the Nineteenth and Early Twentieth Centuries — *Dale, Catherine*

Music and Copyright, 2nd Ed. — *Frith, Simon*

Music and Gender — *Moisala, Pirkko*

Music and Ideology in Cold War Europe — *Carroll, Mark*

Music and Mathematics: From Pythagoras to Fractals — *Fauvel, John*

Music and Medieval Manuscripts: Paleography and Performance: Essays Dedicated to Andrew Hughes — *Haines, John Dickinson*

Music and Nazism: Art under Tyranny, 1933-1945 — *Kater, Michael H.*

Music and Religious Identity in Counter-Reformation Augsburg, 1580-1630 — *Fisher, Alexander J.*

Music and Suicide — *Clark, Jeff*

Music and the Ineffable — *Jankelevitch, Vladimir*

Music and Women of the Commedia dell'Arte in the Late Sixteenth Century — *MacNeil, Anne*

c Music (Illus. by Curto, Rosa Maria) — *Roca, Nuria*

Music Cataloging Bulletin: Index/Supplement to Volumes 21-30, 1990-1999 — *Glennan, Kathryn P.*

Music, Culture, and the Library: An Analysis Of Discourses — *Talja, Sanna*

The Music Festival Guide: For Music Lovers and Musicians — *Pruett, Jon*

c Music for Alice — *Say, Allen*

Music for the People: Popular Music and Dance in Interwar Britain — *Nott, James J.*

Music from the Age of Shakespeare: A Cultural History — *Lord, Suzanne*

Music in European Capitals: The Galant Style, 1720-1780 — *Heartz, Daniel*

Music in Imperial Rio de Janeiro: European Culture in a Tropical Milieu — *Magaldi, Cristina*

Music in the Works of Broch, Mann, and Kafka — *Hargraves, John A.*

Music in West Africa: Experiencing Music, Expressing Culture — *Stone, Ruth M.*

Music Is — *Petie-Roulet, Philippe*

Music Lover's Quotation Book — *Barber, David W.*

Music Makers: Portraits and Songs from the Roots of America — *Duffy, Timothy*

y Music Makers & Toys — *Callihan, Joanna*

Music: Mystery and Memory: Conversations with Claude Glayman — *Dutilleux, Henri*

y The Music of Dolphins — *Hesse, Karen*

The Music of European Nationalism: Cultural Identity and Modern History — *Bohlman, Philip V.*

The Music of Luigi Dallapiccola — *Fearn, Raymond*

Music of Our World: Multicultural Festivals, Songs, and Activities — *Higgins, John*

Music of the Civil War Era — *Cornelius, Steven H.*

Music of the Counterculture Era — *Perone, James E.*

Music of the Primes: Searching to Solve the Greatest Mystery in Mathematics — *Du Sautoy, Marcus*

The Music of the Primes: Searching to Solve the Greatest Mystery in Mathematics — *Sautoy, Marcus du*

Music of the Renaissance — *Ongaro, Giulio*

The Music of the Republic: Essays on Socrates' Conversations and Plato's Writings — *Brann, Eva*

Music on the Frontline: Nicolas Nabokov's Struggle against Communism and Middlebrow Culture — *Wellens, Ian*

Music, Science, and Natural Magic in Seventeenth-Century England — *Gouk, Penelope*

Music, Space and Place: Popular Music and Cultural Identity — *Whiteley, Sheila*

Musica Spirituale, Libro Primo (Venice, 1563). — *Powers, Katherine*

Musical Arts in Africa: Theory, Practice and Education — *Herbst, Anri*

Musical Comedy on the West End Stage, 1890-1939 — *Platt, Len*

c Musical Genius: A Story about Wolfgang Amadeus Mozart (Illus. by Hamlin, Janet) — *Allman, Barbara*

Musical Instruments — *Kuronen, Darcy*

c A Musical Journey: From the Great Wall of China to the Water Towns of Jiangnan (Illus. by Liow, Kah Joon) — *Liow, Kah Joon*

The Musical Lives of Young Children — *Flohr, John W.*

The Musical Madhouse: An English Translation by Alastair Bruce of Berlioz's 'Les Grotesques de la musique' — *Berlioz, Hector*

Musical Migrations: Transnationalism and Cultural Hybridity in Latin/o America, Vol. 1 — *Aparicio, Frances D.*

Musical Theater and American Culture — *Walsh, David F.*

Musician's Guide to Pro Tools — *Keane, John*

The Musician's Handbook: A Practical Guide to Understanding the Music Business — *Borg, Bobby*

c Musicplay for Kindergarten

Musik und Bild im Chorraum Mittelalterlicher Kirchen, 1100-1500 — *Tammen, Bjorn R.*

Musik und Sprache — *Kaiser-El-Safi, Margret*

Musik-Zeit-Geschehen. Zu den Musikverhaltnissen in der SBZ/DDR 1945 bis 1952 — *Koster, Maren*

Musils Philosophie. Essayismus und Dichtung im Spannungsfeld der Theorien Nietzsches und Machs — *Pieper, Hans-Joachim*

Musings: An Anthology of Greek-Canadian Literature — *Fragoulis, Tess*

Musique Secrete — *Millet, Richard*

Musiqueet et poesie dans l' Antiquite — *Pinault, G.-J*

Muskekowuck Athinuwick: Original People of the Great Swampy Land — *Lytwyn, Victor P.*

Muskox Land: Ellesmere Island in the Age of Contact — *Dick, Lyle*

c Muskrats — *Hall, Margaret*

c Muslim Child: Understanding Islam through Stories and Poems (Illus. by Gallinger, Patty) — *Khan, Rukhsana*

c Muslim Festivals throughout the Year — *Ganeri, Anita*

Muslim Modernity in Postcolonial Nigeria: A Study of the Society for the Removal of Innovation and Reinstatement of Tradition — *Kane, Ousmane*

c Muslim Mosque — *Wood, Angela*

Muslim Societies in African History — *Robinson, David Maurice*

Muslims and Christians in Norman Italy: Arabic Speakers and the End of Islam — *Metcalfe, Alex*

Muslims in Medieval Italy: The Colony at Lucera — *Taylor, Julie*

Muslims in the Enlarged Europe: Religion and Society — *Marechal, Brigitte*

Muslims in the United States: The State of Research — *Leonard, Karen Isaksen*

Muslims in the West: Redefining the Separation of Church and State — *Abu-Sahlieh, Sami A.*

Muslims' Place in the American Public Square: Hope, Fears, and Aspirations — *Bukhari, Zahid H.*

Musqueam Reference Grammar — *Suttles, Wayne*

Mussolini: A New Life — *Farrell, Nicholas*

Mussolini and the Origins of the Second World War, 1933-1940 — *Mallett, Robert*

Mussolini — *Bosworth, R.J.B.*

Mussolini — *Neville, Peter*

Mussolini: The Secrets of His Death — *Garibaldi, Luciano*

Mussolini's Fascist Philosopher: Giovanni Gentile Reconsidered — *Moss, M. E.*

Must Christianity Be Violent? Reflections on History, Practice, and Theology — *Chase, Kenneth B.*

A Must See! Brilliant Broadway Artwork — *Suskin, Steven*

Mustang Legends: The Power, the Performance, the Passion — *Dregni, Michael*

Mustin: A Naval Family of the Twentieth Century — *Morton, John Fass*

Mutants: On Genetic Variety and the Human Body — *Leroi, Armand Marie*

Mutants: On the Form, Varieties and Errors of the Human Body — *Leroi, Armand Marie*

Mutating Concepts, Evolving Disciplines: Genetics, Medicine, and Society — *Parker, Lisa S.*

Muted Voices: Latinos and the 2000 Elections — *de la Garza, Rodolfo O.*

Muted Voices: Latinos and the 2000 Elections — *Garza, Rodolfo O. de la*

Mutilation and Transformation: Damnatio Memoriae and Roman Imperial Portraiture — *Varner, Eric R.*

c Mutt Dog! — *King, Stephen Michael*

Mutter Ledig-Vater Staat: Das Gebar-und Findelhaus in Wien, 1784-1910 — *Pawlowsky, Verena*

c Mutton Soup: More Adventures of Johnny Mutton — *Proimos, James*

c Mutton Soup: More Adventures of Johnny Mutton

The Mutual-Aid Approach to Working with Groups: Helping People Help One Another, 2nd Ed. — *Steinberg, Dominique Moyse*

Mutual Empowerment of State and Peasantry: Village Self-Government in Rural China — *Wang, Xu*

Mutual Life & Casualty — *Poliner, Elizabeth*

Mutuality Matters: Family, Faith, and Just Love — *Anderson, Herbert*

Muwassah, Zajal, Kharja: Bibliography of Strophic Poetry and Music from al-Andalus and Their Influence on East and West — *Heijkoop, Henk*

y MVP (Illus. by Shelley, John) — *Evans, Douglas*

c My Amazing Body -- Moving — *Royston, Angela*

My Anecdotal Life: A Memoir — *Reiner, Carl*

My Architect: A Son's Journey — *Kahn, Nathaniel*

My Army Life and the Fort Phil Kearney Massacre — *Carrington, Frances C.*

My Baby's Father: Unmarried Parents and Paternal Responsibility — *Waller, Maureen Rosamond*

c My Beautiful Child (Illus. by Mahurin, Matt) — *Desimini, Lisa*

c My Big Brother (Illus. by Himler, Ronald) — *Cohen, Miriam*

c My Birthday Party — *Wade, Barrie*

c My Bodyworks (Illus. by Fisher, Cynthia) — *Schoenberg, Jane*

c My Bones and Muscles — *Rau, Dana Meachen*

My Boyfriend's Back: True Stories of Rediscovering Love with a Long-Lost Sweetheart — *Hanover, Donna*

The Mysterious Flame of Queen Loana — *Eco, Umberto*

Mysterious Lands — *O'Connor, David B.*

c Mysterious Monsters — *O'Neill, Terry*

c Mysterious Monsters — *Townsend, John*

c Mysterious Mummer — *Falcone, L.M.*

y Mysterious Signs — *Townsend, John*

c Mysterious Urban Myths — *Townsend, John*

Mysterious Ways — *Burns, Terry*

Mysterious You

y Mystery and Terror: The Story of Edgar Allan Poe — *Schoell, William*

y Mystery at Blackbeard's Cove (Illus. by Miller, Joshua) — *Penn, Audrey*

c Mystery at the Club Sandwich (Illus. by Cushman, Doug) — *Cushman, Doug*

c The Mystery Bear: A Purim Story (Illus. by Howland, Naomi) — *Adelson, Leone*

The Mystery of Breathing — *Klass, Perri*

c The Mystery of Eatum Hall (Illus. by Kelly, John) — *Kelly, John (b. 1964 -)*

c The Mystery of Eatum Hall (Illus. by Kelly, John (b. 1964 -)) — *Kelly, John (b. 1964 -)*

The Mystery of Economic Growth — *Helpman, Elhanan*

The Mystery of Olga Chekhova — *Beevor, Antony*

c The Mystery of the Dead Sea Scrolls (Illus. by Abolafia, Yossi) — *Allon, Hagit*

The Mystery of the Egyptian Mummy — *Filer, Joyce*

c The Mystery of the Frozen Brains — *Chan, Marty*

c Mystery of the Lake (Illus. by Krystoforski, Andrej) — *Thomas, Cameron*

c Mystery of the Missing Candlestick — *Weltman, June*

c The Mystery of the Missing Dog (Illus. by Devard, Nancy) — *Hooks, Gwendolyn*

y The Mystery of the Missing Mini-Cons — *Motohira, Ryo*

Mystery of the Nile: The Epic Story of the First Descent of the World's Deadliest River — *Bangs, Richard*

The Mystery of the Portland Vase — *Brooks, Robin*

c The Mystery of the Swimming Gorilla, Vol. 1 (Illus. by Manders, John) — *McMahon, P.J.*

The Mystery of Things — *Grayling, A.C.*

Mysterymania: The Reception of Eugene Sue in Britain 1838-1860 — *Chevasco, Berry Palmer*

Mystic and Rider — *Shinn, Sharon*

Mystic Galveston: Reinventing America's Third Coast — *Hardwick, Susan Wiley*

The Mystic Hours: A Daybook of Interspiritual Wisdom and Devotion — *Teasdale, Wayne*

Mystic: Master Class — *Ryan, Matt*

Mystic: Out All Night — *Ryan, Matt*

The Mystic Poets — *Hopkins, Gerard Manley*

Mystic: Rite of Passage — *Peterson, Brandon*

Mystic: Siege of Scales — *Peterson, Brandon*

Mystic: The Demon Queen — *Peterson, Brandon*

Mystic Warrior (Read by James, Lloyd). Audiobook Review — *Hickman, Tracy*

Mystical Consciousness: Western Perspectives and Dialogue with Japanese Thinkers — *Roy, Louis*

Mystical Language of Sensation in the Later Middle Ages — *Rudy, Gordon*

Mysticism and Social Transformation — *Ruffing, Janet K.*

Mystics, Monarchs, and Messiahs: Cultural Landscapes of Early Modern Iran — *Babayan, Kathryn*

Mystics: Presence and Aporia — *Kessler, Michael*

Mystique: Dead Drop Gorgeous — *Vaughan, Brian K.*

Myterious Ways — *Burns, Terry*

Myth: A Handbook — *Doty, William G.*

Myth and History in Ancient Greece: The Symbolic Creation of a Colony — *Calame, Claude*

Myth and History in the Creation of Yellowstone National Park — *Schullery, Paul*

Myth and the limits of reason, Rev. Ed. — *Stambovsky, Phillip*

Myth, Montage & Visuality in Late Medieval Manuscript Culture: Christine de Pizan's Epistre Othea — *Desmond, Marilynn*

The Myth of 1648: Class, Geopolitics and the Making of Modern International Relations — *Teschke, Benno*

The Myth of Civil Society: Social Capital and Democratic Consolidation in Spain and Brazil — *Encarnacion, Omar G.*

The Myth of Decline: The Rise of Britain Since 1945 — *Bernstein, George L.*

The Myth of Elizabeth — *Doran, Susan*

The Myth of Greater Albania — *Kola, Paulin*

The Myth of Islamic Tolerance: How Islamic Law Treats Non-Muslims — *Spencer, Robert*

The Myth of Leadership: Creating Leaderless Organizations — *Nielsen, Jeffrey S.*

The Myth of Ownership: Taxes and Justice — *Murphy, Liam*

The Myth of Print Culture: Essays on Evidence, Textuality, and Bibliographical Method — *Dane, Joseph A.*

The Myth of Representatives and the Florida Legislature: A House of Competing Loyalties, 1927-2000 — *Prier, Eric*

The Myth of Solid Ground: Earthquakes, Prediction, and the Fault Line between Reason and Faith — *Ulin, David L.*

The Myth of the Birth of the Hero: A Psychological Exploration of Myth, Updated Ed. — *Rank, Otto*

The Myth of the French Bourgeoisie: An Essay on the Social Imaginary, 1750-1850 — *Maza, Sarah*

The Myth of the Non-Russian: Iskander and Aitmatov's Magical Universe — *Harber, Erika*

The Myth of the Perfect Mother: Rethinking the Spirituality of Women — *Barnhill, Carla*

The Myth of the Sacred: The Charter, the Courts, and the Politics of the Constitution in Canada — *James, Patrick*

Myth of the Year: Returning to the Origin of the Druid Calendar — *Benigni, Helen*

The Mythiambi of Babrius. Notes on the Constitution of the Text — *Vaio, J*

Mythic Galveston: Reinventing America's Third Coast — *Hardwick, Susan Wiley*

Mythic Giacometti — *Lord, James*

Mythic Paradigms in Literature, Philosophy, and the Arts — *Eisenhauer, Robert*

The Mythical Detective Loki Ragnarok, Vol. 1 — *Kinoshita, Sakura*

Mythistory: The Making of a Modern Historiography — *Mali, Joseph*

Mythology A to Z

Mythology and Lament: Studies in the Oracles About the Nations — *Geyer, John B.*

Mythology for Storytellers: Themes and Tales from Around the World — *Sherman, Josepha*

Mythology in Our Midst: A Guide to Cultural References — *Peterson, Amy T.*

y Mythology of the World (Illus. by Palin, Nicki) — *Philip, Neil*

Mythology: The DC Comics Art of Alex Ross — *Ross, Alex*

Mythos and Logos: How to Regain the Love of Wisdom — *Anderson, Albert A.*

Mythos Schweiz. Zum Deutschen Literarischen Philhelvetismus Zwischen 1700 und 1850 — *Hentschel, Uwe*

Myths America Lives By — *Hughes, Richard (b. 1941 -)*

Myths and Legends of the Australian Aborigines — *Smith, W. Ramsay*

Myths and Misconceptions Surrounding Opioids in Pain Management — *Cicala, Roger*

c Myths and Monsters: Secrets Revealed (Illus. by Mendez, Simon) — *Edwards, Katie*

Myths of Renaissance Individualism — *Martin, John Jeffries*

Myths of the Plantation Society: Slavery in the American South and the West Indies — *Dessens, Nathalie*

Myths of the Self: Narrative Identity and Postmodern Metaphysics — *Smith, Olav Bryant*

Mzungu Mjinga: A Memoir of a Hunter's First Safari to Tanzania's Masai-Mara — *Boyer, Rick*

N

Nothingness and the Quarrel between Faith and Reason — *Cubbage, Norman Brian*

Nothing's Sacred — *Black, Lewis*

Nothing's Too Small to Make a Difference — *Urbanska, Wanda*

Notice — *Lewis, Heather*

Notorious H.I.V.: The Media Spectacle of Nushawn Williams — *Shevory, Thomas C.*

Notorious in the Neighborhood: Sex and Families Across the Color Line in Virginia, 1787-1861 — *Rothman, Joshua D.*

Notorious Muse: The Actress in British Art and Culture 1776-1812 — *Asleson, Robyn*

Notre Dame vs. the Klan: How the Fighting Irish Defeated the Ku Klux Klan — *Tucker, Todd*

Nous — *Jaegwon, Kim*

Nouvelle Bibliographie refondue et augmentee de la critique sur Francois-Rene de Chateaubriand: 1801-1999 — *Dube, Pierre H.*

Nouvelles — *De Musset, Alfred*

Nouvelles du XVIII siecle — *Coulet, Henri*

Nouvelles ecrivaines: nouvelles voix? — *Rodgers, Catherine*

The Novel 100: A Ranking of the Greatest Novels of All Time — *Burt, Daniel S.*

The Novel and American Left: Critical Essays on Depression-Era Fiction — *Casey, Janet Galligani*

Novel Metathesis Chemistry: Well-Defined Initiator Systems for Specialty Chemical Synthesis, Tailored Polymers, and Advanced Material Applications — *Imamoghu, Y.*

Novel Relations: The Transformation of Kinship in English Literature and Culture, 1748-1818 — *Perry, Ruth*

Novel & Short Story Writers Market 2004: 2,000+ Places to Get Your Fiction into Print — *Bowling, Anne*

The Novel, Spirituality and Modern Culture: Eight Novelists Write about Their Craft and Their Context — *Fiddes, Paul S.*

Novel Technologies for Microwave and Millimeter-Wave Applications — *Kiang, Jean-Fu*

Novel Vaccination Strategies — *Kaufmann, Stefan H.E.*

Novell's Guide to Troubleshooting eDirectory — *Kuo, Peter*

The Novels and Selected Works of Maria Edgeworth, Vols. 1-12 — *Butler, Marilyn*

c Novelties and Souvenirs: Collected Short Fiction — *Crowley, John*

c Now and Then: The Coolest Scrapbook for School-Aged Children — *Shecter, Lara*

Now Go Home: Wilderness, Belonging, and the Crosscut Saw — *Spagna, Ana Maria*

c Now I Eat My ABC's (Illus. by Wolf, Bruce) — *Abrams, Pare*

Now Is the Time To Open Your Heart (Read by Woodard, Alfre). Audiobook Review — *Walker, Alice*

Now is the Time to Open Your Heart — *Walker, Alice*

c Now It Is Winter (Illus. by DePalma, Mary Newell) — *Spinelli, Eileen*

Now That My Father Lies Down Beside Me: New and Selected Poems, 1970-2000 — *Plumly, Stanley*

Now the Green Blade Rises — *Spires, Elizabeth*

Now, Voyager — *Prouty, Olive Higgins*

c Now We Have a Baby (Illus. by Massey, Jane) — *Rock, Lois*

Now You Know: The Book of Answers — *Lennox, Doug*

Now You Know: The Book of Answers. Vol. 2 — *Lennox, Doug*

Now You Know Zire — *Overton, Rick*

Now You See Her — *Tishy, Cecelia*

Now You See Him — *Cameron, Stella*

y Now You See It: A Toby Peters Mystery — *Kaminsky, Stuart M.*

Now You See It — *Lynn, Allison*

y Now You See It... — *Vande Velde, Vivian*

y Nowhere Again — *Sullivan, Jenny*

Nowhere Fast — *Blake, Yashin*

Nowhere Man: The Pronek Fantasies — *Hemon, Aleksandar*

NOX: Machining Architecture — *Spuybroek, Lars*

Nuclear Cardiology: Practical Applications — *Heller, Gary V.*

Nuclear Cardiology: The Basics: How to Set Up and Maintain a Laboratory — *Wackers, Frans J. Th.*

Nuclear, Chemical, and Biological Terrorism: Emergency Response and Public Protection — *Byrnes, Mark E.*

Nuclear Energy Data/Donnees Sur L'Energie Nucleaire 2003

Nuclear Energy: Principles, Practices, and Prospects, 2nd Ed. — *Bodansky, David*

Nuclear Envelope — *Evans, D.E.*

Nuclear Factor kB: Regulation and Role in Disease — *Beyaert, Rudi*

Nuclear North Korea: A Debate on Engagement Strategies — *Cha, Victor D.*

Nuclear North Korea: A Debate on Engagement Strategies — *Kang, David C.*

Nuclear Physics, Large and Small: Proceedings — *Rijker, Roelof*

Nuclear Physics V: Proceedings — *Arnould, M.*

c Nuclear Power — *Sherman, Josepha*

Nuclear Terrorism: The Ultimate Preventable Catastrophe — *Allison, Graham*

The Nuclear Tipping Point: Why States May Reconsider Their Nuclear Choices — *Campbell, Kurt M.*

Nuclear Waste: A Technological and Political Challenge — *Risoluti, Piero*

Nucleic Acids: Curvature and Deformation, Recent Advances and New Paradigms — *Stellwagen, Nancy C.*

The Nude: Ideal and Reality Painting and Sculpture — *Weiermair, Peter*

The Nude in French Art and Culture, 1870-1910 — *Dawkins, Heather*

Nudity: A Cultural Anatomy — *Barcan, Ruth*

Nuendo Power! — *Shepherd, Ashley*

Nuendo Power! — *Smithers, Brian*

Nuevas perspectivas desde/sobre America Latina: El desafio de los estudios culturales — *Morana, Mabel*

Nugget Coombs: A Reforming Life — *Rowse, Tim*

c The Number Devil (Illus. by Berner, Rotraut Susanne) — *Enzensberger, Hans Magnus*

c Number Four, Bobby Orr! (Illus. by Letain, Shayne) — *Leonetti, Mike*

c Number Rhymes to Say and Play! (Illus. by Gon, Adriano) — *Dunn, Opal*

c Number the Stars (Read by Brown, Blair). Audiobook Review — *Lowry, Lois*

c Number the Stars — *Lowry, Lois*

Number Theory: Proceedings — *Kisilevsky, Hershy*

Number Wonder: Book 1 of the Series Real Mathematics — *Koetke, Walter*

c Numbers — *Shannon, Rosemarie*

c Numbers — *Watt, Melanie*

y The Numbers Game: Baseball's Lifelong Fascination with Statistics — *Schwarz, Alan*

Numbers Games: Measuring and Mandating American Education — *Thomas, P.L.*

Numbers Guide: The Essentials of Business Numeracy, 5th ed. — *Stutley, Richard*

Numerical Analysis: A Mathematical Introduction — *Allgower, Eugene L.*

Numerical Analysis and Modelling in Geomechanics — *Bull, John W.*

Numerical and Analytical Methods for Scientists and Engineers Using Mathematica — *Dubin, Daniel*

Numerical Computing With MATLAB — *Moler, Cleve B.*

Numerical Methods for Delay Differential Equations — *Bellen, Alfredo*

Numerical Methods for Nonlinear Estimating Equations — *Small, Christopher G.*

Numerical Modeling of Water Waves, 2nd Ed. — *Mader, Charles L.*

Numerical Modelling in Geomechanics — *Pastor, Manuel*

Numerical Optimization — *Bonans, J. Frederic*

Numerical Polynomial Algebra — *Stetter, Hans J.*

Numerical Solution of Time-Dependent Advection-Diffusion-Reaction Equations — *Hundsorfer, W.*

Nunavik: Inuit-Controlled Education in Arctic Quebec — *Vick-Westgate, Ann*

c Nunca jamas comere tomates/I Will Never Not Ever Eat a Tomato — *Child, Lauren*

Nuns as Historians in Early Modern Germany — *Woodford, Charlotte*

Nuns' Chronicles and Convent Culture in Renaissance and Counter-Reformation Italy — *Lowe, Kate*

nuovo ordine mediterraneo: Le politiche di occupazione dell'Italia fascista in Europa, 1940-1943 — *Rodogno, Davide*

Nur leere Reden: Politischer Diskurs und die Shanghaier Presse im China des spaten 19 — *Janku, Andrea*

The Nuremberg Interviews: An American Psychiatrist's Conversations with the Defendants and Witnesses — *Goldensohn, Leon*

The Nuremberg Interviews — *Gellately, Robert*

The Nuremberg Medical Trial: The Holocaust and the Origin of the Nuremberg Medical Code — *Freyhofer, Horst H.*

Nureyev — *Solway, Diane*

c Nurse Matilda: The Collected Tales — *Brand, Christianna*

Nurse Practitioner's Business Practice and Legal Guide, 2nd Ed. — *Buppert, Carolyn*

Nurse Practitioners: Evolution of Advanced Practice, 4th Ed. — *Mezey, Mathy D.*

Nurse Practitioner's Quick Reference to Clinical Facts

Nurse's Fast Facts: Your Quick Source for Core Clinical Content, 3rd Ed. — *Holloway, Brenda Walters*

A Nurse's Handbook of Spiritual Care: Standing on Holy Ground — *O'Brien, Mary Elizabeth*

Nursing 2005 Drug Handbook

Nursing America: One Year Behind the Nursing Stations of an Inner-City Hospital — *Balfour, Sandy*

Nursing Assisting: Essentials for Long-Term Care, 2nd Ed. — *Acello, Barbara*

Nursing Diagnoses in Psychiatric Nursing: Care Plans and Psychotropic Medications, 6th Ed. — *Townsend, Mary C.*

Nursing Diagnosis: Application to Clinical Practice, 10th Ed. — *Carpenito-Moyet, Lynda Juall*

Nursing Documentation in Aged Care: A Guide to Practice — *Crofton, Christine*

Nursing Health Assessment: Student Applications — *Dillon, Patricia M.*

Nursing Home Litigation: Pretrial Practices and Trial, 2nd Ed. — *Krisztal, Ruben*

Nursing in Today's World: Trends, Issues, and Management, 8th Ed. — *Elllis, Janice Rider*

Nursing Interventions Classification (NIC) 4th Ed. — *Dochterman, Joanne McCloskey*

Nursing Outcomes Classification (NOC), 3rd Ed. — *Moorhead, Sue*

Nursing Pharmacology Made Incredibly Easy

Nursing Preceptorship: Connecting Practice and Education — *Myrick, Florence*

Nursing Rapid-fire Drug Facts

Nursing Student Retention: Understanding the Process and Making a Difference — *Jeffreys, Marianne R.*

Nurturing Hidden Resilience in Trouble Youth — *Ungar, Michael*

Nurturing Your Teenager's Soul: A Practical Approach to Raising a Kind, Honorable, Compassionate Teen — *Doe, Mimi*

c The Nutcracker Ballet Theatre (Illus. by Seddon, Viola Ann) — *Mahoney, Jean*

c The Nutcracker (Illus. by Beck, Ian) — *Doherty, Berlie*

c Nutcracker (Illus. by Zwerger, Lisbeth) — *Hoffmann, E.T.A.*

Nutcracker Nation: How an Old World Ballet Became a Christmas Tradition in the New World — *Fisher, Jennifer*

Nuthin' but a "G" Thang: The Culture and Commerce of Gangsta Rap — *Quinn, Eithne*

Nutrient Cycling and Limitation: Hawai'i as Model System — *Vitousek, Peter*

Nutrients A to Z: A User's Guide to Foods, Herbs, Vitamins, Minerals and Supplements, 3rd Ed. — *Sharon, Michael*

Nutrients Valorisation via Duckweed-Based Wastewater Treatment and Aquaculture — *El-Shafai, Saber Abdel-Aziz Abdel Salam Mohamed*

Nutrition and Alcohol: Linking Nutrient Interactions and Dietary Intake — *Watson, Ronald R.*

Nutrition and Bone Health — *Holick, Michael G.*

Nutrition and Health of the Gastrointestinal Tract — *Blok, M.C.*

y Nutrition and Well-Being A to Z — *James, Delores C.S.*

c Nutrition Anyone? — *Petrie, Kristin*

Nutrition Care of the Older Adult: A Handbook for Dietetics Professionals Working Throughout the Continuum of Care, 2nd Ed. — *Niedert, Kathleen C.*

Nutrition Through the Life Cycle, 2nd Ed. — *Brown, Judith E.*

Nutritional Ergogenic Aids — *Wolinsky, Ira*

c Nuts to You! — *Ehlert, Lois*

The Nutshell Studies of Unexplained Death — *Botz, Corinne May*

c The Nutty Nut Chase (Illus. by Cabban, Vanessa) — *White, Kathryn*

Nuvisavik: The Place Where We Weave — *Finckenstein, Maria von*

c Nzingha: Warrior Queen of Matamba — *McKissack, Patricia*

O

c **Old Coyote (Illus. by Grafe, Max)** — *Wood, Nancy*
c **Old Coyote (Illus. by Grafe, Max)** — *Wood, Nancy C.*
Old English Glossed Psalters: Psalms 1-50 — *Pulsiano, Phillip*
The Old English Life of St Mary of Egypt: An Edition of the Old English Text with Modern English Parellel-Text Translation — *Magennis, Hugh*
Old English Literature: A Short Introduction — *Donoghue, Daniel*
Old-Fashioned and David Austin Roses — *Taylor, Barbara Lea*
Old Filth — *Gardam, Jane*
The Old Friends — *Dixon, Stephen*
Old Glory: American War Poems from the Revolutionary War to the War on Terror — *Hedin, Robert*
y **Old Hickory: Andrew Jackson and the American People** — *Marrin, Albert*
The Old Iron Road: An Epic of Rails, Roads, and the Urge to Go West — *Bain, David Haward*
Old Ironsides: The Military Biography of Oliver Cromwell — *Kitson, Frank*
c **Old MacDonald Had a Woodshop (Illus. by Wolff, Ashley)** — *Shulman, Lisa*
Old Magazines: Identification & Value Guide — *Clear, Richard E.*
The Old Man and the Tee: How I Took Ten Strokes Off My Game and Learned to Love Golf All Over Again — *Pipkin, Turk*
Old Man on His Back: Portrait of a Prairie Landscape — *Butala, Sharon*
Old Man's War — *Scalzi, John*
c **Old Mr. Mackle Hackle (Illus. by Shepherd, Irana)** — *Madsen, Gunnar*
Old Muskoka: Century Cottages and Summer Estates — *Lundell, Liz*
Old Norse Myths, Literature and Society — *Ross, Margaret Clunies*
The Old Norse Poetic Translations of Thomas Percy: A New Edition and Commentary — *Clunies, Margaret*
The Old Norse Poetic Translations of Thomas Percy — *Ross, Margaret Clunies*
Old School: A Novel (Read by Cashman, Dan). Audiobook Review — *Wolff, Tobias*
y **Old School: A Novel** — *Wolff, Tobias*
c **The Old Shepherd's Tale (Illus. by Sorensen, Henry)** — *Nye, Christopher*
Old Spain and New Spain: The Travel Narratives of Camilo Jose Cela — *Henn, David*
c **The Old Stories (Illus. by Lawrence, John)** — *Crossley-Holland, Kevin*
Old Testament Figures in Art — *De Capoa, Chiara*
Old Testament Research for Africa: A Critical Analysis and Annotated Bibliography of African Old Testament Dissertations, 1967-2000 — *Holter, Knut*
The Old Testament Story — *Benjamin, Don C.*
Old Testament Theology: Flowering and Future — *Ollenburger, Ben C.*
Old Testament Theology Vol. 1 — *Goldingay, John*
c **Old Testament Women** — *Ward, Elaine*
c **Old Tom's Holiday (Illus. by Hobbs, Leigh)** — *Hobbs, Leigh*
Old Toronto Houses — *Cruickshank, Tom*
Old Virginia: The Pursuit of a Pastoral Ideal — *Rasmussen, William M.S.*
c **The Old Willis Place: A Ghost Story** — *Hahn, Mary Downing*
y **Olden Days Locket** — *Chamberlain, Penny*
Older Americans: A Changing Market, 4th Ed.
Older Americans: A Changing Market, 4th Ed. — *New Strategist Editors*
Older Americans Information Directory 2004.
The Oldest Cuisine in the World: Cooking in Mesopotamia — *Bottero, Jean*
Oldman's Guide to Outsmarting Wine: 108 Ingenious Shortcuts to Navigate the World of Wine with Confidence and Style — *Oldman, Mark*
Olga Freidenberg's Works and Days — *Perlina, Nina*
Olga Rudge and Ezra Pound: "What Thou Lovest Well..." — *Conover, Anne*
Oligonucleotide Synthesis: Methods and Applications — *Herdewijn, Piet*
The Oliphant: Islamic Objects in Historical Context — *Shalem, Avinoam*
The Olive and the Caper: Adventures in Greek Cooking — *Hoffman, Susanna*
c **Olive, My Love (Illus. by Seibold, J. Otto)** — *Walsh, Vivian*
Olive Propagation Manual — *Fabbri, Andrea*

Olive Schreiner and the Progress of Feminism: Evolution, Gender, Empire — *Burdett, Carolyn*
Oliver Cat on Planet B — *Kettner, Christine*
y **Oliver Cromwell** — *Gaunt, Peter*
Oliver Cromwell: Soldier: The Military Life of a Revolutionary at War — *Marshall, Alan*
c **Oliver the Mighty Pig (Illus. by Schweninger, Ann)** — *Van Leeuwen, Jean*
c **Oliver's Game (Illus. by Tavares, Matt)** — *Tavares, Matt*
c **Olive's Ocean** — *Henkes, Kevin*
Olivia Joules and the Overactive Imagination (Read by Bailey, Josephine). Audiobook Review — *Fielding, Helen*
Olivia Joules and the Overactive Imagination — *Fielding, Helen*
Olivia Kidney and the Exit Academy (Illus. by Reynolds, Peter H.) — *Potter, Ellen*
y **Olivia Kidney (Illus. by Reynolds, Peter H.)** — *Potter, Ellen*
Olivia Manning — *Braybrooke, Neville*
Olivier Mosset: Works, 1966-2003 — *Gauthier, Michel*
c **Ollie the Stomper** — *Dunrea, Olivier*
Olympic Games — *What, Leslie*
The Olympic Odyssey: Rekindling the True Spirit of the Great Games — *Cousineau, Phil*
Olympics in Athens, 1896: The Invention of the Modern Olympic Games — *Smith, Michael Llewellyn*
Olympics in Athens 1896: The Invention of the Modern Olympic Games
Olympus Heights — *Munroe, Kevin*
OMAE 2003, Vol. 1 — *Chakrabarti, Subrata*
Omaeluloolisus ja alltekst — *Kross, Jaan*
Omaha Blues: A Memory Loop — *Lelyveld, Joseph*
The Ombudsman, Good Governance, and the International Human Rights System — *Reif, Linda C.*
Omelettes: Perfect Anytime — *Candian Egg Marketing Agency*
Omero tremila anni dopo. Atti del Congresso di Genova 6-8 luglio 2000. Con la collaborazione di P. Ascheri — *Montanari, F.*
Omnia homini simila sunt: Eine Interpretation von Giordano Brunos Artificium perorandi — *Spang, Michael*
c **Omnibeasts: Animal Poems and Paintings (Illus. by Florian, Douglas)** — *Florian, Douglas*
y **On a Good Day** — *Burnside, Deborah*
On a Night Like This (Read by Gough, Michael). Audiobook Review — *Sussman, Ellen*
c **On a Tall Cliff** — *Murray, Andrew*
On a Wing of the Sun — *Barnes, Jim*
On Adam Smith's Wealth of Nations — *Fleischacker, Samuel*
On Alexander's Track to the Indus: Personal Narrative of Explorations on the North-West Frontier of India — *Stein, Aurel, Sir*
On American Soil: Murder, the Military, and How Justice Became a Casualty of World War II — *Hamann, Jack*
On Angel's Eve: Making the Most of Your Final Time Together — *Arledge, Garnette*
On Apology — *Lazare, Aaron*
On Architecture — *Loos, Adolf*
On Barbarian Identity: Critical Approaches to Ethinicity in the Early Middle Ages — *Gillett, Andrew*
On Beauty — *Eco, Umberto*
On Becoming an Artist: Reinventing Yourself through Mindful Creativity — *Langer, Ellen J.*
On Becoming an Indian Muslim: French Essays on Aspects of Syncretism — *Waseem, M.*
On Being Authentic — *Guignon, Charles B.*
On Being Born — *Gonzalez-Crussi, F.*
On Being John McEnroe — *Adams, Tim*
On Being Liked — *Alison, James*
On Being Nonprofit: A Conceptual and Policy Primer — *Frumkin, Peter*
On Borrowed Time? Assessing the Threat of Mineral Depletion — *Tilton, John E.*
On Broadway: Art and Commerce on the Great White Way — *Adler, Steven*
On Broadway, Men Still Wear Hats: Unusual Lives Led on the Edges of Broadway — *Simonson, Robert*
On Broken Legs: A Shattered Life, a Search for God, a Miracle That Met Me in a Cave in Assisi — *Zoba, Wendy Murray*
On Call: A Doctor's Days and Nights in Residency — *Transue, Emily R.*
On Call: Principles and Protocols, 4th Ed. — *Marshall, Shane A.*

On Capitol Hill: The Struggle to Reform Congress and Its Consequences, 1948-2000 — *Zelizer, Julian E.*
On Cloning — *Harris, John (b. 1945 -)*
On Consciousness — *Honderich, Ted*
On Creating Competition and Strategic Restructuring: Regulatory Reform in Public Utilities — *Wubben, Emiel F.M.*
On Creation, Conservation, and Concurrence: Metaphysical Disputations 20, 21 and 22 — *Suarez, Francisco*
On Deaf Ears: The Limits of the Bully Pulpit — *Edwards, George C.*
On Discovery — *Vergil, Polydore*
On Doing Local History. 2nd Ed. — *Kammen, Carol*
On Evil — *Morton, Adam*
On Film-Making: An Introduction to the Craft of the Director — *Mackendrick, Alexander*
On Food and Cooking: The Science and Lore of the Kitchen — *McGee, Harold*
On Foot, in Flames — *McDowell, Robert*
On Foundationalism: A Strategy for Metaphysical Realism — *Rockmore, Tom*
On Gandhi — *Gruzalski, Bart*
On Global Aging: Old-Age Income Systems in the EU and Other Major Parts of the World — *Kune, Jan B.*
On Hallowed Ground: The Last Battle for Pork Chop Hill — *McWilliams, Bill*
y **On Her Way: Stories and Poems About Growing Up Girl** — *Asher, Sandy*
On Hitler's Mountain: Overcoming the Legacy of a Nazi Childhood — *Hunt, Irmgard A.*
On Human Nature: An Introduction to Philosophy — *Wall, Thomas F.*
On Human Nature — *Wilson, Edward O.*
On Humanism — *Norman, Richard*
On Imperialist Globalization: Two Speeches — *Castro, Fidel*
On Improvisation: Nine Conversations with Roberto Ciulli — *Malgorzata, Bartula*
On Intelligence: How a New Understanding of the Brain Will Lead to the Creation of Truly Intelligent Machines — *Hawkins, Jeff*
On Jean-Jacques Rousseau, Considered as One of the First Authors of the Revolution — *Swenson, James*
On Land and Sea: Native American Uses of Biological Resources in the West Indies — *Newsom, Lee A.*
On Language and Linguistics — *Halliday, M.A.K.*
The On-Line Study of Sentence Comprehension: Eyetracking, ERP, and Beyond — *Carreiras, Manuel*
On-Line Testing Symposium (IOLTS 2004): Proceedings — *Metra, C.*
On Maimonides — *Manekin, Charles H.*
On Medieval Philosophy — *Epicetus*
On Medieval Philosophy — *Inglis, John*
On Modern Origins: Essays in Early Modern Philosophy — *Kennington, Richard*
On Modern Philosophy — *Thomson, Garrett*
On Mourning: Theories of Loss in Modern Literature — *Watkin, William*
On My Own (Read by Toren, Suzanne). Audiobook Review — *Alexander, Sally Hobart*
On My Way to Buy Eggs — *Chen, Zhi Yuan*
On Noah's Ark (Illus. by Brett, Jan) — *Brett, Jan*
On Not Being Able to Sleep — *Rose, Jacqueline*
On Ordered Liberty: A Treatise on the Free Society — *Gregg, Samuel*
On Our Minds: How Evolutionary Psychology Is Reshaping the Nature-Versus-Nurture Debate — *Gander, Eric M.*
On Our Way: The Final Passage through Life and Death — *Kastenbaum, Robert*
c **On Our Way to the Beach (Illus. by McLean, Andrew)** — *Laguna, Sofie*
On Paradise Drive: How We Live Now (and Always Have) in the Future Tense — *Brooks, David*
On Paul Ricoeur: The Owl of Minerva — *Kearney, Richard*
On Personality — *Goldie, Peter*
c **On Pointe** — *Grover, Lorie Ann*
On Pragmatism — *de Waal, Cornelis*
On Sacred Ground: The Spirit of Place in Pacific Northwest Literature — *O'Connell, Nicholas*
On Sacred Grounds: Culture, Society, Politics, and the Formation of the Cult of Confucius — *Wilson, Thomas A.*
c **On Sand Island** — *Johnson, David A.*
On Staffing: Advice and Perspectives from HR Leaders — *Burkholder, Nicholas*
y **On Stony Ground** — *Mason, Gordon*

On Stories — *Kearney, Richard*
On the Banks of the Amazon/En Las Orillas del Amazonas (Illus. by Driessen, Elizabeth) — *Driessen, Elizabeth*
'On the Beliefs of the Greeks': Leo Allatios and Popular Orthodoxy — *Hartnup, Karen*
On the Bloody Road to Jesus: Christianity and the Chiricahua Apaches — *Stockel, H. Henrietta*
On the Border: An Environmental History of San Antonio — *Miller, Char*
On the Brink: The Great Lakes in the 21st Century — *Dempsey, Dave*
On the Cutting Edge: The Study of Women in Biblical Worlds, Essays in Honor of Elisabeth Schussler Fiorenza — *Schaberg, Jane*
On the Death of Childhood and the Destruction of Public Schools: The Folly of Today's Education Policies and Practices — *Bracey, Gerald W.*
On the Down Low: A Journey into the Lives of "Straight" Black Men Who Sleep with Men — *King, J.L.*
On the Edge of Empire: Gender, Race and the Making of British Columbia 1849-1871 — *Perry, Adele*
On the Edge of the Banda Zone: Past and Present in the Social Organization of a Moluccan Trading Network — *Ellen, Roy*
On the Edge: The United States in the Twentieth Century, 3rd Ed. — *Horowitz, David A.*
On the Essence of Language: The Metaphysics of Language and the Essencing of the World: Concerning Herder's Treatise On the Origin of Language — *Heidegger, Martin*
c On the Far Side of the Mountain — *George, Jean Craighead*
On the Farm Front: The Women's Land Army in World War II — *Carpenter, Stephanie A.*
On the Fiery March: Mussolini Prepares for War — *Strang, G. Bruce*
c On the First Day of Grade School (Illus. by Whatley, Bruce) — *Brenner, Emily*
On the Forefront of Educational Psychology — *Waugh, Russell F.*
On the Front Line of Life: Stephen Leacock: Memories and Reflections, 1935-1944 — *Bowker, Alan*
On the Future of History: The Postmodernist Challenge and Its Afternoon — *Breisach, Ernst*
On the Ground — *Howe, Fanny*
On the Journey Home: The History of Mission of the Evangelical United Brethren Church, 1946-1968. — *O'Malley, J. Steven*
On the Justice of Roosting Chickens: Reflections on the Consequences of U.S. Imperial Arrogance and Criminality — *Churchill, Ward*
y On the Land
On the Line — *Shay, Kathryn*
On the Mathematical Method and Correspondence with Exner — *Bolzano, Bernard*
c On the Moon — *Milbourne, Anna*
On the Move: Women and Rural-to-Urban Migration in Contemporary China — *Gaetano, Arianne M.*
On the Music of Stefan Wolpe: Essays and Recollections — *Clarkson, Austin*
c On the Night of the Comet (Illus. by Watts, Leslie Elizabeth) — *Coakley, Lena*
On the Origin of Phyla — *Valentine, James W.*
On the Outside Looking In(dian): Indian Women Writers at Home and Abroad — *Kafka, Phillipa*
On the Philosophy of Communication — *Radford, Gary P.*
On the Properties of Foodstuffs. Introduction, Translation and Commentary — *Powell, O.*
On the Reliability of the Old Testament — *Kitchen, K.A.*
On the River with Lewis and Clark — *Huser, Verne*
On the Road — *Steggall, Susan*
On the Road to Armageddon: How Evangelicals became Israel's Best Friend — *Weber, Timothy P.*
On the Road to Perdition: Detour — *Collins, Max Allan*
On the Run: A Mafia Childhood — *Hill, Gregg*
y On the Run — *Coleman, Michael*
On the Side: More Than 100 Recipes for the Sides, Salads, and Condiments That Make the Meal — *Harris, Jessica B.*
On the Spur of Speed — *Fender, J.E.*
On the Strange Place of Religion in Contemporary Art — *Elkins, James*
"On the Subject of the Feminist Business," Re-Reading Flannery O'Connor — *Caruso, Teresa*

On the Take: How Medicine's Complicity with Big Business Can Endanger Your Health — *Kassirer, Jerome P.*
On the Threshold: Home, Hardwood, and Holiness — *Andrew, Elizabeth J.*
On the Twelfth Day of Christmas — *Gedney, Mona*
On The War for Greek Freedom: Selections from the Historians — *Herodotus*
On the Warpath: An Anthology of Australian Military Travel — *Gerster, Robin*
c On the Waters of the USA: Ships and Boats in American Life — *Sandler, Martin W.*
On the Way Home — *Fishbein, Amy*
On the Way to My Father's Funeral: New and Selected Stories — *Baumbach, Jonathan*
On the Wild Edge: In Search of a Natural Life — *Petersen, David*
On The Wild Side — *Wiley, Keith*
y On the Wing: To the Edge of the Earth with the Peregrine Falcon — *Tennant, Alan*
On the Wings of Checkerspots: A Model System for Population Biology — *Ehrlich, Paul R.*
On the Wings of Checkerspots A Model System for Population Biology — *Ehrlich, Paul R.*
On Their Own Terms: The Legacy of National Socialism in Post-1990 German Fiction — *Schmitz, Helmut*
y On Their Own: What Happens to Kids When They Age Out of the Foster Care System — *Shirk, Martha*
On Thin Ice — *Adair, Cherry*
On Thinking the Human: Resolutions of Difficult Notions — *Jenson, Robert W.*
c On This Spot: An Expedition Back Through Time (Illus. by Christiansen, Lee) — *Goodman, Susan E.*
On Translating Signs: Exploring Text and Semio-Translation — *Gorlee, Dinda L.*
On Trial: From Adam and Eve to O.J. Simpson. — *Anastaplo, George*
On Weaving — *Albers, Anni*
y On Writing for Children and Other People. — *Lester, Julius*
The Once and Future Army: A History of the Citizen Military Forces 1947-1974 — *McCarthy, Dayton*
Once Intrepid Warriors: Gender, Ethnicity, and the Cultural Politics of Maasai Development — *Hodgson, Dorothy L.*
Once Saved, Always Saved?: A New Testament Study of Apostasy — *Claybrook, Frederick W.*
Once Upon a Bride — *Stone, Jean*
y Once upon a Childhood: Stories and Memoirs of American Youth — *Solomon, Barbara H.*
c Once Upon a Cloud (Illus. by Mahurin, Matt) — *Walker, Rob D.*
c Once upon a Cool Motorcycle Dude (Illus. by O'Malley, Carol) — *O'Malley, Kevin*
c Once upon a Curse — *Baker, E.D.*
c Once upon a Marigold — *Ferris, Jean*
y Once Upon a Poem: Favorite Poems That Tell Stories (Illus. by Bailey, Peter)
Once Upon a Poem: Favorite Poems That Tell Stories (Illus. by Bailey, Peter) — *Crossley-Holland, Kevin*
c Once Upon a Rhyme: Story Rhymes (Illus. by Banta, Susan) — *Mitter, Matt*
c Once Upon a Starry Night: A Book of Constellation Stories — *Mitton, Jacqueline*
Once Upon a Summer Day — *McKiernan, Dennis L.*
c Once Upon a Time — *Daly, Niki*
Once Upon a Time in Paradise: Canadians in the Golden Age of Hollywood — *Foster, Charles*
Once Upon a Time in the Italian West: A Filmgoer's Guide to Spaghetti Westerns — *Hughes, Howard*
c The Once Upon a Time Map Book (Illus. by Joyce, Peter) — *Hennessy, B.G.*
c Once upon a Time, upon a Nest — *Emmet, Jonathan*
Once Upon A Universe: Not-so-Grimm Tales of Cosmology — *Gilmore, Robert*
Once Upon a Virus: AIDS Legends and Vernacular Risk Perception — *Goldstein, Diane E.*
c Once upon a Wedding — *Milde, Jeanette*
c Once Upon an Ordinary School Day (Illus. by Kitamura, Satoshi) — *McNaughton, Colin*
Oncology Nursing Clinical Reference — *Otto, Shirley E.*
Oncology Nursing Drug Handbook — *Wilkes, Gail M.*
Oncology Nursing in the Ambulatory Setting: Issues and Models of Care, 2nd Ed. — *Buchsel, Patricia C.*
The One and the Many: English-Canadian Short Story Cycles — *Lynch, Gerald*
One Another — *Coady, Michael*

The One Best System: A History of American Urban Education — *Tyrack, David B.*
One Body, One Spirit: Principles of Successful Multiracial Churches — *Yancey, George A.*
One Building in the Earth: New and Selected Poems — *Helwig, Maggie*
One Car Caravan: On the Road with the 2004 Democrats before America Tunes In — *Shapiro, Walter*
One, Catholic, and Apostolic: Samuel Seabury and the Early Episcopal Church. — *Marshall, Paul Victor*
One China, Many Paths — *Wang, Chaohua*
c One Christmas in Lunenburg (Illus. by Kilby, Don) — *Bennet, Amy*
c One Dark and Dreadful Night (Illus. by Cecil, Randy) — *Cecil, Randy*
One Day at Fenway: A Day in the Life of Baseball in America — *Kettmann, Steve*
One Day My Sister Disappeared — *Orban, Christine*
One-Dimensional Metals: Conjugated Polymers, Organic Crystals, Carbon Nanotubes, 2nd Rev. Ed. — *Roth, Seigmar*
One Electorate Under God? A Dialogue on Religion & American Politics — *Elshtain, Jean Bethke*
One Electorate under God?: A Dialogue on Religion and American Politics — *Dionne, E.J.*
One Electorate under God?: A Dialogue on Religion and American Politics — *Patterson, Stephen J.*
y One False Move (Read by Reed, Maggi-Meg). Audiobook Review — *Kava, Alex*
One False Move — *Kava, Alex*
One Family: Before and During the Holocaust, 2nd Ed. — *Kolin, Andrew*
The One Fatal Flaw in Anselm's Argument — *Millican, Peter*
c One Fine Day (Illus. by Farnsworth, Bill) — *Van Steenwyk, Elizabeth*
One Flag, One Queen, One Tongue: New Zealand, the British Empire and the South African War, 1899-1902 — *Crawford, John*
One Foot in Eden — *Rash, Ron*
One Foot in Love — *Wright, Bil*
One for Sorrow, Two for Joy — *Woodall, Clive*
One Fourteenth of an Elephant: A Memoir of Life and Death on the Burma-Thailand Railway — *Peek, Ian Denys*
One God or Many? Concepts of Divinity in the Ancient World — *Porter, Barbara Nevling*
One God: The Political and Moral Philosophy of Western Civilization — *Lorca, Ernesto*
One Good Marriage — *Reycraft, Sean*
One Heart: Universal Wisdom from the World's Scriptures — *Kuchler, Bonnie Louise*
One Hundred and Fifty Years of The Daily Telegraph — *Howse, Christopher*
One Hundred and One Beautiful Small Towns in Italy — *Lazzarin, Paolo*
One Hundred Million Hearts. Audiobook Review — *Sakamoto, Kerri*
One Hundred Shades of White — *Nair, Preethi*
One Hundred Years of American Archaeology in the Middle East: Proceedings — *Clark, Douglas R.*
One Hundred Years of Canadian Cinema — *Melnyk, George*
One Hundred Years of Chromosome Research and What Remains to be Learned — *Lima-de-Faria, A.*
One Hundred Years of Old Man Sage: An Arapaho Life — *Anderson, Jeffrey D.*
One Hundred Years of Russell's Paradox — *Link, Godehard*
One Hundred Years of World Military Aircraft — *Polmar, Norman*
One Kind of Faith — *Soto, Gary*
One King, One Soldier — *Irvine, Alexander C.*
One Knight Only — *David, Peter*
One Large Coffin to Go — *Maltori, H. Mel*
y One Last Look — *Moore, Susanna*
One Life — *Lampert, Tom*
One Little Bug — *van Turennout, Paola*
c One Little Lamb (Illus. by Greenstein, Elaine) — *Greenstein, Elaine*
c One Little Seed (Illus. by Greenstein, Elaine) — *Greenstein, Elaine*
One Magical Sunday: But Winning Isn't Everything — *Mickelson, Phil*
One Man's Castle: Clarence Darrow in Defense of the American Dream — *Vine, Phyllis*
One Man's Documentary: A Memoir of the Early Years of the National Film Board — *McInnes, Graham*
One Man's Vision: The Life of Automotive Pioneer Ralph R. Teetor — *Meyer, Marjorie Teetor*

P

The Particulars of Rapture: An Aesthetics of the Affects — *Aliteri, Charles*

Parties and Elections in America: The Electoral Process, 4th Ed. — *Maisel, L. Sandy*

Parties and Politics: A Study of Opposition Parties and the PAP in Singapore — *Mutalib, Hussin*

Parties Long Estranged: Canada and Australia in the Twentieth Century — *MacMillan, Margaret*

The Parting of the Ways: The Roman Church as a Case Study — *Spence, Stephen*

Parting the Desert: The Creation of the Suez Canal — *Karabell, Zachary*

The Partisan Paradox: Religious Commitment and the Gender Gap in Party Identification — *Kaufmann, Karen M.*

Partisanenkrieg in Jugoslawien 1941-1944 — *Schmider, Klaus*

The Partitions of Memory: The Afterlife of the Division of India — *Kaul, Suvir*

Partnering for Change: Unions and Community Groups Build Coalitions for Economic Justice — *Reynolds, David B.*

Partnering for the Environment: Multistakeholder Collaboration in a Changing World — *Poncelet, Eric C.*

Partnering Intelligence: Creating Value for Your Business by Building Strong Alliances — *Dent, Stephen M.*

Partners at the Creation: The Men Behind Postwar Germany's Defense and Intelligence Establishments — *Critchfield, James H.*

Partners in Conflict: The Politics of Gender, Sexuality, and Labor in the Chilean Agrarian Reform, 1950-1973 — *Tinsman, Heidi*

y Partners to History: Martin Luther King Jr., Ralph David Abernathy, and the Civil Rights Movement — *Abernathy, Donzaleigh*

The Parts — *Ridgway, Keith*

Party Dips!: 50 Zippy, Zesty, Spicy, Savory, Tasty, Tempting Dips — *Sampson, Sally*

Party Drinks!: 50 Classic Cocktails and Lively Libations — *Rathbun, A.J.*

Party Games: Getting, Keeping, and Using Power in Gilded Age Politics — *Summers, Mark Wahlgren*

Party of the People: A History of the Democrats — *Witcover, Jules*

Party, Process and Political Change in Congress: New Perspectives on the History of Congress — *Brady, David W.*

Party, Process, and Political Change in Congress: New Perspectives on the History of Congress — *Brady, David W.*

Party Punches: Punch Recipes from Around the World — *Page, Tim*

y The Party Room #1: Get It Started — *Burke, Morgan*

The Party That Came out of the Cold War: The Party of Democratic Socialism in United Germany — *Oswald, Franz*

Party Without Bosses: Lessons on Anti-Capitalism from Felix Guattari and Luis Inacio 'Lula' da Silva — *Genosko, Gary*

The Party's Over: Blueprint for a Very English Revolution — *Sutherland, Keith*

y Parvana's Journey — *Ellis, Deborah*

Parzival — *Wolfram, von Eschenbach*

PAS Proteins: Regulators and Sensors of Development and Physiology — *Crews, Stephen T.*

Pasardhesi — *Kadare, Ismail*

Pascal: New Trends in Port-Royal Studies: Actes du 33 congres annuel de la North American Society for Seventeenth-Century French Literature — *Sellier, Philippe*

c Pascual and the Kitchen Angels (Illus. by DePaola, Tomie) — *DePaola, Tomie*

Pashazade: The First Arabesk — *Grimwood, Jon Courtenay*

y Pass It On: An Insiders Novel — *Minter, J.*

Passage — *Goldsworthy, Andy*

Passages — *Olivier, Emile*

Passages: Explorations Of The Contemporary City — *Livesey, Graham*

y Passages to Freedom: The Underground Railroad in History and Memory — *Blight, David W.*

Passages: Welcome Home to Canada

Passed On: African American Mourning Stories — *Holloway, Karla F.C.*

The Passeggiata and Popular Culture in an Italian Town: Folklore and the Performance of Modernity — *Del Negro, Giovanni P.*

Passiflora: Passionflowers of the World — *Ulmer, Torsten*

Passing for White: Race, Religion, and the Healy Family, 1820-1920 — *O'Toole, James M.*

Passing for White--Race, Religion, and the Healy Family 1820-1920 — *O'Toole, James M.*

Passing the Buck: Congress, the Budget, and Deficits — *Farrier, Jasmine*

Passing Through — *Channer, Colin*

Passing Through: The End-of-Life Decisions of Lesbians and Gay Men — *Auger, Jeanette*

Passing under Heaven — *Hill, Justin*

Passion and Pathology in Victorian Fiction — *Wood, Jane (b. 1943 -)*

A Passion for Antiques — *Ohrbach, Barbara Milo*

A Passion for Freedom: My Encounters with Extraordinary People — *Sussman, Leonard R.*

A Passion for Opera: Learning to Love It: The Greatest Masters, Their Greatest Music — *Smith, Peter Fox*

Passion for Survival: The True Story of Marie Anne and Louis Payzant in 18-Century Nova Scotia — *Layton, Linda G.*

A Passion for the Impossible: John D. Caputo in Focus — *Dooley, Mark*

Passion for Wildlife: The History of the Canadian Wildlife Service — *Burnett, J. Alexander*

Passion Is a Fashion: The Real Story of the Clash — *Gilbert, Pat*

The Passion of Abby Hemenway: Memory, Spirit, and the Making of History — *Clifford, Deborah Pickman*

The Passion of Ayn Rand's Critics — *Valliant, James Stevens*

The Passion of My Times: An Advocate's Fifty-Year Journey in the Civil Rights Movement — *Carroll, William L. Taylor*

The Passion of My Times: An Advocate's Fifty-Year Journey through the Civil Rights Revolution — *Taylor, William L.*

Passion, Politics and Philosophie: Rediscovering — *Loft, Leonore*

A Passion to Preserve: Gay Men as Keepers of Culture — *Fellows, Will*

The Passionate Collector: Eighty Years in the World of Art — *Neuberger, Roy R.*

A Passionate Endeavor — *Nash, Sophie*

A Passionate Pilgrim: A Biography of Bishop James A. Pike — *Robertson, David M.*

Passionate Spectator — *Kraft, Eric*

Passionate Spirituality: Hildegard of Bingen and Hadewijch of Brabant — *Dreyer, Elizabeth A.*

The Passionate Troubadour — *Hays, Edward*

A Passionate Usefulness: The Life and Literary Labors of Hannah Adams — *Schmidt, Gary D.*

Passions of the Soul in the Metamorphosis of Becoming — *Tymieniecka, Anna-Teresa*

c Passover Is Here! (Illus. by Desmoinaux, Christel) — *Pearlman, Bobby*

Passport Photos — *Kumar, Amitava*

Past Due — *Lashner, William*

Past Futures: The Impossible Necessity of History, Based on the 1996 Joanne Goodman Lectures — *Martin, Ged*

Past Imperfect: Facts, Fictions, and Fraud in the writing of American History — *Hoffer, Peter Charles*

The Past in Question: Modern Macedonia and the Uncertainties of Nation — *Brown, Keith*

Past Judgement: Social Policy in New Zealand History — *Dalley, Bronwyn*

Past Mortem — *Elton, Ben*

c Past Perfect, Present Tense: New and Collected Stories — *Peck, Richard*

Past Things and Present: Jasper Johns Since 1983 — *Rothfuss, Joan*

The Paston Family in the Fifteenth Century: Endings — *Richmond, Colin*

The Pastor Bonus: Proceedings — *Clemens, Theo*

Pastoral Counselor's Model for Wellness in the Workplace: Psychergonomics — *Menz, Robert L.*

Pastoralists: Equality, Hierarchy, and the State — *Slazman, Philip Carl*

Pastorelles — *Taggart, John*

The Pastry Queen — *Rather, Rebecca*

c Pat-a-Cake — *Collins, Heather*

The Pat Conroy Cookbook: Recipes of My Life — *Conroy, Pat*

Pat Schroeder: A Woman of the House — *Lowy, Joan A.*

c Pat the Bunny — *Kunhardt, Dorothy*

Patagonia: Land of Giants — *Winograd, Alejandro*

Pataphysics: The Poetics of Imaginary Science — *Bok, Christian*

Patchwork Nation: Sectionalism and Political Change in American Politics — *Gimpel, James G.*

c The Patchwork Path: A Quilt Map to Freedom (Illus. by Bennett, Erin Susanne) — *Stroud, Bettye*

Patent and Trademark Information: Uses and Perspectives — *Baldwin, Virginia A.*

Patent Inventions: Intellectual Property and the Victorian Novel — *Pettitt, Clare*

Patent It Yourself, 10th Ed. — *Pressman, David*

Patent Law and Practice, 4th Ed. — *Schwartz, Herbert F.*

Patent Law Essentials: A Concise Guide, 2nd Ed. — *Durham, Alan L.*

Patent Pending in 24 Hours, 2nd Ed. — *Stim, Richard*

Patenting Art and Entertainment: New Strategies for Protecting Creative Ideas — *Aharonian, Gregory*

Patents, Citations, and Innovations: A Window on the Knowledge Economy — *Jaffe, Adam B.*

y Patents: Ingenious Inventions: How They Work and How They Came to Be — *Ikenson, Ben*

Pater to Forster, 1873-1924 — *Robbins, Ruth*

Paternalism in a Southern City: Race, Religion and Gender in Augusta, Georgia — *Cashin, Edward J.*

Paternalism Incorporated: Fables of American Fatherhood, 1865-1940 — *Leverenz, David*

Path Breakers: The Eiteljorg Fellowship for Native American Fine Art, 2003 — *Lippard, Lucy R.*

Path Integrals and Quantum Anomalies — *Fujikawa, Kazuo*

The Path of Compassion: The Bodhisattva Precepts, the Chinese Brahma's Net Sutra — *Batchelor, Martine*

Path of Handsome Lake: A Model of Recovery for Native People — *Walle, Alf H.*

y Path of Honor — *Francis, Diana Pharaoh*

The Path to Geneva: The Quest for a Permanent Agreement, 1996-2004 — *Beilin, Yossi*

The Path to Mass Rebellion: An Analysis of Two Intifadas — *Beitler, Ruth Margolies*

The Path to Partnership: A Guide for Junior Associates — *Bennett, Steven C.*

The Path to Victory: The Mediterranean Theater in World War II — *Porch, Douglas*

c The Path Winds Home — *DeVos, Janie*

Pathfinder: John Charles Fremont and the Course of American Empire — *Chaffin, J. Thomas*

Pathogenesis of Bacterial Infections in Animals, 3rd Ed. — *Gyles, Carlton L.*

Pathogenic Fungi: Host Interactions and Emerging Strategies for Control — *Calderone, Richard A.*

Pathogenic Fungi: Structural Biology and Taxonomy — *San-Blas, Gioconda*

The Pathological Protein: Mad Cow, Chronic Wasting, and Other Deadly Prion Diseases — *Yam, Philip*

Pathologies of Power: Health, Human Rights and the New War on the Poor — *Farmer, Paul*

Pathology: Clinicopathologic Foundations of Medicine, 4th ed. — *Rubin, Emanuel*

Pathology: PreTest Self-Assessment and Review, 11th Ed. — *Brown, Earl J.*

Pathophysiology: Clinical Concepts of Disease Processes, 6th Ed. — *Price, Sylvia Anderson*

Pathophysiology, Evaluation and Management of Valvular Heart Diseases. Vol. 2 — *Borer, Jeffrey S.*

Pathophysiology of Cardiovascular Diseases: Proceedings — *Dhalla, Naranjan S.*

Pathophysiology: PreTest Self-Assessment and Review, 3rd Ed. — *Mufson, Maurice A.*

Paths of Origin, Gates of Life: A Study of Place and Precedence in Southwest Timor — *McWilliam, Andrew*

Paths to Contemporary French Literature — *Taylor, John*

Paths to God: Living the Bhagavad Gita — *Ram, Dass*

Paths to the Professoriate: Strategies for Enriching the Preparation of Future Faculty — *Austin, Ann E.*

Pathway to Purpose for Women — *Brazelton, Katie*

Pathways Out of Poverty: Private Firms and Economic Mobility in Developing Countries — *Fields, Gary S.*

Pathways to Artistry: A Method for Comprehensive Technical and Musical Development; Technique 2 and Repertoire 2. — *Rollin, Catherine*

Pathways to Bliss: Mythology and Personal Transformation — *Campbell, Joseph*

Pathways to Nursing: A Guide to Library and Online Research in Nursing and Allied Health — *Tucker, Dennis C.*

Pathways to Prohibition: Radicals, Moderates, and Social Movement Outcomes — *Szymanski, Ann-Marie E.*

Preaching Eugenics: Religious Leaders and the American Eugenics Movement — *Rosen, Christine*

Preaching the Gospel of John: Proclaiming the Living Word — *Williamson, Lamar*

Preaching the Gospels without Blaming the Jews: A Lectionary Commentary — *Allen, Ronald J.*

Prebisch y Furtado: El Estructuralismo Latinoamericano — *Lora, Jorge*

Precalculus: Graphing, Data, and Analysis. 3rd Ed. — *Sullivan, Michael*

Precarious Life: The Power of Mourning and Violence — *Butler, Judith*

y Precious and the Boo Hag (Illus. by Brooker, Kyrsten) — *McKissack, Patricia*

c Precious and the Boo Hag (Illus. by Brooker, Kyrsten) — *McKissack, Patricia C.*

Precious Fire: Maud Russell and the Chinese Revolution — *Garner, Karen*

The Precisianist Strain: Disciplinary Religion & Antinomian Backlash in Puritanism to 1638 — *Bozeman, Theodore Dwight*

Precision Pendulum Clocks: France, Germany, America, and Recent Advancements — *Roberts, Derek*

The Precision Revolution: GPS and the Future of Aerial Warfare — *Rip, Michael Russell*

Preconcentration Techniques for Natural and Treated Waters: High Sensitivity Determination of Organic and Organometallic Compounds, Cations and Anions — *Crompton, T.R.*

y Predator's Gold — *Reeve, Philip*

Predictable Surprises: The Disasters You Should Have Seen Coming, and How to Prevent Them — *Bazerman, Max H.*

Predicting Chemical Toxicity and Fate — *Cronin, Mark T.D.*

The Prediction and Control of Organized Crime: The Experience of Post-Soviet Ukraine — *Finckenauer, James O.*

Predictions

Predictive Material Modeling: Combining Fundamental Physics Understanding, Computational Methods and Empirically Observed Behavior: Proceedings — *Kirk, Mark T.*

Prefab Home — *Buchanan, Michael.*

A Preface to Politics, 6th Ed. — *Schuman, David*

Prefiguring Cyberculture: An Intellectual History — *Tofts, Darren*

Pregnancy and Birth Sourcebook, 2nd Ed. — *Sutton, Amy L.*

Pregnancy Sucks for Men: What to Do When Your Miracle Makes You Both Miserable — *Kimes, Joanne*

Pregnant Bodies, Fertile Minds: Gender, Race, and the Schooling of Pregnant Teens — *Luttrell, Wendy*

Pregnant Fictions: Childbirth and the Fairy Tale in Early-Modern France — *Tucker, Holly*

Pregnant Passion: Gender, Sex, and Violence in the Bible — *Kirk-Duggan, Cheryl A.*

Preharvest and Post-Harvest Food Safety: Contemporary Issues and Future Directions — *Beier, Ross C.*

c Prehistoric Animals Series

Prehistoric California: Archaeology and the Myth of Paradise — *Raab, L. Mark*

c Prehistoric Life Series

Prehistoric Past Revealed: The Four Billion Year History of Life on Earth — *Palmer, Douglas*

Prehistoric Steppe Adaptation and the Horse — *Levine, Marsha*

Prehistory of the Carson Desert and Stillwater Mountains: Environment, Mobility, and Subsistence in a Great Basin Wetland — *Kelly, Robert L.*

Prehospital Systems and Medical Oversight, 3rd Ed. — *National Association of EMS Physicians*

Prelude to Political Economy: A Study of the Social and Political Foundations of Economics — *Basu, Kaushik*

Preludios y estudios — *Segovia, Andres*

Premature Birth: A Family Survival Guide — *Clancy, Jo*

"The Premier Oboist of Europe": A Portrait of Gustave Vogt — *Burgess, Geoffrey*

Premiere poesie francaise de la Renaissance: Autour des Puys poetiques normands — *Arnould, Jean-Claude*

The Premodern Teenager: Youth in Society, 1150-1650 — *Eisenbichler, Konrad*

Premonitions — *Watson, Jude*

Prenuptial Agreements: How to Write a Fair and Lasting Contract — *Irving, Shae*

y Prep — *Sittenfeld, Curtis*

Preparing for the ACSM Health/Fitness Instructor Certification Examination, 2nd Ed. — *Isaacs, Larry D.*

Preparing Mathematics and Science Teachers for Diverse Classrooms: Promising Strategies for Transformative Pedagogy — *Rodriguez, Alberto J.*

Preparing Reading Professionals: A Collection from the International Reading Association

Preparing School Leaders for the 21st century: an International Comparison of Development Programs in 15 Countries — *Huber, Stephan Gerhard*

Preparing Teachers around the World — *Wang, Aubrey H.*

Prepiska: Priredila i komentare napisala Radmila Suljagic — *Petrovic, Rastko*

c Prepositions — *Heinrichs, Ann*

Presbyterian Beliefs: A Brief Introduction — *McKim, Donald K.*

Prescription for Excellence: How Innovation Is Saving Canada's Health Care System — *Rachlis, Michael*

Prescription for Natural Cures: A Self-Care Guide for Treating Health Problems with Natural Remedies, Including Diet and Nutrition, Nutritional Supplements, Bodywork, and More — *Balch, James F.*

Prescription Pot: A Leading Advocate's Heroic Battle to Legalize Medical Marijuana — *McMahon, George*

c The Presence (Read by Bresnahan, Alyssa). Audiobook Review — *Bunting, Eve*

c The Presence — *Bunting, Eve*

The Presence — *Graham, Heather*

Presence, Prevention, and Persuasion: A Historical Analysis of Military Force and Political Influence — *Rhodes, Edward*

Present Moment Awareness: A Simple, Step-by-Step Guide to Living in the Now — *Duncan, Shannon*

Present Pasts: Urban Palimpsets and the Politics of Memory — *Huyssen, Andreas*

Present Tense: Poets in the World — *Pawlak, Mark*

Present Value — *Willett, Sabin*

Presentation Planning and Media Relations for the Pharmaceutical Industry — *Lidstone, John*

Presenting Celia Cruz — *Rodriguez-Duarte, Alexis*

Preservation of Fertility — *Tulandi, Togas*

The Preservationist (Read by Bunch, Tyler). Audiobook Review — *Maine, David*

y The Preservationist (Read by Tyler, Bunch). Audiobook Review — *Maine, David*

The Preservationist — *Maine, David*

Preserved — *Sandler, Nick*

Preserving Power Through Coalitions: Comparing the Grand Strategy of Great Britain and the United States — *Sampanis, Maria*

Preserving the Sacred: Historical Perspectives on the Ojibwa Midewiwin — *Angel, Michael*

Preserving the Self in the South Seas, 1680-1840 — *Lamb, Jonathan*

The Presidency A to Z — *Nelson, Michael*

The Presidency and Political Science: Two Hundred Years of Constitutional Debate — *Tatalovich, Raymond*

The Presidency and the Law: The Clinton Legacy — *Adler, David Gray*

The Presidency and Women: Promise, Performance and Illusion — *Martin, Janet M.*

The Presidency, Congress, and Divided Government: A Postwar Assessment — *Conley, Richard S.*

c The Presidency of the United States — *Heath, David*

c The President Is Shot: The Assassination of Abraham Lincoln — *Holzer, Harold*

y The President Is Shot! The Assassination of Abraham Lincoln — *Holzer, Harold*

President Kennedy Has Been Shot — *Newseum*

The President of Good and Evil: The Ethics of George W. Bush — *Singer, Peter (b. 1946 -)*

Presidential Campaigns: From George Washington to George W. Bush — *Boller, Paul F.*

The Presidential Companion: Readings on the First Ladies — *Watson, Robert P.*

Presidential Decisions for War: Korea, Vietnam and the Persian Gulf — *Hess, Gary R.*

The Presidential Difference: Leadership Style from FDR to George W. Bush — *Greenstein, Fred I.*

Presidential Elections, 1789-2000 — *CQ Press*

c Presidential Elections and Other Cool Facts — *Sobel, Sylvan*

Presidential Elections: Strategies and Structures of American Politics, 11th Ed. — *Polsby, Nelson W.*

Presidential Leaders

The Presidential Nominating Process: A Place for Us? — *Cook, Rhodes*

Presidential Performance: A Comprehensive Review — *Skidmore, Max J.*

Presidential Power: The Politics of Leadership — *Neustadt, Richard E.*

The Presidential Recordings: Lyndon B. Johnson: The Kennedy Assassination and the Transfer of Power, November 1963-January 1964 — *Holland, Max*

Presidential Speechwriting: From the New Deal to the Reagan Revolution and Beyond — *Ritter, Kurt*

Presidential Voices — *Metcalf, Allan*

Presidential War Power, 2nd Ed. — *Fisher, Louis*

Presidents and the Politics of Agency Design: Political Insulation in the United States Government Bureaucracy, 1946-1997 — *Lewis, David E.*

The Presidents and the Prime Ministers--Washington and Ottawa Face to Face: The Myth of Bilateral Bliss 1867-1982 — *Martin, Lawrence*

Presidents as Candidates: Inside the White House for Presidential Campaign — *Tenpas, Kathryn Dunn*

The President's Assassin — *Haig, Brian*

y The President's Daughter — *Bradley, Kimberly Brubaker*

c Presidents' Day — *Hamilton, Lynn*

c Presidents' Day — *Roslnsky, Natalie M.*

Presidents Every Question Answered: Everything you Could Possibly Want to Know About the Nation's Chief Executives — *Smith, Carter*

The Presidents Fact Book — *Matuz, Roger*

Presidents from Hayes Through McKinley: Debating the Issues in Pro and Con Primary Documents — *Sturgis, Amy H.*

y The President's House: A First Daughter Shares the History and Secrets of the World's Most Famous Home — *Truman, Margaret*

y The President's House: A First Daughter Shares the History and Secrets of the World's Most Famous House (Read by Burr, Sandra). Audiobook Review — *Truman, Margaret*

The Presidents: The Transformation of the American Presidency from Theodore Roosevelt to George W. Bush — *Graubard, Stephen*

Presidio, Mission, and Pueblo: Spanish Architecture and Urbanism in the United States — *Early, James*

Presidio Santa Maria de Glave: A Struggle for Survival in Colonial Spanish Pensacola — *Bense, Judith A.*

Prespectives of Learning — *Phillips, D.C.*

Press Censorship in Jacobean England — *Clegg, Cyndia Susan*

Press Gang: How Newspapers Make Profits from Propaganda — *Greenslade, Macmillan*

Press, Revolution, and Social Identities in France, 1830-1835 — *Popkin, Jeremy D.*

Pressepolitik als Chance: Staatliche Oeffentlichkeitsarbeit in den Laendern der Weimarer Republik — *Lau, Matthias*

Pressure Golf: Overcoming Choking and Frustration — *Clarkson, Michael*

Pressure Systems Casebook: Causes and Avoidance of Failures and Defects — *Wintle, J.B.*

Pressure Systems Safety Regulations: PSSRs, SI 128 — *Matthews, Clifford*

Pressure Vessel and Piping Codes and Standards: Proceedings — *Chakrabarti, G.S.*

The Pressured Child: Helping Your Child Find Success in School and Life — *Thompson, Michael*

y Pretear: The New Legend of Snow White, Volume 1 (Illus. by Naruse, Kaori) — *Naruse, Kaori*

A Pretext for War: 9/11, Iraq, and the Abuse of America's Intelligence Agencies — *Bamford, James*

Pretres en Gaule merovingienne — *Godding, Robert*

Pretty Woman — *Michaels, Fern*

Prevent and Reverse Heart Disease, Arthritis, Diabetes, Allergies, and Asthma — *Challem, Jack*

Preventing and Managing Disabling Injury at Work — *Sullivan, Terrence*

Preventing and Responding to Violence at Work — *Rogers, Kimberly Ann*

Preventing Currency Crises in Emerging Markets — *Edwards, Sebastian*

Preventing Earth Defects — *Haldeman, Joe W.*

Preventing Eating Disorders among Pre-Teen Girls: A Step-by-Step Guide — *Menassa, Beverly Neu*

Preventing Harassment: Federal Employment Law, Vol. III — *Shrm Information Center*

Prevention and Cure: The London School of Hygiene and Tropical Medicine: A Twentieth-Century Quest for Global Public Health — *Wilkinson, Lise*

Prevention and Health Promotion for the Excluded and the Destitute in Europe — *Chauvin, Pierre*

Q R

Q.E.D.: Beauty in Mathematical Proof — *Polster, Burkard*

Q Road — *Campbell, Bonnie Jo*

QBQ!: The Question Behind the Question: Practicing Personal Accountability at Work and in Life — *Miller, John G.*

Qoheleth: A Continental Commentary — *Lohfink, Norbert*

Q'sapi: A History of Okanagan People as Told by Okanagan Families — *Louis, Shirley*

c Quackadack Duck (Illus. by Beder, John) — *Morgan, Allen*

Quadratura americana: essai d'anthropologie levi-straussienne — *Desveaux, Emmanuel*

The Quakers in America — *Hamm, Thomas D.*

The Quakers in South Africa: A Social Witness — *Tonsing, Betty K.*

A Qualified Teacher in Every Classroom?: Appraising Old Answers and New Ideas — *Hess, Frederick M.*

Qualitative Analysis: Practice and Innovation — *Ezzy, Douglas*

Qualitative Data: An Introduction to Coding and Analysis — *Auerbach, Carl F.*

Qualitative Methods and Health Policy Research — *Murphy Elizabeth*

Qualitative Methods for Health Research — *Rodriguez, Judith Green*

Qualitative Research in Journalism: Taking It to the Streets — *Iorio, Sharon Hartin*

Qualitative Research Practice — *Seale, Clive*

Quality Across The Curriculum: Integrating Quality Tools and PDSA with Standards, K-5 — *Marino, Jay*

Quality and Accountability in Higher Education: Improving Policy, Enhancing Performance — *Bogue, E. Grady*

The Quality and Quantity of Contact: African Americans and Whites on College Campuses — *Moore, Robert M., III*

Quality Control. 7th Ed. — *Besterfield, Dale H.*

Quality Essentials: A Reference Guide from A to Z — *ReVelle, Jack B.*

The Quality Improvement Glossary — *Siebels, Don*

The Quality of Freedom — *Kramer, Matthew H.*

Quality of Life Research: A Critical Introduction — *Rapley, Mark*

Quality of Service in Heterogeneous Wired/Wireless Networks: Proceedings — *Boukerche, Azzedine*

Quality Popular Television — *Jancovich, Marc*

Quality Software (QSIC 2004): Proceedings — *International Conference on Quality Software*

Quality Teaching and Learning: Challenging Orthodoxies — *Crebbin, Wendy*

Quand la jeunesse entre en scene: l'Action catholique avant la Revolution tranquile — *Bienveue, Louise*

Quand Les Sumos Apprennent a Danser: la fin du modele Japonais — *Bouissou, Jean-Marie*

Quand on refuse on dit non — *Kourouma, Ahmadou*

Quando Dio ballava il tango — *Pariani, Laura*

c The Quangle Wangle's Hat (Illus. by Voce, Louise) — *Lear, Edward*

Quantico: Semper Progredi-Always Forward — *Gernard, Bradley E.*

Quantification of Tannins in Tree and Shrub Foliage: A Laboratory Manual — *Makkar, Harinder P.S.*

Quantifying the Benefits of Liberalising Trade in Services — *Organisation for Economic Co-operation and Development*

Quantifying the World: UN Ideas and Statistics — *Ward, Michael*

Quantitative Evaluation of Systems: Proceedings

Quantitative Level of Chemical Reactions — *Efremovich, G.E.*

Quantitative Methods in Population Health: Extensions of Ordinary Regression — *Palta, Mari*

Quantitative Methods In Social Science Research — *Gorard, Stephen*

Quantitative MRI of the Brain: Measuring Changes Caused by Disease — *Tofts, Paul*

Quantitative Psychological Research: A Students Handbook. 2nd Ed. — *Clark-Carter, David*

Quantitative Remote Sensing of Land Surfaces — *Liang, Shunlin*

Quantitative Structure-Activity Relationships for Pollution Prevention, Toxicity Screening, Risk Assessment, and Web Applications — *Walker, John D.*

Quantitative Zoology, Rev. Ed. — *Simpson, George Gaylord*

Quantum Chemistry; The Development of 'Ab Initio' Methods in Molecular Electronic Structure Theory — *Schaefer, Henry F.*

Quantum Chromodynamics: High Energy Experiments and Theory — *Dissertori, Gunther*

Quantum Communication and Information Technologies — *Shumovsky, A.S.*

Quantum Computing: A Short Course from Theory to Experiment — *Stolze, Joachim*

Quantum Control: Mathematical and Numerical Challenges — *Bandrauk, Andre D.*

Quantum Dot Lasers — *Ustinov, Victor M.*

Quantum Dots, Nanoparticles and Nanowires: Proceedings — *Guyot-Sionnest, P.*

Quantum Field Theory of Many-Body Systems: From the Origin of Sound to an Origin of Light and Electrons — *Wen, Xiao-Gang*

Quantum Gravity — *Kiefer, Claus*

Quantum Hall Systems: Braid Groups, Composite Fermions, and Fractional Charge — *Jacak, Lujan*

Quantum Leadership: A Textbook of New Leadership — *Porter-O'Grady, Timothy*

Quantum Mechanics: A Conceptual Approach — *Hameka, Hendrik F.*

Quantum Mechanics: A Modern and Concise Introductory Course — *Bes, Daniel R.*

Quantum Mechanics and Gravity — *Sachs, Mendel*

Quantum Mechanics and the Philosophy of Alfred North Whitehead — *Epperson, Michael*

Quantum Mechanics: Fundamentals — *Gottfried, Kurt*

Quantum Mechanics: Theory and Applications — *Ghatak, Ajoy*

Quantum Theory as an Emergent Phenomenon: The Statistical Mechanics of Matrix Models as the Precursor of Quantum Field Theory — *Adler, Stephen L.*

Quantum Theory of Fields — *Wentzel, Gregor*

Quantum Theory of the Optical and Electronic Properties of Semiconductors, 4th Ed. — *Haug, Hartmut*

Quantum Transport in Mesoscopic Systems: Complexity and Statistical Fluctuations, a Maximum-Entropy Viewpoint — *Mello, Pier A.*

The Quantum World: Quantum Physics for Everyone — *Ford, Kenneth W.*

c The Quark — *Bortz, Fred*

Quark Confinement and the Hadron Spectrum V: Proceedings — *Brambilla, Nora*

The Quarry — *Galgut, Damon*

Quarter Notes and Bank Notes: The Economics of Music Composition in the Eighteenth and Nineteenth Centuries — *Scherer, F.M.*

Quaternary Glaciations: Extent and Chronology, Pt. 1 — *Ehlers, Jurgen*

The Quaternary Period in the United States — *Gillespie, A.R.*

Quebec, 1775: The American Invasion of Canada — *Morrissey, Brendan*

Quebec City: A Visual Testimony (Illus. by Paquet, Jocelyn) — *Provencher, Jean*

Queen — *Chodas, Nadine*

Queen Cocaine — *Amat, Nuria*

Queen Elizabeth I — *Doran, Susan*

y Queen Isabella and the Unification of Spain — *Whitelaw, Nancy*

The Queen Jade — *Murray, Maya*

The Queen Jade — *Murray, Yxta Maya*

Queen Margrete I, 1353-1412, and the Founding of the Nordic Union — *Etting, Vivian*

The Queen Mary Psalter: A Study of Affect and Audience — *Stanton, Anne Rudloff*

Queen of Dreams: A Novel — *Divakaruni, Chitra Banerjee*

Queen of Dreams — *Divakaruni, Chitra Banerjee*

The Queen of Education: Rules for Making School Work — *Johnson, LouAnne*

c Queen of Hearts — *Engelbreit, Mary*

Queen of Scots: The True Life of Mary Stuart — *Guy, J.A.*

Queen of Scots: The True Life of Mary Stuart — *Guy, John*

The Queen of Subtleties — *Dunn, Suzannah*

y The Queen of the Big Time (Read by Campbell, Cassandra). Audiobook Review — *Trigiani, Adriana*

The Queen of the Big Time — *Trigiani, Adriana*

c Queen of the Class (Illus. by Engelbreit, Mary) — *Engelbreit, Mary*

Queen of the Night: Rediscovering the Celtic Moon Goddess — *NicMhacha, Sharynne MacLeod*

The Queen of the South (Read by Patel, Lina). Audiobook Review — *Perez-Reverte, Arturo*

y Queen of the South (Read by Patel, Lina). Audiobook Review — *Reverte, Arturo Perez*

The Queen of the South — *Perez-Reverte, Arturo*

Queen: The Life and Music of Dinah Washington — *Cohodas, Nadine*

y Queen Victoria and the British Empire — *Whitelaw, Nancy*

Queen Victoria and the Theatre of Her Age — *Schoch, Richard W.*

Queen Victoria: First Media Monarch — *Plunkett, John*

Queenan Country: A Reluctant Anglophile's Pilgrimage to the Mother Country — *Queenan, Joe*

c The Queen's Dragon (Illus. by Williamson, Gwyneth) — *Cassidy, Anne*

The Queen's Majesty's Passage and Related Documents — *Warkentin, Germaine*

c The Queen's Progress: An Elizabethan Alphabet (Illus. by Ibatoulline, Bagram) — *Mannis, Celeste Davidson*

The Queen's Slave Trader: John Hawkyns, Elizabeth I, and the Trafficking in Human Souls — *Hazlewood, Nick*

Queenship in Europe, 1660-1815: The Role of the Consort — *Orr, Clarissa Campbell*

Queer Beats: How the Beats Turned America on to Sex — *Marler, Regina*

The Queer Composition of America's Sound: Gay Modernists, American Music, and National Identity — *Hubbs, Nadine*

Queer Crips: Disabled Gay Men and Their Stories — *Guter, Bob*

The Queer Encyclopedia of the Visual Arts — *Summers, Claude J.*

y Rattlesnake Mesa: Stories from a Native American Childhood (Illus. by Renkun, Richela) — *Weber, EdNah New Rider*

Rattlesnake Plantain — *Green, Heidi*

c The Rattlesnake Who Went to School (Illus. by Cravath, Lynne) — *Strete, Craig*

Rauschenberg: Art and Life — *Kotz, Mary Lynn*

A Ravel Reader: Correspondence, Articles, Interviews — *Ravel, Maurice*

y Raven Quest — *Stewart, Sharon*

y Raven's Point — *Metz, Melinda*

c The Raven's Ring Pin — *Anacker, John*

The Raw Deal: How Myths and Misinformation about Deficits, Inflation, and Wealth Impoverish America — *Frank, Ellen*

Raw Silk — *Alexander, Meena*

Ray: A Tribute to the Movie, the Music, and the Man — *White, James L.*

y Ray Bradbury: Master of Science Fiction and Fantasy — *Mass, Wendy*

Ray Bradbury: The Life of Fiction — *Eller, Jonathan R.*

Ray Harryhausen: An Animated Life — *Harryhausen, Ray*

Ray, Vol. 1 — *Yoshitomi, Akihito*

c Raymie, Dickie, and the Bean: Why I Love and Hate My Brothers (Illus. by Locke, Gary) — *Romano, Ray*

The Raymond and Frances Bushnell Collection of Netsuke: A Legend at the Los Angeles County Museum of Art — *Goodall, Hollis*

Raymond and Hannah — *Marche, Stephen*

Raymond Loewy: Designs for a Consumer Culture — *Porter, Glenn*

Raymond Williams's Sociology of Culture: A Critical Reconstruction — *Jones, Paul*

c Rays

A Razor for a Goat: Problems in the History of Witchcraft and Diabolism — *Rose, Elliot*

c Razzamadaddy (Illus. by Yoshikawa, Sachiko) — *Walvoord, Linda*

c The RCMP Musical Ride (Illus. by Newhouse, Maxwell) — *Newhouse, Maxwell*

RCRA Regulations and Keyword Index, 2004 Ed. — *Almeria, Sally*

Re-Educating German Women: The Work of the Women's Affairs Section of the British Military Government 1946-1951 — *Tscharntke, Denise*

Re-Enacting the Past: Essays on the Evolution of Modern English Historiography — *Levine, Joseph M.*

Re-Engineering the Chemical Processing Plant: Process Intensification — *Stankiewicz, Andrzej*

Re-Examining Liberation in Namibia: Political Culture Since Independence — *Melber, Henning*

Re-Examining the Cold War: U.S.-China Diplomacy, 1954-1973 — *Ross, Robert S.*

Re-Imagining Justice: Progressive Interpretations of Formal Equality, Rights, and the Rule of Law — *West, Robin L.*

Re-Imagining the Museum: Beyond the Mausoleum — *Witcomb, Andrea*

Re-Inventing the Asian Model: The Case of Singapore — *Bhaskaran, Manu*

Re-Orienting Australia-China Relations: 1972 to the Present — *Thomas, Nicholas*

Re-Orienting Fashion: The Globalization of Asian Dress — *Niessen, Sandra*

Re-presenting the Shoah for the Twenty-First Century — *Lentin, Ronit*

Re-Situating Folklore: Folk Contexts and Twentieth-Century Literature and Art — *De Caro, Frank*

Re-Thinking Aesthetics: Rogue Essays on Aesthetics and the Arts — *Berleant, Arnold*

Re-Understanding Japan: Chinese Perspectives, 1895-1945 — *Lu, Yan*

Re-viewing the Passion: Mel Gibson's Film and its Critics — *Plate, Brent*

Re-Writing the French Revolutionary Tradition — *Alexander, Robert*

(Re)constructing Cultures of Violence and Peace — *Jackson, Richard, (b. 1966 -)*

(Re)productions: Autobiography, Colonialism, and Infanticide — *Miller, Mary-Kay F.*

c Reach for the Stars: A Little Torah's Journey (Illus. by Ofer, Rosalie) — *Rouss, Sylvia*

Reaching for the Stars: A New History of Bomber Command in World War II — *Connelly, Mark*

Reaching out to Religious Youth: A Guide to Services, Programs, and Collections — *Carman, L. Kay*

Reaching the Rural Poor: A Renewed Strategy for Rural Development — *Csaki, Csaba*

Reactions to the Master: Michelangelo's Effect on Art and Artists in the Sixteenth Century — *Ames-Lewis, Francis*

Reactive Intermediate Chemistry — *Moss, Robert A.*

c Read A Zillion Books — *Pallotta, Jerry*

c Read about Abraham Lincoln — *Feinstein, Stephen*

c Read about Cesar Chavez — *Feinstein, Stephen*

c Read about Martin Luther King — *Feinstein, Stephen*

c Read about Sacagawea — *Feinstein, Stephen*

Read-Alouds and Performance Reading: A Handbook of Activities for the Middle School Classroom — *Moen, Christine Boardman*

Read and Do Science Discovery Library

Read It Again! Standards-Based Literature Lessons for Young Children — *Ayes, Linda*

c Read Me a Book — *Reid, Barbara*

c Read, Stick and Learn about Animals (Illus. by Boos, Andre)

Read This!: Why Books Matter — *Zoppa, Karen*

A Reader for the Politically Incorrect — *Zilbergeld, George*

Reader, I Married Him — *Roberts, Michele*

A Reader in Latina Feminist Theology: Religion and Justice — *Aquino, Maria Pilar*

The Reader of Gentlemen's Mail: Herbert O. Yardley and the Birth of American Codebreaking — *Kahn, David*

Reader of the Purple Sage: Essays on Western Writers and Environmental Literature — *Ronald, Ann*

Readers and Writers in Ovid's Heroides: Transgressions of Genre and Gender — *Spentzou, E.*

Reader's Digest Illustrated World Atlas

Reader's Guide to British History, Vols. 1-2 — *Loades, David*

Reader's Guide to British History; Vols. 1-2 — *Loades, David*

A Reader's Guide to William Faulkner: The Short Stories — *Volpe, Edmond Loris*

Readers in Wonderland: The Liberating Worlds of Fantasy Fiction from Dorothy to Harry Potter — *O'Keefe, Deborah*

Reading 1 Corinthians in the Twenty-First Century — *Crocker, Cornelia Cyss*

Reading Across Borders: Storytelling and Knowledges of Resistance — *Stone-Mediatore, Shari*

Reading Across Cultures — *Goody, Joan*

Reading Africa into American Literature: Epics, Fables, and Gothic Tales — *Cartwright, Keith*

Reading Aloud and Beyond: Fostering the Intellectual Life with Older Readers — *Serafini, Frank*

Reading and Literacy in the Middle Ages and Renaissance — *Moulton, Ian Frederick*

The Reading and Preaching of the Scriptures in the Worship of the Christian Church, Vol.4 — *Old, Hughes Oliphant*

Reading and Reader Development: The Pleasure of Reading — *Elkin, Judith*

Reading and the Reference Librarian: The Importance to Library Service of Staff Reading Habits — *Dilevko, Juris*

Reading and the Reference Librarian: The Importance to Library Service of Staff Reading Habits — *Dilveko, Juris*

Reading and Understanding Research. 2nd Ed. — *Locke, Lawrence F.*

Reading Assessment for Diagnostic-Prescriptive Teaching, 2nd Ed. — *Manzo, Anthony V.*

Reading Bayle — *Lennon, Thomas M.*

Reading between the Signs Workbook: A Cultural Guide for Sign Language Students and Interpreters — *Mindess, Anna*

Reading Beyond the Alphabet: Innovations in Lifelong Literacy — *Kothari, Brij*

c The Reading Bug — *Jennings, Paul*

Reading Context — *Stygall, Gail*

Reading Culture: Contexts for Critical Reading and Writing, 5th Ed. — *George, Diana*

Reading Cusanus: Metaphor and Dialectic in a Conjectural Universe — *Miller, Clyde Lee*

A Reading Diary: A Passionate Reader's Reflections on a Year of Books — *Manguel, Alberto*

A Reading Diary: A Year of Favourite Books — *Manguel, Alberto*

Reading Doctors' Writing: Race, Politics and Power in Indigenous Health Research, 1870-1969 — *Thomas, David Piers*

Reading Economic Geography — *Barnes, Trevor J.*

Reading Families: Women's Literate Practice in Late Medieval England — *Krug, Rebecca*

Reading from Right to Left: Essays on the Hebrew Bible in Honour of David J.A. Clines — *Exum, J. Cheryl*

The Reading Group — *Noble, Elizabeth*

Reading Harry Potter: Critical Essays — *Anatol, Giselle Liza*

Reading History in Early Modern England — *Woolf, D.R.*

Reading Humanitarian Intervention: Human Rights and the Use of Force in International Law — *Orford, Anne*

Reading in Alice Munro's Archives — *McCaig, JoAnn*

Reading in the Classroom: Systems for the Observation of Teaching and Learning — *Vaughn, Sharon*

Reading Irish Histories: Texts, Contexts, and Memory in Modern Ireland — *McBride, Lawrence W.*

Reading Is Seeing: Learning to Visualize Scenes, Characters, Ideas, and Text Worlds to Improve Comprehension and Reflective Reading — *Wilhelm, Jeffrey D.*

Reading Lolita in Tehran: A Memoir in Books (Read by Lecat, Lisette). Audiobook Review — *Nafisi, Azar*

Reading Monarch's Writing: The Poetry of Henry VII, Mary Stuart, Elizabeth I, and James VI/I — *Herman, Peter C.*

The Reading Nation in the Romantic Period — *St. Clair, William*

Reading Native American Literature: A Teacher's Guide — *Goebel, Bruce A.*

Reading "Paradise Lost" — *Woof, Pamela*

Reading Psychoanalysis: Freud, Rank, Ferenczi, Groddeck — *Rudnytsky, Peter L.*

Reading Rants! — *Hubert, Jennifer*

Reading Sites: Social Difference and Reader Response — *Schweickart, Patrocinio P.*

Reading, Society, and Politics in Early Modern England — *Sharpe, Kevin*

The Reading Specialist: Leadership for the Classroom, School and Community — *Bean, Rita M.*

Reading Sulpicia: Commentaries, 1475-1990 — *Skoie, M.*

Reading Teacher's Handbook — *Phenix, Jo*

Reading Texts, Seeking Wisdom: Scripture and Theology — *Ford, David F.*

Reading the Bible in the Strange World of Medicine — *Verhey, Allen*

Reading the Bible Today: A 21st Century Appreciation of Scripture — *McKnight, Edgar V.*

Reading the Body in the Eighteenth-Century Novel — *McMaster, Juliet*

y Reading the Bones — *Finch, Sheila*

Reading the Book of Revelation: A Resource for Students — *Barr, David L.*

Reading the Early Republic — *Fugerson, Robert A.*

Reading the East India Company, 1720-1840: Colonial Currencies of Gender — *Joseph, Betty*

Reading the Fascicles of Emily Dickinson: Dwelling in Possibilities — *Heginbotham, Eleanor Elson*

Reading the Gospels in the Dark: Portrayals of Jesus in Film — *Walsh, Richard*

Reading the Medieval Book — *Starkey, Kathryn*

Reading the Modern British and Irish Novel, 1890-1930 — *Schwartz, Daniel R.*

Reading the Naked Truth: Literacy, Legislation, and Lies — *Coles, Gerald*

Reading the New Testament Today — *Voorst, Robert E. van*

Reading the Renaissance: Ideas and Idioms from Shakespeare to Milton — *Berley, Marc*

Reading the Right Text: An Anthology of Contemporary Chinese Drama — *Chen, Xiaomei*

Reading the River: Selected Poems — *Adamson, Robert*

Reading the Rocks: The Autobiography of the Earth — *Bjornerud, Marcia*

Reading the Roots: American Nature Writing Before Walden — *Branch, Michael P.*

Reading The Virginian in the New West — *Graulich, Melody*

Reading The Women Of The Bible: A New Interpretation Of Their Stories — *Frymer-Kensky, Tikva*

Reading the World of Work: A Learner-Centered Approach to Workplace Literacy and ESL — *Gallo, Melina L.*

Reading with Meaning: Teaching Comprehension in the Primary Grades — *Miller, Debbie (b. 1948 -)*

Resurgence — *Sheffield, Charles*

Resurgence of Jewish Life in Germany — *Kahn, Charlotte*

The Resurrected Man — *Williams, Sean*

Resurrecting Empire: Western Footprints and America's Perilous Path in the Middle East — *Khalidi, Rashid*

The Resurrection of Christ: A Historical Inquiry — *Ludemann, Gerd*

The Resurrection of God Incarnate — *Swinburne, Richard*

The Resurrection of Ireland: The Sinn Fein Party, 1916-1923 — *Laffan, Michael*

The Resurrection of the Body and the Ruin of the World — *Guest, Paul*

Resurrection of the Body in Early Judaism and Early Christianity: Doctrine, Community, and Self-Definition — *Setzer, Claudia*

The Resurrection of the Son of God — *Wright, N.T.*

Resynchronization and Defibrillation for Heart Failures: A Practical Approach — *Hayes, David L.*

The Retablo de Isabel la Catolica by Juan de Flandes and Michel Sittow — *Ishikawa, Chiyo*

Retail Therapy — *Bailey, Roz*

Retailing. 5th Ed. — *Dunne, Patrick M.*

Retaining Your Best Employees: Nine Case Studies from the Real World of Training — *Phillips, Jack J.*

Retaking the Universe: William S. Burroughs in the Age of Globalization — *Schneiderman, Davis*

Rethinking AIDS Prevention: Learning from Successes in Developing Countries — *Green, Edward C.*

Rethinking American History in a Global Age — *Bender, Thomas*

Rethinking Anti-Racisms: From Theory to Practice — *Lloyd, Cathie*

Rethinking Childhood — *Bain, Ken*

Rethinking Childhood — *Moss, Wendy L.*

Rethinking Childhood — *Pufall, Peter B.*

Rethinking Classroom Management: Strategies for Prevention, Intervention, and Problem Solving — *Belvel, Patricia Sequiera*

Rethinking Confucianism: Past and Present in China, Japan, Korea, and Vietnam — *Elman, Benjamin A.*

Rethinking Development Economics — *Chang, Ha-Joon*

Rethinking Globalization — *Steger, Manfred B.*

Rethinking Globalization: Teaching for Justice in an Unjust World — *Bigelow, Bill*

Rethinking Humanitarian Intervention: A Fresh Legal Approach Based on Fundamental Ethical Principles in International Law and World Religions. — *Lepard, Brian D.*

Rethinking Learner Support in Distance Education: Change and Continuity in an International Context — *Tait, Alan*

Rethinking Nasserism: Revolution and Historical Memory in Modern Egypt — *Podeh, Elie*

Rethinking R.G. Collingwood: Philosophy, Politics, and the Unity of Theory and Practice — *Browning, Gary K.*

Rethinking Reading Comprehension — *Sweet, Anne Polselli*

Rethinking Reality: Lucretius and the Textualization of Nature — *Kennedy, Duncan F.*

Rethinking Rights and Regulations: Institutional Responses to New Communication Technologies — *Cranor, Lorrie Faith*

Rethinking Scientific Literacy — *Roth, Wolff-Michael*

Rethinking Social Movements: Structure, Meaning, and Emotion — *Goodwin, Jeff*

Rethinking Social Theory — *Sibeon, Roger*

Rethinking Strategic Compensation — *Longnecker, Brent M.*

Rethinking Strategic HR — *Sullivan, John*

Rethinking Student Affairs Practice — *Love, Patrick G.*

Rethinking Teacher Education: Collaborative Responses to Uncertainty — *Edwards, Anne*

Rethinking the Great Depression: A New View of Its Causes and Consequences — *Smiley, Gene*

Rethinking the Korean War: A New Diplomatic and Strategic History — *Struek, William*

Rethinking the Korean War: A New Diplomatic and Strategic History — *Stueck, William*

Rethinking the Labour Movement in the 'New South Africa' — *Bramble, Tom*

Rethinking the Red Scare: The Lusk Committee and New York's Crusade Against Radicalism, 1919-1923 — *Pfannestiel, Todd J.*

Rethinking the Renaissance: Burgundian Arts across Europe — *Belozerskaya, Marina*

Rethinking the SAT: The Future of Standardized Testing in University Admissions — *Zwick, Rebecca*

Rethinking the Welfare State: The Political Economy of Pension Reform — *Rein, Martin*

Rethinking Urban Transport after Modernism: Lessons from South Africa — *Dewar, David*

Retieving the Ancients: An Introduction to Greek Philosophy — *Roochnik, David*

Retina and Optic Nerve Imaging — *Ciulla, Thomas A.*

Retirement for Two: Everything You Need to Know to Thrive Together as Long as You Both Shall Live — *Vandervelde, Maryanne*

Retiring as a Career: Making the Most of Your Retirement — *Newman, Betsy Kyte*

Retiring the State: The Politics of Pension Privatization in Latin America and Beyond — *Madrid, Raul L.*

Retorica — *Trejo, A.E. Ramirez*

Retransmission and U.S. Compliance with TRIPS — *Brennan, David J.*

Retratos: 2000 Years of Latin American Portraits — *Benson, Elizabeth P.*

Retratos: 2,000 Years of Latin American Portraits — *Oettinger, Marion*

The Retreat — *Rambaud, Patrick*

The Retreat from Organization: U.S. Feminism Reconceptualized — *Armstrong, Elisabeth*

The Retreat of the Elephants: An Environmental History of China — *Elvin, Mark*

Retrenchment and Regeneration in Rural Newfoundland — *Byron, Reginald*

Retribution (Read by Mazur, Kathe). Audiobook Review — *Hoffman, Jilliane*

Retribution — *Hoffman, Jilliane*

Retribution — *Ingermanson, Randall Scott*

Retribution: The Jiling Chronicles — *Li, Yong-ping*

Retrieving Experience: Subjectivity and Recognition in Feminist Politics — *Kruks, Sonia*

Retrieving the Tradition and Renewing Evangelicalism: A Primer for Suspicious Protestants — *Williams, D.H.*

Retro (Read by Foster, Mel). Audiobook Review — *Estleman, Loren D.*

Retro Chic — *Eden, Diana*

Retro Luau: Planning the Perfect Polynesian Party — *Perry, Richard*

Retrospect and Prospect in Celtic Studies: Proceedings — *International Congress of Celtic Studies*

Retrospect and Prospect in Celtic Studies: Proceedings of the 11th International Congress of Celtic Studies Held in University College, Cork, 25-31 July 1999 — *Herbert, Maire*

Return, Afghanistan — *Ahad, Zalmai*

Return from the Archipelago — *Toker, Leona*

Return Migration in the Asia Pacific — *Iredale, Robyn*

Return Migration: Policies and Practices in Europe — *International Organization for Migration*

The Return of Cosmopolitan Capital: Globalisation, the State and War — *Harris, Nigel*

y The Return of Gabriel — *Armistead, John*

The Return of Inspector Banks — *Robinson, Peter*

The Return of Nightfall — *Reichert, Mickey Zucker*

The Return of Sara Bartman — *Maseko, Zola*

The Return of Storytelling in Contemporary German Literature and Film: Peter Handke and Wim Wenders — *Coury, David N.*

The Return of the Amami Islands: The Reversion Movement and U.S.-Japan Relations — *Eldridge, Robert D.*

Return of the Black Death: The World's Greatest Serial Killer — *Scott, Susan*

y Return of the Grudstone Ghosts — *Slade, Arthur G.*

c The Return of the King — *Tolkien, J.R.R.*

Return of the Peregrine: A North American Saga of Tenacity and Teamwork — *Burnham, William*

y Return of the Peregrine: A North American Saga of Tenacity and Teamwork — *Cade, Tom J.*

The Return of the State: Protesters, Power-Brokers and the New Global Compromise — *Harmes, Adam*

The Return of the White Plague: Global Poverty and the 'New' Tuberculosis — *Gandy, Matthew*

Return on Software: Maximizing the Return on Your Software Investment — *Tockey, Steve*

Return: The Holocaust and Dutch Anti-Semitism — *Dienke, Honjus*

c Return to Evergreen — *Cincotta, Wendy*

Return to Greatness: How America Lost Its Sense of Purpose and What It Needs to Do to Recover It — *Wolfe, Alan*

Return to Reason — *Toulmin, Stephen*

Return to the City of White Donkeys — *Tate, James*

Return to Titanic: A New Look at the World's Most Famous Lost Ship — *Ballard, Robert D.*

y Return to Warrah — *McGahey, Jo*

Returning Home: Housing and Property Restitution Rights of Refugees and Displaced Persons — *Leckie, Scott*

Reuben Fine: A Comprehensive Record of an American Chess Career, 1929-1951 — *Woodger, Aidan*

y Reunion, a Novel — *Oren, Michael B.*

Reunion at Cottonwood Station — *Flynn, T.T.*

Reunion — *Lightman, Alan*

y Reunion — *Pearce, Jacqueline*

y The Reunion — *Walker, Sue*

Revaluing Ethics: Aristotle's Dialectical Pedagogy — *Smith, T.W.*

The Revealers — *Wilhelm, Doug*

Revealing the Inner Worlds of Young Children: The MacArthur Story Stem Battery and Parent-Child Narratives — *Emde, Robert N.*

Revelation and the End of All Things — *Koester, Craig R.*

Revelation — *Kovacs, Judith*

y Revenge and Forgiveness: An Anthology of Poems — *Vecchione, Patrice*

Revenge — *Morris, Mary*

Revenge — *Schooley, Kerry J.*

The Revenge of Anguished English — *Lederer, Richard*

y Revenge of the Whale: The True Story of the Whaleship Essex (Read by Mali, Taylor). Audiobook Review — *Philbrick, Nathaniel*

Revenge of the Windigo: The Construction of the Mind and Mental Health of North American Aboriginal Peoples — *Waldram, James B.*

Reverse Discrimination: Dismantling the Myth — *Pincus, Fred L.*

Reverse Engineering: Proceedings — *IEEE Computer Society*

Reversible Destiny: Antimafia, and the Struggle for Palermo — *Schneider, Jane C.*

Reversible Protein Acetylation: Proceedings — *Bock, Gregory*

Reversing the Curse: Inside the 2004 Boston Red Sox — *Shaughnessy, Dan*

A Review Guide for Fundamentals of Criminal Investigation, 7th Ed. — *O'Hara, Gregory L.*

Review of Fisheries in OECD Countries: Country Statistics: 1990-2001/Examen des Pecheries Dans les Pays De L'OCDE: Statisques Nationales: 1999-2001 — *Organisation for Economic Co-operation and Development*

Review of Fisheries in OECD Countries: Policies and Summary Statistics — *Organisation for Economic Co-operation and Development*

Review of Hand Surgery — *Beredjiklian, Pedro K.*

Review of Maritime Transport, 2003 — *United Nations Conference on Trade and Development*

Review of Middle East Economics and Finance — *Routledge*

Review of Orthopaedics, 4th Ed. — *Miller, Mark D.*

Reviewing Basic Grammar: A Guide to Writing Sentences and Paragraphs, 6th Ed. — *Yarber, Mary Laine*

Reviewing Delegation: An Analysis of the Congressional Reauthorization Process — *Cox, James H.*

Reviews in Computational Chemistry, Vol. 20 — *Lipkowitz, Kenny B.*

Reviews in Food and Nutrition Toxicity: Vol. 1 — *Preedy, Victor R.*

Reviews in Food and Nutrition Toxicity, Vol. 2 — *Preedy, Victor R.*

Revising Romance — *Dugan, Melanie*

Revising Women: Eighteenth Century "Women's Fiction" and Social Engagement — *Backscheider, Paula R.*

ReVisions — *Czerneda, Julie*

Revisiting Mary Higgins Clark: A Critical Companion — *De Roche, Linda*

Revisiting the Legacy of Edward Bellamy (1850-1898), American Author and Social Reformer — *Widdicombe, Toby*

Revisiting Universalism — *Assiter, Alison*

Revitalizations and Mazeways, Vol. 1 — *Wallace, Anthony F.C.*

The Revival of the Olympian Gods in Renaissance Art — *Freedman, Luba*

Reviving America's Forgotten Neighborhoods: An Investigation of Inner City Revitalization Efforts — *Bright, Elise M.*

Reviving Phoenicia: In Search of Identity in Lebanon — *Kaufman, Asher*

Riding Buffaloes and Broncos: Rodeo and Native Traditions in the Northern Great Plains — *Mellis, Allison Fuss*

Riding for Kids — *Richter, Judy*

y Riding Low on the Streets of Gold: Latino Literature for Young Adults — *Ortiz Cofer, Judith*

Riding the Roller Coaster: A History of the Chrysler Corporation — *Hyde, Charles K.*

Riding the World: The Biker's Road Map for a Seven-Continent Adventure — *Frazier, Gregory W.*

Riding with Reagan: From the White House to the Ranch — *Barletta, John R.*

The Riemann Hypothesis: The Greatest Unsolved Problem in Mathematics — *Sabbagh, Karl*

Rift Zone — *Hillhouse, Raelynn*

Rift Zone — *House, Raelynn Hill*

Rigged Rules and Double Standards: Trade, Globalization, and the Fight Against Poverty — *Oxfam International*

Right and Left — *Roth, Joseph*

Right and Prejudice: Prolegoma to a Hermeneutical Philosophy of Law — *Tontti, Jarkko*

The Right Fight: Bernard Lord and the Conservative Dilemma — *Poitras, Jacques*

Right Ho, Jeeves. Audiobook Review — *Wodehouse, P.G.*

Right Living: An Anglo-American Tradition of Self-Help Medicine and Hygiene — *Rosenberg, Charles E.*

Right Man: An Inside Account of the Bush White House — *Frum, David*

The Right Nation: Conservative Power in America — *Micklethwait, John*

The Right Nation: Why America Is Different — *Micklethwait, John*

The Right to Die: The Law of End-of-Life Decisionmaking, 3rd Ed — *Meisel, Alan*

Right to Exist: A Moral Defense of Israel's Wars — *Lozowick, Yaacov*

Right to Rock: The Black Rock Coalition and the Cultural Politics of Race — *Mahon, Maureen*

c The Right to Speak Out — *King, David C.*

The Right to the City: Social Justice and the Fight for Public Space — *Mitchell, Don*

Right Turns: Unconventional Lessons from a Controversial Life — *Medved, Michael*

y Right Whales: Natural History and Conservation — *Clapham, Phil*

Right-Wing Extremism in the Twenty-First Century, 2nd Rev. Ed. — *Merkl, Peter H.*

Right Wing Women: From Conservatives to Extremists around the World — *Bacchetta, P.*

Right-Wing Women in Chile: Feminine Power and the Struggle Against Allende, 1964-1973 — *Power, Margaret*

A Right Worthy Grand Mission: Maggie Lena Walker and the Quest for Black Economic Empowerment — *Marlowe, Gertrude Woodruff*

Righteous Gentiles of the Holocaust: Genocide and Moral Obligation, 2nd Ed. — *Gushee, David P.*

Righteous Riches: The Word of Faith Movement in Contemporary African American Religion — *Harrison, Milmon F.*

Rights and the Politics of Recognition in Africa — *Englund, Hari*

Rights, Democracy, and Fulfillment in the Era of Identity Politics: Principled Compromises in a Compromised World — *Ingram, David*

Rights for a Season: The Politics of Race, Class, and Gender in Richmond, Virginia — *Randolph, Lewis A.*

Rights for Aborigines — *Attwood, Bain*

Rights from Wrongs: A Secular Theory of the Origins of Rights — *Dershowitz, Alan M.*

Rights from Wrongs: The Origins of Human Rights in the Experience of Injustice — *Dershowitz, Alan M.*

Rights of Inclusion: Law and Identity in the Life Stories of Americans with Disabilities — *Engel, David M.*

Rights of Passage: The Passport in International Relations — *Salter, Mark B.*

y Rights of Students — *Hudson, David L., Jr.*

Rights, Resources and Rural Development: Community-Based Natural Resource Management in Southern Africa — *Fabricius, Christo*

Rigor of Beauty: Essays in Commemoration of William Carlos Williams — *Copestake, Ian D.*

Rimbaud Complete — *Rimbaud, Arthur*

Rinck, Maranke. The Prince Child (Illus. by Linden, Martijn van der) — *Rinck, Maranke*

Ring around My Heart — *White, Pat*

c The Ring Bear: A Rascally Wedding Adventure (Illus. by Brooks, S.G.) — *Slater, David Michael*

Ring Road — *Sansom, Ian*

The Ring, Vol. 4 — *Mizuki, Sakura*

The Ringering Site and the Archaic-Woodland Transition in the American Bottom — *Evans, J. Bryant*

Ringworld's Children — *Niven, Larry*

c Rio de Janeiro — *Morrison, Marion*

Rio de Janeiro: Carnival under Fire — *Castro, Ruy*

Rio Plus Ten: Politics, Poverty and the Environment — *Middleton, Neil*

Riot and Great Anger: Stage Censorship in Twentieth-Century Ireland — *Dean, Joan Fitzpatrick*

c Ripley's Believe It or Not! — *Packard, Mary*

Ripley's Believe It or Not — *Rainford, Jenni*

y Ripped at the Seams — *Krulik, Nancy*

Ripples of Hope: Great American Civil Rights Speeches — *Gottheimer, Josh*

Ripples on the Water: Believers in the Orang Asli's Struggle for a Homeland of Equal Citizens — *Fung, Jojo M.*

The Rise and Demise of the UC Santa Cruz Colleges — *Norena, Carlos G.*

Rise and Fall of a Political Animal: A Memoir — *Green, Sidney*

The Rise and Fall of American Public Schools: The Political Economy of Public Education in the Twentieth Century — *Franciosi, Robert J.*

y The Rise and Fall of American Slavery: Freedom Denied, Freedom Gained — *McNeese, Tim*

The Rise and Fall of Ancient Israeli States — *Sicker, Martin*

The Rise and Fall of Anglo-America — *Kaufmann, Eric P.*

The Rise and Fall of Communism in Sarawak 1940-1990 — *Porritt, Vernon L.*

The Rise and Fall of Czech Capitalism: Economic Development in the Czech Republic Since 1989 — *Myant, Martin*

Rise and Fall of HMOs: An American Health Care Revolution — *Coombs, Jan Gregoire*

The Rise and Fall of Satellite Personal Communication Systems: Business and Legal Issues — *Chioni, Georgia*

The Rise and Fall of the Broadway Musical — *Grant, Mark N.*

The Rise and Fall of the White Republic: Class Politics and Mass Culture in Nineteenth-Century America — *Saxton, Alexander*

The Rise and Fall of the Woman of Letters — *Clarke, Norma*

Rise, Let Us Be on Our Way — *John Paul II, Pope*

The Rise of a Jazz Art World — *Lopes, Paul*

The Rise of Aggressive Abolitionism: Addresses to the Slaves — *Harold, Stanley*

The Rise of Aggressive Abolitionism: Addresses to the Slaves — *Harrold, Stanley*

y The Rise of American Capitalism: The Growth of American Banks — *Moriarty, J.T.*

The Rise of Cable Programming in the United States. — *Mullen, Megan*

The Rise of Commercial Empires: England and the Netherlands in the Age of Mercantilism, 1650-1770 — *Ormrod, David*

The Rise of Conservation in South Africa: Settlers, Livestock, and the Environment, 1770-1950 — *Beinart, William*

The Rise of Evangelicalism: The Age of Edwards, Whitefield and the Wesleys — *Noll, Mark A.*

The Rise of Judicial Management in the U.S. District Court, Southern District of Texas, 1955-2000 — *Wilson, Steven Harmon*

The Rise of Management Consulting in Britain — *Ferguson, Michael*

The Rise of New Woman: The Women's Movement in America, 1875-1930 — *Mathews, Jean V.*

The Rise of Oriental Travel: English Visitors to the Ottoman Empire 1580-1720 — *MacLean, Gerald*

The Rise of Professional Women in France: Gender and Public Administration Since 1830 — *Clarke, Linda*

The Rise of Pseudo-Historical Fiction: Fray Antonio de Guevara's Novelizations — *Rivero, Horacio Chiong*

The Rise of Southern Republicans — *Black, Merle*

The Rise of the Creative Class ... and How It's Transforming Work, Leisure, Community, & Everyday Life — *Florida, Richard*

The Rise of the Hispanic Market in the United States: Challenges, Dilemmas, and Opportunities for Corporate Management — *Nevaer, Louis E.V.*

c The Rise of the House of McNally — *Ardagh, Philip*

The Rise of the Indian Rope Trick: How a Spectacular Hoax Became History — *Lamont, Peter*

The Rise of the New Woman: The Women's Movement in America, 1875-1930 — *Matthews, Jean V.*

The Rise of the New Woman: The Women's Movement in America, 1875 to 1930 — *Matthews, Jean V.*

The Rise of the States: Evolution of American State Government — *Teaford, Jon C.*

Rise of the Vulcans: The History of Bush's War Cabinet — *Mann, James*

The Rise of Viagra: How the Little Blue Pill Changed Sex in America — *Loe, Meika*

y Rise to Rebellion — *Shaara, Jeff*

Rise Up: A Call to Leadership for African American Women — *Rose, Sylvia*

Rise Up, O Men of God: The "Men and Religion Forward Movement" and the "Promise Keepers" — *Allen, L. Dean*

Risen Jesus and Future Hope — *Habermas, Gary R.*

Rising '44: The Battle for Warsaw — *Davies, Norman*

Rising Above Sweatshops: Innovative Approaches to Global Labor Challenges — *Hartman, Laura P.*

The Rising — *Keene, Brian*

Rising Elephant: The Growing Clash with India over White-Collar Jobs and Its Meaning for America and the World — *Sheshabalaya, Ashutosh*

Rising Fire: Volcanoes and Our Inner Lives — *Calderazzo, John*

Rising from the Muck: The New Anti-Semitism in Europe — *Taguieff, Pierre-Andre*

Rising from the Muck: The New Anti-Semitism in Europe — *Tguieff, Pierre-Andre*

Rising from the Rails: Pullman Porters and the Making of the Black Middle Class — *Tye, Larry*

Rising Life Expectancy: A Global History — *Riley, James C.*

The Rising of the Moon: The Language of Power — *O'Dwyer, Ella*

Rising Tide: Lessons from 165 Years of Brand Building at Procter & Gamble — *Dyer, Davis*

y Rising Tide: The Untold Story of the Russian Submarines That Fought the Cold War — *Weir, Gary E.*

Rising Up and Rising Down: Some Thoughts on Violence, Freedom, and Urgent Times — *Vollmann, William T.*

Risk Analysis and Society: An Interdisciplinary Characterization of the Field — *McDaniels, Timothy*

Risk Analysis in Finance and Insurance — *Melnikov, Alexander*

Risk and Morality — *Ericson, Richard V.*

Risk and Performance Evaluation with Skewness and Kurtosis for Conventional and Alternative Investments — *Berenyi, Zsolt Endre*

Risk and Reason: Law and the Environment — *Sustein, Cass R.*

Risk and Resilience in Childhood: An Ecological Perspective, 2nd Ed. — *Fraser, Mark W.*

Risk and Technological Culture: Towards a Sociology of Virulence — *Loon, Joost van*

Risk Communication: A Handbook for Communicating Environmental, Safety, and Health Risks, 3rd Ed. — *Lundgreen, Regina E.*

Risk, Culture, and Health Inequality: Shifting Perceptions of Danger and Blame — *Harthorn, Barbara Herr*

Risk Management in Orthodontics: Experts' Guide to Malpractice — *Graber, Thomas M.*

Risk Measures for the 21st Century — *Szego, Giorgio*

Risking Difference: Identification, Race, and Community in Comtemporary Fiction and Feminism — *Wyatt, Jean*

Risking Difference: Identification, Race, and Community in Contemporary Fiction and Feminism — *Wyatt, Jean*

Risking It All: My Student, My Lover, My Story — *Ingram, Heather E.*

Risks and Legal Theory — *Steele, Jenny*

Risks, Reputations, and Rewards: Contingency Fee Legal Practice in the United States — *Kritzer, Herbert M.*

Risky Business: Corruption, Fraud, Terrorism and Other Threats to Global Business — *Poole-Robb, Stuart*

Risky Business: Financing and Distributing Independent Films — *Litwak, Mark*

S

Title Index

The SMS Blackwell Handbook of Organizational Capabilities: Emergence, Development, and Change — *Helfat, Constance E.*

y The Smugglers — *Lawrence, Iain*

Smut: A Sex Industry Insider (and Concerned Father) Says Enough Is Enough — *Reavill, Gil*

c The Snail and the Whale — *Donaldson, Julia*

Snail Boy — *McGuirk, Leslie*

Snake Eyes — *Wright, Charles*

The Snake Pit Book (Illus. by Snakepit, Ben) — *Snakepit, Ben*

c Snake Pits, Talking Cures, and Magic Bullets: A History of Mental Illness — *Kent, Deborah*

The Snake That Swallowed Its Tail: Some Contradictions in Modern Liberalism — *Garnett, Mark*

y Snakecharm — *Atwater-Rhodes, Amelia*

Snakepit — *Isegawa, Moses*

c Snakes (Illus. by McDonald, Joe) — *Markle, Sandra*

c Snakes Don't Miss Their Mothers — *Kerr, M.E.*

Snakes of the United States and Canada: Natural History and Care in Captivity — *Rossi, John V.*

Snakes of Virginia — *Linzey, Donald W.*

c Snakes!: Strange and Wonderful (Illus. by Henderson, Meryl) — *Pringle, Laurence*

y Snap (Read by Moore, Christina). Audiobook Review — *McGhee, Alison*

y Snap — *McGhee, Alison*

c Snarf Attack, Underfoodle, and the Secret of Life: The Riot Brothers Tell All (Illus. by Long, Ethan) — *Amato, Mary*

Sneaking a Look at God's Cards: Unraveling the Mysteries of Quantum Mechanics — *Ghirardi, Giancarlo*

Sneaky Kid and Its Aftermath: Ethics and Intimacy in Fieldwork — *Wolcott, Harry F.*

Sneaky Uses for Everyday Things — *Tymony, Cy*

Snobbery: The American Version — *Epstein, Joseph*

y Snobbery with Violence — *Beaton, M.C.*

Snobs — *Fellowes, Julian*

c Snog the Frog — *Bonning, Tony*

c Snooze-a-Palooza! More than 100 Slumber Party Ideas (Illus. by Yoshizmni, Carol) — *Yoshizmni, Carol*

Snort 2.1: Intrusion Detection, 2nd Ed. — *Baker, Andrew R.*

Snort 2.1 Intrusion Detection — *Beale, Jay*

c Snot Fair! — *Montano, Josie*

y Snow Amazing: Cool Facts and Warm Tales (Illus. by Thurman, Mark) — *Drake, Jane*

c Snow and More Snow! — *Salzmann, Mary Elizabeth*

Snow Bodies: One Woman's Life on the Streets — *Hudson, Elizabeth*

c Snow — *Frost, Helen*

Snow — *Pamuk, Orhan*

c Snow Dude (Illus. by Kirk, Daniel) — *Kirk, Daniel*

Snow Formations — *Souaid, Carolyn Marie*

The Snow Ghosts — *Landry, Leo*

Snow in July — *Barbieri, Heather*

Snow Loads: A Guide to the Use and Understanding of the Snow Load Provisions of ASCE 7-02 — *O'Rourke, Michael*

Snow Man — *Albahari, David*

Snow Melting in a Silver Bowl: A Book of Active Meditations — *Cunningham, Nancy Brady*

Snow Music — *Perkins, Lynne Rae*

c The Snow Princess (Illus. by Sanderson, Ruth) — *Sanderson, Ruth*

Snow — *Freely, Maureen*

Snow — *Pamuk, Orhan*

y Snow-Walker — *Fisher, Catherine*

The Snow Walker — *Mowat, Farley*

Snow Water — *Longley, Michael*

Snow White and Russian Red — *Maslowska, Dorota*

c Snowbear's Christmas Countdown (Illus. by Smythe, Theresa) — *Smythe, Theresa*

The Snowbird Poems — *Kroetsch, Robert*

Snowboard Champ — *Christopher, Matt*

c Snowboard Twist (Illus. by Minor, Wendell) — *George, Jean Craighead*

Snowed In — *Bartolomeo, Christina*

c Snowed in with Grandmother Silk (Illus. by Harvey, Amanda) — *Fenner, Carol*

c The Snowflake: A Water Cycle Story — *Waldman, Neil*

c A Snowflake Fell: Poems About Winter (Illus. by Huri, Hatsuki) — *Whipple, Laura*

The Snowflake: Winter's Secret Beauty — *Libbrecht, Kenneth*

Snowleg — *Shakespeare, Nicholas*

Snowman — *Fauser, Jorg*

c Snowman in Paradise (Illus. by Roberts, Michael) — *Roberts, Michael*

Snowshoes and Spotted Dick: Letters from a Wilderness Dweller — *Czjakowski, Chris*

c Snug in Mama's Arms (Illus. by Sandford, John) — *Medearis, Angela Shelf*

c Snuggle Me Snuggly! — *Baicker, Karen*

c So 5 Minutes Ago: A Novel (Read by Hamilton, Laura). Audiobook Review — *De Vries, Hilary*

So 5 Minutes Ago (Read by Hamilton, Laura). Audiobook Review — *De Vries, Hilary*

c So B. It — *Geringer, Laura*

y So B. It — *Weeks, Sarah*

So Beautiful — *Dearing, Ramona*

So Black and Blue: Ralph Ellison and the Occasion of Criticism — *Warren, Kenneth W.*

y So Cool — *Lee, Dennis*

So Dance the Lords of Language — *Kociejowski, Marius*

c So Happy! (Illus. by Lobel, Anita) — *Henkes, Kevin*

y So Hard to Say — *Sanchez, Alex*

y So Long Been Dreaming: Postcolonial Science Fiction & Fantasy — *Hopkinson, Nalo*

So Long! Walt Whitman's Poetry of Death — *Aspiz, Harold*

So Many Books, So Little Time: A Year of Passionate Reading — *Nelso, Sarah*

So Me — *Norton, Graham*

So Much More: An Invitation to Christian Spirituality — *Rienstra, Debra*

y So Much to Tell You — *Marsden, John*

So Much Weather!: Facts, Phenomena and Weather Lore from Atlantic Canada — *Saunders, Gary L.*

So Now Who Do We Vote For? — *Harris, John (b. 1964 -)*

So Others Might Live: A History of New York's Bravest; the FDNY From 1700 to the Present — *Golway, Terry*

y So Super Starry — *Wilkins, Rose*

So They Understand: Cultural Issues in Oral History — *Schneider, William*

So This is Love: Lollipop and Other Stories — *Reid, Gilbert*

y So What! The Good, the Mad and the Ugly — *Chirazi, Steffan*

y So Yesterday — *Walters, Eric*

y So Yesterday — *Westerfeld, Scott*

So You Think You're Human? A Brief History of Humankind — *Fernandez-Armesto, Felipe*

So ... You Wanna Buy a Used Car? — *Ann, Susan*

So You Want to Be a Canadian: All about the Most Fascinating People in the World and the Magical Place We Call Home — *Colburn, Kerry*

c So You Want to Be an Inventor? (Illus. by Small, David) — *St. George, Judith*

The Soap Opera Paradigm: Television Programming and Corporate Priorities — *Wittebols, James H.*

SOAS since the Sixties — *Arnold, David*

Soay Sheep: Dynamics and Selection in an Island Population — *Clutton-Brock, Tim*

Sober Justice — *Hilley, Joseph H.*

Soccer Counts! — *McGrath, Barbara Barbieri*

c Soccer Dreams — *Lauber, Leah*

Soccer: Guarding the Goal — *Brodsgaard, Shel*

c Soccer Star! — *Guest, Jacqueline*

y Soccer: The Ultimate Guide to the Beautiful Game — *Gifford, Clive*

Soccer, Women, Sexual Liberation: Kicking off a New Era — *Hong, Fan*

Social Aggression among Girls — *Underwood, Marion K.*

The Social Amplification of Risk — *Pidgeon, Nick F.*

Social and Cultural Lives of Immune Systems — *Wilce, James M. Jr.*

Social and Economic Policies in Korea: Ideas, Networks and Linkages — *Shin, Dong-Myeon*

Social and Economic Transformation in the Digital Era — *Doukidis, Georgios*

Social and Emotional Prevention and Intervention Programming for Preschoolers — *Denham, Susanne A.*

Social and Personal Ethics, 5th Ed. — *Shaw, William H.*

Social and Personal Identity: Understanding Yourself — *Layder, Derek*

Social and Personality Development, 5th Ed. — *Shaffer, David R.*

Social Anxiety Disorder — *Bandelow, Borwin*

Social Capital: A Theory of Social Structure and Action — *Lin, Nan*

Social Capital and Democratization: Roots of Trust in Post-Communist Poland and Ukraine — *Aberg, Martin*

Social Capital and Social Cohesion in Post-Soviet Russia — *Javeline, Debra*

Social Capital and Social Cohesion in Post-Soviet Russia — *Twigg, Judyth*

Social Capital and the Transition to Democracy — *Badescu, Gabriel*

Social Challenges and Organising Capacity in Cities: Experiences in Eight European Cities — *Berg, Leo van den*

Social Challenges and Organising Capacity in Cities: Experiences in Eight European Cities — *Van Den Berg, Leo*

Social Change in America: The Historical Handbook, 2004 — *Becker, Patricia C.*

The Social Circulation of the Past: English Historical Culture, 1500-1730 — *Woolf, Daniel*

Social Class, Politics and Urban Markets: The Making of Bias in Policy Outcomes — *Boschken, Herman L.*

Social Cognition — *Brewer, Marilynn*

Social Cognition — *Brewer, Marilynn B.*

Social Connections in China: Institutions, Culutre, and the Changing Nature of Guanxi — *Hwang, K.K.*

The Social Conscience of the Early Victorians — *Roberts, F. David*

The Social Consequences of Methamphetamine Use — *Sommers, Ira Brant*

Social Construction: A Reader — *Gergen, Mary*

The Social Construction of Diversity: Recasting the Master Narrative of Industrial Nations — *Harzig, Christiane*

The Social Construction of Educational Leadership: Southern Appalachian Ceilings — *McFadden, Anna Hicks*

The Social Construction of Intellectual Disability — *Rapley, Mark*

The Social Construction of International News: We're Talking about Them — *Wasburn, Philo C.*

The Social Construction of Sexuality — *Seidman, Steven*

Social Constructivism and the Philosophy of Science — *Kukla, Andre*

The Social Context of Innovation: Bureaucrats, Families and Heroes in the Early Industrial Revolution — *Wallace, Anthony F.C.*

Social Democracy and the Aristocracy — *Kautsky, John H.*

Social Differentiation: Patterns and Processes — *Juteau, Danielle*

Social Education in the Twentieth Century: Curriculum and Context for Citizenship — *Woyshner, Christine*

Social Empiricism — *Solomon, Miriam*

Social Equity and the Funding of Community Policing — *Gutierrez, Ricky S.*

Social, Ethical, and Policy Implications of Information Technology — *Brennan, Linda L.*

Social Ethics: Sociology and the Future of Society — *Gilman, Charlotte Perkins*

Social Europe: Living Standards and Welfare States — *Berthoud, Ricard*

Social Exclusion: An Approach to the Australian Case — *Weiss, Doris*

Social Experimentation and Public Policymaking — *Greenberg, David H.*

Social Foundations of Markets, Money and Credit — *Lapavitsas, Costas*

Social Funds: Lessons for a New Future — *Garnier, Philippe*

Social History & African Environments — *Beinart, William*

A Social History of Medicines in the Twentieth Century: To Be Taken Three Times a Day — *Crellin, John K.*

A Social History of Milton Keynes: Middle England/ Edge City — *Clapson, Mark*

A Social History of Soviet Trade: Trade Policy, Retail Practices, and Consumption, 1917-1953. — *Hessler, Julie*

A Social History of the Disciples of Christ, Vols. 1-2 — *Harrell, David Edwin*

Social Inequalities in Comparative Perspective — *Devine, Fiona*

Social Inequality and Social Injustice: A Human Rights Perspectives — *Kallen, Evelyn*

Social Interaction and the Development of Knowledge — *Carpendale, Jeremy I.M.*

Social Issues in the Provision and Pricing of Water Services — *Organisation for Economic Co-operation and Development*

Social Justice and the Politics of Community — *Everingham, Christine*

Social Learning and the History of U.S. Telecommunications Policy, 1900-1996: Creating the Telecommunications Act of 1996 — *Zarkin, Michael J.*

Social Learning Theory and the Explanation of Crime: A Guide for the New Century — *Akers, Ronald L.*

The Social Life of Painting in Ancient Rome and on the Bay of the Naples — *Leach, Eleanor Winsor*

The Social Life of the State in Subarctic Siberia — *Ssorin-Chaikov, Nikolai V.*

Social Lives of Medicines — *Whyte, Susan Reynolds*

Social Movements, 1768-2004 — *Tilly, Charles*

Social Movements and Networks: Relational Approaches to Collective Action — *Mertig, Angela G.*

Social Movements in France: Towards a New Citizenship — *Waters, Sarah*

Social Movements in India: A Review of Literature, 2nd Ed. — *Shah, Ghanshyam*

Social Networks and Organizations — *Kilduff, Martin*

Social Networks and Social Exclusion: Sociological and Policy Perspective — *Phillipson, Chris*

The Social Organization of Law: Introductory Readings — *Sarat, Austin*

The Social Organization of Sexuality: Sexual Practices in the United States — *Laumann, Edward O.*

The Social Origins of the Urban South: Race, Gender and Migration in Nashville and Middle Tennessee, 1890-1930 — *Kyriakoudes, Louis M.*

The Social Origins of the Urban South: Race, Gender, and Migration in Nashville and Middle Tennessee, 1890-1930 — *Kyriakoudes, Louis M.*

Social Partnerships and Social Relations: New Strategies in Workforce and Economic Development — *Boguslaw, Janet*

A Social Philosophy of Housing — *King, Peter*

Social Policy Reform in China: Views from Home and Abroad — *Finer, Catherine Jones*

Social Policy Reform in Hong Kong and Shanghai: A Tale of Two Cities — *Wong, Linda*

Social Problem Solving: Theory, Research, and Training — *Chang, Edward C.*

Social Problems Across the Life Course — *Lopata, Helena Z.*

Social Problems, Law, and Society — *Stout, A. Kathryn*

Social Protest and Policy Change: Ecology, Antinuclear, and Peace Movements in Comparative Perspective — *Giugni, Marco*

The Social Psychology of Fundraising, 4th Ed. — *Bell, Brad*

The Social Psychology of Good and Evil — *Miller, Arthur G.*

Social Relations and the Life Course — *Allan, Graham*

Social Research Methodology: A Critical Introduction, 1st ed. — *Gomm, Roger*

Social Research: The Basics — *David, Matthew*

Social Responsibility: Corporate Governance Issues — *Batten, Jonathan A.*

Social Science: An Introduction to the Study of Society, 12th Ed. — *Hunt, Elgin F.*

Social Science Resources in the Electronic Age, Vol. 5 — *Oakes, Elizabeth H.*

Social Science Resources in the Electronic Age. Vols. 1-5 — *Oakes, Elizabeth H.*

Social Science Resources in the Electronic Age, Vols. 1-5 — *Oakes, Elizabeth H.*

The Social Sciences Go to Washington: The Politics of Knowledge in the Postmodern Age — *Cravens, Hamilton*

The Social Sciences in Modern Japan: The Marxian and Modernist Traditions — *Barshay, Andrew E.*

Social Security and Its Discontents: Perspectives on Choice — *Tanner, Michael*

Social Security in the Global Village — *Sigg, Roland*

Social Security Pension Reform in Europe — *Feldstein, Martin S.*

Social Security reform in Advanced Countries: Evaluating Pension Finance — *Ihori, Toshihro*

Social Skills Training for Schizophrenia: A Step-by-Step Guide, 2nd Ed. — *Bellack, Alan S.*

Social Statistics: An Introduction Using SPSS for Windows, 2nd Ed. — *Kendrick, J. Richard*

Social Stories: The Magazine Novel in the Nineteenth-Century America — *Okker, Patricia*

The Social Studies Wars: What Should We Teach the Children? — *Evans, Ronald W.*

Social Support and Physical Health: Understanding the Health Consequences of Relationships — *Uchino, Bert N.*

Social Theory and Later Modernities: The Turkish Experience — *Kaya, Ibrahim*

Social Theory and Religion — *Beckford, James A.*

A Social Theory of International Law: International Relations as a Complex System — *Kawaguchi, Kazuko Hirose*

The Social Theory of W.E.B. Du Bois — *Du Bois, W.E.B.*

Social Transformation in Modern China: The State and Local Elites in Henan, 1900-1937 — *Zhang, Xin*

Social Welfare: A History of the American Response to Need, 6th Ed. — *Axinn, June*

Social Work: A Profession of Many Faces, 10th Ed. — *Morales, Armando T.*

Social Work: An Empowering Profession, 5th Ed. — *DuBois, Brenda*

Social Work and Human Development, 1st Ed. — *Crawford, Karin*

Social Work and Mental Health, 1st ed. — *Golightley, Malcolm*

Social Work, Critical Reflection, and the Learning Organisation — *Gould, Nick*

Social Work in the Health Field: A Care Perspective, 2nd Ed. — *Cowles, Lois A. Fort*

Social Work Malpractice and Liability: Strategies for Prevention, 2nd Ed. — *Reamer, Frederic G.*

Social Work Practice: Assessment, Planning, Intervention and Review, 1st Ed. — *Parker, Jonathan*

Social Work Practice with Children, 2nd Ed. — *Webb, Nancy Boyd*

The Social Work Practicum: A Guide and Workbook for Students, 3rd Ed. — *Garthwait, Cynthia L.*

The Social Work Student's Research Handbook — *Steinberg, Dominique Moyse*

Social Work: Theory and Practice for a Changing Profession, 1st Ed. — *Dominelli, Lena*

Social Work with Elders: A Biopsychosocial Approach to Assessment and Intervention, 2nd Ed. — *McInnis-Dittrich, Kathleen*

Social Work with Multicultural Youth — *De Anda, Diane*

Social Work with Older People, 1st Ed. — *Crawford, Karin*

Social Youth Entrepreneurship: The Potential for Youth and Community Transformation — *Delgado, Melvin*

Socialism Betrayed: Behind the Collapse of the Soviet Union — *Keeran, Roger*

Socialist Emigre: Marxism and the Later Tillich — *Donnelly, Brian*

Socialist Register 2004: The New Imperial Challenge — *Leys, Colin*

Socialist Women: Britain, 1880s to 1920s — *Hannam, June*

The Societe des Concerts du Conservatoire, 1828-1967 — *Holoman, D. Kern*

Society and Culture in the Huguenot World, 1559-1685 — *Mentzer, Raymond A.*

Society and Health: Sociology for Health Professionals — *Thomas, Richard K.*

Society and Individual in Renaissance Florence — *Connell, William J.*

Society and Its Metaphors: Language, Social Theory, and Social Structure — *Lopez, Jose*

y The Society (Read by Charles, J.). Audiobook Review — *Palmer, Michael*

The Society — *Palmer, Michael*

Society Must Be Defended: Lectures at the College de France, 1975-76 — *Foucault, Michel*

The Society of Others — *Nicholson, William*

The Society of Others — *Nicholson, William (British writer and movie director)*

Society Online: The Internet in Context — *Howard, Philip N.*

Society under Siege — *Bauman, Zygmunt*

Society's Sisters: Stories of Women Who Fought for Social Justice in America — *Gourley, Catherine*

Socioeconomic Democracy: An Advanced Socioeconomic System — *George, Robley E.*

The Socioeconomic Well-Being of California's Immigrant Youth — *Hill, Laura E.*

Socioliterary Practice in Late Medieval England — *Barr, Helen*

Sociological Analysis of Aging: The Gay Male Perspective — *Cruz, J. Micheal*

Sociological Snapshots 4: Seeing Social Structure and Change in Everyday Life — *Levin, Jack*

Sociological Theory and the Environment: Classical Foundations, Contemporary Insights — *Dunlap, Riley E.*

Sociology, 9th Ed. — *Shepard, Jon M.*

Sociology and Ideology — *Ben-Rafael, Eliezer*

Sociology and Mass Culture: Durkheim, Mills, and Baudrillard — *Cormack, Patricia*

Sociology — *Abercrombie, Nicholas*

Sociology: Exploring the Architecture of Everyday Life, 5th Ed. — *Newman, David M.*

Sociology: Exploring the Architecture of Everyday Life, Readings, 5th Ed. — *Newman, David M.*

Sociology for Pharmacists: An Introduction, 2d ed — *Taylor, Kevin*

Sociology for Pharmacists: An Introduction, 2nd Ed. — *Taylor, Kevin*

Sociology in Government: The Galpin-Taylor Years in the U.S. Department of Agriculture, 1919 to 1953 — *Larson, Olaf F.*

Sociology in Our Times, 4th Ed. — *Kendall, Diana*

Sociology in the Soviet Union and Beyond: Social Enquiry and Social Change — *Weinberg, Elizabeth A.*

The Sociology of Childhood, 2nd Ed. — *Corsaro, William A.*

Sociology of Crime Law, and Deviance, Vol. 4 — *Athens, Lonnie*

Sociology of Deviant Behavior, 12th Ed. — *Clinard, Marshall B.*

The Sociology of Ethnicity — *Malesevic, Sinisa*

The Sociology of Gender: A Brief Introduction, 2nd Ed. — *Kramer, Laura*

Sociology of Gender: The Challenge of Feminist Sociological Knowledge — *Rege, Sharmila*

Sociology of Religion in India — *Robinson, Rowena*

Sociology of the Arts: Exploring Fine and Popular Forms — *Alexander, Victoria D.*

Sociology: The Essentials, 3rd Ed. — *Andersen, Margaret L.*

Sociology: Your Compass for a New World, 2nd Ed. — *Brym, Robert J.*

The Sociopath Next Door: The Ruthless versus the Rest of Us — *Stout, Martha*

Sock — *Jillette, Penn*

c Sock Monkey Boogie-Woogie: A Friend Is Made (Illus. by Bell, Cece) — *Bell, Cece*

Sock Monkeys — *Svenson, Arne*

Sodom and Gomorrah — *Proust, Marcel*

Sodom's Sin: Genesis 18-19 and Its Interpretation — *Noort, Ed*

Sodomy in Early Modern Europe — *Betteridge, Tom*

Sodomy in Reformation Germany and Switzerland, 1400-1600 — *Puff, Helmut*

SOE in France: An Account of the Work of the British Special Operations Executive in France 1940-1944 — *Cass, Frank*

SOE: The Scientific Secrets — *Boyce, Fredric*

Soekarno: Founding Father of Indonesia, 1901-1945 — *Hering, Bob*

The Soft Cage: Surveillance in America from Slavery to the Patriot Act — *Parenti, Christian*

The Soft Drink Companion: A Technical Handbook for the Beverage Industry — *Shachman, Maurice*

Soft Machines: Nanotechnology and Life — *Jones, Richard A.L.*

Soft News Goes to War: Public Opinion and American Foreign Policy in the New Media Age — *Baum, Matthew A.*

Soft Patriarchs, New Men: How Christianity Shapes Fathers and Husbands — *Wilcox, W. Bradford*

Soft Power: The Means to Success in World Politics — *Nye, Joseph S.*

Soft Targets: A Woman's Guide to Survival — *Varando, Michael L.*

Software Architecture Design Patterns in Java — *Kuchana, Partha*

Software Architecture: Proceedings — *Magee, Jeff*

Software Engineering, 7th Ed. — *Sommerville, Ian*

Software Engineering and Formal Methods: Proceedings — *International Conference on Software Engineering and Formal Methods*

Software Engineering Handbook — *Keyes, Jessica*

Software for Indexing — *Schroeder, Sandi*

Software Metrics: Proceedings — *International Software Metrics Symposium*

The Software Project Manager's Handbook: Principles That Work at Work, 2nd Ed. — *Phillips, Dwayne*

Software Reliability Engineering: Proceedings — *International Symposium on Software Reliability Engineering*

Software Technologies for Future Embedded and Ubiquitous Systems: Proceedings — *Nakajima, Tatsuo*

Software Technology and Engineering Practice (STEP 2003). — *O'Brien, Liam*

Sports Illustrated 50 Years: The Anniversary Book: 1954-2004 — *Fleder, Rob*

c Sports in America — *Buckley, James*

Sports in Zion: Mormon Recreation, 1890-1940 — *Kimball, Richard Ian*

Sports Inc.: 100 Years of Sports Business — *Schaaf, Phil*

y Sports Injuries — *Lennard-Brown, Sarah*

y Sports Injuries Information for Teens — *Brennfleck, Joyce*

y Sports Injuries Information for Teens: Health Tips about Sports Injuries and Injury Prevention — *Shannon, Joyce Brennfleck*

c Sports Jokes — *Moore, Hugh*

c Sports Machines

Sports Market Place Directory, 2003 Ed. — *Myers, K. Jaguar*

Sports Market Place Directory, 2004 Ed. — *Gottlieb, Richard*

Sports Marketing and the Psychology of Marketing Communication — *Kahle, Lynn R.*

Sports Matters: Race, Recreation, and Culture — *Bloom, John*

Sports Medicine for the Primary Care Physician, 3rd Ed. — *Birrer, Richard B.*

Sports Medicine: Just the Facts — *O'Connor, Francis G.*

Sports Scholarships and College Athletic Programs, 5th ed. — *Walker, Ron*

Sports: The First Five Millennia — *Guttmann, Allen*

c Spot the Differences: Animals: 50 Mind-Bending Photographic Puzzles — *Reguigne, Christine*

c Spot the Differences: Vehicles: 50 Mind-Bending Photographic Puzzles — *Reguigne, Christine*

Spreading the "Burden"?: A Review of Policies to Disperse Asylum Seekers and Refugees — *Robinson, Vaughan*

Spreading the Gospel in Colonial Virginia: Sermons and Devotional Writings — *Bond, Edward L.*

Spreadsheet Exercises in Ecology and Evolution — *Donovan, Therese M.*

Spreadsheet Modeling and Applications: Essentials of Practical Management Science — *Albright, S. Christian*

Spreadsheets Made Simple for Administrators, Teachers, and School Board Members — *Singer, Harvey*

c Spring (Illus. by Curto, Rosa Maria) — *Roca, Nuria*

Spring Forward: The Annual Madness of Daylight Saving Time — *Downing, Michael*

Spring Night — *Vesaas, Tarjei*

The Spring Will Be Ours: Poland and the Poles from Occupation to Freedom — *Paczkowski, Andrzej*

Springer Handbook of Nanotechnology — *Bhushan, Bharat*

Springhouse Nurse's Drug Guide 2005, 6th Ed.

SPSS 12 made simple — *Kinnear, Paul R.*

Sputnik and the Soviet Space Challenge — *Siddiqi, Asif A.*

A Spy at the Heart of the Third Reich: The Extraordinary Story of Fritz Kolbe, America's Most Important Spy in World War II — *Delattre, Lucas*

Spy Book: The Encyclopedia of Espionage — *Polmar, Norman*

Spy Goddess, Bk. 1 — *Spradlin, Michael P.*

Spy Handler: Memoir of a KGB Officer: The True Story of the Man Who Recruited Robert Hanssen and Aldrich Ames — *Cherkashin, Victor*

y Spy High: Mission One — *Butcher, A.J.*

Spy High: Mission Three: The Serpent Scenario. — *Butcher, A.J.*

Spy High: Mission Two: Chaos Rising — *Butcher, A.J.*

c Spy Hops and Belly Flops: Curious Behaviors of Woodland Animals (Illus. by Lies, Brian) — *Graham-Barber, Lynda*

y Spy in the Alley — *Jackson, Melanie*

Spy Television — *Britton, Wesley*

Spying 101: The RCMP's Secret Activities at Canadian Universities, 1917-1997 — *Hewitt, Steve*

Spying with Maps: Surveillance Technologies and the Future of Privacy — *Monmonier, Mark S.*

Spymaster: Dai Li and the Chinese Secret Service — *Berkeley, Frederick Wakeman, Jr.*

Spymaster: Dai Li and the Chinese Secret Service — *Wakeman, Frederic E.*

A Spy's Journey: A CIA Memoir — *Paseman, Floyd L.*

SQL in a Nutshell, 2nd Ed. — *Kline, Kevin E.*

c Squanto, 1585?-1622 — *Hirschfelder, Arlene B.*

c Squash the Spider! — *Ward, Nick*

---

c Squeaky Clean (Illus. by McQuillan, Mary) — *Puttock, Simon*

c Squeal and Squawk: Barnyard Talk (Illus. by Slonim, David) — *Pearson, Susan*

SQUID Handbook, Vol. 1 — *Clarke, J.*

c Squirrel and John Muir (Illus. by McCully, Emily Arnold) — *McCully, Emily Arnold*

Squirrel Inc.: A Fable of Leadership through Storytelling — *Denning, Stephen*

c Squirrels and Their Nests — *Rustad, Martha E.H.*

c A Squishy Exterior, Velcro Buckles and a Convenient Handle Make My Sleepover Bag (Illus. by Smith, Tammy) — *Held, Elissa*

Sri Lanka: Ethnic Fratricide and the Dismantling of Democracy — *Tambiah, Stanley J.*

Sri Ramakrishna and His Divine Play — *Saradananda, Swami*

St. Dale — *McCrumb, Sharyn*

St. James Encyclopedia of Labor History Worldwide: Major Events in Labor History and Their Impact — *Schlager, Neil*

St. John Damascene: Tradition and Originality in Byzantine Theology — *Louth, Andrew*

St. John of the Cross: Songs in the Night — *Thompson, Colin*

St. John the Divine: The Deified Evangelist in Medieval Art and Theology — *Hamburger, Jeffrey F.*

St. Joseph in Italian Renaissance Society and Art: New Directions and Interpretations — *Wilson, Carolyn C.*

St. Katherine of Alexandria — *Jenkins, Jacqueline*

St. Louis in the Century of Henry Shaw: A View Beyond the Garden Wall — *Sandweiss, Eric*

St. Patrick of Ireland: A Biography — *Freeman, Philip*

St. Paul's: The Cathedral Church of London, 604-2004 — *Keene, Derek*

St Paul's: The Cathedral Church of London, 604-2004 — *Keene, Derek*

St. Petersburg, 1703-1825 — *Cross, Anthony*

St Petersburg, 1703-1825 — *Cross, Anthony Glenn*

St. Petersburg: Russia's Window to the Future, the First Three Centuries — *George, Arthur L.*

y St. Ursula's Girls Against the Atomic Bomb — *Hurley, Valerie*

Stability of Strong Discontinuities in Magnetohydrodynamics and Electrohydrodynamics — *Blokhin, Alexander*

Stability Domains — *Gruyitch, L.*

Stability-Indicating HPLC Methods for Drug Analysis, 2nd Ed. — *Xu, Quanyun A.*

The Stability of Currency Boards — *Stukenbrock, Kai*

Stability of Life on Earth: Principal Subject of Scientific Research in the 21st Century — *Kondratyev, Kirill Ya.*

Stable Isotopes in Human Nutrition: Laboratory Methods and Research Applications — *Abrams, S.A.*

Stable Strategies and Others — *Gunn, Eileen*

Stadtbild und Elite: Tarraco, Corduba und Augusta Emerita Zwischen Republik und Spatantike — *Panzram, S.*

Stadur i nyjum Heimi: Konungasagan Morkinskinna — *Jakobsson, Armann*

Staff Officers in Gray: A Biographical Register of the Staff Officers in the Army of Northern Virginia — *Krick, Robert E.L.*

The Stag Hunt and the Evolution of Social Structure — *Skyrms, Brian*

Stage-Bound: Feature Film Adaptions of Canadian and Quebecois Drama — *Loiselle, Andre*

The Stage Life of Props — *Sofer, Andrew*

Stage, Page, Scandals, and Vandals: William E. Burton and Nineteenth-Century American Theatre — *Rinear, Davis L.*

Stage Presence from Head to Toe: A Manual for Musicians — *Hagberg, Karen A.*

Staged Diabetes Management: A Systematic Approach, 2d. ed. — *Mazze, Roger S.*

Staged Narrative: Poetics and the Messenger in Greek Tragedy — *Barrett, James*

Stages and Pathways of Drug Involvement. Examining the Gateway Hypothesis — *Kandel, Denise B.*

Stages and Playgoers: From Guild Plays to Shakespeare — *Hill, Janet*

Stages to Saturn: A Technological History of the Apollo/Saturn Launch Vehicles — *Bilstein, Roger E.*

c Stagestruck (Illus. by De Paola, Tomie) — *De Paola, Tomie*

Stagestruck Vampires and Other Phantasms — *Charnas, Suzy McKee*

The Staggerford Murders — *Hassler, Jon*

Staging a Cultural Paradigm: The Political and the Personal in American Drama — *Ozieblo, Barbara*

Staging America: Cornerstone and Community-Based Theater — *Kuftinec, Sonja*

Staging Consciousness: Theater and the Materialization of Mind — *Demastes, William W.*

Staging Desire: Queer Readings of American Theater History — *Marra, Kim*

Staging Growth: Modernization, Development, and the Global Cold War — *Engerman, David C.*

Staging Modern Playwrights: From Director's Concept to Performance — *Homan, Sidney*

The Staging of Drama in the Medieval Church — *Ogden, Dunbar H.*

Staging the Holocaust: The Shoah In Drama and Performance — *Schumacher, Claude*

Staging the Salvage God: The Grotesque in Performance — *Remshardt, Ralf*

Staging the War: American Drama and World War II — *Wertheim, Albert*

Staging the World: Chinese Nationalism at the Turn of the Twentieth Century — *Karl, Rebecca E.*

Stagolee Shot Billy — *Brown, Cecil*

Stain of Guilt — *Collins, Brandilyn*

y Stained — *Jacobson, Jennifer Richard*

Stained Glass: From Its Origins to the Present — *Raguin, Virginia Chieffo*

Stakeholder Theory and Organizational Ethics — *Phillips, Robert*

Stakeholding and the New International Order — *Maile, Stella*

Stalin: A Biography — *Service, Robert*

Stalin: An Unknown Portrait — *Kun, Miklos*

Stalin and His Hangmen: An Authoritative Portrait of a Tyrant and Those Who Served Him — *Rayfield, Donald*

Stalin and His Hangmen: The Tyrant and Those Who Killed for Him — *Rayfield, Donald*

Stalin and the Inevitable War, 1936-1941 — *Pons, Silvio*

Stalin i soiuzniki, 1941-1945 — *Ivanov, Steven I.*

The Stalin-Kaganovich Correspondence, 1931-36 — *Werstch, James V.*

The Stalin-Kaganovich Correspondence 1931-1936 — *Davies, R.W.*

Stalin: The Court of the Red Tsar — *Montefiore, Sebag*

Stalin, the Russians, and Their War — *Broekmeyer, M. J.*

The Stalin Years: The Soviet Union, 1929-1953 — *Mawdsley, Evan*

Stalinism for all Seasons: A Political History of Romanian Communism — *Tismaneanu, Vladimir*

Stalinist Values: The Cultural Norms of Soviet Modernity, 1917-1941 — *Hoffmann, David L.*

Stalin's British Victims — *Beckett, Francis*

Stalin's 'cordon sanitaire': Die sowjetische Osteuropapolitik und die Reaktionen des Westens 1939-1949 — *O'Sullivan, Donal*

Stalin's Empire of Memory: Russian-Ukrainian Relations in the Soviet Historical Imagination — *Yekelchyk, Serhy*

Stalin's Holy War: Religion, Nationalism, and Alliance Politics, 1941-1945 — *Miner, Steven Merritt*

Stalin's Holy War: Religion, Nationalism, and Alliance Politics, 1941-1945 — *Stalin*

Stalin's Loyal Executioner: People's Commissar Nikolai Ezhov, 1895-1940 — *Jansen, Marc*

Stalin's Other War: Soviet Grand Strategy, 1939-1941 — *Weeks, Albert Loren*

Stalin's Outcasts: Aliens, Citizens, and the Soviet State, 1926-1936 — *Alexopoulos, Golfo*

Stalin's Railroad: Turksib and the Building of Socialism — *Payne, Mathew J.*

Stalin's Slave Ships: Kolyma, the Gulag Fleet, and the Role of the West — *Bollinger, Martin J.*

Stalin's Terror: High Politics and Mass Repression in the Soviet Union — *McLoughlin, Barry*

Stalking the Big Bird: A Tale of Turkeys, Biologists, and Bureaucrats — *Shaw, Harley G.*

Stalking the Divine — *Ohlson, Kristin*

Stalking the Riemann Hypothesis: The Quest to Find the Hidden Law of Prime Numbers — *Rockmore, Dan*

y Stan Lee and the Rise and Fall of the American Comic Book — *Raphael, Jordan*

c Stan Lee's Superhero Christmas (Illus. by Jessell, Tim) — *Lee, Stan*

Stand and prosper: Private Black Colleges and their Students — *Drewry, Henry N.*

The Striking Cabbies of Cairo and Other Stories: Crafts and Guilds in Egypt, 1863-1914 — *Chalcraft, John T.*

Striking Terror: America's New War — *Silvers, Robert B.*

Stringing Together a Nation: Candido Mariano da Silva Rondon and the Construction of a Modern Brazil, 1906-1930 — *Diacon, Todd A.*

Strip City: A Stripper's Farewell Journey Across America — *Burana, Lily*

Strip Show: Performances of Gender and Desire — *Liepe-Levinson, Katherine*

y Stripes of the Sidestep Wolf — *Hartnett, Sonya*

Striptease Culture: Sex, Media, and the Democratization of Desire — *McNair, Brian*

Striptease: The Untold History of the Girlie Show — *Shteir, Rachel*

Striving for Excellence: Ancient Greek Childhood and the Olympic Spirit — *Neils, Jenifer*

Stroke and the Family: A New Guide — *Stein, Joel*

Stroke of Midnight — *Phillips, Carly*

Strolling through Athens: Fourteen Unforgettable Walks through Europe's Oldest City — *Freely, John*

Strong and Electroweak Matter: Proceedings — *Schmidt, Michael G.*

Strong Medicine: Creating Incentives for Pharmaceutical Research on Neglected Diseases — *Kremer, Michael*

Strong Religion: The Rise of Fundamentalisms around the World — *Almond, Gabriel A.*

The Strong, Silent Type — *Robinson, C. Kelly*

The Strong, Silent Type: Over 100 Screen Cowboys, 1903-1930 — *Rainey, Buck*

Strong Women Stories: Native Vision and Community Survival — *Anderson, Kim*

Strong Words: Winning and Social Strain in the Italian Renaissance — *Martines, Lauro*

Struck — *Bromhead, Geoffrey*

A Structural Account of Mathematics — *Chihara, Charles S.*

Structural Analysis of Polymeric Composite Materials — *Tuttle, Mark E.*

Structural Dynamics: Theory and Computation, 5th ed. — *Paz, Mario*

Structural Engineering Formulas — *Mikhelson, Ilya*

Structural Equation Modeling: Applications in Ecological and Evolutionary Biology — *Pugesek, Bruce H.*

The Structural Foundations of International Finance: Problems of Growth and Stability — *Padoan, Pier Carlo*

Structural Health Monitoring and Intelligent Infrastructure: Proceedings, Vols. 1-2 — *Wu, Z.S.*

Structural Impediments to Growth in Japan — *Blomstrom, Magnus*

Structural Statistics for Industry and Services/Statistiques des Structures de L'Industrie et des Services — *Organization for Economic Co-Operation and Development*

Structure, Agency, and the Internal Conversation — *Archer, Margaret S.*

Structure and Agency in Everyday Life: An Introduction to Social Psychology — *Musolf, Gil Richard*

Structure and Function of the Body, 12th Ed. — *Thibodeau, Gary A.*

Structure and Meaning in English: A Guide for Teachers — *Kennedy, Graeme D.*

Structure and Reactions of Light Exotic Nuclei — *Suzuki, Yasuyuki*

Structure of Being in Aristotle's 'Metaphysics' — *Yu, Jiyuan*

Structure of Biological Membranes, 2nd Ed. — *Yeagle, Philip L.*

The Structure of Coordination: Conjunction and Agreement Phenomena in Spanish and Other Languages — *Camacho, Jose*

The Structure of Detachment: The Aesthetic Vision of Kuki Shuzo — *Shuzo, Kuki*

The Structure of Slavery in Indian Ocean Africa and Asia — *Campbell, Gwyn*

The Structure of Soviet History: Essays and Documents. 1st Ed. — *Suny, Ronald Grigor*

c Structure of the Body — *Fortin, Francois*

The Structure of the Mind: Outlines of Philosophical System — *Belfiore, Francesco*

Structured Fluids: Polymers, Colloids, Surfactants — *Witten, T.*

Structured Writing II: Using Inspiration Software to Teach Essay Development — *McMurdo, Kathleen*

Structures Under Shock and Impact VIII: Proceedings — *Jones, Norman*

Structuring Mergers and Acquisitions: A Guide to Creating Shareholder Value, 2nd Ed. — *Hunt, Peter A.*

Structuring Venture Capital, Private Equity, and Entrepreneurial Transactions, 2004 Ed. — *Levin, Jack S.*

c Strudel Stories — *Rocklin, Joanne*

The Struggle Against the Bomb, Vol. 1 — *Wittner, Lawrence S.*

The Struggle Against the Bomb, Vol. 2 — *Maddock, Shane J.*

The Struggle Against the Bomb, Vol. 2 — *Wittner, Lawrence S.*

The Struggle Against the Bomb, Vol. 3 — *Wittner, Lawrence S.*

The Struggle Against Violence — *Datar, Chhaya*

The Struggle for Education in Modern Tibet: The Three Thousand Children of Tashi Tsering — *Siebenschuh, William R.*

The Struggle for Independence 1939-1947: A History of the Hashemite Kingdom of Jordan — *Nowar, Maan Abu*

Struggle for Life: A Psychological Perspective of Kidney Disease and Transplantation — *Baines, Lyndsay S.*

The Struggle for Mastery: Britain, 1066-1284 — *Carpenter, David*

The Struggle for Meaning: Reflections on Philosophy, Culture, and democracy in Africa — *Hountondji, Paulin J.*

The Struggle for Modernity: Nationalism, Futurism, and Fascism — *Gentile, Emilio*

The Struggle for the Health and Legal Protection of Farm Workers: El Cortito — *Jourdane, Maurice*

The Struggle for the Soul of the Nation: Czech Culture and the Rise of Communism — *Abrams, Bradley F.*

The Struggle for Water in Peru: Comedy and Tragedy in the Andean Commons — *Trawick, Paul B.*

Struggles for Social Rights in Latin America — *Eckstein, Susan Eva*

Struggling for Perfection: The Story of Glenn Gould (Illus. by Wysotski, Chrissie) — *Konieczny, Vladimir*

Struggling Readers: Assessment and Instruction in Grades K-6 — *Balajthy, Ernest*

Struggling with Forgiveness: Stories from People and Communities — *Self, David*

Struggling with Tradition: Reservations About Active Martyrdom in the Middle Ages — *Gross, Abraham*

Struts Survival Guide: Basics to Best Practices — *Shenoy, Srikanth*

Struts: The Complete Reference — *Holmes, James*

The Stuart Court in Rome: The Legacy of Exile

c Stuart Goes to School — *Pennypacker, Sara*

Stuart Symington: A Life — *Olson, James C.*

Stubbs and the Horse — *Warner, Malcolm*

Student Almanac of African American History — *Media Projects Incorporated*

y Student Almanac of Asian American History — *Media Projects Incorporated*

y Student Almanac of Hispanic American History — *Media Projects Incorporated*

y Student Almanac of Hispanic American History — *Smith, Carter*

Student Almanac of Native American History — *Media Projects Incorporated*

c Student Companion to Edith Wharton — *Pennell, Melissa McFarland*

Student Companion to Elie Wiesel — *Sternlicht, Sanford*

Student Diversity, Choice and School Improvement — *Willie, Charles Vert*

Student Success and Library Media Programs: A Systems Approach to Research and Best Practice — *Farmer, Lesley S.J.*

Student Workshop--Taunting, Gossiping, Hazing: It's Harassment

y The Student's Encyclopedia of Judaism — *Wigoder, Geoffrey*

y Student's Guide to Earth Science

y A Student's Guide to Earth Science, Vols. 1-4 — *Creative Media Applications*

y A Student's Guide to F. Scott Fitzgerald — *Weisbrod, Eva*

y A Student's Guide to Mental Health & Wellness — *Creative Media Applications*

y A Student's Guide to Nathaniel Hawthorne — *Diorio, Mary Ann L.*

A Student's Guide to the Study of African American Literature, 1760 to the Present — *King, Lovalerie*

Studi Su Clemente Romano: Atti Degli Incontri di Roma, 29 Marzo e 22 Novembre 2001 — *Luisier, Philippe*

Studi sull'Aristotelismo del Rinascimento — *Bianchi, Luca*

Studia Albertana: Lectures et lecteurs de L.B. Alberti — *Furlan, Francesco*

Studia Borromaica, Saggi e documenti di storia religiosa e civile della prima eta moderna. Vols. 1-16 — *Burgio, Santo*

Studia Borromaica: Saggi e documenti di storia religiosa e civile della prima eta moderna, Vols. 14-15

Studia Niemcoznawcze/Studien zur Deutschkunde — *Kolago, Lech*

Studien zum Pramonstratenserorden — *Crusius, Irene*

Studies in Behavioral Anthropology (reprint, 2002). — *Graves, Theodore D.*

Studies in Children's Literature, 1500-2000 — *Keenan, Celia*

Studies in Classic American Literature — *Greenspan, Erza*

Studies in Classic American Literature — *Lawrence, D.H.*

Studies in Educational Learning Environments: An International Perspective — *Goh, Swee Chiew*

Studies in Eighteenth-Century Culture, Vol. 31 — *Mostefai, Ourida*

Studies in Eighteenth-Century Culture, Vol. 32 — *Mostefai, Ourida*

Studies in Hysteria — *Freud, Sigmund*

Studies in International Law and History: An Asian Perspective — *Anand, R.P.*

Studies in Italian Sacred and Instrumental Music in the 17th Century — *Bonta, Stephen*

Studies in Language and Social Interaction: In Honor of Robert Hopper — *Glenn, Phillip*

Studies in Law, Politics, and Society, Vol. 26 — *Sarat, Austin*

Studies in Law, Politics, and Society, Vol. 29 — *Sarat, Austin*

Studies in Modern Islamic Law and Jurisprudence — *Arabi, Oussama*

Studies in Poetry, the Visionary — *Beach, J.M.*

Studies in Public Opinion: Attitudes, Nonattitudes, Measurement Error, and Change — *Saris, William E.*

Studies in Symbolic Interaction. Vol. 25 — *Denzin, Norman K.*

Studies in the Formation of the Nation-State in Latin America — *Dunkerley, James*

Studies in the History of Central Nigeria Area: Volume 1 — *Idrees, Aliyu A.*

Studies in the History of the English Language: A Millennial Perspective — *Minkova, Donka*

Studies in the Judicial Methodology of Rabbi David Ibn Abi Zimra — *Morell, Samuel*

Studies in the Origins of Early Islamic Culture and Tradition — *Cook, Michael*

Studies of Chinese Bond Markets: An Empirical Approach — *Wang, Anxing*

Studies of High-Temperature Superconductors: Advances in Research and Applications, Vol. 46 — *Narlikar, Anant*

Studies of High Temperature Superconductors: Advances in Research and Applications, Vol. 47 — *Narlikar, Anant*

Studies of How the Mind Publicly Enfolds into Being — *Smythe, William*

Studies on Astral Magic in Medieval Jewish Thought — *Schwartz, Dov*

Studies on the History of Late Antique and Christian Nubia — *Kirwan, Laurence*

Studies on the Jews of Venice, 1382-1797 — *Ravid, Benjamin*

Studies on the Transmission of Medieval Mathematical Astronomy — *Mercier, Raymond*

Studio A: The Bob Dylan Reader — *Hedin, Benjamin*

Studio Practices, Techniques and Tips: A Collection of Articles from Ceramics Monthly — *Turner, Anderson*

Study of Culture, 3rd Ed. — *Langness, L.L.*

The Study of European Ethnology in Austria — *Dow, James R.*

The Study of Hinduism — *Sharma, Arvind*

A Study of Liberation Discourse: The Semantics of Opposition in Freire and Gutierrez — *Rivera, Roberto*

A Study of Major Political Thinkers in France from the Seventeenth to the Twentieth Century: From Absolutism to Socialism — *Addinall, Nigel*

T

U

V

W

c The World Almanac for Kids 2005
y World Almanac Library of the Civil War
     — *Anderson, Dale*
c World Almanac Library of the Civil War
World Art And Culture
The World As It Shall Be — *Souvestre, Emile*
The World As It Shall Be — *Souvestre, Emile*
World Atlas of Seagrasses — *Green, Edmund P.*
World Authors 1995-2000 — *Rich, Mari*
World Authors, 1995-2000 — *Thompson, Clifford*
World Bank Annual Report 2003, Vol. 1
World Bank Annual Report 2003, Vol. 2
World Bank Atlas, 36th ed. — *International Bank for
     Reconstruction and Development*
World Bank Atlas 2003
The World Bank Group Directory, November 2003
     — *World Bank Group*
World Bank Operations Evaluation Department: The
     First Thirty Years — *Grasso, Patrick G.*
The World Bank Research Program: Abstracts of
     Current Studies, 2002-03
The World Beneath Our Feet: A Guide to Life in the
     Soil — *Nardi, James B.*
The World Book Encyclopedia
World Book of America's Multicultural Heritage
World Book Online Reference Center
World Book's Biographical Encyclopedia of Scientists
World Business: Globalization, Analysis, and Strategy
     — *Hill, John S.*
World Capital Markets: Challenge to the G-10
     — *Dobson, Wendy*
A World Challenged: Fighting Terrorism in the
     Twenty-First Century — *Primakov, Yevgeny M.*
World, Class, Women: Global Literature, Education,
     and Feminism — *Goodman, Robin Truth*
World Commodity Survey: 2003-2004: Markets,
     Trends and the World Economic Environment
     — *Prager, Charles*
The World Court in Action: Judging among the
     Nations — *Meyer, Howard N.*
The World Court Reference Guide: Judgments,
     Advisory Opinions, and Orders of the Permanent
     Court of International Justice and the International
     Court of Justice — *Patel, Bimal N.*
World Development Indicators 2004
World Development Report 2004: Making Services
     Work for Poor People
World Directory of Trade Promotion Organizations
     and Other Trade Support Institutions
     — *International Trade Centre*
World Drug Report 2004, Vols. 1-2
World Economic and Social Survey, 2003: Trends and
     Policies in the World Economy — *United Nations.
     Department of Economic and Social Affairs*
World Economics 2: The Political Economy of
     Development Globalization and System
     Transformation — *Szentes, Tamas*
The World Economy and National Economies in the
     Interwar Slump — *Balderston, Theo*
The World Economy: Historical Statistics
     — *Maddison, Angus*
The World Encyclopedia of Christmas — *Bowler,
     Gerry*
World Energy Investment Outlook: 2003 Insights
World Englishes: A Resource Book for Students
     — *Jenkins, Jennifer*
World Epidemics: A Cultural Chronology of Disease
     from Prehistory to the Era of SARS — *Snodgrass,
     Mary Ellen*
World Federation of Societies of Anaesthesiologists: 50
     Years — *Gullo, A.*
World Finance and Economic Stability: Selected
     Essays of James Tobin — *Tobin, James, (1918 -)*
World Graphic Design: Contemporary Graphics from
     Africa, the Far East, Latin America and the Middle
     East — *Caban, Geoffrey*
World Health Organization — *Gian Luca, Burci*
World Health Report 2004: Changing History
     — *World Health Organization*
World History: Ancient and Medieval Eras
c World History. Audiobook Review
World History in Brief: Major Patterns of Change
     and Continuity, 5th Ed. — *Stearns, Peter N.*
World History: Lives and Times in Egypt, Greece and
     the Roman Empire. Audiobook Review
A World History of Tax Rebellions: An Encyclopedia
     of Tax Rebels, Revolts, and Riots from Antiquity to
     the Present — *Burg, David F.*
World History of Warfare — *Archer, Christon I.*
c World History on File: The 20th Century, Updated
     Ed. — *Chapman, Victoria L.*
The World I Live In — *Keller, Helen*

The World in a Box: The Story of an
     Eighteenth-Century Picture Encyclopedia
     — *Heesen, Anke te*
The World in a City — *Anisef, Paul*
A World in Chaos: Social Crisis and the Rise of
     Postmodern Cinema — *Boggs, Carl*
The World in the Year 1000 — *Heitzman, James*
World Investment Directory, Vol. 8 — *United Nations
     Conference on Trade and Development*
World Investment Directory, Vol. 9, Pts. 1-2 — *United
     Nations Conference on Trade and Development*
World Investment Report 2003: FDI Policies for
     Development: National and International
     Perspectives
World Investment Report 2003: FDI Policies for
     Development, National and International
     Perspectives — *United Nations Conference on Trade
     and Development*
The World Is Flat: A Brief History of the
     Twenty-First Century (Read by Wyman, Oliver).
     Audiobook Review — *Friedman, Thomas L.*
The World Is Flat: A Brief History of the
     Twenty-First Century — *Friedman, Thomas L.*
The World Is Not for Sale: Farmers Against Junk
     Food — *Bove, J.*
World List of Universities and Other Institutions of
     Higher Education, 24th Ed.
"The World Must Be Peopled": Shakespeare's
     Comedies of Forgiveness — *Friedman, Michael D.*
The World Next Door: South Asian American
     Literature and the of America — *Srikanth, Ranjini*
World Of Animals: Birds
The World of Bertoia — *Schiffer, Nancy N.*
The World of Christopher Marlowe — *Riggs, David*
The World of Cities: Places in Comparative and
     Historical Perspective — *Orum, Anthony M.*
The World of Deaf Infants: A Longitudinal Study
     — *Meadow-Orlans, Kathryn P.*
A World of Festivals
The World of Gerard Mercator: The Mapmaker Who
     Revolutionalized Geography — *Taylor, Andrew*
The World of Gerard Mercator: The Mapmaker Who
     Revolutionized Geography — *Taylor, Andrew*
The World of Gregory of Tours — *Mitchell, Kathleen*
World of Hannah Heaton: The Diary of an
     Eighteenth-Century New England Farm Woman
     — *Heaton, Hannah*
A World of Hurt — *Sherman, David*
The World of Music According to Starker — *Starker,
     Janos*
The World of Mykola Lysenko: Ethnic Identity,
     Music, and Politics in Nineteenth and Early
     Twentieth Century Ukraine — *Filenko, Taras*
World of Myths, Vol. 2 — *Fernandez-Armesto, Felipe*
The World of Obituaries: Gender Across Cultures and
     over Time — *Eid, Mushira*
The World of Paperbacks
The World of Perception — *Merleau-Ponty, Maurice*
A World of Presidia — *Fernald, Anya*
The World of the Paranormal: The Next Frontier
     — *LeShan, Lawrence*
The World of the Rings: Language, Religion, and
     Adventure in Tolkien — *Lobdell, Jared*
c A World of Wonders (Illus. by Jay, Alison) — *Lewis,
     J. Patrick*
World on Fire: How Exporting Free Market
     Democracy Breeds Ethnic Hatred and Global
     Instability — *Chua, Amy*
World Peace, Mass Culture, and National Policies
     — *Over, William*
World Peacemakers
A World Perhaps: New and Selected Poems — *Lucas,
     John*
World Population Monitoring, 2002: Reproductive
     Rights and Reproductive Health — *United Nations.
     Dep. of Economic and Social Affairs. Population
     Division*
World Population Policies 2003 — *United Nations.
     Department of Economic and Social Affairs*
World Population Prospects: The 2002 Revision, Vol. 1
     — *United Nations. Dep. of Economic and Social
     Affairs. Population Division*
World Population Prospects: The 2002 Revision, Vol. 2
     — *United Nations. Dep. of Economic and Social
     Affairs. Population Division*
World Poverty: A Reference Handbook — *Gilbert,
     Geoffrey*
World Press Photo 2004
World Public Sector Report 2003: E-Government At
     the Crossroads — *United Nations. Department of
     Economic and Social Affairs*

World Religions and Social Evolution of the Old
     World Oikumene Civilizations, a Cross-Cultural
     Perspective — *Korotaev, Andrey V.*
The World Republic of Letters — *Casanova, Pascale*
World Robotics 2003 — *UN Economic Commission for
     Europe and the International Federation of Robotics*
A World Safe for Capitalism: Dollar Diplomacy and
     America's Rise to Global Power — *Veeser, Cyrus*
The World Since World War II — *Duiker, William J.*
The World Still Melting — *Wilson, Robley*
World Textiles: A Concise History — *Schoeser, Mary*
y World Textiles: A Visual Guide to Traditional
     Techniques — *Gillow, John*
c World That Loved Books — *Parlato, Stephen*
The World That Was Ours — *Bernstein, Hilda*
The World the Sixties Made: Politics and Culture in
     Recent America — *Gosse, Van*
World Trade Review
World Trends in Environmental Education
     — *Azeiteiro, Ulisses*
y The World Turned Upside Down — *Drake, David*
The World Unclaimed: A Challenge to Heidegger's
     Critique of Husserl — *Alweiss, Lilian*
World-Walker — *Michaels, Melisa*
c World War I — *Feldman, Ruth Tenzer*
World War I Memories: An Annotated Bibliography
     of Personal Accounts Published in English Since
     1919 — *Lengel, Edward G.*
World War II — *Willmott, H.P.*
c World War II: Europe — *Goldstein, Margaret J.*
c World War II Home Front — *Barr, Gary E.*
y The World War II Memorial: A Grateful Nation
     Remembers — *Brinkley, Douglas*
World War II: Neuropsychiatric Casualties, Out of
     Sight, Out of Mind — *Gottschalk, Louis A.*
c World War II: Pacific — *Williams, Barbara*
World Water Resources at the Beginning of the
     Twenty-First Century — *Shiklomanov, I.A.*
World Wide Search: The Savvy Christian's Guide to
     Online Dating — *Green, Cheryl*
World Wide Wi-Fi: Technological Trends and Business
     Strategies — *Tan, Teik-Kheong*
A World Without Time: The Forgotten Legacy of
     Godel and Einstein — *Yourgrau, Palle*
A World Without Walls: Freedom, Development, Free
     Trade and Global Governance — *Moore, Mike*
World Writers in English, Vols. 1-2 — *Parini, Jay*
World Youth Report 2003: The Global Situation of
     Young People — *United Nations. Department of
     Economic and Social Affairs*
World Youth Report: The Global Situation of Young
     People — *United Nations. Department of Economic
     and Social Affairs*
Worldly and Heavenly Wisdom of 4QInstruction
     — *Goff, Matthew J.*
The World's 20 Greatest Unsolved Problems — *Vacca,
     John R.*
Worlds Afire — *Janeczko, Paul B.*
Worlds Apart: Civil Society and the Battle for Ethical
     Globalization — *Clark, John D.*
c Worlds Apart: Traveling with Fernie and Me (Illus.
     by Clarke, Greg) — *Soto, Gary*
The World's Banker: A Story of Failed States,
     Financial Crises, and the Wealth and Poverty of
     Nations — *Mallaby, Sebastian*
The World's Best Book: Taste, Culture, and the
     Modern Library — *Satterfield, Jay*
Worlds Beyond: The Thrill of Planetary Exploration
     — *Stern, S. Alan*
The World's Children and Their Companion Animals:
     Developmental and Educational Significance of the
     Child/Pet Bond — *Jalongo, Mary Renck*
Worlds Collide — *Strobel, Alison*
World's End — *Sinclair, Upton*
The World's Finest Mystery and Crime Stories: Fifth
     Annual Collection — *Gorman, Ed*
The World's Greatest Fix: A History of Nitrogen and
     Agriculture — *Leigh, G.J.*
The World's Greatest Letters: From Ancient Greece
     to the Twentieth Century — *Lovric, Michelle*
The World's Hot Spots
The Worlds Most Haunted Places: From the Secret
     Files of Ghostvillage.com — *Belanger, Jeff*
The World's Most Powerful Leadership Principle:
     How to Become a Servant Leader — *Hunter, James
     C.*
The Worlds of Herman: the Intuitive Science of
     Thermonuclear War — *Ghamari-Tabrizi, Sharon*
Worlds of Music: An Introduction to the Music of the
     World's Peoples, Shorter Version, 2nd Ed. — *Titon,
     Jeff Todd*

X Y Z